AMERICAN ART DIRECTORY

AMERICAN ART DIRECTORY

1980

Edited and Compiled by
JAQUES CATTELL PRESS

R. R. BOWKER COMPANY
New York & London

Published by R. R. Bowker Co.
1180 Avenue of the Americas, New York, NY 10036

Copyright © 1980 by Xerox Corporation

Contents

Advisory Committee

Paul B Arnold, Past President
National Association of Schools of Art
c/o Sarah Lawrence College
84710 LaCoste (Vaucluse) France

Mario Cooper, President
American Watercolor Society
1083 Fifth Avenue
New York, New York 10028

Mark Freeman, President
National Society of Painters
  in Casein & Acrylic
225 West 34th Street
New York, New York 10001

William V Gallo, Past President
National Cartoonists Society
1 Mayflower Drive
Yonkers, New York 10710

Judith Hoffberg, Editor
Umbrella
PO Box 773-C
Pasadena, California 91104

Konrad Kuchel, Coordinator of Loans
The American Federation of Arts
41 East 65th Street
New York, New York 10021

John J Mahlmann, Executive Director
National Art Education Association
1916 Association Drive
Reston, Virginia 22091

Laurence McGilvery
Rare Art Book Dealer
PO Box 852
La Jolla, California 92037

Margaret Mills, Executive Director
American Academy & Institute of
  Arts & Letters
633 West 155th Street
New York, New York 10032

Paul C Mills, Secretary
Association of Art Museum Directors
c/o Santa Barbara Museum of Art
1130 State Street
Santa Barbara, California 93101

Claire Stein, Executive Director
National Sculpture Society
15 East 26th Street
New York, New York 10010

Preface

Revised biennially, this 48th edition of the *American Art Directory* lists art museums, associations, and schools located in the United States and Canada; major art museums and schools abroad are also included. Questionnaires were sent to each organization listed. When neither the original questionnaire nor follow-up requests were answered, entries were updated from secondary sources. These organizations are identified by an asterisk (*) following their names.

Sections I and II are arranged geographically and each is preceded by an outline of the data included in the entries and a list of the abbreviations used. The first section includes entries from 2,327 museums and associations in the United States, 194 in Canada, and 428 abroad. Entered in this count are approximately 100 corporations which have art holdings or which actively support the visual arts. Additionally, statistics on over 1,536 art libraries are presented.

For the first time, each entry is introduced by a classification key, designating the type of entry:

C — Corporate Art
L — Library
M — Museum or Gallery
O — Organization or Association

The key "M" was assigned to organizations with the primary function of gathering and preserving the visual arts. Key "O" was given to organizations that function to support the arts through sponsoring artists and art activities.

The second section gives information on 1,492 art schools in the United States, 48 in Canada, and 98 abroad. This year, a special effort was made to contact departments of art history and to list the title and the highest degree achieved for each faculty member.

Section III provides reference to state art councils, directors and supervisors of art education in major school systems, art magazines, newspapers carrying art notes, scholarships and fellowships, open exhibitions, and traveling exhibition booking agencies.

Section IV consists of three alphabetical indexes. While the Organization Index includes museums, libraries, associations, and schools, the Personnel Index lists the people affiliated with them. New to this edition is the two-part Subject Index. It begins with a list of general subject categories and ends with a separate list of named and specialized collections. Each section provides the name and location of museums with such collections.

For this edition and the previous, the *American Art Directory* and its companion volume, *Who's Who in American Art,* have had an advisory committee whose main function was to nominate new artists and organizations for inclusion in the directories. In addition, committee members provided suggestions for changes in format and data presented. The editors thank this committee for the help they have offered.

The editors have made every effort to include all material submitted as accurately and completely as possible within the confines of format and scope. However, the publishers do not assume and hereby disclaim any liability to any party for any loss or damage caused by errors or omissions in the *American Art Directory* whether such errors or omissions resulted from negligence, accident or any other cause. In the event of a publication error, the sole responsibility of the publisher will be the entry of corrected information in succeeding editions.

John Cattafe, design and production manager of Jaques Cattell Press, died shortly before the *American Art Directory* was completed. To him, in recognition of his talents and many contributions, and in appreciation of his good and generous nature, we dedicate this book.

In our ongoing effort to improve this directory so that the user can be assured of its continuing usefulness, we welcome your comments and suggestions along with notes of omissions and errors; these should be addressed to The Editors, *American Art Directory,* P.O. Box 25001, Tempe, Arizona 85282.

Carol Borland, *Editorial Assistant*
Linda Burns, *Editor*
Anne Rhodes, *Managing Editor*
    Information Directories
Steve Nichols, *General Manager*

JAQUES CATTELL PRESS

May 1980

I ART ORGANIZATIONS

Arrangement and Abbreviations

National and Regional Organizations in the U.S.

Museums, Libraries and Associations in the U.S.

National and Regional Organizations in Canada

Museums, Libraries and Associations in Canada

Major Museums Abroad

ARRANGEMENT AND ABBREVIATIONS
KEY TO ART ORGANIZATIONS

ARRANGEMENT OF DATA

Name and address of institution; telephone number, including area code.

Names and titles of key personnel.

Hours open; admission fees; date established and purpose; average annual attendance; membership.

Annual figures on income and purchases.

Collections, with enlarging collections indicated.

Exhibitions scheduled for 1978-80.

Activities sponsored, including classes for adults and children, dramatic programs and docent training; lectures, concerts, gallery talks and tours; competitions, awards, scholarships and fellowships; lending programs; museum or sales shops.

Libraries also list number of book volumes, periodical subscriptions, and audiovisual and micro holdings; subjects covered by name of special collections.

ABBREVIATIONS AND SYMBOLS

Admin — Administration, Administrative
Adminr — Administrator
Admis — Admission
A-tapes — Audio-tapes
Adv — Advisory
AM — Morning
Ann — Annual
Approx — Approximate, Approximately
Asn — Association
Assoc — Associate
Asst — Assistant
AV — Audiovisual
Ave — Avenue
Bldg — Building
Blvd — Boulevard
Bro — Brother
c — circa
Chap — Chapter
Chmn — Chairman
Circ — Circulation
Cl — Closed
Coll — Collection
Comt — Committee
Coordr — Coordinator
Corresp — Corresponding
Cur — Curator
Dept — Department
Dir — Director
Dist — District
Div — Division
Dr — Drive
E — East
Ed — Editor

Educ — Education
Enrl — Enrollment
Ent — Entrance
Estab — Established
Exec — Executive
Exhib — Exhibition
Exten — Extension
Fel(s) — Fellowship(s)
Fri — Friday
Fs — Filmstrips
Ft — Feet
Gen — General
Hon — Honorary
Hr — Hour
Hwy — Highway
Inc — Incorporated
Incl — Including
Jr — Junior
Lect — Lecture(s)
Lectr — Lecturer
Librn — Librarian
Mem — Membership
Mgr — Manager
Mon — Monday
Mss — Manuscripts
Mus — Museums
N — North
Nat — National
Per subs — Periodical subscriptions
PM — Afternoon
Pres — President
Prin — Principal
Prof — Professor

Prog — Program
Pub — Public
Publ — Publication
Rd — Road
Rec — Records
Res — Residence, Resident
S — South
Sat — Saturday
Schol — Scholarship
Secy — Secretary
Soc — Society
Sq — Square
Sr — Senior, Sister
St — Street
Sun — Sunday
Supt — Superintendent
Supv — Supervisor
Thurs — Thursday
Treas — Treasurer
Tues — Tuesday
Tui — Tuition
TV — Television
Univ — University
Vol — Volunteer
Vols — Volumes
VPres — Vice President
V-tapes — Videotapes
W — West
Wed — Wednesday
Wk — Week
Yr — Year(s)

*No response to questionnaire
† Denotes collections currently being enlarged
C Corporate Art Holding
L Library
M Museum
O Organization

National and Regional Organizations In The United States

O **ALLIED ARTISTS OF AMERICA, INC,** 15 Gramercy Park S, New York, NY 10003. *Pres* William D Gorman; *VPres* Moses Worthman; *Treas* Mare Brutus; *Corresp Secy* Reta Soloway
Estab 1914, incorporated 1922, as a self-supporting exhibition cooperative, with juries elected each year by the membership, to promote work by American artists.
Mem: Active 350, assoc 250; dues active $20, assoc $15
Exhibitions: Members' exhibitions; annual exhibition in the fall. 1980 Annual held at American Academy and Institute of Arts and Letters; numerous awards and medals; prizes total approx $10,000 each year
Publications: Newsletter
Activities: Demonstrations; scholarships

O **AMERICAN ABSTRACT ARTISTS,** 41 Sunset Dr, Summit, NJ 07901. *Pres* Dr Irene Rousseau; *Secy* Ruth Eckstein; *Treas* Esphyr Slobodkina; *Membership Chmn* Ward Jackson
Estab 1936, active 1937, to further cause; develop and educate through exhibitions and publications. Mem: 60; quarterly meetings
Income: Financed by membership
Exhibitions: Held at Betty Parsons Gallery and Marilyn Pearl Gallery
Publications: Books and catalogs
Activities: Originate traveling exhibitions

O **AMERICAN ACADEMY AND INSTITUTE OF ARTS AND LETTERS,** 633 W 155th St, New York, NY 10032. Tel 212-368-5900. *Pres* Barbara W Tuchman; *Exec Dir* Margaret M Mills
Open Tues - Sun 1 - 4 PM during exhibitions, by appointment other times. Estab 1898 as an honorary society of artists, writers and composers whose function it is to foster, assist and sustain an interest in literature, music and the fine arts. Formed by 1976 merger of the American Academy of Arts and Letters and the National Institute of Arts and Letters. Maintains two galleries separated by a terrace. Average Annual Attendance: 6000. Mem: 250; membership is by election; no dues; annual meeting May
Income: $750,000 (financed by endowment)
Purchases: $50,000
Collections: Works by members
Exhibitions: Exhibition of Candidates for Art Awards; Exhibition of Paintings Eligible for Hassam Fund Purchase; Memorial Exhibitions for Deceased Artist Members; Newly Elected Members Exhibitions; Recipients of Honors and Awards
Publications: Proceedings; exhibition catalogs
Activities: Awards given: Gold Medal, Richard and Hinda Rosenthal Foundation Award, Marjorie Peabody Waite Award, Arnold W Brunner Memorial Prize in Architecture, and Award of Merit of the Academy
L **Library,** 633 W 155th St, 10032. *Librn* Casindania P Eaton; *Research Librn* Nancy Johnson
Open Mon - Fri 10 AM - 5 PM. Estab to collect books, papers and related articles concerning the members of the Academy-Institute. For reference only
Library Holdings: Vols 15,500; Other—Clipping files, exhibition catalogs, prints, manuscripts, memorabilia, original art works, pamphlets, photographs, reproductions, sculpture
Special Subjects: Literature and music of past and present members
Collections: Books by and about members; manuscripts

O **AMERICAN ANTIQUARIAN SOCIETY,** 185 Salisbury St, Worcester, MA 01609. Tel 617-755-5221. *Dir* Marcus A McCorison; *Cur Graphic Arts* Georgia B Bumgardner
Open 9 AM - 5 PM; cl Sat, Sun & holidays. No admis fee. Incorporated 1812 to collect, preserve and encourage serious study of the materials of American history and life through 1876. Mem: 360 honorary; meetings third Wed in April & Oct
Income: $805,389
Purchases: $141,000
Collections: Early American Portraits; Staffordshire Pottery; †bookplates, †prints, †lithographs, †cartoons, †engraving; Colonial furniture
Exhibitions: Temporary exhibitions
Publications: Proceedings, semi-annually; monographs
Activities: Lect; sponsors fellowships
L **Library,** 185 Salisbury St, 01609.
Collections: 750,000 titles dating before 1877, including early American books on art and 20th century books and periodicals relating to the history and culture of the United States

O **AMERICAN ARTISTS PROFESSIONAL LEAGUE, INC,** 215 Park Ave S, New York, NY 10003. Tel 212-475-6650. *Pres* Angelo John Grado; *Recording Secy* John Damron
Estab 1928 to advance the cause of fine arts in America, through the promotion of high standards of beauty, integrity and craftsmanship in painting, sculpture and the graphic arts; to emphasize the importance of order and coherent communication as prime requisites of works of art through exhibitions and publications. Mem: 1000; monthly meetings Oct through May
Income: $800 - $10,000 (financed by membership)

Exhibitions: Annually
Publications: AAPL News Bulletin, annually

O **AMERICAN ASSOCIATION OF MUSEUMS,** 1055 Thomas Jefferson St NW, Washington, DC 20007. Tel 202-338-5300. *Pres* Kenneth Starr; *Dir* Lawrence L Reger; *Deputy Dir Admin* James Thomas; *Asst Dir Programs* Pamela Johnson; *Ed* Ellen C Hicks
Open Mon - Fri 9 AM - 5 PM. Estab 1906, to promote the welfare and advancement of museums as educational institutions, agencies of scientific and academic research and as cultural centers of the community; to encourage interest and inquiries in the field of museology; to increase and diffuse knowledge of all matters relating to museums. Average Annual Attendance: 6000
Publications: Aviso, monthly; books; Museum News, six per year; Official Museum Directory, annually; reprints

O **AMERICAN ASSOCIATION OF UNIVERSITY WOMEN,** 2401 Virginia Ave NW, Washington, DC 20037. Tel 202-785-7700. *Gen Dir* Open
Estab 1882 to unite alumnae of different institutions for practical educational work; to further the advancement of women, lifelong learning, and responsibility to society expressed through action, advocacy, research and enlightened leadership. Mem: 190,000; holds biennial conventions
Publications: Graduate Woman (magazine), 6 times per year, often features art subjects
Activities: Association's Educational Center has available guidance in a wide range of the arts, including music structure, acting, dance, development of environmental awareness and action

O **AMERICAN CERAMIC SOCIETY,** 65 Ceramic Dr, Columbus, OH 43214. Tel 614-268-8645. *Pres* William Prindle; *VPres* Steven C Carniglia; *Executive Dir* Arthur L Friedberg
Open Mon - Fri 8:30 AM - 5 PM. No admis fee. Estab 1899 to promote the arts, science and technology of ceramics. Average Annual Attendance: 8000. Mem: Dues $40; annual meeting May
Income: $1,000,000 (financed by membership)
Publications: American Ceramic Society Bulletin, monthly; Ceramic Proceedings, bi-monthly; Journal and Abstracts, bi-monthly

O **AMERICAN COLOR PRINT SOCIETY,** c/o Philadelphia College of Art, Broad & Spruce Sts, Philadelphia, PA 19102. Tel 215-893-3160. *Pres* Richard Hood; *VPres* Mildred Dillon; *VPres* Lois Johnson; *Treas* Bernard A Kohn; *Secy* Naomi Limonte
Estab 1939 to exhibit and sell color prints. Mem: 150; dues $10; annual meeting Oct
Exhibitions: National members exhibition held at Philadelphia Art Alliance in October; awarded exhibition prints become a part of the American Color Print Society's Collection housed in the Philadelphia Museum of Art and the National Gallery of Art
Activities: Sponsors annual national members exhibition of all media color prints; 6 annual prizes, 3 of which are purchase prizes

O **AMERICAN COUNCIL FOR THE ARTS,** 570 Seventh Ave, New York, NY 10018. Tel 212-354-6655. *Pres* Anne Bartley; *Dir* W Grant Brownrigg; *Chmn* Louis Harris; *Prog Dir* Annette Covatta; *Ed* Bill Keens; *Publications Mgr* Bob Porter
Estab 1960 as a national organization to provide management training, advocacy, news and publications services which address needs that cut across art forms. Mem: 3500; dues councils $60-$500 (depending on size of budget), business $200, universities and art organizations $100, library $35, individual $30, student $20
Publications: ACA Reports, 8 times a year; Word from Washington, 10 times a year
Activities: Sponsors competitions
L **Library,** 570 Seventh Ave, 10018.
Open Mon - Fri 9 AM - 5 PM. Estab 1965 to serve as a resource for a program of information services to the arts administration field. For reference only
Library Holdings: Vols 1100; Per subs 100; Other—Clipping files, manuscripts, documents
Special Subjects: Cultural policy and management

O **AMERICAN COUNCIL FOR THE ARTS IN EDUCATION,*** 1704 Bolton St, Baltimore, MD 21217. Tel 301-383-0948. *Pres* Eldon Winkler; *VPres* Robert Glidden; *Secy-Treas* Gerry J Martin
Estab 1957, a federation of national organizations concerned with furthering the cause of all the arts in American education. Mem: 25; meetings winter Jan or Feb, summer June or July
Income: Financed by membership, Foundation grants, federal grants and contract research

O **AMERICAN CRAFT COUNCIL,** 22 W 55th St, New York, NY 10019. Tel 212-397-0600. *Board Chmn* Robert O Peterson; *Vice Chmn* Adele Greene; *Vice Chmn* Jack Lenor Larsen; *Executive Dir of Council* Lois Moran; *Secy* Sidney Rosoff; *Editor-in-Chief American Craft Magazine* Pat Dandignac
Estab 1943 to stimulate interest in and appreciation of contemporary American crafts. The Council maintains the American Craft Museum (see entry under

Museums). Mem: 35,000; dues $27.50 and higher; national conference every 3-4 years
Income: $1,2000,000 (financed by membership, private donations and government grants)
Publications: American Craft Magazine (formerly Craft Horizons), bimonthly; exhibition catalogues
Activities: Regional workshops and conferences; sponsors Young Americans, a crafts competition every 6 years for persons 18-30 years old; lending collection contains over 100 slide kits, a national audio-visual service called Your Portable Museum; originate traveling exhibitions
L **American Craft Council Library,** 44 W 53rd St, 10019. Tel 212-397-0637, 397-0638. *Librn* Joanne Polster
See entry under Museum section

O **AMERICAN FEDERATION OF ARTS,** 41 E 65th St, New York, NY 10021. *Pres Board of Trustees* Bayard Ewing; *VPres* Arthur D Emil; *Secy* Francis E Brennan; *Dir* Wiler Green; *Asst Dir & Dir Exhib* Jane S Tai; *Coordr Loans* Konrad G Kuchel; *Exhib Coordr* Susanna D Alton; *Registrar* Melissa Meigham; *Dir Film Prog* Steven Aronson; *Dir Membership* Margot Linton; *Graphic Designer* Pauline DiBlasi; *Assoc Dir Finance & Development* Walter Poleshuck
Estab 1909, a nonprofit educational institution which organizes circulating art exhibitions and film programs for museums, art centers, universities, colleges, schools and libraries. Mem: 1600; dues individual $35-$1000, institutions $75 and up
Income: Financed by endowment and membership
Exhibitions: African Furniture and Household Objects; The Boston Tradition: Paintings, Drawings and Watercolors from the Museum of Fine Arts in Boston; British Art Now: An American Perspective; Court House, A Photographic Document; Generations in Clay, Pueblo Pottery of the American Southwest; History of the American Avant-Garde Cinema; Imperial China: Photography 1846-1912; Italian Drawings 1780-1890; Japan: Photographs 1854-1905; Master Drawings and Watercolors of the 19th and 20th Centuries (Baltimore Museum of Art); Murals Without Walls, Arshire Gorky's Aviation Murals Rediscovered; Objects of Bright Pride, Northwest Coast Indian Art from the American Museum of Natural History; Prints from the Guggenheim Collection; Room for Wonder: Indian Painting During the British Period, 1760-1880; Selections from Alex Hillman Family Foundation Collection; Selections from Sara Roby Foundation Collection; Silver in American Life: Selections from the Mable Brady Garvan and Other Collections at Yale University; Tibet: A Lost World (Newark Museum); Vuillard Drawings 1885-1930; Works on Paper: American Art 1945-1975; Young Americans: Fiber-Wood-Plastic-Leather
Publications: Exhibition catalogs
Activities: Originate traveling exhibitions

O **AMERICAN FINE ARTS SOCIETY,** 215 W 57th St, New York, NY 10019. Tel 212-247-4510. *Pres* Stewart Klonis; *Secy* Arthur J Foster
Incorporated 1889 to provide facilities for art activities. Mem: Annual meeting Jan
Activities: Sponsors lect by prominent persons in the art world

O **AMERICAN INSTITUTE FOR CONSERVATION OF HISTORIC AND ARTISTIC WORKS (AIC),** 1522 K St NW, Suite 804, Washington, DC 20005. Tel 202-638-1444. *Pres* Paul N Banks; *VPres* Perry C Huston; *Secy* Katherine Eirk
Open 8 AM - 4 PM. Estab 1973 for professional organization of Conservators, people who take care of our cultural and historical patrimony. Mem: 1400; dues institutions $40, fellows $30, associates $20; annual meeting late May
Income: Financed by membership
Publications: Directory, annually; Journal, semi-annually; Newsletter, quarterly
Activities: Educ Committee to keep abreast of all conservation education facilities, programs; lect open to public
L **Library,** 1522 K St NW, Suite 804, 20005. *In Charge* Martha Morales
Open 8 AM - 4 PM. For member's use and for students of Conservation
Special Subjects: Conservation of artistic and historic works

O **AMERICAN INSTITUTE OF ARCHITECTS,** 1735 New York Ave NW, Washington, DC 20006. Tel 202-785-7300. *Pres* Charles E Schwing; *First VPres* R Randall Vosbeck; *Secy* Robert M Lawrence; *Exec VPres* David Olan Meeker Jr
Open Mon - Fri 8:30 AM - 5 PM. No admis fee. Estab 1857 to organize and unite the architects of the United States and to promote the esthetic, scientific and practical efficiency of the profession. The Octagon, town house for Colonel John Tayloe, built in 1800 and designed by architect William Thornton serves as a gallery owned and operated by the American Institute of Architects Foundation
Income: Financed by membership
Collections: The Octagon has collections of period paintings and furniture
Exhibitions: Just for Fun: A Celebration of Diversity; Selections from the AIA Architectural Archives; special Christmas exhibition
Publications: AIA Journal, monthly; AIA Memo (newsletter), biweekly
Activities: Continuing education program; awards given, Gold Medal, Kemper Award, Architectural Firm Award, R S Reynolds Memorial Award and Reynolds Aluminum Prize Citation of Honor
L **Library,** 1735 New York Ave NW, 20006. *Librn* Susan Holton
Open to the public, lending provided for members
Library Holdings: Vols 20,000; Per subs 150
Special Subjects: Architecture, architectural history

O **AMERICAN INSTITUTE OF GRAPHIC ARTS,** 1059 Third Ave, New York, NY 10021. Tel 212-752-0813. *Pres* James K Fogleman; *Exec Dir* Caroline Hightower
Open Mon - Fri 9:30 AM - 4:45 PM. No admis fee. Estab 1914 as a national nonprofit educational organization devoted to raising standards in all branches of the graphic arts. Gallery maintained. Mem: 1700; dues resident $100, nonresident $50, student $20
Income: Financed by membership
Exhibitions: Book Show; Communication Graphics
Publications: 1980 AIGA Graphic Design USA:1 (hardbound annual)
Activities: Clinics on aspects of book production and seminars on design and production problems; plant tours; awards AIGA Medal for distinguished contributions to the graphic arts; originate traveling exhibitions

O **AMERICAN INTERNATIONAL SCULPTORS SYMPOSIUMS, INC,*** 799 Greenwich St, New York, NY 10014. Tel 212-242-3374. *Pres & Executive Dir* Verna Gillis; *VPres* Bradford Graves; *Secy* Benay Rubenstein
Estab 1971 to promote art in public places
Income: $45,000 (financed by state appropriation and NEA-corporate support)
Publications: Poem cards
Activities: Lect, 10 visiting lectr per year; Poetry in Public Places, placement of poem cards in buses throughout New York; competitions; awards; originate traveling exhibitions; sales shop sells slides and poem cards

O **AMERICAN NUMISMATIC ASSOCIATION,** 818 N Cascade, Colorado Springs, CO 80903. Tel 303-473-9142. *Pres* George D Hatie; *Exec VPres* Edward C Rochette; *Asst to Exec VPres & Acting Mus Cur* Kenneth L Hallenbeck; *Asst to Exec VPres* Ruthann Brettell
Open Mon - Fri 10 AM - 5 PM. No admis fee. Estab 1891 as an international organization to promote numismatics as a means of recording history. Maintains a museum and library; seven galleries display numismatic material from paper money through coins and art medals. Average Annual Attendance: 3000. Mem: 34,000 to qualify for membership, a person must be at least eleven years of age and interested in coin collecting; dues $15 plus one-time initiation fee of $5; annual meeting second or third week of August
Income: $500,000 - $1,000,000 (financed by endowment, donations and miscellaneous sources)
Collections: Robert T Herdegen Memorial Collection of Coins of the World; Norman H Liebman Collection of Abraham Lincoln on Paper Money; Elliott Markoff Collection of Presidential Memorabilia; several other collections from donations by members
Exhibitions: Three galleries open to the public during the year with permanent exhibits. Colonial Gallery exhibiting coins of the American Colonial period. Americana Galleries exhibiting United States coins, 1792 to date. Gallery of Modern Medallic Art exhibiting contemporary medals
Publications: The Numismatist, monthly
Activities: Classes for adults and children; annual seminar on campus of Colorado College, Colorado Springs; lect open to public, 6 visiting lectr per year; tours; sponsors National Coin Week third week in April when members throughout the United States promote their avocations through exhibits in local areas; awards given; scholarships; sales shop selling books, magazines, slides, medals and souvenir jewelry
L **Library,** 80903. *Librn* Nancy W Stith
Open Mon - Fri 10 AM - 5 PM. Estab 1891 to provide research materials to the members of the Association and the general public. Circ 4500. Open to the public for reference; lending restricted to members
Library Holdings: Vols 7500; Per subs 100; Micro—Reels; AV—Motion pictures, slides; Other—Clipping files

O **AMERICAN NUMISMATIC SOCIETY,** Broadway at 155th St, New York, NY 10032. Tel 212-234-3130. *Pres* Harry W Bass Jr; *VPres* Harry W Fowler; *Dir & Secy* Leslie A Elam; *Chief Cur* William E Metcalf
Open Tues - Sat 9 AM - 4:30 PM, Sun 1 - 4 PM, cl Mon. No admis fee. Estab 1858 as an international organization for the advancement of numismatic knowledge. Maintains museum and library; two exhibition halls, one devoted to medals and decorations, the other to money in early America. Average Annual Attendance: 15,000. Mem: 1902; dues assoc $15; annual meeting second Sat in January
Income: Financed by endowment
Collections: Universal numismatics
Publications: Numismatic Literature, semi-annually; MuseumNotes, annually
Activities: Lect open to public, 2 visiting lectr per year; scholarships
L **Library,** Broadway at 155th St, 10032. *Librn* Francis D Campbell Jr
Open to the public
Library Holdings: Vols 50,000; Per subs 300; AV—Slides; Other—Manuscripts, auction catalogs

O **AMERICAN RED CROSS,** 17th & D Sts NW, Washington, DC 20006. Tel 202-737-8300. *Pres* George M Elsey
Open Mon - Fri 8:30 AM - 4:45 PM. No admis fee. Estab 1881 to improve the quality of human life and enhance individual self-reliance and concern for others. International-Intercultural Art Exchange Program designed to foster human understanding through the arts by providing children and youth the opportunity to share art education and social service experiences with young people in the United States and in countries served by other Red Cross societies
Income: Financed mostly by public contributions
Collections: Oil and Poster Paintings
Activities: Occasionally sponsors art competitions by youth

O **AMERICAN SOCIETY FOR AESTHETICS,** c/o Arnold Berleant, C W Post Center of Long Island Univ, Greenvale, NY 11548. Tel 203-485-3016. *Pres* Rudolf Arnheim; *Journal Ed* John J Fisher
Estab 1942 for the advancement of philosophical and scientific study of the arts and related fields
Publications: Journal of Aesthetics and Art Criticism, quarterly

O **AMERICAN SOCIETY OF ARTISTS, INC,** 1297 Merchandise Mart Plaza, Chicago, IL 60654. Tel 312-751-2500. *Pres* Nancy J Fregin; *VPres* Helen DelValle; *Secy* Arnold Jackson; *American Artisans Dir* Judy A EdBorg; *Festivals Committee Dir* Kathy Chan Barnes; *Dir Lecture & Demonstration Service* Charles J Gruner; *Special Arts Services Dir* Patricia E Nolan
Estab 1972, membership organization of professional artists - American Artisans Division is professional craftspeople. Showroom for stores, shops, designers, and galleries contain original art work by American member artists and artisans. Mem: 600; qualifications for mem, must have work juried and pass jury to be accepted; dues $40, plus one initiation fee of $10
Income: Financed by membership
Exhibitions: Approximately 15 indoor and outdoor juried shows per year
Publications: Art Lovers' Art and Craft Fair Bulletin, quarterly; Members' Bulletin, quarterly
Activities: Lect and Demonstration Service; lect; lending collection contains photographs and slides of members works

L **Library**, 1297 Merchandise Mart Plaza, 60654. *Librn* Don Metcoff
Estab 1978 to provide reference material for member artists. For members only
Library Holdings: Per subs 8; AV—Lantern Slides; Other—Photographs
Special Subjects: Art and craft supplies, exhibition and gallery information

O **AMERICAN SOCIETY OF BOOKPLATE COLLECTORS AND DESIGNERS,** 1206 N Stoneman Ave, 15, Alhambra, CA 91801. Tel 213-283-1936. *Dir & Ed* Audrey Spencer Arellanes
Estab 1922 as an international organization to foster an interest in the art of the bookplate through the publication of a yearbook, and to encourage friendship and a greater knowledge of bookplates among members by an exchange membership list. Mem: 200 who are interested in bookplates as either a collector or artist, of just an interest in bookplates and graphic arts; dues $27.50 which includes yearbook and quarterly newsletter
Income: Financed by membership
Publications: Bookplates in the News, quarterly newsletter; Yearbook, annually
Activities: Lect given upon request; contributes bookplates to the Prints and Photographs Division of the Library of Congress and furnishes them with copies of Newsletter and Yearbook; originate traveling exhibitions

O **AMERICAN SOCIETY OF CONTEMPORARY ARTISTS,** c/o Harold M LeRoy, 1916 Ave K, Brooklyn, NY 11230. *Pres* Harold M LeRoy
Estab 1917. Mem: 130 elected on basis of high level of professional distinction; annual meeting Apr
Exhibitions: 60th & 61st annual at National Arts Club; 62nd annual at Salmagundi Club; exhibitions at Lever House Gallery and US Customhouse Museum
Activities: Demonstrations of graphic technique, watercolor, oil and sculpture; citations to individuals dedicated to arts

O **AMERICAN WATERCOLOR SOCIETY,** 1083 Fifth Ave, New York, NY 10028. Tel 212-876-6622. *Pres* Mario Cooper; *VPres* Samuel Leitman; *Second VPres* William Strosahl; *Corresp Secy* Janet Walsh; *Treas* Elsie Ject-Key; *Recording Secy* Mina Kocherthaler
Open during exhibitions 1 - 5 PM, cl Mon. Estab 1866 as a national organization to foster the advancement of the art of watercolor painting and to further the interests of painters in watercolor throughout the United States; rests the National Academy Galleries for four weeks each year for annual exhibition. Average Annual Attendance: 1200. Mem: Approx 550; to qualify for membership, an artist must exhibit in three annuals within past ten years, then submit application to membership chairman; dues $20; annual meeting in April
Income: Financed by membership
Publications: AWS Newsletter, semi-annually; exhibition catalog
Activities: Demonstrations during annual exhibitions; awards given at annual exhibitions (approx $15,000 in 1980); originate traveling exhibitions

O **ARCHAEOLOGICAL INSTITUTE OF AMERICA,** 53 Park Place, Room 802, New York, NY 10007. Tel 212-732-6677. *Pres* Robert H Dyson Jr; *VPres* Machteld Mellink; *Exec Dir* Eugene L Sterud; *Exec Assts* Carol Smallman; *Exec Assts* James G Hamilton Jr
Estab 1879 as an international organization concerned with two major areas of responsibility: facilitating archaeological research and disseminating the results to the public. Mem: 7445 consisting of professionals and laypersons interested in archaeology; dues $25; annual meeting Dec 27-30
Income: Financed by endowment and membership
Publications: Archaeology Magazine, bimonthly; American Journal of Archaeology, quarterly
Activities: Lect open to the public, 270 visiting lectr per year; annual award given for distinguished archaeological achievement; one or more fellowships awarded for an academic year

O **ART DEALERS ASSOCIATION OF AMERICA, INC,** 575 Madison Ave, New York, NY 10022. Tel 212-940-8590. *Pres* Leo Castelli; *VPres* Norman Hirschl; *VPres* William Acquavella; *Secy* Gilbert S Edelson; *Admin VPres & Counsel* Ralph F Colin
Estab 1962 as a national organization to improve the stature and status of the art-dealing profession. Mem: 110, membership by invitation
Income: Financed by membership
Publications: Activities and Membership Roster
Activities: Gives ADA Award for Excellence in Art History; appraisal service for donors contributing works of art to nonprofit institutions; international art theft service including monthly publication of notices

O **ART DIRECTORS CLUB, INC,** 488 Madison Ave, New York, NY 10022. Tel 212-838-8140. *Pres* William Taubin; *VPres* Walter Kaprielian; *Secy* Blanche Florenza; *Exec Dir* Diane Herzman
Estab 1920 as an international organization to protect, promote and elevate the standards of practice of the profession of art directing. Owns gallery. Mem: 620, criteria for membership: qualified art director, at least 21 years of age, of good character and at least two years of practical experience in creating and directing in the visual communication of graphic arts industry. Dues regular $150, nonresident $75, junior $25
Income: Financed by membership
Exhibitions: Art Directors' Annual Exhibition of Advertising, Editorial and Television Art and Design. Bimonthly shows conceived to provide a showcase for works and ideas not readily viewed otherwise. They cover new art, design, lettering and graphics by illustrators, alumni art directors, ad agencies and individuals
Publications: The Art Directors Annual; Newsletter, bimonthly
Activities: Portfolio Review Programs; seminars; lect open to public; gallery talks; annual exhibition with Gold & Silver Medals, Gold, Silver and Distinctive Merit Certificates; scholarships; originate traveling exhibitions
L **Library,** 488 Madison Ave, 10022.
Open to the public for reference
Library Holdings: Vols 58

O **ARTISTS EQUITY ASSOCIATION, INC,** 3726 Albemarle St NW, Washington, DC 20016. Tel 202-244-0209. *Pres* Michael Gast; *Secy* George Koch; *Exec Dir* Gail Rasmussen
Estab 1947 as a national nonprofit, aesthetically nonpartisan organization working for social, economic and legislative change for all artists. Mem: 3500 who have given evidence of professional status; dues $20 and $30; annual meeting
Income: $50,000 (financed by membership and grants)
Publications: AEA News, quarterly; Legislative Update, bimonthly
Activities: Lect open to the public at annual meeting only; chapter occasionally organize and circulate traveling exhibitions

O **ARTISTS' FELLOWSHIP, INC,** 47 Fifth Ave, New York, NY 10003. *Pres* Michael Engel II; *VPres* Arthur Harrow; *Treas* John R McCarthy; *Correspondence Secy* Robert J Riedinger; *Recording Secy* Sidney H Hermel; *Historian* Russell Rypsam
Estab 1859, reorganized 1889 as Artists' Aid Society, incorporated 1925 as Artists' Fellowship, Inc; to aid artists in need because of death, illness or financial reverses. Controls an endowed bed in Columbia. Mem: 200; annual meeting Dec
Activities: Presbyterian Hospital awards the Gari Melchers Gold Medal for distinguished service to the arts, and Benjamin West Clinedinst Memorial Medal for outstanding achievement in the arts

O **ARTISTS GUILD INC OF NEW YORK,** 25 W 36th St, New York, NY 10018. Tel 212-239-1348. *Chmn* John Josephs; *Pres* Dean Powell; *Secy* Joan De Katch; *Treas* Thomas Connolly
Estab 1920 as a national organization to help establish better business relations between the buyers and sellers of art; charter member of Joint Ethics Committee formed in 1945. Mem: 200 - 300; membership open to professional commercial and fine artists, salaried or free-lance; dues active $25, assoc $15, nonresident $15, student $15
Income: Financed by membership
Activities: Artist of the Year Award given yearly since 1960

O **ART LIBRARIES SOCIETY-NORTH AMERICA,** 143 Bowling Green Place, Iowa City, IA 52240. Tel 319-351-2078. *Chmn of Board* Wolfgang Frietag; *Executive Secy* Pamela Jeffcott Parry
Open 8 AM - 5 PM, cl Sat & Sun. Estab 1972 to promote the profession of art librarians in the country. Mem: 1000; qualification for mem degree in art librarianship or related courses; dues $25; annual meeting Jan
Income: Financed by membership
Publications: Newsletter, 5 per year

O **ASSOCIATION OF AMERICAN EDITORIAL CARTOONISTS,** c/o Jim Lange, 500 N Broadway, Oklahoma City, OK 73125. *Pres* Bob Taylor; *VPres* Sandy Campbell; *Secy & Treas* Jim Lange
Estab 1957 by John Stampone of the Army Times, Washington, DC, as an international organization of professional editorial cartoonists for newspapers and newspaper syndicates. Mem: 225; to qualify for membership, an editorial cartoonists must produce at least three editorial cartoons per week for publication; dues $25
Income: Financed by membership
Exhibitions: University of Southern Mississippi Touring Exhibition of Association's editorial cartoons
Publications: Notebook, AAEC news magazine; Best Editorial Cartoons of the Year

O **ASSOCIATION OF ART MUSEUM DIRECTORS,** PO Box 10082, Savannah, GA 31402. *Executive Secy* Millicent Hall Gaudieri
Estab 1916. Mem: 118; meets twice a year for discussion of the work of art museum executives
Publications: Conference Proceedings; Professional Practices in Art Museums

O **ASSOCIATION OF COLLEGIATE SCHOOLS OF ARCHITECTURE,** 1735 New York Ave NW, Washington, DC 20006. Tel 202-785-2324. *Pres* R Burns; *VPres* R Peters; *Secy* A Vernez-Moudon; *Treas* E Kremer; *Exec Dir* R Schluntz; *Asst Dir & Journal Managing Ed* J Chusid; *Office Mgr* M Colin
Open daily 9 AM - 5 PM. No admis fee. Estab 1912 as an international organization furthering the advancement of architectural education. Mem: 3400 faculty members; membership open to schools (and their faculty) which offer professional degrees in architecture; school dues $650-$900; annual meeting in April
Income: $400,000 (financed by endowment, membership, state appropriation and grants)
Publications: ACSA News, 6 times per year; Journal of Architectural Education, quarterly; Annual Meeting Proceedings; Architecture Schools in North America, biennially
Activities: Educational seminars; institutes; publications; services to member schools; sponsor competitions; awards; sales shop selling books and magazines

O **ASSOCIATION OF MEDICAL ILLUSTRATORS,** 5820 Wilshire Blvd, Suite 500, Los Angeles, CA 90036. Tel 213-937-5514. *Pres* Ruth Wakerlin; *Chmn of Board* Alan Cole; *Corresp Secy* Barbara Rankin; *Exec Dir* Jean Replogle
Estab 1945 as an international organization to encourage the advancement of medical illustration and allied fields of visual education; to promote understanding and cooperation with the medical and related professions. Mem: 514; dues active $75; annual meeting Oct
Income: Financed by membership
Exhibitions: Members' work is exhibited at annual meeting
Publications: Journal of Biocommunications, 3 times per year; Medical Illustration, brochure; Newsletter, 6 times per year
Activities: Individual members throughout the world give lectures on the profession; awards given for artistic achievements submitted to salon each year; scholarships to members of AMI accredited schools only; originate traveling exhibition

O **AUDUBON ARTISTS, INC,** 225 W 34th St, New York, NY 10001. Tel 212-759-2164. *Pres* Renee McKay; *VPres* Howard Mandel; *Secy* Mervin Honig
Open during annual exhibition. Admis 50¢. Estab 1944 as a national organization for the presentation of annual exhibitions in all media, oil, acrylics, watercolors, graphics, sculpture; open to nonmembers. Gallery not maintained; exhibitions held at the National Art Club. Average Annual Attendance: 1350 during three weeks of exhibition. Mem: 400; membership by invitation; dues $20; annual meeting April
Income: $15,000 (financed by membership and exhibition admission)

Exhibitions: Annual exhibition lasting three weeks
Publications: Illustrated catalog
Activities: Demonstrations in all media; medals and $4000 in cash prizes

O **COLLEGE ART ASSOCIATION OF AMERICA,** 16 E 52nd St, New York, NY 10022. Tel 212-755-3532. *Pres* Joshua C Taylor; *VPres* Lucy Freeman Sandler; *Secy* John Rupert Martin; *Exec Secy* Rose R Weil
Estab 1912 as a national organization to further scholarship and excellence in the teaching and practice of art and art history. Average Annual Attendance: 5000 at annual meeting. Mem: 9200; open to all individuals and institutions interested in the purposes of the Association; dues life $1000, institution $50, individual $30-$40 (scaled to salary), student $17.50; annual meeting end of Jan or beginning of Feb
Income: Financed by membership
Publications: Art Bulletin, quarterly; Art Journal, quarterly; CAA Newsletter, 4-5 times per year
Activities: Awards: Distinguished Teaching of Art History Award; Distinguished Teaching of Art Award; Charles Rufus Morey Book Award; Frank Jewett Mather Award for Distinction in Art and Architectural Criticism; Arthur Kingsley Porter Prize for Best Article by Younger Scholar in The Art Bulletin

O **COUNCIL OF AMERICAN ARTIST SOCIETIES,** 215 Park Ave S, New York, NY 10003. Tel 212-475-6650. *Pres* Frank C Wright; *First VPres* Donald DeLue; *Treas & Gen Counsel* John S Dole; *Recording Secy* Florence Whitehill
Estab 1962, a national, tax-free, nonprofit incorporated educational council to educate, motivate and protect art and artists; to further traditional art at the highest esthetic level; policies and management controlled by artists. Mem: 100 societies; no dues; annual meeting in May
Income: Financed by endowment
Publications: Annual Report; monographs
Activities: Presents awards to art organizations; awards and citations for excellence in art; medals and awards; provides some scholarships

O **THE DRAWING SOCIETY,** 41 East 65th St, New York, NY 10021. Tel 212-861-8162. *Pres* Paul Cummings; *VPres* Wilder Green
Estab 1959 to encourage interest in, and understanding of drawing of all periods and cultures. Mem: Dues $100 and up for patrons, institutional $75, associate $25
Publications: Books and catalogues; Drawing, bi-monthly

O **FEDERATION OF MODERN PAINTERS AND SCULPTORS,** * 340 W 72nd St, New York, NY 10023. Tel 212-787-1948. *Pres* Ahmet Gursoy; *VPres* Theo Hios; *VPres* Barbara Krashes; *VPres* Louise Nevelson; *Secy* Elisabeth Model
Estab 1940 as a national organization to promote the cultural interests of free progressive artists working in the United States. Mem: 70; selected by membership committee; dues $10; meeting every two months
Income: Financed by membership and New York State Council on the Arts
Exhibitions: 35th Annual Exhibition traveling in New York State
Activities: Lect open to public, 1 - 2 visiting lectrs per year; originate traveling exhibitions

O **GENERAL SERVICES ADMINISTRATION,** * Public Bldgs Service Fine Arts Program, F St between 18th & 19th NW, Washington, DC 20405. Tel 202-472-1891. *Dir Fine Arts Program* Donald W Thalacker
The Fine Arts Program office directs the work of artists commissioned to design and execute sculpture, murals, tapestries and other art work incorporated as part of the design of new Federal Buildings, except Post Offices and Veterans Administration Buildings. The scope of work is determined by the size and character of the building with allowances up to .5 percent of the estimated construction cost. Artists are commissioned by direct selection by agency upon recommendation by a panel of distinguished art professionals appointed by the National Endowment for the Arts and the Architect for the building
Income: $1,000,000

O **GUILD OF BOOK WORKERS,** 663 Fifth Ave, New York, NY 10022. Tel 212-757-6454. *Pres* Mary C Schlosser; *VPres* Jeanne F Lewisohn; *Secy* Diane C Burke
Estab 1906 as a national organization to establish and maintain a feeling of kinship and mutual interest among workers in the several hand book crafts. Mem: 350; membership open to all interested persons; dues New York City area $50, national $30; annual meeting May or June
Income: Financed by membership
Exhibitions: Held every two or three years; hand bookbinding; calligraphy; decorated papers
Publications: Guild of Book Workers Journal, 2 times per year; Membership List, annually; Newsletter, quarterly; Supply List, biennially; Opportunities for Study in Hand Bookbinding and Calligraphy, directory and supplement
Activities: 2 - 4 lect annually, some open to public and some for members only
L **Library,** c/o Boston Athenaeum, 10 1/2 Beacon St, Boston, MA 02108. *Librn* Stanley E Cushing
Open to Guild members for lending and reference; by appointment to others
Library Holdings: Vols 500
Special Subjects: Related to the hand book crafts

O **INDUSTRIAL DESIGNERS SOCIETY OF AMERICA,** 1717 N St NW, Washington, DC 20036. Tel 202-466-2927. *Pres* Carroll M Gantz; *Exec VPres* Paul Specht; *Secy-Treas* Wallace H Appel; *Exec Dir* Brian J Wynne
Open daily 8 AM - 5 PM. No admis fee. Estab and incorporated 1965 as a nonprofit national organization representing the profession of industrial design. Mem: 1600; dues full, assoc, affiliate, sustaining and student from $25 to $125; annual meeting Oct 1-4, 1980
Publications: IDSA Newsletter, monthly; Membership Directory; other surveys and studies
Activities: IDSA Student Chapters; IDSA Student Merit Awards; lect; competitions

O **INTERMUSEUM CONSERVATION ASSOCIATION,** Allen Art Bldg, Oberlin, OH 44074. Tel 216-775-7331. *Pres* Budd Bishop; *VPres* Bruce Evans; *Secy-Treas & Dir* Thorn Gantle; *Admin & Cur Asst* Ricardo Barreto
Estab 1952 as a non-profit conservation laboratory to aid in the maintenance of the collections of its member museums. Not open to public. Mem: 18; must be a nonprofit cultural institution

O **INTERNATIONAL COUNCIL OF MUSEUMS COMMITTEE OF THE AMERICAN ASSOCIATION OF MUSEUMS,** 1055 Thomas Jefferson St NW, Washington, DC 20007. Tel 212-338-5300. *Prog Coordr* Maria Papageorge
Open 9 AM - 5 PM. No admis fee. Estab 1973, the AAM represents international museum interests within the United States through the AAM-ICOM office which disseminates information on international conferences, publications, travel and study grants and training programs. The AAM-ICOM office also maintains an international network of museum contacts around the world. Mem: 900; members must be museum professionals or institutions holding membership in the American Association of Museums
Income: Financed by membership
Publications: AAM-ICOM Newsletter, quarterly; ICOM News, quarterly
Activities: Specialty committees; serves as liaison for the organization and circulation of traveling exhibitions

O **INTERNATIONAL FOUNDATION FOR ART RESEARCH, INC,** 46 E 70th St, New York, NY 10021. Tel 212-879-1780. *Pres* Edwin L Weisl Jr; *Executive Dir* Bonnie Burnham; *Research Assoc, Art Theft Archive* Mary Ellen Guerra; *Research Assoc, Authentication Service* Virgilia Pancoast
Open Mon - Fri 9:30 AM - 5 PM. Estab 1968 to provide a framework for impartial consideration by experts of questions concerning attribution and authenticity of major works of art; expanded in 1975 to include an Art Theft Archive for collection and cataloguing of information on art theft
Income: Financed by donations, memberships and fees
Publications: Art Theft, Its Scope, Its Impact and Its Control; IFAR Bulletin; Stolen Art Alert; Stolen Art Alert Annual
Activities: Authentication Service. The Foundation examines art objects in order to resolve questions of authenticity and proper attribution. The Foundation accepts works of art in all media for study. Its examinations include complete laboratory tests and stylistic examination by leading scholars or experts in the field. A written report of the experts' conclusions is issued to the owner in the name of the Foundation. Fees range from $200 for a preliminary opinion to $500 - $1000 for a full-scale technical and stylistic examination. Funds are available to museums for IFAR authentications through the New York State Council for the Arts and the National Endowment for the Arts.
Art Theft Archive. A research program of the Foundation, the Art Theft Archive is devoted to collecting and cataloguing records of art thefts, and providing information on stolen objects to individuals, institutions, government agencies, and others in order to prevent the circulation of stolen art and aid in its recovery. The Archive contains reports from a wide range of domestic and international sources. Stolen art reports are published free of charge in its monthly Stolen Art Alert and its Stolen Art Alert Annual. A comprehensive report on the problem of art theft, entitled Art Theft, Its Scope, Its Impact, and Its Control, is a report that includes museum and dealer surveys, international statistics, and an evaluation of the legal context of the problem.
Collection Cataloguing and Research. At the request of collectors or institutions, IFAR will provide cataloguing and inventory system, and create written, automated, and visual records of the collection. Fees on a per-diem basis; estimates free of charge

O **INTER-SOCIETY COLOR COUNCIL,** c/o Dr Fred W Billmeyer Jr, Rensselaer Polytechnic Institute, Troy, NY 12181. Tel 518-270-6458. *Pres* William D Schaeffer; *Secy* Dr Fred W Billmeyer Jr
Estab 1931 as a national organization to stimulate and coordinate the study of color in science, art and industry. Mem: 850; members must show an interest in color and in the aims and purposes of the Council; dues $15; annual meeting usually in April
Income: $10,000 (financed by membership)
Publications: Inter-Society Color Council Newsletter, bimonthly
Activities: Lect open to public; lect at meetings; gives Macbeth Award and Godlove Award

O **KAPPA PI INTERNATIONAL HONORARY ART FRATERNITY,** PO Box 7843, Midfield, Birmingham, AL 35228. Tel 205-428-4540. *Pres* Garnet R Leader; *VPres* Dr Ralph M Hudson; *Secy* Elmer J Porter; *Treas* Myrtle Kerr; *Ed* Arthur Kennon
Estab 1911 as an international honorary art fraternity for men and women in colleges, universities and art schools
Income: Financed by membership
Publications: Bulletin, annually in the fall; Sketch Book, annual spring magazine
Activities: Sponsors competition in photography; annual scholarships available to active members
Alpha, University of Kentucky, Lexington, KY 40506.
Theta, Birmingham Southern College, Birmingham, AL 35204.
Iota, Iowa Wesleyan College, Mount Pleasant, IA 52641.
Kappa, Lindenwood College, Saint Charles, MO 63301.
Lambda, Oklahoma City University, Oklahoma City, OK 73106.
Mu, Western New Mexico University, Silver City, NM 88061.
Nu, Fort Hays State College, Hays, KS 67601.
Xi, University of Montevallo, Montevallo, AL 35115.
Omicron, Western Montana College, Dillon, MT 69725.
Pi, University of Georgia, Athens, GA 30602.
Rho, Mississippi University for Women, Columbus, MS 39701.
Sigma, Huntingdon College, Montgomery, AL 36106.
Phi, Central State University, Edmond, OK 73034.
Chi, Eastern Illinois University, Charleston, IL 61920.
Psi, Southern Illinois University, Carbondale, IL 62901.
Omega, Indiana State University, Terre Haute, IN 47809.
Alpha Alpha, Samford University, Birmingham, AL 35209.
Alpha Beta, Central Washington State College, Ellensburg, WA 98926.
Alpha Delta, University of Arkansas, Fayetteville, AR 72701.
Alpha Epsilon, Mary Hardin Baylor College, Belton, TX 76513.
Alpha Eta, Florida Southern College, Lakeland, FL 33802.

Alpha Theta, Winthrop College, Rock Hill, SC 29733.
Alpha Iota, DePauw University, Greencastle, IN 46135.
Alpha Kappa, Baylor University, Waco, TX 76703.
Alpha Lambda, Sam Houston State University, Huntsville, TX 77340.
Alpha Mu, University of Minnesota, Duluth, MN 55812.
Alpha Xi, Kansas Wesleyan University, Salina, KS 67401.
Alpha Omicron, Georgetown College, Georgetown, KY 40324.
Alpha Pi, Southwest Texas State University, San Marcos, TX 78666.
Alpha Rho, Brenau College, Gainesville, GA 30501.
Alpha Sigma, Our Lady of the Lake University, San Antonio, TX 78207.
Alpha Tau, John B Stetson University, DeLand, FL 32720.
Alpha Upsilon, Winona State University, Winona, MN 55987.
Alpha Chi, Black Hills State College, Spearfish, SD 57783.
Alpha Psi, University of South Carolina, Columbia, SC 29208.
Alpha Omega, Wichita State University, Wichita, KS 67208.
Alpha Alpha Alpha, Oregon College of Education, Monmouth, OR 97361.
Alpha Alpha Beta, Oklahoma Baptist University, Shawnee, OK 74801.
Alpha Alpha Delta, Western State College, Gunnison, CO 81230.
Alpha Alpha Epsilon, Southwestern College, Winfield, KS 67156.
Alpha Alpha Zeta, Carthage College, Kenosha, WI 53140.
Alpha Alpha Eta, University of Southern California, Los Angeles, CA 90007.
Alpha Alpha Theta, University of Tampa, Tampa, FL 33606.
Alpha Alpha Iota, University of Miami, Coral Gables, FL 33124.
Alpha Alpha Kappa, Arkansas State University, Jonesboro, AR 72467.
Alpha Alpha Lambda, Southwestern Oklahoma State University, Weatherford, OK 73096.
Alpha Alpha Mu, Eastern Washington State College, Cheney, WA 99004.
Alpha Alpha Nu, University of Texas at El Paso, El Paso, TX 79968.
Alpha Alpha Xi, Phillips University, Enid, OK 73701.
Alpha Alpha Omicron, Eastern New Mexico University, Portales, NM 88130.
Alpha Alpha Pi, Oregon State University, Corvallis, OR 97331.
Alpha Alpha Rho, University of Southern Mississippi, Hattiesburg, MS 39401.
Alpha Alpha Sigma, New Mexico Highlands University, Las Vegas, NM 87701.
Alpha Alpha Tau, West Liberty State College, West Liberty, WV 26074.
Alpha Alpha Upsilon, St Cloud State University, Saint Cloud, MN 56301.
Alpha Alpha Phi, University of North Carolina, Chapel Hill, NC 27514.
Alpha Alpha Chi, Murray State University, Murray, KY 42071.
Alpha Alpha Psi, Eastern Kentucky University, Richmond, KY 40475.
Beta Beta, Kearney State College, Kearney, NE 68847.
Beta Gamma, Southeast Missouri State University, Cape Girardeau, MO 63701.
Beta Delta, University of Alabama, University, AL 35486.
Beta Epsilon, North Texas State University, Denton, TX 76203.
Beta Zeta, Heidelberg College, Tiffin, OH 44883.
Beta Theta, Wayne State College, Wayne, NE 68787.
Beta Iota, Stephen F Austin State University, Nacogdoches, TX 75961.
Beta Kappa, Queen's College of the City University of New York, Flushing, NY 11367.
Beta Lambda, Hofstra University, Hempstead, NY 11550.
Beta Mu, Frostburg State College, Frostburg, MD 21532.
Beta Nu, Hunter College of the City University of New York, New York, NY 10021.
Beta Xi, University of Evansville, Evansville, IN 47702.
Beta Omicron, Lewis and Clark College, Portland, OR 97219.
Beta Pi, West Texas State University, Canyon, TX 79016.
Beta Rho, University of Northern Iowa, Cedar Falls, IA 50613.
Beta Sigma, Drew University, Madison, NJ 07940.
Beta Tau, Lamar University, Beaumont, TX 77710.
Beta Upsilon, Harris Teachers College, Saint Louis, MO 63103.
Beta Phi, Texas Wesleyan College, Fort Worth, TX 76105.
Beta Chi, Hardin-Simmons University, Abilene, TX 79601.
Beta Psi, Concord College, Athens, WV 24712.
Beta Omega, Seattle Pacific College, Seattle, WA 98119.
Gamma Alpha, Northwest Missouri State University, Maryville, MO 64468.
Gamma Beta, Fairmont State College, Fairmont, WV 26554.
Gamma Gamma, Union College, Barbourville, KY 40906.
Gamma Delta, University of Wisconsin, Eau Claire, 54701.
Gamma Epsilon, University of Houston, Houston, TX 77004.
Gamma Zeta, Hastings College, Hastings, NE 68901.
Gamma Eta, Chadron State College, Chadron, NE 69337.
Gamma Theta, Montclair State College, Upper Montclair, NJ 07043.
Gamma Iota, Eastern Oregon College, LaGrande, OR 97850.
Gamma Kappa, James Madison University, Harrisonburg, VA 22801.
Gamma Lambda, Abilene Christian University, Abilene, TX 79601.
Gamma Mu, Northwestern State University, Natchitoches, LA 71457.
Gamma Nu, University of Southwestern Louisiana, Lafayette, LA 70504.
Gamma Xi, Louisiana College, Pineville, LA 71360.
Gamma Omicron, Centenary College of Louisiana, Shreveport, LA 71104.
Gamma Pi, Western Kentucky University, Bowling Green, KY 42101.
Gamma Rho, Northwestern Oklahoma State University, Alva, OK 73717.
Gamma Sigma, Adelphi University, Garden City, NY 11530.
Gamma Tau, California State University, Los Angeles, CA 90032.
Gamma Upsilon, University of Alaska, Fairbanks, AK 99506.
Gamma Phi, National Photographic, Box 7843, Midfield, Birmingham, AL 35228.
Gamma Chi, Alaska Methodist University, Anchorage, AK 99504.
Gamma Psi, San Diego State University, San Diego, CA 92812.
Gamma Omega, West Virginia Wesleyan College, Buckhannon, WV 26201.
Delta Alpha, Northeast Louisiana University, Monroe, LA 71201.
Delta Beta, Mississippi College, Clinton, MS 39058.
Delta Gamma, Mankato State University, Mankato, MN 56001.
Delta Delta, Western Illinois University, Macomb, IL 61455.
Delta Epsilon, University of Bridgeport, Bridgeport, CT 06602.
Delta Zeta, State University of New York College at New Paltz, New Paltz, NY 12561.
Delta Eta, Northern Montana College, Havre, MT 59501.
Delta Iota, Morehead State University, Morehead, KY 40351.

Delta Kappa, University of the Philippines, Quezon City, PHILIPPINES.
Delta Lambda, Delta State University, Cleveland, MS 38732.
Delta Mu, University of North Alabama, Florence, AL 35630.
Delta Nu, Belhaven College, Jackson, MS 39202.
Delta Xi, Arkansas Tech University, Russellville, AR 72801.
Delta Omicron, Long Island University, C W Post Center, Greenvale, NY 11548.
Delta Pi, University of North Carolina, Asheville, NC 28801.
Delta Rho, Ottawa University, Ottawa, KS 66067.
Delta Sigma, Keuka College, Keuka Park, NY 14478.
Delta Tau, Alabama State University, Montgomery, AL 36101.
Delta Upsilon, Troy State University, Troy, AL 36081.
Delta Phi, College of Mount Saint Vincent, Riverdale, NY 10471.
Delta Chi, California State University, Fullerton, CA 92634.
Delta Psi, Waynesburg College, Waynesburg, PA 15370.
Delta Omega, Louisiana Tech University, Rushton, LA 71270.
Epsilon Alpha, Baldwin-Wallace College, Berea, OH 44012.
Epsilon Gamma, Middle Tennessee State University, Murfreesboro, TN 37130.
Epsilon Delta, Minot State College, Minot, ND 58701.
Epsilon Zeta, Dickinson State College, Dickinson, ND 58601.
Epsilon Eta, University of Central Arkansas, Conway, AR 72032.
Epsilon Theta, McMurray College, Abilene, TX 79605.
Epsilon Iota, Harding College, Searcy, AR 72143.
Epsilon Kappa, Montreat-Anderson College, Montreat, NC 28757.
Epsilon Lambda, University of Wyoming, Laramie, WY 82071.
Epsilon Mu, Boise State University, Boise, ID 83725.
Epsilon Xi, John F Kennedy College, Wahoo, NE 68066.
Epsilon Omicron, Herbert H Lehman College of the City University of New York, Bronx, NY 10468.
Epsilon Pi, Carson Newman College, Jefferson City, TN 37760.
Epsilon Rho, Friends University, Wichita, KS 67213.
Epsilon Sigma, Ohio Northern University, Ada, OH 45810.
Epsilon Tau, University of Alabama in Huntsville, Huntsville, AL 35807.
Epsilon Upsilon, Saint Mary's College, Saint Mary's City, MD 20686.
Epsilon Phi, Mississippi State University, Mississippi State, MS 39762.
Epsilon Chi, Bethany College, Bethany, WV 26032.
Epsilon Psi, University of Mississippi, University, MS 38677.
Epsilon Omega, Instituto Allende, San Miguel de Allende GTO, MEXICO.
Zeta Alpha, Austin College, Sherman, TX 75090.
Zeta Beta, Annhurst College, Woodstock, CT 06281.
Zeta Gamma, Union University, Jackson, TN 38301.
Zeta Delta, Oklahoma Christian College, Oklahoma City, OK 73111.
Zeta Epsilon, Brescia College, Owensboro, KY 42301.
Zeta Zeta, University of Texas, Austin, TX 78712.
Zeta Eta, Kilgore College, Kilgore, TX 75662.
Zeta Theta, Bellevue College, Bellevue, NE 68005.
Zeta Iota, Meridian Junior College, Meridian, MS 39301.

O **MID-AMERICA ARTS ALLIANCE**, Suite 550, 20 W Ninth St, Kansas City, MO 64105. Tel 816-421-1388. *Chmn* James C Olson; *Vice Chmn* Mary De Hahn; *Secy* Marion Andersen; *Executive Dir* Henry Moran; *Dir Programs, Planning and Services* Robert Pierle; *General Mgr* Will Conner; *Visual Arts Coordr* David Smith
Estab 1973 to coordinate touring arts events and services (performing and visual arts), for people of Arkansas, Kansas, Missouri, Nebraska and Oklahoma. Average Annual Attendance: 600,000
Income: $1,800,000 (financed by federal and state grants, private contributions and sponsorship fees)
Exhibitions: American Abstraction; Thomas Hart Bentons' Illustrations from Mark Twain; Daisy Cook Remembers; Crying for a Vision; Goin' to Kansas City; Magic Carpets; Masters of American Watercolor; Native American Paintings; State of the Print; Things Seen; Twelve Photographers; Watercolor USA; biennial exhibition, 4 juried of contemporary visual artists in region
Publications: Exhibition catalogues
Activities: Lect open to public in conjunction with selected touring exhibitions; concerts; competitions; awards; book traveling exhibitions; originate traveling exhibitions

O **MID-AMERICA COLLEGE ART ASSOCIATION**, Univ of Houston, Dept of Art, 4800 Calhoun Blvd, Houston, TX 77004. *Pres* Prof David Hickman
Estab 1938 to promote better teaching of art and art history in colleges and universities. Average Annual Attendance: 700. Mem: 200, college and university art departments in 24 states and 4 Canadain provinces; annual meeting and elections in Oct

O **MID-SOUTHERN WATERCOLORISTS**, 3 Pleasant Place Circle, Little Rock, AR 72205. Tel 501-664-6784. *Pres* Peggy Johnston; *VPres* Dr Howard Stern; *Secy* Norma Brill
Estab 1970 to elevate the stature of watercolor and to educate the public to the significance of watercolor as an important creative permanent painting medium. Gallery not maintained. Mem: 218; approval of membership qualification; dues $20
Income: Financed by membership
Publications: Newsletter, monthly
Activities: Competitions; scholarships; originate traveling exhibitions

O **MIDWEST ART HISTORY SOCIETY**, Dept of Art History, Northwestern University, Evanston, IL 60201. Tel 312-492-3741. *Pres* James D Breckenridge; *VPres & Secy* Edward J Olszewski
Estab 1973 to further art history in the Midwest as a discipline and a profession. Average Annual Attendance: 150 at meetings. Mem: 550; membership is open to institutions, students and academic and museum art historians in the Midwest; dues institution $10, professional $5; annual meeting March 29th-31st
Income: $1200 (financed by membership)
Publications: Midwest Art History Society Newsletter, Oct & April
Activities: Lect provided

O **NATIONAL ACADEMY OF DESIGN**, Fifth Ave & 89th St, New York, NY 10028. Tel 212-369-4880. *Dir* John H Dobkin; *Asst* Barbara Krulik
Open Tues - Sun 1 - 5 PM, cl New Year's, Thanksgiving & Christmas. Admis $1.
Estab 1825, Honorary Arts organization for American artists and architects

Collections: Permanent collection consists of 250 architectural drawings and portfolios, 1200 drawings and graphics, 2000 paintings, 500 sculptures, the gifts of the artist and architectural members of the Academy from 1825 to present
Exhibitions: Annual juried exhibition of contemporary art, exhibitions of permanent collection, loan exhibitions
Publications: Annual exhibition catalogue; catalogues of exhibitions of permanent collection

L **Archives,** Fifth Ave & 89th St, 10028.
Library Holdings: Other—Biographical files on all members, correspondence, exhibition records, news clips from 1826 to present

O **NATIONAL ANTIQUE AND ART DEALERS ASSOCIATION OF AMERICA,** 59 E 57th St, New York, NY 10022. Tel 212-355-0636. *Pres* Edward Munves; *VPres* Emily M Manheim; *VPres* Philip Colleck; *Secy* James Berry Hill; *Treas* Christian Jussel
Estab 1954 to promote the best interests of the antique and art trade; to collect and circulate reports, statistics and other information pertaining to art; to sponsor and organize antique and art exhibitions; to promote just, honorable and ethical trade practices
Activities: Lect

O **NATIONAL ARCHITECTURAL ACCREDITING BOARD, INC,** 1735 New York Ave NW, Washington, DC 20006. Tel 202-833-1180. *Exec Dir* Dr Hugo G Blasdel
Estab 1940 to produce and maintain a current list of accredited programs in architecture in the United States and its jurisdictions, with the general objective that a well-integrated program of architectural education be developed which will be national in scope
Publications: Criteria and Procedures, pamphlet; List of Accredited Programs in Architecture, annually

O **NATIONAL ART EDUCATION ASSOCIATION,** 1916 Association Dr, Reston, VA 22091. Tel 703-860-8000. *Exec Dir* John J Mahlmann; *Pres* Dr Kent Anderson; *Pres-Elect* Dr Edmund B Feldman
Estab 1947 through the affiliation of four regional groups, Eastern, Western, Pacific and Southeastern Arts Associations. The NAEA is a national organization devoted to the advancement of the professional interests and competence of teachers of art at all educational levels. Promotes the study of the problems of teaching art; encourages research and experimentation; facilitates the professional and personal cooperation of its members; holds public discussions and programs; publishes desirable articles, reports, and surveys; integrates efforts of others with similar purposes. Mem: 10,000 art teachers, administrators, supervisors and students; fee institutional comprehensive $100, active $35; National Conference held 1980 in Atlanta, GA, 1981 in Chicago, IL
Income: Programs financed through membership, sales of publications, and occasional grants for specific purposes
Publications: Art Teacher, 3 times per year; Journal of Art Education, 8 issues per year; Studies in Art Education, 3 times per year; special publications

O **NATIONAL ASSEMBLY OF COMMUNITY ARTS AGENCIES,** 1625 Eye St NW, Suite 725A, Washington, DC 20006. Tel 202-293-6818. *Pres* Elizabeth Howard; *VPres* Geoffrey Platt Jr; *Secy* Romalyn Tilghman; *Executive Dir* Charles F Dambach; *Assoc Dir* Gretchen Wiest; *Admin Mgr* Nancy Hicks; *Secy* Veronica Maynard
Open Mon - Fri 9 AM - 5 PM. No admis fee. Estab 1978 to provide services for and represent the interests of community arts agencies. Mem: 500; annual meeting June
Income: $165,000 (financed by membership, grants and contracts)
Publications: Newsletter, semi-monthly

O **NATIONAL ASSEMBLY OF STATE ARTS AGENCIES,** 1010 Vermont Ave NW, Washington, DC 20005. Tel 202-347-6352. *Chmn* Peter de Chero; *VPres* Robert Yegge; *Secy* Ellen McCulloch-Lovell; *Executive Dir* Roy H Helms
Estab 1975 to enhance the growth and development of the arts through an informed and skilled membership; to provide forums for the review and development of national arts policy. Mem: 56; members are the fifty-six state and jurisdictional arts agencies, affiliate memberships are open to public; annual meeting mid-Sept
Income: Financed by membership and federal grants
Publications: Annual survey of state appropriations to arts councils; newsletter, monthly

O **NATIONAL ASSOCIATION OF SCHOOLS OF ART,** 11250 Roger Bacon Dr, 5, Reston, VA 22090. Tel 703-437-0700. *Pres* Paul B Arnold; *Exec Dir* Samuel Hope
Formerly the National Conference of Schools of Design, holding its first conference in 1944. Changed name in 1948, at which time its constitution and by-laws were adopted. Changed its name again in 1960 from National Association of Schools of Design to National Association of Schools of Art.
NASA is the national accrediting agency for higher educational institutions in the visual arts and is so recognized by the US Office of Education and the Council on Postsecondary Accreditation. The organization was established to develop a closer relationship among schools and departments of art for the purpose of examining and improving their educational practice and professional standards in design and art. Membership is open to schools and departments of art established for the purpose of educating designers and artists in the visual arts, and giving evidence of permanence and stability; possessing an approved organization, administration, faculty and facilities, and maintaining standards agreed upon by the Association

O **NATIONAL ASSOCIATION OF WOMEN ARTISTS, INC,** 41 Union Square, New York, NY 10003. Tel 212-675-1616. *Pres* Mabel H Morand
Estab 1889 as a national organization to provide opportunities for member women artists, to exhibit and sell their work. Mem: 650; member work is juried prior to selection; dues $25; meetings Nov and May
Income: Financed by membership
Exhibitions: Annual members' exhibition in spring with awards; annual traveling exhibitions of oils, watercolors and graphics; annual New York City shows of oils, watercolors, graphics and sculpture
Publications: Annual Exhibition Catalog

Activities: Lect open to the public, 1 visiting lectr per year; awards given during annual exhibition; originate traveling exhibitions

O **NATIONAL CARTOONISTS SOCIETY,** 9 Ebony Court, Brooklyn, NY 11229. Tel 212-743-6510. *Pres* John Cullen Murphy; *Secy* Frank Springer; *Scribe* Marge Duffy Devine
Estab 1946 to advance the ideals and standards of the profession of cartooning; to assist needy, or incapacitated cartoonists; to stimulate interest in the art of cartooning by cooperating with established schools; to encourage talented students; to assist governmental and charitable institutes. Mem: 525; annual Reuben Awards Dinner in April
Collections: Milt Gross Fund; National Cartoonists Society Collection
Publications: Newsletter, monthly; The Cartoonist; annually
Activities: Educ dept to supply material and information to students; individual cartoonists to lect, chalktalks can be arranged; cartoon auctions; proceeds from traveling exhibitions and auctions support Milt Gross Fund assisting needy cartoonists, widows and children; gives Reuben Award to Outstanding Cartoonist of the Year, Silver Plaque Awards to best cartoonists in individual categories of cartooning; original cartoons lent to schools, libraries and galleries; originate traveling exhibitions

O **NATIONAL COUNCIL OF ARCHITECTURAL REGISTRATION BOARDS,** 1735 New York Ave NW, Suite 700, Washington, DC 20006. Tel 202-659-3996. *Executive Dir* Samuel T Balen
Estab 1920 as a clearinghouse for architects registering from state to state. All now have laws regulating the practice of architecture. Mem: 55 officials of state architectural registration boards of the United States, Puerto Rico, Virgin Islands and Guam; annual meeting June 1979 in Cambridge, MA
Publications: Annual Report; Architectural Registration Handbook, annually; Newsletter, quarterly

O **NATIONAL ENDOWMENT FOR THE ARTS,** 2401 E St NW, Washington, DC 20506. Tel 202-634-6372. *Chmn* Livingston L Biddle Jr
Open 9 AM - 5:30 PM. No admis fee. Estab 1965 as a national organization to make the arts available to more people across the country; to strengthen cultural institutions so they can better serve the people; to advance cultural legacy
Income: $139,660,000 appropriation for fiscal year 1979, for programming Federal funds that are given through grants to individuals and non-profit organizations. Grants to organizations must be matched at least dollar for dollar by private, state or local funds
Publications: Annual Report; Cultural Post, bi-monthly; Guide to Programs
L **Library,** 2401 E St NW, 20506. Tel 202-634-7640. *Librn* M Christine Morrison
Open Mon - Fri 9 AM - 5:30 PM. Estab 1971 to provide an effective information service which will support program and division activities and contribute to the accomplishment of Agency goals
Income: Financed by federal appropriation
Library Holdings: Vols 5000; Per subs 500; AV—A-tapes; Other—Clipping files, exhibition catalogs
Special Subjects: Arts in contemporary America, arts administration, cultural policy; government and the arts

O **NATIONAL INSTITUTE FOR ARCHITECTURAL EDUCATION,** 139 E 52nd St, New York, NY 10022. Tel 212-759-9154. *Chmn Board* John J Stonehill; *VChmn* Raymond F Pavia; *Treas* Byron Bell; *Secy* James R Jarrett; *Dir Education* Stanley Salzman; *Executive Secy* Lilian Marus
Open Mon - Fri 9 AM - 5 PM. Incorporated 1894 as Society of Beaux-Arts Architects, which was dissolved Dec 1941; Beaux-Arts Institute of Design estab 1916, name changed 1956 to present name. Mem: Approx 250; dues $20; annual meeting first week in Dec
Exhibitions: Prize-winning drawings of competitions held during year
Publications: Yearbook, annually in October
Activities: Trustee for the Lloyd Warren Fellowship (Paris Prize in Architecture) for study and travel abroad; William Van Alen Architect Memorial Award (international competition) annual scholarship for further study or research project of some architectural nature; and other trust funds for prize awards for study and travel abroad and educational activities in the United States

O **NATIONAL SCULPTURE SOCIETY,** 15 E 26th St, New York, NY 10010. Tel 212-889-6960. *Pres* Granville W Carter; *VPres* Charlotte Dunwiddie; *Secy* Laci de Gerenday; *Executive Dir* Claire A Stein
Open Mon - Fri 9 AM - 5 PM. No admis fee. Estab 1893 as a national organization to spread the knowledge of good sculpture. Average Annual Attendance: 4000 at annual exhibition. Mem: 350; work juried for sculptor membership; vote of Board of Directors for allied professional and patron membership; dues $10-$50; annual meeting second Tues in Jan
Income: Approx $80,000, not counting magazine income (financed by endowment, membership, state appropriation and donations)
Exhibitions: Annual juried exhibition open to all United States residents
Publications: Exhibition catalog, annually; membership book; National Sculpture Review, quarterly
Activities: Lect open to the public, 5 visiting lectr per year; gallery talks and tours with annual exhibition; youth awards annually; exhibition prizes in the past provided consultation for large annual competitions; Education Committee chooses recipients for NSS scholarships; scholarships offered to accredited art schools; exhibitions organized for other institutions
L **Library,** 15 E 26th St, 10010.
Open to the public for reference; a few volumes and periodicals, photographic and original archival materials
Special Subjects: American sculpture, biography, history

O **NATIONAL SOCIETY OF MURAL PAINTERS, INC,** 41 E 65th St, New York, NY 10021. Tel 212-787-7063. *Pres* Dean Fausett; *Secy* Lloyd Lozes Goff
Estab and incorporated 1895 to encourage and advance the standards of mural painting in America; to formulate a code for decorative competitions and by-laws to regulate professional practice. Mem: 200; dues $20, non-resident $15
Publications: Biographies and articles pertinent to the mural painting profession; Press Sheets of photographs and articles of the executed work of the members of society

Activities: Exhibitions held in collaboration with allied professions; available for booking - a traveling show of color sketches for murals on the subject of momentous events in American History

O **NATIONAL SOCIETY OF PAINTERS IN CASEIN AND ACRYLIC, INC,** 225 W 34th St, New York, NY 10001. Tel 212-686-2659. *Pres* Mark Freeman; *VPres* Mina Kocherthaler; *VPres* Howard Mandel; *Secy* Lily Shuff
Open in March during annual exhibition. Admis 50¢. Estab 1952 as a national organization for a showcase for artists in casein and acrylic. Galleries rented from National Arts Club. Average Annual Attendance: 800 during exhibition. Mem: 120; membership by invitation, work must pass three juries; dues $15; annual meeting April
Income: $3000 (financed by membership)
Publications: Exhibition Catalog, annually
Activities: Demonstrations; medals and $2500 in prizes given at annual exhibition; originate traveling exhibitions

O **NATIONAL WATERCOLOR SOCIETY,** c/o Dr Jae Carmichael, 985 San Pasqual, Pasadena, CA 91106. *Pres* Dr Jae Carmichael; *First VPres* Pat Cox; *Treas* Betty Rodbard; *Correspondence Secy* Kathryn Chang Liu
Estab 1921 to sponsor art exhibits for the cultural and educational benefit of the public. Mem: 530; dues $25 beginning each year in March (must be juried into membership); annual meeting Jan
Collections: Purchase award-winning paintings from 1954 to present
Exhibitions: All membership exhibition in Spring; national annual exhibition each Nov
Activities: Docent training; slide-cassette program of members' works; competitions; cash awards; originage traveling exhibitions

O **PRINT CLUB,** 1614 Latimer St, Philadelphia, PA 19103. Tel 215-735-6090. *Pres* Donald W McPhail; *VPres* Cynthia Lister; *VPres* Ruth Fine; *VPres* Richard Jaffe; *Secy* Lois Johnson; *Dir* Ofelia Garcia; *Asst to Dir* Blanche Moore
Open Tues - Sat 10 AM - 5 PM. No admis fee. Estab 1915 as a non-profit, educational organization dedicated to the promotion of fine prints and the support and encouragement of printmakers and print collectors. Average Annual Attendance: 2000. Mem: 2000; dues contributing $50, family $30, individual $20, artists $12.50; annual meeting in Feb
Income: $70,000 (financed by endowment, membership and private and government grants for some activities)
Collections: Bookplates, bindings and prints collection held at the Philadelphia Museum of Art
Exhibitions: American Masterprints; Peter Milton - major retrospective; Members' Show; New Directions in Printmaking, recent monoprints; Philadelphia teaches printmaking; exhibit of important prints to be at Print Club Auction
Publications: Newsletter, quarterly
Activities: Workshops for artists; lect series for print collectors; lect open to public, 25 visiting lectr per year; gallery talks; competitions; various prizes and purchase awards; originate traveling exhibitions
L **Library,** 1614 Latimer St, 19103.
Open to members for reference
Special Subjects: Auction information, catalogs raisonnes, exhibitions, history of prints, printmaking

O **PRINT COUNCIL OF AMERICA,** National Gallery of Art, Constitution Ave at Sixth St NW, Washington, DC 20565. Tel 202-737-4215. *Pres* Andrew Robison; *Treas* Janet Flint
Estab 1956 as a nonprofit organization fostering the study and appreciation of fine prints, new and old. Mem: 100 museum and university professionals interested in prints; annual meeting April or May
Publications: Occasional publications on old and modern prints

O **PROFESSIONAL ARTISTS GUILD,** 69 Shelter Lane, PO Box 11, Roslyn Heights, NY 11577. Tel 516-621-4792. *Pres* Anne Orling; *VPres* Rhoda Sherbell; *Secy* Lucille Orzack; *Treas* Ruth Thaler
Estab 1963 as an international nonprofit organization that has been serving the artist, the public and educational institutions through exhibitions, lectures, public meetings and demonstrations of the various art media. Mem: 90; membership is juried and must have had shows in a professional gallery or museum or educational institution; dues $20; meeting first Mon every month except summer
Income: $2500 (financed by membership and sales)
Exhibitions: Held at Royal Academy, Stockholm, Sweden; Lincoln Center, New York, NY; C W Post College Art Center, Greenvale, NY; Union Carbide Building Gallery, New York, NY; Adelphi University, Garden City, NY
Publications: Newsletter, monthly except during summer
Activities: Lect open to public, 10-12 visiting lectr per year; individual paintings lent to public institutions; originate traveling exhibitions

O **SALMAGUNDI CLUB,** 47 Fifth Ave, New York, NY 10003. Tel 212-255-7740. *Chmn of Board* William C W Fames; *Corresp Secy* Linda E Scher
Gallery open during exhibitions 1 - 5 PM. No admis fee. Estab 1871, incorporated 1880, building purchased 1917. Clubhouse with living quarters for men, restaurant, gallery and library. Mem: 600; dues resident layman $288, resident artist $212, nonresident layman $174, nonresident artist $162, junior $120; scholarship graduated to scale
Exhibitions: Sever per year by artist members with cash awards
Publications: Centennial Roster published in 1972; Salmagundi Membership Roster, biennially; Salmagundian, monthly except for summer
Activities: Lect; art classes; awards; scholarships and prizes; acts as organizing and screening agency between the US Navy and all qualified American artists; under its Naval Art Cooperation and Liaison (NACAL) Committee, artists are chosen and sent on short painting trips around the world to interpret the daily life and traditions of the US Navy; buys paintings to present to museums
L **Library,** 47 Fifth Ave, 10003.
For reference only
Library Holdings: Vols 6000

O **SCULPTORS GUILD, INC,** 10 E 53rd St, New York, NY 10022. Tel 212-752-2160. *Pres* Roy Gussow; *Executive VPres* Renata M Schwebel; *VPres Exhib & Special Programs* Richard M Miller; *VPres Members* Helen Beling; *Treas* Chaim Gross; *Secy* Legh Myers
No admis fee. Estab 1937 as a non-profit organization to maintain a high standard in presenting works expressing all aspects of the constantly evolving and varing sculptural scene; to present a wide variety of excellent contemporary sculpture. Mem: 100; dues $25; annual meeting May
Exhibitions: Bi-annual exhibition (Oct - Nov) held at Lever House, New York; series of large outdoor exhibitions in central New York City locations
Publications: Sculpture, fully illustrated catalog of yearly exhibition
Activities: Educ programs connected with sculpture; maintains office for public, with files on members' works; lect; competitions; originate traveling exhibitions

O **SOCIETY OF AMERICAN GRAPHIC ARTISTS,** Room 1214, 32 Union Square, New York, NY 10003. Tel 212-260-5706. *Pres* Gerson Leiber; *VPres* George Nama; *VPres* Anne Youkeles; *Treas* Helen Gerardia; *Recording Secy* Christine Engler
Estab 1915 as a society of printmakers. Mem: Over 200 voted in by merit; dues $10; annual meeting May
Income: Financed by membership and associate memberships
Exhibitions: Semi-annual Open Competition National Print Exhibition; Semi-annual Closed Members Exhibit; National Traveling Exhibitions every two years
Publications: Exhibition Catalog, annually; Presentation Prints for Associate Membership
Activities: Lect open to public, 1 visiting lectr per year; sponsors competitive and members' exhibits with awards; original objects of art lent, lending collection contains original prints; originate traveling exhibitions

O **SOCIETY OF ANIMAL ARTISTS, INC,** 151 Carroll St, City Island, Bronx, NY 10464. Tel 212-885-2181. *Pres* Albert Gilbert; *Treas* Joseph Vance Jr; *Secy* Patricia Allen Bott
Open during exhibitions. No admis fee. Estab 1960 to make the people of the United States and Canada more aware of the artists who explore the beauty and habits of animals, and by so doing, help ecology and the environment. Mem: 150; artists must pass jury of admissions to become a member; dues $75, initiation fee $100; meetings twice a year, or more often if needed
Income: Financed by membership
Exhibitions: 1978 held at Sportsmans Edge, New York City and Owens Gallery, Oklahoma City
Publications: Newsletter, every other month
Activities: Lect for members only, 3 visiting lectr per year; gallery talks; conventions arranged with film lect and instruction; slide lect of trips with animal art by members; advisory board for those who want to study animal art and wildlife; paintings and individual objects of art lent to members, wildlife organizations, Audubon, World Wildlife Special Exhibitions; lending collection consists of catalogs, prints, color and framed reproductions, sculpture, photographs and slides; originate traveling exhibitions; prints, reproductions and original art sold at gallery shows

O **SOCIETY OF ARCHITECTURAL HISTORIANS,** 1700 Walnut St, Suite 716, Philadelphia, PA 19103. Tel 215-735-0224, 735-0246. *Pres* Adolf K Placzek; *First VPres* David Gebhard; *Second VPres* Damie Stillman; *Secy* David T VanZanten; *Executive Secy* Rosann S Berry
Open daily 8:30 AM - 4:30 PM. No admis fee. Estab to provide an international forum for those interested in architecture and its related arts, to encourage scholarly research in the field and to promote the preservation of significant architectural monuments throughout the world. Mem: 4500 who show an interest in architecture, past, present and future; dues $30; annual meeting April (Madison, WI, April 23-27, 1980; Victoria, BC, April 1-5, 1981; New Haven, CT, April 21-25, 1982)
Income: Financed by membership
Publications: Journal, quarterly; Newsletter, bimonthly
Activities: Sponsors competitions; Alice Davis Hitchcock Book Award and Founders' Award given annually; scholarships given to student members for graduate work in architecture and architectural history; sales shop sells architectural guides and booklets and also back issues of the Journal

O **SOCIETY OF ENVIRONMENTAL GRAPHICS DESIGNERS,** 228 N LaSalle St, Suite 1205, Chicago, IL 60601. Tel 312-372-2095. *Pres* Richard Burns; *Secy* Wayne J Kosterman; *Dir* John Berry; *Dir* John Follis; *Dir* Jeff Corbin; *Dir* Bob Lane
Estab 1973 to further environmental graphics. Mem: 70; dues trade mem $220, professional $55, associate $40, student $20
Income: $3000 (financed by membership)
Exhibitions: Images: An International Signage Exhibit, 1978 at Chicago Public Library Cultural Center
Publications: SEGD Sourcebook
Activities: Competitions; awards

O **SOCIETY OF ILLUSTRATORS,** 128 E 63rd St, New York, NY 10021. Tel 212-838-2560. *Pres* Warren Rogers; *Executive Dir* Arpi Ermoyan; *Cur* Terry Brown
Open Mon - Fri 10 AM - 5 PM. No admis fee. Estab 1901 as a national organization of professional illustrators and art directors. Gallery has group, theme, one-man and juried shows, approx every three weeks. Mem: 780
Publications: Illustrators Annual
Activities: Lect open to public; holds annual national juried exhibition of best illustrations of the year; awards scholarships to college level art students

O **SOCIETY OF MEDALISTS,** c/o Donald A Schwartz, Old Ridgebury Rd, Danbury, CT 06810. Tel 203-792-3000. *Pres* Donald A Eifert; *Art Advisory Board* Elvira Clain-Stefanelli; *Art Advisory Board* Frank Eliscur; *Art Advisory Board* Marcel Jovine; *Art Advisory Board* Eric Sloane; *Art Advisory Board* Albert Weinman
Estab 1930 by the late art patron, George DuPont Pratt, to stimulate interest in medallic sculpture. The Society of Medalists has granted two commissions annually since 1930 to American sculptors to execute basrelief medallic sculpture. The finished high-relief fine art medals struck by the Society are then distributed to dues paying members of the non-profit organization. Mem: 1200
Collections: Complete collections of Society medals are on permanent exhibition at the R W Norton Gallery, 4747 Creswell Ave, Shreveport, LA 71106 and the World

Heritage Museum, University of Illinois, 484 Lincoln Hall, Urbana, IL 61801
Publications: News Bulletin, annually

O **SOCIETY OF NORTH AMERICAN ARTISTS, INC**, PO Box 37072 Millard
Station, Omaha, NE 68137. Tel 402-895-5745. *Pres* Eugene H Grimm; *VPres* Gloria
D Grimm; *Secy* Michele K Berry
Open Mon - Fri 9 AM - 4 PM. Estab 1970 as an international organization, founded
to provide all artists a simplified, expedient and low-cost method to register their
original work in a permanent public record for the immediate and long range future.
Mem: 650; a minimum of three registrations required, original work only
Publications: Fine Art Registry, distributed annually to members and selected
public libraries

O **SOUTHEASTERN COLLEGE ART CONFERENCE**, c/o Anne W Thomas,
Dept of Art, University of North Carolina, Chapel Hill, NC 27514. *Pres* John
Schnorrenburg; *VPres* Jeff Bayer; *Second VPres* Martha Caldwell; *Second VPres*
James Madison; *Secy* Anne W Thomas; *Staff Asst* Marion Kay Smith
Estab as a regional organization to promote art at higher education level. Mem: 300;
dues institutional $50, regular $12, student $5
Publications: Annual Review

O **SOUTHERN ASSOCIATION OF SCULPTORS, INC**, c/o Tim Murray,
University of Alabama, Huntsville, AL 35805. Tel 205-895-6114.
Estab 1965, incorporated 1967, to promote the exchange of ideas and information
among its members; assist institutions, museums and the public in developing and
understanding of sculpture through exhibitions, demonstrations and publications.
Mem: 210; mem open to any United States sculptor; annual meeting in Fall
Exhibitions: Annual National Juried Sculpture Traveling Exhibition
Publications: Illustrated Sculptors Directory; Job Information Center Bulletin, 9
per year; periodic technical publications; Presidents Newsletter, quarterly
Activities: Competitions; originate traveling exhibitions

O **SPECIAL LIBRARIES ASSOCIATION**, Museum, Arts and Humanities
Division, 235 Park Ave S, New York, NY 10003. *Chmn* Sharon
Howe Sweeting; *Chmn-elect* Daphne Roloff; *Past-Chmn* Grant Dean; *Secy Treas*
Roberta Hankamer; *Bulletin Ed* William B Neff
Estab 1928 to provide an information forum and exchange for Librarians in the
specialized fields of Museums, Arts and Humanities. Mem: 785; dues $40; annual
meeting early June
Publications: Museums, Arts and Humanities Division Bulletin, semi-annual

O **STAINED GLASS ASSOCIATION OF AMERICA**, c/o Norman Temme, PO
Box 734, Bronxville, NY 10708. *Pres* Helen C Hickman; *First VPres* Richard
Millard; *Second VPres* John Kebrle; *Treas* Otto C Winterich; *Ed* Norman Temme
Estab 1903 as an international organization to promote the development and
advancement of the stained glass craft. Mem: 500; there are four categories of
membership - active member, active artist member, craft supplier member, and
associate member (various criteria apply to each membership); dues vary for
members with size of studio; associate members $30; semi-annual meetings Jan and
June
Publications: Stained Glass magazine, quarterly
Activities: Educ dept with two and three week courses; apprenticeship program;
competitions sponsored for apprentices only, every two years; cash prizes

O **UNITED STATES COMMITTEE OF THE INTERNATIONAL
ASSOCIATION OF ART, INC,*** c/o Helen Treadwell, 33 W 67th St, New York,
NY 10023. Tel 212-787-7063. *Pres* Helen Treadwell
Estab 1952, incorporated 1955, to promote greater appreciation of contemporary
fine arts, regardless of genre; to uphold the status of the artists and to defend their
rights, primarily on the national level, then on the international level, evaluating by

comparison and appraisal; also to stimulate international cultural relations and
exchanges of art and artists free of any aesthetic or other bias. Mem: Twelve national
art organizations of painters, sculptors and graphic arts in the United States;
triennial congress - West Germany, 1982
Publications: Information, three per year

O **UNITED STATES DEPARTMENT OF THE INTERIOR**, Indian Arts and
Crafts Board, C St between 18th & 19th Sts. (Mailing Add: United States Dept
Interior, Room 4004, Washington, DC 20240) Tel 202-343-2773. *Chmn* Lloyd
New; *General Mgr* Robert G Hart; *Dir of Museums, Exhib & Publications* Myles
Libhart
Open Mon - Fri 8 AM - 5 PM, cl legal holidays, Sat & Sun. No admis fee. Estab
1936 to promote contemporary arts by Native Americans of the United States.
Board administers the Southern Plains Indian Museum, Anadarko, OK; Museum
of the Plains Indian, Browning, MT; Sioux Indian Museum, Rapid City, SD.
Average Annual Attendance: 80,000
Income: Financed by federal appropriation
Collections: Contemporary Native American Arts
Exhibitions: 27-30 one-person exhibitions among the three museums
Publications: Exhibition brochures
Activities: Gallery talks; tours; originate traveling exhibitions; sales shop sells
Contemporary Native American Art

O **VISUAL ARTISTS AND GALLERIES ASSOCIATION, INC**, One World Trade
Center, Suite 1535, New York, NY 10048. Tel 212-466-1390. *Executive Dir*
Dorothy M Weber
Open daily 9 AM - 5 PM. Estab 1976 as a nonprofit venture to help artists control
and police the reproduction of their works, from textile designs to photographs in
textbooks; to act as a clearinghouse for licensing reproduction rights and set up a
directory of artists and other owners of reproduction rights for international use.
Mem: European 10,000, American 500; dues gallery and associate $50, artist $10
Income: Financed by membership

O **WESTERN ASSOCIATION OF ART MUSEUMS**, 270 Sutter St, San Francisco,
CA 94108. Tel 415-392-9222. *Pres* Thomas H Garver; *VPres* Mary Beebe; *VPres*
Don Jones; *Secy* Ric Collier; *Executive Dir* Lynn Jorgenson; *Exhib Prog Dir* Gigi
Dobbs; *Exhib, Education & Circulation Coordr* Christine Magdanz-Robbins
Open Mon - Fri 9 AM - 5 PM. No admis fee. Estab as an international nonprofit
membership organization which circulates traveling exhibitions, offers fine art
insurance, and organizes educational seminars for museum professionals. Mem:
Over 500, members selected by accreditation and approval of membership
committee; dues active $150; annual meeting Oct
Publications: Exhibition Catalogs; educational publications printed in conjunction
with seminars
Activities: Seminars for museum professionals; lect; Ilo Liston Publication Award
competition is sponsored annually to award graphic design excellence in museum
publications including posters, books, catalogs, annual reports, and others;
scholarships and fellowships offered; member and non-member institutions may
rent exhibitions organized for circulation

O **WESTERN STATES ARTS FOUNDATION**, 428 E 11th Ave, Denver, CO
80203. Tel 303-832-7979. *Executive Dir* Bill Jamison
Open daily 8 AM - 5:30 PM. No admis fee. Estab 1974 to increase the accessibility
of quality arts through cost-effective, cooperative multi-state programs and services
which expand and work in conjunction with state arts agency programs
Income: Financed by NEA, private funds
Exhibitions: (1978-79) Contemporary Crafts Touring Exhibition. (1979-80) First
Western States Biennial. (1980-81) Western Printmakers
Publications: Annual program brochure; Emphasis, monthly newsletter
Activities: Competitions with cash prizes; fels; originate traveling exhibitions

Museums, Libraries and Associations In The United States

ALABAMA

BIRMINGHAM

M ALABAMA MUSEUM OF PHOTOGRAPHY, 4322 Glenwood Ave, 35222. Tel 205-595-6980. *Pres & Cur* Ed Willis Barnett; *VPres* James S Larkin
Open by appointment and invitation. No admis fee. Estab 1974 to promote photography as a fine art; to procure outstanding photographs from over the world and mount exhibitions in America; to maintain a laboratory for experimentation. Collections are housed in a residence, on display for students and small groups
Income: Financed by donations, grants from National Endowment for the Arts, and Alabama State Council
Collections: Ed Willis Barnett (many photographs, color and black and white); Samuel Chamberlain (30 photographs used to illustrate his books); Man Ray (rayographs, portraits, scenes); collection of Enos, Fassbender, Fincken, Fisher, Gore, Litzel, Underwood, Widder and others
Activities: Organize and circulate traveling exhibitions

M BIRMINGHAM MUSEUM OF ART, 2000 Eighth Ave N, 35203. Tel 205-254-2565. *Dir* Richard V Murray; *Cur* Edward F Weeks; *Cur Decorative Arts* Gail C Andrews; *Registrar* Betty Keen
Open Tues, Wed, Fri, & Sat 10 AM - 5 PM, Thurs 10 AM - 9 PM, Sun 2 - 6 PM. No admis fee. Estab 1959 as a general art museum with collections from earliest manifestation of man's creativity to contemporary work. Its goal is to illustrate the highest level of man's artistic work in an art historical context. The 36 galleries are climate controlled; lighting system is modern and controlled to latest safety standards. Average Annual Attendance: 100,000. Mem: 1000; dues $5 - $100
Income: $600,000 (financed by membership, city appropriation and annual donations)
Purchases: $80,000
Collections: †American and English Silver; American Indian art; Ancient art; †art of the American West; †Asian art; †contemporary American art; †old masters painting and sculpture; †Pre-Columbian; †prints and drawings; †Beeson Collection of Wedgwood; Lamprecht Collection of 19th century German Cast Iron; Frances Oliver Collection of Porcelain; Rives Collection of Palestinian Art
Exhibitions: Birmingham Collections; Man Ray Photographs; Sylvia Pizitz Collection; The Tiepolos: Painters to Princes and Prelates, Rubens and Humanism; William Spratting Silver; drawings; French Painting: 1870 - 1920; 20th Century Art
Publications: Bulletin, quarterly; Calendar, monthly
Activities: Classes for adults and children; docent training; lect open to the public, 12 - 15 vis lectr per year; concerts; gallery talks; tours; competitions; artmobile; individual paintings lent to city offices; organize and circulate traveling exhibitions; museum shop sells reproductions, prints and gifts
L Library, 2000 Eighth Ave N, 35203.
Open to the public by request
Library Holdings: Vols 10,000

L BIRMINGHAM PUBLIC LIBRARY, Art and Music Department, 2020 Park, 35203. Tel 205-254-2551. *Head* Jane Greene; *Librn* Patricia Sweeney; *Librn* Norma Parsons
Open Mon - Thur 9 AM - 9 PM, Fri 9 AM - 6 PM. Estab 1909 to serve the Jefferson County area. For reference and lending
Income: $27,000
Library Holdings: Vols 25,000; Per subs 1500; AV—A-tapes, cassettes, rec, slides; Other—Clipping files, exhibition catalogs, memorabilia, pamphlets, photographs
Special Subjects: Architecture, Art History, Crafts, Photography
Collections: Small permanent collection of prints, paintings and Mexican pottery

KAPPA PI INTERNATIONAL HONORARY ART FRATERNITY
For further information, see National and Regional Organizations

DECATUR

M JOHN C CALHOUN STATE COMMUNITY COLLEGE, Art Gallery, Highway 31 North, PO Box 2216, 35602. Tel 205-353-3102. *Pres* Dr James Chasteen; *Dir* Helen C Austin; *Cur* Richard Green; *Head Art Dept* Arthur Bond
Open Mon - Fri 8 AM - 3 PM, special weekend openings. No admis fee. Estab 1965 to provide temporary exhibits of fine art during the school year for the benefit of the surrounding three county area and for the students and faculty of the college. In a new fine arts building completed June 1979, the gallery has 105 lineal feet of carpeted wall space with adjustable incandescent track lighting and fluorescent general lights in a controlled and well-secured environment. Average Annual Attendance: 20,000
Collections: Permanent collection consists of selected student and faculty works as well as a †graphics collection
Exhibitions: Fibers and Pots (works of Barbara Allbritton and Tim Weber); Five Centuries of Graphic Arts (collection on loan); William Nichols, Early Alabama Architect; Student Art Exhibit; Student Photographs
Publications: Announcements; exhibition catalogs
Activities: Classes for adults; lect open to the public, 3 visiting lectr per year; gallery talks; tours; competitions with awards; scholarships and fellowships; individual paintings and original objects of art lent to museums, galleries and college art departments; lending collection contains 40 original art works and 24 original prints; book traveling exhibitions, biannually; originate traveling exhibitions

FAIRHOPE

O PERCY H WHITING ART CENTER, 401 Oak St, 36532. Tel 205-928-2228, 928-5188. *Pres* Robert Thompson; *Dir* Mary D Foreman; *Registrar* Fydella Evans
Open Mon - Sat 10 AM - Noon, 2 - 5 PM, cl New Years Day, Thanksgiving, Christmas. No admis fee. Estab 1952 to sponsor cultural, educational and social activities for members. Center for Eastern Shore Art Association and Eastern Shore Art Academy; four galleries change exhibits monthly. Mem: 1000; dues: Benefactor: Life $500; Patron: Individual $50, Married Couple $100; Sustaining: Individual $15, Married Couple or Civic Organization $30 - $49; Regular: Individual $8, Married Couple (including children under 18) $15; Junior (no parent membership) $2; Sponsoring Memberships: Business and Professional (includes one single membership) $25
Activities: Courses in composition, drawing, life drawing, oil, watercolor, acrylic, sculpture, pottery and photography; workshops; outreach educational program arranges gallery tours, slide programs, and portable exhibits

FAYETTE

M FAYETTE ART MUSEUM, 2nd Ave SE, Box 189, 35555. Tel 205-932-3300. *Board Chmn* Jack Black
Open Mon - Fri 8 AM - 5 PM. No admis fee. Estab 1969 to offer on continuous basis exhibits of visual arts free to the public. Fayette City Hall auditorium and other wall space in the building serve as a gallery
Collections: Present collection consists of about 200 paintings, mostly from local and regional artists
Activities: book traveling exhibitions, 1 per year; originate traveling exhibitions

HUNTSVILLE

O HUNTSVILLE ART LEAGUE AND MUSEUM ASSOCIATION INC, Von Braun Civic Center, 700 Monroe NW, 35801. *Pres* Keith Berg; *VPres* Shirley Feaux; *Secy* Moira Cumming; *Gallery Exhibits Chmn* Louise Hope; *Educational Chmn* Louise Smith; *Educational Chmn* Gail Hansen; *Treas* Sylvia LeBlanc; *Planning* Shirley Brown; *Gallery Exhibits Chmn* Ophelia Ealy
Estab 1957. The League is a nonprofit organization dedicated to promoting and stimulating the appreciation of the visual arts. Mem: Dues adults $10 and higher for additional members of family, student $5; annual meeting August
Exhibitions: Annual Clothesline Shows; annual juried show; continuous exhibitions throughout Huntsville
Publications: Newsletter on activites and exhibition opportunities in the Southeast, monthly
Activities: Classes for adults and children; film series; competitions

M HUNTSVILLE MUSEUM OF ART, 700 Monroe St SW, 35801. Tel 205-534-4566. *Chmn Board* Tennent Lee III; *Vice Chmn Board* William L Marks; *Secy Board* Dr Clifton Pearson; *Treas Board* Dr Ernst Stuhlinger; *Dir* Donald E Knaub; *Asst Dir Finance & Development* Carter Sibley; *Cur of Exhib & Coll* Michael Preble
Open Tues - Sat 10 AM - 5 PM; Sun 1 - 5 PM; Thurs Evening 7 - 9 PM; cl Mon and month of January. No admis fee, donations. Estab 1970 to provide art and educational exhibitions to the city of Huntsville, surrounding counties and

educational districts; to encourage by appropriate means the cultivation of artistic talents and recognition of artistic achievements. Museum is located in the Von Braun Civic Center; 17,000 sq ft total including 8,000 flex exhibition space. Atmospherically controlled galleries, art storage and vault, research library and museum shop included. Average Annual Attendance: 35,000. Mem: Dues patron $100, sustaining $50, contributing $25, family $15, individual $10, student $5
Income: $500,000 (financed by membership, city appropriation, grants and support groups)
Collections: Works of art on paper with emphasis on 19th and 20th century graphics and drawings Images for Eternity; Jewels of Peter Carl Faberge and Other Master Jewelers; Pre-Columbian Art in Southern Collections; Royal Copenhagen Porcelain; 3000 Years of Egyptian Art; Theodore Wores Retrospective
Exhibitions: Approaches to Photography; Art of China and Japan; Art of the Space Era; Black Artists-South; California Bay Area Art; City of Huntsville Bicentennial Exhibition;
Publications: Catalogues, occasionally; Museum Newsletter, quarterly
Activities: Docent training; educational programs; lect; gallery talks; collection loan program; traveling exhibitions organized and circulated; sales shop selling books, catalogues, reproductions and seasonal items
L **Library,** 700 Monroe St SW, 35801. *Librn* Sophye Lowe Young
Open to public and members upon appointment. For reference only
Library Holdings: Vols 1000; Per subs 12; Other—Exhibition catalogs

SOUTHERN ASSOCIATION OF SCULPTORS, INC
For further information, see National and Regional Organizations

M **UNIVERSITY OF ALABAMA IN HUNTSVILLE,** Gallery of Art, PO Box 1247, 35807. Tel 205-895-6078. *Faculty Advisor* Dr John Sarn; *Cur* Tim Cash; *Student Dir* Michael Cissell
Open Mon - Thurs 1 - 5 PM, Sun 1 - 4 PM. No admis fee. Estab 1975. An intimate and small renovated chapel with a reserved section for exhibits. Average Annual Attendance: 1800
Income: Financed by administration
Exhibitions: Contemporary artwork (US and international); Annual Juried Exhibition
Activities: Lect open to the public, 7-10 visiting lectr per year; gallery talks; competitions with awards; individual paintings and original objects of art lent; book traveling exhibitions, 3 times per year; originate traveling exhibitions

MOBILE

O **ART PATRONS LEAGUE OF MOBILE,** Box 8055, 36608. Tel 205-342-0749. *Pres* Mrs E S McLaughlin Jr; *VPres* Mrs Ramsey McKinney; *Secy* Mrs J Merig
Estab 1964 to promote the education and appreciation of the visual and graphic arts in the Mobile area. Mem: 435; dues associate $25, active $15
Income: $50,000 (financed by membership)
Purchases: $28,000
Exhibitions: Outdoor Arts and Crafts Fair; Christmas Tree Exhibit; Holiday House; Public Sculpture Program
Activities: Classes for adults and children; workshops; lectures open to the public, three visiting lecturers per year; gallery talks; tours; sales shop sells original art, reproductions and prints

M **FINE ARTS MUSEUM OF THE SOUTH,** Langan Park, PO Box 8426, 36608. Tel 205-342-4642. *Chmn of the Board* Charles R Butler; *Dir* Mary O'Neill Victor; *Asst Dir* Harold M Wittmann; *Registrar* David McCann; *Secy* Hazel Mims
Open Tues - Sat 10 AM - 5 PM, Sun Noon - 5 PM, cl Mon. Estab 1964 to foster the appreciation of art and provide art education programs for the community. Average Annual Attendance: 100,000. Mem: 1800; dues associate $250, patron $100, supporting $50, family $25, individual $15
Income: Financed by membership and city appropriation
Collections: American Crafts; African Art; 19th and 20th century American and European paintings, sculpture, prints, and decorative arts; Oriental art; Miller Collection of Oriental Porcelain, Indian Miniatures, Chinese Ceramics, Medieval Art, European Paintings and Sculpture, 16th to 20th century and classical art; Wellington Collection of wood engravings
Exhibitions: American Impressionist; Anchutz Collection of Western Art; Duveneck and Chase; Ripening of American Art
Publications: Calendar, quarterly
Activities: Classes for adults and children; docent training; lect open to the public; competitions; Junior Discovery Museum
L **Library,** Langan Park, PO Box 8426, 36608. *Librn* Iras Smith
For reference only
Library Holdings: Vols 850; AV—Slides; Other—Clipping files, exhibition catalogs, framed reproductions, pamphlets, photographs, reproductions

M **MUSEUM OF THE CITY OF MOBILE,** 355 Government St, 36602. Tel 205-438-7569. *Dir* Caldwell Delaney
Open Tues - Sat 10 AM - 5 PM, cl Mondays and city holidays. Museum is located in the elegantly restored Bernstein-Bush townhouse, the museum houses exhibits bearing upon the history of Mobile and the Gulf Coast area since its founding as a French colony in 1702. This building is listed on the National Register of Historic Places. Displays illustrate life in Mobile under French, British and Spanish colonial rule; the rapid growth of the city in the pre-Civil War period; the rise and fall of the fortunes of Mobile as the best defended Confederate city; and the ever increasing importance of the city as an international seaport and center of culture, business and scholarly institutions
Income: $230,942 (financed by city appropriation)
Collections: Fenollosa Room collection of books, manuscripts and family photographs, Japanese photographs, paintings, prints, china and textiles; Roderick D MacKenzie Room; McMillan Room; Queens of Mobile Mardi Gras; Admiral Raphael Semmes collection includes probably the finest Confederate presentation sword in existence, along with a presentation cased revolver and accessories, books, paintings, documents, personal papers and ship models; Alfred Lewis Staples Mardi Gras Gallery; Eighty thousand items reflecting the entire span of the history of Mobile

L **Reference Library,** 355 Government St, 36602.
For research only
Library Holdings: Vols 1500
M **Carlen House,** 54 Carlen St, 36606.
The Carlen House is an important representation of Mobile's unique contribution to American regional architecture. It is a fine example of the Creole Cottage as it evolved from the French Colonial form and was adapted for early American use. The house was erected in 1842; furnishings are from the collections of the Museums of the City of Mobile and are typical of a house of that period
Activities: Group tours are conducted by guides in period costumes who emphasize aspects of everyday life in Mobile in the mid-nineteenth century. The making of material is demonstrated by the guide who cards wool, spins fibers and weaves cloth

L **UNIVERSITY OF SOUTH ALABAMA,** Ethnic American Slide Library, College of Arts & Sciences, University Blvd, 36688. Tel 205-460-6337. *Head* James E Kennedy
Open daily 8 AM - 5 PM. Estab for the acquisition of slides of works produced by Afro-American, Mexican American and native American artists and the distribution of duplicate slides of these works to educational institutions and individuals engaged in research
Library Holdings: AV—Slides
Collections: 19th and 20th century ethnic American art works in ceramics, drawing, painting, photography, printmaking, sculpture
Publications: Slide Catalog

MONTEVALLO

M **UNIVERSITY OF MONTEVALLO,** The Gallery, 35115. Tel 205-665-2521, Ext 285. *Art Department Chmn* Dr Frank McCoy; *Dir of Gallery* Patricia Johnston
Open Mon - Fri 9 AM - 5 PM. No admis fee. Estab Sept 1977 to supply students and public with high quality contemporary art. The gallery is 27 x 54 ft with track lighting; floors and walls carpeted; no windows. Average Annual Attendance: 2500 - 3000
Income: $2000 - $2500 (financed by state appropriation and regular department budget)
Publications: High quality catalogs and posters
Activities: Management classes; lect open to the public, 6 vis lectr per year; gallery talks: organize and circulate traveling exhibitions

MONTGOMERY

M **ALABAMA DEPARTMENT OF ARCHIVES AND HISTORY MUSEUM,** 624 Washington Ave, 36130. Tel 205-832-6510. *Dir* Milo B Howard Jr; *Museum Cur* Robert A Cason
Open Mon - Fri 8 AM - 5 PM, Sat & Sun 8 AM - Noon and 1 - 5 PM. No admis fee. Estab 1901. Average Annual Attendance: 78,000
Income: Financed by state appropriation
Collections: William Rufus King Collection; Hank Williams; Fine Arts Room; French Room; Music Room
Exhibitions: Hank Williams; History of Alabama
L **Library,** 624 Washington Ave, 36130. *Librn* Albert K Craig
Open Mon - Fri 8 AM - 5 PM. Estab 1901. Department has a Manuscripts Division where original manuscript collections are maintained
Library Holdings: Other—Clipping files, pamphlets, photographs

C **BLOUNT INC,** 4520 Executive Park Dr, PO Box 949, 36102. Tel 205-272-8020. *In Charge Art Coll* Charles R Barnette
Open 8 AM - 5 PM. No admis fee. Estab 1973, original collection began in response to commemorate America's bicentennial. Collection displayed at Corporate Headquarters Building
Collections: Works by American artists from Revolutionary period to present
Activities: Tours; art works lent to museums occasionally; instrumental in the formation of Art, Inc, a traveling exhibition of corporate art

M **MONTGOMERY MUSEUM OF FINE ARTS,** 440 S McDonough St, 36104. Tel 205-834-3490. *Pres* Jim Sabel; *First VPres* Philip T Murkett Jr; *Second VPres* Mrs W K Upchurch Jr; *Secy* Mrs Robert Gallagher; *Treas* Mrs Jack P Evans; *Dir* Philip A Klopfenstein; *Cur* Mitchell D Kahan; *Cur of Education* Kathreen Campbell; *Registrar* Edward Quick
Open Tues - Sat 10 AM - 5 PM, Thurs 10 AM - 9 PM, Sun 1 - 6 PM, cl Mon. No admis fee. Estab 1930 to generally promote the cultural artistic and higher education life of the city of Montgomery by all methods that may be properly pursued by a museum or art gallery. Gallery occupies the upper floor of a two-story museum-library structure built by the city in the late 1950's. Five galleries provide the necessary space for displaying the permanent collection and circulating shows; 180 seat auditorium. Average Annual Attendance: 80,000. Mem: 1700; dues leadership $250 - $5000, associate $50 - $150, individual $10 - $30; annual meeting Oct
Income: Financed by membership, city and county appropriations and grants
Collections: †Contemporary graphics and other works on paper by artists living in the South; decorative arts; master prints of the 15th and 19th Centuries; †paintings by American artists from early 19th Century through the present
Publications: Annual Report; Calendar of Events, quarterly; exhibitions catalogs for selected shows
Activities: Classes for children; docent training; lect open to public, 4 - 8 visiting lectr per year; films; concerts; gallery talks; tours; competitions; individual paintings and original objects of art lent to museums and art galleries; lending collection contains cassettes, film strips, 275 original prints, 450 paintings, 1300 slides; originate traveling exhibitions; museum shop sells books, original art, reproductions, prints, crafts, stationery and jewelry
L **Library,** 440 S McDonough St, 36104. *Librn* Elizabeth B Brown
Open Tues - Fri 10 AM - 5 PM. Estab 1975 to assist the staff and community with reliable art research material. For reference
Library Holdings: Vols 1200; Per subs 25; AV—Fs, motion pictures, slides; Other—Clipping files, exhibition catalogs, prints, pamphlets, photographs
Special Subjects: American Art

SELMA

M STURDIVANT HALL, 713 Mabry St, PO Box 1205, 36701. Tel 205-872-5626. *Pres* J Mel Gilmer; *Cur* Mrs Jefferson Ratcliffe
Open Tues - Sat 9 AM - 4 PM; Sun 2 - 4 PM. Admis adults $2, student $1. Estab 1957 as a museum with emphasis on the historical South. Period furniture of the 1850's in a magnificent architectural edifice built 1852-53. Average Annual Attendance: 10,000. Mem: 480; dues $10 - $1000; annual meeting April
Income: Financed by membership, city and state appropriations
Collections: Objects of art; †period furniture; textiles
Publications: Brochure
Activities: Lect open to public; tours

TALLADEGA

M TALLADEGA COLLEGE, Savery Art Gallery,* 627 W Battle St, 35160. Tel 205-362-2752. *Cur* Edward Jennings
Open 9 AM - 5 PM. No admis fee. Estab to exhibit student art work, faculty art work and traveling exhibitions. Gallery, located in Library Building basement, is 25 x 35 ft and has adjustable lights. Average Annual Attendance: 1500
Income: Financed by college funds
Collections: Permanent collection maintained in the gallery
Exhibitions: Art Instructor Exhibit; Arts Festival Exhibit; Photo Exhibit; Student Exhibit
Activities: Lect open to the public, 12 visiting lectrs per year; concerts; gallery talks; individual paintings lent to faculty, students and administration personnel; lending collection contains prints of paintings; traveling exhibitions organized and circulated; museum shop and sales shop

THEODORE

M BELLINGRATH GARDENS AND HOME, Route 1, Box 60, 36582. Tel 205-973-2217. *General Mgr* John M Brown
Open daily 7 AM to dusk. Admis Gardens $3; Home $3.75. Estab 1932 to perpetuate and educate appreciation of nature, and display man-made objects d'art. The gallery houses the world's largest public display of Boehm porcelain, and the Bellingrath Home contains priceless antiques. Average Annual Attendance: 250,000
Income: Financed by Foundation
Collections: Antiques from Europe and America; Boehm Porcelain
Activities: Classes for children; tours; lending collection contains Kodachromes, motion pictures, slides; sales shop sells books, magazines, prints, reproductions and slides

TUSCALOOSA

O ARTS AND HUMANITIES COUNCIL OF TUSCALOOSA COUNTY, INC, Box 1117, 35401. Tel 205-758-5195. *Pres* John Owens; *Executive* Doug Perry
Open Mon - Fri 8 AM - 5 PM. No admis fee. Estab 1970 for the development, promotion and coordination of educational, cultural and artistic activities of the city and county of Tuscaloosa. Mem: 410 individual, 30 organization; dues organization $25, individual $10; annual meeting June, meetings quarterly
Income: Financed by endowment, membership, city, state and county appropriations
Publications: Arts Calendar, monthly; Newsletter - Arts Update, quarterly
Activities: Dramatic programs; concert series, Stars Fall on Ubama; sponsor of educational program called Sugar (Schools using greater Arts Resources)

TUSCUMBIA

O TENNESSEE VALLEY ART CENTER, 511 N Water St, PO Box 474, 35674. Tel 205-383-0533. *Chmn of Board* John Troy; *Pres* Betty Dardess; *VPres* Ann McCutchen; *Arts Coordinator* Shirley Maize; *Treas* Louis Mays; *Secy* Ina Geise
Open Tues - Sat 1 - 5 PM, Sun 1:30 - 5 PM. No admis to members; adults $.50, children $.25. Chartered 1963 to promote the arts in the Tennessee Valley. Building completed 1973. Main Gallery 60 x 40 ft; West Gallery for small exhibits, meetings and arts and crafts classes. Located one block from the birthplace of Helen Keller in Tuscumbia. During the Helen Keller Festival, TVAC sponsors the Arts and Crafts Fair. Average Annual Attendance: 5000. Mem: 300; dues patron $100, family $25, adult $10, student $5
Income: $15,000
Exhibitions: Exhibits change each month and feature work by national artists, members and students; handcraft exhibits; exhibit of art work by blind and handicapped individuals; Exhibit South and Spring Photo Show (annual, juried)
Activities: Class instruction in a variety of arts and crafts; String School provides music instruction for children and adults; workshops and performances in ballet and drama with special emphasis on children's theater; illustrated slide lecture; Sunday Concert Series; book traveling exhibits

TUSKEGEE

M TUSKEGEE INSTITUTE, George Washington Carver Museum, 36088. Tel 205-727-8911. *Dir & Cur* Elaine F Thomas; *Art Gallery Dir* Stefania Jarkowski
Gallery and Museum will be closed for one year for renovations

UNIVERSITY

M UNIVERSITY OF ALABAMA, Art Gallery, Garland Hall, Box F, 35486. Tel 205-348-5967. *Dir* Angelo Granata
Open Mon - Sat 8 AM - 5 PM, Sun 2 - 5 PM. No admis fee. Estab 1946
Collections: Small collection of paintings, prints, photography, drawings, sculpture and ceramics; primarily modern
Exhibitions: Approx 15 exhibitions per year

ALASKA

ANCHORAGE

O ALASKA ARTISTS GUILD, PO Box 1888, 99510. *Pres* San McClain; *VPres* Teri Jo Hedman; *VPres* Lise Thompson; *Secy* Betty Atkinson; *Treasurer* Dieter Doppelfeld; *Funding* Marie Shaughnessy; *Program* Mary Jean Sommer; *Publicity* Diane Barske; *Newsletter* John Peirce
Estab 1972 to provide an association for the educational interaction of qualified artists and to provide an education focus for the visual arts in the community. Mem: 110; qualifications for membership include talent and training or experience in the visual arts; dues $15; meetings second Tues each month
Income: $1500 (financed by membership)
Exhibitions: Alaska Juried Art Show; Alaska Festival of Music Art Exhibit
Publications: Alaska Artists Guild Newsletter, monthly except July and August
Activities: Lectures open to the public, three or four visiting lecturers per year; gallery talks; competitions; Betty Park Memorial painting award given; scholarships; individual paintings and original objects of art lent to colleges and schools by members

M ANCHORAGE HISTORICAL AND FINE ARTS MUSEUM, 121 W Seventh Ave, 99501. Tel 907-264-4326. *Dir* R L Shalkop; *Cur of Education* Patricia Wolf; *Cur of Exhibits* Gary Webernick; *Cur of Coll* Walter VanHorn
Open Sept - May, Tues - Sat 9 AM - 5 PM, Sun 1 - 5 PM; June - Aug, Mon, Wed, Fri & Sat 9 AM - 5 PM, Tues & Thurs 9 AM - 9 PM, Sun 1 - 5 PM. No admis fee. Estab 1968 to collect and display Alaskan art and artifacts of all periods; to present changing exhibitions of the art of the world. Average Annual Attendance: 138,000. Mem: 900; dues $10 and up
Income: $760,000 (financed by city appropriation)
Collections: Alaskan art; Alaskan Eskimo and Indian art; Alaskan history; American art; Primitive Art (non-American)
Exhibitions: (1978-79) All Alaska Exhibition; Bay area Painters; Contemporary Canadian art; Contemporary Native Art of Alaska; Earth, Fire and Fibre Craft Annual; Polish Textiles; Prints from the Guggenheim Museum; Recent Latin American Drawings; Survival: Art and Life of the Alaskan Eskimo; With Captain Cook in the North Pacific
Publications: Exhibition catalogs; Newsletter, monthly; occasional papers
Activities: Classes for children; dramatic programs; lect open to the public, 10 vis lectr per year; concerts; tours; competitions; individual paintings lent to municipal offices; organize and circulate traveling exhibitions; museum shop sells books, magazines, original art, prints, slides and Alaskan Native art
L Archives, 121 W Seventh Ave, 99501. Tel 907-264-4326. *Museum Archivist* M Diane Brenner
Open Tues - Fri 9 AM - 5 PM. Estab 1968 to maintain archives of Alaska materials, chiefly the Cook Inlet area
Income: Financed by city appropriation
Purchases: $3600
Library Holdings: Vols 2000; Per subs 28; AV—A-tapes, cassettes, motion pictures, rec, slides; Other—Clipping files, exhibition catalogs, memorabilia, photographs 5000, original documents
Special Subjects: American art, Alaska history and culture, Alaska Native peoples, museum techniques
Collections: Hinchey Alagco Photograph Collection of approximately 4000 pictures of the Copper River area; photograph collections

BETHEL

M YUGTARVIK REGIONAL MUSEUM, Third Ave, PO Box 388, 99559. Tel 907-543-2098. *Cur* Susan M Dreydoppel; *Arts & Crafts Dir* Brook B Kristovich
Open Tues - Sat 10 AM - 6 PM. No admis fee. Estab 1967 to help preserve the native culture and lifestyle of the people of the Kuskokwim River. Average Annual Attendance: 1500. Mem: 25; dues $25
Income: $35,000 (financed by city appropriation)
Purchases: $2000
Collections: †Native handmade objects of the Yupik Eskimo, both artifacts and contemporary art objects (included are full-size kayak, ivory carvings and wooden masks)
Activities: Classes for adults and children; lect open to the public; book traveling exhibitions, 3-4 times per year; museum shop selling baskets, ivory jewelry, beaded work, skin and fur items

FAIRBANKS

O ALASKA ASSOCIATION FOR THE ARTS, PO Box 2786, 99707. Tel 907-456-6485. *Pres* Ronald Inouye; *VPres* Susie Hackett; *VPres* Mardee Roth; *Secy* Renata Van Enkevort; *Treas* Terry Dickey; *Historian* Les Rogers; *Executive Dir* Robert A Vaughn
Office open Mon - Fri, 9 AM - 5 PM, gallery Tues - Sat 12:30 - 8:30 PM, Sun 12:30 - 6:30 PM. Estab 1965 to provide assistance and to help coordinate and promote the programs of other arts organizations, to encourage and develop educational programs designed to strengthen and improve the climate for the arts. To stimulate and facilitate the touring of professional and amateur performances and exhibits in

the Fairbanks area, to inform the community of performing and creative arts awareness and development in the Fairbanks area. Average Annual Attendance: 50,000. Mem: 600; comprised of individuals, businesses and art groups; annual meeting in Spring
Income: $192,000 (financed by city and state appropriations, national grants)
Exhibitions: Subscription performing arts series
Publications: Arts in Fairbanks cultural calendar and newsletter each month; Envoy: literary arts statewide newsletter, monthly
Activities: Workshop program; poetry readings; arts education program in the schools

UNIVERSITY OF ALASKA
M **Museum,** 99701. Tel 907-479-7505. *Dir* L J Rowinski; *Cur* D Larsen; *Coordr Exhib & Educational Programs* T Dickey
Open Summer 9 AM - 5 PM, Winter 1 - 5 PM. No admis fee. Estab 1929 to collect, preserve and interpret the natural and cultural history of Alaska. Gallery contains 6000 sq ft of exhibition space. Average Annual Attendance: 78,000
Income: Financed by state appropriation
Activities: Education department; lectures open to the public, one or two visiting lecturers per year; tours; traveling exhibitions organized and circulated; museum shop sells pamphlets
L **Elmer E Rasmuson Library,** 99701. Tel 907-479-7224. *Dir* H Theodore Ryberg; *Head Catalog Department* Sharon West; *Head Reader Services* David A Hales; *Head Archives* Paul McCarthy; *Head Acquisitions Department* William Smith; *Head Media Services* Edmund Cridge
Open Mon - Thurs 7:30 AM - 10 PM, Fri 7:30 AM - 6 PM, Sat 1 - 6 PM, Sun 1 - 8 PM, when school is not in session 8 AM - 5 PM. Estab 1922 to support research and curriculum of the university. Circ 57,000
Income: Financed by state appropriation
Library Holdings: Vols 500,000; Per subs 2500; Micro—Fiche, reels; AV—A-tapes, cassettes, fs, motion pictures, rec, slides, v-tapes; Other—Photographs, original documents
Collections: Lithographs of Fred Machetanz; paintings by Alaskan artists: Claire Fejes, C Rusty Heurlin; photographs of Early Alaskan bush pilots; print reference photograph collection on Alaska and the Polar Regions

HAINES

M **SHELDON MUSEUM AND CULTURAL CENTER,** 25 Main St, Box 236, 99827. Tel 907-766-2128. *Dir Sheldon Museum* Elisabeth S Hakkinen; *Pres Chilkat Valley Historical Society* Karl Ward; *VPres* Carl Heinmiller; *Secy* Jean Smith; *Treas* Retha Young
Open daily 2 - 4 PM. Admis adults $1, children free if with adult. Estab 1925, under operation of Chilkat Valley Historical Society since 1975, for the purpose of collecting, displaying and explaining local and Alaskan history, artifacts and mementoes. Average Annual Attendance: 4000. Mem: 74; dues $5; annual meeting second Thurs of Jan
Income: Financed by membership and other sources
Collections: Indian artifacts, basically Tlingit
Publications: Historical column in newspaper, weekly
Activities: Lect open to the public; sales shop sells books; Children's Corner
L **Library,** 25 Main St, Box 236, 99827. *Dir* Elisabeth S Hakkinen
Open to the public for reference only
Library Holdings: Vols 400

JUNEAU

M **ALASKA STATE MUSEUM,** Whittier St, Pouch FM, 99811. *Dir* Alan Munro; *Deputy Dir* Dan Monroe; *Cur Collections* Bette Hulbert; *Cur Visual Arts* Kesler Woodward; *Cur Education* Martha Stevens; *Conservator* Alice Houeman
Open Weekdays 9 AM - 5:30 PM, weekends 1 - 5:30 PM, summer weekdays 9 AM - 9 PM. No admis fee. Estab 1900 to collect, preserve, exhibit and interpret objects of special significance or value in order to promote public appreciation of Alaska's cultural heritage, history, art and natural environment. Gallery occupies two floors; first floor houses permanent and temporary exhibits on 1400 sq ft with 14 foot ceiling; second floor houses permanent exhibits. Average Annual Attendance: 80,000 with more than 150,000 including outreach program
Income: Financed by state appropriation and grants
Purchases: $50,000
Collections: †Alaskan ethnographic material including Eskimo, Aleut, Athabaskan, Tlingit, Haida and Tsimshian artifacts; †Gold Rush and early Alaskan industrial and historical material; †historical and contemporary Alaskan art
Exhibitions: Roy DeForest and Clayton Bailey; Judith Currelly Paintings
Publications: Museum Alaska, periodic
Activities: Education department; docent training; curculate learning kits to Alaska public schools; concerts; gallery talks; tours; competitions; individual paintings and original objects of art lent to other museums, libraries, historical societies; lending collection contains original prints, photographs; traveling exhibits of photographs and prints organized and circulated
L **Library,** Whittier St, 99811. *Cur of Education* Martha Stevens
Open to staff and other upon request
Library Holdings: Vols 1500; Per subs 25

NOME

M **CARRIE MCLAIN MUSEUM,** (Formerly Nome Museum) Box 53, 99762. Tel 907-443-2566. *Dir* Terry L Gacke
Open Winter Mon - Fri 10 AM - 6 PM, Summer Tues, Wed, Thurs, Sat, Sun 12 - 8 PM
Income: Financed by City of Nome and supplemental grant projects and donations
Collections: Permanent collection includes examples of art from 1890—1980, including basketry, block prints, carved ivory, ink, oil, skin drawings, stone carving, watercolor paintings, woodworking
Exhibitions: Permanent exhibitions, with a large number of rotating exhibits plus temporary exhibits every other month; Annual Competitions include: Arts and

Crafts Fair in March and Photographic Competition in April
Activities: Demonstrations; workshops; lect; film series
L **Library,** Box 53, 99762.
Open to the public
Library Holdings: Vols 4000

SITKA

M **SHELDON JACKSON COLLEGE,** Sheldon Jackson Museum, Lincoln St, PO Box 479, 99835. Tel 907-747-5228. *Dir, Cur* Peter L Corey
Open summer May 15 - Sept 15, 8 AM - 5 PM daily, winter hours Sept 16 - May 14, 1 - 4 PM Tues - Fri and Sun, cl Mon and Sat. Admis $1 over 18. Estab 1888, the first museum in Alaska, for the purpose of collecting and preserving the cultural remains of the Alaskan natives in the form of artifacts. The museum occupies one room with permanent displays concerned with Tlingit, Haida, Aleut, Athabascan, and Eskimo culture. Average Annual Attendance: 35,000
Income: $30,000 (financed by admission fee, sales, donation and college support)
Purchases: $500
Collections: Ethnographic material from Tlingit, Haida, Aleut, Athabascan, Eskimo and some Russian
Publications: Brochures; catalogs of Ethnological Collection
Activities: Lect open to the public, 1 - 2 vis lectr per yr; gallery talks; tours; traveling exhibitions organized and circulated; museum shop sells books, magazines, original art, prints, slides
L **Stratton Library,** Lincoln & Jeff David Sts, Box 479, 99835. *Dir Library Services* Evelyn K Bonner; *Assoc Librn* Mary Gutteridge; *Library Asst In Charge of Interlibrary Loan & Periodicals* Nancy Ricketts; *Library Asst In Charge of Circulation & State Documents* Deborah Saito
Estab 1944 with Collection Library for curriculum support and meeting the needs of patrons interested in the arts. Circ 600
Purchases: $500
Library Holdings: Vols 5559; Per subs 25; Micro—Reels; AV—A-tapes, cassettes, fs, Kodachromes, lantern slides, motion pictures, rec, slides, v-tapes; Other—Clipping files, exhibition catalogs, framed reproductions, memorabilia, original art works, pamphlets, photographs, reproductions, sculpture
Special Subjects: Alaskan and Native American Art Books, Alaska and the Northwest Pacific Coast, Harmon original pictures
Collections: Alaska Reference Collection (containing works on Native Arts and Crafts); E W Merrill Glass Plate Photo Collection (representative of Sitka at the turn of the century)
Activities: Annual programs held in April, includes dramatic presentations; lect; demonstrations

O **SOUTHEAST ALASKA REGIONAL ARTS COUNCIL, INC,** PO Box 2133, 99835. Tel 907-747-8177. *Executive Dir* Marlene Lund; *VPres* Dr Randall Ackley; *Admin Asst* Jan Cunningham; *Secy* Roxana Adams; *Treas* Vivian Poon
Open 8 AM - 5 PM. Estab in 1973 as a not-for-profit coordinating agency for arts organizations and community arts councils in Southeast Alaska. Mem: Arts councils from southeast communities
Income: Financed by membership dues, local school districts and municipalities, private contributions, and grants from the Alaska State Council on the Arts and National Endowment for the Arts
Publications: Annual regional arts directory listing of Southeast Alaska arts council and organizations; booklet of stories and poems by young people; The Panhandle Post (newsletter on art happenings throughout the region and state)

ARIZONA

DOUGLAS

L **COCHISE COLLEGE LIBRARY,** 85607. *Librn* Kathy Lincer
Open Mon, Wed & Fri 8 AM - 9 PM, Sat as posted. Estab 1965. Circ 35,000
Purchases: $36,000
Library Holdings: Vols 50,000; Per subs 236; Micro—Cards, fiche, reels, prints; AV—A-tapes, cassettes, fs, lantern slides, motion pictures, rec, slides, v-tapes; Other—Clipping files, exhibition catalogs, framed reproductions, prints, memorabilia, original art works, photographs, reproductions, sculpture
Collections: A Comprehensive Collection of Oriental Originals (ceramics and paintings); Collection of 19th Century American and European Impressionists

O **DOUGLAS ART ASSOCIATION,** Little Gallery, 11th St at Pan American Ave, PO Box 256, 85607. Tel 602-364-2633. *Pres* Joyce Smith; *First VPres* Terry Mason; *Second VPres* Gayle Bell; *Secy* Jennie Welcome; *Treas* Carol Beeman
Open Tues - Sat 1:30 - 4 PM. No admis fee. Estab 1960 as a non-profit tax exempt organization dedicated to promoting the visual arts and general cultural awareness in the Douglas, Arizona and Agua Prieta, Sonora area. Little Gallery is operated in a city owned building with city cooperation. Average Annual Attendance: 2000. Mem: 100; dues $7.50 and $10
Income: Financed by membership and fund raising events
Collections: †Two Flags Festival International Collections for the cities of Douglas and Agua Prieta, Mexico
Exhibitions: Annual Two Flags Festival exhibit; Monthly exhibits by local and regional arts and craftsman; Outdoor Show
Publications: Newsletter, monthly
Activities: Classes for adults and children; workshops in painting and various art activities; lect open to the public; gallery talks; competitions with cash awards; sales shop sells books and donated items

DRAGOON

O **AMERIND FOUNDATION, INC**, Dragoon Rd, PO Box 248, 85609. Tel 602-586-3003. *Pres* William Duncan Fulton; *VPres* Peter L Formo; *Secy* Elizabeth F Husband; *Treas* Michael W Hard; *Foundation Dir* Dr Charles C Di Peso
Open Mon - Fri 8 AM - Noon and 1 - 5 PM, tours Sat & Sun 10:30 AM & 1 PM by appointment. No admis fee. Estab 1937 for archaeological research of the American Southwest and northern Mexico; maintenance of Museum and Art Gallery on Indians of the Americas. Average Annual Attendance: 6000. Mem: Annual meeting Nov
Income: $241,333 (financed by endowment)
Collections: Archaeological and ethnographic specimens of Native Americans of the Americas; Art of the Southwest; miscellaneous collections of Dr and Mrs William Shirley Fulton
Publications: Amerind Publications on Arizona
Activities: Docent training; lect; tours; individual paintings and original objects of art lent, subject to Board of Directors approval, for temporary exhibitions; lending collection contains original art works and paintings; Brochure of Amerind and postcards available
L **Fulton-Hayden Memorial Library**, Dragon Rd, PO Box 248, 85609. Tel 602-586-3003. *Librn* Mario N Klimiades
Estab 1961. Open to scholars by appointment
Purchases: $1500
Library Holdings: Vols 16,000; Per subs 350; Micro—Reels; AV—Slides; Other—Clipping files, manuscripts, photographs
Special Subjects: Archaeology, Ethnology, Pre-Columbian and post-Columbian history and ethnology of Western Hemisphere
Collections: Parral Archives on microfilm; collections of research and technical reports

FLAGSTAFF

M **MUSEUM OF NORTHERN ARIZONA**, Route 4, Box 720, 86001. Tel 602-774-5211. *Dir* Dr Hermann K Blebtreu; *Pres Board of Trustees* Dr David Chase; *Cur of Archaeology* Dr Alexander J Lindsay
Open Mon - Sat 9 AM - 5 PM, Sun 1:30 - 5 PM. Donation requested. Estab 1928 to maintain a museum where the story of the geological history and pre-history of northern Arizona can be told and where archaeological and ethnological treasures of northern Arizona can be preserved; to protect our historic and prehistoric sites, works of art, scenic places and wildlife from needless destruction; to provide facilities for research and to offer opportunities for aesthetic enjoyment. Average Annual Attendance: 100,000. Mem: 1550; dues $25 - $100
Income: $2,500,000 (financed by endowment, membership and earned income)
Collections: Archaeological collection; art collection, ethnographic collection
Exhibitions: Arizona Sculpture Invitational; Batik Show; Form and Function (science show); Hopi Show; Navajo Blanket Show; Navajo Show; Student Art Exhibition of Northern Arizona; Tribute to Edward B Danson; Walpi Show;
Publications: Museum Notes, bimonthly; Plateau, quarterly
Activities: Classes for adults and children; docent training; expeditions; lect open to public, 25 vis lectr per year; tours; competitions; exten dept serves the Southwestern states; individual paintings and original objects of art lent to various institutions; lending collection contains nature artifacts, original art works, original prints, paintings, photographs, and sculpture; organize and circulate traveling exhibitions; museum shop sells books, magazines, original art and crafts
L **Harold S Colton Memorial Library**, Route 4, Box 720, 86001. Tel 602-774-5211, Ext 56.
Open Mon - Fri 9 AM - 5 PM. Estab 1928, library is a repository of material relating to the Colorado Plateau, with its primary function to serve the needs of the Museum's research staff, although visiting scholars are welcome. Circ 4000 (limited to Museum staff)
Income: Financed by endowment
Library Holdings: Vols 18,000; Other—Clipping files, manuscripts, photographs
Collections: Navajo sandpainting reproductions

M **NORTHERN ARIZONA UNIVERSITY**, Art Gallery, Creative Arts Building, Room 231, Box 6021, 86011. Tel 602-523-3471. *Dir Art Gallery* Joel S Eide; *Dean College Creative Arts* Charles H Aurand
Open Mon - Fri 9 AM - 5 PM, Tues 6:30 - 8:30 PM, Sun 3 - 5 PM, cl Sat. No admis fee. Estab 1968 for the continuing education and service to the students and the Flagstaff community in all aspects of fine arts
Collections: Master prints of the 20th century and American painting of the Southwest
Activities: Concerts; gallery talks; competitions; annual toy show; visiting artist workshop

JEROME

O **VERDE VALLEY ART ASSOCIATION, INC**, Main Street, PO Box 985, 86331. Tel 602-634-5466. *Pres* Elizabeth D Smith; *VPres* Tom Schumacher; *Dir* Hand Chaikin; *Secy* Katherine Hampson; *Treas* Alison Weinberg
Open daily 10 AM - 5 PM. Admis by donation. Estab 1954 to promote and further the arts in Northern Arizona, particularly the Verde Valley, in all its forms; visual arts, performing arts and educational programs. Gallery is 1000 sq ft; changing monthly exhibitions. Average Annual Attendance: 30,000. Mem: 250; dues vary; annual meeting third Tues in June
Income: Financed by membership, federal and state grants, corporate gifts, foundation gifts, donations, fund raising projects
Collections: Small permanent collection of original works and prints
Exhibitions: Jerome Theme and Memorabilia Show; Northern Arizona Invitational; Verde Valley Christmas Exhibition and Sale; Wearable Crafts Exhibition; Young Artists Exhibition and Tour; one-artist shows and group shows of Arizona artists and craftspersons; monthly visual art exhibitions
Publications: Verde Artists Bulletin, monthly
Activities: Performing arts and educational programs; annual Summer Youth Enrichment Program; Verde Valley Visual Artists Slide Registry

PATAGONIA

M **STRADLING MUSEUM OF THE HORSE, INC**, Box 413, 85624. Tel 602-394-2264. *Dir* Anne C Stradling; *Cur* Marianna Rider
Open daily & holidays 9 AM - 5 PM, cl Thanksgiving & Christmas. Admis adults $1, no admis children and special groups. Estab 1960
Collections: Bronzes, china, glass, paintings, prints, saddles, silver; Indian Painting and Kachinas
Activities: Guided tours; sales shop sells saddlery, Indian rugs, art, china and jewelry
L **Library**, Box 413, 85624.
For reference only
Library Holdings: Vols 800
Special Subjects: Art History, Indian history, horses

PHOENIX

O **ARIZONA ARTIST GUILD**, 8912 N Fourth St, 85020. Tel 602-944-9713. *Pres* L Don Miller; *First VPres Membership* Jean Thomas; *Second VPres Exhibitions* Fred Krueger; *Recording Secy* Jean Harney; *Corresponding Secy* Diane Maxey
Estab 1928 to foster guild spirit, to assist in raising standards of art in the community, and to assume civic responsibility in matters relating to art. Average Annual Attendance: 500. Mem: 210, dues $15; membership by jury; monthly meetings
Income: Financed by endowment and membership
Exhibitions: Dimensions (open to whole state); Horizons (annually in spring, members only); fall exhibition for members only
Publications: AAG news, monthly
Activities: Classes for adults; lect sometimes open to the public, 12 or more vis lectrs per year; gallery talks; competions with awards; schol offered
L **Library**, 8912 N Fourth St, 85020.
Open to members for reference only

C **THE ARIZONA BANK**, 101 N First Ave, PO Box 2511, 85003. Tel 602-262-2826. *Chmn & Chief Executive Officer* Don B Tostenrud
Open Mon - Thurs 9 AM - 3 PM, Fri 9 AM - 6 PM. Estab to provide an opportunity for Southwest art to be seen by customers and others in downtown Phoenix. Collection displayed in the Galleria, and in offices statewide. Galleria exhibits, including parts of permanent collection, change monthly
Collections: Approximately 400 Hopi Indian Kachinas; 350 paintings and sculpture
Activities: Gallery talks; tours; sponsor purchase prizes; individual objects of art lent to specific museums upon request; originate traveling exhibitions to museums and art associations within state of Arizona

O **ARIZONA COMMISSION ON THE ARTS**, 6330 N Seventh St, 85014. Tel 602-255-5882. *Chmn* Dino DeConcini; *Vice Chmn* Richard H Whitney; *Executive Dir* Louise C Tester; *Deputy Dir* Adrienne Hirsch; *Education Coordr* Shelley Cohn; *Expansion Arts Coordr* Louis Leroy; *Arts Services Coordr* Tonda Gorton; *Community Development Coordr* Mollie Trivers; *Visual Arts Coordr* Rex Gulbranson; *Museum Cur* Deborah Whitehurst
Open 8 AM - 5 PM. No admis fee. Estab 1966 to promote and encourage the arts in the State of Arizona. Mem: Meetings, quarterly
Income: $1,088,6000 (financed by state and federal appropriation)
Exhibitions: Traveling exhibitions program
Publications: Annual Report; Artists' Guide to Programs; monthly bulletin
Activities: Workshops; lect open to public; fels

O **ARIZONA WATERCOLOR ASSOCIATION**, PO Box 7494, 85011. Tel 602-942-3365. *Pres* Anna Mary Seyfert; *Dir* Jack Ricard; *First VPres* Jannie Mitchell; *Second VPres* Colleen Gustaferro; *Third VPres* Rick Lussier; *Recording Secy* Audrey Urry; *Corresponding Secy* Lois Halle; *Treas* Elsie Goldstein
Estab 1960 to further activity and interest in the watercolor medium, promote growth of individuals and group and maintain high quality of professional exhibits. Mem: 250; qualifications for juried membership, Fall jurying by Membership Committee; for Associate membership, application through First VPres; dues $12; meetings second Mon each month at AAG building
Publications: AWA Newsletter, every two months
Activities: Workshops; lect; demonstrations; paint outs; competitions; traveling exhibitions organized and circulated

M **HEARD MUSEUM**, 22 E Monte Vista Rd, 85004. Tel 602-252-8848. *Dir* Patrick T Houlihan; *Cur Anthropology* H Thomas Cain; *Cur Tech* Jon T Erickson; *Cur Exhib* Patrick Neary; *Cur Education* Camille Tumolo; *Cur Harvey Coll* Cynthia Davies; *Cur Art* Erin Younger; *Asst Cur* Diana Pardue; *Registrar* Nicolette Teufel; *Publicist* Katherine Coe; *Business Mgr* Michael Fox
Open Mon - Sat 10 AM - 5 PM, Sun 1 - 5 PM. Admis adult $1.50, senior citizen $1, student and children 50¢. Estab 1929 to collect and exhibit anthropology and art; collections built around works of Indians of the Americas. Average Annual Attendance: 250,000
Income: $600,000 (financed by membership)
Collections: Archeology, ethnology paintings, sculpture, primitive arts from the cultures of Africa, Asia and Oceania; American Indian; African; Fred Harvey Fine Arts Collection
Exhibitions: African Art; Dancing Kachinas; Fred Harvey Fine Arts Collection; Heard Museum Book; Guatemalan Costumes: The Heard Museum Collection; Indian Art of the Americas; Indian Arts and Crafts of Northwest Mexico; Kachinas: An Evolving Hopi Art Form; Kachinas, a Hopi Artist's Documentary; Kachinas, the Goldwater Collection at the Heard Museum; Loloma: A Retrospective View; Navajo Textiles from the Read Mullan Collection; The CG Wallace Collection of American Indian Art; The Other Southwest
Activities: Docent training; lect open to public, 15 vis lectr per year; lect at schools; original objects of art lent to accredited museums; lending collection contains framed reproductions, original prints, 1000 paintings, photographs, sculpture, and 600 slides; organize and circulate traveling exhibitions; museum shop sells books, original art, prints, reproductions and slides

L **Heard Museum Library**, 22 E Monte Vista Rd, 85004. Tel 602-252-8848. *Librn* Mary E Graham; *Librn Asst* Margaret Myers
Open Mon - Fri 10 AM - 5 PM. Estab 1929 as a research library for museum staff, members and the public (in-house only)
Income: $10,000 (financed by membership and museum budget)
Library Holdings: Vols 50,000; Micro—Fiche, reels; AV—A-tapes, motion pictures, v-tapes; Other—Clipping files, exhibition catalogs, prints, memorabilia, pamphlets, photographs
Special Subjects: Primitive Art, American Indian

M **PHOENIX ART MUSEUM**, 1625 N Central Ave, 85004. Tel 602-257-1222. *Dir* Robert A Applewhite; *VPres* Rae Ludke; *Secy* Thomas W Richardson; *Treas* Howard McCrady; *Dir* Ronald D Hichman; *Asst Dir* Robert H Frankel
Open Mon - Sat 10 AM - 5 PM, Wed 10 AM - 9 PM, Sun 1 - 5 PM. No admis fee. Estab 1925; museum constructed 1959. Average Annual Attendance: 200,000. Mem: 4300; dues $20 and up; annual meeting April
Income: $625,000
Collections: Contemporary paintings, sculptures and graphics; 19th century; Baroque; Mexican art; Oriental arts collection; Renaissance; Thorne Miniature rooms; Western art; Medieval art
Exhibitions: Changing exhibitions in all areas of art including photography and graphics
Publications: Annual report; Calendar, monthly; catalog of permanent collection; exhibition catalogs
Activities: Classes for adults; docent training; lect open to public; concerts; movie series; tours; museum shop; junior museum

L **Art Research Library**, 1627 N Central Ave, 85004. Tel 602-257-1222. *Librn* Annette E Erkin
Open Tues, Thurs, Fri 10 AM 4:30 PM. Estab 1959 to serve reference needs of the museum staff, docents, membership and students. For reference only
Income: Financed by endowment and membership
Purchases: $6000
Library Holdings: Vols 4000; Per subs 49; Other—Clipping files, exhibition catalogs, pamphlets, reproductions
Special Subjects: American Painting, Prints
Collections: Ambrose Lansing Egyptian Collection; Arizona Artist Index; auction catalogs; museum archives; Rembrandt etching catalogs

C **VALLEY NATIONAL BANK OF ARIZONA**, Fine Arts Department, PO Box 71, 85001. Tel 602-261-2966. *Cur Art* Judy Brown
Open to public. Estab 1933 to support emerging artists throughout the state; encourage and promote talented high school students with Scholastic Art Awards; provide the public with beautiful, integrated art in branch banks. Several thousand pieces of art collection displayed in over 200 branches, business offices, and support facilities throughout the state of Arizona
Purchases: $100,000
Collections: Primarily Western, Southwestern art featuring many of the now classic Western artists; earliest lithograph dates back to the 1820's and collection continues through the present
Exhibitions: Employee's Art Show
Activities: Lect; gallery talks; tours by appointment; competitions, since 1942 state sponsor for Scholastic Art Awards throughout Arizona; purchase awards throughout the state, sponsor Employees' Art Show annually, with juried and popular choice awards, underwrite local art exhibitions on the Concourse of the Home Office Building; individual objects of art lent contingent upon bank policy

PRESCOTT

O **PRESCOTT FINE ARTS ASSOCIATION**, 202 North Marina St, PO Box 1267, 86301. Tel 602-445-9853. *Pres* Pat Patton; *VPres* Jesse Thomas; *Secy* Joella Willey
Open Wed - Sun 1 - 5 PM. No admis fee, donations accepted. Estab to promote arts within the county and local community. One room below theater section in what was previously a Catholic Church. Average Annual Attendance: 900. Mem: 318; dues family $15, individual $10; annual meeting first Thurs of Dec
Income: $23,000 (financed by membership and grants from Arizona Arts and Humanities Council)
Activities: Docent training; lect open to public; concerts; competitions

SCOTTSDALE

O **COSANTI FOUNDATION**, 6433 Doubletree Ranch Rd, 85253. Tel 602-948-6145. *Pres* Paolo Soleri; *VPres & Secy* Corolyn Soleri
Open Mon - Sun 9 AM - 5 PM. Admis $1. Estab 1956 as a non-profit educational organization by Paolo Soleri pursuing the research and development of an alternative urban environment. Gallery, the North Studio has on display original sketches, sculptures, and graphics by Paolo Soleri. Average Annual Attendance: 40,000
Income: Financed by state appropriation and sales of art objects
Collections: Permanent collection of architectural designs and drawings by Paolo Soleri
Exhibitions: Permanent exhibit in North Studio; Toward Arcology, Works in Progress, traveled to thirty-five colleges and universities; Two Sun Arcology, The City Energized by the Sun, sponsored by Xerox Corporation, traveled to three East Coast Museums
Activities: Classes for adults; docent training; Arcosanti Workshop Program, experiential workshops; lectures open to the public; gallery talks; tours; scholarships; traveling exhibits organized and circulated; sales shop sells books, original art, prints, reproductions, slides

O **SCOTTSDALE ARTISTS' LEAGUE**, PO Box 1071, 85252. Tel 602-948-3560. *Pres* Maxine Johnston
Estab 1961 to encourage the practice of art and to support and encourage the study and application of art as an avocation, to promote ethical principals and practice, to advance the interest and appreciation of art in all its forms and to increase the usefulness of art to the public at large. Maintains Upstairs Gallery in Camelview

Plaza Mall and gallery in Scottsdale Hospital. Mem: 553; dues individual $10, family $15; monthly meetings first Tues
Exhibitions: Yearly juried exhibition for members only; yearly juried exhibition for all Arizona artists (open shows)
Publications: Art Beat, monthly
Activities: Lect and demonstrations for members and guests

TEMPE

ARIZONA STATE UNIVERSITY

M **University Art Collections**, Mathews Center, 85281. Tel 602-965-2874. *Dir* Rudy H Turk; *Registrar* Mary Jane Williams
Open Mon - Fri 8 AM - 5 PM, Sun 1 - 5 PM. No admis fee. Estab 1950 to provide esthetic and educational service for student and the citizens of the state. Three permanent exhibition galleries featuring American, European and Latin American art; two changing galleries and two changing areas; 48 shows annually. Average Annual Attendance: 40,000
Income: $100,000 (financed by city and state appropriations, donations and earnings)
Purchases: $25,000
Collections: †American crafts, especially ceramics; †American painting and sculpture 18th Century to present; †print collection 16th Century to present
Exhibitions: The Flue and the Brush: Indian Miniatures; Paintings and Prints by Dosamantes; Wood-In-Art Invitational; Wood-In-Art State Competition; continuous showing of Historical and Contemporary Print Exhibitions
Activities: Educ dept; dramatic programs; docent training; special events; lect open to public, 12 visiting lectr per year; gallery talks; tours; competitions; individual paintings and original objects of art lent to campus offices; originate traveling exhibitions; museum shop sells books, original art, slides and crafts

L **Hayden Library**, Arizona State University, 85201. Tel 602-965-3605. *Chief Librn* Don Riggs; *Assoc Librn* Helen Gates; *Acting Asst Librn* Constance Corey
Open Mon - Thurs 7 AM - Midnight, Fri 7 AM - 10 PM, Sat 9 AM - 5 PM, Sun 10 AM - Midnight
Library Holdings: Vols 1,330,515; Per subs 15,020

M **Memorial Union Gallery**, 85281. Tel 602-965-6649. *Dir* Mark Miller
Open Mon - Fri 9 AM - 5 PM. Estab to exhibit work that has strong individual qualities from the United States, also some Arizona work that has not been shown on campus. Gallery is contained in two rooms with 1400 sq ft space; fireplace; one wall is glass; 20 ft ceiling; 26 4 x 8 partitions; track lighting; one entrance and exit; located in area with maximum traffic. Average Annual Attendance: 30,000
Income: $400 (financed by city appropriation)
Purchases: $2000
Collections: Painting and print, primarily Altman, Gorman, Mahaffey and Schoulder
Exhibitions: Barbara MacCallum; Linda S Munswiler; New Southwest Landscapes; Dan O'Dowdy; The Shamen and the Goddess an Environment; Beth Ames Swartz; Jim Waid; Marcia Wallace; Adrianne Wartzel; Edith Weff; Susan Weil; Dina Yellen
Activities: Educ dept; internships; lect open to public, 4 visiting lectr per year; gallery talks; competitions; originate traveling exhibitions

L **Howe Architecture Library**, College of Architecture, Planning & Design Sciences, 85281. Tel 602-965-6400. *Head Librn* Don Riggs; *Acting Department Librn* Open
Open Mon - Thurs 8 AM - 10 PM, Fri 8 AM - 5 PM, Sat Noon - 5 PM, Sun 5 - 10 PM. Estab 1959 to serve the architecture college and the university community with reference and research material in the subject of architecture. Circ 13,500
Income: Financed by state appropriation
Library Holdings: Vols 15,000; Per subs 180; Micro—Reels; AV—A-tapes, cassettes, motion pictures, v-tapes; Other—Prints, manuscripts, memorabilia, original art works, pamphlets, photographs, original documents
Collections: Paola Soleri Archive; Frank Lloyd Wright Rare Material
Publications: Guide to the Library, annually; Information Brochure, annually; New Books List, semi-annual

TUBAC

O **TUBAC CENTER OF THE ARTS**, Santa Cruz Valley Art Association, Box 1314, 84540. *Pres* Robert Lasch; *Dir* Doris Fouch
Open Tues - Sat 1 - 5 PM, Sun & holidays 1 - 5 PM, cl Mon. No admis fee. Estab 1963 to exhibit local artists works
Collections: Works by present and former Tubac artists
Activities: Docent training; lectures; guided tours; films; art festivals; sales shop open

TUCSON

M **CENTER FOR CREATIVE PHOTOGRAPHY**, University of Arizona, 843 E University, 85710. Tel 602-884-4636. *Dir* James Enyeart; *Cur & Libr Photography Archive* Terence R Pitts
Open Mon - Fri 9 AM - 6 PM, Thur 9 AM - 9 PM. Estab 1975 to house and organize the archives of numerous major photographers and to act as a research center in 20th century photography. Gallery exhibitions changing approximately every six weeks. Average Annual Attendance: 15,000
Income: Financed by State appropriation, grants and donations
Collections: Archives of Ansel Adams, Wynn Bullock, Harry Callahan, Aaron Siskind, W Eugene Smith, Frederick Sommer, Paul Strand and others
Publications: Center for Creative Photography, approx 5 times per yr
Activities: Lect open to public, 12 - 15 vis lectr per yr; gallery talks; tours; traveling exhibitions organized and circulated

L **Library**, 843 E University, 85710. *Librn* Terence R Pitts
Open to the public for lending and reference
Library Holdings: Vols 3000; Per subs 60
Collections: Limited edition books; hand-made books; books illustrated with original photographs

M TUCSON MUSEUM OF ART, 235 West Alameda, 85701. Tel 602-624-2333. *Dir* R Andrew Maass; *Cur Educ* David L Jones; *Cur Historic Sites* Bettina Lyons; *Registrar* Rene Verdugo; *Museum Educ Coordr* Toby Falk; *Public Relations Coordr* Diana Hunter; *Development Coordr* Marjorie Sherrill; *Bus Secy* M E Thompson; *Asst to Dir* Toby Engler
Open Tues - Sat 10 AM - 5 PM, Sun 1 - 5 PM. No admis fee. Estab 1924 to operate a nonprofit civic art gallery to promote art education, to hold art exhibitions and to further art appreciation for the public. Upper gallery has changing exhibitions; sales gallery displays contemporary crafts by Arizona artists and the lower galleries hold the permanent collection. Average Annual Attendance: 75,000. Mem: 2450; dues league $6, student $10, individual $20, family $25, donor $50, sponsor $100, patron $250, benefactor $500, Angel $1000 or more; annual meeting May
Income: $500,000 (financed by endowment, membership, city and state appropriations and contributions)
Purchases: $5000
Collections: †Art of the Americas; †European painting and sculpture; †19th and 20th century American; †Oriental; †Pre-Columbian; †Spanish Colonial; †Western
Publications: Calendar, monthly; exhibition catalogs; Arizona Artist Newsletter, six times a yr
Activities: Classes for adults and children; docent training; lect open to public; concerts; gallery talks; tours; competitions; exten department serving Tucson school districts; traveling exhibitions organized and circulated; museum shop features contemporary crafts by Arizona artists
L Tucson Museum of Art Library, 120 North Main Ave, 85705. *Librn* Dorcas Worsley; *Cataloger* Dorothy Siebecker; *Slide Librarian* Elinore Smith; *Bibliographer* Donald Powell; *Asst* Margaret Peck
Open Mon - Fri 10 AM - 3 PM. Estab 1974 for bibliographic and research needs of Museum staff, faculty, students and docents. Open to public for research and study
Library Holdings: Vols 6000; Per subs 13; AV—Cassettes, slides 18,000; Other—Clipping files, exhibition catalogs, pamphlets, photographs
Special Subjects: Pre-Columbian Art, Art of Africa, Oceania, Western art, Contemporary Art
Collections: Biographic material documenting Arizona artists for the Archives of Arizona Art

UNIVERSITY OF ARIZONA
M Museum of Art, Olive & Speedway Sts, 85721. Tel 602-626-2173. *Dir & Chief Cur* Dr Peter Bermingham
Open Mon - Sat 9 AM - 5 PM, Sun 12 - 5 PM. Estab 1955 to share the treasures of three remarkable permanent collections; the C Leonard Pfeiffer Collection, Samuel H Kress Collection and the Edward J Gallagher Jr Collection with the Tucson community, visitors and the university students. One of the most important functions is to reach out to schools around Tucson through the education department. Special exhibitions are maintained on the first floor of the museum; the permanent collections are housed on the second floor. Average Annual Attendance: 80,000
Income: Financed by state appropriation
Collections: Edward J Gallagher Collection of over a hundred paintings of national and international artists; Samuel H Kress Collection of 26 Renaissance works and 26 paintings of the 15th century Spanish Retablo by Fernando Gallego; C Leonard Pfeiffer Collection of American Artists of the 30s, 40s and 50s; Jacques Lipchitz Collection of 70 plaster models
Exhibitions: Arizona and New Mexico; Art and the Law; Contemporary Mexican Artists; Copper II; Paul Delvaux; Ernest Lawson; Peter Milton Prints; The New Deal in the Southwest
Publications: Fully illustrated catalogs on all special exhibitions
Activities: Docent training; tours of museum; lectr; gallery talks; out reach tours; traveling exhibitions organized and circulated; sales shop sells books, reproductions and poster reproductions
L Main Library, Cherry and University Mall, 85721. *Univrsity Librn* W David Laird; *Asst Librn for Public Service* Mary Dale Paisson; *Central Reference Librn* Paul Barton
Open Mon - Fri 7 AM - 3 AM, academic year; summer and holiday hours posted. Estab 1891 to assist instruction and provide basis for research
Purchases: $175,000
Library Holdings: Vols 50,000; Per subs 200; Micro—Cards, fiche, reels, prints; AV—A-tapes, cassettes, fs, Kodachromes, motion pictures, rec, slides, v-tapes; Other—Exhibition catalogs, prints, manuscripts, memorabilia, original art works, pamphlets, photographs, reproductions
Collections: Center for Creative Photography; Regional interests
L Fine Arts Library, Speedway & Olive, 85721. *Librn* Barbara Kittle
Estab to assist staff and students working at museum with reference information. Not open to public; telephone requests for information answered
Library Holdings: Vols 1000; Per subs 16; AV—Cassettes, slides; Other—Clipping files, exhibition catalogs, pamphlets

WICKENBURG
M DESERT CABALLEROS WESTERN MUSEUM, 20 N Frontier St, Box 1446, 85358. *Pres* Roy Coxwell; *Exec VPres and Cur* Harry T Needham; *Asst Cur* Veeva Peabody; *Chmn of the Board* H K MacLennan; *Treas* H D Murphy
Open Tues - Sat 10 AM - 4 PM, cl Mon. Admis by donation. Estab 1975 to show the development of Wickenburg from prehistoric to present day. The museum houses western art gallery, mineral room, Indian room, period rooms and gold mining equipment. Average Annual Attendance: 16,000. Mem: 200; dues vary; annual meeting 2nd Mon in April
Income: $25,000 - $35,000 (financed by membership)
Collections: Indian artifacts; period rooms; western art; George Phippen display of western bronzes
Activities: Museum shop sells books and prints
L Library, 20 N Frontier St, Box 1446, 85358.
Open to members for reference only
Library Holdings: Vols 200; Per subs 6

WINDOW ROCK
M NAVAJO TRIBAL MUSEUM, Highway 264, PO Box 308, 86515. Tel 602-871-6457. *Acting Dir* Russell P Hartman
Open Mon - Sat 8 AM - 5 PM, Sun 1 - 5 PM, cl Sat & Sun, Dec - March, & national & tribal holidays. No admis fee. Estab 1961 to collect and preserve items depicting Navajo history and culture and natural history of region. Exhibit area approx 2500 ft. Average Annual Attendance: 10,000
Income: Financed by tribal budget
Collections: Works in all media by Southwest Indian artists, with emphasis on Navajo artists and subject matter
Exhibitions: (1978) R C Gorman Prints sponsored by Arizona Commission for the Arts and Humanities; (1978-79) Handpainted ceramics by Mary Saxon (Navajo); (1979) Selections from permanent collections
Activities: Individual paintings and original works of art available for loan to other museums; lending collection contains original works of art
L Navajo Nation Library, Highway 264, Box 308, 86515. Tel 602-871-6457. *Librn* Richard Heiser
Open to public for reference only
Library Holdings: Vols 3000

YUMA
O YUMA ART CENTER, 281 Gila St, PO Box 1471, 85364. Tel 602-783-2314. *Dir* Nancy Holmes Ghigna
Open Tues - Sun 10 AM - 5 PM. No admis fee. Estab 1962 to foster the arts in the Yuma area and to provide a showing space for contemporary Arizona artists. Gallery is housed in restored Southern Pacific Railway depot built in 1926. Average Annual Attendance: 12,000. Mem: 500, dues, $5 - $1000
Income: $100,000 (financed by endowment, membership and city appropriation)
Purchases: $3000
Collections: Contemporary Arizona
Exhibitions: Spotlight Artist Gallery: Changing Exhibitions of Contempory Art; 10th, 11th, 12th, and 14th Southwestern Invitational; The Railroad: Focus on the Southwest
Publications: Membership bulletin, bimonthly
Activities: Classes for children; dramatic programs; docent training; lect open to public, 10 - 12 vis lectr per year; concerts; gallery talks; tours; individual painting and original objects of art lent to members and businesses; organize and circulate traveling exhibitions; museum shop sells original art, prints, and reproductions

ARKANSAS

CLARKSVILLE
L COLLEGE OF THE OZARKS LIBRARY, Ward and College Ave, 72830. *Head Art Dept* Lyle Ward; *Librn* Carolyn Harris
No admis fee. Estab 1834
Income: $1000 (financed by endowment)
Purchases: $100 - $200
Library Holdings: Vols 1500
Collections: Original print collection; graduate students painting collection
Activities: Dramatic programs; Lect open to the public, 9 vis lectr per yr; Scholarships offered; individual paintings lent to schools; lending collection contains 100 color reproductions, 16mm films

CROSSETT
O CROSSETT ART LEAGUE, 125 Main, 71635. Tel 501-364-3606. *Pres* Mrs Robert Parkhill; *Secy* Olivia Bingham
Estab to promote and encourage art skills and art appreciation. Mem: 62; dues $5
Income: Financed by membership and federal matching funds
Exhibitions: Junior League Arts and Crafts Fair; Ashley County Fair (held at El Dorado Art Center, Arkansas)
Publications: Monthly newsletter
Activities: Classes for adults and children; field trips; workshops; lect; concerts

EL DORADO
O SOUTH ARKANSAS ART CENTER, 110 E Fifth St, 71730. Tel 501-862-5474. *Executive Dir* Pamela A Bosanko; *Pres* Penny Ralston; *Secy* Lilla Johnston
Open 9 AM - 5 PM. No admis fee. Estab 1965 for the promotion, enrichment and improvement of the visual arts by means of exhibits, lectures and instruction, and through scholarships to be offered whenever possible. Gallery maintained. Mem: 350; dues $5; annual meeting second Tues every month
Income: Financed by membership, city and state appropriation
Collections: All paintings and collections are under jurisdiction of South Arkansas Arts Center
Exhibitions: Various art shows in this and surrounding states; gallery shows, ten guest artists annually, two months dedicated to local artists, works by local artists displayed in corridor year-round
Publications: Newsletter, quarterly
Activities: Classes for adults and children; theater and dance workshops; lect open to public; gallery talks; competitions; scholarships
L Library, 110 E Fifth St, 71730.
Library Holdings: Vols 200

EUREKA SPRINGS

O **EUREKA SPRINGS GUILD OF ARTISTS AND CRAFTS PEOPLE,** PO Box 182, 72632. *Chairperson* Bettina Byrd Jiversen; *VChairperson* Roger Pettit; *Secy* Betty Rotramel; *Treas* Charles Gay
Estab 1976 to encourage quality art work and to provide various art oriented services. Mem: Approx 60; dues $20 - $32; monthly meetings
Income: Approx $6000 (financed by membership)
Exhibitions: Spring Art Fair
Publications: Directory
Activities: Educ dept; workshops; films; lect open to public, 2 - 3 vis lectrs per yr; gallery talks; competitions; lending collections contains 200 books; traveling exhibitions organized and circulated
L **Library,** PO Box 182, 72632.
Library Holdings: Vols 300; Per subs 12

FAYETTEVILLE

UNIVERSITY OF ARKANSAS

M **Fine Arts Center Gallery,** Garland St, 72701. Tel 501-575-3706. *Gallery Coordinator* Martha Sutherland
Open August - May weekdays 9 AM - 4 PM. No admis fee. Estab 1950 as a teaching gallery in fields of painting, drawing, sculpture and architecture, through inreach and outreach programs. One gallery with moveable display panels covers 80 x 80 ft
Income: Financed by state appropriation
Collections: Permanent collection of †paintings, photographs, prints and sculpture
Exhibitions: Sixteen exhibitions per year, of which eight are in-house, art department related; one regional exhibit; one public school exhibit; one architecture exhibit
Activities: Classes for adults; lect open to the public, 4 - 6 vis lectr per year; concerts; gallery talks; competitions with awards; exten dept; traveling exhibitions
L **Fine Arts Library,** FA-103, 72701. Tel 501-575-4708. *Librn* Eloise E McDonald
Open Mon - Thurs 8 AM - 10 PM, Fri 8 AM - 5 PM, Sat noon - 4 PM, Sun 2 - 10 PM. Estab 1951 to support the curriculum in music, art and architecture. Circ 32,900
Library Holdings: Vols 33,000; Per subs 155; AV—Slides; Other—Clipping files, exhibition catalogs

FORT SMITH

O **FORT SMITH ART CENTER,** 423 N Sixth St, 72901. Tel 501-782-6371. *Dir* Polly Crews; *Pres* Marcia Edwards
Open daily 10 AM - 4 PM, Sun 2 - 4 PM, cl Mon, New Years, July 4, Labor Day, Thanksgiving and Christmas. No admis fee. Estab 1957 to provide art museum, art association and art education. Library maintained. Average Annual Attendance: 10,000. Mem: 889; dues $15
Income: $25,000 (financed by endowment)
Collections: †American painting, graphics and drawings
Publications: Bulletin, monthly
Activities: Classes for children; lect open to the public; competitions; traveling exhibitions organized and circulated; sales gallery

HELENA

M **PHILLIPS COUNTY MUSEUM,** 623 Pecan St, 72342. *Pres* Mrs Dale Kirkman
Open Mon - Sat 9 AM - 5 PM, cl national holidays. Estab 1929 as an educational and cultural museum to impart an appreciation of local history and to display objects of art from all over the world. Average Annual Attendance: 5000. Mem: 250; dues $2; annual meeting May
Income: Financed by endowment, membership and city appropriation
Collections: China, glassware, paintings

HOT SPRINGS

O **SOUTHERN ARTISTS ASSOCIATION,** Fine Arts Center,* 815 Whittington Ave, 71901. Tel 501-624-9836. *Pres* Margaret Pedersen; *VPres* Bruce Richards; *Secy* Theresa Kosics; *Staff Secy* Lucille Chick; *Gallery Dir* Violet Richard
Open Wed - Sat 10 AM - 4 PM, Sun 1:30 - 5 PM, cl Mon & Tues. Estab 1951 to provide the community with a yearly calendar of art exhibitions, to provide gallery space for members, to provide educational program in art for the community and serve as a statewide art association. Mem: 137; dues $15; meetings monthly
Income: Financed by membership, city appropriation and commission from sales of artwork
Exhibitions: (1978) Annual Arts Festival; Semiannual Outdoor Exhibitions; one-man shows, traveling Exhibitions
Activities: Classes for adults and children; art films; workshop; lect open to the public, 3-4 visiting lectrs per year; gallery talks; competitions with prizes, awards and honorable mentions given; book traveling exhibitions

JONESBORO

M **ARKANSAS STATE UNIVERSITY ART GALLERY, JONESBORO,** Caraway Rd, Jonesboro. (Mailing Add: Box 846, State University, AR 72467,) *Dir* Evan Lindquist; *Chmn Department of Art* Karl Richards; *Chmn Exhib* John Keech
Open weekdays 8 AM - 4 PM. No admis fee. Estab 1967 for education objectives; recognition of contemporary artists and encouragement to students. Located in the Fine Art Center, the well-lighted gallery measures 45 x 45 ft plus corridor display areas. Average Annual Attendance: 10,500
Income: $3000 (financed by state appropriation)
Collections: Contemporary paintings; contemporary sculpture; historial and contemporary prints
Exhibitions: Duane Criger-Jerry; Michael Dicken; Jim Eisentrager; Ray George; Dona Hedmann; Steve and Susan Kemenyffee; Virginia Myers; Patrick Rowan; Thom Seawell; Hatch-John Walker; Robert Winokur
Publications: Exhibition catalogs
Activities: Lect open to public, 4 - 6 visiting lectr per year; gallery talks; competitions; originate traveling exhibitions

LITTLE ROCK

M **ARKANSAS ARTS CENTER,** MacArthur Park, PO Box 2137, 72203. Tel 501-372-4000. *Exec Dir* Townsend D Wolfe III; *Asst to the Dir* Leon Kaplan; *Dir State Services* June Freeman; *Dir Neighborhood Arts* Brenda Reese; *Dir Special Projects* Evelyn McCoy; *Dir Childrens Theatre* Bradley Anderson; *Dir Education* Anne Pappas; *Registrar* Margaret Wickard
Open Mon - Sat 8 AM - 5 PM, Sun & holidays Noon - 5 PM. No admis fee to galleries, admission charged for theatre activities. Estab 1960 to further the development, the understanding and the appreciation of the visual and performing arts. Five galleries; four used for circulating exhibitions, one for art educational gallery for young people. Average Annual Attendance: 533,000. Mem: 3452; dues from benefactor $20,000 to student $5; annual meeting in July
Income: Financed by endowment, membership, city and state appropriation and earned income
Collections: Paintings, prints and drawings prior to the 20th century; †drawings; †prints; decorative arts
Publications: Members Bulletin, monthly; Annual Catalog; Annual Report
Activities: Classes for adults and children; docent training; lect open to the public, 6 - 10 visiting lectr per year; concerts; gallery talks; tours; competitions; childrens' theatre; dance; exten department serving the state of Arkansas; artmobile; individual paintings and original objects of art lent to schools, civic groups and churches; lending collection contains motion pictures, original prints, paintings, 4300 phonorecords and 16,000 slides; originates traveling exhibitions; museum shop sells books, slides, gifts, jewelry and crafts; junior museum
L **Elizabeth Prewitt Taylor Memorial Library,** Arkansas Arts Center, MacArthur Park, 72203. *Special Programs Adminr* Evelyn McCoy; *Art Librn* Nancy Delamar
Open 10 AM - 5 PM, Sun 12 PM - 5 PM. Estab 1963 to provide resources in the arts for students, educators, and interested public
Income: $25,120
Purchases: $6800
Library Holdings: Vols 6000; Per subs 104; AV—Cassettes, fs, Kodachromes, motion pictures, rec, slides; Other—Clipping files, exhibition catalogs, memorabilia, pamphlets
Collections: George Fisher Cartoons

M **ARKANSAS TERRITORIAL RESTORATION,** Territorial Square, 72201. Tel 501-371-2348. *Dir* Bill Worthen
Open daily 9 AM - 5 PM, Sun 1 - 5 PM, cl New Year's, Easter, Thanksgiving, Christmas Eve and Christmas Day. Admis to museum houses adults $1, senior citizens (65 and over) and children 6 - 16 25¢, children 5 and under free; admis to Reception Center free. Restoration completed 1941. The Restoration is a group of homes including a recently restored log house, that represent the early and mid 19th century of Arkansas history. Average Annual Attendance: 40,000
Collections: Audubon prints; furnishing of the period; porcelain hands, prints and maps from the 19th century; silver collection; watercolors
Activities: Log House activities include educational program for students and adults in candle dipping, cooking and needlework; Reception Center has slide show, exhibits and art gallery; craft store sells early Arkansas crafts
L **Library,** Territorial Square, 72201.
Special Subjects: Furniture, Historical Material, art, gardening, houses

C **FIRST NATIONAL BANK IN LITTLE ROCK,** Capitol & Broadway, PO Box 1471, 72203. Tel 501-371-7284. *In Charge Art Coll & Program* Joy Greer
Open Mon - Fri 9 AM - 4 PM. Estab 1970 to support art community. Collection displayed in main bank building and 12 branch offices; annual amount of contributions and grants $5000 - $15,000
Purchases: $5000
Collections: Arkansas art, chiefly paintings; some sculpture and weavings
Exhibitions: One major exhibit per year
Activities: Tours; purchase awards in two annual festivals; individual objects of art lent to new museums for one year

MID-SOUTHERN WATERCOLORISTS
For further information, see National and Regional Organizations

M **QUAPAW QUARTER ASSOCIATION, INC,** Villa Marre, 1321 Scott St, PO Box 1104, 72203. Tel 501-371-0075, 374-9979. *Pres* Mark Stodola; *VPres* Sandra Hanson; *Secy* Charlotte Brown; *Executive Dir* Ralph J Megna; *Operations Mgr* JoAnne Jennings; *Public Programs Coordr* Pamela Boyd
Open Sun - Fri Noon - 4 PM. Admis adults $1, students 50¢. Estab 1966. The Villa Marre is a historic house museum which, by virtue of its extraordinary collection of late 19th Century decorative arts, is a center for the study of Victorian styles. Average Annual Attendance: 5000. Mem: 1000; dues $15 - $1000; annual meeting Nov
Income: $107,000 (financed by membership, corporate support, grants and fund raising events)
Collections: Permanent Collection principally consists artwork, curioes appropriate

to an 1881 Second Empire Victorian home, late 19th and early 20th Century furniture, textiles
Publications: Quapaw Quarter Chronicle, bi-monthly
Activities: Classes for adults and children; docent training; lect open to public, visiting lectr; tours; book traveling exhibitions; sales shop sells books and magazines

L **Preservation Resource Center,** 308 E Eighth St, 72202.
Open Mon - Sat 9 AM - 5 PM. Estab 1976 for the assembly of materials relevent to the design and furnishing of Victorian period homes
Purchases: $500
Library Holdings: Vols 130; Per subs 12; AV—Kodachromes, lantern slides; Other —Clipping files, manuscripts, pamphlets, photographs

L **UNIVERSITY OF ARKANSAS,** Art Slide Library, Fine Arts Building, Room 159, Art Department, 33rd & University Ave, 72204. *Slide Cur* Susan Terry Borne
Open Mon - Fri 9 AM - 5 PM. Estab 1975. For reference only
Income: $10,000
Purchases: $22,000
Library Holdings: Per subs 10; AV—Fs, Kodachromes, slides; Other—Clipping files, exhibition catalogs, pamphlets
Special Subjects: Dutch, Renaissance, Baroque, Contemporary art

PINE BLUFF

O **SOUTHEAST ARKANSAS ARTS AND SCIENCE CENTER,*** Civic Center, 200 E Eighth Ave, 71601. Tel 501-536-3375. *Dir* Joe Kagle; *Asst Dir* Bill Woodell; *Performing Art Dir* Paul Owens
Open Mon - Fri 8 AM - 5 PM, Sat 10 AM - 4 PM, cl Sun and holidays. No admis fee. Opened in 1968 in Civic Center Complex; governing authority, city of Pine Bluff. Average Annual Attendance: 55,000. Mem: 750; dues family $15
Income: $150,000 (budget)
Collections: Contemporary art assembled by gifts and purchases; prints of American college professors
Exhibitions: Annual Art Festival; Annual Statewide Competition; Art Gallery Exhibitions
Activities: Workshops; regional advisory activities for cultural programs in 11 counties; concerts; film series for adults and children; sales shop selling original art prints, publications

L **Library,*** Civic Center, 200 E Eighth Ave, 71601.
Open to the public, for reference
Library Holdings: Vols 200

SEARCY

L **HARDING UNIVERSITY,** Beaumont Memorial Library, Art Department, Box 938, 72143. *Librn* Winnie Bell
Open daily 8 AM - 10 PM. Circ 200,000
Library Holdings: Per subs 15; Micro—Cards, fiche, prints; AV—Rec; Other— Pamphlets, photographs

SPRINGDALE

O **COUNCIL OF OZARK ARTISTS AND CRAFTSMEN, INC,** Arts Center of the Ozarks, Arts Bldg, 216 W Grove Ave, PO Box 725, 72764. *Pres* Mrs Fred McCuistion; *VPres Arts Division & Exhibit Chmn* Mrs Nicks Matthews; *Prog Dir* Kathi Blundell; *Dir of Theatre* Harry Blundell
Open Mon - Fri 1 - 5 PM, gallery open Wed - Fri noon - 4 PM. No admis fee. Estab 1948, merged with the Springdale Arts Center to become Arts Center of the Ozarks in 1973 to preserve the traditional handcrafts, to promote all qualified contemporary arts and crafts, to help find markets for artists and craftsmen. Mem: 70; annual meeting third Mon in Aug
Income: Financed by membership and city and state appropriations
Exhibitions: Prairie Grove Clothesline Fair (annually on Labor Day weekend); Exhibitions change monthly
Publications: Arts Center Events, monthly; newsletter, bimonthly
Activities: Adult and children's workshops; instruction in the arts, music, dance and drama run concurrently with other activities; evening classes in painting; five theater productions per year

STUTTGART

O **GRAND PRAIRIE ART COUNCIL, INC,** PO Box 65, 72160. Tel 501-673-2874. *Pres* Mrs Neil Maynard; *Secy* Mrs Robert L Fischer
Estab 1956, inc 1964, to encourage cultural development in the Grand Prairie area; to sponsor the Grand Prairie Festival of Arts held annually in September at Stuttgart; and to work toward the establishment of an arts center for junior and senior citizens. Average Annual Attendance: Approx 9000. Mem: 17; annual meeting Jan
Income: $3000 - $4000 (financed by contributions)
Collections: Very small permanent collection started by donations
Publications: Festival invitations in July; programs in Sept

CALIFORNIA

ALHAMBRA

AMERICAN SOCIETY OF BOOKPLATE COLLECTORS AND DESIGNERS
For further information, see National and Regional Organizations

BAKERSFIELD

M **KERN COUNTY MUSEUM,*** 3801 Chester Ave, 93309. Tel 805-861-2132. *Dir* Richard C Bailey; *Secy* Patti Binns

Open Mon - Fri 8 AM - 3:30 PM, Sat, Sun & holidays 10 AM - 3:30 PM. Admis Pioneer Village: adults $1, children 75¢. Estab 1945. Average Annual Attendance: 150,000
Collections: California primitive paintings; 60-structure Pioneer Village covering 12 acres; Photographic Image Collection; Photography
Publications: Guide to the Museum

L **Library,*** 3801 Chester Ave, 93309.
Open for reference only
Library Holdings: Vols 2000; Other—Photographs

M **MARIAN OSBORNE CUNNINGHAM ART GALLERY,** 1930 R St, 93301. Tel 805-323-7219. *Pres* Virginia Cimental; *VPres* Betty Gravis; *Second VPres* Eileen Meyer; *Secy* Jean Reimer; *Treas* Phil Urner; *Dir* Genell Swan; *Recording Secy* Zola Hylton
Open daily Noon - 3:30 PM, cl Mon. No admis fee. Estab to provide art culture to community; encourage and educate amateur artists; assist artists in selling work. Gallery is a one story building located in Camellia Garden of Central Park. Average Annual Attendance: 7500. Mem: 300; dues $7.50; annual meeting second Mon each month 8 PM, except July & Aug
Income: $9500 (financed by membership, fund raising events, dues and donations)
Purchases: $500
Exhibitions: Guest artists, membership shows, past-presidents show
Publications: Perspective, monthly
Activities: Lect open to public (non-members pay fee), 9 visiting lectr per year; demonstrations; tours; fels

BERKELEY

O **BERKELEY ART CENTER,** 1275 Walnut St, 94709. Tel 415-644-6893. *Dir & Cur* Robbin Henderson
Open Wed - Sun 11 AM - 5PM, cl Mon & Tues
Income: Financed by city appropriation and other grants
Exhibitions: Loan exhibitions and shows by Bay Area artists
Activities: Dramatic prog; films; gallery talks; concerts

L **BERKELEY PUBLIC LIBRARY,** Art and Music Division, 2090 Kittredge St, 94704. Tel 415-664-6787, 644-6785. *Head Art & Music Division* Anne C Nutting
Open Mon & Wed 9 AM - 9 PM; Tues, Fri & Sat 9 AM - 6 PM; Thurs 12 - 9 PM; Sun 1 - 5 PM; cl third Sun in June through first Sun in Sept
Income: $37,607
Library Holdings: Vols 19,555; Per subs 93; Micro—Reels; AV—Cassettes, slides; Other—Framed reproductions

M **JUDAH L MAGNES MEMORIAL MUSEUM,** Western Jewish History Center, 2911 Russell St, 94705. Tel 415-849-2710. *Dir* Seymour Fromer; *Cur* Ruth Eis; *Registrar* Ted A Greenberg
Open Sun - Fri 10 AM - 4 PM, cl Jewish and legal holidays. No admis fee. Estab 1962 to preserve, collect and exhibit Jewish artifacts and art from around the world; the museum also does research in the establishment of the Jewish community in the Western part of the United States from 1849 to the present. Museum's first floor has changing exhibition space and painting gallery, and the second floor contains the permanent exhibition area. Average Annual Attendance: 5100
Income: Financed by membership and donations
Collections: †Hannukah lamps; Synagogue art and objects; †spice boxes; †graphics, †manuscripts, †prints, †rare books, †textiles
Exhibitions: (1978 to date) Zmira Alfi: Israel Landscapes; Janet Berg: Engraved Crystal; Calligraphy; The Decorative World of Ori Sherman: Furniture by Ori Sherman, Masks, Paintings, Picture Frames, Wall Hangings; From the Ashes: Holocaust Yahrzeit; Heirlooms of our People, Jewish History through Private Collections; Image Before My Eyes: Photographic Exhibition of Polish Jews 1864-1939; Israel at 30: A Photo Essay: Rafi Magnes; Illustrations from the Bible: Prints by David Bennett; Jewish Ceremonial Textiles: Old & New, A Collection of German Torah Binders and Contemporary Tapestries by Lillian Elliott; Peter Krasnow: Retrospective; Jewelers' Arts; Abraham Rattner: Stained Glass Studies; Yehudit Shadur: Paper Cuts; Norman Solomon: Paintings; Solomon Shukman: Side by Side with America 1974-1978; Spiritual Resistance 1940-1945: Art from Concentration Camps; Thirty by Fifteen: Works by fifteen California Jewish Faculty; Threads of Time, Artistry in Jewish Costume
Publications: Bibliographies; books of Western Jewish Historical themes; exhibition catalogs; pamphlets
Activities: Classes for adults; lect open to the public; gallery talks; tours; individual paintings and original objects of art lent to museums, synagogues, exhibition halls and Jewish organizations; traveling exhibitions organized and circulated; museum shop selling books, magazines, original art, reproductions, prints, original jewelry, note cards, posters, postcards

L **Morris Goldstein Library,** 2911 Russell St, 94705. Tel 415-849-2710. *Librn* Libby Fleischmann
Open Tues & Thurs 10 AM - 3 PM, other days by appointment. Estab 1966 as a center for the study and preservation of Judaica. For reference only
Library Holdings: Vols 10,000; Per subs 15; AV—Fs, motion pictures, slides; Other —Clipping files, exhibition catalogs, manuscripts, memorabilia, pamphlets, reproductions, original documents
Special Subjects: Ethics, Hebraica, Jewish art and music, Judaicaliterature in English, Hebrew, Yiddish and Ladino, mysticism, music of the Yiddish theater, philosophy, rare book and manuscripts, religious thought
Collections: Community collections from Cochin, Czechoslovakia, Egypt, India and Morocco; Holocaust Material (Institute for Righteous Acts); Karaite Community (Egypt); Passover Haggadahs (Zismer); 16th to 19th century rare printed editions, books and manuscripts; Ukrainian programs (Belkin documents)

UNIVERSITY OF CALIFORNIA

M **University Art Museum,** 2626 Bancroft Way, 94720. Tel 415-642-1207. *Dir* James Elliott; *Asst Dir for Admin* Ronald Egherman; *Chief Cur* David Ross; *Cur of Coll* Mark Rosenthal; *Registrar* Gretchen Glicksman
Open Wed - Sun 11 AM - 5 PM. No admis fee. Estab 1965, new museum bldg

opened in 1970. Museum designed by Mario Ciampi, Richard Jorasch and Ronald E Wagner of San Francisco; eleven exhibition galleries, a sculpture garden and a 200 seat theatre. Average Annual Attendance: 300,000. Mem: 1800; dues vary
Income: $1,743,000 (financed by university income programs, Federal and other grants)
Collections: Gift of 45 Hans Hofmann paintings housed in the Hans Hoffman Gallery; Pre-20th century paintings and sculpture; Chinese and Japanese paintings; 20th century European and American painting and sculpture
Exhibitions: Twenty exhibitions annually; Matrix Project (a changing exhibition of contemporary art)
Publications: The Calendar, catalogs, handbills, exhibition brochures, Matrix artist sheets
Activities: Lectures open to the public; gallery talks; film programs for classes and research screenings; traveling exhibitions organized and circulated; museum shop sells books, magazines, crafts, posters, jewelry, art materials
M **R H Lowie Museum of Anthropology,** 103 Kroeber Hall, 94720. Tel 415-642-3681. *Dir* William Bascom; *Asst Dir* Frank A Norick; *Senior Cur Anthropologist* Dave D Herod
Open Mon - Fri 10 AM - 4 PM, Sat and Sun Noon - 4 PM, cl major national holidays. Admis adults 25¢, children 10¢. Estab 1901 as a research museum for the training and educating of undergraduate and graduate students, a resource for scholarly research and to collect, preserve, educate and conduct research. Average Annual Attendance: 65,000
Income: $250,000 (financed by city and state appropriations)
Collections: Over three million objects of anthropological interest, both archeological and ethnological. Ethnological collections from Africa, Oceania, North America (Plains, Arctic and Sub-Arctic); Archaeological collections from Egypt, Peru, California and Africa
Exhibitions: Traditions in Transition; Games of Skill, Chance and Strategy; Indians of Panama; Artisans of India; Ishi, The Last Survivor of a California Indian Tribe; Sons of Vishvakarma, Artisans of India
Publications: Annual Report; Exhibition Guides
Activities: Classes for adults; lectures open to the public; gallery talks; tours; book shop
L **Museum of Anthropology Library,** 103 Kroeber Hall, 94720.
Open for reference and research
Library Holdings: Vols 2000; Other—Prints 20,000, photographs
L **Pacific Film Archive,** 2625 Durant Ave, 94720. Tel 415-642-1412. *Cur Film* Tony Luddy; *Film Consultant* Linda Artel; *Technical Dir* Daniel Tanner; *Librn* Linda Provenzano; *Asst Programmer* Edith Kramer
Open Mon - Fri 8 AM - Noon, 1 - 5 PM. Estab 1971, the Archive is a cinematheque showing a constantly changing repertory of films; a research screening facility; a media information service and an archive for the storage and preservation of films
Income: Financed by endowment, membership and student fees
Library Holdings: Vols 500; Per subs 30; AV—Cassettes, motion pictures; Other—Clipping files, Stills and posters
Collections: Japanese film collection; Soviet Silents; experimental and animated films
Publications: Monthly calendar
Activities: Dramatic programs; special daytime screening of films; lectures, fifty - seventy-five visiting filmmakers per year
L **Visual Aids Collection,** Berkeley, Wurster Hall, 94107. Tel 415-642-3439. *Librn* Maryly Snow
Open Mon - Fri 10 AM - 12 Noon, 1 - 5 PM. Estab 1951 for instructional support for the Department of Architecture. Circ 15,000
Income: Financed by state appropriation
Library Holdings: AV—Lantern Slides, slides; Other—Photographs
Special Subjects: History of Architecture, Slides and Photographs
Collections: Denise Scott Brown and William C Wheaton Collections: city planning, 35 mm slides; Herwin Schaefer Collection: visual design, 35 mm slides

BEVERLY HILLS

L **BEVERLY HILLS PUBLIC LIBRARY,** Fine Arts Library, 444 N Rexford, 90201. Tel 213-550-4720. *Fine Arts Librn* Nicholas Cellini; *AV Librn* Camille Razadi
Open Mon - Thurs 10 AM - 9 PM, Fri & Sat 10 AM - 6 PM. Estab 1973 to make art materials available to the general public. The library concentrates on 19th and 20th Century Art
Income: Financed by city appropriation and Friends of Library
Library Holdings: Vols 20,000; Per subs 200; Micro—Fiche, reels; AV—Cassettes, Kodachromes, motion pictures, slides; Other—Clipping files, exhibition catalogs, prints, pamphlets, photographs
Special Subjects: Architecture, Film, Art, costume, dance
Collections: Dorthai Bock Pierre Dance Collection; Will Rogers Collection
Activities: Lect open to the public, 3 vis lectr per year; gallery talks; tours

M **FRANCIS E FOWLER JR FOUNDATION MUSEUM,*** 9215 Wilshire Blvd, 90210. Tel 213-278-8010. *Cur* Basil W R Jenkins
Open Mon - Sat 1 - 5 PM, cl Sun & holidays. No admis fee. Estab 1953
Collections: Antique European and American Paperweights; drinking cups; European & Asiatic Decorative Arts; 15th - 19th century English, early American and Continental Silver; Oriental Art; Russian Art
Activities: Lect; guided tours

CARMEL

M **CARMEL MISSION BASILICA,** 3080 Rio Rd, 93921. Tel 408-624-9848. *Mgr* Katie Ambrosio; *Cur* Harry Downie
Open Mon - Sat 9:30 AM - 5 PM, Sun 10:30 AM - 5 PM, cl Thanksgiving and Christmas. No admis fee; donations accepted. Estab 1770
Collections: California's first library, founded by Fray Junipero Serra, 1770; Library of California's first college, founded by William Hartnell, 1834; Munras Memorial Collection of objects, papers, furnishings of early California; large collection of ecclesiastical art of Spanish colonial period; large collection of ecclesiastical silver and gold church vessels, 1670 - 1820; paintings, sculpture, art objects of California

Mission period
Activities: Sales shop sells religious articles, souvenir books and postcards
L **Archive of Old Spanish Missions, Diocese of Monterey,** 3080 Rio Rd, 93921. *Cur* Harry Downie; *Asst Curator* Richard Joseph Menn
Estab 1931 for research for Mission Restoration and Documents. Open to scholars by special appointment
Library Holdings: Vols 100; AV—Cassettes; Other—Clipping files, manuscripts, pamphlets, photographs
Special Subjects: Early California reference and photo library
Collections: California's first library

O **FRIENDS OF PHOTOGRAPHY,** Ninth and San Carlos, PO Box 239, 93921. Tel 408-624-6330. *Chmn* Ansel Adams; *Pres* Peter C Bunnell; *VPres* James L Enyeart; *Executive Dir* James Alinder; *Executive Asst* David Featherstone; *Treas* Robert K Byers; *Secy* Julia Siebel
Open daily 1 - 5 PM. No admis fee. Estab 1967 to serve the field of serious art photography through exhibitions, workshops, publications and critical inquiry. Maintains an art gallery with continuous exhibitions. Average Annual Attendance: 10,000. Mem: 3500; dues $22; annual meeting Feb
Income: $235,000 (financed by endowment, membership, city and state appropriations, federal grants and Patrons)
Exhibitions: Annual Member's Exhibition; Ansel Adams; Ruth Bernhard; Michael Bishop; Francis J Bruquiere; Color Photographs of Divola, Fitch, North, Ollman and Pfahl; Robert Cumming; Judy Dater; Roy DeCarava; The Diana Show; Mary Estrin; Bernard Freemesser; Klaus Frahm; Gretchen Garner; Vilem Kriz; Jerome Liebling; Tom Millea; Wright Morris; Olivia Parker; Photograph as Artifice; Edmund Teske; Philip Trager; Arthur Tress; Stephanie Torbert; Carleton E Watkins
Publications: Journal of the Friends, quarterly; Newsletter, monthly
Activities: Classes for adults; workshops; lect open to the public; competitions with cash awards; sales shop sells books and prints

CHERRY VALLEY

M **RIVERSIDE COUNTY ART AND CULTURAL CENTER,** Edward-Dean Museum of Decorative Arts, 9401 Oak Glen Rd, 92223. Tel 714-845-2626. *Dir* Mary Jo O'Neill
Open Tues - Sat 10 AM - 5 PM; Sun 1 - 5 PM. Admis fee. Built in 1957 and given to the county of Riverside in 1964, and is a division of the Parks Dept. The South Wing of the gallery displays antiques and decorative arts as permanent collections; the North Wing has monthly exhibits by contemporary artists. Average Annual Attendance: 55,000. Mem: 250; monthly meetings
Income: Financed by county funding
Collections: Antiques; Boulle Cabinet; Capo di Monte; Chinese export wares and other fine porcelains; decorative arts; Lowestoft; Meissen; David Roberts (original watercolors); Sevres; Wedgwood
L **Library,** 9401 Oak Glen Rd, 92223
Open to the public for reference only
Library Holdings: Vols 1200; Per subs 10
Special Subjects: Decorative Arts, Furniture, Glass, Porcelain, David Roberts (original lithograph set of Holy Land)

CHICO

M **CALIFORNIA STATE UNIVERSITY, CHICO,** Art Gallery, Normal & Salem Sts, 95929. Tel 916-895-5331, 895-5218. *Chmn* Richard Hornaday; *Secy* Janet Karolyi
Open daily 8 AM - 10 PM. No admis fee. Estab to afford broad cultural influences to the massive North California region. Average Annual Attendance: 15,000
Income: Financed by state appropriations
Collections: The Behrick Oriental Ceramics Collection
Exhibitions: Childrens Art; Graduate Thesis; Richard Hornaday-Drawings; Invitational Drawing; Janet Turner Collection Gift; Stanton MacDonald Wright, Selected Paintings-Watercolors; student exhibitions
Activities: Classes for adults and children; lect open to public; competitions with awards; schol offered; exten dept serving the region
L **Library,** Learning Activities Resource Center, Normal & Salem Sts, 95929. *Dir* P Busch
Open to students and the public

CHULA VISTA

M **SOUTHWESTERN COMMUNITY COLLEGE,** Art Gallery, 900 Otay Lakes Rd, 92010. Tel 714-421-0349, 421-6700, Ext 340. *Dean Fine Arts Div* Ann Stephenson
Open Mon - Fri 10 AM - 2 PM; Wed - Thurs 6 - 9 PM. No admis fee. Estab 1961 to show contemporary artists' work who are of merit to the community and the school, and as a service and an educational service. Gallery is approx 3000 sq ft. Average Annual Attendance: 10,000
Income: Financed by city and state appropriations
Collections: Permanent collection of mostly contemporary work
Exhibitions: Show announcements, every 3 weeks
Activities: Classes for adults; lect open to public, 3 vis lectr per year; gallery talks; competitions; individual paintings and original objects of art lent; lending collection contains color reproductions, photographs, and original art works; junior museum

CLAREMONT

M **GALLERIES OF THE CLAREMONT COLLEGES,** 91711. Tel 714-621-8000, Ext 2241. *Dir* David W Steadman; *Asst Dir* David S Rubin; *Registrar* Kay Koeninger; *Galleries Mgr* Doug Humble; *Galleries Coordr* Charmaine Soldat
Open daily 1 - 5 PM, cl National and school holidays. No admis fee. Estab 1974 to present balanced exhibitions useful not only to students of art history and studio arts, but also to the general public. Average Annual Attendance: 15,000

Income: $80,000 (financed by endowment)
Collections: Samuel H Kress Collection of Renaissance paintings; American painting; Old Master and contemporary graphics; photographs; Oriental art; African Art
Exhibitions: (1978) Art of J M Whistler; Know What You See; Pomona Senior Exhibition; Pomona Student Exhibition; Photographs of Wright Morris; Potter's Art in California 1885-1955; Scripps Senior Exhibition; Scripps Student Exhibition; Seven Colorists: Affinities, Differences; 34th Ceramics Annual; 16th Century Italian Prints; June Wayne: Tapestries, Paintings, Prints. (1979) All Claremont Art Faculty; Black and White Are Colors: Paintings from the 1950s - 1970s; Native American Art from the Permanent Collection; 19th Century American Paintings; Photography Collection of Sam Wagstaff; Pomona Senior Exhibition; Recent Los Angeles Painting; Scripps-Pomona Student Exhibition; Scripps Senior Exhibition. (1980) Ceramics Annual; Life: The First Decade; Senior Exhibition; Student Exhibition
Publications: Art Publications List, annual
Activities: Docent training; lect open to the public, 7 - 10 vis lectr per yr; gallery talks; tours; competitions; individual paintings and original objects of art lent; lending collection contains original art works, original prints, paintings and photographs; originates traveling exhibitions; sales shop sells books, posters, and cards

M **Montgomery Art Gallery of Pomona College,** 91711.
Contains one large and two smaller galleries, with two exhibition corridors
M **Lang Art Gallery of Scripps College,** 91711.
Contains one large and three smaller galleries, one of which can be closed off from the rest of the building

M **SCRIPPS COLLEGE,** Clark Humanities Museum, 91711. Tel 714-621-8000. *Pres* Samella Lewis; *Secy* Nancy Burson; *Cur* Paul Henderson; *Asst Cur* Gwen Storey
Open Mon - Fri 9 AM - Noon and 1 - 5 PM, cl holidays and summer. No admis fee. Estab 1970 to present multi-disciplinary exhibits in conjunction with Scripps College's humanities curriculum, and to maintain a study collection. Museum has large room with storage and study area; reception desk
Income: $5000 (financed by private donations)
Purchases: $344
Collections: Nager Collection of Chinese, Tibetan sculpture and textiles; Wagner Collection of African Sculpture
Exhibitions: Batik Paintings (Cigler); Contemporary Nigerian Art: The Oshogbo Community; Phil Dyke Retrospective; Haitian Art; Japanese Prints; D Jones Chinese Ink Landscapes; Jacob Lawrence - Floyd Coleman; Masks and Musical Instruments; Howard Smith; Stations of the Tokaido
Publications: Exhibition catalogues
Activities: Lect open to public

CYPRESS

M **CYPRESS COLLEGE,** Fine Arts Gallery, 9200 Valley View St, 90630.
Open Mon - Fri 11 AM - 3 PM, Tues & Thurs 7 - 9 PM during exhibitions. No admis fee. Estab 1969 to bring visually enriching experiences to the school and community
Income: Financed by school budget, donations, and sales
Collections: Student works; purchase awards
Exhibitions: (1978) Year of the Horse: 4676 The Horse as design in Oriental Art. (1979) Robert Cremean, Sculpture in Wood; Charles White: Graphics; Animal Kingdom in Art. (1980) Steve Schauer; Stained Glass and Neon Designs; Published Drawings and Paintings

DAVIS

M **PENCE GALLERY,** 212 D St, 95616. Tel 916-758-3370. *Pres* Judy Wydick; *VPres* Shirley Loomis; *Cur* Edelgard Brunelle, PhD; *Secy* Joyce Wade
Open Tues - Sat 12 - 4 PM, except holidays and between shows. Estab 1975. A downtown art space with changing exhibitions of contemporary, historical and ethnic art shows. Gallery has 86 running feet of wall space and 650 square feet of floor space. The walls are 8 feet high and provide 6 ft high exhibition areas. Average Annual Attendance: 2400. Mem: 316; dues business $25, family $15, individual $10
Income: $6000 (financed by membership, city appropriation and fund raisings)
Exhibitions: (1979) Directions (fiber); Robert Hockenos: Recent Oil Painting; Season's Greetings, Victorian Christmas Cards from the collection of Joyce Williams. (1980) A survey of American and Canadian artists; Animals: Celebration and communion (mixed media); Children's Art Exhibit (mixed media); Jorjana Holden: Sculpture from the Seventies; Michaele LeCompte (paintings); Joe Mariscal and Jeff Nebeker (ceramic sculpture)
Activities: lect open to the public, 1 visiting lectr per year; concerts; gallery talks; tours; competitions

UNIVERSITY OF CALIFORNIA
M **Memorial Union Art Gallery,** Fourth Floor Memorial Union, 95616. Tel 916-752-2285. *Dir* Linda Tobin; *Program Coordr* Marilyn Berling Hunt
Open Mon - Fri 9 AM - 5 PM, also by appointment. Estab 1965 to provide exhibitions of contemporary and historical concerns for the students, staff and community. Gallery consists of North Gallery and South Gallery
Exhibitions: (1979) Don Asbill, MRA Show; Steven Mark Craig, Wood Sculpture; Design Department Exhibition; John Droogen, photography; Bella Tabak Feldman, sculpture; Five Fine Printers; Group Photography Exhibition Curated by Marla Katz Westover; Boyd Gavin, painting; Dolores Helweg: Portraits of Urban Women; Mike Henderson: Recent Works; Images of Life and Death: anatomical illustrations; Barbara Capell Lawrence, painting; Pam Maddock, Color-viscosity Prints; Clyde McConnell, Neil MacDonald, Steven Moore, photography; Frank Mestemacher, photography; Mosaic Multi-cultural artists; Jon Palmer, sculpture; Sacramento Valley Landscapes; dele-Seltzer, molded fiber wall pieces; Cornelia Schultz Retrospective paintings; Harold Schlotzhauer, recent work; Madelaine Shellaby, photo-emulsion drawings; Katherine Westphal, recent works; Nancy Worthington: Constructive Criticisms
Publications: Occasional catalogs and brochures

Activities: Classes for adults; lectures; concerts; poetry readings; films; competitions; internships
M **Richard L Nelson Gallery,** Department of Art, 95616. Tel 916-752-0105. *Cur* L Price Anderson Jr
Open Mon - Fri Noon - 5 PM. No admis fee. Estab 1976 to provide exhibitions of contemporary art as well as historical importance as a service to teaching program of the department of art and other departments, the university and the public. Contains main gallery and small gallery. Average Annual Attendance: 5000
Income: Financed by university appropriation
Exhibitions: (1977-78) Artists Working in Wood; Guzel Amalrik and Henry Elinson: Paintings and Drawings by Two Russian Emigre Artists; Ashland Printmakers: Five Years Later; Ceramics: Ann Adair and Richard Shaw; Darrell Forney: Large Letter Postcard Paintings 1968-1978; An Exhibition of Paintings and Works on Paper by Jarrold Hines; Kaplan and Rukhin: Works by Two Contemporary Soviet Jewish Artists; Barbara Kasten: Non-Camera Blueprints; London: From the Great Fire to the Great War; Satire and Caricature of British Prints from Hogarth through Rowlandson; MA MFA: Twenty-four Artists Then and Now; MA Recent Works by First Year MFA Students; Fred Martin: New Paintings; A Mona Lisa Scrapbook; The Nagel Collection of South and East Asian Ceramics and Sculpture; History of Photography: Invention to World War II; History of Photography II: World War I through the Present; Recent photographs: John Spence Weir, Jack Welpott; The Photographer as a Collector; Poetry: The Resurrection of the Body; A Survey of Intaglio Printmaking; A Survey of Relief Printmaking; Garner Tullis: Sculptured Print
Publications: Occasional exhibition catalogs
Activities: lectures open to the public, three to five visiting lecturers per year
L **Art Department Library,** University of California, Davis, 95616. Tel 916-752-3138. *Library Asst* Barbara Hoermann; *Library Asst* Karen Spence
Open Mon - Fri 8 AM - Noon, 1 - 5 PM. Estab 1966 to make readily accessible, reference and research material for Art Department faculty, and students, and the general public. Nelson Gallery has original art works
Income: Financed by State appropriation and college funds
Purchases: $5000
Library Holdings: Vols 2500; Per subs 37; Micro—Fiche; AV—Fs, slides; Other—Exhibition catalogs, photographs, reproductions

DOMINGUEZ HILLS

M **UNIVERSITY ART GALLERY OF CALIFORNIA STATE UNIVERSITY AT DOMINGUEZ HILLS,** (Formerly Art Gallery of California State College) 1000 E Victoria, 90747. Tel 213-515-3310. *Gallery Dir* Evelyn Hitchcock
Open Mon - Fri 11 AM - 5 PM. Estab 1973 to exhibit faculty, student and outside art. New 2000 sq ft gallery in 1978
Income: Financed by yearly grants from CSUDH Student Association; support from Friends of the Gallery
Exhibitions: Artists of local or national reputation

DOWNEY

M **DOWNEY MUSEUM OF ART,** 10419 S Rives Ave, 90241. Tel 213-861-0419. *Dir* Lukman Glasgow
Open Wed - Sun Noon - 5 PM. No admis fee. Estab 1957 as an aesthetic and educational facility. Located in Furman Park, it is the only municipal art museum with a permanent collection in Southeast Los Angeles which includes in its area 27 neighboring communities of such significant ethnic range and a total population close to one million. The Museum is continuing a program for new artists which originally was funded by Los Angeles County but is now paid for by museum operating funds. The facility has four gallery areas plus classroom space. Gallery I covers 15 x 39 ft, Gallery II covers approx 12 x 12 x 24 ft, Gallery III covers 15 x 20 ft, and Gallery IV covers 23 x 39 ft. Average Annual Attendance: 7500. Mem: 110; dues $15; annual meeting April
Income: $20,000 (financed by membership, and city appropriation)
Collections: Many pieces produced by Southern California artists over the past 20 years, including Billy Al Bengston, Corita Kent, Don Emery, Sabato Fiorello, Stephen Longstreet, Anna Mahler, Shirley Pettibone, and Betye Saar
Exhibitions: Twelve to fourteen shows a year featuring painting, sculpture, crafts, prints and other visual forms; Los Angeles Printmaking Society National Exhibition. (1978) Southern California Industrial Ceramics, Part I: 1912-1942 by Ernest Batchelder, Part II: 1927-1942 by Southern California Pottery. (1979) Masterworks (Gordor Wagner); Compositions (Raymond Vander Haegen), painting; Configurations (Don Francis, Mary Trudeau, Joan Salinger and Csaba Markus). (1980) Navaho German-Town Rugs and Chief Blankets; Rembrandt Etchings traveling show; Portraits; Los Angeles Center for Photographic Studies
Activities: Classes for children; lect open to public, 4 vis lectr per year; gallery talks; tours; monthly Round Robin Art Competition; co-sponsored carnival and art fair with Downey Training Center for the Retarded and the Department of Parks and Recreation; traveling exhibitions organized and circulated; museum shop selling reproductions and prints

EL CAJON

M GROSSMONT COMMUNITY COLLEGE GALLERY, 8800 Grossmont College Dr, 92020. *Dir* Geene Kennedy
Open Mon - Thurs 10 AM - 9 PM; Fri 10 AM - 4 PM. No admis fee. Estab 1970 as a co-curricular institution which cooperates with and supports the Art Dept of Grossmont College and which provides a major cultural resource for the general public in the eastern part of the greater San Diego area. Two galleries, one 30 x 40 ft; one 30 x 20 ft. Average Annual Attendance: 20,000
Income: Financed through College
Collections: Prints; photographs; clay objects; large Tom Holland painting
Exhibitions: Robert Bechtle; Fletcher Benton; Cheryl Bowers; Sarah Culotta; Robert Cumming; Tom Holland; Ruth Mayerson Gilbert (photographs); Marj Hyde; Jeff Laudenslager; Helen Levitt Photographs; Ken Light (photographs); Harry Lum; The Photograph as Artifice; Gail Roberts; Josef Sudek; Viewpoint: Ceramics, 1978-80; Judy Wines-Jim Bassler-Richard Baker; Wood Works (furniture); Maiden Voyage (photographs); Forms in Metal
Publications: Exhibition catalogs, 2-3 per year
Activities: Lect open to public, 6 vis lectr per year; concerts; original objects of art lent to institutions; lending collection photographs; originate traveling exhibitions

EUREKA

O HUMBOLDT ARTS COUNCIL, PO Box 221, 95501. *Pres* Barbara Kepon; *Secy* Mid Westfall
Estab 1966 to encourage, promote and correlate all forms of activity in the arts and to make such activity a vital influence in the life of the community. Mem: 250; annual meeting Oct
Income: $10,000 (financed by membership)
Collections: Art Bank, consisting of the yearly award winner from the juried Redwood Art Association Spring Show; other purchases and donated works of art; photograph collection
Activities: Concerts; competitions; schol offered; individual paintings and original objects of art lent; traveling exhibitions organized and circulated

FRESNO

M FRESNO ARTS CENTER, 3033 E Yale, 93703. *Exec Dir* R Andrew Maass; *Asst to Dir* Dorys L Beck
Open Mon - Sun 10 AM - 4:30 PM, Wed 7 - 9:30 PM. No admis fee. Estab 1949 as a visual arts gallery to provide Fresno and its environs with a community oriented visual arts center. The Center exhibits works of internationally known artists, and arranges shows of local artists. Three galleries plus entry for exhibits. Average Annual Attendance: 80,000. Mem: 1400; dues $25; annual meeting March
Income: $200,000 (financed by membership and fund raising efforts)
Purchases: $2250
Collections: Works of prominent Central valley artists; Contemporary American artists; Mexican folk arts; Mexican graphic arts; Oriental art
Exhibitions: Stan Bitters; Jean Charlot; David Gilhooley; Ikebana Gund Collection of Western Art; Jean Ray Lawrey; Nathan Oliviera; Ernest Trova Retrospective; Jack Zajac
Activities: Classes for adults and children; docent training; lect open to public, 12 vis lectr per yr; gallery talks; individual paintings and objects of art lent to city and county offices and other institutions; lending collection contains framed reproductions, original art works, original prints and slides; traveling exhibitions organized and circulated; museum shop sells books, original art, reproductions, prints, cards and local crafts

FULLERTON

M CALIFORNIA STATE UNIVERSITY FULLERTON, Art Gallery, 800 N State College Blvd, 92634. Tel 714-870-3262. *Dir* Dextra Frankel; *Asst to Dir* Barbara McAlpine; *Equipment Technician* Quentin James Brown
Open during exhibits, Mon - Fri 1 - 4 PM, Sun Noon - 4 PM. No admis fee. Estab 1963 to bring to the campus carefully developed art exhibits that instruct, inspire and challenge the student to the visual arts, to present to the student body, faculty and community exhibits of national interest; acting as an educational tool, creating interaction between various departmental disciplines, and promotion of public relations between campus and community. Four to five exhibits each year with organizational activity stemming from a class, Display and Exhibition Design. The students have the opportunity to work in an actual gallery environment rather than one which is only theoretical, designing, constructing and installing. The Art Department as a whole, not the Gallery is the holder of the permanent collection. Average Annual Attendance: 5000 - 7000
Income: Financed by state appropriation, grants and donations
Exhibitions: California Perceptions: Selections from the Wortz Collection; Itchiku Kubota: Kimono in the Tsujigahana Tradition; Juan Quezada and the New Tradition; Teaching Artists
Publications: Exhibition catalogs
Activities: Four - six major exhibitions per year; traveling exhibitions
L Library, 800 N State College Blvd, Fullerton, 92634. *Librn* Ernest Toy Jr
Open to students for reference only
Library Holdings: Other—Exhibition catalogs

O MUCKENTHALER CULTURAL CENTER, 1201 W Malvern, 92633. Tel 714-738-6595. *Pres* Margaret Hammon; *Dir Civic Arts* Donald E Knaub; *Program Coordr* Martha L Bartholomew; *Gallery Dir* Ronald Salgado; *Exec Secy* Norman Bricker
Open Tues - Sun Noon - 5 PM. No admis fee. Estab 1966 for the promotion and development of a public cultural center for the preservation, display and edification in the arts for the purpose of encouraging aesthetic appreciation and creative expression, particularly in the field of fine arts. Gallery contains 2500 sq ft; three galleries, the larger also used for the performing arts. Average Annual Attendance: 60,000. Mem: 450; dues $10 and up; annual meeting in June

Income: $130,000 (financed by endowment, membership, and city appropriation)
Exhibitions: (1978-79) 6 Fine Arts Exhibitions
Publications: Exhibition catalogs
Activities: Classes for adults and children; lect open to public, 40 vis lectr per year; concerts; 4 theatre productions annually; gallery talks; tour; competitions; individual paintings lent; traveling exhibitions organized and circulated; sales shop selling books, magazines and original art

GARDEN GROVE

M MILLS HOUSE VISUAL ARTS COMPLEX, 12732 Main St, 92640. Tel 714-638-6707. *Dir* Dorothy M Berry; *Pres Mills House Volunteers* Valencia Burt; *Dir Human Servs* Michael Fenderson
Open Wed - Sun Noon - 4 PM, cl Mon & Tues. No admis fee. Estab 1974 to promote the visual arts in the city of Garden Grove. Mills House West features 8 regional, local and student shows. Mills House East features 3 shows per year of on-loan artifacts and major collections. Average Annual Attendance: 12,000. Mem: 50
Income: Financed by city appropriation
Activities: Lect open to public; gallery talks; tours; gift shop

GILROY

M GAVILAN COLLEGE, Art Gallery, 5055 Santa Therese Blvd, 95020. Tel 408-847-1400. *Gallery Advisor & Humanities Division Dir* Kent Child; *Community Services Dir* Ken Cooper
Open Mon - Fri 8 AM - 9:30 PM. No admis fee. Estab 1967 to serve as a focal point in art exhibitions for community college district and as a teaching resource for the art department. Gallery is in large lobby of college library with 25 ft ceiling, redwood panelled walls and carpeted floor
Income: Financed through college
Collections: Approx 25 paintings purchased as award purchase prizes in college art competitions
Exhibitions: Monthly exhibits of student, local artist and traveling shows
Activities: Lending collection contains books, cassettes, color reproductions, film strips, Kodachromes, paintings, sculpture

GLENDALE

L BRAND LIBRARY AND ART CENTER,* 1601 W Mountain St, 91201. Tel 213-956-2051. *Librn* Jane Hagan; *Gallery Dir* Burdette Peterson; *Asst Librn* Ellen Dworkin
Open Tues & Thurs 12 - 9 PM, Wed, Fri, Sat 12 - 6 PM. No admis fee. Estab 1956 as art and music departments of the Glendale Public Library. Two galleries maintained with contemporary art program and crafts. Average Annual Attendance: 72,000. Mem: Dues $15 - $500
Income: Financed by city and state appropriations
Library Holdings: Vols 28,000; AV—Cassettes, rec; Other—color slides
Collections: Indexes and other guides to art and music literature; Dieterle picture collection; early photography journals
Activities: Lect open to the public; tours; concerts; competitions; lending collection contains color reproductions, Kodachromes

M FOREST LAWN MUSEUM, 1712 Glendale Ave, 91209. Tel 213-254-3131. *Dir* Frederick Llewellyn; *Mgr* Jane E Llewellyn
Open daily 10 AM - 6 PM. No admis fee. Estab 1951 as a community museum offering education and culture through association with the architecture and the art of world masters. There are four galleries in the museum and several smaller galleries in buildings throughout the four parks. Recreation of room under the Medici Chapel in Florence, Italy, where Michelangelo's drawings were recently discovered. Average Annual Attendance: 200,000
Collections: American Western Bronzes; Ancient Biblical and Historical Coins; Crucifixion by Jan Styka (195 x 45 ft painting); Resurrection (Robert Clark), painting; reproductions of Michelangelo's greatest sculptures; stained glass window of the Last Supper by Leonardo da Vinci; originals and reproductions of famous sculptures, paintings, and documents
Activities: Schol offered; lending collection contains reproductions of the crown jewels of England; memento shop selling books and art works
L Library, 1712 Glendale Ave, 91209.
For use of employees
Library Holdings: Vols 3000

C GLENDALE FEDERAL SAVINGS, 201 W Lexington Dr, 91209. Tel 213-956-4624. *In Charge Art Coll* Barbara Cassel
Open 9 AM - 4 PM. Collection displayed in branches

GLEN ELLEN

M JACK LONDON STATE HISTORIC PARK, London Ranch Rd, PO Box 358, 95442. Tel 707-938-5216.
Open daily 10 AM - 5 PM; cl Thanksgiving, Christmas, New Year's Day. Admis adults 50¢. Estab 1959 for the interpretation of the life of Jack London; the fieldstone home was constructed in 1919 by London's widow. The collection is housed on two floors in the House of Happy Walls, and is operated by Calif Dept of Parks & Recreation. Average Annual Attendance: 125,000
Income: Financed by state appropriation
Collections: Artifacts from South Sea Islands; original illustrations
Activities: Museum shop sells books

IRVINE

M UNIVERSITY OF CALIFORNIA IRVINE ART GALLERY, 92717. *Dir* Melinda Wortz; *Admin Asst* Leah Vasquez
Open Sept - June, Tues - Sat Noon - 5 PM. No admis fee. Estab 1965 to house changing exhibitions devoted to contemporary art
Income: Financed by city and state appropriations and by interested private collectors
Exhibitions: Jerry Anderson Paintings; Susan Kaiser Vogel Installation; Situational Imagery
Publications: Exhibition catalogs; mailers
Activities: Monthly lect on each exhibit; performances

KENTFIELD

M COLLEGE OF MARIN, Art Gallery, 94904. *Dir* Ann L Jack
Open Mon - Fri 8 AM - 10 PM; open also during all performances for Drama, Music and Concert-Lecture Series. No admis fee. Estab 1970 for the purpose of education in the college district and community. Gallery is housed in the entrance to Fine Arts Complex, measures 3600 sq ft of unlimited hanging space; has portable hanging units and locked cases. Average Annual Attendance: 100 - 300 daily
Income: Financed by state appropriation and community taxes
Purchases: $300
Collections: Art Student Work; miscellaneous collection
Exhibitions: Eight yearly; Faculty and Art Student; Fine Arts and Decorative Arts
Publications: Catalogs, 1-2 per year
Activities: Gallery Design-Management course; gallery talks; tours

LAGUNA BEACH

M LAGUNA BEACH MUSEUM OF ART, Pacific Coast Highway at Cliff Dr, 92651. Tel 714-494-6531. *Dir* Tom K Enman; *Curator* Jeannette Leeper; *Secy* Vonnie Crutchfield; *Docent Chmn* Suzanne Paulson; *Bookstore Mgr* Ruth Boyle
Open six days a week 11:30 AM - 4:30 PM. No admis fee. Estab 1918 as an art association. Two large galleries, two small galleries, museum store and offices. Average Annual Attendance: 60,000. Mem: 1400; dues $20; annual meeting September
Income: $127,000 (financed by endowment and membership)
Collections: Emphasis on early 20th century California painting
Exhibitions: Picasso and Goya Etchings from the Norton Simon Museum; The Renaissance and its Legacy; Virginia Steele Scott Gift and Selections from the Permanent Collection; Southern California Artists: 1890- 1940; Southern California Artists: 1940 - 1980
Activities: Classes for adults and children; docent training; lect open to public; museum shop sells books, magazines, original art, reproductions and prints

LA JOLLA

M LA JOLLA MUSEUM OF CONTEMPORARY ART, 700 Prospect St, 92037. Tel 714-454-3541. *Dir* Sebastian Adler; *Pres Board of Trustees* Lynn G Faymann; *Comptroller* Racthel Lindgren; *Sr Cur* Robert McDonald; *Educational Cur* Martha Winans
Open Tues - Fri 10 AM - 5 PM, Sat & Sun 12:30 - 5 PM, cl Mon, New Years, Thanksgiving & Christmas. No admis fee, suggested contribution adults $1, children 50¢. Founded 1941, to provide exhibitions and understanding of the visual arts. Museum is a non-profit organization, tax exempt, and maintains a 500-seat auditorium, classrooms and exhibition space; six-acre sculpture garden is under development. Average Annual Attendance: 100,000. Mem: 2000; dues $15 - $1000; annual meeting Oct
Income: $700,000 (financed by endowment, membership and Combined Arts and Education Council of San Diego County)
Collections: Substantial representation from all major painting and sculptural styles since 1930
Exhibitions: Angel of Mercy: Eleanor Antin; Richard Anuszkiewicz: Retrospective; A View of California Architecture 1965-75; Four Californians: Georgesco, Krebs, Spence, Therrien; The Modern Chair: Its Origins and Evolution; Rope Drawings: Patrick Ireland
Publications: Calendar of events; exhibition catalogs; newsletter, monthly
Activities: Dramatic programs; lect open to the public; films; gallery talks; tours; docent program; scholarships; individual paintings lent; intermuseum loans; traveling exhibitions organized and circulated; museum shop

L Helen Palmer Geisel Library, 700 Prospect St, 92037. *Librn* Gail Richardson
Open Tues - Fri 10 AM - 5 PM, Sat & Sun 12:30 - 5 PM. Estab 1941. For reference use by staff and docents; by appointment only to other persons
Income: Financed by membership, gifts and grants
Library Holdings: Vols 4000; Per subs 30; AV—Slides; Other—Clipping files, exhibition catalogs, pamphlets, artist information
Special Subjects: Contemporary art, international in scope
Exhibitions: (1978) Paintings by Manny Farber; Probing the Earth: Contemporary Land Projects; Recent Acquisitions; Herbert Rockere: Recent Work. (1979) Industrial Design Collection; Italy by Design; Sol LeWitt. (1980) Richard Artschwager's Theme(s); Lynn Fayman Photography; Sidney and Harriet Janis Collection; The McCrory Corporation Collection; Roman Opalka; Selections from Permanent Collection

L LIBRARY ASSOCIATION OF LA JOLLA, Athenaeum Music and Arts Library, 1008 Wall St, 92037. Tel 714-454-5872. *Adminr* Lynn Neumann
Open Tues - Sat 10 AM - 5:30 PM; Wed 10 AM - 8:30 PM. Estab 1899 for the use of the people in the community, endeavoring to provide material not otherwise available. Circ 15,000. No established gallery
Library Holdings: Vols 4500; Per subs 42; AV—Cassettes, rec; Other—Clipping files, memorabilia, pamphlets
Exhibitions: Monthly one-man shows
Activities: Lect open to public, 10 vis lectr per year; concerts; library tours

UNIVERSITY OF CALIFORNIA-SAN DIEGO

M Mandeville Art Gallery, B-027, 92093. Tel 714-452-2864. *Dir* Gerry McAllister
Open Sun - Fri Noon - 5 PM, Wed 7 - 9 PM. No admis fee. Estab 1967 to provide changing exhibitions of interest to the visual arts majors, university personnel and the community at large, including an emphasis on contemporary art. Located on the west end of Mandeville Center, flexible open space approximately 40 x 70 ft. Average Annual Attendance: 12,000
Income: Financed by state appropriations and student registration fees
Collections: Small Impressionist Collection owned by UC Foundation, presently on loan to San Diego Fine Arts Gallery, Balboa Park
Exhibitions: Artists in the Courtroom; The Decorative Impulse; R Henry Photography Exhibit; Douglas Huebler: New Work; Images of Mexico; Juan Downey; Yanomami Indians, videotapes, paintings and drawings; Alfred Jensen: Paintings and Diagrams 1957-1977; Autochromes from the Albert Kahn Collection: Tonkin 1915-1916; Los Angeles Women, Narrations: seven Los Angeles women artists; Micro-sculpture: Small scale tableaux and architectural sculptures, group exhibition; Betye Saar Exhibition; Raymond Saunders: New Work
Publications: Exhibitions announcements
Activities: Ten visiting lecturers per year sponsored by the Department of Visual Arts

L Library, B-027, 92093.
Gallery contains current periodical library

L Central University Library, B-027, 92093. Tel 714-452-3336. *Art Librn* Donald McKie
Open Mon - Fri 8 AM - 10 PM; Sat 8 AM - 5 PM, Sun 2 - 10 PM. Estab 1960 as a general university library
Income: Financed by state appropriation
Purchases: $40,000
Library Holdings: Vols 25,000; Per subs 160; AV—Slides
Special Subjects: Architecture, Renaissance Art, 19th and 20th century art

LONG BEACH

CALIFORNIA STATE UNIVERSITY, LONG BEACH

M The Art Museum and Galleries, 1250 Bellflower Blvd, 90840. Tel 213-498-5761. *Administrative Dir* Jane K Bledsoe; *Dir* Constance W Glenn
Open Mon - Fri Noon - 4 PM, Sun 1 - 4 PM. No admis fee. Estab 1949 to be an academic and community visual arts resource. Three galleries situated adjacent to the fine arts patio. Average Annual Attendance: 30,000
Income: Financed by university appropriation
Collections: 1965 Sculpture Symposium; contemporary prints
Exhibitions: Jim Dine Figure Drawings: 1975-1979; Kathe Kollwitz at the Zeitlin Bookshop 1937; CSULB 1979; Roy Lichtenstein: Ceramic Sculpture; Nathan Oliveira Print Retrospective; Lucas Samaras: Photo Transformations; George Segal: Pastels 1957-1965; Frederick Sommer at Seventy-five; The Photograph as Artifice
Publications: Exhibition catalogs, five or six per year
Activities: Docent training; scheduled tours; lectures, ten visiting lecturers per year; traveling exhibitions organized and circulated

L Library, 90840. Tel 213-498-4047. *Dir* Peter Spyers-Duran
Open Mon - Thurs 7:30 AM - Midnight, Fri 7:30 AM - 5 PM, Sat 9 AM - 5 PM, Sun 1 - 10 PM. Estab 1949 to support and augment the curriculum offered by the University's Art Department and to provide enrichment and recreational materials for all the campus community
Income: Financed by university's appropriation
Purchases: $18,500
Library Holdings: Micro—Fiche; AV—A-tapes, cassettes, fs, rec, slides, v-tapes; Other—Clipping files, pamphlets, reproductions

M JEWISH COMMUNITY CENTER, Center Lobby Gallery, 3801 East Willow St, 90815. Tel 213-426-7601. *Pres* Bonnie Krasner; *Executive Dir* Joseph Parmet; *Program Dir* Rhoda Wolfson; *Gallery Dir* Beverly Schreiber
Open Sun - Fri 9 AM - 5 PM, Mon - Thurs evening 7:30 - 10 PM. Estab to provide a community service for local artists and the broader community as well as offering exhibits of particular interest to the Jewish Community. The gallery is the large lobby at the entrance to the building; panels and shelves are for exhibit displays
Income: Finance by membership, United Jewish Welfare Fund, United Way and Fund Raising Events
Exhibitions: Monthly exhibits throughout the year; Annual Holiday Gift Show; Annual Youth Art Show; Paintings; Photography; Portraits; Sculpture; Soft Sculpturing
Publications: Center Services, bimonthly; Jewish Federation News, bimonthly
Activities: Classes for adults and children; dramatic programs; lect open to the public; concerts; competitions with awards; sales shop selling books, Israeli and Jewish Holiday art objects and gift items

M LONG BEACH MUSEUM OF ART, 2300 E Ocean Blvd, 90803. Tel 212-439-2119. *Dir* Russell J Moore; *Cur* Kathy Huffman; *Asst Cur* Kent Smith; *Mgr Publications* Barbara Hendrick
Open Wed - Sun Noon - 5 PM; cl New Year's, Thanksgiving and Christmas. No admis fee. Opened in 1951 as a Municipal Art Center under the city library department; in 1947 the Long Beach City Council changed the center to the Long Beach Museum of Art, a department of municipal government. Average Annual Attendance: Approx 60,000
Collections: †Paintings, †sculpture, †prints, †drawings, crafts and photography; 850 items with emphasis on West Coast and California contemporary art; small collection of African artifacts; sculpture garden; Milton Wichner; Kandinsky; Jawlensky; Feininger; Maholy-Nagy
Exhibitions: Laurie Anderson: Handphone Table; Eleanor Antin: the Nurse and the Highjackers; Children's Choice: International Year of the Child; Currier and Ives Prints; Fifth Annual Ithaca Video Festival; Robert Frank: Photographer-Filmmaker; From Tokyo to Fukui and Kyoto: Contemporary Japanese Videotapes; Japanese Screens; Masks the Other Face; Master French Drawings, 17, 18 & 19th Centuries, E B Crocker Gallery; National Watercolor Society; Slott Collection: Amish Quilts; Videothos: Cross Cultural Video by Artists; Willmore City: Residential Origins of Long Beach; New Work: John Caldwell, Peter D'Agostino, Charlemagne Palestine, Video in Artist Designed Gallery Spaces;

continuous exhibition of permanent collection
Publications: Quarterly bulletin, catalogs, announcements
Activities: Lect series; gallery talks; docent tours; films; art festivals; art rental and sales service; Carriage House Bookshop-Gallery features original folk art, ceramics, jewelry, posters, and changing gallery shows
L **Library,** 2300 E Ocean Blvd, 90803.
Open for staff reference with restricted lending of books, publications and slides
Library Holdings: Vols 1500

L **LONG BEACH PUBLIC LIBRARY,** 101 Pacific Ave, 90802. Tel 213-437-2949. *Dir Libr Servs* Carolyn Sutter; *Head Performing Arts Dept* Natalee Collier; *Assoc Dir Main Adult Servs* Peggy Holmes
Open Mon 10 AM - 8 PM; Tues - Sat 10 AM - 5 PM; Sun 1:30 - 5 PM. Estab 1897. Administers Long Beach Museum of Art
Library Holdings: Vols 734,009; Micro—Fiche, reels; AV—A-tapes, cassettes, rec, v-tapes; Other—Clipping files, exhibition catalogs, framed reproductions, prints, memorabilia, original art works, pamphlets, photographs
Collections: Miller Special Collections Room housing fine arts books and Marilyn Horne Archives

LOS ANGELES

O **ADVOCATES FOR THE ARTS,** University of California School of Law, 405 N Hilgard Ave, 90024. Tel 213-825-4935. *Dir* Monroe E Price; *Coordr* Larry Jacobson
Founded 1974 to provide free legal assistance to visual and performing artists, and art organizations who otherwise would be unable to afford counsel. Besides providing legal support to art groups and individuals, the program seeks to encourage research and understanding of arts-related issues by University of California, Los Angeles students. Over 100 volunteer lawyers
Activities: Research in arts-related topics and historic preservation, copyright, contracts, and libel; legal seminars; research into funding sources for community art; voluntary legal services and assistance to community groups fostering public arts

C **ARCO CENTER FOR VISUAL ART,** 505 S Flower St, 90071. Tel 213-488-0038. *Gallery Asst* Deborah Perrin; *Cur* Fritz A Frauchiger
Estab 1976; the Atlantic Richfield Company is the corporate sponsor of the center, which is a nonprofit gallery for changing exhibitions. The gallery has two show spaces, the larger used for painting, sculpture and installations; the smaller for photography and drawing. Shows are changed every six weeks, with a staggered opening schedule so that there is something new every three weeks. Average Annual Attendance: Approx 75,000
Exhibitions: Contemporary California artists; William Crutchfield (painting, print, sculpture); George Herms (installation); Craig Kauffman (painting); Hassel Smith (painting); Michael Todd (sculpture)

L **ART IN ARCHITECTURE - JOSEPH YOUNG LIBRARY,** 1434 S Spaulding Ave, 90019. *Dir* Dr Joseph L Young
Estab 1955 to provide background to history of art in architecture. Only available to students, associates and apprentices for reference only
Purchases: $2000
Library Holdings: Vols 1000; Per subs 10; AV—Kodachromes, slides; Other—Clipping files, exhibition catalogs, prints, original art works, pamphlets, photographs, reproductions

ASSOCIATION OF MEDICAL ILLUSTRATORS
For further information, see National and Regional Organization

M **CALIFORNIA MUSEUM OF SCIENCE AND INDUSTRY,** 700 State Dr, Exposition Park, 90037. Tel 213-749-0101. *Dir* William J McCann; *Dir Public Relations* Bud Hopps
Open daily 10 AM - 5 PM. Dynamically tells the story of science, industry and commerce to the public by tempting each visitor to take part in a sensory learning experience and education adventure. The museum has 9 halls housing 20 permanent exhibits and more than 60 temporary exhibits among which are Sister Cities Youth Art Exhib and Sister Cities in Focus which appear throughout the year; auditorium seating 500
Income: Financed by state appropriation and California Museum Foundation
Exhibitions: Permanent—Art Hall of Fame. Temporary—Annual Union Artist (paintings and sculpture by all unions in AFL-CIO); Bonsai, Care and Growing; children's Gametime playground exhibit; Key Art Awards (annual showing of posters, logos, word-styles promoting movies or TV shows); props from motion picture Alien
Publications: Notices of temporary exhibits, maps, pamphlets
Activities: Formal science-art education programs for school groups and the public; competitions; scholarships

M **CALIFORNIA STATE UNIVERSITY, LOS ANGELES,** Fine Arts Gallery, 5151 State University Dr, 90032. Tel 213-224-3521. *Dir* Daniel Douke; *Asst to Dir* John Cullen; *Gallery Asst* Fred Daniel
Open Mon - Thurs Noon - 5 PM; Sun 1 - 5 PM. No admis fee. Estab 1954 as a forum for advanced works of art and their makers, so that education through exposure to works of art can take place. Gallery has 1400 sq ft, clean white walls, 11 ft high ceilings with an entry and catalog desk. Average Annual Attendance: 30,000
Income: Financed by endowment and state appropriation
Publications: Exhibition catalogs, 3 per year
Activities: Educ dept; lect open to public, 10 - 20 per year; gallery talks; exten dept

M **CITY OF LOS ANGELES,** Municipal Arts Dept, Room 1500 City Hall, 90012. Tel 213-485-2433. *General Mgr* Rodney L Punt; *Dir Municipal Art Gallery* Josine Ianco-Starrels; *Dir Junior Arts Center* Claire Isaacs; *Dir Bureau of Music* George Milan; *Dir Cultural Heritage* Ileana Welch; *Dir Watts Towers Arts Center* John Outterbridge; *Dir William Grant Still Community Arts Center* Hakim Ali; *Pres Municipal Arts Commission* Jon Lappen; *Pres Cultural Heritage Board* Carl Dentzel
Estab 1925 to bring to the community the cultural and aesthetic aspects of Los Angeles; to encourage citizen appreciation and participation in cultural activities

and developing art skills. The art areas are the Municipal Arts Dept, the Junior Arts Center Gallery, and the Watts Towers Art Center Gallery. Average Annual Attendance: 250,000
Income: $1,125,000 (financed by city appropriation)
Collections: Works by local area artists; Portraits of Mayors of Los Angeles; gifts to the city from other countries
Exhibitions: Abstractions-Sources-Transformations; Approaches to Xerography; Artist as Social Critic 1979; The Blimp Show; Ideas Work-Art Works; Magical Mystery Tour; Newcomers; Portraits-1979; Secrets & Revelations II; Robert Sengstacke and Larry Sykes; The Stamp Act of 1979; Ruth Weisberg 1971-79
Activities: Classes for adults and children; dramatic programs; docent training; lect open to public; concerts; gallery talks; tours; competitions; sales show selling books, original art, reproductions, and prints; Junior Arts Center Gallery at Barnsdall Park

M **CRAFT AND FOLK ART MUSEUM,** 5814 Wilshire Blvd, 90036. Tel 213-937-5544. *Prog Dir* Edith R Wyle; *Asst to Prog Dir* Sharon Emanuelli; *Registrar* Marcia Page; *Education Cur* Karen Copeland; *Executive Secy* Laurie May; *Graphic Designer* Max King; *Publicist* Nina Green; *Preparator* Gustavo Montoya; *Folklorist* Reba Bass; *Special Events Coordr* Willow Young
Open Sat - Wed 11 AM - 5 PM; Fri 11 AM - 8 PM. No admis fee. Estab 1965 as The Egg and The Eye
Collections: Contemporary American Crafts; Mexican Folk Art
Publications: Newsletter, quarterly; exhibition catalogs
Activities: Educ programs; workshops; films; lectures; exhibitions; community outreach programs
L **Library and Media Resource Center,** 5814 Wilshire Blvd, 90036. *Librn* Joan M Benedetti; *Asst Librn* Marisha Laszczoki
Open Wed 11 AM - 5 PM and by appointment. Estab 1975 to support and supplement the documentation and information activities of the Museum in regard to contemporary crafts and international folk art; visual material collected equally with print. For reference only; limited to staff use
Library Holdings: Vols 1000; Per subs 60; AV—Cassettes, slides; Other—Clipping files, exhibition catalogs, memorabilia, pamphlets, photographs
Special Subjects: Architecture, Crafts, Decorative Arts, Folk Art, Handicrafts
Collections: Los Angeles Community Crafts Research Archive (slides, cassette, a-tapes, and reports); Slide Registry of Contemporary Craftspeople
Activities: Los Angeles Community Crafts Research, co-sponsored with Los Angeles Junior League

C **GOLDEN STATE MUTUAL LIFE,** 1999 W Adams Blvd, 90018. Tel 213-731-1131. *Correspondence Secy & Dir Program Advisor* William Pajaud
Open to public by appointment through Personnel Department. No admis fee. Estab 1965 to provide a show place for Afro-American Art; to assist in the development of ethnic pride among the youth of our community. Collection displayed throughout building
Purchases: $5000
Collections: Drawings, lithographs, paintings and sculpture
Activities: Tours by appointment

M **HEBREW UNION COLLEGE,** Skirball Museum, 32nd & Hoover Sts. (Mailing Add: 3077 University Ave, Los Angeles, CA 90007,) Tel 213-749-3424. *Dir* Nancy Berman; *Cur* Alice Greenwald; *Education Cur* Ester Duenyas; *Registrar* Georgia Harvey; *Cataloger* Leslie Blacksberg; *Slide Librn* Cathy Bernbach; *Slide Librn* Sandy Bogin; *Admin Secy* Shirley Taylor
Open Tues - Fri 11 AM - 4 PM; Sun 10 AM - 5 PM. No admis fee. Estab 1913 as part of library of Hebrew Union College in Cincinnati, Ohio, and moved in 1972 to the California branch of the college, and renamed the Hebrew Union College Skirball Museum; to collect and display artifacts of Jewish culture. 5575 sq ft in gallery, divided into four rooms, which are: main or permanent installation, mini-exhibit room (changing gallery), large changing exhibits gallery (north gallery), and ceremonial art gallery (northeast gallery). Average Annual Attendance: 20,000. Mem: 1300; dues varied, contributions
Income: Financed by college appropriation; some private and public grants
Collections: 2000 archaeological objects from the Near East, primarily Israeli; 6000 ceremonial objects, primarily Western European, but some exotic Oriental and Indian pieces as well; Chinese Torah and India Torah cases; 4000 prints and drawings from Western Europe, spanning 4 - 5 centuries
Exhibitions: A Centennial Sampler-One Hundred Years of Collecting at Hebrew Union College; A Disappearing Community: Jewish Life on New York's Lower East Side (photographs, by Bill Aron); And There Was Light, Studies by Abraham Rattner for the Stained Glass Windows of the Chicago Loop Synagogue (selections from the Louis & Jennie Rattner Allen Collection); David Bennett: Illustrations to the Bible; The Custom Cut: Jewish Papercuts, Past & Present; For Meyer Shapiro: $38; Jerusalem—City of Mankind (photographs); Jewish Marriage Contracts: a Celebration in Art; Jews of Yemen, a Retrospective (textiles & ceremonial art); Krasnow: A Retrospective Exhibition of Paintings, Sculpture, and Graphics; Los Angeles Collects: Works on Paper and Graphic Art from Israel; Maranova: A Modern Graphic Interpretation of Kafka's The Trial; Mark Podwal: Drawings from A Book of Hebrew Letters; Segal: Praise Him with the Psaltery and the Harp (sculptural interpretation of Psalm 150); Spiritual Resistance: Art from Concentration Camps 1940-45; Twelve from the Soviet Underground; Ludwig Yehuda Wolpert. Permanent—A Walk Through the Past; The Five Sense Show (ceremonial art)
Publications: Museum News
Activities: Docent training; lect open to public; children's workshops; lending collection contains 1200 slides; museum shop selling books, reproductions, prints, and ceremonial objects; lobby-gift shop area
L **Frances Henry Library,** 3077 University Ave, 90007. Tel 213-749-3424. *Librn* Harvy Horowitz
Open to public
Library Holdings: Vols 60,000; Per subs 250

O **JUNIOR ARTS CENTER,** 4814 Hollywood Blvd, 90027. Tel 213-666-1093. *Chmn Bd Trustees* Marjorie Fasman; *Dir* Claire Isaacs; *Art Cur* James Volkert; *Educ Coordr* Juan Geyer; *Special Events Coordr* Eugene Miller; *Handicapped Services Coordr* Riua Akinshegun
Open Mon - Sat 9 AM - 5 PM. No admis fee. Estab 1967 to stimulate and assist in the development of art skills and creativity. A Division of Municipal Arts

Department, City of Los Angeles. The gallery offers exhibitions of interest to children and young people and those who work with the young. Average Annual Attendance: 50,000. Mem: 350; dues $10 - $1000; annual meeting of Friends of the Junior Arts Center, May
Income: Financed by city appropriation and Friends of the Junior Arts Center
Collections: Two-dimensional works on paper; 8mm film by former students
Publications: Schedules of art classes, quarterly; exhibition notices
Activities: Art classes for young people in painting, drawing, etching, general printmaking, photography, filmmaking, photo silkscreen, ceramics, film animation; workshops for teachers; lectures; films; concerts; musical instrument making, design, video festivals for students and the general public

L **Library,** 4814 Hollywood Blvd, 90027.
Staff use only
Library Holdings: Vols 700; AV—Slides 15,000

O **LOS ANGELES ART ASSOCIATION AND GALLERIES,** 825 N LaCienega Blvd, 90069. Tel 213-652-8272. *Pres* Stephen Longstreet; *Dir* Helen Wurdemann; *VPres* Shirley Burden; *Treas* Oscar Grossman
Open Tues - Fri Noon - 5 PM, Sat Noon - 4 PM, Sun 2 - 4 PM, cl Mon. Estab 1925 to discover and present young professional artists, and to exhibit the work of established California artists. North and South galleries and little gallery. Average Annual Attendance: 25,000. Mem: 600; dues $30; annual meeting April
Income: Financed by membership
Exhibitions: (1980) All Creatures Great and Small; The Animal in Art; Avery Collection of Famous Photographers; Fantasy and Allegory; Los Angeles, Yesterday and Today
Publications: Announcements of exhibitions; pamphlets; folders

M **LOS ANGELES COUNTY MUSEUM OF ART,** 5905 Wilshire Blvd, 90036. Tel 213-937-4250. *Chmn* Richard E Sherwood; *Pres* Mrs F Daniel Frost; *VPres* Charles E Ducommun; *VPres* Hoyt B Leisure; *Treas* Daniel H Ridder; *Secy* Anna Bing Arnold; *Dir* Earl A Powell; *Deputy Dir Admin* Morton Golden; *Cur Exhib and Publications* Jeanne D'Andrea; *Sr Cur of Prints and Drawings* Ebria Feinblatt; *Cur of European Sculpture* Peter Fusco; *Cur of Decorative Arts* William E Jones; *Sr Cur of Far Eastern Art* George Kuwayama; *Cur of American Art* Michael Quick; *Sr Cur of Modern Art* Maurice Tuchman; *Registrar* Patricia Nauert; *Dir of Public Information* Philippa Calnan; *Dir of Film Programs* Ronald Haver
Open Tues - Fri 10 AM - 5 PM, Sat & Sun 10 AM - 6 PM, 2nd Tues of each month 12 - 9 PM, cl Mon, Thanksgiving, Christmas and New Years Day. Admis adults $1, students and senior citizens with ID, young people 5 - 17, 50¢; free day, second Tuesday of each month; museum members and children under 5 admitted free. Estab 1910 as Division of History, Science and Art; estab separately in 1961, for the purpose of acquiring, researching, publishing, exhibiting and providing for the educational use of works of art from all parts of the world in all media, dating from prehistoric times to the present. Complex of three buildings and Sculpture Garden. Average Annual Attendance: 1,500,000. Mem: 45,000; dues $30 - $1000
Income: $5,500,000 (financed by endowment, membership and county appropriation)
Purchases: $2,000,000
Collections: †American Art; †Ancient art; †contemporary art; †decorative arts; †European painting and sculpture; †Far Eastern art; †Indian and Islamic art; †textiles and costumes; †modern art; †prints and drawings
Exhibitions: (1979) Honore Daumier: The Armand Hammer Collection; The Golden Century of Venetian Painting; From Leonardo to Titian: Italian Renaissance Paintings from the Hermitage; Mark Rothko, 1903 - 1970: A Retrospective; Seven Artists in Israel: 1948 - 1978; (1980-81) The Bronze Age of China: An Exhibition from The People's Republic of China; Ceramics from the Permanent Collection; From East to West; The Golden Century of Venetian Painting; The Armand Hammer Collection; The Joy of Collecting: Far Eastern Art from the Lidow Collection; Kokoschka at 94: Seventy Years of his Graphic Art; Monotypes by Sam Francis; Monumental Silver: Selections from the Gilbert Collection; The Art of Mosaics: Selections from the Gilbert Collection; Pictures by Thomas Nast from the George and Betty Longstreet Collection; Old Master Paintings from the collection of Baron Thyssen-Bornemisza; Peruvian Textiles: Selections from the John Wise Collection; Recent Prints and Drawings Acquisitions; Renaissance Costumes and Textiles: 1450 - 1620; The Romantics to Rodin: French Nineteenth-Century Sculpture from North American Collections; Traditional Japanese Designs: The Tom and Francis Blakemore Collection of Textiles, Stencils and Costumes; The Russian Avant-Garde: 1910 - 1930
Publications: Members Calendar, monthly; Bulletin, annually; Biennial Report; exhibition catalogs, 3 - 4 yearly; special installation brochures, 10 - 12 yearly
Activities: Classes for adults and children; dramatic programs; docent training; lect open to the public, 50 vis lectr per yr; concerts; gallery talks; tours; films; competitions with awards; individual paintings and original objects of art lent to other AAM-accredited museums for special exhibitions; lending collection contains original art works, original prints, paintings and 130,000 slides; traveling exhibitions organized and circulated; museum shop sells books, magazines, reproductions, prints, slides, gifts, posters, postcards and antiquities

L **Library,** 5905 Wilshire Blvd, 90036. *Librn* Eleanor C Hartman
Open Tues - Fri 10 AM - 4:30 PM. For reference only
Library Holdings: Vols 55,000; Per subs 269; Other—Clipping files, exhibition catalogs, pamphlets, auction catalogues 19,500

M **LOS ANGELES INSTITUTE OF CONTEMPORARY ART,** 2020 S Robertson Blvd, 90034. Tel 213-559-5033. *Dir* Bob Smith; *Gallery Coordr* Debra Borchett-Lere; *Dir Develop* Tobi Smith; *Admin Asst for CETA Programs* Terrell Anderson; *Gallery Preparator* J D Page; *Film & Video Coordr* Carol Mike; *Information Specialist* Marlene Bleich
Open Tues - Sat Noon - 6 PM. No admis fee. Estab 1974 to be a major resource for exhibition of contemporary art. The gallery maintains 4500 sq ft of exhibition space to be used for static and temporary work; film and video facilities. Average Annual Attendance: 50,000. Mem: 1500; dues active $25, contributing $50, sponsor $100, patron-corporate $500
Income: $105,000 (financed by membership, city appropriation and state appropriation, NEA and CETA)
Exhibitions: Artwords-Bookworks; William Brice; Clothing Constructions; One of a Kind; Pistoletto; Social Works; Sound; Survey Australia; Tableau
Publications: LAICA Newsletter, monthly; Journal: Southern California Art Magazine, bimonthly
Activities: Lect open to the public; concerts; gallery talks; artists performances

M **Downtown Gallery,** 815 Traction Ave, 90013. *Cur* Charles Hill
Estab March, 1980
Exhibitions: Cho Kawai; Joan Watanabe; Richard Yokomi

L **Art Information Center,** 2020 S Robertson Blvd, 90034.
Open to public for reference
Special Subjects: Art catalogs; periodicals on contemporary art, painting, sculpture, installation, performance, photography and video
Collections: Documentation of 34 arts groups covered by CETA Title VI grants

L **Artists Registry,** 2020 S Robertson Blvd, 90034.
Collections: Slides and biographical data of over 1500 Southern California artists

L **LOS ANGELES PUBLIC LIBRARY,** Art and Music Department, 630 West Fifth St, 90071. Tel 213-626-7461. *Art & Music Librn* Katherine Grant
Open Mon - Thurs 10 AM - 8 PM, Fri & Sat 10 AM - 5:30 PM, cl Sun. No admis fee. Established 1872
Income: Financed by municipality
Library Holdings: Vols 180,000; Per subs 500; Other—Clipping files, exhibition catalogs, framed reproductions, prints, original art works, photographs, recreation materials, prints including original etchings, woodcuts, lithographs and drawings
Collections: Twin Prints; Japanese prints, including a complete set of Hiroshige's Tokaido Series

L **LOS ANGELES TRADE-TECHNICAL COLLEGE LIBRARY,*** 400 W Washington Blvd, 90015. Tel 213-746-0800, Ext 217. *Dir* Harold Eckes
Open daily 7 AM - 8:30 PM. Estab 1920 for academic, vocational, trade and technical education. Circ 21,500. Mini-gallery is located in new Learning Resources Center
Income: $500,000 (financed by district tax base)
Purchases: $125,000
Library Holdings: Vols 70,000; Per subs 550; Micro—Fiche, reels; AV—A-tapes, cassettes, fs, Kodachromes, motion pictures, rec, slides, v-tapes; Other—Prints, memorabilia, pamphlets, photographs
Special Subjects: Art History, Graphic Arts, Illustration, Photography, Apparel Arts, Art Trades
Collections: Career Information; Vocational-Trade-Technology Education
Publications: LATTC Learning Resources Center Newsletter
Activities: Classes for adults; competitions; scholarships

M **LOYOLA MARYMOUNT UNIVERSITY,** Art Gallery, Loyola Blvd at W 80th, 90045. Tel 213-642-2880. *Dir* Ellen Ekedal
Open Mon - Fri 11 AM - 4 PM; Sun 1 - 4 PM; Thurs eve 6 - 9 PM. No admis fee. Estab 1971 to hold exhibitions. Gallery is 20 x 60 ft with 15 ft ceilings, track lighting and carpeted floors. Average Annual Attendance: 10,000
Income: $10,000 (financed by university)
Exhibitions: (1979-80) Contemporary L A Drawings; Edward Curtis-Image of the North American Indian; Faces of Jesus 1500-1978 (all media); Francoise Girot: A Retrospective
Publications: Catalogs
Activities: Lect open to public, 2 vis lectr per year; concerts; gallery talks; films

M **MOUNT SAINT MARY'S COLLEGE FINE ARTS GALLERY,*** Art Dept, 12001 Chalon Rd, 90049. Tel 213-476-2237. *Gallery Dir* Jim Murray
Open Wed - Sun 12 - 4 PM. No admis fee. Estab to present works of art of various disciplines for the enrichment of students and community
Income: Financed by College
Collections: Collection of and by Jose Drudis-Blada
Publications: Exhibitions Catalogs, 2-3 per year
Activities: Lect open to public, 2-3 visiting lectrs per year; scholarships

M **NATURAL HISTORY MUSEUM OF LOS ANGELES COUNTY,** 900 Exposition Blvd, 90007. Tel 213-744-3411. *Acting Dir* Leon Arnold; *Pres Bd of Governors* Ed Harrison; *Acting Chief of Exhib* Robert Spangenberg
Open daily 10 AM - 5 PM. Admis adults $1, children, Senior Citizens and Students 50¢. Estab 1913 to collect, hold and research collection in life science, earth science and history, and to exhibit these collections for public education. Average Annual Attendance: 1,500,000. Mem: 11,000; dues $15 - $100
Income: Financed by county appropriation
Collections: Pre-Columbian artifacts
Exhibitions: American Indian images of Edward S Curtis
Publications: Science Bulletin; Contributions in Science; Terra Quarterly Magazine; Terra Monthly Calendar
Activities: Classes for adults and children; docent training; school tours; film program; Saturday workshops; concerts; galley talks; tours; museum shop sells books, original art, reproductions, prints and slides

L **Library,** 900 Exposition Blvd, 90007. *Librn* Katherine Donohue
Open to staff and to the public by appointment for reference only
Library Holdings: Vols 30,000

M **OCCIDENTAL COLLEGE GALLERY,** Thorne Hall, 1600 Campus Rd, 90041. Tel 213-259-2737. *Dir* Constance M Perkins
Open Mon - Fri 9 AM - 3 PM. No admis fee. Estab 1938 to support the academic program of the College and the community. Gallery is located in the foyer of the auditorium. Average Annual Attendance: 19,500
Income: $2600
Activities: Lect open to public; gallery talks

M **OTIS ART INSTITUTE OF PARSONS SCHOOL OF DESIGN GALLERY,** 2410 Wilshire Blvd, 90057. Tel 213-388-3128.
Open Tues - Sat 10:30 AM - 5 PM, Sun 1 - 5 PM. No admis fee. Estab 1954 as a forum for contemporary art. Gallery is flawless white drywall; two rooms measuring 35 x 40 ft each with 16 ft ceilings. Average Annual Attendance: 20,000. Mem: 670; dues $25 and up; meeting May and Dec
Income: Financed by endowment, membership
Exhibitions: Wallace Berman Retrospective on Kawara - Today's Theory (paintings); Beyond Realism (group show); Daniel Buren - Frost and Defrost
Publications: On Kawara, 2 per yr; posters

Activities: Classes for adults; lect open to public and/or members, 2-3 visiting lectr per yr; gallery talks; individual paintings and original objects of art lent; museum shop sells books, magazines, posters, postcards

L **Library,** 627 S Carondelet St, 90057. *Librn* Joan Hugo; *Asst Librn* Neal Menzies
Open daily 9 AM - 5 PM, cl weekends. Estab 1918 as a visual arts library
Library Holdings: Vols 30,000; Per subs 228; AV—Cassettes, motion pictures, rec, slides, v-tapes; Other—Clipping files, exhibition catalogs, prints, original art works, pamphlets, reproductions

O **RUSKIN ART CLUB,** 800 S Plymouth Blvd, 90005. Tel 213-937-9641.
Estab 1888, inc 1905. Owns club building. Mem: Limited to 100 members; dues $10, must have two sponsors; annual meeting April

M **SOUTHWEST MUSEUM,** 234 Museum Drive, PO Box 42128. Tel 213-221-2163. *Pres* C Allan Braun; *VPres* Dr Norman Sprague Jr; *Dir* Dr Carl S Dentzel; *Cur* Bruce Bryan; *Secy* Louise Maynard; *Registrar* Dee Ulrich; *Controller* Valerie F Dembrowski
Open Tues - Sun 1 - 4:45 PM, cl Mon. No admis fee. Estab 1907. Average Annual Attendance: 50,000. Mem: 1500; dues $15 and up
Income: $350,000 (financed by endowment and membership)
Collections: Anthropology and the Science of Man in the New World; Prehistorical, historical, Spanish Colonial and Mexican Provincial Arts; 20 galleries contain various collections
Exhibitions: Hopi Painting; Masterpieces of American Indian Painting; Painted Bronzes by Harry Jackson
Activities: Classes for children and adults; docent training; lect; individual paintings and original objects of art lent to authorized museums; lending collection contains books, color reproductions, framed reproductions, motion pictures, original art works, original prints, paintings, photographs and slides; originate traveling exhibitions; museum and sales shop selling books, magazines, original art, reproductions, prints and slides

L **Braun Research Library,** 234 Museum Drive, 90065. *Librn* Ruth Christensen
Open Tues - Sat 1 - 4:45 PM, cl Sun & Mon. Estab 1897.
For reference only
Library Holdings: Vols 500,000; Micro—Cards; Other—Clipping files, exhibition catalogs, framed reproductions, prints, manuscripts, memorabilia, original art works, pamphlets, photographs, reproductions
Special Subjects: Man in the New World, Indians of the Western Hemisphere, Anthropology of the Americas, Western Americana
Collections: George Wharton James's Collection; Joseph Amasa Munk's Collection; Charles F Lummis's Collection

C **TIMES MIRROR COMPANY,** Times Mirror Square, 90053. Tel 213-972-3977. *Secy of Foundation* Charles R Redmond
Estab as part of Corporate philanthropic activities. Annual amount of contributions and grants $100,000; supports museums by providing funds for acquisitions, constructions and operating (mostly in Southern California)

UNIVERSITY OF CALIFORNIA, LOS ANGELES

M **Grunwald Center for the Graphic Arts,** 405 Hilgard Ave, 90024. Tel 213-825-3783. *Dir & Cur* Dr E Maurice Bloch; *Asst to Dir* Michael W Schantz; *Cur Asst* Cindy Gedeon
Open Mon - Fri 9 AM - Noon and 1 - 5 PM. No admis fee. Estab 1956 as a research and study center for the graphic arts
Collections: French Impressionism; German Expressionism; Japanese Woodblock; Matisse, Picasso, Ornament, Renoir, Rouault; prints and drawings 15th Century to present; Tamarind Lithography Workshop Impressions (complete)
Activities: Original objects of art lent; lending collection contains 25,000 original prints

M **Museum of Cultural History,** 55A Haines Hall, 405 Hilgard Ave, 90024. Tel 213-825-4361. *Dir* Dr Christopher B Donnan; *Asst Dir & Cur Africa, Oceania & Indonesia* George R Ellis; *Admin Asst* Barbara Underwood; *Admin Asst* Kathleen Zernicke; *Publication Dir* Robert W Woolard; *Grants & Accessibility Coordr* Emily M Woodward; *Cur of Textiles & Folk Art* Patricia B Altman; *Consulting Cur of Costumes & Textiles* Patricia Anawalt; *Registrar* Nancy L Ellis; *Conservator* Benita Dumpis; *Photographer* Antonia Graeber; *Collections Mgr* Michael Gowen; *Exhib Coordr* Betsy Quick; *Exhib Designer* George Johnson; *Museum Education* Marjorie Rogers
Scholars or students with special interests may make arrangements to view the collections with the appropriate curator. Estab in 1963 to collect, preserve and make available for research and exhibition objects and artifacts from cultures considered to be outside the Western tradition. Changing exhibitions on view Wed - Sun Noon - 5 PM. Museum's annual major exhibition opens at the UCLA Frederick S Wight Art Gallery, Tues - Fri 11 AM - 5 PM, Sat & Sun 1 - 5 PM
Income: Financed by endowment, state appropriation and private donations
Collections: Archaeological and ethnographic collections; 120,000 objects primarily from non-Western cultures - Africa, Asia, the Americas, Oceania, The Near East and parts of Europe
Exhibitions: (1978) Agbaye: Yoruba Art in Context; Batik: Kains, Sarongs and Slendangs from Northern Java; Dowries from Kutch: A Women's Folk Art Tradition in India (Wight Art Gallery); Fighting with Art: Appliqued Flags of the Fante Asafo; From the Hands of Lawrence Ajanaku: Appliqued Costumes of the Edo of Southern Nigeria; Art of the Native North Americans; Cross-cultural Perspectives of Women; Moche Art of Peru: Pre-Columbian Symbolic Communication (Wight Art Gallery); The Art and Material Culture of the Zulu-speaking Peoples; Artistic Traditions of Santos: Saint Images of Guatemala; (1980-81) Afro-American Arts of the Suriname Rain Forest (Wight Art Gallery); The Art of the Mennonites; Art of the Tropical Rain Forest; Material Cultures of the Middle East; Paper Cuts; The People and Art of the Philippines (Wight Art Gallery); Pupper Festival
Publications: Exhibition catalogues; filmstrips; monographs; pamphlets; papers; posters; slide sets
Activities: Satellite Museum Program; Hall Case Program; Early Man Program; Chumash Indian Program; Publications Program; lect open to public, 1 - 3 visiting lectr per year; seminars; symposia; book traveling exhibitions; originate traveling exhibitions

L **Library,** 55A Haines Hall, 405 Hilgard Ave, 90024.
Open for reference to UCLA students and public
Library Holdings: Vols 5000; Per subs 30
Special Subjects: Art, anthropology and archaeology of non-Western cultures

M **Frederick S Wight Art Gallery,** 405 Hilgard Ave, 90024. Tel 213-825-1461. *Acting Dir* Jack Carter; *Admin Asst* Marian Eber
Open Tues - Fri 11 AM - 5 PM, Sat & Sun 1 - 5 PM, cl Mon and during Aug. No admis fee. Estab 1952. Gallery serves the university and public; program is integrated with the curricula of the Art Department. Average Annual Attendance: 175,000
Collections: The Willitts J Hole Collection of approximately 50 Paintings of the Italian, Spanish, Dutch, Flemish and English schools from the 15th - 19th Century; Franklin D Murphy Sculpture Garden; 20th Century painting, sculpture and photographic collections; 54 sculptures from the 19th - 20th Centuries, including Arp, Calder, Lachaise, Lipchitz, Moore, Noguchi, Rodin and Smith
Exhibitions: Twelve exhibitions annually. Architecture and design: operates in close conjunction with the Museum of Cultural History, and the Grunwald Center for the Graphic Arts; drawings, painting, prints and sculpture

M **Exploratorium, University Student Union,** 5154 State University Dr, 90039. Tel 213-224-2189. *Exploratorium Mgr* Lynda Lyons
Open Mon - Thurs 11 AM - 7 PM, Fri 11 AM - 1 PM. No admis fee. Estab 1975 as a fine art gallery-alternative space
Income: Financed by city and state appropriations
Exhibitions: Works by new and established professional artists; art, cultural and scientific exhibitions
Publications: Catalogs, 3 - 4 per year
Activities: Hosts artists' performances; dance groups; dramatic productions

L **Slide Library,** Art Department, 405 Hilgard Ave, 90024.
Library Holdings: AV—Slides 210,000

L **Art Library,** 2250 Dickson Art Center, 90024. Tel 213-825-3817. *Art Librn* Joyce P Ludmer
Founded 1952
Library Holdings: Vols 56,631
Collections: A copy of Princeton's Index of Christian Art

L **Architecture and Urban Planning Library,** 1302 Architecture Bldg, 90024. Tel 213-825-2747. *Head Librn* Jon S Greene
Open Mon - Thurs 8:30 AM - 9 PM, summer and intersessions Mon - Fri 9 AM - 5 PM, cl Sat, Sun & evenings. Estab 1969 to provide the basic materials for the study of architecture and urban planning at the professional graduate level. Circ 21,000
Income: Financed by endowment and state appropriation
Purchases: $20,000
Library Holdings: Vols 13,000; Per subs 250

L **Elmer Belt Library of Vinciana,** 405 Hilgard Ave, 90024. Tel 213-825-3817. *Belt Library Asst* Victoria Steele
Open Mon - Fri 9 AM - 5 PM. Estab 1961
Income: Financed by state appropriation
Library Holdings: Vols 9000; Other—Clipping files, exhibition catalogs, framed reproductions, manuscripts, original art works, pamphlets, photographs, reproductions, original documents
Special Subjects: Leonardo da Vinci
Collections: Special collection of rare books, incunabula, and related materials in Renaissance studies, with a focus on Leonardo da Vinci, his manuscripts, milieu, art and thought

UNIVERSITY OF SOUTHERN CALIFORNIA

M **University Galleries,** 823 Exposition Blvd, 90007. Tel 213-741-2799, 741-7624. *Dir* Donald Brewer; *Registrar* Bruce Hiles; *Admin Asst* Kay Allen
Open Mon - Fri noon - 5 PM, cl Sat & Sun except for special exhibitions. No admis fee. Estab 1939 as an educational department of the University. Fisher Gallery consists of three rooms, two for changing exhibitions, the third for permanent collection display; Lindhurst Gallery displays student work. Average Annual Attendance: 18,000. Mem: Dues $100; meeting second Tues every month
Income: Financed by endowment
Collections: Galleries house the permanent collections of paintings of 17th Century Dutch, Flemish and Italian, 18th Century British, 19th Century French and American landscape and portraiture schools
Exhibitions: Walter Askin - A Ten Year Survey of Work; Reality of Illusion
Publications: Exhibition catalogs, three annually
Activities: Lect open to public; films; gallery talks

L **Architecture and Fine Arts Library,** Watt Hall, University Park, 90007. Tel 213-741-2798. *Librn* Alson Clark; *Library Asst* Helen Robischon; *Slide Cur* Justine Clancy
Open Mon - Thurs 8:30 AM - 10 PM, Fri 8:30 AM - 5 PM, Sat Noon - 5 PM, Sun 1 - 8 PM. Estab 1925 to provide undergraduate and graduate level students and the teaching and research faculty materials in the areas of architecture and fine arts needed to achieve their objectives. Circ 65,000. Branch library in the central library system is supported by the University
Income: Financed by University funds
Purchases: $35,000
Library Holdings: Vols 35,000; Per subs 200; Micro—Reels; AV—Slides 105,000; Other—Exhibition catalogs, pamphlets, photographs, architectural drawings 1000
Activities: Tours

L **WOODBURY UNIVERSITY LIBRARY,** 1027 Wilshire Blvd, 90017. *Dir* Dr Everett L Moore
Open Mon - Fri 7 AM - 10 PM. Estab 1884 to meet curriculum needs of faculty and students. Circ 65,000
Library Holdings: Vols 42,500; Per subs 464; AV—Cassettes, fs, slides

MALIBU

M J **PAUL GETTY MUSEUM,** 17985 Pacific Coast Highway, 90265. Tel 213-459-2306. *Dir* Stephen Garrett; *Cur of Paintings* Burton Fredericksen; *Cur of Antiquities* Dr Jiri Frel; *Cur of Decorative Arts* Gillian Wilson; *Head Public Information* Cathy LaScola
Open Tues - Sat (summer Mon - Fri) 10 AM - 5 PM. No admis fee. Estab 1953

to display art objects for public viewing and to promote scholarly research in the fields represented. The museum building is a recreation of an ancient Roman villa, and consists of 38 galleries. Average Annual Attendance: 300,000

Income: Financed by endowment

Collections: †Greek and Roman antiquities; †French decorative arts; †Western European paintings

Publications: Calendar, quarterly; Museum Journal

Activities: Docent training; slide show for children; classroom materials; lect open to public, 10 - 12 vis lectr per year; concerts; original objects of art lent occasionally to other museums for special exhibitions; museum shop selling books, reproductions, slides, and museum publications

L **Research Library,** 17985 Pacific Coast Hwy, 90265. *Head Librn* Anne-Mieke Halbrook; *Assoc Librn* Bethany Mendenhall

Open by appointment only Tues - Fri 10 AM - 5 PM. Estab 1973 to support research by curatorial and other professional museum staff. For reference only; noncirculating

Income: Financed by endowment

Library Holdings: Vols 12,000; Per subs 90; Micro—Fiche, reels; AV—V-tapes; Other—Clipping files, exhibition catalogs, pamphlets

Special Subjects: Classical archeology, 18th century French decorative art, Western European painting

Collections: Auction-sales catalogs (approx 14,000)

L **Photo Archives,** 17985 Pacific Coast Hwy, 90265. Tel 312-459-2306. *In Charge* George Goldner

Open Tues - Fri 10 AM - 5 PM; summer hours Mon - Fri 10 AM - 5 PM by appointment. Estab 1972 to provide scholars with a research facility of photographs of works of art in international collections. Non-circulating

Income: Financed by endowment

Library Holdings: Other—Photographs 34,000 cataloged, 20,000 uncataloged

Special Subjects: Ancient art (Greek, Etruscan and Roman); Western European painting (14th - 19th centuries); Western European decorative arts, particularly French 18th century

Collections: Bartsch series of early prints; Courtauld Institute of Photo Survey of private collections; Decimal Index of the art of low countries; paintings and decorative arts from major auction houses

MENDOCINO

O **MENDOCINO ART CENTER,** 45200 Little Lake St, Box 765, 95460. Tel 707-937-5818. *Pres Board Trustees* Elaine Lackey; *Executive Dir* Karen Kesler; *Gallery Mgr* Grace Rubasamen

Open Mon - Fri 10 AM - 4 PM; Sat & Sun 10 AM - 5 PM. No admis fee. Estab 1959 as a rental-sales gallery for exhibition and sales of member work; also to sponsor traveling and museum exhibits. Two major gallery rooms, 1 gallery room available for rental of one-man shows. Average Annual Attendance: 10,000. Mem: 900; dues $15

Collections: Graphics, paintings and sculpture

Publications: Arts & Entertainment, monthly

Activities: Classes for adults and children; lect open to public, 4-10 visiting lectr per year; concerts; gallery talks; tours; competitions with awards; individual paintings and original objects of art lent to businesses and public places; sales shop sells books, original art, reproductions, and crafts

L **Library,** 45200 Little Lake St, Box 765, 95460. *Librn* Joan Burleigh

Open Mon - Fri 9 AM - 1 PM for members only. Estab 1975 to provide members with access to art books and magazines. Circ 600 books & 75 magazines

Library Holdings: Other—Framed reproductions, prints, reproductions

Special Subjects: Architecture

MISSION HILLS

O **SAN FERNANDO VALLEY HISTORICAL SOCIETY,** 10940 Sepulveda Blvd, 91345. Tel 213-365-7810. *Cur* Elva Meline

Open Sat & Sun 1 - 4 PM, weekdays by appointment, cl holidays. No admis fee. Estab 1943. The Society manages the Andres Pico Adobe (1834) for the Los Angeles City Department of Recreation, where they house their collection. Mem: Dues; active, sustaining and organization $10, Life $100

Income: Financed by membership and donations

Collections: Historical material; Indian artifacts; paintings; costumes; decorative arts; manuscripts

Activities: lectures; films; guided tours; permanent and temporary exhibitions

L **Library,** 10940 Sepulveda Blvd, 91345.

Open to the public for research on the premises

Library Holdings: Vols 3500

MONTEREY

M **CASA AMESTI,*** 516 Polk St, 93940. Tel 408-372-8173. *Chmn Monterey Council* Frederick S Farr

Open Sat & Sun 2 - 4 PM, cl 3 wks July. Admis adults 50¢, students 25¢. Bequeathed to the National Trust in 1953 by Mrs Frances Adler Elkins. It is an 1833 adobe structure reflecting phases of the history and culture of the part of California owned by Mexico, after the period of Spanish missions and before development of American influences from the Eastern seaboard. It is a prototype of what is now known as Monterey style architecture. The Italian-style gardens within the high adobe walls were designed by Mrs. Elkins, an interior designer, and her brother, Chicago architect David Adler. The furnishings, largely European, collected by Mrs. Elkins are displayed in a typical 1930's interior. The property is a National Trust historic house. The Old Capital Club, a private organization, leases, occupies and maintains the property for social and educational purposes

Collections: Elkins Collection of largely European furnishings

Activities: Monterey History and Art Association volunteers provide interpretive services for visitors on weekends

O **MONTEREY HISTORY AND ART ASSOCIATION,** 550 Calle Principal, PO Box 805, 93940. Tel 408-372-2608. *Pres* Harold C Hallett

Casa Serrano Open Sat & Sun 1 - 4 PM, cl holidays. No admis fee. Estab 1931. The association owns the 1845 Casa Serrano Adobe; the 1865 Doud House; the 1845 Fremont Adobe and the Mayo Hayes O'Donnell Library. They operate and maintain the Allen Knight Maritime Museum, but do not own the premises. The association celebrates the birthday of Monterey (June 3, 1770) with the Merienda each year on June 3. The association commemorates the landing at Monterey by Commodore John Drake Sloat in 1846. Mem: Dues individual life membership $250, sustaining couple $30, sustaining single $20, couple $15, single $10, junior $1

Collections: Costumes, manuscripts and paintings

Exhibitions: Permanent and temporary exhibitions

Publications: Noticias Del Puerto De Monterey, quarterly bulletin

Activities: Guided tours

L **Mayo Hayes O'Donnell Library,** 550 Calle Principal, 93940.

Open Wed, Fri, Sat 1 - 4 PM, Sun 1:30 - 4 PM

Library Holdings: Vols 2500

M **Allen Knight Maritime Museum,** 550 Calle Principal, 93940. Tel 408-375-2553. *Dir* Earl E Stone

Open Summer Tues - Fri 10 AM - 12 PM, 1 - 4 PM, Sat & Sun 2 - 4 PM, Sept 1 - June 15 afternoons only, cl Mon and National holidays. No admis fee. Estab 1971. Mem: Dues individual life membership $250, sustaining couple $30, sustaining single $20, couple $15, single $10, junior $1

Collections: Marine Artifacts, ship models, paintings, photographs, Fresnel First Order Lens from Point Sur, California (on loan from US Coast Guard)

Exhibitions: Permanent and temporary exhibitions

Activities: Lectures; guided tours

L **Museum Library,** 550 Calle Principal, 93940. *Librn* Mrs George St Jean

Open for research on the premises

Library Holdings: Vols 400-500; Other—Manuscripts

Publications: Brochure of Museum with map

M **MONTEREY PENINSULA MUSEUM OF ART,** 559 Pacific St, 93940. Tel 408-372-5477. *Pres* Theodore Calhoon; *VPres* Steven Sassoon; *VPres* Mrs Rodger Bailey; *VPres* Mrs Charles Wilber; *Recording Secy* William F Stone Jr; *Corresp Secy* Mrs Robert Bonner; *Treas* David McAlpine; *Dir* June Elder Braucht; *Museum on Wheels Coordr* Ilene Tuttle; *Museum on Wheels Dir* Kay Cline

Open Tues - Fri 10 AM - 4 PM; Sat & Sun 1 - 4 PM; cl Mon and holidays. No admis fee. Estab 1959 to perpetuate knowledge of and interest in the arts; to encourage a spirit of fellowship among artists and to bring together the artist and the community at large. It recognizes the need for the collection, preservation and exhibition of art works, especially the best of those done in the area. The main gallery (30 x 60 ft) houses monthly temporary exhibitions, Leonard Heller Memorial Gallery, revolving permanent collection, Armin Hansen Gallery, William Ritschel Memorial Gallery, Folk Art Gallery for collection of international folk arts and hallways which are used to show permanent collection. Average Annual Attendance: 35,000. Mem: 2200; dues individual $10; annual meeting Jan

Income: $120,000 (financed by endowment, membership and fund-raising functions)

Collections: Armin Hansen Collection; international folk art, photography and graphics; regional art, past and present; William Ritschel Collection

Exhibitions: (1978) American Carousel Art; The California Craftsman; The Helen Colby Retrospective; Drawings by Christine Lardon; Drawings by Michael & Melinda Wright; Fire Paintings by Rahel Bashe; New Graphics from the Permanent featuring Angel Ramano; Paintings & Drawings by Christine Fry-Loftis and Stephen Lang; Paintings by Jeanne D'Orge Cherry; Paintings by Richard Lofton; Paintings by Rollin Pickford; Paintings by Robert A Graham; Paintings by Marjorie Berry Faris; Photographs by Joel Pickford; Photographs by Edward Weston; Photographs by Manuel Alvarez Bravo; Photographs by Elliott Erwitt; Photographs by Jerry Takigawa; Photography by Betty Peckinpah; Recent Additions to the Permanent Collection featuring Chang Dai-Chien; Sculpture by Doug Walla; Watercolors by Richard Bennett; Watercolors of Organic Forms by Anita Tortoricia; Works by Jo Mora; Works by Eugene Newmann. (1979) Anatomical Signitures, Paintings by Caroline Seibert; Louise Cardeiro Boyer Retrospective; Ceramics by David Bigelow; Drawings by Fulvio Testa; Monterey County Art; Morris and Co: The Stained Glass; Paintings by Frank Duveneck; Paintings by Thomas McGlynn; Paintings by James Fitzgerald; Paintings by Mirek; Paintings by Jean La Fond; Photographs by Dick Arentz; Photographs by Martha Pearson; Photograms by Arnold Gilbert; Toward Tranquility, Paintings by Richard Young; Treasures and Tools of the Artists Studio. (1980) Fluoro Paint and Printers Ink. featuring Irene Lagorio; Paintings by Craig Antrim; Paintings by Luis Filcer; Saltillo Sarapes; Works by Gloria Alford; Xerox Prints by Steve Vanoni

Publications: Courier, monthly; Yesterday's Artists on the Monterey Peninsula, book; exhibition catalogs

Activities: Classes for adults and children; docent training; lect open to public, 4 visiting lectr per year; concerts; gallery talks; tours; competitions; exten dept serves three rural county areas; Museum on Wheels teaches craft classes in schools; museum shop sells books, reproductions, prints, and museum replicas and folk art objects

L **Library,** 93940. *Librn* Ethel Solliday

Open to the public for reference when supervised, or by appointment

Library Holdings: Vols 1300; Per subs 3; Other—Exhibition catalogs

L **MONTEREY PUBLIC LIBRARY,** 625 Pacific St, 93940. Tel 408-646-3930.

Open Mon - Thurs 9 AM - 9 PM; Fri 9 AM - 6 PM; Sat 9 AM - 5 PM; Sun 1 - 5 PM. Estab 1849 as a library for the city of Monterey. Circ 300,000

Income: Financed by membership and city appropriation

Library Holdings: Vols 114,000; Per subs 200; Micro—Reels; AV—Cassettes, motion pictures, rec, slides; Other—Clipping files, manuscripts, original art works, pamphlets, photographs, reproductions

Special Subjects: Local history

Collections: Adler; Elkins Collection on Architecture and Interior Design, especially 17th - 19th century English, Italian and French; Raiquei

M **PRESIDIO OF MONTEREY ARMY MUSEUM,** 93940. Tel 408-242-8414. *Dir & Cur* Margaret B Adams

Open Thurs - Mon 9 AM - 12:30 PM & 1:30 - 4 PM. No admis fee. Estab 1965. Outlines Presidio Hill from Indian, Spanish and Mexican eras to present United

States Army base. One gallery of historical artifacts. Average Annual Attendance: 50,000

Income: Financed by federal appropriations

Collections: Local Artifacts: Rumsen Indian Tools & Decorations; Spanish and Mexican Military Items; Spanish Paintings and Utensils from Governor Argurlo's Residence; United States Military Items 1846 to Present with Emphasis on the Pre-1940 Horse Cavalry

Exhibitions: (1978) China-Town Before 1906. (1979) American Indian Baskets of the Pacific Coast; Black Buffalo Soldiers at the Presidio

Activities: Docent training; lect open to the public, 15-20 visiting lectr per year; gallery talks; tours; individual paintings and original objects of art lent to other museums and valid private organizations

L Library, 93940.
Estab 1905 to offer military historical library to professional scholars. Open museum hours with advance arrangements for reference only
Library Holdings: Vols 300; Per subs 5; Micro—Fiche; AV—A-tapes, fs, motion pictures, slides; Other—Clipping files, exhibition catalogs, framed reproductions, manuscripts, memorabilia, original art works, pamphlets, photographs
Special Subjects: History of Monterey, United States Army

M SAN CARLOS CATHEDRAL,* 550 Church St, 93940. Tel 408-373-2628. *Rector Msgr* Brendan McGuiness
Open daily 8 AM - 6 PM. No admis fee. Built in 1970, now a branch of the Monterey Diocese. The art museum is housed in the 1794 Royal Presidio Chapel
Collections: Spanish religious paintings and sculpture of the 18th and 19th century
Activities: Guided tours

MORAGA

M SAINT MARY'S COLLEGE OF CALIFORNIA, Hearst Art Gallery, Box AE, 94575. Tel 415-376-4411, Ext 379. *Pres* Bro Mel Anderson; *Gallery Dir* Janice P Alvarez
Open Sun - Wed Noon - 4 PM. No admis fee. Estab 1977 to exhibit a variety of the visual arts for the benefit of college students, staff and members of surrounding communities. Maintains two 30 x 30 ft rooms with connecting rampway. Average Annual Attendance: 2000. Mem: 105; dues patron $50 and up, family $15, students and senior citizens $5; annual meeting in May
Collections: Paintings by William Keith (1838-1911); East European icons; medieval sculpture
Exhibitions: (1978) Art of the Etruscans; Contemporary Pots. (1979) Ancient and Traditional Ceramic Forms; Art of the Printed Book; Prints from the Kala Institute; Watercolors of William Keith. (1980) Landscapes by Linda K Smith; Portraits by Carole Peel
Publications: Catalogue; newsletter, occasionally
Activities: Book traveling exhibitions

NATIONAL CITY

M MUSEUM OF AMERICAN TREASURES, 1315 E Fourth St, 92050. Tel 714-477-7489. *Owner & Founder* Hans K Lindemann
Open Sun 10 AM - 5 PM. Estab 1954 as the Museum of Glass
Collections: Artillery shells hammered into vases and ashtrays; Bronze Buddha; campaign buttons from presidential candidates, including Ulysses S Grant; clock called the Goddess of Fortune with coins from various countries; commemorative medals, plates and ashtrays; door knockers in likenesses of lions, eagles, Egyptians and Abraham Lindoln; documents signed by several presidents; 82 ft elephants tusk carving; handblown glass replica of the royal barge of the King of Siam; Imarivase from Japan; world's largest ivory carved chess set; world's largest bust of Princess Piccarda of the Medici family; woodcarvings; world's largest desert glass collection (10,000 items); old books dating back as far as 1508

NEWHALL

M WILLIAM S HART MUSEUM, William S Hart Park, 24151 N Newhall Ave, 91321. Tel 805-259-0855. *Regional Park Supt* Mike Dortch
Open Wed - Fri 10 AM - 3 PM; Sat & Sun 10 AM - 5 PM. No admis fee. Estab 1958 to maintain the park and museum as center for leisure enjoyment to the population of Southern California. The retirement home of William S Hart is full of Western art. Average Annual Attendance: 120,000
Income: Financed by county appropriation
Collections: Christadoro; Joe de Yong; James M Flagg; Robert L Lamdin; Remington; Charles M Russell (bronzes, oils, watercolors, grisalle, pen & ink); Schrezvogel; Western art
Activities: Classes for children

NEWPORT BEACH

M NEWPORT HARBOR ART MUSEUM, 850 San Clemente Dr, 92660. Tel 714-759-1122. *Pres* John Martin Shea; *Dir* Thomas H Garver; *Secy* Jane Rhodes; *Treas* Charles Hester; *Cur Exhib & Col* Betty Turnbull; *Cur Education* Phyllis Lutjeans; *Adminr* Jean Smock; *Dir Development & Community Relations* Gary Wheelock
Open Tues - Sun 11 AM - 5 PM, Wed 6 - 9 PM. Admis by contribution. Estab 1962 as a museum of the Art of our Time serving Orange County and Southern California. Building completed in 1977 contains four galleries of various sizes; 5000; 1600; 1200; 500 sq ft plus lobby and sculpture garden area. Average Annual Attendance: 80,000. Mem: 3000; dues range from $1000 to $7.50
Income: $600,000
Purchases: $50,000
Collections: Collections of contemporary American art: Walter Darby Bannard; Paul Brach; John Clem Clark; Jim Dine; Mark Tobey; California artists: John Baldessari; Larry Bell; Karl Benjamin; Elmer Bischoff; Vija Celmins; Tony DeLap; Sam Francis; Loren Madsen; David Park; Paul Wonner; Jack Zajac; Photographers: Lewis Baltz; Harry Callahan; William Eggleston; Robert Heinecken; Leland Rice;

Garry Winogrand
Exhibitions: William Baziotes Retrospective: Paintings, Drawings, and Watercolors; Tony Berlant: The Eccentric Image; Tony DeLap: New Work; David Park Retrospective; Rooms: Moments Remembered (Installation); The Prometheus Archives: A Retrospective Exhibition of Work by George Herms; Our Own Artists: Contemporary Art in Orange County; George Segal: Two New Sculptures; Vija Celmins: A Survey Exhibition
Publications: Bimonthly calendar; exhibition catalogs; posters
Activities: Classes for adults and children; docent training; in-training session for teachers; lect open to the public and occasionally for members only, 15 vis lectr per yr; concerts; gallery talks; tours; film programs; individual paintings and original objects of art lent to qualified art museums; lending collection contains original prints; paintings and sculptures; traveling exhibitions organized and circulated; museum shop selling books, magazines, original art
L Library, 850 San Clemente Dr, 92660. *Librn* Ruth Roe
Open for reference by appointment
Library Holdings: Vols 1500; Per subs 6; Other—Exhibition catalogs
Special Subjects: contemporary art

NORTHRIDGE

M CALIFORNIA STATE UNIVERSITY, NORTHRIDGE, Fine Arts Gallery, 18111 Nordhoff St, 91330. Tel 213-885-2192. *Dir* Jean-Luc Bordeaux; *Assoc Dir* Louise Lewis; *Installations Dir* Phil Morrison; *Gallery Asst* Tjimkje Singerman
Open Mon Noon - 4 PM; Tues - Fri 10 AM - 4 PM. No admis fee. Estab 1971 to serve the needs of the four art departments and to provide a source of cultural enrichment for the community at large. Exhibitions in main gallery have average duration of four weeks. Gallery II for weekly MA candidate solo exhibitions. Average Annual Attendance: 35,000. Mem: Arts Council for CSUN 300; dues $25; annual meeting June
Income: $10,000 (financed by city and state appropriation)
Exhibitions: Americans in Paris: the Fifties; Art of the Upper and Lower Niger; Harry Callahan; Fundamental Aspects of Modernism; Recent Abstract Painting from New York; Ukiyo-e and the Feminine Mystique
Publications: Catalogs of exhibitions, average 2 per year
Activities: Docent training; gallery talks; tours; competitions; sales shop selling books, magazines, reproductions and slides

OAKLAND

L CALIFORNIA COLLEGE OF ARTS & CRAFTS, Meyer Library, Broadway & College Aves, 94618. Tel 415-653-8118. *Head Librn* Robert L Harper; *Asst Librn* Fraiser McConnell
Open Mon - Thurs 8 AM - 7 PM, Fri 8 AM - 5 PM. Estab 1907 to support the studio and academic requirements for BFA and MFA
Income: $100,000(financed by tuition)
Purchases: $15,000
Library Holdings: Vols 25,000; Per subs 192; Micro—Reels; AV—Rec; Other—Clipping files, exhibition catalogs, prints, manuscripts, original art works, pamphlets, photographs, reproductions
Collections: Jo Sinel Collection of pioneering work in industrial design
Exhibitions: Small exhibitions mounted on free standing panels

M CENTER FOR THE VISUAL ARTS, 1333 Broadway, 94612. Tel 415-451-6300. *Pres* Tom Martin Browne; *VPres* Virginia Lloyd; *Secy* Altona Anderson; *Executive Dir* Linda E Evans
Open Mon - Sat 9 AM - 5 PM; Registry open Mon - Fri Noon - 4:30 PM. No admis fee. Estab 1972 to serve artists in the contemporary Bay area art scene through exhibitions and referrals; and to serve the community through art and education programming. Average Annual Attendance: 10,000. Mem: 650; dues community $30, artists $20; annual meeting Nov
Income: $200,000 (financed by endowment, membership, city and state appropriation and private donations)
Exhibitions: Children's Art Show; The Figure Redefined; Paper, Wood and Fiber; Art and Technology; Irving Penn Photographs in Platinum-Metals, memberships' shows, national photography
Publications: Newsletter, bi-monthly
Activities: Classes for children; lect open to public; gallery talks; competitions
L Slide Library, 1333 Broadway, 94612. *Librn* Lucinda Lake
Open Mon - Fri 12:30 - 4:30 PM. Estab 1972 to provide data bank of visual materials representing contemporary artist
Library Holdings: AV—Slides 18,000; Other—Exhibition catalogs, pamphlets, photographs

O JUNIOR CENTER OF ART AND SCIENCE, 3612 Webster St, 94609. *Dir* Nancy M Walton
Open Tues - Fri 10 AM - 5 PM, Sat 10 AM - Noon. Estab 1949 as a non-profit organization existing for the benefit of children of the community. Mem: Membership dues Business $100 and up, family $25, individual $15
Income: Financed by membership, donations, memorial gifts and fund-raising
Activities: Classes for children; outreach program provides art and science mini-courses to schools

L LANEY COLLEGE LIBRARY, Art Section, 900 Fallon St, 94607. *Art Librn* Lucy Wilson
Open daily 8 AM - 8:45 PM. Estab 1954. Circ 78,000
Library Holdings: Vols 61,000; AV—A-tapes, cassettes, fs, Kodachromes, lantern slides, motion pictures, rec, slides, v-tapes; Other—Prints, reproductions
Exhibitions: Paintings, sculpture, ceramics, fabrics, photography by students, faculty and community persons

M MILLS COLLEGE, Art Gallery, Seminary & MacArthur Blvd, PO Box 9973, 94613. Tel 415-632-2700, Ext 310. *Dir* Philip E Linhares; *Asst to the Dir* Ann Harlow
Open Tues - Sun 10 AM - 4 PM. No admis fee. Estab 1925 to show contemporary painting, sculpture, and ceramics, exhibitions from permanent and loan collections.

Gallery is Spanish-type architecture and has 4500 sq ft main exhibition space, with skylight full length of gallery. Average Annual Attendance: Approx 12,000
Income: Financed by college funds
Purchases: $1500
Collections: †Regional collection of California paintings, drawings and prints; †extensive collection of European and American prints and drawings; Guatemalan textiles; photographs and slides
Activities: Lect open to the public, 3 vis lectr per yr; gallery talks

M **OAKLAND MUSEUM,*** Art Department, 1000 Oak St, 94607. Tel 415-273-3402. *Dir & Chief Exec Officer* John E Peetz; *Cur Art* George W Newbert; *Deputy Cur Art* Harvey L Jones; *Sr Cur Prints & Photographs* Therese Heyman; *Registrar* Barbara Savinar
Open Tues - Sat 10 AM - 5 PM, Sun 12 - 7 PM, cl Mon, New Year's, Thanksgiving and Christmas. No admis fee. The New Oakland Museum is comprised of three departments: Natural Sciences (formerly the Snow Museum of Natural History, founded 1922); History (formerly the Oakland Public Museum, founded 1910); and the Art Department (formerly the Oakland Art Museum, founded 1916). Internationally recognized as a brilliant contribution to urban museum design. The Oakland Museum occupies a four-square-block, three studded site on the south shore of Lake Merritt. Designed by Kevin Roche, John Dinkeloo and Associates, the Museum is a three-tiered complex of exhibition galleries, with surrounding gardens, pools, courts and lawns, constructed so that the roof of each level becomes a garden and a terrace for the one above. The Art Department has a large hall with 20 small exhibition bays for the permanent collection and a gallery for one-person or group shows as well as the Oakes Art Observatory and Gallery
Collections: Paintings, sculpture, prints, illustrations, photographs, artists dealing with California subjects, in a range that includes sketches and paintings by early artist-explorers; Gold Rush genre pictures; massive Victorian landscape; examples of the California Decorative Style, Impressionist, Post-Impressionist, Abstract Expressionist, and other contemporary works
Exhibitions: Photography and Print Collections; Study Collections: A Multimedia Presentation in the Oakes Art Observatory and Gallery; a wide variety of temporary monthly exhibitions
O **Oakland Museum Association,*** 1000 Oak St, 94607.
A separately incorporated auxiliary for all three departments with over 5000 members. From its membership, the OMA provides assistance and support for museum educational and cultural programs, through its Women's Board, Docent Council, and its Art, History, and Natural Sciences Guilds, which coordinate volunteer activities in the museum's three Departments. Mem: 5000
L **Library,*** 1000 Oak St, 94607.
Library maintained on archives of California art and artists
Library Holdings: Vols 1500

L **OAKLAND PUBLIC LIBRARY,** Fine Arts Section, Main Library, 125 14th St, 94612. Tel 415-273-3178. *Dir Library Services* Lelia White; *Sr Librn in Charge* Richard Colvig
Open Mon 12 - 8:30 PM, Tues, Wed & Thurs 9 AM - 8:30 PM, Fri & Sat 9 AM - 5:30 PM, cl Sun & holidays. Library cooperates with the Oakland Museum and local groups
Purchases: $24,000
Library Holdings: AV—A-tapes, cassettes, rec; Other—Framed reproductions, reproductions, posters
Collections: Picture Collections
Publications: museum catalogs

OJAI

O **OJAI VALLEY ART CENTER,*** 113 S Montgomery, 93023. Tel 805-646-0117. *Pres* Lee Horovitz; *Dir* Rick Hallmark
Open Mon - Sat 9 AM - 5 PM. No admis fee. Estab 1939, dedicated to the advancement and development of the arts. Gallery is 40 x 50 ft, high ceilings, with a large hanging area. Average Annual Attendance: 52,000 - 60,000. Mem: 300; dues family $25, single $10; annual meeting first Mon in Jan
Income: $50,000 (financed by membership, class and special event fees)
Exhibitions: Twelve monthly exhibitions
Publications: Newsletter, monthly
Activities: Classes for adults and children; dramatic programs; workshops; craft fair; competitions

ONTARIO

L **ONTARIO CITY LIBRARY,** 215 East C St, 91764. Tel 714-984-2758. *Supervisor Librn* Barbara Flynn; *Sr Librn Adult Services* Waynn Pearson; *Sr Librn Technical Services* Kay Pearlman
Open Mon - Thurs 9 AM - 9 PM, Fri & Sat 9 AM - 6 PM, Sun 12 - 5 PM. Circ 500,000. Gallery maintained to display local artists' works
Library Holdings: Vols 172,000; Per subs 529; Micro—Fiche, reels; AV—Cassettes, fs, motion pictures, rec, slides, v-tapes; Other—Clipping files, exhibition catalogs, framed reproductions, prints, memorabilia, original art works, pamphlets, photographs, original documents
Exhibitions: Monthly art exhibits, occasional sculpture exhibits
Activities: Lect open to public; gallery talks; tours

PACIFIC GROVE

O **PACIFIC GROVE ART CENTER,** 568 Lighthouse Ave, PO Box 633, 93950. Tel 408-375-2208. *Pres* Elmarie Dyke; *Dir* Patty Morton Davis; *Recording Secy* Constance Callas; *Secy* Connie Callas
Open Tues - Sat 1 - 5 PM; cl Sun, Mon and holidays. No admis fee. Estab 1968 to promote the arts and encourage the artists of the Monterey Peninsula; galleries are available to organizations to exhibit their work; Main Gallery used for exhibiting the works of individuals, organizations, or community oriented shows while Photo Gallery is used primarily for photography. Mem: 250; dues business and club $25, family $10, single $6

Income: Financed by membership, rental or donations
Publications: Newscalendar, monthly
Activities: Museum shop selling original art
L **Library,** 568 Lighthouse Ave, PO Box 633, 93950.
Open to members for reference only

PALM SPRINGS

M **PALM SPRINGS DESERT MUSEUM, INC,** 101 Museum Dr, PO Box 2288, 92262. Tel 714-325-7186. *Pres* H Earl Hoover, II; *Exec Dir* Frederick W Sleight; *Secy* Mrs Hal Wallis
Open Sept - May Tues - Sat 10 AM - 5 PM, Sun 1 - 5 PM, cl Mon. Admis adults $1.50, members, students, children no charge, first Tues of each month no charge. Estab and inc 1938. Mem: 3500; dues $25 - $5000; annual meeting March
Collections: Interpretation of natural sciences of the desert; modern American painting, prints and sculpture, specializing in California artists; Southwestern Indian crafts
Exhibitions: Approx 30 per year
Publications: Calendar of Events, monthly; Parade, seasonal newsletter; special exhibition catalogs
Activities: Classes for adults and children; docent training; lect; films; gallery talks; tours; concerts
L **Library,*** 101 Museum Dr, PO Box 2288, 92262.
Open for reference only; art and natural science books available for use on premises
Library Holdings: Vols 3000; Other—Photographs

PALO ALTO

O **PALO ALTO CULTURAL CENTER,** 1313 Newell Rd, 94303. Tel 415-329-2366. *Dir* Candace Carpenter; *Vol Coordinator* Beth Fair; *Coordinating Cur* Linda Langston; *Workshop Supv* Gary Clarien; *Office Mgr* Beverly Michaud
Open Tues - Sat 10 AM - 5 PM. Thurs 7 - 9 PM, cl Mon. No admis fee. Estab 1971 to serve and inform the entire community in the area of visual arts and their purpose. Maintains California Crafts Museum
Income: Financed by city appropriation
Publications: Exhibition announcement, 4-8 weeks
Activities: Classes; docent training; Preview receptions; concerts; films; lect; special events

M **PALO ALTO JUNIOR MUSEUM,*** 1451 Middlefield Rd, 94301. Tel 415-329-2111. *Supv* Mearl Carson; *Instructor Arts & Crafts* Gale Bruce
Open Tues - Fri 10 AM - Noon, 1 - 5 PM, Sat 10 AM - 5 PM, Sun 1 - 4 PM, cl New Years, Easter, July 4, Thanksgiving, Christmas; Baylands Interpretive Center Wed - Fri 2 - 5 PM, Sat & Sun 10 AM - 5 PM, cl Thanksgiving, Christmas. No admis fee. Estab 1932, completely renovated in 1969. Average Annual Attendance: 100,000
Income: $60,000 (financed by city appropriation)
Collections: Art and artifacts
Publications: Notes, monthly; Prehistoric Palo Alto (brochure)
Activities: Classes; guided tours; exten dept; sciencemobile
L **Library,*** 1451 Middlefield Rd, 94301.
Special Subjects: Crafts, Ethnology

PASADENA

L **ART CENTER COLLEGE OF DESIGN,** James Lemont Fogg Memorial Library, 1700 Lida St, 91103. *Dir* Elizabeth Stockly; *Asst Librn & Cataloger* Carl Baker; *Slide Librn* Marie Jordan; *Acquisitions Librn* Margaret Rose; *Circulation Supv* Maria Elena Aguilar
Open Mon - Thur 8:30 AM - 9 PM, Fri 8:30 AM - 5 PM, Sat 8:30 AM - 1:30 PM. Estab to provide reference and visual resources for the designers who study and teach at Art Center College of Design. Circ 24,541. For lending and reference
Income: $83,764
Purchases: $24,166
Library Holdings: Vols 19,063; Per subs 272; AV—Motion pictures, slides; Other —Clipping files, exhibition catalogs, reproductions
Special Subjects: Commercial Art, Graphic Design, Illustration, Industrial Design, Photography, Fine arts, history of design, moving-pictures, product design, transportation design

M **CALIFORNIA INSTITUTE OF TECHNOLOGY,** Baxter Art Gallery, 91125. Tel 213-795-6811, Ext 1371. *Dir* Michael H Smith; *Asst Dir & Registrar* Wendy Brodhead
Open daily Noon - 5 PM. No admis fee. Estab 1968 to exhibit comtemporary art. Maintains 3,000 sqare feet on campus of Cal Tech in the Humanities Department. Average Annual Attendance: 25,000. Mem: 300; dues $25 - $500
Income: $115,000; (financed by membership, Cal Tech and Pasadena Art Alliance)
Exhibitions: (1980) Michael Brewster; Robert Cumming and William Wegmer; Laddie John Dill; Hans Haacke; Nathan Oliveira: Survey of Monotypes; Bruce Richards; Richard Tuttle; Visionary Drawings of Architecture; Watercolors: Ed Ruscha, Sam Francis, Diebenkorn
Publications: Exhibition catalogs
Activities: Lect open to the public, 10 visiting lectr per year; gallery talks; tours; originate traveling exhibitions

NATIONAL WATERCOLOR SOCIETY
For further information, see National and Regional Organizations

M **PACIFIC - ASIA MUSEUM,** 46 N Los Robles Ave, 91101. Tel 213-449-2742. *Dir* David Kamansky
Open Wed - Sun Noon - 5 PM. Estab 1971 to promote understanding of the cultures of the Pacific and Far East through exhibitions, lectures, dance, music and concerts. Through these activities, the museum helps to increase mutual respect and appreciation of both the diversities and similarities of Eastern and Western cultures. The building was designed by Marston, Van Pelt and Mayberry, architects

for Grace Nicholson. The building is listed in the national register of historic places as the Grace Nicholson Building. Mem: dues benefactor $1000, donor $500, sponsor $250, patron $100, contributor $50, active $25
Collections: Oriental art objects
Exhibitions: Art of Indian Asia; Captain Cook and the Islands of the Pacific; Collector's Choice: Objects of Japan and China, from Southern California collectors; Indonesia: The Fabled Islands of Spice; Japan Day by Day
Activities: Classes for adults; docent training; lectures; museum shop sells art objects and Asian art books

M **PASADENA CITY COLLEGE,** Art Gallery, 1570 E Colorado Blvd, 91106. Tel 213-578-7238. *Dir* John H Jacobs
Open Mon - Thurs 11 AM - 4 PM; Evenings Mon, Tues & Wed 7 - 9 PM. No admis fee. Estab to show work that relates to class given at Pasadena City College. Gallery is housed in separate building; 1000 sq ft. Average Annual Attendance: 20,000. Mem: 2800 (financed by school budget)
Exhibitions: Clothing design; painting; sculpture; Faculty Show; advertising design Student Show
Publications: Mailers for each show

L **PASADENA PUBLIC LIBRARY,** 285 E Walnut St, 91101. Tel 213-577-4049. *Library Dir* Robert Conover; *Head Fine Arts Division* Josephine Pletscher
Open Mon - Thurs 9 AM - 9 PM, Fri & Sat 9 AM - 6 PM, Sun 1 - 5 PM. No admis fee. Art department estab 1927
Income: $24,000 (financed by endowments and gifts, for materials only)
Library Holdings: Vols 25,328; Per subs 133; AV—Motion pictures, rec 13,605; Other—Pamphlets, photographs, scrapbooks on local architecture and artists

M **NORTON SIMON MUSEUM,** Colorado & Orange Grove Blvds, 91105. Tel 213-449-6840. *Pres* Alvin E Toffel; *Dir* David Bull; *Cur* Selma Holo; *Research Cur* David Steadman; *Deputy Cur of Education* Althea B Williams
Open Thurs - Sun Noon - 6 PM. Adults $2, students and sr citizens 75¢, members free. Estab 1924; this museum brings to the Western part of the United States one of the worlds great collections of paintings, tapestries, prints, and sculptures for the cultural benefit of the community at large; the museum is oriented toward the serious and meticulous presentation of masterpiece art. Mem: dues $35 - $1000
Income: Finance by endowment, membership and city appropriation
Collections: Art spanning 14 centuries: including paintings, sculptures, tapestries and graphics from the early Renaissance through the 20th century; Blue Four Galka Scheyer Collection of German Expressionism; Goya Graphics; Indian and Southeast Asian sculpture; masterpieces by Cezanne, Degas, Matisse, Monet, Henry Moore, Raphael, Rembrandt, Rodin, Rubens, Tiepolo, Van Gogh, Zurbarin and others; paintings, etchings and lithographs by Picasso; Photography of Weston, Cunningham and others
Exhibitions: Degas bronze sculptures; Goya prints; Claude Lorrain drawings; Picasso; etchings of Rembrandt; Southeast Asian and Indian Sculpture
Activities: Private guided tours; museum shop sells books, original art, reproductions, prints, slides and postcards
L **Library,** Colorado & Orange Grove Blvds, 91105. *Librn* Amy Navratil
Open to staff for reference & to scholars by appointment
Library Holdings: Vols 5000; Per subs 34
Collections: Knoedler library on micro-fiche; auction and exhibition catalogues dating from the 18th century to 1970; Archival material and books relating to the Blue Four

PLEASANT HILL

M **DIABLO VALLEY COLLEGE MUSEUM,*** 321 Golf Club Rd, 94523. Tel 415-685-1230. *Dir* J S Byrne; *Cur* Erda Labuhn
Open Mon - Fri 9 AM - 4 PM, cl national holidays, Admissions Day, July, August. No admis fee. Estab 1959 as a community service to the public, and to schools, and as a resource for the college. Gallery is maintained; dimensions 85 x 60 ft. Average Annual Attendance: 11,621
Income: Financed by county taxes
Purchases: $2000-$4000
Activities: Classes for children; docent training; individual paintings lent to college students, faculty and staff; lending collection contains nature artifacts, original prints, paintings, sculpture
L **Library,*** 321 Golf Club Rd, 94523.
For reference only
Library Holdings: Vols 150; Per subs 8

RANCHO PALOS VERDES

O **PALOS VERDES ART CENTER,*** 5504 W Crestridge Rd, 90274. Tel 213-541-2479. *Exec Dir* Susan Heinz; *Secy* Carol Ritscher; *Exhib Coordr* Pam Merrill
Open Tues - Fri 10 AM - 4 PM, Sat 11 AM - 2 PM, Sun 1 - 4 PM, cl Mon, Christmas, New Years. No admis fee. Estab 1974, to provide a multifaceted program of classes, exhibits and lectures in the visual arts. Rental-Sales Gallery; also changing exhibits gallery. Mem: 1775; dues $15 - $100
Income: Fianced by membership
Collections: Small purchase prize collection
Exhibitions: Eight museum exhibits per year
Publications: Chronicle, bimonthly
Activities: Classes for children; docent training; lect open to public; gallery talks

RED BLUFF

M **KELLY-GRIGGS HOUSE MUSEUM,** 311 Washington St, Red Bluff, CA. (Mailing Add: 1248 Jefferson St, Red Bluff, CA 96080) Tel 916-527-1129. *Pres* Helen McKenzie Owens; *Pres Emeritus* Fred B Godbolt
Open Thurs - Sun 2 - 5 PM, cl holidays. Donations welcome. Estab 1965, a history museum in a home built in 1880. Mem: Dues associate $10, sustaining $50, charter $100 plus $10 annually, memoriam $100, life $200, patron $500, benefactor $1000
Collections: Pendleton Art Collection spanning over a century of art; Indian artifacts; antique furniture; Victorian costumes
Exhibitions: permanent and temporary exhibitions
Publications: Brochure; Kellygram (guides' newsletter and schedule)
Activities: Guided tours

REDDING

M **REDDING MUSEUM & ART CENTER,** 1911 Rio Dr, PO Box 427, 96001. Tel 916-243-4994. *Pres* Noreen Braithwaite; *VPres* Richard B Eaton; *Secy* Betty Carrick; *Treas* Cindy Howland; *Dir* Carolyn Bond; *Arts Cur* John Harper
Open Summer Tues - Sat 10 AM - 5 PM, Winter Tues - Fri Noon - 5 PM, Sat & Sun 10 AM - 5 PM, cl Mon. Estab 1963 to encourage the understanding of and appreciation for, man's accomplishments throughout history and pre-history. two galleries present changing monthly contemporary art exhibits. Average Annual Attendance: 25,000. Mem: 500; dues $10 - $100; annual meeting second Wed June
Income: Financed by membership, city appropriation
Collections: Central American Pre-Columbian pottery; Native American baskets; Shasta County historical artifacts and documents
Exhibitions: Roberta Aase; Art Faire Winners; Bay Area Painters; David Castleberry, weavings; Christmas Art and Craft Show; Mike Cooper, wood sculpture; Jim Crabb, Intaglio prints; Funnies U S A; Charles Harper (U S Parks Service); John Hunter, lithographs; Dick Kakuda, ceramics; Frank LaPena, oils; Local High School Art; Loom, Needle & Die Pot; Cindy Miracle, fabric wall hangings; Daniel Murphy, airbrush paintings; Nancy Newman, ceramics; India Newton and Ann McGraw Collection; Jan Sousa, handmade paper images; the Upstarts, six Bay Area painters; Visionary painters; Women in Watercolor; I-Chen-Wu Oriental Paintings
Publications: The Covered Wagon, published by Shasta Historical society, an affiliated organization
Activities: Classes for adults and children; docent training; lect open to the public; gallery talks; competitions; Children's Lawn Festival April; Art Faire Oct; Native American Heritage Day Nov; junior museum
L **Museum Research Library,** 1911 Rio Dr, PO Box 427, 96001.
Open for reference only by appointment
Collections: Carousel Animals; Steve French—paintings and prints; Historical Society Show; Dan Ralston—Military Miniatures; Photographs of Shasta County

REDLANDS

L **LINCOLN MEMORIAL SHRINE,** Eureka & Vine, PO Box 751, 92373. Tel 714-793-6622. *Cur* Larry E Burgess
Open Tues - Sat 1 - 5 PM, other hours by appointment; cl Sun, Mon & holidays. No admis fee. Estab 1932, operated as a section of the Smiley Public Library. Reference use only
Library Holdings: Vols 4500
Collections: Sculptures, paintings, murals
Activities: Docent training; temporary art exhibitions; lectures; guided tours

O **REDLANDS ART ASSOCIATION,** 12 E Vine St, 92373.
Open Tues - Sat 11 AM - 3 PM. No admis fee. Estab 1964 to promote interest in the visual arts and to provide a gallery for artists. Mem: 265
Exhibitions: Lyon Gallery exhibitions, 3 times per yr; many media juried shows
Publications: Bulletin, monthly
Activities: Classes for children through teens; lect open to public, 4 vis lectr per yr; tours; competitions; scholarships

M **SAN BERNARDINO COUNTY MUSEUM AND SATELLITES,** Fine Arts Institute, 2024 Orange Tree Lane, 92373. Tel 714-825-4825, 792-1334. *Pres* Bee Walsh; *VPres* Elizabeth Hopkins; *Dir* Dr Gerald Smith; *Asst Dir* Skip Pohl; *Cur Natural History* Gene Cardiff; *Cur Geology* Robert Reynolds; *Cur Archaeology* Ruth D Simpson; *Cur Herpetology* Robert Sanders; *Cur Entomology* Dr Charles Howell; *Cur Entomology* Vicky Hipsley; *Secy* Bobbie Miller; *Cur of Education* Ann Quinn
Open Tues - Sun 10 AM - 5 PM. No admis fee. Estab 1952 for education. Maintains upper and lower dome auditoriums and foyer. Average Annual Attendance: 300,000. Mem: 2100; dues Fine Arts Institute $30, Museum Association $15 and up; annual Fine Arts Institute meeting June; annual Museum Association meeting May
Income: $280,000 (financed by membership)
Purchases: $1000 - $2000
Collections: Collection established through Annual Heritage Awards Exhibit Purchase Awards and Fine Arts Institue Exhibits
Publications: Newsletter, monthly; Quarterly
Activities: Classes for adults and children; docent training; lect open to the public, 150 visiting lectr per yr; competitions with awards; individual paintings and original objects of art lent to various schools and county organizations; lending collection contains books, nature artifacts, original art works, original prints, paintings, photographs, sculpture, slides; originate traveling exhibitions; museum shop selling books, original art, reproductions, prints and slides

M **UNIVERSITY OF REDLANDS,** Peppers Art Center and Gallery, 1200 W Colton Ave, 92373. Tel 714-793-2121. *Chmn Art & Exhib Dir* John Nava
Open daily 1 - 5 PM. No admis fee. Estab 1909
Income: Financed by endowment
Collections: Ethnic Art; graphics; a few famous artists works
Exhibitions: Exhibitions during Fall, Winter, Spring
Activities: Art classes; art sale, student & faculty, May & Dec

RICHMOND

O **RICHMOND ART CENTER,*** Civic Center, 25th and Barrett Ave, 94804. Tel 415-234-2397, Ext 370. *Acting Cur* Clayton Pinkerton
Open Mon - Wed, Fri 10 AM - 4:30 PM, Thurs 10 AM - 4:30 PM, 7 - 9:30 PM, Sun 12 - 4:30 PM, cl Sat & holidays. No admis fee. Estab preliminary steps 1936-44; formed in 1944 to establish community center for Arts; to offer to the community an opportunity to experience and to improve knowledge and skill in the arts and crafts at the most comprehensive and highest level possible. A large gallery, small gallery and entrance corridor total 4757 sq ft, and a rental gallery covers 1628 ft; an outdoor sculpture court totals 8840 sq ft. Average Annual Attendance: 7000. Mem: 1300; dues $10 up; annual meeting fourth Wed in May
Income: $175,000 (financed by membership, city and state appropriations, and Art Center Association)
Collections: †Primarily contemporary art and crafts of Bay area
Publications: Catalog for Designer-Craftsman Show; newsletter, bimonthly; show announcements for exhibitions
Activities: Classes for adults and children; docent training; lect open to the public, 6 visiting lectrs per year; gallery talks; exten dept serving community; individual paintings and original objects of art lent to offices, businesses and homes; museum shop selling crafts, some prints, vignette paintings, cards
L **Library,*** 25th and Barrett Ave, 94804. *Class Supv* A Martin Cooke
Open to Art Center members
Library Holdings: AV—Slides; Other—books on paintings and crafts

RIVERSIDE

M **RIVERSIDE ART CENTER AND MUSEUM,** 3425 Seventh, 92501. Tel 714-684-7111. *Pres* William Engel; *Dir* Poppy Solomon; *Exec Secy* Paula Rhinehart; *Cur of Educ* William Haulicek
Open Tues - Sat 10 AM - 5 PM, cl Mon, August and holidays. No admis fee. Estab 1931 to enlighten and refine the thinking of interested people through the visual arts and crafts. Two galleries for changing exhibitions; permanent collection in lobby areas, members' sales and rental gallery. Mem: 1000; dues student and senior citizen $7.50, general $20, family $30, supporting $40, patron $75 and up
Income: Financed by membership, grants and donations
Collections: Mixture of media dating from the late 1800s to the present; 50 pieces
Activities: Art classes, beginning to advanced studio instruction; art program presented in public school system
L **Library,** 3425 Seventh, 92501.
Open for reference upon request
Library Holdings: Vols 500; Per subs 5; Other—Exhibition catalogs, framed reproductions, pamphlets, photographs, reproductions

M **UNIVERSITY OF CALIFORNIA,** University Art Galleries and California Museum of Photography, 3401 Watkins Dr, 92521. Tel 714-787-4636. *Acting Dir* Kirk de Goyer; *Admin Asst Art Galleries* Phyllis Gill; *Cur Slide Libr* Helene Kosher; *Asst Cur Slide Libr* Barbara Frank; *Cur of Collections* Joe Deal; *Asst Cur of Prints & Education* Katherine V Coy; *Registrar* Daniel McCurdy; *Archivist of the Keystone Mast Collection* Chris Kenney; *Special Projects Dir* Kenda North
Open Mon - Fri 10 AM - 4 PM, Sun 1 - 5 PM. Gallery estab 1963, museum 1972; the galleries present major temporary exhibitions; the museum program has both temporary exhibits and permanent installation; the museum is also a major research center. The main gallery contains 1500 sq ft; Gallery B has 250 sq ft and the museum gallery is 18,000 sq ft. Average Annual Attendance: Galleries 28,000, Museums 35,000
Income: Financed by endowment and university funds
Collections: †Bingham Collection of photographic apparatus; Walker Evans Print Collection; Keystone Mast Collection of stereoptics and stereographs, 340,000 items; Raoul Collection of prints; †19th & 20th Century print collection; Setzer-Alexander Friends of Photography Collection
Exhibitions: Anni Albers; Bowers, Foster & Schutte—three Bay Area artists; Walker Evans; Kaethe Kollwitz; Alma Lavenson; L A Abstract Paintings
Publications: Exhibition catalogs
Activities: Classes for adults; lect open to the public, 6 vis lectr per yr; gallery talks; tours; competitions; original objects of art lent to museums and art center; lending collection contains 17,000 color reproductions, 60,000 photographs and 75,000 slides; traveling exhibitions organized and circulated
L **Library,** 3401 Watkins Dr, 92521. *Librn* Lyndy K Zoeckler
Open to staff and selected private researchers for reference only

ROHNERT PARK

M **SONOMA STATE COLLEGE ART GALLERY,** 1801 E Cotati Ave, 94928. Tel 707-664-2054. *Acting Gallery Dir* Susan Moulton
Open Mon - Fri 10 AM - 4 PM. No admis fee. Estab 1978 to provide exhibitions of quality to the college and northern California community. 2800 sq ft of exhibition space designed to house monumental sculpture and painting
Income: Financed through College
Collections: Asnis Collection of Prints; Garfield Collection of Oriental Art
Exhibitions: Major Artists from Northern California: Bill Allen, Fletcher Benton, Joan Brown, de Forest, Diebenkorn, Sam Francis, Bill Geis, Wally Hendrick, Ed Moses, Harold Paris, Sam Richardson, Cornelia Schultz, Mark deSovero, Peter Voulkos, William Wiley; Thematic Exhibitions of Regional and National Art
Publications: Bulletins and announcements of exhibitions
Activities: Classes for adults; lect open to public, 30 vis lectr per yr; gallery talks; tours; competitions; exten dept

ROSS

O **MARIN SOCIETY OF ARTISTS INC,** Sir Francis Drake Blvd, PO Box 203, 94957. Tel 415-454-9561. *Pres* Malcolm McVickar; *VPres* Jean Allen; *Office Mgr* Deborah Humphrey; *Secy* Helen Loudon
Open Mon - Fri 11 AM - 4 PM; Sat & Sun 1 - 4 PM. No admis fee. Estab 1926 to foster cooperation among artists and to continually develop public interest in art. Gallery is located in a garden setting. It is approximately 3500 sq ft of well lighted exhibit space. Average Annual Attendance: 75,000. Mem: 600; Qualifications for membership: Previous exhibition in a juried show, and must reside in Bay Area if active; dues $20; meeting May & Sept
Income: Financed by membership, sale and rental of art
Exhibitions: Ten exhibitions annually, some are open to non-member artists residing in San Francisco - Bay Area
Activities: Lect open to the public, 2-3 vis lectr per yr; competitions with cash awards; scholarships; sales shop selling original art, original prints, handcrafted jewelry, ceramics and fiberworks

SACRAMENTO

O **CALIFORNIA STATE FAIR AND EXPOSITION ART SHOW,** 1600 Exposition Bldg, 95815. Tel 916-641-2592. *Prog Mgr* Gregg Loeser; *Exhibit Supv* Pete Scott
Open Aug 15- Sept 2, 10 AM - 10 PM. Estab 1854 to exhibit the work of artists of the State of California. Average Annual Attendance: 600,000
Income: $20,000
Collections: Ceramics and enameling; photograph; prints; oils; sculpture; textiles; watercolors
Publications: Art catalog, annually; Premium Book
Activities: Art in Action demonstrations, dramatic programs; individual paintings and original objects of art lent; traveling exhibitions organized and circulated

L **CALIFORNIA STATE UNIVERSITY, SACRAMENTO, LIBRARY,** Humanities Reference Media Services Ctr, 2000 Jed Smith Drive, 95819. Tel 916-454-6291. *University Librn* Gordon P Martin; *Assoc Humanities Reference Librn* Eugene N Salmon; *Sr Asst Humanities Reference Librn* Clifford P Wood; *Asst Humanities Reference Librn* Donna Ridley Smith; *Slide Cur* Delia Schlansky
Open Mon - Thurs 7:45 AM - 11 PM, Fri 7:45 AM - 5 PM, Sat 9 AM - 5 PM, Sun 1 - 9 PM (during Semester and Summer Sessions). Estab 1947. Circ 400,858. The Art Department maintains a gallery in the Art Bldg and a gallery in the University Union
Income: Financed through the University
Library Holdings: Vols 663,000; Micro—Fiche, reels; AV—Cassettes, fs, slides, v-tapes; Other—Clipping files, exhibition catalogs, original art works, pamphlets, reproductions
Special Subjects: Book Arts
Publications: Women Artists: A Selected Bibliography; bibliographic handouts

M **CROCKER ART MUSEUM,** 216 O St, 95814. Tel 916-446-4677. *Dir* Richard Vincent West; *Chief Cur* Roger D Clisby; *Registrar* Joanna Ownby; *Mus Serv* Susan von Berckefeldt
Open Wed - Sun 10 AM - 5 PM, Tues 2 - 10 PM, cl Mon. Admis adults 50¢, children under 12 free. Estab 1873; municipal art museum since 1885; original gallery building designed by Seth Babson completed in 1873; R A Herold Wing opened in 1969. Average Annual Attendance: 100,000. Mem: 1700: annual meeting June
Income: $500,000 (financed by membership and city appropriation)
Purchases: $30,000 - $50,000 per annum
Collections: American Decorative Art and Costumes 1850-1900; †American painting of the 19th century, with emphasis on California painting 1850-1900; †Contemporary California painting, sculpture and crafts; †Prints and photographs; †European decorative arts; †European painting 1500 - 1900; †Old Master drawings; Oriental art
Exhibitions: Aspects of abstract; 40 American photographers; California crafts; Crocker—Kingsley Annual (juried); The Huichol creation of the World; Hungarian Art Noveau; Munich and American realism in the 19th Century; The Santa Show
Publications: Calendar, 10 times per annum: Report; biannually
Activities: Classes for children; docent training; lect open to the public; concerts; gallery talks; tours; annual juried competitions; museum shop selling books, magazines, original art, reproductions and slides
L **Library,** 216 O St, 95814. *Librn* Ellen Schwartz
Open to staff, docents and others upon application
Library Holdings: Vols 1400; Per subs 24; Micro—Fiche; Other—Exhibition catalogs, Dissertations

SAINT HELENA

M **SILVERADO MUSEUM,** 1490 Library Lane, PO Box 409, 94574. Tel 707-963-3757. *Dir* Norman H Strouse; *Cur* Ellen Shaffer
Open Tues - Sun Noon - 4 PM, cl Mon & holidays. No admis fee. Estab 1969; the museum is devoted to the life and works of Robert Louis Stevenson, who spent a brief but important time in the area; the object is to acquaint people with his life and works and familiarize them with his stay. The museum has five wall cases and three large standing cases, as well as numerous bookcases. Average Annual Attendance: 8700
Income: Financed by the Vailima Foundation, set up by Mr & Mrs Norman H Strouse
Exhibitions: A different exhibition devoted to some phase of Stevenson's work is mounted every two months
Activities: Lect open to public; gallery talks; sales shop sells books, postcards
L **Library,** 1490 Library Lane, PO Box 409, 94574.
For reference only
Library Holdings: Vols 2500
Collections: First editions, variant editions, fine press editions of Robert Louis Stevenson, letters, manuscripts, photographs, sculptures, paintings and memorabilia

SALINAS

M HARTNELL COLLEGE GALLERY, 156 Homestead Ave, 93901. Tel 408-758-8211, Ext 250 & 261. *Dir* Gary T Smith
Open Mon - Thur 10 AM - 4 PM & 6 - 9 PM, Fri 10 AM - 4 PM. No admis fee. Estab 1959 to bring to students and the community the highest quality in contemporary and historical works of all media. Main gallery is 40 by 60 ft, south gallery is 15 by 30 ft, brick flooring. Average Annual Attendance: 7500
Collections: Approx 45 works on paper from the San Francisco Bay Area WPA
Exhibitions: Michael Arntz; Bolivian Textiles from the Collection of Jonathan S Hill; Children's Art; Classical Narratives in Master Drawings; Helen Escobedo; Faculty Show; Historical and Contemporary Objects; Alex Katz: cutouts; Barry Le Va: Ten Years of Drawings; Ralph Eugene Meatyard; Orozco and Rivera: Prints and Drawings; Retablos; Selection; Student Show; Marioj Post Woolcott
Publications: Three small catalogs per yr
Activities: Classes for adults; dramatic programs; gallery management training; individual paintings lent to qualifying educational institutions; lending collection contains original art works; traveling exhibitions organized and circulated

SAN BERNARDINO

M CALIFORNIA STATE COLLEGE SAN BERNARDINO, College Art Galleries,* 5500 State College Parkway, 92407. Tel 714-887-7459. *Chmn Art Dept* Julius Kaplan
Open Mon - Fri 9 AM - Noon, 1 - 3 PM, Sat 1 - 4 PM. No admis fee. Estab 1972 for the purpose of providing high quality exhibitions on varied subjects suitable for both campus and community. Gallery 2 opened 1978 as an exhibit area for senior shows and student work. Average Annual Attendance: 5500
Income: Financed by membership, city and state appropriations
Collections: Small collection of prints
Publications: Catalogs; Personas de los Tumbas - West Mexican tomb sculpture
Activities: Classes for adults; lect open to the public, 1-3 visiting lectrs per year; gallery talks; competitions

O SAN BERNARDINO ART ASSOCIATION, INC, 1640 E Highland Ave, 92404. *Pres* Mrs K G Stone; *First VPres* Majorie Mills; *Second VPres* Mrs P S Monroe; *Secy* Mrs Glen Stirnaman: *Corresp Secy* Mrs John Lawson; *Treas* John Lawson
No admis fee. Estab 1934 as a non-profit organization. Open to the public; maintains gallery. Mem: 130; dues $10; monthly meetings
Exhibitions: Inland Exhibit
Publications: Newsletter
Activities: Lect open to public, vis lectr; tours; competition with awards; Scholarships; sales shop sells original art

SAN DIEGO

M MARITIME MUSEUM ASSOCIATION OF SAN DIEGO,* 1306 N Harbor Dr, 92101. Tel 714-234-9153. *Pres & Exec Dir* Carl G Bowman; *Fleet Capt* Kenneth D Reynard
Open daily 9 AM - 8 PM. Admis family $5, adults $2, service personnel $1.50, children under 12 50¢, in groups 25¢, discount to adult groups. Estab 1948. A maritime museum in a fleet of three ships: Star of India (1863); Berkeley (1898 steamer); and Medea (1904 steam yacht). Mem: Dues life $250, development $50, supporting $25, regular $12
Collections: Antiques; maritime art; maritime artifacts
Exhibitions: Temporary exhibitions
Publications: Mains'l Haul, quarterly newsletter; Star of India, They Came by Sea
Activities: Lect; guided tours; films; book traveling exhibitions; sales shop selling maritime books, artifacts and souvenirs

M SAN DIEGO MUSEUM OF ART, Balboa Park, PO Box 2107, 92112. Tel 714-232-7931. *Acting Dir* Steven L Brezzo; *Cur Exhib* Darcie Fohrman; *Cur Paintings* Martin E Peterson; *Business Adminr* C Curtis Champlin; *Mgr Book Store* J Couric Payne; *Cur Education* Roger C Rose; *Cur Secy* Michaleen Sawka; *Activities Coordr* Sharon Hemus; *Secy to Dir* Sandra Erb; *Membership Secy* Sheila Hittle; *Mgr Art Sales & Rental* Denise Draper
Open Tues - Sun 10 AM - 5 PM; cl Mon. Admis general public $1, students and children under 16 50¢. Estab 1925. Gallery built in 1926 by a generous patron in a Spanish Plateresque design; the West wing was added in 1966 and the East wing in 1974. Average Annual Attendance: 370,000. Mem: 5000; dues sustaining friend $1000, sponsoring friend $500, friend of museum $100, family $25, individual $20, senior citizens $15, student $10, junior under 18 $5; annual meeting May
Income: $750,000 (financed by endowment, membership, city and county appropriations)
Purchases: $175,000
Collections: Italian Renaissance and Baroque Paintings; 19th and 20th Century American and European Sculpture and Paintings; Oriental Arts - sculpture, paintings, ceramics, decorative arts, American furniture and glass, English and Georgian silver; Spanish Baroque, Flemish, Dutch and English Schools; extensive print collection containing American, European and Oriental schools
Exhibitions: (1979) Art Inc; Art of the Muppets; Beyond the Endless River; Covers & Containers; Irving Gill; Mathes Collection of Antique Toys; Arthur Putnam; Rare Books
Publications: Annual Report; catalogs of collections; exhibition catalogs; membership calendar, monthly
Activities: Classes for adults and children; docent training; lectr open to the public; gallery talks; tours; competitions; original objects of art lent to city and county offices; traveling exhibitions organized and circulated; museum and sales shops selling books, original art, reproductions, prints, cards, jewelry and ceramics
L Art Reference Library, Balboa Park, PO Box 2107, 92112. *Librn* Nancy Andrews
Open Tues - Fri 10 AM - 3 PM. Estab 1925 for curatorial research and members reference. For reference only
Library Holdings: Vols 40,000; Per subs 35; AV—Slides; Other—Clipping files,

exhibition catalogs, pamphlets
Special Subjects: Asian Art, , Italian Renaissance, Spanish Baroque
Collections: Bibliography of artists in exhibition catalogues
Activities: Reading Club

L SAN DIEGO PUBLIC LIBRARY, Art & Music Section, 820 E St, 92101. Tel 714-236-5810. *Supv Librn* Barbara A Tuthill; *Picture Specialist* Gale Griffin; *Librn* Evelyn Cooperman
Open Mon - Thurs 10AM - 9 PM, Fri & Sat 9:30 AM - 5 PM. Estab 1954 to provide information and reference service in the fine arts; an expanding collection of reference and circulating books available. Corridor Gallery exhibits work by local artists and art groups each month
Income: Financed by city and state appropriation
Purchases: $32,000
Library Holdings: Vols 73,000; AV—Rec 21,406; Other—Clipping files, exhibition catalogs, pamphlets, photographs, postcards
Collections: Former libraries of William Templeton Johnson, architect, and Donal Hord, sculptor; emphasis is on Spanish, Mediterranean, Italian and French Renaissance architecture and Oriental art, sculpture and ceramics; books on the theatre including biographies of famous actors and actresses as well as histories of the American, London and European stages, gift of Elwyn B Gould, local theatre devotee
Exhibitions: Creative Embroiders Guild; Foothills Art Association; San Diego Stitchery Guild California Woodcarvers Association
Activities: Lect open to public,; concerts; opera previews

M SAN DIEGO STATE UNIVERSITY, Art Gallery, 5402 College Ave, 92182. *Chmn Dept Art* Fredrich Orth; *Dir* Dennis Komal
Open Wed - Sun noon - 4 PM. No admis fee. Estab to provide exhibitions of importance for the students, faculty and public of the San Diego environment; for study and appreciation of art and enrichment of the University. Average Annual Attendance: 35,000
Income: Supported by student fees and S D S U Art Council
Collections: Crafts collection; contemporary print collection; graduate student sculpture and painting
Exhibitions: Graduate and undergraduate students exhibitions; National Printmaking Annual
Activities: Lect open to the public; original art objects lent to University
L Love Library and Art Department Slide Library, San Diego State University, 5402 College Ave, 92182. *Art Librn* Lee Sandelin; *Slide Cur* Lilla Sweatt
Love Library open Mon - Thurs 7:30 AM - 11 PM, Fri 7:30 AM - 5 PM, Sat 10 AM - 5 PM, Sun Noon - 10 PM; Slide Library open Mon - Fri 8 AM - 4:30 PM. Estab 1957 to aid and facilitate the faculty in teaching art and art history as well as aiding students in class reports
Library Holdings: Micro—Cards, fiche, reels, prints; AV—Cassettes, Kodachromes, slides 120,000; Other—Clipping files, exhibition catalogs, framed reproductions, manuscripts, memorabilia, pamphlets, reproductions
Exhibitions: Special Art collections, student and women's art shows

M TIMKEN ART GALLERY, Balboa Park, 92101. Tel 714-239-5548. *Chmn Bd* Walter Ames; *Pres Bd* A J Sutherland; *VPres* K R Rearwin; *Exec Asst* Nancy A Petersen
Open Tues - Sat 10 AM - 4:30 PM, Sun 1:30 - 4:30 PM, cl Mon. No admis fee. Estab to display and preserve Old Master's paintings. six galleries. Average Annual Attendance: 75,000
Income: Financed by endowment
Collections: †Dutch and Flemish, †French, †Spanish; American paintings and Russian Icons; all paintings owned by Putnam Collection are on permanent display
Publications: Pamphlets which are distributed free to visitors
Activities: Docent training; tours

M UNIVERSITY OF SAN DIEGO, Founders' Gallery, Alcala Park, 92110. Tel 714-291-6480. *Dir* Therese T Whitcomb
Open Mon - Fri 10 AM - 4 PM. Estab 1971 to enrich the goals of the art department and university by providing excellent in-house exhibitions of all eras, forms and media, and to share them with the community. Gallery is an architecturally outstanding facility with foyer, display area and patio, parking in central campus. Average Annual Attendance: 1500
Collections: †19th & 20th century American folk sculpture; 17th, 18th & 19th century French tapestries and furniture; South Asian textiles and costumes of 19th and 20th centuries; Tibetan and Indian looms, Ghandi etc, spinning wheels
Exhibitions: Seven shows each year
Activities: Lect open to the public; tours; competitions with awards; scholarships offered; original objects of art lent

SAN FRANCISCO

O ACADEMY OF THE MUSEUM OF CONCEPTUAL ART, 75 Third St, 94103. Tel 415-495-3193. *Dir* Tom Marioni; *Preparator* Tony Labot; *Video Cur* Burt Arnowitz
Open Wed PM or for events. Estab 1970 for actions and situational art, preservation of old site, and social activities for artists. gallery maintained and covers 10,000 sq ft on two floors
Income: Financed by endowment
Exhibitions: Vito Acconci; Robert Barry; Bar Room Video; Chris Burden; Lowell Darling; Howard Fried; Paul Kos; Masashi Matsumoto; Restoration of Back Wall; Irv Tepper
Publications: Vision, annually
L Library, 75 Third St, 94103.
For reference only
Library Holdings: Micro—Reels; AV—A-tapes, cassettes, fs, Kodachromes, motion pictures, rec, slides, v-tapes; Other—Exhibition catalogs, prints, original art works, pamphlets, photographs, sculpture, original documents

M ASIA FOUNDATION GALLERY, The Asia Foundation, 550 Kearny St, 5th Floor, PO Box 3223, 94119. Tel 415-982-4640. *Pres* Dr Haydn Williams
Open 9 AM - 5 PM. No admis fee. Estab 1954; The Foundation's gallery is made

available to Asian artists to give them the opportunity to display their works. The gallery also is open to art collections of Asian related works. At Foundation headquarters, long hallway especially constructed to display works of art. Average Annual Attendance: 500

Collections: Batik, oil paintings, traditional and modern art
Exhibitions: Chinese Calligraphy and Painting exhibits; Photographs of Asia
Publications: Rarities of the Asian Art Museum: The Avery Brundage Collection; TAF News

M **ASIAN ART MUSEUM OF SAN FRANCISCO,** Avery Brundage Collection, Golden Gate Park, 94118. Tel 415-558-2993. *Dir & Chief Cur* Rene Yvon Lefebvre d'Argence; *Sr Cur* Clarence F Shangraw; *Cur Chinese Art* Stephen Little; *Cur Indian Art* Terese Tse Bartholomew; *Cur Japanese Art* Yoshiko Kakudo; *Cur Educ* Diana Turner

Open daily 10 AM - 5 PM. Adult(18-64) $1, Youth(12-17) 50¢, senior citizen and children free; recognized educational group free; first day of each month free. Founded in 1969 by the City and County of San Francisco. Branch Museum: Japan Center Extension, Japan Cultural and Trade Center, Webster Street Bridge
Collections: Nearly 10,000 objects of Asian art, including the Avery Brundage Collection and the Roy C Leventritt Collection
Exhibitions: 5000 Years of Korean Art; Folk Traditions in Japanese Art
Publications: handbooks and catalogs on museum collections
Activities: Classes for adults and children; docent training; intern prog for graduate students; lect open to public, 20 visiting lectr per year; gallery talks; tours; films; scholarships; inter-museum loan; originate traveling exhibitions
L **Library,** Golden Gate Park, 94118. *Librn* Fred A Cline Jr
Open Mon - Fri 1 - 4:45 PM. Estab 1967. For reference only
Income: $26,000(financed by membership, city appropriation and private gifts)
Purchases: $20,000
Library Holdings: Vols 12,926; Per subs 120; Micro—Fiche, reels, prints; AV—A-tapes, cassettes, Kodachromes, lantern slides, motion pictures, rec, slides; Other—Clipping files, exhibition catalogs, prints, pamphlets, photographs, reproductions
Special Subjects: Oriental Art

C **BANK OF AMERICA,** 555 California St, Department 3025, 94104. Tel 415-622-1265. *Art Cur* Bonnie Earls-Solari
Estab 1969 to enhance environment for employees; investment; support of art community. Collection displayed in offices. Three galleries usually have one-person shows of painting, photography, prints, tapestries and sculpture, occasionally with collection shows
Collections: Predominantly 20th Century, including Oriental and South American
Activities: Lect; individual objects of art lent to museum exhibitions

O **BAY AREA ART CONSERVATION GUILD,** Conservation Laboratory, Asian Art Museum of San Francisco, 94118. *Pres* Stephen Shapiro; *VPres* Judy Reinits; *Secy* Bruce Hutcheson; *Chief Conservator* Roger Broussal
Estab 1974 to promote ethical preservation of art and artifacts and to carry on educational programs. Mem: 130; dues $10; 6 meetings per year
Income: $1300 (financed by membership)
Publications: Periodic Newsletter
Activities: Presentations; lect; exten dept serves San Francisco Bay Area

O **CALIFORNIA HISTORICAL SOCIETY,** 2090 Jackson Street, 94109. Tel 415-567-1848. *Pres* North Baker; *VPres* Robert J Banning; *Treas* George N Hale Jr; *Exec Dir & Secy* James E Moss; *Dir of Administrative Services* Pamela L Seager; *Dir for Southern California* Dr Carolyn Ditte Wagner; *Accountant* James E Ostrom; *Programs Dir* Renee Eaton; *Membership* Abby Margolis
Estab in 1871 (reorganized in 1922), to collect, preserve and disseminate information pertaining to history of California and the West. Organization designated California's state historical society in 1979
Income: $560,000(Financed by endowment, membership and funding from private, corporate and public agencies)
Collections: Fine Arts includes California lithography and other graphics; oils; watercolors; drawings; furniture and artifacts to 1915
Exhibitions: National traveling photographic exhibitions The American Farm and Executive Order 9066 Permanent exhibition in San Francisco from the Society's collections
Publications: California History, quarterly; California Historical Courier(newspaper), six times per yr
Activities: Classes for adults; docent training; programs; lectures, tours and films throughout the state; lectures open to the public; concerts; gallery talks; tours; awards given for participation in the field of California history; traveling exhibitions organized and circulated; bookshop
M **History Center,** 6300 Wilshire Blvd, Los Angeles, CA 90048. Tel 213-651-5655. *Dir* Dr Carolyn Wagner
Open (archive) Mon - Fri 1 - 4 PM; (Exhibit gallery) Mon - Sat 9 - 5. Primarily photo archive, based on Title Insurance and Trust Los Angeles Collection; changing exhibition gallery
M **El Molino Viejo,** 1120 Old Mill Rd, San Marino, CA 91108. Tel 213-449-5450. *Dir* Margaret Eley
Open Tues - Sun 10 AM - 4 PM. Historic adobe grist mill with changing exhibit room
L **Library,** 2099 Pacific Ave, 94109. *Head Librn* Natalie J Cowan; *Manuscripts* Karl Feichtmeir; *Genealogy* Gerry Wright; *Kemble Coll* Bruce Johnson
Open Wed - Sat, 10 AM - 4 PM. Estab 1922 to collect books, manuscripts, photographs, ephemera, maps and posters pertaining to California and Western history. for reference and research only
Library Holdings: Vols 25,000; Micro—Reels; Other—Clipping files, exhibition catalogs, manuscripts, memorabilia, pamphlets, photographs 200,000, original documents
Special Subjects: Early California imprints county and municipal histories; early voyages of exploration Gold Rush, Mexican War missions, Overland journeys; transcontinental railroad
Collections: C Templeton Crocker Collection; Florence Keen Collection of California Literature; Kemble Collection of California Printing and Publishing

O **CHINESE CULTURE FOUNDATION,** Chinese Culture Center Gallery, 750 Kearny St, 3rd Floor, 94108. Tel 415-986-1822. *Pres* Rosalyn Koo; *VPres* Rolland Lowe; *VPres* James Frolik; *Acting Dir* Vivian Chiang; *Secy* Lillian Sing; *Admin Asst* Lee Foster; *Secy* Marijane Lee
Open Tues - Sat 10 AM - 5:30 PM. No admis fee. Estab 1965 to promote the understanding and appreciation of Chinese and Chinese-American culture in the United States. Traditional and contemporary paintings and sculpture by Chinese and Chinese-American artists, photographs and artifacts illustrating Chinese-American history, and major international and cultural exchanges from China make the center a local and national focus of Chinese artistic activities. Mem: 1500
Income: Financed by membership, city appropriation and grants
Exhibitions: China Observed: Drawings and Paintings of Jack Chen; Modern Chinese Woodcuts
Activities: Classes for adults and children; dramatic programs; docent training; lect open to the public; concerts; gallery talks; tours; museum shop selling books, original art, reproductions, prints, jewelry, pottery, jade, material and papercuts

C **CROCKER NATIONAL BANK,** 1 Montgomery St, San Francisco, CA. (Mailing Add: 111 Sutter St, Suite 1300, San Francisco, CA 94104) Tel 415-983-0389. *Art Coordr* Felicia Cansino
Open 9 AM - 4 PM. No admis fee. Crocker Collection is centered around prominent California artists as well as work that depicts the history of California. Collection displayed in various administrative offices and branches in California
Collections: Variety of pieces from priceless Bierstadt Oils, Oriental Screens, vintage photographs of California and outstanding contemporary graphics by Willard Dixon, Joseph Raffael, Wayne Thiebaud, and others
Activities: Originate traveling exhibitions featuring the art of California 1870-1970

C **EMBARCADERO CENTER MANAGEMENT,** Three Embarcadero Center, Suite 2360, 94111. Tel 415-772-0585, 772-0500. *Executive Dir* Jim Bronkema
Open to public at all hours. No admis fee. Estab 1971, modern art has been a key element in the planning and development of the Embarcadero Center complex; evidence of a desire to provide beauty on a smaller scale amid the harmony of its massive structures; to enhance the total environment, and provide a variety of dramatic views for pedestrians as they circulate through the complex. Collection displayed throughout the Center complex; Center supports San Francisco DeYoung Museum, Fine Arts Museum Downtown Center, American Conservatory Theatre, San Francisco Symphony, San Francisco Center for the Performing Arts, and others
Collections: Citrus Wall by Olga de Amaral; Willi Gutmann's Two Columns With Wedge (stainless steel sculpture that rises eight stories); two macrame-weave pieces by Francoise Grossen; Space Continuum II (handwoven red-and-blue tapestry) by Lia Cook; paintings, sculptures and four vast tapestries three stories high and up to 14 ft wide

O **EXPLORATORIUM,** 3601 Lyon St, 94123. Tel 415-285-8953. *Dir* Frank Oppenheimer; *Admin Asst* Rob Semper; *Executive Asst* Virginia Rubin; *Admin Asst Exhibit Design* Bob Miller; *Biology Lab* Charles Carlsen; *Artist Coordr* Peter Richards
Open Wed - Sat 1 - 5 PM. No admis fee. Estab 1969 to provide exhibits and art works centering around the theme of perception, which are designed to be manipulated and appreciated at a variety of levels by both children and adults. Average Annual Attendance: 500,000
Income: Financed by endowment, membership, city and state appropriation, private foundations and corporation contributions
Publications: The Exploratorium Magazine, monthly
Activities: Docent training; classes for children; lect open to the public; concerts; tours; scholarships and fellowships; lending collection contains science exhibits; book traveling exhibitions, 1-2 per year; museum shop selling books, slides and science related material

M **FINE ARTS MUSEUMS OF SAN FRANCISCO,** M H de Young Memorial Museum and California Palace of the Legion of Honor, Lincoln Park, 94121. Tel 415-558-2881. *Pres* Walter S Newman; *Secy* Delores Malone; *Dir* Ian M White; *Deputy Dir for Admin* Stephen Dykes; *Deputy Dir Education & Exhib* T K Seligman; *Deputy Dir Operations* Gus Teller; *Cur Painting* Thomas P Lee; *Cur Sculpture & Decorative Arts* Michael Conforti; *Cur Prints & Drawings* Robert F Johnson; *Development Officer* Helen Moss; *Cur in Charge Exhib* Susan Levitin; *Asst Cur Exhib* Susan Melim; *Asst Cur Prints & Drawings* Aimee Troyen; *Cur in Charge of Art School* Elsa Cameron; *Asst to Dir* Bruce Merley; *Cur in Charge Department Textiles* Anna Bennet; *Registrar de Young Museum* DeRenne Coerr; *Registrar Legion of Honor* Paula March; *Public Relations Officer* Gail Docktor; *Public Information Officer* Charles Long; *Conservator Paper* Robert Futernick; *Conservator Painting* Teri Oikawa-Picante; *Conservator Furniture* Gene Munsch
Open daily 10 AM - 5 PM. Admis adults $1, youth 75¢. Estab 1895 to provide museums of historic art from ancient Egypt to the 20th century. Two separate buildings are maintained, one in the Golden Gate Park (de Young museum) with 65 galleries, and the other in Lincoln Park (California Palace of the Legion of Honor) with 22 galleries. Average Annual Attendance: 750,000. Mem: 35,000; dues guarantor $1000, sponsor $500, donor $250, supporting $100, sustaining $50, contributing $30, active $20, senior & junior $10
Income: $3,000,000 (financed by endowment, membership, city appropriations)
Collections: American painting and decorative arts; ancient Egypt, Greece and Rome; Europe from the middle ages; graphic arts of all schools and eras; primitive arts of Africa, Oceania and the Americas
Exhibitions: The Hermitage of Leningrad; The Splendor of Dresden: Five Centuries of Art Collecting from the German Democratic Republic; Treasures of Early Irish Art; Treasure of Tutankhamun
Publications: Exhibition and collection catalogues; members' monthly calendar and quarterly
Activities: Classes for adults and children; dramatic programs; docent training; lect open to the public; concerts; gallery talks; tours; extension department serves downtown San Francisco; artmobile; individual paintings and original art objects are lent to other museums; book traveling exhibitions; originate traveling exhibitions to other museums; museum shop sells books, magazines, reproductions, prints, and slides

L **Library,** Golden Gate Park, 94118. Tel 415-558-2887. *Librn* Jane Nelson
Estab 1955 to serve museum staff in research on collections, conservation, acquisition, interpretations. Graphic arts are housed in the Achenbach Foundation Library in the California Palace of the Legion of Honor
Income: Financed by membership and city appropriation
Library Holdings: Vols 25,000; Per subs 50; AV—Slides
Special Subjects: American Indian Art, African, American, French and Oceanic art
Collections: Achenbach Foundation for Graphic Arts (prints and drawings)

O **The Museum Society,** c/o de Young Museum, Golden Gate Park, 94118. Tel 415-752-2800. *Chmn* John L Jones; *Vice Chmn* Cathy Bellis; *Vice Chmn* Florence Wong; *Secy* Patsy Jo Hilliard; *Treas* William A Stimson II; *General Mgr* Nativity D'Souza; *Executive Secy* Alice S Fischer; *Membership Coordr* Ann Knauber; *Mgr de Young Bookshop* Leroy Detro; *Mgr Legion Bookshop* Lewis Thomas
Open 10 - 5. Admis adults $1, juniors 12 - 17 years 50¢ senior citizens and children free. Estab 1971 as a membership organization for Fine Arts Museums of San Francisco and the Asian Art Museum of San Francisco. Mem: 45,000; dues $10 to $1000; annual meeting in May
Income: $2,450,000 (financed by membership and bookshop revenues)
Publications: Museum Calendar, monthly; magazine, quarterly
Activities: museum shop sells books, reproductions, prints and slides

M **GALERIA DE LA RAZA,** Studio 24, 2851 & 2857 24th St, 94110. Tel 415-826-8009. *Co-Dir* Ralph Maradiaga; *Co-Dir* Rene Yanez; *Cur & Education Coordinator* Carmen Lomas Garza; *Cur & Education Coordinator* Maria V Pinedo
Open Wed - Sun 1 - 5 PM, Galeria; Mon - Fri noon - 6 PM, Studio 24. Estab 1969 as a community gallery and museum to exhibit works by Chicano-Latino artists, contemporary as well as cultural folk art. Average Annual Attendance: 35,000
Income: Financed by NEA, California Arts Council and private foundations
Exhibitions: Changing monthly with one traveling per year
Publications: Exhibition catalogs, small publications, yearly calendar, children's coloring book and postcards
Activities: Art classes for adults and children; galeria tours, some lectures; small outlet for books, posters, T-shirts and other culture materials

L **Chicano-Latino Arts Resource Library,** 2857 24th St, 94110. *Dir* Maria V Pinedo
Open Mon - Fri Noon - 6 PM. Estab 1978 as a reference and archive of Chicano and Latino arts
Income: $1000
Purchases: $500
Library Holdings: Vols 100; Per subs 5; AV—Slides; Other—Clipping files, exhibition catalogs, prints, memorabilia, original art works, pamphlets, photographs, reproductions
Special Subjects: El Dia de Los Muertas artifacts and resources
Collections: Chicano and Latino murals; Chicano Latino Youth; car clubs

O **LA MAMELLE INC,** 70 12th St, Box 3123 Rincon, 94119. Tel 415-431-7524. *Pres* Carl E Loeffler
Estab 1975 to support network for contemporary art. gallery houses new contemporary art
Income: Financed by endowment, membership and state appropriation
Exhibitions: Davi-Det-Hompson; Ecart; Photography and Language; Recorded Works; Rubber Stamp Art; Endre Tot; West Coast Conceptual Photographers; Women in the Printing Arts; All Xerox
Publications: Art Contemporary, quarterly; La Mamelle Magazine; Performance Anthology: Source book for a decade of California performance art; Videozine; Audiozine
Activities: Lect open to public; concerts; gallery talks; original objects of art lent; lending collection contains video tapes; traveling exhibitions organized and circulated; sales shop sells books, magazines, original art

L **Contemporary Art Archives,** 70 12th St, Box 3123 Rincon, 94119.
For reference only

M **MEXICAN MUSEUM,** 1855 Folsom St, 94103. Tel 415-621-1224. *Pres* Jesse Aguirre; *Secy* Karen Sullivan; *Founder & Dir* Peter Rodriquez; *Adminr* Alison S Wilbur; *Education Dir* Nora Wagner; *Education Coordr* Bea Carrillo Hocker; *Hispanic Community Coordr* Carmen Carrillo; *Registrar* Gloria Jaramillo
Open Tues - Sun Noon - 5 PM. No admis fee. Estab 1975 to foster the exhibition, conservation and dissemination of Mexican and Mexican American art and culture for all people. Museum has two large gallery spaces plus five large display cases in lobby. Average Annual Attendance: 30,000. Mem: 600
Income: Financed by membership, city and state appropriation, federal grants and corporate support
Collections: Colonial and Mexican Fine Art; Folk Art; early 20th Century collection of ceramics and textiles
Exhibitions: (1979) Las Amigas del Museo of Pre-Hispanic Ceramic; El Dia de Los Muertos Exhibit (day of the Dead Exhibit); Gordo's World by Gus Arriola; Los Regalos III; Paintings by Alex Maldonado; (1980) Edmundo Aquino; Christmas in Mexico; Christmas Nativity Scene; Xavier Viramontes
Publications: Newsletter, quarterly
Activities: Outreach Art Program for schools; workshops; lect open to public, 8 visiting lectr per year; tours; exten dept serves San Francisco Bay area; lending collection contains slides and educational kits

M **NATIONAL MARITIME MUSEUM,** (Formerly San Francisco Maritime Museum Association) Foot of Polk St, 94109. Tel 415-556-8177. *Chief Cur* Karl Kortum; *Cur* Harlan Soeten; *Photograph Librarian* John Maounis
Open daily 10 AM - 5 PM. No admis fee. Estab 1951; museum built in 1939; a terazzo and stainless steel structure with a nautical theme
Collections: Over 100,000 photographs and negatives of ships and other memorabilia; ship models; paintings; recordings; sailing ship and paddlewheeler
Publications: Newsletter; booklets

L **Library,** Foot of Polk St, 94109. *Librn* David Hull
Open to the public for research on premises
Library Holdings: Vols 12,000

M **JOSEPHINE D RANDALL JUNIOR MUSEUM,** 199 Museum Way, 94114. Tel 415-863-1399. *Dir* Dr A Kirk Conragan; *Cur Arts & Crafts* Dennis Treanor
Open Tues - Sat 10 AM - 5 PM, Sun 11 AM - 5 PM, cl Mon, New Year's Day and Christmas. No admis fee. Estab 1945 as part of the San Francisco Recreation and Park Dept. Average Annual Attendance: 120,000
Collections: Children's Art Indian Artifacts
Activities: Classes in ceramics, weaving, leaded glass, painting, art history, jewelry, stitchery; tours; lect; films; individual paintings and original objects of art lent to other museums; traveling exhibitions organized and circulated

L **Library,** 199 Museum Way, 94114.
Open for reference
Library Holdings: Vols 8500; Other—Map files

L **SAN FRANCISCO ACADEMY OF COMIC ART LIBRARY,** 2850 Ulloa St, 94116. Tel 415-681-1737. *Dir* Bill Blackbeard; *Dir* Barbara Tyger
Open daily by appointment 10 AM - 10 PM. Estab 1967 to locate, preserve and house all elements of American popular narrative culture in danger of destruction through oversight or misunderstanding. Gallery maintained
Income: Financed by grants, donations, fees from personnel writing and lect, research charges, etc
Library Holdings: Vols 25,000; AV—Cassettes, motion pictures, rec, slides, v-tapes; Other—Clipping files, exhibition catalogs, framed reproductions, prints, manuscripts, memorabilia, original art works, pamphlets, photographs, reproductions
Collections: Adventure fiction; the American comic strip; the American newspaper; the American popular fiction magazine; children's books since 1850; detective fiction; motion pictures; the popular illustrated periodical; radical and underground publications; science fiction; Victorian illustrated book; western fiction
Exhibitions: Permanent collection: Original art in the comic strip and popular fiction; comic strip exhibit; national science fiction
Activities: Lect, 10 visiting lectr per year; gallery talks; tours; originate traveling exhibitions

M **SAN FRANCISCO ART INSTITUTE,** 800 Chestnut St, 94133. Tel 415-771-7020. *Public Information Mgr* Linda Dachman
Open daily, 10 - 4 PM. No admis fee. Estab 1871, inc 1889 to foster the appreciation and creation of the fine arts and maintain a school and museum for that purpose. Atholl McBean Gallery and Emanuel Walter Gallery for exhibitions of contemporary art; Diego Rivera Gallery for exhibitions of work by SFAI students; SFAI Photo Gallery for exhibition of photographs by participating photographers invited by SFAI Photo Dept. Average Annual Attendance: 60,000. Mem: 1300; dues $15 - $100 and up; annual meeting June
Activities: Traveling exhibitions organized and circulated

L **Anne Bremer Memorial Library,** 800 Chestnut St, 94133. *Media Dir* C Stephanian; *Catalog Librn* S Chickanzeff; *Reference Librn* M Cleaver
Open Mon - Thurs 9 AM - 8 PM, Fri 9 AM - 5 PM during school sessions. Estab 1871 to develop a collection and services which will anticipate, reflect and support the objectives and direction of the San Francisco Art Institute and the contemporary arts community. Circ 12,795
Library Holdings: Vols 22,500; Per subs 250; Micro—Fiche; AV—Cassettes, fs, Kodachromes, motion pictures, slides 6500; Other—Clipping files, exhibition catalogs, manuscripts, memorabilia, pamphlets, photographs, reproductions 2000
Collections: Archives documenting the history of the Art Institute; artists' books; audio-tapes of artists working in sound (experimental music, etc)
Activities: Library holds tropical spring brunch; Artists' book parties; lect

O **SAN FRANCISCO CITY AND COUNTY ART COMMISSION,** 165 Grove St, 94102. Tel 415-558-3465. *Pres Commission* Ray Taliaferro; *Dir Cultural Affairs* Martin Snipper; *Asst Dir* Joan Ellison; *Dir Neighborhood Art Program* Mark Denton; *Coordr Street Artist Program* Howard Lazar; *Visual Arts Dir* Elio Benvenuto; *Cur Capricorn Asunder Gallery* Ansel Wettersten
Open daily 10 AM - 4:30 PM. No admis fee. Estab 1932. Mem: Consists of 9 professional and 3 lay-members appointed by the Mayor with advice of art societies, and 5 ex-officio members; monthly meetings.
Passes on all buildings and works of art placed on property of City or County; supervises and controls all appropriations made by the Board of Supervisors of music and the advancement of art and music; may volunteer advice to private owners who submit plans for suggestions; maintains a Civic Chorale and Neighborhood Arts Program; administers ordinance providing two percent of cost of public construction for art; also, a municipal collection for art for embellishing public offices purchases for enlarging collection are made from the Annual Art Festival; maintains art gallery and presents various concerts; licenses street artists; responsible for cataloging and maintaining all public works of art
Purchases: $5000

M **SAN FRANCISCO MUSEUM OF MODERN ART,** Van Ness at McAllister, 94102. Tel 415-863-8800. *Dir* Henry T Hopkins; *Deputy Dir* Michael McCone; *Chief Cur* Suzanne Foley; *Controller* S C St John
Open Tues - Fri 10 AM - 10 PM, Sat & Sun 10 AM - 5 PM, cl Mon. No admis fee for permanent collections, $1.50 for temporary exhibitions. Estab 1935 to collect and exhibit art of the 20th century. Museum occupies two floors; four major galleries 35 x 180 ft; six corridor galleries; six smaller galleries. Average Annual Attendance: 300,000. Mem: 8000; dues $25
Income: $1,200,000 (financed by endowment, membership, city appropriation, earnings and grants)
Purchases: $60,000
Collections: Clyfford Still; †California clay; †painting, †photography, †sculpture
Exhibitions: Clyfford Still; Fauvism and its Affinities; The Modern Era: A View of California Architecture 1960-1976; Painting and Sculpture in California; People's Murals; Photographs by John Gutmann; Picasso-Braque-Leger; The Wild Beasts
Publications: Calendar, monthly
Activities: Classes for adults and children; docent training; lect open to public, 6-8 visiting lectrs per year; concerts; gallery talks; tours; traveling exhibitions organized and circulated; museum shop selling books, magazines, reproductions and slides

L **Louise Sloss Ackerman Fine Arts Library,*** Van Ness at McAllister, 94102. *Librn* Eugenie Candau
Open to the public for reference
Library Holdings: Vols 6000; Per subs 100; Other—Exhibition catalogs, artists files;

museum archives

Special Subjects: Modern and contemporary art including photography and architecture
Collections: Margery Mann Collection of books in the history of photography

L **SAN FRANCISCO PUBLIC LIBRARY,** Art and Music Department,* Civic Center, 94102. Tel 415-558-3687. *Dir* John C Frantz; *Art & Music* Mary Ashe
Open Mon - Thurs 9 AM - 9 PM, Fri & Sat 9 AM - 6 PM. Estab 1878
Income: Financed by city and state appropriations
Library Holdings: AV—Rec; Other—Framed reproductions, prints

L **SAN FRANCISCO STATE UNIVERSITY,** Paul J Leonard Library, 1600 Holloway, 94132. *Acting Dir* Dr Eric Solomon; *Assoc Dir* Dr Mary MacWilliam
Open Mon - Thur 8 AM - 9:50 PM, Fri 8 AM - 4:50 PM, Sat 8:30 AM - 4:50 PM, Sun 1 - 4 PM. Estab 1890. Circ 742,753
Income: $2,450,241
Purchases: $645,472
Library Holdings: Vols 558,732; Per subs 3123; Micro—Cards, fiche, reels, prints; AV—A-tapes, cassettes, fs, motion pictures, rec, v-tapes; Other—Clipping files, exhibition catalogs, framed reproductions, manuscripts, memorabilia, original art works
Collections: John Magnam Collection of Arts and Crafts; Frank Oebeuis Collection on Italian Culture

WESTERN ASSOCIATION OF ART MUSEUMS
For further information, see National and Regional Organizations

M **WINE MUSEUM OF SAN FRANCISCO,** 633 Beach St, 94109. Tel 415-673-6990. *Dir* Ernest G Mittelberger; *Asst to Dir* Mary M Rodgers; *Dir of Visitor Services* Kip Lee-Bevier; *Preparator* Karl L Folsom
Open Tues - Sat 11 AM - 5 PM, Sun Noon - 5 PM, cl Mon. No admis fee. Estab 1974 for the purpose of learning about the rituals and history of wine and its enjoyment, and as a demonstration of the quality and diversity of artistic expressions created by man as a record of his appreciation of wine from the earliest times to the present. One large room is divided into following sections: Grape, Vineyard and Harvest; Winemaking and the Vintner; Ancient Drinking Vessels; Wine in Mythology; In Celebration of Wine and Life; and a changing exhibition area. Average Annual Attendance: 100,000
Income: Financed by private sponsor
Collections: †Christian Brothers Collection of original graphics and decorative arts; Franz W Sichel Collection of glass drinking vessels spanning 2000 years
Exhibitions: (1978) 2000 Years: Evolution of the Wine Bottle; (1979) Roots of Heaven: Wine and Religion from the Ancient World to the present
Publications: The Wine Museum of San Francisco, brochure
Activities: Docent training; lect open to the public, 5 vis lectr per yr; gallery talks; tours; individual objects of art and individual prints lent to other museums who have proper security and insurance systems; originates traveling exhibitions; museum shop sells books, reproductions

L **Alfred Fromm Rare Wine Books Library,** 633 Beach St, 94109. *Librn* Mary M Rodgers
Open to writers, researchers, and scholars for reference only
Library Holdings: Vols 1000

SAN JOSE

M **ROSICRUCIAN EGYPTIAN MUSEUM AND ART GALLERY,** Park and Naglee, 95191. Tel 408-287-9171, Ext 229. *Dir* Ralph M Lewis; *Cur* Curt Schild
Open Tues - Fri 9 AM - 4:45 PM. No admis fee. Estab 1929, in present location 1966, to publicly show a collection of the works of the ancient Egyptians, reflecting their lives and culture. A Gallery contains the Babylonian and Assyrian collection of funeral works; B Gallery contains tomb replicas and mummies; C Gallery, Tel-El-Armana room with amulets, cosmetics and writing implements; D Gallery has jewelry, pottery, and King Zoser's tomb complex. Average Annual Attendance: 500,000
Income: Financed by Rosicrucian Order
Collections: Egyptian antiquities; French Room with Louis XIV - Louis XVI furniture
Exhibitions: Monthly exhibitions, mainly one-man
Activities: Sales shop sells books, reproductions, prints, slides, jewelry, records and posters

M **SAN JOSE MUSEUM OF ART,** 110 S Market St, 95113. Tel 408-294-2787. *Dir* Albert G Dixon Jr; *Cur* Martha L Manson; *Office Mgr* Judith Bolin; *Development Officer* Charlotte Wendel; *Admn Asst* Donna Carneghi
Open Tues - Sat 10 AM - 4:30 PM; Sun Noon - 4 PM. No admis fee. Estab 1968 to provide the citizens of San Jose and the South Bay region with a changing exhibition schedule featuring local, regional, national and international exhibitions. the museum is housed in an 1892 sandstone structure in the Romanesque style; it was a federal post office building in San Jose, and was renovated for museum use in 1975-76. Average Annual Attendance: 90,000. Mem: dues $8 - $1000; annual meeting June
Income: Financed by memebership, city appropriation
Collections: Principally California paintings, sculptures, prints and drawings
Exhibitions: Approx 55 - 60 exhibitions per yr
Publications: Newsletter monthly; exhibition catalogs
Activities: Docent training; lect open to the public; concerts; traveling exhibitions organized and circulated; museum shop sells books, original art, reproductions

L **Library,** 110 S Market St, 95113.
Open to the museum staff and volunteers for reference only
Library Holdings: Vols 200

SAN JOSE STATE UNIVERSITY

M **Art Gallery,** Ninth and San Carlos, 95192. Tel 408-277-2716. *Dir* Michael Crane
Open Mon - Fri 11 AM - 4 PM during term. No admis fee. Estab 1960 as part of the university Art Dept. Gallery is 34 x 28 ft with 12 ft ceiling. Average Annual Attendance: 9000
Income: Financed by city and state appropriations

Collections: †Contemporary and historical graphics; †work by faculty, students and alumni
Publications: Exhibition catalogs
Activities: Lect open to public; paintings and original art objects lent to university offices; lending collection contains original prints, paintings (including Klee and Chagall), sculpture; originate traveling exhibitions; catalogs sometimes sold

M **Union Gallery,** S Ninth St, Student Union, 95192. Tel 408-277-3221. *Dir & Cur* Stephen Moore; *Asst Dir* Dorothy Torres; *Registrar* Bonnie Cook; *Exhib Coordr* Gratia Rankin
Open Mon - Fri 10:30 - 4 PM, Wed & Thurs 6 - 8 PM. No admis fee. Estab 1968 to supplement the available art at San Jose State and to broaden the student's appreciation of art. The Gallery consists of two main spaces: Main Gallery, with an additional entrance Gallery for smaller exhibitions. Average Annual Attendance: 30,000
Income: Financed by state appropriation and through the University
Exhibitions: Drawings: Bruce Fier; Darryl Sapien: Configuration; Juried Student Art Exhibition
Publications: Exhibition catalogs
Activities: Lect open to public, 9 visiting lectr per year; gallery talks; competitions; paintings and original art objects lent to other galleries or museums; lending collection contains cassettes, original prints and art works, records, photographs, sculpture, slides; originate traveling exhibitions; sales shop

L **Art Department Library,** Art Building, Room 135, 95192. *Art Reference Librn* Edith Crowe
Purchases: $26,000
Library Holdings: Vols 31,000; Per subs 134; Micro—Prints; AV—Lantern Slides, motion pictures, rec, slides; Other—Exhibition catalogs, prints, original art works, photographs, reproductions, sculpture

SAN LUIS OBISPO

L **CUESTA COLLEGE LIBRARY, ART DEPARTMENT,** PO Box J, 93406. *Dir* Mary Lou Wilhelm
Open Mon - Thur 7:30 AM - 9 PM, Fri 7:30 AM - 4:30 PM, vacation hours vary. Estab 1965 to support the educational program of the college
Income: $305,970
Purchases: $26,610
Library Holdings: Vols 1304; Per subs 12; Micro—Fiche, reels; AV—A-tapes, cassettes, fs, slides, v-tapes; Other—Pamphlets
Activities: Flea market; originate traveling exhibits

SAN LUIS REY

M **MISSION SAN LUIS REY MUSEUM,** 4050 Mission Ave, 92068. Tel 714-757-3651. *Local Minister* Bro Christian Ofm; *Mgr* Bro Marion Ofm; *Asst Mgr* Sr Edith Eddy
Open 9 AM - 4:30 PM. Admis adults $1, 12 - 18 50¢, 6 - 12 25¢. Estab 1798 to protect, conserve and show Mission history and artifacts
Income: Financed by property of Franciscan Friars inc, of California
Collections: Artifacts, furniture, paints, statuary, religious vestments and vessels and other historical objects from early mission days in California

SAN MARCOS

M **PALOMAR COMMUNITY COLLEGE,** Boehm Gallery, 1140 W Mission Rd, 92069. *Gallery Dir* Russell W Baldwin; *Gallery Asst* Laurie A Brindle; *Gallery Secy* Dori Marzkiw
Open Mon - Thurs 8:00 AM - 8:30 PM, Fri 8 AM - 4 PM, Sat 10 AM - 2 PM, cl Sun & holidays. No admis fee. Estab 1964 to provide the community with fine art regardless of style, period or approach. The gallery is 35 x 35 ft, no windows, 18 in brick exterior, acoustic ceiling and asphalt tile floor. Average Annual Attendance: 50,000
Income: $8000 (exhibition budget). Financed by city and state appropriations
Collections: †Contemporary art by nationally acclaimed artists
Exhibitions: Annual Student Art Show; Tony deLap: Selection of Work 1962 - 1976; Richard Allen Morris: Painting Retrospective; Christine Oatman: Fantasy Landscapes; Sam Richardson: Ten Year Retrospective of Sculpture and Drawing; Italo Sconga: Recent Sculpture; Masami Teraoka: Recent Paintings and Prints; Wayne Theibaud: Recent Paintings and Drawings; William Wiley: Recent Sculpture and Drawings
Activities: Lect open to public, 12 vis lectr per year; competitions; individual paintings and original objects of art lent to reputable museums and galleries; lending collection contains original paintings, prints and sculpture

L **Fine Arts Library,** 1140 W Mission Rd, 92069. Tel 714-744-1150. *Reference Librn* Judy Jerstad Carter; *Library Technical Asst* Doris C Duel
Open Mon - Thurs 8 AM - 8:30 PM, Fri 8 AM - 4 PM, Sat 10 AM - 2 PM. Estab 1967 to support the curriculum offered by the departments of Art and Music; to provide community access to crafts and fine arts materials. Circ 16,000
Library Holdings: Vols 11,000; Per subs 100; AV—Rec; Other—Clipping files, exhibition catalogs, pamphlets
Collections: Sheet music from the 1890's - 1950's

SAN MARINO

M **HUNTINGTON LIBRARY, ART GALLERY AND BOTANICAL GARDENS,** 1151 Oxford Rd, 91108. Tel 213-792-6141. *Dir* James Thorpe; *Cur Art Coll* Robert R Wark
Open Tues - Sat 1 - 4:30 PM, Sun Noon - 4:30 PM. No admis, call (213) 449-3901 for information regarding free Sun tickets. Estab 1919 by the late Henry E Huntington as a free research library, art gallery, museum and botanical garden; exhibitions open to the public in 1928 for educational and cultural purposes. Average Annual Attendance: 600,000. Mem: 2000, supporters of the institution who give $25 or more annually are known as the Friends of the Huntington Library
Income: Financed by endowment and gifts

Collections: British and European art of the 18th and early 19th centuries with a strong supporting collection of French furniture, decorative objects and sculpture of the same periods
Exhibitions: Rotating exhibitions from the permanent collection
Publications: The Calendar, every other month
Activities: Lect open to public; gallery talks; tours; dramatic programs; fels offered; sales shop sells books, postcards, prints, reproductions and slides
L **Library,** 1151 Oxford Road, 91108. Tel 213-792-6141.
Open to qualified scholars for reference
Special Subjects: British art of the 18th and early 19th centuries
Collections: British drawings and watercolors; probably the largest collection of books, photographs and other materials for the study of British Art that exist outside London

SAN MATEO

L **COLLEGE OF SAN MATEO LIBRARY,*** 1700 W Hillsdale Blvd, 94402. Tel 415-574-6100. *Chief Librn* Gladys Chaw
Open Mon - Fri 7:30 AM - 10 PM, Sun 1 - 5 PM, cl Sat. Estab 1922. An art gallery maintained with monthly exhibits
Income: Financed by state appropriation
Library Holdings: Vols 110,000; Per subs 800; Micro—Fiche, reels; AV—A-tapes, cassettes, fs, Kodachromes, lantern slides, motion pictures, rec, slides, v-tapes; Other—Pamphlets, photographs, reproductions, original documents
Special Subjects: Crafts, European and Oriental art
Exhibitions: Community College Student Show; Faculty Art Show; Mexican folklore; student prints from Ljubljana, Yugoslavia; young European artists

SAN MIGUEL

M **MISSION SAN MIGUEL,** Mission St, 93451. Tel 805-467-3256. *Superior Reverend* Reginald McDonough; *Pastor Reverend* Hilary Hobrecht
Open daily 10 AM - 5 PM, cl New Year's, Easter, Thanksgiving and Christmas. Admis by donation. Estab 1797 as The Old Mission church, the original still in use as the parish church, and the entire Mission has been restored. The Mission contains paintings dating back to the 18th century, also original, untouched frescoes.
Average Annual Attendance: 50,000
Income: Financed by Franciscan Friars
Activities: Concerts; Shop sells books, reproductions, prints, slides and gifts

SANTA ANA

M **BOWER'S MUSEUM,** 2002 N Main St, 92706. Tel 714-972-1900. *Dir* Reilly P Rhodes; *Registrar* Margaret A Key; *Admin Aide* Albert Stein; *Cur Natural History* Peter Barlett; *Cur of Education* Joan Primm; *Exhibit Specialist* Paul John
Open Tues - Sat 9 AM - 5 PM, Sun 1 - 5 PM, cl Mon. No admis fee. Estab 1934 to provide an active general museum for the community. The Charles W Bower Museum is housed in an authenic California mission-style structure amid expansive fountain-studded grounds, originally devoted to the display of antique furniture, Indian relics and historical items of early California families. A new wing has been added with an exhibition program of contemporary art. Average Annual Attendance: 141,996. Mem: 1231; dues from student $5 - life $1000
Income: Financed by city appropriation supplemented by Foundation Board
Collections: Asian, African and contemporary American Art; early California history; Indian artifacts; Late 19th Century Oriental Costumes; 19th & Early 20th Century North and South American Costumes; 19th & 20th Century American Indian Baskets; 19th Century American Textiles, Decorative Arts and Patterned Glass; Pre-Columbia Ceramics
Exhibitions: (1979) Basketry Around the World; Paintings from the J Paul Getty Museum Collection; Ruth and George C Kennedy Collection of Ethnic Arts; Reuben Nakian, Terra Cotta Drawings and Bronze Sculptures; Southeast Asian Stone Sculptures; (1980) Charles Burchfield: The Charles Rand Penny Collection; The Gray Whale; The Gund Collection of Western Art; Paintings on Vases in Ancient Greece; The Phillips Collection in the Making: 1920 - 1930
Publications: Brochures; Calendar, monthly; exhibition catalogs
Activities: Classes for adults and children; docent guild; lect open to public; films; gallery talks; tours; study clubs; paintings and original art objects lent to other museums and to public; organize and circulate traveling exhibitions

SANTA BARBARA

M **SANTA BARBARA MUSEUM OF ART,** 1130 State St, 93101. Tel 805-963-4364. *Dir* Paul C Mills; *Deputy Dir* Carl Vance; *Asst Dir Activities* Shelley Ruston; *Cur Coll* Katherine H Mead; *Cur Exhib* William Spurlock; *Cur Education* Penny Knowles; *Registrar* Elaine Dietsch
Open Tues - Sat 11 AM - 5 PM, Sun Noon - 5 PM, cl Mon. No admis fee. Estab 1941 as an art museum. Average Annual Attendance: 200,000. Mem: 3000; dues $15 and up; annual meeting Jan
Income: $850,000 (financed by endowment, membership, state and federal grants)
Collections: Henry Eichheim Collection of Oriental Musical Instruments; Alice F Schott Doll Collection; American and European paintings, sculpture, drawings, prints; Greek and Roman art; Oriental ceramics, paintings and sculpture
Exhibitions: Change throughout the year
Publications: Calendar and exhibition and collection catalogs monthly
Activities: Classes for adults and children; docent training; lect open to the public, 12 visiting lectr per year; concerts; gallery talks; tours; films; paintings and original art objects lent to museums and University galleries; originate traveling exhibitions
L **Library,** 1130 State St, 93101. *Librn* John Crozier
Open to public on an appointment basis. For reference only
Library Holdings: Vols 2000; Per subs 35; Other—Exhibition catalogs, pamphlets

L **SANTA BARBARA PUBLIC LIBRARY,** Faulkner Memorial Art Wing, 40 E Anapamu St, Box 1019, 93102. *Dir* Robert A Hart; *Reference Librn* Myra J Nicholas

Open Mon - Thurs 10 AM - 9 PM, Fri & Sat 10 AM - 5:30 PM, Sun 1 - 5 PM. Estab 1930 and administered by the library trustees as a municipal art reading room and gallery
Exhibitions: Local contemporary paintings and sculpture
Activities: Lectures, programs and meetings

UNIVERSITY OF CALIFORNIA, SANTA BARBARA
M **Art Museum,*** Arts Bldg, 1626-B, 93106. Tel 805-961-3013, 961-2951. *Dir* David Gebhard; *Cur* Phyllis Plous; *Designer of Exhib* Steven Slaney; *Admin Asst-Registrar* Pamela Koe
Open Tues - Sat 10 AM - 4 PM, Sun & holidays 1 - 5 PM, cl Mon, New Year's, Thanksgiving, Christmas and between exhibits. No admis fee. Estab 1961 and directed at both the needs of university students of art and the community, trying for a wide range of exhibitions both contemporary and historical. Located on the UCSB campus and within the Museum complex; three galleries for changing exhibits; three which exhibit part of the permanent collection. Average Annual Attendance: 30,000
Income: Financed by university funds
Collections: Collection of Architectural Drawings by Southern California Architects, including Irving Gill, R M Schindler, George Washington Smith and Kem Weber; Morgenroth Collection of Renaissance Medals; Sedgwick Collection of 16th - 18th Century Italian, Flemish and Dutch Artists; Ala Story Print Collection
Exhibitions: Each exhibition year includes an annual undergraduate and graduate exhibition and exhibits by MFA candidates, all from the Art Department, UCSB. (1977-78) Contemporary Drawing-New York; Contemporary Tableaux-Constructions; Contemporary-Traditional Chicano and Latino Art; Palladip; Prelude to the Fifth Sun
Publications: Exhibition catalogs, 3 - 6 per year
Activities: Lect upon request; lending collection contains 3000 original art works, 800 original prints, 300 paintings, sculpture, 100,000 architectural drawings; originate traveling exhibitions; sales shop sells exhibition catalogs
L **Arts Library,** University of California, Santa Barbara, 93106. Tel 805-961-2850. *Head Arts Library* William R Treese
Open Mon - Thurs 9 AM - 11 PM, Fri & Sat 9 AM - 6 PM, Sun 2 - 11 PM. Estab 1969 to support academic programs. Circ 57,000
Income: Financed by city appropriation
Purchases: $140,000
Library Holdings: Vols 52,500; Per subs 250; Micro—Fiche, reels; AV—V-tapes; Other—Exhibition catalogs, pamphlets, photographs
Special Subjects: Architecture, Oriental Art, Greek, Roman and Etruscan art, Medieval Art, Renaissance and Baroque Art, 18th, 19th and 20th Century Art, primitive and exotic arts
Collections: Auction catalog collection (6000 titles); exhibition catalog collection (31,000 titles)
Publications: Catalogs of the Art Exhibition Catalogs of the Arts Library, University of California, Santa Barbara; Teaneck, New Jersey, Somerset House, 1978
Activities: Tours

SANTA CLARA

M **TRITON MUSEUM OF ART,** 1505 Warburton Ave, 95050. Tel 408-248-4585. *Dir* Jo Farb Hernandez; *Asst Dir* Marc D'Estout; *Pres* Austen Warburton; *VPres* Shu-Park Chan; *Treas* L Katherine Wasserman; *Secy* Shirley Reich
Open Tues - Fri noon - 4 PM, Sat - Sun noon - 5 PM. No admis fee. Estab 1956 to offer a rich and varied cultural experience to members of the community through the display of works of art by American artists, particularly Artists of California, and through related special events and programs. The museum consists of four buildings constructed in an architectural style that blends Oriental and Spanish elements; each pavilion is designed somewhat differently so as to lend variety to the gallery space. Average Annual Attendance: 15,000. Mem: 500; dues $5 - $1000
Income: $61,065 (financed by endowment, membership and city appropriation)
Collections: American Ceramics and Glass Collection, the heart of which is the Vivian Woodward Elmer Majolica Collection; American painting and sculpture; Oil paintings by Theodore Wores
Exhibitions: Allan Adams; David Hockney; Freidensreich Hundertwasser; Denny Nechuatal; The Day of the Dead: Tradition and Change in Contemporary Mexico; Irv Tepper and Kristi Hager: Stereo Views; The World of Haitian Painting
Publications: Exhibition catalogs; newsletter, bimonthly
Activities: Classes for children; dramatic prog; docent training docent training; lect open to public, 10 per year; concerts; gallery talks; tours; museum shop sells books, postcards and reproductions
L **Library,** 1505 Warburton Ave, 95050. Tel 408-248-4585. *Librn* Jo Farb Hernandez
Open to members for reference
Library Holdings: Vols 150; Per subs 5

M **UNIVERSITY OF SANTA CLARA,** de Saisset Art Gallery and Museum, 95053. Tel 408-984-4528. *Academic VPres* Paul Locatelli; *Dir* Brigid S Barton; *Gallery Coordr* Georgianna Lagoria; *Preparator* Fred Shepard; *Secy & Budget Officer* Roberta Rambeau
Open Tues - Fri 10 AM - 5 PM, Sat & Sun 1 - 5 PM, cl Mon and all holidays. No admis fee. Estab 1955 as a major cultural resource in Northern California. In recent years the art gallery and museum have dramatically broadened their scope, exhibiting some of the world's leading avant-garde artist while not losing sight of the traditional. The gallery has 20,000 sq ft of floor space in a concrete structure adjacent to the Mission Santa Clara, two stories of galleries with a balcony for small exhibitions, plus offices and a gallery shop along with workrooms. Average Annual Attendance: 250,000. Mem: Dues patron $500, benefactor $250, sponsor $100, sustaining $25, annual $15, senior or student $7.50
Income: $100,000 (financed by endowment, membership)
Purchases: $2000
Collections: Kolb Collection of 17th and 18 century graphics; Arnold Mountfort Collection; D'Berger Collection of French furniture and ivories; African collection; New Deal art repository; paintings, antiques, sculture, graphics, china, silver and ivory collections; 17th and 18th century tapestries; photography
Exhibitions: (1978 - 1980) Donald Blumber: Photographs; Christopher Brown:

Paintings; The Candy Store Gallery; Marc d'Estout: Recent Work; Expressions and Impressions: Five Contemporary Belgians; German Expressionist Woodcuts from the Robert Gore Rifkind Collection; Heads: Ceramic Sculpture by Bruria and Paintings by Raimonds Staprans; Graham Nash Collection of rare and vintage photographs; Paper: Images and Constructions; The Permanent Collection; Sixteenth Century Italian prints; Steve Strong: Photographs; Venice in Winter: photographs by Gerri Della Rocca de Candal

Publications: Calendar, quarterly; exhibition catalogs

Activities: Lect open to public, 15 visiting lectr per year; gallery talks;; paintings lent to campus offices; originate traveling exhibitions; museum shop sells books, original art, prints, jewelry, antiques and artifacts

L **Library,** 95053. *Dir* Brigid S Barton
Open for reference only
Library Holdings: Vols 1500; Per subs 25; AV—A-tapes, cassettes, slides, v-tapes; Other—Exhibition catalogs, framed reproductions, prints, manuscripts, memorabilia, photographs, sculpture
Collections: California mission period manuscripts and books

SANTA CRUZ

O **SANTA CRUZ ART LEAGUE, INC,** 526 Broadway, 95060. Tel 408-426-5787. *Pres* Geneva Heald; *VPres* Gorman Woody; *Secy* Ann Frohn; *Treas* Gisela Embree; *Cur* June Baker
Open daily 1 - 5 PM. No admis fee. Estab 1919, Incorporated 1949, to further interest in art;. Monthly gallery displays of paintings by members. Average Annual Attendance: 11,000. Mem: 225; membership qualifications, Evecutive Board of Art League judge three original artworks; dues Active $15, Associate $10, Lay $7; annual meeting second Wed in May, monthly meetings
Income: Financed by donations
Collections: Permanent display of wax figures of Last Supper from DaVinci painting
Exhibitions: 50th Annual Statewide Juried Show
Publications: Bulletin, monthly
Activities: Classes for adults; classes in painting; demonstration by professional artist at monthly meetings; 12 vis lectrs per year; gallery talks; Scholarships offered

L **SANTA CRUZ PUBLIC LIBRARY,** Art, Music, Film Department,* 224 Church St, 95060. Tel 408-429-3530. *Dir* Charles K Atkins; *Art & Music Librn* Alma Westberg; *Reference* Ruth Collins
Open Mon - Fri 9 AM - 9 PM, Sat 9 AM - 5 PM. Estab 1881 for the cultural enrichment and enjoyment of the citizens. Circ 11,000. Gallery maintained in local and western art of variety of media
Income: $10,000 (financed by city and state appropriations)
Purchases: $10,000
Library Holdings: Vols 11,000; Micro—Reels; AV—A-tapes, cassettes, fs, motion pictures, rec, slides; Other—Clipping files, framed reproductions, prints, pamphlets
Activities: Classes for children; film programs; tours; exten dept serving Santa Cruz County

SANTA MONICA

M **SANTA MONICA COLLEGE ART GALLERY,** 1900 Pico Blvd, 90405. Tel 213-450-5150, Ext 340. *Dir* William M Hill; *Technical Asst* Camille Gonzales
Open Mon - Fri 10 AM - 3 PM, Thurs 7 - 9 PM, cl academic holidays. No admis fee. Estab 1973 to provide a study gallery for direct contact with contemporary and historic works of art. Average Annual Attendance: 25,000
Income: Financed by membership, city and state appropriations
Purchases: $1000
Collections: Southern California prints and drawings
Exhibitions: 8 per year
Activities: Lect open to public; gallery talks; tours; original art objects lent

SANTA ROSA

M **SANTA ROSA JUNIOR COLLEGE ART GALLERY,** 1501 Mendocino Ave, 95401. Tel 707-527-4011. *Chief* Lois Newman
Open Mon - Fri 12 - 4 PM, Sat & Sun 1 - 4 PM. No admis fee. Estab 1973. Gallery is 40 x 42 ft, 12 ft walls, peaked roof with four skylights. Average Annual Attendance: 9000
Publications: Annual Report
Activities: Lect open to public, six visiting lectrs per year; concerts; gallery talks; traveling exhibitions organized and circulated

L **Library,** 1501 Mendocino Ave, 95401.
For reference only
Library Holdings: Vols 100; Per subs 2

SARATOGA

O **VILLA MONTALVO CENTER FOR THE ARTS,** 15400 Montalvo Rd, PO Box 158, 95070. Tel 408-867-3421. *Executive Dir* Patricia Oakes
Open Tues - Sun 1 - 4 PM, cl Mon and holidays. Admis Tues - Fri free, Sat & Sun 25¢. Estab 1953; administered by Montalvo Association, Villa Montalvo is part of a cultural center for the development of art, literature, music and architecture by artists and promising students. There are facilities for artists in residence. The home of the late US Senator and Mayor of San Francisco, James Duval Phelan, was bequeathed as a cultural center, and is conducted as a non-profit enterprise by the Board of Trustees of the Montalvo Association. Average Annual Attendance: 50,000. Mem: 800; dues $15 and up; annual meeting in Nov
Collections: Decorative arts, graphics, manuscripts, paintings, and sculpture
Exhibitions: Monthly exhibitions of ceramics, drawings, crafts, jewelry, paintings, photography; graphic arts by California and other artists; student and faculty exhibitions
Publications: Calendar, monthly; James D Phelan, pamphlet
Activities: Classes for adults and children; dramatic programs; lect open to public; films; gallery talks; concerts; organize and circulate traveling exhibitions

SIERRA MADRE

O **DWELLING SCULPTURE INSTITUTE,** 431 Crestvale Dr, 91024. *Dir* Daniel Nign III
Estab 1978 to provide information and promote the concept of Dwelling Sculpture; a blend of architecture and free-form sculpture. Mem: 22
Income: Financed by private funds
Activities: Educ dept

STANFORD

M **STANFORD UNIVERSITY,** T W Stanford Art Gallery & Museum of Art, Museum Way & Lomita Dr, 94305. Tel 415-497-4177. *Dir* Dr Lorenz Eitner; *Asst Dir* Dr Carol Osborne; *Cur of Prints & Drawings* Betsy G Fryberger; *Dir of Oriental Art* Dr Patrick Maveety; *Cur of Photography* Anita V Mozley; *Registrar* Katherine Garrett
Open Tues - Fri 10 AM - 4:45 PM, Sat & Sun 1 - 4:45 PM. No admis fee. Estab 1891 as a teaching museum and laboratory for University's Department of Art. Average Annual Attendance: 85,000. Mem: 1600; dues $10 - $100; annual meeting in May
Income: Financed by endowment, membership and university funds
Collections: †American Indian Art; †Ancient Art; †B G Canton Gallery of Rodin Sculpture; †Contemporary Art; †Oriental Art; †20th Century Art; Stanford Family Collection; †Western Art of the 20th Century
Exhibitions: Ansel Adams Portraits; Art about Artists; TUT - TUT: A Survey of Egyptomania; Joachim Bethold Sculpture; Camera Work; Bloomsbury: prints, drawings, paintings; Blue and White Ceramics of the Far East; The Grand Tour (photographs); In Celebration of Paul Klee: Fifty Prints; Japonisme; Killing Likeness: Caricature and Satire; Nadar Portraits; Thomas Rowlandson: Drawings and Illustrated Books; Giovanni Domenico Tiepolo: The Punchinello Drawings; Seventeenth Century Italian Prints; Some Twenty Odd Visions (contemporary photographs); Whistler: Themes and Variations; recent acquisitions; two exhibitions every two months
Publications: The Stanford Museum, biennially; exhibition catalogs
Activities: Docent training; lect open to the public, 15 vis lectr per year; gallery talks; tours; exten dept serving the community; originate traveling exhibitons; museum shop sells books, cards, prints, reproductions

L **Art Library of the Stanford University Libraries,** Museum Way & Lomita Dr, 94305. Tel 415-497-3408. *Librn* Alex Ross
Open to the public for reference only

STOCKTON

M **PIONEER MUSEUM AND HAGGIN GALLERIES,** 1201 N Pershing Ave, 95203. Tel 209-462-4116. *Pres* E Urban Ernst; *Secy* Constance Miller; *Treas* Dahl C Burnham; *Dir* Keith E Dennison; *Admin Asst* Setsuko Ryuto; *Cur of History* Raymond Hillman; *Registrar* Phyllis G Allen
Open Tues - Sun 1:30 - 5 PM. No admis fee. Estab 1928 to protect, preserve and interpret for present and future generations historical and fine arts collections that pertain to the museum's disciplines. The gallery covers 34,000 sq ft of exhibit space housing art and history collections. Average Annual Attendance: 50,000. Mem: 1075; dues $15 and up; annual meeting third Tues in Jan
Income: $250,000 (financed by endowment, membership, city and county appropriation)
Collections: 19th Century French, American and European paintings; decorative arts; graphics
Publications: Museum Calendar, bimonthly
Activities: Classes for children; docent training; lect open to the public, 4 - 5 vis lectr per year; concerts; gallery talks; tours; competitions; individual paintings and original objects of art lent

L **Petzinger Memorial Library,** 95203. *Librn* Phyllis G Allen
Open Tues, Thurs & Sat by appointment only. Estab 1941 to supply material to those interested in the research of California and San Joaquin County history as well as the history of Stockton
Income: $5400
Purchases: $700
Library Holdings: Vols 7000; AV—Lantern Slides, motion pictures, slides; Other—Clipping files, exhibition catalogs, prints, manuscripts, memorabilia, original art works, pamphlets, photographs, reproductions, original documents
Collections: Roland Art Collection
Activities: Lect open to the public, 3 vis lectr per year; concerts; gallery talks

M **UNIVERSITY OF THE PACIFIC,** University Center Gallery, 3601 Pacific Ave, 95211. *Dir* James F Paull

Open 9 AM - 5 PM. No admis fee. Estab 1975 to expose the University community to various art forms
Activities: Lect open to the public, 2 vis lectr per year

TORRANCE

M EL CAMINO COLLEGE ART GALLERY,* 16007 Crenshaw Blvd, 90506. Tel 213-532-3670. *Dean Fine Arts* Dr Lewis Hiigel
Open Mon - Fri 9 AM - 3 PM, Mon & Thurs 6 - 9 PM, Sun Noon - 4 PM. No admis fee. Estab 1970 to exhibit professional, historical and student art. Larger main gallery is 50 ft sq; smaller lounge gallery is 18 x 22 ft
Collections: Small print collection; small sculpture collection
Publications: Exhibit catalogs
Activities: Lect open to public; concerts; gallery talks; tours

TURLOCK

CALIFORNIA STATE COLLEGE, STANISLAUS
M Art Gallery,* 800 Monte Vista, 95380. Tel 209-633-2122. *Chmn of Art Dept* Winston McGee; *Dir of Gallery* Martin Camarata
Open Mon - Fri 11 AM - 4 PM. No admis fee. Estab 1967, for the purpose of community and cultural instruction. Gallery is small, covering 250 ft running. Average Annual Attendance: 10,000
Income: $500 (financed by state appropriation)
Purchases: $500
Collections: Permanent collection of graphics and small contemporary works
Publications: Exhibition catalogs
Activities: Classes for adults; lect open to the public, 11 visiting lectrs per year; concerts; gallery talks; tours; exten dept serving summer school; individual paintings and original objects of art lent to the campus community; lending collection contains film strips, 35mm lantern slides, motion pictures, original art works, original prints; traveling exhibitions organized and circulated
L Vache Library,* 800 Monte Vista, 95380. Tel 209-633-2232. *Librn* R Dean Galloway
Open daily 8 AM - 10 PM. Estab 1967, as a college resource for liberal arts. Circ 129,000
Income: $5600 (financed by state appropriation)
Purchases: $5600
Library Holdings: Vols 7000; Per subs 77; Micro—Fiche, reels, prints; AV—A-tapes, cassettes, fs, Kodachromes, motion pictures, slides, v-tapes; Other—Framed reproductions, original art works, reproductions
Special Subjects: Emphasis on 19th and 20th century art
Collections: Art History Slide Library Collection; Contemporary American Prints

VALENCIA

L CALIFORNIA INSTITUTE OF THE ARTS LIBRARY, 24700 McBean Parkway, 90038. Tel 805-255-1050. *Dir* Elizabeth Armstrong; *Assoc Librn & Head, Technical Processes* James Elrod; *Cataloger* Joan Anderson; *Head, Public Services* Frederick Gardner; *Film Librn* Margie Hanft; *Art & Slide Librn* Evelyn White
Open Mon - Thurs 10 AM - Midnight, Fri 10 AM - 5 PM, Sun Noon - 9 PM, cl Sat. Estab 1961, first classes 1970, designed to be a community of practicing artists working in schools of art, design, film, music, theatre and dance
Income: Financed by endowment
Library Holdings: Vols 87,702; Per subs 550; Micro—Fiche, reels; AV—A-tapes, cassettes, motion pictures, rec, slides, v-tapes; Other—Exhibition catalogs
Special Subjects: Film, Theatre Arts, Video, art and design, critical studies, dance, music,
Exhibitions: Student work, approximately 20 per year

VICTORVILLE

L VICTOR VALLEY COLLEGE LIBRARY, 92392. *Librn* Kim King
Open daily 9 AM - 5 PM. Estab 1961
Income: $1000
Library Holdings: Micro—Cards, fiche, reels, prints; AV—A-tapes, cassettes, fs, motion pictures, rec, slides, v-tapes; Other—Prints, photographs
Special Subjects: Ceramics
Collections: Japanese Ceramics & Lithography

WALNUT CREEK

M WALNUT CREEK CIVIC ARTS GALLERY,* 1641 Locust St, Walnut Creek, CA. (Mailing Add: 1445 Civic Dr, Walnut Creek, CA 94596) Tel 415-935-3300. *Cur* Carl Worth
Open Tues - Sat 12 - 5 PM, Fri 7 - 9 PM, cl national holidays. No admis fee. Estab 1963, to offer varied and educational changing exhibitions to the community and surrounding area. Gallery contains 396 running ft, 2300 sq ft, including mezzanine gallery. Average Annual Attendance: 24,000. Mem: 500; dues $10
Purchases: $2000
Collections: General city collection consisting of paintings, prints, photographs and crafts
Publications: Artscene (newsletter); three catalogs per year
Activities: Classes for adults and children; dramatic programs; docent training; lect open to public, 6-10 visiting lectrs per year; concerts; gallery talks; tours; competitions; sales shop selling books, original art, slides and catalogs
L Library,* 1445 Civic Dr, 94596.
Open to local schools, docents and civic arts members

WHITTIER

M RIO HONDO COLLEGE ART GALLERY, 3600 Workman Mill Road, 90608. Tel 714-692-0921, Ext 361. *Gallery Dir* Thomas Hawkins
Open Mon - Fri 11 AM - 4 PM & 6:30 - 9 PM. No admis fee. Estab 1967 to bring to the college students a wide variety of art experiences that will enhance and develop their sensitivity and appreciation of art. Small gallery about 1000 sq ft located within the art facility. Average Annual Attendance: 8000
Income: Financed through college
Collections: Contemporary paintings and graphics by Southern California artists
Exhibitions: A Retrospective Show of Drawings and Paintings by Thomas Hawkins; Area High Schools Honor Show; California Japanese Ceramic Art Guild Show; Life Drawing Students of Richard Lopez Show; Painting and Design Students of Jerry Romotsky Show; Rio Hondo Student Honors Exhibition; Whittier Art Association All Media Show
Activities: Classes for adults; lect open to public

WILMINGTON

M LOS ANGELES HARBOR COLLEGE ART GALLERY,* 1111 Figueroa Place, 90744. Tel 213-518-1000, Ext 474. *Dir Art Gallery* Judith Lea Kunda
Open Mon, Wed & Thurs Noon - 4 PM, Wed evenings 7 - 9 PM, Tues & Fri 10 AM - 2 PM. No admis fee. Estab 1960 to educate and elevate mind and spirit. Gallery is approx 28 sq ft. Average Annual Attendance: 1500
Income: Financed by community services
Publications: Catalogs
Activities: Lect open to public, 4 visiting lectr per year; gallery talks; museum and sales shop

YOSEMITE NATIONAL PARK

M YOSEMITE MUSEUM COLLECTIONS, National Park Service, Box 577, 95389. Tel 209-372-4461, Ext 61. *Cur* Jack Gyer
Open on prior request. No admis fee. Estab 1926 to interpret the natural sciences and human history of the Yosemite area. Mem: 1000; dues $5 and up
Income: Financed by federal appropriation
Collections: Indian cultural artifacts; photographs (special collection on early Yosemite); pioneer artifacts
Activities: Lect open to public; paintings and original art objects lent on special exhibits only; lending collection contains prints, photographs; shop sells books; junior museum
L Library, 95289. *Librn* Mary Vocelka
For reference only
Library Holdings: Vols 7000

COLORADO

BLACKHAWK

M BLACKHAWK MOUNTAIN SCHOOL OF ART GALLERY, 251 Main St, 80422. Tel 303-582-5235. *Pres* Michael S Parfenoff; *Dir* Michael J Reardon
Open 10 AM - 5 PM June, July and Aug. No admis fee. Estab 1972 to exhibit works of art by students, faculty and friends of the School. The Gallery is part of the educational experience for the students. They organize exhibits, staff the gallery and carry out all necessary functions of the gallery. There is 300 sq ft of exhibition space

BOULDER

O BOULDER CENTER FOR THE VISUAL ARTS, 1750 13th St, 80302. Tel 303-443-2122. *Dir* Karen Hodge
Open Tues-Sun 11 AM - 5 PM. Gallery maintained to show community art and develop the growth of art in the community
Income: $24,522 (financed by endowment, membership, city appropriation and grants)
Exhibitions: Annual Juried Exhibit - all media; ArtFest 79; Best Wishes - Holiday Show and Sale; Boulder Art 1979 (juried show); Boulder Public School Art Show; Chinese Art from Boulder Collections; Criss-Cross Pattern Project; Exposure: Ideas and Images in Contemporary Colorado Photography (juried); Grassroots People from Colorado; Performance: Art and Artist - A Larger View; Sculpture in the Park; Prints by William T Wiley
Activities: Dramatic programs; lect open to public, 10 visiting lectr per year; gallery talks; tours; competitions; awards; originate traveling exhibitions

L BOULDER PUBLIC LIBRARY AND GALLERY, 1000 Canyon Blvd, PO Drawer H, 80306. Tel 303-441-3100. *Library Dir* Marcelee Gralapp; *Asst to Library Dir* Richard Luce
Open Mon - Thurs 9 AM - 9 PM, Fri & Sat 9 AM - 6 PM, Sun Noon - 6 PM. Estab to enhance the personal development of Boulder citizens by meeting their informational needs. YA Gallery, show changes monthly; Bridge Gallery, show changes monthly; Auditorium Gallery, several shows per year
Library Holdings: Micro—Cards, fiche, prints; AV—A-tapes, cassettes, fs, slides, v-tapes; Other—Clipping files, exhibition catalogs, framed reproductions, prints, manuscripts, original art works, pamphlets, photographs, reproductions, sculpture
Exhibitions: (1979) Art Inspired by Books - Ingrid Asmus; Art of High Mountains by artist Bill Napier; Art of the West; Boulder Landscapes by Diana Kurz; Paintings by Geraldine Brussel; Clay Baskets Pottery Exhibit by Betty Woodman; Colored Pencil Drawings by Vicki Lee Johnston, Virginia Johnson and Marilyn Swartwood; The Creation of A Book: From Beginning to End; Doll Houses; Embroiderers Guild of America Exhibit; First Colorado Art Register Exhibit; Japanese Flower Arrangements by Marcia Livingston; Florence Becker Lennon

Poetry Contest; Photographs and Documents from the Carnegie Library Collection; Photographs of Women of India by Joyce Lebra; George Sand Exhibit; Works of George Woodman - Patterning; photographs
Activities: Classes for adults and children; lect open to public; concerts; tours; competitions; awards

M **UNIVERSITY OF COLORADO ART GALLERIES,** Wolle Fine Arts Building, 80309. Tel 303-492-6504. *Dir Exhib & Cur Permanent Coll* Jean-Edith V Weiffenbach
Open daily 10 AM - 4 PM. No admiss fee. Estab 1939 to maintain and exhibit art collections and to show temporary exhibits. The galleries have 413 linear ft of wall space and a total of 5000 sq ft
Income: Financed through University
Collections: †19th and 20th century paintings and †prints; †prints, drawings, watercolors, sculptures and ceramics of the 15th - 20th centuries
Exhibitions: Artist and the Master Printer; Robert Barry: Prints Drawings and Publications 1968-78; Cynthia Carlson; Luis Eades: recent paintings; The Great West; William Hogarth: Visceral Images; Alfred Jensen: paintings and diagrams from the years 1957-77; Mail, Etc Art; Northern Visions, Grotesqueries and Chimeras: Five Hundred Years of German Art; Prints: Bochner, LeWitt, Mangold, Marden, Martin, Rockburne, Ryman; Ann Leda Shapiro: paintings; Six painters of the figure: Alex Katz, Diana Kurz, Alfred Leslie, Alice Neel, Philip Pearlstein, Sylvia Sleigh
Publications: Brochures; exhibition catalogs
Activities: Lect open to public, 12 visiting artists per year; paintings and original art objects lent to museums; lending collection contains original art works and prints, paintings, photographs, sculpture, original drawings; originate traveling exhibitions

L **Art and Architecture Library,** Box 184, 80309. Tel 303-492-7955. *Head Art and Architecture Library* Prof Lamia Doumato; *Library Technician* Betty Cooney; *Library Asst* Lola Farber
Open Mon - Thurs 8 AM - Midnight, Fri & Sat 8 AM - 5 PM, Sun Noon - Midnight. Estab 1966 to support the university curriculum in the areas of fine arts, art history and architecture. Maintains small gallery devoted to book exhibitions and some photography exhibitions
Income: Financed by state appropriation
Library Holdings: Vols 53,000; Per subs 343; Micro—Fiche, reels; Other—Clipping files, exhibition catalogs, memorabilia
Special Subjects: Photography, Artists books

CENTRAL CITY

O **GILPIN COUNTY ARTS ASSOCIATION,** Eureka St, 80427. Tel 303-582-5952. *Pres* Randall Palser; *VPres* Frances D Hough; *Secy* Mrs John Reutz; *Corresponding Secy* Mrs William Russell; *Gallery Mgr* Richard Emmert
Open daily 11 AM - 5 PM. No admis fee. Estab 1947 to offer a juried exhibition of Colorado artists. A gallery is maintained. Average Annual Attendance: 24,000. Mem: 300; dues $5 - $100; annual meeting third Sun in Aug
Income: Financed by membership, sales and entry fee
Publications: Catalog
Activities: Juried competitions with awards; sponsor elementary school art program; sales shop sells original art

COLORADO SPRINGS

AMERICAN NUMISMATIC ASSOCIATION
For further information, see National and Regional Organizations

M **COLORADO SPRINGS FINE ARTS CENTER,** 30 W Dale St, 80903. Tel 303-634-5581. *Dir* Paul M Piazza; *Adminr* G W Engle; *Cur Fine Arts Coll* William Henning; *Cur Taylor Mus* William Wroth; *Dir Development* Neville Smith; *Dir Educational Prog* Joyce Robinson; *Dir Public Relations* Judith Schreiber; *Dir Sales Shop* Linda Berenson; *Dir Exhib & Physical Plant* Charles Guerin
Open Tues - Sat 10 AM - 5 PM, Sun 1:30 - 5 PM, cl Mon. No admis fee. Estab 1936 as a forum, advocate and programmer of visual and performing arts activities for the community. Eleven galleries range in size from quite small to large. Average Annual Attendance: 150,000. Mem: 2000; dues $25 - $1000; annual meeting Feb
Income: $800,000 (financed by endowment, membership, city and state appropriations, and revenue producing enterprises)
Collections: Taylor Collection of Southwestern Spanish Colonial and native American art; American paintings, sculptures, graphics and drawings with emphasis on art west of the Mississippi; ethnographic collections; fine arts collections; 19th and 20th century art and survey collection of world art
Exhibitions: Bernard Arnest Retrospective; the Arts of the Indians of Northwestern Mexico; Bertoia; Edgar Britton Retrospective; Martin Chambe: Photographs of Cuzco; Cloisonne; Preston Dickinson Retrospective; Enduring Visions: 1000 Years of Southwest Indian Art; Johnson-Hernandez painting and jewelry; Native American Basketry; Pikes Peak: The Ultimate Landmark; Posada's Mexico; Rauschenberg; Charles M Russell: Artist of the American West; Selection of John James Audubon's Birds of America; 20th century Hispanic New Mexican Weaving; Annual Art Auction; Colorado Springs Young People's Art; Gallery of Christmas Trees
Publications: Annual report; Artsfocus; calendar, monthly; educational programs and tours; exhibition catalogs; gallery sheets; scholarly publication
Activities: Art classes for children and adults; dramatic programs; docent training; lect open to public, 12 visiting lectr per year; concerts; gallery talks; competitions; art lent to AAM accredited museums; shop sells books, art and gifts

L **Library,** 30 W Dale St, 80903. Tel 303-634-5481. *Librn* Roderick Dew
Open Tues - Sat 10 AM - 5 PM, cl Mon & Sun. Estab 1936 as a fine arts reference library in support of the museum's collection and activities. Open for public reference, lending is restricted to members of the center and local university students and faculty
Income: Financed by endowment, membership and state appropriation
Purchases: $9000 (1980)
Library Holdings: Vols 15,000; Per subs 100; Other—Clipping files, exhibition catalogs, prints, memorabilia, pamphlets, reproductions

Special Subjects: Art and anthropology of the Southwest
Collections: Taylor Museum Collection on the art and anthropology of the Southwest
Activities: Tours

M **UNITED STATES FIGURE SKATING HALL OF FAME AND MUSEUM,** 20 First St, 80906. Tel 303-635-5200. *Pres* Charles DeMore; *VPres* Joseph Serafine; *Secy* Albert Beard; *Executive Dir* F Don Stoddard; *Museum Dir* Jerry McGaha; *Conservator* Pat Cataldi; *Registrar* Barbara Murphy
Open Mon - Sat 10 AM - 4 PM. Admis adults $1.25, children under 14 75¢. Estab 1979 to preserve the art and history of skating. Maintains 5000 square feet exhibit area. Average Annual Attendance: 90,000
Collections: Skating In Art, the Gillis Crafstrom Collection
Publications: Skating Magazine
Activities: lect; gallery talks; tours; museum shop selling books, jewelry, figurines, medals, decals, cards and decorations

L **Library,** 20 First St, 80906.
Open Tues - Sat 10 AM - 4 PM
Library Holdings: Micro—Reels; AV—A-tapes, cassettes, fs, lantern Slides, motion pictures, rec, slides, v-tapes; Other—Clipping files, exhibition catalogs, framed reproductions, prints, manuscripts, memorabilia, original art works, pamphlets, photographs
Special Subjects: Skating, the best reference collection in the world
Collections: First books published in English, French & German on skating

DENVER

O **COLORADO HISTORICAL SOCIETY,** Colorado Heritage Center, 1300 Broadway, 80203. Tel 303-839-2136. *Executive Dir* Barbara Sudler; *State Historic Preservation Officer* Arthur Townsend; *Cur Documentary Resources* Maxine Benson; *Cur Buildings & Sites* Roger Doherty; *Cur Historic Preservation* James Hartman; *Cur Publications* Cathryne Johnson; *Cur Formal Education* Nancy Markham; *Cur Material Culture* Joseph Morrow; *State Archaeolgist* Bruce Rippeteau
Open Mon - Fri 9 AM - 5 PM, Sat, Sun & Holidays 10 AM - 5 PM, cl Christmas. No admis fee. Estab 1879 to collect, preserve and interpret the history of Colorado. Main level exhibit space of 35,000 sq ft to be developed over the next 5 - 10 years; special exhibit gallery. Average Annual Attendance: 180,000. Mem: 4200; dues $15; annual meeting varies
Income: $1,600,000 (financed by endowment, membership, state and federal appropriations)
Exhibitions: Colorado on Glass (photographs); The Coloradoans: Introduction to the Peoples of Colorado
Publications: The Colorado Magazine, quarterly; Mountain Plain History Notes, monthly
Activities: Classes for children; docent training; lect open to the public; exten dept serving the state; individual paintings and original objects of art lent to museums; originate traveling exhibitions; sales shop sells books, reproductions, slides

L **Documentary Resources Department,** 80203.
Open to public for reference
Library Holdings: Vols 40,000; Micro—Reels 26,000; AV—A-tapes, rec; Other—Manuscripts 1,000,000, photographs 250,000, maps
Collections: William Henry Jacson Glass Plate Negatives of Views West of the Mississippi

M **COLORADO WOMEN'S COLLEGE,** Lyle True Gallery, Montview at Quebec, 80220. Tel 303-394-6012. *Dir* Joyce Eakins
Gallery and Library maintained
Income: Financed by endowment and student tuition
Exhibitions: Six exhibitions per year by nationally-known artists; faculty and student exhibitions
Activities: Classes for adults; field trips to regional and national museums and galleries; dramatic programs; lect open to the public; concerts;; scholarships offered; book shop

M **DENVER ART MUSEUM,** Frederic H Douglas Library, 100 W 14th Ave Parkway, 80204. Tel 303-575-2793. *Dir* Thomas N Maytham; *Assoc Dir* Lewis W Story; *Public Relations Dir* Susan Landess
Open Tues, Thurs, Fri & Sat 9 AM - 5 PM, Wed 9 AM - 9 PM, Sun 1 - 5 PM, cl Mon. No admis fee. Estab 1893, new building opened 1971, to provide a number of permanent and rotating art collections for public viewing, as well a variety of art education programs and services. The Museum is a seven story building composed of two cubes, placed like a square-cornered figure eight. The building contains 210,000 sq ft of space, 117,000 of which is exhibit space. Average Annual Attendance: 500,000. Mem: $10,000; dues family $25, individual $15; annual meeting April
Income: Financed by membership, city and state appropriations and private funding
Collections: American Art; Contemporary Art; European Art; Native American Art; Native Arts; New World Art; Oriental Art; costumes and textiles
Exhibitions: A Century of French Masters: Corot to Braque; Andrew Dasburg Retrospective; Hawaii: The Royal Island; Journey of the Three Jewels; 19th and 20th Century Master Drawings; Song of the Brush; Travels With Pen, Pencil and Ink (David Hockney); Watercolors from the Baltimore Museum of Art; William T Wiley: 12 Years
Publications: Calendar, monthly; catalogues for exhibitions
Activities: Classes for adults and children; dramatic programs; docent training; lect open to the public, 20 vis lectr per year; concerts, gallery talks; tours; art mobile; individual paintings and original objects of art lent to museums; traveling exhibitions organized and circulated; museum shop sells books, jewelry, prints, reproductions, slides, and Native American Art

L **Frederic H Douglas Library,** 100 W 14th Ave Parkway, 80204. Tel 303-575-2256. *Librn* Margaret Goodrich; *Cur Native Arts Department* Richard Conn
Open by appointment only. Estab 1935 to facilitate research in anthropology and native arts
Library Holdings: Micro—Cards, fiche; AV—Slides; Other—Clipping files, exhibition catalogs, framed reproductions, prints, manuscripts, memorabilia, original art works, pamphlets, photographs

Special Subjects: Africa, American Indians, Native American linguistics, Oceania
Collections: Native American linguistics

L DENVER PUBLIC LIBRARY, 1357 Broadway, 80203. Tel 303-573-5152. *Librn* Henry G Shearouse Jr; *Head Arts & Recreation Dept* Georgiana Tiff
Open Mon - Thurs 10 AM - 9 PM, Fri & Sat 10 AM - 5:30 PM. Estab 1889
Library Holdings: Vols 65,391; Micro—Fiche, reels; AV—A-tapes, cassettes, fs, motion pictures, rec, v-tapes; Other—Clipping files, exhibition catalogs, framed reproductions, prints 1384, manuscripts, memorabilia, original art works, pamphlets 177,726, photographs 14,752, reproductions, sculpture, original documents
Exhibitions: Frequent exhibitions from the book and picture collections
Activities: Exten dept serves Denver Art Museum, schools, colleges and clubs throughout the region

M ROCKY MOUNTAIN SCHOOL OF ART GALLERY, 1441 Ogden St, 80218. Tel 303-832-1557. *Dir* Philip J Steele; *Asst Dir* Craig Steele; *Secy & Registrar* June Cranford
Open Mon - Fri 8 AM - 4:30 PM. Vocational School in the Fine Arts
Exhibitions: Annual Art Show; Student Work
Publications: Catalogs; Spectrum, quarterly
L Library, 1441 Ogden St, 80218. *Librn* Mary Ann Burkhardt
Open to students
Library Holdings: Vols 500; Per subs 10

M THE TURNER MUSEUM, 773 Downing St, 80218. Tel 303-832-0924. *Pres & Treas* Douglas Graham; *VPres & Secy* R Canady; *Librn & Registrar* Cynthia Montilla
Open Sun 1 - 6 PM by appointment. No admis fee. Estab 1972 to carry out the last will of T M W Turner and to display his and his principal admirer's (Thomas Moran) works. The Atlantic Richfield Gallery; The Mediterranean Gallery; The Kurt Pantzel Gallery. Average Annual Attendance: 1000. Mem: 800; dues $25; annual meeting first Sun in Dec
Income: $10,000 (financed by endowment and membership)
Collections: Moran Collection; Turner Collection
Exhibitions: Turner & Moran; Turner & Switzerland
Publications: Turner & Moran, yearly; Turner on Paper
Activities: Lect open to the public, 2 visiting lectr per year; concerts; gallery talks; tours; individual paintings and original objects of art lent to other museums and similar organizations; lending collection contains books, color reproductions, original art works, original prints, slides and posters; museum shop selling books, reproductions, prints and posters

WESTERN STATES ARTS FOUNDATION
For further information, see National and Regional Organizations

FORT COLLINS

C FIRST NATIONAL BANK, 205 W Oak, PO Box 578, 80521. Tel 303-482-4861. *Community Relations Officer* Libby Dale
Open 9 AM - 5:30 PM. No admis fee. Estab 1977 to invest in art for enjoyment of bank customers. Collection displayed in lobby and mezzaine of main bank; supports Council on Arts and Humanities, Colorado State University, Symphony, Theater
Collections: Prints by Boulanger, Calder, Sam Francis, Japser Johns, Pali, Rauschenberg, Vasarely, Dave Yust and local artists
Exhibitions: Local one-man shows with receptions for artists
Activities: Originate traveling exhibitions; sponsors Colorado State University Traveling Print Collection

GOLDEN

O FOOTHILLS ART CENTER, INC, 809 15th St, 80401. Tel 303-279-3922. *Executive Dir* Marian J Metsopoulos
Open Mon - Sat 9 AM - 4 PM, Sun 1 - 4 PM. No admis fee. Estab 1968 to provide a cultural center which embrases all the arts, to educate and stimulate the community in the appreciation and understanding of the arts, to provide equal opportunities for all people to participate in the further study and enjoyment of the arts, and to provide artists and artisans with the opportunity to present their work. Housed in the former First Presbyterian Church of Golden, the oldest part was built in 1872, the manse (a part of the whole layout) was built in 1892; there are five galleries, offices, a kitchen and classrooms. Average Annual Attendance: 10,000. Mem: 800; dues $15; annual meeting in December
Income: $71,321 (financed by membership, city appropriation, donations, commissions and rental of rooms)
Collections: Approximately six paintings in permanent collection
Exhibitions: North American Sculpture Exhibition in 1979; Rocky Mountain Watermedia Exhibition; Threads Unlimited; numerous open juried competitions
Publications: Communique; poetry newsletter, monthly
Activities: Classes for adults and children; lect open to the public, 2 - 3 vis lectr per year; concerts; gallery talks; tours; competitions; individual paintings and original objects of art lent to businesses
L Mary S Robinson Art Library, 809 15th St, 80401.
Open to members only
Library Holdings: Vols 2140; Per subs 3

GRAND JUNCTION

L MUSEUM OF WESTERN COLORADO ARCHIVES, Fourth and Ute, 81501. Tel 303-242-0971. *Archivist* Michael J Menard; *Asst Archivist* Inez Dillon Prinster
Open daily 10 AM - 5 PM. Estab 1971 to preserve and collect documents and art concerning Western Colorado. For reference only
Income: Financed by membership and Mesa County
Library Holdings: Vols 3000; Per subs 25; Micro—Reels, prints; AV—Cassettes, lantern slides, motion pictures, slides; Other—Manuscripts, memorabilia, original

art works, pamphlets, photographs
Special Subjects: Social History of Western Colorado
Collections: Frank Dean Collection - 2000 Glass Plates of Western Colorado 1882-1945; Wilson Rockwell Collection - Artwork, Books, Manuscripts and Photographs on the History of Western Colorado
Exhibitions: Grass Roots People - Photo Exhibit by Nancy Wood; Moccasins on Pavement - Photo Exhibit on Urban Indians; Denny Saunders Exhibit
Publications: Museum Notes, quarterly
Activities: Classes for children; docent training; lect open to the public, 10 visiting lectr per year; concerts; gallery talks; tours; awards

O WESTERN COLORADO CENTER FOR THE ARTS, INC, 1803 N Seventh, 81501. Tel 303-243-7337. *Dir* Peter K Faris; *Pres of Board of Trustees* Gary Ashley
Open Tues - Sat 10 AM - 5 PM. No admis fee. Museum incorporated in 1953 to provide an appropriate setting to involve individuals in the appreciation of, and active participation in the arts. One large hexagonal gallery with small stage area; approximately 2048 sq ft of floor space and approximately 1000 sq ft of wall space. No permanent display facilities. Average Annual Attendance: 12,000 - 15,000. Mem: 800; dues family $15, individual $7.50; annual meeting in February
Income: $38,000 (financed by endowment and membership)
Collections: Ceramics, needlework, paintings
Exhibitions: 8-West; monthly exhibitions; changing exhibits only in gallery
Publications: Newsletter for members, monthly
Activities: Classes for adults and children; dramatic programs; Studio Forum Childrens Theatre Company and Class Program; lect open to the public; competitions; book traveling exhibitions; museum shop sells handcrafted jewelry, imports and reproductions
L Library, 1803 N Seventh, 81501.
Open to members and public for reference
Library Holdings: Vols 400; Per subs 4

GREELEY

M UNIVERSITY OF NORTHERN COLORADO, John Mariani Art Gallery,* Department of Fine Arts, Eighth Ave & 18th St, 80639. Tel 303-351-2143. *Dir* Peggy A Ford
Open Mon - Fri 9 AM - 4:30 PM, Sun 1 - 4 PM. No admis fee. Estab 1973, to provide art exhibitions for the benefit of the University and the surrounding community. Average Annual Attendance: 5000
Income: Financed by endowment and city and state appropriations
Publications: Schedule of Exhibitions, quarterly

GUNNISON

M WESTERN STATE COLLEGE, Quigley Hall Art Gallery, 81230. *Dir* Harry Heil; *Dept Head* Pat T Julio
Open Mon - Fri 1 - 5 PM. No admis fee. Estab 1967 for the purpose of exhibiting student, staff and traveling art. Nearly 300 running ft fireproof brick walls, security lock-up iron grill gate is contained in the gallery. Average Annual Attendance: 6000
Income: $500 (financed by state appropriation)
Collections: Original paintings and prints
Activities: Competitions; originates traveling exhibitions

LA JUNTA

M KOSHARE INDIAN MUSEUM, INC, 115 West 18th, 81050. Tel 303-384-4801. *Dir* J F Burshears
Open summer 9 AM - 9 PM, winter 1 - 5 PM. No admis fee. Estab 1949 for the exhibition of Indian artifacts and paintings. Average Annual Attendance: 100,000
Activities: Paintings and original art works lent; museum shop
L Library, 115 West 18th, 81050.
Open for reference only to members
Library Holdings: Vols 2000

LEADVILLE

O LAKE COUNTY CIVIC CENTER ASSOCIATION, INC, Heritage Museum and Gallery, 100-102 W Ninth St, PO Box 962, 80461. Tel 303-486-1878. *Executive Dir* Georgina Brown; *Pres Board of Dir* Neil Reynolds; *Treas Board of Dir* Harold Neufeld; *Secy Board of Dir* Shirley Campbell
Open from Memorial Day through Labor Day Mon - Sun 10 AM - 6 PM. Admis adults $1, children 12 - 18 years 50¢ under 12 free, members free. Estab 1972 to promote the preservation, restoration and study of the rich history of the Lake County area, and to provide display area for local and non-local art work, and also to provide an educational assistance both to public schools and interested individuals. The Museum and Gallery own no art work, but display a variety of art on a changing basis. Average Annual Attendance: 11,000 - 12,500. Mem: 330; dues donor $100, contributing $50, patron $25, associate $10; annual meeting Feb
Income: $7000 - $8000 (financed by membership and admission fees)
Purchases: $500 - $1000
Exhibitions: Changing displays of paintings, photography and craft work
Publications: Mountain Diggings, annual; The Tallyboard, newsletter, quarterly
Activities: Lect open to public; competitions; shop sells books, slides, papers, postcards, rock samples

LOVELAND

M LOVELAND MUSEUM, 503 Lincoln, 80537. Tel 303-667-6070. *Cur & Dir* David S Brandon; *Asst Dir & Cur Educ* Linda Jones; *Cur Coll* Helen Fellows
Open Mon - Wed & Fri 9 AM - 4 PM, Thurs 9 AM - 8 PM, Sat 10 AM - 4 PM, Sun 1 - 4 PM, cl national holidays. No admis fee. Estab 1929. Art gallery located in historic home
Income: Financed by city appropriation
Collections: Archaeology; art; dioramas; historical material; period rooms
Activities: Outreach school programs; lect; guided tours; inter-museum and inter-library loan programs

PUEBLO

O SANGRE DE CRISTO ARTS & CONFERENCE CENTER, 210 N Santa Fe, 81003. Tel 303-543-0130. *Dir* Al Kochka; *Development Mgr* Maggie Divelbiss; *Workshop & Exhibition Coordinator* Susan Ducat; *Rentals Coordinator* Ginny Varney
Open Mon - Sat 9 AM - 5 PM. No admis fee. Estab 1972 to promote the educational and cultural activities related to the fine arts in Southern Colorado and the management of conventions, specifically those which may be concerned with and related to the fine arts. The Studio Gallery in one building has 120 running ft of wall space, 1000 sq ft of floor space ; the Conference Gallery located in another building covers 110 ft x 62 ft. Average Annual Attendance: 120,000. Mem: 550; dues $15 - $500; annual meeting third Wed in Dec
Income: $380,000 (financed by membership, city appropriation and county appropriation)
Exhibitions: (1978) Annual Invitational Pottery Sale; Channel 8 Auction; Colorado Artist Craftsmen Exhibition; Fibers, Sculpture, and Painting (Lin Fife & Ron Snapp); First National Spoon and Ash Tray Show; Harmsen's Navajo Rug Exhibition; Invitational Stained Glass Exhibition; Own Your Own Art Show; Prismatic Reflections in Weaving; The Recent Paintings of Steven Seals; Ten Years of Contemporary Print Making (1967 - 1977). (1979)Hecho En Mexico, Weaving Designs by Lila Clerk; First International Colorado Poster Exhibition; Juried Show of Southern Colorado Photographers; Paintings and Drawings by Pat Garey; Painting Retrospective by Lee Milmon
Publications: Town and Center Mosaic, nine times a year
Activities: Classes for adults and children; dramatic programs, docent training; workshops; lect open to the public; 3 vis lectr per year; concerts; gallery talks; tours

M UNIVERSITY OF SOUTHERN COLORADO, 2200 N Bonforte, 81001. Tel 303-549-2817. *Art Dept Chmn* Ed Sajbel; *Gallery Dir* Robert Hench
Open daily 10 AM - 4 PM. No admis fee. Estab 1972 to provide educational exhibitions for students attending the University. Gallery has a 40 x 50 ft area with 16 ft ceiling; vinyl covered wooden walls; carpeted and adjustable track lighting. Average Annual Attendance: 6000
Income: Financed through University and student government
Purchases: $100,000
Collections: Basketry of the Plains Indian, clothing of the Plains Indian; Orman Collection of Indian Art of the Southwest including Indian blankets of the Rio Grande and Navajo people; pottery of the Pueblo Indians (both recent and ancient)
Exhibitions: (1978-1979) Annual Art Student Exhibit; Cone Ceramic Exhibit; Randy Ford; Midland Collection: Paintings and Sculpture from Denver; Barbara Moore; The New Enamels: Joann Brassill; Poster Exhibit: John Corbie CSU; Senior Exhibit; USC Faculty Show; USC Permanent Collection of Prints and Etchings
Publications: Catalogs
Activities: Lect open to the public; individual paintings and original objects of art lent; book traveling exhibitions 2-6 per year; traveling exhibitions organized and circulated

CONNECTICUT

AVON

O FARMINGTON VALLEY ARTS CENTER, Avon Park North, Box 220, 06001. Tel 203-678-1867. *Pres* Thomas McGee; *VPres* E Barksdale; *Secy* Patricia McGarry; *Executive Dir* Betty Friedman; *Program Dir* Karen Ann Shlomberg; *Admin Coordr* Marie Alipranti
Open Tues - Sat 11 AM - 4 PM, Sun 1-4 PM. No admis fee. Estab 1971 to provide a facility with appropriate environment and programs, to serve as a focal point for public awareness of and participation in the visual arts by furthering quality arts education and exposure to dedicated artists and their works. Maintains 20 studios. Average Annual Attendance: 30,000. Mem: 1200; dues family $20, individual $15; Board of Directors meeting in April
Income: $100,000; (financed by membership, grants, tuitions, donations for corporations and individuals, special event earning)
Exhibitions: Local Artists, 9 exhibitions per year; Regional Crafts
Activities: Classes for adults and children; lect open to the public; gallery talks; tours; competitions; scholarships and fellowships

BRIDGEPORT

O BRIDGEPORT ART LEAGUE,* 528 Clinton Ave, 06605. Tel 203-335-6250. *Pres* Alexander Mazur
Open 10:30 AM - 5 PM, cl Sun. No admis fee. Organized 1895, inc 1916. Average Annual Attendance: 200. Mem: 150; annual meeting May
Exhibitions: Annual exhibition in April with jury and awards, open to non-members; Members Exhibition in May, of work completed in classes during the year; special monthly shows by local artists
Activities: Classes in arts and crafts; lect

M HOUSATONIC COMMUNITY COLLEGE, Housatonic Museum of Art, 510 Barnum Ave, 06608. Tel 203-579-6400. *Dir* Burt Chernow; *Asst Dir* David Kintzler; *Assoc Cur* Ronald Abbe; *Assoc Cur* Michael Stein
Open Mon - Thurs 8 AM - 10 PM, Fri 8 AM - 4 PM. No admis fee. Estab 1968 for educational purposes. Collection is located on five floors throughout college facilities with changing exhibition galleries on the second and fourth floors. Average Annual Attendance: 12,000
Income: Financed by student government, other groups and donations
Collections: Extensive 19th and 20th Century drawings, paintings and sculpture - Avery, Baskin, Calder, Cassat, Chagall, Daumier, DeChirico, Derain, Dubuffet, Gottlieb, Lichtenstein, Lindner, Marisol, Matisse, Miro, Pavia, Picasso, Rauchenberg, Rivers, Shahn, Vasarely, Warhol, Wesselmann and others. Extensive ethnographic collections, including Africa, South Seas and others; smaller holdings from various historical periods
Exhibitions: Allied Sculptors and Painters of Bridgeport; Greater Bridgeport High School Student Show; Rodin Faculty Show; 19th and 20th Century Sculpture
Publications: Exhibition catalogs
Activities: Classes for adults; college art courses; lect open to public, 1 - 3 visiting lectr per year; concerts; gallery talks; tours; individual paintings and original objects of art lent to institutions; lending collection contains 1000 paintings, 20,000 slides; originate traveling exhibitions

L Library, 510 Barnum Ave, 06608. *Librn* Robert Martinson
Extensive art section open to students and community
Library Holdings: Vols 1000; Micro—Fiche

M MUSEUM OF ART, SCIENCE AND INDUSTRY, 4450 Park Ave, 06604. Tel 203-372-3521. *Dir* Christine Stiassni; *Cur Art* Kent dur Russell; *Art Education Coordr* Joan Hackett
Open Tues - Sun 2 - 5 PM, Fri 10 AM - 5 PM. Admis adults $1, children, senior citizens & students 50¢. Estab 1958 to provide exhibitions and educational programs in the arts and sciences for a regional audience. Average Annual Attendance: 164,000. Mem: Dues $10 - $2500; annual meeting June
Collections: Antique furniture; Indian artifacts; paintings
Exhibitions: Temporary and permanent exhibitions
Activities: Classes for adults and children; lect; gallery talks; tours

L UNIVERSITY OF BRIDGEPORT, Magnus Wahlstrom Library, 126 Park Ave, 06602. *Fine Arts Subject Specialist* Rene Boux
Open daily 8:30 AM - 11 PM. Gallery 5 has student exhibitions
Purchases: $2500
Library Holdings: Vols 10,000; Per subs 100
Special Subjects: Architecture

DANBURY

M DANBURY SCOTT-FANTON MUSEUM AND HISTORICAL SOCIETY, INC, 43 Main St, 06810. Tel 203-743-5200. *Pres* Hubert V Morgan; *Dir* Dorothy T Schling
Open Wed - Sun 2 - 5 PM, cl Mon, Tues & holidays. No admis fee. Estab June 24, 1941 as historic house. Merged with Museum and Arts Center by Legislative Act 1947. Operates the 1785 John and Mary Rider House as a museum of early Americana, and the 1790 Dodd Hat Shop with exhibits relating to hatting. Huntington Hall houses frequently changing exhibits. Ives Homestead, located at Rogers Park in Danbury is to be restored and opened to the public as a memorial to American composer Charles Edward Ives. At present there is a Charles Ives Parlor in the Rider House, recreating the period with Ives furnishings and memorabilia. Average Annual Attendance: 5000. Mem: 500; dues student $2 up to life $1000; annual meeting in Nov
Income: Financed by endowment and membership
Publications: Newsletter, monthly; reprints
Activities: Classes for adults and children; lect; concerts; open house; special exhibits

L Library, 43 Main St, Danbury, 06810.
Historic material for reference only
Collections: Photograph collection

SOCIETY OF MEDALISTS
For further information, see National and Regional Organizations

O WOOSTER COMMUNITY ART CENTER, Ridgebury Rd, 06810. Tel 203-743-6311. *Dir* Roger O Prince
Open Mon - Fri 9 AM - 10 PM. Estab 1965 as a Community Art Center for exhibitions and art classes. Average Annual Attendance: 3000
Exhibitions: Sperry Andrews; L Archacki; C Augusine; Will Barnet; Fred Baur; M Carstanjen; George Chaplin; Ed Giobbi; R Hare; Bryan Kay; Mike Nevelson; Andrew Parker; Roger Prince; R Riche; B Roll; Thomas Stearns; A Shundi; Nancy Tholen; P Warfield; A Werner
Activities: Classes for adults, high school and elementary students; 2-year Certificate Program for adults; Advanced Placement

L Library, Ridgebury Rd, 06801.
Library Holdings: AV—Slides 2200; Other—Photographs 170

EAST WINDSOR

M EAST WINDSOR HISTORICAL SOCIETY INC, Scantic Academy Museum, Scantic Road, East Windsor, CT. (Mailing Add: c/o Mrs William T Harrington, 38 Rye St, Broad Brook, CT 06016) Tel 203-623-0937. *Pres* Burton R Wadsworth; *VPres* Flicka Thrall; *Secy* Lillian Osborn; *Cur* Mrs William T Harrington; *Cur* William T Harrington; *Cur* Wanda Mazurek
Open Sundays, May, June, September, October 2 - 5 PM. No admis fee. Estab 1967 to preserve and display items of local history. Average Annual Attendance: 200. Mem: 125; dues $3; annual meeting fourth Wed Evening in May
Income: $1200 (financed by membership and donations)
Collections: Paintings by local artists
Publications: East Windsor, Through the Years: a local history
Activities: Lectures open to the public, 2 vis lectr per yr; individual paintings and original objects of art lent to local library; museum shop sells books

ESSEX

O ESSEX ART ASSOCIATION, INC, N Main St, PO Box 193, 06426. Tel 203-767-8996. *Pres* Jessie Mayer; *Treas* Margaret Wilson; *Secy* Adele Clement
Open daily 1 - 5 PM (June - Labor Day). No admis fee. Estab 1946 as a non-profit organization for the encouragement of the arts and to provide and maintain suitable headquarters for the showing of art. Maintains a small, well-equipped one-floor gallery. Average Annual Attendance: 2500. Mem: 360; dues artists $7.50, associate $10; annual meeting in Sept
Income: $3000 (financed by membership)
Exhibitions: Three annual exhibits each year plus one or two special exhibits; usually one high school or grammer school exhibit

FAIRFIELD

O FAIRFIELD HISTORICAL SOCIETY, 636 Old Post Rd, 06430. Tel 203-259-1598. *Pres* Edward E Harrison
Open Mon - Fri 9:30 AM - 4:30 PM, Sun 1 - 5 PM. No admis fee. Estab 1902 to collect, preserve and interpret artifacts and information relating to the history of Fairfield. Average Annual Attendance: 3000. Mem: 750; dues $10 - $500; meeting date varies
Income: Approx 70,000 (financed by endowment, membership, and city appropriation)
Collections: Ceramics, furniture, greeting cards, jewelry, paintings, photographs, prints, silver; textiles and costumes
Exhibitions: Rotating exhibits
Publications: Newsletter, quarterly
Activities: Classes for children; docent training; lect open to the public, 2 - 4 vis lectr per year; concerts; individual paintings and original objects of art lent to other institutions
L Library, 636 Old Post Rd, 06430.
Open to the public for reference only
Library Holdings: Vols 8000; Per subs 19; Other—Manuscripts, photographs, diaries, documents, maps
Special Subjects: Genealogy

FARMINGTON

M FARMINGTON MUSEUM, Stanley-Whitman House, 37 High St, 06032. Tel 203-677-9222. *Chmn* Mrs William E Sherpick; *Dir* Mary P Spivy
Open April - Nov Tues - Sun 1 - 4 PM, Wed & Sat 10 - Noon, Dec and March Fri, Sat & Sun 1 - 4 PM, cl Jan & Feb except for appointment and holidays. Admis adults $1, children 50¢. Estab 1935. The museum is governed by a branch of the Farmington Village Green and Library Association and is housed in the circa 1660 Stanley-Whitman House
Collections: American costumes and textiles; decorative arts; furniture; musical instruments; 17th century garden
Exhibitions: Permanent and changing exhibitions
Publications: A Guide to Historic Farmington, Connecticut; A Short History of Farmington, Connecticut
Activities: Guided tours; shop sells books and pamphlets

M HILL-STEAD MUSEUM, 671 Farmington Ave, PO Box 353, 06032. Tel 203-677-9064. *Pres* Mrs Erdman Harris; *VPres* George Heard Hamilton; *Secy-Treas* Marguerite Weaver; *Cur* Jarold D Talbot
Open Wed, Thurs, Sat & Sun 2 - 5 PM, cl Thanksgiving & Christmas. Admis adults $1.50, children 75¢. Estab 1946. The art collection is housed in turn-of-the-century house by Stanford White and contains original furnishings and collection of Alfred Atmore Pope. The museum is kept as if lived in by original owners; paintings were collected between 1880 and 1970. Average Annual Attendance: 10,000. Mem: 250; dues $5 - $300; meetings Nov and June
Income: $95,000 (financed by endowment and admissions sales desk)
Collections: French impressionists: Carriere, Cassatt, Degas, Manet, Monet and Whistler; sculpture: Barye, Calder, Manship and others; prints: Durer, Haydon, Hiroshige, Hokusai, Utamara and Whistler; Chinese Porcelains, 18th Century French and English Furniture; Oriental rugs; silver
Publications: Catalog of Hill-Stead Paintings, Hill-Stead Yesterdays; slide brochure
Activities: Docent training; lect for members only, 3 vis lectr per year; guided tours, groups by reservations; sales shop sells books, postcards and slides
L Library, 671 Farmington Ave, 06032.
Open to authorized scholars
Library Holdings: Vols 5000
Collections: An Aquatint by Mary Cassatt; Goya's Disasters of War; Mezzotints by Joshua Reynolds

GREENWICH

O ART BARN, 143 Lower Cross Rd, 06830. *Pres* Mildred Birnbaum; *Secy* Nancy Hamilton; *Exec Dir* Elizabeth P Burt; *Gallery Dir* Shirley Kraus; *Treas* Fred Krasu
Open Tues - Sat 9:30 AM - 3PM, Sun 1 - 4 PM. No admis fee. Estab Mar 1962 to provide a stimulating atmosphere which encourages self-expression and growth without competitive pressures and by bringing sculptors, painters, printmakers and handcrafters from all parts of the country to exhibit at the Art Barn. The gallery is located in a converted dairy barn. Average Annual Attendance: 2500. Mem: 350; dues $20 - $25; annual meeting in Sept
Income: Financed by membership, from workshops, gallery and shop sales
Exhibitions: Ten per year
Activities: Classes for adults and children; demonstrations; scholarships offered
L Library, 143 Lower Cross Rd, 06830.
Library Holdings: Vols 500

M BRUCE MUSEUM, Museum Dr, 06830. Tel 203-869‡0376. *Dir* Jack Clark; *Educational Cur* Andrew Svedlow; *Secy & Asst to Dir* Lee St German
Open Mon - Fri 10 AM - 5 PM, Sat 1 - 5 PM, Sun 2 - 5 PM. No admis fee. Estab 1908 by Robert M Bruce as a natural history, art and historical museum. Average Annual Attendance: 80,000
Income: $115,000 (financed by the Town of Greenwich)
Collections: International porcelain collection; ethnographic art and art objects; 19th and 20th century American and European painting and works on paper; oriental ivories
Activities: lect; weekend and holiday educational programs
L Library, Bruce Park, 06830.
Library Holdings: Vols 1000

O GREENWICH ART SOCIETY AND ART CENTER, 449 Pemberwick Rd, 06830. Tel 203-531-4010. *Dir Art Center* Elaine Huyer; *Publicity* Carol Dixon; *Treas* Barbara Bradbury
Estab 1912, a nonprofit organization to further art education and to awaken and stimulate broader interest in arts and crafts in the town of Greenwich. Art Center studio is used for classes and meetings. Mem: 500; dues family $20, regular $15, student (19 - 24 years) $5, junior (18 and under) $3, annual exhibition fee for exhibiting members $5
Income: Financed by membership
Exhibitions: Annual Sidewalk Show, open to all artists in area; Juried Annual Fall Show; additional exhibitions
Publications: The History of the Greenwich Art Society, booklet; Bulletin of program for the year and class schedule
Activities: Day and evening classes for adults, special classes for children; critiques and demonstrations; lect open to the public: individual paintings lent to schools; scholarships

M PROPERSI SCHOOL OF ART INC GALLERIES, 44 W Putnam Ave, 06830. Tel 203-869-4430. *Pres & Dir* August Propersi; *VPres* Joann Propersi; *Asst Chmn* William Fraccio; *Office Mgr & Admin Asst* Margaret Mujino
Open 10 AM - 5 PM. No admis fee. Estab 1954. Gallery to exhibit professional works of art of Merit, Valve, Investment
Activities: Classes for adults and children; 4 visiting lectr per year; gallery talks; tours; awards; scholarships

HARTFORD

O CONNECTICUT HISTORICAL SOCIETY, 1 Elizabeth St, 06105. Tel 203-236-5621. *Dir* Thompson R Harlow; *Asst Dir* Christopher Bickford; *Cur* Philip H Dunbar
Open Mon - Fri 9 AM - 5 PM, cl Sun, Sat and holidays (June 1 - Sept 1). Estab 1825 to collect and preserve materials of Connecticut interest and to encourage interest in Connecticut history. Exhibition space totals 6500 sq ft, two-thirds of which are devoted to permanent exhibitions; one-third to changing exhibits
Income: $250,000 (financed by endowment and membership)
Purchases: $50,000
Exhibitions: Connecticut antique furniture; folk art, needlepoint, paintings, prints
Publications: Connecticut Historical Society Bulletin, quarterly; Annual Report; Notes and News, five times a year
Activities: Gallery talks; originate traveling exhibitions
L Library, 1 Elizabeth St, 06105. *Librn* Elizabeth Abbe
Library Holdings: Vols 70,000; Per subs 75; Micro—Reels; AV—Kodachromes; Other—Clipping files, exhibition catalogs, prints, manuscripts, original art works, pamphlets, photographs, maps, posters, original documents
Special Subjects: Local Connecticut history and genealogy, Connecticut printing, maps, prints, broadsides, printed ephemerachildren's books and reference books on decorative arts of New England

L CONNECTICUT STATE LIBRARY, Museum of Connecticut History, 231 Capitol Ave, 06115. Tel 203-566-3056. *Museum Dir* David O White
Open Mon - Fri 9 AM - 5 PM, Sat 9 AM - 1 PM, cl holidays. Estab 1910 to collect, preserve and display artifacts and memorabilia reflecting the history and heritage of Connecticut. For reference only
Library Holdings: Vols 500,000; Micro—Fiche, reels; AV—Cassettes, motion pictures, v-tapes; Other—Clipping files, prints, manuscripts, memorabilia, original art works, pamphlets, photographs, original documents
Special Subjects: Coins & Medals, Conneticut, firearms
Collections: Portraits of Connecticut's Governors
Exhibitions: Changing exhibits

L HARTFORD PUBLIC LIBRARY, 500 Main St, 06103. Tel 203-525-9121, Ext 32. *Dept Head* Vernon Martin
Open hours vary. Estab 1774 as a free public library. A gallery is maintained on wall space and glass cases
Income: Financed by endowment, membership, and city appropriation
Library Holdings: AV—Motion pictures, rec; Other—Sculpture, 300,000 pictures

Exhibitions: Changing exhibit each month
Activities: Dramatic prog; concerts

M **OLD STATE HOUSE,** 800 Main St, 06103. Tel 203-552-6766. *Chmn* Wilson Wilde; *Pres* Stanly Schultz; *VPres* Elizabeth Capen; *Secy* Robert H Smith Jr; *Exec Dir* Wilson H Faude; *Exec Secy* Claire Nicoll; *Dir Education* Marie D Meyer; *Museum Shop Mgr* Nancy Stevens; *Membership Coordr* Ruth Shulansky
Open Mon - Sat 10 AM - 5 PM, Sun 12 - 5 PM. Admis adults 50¢, children 10¢, Wed free. Estab 1975 to preserve oldest state house in the nation and present variety of exhibitions on historic and contemporary subjects. Former executive wing is used for exhibitions of contemporary artists and craftsmen, paintings, decorative arts on a rotating basis. Average Annual Attendance: 60,000. Mem: 1500; dues individual $10, family $15, life $1000; annual meeting in the Fall
Income: $100,000 (financed by endowment, membership and appeals)
Collections: †Connecticut portraits; documents; Restored Senate Chamber
Activities: Education department; lect open to the public, 25 vis lectr per yr; concerts; gallery talks; tours; individual paintings and original objects of art lent to museums for special exhibitions; museum shop sells books, magazines, original art, reproductions, prints, slides, Connecticut arts and crafts

O **STOWE-DAY FOUNDATION,** 77 Forest St, 06105. Tel 203-522-9258. *Pres* H Burton Powers; *VPres* Helen D Perkins; *VPres* Mrs Ellsworth Grant; *Secy* Thomas L Archibald; *Dir* Joseph S Van Why; *Cur* Ellice Schofield; *Vistors Center Adminr* Andrea Rudy
Open daily June - Aug 10 AM - 4:30 PM, Sept - May Tues - Sat 9:30 AM - 4 PM, Sun 1 - 4 PM. Estab 1941 to maintain and open to the public the restored Harriet Beecher Stowe House. The Foundation operates the Stowe-Day Library, oversees a publishing program of reprints of H B Stowe's works and new books and provides workshops and lectures. Average Annual Attendance: 22,000. Mem: 210; dues special $25, couple $15, single $12; fall and spring meetings
Income: $200,000 (financed by endowment)
Collections: †Architecture of 19th century: books, plans, drawings, trade catalogs; †decorative arts; study samples of wallpaper
Exhibitions: George Keller, Architect; 'Kaleidoscope' Selection of 150 Early Photographs; Nook Farm: Corner on the World; Portraits of a 19th Century Family (Lyman Beecher and Children); Trade Cards and Catalogs of the 19th Century; Victorian Christmas
Publications: The American Woman's Home; Eminent Victorian Americans; Joan of Arc (reprint of Mark Twain's work); George Keller, Architect; The Minister's Wooing; The Papers of Harriet Beecher Stowe; The Pearl of Orr's Island; Pognauc People; Portraits of a 19th Century Family; H B Stowe and American Literature
Activities: Classes for adults; teacher worshops; lect open to public, 1 - 2 visiting lectr per year; paintings and original art objects lent to institutions; shop sells books, prints, slides, Victorian game reproductions, stencil patterns and needlework

L **Stowe-Day Library,** 77 Forest St, 06105. *Dir* Joseph S Van Why; *Head Librn* Diana Royce; *Asst Librn* Roberta Bradford; *Catalogue Librn* Marion Carmichael
Open Mon - Fri 9 AM - 5 PM, cl national holidays. Estab 1965 to concentrate on the architecture, decorative arts, history and literature of the United States in the 19th century emphasizing a Hartford neighborhood known as Nook Farm
Purchases: $14,500
Library Holdings: Vols 15,000; Per subs 18; Micro—Fiche, reels; AV—Lantern Slides, slides; Other—Clipping files, exhibition catalogs, prints, manuscripts, memorabilia, original art works, pamphlets, photographs, sculpture, original documents

M **TRINITY COLLEGE,** Austin Arts Center, Summit St, 06106. Tel 202-527-3151. *Chmn Dept Fine Arts* Michael Mahoney; *Dir Studio Arts Program* George Chaplin; *Adminr & Technical Dir* John Woolley
Open daily 1 - 5 PM (when college is in session). No admis fee. Estab 1957. A building housing the teaching and performing aspects of music, theater and studio arts at a liberal arts college. Widener Gallery provides exhibition space mainly for student and faculty works, plus outside exhibitions
Income: Financed by college appropriation
Collections: Edwin M Blake Memorial and Archive; College Collection; Samuel H Kress Study Collection; George F McMurray Loan Collection
Exhibitions: American Paintings from the McMurray Collection; Connecticut Invitational; Carol Kreeger Davidson; Denis Farber; Mary Kenealy; Tom Lamb; Winifred Lutz; Andrew Stasik
Activities: Lect open to public, 6 vis lectr per year; lending collection contains 500 original art works and 90,000 slides

M **MARK TWAIN MEMORIAL,** 351 Farmington Ave, 06105. Tel 203-247-0998. *Dir & Cur* Wynn Lee
Open June - Aug 10 AM - 4:30 PM; Sept - May Tues - Sat 9:30 AM - 4 PM; Sun 1 - 4 PM; cl Mon, Jan 1, Easter, Labor Day, Thanksgiving and Dec 25. Guided tours adults $2, children 16 and under $1; special group tour rates with advance arrangements. Estab 1929 to restore and maintain Mark Twain's Hartford home, to collect research materials needed for the project and to keep before the public the life and work of Mark Twain. Maintains Historic House Museum with period interiors, museum room of memorabilia. National Shrine status, US Dept of Interior. Average Annual Attendance: 70,000. Mem: Approx 1000; dues $15 and higher; annual meeting May
Collections: Lockwood deForest Collection; Mark Twain Memorabilia (photographs, manuscripts); Period and Original Furnishings; Tiffany Collection; Candace Wheeler Collection
Exhibitions: occasional exhibits
Activities: Group tours; open house; Victorian Christmas; museum shop

L **Nook Farm Research Library,** 351 Farmington Ave, 06105.
Library Holdings: Vols 13,000; Other—Manuscripts, pamphlets

M **WADSWORTH ATHENEUM,** 600 Main St, 06103. Tel 203-278-2670. *Dir* Tracy Atkinson; *Exec Asst to Dir* Lucia Williams; *Chief Cur & Cur Decorative Arts* Phillip Johnston; *Cur Textiles & Costume* J Herbert Callister; *Cur American Paintings, Sculpture, Drawings & Prints* Richard Saunders; *Cur European Paintings, Sculpture, Drawings & Prints* Jean Cadogan; *Cur of Education* Danielle Rice; *Conservator* Roland C Cunningham; *Assoc Conservator* Patricia Garland; *Cur of Matrix* Andrea Miller-Keller; *Cur Lion's Gallery of the Senses* Sally Williams; *Public Information Officer* Open; *Registrar* David Parrish
Open Tues, Wed & Fri 11 AM - 3 PM; Thurs 11 AM - 8 PM; Sat & Sun 11 AM - 5 PM (during July & August, Thurs hours are 11 AM - 3 PM). Cl Mon, New Year's Day, July 4, Thanksgiving & Christmas. Voluntary admis contribution. Estab 1842 by Daniel Wadsworth as Atheneum Gallery of Fine Arts. There are more than 60 galleries in 5 interconnected buildings, plus lecture room, classrooms and 299-seat theater. 1968 renovation of facilities includes James Lippincott Goodwin Building, along with sculpture court, restaurant, additional classrooms, and offices. Average Annual Attendance: 150,000. Mem: 4000; dues $15 and higher; annual meeting Nov
Income: Financed by private funds
Collections: American and European Costumes; †American Decorative Arts; Arts of Europe, Asia, Africa and the Americas Illustrated; Ceramics; Continental Decorative Arts; †European and American Painting from 1400 to Present, including fine examples of Baroque painting and arts of the Middle Ages and the Renaissance; European and American prints and drawings; European Tapestries; Glass; Lifar Collection of Ballet Designs; †Modern Art; Wallace Nutting furniture; J P Morgan Collection of antique bronzes, silver and porcelain Oriental Art; Pre-Columbian Art; Sculpture
Exhibitions: Major exhibitions of art of all periods; Lion's Gallery of the Senses: changing exhibitions which explore the visual arts through senses other than sight; MATRIX: changing exhibitions of contemporary art
Publications: Newsletter, monthly to members; collections and exhibitions catalogs
Activities: Lect and gallery talks by staff; docent talks; seasonal concerts; gallery tours; outside lect; members' exhibition previews and various special events; Atheneum Shop selling books, reproductions, photographs, cards and gifts

L **Auerbach Art Library,** 600 Main St, 06103. Tel 203-278-2670, Ext 257. *Librn* Elizabeth G Hoke; *Asst Librn* John W Teahan
Open Tues, Wed & Fri 11 AM - 3 PM; Thurs 11 AM - 5 PM; and by appointment. Estab 1933 as a reference service to the museum staff, members and public; to provide materials supporting work with museum collection. For reference only
Income: $11,250 (financed by endowment and membership)
Purchases: $9700
Library Holdings: Vols 17,000; Per subs 150; Micro—Fiche, reels; AV—Lantern Slides, rec; Other—Clipping files, exhibition catalogs, pamphlets
Special Subjects: Decorative Arts, Art sales and collections, museology
Collections: Sol Lewitt (contemporary art); Elizabeth Miles (English silver); Watkinson Collection (pre-1917 art reference)

KENT

O **KENT ART ASSOCIATION, INC GALLERY,** Box 202, Route 7, 06757. Tel 203-927-4289. *Pres* Barbara Goodspeed; *VPres* Frances Townley; *VPres* Norman Gardner; *Recording Secy* Maggie Smith; *Corresponding Secy* Helen Stockli; *Treas* Jayne McGarvey
Open during exhibitions only, 2 - 5 PM. Estab 1923, incorporated 1935. Maintains gallery for changing exhibitions. Average Annual Attendance: 2500. Mem: 375; dues assoc $5, sustaining $15, patron $25, life $100; annual meeting Oct
Exhibitions: Fall Show; Member's Show; President's Show; Spring Show
Activities: Lect; demonstrations

M **SLOANE-STANLEY MUSEUM,** Rt 7, Kent, CT. (Mailing Add: Connecticut Historical Commission, 59 S Prospect St, Hartford, CT 06106,) Tel 203-566-3005, 927-3849. *Dir* John W Shannahan; *Supt Historical Properties* Marion K Leonard
Open May - Oct, Wed - Sun 10 AM - 4:30 PM. Admis adults 50¢, children 25¢. Estab 1969 to collect, preserve, exhibit historic American tools, implements and paintings of American scenes. Average Annual Attendance: 8000
Income: Financed by state appropriation
Collections: Paintings by Eric Sloane; American tools and implements

LITCHFIELD

O **LITCHFIELD HISTORICAL SOCIETY,** On-the-Green, PO Box 385, 06759. Tel 203-567-5862. *Pres* Mrs H C Seherr-Thoss; *VPres* Mrs C A MacDonald; *Secy* Charles A Shields; *Dir* Neil G Larson
Open Tues - Sat 11 AM - 5 PM; Apr 1 - Nov 30. No admis fee. Estab 1856, incorporated 1897 for the preservation and interpretation of local historical collections. A gallery of portraits by Ralph Earl is maintained. Average Annual Attendance: 8000 - 10,000. Mem: 500; dues benefactor $100, donor $50, contributing $25, family $10, individual $6, senior citizen $4, student (under 21) $2; annual meeting second Fri in Sept
Income: $40,000 (financed by endowment and membership)
Collections: American and Connecticut decorative arts, pewter, costumes, textiles, paintings, silver, pottery, and graphics
Exhibitions: (1978) The 19th Century (paintings, graphics, minatures, daguerreotypes and costumes). (1979) Pottery and objects from the Historical Collections; 19th Century lack and costumes. (1980) Three Centuries of Connecticut Folk Art, contemporary art from local collections; local architecture and preservation exhibits. (1981) Adelaide Deming, Impressionist Painter of Litchfield
Activities: Lect open to public, 8 vis lectr per year

L **Ingraham Memorial Research Library,** On-the-Green, PO Box 385, 06759. Tel 203-567-5862. *Librn* Mrs Hugh Todd
Open Tues - Sat 9 AM - 5 PM. Estab 1856 as a center of local history and genealogy study
Income: $10,000 (financed by endowment and membership)
Library Holdings: Vols 10,000; Per subs 35; AV—Kodachromes, slides; Other—Clipping files, exhibition catalogs, prints, manuscripts, memorabilia, original art works, pamphlets, photographs, sculpture, original documents
Collections: 40,000 manuscripts in local history

MERIDEN

O **ARTS AND CRAFTS ASSOCIATION OF MERIDEN INC,** PO Box 348, 06450. *Pres* Irma P Morse; *VPres* James Donnelly; *Secy* Marie LeVan
Open daily 2 - 5 PM & 7 - 9 PM. No admis fee. Estab 1907 to encourage appreciation

of the arts in the community. Mem: 300; dues $5 and up; annual meeting May
Income: Financed by membership and fund raising
Collections: Permanent Museum Collection (130 pieces to date)
Exhibitions: (1978) 54th Annual Exhibition of paintings, crafts, sculpture, prints, drawings and photography
Activities: Classes for adults and children; dramatic programs; lect open to public, 9 vis lectr per yr; gallery talks; tours; competitions with awards; individual paintings and original objects of art lent to public
L **Library,** PO Box 348, 06450.
    Library Holdings: Vols 250
    Collections: Indiana Thomas Book Collection

MIDDLETOWN

M **WESLEYAN UNIVERSITY,** Davison Art Center, 301 High St, 06457. Tel 203-347-9411. *Cur* Ellen G D'Oench; *Admin Asst* Janette J Brothby
Open Tues - Fri 12 - 4 PM, Sat & Sun 2 - 5 PM cl Mon and academic vacations. No admis fee. Much of the collection was presented to Wesleyan University by George W and Harriet B Davison. Since 1952 the collection with its reference library has been housed in the historic Alsop House, now the Davison Art Center
Collections: Millet Print Collection; the print collection, extending from the 15th century to present day includes Master E S Nielli, Mantegna, Pollaiuolo, Durer, Cranach, Rembrandt, Canaletto, Piranesi, Goya, Meryon and others; Japanese prints collection; Old Masters and contemporary art work
Exhibitions: Print exhibitions arranged
O **Friends of the Davison Art Center,** 301 High St, 06457.
Estab 1961 for the support and augmentation of the activities and acquisition fund of the Davison Art Center by its members

MYSTIC

O **MYSTIC ART ASSOCIATION, INC,** Water St, PO Box 259, 06355. Tel 203-536-7601. *Pres* Paul L White; *VPres* Gerald Caron; *Treas* John Lazerek
Open daily 11 AM - 5 PM. No admis fee. Estab 1920 to maintain an art museum to promote cultural education, local philanthropic and charitable interests. The association owns a colonial building on the bank of Mystic River with spacious grounds; there is one small gallery and one large gallery with L-shaped corridor. Average Annual Attendance: 2000 - 3000. Mem: 450, active mem must have high standards of proficiency and be elected by 2 3 vote; dues active $10, assoc $7 - $15; meetings held May and Sept
Income: $10,000 - $15,000 (financed by membership)
Collections: Works donated by deceased members, shown in Groton Savings Bank
Exhibitions: (1980 - all juried) Crafts Show; Members' Show (all media); Photo II; 24th Annual Regional (all media)
Activities: Occasional classes; lect open to public, 3 or 4 vis lectr per year; concerts; gallery talks; competitions with cash awards; individual paintings lent

M **MYSTIC SEAPORT MUSEUM, INC,** Greenmanville Ave, 06355. Tel 203-536-2631. *Chmn Bd Trustees* William C Ridgway; *Pres* Clifford D Mallory; *Dir* J Revell Carr; *Deputy Dir* Franklin Kneedler; *Munson Institute Dir* Benjamin Labaree; *Dir Resource Development & Cur* Benjamin Fuller
Open daily 9 AM - 5 PM (Apr-Nov); 9 AM - 4 PM (Dec-Mar). Admis adult $6.50, child (6-12 yrs) $3.25. Estab 1929 to preserve America's maritime heritage. This is an outdoor museum of about forty buildings which include approx sixty exhibits; three areas are for formal exhibits. Average Annual Attendance: 500,000. Mem: 17,000; dues family $25, individual $15; annual meeting Sept
Income: Financed by endowment, membership, admissions
Collections: Village Area—historic shops and homes in which craft demonstrations take place and appropriate artifacts are on view; shipcarver, smith, cooper, chandler, ropewalk, sailmaker's loft
Exhibitions: Pieces brought out of reserve collections for exhibit periodically; R J Schaeffer Gallery features two exhibits of maritime art per year
Publications: The Log, quarterly; The Windrose, eight times per year; books
Activities: Classes for adults and children; six-week university courses in American maritime history; lect open to public, 3 vis lectr per year; tours; originate traveling exhibitions; museum shop selling books, magazines, crafts, reproductions, prints, and slides; junior museum
L **G W Blunt White Library,** Greenmanville Ave, 06355. *Librn* Gerald E Morris
Open to members, serious researchers, and students
Library Holdings: Vols 30,000; Per subs 300; Other—Manuscripts 250,000
M **Children's Museum,** Greenmanville Ave, 06355. Tel 203-536-2631. *Dir* J Revell Carr
Open daily summer 9 AM - 5 PM, grounds close at 6 PM; winter 10 AM - 4 PM, grounds close at 5 PM; cl Christmas & New Year's Day. Admis adults $6.50, children (6-12) $3.25; group rates on request. Estab as a view into the life of children who went to sea in the late 19th century. A representation of a ship's cabin depicts the living quarters of a captain's family, complete with furnishings typical of a large sailing vessel. Yard with a boat and mast for climbing
Exhibitions: Children Who Went to Sea

NEW BRITAIN

M **CENTRAL CONNECTICUT STATE COLLEGE MUSEUM,** 1615 Stanley St, 06050. Tel 203-287 7325. *Dir* Isabel S Fairchild
Estab to collect, display and interpret works of art and ethnic materials relating to the art education program
Collections: Collection is currently in storage awaiting construction of a fine arts center, with some pieces on loan

M **NEW BRITAIN MUSEUM OF AMERICAN ART,** 56 Lexington St, 06052. Tel 203-229-0257. *Dir* Charles B Ferguson; *Asst to Dir* Lois L Blomstrann
Open Tues - Sun 1 - 5 PM; Wed Noon - 5 PM. No admis fee. Estab 1903 to exhibit, collect and preserve American art. 18 galleries. Average Annual Attendance: 20,000. Mem: 1000; dues $10

Income: Financed by endowment
Collections: American Art from Colonial Period (1740) to Contemporary (Copley, West, Bierstadt, Church, Homer, Eakins, Sargent, Whistler, Cassatt, Wyeth); Murals by Thomas Hart Benton
Publications: Newsletter, quarterly
Activities: Docent training; lect open to public, 4 vis lectr per year; gallery talks; tours; competitions; individual paintings and original objects of art lent to other museums and institutions; originate traveling exhibitions; museum shop selling books, reproductions, prints, slides and postcards

NEW CANAAN

O **SILVERMINE GUILD SCHOOL OF THE ARTS,** Silvermine Guild, 1037 Silvermine Rd, 06840. Tel 203-866-0411, 966-5617. *Pres Bd Trustees* Michael G Allen; *Gallery Dir* Virginia Mann; *School Dir* Robert Franco; *Publicity Dir* Shirley Land
Open daily 12:30 - 5 PM; cl Mon. No admis fee. Estab 1922 as an independent art center for the exchange of ideas, to provide a place for member artists to show and sell their work, and to offer the community a wide variety of artistic and cultural activities. Four exhibition galleries and Farrell Gallery which contains paintings and sculpture for purchase. Average Annual Attendance: 18,000. Mem: 800; dues sustaining $125, individual $35
Income: Financed by membership and contributions
Collections: Permanent print collection containing purchase prizes from National Print Exhibition
Exhibitions: Biennial National Print Exhibition; New England Exhibition of Painting and Sculpture
Publications: Quarterly newsletter for members
Activities: Classes for adults and children; lect; concerts; competitions; individual paintings and original objects of art lent to corporations and banks

NEW HAVEN

M **MUNSON GALLERY,** 33 Whitney Ave, 06511. Tel 203-865-2121. *Pres* Richard M Pelton
Open Mon - Sat 9:30 AM - 5:30 PM. No admis fee. Estab 1860 to encourage interest in the arts by regular exhibitions of painting, sculpture, graphics, framing and restoration. Located in restored foundry building in New Haven Audubon Street Arts complex
Exhibitions: Gold Jewelry by Claire Martin; Sheridan Gustin; William Harris; Richard Lytle; Orsini; Peter Paskas; Nicholas Von Bydoss

O **NEW HAVEN COLONY HISTORICAL SOCIETY,** 114 Whitney Ave, 06510. Tel 203-562-4183. *Pres* Mrs Frank C Hepler; *Secy* Mrs Ward S Becker Jr; *Dir* Floyd M Shumway; *Cur* Robert Egleston
Open Tues - Fri 10 AM - 5 PM; Sat, Sun & major holidays 2 - 5 PM; cl Mon. No admis fee. Estab 1862 for the preservation, exhibition and research of local scholarly materials, memorabilia and arts. Average Annual Attendance: 15,000. Mem: 1000; dues others $15 - $50, students $7.50; annual meeting Nov
Collections: Morris House (c 1685-1780); †Connecticut Pewter; †New Haven silver, local furniture, paintings, drawings and graphics, and items of local historic interest
Publications: Newsletter; Quarterly Journal
Activities: Active school program; Exhibitions; morning and evening lect series; gift shop
L **Reference Library,** 114 Whitney Ave, 06510. Tel 203-562-4183. *Librn & Manuscripts Cur* Ottilia Koel; *Ref Librn* Lysbeth Andrews-Zike; *Archivist* I O Gould
Open Tues - Fri 10 AM - 5 PM. Estab 1862 to collect, preserve, make available, and publish historical and genealogical material relating to the early settlement and subsequent history of New Haven, its vicinity and incidentally, other parts of the USA. The Society has three departments: museum, library-archives, and educational, with the museum staff taking care of the gallery
Income: Financed by endowment, membership, and grants
Library Holdings: Vols 25,000; Per subs 55; Micro—Fiche, reels; AV—Lantern Slides; Other—Clipping files, exhibition catalogs, prints, manuscripts, memorabilia, pamphlets, photographs, original documents; 30,000 glass plate negatives
Special Subjects: Decorative Arts, Historical Material, Photography
Collections: Noah Webster Collections; John W Barber Collection
Publications: Journal, quarterly-irregular; News and Notes, monthly; monographs; exhibition catalogs
Activities: Arrangement with local colleges for internship programs and work-study programs; students from Southern Connecticut State College Library School do on-site field work and give seminars for graduate students in library science; tours

O **NEW HAVEN PAINT & CLAY CLUB, INC,** The John Slade Ely House, 51 Trumbull St, 06510. Tel 203-624-8055. *Pres* Elizabeth Greeley; *Secy* Donna Infantino
Open Tues - Fri 1 - 4 PM; Sat & Sun 2 - 5 PM; cl Mon. Estab 1900, incorporated 1928. Permanent collection is on display in the Upstairs Galleries of the John Slade Ely House at all times when the house is open. Mem: 290; open to artists working in any media whose work has been accepted two times in the Annual Juried Show; dues life $200, sustaining $20, assoc $5, active $10; annual meeting May
Income: $1000
Purchases: $1000
Exhibitions: Annual exhibition in spring open to all artists, working in any medium; selection and award of prizes by jury. Fall exhibition for members only

M **SOUTHERN CONNECTICUT STATE COLLEGE,** Art Gallery, 501 Crescent St, PO Box 3144, 06515. Tel 203-397-4262. *Dir* Olafs Zeidenbergs
Estab 1976 to build a collection of works of art for educational purposes, gallery developing now. Mem: 300; dues $4 and up
Income: $7500 (financed by membership, state appropriation, and fund raising)
Activities: Lect open to public, 6 visiting lectr per year; gallery talks; national and international tours; exten dept; paintings and objects of art lent to administrative offices

YALE UNIVERSITY

M **Art Gallery,** 1111 Chapel St, Box 2006 Yale Station, 06520. Tel 203-436-0574. *Dir* Alan Shestack; *Cur Education* Janet S Dickson; *Cur Oriental Art* Mary G Neill; *Cur Prints, Drawings & Watercolors* Richard S Field; *Registrar* Fernande Ross; *Membership, Sales & Information* Caroline Rollins; *Supt* Robert Soule
Open Tues - Sat 10 AM - 5 PM, Sun 2 - 5 PM, cl Mon. No admis fee. Estab 1832 to exhibit works of art from ancient times to present. Building designed by Louis Kahn and completed in 1953. Average Annual Attendance: 100,000. Mem: 1200; dues $25 and up
Income: Financed by endowment, membership and annual fund-raising
Collections: American and European painting and sculpture; Garvan Collection of Decorative Arts; Jarves Collection of Italian Renaissance Painting; Stoddard Collection of Greek Vases; History Paintings and Miniatures by John Trumbull; 20th Century Art
Exhibitions: American Watercolors from the Collection of George Hopper Fitch; 50 Years of the Garvan Collection; Real and Imaginary Beings: The Netsuke Collection of Mr and Mrs Joseph Kurstin
Publications: Exhibition catalogues; Yale University Art Gallery Bulletin
Activities: Sunday programs; gallery tours three times per week; Art a la Carte (lunchtime mini-lect); sales desk sells books, catalogues, reproductions, jewelry and postcards

M **Yale Center for British Art,** 1080 Chapel St, Box 2120 Yale Station, 06520. Tel 203-432-4594. *Dir* Edmund P Pillsbury; *Asst Dir Academic Programs* T J Edelstein; *Asst Dir Publications & Information* Constance Clement; *Cur Paintings* Malcolm Cormack; *Cur Prints & Drawings* Andrew Wilton; *Cur Rare Books* Joan Friedman; *Librn* Anne-Marie Logan; *Registrar* Timothy Goodhue; *Conservator Paper* Ursula Dreibholz
Open Tues - Sat 10 AM - 5 PM, Sun 2 - 5 PM, cl Mon. Estab 1977 to foster appreciation and knowledge of British art; to encourage interdisciplinary use of the collections
Income: Financed by endowment and annual gifts
Collections: Drawings, paintings, rare books and sculpture
Exhibitions: Thomas Bewick 1753-1828; Color Printing in England 1486-1870; The Cottage of Content; Prints and Drawings by David Hockney; Augustus John; Prints and Drawings-Recent Acquisitions; Room for Wonder (Indian Miniatures); Rowlandson Drawings from The Paul Mellon Collection; Toys, Games and Amusements of 19th Century England; Wildlife in British Art
Publications: Calendar of Events-Preview of Exhibitions, bi-annually; exhibition catalogues, five per year
Activities: Docent training; lect open to public; concert series; gallery talks; tours; films; symposia; colloquia; scholarships

L **Art and Architecture Library,*** 180 York St, 06520. *Art & Architecture Librn* Nancy Sifferd Lambert; *Slide & Photograph* Helen Chillman
Estab 1868 to serve as the working library for the School of Art, the History of Art department, and the Yale University Art Gallery
Library Holdings: Vols 65,000; AV—Slides 190,000; Other—Photographs and color prints 148,000
Collections: Primarily architecture and contemporary art

NEW LONDON

M **LYMAN ALLYN MUSEUM,** 625 Williams St, 06320. Tel 203-443-2545. *Dir* Dr Edgar DeN Mayhew; *Secy* Mrs Willard Shepard; *Cur* Mrs Arvin Karterud; *Educ Coordinator* Mrs James McGuire; *Conservator* David Kolch; *Docent* Mrs Edward Gipstein
Open Tues - Sat 1 - 5 PM; Sun 2 - 5 PM; cl Mon. No admis fee. Estab 1932 for the education and enrichment of the community and others. The current building consists of nine permanent and four galleries for changing exhibitions. Average Annual Attendance: 22,000. Mem: 750; dues range from individual $10 to life $1000
Income: $133,951 (financed by endowment, membership, and gifts)
Purchases: $6000
Collections: Decorative Arts; Drawings; Paintings; Prints; Sculpture
Exhibitions: New London Art Students Show; New London Bicentennial Exhibition; Photographs by Trager; Aaron Draper Shattuck Collection; Jan Werle One-Man Show; Young Peoples Art Classes Show
Publications: Handbook of the Museum's Outstanding Holdings; New London County Furniture from 1640-1840; New London Silver
Activities: Classes for adults and children; docent training; school tours and programs; lect for members; museum shop sells small antiques

L **Library,** 625 Williams St, 06320. *Librn* Marianne Dinsmore
Open Tues - Sat 1 - 5 PM. Estab 1932 to provide an art reference library as an adjunct to the material in the Lyman Allyn Museum
Income: $2000
Purchases: $2000
Library Holdings: Vols 10,000; Per subs 20; Other—Exhibition catalogs

NORWALK

M **LOCKWOOD-MATHEWS MANSION MUSEUM,** 295 West Ave, 06850. Tel 203-838-1434. *Chmn* Mrs Moreau D Brown; *Pres* Mrs Andrew A Rooney; *Dir* Mrs S B Hamilton Jr
Open Mon - Thurs 9:30 AM - 2:30 PM; Sun 1 - 4 PM. Admis, suggested donation $2, students & senior citizens $1. Estab 1968 to completely restore this 19th century 50-room mansion as a historic house museum. Now a registered National Historic Landmark. Average Annual Attendance: 10,000. Mem: 500; annual meeting May
Income: $29,000 (financed by membership, city and state appropriation, federal grant)
Publications: Newsletter, quarterly
Activities: Docent training; lect open to public, 6 vis lectr per year; gallery talks; tours; museum shop selling books, reproductions, prints, Victorian toys and games

NORWICH

M **NORWICH FREE ACADEMY,** Slater Memorial Museum & Converse Art Gallery, 108 Crescent St, 06360. Tel 203-887-2505, Ext 218. *Dir* Joseph P Gualtieri; *Asst to Dir* Marie E Noyes; *Docent* Mary-Anne Hall; *Registrar* Judith Hamblen
Open Sept - May Mon - Fri 9 AM - 4 PM; Sat & Sun 1 - 4 PM; June - Aug Tues - Sun 1 - 4 PM; cl holidays throughout the year. No admis fee. Estab 1888. The collection is housed in two buildings. Average Annual Attendance: 34,000. Mem: 400; sustaining over $25, patron $25, contributing $15, family $10, single $6; annual meeting usually April
Income: Financed by endowment, student tuition paid by towns
Collections: Vanderpoel Collection of Oriental Art; African Art; American Art and Furniture from the 17th - 20th Centuries; American Indian Artifacts; Egyptian Art Objects and Textiles
Exhibitions: Special exhibitions changed monthly
Publications: Exhibition catalogs
Activities: Lect open to public; competitions; individual paintings and original objects of art lent to museums and historical societies; shop sells postcards

OLD LYME

O **LYME ART ASSOCIATION, INC,** Lyme St, PO Box 222, 06371. Tel 203-434-7802. *Pres* H Gil-Roberts; *VPres* Thomas Torrenti; *Corresp Secy* Ruth Avery; *Recording Secy* Sultana Hanniford; *Treas* Ina Karr
Open seasonally 12 - 5 PM, Sun 1 - 5 PM. Admis 50¢. Estab 1901 to present fine arts in the traditional manner. Four large sky-lighted galleries are maintained. Mem: qualifications for mem is invitational, following acceptance by full mem jury; dues $25; annual meeting Sept
Income: Financed by membership and associate members
Exhibitions: (1980) Three annual exhibitions: 2 open, 1 member only

O **LYME HISTORICAL SOCIETY, INC,** Florence Griswold House, 96 Lyme St, 06371. Tel 203-434-5542. *Pres* George B Tatum; *Dir* Jeffrey W Andersen; *Cur* Bonnie MacAdam
Open (June - Aug) Tues - Sat 10 AM - 5 PM; Sun 1 - 5 PM; (Sept - May) Wed - Fri & Sun 1 - 5 PM. No admis fee. Estab 1953 for the purpose of collecting, preserving and exhibiting the art and history of the Lyme region. Average Annual Attendance: 3500. Mem: 870; dues family $20, individual $10; annual meeting May
Income: $85,000 (financed by endowment, membership, grants, and town appropriation)
Purchases: $1500
Collections: Clara Champlain Griswold Toy Collection; Decorative Arts and Furnishings; Local Historical Collections; Old Lyme Art Colony Paintings
Exhibitions: The Ancient Town of Lyme; The Art Colony at Old Lyme; A Child's World; 19th Century Period Rooms
Publications: The Lyme Ledger, quarterly
Activities: Classes for adults and children; docent training; lect open to public; tours; museum show selling books

L **Lyme Historical Society Archives,** 96 Lyme St, 06371. *Librn* Bonnie MacAdam
Open Mon -Fri 10 AM - 5 PM. Estab 1953 as a research facility for museum programs and for the public. Open to the public for reference
Purchases: $1200
Library Holdings: Vols 900; Per subs 15
Special Subjects: The Art Colony at Old Lyme, American landscape paintings, local history

RIDGEFIELD

M **ALDRICH MUSEUM OF CONTEMPORARY ART,** 258 Main St, 06877. *Pres* Richard E Anderson; *Dir* Dorothy Mayhall; *Cur Education* Jacqueline Moss
Open Wed, Sat & Sun 1 - 5 PM; group visits by appointment. Admis adults $1, students, children and senior citizens 50¢. Estab 1964 for the presentation of contemporary painting and sculpture and allied arts; to stimulate public awareness of contemporary art through exhibitions and education programs. Nine galleries on three floors of a totally renovated colonial building provide well-lit exhibition space; outdoor sculpture garden. Average Annual Attendance: 12,000. Mem: 450; dues $25 - $1000
Income: $130,000 (financed by membership, federal and state grants, corporate and private foundations)
Collections: Aldrich Collection; †extended loan collection; †museum collection of emerging artists; print collection
Exhibitions: (1978-80) Art in the Seventies; Contemporary Reflections: The Sixties Revisited; 15 New Talents; Magical Realism; The Minimal Tradition; Sculptural Forms
Publications: Exhibition catalogs; Newsletter, quarterly
Activities: Classes for adults; docent training; lect open to public, 20 vis lectr per year; concerts; gallery talks; tours; individual paintings lent to museums, university galleries, and corporate patrons; Artreach Program sends docents with slide lect into Fairfield County art classes

ROWAYTON

O **ROWAYTON ARTS CENTER,** 145 Rowayton Ave, 06853. Tel 203-866-2744.
Open daily 2 - 5 PM. No admis fee. Estab 1960 as a non-profit association, to promote arts in the area and to give members an opportunity to exhibit. Exhibition gallery downstairs; upstairs studio room used for classes, slide shows, etc. Mem: 500; dues family $20, single $15; annual meeting in April
Income: Financed by membership, sales and fund raising events
Exhibitions: Changed monthly and remain approximately three weeks
Publications: Arts Center (newsletter), bi-monthly
Activities: Classes for adults and children; workshops; individual paintings and original objects of art lent to local banks for monthly display

STAMFORD

C CHAMPION INTERNATIONAL CORPORATION, 1 Landmark Square, 06921. Tel 203-358-7695. *Interior Design Consultant* Mrs Vibeke Simonsen
Estab 1975 to create a pleasant environment and expose employees to art. Collection displayed on most floors and in executive offices
Collections: Antique European Oils; A Calder; large Helena Hernmark Tapestry; two Henry Moore Lithographs
Exhibitions: Sponsoring a year-long program of exhibitions entitled Concentrations at Whitney Museum of American Art, (main-floor at 71st St and Madison Ave in New York City). Concentrations will consist of one-man exhibitions of eight of America's most outstanding 20th Century artists, such as Alexander Calder, Stuart Davis, Gaston Lachaise and Maurice Prendergast (American Post-Impressionism)

M COUTURIER GALERIE, 1814 Newfield Ave, 06903. Tel 203-322-2405. *Dir* Marion B Couturier; *Assoc Dir* Darrell J Couturier
Open Mon, Thurs, Fri & Sat 11 AM - 4 PM, cl Tues, Wed & Sun, open evening & Sun by special appointment. No admis fee. Estab 1961 to promote and exhibit quality fine art by young artists from around the world with occasional special exhibitions by well established artists
Exhibitions: Christmas From Around the World; International Guest Exhibition of Paintings and Sculpture; Native Painters and Canadian Indian Graphics; Pre-Columbian Art; Sculpture by Francois and Bernard Baschet from France (kinetic, musical); Two Painters and a Sculptor (Favus, Paskin, Bezalel); at Christmas time original ceramics and handblown glass are featured; paintings, sculptures, original graphics. (1980)Josh Paskin Retrospective (American Impressionist Painter); Sculpture by Aharon Bezalel
Activities: Classes for adults, some courses on art history; original objects of art lent to schools, museums and occasional fund raising projects; lending collection contains original art works and prints, paintings, sculpture and Pre-Columbian Art

L FERGUSON LIBRARY, 96 Broad St, 06901. Tel 203-325-4354. *Dir* Ernest A DiMattia Jr; *Art & Music Librn* Phyllis Massar
Open Mon - Fri 9 AM - 9 PM, Sat 9 AM - 5:30 PM. Estab 1880 as a public library dedicated to serving the information needs of the community
Income: Financed by city appropriation
Purchases: $10,000 (art and music books), $16,000 (films), $7500 (records)
Library Holdings: Vols 12,600; AV—Cassettes, motion pictures, rec, slides
Collections: Comprehensive reference collection of photography of Old Stamford
Exhibitions: The Stamford Collection; occasional Community sponsored displays

M STAMFORD MUSEUM AND NATURE CENTER, 39 Scofieldtown Rd, 06903. Tel 203-322-1646. *Pres* Haynes Johnson; *Dir* Gerald E Rasmussen; *Asst Dir* Philip Novak; *Art Dir* Dr Robert Metzger
Open Mon - Sat 9 AM - 5 PM, Sun & holidays 1 - 5 PM, cl Thanksgiving, Christmas & New Year's Day. Admis Stamford residents adults $1, children & senior citizens 50¢, nonresidents adults $2, children & senior citizens 75¢. Estab 1936, Art Department 1955. Average Annual Attendance: 250,000. Mem: 3000; dues $15 and up; annual meeting June
Income: $360,000
Collections: American crafts, American Indian, painting, sculpture, sculpture garden
Exhibitions: (1978-79) Connecticut Painters and Sculptors; 100 Drawings of the 1970's - from collection of Richard Brown Baker; The Eye of the Collector - Dine, Johns, Lichtenstein, Oldenberg, Rauchenberg, Rosenquist, Valenta, Warhol and Wesselmann; The Faces of Ireland - Paintings of Jack B Yeats and sculpture of Helen O'Malley Roelofs; Lifelines: Two Generations - Stallknecht and Wight; Hans Richter - First posthumous retrospective of artist and filmmaker; Stamford Art Association; Stamford Museum Studio Art School Faculty; Stamos - First exhibition of 43 acrylics on paper; Hubert Vos - Retrospective of Dutch-American painter (organized and circulated to Maastricht, Holland)
Publications: Brochure; Newsletter, monthly
Activities: Classes in painting, drawing, sculpture, ceramics and modern dance; lect to school groups; museum shop sells books, prints and crafts

C XEROX CORPORATION, Art Collection, High Ridge Park, 06904. Tel 203-329-8711. *VPres* Robert M Schneider; *Program Consultant* Betty Kuchlich
Collection on display at Xerox Headquarters
Collections: The art collection represents a broad spectrum of American fine art as well as art forms from other countries. The works range from abstraction to realism and consist of sculpture by David Lee Brown located in the lobby, fiberwork by Gerhardt Knodel located in the dining facility, collages, etchings, lithographs, graphics, mezzotints, mono-prints, montages, pastels, photography, pochoir, silkscreens, watercolors and xerography

STONY CREEK

L WILLOUGHBY WALLACE MEMORIAL LIBRARY, 146 Thimble Islands Rd, 06405. Tel 203-488-8702. *Chmn of the Art Committee* D Craig Newton; *Librn* Annelaine Lotreck
Open Mon - Fri 2 - 5 PM and 7 - 9 PM, Sat 10 AM - 5 PM. Estab 1958 to collect, organize and make available print and nonprint resources; provide information, education and recreation for all members of the community. Circ 25,000. Art gallery is maintained
Income: Financed by endowment, city and state appropriation
Library Holdings: Vols 21,000; Per subs 70; AV—Cassettes, rec; Other—Framed reproductions, pamphlets
Collections: Old Photographs of the Area; Stony Creek: Historic Shots of Community
Exhibitions: Christmas Craft Show; Stony Creek Art Show; Stony Creek Photography Show; one-man shows every three weeks
Activities: lect; concerts; movies; reading to children

STORRS

UNIVERSITY OF CONNECTICUT

M William Benton Museum of Art, 06268. Tel 203-486-4520. *Dir* Paul F Rovetti; *Asst Dir* Stephanie Terenzio; *Cur* Thomas P Bruhn; *Exhib Coordr* Hildegard Cummings; *Registrar* George Mazeika
Open during exhibitions Mon - Sat 10 AM - 4:30 PM, Sun 1 - 5 PM, cl summers. No admis fee. Estab 1966, a museum of art, operating as an autonomous department within the University, serving the students, faculty and general public; contributing to the field at large through research, exhibitions and publications and by maintaining a permanent collection of over 2000 objects. The main gallery measures 36 x 116 ft with a balcony (with exhibit walls) running on three walls and two small pendant galleries 20 x 31 ft. Average Annual Attendance: 25,000. Mem: 1200; dues double $12
Income: $9000 (financed by membership and state appropriation)
Collections: †American painting and graphics early 20th Century; †German and French graphics late 19th and 20th Century; †selected 17th and 18th Century European paintings, sculptures and graphics; Western European and American 1600 to Present; paintings, graphics
Exhibitions: American Decorative Tiles (1870 - 1915); The Artist and the Landscape; Robert Motherwell in Black; Connecticut and American Impressionism
Publications: Annual report; Bulletin, annually; Exhibition Catalogs
Activities: Lect open to the public, 4 - 5 vis lectr per year; concerts; gallery talks, tours; individual paintings and original objects of art lent to accredited institutions for exhibition purposes; lending collection contains original prints, paintings and sculpture; originate traveling exhibitions; sales shop sells books, original art, prints, reproductions and museum related art objects and jewelry

M Jorgensen Gallery, U-104, 06268. Tel 203-486-4226. *Mgr Jorgensen Auditorium* Jack Cohan; *Assoc Mgr* Edmund O Seagrave; *Coordr* Stephen E Gerling
Open Mon - Fri 10 AM - 5 PM, Sat - Sun 1 - 5 PM. No admis fee. Estab 1967 to present work by leading contemporary artists of contemporary trends chiefly in American Art. Serves the public as well as the University community. The gallery is 80 X 45 ft with 11 ft ceiling with six portable, self-lit room dividers, track type incandescent lighting, off-white tile floor, neutral colored burlap walls. Average Annual Attendance: 25,000
Exhibitions: Frank Ballard Puppertry; Richard Blake Sculpture; Martha and Walter Erdebacher Painting and Sculpture; Philip Gravsman Sculpture; Stephen Green Photography; Jan Groover Photography; Clinton Hill Prints; Alfred Leslie Drawing; John Matt Sculpture; Peter Mihon Prints; Larry Miller Photography; Renda North Photography; Nathan Olivers Painting; John Pfahl Photography; Jerry Pojo Theatre Design; Richard Yorde Painting; Push-Pin Studios
Publications: Season Announcement; Show Announcement
Activities: Dramatic programs; lect open to the public, 10 vis lectr per year; concerts; gallery talks

L Art and Design Library, Box U-5E, 06268. *Head* Thomas J Jacoby; *Asst Head* Tim Ann Parker
Open Mon - Thurs 9 AM - 10 PM, Fri 9 AM - 5 PM, Sat noon - 6 PM, Sun noon - 10 PM. Estab 1979 to support the Departments of Art, Interior and Textile Design. Circ 14,000
Purchases: $10,000
Library Holdings: Vols 23,000; Per subs 110; Micro—Fiche; Other—Exhibition catalogs
Exhibitions: Continuing exhibits of faculty and student work

WALLINGFORD

O WALLINGFORD ART LEAGUE, Box 163, 06492. *Pres* B Jeanne Kovacs; *VPres* Ray Lynn Farkas; *Secy* Carol Carr
Estab 1945. Average Annual Attendance: Approx 200. Mem: 62; dues $5; meetings Oct - June, second Thurs each month
Income: Approx $500 (financed by membership)
Activities: Classes for adults; lect open to public, 4 visiting lectr per year; scholarships

WASHINGTON DEPOT

O WASHINGTON ART ASSOCIATION, 06793. Tel 203-868-2878. *Pres* Donald Harrison; *VPres* Mrs Robert Middlebrook; *VPres* Mrs Robert Frost; *Executive Secy* Mrs William Talbot; *Secy* Mrs Harold Kihl
Open Mon, Tues, Thurs & Fri 2 - 5 PM, Wed 10 AM - Noon, Sat & Sun 2 - 5 PM. Estab 1952 to make available to the community a variety of art experiences through exhibitions and activities. Gallery is located in three rooms downstairs and one room upstairs for temporary exhibitions. Average Annual Attendance: 4000. Mem: 500; dues family $15, individual $10; annual meeting third week in Aug
Income: $18,000 (financed by endowment, membership and fund-raising events)
Exhibitions: (1978) Lorraine Archacki (drawings & prints); Mary Bonkemeyer (figure drawing); Christmas Show; Anne Close (watercolors): Art in Bloom; Craft Show; Karen DiMeglio (acrylics); Helene Glass (watercolors on Oriental paper); Philip Grausman (sculpture); Eleanor Hubbard (paper sculpture); Marion Humfeld (painting); Humor Show (cartoonists); Kathryn Lipke (handmade paper works); Mercedes Matter (drawings); Members Show; Georgia Middlebrook (drawing & painting); Jane Morse (sculpture & drawings); M Lowell Peyton (watercolors); Photography Show (Reeves, Russell, McGovern); Peter Poskas (painting); Wykeham Rise Alumni
Publications: Events Bulletin, biannually
Activities: Classes for adults and children; trips to major museums and Tanglewood concerts; lect open to the public, 2-3 visiting lectrs per year; competitions

L Library,* 06793. *Librn* Mrs Theodore Fowler
Open to members and teachers for reference
Library Holdings: Vols 250

WATERBURY

L SILAS BRONSON LIBRARY, 267 Grand St, 06702. Tel 203-574-8200. *Dir* Stanford Warshasky; *Head Art Music & Theatre Dept* Patricia Veneziano
Open Mon & Wed 9 AM - 9 PM, Tues Thurs, Fri & Sat 9 AM - 5:30 PM. Estab 1869 to provide a free public library for the community. A spotlighted gallery wall and locked glass exhibition case used for art exhibits
Income: Financed by endowment and city appropriation
Library Holdings: Vols 164,204; Other—34,000 pictures in children's department
Exhibitions: local artists in various media
Activities: Lect open to the public; concerts; individual paintings lent

O MATTATUCK HISTORICAL SOCIETY, Mattatuck Museum, 119 W Main St, 06702. Tel 203-753-0381. *Pres* Orton P Camp Jr; *VPres* W Fielding Secor; *Secy* Mrs William W Brown; *Dir* Ann Smith; *Educ Dir* Dorothy Cantor
Open Tues - Sat noon - 5 PM, Sun 2 - 5 PM, cl Mon. No Admis fee. Estab 1877 to collect and preserve the arts, history of the state of Connecticut, especially of Waterbury and adjacent towns. An art gallery is maintained. Average Annual Attendance: 25,000. Mem: 1000; dues $10 - 500; annual meeting in Nov
Income: $65,000 (financed by endowment, membership and grants)
Collections: Connecticut Artists Collection; Decorative Arts Collection; local history and industrial artifacts; period rooms
Publications: Annual Report
Activities: Classes for adults and children; lect open to the public, 5 vis lectr per year; gallery talks; tours; lending collection contains photographs and slides

WATERFORD

M HARKNESS MEMORIAL STATE PARK, 275 Great Neck Rd, 06385. Tel 203-443-5725. *Park Manager* Theodore J Tetreault Jr
Grounds open 8 AM - Sunset year round; buildings open Memorial Day to Labor Day 10 AM - 5 PM. Parking fee $1. Estab 1954. Average Annual Attendance: 125,000
Income: Financed by state appropriation
Collections: Complete collection of artist Rex Brasher: Birds of North American, (874 watercolor paintings)
Activities: Sales shop sells black and white prints of the paintings

WEST HARTFORD

M UNIVERSITY OF HARTFORD, Joseloff Gallery, Hartford Art School, 200 Bloomfield Ave, 06117. Tel 203-243-4393. *Dean* Edwin E Stein; *Gallery Coordr* Joan Saunders
Open Mon - Fri 9 AM - 4:30 PM. No admis fee. Estab 1964 primarily for the education of the students, but is also for the aesthetic enjoyment of the art interested public. The gallery is 40 x 60 x 13 ft high and can be divided into two rooms. Average Annual Attendance: Several thousand
Exhibitions: American Indian Exhibit (Martinez Family pottery, Navajo Rugs, Hopi Kachina Dolls); Connecticut Illustrators Exhibition; The Early Years (Hartford Art School 1877 - 1940); Faculty Exhibition; Graduate Thesis Exhibition; Installation (Andrea Blum, Stephen Zalma and Elyn Zimmerman); Juried Student Exhibition; The Reproductive Media (film, photography, video); various student exhibitions
Publications: The Hartfor Art School: The Early Years
Activities: Classes for adults; lectures open to the public, 20 - 30 vis lectr per yr; concerts; gallery talks; tours; competitions; individual paintings and original objects of art lent to area businesses and institutions; book traveling exhibitions; traveling exhibitions organized and circulated

L Anne Bunce Cheney Library, University of Hartford, 200 Bloomfield Ave, 06117. Tel 203-243-4397. *Art Librn* Jean J Miller; *Library Asst* Anna Bigazzi
Open Mon - Thurs 8:30 AM - 10 PM, Fri 8:30 AM - 5 PM, Sat & Sun Noon - 5 PM. Estab 1964. Circ 9689
Income: Financed through University Library
Library Holdings: Vols 11,000; Per subs 83; Other—Exhibition catalogs, pamphlets, reproductions

WILTON

M CRAFT CENTER MUSEUM, 80 Danbury Rd, 06897. Tel 203-762-8363. *Pres* Kenneth Lynch; *Secy* Otto Gust; *Dir* Carroll Cavanaugh; *Dir* Harvey Muston; *Cur* Joseph Henry
Open Mon - Fri 10 AM - 4 PM (Mar - Dec), cl Jan & Feb. No admis fee. Estab 1956 to exhibit and explain 17th - 19th Century handwork, blacksmithing, casting and woodwork. Maintains gallery for exhibitions. Mem: 12; annual meeting in April
Library Holdings: Vols 3000; Other—Photographs
Collections: Armor, brass casting, copper, furnishing, lead, leather, lighting, silversmithing, wood, tools and finished products in areas of metal spinning

DELAWARE

DOVER

M DIVISION OF HISTORICAL AND CULTURAL AFFAIRS, Bureau of Museums and Historic Sites, Court Street and Legislative Ave, PO Box 1401, 19901. Tel 302-678-5314. *Division Dir* Lawrence Henry; *Chief Bureau of Museums and Historic Sites* Michael Shapiro; *Cur Coll* Ann Horsey; *Cur Exhib* Mrs Dominique C Western; *Cur Education* Madeline Hite; *Cur Historic Buildings* James Stewart; *Cur Archaeology* Merrilea Cowan
Delaware State Museum, John Dickinson Mansion, Old State House, Zwaanendael Museum, Island Field Museum, New Castle Court House, Fort Christina; Tues - Sat 10 AM - 4:30 PM, Sun 1:30 - 4:30 PM; Prince George's Chapel, Fri & Sat 10 AM - 4:30 PM, Sun 1:30 PM - 4:30 PM; Allee House, Octagonal School, Sat & Sun 1:30 - 4:30 PM; Hale-Byrnes House open by appointment only; The Lindens, daily 10 AM - 4:30 PM; Robinson House, Wed 11 AM - 4 PM, first Sun of month, 1 - 4 PM, cl State Legal Holidays. No admis fee. Historic house museums were opened in the 1950s, Zwaanendael Museum 1931, to reflect the pre-historic and historic development of Delaware by exhibiting artifacts and interpreting the same through various facilities. Delaware State Museum, General Museum, housed in c1790, Old Presbyterian Church; Old State House, historic building, c1792, second oldest State House in continuous use, second State House of Delaware and site of first State Constitutional Convention; John Dickinson Mansion, historic house c1740, boyhood home of John Dickinson who drafted the Articles of Confederation; Octagonal School, 1836 schoolhouse, one of the earliest remaining educational structures; Allee House, historic house, c1753, example of vernacular architecture of 18th century Delaware; Hale-Byrnes House, historic house and site, c1750, house where General George Washington and Lafayette met for war council before the Battle of Brandywine; New Castle Court House, historic buildings and site, constructed in 1730 and located on the Green laid out by Peter Stuyvesant in 1655; in 1776 the Declaration of Independence and the first constitution of Delaware were approved; in 1777 the first president of the State of Delaware, John McKinley was elected there; Zwaanendael Museum, history museum, house in an adaptation of the Old Town Hall in Hoorn, Holland; Fort Christina Monument and Park, historic site, 1836 site of the first landing of the Swedish in North America; Island Field Museum, Anthropology and Archaeology Museum, located on the site of prehistoric Indian cemetery, circa 600 - 900 AD; Prince George's Chapel, historic building, 1755 chapel built by the Church of England; The Lindens, historic house, begun in 1705, one of the oldest surviving structures related to a mill village in northern Kent County; Robinson House, historic C1723, used as an inn and visited by General George Washington in 1777
Income: $650,000
Collections: Allee House—furniture and decorative arts; Delaware State Museum—work of Delaware and US silversmiths, ceramics, furnishings, costumes, Indian artifacts; John Dickinson Mansion—Dickinson family furnishings; Hale-Byrnes House—furnishings and decorative arts; Island Field Museum—archaeological remains, artifacts; The Lindens—furniture and decorative arts; New Castle Court House—portraits of famous Delawareans, archaeological artifacts, furniture and maps; Old State House—legislative, judicial and governmental furniture and decorative arts; Prince George's Chapel—ecclesiastical furniture and decorative arts; Robinson House—furniture and decorative arts; Zwaanendael Museum—Indian artifacts and Colonial items pertaining to the early history of Lewes and lower Delaware, commemorative gifts to the State of Delaware from Holland, china, glass, and silver
Publications: Delaware State Museum Bulletins; Delaware History Notebook; miscellaneous booklets and brochures
Activities: Classes for children; docent training; special educational programs for school groups and adults which reflect the architecture, government, education and aspects of social history relevant to Delaware; Artmobile; individual paintings are lent to governmental facilities; traveling trunk program originated and circulated to elementary schools; museum shop sells books, magazines, prints, slides

NEWARK

UNIVERSITY OF DELAWARE
M Student Center Art Gallery,* 19711. Tel 302-738-2630. *Dir* Jack S Sturgell
Open daily Noon - 5 PM, shorter hours during vacation. Estab 1926 to enlarge the student's acquaintance with art in its various aspects. Average Annual Attendance: 10,000
Exhibitions: Change monthly; include traveling exhibitions from prominent museums and organizations as well as from the University collections; annual exhibition of University students' work; yearly juried show of regional artists
Activities: Book traveling exhibitions
M University Art Collections,* 19711. Tel 302-Archivist's Office 738-2750; Art History Collection 738-2418. *University Archivist & Dir Permanent Coll* John M Clayton; *Cur Slide & Photograph Library & Art History Teaching Coll* Charlotte Kelly
No admis fee. Estab to consolidate the gifts of art to the University and to provide exhibitions of art objects from these collections to increase visual awareness on the campus. Several exhibition areas around campus Morris Library, Clayton Hall, Smith Hall mini-exhibition cases. Average Annual Attendance: 4000
Income: Financed by state appropriation
Collections: Art History Teaching Collection of 600 art objects, including painting, sculpture (primarily American, African and pre-Columbian), and prints; permanent collection of 500 art objects including painting, sculpture and prints
Publications: Bulletins
M University Gallery, Museum Studies Department, University of Delaware, 19711. Tel 302-738-1251, 738-1117. *Dir Museum Studies & Art Conservation* William T Alderson
Estab 1978
L Morris Library,* South College Ave, 19711. Tel 302-738-2231. *Dir of Libraries* Dr John M Dawson; *Chief Reference Librn* Katharine M Wood; *Reference Librn (Art & Art History)* Susan A Davi
Open Mon - Thurs 8 AM - 1:30 PM, Fri 8 AM - 10 PM, Sat 9 AM - 5 PM, Sun

1 - 11:30 PM (when in session). Estab 1834 as University Library
Income: Financed through the University
Purchases: $56,000
Library Holdings: Vols 30,000; Per subs 100; Micro—Fiche, reels; AV—Rec; Other —Exhibition catalogs, pamphlets
Collections: American Art and Architecture; Early 20th Century European Art; material on Ornamental Horticulture

REHOBOTH BEACH

O **REHOBOTH ART LEAGUE, INC,*** Henlopen Acres, PO Box 84, 19971. Tel 302-227-8408. *Pres* Lucile K Megee; *Exec VPres* Sandford B Leach; *Exec Secy* Ruth Chambers Stewart
Open March 30 - Sept 30 daily 10 AM - 5 PM. No admis fee. Estab 1938 to provide art education and creative arts in Rehoboth Beach community and Sussex County, Delaware. Two galleries display members' works and outstanding invited artists; one small sales gallery maintained for members' works. Mem: 1050; dues $15 and up; annual meeting last Mon in Aug
Income: Financed by membership, donation and fund raising sales of paintings
Collections: Small permanent collection from gifts
Exhibitions: Bicentennial Exhibition; annual exhibitions
Publications: Brochure of yearly events; newsletters
Activities: Classes for adults and children; lect open to public; concerts; competitions; scholarships; artmobile; sales shop selling original art and prints

WILMINGTON

O **COUNCIL OF DELAWARE ARTISTS,** c/o Vernon L Good, 910 Orange St, 19801. Tel 302-655-8935. *Pres* Vernon L Good; *VPres* Connie Wahl; *Secy* Betty Blumenburg
Estab 1955 to educate the membership and the public about significant aspects of the creative arts including discussions, lectures and exhibitions pertaining to the visual arts and to provide continuous exposure of member's work through exhibitions; to establish an atmosphere of fellowship and cooperation among professional artist members. Mem: 60; dues $10; annual meeting in May
Publications: Newsletter
Activities: Lect open to public; 9 vis lectr per year; individual paintings lent to schools, public offices, retirement homes and banks; originate traveling exhibitions

M **DELAWARE ART MUSEUM,** 2301 Kentmere Parkway, 19806. *Acting Dir & Cur* Rowland P Elzea; *Asst Cur & Cur John Sloan Archives* Elizabeth Hawkes; *Cur of Education* Diane B Stillman; *Dir of Development* Thomas L Sherman; *Mgr Supv Services* Stephen Bruni; *Registrar* Mary Holahan
Open Mon - Sat 10 AM - 5 PM, Sun 1 - 5 PM. Admis adults $1, students 50¢, persons under 12 and over 65 free. Incorporated 1912 as the Wilmington Society of Fine Arts; present building completed in 1935; a privately funded, non-profit cultural and educational institution dedicated to the increase of knowledge and pleasure through the display and interpretation of works of art and through classes designed to encourage an understanding of and a participation in the fine arts. Six galleries are used for exhibitions; five usually hold permanent or semi-permanent exhibitions which change at approximately six week intervals. Exhibitions are also held in the library and the education wing. Average Annual Attendance: 35,000. Mem: 2000; dues family $25, individual $15; annual meeting third Tues in Oct
Income: $552,000 (financed by endowment, membership and grants)
Purchases: $6500
Collections: Bancroft Collection of English Pre-Raphaelite Paintings; †Copeland Collection of Work by Local Artists Phelps Collection of Andrew Wyeth Works; †American Paintings and Sculpture, including many Howard Pyle works and complete etchings and lithographs of John Sloan
Exhibitions: (1977-78) American Art Pottery; Art Off the Picture Press; Accessible Arts; Bertha Corson Day; Delaware Exhibition Prizewinners: Frederick Guthrie, Stephen Tanis, Donna Usher; Flaking, Foxing and Fine Works: A Conservative Exhibition; France Views America; New Deal for Art; Photographs by Arnold Newman; Chalres Lee Reese, Print Collector; 63rd Annaul Delaware Exhibition; 64th Annual Delaware Exhibition; Kirk Sterling: Craftmanship in Silver; Stichery 77; 21st Annual Contemporary Crafts Exhibition; 22nd Annual Contemporary Crafts Exhibition; Julio DaCunha; F O C Darley; Hayiey Lever Russell Patterson. (1979)The American Magazine: 1890 - 1940; Edward Moran
Publications: DAM Bulletin, monthly
Activities: Classes for adults and children; docent training; workshops; lect open to the public and occasionally to members only, 6 vis lectr per year; concerts; gallery talks; tours; competitions; exten dept serving schools and community groups offering two-week programs in visual education; originate traveling exhibitions; museum and sales shops sell books, candles, jewelry, note cards, paper, original art, prints, reproductions, slides and crafts

M **Downtown Gallery,** Bank of Delaware, 901 Market St, 19801. *Mgr* Eric Robinson
Serves businessmen and shoppers in downtown area

L **Library,** 2301 Kentmere Parkway, 19806. *Librn* 10; *Library Asst* Deborah Litwack
Open Mon - Fri 10 AM - 4:30 PM. Estab 1923. Open to students, scholars for reference only
Library Holdings: Vols 20,000; Micro—Reels; Other—Clipping files, exhibition catalogs, prints, manuscripts, memorabilia, original art works, pamphlets, photographs
Special Subjects: American Art 19th - 20th Century, American Illustration, Pre-Raphaelite Art
Collections: John Sloan Archives

M **HAGLEY MUSEUM,** Eleutherian Mills-Hagley Foundation, Barley Mill Rd & Brandywine Creek, Wilmington, DE. (Mailing Add: PO Box 3630, Greenville, DE 19807) Tel 302-658-2401. *General Dir* Dr Walter J Heacock
Open Tues - Sat 9:30 AM - 4:30 PM; Sun 1 - 5 PM. Admis adults $2.50, senior citizens $1.25, students $1, children under 14 with adults free. Estab 1952; museum first opened to public in 1957, to preserve and interpret the site of the original Du Pont black powder works and tell the story of the early history of industry on the Brandywine. The 1803 home of E I duPont, furnished to illustrate the lifestyle of five generations of duPonts, is open year round. Average Annual Attendance:

100,000. Mem: 600; dues family $25, single $15
Income: Financed by endowment and grants
Exhibitions: Changing exhibits
Publications: Annual Report; Guide Books; Newsletter, three per year
Activities: Lect for members; tours; museum shop selling books, reproductions, prints, slides

L **Eleutherian Mills Historical Library,** PO Box 3630, 19807. *Dir* Dr Richmond Williams
Open Mon - Fri to students, and to researchers by appointment
Library Holdings: Vols 120,000; Other—Manuscripts 10 million, photographs 246,000

HISTORICAL SOCIETY OF DELAWARE

M **Old Town Hall Museum and Dingee House Gallery,*** Sixth & Market Sts, 19801. Tel 302-655-7161.
Open Tues - Fri Noon - 4 PM, Sat 10 AM - 4 PM. No admis fee

M **Read House, The Strand,*** Sixth & Market Sts, 19801. Tel 302-322-8411. *Acting Dir* James R Lacey; *Museum Cur* Roland H Woodward
Open Tues - Sat 10 AM - 4 PM, Sun Noon - 4 PM, cl New Year's, Thanksgiving and Christmas. Admis adults $2, sr citizens and children 75¢. Estab 1864 to record and preserve Delaware History. Average Annual Attendance: 15,000. Mem: 1200; dues $10 and up
Income: $100,000
Collections: Costumes; †Delaware pictures; †furniture; manuscripts; †silver
Activities: Educ programs; special programs arranged; lect; tours

L **Library,*** 505 Market St, 19801. Tel 302-655-7161. *Dir of Libraries* Gladys M Coghlan
Open Mon 1 - 9 PM, Tues - Fri 9 AM - 5 PM
Library Holdings: Vols 75,000
Special Subjects: American and Delaware history

C **WILMINGTON TRUST COMPANY,** 100 W Tenth St, 19899. *VPres* C R McPherson
Open to public by appointment only. No admis fee. Estab 1942 to support Delaware artists in watercolors. Collection displayed statewide in branch offices
Collections: Primarily Delaware scenes by Delaware artists

WINTERTHUR

M **WINTERTHUR MUSEUM AND GARDENS,** Route 52, 19735. Tel 302-656-8591. *Pres* John A Herdeg; *Dir* James Morton Smith; *Deputy Dir Collections* Charles F Hummel; *Deputy Dir Interpretation* Scott T Swank; *Deputy Dir Finance & Administration* Wesley A Adams; *Asst to the Dir* John A H Sweeney; *Cur* Nancy E Richards; *Registrar* Nancy Goyne Evans; *Editor Publications Office* Ian M G Quimby; *Head of Public Relations* Catherine Wheeler
Main Museum tours by reservation only early June - mid April daily except Mon & major holidays; non-reserved tours Tues - Sat 10 AM - 4 PM, Sun noon - 4 PM, cl major holidays except Mon holidays when open noon - 4 PM. Admis reserved tour $6, $3 for ages 12 - 16, under 12 not admitted to the Main Museum; non-reserved tour price vary with season. Corporation estab in 1930, museum opened in 1951. Two hundred rooms and display areas featuring decorative arts made or used in America between 1640 and 1840; sixty acres of horticultural displays in the Gardens. Average Annual Attendance: 120,000. Mem: 2300; dues $25 - $35
Income: Approximately $5,000,000 (financed by endowment, membership, grants for special projects)
Collections: Pennsylvania German Folk Art; ceramics, furniture, glassware, interior architecture, metals, needlework, paintings, prints and textiles
Publications: Publications and articles by staff, including Winterhur Portfolio, quarterly; Annual Report
Activities: Docent training; Winterthur Program in Early American Culture, a graduate program sponsored with the University of Delaware; Winterthur Program in the Conservation of Artistic and Historic Objects, a graduate program co-sponsored by the University of Delaware; lect open to the public and to members only; yuletide tours; individual paintings and original objects of art lent to museums and historical societies; museum shop sells books, gifts, postcards, plants and slides

M **Historic Odessa,** Rte 52, 19730. *Cur Corbit-Sharp & Wilson-Warner Houses* Horace L Hotchkiss
Open Tues - Sat 10 AM - 5 PM, Sun 2 - 5 PM, cl National holidays. Located 23 miles south of Wilmington, Odessa is a community of restored 18th and 19th century houses, including many fine examples of early Delaware Valley architecture such as the Corbit-Sharp House (1774) and Wilson-Warner House (1769)

L **Library,** Route 52, 19735. *Head, Library Division* Dr Frank H Sommer III; *Printed Books & Periodicals* Eleanor Thompson; *Slides* Kathryn McKenney; *Manuscripts & Microfilm* Mrs James Taylor; *Archivist* Barbara Hearn; *Decorative Arts Photographic Collections* Deborah D Waters
Open Mon - Fri 8:30 AM - 4:30 PM, 1st Sat of Month, March - Dec. Estab for research in American Decorative Arts and their European antecedents through World War I. For reference only
Library Holdings: Vols 50,000; Micro—Fiche, reels; AV—Motion pictures, rec, slides; Other—Exhibition catalogs, prints, manuscripts, memorabilia, original art works, pamphlets, photographs, reproductions, auction catalogues; architectural drawings
Special Subjects: , American decorative arts, museology
Collections: Belknap Library; Edward Deming Andrews Memorial Shaker Collection; Decorative Arts Photographic Collection; Henry A duPont and Henry F duPont Papers; Thelma S Mendsen Card Collection; Maxine Waldron Collection of Children's Books and Paper Toys

DISTRICT OF COLUMBIA

WASHINGTON

AMERICAN ASSOCIATION OF MUSEUMS
For further information, see National and Regional Organizations

AMERICAN ASSOCIATION OF UNIVERSITY WOMEN
For further information, see National and Regional Organizations

AMERICAN INSTITUTE FOR CONSERVATION OF HISTORIC AND ARTISTIC WORKS (AIC)
For further information, see National and Regional Organizations

AMERICAN INSTITUTE OF ARCHITECTS
For further information, see National and Regional Organizations

M **AMERICAN INSTITUTE OF ARCHITECTS FOUNDATION,** The Octagon, 1799 New York Ave NW, 20006. Tel 202-638-3105. *Pres* Jeanne B Hodges; *Cur Octagon* Alison M MacTavish
Open Tues - Fri 10 AM - 4 PM; Sat & Sun 1 - 4 PM. Admis by donation; groups over 10 charges $1 per person except student and senior citizens groups 50¢ per person. Opened as house museum in 1970; formerly a federal townhouse built by Col John Tayloe III to serve as a winter home; used by President & Mrs Madison as temporary White House during war of 1812. Furnished with late 18th and early 19th century decorative arts; changing exhibition program in second floor galleries. Average Annual Attendance: 18,000
Collections: Permanent collection of furniture, paintings, ceramics, kitchen utensils
Exhibitions: Changing exhibitions - A Celebration of Diversity: Planning the International Center; A Child's Christmas - Toys & Traditions; A Gift to the Street: A Pattern Book of Victorian Architecture; Capitol Losses - A Eulogy; Just for Fun; Two on Two at the Octagon
Publications: Competition 1792-Designing a Nation's Capitol, book; Dolley and the Great Little Madison, book; exhibition catalogs; Octagon Being an Account of a Famous Washington Residence: Its Great Years, Decline and Restoration, book; Selections from the AIA Architectural Archives, book; William Thornton: A Renaissance Man in the Federal City, book
Activities: Educ dept; docent training; tours; lectr for members only, 2-3 vis lectr per yr; sales shop selling books, prints and slides
L **Library,** The Octagon, 1799 New York Ave, NW, 20006. *Librn* Alison M MacTavish
Open to the public for reference but primarily used by staff
Library Holdings: Vols 200; Per subs 10
Special Subjects: Architecture, Decorative Arts, History of the Octagon and the Tayloe Family

AMERICAN RED CROSS
For further information, see National and Regional Organizations

M **AMERICAN UNIVERSITY,** Watkins Art Gallery, Massachusetts and Nebraska Ave NW, 20016. Tel 202-686-2114. *Chmn* Robert D'Arista
Open Mon - Fri 10 AM - Noon & 1 - 4 PM. No admis fee. Estab 1943 to exhibit art of interest to public and university art community; schedule includes occasional education or theme shows and student exhibits. Maintains large room with moveable panels and one small exhibit room with attendant's desk. Average Annual Attendance: 2000 plus art students
Collections: Watkins Collection of 19th and 20th century American and European paintings
Exhibitions: (1979-80) Jack Boul; Leonard Maurer; Selections from the Watkins Collection; Faculty Exhibition
Activities: Educ dept; docent training; lect open to the public, 3-5 vis lectr per yr; individual paintings and original objects of art lent to museums and university galleries; traveling exhibitions organized and circulated on occasion

M **ANACOSTIA NEIGHBORHOOD MUSEUM,*** 2405 Martin Luther King, Jr Ave SE, 20020. Tel 202-381-5656. *Dir* John R Kinard; *Exhib Program Dir* Victor M Govier
Open Mon - Fri 10 AM - 6 PM, Sat, Sun and holidays 1 - 6 PM, cl Christmas. No admis fee. Estab 1967, as a non-profit federally chartered corporation to record and research African, Black American and Anacostia history and urban problems
Collections: Afro-American and African Art; Afro-American History
Publications: Educational booklets; exhibit programs; museum brochures
Activities: Programs for children and adults; lect; tours; gallery talks; art festivals; traveling exhibitions organized and circulated; sales shop
L **Library,*** 2405 Martin Luther King, Jr Ave SE, 20020.
Open to the public for research on the premises
Library Holdings: Vols 1000

M **ANDERSON HOUSE MUSEUM,** Society of the Cincinnati, 2118 Massachusetts Ave NW, 20008. Tel 202-785-2040. *Dir* John D Kilbourne
Open Tues - Sat 2 - 5 PM, special hours on request by groups for guided tours, cl National holidays. No admis fee. The Society of the Cincinnati was founded in May 1783; the museum was opened to the public in 1938. Anderson House Museum is a National museum for the custody and preservation of historical documents, relics and archives, especially those pertaining to the American Revolution. Because of its superb building (1905, Little and Browne, Boston architects), original furnishings and collections of Western and Oriental art, Anderson House Museum is also a Historic House Museum. On the first floor of the house are portraits of founding members of the Society by Gilbert Stuart, George Catlin, Ezra Ames and other early American painters. Average Annual Attendance: 12,000
Collections: Figureines of the French regiments that fought at Yorktown, Virginia in 1781 and others; †historical material; Japanese screens, bronzes, ceramics, jade; Oriental works of art; 16th and 17th Century Flemish tapestries, sculpture and period furniture; paintings
Exhibitions: Rotating exhibitions; the permanent collection
Publications: Annual Report of the director; A Few Questions and Answers regarding the Society of the Cincinnati, Brochures; George Rogers Clark Lectures on American History (3 volumns published); The Sword and Firearm Collection of the Society of the Cincinati

ARTISTS EQUITY ASSOCIATION, INC
For further information, see National and Regional Organizations

M **ARTS CLUB OF WASHINGTON,** James Monroe House, 2017 Eye St NW, 20006. Tel 202-331-7282. *Pres* Dr Henry Lea Mason; *VPres* C Dudley Brown; *Treas* Albert L Yarashus; *Recording Secy* Mary Cates; *Corresp Secy* Jeanne Rose
Open daily 11 AM - 5 PM; cl holidays. Founded 1916. The James Monroe House (1803-1805) was built by Timothy Caldwell of Philadelphia. It is registered with the National Register of Historic Places, the Historical Survey 1937 and 1968, and the National Trust for Historic Preservation. James Monroe, fifth President of the United States, resided in the house while he was Secretary of War and State. During the first six months of his Presidency (1817-1825) the house served as the Executive Mansion, since the White House had been burned in the War of 1812 and had not yet been restored. Mem: 250; annual meeting April
Activities: Monthly lect; exhibitions; scholarships

ASSOCIATION OF COLLEGIATE SCHOOLS OF ARCHITECTURE
For further information, see National and Regional Organizations

M **B'NAI B'RITH EXHIBIT HALL,** 1640 Rhode Island Ave, Northwest, 20036. Tel 202-857-6583. *Dir* Anna R Cohn
Open Sun - Fri 10 AM - 5 PM, cl Sat and Jewish holidays. No admis fee. Estab 1957 for exhibits by Jewish artists. Five galleries
Income: Financed by B'nai B'rith International
Collections: Permanent collection of pre-twentieth century Jewish ceremonial and folk art; ancient coins; archives of B'nai B'rith
Exhibitions: Two to four changing exhibitions annually
Publications: Exhibitions brochures
Activities: Holiday family education program; children's program; lect; films
L **Library,** 20036.
Library Holdings: Vols 8000; Other—Manuscripts, photographs

L **CATHOLIC UNIVERSITY OF AMERICA,** Humanities Division, Mullen Library,* 620 Michigan Ave NE, 20064. Tel 202-635-5075. *Head Humanities Division* B Gutekunst
Open fall & spring terms Mon - Thurs 9 AM - 10 PM, Fri & Sat 9 AM - 5 PM, Sun 1 - 10 PM. Estab 1958 to offer academic resources and services that are integral to the work of the institution
Library Holdings: Vols 6700; Other—Prints

O **COMMISSION OF FINE ARTS,*** 708 Jackson Place NW, 20006. Tel 202-566-1066. *Chmn* J Carter Brown
Open daily 8 AM - 4:30 PM. Estab by Act of Congress in 1910 to advise the President, Members of Congress, and various governmental agencies on matters pertaining to the appearance of Washington, DC. The Commission of Fine Arts is composed of seven members, three architects, one landscape architect, one painter, one sculptor, and one layman, who are appointed by the President for four-year terms. Report issued periodically. Plans for all new projects in the District of Columbia under the direction of the Federal and District of Columbia Governments which in any important way affect the appearance of the city, and all questions involving matters of art with which the Federal Government is concerned must be submitted to the Commission for comment and advice before contracts are made. Also gives advice on suitability of designs of private buildings in certain parts of the city adjacent to of the various departments and agencies of the District and Federal Governments, the Central Mall, Rock Creek Park, and Georgetown

M **CORCORAN GALLERY OF ART,** 17th St and New York Ave NW, 20006. Tel 202-638-3211. *Pres* David Lloyd Kreeger; *Dir* Peter C Marzio; *Assoc Dir* Jane Livingston; *Cur* Edward J Nygren; *Registrar* Susan Williams
Open Tues - Sun 10 AM - 4:30 PM cl Mon and holidays. No admis fee. Founded 1869 primarily for the encouragement of American art. The nucleus of the collection of American Paintings was formed by its founder, William Wilson Corcoran, early in the second half of the 19th century. In 1925 a large wing designed by Charles A Platt was added to house the European collection bequested by Senator William Andrews Clark. The Walker Collection, formed by Edward C and Mary Walker, added important French Impressionists to the collection upon its donation in 1937. Average Annual Attendance: 200,000. Mem: 3000; dues contributing $500 and up, sponsor $250, Friends of the Corcoran $100, family $35, single $25, student and senior citizen $15
Collections: The American collection of paintings, watercolors, drawings, sculpture and photgraphy from the 18th through 20th centuries; The European Collection includes paintings and drawings by Dutch, Flemish, English and French artists; 18th century French salon, furniture, laces, rugs, majolica; Gothic and Beauvais tapestries; Greek antiquities; 13th century stained glass window and bronzes by Antoine Louise Barye; tryptich by Andrea Vanni; Walker Collection of French Impressionists
Exhibitions: Changing exhibitions of Contemporary Art; Fine Art Photography; Works by regional artists; works drawn from the permanent collection
Publications: Calendar of Events (for members)
Activities: Docent service; children's programs; tours; lect; concerts; shop sells exhibition catalogs, books, notecards, reproductions and art periodicals
L **Library,** 17th St and New York Ave NW, 20006. *Archivist* Katherine M Kovacs
Available for inter-library loan and for public use by appointment only
Library Holdings: Vols 4500
Special Subjects: Art History

M **DAR MUSEUM,** National Society Daughters of the American Revolution, 1776 D St NW, 20006. Tel 202-628-1776. *Cur* Jean Taylor Federico
Open Mon - Fri 9 AM - 4 PM. No admis fee. Estab 1890 for collection and exhibition of decorative arts used in America from 1700 - 1840, for the study of objects, and preservation of Revolutionary artifacts (including uniforms and weapons), and documentation of American life. There are 29 period rooms which reflect the decorative arts of particular states, also a museum which houses large collections grouped by ceramics, paintings, glass and furniture. Average Annual

Attendance: 12,000. Mem: 205,000; dues $15 - $17; annual meeting in April
Income: Under $100,000 (financed by membership)
Purchases: Under $20,000
Collections: †Ceramics, †paintings, †prints, †furniture
Exhibitions: Special exhibitions arranged and changed periodically, usually every 2 - 3 months
Activities: Classes for children; docent training; lectures, 3 - 4 vis lectr per year; gallery talks; tours; exten dept serves third to sixth grades; A Suitcase is a traveling museum for local schools; paintings and original art works lent to museums; sales shop sells books, slides, stationery, dolls and DAR souvenirs
L Library, 1776 D St NW, 20006.
Open to public by advance notice; for reference only
Library Holdings: Vols 2000; Per subs 4
Special Subjects: American Decorative Arts

M DECATUR HOUSE, 748 Jackson Pl NW, 20006. Tel 202-387-4062. *Adminr* Earl James; *Asst Adminr* Robert Mawson; *Admin Asst* Vicki Sopher
Open Tues - Fri 10 AM - 2 PM, Sat & Sun Noon - 4 PM, cl Mon. Admis adults $1.50, students & senior citizens 50¢, National Trust Members free. Estab 1958, bequeathed to National Trust for Historic Preservation by Mrs Truxton Beale to foster appreciation and interest in the history and culture of the city of Washington, DC. The House is a Federal period townhouse designed by Benjamin Henry Latrobe and completed in 1819. Average Annual Attendance: 15,000. Mem: National Trust members
Income: Financed by endowment and membership
Collections: Furniture and memorabilia of the Federal period; Victorian house furnishings
Exhibitions: Special exhibits
Activities: Tours; summer lunchtime concerts; workshops; sales shop

M DEPARTMENT OF STATE, Diplomatic Reception Rooms, 2201 C St NW, 20520. Tel 202-632-0298. *Cur* Clement E Conger; *Asst Cur* Gail F Serfaty; *Staff Asst* Patricia Heflin; *Cur Asst* Kathryn McCutchen
Open for 3 public tours by reservation only Tues - Fri. No admis fee. Estab unofficially 1961, officially 1971 to entertain foreign dignitaries. These rooms allow foreign visitors to view furniture of the American Colonies period handcrafted by the colonists. Nine rooms are furnished in 18th century American furniture and silver, Chinese porcelain and antique Persian rugs. Average Annual Attendance: 70,000
Collections: Antique Persian rugs; 18th century American furniture, silver and Chinese porcelain
Publications: Guidebook; Silver Supplement to the Guidebook
Activities: tours given Tues through Fri; Paintings and original art objects lent to special national antique furniture and art gallery exhibitions

O FEDERAL DESIGN COUNCIL,* PO Box 7537, 20044. Tel 202-755-8332. *Pres* Robert Schulman
Organized in 1970 by a group of Federal art directors and design managers concerned with the design image of the Government. The Council has worked with the National Endowment for the Arts; with the Civil Service Commission; with the Government Printing Office and the General Services Administration. Mem: Dues $20; regular meetings held
Income: Financed by membership
Exhibitions: Federal Design Response Exhibition
Publications: Next Issue (newsletter), 4-6 issues
Activities: Visual communications programs; lect open to members only, 5-8 visiting lectrs per year; tours

L FOLGER SHAKESPEARE LIBRARY, 201 E Capitol St SE, 20003. Tel 202-546-4800. *Dir* O B Hardison Jr; *Assoc Dir* Philip A Knachel; *Dir Research Activities* John F Andrews
Open (exhibition gallery) Mon - Sat 10 AM - 4 PM, Sun also from April 15 - Labor Day. Estab 1932 as an international center for the study of all aspects of the European Renaissance and civilization in the 16th and 17th centuries. Maintains an art gallery and a permanent display of Shakespearean items and changing topical exhibits of books, manuscripts, paintings and sculpture. Contemporary art is exhibited in the lower gallery
Income: Financed by endowment
Library Holdings: Vols 220,000; Per subs 180; Micro—Reels; AV—A-tapes, fs, motion pictures, rec, slides; Other—Exhibition catalogs, prints, manuscripts, memorabilia, original art works, pamphlets, photographs, reproductions, sculpture, Original documents
Collections: Shakespeare, playbills and promptbooks
Exhibitions: Decade of Folger Acquisitions; Medicine and Health in the Renaissance; Renaissance Art of War; Shakespeare in American; Sir Thomas More, the Man and His Age
Publications: Newsletter, five times yearly; Shakespeare Quarterly
Activities: Seminars for advanced graduate students; lect open to public; concerts; gallery talks; scholarships offered; originate traveling exhibitions

M FRANCISCAN MONASTERY, Holy Land of America, 14th & Quincy St, NE, 20017. Tel 202-526-6800. *Cur* Bro Joseph Pounds
Open daily 8 AM - 5 PM, cl New Year's, Good Friday, Thanksgiving, & Christmas. No admis fee. Estab 1898, affiliated with the Franciscan Custody of the Holy Land. The Monastery covers 44 acres with rose gardens and replicas of the Roman Catacombs with ancient Christian art and frescoes, along with replicas of principal Christian Shrines of the Holy Land and Assisi, Italy
Collections: Holy Land Arts and Crafts; antiquities, silver, bronzes, ceramics, coins, crusader artifacts, glassware, gold, icons, jewelry, pearl carvings, and pottery
Publications: The Crusader's Almanac, quarterly
Activities: Guided tours; gift shop

M FREER GALLERY OF ART, Twelfth and Jefferson Drive, Southwest, 20560. Tel 202-381-5344. *Dir* Thomas Lawton; *Head Conservator, Technical Laboratory* W T Chase; *Assoc Cur Near Eastern Art* Dr Esin Atil; *Assoc Cur Chinese Art* Dr Shen Fu; *Assoc Cur Japanese Art* Yoshiaki Shimizu; *Asst Cur Japanese Art* Ann Yonemura
Open daily 10 AM - 5:30 PM, cl Christmas. No admis fee. Estab 1906 under

Smithsonian Institution to exhibit its outstanding masterpieces of American and Oriental art; to carry out research and publication in the history of civilizations represented by objects in the collections. Average Annual Attendance: 290,000
Income: Financed by endowment and Federal appropriation
Collections: †Art of the Near and Far East: paintings, sculpture, objects in stone, wood, jade, glass, porcelain, bronze, gold, silver, lacquer, metalwork; manuscripts (early Christian); Collection of works by James McNeill Whistler and some of his contemporaries
Activities: Lectures, six visiting lecturere per year; tours; museum shop sells books, reproductions, slides, needlepoint, objects in the round, desk accessories and postcards
L Library, Twelfth and Jefferson Dr, Southwest, 20560. *Librn* Priscilla Smith
Open to the public for reference
Library Holdings: Vols 25,000; Per subs 100
Special Subjects: Volumes related to cultural and historical background of the collection

GENERAL SERVICES ADMINISTRATION
For further information, see National and Regional Organizations

M GEORGETOWN UNIVERSITY, Art and History Museum, Box 1595, Hoya Station, 20007. *Cur* Clifford T Chieffo; *Assoc Cur* Patricia H Chieffo
Open during University hours according to yearly schedule, cl holidays. No admis fee. University estab 1789. The museum is on the Georgetown University campus in Healy Hall (1879)
Collections: American portraits; Works by Van Dycke and Gilbert stuart; graphics, historical objects, paintings, religious art, paintings
Publications: Collection catalog, exhibit catalogs
Activities: Educational programs for undergraduate students; gallery talks, guided tours; art festivals, temporary exhibitions

M GEORGE WASHINGTON UNIVERSITY MUSEUM & ART GALLERIES, Lower Lisner Auditorium, 20006. Tel 202-676-7091. *Cur* Lenore D Miller
Open Mon - Fri 10 AM - 5 PM, cl Sat, Sun & national holidays. No admis fee. Estab 1964 to provide graduate and undergraduate programs in museum problems, research in art history and documentation of permanent collections
Collections: U S Grant Collection of Photographs; W Lloyd Wright Collection of Washingtoniana; Collection of Prints by Joseph Pennell; Graphic Arts from the 18th, 19th and 20th Centuries, with special emphasis on American art; Historical Material; Paintings; Prints; Sculpture; Works Pertaining to George Washington
Exhibitions: Temporary exhibitions staged during academic year
M Dimock Gallery, 730 21st St NW, 20052. Tel 202-676-7091.
Open Mon - Fri 10 AM - 5 PM. No admis fee. Estab 1966. Average Annual Attendance: 10,000
Exhibitions: (1978-80) Michael Clark: Picture Windows; 400 Years of Art: G W Collects; German Expressionism: Die Brucke; Lowell Nesbitt Paintings; Paintings by Mitchell Jamieson; Douglas H Teller and H Irving Gates; Textural Renderings: Works on Paper; 20th Century American Prints; annual awards, faculty, student, and thesis shows
Publications: Exhibition catalogs
Activities: Lect open to public, 5 visiting lectr per year; gallery talks; individual paintings and original objects of art lent; book traveling exhibitions
M Cloyd Heck Marvin Center Art Gallery.
Exhibitions: Monthly exhibitions of local, national and international artists

M HARVARD UNIVERSITY, Dumbarton Oaks Research Library and Collections, 1703 32nd St NW, 20007. Tel 202-342-3200. *Dir* Giles Constable
Open daily (Gardens) 2 - 5 PM, (Collections) Tues - Sun 2 - 5 PM, cl holidays. Conveyed in 1940 to Harvard University by Mr and Mrs Robert Woods Bliss as a research center in the Byzantine and Medieval humanities and subsequently enlarged. Average Annual Attendance: 100,000
Collections: †Byzantine devoted to Early Christian and Byzantine mosaics, textiles, bronzes, sculpture, ivories, metalwork, jewelry, glyptics, and other decorative arts of the period; European and American paintings, sculpture and decorative arts; Pre-Columbian devoted to sculpture, textiles, pottery, gold ornaments and other objects from Middle and South America, dating from 800 BC to early 16th century
Publications: Handbooks and catalogs of the Byzantine and Pre-Columbia collection; scholarly publications in Byzantine, Pre-Columbian and landscape architecture studies
Activities: Lect; conferences
L Library, 1703 32nd St NW, 20007.
Important resources for Byzantine research
Library Holdings: Vols 85,000
Collections: Dumbarton Oaks Census of Early Christian and Byzantine Objects in American Collection; Photographic copy of the Princeton Index of Christian Art; collection of photographs
L Pre-Columbian Library, 1703 32nd St NW, 20007.
Library Holdings: Vols 8000
L Garden Library, 1703 32nd St NW, 20007.
Library Holdings: Vols 10,000; Micro—Prints; Other—Drawings
Collections: Rare books (2400)

M HIRSHHORN MUSEUM AND SCULPTURE GARDEN, Eighth & Independence Aves SW, 20560. Tel 202-381-6512. *Dir* Abram Lerner; *Deputy Dir* Stephen Weil; *Adminr* Nancy Kirkpatrick; *Chief Cur* Charles Millard; *Cur* Cynthia McCabe; *Cur Inex* Garson; *Chief Education Dept* Edward P Lawson; *Registrar* Douglas Robinson; *Chief Exhib* Joseph Shannon; *Chief Conservator* Laurence Hoffman
Estab 1966 under the aegis of the Smithsonian Institution; building designed by Gordon Bunshaft of the architectural firm of Skidmore, Owings & Merrill. Opened in 1974
Collections: Approx 6500 paintings and sculptures, the majority donated to the nation by Joseph H Hirshhorn, emphasizing the development of modern art from the latter half of the 19th century to the present; American art beginning with a strong group of Thomas Eakins' and going on to Sargent, Chase, Hartley, Gorky, De Kooning, Rothko, Noland, Rivers and Frank Stella; European paintings of the last 3 decades represented by Agam, Bacon, Balthus, Leger, Miro and Vasarely; sculpture collection includes works by Arp, Caro, Daumier, Brancusi, Degas,

Giacometti, Manzu, Moore, Nadelman, Rodin and David Smith
Exhibitions: Permanent collection and special loan exhibitions
Activities: Lect, concerts, films, and docent tours
L **Library,** Eighth & Independence Ave SW, 20560. Tel 202-381-6702. *Librn* Anna Brooke
Estab 1974. For reference only by appointment
Income: Financed by federal funds
Library Holdings: Vols 8000; Per subs 60; Micro—Fiche, reels; AV—Cassettes, slides; Other—Exhibition catalogs, memorabilia, Auction Cats
Special Subjects: American painting 1850 to the present, international modern sculpture
Collections: Armory Show Memorabilia; Eakins Memorabilia; Samuel Murray Scrapbooks

M **HOWARD UNIVERSITY GALLERY OF ART,** College of Fine Arts, Sixth and Fairmont Sts NW, 20001. Tel 202-636-7047. *Dir* Starmanda Bullock
Open Mon - Fri 9 AM - 4 PM, cl Sat & Sun. No admis fee. Estab 1928 to stimulate the study and appreciation of the fine arts in the University and community. Three air-conditioned art galleries are in Childers Hall, James V Herring Heritage Gallery, James A Porter Gallery, and the Student Gallery along with Gumbel Print Room. Average Annual Attendance: 24,000
Collections: †Agnes Delano Collection of contemporary American watercolors and prints; Irving R Gumbel Collection of prints; Kress Study Collection of Renaissance paintings and sculpture; Alain Locke Collection of African art; †University collection of painting, sculpture and graphic arts by Afro-Americans
Exhibitions: Changing monthly exhibits
Publications: Catalogue of the African and Afro-American collections; exhibition catalogues; informational brochures; Native American Arts (serial)
Activities: Bimonthly gallery lect and community programs
L **Art Seminar Library,** Sixth and Fairmont Sts NW, 20001.
Library Holdings: Vols 2100; AV—Slides; Other—Photographs

INDUSTRIAL DESIGNERS SOCIETY OF AMERICA
For further information, see National and Regional Organizations

INTERNATIONAL COUNCIL OF MUSEUMS COMMITTEE OF THE AMERICAN ASSOCIATION OF MUSEUMS
For further information, see National and Regional Organizations

O **JOHN F KENNEDY CENTER FOR THE PERFORMING ARTS,** 20566. Tel 202-872-0466. *Chmn of the Board of Trustees* Roger L Stevens
The center opened in Sept 1971. Facilities include the 2200-seat Opera House, 2750-seat Concert Hall, 1130-seat Eisenhower Theater and 224-seat film theater operated by the American Film Institute.
Estab in 1958 by Act of Congress as the National Cultural Center. A bureau of the Smithsonian Institution, but administered by a separate Board of Trustees; the Center is the sole official memorial in Washington to President Kennedy. Although the center does not have an official collection, gifts in the form of art objects from foreign countries are on display throughout the Center
Exhibitions: Changing exhibits on the performing arts are displayed in the Center's Performing Arts Library, a cooperative effort between Kennedy Center and the Library of Congress. Exhibits frequently include portraits, prints, engravings, sketches, etc, of relevance to the performing arts
L **Performing Arts Library,** John F Kennedy Ctr for the Performing Arts, Roof Terrace Level, 20566. *Deputy Dir of Operations & Center Liaison with the Library of Congress* Dr Geraldine M Otremba; *Head Librn* Peter Fay
Open Tues, Thurs & Sat 10 AM - 6 PM; Wed & Fri 10 AM - 8:30 PM. Estab 1979 to provide a national information and reference facility for all areas of the performing arts, including film and broadcasting. For reference only. Access to all Library of Congress collections
Library Holdings: Vols 4000; Per subs 300; Micro—Fiche, reels; AV—A-tapes, cassettes, v-tapes; Other—Clipping files, exhibition catalogs

L **LIBRARY OF CONGRESS,** Prints and Photographs Division, First St Between E Capitol St & Independence Ave, 20540. Tel 202-287-6394 (reference), 287-5836 (offices), 287-5840 (motion pictures). *Librn of Congress* Daniel J Boorstin; *Reference Section* Jerry L Kearns; *Acting Head, Motion Picture Section* Paul Spehr; *Coll Planner & Coordr* Jerald C Maddox
Open Exhib Halls 8:30 AM - 9:30 PM; Sat & Sun 8:30 AM - 6 PM; Reading Room of the Division open Mon - Fri 8:30 - 5 PM; cl legal holidays. Estab 1897. For reference only
Library Holdings: Other—Prints 110,000, photographs 9,000,000, architectural items 100,000; posters 70,000; popular and applied graphic art items 40,000; master photographs 3500
Collections: Archive of Hispanic Culture; Japanese Prints; †Pennell Collection of Whistleriana; †Civil War drawings, prints, photographs and negatives; †early American lithographs; †pictorial Archives of early American architecture including the Historic American Buildings Survey; †original drawings by American illustrators; original prints of all schools and periods, increased annually by the Gardiner Greene Hubbard and J & E R Pennell Endowments; †outstanding among the collection of photographs and photographic negatives are the Farm Security Administration Collection, Red Cross Collection, Arnold Genthe, F B Johnston, Toni Frissell
Publications: A Century of Photographs, 1846-1946; America 1935-1945; American Prints in the Library of Congress; American Revolution in Drawings and Prints; Graphic Sampler; Historic American Buildings Survey; Middle East in Pictures; Viewpoints; Special Collections in the Library of Congress
Activities: Internship program for advanced undergraduate and graduates who wish to work with and study the collections of the division

M **MUSEUM OF AFRICAN ART,** Smithsonian Institution, 316-332 A St NE, 20002. *Dir* Warren M Robbins; *Deputy Dir* Jean Salan; *Cur Coll* Lydia Puccineli; *Program Dir* Amina Dickerson; *Acad Coordr* Ed Lifschitz
Open Mon - Fri 11 AM - 5 PM; Sat & Sun Noon - 5 PM. Admis voluntary contribution. Estab 1963, open 1964 to reveal African art as one of the great cultural heritages of mankind; to help replace myth and misconception with valid scientific and historical information; to provide proper representation of African art in the spectrum of museums of Washington. 12 galleries display 500 objects of traditional African sculpture, plus a period-furnished memorial room to Frederick Douglass, 19th century abolitionist, orator, publisher, statesman in whose first Washington residence the Museum is located. Average Annual Attendance: 100,000. Mem: 1100; dues $15 - $5000
Income: $1,200,000 (federal funding, membership and contributions)
Collections: African sculpture, textiles, crafts, musical instruments (8000 items); 19th Century Afro-American Art; Eliot Elisofon Memorial Archives of 100,000 photos, slides and films
Exhibitions: The African Photography of Eliot Elisofon; The Influence of African Sculpture on Modern Art; Traditional African Art; Permanent Outdoor color wall mural of the N'Debele villages of South Africa
Publications: Exhibition Catalogs; multimedia slide kit; pamphlets; booklets
Activities: Credit courses in cooperation with area universities; classes for adults and children; docent training; lect open to public, 12 vis lectr per year; concerts; gallery talks; tours; individual paintings and original objects of art lent to museums, universities, public officials and conferences; lending collection contains motion pictures, paintings, photography, sculpture, slides and textiles; museum and sales shop selling books, magazines, reproductions, prints, and slides; Boutique Africa featuring quality crafts, original art, jewelry and other imports from Africa
L **Library,** 318 A St NE, 20002. *Librn* Janet L Stanley
Open Mon - Fri 11 AM - 5 PM; Sat 10 AM - 2 PM. Estab 1969 to provide major resource center for African art and culture. For reference only
Library Holdings: Vols 7500; Per subs 25; Other—Clipping files, exhibition catalogs, pamphlets
Special Subjects: Afro-American Art, Historical Material
Collections: African Maps

M **MUSEUM OF MODERN ART OF LATIN AMERICA,** 201 18th St, NW, Washington, DC. (Mailing Add: 7th and Constitution, NW, Washington, DC 20006) Tel 202-331-1010. *Dir* Jose Gomez-Sicre; *Exhib Coordr* Jane Harmon de Ayoroa; *Public Relations Coordr* Rafael Sarda
Open Tues - Sat 10 AM - 5 PM. No admis fee. Estab 1976 to bring about an awareness and appreciation of contemporary Latin American art. The museum maintains an art gallery with the focus on contemporary Latin American art. Average Annual Attendance: 100,000
Collections: Contemporary Latin American Art
Activities: Lect open to public, 4 visiting lectr per year; gallery talks; tours; paintings and original art objects lent to museums; originate traveling exhibitions
L **Archive of Contemporary Latin American Art,** 201 18th St NW, 20006.
Open to scholars for research only
Special Subjects: Latin American Art

M **MUSEUM OF THE UNITED STATES DEPARTMENT OF THE INTERIOR,** C St between 18th & 19th Sts NW, 20240. Tel 202-343-5016. *Exhib Specialist* Herbert Hallman
Open Mon - Fri 8 AM - 4 PM. No admis fee. Estab 1938 to visualize and explain to the public through works of art and other media the history, aims and activities of the Department. Museum occupies one wing on the first floor of the Interior Department Building. Average Annual Attendance: 100,000
Collections: Antarctic Painting by Leland Curtis; Colburn Collection of Indian basketry; †general collection of Indian, Eskimo, South Sea Islands and Virgin Islands arts and crafts, documents, maps, charts, etc.; Gibson Collection of Indian materials; Indian arts and crafts; murals; miniature dioramas; oil paintings of early American Explorers by William Henry Jackson; oil paintings of Western Conservation Scenes by Wilfrid Swancourt Bronson; sculpture groups; watercolor and black and white illustrations; Wildlife Paintings by Walter Weber
Publications: Illustrated museum brochure

M **NATIONAL AIR AND SPACE MUSEUM,*** 7th & Independence Ave SW, 20560. Tel 202-628-4422 or 381-6264. *Dir* Noel W Henners; *Cur of Art* James Dean
Open daily 10 AM - 5:30 PM, cl Christmas. No admis fee. Estab 1946 to memorialize the national development of aviation and space flight. Gallery comprised of 5000 sq ft devoted to the theme, Flight and the Arts
Income: Financed through the Smithsonian Institution
Collections: Paintings, Prints and Drawings include: Alexander Calder, Lamar Dodd, Richard Estes, Audrey Flack, Francisco Goya, Henri Mattise, Lowell Nesbitt, Georgia O'Keefe, Robert Rauschenberg, James Wyeth; Major Sculptures by Richard Lippold, Alejandro Otero, Charles Perry; the Stuart Speiser Collection of Photo Realist Art (now on loan)
Exhibitions: Art exhibitions; permanent, temporary and traveling exhibitions
Activities: Special educational activities; guided tours; gallery talks; lect open to the public; traveling exhibitions organized and circulated; museum shop selling books
L **Library,*** 7th & Independence Ave SW, 20560.
Library Holdings: Vols 24,000; Other—Manuscripts, photographs

NATIONAL ARCHITECTURAL ACCREDITING BOARD, INC
For further information, see National and Regional Organizations

NATIONAL ASSEMBLY OF COMMUNITY ARTS AGENCIES
For further information, see National and Regional Organizations

NATIONAL ASSEMBLY OF STATE ARTS AGENCIES
For further information, see National and Regional Organizations

M **NATIONAL COLLECTION OF FINE ARTS,** Eighth & G Sts NW, 20560. Tel 202-381-5180. *Dir* Joshua C Taylor; *Asst Dir* Harry Lowe; *Adminr* H Eugene Kelson; *Registrar* W Robert Johnston; *Cur 20th Century Painting & Sculpture* Harry Rand; *Cur 18th & 19th Century Painting & Sculpture* William H Truettner; *Assoc Cur 18th & 19th Century Painting & Sculpture* Robin Bolton-Smith; *Cur Prints & Drawings* Janet A Flint; *Cur Education* Barbara Shissler; *Research Cur* Lois M Fink; *Consultant 20th Century Painting & Sculpture* Adelyn D Breeskin; *Coordr Inventory of American Paintings* Martha Andrews; *Chief Office of Exhib & Design* David Keeler; *Conservator* Ann Creager; *Conservator* Stefano Scafetta; *Conservator* Katherine Eirk; *Editor Office of Publications* Carroll Clark; *Chief Office of Public Affairs* Margery Byers; *Chief Office Visual Resources* Eleanor Fink
Open daily 10 AM - 5:30 PM; cl Christmas. Estab 1829, and later part of the Smithsonian Institution, it was designated the National Gallery of Art in 1906. The title was changed to the National Collection of Fine Arts in 1937: The museum is

now primarily concerned with the study and presentation of American art from its beginning to the present. The Explore Gallery on the first floor offers a stimulating range of exploratory experiences in art both for children and adults. An adjacent gallery, Discover, is devoted to challenging exhibitions of various kinds. Average Annual Attendance: 450,000

Collections: The collection of paintings, sculpture, prints and drawings number over 23,000. It represents a wide range of American work, particularly late 19th and early 20th century. Major collections include those of Harriet Lane Johnston (1906), William T Evans (1907), John Gellatly (1929), and more recently the S C Johnson and Son Collection of paintings from the 1960s. There is a sizeable collection of portrait miniatures. All works not on display are available for examination by scholars

Exhibitions: A representative selection of works from the collection are on permanent display in the galleries, providing a comprehensive view of the varied aspects of American art. Most temporary exhibitions, some twenty-five a year, are originated by the staff, many as part of the program to investigate less well-known aspects of American art. They include both studies of individual artists, such as W H Johnson, Ilya Bolotowsky and Lilly Martin Spencer, and thematic studies such as Art of the Pacific Northwest, Pennsylvania Academy Moderns, and the Academic Tradition in American Art. A small area is devoted to a representation of other than American works. Major exhibitions for 1980 include: American Renaissance, 1876-1917; David Gilmour Blythe (1816-1865); GSA Maquettes; Jan Matulka, 1890-1972

Publications: Major exhibitions are accompanied by authoritative publications; small exhibitions are accompanied by checklists

Activities: The Department of Education carries on an active program with the schools and the general public, offering imaginative participatory tours for children, a Discover Graphics program which includes a print workshop and varied presentations of exhibitions, lectures, symposia and concerts. A research program in American art is maintained for visiting scholars and training is carried on through internship in general museum practice and conservation; the Inventory of American Paintings Executed Before 1914 is compiling a computer list of largely uncatalogued works from throughout the country; the museum also circulates exhibitions throughout the United States on a regular basis

L Library of the National Collection of Fine Arts and the National Portrait Gallery, Eighth & G Sts NW, 20560. Tel 202-381-5118, 381-5853. *Chief Librn* William B Walker; *Asst Librn* Katharine M Ratzenberger; *Cataloger* Charles H King Jr
Open Mon - Fri 10 AM - 5 PM. Estab 1964 to serve the reference and research needs of the staff and affiliated researchers of the National Collection of Fine Arts, the National Portrait Gallery, the Archives of American Art, and other Smithsonian bureaus. Circ 7940. Open to graduate students and other qualified adult researchers

Income: $160,000 (financed by federal appropriation)

Purchases: $30,000

Library Holdings: Vols 38,000; Per subs 900; Micro—Fiche, reels; Other—Clipping files, exhibition catalogs, manuscripts, pamphlets, reproductions, Original documents

Special Subjects: American art, especially printing, drawing, sculpture and graphic arts, contemporary art, American history and biography

Collections: Ferdinand Perret Art Reference Library: collection of scrapbooks of clippings and pamphlets; special section on California art and artists consisting of approx 325 ring binders on art and artists of Southern California; vertical file of 300 file drawers of material on art and artists, with increasing emphasis on American art and artists

Activities: Library tours by appointment only

M Renwick Gallery, 17th St & Pennsylvania Ave NW, 20560. Tel 202-381-5811. *Dir* Lloyd E Herman; *Cur* Michael Monroe
Open daily 10 AM - 5:30 PM; cl Christmas. Designed in 1859 by architect James Renwick, Jr, as the Corcoran Gallery of Art, the building was renamed for the architect in 1965 when it was transferred by the Federal government to the Smithsonian Institution for restoration. Restored to its French Second Empire elegance after 67 years as the United States Court of Claims, the building has two public rooms with period furnishings, the Grand Salon and the Octagon Room, as well as eight areas for temporary exhibitions of American crafts and design

Collections: Since its opening, the Renwick Gallery has presented 62 special exhibitions. 1980 exhibitions include: American Porcelain; Berlin Porcelain; Georg Jensen Silversmithy

Publications: Major exhibitions are accompanied by publications, smaller exhibitions by checklists

Activities: Docent training; film programs; lect and demonstrations emphasizing the creative work of American designers and craftsmen as well as complementing the exhibitions from other countries; tours

NATIONAL COUNCIL OF ARCHITECTURAL REGISTRATION BOARDS
For further information, see National and Regional Organizations

NATIONAL ENDOWMENT FOR THE ARTS
For further information, see National and Regional Organizations

M NATIONAL GALLERY OF ART, Constitution Ave at Fourth St NW, 20565. Tel 202-737-4215. *Bd of Trustees* Chmn Paul Mellon; The Chief Justice of the United States; The Secretary of State; The Secretary of the Treasury; The Secretary of the Smithsonian Institution; John R Stevenson, Carlisle H Humelsine, Franklin D Murphy and Ruth Carter Johnson; *Chmn Board of Trustees* Paul Mellon; *Pres* John R Stevenson; *VPres* Carlisle H Humelsine; *Dir* J Carter Brown; *Asst to Dir Music* Richard Bales; *Asst to Dir Public Information* Katherine Warwick; *Asst to Dir* Carol Fox; *Admin Asst* Elizabeth J Foy; *Asst Dir & Chief Cur* Charles P Parkhurst; *Executive Cur* Earl A Powell III; *Cur American Art & Sr Cur* John Wilmerding; *Cur Dutch & Flemish Painting* Arthur K Wheelock Jr; *Cur French Painting* David E Rust; *Cur Early Italian Painting* David Alan Brown; *Cur Northern & Later Italian Painting* Sheldon Grossman; *Cur Northern European Painting* John Hand; *Cur Prints & Drawings* Andrew Robison Jr; *Cur Sculpture* Douglas Lewis Jr; *Cur Spanish Painting* Anna M Voris; *Cur 20th Century Art* E A Carmean Jr; *Chief Design & Installation* Gaillard F Ravenel; *Chief Exhib, Loans & Registration* Jack C Spinx; *Cur Education* Margaret I Bouton; *Head Extension Prog Development* Joseph J Reis; *Head Art Information Service* Elise V H Ferber; *Editor* Theodore S Amussen; *Sr Conservator* Victor C B Covey; *Registrar* Peter Davidock; *Chief Photographic Laboratory* William J Sumits; *Treas* Robert C Goetz; *Adminr* Joseph G English; *Asst Adminr* George W Riggs; *Planning Consult* David W Scott;

Construction Mgr Hurley Offenbacher; *Secy & Gen Counsel* Robert Amory Jr; *Assoc Secy & Assoc Gen Counsel* Carroll J Cavanagh
Open Mon - Sat 10 AM - 5 PM; Sun Noon - 9 PM; (Apr 1 through Labor Day) Mon - Sat 10 AM - 9 PM; Sun Noon - 9 PM; cl Christmas & New Year's Day. No admis fee. Estab 1937; West Building opened 1941; East Building opened 1978. The West Building was a gift from Andrew W Mellon; the East Building is a gift of Paul Mellon, Ailsa Mellon Bruce, and The Andrew W Mellon Foundation. Average Annual Attendance: 5,500,000

Income: Financed by private endowment and federal appropriation

Collections: The Andrew W Mellon Collection of 126 paintings and 26 pieces of sculpture includes Raphael's Alba Madonna, Niccolini-Cowper's Madonna, and St George and the Dragon; van Eyck Annunciation; Botticelli's Adoration of the Magi; nine Rembrandts. Twenty-one of these paintings came from the Hermitage. Also in the original gift were the Vaughan Portrait of George Washington by Gilbert Stuart and The Washington Family by Edward Savage The Samuel H Kress Collection, given to the nation over a period of years, includes the great tondo The Adoration of the Magi by Fra Angelico and Fra Filippo Lippi, the Laocoön by El Greco, and Fine examples by Giorgione, Titian, Grünewald, Düer, Memling, Bosch, Francois Clouet, Poussin, Watteau, Chardin, Boucher, Fragonard, David and Ingres. Also included are a number of masterpieces of Italian and French sculpture. In the Widener Collection are paintings by Rembrandt, van Dyck, and Vermeer, as well as major works of Italian, Spanish, English and French painting and Italian and French sculpture and decorative arts. The Chester Dale Collection includes masterpieces by Braque, Cezanne, Degas, Gauguin, Manet, Matisse, Modigliani, Monet, Picasso, Pissarro, Renoir, Toulouse-Lautrec, van Gogh, and such American painters as George Bellows, Childe Hassan, and Gilbert Stuart. Several major works of art by Cezanne, Gauguin, Picasso and the American painter Walt Kuhn were given to the Gallery in 1972 by the W Averell Harriman Foundation in memory of Marie N Harriman. Paintings to round out the collection have been bought with funds provided by the late Ailsa Mellon Bruce. Most important among them are: portrait of Ginevra de' Benci (the only generally acknowledged painting by Leonardo da Vinci outside Europe), Georges de la Tour's Repentant Magdalen, Picasso's Nude Woman-1910, Rubens' Daniel in the Lions' Den, Claude Lorrain's Judgment of Paris, St George and the Dragon attributed to Rogier van der Weyden, and a number of American paintings, including Thomas Cole's second set of the Voyage of Life. The National Gallery's rapidly expanding graphic arts holdings, in great part given by Lessing J Rosenwald, numbers about 50,000 items and dates from the 12th century to the present. The Index of American Design contains over 17,000 watercolor renderings and 500 photographs of American crafts and folk arts. The National Gallery's Collection continues to be built by private donation, rather than through government funds, which serve solely to operate and maintain the Gallery

Exhibitions: Temporary exhibitions from collections both in the United States and abroad

Publications: National Gallery of Art-Kress Foundation Studies in the History of European Art; Ailsa Mellon Bruce Studies in the History of American Art; A W Mellon Lectures in the Fine Arts; Studies in the History of Art; exhibition catalogs; Annual Report; monthly calendar of events

Activities: Sunday lect by distinguished guest speakers and members of the staff are given throughout the year; the A W Mellon Lect in the Fine Arts are delivered as a series each spring by an outstanding scholar; concerts are held in the East Garden Court each Sunday evening between September and June at 7 PM without charge; general tours and lect are given in the Gallery by members of the Education Department throughout the week; special tours are arranged for groups; films on art are presented on a varying schedule; provides art loans and multimedia programs to 4000 communities throughout the country; originates traveling exhibitions

L Library, Constitution Ave at Fourth St NW, 20565. Tel 202-737-4215. *Chief Librn* J M Edelstein; *Reader Services Librn* Caroline H Backlund
Open Mon - Fri 10 AM - 5 PM. Estab 1941 to support the national curatorial, educational and research activities and serve as a research center for graduate students, visiting scholars and researchers in the visual arts. For reference only

Income: Financed by federal appropriations and trust funds

Library Holdings: Vols 65,000; Micro—Fiche, reels; Other—Clipping files, exhibition catalogs

Special Subjects: Western European and American art

Collections: Art exhibition, art sales and private art collection catalogs; artist monographs; Leonardo da Vinci

Activities: Library tours on request

L Photographic Archives, Constitution Ave at 6th NW, 20565. *Cur* Ruth Philbrick

Library Holdings: Other—Photographs 900,000

Special Subjects: Black-white photographs of American and Western European art

M NATIONAL MUSEUM OF HISTORY AND TECHNOLOGY, Smithsonian Institution, Constitution Ave between 12th & 14th Sts NW, 20560. Tel 202-628-4422. *Dir* Roger G Kennedy; *Deputy Dir* Douglas E Evelyn; *Asst Dir for Exhibits* Benjamin W Lawless
Open daily 10 AM - 5:30 PM, Apr 1 - Labor Day 10 AM - 9 PM, cl Christmas Day. No admis fee. Estab 1964. The museum tells the story of American achievements from Colonial Times to the present, from man's basic needs of food, clothing and shelter, to the men and women who shaped our heritage and our progress in science and technology. Average Annual Attendance: 6 million

Collections: Archaeology, ceramics, glass, graphic arts, numismatics, photography, textiles

Exhibitions: Atom Smashers; A Nation of Nations; We the People

Publications: Exhibition catalogs; Studies in History and Technology Series

Activities: Docent training; museum shop selling books, prints and slides

L NMHT Branch of Smithsonian Institution Libraries, Constitution Ave between 12th & 14th Sts NW, 20560. *Librn* Frank Pietropaoli
Open to staff and visiting scholars

M NATIONAL PORTRAIT GALLERY, F St at Eighth NW, 20560. Tel 202-381-5380. *Dir* Marvin Sadik; *Prog Management Officer* Harold Francis Pfister; *Admin Officer* Barbara A Faison; *Cur Paintings & Sculpture* Robert G Stewart; *Chief Design & Production* Nello Marconi; *Historian* Marc Pachter; *Cur Exhib* Beverly Cox; *Cur Education* Kenneth A Yellis; *Cur Photographs* William F Stapp; *Cur Prints* Wendy C Wick; *Registrar* Suzanne Jenkins; *Keeper Catalog of American Portraits* Mona Dearborn; *Catalog of American Portraits Survey Coordr* Richard K

Doud; *Sr Conservator* Felrath Hines; *Historian American Culture* Lillian B Miller; *Audiovisual Media Coordr* Eugene Mantie; *Public Affairs Officer* Sandra Westin; *Librn* William B Walker; *Ed* Frances Wein

Open daily 10 AM - 5:30 PM; cl Christmas. No admis fee. The National Portrait Gallery was estab by Act of Congress in 1962 as a museum of the Smithsonian Institution for the exhibition and study of portraiture depicting men and women who have made significant contributions to the history, development, and culture of the people of the United States. The Gallery is housed in one of the oldest government structures in Washington, the former US Patent Office Building constructed between 1836 and 1867, on the very site which Pierre L'Enfant, in his original plan for the city, had designated for a pantheon to honor the nation's immortals. The first floor of the Gallery is devoted to major loan exhibitions and photographs, prints, and drawings from the permanent collection. There are special galleries housing a collection of portrait engravings by C B J F de Saint-Memin, silhouettes by Auguste Edouart, and portrait sculptures by Jo Davidson. On the second floor are featured the permanent collection of portraits of eminent Americans and the Hall of Presidents containing portraits and associative items of our Chief Executives. The two-story Victorian Renaissance Great Hall on the third floor is used for special events and exhibitions. Average Annual Attendance: 500,000

Income: Approx $2,500,000 (financed by federal appropriation)
Collections: The collections, which are constantly being expanded, include portraits of significant Americans, preferable executed from life, in all traditional media: oils, watercolors, charcoal, pen and ink, daguerreotypes, photographs; portraits of American Presidents from George Washington to Jimmy Carter. 900 original works of art from the Time Magazine Cover collection
Exhibitions: (1978-1979) American Portrait Prints: A Survey; Chester Alan Arthur: From Spoilsman to Statesman 1871-1885; Black Hawk and Keokuk: Prairie Rivals; The Great Crash; Robert Edge Pine: A British Portrait Painter in America 1784-1788; Return to Albion: Americans in England 1760-1940; Selections from the National Portrait Gallery Photography Collection; They Have Made a Nation; Time: Arts & Entertainment; Translations: Lithographs After Daguerreotypes; The Whiskey Rebels
Publications: Large-scale, richly illustrated publications to accompany major shows and provide comprehensive analysis of exhibition themes; pamphlets highlighting features of the permanent collection; documentary, audio, and visual materials designed to be used as teaching guides; illustrated checklist; American portraiture; biographies
Activities: Outreach programs for elementary and secondary schools, senior citizens groups, hospitals, and nursing homes; docent training; teacher workshops; scheduled walk-in tours for special groups, adults, families, and schools; programs for handicapped audiences; Haptic Gallery for the visually impaired; Faces of Freedom film; Speakers Bureau; Living Self-Portrait lect series; Portraits In Motion (special weekend events); museum shop selling books, magazines, reproductions, prints, and slides
L **Library,** F St at Eighth NW, 20560.
Shared with the National Collection of Fine Arts
Library Holdings: Vols 38,000

M **NATIONAL TRUST FOR HISTORIC PRESERVATION,*** 740-748 Jackson Place NW, 20006. Tel 202-638-6200. *Pres* James Biddle
Open to the public, hours and fees vary with the property, cl Christmas, New Years. Founded 1949, the National Trust for Historic Preservation is the only national, non-profit, private organization chartered by Congress to encourage public participation in the preservation of sites, buildings and objects significant in American history and culture. Its services, counsel and education on preservation, and historic property interpretation and administration, are carried out at national and regional headquarters in consultation with advisors in each state and U.S. Territory. Mem: 155,000; dues sustaining $100, active $15, student $5
Income: Financed by membership dues, contributions and matching grants from the U.S. Department of the Interior, National Park Service, under provision of the National Preservation Act of 1966
Collections: Fine and decorative arts furnishing nine historic house museums: Chesterwood, Stockbridge, MA; Cliveden, Philadelphia, PA; Decatur House and Woodrow Wilson House, Washington, DC; Drayton Hall, Charleston, SC; Lyndhurst, Tarrytown, NY; Oatlands, Leesburg, VA; The Shadows-on-the-Teche, New Iberia, LA; Woodlawn Plantation, Mt Vernon, VA. (For additional information, see separate listings)
Publications: Historic Preservation, quarterly; Preservation News (newspaper), monthly
L **Library,*** 740-748 Jackson Place NW, 20006. *Librn* Brigid Rapp
For reference only
Library Holdings: Vols 6000

M **PHILLIPS COLLECTION,** 1600-1612 21st St NW, 20009. Tel 202-387-2151. *Dir* Laughlin Phillips; *Cur* James McLaughlin; *Registrar & Archivist* John Gernand; *Dir Music* Charles Crowder; *Assoc Cur* Willem de Looper; *Preparator* William Koberg; *Exec Asst* Louise Steffens
Open Tues - Sat 10 AM - 5 PM, Sun 2 - 7 PM, cl Mon. No admis fee. Opened to the public 1921 to show and interpret the best of contemporary painting in the context of outstanding works of the past; to underscore this intent through the presentation of concerts and lectures. The original building, a Georgian Revival residence designed in 1897 by Hornblower & Marshall, was added to in 1907. A modern annex connected by a double bridge to the old gallery was opened to the public in 1960. Average Annual Attendance: 80,000
Collections: 19th and 20th century American and European painting with special emphasis on units of particular artists such as Bonnard, Braque, Cezanne, Daumier, de Stael and Rouault, and Americans such as Avery, Dove, Gatch, Knaths, Marin, O'Keeffe, Prendergast, Rothoko and Tack. The best known painting is Renoir's Luncheon of the Boating Party
Exhibitions: Loan exhibitions and changing hangings of the Permanent Collection. Some recent exhibitions include: American Monotypes; Avery; Color Paintings of Franz Kline; William Dole; Kokoschka Drawings and Prints; Horace Pippin; Okada, Shinoda and Tsutaka; Tamayo; Wotruba
Activities: Lect; concerts; tours; museum shop sells books, postcards, small and large color reproductions, slides and exhibition catalogs

L **Library,** 1600-1612 21st St NW, 20009. *Librn* Judith Richelien
Available to serious students, researchers and museum professionals, by appointment

PRINT COUNCIL OF AMERICA
For further information, see National and Regional Organizations

PUBLIC LIBRARY OF THE DISTRICT OF COLUMBIA
L **Art Division,** Martin Luther King Memorial Library, 901 G St NW, 20001. Tel 202-727-1101. *Dir Libr* Dr Hardy R Franklin; *Chief Art Div* Lois Kent Stiles
Open Mon - Thurs 9 AM - 9 PM, Fri & Sat 9 AM - 5:30 PM. No admis fee
Collections: †Reference and circulating books and periodicals on architecture, painting, sculpture, photography, graphic and applied arts; †extensive pamphlet file including all art subjects, with special emphasis on individual American artists and on more than 400 artists active in the area; †circulating picture collection numbering over 65,000 mounted reproductions and 290 framed prints
Exhibitions: Special exhibitions held occasionally
L **Audiovisual Division,** Martin Luther King Memorial Library, 901 G St NW, 20001. Open Mon - Thurs 9 AM - 9 PM, Fri & Sat 9 AM - 5:30 PM
Library Holdings: AV—Fs, motion pictures

M **SMITH-MASON GALLERY AND MUSEUM,** 1207 Rhode Island Ave NW, 20005. Tel 202-462-6323. *Dir* Helen S Mason; *Cur Graphics* James L Wells; *Cur Painting* Delilah W Pierce; *Cur Ceramics & Sculpture* Dr Leroy Gaskin
Open Tues - Fri Noon - 4 PM, Sat 10 AM - 5 PM, Sun 2 - 5 PM. No admis fee. Estab 1967 for the preservation and research of ethnology. Mem: Dues life $500, donor $250, contributing $100, supporting $25, sustaining $15, individual $10
Collections: Ethnology; decorative arts; graphics; paintings; sculpture; textiles
Publications: Exhibition brochures; newsletter, annually
Activities: Lect; gallery talks; tours; films
L **Library,** 1207 Rhode Island Ave NW, 20005.
Open to public for research and on premises reading only
Library Holdings: Vols 300

M **SMITHSONIAN INSTITUTION,** 1000 Jefferson Dr SW, 20560. Tel 202-628-4422. *Secy* S Dillon Ripley; *Under Secy* Phillip Samuel Hughes; *Asst Secy for Art & History* Charles Blitzer; *Asst Secy Science* David Challinor; *Asst Secy for Public Service* Julian Euell; *Asst Secy for Museum Programs* Paul N Perrot; *Writer & Editor* Kathryn B Lindeman
Open daily 10 AM - 5:30 PM, extended spring and summer hours determined yearly, cl Christmas. Estab 1846, when James Smithson bequeathed his fortune to the United States, under the name of the Smithsonian Institution, an establishment in Washington for the increase and diffusion of knowledge among men. To carry out the terms of Smithson's will, the institution performs fundamental research; preserves for study and reference about 78 million items of scientific, cultural and historical interest; maintains exhibits representative of the arts, American history, aeronautics and space exploration; technology; natural history; and engages in programs of education and national and international cooperative research and training. Responsibility for the administration of the trust is vested in the Board of Regents, which is comprised of the Chief Justice of the United States (Chancellor of the Board of Regents), the Vice President of the United States, three members of the Senate, three members of the House of Representatives and nine citizen members. Average Annual Attendance: 23,000,000
Income: Board of Regents meets three times yearly, Jan, May and Sept. The individual bureaus concerned with art under the Smithsonian Institution are as follows. For complete information see separate listings.
—**Archives of American Art,** Eighth & G Streets, NW, 20560.
—**Cooper-Hewitt Museum of Decorative Arts and Design,** 2 East 91st St, 20560.
—**Freer Gallery of Art,** 12th & Independence Ave, SW, 20560.
—**Hirshhorn Museum and Sculpture Garden,** Eighth & Independence, SW, 20560.
—**John F Kennedy Center for the Performing Arts,** 20560
Administered under a separate Board of Trustees
—**National Air and Space Museum,** Seventh & Independence Ave, SW, 20560.
—**National Collection of Fine Arts,** Ninth & G Streets, NW, 20560.
Includes the Renwick Gallery
—**National Gallery of Art,** Constitution Ave at Sixth St, NW, 20565.
Administered under a separate Board of Trustees
—**National Museum of History and Technology,** Constitution Ave between 12th & 14th Streets, NW, 20560.
—**National Portrait Gallery,** Eighth & F Streets, NW, 20560.

M **TEXTILE MUSEUM,** 2320 S St NW, 20008. Tel 202-667-0441. *Dir* Andrew Oliver Jr; *Exec Asst* Mary Lee Berger-Hughes; *Cur Old World* Louise W Mackie; *Asst Cur New World* Ann P Rowe; *Asst Cur Old World* Patricia L Fiske; *Cur Emeritus* Irene Emery; *Conservator* Clarissa Palmai; *Museum Shop Mgr* Lilo Markrich
Open Tues - Sat 10 AM - 5 PM. No admis fee. Estab 1925 for the acquisition, study and exhibition of rugs and textiles. The gallery contains eight rooms for exhibition, storage areas, museum shop, conservation laboratory, library and offices. Average Annual Attendance: 20,000. Mem: 1500; dues $25
Income: Financed by endowment, membership and grants
Collections: Oriental rugs from antiquity to the present, as well as rugs and textiles from the Old and New Worlds with the general exception of Western Europe and the United States. The collection contains approximately 9000 textiles and 700 rugs
Exhibitions: Caucasian Rugs; China Looms Resplendent; Ethnographic Textiles of the Western Hemisphere; History of Knitting; Masterpieces in the Textile Museum from 3 AD to 20th Century; Molas; Quilts; Spanish Silks and Carpets, 13th - 17th Centuries; Structures of Fabrics; Tribal Weavers of the Andes-a Fanfare of 19th and 20th Century Rugs; Uzbek Textiles; White-Ground Turkish Rugs
Publications: Newsletter, quarterly; The Textile Museum Journal, annually
Activities: Dramatic programs; docent training; internships in conservation and museum studies; lect open to public, 40 visiting lectr per year; concerts; gallery talks; tours; original objects of art lent to other museums for special exhibitions; originate traveling exhibitions; museum shop and sales shop selling books, original art, patterns, yarn and floss, ethnic folk jewelry, woven and knitted articles
L **Arthur D Jenkins Library,** 2320 S St NW, 20008. Tel 202-667-0442. *Librn* Katherine T Freshley
Open Wed - Fri 10 AM - 5 PM, Sat 10 AM - 1 PM. Estab 1925 as a reference library dealing with ancient and ethnographic textiles and rugs of the world

Income: Financed by endowment, membership and gifts
Library Holdings: Vols 7000; Per subs 30; Other—Clipping files, exhibition catalogs, pamphlets, photographs
Collections: Oriental rugs; Peruvian, Indonesian, American Indian and Indian Textiles

L **TRINITY COLLEGE LIBRARY,** Michigan Ave & Franklin St NE, 20017. Tel 202-269-2252. *Theresa* Librn; *Readers Services* Vivian Templin; *Acquisitions* Therest Marie Gaudreau; *Cataloger* Karen Leider; *Periodicals* Doris Gruber
Open during school semesters, Mon - Thurs 9 AM - 11 PM, Fri 9 AM - 5 PM, Sat 10 AM - 5 PM, Sun 1 - 11 PM. Estab 1897 as an undergraduate college library, serving the college community
Income: $105,000 (financed by college budget)
Purchases: $39,000 for all library materials
Library Holdings: Vols 144,000; Per subs 684; Micro—Reels; AV—Slides
Special Subjects: Art collection in both books and slides is general in content, including works on painting, sculpture and architecture principally

M **TRUXTUN-DECATUR NAVAL MUSEUM,** 1610 H St NW, 20006. Tel 202-842-0050. *Pres* W S DeLany
Open daily 10 AM - 4 PM, cl national holidays. No admis fee. Estab 1950, the Museum is located in the carriage house adjoining the historic home of Stephen Decatur, who distinguished himself in the Tripolitan War. It is also named for Commodore Thomas Truxtun, another naval figure of that period. Sponsored by the Naval Historical Foundation, the exhibits cover the Merchant Marine, US Marine Corps, and Coast Guard in addition to the US Navy. Mem: Dues $7.50 - $2000
Collections: Documents; Navy Memorabilia; Nautical Paintings; Prints; Photographs; Ship Models
Exhibitions: Permanent and temporary exhibitions
Publications: Newsletter, semi-annually; Naval Historical Foundation Report; historical pamphlets, semi-annually
Activities: Lect; films; gift shop
L **Library,** 1610 H St NW, 20006.
Library Holdings: Vols 1000; Other—Manuscripts
Collections: Rare books on naval history

M **UNITED STATES CAPITOL MUSEUM,** 20515. Tel 202-225-1222. *Architect of the Capitol* George M White; *Chief Cur* Dr David Sellin; *Architectural Historian* Dr Anne Imelda Radice
Open daily 9 AM - 4:30 PM, summer and when in session 9 AM - 10 PM. No admis fee. Estab 1793 as a National agency and Historic museum. restored historic chambers. Average Annual Attendance: 7 - 10,000,000
Income: Financed by United States Congressional appropriation and appropriate donations
Collections: Works by Andrei; Brumidi; Crawford; Costaggini; Cox; Franzoni; French; Greenough; Leutze; Peale; Powers; Rogers; Trumbull; Vanderlyn; Weir; 18th, 19th and 20th century paintings, sculpture and decorative arts
Exhibitions: Architectural drawings relating to the Capitol
Publications: Catalog of collections; occasional pamphlets
Activities: Individual paintings and original art objects lent to qualified museums
L **Art Reference Library,** Office of the Architect, 20515. *Art Reference* Florence H Thayn
Open 9:30 AM - 5 PM. Estab for research on United States Capitol, its art and artists
Library Holdings: Vols 5000; Micro—Fiche; AV—Kodachromes, slides; Other—Clipping files, prints, manuscripts, memorabilia, original art works, pamphlets, photographs, sculpture
Collections: 55,000 Architectural drawings; 50,000 photographs; Archives pertaining to Capitol art and architecture 1793 - to present

UNITED STATES DEPARTMENT OF THE INTERIOR
For further information, see National and Regional Organizations

M **UNITED STATES NAVY,** Combat Art Gallery, 9th and M Sts, Bldg 67 Washington Navy Yard, 20374. Tel 202-433-3816. *Cur* Charles D Lawrence; *Asst Cur* John D Barnett
Open Monday - Friday 8AM - 4PM. Estab 1941. Average Annual Attendance: 3000
Collections: Graphic arts, paintings, sketches
Exhibitions: Quarterly exhibits of art work from WWII through 1979 from the permanent collection
Publications: United States Navy Combat Art

M **UNITED STATES NAVY MEMORIAL MUSEUM,** Washington Navy Yard, Ninth & M Sts SE, 20374. Tel 202-433-2651. *Dir* T A Damon; *Assoc Dir* Dr Oscar Fitzgerald
Open Mon - Fri 9 AM - 4 PM, Sat & Sun 10 AM - 5 PM, cl Thanksgiving, Christmas Eve & Day, New Year's Day. Parking and admis free
Collections: History of US Navy from 1775 to Space Age; Naval Combat Art; Paintings; Prints; Watercolors
Exhibitions: Changing art exhibitions

O **UNITED STATES SENATE COMMISSION ON ART AND ANTIQUITIES,** United States Capitol Bldg, Room S-411, 20510. Tel 202-224-2955. *Chmn* Robert C (Senator) Byrd; *VChmn* Howard H (Senator) Baker; *Exec Secy* J S Kimmitt; *Cur* James R Ketchum; *Registrar* James S Haugerud; *Museum Specialist* Diane K Skvarla
Open daily 9 AM - 4:30 PM. No admis fee. Estab 1968 to accept, supervise, hold, place and protect all works of art, historical objects, and exhibits within the Senate wing of the United States Capitol and Senate Office Buildings. Average Annual Attendance: 1,000,000
Income: Financed by United States Senate appropriation
Collections: Old Senate and Supreme Court chambers restored to their appearances c1850; Paintings, sculpture, historic furnishings and memorabilia
Exhibitions: Disputed Election of 1877; Manners in the Senate Chamber; 19th century Women's views; Senate Art in Stamps
Publications: Publications on restored Old Senate and Old Supreme Court chambers; exhibit brochures

L **Library,** United States Capitol Bldg Room S-411, 20510.
A reference collection on fine and decorative arts; supplemented by the United States Senate Library

M **WHITE HOUSE,** 1600 Pennsylvania Ave NW, 20500. Tel 202-456-1414. *Cur* Clement E Conger; *Registrar* Betty C Monkman
Open winter Tues - Fri 10 AM - Noon; summer Tues - Sat 10 AM - Noon; cl Sun, Mon, most holidays. No admis fee
Collections: 18th and 19th Century Period Furniture; 18th, 19th and 20th Century Paintings and Prints; glassware; porcelain; sculpture
Publications: The White House: An Historic Guide; The Presidents of the United States; The Living White House; The First Ladies

M **WOODROW WILSON HOUSE,** 2340 South St, NW, 20008. Tel 202-387-4062. *Adminr* Earl James; *Asst Adminr* Robert Mawson; *Admin Asst* Vicki Sopher
Open Tues - Fri 10 AM - 2 PM, Sat & Sun Noon - 4 PM, cl Mon. Admis $1.50, students and senior citizens 50¢, National Trust Members free. Estab 1968, owned by the National Trust for Historic Preservation, it works to foster interest and appreciation of the history and culture of the City. Wilson House is a 1915 Georgian-Revival townhouse designed by Waddy B Wood, with formal garden. From 1921 it served as the retirement home of President Wilson and Mrs Wilson. Average Annual Attendance: 10,000
Income: Financed by endowment and membership
Collections: Early 20th century clothing, furnishings, utensils
Exhibitions: The Architectural Drawings of Waddy Butler Wood; Civil Liberties in Washington, DC during the First World War; Kalorama: From Country Estate to Urban Elegance; Hornblower & Marshall, A 25¢ Discovery; The War Against Freedom
Activities: Concerts; films; individual paintings and objects of art lent to qualified museums and non-profit corporations

FLORIDA

BOCA RATON

O **BOCA RATON CENTER FOR THE ARTS, INC,** 801 W Palmetto Park Rd, 33432. *Pres* Thomas M O'Leary; *VPres* David Laub; *Secy* Helen Bramhall; *Dir* Maria Lawton; *Executive Secy* Dorothy Christenson
Open Mon - Fri 10 AM - 4 PM, Sat & Sun 1 - 4 PM. No admis fee. Estab 1951 to foster and develop the cultural arts. Large Main Gallery, museum shop contained in one building. Second building houses art school and storage. Average Annual Attendance: 25,000. Mem: 1050; annual dues single $20, family $35; annual meeting April 15
Income: $50,000 (financed by membership and school)
Exhibitions: Craft Show; Contemporary Painting and Sculpture: August Rodin, Hans Hoffman, Alexander Calder; Members Show; Photography Show; Statewide Competition; One Man Show, D Kingman; Two Man Show, Jill Cannady, Painter, Phillip Crangi, Sculptor; Student show
Publications: Exhibition catalogues; newsletter, 10 per year
Activities: Classes for adults and children; docent training; lect for members and guests, 2 vis lectr per yr; tours; two statewide competitions per year and National outdoor art festival with awards given for Best in Show and Merit; scholarships offered; museum shop sells books, original art, reproductions, prints
L **Library of the Center,** 801 W Palmetto Park Rd, 33432. *Personnel* Louise McKenzie
Open Mon - Fri 10 AM - 4 PM, Sat & Sun 1 - 4 PM. Estab 1970
Library Holdings: Vols 1000; Per subs 3

M **FLORIDA ATLANTIC UNIVERSITY ART GALLERY,** * Art Department, 33431. Tel 305-395-5100, Ext 2673. *Chmn Dept Art* Tal Mason
Open Mon - Thurs 8 AM - 11 PM, Fri 8 AM - 5 PM, Sat 9 AM - 5 PM, Sun Noon - Midnight. No admis fee. Estab 1970 to provide exhibit space for faculty and students and to provide an opportunity to bring to the area exhibits which would expand the cultural experience of the viewers. Gallery is located in the University library
Income: Financed by city and state appropriations and student activities fees
Collections: Slide collection; student work
Exhibitions: Annual Juried Student Show; faculty and former students; work from area junior colleges; traveling exhibitions
Activities: Workshops sponsored by Student Art Society; lect open to public; scholarships; traveling exhibitions organized and circulated

BRADENTON

O **ART LEAGUE OF MANATEE COUNTY,** Art Center, 209 Ninth St W, 33505. Tel 813-746-2862. *Office Mgr* Marie Collins
Open Sept - May, Mon - Fri 9 AM - 4:30 PM, Sat 9 AM - noon, Sun 2 - 4 PM, cl June July, Aug and holidays. No admis fee. Estab 1937. Average Annual Attendance: 25,000. Mem: 600; dues $5 and up; annual meeting in April
Exhibitions: Work by members, one person shows and circulating exhibitions changing at three week intervals from Oct to May
Activities: Art school instruction in painting, drawing, clay techniques and variety of handcrafts; creative development for children; special art programs; gallery talks
L **Library,** Art Center, 209 Ninth St W, 33505.
Library Holdings: Vols 850

CLEARWATER

O **FLORIDA GULF COAST ART CENTER, INC,** 222 Ponce De Leon Blvd, 33516. Tel 813-584-8634. *Managing Dir* Judith Boodon Powers; *President* Donald Ehrmann; *VPres* Mrs Gerald Keefe; *Treas* William Crown III; *Sr Secy* Emil

Marquardt; *Cur Education* Karen Tucker Kuykendall
Open Tues - Sat 10 AM - 4 PM, Sun 2 - 5 PM, cl Mon. No admis fee, donations accepted. Estab 1948 as a Regional Center for the visual arts. Gallery has 1800 sq ft of space, carpeted walls, track lighting and a security system. Average Annual Attendance: 10,000. Mem: 1000; dues patron $100, contributing $50, family $30, individual $20; annual meeting in March
Income: Financed by membership and grants
Exhibitions: Average ten exhibitions a year including regional artists, traveling exhibits, permanent collections and those organized by Art Center Staff
Activities: Classes for adults and children; workshops; lectures; films, concerts
L **Art Reference Library,** 222 Ponce de Leon Blvd, 33516.
Open Tues - Fri 10 AM - 4 PM. Estab 1948 to provide reference material and current periodicals to Art Center members and students
Library Holdings: Vols 2500; Per subs 10; AV—Slides; Other—Exhibition catalogs, pamphlets

CORAL GABLES

M **METROPOLITAN MUSEUM AND ART CENTERS,** 1212 Anastasia Ave, 33134. Tel 305-442-1448. *Dir* Dr Arnold L Lehman; *Asst Dir* Tom Schmitt; *Dir School* Juanita May; *Adminr* Dorothy Connors; *Registrar* Cynthia Sottile; *Educ Coordr* Phyllis Reischer; *Pres Board Trustees* Raymond Mathisen; *Chmn Board Trustees* Joseph R Harrison; *Chmn Board Governors* J Deering Danielson; *Education Coordr Programs* Mark Ormand; *School Registrar* Betty Buckalew; *Volunteer Coordr* Caryl Aberl
Open Tues, Wed 10 AM - 10 PM, Thurs, Fri 10 AM - 6 PM, Sat, Sun 1 - 6 PM, cl New Years, Memorial Day, July 4, Labor Day, Thanksgiving, Christmas. No admis fee. Estab 1962 as a general museum of visual arts with emphasis on Latin America, 20th century sculpture and traveling exhibitions. Six gallery spaces are devoted to both temporary and permanent exhibitions. Average Annual Attendance: 150,000. Mem: 5000; dues Life $5000, individual $15, student $10; annual meeting Sept
Income: $500,000 (financed by membership, contributions and grants)
Collections: Contemporary American painting and graphics; Fashion Group Collection of Historic Costumes; Jacques Lipchitz Sculpture Center; Martinez-Canas Collection of Contemporary Latin American Paintings; Oriental; Pre-Columbian
Exhibitions: African Art from South Florida Collections; American Magic Realists; Art De Deco; Cobra paintings and sculpture; Joseph Cornell: Collages; Image Before My Eyes: A Photographic History of Jewish Life in Poland; Roy Lichtenstein (drawings and paintings); John Marin: Watercolors; Amelia Paleaz: Retrospective; Silver from the Rio de la Plata; Third Miami International Graphics Biennial
Publications: Catalogs for exhibitions; newsletter, bimonthly
Activities: Classes for adults and children; docent training; programs for schools; lect open to public, 8 visiting lectrs per year; gallery talks; competitions; exten dept serving North Miami and Miami Beach; individual paintings and original objects of art lent to museums, libraries and educational institutions; traveling exhibitions organized and circulated; museum shop selling books, magazines, original art, reproductions, prints and slides; junior museum
L **Library,** 1212 Anastasia Ave, 33134.
Open to members for reference only
Library Holdings: Vols 2000; Per subs 6
Collections: Fern B Muskat Collection

M **UNIVERSITY OF MIAMI,** Lowe Art Museum, 1301 Miller Dr, 33146. Tel 305-284-3535. *Dir* Ira Licht; *Asst to Dir & Cur of Oriental Art* Brian A Dursum; *Cur* Jay Richard DiBiaso; *Registrar* Arlene B Dellis
Open Tues - Fri noon - 5 PM, Sat 10 AM - 5 PM, Sun 2 - 5 PM, Wed eve to 8 PM. No admis fee. Estab 1952 to bring outstanding exhibitions and collections to the community and to the University; gallery maintained
Collections: African Art; Washington Allston Trust Collection; Virgil Barker Collection of 19th & 20th Century American Art; Alfred I Barton Collection of Southwestern American Indian Textiles; Decorative Arts; Esso Collection of Latin American Art; Samuel H Kress Collection of Renaissance and Baroque Art; Samuel K Lothrop Collection of Guatemalan Textiles; Oriental Art; Pre-Columbian Peruvian Arts
Exhibitions: (1979-1980) Arms and Armor; The Art of Opinion: Don Wright and the Polemic Tradition; Erte On Stage; Red Grooms Discount Store; Jade East and West; Morris Hirshfield; Roy Lichtenstein: Recent Work; Masterworks of 19th Century; Selections from Museum of Modern Art of Latin America of OAS
Publications: Newsletter, bimonthly
Activities: Classes for adults and children; lect open to the public and for members only; Outreach program to Dade County Schools
L **Library,** 1301 Miller Dr, 33146.
For reference only

DAYTONA BEACH

M **MUSEUM OF ARTS AND SCIENCES,** Cuban Museum, Planetarium, 1040 Museum Blvd, 32014. Tel 904-255-0285. *Dir* Gary Russell Libby
Open Tues - Fri 9 AM - 5 PM, Sat Noon - 5 PM, Sun 1 - 5 PM, cl Mon & national holidays. Admis family $1, individual 50¢, museum members free. Estab 1955 to offer both educational and cultural services to the public. Large hexagonal main exhibition gallery, hall gallery and lobby gallery are maintained. Average Annual Attendance: 50,000. Mem: 1185; dues family $20; annual meeting Nov
Income: $83,000 (financed by endowment, membership, city and county appropriations and donations)
Collections: Aboriginal art including Florida Indian; American Illustration: Norman Rockwell; Cuban Collection; decorative arts including silver and furniture; Florida Contemporary Collection
Exhibitions: Great American Illustrations; Indian Cultures Exhibit; Masterpieces of Modern Art; Rockwell's America
Publications: Catalogs, monthly; newsletter, bimonthly
Activities: Classes for adults and children; dramatic programs; docent training; lect open to public, 15 visiting lectrs per year; gallery talks; concerts; tours; competitions; exten dept serving area schools; individual paintings and original objects of art lent to other museums and educational institutions; lending collection contains books, nature artifacts, original art works, original prints, paintings and sculpture; traveling exhibitions organized and circulated; sales shop selling books, magazines, reproductions, children and adult gifts
L **Library,** 1040 Museum Blvd, 32014. *Librn* Marge Segerson
Open to members and school children
Library Holdings: Vols 2500; Per subs 5
Collections: Cuban: Jose Marti Library

DELAND

M **STETSON UNIVERSITY,** Art Gallery, 32720. Tel 904-734-4121, Ext 208. *Dir* Fred Messersmith
Open Mon - Fri 9 AM - 4:30 PM. No admis fee. Estab 1964 as an educational gallery to augment studio teaching program. There is a large main gallery, 44 x 55 ft, with a lobby area 22 x 44 ft. Average Annual Attendance: 5000
Income: University art budget
Purchases: $1000
Collections: 20th Century American Prints, Oils, Watercolors
Exhibitions: American Watercolor Traveling Show; various regional artists exhibitions
Publications: Exhibition announcements, monthly
Activities: Lect open to public, 3 vis lectr per year, gallery talks; competitions

DELRAY BEACH

M **PALM BEACH COUNTY PARKS AND RECREATION DEPARTMENT,** Morikami Museum of Japanese Culture, 4000 Morikami Park Rd, 33446. Tel 305-499-0631. *Pres* Robert S Slater; *VPres* Dean Kutchera; *Secy* Mrs Clarence Plume; *Cur* Larry Rosensweig; *Asst Cur* Thomas Gregersen
Open Tues - Sun 10 AM - 5 PM. No admis fee; donations accepted. Estab 1977 to preserve and interpret Japanese culture and Japanese-American culture. Five small galleries in Japanese style building. Average Annual Attendance: 45,000. Mem: 200; dues $15; annual meeting March
Income: $45,000 (financed by membership and County appropriation)
Purchases: $3000
Collections: †Japanese folk arts (ceramics, dolls, tools, baskets, home furnishings); Japanese art (paintings, prints, textiles)
Exhibitions: Bamboo; Experience Japan; Japanese Posters: Dolls of Hakata; Kites of Japan; Sumie: Aiko Low; Yakimono: The World of Japanese Ceramics; Yamato Florida: A Photographic Essay
Publications: Newsletter, quarterly; Calendar bi-monthly; Exhibition catalogs 2 - 3 annually
Activities: Classes for children; docent training; lect open to the public, 2 - 3 vis lectr per yr; concerts; tours; book traveling exhibitions biannually; museum shop sells books, original art, postcards, Japanese items
L **Donald B Gordon Memorial Library,** Morikami Museum, 33446. *Librn* Tobie Heller
Open Tues morning and by appointment. Estab 1977 to provide printed and recorded materials on Japan
Purchases: $600
Library Holdings: Vols 300; Per subs 10; AV—Fs, Kodachromes, motion pictures, rec; Other—Exhibition catalogs, manuscripts, memorabilia, pamphlets
Special Subjects: Japan, Japanese-Americans
Collections: Memorabilia of George S Morikami

ENGLEWOOD

O **FLORIDA ARTIST GROUP INC,** PO Box 777, 33533. Tel 813-474-2644. *Pres* Lee Lasbury; *VPres* Dorothy Stewart; *Recording Secy* Margaret Kelly; *Correspondence Secy* Anne Atz; *Immediate Past Pres* Reyha Youngerman; *Member Chmn* Bunny Coppe; *Treas* Marcelle Bear
Estab 1949 for the stimulation of finer standards of the creative effort within the state of Florida. Mem: 200, qualification for mem by invitation based on artistic merit; dues $20; annual meeting April or May
Income: $4700 (financed by membership and donations)
Exhibitions: (1978) Harmon Gallery, Naples, FL; (1979) Daytona Beach Museum of Arts and Science; (1980) Sarasota Art Association Galleries
Publications: Newsletter, 3 per year
Activities: Lect open to members and public; competitions, one annual competition open to members only; Genievieve Hamel, Robert Carson and 2 Hilton Leech Memorial awards; originate traveling exhibitions

FORT LAUDERDALE

L **ART INSTITUTE OF FORT LAUDERDALE,** 3000 East Las Olas Blvd, 33316. *Personnel* Brian McKinney
Open daily 7:45 AM - 5:15 PM. Estab 1973 as a technical library for the applied and fine arts
Purchases: $8000
Library Holdings: Vols 500; Per subs 16; AV—A-tapes, cassettes, fs, motion pictures, slides, v-tapes; Other—Clipping files, prints, memorabilia, pamphlets, reproductions

M **FORT LAUDERDALE MUSEUM OF THE ARTS,** 426 E Las Olas Blvd, 33301. Tel 305-463-5184. *Dir* George S Bolge
Open Tues - Sat 10 AM - 4:30 PM, Sun Noon - 5 PM, cl Mon & national holidays. No admis fee. Estab 1958 to bring art to the community and provide cultural facilities and programs. Library, reading room, exhibit space and classrooms are maintained. Average Annual Attendance: 14,000. Mem: 1000; dues $20; annual meeting April
Income: $190,650
Purchases: $20,000

Collections: American and European Graphics; American Indian Ceramics, Stone and Basketry; paintings and sculpture from late 19th century to present; Pre-Columbian Ceramics and Stone Artifacts; West African Tribal Sculpture
Exhibitions: Annual M Allen Hortt Memorial Competition; changing monthly exhibitions
Publications: Annual Report; Bulletin, quarterly; Calendar of Events, monthly; Exhibition Catalogs
Activities: Classes for adults and children; docent training; slide lecture program in schools by request; lect; gallery talks; tours; films; competitions; individual paintings and original objects of art lent to other museums; sales shop
L **Library,*** 426 E Las Olas Blvd, 33301.
Library Holdings: Vols 1000; AV—Slides

GAINESVILLE

UNIVERSITY OF FLORIDA
M **University Gallery,** 32611. Tel 904-392-0201. *Dir* Roy C Craven Jr; *Secy* Marjorie Z Burdick
Open Mon - Fri 9 AM - 5 PM, Sun 1 - 5 PM, cl Sat and holidays. No admis fee. Estab 1965 as an arts exhibition gallery, open 11 months of the year, showing monthly exhibitions with contemporary and historical content. Gallery located in independent building with small lecture hall, limited access and completely secure with temperature and humidity control, carpet covered walls and adjustable track lighting; display area is in excess of 3000 sq ft. Average Annual Attendance: 40,000. Mem: 200; dues professor $100 and up, family $20, individual $10; annual meeting May
Income: $70,000 (financed by state appropriation)
Purchases: $2000
Collections: †European and American prints, paintings and photographs; †Oriental (India) miniatures and sculptures; †Pre-Columbian and Latin American art (also folk art)
Exhibitions: Changing monthly exhibitions; Annual University of Florida Art Faculty (January)
Publications: Bulletins; exhibitions catalogs
Activities: Docent training; lect open to public; exten dept serving area schools; lending collection contains cassetts, original art works, photographs and slides; traveling exhibitions organized and circulated
L **Architecture and Fine Arts Library,** 32611. *Librn* Anna Weaver
Library Holdings: Vols 30,000
Special Subjects: Architecture, Art Education

JACKSONVILLE

M **CUMMER GALLERY OF ART,** DeEtte Holden Cummer Museum Foundation, 829 Riverside Ave, 32204. Tel 904-356-6857. *Dir* 10; *Asst to Dir* L Vance Shrum
Open Tues - Fri 10 AM - 4 PM, Sat noon - 5 PM, Sun 2 - 5 PM, cl Mon and national holidays. No admis fee. Estab 1961 as a general art museum, collecting and exhibiting fine arts of all periods and cultures. Average Annual Attendance: 45,000
Collections: †European and American Painting, Sculpture, Graphic Arts, Tapestries and Decorative Arts; Netsuke, Inro and Porcelains; Oriental Collection of Jade, Ivory; Early Meissen Porcelain
Exhibitions: 6 - 8 special exhibitions annually
Publications: Exhibition catalogs; Handbook of the Permanent Collections
Activities: Lectures; concerts; gallery tours; gift shop
L **Library,** 829 Riverside Ave, 32204.
Open for reference
Library Holdings: Vols 4000; AV—Slides 10,000

M **JACKSONVILLE ART MUSEUM,** 4160 Boulevard Center Dr, 32204. Tel 904-398-8336. *Dir* Bruce H Dempsey
Open Tues, Wed & Fri 10 AM - 4 PM, Thurs 10 AM - 10 PM, Sat & Sun 1 - 5 PM, cl Mon, holidays and month of Aug. No admis fee. Estab 1947 as an art center for the greater Jacksonville area. Average Annual Attendance: 65,000
Income: Financed by membership and city appropriation
Collections: Pre-Columbian Art; Oriental Porcelains and Ceramics; 20th Century Paintings and Prints
Exhibitions: The American Landscape (photographs); Art of India; Elizabethan Portraiture; The Florida Connection; Florida Photographers; Helen Frankenthaler; New Realism; Rosenquist and Rauschenberg; Talent USA
Publications: Calendar, monthly; exhibition catalogues
Activities: Classes for adults and children; docent training; art enrichment program; lect open to the public, 4 - 5 vis lectr per year; concerts; gallery talks; tours; competitions; originate traveling exhibitions; museum shop sells books, magazines, original art, prints and magazines
L **Library,** 4160 Boulevard Center Dr, 32204.
Open to teachers in Duval County Schools

M **JACKSONVILLE MUSEUM OF ARTS AND SCIENCES,** 1025 Gulf Life Dr, 32207. Tel 904-396-7061. *Dir* Doris L Whitmore; *Admis Asst* Sally Taylor; *Program Developer* Michael Coffman; *Cur Coll* Nada Wineman
Open Mon - Fri 9 AM - 5 PM; Sat 11 AM - 5 PM; Sun 1 - 5 PM; cl Mon, Sept and major holidays. No admis fee. Estab 1941. Lobby and three floors contain exhibit areas, classrooms, and studios. Average Annual Attendance: 225,000. Mem: 825; dues vary
Income: Financed by membership, city appropriation, and grants
Exhibitions: Ancient Egypt; Country Store; Early Jacksonville (Cowford) during Revolution; Florida Indians of the Everglades; On the Banks of the St Johns River; dolls; health; wildlife
Publications: Teacher's Guide, annually; brochures, bimonthly; annual report
Activities: Classes for adults and children; dramatic programs; docent training; lect open to public; tours; Art in the Park; traveling exhibitions organized and circulated; museum shop and sales shop selling books, prints, museum-oriented items and toys for children

L **Library,** 1025 Gulf Life Dr, 32207.
Open to staff, docents and volunteers for reference

L **JACKSONVILLE PUBLIC LIBRARY,** Art and Music Department, 122 North Ocean St, 32201. Tel 904-633-6870. *Dir* Harry Brinton; *Art and Music Dept Librn* Jeff Driggers
Open Mon - Fri 9 AM - 9 PM, Sat 9 AM - 6 PM. No admis fee. Estab 1905 to serve the public by giving them free access to books, films, phonograph recordings, pamphlets, periodicals, maps, plus informational services and free programming. Open area on the mezzanine of the building serves as a display area for local artists
Income: Financed by city appropriation
Library Holdings: Vols 31,000; AV—Motion pictures 1935, rec 10,588, slides 5100; Other—Framed reproductions, photographs 3000, color reproductions
Publications: Annual Report
Activities: Classes for adults; weekly film programs

KEY WEST

O **KEY WEST ART AND HISTORICAL SOCIETY,** S Roosevelt Blvd, 33040. Tel 305-296-3913. *Pres* Jack Church; *VPres* Frederic Cole; *Second VPres* Margaret Foresman; *Treas* Gus Mirzaoff; *Recording Secy* Bea Howton; *Corresp Secy* Collin Jameson; *Exec Dir* Ida W Barron
Open Sun - Sat 9:30 - 5 PM. Admis $1.50 adults. Estab 1966. The gallery is located in a restored 1861 brick fort; there are three larger and four smaller galleries, all contiguous. These galleries have arched ceilings, are air conditioned and have moveable track lighting. Average Annual Attendance: 40,000. Mem: 1100; dues couple $20, individual $15, student $5; annual meeting first Wed in April
Income: $55,000 (financed by membership)
Collections: Small collection
Exhibitions: (1977-78) Annual County Schools Exhibition; American Watercolor Society Exhibition; Local-Regional Artists Exhibitions; Membership Exhibition
Publications: Martello
Activities: Sales shop sells books, magazines, original art, prints, reproductions and slides
L **Library,** S Roosevelt Blvd, 33040.
There are approximately 250 hisortical items, such as ledgers, property abstracts, books on history, and others

LAKELAND

M **FLORIDA SOUTHERN COLLEGE,** Melvin Art Gallery, Ludd M Spivey Fine Arts & Humanities Bldg, 33802. Tel 813-683-5521, Ext 431 or 244. *Coordr Art* Donna M Stoddard
Open Mon - Fri 1 - 3:30 PM. No admis fee. Estab 1971 as a teaching gallery. Small gallery dedicated to Frank Lloyd Wright (architect for college) covers 2000 running sq ft
Collections: Brass Rubbings Collection in Ronx Library; Laymon Glass Collection in Annie Pfeiffer Chapel; Permanent Collection in various offices and buildings
Exhibitions: (1978) Juried Show Number Seven (Lakeland Art Guild); Phantasies in Watercolor by Calum Darren; Recent Paintings and Drawings by Downing Barnitz; Student Honors Exhibition. (1979-80) Decade Memorial Exhibition (Eliot O'Hara Watercolors); Depression Glass Show and Sale; Juried Show Number Nine (Lakeland Art Guild); Oriental Print Show; Original Graphics; Painted Fabrics (Cloth Show, Pat Nichelson); Photography by Roger Early; Plexiglass Wall Hangings (Leonard Janklow); Pottery by Stephen Jepson; student honors exhibit

M **POLK PUBLIC MUSEUM,** 800 E Palmetto, 33801. Tel 813-688-7744. *Dir* Nancye Thornbery; *Cur Education* Barbara Adams; *Cur Exhib* Kurt Gibson; *Registrar* Katherine B Boone; *Pres* Frances S Williams; *Secy* Ellen McKeel
Open Mon - Fri 10 AM - 5 PM, Sat 10 AM - 4 PM, Sun 1 - 4 PM. No admis fee. Estab 1966 to bring changing exhibits of art, history and science to community; to provide cultural enrichment to the area. Average Annual Attendance: 16,000. Mem: 850; dues sponsor $500, sustaining $100, patron $50, family $25, individual $15, teacher $10, sr citizen and student $5
Income: Financed by membership
Purchases: $200
Collections: Barnum Collection (outstanding regional artists); Ellis Verink Photographs; 14th - 19th Century stoneware and pottery, various individual pieces of notable art and furniture
Activities: Classes for adults and children; workshops; dramatic programs; Suitcase Museum Program; lect open to public, 6 visiting lectr per year; tours; concerts
L **Library,** 800 E Palmetto, 33801. *Librn* Marjorie Givins
Open Mon - Fri 10 AM - 5 PM, Sat 10 AM - 4 PM, Sun 1 - 4 PM. Estab 1970 as Memorial Reference Library for Polk County residents. Open for reference
Income: $400
Purchases: $200
Library Holdings: Vols 500; Per subs 4; Other—Prints, photographs

MAITLAND

O **MAITLAND ART CENTER RESEARCH STUDIO,*** 231 W Packwood Ave, 32751. Tel 305-645-2181. *Dir* Charles L Baker
Open Tues - Sat 10 AM - 4 PM, Sun 1 - 5 PM, cl Mon. No admis fee. Estab 1939 to promote exploration and education in the visual arts and contemporary crafts. Gallery is maintained. Average Annual Attendance: 7500. Mem: 780; dues $10; annual meeting May
Income: Over $50,000 (financed by membership; city and state appropriations)
Purchases: Over $50,000
Collections: Architectural work including 9-acre compound and memorial chapel designed by Smith; Graphics-Paintings of Andre Smith
Publications: Imagination, bimonthly
Activities: Classes for adults and children; art training classes; lect open to public, 4 visiting lectrs per year; gallery talks; tours; concerts; competitions; scholarships; book shop

L **Library,*** 231 W Packwood Ave, 32751.
Open for reference
Library Holdings: Vols 430

MELBOURNE

M **BREVARD ART CENTER AND MUSEUM, INC,** 1510 Highland Ave, P O Box EG 782, 32935. Tel 305-254-7782. *Pres* Mrs E W Ritter; *VPres* Mrs M Scafati; *Secy* Mrs W M Braselton Jr; *Exec Dir* Robert A Gabriel; *Program Specialist* Burton B Van Scoy; *Office Mgr* Barbara Bannister
Open daily 10 AM - 5 PM, Sun 1 - 5 PM, cl Mon. No admis fee. Estab 1978 to exhibit art for the education, information, and enjoyment of the public. One story building with three galleries with approximately 5000 sq ft of exhibition space for changing exhibits; a please touch gallery for the blind. Average Annual Attendance: 20,000. Mem: 800; dues individual $15, family $25, patron $100 and up; annual meeting third Tues in May
Income: $90,000 (financed by membership, city and county appropriation, corporate gifts and grants)
Purchases: $1500
Collections: †Contemporary Regional Artists; Pre-Columbian Art
Exhibitions: Members Exhibition; Regional Art Annual
Publications: Monthly newsletter; calendar for members
Activities: Classes for adults and children; docent training; lectures open to the public, 4 vis lectr per yr; concerts; gallery talks; tours; competitions with awards; book six - eight traveling exhibitions per yr; museum shop sells books, magazines, original art, reproductions prints

MIAMI

M **DADE COUNTY ART MUSEUM,** Vizcaya Museum and Gardens, 3251 S Miami Ave, 33129. Tel 305-579-2708. *Dir* Carl J Weinhardt Jr; *Cur Education* Louise Drake; *Cur Coll* Susan W Reiling; *Research Cur* Doris B Littlefield; *Conservator* Emilio Cianfoni
Open daily 10 AM - 5 PM, cl Christmas. Admis $3.50 house and gardens, $1.50 garden only, children $1. Estab 1952 to increase the general public's appreciation of the European decorative arts, architecture and landscape design through lectures and visits conducted by trained volunteer guides. Vizcaya is a house museum with a major collection of European decorative arts and elaborate formal gardens. The Villa, formerly the home of James Deering, was completed in 1916 and contains approximately 70 rooms. Average Annual Attendance: 225,000. Mem: 1500; dues $25 and up; annual meeting fourth Wed in April
Income: $1,000,002 (financed by admission fees)
Collections: Italian and French Furniture of the 16th - 18th and Early 19th Centuries; Notable Specialized Collections of Carpets, Tapestries, Roman Antiques and Bronze Mortars
Publications: Vizcayan Newsletter, quarterly
Activities: Docent training; lect open to the public, 6 vis lectr per year; concerts; individual paintings and original objects of art lent to accredited museums; museum shop sells original art, prints and slides

L **Library,** 3251 S Miami Ave, 33129. *Vol Librn* Mrs A Miller
Open to volunteers and students of the decorative arts for reference only
Library Holdings: Vols 1500; Per subs 10; Other—archival material
Special Subjects: Decorative Arts, Furniture, Inter Design
Collections: Slide collection for reference and teaching

L **FLORIDA INTERNATIONAL UNIVERSITY LIBRARY,** Art Department, Tamiami Trail, 33199. *Dir* Howard Cordell
Open 9 AM - 9 PM. Estab 1972
Library Holdings: Vols 8000; Per subs 22; AV—Cassettes, rec, slides, v-tapes; Other—Exhibition catalogs, framed reproductions, reproductions

M **MIAMI-DADE COMMUNITY COLLEGE,** South Campus, Art Gallery,* 11011 SW 104th St, 33176. Tel 305-596-1281. *Dir Cur* Karen Valdes
Open Mon - Fri 8 AM - 4 PM, Tues & Wed 6 - 8 PM. No admis fee. Estab 1970 as a teaching laboratory and public service
Income: Financed by state appropriation
Purchases: $75,000
Collections: Contemporary American paintings, photographs, prints, sculpture includes: Beal, Boice, Bolotowsky, Christo, Fine, Hepworth, Hockney, Judd, Oldenburg, Pearlstein, Remington
Exhibitions: Bruce Boice; Bolotowsky; Mark Cohen; Five Washington Artists; Audrey Flack; Bob Thiele; Hap Tivey; Deborah Remington; Willia T Williams
Activities: Lect open to public, 6-7 visiting lectrs per year; gallery talks; individual paintings and original objects of art lent; lending collection contains original art works, original prints, paintings, photographs, sculpture; traveling exhibitions organized and circulated

L **MIAMI-DADE PUBLIC LIBRARY,** One Biscayne Blvd, 33132. Tel 305-579-5001. *Dir* Edward F Sintz; *Asst Dir* Ben J Guilford II; *Supv Processing Center* Lilliam Conesa; *Supv Traveling Libraries* Carol Gawron; *Public Relations Coordr* Mrs Micki Carden; *Supv Branches* Eleanor McLaughlin; *Coordr Work with Children and Young Adults* Anne Boegen; *Art Librn* Margarita Cano; *Artmobile Librn* Barbara Edwards
Open Mon - Fri 10 AM - 9 PM, Sat 10 AM - 6 PM, Sun 1 - 5 PM. Estab 1947 to provide the informational, educational and recreational needs of the community. Circ 2,659,312. Gallery maintained
Income: $10,400,150 (financed by special millage)
Library Holdings: Vols 1,238,352; Per subs 2900; Micro—Fiche, reels; AV—Motion pictures, rec; Other—Clipping files, exhibition catalogs, framed reproductions, original art works, photographs, reproductions, sculpture
Special Subjects: Latin American Art
Collections: Black American Original Graphics; Latin American Original Graphics; Oriental Collection of Original Graphics
Exhibitions: African Art; Venezuelan Artists of Today
Publications: Exhibition catalogs

Activities: Lect open to public; concerts; gallery talks; tours; competitions; exten dept; artmobile; originate traveling exhibitions

C **SOUTHEAST BANKING CORPORATION,** 100 S Biscayne Blvd, 33131. Tel 305-577-4033. *In Charge Art Coll* Jean H Johnson
Estab 1974 to benefit and provide an attractive working environment for employees and bank customers; belief that support of the arts is one of the corporation's links to the community. Collection displayed throughout banks in Florida
Collections: Mostly contemporary pieces consisting of graphics, oils, sculpture and works on paper (1600 pieces)
Activities: In-house art department works closely with the local visual and performing art organizations in the community

MIAMI BEACH

M **BASS MUSEUM OF ART,** 2100 Collins Ave, 33139. Tel 305-673-7530. *Adminr* Phyllis A Gray; *Chmn of the Board* Harold T Toal
Open Tues - Sat 10 AM - 5 PM. No admis fee. Estab 1963 to provide a pleasant atmosphere for the viewing of the various art and artifacts that have been donated to the city; all of the art in the museum was donated by Mr John Bass. The museum is a two-story building comprising of seven gallery rooms. Average Annual Attendance: 21,000
Income: $67,000 (financed by city appropriation)
Collections: Permanent collection of church vestments, Old Master paintings, Renaissance sculpture, and others
Activities: sales shop selling photographs and postcards

L **MIAMI BEACH PUBLIC LIBRARY,** 2100 Collins Ave, 33139. *Chief Librn* Phyllis A Gray
Open Mon - Wed 10 AM - 9 PM, Thurs - Sat 10 AM - 5:30 PM. Estab 1927 to serve the citizens of Miami Beach. Circ 425,000. Maintains an art gallery. The Library Department manages the Bass Museum of Art which is housed in the former library building
Income: $400,000 (financed by city appropriation)
Purchases: $38,500
Library Holdings: Vols 186,000; Per subs 250; AV—Rec; Other—Clipping files, pamphlets

M **SAINT BERNARD FOUNDATION AND MONASTERY,** 16711 W Dixie Hwy, 33139. Tel 305-945-1462. *Exec Dir* Bruce E Bailey
Open Mon - Sat 10 AM - 5 PM; Noon - 5 PM Sun. Admis adults $3, children 6-12 75¢, under 6 free. Estab 1141. A reconstruction of a monastery built in Segovia, Spain, in 1141, with original stones brought to the United States by William Randolph Hearst
Income: Financed by members and donations of visitors
Collections: Historic and Religious Material; paintings; sculpture
Activities: Tours; museum loan exhibitions; arts festivals; sales shop

OCALA

M **CENTRAL FLORIDA COMMUNITY COLLEGE ART COLLECTION,** 3001 SW College Rd, Box 1388, 32670. Tel 904-237-2111. *Pres* Henry Goodlett; *Gallery Dir* Cramer Swords
Open Mon - Fri 8 AM - 9:30 PM. No admis fee. Estab 1967 as a service to the community. Gallery is the lobby to the auditorium. Average Annual Attendance: 5000
Income: Financed by state appropriations
Collections: Contemporary Artists of Varied Media
Exhibitions: Changing monthly shows, with one show for the summer
Publications: Windfall
Activities: Classes for adults; scholarships

ORLANDO

O **LOCH HAVEN ART CENTER, INC,** 2416 N Mills Ave, 32803. Tel 305-896-4231. *Dir* Marena R Grant; *Cur Education* Maralynn Troutman
Open Tues - Sat 10 AM - 5 PM, Sun 2 - 5 PM. Generally no admis fee. Estab 1926 to encourage the awareness of and participation in the visual arts. Accredited by the American Association of Museums. Average Annual Attendance: 200,000. Mem: 1800; dues vary; annual meeting in May
Income: Financed by membership, city appropriation and grants
Collections: 20th Century American, Pre-Columbian and African Art
Exhibitions: Major exhibitions in various media and styles
Publications: Bulletin and various catalogs
Activities: Classes for adults and children; docent training; workshop; lect open to public, 3 - 5 vis lectr per year; concerts; gallery talks; tours; film series; visiting artists; exten dept serving central Florida; individual paintings and original objects of art lent to organizations within central Florida; lending collection contains original prints; originate traveling exhibitions; museum and sales shop sells books, cards, original art, prints and reproductions

L **Library,** 2416 N Mills Ave, 32803.
Library Holdings: Vols 1000; Per subs 5

O **PINE CASTLE CENTER OF THE ARTS, INC,** 5903 Randolph St, 32809. Tel 305-855-7461. *Executive Dir* Suzanne Nicola; *Music Dir* Constance King; *Accountant* Alice W Arnold; *Secy* Pauline O Pitter
Open 9 AM - 5 PM. No admis fee. Estab 1965 as a non-profit community cultural center which provides programs in visual arts, folk crafts, local history, music and drama, and sponsors special projects for handicapped and senior citizens. One room 15 x 15 ft in main building; 85 yr old cracker farm house. Average Annual Attendance: 19,000. Mem: Annual meeting in March
Income: $96,000 (financed by membership, private foundation, state and county grants)
Collections: Oral histories of area Old-timers, along with photographs, memorabilia and antiques

Exhibitions: Members' Exhibition
Publications: Pioneer Days Historical Quarterly; Quarterly Newsletter
Activities: Classes for adults and children; dramatic programs; lect open to the public, 2 vis lectr per yr; Folk Art Events; concerts

ORMOND BEACH

M TOMOKA STATE PARK MUSEUM, N Beach St, 32074. Tel 904-677-9463. *Museum Guide* Leanna W Ray
Open Wed - Sun 9 AM - 5 PM; cl Mon & Tues. Admis 25¢. Estab 1967
Income: Financed by state appropriation
Collections: Indian Artifacts; Paintings and Sculptures by Fred Dana Marsh
Exhibitions: Florida Geology; Florida History; Indian Artifacts; Paintings and Sculptures by Fred Dana Marsh; wildlife
Publications: Richard Oswald: Tomoka State Park's Hero of the Revolution (brochure)
Activities: Tours

PALM BEACH

M HENRY MORRISON FLAGLER MUSEUM, Whitehall Way, Box 969, 33480. Tel 305-655-2833. *Pres & Trustee* George G Matthews; *Executive Dir* Charles B Simmons; *Asst to Dir* Nan Dennison
Open Tues - Sun 10 AM - 5 PM, cl Mon. Admis adults $2.50, children 6 - 12 $1. Estab 1960 for preservation and interpretation of the Whitehall mansion, the 1901 residence built for Standard Oil partner and pioneer developer of Florida's east coast, Henry Morrison Flagler. Fifty room historic house with restored rooms and special collections, plus addition used for Junior League, Historical Society and special events and exhibitions. Average Annual Attendance: 96,337. Mem: 550; dues $25; annual meeting Fri preceding first Sat in Feb
Income: Financed by endowment, membership
Collections: Original family furnishings, costumes; ceramics, lace, paintings and silver
Exhibitions: Various temporary exhibits
Publications: The Henry Morrison Flagler Museum
Activities: Docent training; lect open to public, 2 - 5 vis lectr per year; gallery talks; tours; individual paintings and original objects of art lent by request; museum shop sells books, slides and postcards
L Library, Whitehall Way, Box 969, 33480.
For reference and by appointment only, in conjunction with Historical Society
Collections: Archives

O SOCIETY OF THE FOUR ARTS, Four Arts Plaza, 33480. Tel 305-655-7226. *Pres* Walter S Gubelmann; *VPres* Mrs James A dePeyster; *Vpres* Philip Hulitar; *VPres* Mrs Robert A Magowan; *VPres* Wiley R Reynolds; *Secy-Treas* William E P Doelger; *Dir* James M Brown; *Asst to Dir* Gabrielle Summerville
Open Dec to mid-April Mon - Sat 10 AM - 5 PM, Sun 2 - 5 PM. Admis to exhibition galleries free. Estab 1936 to encourage an appreciation of the arts by presentation of exhibitions, lectures, concerts, films and programs for young people and the maintenance of a fine library and gardens. Five galleries for exhibitions, separate general library, gardens and auditorium. Average Annual Attendance: 72,000 (galleries and library). Mem: 1500; dues life $5,000, sustaining $225, double $175, single $115; annual meeting third Fri in March
Income: $609,000 (Financed by endowment, membership, city appropriation toward maintenance of library and contributions)
Collections: Small collection of approximately 20 works
Exhibitions: Ansel Adams: A Survey (1979-1980); Charles Burchfield: Drawings and Paintings from the Charles Rand Penney Collection; California Landscape Painting From the early 1860's through 1915 from the Collections of the Oakland Museum and John Garzoli of San Francisco; 40th Annual Exhibition of Contemporary American Paintings; 41st Annual Exhibition of Contemporary American Paintings; La Belle Epoque: Drawings, watercolors and posters by three of the most important artists of the Art Nouveau style in Belgium and Europe at large from the Collection of Mr and Mrs Wittamer de Camps; The Meadows Collection (Impressionist and Early Modern Masters loaned through the courtesy of Mrs Algur H Meadows and the Meadows Foundation); The Painter's West (Selections from the Rockwell-Corning Collection including Remington, Russell, Bierstadt, Catlin and others); Rites of Passage (Textiles of the Indonesian Archipelago from the Collection of Mary Hunt Kahlenberg); The Sensuous Line (Indian drawings of the 17th, 18th and 19 centuries from the Paul F Walter Collection); Twentieth Century Master Photographers From the Collection of the Virginia Museum of Fine Arts; Twentiey Century Sculptors and Their Drawings (Selected works from the Hirshhorn Museum and Sculpture Garden)
Publications: Calendar; Jan, Feb and March; Schedule of Events, annual
Activities: Programs for young people; lect open to the public when space permits; otherwise limited to members, 13 vis lectr per year; concerts; films; competitions open to artists resident in United States; juror selects about 90 paintings for inclusion in annual exhibition; $5000 cash awards are given
L Library, Four Arts Plaza, 33480. *Librn* Helen McKinney; *Cir Librn* Irene D Stevenson; *Children's Librn* Evelyn Rand
Open Mon - Fri 10 AM - 5 PM, cl Sat May to Nov. Circ 38,000
Income: $84,000 (financed by endowment, membership and city appropriation)
Purchases: $12,000
Library Holdings: Vols 28,000; Per subs 56
Collections: Addison Mizner Collection which consists of over 300 reference books and scrapbooks in Mizner's personal library
Activities: Library tours

PENSACOLA

O HISTORIC PENSACOLA PRESERVATION BOARD, West Florida Museum of History,* 205 E Zaragoza St, 32501. Tel 904-434-1042. *Dir* James W Moody Jr; *Chief Cur* Russell Belous
Open Mon - Sat 10 AM - 4:30 PM, Sun 1 - 4:30 PM, cl New Years, Thanksgiving, Christmas. No admis fee, Walton House 25¢. Estab 1967 for collection,

preservation, and interpretation of artifacts dealing with the history and culture of Pensacola and West Florida. Main gallery includes history of development of West Florida as well as area for temporary exhibits. Average Annual Attendance: 60,000
Income: Approx $350,000 (financed by city, county, and state appropriations, sales and rentals)
Collections: Costumes; decorative arts; local artists
Exhibitions: Clockwork Music and Talking Machines; The Seat of American Invention, The World of Lilliput, and American Agriculture (SITES)
Activities: Educ dept; docent training; sales shop selling books, reproductions and local crafts
L Library,* 200 E Zaragoza St, 32501.
Open to the public for reference
Library Holdings: Vols 800; Per subs 15; AV—Slides; Other—Photographs
Special Subjects: Architecture, Decorative Arts, Historical Material, Regional history

M PENSACOLA JUNIOR COLLEGE, Visual Arts Gallery, 1000 College Blvd, 32504. Tel 904-476-5410, Ext 268. *Dir* Allan Peterson; *Secy* Cindy Hill
Open Mon - Thurs 8 AM - 9 PM, Fri 8 AM - 3:30 PM, cl weekends. No admis fee. Average Annual Attendance: 15,000
Income: Financed by state appropriation
Collections: †Contemporary ceramics, glass, drawings, paintings, prints, photographs, sculpture
Exhibitions: Five Printmakers; The Glassmaker: Historic and Contemporary; Old Masters: Selections from the Ringling Museum; Pensacola National Crafts Exhibition; Pensacola National Printmaking Exhibition; Three Florida Painters
Publications: Catalog, Brochure or Poster for each Exhibition; (seven annually)
Activities: lectures open to the public, 3 - 6 vis lectr per yr; workshops; gallery talks; competitions with awards given; scholarships offered for second year students; individual paintings and original objects of art lent to other museums and lending collection contains original art works; book traveling exhibitions; traveling exhibitions organized and circulated

M PENSACOLA MUSEUM OF ART, 407 S Jefferson St, 32501. Tel 904-432-6247. *Pres* Marilyn O Godwin; *Secy* Sarah J Doyle; *Treas* Joseph J Campus III; *Dir* Mary H Takach; *Cur Education* Charley M Harris
Open Tues - Sat 10 AM - 5 PM, cl Sun & Mon. No admis fee. Estab 1954 to further and disseminate information and instruction with regard to all of the Fine Arts and to increase knowledge and appreciation thereof. Museum is a historical building, old city jail built in 1908, and has 13,000 sq ft of exhibition area. Average Annual Attendance: 12,000. Mem: 550; dues $7.50 and up; annual meeting Oct
Income: $62,000 (financed by membership, city and state appropriation and private business)
Collections: Contemporary Art
Exhibitions: Changing displays of permanent collection; In-house organized exhibitions; traveling exhibitions
Activities: Classes for adults and children; docent training; lect open to public; competitions; book traveling exhibitions; originate traveling exhibitions; museum shop sells books, reproductions, crafts and jewelry; junior museum
L Harry Thornton Library, 407 S Jefferson St, 32501. Tel 904-432-6247.
Open Tues - Sat 10 AM - 5 PM, Sun 1 - 4 PM. Estab 1968 to provide reference material for public and members
Income: Financed by membership, city appropriation and grants by state and federal government
Purchases: $250
Library Holdings: Vols 200; Per subs 10; AV—Cassettes, slides; Other—Exhibition catalogs
Collections: Complete set of E Benezit's Dictionaire des Peintres, Sculpteurs, Dessinateurs et Graveurs; Encyclopedia of World Art and other art references books
Exhibitions: (1978) North American Indian Art; (1979) East Hampton Art Colony; (1980) The Impressionist Vision in American Art; high school art show, member artist show
Publications: Exhibitions catalogs; Newsletter, 6 per year
Activities: Classes for adults and children; docent tours; lect open to public, 5 visiting lectr per year; films; concerts; tours; competitions; purchase and category awards; fels; originate traveling exhibitions

M UNIVERSITY OF WEST FLORIDA, Art Gallery, 32504. Tel 904-476-9500. *Dir* Duncan E Stewart; *Chmn* Robert L Armstrong
Open Mon - Thurs 9:30 AM - 7:30 PM; Fri 9:30 AM - 4 PM; cl Sat & Sun. No admis fee. Estab 1975 to hold exhibitions which will relate to our role as a senior level university. Gallery includes a foyer gallery 10 x 40 ft, and a main gallery of 1500 sq ft. It is fully air-conditioned and has carpeted walls with full facilities for construction and display. Average Annual Attendance: 3000
Income: $4000 (financed by state appropriation)
Collections: Photographs and prints by a number of traditional and contemporary artists
Activities: Lect open to public, 3 vis lectr per year; gallery talks; tours; competitions; originate traveling exhibitions

M T T WENTWORTH, JR MUSEUM, 8382 Palafox Highway, PO Box 806, 32594. Tel 909-438-3638. *Dir & Cur* T T Wentworth Jr; *Deputy Dir & Secy* T W Wentworth
Open Sat - Sun 2 - 6 PM. No admis fee. Estab 1957 to conserve historical items and make them available to the public; art sections to encourage art and exhibit local art work. Mem: Annual meeting Aug
Income: Financed by membership and founder's contributions
Collections: Works of local and some nationally famous artists; Indian artifacts; coins; porcelain
Exhibitions: Special yearly art exhibit of some distinguished local artist

SAFETY HARBOR

M SAFETY HARBOR MUSEUM OF HISTORY AND FINE ARTS, 329 S Bayshore Dr, Box 141, 33572. *Pres* H G Pilcher; *VPres* J W McCain; *Secy & Treas* Thelma H Bull; *Dir* Charles C Styron; *VPres* Neal Lube; *Cur* James R Miller; *Asst Cur* Sandra Matos; *Secy* Georgia Miller
Open Mon, Wed & Fri 2 - 5 PM, Sat & Sun 1 - 5 PM. No admis fee. Estab 1977 to promote, encourage, maintain and operate a museum for the preservation of knowledge and appreciation of Florida's history; to display and interpret historical materials and allied fields. Average Annual Attendance: 10,000. Mem: 140; dues $10; annual meeting July
Income: $2000 (financed by membership, city appropriation and donations)
Collections: Fossils; dioramas, Indian artifacts; natural history exhibits
Activities: Classes for adults and children; docent training; slide and narrative programs; lect open to public; tours; individual paintings and original objects of art lent

SAINT AUGUSTINE

O SAINT AUGUSTINE ART ASSOCIATION GALLERY, 22 Marine St, 32084. Tel 904-824-2310. *Pres* Kay Huppi; *VPres* Joe Horn; *Secy* Jean Troemel; *Treas* Enzo Torcoletti; *Gallery Dir* Lee Chellemi
Open Tue - Sat 11 AM - 3 PM, Sun 2 - 5 PM. Estab 1924, inc 1934 as a non-profit organization to further art appreciation in the community by exhibits and instruction. Average Annual Attendance: 8000. Mem: 425; dues $10 and up
Collections: Permanent collection of donated and purchased works
Exhibitions: Oct to June changing monthly
Activities: Classes; demonstrations; lectures; social events

SAINT AUGUSTINE HISTORICAL SOCIETY

M Oldest House and Museums, 14 Saint Frances St, 32084. Tel 904-829-9624. *Pres* Carleton Calkin; *VPres* Hubert W Carcaba; *Secy* W J Winter; *Treas* Charles Coomes; *Mgr* Virginia Solana
Open Mon - Fri 9 AM - 5:30 PM; cl Christmas Day. Admis adults $1, students 50¢. Estab 1883 to preserve the Spanish heritage of the United States through exhibits in historic museum with collection of furnishings appropriate to the periods in Saint Augustine history (1565 to date). The Oldest House was acquired in 1918; it is owned and operated by the Saint Augustine Historical Society; it has been designated a National Historic Landmark by the Department of the Interior and is listed in the national register of historic sites and places. Average Annual Attendance: 105,000
Income: Financed by admissions
Collections: Archaeological Material recovered from this area, both aboriginal and colonial; Period Furnishings
L Library, 271 Charlotte St, 32084. Tel 904-829-5512. *Mgr* J Carver Harris; *Admin Asst* Jacqueline Bearden
Open Mon - Fri 9 AM - Noon and 1 - 5 PM; cl holidays. Research library
Income: Financed by endowment and admissions from Oldest House
Library Holdings: Vols 5500; Per subs 40; Micro—Reels; AV—A-tapes, cassettes, Kodachromes, motion pictures, rec, slides; Other—Clipping files, prints, manuscripts, memorabilia, original art works, pamphlets, photographs, reproductions, sculpture, original documents
Special Subjects: Florida history (to 1821) with emphasis on early periods of Saint Augustine history to the present
Collections: Paintings of early artists and of early Saint Augustine; 200 linear feet of maps, photographs, documents and photostats of Spanish Archival Materials as touching directly on Saint Augustine's History during the early Spanish, British and American periods (1565 to present)
Publications: East Florida Gazette, quarterly; El Escribano, annually
Activities: Lect open to public, 4 vis lectr per year

SAINT PETERSBURG

M MUSEUM OF FINE ARTS OF SAINT PETERSBURG, FLORIDA, INC, 255 Beach Dr N, 33701. Tel 813-896-2667. *Dir* Marion L Grayson; *Asst Dir* Alan Du Bois; *Exec Secy* Mrs Robert S Baer; *Mem & Museum Shop* Mrs Edgar Andruss; *Registrar* Mrs Thomas C Laughlin
Open Tues - Sat 10 AM - 5 PM; Sun 1 - 5 PM; cl Mon. Admis by voluntary donation. Estab 1961 to increase and diffuse knowledge and appreciation of art; to collect and preserve objects of artistic interest; to provide facilities for research and to offer popular instruction and opportunities for esthetic enjoyment of art. Nine galleries of works including American and European paintings, drawings, prints and photographs; French, American, Oriental sculpture; decorative arts; pre-Columbian art. Average Annual Attendance: 40,978. Mem: 3100; dues $5 and higher; annual meeting April or May
Income: $360,000 (financed by endowment, membership, city and state appropriation)
Purchases: $50,000
Collections: Decorative arts; drawings; paintings; photographs; prints; sculpture
Exhibitions: (1978) Campbell Collection; Glass of the Art Nouveau Period; The History of Fashion Photography; Master Prints from the 15th through 18th Century; New Washington Painters; On Assignment: Photography by Sam Shere; Photo Realism; Prints from the Noel Wisdom Collection; Sringar: A Pageantry of Indian Costumes; VanDongen; West Meets East: Impressionism in 19th Century Prints; (1979) The American Scene; An Opera Design by Dali; Antique American Toy Show; Ilya Bolotowsky; Charles Burchfield: His Painting and Related Works; Changing Colors of Stained Glass; Contemporary Silversmiths: Holloware; Lila Katzen Sculpture Show: Plates, Ribbons and Fans; Mask Exhibition; One Man's Vision: The Graphic Works of Odilon Redon; Paintings by Sebastian Matta; Pre-Columbian and African Art from the Pollack Collection; Prints from the Guggenheim Museum Collection; Syd Solomon: The Seventies; Wedgwood from a Local Collection
Publications: Mosaic, quarterly newsletter; Pharos, scholarly magazine
Activities: Classes for adults and children; docent training; films; lectures; Brownbagger Special Lunch; concerts; videocassettes; 3 vis lectr per year; gallery talks; tours; individual paintings and original objects of art lent to other museums;

lending collection contains color reproductions, framed reproductions, motion pictures, original art works and prints, photographs; originate traveling exhibitions; museum shop sells books, reproductions, prints, museum replicas, jewelry, pottery and crafts by local artisans
L Art Reference Library, 255 Beach Dr N, 33701. Tel 813-896-2667. *Dir* Lee Malone; *Asst Dir* Alan Du Bois
Open Tues - Fri 10 AM - 5 PM; cl Mon; special arrangements for Sat or Sun hours. Estab 1965 to promote the appreciation of art and Art Reference
Income: $3500
Purchases: $3500
Library Holdings: Vols 5500; Per subs 30; AV—A-tapes, motion pictures, slides, v-tapes; Other—Exhibition catalogs, reproductions
Collections: Photography
Activities: Classes for adults and children; lect open to the public, 6 vis lectr per year; concerts; gallery talks; exten dept serves public schools

SARASOTA

M JOHN AND MABLE RINGLING MUSEUM OF ART, 5401 Bayshore Rd, Box 1838, 33578. *Dir* Richard S Carroll; *Admin* Gerald Gartenberg; *Cur of Collections* William H Wilson; *Cur Contemporary Art* Elayne H Varian; *Registrar* Elizabeth S Telford; *Cur Ringling Museum of the Circus* John H Hurdle; *Head Education & State Service* John P Daniels; *Chief Public Information* Robert K Ardren; *Comptroller* George D Porter; *Conservator* G Theodore Nightwine
Open Mon - Fri 9 AM - 10 PM; Sun 11 AM - 6 PM. Admis $3.50, children under 12 free; Museum of Art free on Sat. Estab 1946. Bequeathed to the State of Florida by John Ringling and operated by the state; built in Italian villa style around sculpture garden on 38 landscaped acres; original 18th century theater from Asolo, near Venice, in adjacent building; Ringling Residence and Ringling Museum of the Circus on grounds. Mem: Dues individual $15, family $25
Collections: Archaeology of Cyprus; Baroque Pictures, especially those of Peter Paul Rubens; †European Painting, Sculpture, Drawings and Prints from the 16th, 17th & 18th Centuries; Medals and 18th Century Decorative Arts; †developing Collection of 19th & 20th Century Painting, Sculpture, Drawings and Prints
Exhibitions: Richard Anuszkiewicz, retrospective; Cuban Art, 1759-1959; Raoul Dufy, retrospective; Dutch 17th Century Portraiture: The Golden Age; Marca-Relli, retrospective; Masterworks on Paper: Prints and Drawings from the Ringling Museum 1400-1900; James Rosenquist, graphics
Publications: Calendar, monthly; Collection Catalogues; Exhibition Catalogues; Newsletter, quarterly; Program Schedule, annually
Activities: Dramatic prog; docent training; lect series; concerts; art carnival; crafts festival; medieval fair; classic and foreign film series; winter opera season; statewide programs of exhibitions and lectures
L Art Research Library, 5401 Bayshore Rd, 33578. *Librn* Valentine L Schmidt
Open to public for reference
Library Holdings: Vols 8000; Per subs 50
Special Subjects: Art History, emblematics, iconography, Renaissance and Baroque Art

L RINGLING SCHOOL OF ART LIBRARY, 1191 27th St, 33580. Tel 813-355-1232. *Head Librn* Elsie H Straight; *Slide Cur* Martin L Gerbens; *Periodicals Librn* Nan Gebhart
Open 9 AM - 4:30 PM, 7 - 9 PM. Estab 1932 to serve the curriculum needs of this school, Visual Art being the exclusive purpose of the school, therefore the library collection is built on that premise. Circ 12,000. Art gallery is maintained
Income: $10,000 (financed by a library association)
Purchases: $10,000
Library Holdings: Vols 9000; Per subs 90; AV—Fs, slides; Other—Clipping files, exhibition catalogs, prints, original art works, pamphlets, reproductions, sculpture
Special Subjects: Art History, Graphic Design, Illustration, Inter Design, Fine Arts
Collections: Jackson Collection of Japanese Books and Prints; Simmens Collection of 17th, 18th and 19th Century Prints and Engraving (contains 500 portrait engravings of French Revolutionary characters) Cecil Duff-Stevens Collection of 17th and 18th Century Copper and Steel Engravings

O SARASOTA ART ASSOCIATION, Civic Center, 707 N Tamiami Trail, 33577. Tel 813-365-2032. *Pres* Orodon Hobbs; *Gallery Dir* Virginia Klemmer
Open Oct - May, Mon - Fri 10 AM - 5 PM; Sat & Sun 1 - 4 PM. No admis fee. Estab 1926, inc 1940. Average Annual Attendance: 17,000. Mem: Over 1000; dues $5 - $1000; annual meeting Spring
Exhibitions: Ten to twelve exhibitions
Publications: Bulletin, monthly; yearbook
Activities: Lect; demonstrations; competitions with cash awards
L Library, Civic Center, 707 N Tamiami Trail, 33577.
Open for art reference
Library Holdings: Vols 200

STUART

O MARTIN COUNTY HISTORICAL SOCIETY, Elliott Gallery, 825 NE Ocean Blvd, 33494. *Dir* Janet Hutchinson
Open daily 1 - 5 PM. No admis fee to gallery, museum admis adults $1, children 6 - 13 50¢. Society estab 1955; gallery estab 1965. Gallery exhibits contemporary artists of prominence. Average Annual Attendance: 50,000. Mem: 1040
Collections: Small collection of original art works and sculpture not on public display
Exhibitions: Four exhibitions a year
Publications: Progress Report, quarterly
Activities: Dramatic programs; lectr open to public; concerts; receptions; sales shop sells books and gifts
L Library, 825 NE Ocean Blvd, 33494.
Open to members for reference
Library Holdings: Vols 1000; Per subs 5

TALLAHASSEE

M FLORIDA STATE UNIVERSITY, Art Gallery, Fine Arts Building, 32306. Tel 904-644-6836. *Dir* Albert Stewart
Open Mon - Fri 10 AM - 4 PM; Sat - Sun 1 - 4 PM; cl school holidays. Estab 1950. Average Annual Attendance: 60,000
Income: Financed by state appropriations
Collections: Asian Prints; Carter Collection of Peruvian Art; Contemporary American Graphics and Paintings; European Painting; Old Master Works on paper
Exhibitions: Permanent Collections; changing exhibition schedule of Major Art Historical Works and Contemporary American Art
Activities: Docent training; workshops; internships for graduate students; Lect; gallery talks; volunteer program

M LEMOYNE ART FOUNDATION, 125 N Gadsden St, 32301. Tel 813-222-8800. *Dir* Nancy J McIntyre; *AsstDir* Stephen Oakley; *Business Mgr* Charlene Williams
Open Tues - Sat 10 AM - 5 PM; Sun 2 - 5 PM; cl Mon. No admis fee. Estab 1963 as a non-profit organization to serve as gallery for contemporary, quality art; class center; sponsor the visual arts in Tallahassee; an educational institution in the broadest sense. Located in Meginnes-Munroe House, built c 1840; five main galleries and gallery shop. Average Annual Attendance: 7000. Mem: 976; dues $15
Income: $100,000 (financed by membership, sales, classes and fund raisers)
Collections: William Watson Collection of Ceramics; Karl Zerbe Serigraphs
Publications: Newsletter, monthly
Activities: Classes for adults and children; lect open to public, 10 vis lectr per year; gallery talks; tours; competitions; exten dept serving surrounding rural counties; individual paintings and original objects of art lent to businesses and members; lending collection contains original art works, original prints; paintings and sculpture; sales shop sells original art and prints

M TALLAHASSEE JUNIOR MUSEUM, 3945 Museum Dr, 32304. Tel 904-576-1636.
Open Tues - Sat 9 AM - 5 PM; Sun 2 - 5 PM. Admis adults $1.50, children 3 - 16 50¢; members free. Estab 1957 to educate children and adults about natural history, native wildlife, North Florida history, art and culture. Facilities include 1880's farm, historic buildings, exhibit and class buildings, 40 acres of nature trails, and animal habitats. Average Annual Attendance: 100,000. Mem: 1582; dues $10 - $100; annual meeting third Thurs in Jan
Income: $188,000 (financed by membership, fund raisers and county school board appropriations)
Collections: Decorative Arts; Figurines; Oriental Items; Pre-Columbian Florida Indian Pottery
Exhibitions: Changing exhibit on art, clothing, crafts, history, and science; permanent or semi-permanent (3 years) exhibits on local history and natural history
Publications: Guidebook Series; Newsletter, monthly; School Handbook
Activities: Classes for adults and children; lect open to public, 8-12 vis lectr per year; concerts; tours; original objects of art lent to local school groups, and to civic organizations occasionally; lending collection contains 150 boxed exhibits on art, culture, history and science; sales shop sells books, and mainly science and history objects
L Library, 3945 Museum Dr, 32304.
Open to members
Library Holdings: Vols 300; Per subs 7
Collections: Ivan Gundrum Pre-Columbian Florida Indian Artifacts (reproductions) representing the Weeden Island culture 500 - 1500 AD

TAMPA

C FIRST NATIONAL BANK OF FLORIDA, 111 Madison St, PO Box 1810, 33601. Tel 813-224-1427. *In Charge Art Coll* Art Wiggins
Open 8:30 AM - 5 PM. Estab 1973. Collection displayed on all floors of bank
Collections: Acrylic on canvas, aluminum sculpture, ceramic raku, collages (paper, Plexiglas and serigraph), lithographs, oils, silk screen, silk screen on mirrored Plexiglas and plastic, sculpture, serigraphs and wool tapestries
Activities: Tours; individual objects of art lent to Tampa Museum

M HENRY B PLANT MUSEUM, 401 W Kennedy Blvd, 33606. Tel 813-253-8861, Ext 400. *Dir* Doris J Dickson
Open Tues - Sat 10 AM - 4 PM; cl holidays. No admis fee. Estab 1933 in the old Tampa Bay Hotel built in 1891
Income: Financed by city appropriation, University of Tampa and donations
Collections: Late Victorian Furniture and Objects d'Art of Same Period; Venetian Mirrors; Wedgwood, Oriental Porcelains
Exhibitions: Exhibits relating to 19th Century
Publications: Collections of the Henry B Plant Museum
Activities: Antique evaluation clinic: survey of antiques and collectibles (8 week course); Monthly lect for adults, programming for children; tours; originate traveling exhibitions

M TAMPA MUSEUM, (Formerly Tampa Bay Art Center) 601 Doyle Carlton Dr, 33602. Tel 813-223-8128. *Dir* Shirley R Howarth; *Cur* Genevieve Linnehan; *Development Coordr* Susan Taylor; *Preparator* Bob Hellier; *Store Mgr* Lynn Boger; *Membership Coordr* Molly Jensen; *Executive Secy* Beverly Coe; *Education Coordr* Annette D Jones
Open Mon, Tues, Thurs & Fri 10 AM - 6 PM, Wed 10 AM - 9 PM, Sat 9 AM - 5 PM, Sun 1 - 5 PM, cl New Years, Memorial Day, July 4, Labor Day, Thanksgiving, Christmas. No admis fee. Estab 1979. Mem: 2000, dues vary
Income: Financed by membership, city and state appropriation and grants
Collections: C Paul Jennewein Collection of Sculpture; Pre-Columbian Sculpture; 20th century paintings and prints
Exhibitions: Arts of Europe: 1600 - 1780; Circus in America; Reflections: The Child in America; Romantic America: The Middle Decades of the 19th Century
Publications: Annual Report, Exhibition catalogs; Newsletter, monthly
Activities: Classes for adults and children; workshops; docent training; lectures open to the public, 5 visiting lectr per year; concerts; gallery talks; tours; competitions with awards; book traveling exhibitions; originate traveling

exhibitions; museum shop sells ceramics, original art, paintings, prints and reproductions
L Library, 601 Doyle Carlton Drive, 33602. *Dir* Shirles Howarth
For reference only
Library Holdings: Per subs 25; Micro—Fiche; AV—A-tapes, cassettes, fs, Kodachromes, slides; Other—Clipping files, exhibition catalogs, prints, original art works, pamphlets, photographs, sculpture

M UNIVERSITY OF SOUTH FLORIDA, University Galleries, College of Fine Arts, Art Dept, 4202 E Fowler Ave, 33620. Tel 813-974-2375. *Dir* Margaret A Miller; *Mgr* Pamela Miles; *Asst Cur* Michelle S Juristo; *Museum Supv* Roy Trapp; *Dir Fine Arts Events* John Coker; *Exhib Coordr* Jerry Bassett
Open Mon - Fri 10 AM - 5 PM; Sat 1 - 4 PM; cl Sun. No admis fee. Estab 1961 to provide visual art exhibitions covering a broad range of media, subject matter, time periods for the university community and general public. Fine Arts Gallery, Student Services Center, Teaching Gallery, Fine Arts Building, 110, Theatre Gallery, Theatre Building are all maintained. Average Annual Attendance: 33,000
Income: Financed by state appropriation and grants
Collections: †African Art; Pre-Columbian Artifacts; Folk and Ethnic Arts; Art Bank Collection of free loan traveling exhibitions (approx 60 small package exhibitions); †Contemporary Photography; Contemporary Works on Paper; painting, sculpture, ceramics
Exhibitions: (1976-78) Annual Juried Student Exhibition; major exhibitions consist of contemporary painting, photography, sculpture, pre-Columbia art, African art; faculty and student group and one-person shows
Publications: Exhibition catalogs
Activities: Lect open to public, approx 4 vis lectr per yr; gallery talks; tours; competitions; exten dept serving state art organizations; individual paintings and original objects of art lent to institutions within the state of Florida and major institutions outside of the state by special requests; lending collection contains original art works and prints, paintings, photographs, sculpture, pre-Columbian art, African art and folk and ethnic art through the Art Bank Program; traveling exhibitions organized and circulated; shop selling prints, permanent collection and exhibition installations
L Library, 4202 E Fowler Ave, 33620. *Librn* Mary Lou Harkness
Open to students and public
Special Subjects: Historical Material, contemporary
Collections: Rare art books

TEQUESTA

M LIGHTHOUSE GALLERY, 373 Gallery Square N, Tequesta Dr, 33458. Tel 305-746-3101. *Pres* C D Norton; *Secy* Augusta Wells; *Admin Dir* Elizabeth Long
Open Tues - Sat 10 AM - 4 PM; cl Mon. No admis fee. Estab 1964 to create public interest in all forms of the fine arts. Mem: Dues $35 and up
Exhibitions: Temporary and Traveling Exhibitions
Publications: Calendar of Events, monthly
Activities: Classes for adults and children; lect; competitions
L Library, 373 Gallery Square N, Tequesta Dr, 33458.
Small library of art books and art magazines

WEST PALM BEACH

M NORTON GALLERY AND SCHOOL OF ART, 1451 S Olive Ave, 33401. Tel 305-832-5194. *Dir* Richard A Madigan; *Pres* Jane Volk; *Asst Dir* Flanders Holland; *Treas* R Brant Synder; *Cur* Thomas Holman; *Mem Secy* Theresa Hickman; *Pub Relations Dir* Sue Whitman; *Supt* C Phelps Merrell
Open Tues - Fri 10 AM - 5 PM; Sat & Sun 1 - 5 PM. Admis donation required, $1 per person suggested. The Norton Gallery of Art was founded in 1940, dedicated in 1941 for the education and enjoyment of the public; additions were made in 1946, 49, 52 and 66. Acquisitions and gifts are continually being made to the museum. Building and major collections were given by Ralph Hubbard Norton and Elizabeth Calhoun Norton. The Gallery, designed by the Palm Beach architects, Wyeth, King and Johnson, opened to the public in 1941, with an original collection of one hundred paintings. Mr Norton continued to acquire works of art for the museum until his death in 1953, when the remainder of his private collection was given to the museum. Average Annual Attendance: 80,000. Mem: 1600; dues family $50 & $35; annual meeting Apr
Income: Financed by endowment, membership, city appropriation
Collections: Chinese Collection includes Buddhist Sculpture, Ritual Bronzes, Archaic Jades, Tomb Statuettes, Porcelain and Pottery; Norton Collection of Paintings and Sculpture includes European and American Oils and Watercolors, Late 19th and early 20th Century French Paintings and Sculpture
Exhibitions: Annual Members' Exhibition; regular schedule of special exhibitions; students' work
Publications: Monthly calendar
Activities: Classes for adults and children; dramatic programs; docent training; lect for members only; concerts; gallery talks; tours; individual paintings and original objects of art lent to museums around the world; museum shop
L Library, 1451 S Olive Ave, 33401. *Consulting Librn* Hilda Scott
Purchases: $3000
Library Holdings: Vols 3500; Per subs 30; AV—Cassettes, Kodachromes, slides, v-tapes; Other—Clipping files, exhibition catalogs, prints, pamphlets, photographs

WHITE SPRINGS

O FLORIDA FOLKLIFE PROGRAM, Box 265, 32096. Tel 904-397-2192. *Dir* Phillip A Werndli; *Folklife Adminr* Margaret Ann Bulger
The new Department is under Secretary of State George Firestone, and carries on a year-round calendar of folk activities in an effort to encourage statewide public interest and participation in the folk arts and folklore
Activities: Folk festival; folk art conferences (presented at Center and throughout the state)

M Stephen Foster State Folk Culture Center, Box 265, 32096.
Open 8:30 Am - 5 PM daily. Admis adults $2, children $1. Estab 1950 as a memorial to Stephen Collins Foster; operated by the Department of Natural Resources, a Division of Recreation and Parks. Museum contains eight dioramas of Foster's best known songs. The north wing is a collection of minstrel materials; south wing contains 19th century furniture and musical instruments; the 200 foot tall Foster Tower contains a collection of bells and pianos. Average Annual Attendance: 90,000
Income: Financed by state appropriation and receipts
Collections: Art; Gardiner Doll Collection
Publications: Florida Folk Arts Directory, annual; Florida Folklife Newsletter, six times annually
Activities: Concerts; tours; sales shop
L Library, Box 265, 32096. *Librn* Margaret Bulger
Open to public for reference
Library Holdings: Vols 500; Per subs 12; AV—V-tapes

WINTER PARK

M MORSE GALLERY OF ART, 133 E Welbourne Ave, Winter Park, FL. (Mailing Add: 151 E Welbourne Ave, Winter Park, FL 32789) Tel 305-645-5311. *Pres* Reid Ewing; *VPres* Bill Miller; *Secy & Dir of Gallery Activities* Nancy Abberger; *Dir* Hugh F McKean; *Cur* David Donaldson; *Gallery Mgr & Public Relations* Nancy Long
Open Tues - Sat 9:30 AM - 4 PM, Sun 1 - 4 PM, cl Mon. Admis adult $1, students & children 50¢. Estab to display work of Louis Comfort Tiffany and his contemporaries from an extensive collection on a rotating basis. A small, intimate jewel box of a gallery, one block off Park Avenue in downtown Winter Park; consisting of nine rooms and display areas. Mem: 345; dues family $15, individual $10, student $2.50; annual meeting third Wed in Feb
Income: $141,000 (financed by endowment and membership)
Collections: Art Nouveau Furniture by Galle, Guimard, Majorette, and others; Louis Comfort Tiffany: lamps, paintings, personal correspondence and effects, personal windows and photographs; Tiffany and other American art pottery numbering several hundred items; Tiffany studios photographers; items of blown glass; complete inventory of metalware desk sets; paintings by Tiffany's contemporaries; personal windows of others; photographs
Publications: MORSELS, monthly newsletter to members
Activities: Classes for adults and children; docent training; Morse Reader Series; lect, 5 visiting lectr per year; preview lect of new exhibits; concerts; gallery talks; tours; exten dept serves public parks, nursing homes, etc; individual paintings and original objects of art lent; lending collection contains 160 slides and stained glass windows; suitcase exhibit containing Tiffany glass and slide lect programs are presented in the Orange County Schools; originate traveling exhibitions; gallery desk sells docent-designed hand-tinted stationery

M ROLLINS COLLEGE, George D and Harriet W Cornell Fine Arts Center Museum, Holt Ave, 32751. Tel 305-646-2526. *Adminr* Joan B Wavell
Open Tues - Fri 10 AM - 5 PM; Sat & Sun 1 - 5 PM; cl Mon. No admis fee. Estab 1925 when art collection was started. New Fine Arts Center completed in 1976 and dedicated and opened on Jan 29, 1978. Rollins college is a liberal arts college and the Cornell Fine Arts Center is part of this process. The museum houses the college's permanent collection and provides a focus for the arts in central Florida. Museum consists of the Jeannette Genius McKean, the Yust and Knapp Galleries. Average Annual Attendance: 10,000
Income: $50,000 (financed by endowment)
Collections: Smith Watch Key Collection of 1200 watch keys; American Paintings and Portraits; European Paintings from the 15th to 20th Centuries, prints, bronzes; Decorative Arts
Exhibitions: Esmark Collection of Currier and Ives; The Ralph E Kaschai Collection of American Western Art; Bill Loving (photographs); The Terry Collection of Hungarian and Central European Paintings; A Review Exhibition of Drawings, Watercolors and Oils (Daniel Putnam Brinley 1879 - 1963, An American Impressionist); Containers and Photography (sculpture by Ronald Larned, Rollins Faculty); Daytona Museum Collection of Cuban Art; The International Business Machines Touring Exibition of Leonardo da Vinci Models; National Association of Women Artists Traveling Painting Exhibition; North Carolina National Bank Comtemporary American Graphics and Watercolors; Photography of the Dance (Jon Baronn Farmer II); The Mr & Mrs T W Miller Collection of British Royal Memorabilia; The Smith Watch Key Collection; American Landscapes and Portraits; An American Historical Exhibit; Collection of Presidents of the United States; European Paintings and Bronzes; European Paintings 15th - 20th Century; Exhibit of Religious Art; French Paintings, Prints and 19th Century Bronzes; 19th Century American and European Paintings

GEORGIA

ATHENS

UNIVERSITY OF GEORGIA
M Georgia Museum of Art, Jackson St, 30602. Tel 404-542-3254. *Dir* William D Paul Jr; *Cur* Ethel Moore; *Cur Graphic Arts* Richard Schneiderman; *Preparator* Ronald Lukasiewicz
Open Mon - Fri 8 AM - 5 PM; Sat 9 AM - Noon; Sun 2 - 5 PM. No admis fee. Estab 1945; open to the public 1948 as a fine arts museum. Five exhibition galleries. Mem: 250; dues $10 - $500; annual meeting May
Income: Financed through university
Collections: American Paintings, †Drawings; †European and American Graphics, 15th century to the present
Exhibitions: Pol Bury; Danish Expressions in Textiles; Edvard Munch: The Major Graphics; From Type to Landscape: Design, Projects and Proposals by Herbert Bayer, 1923-73; George Grosz: Works in Oil; Gregory Gillespie; Jasper Johns: Prints 1970-1977; Jiri Kolar: Transformations; Landscape Etching in the

Ninetennth Century; Lithographs by Richard Hunt; MFA Thesis Exhibition; Michelangelo Pistoletto: On-Site Works; Photographs by Moholy-Nagy; Photographs by Robert Demachy; The Cuzco Circle: Treasure of Cyprus; The Human Form: Sculpture, Prints and Drawings by Fritz Wotruba; The Sculptor's Eye: The African Art Collection of Mr & Mrs Chaim Gross; Wright Morris: Structures and Artifacts - Photographs 1933-54
Publications: Bulletin, biannual; exhibition catalogs
Activities: Docent training; volunteer docents program; lect open to the public 3 - 5 vis lectr per year; tours; individual paintings and original objects of art lent to other museums and galleries; traveling exhibitions organized and circulated
L Library, Jackson St, 30602.
Library Holdings: Vols 40,000
Special Subjects: Art History

ATLANTA

O ATLANTA ART WORKERS COALITION, Suite 214, 972 Peachtree St NE, 30309. Tel 404-876-4096. *Pres* George Warren; *Gallery Cur* Dan R Talley
Open Tues - Sat Noon - 4 PM. No admis fee. Maintains art gallery. Average Annual Attendance: 1500. Mem: 150; dues $15
Income: Financed by membership, city and state appropriations, NEA, and gifts
Exhibitions: By Way of Explanation (Katherine Mitchell); Converge-Converse (Maria Artemis & Marcia Cohen); Dual Language-Language Duel (Michaelangelo Pistoletto & Dan R Talley); Fluxus Drawings (Ken Friedman); Love Maria (John Turturro); Pursuit (Stan Sharshal); The Rainbow Panels (K S McKend); Recent Work (Andy Nasissee); Sound Structures (Sarah Armstrong); Two Balls (Paul Aho & William Miles)
Publications: Newspaper, bimonthly
Activities: Lect open to public, 4 vis lectr per year; concerts; gallery talks; originate traveling exhibitions; sales shop sells books and magazines

L Information Resource Center, Suite 214, 972 Peachtree St NE, 30309. *Dir* Julia A Fenton; *Assoc Dir* Alison Somogy; *Coordinator of Artists Directory* Victoria Bugbee
Open Tues - Sat Noon - 4 PM. Estab 1978 to provide specialized information to artists on exhibition opportunities, copyright, health hazards in the arts, contracts, arts organizations, grant opportunities
Income: $6000
Purchases: $3000
Library Holdings: Vols 200; Per subs 30; AV—A-tapes, cassettes, slides, v-tapes; Other—Clipping files, exhibition catalogs, memorabilia, original art works, pamphlets, photographs
Special Subjects: Art and the law, Women in Art

L ATLANTA COLLEGE OF ART LIBRARY, 1280 Peachtree St NE, 30309. Tel 404-892-3600, Ext 210. *Dir* JoAnne Paschall; *Visual Coll Cur* Jan Avgikos; *Circulation-Periodicals Librn* Starr Kirkland
Open Mon & Fri 9 AM - 5 PM, Tues, Wed, Thurs 9 AM - 8 PM. Estab 1950 to provide art information and to be a research facility to the Atlanta College of Art community and the southeast art community. Circ 7900. Library has a small exhibition space for art
Income: $23,000
Purchases: $17,800
Library Holdings: Vols 13,000; Per subs 250; Micro—Fiche; AV—Cassettes, motion pictures, rec, slides, v-tapes; Other—Clipping files, exhibition catalogs, prints, memorabilia, original art works, pamphlets, photographs, reproductions, artists' book collection
Special Subjects: , 20th century American art, with emphasis on art since 1950
Collections: Artists' Books; rare books
Exhibitions: Monthly exhibitions of art by students and faculty
Activities: Films; visiting artists program; weekly slide displays

M ATLANTA MUSEUM, 537-39 Peachtree St NE, 30308. Tel 404-872-8233. *Dir* J H Elliott Jr
Open Mon - Fri 10 AM - 5 PM; cl Sat, Sun & holidays. Admis adults $1, children 50¢, special group rates. Estab 1938
Collections: Bronzes; Confederate Money; Decorative Arts; Early Chinese Art; Furniture; Indian Artifacts; Paintings; Porcelains; Sculpture; Glass
Activities: Lect; tours; sales shop sells antiques, china, furntiure, gifts, glass, paintings, porcelain, rugs and silver

L ATLANTA PUBLIC LIBRARY, Fine Arts Department, 10 Pryor St SW, 30303. Tel 404-688-4636. *Head Fine Arts Department* Julie M Compton; *Librn* Ella Gaines Yates
Open weekdays 9 AM - 9 PM; Sat 9 AM - 6 PM. Estab 1950 to provide materials in the fine arts. Some exhibit space maintained
Income: Financed by city and state appropriation
Library Holdings: AV—Cassettes, motion pictures 1100, rec; Other—Prints
Activities: Classes for adults; lect open to the public

L GEORGIA INSTITUTE OF TECHNOLOGY, College of Architecture Library, 225 North Ave NW, 30332. Tel 404-894-4877. *Librn* Frances K Drew; *Library Asst* Shawn Beaty; *Library Asst for Slides* Elsie Harper
Open daily 8 AM - 9:30 PM. Estab 1924 to give good library service to the college faculty and students. Circ 21,000
Income: Financed by state appropriation
Purchases: $6000
Library Holdings: Vols 20,000; Per subs 100; Micro—Fiche; AV—Slides; Other—Exhibition catalogs, pamphlets
Special Subjects: Art nouveau, Greek art and architecture

L GEORGIA STATE UNIVERSITY, Arthur I and Irma L Harris Reading Room and Visual Resource Library, Art Department, University Plaza, 30303. *Cur* Temme Barkin Leeds; *Asst* Joan Tysinger
Open Mon - Fri 9 - 5:30 PM. Estab 1970 to make visual and literary resource materials available for study, teaching and research
Library Holdings: Vols 2000; Per subs 20; AV—A-tapes, slides 90,000; Other—Exhibition catalogs, original art works, pamphlets, reproductions

M HIGH MUSEUM OF ART, 1280 Peachtree St NE, 30309. Tel 404-892-3600. *Dir* Gudmund Vigtel; *Cur Educ* Paula Hancock; *Cur Decorative Arts* Donald Pierce; *Cur of 20th Century Art* Peter Morrin; *Cur European Art* Dr Eric Zafran; *Pres Bd of Sponsors* William B Astrop
Open Mon - Sat 10 AM - 5 PM; Sun Noon - 5 PM. No admis fee. Estab 1929 to make the best in the visual arts available to the Atlanta public in exhibitions and supporting programs. The Museum building, 50,000 sq ft, was completed in 1968. Average Annual Attendance: 300,000. Mem: 10,000; dues $15 and up
Income: $937,000 (financed by endowment, membership, city and state appropriations, grants, and operating income)
Collections: African Objects; American Paintings, Sculpture, Graphics; European Paintings, Sculpture, Graphics; Havery Collection; Kress Collection of Paintings and Sculpture from the 14th - 18th Centuries; Oriental, Pre-Columbian, European and American Decorative Arts; Uhry Collection of Prints after 1850; photography
Exhibitions: (1980) A Thing of Beauty: Art Nouveau; Artists in Georgia; Art of the Yoruba; Barber-Robinson: Photographs; Contemporary Art from Senegal; Contemporary Art from Southern California; Contemporary Classics: Designer Furniture of the Modern Movement; Flemish Expressionists; Flemish Master Drawings; I Shall Save One Land Unvisited: 11 Photographers in South; Marty Emanuel; Paul Kwilecki, Photographs; The Black Photographer
Publications: Calendar of Events, monthly; exhibition catalogues
Activities: Classes for children; docent training; lect open to public, 20 vis lectr per year; gallery talks; tours; exten dept serving city of Atlanta; individual paintings and original objects of art lent; traveling exhibitions organized and circulated; museum shop selling books, magazines, reproductions, slides and gift items; junior museum

AUGUSTA

M AUGUSTA RICHMOND COUNTY MUSEUM, 540 Telfair St, 30901. Tel 404-722-8454. *Interim Dir* Betty Jo Carroll
Open Tues - Fri 11 AM - 5 PM; Sat 1 - 5 PM— Sun 2 - 5 PM; cl most National Holidays. No admis fee. Estab 1937; owns 1850 historic Brahe House at 426 Telfair St
Collections: Archaeology; Decorative Arts; Graphics; Historical Material; Paintings; Sculpture
Activities: Training program for professional museum personnel; workshops; films; lect; guided tours; volunteer council; book traveling exhibitions

M GERTRUDE HERBERT MEMORIAL INSTITUTE OF ART, 506 Telfair St, 30901. Tel 404-722-5495. *Dir* Ed Rice
Open Tues - Fri 10 AM - Noon, 1 - 4 PM, Sat 4 - 6 PM, groups by special arrangement, cl Sun, Mon, Christmas and New Years. Estab 1937. Mem: 250
Income: $10,000
Collections: European Renaissance; modern paintings, sculpture, graphics
Exhibitions: Circulating exhibitions; monthly exhibitions; one-person and group exhibitions
Activities: Art classes; lect; films

COLUMBUS

M COLUMBUS COLLEGE, Experimental Gallery, Art Department, 31907. Tel 404-568-2047. *Pres* Jamie Howard; *VPres & Gallery Coordr* Zoe Allison; *Secy* Judy Templeton
Open 10 AM - 4 PM during exhibits
Exhibitions: Annual art students show
Activities: Lectures open to the public, 4 - 5 vis lectr per yr; gallery talks; competitions with awards; scholarships offered

M COLUMBUS MUSEUM OF ARTS AND SCIENCES, 1251 Wynnton Rd, 31906. Tel 404-323-3617. *Chmn of Board* Dr Phillip Brewer; *Dir & Secy Board* William F Scheele
Open Mon - Sat 10 AM - 5 PM; Sun 2 - 5 PM; cl Thanksgiving, Christmas, New Year's. No admis fee. Estab 1953 to build a permanent collection; encourage work by Georgia and Southern artists; establish loan shows and traveling exhibitions in all fields of art. Mem: dues $25 and up; annual meeting Jan
Collections: †American Art; American and Foreign Doll Collection; †Early Masters; †Georgia Artists; †Indian section with extensive Collection of Ethnological and Archaeological Material relating to local Indians; †Prints; reconstructed pre-Civil War Log House on Museum grounds; †Sculpture; permanent collection includes Landscapes, Paintings and Portraits by Dutch, Early and Contemporary American Painters, English, Flemish, and Italian
Publications: Newsletter
Activities: Workshops for adults and children; gallery talks; tours; lectr; active Museum Guild; originate traveling exhibitions
L Library, 1251 Wynnton Rd, 31906.
Special Subjects: All phases of Art, Indian History

DALTON

O CREATIVE ARTS GUILD, The Old Firehouse on Pentz St, 30720. Tel 404-278-0168. *Pres* George Spence; *Dir* Bernice Spigel
Open Mon - Fri 9 AM - 5 PM; Sat 11 AM - 2 PM. No admis fee. Estab 1963 to recognize, stimulate and popularize the arts. Gallery is located on the ground floor of The Old Firehouse. Average Annual Attendance: 12,000. Mem: 550; dues family $15, individual $10; annual meeting Dec
Income: $100,000 (financed by membership, commissions and fund raising events)
Exhibitions: Changing monthly shows of Crafts; Graphics; Photography; Original Art; Sculpture
Publications: Bulletins to members, monthly
Activities: Classes for adults and children; dramatic programs; visual and performing arts programs for schools; concerts; gallery talks; competitions with awards; arts and crafts festivals; originate traveling exhibitions

DECATUR

M AGNES SCOTT COLLEGE, Dalton Gallery, College Ave & Candler St, 30030. Tel 404-373-2571. *Cur* Leland Staven
Open Mon - Fri 9 AM - 9 PM; Sat 9 AM - 5 PM; Sun 2 - 5 PM. No admis fee. Estab 1965 to enhance art program. Gallery consists of 4 rooms, 300 running ft of wall space, light beige walls and rug; Dana Fine Arts Bldg designed by John Portman
Income: Financed by endowment
Collections: Clifford M Clarke; Harry L Dalton; Steffen Thomas; Ferdinand Warren
Exhibitions: Art Faculty Exhibition; Georgia Designer Craftsmen; Student Art Exhibition; Western Carolina Invitational Fibre Exhibition
Activities: Lect open to public

FORT BENNING

M NATIONAL INFANTRY MUSEUM, Bldg 396, Baltzell Ave, 31905. Tel 404-545-2958. *Registrar* C Clay Aldridge; *Exhibits Specialist* James Lett
Open Tues - Fri 10 AM - 4:30 PM; Sat - Sun 12:30 - 4:30 PM. No admis fee. Estab 1959 to honor the infantryman and his two centuries of proud history. Gallery contains 50,000 sq ft; Hall of Flags, Gallery of Military Art, Benning Room, West Gallery: 1750 - 1865, Center Galleries 1870 - 1970, Medal of Honor Hall and Airborne Diorama. Average Annual Attendance: 150,000. Mem: 9000; dues $20
Income: $100,000 (financed by state appropriation and federal funds)
Collections: Military related Art; Presidential Documents and Memorabilia; 1896 Vintage Sutler's Store
Exhibitions: Hail to the Chief; Minority Art and the Military; Mobil Museum: Two Centuries of Proud History
Activities: Lectr open to public; artmobile
L Library, Bldg 396, Baltzell Ave, 31905. *Cur* Dick D Grube
Open Tues - Fri 1 - 4:30 PM, Sat & Sun 12:30 - 4:30 PM. Estab 1959 to preserve the collection of field manuals and other military information. For reference only
Library Holdings: Vols 20,000; AV—Fs, motion pictures, slides; Other—Clipping files, manuscripts, memorabilia, original art works, pamphlets, photographs, sculpture

JEKYLL ISLAND

M JEKYLL ISLAND NATIONAL HISTORIC LANDMARK, Millionaire's Village, 375 Riverview Dr, 31520. Tel 912-635-2727. *Village Dir* Diane Ashley; *Dir of Jekyll Island Authority* Robert Case; *Dir Restoration* R K Beedle; *Mgr State Park Authority* Robert C Anderson
Open Mon - Sat 9:15 AM - 5 PM; Sun 11 AM - 5 PM. Admis adults $3, students $2 (10-18 years)
Collections: 1890 Furniture; Tiffany Stained Glass Windows; portraits

MACON

M MUSEUM OF ARTS AND SCIENCES, INC, 4182 Forsyth Rd, 31210. Tel 912-477-3232. *Dir* Douglas R Noble; *Class Coordr* Blake Zachritz
Open Mon - Fri 9 AM - 5 PM; Sat 11 AM - 5 PM; Sun 2 - 5 PM; cl National Holidays
Collections: European and American Drawings, Paintings, Prints and Sculpture; Historical Material
Activities: Classes for adults and children; arts festivals; guided tours; lectr; movies; special events; traveling art exhibits in Main Exhibit Hall

MOUNT BERRY

M BERRY COLLEGE, Art Department, 30149. Tel 404-232-5374, Ext 219. *Pres* Dr Gloria Shatto; *VPres* Dr Doyle Mathis; *Secy* Joyce Morris; *Chmn* Dr T J Mew III
Open weekdays 9 AM - 4 PM. No admis fee. Estab 1971. Medium size gallery, carpeted floors and walls, tracking spots. Average Annual Attendance: 3500
Exhibitions: Ken Friedman, works on paper; Dan Talley, conceptual pieces
Activities: Classes for adults and children; lectures open to the public, 8 - 10 vis lectr per yr; gallery talks; competitions with awards; scholarships offered; individual paintings and original objects of art lent; lending collection contains books, cassettes, color reproductions, 20 original prints, paintings, records, photographs and 5000 slides; book traveling exhibitions; originate traveling exhibitions
L Moon Library, 30149. *Chmn* Dr T J Mew III
Open daily 9 AM - 4 PM. Estab 1972 for educational purposes
Income: $1000
Purchases: $1000
Library Holdings: Vols 50; Per subs 25; AV—A-tapes, cassettes, fs, motion pictures, rec, slides, v-tapes; Other—Clipping files, exhibition catalogs, prints, manuscripts, memorabilia, original art works, pamphlets, photographs
Special Subjects: Ceramics, Contemporary women artists

SAVANNAH

ASSOCIATION OF ART MUSEUM DIRECTORS
For further information, see National and Regional Organizations

M KIAH MUSEUM, 505 W 36th St, 31401. Tel 912-236-8544. *Dir & Founder* Virginia J Kiah; *Asst Cur* Nancy H Walker
Open Tues - Thurs 11 AM - 5 PM. No admis fee. Estab 1959 to expose this type of culture to the masses; to teach the relationship of art to everyday life
Collections: Civil War Period Collection; Harmon Foundation Collection of African Wood Carvings; Howard J Morrison Jr Osteological Collection; Marie Dressler Collection Fine arts exhibit of all art work of students and adult artists from 18 countries; Folk Art; 18th, 19th & 20th Century Furniture; Hobby

Collection; Indian Artifacts
Activities: Docent training; gallery talks; tours; paintings and original art objects lent to schools
L **Library,** 505 W 36th St, 31401.
Open to adults and students for reference
Collections: John Speight Simpkins

M **SHIPS OF THE SEA MUSEUM,** 503 E River St, 31401. Tel 912-232-1511. *Dir* Biddy Osbun; *Asst Dir* Deborah Helmken; *Gift Shop Mgr* Mary Ed Kennard; *Museum Asst* Shirley Cunningham; *Museum Asst* Christie Kinzie
Open Tues - Sat 10 AM - 5 PM; cl Mon Sept - Feb. Admis adults $2, children 7 - 12 75¢, group rates available. Estab 1966 to bring a greater awareness to the general public of the great part in history that ships have played. Four floors of ship models and items which pertain to the sea with an outstanding exhibit of ships-in-bottles and scrimshaw. Average Annual Attendance: 36,000
Income: Financed privately
Collections: Figureheads; Porcelains; Scrimshaw; Ships Models
Exhibitions: Scrimshaw Exhibit; Ships-in-a-Bottle
Activities: Classes for children; sales shop sells books and gifts
L **Library,** 503 E River St, 31401. *Librn* Lee Vanger
Reference only
Library Holdings: Vols 350; Per subs 10; Other—Clipping files, framed reproductions, prints, memorabilia, original art works, pamphlets, photographs
Special Subjects: Maritime
Activities: Children summer classes in nautical lore

M **TELFAIR ACADEMY OF ARTS AND SCIENCES INC,** 121 Barnard St, PO Box 10081, 31401. Tel 912-232-1177. *Dir* Alexander V J Gaudieri; *Cur of Coll* Feay Shellman; *Asst Cur of Education* Benjamin F Moore
Open Tues - Sat 10 AM - 5 PM; cl Mon. Admis adults $2, students $1, children under 12 50¢; free on Sun. Estab 1875 to preserve, exhibit and interpret the works of art forming the collections; to preserve and interpret our two National Historic Landmark edifices, the Telfair Academy and the Owens-Thomas House; to enlighten and to educate all groups through art related programs and services; to enrich the quality of life through offering a total cultural resource for the entire region; and to maintain a standard of the highest order throughout the museum. The museum is housed in an 1817 American Regency Mansion (with an 1880's addition of the Rotunda and Sculpture Galleries) which has been designated a National Historic Landmark; designed by the famous English architect, William Jay. Average Annual Attendance: 35,000. Mem: 1675; dues family $25, individual $15, junior citizen and senior citizen $5; annual meeting spring
Income: Financed by endowment, membership, city and state appropriation, banks and corporate foundations and federal government
Collections: American Impressionism; Ash Can Realism; Collections of 18th and 19th Century American Portraiture; Decorative Arts and Period Rooms; Kahlil Gibran's Paintings, Drawings and Costumes; 19th and 20th Century French and German Paintings; prints
Exhibitions: Judges Choice; Savannah Art Association; (1978-79) Acquisitions of 1978; Patterns and Games (Gallery of Interpretation); Varieties of Victorian Dress
Activities: Classes for children; docent training; special tours; lect open to the public, 5 vis lectr per yr; concerts; gallery talks; exten dept serving public schools and Retired Citizens Centers; lending collection contains motion pictures, 1500 slides; museum shop selling books, magazines, original art, reproductions, prints, slides, jewelry, small sculpture, pottery and decorative items; The Gallery of Interpretation, junior museum
L **Library,** 121 Barnard St, PO Box 10081, 31401. *Librn* Wilma Wierwill
For reference only, for scholars and the public
Library Holdings: Vols 1200

VALDOSTA

M **VALDOSTA STATE COLLEGE,** Art Gallery, N Patterson St, 31601. Tel 912-247-3319, 247-3330. *Head Art Department* Irene Dodd
Open Mon - Fri 9 AM - Noon & 1 - 5 PM. No admis fee. Estab to expose both art and general education students to a variety of visual expressions. Gallery is an open rectangular room with approximately 122 running ft of exhibition space. Average Annual Attendance: 12,000
Income: Financed by state appropriations
Exhibitions: Approx 10 - 12 exhibitions per year·
Activities: Lectr; tours to museums in New York, Washington, Boston, etc

HAWAII

HONOLULU

O **ASSOCIATION OF HONOLULU ARTISTS,*** 2417A University Ave, PO Box 10202, 96822. Tel 808-988-2373. *Pres* Ernest Brickman; *VPres* Joyce Mary Ott; *Second VPres* Christine Evans; *Secy* Helen Iaea; *Corresponding Secy* Edna Loo; *Treas* Michael Kiyuan; *Asst Treas* Lilly R Abbott
Estab 1934 to promote congeniality and stimulate growth by presenting programs; to contribute to the cultural life of the State of Hawaii. Average Annual Attendance: 1000. Mem: 350; dues $12; monthly meeting every third Tues
Income: $4200 (financed by membership)
Publications: Paint Rag, monthly
Activities: Lect open to public, 12 visiting lectr per year; demonstrations; competitions; cash awards, plaques and rossettes; scholarships

M **CONTEMPORARY ARTS CENTER OF HAWAII,** 605 Kapiolani Blvd, 96813. Tel 808-525-8047. *Dir* Laila Roster; *Asst Dir* Roy Venters; *Chmn of Board* Russell Cades; *Asst Dir* Mary Mitsuda
Open Mon - Fri 8 AM - 5 PM; Sat 8 AM - Noon; cl Sun. No admis fee. Estab 1960 to provide a showcase for artists living and working in the Hawaiian Islands.

Gallery occupies 1800 sq ft of space in the center of the newspaper building. Average Annual Attendance: 25,000
Income: Approx $10,000 (financed by endowment)
Purchases: $20,000
Collections: Permanent Collection hangs throughout the building and is continually augmented by purchase from ongoing exhibitions
Exhibitions: (1978) Les Biller, Russell Davidson (painters); Gilbert and Marcus (production and performance art); Francis Haar and family (photographers); Honolulu Printmakers Invitational Print Show; Lam Oi Char (Chinese Brush painter); Hiroki Morinoue (paintings from Japan); Marci Morse (printmaker); Frank Salmoiraghi (photographer); works of Balinese artists. (1979) August Becker (painting); Martin Charlot (painting); Amos Kotomori (batik); David Kuraoka (ceramics); Alan Leitner (mixed media); Sharon Smith (drawings); Donna Stoner (painting); Brett Weston (photography); In-house group show; Youth Art; (1980) Lee Chesney (prints, painting); Denise DeVone (mixed media); Don Dugal (drawing); Jonelle Gillette (mixed media); Pegge Hopper (painting); Ken Ibaraki (sculpture); Marie Kodama (mixed media); Yukio Ozaki (ceramics); Julie Scrafford (painting); Jay Wilson (weaving); John Young (painting)
Activities: Individual paintings and original objects of art lent; lending collection contains slides of complete exhibitions as well as permanent collection

L **HAWAII STATE LIBRARY,** Fine Arts-Audiovisual Section, 478 S King St, 96813. Tel 808-548-5913. *Head Fine Arts-AV Section & Art Spec* Chitra Stuiver; *Head AV Unit* Mary Lu Kipilii
Open Tues - Thurs 9 AM - 8 PM, Mon, Wed, Fri and Sat 9 AM - 5 PM. No admis fee. Estab 1930 as central reference and circulating collection for both city and county of Honolulu and for state of Hawaii
Library Holdings: Vols 13,000; Micro—Reels; AV—Fs, motion pictures; Other—Photographs, Pictures 68,000; reproductions 34,000
Special Subjects: Costume Design & Construction, Handicrafts, Photography
Exhibitions: Various local artists exhibited in the courtyard area; special displays in the lobby
Activities: Approx 8000 art items lent yearly

M **HONOLULU ACADEMY OF ARTS,** 900 S Beretania St, 96814. Tel 808-538-3693. *Dir* James W Foster; *Asst Dir* Selden Washington; *Asst Cur Western Art & Publications* Ed James F Jensen; *Senior Cur & Cur Graphic Arts & Studio Programmer* Joseph Feher; *Cur Asian Art & Keeper of Ukiyo-e Center* Howard A Link; *Cur Asian Art* Marshall P Wu; *Consultant for Western Art* Gertrude Rosenthal; *Cur Exten Services* Ruth Tamura; *Cur Gallery Program* Roger Dell; *Cur Program Development* James H Furstenberg; *Cur Art Center* Violet A Scott; *Keeper AV Center* Brone Jameikis; *Keeper, Lending Coll* Barbara F Hoogs; *Consultant for Chinese Art* Tseng Yu-ho; *Registrar* Sanna Deutsch; *Fund Development & Public Relations Officer* Gail Pratt
Open Tues, Wed, Fri & Sat 10 AM - 4:30 PM, Thurs 11 AM - 4:30 PM and 7 - 9 PM, Sun 2 - 5 PM, cl Mon & major holidays. No admis fee. Estab 1927 as the only art museum of a broad general nature in the Pacific; to provide Hawaii's people of many races with works of art representing their composite cultural heritage from both East and West. Main building is a Registered National Historic Place. Average Annual Attendance: 124,000. Mem: 4500; dues $8 and up
Income: $1,710,949
Purchases: $360,500
Collections: Kress Collection of Italian Renaissance Painting; Ancient Mediterranean and Medieval Christian Art; Chinese Bronze, Ceramics, Furniture, Lacquerware, Painting, Sculpture; European and American Decorative Arts, Painting, Prints, Sculpture; Islamic Ceramics; Japanese Ceramics, Folk Arts, Painting, Prints, Screens, Sculpture; Korean Ceramics; Traditional Arts of Africa, Oceania and the Americas; Western and Oriental Textiles
Exhibitions: Approx 35 temporary exhibitions annually
Publications: Art Books and Pamphlets; Catalogs of Special Exhibitions; Honolulu Academy of Arts Journal, biennially
Activities: Classes for children; lectr; films; guided tours; gallery talks; arts festivals; workshops; exten dept serves neighbor islands, resident artist program, research in Asian art; lending collection contains paintings, prints, textiles, reproductions, photographs, slides and miscellaneous objects (about 21,000); originate traveling exhibitions; sales shop sells books and gifts
L **Library,** 900 S Beretania St, 96814. *Librn* Anne T Seaman
Library Holdings: Vols 23,000
Special Subjects: Art History, Oriental Art

M **SCHOFIELD BARRACKS,** Tropic Lightning Historical Center, 25th Infantry Division Headquarters, 96857. Tel 808-655-0438. *Cur* Steve H Kongshaug
Open Wed - Sun 10 AM - 4 PM. No admis fee. Estab 1958 to preserve the military historical background in Hawaii. The Friends of the Tropic Lightning Historical Center render assistance for acquiring and displaying new exhibits; the 25th Infantry Division Headquarters is charged with management and final directives. Average Annual Attendance: 13,000 - 15,000
Income: Financed by military appropriations
Collections: Banners; flags; manuals; military art; military weapons, past and present (many captured in combat); photograph collections of early military installations on Oahu

M **TENNENT ART FOUNDATION GALLERY,** 203 Prospect St, 96813. Tel 808-531-1987. *Dir* Elaine Tennent
Open Tues - Sat 10 AM - Noon; Sun 2 - 4 PM or by appointment. No admis fee. Estab 1954; dedicated to aesthetic portrayal of Hawaiian people and to house works of Madge Tennent. Gallery on slopes of Punchbowl below National Cemetery of Pacific. Average Annual Attendance: 1000-15000. Mem: Dues $8
Income: Financed by trust
Publications: Prospectus, quarterly newsletter
Activities: Special exhibitions and social events sponsored by Friends of Tennent Art Gallery; lect; tours
L **Library,** 203 Prospect St, 96813.
Open for reference
Library Holdings: Vols 350

M UNIVERSITY OF HAWAII AT MANOA, Art Gallery, 2535 The Mall, 96822. Tel 808-948-6888. *Dir* Tom Klobe; *Chmn Department Art* John Wisnosky
Open Mon - Fri 10 AM - 4 PM; Sun Noon - 4 PM; cl Sat. No admis fee. Estab 1976 to present a program of local, national and international exhibitions. Gallery is seen as a major teaching tool for all areas of specialization. It is located in the center of the new art building and is designed as a versatile space with a flexible installation system that allows all types of art to be displayed according to their own requirements. Average Annual Attendance: 25,000
Exhibitions: Akari by Noguchi; The Art of Korea; Pranas Domsaitis; First Western States Biennial American Watercolor Exhibition; Outside-In (Bochner, Yacoe, Rodeck, Lunetta); Spectrum: New Directions in Color Photography; student and faculuty exhibtions
Publications: Exhibition Catalogs
Activities: Lect open to public; gallery talks; originate traveling exhibitions

KAHULAI

L MAUI COMMUNITY COLLEGE LIBRARY, 310 Kaahumanu Ave, 96732. *Head Librn* Bill Lindstrom
Open Mon - Fri 8 AM - 9 PM. Estab 1968 to serve the community and students
Library Holdings: Vols 2000; Micro—Fiche; AV—A-tapes, cassettes, fs, Kodachromes, motion pictures, slides, v-tapes; Other—Clipping files, pamphlets
Exhibitions: Five gallery exhibits of National importance borrowed from Honolulu Art Museum

KAILUA

O WINDWARD ARTISTS GUILD, PO Box 851, 96734. *Pres* Diana Lockwood; *Secy* Marilyn Davidson; *Treas* Shirley Hasenyager
Estab 1961 to promote art and art appreciation in Hawaii. Mem: 100; meeting six times per year
Income: Financed by membership, private donations and state education grants
Exhibitions: Annual Windward Young Artists Show; Easter Art Festival, annually; Guild Members Show
Publications: Windward Artists Guild Bulletin, monthly
Activities: Classes for adults; art demonstrations in schools; lect open to the public, 5 visiting lectrs per year; competitions with cash awards; scholarships

LAHAINA

O LAHAINA ARTS SOCIETY, 649 Wharf St, 96761. Tel 808-661-0111. *Pres* George Allan; *Cur* Rogene Radner
Open daily 10 AM - 4 PM. No admis fee. Estab 1964 as a nonprofit organization interested in perpetuating native culture, art and beauty by providing stimulating art instruction, lectures and art exhibits. Gallery located in old lahaina Courthouse; Main Gallery is on ground floor; Old Jail Gallery is in the basement. Average Annual Attendance: 25,000. Mem: 310; dues family $20, single $15; annual meeting Sept
Income: $12,000 (financed by membership and annual fundraising event, Beaux Arts Ball)
Exhibitions: Honolulu Academy of Arts Annual Traveling Exhibit; exhibits change each month; group, special or theme exhibits in Main Gallery; one or two-person shows are in Old Jail Gallery
Publications: Newsletter, monthly
Activities: Classes for adults and children; lect open to public, 4 vis lectr per year; gallery talks; competitions; scholarships
L Library, 649 Wharf St, 96761.
Open for reference
Library Holdings: Vols 100

LAIE

O POLYNESIAN CULTURAL CENTER,* 96762. Tel 808-293-9291. *Chmn Board* Marvin J Ashton
Open Mon - Sat 10:30 AM - 7 PM, cl Thanksgiving & Christmas. Admis adults $4.50, children $2.25. Estab 1963 by the Church of Jesus Christ of Latter Day Saints as an authentic Polynesian village
Collections: Decorative arts, ethnic material, graphics, paintings and sculpture
Publications: Polynesia in a Day, magazine
Activities: Lect; guided tours; films; sales shop sells Polynesian artifacts and souvenirs

LIHUE

M KAUAI MUSEUM, PO Box 248, 96766. Tel 808-245-6931. *Pres* Hilda Cannon; *Secy* Maureen Morrison; *Dir* Robert A Gahran; *Cur* David Penhallow; *Researcher* Catherine Stauder; *Mgr Museum Shop* Hazel Ward Gahran
Open Mon - Fri 9:30 AM - 4:30 PM; Sat 9 AM - 1 PM; cl Sun. Admis adults $2, children free when accompanied by an adult. Estab 1960 to provide the history through the permanent exhibit, the story of Kauai and through art exhibits; ethnic cultural exhibits in the Wilcox Building to give the community an opportunity to learn more of ethnic backgrounds. Average Annual Attendance: 23,000. Mem: 500; dues $100, $50, $25, $10 and $5; annual meeting Nov
Exhibitions: Annual Artists of Hawaii Exhibit; Annual Elementary and Senior Division School Art Exhibit; Attempted Russian Expansion of Kauai, 1815 - 1817; Captain James Cook Bicentennial Exhibit; Filipino Cultural Heritage Exhibit Featuring the Badillo Collection; Hawaiian Quilts; Oils by John Young; Pacific Northwest Indian Exhibit (watercolors by Wai Hang Lai); The First Americans; The First American Indain Exhibit in Hawaii; Watercolors and Prints of Emily Ehlinger; Watercolors by Hubert Buel
Publications: Hawaiian Quilting on Kauai; Early Kauai Hospitality; Amelia

L Library, PO Box 248, 96766.
For reference only
Library Holdings: Vols 2600; Other—Prints
Collections: Photograph Collection

L KAUAI REGIONAL LIBRARY, 4344 Hardy St, 96766. Tel 808-245-3617. *District Adminr* Donna Marie Garcia
Open Mon - Wed 8 AM - 8 PM, Thurs - Fri 8 AM - 4:30 PM, Sat 8 AM - noon. Estab 1922 to serve the public of Kauai through a network of a regional library, three community libraries, community-school library, reading room in community center and a bookmobile service. Circ 410,000. These libraries provide exhibition space for a variety of art works and individual art shows as well as participate in joint art exhibits with the local schools, community college and museum. Gallery provides display and exhibit area for one-man and group art shows
Income: $566,107 (financed by state appropriation)
Library Holdings: Vols 158,061 (includes all volumes in all public libraries); AV—A-tapes, cassettes, fs, rec, v-tapes; Other—Clipping files, pamphlets
Collections: Curator for art in State Buildings Collection for the Island of Kauai funded through the statewide program by the State Foundation on Culture and the Arts. This collection is a revolving collection available for all state buildings and public schools
Exhibitions: Series of small one-man exhibits; average thirteen per year
Activities: Dramatic programs; film programs; lectr open to public, 4 - 8 vis lectr per year; library tours; craft exhibits; contests

WAILUKU

O MAUI HISTORICAL SOCIETY, Hale Hoikeike, 2375A Main St, PO Box 1018, 96793. Tel 808-243-3326. *Pres* Ben Baldwin; *VPres* James Luckey; *Secy* Polly Purdy; *Treas* Alan Brown; *Mus Dir* Virginia Wirtz
Open Mon - Sat 10 AM - 3:30 PM. Admis adults $2; students 50¢. Estab 1957 to preserve the history of Hawaii, particularly Maui County; housed in former residence of Edward Bailey (1814-1903). Average Annual Attendance: 5000. Mem: 400; dues couple $7.50, individual $5; annual meeting Mar
Income: $25,000 (financed by membership and gift shop purchases)
Collections: Landscape Paintings (1860-1900); Paintings of Hawaiian Scenes by Edward Bailey; Prehistoric Hawaiian Artifacts
Publications: LaHaina Historical Guide; La Perouse on Maui; Hale Hoikeike - A House and Its People
Activities: Lect open to the public, 5 vis lectr per year; sales shop selling books, slides, postcards, notepaper, jewelry and souvenirs

IDAHO

BOISE

M BOISE GALLERY OF ART, c/o Julia Davis Park, Box 1505, 83701. Tel 208-345-8330. *Dir* Richard L Collier; *Asst Dir* Sally Casler; *Admin Asst* Barbara Streng
Open Tues, Thurs, Fri 10 AM - 5 PM; Wed 10 AM - 9 PM; Sat - Sun Noon - 5 PM; cl Mon and holidays. Estab 1931, incorporated 1961, gallery opened 1936. Average Annual Attendance: 147,000. Mem: 170,000
Collections: American, European and Oriental Collections of Painting, The Minor Arts, Sculpture; Collection of works by Idaho Artists
Exhibitions: Biennial exhibition for Idaho Artist; 10 exhibitions annually of all media, regional to international
Publications: Annual Report; Bulletin; Catalogs of Exhibitions, occasionally
Activities: Classes in art and art appreciation; lect open to public; docent tours; concerts; films; arts festival; Beaux Arts Societe (fund raising auxiliary); gallery shop
L Library, c/o Julia Davis Park, 83701.
Library Holdings: Other—4000 items

C FIRST SECURITY BANK OF IDAHO, 119 N Ninth St, PO Box 7069, 83730. Tel 208-384-6877. *In Charge Art Coll* Glenn Lungren
Open Mon - Fri 10 AM - 5 PM. Estab 1967. Collection displayed in 140 banks on a monthly basis
Activities: Underwrite for all kinds of performing art activities all over the state; fels through our Foundation

CALDWELL

M COLLEGE OF IDAHO, Blatchley Gallery, 83605. *Dir & Exhibits Chmn* Max Peter
Open Sun - Thurs 1 - 4 PM; cl academic holidays. No admis fee. Estab 1980, (formerly Jewett Exhibition Center 1962)
Collections: Paintings; Prints Collection
Exhibitions: Temporary and traveling exhibitions on an inter-museum loan basis
Publications: Exhibit Brochures
Activities: Lect; gallery talks; guided tours; films

MOSCOW

M UNIVERSITY OF IDAHO MUSEUM, FOC-W, 83843. Tel 208-885-6480. *Dir* G Ellis Burcaw
Open Mon - Fri 9 AM - 4 PM (when University is in session). No admis fee. Estab 1963 mainly as a training laboratory for students in museum training courses, but also to serve the University and the community by providing exhibits in a variety of fields. One room on the second floor of the Faculty Office Complex West is used as a gallery; exhibits also in the lobby and in the Administration Building. Average Annual Attendance: 1500
Income: $35,000 (financed by state appropriation and through the University)
Collections: American Indian and Eskimo Objects; Arab Objects from North Africa; West African Masks and Figurines
Exhibitions: Temporary, rotating exhibitions

POCATELLO

M IDAHO STATE UNIVERSITY, John B Davis Gallery of Fine Art, 83209. Tel 208-236-2361. *Dir* Gail Larson
Open Mon - Fri Noon - 5 PM. No admis fee. Estab 1956 to exhibit art. Gallery contains 130 running ft of space with 8 ft ceilings. Average Annual Attendance: 2600
Income: $2600 (financed by city appropriation)
Purchases: $350
Collections: †Permanent collection
Exhibitions: Ann Baddley-Fiberforms; Robert Barnum-Prints & Drawings; Group Graduate Exhibit; Anita Kapaun-Fiberforms; Marilyn Levine-Ceramics; MFA Thesis Exhibits, weekly one-man shows; Northwest Eccentric Art; Lorna Obermayr-Paper Pieces; Paper as Medium (from Smithsonian Institute); Mike Phippen-Ceramics; The Production Potter: A Question of Quality; Jacqui Steinberg-Metalsmithing; Undergraduate Exhibit; Janet Wright-Metalsmithing

TWIN FALLS

M COLLEGE OF SOUTHERN IDAHO, Art Gallery, Box 1238, 83301. Tel 208-733-9554. *Chmn Art Dept* La Var Steel; *Gallery Dir* Mike Green
Open Mon - Sat 8 AM - 5 PM, cl Sun. No admis fee. Estab 1967 as a college gallery for student and public enjoyment. Included is a fine arts building and auditorium. Average Annual Attendance: 15,000
Income: Financed by community college and local support
Purchases: $1000
Exhibitions: Alexander Napote; Arthur Okamura; various Waam Shows
Activities: Classes for adults and children; dramatic programs; lect open to public; scholarships
L Library, Administration Bldg, Box 1238, 83301. *Head Librn* Steve Preston; *Reference Librn* Bill Beal
Open Mon - Fri 8 AM - 10 PM. Estab 1965
Library Holdings: Vols 100,000; Per subs 95; Micro—Cards, fiche, reels, prints; AV —A-tapes, cassettes, fs, motion pictures, slides, v-tapes; Other—Framed reproductions, prints, manuscripts, original art works, photographs

ILLINOIS

BISHOP HILL

M BISHOP HILL HISTORIC SITE,* PO Box O, 61419. Tel 309-927-3520. *Historian* Ronald E Nelson; *Site Supt* Edward J Hepner; *Asst Supt* James Likes
Open daily 9 AM - 5 PM, cl Thanksgiving, Christmas and New Years. No admis fee. Estab 1946 to interpret history of Bishop Hill Colony. Average Annual Attendance: 60,000
Income: Financed by state appropriation
Purchases: $25,000
Collections: Artifacts pertaining to Bishop Hill Colony 1846-1861; primitive paintings
Activities: Lect open to public

BLOOMINGTON

M ILLINOIS WESLEYAN UNIVERSITY, Merwin Gallery, Alice Millar Center for Fine Arts, 210 E University St, 61701. Tel 309-556-3077. *Dir School of Art* Miles Bair
Open Tues - Sun 1 - 4 PM & 7 - 9 PM, cl Mon. Estab 1945
Income: Financed by endowment, and membership
Collections: 250 drawings, paintings and prints including works by Baskin, Max Beckmann, Helen Frankenthaler, Philip Guston, John Ible, Oliviera, Larry Rivers and Whistler
Exhibitions: Annual Illinois High School Art Exhibition; School of Art Faculty Exhibition; School of Art Student Exhibition
Publications: Exhibition Posters; Gallery Schedule, monthly
Activities: Dramatic programs; concerts; lect open to public, 5 vis lectr per year; tours; competitions; original objects of art lent, on campus only; book traveling exhibitions; traveling exhibitions organized and circulated
L Slide Library, 210 E University St, 61701.
Library Holdings: AV—Slides 30,000

O MCLEAN COUNTY ART ASSOCIATION, 601 N East St, 61701. Tel 309-827-8621. *Pres* Nancy S Merwin; *Secy* Margot Mendoza; *Dir McLean County Arts Center* Terry M Bush; *Educ Coordinator* John L Holechek; *Gallery Cur* John R Davis; *Admin Asst* Janan Hudek
Open Mon - Sat Noon - 4 PM. No admis fee. Estab 1922 to enhance the arts in McLean County by providing display gallery and sales and rental gallery to aid local professional artists. Gallery is 2500 sq ft and hosts local shows and traveling exhibits. Mem: 425; dues family $15, single $10, students $5; annual meeting first Fri in May
Income: $77,000 (financed by membership, art and book sales)
Exhibitions: (1979-80) Ken Kashian-Photography; Arthur T Towata-Pottery Paintings, Prints; 53rd Annual Amateur Competition and Exhibition; 4th Annual Holiday Sale; Arts Center Staff Exhibition
Activities: Classes for adults and children; Outreach Project providing art instruction to low income individuals; lect open to public; gallery talks; tours; competitions; Merwin Medal for best in show, first through third in each category; sales shop selling books, magazines, original art; operates both a used book store and art sales gallery

CARBONDALE

M SOUTHERN ILLINOIS UNIVERSITY MUSEUM AND ART GALLERIES, Faner 2469, 62901. Tel 618-453-5388. *Dir* John J Whitlock; *Cur Art* Evert A Johnson; *Cur Exhibits* Eugene P Moehring; *Cur History* Marjorie Frankel Nathanson; *Prog Educational Services Coordr* Geraldine Kelley; *Educational Asst* Sherry Delmastro; *Registrar* Lorilee Huffman; *Exhibits Designer* Kathleen Giencke; *Preparator* Alan Harasimowicz; *Secy* Carolyn Taylor; *Adj Cur Archaeology* Dr Robert L Rands; *Adj Cur Anthropology* Dr Carroll L Riley; *Adj Cur Geology* Dr George Fraunfelter; *Adj Cur Art History* Dr Sherwood A Fehm Jr
Open Mon - Fri 10 AM - 4 PM; Sun 1:30 - 4:30 PM. No admis fee. Estab 1874 to reflect the history and cultures of southern Illinois and promote the understanding of the area; to provide area schools and the University with support through educational outreach programs; to promote the fine arts in an unrestricted manner through exhibitions and provide support to the School of Art MFA program through exhibition of MFA graduate students. Two art galleries totaling 3500 sq ft and one semi-permanent exhibit hall featuring exhibits on southern Illinois. Average Annual Attendance: 50,000
Collections: Decorative Arts; European and American Paintings, Drawings, Prints from 13th to 20th Century with emphasis on 19th and 20th century photography; Extensive Oceanic Collection; Southern Illinois History; 20th Century Sculpture, Metals, Ceramics; Various Asiatic Holdings; archaeology; costumes
Activities: Formally organized education programs for children; museum studies program; tours; lect; films; inter-museum loan; public outreach programs; active volunteers program; originates traveling exhibitions

CARLINVILLE

L BLACKBURN COLLEGE, Lumpkin Library, 62626. *Head Librn* Robert Underbrink
Open Mon - Fri 8 AM - 10 PM, Sat 8 AM - 6 PM, Sun 2 - 10 PM. Estab 1958 as a general college library
Library Holdings: Vols 67,000; Per subs 400; Micro—Cards, fiche, reels, prints; AV —A-tapes, cassettes, fs, Kodachromes, lantern slides, motion pictures, rec, slides, v-tapes; Other—Exhibition catalogs, prints, memorabilia, original art works, pamphlets, photographs, reproductions
Collections: Duncan Memorial Art Collection; 19th century European and American artists

CHAMPAIGN

UNIVERSITY OF ILLINOIS

M Krannert Art Museum,* 500 Peabody Dr, 61820. Tel 217-333-1860. *Dir* Muriel B Christison; *Asst Dir* Leonard N Amico; *Research Cur* Margaret Sullivan; *Registrar* Diane Waaler
Open Mon - Sat 9 AM - 5 PM, Sun 2 - 5 PM. No admis fee. Estab 1961 to house and administer the art collections of University of Illinois, to support teaching and research program, and to serve as an area art museum. Average Annual Attendance: 190,000. Mem: 600; dues $15 and up
Income: $350,000 (financed by endowment, membership, state appropriation)
Purchases: $50,000
Collections: †American paintings, sculpture, prints and drawings; †Ancient Near Eastern Classical and Medieval Art; Krannert Collection of Old Masters; Moore Collection of European and American Decorative Arts; Olsen Collection of Pre-Columbian Art; †Oriental Arts: Class of 1908; Trees Collection
Publications: Catalogs; Krannert Art Museum Bulletin, semi-annually
Activities: Classes for children; docent training; lect open to the public, 5-10 visiting lectrs per year; tours; original objects of art lent to museums and university galleries
M World Heritage Museum,* College of Liberal Arts & Sciences, 499 Lincoln Hall, 61801. Tel 217-333-2360. *Dir* Georgette Meredith; *Cur* Shin Theke Kang
Open daily & Sun 2:30 - 5 PM, Sat (during school term) 9:30 - 12 Midnight. No admis fee
Collections: Originals and reproductions of Greek, Roman, Egyptian, Mesopotamian, African, Oriental and European art objects, including sculpture, pottery, glass, implements, coins, seals, clay tablets, inscriptions and manuscrips
M Museum of Natural History,* 438 Natural History Bldg, 61800. Tel 217-333-2517. *Dir* Donald F Hoffmeister

CHARLESTON

M **EASTERN ILLINOIS UNIVERSITY,** Paul Turner Sargent Gallery, Lincoln & Seventh Sts, 61920. Tel 217-581-3410. *Dir* Rodney Buffington
Open daily 9 AM - 5 PM, cl Sat, open Sun 12 - 4 PM. No admis fee. Estab 1948 as an exhibition gallery
Income: Financed by state appropriation and through the University
Exhibitions: Temporary exhibition including ceramics, jewelry, paintings, photography, prints, sculpture and textiles
Publications: Exhibition catalogs
Activities: book traveling exhibitions

CHICAGO

AMERICAN SOCIETY OF ARTISTS, INC
For further information, see National and Regional Organizations

M **ARTEMISA GALLERY,*** 9 W Hubbard St, 60610. Tel 312-751-2016.
Open Tues - Sat 10 AM - 5 PM. No admis fee. Estab 1973, as a non-profit women's cooperative to exhibit members' work, to provide an alternative to commercial galleries, to encourage the development of art created by women, and to offer the community an opportunity to understand and appreciate the artist and art as valuable to society. Photography gallery is maintained. Mem: Dues benefactor $100 or more, patron $50, sponsor $25, members $10
Exhibitions: Regular exhibitions by members
Activities: Visits to artists studios; video programs; evening programs; mini-seminars

L **Learning Resource Center,*** 9 W Hubbard St, 60610.
Open to school groups, organizations and the public, the Learning Resource Center houses a collection of video and audio tapes of locally and nationally known artists, with emphasis on women. A video monitor and replay equipment makes the tapes available for viewing during regularly scheduled hours (4 - 5 PM Tues - Sat) or at other times by appointment
Library Holdings: AV—A-tapes, slides, v-tapes

M **ART INSTITUTE OF CHICAGO,** Michigan Ave at Adams St, 60603. Tel 312-443-3600. *Chmn Board of Trustees* Arthur M Wood; *Dir* James N Wood; *Pres* E Laurence Chalmers Jr; *VPres Admin Affairs* Robert E Marrs; *VPres Develop & Public Relations* Larry Ter Molen; *VPres Academic Affairs* Donald J Irving; *Secy* Linda Starks; *Cur American Art* Milo M Naeve; *Asst Cur Earlier Paintings & Sculpture* Susan Wise; *Conservator* Alfred Jakstas; *Assoc Conservator* Timothy Lenon; *Asst Cur Classical Art* Louise Berge; *Cur Oriental Art* Jack Sewell; *Assoc Cur Oriental Art* Osamu Ueda; *Dir Museum Education* Rex Moser; *Dir Museum Photography* Howard Kraywinkel; *Assoc Cur Photography* David Travis; *Cur Primitive Art* Evan Maurer; *Cur Prints & Drawings* Harold Joachim; *Assoc Cur Prints & Drawings* Anselmo Carini; *Cur Textiles* Christa C Mayer Thurman; *Cur 20th Century Painting & Sculpture* A James Speyer; *Assoc Cur 20th Century Painting & Sculpture* Anne Rorimer; *Museum Registrar* Wallace Bradway; *Dir Museum Education* Barbara Wriston; *Dir Libraries* Daphne Roloff; *Dir Public Relations* Helen M Lethert; *Dir Publications* Margaret Blasage; *Dir Annual Programs* Edith B Gaines
Open Mon - Wed & Fri 10:30 AM - 4:30 PM, Thurs 10:30 AM - 8 PM, Sat 10 AM - 5 PM, Sun & holidays Noon - 5 PM, cl Christmas. Discretionary admission fee, no admis fee on Thurs. Estab and incorporated 1879. Mem: 68,132; dues family $30, individual single member $20
Collections: Paintings, sculpture, oriental art, prints and drawings, photographs, decorative arts, primitive art and textiles; The painting collection reviews Western art, with an especially fine sequence of French Impressionists and Post Impressionists; the print collection illustrates the history of printmaking from the 15th - 20th centuries with important examples of all periods. It is particularly rich in French works of the 19th century including Meryon, Redon, Millet, Gauguin and Toulouse-Lautrec; The Thorne Miniature Rooms are on permanent view; textiles are displayed in the Agnes Allerton Textile Galleries, which includes a study room and new conservation facilities; the collection of primitive art consists of African, Oceanic and ancient American objects; The Columbus Drive Facilities include the reconstructed Trading Room from the Chicago Stock Exchange; Arthur Rubloff Paperweight collection is on view in Gunsaulus Hall; the America Windows, monumental stained glass windows designed by Marc Chagall, are on view in the gallery overlooking McKinlock Court
Exhibitions: American Institute of Architects: 1979 Honor Awards; Chicago Architects: Selections from the Permanent Collection; Contemporary Chinese Paintings; Greek Vase Painting in Midwestern Collections; Japanese Prints, Recent Acquisitions; Toulouse-Latrec: Paintings; Master Prints of Six Centuries; Needlework from the Permanent Collection; 100 Artists, 100 Years; Photography Rediscovered; Plan of Chicago 1909-1979; Rapacious Birds and Severed Heads; Early Bronze Rings from Nigeria; Roman Drawings of the Sixteenth Century from the Louvre; Tapestries from the Permanent Collection; The Joseph Winterbotham Collection; Weekly Film Series at the Film Center
Publications: Bulletin; Museum Studies; catalogs; Annual Report
Activities: Museum Education programs for adults; Lectures, films, discussions, Goodman Theatre Center presents Chicago's only resident theatre company produced by the Chicago Theatre Group; art rental and sales gallery, museum store

L **Ryerson and Burnham Libraries,** Michigan at Adams St, 60603. *Dir of Libraries* Daphne Roloff; *Assoc Librn and Head Reference Dept* Cecilia H Chin; *Architectural Archivist* John Zukowsky; *Head Technical Services* Karen Muller; *Slide Librn* Rosann Auchstetter
Open to museum members, staff of museum, students and faculty of the School of Art Institute and visiting curators only; Open Mon - Sat 10:30 AM - 4:30 PM, cl Sat in June, July & August
Income: $396,100
Purchases: $86,500
Library Holdings: Vols 126,000; Per subs 800; Micro—Fiche, reels; AV—Lantern Slides, slides; Other—Clipping files, exhibition catalogs, manuscripts, memorabilia, pamphlets, photographs, architectural drawings
Special Subjects: Architecture, Photography
Collections: Burnham Archive: 10,000 American architectural drawings, letters, reports; including special Louis Sullivan, Frank Lloyd Wright, and D H Burnham

collections; Percier and Fontaine Collection; Chicago Art and Artists Scrapbook: newspaper clippings from Chicago papers from 1880 to present; Ryerson Collection of Japanese and Chinese Illustrated books; Gary Reynolds Collection: Surrealism
Exhibitions: Exhibition of architectural drawings

O **Woman's Board,** 60603. *Pres* Mrs James P Baxter
Estab 1952 to supplement the Board of Trustees in advancing the growth of the Institute and extending its activities and usefulness as a cultural and educational institution. Mem: 78; annual meeting May

O **Auxiliary Board,** 60603. *Pres* Mrs Jeffrey C Ward
Estab 1973 to promote interest in programs and activities of the Art Institute amoung younger men and women. Mem: 58; dues $25; annual meeting June

O **Antiquarian Society,** 60603. *Pres* Mrs Harold T Martin
Estab 1877. Makes gift of decorative arts to the Institute. Mem: 475; by invitation; annual meeting Nov
Activities: Lectures and seminars for members; tours; trips

O **Print and Drawing Club,** 60603. *Pres* Edward A Bergman
Estab and incorporated 1922 to study prints and drawings and their purchase for the institute. Mem: 190; dues $25

O **Society for Contemporary Arts,** 60603. *Pres* Phil Shorr
Estab and incorporated 1940 to assist the Institute in acquisition of contemporary works. Mem: 190; annual meeting May
Activities: Lectures, seminars and annual exhibition at the Institute

O **Orientals,** 60603. *Secy Treas* Jack Sewell
Estab 1925 to promote interest in the Institute's collection of Oriental art. Mem: 50; dues $25 and $10

O **Textile Society,** 60603. *Pres* Mrs Don S Reuben
Estab 1978 to promote appreciation of textiles through lectures, raising of funds, special publications and exhibitions for the Department of textiles

O **Old Masters Society,** 60603. *Pres* Mrs John A Bross Jr
Estab 1977 to promote interest in the Department of Earlier Painting, through lectures and fund raising for acquisitions. Mem: Dues $100 and $35

M **Junior Museum,** Michigan Ave at Adams St, 60603. Tel 312-443-3680. *Dir* L Raasch
Open Mon - Wed and Fri 10:30 AM - 4 PM, Thurs 10:30 AM - 7 PM, Sat 10 AM - 4:30 PM, Sun & holidays Noon - 4:30 PM. Admission discretionary, no admis fee Thursday. Estab 1964. A facility including auditorium, lunchroom, galleries, offices and library. One main gallery with exhibits changing every two or three years and two corridor galleries changed every six months; Picnic Room for children. Average Annual Attendance: 150,000
Income: Financed by endowment
Exhibitions: Drawings for World Exchange Film Fun; Horses; Make-In: The Pinhole Camera; Photography: Smile for the Birdie; Photography by Students of South Shore and Lane Technical High Schools; Special Faces: A Drawing Box
Publications: A People Watcher: Toulouse-Lautrec Paintings; Forms in Space; Heritage Hike I, II, III; I Spy and Bits and Pieces Gallery Games; Kaleidoscope; The Lion's Pride; Needlework Patterns; preparatory material sent to schools in advance of certain tours; Round Up; This Colorful World; Tracing Holiday Symbols; Volunteer Directory; What is American About American Art
Activities: Docent training; lectures open to the public; gallery games; traveling exhibitions organized and circulated; museum shop sells books, reproductions, prints and slides

L **Little Library,** Michigan Ave at Adams St, 60603.
Open for reference only
Library Holdings: Vols 1500

O **ARTISTS GUILD OF CHICAGO,** 54 East Erie St, 60611. Tel 312-787-6116. *Pres* Corrie Glass; *VPres* Shlomo Krudo; *Secy* Gordon Hempel; *Executive Dir* M Gleeson
Open 10 AM - 4 PM Mon - Fri. No admis fee. Estab 1922 to secure and protect the independence of our members, to prevent their exploitation, to cooperate with groups with similar aims, to further the communicating arts and public knowledge and understanding of same. Galleries are located in headquarters building. Average Annual Attendance: 2000. Mem: 750; dues $65; annual meeting first Tues in Oct
Income: Financed by membership, employment service for artists, social and educational programs, exhibits
Purchases: Approx $2000
Collections: AGC Permanent Collection of over seventy fine art works
Exhibitions: Eight or nine juried shows each year; Members exhibitions; Annual Chicago Show

O **ARTS CLUB OF CHICAGO,** 109 E Ontario St, 60611. Tel 312-787-3997. *Pres* James P Baxter; *First VPres* Mrs George P Rogers; *Secy* Franklin D Trueblood; *Dir* Patricia M Scheidt
Open 10 AM - 5:30 PM. No admis fee. Estab 1916 to maintain club rooms for members and provide galleries for changing exhibitions. Gallery has 200 running ft of wall space. Average Annual Attendance: 15,000. Mem: 1150; annual meeting in Nov
Income: Financed by membership
Purchases: Occasional purchases from bequests
Exhibitions: (1979-80) Fletcher Benton, Sculpture; Elmer Bischoff, Recent Paintings; Vija Celmins, Drawings, Objects, Paintings; David Diao, Paintings; 60th Professional Members Exhibition; E Vuillard, Drawings and Lithographs
Publications: Exhibition Catalogs
Activities: Dramatic programs; lect; concerts; traveling exhibitions organized and circulated

L **Reference library,** 109 E Onario St, 60611.
Library Holdings: Vols 2,000

M **BALZEKAS MUSEUM OF LITHUANIAN CULTURE,** 4012 Archer Ave, 60632. Tel 312-847-2441. *Pres* Stanley Balzekas Jr; *VPres* Casimir Baltramaitis; *Secy* Stanley Balzekas III
Open seven days a week 1 - 4 PM. Admis adults $1, children and senior citizens 50¢. Estab 1966 as a repository for collecting and preserving Lithuanian cultural treasures. Mem: 950; annual dues $10
Income: $5000 (financed by membership and donations)
Collections: Amber, Philately, †Coins, Textiles, Wooden folkart, †Art
Exhibitions: Will exhibit twenty-five paintings
Publications: Lithuanian Museum Review, bi-monthly
Activities: Classes for adults and children; lectures open to the public; gallery talks;

tours; competitions with awards; scholarships offered; individual paintings are lent to the University and other institutions; book traveling exhibitions; Sales shop sells books, reproductions, textiles, amber, Lithuanian dolls, philately, numismatics

L Balzekas Museum Research Library, 4012 Archer Ave, 60632. *Head Librn* Jurgis Kasakaitis
Open Seven days 1 - 4 PM. Estab 1966. Open to public for reference; lending restricted to members
Collections: Folk art; Reproductions of Lithuanian artists; Information on Lithuanian artists and their works
Exhibitions: Rare Book Exhibits
Publications: Books

L BOONE ORIENTAL LIBRARY AND FINE ARTS COLLECTION, Roosevelt Rd & Lakeshore Dr, 60605.
A Substantial private collection has been made available to the college by its owners, Commander and Mrs G E Boone. The collection is designed for study and display, and is located in Field Museum of Natural History
Library Holdings: Vols 5000
Activities: Guest artists; films; gallery critiques; special exhibitions

CHICAGO ARCHITECTURE FOUNDATION
M Glessner House, 1800 S Prairie Ave, 60616. Tel 312-326-1393. *Pres Board Trustees* Franklin Orwin; *Cur* Jethro M Hurt III; *Business Mgr* Richard Combs
Guided tours Tues, Thurs & Sat 10 AM - 3 PM, Sun, May 1 - Aug 31, 11 AM - 4 PM, Sept 1 - Apr 30, 1 - 4 PM. Admis adults $2, students and senior citizens $1, members free; group rates available. Estab 1966 for the restoration of the main floor of this architecturally significant residence, and for the promotion of good architecture in general. Designed by world-famous Henry Hobson Richardson, often known as the Father of Modern Architecture, Glessner House was completed in 1886. Its period furnishings give visitors an excellent idea of what Victorian life was like on this street once known as Millionaires' Row. Average Annual Attendance: 5000. Mem: 1800; dues life $500, contributing $100, family $30, individual $20, students and seniors $10
Income: Financed by membership, tours, and rentals of house
Collections: †House Furnishings
Publications: Chicago Architecture Foundation Members' Newsletter, bimonthly
Activities: Classes for adults and children; docent training; public service; visiting lectrs; tours; original objects of art lent to galleries which are mounting exhibitions on architecture; lending collection contains architectural ornaments; sales shop selling books, posters, stationery, small gift items
M ArchiCenter, 310 S Michigan Ave, 2nd Floor, 60604. Tel 312-782-1776. *Mgr* Alice Sinkevitch
Open Mon - Sat 9 AM - 5 PM. No admis fee. Estab 1976 to make people more aware of the build environment through exhibits, lectures, films and tours. Approx 2500 sq ft of exhibit space offers a permanent exhibit chronicling Chicago's contributions to the modern building arts. Average Annual Attendance: 40,000
Income: Financed by membership, book shop, and federal grant
Exhibitions: (1979) America's Architectural Heritage; Cornell University Alumni Architects; FIRE: What Architects Have Done About It; Graphics in Architecture; Living Here and Liking It; Louis Sullivan in St Louis; Lorado Taft in Illinois; McDonalds of the Future; The Wasmuth Edition; The World's Fair of 1893
Activities: 30 visiting lectrs per year; sales shop selling books, magazines, slides, small gift items, stationery and posters

O CHICAGO HISTORICAL SOCIETY, Clark St at North Ave, 60614. Tel 312-642-4600. *Pres* Theodore Tieken; *VPres* Stewart S Dixon; *Secy* Bryan S Reid Jr; *Dir* Harold K Skramstad Jr; *Cur Painting & Sculpture* Joseph B Zywicki; *Cur Decorative Arts* Sharon Darling; *Cur Costumes* Elizabeth Jachimowicz; *Editor* Fannia Weingartner; *Chief, Education and Public Programs* Judy Weisman
Open Mon - Sat 9:30 AM - 4:30 PM; Sun & holidays 12:00 - 5 PM; Library open Tues - Sat 9:30 AM - 4:30 PM, except for July and August, when it is open Mon - Fri, cl Christmas, Thanksgiving, and New Year's Day. Admis adults $1, children (6-17) 50¢, senior citizens 25¢; no admis fee Mon. Estab 1856 to maintain a museum and library of American history with special emphasis on the Chicago region. Average Annual Attendance: 200,000. Mem: 4500; dues $20; annual meeting in Oct
Income: $1,500,000 (financed by endowment, membership, city and state appropriations and public donations)
Collections: Chicago Decorative Arts; Civil War; Costumes; Graphics; Lincoln collection; Manuscripts; Pioneer Life
Exhibitions: Chicago Ceramics & Glass; Chicago History Galleries; Chromolithography in America 1840-1900; The Working American continuing program of craft demonstrations and exhibits from the Collections
Publications: Books; Calendar of Events, quarterly; Catalogs; Chicago History, quarterly
Activities: Classes for adults and children; lect open to public, 8-10 vis lectr per year; gallery talks; tours; sales shop selling books, magazines, prints, reproductions, slides
L Library, Clark St at North Ave, 60614.
Open Tues - Sat 9:30 AM - 4:30 PM, except July & August when it is open Mon - Fri
Library Holdings: Vols 120,000; Micro—Reels; Other—Prints, manuscripts 4,000,000, photographs

L CHICAGO PUBLIC LIBRARY, Art Section, Fine Arts Division, Cultural Center, 78 E Washington St, 60602. Tel 312-269-2858. *Commissioner* Donald J Sager; *Chief Fine Arts Division* Marjorie R Adkins; *Asst Division Chief* Nancy E Harvey; *Head Art Section* Patricia E Keane; *Picture Coll Librn* Virginia R Smith; *Coll Development* Yvonne S Brown
Open Mon - Thurs 10 AM - 8 PM, Fri 10 AM - 6 PM, Sat 10 AM - 5 PM, Sun 1 - 5 PM. Estab 1872 as a free public library and reading room. The present building was built in 1897. Audio-visual materials are restricted for use by Chicago area residents
Income: $71,150 (financed by city and state appropriations)
Library Holdings: Vols 41,600; Per subs 285; Micro—Fiche, reels; AV—A-tapes, motion pictures, rec, slides, v-tapes; Other—Clipping files, exhibition catalogs, pamphlets, photographs
Special Subjects: Architecture, Costume Design & Construction, Crafts, Decorative Arts, Film, Photography, Theatre Arts, Chicago Architecture
Collections: Exhibitions catalogues beginning in 1973, primarily English language

catalogues; Folk Dance collection of 50 loose leaf volumes; picture collection of over one million items of secondary source material covering all subject areas
Activities: Dramatic programs; lect open to public; concerts; interlibrary loan
M Cultural Center, 78 E Washington St, 60602. Tel 312-269-2820. *Board Pres* Camille Hatzenbuehler; *VPres* Bruce Sagan; *Secy* Stanley Balzekas Jr; *Dir* Janet R Bean; *Cur Special Coll* Tom Orlando; *Head Audio-visual Center* Barbara Flynn; *Coordr of Programs & Exhibits* Janet Carl Smith
Open Mon - Thurs 10 AM - 8 PM, Fri 10 AM - 6 PM, Sat 10 AM - 5 PM, Sun 1 - 5 PM. No admis fee. Estab 1977 to integrate in a single facility the functions of library gallery, museum and center for the arts and humanities. The Center maintains the Randolph Gallery, 2025 sq ft, the West Gallery, 92 running ft, the East Gallery, 150 running ft, Thomas Hughes Gallery, 576 sq ft, G A R Memorial Hall, 5088 sq ft, and the Exhibit Hall, 6004 sq ft. Average Annual Attendance: 1,200,000
Income: Financed by city and state appropriations, grant monies and corporate support
Exhibitions: (1978) The Art of Playboy from the First 25 Years; Great Ideas; Laliberte: An Artist's Retrospective; Mexposicion La Mujer: A Visual Dialogue; 100 Years of Posters of the Folies Bergere; Posters of Paul Colin; Red Groom's Chicago; Sculptures of Nick De Vries; WPA and the Black Artist: Chicago and New York. (1979) The Art of Victor Vasarely; Graficas: Contemporary Latin American Prints; Graphics by Marcell Jensen; Greetings from Ed Weiss; Japan Today Photo Exhibit; Jazz - Seen; Jerry Dantzic and Cirkut Camera; Quilts: A Tradition in Southern Illinois; The Results of a Bizarre Activity; The Sculpture of Carol Hammerman; The Sculpture of Marion Perkins; 21 Views of China; The Way of Stone: The Tomihisa Handa Sculpture Exhibit; The World of Ceramics by Anna Tate
Publications: Calendar of Events, monthly
Activities: Dramatic programs; lect open to public; concerts; tours; book traveling exhibitions; originate traveling exhibitions

O CONTEMPORARY ART WORKSHOP, 542 W Grant Place, 60614. Tel 312-525-9624. *Dir* John Kearney; *Admin Dir* Lynn Kearney
Open daily 9 AM - 5:30 PM, Sat Noon - 5 PM. No admis fee. Estab 1951 as an art center and a Workshop-Alternative Space for artists; it is the oldest artist-run art workshop in the country. Studios for approximately 26 artists and gallery for exhibition of developing and establishing artists from Chicago and other parts of the country are maintained. Average Annual Attendance: 4000
Income: $75,000 (financed by contributions, foundations, Illinois Arts Council, National Endowment for the Arts, and earnings by the workshop fees)
Exhibitions: Joe Agate; Roger Akers; Carol Bendell; Norbert Brown; Nancy Burket; Bob Dixon; Mimi Dolnick; Michael Dunbar; Walter Eydryck; Diana Foster; Julian Harr; W A S Hatch; Irmfriede Hogan; Amy Kaiser; John Kearney; Mark Krastoff; Gail Sherman Kritlow; Steven Lowery; Robert McCauley; Steve Mercer; John Mishler; Renate Ponsold Motherwell; Suzanne Peters; Jacqueline Ruttinger; Suzanne Seed; Diana Shaffer; Bill Stipe; Marilyn Sward; Emerson Woelffer; Michael Wrabak; Paul Zakoian; Peter Zettler
Activities: Classes for adults and children; lect open to the public; gallery shop selling artwork

M DUSABLE MUSEUM OF AFRICAN AMERICAN HISTORY, 740 E 56th Pl, 60637. Tel 312-947-0600. *Dir* Margaret T Burroughs; *Cur* Charles G Burroughs; *Resident Dir* Eugene P Feldman
Open Mon - Fri 9 AM - 5 PM, Sat & Sun 1 - 5 PM, cl Mon last two weeks of Aug & National holidays. Admis adults 50¢, children & students 25¢, groups by appointment. Estab 1961 as history and art museum on African American history. Mem: Dues life $100, general $15
Collections: Historical archives; paintings; photographs; prints; sculpture
Publications: Books of poems, children's stories, African and Afro-American history; Heritage Calendar, annually
Activities: Lect; guided tours; book traveling exhibitions; sales shop selling curios, sculpture, prints, books and artifacts

C EXCHANGE NATIONAL BANK OF CHICAGO, 130 S LaSalle St, 60603. Tel 312-781-8076. *Cur* Herbert Kahn
Open to public. Estab 1968 as a community service by making a meaningful cultural contribution to the community. Collection displayed in public areas of the bank
Collections: Approximately 2000 photographs by important photographers since the founding of photography up to the present
Activities: Tours

M FIELD MUSEUM OF NATURAL HISTORY,* Roosevelt Rd at Lake Shore Dr, 60605. Tel 312-922-9410. *Pres & Dir* E Leland Webber; *Asst Dir Science & Educ* Lorin I Nevling; *Chmn Anthropology* Phillip Lewis
Open winter daily 9 AM - 4 PM, spring & fall daily 9 AM - 5 PM, summer daily 9 AM - 6 PM, cl Christmas, New Years. Admis family $3.50, adults $1.50, students 50¢, senior citizens 35¢, no charge on Fri. Estab 1893 to preserve and disseminate knowledge of natural history. 22 anthropological exhibition halls, including a Hall of Primitive Art are maintained. Average Annual Attendance: 1,200,000. Mem: 74,621; dues $15
Income: $8,000,000 (financed by endowment, membership, city and state appropriations and federal and earned funds)
Collections: Anthropological collections totaling over one third million specimens, including approx 100,000 art objects from North and South America, Oceania, Africa, Asia and prehistoric Europe
Exhibitions: Basketry of the Northwest Coast Indians; Between Friends -Entre Amis; Chinese Folk Art; Field Museum Gamelan; I Wear the Morning Star; 19th century Alaskan Eskimo Art; Peru's Golden Treasures; Treasures of Tutankhamun
Publications: Bulletin, monthly; Fieldiana (serial)
Activities: Classes for adults and children; lect open to the public, 25 visiting lectrs per year; concerts; gallery talks; tours; exten dept serving Chicago area; original objects of art lent to qualified museum or other scholarly institutions; traveling exhibitions organized and circulated; museum shop selling books, magazines, prints, slides
L Library,* Roosevelt Rd at Lake Shore Dr, 60605. *Librn* W Peyton Fawcett
Library Holdings: Vols 197,000; Per subs 2000

C **THE FIRST NATIONAL BANK OF CHICAGO,** One First National Plaza, 60670. Tel 312-732-8939. *Cur* Robert Middaugh
Open to public by appointment only. No admis fee. Estab 1968 to assemble works of art to serve as a permanent extension of daily life. Collection displayed throughout bank building and overseas offices
Collections: Art from Africa, America, Asia, Australia, the Caribbean Basin, Europe, Latin America, Near East and the South Seas ranging from 6th Century BC to the present
Activities: Individual objects of art lent only to major exhibitions in museums

L **HARRINGTON INSTITUTE OF INTERIOR DESIGN LIBRARY,** 410 S Michigan Ave, 60605. *Librn* Adeline Schuster
Open daily 8:30 AM - 5 PM, Tues & Thurs 8:30 AM - 9 PM. Estab 1960 to support the Harrington Institute Curriculum Research requirements as well as student reference
Purchases: $10,000
Library Holdings: Vols 2500; Per subs 55
Special Subjects: Architecture

C **ILLINOIS BELL,** 225 W Randolph St, 60606. Tel 312-727-2158. *Mgr Art Program* Marion Butler
Lobby gallery open 8 AM - 5 PM. Estab 1967 to support the arts; to make the company a responsive member of the community; to provide uplifting atmosphere for employees. Collection displayed throughout building and in offices; Lobby exhibits art (not from company collection)
Collections: Approximately 2000 pieces, multi-media, mostly modern, non-representational works, many by Illinois artists
Activities: Gallery talks; tours for groups; originate traveling exhibitions from Lobby exhibits to various galleries and other public locations in Illinois

M **LOYALA UNIVERSITY OF CHIGAGO,** Martin D'Arcy Gallery of Art, 6525 N Sheridan Rd, 60626. Tel 312-274-3000, Ext 786. *Dir* Donald F Rowe
Open Mon - Fri 1 - 4 PM, Tues & Thurs 6:30 - 9:30 PM, Sun 1 - 4 PM. No admis fee. Estab 1969 to display the permanent university collection of Medieval, Renaissance and Baroque decorative arts and paintings. One gallery set up as a large living room with comfortable seating, classical music, fresh flowers, view of Lake Michigan, and art objects in view. Average Annual Attendance: 10,000
Income: Financed by gifts
Purchases: $200,000
Collections: †Bronze, †enamel, †gold, †ivory, paintings, †sculpture, †silver, †textiles, †wax
Publications: Annual Report; The Art of Jewelry, 1450 to 1650; Enamels, the XII to the XVI century; The First Ten Years, Notable Acquisitions of Medieval, Renaissance and Baroque Art
Activities: Gallery talks; tours on request; paintings and original objects of art lent to qualified museums; lending collection contains original art works, paintings and sculpture
L **Library,** 6525 N Sheridan Rd, 60626.
Open to university students and scholars
Library Holdings: Vols 15,000; Per subs 40

M **MUSEUM OF CONTEMPORARY ART,** 237 E Ontario St, 60611. Tel 312-280-2660. *Pres* Lewis Manilow; *Dir* John H Neff; *Dir Business Services* Helen Dunbeck; *Treas* John Cartland; *Cur* Judith Russi Kirshner; *Secy* Donald Ludgin
Open Tues - Sat 10 AM - 5 PM, Sun 12 - 5 PM, cl Mon. Admis general $2. Estab 1967 as a forum for contemporary arts in Chicago. Average Annual Attendance: 100,000. Mem: 5000
Income: $100,000 (financed by endowment, membership, public and private sources)
Collections: †Permanent collection is mainly contemporary, constantly growing through contributions and purchases
Exhibitions: (1978) Art in a Turbulent Era (Expressionism Festival); Frida Kahlo; (1979) Concept, Narrative, Document; New Dimensions (Chicago artists series); Options Series; Wall Painting (1980) Vito Acconci Retrospective
Publications: Bimonthly calendar, exhibition and program catalogs
Activities: Poetry readings, docent training; lect; performance, tours, films; museum store selling books, designer jewelry and other gifts, magazines, original art & reproductions
L **Library,** 237 E Ontario St, 60611.
Under supervision of education department, for reference only

M **N.A.M.E. GALLERY,** 9 W Hubbard St, 60610. Tel 312-467-6550. *Pres* Michiko Itatani; *VPres* Paul Krainak; *VPres* Terrence Karpowicz; *VPres* Michael Brakke; *Treas* Guy Whitney; *Treas* Othello Anderson; *Gallery Dir* Krystin Grenon; *Adminr Dir* Marcia Bernstein; *Performance Dir* Jean Sousa
Open Tues - Sat 11 AM - 5 PM. Estab 1973, a non-profit, tax exempt, artist-run gallery with exhibition space dedicated to the encouragement of ideas and communication. Gallery has 4000 sq ft of space with one main show area of 3200 sq ft, 210 ft running wall; first floor-loft building. Average Annual Attendance: 22,000. Mem: 6; dues $100; weekly Board of Directors' meetings
Income: Financed by endowment, membership, city and state appropriation, private donations and corporate-foundation grants
Exhibitions: Chicago Video Artists, 1980
Activities: Lect open to public, 12 visiting lectr per year; concerts; gallery talks; tours; panel discussion of current issues; competitions; individual paintings and original objects of art lent to Art Institute of Chicago, Museum of Contemporary Art, Chicago; originate traveling exhibitions
L **N.A.M.E. Documents,** 9 W Hubbard St, 60610.
Open Tues - Sat 11 AM - 5 PM. Estab 1974 to preserve the history of N.A.M.E. Gallery
Library Holdings: AV—Lantern Slides, slides; Other—Clipping files, exhibition catalogs, prints, memorabilia, original art works, photographs

M **NORTHESTERN ILLINOIS UNIVERSITY,** North River Community Gallery, 3307 W Bryn Mawr, 60659. Tel 312-583-4050, Ext 586. *Gallery Coordr* Frank J Fritzmann; *Dept Chmn* Russell Roller
Open weekdays 1 - 5 PM. No admis fee. Estab Feb 1973 for the purpose of providing a link between the University and the local community on a cultural and aesthetic level, to bring the best local and Midwest artists to this community. Gallery is located in a relatively small storefront, on a commercial street, three blocks from the University. Average Annual Attendance: 500-900
Income: Financed by Department of Art funds and personnel
Exhibitions: (1979) Michael Dickens: Printmaking, Intaglio Prints, Serigraphs; David Packer: Retrospective; Spirit of Alumni Exhibit; Bill Whorrall: Indiana Painter
Publications: Flyers on each show
Activities: Competitions

M **PALETTE AND CHISEL ACADEMY OF FINE ARTS GALLERY,*** 1012 N Dearborn St, 60610. Tel 312-337-9889. *Pres* Alfred Alfredson; *Secy* Elsie T Lowe
Open daily 2 - 5 PM, Tues & Thurs evenings 7 - 9 PM. No admis fee. Estab and incorporated 1895. Gallery owns building containing galleries, classrooms, studios and library. Mem: 100; dues $84; annual meeting Jan
Collections: Oil paintings by members
Exhibitions: Annual juried exhibition of members' work in oils, watercolors and mixed media; regular exhibit of members' work; special and one-person shows
Activities: Educ events; lect; competitions; awards

C **PLAYBOY ENTERPRISES, INC,** 919 N Michigan Ave, 60611. Tel 312-751-8000. *VPres, Corporate Art & Graphics Dir* Arthur Paul
Open to public by appointment only in groups. No admis fee. Estab 1953 to gather and maintain works commissioned for reproduction by Playboy Magazine
Collections: Selected works from 4000 illustrations and fine art pieces, works include paintings and sculpture representing 20th Century artists such as Robert Ginzel, Roger Hane, Larry Rivers, James Rosenquist, Seymour Rosofsky, Roy Schnackenberg, George Segal, Andy Warhol, Robert Weaver, Tom Wesselman, Karl Wirsum, and others
Publications: Catalogs pertaining to Beyond Illustration - The Art of Playboy; The Art of Playboy - from the First 25 Years
Activities: Lect; tours; Annual Illustration Awards; individual objects of art lent for exhibitions; originate traveling exhibitions to galleries, universities, museums and cultural centers

M **POLISH MUSEUM OF AMERICA,** 984 N Milwaukee Ave, 60622. Tel 312-384-3352. *Dir* Donald Bilinski; *Pres* Edwin Cudecki
Open daily 1 - 4 PM. No admis fee. Estab 1937, to gather and preserve items and records pertaining to Polish culture as well as Polish American culture. A specialized Museum and Gallery containing works of Polish artists, and Polish-American artists is maintained. Average Annual Attendance: 7000
Income: Financed by donations
Collections: Originals dating to beginning of 20th century, a few older pieces; Pulaski at Savannah (Batowski); works of Polish artists, Polish-American artists and works on a Polish subject
Publications: Polish Museum Quarterly
Activities: Traveling exhibitions organized and circulated; museum shop
L **Research Library,*** 984 N Milwaukee Ave, 60622.
Library Holdings: Vols 25,000; Per subs 65
Special Subjects: Poland and works by Polish-American authors
Collections: Haiman

L **ROSENTHAL ART SLIDES,** 5456 South Ridgewood Court, 60615. Tel 312-324-3367. *Dir* John W Rosenthal; *Librn* Mark M Braunstein
Open Mon - Fri 9 AM - 5 PM. Estab 1950, to make available for purchase or perusal slides of architecture and art, for educational use. Slide library open to the public
Income: Financed through sales
Library Holdings: AV—Slides
Special Subjects: World art history
Collections: Commissioned slide sets from many major museums, including the Metropolitan Museum of Art, the Art Institute of Chicago, the National Collection of Fine Arts, the Phillips Collection, the Albright-Knox Art Gallery, the Cincinnati Art Museum, and many others; also, many slides directly from major artists or their galleries

M **SCHOOL OF HOLOGRAPHY,** Fine Arts Research and Holographic Center Museum, 1134 W Washington Blvd, 60607. Tel 312-226-1007. *Pres* Loren Billings; *VPres* Al Ornelas; *Secy* Robert Billings; *Dir Research* John Hoffmann; *Dir Display and Design* Victor Heredia; *Dir Education* Richard Stevens; *Dir Development* Dr T H Jeong; *Dir Development* Prof D Wender
Open 12 - 5 PM. Admis $1. Estab 1976 to display Holographic works; to carry on public education; to operate a school of Holography. 15,000 sq ft of exhibition space, oak panel walls, special display wings, sales gallery; school facilities comprise 4600 sq ft of fully equipped laboratories and darkrooms with additional lecture facilities. Average Annual Attendance: 5000
Exhibitions: Chicagofest
Activities: Classes for adults; lectures open to the public, 10 visiting lecturers per year; gallery talks; tours; museum shop sells books, magazines, slides
L **David Wender Library,** 1134 W Washington Blvd, 60607. *In Charge* David Wender; *Dir* Loren Billings
Open by appointment only
Library Holdings: Other—Clipping files, exhibition catalogs, photographs
Collections: Historic Collection of Holograms; Extensive collection of Russian Holograms

L **SCHOOL OF THE ART INSTITUTE OF CHICAGO LIBRARY,** 280 S Columbus Dr, 60603. Tel 312-443-3748. *Dir* Nadene Byrne; *Head Readers Services* Rochelle Goldberg; *Head Technical Services* Fred Hillbruner; *Video Data Bank* Lyn Blumenthal; *Video Data Bank* Kate Horsfield; *School Slide Service* Rudy Guernica
Open Mon - Thurs 8:30 AM - 9 PM, Fri 8:30 AM - 5 PM, Sun 10 AM - 6 PM. Estab 1967 to provide a strong working collection for School's programs in the visual and related arts. Circ 30,000
Income: $184,400 (financed through the operational budgets of the School of Art

Institute of Chicago)
Purchases: $44,700
Library Holdings: Vols 12,000; Per subs 141; AV—Cassettes, motion pictures, rec, v-tapes; Other—Exhibition catalogs, prints, pamphlets
Special Subjects: Art, Humanities
Collections: Erens Film Scripts; Whitney Halstead Art History; Film Study Collection; Artists Interview Series
Publications: Library Handbook for patrons, annually
Activities: Scholarships offered

C **SEARS ROEBUCK AND COMPANY,** Sears Tower D 731-H, 60684. Tel 312-875-8570. *In Charge Art Coll* Michael C Lucia
No admis fee. Estab 1972 to present a comprehensive collection of original art of the highest quality, while providing additional decorative and color schemes throughout the Tower complex. Collection displayed throughout building; the gallery within the Tower is for the selection of art by employees for their own office. Tower is worlds tallest building
Collections: Approximately 7000 pieces of art: etchings, lithographs, master graphics, oils, serigraphs and watercolors
Exhibitions: Annual Sear Employee Art Show
Activities: Tours of special events only; competitions with awards; Calders universe sculpture (Marquette 1/3 scale) on loan to Whitney Museum of Art, New York City

SOCIETY OF ENVIRONMENTAL GRAPHICS DESIGNERS
For further information, see National and Regional Organizations

M **SPERTUS MUSEUM OF JUDAICA,** 618 S Michigan Ave, 60605. Tel 312-922-9012, Ext 60. *Dir* Arthur M Feldman; *Cur* Grace Cohen Grossman; *Registrar* Mary Larkin; *Educational Coordr* Randi Sherman; *Asst to Dir* Bernadine Gierut
Open Mon - Thurs 10 AM - 5 PM, Fri 10 AM - 3 PM, Sun 10 AM - 4 PM. Admis adults $1, children, students and senior citizens, 50¢, Fri free. Estab 1967 for interpreting and preserving the 3500-year-old heritage embodied in Jewish history. Museum houses a distinguished collection of Judaica from many parts of the world, containing exquisitely designed ceremonial objects of gold, silver, bronze and ivory. Average Annual Attendance: 20,000
Income: Contributions and subsidy from Spertus College
Collections: A pertinent collection of sculpture, paintings and graphic art; ethographic materials spanning centuries of Jewish experience; a permanent holocaust memorial; Judaica, paintings, ceremonial silver, textiles, archaeology
Publications: Catalog of Collection; special publications with exhibits; yearly Calendar of Events
Activities: Educ dept; docent training; exten dept serving the faculty; original objects of art lent to the faculty for study purposes; lending collection, 1500 slides and archaeological replicas; traveling exhibitions organized and circulated; museum store selling books, original art reproductions, slides and jewelry from Israel
L **Helen Asher and Norman Asher Library of Spartus College,** 618 S Michigan Ave, 60605. *Librn & Dir* Richard Marcus
Reference library open to students and members
Library Holdings: Vols 70,000; art 5000; Per subs 560
Special Subjects: Judaica
Collections: Badona Spertus Library of Art and Judaica

M **SWEDISH AMERICAN MUSEUM ASSOCIATION OF CHICAGO,** 5248 N Clark St, 60640. Tel 312-728-8111. *Pres* Sven Flodstrom; *First VPres & Mgr* Kurt Mathiasson; *Second VPres, Archivist & Board of Dir* Selma Jacobson; *Secy & Treas* Edith Johnson
Open Mon - Fri 11 AM - 2 PM, Sat 11 AM - 3 PM, cl Sun except by appointment. No admis fee, donations appreciated. Estab 1976 to display Swedish arts, crafts, artists, scientists, and artifacts connected with United States, especially Chicago. Material displayed in a store front in Andersonville, once a predominantly Swedish area in Chicago. Average Annual Attendance: 10,000. Mem: 210; dues $5 - $500; annual meetings April, June and Oct
Income: $10,000 (financed by membership)
Collections: Artifacts used or made by Swedes, photographs, oils of or by Swedes in United States
Publications: Bulletins, bi-monthly
Activities: Educ dept for Swedish language and culture study; classes for adults and children; dramatic programs; lect open to public, visiting lectr; concerts; tours; sales shop sells books

M **UKRAINIAN NATIONAL MUSEUM & LIBRARY,** 2453 W Chicago Ave, 60622. Tel 312-276-6565. *Pres* Emil Basiuk; *Cur* Jerry Miakush
Open Mon - Fri 10 AM - 2 PM, Sun 12 - 3 PM. Estab 1954, to collect and preserve Ukrainian documents, books, etc. Gallery is maintained
Income: Approx $30,000 (financed through membership and donations)
Library Holdings: Vols 15,000; Per subs 100; Micro—Cards; AV—Kodachromes, slides; Other—Clipping files, framed reproductions, manuscripts, memorabilia, original art works, pamphlets, photographs, sculpture
Special Subjects: Large collection of Ukrainian Folk Arts: easter egg painting, embroidery, woodcarving
Activities: Book traveling exhibitions; traveling exhibitions organized and circulated

UNIVERSITY OF CHICAGO
M **Bergman Gallery,** Renaissance Society, 5811 S Ellis, 60637. Tel 312-753-2886. *Asst Dir* Richard Born; *Dir* Susanne Ghez
Open daily 11 AM - 4 PM, during academic year, cl during summer. Founded 1915 to advance the understanding and appreciation of the arts in all forms. Gallery houses the Renaissance Society
Exhibitions: Changing, about 6 per year; annual art for young collectors; sales exhibitions
Activities: Lect; gallery talks
M **Lorado Taft Midway Studios,** 6016 Ingleside Ave, 60637. Tel 312-753-4821. *Dir* Thomas Mapp
Open Mon - Fri 9 AM - 5 PM, cl Sun. Studios of Lorado Taft and Associates, a Registered National Historic Landmark; now University of Chicago, Department of Art

Exhibitions: Maquettes and Portraits by Lorado Taft; student work in ceramics, graphics, painting and sculpture held in the Court Gallery
Activities: Special performances
M **David and Alfred Smart Gallery,** 5550 S Greenwood Ave, 60637. Tel 312-753-2121. *Dir* Prof Edward A Maser; *Admin Secy* Jean Hall; *Acting Cur* Richard Born; *Dir of Public Relations* Fran Fanta; *Preparator* Rudy Bernal; *Registrar* Rolf Achilles
Open Tues - Sat 10 AM - 4 PM, Sun Noon - 4 PM, cl Mon. No admis fee. Estab 1974 to assist the teaching program of the Art Department of the University by maintaining a permanent collection and presenting exhibitions of scholarly and general interest. Gallery designed by E L Barnes; exhibit space covers 7000 sq ft and also contains conservation room, print and drawing study room, sculpture garden, storage and preparator's workroom. Average Annual Attendance: 18,000.
Mem: 325; dues individual $15; annual meeting in Spring
Income: Financed by membership, university and special funds
Collections: †American, †Ancient, †Baroque, †Medieval, Modern European, †Oriental and †Renaissance paintings, sculpture and decorative arts
Exhibitions: 1800-1850 Abstract Expressionism Vienna Moderne; Decorative Designs, Jackson Tollock and Frank Lloyd Wright; Development of a Sign Language; 1898-1918 Master Prints from Landfall Press; Joan Miro; New Found Works Art of Russia
M **Oriental Institute,** 1155 E 58th St, 60637. *Dir* John A Brinkman; *Cur* John Carswell; *Assoc Cur* Barbara Hall
Open Tues - Sat 10 AM - 4 PM, Sun Noon - 4 PM, cl Mon. No admis fee. Estab 1919 as a Museum of Antiquities excavated from Egypt, Mesopotamia, Assyria, Syria, Palestine, Persia, Anatolia and Numbia, dating from 7000 years ago until the 10th Century AD. Average Annual Attendance: 83,804. Mem: 2000; dues $15
Income: $174,000 (financed by membership and university)
Collections: Ancient Near Eastern antiquities from pre-historic times to the beginning of the present era plus some Islamic artifacts; Egypt: colossal statue of King Tut, mummies, Assyrian bullman (40 tons); Mesopotamian temple interior, house interior, jewelry; Persian bull; column and capital from Persepolis; Megiddo ivories and horned alter
Exhibitions: Archaeology of Carthage; The Art of Tutankhamen; Coptic Art; Mesopotamia; A Photographer's World
Publications: Annual report; News and Notes, monthly
Activities: Classes for adults; lect open to public, 8 visiting lectr per year; gallery talks; tours; original objects of art lent to museums and institutions; museum shop sells books, reproductions, prints, slides and near Eastern jewelry
L **Research Archives,** 60637. *Librn* Alice Figundio
Open to staff, students and members for reference
Library Holdings: Vols 9989; Per subs 74; Other—Pamphlets 5715
Special Subjects: The ancient Near East
L **Art Library,** 1100 E 57th St, 60637. Tel 312-753-3439. *Asst Art Library* Scott O Stapleton
Open Mon - Thurs 8:30 AM - 9 PM, Fri & Sat 9 AM - 5 PM, Sun 1 - 5 PM, hours vary in summer quarter. Art Library now merged with Regenstein Library
Library Holdings: Vols 55,000; Other—Pamphlets, Auction sales catalogs, Union Catalog of Art Books in Chicago
L **Art Slide Collection,** 60637. Tel 312-753-3896. *Cur* Olivera Mihailovic
Open Mon - Fri 8:30 AM - 4 PM; cl Sat & Sun. Estab 1938. For reference only
Library Holdings: AV—Slides 125,000
L **Max Epstein Archive,** 60637. Tel 312-753-2887.
Open Mon - Fri 9 AM - 5 PM; cl Sat & Sun. Estab 1938. For reference only
Library Holdings: Other—400,000 mounted photographs of art; 8000 catalogued and mounted photographs added annually

CLINTON

O **FINE ARTS CENTER OF CLINTON,** 119 W Macon St, 61727. Tel 217-935-5055. *Pres* Mrs William B Smith; *Dir* Vera MacGillivray; *Secy* Margaret Peltz; *Treas* John Warner III
Open Sept - Aug 1, Mon - Fri 10 AM - Noon, 1 - 5 PM, cl Holidays. Estab 1960 in memory of John Smoot DeQuoin whose conviction it was that almost everyone is born with a latent talent and that developing that talent could be most rewarding. Average Annual Attendance: 1550
Income: Financed by tuition fees and supported by J Warner, III
Collections: Contemporary art, Aaron Bohrod, Emil Gruppe, et al
Exhibitions: Batik; ceramics; needlework; oils; sculpture; watercolors; weaving
Publications: Bulletin of Center activities, annually
Activities: Classes for adults and children; dance, painting and writing workshops; school programs; concerts; scholarships offered

DANVILLE

M **VERMILION COUNTY MUSEUM SOCIETY,** 116 N Gilbert St, 61832. Tel 217-442-2922. *Dir* Ann Bauer
Open Tues - Sat 10 AM - 5 PM, Sun and Holidays 1 - 5 PM, cl Mon, Thanksgiving, Christmas. Admis 15 years over $1, 6 - 14 50¢, under 6 years, no admis fee, school and scout groups no admis fee. Estab 1964 in 1855 doctor's residence and carriage house. Mem: Dues Life $150, patron $50, contributing $25, organization $10, family $10, individual $4, student $4
Collections: Costumes; decorative arts; graphics; historical material; paintings; sculpture
Exhibitions: Temporary exhibitions
Publications: Heritage, quarterly magazine
Activities: Lect; guided tours; arts festivals; book traveling exhibitions; gift shop
L **Library,** 116 N Gilbert St, 61832.
Open to the public and for inter-library loan
Library Holdings: Vols 300

DECATUR

M **MILLIKIN UNIVERSITY,** Kirkland Gallery, Kirkland Fine Arts Center, 1184 W Main St, 62522. Tel 217-424-6227. *Dir* Marvin L Klaven; *Asst Dir Kirkland Gallery & Art Prof* Ted Wolter
Open Mon - Fri Noon - 5 PM, Sat Noon - 4 PM. No admis fee. Estab 1970. Gallery has 3200 sq ft and 224 running ft of wall space
Income: Financed by university appropriation
Collections: Drawings; painting; prints; sculpture; watercolors
Exhibitions: African Artists; American Drawings I and II; American Graphics of 20's and 30's; Frank Berkenkotter; Children's Tapestries from Egypt; Collographs; Continued Prints from Canada; Fritz Eichenberg Prints; Japanese Posters; Peter Milton Prints; student exhibit
Publications: Annual bulletin; Center Activities
Activities: Classes for adults and children; guided tours; lect; gallery talks; junior museum

DE KALB

M **NORTHERN ILLINOIS UNIVERSITY,** Swen Parson Gallery and Gallery 200, Art Department, 60115. *Dir* Sam Yates; *Chmn Dept* Robert L Even
Open Mon - Fri 9 AM - 4 PM; Tues & Wed 7 - 9 PM; Sun 1 - 4 PM. No admis charge. Estab 1898. Two large galleries for general exhibitions; one small gallery for graduate student shows
Income: Financed by state appropriation
Collections: Harold Gross Collection (Indian art); Mel Pfaelzer Collection (prints, surrealist); Nause & Graff Collection (prints, contemporary)
Exhibitions: Changing exhibitions in both galleries
Publications: Show catalogs, four per year
Activities: Lect open to the public; gallery talks; workshops; tours; competitions; exten dept serving Northern Illinois; individual paintings and original art works lent within the University

EDWARDSVILLE

L **SOUTHERN ILLINOIS UNIVERSITY,** Lovejoy Library, Art Department, 62026. *Humanities & Fine Arts Librn* John Dustin
Open Mon - Thurs 8 AM - 11 PM, Fri 8 AM - 5 PM, Sat 9 AM - 5 PM, Sun 2 - 9 PM. Estab 1957, as a source for general University undergraduate and graduate instruction, and faculty research
Purchases: $8200
Library Holdings: Vols 16,700; Per subs 49

ELGIN

M **ELGIN ACADEMY,** Laura Davidson Sears Fine Arts Gallery,* 350 Park St, 60120. Tel 312-695-0300 (Academy). *Headmaster* Robert Haggemann; *Fine Arts Chmn* D Scott Irving
Academy founded 1839, chartered 1856, for the purpose of educational art and theater. Open during drama presentations; one room gallery is dedicated primarily to 20th century local artists
Collections: Decorative articles; furniture; sculpture; Gilbert Stuart's George Washington; Victorian silverplated items
Publications: Museum publication, semi-annual
Activities: Classes; dramatic programs; lect open to public, 6 visiting lectrs per year; tours; traveling exhibitions organized and circulated; museum shop selling books, magazines, slides, minerals, fossils and carvings
L **Library,*** 350 Park St, 60120.
Open for research
Library Holdings: Vols 750; Per subs 3; Other—Prints, photographs

ELMHURST

M **LIZZADRO MUSEUM OF LAPIDARY ART,** 220 Cottage Hill Ave, 60126. Tel 312-833-1616. *Dir* John S Lizzadro; *Exec Secy* Judith Greene
Open Tues - Fri & Sun 1 - 5 PM, Sat 10 AM - 5 PM, cl Mon. Admis adults 50¢, ages 13-18 25¢, under 13 free, no charge on Fri. Estab 1962 to promote interest in the lapidary arts and the study and collecting of minerals and fossils. Main exhibit area contains hardstone carvings, gemstone materials, minerals; lower level contains education exhibits. Average Annual Attendance: 45,000. Mem: 600; dues $20 per year
Income: Financed by endowment
Collections: Hardstone Carving Collection
Exhibitions: Educational exhibits

ELSAH

M **PRINCIPIA COLLEGE,** School of Nations Museum, 62028. Tel 618-466-2131. *Cur* Bonnie Gibbs
Open Tues & Fri 10 AM - 4 PM
Collections: American Indian collection including baskets, bead work, blankets, leather, pottery, quill work and silver; Asian Art collection includes arts and crafts, ceramics, textiles from China, Japan and Southeast Asia; European collections include glass, metals, patch, snuff boxes, textiles and wood; costumes and dolls from around the world
Exhibitions: Changing exhibits on campus locations; permanent exhibits in School of Nations lower floor
Activities: Special programs offered throughout the year; objects available for individual study

EVANSTON

O **EVANSTON ART CENTER,** 2603 Sheridan Rd, 60201. Tel 312-475-5300. *Pres* Virginia Samter; *Dir* Edward J Bania
Open Mon - Sat 10 AM - 4 PM, Mon - Thurs 7 - 10 PM, Sun 2 - 5 PM. No admis fee. Estab 1929 as a community visual arts center with exhibits, instruction, and programs. Includes Wieghardt Memorial Gallery, West Gallery for prints and drawings and Photography Gallery. Average Annual Attendance: 15,000. Mem: 2000; dues $20; annual meeting in April
Income: Financed by membership
Exhibitions: Berenice Abbott, The Red River Series (photography); Manuel Alvarez Bravo (photography; The Chicago Photographer; Chicago Prints; Collage I, Invitational, Gretchen Garner (photography); FigureWorks, Fred Berger, Paula Gerard, and Anita Johnson; The Grid; Anne Grill, Liturgical Art; Jerry Gordon (photography); The Homecoming-50th Anniversary Exhibition; David Plowden (photography); Recent paintings by Amy Shen-Kohler, 50th Anniversary Members Exhibition; Paul Wieghardt, Large Works; Works on Paper, Annette Turow
Publications: Concentrics, monthly
Activities: Classes for adults and children; lect, 6 vis lectr per year; sales shop

MIDWEST ART HISTORY SOCIETY
For further information, see National and Regional Organizations

NORTHWESTERN UNIVERSITY
M **Mary & Leigh Block Gallery,** 60201. Tel 312-492-5209. *Dir* Kathy Kelsey Foley
Open Tues - Sat 10:30 AM - 4:30 PM, Sun 12 - 5 PM. No admis fee. Estab 1980, to serve the university
Exhibitions: Temporary, traveling and loan exhibitions to begin in Spring 1980
Activities: Classes for adults and children; docent training; lect open to public; concerts; gallery talks; tours; book traveling exhibitions; originate traveling exhibitions circulated through other university galleries and museums; sales shop will sell catalogs and posters
L **Library,** Art Collection, 60201. Tel 312-492-7484. *Cur Special Coll* R Russell Maylone; *Art Coll Supv* John Hutton
Open Mon - Thurs 8:30 AM - 10 PM, Fri & Sat 8:30 AM - 5 PM, Sun 1 - 10 PM (Use during other hours limited to staff, faculty, and students. Hours vary during summer). No admis fee. Estab 1970 as a separate collection. It serves curriculum and research needs of the Art and Art History departments
Income: Financed through the University
Library Holdings: Vols 44,000
Special Subjects:

C **WASHINGTON NATIONAL INSURANCE COMPANY,** 1630 Chicago Ave, 60201. Tel 312-866-3084. *Dir Public Relations* Ferrell E White
Estab early 1930's to portray the more human aspects of the life of George Washington. Collection displayed in executive corridor area
Collections: Series of 20 paintings by the American artist Walter Haskell Hinton
Activities: Lect; tours, once per year for invited school classes; competitions; Community Action Awards

FREEPORT

M **HIGHLAND AREA ARTS COUNCIL,** Freeport Art Museum, 511 S Liberty, 61032. Tel 815-235-9755. *Cur and Dir* Linda Prestwich
Open Wed - Sun 10 AM - 5 PM. No admis fee. Estab 1975 to house W T Rawleigh Art Collection and to promote the arts in the region. Nine galleries, 30 x 24 ft with 12-ft ceilings, auditorium, two classrooms and a lounge. Average Annual Attendance: 10,000. Mem: 400; dues $20; annual meeting Jan
Income: $100,000 (financed by endowment, membership, city and state appropriations, and other grants)
Purchases: $3000
Collections: American Indian Pottery, Basketry and Beadwork; Art from Madagascar; Art Nouveau Pottery; European 19th Century Oil Paintings; †Oil Paintings; †prints; sculpture; textiles
Exhibitions: Aaron Bohrod retrospective; Best of the W T Rawleigh Collection; Faraway Places (W T Rawleigh); Oriental Art from the Collection; Phealzer Collection from Northern Illinois University; Professional Artists of Northwest Illinois; numerous one-person shows
Publications: Newsletter, monthly
Activities: Classes for adults and children; dramatic programs; docent training; film festival; lect open to public, 6 vis lectr per year; concerts; gallery talks; tours; competitions; exten dept serving Ogle, Carroll, Jo Daviess Counties; individual paintings and original objects of art lent to bona fide galleries with full insruance; lending collection conatins original art works, paintings, sculpture; traveling exhibitions organized and circulated
L **Library,** 511 S LIberty, 61032.
Open to members for research and reference
Library Holdings: Vols 200; Per subs 10; Other—US Government materials

GALESBURG

O **GALESBURG CIVIC ART CENTER,** 114 E Main, 61401. Tel 309-342-7415. *Pres* LaVonne Bourdeau; *VPres* Richard Lindstrom; *Treas* Rose Sampson; *Secy* Dorothy Kennedy; *Dir* Sue Anne Fones
Open Tues - Fri 10:30 AM - 4:30 PM, Sat 10:30 AM - 3 PM. No admis fee. Estab 1965 as a non-profit organization for the furtherance of art. The main gallery has about 80 running feet of wall space for the hanging of exhibits. The sales-rental gallery runs on a commission basis and is open to professional artists as a place to sell their work under a consignment agreement. Average Annual Attendance: 2500. Mem: 300; dues begin at $6
Income: Financed by membership and grants
Collections: Some paintings and sculpture
Exhibitions: Annual Competitions: Galex, High School Invitational, Members & Friends; Isabelle Pera, Sculpture, Spaces-Places; Recent Etchings by Pam Carson and Robert McCauley; Ellen Sovony, Paintings; Gunther Wittenberg
Publications: The Artifacts, newsletter
Activities: Classes for adults and children; lect open to public, 4 vis lectr per year; gallery talks; tours; competitions; individual paintings and original objects of art lent to schools, library, activity centers; lending collection contains original art works; museum shop selling magazines and original art

GREENVILLE

M **GREENVILLE COLLEGE,** Richard W Bock Sculpture Collection, 62246. Tel 618-664-1840, Ext 321. *Dir & Cur* Donald P Hallmark
Open Mon, Wed, Fri 1:30 - 4:30 PM, Sun 2 - 4 PM, cl August & holidays. Admis adults 50¢, students & senior citizens 25¢. Estab 1975 to display an extensive collection of the life work of the American sculptor in a restored home of the mid-19th Century period. Five large rooms and two hallways have approximately 320 running ft of exhibition space. Average Annual Attendance: 5000
Income: $8000 (financed by future endowment, college appropriation, gifts and donations)
Collections: Furniture and furnishings of the 1850-1875 era; Japanese prints; late 19th and early 20th century drawing, painting and sculpture; late 19th and early 20th century posters; Frank Lloyd Wright artifacts, designs and drawings
Publications: General museum brochures
Activities: Lect open to the public, 1-2 vis lectr per year; gallery talks; individual paintings and original objects of art lent to museums only; lending collection contains original art works, paintings, photographs, sculpture and drawings; traveling exhibitions organized and circulated; museum shop selling books, magazines

L **Research Library,** 62246. *Librn* Donald P Hallmark
For reference only
Library Holdings: Vols 1000
Special Subjects: Richard W Bock, The Prairie School of Architecture, Frank Lloyd Wright

JACKSONVILLE

M **ART ASSOCIATION OF JACKSONVILLE,** David Strawn Art Gallery, 331 W College, 62650. Tel 217-245-4950. *Dir* Barbara B Crouse; *Asst Dir* Michael G Crouse; *Pres* Loren Becker
Open (Sept - May) Tues - Sun 2 - 5 PM; Fri 7 - 9 PM; cl Mon. No admis fee. Estab 1873, endowed 1915, to serve the community by offering monthly shows of visual arts and weekly classes in a variety of media. The two main rooms house the monthly exhibitions and a third large room houses a collection of Pre-Columbian pottery. The Gallery is in a large building, previously a private home. Average Annual Attendance: 1200. Mem: 285; dues $3 and up; annual meeting June
Income: Financed by endowment and membership
Collections: Pre-Columbian Pottery; pottery discovered in the Mississippi Valley
Exhibitions: Barbara & Michael Crouse Director's Show: Fibers-Constructions; Batiks by Kristine Lindahl Northcutt; Carole Henry, Enamels; Ceramics by Bob Dixon; David Robinson, Paper, Paintings; Fred Jones, Prints; John Hawkins: Woodcuts; Katie Sjursen, Paintings; Kelley Hersey, Photographs; Larry Calhoun, Ceramics; Paintings & Drawings by Noreen Ten Eyck; Paintings by Susan Sensemann; Recent Works by Peter & Ann Cohan; Sculpture by Four Midwestern Artists; Watercolors by Jack Madura
Activities: Classes for adults and children; lect open to public, 2 vis lectr per year; concerts

JOLIET

M **JOLIET JUNIOR COLLEGE,** Laura A Sprague Art Gallery, 1216 Houbolt Ave, 60436. Tel 815-729-9020, Ext 423. *Gallery Dir* Joe Milosevich
Open Mon - Fri 9 AM - 2 PM, Wed 5:30 PM - 7:30 PM. Estab 1978, to provide the college and community with a wide variety of artistic experiences. Gallery, approx 20 x 25 ft, has burlap covered panels mounted on the walls, and also has track lighting
Income: Financed by state appropriations
Exhibitions: Faculty, group, student, one-person, two-person exhibitions

LAKE FOREST

L **LAKE FOREST LIBRARY,** 360 E Deerpath, 60045. Tel 312-234-0636. *Librn* Sydney S Mellinger; *Reference Librn* Nancy G Wallens; *Circulation Head* Judy Gummere
Open Mon - Fri 9 AM - 9 PM, Sat 9 AM - 5 PM. Estab 1898 to make accessible to the residents of the city, books and other resources and services for education, information and recreation. Circ 175,000. Gallery carries sculptures and minimasters (framed art prints)
Income: $350,000 (financed by city and state appropriations)
Purchases: $41,500
Library Holdings: Vols 83,000; Per subs 215; AV—Rec; Other—Clipping files, framed reproductions, pamphlets, reproductions, sculpture
Collections: Folk art; painting

LONG GROVE

C **KEMPER GROUP,** Kemper Dr, 60049. Tel 312-540-2502. *Art Cur* Joan E Robertson
Open to public in groups of 5 - 25, by three weeks prior appointment. No admis fee. Estab 1973 to provide a better working environment for employees and to support Chicago and Midwest artists. Collection displayed in halls and offices of headquarters
Purchases: $20,000 - $57,000
Collections: Approximately 70% Chicago and Midwest artists, contemporary, with many young up-and-coming artists
Exhibitions: One-person shows in private exhibition area
Activities: Lect; gallery talks; purchase awards at Chicago area shows and art fairs; individual objects of art lent to artists of works for retrospectives and shows, or works to institutions

MACOMB

M **WESTERN ILLINOIS UNIVERSITY,** Browne Hall Gallery, 61455. Tel 309-298-1355. *Pres* Leslie Malpass; *VPres* Bruce Carpenter; *Secy* Roseanne Ledbetter; *Acting Chmn Art Dept* Daniel Kuruna
Open weekdays 8:30 AM - 4:30 PM. No admis fee. Estab 1945 to present art as an aesthetic and teaching aid. Gallery in one room with 200 running ft. Average Annual Attendance: 2000
Income: Financed through state appropriation
Activities: Classes for adults; lect open to the public, 8 visiting lectrs per year; concerts; gallery talks; tours; competitions with awards; individual paintings lent; lending collection contains 30 paintings; traveling exhibitions organized and circulated

MOLINE

C **DEERE & COMPANY,** John Deere Rd, 61265.
Guided tours Mon - Fri 10:30 AM - 1:30 PM. No admis fee. Estab 1964 to complement the offices designed by Eero Saarinen and Kevin Roche; to provide opportunities for employees and visitors to view and enjoy a wide variety of art pieces from many parts of the world. Collection displayed at Deere & Company Administrative Center
Collections: Artifacts, paintings, prints, sculpture and tapestries from over 25 countries

MOUNT VERNON

M **MITCHELL MUSEUM,** Richview Rd, Box 923, 62864. Tel 618-242-1236. *Pres* Jerome Glassman; *Secy* Ruby Miller; *Exec VPres* Kenneth R Miller
Open Tues - Sun 1 - 5 PM, cl Mon. No admis fee. Estab 1973 to present exhibitions of paintings, sculpture, graphic arts, architecture and design representing contemporary art trends; to provide continued learning and expanded education. Museum has three galleries: Main Gallery, Hall Gallery and Lecture Gallery. Average Annual Attendance: 50,000. Mem: 725; dues $25; annual meeting in Nov
Income: Financed by endowment and membership
Collections: Paintings by late 19th and early 20th century American artists; some drawings and small sculptures; silver, small stone, wood and ivory carvings; vases; jade; cut glass; small bronzes
Exhibitions: Changing exhibits
Publications: Calendar of Events, quarterly; newsletter, quarterly
Activities: Classes for adults and children; dramatic programs; docent training; lect open to public, 10 vis lectr per year; concerts; gallery talks; tours; competitions; individual paintings and original objects of art lent to museums and universities; sales shop selling books, magazines, reproductions, prints and slides

L **Library,** Richview Rd, Box 923, 62864. *Dir* K R Miller
Open to public for reference only
Library Holdings: Vols 1100; Per subs 12; Other—Photographs

NILES

M THE BRADFORD MUSEUM, 9333 Milwaukee Ave, 60648. Tel 312-966-2770; Telex 72-4407. *Museum Dir* Diana Gordon; *Museum Cur* Lisa Hill; *Public Relations Coordr* Eloise Bartlebaugh
Open Mon - Fri 9 AM - 4 PM, Sat & Sun 10 AM - 5 PM. Admis adult $2, sr citizens $1, children under 12 accompanied by adult free. Estab 1977 to house and display limited-edition collector's plates for purposes of study, education and enjoyment. Average Annual Attendance: 10,000
Income: Financed by The Bradford Exchange
Purchases: $2500
Collections: Traded Limited-Edition Collector's Plates, including Bing and Grondahl, Haviland, Lalique, Lenox, Rosenthal, Royal Copenhagen, Royal Doulton, and many more; †plates produced by more than 60 makers from 12 different countries, each plate series is updated yearly
Exhibitions: (1979) The Originals (major exhibit of original art used to create collector's plates); (1980) Christmas Traditions Around the World (exhibit showing Christmas internationally as depicted on collector's plates)
Publications: The Bradford Book of Collector's Plates, annually
Activities: Docent training; lect open to public; tours; original objects of art lent for temporary exhibition purposes for banks, conventions and museums; lending collection contains motion pictures and limited-edition collector's plates; book traveling exhibitions; originate traveling exhibitions

NORMAL

ILLINOIS STATE UNIVERSITY
M University Museums, 61761. Tel 309-829-6331. *Dir* Roslyn A Walker-Oni; *Secy & Registrar* Arlene A Boggs; *Exhibits Designer* David L Kuntz; *Cur International Coll of Child Art* Dr Barry E Moore; *Curatorial Asst* Jeani Shepherd; *Curatorial Asst* Virgina M Wright; *Cur Graphic Reproduction Coll* William V White
Ewing Museum of Nations, open year round, Tues, Thurs, Sat, Sun 1 - 5 PM; Eyestone School Museum, Fall and Spring, Sun only 1 - 5 PM, Summer, Tues, Thurs, Sun 1 - 5 PM; Funk Gem and Mineral Museum, year round, Tues, Thurs, Sun 1 - 5 PM; Hudelson Museum of Agriculture, Fall and Spring, Sun only 1 - 5 PM, Summer, Tues, Thurs, Sun 1 - 5 PM; Stevenson Memorial Room, Fall and Spring, Mon - Fri 10 AM - 5 PM, Summer, Tues, Thurs, Sun 1 - 5 PM; University Historical Museum, year round, Mon - Fri 10 AM - 5 PM, Sat, Sun 1 - 5 PM. Estab 1872, re-estab 1945 to collect, preserve and interpret museum objects directly related to academic programs of the university and the public schools; to support research related to exhibit collections; and to maintain general interest collections. The six museums house temporary and permanent exhibits on loan and from the permanent collection. Average Annual Attendance: 28,000
Income: Financed by state appropriation
Collections: †African art; decorative arts; International Collection of Child Art; †international dolls; native American Art; †Pre-Columbian Art of Middle America; Southeast Asian Artifacts
Exhibitions: Animal Representations in Primitive Art; Art of the First Australians; Art and Community a Senufo Example; Art of Mexico Before Columbus; Children Draw Animals; Ravca Dolls; temporary and permanent exhibits from permanent collections; A Turn of the Century Printing Shop
Publications: Annual Report; exhibit brochures and catalogs
Activities: Lect open to the public; gallery talks; tours; original objects of art lent to local and county schools and local exhibits; lending collection contains cassettes, original art works, sculpture and slides; traveling exhibitions organized and circulated
L Museum Library, 61761. *Librn* Arlene A Boggs
Museum library open to scholars, students and staff
Library Holdings: Vols 201; Per subs 22
Special Subjects: Decorative Arts, American Indian Art, Pre-Columbian Art, African Art and History
M Center for the Visual Arts Gallery, Beaufort St, 61761. Tel 309-436-5487. *Dir* Tom R Toperzer; *Asst Dir* Barry D Weer; *Registrar* Janet L Bertagnolli
Open Tues 9 AM - 10 PM, Wed - Fri 9 AM - 4:30 PM, Sat & Sun 1 - 4:45 PM. No admis fee. Estab 1973 to provide changing exhibits of the visual arts for the students and community at large; also display student art work. The main Gallery I contains rotating exhibitions; Galleries II and III display student work, graduate exhibitions, studio area shows and works from the permanent collection. Average Annual Attendance: 50,000
Income: $100,000
Collections: †20th century American art emphasis
Exhibitions: (1980) Gallery I, Eighth Biennial National Invitational Crafts Exhibition; William T Wiley Prints; Illinois State University Student Annual Exhibition; Selections from the Permanent Collection; First Western States Biennial; Jasper Johns Screenprints; Gallery II and III Graduate Comprehensive Thesis Exhibitions; First Western States Biennial
Activities: Individual paintings and original objects of art lent for other exhibitions; lending collection contains original art works, original prints, paintings, photographs and sculpture; originate traveling exhibitions organized and circulated

PEORIA

M BRADLEY UNIVERSITY GALLERY, Division of Art, 61625. Tel 309-676-7611. Open Wed - Sun 1 - 4 PM. Exhibition space 45 x 25 ft; new gallery: Hartmann Center. Average Annual Attendance: 2000
Income: Financed by University
Exhibitions: Bradley National Print & Drawing Exhibition; ellen Lanyon; Peoria Collects
Activities: Classes for adults; lect open to the public, 10 vis lectr per year; gallery talks; tours; competitions

M LAKEVIEW MUSEUM OF ARTS AND SCIENCES,* (Formerly Lakeview Center for the Arts and Sciences) 1125 W Lake Ave, 61614. Tel 309-686-7000. *Exec Dir* John D Peterson; *Cur Coll* Virginia Najmi
Open Tues - Sat 9 AM - 5 PM, Sun 1 - 6 PM, Wed 7 - 9 PM, cl Mon. Estab 1960, new building opened 1965, to provide enjoyment and education by reflecting the historical, cultural and industrial life of the Central Illinois area. Average Annual Attendance: 150,000. Mem: Dues individual $15, student $10
Income: $220,000
Collections: Archaeological; paintings and graphics
Exhibitions: Monthly exhibitions dealing with the arts and sciences
Publications: Bulletin, bimonthly
Activities: Art classes; demonstrations; lect; concerts

O PEORIA ART GUILD, 1831 N Knoxville, 61603. Tel 309-685-7522. *Pres* B A Drake; *VPres* Charles Schoenheider; *Personnel Coordr* Janet M Jensen; *Sales & Rental Chmn* R Howard Courtney
Open Tues - Sat 10 AM - 4 PM, Sun 1 - 4 PM, cl Mon. No admis fee. Estab 1878 to encourage development of the arts. Average Annual Attendance: 5000. Mem: 500; dues $10 - $15
Income: Financed by membership and Illinois Arts Council
Collections: Framed and unframed two-dimensional work, ceramics, sculpture, jewelry, weaving and wood designs; Winning works from the Bradley Print and Drawing Exhibition
Exhibitions: One-person shows; group theme shows
Activities: Classes for adults and children; workshops; lect open to public; gallery talks; competitions with cash and purchase awards; scholarships offered; individual paintings and original objects of art lent to members of the community; lending collection contains original art works

QUINCY

M HISTORICAL SOCIETY OF QUINCY AND ADAMS COUNTY, 425 S 12th St, 62301. Tel 217-222-1835. *Pres* Charles Barnum; *VPres* Mrs William Sexauer; *Secy* Nona Crawley
Estab 1896, to preserve and collect items of local history and to maintain the home of Governor John Wood, Governor of Illinois 1859. Gallery contains oil paintings and prints of local personages from early 1800's. Mem: Approx 200; dues commercial $100, family $29, single $10, senior citizen $5; annual meeting in Spring
Income: $8500 (financed through membership)
Collections: Artifacts of local history; manuscripts; portraits (mostly oils) of pioneers
Activities: Lect open to the public, 1-3 visiting lectrs per year
L Library, 425 S 12th St, 62301.
For reference only
Library Holdings: Vols 500; Per subs 3; Micro—Fiche

O QUINCY ART CENTER, 1515 Jersey St, 62301. Tel 217-223-5900. *Pres* Magdalene Kuna
Open 1 - 4 PM, Tues - Fri, 2 - 5 PM Sat and Sun, cl on Mon and holidays, cl Jan, Feb, July, August. Estab 1923, incorporated 1951 to foster public awareness and understanding of the visual arts. Average Annual Attendance: 6000. Mem: 400; dues life membership $250, sustaining $100, annual patron $25, family $12, individual $8, student $2; annual meeting in July
Collections: Crafts, graphics, †painting and sculpture by contemporary American and European artists
Exhibitions: Annual Quincy Art Show held in April and open to artists living within a 200 mile radius of Quincy; annual Students Art Show in May and the Art Club's Artist Guild Show in June
Publications: Calendar, brochures and or catalogs for temporary exhibitions; Quarterly Bulletin
Activities: Classes for adults and children; lect; films; gallery talks; concerts; tours; inter-museum loan; traveling exhibitions organized and circulated
L Library, 1515 Jersey St, 62301.
Library Holdings: Vols 350

M QUINCY COLLEGE, Art Gallery, 1831 College Ave, 62301. Tel 217-222-8020. *Gallery Dir* Robert Lee Mejer
Open 8 AM - 10 PM. No admis fee. Estab 1968 as a cultural enrichment and artistic exposure for the community. Exhibitions are held in the library foyer and the foundation room. Average Annual Attendance: 5000
Income: Financed through the College
Collections: 19th century Oriental and European prints; permanent collection of student and faculty works; 20th century American prints and drawings
Exhibitions: (1978) Art of the Comic Book; Connor, Raymond, Redmond, Toth (photographs); German War Art (paintings); Richard Haas (prints and drawings); Winifred Lutz (paperworks); Jack Madura (watercolors); Robert Nelson (drawings, prints and paintings); Dan Socha (drawings). (1979) Irvin Amen (woodcuts); Chuck Evans (ceramic sculptures); Ed and Charlotte Rollman-Shay (watercolors and workshop); Survey of Intaglio Printmaking: Will Barnet, Michael Mazur, Richard Haas, Krishna Reddy, etc; Studio Faculty Show, University of Nebraska, Omaha; Young American Printmakers (prints). (1980) John Grazier and Kevin MacDonald (drawings); Clare Romano (recent collagraphs); Take A Good Look (contemporary works by Pennsylvania, Ohio and New York artists); Annual Alumni, Faculty, Senior, and Student Exhibits
Publications: Brochures, 3-5 times annually; gallery calendars, annually
Activities: Classes for adults; lect open to public, 2 - 3 visiting lectrs per year; scholarships; individual paintings and original objects of art lent; lending collection contains 20,000 Kodachromes and a photograph collection; originate traveling exhibitions; book shop
L Library, 1831 College Ave, 62301.
Library Holdings: Vols 6800

O QUINCY SOCIETY OF FINE ARTS,* 1624 Main St, 62301. Tel 217-222-3432. *Dir* Sam W Grabarski
Open Mon - Fri 9 AM - 5 PM. Estab 1948 as a community arts council to coordinate and stimulate the visual and performing arts in Quincy and Adams County. Mem: 12 art organizations
Income: Financed by endowment, membership and contribution
Publications: Cultural Calendars, quarterly; pamphlets and catalogs
Activities: Workshops for adults and students in visual and performing arts

ROCKFORD

O **ROCKFORD ART ASSOCIATION,** Burpee Art Museum, 737 N Main St, 61103. Tel 815-965-3131. *Pres* Mrs A Pang; *VPres* Mrs C Galloway; *Exec Secy* Mrs Roger Harlan
Open Tues - Fri Noon - 5 PM, Sat & Sun 1 - 5 PM, cl Mon and holidays. No admis fee. Estab 1914 to promote and cultivate an active interest in all fields of fine and applied art, past and present, in the surrounding area. The main building is an Italian style villa which was redecorated and renovated to house six rooms for exhibition space; an auditorium was added later. Average Annual Attendance: 4000. Mem: 400; dues benefactor $1000, individual $20, young adult & senior citizens, $5
Income: Financed by membership and state appropriation
Collections: Permanent collection Early American oil paintings, graphics, sculpture, photography, ceramics, glassware, textiles, watercolors and mixed media
Exhibitions: Annual Rockford and Vicinity Show; Annual Young Artist's Exhibition; numerous one-person and group shows
Publications: Exhibition brochures and catalogs; newsletter, quarterly
Activities: Classes for adults and children; lect open to public, 6 vis lectr per year; gallery talks; tours; competitions with cash awards; scholarships offered; Book traveling exhibitions

L **Katherine Pearman Memorial Library,** 737 N Main St, 61103.
Open to the public and members by appointment. For reference only
Library Holdings: Vols 500; Per subs 15
Special Subjects: The visual arts

ROCK ISLAND

M **AUGUSTANA COLLEGE,** Bergendorf Fine Arts Gallery, 61201. Tel 309-794-7000. *Head Art Dept* A Ben Jasper; *Secy* Carol Peterson
Open Mon - Sat 10 AM - 4 PM. No admis fee. Estab to exhibit contemporary visual arts of local and regional artists. Main gallery serves as an extrance to large auditorium; lower gallery is much smaller than main gallery
Income: $3000
Purchases: $1000
Collections: Contemporary eastern and western prints
Exhibitions: (1979) Charles Barth: Viscosity Prints; Ray George: Lithographs and Drawings; Susan Knopka: Paintings; Jean Serrani: Conceptual Drawings. (1980) Michael Dunbar: Steel Sculpture; Fourth Annual Rock Island Fine Arts Exhibition; Thomas Nawrocki: Color Blend Relief Prints; Jackie Olson: Pastels; Senior Art Majors' Retrospective
Activities: Classes for children; competitions; awards; art works lent to campus offices for display

SPRINGFIELD

L **ILLINOIS STATE LIBRARY,*** Centennial Bldg, 62756. Tel 217-782-2994. *Dir* Kathryn J Gesterfield; *Assoc Dir Library Development* Bridget Lamont; *Asst Dir* Albert Halcli
Open weekdays 8 AM - 4:30 PM, cl Sat & Sun. Estab 1839, Art Service 1916. Reference services are available to patrons of Illinois public libraries on inter-library loan requested through library systems
Library Holdings: Vols 759,004
Collections: Extensive collection of †art books, †magazines, †vertical file prints 54,800 covering painting, sculpture, architecture, theatre, maps and other items; †framed art prints; collection of original lithographs, etchings, and block prints
Exhibitions: Framed art prints continuously displayed within the library

M **ILLINOIS STATE MUSEUM OF NATURAL HISTORY AND ART,** Spring & Edwards St, 62706. Tel 217-782-7125. *Dir* R Bruce McMillan; *Asst Dir* Basil C Hedrick; *Cur Art* Robert J Evans; *Cur Decorative ARts* Susan Pickel; *Cur Asst* Maureen McKenna; *Cur Asst* Larry Rhoads
Open Mon - Sat 8:30 AM - 5 PM; Sun 1:30 - 5 PM. No admis fee. Estab 1877 as museum of natural history, art added in 1928. Collection and display of items related to or of interest to Illinois and its citizens; art program is specialized in Illinois to a great degree. Four changing exhibit galleries of approx 400 running feet of display. Permanent collection galleries of fine and decorative arts, and a gallery for ethnographic arts. Average Annual Attendance: 300,000. Mem: 900; dues $10 - $300
Income: $1,400,000 (financed by state appropriation)
Purchases: $20,000
Collections: Folk and Decorative Art including ceramics, metal work, textiles, glass, clocks and furniture
Exhibitions: Approx 14 exhibitions each year featuring crafts decorative arts, graphics, paintings, photography, sculpture
Publications: Living Museum (also in Braille), bimonthly; exhibit and collection catalogs
Activities: Docent training; lect open to public and members; tours; competitions; exten dept; original objects of art lent to museums and art galleries; traveling exhibitions organized and circulated; museum shop selling books, reproductions and other miscellaneous items

L **Library,** Spring & Edwards St, 62706. Tel 217-782-6623. *Librn* Orvetta Robinson; *Library Asst* Ronald Sauberli
Open Mon - Fri 8:30 AM - 5 PM. Estab to provide informational materials and services to meet the requirements of the Museum Staff in fields pertinent to the purpose and work of the Museum. Circ 100 per month
Income: Financed by state appropriation
Purchases: $2600
Library Holdings: Vols 10,000; Per subs 150; AV—Rec; Other—Clipping files, manuscripts
Special Subjects: Anthropology, art and natural sciences
Collections: Anthropology and Ornithology

O **SPRINGFIELD ART ASSOCIATION OF EDWARDS PLACE,** 700 N Fourth, 62702. Tel 217-523-2631. *Executive dir* William Bealmer
Open daily 2 - 4 PM, cl Mon. No admis fee. Estab 1913 to foster appreciation of art, to instruct people in art and to expose people to quality art. Mem: 3000; dues $20 - $2000; annual meeting May
Income: $90,000 (financed by membership and grants, interests, tuition, and benefits)
Collections: †Contemporary American Indian; African sculpture; early American Paintings; furniture; Mexican; Oriental and Japanese artifacts and textiles; †paintings; †pottery; †prints; †textiles
Exhibitions: Twelve to fifteen exhibitions are scheduled annually with 2 or 3 juried exhibitions; Work is borrowed from museum and artist nationwide
Publications: Newsletters, membership brochures, membership roster, 12 - 15 per year
Activities: Classes for adults and children; docent training; art outreach program in school in community funded through CETA; lectr open to the public; gallery talks; tours; competitions with cash awards of $50 - $100; individual paintings and original objects of art lent to businesses for displays; lending collection contains 300 framed reproductions, original art works, 1500 original prints and paintings, sculpture, pottery, furniture, textiles, craft items; sales shop selling original art

L **Michael Victor II Art Library,** 700 N Fourth, 62702. *CETA Librn* Jenny Charles
Open 9 AM - 4 PM daily, 7 PM - 10 PM Tues, 10 AM - 4 PM Sat, cl Sun. Estab 1965 to provide total community with access to art and art related books
Income: $900
Purchases: $700
Library Holdings: Vols 450; Per subs 12; Micro—Cards; AV—Slides; Other—Clipping files, exhibition catalogs, pamphlets, reproductions
Activities: Film program; lecture series

URBANA

M **UNIVERSITY OF ILLINOIS AT URBANA-CHAMPAIGN,** World Heritage Museum, 484 Lincoln Hall, 61801. *Dir* Georgette Van Buitenen; *Exhib Designer* Theodore Odenweller; *Cur Numismatics* James Dengate; *Asst Dir* Betty Wendland
Open Mon - Fri 9 AM - 5 PM (when University is in session). No admis fee. Estab 1912. The Museum has Egyptian Room, Minoan and Mycenaean Room, Greek and Roman Rooms, The Hall of Writing, The European Wing, Ethnographic Section, Temporary Display Area, and Illinois Indian Room. Average Annual Attendance: 10,500
Income: Financed by state appropriation
Activities: Conducted tours for classes and public groups

L **Ricker Library of Architecture and Art,** 208 Architecture Bldg, 61801. *Librn* Dee Wallace; *Asst Librn* Lysbeth Wilson
Open Mon - Thur 8 AM - 10 PM, Fri 8 AM - 6 PM, Sat 9 AM - 5 PM, Sun 1 - 10 PM. Estab to serve the study and research needs of the students and faculty of the University and the community. Ricker Library lends materials through UIUC Interlibrary loan
Income: $22,000
Purchases: $42,000
Library Holdings: Vols 40,000; Per subs 515; Micro—Fiche; AV—Lantern Slides; Other—Clipping files, exhibition catalogs, pamphlets, photographs, reproductions
Activities: Tours

WHEATON

O **DUPAGE ART LEAGUE,** 219 West Front St, 60187. Tel 312-653-7090. *Pres* Vickie Brucciani; *VPres* Edna Garner; *Secy* Fran Jungblut; *Treas* Henrietta Tweedie; *Pres Emeritus* Dorothy Hvale
Open daily 9 AM - 5 PM. No admis fee. Estab 1957, is primarily an educational organization founded to encourage artists and promote high artistic standards through instruction, informative programs and exhibits. Gallery is maintained where members exhibit and sell their work. Shows change monthly and based on a theme. Mem: 425; dues $15; annual meeting May
Income: Financed through membership, gifts and donations
Publications: Newsletter, monthly
Activities: Classes for adults and children; programs; demonstrations; lect open to the public, 6-7 visiting lectrs per year; gallery talks; competitions; awards; scholarships; traveling exhibitions organized and circulated; sales shop selling original art and prints

WINNETKA

O **NORTH SHORE ART LEAGUE,** Winnetka Community House, 620 Lincoln, 60093. Tel 312-446-2870. *Pres* Lois Verb; *First VPres* Ric Benda; *Second VPres* Paul Weinger; *Recording Secy* Lois Simon
Open Mon - Sat 9 AM - 6 PM. Estab 1924, inc 1954, to promote interest in creative art through education, exhibition opportunities, scholarship and art programs. Mem: 1100; dues $20; annual meeting May
Exhibitions: Annual Members Fair; annual Members Show; annual Midwest Crafts Festival; Faculty Show; Illinois Regional Print Show, juried; Midwest Craft Festival Horizons in Painting and Sculpture Shows, juried for entry, nonmember; Old Orchard Art Festival, juried for entry, nonmember; Student Show
Publications: Art League News, quarterly

INDIANA

ANDERSON

O **ANDERSON FINE ARTS CENTER,** 226 W Historical Eighth St, 46016. Tel 317-649-1248. *Executive Dir* Deborah McBratney; *Pres Board of Trustees* Mrs Robert Hackler; *Cur* Laura Sanchez; *Education Coordr* Austin Custer; *Admin Asst* John Poling
Open Sept - July Tues - Sat 10 AM - 5 PM, Sun 2 - 5 PM, cl Mon, national holidays. No admis fee. Estab 1966 to serve the community by promoting and encouraging

interest in the fine arts through exhibitions, programs and education activities and the development of a permanent collection. Three galleries contain 1705 sq ft; also a small sales and rental gallery. Average Annual Attendance: 30,000. Mem: 700; dues benefactor $5000, student $5; annual meeting first Fri in May

Income: Financed by memberships, endowments, grants, individual and corporate contributions

Purchases: $2000

Collections: Primarily Indiana, †Mid-West and †American art; small number of works by European artists

Exhibitions: Anderson Area Annual; Anderson Art League; Anderson Society of Artists; Anderson Winter Show; Madison County Photography; Student Art Competition; variety of regional and national one-man shows; traveling exhibitions; special exhibitions organized by Anderson Fine Arts Center

Publications: Calendar of Events, quarterly; various exhibitions catalogs

Activities: Classes for adults and children; dramatic programs; docent training; monthly film series; Lect open to the public, 4-6 visiting lectrs per year; concerts; tours; competitions; individual paintings and original objects of art lent to other art museums; lending collection contains books, Kodachromes, motion pictures, original art work, slides; traveling exhibitions organized and circulated; museum and sales shop selling books, original art, reproductions, prints and original crafts, children's gifts, postcards, and gift items

L **Library,** 226 W Historical Eighth St, 46016. *Librn* John Poling

Open Tues - Sat 10 AM - 4 PM, Sun 2 - 5 PM. Estab 1967 for reference needs and enjoyment by members of Arts Center and the community

Purchases: $500

Library Holdings: Vols 300; Per subs 11; AV—Cassettes, Kodachromes, motion pictures, slides; Other—Clipping files, exhibition catalogs, pamphlets

Collections: Main emphasis on Contemporary American Art

BLOOMINGTON

INDIANA UNIVERSITY

M **Art Museum,** Fine Arts 007, 47405. Tel 812-337-5445. *Dir* Thomas T Solley; *Cur Western Art to 1800* Adelheid Gealt; *Cur Modern Art* Constance L Bowen; *Research Ancient Art* Jane E H Leslie; *Research Ancient Art* Adriana Calinescu; *Researcher Asian Art* Pamela Buell; *Registrar* Sarah M Ulen; *Editor* Linda Baden

Open Tues 9 AM - 9 PM; Wed - Sat 9 AM - 5 PM; Sun Noon - 5 PM; cl Mon. No admis fee. Estab 1962 to serve as a teaching adjunct to the Fine Arts Department and as a cultural resource for the University community and the public at large. Average Annual Attendance: 35,000

Income: $326,000 (financed by state appropriation and gifts)

Collections: †Ancient to Modern, Far Eastern and Primitive Prints, Drawings, and Photography

Exhibitions: Burton Y Berry Collection; Contemporary Glass; Royal Benin; Tiepolo's Punchinello Drawings; Italian Majolica from Midwestern Collection; German and Austrian Expressionism, 1900-1920;

Activities: Lect open to public; gallery talks; tours; lending collection contains Kodachromes, lantern slides, photographs; sales show sells books

M **University Museum,** Student Bldg 209, 47401. Tel 812-337-7224. *Dir* Wesley R Hurt; *Cur Coll* Peter Gold; *Cur Exhib* David Schalliol; *Registrar* JoAnne Powell

Open Mon - Sat 9 AM - 5 PM; Sun 1 - 5 PM. No admis fee. Estab 1964. Presently a temporary gallery is being used while plans for a new building are being finalized

Purchases: $3783

Collections: Primitive Paintings; anthropology

Activities: Informal education department conducts tours and handles a small school loan collection; film series; scholarships; originate traveling exhibitions in State of Indiana

L **University Museum Library,** Student Bldg 209, 47401.

Mon - Fri 9 AM - 5 PM. Estab 1964 to assist in research of collections and educate students studying museum training. For reference only

Library Holdings: Vols 1500

Special Subjects: Antropology, Folk Art, Historical Material

Collections: American Indian

CRAWFORDSVILLE

M **HENRY S LANE HOME,** 212 S Water St, 47933. Tel 317-362-3416. *Pres* John Bowerman; *Treas* Maude Arthur

Open (summer) 1:30 - 4:30 PM, (winter) 1 - 4 PM. Admis adults 75¢, children under twelve 15¢. Estab 1933 as a museum. Average Annual Attendance: 1000. Mem: 250; dues $10.00, $7.00, and $4.50

Income: Financed by mem, city and county appropriation

Collections: Antique furniture, artifacts, and china

ELKHART

M **MIDWEST MUSEUM OF AMERICAN ART,** 429 S Main St, PO Box 1812, 46515. Tel 219-293-6660. *Pres* Dr Richard D Burns; *VPres* Michael Nickol; *Secy* Jane Burns; *Dir* Mark J Meister; *Cur Exhib & Registrar* E Michael Flanagan III; *Asst Cur Educ* Karen Karmel

Open Tues - Sat 11 AM - 5 PM, Thurs Eve 7 - 9 PM, Sun 1 - 5 PM. Admis adults $1.50, children 75¢, senior citizens 75¢, members free, Thurs eve free. Estab 1978, to promote the exhibitions and understanding of American art. Three galleries are maintained for changing exhibitions; and five galleries are maintained for the permanent collection. Average Annual Attendance: 20,000. Mem: 900; dues $10 - $250

Income: $100,000 (financed through membership, grants, foundations, contributions

Collections: Paintings: Thomas Hart Benton; Albert Bierstadt; Arthur Bowen Davies; Adolph Gottlieb; Grace Hartigan; Childe Hassam; Conrad Marca-Relli; Joan Mitchell; Robert Natkin; Maurice Pendergast; Robert Reid; Sculpture: Louise Nevelson; Photographs: Ansell Adams; Imogen Cunningham; Walker Evans; W Eugene Smith; Edward Steichen; Alfred Stieglitz; Clarence White; Minor White

Exhibitions: (1979) Panorama of American Art; Carl Toth: Photographs; Emma Schrock: Folk Paintings. (1980) Changing Walls: Tactile Environment; Midwest Photo '80

Publications: Midwest Museum Bulletin, bimonthly

Activities: Classes for adults and children; dramatic programs; docent training; lect open to the public, 6 visiting lectrs per year; concerts; gallery talks; tours; competitions with awards; individual paintings and original objects of art lent; book traveling exhibitions, 8 per year; traveling exhibitions organized and circulated

EVANSVILLE

M **EVANSVILLE MUSEUM OF ARTS AND SCIENCE,** 411 SE Riverside Dr, 47713. Tel 812-425-2406. *Pres Bd Dir* Darrell Bigham; *Dir* John W Streetman; *Dir Emeritus* Siegfried Weng; *Cur Exhib* Mark A Schnepper; *Research Cur* Frances Martin; *Cur of Coll* Mary S McNamee; *Registrar* Cynthia K Cart

Open Tues - Sat 10 AM - 5 PM, Sun Noon - 5 PM, cl Mon. No admis fee. Estab 1926 to maintain and perpetuate a living museum to influence and inspire the taste and cultural growth of the community, to provide facilities for the collection, preservation and exhibition of objects and data and programs related to the arts, history, science and technology. Lower Level: 19th century village of homes, shops, offices and town hall, arms and armor gallery, science and technology gallery; Main Level: River Room Gallery, furnished Gothic Room with linenfold paneling; Sculpture Gallery: Galleries for Dutch & Flemish Art, American Art and English Portraits; Gallery for arts and crafts of Egypt, the Orient, Black Africa and the American Indian; Gallery for monthly exhibits; Upper Lever: Planetarium and corridor display area. Average Annual Attendance: 100,000. Mem: 896; dues donor $250, patron $100, contributing $50, participating $25, family $15, adult $8, and collegiate $5; annual meeting third Tues in May

Income: $174,000 (financed by membership, city and state appropriations)

Collections: American and European graphics; †American Art; American paintings; arts and crafts of Black Africa, Egypt, Oceania and the American Indian; †18th & 19th century American Crafts; European paintings; history archives; oriental art; sculpture from BC to contemporary; Victorian decorative arts

Exhibitions: American Watercolor Society Traveling Exhibition, Annual Mid-States Art Exhibition, Annual Mid-States Craft Exhibition, Art from Indiana State University Evansville, Audubon Revisited, Carolyn Plochmann Restrospective, Folk Art of the Deep South; Master Printers of Japan; Orozco & Rivera, drawings and paintings; Photographs by Yousuf Karsh; The Mighty Pen (Calligraphy Exhibit); They Made them Laugh, Wince and Worry

Publications: Bulletin, monthly; catalogs of exhibitions

Activities: Classes for adults and children; dramatic programs; docent training; lect open to public; concerts; gallery talks; tours; competitions; exten dept serving area schools; individual paintings and original objects of art lent to institutions; lending collection contains nature artifacts, original art works, original prints, paintings, photographs and sculpture; traveling exhibitions organized and circulated; museum shop selling books, original art, reproductions, prints, jewelry, and pottery

L **Henry R Walker Jr Memorial Art Library,** 411 SE Riverside Dr, 47713. Tel 812-425-2406.

Open Tues - Sat 10 AM - 5 PM, Sun Noon - 5 PM. For reference only

Library Holdings: Vols 4000; AV—Slides; Other—Clipping files, exhibition catalogs, prints, manuscripts, memorabilia, original art works, pamphlets, photographs, reproductions, sculpture

UNIVERSITY OF EVANSVILLE

M **Krannert Gallery,** Lincoln Ave, PO Box 329, 47702. *Chmn Art Dept* Les Miley; *Gallery Coordr* Bill Richmond

Open Mon - Sat 9 AM - 5 PM. No admis fee. Estab 1969-70 to bring to the University and public communities exhibitions which reflect the contemporary arts, ranging from crafts through painting and sculpture. Public access exhibition space 80 x 40 ft and located in Fine Arts Building

Income: Financed by Department of Art funds

Collections: 20th century art primarily centered around paintings and prints acquired through purchase awards and private gifts

Exhibitions: (1979-80) Drawing & Sculpture Exhibition; Indiana Ceramics; Jim Pearson-Prints & Painting; New Aquisitions; Ohio River Art Teachers Exhibition; Student Scholarship Exhibition; Undergraduate BFA Exhibition; University of Evansville Alumni Exhibition; University of Evansville Faculty Exhibition

Activities: Competitions; individual paintings and original objects of art lent to university community

L **Clifford Memorial Library,** 1800 Lincoln Ave, PO Box 329, 47702.

Open 8 AM - 12 PM

Library Holdings: Vols 3,550; Per subs 15; Micro—Cards, fiche, prints; Other— Exhibition catalogs, prints, manuscripts, memorabilia, original art works, pamphlets

FORT WAYNE

O FORT WAYNE FINE ARTS FOUNDATION, INC, The Canal House, 114 E Superior St, 46802. Tel 219-424-0646. *Executive Dir* John V McKenna; *Pres* Darrell W Huntley; *Secy* Jean Greenlee; *Mgr Community Arts Center* Mary Brant
Estab 1955 to raise funds for cultural organizations in Fort Wayne and to foster a positive atmosphere for arts growth
Income: Financed by public allocations and private donations
Collections: Bicentennial Collection
Publications: Discovery, quarterly newspaper; fine arts calendar
Activities: Own and manage Community Center for the Performing Arts

M FORT WAYNE MUSEUM OF ART, 1202 W Wayne St, 46804. Tel 219-422-6467. *Dir* James M Bell
Open Sun, Tues - Thur 1 - 5 PM, Fri 11 AM - 5 PM, Sat 10 AM - 5 PM, cl Mon. No admis fee. Estab 1921 to heighten visual perception of fine arts and perception of other disciplines. Two buildings - Main Building, Young People's Wing, sculpture garden. Average Annual Attendance: 30,000. Mem: 1200; dues $20 for an individual and up, $7.50 for full-time students; annual meeting May
Income: Financed by endowment, mem, fine arts foundation and grants
Collections: Paintings, prints, sculpture and minor arts; Dorsky and Tannenbaum Collection of Contemporary Graphics; Fairbanks Collection of paintings and prints; Hamilton Collection of paintings and sculpture; Thieme Collection of paintings; Weatherhead Collection of contemporary paintings and prints; William Moser Collection of African art
Exhibitions: Annual Tri Kappa (Indiana, Ohio, Michigan artists juried show); Contemporary Prints from the Ashland Oil Coll; Egyptian Tapestries; Landon Coll of American Masters; Magic Realism of Frank Liljegren; Narendra Patel Sculpture; West Meets East . . . Impressionism in 19th Century Prints; Western Artists; Ilya Bolotowsky; Alan Fenton; Dorothy Gillespie; Phyllis Mark; Alice Neel; John Ross; Julius Tobias
Publications: Calendar, bi-monthly; catalogs; fact sheets; posters
Activities: Educ dept; docent training; lect open to the public; competitions; originate traveling exhibitions; museum and sales shop selling books, original art, ceramics and other gift items; junior museum in Young People's Wing

M LINCOLN NATIONAL LIFE FOUNDATION, INC, Louis A Warren Lincoln Library and Museum, 1300 S Clinton St, 46801. Tel 219-424-5421, Ext 7864. *Dir* Mark E Neely Jr; *Asst* Mary Jane Hubler
Open Mon - Thurs 8 AM - 4:30 PM, Fri 8 AM - 12:30 PM, May - Nov Mon - Fri 8 AM - 4:30 PM, Sat 10 AM - 4:30 PM. No admis fee. Estab 1928 for collection of Lincolniana; as research library and museum. Average Annual Attendance: 15,000
Collections: †Lincoln Portraits, mostly †lithographs and †engravings, including †paintings, †photographs
Publications: Lincoln Lore, monthly; R Gerald McMurry Lecture, annually
Activities: Lect open to public with visiting lectr; original objects of art lent to museums and libraries

L PUBLIC LIBRARY OF FORT WAYNE AND ALLEN COUNTY, 900 Webster St, 46802. Tel 219-424-7241. *Dir* Robert H Vegeler; *Asst Dir* Rick J Ashton; *Head Fine Arts Dept* Helen Colchin; *Financial Secy* Mrs Richard Belschner
Open Mon - Fri 9 AM - 9 PM, Sat 9 AM - 6 PM. Estab 1968 to provide a reference collection of the highest quality and completeness for the community and its colleges, and a place where local artists and musicians could exhibit their works and perform; and to provide a circulating collection of art prints, slides and musical scores sufficient to meet the demand. The gallery is reserved for painting, sculpture, graphics, ceramics and other art crafts; photography exhibits are held in the lobby area
Income: $100,000 (financed by city appropriation)
Library Holdings: Vols 12,824; Per subs 167; AV—Cassettes, motion pictures, rec, slides, v-tapes; Other—Clipping files, exhibition catalogs, framed reproductions, prints, pamphlets, reproductions
Activities: Concerts

M SAINT FRANCIS COLLEGE, Lakeview Gallery, 1901 Spring St, 46808. Tel 219-432-3551, Ext 236.
Open Mon - Fri 10 AM - 5 PM. No admis fee. Estab 1965, to provide art programs to students and community. Gallery, approx 35 x 40 ft each, is maintained in two rooms, located on the third floor, Bonaventure Hall. Average Annual Attendance: 500-750
Collections: American Indian Collection; †Oriental Collection
Exhibitions: (1980) Art Major Exhibit; Children's Art Classes, Regional High School Exhibit; The City on Paper; Contemporary Prints by Contemporary Women; St Francis Alumni
Activities: Competitions with awards; traveling exhibitions organized and circulated

GARY

O GREATER GARY ARTS COUNCIL, 504 Broadway, Suite 1037, 46402. Tel 219-885-8444. *Pres* Richard Hagelberg; *First VPres* Luci Horton; *Second VPres* Josephine Johnson; *Secy* Carolyn McCrady; *Treas* Maxine Young; *Executive Dir* John H Cleveland Jr
Open 9 AM - 5 PM. Estab 1967 to sponsor and encourage cultural and educational activities in the city of Gary and Lake County. Average Annual Attendance: 20,000. Mem: 500; dues individual $5, head of family $5, student $2.50
Income: $34,000 (financed by endowment, membership, city and state appropriations)
Publications: Greater Gary Arts Council's Artsgram, quarterly
Activities: Classes for children; sponsored several arts projects and are now planning a Community Multi-Arts program which will feature instructions in music, art, theatre, and creative writing; competitions with awards; scholarships

HAMMOND

M PURDUE UNIVERSITY, CALUMET CAMPUS, Bicentennial Library Gallery, 46323. Tel 219-844-0520, Ext 422. *Head Dept Art* Edwin Cohen. PhD; *Chmn Gallery Committee* Barbara M Meeker
Collections: 19th century Chinese Scroll Collection
Exhibitions: Area Professional Artists and Students Shows; group shows; traveling shows (Smithsonian Institution)
Activities: book traveling exhibitions

INDIANAPOLIS

C ELI LILLY AND COMPANY, 307 E McCarty St, 46285. Tel 317-261-2489. *Department Head Community Relations* Priscilla M Gerde
Supports museums, including Indianapolis Museum of Art and The Children's Museum
Activities: Supports construction, special projects and general operating

O HOOSIER SALON PATRONS ASSOCIATION, Hoosier Salon Art Gallery, 143 N Meridian St, 46202. *Pres* Ardath Burkhart; *Secy* Mrs G W Foster; *First VPres* Harry Riser; *Tres* David Shea; *Executive Dir* Mary Beck
Main gallery open Tues - Fri 9:30 AM - 4:30 PM. Estab 1925 to promote work of Indiana artists. Mem: dues mem $10 and up, artist $5, annual meeting June
Collections: Paintings, prints, sculpture
Exhibitions: Annual Hoosier Salon in April then on tour, over $15,000 in prize money
Publications: Annual Salon Catalog; History of the Hoosier Salon; Hoosier Salon Newsletter, three times a year
Activities: Loan service to members

M INDIANA CENTRAL UNIVERSITY, Leah Ransburg Art Gallery, 1400 E Hanna Ave, 46227. Tel 317-788-3253. *Dir* Gerald G Boyce
Open daily 9:30 AM - 4 PM. No admis fee. Estab 1964 to serve the campus and community. Average Annual Attendance: 25,000 - 30,000
Income: Financed by institution support
Purchases: $15,000
Collections: †Art Department Collection; †Krannert Memorial Collection
Publications: Announcements; annual catalog and bulletin

C THE INDIANA NATIONAL BANK, One Indiana Square, 46266. Tel 317-266-5269. *In Charge Art Coll* John R Walsh
Open 9 AM - 2:30 PM. No admis fee. Estab 1970 to give visibility to Indiana artists and their work, starting with the 1834 founding of our bank. Collection displayed in public areas of the bank; Indiana Art Since 1834 Collection is displayed in the Executive offices, Auditorium Lobby, Trust, Corporate Banking
Collections: Permanent collection includes oil and watercolor paintings, traditional and contemporary sculpture
Activities: Gallery talks; tours; purchase prizes in state competitions, some merit awards; Individual objects of art lent to special exhibits in Indianapolis

L INDIANAPOLIS MARION COUNTY PUBLIC LIBRARY, 40 E St Clair St, 46204. Tel 317-635-5662. *Dir* Raymond Gnat
Open Mon - Fri 9 AM - 9 PM, Sat 9 AM - 5 PM, Sun 1 - 5 PM. Estab 1873. Circ 3,540,000 (1978)
Income: $6,889,436 (financed by state appropriation and county property tax)
Library Holdings: Vols 1,350,000; Micro—Reels; AV—Motion pictures, rec; Other —Clipping files, exhibition catalogs, prints, pamphlets
Activities: Lect open to public; concerts; tours; competitions

M INDIANAPOLIS MUSEUM OF ART, 1200 W 38th St, 46208. Tel 317-923-1331. *Chmn Board of Trustees* Harrison Eiteljorg; *Pres Board of Trustees* Clarence W Long; *Dir* Robert A Yassin; *Senior Cur* Dr Anthony F Janson; *Cur Oriental Art* Dr Yutaka Mino; *Cur Textiles and Ethnographic Art* Peggy S Gilfoy; *Assoc Cur Painting & Sculpture* Ellen W Lee; *Assoc Cur Decorative Arts* Catherine Beth Lippert; *Asst Cur Prints & Drawings* Martin F Krause; *Dir Education* Donna B Ari; *Conservator* Martin J Radecki; *Registrar* Hilary D Bassett; *Public Relations* Albert O Louer; *Asst Cur J M W Turner Collection* Kurt F Pantzer Jr; *Asst Cur J M W Turner Collection* Grace Ritchie
Open Tues - Sun 11 AM - 5 PM; cl Mon, Thanksgiving, Christmas & New Year's Day. No admis fee. Estab 1883 to maintain a museum, the grounds, pavilions, and other facilities for the display of art of all kinds; a library for the collection of books, manuscripts, periodicals, photographs and other similar data or facilities relating to art of all kinds; to promote interest in art of all kinds by lectures, exhibitions, publications, programs and general sponsorship of art and artists in the City of Indianapolis and State of Indiana; to cooperate with national state and city government and civic, educational and artistic groups foundations. Maintains three galleries, the Krannert, Clowes and Lilly Pavilions. Average Annual Attendance: 500,000. Mem: 12,000; dues reciprocal $100, sustaining $50, family-double $25, individual $15, student $12.50
Collections: Classical to contemporary watercolors, including JMW Turner Collection; American period rooms, costumes and textiles; †decorative arts, including watch collection; †18th Century English portraiture; 18 - 19th Century European porcelain and furniture; †ethnographic art of North and South America, Africa and Oceania; Indiana paintings; †Oriental bronzes, ceramics, jade and paintings; 19 - 20th Century American and European paintings; 17th Century European paintings; Renaissance to contemporary drawings and prints; Western American art
Exhibitions: (1979) A Bevy of Beasts: Animals in Print; Art Inc: American Paintings from United States Corporate Collections; Christmas at Oldfields; Contemporary Japanese Prints; Contemporary Prints by Contemporary Women; Contemporary Western American Art in Eiteljorg Gallery; Costumes from the Estate of Caroline Burford Danner; Fabric of Jewish Life: Textiles from The Jewish Museum Collection; Garo Antreasian Lithographs; Indiana Earthenware and Stoneware: 1840-1910; Karel Appel Portfolio; Mark Tobey Graphics; Okada, Shinoda and Tsutaka; Old Sheffield Plate - The Collection of Mr and Mrs W Earl Capehart Jr; Paintings by Hung Hsien; Portraits and Painters of the Governors of Indiana: 1800-1978; Prints from Indianapolis Collections; Selections from the

Campbell Museum Collection; 67th Indiana Artists Show; Symphony in Color; The Allen Whitehill Clowes Collection of Bronzes; The American Farm: A Photographic History; The Western Art and Sculptures of George Carlson; Villa and Cottage: The English Picturesque: William Dole Collages; World of Hiroshige; (1980) Accessions from the Contemporary Art Society: 1963-1978; Accessions 1979: European, American and Oriental Art - and - Decorative Arts Potpourri; African Furniture and Household Objects; British Watercolors and Watercolorists; Christmas at Oldfields; Classical Tradition in Rajput Painting; Herbert Bayer Photographs; Key Acquisitions Since 1970; Mid-America Orchid Congress; North German Folk Pottery; Painting & Sculpture Today 1980; Tz'u-chou Ware
Publications: Catalogs of permanent collection; brochures; newsletters and calendars of events, bimonthly
Activities: Classes for adults and children; dramatic programs; docent training; lect open to the public and for members only; concerts; gallery talks; tours; competitions; originate traveling exhibitions; museum shop and sales shop selling books, magazines, original art, reproductions, prints, slides; Alliance Art Rental Gallery rents paintings to members and sells to members and public
M **Clowes Fund Collection,** Clowes Pavilion, 1200 W 38th St, 46208. Tel 317-923-1331. *Cur* Allen W Clowes; *Research Cur* Alan Fraser
Open Tues - Sun 11 AM - 5 PM, cl Mon. No admis fee. Estab 1958 to display paintings of the Old Masters from the collection of the late Dr G H A Clowes. Average Annual Attendance: 62,000
Income: Financed by endowment
Collections: Italian Renaissance: Duccio, Fra Angelico, Bellini, Luini, Tintoretto, and others; Spanish-El Greco, Goya and others; Northern Renaissance-17th and 18th century Dutch, Hals, Rembrandt and others; French-Clouet, Corneille de Lyon; English-Reynolds, Constable and others; Flemish-Breughel, Bosch and others
M **Downtown Gallery,** American Fletcher National Bank, 101 Monument Circle, 46204.
L **Stout Reference Library,** 1200 W 38th St, 46208. *Head Librn* Martha G Blocker; *Cataloger* Julie C Su
Open Tues - Fri 11 AM - 5 PM, Sat & Sun 1 - 4 PM. Estab 1908 to serve needs of Museum staff and Indianapolis community. For reference only
Income: $12,000 (financed by mem)
Purchases: $12,000
Library Holdings: Vols 20,000; Per subs 75; Micro—Fiche, reels; Other—Clipping files, exhibition catalogs
Special Subjects: Architecture, Decorative Arts, American Painting, Sculpture
Collections: Indiana artists
Publications: Exhibition catalogs as needed; Indianapolis Museum of Art Bulletin, irregularly; Newsletter, bimonthly
L **Slide Collection,** 1200 W 38th St, 46208. Tel 317-923-1331, Ext 35. *Head* Carolyn J Metz
Open Tues - Sat 1 - 5 PM. Estab 1972 to provide visuals on the history of art and to document and record the museum programs and activities. Circ 30,000
Income: Financed by endowment and museum budget
Purchases: $6000
Library Holdings: AV—Slides 60,000
Special Subjects: Art History
Collections: Exhibits and installation documentation of programs
M **Indianapolis Museum of Art at Columbus Ind,** Fifth and Franklin Sts, 47201.
Exhibitions: Usually exhibitions from the permanent collection quarterly
M **INDIANA STATE MUSEUM,** 202 N Alabama St, 46204. Tel 317-633-4948. *Dir* Carl H Armstrong; *Asst Dir* Richard Hurst; *Cur Coll* Paul Richard; *Cur Exhib* David McLary; *Exhib Design Coordr* Wade Carmichael; *Cur Educ* Kathleen Cooper; *Pub Relations Coordr* Shirley Boltz; *Grants & Memorial Liaison* Gregg Jackson
Open daily 9 AM - 5 PM. No admis fee. Estab 1869 for collections; current museum building opened 1967 to collect, preserve and interpret the natural and cultural history of the state. Numerous galleries: Woodland Habitat; Indiana Wildlife; Earth Science; Pioneer Lifestyles and Fashions; Hoosier Artists; Modes of Travel; and Abraham Lincoln. Average Annual Attendance: 130,000. Mem: 1300; dues $5 and up; annual meeting Apr
Income: Financed by state appropriation
Exhibitions: Three Indiana art shows annually
Publications: History-on-the-Move, bimonthly
Activities: Docent training; in-school programs; lect open to public, 4 vis lectr per year; sales shop selling books, reproductions and prints
L **Library,** 202 N Alabama St, 46204.
Open to staff for reference
Library Holdings: Vols 1000

INDIANA UNIVERSITY - PURDUE UNIVERSITY AT INDIANAPOLIS
M **Herron School of Art, Art Gallery,** 1701 N Pennsylvania St, 46202. Tel 317-923-3651. *Dean* Arthur H Weber; *Asst Dean & Dir Admissions* Ralph R Thomas; *Asst to Dean, Business Affairs* Karl E Ralph; *Cur* 10; *Asst Cur* Patrick King
Open Mon - Thurs 9 AM - 7 PM; Fri 9 AM - 5 PM. No admis fee. Estab 1877 to educate those students seeking professional careers in fine arts, visual communication and the teaching of art. Emphasis is placed on studio instruction provided by practicing professional artists, designers, and educators. The Gallery is located in the Museum Building and is part of the original John Herron Art Institute
Income: Financed by state appropriation
Collections: Student and faculty exhibits; temporary contemporary arts installations with documentation
Activities: Classes for adults and children; lect; tours; film series; workshops; exten dept serving Indianapolis and surrounding communities
L **Herron School of Art Library,** 1701 N Pennsylvania St, 46202. *Head Librn* Maudine B Williams; *Asst Librn* Jane Anne Snider
Open Mon, Tues, Thurs 8 AM - 7 PM; Wed 8 AM - 9 PM; Fri 8 AM - 5 PM; cl Sat & Sun. Estab 1970 as a visual resource center for the support of the curriculum of the Herron School or Art. Circ 38,101
Income: $10,000 (financed by state appropriation)
Purchases: $10,000
Library Holdings: Vols 10,000; Per subs 170; AV—Fs, lantern slides, rec, slides; Other—Clipping files, prints, photographs, reproductions

Special Subjects: Art History, Art Education, Photography, Printmaking, Sculpture, visual communication, painting

C **LAUGHNER BROTHERS, INC,** 4004 S East St, 46227. Tel 317-783-2907. *Pres* Charles Laughner
Open 11 AM - 2:30 PM and 4 - 8 PM. No admis fee. Estab 1963 to promote artists and their original paintings. Collection displayed in cafeterias. Mr Laughner uses original paintings from several artists as his main decor in all 9 locations in Indiana
Purchases: $2000

M **MARIAN COLLEGE,** Art Department,* Allison Mansion, 3200 Cold Spring Rd, 46222. *Prof Emeritus of Art* Sr Mary Jane Peine
Open Sun 2 - 4 PM. No admis fee, donations accepted. Estab 1970, in the National Register of Historical Places, Allison Mansion houses the Art Department of Marian College, a four-year Liberal Arts College. The interior of the mansion is a work of art with its magnificent treatment of walls of hand carved marble and wood: oak, white mahogany and walnut. The grand stairway in the main hall leads to the balcony overlooking the hall, all hand-carved walnut. A private collection of 17th century paintings complement its beauty

M **MORRIS-BUTLER MUSEUM OF HIGH VICTORIAN DECORATIVE ARTS,** 1204 N Park Ave, 46202. Tel 317-636-5409. *Supv* Barbara E Carson
Open Wed - Sun 1 - 5 PM; other times by appointment for groups; cl Mon & Tues. Home built 1865 and restored by Historic Landmarks Foundation of Indiana. Twenty-one rooms completely furnished. Facilities for receptions and meetings
Collections: Belter furniture; flint glass; paintings by early Indiana artists; Victorian sculpture; Wooton desk

LAFAYETTE

O **LAFAYETTE ART CENTER,** 101 S Ninth St, 47901. Tel 317-742-1128. *Pres* Ken Knevel; *VPres* Lowell Horwedel; *Secy* Manya Fan; *Treas* Bill Bache; *Dir* Sharon A Theobald
Open daily 1 - 5 PM, cl Mon. No admis fee. Estab 1909 to encourage and stimulate art and to present exhibitions of works of local, regional and national artists and groups as well as representative works of American and foreign artists. Size of gallery is 24 x 60. Average Annual Attendance: 3000. Mem: 1300; dues family $15, individual $10, student and senior citizen $5; annual meeting Oct
Income: Financed by endowment and membership
Collections: Permanent collection of over 250 works of art obtained through purchase or donation since 1909
Exhibitions: Monthly exhibitions
Publications: Newsletter, quarterly
Activities: Classes for adults and children; docent training; lect open to the public, gallery talks, tours, competitions with awards; scholarships; individual paintings and original objects of art lent to members; lending collection contains books, original art works, original prints and paintings; originates traveling exhibitions; sales shop selling books, original art, prints, reproductions
L **Library,** 101 S Ninth St, 47901.
Open to members

M **TIPPECANOE COUNTY HISTORICAL MUSEUM,** 909 South St, 47901. Tel 317-742-8411. *Dir* John M Harris; *Asst Dir* Carol N Waddell; *Cur of Coll* Mildred Paarlberg; *Cur of Educ* Paula Woods; *Cur of Genealogy* Lyda Hilt
Open daily 1 - 5 PM, cl Mon. No admis fee. Estab 1925 to collect, preserve, research and interpret the history of Tippecanoe County and the immediate surrounding area. Housed in a Victorian house (1851-52), there are exhibits of various phases of county history in nine rooms. Average Annual Attendance: 20,000. Mem: 1000; dues $5 - $25; annual meeting Jan
Income: $235,000 (financed by endowment, mem, county and state appropriation, sales and programs)
Collections: Broad range, incorporating any object relative to county history
Exhibitions: Changing exhibits; fixed exhibits include Pioneer Development, miniature rooms, paintings and porcelains
Publications: Tippecanoe Tales, occasional series on various phases of Tippecanoe County history; Weatenotes, nine times a year
Activities: Classes for adults and children; docent training; lect open to the public; tours; individual paintings and original objects of art lent to other museums; sales shop selling books, reproductions, original crafts on consignment
L **Alameda McCollough Library,** 909 South St, 47901. *Librn Historical Section* Carol Waddell; *Librn Genealogical Section* Lyda Hilt
Open to serious researchers for reference only
Library Holdings: Vols 2000; Per subs 15; Other—Photographs, maps

MUNCIE

BALL STATE UNIVERSITY
M **Art Gallery,** 47306. Tel 317-285-5242. *Dir* William E Story; *Asst to Dir* Dolores Terhune; *Secy* Betty Magill
Open Mon - Fri 9 AM - 4:30 PM & 7 - 9 PM; Sat & Sun 1:30 - 4:30 PM; cl legal & school holidays and evenings June - Aug. Estab 1936 as a university and community art museum with special emphasis on the art department. Eight large galleries, sculpture court, mezzanine and reception lounge. Average Annual Attendance: 36,000
Collections: Kraft-Ball Collection of Roman and Syrian glass; Italian Renaissance art and furniture; 19th & 20th century American paintings, prints, and drawings
Exhibitions: Annual Art Faculty Exhibit; Annual Art Student Exhibit; Annual Drawing and Small Sculpture Show; Metalworks Invitational, 1979
Publications: Newsletter, occasionally
Activities: Lect open to public, 2 - 3 vis lectr per year; concerts; gallery talks; competitions; individual paintings and original objects of art lent to other art galleries and museums, and to offices and special buildings on campus; originate traveling exhibitions

L **Architecture Library,** College of Architecture & Planning, McKinley at Neely, 47306. Tel 317-285-4760. *Librn* Marjorie Hake Joyner; *Clerical Asst* Barbara Ballinger
Open (Academic year) Mon - Fri 8 AM - 8 PM, Sat 9 AM - 5 PM, Sun 2 - 10 PM; (Summer) Mon - Fri 8 AM - 5 PM. Estab 1965 to provide materials necessary to support the academic programs of the college of Architecture & Planning. Circ 25,000
Income: Financed through University
Library Holdings: Vols 18,000; Per subs 180; Micro—Reels; AV—Slides; Other— Clipping files, pamphlets, Manufacturers' catalogs; architectural drawings; maps and student theses
Special Subjects: Architectural history

NASHVILLE

O **BROWN COUNTY ART GALLERY ASSOCIATION INC,** 1 Artist Dr, PO Box 443, 47448. Tel 812-988-4609. *Pres* Phyllis Whitworth; *VPres* Dwight F Steininger; *Executive Secy* Merwin Bugher
Open Mid-March - Mid-Dec 10 AM - 5 PM. Admis adult 50¢. Estab 1926 to unite artists and laymen in fellowship; to create a greater incentive for development of art and its presentation to the public; to estab an art gallery for exhibition of work of members of the Association. Average Annual Attendance: 35,000. Mem: 53 artists; 750 supporting members; dues individual $10 - life $500; annual meeting Oct
Income: Financed by memberships, foundation and trust
Collections: 75 oil paintings and pastels by the late Glen Cooper Henshaw
Exhibitions: 3 exhibits each year by the Artist members
Activities: Competitions with awards

NEW ALBANY

M **FLOYD COUNTY MUSEUM,** 201 E Spring St, 47150. Tel 812-944-7336. *Pres* Frances Pallant; *VPres* Dr Richard Smith; *Secy* Stephen Beardsley; *Dir* Gerri Samples-Kelley
Open Tues - Sat 10 AM - 4 PM, Sun 2 - 5 PM. No admis fee. Estab 1971, to exhibit professional artists work on a monthly basis. Two galleries are maintained, approx dimensions: 18 x 25 ft and 15 x 25 ft. Average Annual Attendance: 7000. Mem: 300; dues $10 - $25
Income: $10,000 (financed through membership)
Collections: Permanent collection of †historical items
Exhibitions: (1979) General Art Show: All Medias; July Juried Exhibit
Publications: Bulletins
Activities: Classes for adults and children; lect open to the public; gallery talks; tours; competitions; awards; book traveling exhibitions, 2-4 per year; museum shop sells books, original art, reproductions, prints

NOTRE DAME

SAINT MARY'S COLLEGE
M **Moreau Gallery Three,** Art Department, 46556. Tel 219-284-4074. *Chmn, Ceramics & Sculpture* H James Paradis; *Gallery Dir* Michele Fricke
Open Mon - Fri 9 - 11 AM & 12:30 - 3 PM, Sat - Sun 12:30 - 4 PM, cl Mon. Estab 1956 for education and community-related exhibits. Gallery presently occupies three rooms; all exhibits rotate. Average Annual Attendance: 6000
Collections: Cotter Collection; Dunbarton Collection of prints; Norman LaLiberte; various media
Exhibitions: Annual High School Art Exhibition, Faculty-Student Exhibition (all media), Elena Borstein (painting), Gregory Huebner (painting), Richard Margolis (photography), Lee Sido (sculpture), Mahboob Shahzaman (fiber)
Publications: Catalogs, occasionally
Activities: Classes for adults; dramatic programs; lect open to public; tours; concerts
L **Alumnae Centennial Library,** 46556. *Head Librn* Sr Bernice Hollenhorst; *Head Cataloguer* Sr Marjorie Johnes; *Reference Librn* Robert Hohl; *Periodicals Librn* Ann Johnson
Open Mon - Fri 7:45 AM - 11 PM, Sat 9 AM - 11 PM, Sun 1 - 11 PM. Estab 1855
Income: Financed through the University
Library Holdings: Vols 5600; Per subs 32; Micro—Reels; AV—A-tapes, cassettes, fs, Kodachromes, motion pictures, rec, slides

UNIVERSITY OF NOTRE DAME
M **Snite Museum of Art,** 46556. Tel 219-283-4266. *Dir* Dean A Porter; *Cur* Stephen B Spiro; *Cur* Douglas Bradley; *Admin Asst to Dir* Lynda Halley; *Admin Asst to Dir* Cynthia Huff; *Registrar* Susan Bastian; *Preparatorial* Greg Denby; *Preparatorial* John Phegley; *Secy* Gail Jones
Open Mon - Fri 10 AM - 4:45 PM; Thurs 7 - 9 PM; Sat & Sun 1 - 5 PM. No admis fee. Estab 1842; Wightman Memorial Art gallery estab 1917; O'Shaughnessy Hall Art Gallery estab 1951; to educate through the visual arts; during a four year period it is the objective to expose students to all areas of art including geographic, period and media. Galleries consist of 52,000 sq ft. Average Annual Attendance: 40,000
Income: $120,000 (financed by endowment and university appropriation)
Purchases: $15,000
Collections: African art; American Indian and pre-Columbian art; Baroque paintings, northern and Italian; †18th and 19th century American, English and French paintings and drawings; Kress Study Collection; Oriental porcelains and sculpture; western sculpture; medieval, modern, and contemporary paintings; †15th century contemporary prints; †photographs
Publications: Exhibition catalogs, 3-5 times per yr
Activities: Educ dept; docent training; lect open to the public; gallery talks; tours; individual paintings and original objects of art lent to qualified institutions; traveling exhibitions organized and circulated; sales shop selling books, catalogs and note cards
L **Catalog Library,** 46556.
Open to students and faculty for reference only
Library Holdings: Vols 20,190; Per subs 30; Other—Exhibition catalogs

L **Architecture Library,** 46556. Tel 219-283-6654. *Librn* Geri Decker; *Library Asst* Charles Early
Open Mon - Thurs 8 AM - 10 PM; Fri 8 AM - 5 PM; Sat 9 AM - 5 PM; Sun 1 - 10 PM; Vacations Mon - Fri 8 AM - 5 PM. Estab 1890 as a branch of the university library. Circ 15,000
Income: $34,500 (financed by University)
Purchases: $8000
Library Holdings: Vols 13,000; Per subs 100; AV—Motion pictures, rec, slides; Other—Clipping files
Special Subjects: Architecture, art, engineering, planning environment
Collections: Rare folio books on architecture
Exhibitions: Art of Robert Schultz; Models of Major Buildings; Models of Student Booths for School Mardi Gras; Student Thesis Projects

OAKLAND CITY

L **OAKLAND CITY COLLEGE LIBRARY,** Art Department, Division of Fine Arts, 47660.
Estab 1890. Circ 3745. Open to the public
Income: $1400
Purchases: $1400
Library Holdings: Vols 3300; Per subs 20; AV—A-tapes, cassettes, fs, Kodachromes, motion pictures, slides, v-tapes; Other—Framed reproductions, original art works, sculpture

RICHMOND

O **ART ASSOCIATION OF RICHMOND,** McGuire Memorial Hall, 350 Whitewater Blvd, 47374. Tel 317-966-0256. *Pres* Dr William Christopher; *VPres* Mrs Walter Lakoff; *Secy* Dr Denney French; *Dir* Mrs James Lemon
Open Mon - Fri 9 AM - 4 PM, Sun 1 - 4 PM, cl Sat and school holidays. No admis fee. Estab 1898 to promote creative ability, art appreciation and art in public schools. Maintains an art gallery with four exhibit rooms: 2 rooms for permanent collection and 2 rooms for current exhibits. Average Annual Attendance: 10,000. Mem: 600; dues from student $1 - $1000; annual meeting second Wed in Oct
Income: Financed by membership and city appropriation
Collections: Regional and state art; American, European, Oriental art
Exhibitions: Annual photography exhibit; crafts and prints; high school art
Publications: Art in Richmond - 1898 - 1978; newsletter, quarterly
Activities: Docent training; lect open to public, 2 vis lectr per year; gallery talks; tours; competitions with merit and purchase awards; scholarships; individual paintings and original objects of art lent to businesses and schools; lending collection contains books, original art works, original prints and photographs; originate traveling exhib; sales shop selling original art
L **Library,** McGuire Memorial Hall, 350 Whitewater Blvd, 47374.
Open to members
Library Holdings: Vols 200; Per subs 3
Special Subjects: Art museums, art techniques

M **EARLHAM COLLEGE,** Leeds Gallery, National Road W, 47374. Tel 317-962-6561. *Pres College* Franklin Wallin; *Chmn Art Dept* Garret J Boone
Open daily 8 AM - Noon. No admis fee. Estab 1847 as a liberal arts college; Leeds Gallery estab 1970
Income: $2500
Purchases: $500 - $800
Collections: Regional artist: George Baker, Bundy (John Ellwood), Marcus Mote; prints by internationally known artists of 19th & 20th centuries; regional artists
Exhibitions: One-man shows, mostly regional; some traveling shows
Activities: Dramatic programs; lect open to public, 5-6 vis lectr per yr; concerts; individual paintings and original objects of art lent; traveling exhibitions organized and circulated; sales shop selling books
L **Library,** 47374.
Library Holdings: Vols 220,000; Other—Photographs
Special Subjects: Art

SOUTH BEND

O **ART CENTER, INC,** 120 S Saint Joseph St, 46601. Tel 219-284-9102. *Dir* Thomas B Schorgl; *Cur* Judy Oberhausen; *Executive Secy* Barbara Dzikowski; *Accountant* Peggy Barnhart
Warner Gallery open Tues - Sun 12 AM - 5 PM; WAL Gallery open Tues - Fri 12:30 AM - 4:00 PM, Sat & Sun 12 AM - 5 PM. No admis fee. Estab in 1947 for museum exhibitions, lectures, film series, workshops, and studio classes. The Art Center is located in a three-story building designed by Philip Johnson. There are two galleries: the Warner Gallery features travelling shows or larger exhibits organized by the Art Center, and The WAL Upper Level Gallery features one or two-person shows by local or regional artists. Average Annual Attendance: 40,000. Mem: 1,000; dues sustaining $100, family $35, active $20, student & senior citizens $10
Income: Financed by membership, corporate support, city and state appropriations
Collections: European and American paintings, drawings, prints and objects; †20th century American art
Exhibitions: Cut on Wood; Dubuffet Texturologies and Materiologies from the Milton D Ratner Collection; Impressionistic Trends in Hoosier Painting; Michiana Collects; Prints by Peter Milton; Rouault's Miserere Series; The Graham Nash Photography Collection; The Holocaust: Mauricio Lasansky's Nazi Drawings; Works on Paper from the Collections of the Art Center, Inc and the Snite Museum of Art, University of Notre Dame
Publications: Bi-monthly newsletter, exhibition catalogues, and checklists
Activities: Studio classes for adults and children; docent training and tours; outreach educational program conducted by Women's Art League; workshops; lecture series; artist studio tours; film series; museum shop offering gifts and original works of art for sale

L **Library,** 120 S Saint Joseph St, 46601.
Estab 1947 to provide art resource material to members of the Art Center. Open to public on request; for reference only
Library Holdings: AV—Motion pictures, rec; Other—Exhibition catalogs

TERRE HAUTE

M **INDIANA STATE UNIVERSITY,** Turman Gallery, 47809. Tel 812-232-6311. *Chmn Art Dept* Jack Stewart
Open Mon - Fri 8 AM - 5 PM, cl last two weeks Aug. No admis fee
Collections: Paintings and sculpture
Exhibitions: Regular traveling exhibitions for short periods during school terms; student and faculty exhibitions
Activities: Classes for children; lect

M **SHELDON SWOPE ART GALLERY,*** 25 S Seventh St, 47807. Tel 812-238-1676. *Dir* Robert D Kinsman
Open Sept 4 - July 31 Tues - Fri 10 AM - 5 PM, Sat 12 - 5 PM, Sun 2 - 5 PM, cl national holidays. No admis fee. Estab 1942 to present publicly and free of charge fine works of art. Average Annual Attendance: 12,000. Mem: 750; dues individual $12.50; annual meeting Third Wed in Sept
Income: $72,000 (financed by membership, city appropriation and trust fund)
Collections: African Art; extensive American Realism Collections; artifacts; dolls; glass; Hudson River School art; Old Masters; Oriental Art; extensive print collections
Publications: Membership newsletter, bimonthly
Activities: Classes for children; dramatic programs; docent training; lect open to the public, 15 visiting lectrs per year; concerts; gallery talks; tours; competitions; artmobile; individual paintings and original objects of art lent to other museums, banks, country clubs and retirement homes; sales shop selling books, magazines, original art, reproductions and prints

L **Research Library,*** 25 S Seventh St, 47807.
Open to the public
Library Holdings: Vols 3000; Per subs 24

UPLAND

M **TAYLOR UNIVERSITY,** Chronicle-Tribune Art Gallery, Art Dept, 46989. Tel 317-998-2051. *Dir* Dr Ray E Bullock
Open Mon - Sat 11 AM - 4 PM and Mon, Wed and Fri 7 - 9 PM, cl Sun. No admis fee. Estab 1972 as an educational gallery
Activities: Classes for children; competitions

VALPARAISO

M **VALPARAISO UNIVERSITY,** University Art Galleries and Collections, 46383. Tel 219-464-5365 or 464-5364. *Chmn* Dr Jack Hiller; *Dir* Richard Brauer
Open Mon - Fri 8 AM - 10 PM, Sat 9 AM - 5 PM, Sun 1 - 10 PM. No admis fee. Estab 1953 to present significant art to the student and citizen community for their education in the values of art. A 600 sq ft area off the check-out room of the university library; similar gallery spaces are available in the Christ College Building and the Union
Income: $14,000 (financed by endowment)
Purchases: $10,000
Collections: †Sloan Collection: 19th and 20th Century American Landscape Paintings, Prints, and Drawings; Valparaiso University Collection: Art on Biblical Themes
Activities: Lectures open to the public; gallery talks; individual paintings and original objects of art lent to museums and art centers

VINCENNES

L **VINCENNES UNIVERSITY,** Art Slide Library, Shircliff Humanities Bldg, 47591. *Librn* Mary B Gorman
Open Mon - Fri 9 AM - 4 PM. Estab to provide audio-visual and tutorial student aides to University students
Library Holdings: AV—A-tapes, cassettes, fs, Kodachromes, slides, v-tapes; Other—Exhibition catalogs, original art works
Collections: Slide collection of contemporary art

WEST LAFAYETTE

M **PURDUE UNIVERSITY,** Gallery I, Gallery II, Union Gallery & Stewart Center Gallery, Creative Arts Bldg 1, 47907. *Head Dept Creative Arts* Ralph Beelke; *Chmn Art & Design* Robert B Reed; *Gallery Dir* Mona Berg; *Chmn Faculty Gallery Comt* Richard Paul
Open Gallery I, Mon - Fri 8 AM - 5 PM; Gallery II, Mon - Fri 9:30 AM - 4:30 PM, Sun 12:30 - 4:30 PM; Stewart Center Gallery, Mon - Fri 9:30 AM - 4:30 PM & 7 - 9 PM, Sun 12:30 - 4:30 PM, Union Gallery, Mon - Fri 9:30 AM - 4:30 PM, Sun 12:30 - 4:30 PM. No admis fee. The exhibition schedule is designed to provide an aesthetic and educational experience for the art students with programs relating to courses taught in the Dept of Creative Arts, as well as to present exhibitions relevant to the University and Greater Lafayette Community. Average Annual Attendance: 20,000
Income: Financed through the University
Purchases: $1500
Collections: Contemporary paintings, prints, sculpture
Exhibitions: Approximately 40 per year, including work by faculty, students, regionally & nationally prominent artists, and loans from private collectors and other institutions; Al Blaustein (etchings & drawings); Sid Chafetz (satires & portraits); John Cook (sculpture); The Charles Pankow Collection; Joseph & Judy Raffael; Maxine Olson - Stuart Caswell (drawings); Big 10 Student Drawing Show; Editorial Cartoons; Egyptian Antiquities; Four In Focus - Photo Invitational; 60 Square Maximum, Small Print Competition; The Contemporary Basket Maker; 22 x 30 Works on Paper
Publications: Exhibit catalogs
Activities: Lect open to public, 2-4 lectr per yr; competitions; individual paintings and original objects of art lent to university administrarive offices; lending collection contains original prints, paintings, sculpture; traveling exhib organized and circulated

IOWA

AMES

M **IOWA STATE UNIVERSITY,** Brunnier Gallery, Scheman Bldg, Iowa State Center, 50011. Tel 515-294-3342. *Dir & Cur* Nancy Gillespie; *Asst Dir & Asst Cur* Lynette Pohlman; *Registrar & Secy* Mary Atherly
Open Tues - Sun 12:30 - 5 PM, cl Mon. No admis fee. Estab 1975, to provide a high level of quality, varied and comprehensive exhibits of national and international scope; and to develop and expand a permanent decorative arts collection of the western world. Gallery is maintained and comprised of 10,000 sq ft of exhibit space, with flexible space arrangement. Average Annual Attendance: Approx 30,000-50,000
Income: $90,000 (financed through state appropriations)
Collections: Permanent collection of ceramics, dolls, furniture, glass, ivory, wood
Exhibitions: (1978) Andrea Palladio: Villas & Public Buildings. (1979) Beds: Sweet Dreams & Other Things; Benton-Curry Wood Lithographs; Design Center Faculty Show; Iowa College Salon; Jasper Johns: Prints 1970-1977; One Man's Vision: Prints by Redon; Young Americans
Activities: Classes for children; docent training; lect open to the public, 1-2 visiting lectrs per year; competitions; awards; original objects of art lent; lending collection contains decorative arts, original prints; book traveling exhibitions, 3-4 per year; traveling exhibitions organized and circulated; sales shop sells books, slides, catalogs

O **OCTAGON CENTER FOR THE ARTS,** 427 Douglas, 50010. Tel 515-323-5331. *Pres* John Mason; *VPres* Robert Stewart; *Secy* Robert Hoover; *Treas* Paul Gergen; *Dir* Martha Benson; *Dir Educ* David Williamson
Open Mon 1 - 9 PM, Tues - Fri 1 - 5 PM, Sat 10 - 5 PM, Sun 2 - 5 PM. Estab 1966 to provide year-round classes for all ages; exhibitions of the work of outstanding artists from throughout the world and also special programs in the visual and performing arts. Average Annual Attendance: 25,000. Mem: 500, open to anyone who is interested in supporting or participating in the arts; dues $8 - $1000; annual meeting second Sun in Oct
Income: $110,000 (financed by membership, city and state appropriations, class fees and fund raising)
Exhibitions: (1978) A Time of Malfeasance; Aspects of Light by Nancy Teague; Batiks by Vickie Roth; Drawings USA-77; Fantasies on a Withering Tulip by Jeanine Coupe Ryding; Iowa Photography Invitational; Iowa's Fair by William Woolston; Octagon People; Pottery of Mary Weisgram; Real and Imagined Aspects of the State Capitol Building by Amy Worthen; Recent Work: Dean Daas and Sarah Grant; The Clay and Fiber Show; Ways of Seeing by Linda Hodges. (1979) Ames High School Seniors Art Show; Clay and Paper Show; Electrographics; Landscape Architecture by James Sinatra; Surface Design - Four Views. (1980) Ames High School Seniors Art Show; British Ceramics Today; Clay-Fiber-Glass-1980; News Photography as Art by Gary Clarke; Paintings by Nick Friess; Prints by Jeanine Coupe Ryding; Third International Exhibition of Miniature Textiles; Two Honest Pieces by Iowa Designer Craftsmen
Publications: Newsletter, monthly
Activities: Classes for adults and children; dramatic programs; special workshops; film, poetry and music programs; gallery talks; tours; an annual regional juried show, awards given in each category and best in show; lending collection of 500 lantern slides; originate traveling exhibitions; sales shop selling books, magazines, original art, prints, reproductions. Fiber to Fabric Shop carries materials and tools for weaving, spinning, basketry and all fiber arts

ANAMOSA

O **PAINT 'N PALETTE CLUB,** RR 3 - 204 N Huber St, 52205. Tel 319-462-2601, 462-2680. *Pres* Mildred B Brown; *VPres* Betty Christophersen; *Executive Dir* Dr Gerald F Brown; *Executive Dir* Wilbur Evarts; *Secy* Malinda Derga
Open June 1 - Oct 15; Sun 1 - 5 PM; other times by appointment. No admis fee (donations accepted). Estab 1955 to maintain Antioch School, the school attended by Grant Wood, a famous Iowa artist; to provide a studio and gallery for local artists and for public enjoyment. A log cabin art gallery on the grounds of the Grant Wood Memorial Park contains the work of some local and visiting artists. Average Annual Attendance: 2000 - 3000. Mem: 32, members must have art experience; dues $10
Income: $700 - $800 (financed by endowment and donations)
Collections: Prints of Grant Wood, Iowa's most famous artist
Exhibitions: Amateur Art and Craft Show; Grant Wood Art Festival; art sale and exhibit
Activities: Occasional classes for adults and children; films; lect open to public, 6-7 vis lectr per yr; tours; competitions; sales shop selling magazines, original art, prints, reproductions, memorial plates and coins, postcards and used books

BURLINGTON

O **ARTS FOR LIVING CENTER,** Seventh & Washington St, PO Box 5, 52601. Tel 319-754-8069. *Dir* Grant Marshall; *Pres* Jerry Rigdon; *Pres Elect* B K Wilson; *VPres* Robert Matsch; *Treas* Leonard Lane; *Secy* Jean Anderson; *Corresponding Secy* Margaret Rutherford
Open Mon - Fri 1 - 5 PM, special openings Sun 2 - 5 PM, cl Sat and all major holidays, with the exception of Thanksgiving. No admis fee. Estab 1966, the Art Guild purchased the Center (a church building built 1868) in 1974, and has now been placed on the National Register of Historic Places. Mem: 426: dues student $5.00 up to benefactor $1000, meeting first Thurs monthly
Income: Financed by membership and donations
Publications: Newsletter, once-twice monthly
Activities: Classes for adults and children; lect open to the public; competitions; traveling exhibitions organized and circulated; sales shop selling original art, reproductions, prints

CEDAR FALLS

M **UNIVERSITY OF NORTHERN IOWA,** Gallery of Art, 27th st at Hudson Rd, 50613. Tel 319-273-6114. *Dir* Sanford Sivitz Shaman
Open Tues 10 AM - 9 PM, Wed - Sat 10 AM - 3 PM, Sun 1 - 5 PM, cl Mon. No admis fee. Estab 1978 to bring to the University and the community at large the finest quality of art from all over the world. One main gallery with 365 running feet; two upstairs galleries, each with 100 running feet and a photographic exhibition corridor
Income: Financed by state appropriation
Collections: 20th century American & European Art
Exhibitions: Current Clay Works by Barbara Cassino and Ed Harris; Drawings and Sculpture of Gaston Lachaise; Mark Tobey, graphics; Annual Student Exhibition; Bi-Annual Faculty Group Exhibition; Colorado Photographers; The Contemporary American Potter; The Great West; The International Year of the Child; The Right to Art; The Stock Show
Publications: Exhibition catalogs
Activities: Lect open to public, 20 vis lectr per year; concerts; gallery talks; tours; competition
L **Art and Music Dept Library,** 50613. Tel 319-273-6252; TWX 910-525-2450. *Dir* Donald O Rod; *Asst Dir* Donald Gray; *Librn* Verna Ford Ritchie
Open Mon - Thurs 7:30 AM - Midnight, Fri 7:30 AM - 6 PM, Sat 10 AM - 6 PM, Sun 1:30 PM - Midnight. Estab 1964, addition 1975, to serve art and music patrons. Circ 20,900. For lending and reference
Income: $31,000
Purchases: $31,000
Library Holdings: Vols 38,500; Per subs 165; Micro—Fiche, prints; AV—A-tapes, cassettes, rec, slides; Other—Clipping files, exhibition catalogs, prints, original art works, pamphlets, reproductions

CEDAR RAPIDS

O **CEDAR RAPIDS ART CENTER,** 324 Third St SE, 52401. Tel 319-366-7503. *Pres* Jerry Maples; *VPres Finance* Peter Bryant; *VPres Planning* John Bickel; *VPres Programs* Joan Clark; *Secy* Winifred Shuttleworth; *Dir* Joseph Czestochowski; *Cur* Sherry Maurer
Open Tues - Sat 10 AM - 5 PM, Thurs 10 AM - 8:30 PM, Sun 2 - 5 PM. Estab art association 1905, art center 1966. Mem: Dues family $25, individual $15
Income: Financed by endowment, membership, city and state appropriations
Collections: Largest concentrated collection of Grant Wood art in existence; print collection
Exhibitions: Rotating exhibitions
Publications: Newsletter, bi-monthly
Activities: Classes for adults and children; dramatic programs; docent training; competitions; individual paintings and original objects of art lent on request; sales shop sells books, magazines, original art, prints, reproductions and other merchandise
L **Stamats Library,** 324 Third Ave SE, 52401.
Open Tues - Sat 10 AM - 5 PM, Thurs 10 AM - 8:30 PM, Sun 2 - 5 PM. For reference
Library Holdings: AV—Cassettes, fs, Kodachromes, slides; Other—Exhibition catalogs, framed reproductions, manuscripts, photographs

M **COE COLLEGE,** Art Galleries, 1221 First Ave NE, 52402. Tel 319-398-1669. *Chmn Art Dept* Charles Stroh; *Gallery Dir* Shirley Donaldson
Open Mon - Fri 7 - 9 PM, Sat 10 AM - Noon, Sun 2 - 4 PM. No admis fee. Estab 1942 to exhibit traveling exhibitions and local exhibits. Two galleries, both 60 x 18 ft with 125 running ft of exhibit space. Average Annual Attendance: 5000
Income: $3500 (financed through College)
Collections: Coe Collection of art works; Marvin Cone Alumni Collection; Marvin Cone Collection of oils; Conger Metcalf Collection of paintings; The Hinkhouse Collection of contemporary art
Exhibitions: Circulating exhibits; one-person and group shows of regional nature; rental print exhibitions
Publications: exhibit brochures, 6 - 8 per year
Activities: Lect open to public, 5 - 6 vis lectr per year; gallery talks; tours; competitions; individual paintings and original objects of art lent to colleges and local galleries; lending coll contains framed reproductions, original art works, original prints, paintings, sculpture and slides; traveling exhib organized and circulated

M **MOUNT MERCY COLLEGE,** McAuley Gallery, 1330 Elmhurst Dr NE, 52402. Tel 319-363-8213. *Dir* Jane E Gilmor
Open 8 AM - 5 PM & 7 - 9 PM. No admis fee. Estab to show work by a variety of fine artists. The shows are used by the art department as teaching aids. They provide cultural exposure to the entire campus. One room 22 x 30 ft; one wall is glass overlooking a small courtyard. Average Annual Attendance: 900
Income: Financed through the college
Purchases: $300
Collections: Small print collection
Exhibitions: Fibers, Paula Benfer, Jayne Inktlekofer; Reed Estabrook: Photographs; Paintings by Duane Noblett; Lithography: An Introduction by Bela Petheo; Christmas Invitational; Cornell College Faculty Exhibit; Fourth Annual High School Exhibit; Senior Thesis Exhibition

CHEROKEE

M **SANFORD MUSEUM AND PLANETARIUM,** 117 E Willow St, 51012. Tel 712-225-3922. *Dir* Robert W Hoge; *Admin Asst* Linda Burkhart
Open Tues - Fri 9 AM - 5 PM; Sat & Sun 2 - 5 PM. No admis fee. Estab 1951 for collection, preservation and interpretation of historical, archaeological and biological specimens from the region; educational programs; community involvement. Contains Natural History Hall (archaeology, paleontology, geology, biology), combination auditorium, art display wall area and local history hall, temporary exhibitions gallery, and Sanford Room (historical period room). Average Annual Attendance: 15,000. Mem: 150; dues $7.50 - $100; annual meeting-banquet April or May
Income: Approx $35,000 (financed by endowment and donations)
Purchases: Under $100
Collections: Archaeological and ethnographic materials from other regions; archaeological materials from local cultures; historical collections, mostly from the county, but including Civil War memorabilia; mounted African big game animals; mounted local faunal specimens; vertebrate and invertebrate paleontological specimens, mostly from the region
Exhibitions: (1978-80) Hunters of The Valley: Iowa's First People (archaeological interpretation of Cherokee sewer site, earliest dated find in Iowa); S.P.Q.R.: The Romans (life of imperial Rome) Surprising Saurians (life and times of dinosaurs); Trading and Trapping in the Early West (American Indian culture contact and frontier history)
Publications: Northwest Chapter of Iowa Archaeological Society Newsletter, bimonthly
Activities: Classes for adults and children; dramatic programs; lect open to public, 3 vis lectr per yr; concerts; gallery talks; tours; individual paintings and original objects of art lent to responsible parties and institutions at the discretion of the director; traveling exhibitions organized and circulated; museum shop selling books, reproductions, natural science and historical souvenirs and jewelry
L **Sanford Museum Library,** 117 E Willow St, 51012.
Open to public upon approval of the director for reference on;y
Library Holdings: Vols 2000; Per subs 10; Micro—Reels; AV—A-tapes, rec, slides; Other—Photographs
Special Subjects: Archaeology, Herrick Quilt Collection materials, Herrick Cross Collection materials
Collections: Archives Collection; Brown-Fisher-Yates Collection; Herrick Cross Collection; Herrick Quilt Collection; Kirkpatrick Collection; Sanford Collection; Vandercook-Green Collection

CLINTON

O **CLINTON ART ASSOCIATION GALLERY,** 708 25th Ave N, PO Box 132, 52732. Tel 319-242-9635. *Dir* Hortense Blake
Open Sat & Sun 1 - 5 PM, cl Christmas and New Years. No admis fee. Estab 1968 to bring visual art to the community. Small gallery is housed in an abandoned building of an army hospital complex and is loaned to the association by the Clinton Park and Recreation Board. A separate Pottery School has been maintained since 1975. Average Annual Attendance: 15,000. Mem: 400; dues single membership $5; annual meeting first Tues in May
Income: $4500 (financed by membership and through grants from the Iowa Arts Council)
Publications: Newsletter every two months
Activities: Classes for adults and children in watercolor, oil, rosemaling, macrame, photography and pottery making; docent training; lectr open to the public, 3 - 5 vis lectr per year; gallery talks; tours; individual paintings lent by members to businesses; lending collection contains books, lantern slides and slides; sales shop selling original art and prints

DAVENPORT

M **DAVENPORT MUNICIPAL ART GALLERY,** 1737 W 12th St, 52804. Tel 319-326-7804. *Dir* L G Hoffman; *Admin Secy* Marielow Lee; *Arts Specialist* Ray Bouslough; *Dir Educ* Gaile Gallatin; *Registrar* Mitchell Cohen; *Cur* Ann C Madonia
Open Tues - Sat 10 AM - 4:30 PM, Sun 1 - 4:30 PM. No admis fee. Estab 1925 as a museum of art and custodian of public collection and an education center for the visual arts. Consists of three levels including a spacious main exhibition display

area; upper and lower level galleries are art reference library, six multipurpose art studies, gift shop, mechanical shop and storage area; 400 seat auditorium; childrens gallery; studio workshop; registrar center and an outdoor studio-plaza on the lower level. Average Annual Attendance: 131,000. Mem: 1009; dues $10 and up, annual meeting April
Income: $512,000 (financed by city appropriation)
Purchases: $40,000
Collections: European art including English, French, German and Italian; Grant Wood; Haitian; 19th and 20th century American art; Spanish-Colonial
Exhibitions: Douglas Abdel; John Steuart Curry; L'Esprit Noir-Art Haitien; Mississippi Corridor; Native American Arts
Publications: Bulletin, quarterly; catalogs
Activities: Classes for adults and children; docent training; lect open to the public; concerts; gallery talks; tours; competitions; artmobile; traveling exhibiton organized and circulated; sales shop selling original art; junior museum called Arterarium
L **Art Reference Library,** 1737 W 12th St, 52804. *Librn* Gladys Hitchings
Open for reference
Library Holdings: Vols 6000; Per subs 17
Special Subjects: General visual arts

M **PUTNAM MUSEUM,** 1717 W 12th St, 52804. Tel 319-324-1933. *Dir* Joseph L Cartwright; *Cur of Coll* Janice Hall; *Cur of Education* Peter Petersen; *Cur of Exhibits* AnnaBelle Cartwright; *Dir of Development* Joyce Georlett; *Registrar* Carol Hunt
Open Tues - Sat 9 AM - 5 PM, Sun 1 - 5 PM, cl Mon and national holidays. Adults $1, ages 13-18 50¢, ages 5-12 25¢, no admis fee Sat 9 AM - Noon. Estab 1867 as Academy of Science. Average Annual Attendance: 150,000. Mem: 3000; dues life $500, sustaining $100, contributing $50, family $25, individual $15, senior citizen $10, youth $5
Income: $250,000
Collections: Natural History; American Indian, pre-columbian; anthropology; arts of Asia, Near and Middle East, Africa, Oceanic; botany; ethnology; paleontology
Exhibitions: Permanent and changing exhibition programs
Activities: Formally organized education programs for children and adults;.films; lect; gallery talks; guided tours
L **Library,** 1717 W 12th St, 52804.
Available for use by special request
Library Holdings: Vols 40,000

DECORAH

M **VESTERHEIM,** Norwegian-American Museum, 502 W Water St, 52101. Tel 319-382-9682. *Dir* Marion John Nelson; *Cur* Darrell Henning; *Dir in Charge of Academic Relations* John Christianson; *Textiles Cur* Lila Nelson
Open May - Oct 9 AM - 5 PM daily, Nov - Apr 10 AM - 4 PM, cl Thanksgiving, Christmas & New Years. Admis adults $2, children 75¢, (summer), adults $1.50, children 75¢ (winter). Estab 1877 for the collection, preservation and exhibition of all artifacts on the life of the people in the United States of Norwegian birth and descent, in their home environment in Norway and in their settlements in America. Numerous historic buildings, including two from Norway, make up the complex of Vesterheim. Average Annual Attendance: 30,000. Mem: 6000; dues $5; annual meeting Oct
Income: $175,000 (financed by endowment, membership, donations, admissions, sales)
Collections: Extensive collections combine those of Luther College and the Museum Corporation through house furnishings, costumes, tools and implements, church furniture, toys and the like, the Museum tells the story of the Norwegian immigrant
Exhibitions: National Rosemaling Exhibition
Publications: Newsletter, quarterly; Norrona Sketchbook; Norwegian Tracks, quarterly; Pioneer Cookbook, Time Honored Norwegian Recipes; Rosemaling Letter, quarterly; Vesterheim: Samplings from the Collection
Activities: Classes for adults; competitions; museum shop sells books, original art, prints, and slides, related gift items, woodenware, artist supplies for rosemaling
L **Library,** 502 W Water St, 52101.
Reference library open to the public
Library Holdings: Vols 800
Special Subjects: Norwegian history, culture, crafts, genealogy

DES MOINES

M **DES MOINES ART CENTER,** Greenwood Park, 50312. Tel 515-277-4405. *Dir* James T Demetrion; *Asst Dir* Peggy Patrick; *Dir of Educ* Georgeann Kudron; *Pres Bd of Trustees* Robert Lubetkin; *VPres & Treas* Arnold E Levine
Open Tues - Sat 11 AM - 5 PM, Sun Noon - 5 PM, cl Mon. No admis fee. Estab 1948 for the purpose of displaying, conserving and interpreting art. large sculpture galleries in I M Pei-designed addition; the main gallery covers 36 x 117 ft area. Average Annual Attendance: 120,100. Mem: 2859, dues $20 and up
Income: $725,000 (financed by endowment, membership, city and state appropriation)
Collections: African art and graphics †American and European sculpture and painting of the past 200 years
Exhibitions: George Bellows, Vision of America; Mrs Fred Bohen Collection; European Art - The Postwar Decade; Iowa Artists Exhibition; Jess: Translations, Salvages, Paste-ups; Northwest Coast Artists; Joseph Raffael; Synchromism and Color Abstraction; Antoni Tapies; H C Westerman: Retrospective; Art of Adolf Woelfil
Publications: Bulletin, bimonthly; annual report; catalogs of exhibitions
Activities: Classes for adults and children; docent training; lect open to members only, 6 visiting lectr per year; concerts; gallery talks; tours; competitions; traveling exhibitions organized and circulated; museum shop sells books, original art, prints, and postcards; Junior Museum
L **Library,** Greenwood Park, 50312. *Librn* Margaret Buckley
11 AM - 5 PM Tues - Sat. Estab 1948 for research for permanent collection, staff for class preparation and lectures. Open to the public for reference only
Income: $10,400
Purchases: $2000

Library Holdings: Vols 7350; Per subs 21; Other—Exhibition catalogs
Special Subjects: 20th Century Art
Collections: Pennington Collection of weaving samples

M **IOWA STATE EDUCATION ASSOCIATION,** Salisbury House, 4025 Tonawanda Drive, 50312. Tel 515-279-9711. *Exec Dir* Beverly Wolkow; *Museum Coordr* Caroline Moon; *Mgr Business Operations* C William Pritchard
Open daily 8 AM - 4:30 PM. Admis adults $1.50, 12 years and under 75¢, mini-tour 50¢. Estab 1954 as a cultural center. Gallery is maintained as a replica of King's House in Salisbury, England and contains Tudor age furniture, classic paintings, and sculpture from East and West, tapestries, Oriental rugs. Average Annual Attendance: 17,000
Income: Financed through membership and endowment
Collections: Collection of paintings by Hogarth, Raeburn, Romney, Sir T Lawrence, Van Dyck; permanent collection of tapestries by Brussels Brabant, Flemish, French Verdure; permanent collection of sculpture by Archapinko, Bordelle, Martini; permanent collection of Chinese, India and Oriental (Persian) rugs
Activities: Lect; tours; individual paintings and original objects of art lent; lending collection contains motion pictures, original art works, paintings; museum shop sells reproductions, brochures, postcards, stationery

DUBUQUE

M **DUBUQUE ART ASSOCIATION,** Old Jail Gallery, Eight & Central, 52001. Tel 319-557-1851. *Pres* C Robert Justmann
Open daily Noon - 5 PM, cl Mon. Estab 1910, incorporated 1956. Mem: Dues $6 and up; annual meeting May
Collections: Permanent collection consists of ceramics, drawings, paintings, prints and sculptures (hard and soft)
Exhibitions: Crafts show
Activities: Classes; lect; gallery talks; films; slides; new shows monthly; luncheon program Fri; yearly Art Auction

FAIRFIELD

L **FAIRFIELD PUBLIC LIBRARY AND MUSEUM,** Fairfield Art Association,* Court & Washington, 52556. Tel 515-472-6551. *Librn* James Rabis; *Chmn Museum Committee* Ben Taylor; *Chmn Art Gallery* Dr Paul Selzi
Open Mon - Fri 9 AM - 6 PM, Sat 9 AM - 1:30 PM, Winter Sun 1:30 - 4:30 PM, cl national holidays. No admis fee
Income: Library and museum financed by endowment and city appropriation; Art Association financed by endowment and membership
Library Holdings: Vols 45,000; Per subs 90
Collections: †graphics; Indian art; †paintings
Activities: Classes for adults and children; lect open to the public; competitions

FORT DODGE

M **BLANDEN MEMORIAL ART GALLERY,** 920 Third Ave S, 50501. Tel 515-573-2316. *Dir* M Jessica Rowe; *Asst Dir* Cheryl Ann Parker; *Admin Secy & Bookkeeper* Penny Sue Skeie; *Membership* Catherine Deardorf; *Security* L Nelson; *Security* A Dopita
Open Tues, Wed, Fri, Sat & Sun 1 - 5 PM, Thurs 1 - 8:30 PM, cl Mon. No admis fee. Estab 1932; houses works of art in permanent collection. Neo-Italian Renaissance architecture. Average Annual Attendance: 12,000. Mem: dues $3 - $100; annual meeting July
Income: $70,000 (financed by City & State appropriation, membership, Blanden Art Gallery Charitable Foundation)
Collections: American and European paintings and sculpture; 19th & 20th Century graphic art; 17th Century Oriental arts
Publications: Tri-monthly bulletin, BAG Charitable Foundation brochure; exhibition catalogues; annual report; membership information
Activities: Art classes and programs for children, adults, and handicapped; docent programs; museum internship program; guided tours; lectures; films; Art Appreciation program; slide programs for schools and community groups; book traveling exhibitions; Museum sales shop
L **Library,** 920 Third Ave S, 50501.
Open to public for reference only
Library Holdings: Vols 1000; Per subs 10

INDIANOLA

M **SIMPSON COLLEGE ART GALLERY,** 50125. Tel 515-961-6251. *Head Art Dept* Gaile Gallatin
Estab 1860 as a four-year liberal arts college
Collections: Creche figures from 18th century Italy; small permanent collection
Exhibitions: Student shows; visiting exhibits from Iowa Arts Council
Activities: Lect open to public, 2 visiting lectrs per year; concerts

IOWA CITY

ART LIBRARIES SOCIETY-NORTH AMERICA
For further information, see National and Regional Organizations

UNIVERSITY OF IOWA
M **Museum of Art,** Riverside Dr, 52242. Tel 319-353-3266. *Acting Dir & Cur Collections* Joann Moser; *Cur of Education* Honee Hess; *Installation Coordr* David Dennis; *Registrar* Hugo Ruiz-Avila
Open Mon - Sat 10 AM - 5 PM, Sun noon - 5 PM, cl Thanksgiving, Christmas & New Year's Day. No admis fee. Estab 1969 to collect, exhibit and preserve for the future, works of art from different cultures; to make these objects as accessible as possible to people of all ages in the state of Iowa; to assist the public, through

educational programs and publications, in interpreting these works of art and expanding their appreciation of art in general. 48,000 sq ft in 16 galleries, including a central sculpture court. Average Annual Attendance: 50,000. Mem: 780; dues family $25, individual $15, student $5; annual meeting
Income: Financed by membership, state appropriation and private donations
Collections: African and Pre-Columbian Art; Chinese and Tibetan Bronzes; Oriental Jade; 19th and 20th Century European and American paintings and sculpture; prints, drawings, photography, silver
Exhibitions: The Elliott Collection of 20th Century European paintings, silver and jade; a major collection of African sculpture and a selection of prints by Mauricio Lasansky are on permanent exhibition. Approximately 14 changing exhibitions each year, both permanent collection and traveling exhibitions
Publications: Bulletin (small magazine), biannually; Calendar (brochure), monthly; Exhibition catalogs
Activities: Docent training; lect open to the public, 8 visiting lectr per year; concerts; gallery talks; tours; works of art lent to other museums; originate traveling exhibitions; sales area selling posters, postcards and catalogs
L **Art Library,** Riverside Dr, 52242. Tel 319-353-4440. *Librn* Harlan L Sifford
Open Mon - Fri 8 AM - 5 PM, Mon - Thurs 7 - 10 PM, Sat & Sun 1 - 4 PM. Estab 1937 to support the University programs, community and state needs. Circ 32,000
Income: Financed by city appropriation
Purchases: $65,000
Library Holdings: Vols 50,000; Per subs 230; Micro—Fiche, reels; Other—Clipping files, exhibition catalogs, memorabilia, pamphlets

KEOKUK

O **KEOKUK ART CENTER,** 9 1/2 7th St, Box 862, 52632. Tel 319-524-8354. *Pres* Martha Johnstone; *VPres* Peter Wulfing; *Secy* Kathy Galles; *Treas* Tyler Tibbetts; *Dir* Tom Seabold
Open Mon - Sat 9 AM - 4 PM. No admis fee. Estab 1954 to promote art in tri-state area. Gallery maintained in Keokuk Public Library, 210 N Fifth St. Average Annual Attendance: 2000. Mem: Dues sustaining $50, patron$25, family $12, individual $6, student $2; annual meeting first Mon in May
Income: $20,000
Collections: Paintings, sculpture
Exhibitions: Two per month, run for three weeks, all media
Publications: Newsletter, quarterly
Activities: Classes for adults and children; lect open to the public; gallery talks; competitions

LEMARS

M **WESTMAR COLLEGE,** Weidler Art Gallery, 51031. Tel 319-546-7081, Ext 231. *Dir* Laurel Nelson
Open daily 8 AM - 5:30 PM; inactive during summer. No admis fee. Estab 1973. The purpose of the gallery is to provide a forum for cultivating the sensitivity of our student body and the community to a variety of visual arts through a regular schedule of art exhibits. Gallery covers 2000 sq ft floor space, 170 linear feet of display space, with track lighting. Average Annual Attendance: 7500
Income: Financed by endowment, college appropriation and private gifts
Publications: Westmar College Fine Arts Schedule of Events
Activities: Lect open to the public, 1-3 vis lectr per yr; tours
L **Mock Library,** 51031. *Librn* Robert Yontz
Open to students
Library Holdings: Vols 1600; Per subs 9; AV—Slides

MARSHALLTOWN

O **CENTRAL IOWA ART ASSOCIATION, INC,** Fisher Community Center, 50158. Tel 515-753-9013. *Pres* Diana DuBois; *Secy* Flo Patterson
Open 1 - 4 PM. Inc 1959. Average Annual Attendance: 30,000. Mem: 600; dues student $5, individual $7.50; annual meeting May
Collections: Fisher Collection—Utrillo, Cassatt, Sisley, Vuillard, Monet, Degas, Signac, Le Gourge, Vlaminck and Monticelli; sculpture—Christian Petersen, Rominelli, Bourdelle; ceramic study collection—Gilhooly, Arneson, Nagle, Kottler, Babu, Geraedts, Boxem, Leach, Voulkos; traditional Japanese wares
Exhibitions: Monthly exhibits beginning the first Sun of the month and open weekdays thereafter
Activities: Classes for adults and children in ceramics, sculpture, jewelry, painting; gallery talks
L **Art Reference Library,** Fisher Community Center, 50158.
For reference only

MASON CITY

M **CHARLES H MACNIDER MUSEUM,** 303 Second St SE, 50401. Tel 515-423-9563. *Dir* Richard E Leet; *Dir Education & Special Programs* Robert C Christensen
Open Tues & Thurs 10 AM - 9 PM; Wed, Fri, Sat 10 AM - 5 PM; cl Mon & holidays. No admis fee. Estab 1964, opened 1966 to provide experience in the arts through development of a permanent collection, through scheduling of temporary exhibitions, through the offering of classes and art instruction, through special programs in film, music and other areas of the performing arts. The museum was estab in an English-Tudor style of brick and tile. It is located in a scenic setting, 2 1 2 blocks from the main thoroughfare of Mason City. Gallery lighting and neutral backgrounds provide a good environment for exhibitions. Average Annual Attendance: Over 28,000. Mem: 730; dues from contributions $3 - $100 or more
Income: $165,000 (financed by membership and city appropriation)
Collections: Permanent collection being developed with an emphasis on American art, with some representation of Iowa art; contains paintings, prints, pottery; artists represented include Baziotes, Benton, Burchfield, Burford, Davies, Dove, Francis, Graves, Healy, Lasansky, Levine, Maurer, Metcalf and Oliveira
Exhibitions: American View - American Paintings; Annual Area Competitive

Show; Annual Iowa Crafts Competition; Art of the Puppet by Bil Baird; John Flannanan: Sculpture and Works on Paper; Gund Collection of Western Art; Magic Carpets - Rugs of the Orient; Weathervanes, Carvings and Quilts, from the Chase-Manhattan Bank
Publications: Newsletter, monthly; occasional exhibit fliers or catalogs
Activities: Classes for adults and children; docent training; seminars and workshops; lect open to public, 2-4 vis lectr per yr; concerts; gallery talks; tours; competitions; individual paintings and original objects of art lent to other museums and art centers; museum shop selling original art
L **Library,** 303 Second St SE, 50401.
Reference library with the structure of the museum. For reference only
Library Holdings: Vols 500; Per subs 24; AV—Slides
Special Subjects: American art

L **MASON CITY PUBLIC LIBRARY,** 225 Second St SE, 50401. Tel 515-423-7552. *Dir* Steve Rogge; *Reference* Jean Casey; *Childrens Room* Lisa Hoyman; *Young Adult* Judy Werner
Open Mon - Thurs 9 AM - 9 PM; Fri & Sat 9 AM - 5 PM; Sun 1 - 5 PM. Estab 1869 to service public in providing reading material and information. Circ 167,509. Gallery maintained in auditorium
Income: $268,648 (financed by city, county appropriation and Federal Reserve Sharings)
Purchases: $39,110
Library Holdings: Vols 127,146; Micro—Reels; AV—Cassettes, fs, motion pictures, rec; Other—Clipping files, framed reproductions, prints, original art works, pamphlets, original documents
Collections: Permanent collection of regional artists; signed letters of authors
Exhibitions: (1978) Permanent Collection; Burington (painting); Chicken Coop Gang; Hanes & Wagnor (mixed media); Losterbour (watercolor); New Reproductions; Northern Iowa Artists League; Polster (stitchery); Schuler (painting); Timmeracle (graphics); Youth Art Month; (1980) Joe Bittner (oil portraits); Jan Bowman (needlecraft); Larry Gregson (painting); Howard Hof and Ken McClemmons (painting); Pearl Krager (paintings); Josephine Olsen (painting); Fred Peterson (ceramics); Mike Sharp (painting); Mary Siberell (watercolor); Terry Vlademar (wild-life works)

MOUNT VERNON

M **CORNELL COLLEGE,** Armstrong Gallery, 52314. Tel 319-895-8811. *Dir Gallery & Chmn Dept of Art* Hank Lifson
Open Mon - Fri 7:30 AM - 4:30 PM. Estab to display artists work
Income: Financed by Cornell College
Collections: Thomas Nast Drawings and Prints; Sonnenschein Collection of 57 European Drawings of the 15th - 17th century
Exhibitions: Four exhibits per yr plus 10-20 student thesis shows
Activities: Lect open to public, 1 vis lectr per yr

MUSCATINE

M **MUSCATINE ART CENTER,** (Formerly Laura Musser Art Gallery and Museum) 1314 Mulberry Ave, 52761. Tel 319-263-8282. *Dir* Linda Dagel
Open Tues - Fri 11 AM - 5 PM, Sat & Sun 1 - 5 PM, Thurs Eve 7 - 9 PM, cl Mon and legal holidays. No admis fee. Estab 1965. Mem: Dues, single $5, family $10, sustaining $25, life $100
Income: Financed by city appropriation
Collections: African Collection; Civil War Collection; Muscatine History; Button Collection; Paperweight Collection; decorative arts, graphics, paintings
Publications: Newsletter, quarterly; catalogs
Activities: Classes for children and adults; lectures; gallery talks; guided tours; concerts; films; book traveling exhibitions; Sales shop
L **Library,** 1314 Mulberry Ave, 52761.
Library Holdings: Vols 300

ORANGE CITY

M **NORTHWESTERN COLLEGE,** Ramaker Library Art Gallery, 101 Seventh St SW, 51041. Tel 712-737-4904. *Exhib Coordr* Rein Van Derhill; *Coll Coordr* John Kaericher
Open Mon - Fri 8 AM - 5 PM. No admis fee. Estab 1968 to promote the visual arts in northwest Iowa and to function as a learning resource for the college and community. College art gallery for traveling exhibitions, Local artists are sometimes invited. Average Annual Attendance: approx 2000
Collections: Approx 75 original works of art: etchings, woodcuts, serigraphs, lithographs, mezzotints, paintings, sculpture and ceramics by modern and old masters of Western World and Japan
Exhibitions: Contemporary American Artists Series; student and faculty shows
Activities: Classes for adults; lect open to the public, 2 - 3 vis lectr per yr; gallery talks; competitions; individual prints and original objects of art lent to schools and libraries
L **Library,** 101 Seventh St SW, 51041. *Librn* Arthur Hielkema

SIOUX CITY

M **BRIAR CLIFF COLLEGE,** Gallery 147, 3303 Rebecca St, 51104. Tel 712-279-5321, Ext 452. *Chmn Dept Art* William Welu
Open all week 9 AM - 5 PM. Estab 1971 as a working gallery for students and staff. One room gallery
Exhibitions: Student Work
Activities: Educ dept
L **Library,** 3303 Rebecca St, 51104. *Librn* Sr Mary Joanice
Open to students

O SIOUX CITY ART CENTER, 513 Nebraska St, 51101. Tel 712-279-6272. *Pres* Dr Al Blenderman; *VPres* Robert Anderson; *Dir* Bruce Bienemann; *Asst Dir* Tom Butler; *Educ Coordr* Dianne Mumm; *Secy* Cetta Blair; *Mem Secy* Marilyn Laufer; *Cur* Ernest Ricehill Jr
Open Tues - Sat 10 AM - 5 PM, Sun 1 - 5 PM, Mon 5 - 9:30 PM, cl holidays. No admis fee. Estab 1938 to provide art experiences to the general public. Gallery is 3 floors of exhibitions consisting mainly of artists from the midwest regional area; includes a photogallery. Average Annual Attendance: 30,000. Mem: 509; dues $5 - $250; monthly meetings
Income: Financed by membership, city and state appropriation
Collections: Permanent collectionof over 400 works; consists mainly of regional artists
Activities: Classes for adults and children; docent training; lect open to public, 6 vis lectr per yr: gallery talks, tours; competitions; Annual Fall Show with Purchase Award; scholarships; traveling exhibitions organized and circulated; sales shop sells original art

WATERLOO

O WATERLOO ART ASSOCIATION, 420 W 11th St, 56702. Tel 319-232-1984. *Pres* James L Smith; *VPres* Ginny Nutt; *Secy* Sue Davis; *Gallery Dir* Edna Reeck; *Dir Exhib* Doris Frandsen
Open Wed 10 AM - 4:30 PM, Sat & Sun 2 - 4 PM. No admis fee. Estab 1960 to encourage area artists and provide for the exhibition of their work. Gallery is maintained in a rented building providing three gallery rooms, workshop, art supply sales room and storage. Average Annual Attendance: 1200. Mem: 175; dues $10; annual meeting last Tues Jan
Income: $4000 (financed by membership)
Collections: Small collection of work by former members
Exhibitions: Amateur Iowa Artists Regional Show; Black Hawk County Art Show; Monthly exhibits by area professionals
Publications: Bulletin published six times a yr
Activities: Lectr open to the public, 2 vis lectr per yr; gallery talks; competitions; sales and rental gallery for members; sales shop sells original art and art supplies

M WATERLOO MUNICIPAL GALLERIES, 225 Cedar St, 50704. Tel 319-291-4491. *Gallery Dir* Clarence Alling
Open Mon - Fri 9 AM - 5 PM; Sat 9 - Noon; Sun 2 - 5 PM. No admis fee. Estab 1957 to provide an art forum for the Waterloo area. Average Annual Attendance: 35,000, plus junior museum attendance of 16,000. Mem: 500; dues single $3 and up; annual meeting second Thurs of Jan
Collections: Small new collection of contemporary American paintings, prints and sculpture
Exhibitions: Monthly exhibitions of regional painting, sculpture, prints and fine crafts
Activities: Classes for adults and children; dramatic programs; lect open to the public; gallery talks; competitions; junior museum

WEST BRANCH

L HERBERT HOOVER PRESIDENTIAL LIBRARY, 234 S Downey, 52358. Tel 319-643-5301.
Open May - Labor Day Mon - Sat 9 AM - 6 PM, Sun 10 AM - 6 PM, Sept - April Mon - Sat 9 AM - 5 PM, Sun Noon - 5 PM. Estab 1962 as a research center to service the papers of Herbert Hoover and other related manuscript collections; a museum to exhibit memorabilia from Herbert Hoover's 90 years of life and accomplishments
Income: $309,000 (financed by federal appropriation)
Library Holdings: Vols 22,000; Per subs 67; Micro—Reels; AV—A-tapes, motion pictures, rec, slides; Other—Clipping files, manuscripts, memorabilia, pamphlets, original documents, still photographs
Collections: 64 Chinese porcelains; oil paintings; 190 Original Editorial Cartoons; 340 posters; 26 World War I Food Administration; 464 World War I Painted and Embroidered Flour Sacks

KANSAS

ABILENE

L DWIGHT D EISENHOWER PRESIDENTIAL LIBRARY, 67510. Tel 913-263-4751. *Dir* Dr John E Wickman; *Museum Cur* Dennis Medina
Open daily 9 AM - 5 PM, cl Thanksgiving, Christmas Day, New Year's Day. Admis 75¢, children accompanied by parents free. Estab 1962 as library, in 1954 as museum. Average Annual Attendance: 400,000
Income: Financed by Federal Government appropriation
Library Holdings: Vols 23,000; Other—Prints 75,000
Collections: Research Library and Museum contains papers of Dwight D Eisenhower and his associates, together with items of historical interest connected with the Eisenhower Family. Mementos and gifts of General Dwight D Eisenhower both before, during, and after his term as President of the United States

ATCHISON

M MUCHNIC FOUNDATION AND ATCHISON ART ASSOCIATION, Muchnic Gallery, 704 N Fourth St, Box 12, Route 2, 66002. Tel 913-367-1317. *Cur* Mrs Pennell Snowden
Open weekends 1 - 5 PM. No admis fee. Estab 1970 to show a 19th century home and furnishings. Gallery comprised of four rooms is maintained for visiting artists shows and occasional senior exhibits from Benedictine College students. Average Annual Attendance: 1000. Mem: Monthly meeting, first Tues Sept - May
Income: Financed by Muchnic Foundation membership
Purchases: $7000 (1979)
Collections: †Paintings by regional artists: Don Andorer; Thomas Hart Benton; John Stuart Curry; Raymond Eastwood; John Falter; Jim Hamil; Wilbur Niewald; Jack O'Hara; Roger Shimomura; Robert Sudlow; Grant Wood; Jamie Wyeth; Walter Yost
Exhibitions: Christmas Exhibition; exhibitions two weekends per month, Sept - May
Activities: Lect open to the public; gallery talks; tours; book traveling exhibitions, annually; sales shop sells original art

COLBY

M COLBY COMMUNITY COLLEGE, Northwest Kansas Cultural Arts Center, 1255 S Range, 67701. Tel 913-462-3984. *Mgr Cultural Arts Center* Brian Foster
Open Mon - Fri 9 AM - 5 PM, other for special showings. Large secure gallery and small open gallery, small glass display cases. Average Annual Attendance: 10,000
Income: Financed by college general fund
Collections: Permanent collections of student two dimensional work
Exhibitions: (1978-79) Kansas University Traveling Museum Thomas Moran Selling the West—Yellowstone from Mid America Arts Alliance and the Jefferson National Expansion Historical Association National Cone Box III Traveling Show Rocky Mountain Weavers Guild Annual Childrens Exhibit; Annual Graduate Show; Annual High School Show; local artists exhibits
Activities: Lect open to public, 2 vis lectr per yr; gallery talks; tours; competitions; individual paintings lent

L H F Davis Memorial Library, 1255 S Range, 67701. *Dir* Ruth Lowenthal
Mon - Thurs 8 AM - 9 PM, Fri 8 AM - 4 PM, Sat 8 AM - Noon
Library Holdings: Micro—Cards, fiche, reels, prints; AV—A-tapes, cassettes, fs, rec, slides; Other—Clipping files, framed reproductions, prints, original art works, pamphlets, reproductions, sculpture

ELLSWORTH

M ROGERS HOUSE MUSEUM GALLERY, Snake Row, 67439. Tel 914-472-3255. *Dir* Charles B Rogers
Open Mon - Sat 10 AM - 5 PM, Sun & holidays 1 - 5, cl Christmas. Adults 50¢, children 6-12 25¢. Estab 1968 in a historic cowboy hotel
Collections: Original paintings, prints; miscellaneous art
Exhibitions: Traveling exhibitions
Publications: Country Neighbor; The Great West; Quill of the Kansan (books)
Activities: Sales shop sells original paintings and prints

HAYS

M FORT HAYS STATE UNIVERSITY, Visual Arts Center, 67601. Tel 913-628-4247. *Dir of Exhib* Zoran Stevanov; *Chmn Art Dept* John C Thorns Jr
Open Mon - Fri 8 AM - 5 PM, weekends on special occasions. No admis fee. Estab 1953 to provide constant changing exhibitions for the benefit of students, faculty and other interested people in an education situation. A new gallery is being constructed with 2200 sq ft plus adequate storage
Income: Financed by state appropriation
Purchases: $2000
Collections: Vyvyan Blackford Collection; †Contemporary Prints; †National Exhibition of Small Paintings, Prints and drawings; Regionalist Collection (1930s)
Exhibitions: (1979-80) Art & Fantasy, Dr. Caligari Festival; Jim Estes, Sculptor; Young American Printmakers, Pratt Art Graduate Thesis Shows; Annual Faculty Exhibition; Annual Undergraduate Exhibition; Annual High School Exhibition & Art Conference; Annual Smoky Hill (State) Exhibition; Kansas Fifth National Small Paintings, Drawings & Prints Show
Publications: Exhibitions brochures; Art Calendar, annually
Activities: Lectr open to public, 4 vis lectr per yr; gallery talks; tours; competitions; Exten dept serving western Kansas; individual paintings and original objects of art lent to individuals, organizations and institutions; lending collection of original art works and prints, paintings, sculpture and slides; traveling exhibitions organized and circulated

HUTCHINSON

O HUTCHINSON ART ASSOCIATION, 1520 North Main, 67501. *Pres* Marvel Senti; *VPres* Del Kaaver; *Dir of Gallery* Edith M Symns; *Treas* Louise Zink; *Secy* Lucille Glynn
Estab 1949 to bring exhibitions to the city of Hutchinson and maintain a permanent collection in the public schools. Mem: 125; dues $5 and up
Collections: Permanent collection of watercolors, prints, and oils circulated in the public schools
Exhibitions: Includes an all-member show
Activities: Annual Art Fair with prizes

INDEPENDENCE

O **LADIES LIBRARY AND ART ASSOCIATION,** Independence Museum, 123 N Eighth, 67301. Tel 316-331-3515. *Pres* Mrs Earl B Myers Jr
Open Wed, Sat & Sun 1 - 4:30 PM. Admis 25¢. Inc 1882 to provide library facilities and the secure an art collection for the community. The museum has a large gallery which contains original paintings; Indian art and artifacts; Mexican Room, late 1800 and early 1900 costume room, country store, War and Peace Room, presently establishing an historical oil room with the assistance of Arco Pipeline Company.
Mem: 150; dues $5 - $25; meetings monthly Oct - May
Income: Financed by membership, bequests, gifts, art exhibits and various projects
Collections: William Inge Memorabilia Collection; Oriental Collection
Exhibitions: Annual Art Exhibit; Annual Arts and Crafts Fair; Photography Shows; various artists and craftsmen exhibits
Activities: Competitions with awards

LAWRENCE

M **SPENCER MUSEUM OF ART,** The University of Kansas, 66045. Tel 913-864-4710. *Dir* Dr Charles C Eldredge; *Asst Dir Admin* Douglas Tilghman; *Cur Western Art* Douglas Hyland; *Cur Prints & Drawings* Dr Elizabeth Broun; *Cur Photography* Thomas Southall; *Dir Educ* Dolores Brooking; *Research Cur* Dr Marilyn Stokstad; *Registrar* Janet Dreiling; *Exhib Designer* Mark Roeyer; *Publishing Editor* Ruth Lawner; *Membership* Ann Wiklund; *Public Service* Sally Hoffmann; *Public Relations* Carol Shankel
Open Tues - Sat 9:30 - 4:30, Sun 1 - 4:30, cl Mon. No admis fee. Dedicated in Spooner Hall 1928, Spencer dedicated 1978. The Museum has traditionally served as a laboratory for the visual arts, supporting curricular study in the arts. Primary emphasis is placed on acquisitions and publications, with a regular schedulte of changing exhibitions. Museum has a two level Central Court, seven galleries devoted to the permanent collections, and three galleries for temporary exhibitions; altogether affording 29,000 sq ft. Mem: 800; dues $25
Income: Financed by endowment, membership, state appropriation and grants
Collections: †American Paintings; †ancient art; †graphics; †Medieval art; †17th and 18th Century art, especially German; †19th century European and American art; †Oriental art; †20th Century European and American Art
Exhibitions: Artists Look at Art; Chinese Paintings from the Sackler Collection; Court House Photographs; Jim Dine: New Drawings; The Dyer's Art; The Hidden World of Misericords; Obaku; Paintings by Hung Hsien; The Photograph as Artifice; Photographs from the Collection; Prints from the Collection; Quilts from the Collection; Reverse Painting on Glass; Second View: A Rephotographic Survey; Zen Painting & Calligraphy
Publications: The Register of the Spencer Museum of Art, annually; Calendar, bimonthly
Activities: Classes for children, docent training; lect open to the public, 24 vis lectr per yr; concerts; gallery talks; tours; traveling exhibitions organized and circulated; museum shop sells books, magazines and postcards

L **Art Library,** University of Kansas, 66045. *Librn* Paul Bobo
Mon - Thurs 8 AM - Midnight, Fri 8 AM - 10 PM, Sat 9 AM - 5 PM, Sun noon - midnight. Estab 1970 to support academic programs and for research. Open to faculty, students and public
Library Holdings: Vols 40,000; Per subs 700; Micro—Fiche, reels; AV—Slides; Other—Clipping files, exhibition catalogs, pamphlets, photographs
Special Subjects: Oriental Art, Photography

LINDSBORG

BETHANY COLLEGE
M **Birger Sandzen Memorial Gallery,** 401 N First St, 67456. Tel 913-227-2220. *Co Dir* Dr C P Greenough III; *Co Dir* Carl William Peterson
Open Wed - Sun 1 - 5 PM, cl Mon & Tues. Admis adults 50¢, grade and high school students 25¢. Estab 1957 to permanently exhibit the paintings and prints by the late Birger Sandzen, teacher at Bethany College for 52 years. Ten exhibition areas. Average Annual Attendance: 7000 - 9000. Mem: 350; dues $5 - $100; annual meeting April for Board of Directors
Income: Financed by admission fees, sales and membership
Collections: Poor, Raymer, Sandzen
Exhibitions: (1978-79) Glass by Vernon Brejcha; engravings by Evan Lindquist; graphics by National Association of Women ARtists; Paintings by Salvador Estradas, Ken Shen Huang, Albert Krehbiel, Tim Saska; Kansas Painters West Exhibit; Little People Paintings by Lucille Dunn; Photography by Jim Turner; Wall Sculpture by Carl Queen
Publications: The Graphic Work of Birger Sandzen
Activities: Lect open to the public; concerts; gallery talks; tours; lending collection contains books, color reproductions; sales shop sells books, reproductions

L **Library,** 401 N First St, 67456.
Wed - Sun 1 - 5 PM. Estab 1957 for use by art students. For reference only
M **Mingenback Art Center,** 401 N First St, 67456. *Department Head* Daniel Mason
Materials are not for public display, for educational reference only
Exhibitions: Oil paintings, watercolors, prints, etchings, lithographs, wood engravings, ceramics and sculpture

MANHATTAN

L **KANSAS STATE UNIVERSITY,** Paul Weigel Library, College of Architecture and Design, 66506. Tel 913-532-5968. *Dir* Dorothy Leonard; *Asst Dir* Patricia Weisenburger
Open Mon - Thurs 8 AM - 10 PM, Fri 8 AM - 5 PM, Sat 10 AM - 2 PM, Sun 2 - 10 PM. Estab 1917. Circ 31,200
Income: $12,500 (financed by state appropriations and gifts)
Library Holdings: Vols 24,500; Per subs 190
Special Subjects: Architecture, Landscape Architecture, Pre-Design Professions, Interior Architecture, Community and Regional Planning

MCPHERSON

M **MCPHERSON COLLEGE,** Friendship Hall, 1600 E Euclid, 67460. Tel 316-241-0731. *Chmn Art Dept* Mary Ann Robinson
Open Mon - Fri 8 AM - 10 PM. No admis fee. Estab 1960 to present works of art to the college students and to the community. a long gallery which is the entrance to an auditorium, has four showcases and 11 panels 4 x 16 ft. Average Annual Attendance: 2500
Income: Financed through College
Collections: Oils, original prints, watercolors

TOPEKA

O **ARTS COUNCIL OF TOPEKA,*** 215 SE Seventh St, 66603. Tel 316-295-3808. *Pres* Marlyn Burch; *Exec Dir* Don Lambert
Open Mon - Fri 9 AM - 5 PM. Estab 1959, an organization serving more than 70 organization members and 300 individual members in promoting the arts in Topeka.
Mem: 370; dues $10; annual meeting Mar
Income: Financed by membership and city appropriation
Publications: Newsletter, monthly
Activities: Resource fair; competitions; art contest

M **KANSAS STATE HISTORICAL SOCIETY MUSEUM,** 120 W Tenth, 66612. Tel 913-296-4782. *Museum Dir* Mark A Hunt; *Asst Museum Dir* James H Nottage; *Executive Dir* Joseph W Snell; *Cur of Art* Peter C Welsh Jr; *Cur of Decorative Art* Mary Ellen Hennessey Nottage
Open Mon - Sat 8 AM - 5 PM, Sun 1:30 - 5 PM. No admis fee. Estab 1875 to collect, preserve and interpret the historical documents and objects of Kansas history. Average Annual Attendance: 70,000. Mem: 3500; dues life $100; regular $10; annual meeting in spring and fall
Income: $350,000 (financed by endowment and state appropriation)
Collections: Regional collection for period from middle 19th Century to present, especially portraiture and political cartoons
Publications: Kansas History: Journal of the Great Plains, quarterly
Activities: Classes for children; docent training; annual film program; lect open to public; lect provided by staff to public organizations on request; tours; annual folk arts festival; originate traveling exhibitions; sales shop sells books, prints, cards, souveners and jewelry

L **Library,** 120 W Tenth, 66612. *Head Librn* Portia Albert; *Librn* Margaret Briggs
Open Mon - Fri 8 AM - 5 PM, Sat 8 AM - Noon. Estab 1875 to collect and preserve published material on Kansas and the West. Reference only
Purchases: $10,000
Library Holdings: Vols 137,000; Per subs 1200; Micro—Fiche, reels; Other—Clipping files, exhibition catalogs, pamphlets 180,000
Special Subjects: Genealogy, Indians, Kansas, Kansas biography, material culture, the West

O **TOPEKA ART GUILD,** PO Box 701, 66601. *Pres* John D Minnick
Estab 1916, inc 1936. Mem: 250; dues $1 and up
Exhibitions: Various well known artists throughout the year
Activities: Lect; demonstrations;trips and social functions

L **TOPEKA PUBLIC LIBRARY,** 1515 W Tenth St, 66604. Tel 913-233-2040, Ext 330. *Dir* James C Marvin; *Asst Dir* Tom J Muth; *Fine Arts Chmn* Robert H Daw; *Circ Dept Head* Alene Giesy; *Adult Serv Dept* Jim Rhodes; *Childrens Dept Head* Sheila Radell; *Exten Head* Dick Brown; *Tech Serv Head* Helen Spencer
Open Mon - Fri 9 AM - 9 PM; Sun in winter 2 - 6 PM. Estab 1870 to serve the city and the Northeast Kansas Library System residents with public information, both educational and recreational; to be one of the areas cultural centers through services from the unique Fine Arts Dept and Gallery of Fine Arts within the library. Circ 784,091
Income: $653,000 (financed by endowment, city appropriation)
Purchases: $72,713
Library Holdings: Vols 267,782; Per subs 497; Micro—Fiche, reels; AV—Cassettes, fs, motion pictures, rec, slides; Other—Clipping files, exhibition catalogs, framed reproductions, manuscripts, memorabilia, original art works, pamphlets, photographs, reproductions, sculpture, documents, postcards
Special Subjects: Topeka Room of Topeka artists and authors
Collections: Rare book room
Activities: Lectures open to public; concerts; gallery talks; library tours; competitions; exten dept

M **Gallery of Fine Arts,** 1515 W Tenth St, 66604. Tel 913-233-2040, Ext 26. *Dir* Larry D Peters; *Head of Maintenance Dept* Michael Kasson
Open Mon - Fri 9 AM - 9 PM, Sat 9 AM - 6 PM, Sun in winter 2 - 6 PM. No admis fee. Estab 1886 to provide exhibitions for the public and to collect and conserve works of art for future public viewing
Income: $3000 (financed by city appropriation)
Purchases: $1645
Collections: †Glass; †pottery; †paintings; †limited prints; West African art
Exhibitions: American Craftsmanship in Silver, The Samuel Kirk Collection; A Second Chance, Solomon Butcher Photographs; Jewelry of Robert Ebendorf and James Bennett; 19th Century Decorative Arts of China; Pre-Columbian Figuritive Ceramics of Mexico; Topeka Crafts Exhibition III, 1979; Topeka Craft Exhibition II, 1978; Bernard Stone, Jim Bass, L Brent Kington
Activities: Lect open to public, 1 - 3 vis lectr per yr; concerts; gallery talks; tours; competitions, juried crafts exhibition, media: jewelry, pottery, weaving, textiles, glass work, enamels and wood; lending collection contains 150 cassettes, 9000 color reproductions, 50 film strips, 1500 framed reproductions, 200 motion pictures, 700 art works, 300 original prints, 100 paintings, 3734 records, 12,000 slides, sculpture

M **WASHBURN UNIVERSITY,** Mulvane Art Center, 17th & Jewell, 66621. *Dir & Head Art Dept* R J Hunt; *Asst Dir* Edward Navone
Open 9 AM - 5 PM, Sun 2 - 5 PM, cl Sat & holidays. Estab 1924. Building gift of Margaret Mulvane: provides three galleries, studios and classrooms for Department of Art. Average Annual Attendance: 20,000. Mem: 750; dues $7.50 and up
Income: Approx $60,000

Purchases: Approx $2000
Collections: International paintings, sculpture, prints and ceramics
Exhibitions: Continuous program of exhibitions; students exhibition in May
Publications: Exhibition brochures
Activities: Classes for adults and children; popular art lectures in Topeka by staff and visiting artists; frequent gallery programs; films open to the community without charge
L **Library,** 17th & Jewell, 66621.
Library Holdings: Vols 3000

WICHITA

O **KANSAS WATERCOLOR SOCIETY,** 10414 E Harry, 67207. Tel 316-683-9346. *Pres* Barbara Bulloch; *Secy* Jean Shellito
Estab 1968 to promote watercolor in Kansas. Mem: 182; initiation dues; annual meeting
Income: Financed by membership and entry fees
Exhibitions: Annual Tri-State (Kansas, Oklahoma, Missouri) Exhibition; traveling and invitational exhibitions in Kansas
Activities: Demonstrations and workshops; lect open to the public; competitions; scholarships; materials lent; traveling exhibitions organized and circulated

O **WICHITA ART ASSOCIATION INC,** 9112 E Central, 67206. Tel 316-686-6687. *Chmn of Board* Olive Ann Beech; *Dir & Cur* John R Rouse; *Treas* John T Sheffield
Open Tues - Sun 1 - 5 PM, cl Mon, August, National holidays. No admis fee. Estab 1920, inc April 1932. Average Annual Attendance: 25,000. Mem: 1000; dues $25 and up, annual meeting May
Collections: Prints and drawings, paintings, sculpture, decorative arts and crafts
Exhibitions: Traveling exhibitions change each month; one man shows, special programs
Publications: Newsletter, monthly
Activities: Lectures; concerts; gallery talks; workshops; films; demonstrations; Sales gallery
L **Maude Schollenberger Memorial Library,** 9112 East Central, 67206. *Dir* John R Rouse
Open 1 - 5 PM daily, cl Mon. Estab 1965. For reference
Library Holdings: Vols 3000

M **WICHITA ART MUSEUM,** 619 Stackman Dr, 67203. Tel 316-268-4621. *Dir* Howard E Wooden; *Cur of Coll-Exhib* Howard D Spencer; *Admin Asst* Mary Lee Archer; *Financial Officer* Alma Gilley; *Registrar* Barbara Odevseff
Open Tues - Sat 10 AM - 4:50 PM, Sun 1 - 4:50 PM, cl Mon and holidays. No admis fee. Estab 1935 to house and exhibit art works belonging to permanent collection; to present exhibits of loaned art works, to ensure care and maintain the safety of works through security, environmental controls and appropriate curatorial functions and to interpret collections and exhibitions through formal and educational presentations. facility designed by Edward Larrabee Barnes opened Oct 1977. Average Annual Attendance: 60,000 - 75,000. Mem: Dues $2 - $1000; annual meeting May
Income: $600,000 Financed by endowment, membership, city appropriation, restricted gifts for art acquisition
Collections: Florence Naftzger Evans Collection of Porcelain and Faience Kurdian Collection Pre-Columbian Mexican Art; Roland P Murdock Collection of American Art; Gwen Houston Naftzger Collection of Boehm and Doughty Porcelain Birds; M C Naftzger Collection of Charles M Russell Paintings, Drawings and Sculpture; L S and Ida L Naftzger Collection of Prints and Drawings
Exhibitions: 5000 Years of Art from the Metropolitan Museum of Art; Annual Kansas Watercolor Society Competition; Kansas Artists Biennial; Paintings and Drawings of Mary Joan Waid
Publications: Monthly Newsletter; Catalog of Roland P Murdock Collection; exhibition brochures
Activities: Classes for children; dramatic prog; lect open to public; concerts; gallery talks; tours; competitions; individual paintings and original objects of art lent; sales shop sells books, magazines, original art, reproductions, prints, slides, also a sales-rental gallery
L **Library,** 619 Stackman Drive, 67203. *Cur of Education* Novelene Ross
Open by appointment or request. Estab 1935 to provide reference material on Museum collections
Income: $3500
Library Holdings: Vols 2000; Per subs 13; Other—Exhibition catalogs, pamphlets, auction catalogs, museum handbooks
Special Subjects: History of American Art
Collections: Gene Morse Memorial Collection Interior Decoration

L **WICHITA PUBLIC LIBRARY,** 223 S Main, 67202. Tel 316-262-0611. *Head Librn* Richard J Rademachery; *Asst Librn* Gary D Hime; *Circulation Dept Head* Virginia Dillon; *Reference Dept Head* Viola Tidemann; *Acquisitions Dept Head* Bonnie Rupe; *Art & Music Dept Head* Len Messineo Jr; *Children's Room Dept Head* Barbara Fischer; *Business & Technical Dept Head* William Hoffman; *State-Wide Film Service* Sondra Koontz; *Talking Books for the Blind* Betty Spriggs
Open Mon - Thurs 8:30 AM - 9 PM, Fri & Sat 8:30 AM - 5:30 PM, Sun 1 - 5 PM. Estab 1876 and grown to be informational center and large free public library to improve the community with educational, cultural and recreational benefits through books, recordings, films, art works and other materials. Circ 1,100,000
Income: $1,400,000 (from local taxes)
Library Holdings: Micro—Reels; AV—Motion pictures, rec; Other—Framed reproductions
Collections: Kansas Book Collection; John F Kennedy Collection; Harry Mueller Philately Book Collection; Driscoll Piracy Collection
Exhibitions: Annuals, Kansas Scholastic Art Awards Show; Best News Photographs Exhibit; Senior High School Students Spring Exhibit; Wichita Area Girl Scout Exhibit; Wichita Women Artists; plus numerous other exhibits throughout the year
Activities: Lect; tours

M **WICHITA STATE UNIVERSITY,** Edwin A Ulrich Museum of Art, McKnight Art Center - Box 46, 67208. Tel 316-689-3664. *Dir* Dr Martin H Bush; *Cur* Gary Hood; *Admin Asst* Deborah Dodge; *Asst Cur* Robert Workman; *Asst Cur* Gary Buettgenbach
Open Wed 9:30 AM - 8 PM, Thur & Fri 9:30 AM - 5 PM, Sat, Sun & holidays 1 - 5 PM. No admis fee. Estab 1974 to provide exhibitions of major artists for the benefit of the university and community by accepting and putting together traveling shows and to build and exhibit a permanent collection of outstanding quality. A 6000 sq ft main gallery has movable walls that can be changed to accomodate different exhibitions
Income: Financed by endowment
Collections: The Outdoor Sculpture Collection of 22 pieces featuring a 28 by 52 ft mosaic mural designed by Joan Miro; The Permanent Collection, with emphasis on 20th Century American and European artwork; Ulrich Collection of Frederick J Waugh paintings; collection of prints by Honore Daumier, Albrecht Altdorfer, Harry Sternberg, Anthony van Dyck; collections of sculpture by Ernest Trova and Charles Grafly
Exhibitions: Milton Avery (paintings, drawings, prints), Frederic Church (paintings), John DeAndrea (sculpture) Honore Daumier (Prints), Alberto Giacometti (sculptures, drawings, prints), George Grosz (paintings, drawings, prints), Duane Hanson (sculpture), David Hockney (drawings, paintings), Andre Kertesz and France (photographs), Kathe Kollwitz (drawings and prints), Oskar Kokoschka (prints), Dorothea Lange (photographs), Henry Manguin Retrospective (paintings), Joan Miro(paintings), Robert Motherwell (paintings, prints), Moses Soyer (paintings), Joseph Presser (paintings), Realists in Hamburg (paintings), Pierre Alechinsky (prints), Joseph Cornell (box constructions), Holography: Through the Looking Glass (holograms); Georges Rouault (prints), Gustav Klimt and Egon Schiele (drawings) Abraham Walkowitz Retrospective (paintings), Antwerp's Golden Age, as well as various visiting artists
Activities: Lect open to public; concerts; gallery talks; tours by arrangement; traveling exhibits organized and circulated; sales shop sells books

WINFIELD

L **SOUTHWESTERN COLLEGE,** Memorial Library,* 100 College, 67156. Tel 316-221-4150, Ext 25, (after 5 PM & weekends 316-221-3400). *Dir* Daniel L Nutter
Open school year Mon - Thurs 8 AM - 10 PM, Fri & Sat 9 AM - 4 PM, Sun 1 - 10 PM, summer Mon - Fri 8 AM - 4 PM. Estab 1885 as a four-year Liberal Arts College. Circ 30,000
Income: $65,000 (financed by college budget)
Purchases: $40,000
Library Holdings: Vols 100,000; Per subs 500; Micro—Fiche, reels; AV—Cassettes
Collections: Arthur Covey Collection of paintings, mural sketches, etchings, lithographs, drawings and watercolors
Exhibitions: Arthur Covey Centennial Exhibit
Activities: Tours

KENTUCKY

ANCHORAGE

M **LOUISVILLE SCHOOL OF ART GALLERY,** 100 Park Rd, 42023. Tel 502-245-8836. *Dir* Bruce Yenawine; *Assoc Dir* Diana Arcadipone; *Registrar* Carolynn Stephenson
Open 9 AM - 5 PM. Estab 1909 to enrich human life and to provide for the transmission of knowledge and technique; encourage original research and inquiry; promote personal growth and experience. Located in an old, elaborately decorated space, it offers exhibitions of local and nationally-known artists
Income: Financed by endowment, tuition and fees
Exhibitions: Contemporary art, local and nationally-known artists
Publications: Announcements; catalogs; newsletter
Activities: Classes for adults and children; summer workshops; visiting artist program; lect open to public; 12 - 15 visiting lectr per year; gallery talks; tours; competitions; annual auctions; artmobile; originate traveling exhibitions
L **Library,** 100 Park Rd, 40223. *Librn* Mary Jane Benedict
Open Mon - Thurs 9 AM - 9 PM, Fri 9 AM - 5 PM, Sat 10 AM - 2 PM. Estab 1909 to support the curriculum and to stimulate a continuous interest in learning
Income: $6000
Purchases: $6000
Library Holdings: Vols 7458; Per subs 63; AV—Slides; Other—Clipping files, exhibition catalogs, prints, pamphlets
Special Subjects: Decorative Arts
Collections: History of arts in Louisville; textile arts

BEREA

M **BEREA COLLEGE,** Art Department Gallery, 40404. Tel 606-986-9341, Ext 292. *Chmn Art Dept* Lester F Pross
Open Mon - Fri 8 AM - 5 PM. No admis fee. Estab 1936 for educational purposes. Three gallery areas; exhibitions change monthly; loan and rental shows, regional artists, work from Berea College collections
Income: Financed by college budget
Collections: Kress Study Collection of Renaissance art Doris Ullman photographs prints, textiles, paintings, sculpture, ceramics Asian Art
Exhibitions: (1978-80) Berea Faculty Exhbition; Joe and Margaret Cantieni; Nell Connor Here by Ron Fouts; Durer's Life of the Virgin; Robert James Foose:Twenty Years of Graphic Design; Far Eastern Ceramics from the Marsh Collection; Glass and Textiles; Greek and Roman Antiquities; Graduating Seniors; Sculpture by Malcolm Gimse; Photographs by Larry Hunsucker; Photographs by Gerry Munoff; Photographs by Doris Ullman; Drawings by Tom Walsh; international Year of the Child; Islamic Art; Contemporary Color, Four Photographers; Arts from India;

Nigerian Textiles and Crafts; Selections from the Department Collections; Southeastern Crafts; Renaissance and Baroque Textiles
Activities: Education Dept; lect open to the public, 3 - 4 vis lectr per yr; gallery talks; competitions; regional drawing; textiles; individual paintings and original objects of art lent to other colleges, museums, and galleries; lending collection contains 400 framed reproductions
L **Art Department Library,** 40404.
Open Mon - Fri 8 AM - 5 PM. Estab 1936. Reference Library only
Income: Financed by college budget
Purchases: $1000 annually
Library Holdings: Vols 2500; Per subs 30; AV—Fs, Kodachromes, lantern slides, rec, slides; Other—Clipping files, exhibition catalogs, framed reproductions, prints, manuscripts, memorabilia, original art works, pamphlets, photographs, reproductions, sculpture

O **KENTUCKY GUILD OF ARTISTS AND CRAFTSMEN INC,** 213 Chestnut St, PO Box 291, 40403. Tel 606-986-3192. *Executive Dir* Garny Barker; *Admin Asst & Secy* Maggie Rifai
Open Mon - Sat 8 AM - 5 PM. No admis fee. Estab 1961 for the pursuit of excellence in the arts and crafts and to encourage the public appreciation thereof. Maintains an art gallery. Mem: 500; must be a Kentucky resident and be juried for exhibiting status; dues individual $7.50; annual meeting Nov
Income: $250,000 (financed by endowment and state appropriation, sales and admissions)
Collections: Two annual Fairs include a Members Exhibit, Holiday Market
Publications: The Guild Record, 7 times per yr
Activities: Classes for adults; docent training; workshops; lect open to public; competitions; traveling exhibitions organized and circulated; Sales shop sells original art, prints, slides and crafts

BOWLING GREEN

WESTERN KENTUCKY UNIVERSITY
M **Kentucky Museum,** 42101. Tel 502-745-2592. *Cur* Bruce MacLeish; *Cur Exhib* Ira Kohn; *Public Information Officer* Anne Johnston; *Registrar* Patricia MacLeish
Open Tues - Sat 11 AM - 4 PM. No admis fee. As well as offering exhibits and programs of wide interest, the museum also serves as a research and educational resource for scholars, specialists, and academic units of the University. The museum's subject area is the history and art of Kentucky, with supportive areas in American art and decorative arts, and European art. Average Annual Attendance: 10,000
Income: Financed by state appropriation and University
Exhibitions: (1980) Early American Furniture; Historic Costumes; Kentucky Artists; Main Street: Mirror of Change; Old Art Recovered
Activities: Educ programs; lect open to the public; gallery talks; tours; competitions
L **Kentucky Library,** 42101.
Open to the public for reference
Library Holdings: Vols 30,000; Per subs 35; Other—Clipping files, manuscripts, photographs, Maps, broadsides, postcards
Collections: Ellis Collection of steamboat pictures; Gerard Collection of Bowling Green Photographs; McGregor Collection of rare books; Neal Collection of Utopian materials
M **Ivan Wilson Center for Fine Arts Gallery,** Room 200, 42101. *Dir* John Warren Oakes
Open Mon - Fri 8:30 AM - 4 PM, Wed 5:30 - 8:30 PM, Sat 2 - 9 PM, Sun 2 - 5 PM. No admis fee. Estab 1973 for art exhibitions relating to university instruction and regional cultural needs. Average Annual Attendance: 12,000
Income: Financed by city appropriation
Exhibitions: First National College Student Print Invitations; 18th Annual Student Art Competition; Sam Hunt and Robert Love; Neil Peterie: Sabbatical Work; Photo 77 Graphic; Prints by Peter Milton; Selected WKU Seniors Art Exhibit; Walter Stomps: Recent Work; 10th Annual High School Art Competition; The Transforming Eye Photography by Clarence John Laughlin; Twenty-Five years of Prints by Adja Yunkers; WKU Art Faculty: Recent Work; WKU Senior Art Exhibits

FRANKFORT

M **KENTUCKY HISTORICAL SOCIETY MUSEUM,*** Broadway at Saint Clair, PO Box H, 40602. Tel 502-564-3016. *Dir* General William R Buster; *Cur Old Capitol* Willia Long; *Cur Museum* Elizabeth Perkins
Open Mon - Sat 9 AM - 4 PM, Sun 1 - 5 PM. No admis fee. Estab 1836 as a general history and art museum emphasizing the history, culture and decorative arts of the Commonwealth of Kentucky and its people. The Old Capitol Galleries located in the Old State House consist of two rooms totaling 2740 sq ft which are used by the Museum to display its fine arts exhibitions, painting, silver, furniture and sculpture. Average Annual Attendance: 90,000. Mem: 9000; dues from life $100 to individual $10
Income: $160,000 (financed by state appropriation)
Collections: Kentucky and American china, coverlets, paintings, quilts, silver, textiles
Exhibitions: Mr Audubon and Mr Bien: An early phase in American Chromolithography; Contemporary Kentucky Cabinetmakers; Pageant of the Bluegrass; Painting in Kentucky Collections 1400-1914
Activities: Lect open to public, 3-5 visiting lectrs per year; concerts; traveling exhivitions organized and circulated; museum shop selling books, prints, slides and gift items
L **Library,*** Broadway at Saint Clair, PO Box H, 40602.
Library Holdings: Vols 50,000

M **KENTUCKY STATE UNIVERSITY,** Jackson Hall Gallery, Art Department, E Main St, 40601. Tel 502-564-5995. *Gallery Coordr* Jo Leadingham; *Chmn Art Dept* Homer Allen
Open daily 1 - 4:30 PM. No admis fee. Gallery. Average Annual Attendance: 2000
Income: $2000 (financed through small grants and University appropriations)
Collections: A small permanent collection of graphic arts

Exhibitions: (1979) Annual Faculty and Student Exhibitions; Elen Lanyon: Prints and Drawings; temporary exhibitions
Activities: Lect open to the public, 4 visiting lectrs per year; competitions; scholarships; book traveling exhibitions, 2-3 per year

M **LIBERTY HALL MUSEUM,** 218 Wilkinson St, 40601. Tel 502-277-2560. *Chmn* Mary McDowell Boone; *Cur* Mrs Harvey R Bixler
Open Tues - Sat 10 AM - 5 PM, Sun 2 - 5 PM, cl Mon and holidays. Admis adults $1.50, children and students 50¢. Estab 1937 as an historic museum. A Georgian house built in 1796, named Historic Landmark in 1972
Collections: 18th century furniture; china; silver; portraits
Activities: Guided tours
L **Library,** 218 Wilkinson St, 40601.
Open to the public during scheduled hours, with supervision
Library Holdings: Vols 6000
M **Orlando Brown House** 202 Wilkinson St, 40601. Tel 502-875-4952. *Chmn* Mrs Charles W Metcalf; *Cur* Mrs Joseph Taylor
Open Tues - Sat 10 AM - 5 PM, Sun 2 - 5 PM, cl Mon and holidays. Admis adults $1.50, children 50¢. Estab 1956. Built in 1835 by architect Gilbert Shryock
Collections: Paul Sawyier paintings; original furnishings
Activities: Guided tours
L **Orlando Brown House Library,** 202 Wilkinson St, 40601.
Open to public
Library Holdings: Vols 500

HENDERSON

M **AUDUBON STATE PARK,** John James Audubon Museum, U S 41 N, PO Box 576, 42420. Tel 502-826-2247. *Supt* Marianna Buckles
Open 9 AM - 5 PM. Admis adults $1, children 12 and under 35¢. Average Annual Attendance: 12,000
Collections: John James Audubon's original paintings

HIGHLAND HEIGHTS

M **NORTHERN KENTUCKY UNIVERSITY GALLERY,** 41075. Tel 606-292-5420.
Open Mon - Fri 9 AM - 9 PM, Sat & Sun 9 AM - 5 PM. No admis fee. Estab 1968, new location 1976, to provide an arts center for the University and community area. Two galleries maintained, with glass wall; walls are covered with two layers of carpet
Purchases: $3000 (1979)
Collections: Permanent collection of Red Grooms Monumental Sculpture in Metal; Donald Judd Monumental Sculpture; earth works, other outdoor sculpture, prints, painting, photographs, folk art
Exhibitions: Student exhibitions
Publications: Bulletins, 4-5 per year
Activities: Educ Dept; lect open to the public, 5-10 visiting lectrs per year; gallery talks; competitions; scholarships; individual paintings and original objects of art lent; lending collection contains original art works, original prints, paintings, slides

LEXINGTON

M **HEADLEY-WHITNEY MUSEUM,** 4435 Old Frankfort Pike, 40511. Tel 606-255-6653. *Pres* Claude W Trapp; *VPres* William Bagby; *Secy & Operations Mgr* John McKinstry III; *Cur* Anne Gobar
Open Wed - Sun 10 AM - 5 PM. Admis adults $2, students $1, children 5 and under free. Estab 1968, for the collection and dissemination of art in central Kentucky, with emphasis on small works. Five principal galleries are maintained. Average Annual Attendance: 20,000. Mem: 200; dues $25
Income: $100,000 (financed by admissions, membership, benefits, sales)
Collections: Permanent collections of Cornelia Vanderbilt Whitney Doll Houses; European and American paintings; antique boxes, gemstones, jeweled bibelots, minerals; Oriental Porcelains; seashells
Exhibitions: (1979) Changing temporary exhibitions; Rosemary Stahl Combs: Enamels; Fleischmann Collection of Paintings, selected exhibits; The Art of Victor Hammer; McCauley-Conner Paintings; North American Indian Artifacts; Painting of George Claxton; Painting of Elli Samuelson; Claude Trapp: Jade Collection; Herman Wieck: Photography
Publications: Headley Treasure of Bibelots & Boxes (catalog of Bibelot Collection); newsletters, quarterly
Activities: Docent training; lect open to the public; tours; individual paintings and original objects of art lent; lending collection contains selected works from permanent collections by special arrangement; book traveling exhibitions; museum shop sells books, magazines, original art, reproductions, slides, shell items, jewelry, miniatures
L **Library,** 4435 Old Frankfort Pike, 40511. *Cur* Anne Gobar
Open Wed - Sun 10 AM - 5 PM. Estab 1968. For reference, research and visitors' use
Library Holdings: Vols 1400; Per subs 14; Other—Exhibition catalogs, memorabilia, original art works, pamphlets, photographs, reproductions, sculpture
Special Subjects: Goldsmithing, Oriental Art, Gemstones, minerals, seashells

O **LEXINGTON ART LEAGUE, INC,** 1517 S Limestone St, PO Box 5006, 40505. Tel 606-277-9262. *Pres* Lillian Boyer; *VPres* William McFarland; *Secy* Joan Oexmann
Open Mon - Fri 9 AM - 5 PM, 1st Sun of month 3 - 5 PM. No admis fee. Estab 1957, to engender and encourage an active interest in the creative arts among its members and the community as a whole. Average Annual Attendance: 1200. Mem: 400; dues $10; annual meeting April
Income: Approx $4000 (financed by membership, art fairs, donations)
Exhibitions: Changing monthly exhibitions; member, group, one person exhibitions
Publications: Annual Membership Book; newsletter, monthly
Activities: Demonstrations; programs; workshops; lect open to the public; competitions; awards

L **LEXINGTON PUBLIC LIBRARY,** 251 W Second St, 40507. Tel 606-254-8347. *Dir* Ronald Steensland; *Head Information Center* Rebecca Croft; *Gallery Dir* Diane Blazy
Open Mon - Thurs 9 AM - 9 PM, Fri & Sat 9 AM - 5 PM, Sun 1 - 5 PM. Estab 1798 to provide books, periodicals and audiovisual materials for the community. Circ 700,000. Gallery is maintained
Income: $1,200,000 (financed by city, state and federal appropriations)
Library Holdings: Vols 200,000; Per subs 800; Micro—Fiche, reels, prints; AV—Cassettes, fs, motion pictures, rec, slides; Other—Framed reproductions, manuscripts, original art works, photographs, sculpture
Special Subjects: Photograph Collection of early Lexington Audubon Prints
Collections: 19th century American Portraits
Exhibitions: Art, Inside & Out (Inmates); Color Work by Women; Creative Forces: Marie Ebbesen; Lexington Herald Leading Photographer: Richard Smithers; Monthly exhibits of regional artists; Multi-Media Show; Quilts Up-To-Date; Steve Tucker: Fibers
Activities: Artist in residence programs; demonstrations; lect open to the public, 50 visiting lectrs per year; concerts; gallery talks; tours; competitions; exten dept serves inmates, elderly and hospitalized

M **TRANSYLVANIA COLLEGE,** Morlan Gallery, Mitchell Fine Arts Center, 40508. Tel 606-255-6861. *Coordr* Nancy Wolsk
Open Mon - Fri 11:30 AM - 3 PM, Sun 1 - 5 PM, cl Sat
Income: Financed by endowment
Exhibitions: Debbie Fredricks; Hume Collection Textile Art; Alma Lesch Collage in Cloth - Tapestry; Terrie Mangat - Quilts and Prints; Oriental Shadow Puppets; Arturo Sandoval; Soft Sculpture and Woven Collage

UNIVERSITY OF KENTUCKY
M **Art Museum,** Center for the Arts 02410, 105 Fine Arts Bldg, 40506. Tel 606-258-5716. *Dir* Priscilla Colt; *Registrar* Robin Mitchell; *Cur* Bruce Weber; *Admin Asst* Sandi Gamlin; *Preparator* Michael Brechner; *Asst Preparator and Designer* Tom Baker
Estab 1975 to collect, preserve, exhibit and interpret world art for the benefit of the University community and the region. new building completed and opened November 1979; 20,000 sq ft of galleries and work space
Income: $140,000 (financed by state appropriation and gifts)
Collections: African; American Indian; European and American paintings, sculpture and graphics, 15th - 20th century; Oriental; Pre-Columbian
Exhibitions: Beginnings: A University Art Museum Collects
Publications: Art Museum Notes; exhibition catalogs; posters
L **Art Library,** M I King Library, North, 40506. *Librn* Mary Davis
Open to students and the general public
Library Holdings: Vols 18,644; Per subs 149

LOUISVILLE

O **ART CENTER ASSOCIATION,** The Water Tower, 3005 River Rd, 40206. Tel 502-583-6300. *Pres* Donald McClintory; *Secy* Allison Maggiolo; *Executive Dir* Robert A Gottliets; *Executive Secy* Lois Madden; *Asst Dir* Julia Bader
Open Mon - Fri 9 AM - 5 PM, Sat & Sun Noon - 5 PM. No admis fee. Estab 1907 to serve area artists and citizens. Gallery area approx 40 x 60 ft; exhibition space to open Sept 1980. Mem: 368; dues $10 - $50; monthly meeting of Board of Dir
Income: $60,000 (financed by endowment, membership, state appropriation, Greater Louisville Fund for the Arts, grants and rental of space)
Exhibitions: (1980) Aqueons 1980 (Kentucky Watercolor Society Annual Competition); History of Art Center Association: 70 Years Art; local and regional artists
Activities: Classes for children; docent training; information number program; technical assistance programs; lect open to public; competitions; annual cash prize to the Crit Club; fels; originate traveling exhibitions; sales shop sells books, original art, reproductions and prints

O **FILSON CLUB,*** 118 W Breckinridge St, 40203. Tel 502-582-3727. *Secy & Cur Manuscript* James R Bentley
Open Mon - Fri 9 AM - 5 PM, Sat 9 AM - Noon, cl Sats July - Sept and national holidays. No admis fee. Estab 1884 to collect, preserve and public historical material, especially pertaining to Kentucky. Mem: 2200; dues life $300, $15; monthly meeting Oct - June
Collections: †Books and manuscripts, family heirlooms, large collection of portraits of Kentuckians
Publications: Filson Club History Quarterly; Series 1 and Series 2 Publications (38 volumes)
L **Reference and Research Library,*** 118 W Breckinridge St, 40203. *Pres* Charles P Farnsley; *Librn* Martin F Schmidt
Library Holdings: Vols 38,000; Other—Photographs

M **JUNIOR ART GALLERY,** 301 York St, 40203. Tel 502-583-7062. *Exec Dir* Roberta L Williams
Open Mon - Sat 9 AM - 5 PM. cl Sun and holidays. No admis fee. Estab 1950 to develop understanding and appreciation of mans effort to communicate visually. The Gallery attempts to achieve this goal through exhibitions, workshops for adults and children, and special events. The Gallery is housed in the Louisvill Free Public Library. There is a 1500 sq ft exhibition area. Five or six exhibitions a year of work by professional artists. Each exhibition is planned around a theme and in context for special interest to school-age children as well as adults. Average Annual Attendance: 27,000. Mem: 81; dues $5 individual, $10 family
Income: $90,100 (Financed by membership, united arts fund, grants)
Collections: Small permanent collection consists of drawings, paintings, prints, sculptures, ceramics, photographs, textiles and other miscellaneous items
Exhibitions: Another Point of View; Close Encounters with Art and Technology; The Art of Advertising; Made to Wear Printmaking; Silkscreen on Linen
Activities: Classes for adults and children; dramatic programs; docent training; lect open to public; gallery talks; tours; staff member visits schools in area planning a visit to the gallery; lending collection contains 6000 slides

M **SOUTHERN BAPTIST SEMINARY MUSEUM,** 2825 Lexington Rd, 40206. Tel 502-897-4807. *Cur* Dr Ronald F Deering
Open Mon - Sat 9:30 AM - 10 PM, cl Sun & national holidays. No admis fee. Estab 1961
Collections: Archeology; glass; numismatics; religious materials from Caesarea, Machaerus; sculpture; textiles
Activities: Guided tours; films
L **Library,** 2825 Lexington Rd, 40206.
Open to the public and for inter-museum loan
Library Holdings: Vols 250,000; Other—Manuscripts

M **J B SPEED ART MUSEUM,** 2035 S Third St, P O Box 8345, 40208. Tel 502-637-1925. *Chmn Board of Governors* Dillman A Rash; *Pres Board Governor* W L Lyons Brown Jr; *Dir & Cur* Addison Franklin Page; *Cur Asst & Registrar* Mary E Carver; *Communications Officer* Reva Crumpler; *Technician* William E Kruetzman; *Cur Film & Photography* Scott Hammen
Open Tues - Sat 10 AM - 4 PM, Thurs 10 AM - 10 PM, Sun 2 - 6 PM. No admis fee. Estab 1925 for the collection and exhibition of works of art of all periods and cultures, supported by a full special exhibition program and educational activities. Galleries are arranged to present painting, sculpture and decorative arts of all periods and cultures; special facilities for prints and drawings. Average Annual Attendance: 108,000. Mem: 2800; dues $15; annual meeting Jan
Income: $350,000 (financed by endowment)
Purchases: $2,000,000
Collections: Comprehensive permanent collection
Exhibitions: Matthew Boulton Silver; Retrospective of Paintings by Sam Gilliam; An Auditory Environment by Joe Moss; An Exhibition for Corporate Collecting; British Watercolors: A Golden Age 1750-1850; French 19th Century Landscape Watercolors; Ruskin and Venice
Publications: Calendar, monthly; Bulletin, semiannually
Activities: Classes for children; docent training; lect open to public, 10 - 12 vis lectr per yr; concerts; gallery talks; tours; competitions; individual paintings and original objects of art lent to members; lending collection contains 200 paintings; museum shop sells books, original art, reproductions
L **Art Reference Library,** 2035 S Third St, PO Box 8345, 40208. *Librn* Frances Whitfield
Open to public
Library Holdings: Vols 12,000; Per subs 25; Other—picture files

UNIVERSITY OF LOUISVILLE
M **Allen R Hite Art Institute,** Belknap Campus, 40208. Tel 502-588-6794. *Dir* Donald P Anderson; *Secy* Dorothy Jared; *Art Librn* Gail R Gilbert
Estab 1935 for education and enrichment. Open by appointment
Income: Financed by endowment, and state appropriation
Collections: drawings; paintings; †prints
Publications: Exhibition catalogs, occasionally
Activities: Lect open to public; individual paintings lent to University offices
L **Margaret M Bridwell Art Library,** Belknap Campus, 40208. Tel 502-588-6741. *Head Art Library* Gail R Gilbert; *Asst to Art Librn* Kathleen Moore
Open Mon - Thurs 8 AM - 10 PM; Fri 8 AM - 5 PM; Sat 9 AM - 5 PM, Sun 2 - 10 PM. Estab 1956 to support the programs of the art department. For reference only
Income: Financed by endowment and state appropriation
Purchases: $36,300
Library Holdings: Vols 34,600; Per subs 210; Micro—Fiche, reels; AV—Rec; Other—Clipping files, exhibition catalogs, prints, manuscripts, memorabilia, pamphlets
Special Subjects: Photography, American Art and Architecture, German Gothic Sculpture
Collections: Original Christmas cards; original prints; posters
L **University of Louisville Photographic Archives,** 40208. *Cur* James C Anderson; *Asst Cur* David Horvath
Open Mon - Fri 8:30 AM - Noon, 1 - 5 PM. Estab 1967 to collect, preserve, organize photographs and related materials; primary emphasis on documentary photography
Income: Financed through the University
Library Holdings: Vols 500; Micro—Reels; Other—Clipping files, exhibition catalogs, photographs
Activities: Lect open to public; traveling exhibitions organized and circulated
L **Slide Collection,** 40208. Tel 502-588-5917. *Cur Slides* Ann S Coates; *Asst to Cur* Eileen Toutant
Open Mon - Fri 8:30 AM - 4:30 PM. Estab 1930's to provide comprehensive collection of slides for use in the University instructional program; 200,000 catalogued slides illustrating history of Western art. Circ 40,000
Library Holdings: AV—Kodachromes, slides; Other—Clipping files
Special Subjects: Architecture, Furniture, American Painting, Photography, Porcelain, Pottery
Collections: American Studies; Calligraphy; Manuscript of Medieval Life

MOREHEAD

M **MOREHEAD STATE UNIVERSITY,** Claypool-Young Art Gallery,* Art Dept, PO Box 714, 40351. Tel 606-783-2193. *Head Dept Art* Dr Bill R Booth
Open Mon - Fri 8 AM - 4:30 PM, Sat & Sun 1 - 4 PM, by appointment. Estab 1922 to provide undergraduate and graduate programs in studio and art education. An exhibition gallery is maintained for traveling exhibitions, faculty and student work. The Claypool-Young Art Gallery is tri-level with 2344 sq ft of exhibition space
Income: $4000 (financed by appropriation)
Collections: Establishing a permanent collection which to date consists principally of prints by major contemporary figures; several works added each year through purchase or bequest. Additions to lending collection include: The Maria Rilke Suite of lithographs by Ben Shahn consisting of 23 pieces; the Laus Pictorum Suite by Leonard Baskin, consisting of 14 pieces; and three lithographs by Thomas Hart Benton: Jesse James, Frankie and Johnny, and Huck Finn
Exhibitions: A large number of one-man exhibitions along with invitational shows and group exhibits
Activities: Lect open to the public, 5 visiting lectr per year; concerts; gallery talks; tours; competitions; individual paintings lent to schools; lending collection contains 200 items, prints, photographs; traveling exhibitions organized and circulated

L Library,* Art Dept, PO Box 714, 40351.
Library Holdings: Vols 5000

MURRAY

M MURRAY STATE UNIVERSITY, Clara M Eagle Gallery, Price Doyle Fine Arts Center, 42071. Tel 502-762-3784. *Chmn* Robert W Head; *Gallery Dir* Richard G Jackson
Open Mon - Fri 7:30 AM - 9 PM, Sat 10 AM - 4 PM, Sun 1 - 4 PM. No admis fee. Estab 1970, as an educational gallery, part of curriculum of Art Department. Gallery houses the permanent collection of the University; the Main Gallery is located on the first floor and its dimensions are 100 x 40 ft; the second floor is divided into three small galleries that may be used as one or three. Average Annual Attendance: 100,000
Income: Financed by state appropriation and grants
Collections: Asian Collection (given by Asian Cultural Exchange Foundation); Collection of Clara M Eagle Gallery; Harry L Jackson Print Collection
Exhibitions: Alumni Invitational; American Drawing II (Smithsonian); Annual Magic Silver Show; Annual Student Exhibition; Fibers Art; Kentucky Watercolor Society Show 'Aquarius II'; Metals from Southern Illinois University; Mix Master - 10 State Competition; monte Gerlach: Photography; New Faculty - Bishop, Himel, Rigsby; Painting Invitational; win Bruhl - Printmaking
Publications: Brochures and posters for individual shows
Activities: Classes for adults and children; films; visiting artists; lect open to public, 8 visiting lectr per year; gallery talks; tours; competitions; exten dept serving Jackson Purchase Area of Kentucky; individual paintings and original objects of art lent; traveling exhibitions organized and circulated

OWENSBORO

M OWENSBORO MUSEUM OF FINE ART, 901 Frederica St, 42301. Tel 502-685-3181. *Dir* Mary Bryan Hood; *Design & Exhib Dir* Robert Croy; *Educ Dir & Registrar* Jane Wilson; *Business Mgr* Mary Ellen Clark
Open Mon - Fri 10 AM - 4 PM, Sat & Sun 1 - 4 PM. No admis fee. Estab 1977. Average Annual Attendance: 31,000
Income: Financed by endowment, membership, city and state appropriations
Collections: 14th - 18th century Drawings, Graphics, Decorative Arts; 19th - 20th century American and English Paintings
Exhibitions: (1979) Abstract Paintings: Carol Berry; The Art of Cartooning: Original drawings from Jerry Muller Collection; Carson Newman University Faculty: Ceramics and Mixed Media Paintings; Christian Works of Art; Kentucky Folk Art; Kentucky Watercolor Society's 2nd Annual Juried Exhibition; Kanti Lall: Encaustic Paintings; John McNaughton: Sculptor; 19th century American and English Paintings; Rex Robinson: Watercolorist; 2nd Annual Youth Arts Exhibition; Irvin Shapiro: Watercolorist; 3rd Annual Holiday Forest; Western Kentucky University Faculty Show: Mixed Media; three one-person exhibitions by Owensboro artists
Publications: Catalogues; newsletters
Activities: Classes for adults and children; docent training; lect open to the public, 8-10 visiting lectrs per year; concerts; gallery talks; tours; competitions; awards; book traveling exhibitions; traveling exhibitions organized and circulated; museum shop sells books, original art, reproductions, prints
L Library, 901 Frederica Street, 42301.
Open Mon - Fri 10 AM - 4 PM, Sat & Sun 1 - 4 PM. Estab 1977
Library Holdings: Vols 2,000; Per subs 30; AV—Slides, v-tapes; Other—Clipping files, exhibition catalogs, manuscripts, pamphlets, photographs, reproductions

PADUCAH

O PADUCAH ART GUILD, 200 Broadway, PO Box 634, 42001. Tel 502-442-2453. *Pres* Marian Widener; *Dir* R Michael Watts; *VPres* Jerry Streetman; *Secy* Judith Milford; *Treas* T A Paxton
Open Tues - Sat Noon - 4 PM, Sun 1 - 5 PM, cl Mon & major holidays. No admis fee. Estab 1957 as a non profit cultural and educational institution to provide the community and the membership with visual art exhibitions, classes and related activities of the highest quality. Average Annual Attendance: 10,000. Mem: Monthly programs and membership meetings
Income: $12,000 (membership fees, donations, commissions, grants)
Exhibitions: Changing exhibitions of historical and contemporary art of regional, national, and international nature; Two member exhibitions and Regional Juried Craft Show held annually
Publications: Monthly Newsletter
Activities: Classes for children and adults; workshops; lectures; demonstrations; gallery talks; receptions; special fund raising events

RUSSELL

C ASHLAND OIL, INC, Ashland Dr, Russell, KY. (Mailing Add: PO Box 391, Ashland, KY 41101) Tel 606-329-3504. *Art Cur* Mary Pritchard
Collection may be viewed through special arrangement with curator. Estab 1972, primary function is decorative art, but also to establish a creative atmosphere; to enhance community cultural life. Collection displayed in public areas of corporate office buildings
Collections: Mainly contemporary printmaking, empahsis on Americans; paintings, sculpture, wall hangings
Activities: Tours; competitions, sponsorship consists of purchase awards for local art group and museum competitions; provides purchase and merit awards for certain museum and university competitions; individual objects of art lent; originate traveling exhibitions to museums, colleges, universities and art centers in general marketing areas

WILMORE

M ASBURY COLLEGE, Student Center Gallery, Lexington Ave, 40390. Tel 606-858-3511. *Head Art Dept* Dr Gilbert Roller
Open 1 - 9 PM. No admis fee. Estab 1976 for the purpose of exhibiting the works of national, local, and student artists. Carpeted walls, and tract lighting in a 20 by 20 ft space. Average Annual Attendance: 2000
Publications: Newsletter
Activities: Classes for children; dramatic programs; lect open to public, 6 vis lectr per yr; gallery talks; competitions

LOUISIANA

ALEXANDRIA

M CENTRAL LOUISIANA ART ASSOCIATION, Alexandria Museum Visual Art Center, 933 Main St, PO Box 1028, 71301. Tel 318-443-3458. *Pres* Mrs Norman Gunn; *VPres* Richard B Crowell; *Secy* Mrs Graham Kramer; *Dir* Timothy S Allen; *Chief Cur & Registrar* Steve St John; *Cur Educ* Jill McCary
Open Tues - Fri 9 AM - 5 PM, Sat 10 AM - 2 PM. No admis fee. Estab 1977, to encourage appreciation, education and active participation in art and culture; and to sponsor exhibitions. Gallery is located in an 1890's bank with 2014 sq ft of installation space, with a 20 ft ceiling and track lighting; gallery is the only facility in Central and North Louisiana for hanging exhibits of major size. Average Annual Attendance: 10,000. Mem: 550; dues Presidents Club $1000, to individual $10; annual meeting May
Income: $110,000 (financed by membership, grants, state appropriations)
Purchases: $2000
Collections: Permanent collection of art work by 20th century artists
Exhibitions: (1978) Calligraphic Paintings: Robert Berguson; Contemporary 4 - State Photo Competition; Indonesian Batiks; Pre-Columbian Artifacts. (1979) Architectural Exhibit; Bronze Sculpture: Tom Knapp; Ceramic Sculpture Invitational; Discovery I (Tactile - Visual Exhibit); Four State Biennial Thread & Fiber Competition; Invitational Water Color Exhibit; Junior League's Color Exhibit for Children; Louisiana Tech Faculty Exhibit; Mixed Media: Gregor Goethals & C Jackson Brockette; Paintings by Stuart & Mary Purser; Rope Sculpture: Bill Lockhart; 3rd Annual Juried Members Show Show. (1980) Contemporary Prints Show; Junior League Exhibit for Children; Louisiana Collegiate Fine Arts Competition; Paper Making & Paper Works; Stained Glass: Contemporary
Publications: Museum News, monthly; newsletter, quarterly
Activities: Classes for adults and chilren; docent training; workshops; demonstrations; lect open to the public, 6 visiting lectrs per year; gallery talks; tours; competitions; awards; individual paintings and original objects of art lent; lending collection contains original art works, original prints, paintings; traveling exhibitions organized and circulated; museum shop sells books, original art, reproductions, prints, crafts

BATON ROUGE

M JAY R BROUSSARD MEMORIAL GALLERIES,* Old State Capitol, Corner North Blvd & River Rd, PO Box 44247, 70804. Tel 504-342-6480. *Dir* Albert B Head; *Exhib Coordr* Charles Ford
Open Mon - Sat 10 AM - 4:30 PM, Sun 1 - 5 PM. No admis fee. Estab 1938 to promote contemporary art throughout the State. Average Annual Attendance: 85,000
Income: $30,000 (financed by state appropriation)
Purchases: $2000
Exhibitions: Amateur Artist (in Spring); Annual Competitions; International Watercolor Exhibition; Photography (in Spring); Professional Artists (in Fall)
Publications: Exhibition Catalogs

M LOUISIANA ARTS AND SCIENCE CENTER, 100 S River Rd, PO Box 3373, 70821. Tel 504-344-9463. *Pres Board Trustees* George Connor; *Dir* Mrs Allen R Brent
Open Tues - Sat 10 AM - 5 PM; cl Mon. Admis Planetarium only adults $1, children 50¢. Estab 1960. General museum - art, history and science. Center also administers a restored Historic House Museum (Old Governor's Mansion) and a restored four-car train with engine. Average Annual Attendance: 200,000. Mem: dues $2 - $250
Income: Financed by membership, city appropriation and donations
Collections: Richard Balzer (photography); Francois Brochet (sculpture); Turner Browne (photography); Lynn Lennon (photography); Ivan Mestrovic (sculpture); Eskimo Soapstone Carvings and Graphics; Graphics; North American Indian Crafts; Tibetan Religious Art
Exhibitions: Changing; permanent collection. Audio-Visual Man and the Mississippi; Country Store and Acadian House; Egyptian Mummies and Artifacts; Miniature Train, City and Railroad Memorabilia; Replica of River Boat Pilot House
Publications: Happenings, Heavenly Facts, quarterly; Newsletter; Planetarium Schedule Brochure
Activities: Docent training; workshops; school tours; lect for members only, 3 vis lectr per year; sales shop sells reproductions, handicrafts, local pottery, Eskimo carvings
L Library, 100 S River Rd, 70821.
Small reference library open to staff only

LOUISIANA STATE UNIVERSITY
M Anglo-American Art Museum, 114 Memorial Tower, 70803. Tel 504-388-40003. *Pres* Katherine H Long; *Secy* John C Fisher; *Dir* Oscar G Richard; *Cur* H Parrott Bacot
Open Mon - Fri 8 AM - Noon & 12:30 - 4:30 PM; Sat 9 AM - Noon & 1 - 4 PM;

Sun 1 - 4 PM. No admis fee. Estab 1959 to serve as a constant reminder of the major cultural heritage the United States received from the British People. Two temporary galleries house loan exhibitions and local art work. Average Annual Attendance: 25,000. Mem: 400; dues $10 - $25

Income: Financed by endowment, membership

Special Subjects: Hogarth and Caroline Durieux Graphics Collection, New Orleans Silver

Collections: Hogarth & Caroline Durieux (largest collection of graphic works); Early Baton Rouge Subjects; Early New Orleans made Silver (largest public collection); English and American Drawings, Decorative Arts, Paintings, Watercolors

Exhibitions: (1978 - 1980) Nature Painters John O'Neill and Doug Pratt; Childs Gothic Revival Print Show; First and Second Annual Contemporary Metalsmithing Show; New Orleans made Silver Exhibition; SITES Know What You See; Toys From The Attic

Publications: Catalogues; newsletter

Activities: Lect, 2 vis lectr per year; gallery talks; tours; competitions; originate traveling exhibitions

L **Anglo-American Art Museum Library,** 114 Memorial Tower, 70803.
Reference library
Library Holdings: Vols 600; Per subs 7
Special Subjects: Anglo-American decorative arts, drawings, paintings

M **Union Art Gallery,** PO Box BU, 70803. Tel 504-388-5117. *Art Dir* Judith R Stahl
Open daily 9 AM - 9 PM. Estab 1964, designed for exhibitions for university and community interests. Gallery is centrally located on the main floor of the LSU Union with 1725 sq ft. Average Annual Attendance: 55,000
Publications: Brochures for local exhibitions, quarterly
Activities: Lect open to public, 2 vis lectr per year; free art films

L **Union Art Gallery Library,** PO Box BU, 70803.
Collections: Photography Collection

M **Department of Fine Arts,** 114 Memorial Tower, 70803. Tel 504-388-5402. *Head Department* Walter E Rutkowski
Open daily 8 AM - 5 PM. No admis fee. Estab 1934 for special exhibitions planned by faculty committee. Circulates exhibitions of student's arts consisting of 30 - 40 works by students. Average Annual Attendance: 10,000
Collections: Department Collection of Contemporary Graphic Works, Prints and Drawings
Activities: Lect; gallery talks

L **SOUTHERN UNIVERSITY,** Art and Architecture Library, Southern University Post Office Branch, 70813. Tel 504-771-3290. *Librn* Doris Graham
Open Mon - Fri 8 AM - 10:45 PM. Estab 1971, to encourage support of fine arts and architecture. Circ 12,000
Income: Financed by state appropriation
Library Holdings: Vols 5200; Per subs 92; Micro—Fiche, reels; AV—Cassettes, motion pictures, slides; Other—Pamphlets

JENNINGS

M **ZIGLER MUSEUM,** 411 Clara St, 70546. Tel 318-824-0114. *Chmn Board Trustees* Mrs C A Storer; *Pres Board Trustees* Walter C Peters; *Co-Dir* Donn C Allison; *Co-Dir* Frances H Allison
Open Tues - Fri 10 AM - Noon & 2 - 5 PM; cl Mon. No admis fee. Estab 1963 to create an art gallery for Southwest Louisiana. West Wing has permanent collection of American and European paintings and sculptures. East Wing contains nine dioramas of Southwest Louisiana wild life. Central Galleries are reserved for a new art exhibit each month. Average Annual Attendance: 15,000
Collections: Bierstadt; Chierici; Constable; Crane; Gay; Heldner; George Inness Jr; Pearce; Pissarro; Reynolds; Sloan; Frank Smith; Vergne; Whistler; Gustave Wolff; Robert Wood; Sculpture: Euphemia Glover; Charles Parks
Exhibitions: Twenty-four Louisiana Artists
Publications: Brochure
Activities: Docent training, art appreciation

LAFAYETTE

UNIVERSITY OF SOUTHWESTERN LOUISIANA

M **Art Center for Southwestern Louisiana,** PO Drawer 4-4290, University of Southwestern Louisiana Station, 70504. Tel 318-232-1169. *Dir* Frances Love; *Dir Foundation* Nancy Porter Johnson; *Pres Foundation* J Rayburn Bertrand; *Special Projects* Claudia Trevithick; *Secy* Marguerite Landry
Open Mon - Fri 10 AM - 5 PM, Sun 2 - 5 PM, cl Sat. No admis fee. Estab 1968 as an art museum, for education and entertainment. First floor; permanent collection. Average Annual Attendance: 25,000. Mem: 1500; dues $400 - $25
Collections: †American Slag Glass; †ceramics and sculpture; †Hand engraved silver, bronze and copper intaglios; Paintings by 19th & 20th century American artists
Exhibitions: America Through European Eyes: the Graphic Image; Haiti: Voodoo Art; Victorian Decorative Arts in Louisiana (1837-1901)
Publications: Newsletter, every other month; major catalogs, one or two a year
Activities: Classes for adults and children; docent training; lectures open to the public, 25 - 50 visiting lecturers per year; concerts; gallery talks; tours; competitions; extension department serving Lafayette parish schools; individual paintings and original objects of art lent; traveling exhibitions organized and circulated; museum shop sells books, original art, prints, catalogs and postcards

M **Union Art Gallery,** PO Box 4-2611, 70504. Tel 318-233-3850, Ext 779. *Dir Student Union* Glenn Menaro; *Dir Programming* Julie Calzand; *Program Advisor* Martha Hoover; *Program Advisor* Earnie Dannials; *Craftshop Dir* Michael Flaherty
Open Mon - Fri 10 Am - 4 PM and by appointment. No admis fee. Estab 1970 to expose the area and the campus to new ideas through the arts. The gallery has 1500 sq ft of floor area and 153 running feet of wall space. Average Annual Attendance: 12,000
Exhibitions: Lee J Sonniel; Dutch Kepler; Allan Jones; Annual Faculty Show; Biannual Student Show; Tom Secrest; Herman M Hire; Charles Richardson; Gene Koss; David Wortman; Julie Pacaro; David Fox; The Graphics Group
Publications: Gallery schedule, each semester

Activities: Classes for adults and children; lectures open to the public; sales shop sells books, magazines and reproductions; junior museum

L **Art Center Library,** PO Drawer 44290, 70505. *Librn* Kathleen Crain
Open Mon - Fri 10 AM - 5 PM, Sun 2 - 5 PM, cl Sat. Estab 1979 to provide art information, still in formative stage. For reference only
Library Holdings: AV—A-tapes, cassettes, fs, lantern Slides, motion pictures, slides; Other—Clipping files, exhibition catalogs, pamphlets, photographs, reproductions, sculpture
Special Subjects: Louisiana and Acadiana artists and craftsmen

LAKE CHARLES

M **IMPERIAL CALCASIEU MUSEUM,** 204 W Sallier St, 70601. Tel 318-439-3797. *Dir* Amy S Boyd
Open Mon - Fri 10 AM - Noon & 2 - 5 PM, Sun 2 - 5 PM. No admis fee. Estab March 1963 by the Junior League of Lake Charles and housed in City Hall. After several moves in location, the museum is now housed in a building of Louisiana Colonial architecture which incorporates in its structure old bricks, beams, balustrades, and columns taken from demolished old homes. In December 1966 administration was assumed by The Fine Arts Center and Museum of Old Imperial Calcasieu Museum, Inc, with a name change in 1971. Site of the building was chosen for its historic value, having been owned by the Charles Sallier family, the first white settler on the lake, and the town named for him. The museum depicts the early history of the area. Average Annual Attendance: 10,000
Income: Financed by membership
Exhibitions: Exhibits depict typical rooms of early era; special exhibitions four times a year, with smaller exhibits by other organizations at times
Activities: Classes for children; tours; lending collection contains original prints; museum shop selling books and museum stationery

L **Gibson Library,** 204 W Sallier St, 70601.
Open Mon - Fri 10 AM - Noon & 2 - 5 PM, Sun 2 - 5 PM. Estab 1971, to display early school books, bibles, etc. for viewing in closed glass cases
Collections: Audubon animal paintings; Audubon bird paintings

MONROE

M **IRWIN CITY ART FOUNDATION,** Masur Museum of Art,* 1400 S Grand St, 71201. Tel 318-387-3525. *Dir* William C Pratt
Open Tues - Thurs 10 AM - 6 PM, Fri - Sun 2 - 5 PM. No admis fee. Estab 1963 to encourage art in all media and to enrich the cultural climate of this area. Gallery has 500 running ft hanging space. Average Annual Attendance: 5000. Mem: 250; dues $100, $25, $10
Income: $46,000 (financed by membership and appropriations)
Purchases: $3000
Collections: †Contemporary art all media, approximately 100 works
Publications: Brochures of shows, monthly
Activities: Classes for adults and children; Lect open to the public, four visiting lectrs per year; tours; competitions

NEW IBERIA

M **SHADOWS-ON-THE-TECHE,** 117 East Main St, PO Box 254, 70560. Tel 318-369-6446. *Adminr* Curtis R Thomas
Open daily 9 AM - 4:30 PM, cl Christmas, New Years Day and Thanksgiving Day. Admis adults $2, students or senior citizens $1, group rates available. The Shadows is a property of the National Trust for Historic Preservation. Preserved as a historic house museum; operated as a community preservation center, it is a National Historic Landmark. A townhouse on the Bayou Teche, it faces the main street of modern New Iberia, but is surrounded by three acres of landscaped gardens shaded by live oaks. Built in 1831, the Shadows represents a Louisiana adaptation of classical revival architecture.
Fashionable balls and masquerades as well as everyday activities are reflected in the possessions of five generations of the Weeks family on display in the house.
It fell into ruin after the Civil War, but was restored during the 1920s by Weeks Hall, great grandson of the builder. Mr Hall revived the spark of antebellum hospitality at the Shadows entertaining such celebrities as W C Fields, Mae West and HL H L Mr Hall bequeathed the Shadows to the National Trust in 1958.
Property serves as a focal point for advancement of historic preservation. It develops new relationships among cultural community preservation groups and National Trust members in its area. Responds to community preservation needs by acting as a link between community and appropriate regional or headquarters offices of National Trust. Average Annual Attendance: 30,000
Collections: Two paintings by Louisiana's itinerant artist Adrian Persac (1857-72); Paintings by Weeks Hall; furnishings typical of those owned by a planter's family between 1830 and 1865
Exhibitions: Sidewalk Art Show; Sugar Cane Festival
Activities: Interpretive programs which are related to the Shadows historic preservation program; Members Day during National Historic Preservation Week

NEW ORLEANS

M **HISTORIC NEW ORLEANS COLLECTION,** Kemper and Leila Williams Foundation, 533 Royal St, 70130. Tel 504-523-7146. *Chmn of Board* Benjamin W Yancey; *Dir* Stanton M Frazar; *Asst Dir* Dr Robert D Bush; *Chief Cur* Mrs Ralph V Platou; *Cur* John Mahe; *Assoc Cur* Rosanne McCaffrey; *Asst Cur* John Lawrence; *Registrar* Lisette Carriere; *Education Cur* Ellen Leaman
Open Tues - Sat 10 AM - 4:30 PM. No admis fee to Gallery, admis to Williams Residence and ten gallery tour by guide $1. Building constructed in 1792 by Jean Francois Merieult; recently renovated by Koch and Wilson to accommodate the ten galleries which house a collection of paintings, prints, documents, books and artifacts relating to the history of Louisiana from the time of its settlement, gathered over a number of years by the late L Kemper Williams and his wife. The foundation was established with private funds to keep it intact. Average Annual Attendance:

50,000
Income: Financed by endowment
Collections: James Gallier, Sr and Jr Architectural Drawings (1830-1870); Morris Henry Hobbs (prints 1940); B Lafon Drawings of Fortifications (1841); B Simon Lithographs of 19th Century Businesses; Alfred R and William Waud Drawings of Civil War and post-War; maps, paintings, photographs, †prints, Three-dimensional Objects
Exhibitions: Alfred R Waud, Special Artist on Assignment (Profiles of American Cities 1850-1880); Crescent City Silver (19th Century New Orleans Silver and Silversmiths)
Publications: Exhibition Brochures and Catalogs; Monograph Series
Activities: Docent training; lect open to public; tours; competitions; individual paintings and original objects of art lent to museums, institutions, foundations, libraries and research centers; lending collection contains 5500 books, 70 motion pictures, 2000 original prints, 200 paintings, 25,000 photographs, 100 sculptures, 4500 rare pamphlets and 400 maps; originate traveling exhibitions; sales shop sells books, original art, reproductions and prints

L **Library,** 533 Royal St, 70130. *Head Library & Archives* Kenneth T Urquhart; *Librn* Florence Jumonville
Open to researchers
Library Holdings: Vols 5500; Per subs 100; Other—Rare pamphlets 4500
Collections: Archives Division: unique textural sources on New Orleans and Louisiana History and Culture (broadsides, libretti, newspapers, sheet music)

M **LAMPE GALLERY OF FINE ART,** Lampe School of Art, 3920 Old Gentilly Rd, 70126. Tel 504-949-6387. *Co-Owner* Frederick Lampe; *Co-Owner* June Lampe
Open Mon, Tues, Thurs, Fri 10 AM - 5:30 PM, Sat 10 AM - 3 PM, cl Wed. No admis fee. Estab 1968 to teach art and art appreciation. Gallery handles restoration of old paintings
Collections: Clemintine Hunter; June Lampe; Icart; Calder; Renoir; European paintings
Activities: Classes for adults and children; tours; museum shop selling original art, reproductions, prints, museum replicas in sculpture, jewelry

O **LOUISIANA HISTORICAL ASSOCIATION,** Confederate Museum, 929 Camp St, 70130. Tel 405-523-4522. *Pres* Leonard V Huber; *Chmn Memorial Hall Committee* Henry Morris; *VChmn Memorial Hall Committee* Bernard E Eble; *Cur* Belinda Reuther
Open Mon - Sat 10 AM - 4 PM. Admis adults $1, children 50¢. Estab 1891 to collect and display articles, memorabilia and records from Louisiana history and particularly the era surrounding the Civil War. Gallery is maintained in a one story brick building; one main hall paneled in Cypress, one side hall containing paintings of Civil War figures and display casses containing artifacts. Average Annual Attendance: 13,000. Mem: 2000; dues $8; annual meeting March
Income: Financed by membership and admissions
Publications: Louisiana Historical Association Newsletter; Louisiana History, quarterly
Activities: Lect open to the public; competitions; sales shop sells books, reproductions and novelties

M **LOUISIANA STATE MUSEUM,** 751 Chartres St, PO Box 2458, 70176. Tel 504-568-6968. *Pres* F Clancy Dupepe; *VPres* E F LeBreton; *Secy* George R Montgomery; *Dir* Robert R Macdonald; *Chief Cur* Vaughn Glasgow; *Chief Cur* Dr Edward Haas
Open Tues - Sun 9 AM - 5 PM. Admis adults $1, children 50¢, children under 12 free. Estab 1906, to collect, preserve and present original materials illustrating Louisiana's heritage. Gallery is maintained, and has eight historic buildings containing paintings, prints, maps and photographs. Average Annual Attendance: 320,000. Mem: 2500; dues $10; annual meeting May
Income: $2,100,000 (financed by state appropriation)
Purchases: $60,000
Collections: Permanent collection of ceramics, decorative arts, costumes, glass, maps, paintings photographs, prints, silver, textiles
Exhibitions: GPA Healy: Louisiana Patrons; Louisiana Portrait Gallery Exhibition; Played with Immense Success
Publications: Louisiana's Black Heritage; Louisiana Portrait Gallery, Vol I
Activities: Classes for children; docent training; lect open to the public, 4 visiting lectrs per year; tours; book traveling exhibitions, one per year; originate traveling exhibitions, circulated through SITES; museum shop sells books, original art, reproductions, prints

L **Louisiana Historical Center Library,** 751 Chartres St, 70116. *Librn* Rose Lambert
Open Mon - Fri 9 AM - 5 PM. Estab 1906, to collect materials related to Louisiana heritage
Purchases: $10,000
Library Holdings: Vols 40,000; Per subs 25; Micro—Reels; AV—A-tapes, motion pictures; Other—Exhibition catalogs, prints, manuscripts, pamphlets, photographs

M **NEW ORLEANS MUSEUM OF ART,** Isaac Delgado Museum, Stern Auditorium, Wisner Education Wing. (Mailing Add: Lelong Ave, PO Box 19123, New Orleans, LA 70179) Tel 504-488-2631. *Pres* J Thomas Lewis; *First VPres* Dr Richard W Levy; *Second VPres* Mrs P Roussel Norman; *Secy* Mrs J Frederick Muller Jr; *Treas* Dr Joseph Bonin; *Dir* E John Bullard; *Adminr* Barbara H Neiswender; *Chief Cur* William A Fagaly; *Adjunct Cur of Japanese Art* Stephen Addiss; *Registrar* Charles 1 Mo; *Asst Registrar, Cur of Traveling Exhib* Renee Rodrique Ryan; *Research Cur* Joan Caldwell; *Research Assoc* Hugh J Smith Jr; *Cur of Photography* Tina Freeman; *Cur of Prints and Drawings* Valerie Loupe Olsen; *Principal Cur of Education* Alice Rae Yelen; *Cur of Education* David Swoyer; *Asst for Public Information* Donna Banting; *Asst for Special Projects* Betty McDermott; *Audiovisual Coordr* Marilyn Duckworth; *Membership Secy* Anne Bittel; *Activities Coordr* Carol Leonard; *Preparator* Thomas E Herrington
Open Tues, Wed, Fri - Sun 10 AM - 5 PM; Thurs 1 - 9 PM; cl Mon. Admis adults (18-65) $1, children (12-18) 50¢; Thurs free. Estab 1911; building given to city by Isaac Delgado, maintained by municipal funds to provide a stimulus to a broader cultural life for the entire community. Stern Auditorium, Ella West Freeman wing for changing exhibitions; Wisner Education wing for learning experiences; Delgado Building for permanent display; Hyams Room for Barbizon and late 19th century Salon Painting. Average Annual Attendance: 150,000. Mem: 10,000; dues $15 - $1000; annual meeting Nov
Income: Financed by membership, city appropriation and federal grants
Collections: †Victor Kiam Collection of Fauve and Surrealist Paintings; Samuel H Kress Collection of Renaissance Masterpieces; Latter-Schlesinger Collection of Portrait Miniatures; Stern-Davis Collection of Peruvian Colonial Painting; †African Art; †Graphics; †Latin American Colonial Painting and Sculpture; Japanese Painting of the Edo Period; †19th and 20th Century American Art; 19th and 20th Century Louisiana Painting and Furniture; †Old Masters Paintings of various schools; †Pre-Columbian Masterworks
Exhibitions: Emergence and Progression: Six Contemporary American Artists; The Gold of El Dorado; New Orleans Triennail; Objects of Bright Pride: Northwest Coast Indian Art; Treasures from Chatsworth: The Devonshire In-Heritance
Publications: Arts, quarterly; catalogs of exhibitions
Activities: Classes for children; docent training; lect open to public, 20 vis lectr per year; concerts; gallery talks; tours; competitions; individual paintings and original objects of art lent to museums; book traveling exhibitions 5 per year; originate traveling exhibitions; museum shop sells books, original art, reproductions, prints, cards, toys and jewelry

L **Felix J Dreyfous Library,** Lelong Ave, PO Box 19123, 70179. *Librn* Jeanette Downing; *Library Asst* Wanda Hickerson
Open Mon - Fri 9 AM - 5 PM. Estab 1971 to provide information for reference to the curators, museum members and art researchers. Open to staff and members; general public by appointment
Income: Financed by membership, donations and gifts
Library Holdings: Vols 5000; Per subs 53; AV—Slides; Other—Clipping files, exhibition catalogs, photographs
Special Subjects: Photography, African art, Pre-Columbian art
Collections: WPA Project - New Orleans Artists

TULANE UNIVERSITY

M **Newcomb Art Department Exhibition Gallery,** 60 Newcomb Place, 70118. Tel 504-865-4631. *Chmn Art Department* John Clemmer
Open daily 9 AM - 4:30 PM
Exhibitions: Exhibitions as an integral part of the Art Department Program

L **Architecture Library,** Division of Howard Tilton Library, 60 Necomb Place, 70118. Tel 504-865-4409. *Librn* Elizabeth Gaudit Lockett
Library Holdings: Vols 6208; AV—Slides; Other—Prints, photographs
Collections: Extensive file of pictorial material, including architectural photographs relating to New Orleans; a small working reference library of architectural material is maintained in Richardson Memorial the School of Architecture Building

M **UNIVERSITY OF NEW ORLEANS,** Fine Arts Gallery, Lake Front Dr, 70122. *Chmn Fine Arts* Richard A Johnson; *Gallery Dir* Richard A Johnson; *Secy* Molly Matthews
Open Mon - Fri 8 AM - 4:30 PM. No admis fee. Estab 1974 to expose the students and community to historic and contemporary visual arts. Gallery consists of 1800 sq ft, 112 lineal ft of wall space, 20 ft ceilings, natural and artificial lighting
Income: Financed by state appropriation

PORT ALLEN

M **WEST BATON ROUGE MUSEUM,** 845 N Jefferson Ave, 70767. Tel 504-383-2392. *Pres & Dir Art Exhib* Mrs Booth Kellough; *Chmn Empire Bedroom Coll* Mrs P Chauvin Wilkinson; *Cur* Mary Vlcek Pramuk; *Custodian* Mrs George Lefebre; *Asst Custodian* Dorothy Landry; *Exhib Chmn* Evelyn B Terrill
Open Tues - Sat 10 AM - 4:30 PM. No admis fee. Estab 1968, Museum opened 1970, to foster interest in history, particularly that of West Baton Rouge Parish; to encourage research, collection and preservation of material illustrating past and present activities of the parish; to operate one or more museums; to receive gifts and donations; to accept exhibits and historical materials on loan. One room housing a collection of American Empire (circa 1840) bedroom furniture; a large room housing a parish relief map and parish memorabilia, two old printing presses; a room 31 x 40 ft for art exhibits; restored plantation Quarters Cabin (circa 1850). Average Annual Attendance: 6000. Mem: 275; dues $5; annual meeting Jan
Income: $25,000 (financed by membership and gifts)
Collections: †Art Collection of Parish Artists; †Empire Bedroom Furnishings; †Needlework; †Newcomb Pottery; Old Duck Decoys; †Parish Artifacts
Exhibitions: Savior Faire, The French Taste in Louisiana; Dan Girouard, Blind Sculptor; Angela Gregory & Selima Bres Gregory; David Miller Chess Sets; The Art of David I Norwood; William Warehall Glass; Fonville Willan's Photographs of the 30's; The Animaliers; Annual High School Art Exhibit; The Artist and His Materials; The Child's Image in Art; Juried Parish Art Exhibit; Louisiana Crafts Council; New Directions in Fiber by Louisiana Artists; The Painter Collects; W P A Art; Wooden Imposters
Publications: Ecoutez, twice a year
Activities: Gallery talks; tours; competitions

SHREVEPORT

M **CENTENARY COLLEGE OF LOUISIANA,** Meadows Museum of Art, 2911 Centenary Blvd, PO Box 4188, 71104. Tel 318-869-5169. *Cur* Willard Cooper; *Programs Dir* Carolyn Nelson
Open Tues - Fri 1 - 5 PM, Sat & Sun 2 - 5 PM. No admis fee. Estab 1975 to house the Indo-China Collection of Drawings & Paintings by Jean Despujols. Eight galleries; main gallery on first floor 25 x 80 ft; other galleries 25 x 30 ft; linen walls, track lights and no windows. Average Annual Attendance: 6000
Income: $40,000 (financed by endowment)
Collections: 360 works in Indo-China Collection, dealing with Angkor Region, The Cordillera, Gulf of Siam, Laos, The Nam-Te, The Thai, Upper Tonkin, Vietnam
Exhibitions: (1978-80) Designs of The Ndebele; Etchings and Engravings; Judagan Antiquities; Naive Art of Yugoslavia; Old and Modern Masters; Prints from The Guggenheim; national juried show
Publications: Partial Catalog of Permanent Collection with 21 color plates
Activities: Lect open to public, some for members only, 4 visiting lectr per year; concerts; gallery talks; tours; competitions; cash awards; book traveling exhibitions 3 or 4 per year; sales shop sells catalogs, post cards

M **LOUISIANA STATE EXHIBIT MUSEUM,*** 3015 Greenwood Rd, 71109. Tel 318-635-2323. *Dir* R E Baremore Jr
Open Mon - Sat 9 AM - 5 PM, Sun 1 - 5 PM, cl Christmas. No admis fee. Estab 1939 to display permanent and temporary exhibitions demonstrating the state's history, resources and natural beauty. Art Gallery is maintained. Average Annual Attendance: 600,000
Income: Financed by state appropriation
Collections: Archaeology; china; coins; dioramas; glass; historical relics; Indian artifacts; murals
Exhibitions: Ceramic and china painting shows; approx 15 exhibitions per year by local and regional art groups and artists
Publications: History of Art; brochures
Activities: Art workshops; films; concerts

M **R W NORTON ART GALLERY,** 4747 Creswell Ave, 71106. Tel 318-865-4201. *Pres of the Board* Mrs Richard W Norton Jr; *Secy Registrar* Jerry M Bloomer; *Building & Grounds Supt* Frank Todaro; *VPres of the Board* A W Coon
Open Tues - Sun 1 - 5 PM; cl Mon & holidays. No admis fee. Estab 1946, opened 1966. Founded to present aspects of the development of American and European art and culture through exhibition and interpretation of fine works of art and literature, both from the Gallery's own collections and from those of other institutions and individuals. Average Annual Attendance: 25,000
Collections: Large collections of Paintings and Sculpture by Western American Artists Frederic Remington & Charles M Russell; American Miniatures and Colonial Silver; European Paintings, Sculpture; Paintings and Sculpture relating to Early American History; †Paintings by 19th Century American Artists of the Hudson River School; Portraits of Famous Confederate Leaders; 16th Century Flemish Tapestries; Large Collection of Wedgwood Pottery
Exhibitions: (1978) The Gross Collection of Irish, English & Continental Silver; English Delftware from the Morgan Collection; 11th Annual Christmas Exhibition; (1979) Loren D Adams Jr Retrospective; American Painters of the Impressionist Period Rediscovered; 12th Annual Christmas Exhibition; (1980) 100 Years of Daum Crystal; Porcelains for Children & Other People; 13th Annual Christmas Exhibition
Publications: Announcements of special exhibitions; catalogs (34 through 1980); catalogs of the Frederic Remington & Charles M Russell Collections
Activities: Educ dept; docent training; lect open to public; gallery talks; tours; museum shop sells magazines, slides, exhibition catalogs, catalogs of permanent collection

L **Library,** 4747 Creswell Ave, 71106. *Librn* Jerry M Bloomer; *Asst Librn* Eva W Moses
Open Wed & Sat 1 - 5 PM. Estab 1946 to acquire and make available for public use on the premises, important books, exhibition catalogs, etc relating to the visual arts, literature, American history and genealogy, as well as other standard reference and bibliographic works for reference only
Income: Financed by endowment
Library Holdings: Vols 6000; Per subs 125; Micro—Reels; AV—Slides; Other—Clipping files, exhibition catalogs, manuscripts, memorabilia, pamphlets, photographs, original documents
Special Subjects: Bibliography, fine arts, history, literature, ornithological works by J J Audubon (elephant folio edition of Birds of America) and John Gould (complete set), rare books and atlases
Collections: James M Owens Memorial Collection of Early Americana (725 volumes on Colonial History, particularly on Virginia)

MAINE

AUGUSTA

M **UNIVERSITY OF MAINE AT AUGUSTA GALLERY,** University Heights, 04330. Tel 207-622-7131. *Dir* Patricia McGraw Anderson
Open Mon - Thurs 9 AM - 9 PM; Fri 9 AM - 5 PM. No admis fee. Estab 1970 to provide changing exhibitions of the visual arts for the university students and faculty and for the larger Augusta-Kennebec Valley community; the principal exhibition area is a two level combination lounge and gallery. Average Annual Attendance: 9000
Income: Financed by university budget
Collections: Drawings, Paintings, Prints, Sculpture by students and faculty
Exhibitions: (1978-80) Gallery Figures: Thomas Cornell; Ron Cross, Sculpture; Edward S Curtis; Alex Katz; Frederick Lynch; Denny Winters; Directions Craft Show; Faculty Biennial; The Model: Work from Life; Site Planning; Learning Resources Center: Anne Ayvaliotis; Dianne Ballon; Patricia Gorman; Alison Hildreth; Jane Kinney-Young; Catherine Morgan; Penny Oliphant Parkhurst; Abbott Pattison; Nina Jerome Sutcliffe; Sharon Ventimiglia
Activities: Lect open to public, 2 - 3 vis lectr per year; gallery talks; tours

BATH

M **MAINE MARITIME MUSEUM,** (Formerly Bath Marine Museum) 963 Washington St, 04530. Tel 207-443-6311. *Exec Dir* Ralph L Snow; *Asst Cur Coll* Marnee Lilly; *Asst Cur Exhib* Nathan Lipfert
Open daily 10 AM - 5 PM (mid-May - mid-Oct), Sun only 10 AM - 5 PM remainder of the year. Admis adults $3.24 - $4.50, under 16 $1.25 - $1.50, under 6 free. Estab 1964 for the preservation of Maine's maritime heritage. Average Annual Attendance: 30,000. Mem: 1400; dues $15 and up; annual meeting Oct
Income: $325,000 (financed by membership, gifts and grants)
Collections: Ships portraits and seascapes
Publications: Long Reach Log, quarterly
Activities: Docent training; lect open to public; individual paintings and original objects of art lent; museum shop selling books, reproductions, prints and related novelties

L **Archives Library,** 963 Washington St, 04530. *Cur Emeritus* Harold Brown
Library Holdings: Vols 5000; Per subs 5; AV—Kodachromes, slides; Other—Clipping files, memorabilia, original art works, pamphlets, photographs, original documents
Special Subjects: Maine maritime history, especially shipbuilding
Collections: Marine paintings; photographs of vessels built in Bath; ship models, navigational instruments; shipbuilding tools
Exhibitions: Permanent and changing exhibits concerned with Maine's maritime history

BLUE HILL

M **PARSON FISHER HOUSE,** Jonathan Fisher Memorial, Inc, 04614. Tel 207-374-2780. *Pres* William P Hinckley
Open Tues $ Fri 2 - 5 PM; Sat 10 AM - Noon (summer only). Admis 50¢. Estab 1954 to preserve the home and memorabilia of Jonathan Fisher. The house was designed and built by him in 1815. Average Annual Attendance: 300. Mem: 320; dues $2; annual meeting August
Income: Financed by endowment and membership
Collections: Furniture, Manuscripts, Paintings and Articles made by Fisher

BOOTHBAY HARBOR

O **BOOTHBAY REGION ART GALLERY,** Brick House, Oak St, 04538. Tel 207-633-2703. *Pres* Richard Johnson; *VPres* Eberhard Schmidt; *Secy* Eleanor Miller; *Treas* William Burley
Open Mon - Sat 11 AM - 5 PM; Sun 2 - 5 PM (July 1 through Sept 15). Admis adults 25¢, children free. Estab 1966, originated to help develop an art curriculum in the local schools, presently functions to bring art of the region's artists to enrich the culture of the community. Located in historic Brick House, built in 1807, two exhibition rooms on the first floor and two on the second, one of which features prints, drawings and small watercolors. Average Annual Attendance: 3000. Mem: 475; dues $1 - $25; annual meeting Oct
Income: Financed by memberships, contributions and commissions
Exhibitions: Three juried shows of graphics, paintings and sculpture by artists of the Boothbay Region and Monhegan Island
Activities: Classes for adults

BRUNSWICK

M **BOWDOIN COLLEGE,** Museum of Art & Peary-MacMillan Arctic Museum, 04011. Tel 207-725-8731, Ext 275. *Dir* Katharine J Watson; *Admin Asst to Dir* Lynn C Yanok; *Cur* Margaret B Clunie; *Secy to Dir* Suzanne Bergeron; *Registrar* Brenda Pelletier; *Museum Receptionist & Shop Mgr* Mary Poppe
Open Tues - Fri 10 AM - 4 PM; Sat 10 AM - 5 PM; Sun 2 - 5 PM; cl Mon & holidays. No admis fee. Estab Museum of Art 1894, Peary-MacMillan Artic Museum 1967. The Walker Art Building, designed by McKim, Mead and White, houses a collection begun in 1811 at the bequest of James Bowdoin III. There are eight galleries housing the permanent collection and one for temporary exhibitions. Average Annual Attendance: 50,000. Mem: 800
Collections: Colonial and Federal Portraits by Copley, Feke, Smibert, Stuart; 19th and 20th Century Works by Leonard Baskin, Thomas Eakins, Martin Johnson Heade, Robert Henri, George Inness, John Sloan; The Molinari Collection of Coins, Medals, Plaquettes; The Warren Collection of Classical Antiquities; The Winslow Homer Collection and Memorabilia; Old Master Prints and Drawings
Exhibitions: The Ancient Collection; Daniel Putnam Brinley: The Impressionist Years; Spirit of the New Landscape
Publications: Contemporary Photographers: Colonial and Federal Portraits at Bowdoin College; A Decade of Murals; Ernest Haskell (1876-1925); Medals and Plaquettes from the Molinari Collection; The Persistence of Vision; Howard Warshaw; Photographs: John McKee; Recent Figure Sculpture
Activities: Docent training; concerts; gallery talks; tours; individual paintings and original objects of art lent to qualified institutions; museum shop sells books, magazines, original art, reproductions, prints, slides and jewelry

DEER ISLE

M **HAYSTACK MOUNTAIN SCHOOL OF CRAFTS GALLERY,** 04627. Tel 207-348-2816. *Chmn of Board* Jack Lenor Larsen; *Pres* Charles R Gailis; *Admin Asst* Ethel Clifford; *Dir* Howard M Evans; *Treas* Adam Rhodes
Open Sat & Sun, June - Sept. Estab 1950 for research and instruction in crafts and related extension services of exhibitions, consultation and conferences. Gallery maintained for continuous summer exhibition of important American and other national craftsmen. Average Annual Attendance: 2500
Income: $150,000 (financed by tuition income plus annual donations)
Collections: †American Ceramics; †Jewelry
Publications: Annual brochure
Activities: 12 week summer session in ceramics, graphics, glass, jewelry, weaving and photography; lect; gallery talks; Scholarships; national extension dept; original objects of art lent; crafts and slide material lent to schools, galleries and museums; lending collection contains 1000 Kodachromes; originate traveling exhibitions

L **Library,** 04627.
For reference only
Library Holdings: Vols 500; AV—Kodachromes

ELLSWORTH

M COLONEL BLACK MANSION, 04605. Tel 207-667-8671. *Pres* Ruth Sullivan Foster; *Secy* Mrs Morton C Whitcomb
Open June 1 - Oct 15, Mon - Sat 10 AM - 5 PM; cl Sun. Donations adults $2, children $1. Historical mansion operated by the Hancock County Trustees of Public Reservations. Average Annual Attendance: 5500. Mem: 225; annual meeting second Thurs in August
Collections: Authentic period China, Decorative Objects, Glass, Furniture in their fine original setting
Activities: Guided tours

HALLOWELL

O KENNEBEC VALLEY ART ASSOCIATION, Harlow Gallery, 160 Water St, PO Box 213, 04347. *Pres* Laura Rothstein; *Dir* Adele Nichols; *VPres* Florence Daly; *Treas* Madge Ames
Open Tues - Sat 1 - 4 PM, Sun 2 - 4 PM, cl Mon. No admis fee. Estab 1963 to foster an interest in and appreciation of fine art. Single gallery on ground level having central entrance and two old storefront windows which provide window display space, peg board covering walls, with two large display screens providing extra display area. Average Annual Attendance: 700. Mem: Approx 100; dues $5; annual meeting first Mon in Jan
Income: $5000 (financed by membership and donations)
Exhibitions: Cicily Aikman, oils; Antique-Contemporary Dolls; Jeanna Bearce, Larry Rakovan, oils, prints, drawings; Jan Beerits, drawings; Henry Beerits, watercolors; Anita Bartlett, oils, acrylics, drawings; Porge Buck, etchings; Lewis Buck, acrylics, collages, prints; Linda Burley, oils, watercolors; Marion Dwyer, sculpture; Frances Hodsdon, prints; Richard Lee, collages; Winifred Long, watercolors; Members Annual; July and August Maine Invitational; Margaret Manter, watercolors; Lynn Harwood, oils; National Print Show; Elizabeth O'Malley, oils, acrylics; Fred Scherrer, oils; Antoinette Schultz, sculpture; Sharon Ventimiglia, sculpture; Libby Wohler, oils, prints; Christmas Exhibit and Sale; Holiday Exhibit and Sale
Publications: Newsletter, monthly
Activities: Lectures open to the public, six - eight visiting lecturers per year; museum shop sells original art

KENNEBUNK

M BRICK STORE MUSEUM, 117 Main St, PO Box 177, 04043. Tel 207-985-4802. *Dir* David C Thurheimer; *Cur Registrar* Sandra S Armentrout; *Pres Board* Cyrus Hamlin
Open Tues - Sat 10 AM - 4:30 PM. Admis by donation. The Museum is composed of a block of 19th century commercial buildings, including William Lord's Brick Store (1825), exhibiting fine and decorative arts, historical and marine collections. Average Annual Attendance: 5000. Mem: 400; dues $10 - $35; annual meeting Sept
Income: Financed by endowment, membership, small grants
Collections: Taylor-Barry Period House (circa 1803, sea captain's house); 19th Century Americana; Costumes; Graphics; Household Furnishings; Marine Artifacts; Paintings; Tools
Exhibitions: Crafts, fine arts, local history
Publications: Abbott Graves Exhibition Catalog 1979
Activities: Contemporary craft program at Barry Workshop; lect series; architectural walking tours; teas and receptions at Taylor-Barry House; sales shop sells books, cards, gifts
L Library, 117 Main St, 04043.
Non-circulating reference library only
Special Subjects: Decorative Arts, Fine Arts, Local and State History

LEWISTON

M BATES COLLEGE, Treat Gallery, 04240. Tel 207-783-6535. *Cur* Nancy Carlisle
Open Mon - Fri 1 - 5 & 7 - 8 PM, Sun 2 - 5 PM, open mornings by appointment, cl major holidays. No admis fee. Estab 1955 in honor of Mr & Mrs George W Treat to acquaint the student body and the community with the works of recognized artists. Average Annual Attendance: 6800
Collections: Marsden Hartley Drawings (99) Paintings (2); Freeman Hinckley (former Bates College Trustee) Collection of Chinese Objects; Sylvan Lehman Joseph Collection of Prints including one Rembrandt and 19 Cassattas; Four Thompson Family Portraits (ancestors of George W Treat); One Zorach Sculpture; The Little Family Antique Collection; 19th & 20th Century American and European Paintings and Prints; 17th & 18th Century Dutch, English, French and Italian Landscapes and Portraits
Exhibitions: Changed monthly
Activities: Lect

MACHIAS

M UNIVERSITY OF MAINE AT MACHIAS ART GALLERY, 04654. Tel 207-255-3313. *Dir of Gallery* Dr Mary Leigh Morbey; *Chmn Cultural Affairs* Dr Alvin Bowker
Open 8 AM - 8 PM. No admis fee. Estab 1968. Average Annual Attendance: 1200
Income: Financed by city and state appropriation
Collections: John and Norma Marin Collection
Exhibitions: Annual photography competition; annual student exhibition; one-man shows; traveling exhibitions
Activities: Classes for adults; lect, 12 visiting lectr per year; exten dept serves Washington County; material available to residents and summer visitors; material lent, books, records, prints, slides; individual paintings and original objects of art lent; lending collection contains color reproductions (100), lantern slides (2000), Kodachromes (6400), film strips (1200); traveling exhibitions organized and circulated to Calais Technical Institute

L Library, 04654.
Lending and reference library
Library Holdings: Vols 56,000; Other—Prints

OGUNQUIT

M MUSEUM OF ART OF OGUNQUIT, Shore Rd, Box 815, 03907. Tel 207-646-8827. *Dir* Henry Strater; *Cur* Peter R Mawn; *Asst Dir* John Dirks
Open (July through Labor Day, 10 wks only) Mon - Sat 10:30 AM - 5 PM, Sun 1:30 - 5 PM. No admis fee. Estab 1951. Gallery has 3 large rooms in a cinder-block building overlooking a grove of cedar trees and a rocky cove on the coast of southern Maine. Average Annual Attendance: 16,000. Mem: 200; dues couple $25, individual $15; annual meeting Aug
Income: Financed by endowment, membership
Collections: Paintings and sculpture by Americans of Our Times (1920 on)
Exhibitions: (1978)Permanent Collection plus sculpture by Clark Fitz-Gerald. (1979) Permanent Collection plus William Carlos Williams Exhibition from Whitney Museum of American Art
Publications: Exhibition catalog, annually
Activities: Individual paintings and original objects of art lent (restricted list only, available for short periods to museums and galleries); some color postcard reproductions of permanent collection are sold

O OGUNQUIT ART ASSOCIATION, The Barn Gallery, Bourne's Lane, 03907. Tel 207-646-5370. *Pres* Jayne Dwyer; *VPres* Ron Hayes; *Secy* Sylvia Fullinwider; *Treas* Valfred Thelin; *Cur* Sandra Brennan
Open Mon - Sat 10 AM - 5 PM; Sun 2 - 5 PM (mid-June through mid-Sept). No admis fee. Estab 1928 as a charitable, educational institution. Maintains two main galleries, the Collector's Gallery of unframed works and J Scott Smart outdoor sculpture court. Average Annual Attendance: 15,000. Mem: 59; dues $20; meetings June & Aug
Exhibitions: Exhibitions during the summer
Activities: Classes for adults and children; workshops; films and demonstrations; art auction; lect open to public; concerts; gallery talks

O OGUNQUIT ART CENTER, Hoyt's Lane, 03907. Tel 207-646-2453. *Dir* Florence W Nims
Open daily 10 AM - 5 PM, Sun 2 - 5 PM. No admis fee. Estab 1920, to provide a high quality of paintings on exhibition. Average Annual Attendance: Approx 5000. Mem: 300; dues $12; annual meeting Sept
Income: Financed through patrons
Exhibitions: (1980) 60th Annual National Exhibition of Paintings
Activities: Competitions; awards

ORONO

M UNIVERSITY OF MAINE AT ORONO, Art Collection, Carnegie Hall, 04469. Tel 207-581-7165. *University Pres* Kenneth Allen; *Cur* Vincent A Hartgen
Open Mon - Fri 8 AM - 4:30 PM. Estab 1946 to add to the cultural life of the university student; to be a service to Maine artists; to promote interest in good and important art, both historic and modern. There are seven galleries, four in Carnegie Hall, and three in campus buildings. Average Annual Attendance: 15,000. Mem: 180; dues $100, $50, $25
Income: $40,000 (financed by membership and state appropriation)
Purchases: $1000
Collections: The University Collection has grown to a stature which makes it a nucleus in the state for outstanding contemporary art, in all media. It includes more than 3500 original works of art
Exhibitions: Full schedule of exhibitions of all media by outstanding American and European Artists; Art Program of Exhibitions in Annual Art Festivals and year-round exhibitions; maintains Artists of Maine Gallery to show examples of Maine Art at all times
Publications: Occasional catalogs and exhibition notes
Activities: Individual paintings and original objects of art lent; lending collection contains 1800 original prints and drawings, 925 paintings, 330 manuscripts, photos, sculptures and ceramics; originate traveling exhibitions to Maine Schools
L Fogler Library, Carnegie Hall, 04469. *Dir Libraries* Dr James C MacCampbell
Library Holdings: Vols 537,000; Per subs 3100

PEMAQUID POINT

O PEMAQUID GROUP OF ARTISTS, Lighthouse Park, Pemaquid Point, ME. (Mailing Add: c/o Gene Klebe, Route 130, Bristol, ME 04539) Tel 207-677-3672. *VPres* Ernest Thompson; *VPres* Maurice Day; *Secy* Florence Thompson; *Treas* Cynthia Brackett; *Gallery Hostess* Frances Curtis; *Asst* Jeanette Andrus; *Asst* Helen Strauss
Open Mon - Sat 10 AM - 5 PM; Sun 1 - 5 PM. Admis 25¢. Estab 1929 to exhibit and sell paintings, sculpture, carvings by members. Maintains an art gallery, open July through Labor Day. Average Annual Attendance: 8000. Mem: 35, must be residents of the Pemaquid Peninsula; dues $5; annual meeting the day after Labor Day
Exhibitions: Summer members exhibition
Activities: Scholarships; sales shop sells original art

POLAND SPRING

M SHAKER MUSEUM, Sabbathday Lake, 04274. Tel 207-926-4597. *Dir* Theodore E Johnson; *Cur Graphic Arts & Photography* David W Serette; *Cur Manuscripts* R Mildred Barker; *Archivist* Frances A Carr
Open May 30 - Labor Day, Tues - Sat 10 AM - 4:30 PM; cl Sun & Mon. Admis adults $2, children (6-12) $1, under 6 free with adult. Estab 1931, incorporated 1971, to preserve for educational and cultural purposes Shaker artifacts, publications, manuscripts and works of art; to provide facilities for educational and cultural activities in connection with the preservation of the Shaker tradition; to

provide a place of study and research for students of history and religion

Collections: †Drawings and Paintings by Shaker Artists; Shaker †Textiles; †Community Industries; †Furniture; †Manuscripts; †Metal and Wooden Ware

Publications: The Shaker Quarterly

Activities: Classes for adults; lect open to public; gallery talks; tours; museum shop sells books, prints and slides

L **Shaker Library,** Sabbathday Lake, 04274. *Librn* Theodore E Johnson
Open to qualified scholars by appointment
Library Holdings: Vols 15,363; Per subs 104; Micro—Reels 353, prints 317; Other —Manuscripts, photographs, ephemera
Special Subjects: , American communal societies, early American technology, herbology
Collections: The Koreshan Unity; The Religious Society of Friends

PORTLAND

O **MAINE HISTORICAL SOCIETY,** 485 Congress St, 04101. Tel 207-774-1822. *Acting Dir* Thomas L Gaffney
Open June - Sept Mon - Fri 10 AM - 5 PM, cl State & Federal holidays. No admis fee. Estab 1822, a society that owns and operates a branch museum established in a 1785 historic house, Wadsworth-Longfellow House. Mem: Dues $15-$250
Collections: Maine furniture; glass; historic artifacts; paintings; photographs; pottery; prints; textiles
Exhibitions: Temporary exhibitions
Publications: Maine Historical Society, quarterly; tri-annual monograph
Activities: Classes for local college students; archival training course

L **Library,** 485 Congress St, 04101. *Librn* Mary-Kate Murphy; *Manuscripts Asst* Arthur J Gerrier
Library Holdings: Vols 60,000; Other—Manuscripts

M **PORTLAND MUSEUM OF ART,*** 111 High St, 04101. Tel 207-775-6148. *Dir* John Holverson
Open Tues - Sat 10 AM - 5 PM, Sun 2 - 5 PM, cl Mon & holidays. Admis to Galleries free (voluntary donation), to McLellan-Sweat House adults $1, children & students 50¢. Estab 1882 as a non-profit educational institution based on the visual arts and critical excellence. The Museum includes the McLellan-Sweat House, built in 1800 and Galleries built in 1911. The McLellan-Sweat House is furnished in the style of the Federal period and is a superb example of an early 19th century, three-story mansion; it is a Registered National Historic Landmark. The Museum Galleries, designed by John Calvin Stevens, 1911, consist of five galleries surrounding a central rotunda. Average Annual Attendance: 15,000. Mem: 1200; dues $15 - $1000; annual meeting May
Income: $150,000 (financed by endowment, membership, state appropriation, Federal funds, public support, fund-raising and grants)
Purchases: $7500
Collections: American decorative arts, particularly of the Federal period; neo-classic American sculpture; 19th century American paintings, especially from the Portland and Maine region; Portland pattern glass (1863-1873)
Exhibitions: American Glass; Collection of Contemporary Prints by Living American Artists; Paul Dougherty; Marsden Hartley; Ellen and Chris Huntington Collection; Images of Woman; 58 Maine Paintings; William Manning; Multiple Fields; The Revolutionary McLellans; Andrew Wyeth in Maine
Publications: Bulletin, monthly; exhibition catalogs
Activities: Dramatic programs; docent training; lect open to the public, 6-10 visiting lectrs per year; gallery talks; tours; competitions; individual paintings and original objects of art lent to museums; museum shop selling books, original art, reproductions, prints, posters, cards, jewelry, and gifts

L **Library,*** 111 High St, 04101.
Open to visiting scholars, students and members by appointment
Library Holdings: Vols 1000

L **PORTLAND SCHOOL OF ART LIBRARY,** 93 High St, 04101. *Librn* Joanne Waxman
Open Mon, Tues, Fri 8 AM - 5 PM, Wed & Thurs 8 AM - 9:30 PM. Estab 1973, to support the curriculum and serve the needs of students and faculty. Circ 6253
Income: $12,000
Purchases: $8000
Library Holdings: Vols 10,000; Per subs 34; AV—Cassettes, lantern Slides, slides; Other—Clipping files, exhibition catalogs, pamphlets, photographs, reproductions

M **VICTORIA SOCIETY OF MAINE WOMEN,** Victoria Mansion and Morse Libby Mansion, 109 Danforth St, 04101. Tel 207-772-4841. *Pres* Mrs Howard F Detmer; *Secy* Mrs Ellis Leach; *Cur* Roger D Calderwood
Open mid-June to Labor Day, Tues - Sat 10 AM - 4 PM; cl Sun, Mon & holidays. Admis adults $1, children under 12 50¢. Estab 1943 to display Italian Villa, Victorian Period, built by Henry Austin of New Haven, Connecticut in 1859-1863. Average Annual Attendance: 5000. Mem: 398; annual meeting June
Income: Financed by membership, tours and special activities
Collections: Original Interior-Exterior and Original Furnishings, Gifts and Loans of the Victorian Period
Activities: Lect open to public; tours; individual paintings lent; lending collection contains books

M **WESTBROOK COLLEGE,** Joan Whitney Payson Gallery of Art, 716 Stevens Ave, 04103. Tel 207-797-9546. *Dir* Annie V F Storr; *Asst to Dir* Gael May McKibben
Open Tues - Fri 10 AM - 4 PM, Sat & Sun 1 - 5 PM, cl Mon & holidays. No admis fee. Estab May 1977 for cultural exhibits. Payson Gallery is a tri-level cube 32 x 32 ft
Income: Financed by college operating budget
Collections: American masters of the 19th and 20th century; Impressionist paintings; Post-impressionist
Exhibitions: (1978) Milton Avery, American, 1893-1965. (1979) SPECTRA I, Maine Women: Painting and Graphics. (1980) The Gregorian Collection of Oriental Rugs; there are regularly changing special exhibitions as well as sculpture exhibits
Activities: Museum shop selling catalogs and postcards

ROCKLAND

M **WILLIAM A FARNSWORTH LIBRARY AND ART MUSEUM,** 19 Elm St, Box 466, 04841. Tel 207-596-6457. *Dir* Marius B Peladeau; *Admin Asst* Valerie N Duffy; *Membership Secy* Mary K Wasgatt
Open Tues - Sat 10 AM - 5 PM; Sun 1 - 5 PM; Mon (June - Sept) 10 AM - 5 PM. Admis by donations. Estab 1948 to house, conserve and exhibit American art. Four galleries house permanent and changing exhibitions. Average Annual Attendance: 60,000. Mem: 950; dues $10 and up
Collections: American Art; American Decorative Arts; European Fine Arts and Decorative Arts
Exhibitions: Annual Open Show; Childrens Art Show
Publications: Annual report, quarterly newsletter, exhibit catalogs
Activities: Classes for adults and children; lect open to public; concerts; gallery talks; competitions; individual paintings and original objects of art lent to other museums and galleries; originate traveling exhibitions; museum shop sells books, original art, reproductions, prints

L **William A Farnsworth Library,** 19 Elm St, 04841. *Librn* Anne Wadsworth
Estab 1948. Art reference only
Library Holdings: Vols 4000; Per subs 25; Other—Clipping files, exhibition catalogs
Collections: Nevelson Archives Collection of Material Pertinent to the Life and Works of Louise Nevelson

ROCKPORT

O **MAINE COAST ARTISTS,** Russell Ave, Box 147, 04856. Tel 207-236-2875. *Dir of Exhibits* Benedict Goldsmith; *Gallery Mgr* Sarah Fasoldt
Open Tues - Sat 10 AM - 5:30 PM; Sun 1 - 6 PM; cl Mon (June - Sept). No admis fee. Estab 1958 to show the works of artists who paint in Maine, full or part time. Gallery building was an old large livery stable overlooking Rockport Harbor. Average Annual Attendance: 8000. Mem: dues $15 and up
Income: $30,000 (financed by members, sales, contributions and special events)
Exhibitions: (1980) Invitational - selected Art of best Maine Artists; Off The Wall - a show for three-dimensional art (invitational); Open (juried) Show for all Maine Artists
Activities: Classes for adults and children; lect open to public; studio tours of local artists' studios

SACO

M **YORK INSTITUTE MUSEUM,** 375 Main St, 04072. Tel 207-282-3031. *Executive Dir* Barbara Bond; *Cur* Audrey Milne
Open May - Oct; cl Nov - April. No admis fee. Estab 1867. Mem: Dues, perpetual $1000, life $100, contributing $25, family $10, single $5
Collections: Colonial Decorative Arts; Glass; Historical Material; Paintings; Sculpture
Exhibitions: Temporary Exhibitions
Activities: Guided tours; inter-museum loan

L **Library,** 375 Main St, 04072.
Historical books, early newspapers and manuscripts for use on the premises

SEARSPORT

M **PENOBSCOT MARINE MUSEUM,** Church St, 04974. Tel 207-548-6634. *Dir* C Gardner Lane Jr; *Secy* Marilyn Kenney
Open Memorial Day weekend - Oct 15, Mon - Sat 9:30 AM - 5 PM, Sun 1 - 5 PM. Admis adults $2, senior citizens $1.50, ages 13-17 $1, ages 7-12 50¢, under 7 free. Estab 1936 as a memorial to the maritime record of present and former residents of the State of Maine in shipbuilding, shipping and all maritime affairs. The Museum consists of six buildings, including the Old Town Hall (1845), Nickels-Colcord-Duncan House (circa 1880); small crafts exhibits and a special exhibits building. Average Annual Attendance: 9000. Mem: 450; dues $10 and up; annual meeting July
Income: Financed by endowment, membership and admissions
Collections: Marine Hardware; Oriental Exports; †Paintings; †Ships Models; Small Craft
Exhibitions: Offshore Oil Drilling; permanent exhibit: The Challenge of the Downeasters
Publications: Annual report; newsletter, when appropriate
Activities: Classes for children; individual paintings and original objects of art lent to other institutions

L **Library,** Church St, 04974.
Open for reference to researchers
Library Holdings: Vols 3000; Per subs 10; Other—Photographs, nautical charts

SKOWHEGAN

L **SKOWHEGAN SCHOOL OF PAINTING AND SCULPTURE,** Margaret Day Blake Library, Box 449, 04976.
Estab 1946, to serve the students at the School. For reference only
Purchases: $500
Library Holdings: Vols 2500; Per subs 5; AV—A-tapes, Kodachromes, lantern slides, motion pictures; Other—Exhibition catalogs

SPRINGVALE

L NASSON COLLEGE, Anderson Learning Center, Bradeen St, 04083. Tel 207-324-5340. *Dir* Robert J Berkley; *Cur* George Burk
Open Mon - Fri 8:30 AM - 1 PM, Sat 9 AM - 5 PM, Sun 1 - 10 PM. Estab 1969 to provide facilities for the study of humanities and a location for the display of the college's permanent art study collection. Maintains an art gallery with exhibition and lecture area and an adjoining outdoor sculpture court
Income: Financed by endowment and through college
Library Holdings: Vols 120,000; Per subs 900; Micro—Fiche, reels; AV—A-tapes, fs, lantern slides, motion pictures, rec, slides, v-tapes; Other—Clipping files, exhibition catalogs, framed reproductions, memorabilia
Collections: 20th Century Graphic Works; Paintings; Photographs; Sculpture
Exhibitions: Seven exhibitions of prominent artists per year; Historical Exhibitions; Student Shows
Publications: Posters for each exhibit

WATERVILLE

M COLBY MUSEUM OF ART, 04901. Tel 207-873-1131, Ext 221. *Dir* Hugh J Gourley III
Open Mon - Sat 10 AM - Noon, 1 - 4:30 PM, cl major holidays. No admis fee. Estab 1959 to serve as an adjunct to the Colby College Art Program and to be a museum center for Central Maine. Mem: Friends of Art at Colby, 625; dues $10 and higher
Collections: Bernat Oriental ceramics and bronzes; American Heritage collection; The Helen Warren and Willard Howe Collection of American Art; American Art of the 18th, 19th and 20th centuries; Jette Collection of American painting in the Impressionist Period; John Marin Collection of twenty-five works by Marin; Adelaide Pearson Collection; William J Pollock Collection of American Indian Art; Pulcifer Collection of Winslow Homer; Pre-Columbian Mexico; Etruscan art;
Publications: Newsletter, quarterly
L Library, Waterville, 04901.
For reference only
Library Holdings: Vols 1500

M THOMAS COLLEGE GALLERY, W River Rd, 04901. Tel 207-873-0771. *Pres* John L Thomas; *Dir* Ford A Grant
Open Mon - Fri 8 AM - 5 PM. No admis fee. Estab 1968 for presentation of instructional shows for student audience. Average Annual Attendance: 1500
Exhibitions: One or two exhibitions a month during school year of Maine artists only. Included are: Joan Beuregard; Lois Dodd; David Ellis; Richard Wiggin Johnson; Bernard Langlais; Harry Stump
L Library, W River Rd, 04901.
For reference only
Library Holdings: AV—Slides

M WATERVILLE HISTORICAL ASSOCIATION, 64 Silver St, 04901. Tel 207-872-9439. *Pres* Cyril M Joly; *VPres* Anne Marden; *Secy* Frank Bartlett; *Cur* William B Miller; *Asst Cur* Agatha Fullam
Open May - Oct Tues - Sat 2 - 6 PM. Admis adults $1, under 18 free. Average Annual Attendance: 1500. Mem: Dues couples $8, individual $5
Income: Financed by membership and city appropriation
Collections: 19th Century drug store, 19th Century furniture, portraits of early local residents, early silver and china, Victorian clothing
Activities: Tours

WISCASSET

O LINCOLN COUNTY CULTURAL AND HISTORICAL ASSOCIATION, 04578. *Pres* Prescott Currier
Inc 1954, to preserve buildings of historic interest. Presents 200 years of Maine's crafts and skills including the work of craftsmen who spend part of the year in Maine. Gallery presents the works of contemporary professional artists, working in Maine, by means of two juried summer exhibitions. Three museums and one art gallery maintained. Average Annual Attendance: 3000. Mem: 650; dues $10 and up; annual meeting July
Income: Approx $10,000
Collections: Furniture; hand tools; household articles; prison equipment; textiles
Exhibitions: Changing exhibits on 200 years of Maine crafts and skills; Lincoln County Museum, permanent exhibit on the history of punishment
Publications: Newsletter and occasional monographs
Activities: School programs; tours; slide shows; lect
L Library, 04578.
Open by appointment for reference and research
M Lincoln County Museum, 04578.
Open daily 10 AM - 5 PM, Sun 12:30 - 5 PM Jul 1 - Aug 30
M Lincoln County Fire Museum, 04578.
Open by appointment only 10 AM - 4 PM, Jul 1 - Aug 30
M Maine Art Gallery, Old Academy, Warren St, PO Box 815, 04578. Tel 207-882-7511. *Chmn & Dir* Roger Johnson; *Treas* William Burley; *Secy* Warren Spaulding
Open Summer daily 10 AM - 5 PM, Sun 1 - 5 PM, Winter Sat 10 AM - 4 PM, Sun 1 - 4 PM. No admis fee, donations appreciated. Estab 1958 as a cooperative, non-profit gallery created by the Artist Members of Lincoln County Cultural & Historical Association to exhibit the work of artists living or working in Maine. Gallery occupies a red brick federal two-story building built in 1807 as a free Academy. The building is now on National Historical Register. Average Annual Attendance: 6000. Mem: Annual meeting Sept
Income: Financed by patrons
Exhibitions: Summer Exhibition: A juried show in two parts of 5 weeks each featuring approx 100 painters and sculptors living or working in Maine. Winter series of one-person invited exhibitions

YORK

M OLD GAOL MUSEUM, York St and Lindsay Rd, 03909. Tel 207-363-3872. *Dir & Cur Coll* Eldridge H Pendleton; *Chmn Committee* Mrs John Laurent; *Asst Cur* Mary Pietsch; *Secy* Alice Gates
Open Mon - Sat 10:30 AM - 5:30 PM, Sun 1:30 - 5 PM. Admis $1.50. Estab 1900 as a local history museum to maintain, care for and develop historical collections of a regional nature and to promote historic research and historically educational programs. Museum consists of the oldest jail in the United States and an 18th century tavern arranged as period rooms. Two exhibition rooms house traveling shows and temporary exhibitions of an historical nature. Average Annual Attendance: 10,000. Mem: 600; dues family $8, single $5; annual meeting Aug
Income: $45,000 (financed by endowment)
Collections: Regional Collection of American Furniture and Decorative Arts; Rare Books; Manuscripts
Publications: Old Gaol Newsletter, quarterly
Activities: Classes for adults and children; dramatic programs; lect for members; tours; lending collection contains 4000 original art works, original prints, paintings, sculpture, 500 slides
L Library, Box 188, 30909.
Open daily 10 AM - 4 PM. Reference only
Library Holdings: Vols 3300; Micro—Prints; Other—Clipping files, manuscripts, memorabilia, pamphlets, photographs, original documents
Special Subjects: Decorative Arts, genealogy, local history

O SOCIETY FOR THE PRESERVATION OF HISTORIC LANDMARKS, 03909. Tel 207-363-3200. *Pres* Karen Bowden; *VPres* John Bardwell; *Secy* Nora Clements
Estab 1941 to operate buildings of historic interest. Mem: 150; dues $2; annual meeting August
M Elizabeth Perkins House, 03909.
Open June 16 - Sept 4, Mon - Sat 9:30 AM - 5 PM, Sun 1:30 PM - 5 PM. Admis adults $1. A Colonial house as lived in by a Victorian family, built in 1730; contains 18th and 19th century furniture, china, and prints. Average Annual Attendance: 2300
M Old School House, 03909.
Open May 27 - Sept 30, Mon - Sat 9:30 Am - 5 PM, Sun 1:30 - 5 PM. Original school built in 1745; figures of the schoolmaster and children are in period costumes. Average Annual Attendance: 11,500
M Jefferds Tavern, 03909.
Open May 30 - Sept 30, Mon - Sat 9:30 AM - 5 PM, Sun 1:30 - 5 PM. Admis adults $1. An ancient hostelry built before the Revolution by Captain Samuel Jefferds
M John Hancock Warehouse, 03909.
Open May 27 - Sept 30, Mon - Sat 9:30 AM - 5 PM, Sun 1:30 - 5 PM. Admis adults 50¢. Owned by a signer of the Declaration of Independence at the time of his death; listed in the National Register of Historic Places. Average Annual Attendance: 4500
Exhibitions: Old tools; antique ship models

MARYLAND

ANNAPOLIS

M HAMMOND-HARWOOD HOUSE, 19 Maryland Ave, 21401. Tel 301-269-1714. *Admin* Barbara A Brand
Open Nov - March Tues - Sat 10 AM - 4 PM, Sun 1 - 4 PM, Apr - Oct Tues - Sat 10 AM - 5 PM, Sun 2 - 5 PM. Admis adults $2, students $1, children 50¢. Estab 1938 to preserve the Hammond-Harwood House (1774), a National Historic Landmark; to educate the public in the arts and architecture of Maryland in the 18th century. Average Annual Attendance: 19,000. Mem: 1800; dues varied; meeting May and Nov
Income: Financed by endowment, membership, attendance and sales
Collections: Paintings by C W Peale; Chinese Porcelain; English and American Furnishings especially Maryland; Glasware; Prints; Silver
Publications: Maryland's Way (Hammond-Harwood House cookbook); Historic Booklet on Hammond-Harwood House
Activities: Dramatic programs; docent training; lect open to public; individual paintings and original objects of art lent to bonafide museums within reasonable transporting distance; sales shop sells books, slides, postcards and notepaper

M UNITED STATES NAVAL ACADEMY MUSEUM, 21401. Tel 301-267-2108. *Dir* Dr William W Jeffries; *Senior Cur* James W Cheevers; *Cur of Ship Models* Robert F Sumrall; *Cur of Robinson Coll* Alexandra Welsh; *Senior Exhibit Specialist* Archie M Wild
Open Tues - Sat 9 AM - 5 PM, Sun 11 AM - 5 PM, cl Mon. No admis fee. Estab 1845 as Naval School Lyceum for the purpose of collecting, preserving and exhibiting objects related to American naval history. Museum contains two large galleries totaling 9000 sq ft, with other exhibits in other areas of the campus. Average Annual Attendance: Approx 600,000
Income: Financed by Federal Government appropriations and private donations
Purchases: $70,327 (1978), $46,226 (1979)
Collections: Ceramicwares; Drawings, †Paintings, Prints, Sculpture of Naval Portraits and Events; Medals; Naval Uniforms; Ship Models; Silver; †Weapons
Exhibitions: (1978)Photography of David Douglas Duncan; American Naval Prints; selections from permanent collection; (1979) John Paul Jones' Victory; selections from permanent collection
Publications: Collection catalogs and special exhibition brochures, periodically
Activities: Lect; tours upon request; individual paintings and original objects of art lent to other museums and related institutions for special, temporary exhibitions; originate traveling exhibitions
L Library, 21402.
Open to students, scholars and public with notice, reference only
Library Holdings: Vols 2600; Per subs 24

BALTIMORE

AMERICAN COUNCIL FOR THE ARTS IN EDUCATION
For further information, see National and Regional Organizations

M **ARTS, LIMITED,** 805 N Charles St, 21201. Tel 301-837-3575. *Dir* Judith Lippman; *Gallery Asst* Abbie Chessler; *Advertising* Meredith Lippman
Open Mon - Fri 10 AM - 4 PM, Sun 2 - 5 PM. No admis fee. Estab 1977 to show a variety of contemporary art forms, painting, sculpture, prints, clay, fibre and mixed media. Located on the parlor and second floor of an old structure on one of the oldest streets in Baltimore. Building has been contemporized with as much of the old architective remaining as possible. Average Annual Attendance: 3500
Exhibitions: (1978-79) Ed Baynard, Robert DeNiro, Chiam Gross, Hans Hofmann, Alex Katz, Michael Knigin, Reuben Kraner, Herman Maril, Joseph Solman, Andy Warhol; Photography: Edie Baskin, Ralph Gibson, Eve Sonneman
Publications: Washington Artists: Works on Paper, Works on Clay
Activities: Classes for adults and children; educational lect on current exhibitions; lect open to public; gallery talks; tours; lend complete exhibitions to authorized spaces; book traveling exhibitions; originate traveling exhibitions

M **BALTIMORE MARITIME MUSEUM,*** Pier 4, Pratt St, 21202. Tel 301-837-1776. *Dir* Donald F Stewart
Open Labor Day - June 20 Sat 10 AM - 5 PM, Sun 12 - 5 PM, June 21 - Labor Day daily 10 AM - 6 PM. Admis adults $1.50, children 75¢, under 6 no charge. Estab 1921 in a working lightship. Mem: Dues individual $10
Collections: Flags and trophies; models; paintings; prints; records; sailor art; scrimshaw; shipbuilding memorabilia; 1770-1945 ship lantern display relics of famous ships; woodcarving
Activities: Guided tours; winter festival; sales shop

M **BALTIMORE MUSEUM OF ART,** Art Museum Dr, 21218. Tel 301-396-7101. *Dir* Arnold L Lehman; *Asst Dir of Art* Brenda Richardson; *Asst Dir for Admin* Ann Boyce Harper; *Chmn Curatorial Div & Cur Decorative Arts* William Voss Elder III; *Cur Prints and Drawings* Victor Carlson; *Asst Cur Decorative Arts* M B Munford; *Asst Cur Prints and Drawings* Jay Fisher; *Assoc Cur Painting and Sculpture* Sona Johnston; *Chmn Education Division* Susan Badder
Open Tues - Sat 11 AM - 5 PM, Thurs 7 - 10 PM, Sun 1 - 5 PM, cl Mon & New Year's. No admis fee. Estab 1914 to house and preserve art works, to program art exhibitions and programs and to offer educational programs and events. The building was designed by John Russell Pope in 1929 and houses permanent and temporary galleries and Antioch Court. Average Annual Attendance: 250,000. Mem: 500; dues $15 - $100
Income: $1,602,000 (financed by endowment, membership, city and state appropriation and federal and county funds)
Collections: Abram Eisenberg Collection of Paintings primarily of 19th century French origin; Antioch Mosaics; Blanche Adler Collection of Graphic Art; Charles and Elsa Hutzler Memorial Collection of Contemporary Sculpture; Cone Collection of 19th and 20th Century French Paintings, Sculpture, Drawings and Prints, Near Eastern and European Textiles, Laces, Spanish and French 18th Century Jewelry, Furniture and other Decorative Arts; Edward Joseph Callagher III Memorial Collection of Paintings by American artists executed between 1921 and 1955; Elise Agnus Daingerfield Collection of 18th Century English, French and American Paintings with emphasis on portraiture; Ellen H Bayard Collection of 18th and 19th Century American Paintings, European Ceramics, Chinese Export Porcelain, Irish Glass, 19th Century European Jewelry, and American and English Silver; General Lawrason Riggs Collection of Old Master Prints and Chinese Ceramics; George A Lucas Collection of 19th Century Paintings, Drawings, Prints and Bronzes; Hanson Rawlings Duval Jr Memorial Collection of 19th Century Baltimore Architectural Elements, American Furniture, Paintings, Metalwork and European and Chinese Ceramics; Harry A Bernstein Memorial Collection of Contemporary American Paintings; Jacob Epstein Collection of Old Master Paintings; Janet and Alan Wurtzburger Collection of 20th Century Sculpture by European masters with emphasis on the human figure; J G D'Arch Paul Collection of 18th Century American Furniture; Julius Levy Memorial Fund Collection of Oriental Art; Mary Frick Jacobs Collections of 15th - 18th Century European Paintings, Tapestries, Furniture and Objets d'Art; McLanahan Memorial Collection of Furnishings for and installation of 1720 bedchamber; Nelson and Juanita Greif Gutman Memorial Collection of 20th Century Paintings, Sculpture and Drawings; Peabody Institute Collection of 19th and 20th Century American Paintings; Saidie A May Collection of 20th Century Paintings, Sculpture and Graphics, Ancient, Medieval and Renaissance Sculpture, Textiles; Samuel and Tobie Miller Memorial Collection of Contemporary Painting and Sculpture; T Harrison Garrett Collection of Graphic Art from the 15th through 19th century; Thomas E Benesch Memorial Collection of Drawings by contemporary American and European artists; White Collection of Ceramics, Furniture, Needlework, Glass and Decorative Art Books; White Collection of Early Maryland Silver of outstanding examples of 18th and 19th century work of Maryland silversmiths; William Woodward Collection of 18th and 19th Century Paintings of English sporting life; Wurtzburger Collection of Art from Africa, the Americas and the Pacific
Exhibitions: Painting, sculpture, decorative arts, prints, drawings and photography
Publications: Calendar, monthly; exhibition catalogs
Activities: Classes for children; docent training; lect open to the public; concerts; gallery talks; tours; competitions; exten dept serving Museum in the Mall, Columbia, Maryland; originate traveling exhibitions; museum shop selling books, original art, reproductions, prints, slides

L **Library,** 21218. Tel 301-396-7101. *Librn* Joan Robison
Open by appointment for refernece only
Library Holdings: Vols 25,000; Per subs 62
Special Subjects: American decorative arts, 19th and 20th century French art

M **COMMUNITY COLLEGE OF BALTIMORE,** Art Gallery, 2901 Liberty Heights Ave, 21215. Tel 301-396-7980. *Gallery Dir* David Bahr
Open Mon - Fri 10 AM - 4 PM, Sun 2 - 5 PM. No admis fee. Estab 1965 to bring to the Baltimore and college communities exhibitions of note by regional artists, and to serve as a showplace for the artistic productions of the college art students and faculty. Consists of one large gallery area, approx 120 running ft, well-lighted through the use of both natural light through sky domes and cove lighting which provides an even wash to the walls
Income: Financed through the college
Collections: Graphics from the 16th century to the present; paintings by notable American artists and regional ones
Exhibitions: The Inner Harbor (an invitational theme show); Teachers as Artists; annual art faculty, art student, and one-person faculty exhibits
Activities: Lect open to public; gallery talks

JOHNS HOPKINS UNIVERSITY

M **Archaeological Collection,*** Charles & 34th St, 21218. *Archaeological Coll Cur* Dr John Pollini
Open Mon - Wed 11 AM - 3 PM. Estab 1876. Small exhibit space in Gilman Hall
Collections: Egyptian through Roman material 3500 BC to 500 AD

M **Evergreen House,*** 4545 N Charles St, 21210. Tel 301-338-7641. *Cur* Elizabeth F Hammann
Open Mon - Fri 2 - 5 PM, second Tues every month tours 10 AM - 5 PM. No admis fee. Formerly the house of John W Garrett which he bequeathed to the University
Collections: Fine arts, Rare Book Library, paintings left by Mrs Garrett to the Evergreen House Foundation
Exhibitions: Changing exhibitions

L **Milton S Eisenhower Library Galleries,*** Quadrangle Level, 21218. Tel 301-338-8325; TWX 710-234-4090. *Dir* Susan K Martin
Open Mon - Fri 9 AM - 5 PM
Exhibitions: Changing exhibitions of paintings, photography and sculpture by Baltimore artists

M **MARYLAND HISTORICAL SOCIETY MUSEUM,** 201 W Monument St, 21201. Tel 301-685-3740, Ext 70, 71 & 72. *Pres* Leonard C Crewe Jr; *Recording Secy* Mrs Frederick W Lafferty; *Dir* Mrs Romaine S Somerville; *Gallery Cur* Stiles T Colwill
Open Tues - Sat 11 AM - 4 PM, Sun 1 - 5 PM. Admis contribution for non-members. Estab 1844 to collect, display and interpret the history of the State of Maryland. Average Annual Attendance: 54,000. Mem: 5000; annual meeting Oct
Income: Financed by endowment, membership, city and state appropriations
Collections: Architectural drawings; crystal and glassware; ethnic artifacts, all of Maryland origin or provenance; metalwork; paintings, both portrait and landscape; porcelain and pottery; silver; textiles and costumes
Exhibitions: Continually changing exhibitions reflecting the history and culture of the state
Publications: Maryland Historical Society Magazine, quarterly; News and Notes, bimonthly
Activities: Lect open to the public; gallery talks; tours; individual paintings and original objects of art lent to other organizations; sales shop selling books, magazines, prints and reproductions

L **Library,** 201 W Monument St, 21201. *Librn* Dr Larry Sullivan
Open Tues - Sat 9 AM - 4 PM. Estab 1844 to provide resources for the study of Maryland history, genealogy and resources
Library Holdings: Vols 80,000; Per subs 245; Micro—Reels; AV—Lantern Slides, slides; Other—Clipping files, exhibition catalogs, prints, manuscripts 3,000,000, pamphlets, photographs
Collections: Robert G Merrick Collection of Prints
Activities: Lect open to the public

M **MARYLAND INSTITUTE COLLEGE OF ART,** Decker Gallery,* 1300 W Mount Royal Ave, 21217. Tel 301-669-9200. *Pres* Fred Lazarus IV; *Dir* Robin Coplan
Open Mon - Thurs 10 AM - 4 PM & 6 - 9 PM, Fri - Sat 10 AM - 4 PM, Sun 1 - 4 PM. No admis fee. Estab 1826. Average Annual Attendance: 10,000
Income: Financed by endowment and student tuition
Collections: Maryland Institute-George A Lucas Collection donated in 1909 comprising over 400 paintings and drawings by Corot, Daumier, Delacrox, Greuze, Manet, Millet, Pissarro, Whistler; bronzes by Antoine Barye, and a collection of 17,000 graphics
Publications: Handouts of the works in the Lucas Collection; several small catalogs; two major publications per year
Activities: Dramatic programs; lect open to the public; concerts; gallery talks; tours; original objects of art lent; traveling exhibitions organized and circulated; sales shop selling books

L **Library,*** 1300 W Mount Royal Ave, 21217. *Librn* John Stoneham
Library Holdings: Vols 29,000

M **MORGAN STATE UNIVERSITY GALLERY OF ART,*** Cold Spring Lane & Hillen Rd, 21239. Tel 301-444-3030. *Dir* James E Lewis; *Cur* Gabriel S Tenabe
Open Mon - Fri 9 AM - 5 PM, Sat, Sun, holidays by appointment only, cl Easter, Thanksgiving, Christmas. No admis fee. Estab 1950. Average Annual Attendance: 5000
Income: $5500
Collections: American, European, African, New Guinea; paintings; prints; sculpture
Exhibitions: Exhibitions from the collection; temporary and traveling exhibitions
Publications: Catalogs, monthly
Activities: Lect open to the public, visiting lectrs; lending collection contains 500 Kodachromes; traveling exhibitions organized and circulated

L **Library,*** Cold Spring Lane & Hillen Rd, 21239.
Library Holdings: Other—Photographs

M **MOUNT CLARE MANSION,** Carroll Park, 21230. Tel 301-837-3262. *Chmn House Committee* Mrs Thomas B Cockey III
Open Tues - Sat 11 AM - 4 PM, Sun 1 - 4 PM. Admis adults $1.50, children under 12 25¢. Estab 1917 to demonstrate how wealthy colonial and federal period families lived. Maintained by the National Society of Colonial Dames. Rooms of the house furnished with 18th & early 19th century decorative arts, much of which belonged to the Carroll family who built the house in 1754. Average Annual Attendance: 4500
Collections: American paintings; 18th and early 19th century English and American furniture; English silver; Irish crystal; Oriental export porcelain; other English and American decorative arts
Exhibitions: Changing exhibits

Publications: Brochure on Mount Clare, booklet on the house
Activities: Historical slide shows for schools and organizations; docent training; tours; competitions; individual paintings and original objects of art lent to local museums on occasion; sales shop selling books, prints, slides and gifts
L **Library,** Carroll Park, 21230.
Open to members and the public
Library Holdings: Vols 800
Special Subjects: Decorative Arts, 18th Century Culture
Collections: Part of the library of Charles Carroll, Barrister-at-law, builder of the house, 1754

O **MUNICIPAL ART SOCIETY OF BALTIMORE CITY,** c/o Beverley C Compton Jr, 135 E Baltimore St, 21202. Tel 301-727-1700. *Pres* Beverley C Compton Jr; *Treas* Alan P Hoblitzell
Estab 1899; the society contributes primarily public sculpture. Mem: 150; dues $15
Income: $7000
Activities: Series of lect on art by outstanding critics; annual traveling scholarship

M **PEALE MUSEUM,** 225 Holliday St, 21202. Tel 301-396-3523. *Pres* George D Hubbard; *VPres* Mrs Martin L Millspaugh; *Treas* H Chace Davis Jr; *Dir* Dennis K McDaniel; *Asst Dir* Barry Dressel
Open Tues - Fri 10:30 AM - 4:30 PM, Sat & Sun 2 - 5 PM. No admis fee. Estab 1931 as the museum of the life and history of Baltimore. Built in 1814 as Rembrandt Peal's Baltimore Museum and Gallery of Fine Arts, a national historical landmark. Also operates the Carroll Mansion, historic house built in 1812. Average Annual Attendance: 15,000. Mem: 450; dues $15 - $500
Income: $175,000 (financed by endowment, membership, city appropriation)
Purchases: $5000 - $10,000
Collections: The A Aubrey Bodine Collection; paintings by members of the Peale family; photographs of Baltimore of the 19th and 20th centuries; prints of Baltimore
Activities: Lect open to public, 1 - 2 visiting lectr per year; lending collection contains 350 photographs; museum shop selling books, reproductions, prints, slides
L **Library,** 225 Holliday St, 21202.
Open to staff for reference only
Library Holdings: Vols 2000

L **ENOCH PRATT FREE LIBRARY OF BALTIMORE CITY,** Fine Arts Dept, 400 Cathedral St, 21201. Tel 301-396-5490. *Dir* Ernest Siegel; *Chief Public Relations Division* Howard W Hubbard
Open Mon - Thurs 9 AM - 9 PM, Fri - Sat 9 AM - 5 PM; Oct - May Sun 1 - 5 PM. Estab 1882 to provide materials, primarily circulating on the visual arts and music. Exhibition space in display windows, interior display cases, corridors and special departments
Income: Financed by city and state appropriation
Purchases: $27,500
Library Holdings: AV—Fs, motion pictures, rec, slides; Other—Framed reproductions, reproductions
Publications: Booklets
Activities: Lect and film showings; concerts
L **George Peabody Branch,** 17 E Mount Vernon Place, 21202. Tel 301-396-5540. *Head* Evelyn L Hart
Open Mon - Sat 9 AM - 5 PM, cl Sun

O **STAR-SPANGLED BANNER FLAG HOUSE ASSOCIATION,** 844 E Pratt St, 21202. *Pres* Herbert E Witz; *VPres* Hugh Benet Jr; *VPres* S Vannort Chapman; *VPres* Herbert R Preston Jr; *Treas* John H Ensor; *Secy* Mrs Turner Moore; *Dir* Mrs Hugh Martin
Open Tues - Sat 10 AM - 4 PM, Sun 2 - 4:30 PM. Admis adults $1, students 12 - 18 50¢, under 12 free. Estab 1927 for the care and maintenance of 1793 home of Mary Pickersgill, maker of 15 star, 15 stripe flag used at Fort McHenry during Battle of Baltimore, War of 1812, which inspired Francis Scott Key to pen his famous poem, now our national anthem; also to conduct an educational program for public and private schools. Museum houses artifacts, portraits and library. 1793 house furnished and decorated in Federal period to look as it did when Mary Pickersgill was in residence. Average Annual Attendance: 18,000. Mem: 750; dues vary; annual meeting April
Collections: Flag collection; original antiques of Federal period
Exhibitions: Old and Historic Flag Exhibit
Publications: The Star (newsletter), quarterly
Activities: Classes for adults and children; lect open to public; tours; originate traveling exhibitions; sales shop selling books and souvenirs
L **Library,** 844 E Pratt St, 21202.
Open to public for reference
Library Holdings: Vols 300

M **UNITED METHODIST HISTORICAL SOCIETY,** Lovely Lane Museum, 2200 Saint Paul St, 21218. Tel 301-889-4458. *Pres* William Louis Piel; *Executive Secy* Edwin Schell
Open Mon & Fri 10 AM - 4 PM, Sun after church; groups by appointment. No admis fee. Estab 1855; a religious collection specializing in Methodism. The main museum room contains permanent exhibits; three other galleries are devoted largely to rotating exhibits. Average Annual Attendance: 5000. Mem: 581; dues $3 - $100; annual meeting May
Income: $22,334 (financed by membership, and religious denomination)
Collections: Church edifices, furniture, medallions and emblems, photographs, quilts, and statuary
Exhibitions: Holy Rolling - All the News That's Fit to Print; Our Ethnic Church Heritage
Publications: Third Century Methodism, quarterly; annual report
Activities: Docent training; lect open to public, 1 visiting lectr per year; gallery talks; tours; competitions; sales shop selling books, prints, and cards
L **Library,** Lovely Lane Museum, 2200 Saint Paul St, 21218. *Librn* Edwin Schell; *Asst Librn* Betty Ammons
Open to general public for reference
Library Holdings: Vols 4500; Per subs 30; Other—Manuscripts, Archives

M **WALTERS ART GALLERY,** 600 N Charles St, 21201. Tel 301-547-9000. *Pres Board of Trustees* Jay M Wilson; *Dir* Richard H Randall Jr; *Asst Dir* William R Johnston; *Administrative Officer* Scott Hunter; *Cur Renaissance and Baroque Art* Mary Smith Podles; *Cur of Egyptian and Ancient Near Eastern Art* Jeanny Vorys Canby; *Cur of Greek and Roman Art* Diana M Buitron; *Cur of Manuscripts and Rare Books* Lilian M C Randall; *Dir of Education* Theodore L Low; *Deputy Dir for Development* John H Nozynski; *Editor of Publications* Anne Garside; *Dir of Conservation Dept* Terry Drayman Weisser; *Registrar* Leopoldine Arz; *Sales Mgr* Irene Butterbaugh
Open Mon 1 - 5 PM, Tues - Sat 11 AM - 5 PM, Sun and legal holidays 2 - 5 PM; cl New Year's Day, Fourth of July, Thanksgiving, Christmas Eve, Christmas. No admis fee. Estab 1931 by the will of Henry Walters and opened in 1934 as an art museum. A neoclassic museum of 1905 with a contemporary wing of five floors opened in 1974, covering 126,000 sq ft of exhibition space with auditorium, library and conservation laboratory. Average Annual Attendance: 166,000. Mem: 3000; dues $15 - $500
Income: $1,300,000 (financed by endowment, membership, city and state appropriation and grants)
Collections: The Collection covers the entire history of art from Egyptian times to the beginning of the 20th century. It includes important groups of Roman Sculpture, Etruscan, Byzantine and medieval art; Sevres porcelains; Near Eastern Art and European paintings
Exhibitions: (1978) Ancient Persia; I, Claudius; In Search of Ancient Treasure; Know What You See; Netsuke; Nigeria; Splendor in Books; The Grand Mogul
Publications: Bulletin, monthly Oct through May; journal, annually
Activities: Classes for adults and children; docent training; lect open to the public, 12 visiting lectr per year; concerts; gallery talks; tours; individual paintings and original objects of art lent; lending collection contains 25,000 original art works, 2000 paintings, 2500 sculpture; museum shop selling books, reproductions, slides, Christmas cards, notepaper
L **Library,** 600 N Charles St, 21201. *Librn* Muriel L Gers
Open Mon 1 - 5 PM, Tues - Fri 11 AM - 5 PM. Estab 1934 chiefly to serve the curatorial staff; also provides art reference services for students and the general public. For reference only
Income: $68,000
Purchases: $36,300
Library Holdings: Vols 75,000; Per subs 500; Other—Exhibition catalogs
Special Subjects: History of art from prehistoric times to the end of the 19th century, with emphasis on manuscript illumination and decorative arts

CHESTERTOWN

O **HISTORICAL SOCIETY OF KENT COUNTY,** Church Alley, PO Box 665, 21620.
Estab 1936 to foster an appreciation of our colonial heritage, to encourage restoration, to enlighten and to entertain. Open by appointment only. Headquarters are in an early 18th century town house, beautifully restored and furnished. Mem: 525; dues family $10, single $7; annual meeting Apr
Income: Financed by membership and a Candlelight Tour
Collections: Furniture, pictures, some silver
Exhibitions: Annual Decorative Arts Forum
Activities: Lect for members and guests, 4 visiting lectr per year; tours; open house with traditional costuming

CHEVY CHASE

C **GOVERNMENT EMPLOYEES INSURANCE COMPANY,** 5260 Western Ave, Chevy Chase, MD. (Mailing Add: GEICO Plaza, Washington, DC 20076) Tel 301-986-2042. *In Charge Art Coll* Walter R Tinsley
Open to public by special arrangement. No admis fee. Estab 1959 for edification and pleasure of officers, employees and visitors; to adorn the offices and common areas. Collection displayed throughout office building
Collections: American contemporary art, 19th Century and early 20th Century figurative art
Exhibitions: Exhibitions of works loaned by artists

COLLEGE PARK

M **UNIVERSITY OF MARYLAND,** Art Gallery, 1202 Art-Sociology Bldg, 20742. Tel 301-454-2763. *Dir* Edith A Tonelli; *Dept Chmn* David C Driskell; *Registrar* Susan Worteck
Open Mon - Fri 9 AM - 4 PM, Sat & Sun 1 - 5 PM; check for summer hours. No admis fee. Estab 1966 for exhibitions related to the programs of the Department of Art of the university and to serve the Museum Training Program of the department. Gallery has 4000 sq ft of space, normally divided into one large gallery and a smaller study gallery. Average Annual Attendance: 22,000
Collections: Small collection of 20th century paintings, sculpture and prints, including works executed on the WPA Federal Art Project and the Department of the Treasury, Section of Painting and Sculpture; small collection of West African sculpture
Exhibitions: William Baziotes; Contemporary Photography; Edward Corbett; French Watercolors from Delacroix to Cezanne; Charles Gleyre; Grace Hartigan; 17th Century Dutch Drawings; Selections from Skowhegan; Women Artists in Washington Collections
Publications: Catalogs for exhibitions
Activities: Lect open to public, 8 visiting lectr per year; originate traveling exhibitions; museum shop selling exhibition catalogs
L **Art Library,** Art-Sociology Bldg, 20742. Tel 301-454-2065. *Head Art Library* Courtney Shaw; *Assoc Librn* Patricia Lange
Open Mon - Thurs 8:30 AM - 10 PM, Fri 8:30 AM - 5 PM, Sat 9 AM - 5 PM, Sun 1 - 10 PM. Estab 1979 in new building to serve the needs of the art department and campus in various art subjects
Library Holdings: Vols 37,000; Per subs 185; Micro—Fiche, reels; Other—Exhibition catalogs, reproductions

Publications: Bibliography; Checklist of Useful Tools for the Study of Art
Activities: Tours

EASTON

M **ACADEMY OF THE ARTS,*** Harrison & South Sts, PO Box 605, 21601. *Pres* Esther Henry; *Cur* James Plumb; *Dir* Mrs Kurt L Lederer
Open Mon - Fri 10 AM - 4 PM, Sat & Sun 2 - 4 PM, cl bank holidays. No admis fee. Estab 1958 to enrich the lives of the people in the community with the arts through exposure and instruction. Two galleries are maintained. Average Annual Attendance: 6000. Mem: 900; dues individual $12, junior $5; annual meeting May
Income: Financed by endowment, membership, city and state appropriation
Collections: Permanent art collection
Publications: Newsletter, quarterly
Activities: Classes for adults and children; dramatic programs; docent training; lect open to the public; concerts; gallery talks; tours; competitions; exten dept serving tri-county area; individual paintings lent to different organizations locally and to other galleries; lending collection contains books, original art works, original prints, paintings, photographs
L **Library,*** Harrison & South Sts, PO Box 605, 21601.
Open to members only
Library Holdings: Vols 500
Collections: Print Collection

FORT MEADE

M **FORT MEADE MUSEUM,*** 4674 Griffin Ave, 20755. Tel 301-677-6966. *Cur* David C Cole
Open Wed - Sat 11 AM - 4 PM, Sun 1 - 4 PM, cl Mon, Tues and holidays. No admis. Estab 1963 to collect, preserve, study and display military artifacts relating to the United States Army, Fort Meade and the surrounding region. The gallery is a small post museum with a single display gallery. Average Annual Attendance: 7500
Income: Financed by federal and military funds
Collections: Military art, mostly World War II
Activities: Lect open to the public; gallery talks; tours

FROSTBURG

M **FROSTBURG STATE COLLEGE,** Fine Arts Gallery I, 21532. Tel 301-689-4274. *Gallery Dir* Dustin P Davis
Open Mon - Fri Noon - 5 PM, Sun 2 - 5 PM. No admis fee. Estab 1968 for educational purposes
Income: Financed by state appropriation
Collections: Folk art; prints
Exhibitions: Duane Hanson; Mid-Atlantic Region Print Exhibition; Tenth Street Days
Activities: Lect open to public, 5 visiting lectr per year; gallery talk; competitions

HAGERSTOWN

M **WASHINGTON COUNTY MUSEUM OF FINE ARTS,** City Park, PO Box 423, 21740. Tel 301-739-5727. *Pres Board of Trustees* Richard G Wantz; *Dir* H Paul Kotun; *Cur* Robert E Preszler; *Secy* Rita E Kershner
Open Tues - Sat 10 AM - 5 PM, Sun 1 - 6 PM, cl Mon. No admis fee. Estab 1929 and opened to the public in 1931 for the purpose of preserving, protecting, promoting, displaying and educating through the arts. The museum consists of the William H Singer Memorial Gallery, Sculpture Court, Concert Gallery, two general galleries and the Youth Gallery. Average Annual Attendance: 60,000. Mem: 800; dues family $25, individual $10; annual meeting April and Oct
Income: $116,000 (financed by membership, city and county government)
Collections: American pressed glass; antique laces; †contemporary painting, drawing, prints and sculpture; European, †American sculpture, †prints and drawings; illuminated manuscripts; Oriental jades
Exhibitions: African Sculpture; Albert Decaris Engravings; Americana (carvings) by Wilhelm Schimmel and John Bell (ceramics); American Pressed Glass; Americans Abroad; Annual Exhibition of Cumberland Valley Artists; Annual Photographic Salon; Ansel Adams - A Survey; Antique Laces - The Kimler Collection; Art in Bloom; Cambodian Art from Angkor Wat; Charles Carroll of Carrollton; Clay, Fiber and Metal; Contemporary American Painters; Fiber Art by Thurid Clark; Hagerstown Art Club Annual Exhibition; H I Gates - A Retrospective; Lily Spandorf; Museum's Permanent Collection: Prints, Landscapes, Portraits, Drawings, Contemporary Work, Sculpture, Oriental Objects; New Aspects of Self in American Photography; Old Master Drawings; Paintings by Alice Neel; Paintings by American Indians; Paintings by the Peale Family; Pressed Glass; Public School Art; Royal Watercolor Society; Scouting Through the Eyes of Norman Rockwell; Sea and Shore - 19th Century Views; Stoneware by Jane Larson; Textiles by Maria DeConceicao
Publications: American Pressed Glass; Old Master Drawings; annual reports; bulletin, monthly; catalogs of major exhibitions; catalogue of the permanent collection
Activities: Classes for adults and children; dramatic programs; docent training; lect open to the public, 4 visiting lectr per year; concerts; gallery talks; tours; competitions; exten dept serving Pennsylvania, Virginia, West Virginia, western Maryland; individual paintings and original objects of art lent to other museums and galleries, as per Museum Policy regarding security; originate traveling exhibitions; sales shop selling books, magazines, original art, reproductions, prints, slides and original art objects and hand crafted items
L **Library,** City Park, PO Box 423, 21740.
Open to the public for reference only
Library Holdings: Vols 5000; Per subs 14

MONKTON

M **BREEZEWOOD FOUNDATION MUSEUM AND GARDEN,*** 3722 Hess Rd, 21111. Tel 301-771-4485. *Pres* A B Griswold
Open May - Oct, first Sun each month 2 - 6 PM. Admis $2. Estab 1956 to exhibit Breezewood's collection of sculpture and other art from Southeast Asia. Museum has one large room and two small rooms. Average Annual Attendance: 600
Income: Financed by endowment and private means
Collections: Buddhist art from India; sculpture and art from Southeast Asia

ROCKVILLE

M **CITY OF ROCKVILLE MUNICIPAL ART GALLERY,*** Baltimore Rd, 20853. Tel 301-424-3184. *Dir* Bernard R Loiselle
Open Mon - Fri 1 - 5 PM, Sun 2 - 5 PM. No admis fee. Estab 1959. Average Annual Attendance: 7500
Income: Financed by city appropriation
Collections: Small permanent collection
Exhibitions: Twelve shows per year, including a youth show
Activities: Classes for adults

SAINT MICHAELS

M **CHESAPEAKE BAY MARITIME MUSEUM,** Navy Point, PO Box 636, 21663. *Dir* R J Holt
Open Oct - May, Tues - Sun 10 AM - 4 PM; cl Mon; Jan & Feb weekends only; May - Oct daily 10 AM - 5 PM. Admis adults $2, children 75¢. Estab 1968 as a waterside museum dedicated to preserving the maritime history of the Chesapeake Bay. Consists of fifteen buildings on approximately twelve acres of waterfront property including Hooper's Strait Lighthouse, 1879. Average Annual Attendance: 70,000. Mem: 3000; dues $10 - $35
Income: Financed by membership and admissions
Collections: Paintings; ship models; vessels including skipjack, bugeye, log canoes, and many small crafts; waterfowling exhibits; working boat shop
Publications: Weather Gauge (newsletter), quarterly
Activities: Docent training; museum shop selling books, reproductions, prints
L **Library,** Navy Point, PO Box 636, 21663.
Small library for research only by appointment with curator

SALISBURY

SALISBURY STATE COLLEGE

M **College Gallery,** College & Camden Aves, Art Department, 21801. Tel 301-546-3261, Ext 417 or 441. *Acting Pres* Dr A N Page; *Acting Academic Dean* Dr R A Phipps; *Gallery Dir* John R Cleary; *Dept Chmn* K N Kimmel
No admis fee. Estab 1967, to provide a variety of fine arts to the college and community, with emphasis on educational value of exhibitions. Gallery open to public, and is located on the second floor of Blackwell Library, hours vary. Average Annual Attendance: 3200
Income: Financed by state appropriations
Exhibitions: (1979-80) Alfred Eisenstaedt; Exhibition of Photographs; Images on Exchange; faculty, invitational, senior and student shows
Publications: Announcements
Activities: Classes for adults; dramatic programs; lect open to the public, 3-4 visiting lectrs per year; concerts; gallery talks; tours; competitions; awards; exten dept serves local community
L **Blackwell Library, Art Department,** College & Camden Aves, 21801. *Library Dir* James R Thrash
Open Mon - Thurs 8 AM - Midnight, Fri 8 AM - 10 PM, Sat 10 AM - 5 PM, Sun Noon - Midnight. Estab 1925, to support the curriculum of Salisbury State College. Circ 2500. Library has total space of 66,000 sq ft
Income: $6000
Purchases: $6000
Library Holdings: Vols 128,618; Per subs 36; Micro—Cards, fiche, reels; AV—A-tapes, cassettes, fs, rec; Other—Clipping files, pamphlets
M **Wildfowl Art Museum,** Camden Ave, 21801. Tel 301-742-4988. *Dir* Ken Basile; *Chmn* Tom George; *Vice Chmn* Max Hughes; *Secy* Bill Humphreys; *Treas* Ted Crockett; *Cur* Cindy Doerzbach; *Asst Cur* Katie Fox; *Secy* Barbara Gehrm; *Gift Shop Coordr* Peggy Parsons; *Gift Shop Coordr* Elmer Lowe
Open daily 1 - 5 PM. Admis $1. Estab 1976, a non-profit organization dedicated to the preservation and conservation of wildfowl carving. Main gallery and balcony contains wildfowl carvings, paintings and prints. Average Annual Attendance: 5000. Mem: 1020; dues family $25, individual $15, student $5; annual meeting March
Income: $77,297 (financed by membership, city and state appropriations, grants, donations, gift shop sales)
Collections: Permanent collection of 2300 bird carvings
Exhibitions: (1980) Annual Fall Exhibition (October); Annual Spring Competition (April)
Publications: Newletter, four times per year
Activities: Lect open to the public, 10 visiting lectrs per year; gallery talks; tours; competitions; awards; individual paintings and original objects of art lent; lending collection contains color reproductions, framed reproductions, original art works, original prints, paintings, photographs, sculpture; museum shop sells books, magazines, original art, reproductions, prints

SILVER SPRING

L MARYLAND COLLEGE OF ART AND DESIGN LIBRARY, 10500 Georgia Ave, 20766. Tel 301-649-4454. *Head Librn* Laura C Pratt; *Asst Librn* Gloria Coffman; *Librn* M Elizabeth Stites
Open Mon - Fri 9 AM - 4 PM. Estab 1977 to facilitate and encourage learning by the students and to provide aid for the faculty. Circ 4100. College maintains Gudelsky Gallery
Purchases: $6153
Library Holdings: Vols 6360; Per subs 26; AV—Cassettes, fs, rec, slides; Other—Clipping files
Special Subjects: Drawings, Illustration, Sculpture, Design, painting, visual communications
Collections: Leonardo and The Italian Renaissance Book; Stites Collection

SOLOMONS

M CALVERT MARINE MUSEUM, PO Box 97, 20688. Tel 301-326-3719. *Dir* Ralph E Eshelman; *Registrar* Dave Bohaska; *Exhib Designer* Bette Houseman; *Master Woodcarver* Pepper Langley
Open May - Sept, Mon - Sat 10 AM - 5 PM, Sun 1 - 5 PM, Oct - April, Mon - Fri 10 AM - 4:30 PM, Sat & Sun 1 - 5 PM. No admis fee. Estab 1970, to provide the public with a marine oriented museum on maritime history, esturine natural history and marine paleontology. Gallery is maintained on the history of sail. Average Annual Attendance: 50,000. Mem: 480; dues family $7.50, individual $5, student $2.50
Income: $130,000 (financed by county appropriation)
Purchases: $1000
Collections: J S Bohannon Folk Art Steamboat Collection; †local Chesapeake Bay Ship Portraits; Tufnell Watercolor Collection
Exhibitions: (1980) Fossils of Calvert Cliffs: A 10 x 7 ft mural depicting Marine Miocene life; John Olsen Chapter of American Shipcarving Guild Exhibit
Publications: Newsletter 'Bugeye Times', quarterly; miscellaneous special publications on history
Activities: Classes for adults and children; docent training; lect open to the public, 16 visiting lectrs per year; gallery talks; tours; competitions; awards; individual paintings and original objects of art lent; lending collection contains motion pictures, nature artifacts, photographs, slides; sales shop sells books, prints, slides, hand crafts
L Library, PO Box 97, 20688.
Open May - Sept, Mon - Sat 10 AM - 5 PM, Sun 1 - 5 PM, Oct - April, Mon - Fri 10 AM - 4:30 PM, Sat & Sun 1 - 5 PM. Estab 1974. Library open for research and reference

TOWSON

M GOUCHER COLLEGE, Kraushaar Auditorium Lobby Gallery,* Department of Visual Arts, 1021 Dulaney Valley Rd, 21204. Tel 301-825-3300, Ext 310. *Chmn Dept* Lincoln F Johnson
Open Mon - Fri 9 AM - 5 PM during the academic calendar and on evenings and weekends of public events. No admis fee. Estab 1964 to display temporary and continuously changing exhibitions of contemporary and historically important visual arts. Gallery space located in the lobby of the Kraushaar Auditorium; 150 running feet of wall space. Average Annual Attendance: 15,000
Income: Financed privately
Collections: Elizabeth Morris Collection; ceramics; coins; drawings; paintings; prints; sculpture; textiles containing over 200 objects representing textiles from Egypt, Peru, Java, China, Japan, Europe and America
Exhibitions: Artworks by Jane Kelly Morais; Ceramics from the Goucher Collection; Fiberworks by Sharon Rose; Paintings by Hilton Brown, Lisa Lawrence; Photographs by Barbara Young; Women Artists in Baltimore
Activities: Lect open to public, 3 visiting lectrs per year; gallery talks; individual paintings and original objects of art lent to museums and university galleries

TOWSON STATE UNIVERSITY

M The Holtzman Art Gallery, Osler Dr, 21204. Tel 301-321-2808. *Dir* Christopher Bartlett; *Secy* Joanna Warrington
Open Mon - Fri 11 AM - 4 PM, Tues & Thurs 7 - 9 PM, Sat & Sun 1 - 5 PM. Estab 1973 to provide a wide variety of art exhibitions, primarily contemporary work, for students, faculty and community. The main gallery is situated in the new fine arts building directly off the foyer. It is 30 x 60 ft with 15 ft ceiling and 15 x 30 ft storage area. Average Annual Attendance: 10,000
Income: $10,000 (financed by state appropriation, cultural services fees and private gifts)
Purchases: $1000
Collections: African art; †Asian arts, through Roberts Art Collection; †contemporary painting and sculpture
Exhibitions: Art Department Faculty; Art Student Show; Chinese Brush Painting by Chao-Hwa Tung; Drawings USA 77; Haitian Paintings; John Mitchell (plastics and prints); Leonard Baskin (new graphics and watercolors); Milton Avery Prints; Morningstar Quilts; Native Art in Yugoslavia; National Ceramic Invitational: Function - Non-Function; New American Monotypes; New Directions in Fabric Design (national invitational); Paintings by Colleen Browning; Theatre Design, A Student Perspective; Tyler School of Art Faculty (painting, drawing, sculpture)
Publications: Calendar, each semester; exhibition posters and catalogs
Activities: Lect open to public, 5 - 10 visiting lectr per year; gallery talks; tours; exten dept serves Maryland; artmobile; book 2 - 3 traveling exhibitions per year; originate traveling exhibitions to other universities; sales shop selling exhibition catalogs and posters
L Roberts Room, Fine Arts Building, York Rd, 21204. Tel 301-321-2807. *Cur* Harriet McNamee
Open during academic year Mon - Fri 10 AM - Noon and 2 - 4 PM; summers Mon - Fri 10 AM - Noon and 1 - 3 PM. No admis fee. Estab 1972 to provide an area to display the Asian art collections of the University and for the benefit of both the university community and the public. The gallery is located on the second floor of

---

the Fine Arts Building. Average Annual Attendance: 3000
Income: $33,800 (financed by state appropriation and university budget)

WESTMINSTER

M WESTERN MARYLAND COLLEGE, Gallery One, Department of Art, 21157. *Gallery Dir* Wasyl Palijczuk
Open Mon - Fri 10 AM - 4 PM. No admis fee. Estab to expose students to original works by artists

MASSACHUSETTS

AMHERST

M AMHERST COLLEGE, Mead Art Bldg, 01002. Tel 413-542-2335. *Dir* Frank Trapp; *Cur* Judith Barter
Open Mon - Fri 8:30 AM - 4:30 PM, Sat & Sun 1 - 5 PM (shorter hours during summer); cl Aug. No admis fee. Estab 1949. Average Annual Attendance: 13,500
Collections: †Ancient art; †American art; †English art; Western European and Oriental collections
Exhibitions: American Folk Art; American Painters of the Artic; Fumio Yoshimura: Contemporary Wood Sculpture; Glass by Rene Lalique; War a la Mode; changing exhibitions for college curriculum needs
Publications: American Art at Amherst: A Summary Catalogue of the Collection at the Mead Art Gallery; catalogs for major exhibitions
L Art Library, Mead Art Bldg, 01002.
Library Holdings: Vols 20,000

L JONES LIBRARY, INC, 43 Amity St, 01002. Tel 413-256-0246. *Dir* Anne M Turner; *Asst Dir* Sondra M Radosh; *Reference Librn* Pauline M Peterson; *Adult Service Librn* Catherine B Gannon; *Cur* Anne K Williamson
Open Mon, Wed and Fri 9 AM - 5:30 PM; Tues & Thurs 9 AM - 9:30 PM; Sat 10 AM - 5:30 PM; Sun Mon, Wed - Fri 9 AM - 5 PM; Tues 9 AM - 9 PM; Sat 10 AM - 5 PM. Estab 1919 as a public library. Circ 210,000. Gallery. Average Annual Attendance: 100,000
Income: Financed by endowment and city appropriation
Library Holdings: Vols 93,827; Per subs 295; Micro—Reels; AV—A-tapes, cassettes, Kodachromes, lantern slides, rec, slides; Other—Clipping files, framed reproductions, prints, manuscripts, memorabilia, original art works, pamphlets, photographs, reproductions, sculpture, original documents
Collections: Emily Dickinson; Harlan Fiske Stone; Ray Stannard Baker; Robert Frost; Sidney Waugh liturgical vestments and artifacts; medieval sculpture
Exhibitions: Gallery has monthly exhibits by local artists Picasso traveling exhibitions; New York State Council on the Arts; Smithsonian Institution Traveling Exhibition; local one man shows
Publications: Sun and Balance, three times a year
Activities: Lect open to public; concerts; gallery talks; tours

UNIVERSITY OF MASSACHUSETTS, AMHERST

M University Gallery, Fine Arts Center, 01003. Tel 413-545-3670. *Dir* Hugh M Davies; *Gallery Mgr* Peter J Bena; *Registrar* Betsy Siersma
Open Tues - Fri 11:30 AM - 4:30 PM, Sat & Sun 2 - 5 PM during school year. No admis fee. Estab 1962. Main gallery 60 x 60 ft; East, West and Lower Galleries 20 x 60 ft each. Average Annual Attendance: 10,000. Mem: 150; dues $8 and up
Collections: †20th century American works on paper including drawings, prints and photographs
Exhibitions: Class of 1928 Photography Collection; George Trakas; 19th Century Drawings and Watercolors; Relief Sculpture of the Seventies; Sam Gilliam; Stephen Antonakos
Publications: Exhibition catalogs
Activities: Lect open to the public; gallery talks; tours; film program; individual art works from the permanent collection loaned to other institutions; originate traveling exhibitions
L Art Slide Library, Bartlett Hall, 01003. Tel 413-545-3595. *Cur* Dorothy Perkins
Open Mon - Fri 8 AM - 4 PM
Library Holdings: Vols 24,000; AV—Slides 65,000

ANDOVER

M PHILLIPS ACADEMY, Addison Gallery of American Art, PO Box 48, 01810. Tel 617-475-7515. *Dir* Christopher C Cook; *Cur Photography* James L Sheldon; *Registrar* Antoinette Thiras
Open Tues - Sat 10 AM - 5 PM, Sun 2:30 - 5 PM. No admis fee. Estab 1931 in memory of Mrs Keturah Addison Cobb, to enrich permanently the lives of the students by helping to cultivate and foster in them a love for the beautiful. The gift also included a number of important paintings, prints and sculpture as a nucleus for the beginning of a permanent collection of American art. Average Annual Attendance: 35,000
Income: Financed by endowment
Collections: 18th, 19th and 20th century drawings, paintings, prints, sculpture; photographs; film; videotapes
Exhibitions: The American Still Life, 1835-1979; Photographs by Lotte Jacobi; Urban-Suburban: Photographs in Color
Activities: Lect open to public, 8-10 visiting lectrs per year; concerts

ATTLEBORO

M ATTLEBORO MUSEUM, CENTER FOR THE ARTS, Capron Park, 199 County St, 02703. Tel 617-222-2644. *Pres* Mrs Anthony Nyzio; *VPres* Mrs Charles O'Connell; *Treas* William C Bott; *Dir* Mrs F K Cross
Open Tues - Fri 12:30 - 4 PM, Sat & Sun 2 - 5 PM, cl Mon & holidays. No admis fee. Estab 1927 to exhibit the works of current artists, as well as the art works of the museum's own collection. There are preview openings for members and guests, plus several competitive exhibits with awards and an outdoor art festival. Three galleries, with changing monthly exhibits of paintings, drawings and prints as well as glass cases for jewelry and crafts, are maintained. All three galleries are carpeted with grass cloth walls and excellent track lighting. Average Annual Attendance: 7200. Mem: 300; dues life mem $250, sustaining mem $25, associate mem $15, family $12, individual $8; annual meeting May
Income: Financed by membership, gifts
Purchases: $400
Collections: Paintings and prints
Exhibitions: (1979) The Boston Printmakers; Dedham Art Guild; Holiday Show. (1980) The Alphabet; Annual Area Artist Exhibit; Art in the Park; Competitive Painting Exhibit; Faculty Show; Members Show; Recent Members; Spring Spectacular; Student and Teachers Exhibit
Publications: Newsletter, monthly; school brochures; yearly program booklet
Activities: Classes for adults and children; lect open to public; concerts; gallery talks; competitions, painting and photography; original objects of art lent; museum shop sells original art

BEVERLY

M BEVERLY HISTORICAL SOCIETY, 117 Cabot St, 01915. Tel 617-922-1186. *Pres* Robert Perron; *Treas* Ray Standley; *Chmn Cabot House Museum & Library* Elizabeth Webber; *Chmn Balch House* Roger Hanners; *Chmn Hale House* Esther Herrick
Museum & library open in Mar, Thurs 10 AM - 4 PM; Apr - June, Wed & Thurs 10 AM - 4 PM; July - Aug, Wed & Thurs 10AM - 4 PM, Sat 1 - 4 PM; Sept - mid Dec, Wed & Thurs 10 AM - 4 PM; other times by appointment. Hale House open June 15 - Sept 15 daily 10:30 AM - 4 PM, cl Sun & Mon; other times by appointment. Admis adults $1, children 50¢. The Balch House built in 1636 by John Balch contains old furniture. The Hale House was built in 1694 by the first minister, John Hale. Mem: 380; dues single $5; annual meeting Oct
Collections: Children's toys; military objects; portraits; seamen's instruments; ship models

BOSTON

O ANCIENT AND HONORABLE ARTILLERY COMPANY OF MASSACHUSETTS, Faneuil Hall, 02109. Tel 617-227-1638. *Cur* Sidney M Abbott
Open Mon - Fri 10 AM - 4 PM; cl Sat, Sun, holidays and two weeks in Oct. No admis fee. Estab 1638
Collections: Military historical material; paintings; portraits
Activities: Guided tours
L Library, Faneuil Hall, 02109.
Open to individuals by request for research
Library Holdings: Vols 100

M ART INSTITUTE OF BOSTON, Gallery West, Gallery East, 700 Beacon St, 02215. Tel 617-262-1223. *Pres* William H Willis; *Chmn Gallery* Angelo Ferbitta
Open Mon - Fri 9 AM - 5 PM, Mon - Thurs 6 - 7 PM. No admis fee. Estab 1969 to show work by young New England artists, all disciplines and work by well known artists from any locale, especially in less exhibited disciplines such as graphic design, and to show work by students and faculty of the institute. 3000 sq ft of gallery. Average Annual Attendance: 2500
Exhibitions: (1979)Complete Graphic Works of Hundertwasser; The Illustrators Workshop; Illustrations of LeRoy Nieman; Roswell Angier, photographer; Thirty-one selected shows
Activities: Classes for adults; lectures open to the public, five visiting lecturers per year; lecture series coordinated with exhibitions; gallery talks; competitions, local and regional, usually student oriented; extension department serving metropolitan Boston; individual paintings and original objects of art lent to other galleries
L Library, 700 Beacon St, 02215. *Librn* Susan Sobel
Open Mon - Thurs 9 AM - 9 PM, Fri 9 AM - 5 PM, Sat 9 AM - 3 PM. Estab 1969 to support school curriculum
Library Holdings: Vols 4500; Per subs 55; AV—Slides; Other—Clipping files, exhibition catalogs

O BOSTON ARCHITECTURAL CENTER,* 320 Newbury St, 02115. Tel 617-536-3170.
Open Mon - Thurs 9 AM - 11 PM, Fri - Sun 9 AM - 5 PM. No admis fee. Estab 1883 for education of architects and designers. Small exhibition space on first floor. Average Annual Attendance: 2000. Mem: 300; dues $25; annual meeting June
Exhibitions: Signs and Lights
Activities: Classes for adults; lect open to public, 16 visiting lectrs per year; competitions; exten dept serving professional architects; traveling exhibitions organized and circulated
L Library,* 320 Newbury St. 02115. Tel 617-536-9018. *Librn* Susan Lewis
Open to the public for reference
Library Holdings: Vols 13,000; Per subs 130; AV—A-tapes, fs, v-tapes; Other—Photographs, maps
Special Subjects: Architecture, Solar energy
L Memorial Library,* 320 Newbury St, 02115.
Open by appointment only
Library Holdings: Vols 2000
Collections: 18th, 19th and early 20th century architectural books from the collections of practicing architects

O BOSTON ART COMMISSION OF THE CITY OF BOSTON,* 1 City Hall Square, 02201. Tel 617-725-4551.
Estab 1898 to accept and maintain the art collection owned by the City of Boston. Mem: 5; one representative from each organization: American Institute of Architects, Massachusetts Institute of Technology, Boston Public Library, Copley Society, and Boston Museum of Fine Arts; meetings approx once per month
Income: $3335 (financed by city appropriation)
Collections: City of Boston art collection, including fountains, paintings, sculpture, statuary
Publications: Catalog and guide to the art work owned by the City of Boston, in preparation

L BOSTON ATHENAEUM, 10 1/2 Beacon St, 02108. Tel 617-227-0270. *Dir & Librn* Rodney Armstrong; *Art Librn* Jack Jackson; *Art GAllery Dir* Donald C Kelley; *Print Dept Cur* Pamela Hoyle; *Print Dept Cur* Sally Pierce; *Honorary Cur of Prints* Charles E Mason Jr
Open Mon - Fri 9 AM - 5:30 PM, Sat 9 AM - 4 PM; cl Sun also Sat June 1 - Sept 1. Estab 1807 to serve New England living artists in the fine arts and crafts
Income: $750,000 (financed by endowment and membership)
Purchases: $75,000
Library Holdings: Vols 650,000; Per subs 625; Micro—Reels; Other—Clipping files, exhibition catalogs, prints, manuscripts, memorabilia, original art works, pamphlets, photographs, reproductions, sculpture, original documents
Collections: 19th Century Boston Prints & Photographs
Activities: Lect open to the public, 6 vis lectr per year; concerts; gallery talks; tours; competitions; exhibitions

BOSTON PUBLIC LIBRARY
L Central Library, Copley Square, 02117. Tel 617-536-5400. *Dir & Librn* Philip J McNiff
Building contains mural decorations by Edwin A Abbey, John Elliott, Pierre Puvis de Chavannes, and John Singer Sargent; bronze doors by Daniel Chester French; sculptures by Frederick MacMonnies, Bela Pratt, Louis Saint Gaudens, Francis Derwent Wood; illustrators by Howard Pyle; paintings by Copley and Duplessis; and bust of John Deferrari by Joseph A Coletti
L Fine Arts Department, Copley Square, 02117. *Cur of Fine Arts* G Florence Connolly
Open Mon - Fri 9 AM - 9 PM, Sat 9 AM - 6 PM, Sun 2 - 6 PM in winter, cl summer
Library Holdings: Vols 120,000; Other—Original art works, reproductions
L Albert H Wiggin Gallery (Prints), Copley Square, 02117. *Keeper of Prints* Sinclair H Hitchings
Open Mon - Fri 9 AM - 9 PM, Sat 9 AM - 6 PM, Sun 2 - 6 PM in winter. Print Study Room Mon - Fri 9 AM - 5 PM, cl Sat & Sun
Library Holdings: Vols 1554; Other—Prints, original art works, photographs, sculpture
Exhibitions: Eight or nine per year

C FEDERAL RESERVE BANK OF BOSTON, 600 Atlantic Ave, 02106. Tel 617-973-3454. *In Charge Art Collection* Anne M Belson
Open Mon - Fri 9 AM - 5 PM by appointment only. No admis fee. Estab 1978 for educational and cultural activities. Collection displayed on 3rd, 4th, 31st and 32nd floors and elsewhere throughout building. A permanent gallery, 27 x 178 ft with an adjoining 420-seat auditorium, located on the ground floor; open Mon - Fri 10 AM - 4 PM; is reserved for traveling exhibitions
Collections: Focus of the collection is on United States art since the mid-1950's
Activities: Lect; gallery talks; tours; book traveling exhibitions

M ISABELLA STEWART GARDNER MUSEUM,* 280 Fenway, Boston, MA. (Mailing Add: 2 Palace Rd, Boston, MA 02115,) Tel 617-566-1401. *Dir* Rollin van N Hadley; *Asst Dir* Linda V Hewitt; *Cur* Deborah Gribbon
Open Sept - June Tues 1 - 9:30 PM, Wed - Sun 1 - 5:30 PM, July & Aug Tues - Sun 1 - 5:30 PM, cl Mon, national holidays, Sun before Labor Day. Admis adults $1. Estab 1903, the museum houses Isabella Stewart Gardner's various collections. Museum building is styled after a 16th century Venetian villa; all galleries open onto a central, glass-roofed courtyard, filled with flowers that are changed with the seasons of the year. Mem: 170,000
Income: Financed by endowment and door fee
Collections: Gothic and Italian Renaissance, Roman and classical sculpture; Dutch and Flemish 17th century; Japanese screens; Oriental and Islamic ceramics, glass, sculpture; 19th century American and French paintings
Publications: Fenway Court (annual report)
Activities: Sales shop selling books, reproductions, prints, slides
L Library,* 02115. *Librn* Susan Sinclair
Open to scholars who need to work with museum archives
Library Holdings: Vols 500; Per subs 6

M GIBSON SOCIETY, INC, 137 Beacon St, 02116. Tel 617-267-6338. *Pres* Stephen T Hibbard; *Custodian* Chuck Richards; *Custodian* Pam Richards
Open Tues - Sun 2 - 5 PM; cl Mon and holidays. Admis $2. Estab 1957 as a Victorian House museum. Average Annual Attendance: 1500
Collections: Decorative arts; paintings; sculpture; Victorian period furniture
Activities: Guided tours; sales shop selling books and postcards

O GUILD OF BOSTON ARTISTS, 162 Newbury St, 02116. Tel 617-536-7660. *Pres* Charles A Mahoney; *VPres* Kenneth L Gore; *Secy* Maris Platais; *Cur* Gretchen Knowles Stone
Open Tues - Sat 10:30 AM - 5:30 PM; cl Sun & July & Aug. No admis fee. Estab and incorporated 1914, cooperative organization. Guild owns building; one gallery with continuous exhibitions in which each member is entitled to show one work; second gallery devoted to one-man shows, each member by turn at regular intervals. Mem: Active 65-80, associates under 100; annual meeting April
Exhibitions: Three yearly general exhibitions by entire active membership

M INSTITUTE OF CONTEMPORARY ART, 955 Boylston St, 02115. Tel 617-266-5152. *Dir* Stephen S Prokopoff; *Business Mgr* Jan Chester; *Development Dir* Melissa Carey; *Cur* Elisabeth Sussman; *Cur* Gillian Levine; *Communications* Michelle Satter
Open Tues - Sat 10 AM - 5 PM, Wed 10 AM - 9 PM, Sun Noon - 5 PM. Admis adults $1.25, students and senior citizens 75¢, members free. Estab 1936 to organize,

document, and exhibit works of contemporary masters of new and innovative talents and of artists who have been overlooked. A full range of contemporary working methods including photography and film, crafts and performance are shown. Gallery is comprised of two floors gallery space 4000 sq ft, offices and auditorium are located on the third floor; building is 19th century renovated police station. Average Annual Attendance: 55,000. Mem: 2000; dues $20 and up; annual meeting Jan

Income: $500,000 (financed by membership, city and state appropriations, gifts and grants)

Purchases: $350,000

Exhibitions: American Impressionism; Boston Architecture; Carl Andre; German DaJa; George Platt Lynes; Natural Resources; Jackson Pollock: 1951-1952; Portrait of a New England Village: Alice Stahlknecht; Florine Stettheimer

Publications: Exhibition catalogs; newsletter, bimonthly

Activities: Classes for children; dramatic programs; docent training; lect open to public, 20 visiting lectr per year; concerts; gallery talks; tours; traveling exhibitions organized and circulated; museum shop selling books, catalogs and cards

O **MASSACHUSETTS HISTORICAL SOCIETY,** 1154 Boylston St, 02215. Tel 617-536-1608. *Dir* Louis L Tucker
Open Mon - Fri 9 AM - 4:45 PM, cl Sat, Sun & holidays. No admis fee. Estab 1791
Collections: Archives; historical material; paintings; sculpture
Exhibitions: Temporary exhibitions
Publications: Annual brochure; irregular leaflets; various books
Activities: Lect
L **Library,** 1154 Boylston St, 02215. *Librn* John D Cushing
Library Holdings: Vols 400,000; Other—Manuscripts

M **MUSEUM OF FINE ARTS,** 465 Huntington Ave, 02115. Tel 617-267-9300. *Dir* Jan Fontein; *Assoc Dir* Robert C Casselman; *Dir of Finance* John J Higgins; *Asst Dir Admin* Arthur D Larson; *Registrar* Linda Thomas; *Conservator Asiatic Art* Yashiro Iguchi; *Cur American Decorative Arts* Jonathan Fairbanks; *Cur European Decorative Arts & Sculpture* Robert C Moeller; *Cur Contemporary Art* Kenworth Moffett; *Cur Textiles* Larry Salmon; *Cur Prints & Drawings* Eleanor A Sayre; *Cur Egyptian Art* William Kelly Simpson; *Cur Classical Art* Cornelius C Vermeule
Open daily 10 AM - 5 PM, Tues Eve until 9 PM, cl New Years Day, July 4, Thanksgiving and Christmas. Admis adults $2.50, students and senior citizens $1.50, free Sun 10 AM - 1 PM, children under 16 free, 65 and over free Mon 10 AM - 12 Noon. Estab and inc 1870; present building opened 1909. Average Annual Attendance: 650,000. Mem: 13,000; dues $1000 - $10
Income: $3,500,000
Purchases: $1,000,000
Collections: Outstanding Chinese, Japanese and Indian art; exceptional †Egyptian, †Greek and †Roman art; †master paintings of Europe and America; †superb print collection from 15th century to present; †sculpture, †decorative and minor arts including period rooms, porcelains, †silver, †tapestries, †textiles, †costumes, †musical instruments
Exhibitions: Specially organized exhibitions are continually on view; exhibitions of the permanent collections
Publications: Bulletin, yearly; Calendar of events, monthly
M **William Morris Hunt Memorial Library,** 465 Huntington Ave, 02115. Tel 617-267-9300. *Librn* Nancy S Allen
Open Tues - Fri 10 AM - 4:30 PM, Sat (during academic year) 10 AM - 1 PM. Estab 1879 to support curatorial research. For reference only
Income: $80,000 (financed by endowment and membership)
Library Holdings: Vols 104,000; Per subs 650; AV—Slides 70,000; Other—Clipping files, exhibition catalogs, pamphlets
Publications: The Museum Year; Boston Museum Bulletin; MFA Preview; Calendars; Pompeii AD; Mary Cassatt at Home; A Gallery Guide to American Decorative Arts; Corpus Vasorum Antiquorum: Attic Blackfigured Pelike, Kraters, Dinoi, Hydriai and Kylikes; Application of Science to the Dating of Works of Art; Cape Light: Color Photographs by Joel Meyerowitz; Javanese Batiks; Art and Commerce: American Prints of the Nineteenth Century; Corot to Braque: French Paintings in the Museum of the Fine Arts, Boston; How to Care for Works of Art on Paper; Richard Estes: The Urban Landscape; Morris Louis in the Museum of Fine Arts, Boston; William Morris Hunt: A Memorial Exhibition
Activities: Classes for adults and children; docent training; dramatic programs; lect open to public; concerts; gallery talks; tours; book traveling exhibitions

M **MUSEUM OF THE NATIONAL CENTER OF AFRO-AMERICAN ARTISTS,** 300 Walnut Avenue, 02119. Tel 617-442-8820. *Pres* Adelaide C Gulliver; *Dir* Edmund B Galther; *Secy* Alvin Poussaint; *Artistic Dir* Elma Lewis
Open Tues - Sat 1 - 5 PM, Sun 1 - 7 PM. Admis adult $1.25, children 50¢. Estab 1969 to promote visual art heritage of Black people in the Americas and Africa. Suite of three special exhibition galleries; suite of three African Art Galleries; suite of three permanent collection galleries; one local artist gallery. Average Annual Attendance: 10,000. Mem: 250; annual dues $25
Income: $250,000 (financed by private gifts, contracts, etc)
Collections: Art from Western Africa; Early 20th century Afro-American Prints and Drawings
Exhibitions: African Artists in America; Stone Churches of Ethiopia
Publications: Newsletter, quarterly
Activities: Dramatic programs; lectures open to the public; concerts; gallery talks; tours; competitions with awards (Edward Mitchell Barrister Award); book traveling exhibitions; traveling exhibitions organized and circulated; sales shop sells books, magazines, prints

O **SOCIETY FOR THE PRESERVATION OF NEW ENGLAND ANTIQUITIES,*** Otis House, 141 Cambridge St, 02114. Tel 617-227-3956. *Exec Dir* Abbott L Cummings
Open Mon - Fri 10 AM - 4 PM, cl Sat, Sun & holidays. Admis non-members $1. Estab and inc 1910, the Otis House serves as both headquarters and museum for the Society. Society owns over 60 historic houses throughout New England, which are open to the public. Mem: 3650; dues $10 and up; annual meeting May
Publications: Old Time New England, biannual bulletin
Activities: tours

L **Library,*** Otis House, 141 Cambridge St, 02114. *Librn* Elinor Reichlin
Collections: Study collections of New England Architecture in the form of fragments, measured drawings, 200,000 photographs, pattern books; other collections include textiles and wallpaper

BROCKTON

O **BROCKTON ART CENTER,** Fuller Memorial, Oak St, 02401. Tel 617-588-6000. *Dir* Marilyn Hoffman; *Cur* Richard Minutillo; *Dir of Development and Public Relations* Steve Aton; *Business Mgr* James Keneklis; *Education Coordr* Carol Heepke; *Graphic Designer* Sharon Blagdon; *Museum Technician* Patrick Bell; *Dir Art Workshops* Beverly Edwards
Open Tues - Sat 1 - 5 PM, Sun 1 - 6 PM. Admis donations. Estab 1969 to provide a variety of art exhibitions, performing arts and education programs of regional and national interest. The center houses six galleries; one gallery is reserved for important works of art on loan from the Museum of Fine Arts, Boston. Average Annual Attendance: 28,000. Mem: 1500; dues $20
Income: $784,000 (financed by endowment, membership, state appropriation and grants)
Collections: Contemporary American art; Early American and Sandwich glass; 19th century American and European paintings
Exhibitions: Biennial of Boston painting and sculpture; regional and national contemporary exhibits; temporary exhibits of 19th century American contemporary crafts
Publications: Newsletter and calendar of events, 4 per year
Activities: Classes for adults and children; dramatic programs; docent training; special programs for children; lect open to the public, 4 vis lectr per year; gallery talks; tours; competitions; individual paintings and original objects of art lent to accredited museums of the American Association of Museums; lending collection contains paintings and slides; originate traveling exhibitions; museum shop sells original art, reproductions and contemporary crafts
L **Library,** Fuller Memorial, Oak St, 02401.
Open to members, staff and students
Library Holdings: Vols 1200; Per subs 8

L **BROCKTON PUBLIC LIBRARY SYSTEM,** Municipal Art Gallery,* 304 Main St, 02401. Tel 617-587-2515. *Dir* Ernest J Webby
Open Mon - Fri 9 AM - 9 PM, Sat 9 AM - 6 PM, cl Sun. No admis fee. Special room for monthly art exhibitions. Average Annual Attendance: 20,000
Library Holdings: Vols 5000
Collections: W C Bryant Collection of 19th and 20th century American paintings, chiefly by New England artists; gifts of 20th century paintings which includes four paintings by Hendricks Hallett and an oil painting by Mme Elisabeth Weber-Fulop; loan collection of 20th century painters from the Woman's Club of Brockton; mounted photographs of Renaissance art and watercolors by F Mortimer Lamb
Exhibitions: Monthly exhibitions by local and nationally known artists

BROOKLINE

L **BROOKLINE PUBLIC LIBRARY,** 361 Washington St, 02146. Tel 617-734-0100. *Town Librn* Theresa A Carroll; *Asst Town Librn* Dalija Karoblis; *Supv Loan Dept* Cynthia J Battis; *Head Technical Services* Irene Wilkinson; *Reference Supv* Lois Van Hoesen; *Art & Music Librn* Judith Jackson Long; *Head Adult Services* Barbara H Kohl
Open (Sept - June) Mon - Thurs 9 AM - 9 PM, Fri - Sat 9 AM - 6 PM, Sun 1 - 4 PM; (July - Aug) Mon - Thurs 9 AM - 9 PM, Fri 9 AM - 6 PM. Estab 1857 to provide information, books, records, pictures, for the use of the community. Circ 550,000
Income: $1,200,000 (financed by city appropriation)
Purchases: $175,000
Library Holdings: Vols 375,000; Per subs 700; Micro—Reels; AV—Cassettes, rec; Other—Clipping files, exhibition catalogs, pamphlets, photographs, catalogued maps
Collections: Reference collection of pictures and photographs of Brookline
Publications: Booklists
Activities: Lect open to public, 6 vis lect per year; concerts; tours; film programs; competitions
O **Brookline Art Society,** 361 Washington St, 02146.
Estab 1950. Mem: Dues $20
Exhibitions: Annual juried show; rotating exhibits by individual members, local artists and photographers
Publications: Newsletter, monthly
Activities: Workshops and programs open to public

CAMBRIDGE

O **CAMBRIDGE ART ASSOCIATION,** 23 Garden St, 02138. Tel 617-876-0246. *Acting Dir* Lee MacDonald
Open Tues - Sat 10 AM - 4 PM, cl in Aug. No admis fee. Estab 1944 to exhibit, rent and sell members' work and to encourage an interest in fine arts and crafts in the community. Mem: 350; dues artists $25, friends $20, students $7.50; annual meeting June
Exhibitions: Invited shows in Rental Gallery and Craft Gallery; foreign exhibition each year; members' juried exhibitions in Main Gallery every month
Publications: Bulletin, monthly
Activities: Classes for adults; lect and demonstrations; competitions with prizes; exhibit and sale of books by members; rental services of art works; spring auction; print box

HARVARD UNIVERSITY

M **Busch-Reisinger Museum,** 29 Kirland St, 02138. Tel 617-495-2317. *Asst Cur* Charles W Haxthausen; *Staff Asst* Karen Davidson
Open Mon - Sat 9 AM - 4:45 PM, cl Sun, holidays and Sat in July & Aug. No admis fee. Estab 1901 to collect and preserve art objects and artifacts of central and northern Europe which are of high quality and-or historically and culturally

significant. This collection serves the teaching program of the Department of Fine Arts, outside scholars and the general public. Galleries are divided into three architectural styles: Romanesque, Gothic and Renaissance; in addition, there are galleries for German Expressionist art. Average Annual Attendance: 39,000. Mem: 435; dues $20; annual meeting in Fall
Income: $180,000 (financed by endowment and membership)
Collections: Bauhaus and Lyonel Feininger Archives; extensive collection of Expressionist and Bauhaus works; reproductions of works of Germanic Art of the Middle Ages and Renaissance; works of art of the Middle Ages, Renaissance and Modern Times
Exhibitions: Color of the Middle Ages (facsimiles of illuminated manuscripts); Constructivist Art; German and Netherlandish Art from the time of Durer and Greugel; German Expressionist Arts; Graphic Art from the Romantic Age; Graphic Art in Germany Today; Graphic Works of Max Beckmann; The works of Paul Klee; prints, drawings and sculpture of Kathe Kollwitz; New European Graphics from Bauhaus
Publications: Newsletter, quarterly
Activities: Tours by appointment; lect open to public; concerts; gallery talks; 8000 individual paintings and 4000 original objects of art lent to museums having special exhibitions; originate traveling exhibitions

M **Carpenter Center for the Visual Arts,** 24Quincy St, 02138. Tel 617-495-3251. *Dir & Sr Lecturer-Visual Studies* Robert G Gardner; *Chmn* Lou J Bakanowsky
No admis fee. Estab 1963 as an undergraduate department in visual and environmental studies
Income: Financed by endowment
Publications: Exhibition catalogs
Activities: Individual paintings lent to other Harvard departments or houses; originate traveling exhibitions

M **Harvard Semitic Museum,** 6 Divinity Ave, 02138. Tel 617-495-4631. *Dir* Frank Moore Cross Jr; *Cur* Dr Carney E S Gavin
No admis fee. Estab 1889 to promote sound knowledge of Semitic languages and history; an archaeological research museum. Open by appointment only. Average Annual Attendance: 1000. Mem: 150; dues $20
Income: Financed by endowment, membership, federal research grants and contracts
Collections: †Historic photographs, E E Hale Egyptian Collection; Excavated material from Nuzi and various other Palestinian and Near Eastern sites; Islamic metal, weapons, garments (Ottoman Empire); Phoenician glass
Publications: Harvard Semitic Series
Activities: Classes for adults and children; docent training; lect open to public, 5 visiting lectr per year; tours; exten dept serves Harvard University; original objects of art lent to universities and museums; museum shop sells reproductions, prints, rubbings, jewelry and cards

M **William Hayes Fogg Art Museum,** 32 Quincy St, 02138. Tel 617-495-7768. *Dir* Seymour Slive; *Asst Dir Cultural Affairs & Programs* Gabrilla Jeppson; *Deputy Dir* Suzannah Doeringer; *Budget Officer* Martha Williams; *Archivist* Phoebe Peebles; *Chief Conservator* Arthur Beale; *Assoc Conservator* Greta Andersen; *Assoc Conservator* Marjorie Cohn; *Science Assoc* Eugene Farrell
Open Mon - Fri 9 AM - 5 PM, Sat 10 AM - 5 PM, Sun 2 - 5 PM. No admis fee. Estab 1895, present structure opened 1927; serves both as a public museum and as a laboratory for Harvard's Department of Fine Arts, which trains art historians and museum professionals. The Center for Conservation and Technical Studies operates a training program for conservators and technical specialists. Average Annual Attendance: 80,000. Mem: 2600; dues $10 and $15
Income: Financed by endowment, membership and federal grants
Collections: Ancient coins; Egyptian antiquities; English and American silver; European and American painting and sculpture; Greek and Roman sculpture and vases; Oriental bronzes, ceramics, jades, paintings, prints and sculpture; Romanesque and Gothic sculpture; Sculpture from Persepolis; Wedgwood; Maurice Wertheim Collection of Impressionist and Post-Impressionist Art
Exhibitions: America 1976; Daniel Chester French Retrospective; Stuart Davis: Art and Art Theory; Degas Bronzes; Fogg Master Paintings; Photographs from the Julien Levy Collection; Giovanni Battista Piranesi: Drawings and Prints from the Sackler Collection; Drawings from the Collection of John and Alice Steiner; Studies in Connoisseurship: Chinese Paintings from the Arthur M Sackler Collection; Wash and Gouache: Watercolor at Harvard
Publications: Annual report; newsletter, 4 - 5 per year
Activities: Lect open to public, 30 visiting lectr per year; concerts; gallery talks; tours; individual paintings and original objects of art lent to exhibitions; originate traveling exhibitions; museum shop sells books, reproductions and prints

L **Fine Arts Library,** 02138. Tel 617-495-3373. *Librn* Wolfgang Freitag; *Acquisitions Librn* James Hodgson; *Cur Visual Coll* Helene Roberts; *Chief Cataloguer* Jane Kaufman
Open to Harvard community Mon - Fri 9 AM - 5 PM, Sat 10 AM - 5 PM. Estab 1895 to support the teaching department of fine arts and the research needs of the curatorial department of the Fogg Art Museum and an international community of scholars in art history. Circ 116,000
Income: $460,000 (financed by endowment)
Purchases: $105,000
Library Holdings: Vols 180,000; Per subs 1090; Micro—Fiche, reels; AV—Lantern Slides, slides; Other—Clipping files, exhibition catalogs, pamphlets, photographs
Special Subjects: All areas of art history with emphasis on Italian primitives, architectural history, art and architecture of Eastern Europe, conservation and restoration of works of art, Dutch 17th Century, history of photography, Italian Renaissance, master drawings, Romanesque sculpture
Collections: DIAL Index; Foto Marburg Collection; The Index of Jewish Art; The Knoedler Library Microfiche; Manuscript Archives of American artists and art scholars; Oriental and Islamic Art; Rübel Asiatic Research Collection: Library collection on the arts of the Far East; 25,000 catalogued auction sales catalogs
Publications: Catalog of Auction Sales Catalogs, and First Supplement; Fine Arts Library Catalog

M **LONGFELLOW NATIONAL HISTORIC SITE,** 105 Brattle St, 02138. Tel 617-876-4491. *Supt* James Brown; *Cur* Kathleen Catalano; *Librn* Elizabeth Egbert; *Supervisory Interpreter* Frank Buda
Open daily 10 AM - 4:30 PM. Admis 50¢ (16 years of age and older). Estab 1973 to acquaint the public with the life, work, and time of the American poet Henry W Longfellow
Income: Financed by US Department of the Interior
Collections: Paintings, sculpture, prints, furniture and furnishings once belonging to Henry W Longfellow and his daughter Alice
Activities: Concerts; tours; individual paintings and original objects of art lent to qualified institutions; sales shop selling books, slides and postcards

MASSACHUSETTS INSTITUTE OF TECHNOLOGY

M **MIT Committee on Visual Arts (Hayden Gallery and MIT Permanent Collection),** Hayden Memorial Library Bldg, 160 Memorial Drive, 02139. Tel 617-253-4680. *Dir Exhib* Kathy Halbreich; *Gallery Mgr* Dan Pike
Open daily 10 AM - 4 PM, Wed evening 6 - 9 PM, cl holidays. No admis fee. Estab 1950 to house the Hayden Gallery's and MIT's permanent collection. The MIT Committee on the Visual Arts organizes an active program in contemporary visual arts that includes exhibitions in Hayden Gallery and Hayden Corridor Gallery; more than 800 works of art contained in the permanent collection are sited throughout the Institute's public spaces and offices; the outdoor sculpture collection is on view 24 hours a day to the public. Average Annual Attendance: 20,000
Collections: MIT Permanent Collection of 20th Century painting, sculpture and works on paper
Exhibitions: Twelve exhibitions per year of contemporary art in all mediums
Activities: Symposia; artist-in-residence programs; gallery talks; lect; films

M **Hart Nautical Museum,** Building 5, first floor, 77 Massachusetts Ave, 02139. Tel 617-253-5942. *Cur* William Baker
Open daily 9 AM - 10 PM
Collections: Forbes Collection of whaling prints; rigged models of merchant and warships, engine models, paintings, prints, photos, ship plans and working drawings

M **Compton Gallery,** MIT Alumni Center, Building 10, 02139. Tel 617-253-5075 (gallery), 253-5014 (office). *Dir* Virginia Gunter
Open Mon - Fri 9 AM - 5 PM, cl holidays. No admis fee. Estab 1977
Exhibitions: Several exhibitions each year reflect a wide range of Massachusetts Institute of Technology programs and activities

M **Creative Photography Gallery,** 120 Massachusetts Ave, W31-310, 3rd Floor, 02139. Tel 617-253-4424. *Dir* Starr Ockenga
Open Mon - Fri 9 AM - 10 PM, Sat 10 AM - 6 PM, Sun Noon - 8 PM. No admis fee. Estab 1965
Exhibitions: Seven exhibitions of contemporary photography per year

L **Historical Collections,** Building N52-260, 265 Massachusetts Ave, 02139. Tel 617-253-4444. *Dir* Warren A Seamans
Open Mon - Fri 9 AM - 5 PM. No admis fee. Estab 1971 as a museum facility documenting visually the development of the Institute and of 19th and 20th century science, engineering and architecture. For reference only. Average Annual Attendance: 3100
Library Holdings: AV—A-tapes, cassettes, lantern slides, motion pictures, rec, slides, v-tapes; Other—Clipping files, exhibition catalogs, prints, memorabilia, original art works, pamphlets, photographs, sculpture
Special Subjects: Historical Material
Collections: Architectural drawings; biographical information; furniture; objects d'art; scientific instruments and apparatus; silver
Exhibitions: Twenty exhibitions per year
Activities: Seminars on conservation of works of art

L **Rotch Library of Architecture and Planning,** Room 7-238, 77 Massachusetts Ave, 02139. *Librn* Margaret DePopolo; *Assoc Librn* Micheline Jedrey; *Coll Librn* Rona Gregory; *Librn Aga Khan Program for Islamic Architecture* Richard Dewey; *Visual Coll Librn* Merrill W Smith
Open Mon - Thurs 8:30 AM - 10 PM, Fri 8:30 AM - 8 PM, Sat 10 AM - 6 PM, Sun 2 - 10 PM, special hours when school is not in session. Estab 1868 to serve the students and faculty of the School of Architecture and Planning and other members of the MIT community
Library Holdings: Vols 138,500; Per subs 650; Micro—Fiche, reels; AV—A-tapes, cassettes, Kodachromes, lantern slides, motion pictures, slides, v-tapes; Other—Exhibition catalogs, pamphlets, photographs
Special Subjects: Architecture, Historical Material, Art History, Contemporary Islamic architecture, environmental designs
Exhibitions: Student and faculty work
Publications: Selected Rotch Library Acquisitions; Selected Publications of the Faculty, School of Architecture and Planning, annually

L **Reference Library,** 02139.
Library Holdings: Vols 138,500; AV—Slides 172,750; Other—Prints 41,000, pamphlets 34,100, photographs 43,000

CONCORD

M **CONCORD ANTIQUARIAN SOCIETY MUSEUM,** 200 Lexington Rd, Box 146, 01742. Tel 617-369-9609. *Pres* Frederick W Mears; *VPres* Jonathan M Keyes; *Dir* Mrs William F A Stride; *Corresponding Secy* Rob Roy McGregor; *Treas* William A Lawrence; *Administrator* Mrs Thomas G Doig
Open Mon - Sat 10 AM - 4:30 Pm, Sun 2 - 4:30 PM. Admis adults $2, Children 15 and under $1. Estab 1886 to collect and preserve objects of antiquarian interest to Concord and towns originally a part of Concord; to interpret life in Colonial America, range of American arts, role of Concord in the American Revolution, and contributions of Concord authors-Thoreau, Emerson, Alcotts and Hawthorne-to American literature. Fifteen Period rooms showing life in Concord from 1685 to 1840; Ralph Waldo Emerson study. Average Annual Attendance: 20,000. Mem: 804; dues $15 and up; annual meeting Feb or March
Income: $50,000 (financed by membership, admission)
Publications: Newsletter, quarterly; The Flavour of Concord, cookbook; Concord: Climate for Freedom by Ruth Wheeler
Activities: Classes for adults and children; docent training; lectures open to the public; tours; museum shop sells books, magazines, reproductions, slides, gift items

L **Library,** 200 Lexington Rd, 01742.
Open to members only for lending reference
Special Subjects: Decorative Arts

O **CONCORD ART ASSOCIATION,** 15 Lexington Rd, 01742. *Pres* Maris Platais; *VPres* Loring Coleman; *Cur* Frances P Mellen
Open Tues - Sat 11 AM - 4:30 PM, Sun 2 - 4:30 PM. Admis 50¢. Estab 1916 for

the encouragement of quality art by New England artists. Average Annual Attendance: 10,000. Mem: 500; dues $15 & $20
Income: Financed by membership
Collections: Bronze sculptures; colonial glass; miniatures
Exhibitions: Changing exhibits
Publications: Exhibition notices
Activities: Lect open to public, 4 - 6 vis lectr per year; tours; sales gallery selling original art, prints and reproductions

DEDHAM

O **DEDHAM HISTORICAL SOCIETY,** 612 High St, 02026. Tel 617-326-1385. *Pres* Courtenay P Worthington; *Librn* Muriel N Peters
Open daily 2 - 5 PM; cl Sun, cl Sat during July and Aug. Estab 1859, incorporated 1862 to preserve local material of historical importance, to provide data for historical research and to maintain a library of genealogies and histories. Average Annual Attendance: 2500. Mem: 394; dues life $150, family $8, individual $5; annual meeting first Tues in Mar
Collections: China; Indian relics; 17th century furniture; oil paintings and portraits; pewter; relics pertaining to Dedham history or Dedham families
Publications: A Brief Guide to Dedham Village (pamphlet); Dedham, Massachusetts 1635-1890 (book); Dedham Pottery (book)
L Library, 612 High St, 02026.
Library Holdings: Vols 7000; Other—Manuscripts

DEERFIELD

M **DEERFIELD ACADEMY,** Hilson Gallery, Dept Fine Arts, 01342. Tel 413-772-0241, Ext 221. *Dir* Robert Moorhead
Open Mon - Fri 9 AM - 2 PM, cl weekends. No admis fee. Estab 1955 to exhibit the work of regional artists and members of the Deerfield community; to serve as a focus for visiting lecturers, concerts and similar events; to be a logical extension of the academic program of the Fine Arts Department; to enrich the Academy. A single large exhibition space with its own entrance and central fireplace. Average Annual Attendance: 750 - 1500
Income: Financed through Academy
Exhibitions: David Dickenson (paintings); Elizabeth Fuller, a Memorial Retrospective; Dan Hodermarsky (watercolors); Laura Holland (paintings); David Klopfenstein (photographs); Stuart Salomon (photographs)
Publications: Term schedule, three times a year

M **HISTORIC DEERFIELD INC,** The Street, PO Box 321, 01342. Tel 413-773-5401. *Pres* William E Dwyer; *VPres* Henry N Flynt Jr; *Executive Dir & Secy* Donald R Friary; *Cur* Joseph P Spang; *Dir of Education* J Richie Garrison; *Business Mgr* Hugh D Wharton
Open Mon - Sat 9:30 - 4:30 PM, Sun 1 - 4:30 PM. Admis per house adults $1 - $2.50, children 50¢. Estab 1952 to collect, study and interpret artifacts related to the history of Deerfield, the culture of the Connecticut Valley and the arts in early American life. Maintains 12 historic house museums. Average Annual Attendance: 50,000. Mem: 383; dues $25; annual meeting 2nd Sun in Nov
Income: $683,084 (financed by endowment, membership, rental, royalty and museum store income)
Purchases: $14,262
Collections: †American and English silver; American and European textiles and costume; †American needlework; †American pewter; †Chinese export porcelain; †early American household objects; †early American paintings and prints; †early New England furniture; †English ceramics
Exhibitions: (1978) Folk Selections from the Deerfield Collection; Schoolgirls' Needlework. (1979) French Canadian Furniture at Historic Deerfield. (1980) A Christmas Exhibit of Antique Toys
Publications: Historic Deerfield Quarterly
Activities: Educ dept; Lect open to public, 8 visiting lectr per year; gallery talks; tours; scholarships and fellowships; museum shop selling books, reproductions, slides and local crafts
L Henry N Flynt Library, Memorial Street, 01342. *Librn* David R Proper; *Library Asst* Louise H M Perrin
Open Mon - Fri 9 AM - 4:30 PM. Estab 1970 to support research on local history and the museum collections; also for staff training. Circ 1250
Income: $2157
Purchases: $2679
Library Holdings: Vols 8100; Per subs 30; Micro—Reels; AV—Motion pictures, slides; Other—Clipping files, exhibition catalogs, manuscripts, memorabilia, pamphlets, photographs

O **POCUMTUCK VALLEY MEMORIAL ASSOCIATION,** Memorial Hall, Memorial St, Box 174, 01342. Tel 413-773-9829, 773-5206. *Pres* Rus A Miller; *VPres* William Hubbard; *Secy* Mary Hawkes; *Cur & Dir* Timothy C Neumann; *Asst Cur & Registrar* Ann W duMont
Open daily 11 AM - 4 PM May - Oct. Admis adults $1.50, students $1, children (6-12) 50¢. Estab 1870 to collect the art and other cultural artifacts of the Connecticut River Valley and Western Massachusetts. Maintains 15 galleries. Average Annual Attendance: 10,000. Mem: 800; dues $5; annual meeting last Tues in Feb
Income: $34,000 (financed by endowment, membership and sales)
Collections: Folk art; furniture; Indian artifacts; paintings; pewter; textiles; tools; toys; dolls
Publications: PVMA Newsletter, quarterly
Activities: Classes for children; lect open to the public; concerts; tours; artmobile; individual paintings and original objects of art lent to other museums; lending collection contains original art works, original prints, paintings and artifacts; museum shop selling books, original art, reproductions and slides

DORCHESTER

M **JOHN F KENNEDY LIBRARY AND MUSEUM,** Columbia Point, 02125. Tel 617-929-4546. *Chief Archivist* William W Moss; *Cur* David F Powers
Open daily 9 AM - 5 PM. Admis adult 75¢, children free. Estab 1979 to preserve collections of Kennedy papers and other material pertaining to his career; to educate public about J F Kennedy's career and political system; to make materials available to researchers. Library is a nine-story building overlookinb Boston Harbour, and has two theaters and an exhibition floor. Average Annual Attendance: 270,000,000
Income: Financed by federal and national archives trust fund
Library Holdings: Micro—Cards, fiche, prints; AV—A-tapes, cassettes, fs, lantern slides, motion pictures, slides, v-tapes; Other—Prints, memorabilia, original art works, pamphlets, photographs, reproductions
Collections: 32,000,000 documents and personal papers of John F Kennedy, Robert Kennedy and many others associated with life and career of John F Kennedy; Ernest Hemmingway 6,000,000 ft of film relating to political career, 150,000 photographs, 3000 oral histories, 11,000 paintings and museum objects (personal)
Activities: Tours; museum shop sells books, reproductions, prints and slides

DUXBURY

M **ART COMPLEX MUSEUM AT DUXBURY,** 189 Alden St, PO Box 1411, 02332. Tel 617-934-6634. *Museum Dir* Charles A Weyerhaeuser; *Assoc Dir* Lillian E Bengtz; *Dir Public Affairs* Lanci Valentine; *Librn* Genevieve Tribble
Open Fri - Sun 2 - 5 PM. No admis fee. Estab 1971 to exhibit art. Gallery is 40 x 60 ft; entrance also used for exhibition purposes. Average Annual Attendance: 8000
Collections: American, European and Oriental art; Shaker furniture
Exhibitions: Arts of Japan from museum collection, and others; Boston Printmakers; Boston Watercolor Society; various local artists
Publications: The Lithographs of Ture Bengtz (book)
Activities: Lect open to public, 2-3 visiting lectr per year; concerts; gallery talks; tours of visiting groups
L Library, 189 Alden St, PO Box 1411, 02332. *Librn* Genevieve M Tribble
Open to the public for reference
Library Holdings: Vols 1900
Special Subjects: Asian Art

FALL RIVER

O **GREATER FALL RIVER ART ASSOCIATION,** 80 Belmont St, 02720. Tel 617-673-7212. *Pres* Mrs William Hoyle; *First VPres* Paul J Hughes; *Second VPres* Mrs Roger Buffington; *Clerk* Mrs William Renaud; *Corresp Secy* Shirley Martin; *Treas* Lucille Maynard; *Asst Treas* Paulette Dennis; *Dir* Mrs Edward A Doyle
Open Sept - June daily 1 - 4 PM. Estab 1955 for the cultural enrichment of the community. Seven rooms of large Victorian house are used for art exhibitions. Average Annual Attendance: 10,000. Mem: 310; dues Sustaining $14, Regular $10, Student (college) $6, Student (high school) $5; annual meeting in May
Income: $800 after expenses
Purchases: $100
Collections: †Graphics; †ceramics; slides of paintings of the Fall River School
Exhibitions: Annual Traditional Open Show-New England Artists; Fall River Collects Art, semi-annually; Classes Exhibition; Members Show; National Competitive Exhibition; Sunday Painters Show; three or four one-man shows annually
Publications: Bulletin, bi-monthly
Activities: Classes for adults and children in Pottery, Ceramics, Sculpture, Oil Painting, drawing, quilting; lectures open to the public, eight visiting lecturers per year; Camera Club meeting and competitions; extension department serving Greater Fall River organizations; lending collection contains slides

FITCHBURG

M **FITCHBURG ART MUSEUM,** Merriam Parkway, 01420. Tel 617-345-4207. *Pres* Andre A Gelinas; *VPres* Roger W Foster; *Dir* Peter Timms; *Asst to the Dir* Aliki Katsaros; *Secy* Nelde Drumm; *Treas* Mrytle Parcher; *Exhib Interpreter* Ursula Pitman
Open Tues - Sat 10 AM - 5 PM, Sun 2 - 5 PM. No admis fee. Estab 1925. Two large galleries and entrance hall on the first floor; two large galleries with connecting hall gallery on the second floor. Average Annual Attendance: 10,000. Mem: 900; dues $10 - $500; annual meeting Dec
Income: $85,000 (financed by endowment and membership)
Collections: †Drawings, †paintings, †prints
Exhibitions: (1980) David Hayes (sculpture); Architectural Etchers; 49th Regional Exhibition; Janiye Jewelry; Japanese Prints from the Fogg Art Museum; Prize Award Show
Publications: Catalogs and events notices
Activities: Organized education programs for adults and children; gallery tours; lect; bus tours; inter-museum loans; gift shop; sales gallery

FRAMINGHAM

M **DANFORTH MUSEUM,** 123 Union Ave, 01701. Tel 617-620-0030. *Pres Board of Trustees* Paul B Rosenberg; *Treas* Mitchell Kur; *Dir* Joy L Gordon
Open Wed - Sun 1 - 4:30 PM. No admis fee. Estab 1974 to provide fine arts and art-related activities to people of all ages in the South Middlesex area. There are six galleries. Average Annual Attendance: 50,000
Income: Financed by membership, Framingham State College and Town of Framingham
Collections: †Old master and contemporary prints; turn-of-the-century American paintings
Exhibitions: Jean-Louis Forain: 1852-1931; Eadweard Muybridge Photographs; The Sara Roby Foundation Collection; William Sidney Mount: Paintings, drawings and prints; Abstract Illusionism; Around the Station: The Town and the Train; Art

In Process; Aspects of the Seventies: Directions In Realism; Containers; Eskimos of Alaska: Today and Yesterday; Images of Indian Life: The Plains and the Southwest.
Publications: Calendar of events, monthly; newsletter, three times a year; museum school brochure, quarterly
Activities: Classes for adults and children; docent training; programs for area schools; lect; film series; concerts; gallery talks; museum shop selling original art, prints, ceramics, jewelry and glass
L **Library,** 123 Union Ave, 01701. *Head of the Library Committee* Anna McGovern
Open Wed - Sun 1 - 4:30 PM. Estab 1975 for an educational resource of art books and catalogues. For reference only; research as requested
Purchases: $110
Library Holdings: Vols 1100; Per subs 3; AV—A-tapes, cassettes, slides, v-tapes; Other—Clipping files, exhibition catalogs, pamphlets
Special Subjects: Rare and valuable books
Collections: Bibliographies for the museum exhibitions; museum school book collection

GARDNER

M **MOUNT WACHUSETT COMMUNITY COLLEGE,** Art Galleries, Green St, 01440. Tel 617-632-6600, Ext 180. *Coordinator Dept Art* Jean C Tandy; *Dir Fine Arts Gallery* Gene Cauthen
Open Mon 8 AM - 9:30 PM. No admis fee. Estab 1971 to supply resources for a two-year art curriculum; develop an art collection
Income: Financed by city and state appropriations
Collections: †Approx 80 works; framed color art posters and reproductions
Exhibitions: Annual student competition of painting, sculpture, drawing, ceramics, weaving, printmaking; local, Boston and former students works
Activities: Dramatic program; evening and summer studio courses; workshops; lect open to public, 10 visiting lectr per year; concerts; gallery talks; tours; competitions; art club, visual arts film series
L **Library,** Green St, 01440. *Head Librn* Mason Parker; *Asst Librn* Linda Oldacht
Open Mon - Thurs 8 AM - 9:30 PM, Fri 8 AM - 5 PM, Sun 2 - 6 PM (when school is in session). Estab 1964. Circ 12,998
Income: $30,000 (financed by state appropriation)
Purchases: $30,000
Library Holdings: Vols 51,137; Per subs 256; Micro—Fiche, reels; AV—Cassettes, fs, rec, slides; Other—Memorabilia, pamphlets
Exhibitions: Periodic exhibitions

GLOUCESTER

O **CAPE ANN HISTORICAL ASSOCIATION,** 27 Pleasant St, 01930. Tel 617-283-0455. *Cur* Caroline E Benham
Open Tues - Sat 11 AM - 4 PM, cl Sun, Mon & holidays. Admis adults $2, children no charge if accompanied by adult. Incorporated in 1876 for the preservation of ancient houses. One built in 1650, one in 1750 and one in 1803. Average Annual Attendance: 5000. Mem: 425; dues $5 and up; annual meeting May
Collections: Paintings and drawings by Fitz-Hugh Lane, antique furniture, glass, jewelry, mementos of the Revolutionary period, porcelain, ship models, silver
Activities: Occasional classes; lect
L **Reference Library,** 27 Pleasant St, 01930.
Library Holdings: Vols 500

M **HAMMOND MUSEUM, INC,** Hammond Castle, 80 Hesperus Ave, 01930. Tel 617-283-2080, 283-2081. *Executive Dir* Ben J Deluca Jr; *Cur* Naomi Kline
Open for guided tours (spring - Summer - Fall) daily 10 AM - 4 PM; (Winter) Tues - Fri 10 AM - 3 PM, Sat & Sun 10 AM - 4 PM, cl Mon except holidays, cl during Jan, Thanksgiving Day, New Year's Day and Christmas Day. Admis adults $2.50, children 12 years and under $1; group rates available. Estab 1928 by a famous inventor, John Hays Hammond Jr. Incorporated in 1938 for the public exhibition of authentic works of art, architecture and specimens of antiquarian value and to encourage and promote better education in the fine arts, with particular reference to purity of design and style. Mr Hammond combined elements of Roman, Medieval and Renaissance periods in his attempt to recreate an atmosphere of European beauty. Average Annual Attendance: 67,442. Mem: 126; dues $15 - $100
Income: Financed by tours, concerts, membership and grants
Collections: Rare collection of European artifacts; Roman, Medieval and Renaissance Periods
Publications: Newsletter; Visitor Reference Directory
Activities: Concerts; lect; gift shop

O **NORTH SHORE ARTS ASSOCIAITON, INC,** 197 E Main St (Rear), 01930.
Pres Paul Planchet; *VPres* Elsie Reinert; *Treas* Roger Curtis; *Secy* Winifred Curtis
Open 10 AM - 5:30 PM, Sun 2:30 - 5:30 PM, July, Aug & Sept. No admis fee. Estab and inc 1922. Gallery owned by Association. Average Annual Attendance: 4000. Mem: 300; dues artist $15, patron $10, associate $5; annual meeting Aug
Exhibitions: Summer exhibition of members' work: jury, prizes
Activities: Art classes in painting and drawing from life; demonstrations; lect; Artists-at-Work day in gallery in July and August with artists demonstrating all media; silent auction

GRAFTON

M **WILLARD HOUSE AND CLOCK MUSEUM, INC,** 3 Willard St, 01519. Tel 617-839-3335. *Pres* Dr Roger W Robinson; *VPres* Georgett McEroy; *Dir* Mrs Roger W Robinson; *Secy* Margarita Longstreet; *Resident Hostess* Georgia Maddox
Open Tues - Sat 10 AM - 4 PM, Sun 1 - 5 PM. Admis adults $1.50, children 75¢. Estab 1968 for education in fields of decorative arts and antiques. Maintains seven rooms open in house museum. Average Annual Attendance: 3000. Mem: 200; dues $5; annual meeting Oct
Income: Financed by endowment, membership, admissions, gifts and sales
Collections: Early Country Antique Furniture, 17th & 18th Century; 44 Willard Clocks by Benjamin, Simon, Ephraim and Aaron Willard; 16 paintings of various members of the Willard Clockmaking Family
Exhibitions: Doll Show; Fashion Show of 18th & 19th Century Gowns
Activities: Lect, 4 visiting lectr per year; museum shop selling books and antiques

GREAT BARRINGTON

M **SIMON'S ROCK OF BARD COLLEGE,** Alford Rd, 01230. Tel 413-528-0771. *Chmn Art Dept* William Jackson
Estab 1964 as a liberal arts college
Exhibitions: A continuing exhibition program of professional and student works in drawing, painting, graphics, sculpture and crafts; Graphic Design Workshop of Simon's Rock (poster); Barbara Baranowska (photographs); Jim Cave (prints); Peter Homestead (sculpture); Tom Shepard (sculpture and drawings); Evan Stoller (sculpture)
Activities: Gallery talks; tours
L **Library,** Alford Rd, 01230. *Librn* Karen Carney
Library Holdings: Vols 44,000; Per subs 320

HARVARD

M **FRUITLANDS MUSEUMS,** Prospect Hill, 01451. *Dir* Richard S Reed
Open May 30 - Sept 30, Tues - Sun 1 - 5 PM, cl Mon. Admis adults $2, children 50¢. Estab 1914, incorporated 1930 by Clara Endicott Sears. Fruitlands was the scene of Bronson Alcott's experiment in community life. Old Shaker house contains furniture, household articles, pictures, handicrafts, books and valuable manuscript collection of Alcott family and Transcendental group. American Indian museum contains ethnological exhibits. Picture gallery contains portraits by itinerant artists and landscapes by Hudson River School. Average Annual Attendance: 12,000
Exhibitions: Specimens of Indian Lore, Art, Culture and Dioramas illustrating Historical Events of the Indians of the Region; Sculpture of Philip Sears
L **Library,** Prospect Hill, 01451.
Library Holdings: Vols 10,000; Other—Manuscripts
Special Subjects: Art History, Transcendental Movement, Shakers, American Indian North of Mexico

HAVERHILL

L **HAVERHILL PUBLIC LIBRARY,** 99 Main St, 01830. Tel 617-373-1586. *Librn* Virginia Bilmazes Bernard; *Cur* Howard W Curtis
Open Mon - Thurs 9 AM - 9 PM, Fri & Sat 9 AM - 5:30 PM. No admis fee. Estab 1873
Library Holdings: Vols 8000; Per subs 16; AV—A-tapes, cassettes, fs, Kodachromes, lantern Slides, motion pictures, v-tapes; Other—Prints, manuscripts, original art works, photographs, sculpture
Collections: Illuminated manuscripts; mid-19th century photographs, work by Beato and Robertson, Bourne, Frith, Gardner, Naya, O'Sullivan, and others; 19th & 20th century prints, including Cassatt, Chagall, Daumier, Degas, Dufy, Kollwitz, Legros, Picasso, Renoir, Sloan, Toulouse-Lautrec, Whistler, and others; small group of paintings including Joseph A Ames, Henry Bacon, Sidney M Chase, William S Haseltine, Thomas Hill, Harrison Plummer, Winfield Scott Thomas
Activities: Slide presentations; periodic classes

HOLYOKE

M **CITY OF HOLYOKE MUSEUM-WISTARIAHURST,** 238 Cabot St, 01040. Tel 413-536-6771. *Museum Dir* Marie S Quirk; *Chmn Holoyoke Historical Commission* Philip Cote
Open Tues - Sat 1 - 5 PM, Sun 2 - 5 PM on special event days, cl national and state holidays. No admis fee. Sponsored by the City of Holyoke under the jurisdiction of the Holyoke Historical Commission. Mem: Dues regular $10, active $10 and up, junior $3
Income: $77,000 (financed by city appropriation)
Collections: †Antique furniture; china; glass; historical dioramas; †Oriental art; †paintings; period rooms; silver
Activities: Classes for children; dramatic programs; special art shows; concerts; gallery talks; sponsors films and lectures; special exhibits and festivals of ethnic culture featured periodically; special programs and illustrated lectures planned for visiting school classes; sales shop selling booklets and items relating to exhibitions
M **Youth Museum,** 238 Cabot St, 01040.
Open Mon - Sat 1 - 5 PM, Sun when a concert, special program or opening of art exhibit is scheduled. Opened May 3, 1964 in Carriage House on Wisteriahurst estate; sponsored by the City of Holyoke, under jurisdiction of Holyoke Historical Commission. North American Indian Hall opened May 1973 on the second floor. Average Annual Attendance: 18,000
Exhibitions: Scrimshaw, an Early Folk Art Exhibit; twelve exhibits encompassing Northeast, Southeast, Plains, Southwest, Northwest Coast and California Indian tribes
Activities: Art classes for children; lect on arts and crafts; guided tours including film and slides on Indians; individual paintings and original objects of art lent; traveling exhibitions organized and circulated

LINCOLN

M DECORDOVA AND DANA MUSEUM AND PARK, Sandy Pond Rd, 01773. Tel 617-259-8355. *Exec Dir* William A Bagnall; *Dir DeCordova School* Patricia McMahan; *Dir Outreach Educ* Merrie Blocker
Open Tues - Fri 10 AM - 5 PM, Sat Noon - 5 PM, Sun 1:30 - 5 PM. Admis adults $1.50, under 21 50¢. Estab 1948 to offer a variety of exhibitions, build an important collection of contemporary art and to support living New England artist, in its collecting and exhibitions. 4500 sq ft is broken into five galleries. Average Annual Attendance: 60,000. Mem: 3200; dues $35 - $500
Income: $900,000 (financed by endowment and membership)
Purchases: $20,000
Collections: †Works of living New England artists
Exhibitions: African Art: The Spirit Manifest; An American Dream: The Art of Free Enterprise; Born in Boston; Boston Printmakers National; By the People, For the People: New England; The China Trade: Romance and Reality; Barbara Busteter Falk: Paintings; Finnish Constructivism; Homer to Hopper: Sixty Years of American Watercolors; Peter Milton: Prints; New England in Winter; Patron's Choice: New England Artists Under 36; Donald Stoltenberg: Collagraphs; Francisco Zuniga: Sculpture and Drawing
Publications: Exhibition catalogs; newsletter
Activities: Classes for adults and children; docent training; lect open to public, 6 visiting lectr per year; tours; competitions; paintings and original objects of art lent to corporate membership; traveling exhibitions organized and circulated
L DeCordova Museum Library, Sandy Pond Rd, 01773. *Librn* Bee Warren
Open Mon - Fri 9 AM - 5 PM, for members only
Library Holdings: Vols 1600; Per subs 17; AV—Slides, v-tapes; Other—Exhibition catalogs
Special Subjects: Fine arts and crafts

LOWELL

O LOWELL ART ASSOCIATION, Whistler House and Parker Gallery,* 243 Worthen St, 01852. Tel 716-452-7641. *Pres* Lewis Karabatsos; *VPres* John A Goodwin; *Corresp Secy* Anastasia Porter; *Recording Secy* Arlene Redmond; *Whistler House Dir* Amy Woodfall
Open Whistler House Tues - Sun 1 - 4 PM, Parker Gallery Tues - Sun 1 - 4 PM, cl Mon. Admis adults $1, senior citizens & students 50¢, members no charge. Estab 1878 to preserve the birthplace of James McNeil Whistler; to promote the arts in all its phases; and to maintain a center for the cultural benefit of all the citizens of the community. Mem: 200; dues sustaining $50, individual $10, student $5
Income: Financed by endowment and membership
Publications: Brochures
Activities: Classes for adults and children; lect open to the public

MALDEN

L MALDEN PUBLIC LIBRARY, 36 Salem St, 02148. Tel 617-324-0218. *Librn* Dina G Malgeri; *Art Librn* Frederica de Beurs; *Art & Music Librn* Jane Lawless
Open Mon - Thurs 9 AM - 9 PM, Fri $ Sat 9 AM - 9 PM, cl Sun & holidays, cl Sat during summer months. Estab 1879, incorporated 1885 as a public library and art gallery. Circ 237,733. Maintains an art gallery with three galleries
Income: $437,706 (financed by endowment, city and state appropriations)
Purchases: $428,763
Library Holdings: Vols 201,189; Per subs 350; Micro—Reels; AV—A-tapes, cassettes, fs, motion pictures, rec, slides; Other—Clipping files, exhibition catalogs, framed reproductions, prints, manuscripts, memorabilia, original art works, pamphlets, photographs, reproductions, sculpture
Publications: Annual Report; Thirty Paintings in the Malden Collection (art catalog)
Activities: Lect open to public; concerts; gallery talks; tours; competitions

MARBLEHEAD

O MARBLEHEAD ARTS ASSOCIATION, INC, 8 Hooper St, 01945. Tel 617-631-2608. *Pres* Mary Conant; *VPres* William E McKeon; *Secy* Nathaniel Wetherbee; *Executive Secy* Mrs James Livengood
Open Tues - Sun 1 - 4 PM, cl Mon. Admis $1. Estab 1922. Owns and occupies the historic King Hooper Mansion (1728). Contains fine paneling, ballroom, gallery, and garden by Shurclif. Maintains an art gallery. Average Annual Attendance: 3000
Income: $400; dues $12 and up; annual meeting June
Exhibitions: Continuous exhibitions of members work and invited guest exhibitors
Activities: Special art classes; lect open to the public; tours

O MARBLEHEAD HISTORICAL SOCIETY, 161 Washington St, 01945. Tel 617-631-1069. *Executive Secy* John Merrow, Jr
Open May 15 - Oct 15, Mon - Sat 9:30 AM - 4 PM, cl Sun. Admis $1.50. Estab 1898, incorporated 1902 for the preservation of Lee Mansion and historical material and records of Marblehead. Average Annual Attendance: 3000
Income: Financed by endowment, membership, and admissions
Collections: China and glass; collection of portraits; documents; furniture; pictures of ships
Activities: Lect open to the public; tours; sales shop selling books, prints, reproductions
L Library, 161 Washington St, 01945.
Open to qualified visitors for reference only

MARION

O MARION ART CENTER,* 80 Pleasant, 02738. Tel 617-748-1266. *Pres* Sarah R Brown
Open Tues - Sun 1 - 5 PM. Estab 1957 to provide theater and visual arts exhibitions for the community and to provide studio classes for adults and children. Gallery is 70 ft of wall space, 280 sq ft floor space; indirect lighting; entrance off Main St. Average Annual Attendance: 1200. Mem: 300; dues family $12.50, single $7.50; annual meeting second Tues in July
Publications: Annual membership folder; monthly invitations to opening
Activities: Classes for adults and children; dramatic programs; lect open to the public, 5 visiting lectrs per year; concerts; competitions; scholarships; original objects of art lent; rental of paintings and prints available to anyone for a fee of $10-$20 per two month period

MEDFORD

M TUFTS UNIVERSITY, Gallery Eleven, Cohen Arts Center - Fine Arts Dept, Talbot Ave, 02155.
Open Fall & Spring semesters, Mon - Fri 9:30 AM - 4:30 PM. No admis fee. Estab 1955 to display works of art by University students and faculty and special exhibitions of traditional and experimental works in all visual art media. Average Annual Attendance: 5000
Income: Financed through the Fine Arts Department
Exhibitions: 14 shows annually, including theses exhibits of candidates for the MFA degree offered by Tufts in affiliation with the School of the Boston Museum of Fine Arts; History of Photography; Musical Scores; one-person and group shows of contemporary art

MILTON

M MUSEUM OF THE AMERICAN CHINA TRADE, 215 Adams St, 02186. Tel 617-696-1815. *Pres* Nancy Vappi; *Secy* Joseph Hinkle; *Dir* Betty Wurth Hirsch; *Cur* H A Crosby Forbes; *Asst Cur* William Sargent; *Dir of Development & Public Relations* Deanna S Lackaff; *Registrar* Dana Ricciardi; *Membership Secy* Joanne Kickham
Open Tues - Sun 1 - 4 PM; group tours 9:30 AM - 12:30 PM. Admis adults $3, sr citizens and students (with ID) $1.50, children free. Estab 1964 to promote understanding of the cultural, historical, economic and political implications of the early Western trade with East Asia. Robert Bennet Forbes House 1833, National Historic Landmark, Greek Revival mansion, nine exhibition rooms; Amos Holbrook House 1800, Federalist mansion, exhibition rooms and lecture hall. Average Annual Attendance: 7000. Mem: 1000; dues $25 - $1000; annual meeting March
Income: $275,000 (financed by endowment, membership, contributions and grants from government, private foundations and admission fees)
Purchases: $12,000
Collections: Archives of documents, Chinese art, fancy goods, furniture, Oriental export porcelain, paintings, 19th Century photographs, silver, textiles
Publications: China Trade Register, membership newsletter, quarterly; exhibition catalogs
Activities: Classes for adults and children; school outreach; lect open to public, some for members only, 4 visiting lectr per year; gallery talks; tours; Samuel Shaw Award; fels; exten dept serves nationwide; original objects of art lent to other institutions; lending collection contains original art works, original prints, paintings and decorative arts; originate traveling exhibitions; museum shop sells books, reproductions, prints and imported arts and craft items from Peoples Republic of China
L Library and Archives, 215 Adams St, 02186. *Archivist* Dana D Ricciardi
Open by appointment only. Estab 1965 as reference for staff, members and visitors
Library Holdings: Vols 1500; Per subs 20; Micro—Reels; AV—Slides, v-tapes; Other—Clipping files, exhibition catalogs, manuscripts, memorabilia, pamphlets, photographs
Special Subjects: United States - China Trade
Collections: Documents (letters, logbooks, etc) of the United States - China trade; history of China and China trade; history of art; early photographs of China and Japan

NANTUCKET

O ARTISTS ASSOCIATION OF NANTUCKET, Kenneth Taylor Gallery, 02554. Tel 617-228-0722. *Pres* Louis Roberts
Open daily 9 AM - 10 PM (June - Oct 15). No admis fee. Estab 1944 to provide gallery space to approximately 240 exhibiting artist members, to promote the arts; to provide arts and crafts workshops year round. Maintains two galleries: The Kenneth Taylor Gallery, two floors in historic building, and The Little Gallery, one small floor for one-person shows. Average Annual Attendance: 50,000 - 75,000. Mem: 450; dues patron $25 - $500, artist $20; annual meeting Aug
Income: $12,000 - $15,000 (financed by membership, fund raising and commissions)
Collections: Permanent collection on loan to hospital and town buildings
Exhibitions: Changing one-person and group member shows during summer; occasional off-season shows
Publications: Newsletter, three times per year
Activities: Classes for adults and children; workshops; lect open to public, 3 - 4 vis lectr per year; gallery talks; competitions with awards; scholarships; individual paintings and original objects of art lent to local hospital and public offices

NEEDHAM

O BOSTON PRINTMAKERS, c/o Sylvia Rantz, 299 High Rock St, 02192. Tel 617-444-2692. *Pres* Tim Hamill
Estab 1947 to aid printmakers in exhibiting their work; to bring quality work to the public. Average Annual Attendance: 15,000. Mem: 150; dues $15; annual meeting June
Income: Financed by membership, entry fees, and commission on sales
Purchases: $10,000
Exhibitions: Exhibitions are held at Brockton Art Center, Rose Art Museum, Brandeis University; and Museum of Fine Arts, Boston University
Activities: Lect; gallery talks; competitions with awards and prizes; traveling exhibitions organized and circulated

NEW BEDFORD

L NEW BEDFORD FREE PUBLIC LIBRARY, 613 Pleasant St, 02740. Tel 617-999-6291. *Dir* Laurence H Solomon; *Dept Head Reference* Thelma Paine; *Dept Head Genealogy & Whaling Coll* Paul Cyr; *Dept Head AV* Phillip Dimor; *Dept Head Technical Service* Pauline Bolduc
Open Mon - Thurs 9 AM - 9 PM, Fri & Sat 9 AM - 5 PM, cl Sun & holidays. Estab 1852. Circ 478,828
Income: $640,900 (financed by endowment, city and state appropriation)
Purchases: $111,178
Library Holdings: Vols 375,531; Per subs 281; Micro—Reels; AV—Cassettes, fs, motion pictures, rec, slides, v-tapes; Other—Framed reproductions, photographs
Special Subjects: Whaling, New Bedford Artists
Collections: Paintings by Clifford Ashley, Albert Bierstadt, F D Millet, William Wall
Activities: Scholarships

M NEW BEDFORD WHALING MUSEUM, 18 Johnny Cake Hill, 02740. Tel 617-997-0046. *Dir* Richard C Kugler; *Asst Dir* Barbara H Collins; *Sr Cur* Philip F Purrington; *Cur Coll* Elton W Hall; *Cur Ethnology* John R Bockstoce
Open Mon - Sat 9 AM - 5 PM, Sun 1 - 5 PM, cl Mon Oct - May. Admis adults $1.50, children 6 - 14 75¢. Estab 1903 to interest and educate the public in the history of the whaling industry and the greater New Bedford area. Average Annual Attendance: 100,000. Mem: 1800; dues $10 - $500; annual meeting May
Income: $225,550 (financed by endowment, membership)
Purchases: $12,000
Collections: Russell-Purrington Panorama of a Whaling Voyage; domestic crafts; †furniture and domestic arts; †New Bedford artists; paintings and prints; †scrimshaw; ship models; Whaleship Lagoda (1-2 scale model); †whaling arts and crafts
Exhibitions: (1978) William Allen Wall, an artist of New Bedford; (1979) The Image of the Past: Historic New Bedford Photographs
Publications: Bulletin from Johnny Cake Hill, quarterly; exhibition catalogs
Activities: Classes for children; docent training; lect open to public, 6 vis lectr per yr; tours; individual paintings and original objects of art lent to other museums; traveling exhibitions organized and circulated; museum shop selling books, reproductions, prints

L Old Dartmouth Historical Society and Whaling Museum Library, 18 Johnny Cake Hill, 02740. Tel 617-997-0046.
For reference only
Library Holdings: Vols 20,000; Per subs 12; Other—Manuscripts
Special Subjects: Charles F Batchelder Whaling Collection, Charles A Goodwin Collection, History of Whaling Industry, Andrew Snow Logbook Collection

M SWAIN SCHOOL OF DESIGN, William W Crapo Gallery, 19 Hawthorn St, 02740. Tel 617-997-7831. *Pres* James Davies; *Gallery Dir* Sarah Benham
Open Mon - Fri 10 AM - 4 PM, cl Sat, Sun & holidays. Estab 1881
Exhibitions: Monthly exhibitions; Sigmund Abeles; Leland Bell; Robert DeNiro; Mary Gregory; David Hockney; Arthur Hoener: Works in Color; Richard Hunt; John Matt; Kathrine and Michael McCoy: Visiting Artists; James Rosenquist; John Udvardy; Massimo Vignelli; Photographics: New England Photographers
Publications: Catalogs

L Library, 19 Hawthorn St, 02740. *Library Dir* Angela M Sciotti
Open Mon - Fri 8:30 AM - 4:30 PM and 6 - 9 PM during school term. Estab 1967 for reference and research supporting fine arts curriculum. Circ 800
Purchases: $8000
Library Holdings: Vols 12,000; Per subs 45; AV—Kodachromes, slides; Other—Clipping files, exhibition catalogs
Special Subjects: Art History, Fine arts, Design
Collections: New Bedford Area Artist File

NEWBURYPORT

M CUSTOM HOUSE MARITIME MUSEUM, 25 Water St, PO Box 306, 01950. Tel 617-462-8681. *Pres* Kennard Bowlen; *Dir & Cur* Regina Tracy; *Secy* Jean Murdy
Open Mon - Fri 10 AM - 4 PM Oct - April, Mon - Sat 10 AM - 4:30 PM, Sun 2 - 5 PM April - Oct. Admis adults $1, children to 15 50¢, under 5 free. Estab 1975 to exhibit the maritime heritage of the Memnack Valley; Valley. Housed in an 1835 custom house designed by Robert Mills. The structure is on the National Register of Historic Places. Average Annual Attendance: 8000. Mem: 525; dues $200, $50, $20, $15 or $10; annual meeting March
Income: $30,000 (financed by membership, admission and fundraisers)
Collections: Collection of portraits and decorative art objects 1680-1820; original collection of ethnographic items owned by Newburyport Marine Soceity Members, half hull models of Merrimack River Valley Ships; portraits of sea captains; navigational instrument and models
Exhibitions: Lithographs of George C Wales; Run of the Mill - Photos of New England Milling
Publications: Newsletter, bimonthly
Activities: Classes for adults and children; lect open to the public, 6 visiting lectr per year; gallery talks; tours; individual paintings and original objects of art lent to other museums and historical agencies; museum shop selling nautical items

M HISTORICAL SOCIETY OF OLD NEWBURY, Cushing House Museum, 98 High St, 01950. Tel 617-462-2681. *Cur* Wilhelmina V Lunt
Open May - Oct Tues 10 AM - 4 PM, Sun 2 - 5 PM, cl Nov - Apr, except by appointment. Admis adults $1.50, children under 16 50¢, special group rates. Estab 1877. Mem: Dues individual life $200, annual benefactor $100, annual sustaining $25, family $15, individual $10
Collections: China; dolls; furniture; glass; miniatures; needlework; paintings; paperweights; sampler collection; silver; other historical material
Exhibitions: Temporary exhibitions
Activities: Lect; guided tours
L Library, 98 High St, 01950.
Library Holdings: Vols 5000; Other—Manuscripts, deeds, documents

NORTHAMPTON

L FORBES LIBRARY, 20 West St, 01060. Tel 413-584-8550. *Dir* Blaise Bisaillon; *Art & Music Librn* Daniel J Lombardo
Open Mon - Sat 9 AM - 9 PM, Sun & holidays 2 - 6 PM, cl Memorial Day, July 4, Thanksgiving, Christmas, and New Years Day. Estab 1894 to serve the residential and academic community as a general public library and a research facility. Circ 292,950. Gallery and exhibit cases for regional artists, photographers and craftspeople
Income: $328,050 (financed by endowment, city and state appropriation, federal funds)
Purchases: $59,931
Library Holdings: Vols 312,674; Per subs 312; Micro—Reels; AV—Cassettes, fs, lantern slides, motion pictures, rec, slides; Other—Clipping files, exhibition catalogs, framed reproductions, prints, manuscripts, memorabilia, original art works, pamphlets, photographs, reproductions, sculpture, original documents
Special Subjects: Art, music
Collections: Bien Edition of Audubon Bird Prints; Library of Charles E Forbes; Lyman Collection of Japanese Wood Block Prints and Japanese Books; Walter E Corbin Collection of Photographic Prints and Slides; The Coolidge Collection; Connecticut Valley History; Genealogical Records; Official White House Portraits of President Calvin Coolidge and Grace Anna Coolidge; The Holland House Collection of English Miniatures; World War I and II Poster Collection
Exhibitions: Monthly exhibits of works by regional artists, photographers and craftspeople
Activities: Lect program; concerts; tours; weekly film

M SMITH COLLEGE, Museum of Art, Elm Street at Bedford Terrace, 01063. Tel 413-584-2700, Ext 2236, 740. *Dir & Chief Cur* Charles Chetham; *Assoc Dir & Cur of Paintings* Betsy B Jones; *Acting Asst Cur Prints* Inga Christine Swenson
Open Tues - Sat 11 AM - 4:30 PM, Sun 2 - 4:30 PM, cl Mon & academic holidays; June by appointment; July - August Tues - Sat 1 - 4 PM. No admis fee. Collection founded 1879; Hillyer Art Gallery built 1882; Smith College Museum of Art established 1920; Tryon Art Gallery built 1926; present Smith College Museum of Art in Tryon Hall opened 1973. Average Annual Attendance: 36,000. Mem: 700; dues student $8 and higher
Collections: European and American paintings, sculpture, drawings, prints, photographs and decorative arts of the 17th-20th centuries
Exhibitions: 12-24 temporary exhibitions and installations annually
Publications: Catalogues
Activities: Gallery tours; lectures; gallery talks; concerts; individual works of art lent to other institutions; sales desk selling publications, post and note cards, posters
L Hillyer Art Library, Elm Street at Bedford Terrace, 01063. *Librn* Karen H Harvey
Open Mon - Thurs 8 AM - 11 PM; Fri 8 AM - 10 PM; Sat 10 AM - 10 PM, Sun 12 Noon - 10 PM. Estab 1900 to support courses offered by art department of Smith College
Income: Financed by endowment
Library Holdings: Vols 38,500; Per subs 204; Micro—Fiche; Other—Photographs

NORTH ANDOVER

M MERRIMACK VALLEY TEXTILE MUSEUM, 800 Massachusetts Ave, 01845. Tel 617-686-0191. *Pres* Samuel S Rogers; *Dir* Thomas W Leavitt; *Secy* Clifford E Elias; *Cur* Laurence F Gross; *Supv Education Services* Paul Hudon; *Museum Conservator* Robert A Hauser; *Textile Conservator* Michael Bogle; *Asst Cur Textiles* Katherine R Koob
Open Tues - Fri 10 AM - 5 PM, Sat & Sun 1 - 5 PM. Admis adults $2, minors and senior citizens $1, free to all on Sat. Estab 1960 to preserve artifacts, documents and pictorial descriptions of the American textile industry and related development abroad. Two permanent exhibit galleries: Homespun to Factory Made; Woolen

Textiles in America, 1776-1876. Average Annual Attendance: 6000
Income: Financed by endowment
Collections: Photographs, prints and †textile collection
Activities: Classes for adults; docent training; tours; competitions; lending collection contains slides; originate traveling exhibits; sales desk selling books, prints and postcards
L **Library,** 800 Massachusetts Ave, 01845. *Librn* Helena Wright; *Asst Librn* Eartha Dengler
Open Tues - Fri 10 AM - 5 PM
Income: Financed by endowment
Library Holdings: Vols 35,000; Per subs 30; Micro—Reels; AV—Motion pictures; Other—Exhibition catalogs, prints, manuscripts, original art works, pamphlets, photographs, original documents
Special Subjects: History of textile industry, textile design and manufacturing, textile mill architecture
Publications: Checklist of prints and manuscripts

NORTON

WHEATON COLLEGE
M **Watson Gallery,** East Main St, 02766. Tel 617-285-7722, Ext 428. *Dir* Dr Ann H Murray; *Cur Asst* Susan Werner
Open Mon 10 AM - 12 Noon, 2 - 4 PM, Tues - Sun 1 - 5 PM. No admis fee. Estab 1960, gallery program since 1930 to provide a wide range of contemporary one person and group shows as well as exhibitions from the permanent collections of paintings and graphics. Gallery is of fireproof steel-frame, glass and brick construction; there are no windows. Average Annual Attendance: 4000
Income: Financed by College budget
Collections: Ancient Coins from the Newell Bequest; Ashley Collection of Textiles; Helen Mead Wires Collection of Textiles; Laila G Raab Collection of American Glass; †paintings; †drawings; †prints; †sculpture; †glass and other decorative arts
Exhibitions: (1979) Nancy Hemenway-Teacher, Amy Gray-Student; Anne McQueen, Theo Westenberger: Photographs; Prints of the Nineteenth Century: A selection from the Wheaton Collection. (1980) Collage: An exhibition of eleven contemporary artists; Vaino Kola: Works on Paper; Marcia Marcus: Paintings; Robert Scofield: Sculpture; Seen Elsewhere: An Installation by Frances Torres; Student Exhibition
Publications: Gallery notes, semi-annually; exhibition catalogs; Prints of the Nineteenth Century: A Selection from the Wheaton College Collection; Collage
Activities: Lectures open to the public, five - eight visiting lecturers per year; concerts; gallery talks; tours; individual paintings and original objects of art lent to college and other museums and galleries; traveling exhibitions organized and circulated; Original prints and reproductions for annual rental
L **Fine Arts Collection,** Wheaton College, 02766. *Fine Arts Librn Liaison* Kersti Tannberg
Open Mon - Fri 8:30 AM - 10 PM, Sat 9 AM - 10 PM, Sun 10:30 Am - 10 PM. Estab 1962 in Watson Hall; consolidated in 1980 as special collection in Main library to support curricular and other needs of the Wheaton community. Circ 6000
Library Holdings: Vols 14,350; Per subs 85; Micro—Fiche; AV—Lantern Slides, motion pictures, rec 6600, slides; Other—Clipping files, exhibition catalogs, framed reproductions, prints, manuscripts, memorabilia, original art works, pamphlets, photographs, reproductions, sculpture

PAXTON

M **ANNA MARIA COLLEGE,** Saint Luke's Gallery, Moll Art Center, Sunset Lane, 01612. Tel 617-757-4586. *Chmn Art Dept* David T Green; *First Asst* Alice Jacqmin; *AV Librn* Rebecca Hubert; *Art Librn* Nicholas McCauley
Open 9 AM - 4 PM. No admis fee. Estab 1968 as an outlet for the art student and professional artist, and to raise the artistic awareness of the general community. Main Gallery is 35 x 15 ft with about 300 sq ft of wall space with additional areas adjoining the gallery. Average Annual Attendance: 2000
Income: $90,000 (financed by endowment, city appropriation, federal and state aid (LSA & LSCA), Friends of the Library
Purchases: $90,000
Library Holdings: Vols 80,000; Per subs 400; Micro—Fiche, reels; AV—A-tapes, cassettes, fs, Kodachromes, rec, slides; Other—Clipping files, exhibition catalogs, framed reproductions, pamphlets, reproductions, sculpture, exhibition posters, portrait file, sheet music collection, auction catalogs
Special Subjects: Decorative Arts, Oriental Art
Collections: Small assortment of furniture, paintings, sculpture
Exhibitions: Annual Senior Art Exhibit; local artists, faculty and students shows
Activities: Lect open to public; tours; 80,000

PITTSFIELD

L **BERKSHIRE ATHENAEUM,** Music and Arts Department, 1 Wendell Ave, 01201. Tel 413-442-1559, Ext 26. *Librn* Robert G Newman; *Asst Librn* Larry Price; *Supv Music and Arts Services* Jean Bousquet; *First Asst Music and Arts Services* Mary Ann Knight
Open Mon - Fri 9 AM - 9 PM; Sat 9 AM - 6 PM; summer Mon, Wed & Fri 9 AM - 9 PM; Tues & Thurs 9 AM - 6 PM; Sat 9 AM - 5 PM. Estab 1872, music and arts Dept 1937
Income: Financed by city and state appropriations and gifts
Library Holdings: Vols 5000; AV—Cassettes, rec; Other—Prints
Exhibitions: (1978) An Artist's View of Childhood by Leonard Weber; Bygones - Amusements & Occupations of Children; Handwoven Works by Sharon Steinberg; Paper Sculpture by David Sears; Photography by Paul Rocheleau; South Mountain's Young Audiences Concerts 1955-1978; Prints & Drawings by Barbara Finn Eustace; Stoneware Pottery by Allan Steinberg; (1978-79) Bells - Bells - Bells; Dolls From Storybooks by Berkshire Museum Doll Club; Dolphin Studio Crafts by Primm & John French; 18th Century English Porcelain by Stone House Antiques; Jewelry by Joan A Grant; Paintings by Cathy Porter; Photographs by Warren Fowler; Quilting: Folk Art of the American Woman; Soft Sculpture by Dana Collins; Stained Glass from Cummings Studio; Woodcuts by Norman Folger

Dellert; The Art of Bookbinding by Arno Werner; (1979-80) Batik by Barbara Long Powell; Glass Sculpture by Corey R Powers; Hooked Rugs by Pearl K McGown and Dorothy Lepisto; Illuminated Manuscripts by John Von Kadich; Kitchen Utensils of the Hancock Shakers; Natural Basketry by Joan Patton; Oils and Watercolors by Spencer P Kennard; Portrait Sculpture by Joel Rudnick; Pottery by Thomas A Hoadley; Sandy Vohr's Leather Designs; Woodworks by Brys and Claire Cabiles; Young Musicians and Abstracts in Photographs by Sue Nunley
Activities: Library Arts Series; lect open to public; films; outreach program for the elderly

M **BERKSHIRE MUSEUM,** 39 South St, 01201. Tel 413-443-6721. *Dir* Gary C Burger; *Cur Science* Bartlett Hendricks; *Head Junior Dept* Thomas G Smith; *Financial Secy* Samuel A Spratlin; *Secy-Registrar* Mrs Theodore W Hall; *Mem Secy* Avery Spencer; *Bldg Supt* Joseph A Trassati
Open Tues - Sat 10 AM - 5 PM, Sun 2 - 5 PM, cl Mon. No admis fee. Estab 1903 as a museum of art, science and history. Mem: 1620; dues sustaining $25 and up; family $15; single $7.50; annual meeting February
Income: Financed by endowment, membership and gifts
Collections: American Paintings of the Hudson River School (Inness, Moran, Blakelock, Martin, Wyant, Moran, Church, Knight and others); Chinese objects and two rooms from Aston Magna (home of Albert Spaulding); Early American and European abstracts; early American Portraits; Egyptian, Babylonia and Near East Arts; Giant Redwood Trees of California (Albert Bierstadt); grave reliefs from Palmyra; Paul M Hahn Collection of 18th century English and American Silver; Old Masters (Patinir, Pons, de Hooch, Van Dyck, Reynolds, Raeburn, Lawrence and others); †contemporary sculptures; two Norman Rockwell paintings
Exhibitions: Changing monthly exhibitions
Publications: Schedule of events, quarterly
Activities: Classes for adults and children; lectures open to the public; museum shop sells gifts; junior museum

M **SHAKER COMMUNITY, INC,** US Rte 20, PO Box 898, 01201. Tel 413-443-0188. *Pres* Mrs Lawrence K Miller; *Dir* John Harlow Ott; *Cur Coll* June Sprigg; *Cur Educ Service* Cheryl Anderson
Open June 1 - Oct 31 9:30 AM - 5 PM daily. Admis adult $3.50, children 6 - 12 $1, children under 6 free. Estab 1960 for the preservation and restoration of Hancock Shaker Village and the interpretation of Shaker art, architecture and culture. Period rooms throughout the village. Exhibition Gallery contains Shaker inspirational drawings and graphic materials. Average Annual Attendance: 50,000. Mem: 1000; dues individual $15
Income: Financed by membership, donations
Collections: Shaker architecture, furniture and industrial material; Shaker inspirational drawings
Exhibitions: (1978) Simple Gifts, William Benton Museum of Art. (1979) Gift of Inspiration: The Art of the Shakers
Publications: Newsletter, biannually; specialized publications
Activities: Classes for adults and chilren; workshops, seminars; lect open to public, 6 visiting lectr per year; concerts; tours; original objects of art lent to accredited museums; lending collection contains 1 film strip, 4 motion pictures, 250 photographs, 40 slides; museum shop selling books, magazines, reproductions, prints, slides
L **Hancock Shaker Village Library,** US Rte 20, PO Box 898, 01201. Tel 413-447-7284. *Librn* Robert F W Meader
Reference library open to students and scholars by appointment
Library Holdings: Vols 1000; Other—Manuscripts, photographs, graphic, maps

PLYMOUTH

O **PLYMOUTH ANTIQUARIAN SOCIETY,** 27 North St, 02360. Tel 617-746-9697. *Pres* Hugh M Flick; *VPres* John H G Pell; *Secy* Edward W Stack; *Assoc Dir & Chief Education* Milo V Stewart; *Cur* Bruce MacLeish; *Registrar* Carl Nold; *Chmn Antiquarian House* Mrs Eliot Sargent
Open May - Oct Tues - Sat 9 AM - 5 PM, cl Mon & Sun, Nov & April mornings only, cl winter. Admis adults $1.25, children 25¢. Estab 1919 to maintain and preserve the three museums: Harlow Old Fort House (1677), Spooner House (1747), and Antiquarian House (1809). Average Annual Attendance: 2000. Mem: adults 2800, juniors 5000; dues $15 - $100; annual meeting July
Income: $35,000 (financed by membership)
Collections: Antique dolls
Activities: Classes for children; lect open to the public; sales shop at Harlow House selling hand woven items

PROVINCETOWN

O **PROVINCETOWN ART ASSOCIATION AND MUSEUM,** 460 Commercial Street, 02657. Tel 617-487-1750. *Pres* Ciriaco Cozzi; *VPres* Mischa Richter; *Dir* Annabelle Hebert; *Asst Dir* Ellen O'Donnell
Open daily 12 - 4 PM & 7 - 9 PM Memorial Day to Oct. Estab in 1914 to promote and cultivate the practice and appreciation of all branches of the fine arts, to hold temporary exhibitions, forums, and concerts for its members and the public. Four galleries are maintained. Mem: 500; dues vary
Income: Financed by membership
Exhibitions: Permanent Collection, Members' Exhibitions
Publications: Exhibitions catalogues and newsletters
Activities: Life drawing groups; workshops for children; lect open to the public; concerts; film series; book traveling exhibiton; museum shop selling books, original art, prints, reproductions, slides, postcards and notecards
L **Library,** 460 Commercial Street, 02657.
Open to members only
Library Holdings: Vols 500; Other—Exhibition catalogs
Special Subjects: Provincetown artists
Collections: Memorabilia of WHW Bicknell

QUINCY

M ADAMS NATIONAL HISTORIC SITE, 135 Adams St, PO Box 531, 02269. Tel 617-773-1177. *Supt* Wilhelmina S Harris
Open daily (April 19 - Nov 10) 9 AM - 5 PM. Admis adults 50¢, children under 16 admitted free if accompanied by an adult. Estab 1946. The site consists of a house, part of which dates to 1731; a library containing approx 12,000 books, (most of which belonged to John Quincy Adams); a carriage house; a woodshed and grounds which were once owned and enjoyed by four generations of the Adams family. Average Annual Attendance: 20,000
Income: Financed by Federal Government
Collections: Original furnishings belonging to the four generations of Adamses who lived in the house between 1788 and 1937
Activities: Lectures (one week each spring); tours

ROCKPORT

O ROCKPORT ART ASSOCIATION, Old Tavern, 12 Main St, 01966. Tel 617-546-6604. *Pres & Cur* Isabel LaFreniere; *VPres* Laurence Webster; *Secy* Eleanor Harper; *Dir* Martta Blanchet; *Mgr Tavern Door Card Shop* Mary M Ahearn; *Mem Secy* Marie Smith
Open Summer: daily 9:30 AM - 5 PM, Sun 1 - 5 PM, Winter: daily 9:30 AM - 4:30 PM, Sun 1 - 5 PM. No admis fee. Estab 1921 as a non-profit educational organization established for the advancement of art. Three galleries are maintained in the Old Tavern Building; two large summer galleries are adjacent to the main structure. Average Annual Attendance: 65,000. Mem: 1000; dues artists $35; annual meeting second Thurs in August
Income: Financed by endowment and membership
Collections: Permanent collection of works by former and current association artist members
Exhibitions: Amateur Art Festival; Annual Spring Ten-Man Show; Boston Watercolor Society; bi-monthly one artist shows and monthly one artist revolving screen show; four major summer shows, second & third juried; monthly group shows year-round, representing over 200 artist members; Rockport Public Schools Show; Special Annual Exhibitions: Amateur Members' Show; various community shows
Publications: Exhibition catalogs; Rockport Artist Book (1970); Rockport Sketchbook
Activities: Classes for adults and children; sketch groups; workshops demonstrations; lect open to the public; competitions with awards given; gallery talks; tours; concerts; slide lect; individual paintings and original objects of art lent to colleges, art schools, churches and hospitals for short term exhibition; lending collection contains original art works of paintings, graphics and sculpture; sales shop sells books, cards and notes by artist members
L Library, Old Tavern, 12 Main St, 01966.
Open for reference to members and friends of the association
Library Holdings: Vols 200
Special Subjects: Fine arts especially painting

SALEM

M ESSEX INSTITUTE, 132 Essex St, 01970. Tel 617-744-3390. *Dir* Bryant F Tolles Jr; *Asst to Dir* Katherine W Richardson; *Cur* Anne Farnam; *Librn* Robinson Murray Jr
Open (June 1 - Oct 15) Mon & Tues 9 AM - 4:30 PM, Sun 1 - 5 PM, open Sat all year 9 AM - 4:30 PM. Admis adults $1, children 50¢. Estab 1848 to display the Institute's collections of artifacts and historic houses representing the richness of Salem's and Essex County's material culture from the early 17th into the 20th centuries. The Museum is housed in Plummer Hall built in 1857 and is an excellent example of Victorian Italian Revival architecture. On the first floor is the John A McCarthy Gallery devoted to changing displays and loan exhibitions. The second floor has a portrait gallery, and the main gallery containing three early period rooms; a special collections and print room used for small exhibitions. Average Annual Attendance: 100,000. Mem: 1200; dues from $15 to life $250; annual meeting April
Income: $432,621 (financed by endowment, membership, gifts and admissions)
Collections: Architectural fragments, buttons, ceramics, clocks, dolls, furniture, glassware, pewter, sculpture, silver and toys all associated with the civil history of Essex County and adjacent areas since the early 17th century
Exhibitions: Charles Osgood (1809-1890); Child Life in Early America; Costume Exhibition, CEL Greene; Crazy Quilts (1875-1885); Early American Woodworking Tools; Essex County Landscape artist; Fashions and Draperies for windows and beds; Library Exhibit - Conservation: Some Problems and Solutions; Life and Times in Shoe City: The Shoe Workers of Lynn; Nathaniel Hawthorne exhibition; Olive Prescott: Weaver of Forge Village; Prints at the Essex Institute; Rare Book Exhibit; Recent Acquisitions and Basement Treasures in the Essex Institute Collections; Salem on the Grand Tour; Salem Willows in Retrospect; Salem Witches: Myth and Reality; Sights and Sound from the Past: The Television Age is Born; The First Church of Salem: 350 years; The Prolific Portrait Painter of Salem, MA; The Salem Redevelopment Authority: The Changing Picture of Urban Renewal in an Historic City; To My Valentine (1880-1929)
Publications: Historical Collections, quarterly; newsletter, quarterly; occasional books
Activities: Classes for adults and children; docent training; lect open to public, 6 visiting lectr per year; gallery talks; tours; concerts; films; paintings and original objects of art lent to museums and institutions
L James Duncan Phillips Library, 132 Essex St, 01970. For reference only
Open Mon - Fri 9 AM - 4:30 PM. For reference only
Library Holdings: Vols 400,000; Other—Manuscripts, memorabilia, pamphlets
Collections: Frederick T Ward China Collection, the history of China and Chinese-American relations to the early 20th century
M Gardner-Pingree House, 132 Essex St, 01970.
Open Tues - Sat 10 AM - 4 PM; Sun 1 - 4:30 PM (June 1 - Oct 15). Admis adults $1, children and senior citizens 50¢. Built in 1804-1805 and illustrates the Federal Style of Salem master-builder and carver, Samuel McIntire; furnished in that period

M Crowninshield-Bently House, 132 Essex St, 01970.
Open Tues - Sat 10 AM - 4 PM; Sun 1 - 4:30 PM (June 1 - Oct 15). Admis adults $1, children and senior citizens 50¢. Built in 1727, added to and remodeled after 1800. It illustrates the styles of interior architecture and furnishings of much of the 18th century in Salem
M John Ward House, 132 Essex St, 01970.
Open Tues - Sat 10 AM - 4 PM; Sun 1 - 4:30 PM (June 1 - Oct 15). Admis adults $1, children and senior citizens 50¢. Built 1684, restored 1910-1912 under direction of George Francis Dow, architectural historian. Furnished in the manner of the time. The rear lean-to contains a later apothecary's shop, a weaving room with operable loom and a small cent shop
M Andrew-Safford House, 13 Washington Square, 01970.
Open Thurs 2 - 4:30 PM. Admis $1. Built in 1818-1819, and purchased by the Institute in 1947 for the purpose of presenting a vivid image of early 19th century urban life. It is the residence of the Institute's director
M Peirce-Nichols House, 80 Federal St, 01970.
Open Tues - Sat 2 - 4:30 PM. Admis $1. Built in 1782 by Samuel McIntire. Maintains some original furnishings and a counting house
M Assembly House, 138 Federal St, 01970.
Open Tues - Fri 2 - 4 PM all year; Sat 2:30 (June 1 - Oct 15). Admis $1. Built in 1782 as a hall for social assemblies; remodeled in 1796 by Samuel McIntire as a home residence. The interior features a Victorian sitting room and an unusual Chinese parlor
M Lye-Tapley Shoe Shop (1830) and Vaughan Doll House, 132 Essex St, 01970.
Open Tues - Sat 10 AM - 4 PM; Sun 1 - 4:30 PM (June 1 - Oct 15). Accommodates special collections

M PEABODY MUSEUM OF SALEM, East India Square, 161 Essex St, 01970. Tel 617-745-1876 and 745-9500. *Dir* Ernest S Dodge; *Asst Dir* Peter Fetchko
Open Mon - Sat 9 AM - 5 PM, Sun 1 - 5 PM, cl New Years, Thanksgiving, Christmas. Admis adults $1.50, children 75¢. Estab 1799 for the conservation of American maritime history, art objects; ethnology of non-European peoples; natural history of Essex County. Gallery is a conglomeration of old and new buildings, 45,000 sq ft of exhibit space, 95,000 sq ft total. Average Annual Attendance: 100,000. Mem: 1800; dues $100, $30, $20; annual meeting Sept
Income: $200,000 (financed by endowment, membership)
Collections: American Maritime History (paintings, objects); Ethnology of Pacific Islands and Far East; Natural History of Essex County, Massachusetts
Publications: The American Neptune, quarterly journal of maritime history
Activities: Classes for adults and children; docent training; lect open to public, 4 visiting lectrs per year; gallery talks; tours; museum shop selling books, reproductions, prints
L Phillips Library, East India Square, 161 Essex St, 01970. *Librn* Barbara Edkins
Open Mon - Fri 9 AM - 4:30 PM. Staff library, but open to qualified researchers
Income: Financed by endowment
Library Holdings: Vols 100,000; Per subs 225
Special Subjects: Ethnology of non-European peoples, maritime history of New England, natural history of Essex County, voyages of discovery

SANDWICH

M HERITAGE PLANTATION OF SANDWICH, Grove and Pine Sts, 02563. Tel 617-888-3300. *Dir* Gene A Schott; *Cur Arts & Crafts* Ladd MacMillan; *Cur Military History* James Cervantes; *Cur Botanical Science* Jean Gillis; *Registrar* Allota Lentel
Open daily 10 AM - 5 PM, May 1 - Oct 15. Admis adults $2.50. Estab 1969 as a museum of Americana. Heritage Planation is an educational trust. Maintains three galleries which house collections. Average Annual Attendance: 100,000. Mem: 1200; dues family $25, individual $15; annual meeting May
Income: $400,000 (financed by endowment, membership, admissions)
Collections: †American Indian artifacts; folk art; primitive paintings; †Scrimshaw
Exhibitions: (1978) Arms and Armor; Birds in American Art; (1979) Three American Museums and Egypt; Toys of Transportation; Warriors of the Plains
Publications: The Cupola, quarterly
Activities: Classes for adults and children; lect for members only, 4 - 5 vis lectr per year; concerts; gallery talks; tours; exten dept serving Cape Cod area; artmobile; individual paintings and original objects of art lent
L Library, Grove & Pine Sts, 02563.
Open to staff and members for reference only
Library Holdings: Vols 1000; Per subs 10
Special Subjects: Antique automobile, art, military history

SCITUATE

O BOSTON WATERCOLOR SOCIETY, 748 First Parish Rd, 02066. Tel 617-545-2025. *Pres* Charles A Mahoney; *VPres* Glenn MacNutt; *Secy* Fletcher P Adams
Estab 1886 to advance watercolor proficiency. Mem: 85; dues $15; annual meeting Jan
Income: Financed by membership

SHARON

M KENDALL WHALING MUSEUM, 27 Everett St, PO Box 297, 02085. Tel 617-784-5642. *Dir* Kenneth R Martin; *Cur* Robert H Ellis Jr
Open Mon - Fri 1 - 4 PM, cl holidays. Admis adults $1, children under 14 50¢. Estab 1956 to collect, preserve and interpret materials relating to the history of whaling and the natural history of the whale. Maintains a Dutch-European Gallery, a Japanese Gallery, the scrimshaw exhibit gallery, the whale boat and whaling gear room, along with two large American galleries. Mem: 4000
Income: Financed by foundations, grants, admissions, gifts and publications
Collections: †Paintings; †prints; scrimshaw and other whalemen's folk art; ship models
Exhibitions: Modern Whaling; Save the Whale
Publications: Original publications
Activities: Lect open to public; symposia; museum shop selling books, original art, prints and posters
L Library, 27 Everett St, 02067.
For reference only
Library Holdings: Vols 4000; Per subs 25; Micro—Reels; Other—Pamphlets

SOUTH HADLEY

M MOUNT HOLYOKE COLLEGE ART MUSEUM, 01075. Tel 413-538-2245. *Dir* Jean C Harris; *Chief Cur* Wendy Watson; *Admin Asst* Margery Roy
Open Mon - Fri 11 AM - 5 PM; Sat - Sun 1 - 4 PM; summer Mon - Fri 1 - 4 PM. No admis fee. Estab 1875 to display permanent collection and temporary exhibitions. Building erected in 1971 to house the equipment and collections of the Department of Art of Mount Holyoke College. Contains lecture rooms, painting and sculpture studios, art library; art museum with five galleries houses the permanent collection. Mem: Dues $15 - $100
Income: Financed by endowment, membership, state appropriations and college funds
Collections: †Asian art, European and American paintings, sculpture, prints and drawings; Egyptian, Greek, Roman, Pre-Columbian
Exhibitions: (1979-80) Artcrafts, Images of Italy: Photography in the 19th Century; Baroque Painting in the Low Countries: Selections from the Bader Collection; The Art of the Print: New Dimensions; The Garden in Islamic Art
Publications: Newsletter, twice yearly
Activities: Lect open to the public, 5 - 6 vis lectr per year; individual paintings lent to exhibitions sponsored by museums
L Art Library, 01075.
Open to college community only
Library Holdings: Vols 15,000; Per subs 60; AV—Slides

SOUTH SUDBURY

M LONGFELLOW'S WAYSIDE INN, Wayside Inn Road off Route 20, 01776. Tel 617-443-8846. *Innkeeper* Francis Koppeis; *Chmn Trustees* Lawrence Coolidge
Open daily 9 AM - 9 PM; cl Christmas Day. Admis 50¢; no charge for dining room and overnight guests. Estab c 1702 as the oldest operating Inn in America. The ancient hostelry continues to provide hospitality to wayfarers from all over the world. 18th century period rooms including Old Barroom, Longfellow Parlor, Longfellow Bed Chamber, Old Kitchen, Drivers and Drovers Chambers. Historic buildings on the estate include Redstone School of Mary's Little Lamb fame, grist mill, and Martha Mary Chapel. Average Annual Attendance: 250,000
Collections: Early American furniture and decorative arts; Howe family memorabilia; paintings; photographs of the Inn; prints
Activities: Classes for adults; docent training; colonial crafts demonstrations and workshops; lect open to public, 10 vis lectr per year; gallery talks; tours; sales shop selling books, original art, reproductions, prints and slides

SPRINGFIELD

M CONNECTICUT VALLEY HISTORICAL MUSEUM, 194 State St, 01103. Tel 413-732-3080. *Cur* Gregory Farmer
Open Tues - Sun Noon - 5 PM, cl Mon, New Year's Day, July 4, Thanksgiving & Christmas. No admis fee. Estab 1876
Income: $76,000
Collections: Decorative arts of the Connecticut Valley; furniture; paintings
Exhibitions: Displays of pewter, silver, glass and ceramics; Early photography; paintings by J S Ellsworth, J W Stock and C Harding; 17th and 18th century period rooms

M MUSEUM OF FINE ARTS, 49 Chestnut St, 01103. Tel 413-733-5857. *Dir Public Relations* Patricia Cahil
Open Tues - Sat 1 - 5 PM; Sun 2 - 5 PM; cl Mon & holidays. No admis fee. Estab 1933 as a unit of the Springfield Library and Museums Association through the bequests of Mr & Mrs James Philip Gray. Building contains 18 galleries, library theater, offices
Collections: Gothic to Renaissance; Japanese woodblock prints, paintings and sculpture; Persian miniatures from 10th - 20th century; Prehistoric Chinese to 19th century; primitive to contemporary American paintings, sculpture and graphics; 17th, 18th, 19th and 20th century Italian, Dutch, French and British
Exhibitions: Special exhibitions, historic to contemporary, are continually on view in addition to permanent collection
Activities: Docent training; audio-visual programs; public school programs; lect; films; concerts; tours

L Reference Library, 49 Chestnut St, 01103.
Library Holdings: Vols 5000; AV—Slides

M GEORGE WALTER VINCENT SMITH ART MUSEUM, 222 State St, 01103. Tel 413-733-4214. *Chmn of Trustee Committee* Kathleen Morehead; *Dir* Richard Muhlberger; *Cur Education* Janet Gelman; *Asst Cur Education* Lisa Italiano; *Conservator* Emil G Schnorr
Open Tues - Sat 1 - 5 PM, Sun 2 - 5 PM, cl Mon. No admis fee. Estab 1889 to

preserve, protect, present, interpret, study and publish the collections of fine and decorative arts. Maintains eleven galleries housing permanent collection and one gallery reserved for changing exhibitions. Average Annual Attendance: 35,000.
Mem: 2000; dues $15 and up; annual meeting June
Income: Financed by endowment, membership, city and state appropriations
Collections: American and European Paintings; Near Eastern Carpets; Oriental Arts (calligraphy, ceramics, lacquer, painting, sculpture, textiles); Plaster Casts
Exhibitions: (1979) Marie Danforth Page: Back Bay Portraitist; Calligraphy Exhibition; Japanese Bronzes; Of Town and River: The Art of Springfield's First Golden Era
Publications: Annual report; quadrangle calendar; special exhibition catalogs
Activities: Classes for adults and children; docent training; lect open to public; gallery talks; tours; scholarships; individual paintings and original objects of art lent to museums; originate traveling exhibitions
L Research Library, 222 State St, 01103.
Open to scholars by special arrangement
Library Holdings: Vols 2700
Special Subjects: Related to collections

O SPRINGFIELD ART LEAGUE, GWV Smith Art Museum, 222 State Street, 01103.
Estab 1918 to stimulate art expression and appreciation in Springfield. Mem: Dues $10; annual meeting May
Exhibitions: Non-juried show in Nov open to all members; annual juried exhibition in April open to all artists
Activities: Lect; demonstration; tours

L SPRINGFIELD CITY LIBRARY, Art Department, 220 State St, 01103. Tel 413-739-3871. *Pres* John J Canowan Jr; *Dir* Robert Wagenknecht; *Head Fine Arts Department* Karen A Dorval
Open Mon - Thurs 9 AM - 9 PM, Fri 9 AM - 6 PM, Sat 9 AM - 5 PM, cl Sun and holidays. No admis fee. Estab 1857, Fine Arts Department opened 1905. In addition to the City Library system, the Springfield Library and Museums Association owns and administers, as separate units, the George Walter Vincent Smith Museum, the Springfield Museum of Fine Arts, the Science Museum and the Connecticut Valley Historical Museum
Income: $12,000
Library Holdings: Vols 20,000; Per subs 50; Other—Photographs, reproductions, pictures 125,000; American wood engravings and blockprints
Exhibitions: Monthly exhibitions from the Library's collections and of work by local artists; loan exhibitions
Activities: Book traveling exhibitions

L SPRINGFIELD COLLEGE, Babson Library Art Gallery, 263 Alden St, 01109. Tel 413-787-2340. *Cultural Affairs Committee* Nancy Bower
Open daily 8 AM - 4:30 PM. Estab 1975 to bring a wide range of quality exhibits in all areas of the visual arts to the Springfield College campus and surrounding community
Income: Financed by Cultural Affairs Committee
Purchases: $1000
Library Holdings: Vols 116,000; Per subs 800; Micro—Prints; AV—Cassettes, fs, motion pictures, v-tapes; Other—Prints, original art works
Activities: Lect open to public, 6 vis lectr per year; concerts; tours; gallery talks; competitions

STOCKBRIDGE

M CHESTERWOOD, Box 248, 01262. Tel 413-298-3579. *Adminr* Paul W Ivory; *Admin Asst* Kathleen Oppermann
Open daily 10 - 5, May 1 through Oct 31. Admis adults $2.50, senior citizen $1.25, children $1.00; reserved tours of 10 or more, adults $2.00, students 50¢, free to National Trust Members. Chesterwood, a museum property of the National Trust for Historic Preservation, was the Berkshire Hill summer estate of Daniel Chester French (1850-1931), sculptor of the Lincoln Memorial and Minute Man. The 150 acre property includes: French's studio (1898) and colonial revival residence (1900-1901), both designed by Henry Bacon, architect of the Lincoln Memorial; Barn Sculpture Gallery, a c1825 barn adapted for use as exhibition, museum storage and sales space; a period garden and nature walks laid out by French in the woods to the North of the studio. Average Annual Attendance: 25,000
Collections: Plaster models, marbles and bronze casts of French's work and paintings; decorative arts and furnishings representing his family's taste and lifestyle
Exhibitions: Annual Antique Car Show; Antique Toy Exhibit; special exhibits dealing with aspects of historic preservation in the Berkshire region and French's life, career, social and artistic milieu, and summer estate; outdoor sculpture shows
Activities: College summer intern programs; guide training program; sculptor in residence program; guided and school group tours; National Trust Members Day; Berkshire Day Open House; National Trust Preservation Bookstore
L Chesterwood Library, Box 248, 01262. *Program Asst* Susan Frisch
Open by appointment only. Estab 1969. Library consists of art, reference, gardening, architecture and personal books collected by Daniel Chester French and Margaret French Cresson (Daughter) as well as archival material; serves art, social and architectural historians and historic preservationists
Library Holdings: Vols 5000; Per subs 2; AV—Cassettes, lantern slides, motion pictures, rec, slides; Other—Clipping files, prints, manuscripts, memorabilia, original art works, photographs, sculpture
Special Subjects: Chesterwood, late 19th, early 20th century classical sculpture
Collections: Oral histories; Daniel Chester French and Chesterwood; Berkshire region historic preservation clipping file; blueprints and plans of work; photographs of Daniel Chester French and his family, summer estate and works

O STOCKBRIDGE HISTORICAL SOCIETY, INC,* Main St, 01262. Tel 413-298-3822. *Dir* David H Wood; *Asst Dir* Mrs John T Batty
Open daily 10 AM - 5 PM, cl Tues, Thanksgiving, Christmas, New Years. Admis adults $1, children under 12 25¢, local residents no admis fee. Estab 1967 in The Old Corner House, an 1800 Georgian house located on the original property deeded to successive Mohican Indians under charter granted to town by Queen Anne in 1739

Collections: Historical material; original sketches and paintings by Norman Rockwell
Exhibitions: Temporary exhibitions
Activities: Lect; guided tours; sales shop selling Norman Rockwell books and prints

M **STOCKBRIDGE MISSION HOUSE ASSOCIATION,** Box 422, 01262. Tel 413-3383. *Cur* Carol D Patten
Open Memorial Day through Columbus Day Tues - Sat 10 AM - 5 PM, Sun 11 AM - 4 PM. Admis. Built 1739, restored by Mabel Choate in 1928 as a memorial to her parents, Mr and Mrs Joseph H Choate. Originally the home of John Sergeant, first missionary to the Stockbridge Indians, it is now an Early American Museum containing household objects, portraits and decorations of the period, and Indian relics. Average Annual Attendance: 3000

STURBRIDGE

M **OLD STURBRIDGE VILLAGE,*** 01566. Tel 617-347-3362. *Pres* Crawford Lincoln; *VPres Museum Admin* Darwin P Kelsey; *Dir Cur Dept* John O Curtis; *Dir Research & Librn* Roger Parks
Open daily April - Oct 9:30 AM - 5:30 PM, Nov - Mar 10 AM - 4 PM, cl Mon during Dec - Mar, New Years, Christmas. Admis adults $6, children 6-15 $2.50. Estab 1936 to perpetuate and interpret the New England social, economic and cultural heritage; authentically restored rural village consisting of 43 structures. Average Annual Attendance: 670,000
Collections: Buildings; †clocks; decorative arts; furnishings; †folk arts; †glass; †iron; †New England rural paintings; pewter; †pottery; †textiles; †tin
Publications: Annual Report; Guidebook; The New England Galaxy; pamphlet series; The Rural Visitor, quarterly
Activities: Classes for adults and children; craft demonstrations; lect; films; concerts; tours; internships

L **Research Library,*** 01566. Tel 617-347-3362, Ext 132. *Librn* Etta Falkner; *Asst Librn* Theresa Rini
Open Mon - Fri 8:30 AM - 5 PM. Estab 1946 to serve the museum staff. Open to the public for reference only
Income: Financed through museum
Purchases: $7500
Library Holdings: Vols 25,000; Per subs 165; Micro—Fiche, reels; AV—Slides; Other—Manuscripts
Special Subjects: New England 1790-1850 including law, technology and industry especially textile, agriculture, crafts, fine and decorative arts, music, local history

TYRINGHAM

M **TYRINGHAM ART GALLERIES,** Tyringham Rd, 01264. Tel 413-243-0654, 243-3260. *Dir* Ann Marie Davis; *Dir* Donald Davis
Admis 50¢, children under 12 free. Estab 1953 to exhibit and sell paintings, prints sculptures by recognized artists, including world masters. The building was designed as a sculpture studio by the late Sir Henry Kitson; on three levels, smaller studios on the second level are furnished with trap door facilities for lowering sculpture to the main level; two former silos are involved in the structure. Average Annual Attendance: 30,000
Income: Financed privately
Exhibitions: Frequent one-person shows by established artists from New York City
Publications: Occasional auction catalogs
Activities: Gallery talks; tours

L **TYRINGHAM INSTITUTE,** Jean Brown Archive, Shaker Seed House, 02164. Tel 413-243-3216. *Dir* Mrs Leonard Brown
Open Mon - Fri 2 - 5 PM. No admis fee. Estab 1971 for research in dada, surrealism, fluxus for scholars on graduate and advanced research levels. For reference only. Average Annual Attendance: 100-300
Income: Privately financed
Collections: Concrete Poetry; Dada; Fluxus; Happenings; Intermedia
Activities: Lending collection contains original art works, original prints and photographs
L **Library,** Shaker Seed House, 01264.
Open Mon - Fri 2 - 5 PM. Estab 1971 for reference only
Library Holdings: Vols 30,000; Per subs 25; AV—Cassettes, rec; Other—Clipping files, exhibition catalogs, manuscripts, memorabilia, pamphlets
Special Subjects: Dada, fluxus, mail art, performance art, surrealism, visual art

WALTHAM

O **AMERICAN JEWISH HISTORICAL SOCIETY,** 2 Thornton Rd, 02154. Tel 617-891-8110. *Pres* Saul Viener; *Chmn Executive Council* David R Pokross; *Dir* Bernard Wax
Open (summer) Mon - Fri 8:30 AM - 5 PM, (winter) Mon - Thurs 8:30 AM - 5 PM, Fri 8:30 AM - 2 PM. No admis fee. Estab 1892 to collect, preserve, catalog and disseminate information relating to the American Jewish experience. Two galleries with exhibitions mounted, 15 x 50 ft. Average Annual Attendance: 3000.
Mem: 3400; dues $20; annual meeting May
Income: $200,000 (financed by endowment, membership, city appropriation, grants and donations)
Collections: Manuscripts; Portraits; Yiddish Motion Pictures; Yiddish Theater Posters
Exhibitions: Haym Salomon: A Gentleman of Precision and Integrity; Jews in Colonial America
Activities: Lect open to public, 3 vis lectr per year; gallery talks; individual paintings and original objects of art lent to museums and historical societies; lending collection contains motion pictures and paintings
L **Lee M Friedman Memorial Library,** 2 Thornton Rd, 02154. *Librn* Dr Nathan M Kaganoff
Open to qualified researchers for reference
Library Holdings: Vols 65,000; Per subs 100; Other—Manuscripts, archives
Special Subjects: Colonial American Jewry, philanthropic institutions, synagogues

Collections: The Archives consist of approximately four million items which relate to all areas of American Jewish History

M **BRANDEIS UNIVERSITY,** Rose Art Museum, 415 South St, 02154. Tel 617-647-2404. *Dir* Carl I Belz; *Cur* Michael Leja; *Registrar* Cathleen Calmer; *Preparator* Roger Kizik
Open Tues - Sun 1 - 5 PM, cl Mon and holidays. No admis fee. Estab 1961 for the organization of regionally and nationally recognized exhibits of contemporary painting and sculpture. A additional gallery is located in the Spingold Theatre Building. All galleries are used for changing exhibitions; there are no permanent exhibitions. Average Annual Attendance: 20,000
Collections: The permanent collections consist of: African art; American Indian art; contemporary art (post World War II); Japanese prints; modern art (1800 to World War II), including the Riverside Museum Collections and the Teresa Jackson Weill Collection; Pre-Columbian art; pre-modern art (before 1800); Mr and Mrs Edward Rose Collection of early ceramics; Helen S Slosberg Collection of Oceanic art; Tibetian art
Exhibitions: (1979) David Aronson; Don Nice and John Walker; Frank Stella. (1980) Mavericks, Mel Romos, (Guston, Jensen, Samaras, Golub, etc)
Publications: Exhibition catalogs
Activities: Educ dept; docent training; lect open to public, 6 visiting lectrs per year; gallery talks; tours; individual paintings and original objects of art lent to students and individuals within the university; lending collection contains original art works, original prints, paintings; traveling exhibitions organized and circulated

WELLESLEY

WELLESLEY COLLEGE

M **Museum,** 02181. Tel 617-235-0320, Exten 314. *Dir* Ann Gabhart; *Asst Dir* Judith Woos Fox; *Admin Asst Friends of Art* Marjorie Dings
Open Mon - Sat 10 AM - 5 PM; Sun 2 - 5 PM; cl New Years Day, Thanksgiving, Dec 24, 25 and 31, mid-June, July and Aug. No admis fee. Estab 1899, dedicated to acquiring a collection of high quality art objects for the primary purpose of teaching art history from original works. Main gallery houses major exhibitions; Corridor Gallery, works on paper; Sculpture Court, permanent installation, sculpture, reliefs, works on wood panel. Average Annual Attendance: 8000. Mem: 550; dues donor $100, contributor $50, regular $25
Income: Financed by membership, through college and gifts
Collections: 15th and 20th Century paintings
Exhibitions: American Portraits and Landscapes (includes works by Capley, Sargent, Inness, Rensett, Moran); European Painting: 16th Century - 18th Century (includes works by Amigoni, Vasari, Girodano, Kauffmann, Domenichino); French Paintings of the 19th Century (includes works by Carot, Rousseau, Troyan, Boudin, Millett, Luce, Cezanne, Renoir); Lee Friedlander: Photographs; Ralph Eugene Meatyard: A Retrospective; Sitework (sculpture by Stephen Antonakos, Nancy Holt, Robert Irwin, Ned Smyth)
Publications: Exhibition catalogs; Wellesley College Friends of Art Newsletter, annually
Activities: Docent training; original objects of art lent to students; lending collection contains original prints; originate traveling exhibitions; sales desk sells catalogs, postcards and notecards
L **Art Library,** 02181. *Librn* Katherine D Finkelpearl; *Asst* Susan Farlow; *Asst Librn* Janet Dwyer
Circ 22,000
Income: $20,000 (financed by College appropriation)
Purchases: $15,000
Library Holdings: Vols 28,000; Per subs 75; AV—Kodachromes, lantern Slides; Other—Exhibition catalogs, pamphlets, photographs
Special Subjects: Photography, American art and architecture, Western European art and architecture, Far Eastern art, Ancient art and architecture

WENHAM

O **WENHAM HISTORICAL ASSOCIATION AND MUSEUM, INC,** 132 Main St, 01984. Tel 617-468-2377. *Dir* Eleanor E Thompson; *Doll Cur* Mrs F J Donoghue; *Office Admin* Felicia Connolly; *Office Admin* Mary L Corning; *Pres* Mrs Dean Cogswell
Open Mon - Fri 1 - 4 PM, Sun 2 - 5 PM, mornings by appointment. Admis adults $1, children (6-14) 25¢. Estab 1921 as Historical Society, incorporated 1953, to acquire, preserve, interpret, and exhibit collections of literary and historical interest; to provide an educational and cultural service and facilities. Maintains three permanent galleries and one gallery for changing exhibits. Average Annual Attendance: 8000. Mem: 650; dues family $10, individual $5; annual meeting April
Income: $38,000 (financed by endowment, membership, earned income)
Collections: Dolls; Doll Houses; Figurines; Costumes and Accessories 1800 - 1960; Embroideries; Fans; Needlework; Quilts; toys
Exhibitions: Color Photography; Doll Houses; Grandma's kitchen; landscapes; Model Trains; Needle Artists; Needlecrafts Portraits, Still Lifes; Quilts Old and New; Samplers; Tin and Woodenware; Weavers; Wedding Dresses
Publications: Annual report; newsletter
Activities: Classes for children; lect open to public, 4 vis lectr per year; gallery talks; originate traveling exhibitions; museum shop sells books, miniatures, original needlework and dolls
L **Timothy Pickering Library,** 132 Main St, 01984. *Librn* Mary L Corning
Open to members and the public for reference
Library Holdings: Vols 1000

WESTFIELD

M WESTFIELD ATHENAEUM, Jasper Rand Art Museum, 6 Elm St, 01085. Tel 413-568-7833. *Pres* James P Stow III; *Treas* Leslie A Chapin; *Dir* Franklin P Taplin; *Secy* Nancy C Dalton
Open Mon, Tues, Thurs & Fri 8:30 AM - 8 PM, Wed 9 AM - 6 PM, Sat 8:30 AM - 5 PM, cl Sat in summer. No admis fee. Estab 1927 to provide exhibitions of art works by area artists and other prominent artists. Gallery measures 25 x 30 x 17 feet, with a domed ceiling and free-standing glass cases and wall cases. Average Annual Attendance: 13,500. Mem: 250; no dues; annual meeting fourth Mon Oct
Income: Financed by endowment, city appropriation
Exhibitions: American Indian pottery made by the Indians of Arizona; Bicentennial plaques by Eugene Lederle; original paintings of scenes along the General Knox Trail by Wallace Noel; paintings by eleven members of Springfield Art League; paintings of New England scenes by Joseph R Corish
Activities: Classes for children

WESTON

M REGIS COLLEGE, L J Walters Jr Gallery, 235 Wellesley St, 02193. Tel 617-893-1820, Ext 237. *Dir* Sr Louisella Walters
Open Mon - Fri 9 AM - 4:30 PM. No admis fee. Estab 1964 for education; for visiting exhibits; for student use. Gallery is one room, 20 x 30 ft. Average Annual Attendance: 1500
Exhibitions: Local Painters and Sculptors; Student Exhibits

WILLIAMSTOWN

M STERLING AND FRANCINE CLARK ART INSTITUTE, 225 South St, PO Box 8, 01267. Tel 413-458-8109. *Dir* David S Brooke; *Assoc Dir* John H Brooks; *Cur Prints & Drawings* Rafael A Fernandez; *Asst Cur* David B Cass; *Asst Cur* Beth Carver Wees; *Registrar* Martha Asher; *Asst Comptroller* Virginia Riorden; *Photograph & Slide Librn* J Dustin Wees; *Supt* G Louis McManus
Open Tues - Sun 10 AM - 5 PM, cl Mon, New Year's Day, Thanksgiving & Christmas. No admis fee. Estab 1955 as a museum of fine arts with galleries, art research library and public events in auditorium. Average Annual Attendance: 100,000
Collections: Antique Silver; Dutch, Flemish, French, Italian Old Master Paintings from the 14th - 18th Centuries; French 19th Century Paintings including The Impressionists; 19th Century Sculpture; Old Master Prints and Drawings; Porcelains; Selected 19th Century American Artists (Homer and Sargent)
Exhibitions: The Permanent Collection and Traveling Exhibitions
Publications: Calendar of Events, quarterly
Activities: Docent training; organized educ programs for children; graduate program for MA in art history in collaboration with Williams College; lect; concerts; movies; gallery talks; book traveling exhibitions; museum shop sells books, reproductions, prints, slides and postcards
L Clark Art Institute Library, 225 South St, 01267. *Librn* Michael Rinehart; *Asst Librn* E Marie Wikander
Open Tues - Fri 10 AM - 5 PM. Estab 1962. For reference only
Purchases: $50,000
Library Holdings: Vols 63,000; Per subs 474; Micro—Fiche, reels; Other—Clipping files, exhibition catalogs, pamphlets, photographs, Auction sales catalogues
Special Subjects: Eoropean and American Art
Collections: Mary Ann Beinecke Decorative Art Collection; Duveen Library and Archive; Juynboll Collection

M WILLIAMS COLLEGE, Museum of Art, Main St, 01267. Tel 413-597-2429. *Acting Dir* John W Coffey; *Supt* George T Aitken; *Secy* Elizabeth Kieffer
Open Mon - Fri 9 AM - 5 PM, weekends 1 - 5 PM, summer daily 1 - 5 PM, cl college & legal holidays. No admis fee. Estab 1926 for the presentation of the permanent collection and temporary loan exhibitions for the benefit of the Williams College community and the general public. Maintains a central rotunda, built in 1846 by Thomas Tefft, also other period galleries and loan exhibitions gallery are maintained. Average Annual Attendance: 10,000
Collections: African and Asian Art; Ancient and Medieval Sculpture and Glass; British and American Portraits; Contemporary Art; 19th & 20th Century American Painting and Sculpture; Renaissance and Baroque Paintings; prints and photographs
Exhibitions: All media, with emphasis on contemporary art
Publications: Exhibition catalogs, 3 - 4 per year
Activities: Classes for children; lect open to public, 20 vis lectr per year; concerts; gallery talks; tours; individual paintings and original objects of art lent to museums; originate traveling exhibitions; museum shop sells books
L Sawyer Library, Main St, 01267.
Income: $10,400
Library Holdings: Vols 16,600; Per subs 86; AV—Slides; Other—Reproductions

WORCESTER

AMERICAN ANTIQUARIAN SOCIETY
For further information, see National and Regional Organizations

M CLARK UNIVERSITY, Little Center Gallery, 950 Main St, 01610. Tel 617-793-7260. *Dir* Donald W Krueger; *Intern* Karla Buchinskas; *Intern* Tracey Nurik; *Asst* Stacie Gerard
Open Mon - Fri Noon - 6 PM, Sat & Sun 2 - 6 PM, cl University holidays. No admis fee. Estab 1977 primarily for one and two-person shows of young, unknown artists; to help artists get recognition. Gallery 40 x 50 ft with moveable panels. Average Annual Attendance: 16,400
Income: Financed through the University
Exhibitions: Ten exhibitions a year of young artists
Publications: Announcements of exhibitions
Activities: Vis lectr; gallery talks

M JOHN WOODMAN HIGGINS ARMORY, 100 Barber Ave, 01606. Tel 617-853-6015. *Pres* Roger N Perry Jr; *Dir & Cur* Richard E Ford
Open Tues - Fri 9 AM - 4 PM, Sat 10 AM - 3 PM, Sun 1 - 5 PM, cl Mon and National holidays. Established 1928. Museum is in a Gothic Hall with high vaulted ceilings. Average Annual Attendance: 35,000. Mem: 325; dues $25 & $10; annual meeting May
Income: Financed by admissions, membership, grants, gift shop and endowment
Collections: Arms and armor from Stone Age through the 19th century; artistic objects of the iron smith's craft; art from related periods: paintings; tapestries; stained glass; woodcarvings
Publications: Catalog of Armor; Booklet on Armor; Ventail Voice, quarterly
Activities: Docent training; independent study for college students; audio-visual talks for adults and children; lectures open to the public; concerts; gallery talks; tours; museum and sales shop sells books, reproductions, prints, slides and gifts relating to arms and armor
L Library, 100 Barber Ave, 01606. *Dir* Richard E Ford; *Librn* Erveen C Lundberg
Open for reference Tuesday, Wednesday and Thursday only
Library Holdings: Vols 2500
Special Subjects: Arms and armor, metal craftmanship

M WORCESTER ART MUSEUM, 55 Salisbury St, 01608. Tel 617-799-4406. *Dir* Richard Stuart Teitz; *Development Dir* Steven L Lanier; *Dir Public Relations* William H Toner; *Dir Publications* Gaye L Brown; *Cur Coll* Dagmar E Reutlinger; *Assoc Cur* James Q Welu; *Cur of Education* Ellen R Berezin; *Asst Cur of Education* Jeanne C Pond; *Registrar & Cur Photography* Stephen B Jareckie; *Cur Prints & Drawings* Timothy A Riggs; *Cur Japanese Prints* Alice Mundt; *Adminr* W Arthur Gagne; *Membership Coordr* Jean T Larkin; *Conservator* Norman E Muller; *Slide Librn* Laura Cannamela
Open Tues - Sat 10 AM - 5 PM, Sun 2 5 PM, cl Mon, New Year's, July 4th, Thanksgiving & Christmas. Admis nonmember adults $1, children under 14 and senior citizens 50¢, children under 5 accompanied by adult free, members free. Estab Museum 1896, School 1898. The Museum and School were founded for the promotion of art and art education in Worcester; for the preservation and exhibition of works and objects of art and for instruction in the industrial, liberal and fine arts. l05There are 42 galleries housed in a neoclassical building. The Higgins Education Wing, built in 1970, houses the Museum School and contains exhibition space for shows sponsored by the Education Department and the School. Average Annual Attendance: 95,000. Mem: 3200; dues $8 - $1000 and over; annual meeting Oct
Income: $1,480,000 (financed by endowment, membership, admission fees, private corporate contributions and government grants)
Collections: John Chandler Bancroft Collection of Japanese Prints; †American Paintings of 18th - 20th Centuries; †British Paintings of 18th and 19th Centuries; †Dutch 17th Century Paintings; †Egyptian, Classical, Oriental and Medieval Sculpture; †French Paintings of 16th - 19th Centuries; †Flemish 16th Century Paintings; †Italian Paintings of the 13th - 18th Centuries; †Mosaics from Antioch; †Pre-Columbian Collection; 12th Century French Chapter House
Exhibitions: (1978) For (1978)For Collectors: A Sales Exhibition of Works of Art; Nomadic Weaving Tradition of the Middle East; Two Decades of American Printmaking; (1978-79) John Marin's Maine; (1979) The Admiring Spectator: George Bellows' Vision of America; Courthouse: A Photographic Document; The Newark Museum Collection of Tibetan Art and Ethnography; 17th Century Dutch Painting: Raising the Curtain on New England Private Collections; Tibet: A Lost World; West Comes East: Painting and Sculpture from the Amon Carter Museum; (1980) Sculpture by Hugh Townley; Treasures of the Royal Photographic Society
Publications: Calendar of Events, quarterly
Activities: Classes for adults and children; docent training; lect open to public, 5 - 6 vis lectr per year; concerts; gallery talks; tours; museum shop sells books, reproductions, prints, jewelry, and others
L Library, 55 Salisbury St, 01608. Tel 617-799-4406, Ext 30. *Librn* Hollee Haswell; *Asst* Maureen Killoran
Open Tues - Fri 10 AM - 5 PM, Sun 2 - 5 PM during the academic year. Estab 1909 to provide resource material for the Museum Departments and participate in Worcester Area Cooperating Libraries. Maintains non-circulating collection only
Purchases: $7000
Library Holdings: Vols 35,000; Per subs 90; Micro—Fiche; AV—Lantern Slides, slides; Other—Exhibition catalogs, pamphlets
Special Subjects: Auction Sale Catalogs, Fine Arts, Museum Exhibition Catalogs, Prints and Drawings, Western European Paintings
Activities: Tours

M WORCESTER CRAFT CENTER GALLERY, 25 Sagamore Rd, 01605. Tel 617-753-8183. *Executive Dir* Cyrus D Lipsitt; *Exhib Coordr* John I Russell
Open Mon - Sat 9 AM - 5 PM, Sun 2 - 5 PM. No admis fee. Estab 1952 for educational exhibits of historic and contemporary crafts. Professionally lighted and installed 40 x 60 gallery with four major shows per year. Average Annual Attendance: 5000. Mem: 1100; dues $15 and up
Income: Financed by membership and grants
Collections: Collection contains 200 books, 2000 Kodachromes, 300 photographs
Exhibitions: Objects for an Interior Environment, David Davison; The North American Basket 1790-1970; Its About Time, American Woodcarvers;
Publications: Exhibition catalogs
Activities: Classes for adults and children; lectures open to the public, 12 visiting lecturers per year; gallery talks; tours; traveling exhibitions organized and circulated; museum shop sells books, original art, reproductions and slides
L Library, 25 Sagamore Rd, 01605.
Open Mon - Fri 9 AM - 5 PM. Established 1958. For reference only
Library Holdings: Vols 100; Per subs 50; AV—Slides; Other—Photographs

MICHIGAN

ADRIAN

M **SIENA HEIGHTS COLLEGE,** Little Gallery, Studio Angelico, 1257 Siena Heights Dr, 49221. Tel 313-263-8736. *Dir* Jeannine Klemm
Open Tues - Fri 1 - 9 PM, cl Mon, Easter, Christmas and semester breaks. No admis fee. Estab 1919 as an arts center and institute
Collections: Paintings; sculpture; graphics; decorative arts; art history; textiles; archaeology; paintings and sculpture on loan from the University of Michigan
Exhibitions: Invitational Artists Shows; temporary exhibitions
Activities: Classes for adults and children; lectures; guided tours; competitions

ALBION

M **ALBION COLLEGE,** Bobbitt Visual Arts Center, 49224. Tel 517-629-5511, Ext 246. *Chmn Department Visual Arts* Frank Machek
Open Mon - Thurs 9 AM - 4:45 PM & 6:30 - 10 PM, Fri 9 AM - 4:45 PM, Sat 10 AM - 1 PM, Sun 2 - 5 PM. No admis fee. Estab 1835 to offer art education at college level and general art exhibition program for campus community and public. Four galleries, one large, three small
Income: Privately funded
Purchases: $2000 - $4000
Collections: African Art; ceramics; glass; †prints
Exhibitions: From The Print Collection; Pieces from the Permanent Collection; various one-man and group shows various One-Man and Group Shows
Activities: Lect open to public, 2 - 4 vis lectr per year; gallery talks; original objects of art lent to faculty and students

ALPENA

M **JESSE BESSER MUSEUM,** 491 Johnson St, 49707. Tel 517-356-2202. *Dir* Dennis R Bodem; *Pres* Philip M Park; *VPres* Alan Walker; *Secy* Helen Wilson; *Treas* J Austin Sobczak
Open Mon - Fri 9 AM - 5 PM, Sat & Sun 1 - 5 PM, Thurs evenings 7 - 9 PM. Admis by donation. Estab association 1962, building open to public 1966, a museum of history, science, and art serving northern Michigan. Museum as a planetarium and the Foucault Pendulum. Three galleries are utilized for shows, traveling exhibits, and changing exhibitions of the Museum's collection of modern art and art prints. There is 104 running ft of wall space on lower level, 1250 sq ft and 1645 sq ft on upper level galleries. Average Annual Attendance: 50,000
Income: Financed by Besser Foundation, federal and state grants, private gifts and donations, Museums Founders Society
Collections: Photography of Daniel Farber; †art prints; †modern art
Activities: Classes for adults and children; docent training; lect open to public, 2 - 4 vis lectr per year; gallery talks; tours; book traveling exhibitions; sales shop sells books

L **Library,** 491 Johnson St, 49707.
Open to public for reference only
Library Holdings: Vols 600; Per subs 14

ANN ARBOR

O **ANN ARBOR ART ASSOCIATION,** 117 W Liberty, 48103. Tel 313-994-8004. *Pres* I B Remsen; *VPres* Bettye Elkins; *Secy* Margaret Shelton; *Executive Dir* Marsha Chamberlin; *Asst to the Dir* Susan Monaghan; *Exhibit Gallery Dir* Susan Froelich; *Gallery Shop Dir* Jean Lau; *Gallery Shop Dir* Patricia Due
Open Mon - Sat 10 AM - 5 PM. Estab 1909 to further the welfare of visual art in Ann Arbor by encouraging local art interests. Maintains 750 square feet of exhibit gallery space with monthly shows; sales - rental gallery next to exhibit area. Average Annual Attendance: 10,400. Mem: 475; dues $15; annual meeting May
Income: $150,000 (financed by membership, Michigan Council for the Arts grant, rental of studios and retail sales)
Exhibitions: Monthly Shows
Publications: Class catalog, quarterly; gallery announcements, monthly; lecture listings, quarterly; newsletter, monthly
Activities: Classes for adults and children; lect open to the public, 4-6 visiting lectr per year; gallery talks; tours; awards; scholarships; individual paintings and original objects of art lent to organizations and community facilities; sales shop selling original art

O **ARTWORLDS CENTER FOR CREATIVE ARTS,** 213 S Main St, 48104. Tel 313-994-8400. *Pres* William Bloom; *VPres* Kathryn McGowan; *Secy* James Morse; *Dir* Cecil Taylor; *Program Coordr* Linda Hawkins; *Public Relations* Kathy Manley; *Accountant* Amanda Kelly
Open Mon - Thur 3:30 - 9:30 PM, Sat 9:30 AM - 3:30 PM. Estab 1972 to bring art into peoples' lives through workshops on visual, cultural, performing and other art forms. Average Annual Attendance: 3000. Mem: Annual meeting Oct
Income: $90,000 (financed by workshop fees, facilities rental and donations)
Exhibitions: Photography, drawings, paintings of new and established artists; 2-dimensional visual arts exhibits
Publications: Biannual publication of brochures, news releases and posters
Activities: Lect open to the public; book traveling exhibitions, 2 per year

UNIVERSITY OF MICHIGAN MUSEUM OF ART

M **Alumni Memorial Hall,** 525 S State St, 48109. *Dir* Bret Waller; *Cur of Asian Art* Marshall Wu; *Asst to Dir* Jacquelynn Slee; *Registrar* Carole Cunningham; *Coordr Public Programs* Richard Croake; *Admin Secy* Jo Lau
Open (Sept - May) Mon - Sat 9 AM - 5 PM, Sun 1 - 5 PM; (June - Aug) daily 11 AM - 5 PM. No admis fee. Estab 1946, as a university art museum and museum for the Ann Arbor community. Average Annual Attendance: 55,000. Mem: 1500; dues individual $25
Income: Financed by state appropriation

Collections: Arts of the Western world from the 6th century AD to the present; Asian, Near Eastern, African and Oceanic, including ceramics, †contemporary art, †decorative art, †graphic arts, manuscripts, †painting, †sculpture
Exhibitions: (1978) Art a la Carte: Decorative Imagery in Maps 1600-1800; Atelier 17; Chicago: The City and its Artists; Close Observation: Selected Oil Sketches by Frederick E Church; The Crisis of Impressionism, 1878-1882; Expressionist Drawings from the D Thomas Bergen Collection; French Watercolor Landscapes of the 19th century; Gitter Collection of Japanese Zenga & Nanga Ptg; Image and Life: 50,000 Years of Japanese Pre-History; The Inuit Print & Inuit Sculpture; Ludwig Meidner: an Expressionist Master; John Montresor in America: 18th century military maps; Projects-New Urban Monuments; U-M Art Faculty Exhibition; Whistler: The Later Years
Publications: Bulletin of the Museums of Art and Archaeology, annually
Activities: Educ dept; docent training; 10 visiting lectr per year; gallery talks; tours; museum shop selling publications and posters, postcards

M **Kelsey Museum of Ancient and Medieval Archaeology,** 434 State St, 48109. Tel 313-764-9304. *Dir* John G Pedley; *Asst Cur* Elaine K Gazda; *Asst Cur* John H Humphrey; *Asst Cur* Margaret C Root; *Asst Cur* Amy Rosenberg; *Registrar* Jill B Bace; *Technician* David W Slee
Open Mon - Fri 9 AM - 4 PM, Sat & Sun 1 - 4 PM. No admis fee. Estab 1928. Four small galleries are maintained. Average Annual Attendance: 25,500
Collections: Objects of the Graeco-Roman period from excavations conducted by the University of Michigan in Egypt and Iraq; Greece, Etruria, Rome and provinces: sculpture, inscriptions, pottery, bronzes, terracottas; Egyptian antiquities dynastic through Roman; Roman and Islamic glass, bone and ivory objects, textiles, coins
Exhibitions: Ancient and Modern Revivals; Cathage; The Gods of Egypt; Greek Vases from Boston; Islamic Art from the University of Michigan Collections; Karanis Culpture; The Monastery of St Catharine's on Mt Sinai; Roman Portraiture; Seleucia-on-the-Tigris
Publications: Bulletin of the Museums of Art and Archaeology
Activities: Lect open to the public, 10-12 visiting lectr per year; gallery talks; tours; sales shop selling books and exhibition catalogs

M **Slusser Gallery,** School of Art, 2000 Bonisteel Blvd, 48109. Tel 313-764-0397. *Exhib Dir* Gerome Kamrowski
Open Mon - Fri 9 AM - 5 PM, Sat 9 AM - 12 Noon. No admis fee. Estab 1974, primarily used as an educational facility with high volume of student and faculty participation. Gallery is located on the main floor of the Art & Architecture Building and is comprised of 3,431 sq ft of exhibition space and is a well lighted area. Average Annual Attendance: 4000
Collections: Artifacts of the schools history
Exhibitions: (1979) Bachelor of Fine Arts Exhibition; Photographs & Photo Equipment; Provicetown Artists from Long Point Gallery
Publications: Abstraction-Creation; Harvey Breverman; Catalogs; Sculpture Inside and Out
Activities: Lect open to the public, 10-15 visiting lectr per year; gallery talks

L **Fine Arts Library,** 103 Tappan Hall, 48109. Tel 313-764-5405. *Head Fine Arts Library* Valerie D Meyer
Open Mon - Thurs 8 AM - 5 PM, 7 - 11 PM, Fri 8 AM - 5 PM, Sat 9 AM - 6 PM, Sun 12 - 6 PM; May - Aug 8 AM - 5 PM Mon - Fri. Estab 1949, to support the academic programs of the History of the Art Dept, including research of faculty and graduate students. Circ 15,100
Income: $31,000 (financed by state appropriation)
Library Holdings: Vols 49,000; Per subs 228; Micro—Fiche, reels; Other—Exhibition catalogs, pamphlets, Marburger index of photographic documentation of art in Germany
Special Subjects: Art History, Oriental Art
Collections: Index of Jewish Art

L **Slide and Photograph Collection,** History of Art Department, 107 Tappan Hall, 48109. Tel 313-764-5404. *Cur* Marie Light; *Assoc Cur* Barbara Wagner; *Asst Cur* Joy Alexander; *Photographer* Patrick Young
Open Mon - Fri 8:30 AM - 1 PM, 2 - 5 PM. Estab 1911, as a library for teaching and research collection of slides and photos of art objects; limited commercial distribution (Asian Art Photographic Distribution). Circ 3,600
Income: Financed by state appropriation
Library Holdings: AV—Lantern Slides, slides, v-tapes; Other—Photographs, reproductions
Special Subjects:
Collections: Berenson's I Tatti Archive; Courtauld Institute Illustration Archive; Palace Museum Archive (Chinese painting); Romanesque Archive (sculpture and some architecture concentrating on Burgundy, Southwestern France, Spain and southern Italy; SE Asian and Indian Archives
Activities: Materials lent only to University of Michigan faculty and students

BATTLE CREEK

O **BATTLE CREEK CIVIC ART CENTER,** 265 E Emmett St, 49017. Tel 616-962-9511. *Dir* Darwin R Davis; *Pres* Anita Yannitelli; *Asst Dir* Ruth M Sundberg
Open Tues - Sat 9:30 AM - 4:30 PM, Sun 1 - 4 PM, cl Mon, August & legal holidays. No admis fee. Estab 1947 to offer classes for children and adults, and to plan monthly exhibitions of professional work. Mem: 800; dues $10 and up; annual meeting May or June
Collections: New Michigan Art Collection featuring 19th & 20th Century Michigan Artists
Exhibitions: Crafts; Drawings; Group and One-Man Shows; Paintings; Photography; Prints; Student Exhibits
Activities: Classes for children and adults; lect; demonstrations; movies; talks; gift and rental gallery

BENZONIA

L BENZONIA PUBLIC LIBRARY, Michigan Ave, PO Box I, 49616. Tel 616-882-4111. *Librn & Hostess* Susan Gerhart
Open summer Mon - Sat 1:30 - 5:30 PM, Mon - Thur 7 - 9 PM, winter Mon - Thur 1:30 - 5:30 PM & 7 - 9 PM, Sat 1:30 - 5:30 PM. Estab 1966 to provide educational and cultural services to the people of the village and surrounding area. Circ 14,469. Maintains art gallery
Library Holdings: Vols 11,061; Per subs 50; AV—Cassettes, fs, rec; Other—Clipping files, photographs
Collections: Overleaf Collection - Photographs of Area During Logging Era
Exhibitions: Rosemary Blacklock; Constance Creech; Jim Durrell (photographs); Mike French
Publications: Newsletter, monthly

BIRMINGHAM

O BIRMINGHAM-BLOOMFIELD ART ASSOCIATION, 1516 S Cranbrook Rd, 48009. Tel 313-644-0866. *Pres* Victor L Klein; *VPres* James W Atkinson; *Secy* Mrs Harry Velick; *Executive Dir* Kenneth R Gross; *Asst Dir* Leslie Masters; *Office Mgr* Mrs Douglas Garrison; *Business Mgr* Frances Lawrence
Open Mon - Thurs 9 AM - 10 PM, Fri 9 AM - 7 PM, Sat 9 AM - 5 PM, cl Sun. No admis fee. Estab 1956 to provide a community-wide, integrated studio-gallery art center. Average Annual Attendance: 10,000. Mem: 800; dues $20 and up; annual meeting June
Income: $100,000 (financed by membership, tuitions and special events funding)
Collections: Very small collection of craft objects and prints by local artists
Publications: Newsletter, ten a year
Activities: Classes for adults and children; docent training; Picture Lady Program; Career Program; Teen Volunteer Service; lect open to public, 4 - 8 vis lectr per year; tours; competitions, cash awards, ribbons and certificates; scholarships; exten dept serving public schools; individual paintings and original objects of art lent to public on a rental basis; lending collection contains color reproductions, Kodachromes, original art works and prints, paintings, photographs, sculpture, slides; sales and rental gallery; sales shop sells books, original art, prints, photographs, paintings and crafts

BLOOMFIELD HILLS

M CRANBROOK ACADEMY OF ART MUSEUM, 500 Lone Pine Rd, 48103. Tel 313-645-3300. *Dir Museum* Roy Slade; *Museum Adminr* Linda Dunne Parks; *Admin Asst* Anne Padden; *Cur of Coll* John Gerard
Open Tues - Sun 1 - 5 PM, cl Mon and major holidays. Admis adults $1.50, students & Senior citizens $1, group rates available. Estab 1924 as part of Cranbrook Academy of Art. Average Annual Attendance: 60,000
Collections: Ceramics by Maija Grotell; Decorative Arts by Eliel Saarinen; Porcelains by Adelaide Robineau; Sculpture by Carl Milles; Contemporary Paintings; 19th Century Prints; Study Collection of Textiles
Exhibitions: Annual Student Exhibition; contemporary architecture, crafts, design, paintings and sculpture
Activities: Lect; tours; film program
L Library, 500 Lone Pine Rd, 48103.
Library is for Academy students, faculty and staff use only

DEARBORN

M GREENFIELD VILLAGE AND HENRY FORD MUSEUM, 48121. Tel 313-271-1620, information 271-1976. *Pres* Frank Caddy; *VPres Coll* Robert Wheeler; *VPres Education* David Glick; *VPres Public Affairs* Robert Dawson; *Dir Public Relations* Robert Ritter
Open weekdays 9 AM - 5 PM, weekends and July - Aug 9 AM - 6 PM. Separate admis charges to the Village and Museum, adults $4.25, children 6 - 12 $2.25. Estab 1929 as a general museum of American culture and history for educational purposes. Greenfield Village has over 100 historic buildings, including homes of famous Americans and public and industrial structures. Most buildings are furnished or equipped and many were moved from their original sites to Dearborn. Average Annual Attendance: 1,600,000
Income: Publicly supported through admissions and the Friends of Greenfield Village and Henry Ford Museum
Collections: Crafts; Decorative Arts; Folk Art; Home Art
Publications: The Herald, museum quarterly issued to members; publications on exhibits and individual collections, issued as published
L Library, 48121.
Library Holdings: Vols 30,000; Other—Manuscripts, photographs
Collections: Henry Ford Archives contain some 14 million documents; Rare Book Collections

DETROIT

L CENTER FOR CREATIVE STUDIES - COLLEGE OF ART & DESIGN LIBRARY, 245 E Kirby, 48202. Tel 313-872-3118. *Librn* Jean Peyrat
Open Mon - Thurs 8:30 AM - 1 PM & 2:15 - 7 PM, Fri 8:30 AM - 1 PM & 2:15 - 4:30. Estab 1966 to serve students and faculty of an undergraduate art school. Primarily a how-to collection
Income: Financed by private school
Library Holdings: Vols 10,000; Per subs 72; AV—Slides; Other—Exhibition catalogs

M DETROIT INSTITUTE OF ARTS, 5200 Woodward Ave, 48202. Tel 313-833-7900. *Dir* Frederick J Cumings; *Art Museum Adminr* Robert T Weston; *Cur American Art* Nancy Rivard; *Cur Ancient* William H Peck; *Cur Ethnographic Art* Michael Kan; *Cur European Art* Dewey F Mosby; *Cur Education* Linda Downs; *Graphic Arts* Ellen Sharp; *Cur Modern Art* Jay Belloli; *Cur Oriental Art* Suzanne Mitchell; *Registrar* Susan Weinberg; *Photographer* Nemo Warr; *Head Conservator*

Abraham Joel; *Cur Emeritus Medieval Art* Francis W Robinson
Open Tues - Sun 9:30 AM - 5:30 PM, cl Mon & holidays. Estab and incorporated 1885 as Detroit Museum of Art; chartered as municipal department 1919 and name changed; original organization continued as Founders Society Detroit Institute of Arts; present building opened 1927; South Wing addition completed 1966; North Wing addition opened 1971. Midwest area office of Archives of American Art
Collections: Elizabeth Parke Firestone Collection of 18th Century French Silver; William Randolph Hearst Collection of Arms and Armor and Flemish Tapestries; Grace Whitney Hoff Collection of Fine Bindings; Paul McPharlin Collection of Puppetry, Theatre and Graphic Arts; Robert H Tannahill Bequest of Impressionist and Post-Impressionist Paintings, traditional African Objects, French Silver; Comprehensive Collection of Textiles and of American Decorative Arts; Representative examples of the Arts from prehistory to the present time, including Egypt, Mesopotamia, Greece and Rome, the Orient, Europe, Africa, the South Seas, and the Americas. Central court decorated with Diego Rivera frescoes (1932-33). Whitby Hall, furnished with important collection of furniture
Exhibitions: John Singer Sargent and the Edwardian Age (drawings, paintings, watercolors; will not be shown elsewhere); Michigan Artists and Michigan Artist-Craftsmen (alternate years)
Activities: Workshops; cooperative programs with schools, university and special interest groups; lect series; films (Detroit Youtheatres, Puppetry, Detroit Film Theatre); gallery talks; tours; concerts; two museum shops
L Research Library, 5200 Woodward Ave, 48202. *Librn* F Warren Peters; *Asst Librn & Cataloguer* Constance Wall; *Asst Librn & Reference* Lynne Garza
Open Mon - Fri 9 AM - 5 PM. Estab 1905 to provide material for research, interpretation and documentation of museum collection. For reference only
Income: Financed by city
Library Holdings: Vols 60,000; Per subs 125; Micro—Cards, reels; AV—Slides; Other—Clipping files, exhibition catalogs, pamphlets, photographs
Special Subjects: Archaeology, Architecture, Art History, applied arts
Collections: Albert Kahn Architecture Library; Paul McPharlin Collection of Puppetry; Grace Whitney-Hoff Collection of Fine Bindings
O Detroit Institute of Art Founders Society, 5200 Woodward Ave, 48202. Tel 313-833-7950. *Chmn of Board* Stanford C Stoddard; *Pres* Norman B Weston; *VPres* Mrs Gaylord W Gillis Jr; *Secy* Mrs Alan E Schwatz; *Treas* Alfred M Pelham; *Executive Dir* Frederick J Cummings; *Mgr* Boris Sellers
Estab and incorporated 1885; public membership philanthropic society contributing to the growth of the Detroit Institute of Arts; underwrites Educ Dept activities, publications, special exhibitions and most purchases of works of art. Mem: 12,000; dues corporate patron $10,000, corporate sponsor $5000, corporate contributor $1000, corporate $250, patron $150, family $40, individual $25
Activities: Museum shop rents original work by Michigan artists and reproductions

L DETROIT PUBLIC LIBRARY, Fine Arts Department, 5201 Woodward Ave, 48202. Tel 313-833-1467. *Library Dir* Jane Hale Morgan; *Chief Fine Arts Department* Shirley B Solvick; *First Asst Fine Arts Department* Patricia W McHugh; *Reference Librn* Ruth Barton; *Reference Librn* Winnifred Clark; *Reference Librn* Leonard Parent; *Clerk* Shirlie Morse
Open Mon, Tues, Thurs, Fri & Sat 9:30 AM - 5:30 PM, Wed 9 AM - 9 PM, mid-Oct - mid-May Sun 1 - 5 PM. Estab 1921 to serve residents of Michigan with circulating and reference materials in all fields of art
Income: Financed by city and state appropriation
Purchases: $29,800
Library Holdings: Vols 57,000; Per subs 270; Micro—Fiche, reels; Other—Clipping files, exhibition catalogs, framed reproductions, pamphlets, photographs, reproductions
Activities: Concerts; tours

O MICHIGAN ARTRAIN, INC, 1200 Sixth St, 48226. Tel 313-963-6334. *Pres* W Calvin Patterson III; *VPres* William B Heaton; *Dir* John J Hohmann; *Cur* Julie Hall; *Community Coordr* James Patterson; *Secy* Virginia B Hutcheson
No admis fee. Estab 1971 to take art to areas removed from major institutions and provide catalyst for on-going development. Consists of converted railroad cars with large walls and cases. Average Annual Attendance: 225,000
Income: Financed by endowment, state appropriation, foundation and corporation campaigns
Exhibitions: Changing Canvas; Full Spectrum - Michigan Contemporary Folk Paintings; Michigan Public Sculpture; juried exhibition
Publications: Newsletter; tour catalogs
Activities: Classes for children; docent training; lect open to the public, 10-15 visiting lectr per year; awards competition; book traveling exhibitions; sales shop selling books, prints and slides

M WAYNE STATE UNIVERSITY, Community Arts Gallery,* 450 Reuther Mall, 48202. Tel 313-577-2400. *Dir* Richard J Bilaitis
Open Mon - Fri 9 AM - 5 PM, Sat & Sun 1 - 5 PM. No admis fee. Estab 1956 as a facility for university and community oriented exhibitions and programs
Collections: Small collection of American and European graphics, painting, sculpture
Exhibitions: Monthly exhibitions
Activities: Lect for adults, students and the community; concerts

M YOUR HERITAGE HOUSE, INC, 110 East Ferry Ave, 48202. Tel 313-871-1667. *Chmn of Board* Reginald Wilson; *Dir* Josephine Harrell Love; *Instructor* Jacqueline Edwards; *Instructor* Gloria Hicks; *Instructor* Charles High; *Instructor* Michael Mahoney; *Instructor* Nancy Ann Miller; *Instructor* Mary Bloomer; *Instructor* Terry Kelley; *Instructor* Annette Alexander
Open daily 10 AM - 4 PM. Estab 1980. Average Annual Attendance: 15,000 - 20,000. Mem: 100; dues $50; annual meeting Sept
Income: $164,000 (financed by endowment, membership, city and state appropriation, individuals, groups and business donations)
Collections: †Art for Youth; Black Heritage; graphics; Puppetry; Paintings; objects and works of interest to children
Exhibitions: (1978) From These Roots; Jacob Lawrence: Art of His Youth & Art for Today's Youth; (1979) Elizabeth Catleth; Symposium: Women and the Arts
Publications: Catalogues; imprints; I Remember a Southern Christmas, book
Activities: Classes for adults and children; lect open to the public, 3-6 visiting lectr

per year; concerts; gallery talks; tours; scholarships; artmobile; sales shop selling books, cards and catalogues of exhibits
L Library, 110 East Ferry Ave, 48202.
Open daily 10 AM - 4 PM. Estab 1969 to provide fine arts material for children. For reference only
Library Holdings: Micro—Cards; Other—Clipping files, exhibition catalogs, prints, manuscripts, memorabilia, pamphlets, photographs
Special Subjects: Fine Arts for Youth
Collections: Black Heritage; Music for children by notable French composers; Puppetry of the World

EAST LANSING

M MICHIGAN STATE UNIVERSITY, Kresge Art Center, 48824. Tel 517-355-7610, Gallery 355-7631. *Chmn Department of Art* Roger Funk; *Dir of Gallery* Joseph Ishikawa
Open Mon - Fri 9 AM - 5 PM, Tues 7 - 9 PM, Sat & Sun 1 - 4 PM. No admis fee
Collections: Permanent collection of paintings, †prints, †sculptures
Exhibitions: Rental Shows; Staff and Student Shows making up a yearly calendar of about 14 exhibitions supplementing the permanent collection
Publications: Exhibition calendar, annually; occasional announcements of art lectures and films; catalogs
L Library, 48824. Tel 517-353-4593. *Art Librn* Shirlee A Studt
Open Mon - Fri 8 AM - 11 PM, Sat 9 AM - 11 PM, Sun 1 - 11 PM. Estab 1973 to support the research and teaching needs in the visual arts of Michigan State University
Income: Financed by state appropriation
Library Holdings: Vols 37,000; Per subs 184; Micro—Cards, fiche, reels, prints; Other—Clipping files, exhibition catalogs
Special Subjects: Architecture, Illuminated manuscripts facsimiles, Italian Renaissance art

FLINT

M FLINT INSTITUTE OF ARTS, 1120 E Kearsley St, 48503. Tel 313-234-1695. *Dir* Dr G Stuart Hodge; *Asst Dir* Alain Joyaux; *Cur Coll* Christopher Young; *Program Coordr & Educator* Jean Hagman; *Museum Shop Mgr* Barbara Lippincott
Open Tues - Sat 10 AM - 5 PM, Sun 1 - 5 PM, Tues (May - Oct) 7 - 9 PM. No admis fee. Estab 1928 as a community art museum serving the citizens of the area. Average Annual Attendance: 100,000. Mem: 2200; dues $12 and up; annual meeting third Thurs in June
Collections: African Sculpture; French Paperweights; 19th & 20th Century European & American Art; 19th Century Germanic Glass; Oriental Gallery; Renaissance Gallery of Decorative Arts; furniture; textiles
Exhibitions: Auguste Rodin; Art of the Automobile; Art of the Twenties; Illuminated Manuscripts: The French School
Publications: Exhibition catalogs; monthly Calendar for members
Activities: Classes for adults and children; docent training; lect open to public, 6 - 7 vis lectr per year; concerts; gallery talks; tours; Flint Art Fair; individual paintings and original objects of art lent to other museums; museum shop sells books, gift items, stationery, cards and jewelry
L Library, 48503. *Librn* Christopher Young
Open to members and staff for reference
Library Holdings: Vols 2500; Per subs 15

L FLINT PUBLIC LIBRARY, Fine Arts Department, 1026 East Kearsley, 48502. Tel 313-231-7111. *Asst Dir* John A Oliver; *Head Art, Music & Drama Dept* Forrest Alter
Open Mon - Thurs 9 AM - 9 PM, Fri & Sat 9 AM - 6 PM. Art, Drama, and Music Department established in 1958 a division of Flint Board of Education
Library Holdings: Vols 38,000; Per subs 191; Other—Clipping files, exhibition catalogs, photographs, reproductions

GRAND RAPIDS

M CALVIN COLLEGE CENTER ART GALLERY, 49506. Tel 616-949-4000, Ext 326. *Dir of Exhib* James Kuiper; *Secy* Marlene Vanderhill
Open Sept - May Mon - Fri 9 AM - 9 PM, Sat 10 AM - 4 PM. No admis fee. Estab 1974 to provide the art students, and the college community and the public at large with challenging visual monthly exhibitions. Gallery is well lighted, air-conditioned 40 x 70 ft with 10 ft ceiling along the sides and 8 ft ceiling in the center. Average Annual Attendance: 12,000
Income: Financed through private budget
Collections: Dutch 17th & 19th Century Paintings and Prints; Japanese Prints; †contemporary paintings, prints, drawings, sculpture, weaving and ceramics
Exhibitions: (1979) Lyman Kipp - Kent Floeter; Eight Michigan Photographers; Faculty Exhibit; Japanese Exhibit; Prints by Chicago Artists; various faculty and student exhibits
Publications: ADA (art department activities); various exhibition brochures
Activities: Classes for adults; lect open to public; concerts; gallery talks; competitions; MATRIX - a monthly meeting for art students, faculty and public, with outside lectr and discussions
L Library, 49506. *Librn* Marvin Monsma
Open to students and the public
Library Holdings: Vols 280,000; Per subs 1800; Micro—Cards, fiche, reels; Other—Curriculum Center of demonstration teaching materials
Collections: H H Meeter Calvinism Research Collection; Cayvan Collection of Recordings; Colonial Origins Collection of the Christian Reformed Church; Government Documents

M GRAND RAPIDS ART MUSEUM, 230 E Fulton, 49503. Tel 616-459-4676. *Dir* Robert M Murdock
Open Tues, Thurs, Fri, Sat 9 AM - 5 PM, Wed 9 AM - 9 PM, Sun 2 - 5 PM, cl Mon & legal holidays. No admis fee. Estab 1910, incorporated 1913, to promote an active interest in the fine and applied arts; to establish and maintain an art

collection; and to provide special art exhibits for the enjoyment and education of the public. The building is an 1844 Classical Greek Revival House with additional wings added in 1928 and 1930. Seven galleries are used for exhibitions. Average Annual Attendance: 65,000. Mem: 1300; dues $7.50 - $200; annual meeting May
Income: $435,000 (financed by endowment, membership, state appropriation and Federal grants)
Purchases: $10,000
Collections: Staffordshire Pottery; American 19th & 20th Century Paintings; Decorative Arts; Drawings; French 19th Century Paintings; German Expressionist Paintings; Master Prints of all eras; Renaissance Paintings; Sculpture
Exhibitions: Helen Frankenthaler; Inge Morath: Photographs of China; Roman Opalka: 16 Details; Joan Snyder; Folk Art of Michigan 20th Century; German Expressionism in Western Michigan Collections; Light Spaces (1979); Michigan Artists; The Pastel in America; Recollections: Ten Great Women of Photography; Permanent Collection; Temporary and Traveling Exhibitions
Publications: Catalogs of major exhibitions; newsletter, monthly
Activities: Docent training; lect open to public, 15 vis lectr per year; gallery talks; tours; competitions; artmobile; individual paintings and original objects of art lent to museums; lending collection contains books, color reproductions, framed reproductions, original art works, original prints, paintings, photographs, sculpture and slides; originate traveling exhibitions; museum shop sells books, reproductions, jewelry, arts and crafts objects
L McBride Art Reference Library, 230 E Fulton, 49503.
Open Tue, Thurs, Fri & Sat 9 AM - 5 PM, Wed 9 AM - 9 PM, Sun 2 - 5 PM, cl Mon & legal holidays. Estab 1971. Reference library, members may borrow books
Library Holdings: Vols 2500; Per subs 20; AV—Slides; Other—Clipping files, exhibition catalogs, pamphlets

L GRAND RAPIDS PUBLIC LIBRARY, Music and Art Department, Library Plaza NE, 49503. Tel 616-456-4410. *Dir Library* Robert Raz; *Head Music & Art Dept* Lucija Skuja; *Music Librn* Helen Vanden Engel
Open Mon - Thurs 9 AM - 9 PM, Fri & Sat 9:30 AM - 5:30 PM, Sun 2 PM - 5 PM. Estab 1871 to provide information and library materials for people in Grand Rapids and Lakeland Library Federation area. Circ 871,859
Income: $2,032,478 (financed by city and state appropriations)
Purchases: $1,933,330
Library Holdings: Vols 17,000; Per subs 44; Micro—Reels; AV—Cassettes, motion pictures, rec; Other—Clipping files, pamphlets, sculpture
Collections: The Furniture Design Collection
Activities: Art talks; tours

HARTLAND

O HARTLAND ART COUNCIL, PO Box 127, 48029. Tel 313-632-5200. *Pres* Bruce Sdunek; *VPres* Phyllis Kerslake; *Secy* Brooke Tuck; *Treas* Eleni Lambrecht
Estab 1967 to promote arts in Hartland community. Gallery space in local library and Hartland High School Media Center. Mem: 15; dues $3 - $100
Income: $3000 - $4000 (financed by membership)
Purchases: $1500 - $2000
Collections: †Paintings, †photographs, †sculptures
Exhibitions: Annual Art Show
Activities: Dramatic programs; lect open to public; concerts; competitions; scholarships; exten dept serving Michigan art councils and schools, lending collection contains kodachromes and photographs; originate traveling exhibitions

HOLLAND

M HOPE COLLEGE, DeWitt Cultural Center, Art Department, 49423. Tel 616-392-5111. *Chmn* John M Wilson; *Pres* Gordon Van Wylen; *Secy* Char Mulder; *Provost* David G Marker; *Dean Arts & Humanities* Jacob E Nyenhuis
Open Mon - Fri 9:30 AM - 10:30 PM, Sat & Sun 1:30 - 10:30 PM. No admis fee. Average Annual Attendance: 5000
Activities: Classes for adults and children; lect open to the public; tours; competitions; scholarships and fellowships; individual paintings and original objects of art lent to faculty; lending collection contains original art works; original prints, paintings and sculpture
L Van Zoeren Library, 49423. *Librn* Harry Boonstra
Open Mon - Fri 8 AM - 12 Noon, Sat 10 AM - 10 PM, Sun 1:30 - 12 PM. Estab 1851 for the college
Library Holdings: Vols 190,000; Per subs 1200; Micro—Cards, fiche, reels; AV—A-tapes, cassettes, fs, Kodachromes, lantern slides; motion pictures, rec, slides, v-tapes; Other—Clipping files, manuscripts, memorabilia, pamphlets
Collections: Netherland; Old Dutch Bibles

INTERLOCHEN

L INTERLOCHEN CENTER FOR THE ARTS, Interlochen Arts Academy Library, 49643. Tel 616-276-9221, Ext 320. *Head Librn* Patricia Scheffler
Open daily 8:30 AM - 5 PM & 7 - 9:30 PM. Estab 1963. Circ 9000
Library Holdings: Vols 14,000; Per subs 140; Micro—Reels; AV—Cassettes, fs, rec
Publications: Interlochen Review, annual
Activities: Dramatic programs; lect open to the public, 10 visiting lectr per year; concerts; tours; competitions; awards; scholarships or fellowships; originate traveling exhibitions

JACKSON

M ELLA SHARP MUSEUM, 3225 Fourth St, 49203. Tel 517-787-2320. *Dir* Millie Hadwin; *Cur Historical Educ* Lynn Loftis; *Cur Art Education* Elise Cole; *Conservator* James Richardson
Open Tues - Fri 10 AM - 5 PM, Sat & Sun 1:30 - 5 PM, cl Mon, Jan and major holidays. Admis adults 50¢, children 25¢, school tours free. Estab 1965 to serve the people of Jackson and to provide a place for cultural education in the community and a temporary gallery where a variety of exhibits are held. Included are a large

and small gallery. Average Annual Attendance: 10,000. Mem: 10,000; dues $1000 and up, $500, $125, $65, $35, $20, $15, $5; annual meeting May
Income: Financed by endowment and membership along with grants
Collections: China; coverlets and quilts; furniture from Victorian period; †oil paintings; porcelain; †prints
Exhibitions: (1978) African Art; Dimensions in Fiber, Clay & Metal; FSA Photos for Michigan's people; Handwoven coverlets; Johann Adam List: Frankenmuth Folk Artist; Native Close-ups (photo); Prints of Louise Nevelson; Puppets. (1979) Philip C Curtis Paintings; The Figure in 19th Century French Painting; Michigan Folk Art (paper cutouts); 16th and 17th Century European Prints; Watercolors; Annual Children's Exhibit and Works of Jackson Area Artists
Publications: Annual Report; bulletins and catalogs; newsletter, monthly; research material as requested
Activities: Classes for adults and children; dramatic programs; lect open to public, 7 visiting lectr per year; concerts; gallery talks; tours; competitions; scholarships offered; art objects lent to schools; kits of museum artifacts available; lending collection has photographs; originate traveling exhibitions; gift shop
L **Library,** 3225 Fourth St, 49203.
Library Holdings: Vols 250; Other—Photographs

KALAMAZOO

M **KALAMAZOO INSTITUTE OF ARTS,** Genevieve and Donald Gilmore Art Center, 314 S Park St, 49007. Tel 616-349-7775. *Dir Art Center* Thomas A Kayser
Open Tues - Sat 10 AM - 5 PM, Sun 1 - 5 PM, Thurs evenings 7 - 9 PM, cl last two weeks of Aug, Sun during July & Aug and holidays. No admis fee. Incorporated 1924 to further interest in the arts, especially in the visual arts; new building opened in 1961. There is one large gallery, four small exhibition galleries, with exhibitions changed monthly. One or more galleries always devoted to pieces from the permanent collection. Average Annual Attendance: 80,000. Mem: 1400; dues $15; annual meeting June
Income: $350,000 (financed by endowment, membership)
Collections: †Art on Paper - Drawings, Graphics, Photographs and Watercolors; †Sculpture; †20th Century American Art
Exhibitions: Bronson Park Art Fair; Kalamazoo Area Show; Traveling exhibit program covers all aspects of visual arts
Publications: Exhibition catalogs, issued irregularly; newsletters, monthly
Activities: Classes for adults and children; lect open to public, 5 vis lectr per year; gallery talks; tours; competitions; individual paintings and original objects of art lent to other institutions; lending collection contains books and slides; originate traveling exhibitions; museum shop sells books, reproductions, craft items, jewelry, cards
L **Library,** 314 S Park St, 49007. *Head Librn* Helen Sheridan; *Assoc Librn* Martha Franklin
Open Tues - Sat 10 AM - 5 PM, Sun 1 - 5 PM, Thurs evenings 7 - 9 PM. Estab 1961, reference for Kalamazoo Institute of Arts curatorial staff and school faculty. For public reference only, open to members for circulation
Library Holdings: Vols 5200; Per subs 50; AV—Slides; Other—Clipping files, exhibition catalogs, original art works, pamphlets
Special Subjects: Photography, American art, especially art of the 20th century printmaking, history and technique
Activities: Lect; tours

LANSING

M **LANSING ART GALLERY,** 425 S Grand Ave, 48933. Tel 517-374-6400, 371-2120. *Pres* Dot Riley; *VPres* S J Venable; *Executive Dir* Marte E Milks; *Asst Dir* Jonathon Hansen; *Secy* Barb Anderson; *Field Representative* Pati Brush; *Field Representative* Sheldon Kemp
Open Tues - Fri 10 AM - 4 PM, Sun 1 - 4 PM. No admis fee. Estab 1965 to promote the visual arts in their many forms to citizens of the greater Lansing area. Maintains large exhibit area, gallery shop and rental gallery. Average Annual Attendance: 18,000. Mem: 300; dues $10 - $500; annual meeting May
Income: $90,000 (financed by membership, sales, grants, contributions and fees)
Publications: Gallery News, bimonthly
Activities: Docent training; lect open to the public, 10 visiting lectr per year; gallery talks; tours; competitions with awards; individual paintings and original objects of art lent to other organizations, schools, library, Chamber of Commerce, etc; lending collection contains 350 books, 250 kodachromes, original art works, original prints, paintings, photographs and sculpture; book traveling exhibitions, 1-2 per year; sales shop selling books, jewelry, pottery, original art and prints
L **Art Reference Library,** 425 S Grand Ave, 48933.
Open Tues - Fri 10 AM - 4 PM, Sun 1 - 4 PM. Estab 1965 to enhance the meaning of visual art to our patrons
Library Holdings: Vols 350; Per subs 50; AV—Slides
Special Subjects: History of Macrame, Glass Blowing

MARQUETTE

M **NORTHERN MICHIGAN UNIVERSITY,** Lee Hall Gallery, 49855. Tel 906-227-1000. *Exhib Coordr* Marvin Zehnder
Open Mon - Fri 8 AM - 5 PM. No admis fee. Estab 1975 to bring exhibits of the visual arts to the University, community and the upper peninsula of Michigan. Gallery covers approx 1500 sq ft of space, with security system and smoke detectors. Average Annual Attendance: 4000-6000
Income: $6500 (financed by University funds)
Collections: †Permanent collection; student collection
Exhibitions: Average of one to two major exhibits each month, with a reduction of exhibits during the summer months
Publications: Exhibit Announcement, monthly
Activities: Lect open to the public, 3-4 visiting lectrs per year; gallery talks; competitions; individual paintings and original objects of art lent contains original art works; traveling exhibitions organized and circulated

MIDLAND

L **GRACE A DOW MEMORIAL LIBRARY,** 1710 W Saint Andrews, 48640. Tel 517-835-7151. *Dir* Edward M Szynaka; *Fine Arts Reference Librn* Margaret Allen
Open during school year Mon - Fri 10 AM - 9 PM, Sat 10 AM - 5 PM, Sun 1 - 5 PM. Estab 1953 as a public library. Maintains art gallery
Income: $14,000 (financed by city appropriation and gifts)
Purchases: $20,000
Library Holdings: Vols 10,000; Per subs 75; AV—Cassettes, motion pictures, rec; Other—Clipping files, framed reproductions, original art works, reproductions
Collections: Alden B Dow Fine Arts Collection
Exhibitions: Susan Beyer (silkscreening and photolithography); Biological Photography from the Smithsonian Institution; Central Michigan University Sculpture; Eunice Y Smith Canterbury Tales Etchings; Washington Square Prizewinners; exhibits from local art groups and schools
Publications: Arts Newsletter, 3 times per year
Activities: Films; book traveling exhibitions, 3-4 per year

O **MIDLAND ART COUNCIL OF THE MIDLAND CENTER FOR THE ARTS,** 1801 W St Andrews, 48640. Tel 517-631-3250. *Chmn* Don Peterson; *VChmn* Ken Kerr; *Pres & Acting Dir* Ann Boem; *VPres* Nan Punnet; *Secy* Paulette Moss; *Secy* Beth Stewart; *Public Relations* Mary Dalton; *Studios* Rae Cooker
Open daily 1 - 5 PM, Thurs 7 - 9 PM. No admis fee. Estab 1956. Exhibition space consists of three galleries, one 40 x 80 ft and two smaller 20 x 40 ft space; spot tracking lighting. Mem: 350; dues $25; meetings held in spring and fall
Income: $100,000 (financed by endowment and membership)
Exhibitions: (1978-80) Fiberworks - Cranbrook; Dowries from Kutch; Benny Motzfeldt - Norwegian Pathfinder in Glass; Vuillard Drawings 1885 - 1930; American Painters of the Impressionist Period Rediscovered; Detroit Institute of Art Michigan Artists Exhibition; German Expressionists Art; Japanese Packaging; Midland Public Schools Exhibit; Mid-Michigan all-media exhibit; National Watercolor Society; New Guinea and African Art; Oriental Ceramics; Prints from the Guggenheim; Puppets from the Detroit Institute of Art; Studio Instructors' Show; Styrofoam Sculpture; Tibetan Thankas; Tsutsumu
Publications: Calendar of events; monthly newsletter for members; yearly report
Activities: Classes for adults and children; docent training; Volunteer show me a picture program in public schools; lect open to public; gallery talks; tours; competitions; originate traveling exhibitions; sales shop sells books, magazines, original art and reproductions

MONROE

O **MONROE CITY-COUNTY FINE ARTS COUNCIL,** 1555 S Raisinville Rd, 48161. Tel 313-242-7300. *Pres* Hugh Bakar; *Secy* Viola Switlick; *Treas* Elsie Little
Estab 1967 to promote the arts. Average Annual Attendance: 120. Mem: 50; dues $2
Income: $1000 (financed by endowment, membership, city appropriation)
Activities: Competitions with awards; scholarships

MOUNT CLEMENS

O **ART CENTER,** 125 Macomb St, 48043. Tel 313-469-8666. *Pres Bd of Trustees* Joanne Roskopp; *Adminr* Marjorie U DeFrancis
Open Tues - Sat 11 AM - 5 PM, Sun 1 - 4 PM, cl Mon. No admis fee. Estab 1970 to foster art appreciation and participation for people of Macomb County. The only public facility of its kind in county northeast of Detroit Metro area; center has two rooms, 17 x 27 ft, connected by lobby area in former Carnegie Library Bldg, Historical State Register. Average Annual Attendance: 10,000. Mem: 500; dues individual $10; annual meeting June
Income: $54,400 (financed by membership, city and state appropriation)
Exhibitions: Several all state open competitive exhibitions, including painting and sculpture; crafts; two country wide student shows, one is regional scholastic art awards shows
Publications: Newsletter, semi-monthly
Activities: Classes for adults and children; docent training; tours; competitions; individual paintings lent; sales shop sells original art

MOUNT PLEASANT

M **CENTRAL MICHIGAN UNIVERSITY,** University Art Gallery, S Art Studio, 48859. Tel 517-774-3800. *Dir* Virginia Jenkins
Open Mon - Fri 10 AM - 4 PM, Tues 7 - 9 PM, Sat & Sun Noon - 3 PM. No admis fee. Estab to serve Mount Pleasant and university community; offer contemporary and traditional forms of art. Gallery has 114 ft running space; track lighting in all areas; motion monitoring alarm system. Average Annual Attendance: 4500
Income: $4000 (financed by Art Department)
Exhibitions: (1978-79) Contemporary Prints from Canada - traveling; Frank Eullo; Gary Hallman from Eastman House; David Huling; National Kite Show; Real Fiber Invitational; Work on Paper (drawing competition); faculty exhibit
Activities: Classes for adults; lect open to public, 3 - 5 visiting lectr per year; gallery talks; tours upon request; competitions; cash awards; book traveling exhibitions

MUSKEGON

M **MUSKEGON MUSEUM OF ART,** (Formerly Hackley Art Museum) 296 W Webster Ave, 49440. Tel 616-722-2600. *Dir* Mary Riordan; *Asst Cur* Richard Nelson
Estab 1912, Hackley Gallery designed by S S Beman, Chicago architect
Income: $100,000 (financed by school board and membership)
Collections: American Paintings; Eastern Art; Impressionist Paintings; Modern Master Prints; Old Master Prints
Exhibitions: Recent Works by Elizabeth Aralia; An Artist Collects; Annual Juried Regional Exhibition (all media); Flight Series; German Expressionist Art; Rainbows in the Sky (folk art in Michigan); Watercolors by six Michigan artists;

changing exhibitions from the permanent collection
Publications: Catalogs of American & European paintings from the Permanent Collection
Activities: Docent program; lect; gallery talks; museum shop
L **Library,** 296 W Webster, 49440.
Membership estab 1977. Reference only

OLIVET

M **OLIVET COLLEGE,** Armstrong Museum of Art and Archaeology, 49076. Tel 616-749-7000. *Dir* William Whitney
Estab 1960 to collect artifacts and display for educational purposes. Average Annual Attendance: 1200
Purchases: Approx $1000
Collections: American Indian, Mesopotamian, Philippine and Thailand Artifacts; Modern American Prints; Primitive Art; Sculpture
Exhibitions: Invitational shows; one-man shows; student shows; traveling shows
Activities: Book traveling exhibitions
L **Library,** 49076.
Library Holdings: Vols 70,000; Micro—Prints

ORCHARD LAKE

M **ORCHARD LAKE SCHOOL GALERIA,** 48033. *Dir* Marian Owczarski
Open Mon - Fri 1 - 5 PM, First Sun of the Month 1 - 4 PM and anytime upon request. No admis fee. Estab to house major Polish and Polish-American art. Average Annual Attendance: 8000
Collections: Contemporary Polish Painting by Andrzej Luczynski; John Paul II: The First Year (Pictorial exhibit); Sculpture by Marian Owczarski; History of Polish Printing: Rare Books and Documents; Polish Folk Art; Polish Tapestry
Activities: Lectures open to the public; concerts; tours

PONTIAC

O **PONTIAC ART CENTER,*** 47 Williams St, 48053. Tel 313-333-7849. *Educ Coordr* Carol S Goodale
Open Mon - Sat 9 AM - 5 PM, cl holidays. No admis fee. Estab 1968 to educate and uplift minority and culturally deprived people through the exposure of art. Gallery is maintained. Mem: 400; dues corporation $200, patron $100, family $25, individual $15; annual meeting March
Income: $84,000 (financed by endowment, membership, city and state appropriation)
Activities: Classes for adults and children; dramatic programs; lect open to the public, 4 visiting lectrs per year; gallery talks; competitions; scholarships

PORT HURON

M **MUSEUM OF ARTS AND HISTORY,** 1115 Sixth St, 48060. Tel 313-982-0891. *Pres* Mrs N Fred Haynes; *Dir* Stephen R Williams
Open Wed - Sun 1 - 4:30 PM. No admis fee. Estab 1968 to preserve area historical and marine artifacts; exhibit living regional artists; exhibit significant shows of national and international interest. Two galleries are maintained for loaned exhibitions and the permanent collection; also a decorative arts gallery and a sales gallery. Average Annual Attendance: 18,000. Mem: 500; dues family $15
Income: $59,000 (financed by membership, city and state appropriations)
Collections: Thomas Edison; Civil War; Marine Artifacts; 19th Century American Decorative Arts, Painting and Prints
Exhibitions: Johann Adam List: Frankenmuth Folk Artist; John Berry (photographs); Edison and the Electrical Age: 100 Years; Esmark Collection of Currier and Ives; Hans Hofmann: Colorist in Black and White; Beatrice Thornton Student Art Show; Duane Wakeham (paintings); The Art Company; Bible in Graphic Art; Blue Water Art Club Exhibition; Cybis Porcelains; Decorative Arts of West Africa; Eastern Michigan International Art Exhibition
Publications: Newsletter, monthly
Activities: Classes for adults and children; docent training; lect open to public, 6 vis lectr per year; gallery talks; tours; competitions; museum shop sells books, magazines, original art

M **SAINT CLAIR COUNTY COMMUNITY COLLEGE,** Jack R Hennesey Art Galleries, 323 Erie, 48060. Tel 313-894-3881, Ext 340. *Coordr of Galleries* Ray Pierotti
Open Mon - Fri 8 AM - 5 PM. No admis fee. Estab 1975 to serve the community as an exhibition site and to serve the faculty and students of the college as a teaching tool. Maintains three galleries connected by common hall with approximately 2,000 sq ft. Average Annual Attendance: 3000
Collections: Paintings, print, and sculpture (wood and metal)
Activities: Educ dept; lect open to the public, 6 visiting lectr per year; concerts; competitions with awards; scholarships; artmobile

ROCHESTER

M **OAKLAND UNIVERSITY,** Meadow Brook Art Gallery, 48063. Tel 313-337-3005. *Dir Office Cultural Affairs Oakland Univ* Robert Dearth; *Cur* Kiichi Usui; *Secy* Judith Holmes; *Cur Asst* Stel Toland; *Pres Meadow Brook Gallery Assocs* Mrs David Handleman
Open Tues - Fri 1 - 5 PM, Sat & Sun 2 - 6:30 PM, evening 7:30 - 8:30 PM in conjunction with Meadow Brook Theater Performances. No admis fee. Estab 1962 to provide a series of changing exhibitions and to develop an art collection to serve the university community and the greater community of southern Michigan. Average Annual Attendance: 50,000. Mem: 300; dues $20 - $500
Income: Financed by university budget
Collections: Art of Africa, Oceania and Pre-Columbian America; contemporary art and architecture; Oriental art
Exhibitions: (1978) Return of Realism: Four from the Allan Frumkin Gallery, Jack Beal, Alfred Leslie, William Midgette, Philip Pearlstein. (1979 - 80) America in the 70's as Depicted by Artists in the Richard Brown Baker Collection; Classics in Primitive Art: from the Collection of Professor Harry Bober, New York University; Meadow Brook Hall: Tudor revival Architecture and Decoration
Publications: Exhibition catalogs
Activities: Educ dept; lect open to public, 2 visiting lectr per year; slide presentations in conjunction with exhibitions; paintings and original art objects lent within university; originate traveling exhibitions

SAGINAW

M **SAGINAW ART MUSEUM,** 1126 N Michigan Ave, 48602. Tel 517-754-2491. *Dir* Janie K Chester
Open Tues - Sat 10 AM - 5 PM, Tues Eve 7 - 9 PM, Sun 1 - 5 PM, cl Mon. Estab 1948 to offer the cultural and educational services of an art museum to the regional community and to foster a love and understanding of the visual arts. Historic Georgian Revival Mansion (Charles Adams Platt, architect); approx 2600 sq ft of gallery space; formal outdoor garden. Average Annual Attendance: 12,000. Mem: 520; dues $5 - $500; annual meeting May
Income: $124,000 (financed by endowment, membership)
Collections: American Sculpture and Painting (especially John Rogers sculpture); European painting, sculpture and decorative arts, 1000 AD - present; Oriental prints, decorative arts, and textiles; †contemporary painting, †prints, and sculpture
Publications: Annual report; bulletin, monthly
Activities: Classes for adults and children; docent training; lect open to public, 6 vis lectr per year; talks; tours; competitions; individual paintings and original objects of art lent to other museums and other small extension exhibitions in community; traveling exhibitions organized and circulated; museum shop sells books, original art, reproductions, prints
L **Library,** 1126 N Michigan Ave, 48602. *Librn* Deborah Schell
Open to public for reference only
Library Holdings: Vols 1000; Per subs 8

SAINT JOSEPH

O **SAINT JOSEPH ART ASSOCIATION INC,** Krasl Art Center, 707 Lake Blvd, 49085. Tel 616-983-0271. *Dir* Alan Garfield; *Office Mgr* Vicky Nemethy
Open Tues - Fri 10 AM - 4 PM, Sat & Sun 1 - 4 PM. Estab 1962 to increase the level of aesthetic understanding in the area through exhibitions and studio art history classes. Maintains two galleries, 20 x 20 and 30 x 40 with humidity and temperature controls. Average Annual Attendance: 10,000. Mem: 650; dues family $25, individual $15
Income: Financed by endowment and membership
Exhibitions: Art of China; Clyde & Belva Ball; Crying For a Vision by Don Doll; International Year For Children's Art; Faculty Show; juried exhibitions
Publications: Newsletter, monthly
Activities: Classes for adults and children; lect open to the public, 3 visiting lectr per year; gallery talks; tours; competitions with awards; art fair; museum shop selling original art, reproductions, prints, crafts and gift items

SOUTHFIELD

C **THE BENDIX CORPORATION,** 20650 Civic Center Dr, 48037. Tel 313-827-6101. *In Charge Art Coll* Mary Wilson
Collection may be viewed by arrangement with Mary Wilson. No admis fee. Estab 1979 to enhance office environment. Collection consists of three large steel sculptures by Louise Nevelson, two are indoors and one in outdoor atrium
Collections: Three Steel Sculptures by Louise Nevelson
Activities: Tours

TRAVERSE CITY

L **NORTHWESTERN MICHIGAN COLLEGE,** Mark Osterlin Library, 1701 E Front St, 49684. Tel 616-969-5650, Ext 541. *Library Dir* Bernard C Rink
Open Mon - Thurs 8 AM - 10 PM, Fri & Sat 9 AM - 4 PM, Sun 1 - 5 PM. Estab 1961, the library is charged with providing the resources needed to fulfill the educational and cultural task of the college. Permanent sculpture and print display in lobby and throughout building whenever wall space permits
Income: $245,000 (financed by state and county appropriation)
Purchases: $2000 - $5000
Library Holdings: Vols 43,000; Per subs 400; Micro—Reels; AV—A-tapes, cassettes, fs, Kodachromes, motion pictures, rec, slides, v-tapes; Other—Prints, sculpture
Special Subjects: Italian Renaissance art history
Collections: Canadian Eskimo sculpture and prints collected and for sale
Exhibitions: Annual Eskimo Sculpture and Print Exhibit

YPSILANTI

M **EASTERN MICHIGAN UNIVERSITY**, Sill Gallery, 48197. Tel 313-487-1268.
Dept Head John Van Haren; *Gallery Dir* Jay Yager
Open Mon - Fri 8 AM - 5 PM. No admis fee. Estab 1925, in present building since 1964, for educational purposes. Art Dept gallery is maintained displaying staff and student exhibitions from a wide variety of sources; also one large, well-lighted gallery with lobby and a satellite student-operated gallery are maintained
Income: Financed by city appropriation
Purchases: $500
Exhibitions: Children's art; conceptual art; faculty art; international ceramics; international jewelry and metal; international textiles; National Student Photography Exhibition; student art; G Mennen Williams African art
Publications: Campus Life, bi-annual bulletin
Activities: Classes for adults; lect open to public, 6 visiting lectr per year; gallery talks; concerts; competitions; Community Art House

L **Art Department Book Collection**, Sill Hall, Room 112, 48197. Tel 313-487-1849.
Librn Virginia Stein
Open 9 AM - 5 PM. Estab 1978 as reference source for faculty and graduate students. Open to faculty and students for reference
Library Holdings: Vols 350

MINNESOTA

BROOKLYN PARK

M **NORTH HENNEPIN COMMUNITY COLLEGE**, Art Gallery, 7411 85th Ave N, 55445. Tel 612-425-4541.
Open Mon - Fri 8 AM - 4 PM. Estab to show works of art. Consist of two gallery spaces: small gallery for students, large gallery for local, state and national personalities
Income: $2000 (financed by state appropriation)
Purchases: $1000
Collections: Student works and local artists in Minnesota
Exhibitions: Student Art Show
Activities: Lect open to the pub;ic; concerts; gallery talks; tours; competitions with awards

DULUTH

M **SAINT LOUIS COUNTY HISTORICAL SOCIETY**, 506 W Michigan St, 55802. Tel 218-722-8011. *Dir* Laurence Sommer
Open daily 10 AM - 5 PM. Admis adults $1.50. Estab 1922 as a regional historical museum. Average Annual Attendance: 150,000. Mem: 900; dues individual $5.50; annual meeting Jan
Income: $150,000 (financed by membership, county appropriation and sales)
Collections: E Johnson Collection; drawings; paintings
Publications: Newsletter, quarterly
Activities: Docent training; lect open to the public, 2-3 visiting lectr per year; gallery talks; tours; awards; individual paintings and original objects of art lent to other museums; sales shop sells books, reproductions, prints, miscellaneous merchandise and crafts

M **UNIVERSITY OF MINNESOTA**, Tweed Museum of Art, 55812. Tel 218-726-8222. *Dir* William G Boyce; *Cur* Edna Garte; *Technician* Larry Gruenwald; *Secy* Sharon Alexander; *Secy* Lorainne Morris; *Mgr Tweed Museum Gift Shop* Joyce Nelson
Open Mon - Fri 8 AM - 4:30 PM, Sat & Sun 2 - 5 PM. No admis fee. Estab 1950 to serve both the University and community as a center for exhibition of works of art and related activities. Six galleries within the Museum. Average Annual Attendance: 70,000. Mem: 820; dues $10 - $100
Income: Financed by membership, state appropriation and foundation
Purchases: $30,000
Collections: †Jonathan Sax Collections of 20th Century American prints; George P Tweed Memorial Art Collections of 500 paintings with emphasis on Barbizon School and 19th Century American; †20th century American paintings and sculptures
Exhibitions: American Architecture: Its Roots, Growth & Horizons; American Drawing I & II; American Watercolor Society; Beads: Their Use by Upper Great Lake Indians; Contemporary Egyptian Painting; Coverlets from the Helen L Allen Textile collection; Guthrie Theatre Touring Costume Exhibit; I Wear The Morning Star; Milestone Era Automobiles: 1946-1964; Student and Faculty Exhibitions; Women Artists Today; World Architecture in Minnesota
Activities: Docent training; lect open to public, 1 - 2 vis lectr per yr; concerts; gallery talks; tours; individual paintings and original objects of art lent to qualifying museums and institutions; lending collection contains original art works, original prints and paintings; traveling exhibitions organized and circulated; museum shop sells books, original art, reproductions, craft objects and cards

ELYSIAN

M **LESUEUR COUNTY HISTORICAL SOCIETY MUSEUM**, Box 557, 56028. Tel 507-267-4620, 362-8350. *Pres & Dir* James E Hruska; *VPres* Gene LaFrance; *Secy* Carol Morsching; *Co-Dir & Muzeologist* Dorothy Irene Hruska
Open May - Sept Sat & Sun 1:30 - 5:30 PM. No admis fee. Estab 1966 to show the works of Adolf Dehn, Roger Preuss and David Maass; to preserve early heritage and artifacts of the pioneers of LeSueur County. Museum is depository of Dehn, Preuss and Maass, examples of originals, prints and publications of the Artists are on display. Average Annual Attendance: 5000. Mem: 700; dues life $25, annual $1; annual meeting quarterly
Income: $11,000 (financed by membership, county appropriation, county

government and by grants)
Purchases: $21,000
Collections: †Adolf Dehn; David Maass; Roger Preuss
Exhibitions: (1978-80) Special art exhibition by Virginia Dehn showing over 90 original works of Adolf Dehn; Original works of David Maass; Calendar Original works of Roger Preuss
Publications: Newsletters, quarterly
Activities: Slide carousel to show the sites and early history of the County and works of the Artists; lect open to public; gallery talks; tours; lending collection contains 300 books, cassettes, color reproductions, 400 lantern slides, original prints, paintings, motion pictures and 300 photographs; museum shop sells books, original art and prints

L **Collections Library**, Box 557, 56028.
Open by appointment only. Estab 1970 to collect local and state purposes for geneaology; history of the Artists
Income: $300
Purchases: $450
Library Holdings: Vols 300; Per subs 2; Micro—Reels 42; AV—A-tapes, lantern slides, motion pictures; Other—Clipping files, framed reproductions, prints, manuscripts, original art works, reproductions
Special Subjects: Prints of three Artists
Collections: Adolf Dehn Watercolors and Lithographs; Duck Stamp Prints of Preuss and Maass

MANKATO

L **BETHANY LUTHERAN COLLEGE**, Memorial Library, 734 Marsh St, 56001. Tel 507-625-2977. *Pres* Norman Holte; *Librn* Mary Birmingham
Open Mon - Thur 8 AM - 10 PM, Fri 8 AM - 4 PM, Sat 12 - 3 PM, Sun 2 - 5 PM & 7 - 10 PM. No admis fee. Estab 1927 as a display area
Income: Financed by college
Exhibitions: Old Bergen Art Guild Exhibits
Activities: Dramatic programs; lect, 2-3 visiting lectr per year; concerts; scholarships; book traveling exhibitions, 3 per year

M **MANKATO STATE UNIVERSITY**, Nichols Gallery,* 56001. Tel 507-389-2463.
Gallery Dir Harlan Bloomer
Open Mon - Fri 8 AM - 4:30 PM. No admis fee. Estab 1960 to provide cultural enrichment in the visual arts to the campus and community through a program of exhibitions from local, regional, and national sources, and student exhibitions. Gallery has 180 running feet of carpeted display area, track lighting and climate controlled
Income: $3300 (financed by city appropriation)
Collections: American bookplates; contemporary prints, drawings, paintings, photographs, sculpture and crafts; student works in all media

MINNEAPOLIS

M **AMERICAN SWEDISH INSTITUTE**, 2600 Park Ave, 55407. Tel 612-871-4907. *Dir* William T Hakala; *Pres* Bernhard W LeVander
Open Tues - Sat 1 - 4 PM, Sun 1 - 5 PM, cl Mon and National holidays. Admis adults $1, students under 21 and senior citizens 50¢, children under 6 25¢. Estab and inc 1929. Building donated by Swan J Turnblad and contains, in a home setting, a fine collection of Swedish artifacts, plus many items of general cultural interest pertaining to Scandinavia. The Grand Hall, paneled in African mahogany, is considered to be a fine installation. Throughout the gallery there are eleven porcelain tile fireplaces; nine Swedish and two German design. Average Annual Attendance: 50,000. Mem: dues student attending school, below the age of 21, $5, non-resident single, or husband and wife outside a fifty mile radius of Twin Cities $10, regular (single)$15, regular (husband and wife) $20, sustaining (husband, wife and all children under age 21, living at home) $35, supporting $50, patron $100, life $1000
Collections: Paintings, sculpture, tapestries, ceramics, china, glass, pioneer items and textiles
Publications: Happenings (newsletter), monthly
Activities: Films; lect; concerts; gift shop and bookstore

C **DAYTON HUDSON CORPORATION**, 777 Nicollet Mall, 55402. Tel 612-370-6657. *Arts Grants Adminr* Margaret Wurtele
No admis fee. Estab for works by artists living and working in Minneapolis. Collection displayed on 15th Floor, IDS Building, Minneapolis
Activities: Corporate Giving Program has designated 40% of its funds to community art organizations

C **FEDERAL RESERVE BANK OF MINNEAPOLIS**, 250 Marquette Ave, 55480. Tel 612-340-2279, 340-2443. *Art Dir* Kathy Balkman
Open to public by appointment with Art Dir or Asst. No admis fee. Estab 1973 to enhance the working environment of bank; to support the creative efforts of 9th District artists. Collection displayed throughout the bank in offices, lounges, public areas and work areas
Collections: Regional collection consists of works by artists living and working in the 9th District
Activities: Tours with 10 minute slide presentation; individual objects of art lent for special exhibitions upon request

C **GENERAL MILLS, INC**, 9200 Wayzata Blvd, PO Box 1113, 55440. Tel 612-540-7269. *Art Cur* Donald B McNeil
Open to public by appointment only. No admis fee. Estab 1959 to enhance employee work areas and alternative community art resource. Collection displayed in office building
Collections: 20th Century multi-media works, original prints, paintings and sculptures (1000 pieces)
Activities: Lect; gallery talks; tours; individual objects of art lent at request of museums, galleries, and artists for specific exhibitions; originate traveling exhibitions to colleges, art centers and museums

C **LUTHERAN BROTHERHOOD,** 701 Second Ave S, 55402. Tel 612-340-7261. *In Charge Art Program* Debra Amundson
Annual amount of contributions and grants $3000; gallery maintained; exhibits purchased works of art by local and national artists
Collections: Bing and Grondahl Plate Collection; Martin Luther Coin Collection
Exhibitions: Junior, senior and student exhibitions
Activities: Competitions with awards; purchase awards; originate traveling exhibitions to churches, organizations throughout the United States

O **METROPOLITAN CULTURAL ARTS CENTER,** 1530 Russell Ave N, 55411. Tel 612-522-4111. *Chmn Board* Robert Sampics
Open 9:30 AM - 9 PM. No admis fee. Estab 1967 to offer training in the arts to people who could not afford it otherwise and to bring people of different cultural backgrounds together to experience art. Average Annual Attendance: 400. Mem: 100; dues $10; annual meeting Sept
Income: $50,000 (financed by endowment, membership, state appropriation and grants)
Publications: Newsletter, monthly
Activities: Classes for adults and children; dramatic programs

L **MINNEAPOLIS COLLEGE OF ART AND DESIGN,** Library and Media Center, 200 E 25th St, 55404. Tel 612-870-3291. *Dir* Richard Kronstedt; *Asst Librn* Janet Hennesy; *Slide Librn* Peggy Rudberg; *Media Center Dir* Tim Perkins; *Catalogue Librn* Kathleen Arsenault
Open Mon - Thurs 8 AM - 8 PM, Fri 8 AM - 5 PM, Sat 12:30 - 4:30 PM, summer 8:30 AM - 4:30 PM; slide library and media center have different hours. Estab 1960 to provide library and media center services and materials in support of the curriculum of the College. Circ 40,000; limited to students and staff. 40,000
Income: $131,087 (financed by student tuition, grants and gifts)
Purchases: $18,304
Library Holdings: Vols 46,000; Per subs 180; AV—Cassettes, fs, motion pictures, rec, slides, v-tapes; Other—Clipping files, exhibition catalogs, pamphlets, reproductions
Special Subjects: Drawings, Fashion Arts, Film, Graphic Design, Illustration, Contemporary painting
Collections: College archive

M **MINNEAPOLIS INSTITUTE OF ARTS,** 2400 Third Ave S, 55404. Tel 612-870-3046. *Dir* Samuel Sachs II; *Assoc Dir* Timothy Fiske; *Chmn Communications* Marcy Dahlquist; *Acting Chmn Education* Kathryn C Johnson; *Dir Upper Midwest Conservation Assoc* David Dudley; *Coordr Exhib* Terrell Lucius; *Cur Prints & Drawings* John Ittmann; *Cur Paintings* Gregory H Hedberg; *Cur Photography* Carroll T Hartwell; *Cur Oriental Arts* Robert Jacobsen; *Registrar* Marilyn Bjorkland
Open Tues, Wed, Fri & Sat 10 AM - 5 PM, Thurs 10 AM - 9 PM, Sun Noon - 5 PM cl Mon. Admis adults $1, student 50¢, free to members, senior citizens, those under twelve, school groups. Estab 1883 to foster the knowledge, understanding and practice of the arts. The first gallery was opened in 1889, and the original building was constructed in 1911-15. The south wing was added in 1926, and the entire structure features the classical elements of the day. The museum was expanded to twice the original size in 1972-74, and has incorporated modern themes designed by Kenzo, Tange and URTEC of Tokyo. Average Annual Attendance: 350,000. Mem: 11,862; dues household $25, individual $15; annual meeting in Oct
Income: Financed by endowment, membership, county and state appropriations, and admissions
Collections: Collection representing all schools and periods of art: American and European paintings, decorative arts, period rooms, photography, prints and drawings, sculpture; Ancient, African, Oceanic, Oriental and native North and South American arts
Exhibitions: (1978 - 1980) Arts of China and Japan; Carl Chiarenza: Photographs; Drawings by Arakawa: Mechanism of Meaning; Leger's Grand Dejeuner: a Masterpiece from the Museum of Modern Art; Millet's Gleaners: a Masterpiece from the Louvre; New Treasure at the Institute; Sculpture from the David Daniels Collection; James Jacques Joseph Tissot: The Complete Printer; Victorian High Renaissance Art of Norway 1750 - 1914
Publications: Bulletin, biannually; exhibitions catalogs; member's magazine, monthly
Activities: Classes for adults and children; docent training; workshops; lect open to public, 15 visiting lectr per year; concerts; gallery talks; tours; artmobile; paintings and original art objects lent to other professional arts organizations; originate traveling exhibitions; museum shop sells books, original art, reproductions, prints, slides and jewelry

L **Art Reference Library,** 2400 Third Ave S, 55404. *Librn* Harold Peterson
Open Tues - Sat 10 AM - 5 PM, Sun Noon - 5 PM, cl Mon. Estab 1915 to provide a reference collection based around the museum's collection of works of art for use primarily by curatorial staff but to be available to students and museum visitors. Maintains an art gallery, Leslie Memorial Room and has exhibitions of books and prints
Library Holdings: Vols 30,000; Per subs 100
Special Subjects: History of books, printings, decorative arts, prints and photography
Collections: Leslie Collection: History of Books and Printing; Minnick Collection: Botanical, Floral and Fashion Books
Exhibitions: Artist as Book Illustrator; Artists Books of the Seventies; Eye of the Composer; 19th Century English Book Illustrators; Private Presses; Bruce Rogers: Book Designer

O **Friend of the Institute,** 2400 Third Ave S, 55404. *Pres* Ellie Reid
Estab 1922 to broaden the influence of the Institute in the community and to provide volunteer support within the museum. Mem: 1900; annual meeting May
Activities: Coordinates docent program, museum shop, sales and rental gallery, speaker's bureau, information desk, special lect, exhibitions and fund-raising projects

L **MINNEAPOLIS PUBLIC LIBRARY AND INFORMATION CENTER,** Art, Music and Film Dept, 300 Nicollet Mall, 55401. *Dir* Joseph Kimbrough; *Assoc Dir* Zella Shannon; *Head Art, Music, Films Dept* Marlea Warren; *Films Specialist* Elizabeth Bingaman
Open 9 AM - 9 PM Mon -Thurs, Fri & Sat 9 AM - 5:30 PM, cl Sat, Memorial and Labor Days. Estab 1889
Income: $78,195
Library Holdings: Vols 42,680; Per subs 165; AV—Fs, lantern Slides, motion pictures, slides, v-tapes; Other—Clipping files, exhibition catalogs, original art works, pamphlets

C **THE PILLSBURY COMPANY,** 608 Second Ave S, 55402. Tel 612-330-5442. *Executive VPres* Walter D Scott
Estab to create exciting and attractive environment and support the arts. Collection displayed on internal walls of corporate headquarters building
Purchases: $100,000
Collections: Contemporary and Western American art, primarily oil paintings, prints and watercolors

UNIVERSITY OF MINNESOTA

M **University Gallery,** 110 Northrop Memorial Auditorium, 84 Church St SE, 55455. Tel 612-373-3424, 373-3425. *Acting Dir* Melvin Waldfogel; *Asst Dir* Robert Van Der Wege; *Cur* Charles Helsell; *Editor & Cur* Valerie Tvrdik; *Tour Exhib Coordr* Mary Harvey; *Registrar* Melissa Herrick; *Asst Cur* Lenore Aaseng; *Rental Mgr* Clyde Scroggins; *Preparator* William Lampe
Open Mon, Wed & Fri 11 AM - 4 PM, Tues & Thurs 11 AM - 8 PM, Sun 2 - 5 PM, cl Sat & holidays. Estab 1933; the program of the University Gallery is one which provides for the all-University function of meeting the broad objective of an all University art museum, and for in-service function of meeting the specific teaching and research needs of various University of Minnesota departments. Average Annual Attendance: 50,000
Collections: Paintings, drawings and prints by American artists working in the first half of the 20th century, and contains notable works by Avery, Dove, Feininger, Hartley, MacDonald-Wright, Marin, Maurer and O'Keefe; Nordfeldt collection on extended loan from Mrs. B J O Nordfeldt; print collection includes works by artists of all schools and periods; sculpture collection of major works by contemporary artists including: Baizerman, Bertoia, Richier, David Smith and others
Exhibitions: The University Gallery stresses a program of major loan exhibitions, held concurrently with smaller exhibitions organized for specific teaching purposes or from the permanent collection
Activities: Programs; lending program to University of Minnesota faculty of framed two-dimensional material

M **Coffman Union Gallery,** 110 Northrop Memorial Auditorium, 84 Church St SE, 55455. Tel 612-373-6704. *Coordr* Roselyn Rezac; *Chairperson* Elaine Ward; *Advisor* Marlene Vernon
Open Daily 10 AM - 5 PM. No admis fee. Estab 1976 for campus and local artists
Income: Financed by student fees
Activities: Lect; films; demonstrations

L **Art Library,** 12 Walter Library, 117 Pleasant Street SE, 55455. *Librn* Herbert G Scherer
Open Mon - Thurs 8 AM - 9 PM, Fri 8 AM - 5 PM, Sat & Sun 1 - 5; Summer Mon, Wed, Fri 8 - 4:30, Tues 8 AM - 9 PM. Estab 1950 to serve undergraduate and graduate teaching programs in Art History to PhD level and in Studio Art to MA level. To provide art related books to other departments and to the entire academic community
Library Holdings: Vols 54,267; Per subs 339; Micro—Fiche; AV—Slides; Other—Exhibition catalogs 4701, pamphlets, trade and post card albums
Special Subjects: Scandinavian art history
Activities: Tours; single lectures

M **WALKER ART CENTER,** Vineland Place, 55403. Tel 612-377-7500. *Pres* Alice E Wittenberg; *VPres* C Angus Wurtele; *Chmn Board* Philip Von Blon; *Dir* Martin Friedman; *Admin Dir* D C Borrman; *Chief Cur* Graham W J Beal; *Cur* Lisa Lyons; *Cur Design* Mildred S Friedman; *Registrar* Carolyn Clark DeCato; *Asst Registrar* Gwen Bitz; *Dir Development* Robert Sain; *Acting Cur Education* Emily Kass; *Dir Performing Arts* Nigel Redden; *Dir Learning Museum Program* Melinda Ward; *Cur Film* Richard Peterson; *Public Information* Kathe Kertz Stanton; *Graphic Designer* Robert Jensen
Open Tues - Sat 10 AM - 8 PM; Sun 11 AM - 5 PM, cl Mon. No admis fee. Estab 1879 by T B Walker, reorganized 1939 as Walker Art Center, Inc; building erected 1927; new museum building opened 1971. The Center consists of seven galleries, three sculpture terraces, the Center Bookshop and the Gallery 8 restaurant. Average Annual Attendance: 450,000. Mem: 5000; dues regular $25, non resident $18, student and senior citizens $15; annual meeting Sept
Income: $1,983,625 (financed by endowment, membership, state appropriation, grants and book shop)
Purchases: $2,001,148
Collections: †Graphics; 19th Century American Landscape paintings by Church, Cole, Durand, Kensett, Inness, Ryder; †photography; †sculpture; †20th century paintings
Exhibitions: Architecture of James Stirling: Four Works; Gene Davis: Recent Paintings; Eight Artists: The Flusive Image; Robert Irwin; Morris Louis: The Veil Cycle; Nelson, Eames, Girard, Propst: The Design Process at Herman Miller; Noguchi's Imaginary Landscapes; Picasso: From the Future Musee Picasso, Paris; Press Photography: Minnesota Since 1930; The River: Images of the Mississippi; Scale & Environment: 10 sculptors; Sculpture Made in Place: Dill, Ginnever, Madsen; George Segal Sculptures; William Wiley: Twelve Years
Publications: Brochures; calendar of events, 11 issues a year; Design, quarterly; exhibition catalogs
Activities: Classes for adults and children; docent training; family workshops; lect open to public, 8 vis lectr per yr; concerts; gallery talks; tours; exten dept serving Minnesota and surrounding states; individual paintings and original objects of art lent to schools, community groups, corporation and museums; traveling exhibitions organized and circulated; museum shop selling books, magazines, posters, jewelry and gift items

L **Library,** Vineland Place, 55403. *Library Asst* Geraldine Owens
Open to museum personnel, librarians, graduate students by appointment. For reference only
Library Holdings: Vols 3200; Per subs 95; Other—Clipping files, exhibition catalogs
Special Subjects: Architecture, Decorative Arts, Film, One-man contemporary artist catalog dating back to 1940, Design, Graphics

O **WOMEN'S ART REGISTRY OF MINNESOTA,** 414 First Ave N, 55401. Tel 312-332-5672. *Admin Coordr* Diane E Gorney
Open Tues - Fri 11 AM - 4 PM, Sat 12 - 5 PM. No admis fee. Estab 1975. Maintains gallery. Average Annual Attendance: 4000. Mem: 186; dues $8; annual meeting Feb
Income: Financed by membership and small grants for projects
Collections: Members work on display in one area
Exhibitions: International Women Invite Women Exhibit; Members work plus special shows and theme shows
Publications: W A R M Newsletter
Activities: Educ dept; workshops for public; events-poetry readings; performances; lect open to the public, 4 vis lectr per year; gallery talks; traveling exhibitions organized and circulated

MOORHEAD

PLAINS ART MUSEUM

M **Main Gallery,** 521 Main Ave, PO Box 37, 56560. Tel 218-236-7171. *Dir & Secy Board Dir* James O'Rourke; *Asst Dir* Susan Hunke; *Pres Board Dir* Richard B Crockett; *VPres Board Dir* Richard Moorhead; *Business Mgr* Steven W Illg; *Cur* Roger Sherman; *Photographer & Publisher* Owen K Osten; *Registrar* Tracy Moorhead; *Membership* Lynn Gifford
Open Wed - Sun 9 AM - 5 PM. Admis $1. Estab 1965 to foster and promote a knowledge and love of art in the community and to provide a repository for the artistic heritage of this area; to operate and maintain an art gallery and museum, to promote the extension and improvement of education in the arts; to provide facilities for the exhibition and conservation of the art in this area, past and present. Former Moorhead Federal Building (1913), Oscar Wenderoth, architect, houses the museum. This stately federal style building has a vari-colored marble lobby, ionic columns and tall arched windows. Average Annual Attendance: 26,000. Mem: 1100; dues $10 - $1000; annual meeting June
Income: Financed by membership and foundation grants
Purchases: $3000
Collections: African, Oceanic, Pre-Columbian and North American Indian, Persian and Oriental art; Eskimo sculpture; 19th & 20th century prints and drawings; 19th century decorative arts; 20th century paintings from local, regional and national artists; photography
Exhibitions: Clay at Clay, County, American Artists working in Clay; James Rosenquist Paintings; Bud Shark: Master Lithographer; 21st Midwestern Exhibition; Andre Kertisz and Charles Harbutt (photographs)
Publications: Slaytons Pictorial, monthly
Activities: Classes for adults; docent training; lect open to public, 12 visitng lectr per year; concerts; gallery talks; tours; exten dept serving North Dakota, South Dakota, Western Minnesota; individual paintings and original object of art lent to art galleries, historical museums, colleges and schools; lending collection contains 2000 original art works, 500 original prints, 400 paintings, 300 photographs; museum shop sells books, magazines, original art, prints and slides

M **Rourke Art Gallery,** 523 S Fourth St, 56560. Tel 218-236-7171. *Registrar* Kevin Brown
Open Wed - Sun Noon - 5 PM. No admis fee. Estab 1960 to foster and promote a knowledge and love of art in our community and to provide a repository for the artistic heritage of this area; to operate and maintain an art gallery and museum. Former Martinson family home built in 1884, remodeled 1920, renovations have preserved the period details and historical features; three floors for exhibitions. Average Annual Attendance: 16,000. Mem: 800; dues $10 - $1000; annual meeting June
Income: Financed by membership and foundation grants
Purchases: $5000
Collections: Nineteenth Century Decorative Art; North American Indian Art; Persian Art; Pre-Columbian Art; West African Art
Exhibitions: Cameron Booth Paintings; San Francisco Artists; West African Textiles
Publications: Slaytons Pictorial, monthly

OWATONNA

O **OWATONNA ARTS CENTER,** 435 Dunnel Dr, P O Box 134, 55060. Tel 507-451-4540. *Pres* Mary E Leach; *VPres* Robert Allyn; *Treas* James Birdsall; *Bldg Mgr* John M Spencer; *Secy* Bea Spencer; *Cur* Silvan A Durkin; *Performing Art Chmn* Virginia Birdsall
Open Tues - Sat 1 - 5 PM, Sun 2 - 5 PM. No admis fee except for specials. Estab 1975 to preserve local professional artists' work and promote the arts in the community. The West Gallery (32 x 26 x 12 ft) and the North Gallery (29 x 20 x 12 ft) provide an interesting walk through space and a versatile space in which to display two and three dimensional work; the two galleries can be combined by use of moveable panels; and the Sculpture Garden which was completed in 1979 of multi-level construction. Average Annual Attendance: 5000. Mem: 400; dues, individual $5, family $10; annual meeting first Tues in Oct
Income: $20,394 (financed by membership and fund raising activities plus sustaining fund from industries and business)
Purchases: $500
Collections: Marianne Young World Costume Collection of garments and jewelry from 27 countries; painting, prints, sculpture by local professional artists
Exhibitions: Acrylics, prints and Handmade paper by Charles Putnam; Annual Outdoor Arts Festival; Annual Steel Country Show; Archeology and the Art of China; Contemporary Jewelry by Richard Shea; Steve Delaitsch Painting; Five Women from Texas, textile show; Photography by Roger Kastelle; Living Arts of West Africa; Lutheran Brotherhood Student Traveling Exhibit; Owatonna Watercolorists; An Old Fashioned Christmas; Public School Art; Sculptured Canvases by Helen Kral; Serigraphs and Serigrams by Alice Ottinger and Jean Zamboni; Wood Carving and Pottery, five artists
Publications: Monthly newsletter to members only
Activities: Classes for adults and children; lect open to the public, 2 vis lectr per yr; concerts monthly; tours; traveling exhibitions organized and circulated; sales shop sells original art

L **Library,** 435 Dunnel Dr, 55060.
Open to members only; for reference
Library Holdings: Vols 180

PARK RAPIDS

M **NORTH COUNTRY MUSEUM OF ARTS,** Third and Court Streets, PO Box 328, 56470. Tel 218-732-5237. *Chmn* Grace Privratsky; *Treas* Blanche Szuszitzky; *Secy* John Masog; *Cur* Pamela Teslow
Open Tues - Sun 11 AM - 5 PM May - Oct. Admis adults $1, students 50¢. Estab 1977 to provide a cultural and educational center in which to house our Anchor collection and additional traveling exhibitions from which all ages may benefit by being exposed to and working with art in its many forms. Maintins Great Gallery, Members Gallery, four Revolving Galleries, gift shop and studio. Average Annual Attendance: 6000. Mem: 120; dues family $20, individual $15; annual meeting Oct
Income: $40,000 (financed by membership, individual and corporate grants and gifts)
Collections: †Nigerian arts, crafts and artifacts; †30 †Old School European paintings
Exhibitions: (1980) Drawings by Gendron Jensen; Juried High School Fine Art Exhibition; Learning to See - Conservation of Paintings by Louis Pomerantz Once Upon a Time: Illustrations of Children's Tales from Around the World; Scandinavian Wood, Traditional Scandinavian Woodworking
Activities: Classes for adults and children; docent training; lect open to the public, 2-3 lectr per year; concerts; gallery talks; tours; competitions; book traveling exhibitions, 5-6 per year; museum shop selling original art

ROCHESTER

O **ROCHESTER ART CENTER,** 320 E Center St, 55901. Tel 507-282-8629. *Dir* Betty Jean Shigaki
Open Tues - Sat 10 AM - 4 PM, Sun 1 - 5 PM, cl Mon. No admis fee. Estab 1946 as a center for contemporary arts and crafts of the Upper Midwest region, to sponsor an on-going program of exhibitions, educational classes, lectures, workshops and community services in the arts. Included are the Upstairs Gallery of Contemporary Crafts, and the main exhibitions space, the Holland Gallery. Average Annual Attendance: 30,000. Mem: 350; dues $15 - $100; annual meeting Nov
Income: $115,000 (financed by endowment, membership, city and state appropriations, fund raising and tuition)
Collections: Local and regional artists' work
Exhibitions: Varied exhibits in Contemporary Fine Arts and Crafts
Publications: Newsletter, quarterly
Activities: Classes for adults and children; lect open to public, 2 visiting lectr per year; concerts; gallery talks; tours; competitions; sales shop sells original art

L **Library,** 320 E Center St, 55901.
Open to staff and members only
Library Holdings: Vols 500; Per subs 12

SAINT CLOUD

SAINT CLOUD STATE UNIVERSITY

M **Atwood Center Gallery Lounge,** Atwood Center, 56301. Tel 612-255-2202. *Program Dir* Patricia A Kreuger
Open Mon - Fri 7:30 AM - 11 PM, Sat 8 AM - 11 PM, Sun Noon - 11 PM. No admis fee. Estab 1967 as a university student union facility. Gallery area is part of program, designed for maximum exposure, where students may relax or study while enjoying exhibits; space is flexible; also area for music listening and small theatre; additional exhibits displayed in prominent area
Income: Financed by student enrollment fee assessment
Exhibitions: 1 - 3 exhibits monthly, many by students
Activities: Classes for adults and children; dramatic programs; lect open to public, 10 - 20 vis lectr per year; concerts

M **Kiehle Gallery,** 56301. Tel 612-255-4283. *Dir* Kingsly Dorholt
Open Mon - Fri 8 AM - 4:30 PM. No admis fee. Estab 1974 to expose college community to ideas and attitudes in the field of visual arts and crafts. The gallery has 1600 sq ft of enclosed multi use gallery floor space and 2500 sq ft outside sculpture court. Average Annual Attendance: 15,000
Income: Financed by student fund appropriation
Collections: Works donated by Master of Arts degree program (visual arts)
Activities: Lect open to the public, 5 vis lectr per yr; gallery talks; competitions; individual paintings and original objects of art lent to other departments on campus; lending collection contains original prints, paintings, photographs and sculpture; traveling exhibitions organized and circulated

SAINT JOSEPH

M COLLEGE OF SAINT BENEDICT, Art Gallery, Benedict Arts Center, 56374.
Tel 612-363-5785. *Pres* S Emanuel Renner; *VPres* S Linda Kulzer; *Chmn of Art Dept
& Gallery Dir* Stanley Shafer
Open daily 9 AM - 4:30 PM. No admis fee. Estab 1963
Income: Financed by college
Purchases: $500 - $1000
Collections: Contemporary collection of crafts, drawings, praintings, prints and
sculpture; East Asian Collection of ceramics, crafts, drawings, fibers and prints;
Miscellaneous African, New Guinea, Indian and European
Exhibitions: (1978) African Art (sculpture, fibers, crafts); David Brown Paintings;
Guthrie Theater Props; John Liikala Sculpture; Bob Mattson Drawing; Bill Ryan
Photography; Stanley Shafer & Miles Bair (sculpture, drawing, painting). (1979)
Richard Bresnahan Pottery; CSB Permanent Collection; Carole Fisher Sculpture;
Sister Dennis Frandrup Ceramics; Sister Baulu Kuan (paintings, drawings); Anita
Mills Prints; Selections from the WARM Gallery; Women Look at Women
Photography
Activities: lect open to the public, 8 visiting lectr per year; gallery talks; tours;
scholarships; individual paintings and original objects of art lent to faculty and staff
members of the college

SAINT PAUL

M CATHOLIC HISTORICAL SOCIETY OF SAINT PAUL, 2260 Summit Ave,
55105. Tel 612-690-4355. *Acting Cur* Leo J Tibesar
No admis fee. Estab 1905 to collect and preserve materials of historic interest
relating to the Catholic history of the ecclesiastical province of Saint Paul. Open
by appointment only
Income: Financed by endowment
Collections: Architectural drawings; ecclesiastical memorabilia; liturgical
vestments

C CONTROL DATA ARTS INTERNATIONAL, 474 Concordia Ave, 55103. Tel
612-292-2176. *VPres* R E McElroy
Estab as corporate social responsibility and East-West trade
Exhibitions: Exhibitions sponsored and organized; co-sponsors a tour of some 400
art works from Russia's Hermitage in 1980
Activities: Originate traveling exhibitions to museums

M HAMLINE UNIVERSITY GALLERIES, Dept of Art, 55104. *Cur Permanent
Collection* Roslye Ultan; *Exhib Dir* James Conaway
Open Mon - Fri 9 AM - 4:30 PM, cl Sat & Sun. Estab 1943 to display outstanding
works of art in all media for instruction of and appreciation by the public and
students
Income: Financed by the University
Collections: Paintings, prints, drawings and sculpture
Exhibitions: Continuous exhibitions; annual purchase award exhibits in painting
and graphic arts
L Library, 55104.
Rental Library of original modern works and reproductions; extensive color slide
library of paintings, architecture, sculpture, minor arts and graphics

M MACALESTER COLLEGE GALLERIES, * 1600 Grand Ave, 55101. Tel
612-647-6221. *Cur* Roxann Sorenson
Open Mon - Fri 8 AM - 10 PM, cl Aug, national holidays & school vacations. No
admis fee. Estab 1964 as a college facility to bring contemporary art exhibitions to
the students, faculty and community
Exhibitions: Temporary, traveling and student exhibitions
Activities: Lect; guided tours; gallery talks; traveling exhibitions organized and
circulated; sales shop selling art books and supplies
L Weyerhauser Library, * 1600 Grand Ave, 55101. Tel 612-647-6345.
Library Holdings: Vols 234,439; Per subs 823
Special Subjects: Art History

O MINNESOTA HISTORICAL SOCIETY, * 690 Cedar St, 55101. Tel
612-296-2747. *Pres* Paul L Parker; *Dir* Russell W Fridley; *Assoc Dir* Robert C
Wheeler; *Deputy Dir* John J Wood; *Asst Dir* June Holmquist; *Asst to Dir for Libraries
and Museum Coll* Lila J Goff
Open Mon - Sat 8:30 AM - 5 PM, Sun 1 - 4 PM. No admis fee. Estab 1849 to collect,
preserve and make available to the public the history of Minnesota. Mem: 6000
Income: $5,600,000 (financed by endowment, membership and state appropriation)
Purchases: $30,000
Collections: Archives; †art works; †books; †maps; †manuscripts; †museum artifacts
relating to the history of Minnesota; newspapers; †photographs
Exhibitions: The Clothes Off Our Backs
Publications: Minnesota History, quarterly; Minnesota History News, 6 issues per
year
Activities: Classes for adults; lect open to the public; tours; sales shop selling books,
magazines, prints, reproductions
L Library, * 690 Cedar St, 55101. *Chief Reference Librn* Patricia Harpole
Open to the public for general reference; library contains only a few works relating
to art
Library Holdings: Vols 500,000
Collections: Seth Eastman (watercolors); maps; Minnesota photographs; Edwin
Whitefield (watercolors)

M MINNESOTA MUSEUM OF ART, St Peter at Kellogg Blvd, 55102. Tel
612-224-7431. *Chmn Board Trustees* Richardson B Okie; *Pres* James V Toscano;
Dir Dean R Swanson; *School Coordr* Allyson J Hakes; *Education Asst* Esther Rachel
Holtzer; *Publications & Public Relations* Patricia Heikenen; *Registrar* Leanne Klein;
Acting Dir Education Nell H McClure; *Dir Business Affairs* Ruth H Moran;
Recorder Marina E Pacini; *Development Officer* Lola P Plaisted; *Conservator &
Preparator* Laurel O'Gorman; *Dir Visitor Services* Betty V Runyon; *Coordr After
School Art* Karen Sugerman; *Acting Dir Cur* Otto Theuer; *Asst Registrar* Katherine
Van Tassell; *Photographer* Theresa Wegner; *Programmer & Exhib* Janet Wesle;
Teacher & Education Asst Kathleen Koos; *Exhib* James D Ristine

Open Tues - Sat 10 AM - 5 PM, Sun 1 - 5 PM. Admis by donation. Estab 1927
to act as trustee in preserving important works of art for the benefit of present and
future generations, and to use its resources and collection actively as an educational
force to enrich the community. The museum is housed in a beautiful four-story Art
Deco building built in 1931 by architect Magnus Jemne; his wife did inlays of brass
in foyer floors; designer Frank Post did curving brass stair rail and lighting fixtures;
the fourth floor auditorium has gold leaf on the walls, and the upstairs dining room
sits amid art works. Average Annual Attendance: 25,000. Mem: 1000; dues
household $25, individual $15, special $12; annual meeting Nov
Income: $650,000 (financed by endowment, membership, allocation from United
Arts Fund and foundation grants)
Purchases: $100,000
Collections: American and European lace; Asian sculpture, ceramics, paintings,
prints, screens, drawings, textiles and furniture; contemporary American, African
and Northwest Coast Indian crafts; 20th century drawings, sculpture, paintings and
prints
Exhibitions: (1978-80) Art of Iceland, 1944-79; Brown Wares: East & West;
Celadon: East & West; A Century of Fashion; Chinese Painting, the Flawless Line;
Court House; Dance of the Pen (calligraphy); Finnish Constructivism; The
Goldsmith, '78; Stuart Klipper: Photographs; Jack Levine Retrospective; Life: The
First Decade; Light Abstractions; Minnesota Artists; Molas from the San Blas
Islands; Shamans and Spirits; 20th Century Drawings from the Whitney Museum
of American Art; West'79, The Law; West'80, Art and the Law; (annual) Recent
Acquisitions
Publications: Exhibition catalogues
Activities: Lect open to public, 10 visiting lectr per year; gallery talks; tours;
competitions; art works are lent to businesses and professional offices in the
community for a specified fee; originates traveling exhibitions
L Library, St Peter at Kellogg Blvd, 55102. *Librn* Leanne Klein
Open to members, students and staff for reference only
Library Holdings: Vols 3000; Per subs 15; AV—Slides
Special Subjects: Asian Art, Drawings, Prints, Eskimo Art, Laces, Northwest
Coast Indian Art
M Landmark Center, 75 W Fifth St, 55102.
Open Tues - Sat 10 AM - 5 PM, Sun 1 - 5 PM. No admis fee
Income: Financed with Minnesota Museum of Art
Exhibitions: Changing exhibition of wide community interest

L ST PAUL PUBLIC LIBRARY, * 90 W Fourth St, 55102. Tel 612-224-3383. *Dir
of Libraries* J Archer Eggen; *Librn* Gerald W Steenberg; *Supv Arts & AV Services*
Delores A Sundbye
Open Mon & Thurs 11:30 AM - 8 PM, Tues, Wed, Fri & Sat 9 AM - 5:30 PM.
Estab 1857. Circ 92,642. Gallery has changing exhibitions where various
organizations may hold meetings
Income: Financed by city appropriation
Purchases: $10,000
Library Holdings: Vols 16,000; Per subs 50; AV—Cassettes, fs, motion pictures,
rec, slides; Other—Clipping files, exhibition catalogs, framed reproductions,
sculpture
Collections: Complete collection of first edition Arundel prints
Exhibitions: Open exhibits for local artists, school children, senior citizens, art
therapy
Activities: Lect open to the public; traveling exhibitions organized and circulated

O SAINT PAUL - RAMSEY ARTS AND SCIENCE COUNCIL, 30 E Tenth St,
55101. Tel 612-292-3222. *Executive VPres* Michael D Smith
Estab 1954. Conducts annual federated fund drive (United Arts Fund) for six
member agencies, including: The Saint Paul Chamber Orchestra, Chimera Theater,
Schubert Club, Community Programs in the Arts and Sciences, Minnesota Museum
of Art and Minnesota Landmarks. Five percent of fund drive proceeds designated
for Arts Development Fund to assist local emerging arts organizations. The Council
also provides management planning services for its agencies, administers building
space for arts organizations and serves as an institutional sponsor for KSJN-FM of
the Minnesota Public Radio network

M SCHOOL OF THE ASSOCIATED ARTS GALLERIES, 344 Summit Ave,
55102. Tel 612-224-3416. *Dir* Virginia Rahjd; *Dean* Ronald Swenson
Open Mon - Fri 9 AM - 4 PM. No admis fee. Estab 1948; galleries were established
as an adjunct to, and of, the art education we offer our students. Average Annual
Attendance: 400-500
Income: Financed by endowment
Exhibitions: Ten shows per year of the work of local artists, faculty, students,
traveling shows, and work from our own collection. The emphasis is on Modern
Art
L Library, 344 Summit Ave, 55102.
Estab 1948 to have reference material for our own students. Not open to public.
Maintains an art gallery
Library Holdings: Vols 7500; Per subs 5; AV—Slides; Other—Original art works,
pamphlets, photographs, reproductions

M UNIVERSITY OF MINNESOTA, Student Center Galleries,* 2017 Buford,
55108. Tel 612-373-1046 or 373-1051. *Dir* Paul W Larson; *Asst Dir for Programming*
Timothy L McCarty; *Gallery Cur* Ron Dufault; *Activities Consultant* Ester Neely
Open daily 8 AM - 10 PM, Sun Noon - 10 PM. No admis fee. Estab 1959 to bring
art of great variety into the daily lives of students. Two lounge galleries and one
pedestrian gallery are maintained. Average Annual Attendance: 1,500,000. Mem:
5400; annual meeting last Thurs in Sept
Income: Financed by student fee
Publications: Annual Report and Activity Summary
Activities: Classes for adults; dramatic programs; mini-courses in crafts; lect open
to the public, 10 visiting lectrs per year; concerts; gallery talks; tours; competitions;
exten dept serving Minnesota

WORTHINGTON

O NOBLES COUNTY ART CENTER GALLERY, 407 12th St, PO Box 281, 56187. Tel 507-376-4431. *Pres of Board of Dir* Mrs Tom Anderson; *Cur and Secy* Genevieve Peterson
Open Mon - Sat 2 - 4:30 PM, Mon - Fri in summer. No admis fee. Estab 1961 to nourish the arts and to bring the arts and cultures of other communities, nations and civilizations to Nobles County and the surrounding area, so that its residents may become more universal in their thinking. Room on lower level of building housing county library and information center; 25 x 51 ft. Average Annual Attendance: 1000. Mem: 150; dues family $5; annual meeting January
Income: Financed by county appropriation
Exhibitions: Art in the Park; the work of area artists
Publications: Newsletter monthly, from Sept through June
Activities: Classes for adults; gallery talks; competitions; original art work for sale during exhibitions

MISSISSIPPI

CLEVELAND

M DELTA STATE UNIVERSITY, Fielding L Wright Art Center, Box D-2, 38733. Tel 601-843-2151. *Chmn Dept* Malcolm M Norwood; *Exhib Chmn* Terry K Simmons; *Chmn Art Education* Dr Carolyn Stone
Opem Mon - Fri 8 AM - 5 PM, Sun 3 - 5 PM on opening shows, cl school holidays. No admis fee. Estab 1968 as an education gallery for the benefit of the students, but serves the entire area for changing art shows; it is the only facility of this nature in the Mississippi Delta Region. Three gallery areas; Gallery A carpeted 40 x 22 ft; gallery can accommodate about 25 hangings depending on size. Average Annual Attendance: 2500-3000
Income: Financed by state appropriation
Collections: Delta State University permanent collection; Marie Hull Collection; Smith-Paterson Memorial Collection; Whittington Memorial Collection
Exhibitions: Faculty Exhibitions; Fibrations Traveling Exhibitions from the University of Georgia; Fourth Juried Student Exhibition; Paintings by Mary Sims; Photographs by William Byron McCaslin; Selections from the Permanent Collection; Senior Thesis Show; Third Former Graduates Exhibition: Kay Grabowski, Dick Kelso, Greely Myatt, Frank Neal, Tommy Thurmond
Publications: Announcements of exhibitions, monthly during fall, winter and spring
Activities: Classes for adults; lect open to public, 10 vis lectr per yr; gallery talks; tours; competitions; exten department serving the Mississippi Delta Region; individual paintings and original objects of art lent to offices of campus; lending collection contains color reproductions, film strips, motion pictures, original art works, 6000 slides; traveling exhibitions organized and circulated

CLINTON

L MISSISSIPPI COLLEGE LIBRARY, Art Department, 39058. *Dir* Billy Lytal
Open Mon - Sat 8:30 AM - 10 PM, cl Sun. Estab to serve all departments of college
Library Holdings: Vols 2000; Per subs 16; AV—A-tapes, cassettes, fs, Kodachromes, motion pictures, rec, slides, v-tapes; Other—Original art works
Special Subjects: Architecture, Art Education, Art History, Inter Design, Sculpture

COLUMBUS

M MISSISSIPPI UNIVERSITY FOR WOMEN, Art Gallery and Museum, Fine Arts Bldg, 39701. *Dir of Gallery, Cur of Museum & Permanent Coll* Charles E Ambrose
Open Mon - Fri 8 AM - 5 PM. No admis fee. Estab 1948
Collections: †American Art; †Paintings, drawings, prints; †Permanent collection of Mississippi artists
Exhibitions: Frequent special and circulating exhibitions; International exhibition; Selections from permanent collection, periodically
Activities: Children's art classes; visiting artists program; visiting foreign artists workshops; films

JACKSON

O CRAFTMEN'S GUILD OF MISSISSIPPI, Mississippi Crafts Center, Jackson, MS. (Mailing Add: Natchez Trace Parkway at Ridgeland, PO Box 22886, Jackson, MS 22886,) Tel 601-856-4218. *Executive Dir* Dan Overly
Open daily 9 AM - 5 PM
Activities: Mississippi School of Crafts and Design; summer program; classes for children; exhibits program; marketing assistance

L MISSISSIPPI DEPARTMENT OF ARCHIVES AND HISTORY, 100 State St, PO Box 571, 39205. Tel 601-354-6218, 354-6222. *Pres Board Trustees* William F Winter; *Dir* Elbert R Hilliard; *Dir Old Capitol Museum* Patti Carr Black; *Dir Information and Education* Charlotte Capers; *Dir Archives & Library* Madel Morgan; *Dir Historic Preservation* Robert J Bailey
Open Mon 8 AM - 9 PM, Tues - Sat 8 AM - 5 PM, cl Sun. Estab 1902 for the care and custody of official archives; to collect material relating to the history of the State from the earliest times and to impart a knowledge of the history and resources of the State. Maintains the State Historical Museum. Maintains an art gallery which includes a portrait gallery of distinguished Mississippians and holds monthly exhibitions, folk song and folk crafts programs
Income: Financed by city appropriation
Library Holdings: Vols 33,000; Per subs 250; Micro—Fiche, reels; AV—A-tapes, cassettes, fs, motion pictures, rec, slides, v-tapes; Other—Clipping files, exhibition catalogs, prints, manuscripts, pamphlets, photographs, original documents
Special Subjects: Archaeology, Civil War, genealogy, Mississippiana
Collections: Maps; photographs; newspapers; all pertaining to Mississippi
Publications: Journal of Mississippi History, quarterly; Mississippi Newsletter, monthly
Activities: Folk crafts programs

M MISSISSIPPI MUSEUM OF ART, Pascagoula at Lamar Sts, PO Box 1330, 39205. Tel 601-960-1515. *Chmn Board of Trustees* E B Robinson Jr; *Pres* Mrs Noel Womack; *Dir* M J Czarniecki III; *Dir Admin, Sales & Security* Daniel A Matusiewicz; *Dir Coll & Exhib* John B Henry III; *Dir Education & State Services* W Ray Parish; *Supv Public Services* Cissy Anklam; *Supv Information* Mari Martinez; *Supv Coll & Registrar* Cynthia Lee Warden; *Supv Media Center* Margaret Tucker; *Supv State Services* George Snyder; *Comptroller* Rebecca Jaynes
Open Wed Fri & Sat 10 AM - 6 PM, Tues & Thurs 10 AM - 10 PM, Sun 1 - 5 PM, cl Mon. Admis donation suggested. Chartered in 1911. Museum opened April 22, 1978; East Exhibition Galleries 6400 sq ft; West Exhibition Galleries 2600 sq ft; Graphics Study Center houses exhibition area, study and storage rooms; Open Gallery includes special power, lighting and water requirements for technological media; Upper and Lower Atrium Galleries and outdoor Sculpture Garden; Non-Profit Corporation. Mem: 3000; dues student $5, individual $15, artist $20, family $20, patron $100, donor $250, benefactor $500, grand benefactor $1000
Income: $550,000 (financed by endowment, membership, contributions, public sector, earned income)
Collections: Varied Western art collection, state, regional, national and international artists; smaller non—western art collection
Exhibitions: To Live upon Canvas, the portrait art of Thomas Cantwell Healy (1820-1889)
Publications: Newsletter, bi-monthly; selected exhibition catalogs
Activities: Classes for adults and children; docent training; lect open to public, some for members only, 20 vis lectr per yr; tours; competitions; Outreach programs; Art Cart; Art Lecture Van; travel lecture program; corporate museum membership entitle business to 6 month loans from permanent collection; museum shop selling books, reproductions, prints and fine handmade items
L Media Center Library, Pascagonla at Lamar Sts, 39205. *Media Center Supv* Margaret Tucker
For reference only, open to the general public
Library Holdings: Vols 3000; Per subs 28
Collections: Walter Anderson Collection on Slides; Marie Hull Collection of Art Reference Books; Metropolitan Miniature Album; Museums permanent collection

LAUREL

M LAUREN ROGERS LIBRARY AND MUSEUM OF ART, Fifth Avenue & Seventh St, PO Box 1108, 39440. Tel 601-428-4875. *Dir* Donald D Crawford; *Asst Dir* Amorita Gordon; *Librn* Betty Mulloy
Open Tues - Sat 10 AM - Noon, 1 - 5 PM, Sun 2 - 5 PM, cl Mon. No Admis fee. Estab 1923 as a reference and research library and museum of art for public use and employment. Five smaller galleries open off large American Gallery; these include European room, Contemporary room, Gardiner Basket collection, Western and Indian room, and temporary exhibit gallery. Average Annual Attendance: 7000. Mem: Dues $10 - $100
Income: Financed by endowment
Collections: European Artists of the 19th Century; †Georgian Silver; Indian Basketry; †19th and 20th Century American artists
Exhibitions: Annual schedule of monthly exhibitions by regional and nationally recognized artists
Publications: Exhibition announcements
Activities: Classes for adults and children; docent training; lect open to the public, 2 - 3 vis lectr per yr; concerts; competitions; individual paintings lent to AAM Accredited museums or galleries
L Library, 39440.
For reference only
Library Holdings: Vols 17,000
Special Subjects: Art, genealogy, Mississipiana, Laurel history
Collections: Edward S Curtis books and photogravure portfolios on American Indian

MERIDIAN

M MERIDIAN MUSEUM OF ART, Seventh St at Twenty fifth Ave, PO Box 5773, 39301. Tel 601-693-1501. *Pres* Tom Bordeaux; *Dir* Dan W Griffin; *Secy* Janet Tinnin
Open Tues - Sun 1 - 5 PM, cl Mon and holidays. Estab in 1969 to give cultural enrichment and educational benefits to the people of eastern Mississippi, western Alabama and the South. Five galleries. Average Annual Attendance: 6000. Mem: 350; dues $2 - $1000; annual membership meeting second week of Dec
Income: Financed by membership and appropriation
Collections: Ink drawings; lithographs; paintings (oil, acrylic and water color); photographs; pottery; sculpture
Activities: Classes for adults, teens, children; workshops; lectures and special exhibitions; museum receptions; gallery talks; tours; competitions; Museum Guild for Education gift shop
L Library, Seventh St at Twenty fifth Ave, 39301.
For reference only
Library Holdings: Vols 220

O MISSISSIPPI ART COLONY, c/o Alex M Loeb, 2741 38th St, 39301. Tel 601-482-2827. *Dir* Bess Dawson; *Pres* Alex M Loeb; *VPres* R B Jacoby; *Secy & Treas* Jean R Loeb
Estab 1945 to hold workshops at least twice yearly, for painting instruction and occasionally other areas. To select show, with prizes awarded, which travels state of Mississippi between workshops. Mem: 40; dues $5; annual meetings Oct and May
Income: Financed by membership
Exhibitions: Four exhibitions 1978-1979

Publications: Bulletin, newsletter
Activities: Traveling exhibitions organized and circulated

OXFORD

M UNIVERSITY OF MISSISSIPPI, University Museums, University Ave and Fifth St, 38677. Tel 601-232-7073. *Dir* Valerie V Baybrooke; *Registrar* Jill Thomas; *Honorary Cur of Classics* Lucy Turnbull; *Honorary Cur Millington-Barnard Coll* A B Lewis
Open Tues - Sat 10 AM - 4 PM, Sun 1 - 4 PM, cl Mon. No admis fee. Estab 1977 to collect, conserve and exhibit objects related to history of the University of Mississippi and to the cultural and scientific heritage of the people of the state and region. Main gallery contains 300 sq ft with 12 ft ceilings for permanent collections; the temporary wall hung exhibits has 800 sq ft with 18 ft ceilings for temporary exhibits; Meeting room has 1100 sq ft for temporary wall hung exhibits; each of the four galleries of the Mary Buie Museum contains 400 sq ft for permanent collection.
Mem: 75; dues student $10, individual $15, family $25, contributing $50, patron $100 up
Income: $70,000 (financed by membership and state appropriation)
Collections: Theora Hamblett Collection (paintings, glass, drawings); Millington-Barnard Collection; David Robinson Collection of Greek and Roman antiquities; antique dolls; Victorian memorabilia
Exhibitions: (1980) Archaeology in the Past, Present and Future; Conservation: A Future for the Past; Court Houses: A Photographic Document; Annabelle Meacham paintings; William Nichols Architecture; Southern Realism; Western Carolina Drawing Invitational; World War I Posters; (1981) Artist-Artisan Folkroots; I Shall Save One Land Unvisited (southern photographers); Sea, Earth and Sky: the Art of Walter Anderson; Soviet Exchange Exhibition
Publications: Newsletter, quarterly
L Library, University Ave and Fifth St, 38677.
Open to members, students, researchers for reference
Library Holdings: Vols 600; Per subs 7
Special Subjects: Graphic Arts, Art History, Victorian Decorative Arts, American Art, Philosophy of Art

PASCAGOULA

O SINGING RIVER ART ASSOCIATION INC, L & N Railroad Depot Gallery, PO Box 262, 39567. *Pres* W A Dobbs; *VPres* Gay Thornhill; *Secy* Mrs Harold Jones
Open Mon - Sat 11 AM - 3 PM. No admis fee. Estab 1964 to promote and encourage interest in art and exhibition art works. Gallery exhibits members works in an old railroad station restored as Bicentennial project 1976. Average Annual Attendance: 2000 - 3000. Mem: 125; dues $5 and up, $10 and contributions; monthly meetings second Thurs
Income: $1100 (financed by membership and commissions on sales)
Collections: Paintings by local prominent artists, some purchase prize winners, some by memorial gifts; some donations by artists
Exhibitions: Exhibitions on a six week rotating basis
Publications: Members newsletter, monthly
Activities: Classes for adults; educational workshops; lect open to public; gallery talks; competitions; scholarships; lending collection contains cassettes, film strips, 200 lantern slides, original art work, original prints, paintings, phonorecords, slides; sales shop sells original art, prints, reproductions
L Library, PO Box 262, 39567.
Open to members only for reference
Library Holdings: Vols 50

RAYMOND

M HINDS JUNIOR COLLEGE, Marie Hull Gallery, 39154. Tel 601-857-5261, Ext 274. *Dir* Bob A Dunaway
Open Weekdays 9 AM - 3 PM. No admis fee. Estab 1971 as a community service and cultural agent for the visual arts. Main gallery measures 60 x 60 ft; an adjacent gallery 8 x 45 ft; reception area 15 x 25 ft. Average Annual Attendance: 2500
Income: $700 (financed by Art Department budget)
Collections: †Permanent collection of state artist, with 125 pieces in prints, sculptures and paintings
Exhibitions: The gallery sponsors 4 exhibits during college session, September to May
Activities: Lect open to the public; gallery talks; tours; competitions; individual paintings and original objects of art lent to faculty and staff offices on three campuses; lending collection contains original art works

TOUGALOO

TOUGALOO COLLEGE
M Art Collection, 39174. Tel 601-956-4941, Ext 327. *Pres* Dr George A Owens; *Academic Dean* Dr Nathaniel Pollard; *Photographer* Bruce O'Hara
Open Wed 2 - 5 PM, Sun 1 - 4 PM, and by appointment. No admis fee. Estab 1963 to service the community and the metropolitan Jackson area. Located in Student Union Building and Library. Average Annual Attendance: 1000
Income: Financed by endowment and department budget
Collections: †Afro-American; African; International Print Collection with emphasis on European art; New York School (abstract, expressionism, minimal art, surrealism)
Exhibitions: African Collection; Afro-American Collection; AMISTAD II (originated at Fisk University, Nashville); faculty and student shows, local artists
Publications: Catalog; newspaper of special events
Activities: Dramatic programs; lect open to public, 1 - 2 visiting lectr per year; concerts; gallery talks; tours by appointment; exten dept; individual paintings and original objects of art lent to libraries, universities and museums; lending collection contains 8000 lantern slides, 600 original art works, 300 original prints, 120 paintings, 100 sculpture, industrial designs and typography; originate traveling exhibitions

L Library, 39174. *Librn* Juanetta Roach
Open to students and faculty
Library Holdings: Vols 80,000; Per subs 426
Collections: Tracy Sugerman (wash drawings, civil rights studies 1964)

TUPELO

C BANK OF MISSISSIPPI, 1 Mississippi Plaza, Spring & Troy, PO Drawer 789, 38801. Tel 601-842-6661. *Pres* J W Collins
Open 9 AM - 4:30 PM. Estab to encourage local artists and provide cultural enrichment for customers and friends
Purchases: $500
Collections: Oils, prints, watercolors
Activities: Grants available

L LEE COUNTY LIBRARY, 219 Madison, 38801. Tel 601-844-2377. *Chmn Board of Trustees* Carol S Leake; *Dir* Betty R Kemp; *Technical Services Librn* Barbara Anglin; *Children's Librn* Marion Cagle
Open Mon - Thurs 9 AM - 8PM, Fri & Sat 9 AM - 5 PM, cl Sun. Estab 1941 to provide books and other sources of information to serve the intellectual, recreational and cultural needs of its users. Maintains art gallery; The Mezzanine Gallery and Helen Foster Auditorium are used as exhibit space for works by University Art students, local professional artists and traveling exhibitions
Income: $358,009 (financed by city, state and county appropriations)
Library Holdings: Vols 151,354; Per subs 147; AV—Cassettes, motion pictures, rec; Other—Framed reproductions
Collections: The Tupelo Gum Tree Festival purchase prizes, these include paintings and pottery
Activities: Book traveling exhibitions

UNIVERSITY

M UNIVERSITY OF MISSISSIPPI, University Gallery,* Fine Arts Center, 38677. Tel 601-232-7193. *Dir* Margaret Gorove
Open daily 8:30 AM - Noon & 1 - 4:30 PM. No admis fee. Estab 1954 as a teaching gallery. Average Annual Attendance: 2000
Income: Financed by state appropriation
Collections: Former faculty and student work; some work bought from traveling exhibitions
Publications: Gallery Schedule, yearly
Activities: Lect open to public, 1-2 visiting lectrs per year; gallery talks; individual paintings and original objects of art lent to departments within the University Complex; lending collection contains original art works, original prints, paintings and sculpture

MISSOURI

CAPE GIRARDEAU

L SOUTHEAST MISSOURI STATE UNIVERSITY, Kent Library, 63701. Tel 314-651-2230. *Documents & Reference Librn* Duane Ed Henricks
Open daily. Exhibition areas on second and third levels; Atrium gallery on fourth level. The Jake K Wells Mural, 800 sq ft covers the West wall of the library foyer, one of the largest murals in Missouri, it depicts the nature and the development of the Southeast region of the state
Library Holdings: Vols 300,000; Per subs 2500
Collections: Charles Harrison Collection (rare books including some of the finest examples of the book arts); books and manuscripts from the 13th to the 20th century
Exhibitions: MidAmerica Arts Alliance exhibits: A Second Chance, photographs by Solomon Butcher: 1886-1912; 500 Years of Botanical Illustration; IBM exhibit: Leonardo daVinci Inventions; Alberto Burri Prints; Missouri Arts Council touring exhibits; French Cultural Services, New York; touring shows

COLUMBIA

L DANIEL BOONE REGIONAL LIBRARY, 100 W Broadway, PO Box 1267, 65205. Tel 314-443-3161. *Dir* Gene Martin
Open Mon - Thurs 9 AM - 9 PM, Fri 9 AM - 6 PM, Sat 9 AM - 5 PM, Sun 1 - 5 PM. Estab 1959
Library Holdings: Micro—Reels; AV—Cassettes, fs, motion pictures, rec, slides; Other—Framed reproductions, original art works, pamphlets, photographs, sculpture
Exhibitions: Touring exhibits through the Missouri State Council on the Arts, exhibits by local artists through the year

O STATE HISTORICAL SOCIETY OF MISSOURI, Hitt and Lowry Sts, 65201. Tel 314-443-3165. *Dir* Dr Richard S Brownlee; *Cur* Sidney Larson
Open Mon - Fri 8 AM - 4:30 PM. No admis fee. Estab 1898 to collect, preserve, make accessible and publish materials pertaining to the history of Missouri and Western America. Average Annual Attendance: 800. Mem: 14,000; dues $2; annual meeting held in the fall
Income: Financed by state appropriation
Collections: Works by Thomas H Benton, George C Bingham, Karl Bodmer, Fred Geary, Carl Gentry, William Knox, Roscoe Misselhorn, Frank B Nuderscher, Charles Schwartz, Fred Shane, Frederick Sylvester; contemporary artists collection containing work of over fifty outstanding Missouri related artists; original cartoon collection of works by Tom Engelhardt, Daniel Fitzpatrick, Don Hessee, Bill Mauldin, S J Ray and others
Publications: Missouri Historical Review, quarterly

L Library, Hitt and Lowry Sts, 65201. *Librn* Richard S Brownlee
Open to public
Library Holdings: Vols 420,000; Per subs 200
Special Subjects: Missouri and the midwest
Collections: J Christian Bay Collection; Eugene Field Collection; Mahan Memorial Mark Twain Collection; Bishop William Fletcher McMurray Collection; Francis A Sampson Collection of rare books

M STEPHENS COLLEGE, Lewis James and Nellie Stratton Davis Art Gallery, 65201. Tel 314-442-2211, Ext 302. *Dir & Head Art Dept* Gardiner McCauley
Open Sept 10 - May 10, Mon - Fri 8 AM 5 PM. No admis fee. Estab 1964 to provide exhibitions of art for the general interest of the local community and for the education of the student body in general. Average Annual Attendance: 7000
Income: Operating budget $4000 (financed by endowment)
Purchases: $250
Collections: Modern paintings; †modern graphics; primitive sculpture
Activities: Lect open to the public, 6 vis lectr per yr; gallery talks; exhibitions

UNIVERSITY OF MISSOURI

M Museum of Art and Archaeology, 1 Pickard Hall, 65211. Tel 314-882-3591. *Dir* Osmund Overby; *Asst Dir* Ruth E Witt; *Cur Renaissance & Modern ARt* Richard Baumann; *Cur Ancient Art* Jane C Biers; *Assoc Cur South Asian Art* Sarla Nagar; *Assoc Cur American & Contemporary Art & Registrar* Harold Nelson; *Assoc Cur Exhib* Jeffrey Wilcox; *Assoc Cur Conservation* Maura Cornman; *Asst Cur* John Huffstot
Open Tues - Sun 12 - 5 PM, cl Mon and Holidays. No admis fee. Estab 1957 to exhibit a study collection for students in Art History and Archaeology; a comprehensive collection for the enjoyment of the general area of Missouri. Nine separate galleries, each devoted to specific collections. Average Annual Attendance: 16,000. Mem: 675; dues family $15
Income: $166,000 (financed by membership, and state appropriation)
Purchases: $35,000
Collections: †Ancient Art—Egypt, Near and Middle East, Greek and Roman; †Old Masters, painting and sculpture; †Early Christian—Byzantine and Coptic; †Modern paintings and sculpture; †Prints and drawings; Primitive—Oceanic, African, Pre-Columbian; Oriental—Chinese and Japanese; South Asian—Indian, Thai, Tibetan, Nepalese
Exhibitions: Changing exhibitions from permanent collections, mainly in the archaeological material of the Near East and in Prints and Drawings
Publications: Muse, annually
Activities: Docent training; lect open to public, 6 vis lectr per yr; tours; original objects of art lent to institutions; museum shop sells books, prints, reproductions and slides

L Museum of Art and Archaeology Library, 1 Pickard Hall, 65211.
Open to the public
Library Holdings: Vols 6000; Per subs 2; Other—Sales catalogs of three major auction houses; bulletins; exhibitions catalogs and annual reports of other institutions; coin catalogs and journals in Near Eastern Archaeology

L Art Archaeology and Music Library, 4D32 Ellis Library, Ninth & Lowry St, 65201. Tel 314-882-7634. *Librn* Marcia Collins
Open 8 AM - 5 PM, Mon - Fri. Estab 1841 to house material for the faculty and students of the University
Income: Financed by state appropriation
Library Holdings: Vols 65,000; Per subs 300; Other—Exhibition catalogs
Exhibitions: The Dance of Death in Book Illustration
Publications: The Dance of Death in Book Illustration by Marcia Collins; 1978 University of Missouri Library Series, No 27

FULTON

M WILLIAM WOODS COLLEGE, Art Gallery, 65251. Tel 314-642-2251, Ext 367. *Dir* Paul Clervi
Open Mon - Fri 9 AM - 4:30 PM. No admis fee. Estab 1967 to be used as a teaching aid for the Art Center. Maintains 3200 sq ft sky-lighted gallery with a mezzanine
Income: Financed by endowment
Activities: lect open to the public, 2 per year; gallery talks; scholarships

INDEPENDENCE

O JACKSON COUNTY HISTORICAL SOCIETY, 217 N Main St, 64050. Tel 816-252-1892. *Pres* Mrs William Coleman Branton; *Exec Dir* Mrs Kenneth L Graham; *Secy* Susannah Gentry
Mem: 2500; dues $10 - $100
Income: Financed by membership
Collections: Furnishing and interior decor at 1859 Jail Museum and John Wornall House; original portraits and other materials to 1830s; displays featuring pioneer life in the period of the westward expansion; selected memorabilia of Harry S Truman, 33rd President of the United States
Exhibitions: Mid 19th century Christmas displays and fine early handmade quilts at both museums; 19th century toys and special area history exhibits
Publications: Jackson County Historical Society Journal
Activities: Classes for adults and children; lect open to the public, 3 vis lectr per yr

L Research Library and Archives, Independence Square Courthouse, 64050. *Dir* Nancy Ehrlich
Open Mon - Thurs 11 AM - 3 PM. Estab 1960
Collections: Photograph collection for reference

M 1859 Jail Museum and Marshall's House, 217 N Main St, 64050. *Dir* Mrs J W Schwenk III
Open June, July & Aug, Mon - Sat 9 AM - 5 PM, Sun 1 - 5 PM, Sept - May Tues - Sat 10 AM - 4 PM, Sun 1 - 5 PM. Admis 75¢, children under 12 free. Estab 1959. Average Annual Attendance: 25,000
Activities: Elementary school tours emphasizing local and regional history; sales desk

M John Wornall House, 61st Terrace & Wornall Rd, Kansas City, MO 64113. *Dir* Janet Bruce; *Chmn* Ann Stapleton
Open Tues - Sat 10 AM - 4:30 PM, Sun 1 - 4:30 PM. Admis adults $1, children 50¢. Estab 1972 to familiarize people with how a farm family lived during the 1850s in early Kansas City. Average Annual Attendance: 11,580
Activities: Classes for children; docent training; lectures; traveling exhibitions organized and circulated; museum shop sells books, slides, postcards, pewter, herbs and other gift items

M HARRY S TRUMAN LIBRARY AND MUSEUM, 64050. Tel 816-833-1400. *Dir* Benedict K Zobrist; *Asst Dir* George H Curtis
Open Summer 9 AM - 7 PM, winter 9 AM - 5 PM. Estab 1957 to preserve and make available for study and exhibition the papers, objects and other materials relating to President Harry S Truman and to the history of the Truman administration. Gravesite of President Truman in the courtyard. Administered by the National Archives and Records Service of the Federal Government
Income: Financed by federal appropriation and federal trust fund
Library Holdings: Vols 45,000; Per subs 117; Micro—Reels; AV—A-tapes, motion pictures, rec, slides; Other—Clipping files, framed reproductions, prints, manuscripts, memorabilia, original art works, pamphlets, photographs, sculpture, original documents
Collections: Papers of Harry S Truman, his associates, and of officials in the Truman administration; Portraits of President Truman; paintings, prints, sculptures and artifacts presented to President Truman during the Presidential and Post—Presidential periods; original political cartoons; mural by Thomas Hart Benton
Exhibitions: Permanent and temporary exhibits relating to the life and times of Harry S Truman; the history of the Truman administration; the history and nature of office of the Presidency
Publications: Historical materials in the Truman Library

JEFFERSON CITY

M MISSOURI STATE MUSEUM, State Capitol, 65101. Tel 314-751-2854. *Dir* Clay R Bauske; *Cur* Bill Fannin
Open daily 8 AM - 5 PM, cl holidays. No admis fee. Estab 1920
Income: Financed by state appropriation, affiliated with Missouri Department of Natural Resources
Collections: Art murals by T H Benton, Berninghaus, Frank Brangwyn, N C Wyeth; historical material and natural specimens representing Missouri's natural and man-made resources; Indian artifacts
Exhibitions: Permanent and temporary exhibits
Publications: Pamphlets
Activities: Guided tours of Capitol; audio-visual presentations

JOPLIN

O SPIVA ART CENTER, INC, Newman & Duquesne Rds, Missouri Southern State College Campus, 64801. Tel 417-623-0183. *Dir* V A Christensen; *Exeuctive Secy* Pam Newby
Open Tues - Fri 10 AM - 4 PM, Sat 9 AM - Noon, Sun 2 - 5 PM, cl Mon & National holidays. Estab June 1959, inc 1969, as a non-profit, cultural center with the purpose of increasing knowledge and appreciation of the visual arts in Joplin and surrounding area; to offer educational classes, workshops, and to exhibit works of educational and artistic value. Average Annual Attendance: 15,000. Mem: 650; dues $5 - $1000; annual meeting in March
Collections: American Indian prints; early American glass; Mary Gregory glass; New Guinea sculpture; 19th century paintings
Exhibitions: Annual May Competitive Exhibition; Annual Photospiva Competitive; changing monthly exhibits including one-man and group
Publications: Calendar; newsletter
Activities: Classes in various phases of the visual arts for adults and children; lect; gallery tours; competitions

L Library, Newman & Duquesne Rds, 64801.
Art books for reference only

KANSAS CITY

O ART RESEARCH CENTER, 922 E 48th St, 64110. Tel 816-531-2067. *Coordr* Michael Stephens; *Education Dir* Virginia Hillix; *Public Information* Phyllis Henri; *Photographer* John Baird; *Photographer* Kathryn Howard; *Technical Dir* Jay Heuser
Open Sun - Thurs 3 - 7 PM. No admis fee. Estab 1966 as an independent collective of artists, stressing multi-disciplinary activity and open experiment in the Constructive Arts. Three temporary gallery spaces at 4725 Troost. Average Annual Attendance: 3000. Mem: 30; monthly meetings
Income: $55,000 (financed by grants)
Exhibitions: Process exhibitions are designed to show the working process of a systematic and programmatic artist: Steve Baer, David Barr, Alberto Biasi, Hartmouth Bohm, Lief Brush, Steve Conard, Chas DiJulio, Jay Heuser, Virginia Hillix, Jaya James Kern, Francois Morellet, Willi Otremba, Clark Rickert, Thomas Michael Stephens, Athena Tacha, Jon Thogmartin, Andreas Weininger, Elizabeth Willmott. Tenth Anniversary Exhibition and Symposium; International exhibitions: concerts, films, photographs, prints, symposia, visual poetry (80 artists from 15 countries); International Group Show; International Exhibition, Telic 1980 Group Collaborative Shows; Limen Light and Color; Reflection and Reflaction; Module and Manipulation
Publications: ARC Magazine, regularly; BioMechanic International Journals, annually
Activities: Classes for adults; lect open to public, 6 visiting lectr per year; concerts; gallery talks; films

L Library, 922 E 48th St, 64110.
Library open to members and students
Library Holdings: Vols 2000; Per subs 6
Special Subjects: Photography, Art science in art, art and politics, structuralist activity
Collections: Constructivist catalogs; films (abstract) by contemporary film-makers;

survey of historic and contemporary structural art, architecture, design in slides; also documentary films and video tapes

M AVILA COLLEGE, Art Gallery,* 11901 Wornall Rd, 64110. Tel 816-942-8400. *Dir* Martha Crow; *Pres* Sr Olive Louise Dallavis; *Academic Dean* G Richard Scott; *Chmn Fine Arts* William Louis
Open 10 AM - 4 PM. No admis fee. Estab 1978 to present the visual arts in a contemporary sense to the student community as well as the Greater Kansas City community. Gallery space 60 x 35 ft is maintained with carpeted floor and walls, an Artist-in-Residence studio, and track lighting. Average Annual Attendance: 2000
Income: Financed through school budget
Exhibitions: Susan Cochran, Laura Foster, Lynn Smiser, Eileen Troxell (ceramics and fiber); Martha Crow, Lynn Manos Huber, Judy Kennett, David Melby, Barbara Mueller, Hal Parker (drawings); Richard Gillespie (drawings and sculpture); Bruce Robinson (paintings); Michael Burks (photographs); Stephen Sidelinger (posters); Student Exhibition
Activities: Classes for adults; dramatic programs; lect open to public, 10 visiting lectrs per year; concerts; gallery talks

HALLMARK CARDS, INC
C Hallmark Collections, 25th & McGee, 64108. Tel 816-274-5298. *Cur* Keith F Davis
No admis fee. Circa 1947. Collection displayed in lobby exhibit area
Collections: Antique greeting cards and playing cards; antique toys and Christmas ornaments; drawings; paintings; photographs; prints; slide collection
Activities: Lect; purchase awards for art shows; fels through the Hallmark Foundation; individual objects of art lent to reputable institutions for temporary exhibitions; originate traveling exhibitions from antique cards in retail outlets, to large exhibitions in major museums
L Creative Library, 25th & McGee, 64108. Tel 816-274-5525. *Mgr Library Services* Susan G Duncan
Open to Hallmark personnel only. Estab to provide pictorial research
Income: Financed by state appropriation
Library Holdings: Vols 9000; Per subs 120; AV—Slides; Other—Clipping files

M KANSAS CITY ART INSTITUTE, Charlotte Crosby Kemper Gallery,* 4415 Warwick Blvd, 64111. Tel 816-561-4852. *Chmn Board of Governors* George E Powell; *Vice Chmn Board & Chmn Membership Committee* Mrs Robert G Evans; *Dir* Sherry Cromwell-Lacy
Open Tues - Fri 11 AM - 4 PM, Sat & Sun Noon - 5 PM. Estab 1963 to provide exhibitions of interest to the college and regional community
Exhibitions: Changing exhibitions
L Library, 4421 Warwick Blvd, Box 10360, 64111. Tel 816-561-4852. *Library Dir* Verna B Riddle
Open Mon - Thurs 8:30 AM - 5 PM and 6 - 10 PM, Fri 8:30 - 5 PM, Sun 1 - 6 PM. Estab 1924 to serve students and Faculty of Art Institute
Income: $61,863 (financed by Art Institute budget)
Library Holdings: Vols 28,400; Per subs 80; Other—Clipping files, exhibition catalogs, pamphlets
Special Subjects: Photography, Fine arts

L KANSAS CITY PUBLIC LIBRARY, Art & Music Department, 311 East 12th St, 64106. Tel 816-221-2685. *Librn* Harold R Jenkins; *Reference Supervisor* Christina Gradinger
Open Mon - Sat 9 AM - 5 PM, cl Sun. Established 1873
Income: $2,998,856
Purchases: $13,800
Library Holdings: Vols 30,000; Per subs 1315; Micro—Fiche, reels; AV—Motion pictures, rec, slides; Other—Clipping files, exhibition catalogs, framed reproductions, prints, memorabilia, pamphlets, reproductions

MID-AMERICA ARTS ALLIANCE
For further information, see National and Regional Organizations

O MUNICIPAL ART COMMISSION, City Hall, 415 E 11th St, 64106. Tel 816-274-1866. *Chmn* Richard L Berkley; *VChmn* Lynn Bauer; *Exec Dir* Patti Browne
Created by Charter in 1925; approves all works of art to become property of the city, whether by purchase or gift. Approves design of buildings, bridges, and other structures to be erected upon city property

WILLIAM ROCKHILL NELSON GALLERY OF ART
M Atkins Museum of Fine Art, 4525 Oak St, 64111. Tel 816-561-4000. *Dir* Ralph T Coe; *Sr Cur* Ross E Taggart; *Cur Oriental Art* Marc F Wilson; *Assoc Cur Oriental Art* Jeanne Harris; *Registrar & Cur Prints* George L McKenna; *Adminr Business and Operations* Sherwood Songer; *Cur 20th Century Art* Ellen R Goheen; *Dir Emeritus* Laurence Sickman; *Executive Dir Society of Friends* Dr Nicholas Pickard; *Dir Education* Ann Brubaker; *Designer & Cur Installations* Michael Hagler
Open Tues - Sat 10 AM - 5 PM, Sun 2 - 6 PM. Admis adults $1.50, children under 12 75¢, free Sun. Estab 1933 to enrich and enliven; present the arts of the ancient and modern world to the midwest and the country; develop activities relating to art education, the interpretation of the collections and their general enjoyment. Average Annual Attendance: 300,000. Mem: 7000; dues $15 - $30
Income: Financed by endowment, membership and gifts
Collections: †Burnap Collection of English pottery, Oriental ceramics, paintings, sculpture, bronze, Egyptian tomb sculpture, American painting, period rooms and furniture; Cloisters; †contemporary works of art; †impressionist painting; the finest Oriental furniture collection outside of the Orient; sculpture garden
Exhibitions: Christo's Wrapped Walkways Documentation; Richard Estes Urban Landscape; Monet's Water Lilies Triptych; various loan shows and displays of permanent exhibitions
Activities: Classes for adults and children; docent training; lect open to the public; concerts; gallery talks; tours; competitions; films; individual paintings and original objects of art lent to other museums, city institutions requesting display; traveling exhibitions organized and circulated; museum and sales shops selling books, magazines, reproductions, prints, slides; sales and rental gallery sells or rents original art; junior museum

L Kenneth and Helen Spencer Art Reference Library, 4525 Oak St, 64111. *Librn* open
Open Tues - Fri. For reference only
Library Holdings: Vols 25,000; Per subs 75; AV—Slides; Other—Clipping files, exhibition catalogs, Auction catalogues, international auction records
Special Subjects: Oriental Art
Collections: Bender Library is comprised of books on prints and drawings; Oriental Study houses collection of materials on Oriental art
O Friends of Art, 4525 Oak St, 64111. *Pres* Fred Beihl; *VPres* Mrs Don McGrath; *Secy* Rodger Wilkin; *Executive Secy* Joann Baldwin
Open Tues - Fri 9 AM - 5 PM. Estab 1934 as a non-profit organization supporting the Nelson Gallery and serving as a membership department. Mem: 7000; dues $15-$30; annual meeting Nov
Income: Financed by membership and contributions
Publications: Membership communication
M Junior Gallery and Creative Arts Center, 4525 Oak St, 64111. *Dir* Ann Brubaker
Open Tues - Sat 10 AM - 5 PM, Sun 2 - 6 PM. Estab 1960 to create a greater awareness of the world around us through art. Average Annual Attendance: 144,249
Activities: Creative art classes; adult sculpture, drawing, painting, Oriental brushwork and design classes; workshops; docent training; tours
L Junior Gallery Library, 4525 Oak St, 64111.
Open for children and guides
Library Holdings: Vols 2710; Other—Reproductions

MARYVILLE

M NORTHWEST MISSOURI STATE UNIVERSITY, DeLuce Gallery, 64468. Tel 816-582-7141. *Chmn Dept Art* Lee Hageman; *Cur Gallery Coll & Chmn Division Fine Arts* Robert Sunkel
Open Mon - Fri 1 - 4 PM. No admis fee. Estab 1965 to provide exhibitions of contemporary works in all media as part of the learning experiences in the visual arts. Gallery is maintained with 150 running feet exhibition space with high security, humidity controlled air conditioning and flexible lighting. Average Annual Attendance: 6000
Income: Financed by city appropriation
Collections: Percival DeLuce Memorial Collection consisting of American paintings, drawings, prints and decorative arts; some European furniture and prints
Exhibitions: Craft Multiples; Photography Exhibit; Print Exhibition; Regional artists
Activities: Lect open to public, 6 visiting lectrs per year; gallery talks; lending collection contains original art works, original prints, paintings and drawings

MEXICO

L MEXICO-AUDRAIN COUNTY LIBRARY, 305 W Jackson, 65265. Tel 314-518-4939. *Pres* Mrs Mark Aulbur; *Interim Dir* Mrs Karl Smith; *Secy* Mrs Harold Holsheiser; *Childrens Librn* Mrs Howard Mountcastle; *Acquisitions Librn* Violet Lierheimer; *Reference Librn* Christal Brunner; *Bookmobile Librn* Nancy Archer
Open winter hours, Mon - Thurs 9 AM - 9 PM, Fri & Sat 9 AM - 5:30 PM. No admis fee. Estab 1912 to provide library services to the residents of Audrain County, Missouri. Exhibit room with different exhibits each month; childrens department has a continuously changing exhibit
Income: $198,000
Purchases: $183,600
Library Holdings: Vols 112,529; Per subs 127; AV—Fs, Kodachromes, motion pictures, rec; Other—art print reproductions; newspapers
Exhibitions: Local Federated Womens Club sponsored a different exhibit each month during the fall, winter and spring, these included local artists, both adult and young people, and recognized artists of the area; The Missouri Council of the Arts also provide traveling exhibits that we display
Activities: Classes for children; story hour 45 minutes each Tuesday; individual paintings and original objects of art lent

SAINT CHARLES

M LINDENWOOD COLLEGES, Harry D Hendren Gallery, Department of Art, 63301. Tel 314-723-7152, Ext 241 or 946-6912, Ext 241. *Chmn* W Dean Eckert
Open Mon - Fri 9 AM - 10 PM, Sat 9 AM - 4 PM, Sun Noon - 4 PM. No admis fee. Estab 1969 as a college exhibition gallery. Gallery is approximately 3600 sq ft with skylight and one wall of side light. Average Annual Attendance: 4000
Income: Financed by endowment
Collections: Contemporary American and European prints in various media including works by Paul Jenkins, William Hayter, Picasso, Villon and others
Activities: Classes for adults; lect open to the public, 5-6 visiting lectr per year; gallery talks; tours; scholarships; original objects of art lent; lending collection contains photographs; traveling exhibitions organized and circulated through the Missouri State Council on the Arts; book shop

SAINT JOSEPH

M ALBRECHT ART MUSEUM, 2818 Frederick Blvd, 64506. Tel 816-233-7003. *Dir* Jim Ray; *Secy Registrar* Margo Prentiss
Open Tues - Fri 10 AM - 4 PM, Sat & Sun 1 - 5 PM, cl Mon. Admis adults 50¢, children 10¢, free to members. Estab 1914 to increase public knowledge and appreciation of the arts. Average Annual Attendance: 12,000. Mem: 600; dues $15 up; annual meeting second Wed in April
Income: $70,000 (financed by membership)
Collections: †Henry D Bradley Memorial Collection of Prints; Forrest C Campbell Collection of Prints; †Drawing America Collection; †Hax Memorial Collection; Eugene S Juda Jr Memorial Collection of American Engravings; Kemper Collection of American Paintings; Saint Joseph Photographic Collection of Architecture and Stained Glass Windows; William Toben Memorial Collection
Exhibitions: Thomas Hart Benton's Illustrations from Mark Twain; Drawing

Missouri 1976; Magic Carpets; Rugs of the Orient; Stained Glass Windows of St Joseph
Publications: Calendar of events, monthly
Activities: Classes for adults and children; lect open to public; competitions

L **Library,** 2818 Frederick Blvd, 64506.
Library open to museum members only
Library Holdings: Vols 500; Per subs 4

M **MISSOURI WESTERN STATE COLLEGE,** Fine Arts Gallery, Downs Dr, 64507. Tel 816-271-4282. *Pres* Dr M O Looney; *VPres* Dr Robert Nelson; *Chmn Department of Art* Dr William Eickhorst; *Gallery Coordr* Prof John T Hughes
Open 8 AM - 4:30 PM. No admis fee. Estab 1971 to bring an awareness of contemporary directions in art to students and to the community. Gallery is in front of building, next to theater; 120 ft long, 30 ft wide, with 25 ft high ceiling; rug paneling on walls; modern decor. Average Annual Attendance: 10,000
Income: Financed by state appropriation
Exhibitions: Invitational or juried art exhibitions
Activities: Classes for adults; lect open to public; gallery talks; tours; competitions; scholarships; exten dept; individual paintings and original objects of art lent to staff offices within college; lending collection contains original art works, original prints, paintings and sculpture; book traveling exhibitions

M **SAINT JOSEPH MUSEUM,** 11th and Charles, 64501. Tel 816-232-8471. *Dir* Richard A Nolf; *Asst Dir & Cur Pony Express Stables* Don L Reynolds; *Executive Secy* June M Swift; *Registrar* Bonnie K Harlow; *Conservator and Cur Coll* Marilyn S Taylor
Open April to Oct Mon - Sat 9 AM - 5 PM, Sun & holidays 2 - 5 PM, Oct to April Tues - Sat 1 - 5 PM, cl Mon, Christmas, Thanksgiving and New Years Day. Admis adults 50¢, children 12 and under 25¢. Estab 1926 to increase and diffuse knowledge and appreciation of history, art and the sciences and to aid the educational work that is being done by the schools of Saint Joseph and other educational organizations. Mini-gallery, usually for small, low security traveling exhibits. Average Annual Attendance: 100,000. Mem: 209; dues $15 and up; annual meeting Jan
Income: $100,000 (financed by membership, and city appropriation)
Publications: The Happenings (newsletter), bimonthly
Activities: Classes for children; craft program; lect open to public; museum shop selling books, reProductions, prints, slides, gift items

L **Library,** 11th & Charles, 64501. *Librn* Lucile Rush
Library open during museum hours for research purposes only
Library Holdings: Vols 5000; Per subs 40

SAINT LOUIS

O **ACADEMY OF PROFESSIONAL ARTISTS,** 4 Daniel Rd, 63124. *Executive Dir* Ruth Keller Schweiss
Estab 1968 to provide for the aesthetic needs of a human community irrespective of any and all persuasions by the exhibition of visual works of fine art; art work displayed in variety of locations. Average Annual Attendance: 100,000 - 500,000. Mem: 82; dues $35; annual meeting Jan
Income: Financed by membership and Arts & Education Council of St Louis
Exhibitions: Fine art by the membership presented in pub lic area, such as malls, banks, universities, government centers, etc
Activities: Lect open to members; competitions

O **ART AND EDUCATION COUNCIL OF GREATER SAINT LOUIS,** 40 N Kings Hwy, 63103. Tel 314-367-6330. *Chmn* Donald N Brandin; *Pres* Mrs John Peters MacCarthy; *VPres* Homer E Sayad; *Secy* Robert S Edwards
Estab 1963 to coordinate, promote and assist in the development of cultural and educational activities in the Greater St. Louis area; to offer generally, planning, coordinating, promotional and fund-raising service to eligible organizations and groups, thereby creating a valuable community-wide association. Mem: 130
Publications: Calendar of Cultural Events, monthly

M **CONCORDIA HISTORICAL INSTITUTE,** 801 DeMun Ave, 63105. Tel 314-721-5934. *Dir* Dr August R Suelflow
Open Mon - Fri 8 AM - 5 PM, cl national holidays. No admis fee. Estab 1847, affiliated with The Lutheran Church, Missouri Synod. Mem: Dues Life $300, corporation $200, organization $75. patron $35, sustaining $15, active $10
Collections: Church archives and vast historical materials; crafts; handcrafts; Reformation and Lutheran coins and medals; Works by Lutheran artists and paintings and artifacts for Lutheran worship
Exhibitions: Temporary exhibitions
Publications: Bulletins; Concordia Historical Institute, quarterly; Historical Footnotes, a quarterly newsletter; Regional Archivist, a newsletter and 'how to' serial for archives
Activities: Lect; guided tours; traveling exhibitions organized and circulated; sales shop selling new and used books; arts, crafts and gifts

L **Library,** 801 DeMun Ave, 63105. *Archivist & Librn* Roger Moldenhauer
Open Mon - Fri 8 AM - 5 PM. Estab 1847, to record and exhibit the panorama of Lutheran history in America and to provide reference and research services
Income: $155,000
Purchases: $1500
Library Holdings: Vols 57,200; Per subs 200; Micro—Cards, fiche, reels, prints; AV—A-tapes, cassettes, fs, Kodachromes, lantern slides, motion pictures, rec, slides, v-tapes; Other—Clipping files, prints, manuscripts, memorabilia, original art works, pamphlets, photographs, reproductions
Special Subjects: Lutheran history in America
Collections: Archives of various Lutheran church organizations; manuscript holdings of a large number of Lutheran leaders
Activities: Conferences on archives and history; receptions; Tours

C **EMERSON ELECTRIC COMPANY,** 8100 W Florissant, 63136. Tel 314-553-3614. *Dir Corporate Affairs* Robert B Crane
Estab to enhance the communities in which corporation is located. Emerson Electric Company supports: The Arts, St Louis, Missouri; Bingham Sketches, St Louis, Missouri; Business Committee for the Arts, New York, New York; Children's Art Bazaar, St Louis, Missouri; Greater St Louis Arts & Education Council, St Louis, Missouri; Indianapolis, Indiana Museum of Art; Neshoba Company Library, Philadelphia, Mississippi; St Louis Ambassador's Art & Fountain Foundation, St Louis, Missouri; St Louis Art Museum, St Louis, Missouri; St Louis Conservatory & Schools for the Arts, St Louis, Missouri; St Louis Museum of Science & Natural History, St Louis, Missouri
Purchases: $110,000

M **MISSOURI HISTORICAL SOCIETY,** Jefferson Memorial Bldg, 63112. Tel 314-361-1424. *Dir* Raymond Pisney; *Pres* J Terrell Vaughan; *Assoc Archivist* Beverly Bishop; *Cur* Gary Smith; *Cur Pictures* Judith Ciampoli; *Cur Educ* Linda Claire Kulla
Open daily 9:30 AM - 4:45 PM (library and archives cl Sun & Mon). No admis fee. Estab 1866 to collect and preserve objects and information relating to the history of Missouri and the Louisiana Purchase Territory. Average Annual Attendance: 400,000. Mem: 3000; dues from $25; annual meeting Sept
Income: Financed by endowment, membership and special events
Collections: †Early Midwestern arts and crafts; †manuscripts; †paintings; †photographs; †prints; †other museum objects
Exhibitions: Show of Curtis Indian photographs; special show of Lindbergh memorabilia
Publications: Bulletin, quarterly; newsletter, quarterly
Activities: Classes for children; lect open to public, 3-5 visiting lectr per year; gallery talks; tours; sales shop selling books, prints, slides, souvenirs, china, antique items, miniatures and doll houses

L **Library,** Jefferson Memorial Bldg, 63112. *Librn* Kathleen S Schoene; *Assoc Librn* Catherine Barber
Library open to members for reference; non-members must pay $3 per day
Library Holdings: Vols 120,000; Per subs 250

O **SAINT LOUIS ARTISTS' GUILD,** 227 E Lockwood, 63119. *Pres* Paul F Pattengale; *Secy* Ann Hysmith Wilson; *Treas* Erwin W H Knoeset
Open daily Noon - 4 PM, Sun 1 - 5 PM, cl Tues. No admis fee. Estab for the purpose of exhibiting art. Average Annual Attendance: 5000. Mem: 500; dues $35
Income: Financed by membership
Activities: Lect open to the public; competitions with awards

M **SAINT LOUIS ART MUSEUM,** Forest Park, 63110. Tel 314-721-0067. *Dir* open
Open Tues 2:30 - 9:30 PM, Wed - Sun 10 AM - 5 PM, cl Mon. No admis fee. Estab 1904, erected as Palace of Art for 1904 World's Fair; designed by Cass Gilbert in Beaux Art architecture; the main sculpture hall is fashioned after Roman Baths of Carcalla. Average Annual Attendance: 650,000. Mem: 8000; dues fellow $1000, associate $500, sustaining $100, contributing $50, participating $25, student $15
Income: $4,018,075 (financed by endowment, membership, county, grants, sales and contributions)
Collections: Holdings range from Egyptian to contemporary art. A new department of prints, drawings and photographs displays works from the Museum's 6000 holdings; outstanding art collection of works from Oceania, Africa, Pre-Columbian and American Indian objects; paintings emphasize Northern European works from the Renaissance to Rembrandt as well as colonial to contemporary American, French Impressionist and Post Impressionist and German Expressionist works; 20th century European sculpture, American and European decorative art; Chinese bronzes and porcelains
Exhibitions: (1980-81) Ansel Adams and the West; Joel Meyerowitz: St Louis and the Arch; Ceramics from the Collections of the St Louis Art Museum; Chuck Close; Currents 8, Alfred Lesslie; Marsden Hartley; Lichtenstein, 1970-80; Native American Civilizations Before Columbus; Persian and Mughal Miniatures from the Collections of the St Louis Art Museum; Prints from the Collections of the St Louis Art Museum; Printmaking in the Age of Rembrandt; The Realist Tradition; St Louis Collectors Photography Exhibitions; St Louis Silversmiths; Silver in American Life; Treasures from the Royal Photographic Society; Monet Triptych: Waterlilies
Publications: The St Louis Art Museum Bulletin
Activities: Classes for adults and children; docent training; lect; concerts; gallery talks; tours; individual paintings and original objects of art lent to other museums; traveling exhibitions organized and circulated

L **Richardson Memorial Library,** Forest Park, 63110. *Librn* Ann B Abid; *Cataloguer & Archivist* Gerald Baum; *Library Asst & Slide Collection* Cheryl Vogler
Open Tues 2:30 - 5 PM June-August, 2:30 - 9 PM Sept-May, Wed - Fri 10 AM - 5 PM. Estab 1915 to provide reference and bibliographical service to the museum staff and the adult public; to bibliographically support the collections owned by the museum
Income: Financed by endowment and city appropriation
Library Holdings: Vols 25,000; Per subs 300; Micro—Fiche, reels; AV—Lantern Slides, slides; Other—Clipping files, exhibition catalogs, pamphlets, photographs, reproductions, Art auction catalogs

M **SAINT LOUIS COUNTY DEPARTMENT OF PARKS AND RECREATION,** Laumeier Sculpture Park, 12580 Rott Rd, 63127. Tel 314-821-1209. *Executive Dir* Beej Niergarten-Smith; *Registrar* Ann McKerrow
Park open daily 8 AM - half hour past sunset; Gallery open Wed - Sat 10 AM - 5 PM, Sun 12 - 5 PM. Estab 1976 to exhibit contemporary sculpture by internationally acclaimed artists. Average Annual Attendance: 60,000. Mem: 250; dues corporate $250, patron $100, contributing $50, regular $20 and students $7.50; bi-annual meetings Jan & June
Income: $60,000 (financed by endowment, membership, donations, and affiliated with the Saint Louis County)
Collections: Outdoor contemporary sculpture collection by Anthony Caro, Jean Dubuffet, Richard Hunt, Ellsworth Kelly, Robert Morris, Louise Nevelson, George Rickey, David Von Schlegell, Richard Serra, Michael Steiner, Mark Di Suvero and Ernest Trova
Exhibitions: (1978) Americana Show, Childhood Memorabilia 1910 to 1960; Inside and Outside (sculpture exhibition); Jasper Johns Prints; Lithographs and Sculpture by Louise Nevelson; Recent Works by Ernest Trova. (1979) Artists Photographed by Alexander Liberman; Beginnings masquettes by Chuck Ginnever, Jerald Jacquard, Richard Hunt, Alexander Liberman, Clement Meadmore, Joe Moss, Claes Oldenburg, Beverly Pepper, Tony Smith, Athena Tacha; Environmental Environments (photographs and drawings); Richard Hunt Three Places at One

Time; Sculpture by Marisol

Activities: Classes for adults and children; dramatic programs; docent training; lect open to the public, 4 visiting lectr per year; concerts; gallery talks; tours; competitions with awards; original objects of art lent to established institutions; lending collection contains 40 sculptures; book traveling exhibitions; originate traveling exhibitions; sales shop selling books and posters

L SAINT LOUIS PUBLIC LIBRARY, Art Dept, 1301 Olive St, 63105. Tel 314-241-2288. *Librn* Joan Collett; *Chief Art Dept* Martha Hilligoss
Open Mon 9 AM - 9 PM, Tues - Sat 9 AM - 5 PM. Estab Art Department in 1912
Income: $13,000
Library Holdings: Vols 44,000; Micro—Fiche, reels; AV—Cassettes, motion pictures, rec, slides, v-tapes; Other—Clipping files, exhibition catalogs, framed reproductions, prints, pamphlets, reproductions, sculpture
Collections: Steedman Architectural Library

M UNIVERSITY OF MISSOURI, SAINT LOUIS, Gallery 210, Art Department, 8007 Nahral Bridge Rd, 63121. Tel 314-453-5975. *Chancellor* Arnold Grobman; *Chmn Art Department* Sylvia S Walters
Open Mon - Thurs 9 AM - 9 PM, Fri 9 AM - 5 PM. Estab 1972 to provide visual enrichment to campus and community. Average Annual Attendance: 5000
Income: $2000 (financed by state appropriation)
Exhibitions: Seven shows per year of artists such as Ansel Adams, Hockney, Lichtenstein, Pearlstein; specialized shows in Concept Art
Publications: Exhibition catalogs: Color Photography; Light Abstractions
Activities: Educ dept on art history; studio courses; lect open to public; book traveling exhibitions; originate traveling exhibitions

WASHINGTON UNIVERSITY

M Gallery of Art, Steinberg Hall, Box 1189, 63130. *Dir* Gerald D Bolas; *Asst Cur* Arline Leven; *Admin Secy* Barbara Franck
Open Mon - Fri 9 AM - 5 PM, Sat & Sun 1 - 5 PM. No admis fee. Estab 1879, present building opened 1960, for the students of Washington University and the community at large. A modern building containing two floors of gallery space for exhibit of the permanent collection and special exhibitions. Also houses a library of art, archaeology, architecture, and design
Collections: Emphasis on modern artists, including Miro, Ernst, Picasso, Leger, Moore; many Old Masters, 19th Century
Exhibitions: Leonard Baskin: Images of Man; Larry Bell: The Iceberg and its Shadow; Charles Eames: Iranian Locks; Hugh Ferriss Drawings: An Architect's Vision; Joe Goode: Recent Work; Joan Miro: The Development of a Sign Language
Activities: Lect open to public, 24 visiting lectr per year; traveling exhibitions organized and circulated

L Art and Architecture Library, Steinberg Hall, Box 1189, 63130. Tel 314-889-5268. *Librn* Imre Meszaros; *Circulation Supv* Julie Arnott; *Library Records* Betty Daniel; *Reserve Supv* Madeleine Illies; *Serials and Rare Books* Paula Ferrario
Open Mon - Thurs 8:30 AM - 11 PM, Fri 8:30 AM - 5 PM, Sat 11 AM - 6 PM, Sun 11 AM - 10 PM, cl nights and weekends during vacations and intersessions. Estab 1879 to support the academic programs of the three departments of the University: the School of Fine Arts, the School of Architecture, and the Department of Art & Archaeology. Circ 67,602
Income: $100,000 (financed through the University)
Purchases: $50,000
Library Holdings: Vols 60,000; Per subs 473; Micro—Fiche, reels; Other—Exhibition catalogs, pamphlets, reproductions
Special Subjects: Archaeology, Architecture, Costume Design & Construction
Collections: Baker Collection: 50 examples of fine binding; Bryce Collection: 576 volumes of early books on Architectural History; Eames and Young Collection: 273 volumes of 19th and pre-19th century imprints on architectural history; East Asian Art Collection; Exhibitions: Fashion Design of the 19th century; Eames & Young Architectural Library: Printed Books and Photo-Albums; Rare Book Room; Sorger Collection: 243 volumes of 19th century historic costume books with lithographs and hand-coloured fashion or costume plates, and 4 drawers of plates
Activities: Library tours

M WEBSTER COLLEGE, Loretto-Hilton Center Gallery, 130 Edgar Rd, 63119. Tel 314-968-0500. *Admin* Charles F Madden
Open Mon - Sat 10 AM - 4 PM, Sun 1:30 - 5 PM, cl Christmas. No admis fee. Estab 1966
Publications: Monthly news releases; exhibition catalogs; books
Activities: Classes for adults and children; lectures; gallery talks; guided tours; concerts; films; competitions; temporary and traveling exhibitions
L Library, 130 Edgar Rd, 63119.
Open to the public for researching on the premises
Library Holdings: Vols 300
Special Subjects: , 20th century paintings, prints, sculpture and photography

SPRINGFIELD

O SOUTHWEST MISSOURI MUSEUM ASSOCIATES INC, 1111 Brookside Dr, 65807. Tel 417-866-2716, Ext 2. *Pres* Mrs John White
Estab 1928 to inform and interest citizens in appreciation of art, and to maintain an art museum as an essential public institution. Mem: 1435; dues non-resident $6, resident $10; annual meeting second Wed May
Income: $25,000 (financed by membership)
Publications: Calendar, monthly, in cooperation with the Museum
Activities: Sales shop sells prints, reproductions, stationery

M SOUTHWEST MISSOURI STATE UNIVERSITY, University Gallery, 901 S National, 65802. Tel 417-836-5110. *Dir* Dianne Strickland
Open Mon - Fri 8 AM - Midnight, Sat 8 AM - 5 PM, Sun 2 - Midnight. No admis fee. Estab 1963 to present exhibitions of interest and educational worth to the university community and general public
Income: $4000 (financed by state appropriation)
Collections: †Contemporary and historical prints
Exhibitions: Six-State Regional Photography Competition; student and faculty shows; temporary exhibitions

Publications: Catalogs, 2 or 3 per year
Activities: traveling exhibitions organized and circulated

M SPRINGFIELD ART MUSEUM, 1111 E Brookside Dr, 65807. Tel 417-866-2716. *Dir* William C Landwehr; *Cur of Coll & Registrar* Greg G Thielen; *Cur Education* James D Weaver; *Asst Cur Art & Librn* Faith Ann Yorty; *Admin Asst to Dir* Mary Beth Williams
Open Tues - Sat 9 AM - 5 PM, Tues - Thurs 6:30 - 9 PM, Sun 1 - 5 PM, cl Mon. No admis fee. Estab 1928 to encourage appreciation and foster education of the visual arts. Museum has three temporary exhibition galleries totaling approximately 6500 sq ft; new wing opened in 1975 contains 400-seat auditorium and sales gallery. Average Annual Attendance: 100,000. Mem: 1450; dues $10; annual meeting second Wed in May
Income: $285,000 (financed by membership, city and state appropriations)
Purchases: $15,000 - $20,000
Collections: †American drawing and photography; †American painting and sculpture of all periods; †American and European prints of all periods with emphasis on the 20th Century
Exhibitions: The Etchings of Anders Zorn from the Collection of the Springfield Art Museum; The Lithographs and Etchings of Philip Pearlstein
Publications: Annual Accessions catalog and temporary exhibition catalogs; Watercolor USA, annually
Activities: Classes for adults and children; performing arts programs; lect open to public, 4-6 visiting lectr per year; concerts; gallery talks; tours; competitions; sales shop selling books, original art, prints
L Library, 1111 E Brookside Dr, 65807. *Asst Cur & Librn* Faith Ann Yorty
Open Tues - Fri 1 - 5 PM, Tues - Thurs 6:30 PM - 9 PM, Sat 1 - 5 PM. Estab 1946 to assist those persons interested in securing information regarding art and artists, craftsmen from ancient times to the present. Circ 750-800
Purchases: $2500
Library Holdings: Vols 4000; Per subs 47; AV—Slides; Other—Clipping files, exhibition catalogs, pamphlets

WARRENSBURG

M CENTRAL MISSOURI STATE UNIVERSITY, Grinstead Gallery, 74093. *Dir* Raeford Lewis
Open Mon - Fri 8 AM - 5 PM, cl holidays. No admis fee. Estab 1958 for the purpose of education through exhibition. Small university oriented gallery located in the Art Department. Average Annual Attendance: 2000
Income: Financed by state appropriation and university funding
Activities: Lect open to the public, 2 visiting lectr per year; gallery talks; competitions; traveling exhibitions organized and circulated

MONTANA

ANACONDA

O COPPER VILLAGE MUSEUM AND ARTS CENTER, Eighth and Main St, PO Box 29, 59711. Tel 406-563-8421, Ext 242. *Dir* Mary Dolan; *Admin Asst* Mary Blaskovich; *Gallery Hostess* Kathleen Papich; *Gallery Hostess* Helen Peterson; *Pres Board of Dir* Fred Boyer; *VPres* Millie Avery
Open Sun 1 - 5 PM, Wed 7 - 9 PM. No admis fee. Estab 1971 as Community Arts Center, gallery and local historical museum. Average Annual Attendance: 15,000. Mem: 370; dues family $3-$10; annual meeting Oct
Income: Financed by endowment, membership and city appropriation
Collections: Permanent collection
Exhibitions: Monthly exhibits
Activities: Classes for adults and children; traveling exhibitions organized and circulated; sales shop selling original art, reproductions, prints and pottery
L Library, Eighth and Main St, PO Box 29, 59711.
Library open to the public for reference
Library Holdings: Vols 30; Per subs 3
Special Subjects: Western History and Art

BILLINGS

O YELLOWSTONE ART CENTER, 401 N 27th St, 59101. Tel 406-259-1869. *Dir* Donna M Forbes; *Pres of Board* Larry Siegel; *Cur* Michael Connelly
Open Tues - Fri 11 AM - 5 PM (summer 10 AM - 4 PM), Sat & Sun Noon - 5 PM, Wed & Thurs 7 - 9 PM. No admis fee. Estab 1964 to offer a broad program of art exhibitions, both historical and contemporary, of the highest quality, to provide related educational programs. Two large galleries and four smaller ones in a large brick structure. Average Annual Attendance: 25,000. Mem: 850; dues $10 and up; annual meeting third Wed June
Income: $130,000 (financed by membership and county appropriations)
Collections: †Contemporary Print Collection; Mackay Collection of Olaf Wieghorst Painting; Mary Mulloy Carmichael Collection of 20th Century French Prints; Poindexter Collection of Abstract Expressionists
Exhibitions: The Archie Bray Permanent Collection; The Christmas Story in 14th-16th Century Art from the Metropolitan Museum of Art; Linda Conner; The Cowboy; Imogen Cunningham; Egyptian Children's Tapestries; the Sculpture of Jacob Epstein; the Sculpture of Gaston Lachaise; Prints of the Christmas Theme from the Collection of the William Rockhill Nelson Gallery, Atkins Museum; Shamans and Spirits, Eskimo Art; Western States Contemporary Crafts
Publications: Monthly exhibition announcements; newsletter, monthly
Activities: Classes for adults and children; docent training; lect open to public, 6 visiting lectr per year; gallery talks; tours; competitions; individual paintings and original art objects lent to museums and art centers; museum shop selling books, original art, reproductions, prints, jewelry and pottery

BOZEMAN

O **KETTERER ART CENTER,** 35 N Grand, 59715. *Dir* Ray Campeau; *Cur* Rand Honadel
Open Tues - Sun 1 - 5:30 PM. No admis fee. Estab 1969 as a Fine Arts Center with a gallery and art school
Income: Financed from sales of art and fees
Exhibitions: Monthly shows
Activities: Gallery talks; individual paintings lent; lending collection contains original art works, original prints, paintings and sculpture; traveling exhibitions organized and circulated; sales shop selling original art

MONTANA STATE UNIVERSITY

M **Museum of the Rockies,** 59717. Tel 406-994-2551. *Dir* Michael W Hager; *Construction Specialist* Jim Goosey; *Administrative Asst* Judy Weaver; *Registrar* Jan Postler; *Museum Asst* Jeri Walton
Open Mon - Fri 9 AM - 4:30 PM, 1 - 4:30 PM weekends. No admis fee. Estab in 1958 to interpret the physical and social heritages of the Northern Rockies region. Rotating gallery features monthly showings of local work and traveling exhibits
Collections: Works by R E DeCamp; Edgar Paxton; C M Russell; O C Seltzer; William Standing Geology; paleontology; archaelogy; history and western art
Publications: Quarterly newsletter; papers
Activities: Education department classes; guided tours; monthly gallery openings; lecture series

M **Fine Arts Gallery,** Bozeman, 59717. Tel 406-994-4501. *Pres* William Tietz; *VPres* S Knapp; *Dir* Dennis O'Leary
Open Mon - Fri 8:30 - 4:30, 1 - 4 PM, Sunday. No admis fee. Estab 1894 to present exhibitions of national interest. A new building with a small gallery space adjacent to offices and studio classrooms. Average Annual Attendance: 10,000
Income: Financed by university appropriation
Activities: Lectures open to the public, ten visiting lecturers per year; gallery talks; competitions

L **Creative Arts Library,** Cheever Hall, Creative Arts Complex, Bozeman, 59717. Tel 406-994-4091. *Librn* Ellen Lignell; *Slide Cur* Emily Gadd
Open Mon - Thurs 8 AM - 11 PM, Fri 8 AM - 5 PM, Sat 1 - 5 PM, Sun 1 - 11 PM. Estab 1974 to support the Schools of Architecture and Art. Maintains art gallery
Income: Financed by state appropriation
Library Holdings: Vols 15,000; Per subs 115; Micro—Reels; AV—Slides; Other—Clipping files, exhibition catalogs, framed reproductions, prints, reproductions
Special Subjects: Architecture
Exhibitions: Colored Lithographs: John Mix Stanley; Turn of the Century: Printing and Illustration; Books by Jim Koss; MIA Photographers Show; Montana Authors and Artists
Activities: Book traveling exhibitions

BROWNING

M **MUSEUM OF THE PLAINS INDIAN,** US Hwy 89, PO Box 400, 59417. Tel 406-338-2230. *Acting Cur* Rosemary Ellison
Open June - Sept, daily 9 AM - 5 PM, Oct - May Mon - Fri 10 AM - 4:30 PM, cl New Year's Day, Thanksgiving Day and Christmas. No admis fee. Estab 1941 to promote the development of contemporary Native American arts, administered and operated by the Indian Arts and Crafts Board, US Dept of the Interior. Average Annual Attendance: 80,000
Income: Financed by Federal appropriation and gifts
Collections: Contemporary Native American arts and crafts; historic works by Plains Indian craftsmen
Exhibitions: Contemporary Shoshone Arts and Crafts; permanent exhibit of historic Plains Indian arts; Plains Indian Metalwork; continuing series of one-person exhibitions
Publications: Continuing series of brochures for one-person shows
Activities: Gallery talks; traveling exhibitions organized and circulated; sales shop selling books, original art

BUTTE

M **COPPER KING MANSION,** 219 W Granite, 59701. Tel 406-792-7580. *Dir* Ann Cote Smith; *Deputy Dir* Robert Ross Smith
Open May - Sept Mon - Sat 9 AM - 9 PM, Sun mornings, winter daily 9 AM - 6 PM. Admis adults $2, students $1.50, children $1; tours at discount. Estab 1966 in 1884 mansion built by Senator W A Clark
Collections: Glass (crystal and cut glass); paintings; porcelains; sculpture; silver; Victorian furniture
Activities: Classes for adults and children; lect; gallery talks; guided tours; films; book traveling exhibitions; sales shop selling arts and craft items

DILLON

M **WESTERN MONTANA COLLEGE,** Art Gallery, 59725. Tel 406-683-7232. *Dir* Jim Corr
Open Mon - Fri 8 AM - 10 PM, Sat 2 - 4 PM, Sun 7 - 10 PM. No admis fee. Estab 1970 to display art works of various kinds, used as an educational facility. Art Gallery located in the College library. Average Annual Attendance: 5000
Income: Financed through college funds
L **Library,** 59725. *Librn* Ken Cory
Library open to the public
Library Holdings: Vols 80,000; Per subs 280

GREAT FALLS

M **C M RUSSELL MUSEUM,*** 1201 Fourth Ave N, 59401. Tel 406-452-7369. *Dir* Ray W Steele
Open Mon - Sat 10 AM - 5 PM, Sun 1 - 5 PM, cl Mon during winter. Estab 1953. Museum includes Russell's original studio. Average Annual Attendance: 50,000. Mem: Dues sponsor $500, sustaining $100, supporting $50, associate $35, non-resident and family $20, student $2
Income: $125,000 (financed by operating budget)
Collections: Works by Charles M Russell and other Western works, historical and contemporary
Exhibitions: Traveling exhibitions in contemporary arts; more than a dozen exhibitions are offered yearly, along with related programs within the arts
Activities: Creative dramatics; creative workshops; children's theatre; film program; Arts-Science Fair; Annual C M Russell Auction; traveling exhibitions organized and circulated; gift shop selling books, reproductions, jewelry

HELENA

O **ARCHIE BRAY FOUNDATION,*** 2915 Country Club, 59601. Tel 406-442-2521. *Resident Dir* Kurt Weiser
Open Mon - Sat 9 AM - 5 PM. No admis fee. Estab 1951 to make available a fine place to work for all interested in the ceramic arts. Art gallery is maintained
Income: Self-supporting with occasional aid from National Endowment and State Art Council
Collections: Works by Cushing, Ferguson, Hamady, Higby, Leach, McKinnel, Rhodes, Shanery, Turner, Voulkos
Exhibitions: Resident Potters Show; shows of other outstanding potters
Activities: Classes for adults and children; resident potter program; lect open to the public, 2-3 visiting lectrs per year; lending collection of original art works; traveling exhibitions organized and circulated; sales shop selling original pottery

L **Library,*** 2915 Country Club, 59601. *Librn* David Cornell
Open to resident potters and students
Library Holdings: Vols 300; Per subs 3

O **MONTANA HISTORICAL SOCIETY,** 225 N Roberts, 59601. Tel 406-449-2694. *Dir* Dr Robert Archibald; *Pres* Eric J Myhre; *VPres* Randall Swanberg; *Secy* Joseph E Reber; *Business Mgr* Linda Gamble
Open daily 8 AM - 5 PM (Sept - May), 8 AM - 8 PM (June - August). No admis fee. Estab 1865 to collect, preserve and present articles relevant to history and heritage of Montana and the Northwest. C M Russell Art Gallery, western artists; Poindexter Gallery, contemporary revolving art shows; Haynes Gallery, collection of exceptional western art. Average Annual Attendance: 200,000. Mem: 11,000; dues $10
Income: $512,000 (financed by membership, state appropriation and donations)
Purchases: $400,000
Collections: †Haynes Collection of Art and Artifacts; MacKay Collection of C M Russell Art; Poindexter Collection of Contemporary Art
Exhibitions: Annual Christmas Show and Sale; Haynes Gallery Opening; monthly contemporary art shows
Publications: Montana, Magazine of Western History, quarterly; Montana Post (newsletter), quarterly
Activities: Classes for adults and children; docent training; lect open to public, 2 visiting lectr per year; gallery talks; special guided tours; individual painting and original objects of art lent only with approval of Board of Trustees; traveling exhibitions organized and circulated; sales shop selling books, magazines, original art, prints, reproductions, slides, sculpture, pottery and bronzework

L **Library,** 225 N Roberts, 59601. *Art Cur* Mike McCourt; *Photographs* Lori Morrow
For reference and research only
Library Holdings: Vols 5000; Per subs 100
Collections: Newspaper Collection; Photographic Collection

KALISPELL

O **HOCKADAY CENTER FOR THE ARTS,** Flathead Valley Art Association, Second Ave East and Third St, Box 83, 59901. Tel 406-755-5268. *Dir* John Brice; *Secy* Sue Rolfing
Open Tues - Sat 10 AM - 5 PM. No admis fee. Estab 1968 to foster and encourage a growing interest in and understanding of all the arts; to provide the opportunity to take a place in the main current of the arts today, as well as to observe and learn from the arts of the past. Center is housed in the former Carnegie Library near downtown Kalispell; has two spacious exhibition galleries and a sales gallery. Mem: Dues benefactor $50; patron $25; family $20; individual $10; student $5; senior citizen $5
Income: Financed by membership, county and city funds, state grants, fund raisers and the Kalispell Art Show and Auction
Collections: Main collection includes eight portrait studies by Hugh Hockaday, the center's late namesake, as well as several other of his works
Exhibitions: Changed monthly; include a variety of art forms from Japanese posters to fabric sculptures by Dana Boussard; annual juried art competition with awards History of Art through Printmaking; New Artists (work by local high school students); Six Women, Six Views (local women selected by jury); Watercolor USA
Publications: Bulletin, monthly to members
Activities: Classes for adults and children; drama programs; pottery lab with full-time potter; gallery talks open to public; annual film tour

L **Library,** Second Ave, East and Third St, 59901.
Library Holdings: Vols 100

MILES CITY

O CUSTER COUNTY ART CENTER, PO Box 1284, 59301. Tel 406-232-5841. *Pres* Syd Sonneborn; *VPres* Jess Stickney; *Secy* Kathy Doedon; *Dir* Michael Shaneour
Open Tues- Sun 1 - 5 PM. No admis fee. Estab 1977 to provide an arts program of exhibits and workshops to Southeastern Montana. Maintains The Water Works Gallery, located in the old Miles City pumping plant holding tanks; pottery workshop; printing workshop. Average Annual Attendance: 10,000. Mem: 389; annual meeting Jan
Income: $30,000 (financed by endowment, membership, city and state appropriation
Exhibitions: Custer County Art Show
Publications: Newsletter, monthly
Activities: Classes for adults and children; docent training; lect open to the public, 4 visiting lectr per year; gallery talks; tours; competitions; book traveling exhibitions; originate traveling exhibitions; sales shop selling books, magazines and original art

MISSOULA

M MUSEUM OF THE ARTS FOUNDATION, Missoula Museum of the Arts, 335 N Pattee, 59801. Tel 406-728-0447. *Pres* Carol Orr; *VPres* Jim Sturnaman; *Secy* Patricia Dunkum; *Dir* David C Hunt; *Cur* Lawrence E Eick; *Executive Secy* Billie Blom
Open Mon - Sat Noon - 5 PM. No admis fee. Estab 1975 as public, visual arts facility serving the city and county of Missoula with rotating exhibits, classes, City Spirit-Cultural Commission events. Housed in renovated Carnegie Library (1903) featuring soft-panel covered walls; moveable track lighting; approx 3500 sq ft of exhibits space on two floors; fire and security alarm systems; meeting rooms. Average Annual Attendance: 16,000. Mem: 450; monthly meetings of board on fourth Thurs, monthly meetings of County trustees on second Wed, annual meeting in May
Income: $65,000 (financed by membership and annual permissive mill levy by Missoula County)
Exhibitions: Average of twenty exhibitions, including local, regional, national; local or state juried shows in crafts, painting, photography and printmaking
Publications: Exhibition catalogs; FOCUS, monthly membership newsletter; mailers and posters advertising shows
Activities: Classes for adults and children; lect open to public, 6 - 8 visiting lectr per year; gallery talks; tours; competitions; prize and purchase awards; book traveling exhibitions 4 - 8 per year; originate traveling exhibitions

M UNIVERSITY OF MONTANA, Gallery of Visual Arts, 59801. Tel 406-243-4181. *Chmn Dept* Ken D Little; *Prof in Charge* Mary Warner; *Gallery Clerk* Gayl Teichert
Opem Mon - Fri summer and academic year, 12 - 5 PM. No admis fee. Estab 1970 to provide exhibit space for students and faculty of the Art Department at the University of Montana and for periodical showings of the Universitys' permanent art collection; to sponsor outside exhibitions in an effort to acquaint the community and the university with significant contemporary artists nationwide; to provide guest lecturers to the community. Gallery covers 60 x 40 ft exhibit space with spot and flood lighting, moveable panels and 14 ft ceilings. Average Annual Attendance: 10,000
Income: $3000 (financed by city and state appropriation)
Collections: Dana Collection; Poindexter Collection
Exhibitions: Faculty, student and traveling exhibitions are shown in both galleries; shows from the permanent collection
Activities: Lect open to the public, 5 vis lectr per yr; competitions; Scholarships offered; original objects of art lent; lending collection contains Kodachromes

PRYOR

M CHIEF PLENTY COUPS STATE MONUMENT, Box 35, 59066. *Dir* Robert Wambaug; *Deputy Dir* Fletcher Newby; *Cur* Harley R Sorrells
Open Mon - Sat 9 AM - 5 PM, Sun Noon - 5 PM. No admis fee. Estab 1932
Income: Financed by state appropriation; affiliated with Montana Fish, Wildlife and Parks
Collections: Ethnographic materials of the Crow Indians; paintings; drawings; prehistoric artifacts
Activities: Sales shop sells books, prints, sculpture, and handicrafts of the Crow Indians

SAINT IGNATIUS

M FLATHEAD INDIAN MUSEUM, PO Box 460, 59865. Tel 406-745-2951. *Owner* L Doug Allard; *Mgr* Martena Savage
Open daily 9 AM - 5:30 PM. No admis fee. Estab 1975 for American Indian Art. Average Annual Attendance: 10,000
Income: $8000 (financed by private funds)
Collections: Allard Collection of American Indian Art

SIDNEY

M J K RALSTON MUSEUM AND ART CENTER, 221 Fifth Ave SW, PO Box 50, 59270. Tel 406-482-3500. *Chmn County Museum Board* Dave Torrence; *Dir* Linda K Mann
Open Tues - Fri & Sun 1 - 5 PM, cl Mon & Sat. No admis fee. Estab 1972 to preserve history of area and further interest in fine arts. Average Annual Attendance: 4500.
Mem: 200; dues $5; annual meeting March
Income: Financed by County and State appropriations
Exhibitions: (1979-80) Coe: Oils; Japanese Prints; Katz Photographs; Kuaalen: Oils; Northwest Enamelists; Original Prints; Tombstones Photographs
Activities: Classes for adults and children; dramatic programs; competitions; sales shop sells books, magazines, original art, reproductions, postcards, dolls, minerals and coins

L Willo Ralston Library for Historical Research, 59270. *Librn* Gary Thogerson
Open to the public for historical reference

SOMERS

M KALAMUNDA MUSEUM OF WESTERN ART, 1485 Montana Hwy 208, 59932. Tel 406-857-3802. *Pres* Cecil Smith; *VPres* Marie W Smith; *Secy* Rockwell L Smith; *Museum Attendant* La Priel Smith; *Museum Attendant* Raychelle R Smith; *Framer* Stephen L Smith; *Asst Framer* Carey Smith
Open daily 9:30 AM - 3 PM. No admis fee. Estab 1980 to promote and encourage national interest in Masterpiece Western and Genre Art. Maintains two four wall galleries: one gallery accomodates permanent collection and the other accomodates temporary exhibits
Income: Financed by endowment
Collections: †Buckaroo Artists of America; †Original Art by the Rare Brede Artists; †Work by Renown Painters and Sculptors
Publications: Art Service Associate, catalogue; Full Color Listing of Paintings and Prints
Activities: Individual paintings and original objects of art lent to state and national museums; lending collection contains paintings, photographs and sculpture; museum and sales shop selling original art, reproductions, prints and slides

NEBRASKA

CHADRON

M CHADRON STATE COLLEGE, Arts Gallery, Tenth and Main Sts, 69337. Tel 308-432-4451, Ext 317. *Coordr* Harry E Holmberg
Open Mon - Fri 9 AM - Noon, 1 - 4 PM. No admis fee. Estab 1967 to offer opportunities for students, faculty and local artists to present their works; to bring in shows to upgrade the cultural opportunities of students and the general public. Main gallery has space for traveling and larger shows; little gallery suffices for small shows. Average Annual Attendance: 5000
Income: Financed by college budget and state appropriation
Exhibitions: Arts and Crafts Fair; Bosworth, Rickenbach Exhibits; DaVinci Model show by IBM; Edges: Hard and Soft; Faculty Art Show; Former Students Works; Hands in Clay; Greg Lafler: Handmade Jewelry; Tony Martin: Ceramics and Crafts; Photographs of the Farm Security Administration; Roten Galleries: Graphics Show; National Cone Box Traveling Show; State of the Print; Student Art Show

CHAPPELL

L CHAPPELL MEMORIAL LIBRARY AND ART GALLERY, 289 Babcock, 69129. Tel 308-874-2626. *Head Librn* Doris McFee; *Asst Librn* Gladys Smith
Open Tues & Thurs 2 - 5 PM, 7 - 9 PM, Sat 2 - 5 PM. Estab 1935 by gift of Mrs Charles H Chappell
Income: Financed by city of Chappell
Library Holdings: Vols 10,390; Per subs 34
Collections: Permanent personal collection of art works from many countries, a gift from Mrs Charles H Chappell
Activities: Gallery talks; library tours

GERING

M SCOTTS BLUFF NATIONAL MONUMENT, Department of the Interior, Box 427, 69341. Tel 308-436-4340. *Supt* Robert L Burns; *Supv Park Ranger* Christopher M White; *Admis Officer* Sherry Shelbourn
Open day after Labor Day through May 29 8 AM - 4:30 PM, Memorial Day through Labor Day 8 AM - 8 PM. No admis fee for museum; fee charged for Summit Road. Estab 1919 for commemoration of the Oregon Trail. Gallery has three exhibit rooms: Oregon Trail Room, Landmark Room and William H Jackson Memorial Wing
Income: Financed by Federal Government
Collections: †Original watercolor paintings
L Library, Department of the Interior, Box 427, 69341.
For reference only
Library Holdings: Vols 100

HASTINGS

M HASTINGS MUSEUM, 1330 N Burlington Ave, 68901. Tel 402-463-7126. *Dir* Ed Bisaillon; *Pres Board Trustees* O J McDougal Jr; *Cur Exhib* Burton R Nelson; *Museum Coordr* Geraldine S Shuman; *Cur Astronomy* Elizabeth S Wasiluk; *Exhib Specialist* Jerome Dierfeldt
Open Mon - Sat 8 AM - 5 PM, Sun 1 - 5 PM. Admis adults 75¢, children (6-11) 25¢, tots free. Estab 1926 for a program of service and exhibits to augment and stimulate the total educative program of schools and the general public. Animal displays in natural habitat settings. Average Annual Attendance: 45,000. Mem: 1225; dues life $100, family $4, individual $2
Income: Financed by city appropriation
Collections: American Indian artifacts; glassware; Irma Kruse Collection; Richards Coin Collection
Publications: Yester News, monthly except July-August-Sept
Activities: Sales shop selling books and selected gift items

HOLDREGE

M PHELPS COUNTY HISTORICAL SOCIETY MUSEUM, N Burlington St, PO Box 215, 68949. Tel 308-995-5015. *Pres* Millard Johnson; *VPres* Eileen Schrock; *Secy* Faye Steven
Open June - Aug daily 2 - 5 PM, Sept - May daily 1 - 4 PM. No admis fee. Estab 1966 for preservation of County History and artifacts. Average Annual Attendance: 4000. Mem: 450; dues life $100, annual $5; annual meeting May
Income: $10,000 (financed by membership and County mill levy)
Collections: Agriculture equipment, China, furniture, historical items, photos
Exhibitions: Omaha International Exposition Art Display
Activities: Lect open to public; museum shop sells books

LINCOLN

O LINCOLN COMMUNITY ARTS COUNCIL, Room 508, Lincoln Center Bldg, 68508. Tel 402-477-5930. *Executive Dir* Jackie Hall; *Pres* Keith Heckman; *Sr Arts Coordr* Dixie Moss
Open 8:45 AM - 4:45 PM. Estab 1966 to promote and encourage the community at large and all its arts organizations to grow, develop, use all the resources available, avoid over-lapping of energy, money, talent and to enrich the entire community; clearing house for arts activities scheduling. Mem: 175; 60 groups; dues prorated; meetings monthly
Income: Financed by endowment, membership, city and state appropriation
Publications: Arts calendar; newsletter

M NEBRASKA WESLEYAN UNIVERSITY, Elder Gallery, 50th & Huntington, 68504. Tel 402-466-2371. *Dir* Betty Wallace
Open Tues - Fri 10 AM - 4:30 PM, Sat & Sun 1 - 4:30 PM. No admis fee. Estab 1966 as a cultural addition to college and community. Average Annual Attendance: 10,000
Income: Financed through College
Collections: Campus collection; †permanent collection of prints, paintings and sculpture
Exhibitions: Annual Fred Wells 10-state juried exhibition; Nebraska Art Educators; faculty show; students shows; other changing monthly shows
Activities: Classes for adults

UNIVERSITY OF NEBRASKA LINCOLN
M Sheldon Memorial Art Gallery, 68588. Tel 402-472-2461. *Dir* Norman A Geske; *Asst to Dir* Jon Nelson; *Dir Educational Services* Mrs A Douglas Anderson; *Dir Sheldon Film Theatre* Dan Ladely
Open Tues 10 AM - 10 PM, Wed - Sat 10 AM - 5 PM, Sun 2 - 5 PM. No admis fee. Estab 1888 to exhibit the permanent collections owned by the University and to present temporary exhibitions on an annual basis. These activities to be accompanied by appropriate interpretive programs. The Sheldon Gallery is a gift of Frances and Bromly Sheldon. Opened in 1963 it is the work of Philip Johnson. Facilities in addition to 25,000 sq ft of exhibition galleries include an auditorium, a print study, members room and an outdoor sculpture garden. Average Annual Attendance: 110,000
Income: Financed by endowment, state appropriation and Nebraska Art Association
Purchases: $30,000
Collections: †Frank M Hall Collection of contemporary paintings, sculpture, prints, drawings, photographs and ceramics; †Nebraska Art Association Collection of American paintings and drawings; Bertha Schaefer Bequest
Exhibitions: Annual Faculty Exhibition; Annual Undergraduate Exhibition; Prints and Drawings by Sigmund Abeles; Paintings by James Bama; Photographs by Cirrus Bonneau; Photographs by Jim Butkus; Paintings by John Dawson; Paintings and Drawings by Preston Dickinson; photographs by Elliot Erwitt; Of Dust Bowl Descent, photographs by Bill Ganzel; Kadinsky's Small Worlds, prints; Paintings, drawings and collages by Weldon Kees; Graphics by Michael Mazur; Fiberworks by Trudy Morgenstern; Photographs by Dave Read; Magic Carpets; Paintings and Drawings by David Routon; Graphics by Mark Tobey; Photographs by Kelly Wise
Publications: Exhibition catalogs, 2 per yr
Activities: Classes for adults; docent training; lect opento the public; tours; competitions; individual paintings and original objects of art lent to campus offices; traveling exhibitions organized and circulated; museum shop sells books, original art, prints, jewelry and ceramics
L Love Library, 13th and R Sts, 68588. Tel 402-472-2848; TWX 910-621-8232. *Asst Prof* K A Johnson
Open Mon - Thurs 7:30 AM - 11 PM, Fri 7:30 AM - 5 PM, Sat 10 AM - 5 PM, Sun 1:30 - 11 PM. Estab 1869 contains art books and periodicals to support the BA, BFA and MFA programs at the University
Library Holdings: Vols 20,000; Per subs 85; Micro—Cards, fiche, reels, prints; AV—A-tapes, cassettes, fs, rec, slides; Other—Exhibition catalogs
L Architecture Library, 13th and R Sts, 68588. Tel 402-472-1208. *Asst Prof* Kay Horton
Open Mon - Fri 8 AM - 5 PM, Sat 10 AM - 5 PM, Sun 6 - 10 PM. Architecture supports the College of Architecture. Circ 8700
Purchases: $13,000
Library Holdings: Vols 20,500; Per subs 132; Micro—Cards, fiche, reels, prints; AV—A-tapes, cassettes, fs, rec, slides; Other—Exhibition catalogs, photographs
Special Subjects: Architecture: community and regional planning
Collections: Architecture: Urban Documents Microfiche; Historic American Building Survey Measure and Drawings
O Nebraska Art Association, 68588. *Pres* Elwood N Thompson; *VPres* Mrs William T Griffin; *VPres* Dr Philip Heckman; *VPres* Congdon E Paulson; *Secy* Mrs Barbara Simon
Open Tues 10 AM - 10 PM, Wed - Sat 10 AM - 5 PM, Sun 2 - 5 PM, cl Mon. Estab 1888 as the Haydon Art Club, inc 1900 to study and prepare papers on art, to form a collection, to acquire a suitable art museum, to encourage young artists, to interest public school children and to attract industry and keep abreast of a growing city; a supportive organization to the Sheldon Memorial Art Gallery. Mem: 900; dues family $15; annual meeting May
Income: $18,865 (financed by endowment, membership)

Purchases: $15,000
Collections: Paintings, drawings, prints, photographs, crafts, sculpture
Publications: Annual report; exhibition catalog
Activities: Scholarships offered; individual paintings and original objects of art lent to corporations

MCCOOK

M HIGH PLAINS MUSEUM, 423 Norris Ave, 69001. Tel 308-345-3661. *Pres* Mrs Alan Redfern
Open daily 1:30 - 4:30 PM, cl legal holidays. No admis fee. Estab 1966 to preserve the items pertaining to the local history and to interpret them to the public. Museum is located in former Carnegie Library mission style building. New additions include complete pioneer kitchen; Railroad section (inside and out);complete Old Time Pharmacy. Morning tours by appointment. Average Annual Attendance: 8000. Mem: 230; dues sustaining $125, adults $5, children $2
Income: Financed by membership
Collections: Paintings made on the barracks walls of prisoner of war camp near McCook; paintings donated by local artists
Activities: Lect open to the public; gallery talks; tours; Book shop
L Library, 423 Norris Ave, 69001. *Dir* Dina McDonald Kanowicz
Open 1:30 - 4:30 PM, mornings by appointment. Estab 1966
Library Holdings: Vols 1082; AV—Cassettes; Other—Clipping files, framed reproductions, prints, manuscripts, memorabilia, original art works, photographs, reproductions
Collections: Russian and German bibles and books; Schoolbooks and novels in German

MINDEN

M PIONEER VILLAGE, 58959. Tel 308-832-1181. *Pres* Harold Warp; *Cur* Ruby Warp Nielsen
Open daily. Admis adults $3, children $1, children under 6 free; special rates to groups
Collections: Folk art; graphics; historical materials; paintings; sculpture

NEBRASKA CITY

M GAME AND PARKS COMMISSION, Arbor Lodge State Historical Park, Rural Route Two, 68410. Tel 402-873-3221. *Supt* Randall Fox; *Asst Supt* Kathleen Moore; *Dir* Eugene Mahoney
Open April 15 - May 24 1 - 5 PM, May 24 - Sept 1 10 AM - 8 PM, Sept 2 - Nov 3 1 - 5 PM. Admis adults 50¢, children 25¢. Estab 1923. Art collection of members of the J S Morton family and Outdoor Scenes spread through a 52 room mansion. Average Annual Attendance: 40,000
Income: $20,000 (financed by state appropriation)
Activities: Lect open to public; tours; awards, Arbor Day Tree plantings on April 22; sales shop sells books, Arbor Day Tree and stick pins and postcards

OMAHA

M CREIGHTON UNIVERSITY ART GALLERY, 2602 California St, 68178. Tel 402-449-2509. *Dir* Jim Butkus; *Chmn Fine & Performing Arts Dept* Donald A Doll
Mus estab 1973. Gallery handles 10 exhibits per academic year; space provided for student thesis exhibits
Collections: Ceramics; drawings; graphics; paintings; photography; pottery and sculpture
Activities: Lect open to the public

M JOSLYN ART MUSEUM, 2200 Dodge St, 68102. Tel 402-342-3300. *Dir* Henry Flood Robert Jr; *Assoc Dir* B M Fredrickson; *Cur of American Art* Holliday T Day; *Asst to Dir* Audrey S Gryder; *Registrar* Berneal Anderson; *Research Asst-Director's Office* Jeannie J Egan; *Admin* William Woodall; *Office Mgr* Cheryl Beam; *Cashier-Receptionist* Sherrl Urbanek; *Cur European Art* Open; *Cur Western Art* Open; *Cur of Education* Open; *Assoc Cur-Interpretation* Francine Werthmann; *Head Department of Registration & Preparation* Edward R Quick; *Asst Registrar* Janna Hoffman; *Public Relations* Barbara Wright; *Museum Shop* Evelyn Veach
Open Tues - Sat 10 AM - 5 PM, Sun 1 - 5 PM, cl Mon & holidays. Admis adults 75¢, children under 12 & sr citizens 25¢, members free. Joslyn Art Museum was incorporated 1928, opened 1931, to care for and expand the collections; offer exhibitions; promote education in and cultivation of the fine arts. Museum was a gift of Mrs Sarah H Joslyn in memory of her husband, George A Joslyn. Museum is a marble building covering a two-block area; contains ten large galleries with small exhibit areas surrounding a large central court and 1200-seat Witherspoon Concert Hall on the main floor. The concert hall is used for programs by major community music and cultural organizations. The ground floor includes exhibit areas, library, studios, lecture hall, museum shop, rental and sales gallery and offices. Mem: 5000; dues benefactor $2500, patron $1000, donor $500, sponsor $250, sustainer $100, associate $50, friend $30, family $20, individual $15, student $10; annual meeting 2nd Tues in Dec
Collections: American Art from Colonial to present; European Art from Middle Ages to present; Native American from pre-Columbian to present; works from the Orient and Ancient Mediterranean civilizations
Exhibitions: The Joslyn Biennial Exhibition, a juried show open to artists in a 22 state area around Nebraska, is held in even-numbered years; it includes paintings, sculpture and graphics; additions to the Museum's permanent collection are purchased from the exhibition. Temporary exhibitions include traveling shows of national significance, Joslyn-organized show, one-man and group shows in all media, student art
Publications: Annual Review; brochures; Guide to the Museum; monthly calendar (Sept - June); special exhibition catalogs
Activities: Creative and art appreciation classes for adults and children (pre-school through high school); special workshops; monthly film programs; special tour program of permanent collections and special exhibitions maintained for public

school children; lect and exhibition gallery talks; tours of the collections and special exhibitions; book traveling exhibitions

L **Art Reference Library,** 2200 Dodge St, 68102. *Librn* Mary Kellett
Library Holdings: Vols 17,000; AV—Slides 20,000; Other—Clipping files, pamphlets, circulating material of mounted pictures and folios, 140 vertical files
Collections: Maximilian-Bodmer Collection from the expedition of 1832-34, owned by Northern Natural Gas Company, Omaha, including over 400 watercolors by Karl Bodmer, over 100 works by Alfred Jacob Miller, and over 100 works by artists such as George Catlin, Frederick Remington and Charles Russell

L **NEBRASKA ARTS COUNCIL LIBRARY,** 8448 W Center Rd, 68124. Tel 402-554-2122. *Chmn* Wallace Richardson; *Vice Chmn* Marian Anderson; *Executive Dir* Robin Tryloff
Open Mon - Fri 8 AM - 5 PM. Estab circa 1970 to provide information on arts administration topics to our constituents
Income: $250 (financed by state appropriation and federal grants)
Purchases: $250
Library Holdings: Vols 500; AV—Motion pictures, slides, v-tapes; Other—Pamphlets
Publications: Artists-in-Schools - Communities Guidelines, annually; Guidelines, annually; Newsletters, bi-monthly
Activities: Grants to non-profit community organizations and schools for education projects related to the arts; workshops; lect open to public and some for members only, 2 - 3 visiting lectr per year; grant awards to non-profit organizations in Nebraska for arts projects

M **OMAHA CHILDREN'S MUSEUM, INC,** 515 S 18th, 68102. Tel 402-342-6163. *Pres* Clay Chandler; *VPres* Sheri Hofshire; *Secy* Maria Laas; *Dir* Karen Levin; *Museum Mgr* Daniel L Dixon; *Special Projects* Joletta Hoesing; *Education Specialist* Dorothy M Hill
Open Thurs - Sat 10 AM - 5 PM. Admis over 1 year old 75¢. Estab 1978 to provide hands-on Museum experience for children. Mem: 528; dues $10; annual meeting first Tues in May
Income: Financed by membership, admissions, donations from individuals and corporations
Exhibitions: Series of shows by local professional artists, children and some non-local; traditional gallery shows with related open studio experience
Publications: Bang, bi-monthly National Children's Museum Newspaper; newsletter, tri-monthly
Activities: Classes for adults and children; docent training; gallery talks; exten dept serves Greater Metro Omaha; book traveling exhibitions two per year; originate traveling exhibitions; museum shop sells books, educational games and toys

SOCIETY OF NORTH AMERICAN ARTISTS, INC
For further information, see National and Regional Organizations

UNIVERSITY OF NEBRASKA-OMAHA ART GALLERIES
M **New Gallery,** Annex 22, 133 S Elmwood Rd, 68101. Tel 402-554-2686. *Gallery Dir* Donald Bartlett Doe; *Asst Dir* Kent Rastede; *Dean College Fine Arts* C Murray North
Open weekdays 9 AM - 7:30 PM. No admis fee. Estab 1975 to heighten cultural and aesthetic awareness of the metropolitan and midlands area
Income: Financed by state appropriation
Exhibitions: (1979-80) Bruce Brand & Barbara Tebbitts, Paintings on Paper; Dan Christensen: Paintings in Seventies; Jack Damer, Recent Prints; David Keister Collection, (Printer's Proofs from Landfall Press); Warren Rosser: American Works, 1972-79; Stanley Tigerman - Architect; William Walmsley - Recent Prints; BFA Thesis Exhibit; Faculty Art Exhibit; Juried Art Competition; Student Competition
M **Administration Gallery,** Administration Bldg, Room 371, 68101. Tel 402-554-2420.
Open weekdays 8 AM - 5 PM. No admis fee. Estab 1967 to heighten cultural and aesthetic awareness of the metropolitan and midlands area. Average Annual Attendance: 14,000
Income: Financed by state appropriation
Purchases: $5000
Collections: University Visiting Printmaker's Collection
Activities: Lect open to public, 2 vis lectr per year; gallery talks; tours; competitions; scholarships

SEWARD

M **CONCORDIA COLLEGE,** Koenig Art Gallery, 800 N Columbia Ave, 68434. Tel 401-643-3651. *Dir* Richard Wiegmann
Open weekdays 8 AM - 5 PM, Sun 2 - 5 PM. No admis fee. Estab 1959 to provide the college and community with a wide variety of original art; both monthly exhibitions and permanent collection serve primarily an educational need; spacious gallery has additional showcases
Collections: Ceramics; †Contemporary Original Prints
Exhibitions: Jim Bass: Bronze Sculpture; Alberto Burri Prints 1959-1977; Antonio Frasconi, Graphic Artist; Oscar Howe Paintings; Color Prints by Michael Nushawg; Tom Palmerton; Kathy Sylwester's Fantasies; Portrait Drawings by Pavel Tchelichew; The Nebraska Landscape; Texture: Exploring the Depths of Surface; occasional shows drawn from Permanent Collection and Annual Student Exhibitions
Activities: Gallery talks; original objects of art lent; lending collection of framed reproductions, original prints and paintings

WAYNE

M **WAYNE STATE COLLEGE,** Nordstrand Visual Arts Gallery, Fine Arts Center, 68787. *Division Chmn of Fine Arts* Dr Cornell Runestad
Open Mon - Fri 9 AM - 5 PM. No admis fee. Estab January 1977 to provide art students with a space to display work; to enhance student's education by viewing incoming regional professional work; to enrich cultural atmosphere of college and community. Small gallery, carpeted floors and walls, ceiling spotlights on tracts. Average Annual Attendance: 800
Income: Financed by city and state appropriation, as well as Wayne State Foundation
Collections: †Wayne State Foundation Print Collection
Exhibitions: Faculty exhibitions; student exhibition; visiting artist exhibition
Activities: Lect open to public, 1 - 2 vis lectr per year; competitions

NEVADA

ELKO

M **NORTHEASTERN NEVADA MUSEUM,** 1515 Idaho St, PO Box 503, 89801. Tel 702-738-3418. *Dir* Howard Hickson; *Registrar* Karen Walther; *Office Mgr* Pam Morrison; *Researcher* Claudia Riordan
Open weekdays & Sat 9 AM - 5 PM, Sun 1 - 5 PM. No admis fee. Estab 1968; general museum concentrating on Northeastern Nevada; also area cultural center. Gallery is 30 x 40 ft. Average Annual Attendance: 55,000. Mem: 1600; dues $5 - $1000; annual meeting date varies
Income: $105,000 (financed by private funding)
Publications: Historical, quarterly
Activities: Classes for adults and children; lect open to public, 2 vis lectr per year; gallery talks; competitions; exten dept serving Nevada; lending collection of film strips, slides (complete programs); originate traveling exhibitions; museum shop sells books and local Indian craft items
L **Library,** 1515 Idaho St, 89801.
Open to public for reference
Library Holdings: Vols 1500; Per subs 5; Other—Photographs
Special Subjects: Concentration on Northeastern Nevada History
Collections: Newspaper and negative files

LAS VEGAS

L **CLARK COUNTY LIBRARY DISTRICT,** 1401 E Flamingo Rd, 89109. Tel 702-733-7810. *Dir* Charles W Hunsberger; *Admin* Joel McKee; *Admin* Jack Gardner; *Young People's Coordr* Beryl Andrus; *Reference* Vlasta Honsa; *Head of Circulation* Darlene Warfield; *Exten Service Coordr* Ann Thompson; *Regional Service Librn* Darrell Batson; *Asst Dir* Nancy Hudson
Open Mon - Thurs 9 AM - 9 PM, Fri & Sat 9 AM - 5 PM, Sun 10 AM - 6 PM. Estab 1965 to provide information in all its varieties of form to people of all ages. Circ 600,000. Gallery provides regularly rotating art exhibitions of regional and national repute as well as three solo local shows a year, and a regional mixed media competition every Spring
Income: $1,600,000 (financed by state and county appropriation)
Purchases: $120,000
Library Holdings: Vols 200,000; Per subs 750; Micro—Fiche, reels; AV—Cassettes, fs, motion pictures, rec; Other—Clipping files, framed reproductions, prints, original art works, pamphlets, photographs, sculpture
Collections: Nevada materials
Exhibitions: Rita Abbey: River Trip; Art-a-Fair: Nevada Water Color Society; Arizona Print Competition; Gustaze Baumann: Color Wood Cuts; Art & Poetry: Farrell Walback in retrospect; Tomie de Paola: Childrens' Book of Illustrations; Professional Black American Artists; Roy Pursell: Jesus, a Contemporary Chronicle; Space Art from USSR; Neon Las Vegas
Publications: Coming Soon (Cinema Guide); exhibition brochures, monthly; library program, bimonthly
Activities: Dramatic programs; forums; cinema series; lect open to the public; concerts; gallery talks; library tours; competitions; exten dept and regional service dept serving the area; bookmobiles; artists traveling through Southern Nevada giving demonstrations and lect; traveling exhibitions organized and circulated
M **Flamingo Gallery,** 1401 E Flamingo Rd, 89109. *Dir* Peggy Transatti
Gallery is located in Clark County Library

O **LAS VEGAS ART LEAGUE,** Las Vegas Art Museum, 3333 W Washington, 89107. Tel 702-647-4300. *Pres* Don Trippy; *Secy* Kaye Thompson; *Museum Dir* Barbara A Clark
Open Mon - Sat 10 AM - 5 PM, Sun 1 - 5 PM. No admis fee. Estab 1950 to offer fine arts to the citizens of Las Vegas; to offer artist a place to show, work and study; to offer good education in fine arts to adults and children of the community. Average Annual Attendance: 8000. Mem: 400; dues benefactors $1000, parton $500, sponsor $100, family $25, individual $18, Senior citizens (65 and over) $10
Income: $24,000 (financed by membership)
Purchases: $1000 - $5000
Collections: Present day artists, majority of which have been winners in annual national competition
Exhibitions: Local and out-of-town artists; National Art Roundup and Fall Roundup Exhibits with cash and purchase awards for each show; one, two or three-man juried exhibits for members and non-members held monthly
Publications: Bulletin, monthly
Activities: Classes for adults presented by leading artists and craftsmen; Junior Art League sponsors classes for youths; self-help workshops; competitions

M **UNIVERSITY OF NEVADA, VEGAS, ART GALLERY,** Maryland Parkway, 89109. Tel 702-736-6111, Ext 237. *Chmn Art Department*

Prof Michael McCollum

Open Mon - Sat Noon - 4 PM. Gallery measures 26 x 22 ft. Average Annual Attendance: 5000. Mem: 50; dues $10

Income: Financed by membership and appropriation

Collections: †Ceramics; Oriental Art; †Paintings; Prints; †Sculpture

Exhibitions: Regularly exhibits work by students and faculty; sponsors exhibits throughout the year by several nationally-renowned artists

Activities: Classes for adults and children; dramatic programs; lect open to the public, 2 vis lectr per year; concerts; gallery talks; tours; competitions; scholarships; lending collection contains 15,000 Kodachromes and 70,000 slides; originate traveling exhibitions

RENO

O **SIERRA ARTS FOUNDATION,** 150 S Virginia, PO Box 2814, 89505. Tel 702-329-1324. *Pres* George Aker; *VPres* Carol Mousel; *Secy* Charles D Glattley; *Exec Dir* Don R M Carter

Estab as a service organization and management organization for arts

Income: Financed by endowment, membership, city and state appropriations, and gifts

Publications: Newsletter and calendar, bimonthly

Activities: Educ dept

M **SIERRA NEVADA MUSEUM OF ART,** 549 Court St, 89501. Tel 702-329-3333. *Pres* Dorthy B Newberg; *VPres* John C Deane; *Treas* Clifton Shoolroy; *Dir* Suzanne M Loomis; *Cur* Marcia Cohn Growdon; *Dir of Museum School* William Keith Kays; *Asst Registrar* Bernie Antone; *School Asst* Alice Nuwer; *Admin Secy* Andrea Crowell

Open Tues - Sat 10 AM - 4 PM, Sun 12 - 4 PM, cl Mon. No admis fee. Estab 1931 to collect, conserve, exhibit and interpret art for the enrichment and heritage of the citizens of Nevada. Museum is a nonprofit educational institution operated in the community's interest. Located in the Hawkins House, a Historic Landmark building designed in the Georgian style by Elmer Grey in 1911. Maintains drawing rooms, dining room, library and suite of rooms that house the galleries. Average Annual Attendance: 12,000. Mem: 600; dues corporation $100, family $20 and individual $15; annual meeting April 1

Income: $203,000 (financed by endowment, membership, federal and private foundation grants, individual grants and earned income)

Collections: Charles Cutts Collection (†art glass, †graphic art, †manuscripts, oriental carpets, paintings and †rare books); †Samuel Houghton Great Basin Collection

Exhibitions: Artists in the American Desert; California Landscape Painting; Joseph Cornell - Paintings and Collages; Maynard Dixon - Paintings and Drawings (Second Annual Great Basin Collection Exhibition); Hawkins House by Elmer Grey - A Historic Landmark; Henry Moore; New Realism; Treasures of Medieval Art from the Metropolitan Museum of Art; New York School 1940-60, the First Generation of Abstract Expressionists; Warp and Weft of Islam

Publications: Annual Bulletin; brochures; catalogues; calendar newsletter, bi-monthly

Activities: Classes for adults and children; workshops; docent training; lect open to the public, 12 visiting lectr per year; concerts; gallery talks; tours; competitions with awards; outreach services to schools, senior citizens and other community groups in Greater Reno-Carson-Tahoe area; individual paintings and original objects of art lent to museums and galleries; book traveling exhibitions, 3-4 times per year; originate traveling exhibitions; museum shop selling books, original art, prints, weavings, cards and letter paper

L **Art Library,** 549 Court St, 89501.

Open by arrangement only. Estab 1951. For reference only

Library Holdings: Vols 1000; Other—Exhibition catalogs, manuscripts, memorabilia, pamphlets, photographs, reproductions

NEW HAMPSHIRE

CONCORD

O **LEAGUE OF NEW HAMPSHIRE CRAFTSMEN,** 205 N Main St, 03301. Tel 603-224-3375. *Pres* Ann Margolis; *VPres* Elizabeth Stecle; *Secy* Samuel Azzaro; *Dir* Merle D Walker; *Business Mgr* Brian Curry; *Supv of Standards* Ruth Burt; *Education Coordr* Evelyn Zimmerman

Estab 1932 to encourage the economic development and education of the crafts; small gallery displaying traveling shows (SITES, ACC) and exhibits of members' works. Mem: 3500; dues $6; annual meeting in Oct

Publications: Newsletter, six times per year

Activities: Classes for adults; seminars; lect open to public; tours; competitions with awards; scholarships; lending collection of books and slides

L **Library,** 205 N Main St, 03301.

Open to members

Library Holdings: Vols 1000; Per subs 24

Special Subjects: Crafts

O **NEW HAMPSHIRE HISTORICAL SOCIETY,** 30 Park, 03301. Tel 603-225-3381. *Pres* Richard F Upton; *VPres* Mrs Carl G Gesen; *VPres* Charles E Clark; *Dir & Secy* John F Page; *Cur* James L Garvin

Open Mon, Tues, Thurs, Fri 9 AM - 4:30 PM, Wed 9 AM - 8 PM. No admis fee. Estab 1823 to collect, preserve and make available books, manuscripts and artifacts pertaining to the history of New Hampshire; art gallery maintained. Average Annual Attendance: 10,000. Mem: 1800; dues family $15, active $10; annual meeting first Sat in May

Income: $200,000 (financed by endowment, membership, state appropriation and grants)

Purchases: $10,000

Collections: Artifacts made or used in New Hampshire such as collections of Glass,

Furniture, Metals, Paintings, Silver and Textiles; Fine and Decorative Arts; Historical Memorabilia

Exhibitions: Concord's Count & Countess Rumford; Documented New Hampshire Furniture; Linen Making in New England

L **Library,** 30 Park, 03301. *Asst Librn* William N Copely

Open to public for reference

Library Holdings: Vols 75,000; Per subs 75

M **SAINT PAUL'S SCHOOL,** Art Center in Hargate, 03301. Tel 603-225-3341, Ext 58. *Head Art Dept* Thomas R Barrett

Open Tues - Sat 10 AM - 4:30 PM, during school year. Estab 1967 to house the Art Department of St Paul's School, to provide a cultural center for the school community as well as the central area of New Hampshire. Secure gallery consisting of subdivided room approximately 60 x 40 ft. Average Annual Attendance: 8500

Income: Financed by endowment

Collections: Painting, sculpture, drawings, graphics, chiefly gifts to the school; collection represents varied periods and nationalities

Exhibitions: Faculty and student exhibitions

Activities: Classes for members only, four visiting lecturers per year; galler talks; tours; original objects of art lent

L **Sheldon Library,** 03301. *Librn* J Alden Manly; *Head Art Dept* T R Barrett; *Research Librn* Anne Locke

Open 10 AM - 4:30 PM Tues - Sat during the school year. Estab 1967 for art reference only. Circ 600

Income: Approx $1000

Purchases: Approx $1000

Library Holdings: Vols 350; Per subs 10; AV—Slides

CORNISH

M **SAINT-GAUDENS NATIONAL HISTORIC SITE,** off New Hampshire Route 12A, Cornish, NH. (Mailing Add: RR 2, Windsor, VT 05089) *Supt & Chief Cur* John H Dryfhout

Open daily 8:30 AM - 5 PM (end of May - Oct 31). Admis (16 and over) 50¢. Estab 1926, transferred to Federal Government 1965 to commemorate the home, studios and works of Augustus Saint-Gaudens (1848-1907), one of America's foremost sculptors. The site has historically (1907) furnished rooms, studios and gardens displaying approximately half of the work of Augustus Saint-Gaudens. Sculptor-in-residence program. Average Annual Attendance: 11,000

Income: Financed by federal appropriation (National Park Service)

Collections: Historic furnishings and plaster, bronze and marble works by Augustus Saint-Gaudens

Exhibitions: Contemporary and Historic Paintings; Drawings; Photographs; Prints; Sculpture

Activities: Individual paintings and original objects of art lent to museums and societies; sales shop sells books, slides and souvenir items

L **Library,** off New Hampshire Route 12A, 03102.

Open for reference

Library Holdings: Vols 400

Special Subjects: 19th and early 20th Century American art

DURHAM

M **UNIVERSITY OF NEW HAMPSHIRE,** University Art Galleries, Paul Creative Arts Center, 03824. Tel 603-862-2190. *Dir* Susan Faxon Olney

Open Mon - Thurs 10 AM - 4 PM, Sat & Sun 1 - 5 PM, cl Fri and school holidays. No admis fee

Collections: Small teaching collection of 19th and 20th century paintings and graphics

Exhibitions: temporary exhibitions

Publications: Exhibition catalogs; miscellaneous booklets

Activities: Educational program for area schools; workshops; lectures

L **Dimond Slide Library,** Department of Art, 03824. *Librn* Don Vincent

Estab 1928 as University Library. Slide library art works are part of Department of the Arts

Library Holdings: AV—Slides 60,000

EXETER

M **PHILLIPS EXETER ACADEMY,** Lamont Gallery, 03833. *Principal* Stephen G Kurtz; *Dir* John Wharton; *Asst Dir* Susan MacDougall

Open Mon, Tues, Thurs, Fri, Sat 9 AM - 5 PM, Wed 9 AM - 1 PM, cl Sun. Estab 1953 to provide an Art Center and studios for art instruction Dedicated to the memory of Thomas William Lamont II, lost in action in 1945

Exhibitions: Eight exhibitions per year; John Matt; Photographs by Joel Meyerowitz; Chris Sproat neon Absence; Board Feat - Contemporary Furniture; Building the Surf Dory (construction and exhibition); Cape Light; Design for Speed; 16th Century Illustrated Pages; Still Life - works by nineteen artists; annual student exhibition and ongoing display of student work; New Architectural Vision in Northern New England

Activities: Classes for Academy students; dramatic programs; films; lect; concerts

HANOVER

M **DARTMOUTH COLLEGE MUSEUM & GALLERIES,** Hopkins Center, 03755. Tel 603-646-2808. *Cur* Arthur Blumenthal; *Exhib Coordr* Malcolm Cochran; *Admin Asst* Nancy Tenney; *Asst to Exhib Coordr* Jack Wilson; *Cur of Anthropology* Tamara Northern; *Curatorial Asst* Gregory Schwartz; *Admin Asst* Eva Coutermarsh; *Registrar* Margaret J Moody; *Asst to Exhib Coordr* Benjamin White

Open Mon - Fri 10 AM - 4 PM, 7 - 10 PM, Sat & Sun 2 - 4 PM. No admis fee. Estab 1771. Situated in the Hopkins Center for the Visual and Performing Arts along with extensive facilities for theatre, music, studio, film and workshops. It houses anthropological collection in Wilson Hall; permanent collection in Carpenter Galleries; sculpture court; Barrows print room; lower Jewett corridor;

Beaumont-May, Strauss, Jaffe-Friede Galleries
Income: Financed through Dartmouth College
Collections: American and European paintings, sculpture, drawings and prints; Far Eastern art; Far and near Eastern Art; anthropological artifacts; ethnic arts
Exhibitions: Acquisitions 1974-1978; artist in residence exhibitions; annual student show; exhibits from permanent collection; Gregorian Collection of Armenian Rugs; Nigerian Splendor; outdoor sculpture; Picasso's Vollard Suite; Richard Stankiewicz, Summer 1979 artist in residence; Ralph Steiner: A Retrospective; Theatre Art of the Medici; Women's Clothing and Accessories 1800-1930
Activities: Undergraduate museum studies courses offered; gallery talks; traveling exhibitions
L   **Sherman Art Library,** Carpenter Hall, 03755. Tel 603-646-2305. *Librn* Molly M O'Connor
Open Mon - Fri 8 AM - 12 PM; Sat 9 AM - 5 PM, Sun 1 - 12 PM. Estab 1928
Library Holdings: Vols 50,000; Per subs 450; Micro—Cards, fiche, reels; Other—Exhibition catalogs, pamphlets

KEENE

M   **KEENE STATE COLLEGE,** Thorne-Sagendorph Art Gallery, Appian Way, 03431. Tel 603-352-1909, Ext 382. *Dir* Nancy Doll
Open Mon - Fri Noon - 5 PM, Tues evening till 7 PM, Sun 1 - 5 PM. No admis fee. Estab 1965 to provide a year-round calendar of continuing exhibitions; to sponsor related programs of artistic and educational interest; and to maintain small permanent collection displayed on campus. Two adjacent galleries occupy space in a wing of Mason Library on campus. Average Annual Attendance: 9000. Mem: 400; dues $5
Income: $20,000 (financed by endowment, state appropriation and annual College budget)
Collections: Paintings and Prints of Historical Interest included: Pierre Alechinsky; Milton Avery; Paul Pollaro; Gregorio Prestopino; George Rickey; Sidney Twardowicz; Artists of National Prominence; Paintings by Regional Artists
Exhibitions: Hannes Beckmann: Paintings 1972-75; Tom Blagden - Watercolors; Nancy Brown - Lynda McIntyre (paintings); Hans Hofmann: colorist in Black and White; Works by Nicholas Isaak; Works by Guy Murchie; Annual Keene State College Student Art Exhibition; Artistic Resources in the Community; A Sense of Place; The Billboard Show; Dance Exhibition; Friends Collect; Into the 80's: New England Photography; KSU-UTC Faculty Exchange; MASKS, Contemporary Artists; Tri-State Weaving Show; Work in Fibers and Clay
Publications: Small catalogs or brochures to accompany exhibitions
Activities: Lect open to public, 2 vis lectr per year; concerts; gallery talks; tours; competitions; individual paintings lent to departments on campus, other museums and galleries; lending collection consists of original prints, paintings and sculpture; originate traveling exhibitions

MANCHESTER

M   **CURRIER GALLERY OF ART,** 192 Orange St, 03104. Tel 603-669-6144. *Pres* Kimon S Zachos; *Treas* Ernest A Sweet Jr; *Clerk* Mrs Norman F Milne; *Dir* Robert M Doty; *Dir of Education* Marian D Woodruff; *Cur* Melvin E Watts; *Assoc Cur* Philip D Zimmerman; *Coordr of Public Relations* Barbara Clinton; *Coordr of Membership* Virginia Eshoo; *Supv The Currier Art Center* Robert Eshoo
Open Tues, Wed, Fri, Sat 10 AM - 4 PM, Thurs 10 AM - 10 PM, Sun 2 - 5 PM, cl Mon and national holidays. No admis fee. Estab and incorporated 1915 by will of Mrs Hannah M and Governor Moody Currier, which included endowment. The building opened in 1929, contains six galleries, library and auditorium. Currier Art Center is housed in an adjacent building acquired in 1938, and offers after school and Sat classes for children. Average Annual Attendance: 30,000. Mem: 1000; dues $10 and up; annual meeting in March
Income: Financed by endowment
Collections: †American Paintings and Sculpture 18th Century to present; †European Masters 13th to 20th Century; †Fine American Decorative Art 17th to 19th Century including Furniture, Glass Textiles and Silver
Exhibitions: Decorative and industrial art, painting, sculpture
Publications: Bulletin, annually; exhibition catalogs, sproadically
L   **Library,** 192 Orange St, 03104. *Librn* Maria K Graubart
Open to gallery staff, docents and research students by appointment for reference only
Library Holdings: Vols 5000; Per subs 40

L   **MANCHESTER CITY LIBRARY,*** Carpenter Memorial Building, 405 Pine St, 03104. Tel 603-615-6485; TWX 710-220-6489. *City Library Dir* John J Hallahan; *Fine Arts Librn* Ann Frank
Open Mon - Thurs 9 AM - 9 PM, Fri 9 AM - 6 PM, Sat 9 AM - 5 PM, cl Sun
Library Holdings: Vols 8500; Micro—Reels; AV—Fs; Other—mounted pictures
Activities: Monthly film program to public; Canadian travel films available to groups, cooperative film collection available for loan and interlibrary loan

O   **MANCHESTER HISTORIC ASSOCIATION,** 129 Amherst St, 03104. Tel 603-622-7531. *Pres* Timothy Jones; *Dir* George Comtois; *Librn* Elizabeth B Lessard
Open Tues - Fri 11 AM - 4 PM, Sat 10 AM - 4 PM, cl Sun and Mon, National and state holidays, and Tues following Mon holidays. Inc 1896 to collect, preserve and make known Manchester's historical heritage. Average Annual Attendance: 8000. Mem: 237; dues active $1000, patron $100 or more, contributing $15 - $99
Income: $45,000
Collections: †Furniture, †glass, †pewter, †maps, †prints, †paintings, †ceramics, †costumes, †textiles, †artifacts of all types; †Indian artifact collection of over 10,000 pieces found at Manchester sites; historical material
Exhibitions: Permanent and changing exhibitions reflecting all aspects of Manchester history
Publications: Quarterly Bulletin; Annual Report; Occasional catalogs
Activities: Spring and fall program series
L   **Library,** 129 Amherst St, 03104.
Library Holdings: Other—Prints, manuscripts, photographs, maps; early textiles mill records; swatch sample books

M   **MANCHESTER INSTITUTE OF ARTS AND SCIENCES GALLERY,** 148 Concord St, 03104. Tel 603-623-0313. *Exec Dir* Angelo Randazzo; *Program Coordr* Marc Normand; *Educ Coordr* Pamela Riel; *Registrar* Linda Lord
Open Mon - Thurs 9 AM - 9 PM, Fri & Sat 9 AM - 5 PM, cl Sun. No admis fee. Estab 1898, as a private non-profit educational institution in order to promote, encourage and stimulate education in the arts and sciences. Gallery has limited space which is devoted to a variety of exhibitions including historical as well as contemporary themes. Mem: 450; dues family $25, individual $15, student $10; annual meeting in June
Income: Financed by endowment, membership, tuition and grants
Exhibitions: Arts Biennial and Crafts Biennial; changing exhibitions of fine art and crafts
Publications: Exhibition catalogs; schedule of courses, exhibitions and programs, 2 or 3 times per year
Activities: Classes for adults; films; lect; concerts; sales shop selling handcrafted items

O   **NEW HAMPSHIRE ART ASSOCIATION, INC,** 24 W Bridge St, Box 1075, 03105. Tel 603-622-0527. *Executive Dir* Grace Casey; *Pres* Frank Moulton; *VPres* James Locke; *Treas* Lucie Duhaime; *Correspondence Secy* Alice Coyne; *Recording Secy* Virginia Hurt
Sales and rental gallery open year-round, Mon - Fri 9 AM - 5 PM. Estab 1940, incorporated 1962, as a non-profit organization, to promote the public's understanding and appreciation of the arts; to provide the artist with a forum for his work and ideas. It offers a year-round exhibition and sales gallery at its headquarters in Manchester; a summer gallery in the Joshua Wentworth House, Strawbery Banke, Portsmouth; an August exhibition and sales program at Sunapee State Park. Mem: 300; dues $20; annual meeting June
Exhibitions: Annuals at Currier Gallery of Art; Summer Annual combined with New Hampshire League of Arts and Crafts at Mount Sunapee State Park; Summer Annual Juried Exhibition at Prescott Park; Spring Annual Juried Exhibit at the Nashua Arts and Science Center; various one-man and group shows
Activities: Educ program for schools; patron program; Lect demonstrations by member artists; awards; originate traveling exhibitions

M   **SAINT ANSELM'S COLLEGE,** Chapel Arts Center, 03102. Tel 603-669-1030, Ext 328. *Assoc Dir* Joseph E Scannell; *Assoc Dir* Beverly Zisla Welbur; *Cur* Paul Sullivan; *Docent* Patricia Farrell
Open Mon - Fri 10 AM - 4 PM. No admis fee. Large gallery, formerly college chapel with painted, barrel-vaulted ceiling, stained glass windows; one small gallery. Average Annual Attendance: 2000
Income: Financed through College
Collections: †Photographs; †prints; †New Hampshire artists and craftsmen
Exhibitions: Buildingbooks; Minnesota Landscapes; New Hampshire Clocks; Pieta; permanent collection; Medieval Armor; The Parthenon; Shaker Built; Student Show

NASHUA

O   **ARTS AND SCIENCE CENTER,** 14 Court St, 03060. Tel 603-883-1506. *Pres* William K Phillips; *Chmn Executive Committee* David Cheever; *Admin* Ann L Carner; *DirChildrens Museum* Nancy Fite
Open Mon - Fri 10 AM - 5 PM, Thurs 10 AM - 9 PM, Sat 10 AM - 5 PM, Sun 1:30 - 5 PM; Childrens Museum: Tues - Fri 9:30 - 11:30 AM, 1 - 4:30 PM, Sat 10 - 12 AM, 2 - 4:30 PM, Sun 2 - 4:30 PM, cl Sundays in July & Aug. No admis fee. Inc 1961 to provide performances and exhibitions, lectures, film programs, musical performances and productions by theatre arts groups. New facility opened Nov 1973, includes two large exhibition galleries, rental and sales department, museum shop, theatre with capacity of 250 for performances and productions, six classrooms, coffee shop, large meeting room, storage and office space. The Childrens Museum, the only one of its kind in New Hampshire, is designed to allow children to experience more through participation instead of observation. Special tours and programs for school and childrens groups. There is a nominal admission fee. Average Annual Attendance: 100,000. Mem: 954; dues $10 - $1000; monthly meeting of the Board of Trustees held first Tues of each month; annual meeting of the Board and members held in May
Publications: Newsletters; releases; invitations to openings
Activities: Classes for preschool, primary, secondary and adults in arts and crafts; lectures; films; scholarships offered

PLYMOUTH

L   **PLYMOUTH STATE COLLEGE,** Herbert H Lamson Library, 03264. *Dir Library Services* Janice Gallinger; *Coordr Public Services* Robert V McDermand; *Slide Librn* William Kietzman; *Acquisitions Librn* Peter C Gerdine; *Interlibrary Loan Librn* Michael J Flannery
Open Mon - Thurs 8 AM - 11 PM, Fri 8 AM - 6 PM, Sat 10 AM - 6 PM, Sun 1 - 11 PM. Estab 1871 to serve the academic and personal needs of the college's students and faculty. Circ 80,000. Maintains exhibition space, an 18 ft exhibition wall
Income: $450,000 (one-fourth financed by state appropriation)
Purchases: $69,000
Library Holdings: Vols 200,000; Per subs 1400; Micro—Fiche 200,000, reels 7500; AV—Cassettes 1000, fs 3000, rec 6000, slides 31,000; Other—Pamphlets, audio discs 5900
Exhibitions: Lucien Aigner; Patricia Benson; James Fortune; Margaret Houseworth; Winthrop Pratt; Leslie Snow
Publications: Brochures; Handbook; newsletter and new acquisitions list, bi-weekly
Activities: Lect open to public; library tours

PORTSMOUTH

M   **JOHN PAUL JONES HOUSE,** Middle and State St, 54 Court St, 03801. Tel 603-436-8420. *Pres* Arnold J Grover; *VPres* Wyman P Boynton; *Secy* Mrs Harry Downing

Open June 1st - Oct 15th, Mon - Sat 10 AM - 5 PM, cl Sun. Admis $1.50. Estab 1920 to identify and retain local history. The House was built in 1758 by Gregory Purcell, a merchant sea-captain. Purchased and restored in 1920 by the Portsmouth Historical Society. Average Annual Attendance: 7000. Mem: 245; dues $5; annual meeting May
Income: Financed by membership and investment
Collections: Books, china, costumes, documents, furniture, glass, portraits and silver pertaining to the early history of Portsmouth

M **PORTSMOUTH ATHENAEUM NR, INC 1817,** 9 Market Square, Box 848, 03801. *Pres* John R Maher; *VPres* Azio J Ferrini; *Treas* Prof Leonard N Rhoades; *Secy* Frederick S Gray; *Cur* Joseph P Copley
Open yearly Thurs 1 - 4 PM or by appointment. No admis fee. Estab 1817 to house museum of historical objects of local, statewide and national interest and is listed on National Register of Historical Sites. Average Annual Attendance: 2800. Mem: 185; dues $40; annual meeting 2nd Wed in Jan
Income: Financed by endowment and membership
Collections: American Paintings
Exhibitions: Various
Activities: Lect; individual paintings lent to historical societies; lending collection contains books
L **Library,** 9 Market Square, Box 848, 03801. *Librn* Mrs William Boesch
Open Thurs 1 - 4 PM or by appointment. Estab 1817. For reference only
Library Holdings: Vols 3100; Per subs 36; Micro—Cards; Other—Clipping files, prints, manuscripts, memorabilia, original art works, pamphlets, photographs
Special Subjects: United States Marine History

SHARON

O **SHARON ARTS CENTER, INC,** RFD 2, Box 361, Route 123, 03458. Tel 603-924-7256. *Pres* Bissell Alderman; *Dir* Alan Erdossy
Open daily 10 AM - 5:30 PM, Sun 1 - 5 PM. Estab 1945 to promote appreciation of the arts and crafts in the Monadnock area. Member of the League of New Hampshire Craftsmen. Exhibition gallery and shop. Mem: Dues $10; annual meeting Sept
Income: Financed by endowment and membership
Activities: Arts and crafts classes

NEW JERSEY

ATLANTIC CITY

L **PRINCETON ANTIQUES BOOKSERVICE,** Art Marketing Reference Library, 2915-17 Atlantic Ave, 08401. Tel 609-344-1943. *Pres* Robert E Ruffolo Jr; *Cur* Martha Ireland; *Adminr* Robert Eugene
Estab 1974 for pricing documentation of books and antiques. Open by appointment only; maintains art galery
Income: $25,000 - $30,000
Purchases: $20,000
Library Holdings: Vols 12,500; Per subs 20; AV—Slides; Other—exhibition catalogs, original art works and prints
Special Subjects: The function in US of art and the book market, Price information history from 1900
Collections: 19th century art; Post-card Photo Library Information Bank, 1900 - 1950, consisting 250,000 post-cards

BAYONNE

L **BAYONNE FREE PUBLIC LIBRARY, ART DEPARTMENT,** 697 Avenue C, 07002. Tel 201-858-6981. *Art Music Librn* Michael Loscalzo
Open Mon, Tues, Thurs 9 AM - 12PM, 1 - 5 PM, Wed, Fri, Sat 9 AM - 12 PM, 1 - 5 PM. Estab 1894
Income: $580,000 (financed by city appropriation)
Library Holdings: Vols 10,875; AV—Fs, rec, slides; Other—Clipping files
Activities: Concerts; adult and children film programs weekly

BLOOMFIELD

M **HISTORICAL SOCIETY OF BLOOMFIELD, NEW JERSEY,** 90 Broad St, 07003. Tel 201-429-9292. *Pres* Dorothy E Johnson; *VPres* Richard West; *Corresponding Secy* Betty Kingsley; *Co-Cur* Sallie Black; *Co-Cur* Louise E Greenland
Open Wed 2 - 4:30 PM, Sat 11 AM - 3 PM. No admis fee. Estab circa 1968 to collect, preserve and exhibit items which may help to establish or illustrate the history of the area. Museum located in the gallery of the Bloomfield Public Library. Average Annual Attendance: 1436. Mem: 232; dues life $50, commercial organization $25, non-profit organization $10, couple $8, individual $5, student under 18 $1; meeting second Wed of alternate months Sept - May
Income: $1525 (financed by membership, Ways and Means Committee)
Collections: Miscellaneous items of books, clothing and accessories, deeds and other documents, dioramas, early maps and newspapers, furniture, household articles, letters, memorabilia, paintings, postcards, posters, tools, toys
Exhibitions: Old photographs of Bloomfield and artifacts in connection with Thomas Edison; Embroidery and Handwork, fans, old time toys, old valentines
Activities: Lect open to public, 3 - 5 visiting lectr per year; tours; $100 award to student graduating from Bloomfield Senior High School who has attained an outstanding achievement in American History; sales shop sells books, prints, postcards, medallions, wallets, phonorecords and fruit cake (seasonal)

BURLINGTON

O **BURLINGTON COUNTY HISTORICAL SOCIETY,** 457 High St, 08016. Tel 609-386-4773. *Pres* Susan Bradman; *VPres* Anna Black; *Secy* Anita Parry; *Dir* Rebecca H Siman
Open Wed 1 - 4 PM, Sun 2 - 4 PM. Admis by contribution. Estab 1923 to maintain collections relating to Burlington County History and residents. Average Annual Attendance: 2300. Mem: 350; dues $5; annual meeting May
Income: Financed by endowment
Collections: China; Glass; Quilts; Sampler

CALDWELL

M **CALDWELL COLLEGE ART GALLERY,** 07006. Tel 201-228-4424. *Dir* Sr M Gerardine
Open Mon - Fri 8:30 AM - 5 PM, weekends by appointment. No admis fee. Estab 1970 to provide students and area community with exposure to professional contemporary talent, to afford opporunities for qualified artists to have one-person shows
Exhibitions: Alice Brewster; Zelda Burdick; Ellen Chuse; Jo DeCaro; Gary Erbe; Patricia Garrett; James Gwynne; Jutta Hagen; Patricia Malarcher; Jean Schonwalter; Sy Shames; Perry Zimmerman
Activities: Education department in connection with the college art department; lect open to public, 3 vis lectr per yr; scholarships offered; Lending collection contains 12,000 Kodachromes, motion pictures

CAMDEN

C **CAMPBELL MUSEUM,** Campbell Place, 08101. Tel 609-964-4000. *Pres* Ralph Collier
Open Mon - Fri 9 AM - 5 PM. No admis fee. Estab 1966 to collect soup tureens of silver, porcelain and pewter of the 18th Century. Collection displayed at Campbell Museum. Museum has red velvet walls and Plexiglas cases
Collections: 18th Century soup tureens by leading porcelain makers and silversmiths
Activities: Lect; gallery talks; tours; originate traveling exhibitions to museums only

M **RUTGERS UNIVERSITY,** Stedman Art Gallery, Camden College of Arts & Sciences, Fine Arts Complex, 08102. Tel 609-757-6350, 757-6245. *Dir* Virginia Oberlin Steel
Open Mon - Sat 11 AM - 4 PM. No admis fee. Estab 1975 to serve educational needs of Art Department; to serve community of Southern New Jersey. Gallery is a large open space in the Fine Arts Complex. Average Annual Attendance: 7000
Income: Financed by endowment, state appropriation and grants
Purchases: $5000
Collections: Modern and Contemporary Art, including Artists such as Harvey Breverman; Anne Chapman; Agnes Denes; Sir Jacob Epstein; Ben Kamihira; Jacob Landau; Sandra Lerner; Abraham Rattner; George Rouault; Bruce Samuelson; Charles Schmidt; Burton Silverman; Louis Sloan; Paul Wunderlich
Exhibitions: Changing exhibitions of fine arts in wide range of media
Publications: Catalog for a major exhibition, yearly
Activities: Gallery lect; symposia; concerts; tours; all open to public; biennial national drawing competition with purchase prizes

CLINTON

M **CLINTON HISTORICAL MUSEUM VILLAGE,*** 56 Main St, PO Box 5005, 08809. Tel 201-735-4101. *Dir* Gloria Lazor; *Cur* Claire Young
Open Mon - Fri 1 - 5 PM, Sat & Sun Noon - 6 PM. Admis adults $1.75, seniors $1, children under 12 50¢, pre-schoolers free. Estab 1960 for the preservation and display of artifacts from the 18th and 19th century for educational and cultural purposes. Four-floor grist mill containing pottery shop, blacksmith shop, general store, log cabin and herb garden. Average Annual Attendance: 22,000. Mem: 250; dues $5 - $1000; annual meeting April
Income: $85,000 (financed by membership and donations)
Collections: Artifacts pertaining to 18th and 19th centuries
Publications: The Old Mill Wheel, newsletter, three times a year
Activities: Classes for adults and children; docent training; harvest jubilee; dance; lect; lending collection of slides; sales shop selling books, slides and gift items
L **Library,*** 56 Main St, PO Box 5005, 08809.
For historical reference
Library Holdings: Vols 500

O **HUNTERDON ART CENTER,** 7 Center St, 08809. Tel 201-735-8415. *Pres* Larry Carlbon; *VPres* Helen Axel; *Secy* Richard Dieterly; *Exec Dir* Diane Lazarus; *Admin Asst* Ruth Harrison
Open Tues - Fri 1 - 4 PM, Sat & Sun 1 - 5 PM, cl Mon. No admis fee. Estab 1951 as a non-profit organization to provide opportunity for adults and children to participate in the enjoyment of the arts and crafts in all forms. The first and second floors provide gallery space. The old stone mill has been remodeled retaining the original atmosphere with open broad wooden beams, white walls and plank flooring. Average Annual Attendance: 15,000. Mem: 2000; dues student $5, single $15, family $20, sustaining $25, patron $100; annual meeting April
Income: Financed by membership, city, state and county appropriations, federal funding, donations
Purchases: $100
Collections: †Print collection
Exhibitions: Annual Juried Exhibition; Art and Jazz Celebration; Craft Exhibitions; Invitational Group Shows; Members Show; National Print Exhibition
Publications: Newsletter, bimonthly
Activities: Classes for adults and children; workshops; competitions; lect open to the public; theatre productions; films; museum shop sells prints, pottery, weavings, jewelry and books

CONVENT STATION

L COLLEGE OF SAINT ELIZABETH, Mahoney Library, 07961. Tel 201-539-1600, Ext 365. *Librn* Sr Marie Rousek
Open weekdays 9 AM - 5 PM. Estab 1899 for academic purposes
Income: Financed by private funds
Library Holdings: Vols 145,000; Per subs 1100; Micro—Fiche, reels; AV—Cassettes, fs, rec; Other—Exhibition catalogs, reproductions
Exhibitions: (1978) Recent works in Stoneware and Porcelain by Abigail Brassil Adelman; Illuminated Manuscript Pages from the Collection of the late Dr Raymond Hennessy and from Library's Collection; Sculpture in Wood by John Neonakis

EAST ORANGE

O ART CENTRE OF NEW JERSEY, 16 Washington St, 07017. Tel 201-674-8445. *Pres* George Corning; *VPres* John Watson; *VPres* John Richter; *Treas* Ruth Schwacha; *Recording Secy* Katherine Cantlin
Open daily. Estab 1924 as an art school and as a venue for art events, lectures, etc. Three galleries and one large work studio. Mem: 250; dues $12.50; annual meeting May
Income: Financed by membership and art sales
Exhibitions: Annual Regional and members exhibitions, as well as others
Publications: Quarterly
Activities: Classes for adults; docent training; workshops; lect open to public; gallery talks; competitions

ELIZABETH

L FREE PUBLIC LIBRARY OF ELIZABETH, Fine Arts Dept,* 11 S Broad St, 07202. Tel 201-354-6060. *Library Dir* Hazel Hulbert Elks; *Asst Dir* Roman Sawycky; *Sr Art Librn* Daisy Tamayo
Open Mon - Fri 9 AM - 9 PM, cl Sun. No admis fee. Estab 1913, the art department functions within the area library system; it offers free service to patrons of Elizabeth and also to patrons of neighboring towns, Roselle Park, Kenilworth, Union and Cranford. Special exhibit area displays paintings and miscellaneous objects d'art
Income: Financed by city and state appropriations
Library Holdings: Vols 15,000; Other—Photographs, reproductions
Collections: Japanese prints by various artists
Exhibitions: Works by local artists and photographers; other special exhibitions from time to time
Activities: Dramatic programs; lect open to the public, 15 visiting lectrs per year; concerts; exten dept servicing Elizabeth and towns of Union, Kenilworth, Roselle Park, Cranford; material available to patrons of these municipalities with no fees; individual prints lent to schools; lending collection contains film strips and projection equipment, motion pictures

ENGLEWOOD

L ENGLEWOOD LIBRARY, 31 Engle St, 07631. Tel 201-568-2215. *Dir Library* Patricia Anderson; *Head Programming Dept* Mary Beall
Open Mon - Thurs 9 AM - 9 PM, Fri & Sat 9 AM - 5 PM, Sun 1 - 5 PM (Oct-May). Estab 1901 to establish a free public library for citizens. Area of library is used for exhibitions; special panels and cases
Income: $450,000 (financed by endowment, city and state appropriation)
Library Holdings: Vols 110,000; Per subs 365; Micro—Reels; AV—Cassettes, fs, motion pictures, rec, slides; Other—Clipping files, framed reproductions, original art works, pamphlets
Exhibitions: Faculty of Old Church Cultural Center; Members of Artists File; Photographs of David Jordan; Two Hundred Years of American Painting; Watercolors of Dorothy Dallas
Activities: Lectures open to the public, 5 visiting lecturers per yr; concerts; gallery talks; tours; competitions

HOPEWELL

M HOPEWELL MUSEUM, 28 E Broad St, 08525. Tel 609-466-0103. *Pres* Dr Donald M Bergen; *Cur* Beverly Weidl; *Asst Cur* Betsy Errickson
Open Mon, Wed & Sat 2 - 5 PM, cl national holidays. No admis fee, donations suggested. Estab 1922 as a museum of local history from early 1700 - 1900, to show what this community was like for almost 300 years. Average Annual Attendance: 2000
Income: Financed by endowment, membership and donations
Collections: Antique China, Glass, Silver and Pewter; Colonial Furniture; Colonial Parlor; Early Needlework; Indian Handicrafts; Photograph Collection; Victorian Parlor
Publications: Hopewell Valley Heritage; Pioneers of Old Hopewell; maps

JERSEY CITY

M HUDSON COUNTY COURT HOUSE, Board of Chosen Freeholders, 595 Newark Ave, 07306. Tel 201-792-3737. *Chairman* Hon; *County Executive* Hon
Collections: Mural Paintings—The Coming of the Dutch; The Coming of the English; In Old Dutch Days and decorations in Superior Court Room by Howard Pyle; The Purchase of Pavonia and A Skirmish with the Indians, by Frank D Millett; Washington Watching the Assault on Fort Washington from Fort Lee and the First Trip of the Clermont (in the upper gallery of the Rotunda), by Charles Yardley Turner; dome decorations installed in 1911, by Edwin Howland Blashfield

M JERSEY CITY MUSEUM ASSOCIATION, 472 Jersey Ave, 07302. Tel 201-547-4513. *Pres* J Owen Grundy; *VPres* Theodore Conrad; *Secy* Adelaide Dear; *Treas* Arthur Hansen; *Trustee & Cur* Cynthia Sanford; *Asst Cur* Robert Ferguson
Open Wed 4 - 8 PM, Fri & Sat 11 AM - 4:30 PM. No admis fee. Estab 1932 for the purpose of advancing interest in the Arts, Sciences and History. Maintains an art gallery housing the Will Collection. Average Annual Attendance: 10,000. Mem: 189; dues from Junior $1 to Benefactor $1000; meetings Jan, Mar and Nov
Income: $1000 (financed by endowment)
Collections: Will Collection of Paintings & Drawings (1850's - 1910) of Jersey City Scenes; Antiques; Local Historical Pictures and Artifacts; Modern and Old Paintings; Posters; Sculpture
Publications: Year Book
Activities: Educ dept; lect open to public, 4 - 5 vis lectr per year; competitions

L JERSEY CITY PUBLIC LIBRARY, Fine Arts Department, 678 Newark Ave, 07306. Tel 201-547-4546. *Dir* Ben Grimm; *Librn Fine Arts* Alfred Trattner
Open Mon 1 - 8 PM, Tues - Fri 10 AM - 6 PM, Sat 10 AM - 5 PM. Circ 28,000. Maintains an art gallery of four movable panels totaling 250 sq ft
Income: $16,000
Purchases: $12,000
Library Holdings: Vols 9400; AV—Cassettes, fs, motion pictures, rec, slides; Other—Framed reproductions, prints, reproductions

M JERSEY CITY STATE COLLEGE, Courtney Art Gallery, Dept of Art, 2039 Kennedy Blvd, 07307. Tel 201-547-3214. *Dir* Harold Lemmerman
Open Mon - Fri 10 AM - 5 PM. No admis fee. Estab 1969 to bring examples of professional work to the campus in each of the areas in which students are involved: Painting, sculpture, film, photography, textiles, weaving, ceramics, graphic design. Gallery is operated by students, and with the Jersey City Museum form a student internship training program. Average Annual Attendance: 5000
Income: Financed by city or state appropriation, and Art Department
Collections: Small collection of prints and paintings
Exhibitions: Photography; multi-media exhibitions in painting, sculpture, ceramics, crafts, animation, antiques and prints; Recent Work Annual
Activities: Lect open to public, 5 visiting lectrs per year; gallery talks; exten dept serving community organizations; individual paintings and original objects of art lent; lending collection contains color reproductions, film strips, Kodachromes, motion pictures, photographs; traveling exhibitions organized and circulated
L Forrest A Irwin Library, 2039 Kennedy Blvd, 07307. Tel 201-547-3016 (circulation) or 547-3033 (reference). *Dir* Robert Nugent; *Asst Dir Reader Services* John Luchechko
Open Mon - Thurs 8:30 AM - 9 PM, Fri 8:30 AM - 5 PM, Sat 9 AM - 5 PM. Estab 1927
Library Holdings: Vols 209,010; Per subs 1577; Other—Clipping files, exhibition catalogs, framed reproductions, manuscripts, memorabilia, reproductions
M Zigfelt Gallery, 2039 Kennedy Blvd, 07307
Gallery maintained for student exhibitions

M SAINT PETER'S COLLEGE ART GALLERY,* 2641 Kennedy Blvd, 07306. Tel 201-333-4400. *Dir* Oscar Magnan
Open Mon, Tues, Fri & Sat 11 AM - 4 PM, Wed & Thurs 11 AM - 9 PM. No admis fee. Estab 1971 to present the different art trends. Gallery is maintained with good space, lighting and alarm systems
Income: Financed by the college
Exhibitions: 40 Years of American Collage; The History of the Poster; Puerto Rican Prints; 3D-2D
Activities: Classes for adults; docent training; lect open to public, 20 visiting lectrs per year; concerts; gallery talks; tours; exten dept serving students
L College Library, Art Section,* 2641 Kennedy Blvd, 07306. *Librn* Richard Tetrau
Open to students and faculty

LAKEWOOD

M GEORGIAN COURT COLLEGE GALLERY, Lakewood Ave, 08701. Tel 201-364-2200, Ext 48. *Dir* Sr M Christina Geis
Open Mon - Fri 9 AM - 4 PM. No admis fee. Estab 1964 to offer art students the opportunity to view the works of professional artists and also to exhibit student work. Gallery is one large room with 100 running feet of wall area for flat work; the center area for sculpture. Average Annual Attendance: 1000
Income: Financed through the college
Exhibitions: Arthur Evans (sculpture & paintings); Mary Fleming (paintings & prints); Carla Frumusa (paintings & prints); Pat Kennedy & Deena Kutcher (crafts & paintings); Lynn Lemire (drawings & paintings); Gen Mitchell (color photography); Stephanie Palermo & Nancy Morse (crafts, drawings, paintings); Cheryl Stoeber (paintings); Jean Townsend (paintings); Georgian Court College Alumnae (drawings, paintings, prints)

LAWRENCEVILLE

RIDER COLLEGE

M Rider College Art Gallery, 2983 Lawrenceville Rd, PO Box 6400, 08648. Tel 609-896-5327. *Associate Dir Student Activities* H Donald Thibault
Open 9:30 AM - Noon, 1 - 5 PM, 7 - 11 PM. No admis fee. Estab 1970 to afford members of the Rider College community the opportunity to expand their knowledge and exposure to art. Gallery has 1513 sq ft of space divided into two rooms of different height. Average Annual Attendance: 5000
Income: $500 (financed by college appropriation)
Exhibitions: Peter Ackerman, Steve Mironov, Ron Kress photography; Maryke Seldes, Pen and Ink; Eva Kaplan, Collages; Mariane Aamod, Weaving; Selma Bortuer, George Ivers, Mixed Media
Activities: Dramatic programs; concerts
L Franklin F Moore Library and Art Room, Lawrenceville Rd, 08648. Tel 609-896-5193. *Art Librn* Violet K Devlin
Open 8 AM - 11 PM Mon - Thurs, 8 AM - 9 PM Fri, 10 AM - 5 PM Sat, 1 - 11 PM Sun. Estab 1964 to support the Fine Arts curriculum at the college, and the recreational and cultural needs of the entire college community. Circ 2000
Income: Financed from the general college library budget
Purchases: $15,000
Library Holdings: Vols 12,000; Other—Clipping files, exhibition catalogs, prints,

memorabilia, pamphlets, reproductions
Exhibitions: (1979-80) The Arts of Japan; Arts of Nigeria; The Bookarts: Typography, Illustration, Covers; Baroque Musical Instruments; Model Railroading; Origami; Photography by students

LAYTON

L **PETERS VALLEY CRAFT CENTER LIBRARY,** 07851. *Executive Dir* Philip C Homes
Not open to public. Estab 1978 to serve as resource library for residents, interns and students at Peters Valley Craft Center. Located at Valley Brook Farm Administrative Offices
Purchases: $2500
Library Holdings: Vols 1000; Per subs 5; AV—Slides; Other—Exhibition catalogs, memorabilia, original art works
Special Subjects: Ceramics, Crafts
Collections: Encyclopedias of Japanese wood-fired pottery; slides of contemporary craft work

LINCROFT

M **MONMOUTH MUSEUM AND CULTURAL CENTER,** Brookdale Community College, Newman Springs Rd, 07738. Tel 201-747-2266. *Dir* Dorothy V Morehouse; *Pres* Howard R Berger; *First VPres* Philip C Carling; *Second VPres* Jean Blair; *Program Admnr* Catherine Jahos
Open Mon - Sat 10 AM - 4:30 PM, Sun 1 - 5 PM. Admis adults $1.50 children and Senior citizens 75¢, free to Museum members and students. Estab 1963 to advance interest in art, science and nature in this area. Museum houses two large galleries, a children's gallery, the Wonder Warehouse and the main gallery which changes exhibitions four times yearly; also an educational area and a conference area. Average Annual Attendance: 100,000. Mem: 1600; dues family $25, individual $15; annual meetings Jan
Income: $220,000 (financed by membership, donations and county funds)
Exhibitions: Alternate Energy; Curious Creatures and Bizarre Beasts; Indian Art of the Americas, made in Monmouth; Inuit Eskimo; Year of the Coast
Publications: Calendar of events; catalogues of exhibitions; newsletter
Activities: Classes for adults and children; docent training; lect open to public; artmobile; originate traveling trunks for use in schools; museum shop sells books and gift items

LITTLE SILVER

O **NEW JERSEY WATERCOLOR SOCIETY,** c/o Roberta Carter Clark, 47B Cheshire Square, 07739. Tel 201-747-6141. *Pres* Roberta Carter Clark; *VPres* Rodell Johnson; *Correspondence Secy* June Benson; *Recording Secy* Wini Smart; *Treas* Thomas A Bavolar
Mem: 108; dues $10
Collections: Annual Members Show in spring; Annual Open Statewide Juried Exhibition in fall - alternating between Morris Museum of Arts and Sciences, Morristown NJ and the Monmouth Museum, Lincorft NJ
Publications: Illustrated Catalogue; Newsletter; Open Show
Activities: Annual Dinner; Receptions for Open Show and Members Show

LONG BRANCH

M **LONG BRANCH HISTORICAL MUSEUM,** 1260 Ocean Ave, 07740. Tel 201-229-0600, 222-9879. *Pres* Edgar N Dinkelspiel
Open summers Wed - Sun 10 AM - 5 PM, cl Mon & Tues, other times by appointment. No admis fee. Estab 1953 as post Civil War historical museum. Average Annual Attendance: 10,000. Mem: Dues $1
Income: Financed by Art Shows
Exhibitions: Art Shows for 19 years
Publications: Annual Art Show Book

MADISON

M **DREW UNIVERSITY,** College Art Gallery, 07940. Tel 201-377-3000, Ext 321. *Dean* Robert Ackerman; *Chmn Art Dept* Martyvonne Dehoney
Open weekdays 1 - 4 PM, Sat 9 AM - Noon, and by appointment. Estab 1968 to provide 8 or 9 exhibitions each school year to augment program of courses and to serve the community. Mem: 60
Income: Financed by University instructional budget, general budget and donations
Collections: Study collection of serigraphs, lithographs and intaglio prints; pottery; large sculpture by Robert Mallary
Exhibitions: Aspects of Drawing; Berger Collection of Prints; One person shows; The Printmaking Council of New Jersey Benefit Show; also exhibitions on loan from major New York galleries
L **Library,** 07940
Library maintained for art history courses
Library Holdings: AV—Slides

MONTCLAIR

M **MONTCLAIR ART MUSEUM,** 3 South Mountain Ave, PO Box X, 07042. Tel 201-746-5555. *Pres* James S Vandermade; *Dir* Robert j Koenig; *Coordr Public Relations* Lillian Bristol; *Cur* Maureen C O'Brien; *Curatorial Registrar* Joan Lorenson; *Education Cur* Leone Otis; *Bursar* Adelaide R Birnie
Open Tues - Sat 10 AM - 5 PM, Sun 2 - 5 PM. No admis fee. Estab 1914. Five galleries of changing exhibitions; one gallery of permanent exhibitions; student gallery. Average Annual Attendance: 39,000. Mem: 2500; dues $20
Income: Financed by endowment and membership
Collections: American costumes; The Lang Collection and Tomlin Collection of

Chinese Snuff Bottles; the Rand Collection of American Indian Art; Whitney Silver Collection; †American paintings, 18th - 20th Century; prints and drawings
Exhibitions: Collage: American Masters; Drawing the Line, The Alchemy of Walter Murch; Images of the American Indian, James Brooks and James Opper; Adolf Konrad Retrospective; Robert Rauschenberg: Two Serial Works; The Season Splendid: Paintings by Lee Hall
Publications: Bulletin, bi-monthly, five issues
Activities: Classes for adults and children; docent training; workshops coordinated programs with school groups; lectures open to the public, six to eight visiting lecturers per year; concerts; gallery talks every Sunday; tours; museum shop sells books, reproductions, slides, handcrafted textiles, pottery, jewelry and objects for children
L **LeBrun Library,** 3 South Mountain Ave, PO Box X, 07042. *Librn* Edith A Rights
Open Tues - Fri 10 AM - 5 PM, Sat 10 AM - 1 PM, cl July and August. Estab 1924 to support research and exhibitions of the museum. For reference only
Income: $4000
Purchases: $4000
Library Holdings: Vols 9000; Per subs 50; Micro—Fiche; AV—A-tapes, cassettes, lantern Slides, slides; Other—Clipping files, exhibition catalogs, pamphlets, reproductions
Special Subjects: American Art, American Indian, Japanese Culture
Collections: Bookplates; Posters

MORRISTOWN

M **MORRIS MUSEUM OF ARTS AND SCIENCES,** Normandy Heights & Columbia Rds, PO Box 125, Convent, 07961. Tel 201-538-0452. *Dir* Chester H Newkirk; *Asst Dir* John Krushenick; *Art Cur* Gail Gelburg
Open Mon - Sat 10 AM - 5 PM; Sun 2 - 5 PM. Summer, July and August, Tues - Sat 10 AM - 4 PM; cl major holidays. Admis adults $1, students & senior citizens 50¢, children 25¢, groups 25¢. Inc 1943. Average Annual Attendance: 175,000. Mem: 1550; dues benefactor $100, patron $50, organizations $25 and up, family $25, couple $15, individual $10, students and senior citizens $5; annual meeting third Wed in Jan
Collections: American historic and foreign; decorative arts; dolls; North American Indians
Activities: Dance, music and drama programs; art and nature workshops; (for 3 - 7 year olds) Summer Theater Festival for children; children's theater throughout year; lect; gallery talks; tours; foreign films; sales shop; Five Sense Center
L **Library,** Normandy Heights and Columbia Rds, PO Box 125, Convent, 07961.
Library Holdings: Vols 1000; AV—Slides

M **SCHUYLER-HAMILTON HOUSE,** 5 Olyphant Place, 07960. Tel 201-267-4039. *Regent* Mrs Philip L Rea Jr; *Cur* Mrs Francis Black
Open Sun & Tues 2 - 5 PM, other times by appointment. Admis 50¢, children under 12 free. Estab 1923 for preservation of historical landmark. House is furnished with 18th Century antiques; five large portraits of General & Mrs Philip Schuyler, their daughter, Betsey Schuyler Hamilton, Alexander Hamilton and Dr Jabez Campfield; old lithographs, silhouette of George Washington, needle and petit point. Average Annual Attendance: 350. Mem: 106; dues $20; annual meeting May, Chapter meets Sept - May
Income: Financed by membership
Collections: China - Canton, blue willow, Staffordshire; doll china; pewter; brass candlesticks; rugs; tunebooks
Activities: Docent training; lect open to public; tours; competitions with awards; scholarships; exten dept; sales shop sells colonial dolls, miniature furniture and rugs, stationery, cards and reproductions

MOUNT HOLLY

M **HISTORIC BURLINGTON COUNTY PRISON MUSEUM,** 128 High St, 08060. Tel 609-267-3300, Ext 5806. *Cur* Nicholas Kusti
Open Tues - Sat 10 AM - Noon & 1 - 4 PM, cl National holidays. No admis fee. Estab 1966, built 1811; designed by Robert Mills. Mem: Dues $2
Collections: Glass; graphics; historic military materials; Indian artifacts; paintings
Exhibitions: Historical Exhibits
Activities: Lect; tours; temporary and traveling exhibits
M **Mansion at Smithville,** 49 Rancocas Rd, 08060. *Admin* David A Miller
Open March - Nov, Wed & Sat 10 - 4 PM. Admis adults $1, students and senior citizens 50¢. Victorian house museum, historic industrial village, art gallery
Exhibitions: Permanent and rotating art exhibits
Activities: Tours; festivals; concerts

NEWARK

M **NEWARK MUSEUM,** 49 Washington St, PO Box 540, 07101. Tel 201-733-6600. *Pres* C Malcolm Davis; *Dir* Samual C Miller; *Asst to Dir* Dorothy McNally; *Admin Asst* Wilmot T Bartle; *Business Mgr* Dominic A Lisanti; *Dir Education* Sally O C Townsend; *Lending Dept* Janet E Smerczak; *Public Relations* Walter Newkirk; *Arts Workshop* Jean West; *Program & Publicity* Mary Sue Sweeney; *Cur Classical* Susan Auth; *Cur Coins & Fri Museum* Dorothy B Bartle; *Cur Decorative Arts* Philip H Curtis; *Cur Oriental Coll* Valrae Reynolds; *Cur Ethnology* Anne Spencer; *Cur Painting & Sculpture* Fearn Thurlow
Open Mon - Sun Noon - 5 PM, holidays 1 - 5 PM, cl Christmas, New Year's Day, July 4 & Thanksgiving. No admis fee. Estab 1909 to exhibit articles of art, science, history and technology, and for the study of the arts and sciences. The building was a gift of Louis Bamberger, opened 1926; held in trust by the Museum Association for the City of Newark, which gave the site. The adjoining building purchased by Museum in 1937. Average Annual Attendance: 412,000. Mem: 4700; dues $10 and up; annual meeting Jan
Income: $2,000,000 (financed by city and state appropriations, county funds)
Collections: †American painting and sculpture of all periods with primitives well represented; †African, †American Indian, †Chinese, †Indian, †Islamic, †Japanese, †South Pacific, †Tibetan; †Mediterranean Antiquities, including Eugene Schaefer Collection of ancient glass; †decorative arts; †Pre-Columbian material; †crosses and

crucifixes; †coins

Exhibitions: Abstract Artists from the Collection; As the Seasons Turn: Southwest Indian Easel Painting of the Early 20th Century and Related Traditional Art; Colonial and Federal Portraits from the Collection; Lee Gatch; Myth and Gospel, Art of Coptic Egypt; Murals Without Walls; Survival: Life and Art of the Alaskan Eskimo; Tibet: A Lost World; The Two Worlds of Japenese Art; 2000 Years of Chinese Ceramics; Arshile Gorky's Aviation Murals Rediscovered

Publications: New Notes, monthly; The Newark Museum, quarterly; catalogs and bulletins on major exhibitions

Activities: Classes for adults and children; dramatic programs; docent training; lect open to the public, 15 - 20 vis lectr per yr; concerts; gallery talks; tours; competitions; extention department serving community neighborhoods; individual paintings and original objects of art lent to other museums; lending collection contains nature artifacts; museum shop sells books, magazines, original art, reproductions, prints, original craft items from around the world

L **Library,** 49 Washington St, 07101. Tel 201-733-6640, 733-6584. *Libr Asst* Helen Olsson

Open Mon - Fri 9 Am - 5 PM. Estab 1926 to serve the Museum staff and to provide information on the collections

Library Holdings: Vols 21,000; Per subs 143; AV—Kodachromes, lantern Slides, slides; Other—Clipping files, exhibition catalogs, pamphlets, photographs

Special Subjects: American Indian Art, Decorative Arts, Oriental Art, Primitive Art, American Art, Tibet, general art subjects

Publications: Acquisitions list, bimonthly to staff

M **Junior Museum,** 49 Washington St, 07101. *Supv* Sheryl B Bouler; *Asst Supv* Stephen Kneisel; *Art Asst* Bisa Washington; *Art Asst* Jane Caffrey

Open daily Noon - 5 PM. No admis fee. Estab 1926 to supply art and science programs designed to stimulate the individual child in exploration and discovery of self expression, and to teach effective use of the Museum as a whole, which may lead to valuable lifetime interests. Art and Science education resource information and workshops, after school, Saturday and summer workshops in art for children ages 3 - 18; preschool workshops Tues - Fri mornings; special holiday festivals for children; awards; field trips. Average Annual Attendance: 16,700. Mem: 10,123; dues 10¢; annual meeting May

Income: Financed through The Newark Museum

Exhibitions: Changing exhibitions; annual exhibition of childrens work

Activities: Parents art workshops; special education workshops for exceptional children and adults

L **NEWARK PUBLIC LIBRARY,** 5 Washington St, Box 630, 07101. Tel 201-733-7840. *Prin Art Librn* Joan E Burns; *Supv Art & Music Department* William J Dane

Open Mon, Wed & Thurs 9 AM - 9 PM; Tues & Fri 9 AM - 6 PM; Sat 9 AM - 5 PM. Estab 1888 to provide materials on all aspects of the visual arts to the metropolitan area of New Jersey. Circ 70,000. Maintains an art gallery: three separate galleries with a total of 375 running feet

Income: Financed by city and state appropriations

Purchases: $30,000

Library Holdings: Per subs 200; Micro—Fiche, reels; AV—Cassettes, slides 15,000; Other—Clipping files, exhibition catalogs, prints, manuscripts, original art works, pamphlets, photographs, reproductions, original documents

Special Subjects: Fine Prints, History of Fine Printing, Japanese Books and Prints

Collections: R C Jenkinson Collection of fine printing; Autographs; Bookplates; Fine Print Collection (12,000); Picture Collection (1,000,000 illustrations); Posters

Exhibitions: Rudolph Ruzicka Memorial Show; American Art Magazines; Art and the Urban Experience; Caxton and His Followers; Folk Costume the World Over; Heritage of Italian Printing; It's On The Bag (Shopping Bag Design); Photography in Posters; Posters from Paris 1955-1970; Salute to Picasso; Visuals for Black Studies; The Hoboken Five

Publications: Calendar of events, bimonthly

Activities: Concerts; gallery talks; films; tours; traveling exhibitions organized and circulated

M **NEW JERSEY HISTORICAL SOCIETY MUSEUM,** 230 Broadway, 07104. Tel 201-483-3939. *Pres* Peter Cartmell; *Dir* Joan C Hull; *Chmn of the Board* Milford A Vieser; *Cur - Registrar* Alan D Frazer

Open Mon - Sat Noon - 4:15 PM; from 9:30 AM by appointment for research. No admis fee. Estab 1845 to collect, preserve, exhibit and make available for study the materials pertaining to the history of New Jersey and its people. The gallery has six period rooms and lobby display cases on the main floor; three galleries on second floor totaling 3900 sq ft devoted to permanent or changing exhibitions. Average Annual Attendance: 10,000. Mem: 3600; dues adults $20 and up; annual meeting third Wed in April

Income: Financed by endowment, membership, gifts and grants

Purchases: $500

Collections: Ceramics; glassware; furniture; important technical drawings from 1790-1815; Indian relics; New Jersey portraits, landscapes, prints and photographs; sculpture; silhouettes and miniatures; silver; toys; World War I posters

Exhibitions: (1976-78) A Self-Portrait - The New Jersey Historical Society: 1845-1977; Alone with the Pigeons - Public Sculpture in New Jersey (photographs and graphics); The American Marines in the Revolution; Yearning to Breathe Free; (1978-80) Building New Jersey - Designs by William E Lehman, Architect; Patent Models by Ingenious Jerseymen; An Exhibit on Americans - the Italians in New Jersey; Craftsmen of Elegance - The Newark Jewelry Industry; Gems from the Manuscript Collection; Planned: The Germans of New Jersey

Publications: Exhibition catalogs; New Jersey History, quarterly; New Jersey Messenger, quarterly newsletter; The Cockpit; The Crossroads

Activities: Classes for children; docent training; school history clubs; lectr open to the public; tours; competitions; individual paintings and original objects of art lent to established institutions; traveling exhibitions organized and circulated; sales shop selling books, reproductions, prints and items for children

L **Library,** 230 Broadway, 07104. Tel 201-483-3939. *Library Dir* Barbara S Irwin; *Reference Librn* Patricia Zerbe; *Cataloger* Cynthia E Browne; *Conservator* Janet L Koch; *Keeper of Manuscripts* Carl A Lane; *Field Archivist* Carolyn Ryan

Open Mon - Sat 9:30 AM to 4:15 PM. Estab to collect and make available materials relating to the study of New Jersey and family history. For reference only

Income: Financed by endowment, membership, gifts and grants

Purchases: $5000

Library Holdings: Vols 60,000; Micro—Reels; AV—A-tapes; Other—Clipping files, exhibition catalogs, pamphlets, original documents, maps, broadsides

Collections: Rare books (manuscripts, over 1100 major groups); 18th and 19th century newspapers

Publications: Guide to the Manuscript Collections of The New Jersey Historical Society (1979); Library Acquisitions, quarterly

NEW BRUNSWICK

RUTGERS UNIVERSITY

M **Art Gallery,** Voorhees Hall, Hamilton Street, 08903. Tel 201-932-7237. *Dir & Cur Prints* Phillip Dennis Cate; *Cur Painting & Sculpture* Jeffrey Wechsler; *Admin Asst Education* Stephanie Grunberg; *Cur of Children's Literature* Elaine-Carol Stanis; *Registrar* Marilyn Pruce

Open Mon - Fri 10 AM - 4:30 PM; Sat & Sun noon - 5 PM. No admis fee. Estab 1966 to house Fine Arts Collection and present exhibitions through the school year. Average Annual Attendance: 40,000. Mem: 300; dues corporate & business $250 and up, endowment $100 and up, patron $35 and up, family $20, individual $15, senior citizen $10, student $5

Income: Financed by state appropriation

Purchases: $10,000

Collections: 15th and 17th century Italian; 17th century Dutch; 18th, 19th and 20th century American; 18th and 19th century English paintings; †19th and 20th century French and American prints

Exhibitions: (1978) Contemporary Artists Series 1: Pat Adams, Robert Graham, Norman Tuck; The Color Revolution: Color Lithography in France 1890-1900; Claire Van Vliet: Printmaker and Printer - A selection of her prints and illustrated books from her Janus Press; (1979) The Raymond V Carpenter Collection; Posters by Paul Colin: 1925-1967; David Hare: Color Photography by the Pueblo Indians (1940); Cornelis Ploos Van Amstel (1726-1798); Color Etchings After Seventeenth century Dutch and Flemish Master Drawings; Contemporary American Artists Series II; Eighteenth century French Drawings; Middlesex County Residents - Rutgers Faculty and Staff Collect; Rutgers University Masters of Fine Arts Exhibition; Vanguard American Sculpture: 1913-1939 Paintings by Watanabe Kazan (1793 - 1841); Rutgers-Camden Biennial Drawing Competition

Publications: Exhibition catalogs, annually; Friends Newsletter

Activities: Classes for adults and children; lect open to public; concerts; gallery talks; tours; traveling exhibitions organized and circulated

L **Art Library,** Voorhees Hall, Hamilton St, 08903. Tel 201-932-7739. *Art Librn* Ferris Olin; *Asst to Art Librn* Donna Dunlop

Open Mon - Thurs 9 AM - 12 PM, Fri 9 AM - 5 PM, Sat 12 - 5 PM, Sun 1 - 12 PM. Estab 1966 for academic research. Circ Open stacks. For reference only

Library Holdings: Vols 27,000; Per subs 280; Micro—Fiche; Other—Clipping files, exhibition catalogs, pamphlets

Special Subjects: Architecture, Decorative Arts, Photography, Classical archaeology, graphics

Collections: Mary Bartlett Cowdrey Collection of American Art; Louis E Stern Collection of Contemporary Art; Western Art-Architectural History

Activities: Bibliographic instruction; tours; lect

NORTH BRUNSWICK

M **JOHNSTON NATIONAL SCOUTING MUSEUM,** Routes 1 and 130, 08902. Tel 201-249-6000, Ext 428. *Dir* Ilmar Pleer

Temporarily closed; new facilities being sought

NUTLEY

O **MINIATURE ART SOCIETY OF NEW JERSEY,** 200 Chestnut St, 07110. Tel 201-661-2280. *Pres* John Barnwell; *VPres Publicity* Pat Longley; *VPres Programs* Marilyn Brill; *Secy* Vivian Noyes Fikus; *Treas* V Egan; *Recording Secy* Adele Landfear

Mem: 150; dues $10

Exhibitions: National Show; competitive awards, ten catagories

Publications: Newsletter, four or five times a year

Activities: Competitions; traveling exhibitions organized and circulated

OCEAN CITY

O **OCEAN CITY ARTS CENTER,** 409 Wesley Avenue, 08226. Tel 609-399-7628. *Executive Dir* Frances Taylor; *Asst to Dir* Eunice Bell; *Publicity Coordr* Shirley A Waldron

Open Mon - Sat 9 AM - 4 PM, Evenings Mon - Fri 7 - 10 PM. Estab 1966 to promote the arts. Two galleries are maintained; upper gallery houses the permanent collection; lower gallery is for monthly changing exhibitions throughout the year. Average Annual Attendance: 10,000. Mem: 1059; dues individual $6, family $12; annual meeting in January

Income: $70,000 (financed by membership, city appropriation, New Jersey State Council on the Arts Grant 1980)

Exhibitions: Annual: Membership Show, Juried Show, Boardwalk Art Show Winners Exhibition, December Christmas Card Crafts, Juried Photography Show; Needlework Show in 1980

Publications: Newsletters, quarterly

Activities: Classes for adults and children; dramatic programs; docent training; lectures open to the public, 12 visiting lecturers per year; concerts; gallery talks; tours; competitions with awards; scholarships offered; museum shop sells books, magazines, original art, reproductions, prints

L **Art Library,** 409 Wesley Ave, 08226. Tel 609-399-7628.

Open 9 AM - 4 PM daily, & Mon - Sat, 7 - 10 PM evenings. Estab 1972 to make art and research materials available to instructors, students and members

Income: $70,000
Library Holdings: Vols 700; Per subs 2; AV—A-tapes, fs, lantern Slides, motion pictures, rec, slides; Other—Clipping files, exhibition catalogs, memorabilia, pamphlets, photographs
Special Subjects: Art History, Photography

PARAMUS

M BERGEN COMMUNITY MUSEUM, E Ridgewood and Farview Ave, 07652. Tel 201-265-1248, 265-1255. *Dir* Carol Stahl; *Preparator* Vickie Learner; *Educational Liaison* Linda Nasta; *Secy* Yolanda Tremper
Open Tues - Sat 10 AM - 5 PM; Sun 1 - 5 PM. No admis fee. Estab May 1956 to maintain a museum which will provide a creative and recreative center to stimulate youth and adult interest in arts, science, history and industry
Income: Financed by membership, contributions and country appropriations
Collections: Mainly works of New Jersey artists
Publications: Calendar, bi-monthly
Activities: Classes for children; lect open to the public, 10 vis lectr per yr; concerts; gallery talks; tours; individual paintings lent; museum shop selling lithographs, books, model kits, souvenirs for children

PATERSON

O PASSAIC COUNTY HISTORICAL SOCIETY, Lambert Castle, Valley Rd, 07503.
Open Wed - Sun 1 - 4:45 PM. Admis adults 50¢, children under 15 free. Estab 1926. Located in Lambert Castle built in 1892. Mem: Dues Sustaining $25; family $10; regular $7.50; student $3
Collections: Koemple Spoon collection; Indian art; textiles; local historical material; paintings; sculptures; period furniture
Publications: Castle Lite, bi-monthly newsletter; pamphlets
Activities: Lectures; guided tours; museum shop sells publications, postcards, souvenirs, gifts
L Library, Lambert Castle, Valley Rd, 07503
Open to the public when the museum is open
Library Holdings: Vols 5000

PITTSTOWN

O ASSOCIATED ARTISTS OF NEW JERSEY, RD 1, 08867. Tel 201-735-5831. *Pres* W Carl Burger; *VPres* Joseph Konopka; *Secy* Anne Steele Marsh; *Treas* Hella Bailin
Estab 1941 to hold one or two exhibitions a year, with informatl meetings in summer. Mem: Members selected by invitation of the Board; dues $7; annual meeting April-May
Income: Financed by membership

PLAINFIELD

L PLAINFIELD PUBLIC LIBRARY, Eighth St at Park Ave, 07060. Tel 201-757-1111. *Dir* L A Moore
Open Mon - Fri 9 AM - 9 PM; Sat 9 AM - 5 PM. Estab 1881. Circ 200,000. Maintains an art gallery with original artworks on permanent display, group shows as scheduled
Income: $575,000 (financed by endowment, city and state appropriation, and Federal funds)
Library Holdings: Vols 198,000; Per subs 546; Micro—Fiche, reels; AV—Cassettes, fs, Kodachromes, motion pictures, rec, slides, v-tapes; Other—Exhibition catalogs, original art works, photographs
Collections: Arts of the United States (slides); Lincoln Fine Arts Collection (books & periodicals)
Exhibitions: Annual National Print Exhibition; Associated Artists of New Jersey; Invitational Exhibits; student work
Activities: Dramatic programs; lect open to public, 3-4 vis lectr per yr; gallery talks; tours

PRINCETON

O PRINCETON ART ASSOCIATION, Rosedale Rd, 08540. Tel 609-921-9173. *Pres* Harleston Hall; *VPres* Hope Carter; *Secy* Mary O'Leary; *Treas* Fred Proctor; *Exec Dir* Mary M Ward
Open Seven days a week, hours vary. Estab 1964 to establish and maintain educational and cultural programs dovoted to art. Exhibitions are held at McCarter Theatre and at various locations throughout the community. Average Annual Attendance: 1500. Mem: 1000; annual meeting May
Income: Financed by membership, class fees, workshops and demonstration fees, trip fees, entry fees and donations
Activities: Classes for adults and children; lectures open to the public; competitions with awards; scholarships offered

PRINCETON UNIVERSITY
M Art Museum, 08540. Tel 609-452-3787. *Acting Dir* Allen Rosenbaum; *Cur Coll* Frances F Jones; *Dir Public Relations* Virginia Wageman; *Dir Community Services* JoAnn Carchman; *Registrar* Robert LaFond; *Custodian Prints & Drawings* Barbara T Ross
Open Tues - Sat 10 AM - 4 PM; Sun 1 - 5 PM; Summer 2 - 4 PM; cl Mon & major holidays. No admis fee. Estab 1882 to make original works of art available to students in the Department of Art & Archeology and also for the enjoyment of the University, community and general public. About 24,000 sq ft of gallery space for permanent, semi-permanent and changing installations. Average Annual Attendance: 90,000. Mem: 1200; dues $15 and up
Income: Financed by endowment and University
Purchases: $150,000

Collections: †Ancient Mediterranean; †British and American; †Chinese ritual bronze vessels; †Far Eastern, especially Chinese and Japanese, paintings; †mediaeval and later European; †Pre-Columbian
Publications: Catalogs, occasionally; Record of the Art Museum, semi-annually
Activities: Docent training; lect; gallery talks; tours

L Index of Christian Art, McCormick Hall, 08540. Tel 609-452-3773. *Dir* Rosalie B Green
Open Mon - Fri 9 AM - 5 PM; cl August and holidays. Estab 1917 as a division of the Department of Art and Archaeology. It is a research and reference collection of cards and photographs designed to facilitate the study of Christian iconography in works of art before 1400. Duplicate copies exist in Washington, DC in the Dumbarton Oaks Research Center and in Los Angeles in the Library of the University of California. European copies are in Rome in the Vatican Library and in Utrecht in the University

C E R SQUIBB & SONS, INC, Lawrenceville-Princeton Rd, PO Box 4000, 08540. Tel 609-921-4261. *Dir Community Affairs* Lora W Jones
Estab as a community service, in appreciation of beauty. Maintains a Fine Arts Gallery which mounts 8 exhibitions per year
Activities: Competitions; financial assistance to museums and art association's juried shows throughout New Jersey; for medical charities, have initiated large photograph exhibitions; awards; originate traveling exhibitions

RINGOES

M RELIGIOUS AMERICANA MUSEUM, Van Lieu's Rd, 08551. Tel 201-782-0392. *Cur* Mrs Joseph J Domas; *Trustee* Clyde M McBride; *Secy* Joseph J Domas
Open Mon - Fri 10 AM - 4 PM; weekends to church groups by appointment. No admis fee. Estab 1971 as a corporation under New Jersey laws to preserve our nation's religious heritage in artifacts of the three major faiths. Main gallery 35 x 18 ft, two side galleries 25 x 16 ft. Average Annual Attendance: 200. Mem: Annual meeting May
Income: Financed by donations and lecture fees
Collections: Beadwork; books (pamphlets, broadsides, leaflets); bottles; ceramics; chalkware; cloth; costume; glass; horn; jewelry; metal (brass, copper, iron, pewter, silver, tin); music; needlework; over 450 artifacts, in 23 media, all made in America before 1900; painting; paperwork; parian; perforated cardboard; plaster; pottery; prints (woodcuts, engravings, lithographs); quilts; scrimshaw; shellwork; stone and wood
Exhibitions: Beginnings (founders of sects); Issues (affecting all faiths); folk art; Regional
Activities: Classes for children; lect open to public
L Library, Van Lieu's Rd, 08551
Open to serious students only

RINGWOOD

M RINGWOOD MANOR HOUSE MUSEUM, Sloatsburg Rd, PO Box 1304, 07456. Tel 201-962-7031. *Cur* Elbertus Prol
Open May - Oct Tues - Fri 10 AM - 4 PM; Sat, Sun & holidays 10 AM - 5 PM. No admis fee. Estab 1935
Income: Financed by state appropriation
Collections: Decorative arts; furniture; graphics; historical material; paintings
Activities: Guided tours; sales shop

RIVER VALE

L RIVER VALE PUBLIC LIBRARY, 644 River Vale Rd, 07675. Tel 201-391-2323. *Dir* Dorothy Cornell
Open Mon - Thurs 10 AM - 9 PM, Fri 10 AM - 5 PM, Sat 10 AM - 4 PM, cl Sat July and Aug. Circ 80,000
Income: $90,000 (financed by city appropriation)
Library Holdings: Vols 30,000; Per subs 115; AV—Cassettes, rec, slides; Other—Framed reproductions, prints, sculpture
Collections: Fine arts: music and art, history, artists, techniques; Theatre history: Broadway; movies; Beginning photography collection
Exhibitions: Local artists exhibits

SOUTH ORANGE

M SETON HALL UNIVERSITY, Student Center Art Gallery, S Orange Ave, 07079. Tel 201-762-9000, Ext 675. *Dir* Petra Ten-Doesschate Chu; *Cur Exhib* Barbara W Kaufman
Open daily 9 AM - 10 PM. No admis fee. Estab 1963. Troast Memorial Gallery, estab 1974, houses permanent collection of contemporary American art; Wang Fang-Yu Collection of Oriental art was estab in 1977. Average Annual Attendance: 35,000
Exhibitions: Sculpture: Tony Triano; Miquel Ferreiro-Paz
Activities: Lect open to the public; gallery talks
L Library, S Orange Ave, 07079.
Library Holdings: AV—Slides 11,000

SPRINGFIELD

L SPRINGFIELD FREE PUBLIC LIBRARY, Donald B Palmer Museum, 66 Mountain Ave. Tel 201-376-4930. *Library and Museum Dir* Helen C Francis; *Head Technical Services* Mary Manuel; *Head Reference Department* Joan Meyer; *Head Circulation Department* Rose Searles; *Head Childrens Department* Patricia Fennimore; *Bookeeper* Erna Kitzing; *Cur* Donald Palmer; *Coordr of Public Relations* Iris Goodmen
Open Mon, Wed, Thurs 9 AM - 9 PM, Tues, Fri, and Sat 9 AM - 5 PM. No admis fee. Estab 1975 as a museum addition to a public library established to preserve local

history and to present cultural exhibits throughout the year. The library, including a meeting room with monthly art exhibits and the museum's bimonthly exhibits of art, crafts and history, serves as a cultural center

Income: $1500
Purchases: $5700
Collections: †Permanent collection of circulating framed art reproductions
Exhibitions: Traveling exhibitions from art institutes and galleries; Museum: crafts; ethnic; historicsl; art and design; Meeting Room: exhibits of original oils, watercolors, graphics and cray-pas
Publications: Bulletin, monthly
Activities: Dramatic programs; workshops; programs for adults and children include concerts; films; lectures; puppet shows; lect open to public, 12 visiting lecturers per year; Individual reproductions lent to library patrons; lending collection contains books, framed reproductions, records, photographs, slides and periodicals; book four traveling exhibitions annually; museum shop sells used books, prints and records twice a year

O SPRINGFIELD HISTORICAL SOCIETY, 126 Morris Ave, Box 124, 07081. *Pres* Madeline E Lancaster; *VPres* Howard Wiseman; *Secy* Mildred Levsen
Open Sun 2 - 4 PM, except holidays and storm days. Admis 50¢. Estab 1953, the Society owns and maintains the historic Cannon Ball House, circa 1741, known as Hutchins Homestead, registered as State Historic Site in 1976 and National in 1977. Average Annual Attendance: 500. Mem: 185; dues $5; meeting four times a year
Income: Financed by membership and small donations
Collections: Pictures of Revolutionary soldiers and local history; †furnishings in the home
Activities: Tours; sales shop selling maps, plates and postcards

SUMMIT

AMERICAN ABSTRACT ARTISTS
For further information, see National and Regional Organizations

O SUMMIT ART CENTER, INC, 68 Elm St, 07901. Tel 201-273-9121. *Pres* Mrs Harold Van Tassel; *Dir* Robert Reid
Exhibits open daily Noon - 4 PM, Sat & Sun 2 - 4 PM. Estab 1933. New exhibitions every 3 - 4 weeks. Mem: 2000; dues Friends Membership $35, general membership $25; annual meeting April
Exhibitions: Annual Statewide Juried Show; one and two-man shows
Activities: Art classes for adults and children; lectures; musical events; Art Caravan; art to the elderly (Nursing home project bringing art slides and lecture series to the confined)

TRENTON

L FREE PUBLIC LIBRARY, Art and Music Department, 120 Academy St, PO Box 2448, 08608. Tel 609-392-7188, Ext 24. *Dir* Harold W Thompson Jr; *Head Art and Music Dept* James N Kisthardt
Open Mon, Wed, Thurs 9 AM - 9 PM, Tues, Fri and Sat 9 AM - 5 PM, cl Sun and holidays. Estab 1900
Income: Financed by city appropriation
Library Holdings: Vols 7000; Per subs 92; AV—Motion pictures, rec; Other— Photographs

M MERCER COUNTY COMMUNITY COLLEGE GALLERY, 1200 Old Trenton Rd, 08690. Tel 609-586-4800. *Dir* Frank G Butorac
Open 9 AM - 5 PM. No admis fee. Triangle Gallery primarily for exhibiting student work
Collections: Ceramics collection; Cybis Collection; Kelsey Collection; Mexican art and handicrafts; painting by Wolf Kahn
Exhibitions: Faculty, student and children's art exhibits as well as exhibits from the permanent collection
Activities: Classes for adults and children; lect open to the public; gallery talks; extension dept; lending collection contains motion pictures; book traveling exhibitions

L Library, 1200 Old Trenton Rd, 08690
Estab 1891 to provide library services for the college; portion of the main floor is devoted to permanent display cabinets. In addition display panels are used for faculty exhibits, community exhibits and traveling exhibits
Library Holdings: Vols 70,000; Other—Prints
Publications: Audio-visual materials catalog, biannually; college catalog, every two years; film catalog, annually; library handbook, biannually; library newsletter, quarterly; The Book Bynder

M NEW JERSEY STATE MUSEUM, 205 W State St, 08625. Tel 609-292-6300. *Dir* Leah P Sloshberg; *Asst Dir* Karen Cummins; *Cur Fine Arts* Zoltan Buki; *Cur Cultural History* Suzanne Corlette; *Cur Exhibits* Wallace Conway; *Cur Education* Raymond Howe; *Cur Archaeology-Ethnology* Lorraine Williams
Open Mon, Wed 9 AM - 4:45 PM; Sat, Sun & holidays 1 - 5 PM; cl Christmas, New Year's, Thanksgiving and Fourth of July. No admis fee. Estab 1891 by legislation to collect, exhibit and interpret fine arts, cultural history, archaeology-ethnology and science with a New Jersey focus; changing exhibit gallery, Hall of Natural Science, projected hall for permanent collection. Average Annual Attendance: 425,000. Mem: 1800; dues $25 and up; annual meeting June
Income: $1,300,000 (financed by state appropriation)
Purchases: $60,000, plus $30,000 - $60,000 from Friends
Collections: American fine and decorative arts of the 18th, 19th and 20th century; American painting from 1910-1950 with special emphasis on the †Steiglitz circle, Regionalist, Abstract Artists; †New Jersey fine and decorative arts
Exhibitions: Changing exhibitions focus on New Jersey artists and cultural history; Long-term teaching exhibitions on language of the visual arts and Indian culture
Publications: Bulletins; catalogs and irregular serials; Investigators; reports
Activities: Classes for children; dramatic programs; docent training; lect open to the public; competitions; films; individual paintings and original objects of art lent to other institutions; lending collection contains 1281 motion picture titles, 2613 reels, nature artifacts, original art works, original prints, paintings; traveling exhibitions

organized and circulated; museum shop selling books, international folk crafts or items related to collection

L Library, 205 W State St, 08625
Open to staff for reference only

M OLD BARRACKS, S Willow St, 08608. Tel 609-396-1776. *Dir* Cynthia Koch; *Asst Dir* Alyce Lang
Open April - Oct Mon - Fri 10 AM - 5 PM, Sun 1 - 5 PM, Nov - Mar Mon - Fri 10 AM - 4:30 PM, Sun 1 - 4:30 PM. Admis adults 50¢, children through 12 25¢, student groups free. Estab 1902 as museum of history and decorative arts. Located in English barracks that housed Hessian Soldiers Dec 1776. Average Annual Attendance: 28,000. Mem: 330; dues family $15, individual $10; annual meeting Nov, March, May
Income: Financed by membership and state appropriation
Collections: Mementos of George Washington; China of Colonial and Federal periods; collection of early firearms; diorams: Two Battles of Trenton and Princeton; furniture, silver, restored soldier's room
Activities: Lect for members and guests only; tours for school children; individual paintings and original objects of art lent to museums; book traveling exhibitions; sales shop sells books, reproductions, slides and trinkets for school children

M TRENTON STATE COLLEGE, Holman Gallery, Hillwood Lakes, 08625. Tel 609-771-2198. *Pres* Dr Harold Eickoff; *Art Department Chairman* Dr Norval Kern; *Gallery Coordr* Rotraud Sackerlotzky
Open Mon - Fri 12 - 3 PM, Thurs 7 - 9 PM, Sun 1 - 3 PM. No admis fee. Estab to present students and community with the opportunity to study a wide range of artistic expressions and to exhibit their work. Average Annual Attendance: 2000
Collections: Purchases from National Print and Drawing Show
Exhibitions: Craft Show; Faculty Show; Mercer County Competitive Art; Mercer County Competitive Photography; National Drawing Exhibition; National Print Exhibition; Selections from the State Museum; Sculpture Shows; Student Exhibition
Publications: Catalog for National Print Exhibition; catalog for National Drawing Exhibition
Activities: Classes for adults and children; Lectures open to the public, five visiting lecturers per year; gallery talks; tours; competitions with awards; individual paintings and original objects of art lent to other offices and departments on campus; lending collection contains original art works; original prints; paintings; traveling exhibitions organized and circulated to other state colleges and art schools

UNION

M KEAN COLLEGE OF NEW JERSEY, College Gallery, Morris Avenue, 08063. Tel 201-527-2307, 527-2347. *Pres* Dr Nathan Weiss; *Chmn Art Dept* Dr Robert Coon; *Gallery Dir* Zara Cohan
Open Mon - Fri 10 AM - 2 PM; Tues - Thurs 7:30 - 10 PM; Sat 9 AM - 1 PM; by appointment at other times. No admis fee. Estab 1971 as a forum to present all art forms to students and the community through original exhibitions, catalogues, fine art, art history and museum training. One gallery 22 x 34 ft plus an alcove 8 x 18 ft on first floor of arts and humanities building. Average Annual Attendance: 3000
Income: Financed by state appropriation
Collections: American painting by J Stella, P Jenkins, L Baskin, W Homer, Audubon, W Gropper, Lamar Dodd; prints and photographs
Exhibitions: Good Design Interior Design Projects; John Cotton Dana: Visionary; Italian Baroque Drawings; Major Works Art Faculty; Local Limners; Mount, Homer and their contemporaries; Piranesi: Real and Imaginary; Problems in Connoissenorship; Three Women Graduate Thesis
Publications: Catalogues for exhibitions
Activities: Dramatic programs; lect open to public; individual paintings lent to colleges, institutions, and departments on the campus; lending collection contains original art works, original prints, photographs, sculpture and slides

L Nancy Thompson Library, Morris Avenue, 08063. *Acquisitions Librn* Tamara Avdzej
Open Mon - Thurs 8 AM - 11:30 PM, Fri 8 AM - 10 PM, Sat 9 AM - 4 PM, Sun 1 - 8 PM. Estab 1855 to support instruction
Purchases: $6000
Library Holdings: Vols 200,000; Per subs 57; AV—A-tapes, cassettes, fs, Kodachromes, motion pictures, rec, slides, v-tapes

UPPER MONTCLAIR

M MONTCLAIR STATE COLLEGE, Gallery One, 07043. Tel 201-893-5112. *Dir* Harry Rosenzweig; *Asst Dir* Julie Marchini; *Pres* Dr David W D Dickson; *VPres* Dr Irwin Gawley; *Dean* Dr Donald Mintz; *Chmn Fine Arts Department* William McCreaty
Open Mon - Fri 9:30 AM - 4:30 PM. No admis fee. Estab 1973. Approx 1000 sq ft, at center of Life Hall Arts Center complex. Average Annual Attendance: 5000
Exhibitions: Joanne Segal Brandford; Faculty Biannual; Richard Hunt; Michael Metzger; Micaoros (Smithsonian); Juried Student Work
Activities: Lect open to public, 50 visiting lectrs per year; concerts

L Slide Library, Fine Arts Department, 07043. *Slide Librn* Rosanne Martin
Open Mon - Thurs 8:30 AM - 8 PM, Fri 8:30 AM - 1:30 PM. Estab 1968 to provide audio visual material and information about the art world for faculty, visiting artists and community. Circ 40,000
Library Holdings: Per subs 15; AV—Cassettes, fs, Kodachromes, lantern Slides, slides; Other—Clipping files, exhibition catalogs, framed reproductions, pamphlets, photographs, reproductions, announcements of art shows throughout the country
Special Subjects: Prehistoric to contemporary art

WESTFIELD

O FEDERATED ART ASSOCIATIONS OF NEW JERSEY, INC, 720 Lawrence Ave, 07090. Tel 201-232-7623. *Pres* Jane Whipple Green; *VPres for South Jersey* Barbara L McIlvain; *VPres for North Jersey* W Carl Burger; *Secy* Ruth Crown
Estab 1969 to provide communications and exchange of ideas among visual art groups. Mem: 9000 (50 member groups); dues per club $15, individuals $10; composed of four districts which meet separately, annually
Publications: Directory of Visual Art Organizations in New Jersey; newsletter, quarterly; Views
Activities: Annual Art Seminar; programs open to the public

NEW MEXICO

ABIQUIU

M GHOST RANCH VISITOR CENTER, Carson Nation Forest, Canjilon District, General Delivery, 87510. *Dir* David C Suazo
Open daily 8 AM - 4:30 PM. No admis fee. Estab 1959 as an outdoor interpretive project for the conservation of natural resources. Average Annual Attendance: 90,000
Income: Financed by federal and private contributions
Collections: Paintings and prints related to natural resources conservation; art objects

ALBUQUERQUE

O ALBUQUERQUE ARTS COUNCIL, 5900 Domingo Rd NE, 87108. Tel 505-265-3271. *Executive Dir* Helen A Sidler
Open Mon - Fri 8 AM - 5 PM. No admis fee. Estab 1971 to stimulate and encourage cultural and educational activities. Mem: 450; three categories of membership: individual, art organizations and art related businesses, and business - industry; dues business $50, arts $25, individual $10; annual meeting Oct
Income: $16,737 (financed by membership and state appropriation)
Publications: Cultural Arts calendar, bimonthly
Activities: Open workshops in various areas of concern to the arts community

M ALBUQUERQUE MUSEUM OF ART, HISTORY AND SCIENCE, 2000 Mountain Road NW, PO Box 1293, 87103. Tel 505-766-7878. *Dir* James C Moore; *Cur Art* Ellen Landis; *Cur Exhibits* Ruth Gebel; *Cur Collections* Zana Grant; *Cur History* Byron Johnson; *Cur Education* Patrick McCracken; *Admin Asst* Irene Kersting
Open Tues - Fri 10 AM - 5 PM; Sat & Sun 1 - 5 PM. No admis fee. Estab 1967 as a city museum with Mexico diffusing knowledge and appreciation of history, art and science, establishing and maintaining a museum and related reference library, of collecting and preserving objects of historic, artistic and scientific interest, of protecting historic sites, works of art and works of nature from needless destruction, of providing facilities for research and publication and of offering popular instruction and opportunities for aesthetic enjoyment. Maintains art gallery. Average Annual Attendance: 110,000. Mem: 1075; dues benefactor $1500, individual $10
Income: Financed by city appropriation and Albuquerque Museum Foundation
Collections: Decorative arts; costumes; fine arts and crafts; objects and artifacts relevant to our cultural history from 20,000 BC to present; photography
Exhibitions: Albuquerque Illustrated: New Town and the Railroad Boom Years, 1880-1912; An Automotive History of Albuquerque; Katachi: Form and Spirit in Japanese Art; One Space, Three Visions; Probing Energy Potentials; Reflections of Realism
Publications: Las Noticias, bimonthly
Activities: Classes for children; docent training; lect; monthly vis lectr per year; gallery talks; tours; competitions; extension department serving Albuquerque Public Schools; artmobile; sales shop selling original magazines, reproductions, prints, Indian jewelry and local crafts
L Library, 2000 Mountain Road NW, 87103
Open to staff, docents and volunteers for reference
Library Holdings: Vols 1500; Per subs 20
Special Subjects: New Mexico history, art and material culture

L ALBUQUERQUE PUBLIC LIBRARY, 501 Copper NW, 87102. Tel 505-766-5009. *Dir* Alan B Clark; *Head Fine Arts Dept* Hester Miller
Open Mon - Thurs 9 AM - 9 PM; Fri - Sat 9 AM - 5:30 PM. Estab 1967 to provide study, research, and recreational materials in the arts for the people of the city, county and state
Income: $5000 (financed by city and state appropriations)
Purchases: $5000
Library Holdings: Vols 9000; Other—Clipping files
Collections: Circulating framed print collection (reproductions and originals); recordings collection; picture file (39,500)
Activities: Individual paintings, reproductions and original graphics lent to schools

M CLASSICAL SCHOOL GALLERY, 614 Indian School Rd NW, 87102. Tel 505-843-7749. *Pres* C M Flumiani
Open daily 10 - 12 AM and 3 - 5 PM. No admis fee. Estab 1969 to foster the classical approach to the arts and art education. New 2500 sq ft building. Mem: 15; dues $200
Income: Financed by endowment
Collections: Italian masters
Publications: Art & Life, quarterly
Activities: Classes for adults; lect; book shop
L Library, 614 Indian School Rd NW, 87102.
Library Holdings: Vols 2000

C LOVELACE MEDICAL FOUNDATION, Art Collection, 5400 Gibson Blvd, SE, 87108. Tel 505-842-7000. *Chief Executive Officer* Dr David J Ottensmeyer; *Cur Art Coll* Will Taylor
Open daily. No admis fee. Estab 1940. Foundation utilizes patient waiting lobbies throughout medical clinic and hospital complex to display collection
Collections: Indian (American Southwest) Textiles; Santa Fe School paintings; Taos School paintings
Activities: Tours; individual paintings lent to requesting museums

O NEW MEXICO ART LEAGUE, Ken Roberts Gallery, 3401 Juan Tabo NE, 87111. *Pres* Sandra Quinlan; *VPres* Nancy Golden; *Dir* Maureen Fuertsch; *Secy* Barbara Navratil
Open Mon - Sat 10 AM - 5 PM; Sun 12:30 - 5 PM. No admis fee. Estab 1929 to promote artists of New Mexico; art gallery. Mem: 400; dues $20; monthly meetings
Income: Financed by membership and sales
Collections: Best of show of National Small Painting Show
Exhibitions: National Small Painting Show
Publications: Catalog of National Small Painting Show; newsletter, monthly
Activities: Workshops for adults; lect; competitions; sales gallery selling origina; art, prints, pottery and sculpture

UNIVERSITY OF NEW MEXICO

M University Art Museum, Fine Arts Center, 87131. Tel 505-277-4001. *Acting Dir* Clinton Adams; *Asst Dir* Elizabeth Anne McCauley; *Assoc Cur* Cleta H Downey; *Registrar* Peter S Briggs; *Preparator* William Masterson; *Staff Asst* Kathleen E Christensen; *Receptionist* Sandra Edwards
Open Tues - Fri 10 AM - 5 PM & 7 - 10 PM; Sun 1 - 5 PM. Admis 50¢. Estab 1963. Maintains an upper level gallery; a print and photograph room which is open to the public at certain hours. Mem: 200; dues $10 to $500; annual meeting May
Collections: Contemporary American paintings, drawings, prints, photographs and sculpture with emphasis on artists who have worked in New Mexico; Labhard Collection (photography); 19th & 20th century lithographs; prints by American and European masters
Publications: Bulletin, yearly
Activities: Lect open to public; inter-museum loans; traveling exhibitions organized and circulated; museum shop selling books, magazines, reproductions, cards and newspapers

M Jonson Gallery, 1909 Las Lomas Rd NE, 87106. Tel 505-243-4667. *Dir* Raymond Jonson; *Cur* Arthur H Johnson
Open Tues - Sun Noon - 6 PM, cl Mon. No admis fee. Estab 1948 for the assemblage and preservation of a comprehensive collection of the works of Raymond Jonson; a depository for works of art by other artists and their preservation; the exhibition of works of art. The structure includes a main gallery, four storage rooms, two work shops, studio for Jonson, a museum room and living quarters for the director. Average Annual Attendance: 4000
Income: Financed through University
Collections: Jonson reserved retrospective collection; other artists works by Jonson students
Exhibitions: Joseph A Chavez; Howard Cook; R C Ellis; Vernon Fimple; Catherine Fisher; David Gale; Ed Garman; Raymond Jonson; Casimir Mayshark; Frank McCulloch; Gwen Peterson; Martha Slaymaker; Jeanette Styborski; Frank Walker; Women Contemporary: Peggy Hight-Robb, Ray Jacobsen, Betty J Pritchard, Arthur Sussman, Esther Sutin, Harriet Sutton, Arlene Wackerbarth, Ann Upson
Publications: Exhibition announcements
Activities: Individual paintings and original objects of art lent to museums
L Jonson Gallery Library, 1909 Las Lomas Rd NE, 87106
Open to students and others doing research
Library Holdings: Vols 1000; Per subs 1
Collections: The Jonson Archives containing books and magazines relating to Raymond Jonson, his letters, his diaries, catalogs, clippings, photographs and slides of works
L Fine Arts Library, Fine Arts Center, 87131. *Head Fine Arts Library* James Wright; *Asst Head Fine Arts Library* Nancy Pistorius
Open Mon - Thurs 8 AM - 12 PM; Fri 8 AM - 9 PM; Sat 9 AM - 9 PM; Sun 10 AM - 12 PM. Estab 1963 to provide library assistance and literary, microform and sound recording materials to support the programs of the university in the areas of art, architecture, music and photography
Library Holdings: Vols 78,000; Per subs 180; Micro—Cards, fiche, reels; AV—Cassettes, rec; Other—Exhibition catalogs, pamphlets, photographs
Special Subjects: History of Photography, Modern American & EuropeanNative American, Spanish Colonial

CHURCH ROCK

M GALLUP MUSEUM OF INDIAN ARTS, c/o Red Rock State Park, PO Box 328, 87311. Tel 505-722-6196
Open Mon - Fri 9 AM - 5 PM. No admis fee. Estab 1959 to acquaint visitors with the arts and crafts of the Navajo, Zuni and Hopi Indians. A small museum manned by Red Rock State Park; thirteen cases displaying Indian arts and crafts. Average Annual Attendance: 6000
Publications: Exhibitions catalog

DEMING

M DEMING LUNA MIMBRES MUSEUM, 301 S Silver St, 88030. Tel 505-546-2382. *Dir* Joyce Fawcett
Open daily 1:30 - 4 PM, cl New Year's Day, Thanksgiving and Christmas Day, open by appointment during evenings for special interest groups. Admis free with donations. Estab 1969, moved into Old Armory 1978. Sponsored by Luna County Historical Society, Inc. Mem: Dues $3
Collections: Chuck wagon, clothing, dolls, Frontier life objects and other items on the local history, Indian artifacts, mine equipment, minerals, paintings and saddles

LAS VEGAS

M NEW MEXICO HIGHLANDS UNIVERSITY ART GALLERY, National Ave, 87701. Tel 505-425-7511. *Chmn of Fine Arts* Lawrence Wise
Open Mon - Fri 8 AM - 5 PM. No admis fee. Estab 1956 to acquaint University and townspeople with art of the past and present. Gallery dimensions approximately 100 x 35 ft
Income: Financed by state appropriation
Collections: Very small permanent collection
Publications: University general catalog, annually
Activities: Classes for adults; dramatic programs; concerts; exten dept serving Northern New Mexico

LOS ALAMOS

M FULLER LODGE ART CENTER, 2132 Central Ave, PO Box 790, 87544. Tel 505-662-9331. *Dir* Ann G Barker
Open summer Tues - Fri 10 AM - 4 PM, Sat 10 AM - 2 PM, winter Mon - Fri 10 AM - 4 PM. No admis fee. Estab 1977 to provide an art center to the regional area; to exhibit works of art which otherwise wouldn't be viewed in this region. Center is approx 210 running ft; located in the Fuller Lodge; national Historical Site; gallery area has been renovated. Average Annual Attendance: 263; dues life $1000, patron $100, sponsor $50, contributing $25, family $15, individual $10, sr citizens and student $5
Income: $7800 (financed by membership, state appropriation and grants)
Exhibitions: (1979-80) Art in Public Places; Santa Fe: Andy Burns Sketchbook; Fibercraft; 19th and 20th Century French Illustrators; Laura Gilpin and William Clift; Morning Star Quilts; Frederic Remington; Rental-Sales Gallery Exhibit; Traditional and Contemporary Landscapes; Western Art; juried exhibits
Publications: Bulletin, quarterly
Activities: Classes for children; docent training; lect open to public, 12 visiting lectr per year; concerts; gallery talks; tours; competitions; awards

O LOS ALAMOS ARTS COUNCIL, 223 El Viento, 87544. Tel 505-662-7384. *Pres* Ardyth Hafer; *Secy* Norma Davis
Estab 1967 for coordination of cultural activities in Los Alamos and surrounding areas. Gallery maintained for permanent ?collections and exhibits. Average Annual Attendance: 11,600. Mem: 200; dues $5, $8 and $20; meeting Sept and Mar
Income: Under $5000 (financed by membership, city and state appropriations)
Exhibitions: Annual Arts Festival; Two Northern New Mexico Crafts Fairs
Publications: Look at the Arts; Calendar of Events, monthly

PORTALES

M EASTERN NEW MEXICO UNIVERSITY, Art Gallery, Liberal Arts Bldg 101, 88130. Tel 505-562-2652. *Dir* Chris Gikas
Open 8 AM - 9 PM. No admis fee. Estab 1974 for exhibiting student artwork; gallery is room coverted for student works
Income: Financed by University funds
Collections: Student works in Art Department Collection
Activities: Individual paintings and original objects of art lent to the University

ROSWELL

M ROSWELL MUSEUM AND ART CENTER, 11th and Main Sts, 88201. Tel 505-622-4700. *Pres Board Trustees* Donald B Anderson; *VPres* Robert V Ely; *Secy* Martha Gillespie; *Treas* Ralph McIntyre; *Dir* Wendell Ott; *Asst Dir* William D Ebie; *Registrar & Cur* Wesley A Rusnell
Open Mon - Sat 9 AM - 5 PM, Sun & holidays 1 - 5 PM. Estab 1937 to promote and cultivate the fine arts. The basis of the fine arts collection being paintings and sculptures with emphasis on the artistic heritage of the Southwest. Six galleries are maintained for art works; science display area and Robert H Goddard display areas are also maintained. Average Annual Attendance: 50,000. Mem: 600; dues $10 and up
Income: $200,000 (financed by membership, city and county appropriation)
Purchases: $5000 - $10,000
Collections: Witter Bynner Collection of Chinese Paintings & Jade; ethnological and archaeological collection of Southwestern Indian art; †international graphics collection; New Mexico regional natural history displays; †20th century Southwestern paintings & sculpture
Exhibitions: Permanent collection plus 10-14 temporary exhibitions annually
Publications: Bulletin, quarterly; Exhibition Catalogs
Activities: Classes for adults and children; lect open to public, 2-3 visiting lectrs per year; gallery talks; tours; individual paintings lent to museums; lending collection contains books, Kodachromes, and motion pictures; traveling exhibitions organized and circulated; museum shop selling books, magazines, reproductions, prints, and Indian jewelry
L Library, 11th and Main Sts, 88201.
Library Holdings: Vols 1500; Per subs 6
Special Subjects: Southwestern Art

SANTA FE

M INSTITUTE OF AMERICAN INDIAN ARTS MUSEUM, Cerillos Rd, 87501. Tel 505-988-6281. *Dir* Charles Dailey; *Cur Functions* Manuelita Lovato
Open summer Mon - Sat 9 AM - 5 PM, Thurs Evenings 7:30 - 9:30 PM, Sun 1 - 5 PM, winter daily 9 AM - 5 PM, weekends by appointment only. No admis fee. Estab 1962 to train Native American students to own, operate and manage their own museums; to collect, preserve and exhibit materials relating to the Native American; act as a resource area for Indian Museums nationwide. Small museum of 5 principal galleries; approx 10,000 ft of exhibit area. Average Annual Attendance: 15,000
Income: $11,700 (financed by Bureau of Indian Affairs, Washington DC)
Purchases: $5000

Collections: Only major collection of contemporary Indian arts and crafts in America; Vital and comprehensive collection in fields of paintings, graphics, textiles, ceramics, sculpture, jewelry, photographs, printed textiles, costumes, ethnological materials such as drums and paraphernalia for general living
Exhibitions: Photograph traveling show; yearly student sales exhibit held in June - Sept each year
Publications: How to make a low cost Maniken; One With The Earth (catalog of traveling exhibit)
Activities: Assisting any Indian reservation in setting up their own visitor centers or museums in America; material available to Indian reservations, museum, cultural centers and universities, with fees, transportation and insurance provided; classes for adults; lect open to public, 2-3 visiting lectr per year; concerts; gallery talks; competitions; awards; scholarships; individual paintings and original objects of art lent; book traveling exhibitions 6-8 per year; originate traveling exhibitions; sales shop sells student arts and crafts, books, magazines, original art and prints
L Library, Cerrillos Road, 87501. *Librn* Evelyn Fredericks
Open daily 9 AM - 5 PM, cl weekends. Estab 1962 to support college curriculum. Circ 30,000
Income: $10,000
Purchases: $8000
Library Holdings: Vols 18,000; Per subs 1000; Micro—Fiche; AV—A-tapes, cassettes, fs, Kodachromes, motion pictures, rec, slides, v-tapes; Other—Prints, photographs
Special Subjects: Native American subjects

M MUSEUM OF NEW MEXICO, 105 W Palace, PO Box 2087, 87503. Tel 505-827-2834. *Dir* George Ewing; *Assoc Dir* Michael Weber; *Dir Fine Arts* Ellen Bradbury
Open daily 9 AM - 5 PM, cl Mon in winter. Estab 1909. Museum is a state institution and operates in four major fields of interest: Fine Arts, International Folk Art, History and Anthropology, which are housed in four separate buildings. Average Annual Attendance: 800,000
Income: Financed by state appropriation
Collections: Over 185,000 items in collections
Publications: Annual report; books; El Palacio, quarterly; exhibition catalogs; guides; magazines; monographs; pamphlets
Activities: Educ kits with hands-on materials are sent to schools throughout the state; docent program serving 15,000 school children; originate traveling exhibitions
L Library, 105 W Palace, PO Box 2087, 87503.
Museum houses four separate research libraries on Folk Art, Fine Arts, History and Anthropology
Library Holdings: Vols 24,000
M Museum of Fine Arts, 105 W Palace, PO Box 2087, 87503. *Dir* Ellen Bradbury; *Chief Cur* Don Humphrey; *Cur* Sandra D'Emilio; *Cur* Steve Yates
Open daily 9 AM - 4:45 PM, cl Mon in winter. No admis fee. Estab 1917 to serve as an exhibitions hall, chiefly for New Mexican and Southwestern art. Building is of classic Southwestern design (adobe); attached auditorium used for performing arts presentations. Average Annual Attendance: 290,000
Income: Financed by state appropriation
Collections: Drawings, paintings, photographs, prints and sculpture with emphasis on New Mexican and regional art, including Native American artists
Exhibitions: (1978) Art in Public Places; Fiske and Shonnard Gifts; Donald Graham, Collection of Early Western Prints; Hennings Prints; Fred Kabotie, Paintings; 1978 Southwest Fine Arts Biennial; Roswell Compound; John Sloan Etchings; Paul Strand, Photographs; Jerry Uelsman, Photographs; Video Art; (1979) Prints by Garo Antreasian 1954-1978; Bells, Feathers and Drums; Howard Cook, Drawings and Prints; Barbara Gluck Photographs; Allan Graham: Recent Paintings; Group show of New Mexico Hispanic artists; Luis Jimenez, Sculpture, Drawings and Prints; Paintings by Douglas Johnson; Lippincott Prints; Agnes Martin, Recent Paintings; The Stream: Paints by Forrest Moses; Narcissus Quagliata Stained Glass; Hyde Solomon Paintings; Expanded Horizons, Paintings and Lithos by Earl Stroh; Works on Paper; (1980) Kenneth Adams, Paintings, Drawings and Prints; Harry Callahan Callahan, Photographs in Color; T C Cannon, Paintings, Prints and Drawings (Memorial Exhibition); Laura Gilpin Photographs and Santa Fe Scenes (permanent collection)
Activities: Classes for adults and children; docent training; lect open to public, 10 visiting lectr per year; concerts; gallery talks; tours; competitions; individual paintings and original objects of art lent to art museums; lending collection contains original prints, paintings, photographs and sculpture; originate traveling exhibitions; museum shop sells books, magazines, reproductions and slides
L Museum of Fine Arts Library, 105 W Palace, PO Box 2087, 87503. *Librn* Alberta F Donlan
Open Tues 10 AM - Noon and 2 - 4 PM, Wed 10 AM - Noon. Estab 1917 to provide fine arts research materials to museum staff, artists, writers and community
Purchases: $1500
Library Holdings: Vols 4784; Per subs 29; AV—Slides; Other—Clipping files, exhibition catalogs, manuscripts, memorabilia, pamphlets, photographs
Special Subjects: American art and artists with emphasis on Southwestern art and artists
Collections: Biography files of artists
M Museum of International Folk Art, 706 Camino Lejo, 87501. Tel 505-827-2544. *Dir* Dr Yvonne Lange; *Asst Dir* Paul Winkler; *Cur American & Latin American Coll* Charlene Cerny; *Cur Coll* Carol Steiro; *Cur European Coll* Judith Chiba-Cohen; *Cur Spanish Colonial Coll* Christine Mather; *Cur Textiles* Nora Fisher; *Conservator* Claire Munzenrider
Open daily 9 AM - 4:45 PM, cl Mon in winter. No admis fee. Estab 1953 to collect, exhibit and preserve worldwide folk art. Average Annual Attendance: 80,000
Income: Financed by endowment, grants and state appropriation
Collections: Costumes; International Folk Art, with emphasis on Spanish Colonial and Hispanic-related Culture; textiles; worldwide carvings, ceramics and toys
Exhibitions: (1978-79) Baroque to Folk; Girard Foundation Collection; Palestinian Costumes; Spanish Textiles; 25th Anniversary Show
Publications: Celebrate, 25th anniversary catalog; El Palacio, quarterly
Activities: Docent training; lect open to public; tours; individual paintings and original objects of art lent to responsible museums nationwide; originate traveling exhibitions; museum shop sells books, magazines, original art and reproductions

L **Museum of International Folk Art Library,** 706 Camino Lejo, 87501. *Librn* Judith Sellars; *Librn* Ann Bancroft
Open Mon - Fri 9 AM - Noon and 1 - 4:45 PM, cl Mon in winter. Estab 1953 to support museum's research needs
Income: $20,000
Purchases: $4000
Library Holdings: Vols 5500; Per subs 80; AV—A-tapes, cassettes, rec, slides; Other —Clipping files, exhibition catalogs, manuscripts, pamphlets, photographs
Special Subjects: Costume Design & Construction, Textiles, Folk art of various countries, religious folk art of New Mexico
Collections: Folk literature and music of the Spanish Colonist in New Mexico circa 1800-1971
M **Palace of Governors,*** 87503. Tel 505-827-2921
Built in 1610
Exhibitions: The Palace Press, a working exhibit of Frontier printing; Southwestern History, Spanish-Colonial and Territorial Periods
M **Hall of the Southwestern Indian,** 87503
Collections: Contemporary Indian Civilizations of the Southwest
M **Laboratory of Anthropology,*** 87501. Tel 505-827-3241.
Open Mon - Sat 8 AM - Noon and 1 - 5 PM. Estab 1936 as a research laboratory in archaeology and ethnology
Collections: Materials from various Indian cultures of the Southwest: jewelry, pottery and textiles
Exhibitions: Ceremonial paraphernalia; Indian silverwork

M **SCHOOL OF AMERICAN RESEARCH,** 660 Garcia St, PO Box 2188, 87501. Tel 505-982-3583. *Pres* Douglas W Schwartz; *Mgr Coll* Barbara Stanislawski
Estab 1907. Dedicated to advance studies in anthropology, support advanced seminars for post-doctoral scholars, archaeological research, anthropological publication, and a public education program. Open to members and special scholars by appointment. Southwest Indian Arts Building houses collections for research.
Mem: 1250; dues family $28, individual $18
Income: Financed by endowment, membership, special grants and individuals
Collections: Basketry, paintings, Southwest Indian pottery, silver jewelry, textiles
Publications: Discovery, once a year; Explorations, once a year; Publications of Advanced Seminar Series
Activities: Lect for members only, 5 visiting lectrs per year;; scholarships
L **Library,** 660 Garcia St, PO Box 2188, 87501.
Open to scholars of the School of American Research; staff and members by appointment
Library Holdings: Vols 6000; Per subs 27; Other—Government publications
Special Subjects: Anthropology

M **WHEELWRIGHT MUSEUM,*** 704 Camino Lejo, PO Box 5153, 87502. *Dir* Susan McGreevy; *Cur* LaRayne Parrish
Open Mon - Sat 10 AM - 5 PM, Sun 1 - 5 PM, cl Mon from Nov - May. No admis fee. Estab 1937 to preserve Navajo ceremonialism and promote the culture of the American Indian. Main gallery has changing exhibitions dealing with contemporary Indian themes; lower gallery is a recreation of a turn-of-the-century trading post and functions as a museum shop. Average Annual Attendance: 20,000. Mem: 1000; dues $10 and up; annual meeting
Income: $243,000 (financed by endowment and membership)
Collections: Jewelry; masks; photographs; ritual material; sandpainting reproductions of various Navajo ceremonies; tapes
Exhibitions: American Indian Art Now; Feasts and Ceremonies
Publications: Bulletins and books on Navajo culture
Activities: Lect open to public, 15 visiting lectrs per year; tours; individual paintings and original objects of art lent to museums; lending collection contains books, color reproductions, film strips, framed reproductions, Kodachromes, nature artifacts, original art works, original prints, paintings and phonorecords; museum shop selling books, magazines, original art, reproductions, prints, slides and authentic American Indian arts and crafts
L **Mary Cabot Wheelwright Research Library,*** 704 Camino Lejo, PO Box 5153, 87502.
Open to members for reference
Library Holdings: Vols 2000; Per subs 3000

TAOS

O **KIT CARSON MEMORIAL FOUNDATION,** PO Box B, 87571.
Estab 1949 to maintain and operate the home of Kit Carson and to perpetuate his name and deeds. The Kit Carson Home is now classified as a Registered National Historic Landmark. In 1962 the home of Ernest L Blumenschein was given to the Foundation by Miss Helen C Blumenschein; it is now classified as a Registered National Historic Landmark. In 1967 Mrs Rebecca S James gave the Foundation the Ferdinand Maxwell House and Property. The 6-room house is an excellent example of the New Mexican Territorial Period. In 1972, acquired the Hacienda de Don Antonio Severino Martinez, prominent Taos merchant and official during the Spanish Colonial Period. It is designated a Registered National Historic Landmark. Acquired in 1972, site of the Simeon Turley Trading Post, Grist Mill and Distillery, built in 1830 and destroyed in Taos Rebellion of 1847. Entered in National Register of Historic Places. Acquired in 1977 La Morada de Don Fernando de Taos, Chapel and meeting place of Los Penitentes, an early religious organization. Entered in National Register of Historic Places. Average Annual Attendance: 53,000. Mem: 230; dues patron $1000, sponsor $750, benefactor $500, supporting $250, subscribing $100, sustaining $50, share $25, participating $15, contributing $10; annual meeting March
Income: $33,796
Purchases: $20,840
Collections: †Historical and Archaeological Collection; Western Americana
Activities: Tours; lect
L **Foundation Library,** PO Box B, 87571.
For reference only
Library Holdings: Vols 3600; Other—Photographs, maps

M **Ernest Blumenschein Home,** PO Box B, 87571.
Open daily - summer, spring and autumn 9 AM - 5 PM, winter 10 AM - 4 PM. Admis family rate $2.50, adults $1, youths 50¢, children 25¢, children under 6 years free with parents
Collections: Original antique furniture; pieces of art by the Blumenschein family and members of Taos Society of Artists and other Taos artists - 1890-1930
M **Kit Carson Home and Museum,** PO Box B, 87571.
Open daily - summer 7:30 AM - 6 PM, spring and autumn 8 AM - 6 PM, winter 8 AM - 5 PM. Admis family rate $2.50, adults $1, youths 50¢, children 25¢, under 6 years free with parents

M **HARWOOD FOUNDATION OF THE UNIVERSITY OF NEW MEXICO,** Box 766, 87571. Tel 505-758-3063. *Dean* Dr Rupert A Trujillo; *Pres of Board* Lucy Cruz; *Dir* James Levy; *Cur* David Witt
Open Mon - Fri 11:30 AM - 5 PM, Sat 10 AM - 4 PM, cl Sun & holidays. No admis fee. Buildings and contents given to the University by Elizabeth Case Harwood, 1936, to be maintained as an art, educational and cultural center; maintained by the University with all activities open to the public. Foundation was added to the National Register of Historic Places in 1976
Collections: Old New Mexico Santos; †permanent collection of works by Taos artists; Persian miniatures; wood sculptures by Patrocinio Barela
Exhibitions: Changing exhibits
L **Library,** 25 Ledoux St, 87571. *Dir* James Leuy; *Librn* John Flexner
Open Mon, Thurs 11:30 AM - 8 PM; Tues, Wed, Fri 11:30 AM - 5 PM; Sat 10 AM - 4 PM. Estab 1936 as a public library. Circ 8000
Library Holdings: Vols 25,000; Per subs 10; AV—Slides; Other—Clipping files, exhibition catalogs, framed reproductions, prints, manuscripts, original art works, pamphlets, photographs, reproductions, sculpture
Special Subjects: Southwestern Art
Activities: Lect; concerts; films; plays

M **MILLICENT ROGERS MUSEUM,** Museum Rd, PO Box A, 87571. Tel 505-758-2462. *Pres* Inga Peralta Ramos; *Dir* Arthur H Wolf; *Cur and Registrar* Michael Stephens; *Admin Asst* Christine Bernal; *Membership Coordr* Jennifer Hicks; *Audio-Visual Coordr* Rick Romancito; *Public Information Coordr* Jack Roush; *Bilingual Coordr* Guadalupe Tafoya; *Newsletter Editor* Linda Tasch
Open daily 9 AM - 5 PM, Summer 10 AM - 4 PM, cl Mon, Winter. Admis adults $2 ($1.50 groups of 10 or more), under 6 50¢, family groups $5. Estab 1956 for the preservation and display of art and artifacts of Native American cultures of Western and Southwestern United States, and Hispanic cultures of Northern New Mexico. The museum's permanent home is a traditional adobe building, once the private residence of Claude J K Anderson. Average Annual Attendance: 11,000. Mem: 125; dues individual $15, family $25, contributing $50 and up; semi-annual Board of Directors meeting, Spring and Fall
Income: Financed by endowment, membership, donations, admissions, revenue from Museum Store
Collections: American Indian Art of Western United States, emphasis on Southwestern groups; paintings by contemporary Native American artists; religious arts and non-religious artifacts of Hispanic cultures; Nucleus of collection formed by Millicent Rogers
Exhibitions: (1978-79)Navajo Weaving: A Survey; Spanish New Mexican Woodworking
Publications: Las Palabras, quarterly newsletter for members of the museum
Activities: Lectures open to the public; gallery talks; tours; individual paintings and original works of art lent to similar institutions and special interest groups; book three traveling exhibitions per year; museum shop sells books, magazines, original art, reproductions, prints, art and craft work by contemporary Southwest Indian and Hispanic artisans
L **Library,** Museum Rd, 87571. *Librn* Betty Suttle
Estab 1977 as reference library for members and staff
Library Holdings: Vols 500; Per subs 10; Other—Exhibition catalogs, pamphlets
Collections: Limited edition, special edition and out of print books on Southwestern Americana

O **TAOS ART ASSOCIATION INC,** PO Box 198, 87571. Tel 505-758-2052. *Pres* Ernest S Romero; *Executive Dir* Bill Whaley; *Secy* Johanna Jones; *Dir Stables Gallery* Thom Andriola
Open daily 10 AM - 5 PM. No admis fee. Estab April 1952 as an art association composed of artists and businessmen to encourage the understanding of the arts both plastic and performing; Stables Gallery. Average Annual Attendance: 20,000. Mem: 525; annual meeting April
Income: Financed by memberships, contributions, grants and sales of art works
Exhibitions: Annual Awards Show for Taos County; twelve one-man show exhibitions
Publications: Monthly calendar of events to membership and with map to hotels
Activities: Classes for adults and children; children's program in painting and theater; dramatic programs; lect open to the public; concerts; competitions; traveling exhibitions organized and circulated

TOME

M **TOME PARISH MUSEUM,** PO Box 397, 87060. Tel 505-865-7497. *Dir* Robert M Beach
Open daily dawn to dusk. No admis fee. Estab 1966 as a religious museum
Collections: Paintings; religious material

NEW YORK

ALBANY

M ALBANY INSTITUTE OF HISTORY AND ART, 125 Washington Ave, 12210. Tel 518-463-4478. *Pres* Herbert A Jones; *Dir* Norman S Rice
Open Tues - Sat 10 AM - 4:45 PM, Sun 2 - 5 PM, cl Mon. No admis fee. Estab 1791, inc 1793 as the Society for the Promotion of Agriculture, Arts, and Manufactures; 1829 as Albany Institute; 1900 as Albany Institute and Historical and Art Society. Present name adolpted 1926. Provides curatorial services to Empire State Plaza contemporary art collection. Maintains luncheon gallery. Average Annual Attendance: 80,000. Mem: 2000; dues $15 and up; annual meeting May
Income: $700,000 (financed by endowment, membership, sales, city, county and state appropriations)
Collections: Art and historical material, chiefly related to artists and craftsmen of the region; †ceramics; Chelsea, Bow china; †contemporary paintings and sculpture; †18th & 19th century painting and sculpture by artists of the Hudson River area; English 18th century furnishings and paintings; export ware; †furniture; †glass; †pewter; †silver
Exhibitions: American Decorative Arts Centered Around Albany; Annual Regional Exhibition by Artists of the Upper Hudson; changing exhibition program in contemporary design and fine arts
Activities: Classes for adults and children; dramatic programs; lect open to public; exten dept serving area schools; sales-rental gallery

L McKinney Library, 125 Washington Ave, 12210. *Librn* James R Hobin; *Manuscripts Librn* Christine W Ward
Open Mon - Sat 8:30 AM - 4 PM. Estab 1793 to collect historical material concerning Albany and the Upper Hudson region, as well as books on fine and decorative art related to the Institute's holdings. For reference only
Library Holdings: Vols 9000; Per subs 35; Other—Clipping files, exhibition catalogs, framed reproductions, prints, manuscripts, memorabilia, pamphlets, photographs
Special Subjects: Albany social and political history, American painting and sculpture, Dutch in the Upper Hudson Valley, 17th to 19th century manuscripts
Collections: American Art Collections: Ezra Ames, Frederic Church, Thomas Cole, Sanford Gifford, Will H Low, Erastus D Palmer, Walter L Palmer, John Q A Ward

M COLLEGE OF SAINT ROSE ART GALLERY, 324 State Street, 12210. Tel 518-471-5185. *Dir* Jeanne Flanagan
Open Sun - Fri 12:30 - 4:30 PM, cl Sat. No admis fee. Estab 1969 to provide a facility that presents fine art both to the college community and to the public and provide a place for college art students to display their works
Income: Financed by college funds
Collections: Very small permanent collection consisting of paintings; prints and a few pieces of sculpture
Exhibitions: Faculty and student shows; invitationals
Activities: traveling exhibitions

L NEW YORK STATE LIBRARY, Manuscripts and Special Collections, Eleventh Floor, Cultural Education Center, Empire State Plaza, 12230. Tel 518-474-4461. *State Librn-Assoc Commissioner for Libraries* Joseph Shubert; *Dir* Peter J Paulson; *Manuscripts and Special Coll* Peter Christoph
Open Mon - Fri 9 AM - 5 PM
Collections: Over 50,000 items: black and white original photographs, glass negatives, daguerreotypes, engravings, lithographs, original sketches and drawings, cartoons, stereograms, and extra illustrated books depicting views of New York State and portraits of its citizens past and present
Exhibitions: Exhibit program involves printed and manuscript materials

M NEW YORK STATE MUSEUM, Empire State Plaza, 12230. Tel 518-474-5877. *Asst Commissioner* Open; *Museum Services Bureau Chief* G Carroll Lindsay; *Science Service Bureau Chief* Hugo Jamnback; *Historical Service Bureau Chief* Paul Scudieri
Open 10 AM - 5 PM. No admis fee. Estab 1843 to research, collect, exhibit and educate about the sciences and history of New York State for the people of New York; to function as a cultural center in the Capital District of the Empire State. Museum has 1 1 2 acres of exhibit space; 3 permanent exhibit halls devoted to man & nature (history & science) themes of Adirondack Wilderness, Metro New York, upstate New York; 3 temporary exhibit galleries of art, historical and technological artifacts. Average Annual Attendance: 500,000
Income: $3,500,000 (financed by state appropriation)
Collections: Ethnological artifacts of Iroquois-Algonkian (New York area) Indians; circus posters, costumes, decorative arts, paintings, photographs, postcards, prints, toys, weapons
Exhibitions: Antique Firefighting Equipment and Engines; Black America on Stage; Images of the City (historic prints of New York City); New York Agriculture; New York State of Art; One With The Earth; Treasure House: Museums of the Empire State
Activities: Classes for adults and children; lect open to public; concerts; individual paintings and original objects of art lent to museums and historical societies, primarily in New York; lending collection contains nature artifacts, original art works, original prints, paintings, photographs and slides; book traveling exhibitions 6 per year; originate traveling exhibitions; museum shop sells books, magazines, original art, reproductions, prints, slides, toys, baskets, pottery by local artists, jewelry, stationery and posters

M SCHUYLER MANSION, 27 Clinton St, 12202. Tel 518-474-3953. *Site Mgr* Chris Averill; *Interpretive Programs Asst* Susan L May; *Historic Site Asst* Mary Ellen Latcher; *Historic Site Asst* Joseph Grimaldi; *Historic Site Asst* Norman Coleman
Open Wed - Sun 9 AM - 5 PM, cl Mon & Tues. No admis fee. Estab 1917 for the preservation and interpretation of the 18th century home of Philip Schuyler. Period rooms: informal parlour, formal parlour, dinning room, study, ballroom, young ladies bedroom, master bedroom, summer bedroom. Average Annual Attendance: 9000
Income: Financed by state appropriation

Collections: 18th century American and European antiquities
Activities: Educ dept; lect; tours

O STATE EDUCATION DEPARTMENT, State University of New York, State Educ Bldg, 12234. Tel 518-474-2121. *Pres* Gordon Ambach; *Exec Deputy* Joseph Blaney; *Deputy Commissioner for Elementary, Secondary and Continuing Educ* Robert Spillane; *Asst Commissioner for General Education & Curricular Services* Gordon Van Hooft; *Chief Bureau of Art Educ* Charles Truplo
The State Education Department through its various supervisors determines the policy and direct the courses and the supervision and inspection of work in art in the elementary and secondary schools, including the junior and senior high schools. The Department also passes upon applications for licenses to teach art in the public schools, and upon college programs for teachers of the subject

M STATE UNIVERSITY OF NEW YORK AT ALBANY, University Art Gallery, 1400 Washington Ave, 12222. Tel 518-457-3375. *Dir* Nancy Liddle; *Asst Dir* Marijo Fasulo; *Preparator* Jason Stewart; *Admin Asst* Joanne Lue
Open Tues, Wed & Fri 9 AM - 5 PM; Thurs 9 AM - 8 PM; Sat & Sun 1 - 4 PM; cl Mon. No admis fee. Estab 1968 to augment the teaching program of the Fine Arts Department, to present exhibitions of community interest, and to be of service to the University System, particularly Albany. Gallery has 6400 sq ft on first floor, 3200 sq ft on second floor. Medium security gallery, students as security personnel. Average Annual Attendance: 25,000
Income: Financed by state appropriation
Collections: †Paintings, †prints, †drawings and †sculpture of 20th century contemporary art; photographs. The University Art Gallery is custodian for the Student Art Council Collection, a collection of contemporary art which is available on premises for study purposes
Exhibitions: (1978) Aluntinum Sculpture; Polly Hope; J Pincyck Miller; Stuffed Pictures; (1979) Mauricio Lasansky; Sculpture of Richard Stankiewicz; Tenth Street Days; (1980) Allan D'Arcangelo; Dorothea Lange
Activities: Educ dept; docent training; lect open to public, 5 vis lectr per yr; gallery talks; tours; individual paintings lent to offices on the university campus only; lending collection contains 300 art works, 150 original prints and 75 sculptures

L Art Department Slide Library, Fine Arts Building, Room 121, 12222. *Art Historian* Mojmir Frinta
Open daily 9 AM - Noon. Estab 1967 to provide instruction and reference for the university and community
Purchases: $1000
Library Holdings: Per subs 8; AV—Fs, Kodachromes, lantern slides, slides 80,000; Other—Exhibition catalogs, prints, original art works, pamphlets, photographs, sculpture
Collections: Asian, Russian and Slavic collections

ALBERTSON

L SHELTER ROCK PUBLIC LIBRARY, 165 Searingtown Road, 11507. Tel 516-248-7363, 248-7343. *Dir* Frances M Conrad; *Art Librn* Lenore Anhalt
Open Mon & Tues 10 AM - 9 PM, Wed 2 - 9 PM, Thurs 10 AM - 9 PM, Fri 10 - 6 PM, Sat 9 AM - 5 PM, Sun 1 - 5 PM. Estab 1963 as a Public Library Service. Circ 240,000. Gallery maintained for monthly exhibits
Income: $600,000 (financed by local tax appropriation)
Purchases: $80,000
Library Holdings: Vols 115,000; Per subs 450; Micro—Fiche, reels; AV—Cassettes, fs, motion pictures, rec; Other—Clipping files, framed reproductions, pamphlets
Exhibitions: (1978) Collages Rose Marie Tawfik; Herricks Adult Education Art Class Exhibit; Oils, Harriet Stanton, Walter Smith; Paintings, Iris Kelmenson, Janet Luongo; Circus Posters; Paintings and Sculpture, Seymour and Elsie Nydorf; Sculpture and Oils, Ruth Lee Siegel; Serigraphs and paintings, Shellie Schneider; Watercolors, Keith Hoffman. (1979) Chinese Brushwork, Irving Affias; Herricks Adult Education Art Class Exhibit; Nature Photography, Eugene Cohen; Oils, Edna May Young, Mildred Pawl, Honey Kurlander; Paintings, Rosalyn Murray; Photography, Linda Cohen; Renaissance exhibit from Metropolitan Museum; Watercolors, Joan Sanders; Showcase exhibits changed monthly
Publications: The Scene, three times a year; brochures for each monthly exhibit
Activities: Lectures open to the public; concerts

ALFRED

L NEW YORK STATE COLLEGE OF CERAMICS AT ALFRED UNIVERSITY, Scholes Library of Ceramics, Harder Hall, State St, 14802. Tel 607-871-2494. *Dir and Head Serials Section* Robin B Murray; *Head Readers Services* Martha A Mueller; *Head Technical Services* Bruce E Connolly; *Head Technical Reference* Paul T Culley; *Head Art Reference & Slide Library* Susan S Strong
Open academic year Mon - Thurs 8:30 AM - 10:30 PM, Fri 8:30 AM - 4:30 PM, Sat 10 AM - 10:30 PM, Sun 1 - 10:30 PM, other periods Mon - Fri 8:30 AM - 4:30 PM. Estab 1947 to service art education to the Master's level in fine and art the PhD level in engineering and science related to ceramics. The College has a 2500 sq ft Art Gallery which is managed by the Art and Design Division
Income: $270,000 (financed by endowment, state appropriation, and federal grant)
Purchases: 41,000
Library Holdings: Vols 5,000; Per subs 150; Micro—Fiche, reels; AV—Cassettes, fs, slides; Other—Original art works, pamphlets
Special Subjects: Ceramics, American Painting, Photography, Pottery, Printmaking, Sculpture, Video, Fine art, wood design
Collections: Silverman Collection (glass)
Publications: Books; Library Notes; Reports, all bi-monthly
Activities: Tours

AMENIA

O **AGES OF MAN FELLOWSHIP**, Sheffield Rd, 12501. Tel 914-373-9380. *Pres* Dr Nathan Cabot Hale; *VPres* Don Holden; *Secy* Alison B Hale
Open 10 AM - 5 PM. Estab 1968 for the building and design of a sculpture chapel based on the thematic concepts of the Cycle of Life. Mem: 20; dues $100; meetings May and Nov
Income: Financed by membership and contributions
Collections: Sculpture and architectural models of the chapel
Publications: Project report, yearly
Activities: Art history; apprenticeship and journeyman instruction in Cycle of Life design; lect open to the public, 20 visiting lectr per year; gallery talks; original objects of art lent to museums, art associations, educational institutions; originate traveling exhibitions

AMHERST

M **DAEMEN COLLEGE**, Dun Scotus Gallery, 4380 Main St, 14226. Tel 716-839-3600, Ext 241. *Dir* Liz Simon
Open daily 9 AM - 5 PM. No admis fee. Estab to add dimension to the art program and afford liberal arts students opportunity to view art made by established artists as well as art students. Gallery area is part of main building protected by folding gate. Average Annual Attendance: 1000
Income: Financed by College Art Department
Activities: Lect open to public, 4 - 5 visiting lectr per year; competitions

AMSTERDAM

M **WALTER ELWOOD MUSEUM AND ART GALLERY**, 300 Guy Park Ave, 12010. Tel 518-843-3180, Ext 460, 461. *Coordr* Margery Diamond Zucker
Open weekdays Sept 1 - June 31, 8:30 AM - 4 PM, July 1 - Aug 31, 8:30 AM - 3 PM, cl legal holidays. Estab 1940 by Walter Elwood; sponsored by the Board of Education. Average Annual Attendance: 10,000
Collections: Early American, Victorian, Indian and Natural History material; paintings; period rooms; prints
Activities: Guided tours, special topic tours; multi-media kits on request

ANNANDALE-ON-HUDSON

M **BARD COLLEGE**, William Cooper Procter Art Center, 12504. Tel 914-758-8494, Ext 138. *Cur* Tom Wolf
Open daily 10 AM - 5 PM. Estab 1964 as an educational center. Art center has a gallery, slide library and uses the college library for its teaching
Collections: Assorted contemporary paintings and sculptures; photograph collection of prints
Exhibitions: Two student exhibitions per year; faculty and traveling exhibitions
Publications: Catalogs
Activities: Children's art classes; lect open to the public; gallery talks; scholarships

ARDSLEY

C **CIBA-GEIGY CORPORATION**, 444 Saw Mill River Rd, 10502. Tel 914-478-3131. *In Charge Art Coll* Markus J Low
Open to public by appointment. No admis fee. Estab 1959 to add color and warmth to interior of its new headquarters; since 1966 for support of promising artists. Collection displayed at various company facilities
Collections: New York School of Painting, abstract expressionist, geometric and figurative art; Swiss Art
Activities: Individual objects of art lent upon request to museums and educational institutions for limited periods; originate traveling exhibitions upon request to museums and educational institutions

AUBURN

M **CAYUGA MUSEUM OF HISTORY AND ART**, 203 Genesee St, 13021. Tel 315-253-8051. *Dir* Walter K Long
Open Tues - Fri 9 AM - 5 PM, cl Mon. No admis fee. Estab 1936 for research and Indian history. Average Annual Attendance: 40,000. Mem: 500; dues $10 - $30; annual meeting in Jan
Income: $45,000 (financed by endowment, membership, county and city appropriation)
Collections: Beardsley Filipino; Herter textiles; †sound on film; †permanent paintings by Americans
Exhibitions: Bicentennial, 12 Ethnic Group Shows
Activities: Classes for adults and children; docent training; lect open to public, 6 visiting lectr per year; gallery talks, tours; competitions; lending collection contains motion pictures, paintings, slides; museum shop sells original art, reproductions and small gifts
L **Library**, 203 Genesee St, 13021.
Open to researchers for reference
Library Holdings: Vols 15,000
Special Subjects: Indians, local history
Collections: Clarke Collection

BAYSIDE

L **QUEENSBOROUGH COMMUNITY COLLEGE LIBRARY**, 56th Ave & Springfield Blvd, 11364. Tel 212-631-6226. *Chief Librn* Prof Charles Pappalardo; *Music & Art Librn* Eleanor Eldot
Open Mon - Thurs 8:30 AM - 9 PM, Fri 8:30 AM - 5 PM. Estab 1961 to serve the students and faculty of the college
Income: Budget $750,000
Purchases: $55,000
Library Holdings: Other—book and periodical collection which includes material on painting, sculpture and architecture reproductions of famous paintings on walls throughout the library and reproductions of artifacts and paintings
Collections: Extremely valuable vertical file collection; print collection
Exhibitions: Exhibit cases are changed approximately every two months

BINGHAMTON

M **ROBERSON CENTER**, 30 Front St, 13905. Tel 607-772-0660. *Pres of the Board* Lloyd L Kelly; *VPres* Alice A Wales; *Secy* Patricia Hill; *Treas* John B Cummings; *Dir* Duane P Truex; *Asst Dir* Laura B Martin; *Cur* Robert Aguglia; *Cur* Richard Barons; *Cur* Philip Carey; *Cur* Richard DeLuca; *Cur* Roselyn Tunis
Open Tues - Fri 9 AM - 10:30 PM, Sat 9 AM - 5 PM, Sun Noon - 5 PM, cl Mon. No admis fee. Estab 1954. The Roberson Center is a complex of museums including art, history and science. It is Broome County's Art and Science Council and an education and performing art center. The Roberson Mansion, built in 1910 contains eight galleries, and the Neutra, which was built in 1968 and renamed the Keith Martin Building in 1978, contains five galleries. Average Annual Attendance: 300,000. Mem: 3000; dues $10 - $30
Income: $900,000 (financed by endowment, membership, city, county and state appropriations, federal funds and foundations)
Collections: Decorative art; documents, drawings; furniture; paintings; photographs; prints
Exhibitions: Ancient Idols; Charles Eldred: Sculpture and Drawings; The Examination and Treatment of Paintings; Fine Arts Society Members' Show; The Forest: Cash Crop of Our Early Settlers; Emil Holzhauer retrospective; Made in Broome, Parts I - IV; Photo Exhibition; Scholastic Art; annual student show and Christmas Forest
Publications: Bulletin, monthly; catalogs, 3 major per year
Activities: Classes for adults and children; docent training; lect open to public; competitions; programs sent to schools in ten counties; individual paintings and original objects of art lent; originate traveling exhibitions; museum shop sells books, original art, contemporary crafts, reproductions and prints
L **Broome County Historical Library**, 30 Front St, 13905.
For reference and research only

M **STATE UNIVERSITY OF NEW YORK AT BINGHAMTON**, University Art Gallery, 13901. Tel 607-798-2634. *Gallery* Jill Grossvogel; *Secy* Katherine Gleason; *Technician* Walter Luckert
Open Mon - Fri 9 AM - 4:30 PM, Sat & Sun 1 - 4:30 PM. Estab 1967
Income: Financed by state appropriations and gifts
Collections: †Teaching collection from Egyptian to contemporary art
Exhibitions: Architecture & Urbanism; Recent Works by Appel, Alechinsky, Corneille; Frans Kline; Mirror of Marvelous Rome (16th century engravings); Political Comment in Contemporary Art; Claude-Emile Schuffenecker: Margin and Image
Publications: Art Gallery Bulletin; Ancient Vessels; The Sara Roby Foundation Collection of American Art; Traditional Art of West Africa
Activities: Lect; musical programs; tours; traveling exhibitions organized and circulated
L **Library**, 13901.
The Gallery Library is supplemented with the University Library and is very adequate for research

BLUE MOUNTAIN LAKE

O **ADIRONDACK LAKES CENTER FOR THE ARTS**, 12812. Tel 518-352-7715. *Pres* Johan R Collins Jr; *VPres* Tony Morrow; *Treas* Robert Webb; *Dir* Robert Struthers; *Secy* Susan Martin
Estab 1967; the Community Art Center offers both community and artist - craftsmen the opportunity for creative exchange. Open year round. Mem: Dues associate $25, $50, $75 or more, family $15, students $3
Income: Financed by private contributions, county, state and federal assistance, foundations, local businesses and government
Publications: Newsletter - Program, quarterly
Activities: Artist - residency program; artist presentations; concerts; film series; theatre series; art and craft shop
L **Library**, 12812.
For reference only
Library Holdings: Vols 300

M **ADIRONDACK MUSEUM OF THE ADIRONDACK HISTORICAL ASSOCIATION**, 12812. Tel 518-352-7311. *Pres* H K Hockschild; *Dir* Craig A Gilborn
Open June 15 - Oct 15 daily 10 AM - 6 PM. Admis adults $4, children 7 - 15 $2.25, under 7 free, special group rates. Estab 1955 to show the relationship of man to the Adirondacks. Museum contains two large galleries for paintings. Average Annual Attendance: 90,000. Mem: Annual meeting Aug
Collections: Paintings and prints
Exhibitions: One special exhibition each year (has included the work of Winslow Homer, A F Tait and Eliot Porter)
Activities: Lect; individual objects of art lent to museums and galleries
L **Library**, 12812. Tel 518-352-7312. *Librn* Vijay Nair
Open Mon - Fri 9:30 AM - 4:30 PM by appointment. Estab to provide research materials for museum staff (exhibit documentation) and researchers interested in the Adirondack, and to preserve written materials relating to the Adirondack. For

research only
Library Holdings: Vols 5000; Per subs 90 - 100; Micro—Reels; AV—A-tapes, cassettes, Kodachromes, motion pictures, slides; Other—Exhibition catalogs, manuscripts, pamphlets, photographs, maps
Special Subjects: All Adirondackiana

BRIARCLIFF MANOR

PACE UNIVERSITY
M **The Art Gallery,** Elm Rd, 10510. Tel 914-941-6400, Ext 714. *Gallery Dir* Beth A Treadway
Open Sun - Fri 1 - 5 PM, cl Sat. No admis fee. Estab 1978 to exhibit the works of nationally known professional artists and groups, and to serve as a focal point for artistic activities within the university and surrounding communities. The gallery is located on the ground floor of the Arts Building and has a commanding view of the center of campus; it is both spacious and modern
Income: Financed by the University
Exhibitions: Abraxas; The Art of the Painted Finish; Brenda Bettinson; Briarcliff Manor's Early Days; Creativity, A Juried Show; Imprisoned Art; The Lower East Side: Port to American Life; Mamaroneck Artists' Guild; John Mulgrew; Women Photograph Men
Activities: Lect open to the public, 8 - 10 visiting lectr per year; gallery talks; tours
L **Pace University Library,** Elm Rd, 10510. *Dir* William Murdock
Estab 1963
Library Holdings: Vols 7565; Per subs 40

BRONX

M **BRONX MUSEUM OF THE ARTS,** 851 Grand Concourse, 10451. Tel 212-681-6000. *Chmn Board* Sol Shaviro; *Dir* Luis R Cancel; *Admin Asst* Carmen Rivera-Torres; *Cur Satellite Galleries* Henry Joyce
Open Mon - Fri 9 AM - 5 PM, Sun 12:30 - 4:30 PM. No admis fee. Estab 1971 as a conduit for other museums of the city to bring their works to the community and for local artists to have their works viewed, making art available, free and easily accessible to the Bronx community. Exhibition gallery in Rotunda of Bronx County Courthouse; community gallery in Con Edison Bronx District Office; Bronx Arts Exchange in seven Bronx public places. Mem: 75; dues sponsor $1000, donor $500, contributing $100, sustaining $50, family $15, individual $10, student $5
Income: Financed by membership, city and state appropriations
Collections: Artist's file on Bronx artists
Publications: Catalogs of exhibitions; educational workbooks; walking tours of the Bronx
Activities: Formally organized education programs for children; college internship program; curatorial and administrative appreticeships; film programs; demonstrations; gallery talks; art festivals; concerts; originate traveling exhibitions

L **HUNTINGTON FREE LIBRARY AND READING ROOM,** Depository Library for the Museum of the American Indian, 9 Westchester Square, 10461. Tel 212-829-7770. *Pres Board Trustees* Edward A Morgan; *Librn* Mary B Davis; *Asst Librn* Dorothy Cisneros
Open Mon - Sat 9:30 AM - 4:30 PM by appointment. Estab 1891, the Reading Room was established as a library for the people of Westchester Square. Materials are for reference only
Income: Financed by endowment
Library Holdings: Vols 40,000; Per subs 80; Micro—Fiche; AV—Rec; Other—Clipping files, exhibition catalogs, manuscripts, pamphlets, original documents
Special Subjects: Indians of North, South and Central America

C **PROSPECT HOSPITAL,** 730 Kelly St, 10455. Tel 212-542-1500, Ext 296. *Executive Dir* Dr Jacob B Freedman
Open to public. No admis fee. Estab 1969 to bring joy to the dissadvantaged of the South Bronx; to provide a pleasant and cheerful environment for patients, visitors, staff and employees. Collection displayed throughout hospital
Collections: Lithographs, paintings, posters, reproductions by Calder, Chagal, Matise, Modigliani, Picasso, and others
Exhibitions: Art exhibitions by unknown artists, who hang their works in the lobby of the hospital
Activities: Lect; sponsored art and cultural concerts; individual objects of art lent to Bronx Borough President, Banks in the Bronx, Bronx Museum of Art

SOCIETY OF ANIMAL ARTISTS, INC
For further information, see National and Regional Organizations

M **VAN CORTLANDT MUSEUM,*** Van Cortlandt Park, W 246th St & Broadway, 10471. Tel 212-543-3344.
Open AM - 4:30 PM, Sun 2 - 4:30 PM, cl Mon. Admis adult 50¢, children under 12 free, Fri & Sat free to all. Estab 1898. Average Annual Attendance: 30,000
Collections: Furniture and objects relating to the Colonial period of American history; also Delftware, pottery and glass
Activities: Classes for children; slide programs for visitors

BRONXVILLE

L **BRONXVILLE PUBLIC LIBRARY,** 201 Pondfield Rd, 10708. Tel 914-337-7680. *Dir* Jane Cumming Selvar
Open (Winter) Mon, Wed and Fri 9:30 AM - 5:30 PM, Tues 9:30 AM - 9 PM, Thurs 1 - 9 PM, Sat 9:30 AM - 5 PM, Sun 1 - 5 PM, (Summer) Mon, Wed and Fri 9:30 AM - 5:30 PM, Tues 9:30 AM - 9 PM, Thurs 1 - 9 PM, Sat 9:30 AM - 1 PM. No admis fee
Income: Financed by city and state appropriations
Collections: American painters: Bruce Crane, Childe Hassam, Winslow Homer, William Henry Howe, Frederick Waugh; Japanese Art Prints; 25 Original Currier and Ives Prints
Exhibitions: Current artists, changed monthly; original paintings and prints

L **SARAH LAWRENCE COLLEGE LIBRARY,** Glen Washington Rd, 10708. Tel 914-337-0700. *Librn* Rose Anne Brustein; *Exhibits Librn* Carol Shaner; *Slide Librn* Renee Kent
Open 9 AM - 5 PM. Estab to provide library facilities for students and members of the community with an emphasis on art history. Slide collection closed to the public; non-circulating reference materials available to the public
Library Holdings: Vols 20,000; Per subs 951; AV—Slides
Exhibitions: Changing exhibits
Activities: Tours on request

STAINED GLASS ASSOCIATION OF AMERICA
For further information, see National and Regional Organizations

BROOKLYN

M **BROOKLYN MUSEUM,** 188 Eastern Parkway, 11238. Tel 212-638-5000. *Chmn Board of Governors* Robert A Levinson; *Dir* Michael Botwinick; *Exec Asst* B J van Donme; *Asst Dir Operations* Robert Hayden; *Asst Dir Education & Program Development* David H Katzive; *Adminr Curatorial Affairs* Patrick Cardon; *Asst Dir Financial Aide* John Helmich; *Public Relations Mgr* Judith Schwartz; *Chmn of Dept Egyptian & Classical Art, Keeper of the Wilbur Coll* Bernard V Bothmer; *Cur Egyptian & Classical Art* Richard Fazzini; *Assoc Cur Egyptian & Classical Art* Robert Bianchi; *Asst Cur Egyptian & Classical Art* James Romano; *Cur & Dept Head Paintings & Sculpture* Sarah C Faunce; *Cur Paintings & Sculpture* Linda Ferber; *Asst Cur Paintings & Sculpture* Holly Conners; *Cur Oriental Art* Robert Moes; *Assoc Cur Oriental Art* Amy Poster; *Cur Costumes & Textiles* Elizabeth A Coleman; *Cur Decorative Arts* Dianne H Pilgrim; *Cur African, Oceanic & New World Cultures* Sylvia Williams; *Asst Cur African, Oceanic & New World Cultures* Diana Fane; *Consultant Cur Prints & Drawings* Gene Baro; *Asst Cur Prints & Drawings* Ripley Albright; *Conservator* Suzanne P Sack; *Publications & Marketing Services Mgr* Brian Rushton; *Security* Edward Pisano; *Registrar* Barbara LaSalle; *Librn* Margaret Zorach; *Community Gallery Coordr* Richard Waller; *Graphic Designer* Daniel Weidmann; *Assoc Cur Sculpture Garden* Barbara Millstein
Open Wed - Sat 10 AM - 5 PM, Sun Noon - 5 PM, cl Mon & Tues. No admis fee. Estab 1823 as an art museum with educational facilities. Five floors of galleries maintained, seventh largest museum of art in the United States. Average Annual Attendance: 575,000. Mem: 4500; dues donor $500, patron $250, contributor $100, sustaining $50, family $30
Income: $3,242,400 (financed by endowment, membership, city and state appropriation)
Collections: Art from the Americas and South Pacific; American period rooms; American Renaissance 1876-1970, includes works by John Singer Sargent and Abbott Thayer; Belgian Art 1880-1914, includes works by James Ensor, Ferdinand Knotff and Lewis W Hine; European and American paintings, sculpture, prints and drawings, textiles, decorative arts; Major collections of Egyptian and Classical; Oriental, Middle Eastern and African art; Sculpture Garden of ornaments from demolished New York buildings
Exhibitions: 1874-1940: A Retrospective of Photography
Publications: Annual Report; calendar, monthly; catalogs of major exhibitions; handbooks
Activities: Classes for adults and children; dramatic programs; docent training; lect open to the public, 150 visiting lectr per year; concerts; gallery talks; tours; individual paintings and original objects of art lent to other museums; originate traveling exhibitions; museum and sales shop sells books, original art, reproductions, prints, slides
L **Art Reference Library,** 11238. Tel 212-638-5000, Ext 307, 308, 309. *Principal Librn* Margaret B Zorach
Open Wed 1:30 - 5 PM, Thurs & Fri 1 - 5 PM. Estab 1823 to serve the staff of the museum and local researchers. Circ 3000
Income: $22,000 (financed by city and state appropriation)
Purchases: $15,000
Library Holdings: Vols 100,000; Per subs 600; Micro—Fiche; AV—Slides; Other—Clipping files, exhibition catalogs, original art works, pamphlets
Special Subjects: American painting and decorative arts; Mid-Eastern art and archaeology; Oriental art, African, Oceanic and New World Cultures art; original designer sketches; information on Women's Art
L **Wilbour Library of Egyptology,** 11238. Tel 212-638-5000, Ext 215. *Librn* Diane Guzman
Open Wed - Fri 10 AM - 5 PM, cl Mon & Tues. Estab 1916 for the purpose of the study of Ancient Egypt. For reference by appointment only
Income: Financed by endowment and city appropriation
Purchases: $6000
Library Holdings: Vols 20,000; Per subs 150; Micro—Fiche; Other—Exhibition catalogs, pamphlets, original documents
Collections: Seyffarth papers
Publications: Wilbour Monographs; general introductory bibliographies on Egytian art available to visitors

L **BROOKLYN PUBLIC LIBRARY,** Art and Music Division, Grand Army Plaza, 11238. Tel 212-780-7784. *Dir* Kenneth F Duchac; *Chief Art & Music Division* William R Johnson; *Chief AV Division* Kenneth Axthelm
Open Mon - Thurs 9 AM - 8 PM; Fri & Sat 10 AM - 6 PM; Sun 1 - 5 PM. No admis fee. Estab 1892
Income: Financed by city and state appropriation
Library Holdings: Vols 130,487; Per subs 420; AV—Slides; Other—Framed reproductions, mounted picture
Collections: Checkers Collection; Chess Collection; Costume Collection
Publications: Brooklyn Public Library Bulletin, bimonthly
Activities: Classes for children; programs; films

O **LONG ISLAND HISTORICAL SOCIETY,** 128 Pierrepont St, 11201. Tel 212-624-0890. *Pres* Dwight Demeritt Jr
Open Tues - Sat 9 AM - 5 PM. No admis fee for members, non members $1 per day for library use. Estab in 1863 to discover, procure, and preserve historical and genealogical materials from New York City (especially Brooklyn and Long Island), and the New England vicinity. The exhibition area is on the library floor. Average Annual Attendance: 6200. Mem: 1300; dues $15, annual meeting May

Income: $150,000 (financed by endowment, membership, state appropriation and grants)
Purchases: $10,000
Collections: Artifacts, paintings, photographs and prints
Exhibitions: Battle of Long Island; Conserving Brooklyn's Heritage; Old Brooklyn in Early Photographs (1865 - 1929)
Publications: Journal of Long Island History, biannual
Activities: Lect open to the public, 10 visiting lectr per year; concerts; individual paintings and original objects of art lent to other institutions; lending collection contains 6000 original prints, 275 paintings, 20 sculptures; shop sells books and prints

L **Library,** 128 Pierrepont St, 11201. *Librn* Anne M Gordon; *Asst Librn* Elaine Bak
Open for reference only
Library Holdings: Vols 150,000; Per subs 80

NATIONAL CARTOONISTS SOCIETY
For further information, see National and Regional Organizations

M **NEW MUSE COMMUNITY MUSEUM OF BROOKLYN, INC,** 1530 Bedford Ave, 11216. Tel 212-774-2900, 774-2901. *Chmn Bd of Dir* Joseph Jiggetts; *Exec Dir* Andrew J Gill; *Secy Bd of Dir* Lucille Bell; *Exec Secy* Ima Zawadi; *Coordr Exhib* Teresia Bush; *Coordr of Cultural Arts* Gaylord Hassan; *Coordr Music* Reginald Workman; *Coordr Public Relations* Mark Irving
Open Tues - Fri 2 - 10 PM, Sat and Sun 1 - 5 PM. No admis fee(donations and contributions accepted). Estab 1973 to effect an African-American educational and cultural institution of high calibre in the Crown Heights and Bedford-Stuyvesant sections of Brooklyn. Gallery contains cultural and historic exhibitions; fine art exhibitions. Average Annual Attendance: 650,000. Mem: 150; dues $100 - $5; annual meeting Jan 31
Income: $375,000 (financed by membership, city and state appropriation)
Collections: Small nucleus of Haitian, African and African-American Artifacts
Exhibitions: Black Artists of Brooklyn; Black Contribution to the Development of Brooklyn; Family of Muse Exhibit; Permanent and semi-permanent exhibitions, three to six weeks duration
Publications: Bulletins, announcing activities and workshops, monthly
Activities: Classes for children and adults; dramatic programs; music lectures open to the public

L **NEW YORK CITY COMMUNITY COLLEGE,** Namm Hall Library and Learning Resource Center, 300 Jay Street, 11201. Tel 212-643-5240. *Acting Chief Librn* Prof Catherine T Brody; *Admin Services Librn* Prof Paul T Sherman
Open Mon - Thurs 9 AM - 8 PM, Fri 9 AM - 5 PM. Estab 1947. Circ 31,978
Income: $378,000
Purchases: $57,107
Library Holdings: Vols 120,000; Per subs 376; Micro—Reels; AV—A-tapes, cassettes, rec, v-tapes; Other—Clipping files, pamphlets, reproductions, picture file
Special Subjects: Advertising Design, Graphic Arts
Exhibitions: (1978) The Art of Black America; Kaleidoscope of Color: The Art of Quilts; Medieval Art in Monumental Brasses. (1979) Art Club Photographs
Publications: Library Notes, occasional publication
Activities: Tours

L **PRATT INSTITUTE LIBRARY,** 11205. Tel 212-636-3685. *Dir* Vanessa Lynn; *Dir* George Lowy; *Art and Architecture Librn* Sydney Starr Keaveney
Open Mon - Thurs 9 AM - 9 PM, Fri and Sat 9 AM - 5 PM, Sun 12 AM - 6 PM. Estab 1887 for students, faculty, staff and alumni of Pratt Institute. The school has several galleries, the library has exhibitions in display cases
Income: $80,000 (financed by endowment and tuition)
Library Holdings: Vols 28,000; Micro—Fiche, reels; AV—A-tapes, cassettes, rec, slides; Other—Clipping files, exhibition catalogs, pamphlets, reproductions

O **SCHOOL ART LEAGUE OF NEW YORK CITY,** 131 Livingston St, 11201. Tel 212-875-5381. *Pres* Charles M Robertson; *First VPres* Reynolds Girdler Jr; *Second VPres* Samuel Magdolf; *Treas* George Kaye; *Secy* Dan Tyre; *Exec Dir* Dorothy G Evans; *Asst Dir* Judith Meyers
Estab 1909 to foster art education in the public schools of the City of New York. The League is co-sponsored by a Board of Trustees and the Board of Education of the City of New York. Its purpose is to enrich and enlarge the arts programs available to our young people in our city's schools. Interdisciplinary arts activities are offered as a supplement to existing arts programs through the use of New York City's cultural resources. Support is provided for innovative programs within the schools, and scholarships and grants are given to encourage gifted students. Mem: 3000; junior mem 22,000; dues $5 and up; public school pupils $1 per school term
Activities: Classes; workshops; seminars; in-service training for teachers; Tours; films; annual awards; scholarships

BUFFALO

M **ALBRIGHT-KNOX ART GALLERY,** Buffalo Fine Arts Academy, 1285 Elmwood Ave, 14222. Tel 716-882-8700. *Chmn* Seymour H Know; *Pres* Samuel D Magavern; *VPres* Mrs John T Elfvin; *VPres* Northrup R Knox; *VPres* Robert E Rich; *Secy* Roy W Doolittle Jr; *Treas* William J Magavern II; *Dir* Robert T Buck Jr; *Cur Education* Charlotte B von Wodtke; *Cur* Douglas G Schultz; *Assoc Cur* Charlotta Kotik; *Registrar* Jane Nitterauer
Open Tues - Sat 10 AM - 5 PM, Sun Noon - 5 PM, cl Thanksgiving, Christmas and New Year's Day. No admis fee, voluntary contribution. Estab 1862 as The Buffalo Fine Arts Academy, gallery opened in 1905, with a new wing added in 1962. Average Annual Attendance: 236,463. Mem: 4800; dues $25; annual meeting in Oct
Income: $1,226,433 (financed by endowment and county appropriations)
Collections: †Paintings and drawings; †prints ranging from 3000 BC to the present with special emphasis on American and European contemporary art; †sculpture and constructions
Exhibitions: (1978-79) American painting of the 1970's; Carl Andre: Sculpture 1959 to 1977; The Armand Hammer Collection: Four Centuries of Masterpieces; Richard Artschwager's Theme(s); Donald Blumberg: Recent Photographs in Series; Constructivism and the Geometric Tradition: Selections from the McCrory Corporation Collection; Piero Dorazio: A Retrospective; Eight Sculptors; In Western New York 1979; Modern European Sculpture 1918 to 1945 (Unknown Beings and Other Realities); Ben Nicholson: Fifty Years of His Work; Bridget Riley: Works 1951 to 1978; Clyfford Still: 33 Paintings from the Collection; 37th Western New York Exhibition; Tibet, A Lost World: The Newark Museum Collection of Tibetan Art and Ethnography; The Vasulkas: Steina: Machine Vision; Woody: Descriptions
Publications: Annual report; calendar (monthly); exhibition catalogs
Activities: Classes for adults and children; docent training; lect open to public; concerts; gallery talks; tours; community outreach program; original objects of art lent to members; lending collections contain paintings, photographs and sculptures; originate traveling exhibitions; gallery shop sells books, magazines, original art, reproductions, prints, slides, cards, stationery, toys and jewelry

L **Art Reference Library,** 1285 Elmwood Ave, 14222. Tel 716-882-8700, Ext 225. *Librn* Annette Masling; *Asst Librn* Anita Gilden
Open Tues - Fri 2 - 5 PM, Sat 1 - 3 PM. Estab 1905 to support the staff research and to document the Gallery collection, also to serve the fine art and art history people doing research in the western New York area. Exhibits are prepared in a small vestibule just outside the library, rare items in the library collection and print collection are displayed
Library Holdings: Vols 16,500; Per subs 120; AV—V-tapes; Other—Clipping files, prints, manuscripts, memorabilia, original art works, pamphlets, photographs, original documents

L **BUFFALO AND ERIE COUNTY PUBLIC LIBRARY,** Lafayette Square, 14203. Tel 716-856-7525. *Dir* Paul M Rooney; *Deputy Dir Public Services* Diane S Chrisman; *Deputy Dir Support Services* Donald Cloudsley
Open Mon - Thurs 10 AM - 9 PM, Fri and Sat 9:30 AM - 5:30 PM. Estab 1954 through a merger of the Buffalo Public, Grosvenor, and Erie County Public Libraries. Circ 4,647,000
Income: $10,500,000 (financed by county appropriation)
Purchases: $20,000
Library Holdings: Vols 33,000; Per subs 75; AV—Motion pictures; Other—Exhibition catalogs, prints, manuscripts, original art works, photographs
Collections: Drawings by Fritz Eichenberg; etchings by William J Schwanekamp; Niagara Falls prints; original woodcuts of J J Lankes; posters (mostly WW I); Rare Book Room with emphasis on fine printing
Publications: Library Bulletin, monthly
Activities: Dramatic programs; consumer programs; gallery talks; tours; concerts

M **BURCHFIELD CENTER,** 1300 Elmwood Ave, 14222. Tel 716-878-6011. *Chmn* Peter Vogt; *Dir* Dr Edna M Lindemann; *Registrar* Gary A Dayton; *Education Prog Coordr* Sylvia P Volk; *Education Prog Coordr* Margaret Bauer; *Technical Asst to Dir* Micheline Lepine
Open Mon - Fri 10 AM - 5 PM, Sun 1 - 5 PM. No admis fee. Estab 1966 to develop a total center concept including a regional center for the exhibition, study and encouragement of art expression in the Western New York area. This includes building a permanent collection of works by Charles Burchfield and other artists of the area, both living and historical. Museum has a main gallery with four supplemental galleries and the Burchfield studio gallery. Average Annual Attendance: 40,000. Mem: 1600; dues sustaining $35, regular $20, student $8
Income: Financed by endowment, membership, SUNY and other sources
Collections: †Charles Burchfield collection; †works by contemporary and historical artists of the western New York area
Exhibitions: Charles Burchfield (on loan from the permanent collection); The American Landscape; Language of Clay; Paintings by Allan D'Arcangelo; Six Artists Under 30
Publications: Exhibition catalogues
Activities: Docent training; lect open to the public; concerts; tours; competitions; exten dept serves area schools and community organizations; original objects of art lent to students and teachers; lending collection contains books, cassettes, color reproductions, film strips, framed reproductions, original art works slides, magazine articles, periodicals; Originates traveling exhibitions; shop sells books, magazines, reproductions and wallpapers designed by Charles Burchfield

L **Burchfield Center Resource Room,** RH 317, 1300 Elmwood Ave, 14222. *Librn & Archivist* Gary A Dayton
Open Mon - Fri 9 AM - 5 PM. Estab 1967. For public reference only
Library Holdings: Vols 500; Per subs 3; AV—A-tapes, cassettes, motion pictures, slides, v-tapes; Other—Clipping files, exhibition catalogs, framed reproductions, prints, manuscripts, memorabilia, original art works, pamphlets, photographs, reproductions
Special Subjects: Works of Charles Burchfield, Western New York art and artist, American art
Collections: Charles Burchfield Archive, George William Eggers Archive
Exhibitions: Archive materials relating to the life and career of Charles Burchfield

M **HALLWALLS GALLERY,** 30 Essex St, 14213. Tel 716-885-2852. *VPres* Charles Clough; *Dir and Pres* William Currie; *Asst to Dir* Diane Bertolo
Open Tues - Fri 11 AM - 5 PM, Sun 1 - 4 PM. No admis fee except for special events. Estab 1974 to provide exhibition space for anyone wishing to exhibit. Three large rooms, one small room (the Matrix Room), and office space; the building was originally a 1900's ice factory. Average Annual Attendance: 50,000. Mem: 130; dues $15, $25, $100; meeting dates January and September
Income: Financed by endowment
Collections: Vito Acconci; Jared Bark; Jon Borofsky; Chris Burdon; Rafael Ferrer; Judy Haffif; Suzy Lake; Sol Lewitt; Gregoire Muller; Charles Simonds
Publications: Top Stories; catalog
Activities: Lectures open to the public; internships; concerts; gallery talks; tours; traveling exhibitions organized and circulated throughout the United States and Canada; museum sales shop sells books

L **Library,** 30 Essex St, 14213.
Estab 1977 to provide access to art periodicals. Open to public for viewing video tapes and documentation of work exhibited in the gallery
Library Holdings: Vols 400; Per subs 20; AV—A-tapes, lantern Slides, rec, slides, v-tapes; Other—Clipping files, exhibition catalogs, prints, memorabilia, original art works, pamphlets, photographs

STATE UNIVERSITY OF NEW YORK AT BUFFALO

M **Gallery 219,** University Union Activities Board, Arts Committee. (Mailing Add: Room 106, Talbert Hall, Amherst, NY 14260) Tel 716-636-2748.
Open Mon - Thurs 9 AM - 10 PM, Fri 9 AM - 5 PM, Sat 9 AM - 5 PM. No admis fee. Estab to expose the campus to a wide variety of art, ranging from contemporary painting, sculpture, prints, photographic design, crafts and media related arts; and to give student artists a place to show their works. A small gallery is located in Squire Hall
Income: $1300 (financed by student fees)
Exhibitions: Local artists' shows; student shows; loan exhibitions
Activities: Lect open to public, 4 visiting lectrs per year; competitions
L **Lockwood Memorial Library,** Art Dept, Room 106, Talbert Hall, 14260. Tel 716-636-2748. *Art Librn* Florence S DaLuiso
Open Mon - Thurs 9 AM - 10 PM, Fri 9 AM - 5 PM. Sat 9 AM - 5 PM. Estab 1913 to support curriculum in the history of art and architecture, and in the fine arts. Library has microfiche holdings on a reciprocal exchange basis, of the Albright-Knox Art Gallery catalog
Library Holdings: Vols 38,000; Micro—Fiche
Exhibitions: Monthly exhibitions of bibliothecal interest

CANAJOHARIE

M **CANAJOHARIE LIBRARY AND ART GALLERY,** Erie Blvd, 13317. Tel 518-673-2314. *Pres* Mrs William Crangle; *Cur* Edward Lipowicz; *Secy* Mrs James Dern
Open Mon - Wed and Fri 9:30 AM - 4:45 PM, Thurs 9:30 AM - 8:30 PM, Sat 9:30 AM - 1:30 PM, cl Sun. No admis fee. Estab 1927 as a memorial to Senator James Arkell. Average Annual Attendance: 3000 - 5000. Mem: Annual meeting in Jan
Income: Financed by endowment and village grants
Collections: †Paintings by American artists
Exhibitions: From permanent collection, changed monthly
Activities: Gallery talks; tours; individual paintings and original art objects lent to community residents and business institutions; lending collection contains paintings and sculptures
L **Library,** Erie Blvd, 13317. Tel 518-673-2314. *Librn* Bonnie Young
Library Holdings: Vols 21,000; Per subs 50

CANTON

M **ST LAWRENCE UNIVERSITY,** Richard F Brush Art Gallery, Romoda Dr, 13617. Tel 315-379-6003. *Dir* Dr Paul D Schweizer
Open Mon - Fri 9 AM - 5 PM. No admis fee. Estab 1968 as an adjunct of the Department of Fine Arts. The Gallery's programs are intended to compliment the University's art courses as well as benefit the general public of northern New York state and southern Canada
Income: Financed by university funds
Collections: Contemporary prints, paintings, sculture and photography; 19th century American art; Old Master graphics; Oriental and African art; Frederic Remington collection
Exhibitions: Altered Landscape Photography by John Pfahl; drawings from the permanent collection; Forms and Figures in Canadian art; Paintings by Joseph Piccillo; Prints and paintings by Guy Berard and Roger Bailey; 24 x 24, Video Art Exhibition; Watercolors by Edward Christiana; Student Art Exhibition; Annual Acquisitions
Publications: Annual report; exhibition brochures
Activities: Lect open to public, 4 visiting lectr per year; competitions; individual paintings and original art objects lent to student loan program and museums

CAZENOVIA

M **CAZENOVIA COLLEGE,** Chapman Art Center Gallery, 13035. Tel 315-655-3466. *Dir Art Prog* John Aistars
Open Mon - Fri 1 - 4 PM & 7 - 9 PM, Sat 10 AM - 7 PM, Sun 1 - 5 PM. No admis fee. Estab 1977 as a college gallery for students and community. Gallery is 1084 sq feet with track lighting and movable display panels. Average Annual Attendance: 1000
Income: Financed through College
Collections: A small permanent collect of work donated to college
Exhibitions: (1978) Peter Berg and Gary Trento; Phillip Block and Stephen Callagnino; Gene Gissin and Carol Jenney: Marilyn Lindner; Jerome Malinowski and Bruce Manwaring; 20th century print; sculpture exhibit. (1979-80) Advertising Design; Helen Block and Lawson Smith; Photography exhibit; Rodger and Isabelle Waiting-Mack; Jerome Witkin; Henery Gernhardt and Ann Hartranft Temple Exhibit; Annual shows of faculty, alumni, student and invitational work

CHAUTAUQUA

M **CHAUTAUQUA GALLERY OF ART,** Chautauqua Art Association, Wythe Ave, 14722. Tel 716-357-2771. *Pres & Advisor Dir* Helen B Cleveland; *VPres* George Weaver; *Secy* Suzanne Gray; *Dir* Rob Erdle
Open Mon - Sat 1 - 7:30 PM, Sun 1:30 - 2:30 PM and 4 - 7:30 PM. No admis fee. Estab 1948 to promote quality art, culture and appreciation of the arts. Winter address and phone: 1192 Parkside Dr, Alliance, Ohio 44601, 216-821-0468. Average Annual Attendance: 12,000. Mem: 1200; dues $4; six annual meetings
Income: Financed by membership
Exhibitions: Approximately 68; Chinese Philosophy and Art; Madam Shao Sheng; 23rd National Jury Show; Plaza Festival; sculpture
Publications: Art Gallery Magazine; national jury show program activities schedule
Activities: Classes for adults and children; dramatic programs; art appreciation; lect open to public, 24 visiting lectr per year; concerts; gallery talks; tours; competitions; scholarships; individual paintings lent to schools; lending collection tontains paintings, art magazines; book shop; junior museum

CLINTON

M **HAMILTON COLLEGE,** Edward W Root Art Center, 13323. Tel 315-859-7331. *Dir* Lettie Tourville
Open September - May Mon - Fri, 8:30 AM - 10:30 PM, Sat 9 AM - 6 PM, Sun 1 - 10:30 PM. Estab 1958 to make available to Hamilton College students and to the entire community fine examples of art, music and literature. Housed in 1800 building. Average Annual Attendance: 15,000
Income: Financed by Hamilton College appropriations
Exhibitions: Six exhibitions throughout the academic year arranged under the direction of the Hamilton College Department of Art and the Director of the Art Center
Activities: Lectures; concerts; gallery talks; tours
L **Library,** 13323.
Books on art and related subjects
M **Bristol Campus Center,** 13323. Tel 315-859-7194. *Dir* Andrew W Wertz
Exhibitions: Six throughout the academic year arranged under the direction of a Student Faculty Committee
M **Art Lending Library,** 13323.
Over 200 paintings and prints which may be rented by the semester by students for a nominal fee

O **KIRKLAND ART CENTER,** On-the-Park, 13323. Tel 315-853-8871. *Dir* Cynthia Jones Butcher; *Secy* Susan Elliott White
Open Tues - Fri 11 AM - 5 PM, Sat and Sun 2 - 4 PM, cl Mon, (July and Aug) Tues - Fri 1 - 5 PM, Sat and Sun 2 - 4 PM. No admis fee. Estab 1960 to promote the arts in the town of Kirkland. The center has a large main gallery, small downstairs gallery. Average Annual Attendance: 15,000 - 17,000. Mem: 1100; dues adults $5; annual meeting June
Income: $50,000 (financed by endowment, membership, state appropriation, fund raising events, thrift shop)
Exhibitions: Varied monthly; group shows including painting, sculpture, graphics, photography, crafts and others
Publications: Newsletter, bimonthly
Activities: Classes for adults and children; lect open to the public; gallery talks; competitions; thrift shop sells books, original art, crafts and purchased items

COOPERSTOWN

O **COOPERSTOWN ART ASSOCIATION,*** 22 Main St, 13326. Tel 607-547-9777.
Open Mon - Sat 10 AM - 4 PM, Sun 1 - 4 PM. Estab 1928 to provide a cultural program for the central part of New York State. An art gallery is maintained. Average Annual Attendance: 14,000. Mem: 1284; dues $7.50 and up
Income: Financed by membership
Collections: †Crafts; †paintings; †sculpture
Exhibitions: (1978) Annual National Juried Exhibitions; 50th Anniversary Exhibition
Publications: Newsletter, annual
Activities: Classes for adults; competitions; prizes; individual paintings and original objects of art lent; lending collection contains paintings, sculpture
L **Reference Library,*** 22 Main St, 13326.
For reference only

O **HISTORICAL SOCIETY OF EARLY AMERICAN DECORATION, INC,*** 200 W Market St, 27944. Tel 919-426-5417. *Pres* Mrs Donald Heatherington; *Cur* Mrs Edwin W Rowell
Exhibition Hall in Farmer's Museum of the New York State Historical Association open summer 9 AM - 5 PM, winter Tues - Sat 9 AM - 5 PM, cl Sun AM & Mon. Admis special educational group rate. Estab 1946 to perpetuate Early American decoration as an art, promote research in that field, record and preserve examples of the decorative arts, with emphasis on Americana. Gallery maintains exhibits and publishes works on the subject of early American decoration and the history thereof; to elevate the standards of its reproduction and utilization. Average Annual Attendance: 136,000. Mem: 800; dues $15 and up; annual meeting May
Collections: †Decorated chairs; painted chests; †stenciled and painted tin of all kinds
Exhibitions: Two exhibitions each year, other than that in the permanent gallery at the Farmer's Museum
Publications: The Decorator, twice a year; The Decorator Digest; An Illustrated Glossary of Decorated Antiques; The Ornamented Chair; The Ornamented Tray; also, reprinted from Antiques Magazine, 27 articles by Esther Stevens Brazer
Activities: Lect; exhibitions; awards to members for outstanding craftsmanship
L **Library,*** 200 W Market St, 27944.
Library Holdings: Vols 150; AV—Lantern Slides; Other—Photographs, recordings of original antiques by Esther Stevens Brazer and Walter H Wright, for members use

O **LEATHERSTOCKING BRUSH AND PALETTE CLUB INC,** (Formerly Brush and Palette Club) PO Box 446, 13326. *Pres* Sylvia Woerner; *VPres* Bert Van Duzer; *Secy* Elizabeth Rogers; *Treas* Virginia Hawthrush
Estab 1965 to encourage original arts and crafts work and foster general art appreciation and education. Arts and crafts gallery in local historical building. Mem: 100; dues $3, meetings May and Oct
Income: $2420 (financed by membership and outdoor show)
Library Holdings: Vols 12; Per subs 2
Exhibitions: Annual Fall Fine Arts; Firehouse Arts and Crafts Gallery
Publications: Information Bulletin, quarterly
Activities: Classes for adults; Shop sells original art
L **Cooperstown Art Association Workroom,** PO Box 446, 13326. *Librn* Dorothy V Smith
Open to members only
Special Subjects: Art History, Crafts

NEW YORK STATE HISTORICAL ASSOCIATION

M **Fenimore House,** Rte 80, Lake Rd, 13326. Tel 607-547-2533. *Dir and Chief Cur*

Minor Wine Thomas Jr; *Assoc Dir and Chief Educ* Milo V Stewart; *Cur Exhib* Daniel D Mayer

Open April 1 - Nov 30 daily 9 AM - 5 PM. Admis adults $2.50, children $1.25, members free. Estab 1899 as a historical society whose purpose is to promote the study of New York State through a statewide educational program, the operation of two museums, and graduate programs offering master's degree in conjunction with the State University College at Oneonta. Fenimore House is an art museum with an extensive collection of art. Average Annual Attendance: 55,000. Mem: 7800; dues $12; annual meeting July

Collections: †American folk art; Browere life masks of famous Americans; James Fenimore Cooper (memorabilia); genre paintings of New York State; landscapes; †portraits

Exhibitions: Photographs from the Smith and Telfer Photographic Collection of the New York State Historical Association

Publications: Director's Report, annual; Newsletter, biannual; New York History, quarterly journal; The Yorker, junior magazine

Activities: Classes for adults and children; docent training; seminars on American culture; junior program; conferences; lect open to the public; gallery talks; tours; individual paintings and original objects of art lent to selected museums

M **Farmers' Museum, Inc,** Lake Rd, 13326. Tel 607-547-2593. *Dir & Chief Cur* Minor Wine Thomas Jr; *Cur* David L Parke Jr; *Asst Cur* Virginia P Partridge

Open May - Oct daily 9 AM - 5 PM. Nov - April cl Sun & Mon mornings. Admis adults $3, children $1.25, under 7 and members free. Estab 1943 as an outdoor folk museum of rural life in upstate New York, 1785-1860. Main buildings with collections and craft demonstrations are maintained; recreated Village Crossroads with 13 buildings are brought in from nearby area. Average Annual Attendance: 120,000

Collections: Folk art

L **Library,** Lake Rd, 13326. Tel 607-547-2509. *Ed Assoc & Chief Library Service* Wendell Tripp

Open to public for reference only

Library Holdings: Vols 57,000; Per subs 300; Other—Manuscripts

Special Subjects: Decorative Arts, Folk Art, New York State history, genealogy

CORNING

M **CORNING MUSEUM OF GLASS,** 14830. Tel 607-937-5371. *Dir* Thomas S Buechner; *Deputy Dir Collections* Dwight P Lammon; *Deputy Dir Admin* John H Martin; *Deputy Dir Communications* Anthony E Snow; *Research Scientist* Robert H Brill; *Cur Ancient Glass* Sidney M Goldstein; *Cur American Glass* Jane Shadel Spillman; *Asst Cur 20th Century Glass* William Warmus; *Registrar* Priscilla B Price; *Managing Editor* Charleen K Edwards

Open all year daily 9 AM - 5 PM. Admis family $5, adults $2, children (11-17) $1. Estab 1951 to present to the public the art and history of glass. New building opens May 1980. Average Annual Attendance: 750,000

Income: Financed by state appropriations

Collections: Over 19,000 objects representing all periods of glass history from 1500 BC to the present

Exhibitions: Glassmaking: America's First Industry (traveling); The Great Paperweight Show; New Glass: A Worldwide Survey (traveling)

Publications: Journal of Glass Studies annually; Contemporary Glass, microfiche

Activities: Classes for children; annual seminar on glass; lect open to the public, 20 visiting lectr per year; original art objects lent to other museums; originates traveling exhibitions; sales shop sells books and slides

L **Corning Museum of Glass Library,** 14830. Tel 607-937-5371. *Librn* Norma P H Jenkins; *Reference Librn* Virginia L Wright

Open Mon - Fri 9 AM - 5 PM. Estab 1951 for the purpose of providing extensive and comprehensive coverage of the manufacture of glass. The library is primarily for research reference only

Library Holdings: Vols 25,000; Micro—Fiche, reels; AV—Motion pictures, v-tapes; Other—Clipping files, exhibition catalogs, pamphlets, photographs, Original documents

Special Subjects: Glass history, manufacturing, painting and stainingGlassware, Ornamental glass

Collections: Archival and historical materials relating to glass and its manufactures; 350 manufacturers' trade catalogs on microfiche

M **ROCKWELL-CORNING MUSEUM,** Baron Steuben Place, 14830. Tel 607-937-5386. *Supv Museum Coll* Kristin A Amylon; *Supv Museum Prog* P Jensen Monroe; *Admin Asst* Carolyn Lovejoy; *Vol Services* Marzie Seibert; *Sales Mgr* Ida Brown; *Cataloguing Asst* Cathy Birch; *Dir* Anthony E Snow

Open June - Sept, Mon - Sat 10 AM - 5 PM, Sun Noon - 5 PM, Oct - May, Tues - Sat 10 AM - 5 PM, Sun 1 - 5 PM, cl Mon. Admis adults $1, senior citizens and students 50¢, children 25¢, maximum family rate $3. Estab 1976 to house and exhibit the collections of the Robert F Rockwell Foundation and Family and to serve the Corning community with the funding provided by the Corning Glass Works. Average Annual Attendance: 35,000

Income: $400,000 (financed by a grant from the Corning Glass Works

Purchases: $25,000

Collections: Carder Steuben glass (1903-1933); bronzes; etchings; paintings; Plains Indian beadwork and artifacts; prints; Pueblo Indian pottery; Navajo rugs

Exhibitions: Best of Rockwell's Western Art Collection; seasonal exhibits featuring smaller parts of Rockwell collections

Publications: Exhibition catalog; Newsletter, quarterly

Activities: Classes for children; programs for students; lect open to public and for members only, 2 visiting lectr per year; gallery talks; tours; paintings and original objects of art lent to established museums; lending collection contains reproductions, original art works, original prints, Victorian toys, Carder Steuben Glass; originate traveling exhibitions; shop sells books, magazines, reproductions, prints, Indian jewelry, postcards, needlepoint, T-shirts

L **Library,** Baron Steuben Place, 14830. Tel 607-937-5386. *Librn* Carolyn Lovejoy

Open to the public by prior arrangement for reference only

Library Holdings: Vols 75; Per subs 10

CORTLAND

L **CORTLAND FREE LIBRARY,** Art Gallery, 32 Church St, 13045. Tel 607-753-1042, 753-1043. *Dir* Warren S Eddy

Open Mon - Thurs 10 AM - 9 PM, Fri and Sat 10 AM - 5:30 PM, cl Sun. No admis fee. Estab 1938

Library Holdings: Vols 1300

Exhibitions: Monthly exhibitions held

L **STATE UNIVERSITY OF NEW YORK COLLEGE AT CORTLAND,** Art Slide Library, 13045. Tel 607-753-4316. *Chmn* David L Simon, PhD; *Cur* Jo Schaffer

Open Mon - Fri 8:30 AM - 5 PM, and by appointment. Estab 1967 to provide visual resources to faculty, students and community

Income: Financed by state appropriation

Purchases: $1000

Library Holdings: Vols 300; Per subs 10; AV—Lantern Slides, slides; Other—Exhibition catalogs, photographs

DOUGLASTON

O **NATIONAL ART LEAGUE,** * 44-21 Douglaston Parkway, 11360. Tel 212-229-9495. *Pres* Leo Breslau

Estab 1932, inc 1950, as Art League of Long Island, Inc. Mem: 200

Exhibitions: Two annual major shows, one national; gallery exhibitions

Publications: Brochures; bulletins; catalogs

Activities: Art classes for adults and children; demonstrations; lect

EAST HAMPTON

M **GUILD HALL OF EAST HAMPTON, INC,** Museum Section, 158 Main St, 11937. Tel 516-324-0806. *Chmn* Budd Levinson; *First VChmn* Eloise Spaeth; *Second VChmn* Deborah L Perry; *Secy* Mrs Dana M Raymond; *Treas* Oscar Weinberger; *Dir* Enez Whipple; *Asst to Dir & Publicity Dir* Mildred Granitz; *Office Mgr* Billie Kalbacher; *Secy* Mary Frayher; *Cur* Judith Wolfe; *Assoc Cur* Rae Ferren

Open Mon - Sat 10 AM - 5 PM, Sun 2 - 5 PM (May - Sept), Tues - Sat 10 AM - 5 PM, cl Sun, (Oct - April). No admis fee. Estab 1931 as a cultural center for the visual and performing arts with a State Board of Regents Educational Charter. Emphasis on art collection and exhibitons is chiefly on the many artists who live or have lived in the area. Museum has three galleries and a sculpture garden. Average Annual Attendance: 83,000. Mem: 3200; dues $25 - $1000; annual meeting Nov

Income: $314,857 (financed by membership, state appropriation, benefits, events and fund drives)

Purchases: $70,000

Collections: Mainly American artist associated with the regions of eastern Long Island, including James Brooks, Jimmy Ernst, Adolf Gottlieb, Childe Hassam, Willem de Kooning, Roy Lichtenstein, Thomas Moran, Jackson Pollock and Larry Rivers: paintings, works on paper, prints, sculpture, photographs

Exhibitions: Children of China; Paul Gianfagna: An Anatomical Perspective; Gods of India (sculpture); Thomas Moran, A Search for the Scenic; Kyle Morris, Memorial Exhibition; Alfonso Ossorio, 1940-1980; Paper Works I and II; Photographs by Walter Krajicek; Points of View; the Stereograph in America, A Cultural History (GANYS); Athis Zacharias; Artists of the Region Annual Invitational; Awards Exhibition; 42nd Annual Guild Hall Artist Members' Exhibiton; Prints from the guild Hall Collection

Publications: Guild Hall Newsletter, monthly

Activities: Classes for adults; docent training; cooperative projects with area schools; lect open to public, 12 visiting lectr per year; concerts, gallery talks; tours, competitions; original art objects lent to museums, libraries, schools, public building; lending collection contains cassettes, original art works and prints, paintings, photographs, sculpture, slides; originate traveling exhibitions; shop sells books, prints, hand crafts, posters

ELMIRA

M **ARNOT ART MUSEUM,** * 235 Lake St, 14901. Tel 607-734-3697. *Dir* Kenneth H Lindquist; *Cur Coll* Allen C Smith

Open Tues - Fri 10 AM - 5 PM, Sat 9 AM - 5 PM, Sun 2 - 5 PM, cl Mon & national holidays. No admis fee. Estab 1911 to serve the people of the community with a regular schedule of changing exhibits from the permanent collection and traveling shows, as well as providing other free cultural activities not ordinarily available in the area. Average Annual Attendance: 40,000. Mem: 650; dues $5 and up; annual meeting in May

Collections: †American and European sculpture; †contemporary prints; Flemish, Dutch, French, English, German, Italian, Spanish and †American paintings

Exhibitions: Changed monthly; Annual Regional Exhibition with prizes; Annual Craft Exhibition with prizes

Activities: Classes for adults and children; lect open to public

M **ELMIRA COLLEGE,** Hamilton Art Gallery, Park Place, 14901. *Dir* Jo Ann Smith

Open Mon - Fri 1 - 4:30 PM. No admis fee. The Gallery is located in a Gothic Cathedral-like building with 100 x 35 feet of space. Average Annual Attendance: 1000

Income: Financed by school budget

O **SOUTHERN TIER ARTS ASSOCIATION, INC,** PO Box 641, 14902. Tel 607-737-2071. *Pres* Mary Louise Donovan; *VPres* Cameron Macdonell; *Public Relations and Grants* James L Manning

Estab 1974 to improve the Fine ARts in the Southern Tier of New York State. Mem: 130; dues $12; annual meeting Dec

Income: $5700 (financed by membership, decentralization grants)

Purchases: $5000

Exhibitions: Arts in the Parks

Activities: Lectures open to the public, 2 visiting lecturers per year; gallery talks;

competitions with awards; individual paintings and original objects of art lent to area museums, banks, cultural institutions, businesses

FLUSHING

M BOWNE HOUSE, 37-01 Bowne St, 11354. Tel 212-224-5919. *Pres* Franklin F Regan; *VPres* John H Tennent; *Secy* Mrs E V Bowen
Open Tues, Sat & Sun 2:30 - 4:30 PM. No admis fee. Estab 1945 for historic preservation, education, collection of decorative arts and examples of colonial life. Average Annual Attendance: 5000. Mem: 450; dues $5, $10, $25, $100, $250; annual meeting third Tues in May
Income: $12,000 (financed by membership and contributions)
Collections: Decorative arts from the 17th, 18th and early 19th Centuries Furniture, pewter, fabrics, china, portraits, prints and documents
Publications: Booklets regarding John Bowne and the House; Newsletter every sixty days
Activities: Classes for children; docent training; lectures for members only; tours; museum shop sells books, prints, gift items relating to Bowne House

M QUEENS COLLEGE OF THE CITY UNIVERSITY OF NEW YORK, Art Collection, Kissena Blvd and Long Island Expressway, 11367. Tel 212-520-7243. *Chief Librn* Robert Muller; *Art Librn and Cur* Neal W Richmond; *Art Bibliographer* Gerd Muehsam
Open Mon - Wed 9 AM - 8 PM, Tues and Thurs 9 AM - 6 PM, Fri 9 AM - 5 PM. No admis fee. Estab 1957 for a study collection for Queens College students. Permanent collection exhibited in Art Library reading room, loan shows in adjacent gallery and entrance corridor
Income: Financed by state appropriation
Collections: Ancient and Antique Glass; Egyptian, Greek, Luistan Antiquities, Old Master and WPA Prints; Renassance and Later Bronzes; 16th - 20th Century Paintings
Exhibitions: Anni Albers (prints); Rudolph Baronik (collages); Naomi Boretz (watercolors); Lois Dodd (paintings); Blance Dombek (sculpture); Evelyn Eller (collages); M C Escher (prints); Sally Friedman (paintings); Zofia Griffen (drawings); Richard McDermott Miller (sculpture); Emily Nelligan (prints and drawings); Peri Schwartz (paintings); Zelda Tannenbaum (drawings)
Publications: Brochures; exhibition catalogs
Activities: Lending collection contains 11,000 lantern slides
L Paul Klapper Library, Kissena Blvd and Long Island Expressway, 11367.
Open to City University students for reference
Library Holdings: Vols 22,000; Per subs 100

M QUEENS MUSEUM, New York City Bldg, Flushing Meadow Park, 11368. Tel 212-592-2405. *Dir* Janet Schneider; *Asst Dir* Shelley Grossberg; *Cur* Carlos Gutierrez-Solana; *Prog Coordr* Janet Katz; *Business Officer* Barbara Sperber; *Chmn* Peter Rothholz; *Pres* Geraldine Eiber; *Secy* Rose Ciampa
Open Tues - Sat 10 AM - 5 PM, Sun 1 - 5 PM, cl Mon. No admis fee, contributions requested. Estab 1972 to provide quality art and related programs for residents of Queens and New York City. Museum has approx 13,000 sq ft gallery space, 1776 Panorama Gallery surrounding 18,000 sq ft of Panorama, Theatre, workshops, offices. Average Annual Attendance: 100,000. Mem: 500; dues $5 - $1000
Income: $310,000 (financed by membership, city and state appropriation, Corporation, Foundation, NEH and individual grants)
Collections: Small collection of paintings, photographs and prints
Exhibitions: (1978) Ancient Glass from the Queens College Collection; Symcho Moszkowicz: the Artist in Post War Europe; Photography: Art and Artifacts; Play Ball, A Century of Sports in Art; Private Myth; Queens Artists '78. (1979) The Artistic Discovery of the Little Continent of Long Island; By the Sea; Clay Attitudes; Charles Henry Miller; Jose Orozco and Diego Rivera: drawings and prints; Queens Museum Annual 1979. (1980) Queens Annual 1980
Publications: Catalogs; newsletter, quarterly
Activities: Classes for adults and children; docent training; projects involving elementary school children; lect open to public and some for members only, with visiting lectr; concerts; gallery talks; tours; competitions; originate traveling exhibitions; museum shop sells books, reproductions and children's items

FREDONIA

M STATE UNIVERSITY OF NEW YORK COLLEGE AT FREDONIA, M C Rockefeller Arts Center Gallery, 14063. *Art Gallery Dir* Nancy Weekly; *Art Gallery Asst* Marilyn Bomasuto
Open Mon - Fri 10 AM - noon, 1 - 4 PM and 7 - 9 PM, Sat 1 - 4 PM, schedule subject to change each semester. No admis fee. Estab 1963 and relocated in 1969 to new quarters designed by I M Pei and Partners. The gallery serves as a focal point of the campus, uniting the college with the community. Average Annual Attendance: 20,000
Income: Financed by state appropriation
Collections: Primarily 20 century American art and architectural archival material, with an emphasis on †prints and †sculpture
Exhibitions: Canadian Eskimo Lithographs; Celebrate the Arts Alumni Show; Outside the City Limits; Student and Faculty Exhibitions; Two Approaches to Photography: John Pfahl and W Eugene Smith; Western New York Collegiate Drawing Exhibition; Works on Paper
Publications: Exhibition catalogs
Activities: Small slide library; Lect open to public, 2 - 4 vis lectr per year; gallery talks; tours; competitions; individual paintings and original objects of art lent to offices and public lobbies on campus; lending collection contains framed reproductions original prints, paintings, photographs, sculpture; traveling exhibitions organized and circulated

GARDEN CITY

L ADELPHI UNIVERSITY, Fine Arts Library, 11530. Tel 516-294-8700, Ext 7353. *Head Fine Arts Library* Erica Doctorow; *Fine Arts Librn* Roberta Blitz
Open Mon - Thurs 8:30 AM - 10 PM, Fri & Sat 9 AM - 5 PM, Sun 1 - 5 PM. The Fine Arts Library builds print and nonprint collections and provides reference service in fine and applied arts, music and related performing arts. Maintains an art gallery
Income: Financed by state appropriations and through the University
Library Holdings: Vols 17,000; Per subs 125; Micro—Fiche, reels; AV—Cassettes, rec, slides, v-tapes; Other—Exhibition catalogs, prints, manuscripts, memorabilia, original art works, pamphlets, photographs, reproductions, original documents
Collections: Americana; William Blake; Cuala Press; Expatriate Writers: Cobbett, Morley, Hauptman and Whitman; University Archives
Exhibitions: A Dream Transplanted: Brooklyn-Garden City; A Thousand Words: Early American Photography; Apres-midi d' un faun; Canada: The Art Bank; Dada in Berlin; Hand Bookbinding: The Art and Craft; Images of India; Mind and Hand: Selections from the Adelphi University Art Collection; The Trotsky-Stalin Conflict

GENESEO

M STATE UNIVERSITY OF NEW YORK COLLEGE AT GENESEO, Fine Arts Gallery, 14454. Tel 716-245-5801 and 245-5802. *Coordr Fine Arts Activities* Bertha V B Lederer; *Secy* Dora J Scorsone
Open 2 - 5 PM for exhibitions. No admis fee. Estab 1967; the gallery serves the college and community. Average Annual Attendance: 6000
Income: Financed by state appropriation
Collections: Ceramics, furniture, graphics, paintings, sculpture
Exhibitions: (1979) A Genesee Harvest, A Scene in Time: 1779
Publications: Exhibition catalogs
Activities: Lect open to public, 3 - 4 vis lectr per year; concerts; lending collection contains 400 - 600 books

GLENS FALLS

M HYDE COLLECTION, 161 Warren St, 12801. Tel 518-792-1761. *Dir* Frederick J Fisher; *Cur* James Kettlewell
Open Tues, Wed, Fri, Sat & Sun 2 - 5 PM, cl Mon & Thurs, cl month of Jan. Admis adults $1, children, students, senior citizens 50¢. Average Annual Attendance: 15,000
Collections: Drawings by da Vinci, Degas, Tiepolo, Matisse, Lorraine and others; Paintings by El Greco, Rembrandt, Rubens, Botticelli, Tintoretto, Renoir, Picasso, Homer and others; furniture, sculpture, tapestries
Exhibitions: Eight temporary exhibitions throughout the year
Publications: American Quilts: European and American Samplers; Annual Report; The Art of Henry Ossawa Tanner; Rembrandt's Christ; The Sculpture of John Rogers; David Smith of Bolton Landing; Rockwell Kent (1882-1971); Elihu Vedder
Activities: Classes for high school students; lectures; concerts
L Library, 161 Warren St, 12801.
Library Holdings: Vols 500

GOSHEN

M HALL OF FAME OF THE TROTTER, 240 Main St, 10924. Tel 914-294-6330. *Dir* Philip A Pines; *Graphics Designer* Janet S Hack; *Registrar* Jean E Musgrave; *Asst Secy & Treas* Ellen Nuzzolese; *Staff Asst* Walter Latzko
Open Mon - Sat 10 AM - 5 PM, Sun & holidays 1:30 - 5 PM. No admis fee. Estab 1951 to preserve the artifacts of harness racing. There are two galleries; one usually has the museum's permanent collection; the smaller one is used for visiting art shows. Average Annual Attendance: 27,000 - 35,000. Mem: 1200; dues $100, $30, $15; annual meeting in July
Income: Financed by endowment, membership
Collections: Large collection of lithographs by Currier and Ives pertaining to harness racing, plus other leading printers of the 19th century; bronzes, dioramas, statuary, wood carvings
Exhibitions: Visiting art shows for nine months of the year
Publications: Newsletter, bimonthly
Activities: Classes for children; lect open to public; concerts; tours; museum shop sells books, prints, slides
L Library, 240 Main St, 10924.
Open to the public for reference only

M ORANGE COUNTY COMMUNITY OF MUSEUMS AND GALLERIES, 101 Main St, PO Box 527, 10924. Tel 914-294-5657. *Pres* Philip A Pines; *VPres* R E Kuehne; *Secy* M A Booth
Open Mon - Fri, 9 AM - 5 PM. No admis fee. Estab 1961 to coordinate the programs and activities of the member museums and galleries. Promotional agency for local museums. Mem: 100; dues $10 individual, $25 institutional
Income: $9800 (financed by membership and CTEA)
Activities: Lectures open to the public; Extension department serves Orange County and adjacent areas; museum shop sells books
L Library, 101 Main St, 10924. *Secy* Malcolm Booth
Open Mon - Fri, 9 AM - 5 PM. Estab 1966
Income: $9180 (financed by membership and CTEA)
Purchases: $76
Library Holdings: Vols 200; Per subs 8; AV—Motion pictures, slides; Other—Manuscripts, photographs
Special Subjects: Architecture, Museology
Collections: Dwight Akers (local author); Manuscript notes (local history); Local architecture
Activities: Lectures open to the public; Extension department serving Orange County and adjoining counties

GREAT NECK

O **LOUIS COMFORT TIFFANY FOUNDATION**, PO Box 1088, 11023. *Pres* Lewis Iselin; *VPres* Paul Smith; *Secy* Gerard Jones; *Exec Dir* Elizabeth Stevens
Estab 1918 to give grants to painters and sculptors and in the crafts. Applications available Jan 1981, applications due Sept 1981. Mem: Annual meeting May
Income: Financed by endowment
Activities: Open competition for painters and sculptors every two years; twenty grants of $5000 each are given

GREENVALE

AMERICAN SOCIETY FOR AESTHETICS
For further information, see National and Regional Organizations

M **C W POST CENTER OF LONG ISLAND UNIVERSITY**, Art Gallery,* 11548. Tel 516-299-2788 & 299-2789. *Dir* Joan Vita Miller
Open Mon - Fri 10 AM - 5 PM, Sat & Sun 1 - 5 PM. No admis fee. Estab 1973. Gallery has great appeal to the surrounding North Shore community as well as the student body. The gallery is located in a multimillion dollar student complex; it occupies a space of approx 46 x 92 ft. Average Annual Attendance: 40,000 - 50,000
Income: Financed by university budget, grants and donations
Collections: Contemporary graphics, including works by Rauschenberg, Max Ernst, Pearlstein, Mark di Suvero and Salvador Dali
Exhibitions: (1978). The Unconquered Spirit: American Indian Painting and Objects 1937-1977
Publications: Catalogs: The Arts of China, Marsden Hartley, Louise Nevelson
Activities: Docent training; lect open to public, 4 visiting lectrs per year; concerts; gallery talks; individual paintings lent; lending collection contains original prints, paintings; traveling exhibitions organized and circulated; sales shop selling books, magazines, reproductions

HAMILTON

M **COLGATE UNIVERSITY**, Picker Art Gallery, Charles A Dana Arts Center, 13346. Tel 315-824-1000, Ext 632. *Dir-Cur* Edward Bryant; *Registrar* Leslie Ann Eliet
Open Mon - Fri 10 AM - 5 PM, Sat, Sun, holidays 1 - 5 PM, cl academic recesses. No admis fee. Estab 1966, as an educative adjunct to study in the fine arts and liberal arts curriculum. Building designed by architect Paul Rudolph. Average Annual Attendance: 10,000. Mem: 110; dues $5 and up; annual meeting in the Spring
Income: Financed by the University
Collections: Herman Collection of Oriental Art; Luis de Hoyos Collection of Guerrero Stone Sculpture; paintings; photographs; posters; prints; sculptures
Exhibitions: Folk Art of Central New York State; Luis de Hoyos Collection; Thomas Nast: President Maker; New Deal for Art (GANYS); One-Person Shows: Adal, Steven Barbash, Tom Doyle, Rene Gelpi, Marty Greenbaum, Douglas Holloley, Lynn Itzkowitz, John Koch, Leslie Krims, James Loveless, Neil Spitzer, Frank Lincoln Viner
Publications: Catalogs
Activities: Lect open to public, 10 visiting lectrs per year; gallery talks; individual paintings and original objects of art lent to members of Friends of the Visual Arts

HEMPSTEAD

M **HOFSTRA UNIVERSITY**, Emily Lowe Gallery, Hempstead Turnpike, 11550. Tel 516-560-3275 & 560-3276. *Dir* Kevin E Consey; *Education Specialist* Joan Friedman; *Asst Cur* Manya Balch; *Secy* Mary Wakeford
Open Thurs - Fri 10 AM - 5 PM, Tues - Wed 10 AM - 9 PM, Sun 1 - 5 PM. No admis fee. Estab 1963; a university museum that serves the needs of its student body and the surrounding Nassau County community. Average Annual Attendance: 35,000 - 40,000. Mem: 500; dues $20 - $100
Income: Financed by endowment, membership, foundation and University
Collections: †American Prints; African, Pre-Columbian, New Guinea, Japanese and Indian Art; 17th and 18th Century European Painting; Contemporary Prints, Painting and Photographs
Exhibitions: (1978) The Art of Boxing; New Deal Murals on Long Island. (1979) Focus on India, The Floating World; Remains: The Artist in Environment; Stanley Twardowicz: Thirty Years of Photography. (1980) 18th and 19th Century British Watercolors; Italian Design Now
Publications: Exhibition catalogs
Activities: Classes for children; lect open to public, 10 - 15 vis lectr per year; gallery talks; tours; individual paintings and original objects of art lent; originate traveling exhibitions

HEWLETT

L **HEWLETT-WOODMERE PUBLIC LIBRARY**, 1125 Broadway, 11557. Tel 516-374-1967. *Dir* William H Menear; *Chief of Public Services* Rebecca Rockmuller; *Art Librn* Clarice Henry
Open Mon - Thurs 9 AM - 9 PM, Fri 9 AM - 6 PM, Sat 9 AM - 5 PM, Sun 1 - 5 PM. Estab 1947 as a Co-Center for art and music. Circ 286,819. Gallery maintained
Income: $923,882 (financed by state appropriation and school district)
Purchases: $881,659
Library Holdings: Vols 124,980; Per subs 473; Micro—Reels; AV—Fs, Kodachromes, motion pictures, rec, slides; Other—Clipping files, exhibition catalogs, framed reproductions, prints, pamphlets, photographs, reproductions
Special Subjects: Architecture, Crafts, Film, Photography, antiques
Exhibitions: Hold local exhibits
Publications: Index to Art Reproductions in Books (Scarecrow Press)
Activities: Classes for adults and children; lect open to the public; concerts; gallery talks; tours

HUDSON

M **OLANA HISTORIC SITE**, RD 2, Off Route 9-G, 12534. Tel 518-828-0135. *Pres Governor's Board* Thomas Quinn; *Historic Site Mgr* James Ryan; *Interpretive Programs Asst* Linda McLean
Open Memorial Day weekend to last Sun in Oct Wed - Sun 9 AM - 5 PM by tour (last tour 4:30). Admis 50¢. Estab 1870-74, and opened as a museum June 1967 to promote interest in and disseminate information of the life, works and times of Frederic Edwin Church, landscape painter of the Hudson River School. Managed by New York State Department of Parks and Recreation. The building is a Persian-style castle overlooking the Hudson River. Average Annual Attendance: 30,000 - 70,000. Mem: 150; dues $10; annual meeting May or June
Income: Financed by state appropriation
Collections: Extensive 19th Century Furniture Collection; Oil Sketches, Drawings, and Photographs by Church; Paintings by Church and Other Artists; Textile Collection from all over the World; decorative arts
Publications: The Crayon, quarterly (journal produced by Friends of Olana)
Activities: Classes for children; dramatic programs; docent training; slide programs, lectures; concerts; individual paintings and original objects of art lent to other institutions who qualify; museum shop sells books, postcards, posters and slides
L **Archives**, Rd 2, Off Route 9-G, 12534.
Open to the public with approval of Site Manager; for reference only
Collections: Family papers, photographs, books, correspondence diaries, receipts

HUNTINGTON

M **HECKSCHER MUSEUM**, Prime Ave, 11743. Tel 516-351-3250. *Chairman Board Trustees* Miner D Crary Jr; *Dir* Katherine Lochridge; *Asst Dir* Ruth Solomon; *Registrar* William Titus; *Public Information & Publications Officer* Barbara Press
Open Tues - Fri 10 AM - 5 PM, Sat, Sun & holidays 1 - 6 PM, cl Mon. No admis fee. Estab 1920, inc 1957, for the maintenance, preservation and operation of the museum building together with the preservation, exhibition and display of all objects and works of art therin. Four galleries, each 20 x 40 ft with 15 ft ceilings, track incandescent and diffused ultraviolet-free fluorescent lighting. Two galleries are used for changing exhibition and two for permanent collections. Average Annual Attendance: 50,000. Mem: 675; dues $15 and up; annual meeting in June
Income: Approx $250,000 (financed by endowment, membership, town appropriations and grants)
Collections: Major works by the Moran family, George Grosz, Thomas Eakins, Lucas Cranach the Elder are included; paintings, sculpture, drawings and prints by 16th - 20th century artists, primarily American with some European
Exhibitions: As We See Ourselves: Artists Self Portraits; By A Child's Hand Wrought: American Children's Folk Art; Daumier Lithographs; Drawings: Aspects of Change; Henri Matisse: Jazz and Other Illustrated Books; The Precisionist Painters; The Seeing Eye: Neutron Activation Autoradiography; Target Collection of Photography; Huntington Township Art League sponsors annual Long Island Artists Exhibition; regional artists are featured in contemporary exhibitions
Publications: Heckscher News, quarterly newsletter
Activities: Lect open to public, 9 - 12 vis lectr per year; gallery talks; tours; individual paintings and original objects of art lent to art institutions and galleries; lending collection contains original art works, paintings, sculpture; shop sells magazines, reproductions, slides and catalogues
L **Library**, Prime Ave, 11743.
Open to researchers by appointment for reference only
Library Holdings: Vols 1000; Per subs 15

HYDE PARK

M **FRANKLIN D ROOSEVELT LIBRARY AND MUSEUM**, Albany Post Rd, 12538. Tel 914-229-8114. *Dir* William R Emerson; *Acting Cur Museum* Marguerite B Hubbard
Open daily 9 AM - 5 PM, cl Christmas Day and New Year's Day. Admis adults $1.50 for combination ticket to the Roosevelt Home, Library, Museum and Vanderbilt Mansion, children, senior citizens and school groups free. Estab 1941 to display illustration of President and Mrs Roosevelt's careers and special interest, including personal items, gifts and items collected by President Roosevelt. Average Annual Attendance: 225,000
Collections: Papers of President and Mrs Roosevelts and of various members of his administration; Prints, Paintings and Documents on the Hudson Valley; paintings, prints, ship models, documents and relics of the history of the United States Navy as well as other marine items
Publications: The Franklin D Roosevelt Library and Museum for Visitors; Historical Materials in the Franklin D Roosevelt Library for Researchers
Activities: Sales shop selling books, prints, reproductions and slides
L **Library**, Albany Post Rd, 12538. *Librn* Joseph W Marshall
Open to scholars for reference only
Library Holdings: Vols 38,000; Per subs 45; Other—Pamphlets, Newspapers, maps, broadsides, unbound per 62,000

M **ROOSEVELT-VANDERBILT NATIONAL HISTORIC SITES**, 12538. Tel 914-229-9115. *Superintendent* Warren H Hill
Open 9 AM - 5 PM, summer 9 AM - 6 PM. Admis $1.50, under 16, over 62 and school groups free admis. Estab 1940 to preserve the home of Franklin D Roosevelt and the Frederick W Vanderbilt Mansion. Average Annual Attendance: 300,000
Income: Financed by Federal Government
Collections: Furnishings which are original to the historic periods and owners
Publications: Two park brochures, annually
Activities: Lectures open to the public; tours; sales shop sells books, postcards and slides

M **EDWIN A ULRICH MUSEUM**, Wave Crest on-the-Hudson, Albany Post Rd, 12538. Tel 914-229-7107. *Dir* Edwin A Ulrich
Open May - Oct Thurs - Mon 11 AM - 4 PM. Admis $1.50. Estab 1956 to exhibit three generation of the Waugh family of painters, 1813 - 1973. Average Annual Attendance: 500

Income: Financed by owner and director
Collections: Collections by Samuel Bell Waugh, 1813-1884; Fred J Waugh 1860-1940; Coulton Waugh, 1896-1973
Exhibitions: Fine Art and Works by the Waugh family
Activities: Lect open to the public; individual paintings lent to other recognized museums; lending collection contains 300 Kodachromes; sales shop selling books, reproductions, slides
L **Library,** Wave Crest on-the-Hudson, Albany Post Rd, 12538. *Dir* Edwin A Ulrich
Open Thurs - Mon 11 AM - 4 PM. Estab 1956. For reference only
Library Holdings: Vols 75; Per subs 3; Micro—Prints; AV—Kodachromes, slides; Other—Clipping files, exhibition catalogs, framed reproductions, prints, memorabilia, original art works, pamphlets, photographs, reproductions
Collections: Early Original Drawings by Fred J Waugh

ITHACA

M **CORNELL UNIVERSITY,** Herbert F Johnson Museum of Art, 14853. Tel 607-256-6464. *Dir* Thomas W Leavitt; *Cur Asian Art* Martie Young; *Adjunct Cur Modern Art* Robert Hobbs; *Asst Cur* Gwendolyn Owens; *Coordr Education & Cur Crafts* Nancy S Press; *Registrar* Jill Aszling; *Supt* Donald Feint; *Adminr* Nancy Scoones; *Exhib Coordr* Jill Chambers-Hartz
Open Tues - Sun 10 AM - 5 PM, cl Mon. No admis fee. Estab 1973, replacing the Andrew Dickson Art Museum of Art, originally founded in 1953 as Cornell University's Art Museum to serve students, the Tompkins County community and the Finger Lakes region. The collection and galleries are housed in an I M Pei designed building on Cornell University campus overlooking downtown Ithaca and Lake Cayuga. Average Annual Attendance: 93,000. Mem: 1050; dues $5 - 10
Income: $400,000 (Financed by endowment, membership, state appropriation, grants and university funds)
Purchases: $100,000
Collections: Asian Art; Arts of Primitive Societies; European and American Paintings, Drawings, Sculpture, Graphic Arts and Photographs
Exhibitions: Abstract Expressionism: The Formative Years; Architecture and Media: Visual Communications in Environmental Design; Cornell Then, Sculpture Now; Landscape: New Views
Publications: Annual academic year calandar listing exhibitions and special members' events; exhibition catalogs, approximately 10 a year
Activities: Classes for adults and children; lect open to public, 5 - 10 vis lectr per year; gallery talks; tours; individual paintings and original objects of art lent to Cornell University community upon official permission; lending collection contains paintings, sculpture, drawings; originate traveling exhibitions; museum shop selling exhibition catalogs, postcards, notecards and slides
L **Museum Library,** 14853. *Asst Cur* Gwendolyn Owens
Open to public by appointment only. Estab 1973. For reference only
Income: Financed by gifts
Library Holdings: Vols 4000; Per subs 20; Other—Exhibition catalogs, pamphlets, Monographs
L **Fine Arts Library,** Sibley Dome, 14853. Tel 607-256-3710. *Librn* Judith Holliday; *Asst Librn* Patricia Sullivan
Open Sat 9 AM - 5 PM, Sun 1 - 11 PM, Mon - Thurs 8 AM - 11 PM, Fri 8 AM - 10 PM, hours change for University vacation and summer session. Estab 1871 to serve Cornell students. Circ 56,000
Income: Financed through University funds
Purchases: $61,000
Library Holdings: Vols 100,200; Per subs 1800; Micro—Fiche, reels; Other—Exhibition catalogs

JAMAICA

L **QUEENS BOROUGH PUBLIC LIBRARY,** Art and Music Division, 89-11 Merrick Blvd, 11432. Tel 212-990-0755. *Acting Dir* Constance B Cooke; *Librn* Charles F J Young; *Head, Art & Music Division* Dorothea Wu; *Asst Head Art & Music Division* Esther Lee
Open Mon - Fri 10 AM - 9 PM, Sat 10 AM - 5:30 PM, Sun noon - 5 PM, cl in summer. Estab 1933 to serve the general public in Queens, New York
Income: $42,500
Purchases: $42,500
Library Holdings: Vols 70,000; Per subs 260; Micro—Fiche, reels; AV—Cassettes, rec; Other—Exhibition catalogs, framed reproductions 300, prints, original art works, pamphlets, photographs, reproductions 1,500,000
Collections: The WPA Print Collection

M **SAINT JOHN'S UNIVERSITY,** Chung-Cheng Art Gallery, Sun Yat Sen Hall, Grand Central and Utopia Parkways, 11439. Tel 212-969-8000, Ext 582. *Cur* Abraham P Ho
Open Mon - Sun 10 AM - 8 PM. No admis fee. Estab Oct 1977 to make available Oriental art objects to the public, and to expose the metropolitan area to the Oriental culture through various exhibits and activities. Gallery displays contemporary as well as ancient objects, mainly Oriental with a few western subjects. Average Annual Attendance: 50,000
Income: Financed by the University, endowments and private contributions
Collections: Harry C Goebel Collection containing 595 pieces of rare and beautiful art objects dating from the 7th - 19th century - jades; ivory carvings; netsuke; procelains; lacquerware and paintings from Japan and China; Permanent collection contains 600 pieces of Chinese porcelain, paintings and calligraphy dating from 7th - 20th century
Exhibitions: (1978) 15th Annual Sumi-e Society National Exhibition; Leroy Neiman: Sports Art. (1979)Chinese Currency Through the Dynasties; Chinese Women Artists in America; Three Friends in Winter (three eminent Chinese Calligraphers). (1980) Monkey King: A Celestial Heritage
Publications: Exhibition catalgoues
Activities: Classes for adults; films; demonstrations; lect open to the public, 5 vis lectr per yr; gallery talks; tours; lending collection contains 200 original art works; original prints; 200 paintings; traveling exhibitions organized and circulated

L **Asian Collection,** Saint Augustine Hall, 11439. *Librn* Hou-Ran Ferng
Open to the public for reference only
Library Holdings: Vols 50,000; Per subs 100
Collections: Collected Works of Chinese and Japanese Calligraphy; Japan Foundation Collection includes 200 volumes on various Japanese art subjects; Series of Chinese Arts

M **STORE FRONT MUSEUM,** * 162-02 Liberty Ave, 11433. Tel 212-523-5199. *Dir & Cur* Tom Lloyd; *Asst Dir* Janet DeSisso
Open Tues - Fri 9:30 AM - 4 PM. No admis fee. Estab 1970 to preserve Black art and history, and for use as a cultural center
Collections: Drawings; paintings; sculpture; tribal African art
Exhibitions: temporary exhibitions
Activities: Classes for adults and children; training programs for professional museum workers; lect; gallery talks; guided tours; concerts; competitions; hobby workshops; TV programs; artmobile; traveling exhibitions organized and circulated
L **Library,** * 162-02 Liberty Ave, 11433.
Open to the public; material also for inter-museum loan
Library Holdings: Vols 500
Special Subjects: Black history and culture

JAMESTOWN

L **JAMES PRENDERGAST LIBRARY ASSOCIATION,** 509 Cherry St, 14701. Tel 716-484-7135. *Dir* Murray L Bob
Open Mon - Fri 9 AM - 9 PM, Sat 9 AM - 6 PM, Sun 1 - 4 PM, shorter hours in summer. Estab 1891 as part of library. Maintains art gallery. Mem: 410,173
Library Holdings: Vols 5000; Micro—Prints; AV—Motion pictures, rec, slides; Other—Reproductions, sculpture
Exhibitions: Traveling Exhibitions; local one-person and group shows
Activities: books traveling exhibitions

KATONAH

M **JOHN JAY HOMESTEAD,** Jay St, PO Box AH, 10536. *Site Mgr* Emilie W Gould
Open Wed - Sun 9 AM - 5 PM. No admis fee. Estab 1958 as a New York State Historic Site, the home of the first Chief Justice John Jay and six following generations. Museum contains period furnishings, historic portraits and a library. Average Annual Attendance: 22,000
Income: Financed by state appropriation
Activities: Classes for children; docent training; lect open to the public; tours
L **Library,** Jay St, PO Box AH, 10536.
Open by appointment

M **KATONAH GALLERY,** 28 Bedford Rd, 10536. Tel 914-232-4343. *Dir* Betty Himmel; *VPres* Mrs John McCain; *Secy* Mrs William Cabell; *Treas* Richard Weinland; *Adminr* Mrs Paul Baren
Open Tues - Thurs 2 - 5 PM, Fri & Sat 10 AM - 5 PM, Sun 1 - 5 PM, cl Mon. No admis fee. Estab 1953 to present exhibitions created with loaned works of art, programs for schools, films, lectures, demonstrations and workshops. Located on the ground floor of the Katonah Village Library; the Katonah Gallery consists of 1800 sq ft of exhibition space with a meeting room of 1200 sq ft. Average Annual Attendance: 25,000. Mem: 1000; dues $15 - $500
Income: Approx $117,000 (financed by membership, contributions, and grants)
Exhibitions: American Still Life and Trompe L'Oeil Paintings; Anni Albers Graphics; Jim Dine; Gallery 28; Kenneth Nolan, Ceramics-Handmade Papers; Islamic Insights: An Introduction to Islamic Art; Removed Realities: New Sculpture; Mott B Schmidt: An Architectural Portrait; Shadow Images of Asia; Through English Eyes: Romanticism in British Watercolors; Local Artists; Works From a 20th Century Private Collection
Publications: Exhibition catalogs
Activities: Docent training; teacher workshops; programs for schools; lect open to the public, 5 - 10 vis lectr per year; gallery talks; concerts; tours; competitions; individual paintings and original objects of art lent; lending collection contains motion pictures, photographs, slides; originate traveling exhibitions; sales shop selling books, jewelry, notepaper, postcards, prints and reproductions

KINDERHOOK

M **COLUMBIA COUNTY HISTORICAL SOCIETY,** House of History and Van Alen House, 12106. Tel 518-758-9265. *Pres* William Appell; *VPres* Carl G Whitbeck Jr; *Secy* Jane Mills; *Exec Dir* Ruth Piwonka
Open Memorial Day - Labor Day weekends, Tues - Sat 10:30 AM - 4:30 PM, Sun 1:30 - 4:30 PM, open weekends during Sept and Oct weather permitting. Admis one museum adults $1.25, children over 12 75¢, both museums: adults $2 children over 12 $1. Estab 1924 as restoration museums to interpret local and regional, colonial and federal period history, including art of 18th and 19th century and decorative arts. In large hall, wall space used for exhibition of paintings. Average Annual Attendance: 5000. Mem: 630; dues $75, $35, $25, $10, senior citizen $5; annual meeting first Sat in October
Income: $19,000 (financed by membership, endowment, activities, projects, events and grants)
Purchases: $1800
Collections: Historical objects pertaining to history of county; New York regional decorative arts; paintings of 18th and 19th centuries
Exhibitions: (1978) Emma Cady and Her Contemporaries. (1979) Montgomery Livingston; American Decorative Painting
Publications: Newsletter, five times a year; exhibition
Activities: Classes for adults; docent training; lectures open to the public, 4 - 6 visiting lecturers each year; concerts; tours; individual paintings lent to museums, schools; lending collection contains cassettes, paintings, photographs, slides; museum shop sells books, magazines, gifts

M **Library**, Broad St, 12106.
Open June - August Tues - Sat 10:30 AM - 4:30 PM, Sun 1:30 - 4:30 PM; September - May Mon - Fri 9:30 AM - 5:00 PM, appointment advisable. Estab 1929 to maintain research files on the county and regional art history. For reference only
Library Holdings: AV—Lantern Slides; Other—Clipping files, exhibition catalogs, manuscripts, photographs

KINGSTON

M **PALISADES INTERSTATE PARK COMMISSION**, Senate House State Historic Site, 296 Fair St, 12401. Tel 914-338-2786. *Historic Site Mgr* Leigh Rehner Jones
Open Wed - Sun 9 AM - 5 PM; cl Mon & Tues. No admis fee. Estab 1887. The site is one of 38 New York State historic sites. Senate House is where the first New York State Senate met in 1777; furnished as 18th century middle-class dwelling
Collections: 18th and 19th century decorative arts; 18th and 19th century paintings and other works of art, particularly those by James Bard, Jervis McEntee, Ammi Phillips, Joseph Tubby and John Vanderlyn
Exhibitions: At the Risk of our Lives and Fortunes; Vanderlyn the Artist; 19th Century American Artists
Activities: Classes for children; lect open to public, 4-6 vis lectr per yr; concerts
L **Library**, 12401.
Open by appointment to scholars, students and researchers for reference only
Library Holdings: Vols 2500; Other—Manuscripts
Collections: Collection of letters relating to the artist John Vanderlyn

LAKE PLACID

M **LAKE PLACID SCHOOL OF ART GALLERY**, Saranac Ave, 12946. Tel 518-523-2591. *Dir* Lesley A Cadman; *Mgr Dir Center for Music, Drama & Art* Ken Lawless; *Board Pres* Carolyn Hopkins
Open 9 AM - 6 PM. Estab 1972 to serve as an art resource center for the north country region through school classes and programs. Average Annual Attendance: 6000
Income: Financed by foundation funds, grants and tuition
Exhibitions: Gallery offers 12 - 15 exhibitions a year; approximately half are invitational to artists of national prominence, other shows are group shows from national organizations
Activities: Lect open to the public, 16 vis lectr per year; concerts; gallery talks; competitions
L **Nettie Marie Jones Fine Arts Library**, Saranac Ave, 12946. Tel 518-523-2592 or 523-2593, Ext 31. *Library Dir* Suellen Linn; *Library Asst* Dana Loud; *Library Asst* Sarah Adams
Open Mon & Thurs 9 AM - 8 PM, Tues, Wed & Fri 9 AM - 5 PM, Sat noon - 5 PM. Estab 1972 to serve as a unique resource center for visual and performing arts to the Lake Placid School of Art, the Center for Music, Drama and Art, and the surrounding North County. Circ 1500
Income: $38,000
Purchases: $8100
Library Holdings: Vols 9000; Per subs 120; Micro—Fiche; AV—Motion pictures, rec, slides; Other—Exhibition catalogs, prints, memorabilia, original art works, photographs, sculpture
Collections: Stedman and Kaiser Glass Plate Negative Collection; Victor Herbert Memorabilia
Activities: Summer lect series

LOCUST VALLEY

M **COUNTRY ART GALLERY**, 198 Birch Hill Square, 11560. Tel 516-676-6886. *Dir* Clarissa H Watson
Open Tues - Sat 10 AM - 5 PM. No admis fee. Estab 1953 as dealer in Fine Arts. Average Annual Attendance: 10,000
Collections: Contemporary American and European paintings and sculpture, specializing in American Realism
Exhibitions: (1978-79) Ernest Chiriacks; Christmas Miniature Show; Bet Cottell; Wayne Davis; 19th and 20th Century Drawing; Favorite Americans; Lucy Gould; Realists; Eve Rubins; Marie Stobbe; Reynolds Thomas; A N Wyeth
Activities: Lect open to public, 3 - 4 visiting lectr per year

LONG BEACH

O **LONG BEACH ART ASSOCIATION**, 111 W Park Ave, 11561. Tel 516-432-7201.
Founded in 1952 by a group of interested residents determined to form an organization to promote art activity and appreciation with emphasis on quality. Sponsored by the Long Beach Public Library
Exhibitions: Artists-of-the-Month Shows; July Outdoor Show and Sale, co-sponsored by the City of Long Beach; May Open Juried Show; Material Awards Shows; three Membership Shows annually
Publications: Exhibitions brochures
Activities: Workshops; demonstrations; lect; discussions

L **LONG BEACH PUBLIC LIBRARY,** 111 W Park Ave, 11561. Tel 516-432-7200.
Dir Sylvia Eisen; *Asst Dir* George Trepp; *Adult Services* Norman Kupferman; *Children's Librn* Margaret Ptasinski; *Circulation* Katherine Fanata
Open Mon, Wed, Thurs 9 AM - 9 PM, Tues & Fri 9 AM - 6 PM, Sat 9 AM - 5 PM, Sun 1 - 5 PM. Estab 1928 to serve the community with information and services, including recreational, cultural and informational materials. Circ 263,126. The Long Beach Art Association in cooperation with the library presents monthly exhibits of all types of media in a room 32 ft x 22 ft with seating capacity of 50
Library Holdings: Vols 108,417; Per subs 267; Micro—Fiche, reels; AV—Cassettes, fs, motion pictures, rec; Other—Memorabilia, pamphlets, photographs
Collections: Local history; 300 photographs of Long Beach

Exhibitions: Local talent; membership shows; juried exhibitions; politician myth and reality; Telma Hillman's spectra sculpture
Publications: Monthly newsletter
Activities: Dramatic programs; lect open to public, 18-20 visiting lectrs per year; concerts; gallery talks

LONG ISLAND CITY

O **THE INSTITUTE FOR ART AND URBAN RESOURCES, INC**, 46-01 21st St, 11101. Tel 212-784-2084.
A non-profit organization specializing in matching artists with unused city spaces and establishing artists' compounds with low-rent studios, exhibitions in galleries on the premises and special project rooms in which artists can work out experimental ideas. Project Studios One was rehabilitated from an abandoned 19th century school house in Long Island City with spaces for over 50 artists; The Clocktower, located at 108 Leonard St in Manhattan is on the 13th floor of a city office building where there are 2 exhibitions spaces and more studios for both national and international artists. Both Project Studios One and The Clocktower are opened throughout the year with four main project periods

MOUNTAINVILLE

M **STORM KING ART CENTER**, Old Pleasant Hill Rd, 10953. Tel 914-534-3115. *Dir* David R Collens
Open Mid-May - Oct Mon, Wed - Sun 2 - 5:30 PM, cl Tues, grounds cl Nov - Mar. No admis fee, donation $2 per person will be appreciated. Estab 1959. Average Annual Attendance: 28,000
Collections: 200 acre sculpture garden with over 125 large scale outdoor contemporary sculptures, including works by: Bill, Calder, Caro, Ferber, Ginnever, Grosvenor, Hepworth, LeWitt, Moore, Myers, Rickey, David Smith, Snelson, Stankiewicz, Von Schlegell
Exhibitions: Changing exhibitions in the galleries of paintings, prints and sculpture; permanent sculpture collection, plus loan sculptures in special exhibitions
Publications: Brochures; catalogs
Activities: Gallery and garden tours; lect

MOUNT VERNON

L **MOUNT VERNON PUBLIC LIBRARY**, Fine Art Department,* 28 S First Ave, 10550. Tel 914-668-1840. *Library Dir* Emanuel Dondy
Open Mon - Fri 9 AM - 9 PM, Sat 9 AM - 6 PM, Sun 1 - 5 PM, cl Sat & Sun during July and Aug. No admis fee. Library contains Doric Hall who carries murals by Edward Gay, NA; Exhibition Room with frescoes by Louise Brann Soverns; and Norman Wells Print Alcove, estab 1941
Library Holdings: Vols 4000
Special Subjects: Architecture, Ceramics, Costume Design & Construction, Decorative Arts, American Painting, Photography, Prints
Exhibitions: Costume dolls; fans; metalwork; one-man shows of painting and sculpture; porcelains; silver; woodcarving; semi-annual shows by Mount Vernon Art Association; Other exhibits changing monthly cover a wide range of subjects
Activities: Lending collection contains pictures, framed prints and sculptures

NEW PALTZ

M **STATE UNIVERSITY OF NEW YORK AT NEW PALTZ**, College Art Gallery, Smiley Art Bldg, 12562. Tel 914-257-2493. *Dir* Kathy Zimmerer; *Admin Asst* Priscilla Price
Open Mon - Fri 10 AM - 4 PM. No admis fee. With an exhibition schedule of 12 major shows per year, the College Art Gallery provides support for the various art curricula and serves as a major cultural resource for the College and surrounding community. There are two adjoining galleries, South Gallery 59 x 56 ft, North Gallery 42 x 23 ft. Average Annual Attendance: 15,000 - 20,000
Collections: Oriental Prints, Sculpture, Artifacts, Photographs, Folk Art, Posters; Pre-Columbian Art; Painting, principally 20th Century America; Prints, Primitive African and New Guinea
Exhibitions: (1978) American Art from the Permanent Collection, 1885-1950; Artwomen: A Celebration of Women Working in Ulster County; Faculty Art 1978. (1979) Berenice Abbott: Photographs from Two Series; Ben Bishop Retrospective; CAPS Graphics: 19 Artists; The Female Image in the Greco-Roman World; German Expressionism: Selected Drawings, Prints and Watercolors; Hungarian Art Nouveau (SITES); Language of Clay; Alex Minewski Retrospective; Polish Posters (SITES); Theodoros Stamos: Selected Paintings 1945-1979; Faculty Art: Selected Works; The Faculty Selects Works by New Paltz Students; student show
Activities: Lect open to public; concerts; gallery talks; competitions; individual paintings and original objects of art lent to museums and galleries; lending collection contains artifacts; original prints; paintings, photographs, sculpture, folk art, textiles, drawings, posters

NEW ROCHELLE

M **COLLEGE OF NEW ROCHELLE**, Castle Gallery, Castle Place, 10801. Tel 914-632-5300, Ext 423. *Dir* Ellen Kenny; *Community Relations* Wilma Reid; *Secy and Receptionist* Adele Ingellis
Hours open vary with shows. No admis fee. Estab 1979 as a professional art gallery to serve the college, city of New Rochelle and lower Westchester. Located in Leland Castle, a gothic revival building; gallery is modern facility, with flexible space
Publications: Newsletter, quarterly
Activities: Docent training; lectures; gallery talks; tours

L **NEW ROCHELLE PUBLIC LIBRARY**, Library Plaza, 10801. Tel 914-632-7878. *Dir* Eugene L Mittelgluck; *Head of Reference* Ethelynn Williams
Open Mon - Thurs 9 AM - 9 PM; Fri & Sat 9 AM - 5 PM; Sun 1 - 5 PM; summer hours vary. Estab 1893

Library Holdings: Vols 7800; Other—Clipping files
Exhibitions: All shows, displays and exhibits are reviewed and scheduled by professional advisory panel
Activities: Lect and demonstrations; lending collection contains framed prints and art slides

O **New Rochelle Art Association,** Library Plaza, 10801. Tel 914-632-7878. *Pres* Inga Meyer
Estab 1912. Mem: 200; dues $10; monthly meeting
Activities: Lect

NEW YORK

M **A I R GALLERY,** 97 Wooster St, 10012. Tel 212-966-0799. *Dir* Sally Webster
Open Tues - Sat 10 AM - 6 PM. No admis fee. Estab 1972 as cooperative women's gallery representing 20 American women artists; also provides programs and services to women artists community. Average Annual Attendance: 20,000. Mem: 20; dues $350
Income: $30,000 (financed by membership, city and state appropriation)
Exhibitions: One-woman exhibitions; invitational which can be international, regional and performance or theme shows
Publications: Invitational exhibition catalogues, bi-annually
Activities: Lect open to public

ALLIED ARTISTS OF AMERICA, INC
For further information, see National and Regional Organizations

AMERICAN ACADEMY AND INSTITUTE OF ARTS AND LETTERS
For further information, see National and Regional Organizations

O **AMERICAN ACADEMY IN ROME,** 41 E 65th St, 10021. Tel 212-535-4250.
Chairman Walker O Cain; *Treas* Philip Bastedo; *Secy* J Kellum Smith; *Dir* John D'Arms; *Executive Secy* Ruth D Green
Estab 1884, inc by Congress 1905; consolidated with School of Classical Studies 1913; Dept of Musical Composition estab 1921. Fellowships in architecture, landscape architecture, design-photography, painting, sculpture, musical composition, classical and post-classical studies, medieval studies, history of art, writing, Italian studies are open to citizens of the United States for one year (also six month mid-career fellowships in architecture, landscape architecture and design) beginning in September. Approximately 28 fellowships are awarded each year. Applicants' material is judged by independent juries of professionals in the field of award. Stipend, travel and supplies allowances $7,400; free residence, studio or study, library and other Academy facilities. Applications and supporting material must be received at the Academy's New York office by November 15 of each year. Application forms and information sheets are available from the New York office. There is a $15 application fee payable when completed application is submitted. Mem: Annual meeting Oct; Board in Feb
Activities: 28 fellowships
Library.
See Rome, Italy for information

AMERICAN ARTISTS PROFESSIONAL LEAGUE, INC
For further information, see National and Regional Organizations

AMERICAN COUNCIL FOR THE ARTS
For further information, see National and Regional Organizations

M **AMERICAN CRAFT MUSEUM,** 44 W 53rd St, 10019. Tel 212-397-0630. *Dir* Paul J Smith
Open Tues - Sat 10 AM - 5 PM, Sun 11 AM - 5 PM, cl Mon. Admis adults $1, children under 16, students and senior citizens 50¢. Estab 1956 by the American Craft Council (see National Organizations). Average Annual Attendance: 31,5000
Collections: Contemporary American crafts
Exhibitions: (1978) New Stained Glass; the Great American Foot. (1979) The Harmonious Craft: American Musical Instruments; New Handmade Furniture; Peter Voulkos, A Retrospective 1948-78; Young Americans: Clay and Glass. (1980) Art for Use; Young Americans: Metal; Exhibitions from the Permanent Collection

L **American Craft Council Library,** 44 W 53rd St, 10019. Tel 212-397-0637, 397-0638.
Librn Joanne Polster
Open Tues, Wed & Fri Noon - 4:30 PM. Estab 1956 to promote the work of contemporary American crafts and crafts people. The Library is open to members only, and is owned and maintained by the American Craft Council (see entry under National Organizations)
Library Holdings: Vols 2600; Per subs 40; AV—A-tapes, motion pictures, slides, v-tapes; Other—Clipping files, exhibition catalogs, pamphlets, photographs, data on craft courses, suppliers, organizations and the state arts councils
Collections: Archives of the American Craft Museum; Photo-Archives of the American Craft Museum; Portfolio Files of 2000 contemporary American craftspeople working in all media
Publications: Books; bibliographies; exhibition catalogues; directories; posters
Activities: Gallery talks; competitions with awards; extension department serves greater New York City community; books traveling exhibitions, annually; originates traveling exhibitions to other museums

AMERICAN FEDERATION OF ARTS
For further information, see National and Regional Organizations

AMERICAN FINE ARTS SOCIETY
For further information, see National and Regional Organizations

AMERICAN INSTITUTE OF GRAPHIC ARTS
For further information, see National and Regional Organizations

AMERICAN INTERNATIONAL SCULPTORS SYMPOSIUMS, INC
For further information, see National and Regional Organizations

M **AMERICAN MUSEUM OF NATURAL HISTORY,** Central Park West at 79th St, 10024. Tel 212-873-1300. *Pres* Robert G Goelet; *Dir* Dr Thomas D Nicholson
Open Mon - Sat 10 AM - 4:45 PM, Sun and holidays 11 AM - 5 PM, Wed until 9 PM, cl Thanksgiving and Christmas. Admis by contribution (suggested, adults $1.50, children 75¢). Estab 1869 as a museum for the study and exhibition of all aspects of natural history. Included ceremonial objects, artifacts, clothing, weapons and architecture of primitive peoples and earlier civilizations. Average Annual Attendance: 2,500,000. Mem: 470,000
Exhibitions: Permanent exhibitions of Museum's renowned habitat dioramas of mammals, birds, forest and ocean life; Corridor of Small North American Mammals; Hall of the Biology of Man; John Lindsley Hall of Earth History; Hall of Man in Africa; Hall of Mexico and Central America; Morgan Memorial Hall of Minerals and Gems
Activities: Adult evening lecture series; gallery talks; slide lectures and films

L **Library,** Central Park West at 79th St, 10024.
Library Holdings: Vols 350,000

M **Theodore Roosevelt Memorial,** Central Park West at 79th St, 10024.
Collections: Equestrian statue of Theodore Roosevelt by the late James Earle Fraser, located at the entrance; mural painting by William Andrew Mackay in the hall

AMERICAN NUMISMATIC SOCIETY
For further information, see National and Regional Organizations

AMERICAN SOCIETY OF CONTEMPORARY ARTISTS
For further information, see National and Regional Organizations

AMERICAN WATERCOLOR SOCIETY
For further information, see National and Regional Organizations

ARCHAEOLOGICAL INSTITUTE OF AMERICA
For further information, see National and Regional Organizations

O **ARCHITECTURAL LEAGUE OF NEW YORK,** 457 Madison Ave, 10022. Tel 212-628-4500. *Pres* Jonathan Barrett; *Executive Dir* Marita O'Hare
Open Mon - Fri 10 AM - 5 PM. Admis seminars $5, mem free. Estab 1881 to promote art and architecture; serves as a forum for new and experimental ideas in the arts. Sponsors Archive of Women in Architecture. Mem: 500; dues over 35 years $75, under 35 years $40, students $15; annual meeting April
Exhibitions: Annual Juried Exhibition of Architectural Renderings
Publications: Art tour map of New York City; exhibition catalogues; Membership directory; posters
Activities: Lect; slide lect; walking tours; competitions; awards

M **ARCHIVES OF AMERICAN ART,** Smithsonian Institution, National Headquarters, 41 East 65th St, 10021. Tel 212-826-5722. *Chmn* Mrs Otto L Spaeth; *Pres* Gilbert H Kinney; *Secy* Mrs Dana M Raymond; *Dir* William E Woolfenden; *Cur Manuscripts* Arthur Breton
The Archives of American Art, founded in 1954, has assembled the world's largest collection of material documenting the history of the visual arts in this country. Five million items of original source material are available on microfilm to scholars, students, writers and researchers. Affiliated with the Smithsonian Institution since 1970, the Archives preserves its original documents in Washington with microfilm copies in its regional branches
—**Washington Center,** FA-PG Building, Eighth & F Streets, NW, Washington, DC 20560. Tel 202-381-6174. *Archivist* Garnett McCoy
—**New York Area Center,** 41 East 65th St, 10021. Tel 212-826-5722. *Dir* William McNaught
—**Midwest Area Center,** 5200 Woodward Blvd, Detroit, MI 48202. Tel 313-226-7544. *Dir* Dennis Barrie
—**New England Area Center,** 87 Mount Vernon St, Boston, MA 02108. Tel 617-223-0951. *Dir* Robert Brown
—**West Coast Area Center; de Young Museum,** San Francisco, CA 94118. Tel 414-556-2530. *Dir* Paul Karlstrom
—**Texas Area Center: Museum of Fine Arts,** Houston, TX 77052. Tel 713-526-1361. *Area Collector* Sandra J Curtis

O **ART COMMISSION OF THE CITY OF NEW YORK,** City Hall, 10007. Tel 212-566-5525. *Pres* Muriel R Silberstein-Storfer; *VPres* Norval White; *Secy* Gordon Hyatt; *Adminr* Annette Kuhn
Open by appointment only. No admis fee. Estab 1898 to review designs for city buildings and the works of art proposed for their embellishment. Portraits are installed in Governors Room and other areas in City Hall. Mem: 11
Income: Financed by membership
Collections: 100 portraits of historic figures, state, city and national
Publications: City Hall, Art and Architecture
Activities: Lending collection contains 100 paintings, sculpture

O **Associates of the Art Commission, Inc,** City Hall, 10007. Tel 212-566-5525. *Pres* David Levine; *VPres* Francis D Rogers; *Secy* Allyn Cox
Estab 1913 to advise and counsel Art Commission as requested. Mem: 35; dues $35; annual meeting in Jan
Income: Financed by membership

ART DEALERS ASSOCIATION OF AMERICA, INC
For further information, see National and Regional Organizations

ART DIRECTORS CLUB, INC
For further information, see National and Regional Organizations

O **ART INFORMATION CENTER, INC,** 189 Lexington Ave, 10016. Tel 212-725-0335. *Dir* Betty Chamberlain; *Board Dir Member* Stanley William Hayter; *Board Dir Member* Jacob Lawrence; *Board Dir Member* Mrs Andrew C Ritchie
Open mid-Sept - mid-June Mon - Fri by appointment. Organized 1959, inc 1963, as a free tax-deductible clearing house of contemporary fine arts. Maintains ?files of living artists with their gallery affiliations (c 50,000 artists); files of galleries, their rosters of artists and catalogs of current and recent shows (c 550 in New York, 300 in other US cities, 50 in foreign cities); ?files of slides of work by unaffiliated artists (c 750 artists and 8-12 slides each) for use by dealers looking for new talent. The

Center helps to channel the many artists in New York, and those coming to New York, seeking New York outlets for their work. It aids new galleries to start, helps artists to find out where they can learn special disciplines and skills. Furnishes information on many aspects of contemporary art to museums, art schools, collectors and the public. All documentation kept constantly up-to-date

O **ARTIST-CRAFTSMEN OF NEW YORK,** 130 E 28th St, 10016. Tel 212-679-8154. *Pres* Monona Rossol; *First VPres* Kathy Berle; *Second VPres* Reva Freed; *Treas* Joyce Kaplan
Estab 1958 as successor to New York Society of Craftsmen and New York Society of Ceramic Arts. Exhibitions and demonstrations are arranged for the purpose of broadening public interest in and knowledge of crafts; developing standards of taste in design and workmanship. Affiliated with American Craftsmen's Council. Mem: 300; qualification for mem: by submission of work by artist-craftsman member to membership jury with emphasis laid upon professional standards of craftsmanship and the quality of work; non-craftsman may become associate or contributing member on election by the Board of Governors; annual meeting in March, with six membership meetings per year
Exhibitions: Annual exhibition in New York City; periodic exhibitions at National Design Center and other New York City locations
Publications: Newsletter, 4 - 6 per year

ARTISTS' FELLOWSHIP, INC
For further information, see National and Regional Organizations

ARTISTS GUILD INC OF NEW YORK
For further information, see National and Regional Organizations

O **ARTISTS SPACE,** 105 Hudson St, 10013. Tel 212-226-3970. *Executive Dir* Helene Winer; *Assoc Dir Services* Susan Wyatt; *Assoc Dir Gallery* Ragland Watkins
Open Sept - June Tues - Sat 11 AM - 6 PM. No admis fee. Estab 1972 as a non-profit organization formed to respond to the diverse needs of the artists community in New York. The gallery is devoted exclusively to the exhibition of serious new art that is not given adequate exposure in galleries and museums and, by virtue of its unfamiliarity, transitory form, unconventional media or controversial content, is not readily accommodated by these traditional outlets. Exhibition space includes three gallery spaces for regular exhibitions, project rooms for special installations and a hall gallery for photographic exhibitions. Average Annual Attendance: 10,000
Income: $160,000 (financed by National Endowment for the Arts; New York State Council, corporate and foundation funds and private contributions)
Exhibitions: Artists Film Series; Artists Performance Series; Artists Super 8 Film Exposition; Audio Works; New Art Auction; Pictures; Traditions: Five Painters; One person exhibitions; group shows; exchange shows
Publications: Exhibition catalogs
Activities: Internship program; book traveling exhibitions

L **Unaffilated Artists File,** c/o Committee for the Visual Arts, 105 Hudson St, 10013. *Dir* Cindy Sherman; *Assoc Dir* Susan Wyatt
Open Tues - Sat 11 AM - 6 PM. Estab 1974; maintains slide file of New York artists not affiliated with commercial or cooperative galleries. Available to dealers, critics, curators, artists for reference only
Activities: Grants to artists for independent exhibitions and materials

O **Committee for the Visual Arts, Inc,** 105 Hudson St, 10013. Tel 212-254-8310. *Program Coordr* Cindy Sherman
Open Tues - Sat 11 AM - 6 PM. Estab 1972 to respond to the diverse needs of the artists community in New York. Its programs provide support, assistance and exhibition opportunities as well as audience access to current art work. The Committee for the Visual Arts' role is to diminish the economic and professional difficulties that exist for artists and create a responsible context for the public to become acquainted with current visual arts activity
Activities: Artist performances and artists films; grants and fees to artists

O **ARTISTS TECHNICAL INSTITUTE,*** 207 W 106th St, 10025. Tel 212-749-7819. *Pres* Herb Aach; *VPres & Secy* Bena F Mayer; *Treas* Felicia Van Veen; *Dir* Ralph Mayer
Estab 1959 for the publication of results of scientific laboratory investigations of the materials of creative painting and sculpture
Income: Financed by appropriations and grants from NEA and private donations
Publications: Journal, quarterly; publication of audio-visual materials

O **ART STUDENTS LEAGUE OF NEW YORK,** 215 W 57th St, 10019. Tel 212-247-4510. *Pres* Frank E Field; *Executive Dir* Stewart Klonis; *Recording Secy* Adeia S Lintelmann
Estab 1875 to maintain art school and membership activities. Maintains an art gallery. Average Annual Attendance: 2400. Mem: 5000; dues $5; annual meeting Dec
Exhibitions: Exhibitions by members, students and instructors
Publications: Art Students League News, monthly
Activities: School; lect; 210 scholarships

L **Library,** 215 W 57th St, 10019.
Reference library for students and members

M **ASIA SOCIETY, INC,** Asia House Gallery, 112 E 64th St, 10021. Tel 212-751-3210. *Chmn Board of Trustees, Asia Society, Inc* George W Ball; *Pres, Asia Society, Inc* Phillips Talbot; *Executive VPres, Asia Society, Inc* Lionel Landry; *Dir, Asia House Gallery* Allen Wardwell; *Asst Dir, Asia House Gallery* Sarah Bradley
Open during exhibitions Mon - Sat 10 AM - 5 PM, Thurs until 8:30 PM, Sun 1 - 5 PM. No admis fee. Inc 1957 as a non-profit organization to further greater understanding and mutual appreciation between the US and peoples of Asia. The Asia House Gallery was inaugrated in 1960 to acquaint Americans with the historic art of Asia. In 1981 the Asia Society will move to a new building at 725 Park Ave. At that time it will come into possession of a permanent collection, the John D Rockefeller 3rd Collection of Asian Art, and many of the current programs will be expanded. Average Annual Attendance: 60,000. Mem: 3000; dues $15 and up; annual meeting in May
Income: Financed by membership, contributions and grants
Collections: No permanent collection; loans obtained from the US and foreign collections for special exhibitions
Activities: Three or more lectures for members given by guest specialists in connection with each exhibition and recorded lectures by the gallery director available to visitors; loan exhibitions originated; Sales shop selling exhibition catalogs, cards and other Asia Society publications

M **ATLANTIC GALLERY,** 458 W Broadway, 10012. Tel 212-228-0944. *Dir & Pres* Rich Samuelson; *VPres* Elliott Jacobs; *Secy* Rebecca Leonard
Open Tues - Sun Noon - 6 PM. No admis fee. Estab 1974 as an artist-run gallery presenting the work of members and guests artists in solo exhibitions and group shows. Gallery is 25 x 75 ft seoncd-floor space. Average Annual Attendance: 12,000. Mem: 32; dues $360; monthly meetings
Income: Financed by membership and artists of the gallery
Exhibitions: Continuing series of solo shows
Publications: Periodic flyers
Activities: Life-drawing sessions; concerts; poetry readings, all open to public; sales shop sells original art

AUDUBON ARTISTS, INC
For further information, see National and Regional Organizations

O **CARAVAN OF EAST AND WEST, INC,** Caravan House Galleries, 132 65th St, 10021. Tel 212-744-4793. *Gallery Dir* John Lally; *Asst Dir* Franca P Lally
Open Tues - Sat 11:30 AM - 5:30 PM, cl Sun & Mon. No admis fee. Estab 1929 as a non-profit foundation, chartered to help artists expose their work to the general public. In addition chartered to help communication between peoples of the world. Founded the first Pen Pal Journal. The Caravan House has two galleries designed to show two separate artists at the same time. Located in a town house with a gallery downstairs and one upstairs. Average Annual Attendance: 14,000. Mem: 690; dues $10; annual meeting in April
Income: $100,000 (financed by endowment, membership)
Collections: Two exhibitions every month January to May, September to December
Publications: Pen Friend Guide, biannually
Activities: Classes for adults; lect open to public, 12 vis lectr per year; concerts; gallery talks

M **CATHEDRAL MUSEUM OF RELIGIOUS ART,*** Cathedral of Saint John the Divine, 1047 Amsterdam Ave, 10025. Tel 217-678-6923. *Dir* Richard Mann; *Asst* Thomas Croft
Open Tues - Fri 9 AM - 5 PM, Sat & Sun 12 - 5 PM, cl Mon. No admis fee. Estab 1974, through many different images, to deepen and clarify people's experience of what they believe life and death to be. The museum building was erected in the 1820's and forms part of the complex of the Cathedral of Saint John the Divine. Over the years it has served as an orphanage, offices, religious services and school. The Museum occupies one large room fitted with movable panels. Average Annual Attendance: 250,000
Income: $26,000(financed by state appropriation and Cathedral assistance)
Collections: The Cathedral has a collection of tapestries and religious objects and vestments
Exhibitions: Annual exhibitions planned to demonstrate contemporary art that expresses religious values, the first being the Cartwright Exhibition mounted in 1977 including more than 45 paintings and sculptures by 26 American and European artists; Works by Audrey Flack, Morris Graves, Gyorgy Kepes, Giacomo Manzu, Alfonso Ossorio, Richard Pousette-Dart, Mark Rothko, Mark Tobey are included

M **CENTER FOR INTER-AMERICAN RELATIONS ART GALLERY,** 680 Park Ave, 10021. Tel 212-249-8950. *Dir Visual Arts Program* John Stringer; *Deputy Dir* Sharon L Schultz; *Education Coordr* Mara Garnder; *Installation Designer* J Esteban Perez
Open Tues - Sun noon - 6 PM, cl Mon (during exhibitions). Admis suggested $1 contribution. Estab 1967 to enlarge knowledge and appreciation in the United States of the art and cultural heritage of other areas in the Western Hemisphere. Three galleries with 5 - 6 loan exhibitions a year of Latin American and Canadian art. Average Annual Attendance: 10,000. Mem: 880; dues regular $250, program $100, student $25
Income: $120,500 (financed by endowment and membership)
Collections: 17th and 18th Century Frency, English, Italian and Spanish Furniture and Decorative Arts as House Furnishings; 19th Century Mexican, Colonial and Pre-Columbian Objects on permanent loan; Limited collection of Contemporary Latin American Paintings, Drawings and Prints
Exhibitions: Abstract Currents in Ecuadorian Art; Americas: The Decorative Arts of Latin America in the Era of the Revolution; Aztec Stone Sculpture; Lines of Vision: Recent Latin American Drawings; Ron Martin and Henry Saxe: Two Contemporary Artists from Canada; Objects of Bought Pride: Northwest Coast Indian Art; Pioneer Photographers of Brazil; Warp-patterned Weaves of the Andes
Publications: Exhibition catalogs
Activities: Classes for adults and children; lect open to the public, 20 - 25 vis lectr per year; gallery talks; originate traveling exhibitions; sales shop sells books

C **THE CHASE MANHATTAN BANK, NA,** 410 Park Ave, 10022. Tel 212-223-6131. *VPres & Dir Art Program* Jack Boulton
Estab 1959 to enhance Bank offices world-wide. Collection displayed in branches, offices in New York City, state and world-wide
Collections: Largely contemporary American, approximately 5000 works in all media
Activities: Limited tours; individual objects of art lent to museum and gallery exhibitions; originate traveling exhibitions

M **CHINA INSTITUTE IN AMERICA,** China House Gallery, 125 East 65th Street, 10021. Tel 212-744-8181. *Chmn Art Committee* Gordon B Washburn; *Pres & Dir* F Richard Hsu; *Assoc Dir* Amy V McEwen
Open Mon - Fri 10 AM - 5 PM, Sat 11 AM - 5 PM, Sun 2 - 5 PM Nov - Jan & March - May, cl June - Sept. No admis fee. Estab 1966 to promote a knowledge of Chinese culture. One-room gallery. Average Annual Attendance: 12,000. Mem: 800; dues resident $50, non-resident $35, academic $25
Income: $30,000 (financed by membership government grants and sponsors)
Exhibitions: Art of the Han; Chinese Porcelain in European Mounts; Embroidery of Imperial China; Origins of Chinese Ceramics; Treasures from The Metropolitan Museum of Art; Treasures from The Newark Museum; I-Hsing Ware; Tz'u-chou Ware

Publications: Exhibition catalogs, two a year
Activities: Classes for adults; lect open to the public; gallery talks

C **CITIBANK, NA,** 399 Park Ave, 10043. Tel 212-559-1864. *In Charge Art Coll* Laura Lynn Miner
Estab to enhance the environment. Collection displayed in offices of the corporate headquarters
Collections: Art reflects the working environment of the various departments, including international, American and New York themes
Activities: Individual objects of art lent for museum exhibitions

CITY COLLEGE OF THE CITY OF NEW YORK
M **Eisner Hall Art Gallery,** 133 St and Convent Ave, New York, NY 10031. Tel 212-690-4201. *Chmn Art Department* Jacob Rotherberg
No admis fee. Estab 1960, contains modest collection of paintings and prints acquired by gifts for use by art students and faculty. Open by appointment; gallery is located in two areas in the lobby of the Eisner Hall
Collections: Paintings of Renaissance, Baroque and 19th century America; selection of prints from Renaissance to 20th century
Activities: Individual paintings and original objects of art lent to other museums and galleries; lending collection contains original prints and paintings
L **Morris Raphael Cohen Library,** Arts Division, 135th St and Convent Ave, 10031. Tel 212-690-4268. *Acting Chief Librn* Margaret Kenny; *Co-Chief of Archives & Art Library* Barbara Dunlap; *Head Librn* Sidney Kneebone
Open Mon - Fri 9 AM - 5 PM. Estab as a college library in 1847 and an art division in 1958 to support the education goals of the college. Open to students, faculty and staff only and as reference to others
Income: Financed by city and state appropriation
Library Holdings: Vols 22,000; Per subs 53; Micro—Reels; Other—Clipping files, pamphlets, reproductions
Special Subjects: Art History, Photography, History of costumes
Collections: History of Costume

COLLEGE ART ASSOCIATION OF AMERICA
For further information, see National and Regional Organization

L **COLUMBIA UNIVERSITY,** Avery Architectural and Fine Arts Library, 117th St W of Amsterdam Ave, 10027. *Librn* Adolf K Placzek
Open Mon - Thurs 9 AM - 11 PM; Fri 9 AM - 5 PM; Sat 10 AM - 6 PM; Sun 2 - 10 PM. Estab 1890 for reference only
Library Holdings: Vols 200,000; Per subs 1000; Micro—Fiche, reels; Other—Clipping files, exhibition catalogs, original documents
Special Subjects: Architecture, Art History
Collections: Over 30,000 original architectural drawings, mainly American
Publications: Catalog of Avery Memorial Architectural Library; Avery Index to Architectural Periodicals; supplements

M **COOPER-HEWITT MUSEUM,** Smithsonian Institution National Museum of Design, 2 E 91st St, 10028. Tel 212-860-6868. *Dir* Lisa Taylor; *Asst Dir for Coll* Christian Rohlfing; *Asst Dir Admin* Daniel J O'Leary; *Cur Architecture & Design* Richard B Oliver; *Cur Decorative Arts* David McFadden; *Cur Drawings & Prints* Elaine Evans Dee; *Cur Textiles* Milton Sonday; *Exhib Coordr* Dorothy Twining Globus
Open Tues 10 AM - 9 PM, Wed - Sat 10 AM - 5 PM, Sun Noon - 5 PM, cl Mon and major holidays. Admis $1.50, no admis Tues after 5 PM. Founded 1895 as the Cooper Union Museum, to serve the needs of scholars, craftsmen, students, designers and everyone who deals with man's living world. Museum is based on large and varied collections of decorative arts, architecture and a library strong in those fields. Exhibitions are based on the Museum's vast collections or loan shows illustrative of some phase of design, make available the best examples of man's creative genius from the past and present. Its emphasis on education is expanded by special courses and seminars related to design in all forms and of all periods. The Main galleries occupy the first and second floors; exhibitions relate to the collections and some aspects of design; the Contemporary Design Gallery has changing exhibitions relating to architecture and design. Average Annual Attendance: 200,000. Mem: 5000; dues $25 - $1000
Income: Financed by membership and partly Smithsonian Institution
Collections: Drawings and paintings by Frederic Church, Winslow Homer, Thomas Moran and other 19th Century American artists; ceramics, furniture and woodwork, glass, lace, original drawings and designs for architecture and the decorative arts; 15th - 20th Century prints; textiles
Exhibitions: (1979) Alvar Aalto; The Cooper-Hewitt Collection: Furniture, Glass and Porcelain; Fantastic Design and Illustration in Britain 1850-1930; Indelible Images: Contemporary Advertising Design; Japanese Collections in the Cooper-Hewitt Museum; Ludwig II of Bavaria, The Dream King; Ma, Space-Time in Japan; Roma Interrotta; The Shopping Bag: Portable Graphic Art; Smithsonian (whole show); Streets - Street Graphics and Street Furniture; Take Your Choice: Contemporary Product Design
Publications: Books on Decorative Arts; exhibition catalogues; Newsletter, quarterly
Activities: Classes for adults and children; lect open to public; tours; seminars; concerts; paintings and original objects of art lent to museums and cultural institutions; museum and sales shop sells books, reproductions, prints, slides, posters, postcards and catalogues
L **Doris and Henry Dreyfuss Study Center,** 2 E 91st St, 10028. Tel 212-860-6887. *Librn* Robert C Kaufmann; *Library Technician* Margaret Luchars; *Co-Supv Picture Library* Sheila Smith; *Co-Supv Picture Libr* Jacqueline Rea
Open Mon - Fri 9 AM - 5:30 PM by appointment. Estab 1896 to serve the museum staff in all of its programs and to serve the design field and the design public. For reference only
Income: Financed by federal appropriation
Library Holdings: Vols 32,000; Per subs 80; Other—Exhibition catalogs, prints, manuscripts, memorabilia, photographs, reproductions, pictures and photographs 1,500,900, original documents
Special Subjects: Advertising Design, Decorative Arts, Graphic Design, Industrial Design, Inter Design, Color, materials of design
Collections: Donald Deskey Arach Archive; Henry Dreyfuss Archive; Nancy McClelland Arach; Ladislav Sutnar Arach Archive

O **LOVIS CORINTH MEMORIAL FOUNDATION, INC,** 120 Broadway, 10005. Tel 212-964-4424. *VPres & Dir* H Borchardt; *Treas* M Weinstein; *Secy* Thomas Corinth; *Art Ed* M Klopfer
Open by appointment. No admis fee. Estab 1969-70 as a tax-exempt, non-profit, educational Membership Corporation; organized to dispense information about German Art as represented by the painter Lovis Corinth to the inquiring public at large. Mem: Members must be over 21 years of age; dues $120; annual meeting Oct
Income: Financed by membership
Publications: Bulletin, on special occasions; collaborating in the publishing of the Lovis Corinth Documentary

COUNCIL OF AMERICAN ARTIST SOCIETIES
For further information, see National and Regional Organizations

M **CULTURAL COUNCIL FOUNDATION,** Fourteen Sculptors Gallery, 75 Thompson St, 10012. Tel 212-966-5790. *Board of Dir* Harold Olejarz; *Board of Dir* Jane Schneider; *Board of Dir* Steve Steinman; *Board of Dir* Shaw Stuart
Open Wed - Sun 11 AM - 6 PM. No admis fee. Estab 1973 to offer the artist exhibition space, possible reviews by art periodicals, and a forum for the exchange of ideas and techniques; to offer the public the chance to see fresh new work. Average Annual Attendance: 20,000. Mem: 15; dues $480
Income: Financed by membership
Exhibitions: (1978) Deruck Fraser; Nexus Gallery; Susan Reinhart; Lila Ryan; Shaw Stuart; (1979) Ethel Borg; Elise Gray; Harold Olejarz and Steve Steinman; Tim Pollock; Jane Schneider; group shows
Activities: Originate traveling exhibitions

THE DRAWING SOCIETY
For further information, see National and Regional Organizations

O **ELECTRONIC ARTS INTERMIX, INC,** 84, Room 301, 10011. Tel 212-989-2316, 989-2317. *Pres* Howard Wise; *Distribution* Janice Putney; *Editing Post Production Facility* Ann Volkes
Open daily 9:30 - 5:30. Estab as a non-profit corporation to assist artists seeking to explore the potentials of the electronic media, particularly television as a means of personal expression
Income: Financed by videotape and editing fees and in part by federal and state funds and contributions
Publications: Electronic Arts Intermix Videocassette Catalog, annual

M **EL MUSEO DEL BARRIO,** 1230 Fifth Ave, 10029. Tel 212-831-7272. *Dir* Jack Agueros; *Cur* Jacqueline Biaggi; *Dean Fine Arts School* Carmen Biascoechea
Open Tues - Fri 10:30 AM - 4:30 PM, Sat & Sun 11 AM - 4 PM. No admis fee. Estab 1969. Located on Museum Mile
Collections: 16mm Films on History, Culture and Art; Paintings and Works on Paper, by Puerto Rican and other Latin American Artists; Pre-Columbian Caribbean artifacts; Santos (Folk Religious Carvings); video-tapes
Exhibitions: Permanent and temporary traveling exhibitions
Activities: Lect; film series; artmobile; sales shop sells original prints and objects, catalogues, books, etc

C **EQUITABLE LIFE ASSURANCE SOCIETY,** 1285 Ave of the Americas, 10019. Tel 212-554-1057. *Dir Corporate Support* William P Epke
Annual amount of contributions and grants $75,000; supports employee gifts to all arts organizations; direct grants to 8 national arts service organizations
Activities: Support technical assistance programs

M **FASHION INSTITUTE OF TECHNOLOGY,** Galleries,* 277 W 27th St, 10001. Tel 212-760-7675. *Dir* Marty Bronson
Open Tues & Wed 10 AM - 8 PM, Thurs - Sat 10 AM - 5 PM, cl Sun, Mon and holidays. No Admis Fee. Estab May 1975 to bring to the student body and the community at large a variety of exhibitions in the applied and fine arts. Gallery contains 11,500 sq ft of space divided into four galleries. The gallery on the main floor is used for small exhibits while the three galleries located in the lower level are used for major exhibitions. Average Annual Attendance: 50,000
Income: Financed by endowment and grants
Collections: Largest working costume and textile collection in the world
Publications: Facades by Bill Cunningham (book); Poiret (book)
Activities: Classes for adults; docent training; lect open to the public, 2 visiting lectrs per year; gallery talks; tours; exten dept serving the museum personnel; individual paintings and original objects of art lent to major museums and art institutions; traveling exhibitions organized and circulated
L **Library,** * 277 W 27th St, 10001. Tel 212-760-7695. *Dir* John F Touhey; *Art Librn* Marjorie Miller; *Art Librn* Lorraine Weberg
Open Mon - Fri 9 AM - 10 PM, Sat & Sun Noon - 5 PM. Estab 1948 to meet the academic needs of the students and faculty and to serve as a resource for the fashion industry. Open for reference only
Library Holdings: Vols 56,200; Per subs 492; Micro—Reels; AV—A-tapes, cassettes, fs, motion pictures, rec, slides, v-tapes; Other—Clipping files, exhibition catalogs, memorabilia, pamphlets, sketchbook collections
Special Subjects: Costume Design & Construction, Fashion Arts
Collections: Oral History Project on the Fashion Industry; several sketchbook collections

FEDERATION OF MODERN PAINTERS AND SCULPTORS
For further information, see National and Regional Organizations

M **55 MERCER,** 55 Mercer St, 10013. Tel 212-226-8513. *Pres* Jack Bosson; *Secy* Mimi Smith
Open 11 AM - 6 PM. No admis fee. Estab 1970 for mainly Avant-Garde Art. Mem: 18
Exhibitions: Invitational guest shows
Activities: Apprenticeship program; individual paintings and original objects of art lent to college shows, etc; originate traveling exhibitions

O **FINE ARTS FEDERATION OF NEW YORK,** * 44 W Ninth St, Room 20, 10011. Tel 212-982-7272. *Pres* Margot Gayle; *Secy* Minor Bishop; *Treas* Bradford Greene
Estab 1895, inc 1897, to secure united action by the art societies of New York in

all matters affecting their common interests, and to foster and protect the artistic interests of the community. Members of the Art Commission of the City of New York are appointed by the Mayor from nominations provided to him by the Federation. Mem: 7000; dues each representative $7 ($42 for each society); annual meeting April

L **FRANKLIN FURNACE ARCHIVE, INC,** 122 Franklin St, 10013. Tel 212-925-4671. *Executive Dir* Martha Wilson
A non-profit corporation dedicated to the cataloging, exhibition and preservation of book-like work by artists
Library Holdings: Vols 3000; Per subs 100; AV—A-tapes, slides, v-tapes
Activities: Intern training program; performance program

L **FRENCH INSTITUTE-ALLIANCE FRANCAISE LIBRARY,** 22 E 60th St, 10022. Tel 212-355-6100. *Librn* Fred J Gitner
Open Mon - Thurs 10 AM - 8 PM, Fri 10 AM - 6 PM, Sat 10 AM - 1:30 PM. Estab 1911 to encourage the study of the French language and culture. Circ 27,500. Maintains art gallery
Income: Financed by endowment and membership
Library Holdings: Vols 35,000; Per subs 60; AV—Cassettes, rec; Other—Exhibition catalogs
Special Subjects: French Art
Collections: Architecture, costume, decorative arts, paintings
Exhibitions: Art Deco Posters, 1925-1935; Etchings, Collages and Illustrated Books by Bertrand Dorny; The Golden Age of the Picture Postcard; Louisiana Cajuns (photography)
Publications: Acquisitions list, quarterly
Activities: Classes given; lect open to public, 50 vis lectr per year; concerts; originate traveling exhibitions

L **FRICK ART REFERENCE LIBRARY,** 10 E 71st St, 10021. Tel 212-288-8700. *Librn* Helen Sanger; *Asst Librn & Indexer of Photographs* Marie C Keith; *Cataloguer* Blanche V Houston; *Reference Librn* Paula L Pumplin
Open Mon - Fri 10 AM - 4 PM, Sat 10 AM - Noon; cl Sun, holidays & month of August. Estab 1920 as a reference library to serve adults and graduate students interested in the history of European and American painting, drawing, sculpture, illuminated manuscripts. For reference only
Library Holdings: Vols 82,698; Other—Exhibition catalogs, pamphlets 64,599, photographs 412,443, 51,406 sales catalogs

M **FRICK COLLECTION,** 1 E 70th St, 10021. Tel 212-288-0700. *Pres* Henry Clay Frick II; *Secy* Martha F Symington; *Dir* Everett Fahy; *Cur* Edgar Munhall; *Research Cur* Bernice Davidson; *Bus Adminr* David M Collins; *Mgr Sales & Info* Martha Hackley; *Supt* Fred Jakob
Open (Sept - May) Tues - Sat 10 AM - 6 PM; (June - Aug) Wed - Sat 10 AM - 6 PM, Sun 1 - 6 PM; cl Jan 1, July 4, Thanksgiving, Dec 24 & 25. Admis adults $1, students & senior citizens 50¢ (Sun $2); children under 10 not admitted. Estab 1920; opened to public 1935 as a gallery of art. The Frick Collection is housed in the former residence of Henry Clay Frick (1849-1919), built in 1913-14 and alterations and additions were made 1931-1935 and a further extension and garden were completed in 1977. The rooms are in the style of English and French interiors of the 18th century. Average Annual Attendance: 228,027. Mem: 200 Fellows; dues $250 minimum contribution
Income: $2,500,000 (financed by endowment, membership, admissions)
Collections: 15th-18th century sculpture, of which Renaissance bronzes are most numerous; 14th-19th century paintings, with fine examples of Western European masters and suites of Boucher and Fragonard decorations; Renaissance and French 18th century furniture; 17th-18th century Chinese and French porcelains; 16th century Limoges enamels; 16th-19th century drawings and prints
Publications: Bellini Monograph; The Frick Collection, An Illustrated Catalog (Vols I & II-Paintings, Vols III & IV-Sculpture, Vol VII-Porcelains, Vol VIII-Enamels, Rugs, Silver); Handbook of Paintings; Guide to the Galleries
Activities: Lect open to public; concerts; museum shop selling books, prints, slides, postcards, greeting cards

M **GALERIA VENEZUELA,** 7 E 51st St, 10022. Tel 212-826-1660. *Dir* Marius Sznajderman
Estab 1945 to exhibit the work of prominent Venezuelan artists, painters, sculptors, printmakers, photographers, graphic artists. Administered by the Consulate-General of Venezuela in New York City. There are two galleries, a large one on the ground floor and another smaller one
Exhibitions: One-person shows by: Ismael Anez; Bellorin; Bogarin; J J Castro; Cruz-Diez; Elba Damast; Ephraim Guevara; Milos; Exhibits of Guajiro Tapestries by Tere and Luis Montiel; Luis Guevara Moreno; Thea Segall; Marius Sznajderman; Melida Torres

M **GALLERY OF PREHISTORIC PAINTINGS,** 20 E 12th St, 10003. Tel 212-674-5389. *Dir* Douglas Mazonowicz; *Co-Dir* Susan Dryfoos; *Cur* Sharon Citrin
Open Mon - Fri 9 AM - 5 PM, Sat 9 AM - Noon, other times by appointment. No admis fee. Estab 1975 to make available to the public the art works of prehistoric peoples, particularly the cave paintings of France, Spain and the Sahara Desert. Large display area. Average Annual Attendance: 10,000
Income: Financed by private funds
Collections: Early American Indian Rock Art; Rock Art of Eastern Spain; Rock Art of the Sahara; serigraph reproduction editions of Cave Art of France and Spain
Exhibitions: Three traveling collections circulating the US: Paleolithic Cave Paintings of France and Spain; Rock Art of Eastern Spain; Rock Paintings of the Tassili, Sahara
Publications: Newsletter, quarterly
Activities: Classes for adults and children; Cave Art-in-Schools Program; lect open to the public; gallery talks; tours; lending collection contains books, cassettes, framed reproductions, 1000 kodachromes, motion pictures, original prints, 1000 photographs, 2000 slides; traveling exhibitions organized and circulated; sales shop selling books, magazines

L **Library,** 20 E 12th St, 10003.
Open Mon - Fri 9 AM - 5 PM, Sat 9 AM - Noon. Estab 1975 to make information available to the general public concerning the art works of prehistoric peoples. For reference only
Library Holdings: Vols 200; Per subs 10; AV—Cassettes, Kodachromes, motion pictures, slides; Other—Clipping files, exhibition catalogs, framed reproductions, prints, manuscripts, pamphlets, photographs, reproductions, sculpture

M **GRAND CENTRAL ART GALLERIES, INC,** Biltmore Hotel, 43rd St & Madison Ave, 10017. Tel 212-867-3344. *Pres Board of Trustees* Jack S Parker; *Galleries Dir* James D Cox; *Sales Mgr* John S Evans; *Dir American Masters Dept* Robert R Preato; *Public Affairs Dir* Jeremyn Davern
Mon - Fri 10 AM - 6 PM. No admis fee. Estab 1922 to promote and exhibit oil paintings, sculpture and watercolors by the finest American realist artists, operating from large, well appointed New York showrooms. Sixteen professional staff members and a national board of trustees sustains operation of this non-profit organization, with world-wide shipping and packing capabilities. Mem: 100; dues $500; annual meeting: Founders Festival Dinner & Exhibition
Income: Financed by art commissions, patron memberships, endowment fund
Exhibitions: (1979-1981) A continuing schedule of exhibitions rotating approx monthly by artist members, guest artists and special shows of work by late 19th and early 20th century American Masters; themes include Illustration, Impressionism, Landscape, Marine, Portraits, Still Life, Western (contemporary and classical), Wildlife; featured artists include: Michael Aviano, Mae Bertoni, Sergei Bongart, Chen Chi, Thomas Aquinas Daly, Daniel Greene, Raymond Kinstler, David Leffel, Tom Nicholas, Bruce North, Priscilla Roberts, Richard Schmid, Eric Sloane, Robert Skemp, Robert Sticker, Carl Wuermer
Publications: Illustrated catalogs accompanying shows; The Illuminator, bi-annually
Activities: traveling exhibitions organized and circulated

L **GROLIER CLUB LIBRARY,*** 47 E 60th St, 10022. Tel 212-838-6690. *Pres* H W Liebert; *Secy* F S Streeter; *Librn* Robert Nikirk
Open Mon - Fri 10 AM - 5 PM, Sat 10 AM - 3 PM, cl Sun. Estab 1884, devoted to the arts of the book. Mem: 625
Purchases: $15,000
Library Holdings: Vols 65,000; Per subs 35; Other—Prints
Special Subjects: Bibliography
Collections: Bookseller and auction catalogs from 17th century

C **M GRUMBACHER INC,** 460 W 34th St, 10001. Tel 212-279-6400. *In Charge Art Coll & Dir Public Relations* Dan Daniels
Activities: lect; factory tours; cash awards, medallions, certificates, purchase awards from various shows by Art Societies; film-slide lect on brushes and paints

O **JOHN SIMON GUGGENHEIM MEMORIAL FOUNDATION,** 90 Park Ave, 10016. Tel 212-687-4470. *Pres* Gordan B Ray; *VPres* G Thomas Tanselle; *Secy* Stephen L Schlesinger; *Treas* Robert P Bergin
Estab and incorporated 1925; offers fellowships to further the development of scholars and artists by assisting them to engage in research in any field of knowledge and artistic creation in any of the arts under the freest possible conditions and irrespective of race, color or creed

M **SOLOMON R GUGGENHEIM MUSEUM,** 1071 Fifth Ave, 10028. Tel 212-860-1313. *Dir* Thomas M Messer; *Deputy Dir* Henry Berg; *Secy of Museum* Floyd Lattin; *Exec Asst* Susan L Halper; *Dir Coordr* Vanessa Jalet; *Auditor* Agnes R Connolly; *Sr Cur* Louise Averill Svendsen; *Cur Exhib* Diane Waldman; *Cur* Margit Rowell; *Research Cur* Angelica Rudenstine; *Asst Cur* Linda Shearer; *Assoc Cur* Vivian Endicott Barnett; *Ed* Carol Fuerstein; *Archivist* Ward Jackson; *Conservator* Orrin Riley; *Preparator* Saul Fuerstein; *Photographer* Robert E Mates; *Public Affairs Officer* Mimi Poser; *Public Affairs Coordr* Marianne Collins; *Head Membership Dept* Miriam Emden; *Development Officer* Nancy McDermott; *Development Assoc* Carolyn Porcelli
Open Wed - Sun 11 AM - 5 PM, Tues 11 AM - 8 PM, cl Mon except holidays, and Christmas. Admis students $1.50 with validated ID cards, visitors over 62 75¢; group rates for students when accompanied by a teacher, children under seven free; Tues eve free. Estab 1937 as a nonprofit organization which is maintained by the Solomon R Guggenheim Foundation; founded for the promotion and encouragement of art and education in art; to foster an appreciation of art by acquainting museum visitors with significant paintings and sculpture of our time. The gallery was designed by architect Frank Lloyd Wright. Average Annual Attendance: 530,000. Mem: 990; dues $25 - $250
Income: $2,876,000 (financed by endowment, membership and state and federal appropriations)
Collections: Reflects the creative accomplishments in modern art from the time of the Impressionists to the constantly changing experimental art of today. The collection of nearly four thousand works, augmented by the Justin K Thannhauser Collection of 75 Impressionists and Post-Impressionist masterpieces, including the largest group of paintings by Vasily Kandinsky; one of the largest and most comprehensive collection of paintings by Paul Klee; largest number of sculptures by Constantin Brancusi in any New York museum; paintings by Chagall, Delaunay, Lager, Marc, Picasso, Bacon, Bonnard, Braque, Cezanne, Malevitch, Modigliani, Moore, Reusseau and Seurat, with concentration of works by Dubuffet, Miro and Mondrian among the Europeans; and such Americans as Davis, deKooning, Diebenkorn, Frankenthaler, Gottlieb, Gaston, Johns, Lichenstein, Lonis, Agnes Martin, Motherwell, Nevelson, Noguchi, Pollack, younger artists include Andre, Christensen, Hamilton, Hesse, Norman, Mangold, Nauman, G Richter and Serra; paintings, drawings, sculpture and print collections are being enlarged
Exhibitions: Joseph Beuys; Willem de Kooning in East Hampton; The Planar Dimension: Europe 1912-1932; Mark Rothko, 1903-1970: A Retrospective; Rufino Tamayo: Myth and Magic; small group and one-man shows and periodic selections from the Permanent Collection. International and American talent exhibitions held alternately every year, sponsored by Exxon Corporation
Activities: Docent training; museum training program; lect open to the public, 6 - 10 visiting lectrs per year; concerts; gallery talks; individual paintings and original objects of art lent to other museum and galleries; lending collection contains original art works, original prints, paintings, 4000 photographs, sculpture, 50,000 slides; originates traveling exhibitions; museum shop selling books, reproductions, slides, postcards, catalogs, newsletters and lithographs

L **Library,** 1071 Fifth Ave, 10028. *Librn* Mary Joan Hall; *Asst Librn* Marian Wolf
Open by telephone appointment only, Mon - Fri 11 AM - 5 PM. Estab 1952 to document the Museum's collection of 20th century ary. For reference only
Library Holdings: Vols 15,320; Per subs 50; Micro—Reels; AV—Slides; Other—Clipping files, exhibition catalogs, manuscripts, pamphlets, photographs, reproductions
Collections: Rebay Library; Aye Simon Reading Room

GUILD OF BOOK WORKERS
For further information, see National and Regional Organizations

M **HISPANIC SOCIETY OF AMERICA MUSEUM,** Broadway, Between 155th and 156th Sts, 10032. Tel 212-926-2234. *Pres* A Hyatt May; *Dir* Theodore S Beardsley Jr; *Cur Mus Paintings & Metalwork* Priscilla E Muller; *Cur Archaeology* Vivian A Hibbs; *Cur Costume* Ruth M Anderson; *Cur Iconography* Lydia A Dufour; *Cur Emer Sculpture* Beatrice G Proske; *Cur Textiles* Florence L May
Open Tues - Sat 10 AM - 4:30 PM, Sun 1 - 4 PM. No admis fee. Estab 1904 by Archer Milton Huntingon as a free public museum and library devoted to the culture of Hispanic peoples. Average Annual Attendance: 35,000. Mem: 100 plus 300 corresponding members; membership by election
Income: Financed by endowment
Collections: Archaeology; costumes; customs; †decorative arts of the Iberian peoples; †paintings; †photographic reference files; †sculpture
Exhibitions: Gifts to the Collection; gallery exhibits are representative of the cultures of Iberian Peninsula from prehistory to the present
Publications: Works by members of the staff and society on Spanish art, history, literature, bibliography, with special emphasis on the collections of the society
Activities: Individual paintings and original objects of art lent; sales shop selling books, reproductions and slides

O **INSTITUTE FOR ADVANCED STUDIES IN CONTEMPORARY ART,** Canal St Station, PO Box 600, 10013. Tel 212-226-4469. *Executive Dir* Dr Kenneth S Friedman
Estab 1966 as a research center to provide information and services on contemporary art to arts institutions, artists, publishers, scholars and research specialists in a wide variety of topics. Open by appointment only
Income: Financed by gifts, grant funding, lecture and consulting fees for work by senior staff, and other means
Collections: Contemporary Art, including works by Arman, Joseph Beuys, Don Boyd, Christo, Dick Higgins, Alison Knowles, George Maciunas, Tommy Mew, Julius Schmit and Endre Tot
Activities: Educ program available by arrangement; workshops; lect; seminars; competitions; awards

L **Library,** Canal St Station, PO Box 600, 10013.
Open only to research scholars by appointment or to Institute staff
Library Holdings: Vols 15,000
Special Subjects: Aesthetic anthropology and fine arts administration, arts biographical studies, artists' books, concrete poetry, ephemeral media, European art information, sociology of art

O **INTERNATIONAL CENTER OF MEDIEVAL ART, INC,** The Cloisters, Fort Tryon Park, 10040. Tel 212-923-3700. *Pres* Carl F Barnes Jr; *First VPres* Walter Cahn; *Second VPres* Robert G Calkins; *Treas* Carl D Sheppard; *Secy* Gloria Gilmore House
Estab 1956 as The International Center of Romanesque Art, Inc. The International Center of Medieval ARt was founded to promote greater knowledge of the arts of the Middle Ages, and to contribute to and make available the results of new research. Mem: 850; dues benefactor $1000, contributing $100, institutions $28, active foreign countries $21, active (US, Canada, Mexico) $18, student $15; annual meeting Jan Feb, in conjunction with College Art Association of America
Publications: Gesta (illustrated journal devoted to medieval art history), two issues per year; ICMA Newsletter, 3 issues per year; Romanesque Sculpture in American Collections, Vol I-New England Museums
Activities: Sponsor sessions at the annual conferences of The Medieval Institute of Western Michigan University, Kalamazoo; keeps its members informed as to events of interest to medievalists; public lect, exhibitions and symposia;; financial support given to excavations of important medieval sites

M **INTERNATIONAL CENTER OF PHOTOGRAPHY,** 1130 Fifth Ave, 10028. Tel 212-860-1777. *Executive Dir* Cornell Capa; *Dir Exhib* William Ewing; *Dir Education* Via Wynroth; *Development Dir* Ann Doherty; *Adminr* Nancy Blechman; *Public Information Dir* Phyllis Levine; *Cur of Coll* Miles Barth
Open Tues - Sun 11 AM - 5 PM. Admis adults $1, student 50¢, senior citizens voluntary contributions. Estab 1974 to encourage and assist photographers of all ages and nationalities who are vitally concerned with their world and times, to find and help new talents, to uncover and preserve forgotten archives and to present such work to the public. Maintains four exhibition galleries showing a changing exhibition program of photographic expression and experimentation by over 350 photographers. Average Annual Attendance: 75,000. Mem: 2700; dues $25 and higher
Income: Financed by public and private grants
Exhibitions: Atget's Gardens; Henri Cartier-Bresson: Photographer; Copyright Philippe Halsman; Fotografia Polska: Photography in Poland from 1839 to the Present; Recollections: Ten Women of Photography
Publications: Centernews, 3 times per yr; monographs
Activities: Classes for adults and children; docent training; workshops; lect open to public, 75 vis lectr per yr; gallery talks; tours; museum shop selling books, magazines, original art, reproductions, prints and postcards

INTERNATIONAL FOUNDATION FOR ART RESEARCH, INC
For further information, see National and Regional Organizations

JAPAN SOCIETY, INC
M **Japan House Gallery,** 333 E 47th St, 10017. Tel 212-832-1155. *Pres Japan Society* David MacEachron; *Dir* Rand Castile
Open Mon - Thurs 11 AM - 5 PM, Fri 11 AM - 7:30 PM. No admis fee to members; contribution for nonmembers. Estab 1907, bi-cultural membership organizations to deepen understanding and friendship between Japan and the United States. Average Annual Attendance: 50,000 - 100,000. Mem: 3000 individual; dues $100, $40, $25, $10; annual meeting Oct
Income: Financed by membership, grants and donations
Exhibitions: Shinto Arts; The Tokugawa Collection of No Robes and Masks; Utamaro and Hiroshige prints from the James A Michener Collection; Whose Sleeves . . . Kimono from the Kanebo Collection
Publications: Japan Society Newsletter, monthly; exhibition catalogs
Activities: Classes for adults; concerts; movies; tours

L **Library,** 333 E 47th St, 10017. Tel 212-832-1155. *Librn* Tomie Machizukir
Open Mon - Fri Noon - 5 PM. Estab 1971
Income: Financed by membership
Library Holdings: Vols 6500; Per subs 113; Other—Clipping files, pamphlets

M **JEWISH MUSEUM,** 1109 Fifth Ave, 10028. Tel 212-860-1888. *Dir* Joy Ungerleider-Mayerson; *Adminr* Ruth M Dolkart; *Chief Cur* Susan Goodman; *Cur of Judaica* Vivian Mann; *Dir of Membership & Public Information* Joan M Hartman; *Dir of Education* Andrew Ackerman; *Registrar* Rita Feigenbaum; *Mgr of Museum Shop* Ceil Skydell; *Dir of Development* Virginia Strull
Open Mon - Thurs 12 - 5 PM; Sun 11 AM - 6 PM. Admis adults $2, children (6-16) and students with ID card $1, senior citizens pay-as-you-wish, members free. Estab 1904 to preserve and present the Jewish cultural tradition. Three exhibition floors devoted to the display of ceremonial objects in the permanent collection, special exhibitions from the permanent collections and photographs and contemporary art on loan. Average Annual Attendance: 85,000. Mem: 2000; dues $10 - $250 and up
Income: $800,000 (financed by membership, grants, individual contributions and organizations)
Collections: Contemporary art; graphics; Jewish ceremonial objects; paintings; textiles; comprehensive collection of Jewish ceremonial art
Exhibitions: David Aronson Retrospective; Brauer Retrospective; Ceremonial Art from the Tobe Pascher Workshop; Fabric of Jewish Life: Textiles from The Jewish Museum Collection; Peter Freudenthal: The Silent Prayer; Jack Levine: Retrospective Exhibition; Seymour Lipton: Aspects of Sculpture; Shalom of Safed: Paintings - Stained Glass Windows for Porat Yoseph Yeshiva, Jerusalem; Spiritual Resistance: Art from Concentration Camps 1940-45; Sarah Swenson Revisions
Publications: Calendar, bimonthly; exhibition catalogs; program brochures; posters and graphics
Activities: Classes for children; docent training; lect open to public; traveling exhibitions organized and circulated; museum shop selling books, magazines, original art, reproductions, prints, slides, needlecrafts, posters, catalogs and postcards

L **Library,** 1109 Fifth Ave, 10028.
Reference library open to staff only
Special Subjects: Judaica
Collections: Comprehensive collection of Judaic textiles in the world; Harry G Friedman Collection of ceremonial objects; Samuel Friedenberg Collection of plaques and medals; Rose and Benja min Mintz Collection of Eastern European art; Harry J Stein-Samuel Friedenberg Collection of coins from the Holy Land

M **JAY JOHNSON, AMERICA'S FOLK HERITAGE GALLERY,** 72 E 56th St, 10022. Tel 212-759-7373. *Owner* Jay Johnson
Open Noon - 5 PM. No admis fee. Estab 1977 to further the knowledge and appreciation of the American Folk Art form. The large gallery is exclusively devoted to American Folk Art. Average Annual Attendance: 10,000
Collections: Carvings in wood and stone, fabric crafts; paintings in many media and works in metal
Exhibitions: (1980) Sylvia Alberts; Animals In Folk Art - Group Show; John Cross; Folk Art For Christmas - Group Show; Kathy Jakobsen; Mattie Lou O'Kelley; Quilts and Coverlets (Antique and Contemporary); Mark Sabin; Antionette Schwob; Malcah Zeldis
Activities: Lect open to public, visiting lectr; tours; individual paintings and original objects of art lent

LINCOLN CENTER FOR THE PERFORMING ARTS
M **Amsterdam, Plaza and Main Galleries,** 111 Amsterdam Ave, 10023. Tel 212-877-1800. *Chmn of Board* Amyas Ames; *Pres* John W Mazzola
Open daily 10 AM - Midnight. Admission varies. First building opened in 1962, Center was completed in 1969 to present the performing arts to the broadest cross-section of the community. Average Annual Attendance: Paid audiences 30,000; tours 90,000; one million attend free performances in the parks and on the plaza. Mem: Center has guilds, associations and constituents which support it; dues $1000 - $15
Income: $71,000,000 (financed by endowment, membership, city, state and federal appropriation)
Purchases: $76,000,000
Collections: Painting; sculpture; portraits by such artists as Jasper Johns; Jacques Lipchitz; Elie Nadelman; Seymour Lipton; Auguste Rodin; Henry Moore; Alexander Calder; Marc Chagall; Aristide Maillol; Raoul Dufy; David Smith; Louise Nevelson and Jaacov Agam
Exhibitions: All exhibits relate to the performing arts and change frequently
Publications: Calendar of Events; newsletter or magazines
Activities: Lectures for subscribers; concerts; tours; scholarships; lending collection of photographs

M **Cork Gallery,** Avery Fisher Hall, 10023.
Hall used for community group exhibitions

L **Library,** 111 Amsterdam Ave, 10023. *Chief* Dr Robert M Henderson; *Admin Assoc* Joan R Canale
Open Mon - Thurs 10 AM - 8 PM, Tues 10 AM - 6 PM, Fri and Sat 12 - 6 PM, cl Wed and Sun. Established 1965
Library Holdings: Micro—Cards, fiche, reels, prints; AV—A-tapes, cassettes, fs, motion pictures, rec, slides, v-tapes; Other—Clipping files, exhibition catalogs, framed reproductions, manuscripts, memorabilia
Collections: Americana Collection; Rodgers and Hammerstein Archives of Recorded Sound; Toscanini Memorial Archives

O **LOTOS CLUB,*** 5 E 66th St, 10021. Tel 212-737-7100. *Pres* J Roger Friedman; *Secy* Seymour Udell; *Mgr* Emmanuel Roux
Not open to public. Estab 1870 as a cultural center. Mem: 500; dues $750

Income: $600,000 (financed by membership)
Exhibitions: Antique Quilts; Howard Chandler Christy Oil and Watercolors; Exhibit of Member's Paintings; Posters of World War I and II
Publications: Lotos Leaf, monthly
Activities: Round tables; receptions; state dinners; lect for members only, 20 visiting lectrs per year; concerts; individual paintings and original objects of art lent to museums

C **MCCRORY CORPORATION,** 888 Seventh Ave, 10019. Tel 212-399-4606. *In Charge Art Coll* Celia Ascher
Estab 1968. Collection in traveling exhibitions
Collections: Modern art with special emphasis on Constructivism
Activities: Gallery talks; tours; individual objects of art lent to museum exhibitions; originate traveling exhibitions; previously a two-year exhibition through Europe, at present, two-year exhibition at major United States museums

M **METROPOLITAN MUSEUM OF ART,** Main Bldg, Fifth Ave at 82nd St, 10028. Tel 212-General Information 736-2211, Museum Offices 879-5500. *Pres* William B Macomber Jr; *Dir* Philippe de Montebello; *VPres Public Affairs* Richard Dougherty; *VPres Finance & Treas* Daniel Herrick; *VPres Operations* Richard Morsches; *VPres Architecture & Planning* Arthur Rosenblatt; *VPres, Secy & Counsel* Ashton Hawkins; *Chmn Board Trustees* Dougals Dillon; *Chmn Special Projects* Karl Katz; *Mgr Personnel* John T Conger; *Cur American Paintings & Sculpture* John K Howat; *Cur in Charge American Decorative Arts* Berry B Tracy; *Cur American Decorative Art* Morrison H Hecksher; *Cur in Charge Ancient Near Eastern Art* Vaughn E Crawford; *Cur Ancient Near Eastern Art* Prudence Oliver Harper; *Cur Arms & Armor* Helmut Nickel; *Cur Drawings* Jacob Bean; *Cur Egyptian Art* Christine Lilyquist; *Lila Acheson Wallace Cur Egyptology* Henry G Fischer; *Consultant Department Islamic Art* Stuart Cary Welch; *Cur Robert Lehman Coll* George Szabo; *Cur Medieval Art* Carmen Gomez-Moreno; *Chmn Department Medieval Art* William D Wixon; *Cur European Paintings* Elizabeth E Gardner; *Special Consultant for Far Eastern Affairs* Wen Fong; *Research Fellow Far Eastern Art* Martin Lerner; *Chmn Greek & Roman Art* Dietrich von Bothmer; *Assoc Cur in Charge Musical Instruments* Laurence Libin; *Chmn Primitive Art* Douglas Newton; *Cur Primitive Art* Julie Jones; *Cur Prints & Photographs* Janet S Byrne; *Cur in Charge Prints & Photographs* Colta Feller Ives; *Cur 20th Century Art* Hess Thomas; *Chmn Department 20th Century Art* William Liebermen; *Chmn Sculpture & Decorative Arts* Olga Raggio; *Consultant Sculpture & Decorative Art* Yvonne Hackenbroch; *Cur Western European Arts* James Parker; *Conservator Paintings* John Brealey; *Conservator Prints & Drawings* Merritt Safford; *Special Asst to Dir* John Buchanan; *Assoc Cur Central Catalog* Marcia Vilcek; *Program Mgr Concerts & Lectures* Hilde Limondjian; *Mgr Photograph Studio* Mark Cooper; *Museum Education Community Education* Herbert Scott-Gibson; *Mgr Public Information* Jack Frizzelle; *Publisher* Radford D Kelleher; *Ed Bulletin* Joan Holt; *Ed-in-Chief* John P O'Neill
Open Tues 10 AM - 8:45 PM, Wed - Sat 10 AM - 4:45 PM, Sun 11 AM - 4:45 PM, cl Mon. Admis contribution $2.50 suggested. Estab 1870 to encourage and develop the study of the fine arts, and the application of arts to manufacture and practical life; of advancing the general knowledge of kindred subjects and to that end of furnishing popular instruction and recreation. Average Annual Attendance: 3,000,000. Mem: 70,000; dues patron $2500, sponsor $1000, donor $500, contributing $250, sustaining $100, participating $50, individual $35, student $15
Income: $43,450,379 (financed by endowment, membership, city and state appropriations)
Collections: American decorative arts, paintings and sculpture; Ancient Near East, Egyptian, European, Greek, Islamic and Roman paintings; medieval art; Arms and Armor; Comprehensive collections spanning the Ancient Civilizations of Egypt, the Ancient Near East, the Far East, Greece and Rome; Far East 20th Century Art; Lehman Collection: musical instruments; Primitive Art; Western European decorative arts, paintings and sculpture
Exhibitions: A Faun Teased by Children; Annual Baroque Christmas Tree and Creche Display; Annual Cloisters Christmas Display: Original Silent Night Manuscript; Blue and White; Childe Hassam; Contemporary American Prints; Degas in the Metropolitan; Gustave Dore: Dark Tales and Drolleries; Early Japanese Export Porcelain; Egyptian Reinstallation Phase I; 15th Century Woodcuts and other Relief Prints; Daniel Chester French: an American Sculptor; The Glory of Russian Costume; Liberty or Death; Nadar, Photographer; Five Paintings from the Bavarian State Paintings Collection; Paris-New York, American Cinematheque; Irving Penn: Street Material; Portraits by Stuart and Sully; Maurice Prendergast's Large Boston Public Garden Sketchbook; The Putto With a Dolphin; Roman Artists of the 17th Century: Drawings and Prints; Rubens in Prints; Russian and Soviet Painting; Gifts from the Singer Collection; Thracian Treasures from Bulgaria; Titian and His Circle; Tricolour: 17th Century Dutch, 18th Century English and 19th Century French Drawings from the Robert Lehman Collection; Two Worlds of Andrew Wyeth: Kurners and Olsons; The Wrightsman Galleries; Andrew Wyeth: Drawings and Watercolors
Publications: Bulletin, quarterly; The Journal, annually
Activities: Classes for children; docent training; films; lect open to public and occasionally for members only; concerts; gallery talks; tours; exten dept serves community programs for Greater New York City area; individual paintings and original objects of art lent to other institutions; lending collection contains color reproductions and original art works; originate traveling exhibitions; museum shop sells books, reproductions, prints, slides and postcards

L **Thomas J Watson Library,*** Fifth Ave at 82nd St, 10028. Tel 212-879-5500, Ext 221, 222. *Chief Librn* Elizabeth R Usher; *Museum Librn* Dobrila-Donya Schimansky
Open Tues - Fri 10 AM - 4:45 PM, cl holidays and Aug. Estab 1881 for the use of the curatorial, educational and other staff; privileges are extended to qualified researchers and graduate students with appropriate identification. Circ 208,500
Income: Financed by endowment
Library Holdings: Vols 212,000; Per subs 1200; Micro—Fiche, reels; Other—Clipping files, exhibition catalogs, memorabilia, pamphlets, original documents
Special Subjects: Archaeology, American Painting, Sculpture, Ancient and modern art, industrial art
Collections: Art Auction Catalogs

L **Photograph and Slide Library,*** Fifth Ave at 82nd St, 10028. Tel 212-879-5500, Ext 230, 260. *Chief Librn* Margaret P Nolan
Open Tues - Fri 10 AM - 4:45 PM. Estab 1907 to provide a circulation (rental) library of slides covering the history of art; to provide color transparencies and photographs of the collections of the Metropolitan Museum of Art for publication purposes; to maintain a reference collection of photographs and mounted color prints covering the history of art. Circ 170,000
Library Holdings: AV—Lantern Slides, slides; Other—Prints, photographs
Special Subjects: Collections of the Metropolitan Museum of Art, particularly complete coverage of Western decorative arts
Collections: William Keighley Slide Collection covering Asia Minor, Austria, France, Germany, Italy and Spain; architecture and other arts of various periods

L **Robert Goldwater Library of Primitive Art,*** Fifth Ave at 82nd St, 10028. Tel 212-879-5500. *Museum Librn* Allan D Chapman
Estab 1957 for reference only
Library Holdings: Vols 20,000; Per subs 125; Micro—Fiche, reels; Other—Black and white photographs of primitive art 100,000
Special Subjects: Antropology, Archaeology, Ethnology, African, American Indian, Eskimo, Oceanic, Pre-Columbian and Primitive art
Publications: Primitive Art Bibliographies

L **Robert Lehman Collection Library,*** Fifth Ave at 82nd St, 10028. Tel 212-879-5500, Ext 656. *Asst Cur Research* Victoria S Galban
Open by appointment only
Income: $10,000 (financed by endowment)
Library Holdings: Vols 8000; Per subs 758; Other—Clipping files, exhibition catalogs, manuscripts, pamphlets, photographs, reproductions, original documents
Special Subjects: Western European arts from the 13th - 20th Centuries with special emphasis on the art of Siena, Old Master drawings and Renaissance decorative arts
Collections: Archives containing books, correspondence, manuscripts and reproductions; photograph collection

L **Irene Lewisohn Costume Reference Library,*** Fifth Ave at 82nd St, 10028. Tel 212-879-5500, Ext 628. *Assoc Museum Librn* K Gordon Stone
Open Tues - Fri 10 AM - 1 PM, and 2 - 4:30 PM. Estab 1946 to study costume history, fashion and theatre design and any subject related to the subject of dress. For reference only
Income: Financed by bequest
Library Holdings: Vols 30,200; Per subs 32; Other—Clipping files, prints, memorabilia, photographs, fashion plates, original fashion sketches
Special Subjects: Costume Design & Construction
Collections: Mainbocher Fashion Sketches by Douglas Pollard from 1940-1970

M **Junior Museum,*** Fifth Ave at 82nd St, 10028. Tel 212-879-5500. *Museum Educator* Roberta Paine; *Assoc Museum Educator* Elizabeth Flinn; *Asst* Meera Thompson
Open Tues - Sat 10 AM - 4:45 PM, Sun & holidays 11 AM - 4:45 PM, cl Mon. Estab 1941 as a department of The Metropolitan Museum of Art, and opened in 1957 as the new Junior Museum. Museum has exhibition area, and auditorium seating of 279. Average Annual Attendance: 300,000
Collections: Draws upon the collections of the Metropolitan Museum of Art
Exhibitions: Archaeology-Exploring the Past, 1966-1968; Artist's Workshop-Tools and Techniques; changing exhibitions of children's work
Activities: School programs; auditorium programs; studio hours; treasure hunts; sales desk

L **Junior Museum Library,*** Fifth Ave at 82nd St, 10028. Tel 212-879-5500, Ext 350. Open Tues - Sat 10 AM - 4:45 PM, Sun Noon - 4:45 PM, cl holidays. Estab 1941 for children; an art research library within the Junior Museum. For reference only
Income: Financed by state appropriation and private funds
Purchases: $400
Library Holdings: Vols 5200; Per subs 4
Special Subjects: Archaeology, Art History, Illustration, Applied arts and crafts, children's books, history, juvenile picture books, mythology
Publications: A Selection of Art Books for Young People in the Junior Museum Library, annually

M **Cloisters,** Fort Tryon Park, 10040. Tel 212-923-3700. *Admnr* Timothy Husband; *Consultative Cur* Kurt Weitzmann; *Cur* Jan Hayward; *Cur* Jack Schrader
Open Tues - Sat 10:45 AM - 4:45 PM, Sun & holidays Oct - April 1 - 4:45 PM, May - Sept Noon - 4:45 PM. Estab 1928 to display in an appropriate setting works of art and architecture of the Middle Ages. Medieval French cloisters incorporated into the building, as well as the chapter house, a chapel, and Romanesque apse; also Medieval herb garden. Average Annual Attendance: 200,000
Collections: Frescoes, ivories, precious metalwork, paintings, polychromed statues, stained glass, tapestries, and other French and Spanish architectural elements
Publications: The Cloisters Guidebook
Activities: Classes for adults and children; dramatic programs; lect open to public; concerts; original objects of art lent to other museums; museum shop sells books, reproductions and slides

L **Cloisters Library,*** Fort Tryon Park, 10040. Tel 212-923-3700, Ext 54. *Librn* Suse C Childs; *Library Asst* Daniel Schoonover
Open Tues - Fri 10 AM - 1 PM and 2 - 4:45 PM. Estab 1938 to be used as a small highly specialized reference library for the curatorial staff at the Cloisters; scholars and accredited graduate students are welcome. For reference only
Income: Financed by endowment
Purchases: $12,000
Library Holdings: Vols 5750; Per subs 46; AV—Slides; Other—Exhibition catalogs, photographs, original documents
Collections: George Grey Barnard Archive

L **PIERPONT MORGAN LIBRARY,** 29 E 36th St, 10016. Tel 212-685-0008. *Pres* H S Morgan; *Secy* Haliburton Fales; *Dir* Charles Ryskamp; *Asst Dir* Francis S Mason Jr; *Research Fellow for Texts Emeritus* Curt F Buhler; *Cur Printed Books and Bindings* Paul Needham; *Cur Medieval and Renaissance Manuscripts* Dr John H Plummer; *Assoc Cur Medieval & Renaissance Manuscripts* William M Voelkle; *Cur Drawings and Prints* Felice Stampfle; *Assoc Cur Drawings and Prints* Cara D Denison; *Cur Autograph Manuscripts* Herbert Cahoon; *Asst Cur Autograph and Music Manuscripts* J Rigbie Turner; *Honorary Cur Seals and Tablets* Edith Porada; *Cur of Gilbert & Sullivan Coll* Reginald Allen; *Cur Early Children's Books* Gerald Gottlieb; *Conservator* Alexander J Yow; *Reference Librn* Evelyn Semler; *Registrar* David W Wright
Open Tues - Sat 10:30 AM - 5 PM, Sun 1 - 5 PM, cl Sun during July, cl month

of Aug; reading room open Mon - Fri. Estab 1924 by endowment; collection placed in custody of a Board of Trustees for research and exhibition purposes. The Gallery has changing exhibitions with various types of printed materials, as well as Old Masters' drawings
Income: $770,000 (financed by endowment and membership)
Purchases: $1,050,000
Library Holdings: Vols 45,000; Per subs 170; AV—Slides; Other—Manuscripts, original art works, original documents
Collections: Ancient written records including seals, cuneiform tablets and papyri; art objects; autograph manuscripts; book bindings; early children's books; illuminated manuscripts; later printed books; letters and documents; mezzotints; modern calligraphy; music manuscripts; original drawing from 14th-19th centuries; printed books from 1450; Rembrandt etchings
Exhibitions: (1978-79) British Literary Manuscripts, 800-1800; Classical Style in Rajput Painting; Drawings by Giovanni Battista Piranesi; Letters of Love and Affection; Music Manuscripts from Bach to Stravinsky; The Age of Michelangelo; Twelve Centuries of Fine Bindings; William and Mary and Their House
Publications: Report to the Fellows, biennial; books; catalogs; facsimiles
Activities: Lect open to the public, 8 vis lectr per year; concerts; scholarships

M **MORRIS-JUMEL MANSION,** W 160th St & Edgecombe Ave, 10032. Tel 212-923-8008. *Pres* Mrs Alden O Stanton; *Dir* Jane Sullivan Crowley
Open Tues - Sun 10 AM - 4 PM. Admis 50¢. Estab 1903 as a Historic House Museum. There are 12 rooms furnished in three periods of American history. Average Annual Attendance: 35,000. Mem: 400; dues $10 - $500; annual meeting May
Income: Financed by membership and fund raising
Collections: Art; furniture of 18th and 19th centuries
Publications: Morris-Jumel News, quarterly
Activities: Educ dept; docent training; lect open to public, 4 vis lectr per year; concerts; tours; traveling exhibitions organized and circulated; sales shop selling books, postcards

O **MUNICIPAL ART SOCIETY OF NEW YORK,** 457 Madison Ave, 10022. Tel 212-935-3968. *Pres* Doris C Freedman; *Secy* Gordon Hyatt; *Executive Dir* Margot Wellington
Estab 1892, incorporated 1898. The Society is the one organization in New York where the layman, professional and business firm can work together to encourage high standards for public art, architecture, planning, landscaping and preservation in the five boroughs. Mem: 2800; dues $25 and up; annual meeting June
L **The Information Exchange,** 457 Madison Ave, 10022. *Dir* Darlene McCloud
Open Mon - Fri 9 AM - 5 PM. Estab 1979. For reference only
Library Holdings: Vols 600; Per subs 85; AV—Slides; Other—Clipping files, exhibition catalogs, pamphlets, photographs
Special Subjects: Architecture, Industrial Design, City Planning, Urban and landscape design

M **MUSEUM OF AMERICAN FOLK ART,** 49 W 53rd St, 10019. Tel 212-581-2475. *Chmn* Ralph Esmerian; *VPres* Mrs Ronald Lauder; *VPres* Mrs Richard Taylor; *VPres* Lucy Danziger; *VPres & Secy* Frances S Martinson; *Exec VPres* Alice M Kaplan; *Treas* William I Leffler; *Dir* Dr Robert Bishop; *Asst Dir* Patricia L Coblentz
Open Tues - Sun 10:30 AM - 5:30 PM; cl Mon. Admis $1. Estab 1961, the Museum's primary purpose is to present outstanding exhibitions on specific topics of folk art. Organized by prominent authorities on folk art and dedicated collectors, this unique Museum has become a focal point for the many people who want to explore the folk art traditions in their art, design, and way of life. The gallery has 950 sq ft of floor space; total length of gallery, 76 1 2 ft; width of gallery, 20 ft; height of ceilings, 14 ft. Average Annual Attendance: 50,000. Mem: 2500; dues $20 and up
Income: $300,000 (financed by membership, state appropriation, personal donations)
Collections: Furniture; miscellaneous decorative arts; paintings; prints and drawings; sculpture
Exhibitions: American Folk Paintings from the Collection of Mr & Mrs William E Wiltshire III; Annual Antique Show Preview; Hawaiian Quilts: Treasures of an Island Folk Art; The Art of the Weathervane; The Shakers in New York State; The Woman Folk Artist in America
Publications: The Clarion, quarterly magazine
Activities: Classes for adults and children; docent training; lect open to public; individual paintings and original objects of art lent to sister institutions in the United States; traveling exhibitions organized and circulated
L **Library,** 49 W 53rd St, 10019.
Not open to public
Library Holdings: Vols 300

M **MUSEUM OF HOLOGRAPHY,** 11 Mercer St, 10013. Tel 212-925-0581, 925-0526; Telex 23-6194. *Pres & Dir* Rosemary Jackson; *Dir of Information Services* Laura Mack; *Dir of Educational Services* Edward A Bush; *Dir Traveling Exhibition Services* Paul D Barefoot; *Mgr Museum Bookstore* D Lee Zemann; *Comptroller* Robin Harvey
Open Wed - Sun noon - 6 PM, Thurs 12 - 9 PM. Admis adults $2, children and senior citizens $1, group rates if booked in advance. Estab 1976 to provide a focal point for the growing art form of holography and serve as an information center for the field. Consists of temporary exhibition gallery, permanent historical gallery, and downstairs galleries for the permanent collection. Average Annual Attendance: 100,000. Mem: 450; dues $1000, $500, $100, family $45, individual $25
Income: Financed by membership, federal funds, state appropriation, corporate and foundation grants and admissions
Collections: †Contemporary art holography collection of 400 holograms; †Contemporary and historic commercial holography collection of 250 holograms and data; †Historic collection of 40 early prototypes and firsts, with date, early machines and books, tapes and photographs, major bequest from inventor of the medium, Dr Dennis Gabor and other pioneers of the medium
Exhibitions: (1980-81) One woman retrospective of work by Margaret Benyon, pioneer of holography as art; Its All Waves Anyway, retrospective work of Abe Rezny, holography, neon, photography; Shadowgrams, one man retrospective work of Rick Silberman; Similar Visions, the history and development of dimensional imaging systems, guest curated by Dr Stephen A Benton of Polaroid Corporation
Publications: Holosphere, the newsletter of the art science and industry of

holography, monthly; exhbition catalogs every three months; bookstore mail order catalog every fall, general information on holography and the museum information packet; reprints on holography
Activities: Docent training; study notes for exhibitions; artist in residence program; lectures open to the public, 4 - 8 visiting lecturers per year; gallery talks; tours; scholarships offered; individual holograms and original objects of art lent to museums and other non-profit cultural organizations; lending collection contain photographs, holograms; book traveling exhibitions; traveling exhibitions organized and circulated to Art Museums, Science Centers; museum shop sells books, magazines, holograms, exhibition catalogs, original art objects, postcards, posters, reproductions and optical art objects
L **Reference Library,** 11 Mercer St, 10013. *Librn* Laura Mack; *Admin Asst* Mary Duffy
Open Wed - Sun noon to 6 PM, by appointment only. Estab 1976 to provide data from a wide variety of disciplines that relate to holography, lasers, artists working in the field, equipment and opportunities in holography
Library Holdings: Vols 250; Per subs 18; AV—A-tapes, cassettes, fs, motion pictures, slides, v-tapes; Other—Clipping files, exhibition catalogs, manuscripts, memorabilia, pamphlets, photographs
Special Subjects: Holography
Collections: Nobel Prize for Holography awarded to Dr Dennis Gabor; Papers, technical manuscripts, books and photographs from Dr Dennis Gabor, inventor of holography; early books about holography, including holograms

M **MUSEUM OF MODERN ART,** 11 W 53rd St, 10019. Tel 212-956-6100. *Chmn of Board* William S Paley; *VChmn* Gardner Cowles; *VChmn* Mrs Bliss Parkinson; *VChmn* David Rockefeller; *Pres* Mrs John D Rockefeller III; *VPres* Mrs Frank Y Larkin; *VPres* Donald B Marron; *VPres & Treas* John Parkinson III; *Secy & Gen Counsel* John B Koegel; *Dir Museum* Richard E Oldenburg; *Dir Admin* Edward L Saxe; *Dir Painting & Sculpture Coll* William Rubin; *Dir Drawings* John Elderfield; *Dir Prints & Illustrated Books* Riva Castleman; *Dir Dept Architecture & Design* Arthur Drexler; *Dir Dept Photography* John Szarkowski; *Acting Dir Dept Film* Mary Lea Bandy; *Coordr Planning* James S Snyder; *Dir Exhib* Richard L Palmer; *Dir International Prog* Waldo Rasmussen; *Dir Dept Education* William Burback; *Dir Dept Publication* Martin Rapp; *Dir Membership & Development* John Limpert; *Dir Public Information* Luisa Kreisberg
Open Mon, Tues, Fri, Sat & Sun 11 AM - 6 PM; Thurs 11 AM - 9 PM; cl Wed and Christmas. Admis adults $2.50, students $1.50, children and senior citizens 75¢, Tues pay-what-you-wish. Estab 1929 to help people enjoy, understand and use the visual arts of our time. New gallery addition to be designed by Cesar Pelli. Nonprofit education organization. Average Annual Attendance: 1,200,000. Mem: 40,000; dues $35 and up (student $10)
Income: Financed by admissions, membership, sales of publications and other services and contributions
Collections: Painting and sculptures 3000; drawings 2600; prints 10,000; illustrated books 800; posters and graphics 3000; photographs 14,000; architectural drawings 400; architectural models 60; design objects 2500; films 4500; film stils 3,000,000
Exhibitions: (1978) Joan and Lester Avnet Collection; Matisse in the Collection of the Museum of Modern Art; Mirrors and Windows: American Photography Since 1960; Sollewitt, A Treasury of Modern Drawing. (1979) Ansel Adams and the West; Art of the Twenties; Contemporary Sculpture: Selections from the Permanent Collection; Masterworks of Edvard Munch; Transformations in Modern Architecture. (1980) Printed Art, Eileen Gray
Publications: Book on exhibitions and artists; monographs; catalogs
Activities: Symposia; film showings, international in scope, illustrating the historic and esthetic development of the motion picture; lectr; concerts; art lending service; originates traveling exhibitions; circulating film programs; bookstore selling publications, reproductions, postcards, note and seasonal cards, posters, slides
L **Library,** 11 W 53rd St, 10019. *Reference Librn* Janette Rozene; *Librn* Clive Phillpot
Open Mon - Fri 1 - 5 PM. Estab 1929 as a research library. For museum staff and accredited researchers
Library Holdings: Vols 35,000; Per subs 200; Micro—Reels; AV—Cassettes, v-tapes; Other—Clipping files, exhibition catalogs, manuscripts, memorabilia, pamphlets, photographs
Special Subjects: Architecture, Drawings, Film, Graphic Arts, Mixed Media
Collections: Archive of Museum Publications; Personal Archives of Past Members, Staff and Trustees; Personal Archives of Artists, Writers, Dealers

M **MUSEUM OF THE AMERICAN INDIAN,** Broadway at 155th St, 10032. Tel 212-283-2420. *Dir* Dr Roland W Force; *Asst Dir* George Eager; *Cur North America* Dr James G E Smith; *Cur South America* Dr Anna C Roosevelt; *Registrar* David Fawcett; *Public Information* Nancy Henry; *Development Officer* Elizabeth Beim; *Cur of Exhibits* Tom Martin; *Designer* Don Werner; *Conservator* Phyllis Dillon
Open Tues - Sun 10 AM - 5 PM, cl Mon and holidays. Admis adults $1.50, students with ID 75¢, pre-registered groups 25¢; free to native Americans, members. Estab 1916, building opened 1922. Average Annual Attendance: 75,000. Mem: 1000; dues benefactor $5000, Calumet Circle Corporate Memberships $1000, patron $1000, supporting $500, associate $250, contributing $100, sustaining $50, family $35, regular $20 , senior citizen and student $10
Collections: Decorative arts; numismatic; outstanding collections of pre-Columbian art and historical materials; world's largest collection of art and culture of the Indians of North, Central and South America, West Indies and the Eskimo
Exhibitions: (1978) Echoes of the Drums. (1979) The Ancestors: Native Artisans of the Americas; panoramic survey exhibit. (1980) Artic Art: Eskimo Ivory Carving; Iroquois Silver; hemispheric craft exhibit; permanent exhibits of all phases of Indian life
Publications: Indian News; annual book; annual monograph
Activities: Gallery talks; tours; lending service to schools; originate traveling exhibition

M **MUSEUM OF THE CITY OF NEW YORK,** 1220 Fifth Ave, 10029. Tel 212-534-1672. *Dir* Joseph Veach Noble; *Controller* Thomas McNamara; *Public Affairs* Monika Dillon
Open Tues - Sat 10 AM - 5 PM, Sun & holidays 1 - 5 PM, cl Mon. No admis fee. Estab 1923 to preserve the cultural accomplishments of New York City's ancestors and to meet the needs and interests of the community. Average Annual Attendance: 850,000. Mem: 3200; dues $15 and up
Collections: Costume collection; decorative arts collection; print and photograph

collection; theatre and music collection; toy collection
Exhibitions: (1980) 1880's Costumes; Hundreds of Dolls; Life with Father; New York's Dolls' Houses; The Big Apple: Multi Media
Publications: Annual Report; Bulletin, Fall and Spring
Activities: Dramatic programs; demonstrations; concerts; tours; individual paintings and original objects of art lent to affiliated institutions; museum shop selling books, reproductions, cards

NATIONAL ACADEMY OF DESIGN
For further information, see National and Regional Organizations

NATIONAL ANTIQUE AND ART DEALERS ASSOCIATION OF AMERICA
For further information, see National and Regional Organizations

M **NATIONAL ART MUSEUM OF SPORTS, INC,*** 375 Park Ave, Suite 3408, 10022. Tel 212-472-3775. *Dir* Germain G Glidden
Open Mon - Fri 9:30 AM - 5:30 PM, holidays 10 AM - 5:30 PM, cl Christmas & New Year's Day. Admis adults 50¢, children 25¢. Estab 1959 as an art museum covering sports subjects. Mem: Dues sponsor $5000, general $100, sustaining $25, individual $10
Income: Financed by the State University of New York and governed by the Board of Regents
Collections: Paintings, prints and sculpture of sporting subjects
Exhibitions: Permanent, temporary and traveling exhibitions
Publications: News from the Museum, quarterly newsletter
Activities: Guided tours; rental gallery; book traveling exhibitions

NATIONAL ASSOCIATION OF WOMEN ARTISTS, INC
For further information, see National and Regional Organizations

NATIONAL INSTITUTE FOR ARCHITECTURAL EDUCATION
For further information, see National and Regional Organizations

NATIONAL SCULPTURE SOCIETY
For further information, see National and Regional Organizations

NATIONAL SOCIETY OF MURAL PAINTERS, INC
For further information, see National and Regional Organizations

NATIONAL SOCIETY OF PAINTERS IN CASEIN AND ACRYLIC, INC
For further information, see National and Regional Organizations

M **NEW MUSEUM,** 65 Fifth Ave, 10003. Tel 212-741-8962. *Dir* Marcia Tucker; *Dir Planning & Development* Dieter Morris Kearse; *Adminr* Maureen Stewart
Open Mon - Fri Noon - 6 PM, Wed Noon - 8 PM, Sat Noon - 5 PM; cl Sun. Estab 1977 to present to the public new, provocative art that does not yet have wide public exposure or critical acceptance. The gallery space is 2500 sq ft which has been given to us by the New School for Social Research on an extended basis. Average Annual Attendance: 60,000. Mem: 400; dues $15 and up
Income: Financed by endowment, membership, state appropriation, corporations, foundations and Federal grants
Exhibitions: Dimensions Variable; In a Pictorial Framework; Invented Landscape; Barry Le Va; Outside New York; Sustained Visions
Publications: Newsletter; exhibition catalogs
Activities: Lect open to public; gallery talks

M **NEW SCHOOL FOR SOCIAL RESEARCH ART CENTER GALLERY,*** 65 Fifth Ave, 10003. Tel 212-741-7914. *Art Workshops Dir* Julian Levi; *Dir Art Center* Paul Mocsanyi
Estab 1919, as a university for adults to advance education of both the scholar and the layman, with work centering in the social sciences and the humanities. Gallery includes large non-credit program; Graduate Faculty of Political and Social Science, Center for New York City Affairs and undergraduate New School College. In 1970 the Parsons School of Design affiliated with The New School. Gallery occupies six buildings, dedicated 1931, 1956, 1959, 1969 and 1972. Mural decorations by Thomas Hart Benton, Michael Cadoret, Camilo Egas, Gonzalo Fonseca and Jose Clemente Orozco. Average Annual Attendance: 17,000
Collections: Paintings by Carlo Dolci, Cleve Gray, Rattner, Youngoman; †sculpture including works by Baskin, Gross, King, Konzal, Lipchitz, Lipton, Hadzi, Noguchi, Penalba, Trajan, Zogbaum and others
Publications: Monthly Bulletin; Social Research, quarterly
M **Collectors Institute of the New School,*** 65 Fifth Ave, 10003. *Dir* Paul Mocsanyi
Estab to teach connoisseurship in many fields of art ancient and modern, as well as the ways and means of collecting. Open to members only. Mem: Dues $650 annually or $325 semi-annually

O **NEW YORK ARTISTS EQUITY ASSOCIATION, INC,** 225 W 34th St (Suite 1302), 10001. Tel 212-736-6480. *Pres* Harry Waterston; *VPres* Mark Freeman; *VPres* Howard Mandel; *VPres* Renee McKay; *VPres* Joseph Rothman; *Recording Secy* Helen Gerardia; *Corresponding Secy* Esther K Gayner; *Treas* Meg Weil; *Exec Dir* Eve Wilen
Open 10 AM - 5 PM. Estab 1947 as a politically non-partisan group to advance the cultural, legislative, economic and professional interest of painters, sculptors, printmakers, and others in the field of visual arts. Various committees concerned with aims. Administrators of the Artists Welfare Fund, Inc. Mem: Over 1300; dues $22; meetings Oct, Dec, Feb, Apr
Publications: AEA Newsletter
O **Artists Welfare Fund, Inc,** 225 W 34St, 10001. Tel 212-736-6480. *Exec Officer* Elias Newman
Artists Welfare Fund, Inc is a non-profit tax-deductible service organization, administered by officers of New York Artists Equity Association, Inc primarily to help artists in need of financial emergency assistance to tide them over a critical period with small loans, without interest

O **NEW YORK CHAMBER OF COMMERCE AND INDUSTRY,*** 65 Liberty St, 10005. Tel 212-766-1300.
Open 9:30 - 11:30 AM & 2 - 4:30 PM. No admis fee. Estab 1768. Mem: 1800; annual meeting May

Collections: Portraits of business leaders of the United States from the late 18th century to the present
L **Library,*** 65 Liberty St, 10005. *Librn* Anita Randolfe
Library Holdings: Vols 12,000

O **NEW YORK HISTORICAL SOCIETY,** 170 Central Park W, 10024. Tel 212-873-3400. *Pres* Robert G Goelet; *VPres* R McAllister Lloyd; *Dir* James J Heslin; *Cur Museum* Richard J Koke; *Cur Painting & Sculpture* Mary Black; *Secy* Mrs Robert J Malone
Open Tues - Fri 11 AM - 5 PM; Sat 10 AM - 5 PM; Sun 1 - 5 PM. No admis fee. Estab 1804 to collect and preserve material relating to the history of New York City and State. Maintains art gallery. Average Annual Attendance: 400,000. Mem: 2500; dues corporate member $250, sustaining member $50, annual member $25, research member $10
Income: $750,000 (financed by endowment and membership)
Collections: American landscape and genre paintings; American portraits; European paintings prior to 1850
Publications: The New York Historical Society Quarterly
Activities: Lect for members only, 5 vis lectr per yr; concerts; gallery talks; tours; individual paintings and original objects of art lent to museums; lending collection contains 8000 paintings, 500,000 photographs, 2500 sculptures; sales shop selling books, magazines and prints
L **Library,** 170 Central Park West, 10024. *Librn* James Gregory; *Asst Librn* Sue Gillies
Open Tues - Sat 10 AM - 5 PM. Estab 1804. For reference only
Library Holdings: Vols 600,000; Per subs 350; Micro—Cards, fiche, reels; Other—Exhibition catalogs, prints, manuscripts, memorabilia, original art works, pamphlets, photographs, sculpture
Special Subjects: American Art to 1900
Collections: Civil War material; New York City & State History; 19th century advertising

L **NEW YORK PUBLIC LIBRARY,** Astor, Lennox & Tilden Foundations, Fifth Ave & 42nd St, 10018. Tel 212-790-6262. *Pres* Richard W Couper
Estab 1895. Holdings for entire library contain over 5,607,863 volumes
L **Prints Division,** Fifth Ave & 42nd St, Room 308, 10018. *Keeper of Prints* Elizabeth Roth
Admis by application to Research Libraries. Estab 1899
Library Holdings: Vols 13,000; Other—Prints 160,000
Special Subjects: Graphic artists and catalogs of their works, Original fine prints of the past six Centuries with special emphasis on 19th Century French and American, contemporary American and European, prints, techniques and illustrated books
Collections: Bookplates including Radin Collection of Western European bookplates; British and American caricatures; Beverly Chew bequest of Milton and Pope Portraits; Eno Collection of New York City Views; McAlpin Collection of George Washington Portraits; Smith Collection of Japanese prints; Phelps Stokes Collection of American views
L **Spencer Collection,** Fifth Ave & 42nd St, Room 324, 10018. Tel 212-790-6110. *Cur* Joseph T Rankin
Library Holdings: Vols 8000
Special Subjects: Rare illustrated and illuminated manuscripts and books in fine bindings, in all languages of all countries and of all periods, constituting the development of book illustration and the book arts of the world
L **Art and Architecture Division,** Fifth Ave & 42nd St, Room 313, 10018. *Chief* Donald Anderle
Open Mon, Wed, Fri & Sat 10 AM - 6 PM, Tues 10 AM - 9 PM, cl Sun & Thurs. Estab 1911 for reference
Library Holdings: Vols 100,000; Other—Clipping files, exhibition catalogs, pamphlets
Special Subjects: Ceramics, Costume Design & Construction, Folk Art, Furniture, Glass, Inter Design, Jewelry, Silversmithing, Textiles, Architectural design, history, painting and sculpture of the decorative arts of all countries from prehistoric times to the present, special emphasis on scholarly works in history, post-Columbian American art and Oriental art
Collections: Private and public collection catalogs; individual artists and architects
L **Schomburg Center for Research in Black Culture,** 103 W 135th St, 10030. Tel 212-862-4000. *Chief* Jean B Huston
A reference library devoted to Black people throughout the world
Library Holdings: Vols 70,000; Micro—Reels; AV—Fs, rec; Other—Clipping files, prints, photographs, broadsides, maps, playbills, programs
Special Subjects: Black people throughout the world with major emphasis on Afro-American, Africa and Carribbean, nucleus of collected rarities of Arthur A Schomburg, a Puerto Rican of African descent
Collections: Largest collection in the country of books on Black Culture and Art; permanent collection of African Art
L **Picture Collection,** Fifth Ave & 42nd St, Room 73, 10018. *Cur* Lenore Cowan
Open Mon, Wed & Fri Noon - 5:45 PM, Tues Noon - 7:45 PM, cl Thurs, Sat, Sun & holidays. Estab 1915
Collections: Approximately 2,250,000 classified pictures encyclopedic in subject, copy may be borrowed by those who live, work or study in New York State, except for exhibition or classroom use
L **Donnell Library Center Art Library,** 20 W 53rd St, 10019. *Supervising Librn* Rebecca Siekevitz
Open Mon, Thurs 9:30 AM - 8 PM, Tues, Wed & Fri 9:30 AM - 5:30 PM, Sat 12:30 - 5:30 PM, cl Sun & holidays
Library Holdings: Vols 16,000; Per subs 80; Micro—Reels; Other—Clipping files, Vertical files of catalogs and clippings on contemporary artists and art movements
M **Shelby Cullom Davis Museum of the Performing Arts and: The Library and Museum of the Performing Arts,** at Lincoln Center, 111 Amsterdam Ave, 10024. Tel 212-799-2200. *Head Library & Museum of the Performing Arts* Dr Robert Henderson; *Dir Shelby Cullon Davis Museum of the Performing Arts* Don Vlack
Open Mon & Thurs 10 AM - 8 PM, Tues 10 AM - 6 PM, Fri & Sat Noon - 6 PM, cl Wed. No admis fee. Estab 1964 to present exhibitions of high quality pertaining directly with the performing arts. Main gallery is 140 x 40 x 20 ft and has large glass space designed by Saarinen; Astor Gallery at the rear of Vivian Beaumont Theatre measures 80 x 30 x 30 ft; Amsterdam Gallery 30 x 50 x 10 ft; small plaza gallery 20 x 20 x 20 ft

Income: Financed by endowment and city appropriation

Collections: Maintained by the curators of the various departments. 95% of material is of an archival nature and physically flat, documents and letters, memorabilia, original costumes and scene designs, photographs

Exhibitions: Artistic Adventurer-Animateur - The Muppets; Theatres of New York: Park Theatre; Niblo's Garden; Wallach's-Star Theatre - Duke Ellington - Diaghilev

Activities: Sales shop sells books, magazines, reproductions, prints, slides and various material related to the performing arts

L **NEW YORK SCHOOL OF INTERIOR DESIGN LIBRARY,** 155 E 56th St, 10022. *Librn* Malcolm E Scheer

Open Mon, Thurs, Fri 9 AM - 4 PM, Tues & Wed Noon - 7 PM. Estab 1924 to supplement the courses given by the school and to aid students and faculty in their research and projects

Income: $15,000

Purchases: $5000

Library Holdings: Vols 2000; Per subs 47; AV—Slides; Other—Exhibition catalogs

Special Subjects: Inter Design

O **NEW YORK SOCIETY OF ARCHITECTS,** 16 E 42nd St, 10017. Tel 212-682-3594. *Pres* William R Sachs; *VPres* Donald Freed; *VPres* Peter Goldhammer; *Secy* Samuel Horn; *Treas* Robert A Brisson; *Executive Dir* Margot A Henkel

Open 10:30 AM - 5 PM. Incorporated 1906. Mem: 450; dues $60; meetings third Wed of every month

Income: $32,000 (financed by dues and sales)

Publications: Bulletin, monthly; New York City Building Code Manual; New York City Electrical Code; New York City Fire Prevention Code

Activities: Matthew W DelGaudio Award for Excellence in Design to architectural students, Honorary Membership Certificate to other than architect, Distinguished Service Award to members, Sidney L Strauss Memorial Award to architect or layman

NEW YORK UNIVERSITY

M **Grey Art Gallery and Study Center,** 33 Washington Place, 10003. Tel 212-598-7603. *Dir* Robert R Littman; *Cur* Gary Reynolds; *Asst Dir for Public Affairs* Michael Boodro; *Gallery Mgr* Jim Clearwater

Open Tues & Thurs 10 AM - 6:30 PM; Weds 10 AM - 8:30 PM; Fri 10 AM - 5 PM; Sat 1 - 5 PM. No admis fee. Estab 1975 as university art museum to serve public as well as university community. The New York University Art Collection of approx 3500 works is now under the Grey Art Gallery. Gallery space of approx 4000 sq ft used for changing exhibitions

Collections: American and European 20th Century Paintings, Watercolors, and Prints; Ben and Abby Grey Foundation Collection of Comtemporary Asian and Middle Eastern Art; New York University Art Collection

Exhibitions: American Imagination and Symbolist Painting, Charles Gleyre; American Painting: The Eighties; Balet-Smythe-Palmer; Changes of Perspective: 1880-1925; Decorative Arts of Frank Lloyd Wright; Life: The First Decade; New Deal for Art; Panoramic Photography; Photographs from the Sam Wagstaff Collection; Louis Comfort Tiffany: The Paintings; Wilmarth-Sandman

Publications: Exhibition catalogs

Activities: Individual paintings and original objects of art lent to other cultural institutions; originate traveling exhibitions; sales shop selling exhibition catalogs

L **Stephen Chan Library of Fine Arts,** 1 E 78th St, 10021. *Dir* Evelyn K Samuel; *Cataloger* Francis G Bondurant

Estab to provide scholarly materials for graduate studies in art history and archaeology. Open to the public upon application to the librarian

Library Holdings: Vols 80,000; Per subs 450; Micro—Fiche, reels; AV—Slides

M **92ND STREET YMHA-YWHA,** Weill Art Gallery, 1395 Lexington Ave, 10028. Tel 212-427-6000, exten 722. *Exec Dir* Reynold Levy; *Assoc Exec Dir Admin* Sidney Zachter; *Performing Arts Dir* Omus Hirshbein; *Assoc Dir Performing Arts* Sima Mittman

Open Mon, Wed & Thurs 1 - 6 PM, Tues 2 - 7 PM & other times to ticket holders. No admis fee. Large room with facilities to mount on wall panels; no partitions; track lighting; windows; no humidity control system; minimal security. Average Annual Attendance: 100,000

Income: Financed by state appropriation and NEA

Exhibitions: (1979-80) Haggadah by Ya'akor Bovssidan; Photographs of Famous People by Philippe Halsman; Printmaking in Israel; Purim, courtesy of Yeshira University Museum

Publications: The Y Bulletin, bimonthly

Activities: Classes for adults and children; dramatic programs; lect open to the public, 100 vis lectr per year; concerts

O **PAINTERS AND SCULPTORS SOCIETY OF NEW JERSEY, INC,** c/o May Heiloms, 340 W 28th St, 10001. Tel 212-924-2596. *Honorary Life Pres* May Heiloms

Estab 1941. Average Annual Attendance: 10,000. Mem: 115; dues $20; meetings March and Nov

Exhibitions: Exhibition open to all artists nationally and internationally; nonmembers subject to jury of selection. Exhibitions usually one-third members and two-thirds nonmembers. Next annual will be held at Salmagundi Club (Fifth Ave & 13th St)

L **PARSONS SCHOOL OF DESIGN,** Adam L Gimbel Library, 2 W 13th St, New York, NY. (Mailing Add: 66 Fifth Ave, New York, NY 10011) Tel 212-741-8914, 741-8915. *Head Librn* Christiane C Collins; *Reference Librn & Cataloguer* Grace Anne DeCandido

Open Mon - Thurs 9 AM - 9 PM, Fri 9 AM - 6 PM, Sat 10 AM - 6 PM. Estab as a school in 1896, with the Adam L Gimbel Library moving at present location in 1974, as a support to the curriculum of the school

Library Holdings: Vols 32,000; Per subs 130; Other—Clipping files, exhibition catalogs, prints, memorabilia, original art works

Special Subjects: Architecture, Costume Design & Construction, Crafts, Fashion Arts, Furniture, American Painting, Photography, Sculpture, City planning, environmental design, graphics, typography

O **PEN AND BRUSH, INC,** 16 E Tenth St, 10003. Tel 212-475-3669. *Pres* Margaret Sussman; *First VPres* Helen Slottman; *Recording Secy* Harriet M Hagerty; *Corresp Secy* Arthur Ray Nichols; *Exec Secy* Camilla Belding; *Treas* Jennie M Palen

Open 1 - 5 PM except holidays during exhibitions. Estab 1893, incorporated 1912. The Clubhouse was purchased in 1923, and contains rooms, dining room and exhibition galleries. Mem: Approx 250 professional women writers, artists, sculptors, and craftsmen; annual meeting Feb

Exhibitions: Ten annual exhibitions of members' work; occasional one-man shows

Activities: Workshops; lect

L **Library,** 16 E Tenth St, 10003.

Library Holdings: Vols 1500

C **PHILIP MORRIS INCORPORATED,** 100 Park Ave, 10017. Tel 212-880-3470. *Mgr Cultural Affairs* Odile Basch

Estab 1960's to enhance the creative and aesthetic environments of offices. Collection displayed in offices and corridors; annual amount of contributions and grants $1,000,000; supports museums, exhibitions, theater, groups, symphony orchestras, art associations, libraries, historical societies, opera companies, commissions

Collections: Prints by artists around the world, tobacco memorabilia, works by emerging artists

Activities: Supports arts organizations located in Philip Morris plant communities; individual objects of art lent to museums exhibitions only

M **PRATT INSTITUTE,** Pratt Manhattan Center Gallery, 160 Lexington Ave, 10016. Tel 212-685-3169. *Dir* Andrew Stasik

Open Mon - Fri 10 AM - 7 PM, Sat 10 AM - 5 PM. No admis fee. Estab to present to the public exhibitions of historical interest vital to the concerns of the New York artists and collectors. Average Annual Attendance: 10,000. Mem: 2500; dues $15 and up

Exhibitions: International Miniature Print Competition; Molas: Art of the Cuna Indians; mini-competition and annual exhibition of Artists of the Pratt Graphics Center

Publications: Print Review magazine, semi-annually

Activities: Classes for adults in printmaking only; lect for members only, 5 - 10 lectr visiting per year; gallery talks; competitions; awards; book traveling exhibitions; originate traveling exhibitions

M **PRINCE STREET GALLERY,** 121 Wooster St, 10012. Tel 212-226-9402.

Open Tues - Sat Noon - 6 PM. Estab 1970 to provide a showing place for members, mainly figurative art. Gallery has about 25 members who have shown in New York as well as throughout the Country and internationally. Average Annual Attendance: 6000. Mem: 25; dues $420; monthly meetings

Income: Financed by membership

Exhibitions: Three week shows Sept - June: one-person and group shows

O **PRINTED MATTER INC,** 7 Lispenard St, 10013. Tel 212-925-0324. *Gen Mgr* Nancy Linn

Open Tues - Sat 10 AM - 6 PM. Estab 1976 for the distribution and publishing of artists' books. Average Annual Attendance: 10,000

Exhibitions: Permanent exhibition of all artists' books in stock; largest inventory of artists' books anywhere, with continually changing window shows of artists' books

Publications: Catalog, annually

Activities: Artists' books lent for exhibitions; sales shop selling books, also a mail distribution network, magazines, slides and related artists' records

O **PRINTMAKING WORKSHOP,** 114 W 17th St, 10011. Tel 212-989-6125, 242-9884. *Dir* Robert Blackburn

Open weekdays 8 AM - 11 PM; weekends 9 AM - 5 PM. Estab 1949 as a workshop space for artists to print etchings and lithographs including night classes and edition printing. Gallery is maintained with 2000 contemporary prints for sale and exhibition rental. Mem: 800; dues vary

Income: Financed by endowment, membership, city and state appropriation

Activities: Classes for adults; classes in graphic arts; lect open to the public; scholarship; original objects of art lent; material available to local areas with mobile print programs; traveling exhibitions organized and circulated

O **PUBLIC ART FUND, INC,** 25 Central Park West, 10023. Tel 212-541-8423. *Pres* Doris Freedman; *Acting Dir* Jenny Dixon; *Project Coordr* Jessica Cusick

Open Mon - Fri 10 AM - 6 PM. Estab 1977 as an umbrella organization to fund the activities of the Public Arts Council and City Walls; to bring art outside and into a daily urban environment

Income: $120,000 (financed by National Education Association, New York State Council of the Arts, private contributions)

Exhibitions: F Dubuffet, Richard Sena, Noguchi, Jeffrey Brosh and Linda Howard

Publications: A walking tour guide to Lower Manhattan

Activities: Lectures; competitions to commission new works of art; sales shop sells slides, catalogs and manuals on public art

L **Library,** 25 Central Park West, 10023.

Estab as a reference library on public art

Library Holdings: AV—Slides 4000

Collections: Murals; outdoor sculpture

M **NICHOLAS ROERICH MUSEUM,** 319 W 107th St, 10025. Tel 212-864-7752. *Pres* Katherine Campbell Stibbe; *Secy* Elina Yussupoff; *Exec VPres* Sina Fosdick; *VPres* Robert Leser; *VPres* Dorothy Blalock; *VPres* Dr D Fogel; *VPres* Svetoslav Roerich; *VPres* Edgar Lansbury; *VPres* Ingeborg Fritschi

Open daily 2 - 5 PM; cl Sat & holidays. No admis fee. Estab 1958 to show a permanent collection of paintings by Nicholas Roerich, internationally known artist, to promote his ideals as a great thinker, writer, humanitarian, scientist, and explorer, and to promote his Pact and Banner of Peace. There is a gallery in which works of contemporary artists are shown. Average Annual Attendance: 5000. Mem: Dues sustaining $50, contributing $25, assoc $10

Income: Financed by membership and donations

Collections: Permanent collection of paintings by Nicholas Roerich

Exhibitions: Svetlana I Dalski Exhibition of Paintings; Lily Dimkova Exhibition of Portraits and Landscapes (oil pastel); Charles W Haddock Paintings and Drawings;

Zetun Jebor Exhibition of Paintings; Moisey Kogan Exhibition of Paintings; Lloyd Nich Exhibition of Paintings; Ukrainian Children's Drawings Exhibition; Kenneth Verzyl Progression Drawings
Activities: Lect open to public, 3 vis lectr per year; concerts; tours; museum shop selling books, reproductions and postcards
L **Library,** 319 W 107th St, 10025.
Pamphlets and publications being catalogued for reference

C **RUDER & FINN FINE ARTS,** 110 E 59th St, 10022. Tel 212-593-6475. *In Charge Art Program* Nina Wright
We are in the business of linking corporations with museums and other arts organizations in support of exhibitions; also council both small business and large corporations on how they can contribute to their communities through the visual arts. Ruder & Finn Fine Arts is a division of the public relations firm of Ruder & Finn Inc
Activities: Originate traveling exhibitions to museums nationwide

SALMAGUNDI CLUB
For further information, see National and Regional Organizations

M **SCALAMANDRE MUSEUM OF TEXTILES,** 950 Third Ave, 10022. Tel 212-361-8500. *Founder & Pres* Franco Scalamandre; *Dir* Serena Hortian
Open 9 AM - 5 PM; cl Sat, Sun and National holidays. Estab 1947 to encourage interest in textile design for decoration
Collections: Contemporary textiles showing modern motifs in textured weaves of today; reproductions of old textiles; 2000 old documentary pieces of textile
Exhibitions: 15 small student exhibits for art schools, colleges (must be requested by faculty member); permanent display of textiles used in ?Historic Restorations
Activities: Lect given on history of textile design, including the classification of textiles, both period and modern; traveling exhibits in the various periods of decorative art for circulation throughout the United States to museums only

L **SCHOOL OF VISUAL ARTS LIBRARY,** 209 E 23rd St, New York, NY. (Mailing Add: 380 Second Ave, New York, NY 10010) Tel 212-679-7350, Ext 67. *Chief Librn* Zuki Landau; *Cataloger* Rosemary Pandolfi; *Cataloger* Joan Arnold; *Slide Cur* Cynthia Roberts
Open Mon - Thurs 9 AM - 7:30 PM, Fri 9 AM - 5 PM, Sat 11 AM - 4 PM exculsively for student and faculty use. Estab 1962 to serve needs of School of Visual Arts students and faculty. Circ 32,500. Small gallery space for student work
Income: Financed by tuition
Purchases: $37,785
Library Holdings: Vols 20,000; Per subs 178; AV—Cassettes, rec, slides; Other—Clipping files, exhibition catalogs, framed reproductions, prints 38,000, original art works, pamphlets, photographs 28,000, reproductions, sculpture
Special Subjects: Art History, Film, Photography, Sculpture, media arts, painting
Exhibitions: Master Eagle Family of Companies' exhibition; student exhibitions
Publications: Library Handbook; monthly accessions lists
Activities: Poetry readings are held

SCULPTORS GUILD, INC
For further information, see National and Regional Organizations

M **SCULPTURE CENTER,** 167 E 69th St, 10021. Tel 212-879-0430. *Pres* Arthur F Abelman; *Treas* Victor Tamerlis; *VPres* John Gilman; *VPres* Barbara Lekberg; *Secy* Nancy Russell; *Dir* Mary Stiles; *School Dir* Gary Sussman
Open Tues - Sat 11 AM - 5 PM. No admis fee. Estab 1928 as Clay Club of New York to further the interest of student and professional sculptors. Incorporated in 1944 as the Sculpture Center, a nonprofit organization for the promotion of the art of sculpture and to provide work facilities. Moved into the new building in 1950, when the present name was adopted. A gallery is maintained, and has represented in it approximately 40 professional sculptors. School and studio space can be provided for beginning, intermediate and advanced students. Average Annual Attendance: 35,000
Exhibitions: Solo and group exhibitions throughout the year
Publications: Announcements (for the gallery and school); brochures; exhibition catalogs
Activities: Lectures; special events on Sat
L **Library,** 167 E 69th St, 10021.
Library Holdings: Vols 200

C **JOSEPH E SEAGRAM & SONS, INC,** 375 Park Ave, 10022. Tel 212-572-7379. *In Charge Art Coll* Carla Caccamise Ash
Open to public. No admis fee. Estab 1958 for the enjoyment of Seagram employees. Collection displayed in offices and reception areas; permanent gallery on 4th floor, used for temporary art exhibitions, both loan and in-house
Collections: 19th and 20th Century American photographs of urban life; antique glass, European and American; 20th Century drawings, graphics, paintings, posters and tapestries
Exhibitions: Temporary installations of notable sculpture on Plaza; several loan exhibitions
Activities: Lect; tours Tues 3 PM; individual objects of art lent for selected musuem exhibitions; originate traveling exhibitions

SOCIETY OF AMERICAN GRAPHIC ARTISTS
For further information, see National and Regional Organizations

SOCIETY OF ILLUSTRATORS
For further information, see National and Regional Organizations

O **SOHO CENTER FOR VISUAL ARTISTS,** 110-114 Prince St, 10012. Tel 212-226-1933, 226-1995. *Founder & Pres* Larry Aldrich
Open Tues - Fri Noon - 5 PM, Sat 11 AM - 5 PM, cl Aug. No admis fee. Estab 1974, a non-profit activity sponsored by the Aldrich Museum of Contemporary Art and the Mobil Foundation. An Exhibition Center was established for the purpose of showing the work of new artists who are not represented by a commercial gallery. Average Annual Attendance: 50,000
Exhibitions: Changing monthly

L **Library,** 110-114 Prince St, 10012.
For reference only, and includes materials specifically for the working artist
Library Holdings: Vols 2000; Per subs 40; Other—Pamphlets

M **SOUTH STREET SEAPORT MUSEUM,*** 16 Fulton, 10038. Tel 212-766-9020. *Pres* John B Hightower; *Dir Educ* Jane Clark
Open daily 11 AM - 6 PM. Admis adults $1.50, children 75¢, museum mem free. Estab 1967 to preserve the maritime history and traditions of the Port of New York. Several gallery spaces: The Seaport Gallery for art exhibits; the model ship gallery; the printing press gallery at Bowne & Co Stationers; the museum orientation center. Mem: 9000; dues family $25, individual $15; annual meeting May
Income: Financed by membership and corporate grants
Collections: Collection is mainly the buildings and ships and the neighborhood they define; small permanent collection of marine art and artifacts; Palmer Collection of ship models
Exhibitions: John DePol: The Wood Engraver's Art; In Celebration of Fish; 19th Century prints of fish and fishing scenes, highlighting the Fulton Fish Market
Publications: South Street Packet, bi-monthly; South Street Reporter, quarterly
Activities: Classes for adults and children; walking tours of area; lect open to public, 10 - 15 visiting lectr per year; concerts; individual paintings and original objects of art lent to institutions; lending collection contains 200 original prints, paintings, ship models; museum shop sells books, magazines, original art, reproductions, prints and slides
L **Library,*** 16 Fulton, 10038. Tel 212-766-9047. *Librn* Gerard Boardman
For reference
Library Holdings: Vols 3000; Per subs 20; Other—Photographs, negatives

SPECIAL LIBRARIES ASSOCIATION
For further information, see National and Regional Organizations

M **STUDIO MUSEUM IN HARLEM,** 2033 Fifth Ave, 10035. Tel 212-427-5959. *Executive Dir* Mary S Campbell; *Deputy Dir* William Day; *Membership Dir* Cathy Chance Connors; *Cur* Terrie Rouse; *Registrar* Pat Marian Bell; *Bookkeeper* Angela Sinyda
Open Tues - Fri 10 AM - 6 PM; Sat & Sun 1 - 6 PM. Suggested admis $1. Estab 1968 to exhibit the works of contemporary Black American Artists, mount historical and informative exhibitions, and provide culturally educational programs and activities for the general public. 4500 sq ft of exhibition space. Average Annual Attendance: 100,000. Mem: 400; dues $10 - $1000
Income: Financed by membership, city and state appropriation, and corporate funding
Collections: James Van Der Zee Collection of Photography; 200 works of art by Afro-American artists including sculpture, painting and works on paper
Exhibitions: Impressions-Expressions: A Survey of Blacks in Printmaking; New York - Chicago: The Black Artist and the WPA
Publications: Catalogues of major black artists
Activities: Classes for adults and children; school program; lect open to the public, 5 vis lectr per yr; concerts; gallery talks; tours; museum shop selling books, magazines, original art, reproductions, prints, postcards and pottery

O **FREDERICK THOMPSON FOUNDATION, INC,** 441 E 20th St, 10010. Tel 212-533-6631. ; *Executive Dir* Mrs Frederick Thompson
Open Sat and by appointment. Estab 1956 and incorporated 1962 to provide a center where there may be study, discussion and the production of creative arts. A program of activities planned to create a sense of appreciation of art and particularly the art of painting. Average Annual Attendance: Over 5000; annual meeting Oct; board meets quarterly
Collections: Over 300 paintings by Frederick Thompson, all excellent examples of Trompe L'Oeil technique
Exhibitions: Lincoln Center Museum of the Performing Arts, New York
Activities: Programs with color slides and tapes free to New York City residents for presentations. Instructional outlines also available; slide and film shows; loan collection of color plates from American and European museums on Giotto, Raphael, Halls, Vermeer, Rembrandt, Chardin, Copley, Homer, Cezanne, Eakins and Van Gogh; essays by Frederick Thompson on the above masters available upon request

M **TRAPHAGEN SCHOOL OF FASHION,** Museum Collection, 257 Park Ave S, 10010. Tel 212-673-1300. *Cur Museum Coll* Florita Raupt
Open to public by appointment only. No admis fee. Estab 1923 to record fashion changes through the centuries; to use the collection as another means of teaching history of costume; to use the items as inspiration for new design ideas. Exhibition area in Reception Hall. Trunk showings for students, guests or designers (by appointment) in Museum Workroom are also given
Collections: Bride and bridegroom folk costumes around the world; ethnic dolls in native costume; extensive African and American Indian costumes and jewelry; famous women in history; famous women in the theatre; four doll collections, including children of the 19th and 20th centuries; over 1000 period and ethnic costumes, plus fashion accessories
Exhibitions: Antique Laces; Beaded Chemises of the Twenties; Children of the 19th and 20th Centuries; Gloves and Fans; Period Bridal Gowns; Undercover Fashions 1840-1910
Activities: Educ dept; docent training; tours
L **Library,** 257 Park Ave S, 10010. Tel 212-673-0300. *Librn* Barbara German
Open to public by appointment. Estab 1923 to stimulate inquiry into new areas of fashion and allied fields; to give students of fashion design, illustration, or interior design the opportunity to explore related subjects in depth
Library Holdings: Vols 16,000; Per subs 10; AV—Slides; Other—Clipping files, memorabilia, pamphlets
Special Subjects: Fashion Arts, Inter Design
Collections: Bound volumes of early fashion magazines including: Graham's Magazine; Journal des Dames et Modes (1798-1840); Journal des Demoiselles (1870-1907); La Art et La Mode (1880-1915); Ladies' Companion; Les Medes (1903-1936); Les Modes and Usages du temps de Marie Antoinnette (1787-1792), 2 vols; Studio and Illustration Magazine of Fine and Applied Arts, 41 Vols
Activities: Library tours

M UKRAINIAN MUSEUM, 203 Second Ave, 10003. Tel 212-228-0110. *Pres* Dr B Cymbalsity; *VPres* Dr K Rohozynsky; *Secy* O Bajko; *Secy* Mrs M Sawchak; *Dir* Maria Shust; *Admin Dir* Daria Bajko; *Cur* Oksana Grabowicz; *Development Officer* Natalia Rybak; *Public Relations* Lesia Gajdycz
Open Wed - Sun 1 - 5 PM. Admis adults $1, sr citizens, students & children 50¢. Estab 1976 to preserve, maintain, expand and exhibit its permanent collection of Ukrainian and Folk Art and its photographic and document collection on Ukrainian immigration. Average Annual Attendance: 13,000. Mem: 600; dues family $50, adults $25, sr citizens $10
Income: $94,000 (financed by membership, donations and grants)
Purchases: $2000
Collections: Fine arts, photographs and documents; major crafts in Ukrainian Folk Art; Ukrainian Easter eggs; ceramics, metalwork, woodwork, woven and embroidered textiles (including costumes), kilims
Exhibitions: Children's Art Exhibit; Nikifor, The Naive Painter of Krynica; Pysanka and its Symbols; Pysanka, The Ukrainian Easter Egg; Samvydav, Uncensored Writings from Ukrainian and the Soviet Union; Traditional Designs in Ukrainian Textiles; Ukrainian Embroidery Crafts; Ukrainian Folk Art from the Carpathian Mountains; Ukrainian Folk Ceramics from the Carpathian Mountains
Publications: Annual report; bulletins; bilingual exhibition catalogs or brochures
Activities: Classes for adults and children and workshops on Ukrainian Easter Eggs and Christmas decorations; embroidery and woodcarving courses; lect open to public, 3 visiting lectr per year; tours; original objects of art lent to museums; lending collection contains 300 slides, 200 Ukrainian woven and embroidered textiles; sales shop sells books, reproductions, prints, slides, embroideries, ceramics, wooden inlayed items and jewlery
L Library, 203 Second Ave, New York, NY 10003.
Library for internal use only
Library Holdings: Vols 200; AV—Slides 600; Other—Exhibition catalogs, photographs
Special Subjects: Ukrainian Fine and Folk Art

L UNION OF AMERICAN HEBREW CONGREGATIONS, Synagogue Art and Architectural Library, 838 Fifth Ave, 10021. Tel 212-249-0100. *Dir* Myron E Schoen
Open Mon - Fri 9:30 AM - 5 PM; cl Sat & Sun. Estab 1957. For use on premises only
Library Holdings: Vols 200
Special Subjects: Synagogue Architecture; Ceremonial Objects and Art
Publications: An American Synagogue for Today and Tomorrow (book); Contemporary Synagogue Art (book)
Activities: Slide rental service

UNITED STATES COMMITTEE OF THE INTERNATIONAL ASSOCIATION OF ART, INC
For further information, see National and Regional Organizations

L UNIVERSITY CLUB LIBRARY, 1 W 54th St, 10019. Tel 212-572-3428. *Dir* Guy StClair; *Asst Dir* R Smith
Open to members and qualified scholars (inquire by letter first) Mon - Sat 10 AM - 5 PM. Estab 1865 for the promotion of the arts and culture in post-university graduates. Art is displayed in all areas of the building. Average Annual Attendance: 7000. Mem: 4250
Income: Financed by endowments and membership
Library Holdings: Vols 135,000
Collections: Art; architecture, fine bindings

VISUAL ARTISTS AND GALLERIES ASSOCIATION, INC
For further information, see National and Regional Organizations

M WARD-NASSE GALLERY, 178 Prince St, 10012. Tel 212-925-6950. *Dir* Harry Nasse; *Asst Dir* Maggie Reilly
Open Tues - Sat 11 AM - 5:30 PM. No admis fee. Estab 1969 to provide an artist-run gallery; also serves as resource center for artists and public; to provide internships for students. Cooperative gallery with four-person and larger salon shows. Average Annual Attendance: 7000. Mem: 150; dues four-person $500 1st year, $450 2nd year, salon $250 1st year, $150 2nd year; meeting every 2 months
Income: Financed by membership
Exhibitions: (1980) Siri Berg - Solo Exhibition; three and four person shows
Publications: Gallery catalog, every two years; newsletter, bimonthly
Activities: Lect open to public, lect by artist members; concerts; gallery talks; tours; performances; auctions; book traveling exhibitions 3 per year
L Library, 178 Prince St, 10012.
Open Tues - Sat 11 AM - 5:30 PM. Estab 1969 to provide biographical information and slides of artists' work; to provide information on the art events in the area
Library Holdings: Vols 100; Per subs 4; Other—Clipping files, exhibition catalogs, prints, memorabilia, original art works, pamphlets, photographs, sculpture

M WHITNEY MUSEUM OF AMERICAN ART, 945 Madison Ave, 10021. Tel 212-794-0600. *Dir* Thomas N Armstrong III; *Adminr* Palmer Wald; *Cur* Jennifer Russell; *Cur* Patterson Sims; *Cur* Barbara Haskell; *Cur* Gail Levin; *Cur* Richard Marshall; *Cur* Patricia Hills; *Cur* Paul Cummings; *Educ Head* David Hupert; *Educ Cur* Helen Ferrulli; *Development Officer* Jane E Heffner
Open Tues 11 AM - 9 PM, Wed - Sat 11 AM - 6 PM, Sun Noon - 6 PM. Admis $2, no admis Tues 6 - 9 PM. Estab 1930, incorporated 1931 by Gertrude Vanderbilt Whitney for the advancement of contemporary American art; Museum opened 1931 and moved to 54th Street in 1954; new building opened in 1966
Income: Financed by endowment, admissions, grants, membership
Collections: Drawings, paintings, prints, sculpture; work is mainly 20th century American artists
Exhibitions: (1978-1980) Abstract Expressionism: The Formative Years; New Image Painting; (1979) Edward Hopper: Prints and Illustrations; Photography Rediscovered: American Photographs, 1900-1930; George Segal Sculptures; David Smith: The Drawings; Tradition and Modernism in American Art, 1900-1930; Cy Twombly; Andy Warhol: Portraits of the 70's; Whitney Biennial, 1979; William Carlos Williams and the American Scene (1980) American Sculpture: Gifts of Howard and Jean Lipman; Figurative Paintings and Sculpture in 20th Century American Art; Marsden Hartley; Edward Hopper: The Art and the Artist; Isamu

Noguchi: Imaginary Landscapes; Myron Stout: American Folk Painters of Three Centuries
Activities: Museum studies and studio program for graduate students; courses seminars with artists; lect open to public; weekend lect; concerts; gallery talks; tours; fels; Artreach provides introductory art education to elementary and high school students
L Library, 945 Madison Ave, 10021. Tel 212-570-3649.
Open Tues - Fri 10 AM - Noon & 2 - 5 PM by appointment for advanced research. No admis fee. Estab 1931 for encouragement and advancement of American art and art scholarship
Purchases: $10,000
Library Holdings: Vols 10,000; Per subs 50; Micro—Reels; AV—A-tapes, cassettes, rec, slides; Other—Clipping files, exhibition catalogs, manuscripts, memorabilia, pamphlets, photographs, reproductions
Special Subjects: Focuses on 20th century American drawing, graphics, painting and sculpture
M Downtown Branch, 55 Water St, 10041. *Dir* David Hupert
Open Mon - Fri 11 AM - 3 PM. No admis fee. Operated by students participating in the Education Department Independent Study Program
Income: Financed by the lower Manhattan business community and the National Endowment for the Arts
Exhibitions: (1979-80) Artists by Artists; Auto Icons; Dada and New York; Enclosure and Concealment; Industrial Sights; Making Money; Painting in Relief; Sculpture in the Age of Painting, 1943-57; Stuart Davis, Charles Sheeler, Joseph Stella
Activities: Performances; gallery talks
O Friends of the Whitney Museum of American Art, 945 Madison Ave, 10021.
Since their founding in 1956, the Friends have contributed a large number of important works of art to the permanent collection as well as supporting other parts of the museum's program. Mem: Approx 700; dues Whitney and Corporate members $1000, individual or couple $250, junior members $100 for persons up to age 30

O CATHARINE LORILLARD WOLFE ART CLUB, INC, 802 Broadway, 10003. Tel 212-254-2000. *Pres* Carey Boone Nelson; *First VPres* Cecilia Cardman; *Treas* Sybil D'Orsi; *Recording Secy* Patricia Sprouls; *Corresponding Secy* Jacquie-Louise Gray
Estab 1896, inc 1963, to further fine, representational American Art. A club of professional women painters and sculptors. Mem: 250; dues $15, associate membership $10; monthly meetings
Exhibitions: 84th Open Annual Exhibition; members exhibition
Activities: Metropolitan Museum Benefit, annually; Lect; demonstration programs; scholarships offered

O WOMEN IN THE ARTS FOUNDATION, INC, 325 Spring St, 10013. Tel 212-691-0988. *Pres* Joyce Weinstein; *VPres & Action Chmn* Evelyn Eisgrau; *Secy* Alice Phillips; *Treas* Ann Kronenberg; *Coordr* Joyce Weinstein; *Mem Chmn* Freda Pond; *Public Appearance Chmn* Lisa Shainswit; *Public Appearance Chm* Jackie Skiles; *Publicity Chmn & Funding Chmn* Carol Hamoy; *Slide Registry Chmn* Ruth Jacobsen; *Program Chmn* Jean Zaleski; *Museum Liaison Chmn* Rebecca Weisberg; *In-House Gallery Chmn* Christina Rang; *Area Liaison* Annette Nachumi; *Newsletter Editor* Catherine de Bary
Open Tues & Sat 2 - 5 PM. Estab 1971 for the purpose of overcoming discrimination against women artists both in government and the private sector. Gallery is located in the Soho district of New York City, and exhibits the work of women artists, both established and unknown. Average Annual Attendance: 300. Mem: 300; dues $25
Income: $12,000 (financed by endowment, membership)
Collections: Artists Choice; Eleven Women Artists; Four Artists at WIA; Paintings and Sculpture at Fort Lee
Exhibitions: (1978-80) Lincoln Center Colk Gallery Group Show; Linda Shearer - curator - Group Show; Lucy Lippard Group Show
Publications: Women in the Arts, bulletin-newsletter, monthly
Activities: Classes for adults; public education as to the problems and discrimination faced by women artists; lect open to the public, 10 vis lectr per year; individual paintings and original objects of art lent to museum and university art galleries for special exhibitions; lending collection contains 1500 slides; original art works for exhibitions are obtained from member artists; traveling exhibitions organized and circulated; sales shop selling catalogs of own exhibitions

M WOMEN'S INTERART CENTER, INC, Interart Gallery, 549 W 52 St, 10019. Tel 212-246-1050. *Pres* Marguerite A L Lewitin; *VPres* Stanley Waren; *Secy* Luana Cleveland; *Mgr Dir* Abigail Franklin; *Cur* Francyne de St Amand
Open Mon - Fri Noon - 6 PM. No admis fee. Estab 1970 to present to the public the work of significant, emerging women artists. Average Annual Attendance: 9000. Mem: Dues $25
Income: Financed by state appropriation, National Endowment for the Arts and private foundations
Exhibitions: Helene Brandt, Sculptures; Janet Culbertson, Drawings; Susan Dallas, Light Machines; Wopo Holup, Constructions; Susan Milano, Nancy Cain, Bart Criedman, Backseat Video Installation; Mary Obering Paintings
Activities: Classes for adults; lect open to public, 2 visiting lectr per year; originate traveling exhibitions

NORTHPORT

L NORTHPORT-EAST NORTHPORT PUBLIC LIBRARY, Art Dept, 151 Laurel Ave, 11768. Tel 516-261-6930. *Dir* Victoria Wallace; *Asst Dir* Frances Ingram
Open Mon - Fri 9 AM - 9 PM, Sat 9 AM - 5 PM, Sun 1 - 5 PM, Oct - May. Estab 1914. Circ 476,240
Income: $878,004 (financed by state appropriation, local tax levy)
Purchases: $100,812 (book budget)
Exhibitions: Inga Bassinette (acrylic paintings and sculpture); Sanford Blumenthal (water colors); Eleanor Braun (watercolors); Ruth Brooks (oil paintings); Paula Brown (abstract watercolors); Richard Cardiff (oil & watercolors); Charlene Cawley (acrylics on canvas and wood); Jeanne Cooke (oils); Miriam Dougenis (watercolors); William Dula (sports paintings); Bonnie Gardner (oils, watercolors, sculpture); Eloise Gardner (watercolors); Shirley Geller (oil paintings); Jean Gentile (oils & acrylics); Nicky Goldblatt (ink & color pictures); Donald Holmes (watercolors); Robin Hotchkiss (multi-media); Lois Kfoury (mixed media, sculpture and pottery); Olga Leone (watercolors); Evelyn Lucas (watercolors); Florence Muller (watercolors); Ann-Marie Murphy (watercolors); Tom O'Brien (pewter statuary); Pat Olds (pastels & watercolors, sculpture); Carol Packard (watercolors, acrylics & silk screen); Lucille Pinto (oils and pastels); John M Scarola (nautical oil paintings); Doris Steinman (watercolors); Connie Swanan (oils); Cynthia Tanenbaum (etchings: color, black & white); Ruth Waldenburg (watercolors)

NORTH SALEM

M HAMMOND MUSEUM, Museum of the Humanities, Deveau Rd, 10560. Tel 914-669-5033. *Dir* Natalie Hays Hammond; *Assoc Dir* Elizabeth H Taylor
Open May - Dec, Wed - Sun 11 AM - 5 PM. Admis to Museum, adults $1.50, children $1; to the Gardens, adults $1.50, children $1. Incorporated in 1957 as a non-profit, educational institution; absolute charter from New York State Board of Regents 1962. A Museum of the Humanities, it presents changing exhibitions of international scope and varied historic periods and topics, supplemented by programs of related special events. The Oriental Stroll Gardens comprising 15 individual gardens on 3 1 2 acres, include a lake, a reflecting pool, a dry landscape, a waterfall, and a Zen Garden. Average Annual Attendance: 35,000. Mem: 1800; Qualifications for mem: Open to all who are in sympathy with its aims and purposes
Activities: Dramatic programs; lect open to the public; concerts; documentary films; museum shop; Terrace Restaurant, luncheon by reservation

OGDENSBURG

M REMINGTON ART MUSEUM, 303 Washington St, 13669. Tel 315-393-2425. *Dir* Mildred Dillenbeck; *Secy Receptionist* Ruth Hunter; *Secy Receptionist* Beverly Walker
Open Mon - Sat 10 AM - 5 PM, Sun 1 - 5 PM, cl Sun in winter. Admis adults $1, students 12 and over 50¢. Estab 1923 to house and exhibit the major works of art of Frederic Remington. The museum is in the converted Parish Mansion which was built in 1809-10; the newly constructed Addie Priest Newell Galleries display the major Remington artifacts. Remington's last studio has been reconstructed with most of the original furnishings. Average Annual Attendance: 13,000
Income: Financed by endowment and city appropriation
Collections: Remington artifacts, painting, bronzes, oils and watercolors; studies in plaster by Edwin Willard Deming; sculpture by Sally James Farnham; Haskell collection of 19th century American and European paintings; Parish Collection of Belter furniture; Sharp Collection of period glass, china, silver and cameos
Activities: Tours; sales shop sells prints, slides, post cards, plates, spoons and rings
L Library, 303 Washington St, 13669.
Remington's own personal library for viewing purposes only

OLD CHATHAM

M SHAKER MUSEUM, Shaker Museum Rd, 12136. Tel 518-794-9100. *Dir* Peter Laskovski; *Admin Asst* Claire Wheeler; *Cur* Ruth Roberts; *Registrar* Maria Larsen
Open May - Oct daily 10 AM - 5:30 PM. Admis adults $2.50, Senior citizens $2, youths $1.50, children 75¢. Estab 1950 to promote interest in and understanding of the Shaker cultural heritage. The exhibits are housed in a complex of eight buildings. Average Annual Attendance: 20,000. Mem: 200; dues $15
Income: $150,000 (financed by endowment and membership)
Purchases: $3000
Collections: 19000 artifacts representing 200 years of Shaker history and culture
Exhibitions: Intro to Shaker History; Crafts and Industries; agriculture; workshops and period rooms; changing exhibits
Publications: Newsletter; The Shaker Adventure; Shaker Seed Industry; Pamphlets; booklets; gallery guide; catalogs; postcards, slides, reprints, and broadsides
Activities: Seminars; lect open to public; festivals; craft fairs; gallery talks; tours; community showcase program of regional contemporary art, other special events; traveling exhibitions organized and circulated; museum shop sells books, magazines, original art, reproductions, prints and slides
L Emma B King Library, Shaker Museum Rd, 12136.
Open to qualified persons by appointment
Collections: Manuscripts and records; Photographic and map archive

OLD WESTBURY

M NEW YORK INSTITUTE OF TECHNOLOGY GALLERY, Wheatly Rd, 11568. Tel 516-686-7542. *Associate Dir Fine Arts Dept* John Murray
Open Mon - Fri 9 AM - 5 PM. Estab 1964. Gallery maintained for the many exhibits held during the year
Exhibitions: Annual faculty and student shows; some traveling exhibitions
Activities: Classes in custom silk-screen printmaking

L Art & Architectural Library, Old Westbury, 11771. Tel 516-686-7579. *Librn* Hong Kyung Elizabeth Ahmedi
Open Mon - Thurs 8:30 AM - 9 PM; Fri 8:30 AM - 6 PM. Estab 1976. Maintains an art gallery
Library Holdings: Vols 8800; Per subs 100; Micro—Reels; AV—A-tapes, cassettes, fs, slides, v-tapes; Other—Clipping files, exhibition catalogs, pamphlets, photographs
Special Subjects: Architecture
Activities: Educ dept; classes for children; lect open to public, 10 vis lectr per yr; concerts; gallery talks; tours; competitions with awards; scholarships and fellowships

ONEIDA

M MADISON COUNTY HISTORICAL SOCIETY, 435 Main St, 13421. Tel 315-363-4136. *Pres* F Newberry; *VPres* H Hood; *Secy* D Gradel; *Dir* John H Braunlein; *Cur* Mildred Stress
Open June 1 - Aug 31, daily 9 AM - 5 PM, Sat & Sun 1 - 4 PM, Sept 1 - May 31, Daily Mon - Fri 9 AM - 5 PM. No admis fee. Estab 1898 to collect, preserve and interpret artifacts indigenous to the history of Madison County. 1849 AJ Davis Gothic dwelling with period rooms, library and Craft Archive. Average Annual Attendance: 3500. Mem: 1000; dues $5; annual meeting second Monday of November
Income: $44,000 (financed by endowment, membership, county, city and state appropriation, Annual Craft Fair)
Collections: Locally produced and or used furnishings, paintings, silver, textiles and ceramics
Exhibitions: Forces: Thru forces in the Lives of New Yorkers; The Chittenango Pottery
Publications: Monthly Newsletter; Madison County Heritage, published annually; Studies in Traditional American Crafts, annually
Activities: Educational outreach programs for nursing homes and schools; lectures open to the public, 11 visiting lecturers per year; slides, tapes and movies documenting traditional craftsmen at work; individual paintings and original objects of art lent to qualified museums and galleries for special exhibits; sales shop sells books, magazines, prints and slides
L Library, 435 Main St, 13421.
Open Mon - Fri 9 AM - 5 PM. Estab 1975 as a reference library of primary and secondary sources on Madison County History
Library Holdings: Vols 2500; Per subs 5; AV—Cassettes, lantern Slides, motion pictures, rec, slides, v-tapes; Other—Clipping files, exhibition catalogs, prints, manuscripts, memorabilia, pamphlets, photographs
Special Subjects: Madison County and New York State History, Civil War, Oneida Indians
Collections: Gerrit Smith family papers

ONEONTA

M HARTWICK COLLEGE FINE ART GALLERY, Anderson Center for the Arts, 13820. Tel 607-432-4200. *Cur* K Christine Flom
Open Mon - Fri 1 - 4 PM, or by appointment; cl last half of Dec. No admis fee. Estab 1928, college collections and exhibitions for benefit of faculty, students and community
Collections: Painting, prints, drawings, sculpture, ceramics, and tapestry from 15th through 20th centuries: Van Ess collection of Renaissance and Baroque paintings and drawings; 19th century American Landscapes from Van Ess and Merritt Collections; 260 American political cartoons by John H Cassell
Exhibitions: Changing Exhibitions to meet curriculum needs
Activities: Classes in museum studies; lectures; guided tours; films
M Yager Museum, Hartwick College, 13820. *Dir* Jane des Grange; *Cur* Richard Rose
Open Mon - Fri 10 AM - 4 PM, closed holidays. Estab 1928
Collections: Collection of North American, Mexican and South American Indian Art and artifacts
Exhibitions: Changing exhibitions
Activities: Classes in museum studies; lectures; tours; films
L Yager Museum Library, Anderson Center for the Arts, 13820.
Small collection of books on history of the American Indian can be used on premises upon request

M STATE UNIVERSITY OF NEW YORK COLLEGE AT ONEONTA, * Fine Arts Center, 13820. Tel 607-431-3500. *Chmn Art Dept* James M Mullen
Estab 1972 to offer students, staff and visitors an opportunity to view current as well as past artistic styles and works. Art Gallery and Sculpture Court are major features of the Art Wing
Income: Financed by city and state appropriation
Activities: Lect open to the public, 8 visiting lectrs per year; extensive exhibition program

OSWEGO

M STATE UNIVERSITY OF NEW YORK AT OSWEGO, Tyler Art Gallery, 13126. Tel 315-341-2113. *Dir* Coy L Ludwig; *Gallery Asst* Mindy Ostrow; *Designer* Judith Benedict; *Secy* Ellen Wiggins
Open Mon - Fri 9:30 AM - 4:30 PM, Sept - May; summer hours as posted. No admis fee. Estab as a teaching gallery. Located in Tyler Hall as part of the Fine Arts Complex. Average Annual Attendance: 25,000 - $30,000
Income: Financed by University funds
Collections: Arnold Collection of Fine Prints; Contemporary American Prints and Paintings
Exhibitions: Two galleries show a combined total of 20 exhibitions per school year
Publications: Brochures; occasional catalogs for exhibitions; posters
Activities: Lect; originates traveling exhibitions

PORT CHESTER

M MUSEUM OF CARTOON ART, Comly Ave, 10573. Tel 914-939-0234. *Pres* Mort Walker; *Dir* Charles Green; *Dir* Brian Walker; *Secy* Veronica Nasca
Open Tues - Fri 10 AM - 4 PM, Sun 1 - 5 PM, cl Sat and Mon. Admis adults $1, senior citizens and children under 12 50¢
Collections: Animated Film Collection, videotape; Cartoon Hall of Fame; Comics collection from 1896 to the present; early and contemporary original cartoon art; Walt Disney display showing the various steps used to produce animated cartoons
Publications: Tad Dorgan, Story of America in Cartoons; Dick Tracy: The Art of Chester Gould
Activities: Educ program; lectures; Sales shop
L Library, Comly Ave, 10573.
Collections: Archives collection

L PORT CHESTER PUBLIC LIBRARY, 1 Haselo Ave, 10573. *Dir* 10; *Reference Librn* Carol Woodger; *Art Dir* Winifred DeVeau; *Young Adult Librn* Robin Mendel; *Childrens Librn* Phyllis Kunstler
Open Mon 9 AM - 9 PM, Tues & Wed 9 AM - 8 PM, Thurs - Sat 9 AM - 5 PM. Estab 1876 to circulate books, records, magazines, to the general public to provide reference services. Circ 112,637. Maintains an art gallery. A small gallery with about ten shows per year, mostly local artists
Income: $275,215 (financed by endowment, city and state appropriation)
Purchases: $37,669
Library Holdings: Vols 96,894; Per subs 219; Micro—Reels; AV—Fs, rec, slides; Other—Framed reproductions, prints, pamphlets
Exhibitions: Water colors, oils, acrylics, photographs
Activities: lectures, concerts, films; open to the public

POTSDAM

M POTSDAM PUBLIC MUSEUM, Civic Center, 13676. *Pres of Board* Dr James Levitt; *Dir - Cur* Katherine F Wyant; *Asst Cur* Klara Lovass Nagy; *Registrar* Sharon Dresye; *Secy* Mrs F A Ramsdell
Open Tues - Sat 2 - 5 PM, cl Sun & Mon. No admis fee. Estab 1940 as an educational institution acting as a cultural and historical center for the Village of Potsdam and surrounding area. Educational services taken to area schools. Museum occupies a sandstone building, formerly a Universalist Church built in 1876. Average Annual Attendance: 6500; annual meeting Nov
Income: $35,000 (financed by city and state appropriation)
Collections: Burnap Collection of English Pottery; costumes of the 19th and 20th centuries; Mandarin Chinese hangings, china and costumes; photograph collection and artifacts and material on local history; pressed glass and art glass of the 19th and early 20th century
Exhibitions: Cranberry Glass; Charles Edison Fund Exhibit; Faberge-Style Decorated Eggs; From Old China; Ironside China; History of Lighting; Local History; New York State Forces Exhibit; Wedding Party; Wrapping Up (coats and capes)
Publications: Newsletter, ten times per year
Activities: Classes for adults and children; programs for schools craft days; lect open to public, 8 vis lectr per year; concerts; tours
L Library, Civic Center, 13676.
For reference only
Library Holdings: Vols 300
Special Subjects: Antiques, Local History, Early American Crafts

M STATE UNIVERSITY OF NEW YORK COLLEGE AT POTSDAM, Brainerd Art Gallery, Pierrepont Ave, 13676. Tel 315-268-5040, 268-2710. *Art Department Chmn* Dr Mark Sandler; *Gallery Dir* Dr Kendall Taylor; *Secy* Mary Haught
Open Mon - Fri 1 - 5 PM, 7 - 9 PM, Sat & Sun 1 - 5 PM. No admis fee. Estab 1967 to serve college and community as a teaching gallery. Gallery associated with Art Department. Average Annual Attendance: 18,000
Income: Operating budget $15,000 (financed by state appropriation)
Collections: Roland Gibson Collection, contemporary Japanese, Italian and American Art (painting, sculpture and prints); †contemporary drawing collection; †contemporary painting collection; †contemporary prints collection; †contemporary sculpture collection
Exhibitions: Alumni Show; Annual Sucp Student Show; Black and White: Two views of New York City During the Depression; Clay, Fiber, Metal; 15th National Print Exhibition; Historic Courthouses of New York State; Political Comment in Contemporary Art; student and faculty exhibitions
Activities: Lect open to the public, 6 visiting lectr per year; concerts; gallery talks; tours; competitions; original objects of art lent; traveling exhibitions organized and circulated

POUGHKEEPSIE

M MID-HUDSON ARTS AND SCIENCE CENTER, 228 Main St, 12601. Tel 914-471-1155. *Pres* Leonard Zimmerman; *VPres* David Tucker; *Secy* Josephine Dumas; *Dir* Paul Gershowitz; *Dir of Performing Arts* Joan Sellers; *Dir Education* Laurie Shapiro
Open Tues - Sat 10 AM - 6 PM, Sun Noon - 5 PM, Thurs 10 AM - 9 PM. Admis adults 25¢, children 10¢. Estab 1977 as a museum for all people. Main gallery approx 35 x 60 ft, community gallery approx 15 x 20 ft, theatre gallery approx 35 x 35. Average Annual Attendance: 5000. Mem: 350; dues $15 family, $10 individual, $5 student
Income: $25,000 (financed by membership, state appropriation, and foundation grants)
Exhibitions: (1978) Painting by Chrichlow; Recent Photographs of China; Turn of the Century Posters from France; Three-dimension reproductions of Leonardo daVinci's inventions by IBM; (1979) A Century of Women Artists in Cragsmoor; Comic Book Art; Inside 42nd Street (photographs); Study in Contrast; Two 20th Century Masters (Calder and Frank Lloyd Wright)
Activities: Classes for adults and children; dramatic programs; lectures open to the public; concerts; gallery talks; tours; competitions with awards; Individual paintings and original objects of art lent to local businesses, schools, government buildings;

traveling exhibition organized and circulated to schools, government buildings; museum shop sells books, magazines, original art, reproductions, prints and import gift items

M VASSAR COLLEGE ART GALLERY, Raymond Ave, 12601. Tel 914-452-7000, Ext 2645. *Dir* William J Hennessey; *Cur* Joan Reid; *Secy* Allegra Knight; *Friends of the Art Gallery Exec Dir* Joan Grennan
Open Mon - Sat 9 AM - 5 PM, Sun 1 - 5 PM. No admis fee. Estab 1864 as a college gallery collecting Eastern and Western art of all periods. The gallery has 6000 sq ft of exhibition space in 1915 Gothic style building. Average Annual Attendance: 9000. Mem: 600; dues $15 - $1000; annual meeting Apr
Income: Financed by membership and endowment
Purchases: $15,000
Collections: Charles M Pratt gift of Italian paintings; Matthew Vassar collection of American paintings of Hudson River School and 19th century English architectural watercolors; Mary Thaw Thompson Collection of 17th century French engravings including works of Nanteuil, Morin; Dexter M Ferry Collection of paintings and etchings; Felix M Warbur Collection of medieval sculpture and of graphics including 54 by Durer and 68 by Rembrandt; Olga Hasbrouck Collection of Chinese ceramics; †European paintings, sculpture and drawings ranging from the Renaissance to the 20th century, including Bacchiacca, Valentin de Boullogne, Cezanne, Salvator Rosa, Claesz, Robert, Corot, Courbet, Delacroix, Tiepolo, Van Gogh, Munch, Klee, Bourdelle, Laurent, Kolbe, Gabo, Calder, Moore; †20th Century American and European paintings including Bacon, Nicholson, Rothko de Kooning, Hartley, Weber, Ryder; graphics ranging from Rembrandt to Rouault, Picasso, Matisse and Braque; The Classical Collection, which was established in 1938, includes Greek vases; Egyptian, Etruscan, and Mycenaean objects ranging from a mummy to tiny bronzes; Roman glass; marble portraits; jewelry; other archaeological finds
Exhibitions: Ivor Abrahams: Retreat; Dutch Scripture Painting of Hudson Valley; Patsy Norvell: Ten Years; Recent Latin American Drawings; Works on Paper from Winston-Malbin Coll
Publications: Gallery, biannually
Activities: Lect open to public, 3 - 4 vis lectr per yr; gallery talks; tours; individual paintings and original objects of art lent to other museums
L Art Library, Raymond Ave, 12601. *Librn* Janis Ekdahl
Open Mon - Thurs 8:30 AM - midnight, Fri 8:30 - 10 PM, Sat 9 AM - 10 PM, Sun 10 AM - 12 PM, cl summers. Estab 1937. Circulation to students and faculty only
Library Holdings: Vols 31,000; Per subs 180

PURCHASE

M MANHATTANVILLE COLLEGE, Brownson Art Gallery, 10577. Tel. 914-946-9600, Ext 331. *Pres* Barbara Knowles Debs; *Dean of Faculty* Dr Marlene Fisher
Open during academic year and summer session
Income: Financed by endowment and tuition
Publications: Magazine, bimonthly; catalogs
Activities: Classes for adults; dramatic programs; concerts; tours; gallery talks
L Manhattanville Library, 10577. *Librn* Dr Robert O'Clair
Library Holdings: Vols 200,000; Per subs 800

M STATE UNIVERSITY OF NEW YORK COLLEGE AT PURCHASE, Neuberger Museum, 10577. Tel 914-253-5087. *Pres* Estelle Tanner; *Dir* Suzanne Delehanty; *Asst Dir* Laurence Shopmaker; *Cur Asst* Laurel Addison; *Museum Mgr* Douglas Caulk; *Public Relations* Barbara Schofield; *Chmn Friends of the Neuberger Museum* Melvin Merians
Open Tues 11 AM - 8 PM, Wed - Fri 11 AM - 5 PM, Sat & Sun 1 - 5 PM, cl Mon and major holidays. No admis fee. Estab 1968, opened May 1974 to serve college and residents of New York State and Connecticut. Mem: Dues sustaining $1000, patron $500, donor $250, contributing $100, family $35
Collections: The Neuberger Museum's permanent collection includes nearly 7000 paintings, drawings, prints, photographs, films, and features 20th-century European and American art, largescale sculptures, African art from Roy R Neuberger, George and Edith Rickey, Hans Richter, Eliot Herschberg and other private donors
Exhibitions: Changing contemporary art exhibitions
Activities: Interpretive program for school and community groups; symposia; lectures; films

ROCHESTER

O AMERICAN BAPTIST HISTORICAL SOCIETY,* 1106 S Goodman St, 14620. Tel 716-473-1740. *Acting Dir* W Hubert Porter
Open Mon - Fri 9 AM - 5 PM, cl Sat, Sun & holidays. No admis fee. Estab 1853 as a religious museum affiliated with American Baptist Convention
Collections: Paintings; pewter; religious historical material; silver
Publications: Foundations, quarterly
L Library,* 1106 S Goodman St, 14620.
Open to the public, under staff supervision
Library Holdings: Vols 55,000; Other—Manuscripts
Collections: Archives; Baptistiana; records

M INTERNATIONAL MUSEUM OF PHOTOGRAPHY AT GEORGE EASTMAN HOUSE, 900 East Ave, 14607. Tel 716-271-3361. *Chmn* Dr Wesley T Hanson; *Acting Dir* Dr John Kuiper; *Asst Dir* Andrew Eskind; *Business Mgr* Dan Meyers; *Equipment* Philip Condax; *Cur* Marianne Margolis; *Cur* Robert Sobieszek; *Cur* Janet Buerger
Open Tues - Sun 10 AM - 4:30 PM, cl Mon. Admis adults $2. Estab 1949 for photography exhibitions, research and education. Average Annual Attendance: 125,000. Mem: 1200; dues $20
Income: Financed by membership, grants and earned income
Collections: Equipment (photographic); film; 19th and 20th century photography
Exhibitions: (1979) Auto As Icon; Electroworks; Kodak No 1; Barbara Morgan; Photographers Hand; Steichen
Publications: Image, quarterly
Activities: Classes for children; docent training; teacher workshops; school

exhibition program; lect open to public; concerts; gallery talks; tours; exten dept; lending collection contains photographs; traveling exhibitions organized and circulated; museum shop selling books, original art, reproductions and prints

L **Archives,** 900 East Ave, 14607. Tel 716-271-3361, Ext 235. *Dir* Susan Wyngaard; *Asst Librn* Mary Widger
Open by appointment only
Income: Financed by trust endowment, admission, traveling exhibitions and loan shows
Purchases: $15,000
Library Holdings: Vols 30,000; Per subs 1200; Micro—Fiche, reels; AV—A-tapes, fs, rec, slides; Other—Clipping files, exhibition catalogs, prints, manuscripts, memorabilia, original art works, pamphlets, photographs, reproductions, autochromes
Special Subjects: History and Aesthetics of Photography
Collections: Alvin Langdon Coburn; Lewis W Hine; Nikolas Muray; Edward Muybridge; Edward Steichen
Exhibitions: (1977-78) An American Century of Photography; Alvin Langdon Coburn; History of Fashion Photography

O ROCHESTER HISTORICAL SOCIETY, 485 East Ave, 14607. Tel 716-271-2705. *Pres* Elizabeth G Holahan; *First VPres* James P Carley; *Second VPres* William E Diez; *Cur* Mary R Shannon; *Cur* Virginia Skuse; *Treas* Eric B Hoard; *Secy* Mrs John J Higgins
Open Mon - Fri 10 AM - 4 PM. Admis adults $1, senior citizens and students 50¢. Headquarters at Woodside, Greek Revival Masion built 1839. Maintains major collection of portraits and scenes relating to Rochester, Reference Library and other collections. Average Annual Attendance: 2500. Mem: 600; dues $10 - $500
Income: Financed by membership

UNIVERSITY OF ROCHESTER

M **Memorial Art Gallery,** 490 University Ave, 14607. Tel 716-275-3081. *Pres Bd of Mgrs* Ramsay Lawless; *Acting Dir* Bruce W Chambers; *Asst Dir* Langdon F Clay; *Adminr* Bernice L Meyer; *Develop Officer* Christine D Hyer; *Cur of Coll* Donald A Rosenthal; *Public Relations Coordr* Karreen Roger-Smith; *Head Membership* Margaret Bennett; *Superintendent* Stan Brew
Open Tues 2 - 9 PM, Wed - Sat 10 AM - 5 PM, Sun 1-5 PM, cl Mon. Admis adults $1.25, children 25¢, senior citizens 50¢; No admis fee Tues 5 - 9 PM and to members, students and children accompanied by adults. Estab 1913 as a university art museum and public art museum for the Rochester area involved in a broad variety of community programs. The building is built in an Italian renaissance style, a new wing built in 1968 reflects a comtemporary style. Average Annual Attendance: 200,000. Mem: 8000; dues $25 and up
Income: $1,065,000
Collections: Covers all major periods and cultural area from Assyria and predynastic Egypt to the present, paintings, sculpture, prints, drawings, decorative arts; Special strengths are medieval, renaissance and 17th century art, 19th and early 20th century French painters, American tribal arts, folk art and contemporary prints
Exhibitions: Contemporary Drawings and Watercolors; George Eastman Collections; Erte'; Kuniyoshi Prints; The Working American
Publications: Gallery Notes, nine times yr; bulletin, annually; exhbition catalogs
Activities: Classes for adults and children; docent training; lect open to the public, 30 vis lectr per yr; concerts; gallery talks; tours; exten department serving Rochester area and surrounding nine counties; individual paintings lent and original objects of art lent to cultural institutions; lending collection contains books, cassettes, color reproductions, framed reproductions, kodachromes, motion pictures, original art works, original prints, paintings, photographs, sculpture and slides; Traveling exhibitions organized and circulated; museum and sales shop sells books, magazines, original art, reproductions and prints

M **Memorial Art Gallery Library,** 490 University Ave, 14607. Tel 716-275-4765. *Librn* Mrs Thomas Nesbit; *Libr Clerk* Grace Field
Open Tues 2 - 4 PM, Wed - Sat 10 AM - 4 PM, Sun 1 -5 PM; cl Mon and July and August. Research library for use of the staff and gallery members
Income: Financed by endowment, membership and city appropriation
Library Holdings: Vols 14,000; Per subs 65

L **Fine Arts Library,** River Campus, 14627. Tel 716-275-4476. *Stephanie/Frontz*
Open Mon - Thurs 9 AM - 10 PM, Fri 9 AM - 8 PM, Sat 12 - 5, Sun 2 - 10 PM. Estab to support academic programs of Fine Arts Department and other academic departments within the University. Small gallery is maintained by Fine Arts Department
Income: $10,000 (financed by private funds)
Purchases: $10,000
Library Holdings: Vols 32,000; Per subs 220; Other—Exhibition catalogs

M **VISUAL STUDIES WORKSHOP,** 31 Prince St, 14607. Tel 716-442-8676. *Dir* Nathan Lyons; *Asst Dir* Alan Winer; *Chmn Board of Trustees* William Parker; *Coordr Exhib* Charles Stainback; *Editor Afterimage* Charles Hagen; *Coordr Print Shop* Joan Lyons; *Coordr Research Center* Helen Brunner; *Coordr Book Distribution* Joe Flaherty; *Coordr Summer Institute* Don Russell
Open Mon - Thurs 9:30 AM - 11 PM, Fri 9:30 AM - 5 PM, Sat 12 - 5 PM. No admis fee. Estab 1969 to establish a center for the transmission and study of the visual image. At this time there are three exhibition spaces at the workshop; one for contemporary imagemakers, one for historical material and one for area artists and artists-in-residence. Average Annual Attendance: 250,000. Mem: 2400; dues $15
Income: $450,000 (financed by membership, state appropriation, federal and corporate sources and earned income)
Special Subjects: Posters, Prints, paintings
Exhibitions: (1978) Group Exhibition: Paul Diamond, John Wood, Tom Gibson, Bruce Horowitz, Bart Parker, John Pfahl, Ken Josephson, Keith Smith, Henry Wessel Jr, Bonnie Gordon, Joseph Jachna; Roger Mertin: Photographs; Joseph Jachna; Mario Giacomelli; Joan Lyons; Eric Renner; Murray Riss. (1979) Book Show; John Divola; Jim Henkel; Bart Parker; John Pfahl; E O Goldbeck: Panoramic Views; Lejaren Hiller; The Image Considered: Recent Work by Women. (1980) Contemporary Issues: Visual Articulation of Idea; William Parker, Joyce Niemanas; Paul Diamond; Les Krims; Ongoing Traditions; Freund, Lyons, etc
Publications: Afterimage, monthly
Activities: Classes for adults and children; graduate program in museum studies

that grants a MFA degree; summer Institute program with intensive short term workshops for artists and museum professionals; lectures open to the public, 30 visiting lecturers per year; gallery talks; tours (by appointment); scholarships offered for graduate program; original objects of art lent to institutions with proper exhibition facilities; lending collection contains 15,000 photographs of original artwork; traveling exhibitions organized and circulated to museums, colleges and universities; museum shop sells books, magazines, original art and prints

L **Research Center,** 31 Prince St, 14607. *Coordr Research Center* Helen M Brunner; *Librn* Robert Bretz; *Conservation Asst* Cindy Furlong
Open Mon - Thurs 2 - 5 PM, Mon & Tues 8 - 11 PM. Estab 1971 to maintain a permanent collection for the study of the function and effect of the visual image. For reference only
Library Holdings: Vols 12,000; Per subs 125; AV—A-tapes, cassettes, fs, Kodachromes, lantern Slides, motion pictures, slides, v-tapes; Other—Clipping files, exhibition catalogs, prints, manuscripts, original art works, photographs, reproductions, posters
Special Subjects: Photography
Collections: Illustrated book collection; photographic print collection
Exhibitions: Exhibitions are shown
Publications: Various publications
Activities: Internship programs; workshops; graduate museum studies program

ROME

O ROME ART AND COMMUNITY CENTER, 308 W Bloomfield St, 13440. Tel 315-336-1040. *Dir* Marian B Wedow; *Admin Asst* Katharine J Schlieder; *Gift Shop* Jacqueline Janowicz
Open Tues - Fri 9 AM - 5 PM, Sat & Sun 2 - 4 PM. No admis fee. Estab 1968 for art exhibits and classes. Three galleries. Average Annual Attendance: 30,000. Mem: 1000; dues family with 2 children $10, individual $5
Income: Financed by city appropriation
Exhibitions: Various art and craft exhibitions every six weeks
Publications: Quarterly calendar; invitations to programs, etc
Activities: Classes for adults and children; lectures open to the public; tours; readings; Scholarship offered on occasion to a child

M ROME HISTORICAL SOCIETY, Rome Information and Cultural Center, 113 W Court St, 13440. Tel 315-336-5870. *Pres* Richard F Kahler; *VPres* P F Scripture; *Secy* Mrs F E Henze; *Dir* Joseph G Vincent; *Admin Asst* Mrs C E Flack; *Registrar & Conservator* M L Campbell; *Assoc Dir* W T Macmaster
Open 9 AM - 4 PM. No admis fee. Estab 1936 as a historical museum and society. Average Annual Attendance: 79,000. Mem: 800; dues $7.50; annual meeting in Dec
Income: $61,000 (financed by membership and city appropriation)
Purchases: $1000-2000
Collections: E Buyck; P F Hugunine; Forest Moses; Ann Marriot; Joseph G Vincent; Will Moses; Revolutionary War period paintings
Exhibitions: Statewide tours; local artists on tour
Publications: Annuals and Recollections
Activities: Lectures open to the public, 12 visiting lecturers per year; tours; awards; lending collection contains books, original art works, original prints, paintings, sculpture; traveling exhibitions organized and circulated; museum shop sells reproductions, prints, history related art works

L William and Elaine Scripture Memorial Library, 113 W Court St, 13440.
Open 9 AM - 4 PM, Mon - Fri. Estab 1936 for historical research of Rome and the Mohawk Valley
Purchases: $500
Library Holdings: Vols 2200; Per subs 5; Other—Clipping files, prints, manuscripts, pamphlets, photographs, reproductions
Collections: Area paintings from the Revolutionary War period to the present

ROOSEVELT

M ROOSEVELT PUBLIC LIBRARY ART WORKSHOP GALLERY, 27 W Fulton Ave, 11575. Tel 516-378-1408, 378-9872. *Pres* Eliot Israel; *Dir* Briding Newall
Open Mon - Fri 9 AM - 5 PM, Sat 11 AM - 2 PM. No admis fee. Estab 1972 to develop and maintain a viable art program for education and information of surrounding community and its outside patrons. Small community centered gallery, 88 sq ft of wall space. Average Annual Attendance: 2050
Income: Financed by endowment, state appropriation and Roosevelt Public Library
Collections: Various works of art
Exhibitions: Monthly exhibit
Publications: Press release; invitations to special events
Activities: Classes for adults and children;; Summer festival; lect open to the public, five visiting lectr per year; gallery talks

ROSLYN

M **NASSAU COUNTY MUSEUM OF FINE ART,** Northern Blvd, PO Box D, 11576. Tel 516-484-9337, 484-9338. *Dir Office of Cultural Development* Marcia E O'Brien; *Dir Museum of Fine Art* Charles L Mango
Open Mon - Fri 9:30 AM - 4:30 PM, Sat & Sun 1 - 5 PM. No admis fee. Estab 1975 for exhibits of Historical and Contemporary nature for Nassau County Residents. The building houses ten galleries, three on the first floor, and seven on the second floor, which are utilized for rotating exhibitions. One gallery utilized for Community Artists. Average Annual Attendance: 60,000. Mem: 200; dues $500 - $5
Income: $70,000 (financed by membership and county appropriation)
Collections: Contemporary prints; contemporary sculpture (outdoor)
Exhibitions: Allen Bertoldi: Sculpture; Cristos Gianakos: Sculpture; Monuments and Monoliths: A Metamorphosis
Publications: Catalogs for exhibitions
Activities: Classes for adults and children; dramatic programs; docent training; lectures open to the public, 78 visiting lecturers per year; concerts; gallery talks; tours; original paintings and original objects of art lent to other qualified institutions; book traveling exhibitions; traveling exhibitions organized and circulated to the Gallery Association of New York State

ROSLYN HEIGHTS

PROFESSIONAL ARTISTS GUILD
For further information, see National and Regional Organizations

SAINT BONAVENTURE

M **SAINT BONAVENTURE UNIVERSITY ART COLLECTION,** 14778. Tel 716-375-2323, Ext 6. *Art Cur* Irenaeus Herscher; *Asst Art Cur* Bro John Capozzi
Open Mon - Thurs 8 AM - Midnight, Fri 8 AM - 5 PM, Sat 8 AM - 8 PM, Sun 10 AM - Midnight. No admis fee. Estab 1856 to provide artistic surroundings for students. Average Annual Attendance: 3500
Income: Financed by university budget
Collections: Paintings; porcelains and American Indian pottery; 50 ivories, jade miniatures; 4 cloisonne'
Exhibitions: Rotating exhibitions
Publications: Art Catalog of Collection
Activities: Museum shop selling reproductions
L **Friedsam Memorial Library,** Saint Bonaventure, 14778. *Librn* John Marcik
Open to the public
Library Holdings: Vols 180,000; Per subs 3000; Micro—Cards, fiche, reels; AV—A-tapes, cassettes, Kodachromes, motion pictures, rec, slides, v-tapes; Other—Clipping files, framed reproductions, prints, manuscripts, memorabilia, original art works, pamphlets, photographs, reproductions, sculpture
Collections: Library of American Civilization (20,000 vols on microfiche): Vatican Library Microfilms; NY Times Collection complete on microfilm (1851-1978); Short Title Catalog (1475-1640); Franciscana, art, science, philosophy and theology collections; Historical recordings of events, voices, speeches; Jim Bishop and Thomas Merton Manuscript Collections; Musical recordings; Stamp collections; Gutenberg-Printing; Incunabula; Manuscript collection

SANBORN

M **NIAGARA COUNTY COMMUNITY COLLEGE ART GALLERY,** 3111 Saunders Settlement Rd, 14132. Tel 716-731-3271, Ext 159. *Gallery Dir* Dorothy H Westhafer
Open hours vary from semester to semester, generally, Mon - Fri 11 - 3 PM, Thurs 6 - 9 PM, occasional Sun hours. Estab 1973 for varied exhibits that will be of interest to students and the community. There are two galleries with 270 sq ft of area and approx 250 running ft. Average Annual Attendance: 7500
Income: $2600
Collections: Prints (contemporary)
Exhibitions: Nature Transformed: Gail McCarthy, porcelain, Llana Pejovic, drawings; NCCC faculty; Robert Gulley, sculpture, Wayne Goldstein, photographs; NCCC students; NCCC alumni; 1977-78 CAPS Graphics awardees; Freidus Gallery photographers: Pfahl, Taussig & Patterson; Mortuary Posts of the Giryama; Art as Language; Artists' Books from GANY About Face: Ellen Carrey, photographer and Bruce Morosko, sculptor
Publications: Catalogs
Activities: Classes for adults; dramatic programs; lectures open to the public; tours

SARATOGA SPRINGS

M **NATIONAL MUSEUM OF RACING, INC,** Union Ave, 12866. Tel 518-584-0400. *Chmn* John W Hanes; *VPres* Walter M Jeffords Jr; *Secy-Treas* Paul R Rouillard; *Dir* Elaine E Mann; *Pres* Charles E Mather II
Open all year 9:30 AM - 5 PM, Sat 12 Noon - 5 PM (except Jan, Feb & Mar), Sun 12 Noon - 5 PM (June 15 - Sept 15), August Racing Season 9:30 AM - 7 PM daily. No admis fee, children under 12 must be accompanied by parents. Estab 1950 as a museum for the collection, preservation and exhibition of all kinds of articles associated with the origin, history and development of horse racing. There are 10 galleries of sporting art. The handsome Georgian-Colonial design brick structure houses one of the world's greatest collections of equine art along with trophies, sculptures and memorabilia of the sport from its earliest days. Average Annual Attendance: Approx 45,000. Mem: Annual meeting Aug
Income: Financed through annual appeal and individual contributions
Collections: Oil paintings of thoroughbred horses, trophies, racing silks, bronzes, prints, racing memorabilia
Exhibitions: Special exhibits annually during summer months, loans from private collectors of sporting art
Publications: Catalog; Hall of Fame booklets
Activities: Lect open to public, 2-4 visiting lectrs per year; gallery talks; exten dept

serving Northeast; original objects of art lent on special occasions; museum shop selling books, reproductions, prints, jewelry, figurines and other items
L **Reference Library,** Union Ave, 12866.
Open to researchers, students and authors by appointment
Special Subjects: Thoroughbred racing, horses

M **SKIDMORE COLLEGE,** Art Gallery, North Broadway, 12866. Tel 518-584-5000, Ext 370. *Dir* David Miller
Open Mon - Fri 9 AM - 5 PM, Sat & Sun 12 - 5 PM, cl during Skidmore vacations. No admis fee. Estab 1927 for educational enrichment of the college and community. Exhibitions are intended to bring awareness of both contemporary and historical trends in art. Average Annual Attendance: 6000
Income: Financed through College
Collections: American and European Prints; Saratoga Springs Historical Collection
Exhibitions: Crafts Invitational; NASA Oakleigh Collection; Navajo Art & Ceremony; 20th Century Printmaker's Portfolio; Watercolors, historical and contemporary; student and faculty shows; student drawings
Publications: Exhibition catalogs, occasionally
Activities: Lect open to public, 5-6 visiting lectr per year; gallery talks; traveling exhibitions organized and circulated
L **Lucy Scribner Library,** Art Section, North Broadway, 12866. *Art Librn* Jane Graves
Open Mon - Sat 8 AM - 11 PM, Sun Noon - 11 PM. Estab 1925
Library Holdings: Vols 10,000; Per subs 129; Micro—Cards; AV—Fs, Kodachromes, lantern slides, motion pictures, rec, slides 50,000; Other—Clipping files, exhibition catalogs, framed reproductions 10,000, prints 600, memorabilia, original art works, photographs, reproductions, sculpture
Collections: Anita Pohndorff Yates Collection of Saratoga History

SCHENECTADY

O **SCHENECTADY COUNTY HISTORICAL SOCIETY,** * 32 Washington Ave, 12305. Tel 518-374-0263. *Pres* Larry Hart; *Cur* Elsa Church; *Cur* Jean Thorkildsen
Open Mon - Fri 12:30 - 5 PM, Sat 1 - 5 PM, Sun 2 - 5 PM, cl national holidays. No admis fee. Estab 1906, located within area of original Schenectady stockade by the Dutch in 1661. Mem: Dues life $50, organization $25, patron $10, regular $5
Collections: Decorative arts; historical material; Indian artifacts; paintings; photographs
Exhibitions: Temporary exhibitions from other museums
Publications: Newsletter, monthly
Activities: Lect; guided tours; films; sales shop selling books and postcards
L **Library,** * 32 Washington Ave, 12305.
Library Holdings: Vols 2500

M **SCHENECTADY MUSEUM,** * Nott Terrace Heights, 12308. Tel 518-382-7890. *Dir* Bruce B Eldredge; *Cur Exhib* James Walsh; *Assoc Cur Educ* Constance J Carroll
Open Tues - Fri 10 AM - 4:30 PM, Sat & Sun Noon - 5 PM. No admis fee. Founded 1934, chartered by the New York State Regents in 1937 to increase and diffuse knowledge in appreciation of art, history, industry, and science by providing collections, exhibits, lectures and other programs. Sales and rental gallery is maintained. Average Annual Attendance: 68,000. Mem: 2200; dues annual $60, regular $25, individual $15, student & senior citizens $7.50
Income: $190,000
Collections: African Art; decorative arts; 19th and 20th century art; 19th and 20th century costumes and textiles; North American Indian Art
Exhibitions: Artists of the Mohawk-Hudson Region; Regional Crafts Show, purchases and awards; temporary exhibits of costumes, textiles and art
Publications: Annual Report; Calendar, monthly
Activities: Art and craft classes; Festival of Nations; Crafts Fair; Rock Festival; lect; guided tours; European and Central American tours; loan materials and exhibits for area schools, colleges and libraries; gift shop
L **Library,** * 12308. *Librn* Sue C Welch
For reference and technical information only
Library Holdings: Vols 5000

SKANEATELES

O **SKANEATELES LIBRARY ASSOCIATION,** 49 E Genesee St, 13152. Tel 315-685-5135. *Pres* Windsor M Price; *Secy* Mrs J W Thorne
Open 10 AM - 5:30 PM, cl Sun. Estab 1877
Collections: Paintings by American artists; Etchings by American and foreign artists; 200 paintings by John D Barrow, in separate wing
Exhibitions: Occasional special exhibitions
L **Library,** 49 E Genesee St, 13152. *Librn* Mrs Samuel Townsend; *Asst Librn* Mrs Edward D Ramage
Library Holdings: Vols 27,000

SOUTHAMPTON

M **PARRISH ART MUSEUM,** * 25 Jobs Lane, 11968. Tel 516-283-2118. *Dir* Ronald G Pisano; *Asst Cur* Melinda Brady Munford; *Registrar* Penelope Henry; *Educ Dir* Anke tom Dieck Jackson
Open Tues - Sat 10 AM - 5 PM, Sun 1 - 5 PM, cl Mon, holidays. No admis fee. Estab 1896 to exhibit, care for and research permanent collections and loaned works of art with emphasis on American 19th and 20th century paintings. Three main galleries are maintained; total dimensions 4288 sq ft, 355 running feet. Average Annual Attendance: 50,000. Mem: 1100; dues $15 - $1000 and up; annual meeting Dec
Income: Approx $170,000 (financed by endowment, membership)
Collections: †American paintings, 19th and 20th century; Carney Collection of Chinese Ceramics; D Doughty porcelains; Dunnigan Collection of 19th century Etchings; Japanese woodblock prints and stencils; Oriental decorative arts; Samuel Parrish Collection of Italian Renaissance Panel Paintings; Phillips Collection of 17th and 18th century Portraits
Exhibitions: Clay; G Ruger Donoho Retrospective; Eisenstadt, First Fifty Years;

Fabrications; Lion Rugs; Henry Miller, Abraham Rattner: Our America; Options; Fairfield Porter's Maine; 20th century American Paintings; 24th Annual Juried; Viewpoint: The American Land

Publications: Exhibition Catalogs (10 per year); Newsletter, quarterly

Activities: Classes for adults and children; dramatic programs; films; lect open to public, 3 visiting lectrs per year; concerts; competitions; exten dept serving area schools; lending collection contains color reproductions, film strips, original art works, original prints; traveling exhibitions organized and circulated; museum shop selling books, magazines, reproductions, prints, craft items

L **Aline B Saarinen Library,** * 25 Jobs Lane, 11968. *Librn* Penelope Henry
Reference library is open to the public
Library Holdings: Vols 5300; Per subs 6; Other—Exhibition catalogs
Special Subjects: Architecture, Oriental Art, American Painting
Collections: William Merritt Chase Archives; original documents, photographs, memorabilia, research materials pertaining to the life and work of Chase (1849-1916)

STAATSBURG

M **MILLS MANSION STATE HISTORIC SITE,** Old Post Road, 12580. Tel 914-889-4100. *Historic Site Mgr* John Feeney
Open May 26 - Oct 31, Wed - Sun 9 AM - 4:30 PM. No admis fee. Estab 1938 to interpret lifestyle of the very affluent segment of American society during the period 1890--1929. Average Annual Attendance: 10,000
Collections: Original furnishings, paintings, prints, decorative art objects and tapestries from Mr and Mrs Mills
Activities: Docent training; lectures open to the public; concerts; gallery tours; loans of paintings or original art objects have to be approved by New York State Office of Parks and Recreation, Division of Historic Preservation

STATEN ISLAND

M **JACQUE MARCHAIS CENTER OF TIBETAN ARTS, INC,** 338 Lighthouse Ave, 10306. Tel 212-987-3478. *Dir* Joyce Cini
Open April 1 - November 30, 1 - 5 PM; June, July & Aug, open Thurs & Fri 1 - 5 PM. Admis adults $1, children under 12 50¢. Estab 1946 for maintenance of library and museum in Buddhist philosophy, art and religion, with particular emphasis on Tibetan Buddhism. Buildings planned for and collection amassed by Mrs Harry Klauber, (known professionally as Jacques Marchais) who ran an Oriental art gallery from 1938 until her death in 1948. She never left the United States, but through agents and dealers, built her collection upon original bronzes, a gift from her grandfather. The center is a memorial to her by her husband. Buildings are a facsimile of a Tibetan Lamasery, located in a garden setting. Average Annual Attendance: 4000
Income: Financed by contributions, admissions, some county state and federal appropriations, and gift shop sales
Collections: Jacques Marchais permanent collection of Tibetan and Buddhist Art
Activities: Lect open to the public, 6 vis lectr per year; special lectures and tours are available by appointment; gift shop selling reproductions and woodblock prints, incense, prayer flags
L **Library,** 338 Lighthouse Ave, 10306. *Librn* Sigred Sidrow
For reference only
Library Holdings: Vols 1100; Other—Photographs

M **STATEN ISLAND FERRY MARITIME MUSEUM,** Saint George Ferry Terminal Building, 10301. *Captain and Historian* Theodore Costa; *Registrar* Edith Nilsen
Open Mon - Fri 8 AM - 3 PM, Summer Sat - Tues 9:30 AM - 3 PM, Wed - Fri 8 AM - 3 PM. No admis fee. Estab 1976 to collect and preserve history of ferries and educate the public of their true historic value
Income: Financed by city appropriation
Collections: Permanent historical exhibitions of ferry boat models, a working pilot house, and engineers gauges and signals; series of highly detailed, finely worked color pen and ink drawings of the floating derrick, City of New York, c1876; Artists renderings of boats of the future, a sleek 6000 passenger ferryboat that the city will soon contract for
L **Library,** Saint George Ferry Terminal Building, 10301. *Librn* Gerda Bernhardt
Open to the public for reference only

M **STATEN ISLAND INSTITUTE OF ARTS AND SCIENCES,** 75 Stuyvesant, Saint George, 10301. Tel 212-727-1135. *Pres* William Siebenheller; *Dir* A Mae Seeley; *Cur of Art* Barry Leo Delaney; *Editor & Librn* Gail K Schneider; *Museum Lectr* Freda Mulcahy Esterly
Open Tues - Sat 10 AM - 5 PM, Sun & holidays 2 - 5 PM, cl Mon, Thanksgiving, Christmas, New Years, Fourth of July, Labor Day. No admis fee. Estab 1881, inc 1906. Average Annual Attendance: 105,000. Mem: 900; dues $10 and up
Collections: †American paintings of the 19th and 20th centuries; Oriental, Greek, Roman and primitive art objects; †prints and small sculptures
Exhibitions: Exhibitions in decorative arts; design exhbitions in various media; major loan shows of paintings and prints; special exhibitions of graphic arts and of photography; four Weissglass awardd totaling $400 presented each year
Publications: Proceedings, 3 times a yr; catalogs; Annual Reports
Activities: Fall and spring terms of adult classes; lectures on art and science; complete program of lectures, art and natural history, for school children with annual registration of 30,000
L **Library,** 75 Stuyvesant PL, St George, 10301.
Collections: George W Curtis Collection of books, manuscripts, and memorabilia; reference collection of 30,000 publications in science and art history; a choice collection of Staten Island newspapers from 1834-1934 on microfilm; letters, documents, journals, files of clippings and old photographs relating to the history of Staten Island and the metropolitan region

STONE RIDGE

M **ULSTER COUNTY COMMUNITY COLLEGE,** Visual Arts Gallery,* 12484. Tel 914-687-7621, Ext 76. *Coordr* Allan L Cohan
Open Mon - Fri 10 AM - 4 PM, Fall and Spring semesters, Noon - 3 PM Summer. No admis fee. Estab 1963 as a center for creative activity. Gallery is maintained as an adjunct to the college's cultural and academic program; John Vanderlyn Hall has 40 x 28 ft enclosed space and is located on the campus. Average Annual Attendance: 3000-4000
Income: Financed by college funds
Purchases: $750
Collections: Contemporary drawings, paintings, photographs, prints, sculpture
Publications: Flyers announcing each exhibit, every four to six weeks
Activities: Lect open to the public, 2-3 visiting lectrs per year; concerts

STONY BROOK

M **MUSEUMS AT STONY BROOK,** Route 25A, 11790. Tel 516-751-0066. *Dir* Susan Stitt; *Adminr* Nicholas Langhart; *Public Information Officer* Peter Schaefer
Open Wed - Sun 10 AM - 5 PM, cl Mon & Tues. Admis adults $2, students and Sr. Citizens $1.50, children 6 - 12 $1, under 6 free. Estab 1942 as a nonprofit educational institution whose purpose is to collect and preserve objects of historic and artistic interest. The Museums' 19 buildings, 13.5 acre complex includes a History Museum, Art Museum, Carriage Museum (open Apr - Nov), various period buildings, a museum store, the Stony Brook Grist Mill (open Sundays, June - Oct) and the Hawkins-Mount House (open for one week of guided tours in June and Dec). Average Annual Attendance: 55,000. Mem: 660; dues $10 - $500
Collections: Paintings, drawings and memorabilia of artist William Sidney Mount; other 19th century American artists costumes; dolls; textiles; ceramics
Exhibitions: Changing exhibitions in Art Museum and History Museum; A Time to Mourn, Victorian mourning customs in America, History Museum, Main Gallery
Publications: Annual Report; Quarterly Newsletter; exhibition catalogs; brochures
Activities: Classes for adults and children; docent training; lect open to public; vis lectrs; gallery talks; tours; loans to other museums; museum shop sells books, reproductions, prints, childrens folk toys, early American housewares, miniatures
L **Kate Strong Historical Library,** Route 25A, 11790. *Librn & Registrar* David Cassedy
Reference library open to researchers by appointment
Library Holdings: Vols 1500; Per subs 15; Other—Manuscripts, photographs, trade catalogs
Collections: William Cooper, shipbuilder, 19th century, Sag Harbor; Israel Green Hawkins, Edward P Buffet, Hal B Fullerton; Archives: Papers of William Sidney Mount and family; Daniel Williamson and John Williamson, Stony Brook

M **STATE UNIVERSITY OF NEW YORK AT STONY BROOK ART GALLERY,** 11794. Tel 516-246-7071. *Dir* Lawrence Alloway; *Asst to the Dir* Elizabeth S Boudreau; *Exhibition Coordr* Richard Smith
Open Mon - Fri Noon - 5 PM. No admis fee. Estab 1967 to serve both the campus and the community by exhibitions of professional artists. One gallery 42 x 74 with 22 ft ceiling; second space 22 x 60 ft with 12 ft ceilings. Average Annual Attendance: 1500 students and members of the community per show
Income: Financed by state appropriation
Exhibitions: (1978-79) Sister Chapel; Shirley Goulick, photographs; Roy Lichenstein: Mirrors and Entablatures; Rosemary Mayer; Howardena Pindell: Works on Canvas; Alan Sonfist: An Environmental Sculpture; (1980)Benny Andrews: Bicentennial Series; Alex Katz: Recent Paintings; Otto Piene: Sculpture; Senior Art Show, Mixed Media
Activities: Lectures weekly

SYRACUSE

L **ERNEST STEVENSON BIRD LIBRARY,** Waverly Ave, 13210. Tel 315-423-2440. *Dept Head* Donald C Seibert; *Architecture Librn* Barbara A Opar; *Slide Curator* Johanna W Prins; *Art Librn* Randall I Bond
Open Mon - Thurs 8 AM - 11 PM, Fri 8 AM - 6 PM, Sat 10 AM - 6 PM, Sun 12 PM - 10 PM. Estab to serve faculty and students teaching and studying the fine arts field. Located in Syracuse University Library
Purchases: $30,000
Library Holdings: Vols 40,000; Per subs 130; Other—Exhibition catalogs 5000, Picture file 26,000

M **EVERSON MUSEUM OF ART,** 401 Harrison St, 13202. Tel 315-474-6064. *Pres* Joel Fleming; *VPres* Dr John J Prucha; *VPres* Mrs William Hall; *Dir* Ronald A Kuchta; *Asst Dir* Sandra Trop-Blumberg; *Cur of Collections & Education* Ross Anderson; *Secy* Mrs Richard P Davis; *Treas* Joseph S Vogtle; *Registrar* Linda Steigleder
Open Tues - Fri 12 - 5 PM, Sat 10 AM - 5 PM, Sun 12 - 5 PM, cl Mon. No admis fee. Estab 1968 to present exhibitions by lending artists, chiefly American, free to the public; to serve as an educational element of the cultural and general community. Main Sculpture Court - indoor and 50 x 50 x 40, four large upper galleries 40 x 50 x 28, lower gallery 40 x 50 x 15, four small galleries, Sales Gallery & Luncheon Gallery, Inner Court in Administration Wing 28 x 40 x 32, square block of outdoor Community Plaza with monumental sculpture. Mem: 2609; dues general $25, student $7.50
Income: $822,000; (financed by membership, city and state appropriation, New York State Council on the Arts, National Endowment for the Arts, Institute for Museum Services (HEW), private corporate grants, individual grants)
Collections: African Collection; Contemporary American Ceramics; Contemporary American Painting & Sculpture; 17th, 18th & 19th Century English Porcelain; Traditional American Painting & Portraiture; Video-tape Collection; Cloud Wampler Collection of Oriental Art
Exhibitions: A Century of Ceramics in the US 1878-1978; Ancient Roots - New Visions; Annual Community & Scholastic Shows; Contemporary American Painting & Drawing; Perspective on Portraiture - 18th century to the present; Synchronism and American Color Abstraction; Video Revue (1978-1979)

Publications: Art books; bulletin, monthly; Educational materials; exhibition catalogs

Activities: Educ dept; classes for adults, children and handicapped persons; docent training; lect open to the public, 10 visiting lectr per year; concerts; gallery talks; tours; competitions; exten dept serves public schools of Syracuse; individual paintings and original objects of art lent; originate traveling exhibitions; museum and sales shop selling books, magazines, original art, reproductions, prints, slides, ceramics, local and national arts and crafts

L　**Art Reference Library,** 401 Harrison St, 13202.
Library Holdings: Vols 5200; Micro—Cards, prints; AV—Kodachromes, slides, v-tapes; Other—Clipping files, exhibition catalogs, memorabilia, pamphlets, photographs

M　**LEMOYNE COLLEGE,** Art Gallery, LeMoyhe Heights, 13214. Tel 315-446-2882. *Chairperson & Librn* Dr Tanya Popovic; *Asst Prof of Philosophy* William McKenna; *Asst Prof of Philosophy* Dr Donald Arentz; *Periodical Librn* Lynnette Stevens
Open Mon - Thurs 9 AM - 11 PM, Fri 9 AM - 9 PM, Sat & Sun 9 AM - 5 PM. No admis fee. Estab 1966. Average Annual Attendance: 1500
Income: Financed through the Faculty Art Gallery Committee
Purchases: $250
Collections: Paintings, etchings, prints and watercolors
Exhibitions: (1978) Maxwell Chayat (sculpture and jewelry); Peter Colvin (paintings); Lucinda Devlin (photographs). (1979) Gustave Kaitz Art; James Williams (needlepoint); Charles Wollowitz (graphics); student show
Activities: Individual Painting and original object of art lent

SYRACUSE UNIVERSITY

M　**Joe and Emily Lowe Art Gallery,** College Place, 13210. Tel 315-423-4098. *Dir* Joseph A Scala; *Cur* Jason D Wong; *Secy* Paula Edelsack; *Preparator* Leonard Eichler
Open Tues - Sun Noon - 5 PM, cl Mon. No admis fee. Estab 1952 to present art exhibitions to inform University and communities of central upstate New York areas of international heritage of art, new advances in contemporary art with emphasis on the discovery of regional values, outstanding local art including faculty and student work. Museum Training Program complements our exhibition program. 6300 sq ft of space normally divided into separate galleries by movable walls. Average Annual Attendance: 20,000
Income: Financed through University with additional outside grants
Exhibitions: Winslow Homer Drawings, 1875-1885; Mural Art of Ben Shahn; Margaret Bourke White: The Deco Lens; Le Corbusier: Architectural drawings; Annual Showcase of New York State Artists' Works; Current New York: Relief Sculpture; Alumni Artists Exhibition, 1979; MFA Degree Candidates' Exhibit; Portfolios: In and Out of the 1960s; Record Album Art; West African Sculpture: Traditions in Transition
Publications: Exhibition catalogs each show
Activities: Private tours on request; traveling exhibitions organized and circulated

M　**Art Collection,** Sims Hall, 13210. Tel 315-423-4097. *Dir* Alfred T Collette; *Cur Coll* Domenic J Iancono; *Asst to Registrar* Thomas Piche
The Art Collection is housed in a temperature and humidity-controlled area of Sims Hall, adjacent to the Art Gallery. Used primarily for storage and care of the Collection, this facility also includes a teaching display area to accommodate classes and individuals involved in research
Collections: Andrei Nitecki Collection of West African Tribal Art; Korean, Japanese and American ceramics; Ruth Reeves Collection of Asian-Indian Folk Art; Pre-Columbian and Contemporary Peruvian Ceramics; Scandinavian designs in metal, wood and clay; 20th century American works with an emphasis on the Depression and War years (paintings); 19th century European Salon paintings; history of printmaking (emphasis on American artists); decorative arts

L　**Library,** 13210. *Librn* Randall Bond
Open Mon - Fri 8 AM - 10 PM, Sat 10 AM - 5 PM, Sun 2 - 10 PM. Estab 1870 for reference and research in the history of art
Library Holdings: Vols 45,000; Per subs 145; Micro—Cards, fiche, reels, prints; AV —A-tapes, cassettes, fs, lantern Slides, motion pictures, rec, slides, v-tapes; Other —Exhibition catalogs, manuscripts, photographs
Collections: Manuscript Collections of many American artists

TARRYTOWN

M　**LYNDHURST,** 635 S Broadway, 10591. Tel 914-631-0046. *Administrator* Richard E Slavin III; *Asst Administrator & Cur* Nancy Richards
Open May 1 - Oct 31 10 AM - 5 PM & legal holidays, Nov 1 - April 30 10 AM - 4 PM. cl Thanksgiving, Christmas, and New Years Day. Admis adults $3, senior citizens and students $1.50, group rates by arrangement; free to National Trust members. A property of the National Trust for Historic Preservation, preserved as a historic house museum operated as a community preservation center. It is a National Historic Landmark. Lyndhurst is a Gothic Revival castle designed in 1838 for General William Paulding by Alexander Jackson Davis, one of America's most influential 19th century architects. Commissioned by second owner, George Merritt, to enlarge the house, Davis, in 1865, continued the Gothic revival style in the additions. It was purchased in 1880 by Jay Gould and willed to his daughter, Helen. Later acquired by another daughter, Anna, Duchess of Talleyrand-Perigord Lyndhurst was left to the National Trust in 1964. The property is located on spacious grounds along the Hudson River. Visitors are free to explore the magnificent park which is being restored. Other highlights include a carriage house, stocked with period vehicles, stables, and the remains of private greenhouses. Windows attributed to L C Tiffany. The preservation of Lyndhurst is a composite of the contributions of the three families who lived in it. Property serves as a focal point for advancement of historic preservation. Through it are developed new relationships among cultural, community preservation groups and National Trust members in its area. Responds to community preservation needs by acting as a link between community and appropriate regional or headquarters offices of National Trust. Provides interpretive programs which are related to Lyndhurst's particular case study in historic preservation. The National Trust Restoration Workshop, located in a portion of the stable complex carries out restoration craft services for National trust properties. Average Annual Attendance: 51,000
Collections: Collection of Gothic furniture designed by architect A J Davis in the

1830s and 1870s; 19th century furnishings and paintings
Activities: Summer outdoor concerts; antique and auto shows; Christmas programs

M　**SLEEPY HOLLOW RESTORATIONS INC,** 150 White Plains Road, 10591. Tel 914-631-8200. *Pres* Dana S Creel; *Exec Dir* John W Harbour Jr; *Deputy Dir Admin* Saverio Procario; *Cur* Joseph T Butler
Open 10 -AM - 5 PM, cl Thanksgiving Day, Christmas and New Years. Admis to Sunnyside, Philipsburg Manor and Van Cortland Manor adults $2.25 each property, juniors 6 - 14 $1.50 each property; three visit tickets valid one year, adults $5.75, juniors $3.75; groups of 20 or more must make reservations in advance. Chartered 1951 as a nonprofit educational foundation. Owns and operates historic properties which are Sunnyside in Tarrytown, the home of author Washington Irving; Phillipsburg Manor in North Tarrytown, a Dutch-American gristmill-farm site of the early 1700s; Van Cortland Manor in Croton-on-Hudson, a manorial estate of the Revolutionary War period. Average Annual Attendance: 200,000
Collections: Memorabilia of Washington Irving, Van Cortlandt and Philips families; 17th, 18th and 19th century decorative arts
Exhibitions: Exhibitions of collections
Publications: America's Wooden Age; Aspects of Early New York Society and politics; Family Collections at Van Cortlandt Manor; The Knickerbocker Tradition; Life of George Washington; Life Along the Hudson; The Loyalists Americans; The Mill at Philipsburg Manor; Philipsburg Manor: A Guidebook; Rip Van Winkle and the Legend of Sleepy Hollow; Six Presidents from the Empire State; The Van Cortlands of Croton: York State Patriots; Washington Irving: A Tribute; Washington Irving's Sunnyside; The Worlds of Washington Irving; prints and documents including the Declaration of Independence, Howe Map and A Portfolio of Sleepy Hollow Prints
Activities: Organized education programs; demonstrations of 17th and 18th century arts and crafts; lectures; guided tours

L　**Library,** 150 White Plains Rd, 10591. *Librn* Raissa Fomerand
Specialized reference library with particular emphasis on 17th, 18th and 19th century living in the Hudson River Valley

TICONDEROGA

M　**FORT TICONDEROGA MUSEUM,** 12883. Tel 518-585-2821. *Pres* John G Pell; *Cur* Jane M Lape; *Genl Mgr* Wayne J Morgan
Open daily, mid-May - mid-Oct 9 AM - 4PM. Admis 14 and over $3.50. Estab 1909 to preserve and present the Colonial and Revolutionary history of Fort Ticonderoga. the museum is the restored barracks of the Colonial fort. Average Annual Attendance: 200,000
Income: Financed by admission fees
Collections: Artifacts; manuscripts; paintings
Exhibitions: Exhibitions are held in mid-May - mid-Oct
Publications: Bulletin of the Fort Ticonderoga Museum
Activities: Classes for adults; individual paintings and original objects of art lent to qualified museums; sales shop sells books, reproductions, slides

L　**Library,** 12883. *Librn* Jane M Lape
Open by appointment for reference only
Library Holdings: Vols 5000

TROY

INTER-SOCIETY COLOR COUNCIL
For further information, see National and Regional Organizations

O　**RENSSELAER COUNTY HISTORICAL SOCIETY,** 59 Second St, 12180. Tel 518-272-7232. *Pres* Mrs W E Smith; *VPres* George W Singiser; *Dir* Breffny A Walsh; *Cur* Stacy F Pomeroy; *Secy* Sandra Reizen
Open Tues - Sat 10 AM - 4 PM. Admis donation for adults $1. Estab 1927 to promote historical research and to collect and exhibit materials of all kinds related to the history of the Rensselaer County area including books, papers, fine and decorative arts. An historic house museum with 11 period rooms. Average Annual Attendance: 10,000. Mem: 550; dues $2 - $1000; annual meeting Sept
Income: Approx $60,000 (financed by endowment and membership)
Collections: Ceramics; costumes; Elijah Galusha 19th century furniture; paintings by local artists including C G Beauregard, Joseph Hidley and Abel Buel Moore; portraits; quilts and coverlets; silver
Exhibitions: (1980) Canes; Currier and Ives; Troy-Built Rototiller
Publications: Newsletter, monthly
Activities: Lect open to public, 8 visiting lectr per year; internships; lending collection contains cassettes, motion pictures, slides; traveling exhibitions organized and circulated; sales shop selling books, prints and gifts

L　**Library,** 59 Second St, 12180.
Library Holdings: Vols 1000; Per subs 3; AV—Slides; Other—Photographs
Special Subjects: , 210

M　**RENSSELAER NEWMAN FOUNDATION CHAPEL AND CULTURAL CENTER,** 2125 Burdett Ave, 12180. Tel 518-274-7793. *Pres* Paul Catan; *Dir* David Fletcher; *Secy* Thomas Phelan
Open 8 AM - 11 PM. Estab 1968 to provide religion and culture for members of the Rensselaer Polytechnic Institute and Troy area, a broadly ecumenical service. Gallery maintained. Average Annual Attendance: 100,000
Income: $110,000 (supported by contributions)
Collections: Contemporary paintings, sculpture and needlework; liturgical vestments and artifacts; medieval sculpture
Exhibitions: Laliberte banners; Picasso traveling exhibition New York State Council on the Arts; Smithsonian Institution Traveling Exhibition; local one man shows
Publications: Sun and Balance, three times a year
Activities: Dramatic programs; classes for adults and children; lect open to public, 10 vis lectr per yr; concerts

M　**RUSSELL SAGE COLLEGE,** New Gallery, Schacht Fine Arts Center, 12180. Tel 518-270-2248. *Gallery Dir* Ruth Healey

Open Mon - Fri 9 AM - 5 PM, Sun 2 - 5 PM. No admis fee. Estab 1970 for exhibition of contemporary art for college and public. Gallery is one room, with 150 running ft. Average Annual Attendance: 3000
Income: Financed by the college
Collections: Drawings (contemporary); paintings (contemporary); sculpture of New Guinea and Africa
Exhibitions: Faculty and student shows; paintings, drawings, sculpture from New York City galleries and area artists; photography; traveling exhibitions
Activities: Gallery talks; original objects of art lent on campus; lending collection contains original prints, paintings, sculpture; traveling exhibitions organized and circulated

UTICA

M **CHILDREN'S MUSEUM OF HISTORY, NATURAL HISTORY AND SCIENCE,** (Formerly Mohawk Valley Museum) 311 Main St, 13501. Tel 315-724-2075. *Dr* Eino/Kivisalu ; *Educ Asst* Emily Meyers; *Secy, Receptionist, Bookkeeper* Harriette Tilley
Open Tues - Sat 10 AM - 5 PM, Sun 1 - 5 PM, cl Mon. No admis fee. Estab 1966 to supplement school curricula in history, natural history and science. A classroom contains mini exhibits where children learn by operating pulleys, hydraulic lift, sand pendulum; bee hive for internal exploration. Average Annual Attendance: 30,000.
Mem: 570; dues family $8
Income: $40,000 (financed by membership and state appropriation)
Collections: Major collection of dolls
Exhibitions: Colonial Craftsmen Exhibit; History of the Mohawk Valley in Dioramas; Iroquois Exhibit
Publications: Mohawk Valley Museum Newsletter, monthly
Activities: A state certified educational institution; classroom demonstrations; school tours; museum shop

M **MUNSON-WILLIAMS-PROCTOR INSTITUTE,** Museum of Art, 310 Genesee St, 13502. Tel 315-797-0000. *Pres* Paul J Farinella; *Dir* Edward H Dwight; *Asst to Dir* Joseph S Trovato; *Cur Decorative Arts* Carol Gordon
Open Tues - Sat 10 AM - 5 PM, Sun 1 - 5 PM , cl Mon. No admis fee. Estab 1919 through an endowment granted a provisional charter by the Board of Regents of the University of the State of New York, changed to an absolute charter in 1941, and amended in 1948 to empower the Institute to provide instruction at the college level in the field of fine arts. The Institute became active in 1935 with the purpose of establishing and maintaining a gallery and collection of art; to give instruction; and to have an auxiliary library. It consists of a School of Art estab 1941; a Museum of Art opened in 1960; Fountain Elms, a house-museum was restored in 1960; a Meetinghouse opened in 1963. Average Annual Attendance: 200,000. Mem: 4500; dues $15
Income: Financed by endowment and private contributions
Collections: †Archives of Central New York architecture; †Arts of Central New York; †Contemporary European Paintings and Sculpture; Greek, Persian and pre-Columbian Art; †18th, 19th and 20th Century American paintings, sculpture, and decorative arts; †drawings and prints
Exhibitions: American Art 1945 - 1975; Antwerp Drawings and Prints from the 16th and 17th Centuries; Critics Choice: A Loan Exhibition of Contemporary Paintings from the New York Gallery Season, 1976 - 77; Lines of Vision; The Classical Tradition in Rajput Painting; Paintings from the William H Lane Foundation; Sidewalk Arts Exhibition; Tsutsuma: The Art of the Japanese Package; Utica Art Festival; Works on Paper
Publications: Bulletin, monthly; exhibition catalogues
Activities: Educ dept; docent training; lect open to public; visiting lectureres; concerts; tours; film series; competitions; art and gift shop sells books, original art, reproductions, prints, slides

L **Art Reference Library,** 310 Genessee St, 13502. *Librn* Sylvia S Haq; *Asst to Librn* Resa Holak; *Slide Librn* Kim Wheatley
Open Tues - Sat 10 AM - 5 PM. Estab 1940 to support School of Art, researchers for exhibitions and the community. Circ 3500. Open to members and the public for lending and reference
Income: $25,000
Purchases: $5000
Library Holdings: Vols 12,000; Per subs 50; Micro—Fiche; AV—Rec, slides; Other —Clipping files, exhibition catalogs, manuscripts, pamphlets
Special Subjects: Architecture, Decorative Arts
Collections: Fountain Elms Collection; autographs, books, book plates; 19th century pictorial sheet music covers
Exhibitions: Exhibitions once a year, showing materials related to art in the library collection

WATERTOWN

L **ROSWELL P FLOWER MEMORIAL LIBRARY,** 229 Washington St, 13601. Tel 315-788-2352. *Dir* Anthony F Cozzie
Open (Sept - June) Mon - Fri 8:30 AM - 8:30 PM, Sat 9 AM - 5 PM; (July & Aug) Mon 8:30 AM - 8:30 PM, Tues - Fri 8:30 AM - 5:30 PM, cl Sat. Estab 1904. Circ 176,442. The art gallery contains murals, paintings and sculptures scattered throughout the building
Income: $380,000
Library Holdings: Vols 158,000; Per subs 405; Micro—Fiche, reels; AV—Motion pictures, rec; Other—Framed reproductions
Special Subjects: Murals and paintings of local history and local interest
Collections: Military History (US); New York State material and genealogy
Exhibitions: Local Artists Guild; North Country Artist Guild
Publications: Focus, every other month
Activities: Lectures open to public; concerts; library tours

WESTFIELD

L **PATTERSON LIBRARY,*** 40 S Portage St, 14787. Tel 716-326-2154. *Library Dir* Charles Thompson; *Art Dir* Joseph Koshute
Open Mon - Sat 9:30 AM - 5 PM, Mon, Wed & Thurs 7 - 9 PM. Estab 1896 to provide opportunity for education and recreation through the use of literature, music, films, paintings and other art forms. Circ 100,000. Octagon Gallery has 1115 sq ft with 11 ft ceilings while Members Gallery is 70 ft long with 8 ft high display wall of burlap-covered plywood
Income: $80,000 (financed by endowment, city and state appropriation)
Purchases: $12,500
Library Holdings: Vols 31,773; Per subs 164; AV—A-tapes, cassettes, fs, motion pictures, rec, slides; Other—Framed reproductions, memorabilia, original art works, pamphlets, photographs, sculpture
Special Subjects: Glass plate negatives of local history, WW I posters, seashells, mounted birds
Exhibitions: Traveling exhibits; paintings, sculpture and photography from western New York, Ohio and Pennsylvania artists
Activities: Classes for adults and children; lect open to the public; concerts; gallery talks; tours; traveling exhibitions organized and circulated

WEST POINT

M **UNITED STATES MILITARY ACADEMY,** West Point Museum, 10996. Tel 914-938-2203. *Dir Museum* Richard E Kuehne; *Cur Arms & Armor* Robert W Fisch; *Cur History* Michael J McAfee; *Cur Art* Michael E Moss; *Museum Specialist* Walter J Nock; *Registrar* Rene Klish-Ginsberg
Open 10:30 AM - 4:15 PM. No admis fee. Estab 1854, supplementing the academic, cultural and military instruction of cadets. Collections open to the public. Average Annual Attendance: 370,000
Income: $100,000
Purchases: $5000
Collections: Rindisbacher Watercolors; Sully Portrait Collection; †military paintings and prints; †military artifacts including weapons, flags, uniforms, medals, etc; paintings and prints of West Point
Exhibitions: (1978)Posters for Victory; (1978) The Wars of Napoleon; An exhibition of Uniforms; works of art and weapons associated with these soldiers; (1979) The US Cavalry in the West: Exhibition of Don Spaulding's art and private collection; American and French Zouaves
Publications: Posters for Victory; West Point Museum Bulletin, irregularly

L **Library,** 10996.
Small reference library of military subjects
Activities: photographic collection of 2500 items for lending or reference

WHITE PLAINS

O **HUDSON VALLEY ART ASSOCIATION,** c/o Rayma M Spaulding, 15 Minivale Road, 06907. Tel 203-322-1110. *Pres* Rayma M Spaulding; *Treas* Perry Alley; *Secy* Joan Rudman
Estab 1928, inc 1933 to perpetuate the artistic traditions of American artists such as made famous the Hudson River School of Painting through exhibitions of painting and sculpture with public support. Mem: 300; membership by invitation; dues $15, special exhibits extra; annual meeting May
Exhibitions: Annual juried exhibition each May, open to all artists of the US who work in realistic tradition, to compete for money awards and gold medals of honor; other exhibits from time to time
Activities: Free demonstrations, exhibitions, lectures

YONKERS

M **HUDSON RIVER MUSEUM,** 511 Warburton Ave, Trevor Park-on-Hudson, 10701. Tel 914-963-4550. *Dir* Richard Koshalek; *Planetarium Dir* Robert Klomburg; *Registrar* Craig Flexner; *Pub Information Dir* Judy Matson; *Cur Educ* Richard Carlson; *Development Dir* Julie Hazar
Open Wed - Sat 10 AM - 5 PM, Sun Noon - 5 PM. Admis by voluntary contribution. Estab 1924 as a general museum of art, history and science. Victorian Mansion, Glenview, 300 seat auditorium. Average Annual Attendance: 150,000. Mem: 1600; dues vary
Income: Financed by membership, city and state appropriations, corporations, foundations
Collections: Tom Clancy: Winter; Contemporary Art and Architecture; Dan Flavin: Untitled, Fluorescent light installation Red Grooms: The Bookstore; late 19th century American painting, sculpture, decorative arts and photography
Exhibitions: Harry Callahan: Photographs; Dan Flavin: drawn along the shores; Rufus Porter; 1000 Boxes: an exhibition about Architecture for Kids; An Unprejudiced Eye: The Drawings of Jasper F Cropsey
Publications: Bimonthly calendar of events; special exhibitions catalogs
Activities: Docent training; lectures and special events open to public; art lent to other museums for exhibition purposes; lending collection contains original art works, paintings, photographs, sculpture; traveling exhibitions organized and circulated; museum shop selling books, inexpensive items for children

L **Library,** 511 Warburton Ave, Trevor Park-on-Hudson, 10701.
For staff use only
Library Holdings: Vols 3000

M **PHILIPSE MANOR HALL STATE HISTORIC SITE,** 29 Warburton Ave, PO Box 496, 10702. Tel 914-965-4027. *Historic Site Mgr* Mary Dougal; *Education Dir* Tracy Van Riper
Open Wed - Sun 9 AM - 5 PM. No admis fee. Estab 1908 to preserve Georgian manor house owned by the Frederick Philipse family; to interpret Philipse Manor Halls architecture, its significance as the home of an American Loyalist and its importance as an example of 17th and 18th Century Anglo-Dutch patterns in landholding and development. The State Historic Site is part of the New York State Office of Parks and Recreation; the Hall houses contemporary style exhibits of history, art and architecture hung against a backdrop of fine 18th and 19th Century

architectural carvings
Income: Financed by state appropriation
Collections: Cochran Portrait Collection of Famous Americans
Activities: Classes for children; lectures open to public; concerts; tours; demonstrations; films

L **YONKERS PUBLIC LIBRARY,** Fine Arts Department, 1500 Central Park Ave, 10710. Tel 914-337-1500, Ext 21. *Librn III & Head Department* Marta Schwartz; *Librn II* Alan Beggs; *Librn I* Beverly Katopis
Open Mon, Tues, Wed, Fri 10 AM - 9 PM, Thurs 10 AM - 5 PM, Sat 9 AM - 5 PM. Estab 1962 to serve the general public with a special interest in the arts, especially the fine arts, performing arts, and the decorative and applied arts. Circ Printed material approx 25,000; recorded material approx 63,000
Income: $25,000 (financed by city appropriation)
Purchases: $42,000
Library Holdings: Vols 14,000; AV—Cassettes, rec 15,000, slides; Other—Clipping files, pamphlets

L **Will Library,** 1500 Central Park Ave, 10710.
Exhibitions: Exhibits work by local artists and craftsmen

NORTH CAROLINA

ASHEVILLE

M **ASHEVILLE ART MUSEUM,** Civic Center Complex, Haywood St, 28801. Tel 704-253-3227. *Exec Cur & Acting Dir* Carolyn Williams; *Secy* Karen McKinster; *Chmn Volunteer Service* Estelle Marder; *Pres Board of Dir* Sylvia Fisher; *Production Asst* Dennisse Espina; *Dir* open
Open Tues - Fri 10 AM - 5 PM, Sat & Sun 1 - 5 PM, cl Mon. No admis fee. Estab 1948 to provide educational services to the western North Carolina area through exhibitions. Three galleries maintained, with movable walls. Average Annual Attendance: 45,000. Mem: 1000; dues family $20, single $10, student $5; annual meeting July
Income: Financed by endowment, membership, city appropriation, State Arts Council and auxiliary
Collections: Contemporary Regional Fine Arts $ Crafts
Exhibitions: (1979-80) Antique Dolls & Quilts; British Portraits (NCMA); 50 Contemporary Prints; Frieske: American Impressionist; Metal Sculpture: Bob Gursky; Pottery & Photography: Don Davis, H Witherill; Pre-Columbian Exhibition (Mint); Realists; R J Reynolds Competition; SE Invitational Drawing and Graphics; Bob Timberlake Retrospective; UNC-A Photo Competition; Watercolors: Chris Schink, Buddy Folk (workshop); Woman: Images on Paper; Wood Sculpture: Dirck Cruser
Publications: Bi-monthly membership and affiliate newsletter
Activities: Classes for adults and children; Lect open to the public; concerts; competitions; art auction

O **SOUTHERN HIGHLAND HANDICRAFT GUILD,** 15 Reddick Rd, P O Box 9545, 28805. Tel 704-298-7928. *Dir* Robert W Gray; *Asst Dir* James Gentry
Open Mon - Fri 9 AM - 5 PM. No admis fee. Estab 1930 to encourage wider appreciation of mountain crafts; raise and maintain standards of design and craftsmanship, and encourage individual expression. Mem: 621; open to eligible craftsmen from Southern Appalachian Mountain Region and approval of applicants work by Standards Committee and Board of Trustees; dues group $20, single $6; annual meeting in April
Income: Financed by membership and merchandising
Publications: Highland Highlights, newsletter monthly
Activities: Educational programming will be available in March opening on the Blue Ridge Parkway; workshops; demonstrations; retail shop open

BREVARD

M **BREVARD COLLEGE,** Coltrane Art Center, 28712. Tel 704-883-8292, Ext 245. *Dir* Prof Tom Murray
Open Mon - Thurs 8 AM - 10 PM, Fri 8 AM - 5 PM. No admis fee. Estab 1969 as Art Department with on-going gallery. Center has three areas, 160 ft running space, and 1500 sq ft floor space
Income: Financed by departmental appropriation
Collections: Contemporary art; 1940-1970 paintings and watercolors; print and pottery collection
Exhibitions: Student and visiting artist exhibitions
Activities: Classes for adults; dramatic programs; college classes and continuing education; 4 visiting lectr per year; 4 gallery talks; competitions; cash awards; scholarships; lending collection contains books, cassettes, color reproductions, film strips, photographs, slides

L **Jones Library,** Brevard College, 78712.
Open Mon - Thurs 8 AM - 6:30 PM, Fri 8 AM - 5 PM, Sat 10 AM - Noon and 1 - 4 PM, Sun 2 - 5 PM. Estab 1934
Library Holdings: Vols 3000; Per subs 10; AV—Cassettes, fs, slides; Other—Clipping files, prints, pamphlets
Activities: Film series, weekly; shows

CHAPEL HILL

SOUTHEASTERN COLLEGE ART CONFERENCE
For further information, see National and Regional Organizations

UNIVERSITY OF NORTH CAROLINA
M **The Ackland Art Museum,** Columbia & Franklin Streets, 27514. Tel 919-966-5736. *Dir* Evan H Turner; *Cur* Katharine Lee Keefe
Open Tues - Sat 10 AM - 5 PM, Sun 2 - 6 PM, cl Mon and University holidays.

No admis fee. Estab 1958 as an art museum which serves the members of the university community as well as the public. The Museum houses a permanent collection in two galleries and foyer, a period room, a prints and drawings gallery and an exhibition gallery. Average Annual Attendance: 40,000. Mem: 225, dues $25
Income: $400,000 (financed by endowment, membership and state appropriation)
Collections: †Collection of paintings, sculpture, photographs, prints and drawings covering the history of primarily Western art from ancient Egypt to the present day; decorative arts
Exhibitions: (1978) North Carolina Country Quilts (1978) French 19th Century Oil Sketches; (1979) Drawings about Drawing Today. (1980) New Art from Chicago
Publications: Newsletter, fall and spring
Activities: Docent tours; gallery talks open to public; lectures; films; receptions for members; exhibition catalogs available for sale

L **Art Library,** Columbia & Franklin Streets, 27514. Tel 919-933-2397. *Art Librn* Philip Rees; *Library Asst* Michele Patterson
Open Mon - Thurs 8 AM - 11 PM, Fri 8 AM - 5 PM, Sat 8:30 AM - 5 PM, Sun 2 - 11 PM
Income: Financed by state appropriation
Purchases: $31,000
Library Holdings: Vols 35,000; Per subs 185; Micro—Fiche, reels; Other—Pamphlets

CHARLOTTE

M **CHARLOTTE NATURE MUSEUM, INC,*** 1658 Sterling Rd, 28209. Tel 704-333-0506. *Exec Dir* Russell I Peithman; *Cur Exhib* Jeffery Birch; *Cur Educ* Freda Nicholson
Open Mon - Sat 9 AM - 5 PM, Sun 2 - 5 PM, cl holidays. No admis fee. Inc 1947 to develop an appreciation of man and nature. Average Annual Attendance: 405,000. Mem: 1000; dues $15 - $500; annual meeting May
Income: $228,000
Purchases: $4000
Collections: †Pre-Columbian: Mayan, North America, Peruvian; †Primitive Art: Africa, Alaskan Eskimo, Oceania, South America
Activities: Art workshops in nature sketching and museum methods; lect on African kingdoms, ancient civilizations

M **MINT MUSEUM OF ART,*** 501 Hempstead Place, PO Box 6011, 28208. Tel 704-334-3948. *Dir* Milton J Bloch; *Asst Dir* Stephen W Musgrove; *Cur of Exhib* Jerald Melberg
Open Tues - Fri 10 AM - 5 PM, Sat & Sun 2 - 5 PM. No admis fee. Estab 1936 as an art museum in what was the first branch of the US mint erected in 1837. Museum houses three changing galleries: a permanent gallery, Delhom Decorative Arts Gallery; two Charlotte Gold Rooms; and a sales and rental gallery. Average Annual Attendance: 150,000. Mem: 1850; dues student and senior citizens $7.50, up to $150 for others; annual meeting Jan
Income: Financed by endowment, membership and city appropriation
Collections: Decorative arts, paintings, sculpture with emphasis on Baroque, Renaissance, 18th century English, 19th and 20th century European and American paintings, and pre-Columbian art
Publications: Mint Museum Newsletter and calendar of events, six times a year
Activities: Classes for adults; docent training; lect open to the public, 25 visiting lectrs per year; concerts; gallery talks; tours; competitions; original objects of art lent to other museums; museum shop selling books, original art, prints, gifts, museum replicas, jewelry, cards

L **Library,*** 501 Hempstead Place, PO Box 6011, 28208. *Librn* Sara Wolf
Open to members for reference only
Library Holdings: Vols 6000

L **PUBLIC LIBRARY OF CHARLOTTE AND MECKLENBURG COUNTY,** 310 N Tryon St, 28202. Tel 704-374-2725. *Dir* Arial A Stephens; *Assoc Dir* Judith Sutton; *Art Librn* Carolyn Hunter
Open Mon - Fri 9 AM - 9 PM, Sat 9 AM - 6 PM, Sun 2 - 6 PM, cl Sun June - Aug. Estab 1903 to provide free public library service to citizens of Mecklenburg County. Gallery contains 90 linear feet of wall space
Income: $3,295,482 (financed by state and county appropriations)
Purchases: $461,829
Library Holdings: Vols 689,688; AV—Cassettes, fs, motion pictures 1137, rec 16,018, slides 9261; Other—Prints 262, sculpture, maps 6507
Exhibitions: Local artists exhibit for one month
Activities: Individual paintings loaned to residents

DALLAS

M **GASTON COUNTY ART AND HISTORY MUSEUM,** 131 N Gaston St, PO Box 429, 28304. Tel 704-922-8361. *Pres* Robert Ragan; *VPres* Simeon Adams; *Secy* Dalton Stowe; *Treas* Ralph Robinson; *Dir* Alan D Waufle; *Cur of Education* Melissa Jones; *Chief Art Instructor* Larry Young
Open Tues - Fri 10 AM - 5 PM, Sat 10 AM - 2 PM, Sun 2 - 5 PM. No admis fee. Estab Nov 1975, opened July 1976 to promote the fine arts and local history in Gaston County, through classes, workshops and exhibitions; to preserve Historic Dallas Square; promote the history of the textile industry. The museum is located in an 1848 Greek Revival Courthouse; the Hands-On Gallery includes sculpture and weaving which may be touched; the two small galleries are on local history, with the major gallery for changing and traveling exhibitions. Average Annual Attendance: 20,000. Mem: 400; dues $10 - $35; annual meeting Nov, with monthly meetings the first Thurs in Feb, May, August and Nov
Income: $50,000 (financed by membership and county appropriation)
Purchases: $2000
Collections: †Contemporary Sculpture; †Documents; Objects of Local History; †Paintings by North Carolina Artists living and dead; Photographs; †Textile History
Exhibitions: Frank Creech; Pauline Dove; Annual Crafts Show; Annual Photography Show; Annual Spring Art Show; The Christmas Doll; Gaston Textile History; High School Show; Historic Gaston Churches; Judaic Ceremonial Art; What's in a Map?

Publications: The Register, quarterly newsletter
Activities: Classes for adults and children; docent training; lect open to the public, 4 vis lectr per year; puppet performances; competitions; originate traveling exhibitions; museum shop sells books, slides, stationery, jewelry, maps, decorative art objects
L **Library,** 131 N Gaston St, 28304.
Open to public for reference only
Library Holdings: Vols 50; Per subs 10

DAVIDSON

M **DAVIDSON COLLEGE ART GALLERY,** Box 2495, 28036. Tel 704-892-2000.
Dir Herb Jackson
Open Mon - Fri 10 AM - 5 PM, Sat & Sun 2 - 5 PM. No admis fee. Estab 1952 to provide exhibitions of educational importance. Gallery covers 4000 sq ft. Average Annual Attendance: 6000
Income: Financed by college budget
Collections: Primary emphasis in Graphics
Activities: Lect open to public, 6 vis lectr per year; gallery talks
L **Library,** Box 2495, 28036. *Librn* Dr Leland Park
Open to students and visitors

DURHAM

M **DUKE UNIVERSITY MUSEUM OF ART,** 6877 College Station, 27708. Tel 919-684-5135. *Dir* W K Stars; *Staff Asst* Judith S Markwordt; *Cur Pre-Columbian Coll* Paul A Clifford; *Cur Classical Coll* Dr Keith Stanley; *Honorary Cur Medieval Coll* Dr Elizabeth Sunderland
Open Mon - Fri 9 AM - 5 PM, Sat 10 AM - 1 PM, Sun 2 - 5 PM. No admis fee. Estab 1969 as a study museum with the collections being used and studied by various university departments, as well as the public school system and surrounding communities. The museum is located on the East Campus in a renovated two-story Georgian building; gallery space includes part of the first floor and entire second floor with the space divided into eight major gallery areas. Average Annual Attendance: 8000 - 10,000
Income: Financed by University
Collections: African; Classical; Graphics; Medieval Decorative Art and Sculpture; Oriental Jade and Porcelain; Paintings; †Pre-Columbian; Textiles (Peruvian, Navajo)
Publications: Exhibition catalogs, 1 - 2 per year; Friends of the Museum Newsletter, quarterly
Activities: Lect open to public, 2 - 4 lectr per year; gallery talks; tours; individual paintings and original objects of art lent to other museums which are equipped with proper security and insurance
O **Union Graphic Arts Committee,** Box KM, Duke Station, 27706. Tel 919-684-2911.
Pres Tina I Finkel
Open 8:30 AM - Noon. No admis fee. Estab to bring to the university community exhibits of every type of graphic arts; to bring artists to campus for workshops. Galleries, large room in Union and wall and shelf space in Booklovers Room in East Campus Library. Mem: 15; monthly meetings
Income: Financed by endowment and 10% commission on exhibit works sold
Exhibitions: Professional and Local Artist, approx twice monthly
Activities: Classes for adults; lect open to public, 1 vis lectr per year; competitions
L **East Campus Library,** 6877 College Station, 27708. *Reference Librn* Margaret Knoerr; *Art History Librn* Edith Hassold
Open 8 AM to Noon. Estab 1930 to support the study of art at Duke University
Purchases: $20,000
Library Holdings: Vols 52,000; Per subs 179; Micro—Cards, fiche, reels; Other—Clipping files, exhibition catalogs, pamphlets
Collections: Emphasis on European and American Art

M **NORTH CAROLINA CENTRAL UNIVERSITY,** Museum of Art, Fayetteville St, 27707. Tel 919-683-6211. *Dir* Norman E Pendergraft; *Secy Registrar* Patti Farrior; *Guard Preparator* Terry L Singletary
Open Tues - Fri 9 AM - 4 PM, Sun 2 - 4 PM. No admis fee. Estab 1971 as a predominantly black teaching institution with a collection of contemporary art, many Afro-American artist, reflecting diversity in style, technique, medium and subject. Three galleries are maintained; one houses the permanent collection and two are for changing shows. Average Annual Attendance: 4000
Income: Financed by state appropriation
Purchases: $174,359
Collections: African and Oceanic; †Contemporary American with a focus on minority artists; †Contemporary, non-American
Exhibitions: Alumni Exhibition: Stanley Comer and Walt Davis; Faculty: Mohinder Gill, two-dimensional works; Isabel Levitt, three-dimensional works; American Landscape: East and West 1820 - 1920; The Museum's Choice; University Artists: New Horizons; The World of Haitian Painting
Publications: Exhibition catalog
Activities: Lect open to public; gallery talks; tours

FAYETTEVILLE

M **FAYETTEVILLE MUSEUM OF ART, INC,** 868 Elm St, PO Box 35134, 28303.
Tel 919-485-1395. *Pres* Dell K Hollstein; *VPres* Burt Melton; *Secy* Bruce Pullium; *Dir* Phyllis A McLeod; *Asst Dir* Rebekah K Lee
Open Tues - Fri 10 AM - 5 PM, Sat & Sun 1 - 5 PM. No admis fee. Estab 1971 to promote in the area an active interest in the fine and applied arts; to establish and maintain a permanent collection. Lobby and main gallery is 996 sq ft, 143 ft wall space. Average Annual Attendance: 10,000. Mem: 500; dues $100, $50, $25, $15, $10; annual meeting in the Spring
Income: $60,000 (financed by membership and city appropriation)
Collections: Contemporary Southeastern Artists
Exhibitions: Frederick Carl Frieseke - An American Impressionist; 100 Years of American Art; Kinetic Sculpture and Color Painting by Rudy Ayoroa; 7th and 8th Annual Competitions for North Carolina Artists
Publications: Monthly calendar
Activities: Classes for adults and children; docent training; lect open to public, 12 - 15 visiting lectr per year; concerts; gallery talks; competitions; cash awards; book traveling exhibitions 3 - 4 per year; originate traveling exhibitions

GREENSBORO

M **GREEN HILL ART GALLERY,** 200 N Davie St, 27401. Tel 919-373-4515. *Pres Board Dir* Clifford B Lowery; *VPres* James P Hendrix; *Secy* Dorothy Latham; *Treas* Richard Windham; *Dir* Cynthia K Ference
Open Tues - Fri 10 AM - 5 PM, Sat & Sun 2 - 5 PM, cl Mon and holidays. No admis fee. Estab and incorporated 1974 as a non-profit institution offering exhibitions and educational programming featuring the visual arts of North Carolina. Mem: Dues $5 to patron $100 and up
Income: Financed by memberships, United Arts Council of Greensboro and various grants
Exhibitions: Monthly exhibitions featuring North Carolina Visual Arts: crafts, drawing, film, painting, photography, sculpture and video
Publications: Newsletter
Activities: Junior Curators Program for high school students: Friends classes; concerts; lect; gallery tours; competitions; art referral; Friends of Green Hill Volunteer group; services for corporations and individuals; collectors sales gallery

M **UNIVERSITY OF NORTH CAROLINA AT GREENSBORO,** Weatherspoon Art Gallery, Walker Ave at McIver St, 27412. Tel 919-379-5770. *Dir* Gilbert F Carpenter; *Secy* Scott Keener; *Cur* James E Tucker
Open Tues - Fri 10 AM - 5 PM, Sat & Sun 2 - 6 PM, cl Mon, University holiday periods and between academic sessions. No admis fee. Estab 1942 as a teaching arm of the University Department of Art. The gallery houses modern art for the Greensboro and Piedmont area; the main gallery is large and can exhibit large shows, or several small shows at once; the outer lobby gallery is used mainly for student shows; a sculpture court contains permanently installed modern sculptures. Mem: 500; dues $5 and up; annual meeting April or May
Income: $9200 (financed by university budget)
Purchases: $60,000
Collections: 20th Century American and European Drawings, Paintings, Prints and Sculpture; smaller Collection of Oriental Prints, Scrolls and Snuff Bottles
Exhibitions: (1978) Lee Adler - One-Man Exhibition of Paintings and Prints; African Tribal Art; Art on Paper 1978; Leonard Bocour Gifts to the Weatherspoon Gallery Permanent Collection; Stanley Boxer - Drawings; Christopher Cairns and Jonathan Silver - Sculpture; Eight German Theatre Poster-Makers; Japanese Scrolls; The Robert Marks Photography Collection; Woodcuts. (1979) American Images: Documentary Photographs by the Farm Security Administration 1935-42; Art on Paper 1979; Contemporary Printmaking - selections from the Collection of Ashland Oil, Inc; Domlandschaft - Photographs of the Cologne Cathedral by Winfrid Kralisch; A Doren Photography: Americana Faces and Solarized Nude Studies; Greensboro Collectors; Alex Katz - Prints; Lithography; MFA Thesis Exhibition; Mail Art; Robert Natkin - One-Man Exhibition; North Carolina Sculpture 1979; Architectural Drawings of Matthew Nowicki; Selections from the Permanent Collection featuring Recent Acquisitions; Piranesi Prints; Statewide Touring Black Artist Exhibition; Woman: Images on Paper; Drawings by Sculptors; Scholastic Art Awards; Senior Exhibition; Spring Loan Exhibition; (1980) 500 Years of Wine in the Arts; The Paintings of Yun Gee; MFA Thesis Exhibition; Modern German Drawings; Scholastic Art Awards; Spring Loan Exhibition; selections from the Permanent Collection; Student Exhibitions
Publications: Weatherspoon Gallery Association Bulletin, annually
Activities: Lect open to the public, 6 - 8 vis lectr per year; gallery talks; tours; individual paintings and original objects of art lent to other museums, and local corporate and individual benefactors contributing $1000 or more per year; lending collection consists of original art works, original prints, paintings, photographs, sculpture and videotapes; originate traveling exhibitions

GREENVILLE

M **EAST CAROLINA UNIVERSITY,** Wellington B Gray Gallery, School of Art, 27834. Tel 919-757-6665. *Dean* Richard H Laing; *Gallery & Museum Dir* Randolph Osman
Open Mon - Fri 9 AM - 5 PM. No admis Fee. Estab 1977 as a teaching gallery offering students visual experiences on campus. A new museum section is opening in 1980; the gallery is a large, modern facility
Income: Financed by state appropriation and Friends of Art
Collections: Contemporary American Art
Exhibitions: National and Regional Exhibitions, faculty and student (undergraduate and graduate); permanent collection
L **Art Library,** Leo Jenkins Fine Arts Center, 27834.
Open daily 8 AM - 5 PM. Estab 1977 for Art School study of current and selected periodicals and selected reference books and slides. For lending and reference
Library Holdings: Per subs 60; Micro—Cards; AV—Fs, motion pictures, slides, v-tapes; Other—Exhibition catalogs, manuscripts

O **GREENVILLE ART CENTER,** 802 Evans St, 27834. Tel 919-758-1946. *Dir* Edith G Bradley Walker
Open year round, except for holidays; gallery hours Mon - Fri 9 AM - 5 PM, and by appointment. Estab 1939, incorporated as East Carolina Art Society in 1956, to foster public interest in art and to form a permanent collection. Average Annual Attendance: 20,000. Mem: 1200; dues $10 and higher; annual meeting each Spring
Income: $30,000 (plus Foundation income for acquisition of art)
Collections: Contemporary paintings; graphics; sculpture; weavings
Exhibitions: Exhibitions change monthly, featuring work of regional artists; national traveling exhibits; works from the North Carolina Museum of Art, of which our museum is an Affiliate Gallery
Publications: Periodical newsletter
Activities: Classes for adults and children; demonstrations; workshops; Lect; traveling exhibitions organized and circulated
L **Library,** 802 Evans St, 27834.
Library Holdings: Vols 200; Per subs 150

HICKORY

M **HICKORY MUSEUM OF ART, INC,** Third St & First Ave NW, PO Box 2572, 28601. Tel 704-327-8576. *Pres* Neill W Clark, Jr; *VPres* Dale K Cline; *Secy* Connie Bray; *Treas* Ronald Deal; *Exec Dir* Mildred M Coe; *Asst to Dir* Thelma M Abee
Open Mon - Fri 10 AM - 5 PM, Sun 3 - 5 PM. No admis fee. Estab 1944 to collect and foster American art and serve the western Piedmont area as an exhibiting and training art center. One large gallery is used mainly for traveling exhibitions; eight small galleries are used for permanent collections. Average Annual Attendance: 10,000. Mem: 670; dues $15 - $1000; meetings second Tues of each quarter
Income: $32,500 (financed by membership and donations)
Collections: Small European collection; very fine collection of 19th and 20th century American paintings
Exhibitions: 12 national, regional and local exhibitions per year
Activities: Classes for adults and children; docent training; periodic art classes; lect open to public; gallery talks; tours; competitions; exten dept; individual paintings lent to museums only; traveling exhibitions organized and circulated

LAKE JUNALUSKA

M **UNITED METHODIST CHURCH COMMISSION ON ARCHIVES AND HISTORY,** 39 Lakeshore Dr, Box 488, 28745. Tel 704-456-9433. *Executive Secy* Dr John H Ness Jr; *Admin Asst* Louise Queen
Open Mon - Fri 9 AM - 5 PM, summer Sat 9 AM - 5 PM, cl Sun and holidays, Sept - May cl Sat & Sun. No admis fee. Estab 1885 as a religious history museum
Collections: John Wesley Busts; Paintings of Church Leaders and Historic Buildings; Religious Church Materials
Publications: Historian's Digest, bimonthly; Methodist History, quarterly
Activities: Guided tours in summer; sales shop sells books, plates, cards, slides and prints
L **Library,** 39 Lakeshore Dr, 28745.
Library Holdings: Vols 40,000

NEW BERN

M **TRYON PALACE RESTORATION COMPLEX,** 613 Pollock St, 28560. Tel 919-638-5109. *Dir* Donald R Taylor; *Chmn* Robert L Stallings Jr; *Cur Education* Dabney M Coddington; *Education Specialist* Margaret Wall; *Registrar* Mrs Robert A Ipock; *Maintenance* James A Thomas; *Horticulturist* W H Rea
Open Tues - Sat 9:30 AM - 4 PM, Sun 1:30 - 4 PM, cl Mon. Admis adults $2, children $1. Estab 1959. Maintained are the historic house museums (Tryon Palace, Stevenson House, John Wright Stanly House) with fine portraits, paintings, Federal and Empire antiques, furnishings, silver, porcelain and object d'art. Average Annual Attendance: 47,500. Mem: meetings April & Oct
Collections: Paintings by Nathaniel Dance; Thomas Gainsborough; School of Sir Godfrey Kneller; Claude Lorrain; David Martin; Richard Paton; William Peters; Charles Phillips; Alan Ramsay; Jan Siberechts; E Van Stuven; Richard Wilson; Graphics
Publications: Seven books, many leaflets
Activities: Audio-visual orientation program; annual symposium on 18th century decorative arts; lect open to public; tours; lending collection contains slides; museum shop
L **Library,** 613 Pollock St, 28560.
Open for use with permission
Library Holdings: Vols 3000; Other—Photographs

RALEIGH

O **NORTH CAROLINA ART SOCIETY,*** 107 E Morgan St, 27601. Tel 919-733-4779. *Pres* Mrs Isaac V Manly; *VPres* Mrs Charles M Reeves; *Secy & Treas* Charles Lee Smith; *Exec Secy* Mrs Christopher R Webster
Estab 1927 to formulate programs to promote public appreciation of visual art, to encourage talent, to disseminate information on art through publications, to encourage private acquisition of works of art and to support the State Art Museum's programs by membership. The Art Society's collection has been given to the North Carolina Museum of Art and all purchases are given either to that or other art centers in the state. Mem: 3000; dues student $5 and up; annual meeting Dec
Income: $25,000
Purchases: $50,000 (annually for work of art for State Art Museum; $3000 for NC Artists' Exhibition)
Exhibitions: Annual North Carolina Artists' Exhibition held at North Carolina Museum of Art, including medal awards and purchases, financed by the Art Society

M **NORTH CAROLINA MUSEUM OF ART,** Department of Cultural Resources, 107 E Morgan St, 27611. Tel 919-733-7568. *Assoc Dir* Kenneth M Beam; *Chief Cur* Gay M Hertzman; *Chief Programs* Sterling Boyd; *Education Services* Michael W Brantley; *Exhib & Publications* Dorothy B Rennie; *Conservator* Adele de Cruz;

Registrar Peggy Jo Kirby
Open Tues - Sat 10 AM - 5 PM, Sun 2 - 6 PM, cl Mon & holidays. No admis fee. Estab 1947, open to public 1956, to acquire, preserve, and exhibit works of art for the education and enjoyment of the people of the State; and to conduct programs of education, research, and publications designed to encourage interest in and an appreciation of art, on the part of the people. Average Annual Attendance: 100,000
Income: Financed by state appropriation
Collections: Mary Duke Biddle Gallery for the Blind; Samuel H Kress Collection; African, North American Indian and Pre-Columbian Art; American and European Decorative Arts, Painting, Sculpture; Ancient Art
Exhibitions: Annual Artists North Carolina Exhibition; John J McCurdy: A Memorial Exhibition; A Survey of Zairean Art
Publications: Bulletin, irregular; Calendar, monthly
Activities: Classes for children; docent training; Affiliate Gallery Program; lect open to public, 10 vis lectr per year; concerts; gallery talks; tours; competitions; exten dept serving North Carolina; originate traveling exhibitions; museum shop sells books, gifts
L **Library,** 107 E Morgan St, 27611. *Librn* Dr Anna Dvorak
Open to public for reference
Library Holdings: Vols 15,000; Per subs 50; AV—Slides 13,700; Other—Photographs 18,900, transparencies 1370

O **NORTH CAROLINA MUSEUMS COUNCIL,** PO Box 27647, 27611. Tel 919-733-7450.
Estab 1964 to stimulate interest, support and understanding of museums. Mem: 250; dues individual $5; meetings spring and fall
Income: Financed by membership
Publications: Newsletter, summer and winter

L **NORTH CAROLINA STATE UNIVERSITY,** Harrye Lyons Design Library, 209 Brooks Hall, 27650. *Librn* Maryellen LoPresti; *Library Asst* Lynn Crisp; *Library Asst* Marianne Dale; *Library Asst* Dot Hunt
Open Mon - Thurs 8:30 AM - 9:30 PM, Fri 8:30 - 5 PM, Sat 9 AM - 1 PM, Sun 1 - 5 PM. Estab 1942 to serve the reading, study, reference and research needs of the faculty, students and staff of the School of Design and the University campus, as well as off-campus borrowers. Circ 42,366
Income: Financed by membership, state appropriation and private funds
Purchases: $20,000
Library Holdings: Vols 20,804; Micro—Fiche, reels; AV—Cassettes, fs, motion pictures, slides, v-tapes; Other—Clipping files, exhibition catalogs, prints, pamphlets, photographs, reproductions, trade literature, vertical files
Special Subjects: Art History, Architecture, Historical Material, urban, product, industrial and landscape design
Collections: John L Skinner Collection (etchings of the Raphel Loggia); File on measured Drawings of North Carolina Historic Sites; 1154 maps and plans; 300 bibliographies compiled by the Design Library staff; and a 370 item print collection
Publications: Index to the School of Design, student publication book Vols 1 - 25

REIDSVILLE

M **UNIVERSITY OF NORTH CAROLINA AT GREENSBORO,** Chinqua-Penn Plantation House, Route 3, Box 437, 27320. Tel 919-349-4576. *Executive Dir* George W Hamer; *House Mgr* Vivien Forrester; *Supt of Grounds* Dwight Talley
Open March - third Sun in Dec Wed - Sat 10 AM - 4 PM, Sun 1:30 - 4:30 PM. Admis adults $2, senior citizens $1.50, children $1. Estab 1966 as part of University's total educational program to make the house with its collection and the gardens available to the public. Average Annual Attendance: 37,000
Income: Financed by state appropriation
Collections: Antique European Furniture; Oriental Art Objects
Activities: Sales shop sells Chinqua-Penn Book and postcards

RESEARCH TRIANGLE PARK

C **BURROUGHS WELLCOME COMPANY,** 3030 Cornwallis Rd, 27709. Tel 919-541-9090, Ext 4449. *In Charge Art Coll* Thack Brown
Open 9 AM - 4 PM, groups only by prior arrangement. No admis fee. Estab 1979 to develop a meaningful collection of American Contemporary Art for enjoyment and enrichment for employees and communities. Collection displayed in Corporate Headquarters Building
Collections: Paintings and sculpture from permanent collection and on-loan from The Whitney Museum in New York City
Activities: Tours

ROCKY MOUNT

O **ROCKY MOUNT ARTS AND CRAFTS CENTER,** Old Nashville Rd, PO Box 4031, 27801. Tel 919-977-2111, Ext 377. *Dir* Julia Jordan; *Dir Theatre* William A Rawls
Open Mon - Fri 9 AM - 1 PM and 2 - 5 PM, Sun 3 - 5 PM, cl Sat except for classes. No admis fee. Estab 1957 to promote the development of the creative arts in the community through education, participation and appreciation of music, dance, painting, drama, etc; to provide facilities and guidance for developing talents and enriching lives through artistic expression and appreciation. Average Annual Attendance: 25,000. Mem: 600; dues $7.50 and up
Income: Financed by City Recreation Department with supplemental support by membership
Exhibitions: Outdoor Art Exhibition in the Spring, part of the Arts Festival; Permanent collection and traveling shows change each month
Activities: Conducts art classes; year-round theatre program; classes for adults and children; lect; concerts; book traveling exhibitions

SALISBURY

M SUPPLEMENTARY EDUCATIONAL CENTER, Art Gallery,* 1636 Parkview Circle, 28144. Tel 704-636-3462. *Dir* Herbert C Rhodes; *Cur Visual Art* Rosemary Johnson
Open during school hours. No admis fee. Estab 1968 to exhibit art work of public schools, supplemented by exhibits of local artists from time to time during the school year; primary purpose is to supplement art education activities in the public schools. The Center is comprised of two areas, one approximately 24 x 65 ft, the other 15 x 70 ft with an adjoining classroom for instruction and demonstrations. Average Annual Attendance: 3500
Income: Financed by membership, state and county appropriation, and from local foundations
Activities: Classes for adults and children

WILMINGTON

M SAINT JOHN'S ART GALLERY, 114 Orange St, 28401. Tel 919-763-0281. *Dir* Alan Aiches
Open Tues - Sat 10 AM - 5 PM. No admis fee. Estab 1962 to promote interest in the fine and applied arts; to establish and maintain an art collection; and to provide exhibitions for the enjoyment of creative ability and artistic achievement; the gallery is a non-profit educational and cultural center serving southeastern North Carolina. Average Annual Attendance: 15,000. Mem: 700; dues $15 - $100; annual meeting first Tues in June
Income: Financed by membership, city, county and state appropriation
Collections: Jugtown Pottery; Paintings; Scent Bottles
Exhibitions: Monthly exhibition including Artwork from Regional Artists, and loans from North Carolina Museum of Art
Publications: Bulletin, monthly
Activities: Classes for adults and children; docent training; lect open to public, 2 vis lectr per year; concerts; gallery talks; tours; sales shop sells original art
L Library, 114 Orange St, 28401.
Estab 1962. Open to members by appointment
Library Holdings: Vols 250; Per subs 3; Other—Exhibition catalogs, reproductions

M USS NORTH CAROLINA BATTLESHIP MEMORIAL, Cape Fear River, PO Box 417, 28402. Tel 919-762-1829. *Dir* F S Conlon; *Asst Dir* Charles Peek
Open daily 8 AM to approx sunset. Admis fee. Estab 1961 as historic ship museum
Income: Admissions only
Collections: World War II Battleship Memorabilia
Activities: Open for tours every day; summer months outdoor sound and light show; free brochure on request

WILSON

M ATLANTIC CHRISTIAN COLLEGE, Case Art Gallery, 27893. Tel 919-237-3161. *Museum Dir* Edward Brown
Open Mon - Fri 10 AM - 4:30 PM, Sat 1:30 - 3:30 PM. Estab 1967 to provide art exposure for our students and community. Gallery is 50 x 50 ft. Average Annual Attendance: 2000
Income: Financed by college budget
Purchases: $500
Collections: Ceramics; Recent Drawings; Painting; Prints; Sculpture
Exhibitions: New monthly exhibitions of Painting; Photography; Pottery; Prints; Sculpture; Weaving
Activities: Classes for adults; docent training; lect open to public, 3 vis lectr per year; gallery talks; competitions; lending collections contains cassettes, 750 original art works, prints, sculpture, 4500 slides

WINSTON-SALEM

O ARTS COUNCIL, INC,* 226 N Marshall St, 27101. Tel 919-722-2585. *Pres* Elizabeth M Booke; *Executive Dir* Jesse C Reese Jr
Open Mon - Fri 9 AM - 5 PM. Estab 1949 as a housing, coordinating, promoting and fund-raising organization for 39 member groups, including Associated Artists, Arts and Crafts Association, the Winston-Salem Symphony Association, The Little Theatre, South Eastern Center for Contemporary Art and Childrens' Theatre, member groups are autonomous of Arts Council. Housing facilities include a theatre, rehearsal rooms, art and craft studios and an exhibition gallery. Mem: 15,000; annual meeting May
Income: Financed by endowment, city and state appropriation and fund-drives
Activities: Management counsel, promotion and funds are provided for various arts programs

O ASSOCIATED ARTISTS OF WINSTON-SALEM,* 226 N Marhsall St, 27101. Tel 919-722-2585. *Pres* Agnes David
Open daily 10 AM - 4 PM. the Association rents the walls of the Gallery from the Arts Council. Mem: 300; dues $7
Income: $5000 (financed by membership and funds)
Publications: Newsletter, monthly
Activities: Classes for adults; lect open to public; gallery talks; competitions

M MUSEUM OF EARLY SOUTHERN DECORATIVE ARTS, Old Salem Inc, 924 S Main St, Drawer F, Salem Station, 27108. Tel 919-722-6148. *Secy & Receptionist* Patricia Pruette; *Assoc Educ* Elizabeth Putney; *Dir* Frank L Horton; *Educ Coordr* Sally Gant; *Archivist* Rosemary N Estes; *Asst to Dir* Bryding Adams; *Publications Dir* John Bivins Jr; *Photographer Technician* Wes Stewart
Open Mon - Sat 10:30 AM - 5 PM, Sun 1:30 - 4:30 PM. Admis adult $3, student $1.50. Estab 1965 to bring to light the arts and antiquities produced in Maryland, Virginia, Kentucky, Tennessee, North and South Carolina, and Georgia through the first two decades of the 19th century. Three galleries are furnished with southern decorative arts or imported objects used in the South, and fifteen period settings from southern houses dating from 1680 to 1821. Average Annual Attendance: 21,000. Mem: 650; dues $15 - $500; annual meeting April

Income: $225,000 (financed by endowment, membership, state appropriation, and other funds)
Purchases: Approx $50,000
Collections: †Southern decorative arts in general, and specifically furniture, paintings, silver, ceramics, metalwares, and woodwork of southern origin
Exhibitions: (1979-1981) Ongoing Research in Southern Decorative Arts
Publications: Journal of Early Southern Decorative Arts, semiannually; catalog of the collection 1979, Museum of Early Southern Decorative Arts
Activities: Classes for adults and children; graduate Summer Institute; lect open to public, 25 visiting lectr per year; gallery talks; scholarships; exten dept serves eight Southern States; individual paintings and original objects of art lent to museums and cultural institutions, and with special permission from staff are available for special exhibits; lending collection contains 2000 original art works, 100 paintings, 9000 photographs and 30,000 slides; originate traveling exhibitions; sales shop selling books, slides
L Library, 924 S Main St, Drawer F, Salem Station, 27108. *Librn* Bradford L Rauschenberg
Open 8:30 AM - 5 PM for collectors, students, or MESDA staff for reference only
Library Holdings: Vols 2000; Per subs 15; Micro—Cards, fiche, reels; AV—Lantern Slides; Other—Clipping files, exhibition catalogs, manuscripts, photographs
Special Subjects: County Histories of Southern States, Southern Decorative Arts

M REYNOLDA HOUSE, INC, Reynolda Village, Reynolda Rd, PO Box 11765, 27106. Tel 919-725-5325. *Executive Dir* Nicholas B Bragg; *Cur of Education* Marjorie Northup; *Admin Asst* Linda Grimes; *Development Asst* Elen Knott; *Secy* Marge Wagstaff
Open Tues - Sat 9:30 - 4:30 PM, Sun 1:30 - 4:30 PM, cl Mon. Admis adults $2, Senior citizens $1, students 75¢. Estab 1964 to offer a learning experience through a correlation of art, music and literature using the house and the Collection of American Art as resources. Gallery located in the 40 rooms of the former R J Reynolds mansion. Average Annual Attendance: 38,500. Mem: 600; annual meeting of Board of Directors in May and Nov
Income: $270,000 (financed by endowment, Friends' contributions, local and state government grants for specific programs, as well as foundation grants)
Collections: Doughty Bird Collection; Costume Collection; †Permanent Collection of Paintings and Prints on permanent loan
Publications: Annual Report; Calendar of Events, biannually
Activities: Classes for adults and children; dramatic programs; docent training; lect open to public, 20 vis lectr per year; concerts; gallery talks; tours; individual paintings and original objects of art lent to specific museums with reciprocity agreement; lending collection contains original prints, paintings; slides of paintings are sold
L Library, Reynolda Village, Reynolda Rd, 27106. *Librn* Elen Knott
Open to public
Library Holdings: Vols 1000; Per subs 30

C R J REYNOLDS INDUSTRIES, INC, Reynolds Blvd, World Headquarters, 27102. Tel 919-777-2925. *In Charge Art Coll* Laurie D Triplette
Estab 1977-78 to provide stimulating work environment for employees and visitors; to support artists and resources of R J Reynolds's many communities; to build an art collection of merit that will enhance the company. Collection displayed in corporate offices and operating facilities
Collections: Late 20th Century contemporary collection of all art media by regional, national and international artists
Exhibitions: Sponsors North Carolina Artists Competition; North Carolina Photography Competition
Activities: Competitions with awards; purchase awards at juried exhibitions; individual objects of art lent to arts institutions for specific exhibitions and events; originate traveling exhibitions to arts institutions, educational organizations of R J Reynolds communities

M SOUTHEASTERN CENTER FOR CONTEMPORARY ART, 750 Marguerite Dr, 27106. Tel 919-725-1904. *Pres* Mrs John Willingham; *Dir* Ted Potter; *Asst Dir* McChesney S Dunn; *Business Mgr* Lucy P Wilson; *Education Coordr* Susan B Mickey
Open Tues - Sat 10 AM - 5 PM, Sun 2 - 5 PM, cl Mon. No admis fee. Estab 1956 to identify and exhibit the southeast's major artists of exceptional talent; to present educational programs for children and adults; to bring the viewing public in direct contact with artists and their art. Maintained are nine indoor and outdoor exhibition areas. Average Annual Attendance: 80,000. Mem: 1500; dues varying categories; annual meeting June
Income: Financed by endowment, membership and state appropriation
Publications: Newsletter, quarterly
Activities: Classes for adults and children; docent training; workshops; lect open to public, 12 vis lectr per year; concerts; gallery talks; tours; competitions; originate traveling exhibitions; center shop sells books, magazines, original art, gifts, paper products, crafts

C WACHOVIA BANK & TRUST COMPANY, NA, 300 S Main, PO Box 3099, 27101. Tel 919-748-6143. *Asst VPres* Janet S Walters
Estab to support the arts and enhance the environment for customers and employees. Collection displayed throughout the 204 offices
Collections: Traditional and contemporary work, primarily by North Carolina and Southeastern United States artists

NORTH DAKOTA

DICKINSON

M DICKINSON STATE COLLEGE, Mind's Eye Gallery, Department of Art, 58601. Tel 701-227-2312. *Dir* Gail Ebeltoft; *Gallery Supv* Den Navrat
Open daily during academic year, regular library hours. No admis fee. Estab 1972

as a visual arts gallery presenting monthly exhibits representing the work of local, national and international artists. Gallery is a secure, large room approx 50 x 20 ft, with a 20 ft ceiling and approx 120 running ft of carpeted display space. Average Annual Attendance: 10,000

Income: $8000 (financed by endowment, state appropriation, Badlands Art Association)

Purchases: $Approx $1000

Collections: Zoe Beiler Paintings; †Contemporary Graphics

Exhibitions: Monthly rental exhibits

Publications: Exhibit announcements

Activities: Docent training; lect open to public, 2 - 4 vis lectr per year; gallery talks; originate traveling exhibitions

L **Stoxen Library,** Art Department, 58601. *Librn* Bernnett Reinke
Open to college students
Library Holdings: Vols 3150; Per subs 10

FORT RANSOM

M **SVACA - SHEYENNE VALLEY ARTS AND CRAFTS ASSOCIATION,** Bjarne Ness Gallery, PO Box 52, 58033. *Pres* Wayne Hankel; *VPres* Helen Bjone; *Exec Secy* Mrs Bjarne Ness; *Recording Secy* Mrs Ed Monson
Open Sat, Sun and holidays 1 - 6 PM, June 1 - Sept 30. No admis fee, donations accepted. Estab 1971 to preserve and care for the Bjarne Ness Gallery and to sponsor and promote interest in arts and crafts by conducting seminars, workshops, and an annual festival. The Gallery is the former studio of the late Bjarne Ness. Average Annual Attendance: 2400. Mem: 205; dues couple $5, single $3; annual meeting Nov

Income: Financed by membership and grants

Collections: Paintings of Bjarne Ness; paintings and wood carvings by area artists in SVACA's Bear Creek Hall

Exhibitions: Annual Arts and Crafts Festival; one or two members' shows

Activities: Classes for adults; gallery talks; individual paintings lent to banks, libraries, cafes

L **Bjarne Ness Gallery Library,** PO Box 52, 58033.
Open to members for reference
Library Holdings: Vols 150
Special Subjects: Arts and crafts

GRAND FORKS

M **UNIVERSITY OF NORTH DAKOTA ART GALLERIES,** University Ave, Box 8136, Univ Station, 58202. *Dir & Head Cur* Laurel J Reuter; *Asst Dir* Pat Gimbel
Open Mon - Thurs 10 AM - 9 PM, Fri 10 AM - 5 PM, Sat & Sun 1 - 5 PM. No admis fee. Estab 1971 as an exhibition gallery, historical as well as contemporary arts and crafts; galleries are also involved in educational and humanities projects. Galleries occupy three large sections on third floor of University Center, offices adjacent; mobile gallery housed in trailer. Average Annual Attendance: 18,000

Income: Financed by endowment, state appropriation and grants

Exhibitions: John Batho; Gary Bower; Grey Canyon Artists; Dakota Made; Folk Art; Frank Gohlke; Allen Graham Artists; Grain Elevators; Emily Lunde; John McQueen and Jessie Shefrin; N Scott Momaday; Numerals; Old Friends; Record Album Art; Don Reitz; Sense of the Self; Roger Shimomura; Water Works; North Dakota Annual; Juried Student Show

Publications: Exhibition catalog

Activities: Lect open to public, 6 - 8 vis lectr per year; gallery talks; originate traveling exhibitions

L **Bierce Library,** University Ave, 58202. *Librn* H Paul Schrank Jr
Open Mon - Fri 7:30 AM - Noon, Sat 9 AM - 5 PM, Sun 2 PM - 12 AM. Estab 1870
Library Holdings: Vols 9000
Activities: Classes for adults and children; lect open to public, 12-15 visiting lectr per year; gallery talks; art mobile; paintings lent to University offices; originate traveling exhibitions

MINOT

M **MINOT ART GALLERY,** Minot Art Association,* State Fair Grounds, PO Box 325, 58701. Tel 701-838-4445. *Dir* Beth Kjelson
Open Tues - Sun 1 - 5 PM. Admis adults 50¢, children 14 and under 10¢. Estab 1970 to promote means and opportunities for the education of the public with respect to the study and culture of the fine arts. Average Annual Attendance: 10,000. Mem: 235; dues life members $500 and up, student $5; annual meeting April

Income: $23,000 (financed by endowment, membership, and contributions)

Purchases: $500

Collections: Macrame; paintings; pottery; prints; sculpture; all done by local and national artists

Exhibitions: Art competitions; artfests; one-person exhibits; traveling art exhibits; exhibitions change monthly

Publications: Calendar of Exhibits, five times per year; newsletter

Activities: Classes for adults and children; lect open to public, 3 visiting lectrs per year; concerts; gallery talks; tours; competitions; individual paintings and original objects of art lent to local businesses, schools and libraries; lending collection contains original art works, original prints, paintings; traveling exhibitions organized and circulated; junior museum

M **Downtown Minot Art Gallery,*** 120 Main St, Ellisons 'The Fair', Balcony Floor, 58701.
Estab 1975
Exhibitions: Acrylic Paintings by Ruth Houff; Acrylic and Watercolor Paintings by Betsy Jones; Artwork by Art Students at Magic City Campus; North Dakota Impressions: Color Photography by Dave McGlauchlin; Weavings by Evelyn Souther

VALLEY CITY

M **FINE ARTS CLUB,** Second Crossing Gallery,* Room 210, McFarland Hall, Valley City State College, PO Box 1319, 58072. Tel 701-845-7561 (Art Dept). *Dir* Mrs Riley Rogers
Open Mon - Fri 1 - 4 PM, Mon, Wed 7 - 9 PM, Sun 2 - 4 PM, cl Aug. No admis fee. Estab 1973 to provide local, state, national and international shows for people in this area. Small but professional gallery consists of a room 28 x 40 ft with track lighting and movable standards. Average Annual Attendance: 3500. Mem: 130; dues $15 and up

Income: $12,000 (financed by endowment and membership)

Collections: †The Fine Arts Club has 19 pieces; †Second Crossing Gallery has 25 pieces

Exhibitions: 11 or 12 exhibitions a year of material from American Federation of Arts, Smithsonian, Western Association of Art Museums, local and state shows

Publications: Calendar, annually

Activities: Competitions with cash awards; individual painting and original objects of art lent to various offices on campus

WILLISTON

M **WILLIAMS COUNTY HISTORICAL SOCIETY,** Frontier Museum, 58801. *Pres* Olive Beard
Open May - Labor Day Sun 1 - 5 PM. Admis family $3.50, adults $1.50, children under 12 free, special rates to groups. Mem: Dues life $100, sustaining $25, patron $10, annual $3

Collections: Coins, decorative arts, historical material and buildings, paintings, prints, sculpture, textiles

Activities: Lect; guided tours; sales shop

L **Library,** Frontier Museum, 58801.
Library contains a small collection of historical and biographical publications

OHIO

AKRON

M **AKRON ART INSTITUTE,** 69 E Market St, 44308. Tel 216-376-9185. *Asst Dir* Gregory Allgire Smith; *Cur of Art* Carolyn Kinder Carr; *Cur of Education* Marcianne Herr; *Asst Cur & Registrar* Marjorie Harvey; *Public Information Officer* Cynthia Davidson-Powers
Open Tues - Fri Noon - 5 PM, Sat 9 AM - 5 PM, Sun 1 - 5 PM. No admis fee. Estab 1921 as a museum to exhibit and collect art. A total of four galleries; two house the permanent collection and two have changing exhibitions. Average Annual Attendance: 75,000. Mem: 1200; dues $20; annual meeting May

Income: $400,000 (financed by membership, endowment, corporate, foundation and government grants)

Collections: 19th & 20th Century American and European Art

Exhibitions: (1979) Diane Arbus Photographs; Brancusi Photographs; Brassai Photographs; Mark Cohen Photographs; Willem DeKooning Drawings, Paintings and Sculpture; Fulper Art Pottery; Graef Collection of American Jukeboxes; Jan Groover Photographs; Robert Horvitz Drawings; Jasper Johns Screenprints; Donald Judd Sculpture; Ben Lifson Photographs; Joel Meyerowitz Photographs; Robert Morris Sculpture; NASA Photographs; Alice Neel Portraits; Dennis Oppenheim Sculpture; Robert Rauschenberg Spreads and Scales; Alexander Rodchenko Retrospective; Lucas Samaras Fabric Reconstructions and Phototransformations; Buky Schwartz Videoconstructions; Kurt Schwitters Collages; Joel Shapiro Sculpture; Robert Smithson Sculpture; Southwest Indian Textiles; Jewel Stern Photographs; Athena Tacha Installation; Brinsley Tyrrell Landscapes (drawings); James VanDerZee Photographs; West Coast Ceramics; The Wheeler Album Photographs (O'Sullivan and Bell)

Publications: Calendar, monthly; exhibition catalogs

Activities: Classes for adults and children; docent training; lect open to public, 6 - 8 lectr per year; gallery talks; concerts; tours; artmobile; originates traveling exhibitions

L **Martha Stecher Reed Art Library,** 69 E Market St, 44308.
Open for reference
Library Holdings: Vols 5000; Per subs 50
Special Subjects: Contemporary art
Collections: Edwin Shaw Volumes, to accompany collection of American Impressionistic Art

C **THE FIRESTONE TIRE & RUBBER COMPANY,** 1200 Firestone Parkway, 44317. Tel 216-379-6432. *Chmn Contributions* John F Floberg
Firestone may contribute to the Akron Art Institute $130,000 during the next three-year period (1980-82) to the capital needs of the new location of the Akron Art Institute

M **STAN HYWET HALL FOUNDATION, INC,** 714 N Portage Path, 44303. Tel 216-836-5533. ; *VChmn* Raymond Wernig; *Pres* David C Corbin; *VPres* John L Tormey; *VPres* Robert L Reeves; *Secy* Mrs Albert J Brewster III; *Asst Secy* Mrs Harold W Nolf; *Treas* Howard Milford; *Asst Treas* Frank W Steere Jr
Open Sat 10 AM - 4 PM, Sun 1 - 4 PM, cl Mon & major national holidays. Admis adults $4, children 6 - 12 $1.50. Incorporated 1956, Stan Hywet Hall is a house museum, serving as a civic and cultural center. All restoration and preservation work is carefully researched to retain the original concept of the property, which represents a way of life that is gone forever. The mansion, the focal point of the estate, is a 65-room Tudor Revival manor house, furnished with priceless antiques and works of art dating from the 14th century. The property is the former home of Frank A Seiberling, (Akron rubber industrialist) and was completed in 1915. There are 70 acres of formal gardens, meadows, woods and lagoons. Average Annual Attendance: 135,000. Mem: 2900; dues $20 and up; annual meeting third Sun in March

Income: $600,000 (financed by endowment, membership, admissions, gifts, grants, rentals and special events)
Collections: Antique Furniture; China; Crystal; Paintings; Porcelain; Rugs; Sculpture; Silver; Tapestries
Publications: Stan Hywet Hall Newsletter, monthly
Activities: Classes for children; dramatic programs; docent training; lect open to public, 20 vis lectr per year; concerts; gallery talks; tours; competitions; lending collection contains photographs, slides and slide show with soundtrack, available with operator; sales shop sells books, original art, slides and wide variety of gift items
L **Library,** 714 N Portage Path, 44303.
Currently being developed, with reference materials relative to Stan Hywet Hall and Gardens

UNIVERSITY OF AKRON

M **University Galleries,** 44325. Tel 216-375-7012. *Dir* Donald E Harvey; *Art Dept Chmn* Thomas Morin
Open Mon - Fri 10 AM - 4 PM, Wed 6 - 9 PM. Estab 1974 to exhibit the work of important contemporary artists working in all regions of the United States, as well as to provide a showcase for the work of artists working within the university community. Two galleries: Emily H Davis Art Gallery, 1500 sq ft of wall space; Guzzetta Hall Atrium Gallery, 120 running ft of wall space. Average Annual Attendance: 8000
Income: Financed by university funds
Exhibitions: (1978-79) Recent Fibers by Akers, Grossen, Tawney; E J Bellocq, Photographs; Jack Earl, Ken Little, Ceramics; William King, Sculptures; Karen Shaw, Additional Meanings; William T Wiley Graphics; Editorial Cartoonists from Ohio Newspapers; (1980) Jennifer Bartlett, Paintings; Micha Laury, Sculpture and Drawings; Robert and Paula Winokur, Ceramics; Prints from Tyler Graphics, Ltd
Publications: Catalogs and artists books in conjunction with exhibitions
Activities: Lectures open to the public, six to eight visiting lecturers per year; gallery talks; traveling exhibitions organized and circulated
L **Bierce Library Art Department,** 44325. Tel 716-375-7495. *Librn* H Paul Schrank Jr
Open Mon - Fri 7:30 AM - 12 AM , Sat 9 AM - 5 PM, Sun 2 PM - 12 AM. Estab 1870
Library Holdings: Vols 9000

ASHLAND

M **ASHLAND COLLEGE ARTS AND HUMANITIES GALLERY,** College Ave, 44805. Tel 419-289-4005. *Chmn* Albert W Goad; *Dir Gallery* Carl M Allen
Open Tues - Sun 1 - 4 PM, Tues evenings 7 - 10 PM. No admis fee. Estab 1969-70. Gallery maintained for continuous exhibitions
Income: $2500
Purchases: $20,000
Exhibitions: Mostly contemporary works, some historical, occidental and Oriental
Activities: Classes for children; dramatic programs; lect open to public; 2 - 3 gallery talks; tours and regular tours to leading art museums; concerts; scholarships; original objects of art lent to Akron Art Institute and Cleveland Museum of Art

ASHTABULA

O **ASHTABULA ARTS CENTER,** 2928 W 13th St, 44004. Tel 216-964-3396. *Pres* Daniel Madden; *VPres* Wilbur Shenk; *Secy* Ruth Haskell; *Executive Dir* Caron VanGilder; *Asst Dir* Corinne Loyd; *Music Coordr* Sandy Kasper; *Visual Arts Coordr* Jeff Henning; *Drama* Laura Connors; *Public Relations* Nancy Carroll; *Asst Public Relations* P J Wineberg; *Secy* Rosemary Humphrey; *Dance Coordr* Bobbi Raisanen; *Dance Coordr* Nina Nelson
Open Mon - Fri 8 AM - 9 PM, Sat 9 AM - 5 PM, Sun 1 - 5 PM. No admis fee. Estab 1953 as a non-profit, tax exempt art organization, to provide high quality instruction. One major gallery area with smaller anex-fixed panals on all walls. Average Annual Attendance: 5000. Mem: 1000; dues family $25, individual $15; annual meeting Oct 20th
Income: $350,000 (financed by membership, earned, NEA, OAC, WSL, CETA)
Collections: Local and regional contemporary work, small international contemporary print collection, regional wood sculpture (major portion of collection represents local and regional talent)
Exhibitions: (1978) Christmas Exhibit; Charles McCaughtry (watercolors); Darlene Miller (sculpture); Betty Schabacker - Cloth Collage; 4 artists from Kent, graphics, painting
Publications: Ashtabula Arts Center News, monthly; exhibit information monthly
Activities: Classes for adults and children; dramatic program; lect open to public, 5 - 10 visiting lectr per year; concerts; gallery talks; tours; competitions; cash awards; scholarships; exten dept serves Ashtabula County hospitals and public buildings; individual paintings and original objects of art lent to schools and public buildings; lending collection contains books, cassettes, color reproductions, framed reproductions, original art works, original prints, paintings, phonorecords, photographs, sculpture and slides; book traveling exhibitions; originate traveling exhibitions; museum shop sells books, gift items, jewelry, original art, prints, reproductions and stationary

ATHENS

M **OHIO UNIVERSITY,** Anthony G Trisolini Memorial Gallery, 48 E Union St, 45701. Tel 614-594-5664. *Dir* Henry H Lin; *Asst to Dir* Barbara F Mantel
Open Tues - Sat Noon - 4 PM. No admis fee. Estab 1974 to provide cultural exposure to the university community and to the residents of the surrounding region. Gallery has four rooms with carpeted walls and floors. Average Annual Attendance: 9,000-12,000
Income: Financed by state appropriation
Purchases: $6,000 (plus grant funds)
Collections: †Contemporary prints, some paintings, photographs and sculpture
Exhibitions: African Artists in America; Courtesans of the Floating World; Erte; Nigerian Textiles; Seven Artists at Tyler Graphics Ltd; Skunder Boghossian

Publications: Scholarly exhibition catalogs, two or three times a year
Activities: Lect open to public; traveling exhibitions organized and circulated; museum shop selling original art, prints and crafts
M **Seigfred Gallery,** School of Art, Seigfred Hall 528, 45701. Tel 614-594-5667. *Dir* Erik Forrest; *Gallery Dir* Mary Manusos
Open Mon - Fri 10 AM - 4 PM. No admis fee. Gallery is used for faculty exhibitions, student exhibitions and visiting artist shows
L **Fine Arts Library,** 48 E Union St, 45701. Tel 614-594-5065. *Art Librn* Anne Brazton; *Asst Art Librn* Timothy Daum
Open Mon - Fri 8 AM - 12 Midnight, Sat & Sun 1 - Midnight
Income: Financed by state appropriation
Library Holdings: Vols 30,000; Other—Exhibition catalogs, prints, photographs
Collections: Research collection in history of photography; small collection of original photographs

BEACHWOOD

M **SALVADOR DALI MUSEUM,** 24050 Commerce Park Rd, 44122. Tel 216-464-0372. *Pres* A Reynolds Morse; *Dir* Joan Dropf; *Asst Mgr* Robin Houlas
Open Tues - Sat 10 AM - Noon and 1 - 4 PM, appointments necessary. No admis fee. Estab 1971 to share the private Dali Collection of Mr and Mrs A Reynolds Morse with the public. The collection is housed in a private office building in Commerce Park. Average Annual Attendance: 16,000
Income: Financed by private collector
Collections: †55 Oils and 3 large Masterworks by Dali make up a retrospective of his work from 1914 to the present; numerous Drawings and Watercolors
Exhibitions: Anamorphoses by Dali (graphic); Anthropomorphic Echo; Archaeological Reminiscence of Millet's Angelus; Broken Bridge of the Dream; Classical Series; Les Diners de Gala and Dalivision (graphic); Dali's Surrealist Fruits and Flowers (graphic show); Hiram College Graphic Exhibit; Important Dali Statements & Surrealist Documents; Women - Dali's view Erotic Art by Dali; Dali and Halshan photography
Publications: Dali Adventure; Dali - A Panorama of his Art; Dali Draftmanship; Guide to Works by Dali in Public Museums; Introduction to Dali; Dali-Picasso; Poetic Homage to Gala-Dali; Dali Primer; exhibition catalogues
Activities: Lect open public; gallery talks; tours; lending collection contains color reproductions; museum shop sells books, magazines, original art, reproductions, prints, slides, postcards, collector plates and jewelery
L **Library,** 24050 Commerce Park Rd, 44122.
Restricted use at present; contains references to Dali in books, periodicals and newspapers
Collections: Films and Tapes on or by Dali

BEREA

M **BALDWIN-WALLACE COLLEGE ART GALLERY,** 95 E Bagley Rd, 44017. Tel 216-826-2152. *Head Department Art* Dean Drahos
Open Thur, Fri 2 - 5 PM and 7 - 10 PM, Sat & Sun 2 - 5 PM, cl Mon, Tues, Wed and holidays. No admis fee. The Art Gallery is considered to be a part of the art program of the department of art; its purpose is that of a teaching museum for the students of the college and the general public. Average Annual Attendance: 2500
Income: Financed through budgetary support of the college
Collections: Approx †200 Paintings and Sculptures by Midwest artists of the 20th Century; approx †1900 Drawings and Prints from 16th - 20th Century, with a concentration in 19th & 20th Century examples
Exhibitions: Traveling and student exhibitions
Publications: Exhibition catalogs are published for important exhibitions, 1 - 2 per year
Activities: Lect open to public; gallery talks; tours; competitions; individual paintings lent to schools; book traveling exhibitions

BOWLING GREEN

M **BOWLING GREEN STATE UNIVERSITY,** Fine Arts Gallery, School of Art, 43403. Tel 419-372-2787. *Dir of Gallery* Ralph Warren
Open Mon - Fri 8:30 AM - 5 PM, Sun 2 - 5 PM. Estab 1964 to provide enrichment to School of Art program by furnishing research materials, exhibitions and related events; to provide for the growth of public sensitivity to the visual arts. Gallery is a multi-level facility located in the Fine Arts building with approximately 1500 running feet of exhibition space. Average Annual Attendance: 7500
Income: Financed by state appropriation and foundation

CANTON

M **CANTON ART INSTITUTE,** 1001 Market Ave N, 44702. Tel 216-453-7666. *Pres* Thomas H Horner; *VPres* Mrs Walter H Shealor; *Treas* R Richard Fawcett Jr; *Secy* Mrs Donald C Smith; *Dir* Joseph R Hertzi; *Assoc Dir* M J Albacete; *Admin Asst* Mrs Kenneth D Adams
Open Sept - July 15, Tues - Sat 10 AM - 5 PM, Tues, Wed & Thurs 7 - 9 PM, Sun 2 - 5 PM. Summer, July 15 - Aug 16, Tues - Sat 10 AM - 4 PM. Estab 1935, incorporated 1941. Average Annual Attendance: 75,000. Mem: 1680; dues $10 and higher; annual meeting Oct
Collections: National Stereoscopic Association's, Oliver Wendell Holmes National Stereographic Library estab 1979 (collection of stereo views and viewers); American, Italian, and Spanish Paintings; Art Objects; Costumes; Decorative Arts; 18th & 19th Century English and American Portraiture; Graphics; Sculpture; 20th Century Regional Art
Exhibitions: Approx 40 to 50 traveling or collected exhibitions of Commercial and Industrial Arts; Painting; Sculpture annually
Activities: Formally organized education programs for adults and children; Guided tours; lect; films; gallery talks; arts festivals; book traveling exhibitions

L **Art Library,** 1001 Market Ave N, 44702.
Library Holdings: Vols 4000

CINCINNATI

O **CINCINNATI ART CLUB,** 1021 Parkside Place, 45202. Tel 513-241-4591. *Pres* Louis C Austerman; *Secy* Sherman Peeno; *Treas* Joseph O Emmett
Open Sun afternoon Sept - May. Estab 1890, incorporated 1923. Gallery contains a small collection of paintings by American artists. Average Annual Attendance: 3500. Mem: 250; dues active $45, associate $35
Exhibitions: Exhibition of members' work changed monthly. Annual Club Shows Sept, Jan, and Christmas Art Bazaar.
Activities: Lect and demonstrations by important artists each month (Sept to May); a Forum open to the public each month

M **CINCINNATI ART MUSEUM,** Eden Park, 45202. Tel 513-721-5204. *Dir* Millard F Rogers; *Asst Dir* Betty L Zimmerman; *Business Mgr* Robert J Petersen; *Sr Cur & Cur Decorative Arts* Dr Carol Macht; *Cur Costumes, Textiles, Tribal Arts* Carolyn R Shine; *Cur Prints, Drawings & Photographs* Kristin L Spangenberg; *Cur Ancient, Near and Far Eastern Arts* Daniel S Walker; *Cur Painting* Denny T Carter; *Cur Slides & Photographs* Beth DeWall; *Conservator* Elizabeth Batchelor; *Registrar* Kathryn Taulbee
Open Tues - Sat 10 AM - 5 PM, Sun 1 - 5 PM, cl Mon & holidays. Admis adults $1, children ages 12 - 18 50¢, free to members and scheduled school tours, free to all on Sat. Estab 1881 to collect, exhibit, conserve and interpret works of art from all periods and civilizations (range of 5000 years of major civilizations of the world). Exhibition galleries cover an area of approx 4 acres, occupying two floors, with a few exhibition galleries, assembly areas and social center on ground level; altogether some 118 galleries given over to permanent collections, with additional galleries set aside for temporary exhibitions. Average Annual Attendance: 210,000. Mem: 3700; dues $25 and up; annual meeting March
Income: $1,500,000 (financed by endowment, membership, city appropriation, Cincinnati Fine Arts Fund, museum shop earnings, federal, state and private grants)
Collections: Ancient Musical Instruments; Artists; Art in Cincinnati; the Cincinnati Art Museum; †Egyptian, Greek, Roman, Near and Far Eastern Arts; †Paintings (European and American); †World Costumes, Textiles and Tribal Arts; †World Prints, Drawings and Photographs; †World Sculpture
Exhibitions: Ancient Art in Cincinnati Collections - Ceramics, Metalwork and Sculpture from Near East and Classical World; Antique English Silver Coffee Pots - The Folger Collection (showing designs from Queen Ann through George III); Jim Dine's Etchings - 107 works, 1961-1978 from Museum of Modern Art; 18th Century Master Drawings from the Ashmolean; Germany 1900-1933 (drawings, photographs and prints from museum and private collection); The Golden Age: Cincinnati Painters of the 19th Century represented in Cincinnati Art Museum; Mailers of History - 16th through 20th Century noted World Figures in Prints
Publications: Annual Report; catalogues for exhibitions; Handbook
Activities: Classes for children; docent training; seminars; lect open to public, 8 vis lectr per year; gallery talks; tours; competitions; exten dept serving Greater Cincinnati; individual paintings and original objects of art lent to established art institutions meeting aesthetic and security standards approved by Director and Board of Trustees; museum shop sells books, original art, reproductions, prints, slides, postcards and others

L **Library,** Eden Park, 45202. Tel 513-721-5204, Ext 51 & 52. *Librn* Patricia P Rutledge; *Asst Librn & Museum Archivist* Carole Schwartz; *Reference Librn* Grace S Keam
Open Tues - Fri 10 AM - 4:45 PM
Library Holdings: Vols 42,802; Per subs 98; Other—Clipping files, exhibition catalogs, pamphlets, reproductions
Collections: Files on Cincinnati Artists, Art in Cincinnati, the Cincinnati Art Museum, and the Art Academy of Cincinnati

O **CINCINNATI INSTITUTE OF FINE ARTS,** 2649 Erie Ave, 45208. Tel 513-871-3325. *Pres* Paul George Sittenfeld; *Secy* Fletcher E Nyce
Estab and inc 1927 to provide for the continuance and growth of education and culture in the various fields of fine arts in the metropolitan community of Cincinnati. Mem: Annual meeting Oct
Income: Financed through endowments by Cincinnati Symphony Orchestra, Cincinnati Art Museum, Cincinnati Opera, Taft Museum, May Festival, Cincinnati Ballet, Contemporary Arts Center, Cinnati Playhouse in the Park, Special Projects Pool
Publications: Quarterly Calendar

M **CONTEMPORARY ARTS CENTER,** 115 E Fifth St, 45202. Tel 513-721-0390. *Chmn* Alfred A Moore; *Pres* Toni Birckhead; *VPres* Phillip Long; *Treas* Stuart Schloss; *Secy* K R B Niehoff; *Dir* Robert Stearns; *Asst to Dir* Jean-Marie Baines; *Asst Preparator* Phillip Boyd; *Bookstore Mgr* Carolyn Brown; *Membership & Gallery Coordr* Nancy Glier; *Preparator* Stephen Jenkins; *Cur Asst* Sheri Lucas; *Audience & Program Development Dir* James Rosenberger; *Educ Dir* Pat Thomson
Open Tues - Sat 10 AM - 5 PM, Sun Noon - 5 PM, cl Mon. Admis adults $1, students 50¢. Estab 1939. The Center is a museum for the presentation of current developments in the visual and related arts. It does not maintain a permanent collection but offers changing exhibitions of international, national and regional focus. Average Annual Attendance: 15,000 - 20,000. Mem: 1000; dues from $10 - $100
Income: $375,000 (financed by endowment, city and state appropriations)
Exhibitions: Peter D'Agnostino Coming and Going: Paris (Metro), San Francisco (BART); Alice Aycock: The Angeles Continue Turning the Wheels of the Universe, part III; Peter Berg: Jan and Vern; Ethereat; Cloud Deflected Air: Pat Oleszko, Cecil Taylor; Mildred Fisher: Weaving and Paper; Europe in the Seventies: Aspects of Recent Art; Painting and Sculpture by Willem de Kooning; Prints of the Seventies; Modern Art Society: The Center's Early Years; Terry Ripley, Robert Ashley, John Stewart: Paintings; Strategies: Artists in the 80's; Sandy Rosen: Rooming In; Kes Zapkus: Recent Paintings
Publications: Catalogs of exhibitions
Activities: Docent training; lect, 6 visiting lectr per year; concerts; gallery talks; programs for adults and children; tours; lending collection contains slides and videotapes; traveling exhibitions organized and circulated

L **Library,** 115 E Fifth St, 45202.
Open to members and others by appointment for reference
Library Holdings: Per subs 10; Other—Exhibition catalogs

M **EDGECLIFF COLLEGE,** Emery Galleries, 2220 Victory Parkway, 45206. Tel 513-961-3770. *Dir* Ann Beiersdorfer
Open daily 1 - 5 PM, cl Sat. No admis fee. Estab to present to students and public outstanding artists of local, national and international fame
Income: Privately financed
Exhibitions: Professional artists; qualified students of Edgecliff College

L **PUBLIC LIBRARY OF CINCINNATI AND HAMILTON COUNTY,** Art and Music Department, 800 Vine St, 45202. Tel 513-369-6955, 369-6954. *Head Art & Music Department* Jayne Craven; *Head Librn* James R Hunt
Open Mon - Fri 9 AM - 9 PM, Sat 9 AM - 6 PM, cl Sun. Estab 1872 to provide the community with both scholarly and recreational materials in area of fine arts. Have display cases in the department to exhibit collections
Income: $21,925 (financed by intangible taxes, state and county appropriations)
Purchases: $21,925
Library Holdings: Vols 111,677; Per subs 576; Micro—Cards, fiche, reels, prints; AV—A-tapes, cassettes, fs, Kodachromes, lantern slides, motion pictures, rec, slides; Other—Clipping files, exhibition catalogs, prints, manuscripts, memorabilia, original art works, pamphlets, photographs, reproductions
Special Subjects: Architecture, Costume Design & Construction, Film, Photography
Collections: Langstroth Collection - Chromolithographs of the 19th Century: also scrapbooks on the history of Chromolithography; Eda Kuhn Loeb Collection - The Artist and the Book 1875 to present; 156 Titles with Original signed Lithographs by Artists from Manet to Dali
Exhibitions: Floral Illustrators of the 18th and 19th Century: Chromolithographs of Cincinnati in the mid-19th Century from the Collins Collection; Irish Art; Photographs of Cincinnati by Paul Briol; Toys of Yesteryears; World War II Posters
Activities: Lect open to public, 2 or 3 visiting lectr per year

M **TAFT MUSEUM,** 316 Pike St, 45202. Tel 513-241-0343. *Pres* Morley P Thompson; *Chmn* John W Warrington; *Dir* Katherine Hanna; *Designer* Jan Weigel; *Art Historian & Promotion* Marsha K Semmel
Open Mon - Sat 10 AM - 5 PM, Sun & Holidays 2 - 5 PM, cl Thanksgiving and Christmas. No admis fee. Estab 1927, a gift of Mr and Mrs Charles P Taft's art collection to the Cincinnati Institute of Fine Arts including the house and an endowment fund for maintenance. Active control was taken in 1931; Museum opened in 1932. The historic house, built in 1820, is one of the finest examples of Federal architecture in this country. It has been designated a National Landmark. Its interior is decorated in the style of the period. An architectural formal (green) garden was opened in 1949. Average Annual Attendance: 60,000. Mem: Annual meeting Oct
Income: $250,000 (financed by endowment and annual Fine Arts Fund drive)
Collections: Furnishings include Antique Toiles and Satins and a notable Collection of Duncan Phyfe Furniture; Paintings including works by Rembrandt, Hals, Turner, Goya, Corot, Gainsborough, Raeburn and other Masters; 200 notable Chinese Porcelains K'ang Hsi and Ch'Ien Lung; 120 French Renaissance Enamels; Renaissance Jewelry and 18th Century Watches from many countries
Exhibitions: Antique Dolls: 1820-1920; The Cartoon Show: American Folk Art from the Traditional to the Naive; Chinoiserie: The Chinese Influence; Designing the Nutcracker; Galaxies; What is a Painting; Whimsy
Activities: Docent training; lect open to public, 10 vis lectr per year; gallery talks; tours; individual paintings lent to special museum exhibitions; museum shop sells reproductions, prints, slides, needlework and titles

UNIVERSITY OF CINCINNATI

M **Tangeman Fine Arts Gallery,** 403 Tangeman, 45221. Tel 513-475-3462. *Dir* Lance Kinz; *Co-Dir & Conservator* Gilbert Young
Open Mon - Fri 9 AM - 5 PM, Sat 11 AM - 3 PM. No admis fee. Estab 1967 to preserve and maintain the University's art collection. Gallery is maintained and presents quality contemporary and historical exhibitions of works by artists of local, regional and national reputation. Average Annual Attendance: 10,000
Collections: Indian basketry; Japanese woodblock prints; Persian miniatures; some 250 paintings by European artists executed in the 1950's, donated by Mr and Mrs Julius Fleischmann. early Cincinnati art collection
Activities: Lect open to public, 2 visiting lectr per year; gallery talks; individual paintings and original objects of art lent, 10 items lent in an average year; small traveling exhibitions organized and circulated

L **Design, Architecture and Art Library,** 800 Alms Bldg, 45220. Tel 513-475-3238. *DAA Librn* Elizabeth Douthitt Byrne
Open Mon - Thurs 8 AM - 10 PM, Fri 8 AM - 5 PM, Sat 9 AM - 5 PM, Sun 1 - 8 PM (Academic Year); summer hours vary. Estab 1960 to support the programs of the College of Design, Architecture and Art. Circ 34,000
Purchases: $51,000
Library Holdings: Vols 28,300; Per subs 200; Micro—Fiche, reels; Other—Clipping files, exhibition catalogs, pamphlets
Special Subjects: Architecture

L **Art History Slide Collection Library,** Art History Dept, 45220.
Library contains 125,000 slides

CLEVELAND

C **AMERITRUST COMPANY,** 900 Euclid Ave, 44101. Tel 216-687-5056. *Sr VPres* L Louis Amoroso; *VPres* Charles W Zawadzki
Estab 1971 to enhance the executive offices of the bank; supports and promotes the performing and visual arts. Collection displayed in executive offices
Collections: Primarily 19th Century American oils with few contemporary pieces
Activities: Tours; individual objects of art lent to traveling exhibit touring United States and Europe

M CLEVELAND INSTITUTE OF ART, University Circle, 11141 East Blvd, 44106. Tel 216-421-4322. *Pres* Joseph McCullough; *Dean* Robert D Weitzel, Jr
Open Mon - Fri 9 AM - 4:30 PM, Tues & Wed 7 - 9 PM, Sat 9 AM - noon, Sun 2 - 5 PM. No admis fee. Estab 1882 as a five-year, fully accredited professional college of art. Gallery is maintained with extensive galleries
Exhibitions: (1979) Form & Fiber: Toshiko Taka Ezu; Lenore Tawney; Visual Logic Exhibition
Publications: Link (alumni magazine), quarterly; posters to accompany each exhibit
Activities: Classes for adults and children; lect open to public

L Jessica Gund Memorial Library, University Circle, 11141 East Blvd, 44106. *Librn* Karen Tschudy; *Asst Librn* Kenneth P Goldberg; *Technical Services Librn* Hyosoo Lee; *Media Center Librn* Patricia Lynagh
Open Mon - Thurs 9 AM - 9:30 PM, Fri 9 AM - 5 PM, Sat 9 AM - 4:30 PM, cl Sun. Estab 1882 to select, house and distribute library material in all media that will support the Institute's studio and academic areas of instruction
Library Holdings: Vols 33,000; Per subs 225; AV—A-tapes, slides; Other—Clipping files, exhibition catalogs, prints, manuscripts, memorabilia, original art works, pamphlets, photographs, reproductions, original documents
Special Subjects: Anthropology, art, humanities, natural science, Russian Studiessocial and behavioral sciences, 20th century literature
Collections: Archival collection of clippings and exhibition notices; late 19th and early 20th century textiles; mounted natural history collection; mounted pictures; nature study; posters & graphics
Activities: Library tours

O Cleveland Art Association, University Circle, 11141 East Blvd, 44106. *Pres* Ann Roulet; *Secy* Joseph McCullough
Estab and inc 1916, re-incorporated 1950 as a non-profit organization. Mem: 200; dues $45; annual meeting Nov
Income: $6000 (financed through endowment and donations)
Purchases: $5200
Activities: Competitions; awards; scholarships; individual paintings of local artists lent to members

M CLEVELAND MUSEUM OF ART, 11150 East Blvd, 44106. Tel 216-421-7340. *Pres* Lewis C Williams; *Dir & Chief Cur Oriental Art* Sherman E Lee; *General Mgr* A Beverly Barksdale; *Asst to Dir* Ursula Korneitchouk; *Chief Cur Modern Art* Edward B Henning; *Assoc Cur Modern Art* Tom E Hinson; *Chief Cur Later Western Art* Henry Hawley; *Assoc Cur Paintings* Ann T Lurie; *Assoc Cur Paintings* William S Talbot; *Cur Prints & Drawings* Louise S Richards; *Cur Textiles* Dorothy G Shephard; *Cur Chinese Art* Wai-Kam Ho; *Cur Indian Art* Stansilaw Czuma; *Asst in East Indian Art & Museum Designer* William E Ward; *Assoc Cur in Charge Ancient Art* Arielle P Kozloff; *Cur Education* Gabriel P Weisberg; *Cur Musical Arts* Karel Paukert; *Ed Museum Publications* Merald E Wrolstad; *Mgr Public Relations & Membership* David Patterson; *Registrar* Delbert R Gutridge
Open Tues, Thurs, Fri 10 AM - 6 PM, Wed 10 AM - 10 PM, Sat 9 AM - 5 PM, Sun 1 - 6 PM, cl Mon & national holidays. No admis fee. Estab and incorporated 1913; building opened 1916; New Wing 1958; New Education Wing 1970. Average Annual Attendance: 500,000. Mem: Approx 9700; dues $15 and up; annual meeting Nov
Income: $5,243,708
Purchases: $3,668,972
Collections: †Leonard C Hanna Jr; †Holden; †Mr and Mrs William H Marlatt; Elisabeth Severance Prentiss; Grace Rainey Rogers; †John L Severance; †J H Wade; Classical and Egyptian Art; Drawings and Prints; European and American Decorative Arts of all periods, notably medieval and 18th Century; European and American Paintings of all periods and styles, especially strong in works of 17th and 19th Centuries; Near Eastern Art; Oriental Art, including important Collections of Chinese and Japanese Painting and Ceramics, and Indian Sculpture; Textiles
Exhibitions: Annual exhibition, May Show - work by Artists and Craftsmen of the Western Reserve, awards by jury; Annual exhibition, Year in Review, all acquisitions made during the year, in Jan or Feb
Publications: African Tribal Images; book-catalogs of special exhibitions; bulletin, 10 times a year; Chinese Art Under the Mongols: The Yuan Dynasty (1279-1358); Faberge and His Contemporaries; Lyonel Feininger: a Definitive Catalogue of His Graphic Works; The Many Ways of Seeing; Monographs and Evolution in the Arts: And Other Theories of Culture History; News and Calendar 6 times a year
Activities: Classes; study courses; lect; concerts; gallery talks; films; special exhibits for children; exten exhibitions in schools and other groups

L Library, 11150 East Blvd, 44106. *Librn* Jack Perry Brown
Estab 1916. Open to Museum members, visiting graduate students, faculty, curators only
Library Holdings: Vols 103,000; Per subs 1040; Micro—Fiche, reels; AV—Slides; Other—Clipping files, photographs

O Print Club of Cleveland, 11150 East Blvd, 44106. Tel 216-421-7340. *Pres* Elizabeth Shearer; *VPres* Robert Cavano; *VPres* Robert D Milne; *Secy* John C Bonebrake
Estab 1919 to stimulate interest in prints and drawings through education, collecting and commissioning of new works and enhancement of the museum's collection by gifts and purchases. Mem: 250; dues $85 and up; annual meeting Jan
Income: Financed by membership
Publications: The Print Club of Cleveland 1919-1969. Available at Musuem Sales Desk, $10 plus postage
Activities: Lect open to the public

L CLEVELAND PUBLIC LIBRARY, 325 Superior Ave, 44114. Tel 216-623-2800, 623-2848. *Dir* Ervin J Gaines; *Head Fine Arts Dept* Joan Hoagland
Open Mon - Sat 9 AM - 6 PM, cl Sun. Estab 1869. Circ 2,929,777
Income: $16,860,096 (1979) (financed by state and county appropriations)
Library Holdings: Vols 185,000; Per subs 218; Micro—Fiche, reels; Other—Exhibition catalogs, manuscripts, original art works, pamphlets, photographs, original documents
Special Subjects: Architecture, Art History, Costume Design & Construction, Decorative Arts, Oriental Art, Primitive Art
Collections: Hubbell Architecture Collection; Schweinfurth Architecture Collection; J G White Collection of folklore, orientalia and chess
Activities: Collections open to the public; tours available for groups

L CLEVELAND STATE UNIVERSITY, Library - Art Area, 44115. *Supv Art Area* Candace Shireman
Estab 1973 to house collection of visual arts
Purchases: $18,000
Library Holdings: Vols 9000; Per subs 90; Micro—Fiche, reels; AV—A-tapes, cassettes, fs, motion pictures, slides 70,000; Other—Exhibition catalogs, prints
Special Subjects: Costume Design & Construction, Cleveland and Ohio architecture, environmental art, set design

M COOPER SCHOOL OF ART, Cooper Gallery, 2341 Carnegie Ave SE, 44115. Tel 216-241-1486. *Pres* Donald H Wright; *Secy & Special Consultant* Howard Hammerlund; *Dean of Educ* Charles Bowen
Open 8 AM - 4:30 PM, Mon, Tues & Thurs 6 - 10 PM, Sat 9 AM - 2 PM. No admis fee. Estab 1936 as a private art school with emphasis in communicating visual arts and photography
Income: Financed by tuition and fees
Exhibitions: Eight exhibits plus faculty and student shows; local and regional professional artists showing in one-man or small group exhibits
Activities: Classes for adults and children; lect for students only, 30 visiting lectrs per year; art programs; gallery talks; tours; competitions; scholarships; extension material available to high school art instructors; individual paintings and original objects of art lent; 5000 lantern slides in lending collection; traveling exhibitions organized and circulated; book shop

L Library, 2341 Carnegie Ave SE, 44115. *Head Librn* Barbara Hammerlund
Open to students only, for lending and reference
Library Holdings: Vols 3000; AV—Slides

M DEZIGN HOUSE III, 1701 E Twelfth St, 44114. *Dir* Ramon J Elias; *Assoc* Margery M Elias
Open only to clients. Estab 1962 for the encouragement of original art. Private gallery
Collections: Original American and European

L Library, 44114.
Estab 1953. Open for private research only
Library Holdings: Vols 5000; Per subs 25; AV—Kodachromes 2000; Other—Clipping files, exhibition catalogs, prints, manuscripts, memorabilia, original art works, pamphlets, photographs

M SAINT MARY'S ROMANIAN ORTHODOX CHURCH, Romanian Ethnic Museum, 3256 Warren Rd, 44111. Tel 216-941-5550. *Pres* David Salanty; *VPres* Dan Millau; *Secy* Mabel Barsan; *Dir* Vasile Hategan
Open Sun Noon - 5 PM, other hours by appointment. No admis fee. Estab 1960. Average Annual Attendance: 10,000
Income: Financed by parish appropriation
Collections: Anisoara Stan Collection; O K Colsa Collection; Gunther Collection; Romanian art, artifacts, costumes, ceramics, painters, rugs, silver and woodwork
Activities: Lect open to public; tours; individual paintings and original objects of art lent locally for exhibits; lending collection contains 100 original art works, 250 original prints, 50 paintings, sculpture, 2000 costumes, rugs and artifacts

C THE STANDARD OIL COMPANY (OHIO), Midland Bldg, 44115. Tel 216-575-5700. *In Charge Art Program* C D Shields
Estab to enhance quality of life in communities where the company has employees or operations. Supports performing theatres, museums, orchestras and art education
Activities: Operating support, facilities and production sponsorship

M TEMPLE MUSEUM OF JEWISH RELIGIOUS ART AND MUSIC, University Circle & Silver Park, 44106. Tel 216-791-7755. *Dir* Daniel Jeremy Silver
Open by appointment only. No admis fee. Estab 1950. Branch museum on Shaker Blvd, Beachwood
Collections: Archaelogy; ceremonial art; decorative arts; paintings; prints; sculpture

L Library, University Circle & Silver Pk, 44106.
Small library of art books and manuscripts available for research

M WESTERN RESERVE HISTORICAL SOCIETY, 10825 East Blvd, 44106. Tel 216-721-5722. *Exec Dir* Meredith Colket; *Dir History Museum* Jairus B Barnes; *Dir Auto Museum* Kenneth Gooding; *Dir Development & Communication* David C Twining; *Librn* Kermit Pike; *Chief Cur of Education* Karen Grachaw; *Comptroller* Eugene Huhtala
Open Thurs - Sat & Tues 10 AM - 5 PM, Wed 10 AM - 10 PM, Sun Noon - 5 PM, cl Mon. No admis adult $2, senior citizens, students, children $1. Estab 1867 to collect and preserve items of historical interest to Western Reserve such as antique furniture and cars. Average Annual Attendance: 80,000. Mem: 3500; dues $25 and up; annual meeting Oct
Income: $1,400,000 (financed by endowment, membership, admissions, gifts, county appropriations and special grants)
Collections: Period rooms including: People at the Crossroads: Settling the Western Reserve, and a Renaissance Revival Parlor
Exhibitions: Changing and permanent exhibits
Publications: Books on Regional History; Western Reserve Historical Society News, bi-monthly
Activities: Docent training; classes for adults and children; lect open to public; gallery talks; tours; competitions; individual paintings and objects of art lent to institutions; originate traveling exhibitions; sales shop sells books, magazines and original art

O WOMEN'S CITY CLUB OF CLEVELAND, 322 Superior Ave NE, 44114. Tel 216-696-3760. *Pres* Mrs Frank Kosich; *VPres* Mrs H G Weidner Jr; *Secy* Mrs George S Voinovich; *Exec Dir* Norma Huey
Open Mon - Fri 9 AM - 5 PM, closes at 4:30 PM during July & Aug. No admis fee. Estab 1916 to promote a broad acquaintance, provide a central meeting place, maintain an open forum and promote the welfare of the City of Cleveland. Maintains an art gallery featuring monthly exhibitions by local professional artists. Average Annual Attendance: 25,000. Mem: 1000; dues resident member $100, junior member $50
Income: Financed by membership
Exhibitions: Continous exhibitions changing every four to six weeks

Publications: Bulletin, monthly
Activities: Classes for adults; art appreciation classes;; lect open to public; gallery talks

COLUMBUS

AMERICAN CERAMIC SOCIETY
For further information, see National and Regional Organizations

M **CAPITAL UNIVERSITY,** Schumacher Gallery, 2199 E Main St, 43209. Tel 614-236-7108. *Dir* Prof Richard G Bauer; *Secy* Janet E Popp
Open Mon - Fri 1 - 5 PM, Sat and Sun 2 - 4 PM. No admis fee. Estab 1966 to provide the best available visual arts to the students; to serve the entire community with monthly traveling shows, community programming and permanent collections. Gallery is 16,000 sq ft, that includes six display galleries, fabrication room, community reception room, lecture hall seating 60 and lecture space seating 250.
Average Annual Attendance: 6000 - 7000
Income: Financed by endowment
Collections: †American paintings, sculpture and graphics of 20th century; Flemish paintings from 16th - 17th century; 19th century paintings; Oceanic collection of tribal arts and artifacts; †Ohio painters; †prints
Exhibitions: Nine individual and group visiting shows per year; Group exhibits include Central Ohio Watercolor Society, Bexley Area Art Guild, Ohio Liturgical Art Guild, Senior Student and Alumni Show, Art Faculty Show; Individual exhibits include Aistars Brothers, Men of Art: Chadeayne and Nicodemus, Jack Osbun, Jim Mason, Liz Kregloe Exhibit, Performance-Photography, and Monotypes from Pratt Graphic Center, New York; Selected works from permanent collection are also exhibited
Activities: Lect open to public, 4 visiting lectr per year; concerts; gallery talks; tours; competitions; individual paintings and original art objects lent by special request only;; gallery shop open to the public
L **Library,** 2199 E Main St, 43209. Tel 614-236-7108. *Dir* Dr Albert Maag
Open to students, faculty, staff, and for reference only to the public
Library Holdings: Vols 2000; Per subs 7

L **COLUMBUS COLLEGE OF ART AND DESIGN,** Packard Library, 47 N Washington Ave, 43215. Tel 614-224-9101. *Librn* Chilin Yu
Open Mon & Fri 8:30 AM - 5 PM, Tue - Thurs 8:30 AM - 8 PM. Estab 1879. Open to public for reference only
Income: $80,000 (financed by tuition fees and grants)
Purchases: $20,000
Library Holdings: Vols 16,620; Per subs 127; AV—Cassettes, Kodachromes, lantern Slides, rec, slides; Other—Clipping files, exhibition catalogs, original art works, pamphlets, photographs, reproductions, sculpture
Exhibitions: students' work
Publications: Botticelli, annually
Activities: Classes for adults and children; lect; 25 visiting lectr per year; tours; awards of scholarships to outstanding seniors; scholarships; artmobile

M **COLUMBUS MUSEUM OF ART,** 480 East Broad St, 43215. Tel 614-221-6801. *Pres* John W Kessler; *Dir* Bud Harris Bishop; *Chief Cur* Steven W Rosen; *Cur of Exhib* Mary L Harlan; *Development Dir* James V Buchanan; *Registrar* Susan Visser-Rapp; *Dir Education* Merle S Harbach; *Business Mgr* Herbert Moore; *Public Information Coordr* Bonnie H Mahon
Open Tues, Thurs, Fri & Sat 11 AM - 5 PM, Wed 11 AM - 8:30 PM, cl Mon & holidays. Admis adults $1.50, children (6 - 17) senior citizens and students with valid school ID 50¢, Tues free. Estab 1878. Present main building constructed in 1931 in an Italianate palatial style; addition built in 1974; Sculpture Park and Garden added in 1979. Average Annual Attendance: 100,000. Mem: 4000; dues $25
Income: Financed by annual contributions, endowment, membership, and government appropriations
Collections: 16th - 20th century European paintings, drawings and prints; 19th and 20th century American paintings, works on paper, and sculpture; Chinese and Japanese ceramics; sculpture collection
Exhibitions: (1978-80) Beaux Arts Designer-Craftsman; Wesley Bellows: Paintings, drawings and prints; Masters of the Camera: Steiglitz, Steichen and their Successors; 130 Years of Ohio Photography; Athletes by Warhol; Jamie Wyeth: Recent Paintings; Woman: Artist and Image
Publications: Exhibition and permanent collection catalogs; monthly calendars
Activities: Workshops for adults and youth; docent training; film series; concerts; lectures; gallery talks; guided tours; members trips; lending collection contains original prints, paintings and sculpture; museum shop sells contemporary crafts
L **Columbus Museum of Art Resource Center,** 480 East Broad St, 43215.
Estab 1974 as a reference center for staff
Library Holdings: AV—Slides; Other—Clipping files, exhibition catalogs, pamphlets

O **OHIO HISTORICAL SOCIETY,** I 71 & 17th Ave, 43211. Tel 614-466-1500. *Acting Dir* William G Keener; *Chief Educ Division* Dr Amos Loveday; *Head Archaeology* Martha Otto; *Acting Head History* Don Hutslar; *Head National History* Dr William Schultz
Open Mon - Sat 9 AM - 5 PM, Sun 10 AM - 5 PM. No admis fee. Estab 1885, Ohio Historical Society was chartered on this date, to promote a knowledge of history, natural history and archaeology, especially of Ohio; to collect and maintain artifacts, books and archives relating to Ohio's history. Main gallery covers over one acre of floor space and includes exhibits on history, natural history, archaeology and furniture; also houses a natural history demonstration laboratory and several audio-visual theatres. Average Annual Attendance: 500,000. Mem: 11,350; dues family $15, individual $10; annual meeting September
Income: $4,500,000 (financed by endowment, membership, state appropriation and contributions)
Purchases: $100,000
Collections: Archaeology; †artifacts; ceramics; †clothing; ††furniture; †glassware; †paintings
Exhibitions: The First 50 Years of American Photography; History of American Currency; Images for Everyone; Ohio in the American Revolution; Ohio in the Centennial Year, 1876

Publications: Museum Echoes, newsletter, monthly; Ohio History, scholarly journal, quarterly
Activities: Docent training; lect; individual paintings and original art objects lent; lending collection contains film strips; books traveling exhibitions; originate traveling exhibitions; sales shop sells books, magazines, reproductions, prints, slides and other souvenir items, post cards, jewelry
L **Archives and Library,** 1982 Velma Ave, 43211. Tel 614-466-1500. *Acting Head Librn* Mary Ellen West; *Head of Archives & Manuscripts* Dennis East
For reference only
Library Holdings: Vols 100,000; Per subs 400; AV—A-tapes, motion pictures; Other—maps 3000
Collections: Broadsides; Coonskin Library; lithographs; maps; Ohio government documents and papers from early Ohio leaders; Ohio newspapers, posters; rare books

OHIO STATE UNIVERSITY
M **Gallery of Fine Arts,** 128 North Oval Mall, Hopkins Hall, 43210. Tel 614-422-0330. *Dean, College of the Arts* Andrew J Broekema; *Dir* Betty Collings; *Chief Exhib Preparator* Rick Mayer; *Exhib Preparator* Jim Scott; *Exhib Preparator* Susan Williams
Hopkins Gallery open Mon - Fri 9 AM - 5 PM; Sullivant Gallery open Mon - Fri 9 AM - 5 PM, Tues & Thurs 6 - 8 PM, Sat 10 AM - 2 PM, Sun 2 - 5 PM. No admis fee. Estab 1968 to provide quality contemporary exhibitions for students and faculty, to promote interaction with the regional art community and to maintain and extend our collection of contemporary art. Sullivant Hall, 3500 sq ft, Hopkins Hall 1500 sq ft. Average Annual Attendance: 70,000
Income: $180,000 (financed by state and federal grant, funds raised through the University development fund, and state appropriation)
Purchases: $60,000
Collections: †Contemporary collection; Historical collection
Exhibitions: (Solo Exhibitions) Robert Arnold; Moe Brooker; Joan Brown; Eric Cameron; Peter D'Agostine; Tom Doyle; Benni Efrat; Siah Armajani; Moshe Kupferman; Robert Morris; Elizabeth Murray; William Ramage; Harold Reddicliffe; Robert Rauschenberg; Joel Shapiro; Este Schurr. (Group Exhibitions) Acquisitions 1976-78; Artists' Books; Canadian Paintings; Columbus Focus; Sculpture Projects for the 1970's Summer '78, Six in Ohio; Summer '79 Columbus Focus
Publications: Dialogue, bi-monthly visual arts magazine
Activities: Classes for adults and children; lect open to public, 25 visiting lectr per year; competitions; awards; original objects of art lent to institutions for exhibition; original art and prints are rented to students, staff and faculty through the Circulation Collection
L **Fine Arts Library,** Room 166 Sullivant Hall, 1813 North High St, 43201. *Head Librn* Jacqueline D Sisson; *Asst* Linda L Talmadge
Open Mon - Thurs 8 AM - 10 PM, Fri 8 AM - 5 PM, Sat 10 AM - 4 PM, Sun 2 - 10 PM, while classes are in session; vacation 8 AM - 5 PM daily. Estab during 1930's
Income: $77,000
Purchases: $38,165
Library Holdings: Vols 60,000; Per subs 353; Micro—Fiche, reels; AV—Slides; Other—Exhibition catalogs, original art works
Special Subjects: Medieval and Renaissance, Slavic publications with emphasis on Byzantine painting
Collections: Archival materials on microfiche, such as Victoria and Albert museum collection
M **Visual Resource Collection, Department of History of Art,** 204 Hayes Hall, 108 N Oval Mall, 43210. *Cur* Jennifer Hehman
Open Mon - Fri 8 AM - 5 PM. Estab 1925 to provide visual resources for instruction and research in history of art. Circ 35,000
Library Holdings: AV—Cassettes, slides; Other—Prints, original art works, photographs, reproductions, x-rays
Special Subjects: Art History
Collections: Asian Art photographs; Contemporary African Art; History of Islamic Art; survey sets

L **PUBLIC LIBRARY OF COLUMBUS AND FRANKLIN COUNTY,** Humanities, Fine Arts and Recreation Division, 96 S Grant Ave, Columbus, OH. (Mailing Add: 28 S Hamilton Rd, Columbus, OH 43213,) Tel 614-222-7189. *Dir* Richard Sweeney; *Division Head* Suzanne Fisher; *Exhib Coordr* Patti Kinsinger
Open Mon - Thurs 9 AM - 9 PM, Fri & Sat 9 AM - 6PM, cl Sun. Estab 1873 to serve informational, educational and cultural needs of Columbus and Franklin County. Gallery is 130 running ft
Income: $23,000 (financed by state and county appropriation)
Library Holdings: Vols 33,000; Per subs 112; Micro—Reels; AV—Cassettes, motion pictures, rec, v-tapes; Other—Exhibition catalogs, pamphlets, Classified picture file
Special Subjects: Architecture, Decorative Arts, Film, Photography, Theatre Arts, Antiques, music, television
Exhibitions: Milton Caniff: Art for Everybody; Rock Art; The Wonderful T: The Art of James Thurber; innovative and informative exhibits with emphasis on local professional artists and traveling exhibits
Publications: Librarities, newsletter, monthly
Activities: Classes for adults and children; film series; lect open to public; concerts; tours; exten dept serves Franklin County; book traveling exhibitions 3 - 4 per year; originate traveling exhibitions

COSHOCTON

M **JOHNSON-HUMRICKHOUSE MUSEUM,** 300 Whitewoman St, Roscoe Village, 43812. Tel 614-622-3155. *Dir* Mary M Shaw
Open daily 12:00 - 5 PM May through Oct, 1:30 - 4:30 PM Nov through April, cl Mon, Thanksgiving, Christmas and New Year's Day. No admis fee. Estab 1931, as a gift of two pioneer residents. Museum occupies a school building erected in 1853 and managed by Library Board. Historical Roscoe Village is a restored 19th century canal town
Collections: American Indian baskets and bead work; Aztec, Toltec and Mayan pottery heads; Chinese and Japanese amber, brass, bronze, cloisonne, copper,

embroideries, ivory, jade, lacquers, pewter ware, porcelains, prints, wood carvings; European glass, laces, pewter, porcelains, prints; Eskimo artifacts; material from Coshocton County Mound Builders; Miller-Preston bequest of furnishings and implements used by Coshocton County pioneer families
Exhibitions: Permanent collection exhibitions changed periodically; traveling exhibitions
Activities: Educ Dept; gallery talks, lect
L **Library,** 300 Whitewoman St, Roscoe Village, 43812.
Technical books for research supplied by City Library on permanent loan

CUYAHOGA FALLS

L **CREATIVE SCHOOL OF DESIGN LIBRARY,** 2250 Front St, 44221. *Dir*
Open by appointment only. Estab 1960
Library Holdings: Vols 1000; Per subs 20; AV—Slides; Other—Clipping files, framed reproductions, prints, original art works, photographs, reproductions
Activities: Programs on art

M **RICHARD GALLERY AND ALMOND TEA GALLERY,** Divisions of Studios of Jack Richard, 2250 Front St, 44221. *Dir* Jack Richard; *Agent* Jane Williams
Open weekdays 11 AM - 5:30 PM, Sat 11 AM - 1 PM, other hours by appointment. No admis fee. Estab Richard Gallery 1960, Almond Tea Gallery 1964, for exhibition of local, regional and national works of art
Income: Financed privately
Collections: Ball; Brackman; Cornwell; Grell; Gleitsmann; Loomis; Terry Richard
Exhibitions: Robert Brackman; Dalton Collection of Japanese Art; Mitsuka Hurdina, Miles Palladino Sculpture; Susan Shoemaker; Maria von Trapp; Student exhibits; Japanese prints; members exhibits, Women's City Club Exhibits, 15 one-person exhibits
Activities: Lect open to public; 3 visiting lectrs per year; 20 gallery talks; 20-25 tours; competitions; scholarships; individual paintings and original objects of art lent; lending collection contains 300 paintings and prints; originate traveling exhibitions; book shop; frame shop; art supplies
L **Library,** 2250 Front St, 44221.
For reference and limited lending only
Library Holdings: Vols 1000; Other—Clipping files

DAYTON

M **DAYTON ART INSTITUTE,** Forest & Riverview Ave, PO Box 941, 45401. Tel 513-223-5277. *Dir* Bruce H Evans; *Chief Cur* Kent Sobotik; *Asst Cur European Painting & Registrar* Dominique Vasseur; *Asst Cur Decorative Arts* Sue Walsh; *Acting Dir Development & Public Relations* Linda Steen; *Adminr* Marie D Ferguson; *Chmn Education Dept* Honore S David
Open Tues - Fri & Sun Noon - 5 PM, Sat 9 AM - 5 PM. No admis fee. Estab 1929 for the public benefit. Some of the galleries include: Ancient Gallery, Contemporary Gallery, European 16th-18th Century Gallery, Experience Center Gallery, Medieval Gallery, New Acquisitions Gallery, Print Gallery, Special Exhibitions Gallery and an Asian Wing and an American wing. Average Annual Attendance: 30,000. Mem: 2000; dues $20 - $1000; annual meeting April
Collections: †American Collection; European Art From Medieval Period to Present; Sidney & Frances Lewis Collection; Oriental Collection; †Phillips Collection;
Exhibitions: (1978) Artists, Authors and Others; All-Ohio Paintings, Sculpture, Graphics and Photography Biennial 1979; Drawings by David Levine; The Dyer's Art: Ikat, Batik, Plangi; Paintings by George Cope; Soho: On the Market; Courtesans of the Floating World; Rodin's Burghers of Calais: Sculptural Studies; Edward Weston's Gifts to his Sister: German Expressionist Drawings from the Collection of D Thomas Bergen. (1979) Late 20th Century Art; George Cruikshank, Printmaker; Robert Murray Sculpture; Books forms: Patterns Plus; Japanese House; Containers: Japanese Way of Design. (1980) Brooke Alexander, A Decade of Print Publishing; Americans in Glass; Classical Tradition in Rajput Painting; Louise Nevelson at 80; Surrealism in Photography;
Publications: Annual report, bulletin
Activities: Docent training; classes for adults and children; lect open to public, 3 - 6 per year; gallery talks; tours; individual paintings lent to members; originate traveling exhibitions; sales shop selling books, original art, toys and jewelry
L **Library,** 456 Belmonte Park, N, PO Box 941, 45401. *Librn* Helen L Pinkney
Open Mon - Fri 9 AM - 5 PM. Estab 1922. Open to the public for art reference only
Library Holdings: Vols 21,810; Per subs 73; Micro—Fiche; AV—Slides; Other—Clipping files, exhibition catalogs, pamphlets, reproductions
Special Subjects: Architecture
Collections: Louis J P Lott and Walter G Schaeffer, architecture

C **THE THIRD NATIONAL BANK AND TRUST COMPANY,** 34 N Main St, 45402. Tel 513-226-6144. *In Charge Art Coll* Judith L Mitchell
Open Mon - Fri 9 AM - 2 PM. No admis fee. Estab 1979 for collection dedicated to the people of Dayton; part of renovation of bank's headquarters. Collection displayed in lobbies, offices and public spaces throughout bank
Collections: Collection centers on three major works by Dr R Buckminster Fuller and is augmented by paintings and photographs of Spaceship Earth; paintings, photographs and sculpture
Activities: Tours

WRIGHT STATE UNIVERSITY
M **Fine Arts Gallery,** 45435. Tel 513-873-2896. *Dir* Michael Jones; *Assoc Dir* David Givler; *Admin Asst* Kathleen J Letson
Open Mon - Fri 9:30 AM - 5 PM, Sat 10 AM - 5 PM, Sun 1 - 5 PM, Wed & Thur evenings 5 - 8 PM. No admis fee. Estab 1974, devoted to exhibitions of and research in comtemporary art. The gallery is a multi-level contemporary building with 1500 sq feet on each of two levels and 300 running feet of wall space on each level. Available also are areas outside on the campus and selected sites in Dayton. Average Annual Attendance: 13,000
Income: Financed through the University
Collections: Small collection of contemporary art on paper

Exhibitions: Installation or project works by Cecile Abish, Vito Acconci, Patrick Ireland, Robert Irwin, Barry Le Va, Loren Madsen, Dennis Oppenheim, Athena Tacha, John Willenbecher. Exhibitions of existing works by Rudolf Baranik, Richard Fisher, Simone Forti, Jan Groover, Robert Morris, Michelle Stuart; regional artists and traveling exhibitions
Publications: Artist's books and exhibition catalogs, 6 per year
Activities: Lect open to public, 16 visiting lectr per year; gallery talks; individual paintings and art objects lent to faculty and administrative areas; lending collection contains original art works, original prints, paintings, photographs and sculpture; book traveling exhibitions; originate traveling exhibitions; sales desk sells books
L **Department of Art and Art History Resource Center & Slide Library,** 45435. *Slide Cur* Kimberly Sugrue
Open Mon - Fri 8:30 AM - 5 PM. Estab 1970 to serve Wright State University and art professionals in the greater Dayton area. Circ Approx 200 slides per week. For lending and reference
Library Holdings: Vols 200; Per subs 10; AV—A-tapes, cassettes, slides, v-tapes; Other—Exhibition catalogs, Art school catalogs

DELAWARE

M **OHIO WESLEYAN UNIVERSITY,** Department of Fine Arts Gallery, Humphreys Art Hall, 43015. Tel 614-369-4431, Ext 650. *Chmn & Dir of Exhib* Justin Kronewetter
Open daily 9 AM - 4 PM, Sat 9 AM - Noon. No admis fee. Estab 1915
Collections: †Drawings; †photography; †prints
Exhibitions: (1979-1980) Dorothy Getz: Drawings and Sculpture; Denny Griffith: Painting; Heald, Hoernschemeyer and Jaffe: Faculty; Light Gallery Photographers: Photography; Selby-Boyd: Graphic Designers; Jarvis Stewart: Retrospective Paintings & Photographs; Tomb of Tutankamun: Photographic study with the assistant of The Ohio Foundation on the Arts; Athena Tacha: Environmental Sculpture; Richard Wengenroth: Painting; Roberta Williamson: Metalsmith; exhibitions of professional and student work; annual exhibition of contemporary photography; monthly exhibits in Lynn Mayhew Gallery
Activities: Classes for children; visiting artists workshops; lect open to the public, 10 visiting lectrs per year; art programs; gallery talks; lending collection contains 40,000 slides
L **Beeghly Library,** 43015. Tel 614-369-4431, Ext 650.
Open to the public
Library Holdings: Vols 2200; Per subs 8

FINDLAY

M **FINDLAY COLLEGE,** Egner Fine Arts Center, 1000 N Main St, 45840. Tel 419-422-8313. *Dir* Douglas Salveson
Open Mon - Fri 9 AM - 5 PM. Estab as a college art department. Gallery is maintained
Income: Financed by endowment
Collections: †primarily contemporary prints
Exhibitions: 18 exhibitions of contemporary art and crafts and one retrospective exhibition during last three years
Activities: Classes for adults and children; dramatic programs; concerts; competitions; scholarships; book shop

GALLIPOLIS

O **FRENCH ART COLONY, INC,** 530 First Ave, Box 472, 45631. Tel 614-446-3834. *Pres* Donald M Thaler; *VPres* Jack Hudson; *Secy* Mary B Cherrington; *Acting Dir* Janice M Thaler; *Education* Janet Byers; *Education* Bess Grace; *Gallery* Peggy B Evans
Open Tues & Thurs 10 AM - 3 PM, Sat & Sun 1 - 5 PM. No admis fee. Estab 1964 to promote the arts throughout the region. Mem: 300; dues $12 and up; annual meeting last Thurs in Feb
Income: Financed by membership
Exhibitions: Photography, bi-annual; visual arts - annual
Publications: Newsletter, monthly
Activities: Classes for adults and children; dramatic programs; community programs; creative writing; visual art programs and classes; lect open to public; concerts; tours; competitions; 10 - 12 purchase awards; book traveling exhibitions
L **Library,** 530 First Ave, Box 472, 45631. *Librn; Library* Vilma Pikoja
Open Tues & Thurs 10 AM - 3 PM, Sat & Sun 1 - 5 PM. Estab 1972 as small reference library dealing primarily with visual arts
Library Holdings: Vols 2000; Per subs 5; AV—Lantern Slides; Other—Exhibition catalogs, prints, pamphlets, reproductions

GAMBIER

M KENYON COLLEGE, Colburn Gallery, 43022. Tel 614-427-2244. *Coordr* Florence S Lord
Open Mon - Fri 8:30 AM - 8:30 PM, Sat & Sun 1:30 - 8:30 PM, through school year only. No admis fee. Estab 1973 as teaching arm of the Art Department of Kenyon College. Gallery was built 1904 with neo-gothic architecture, and has 153 ft running space. Average Annual Attendance: 1500
Income: Financed by college
Collections: Art collection and items of some historical importance
Exhibitions: (1977-80) Ardine Nelson: Black and White and Color Photography; Jim Butler Paintings, Prints and Drawings; Capricu Philipp Fehl; Courtesans of the Floating World Photography; Ceramic Sculpture Walter Hyleck; James Jabuson Sculpture; Gerry Kramer Paintings and Drawings; Linda Mahoney Photographs; The Mini-Art Show; Ohio Post Office Murals, Urban Walls and City Canvasses; George Olson Drawings and Constructions; Harold Reddicliffe Paintings and Drawings; Transparent Watercolor Exhibition (from the Schumacher Collection); Two-Man Show: Martin J Garhart and Barry L Gunderson (drawings, prints and sculpture); drawings, faculty exhibition, printmaking, photography, sculpture, senior show
Activities: Lect open to public, visiting lectr; tours; competitions; Honors Day cash awards; individual paintings and original objects of art lent

GRANVILLE

M DENISON UNIVERSITY ART GALLERY, 43023. Tel 614-587-0810, Ext 255. *Dir* Paul J Cardile; *Registrar* Letha Schetzsle; *Cur Burmese Art* Jane Terry Bailey
Open Mon - Fri 10 AM - 4 PM; Sun 1 - 4 PM, cl Sat. No admis fee. Estab 1946 for educational purposes
Income: Financed through University
Collections: American Indian pottery; Burmese sculpture, manuscripts, paintings and crafts; Central American arts and crafts; Chinese ceramics, rubbings, sculpture and crafts; European and American drawings, paintings, prints and crafts
Publications: Catalogs
Activities: Lect open to public; individual paintings and art objects lent
L Art Department Slide Library, 43023.
Open to students and faculty for reference only
Library Holdings: Other—50,000 slides

KENT

KENT STATE UNIVERSITY
M School of Art Gallery, 44242. Tel 216-672-7853. *Dir* Sheila K Tabakoff
Open Mon - Fri 9 AM - 4 PM, Sun 12 - 4 PM, cl school holidays. No admis fee. Estab 1950 as part of the instructional program at Kent State
Collections: Decorative arts; paintings; prints; sculpture
Exhibitions: Annual Invitational Painting and Sculpture Show; exhibitions originating at this gallery; faculty and student one-man and group exhibitions; traveling exhibitions from museums
Publications: Brochures; catalogs
Activities: Classes for students in museum preparation; gallery talks; book traveling exhibitions; traveling exhibitions organized and circulated
L Architecture and Urban Studies Library, 44242. Tel 216-672-2854. *Librn* Edward J Hall Jr; *Supvr* Judy Meyer
Open 8 AM - 5 PM. Estab 1967
Income: Financed by state appropriations
Library Holdings: Vols 6435; Per subs 275; Micro—Reels; AV—Kodachromes; Other—Clipping files
Publications: Urban Scene (newsletter), quarterly

LAKEWOOD

O KENNETH C BECK CENTER FOR THE CULTURAL ARTS, 17801 Detroit Ave, 44107. Tel 216-521-2540. *Pres* Joseph H Albrecht; *VPres* Erna L Berkey; *Secy* Barbara N King; *Managing Dir* Karl A Mackey; *Museum Coordr* Mary G Farr
Open Mon, Wed, Thurs, Fri & Sat 2 - 5 PM, Sun 2 - 5 PM and 6:30 - 8:30 PM, Performance evenings 7:30 - 9:30 PM, cl Tues. No admis fee. Estab 1976 to present a wide variety of the fine and graphic arts including exhibits from the Cleveland Museum of Art. A North and South Gallery separated by an indoor garden under a skylight roof; total sq footage: approx 3400 sq ft; part of a cultural center which includes a legitimate theatre. Average Annual Attendance: 50,000
Income: Financed by operating cost of the center
Collections: Contemporary pieces including acrylics, collages, etchings, oils, sculpture and watercolors
Exhibitions: (1978) American Folk Art from the Traditional to the Naive; The Public Monument and Its Audience (commemorative public art using 23 monuments of Ohio); Repetition: Geometric Forms in Art; Exhibition of Romanian Contemporary Painting; A Study in Regional Taste: The May Show 1919 - 1975 (works by Cleveland area artists); Richard Treaster One-Man Show; faculty exhibitions, Proscenium 78, the second annual juried show. (1979) An Art Deco Exhibit; C I A Faculty Members; The History of the Poster (1870 to early 1900's); Japanese Textile Show (cotton textiles); Photographs from Collection of Cleveland Museum of Art; Proscenium 79, the third annual juried show. (1980) The American Scene - Graphics; First Junior Proscenium 1980 Juried Art Show; The Great American Art Swap; Regional Artists' Summer Sale (works of five professional artists); Surrealism in Perspective; Womansart 1979 (works by professional Ohio women artists); work done by the institute faculty
Publications: Bulletins; Programs, every five weeks
Activities: Classes for adults and children; dramatic programs; concerts; gallery talks; tours; competitions; cash awards; book traveling exhibitions 5 per year; sales shop sells original art and prints

MANSFIELD

O MANSFIELD ART CENTER, Mansfield Fine Arts Guild Inc, 700 Marion Ave, 44903. Tel 419-756-1700. *Dir* H Daniel Butts III; *Exec Secy* Mrs Henry Van Horn
Open Tues - Sat 11 AM - 5 PM, Sun 12 - 5 PM, cl Mon & national holidays. No admis fee. Estab 1945, incorporated 1956, to maintain an art center in which exhibitions, lectures, gallery talks, special programs, symposia and series of classes for adults and children are provided for the North Central Ohio area; maintained by membership, commission on sales and classes. Gallery dimensions 5000 sq ft with flexible lighting, movable walls, props, etc to facilitate monthly exhibition changes. Average Annual Attendance: 15,000. Mem: 1050; dues $3 - $500; annual meeting in April
Income: $45,000
Exhibitions: Changing exhibitions of member artists' work; traveling shows & locally organized one-man, group and theme exhibitions changing monthly throughout the year
Publications: Annual report; class schedules; monthly newsletter
Activities: Classes for adults and children; lect open to public, an average of 6 visiting lectrs per year; film series; gallery talks mainly for school groups; competitions; scholarships
L Library, 700 Marion Ave, 44903.
The library is basically a collection of monographs and studies of styles and periods for teacher and student reference
Library Holdings: Vols 750

MARIETTA

M CAMPUS MARTIUS MUSEUM AND OHIO RIVER MUSEUM, 601 Second St, 45750. Tel 614-373-3750. *Mgr* John B Briley; *Asst Mgr* Juanita Etter
Open daily 9:30 AM - 5 PM, cl Thanksgiving, Christmas, and New Years Day. Admis adult $1.50, children 6-12 75¢, children 5 and underfree. Estab 1920 as part of the Ohio Historical Society to collect, exhibit and interpret historical items, including art and manuscripts, pertaining to Ohio's history, and particularly to Marietta, the Northwest Territory (Ohio portion) and the Ohio River. Campus Martius Museum has 2500 sq ft of exhibition space on two floors plus a two-story home, a portion of the original fort of 1788-91, entirely enclosed within the building. The Ohio River Museum has approximately 1500 sq ft of exhibition space in three separate buildings connected by walkway. Average Annual Attendance: 70,000
Income: Financed by endowment, membership, state appropriation, grants and fund raising
Collections: Tellcity Pilothouse, a replica of the 18th century flatboat; Steamer W P Synder, Jr; decorative arts from 19th century Ohio; early Ohio Paintings, prints, and photographs; items from early Putnam, Blennerhassett and other families; Ohio Company and Marietta materials; Ohio River landscapes
Exhibitions: Ohio Longrifle Exhibit; temporary exhibits
Activities: Classes for adults and children; museum tours; original art objects lent to other museums for exhibitions; sales shop sells books, reproductions, prints, slides, crafts, and souvenir items
L Library, 45750.
Open to the public for reference
Library Holdings: Vols 2000; Per subs 6

M MARIETTA COLLEGE, Grover M Hermann Fine Arts Center, 45750. Tel 614-373-4643. *Chmn Art Dept* M Jeanne Tasse
Open Mon - Fri 8 AM - 10:30 PM, Sat 8 AM - 5 PM, Sun 1 - 10:30 PM. No admis fee. estab 1965. Gallery maintained. Average Annual Attendance: 20,000
Collections: Permanent collection of contemporary American paintings, sculpture and crafts; significant collection of African and pre-Columbian art
Exhibitions: Marietta College Crafts National; student exhibitions, faculty show, art club
Activities: Lect open to public; competitions; book shop

MASSILLON

M MASSILLON MUSEUM, 212 Lincoln Way E, 44646. *Dir* Mary M Merwin; *Education* John Klassen; *Registrar* Margaret Vogt; *Clerk & Treas* Raymond Ruwadi
Open Tues - Sat 9:30 AM - 5 PM, Sun 2 - 5 PM. No admis fee. Estab 1933 as a museum of art and history. The museum places emphasis on the Ohio area by representing the fine arts and crafts and the Massillon area with an historical collection. Average Annual Attendance: 17,000. Mem: 1254; dues $5 and higher
Income: Financed by county appropriations
Collections: †Ceramics, china, costumes, drawings, †glass, †jewelry, ivories, †paintings, prints
Exhibitions: Monthly exhibitions
Publications: Pamphlet of activities and exhibitions, twice yearly
Activities: Classes for adults and children; docent training; tours; competitions; individual paintings and original art objects lent to institutions; sales shop sells crafts, toys and jewelry

MIDDLETOWN

O MIDDLETOWN FINE ARTS CENTER, AIM Bldg, 130 N Verity Parkway, 45042. Tel 513-424-2416. *Pres & Dir* Edith Kohler
Open Mon - Thurs 9 AM - 9 PM, Fri 9 AM - 4 PM, Sat 9 AM - Noon. Estab 1957 to provide facilities program and instruction, for the development of interests and skills in the visual arts, for students of all ages from Middletown and its surrounding communities. Average Annual Attendance: Annual meeting Mar
Income: Endowment through funds donated to Arts in Middletown (funding agency)
Exhibitions: 10 to 12 exhibitions per year including Annual Area Art Show; Annual Clay Day; Annual Student Show; plus one and two-man invitational shows of artists throughout the US
Activities: Classes for adults and children Sat mornings

L **Library**, 130 North Verity Parkway, 45042. *Librn* Louise Kindred
Open Mon - Thurs 9 AM - 9 PM, Fri 9 AM - 4 PM, Sat 9 AM - Noon, cl Sun. Estab 1963, to provide information and enjoyment for students and instructors. Circ 30. Library open for lending or reference
Purchases: $131
Library Holdings: Vols 711; Per subs 4; AV—Slides
Collections: All books pertain only to art subjects: Art history; ceramics; crafts; illustrations; references; techniques; theory

MOUNT SAINT JOSEPH

L **COLLEGE OF MOUNT SAINT JOSEPH ON THE OHIO**, Archbishop Alter Library, Art Department, 45051. *Dir of Library* Sr Elizabeth Brown; *Art Library Asst* Sr Ann Austin Mooney
Open 8:30 am - 10 PM. Estab 1920 primarily to serve the students of the Art Department. Circ 1200
Income: $2500
Purchases: $2500
Library Holdings: Vols 3400; Per subs 24; AV—A-tapes, fs, slides; Other— Exhibition catalogs, prints

NEWARK

M **LICKING COUNTY ART ASSOCIATION GALLERY**, 391 Hudson Ave, 43055. Tel 614-349-8031. *Pres* John K Smart; *VPres* James Elliott; *Secy* Nancy Pennington; *Main Gallery Chairperson* Helen Crumet; *Membership* Polly Manning; *Art Education* Marilyn Herreman; *Planning & Design* Don Gunnerson; *Publicity* J Vivian Smith; *Pres of Art Guild* Helen Phillips; *Docent Chairperson* Carolyn Harper
Open daily 1 - 4 PM, cl Mon. No admis fee. Estab 1959 to offer nine monthly art exhibits of Ohio and mid-west artists. Three large rooms for monthly shows, also a youth gallery, members gallery and a permanent collection. Second building located at 19 North St adjoining, for art classes and houses a large kiln for ceramics. Average Annual Attendance: 4000. Mem: 400; dues life $150, $50, $10; annual meeting third Tues in May
Income: $15,000 (financed by membership, annual art auction and Guild's Craft and Art Fair)
Collections: Paintings
Exhibitions: Robert Eichholt (glass); Mary Sherwood Jones (drawings and watercolors); Ruth Kersteter (watercolors); Richard McMahan (woodcarvings); Carol Raab (acrylic paintings); Christopher Ries (glass sculpture); Richard Wheeler (Denison professor - sculpture); annual juried show
Publications: Art Print, monthly newsletter
Activities: Classes for adults and children; docent training; monthly programs; lect open to public, 4 visiting lectr per year; gallery talks; tours; demonstrations; competitions; cash awards; fellowships; book traveling exhibitions; sales shop sells, books, original art, prints, craft items, ceramics, jewelry, wood mirrors and stitchery

NORTH CANTON

L **NORTH CANTON PUBLIC LIBRARY**, Little Art Gallery, 185 N Main St, 44720. Tel 216-499-4712. *Library Dir* Sara Lee Donze; *Co-Chmn* Mrs Richard Hoover; *Cur Gallery* Mrs John L Zumkehr
Open Mon - Fri 10 AM - 9 PM, Sat 10 AM - 5 PM. No admis fee. Estab 1936 to encourage and promote appreciation and education of fine art, graphic arts, commercial art and other related subjects; also recognizes and encourages local artists by promoting exhibitions of their work. Circ 446. Average Annual Attendance: 5000
Income: Budget $1200 (financed by city and state appropriation)
Purchases: $500
Library Holdings: Vols 54,014; Per subs 180
Collections: †Original works by contemporary artists
Exhibitions: Art from the classrooms of the North Canton Public Schools (April); competitive May show each year, with cash awards totaling $270; monthly shows featuring the works of many northeastern Ohio artists; shows featuring collection of famous reproductions of religious subjects as well as secular
Activities: Classes for adults and children; lect open to the public; gallery talks; tours; competitions; lending collection contains color reproductions

OBERLIN

INTERMUSEUM CONSERVATION ASSOCIATION
For further information, see National and Regional Organizations

M **OBERLIN COLLEGE**, Allen Memorial Art Museum, Main & Lorain Sts, 44074. Tel 216-775-8665. *Dir* Richard E Spear; *Cur Modern Art* Chloe H Young; *Cur Modern Art* William Olander; *Honorary Cur Modern Art* Ellen H Johnson
Open during school year Tues - Fri 11 AM - 5 PM, Sat & Sun 2 - 5 PM, cl Mon; during vacations, summer and spring term Wed - Sun 2 - 5 PM, cl Mon & Tues. No admis fee. Estab 1917 to serve teaching needs of Oberlin College Art Department and other departments of the college and the college community. Original building was designed by Cass Gilbert, a new addition opened in 1977 and was designed by Venturi and Rauch. Average Annual Attendance: 27,000. Mem: 650; dues from $5 for students to $30
Income: Financed by endowment and membership
Collections: †Decorative Arts, †Graphics, †Painting, †Sculpture, from Early Egyptian Period to Present Day
Exhibitions: Frequent traveling exhibitions and specially assembled exhibitions
Publications: Allen Memorial Art Museum Bulletin; catalogues of permanent collections
Activities: Tours; lect open to public; competitions; individual paintings and original objects of art are lent to other institutions for special exhibitions; lending collection contains 250 original art works for lending to students on a semester basis; traveling exhibitions organized and circulated; sales desk selling reproductions, slides and museum publications

L **Clarence Ward Art Library**, Allen Art Bldg, Main & Lorain Sts, 44074. Tel 216-775-8635.
Open Mon - Thurs 8 AM - 5:30 PM and 7 - 11 PM, Fri 8 AM - 5:30 PM and 7 - 10 PM, Sat 9 AM - 5 PM, Sun 1 - 5 PM and 7 - 11 PM. Estab 1917 to serve the library needs of the Art Department, the Allen Memorial Art Museum and the Oberlin College community in the visual arts
Library Holdings: Vols 35,000; Per subs 200; Micro—Fiche, reels; Other—Clipping files, exhibition catalogs, pamphlets, reproductions
Collections: Jefferson Collection of Early Architectural Books
Activities: Tours

OXFORD

M **MIAMI UNIVERSITY ART MUSEUM**, Patterson Ave, 45056. Tel 513-529-2232. *Dir* David Berreth; *Cur* Sterling Cook
Open Tues - Sun 1 - 5 PM, cl Mon and University holidays. Estab 1972, Art Museum facility opened Fall 1978, to care for and exhibit University art collections, to arrange for a variety of exhibitions from other sources, and for the educational and cultural enrichment for the University and community. Gallery is maintained with exhibition space of 6,363 sq ft, 571 lin ft wall space. Average Annual Attendance: 25,000
Income: Financed by gift and state appropriation
Purchases: $10,000 - $30,000
Collections: Decorative Arts; †Folk Art, largely Middle European, Middle Eastern, Mexican, Central and South America; †paintings, †prints and †sculptures
Exhibitions: 6-8 exhibitions per year
Publications: Brochures; catalogs, approx 6-8 per year
Activities: Lect open to public, 8 visiting lectrs per year; gallery talks; tours
L **Library**, Patterson Ave, 45056.
For reference only
Library Holdings: Vols 1500

SPRINGFIELD

M **CLARK COUNTY HISTORICAL SOCIETY**, Memorial Hall, 45504. Tel 513-324-0657. *Pres* Mrs Robert Snodgrass; *Executive Dir & Cur Museum* George H Berkhofer
Open Tues - Fri 9 AM - 4 PM; Sat 9 AM - 1 PM. Estab 1897 for collection and preservation of Clark County history and historical artifacts. Mem: 600; dues family $7.50, individual $5; annual meeting Nov
Income: $20,000 (financed by appropriation)
Purchases: $20,000
Collections: European Landscapes; Oil Paintings, mostly mid-late 19th century, of prominent Springfielders
Publications: Newsletter, monthly; annual monograph
Activities: Monthly meetings and lect open to public; restoration project: The David Crabill House (1826), located at Lake Lagonda in Buck Creek State Park; books for sale
L **Library**, Memorial Hall, 45504.
Open to public
Collections: Photograph Collection

M **SPRINGFIELD ART CENTER**, 107 Cliff Park Rd, 45501. Tel 513-325-4673. *Chmn Board* Ralph H Wetherbee Jr; *Pres* Howard B Noonan; *VPres* Glenn W Collier; *Secy* George McCleary; *Secy* David L Hobson; *Dir* Patricia Catron
Open Tues - Fri 9 AM - 5 PM; Sat 9 AM - 3 PM; Sun 2 - 4 PM; cl Mon. No admis fee. Estab 1951 for educational and cultural purposes, particularly the encouragement of the appreciation, study of, participation in and enjoyment of the fine arts. Average Annual Attendance: 25,000. Mem: 1000; dues benefactor $100, sustaining $35, family $25, individual $15; meetings third Tues in June
Income: $85,000 (financed by endowment, membership, and tuition fees)
Collections: 19th & 20th Century Artists (mostly American, some French)
Exhibitions: Monthly exhibits
Publications: Newsletter, monthly
Activities: Classes for adults and children; lect open to public, 3 - 4 vis lectr per year; tours; sales shop selling original art
L **Library**, 107 Cliff Park Rd, 45501. *Librn* Mary M Miller
Open Tues - Fri 9 AM - 5 PM; Sat 9 AM - 3 PM; Sun 2 - 4 PM. Estab 1970 for art study. For reference only
Library Holdings: Vols 1500; Per subs 12; Other—Clipping files, exhibition catalogs, pamphlets
Special Subjects: Photography

TOLEDO

M **BLAIR MUSEUM OF LITHOPHANES AND CARVED WAXES**, 2032 Robinwood Ave, Toledo, OH. (Mailing Add: 2243 Ashland Ave, Toledo, OH 43620) Tel 419-243-4115. *Cur* Laurel G Blair
Open by appointment for groups of 10-20. Admis $2. Estab 1965 for the purpose of displaying lithophanes and carved waxes; the only museum of its kind in the world. There are five galleries. Average Annual Attendance: 2000. Mem: 145; dues $10
Income: $30,000 (financed by membership and sales to members)
Collections: Lithophane Collection, with 2300 examples is the world's largest (only 1000 can be shown at once); †Wax Collection
Publications: Bulletin, bi-monthly
Activities: Lect open to the public
L **Library**, 2243 Ashland Ave, 43620.
For reference only
Library Holdings: Vols 100; Per subs 30

C **OWENS-CORNING FIBERGLAS CORPORATION**, Fiberglas Tower, corner Jefferson and Saint Clair, 43659. Tel 419-248-6179. *Cur Asst* Penny McMorris
Open to public. Estab 1968 to create a pleasant and stimulating work environment for employees; to provide a focal point for contemporary art; supporting the arts

both through purchase of works and display of the collection. Collection displayed in company offices in Toledo and other cities

Collections: Approximately 1000 works of contemporary art by American artists, many relatively young

Activities: Lect; tours

O **SPECTRUM, FRIENDS OF FINE ART, INC,** 5304 Elmer Dr, 43615. Tel 419-531-7769. *Pres* Dick MacAdams; *VPres* Nelson Thal; *Corresponding Secy* Odessa W Rowan; *Recording Secy* Martin Nagy; *Treas* Gary Armstrong
Open Tues - Sun 1 - 4 PM; cl Mon. No admis fee. Estab 1976 to encourage and support public appreciation of Fine Art and to organize and promote related activities; promote mutual understanding and cooperation among artists, artist groups and the public; promote beautification of Toledo through use of art work. Clubhouse (2 galleries, sales room and office) part of Crosby Village Green in Crosby Gardens; large adjacent Art Education Center. Average Annual Attendance: 1500 - 2000. Mem: 350; dues adult $15 - $25, student $7; annual meeting May

Income: Approximately $6000 - $7000 (financed by membership and fund-raising events)

Exhibitions: Membership Show, Edison Co-juried, Spectrum Touring Show (six locations); Photographic Exhibition; Promenade Park; Scarab Show; Spot Exhibitions; Summer Fiesta

Publications: Spectrum (newsletter), bi-monthly

Activities: Classes for adults and children; lect open to the public, 4-5 vis lectr per year; competitions; traveling exhibitions organized and circulated; sales shop selling original art

O **TOLEDO ARTISTS' CLUB,** 5430 Elmer Dr, PO Box 7430, 43615. Tel 419-531-4079. *Pres* Edith D Shears; *First VPres* Ernest Spring; *Second VPres* Dale Keiser; *Secy* Helen Packard; *Treas* Lowell Skilliter
Open Mon - Fri 12 - 4 PM, Sat 9 AM - 1 PM, July - Oct open Sun. Estab 1943. New Clubhouse-Gallery opened at Crosby Gardens, Toledo in August 1979. Mem: 400-500; dues $15 (variable)

Income: Financed by membership and exhibitions

Exhibitions: Approximately 80 pieces of artwork exhibited each month in new Gallery; includes paintings, pottery, schulpture, stained glass

Publications: Newsletter, monthly

Activities: Classes for adults and children; workshops; demonstrations; lect open to the public; competitions; jointly present Crosby Gardens Arts Festival in June with Crosby Gardens, Toledo Forestry Division and the Arts Commission of Greater Toledo; sales shop selling original art

O **TOLEDO FEDERATION OF ART SOCIETIES,** PO Box 5588, 43613. Tel 419-255-8000. *Pres* Nelson Thal; *First VPres* Edith Franklin; *Second VPres* Eleanor Bacon; *Recording Secy* Beryl Preketes; *Treas* Christine Turnbull; *Corresponding Secy* Peggy Snug
Estab 1917 to arrange for annual area exhibition. Mem: 13 area clubs; dues $10; meetings first Sat after first Fri (Sept - May)

Income: Financed by membership, city appropriation, fund drive and Ohio Arts Council Grant

Collections: †Permanent collection

Exhibitions: Annual Exhibition

Activities: Competitions with cash awards; individual paintings and original objects of art lent to civic organizations; lending collection contains original art works, original prints, paintings and sculpture

M **TOLEDO MUSEUM OF ART,** Monroe St at Scottwood Ave, Box 1013, 43697. Tel 419-255-8000. *Pres* Samuel G Carson; *Dir* Roger Mandle; *Asst Dir Education* Charles F Gunther; *Registrar* Patricia Whitesides; *Chief Cur & Cur of Contemporary Art* Robert F Phillips; *Cur Ancient Art* Kurt T Luckner; *Cur Decorative Arts* Roger M Berkowitz; *Sr Cur* William Hutton; *Cur of Prints* Roberta Waddell; *Supv Music* Joyce Smar; *Supt* Alan Gray
Open Tues - Sat 9 AM - 5 PM; Sun 1 - 6 PM; cl Mon and legal holidays. No admis fee. Estab and incorporated 1901; building erected 1912, additions 1926 and 1933. Average Annual Attendance: 463,000. Mem: 8000; dues $20 and higher

Collections: Ancient and Modern Glass; Contemporary Art in Glass Gallery; European Paintings and Decorative Arts, including Edward Drummond Libbey and Arthur Secor Gifts; Stained Glass; Maurice A Scott Galleries of American Paintings; George W Stevens Collection of Books and Manuscripts; traveling exhibitions; ceramics, prints, sculpture

Exhibitions: Annual exhibitions of the work of Toledo area artists

Publications: Quarterly Museum News; Calendar Guide to the Collections, monthly; Art in Glass

Activities: Classes; lect; talk; concerts; book traveling exhibitions; traveling exhibitions

L **Library,** Box 1013, 43697. *Librn* Anne O Reese; *Asst Librn* Joan L Sepessy
Open Tues - Fri 9 AM - 5 PM (Tues & Thurs 5 - 8:30 PM during university sessions). Estab 1901 to provide resources for the museum's staff

Library Holdings: Vols 35,000; Per subs 300; Micro—Fiche, reels; AV—Lantern Slides, slides; Other—Clipping files, exhibition catalogs, photographs

VERMILION

M **GREAT LAKES HISTORICAL SOCIETY,** 480 Main St, 44089. Tel 216-967-3467. *Pres* Alexander C Meakin; *VPres* Douglas S Keith; *Secy* T A Sykora; *Business Mgr* Arthur N O'Hara
Open daily 11 AM - 5 PM. Admis adults $1.50, children 75¢. Estab 1944 to promote interest in discovering and preserving material about the Great Lakes and surrounding areas. Maintains an art gallery as part of the Maritime History Museum. Average Annual Attendance: 30,000. Mem: 3000; dues from $12 - $500; meetings May and Oct

Income: $100,000 (financed by endowment, membership and sales from Museum Store)

Collections: Collection of Ship Models, Marine Relics, Paintings and Photographs dealing with history of the Great Lakes

Exhibitions: Great Lakes Heritage (Paul C LaMarre Jr); Maritime History in Art (James Clary); Annual Model Boat Show Exhibition

Publications: Chadburn (newsletter), quarterly; Inland Seas, quarterly

Activities: Educ dept; lect open to public, 5 vis lectr per year; tours; competitions; awards; sales shop selling books, magazines, original art, prints, slides and gifts

WELLINGTON

M **SPIRIT OF '76 MUSEUM,** Southern Lorain County Historical Society, 201 N Main, PO Box 76, 44090. Tel 216-647-4531. *Pres* Ralph Miller; *VPres* Clyde Ray; *Secy* Margaret Henes; *Museum Dir* Ernst L Henes
Open April - Nov 2:30 - 5 PM, groups of ten or more by reservation. No admis fee. Estab 1970 to memorialize Archibald M Willard who created the Spirit of '76, nation's most inspirational painting. Average Annual Attendance: 2000. Mem: 237; dues couples $5, individual $3; annual meeting April

Income: $10,000 (financed by membership, city appropriation, gifts and gift shop)

Purchases: $10,000

Collections: Archibald M Willard Paintings; artifacts of local interest

Publications: Newsletters

Activities: Sales shop sells books, reproductions, prints and miscellaneous items

WILLOUGHBY

O **FINE ARTS ASSOCIATION,** School of Fine Arts, 38660 Mentor Ave, 44094. Tel 216-951-7500. *Pres* Brian Sherwin; *Executive Dir* James J Savage; *Secy* Mrs Ronald Chapnick; *Visual Arts Coordr* Doris Foster
Open Weekdays 9 AM - 8 PM, Sat 9 AM - 5 PM, and performance times. No admis fee. Estab 1957 to bring arts education to all people regardless of their ability to pay, race or social standing. Gallery maintained. Average Annual Attendance: 20,000. Mem: 800; dues $15 and up; annual meeting April

Income: Financed by class fees and donations

Exhibitions: Monthly exhibitions, theme, one man and group; Annual juried exhibit for area artists; Annual outdoor Arts Festival

Activities: Art, ballet, theatre and music classes; classes for adults and children; in-school programs; lectures open to the public 10 - 15 visiting lecturers per year; gallery talks; tours; concerts; theatre productions; competitions; scholarships; three county area served by extension department; material available to schools and organizations

L **Library,** 38660 Mentor Ave, 44094.
For reference only

Library Holdings: Vols 5000

WOOSTER

M **COLLEGE OF WOOSTER ART CENTER MUSEUM,** University St, 44691. Tel 216-264-1234, Ext 388. *Dir* Dr Arnold Lewis; *Asst Mus Dir* Phyllis Blair Clark; *Cur* Esther de Vecsey
Open Mon - Sat 9 AM - Noon & 1 - 5 PM; Sun 2 - 5 PM. No admis fee. Estab 1944 to provide an opportunity for students, faculty and the local community to view original works of art. The gallery is housed in a former library; Main floor has large open areas and upper balcony more intimate exhibition space. Average Annual Attendance: 5000

Income: $7000 (financed through College)

Collections: Chinese Bronzes and Porcelains; paintings; prints; sculpture; tapestries

Exhibitions: Invitational Functional Ceramics Exhibition; traveling and monthly exhibitions

Activities: Lect open to public, 10 - 15 vis lectr per year; gallery talks; books traveling exhibitions

YELLOW SPRINGS

M **ANTIOCH COLLEGE,** Noyes, Read and Gray Galleries, 45387. Tel 513-767-7331, Ext 464. *Chmn* Karen Shirley
Open Mon - Fri 1 - 4 PM. No admis fee. Estab 1972. Noyes Gallery to offer works to students and the community that both challenge and broaden their definitions of Art; Gray Gallery is a small photo gallery; Read Gallery is primarily a student gallery. Average Annual Attendance: 3000

Exhibitions: Michael Blaine; Beyond Dada - James Jordan - Ma'aleesh; Nancy Koehler - Photo Performance

YOUNGSTOWN

M **BUTLER INSTITUTE OF AMERICAN ART,** 524 Wick Ave, 44502. Tel 216-743-1711. *Dir & Pres* Joseph G Butler; *Assoc Dir* Clyde Singer; *Cur* Dr Eric C Hulmer; *Education Dir* Alice Goldcamp
Open Tues - Sat 11 AM - 4 PM; Sun Noon - 4 PM; cl Mon. No admis. Estab 1919, and is the first museum building to be devoted entirely to American Art. Average Annual Attendance: 80,000. Mem: 700 (Friends of American Art, art auxilliary organization)

Income: Financed by endowment
Collections: American Paintings Dating from 1719 to Present: †Oils, †Watercolors, †Drawings, †Sculpture and Ceramics; †Paintings and Drawings of the American Indian; Seven Ship Scale Models; †32 Paintings of Clipper Ships from Sail to Steam; prints
Exhibitions: Annual Midyear Show; Area Artists Annual; Ohio Ceramic Annual; Polish Arts Club Show; traveling exhibitions; Youngstown State University Annual
Publications: Catalog of permanent collection with numerous reproductions issued Oct 1979 (60th anniversary edition)
Activities: Classes for children; lect open to the public; concerts; gallery talks; tours; individual paintings and original objects of art lent to qualified museums, institutions; book traveling exhibitions; traveling exhibitions organized and circulated; sales shop selling books, original art, reproductions, slides
L **Library,** 524 Wick Ave, 44502.
For reference only
Library Holdings: Vols 1500; Per subs 15

M **YOUNGSTOWN STATE UNIVERSITY,** Kilcawley Center Art Gallery, 410 Wick Ave, 44555. Tel 216-742-3575. *Prog Dir* David Johnson; *Art Gallery Coordr* June Bennehoof
Open Mon - Thurs 10 AM - 8 PM; Fri 10 AM - 3 PM. Estab 1974 to provide the university and the community with a diversified art program. Gallery is 100 running ft. Average Annual Attendance: 10,000
Income: Financed by university appropriation
Purchases: $1000
Collections: †Kilcawley Collection includes works by Alan Davie, Gene Davis, Jim Dine, Don Eddy, Sam Gilliam, Robert Indiana, Jasper Johns, Alfred Leslie, Roy Lichtenstein, Robert Motherwell, Clas Oldenburg, Robert Rauschenberg, James Rosenquist, Alen Shields, Jack Tworkov, Andy Warhol
Activities: Lect open to the public, 4 vis lectr per year; gallery talks; individual paintings lent on exchange

ZANESVILLE

O **ZANESVILLE ART CENTER,** 620 Military Rd, 43701. Tel 614-452-0741. *Dir* Dr Charles Dietz; *Secy & Registrar* Mrs Joseph Howell; *Pres Board Trustees* Hiram Heck; *Pres Board Dir* Mrs Robert E Raymond; *Cur Oriental Art* Mrs Willis Bailey; *Cur Glass* William Brown
Open daily 1 - 5 PM; cl Fri and holidays. No admis fee. Estab 1936 to provide a public center for the arts and crafts, permanent collections and temporary exhibitions, classes in art and crafts, library of art volumes and a meeting place for art and civic groups. There are five galleries for Old and Modern Masters' paintings, sculpture, prints, ceramics, glass, photography, children's art and gift art. Average Annual Attendance: 25,000. Mem: 300; dues $10 and up
Income: Financed by endowment, membership
Collections: †American, European and †Oriental Paintings, Sculptures, Ceramics, Prints, Drawings, and Crafts; †Children's Art; †Midwestern and †Zanesville Ceramics and Glass
Exhibitions: AAUW Annual Children's Art Show; Annual May Arts & Crafts Exhibition; Ceramics, Jim Betts; Governor's Pre-Columbus Children's Art Show; Jewelry, Paula Dickson; June Salon de Refuses; Ohio Historical Preservation Photos & Architectural Drawings; Oils & Pastels, Cleo Williams; Photos, Charles Colliflower; Soft Sculpture, Vince Carletti; Spring Flower Show; Watercolors, Don Dodrill; Watercolors, George Marquis & Marilyn Phillis; Watercolors, Ohio Watercolor Society; Watercolors, Southeastern Ohio Watercolor Society; Watercolors, Thomas Thierry and Rogers Rusk; Zanesville Art League Spring Show
Publications: Bulletin, monthly
Activities: Classes for adults and children; lect open to public, 5 vis lectr per year; concerts; gallery talks; tours; competitions; individual paintings lent to public institutions; sales shop selling original art, prints, crafts
L **Library,** 620 Military Rd, 43701. *Librn* Mrs Joseph Howell
Open Mon - Thur 1 - 5 PM, cl Fri and major holidays. Estab 1936 to provide fine arts and crafts information
Purchases: $1000
Library Holdings: Vols 4500; Per subs 5; AV—Fs, slides; Other—Exhibition catalogs, prints, original art works, pamphlets, photographs, reproductions, sculpture
Collections: Midwestern & Zanesville Glass

OKLAHOMA

ANADARKO

M **NATIONAL HALL OF FAME FOR FAMOUS AMERICAN INDIANS,** Box 808, 73005. Tel 405-247-3000, 247-5795. *Pres* Allie Reynolds; *Executive VPres & Dir* Paul T Stonum; *Treas* Lorraine Cox; *Secy* Sally Stonum
Open during daylight hours, seven days a week. No admis fee. Estab 1952 to honor famous American Indians who have contributed to the culture of America, including statesmen, innovators, sportsmen, warriors; to teach the youth of our country that there is a reward for greatness. An outdoor Museum in a landscaped area containing bronze sculptured portraits of Honorees. Average Annual Attendance: 10,000. Mem: 1000; dues life $100, family $10, individual $5; annual meeting August
Income: Financed by membership, city and state appropriation and donation
Purchases: $2500 - $5000
Collections: Bronze sculptured portraits and bronze statues of two animals important to Indian culture
Publications: Brochure
Activities: Seminars of American Indian Culture held during dedication ceremonies for Honorees

M **SOUTHERN PLAINS INDIAN MUSEUM,** US Hwy 62, PO Box 749, 73005. Tel 405-247-6221. *Cur* Rosemary Ellison
Open (June - Sept) Mon - Sat 9 AM - 5 PM; Sun 1 - 5 PM; (Oct - May) Tues - Sat 9 AM - 5 PM; Sun 1 - 5 PM; cl New Year's Day, Thanksgiving and Christmas. No admis fee. Estab 1947-48 to promote the development of contemporary native American arts and crafts of the United States. Administered and operated by the Indian Arts and Crafts Board, US Department of the Interior. Average Annual Attendance: 80,000
Income: Financed by federal appropriation
Purchases: Primarily dependent upon gifts
Collections: Contemporary Native American Arts and Crafts of the United States; Historic Works by Southern Plains Indian Craftsmen
Exhibitions: Comtemporary Southern Plains Indian Metalwork; continuing series of one-person exhibitions; changing exhibitions by contemporary native American artists and craftsmen; Historic Plains Indian Arts
Publications: One-person exhibition brochure series, monthly
Activities: Gallery talks; traveling exhibitions organized and circulated

ARDMORE

O **CHARLES B GODDARD CENTER FOR THE VISUAL AND PERFORMING ARTS,** First & D St SW, 73401. Tel 405-226-0909. *Pres* Mrs Leon Daube; *Secy* Richard Colvert; *Managing Dir* Laurence London; *Treas* John Snodgrass; *Dir* Robert Batis; *Dir* James E Thompson; *Office Secy* Eve Putman
Open Mon - Fri 9:30 AM - 4 PM; Sat 11 AM - 4 PM. No admis fee. Estab March 1970 to bring fine art programs in the related fields of music, art and films to local community at minimum cost; gallery to bring traveling exhibitions to Ardmore. Average Annual Attendance: 35,000. Mem: 450; dues $12 - $1000; monthly Advisory Board meeting, and semi-annual Primary Board meeting
Income: $65,000
Collections: Portraits, paintings and drawings
Exhibitions: Ada Art Exhibit; American Watercolor Society; Contemporary Prints from Canada; Paintings by Max Butler; Southwest Graphics Exhibit; Southwestern Watercolor Society; State Sculpture Show; 10th Annual Ardmore Art Exhibit; White House Photographers Exhibit; Wichita Falls Museum Exhibit
Publications: Outlook, monthly
Activities: Classes for adults and children in dancing, art, pottery, piano, adult ballroom dancing, ladies exercise and movement classes; lect open to the public; concerts; books for sale

BARTLESVILLE

M **WOOLAROC MUSEUM,** State Hwy 123, Route 3, 74003. Tel 918-336-6747. *Dir* Robert R Lansdown; *Cur Art* Linda Stone; *Museum Artist* Francis Letchworth
Open daily 10 AM - 5 PM Apr - Oct; cl Mon, and Nov - Mar. No admis fee. Estab 1929 to house art and artifacts of the Southwest. Museum dedicated by Frank Phillips. Gallery has two levels, 6 rooms upstairs and 3 rooms downstairs. Average Annual Attendance: Over 250,000
Income: Financed by endowment
Collections: American Indian Artifacts; Prehistoric Artifacts; paintings, drawings, graphics, sculpture
Activities: Lect open to public; gallery talks; tours; lending collection contains transparencies to be used to illustrate educational publications; museum shop selling books, original art, reproductions, prints, slides, Indian-made jewelry and pottery, postcards
L **Library,** State Hwy 123, Route 3, 74003.
Circ Reference library open to employees only
Library Holdings: Vols 718

CLAREMORE

M **WILL ROGERS MEMORIAL AND MUSEUM,** W Will Rogers Blvd, PO Box 157, 74017. Tel 918-341-0719. *Cur* Dr Reba Neighbors Collins; *Mgr* Delmar L Collins; *Tour Guide* Greg Malek; *Secy* Patricia A Lowe
Open Daily 8 AM - 5 PM. No admis fee. Estab 1938 to perpetuate the name, works, and spirit of Will Rogers. There are three main galleries, diorama room, foyer and gardens. The large Jo Davidson statue of Will Rogers dominates the foyer; the north gallery includes photographs and paintings of Will Rogers and his ancestors (including a family tree, explaining his Indian heritage), and many other personal items; east gallery has saddle collection and other Western things; Jo Mora dioramas. Average Annual Attendance: 500,000
Income: Approx $100,000 (financed by state appropriation)
Collections: Borein Etchings; Bust by Electra Wagoner Biggs; Collection of Paintings by Various ARtists commissioned by a calendar company with originals donated to Memorial; Count Tamburini Oil of Will Rogers; Jo Mora Dioramas (13); Large Equestrian Statue by Electra Wagoner Biggs; Mural by Ray Piercey; Original of Will Rogers by Leyendecker; Paintings of Will's Parents by Local Artists
Publications: Brochures and materials for students
Activities: Lect; films; assist with publishing project of Will Rogers works at Oklahoma State University; lending collection contains motion pictures, 50 photographs, 144 slides, 20 minute documentary of Will Rogers available to nonprofit organizations; originate traveling exhibitions; museum shop selling books, magazines, reproductions of original photographs in sepiatone, slides
L **Library,** W Will Rogers Blvd, PO Box 157, 74017. *Cur-Librn* Dr Reba Collins
Reference library for research by appointment only
Library Holdings: Vols 600; Other—original writings
Collections: Will Rogers Collection

ENID

M **PHILLIPS UNIVERSITY,** Grace Phillips Johnson Art Gallery, University Station, 73701. Tel 405-237-4433. *Cur* Mary E Phillips
Open Tues - Fri 10 AM - 5 PM; Sat, Sun & holidays 2 - 5 PM; cl national holidays. No admis fee. Estab 1966
Collections: Decorative Arts; Historical Material of the University; paintings, prints, sculpture
Exhibitions: Exhibitions from the collection; traveling exhibitions
Activities: Lect; gallery talks; tours; competitions; book traveling exhibitions

GOODWELL

M **NO MAN'S LAND HISTORICAL SOCIETY,** Sewell St, 73939. Tel 405-349-2670. *Pres* Lona Neff Graham; *VPres* Henry C Hitch Jr; *Museum Dir* Dr Harold S Kachel; *Cur & Secy* Joan Overton Kachel
Open Tues - Fri 9 AM - 5 PM, Sat & Sun 1 - 5 PM; cl Mon & holidays. No admis fee. Estab 1934 to procure appropriate museum material with special regard to portraying the history of No Man's Land (Oklahoma Panhandle) and the immediate adjacent regions. The gallery is 14 ft x 40 ft (560 sq ft). Average Annual Attendance: 4000. Mem: 59; dues life $100, organization $10, individual $5
Income: Financed by state appropriation and donations
Collections: Oils by Pearl Robison Burrows Burns
Exhibitions: Nine exhibits each year by local artists; six exhibits by local craftsmen each year
Activities: Lect open to public, 2 vis lectr per year; gallery talks; tours

LANGSTON

M **LANGSTON UNIVERSITY ART GALLERY,** 73050. Tel 918-466-2231. *Chmn* Wallace Owens
Open Mon - Fri 8 AM - 5 PM. No admis fee. Estab 1959 to exhibit pertinent works of art, both contemporary and traditional; to serve as a teaching tool for students. Average Annual Attendance: 6000
Income: Financed by state appropriation
Collections: Award purchases
Activities: Classes for adults; lect, 2 vis lectr per year; gallery talks; tours

LAWTON

M **INSTITUTE OF THE GREAT PLAINS,** Museum of the Great Plains, 601 Ferris, PO Box 68, 73502. Tel 405-353-5675. *Dir* Steve Wilson; *Cur Anthropology* Towana Spivey; *Cur Exhibits* William Austin; *Cur Education* Maryruth Prose; *Archaeologist* John Northcutt; *Exhibits Technician* Kevin Britz; *Photo Technician* Darleen Clifton
Open Mon - Fri 8 AM - 5 PM, Sat 10 AM - 5:30 PM, Sun 1:30 - 5:30 PM. No admis fee. Estab 1961 to collect, preserve, interpret, and exhibit items of the cultural history of man in the Great Plains of North America. Galleries of the Museum of the Great Plains express a regional concept of interpreting the relationship of man to a semiarid plains environment. Average Annual Attendance: 90,000. Mem: 700; dues $7.50
Income: Financed by endowment, city and state appropriations
Collections: Archaeological, ethnological, historical, and natural science collections relating to man's inhabitance of the Great Plains
Exhibitions: Lawton Jr Service League Annual Juried Art Show; history, archaeology, and ethnological exhibits
Publications: Great Plains Journal, annual; Contributions to the Museum of the Great Plains 1-9, irregular; Museum Newsletter, irregular
Activities: Classes for children; dramatic programs; docent training; lect open to public, 6 vis lectr per year; gallery talks; museum shop selling books, magazines, original art, reproductions, prints

L **Research Library,** Sixth & Ferris, 73502. Tel 405-353-5676. *Cur Special Coll* Jeane Bothe
Open Mon - Fri 8 AM - 5 PM. Estab 1961 to provide research materials for the 10-state Great Plains region. Lending to staff only
Income: Financed by endowment, city and state appropriations
Library Holdings: Vols 16,000; Per subs 100; Micro—Reels; Other—Photographs
Special Subjects: Archaeology, Antropology
Collections: Archives; photographic collections

MUSKOGEE

M **BACONE COLLEGE MUSEUM,** Ataloa Lodge, 74401. Tel 918-683-4581, Ext 220. *Dir* Howard L Meredith; *Admin Asst* Pauline Harjo
Open Mon - Fri 10 AM - Noon, 1 - 4:30 PM. No admis fee. Estab to enhance Indian culture by having a collection of artifacts from various Indian tribes. One large room. Average Annual Attendance: 1000
Income: Financed through Bacone College
Collections: Indian crafts and artifacts: silverwork, weapons, blankets, dolls, beadwork, pottery, weaving and basketry; Indian Art
Activities: Tours

M **FIVE CIVILIZED TRIBES MUSEUM,** Agency Hill, Honor Heights Dr, 74401. Tel 918-683-1701. *Pres* John T Griffin Jr; *Secy* Charlene Adair; *Dir* Mrs Spencer Denton
Open Mon - Sat 10 AM - 5 PM, Sun 1 - 5 PM. Admis adults 50¢, students 25¢; group rates available. Estab 1966 to exhibit artifacts, relics, history, and traditional Indian art of the Cherokee, Chickasaw, Choctaw, Creek, and Seminole Indian Tribes. Average Annual Attendance: 33,000. Mem: 1242; dues $5-$300; annual meetings Apr and Oct
Income: $48,000 (financed by membership, and admissions)
Collections: †Traditional Indian art by known artists of Five Tribes heritage
Exhibitions: Annual Judged Exhibition and Sale of Beadwork, Pottery, Basketry and Silver; Competitive Art Show; Students Competitive Show
Publications: Newsletter, bimonthly

Activities: Competitions; museum shop selling books, magazines, original art, reproductions, prints, beadwork, pottery, basketry and other handmade items

L **Library,** Agency Hill, Honor Heights Dr, 74401. *Chmn* Frances R Brown; *Dir* Mrs Spencer Denton
Open Mon - Sat 10 AM - 5 PM, Sun 1 - 5 PM. Estab 1966 to preserve history, culture, traditions, legends, etc of Five Civilized Tribes (Cherokee, Creek, Choctaw, Chickasaw, and Seminole tribes). Maintains an art gallery
Income: Financed by museum
Library Holdings: Vols 3500; Per subs 5; AV—Cassettes, lantern Slides; Other—Clipping files, exhibition catalogs, framed reproductions, prints, manuscripts, memorabilia, original art works, pamphlets, photographs, reproductions, sculpture, original documents

NORMAN

UNIVERSITY OF OKLAHOMA

M **Museum of Art,** 410 W Boyd St, 73019. Tel 405-325-3272. *Dir* Sam Oklinetzky; *Asst Dir* Edwin J Deighton; *Museum Secy* Mary Cook
Open Tues - Fri 10 AM - 4 PM, Sat 10 AM - 1 PM, Sun 1 - 4 PM, cl Mon & holidays. Estab 1936 to provide cultural enrichment for the people of Oklahoma; to collect, preserve, exhibit and provide research in art of all significant periods. Approx 15,000 sq ft for permanent and temporary exhibitions on two indoor levels; 30 ft high, carpeted walls in 3 galleries; 2 galleries 120 sq ft each. Average Annual Attendance: 50,000. Mem: 360; dues $15 - $100; meetings Sept & Jan
Income: Financed by university allocation
Collections: African sculpture; †American all media; †crafts; European all media; oceanic art; †photography
Exhibitions: (1978-1979) African Sculpture; Architecture in Oklahoma: Landmark and Vernacular; Courthouse: A Photographic Document; Egyptian Tapestries; Northwest Eccentric Art; Oklahoma Indian Art: A Continuing Tradition Art; The Lower East Side: Portal to American Life
Publications: Calendar of activities; posters; announcements
Activities: Docent training; lect open to public; concerts; gallery talks; tours; competitions; individual paintings and original objects of art lent to other museums and galleries; lending collection contains original art works and prints, paintings; museum shop selling books, magazines, original art, slides

L **Art Library,** 550 Parrington Oval, Room 203 Jacobson Hall, 73019. Tel 405-325-2841. *Art Librn* Don Koozer
Open Mon - Fri 9 AM - 5 PM, Sat 10 AM - 1 PM, Mon - Thurs 6:30 - 9 PM. Estab to provide instructional support to the academic community of the university and general service to the people of the state. Circ 6900
Income: Financed by state appropriation
Library Holdings: Vols 10,000; Per subs 55; Micro—Fiche, reels

OKLAHOMA CITY

ASSOCIATION OF AMERICAN EDITORIAL CARTOONISTS
For further information, see National and Regional Organizations

M **NATIONAL COWBOY HALL OF FAME AND WESTERN HERITAGE CENTER,** 1700 NE 63rd St, 73111. Tel 405-478-2250. *Exec Dir* Dean Krakel; *Managing Dir* Rich Muno; *Pub Relations Dir* Marsi Thompson
Open daily 9:30 AM - 5:30 PM; summer 8:30 AM - 6 PM; cl New Year's Day, Thanksgiving & Christmas Day. Admis adults $2, children $1, group rates available for 10 or more persons. Estab 1965 as a memorial shrine to great Westerners. Museum includes the Rodeo Hall of Fame and the Hall of Fame of Great Western Performers. Mem: 5000; dues $25 and up; annual meeting Apr
Income: Financed by membership
Collections: Albert K Mitchell Russell-Remington Collection; Albert Bierstadt; contemporary Western Art; Fechin Collection; Thomas Moran; C M Russell Bronzes; Schreyvogel Collection; Taos Collection; John Wayne Kachina Collection; Western Art; James Earle and Laura G Fraser Studio Collection
Exhibitions: National Academy of Western Art Exhibition; special exhibitions throughout year
Publications: Persimmon Hill Magazine, quarterly
Activities: Western Heritage Awards in April; Rodeo Hall of Fame Inductions in December

L **Library,** 1700 NE 63rd St, 73111.
For reference only
Library Holdings: Vols 7000; Per subs 75

L **NATIVE AMERICAN PAINTING REFERENCE LIBRARY,** Box 33123, 73132. *Dir* Arthur Silberman
Established as a privately funded institution committed to the premise that Indian painting is a valuable part of the American cultural heritage. It is a repository for any kind of information having a bearing on the history and development of native American paintings
Library Holdings: Other—Clipping files, photographs, Correspondence catalogues, auction records, interview tapes
Collections: Slides of paintings in private and public museums
Activities: Traveling exhibitions organized and circulated

O **OKLAHOMA ART CENTER,** Plaza Circle-Fair Park, 3113 Pershing Blvd, 73107. Tel 405-946-4477. *Pres* Richard Clements; *VPres* Jerome M Westheimer; *VPres* Richard D Harrison; *VPres* Mrs Dan Hogan; *Treas* H E Boecking Jr; *Secy* C Richard Ford; *Dir* Lowell Adams; *Assoc Dir* Mary Kathryn Adams; *Public Relations Dir* Kate Hammett
Open Tues - Sat 10 AM - 5 PM, Sun 1 - 5 PM, cl holidays. Admis $1. Estab 1936 and incorporated 1946 to encourage regional art activity and to present an educational program for adults and children. Average Annual Attendance: 50,000. Mem: 2500; dues $15 and higher
Collections: †American contemporary paintings and sculpture (including Washington Gallery of Modern Art complete collection and Eight State purchase awards); †American masters paintings; †contemporary prints, drawings, watercolors; †historical survey of prints and drawings
Exhibitions: Annual Eight State Exhibition of Painting and Sculpture; National

Exhibition of Prints and Drawings; Oklahoma Designer-Craftsmen Exhibition; Young Talent in Oklahoma (juried high school show with awards of seven college scholarships)
Activities: Lect; tours; art films; gallery talks; family art events; originate traveling exhibitions; book store, sales and rental gallery
L **Oklahoma Art Center Library,** 3113 Pershing Blvd, 73107. Tel 405-946-4477. *Assoc Dir* M K Adams
Open Tues - Fri 10 AM - 4 PM. Estab 1965 to provide art reference materials,. Art gallery maintained
Income: $300,000 (financed by endowment, membership and Allied Arts contributions)
Library Holdings: Vols 1500; AV—Slides
Collections: Doughty Bird Ceramics; 20th century American art and graphics
Exhibitions: 22nd National Print and Drawing Exhibition; 22nd Eight State Exhibition of Painting and Sculpture
Publications: Catalogues of exhibitions
Activities: Classes for adults and children; dramatic programs; docent training; lect open to public; 5-10 vis lectr per year; concerts; gallery talks; tours; competitions with awards; scholarships; exten dept serves center of metro area, downtown gallery and Artsplace II; originate traveling exhibitions to other regional museums
O **Oklahoma Art Center Annex,** 3000 Pershing Blvd, 73107. *Educ Dir* Michael Sanden
Educational facility with extensive ceramics studio, print making studio and 350 seat auditorium
Activities: Year-round classes in ballet, art and crafts, fencing and modern dance
O **Arts Place II,** 115 Park Ave, 73116. Tel 405-232-1787. *Mgr* June C Parsons; *Dir* Pat Gallagher
Open Mon - Fri 10 AM - 4 PM. No admis fee. Estab 1977 to promote the visual and performing arts by providing these experiences to downtown and offering fine arts and crafts for sale and rental by offices and houses. Exhibition gallery, performing arts area, sales and rental gallery
Income: Financed by membership and donations
Exhibitions: Drawing from the various university art professors and professional artists in Oklahoma; works by 59 artists are offered in sales and rental gallery; regional exhibitions plus permanent collection from OAC featured every three weeks in main gallery
Publications: OAC Bulletin; bi-monthly mailer listing exhibitions and performances
Activities: Classes for adults and children; dramatic programs; docent training; lect open to public, 12-15 vis lectr per year; concerts; gallery talks; tours; competitions; artmobile; individual paintings and original objects of art lent; lending collection contains original art works and prints, paintings, photographs, sculpture; traveling exhibitions organized and circulated; sales shop selling books, magazines, original art, reproductions, prints

M **OKLAHOMA HISTORICAL SOCIETY,** Central Museum, Historical Bldg, 73105. Tel 405-521-2491. *Pres Board Trustees* W D Finney; *Executive Dir* H Glenn Jordan; *Intrepretations* Bruce Joseph; *Museums & Historical Sites* C E Metcalf; *Library Resources* Vickie Sullivan; *Publications* Bob Blackburn; *Preservation Dir* Melvena Thurman; *Preservation Dir* Steve Day
Open Mon - Fri 9 AM - 5 PM. No admis fee. Estab 1893 to provide an overview of the history of the State of Oklahoma presented in graphic and three-dimensional forms through the use of artifacts with which the history was made, to tell the story in chronological order, pointing out the highlights of history. The gallery has a feature of the month program to place focus on prominent Oklahoma artists whose works deal with historical interests. Average Annual Attendance: 50,000. Mem: 2000; dues $5; annual meeting Apr
Income: $1.2 million (financed by state appropriations and membership; society depends on donations for additions to its collections)
Collections: Anthropology; archaeology; art history; costumes; ethnology; folk art; Indian art; numismatic art; specialized collections at historic sites and museums over the state
Exhibitions: Permanent chronological displays depicting pre-history, Plains Indian history, the Five Civilized Tribes' occupancy of Indian territory, the land openings of the late 19th and early 20th centuries, statehood, and progress since statehood
Publications: Mistletoe Leaves, monthly newsletter; The Chronicles of Oklahoma, scholastic quarterly; various brochures and reprints
Activities: Junior historian clubs; special presentations and study programs for children and adults; other interpretative programs; lect open to the public, approx 40 vis lectr per year; gallery talks; tours; book shop
L **Library,** Central Museum, Historical Bldg, 73105. *Dir Reference Library* John Heisch
For reference only
Library Holdings: Vols 40,000; Other—Photographs

M **OKLAHOMA MUSEUM OF ART,** 7316 Nichols Rd, 73120. Tel 405-840-2759. *Pres* John A Taylor; *Secy* Mrs James Randolph; *Dir* James K Reeve; *Bus Mgr* Michael L McGee; *Dir Education* Margaret Flansburg; *Mem Secy* Phylis Powers
Open Tues - Sat 10 AM - 5 PM, Sun 1 - 5 PM, cl Mon & major holidays. Admis adults $1, young people under 18 and members free. Estab 1960 and reorganized 1975; the Museum is committed to those ideals which hold that the great traditional values of art not only provide the soundest basis for continuing artistic expression, but offer a stability against which the merits of contemporary art can be weighed. The Museum sponsors exhibitions and offers studio and lecture art classes which familiarize the visitor and student with all art idioms. Twelve galleries are used for permanent collection and monthly changing temporary loan shows. Average Annual Attendance: 30,000. Mem: 1600; dues $15 - $1000; annual meeting Jan
Income: $200,000 (financed by membership and private contributions)
Collections: Major works include paintings by Crespi, Lawrence, Courbet, Boudin, Blakelock and Benton; 13th-20th century European and American paintings, manuscripts, graphics, decorative art; the museum is expanding collections through purchase and gifts to include works in all media
Exhibitions: Works by major historic and contemporary artists presented in one-man and group shows on monthly and six week basis; recent major shows include American Painters of the Impressionist Period, Oklahoma Sculpture Today, Masters of the Portrait and Magic Carpets; annual competitive juried shows include Statewide High School Drawing Show and Members' Juried Annual
Publications: Monthly calendar; exhibition catalogs and posters; postcards; reproductions of art work
Activities: Studio training for adults and children; fine arts and crafts fairs; lect;

docent program; volunteer program; fund-raising benefits; concerts and dramatic presentation; air and bus tours; film series; gallery talks; competitions; scholarships; museum gift shop and sales-rental gallery
L **Library,** 7316 Nichols Rd, 73120.
Library for reference only
Library Holdings: Vols 1000; AV—Slides

M **OMNIPLEX,** Kirkpatrick Center, 2100 NE 52nd, 73111. Tel 405-424-5545 (Omniplex); 427-5461 (Kirkpatrick Center). *Pres Omniplex Board of Trustees* Ray Ackerman; *Dir Omniplex* Jerry Porter; *Dir Education Omniplex* Sherman Kent; *Coordr Exhib Omniplex* Donald Binkley; *Pres Board of Governors Kirkpatrick Center* John E Kirkpatrick; *Manager Kirkpatrick Center* Dixie Clement; *Cur Kirkpatrick Center* Peggie McCracken; *Coordr Indian Gallery Kirkpatrick Center* Mary Jo Wantland; *Coordr Afro-American Gallery Kirkpatrick Center* Hannah Atkins
Open Mon - Sun 9 AM - 5 PM, including holidays. Admis Omniplex: adults $1.50, children 12 and under 75¢ Planetarium: adults $1.50, children 75¢. Estab 1958 to focus on the inter-relationships between science, arts and the humanities and to supplement educational facilities offered in the public schools in the areas of arts and sciences. The Kirkpatrick Center houses Omniplex, a hands-on science museum; Florence O Wilson Zoological Library; George Sutton Bird Paintings; Oklahoma Aviation and Space Hall of Fame and Museum; North American Indian Gallery; Afro-American Gallery; Oklahoma Zoological Society Offices; Kirkpatrick Planetarium. Average Annual Attendance: 1,000,000. Mem: 900; dues $25 and up
Income: Financed by membership, private donations, Allied Arts Foundation, admission fees, and class tuition
Collections: Kirkpatrick Ivory; George Sutton Paintings; African Artifacts and Paintings; Japanese Woodblock Prints
Exhibitions: Traveling exhibitions every six to ten weeks
Publications: Omniplex Newsletter, monthly
Activities: Classes for adults and children; docent training; lect open to public; tours; book traveling exhibitions; museum shop sells books and prints
L **Florence O Wilson Library,** Kirkpatrick Center, 73111. Tel 405-424-5561. *Librn* Nancy Kempf
Open to public for reference only

OKMULGEE

M **CREEK COUNCIL HOUSE AND MUSEUM,** Council Square, 74447. Tel 918-756-2324. *Dir* Bruce M Shackelford; *Pres* Joehugh Mansfield
Open Tues - Sat 9 AM - 5 PM. No admis fee. Estab 1867, first Council House Built, present Council House erected in 1878, to collect and preserve artifacts from the Creek History. Five rooms downstairs containing artifacts; four rooms upstairs showing art work, early time of Okmulgee; rooms of House of Warriors and House of Kings. Average Annual Attendance: 4000
Income: Financed by membership and city appropriation
Activities: Tours; sales shop selling books, magazines, reproductions
L **Creek Council House Library,** Town Square, 74447. *Cur-Dir* Bruce M Shackelford
Open Tues - Fri 9 AM - 5 PM. Estab to collect Creek and related books and documents for research and historical purposes. For reference only
Library Holdings: Vols 150; Per subs 15; AV—A-tapes, motion pictures; Other—Clipping files, exhibition catalogs, framed reproductions, prints, manuscripts, memorabilia, original art works, pamphlets, photographs, sculpture

PONCA CITY

O **PONCA CITY ART ASSOCIATION,** Box 1394, 819 East Central, 74601. Tel 405-765-9746. *Pres* Judy Tooman; *Secy* Arzella Walz
Open Wed - Sun 1 - 5 PM. No admis fee. Estab 1947 to encourage creative arts, to furnish place and sponsor art classes, art exhibits and workshops. Mem: 600; dues $5 family; annual meeting third Tues in April
Income: $10,000 (financed by membership and flea market)
Collections: Permanent fine arts collection; additions by purchases and donations
Exhibitions: Eight per year
Publications: Association Bulletin, quarterly
Activities: Education Committee has spring and fall classes; lectures; workshops in all media; competitions with awards; scholarships

M **PONCA CITY CULTURAL CENTER MUSEUM,** 1000 E Grand Ave, 74601. Tel 405-762-6123. *Cur* Diane Dembicki
Open Mon, Wed - Sat 10 AM - 5 PM, Sun and holidays 1 - 5 PM; cl Tues, Thanksgiving, Christmas Eve and Christmas Day, New Year's Eve and New Year's Day. No admis fee. The Cultural Center Museum, a National Historic House since 1976, houses the Indian Museum, the Bryant Baker Studio, the 101 Ranch Room, and the DAR Memorial museum. The Indian Museum, established in 1936, places an emphasis on materials from the five neighboring tribes (Ponca, Kaw, Otoe, Osage, and Tonkawa) whose artistic use of beading, fingerweaving and ribbon-work are displayed throughout the Museum. The Bryant Baker Studio is a replica of the New York Studio of Bryant Baker, sculptor of the Pioneer Woman Statue, a local landmark, and the studio contains original bronze and plaster sculpture. The 101 Ranch Room exhibits memorabilia from the world renowned Miller Brothers' 101 Ranch, located south of Ponca City in the early 1900s. The Museum is the former home of Ernest Whitworth Marland, oilman and philanthropist, and the tenth governor of Oklahoma. Average Annual Attendance: 25,000
Income: Financed by the City of Ponca City and donations
Collections: Bryant Baker original sculpture; 101 Ranch memorabilia; Indian ethnography and archeology of Indian tribes throughout the United States
Exhibitions: Smithsonian Indian Images; Indian costumes, jewelry, pottery, baskets, musical instruments and tools
Publications: Brochure
Activities: Fingerweaving lessons; tours; sales shop selling books, calendars, arrowheads, Indian arts and crafts

L **Library,** 1000 E Grand Ave, 74601.
Primarily research library
Library Holdings: Vols 200; Per subs 15
Special Subjects: Anthropology, Archaeology, Indian art

L **PONCA CITY LIBRARY,** 515 E Grand, 74601. Tel 405-762-6311. *Dir* Jane
Northcutt; *Head-Circulation* Marlene Stewart; *Technical Processes* Jean Gilbert
Open Mon - Thurs 9 AM - 9 PM, Fri & Sat 9 AM - 5 PM, cl Sun. Estab 1904 to
serve the citizens of Ponca City. Circ 150,000. Gallery maintained
Income: $146,000 (financed by city appropriation)
Library Holdings: Vols 55,000; Per subs 150; Micro—Reels; AV—Cassettes, fs, rec,
slides; Other—Clipping files, framed reproductions, original art works, pamphlets,
photographs, sculpture
Collections: Oriental Art Collection; Sandzen Collection; paintings

SHAWNEE

M **SAINT GREGORY'S ABBEY AND COLLEGE,** Mabee-Gerrer Museum, 1900
W MacArthur Dr, 74801. Tel 405-273-9870, 273-9878. *Dir* Robert G Dodson; *Chief
Conservator* Martin Wiesendanger; *Assoc Conservators* Margaret Wiesendanger;
Assoc Conservators John Walch; *Staff Asst* Justin Jones
Open daily 1 - 4 PM, cl Mon. No admis fee. Estab 1915 to contribute to the cultural
growth and appreciation of the general public of Oklahoma as well as of the student
body of Saint Gregory's College. A new 16,000 sq foot gallery was completed in
1979. All collections are being enlarged by purchases and by gifts. Average Annual
Attendance: 50,000
Income: Financed by endowment, membership and foundation funds
Collections: †Artifacts from ancient civilizations: Egyptian, Roman, Grecian,
Babylonian, Pre-Columbian North, South and Central American Indian, and South
Pacific; †etchings, †engravings, †serigraphs and †lithographs; †oil paintings by
American and European artists
Exhibitions: Australia: Clay Exhibit; Shirley Bowers Sculpture Exhibit; Far East
Exhibit; Religious Art of Richard C Coones; Santos: New Mexico's Holy Images
in Retablos and Bultos; Shawnee Collects; The Mabee-Gerrer's Collection of
American Indian Art and Artifacts
Activities: Classes for adults and children; docent training; lect open to public;
gallery talks; tours; competitions; individual paintings and original objects of art
lent to other museums and galleries; lending collection contains nature artifacts,
original art works and prints, paintings, sculpture; sales shop selling books,
magazines, original art, reproductions, prints, replicas

L **Library,** Mabee-Gerrer Museum, 1900 W MacArthur Dr, 74801.
Reference library open to art students and researchers
Library Holdings: Vols 1000; Per subs 10

STILLWATER

M **OKLAHOMA STATE UNIVERSITY,** Gardiner Art Gallery, Dept of Art,
Gardiner Hall, Morrill & Knoblock Sts, 74074. Tel 405-624-6016. *Dir* B J Smith
Open Mon - Fri 8 AM - 5 PM, Sun 2 - 5 PM. No admis fee. Estab 1970 as a visual
and educational extension of the department's classes and as a cultural service to
the community and area. One gallery located on the ground floor in the East wing
of the building. 170 running ft of wall space, 16 ft ceiling. Average Annual
Attendance: 5000
Income: Financed by College of A & S
Collections: Fifty plus prints, mostly post World War II
Exhibitions: Exhibitions changed every 3 - 4 weeks year round; faculty, student,
invitational and traveling shows
Publications: Exhibition schedule, annually; exhibition brochures
Activities: book traveling exhibitions

TAHLEQUAH

O **CHEROKEE NATIONAL HISTORICAL SOCIETY, INC,** PO Box 515, 74464.
Tel 918-456-6007. *Pres* Ross O Swimmer; *Exec VPres* M A Hagerstrand; *Secy* James
C Leake; *Office Mgr* Earl E Squyres
Open Mon - Fri 10 AM - 5 PM. Estab 1963 to commemorate and portray the
history, traditions and lore of a great Indian tribe, and to assist in improving local
economic conditions. Maintains an art gallery, primarily Cherokee art. Average
Annual Attendance: 130,000. Mem: 1500; dues $10 and up
Income: Financed by membership, admissions and grants
Publications: The Column, quarterly
Activities: Lect open to public; competitions with cash awards; scholarships; sales
shop selling books, prints, slides

L **Cherokee National Museum Library,** PO Box 515, 74464.
Open Mon - Fri 8 AM - 5 PM. Estab 1976 to preserve remnants of Cherokee history
and to educate the general public about that cultural heritage; a repository of Indian
art and documents. Maintains an art gallery with work by artists of several different
tribes; heavy emphasis given to the Cherokee experience
Income: Financed by membership, admissions and grants
Library Holdings: Vols 2500; Per subs 10; Micro—Reels; AV—Kodachromes,
slides; Other—Clipping files, prints, manuscripts, memorabilia, original art works,
pamphlets, photographs, sculpture, manuscripts; archival materials in excess of 500
cu ft
Special Subjects: Cherokee history
Exhibitions: Annual Trail of Tears Art Show (Indian artists' interpretation of the
Trail of Tears theme); Cherokee Artists Exhibition; rotating exhibitions; special
exhibitions, periodically (primarily Indian artists)

TULSA

C **BANK OF OKLAHOMA,** Williams Plaza, 74136. Tel 918-588-6511. *Chmn
Executive Committee* Eugene Swearingen
Open 8 AM - 5 PM. No admis fee. Estab 1968 to enhance work environment.
Collection displayed on 7 floors of the Bank of Oklahoma Tower

Purchases: $15,000
Collections: Approximately 300 pieces of Modern Art
Activities: Lect; tours; scholarships offered to University of Tulsa

M **THOMAS GILCREASE INSTITUTE OF AMERICAN HISTORY AND ART,***
1400 N 25 West Ave, 74127. Tel 918-581-5311. *Dir* Fred A Myers
Open Mon - Sat 9 AM - 5 PM, Sun & holidays 1 - 5 PM, cl Christmas. No admis
fee. Estab by the late Thomas Gilcrease as a private institution; acquired by the City
of Tulsa 1954 (governed by a Board of Directors and City Park Board); building
addition completed 1963. Average Annual Attendance: 80,000. Mem: 1600; dues
$15 and up
Collections: American art from Colonial period to present, with emphasis on art
of historical significance, sculpture, painting, graphics. Much of the work shown is
of documentary nature, with considerable emphasis on the American Indian and
the opening of the West. Art collections include 4000 paintings by 400 American
artists; artifact collections include 10,000 objects from Mid-Americas, and North
America, and include both prehistoric and historic materials from most of the
Indian cultures of these areas
Exhibitions: Public school art exhibit; special exhibitions periodically; a special or
rotating exhibit during fall, winter, spring seasons
Publications: The American Scene, quarterly; The Curator, bimonthly; The
Gazette, bimonthly
Activities: Film program; lect on art and history; gallery tours; lect to school groups
outside the museum; book shop

L **Library,*** 1400 N 25 West Ave, 74127.
Open daily, cl weekends and holidays. Library open for research contains 65,000
books and documents, many rare books and manuscripts of the American discovery
period, as well as materials concerning the Five Civilized Tribes
Library Holdings: Vols 75,000

M **PHILBROOK ART CENTER,** 2727 S Rockford Rd, PO Box 52510, 74152. Tel
918-749-7941. *Dir* Jay Wright; *Asst Dir* Marcia Manhart; *Chief Cur* John Mahey;
Registrar Christine Knop; *Preparator of Exhib* Charles Taylor; *Dir of Museum
School* Judy Cunningham
Open Mon - Sat 10 AM - 5 PM, Sun 1 - 5 PM. Admis adults $1.50; adults over
65 and students with ID 75¢; children under 15 free. Estab 1939 as a reference and
resource center for exhibiting art of all historical periods including the present;
encourages regional art activity and art education. Average Annual Attendance:
100,000. Mem: Dues $18 and up; annual meeting April
Income: Financed by endowment, membership and earned income
Collections: Laura A Clubb Collection of American & European Paintings; Clark
Field Collection of American Indian Baskets and Pottery; Gillert Collection of
Southeast Asian Ceramics; Gussman Collection of African Sculpture; Samuel H
Kress Collection of Italian Renaissance Paintings and Sculpture; Roberta C Lawson
Collection of Indian Costumes and Artifacts; Tabor Collection of Oriental Art;
American Indian paintings and sculpture; European, early American and
contemporary American oils, watercolors and prints; period furniture
Exhibitions: (1978) Acropolis of Tulsa; America in Black & White: Prints from the
30's and 40's; Associated Artists; E B Delk, Architect; Sybil B Gleason Paintings
& Drawings; Painterly Realism; Wolfgang Pogzeba Sculpture: Figure Fragment
Selections; Sculpture: Modern Works; 33rd Annual American Indian Artists
Exhibition; Trader's Cargo from the China Sea: The Gillert Collection of Southeast
Asian Ceramics; Twelve Photographers: A Contemporary Mid-America
Document; Deja Vu; Glenda Youritzin Paintings (1979) Brooke Alexander: A
Decade of Print Publishing; Americans in Glass; Classic Chairs as Art; Michael
Dwyer Drawings; Five Oklahoma Designer Craftsmen: Clay, Fiber, Wood, Metal,
Glass; Gloria dell'Arte: A Renaissance Perspective; History of the Color Print;
International Chair Design Competition; Robert Rauschenberg: Stoned Moon
Series; 6th Annual Midwestern Printmaking & Drawing Competition & Exhibition;
Taos to Tulsa: 50 Years Later; 34th Annual American Indian Artists Exhibition
Activities: Classes for adults and children; docent training; gallery talks and films;
tours; museum shop

L **Library,** 2727 S Rockford Rd, O Box 52510, 74152. Tel 918-749-7941. *Librn*
Thomas E Young
Open Tues - Fri 10 AM - 1 PM or by appointment. Reference-resource center for
the curatorial staff, teaching faculty, volunteer element and their education, as well
as the membership
Income: $17,5000
Library Holdings: Vols 4500; Per subs 45; AV—Slides; Other—Clipping files,
exhibition catalogs
Collections: Roberta Campbell Lawson Library of source materials on Indians

M **SCHELLSTEDE GALLERY OF FINE ARTS,** (Formerly Green Country Art
Center) 1825 E 15th St, 74104. Tel 918-932-4259. *Pres* Eloise J Schellstede; *VPres
& Dir* Richard L Schellstede
Open 11 AM - 5:30 PM. No admis fee. Estab 1970 to promote the fine arts and the
artists. There is a gallery for continuing exhibit of fine art, and for special exhibitions
Income: Financed by endowment
Collections: Acrylics, graphics, oil paintings, outstanding works, sculptures and
watercolors
Exhibitions: International Works of Art and Artifacts; Western, area group
showings
Publications: Newsletter, 4 - 6 times per year
Activities: Classes for adults; lect open to public; gallery talks; sales shop sells
original art, prints, reproductions

M **WORLD MUSEUM & ART CENTRE,** Osborn Foundation, 1400 E Skelly Dr,
Box 7572, 74105. *Founder* T L Osborn; *Founder* Daisy Osborn; *Mgr* James R Bolley
Open daily 10 AM - 6 PM. Admis adults $2.50, students $1.75, children (6-12) $1,
under 6 free. Estab 1972 to house the ever-increasing art collection of the Osborn
Foundation. It is devoted to preserving, for future generations, great works of art
from many Ages of Man. Over 60,000 sq ft of corridors and galleries. Mem: 70,000
Collections: Bronze, marble and porcelain works by noted sculptors of the last two
centuries; Chinese and Oriental expositions; clocks of distinction; collection of
musical instruments; engravings; etchings; European and American furniture; large
collection of crafts: Stone Age weapons, tools, drums, masks, aboriginal statuary;
oil paintings; primitive bark paintings; primitive sculptures; prints; totem poles

WOODWARD

M PLAINS INDIANS & PIONEER HISTORICAL FOUNDATION, Pioneer Museum & Art Center, 2009 Williams Ave, Box 1167, 73801. Tel 405-256-6136. *Cur* Marcella Plank; *Asst Cur* Maedine Jones; *Art Dir* Mrs C E Williams
Open Mon - Sat Noon - 5 PM; Sun 2 - 5 PM. No admis fee. Estab 1957 to preserve local history and for the purpose of supporting the art movement. Average Annual Attendance: 15,000. Mem: 450; dues $5; annual meeting Nov
Income: Financed by membership and trust fund
Collections: Early day artifacts as well as Indian material
Exhibitions: Bank from Fargo; Early Day Madam Room of Dolly Kezer; Murals on Wall in Rotunda by Paul Laune & Pat Patterson; Supply Post Office; Temple Houston Room; fort supply fire house and room of artifacts pertaining to the old fort
Publications: Woodward County Pioneer Families, before 1915; brochures

OREGON

ASHLAND

SOUTHERN OREGON COLLEGE
M Stevenson Union Art Gallery, 97520. *Dir* Katharine Danner; *Asst Dir* Jerry Findley
Open Mon 8 AM - 8 PM, Tues - Fri 8 AM - 5 PM. No admis fee. Estab 1966 to provide members of the Southern Oregon College community and the greater Ashland area an opportunity to experience a well rounded selection of art and crafts. Average Annual Attendance: 4000
Income: Financed by student fees
Collections: †Small permanent collection of prints, paintings by local artists and a sculpture by Bruce West
Exhibitions: Ceramics, graphic design, paintings, photography, sculpture, weaving, works of professional artists
Activities: Short programs for educ television; exhibiting artists lect to art classes when possible; workshops; special lect; lect open to public, 3 visiting lectr per year; eight gallery talks yearly
M Central Art Gallery, 97520. *Department of Art Chmn* Robert Alston
Open Mon - Fri 8:30 AM - 12 PM, other hours by appointment
Income: Financed by Department of Art
Exhibitions: Primarily students works, also professional and local artists

ASTORIA

M COLUMBIA RIVER MARITIME MUSEUM, 16th & Exchange Sts, 97103. Tel 503-325-2323. *Dir* Rolf Klep; *Cur* Michael Naab
Open May - Sept daily 10:30 AM - 5 PM; Oct - Apr Tues - Sun 10:30 AM - 5 PM. Admis adults $1, children 50¢. Estab 1962 as a maritime museum
Collections: Maritime Paintings, Prints and Photography; Ship Models and Sailing Memorabilia
L Library, 16th & Exchange Sts, 97103.
Library for use on the premises
Library Holdings: Vols 1000

COOS BAY

M COOS ART MUSEUM, 515 Market Ave, 97420. Tel 503-267-3901. *Dir* Maggie Karl; *Pres* Joann Coughlin; *VPres* Saskia Dyer; *Second VPres* Maxeen Wegner; *Treas* Nina Grunwaldt; *Secy* Jean Day
Open Tues - Sun 1 - 4 PM. No admis fee. Estab 1966 to bring contemporary art to southwestern Oregon, and to have classes in related art subjects. There are two large spacious galleries with a wide entrance hall. Average Annual Attendance: 10,000. Mem: 800; dues family $15, single $10; annual meeting first Sat of the year
Income: $5315 (financed by membership)
Collections: †Contemporary American Printmakers; †paintings, †photographs, †sculpture
Exhibitions: Crafts, functional; Sculpture, Painting and Nonfunctional Pottery, Weaving; monthly exhibits; three juried shows a year; one photography show
Publications: Bulletins, monthly
Activities: Classes for adults and children; dramatic programs; film festivals; lect open to the public, 2 - 3 vis lectr per year; concerts; tours; competitions;; individual paintings and original objects of art lent to members; museum and sales shops selling books, original art, prints, photographs, pottery, stained glass, blown glass

COQUILLE

O COQUILLE VALLEY ART ASSOCIATION,* Fairview Route, Box 625, 97423. Tel 503-396-3294. *Pres* Wilma Ryan; *VPres* Darlene Castleman; *Secy* Marilyn Dahlen; *Treas* Evelyn Hunnicutt
Open Tues - Sun 1 - 4 PM, cl Mon. Estab 1950 to teach art and art appreciation. Gallery maintained on main floor of Art Association owned old refurbished schoolhouse
Income: Financed by membership
Exhibitions: Exhibits by local members, as well as by others throughout the state
Activities: Classes for adults and children; lect open to the public, 2-3 visiting lectr per year; traveling exhibitions organized and circulated
L Library,* Fairview Route, Box 625, 97423. *Librn* Sharon Orchard

CORVALLIS

OREGON STATE UNIVERSITY
M Horner Museum, Gill Coliseum, 26th near Western, 97331. Tel 503-754-2951. *Dir* Lucy Skjelstad

Open Tues - Fri 10 AM to 5 PM; Sat 10 AM - 2 PM; Sun 2 - 5 PM; summers, Mon - Fri 10 AM - 5 PM; Sun 2 - 5 PM. No admis fee. Estab 1877 to collect, preserve and exhibit the history and natural history of Oregon. Average Annual Attendance: 12,000. Mem: 100; dues individual $10
Income: Financed by state appropriations and donations
Collections: Ethnographic, Worldwide; Geological and Biological Specimens; Historic Objects, Pioneer Period to Present; Oral History
Publications: Horner Museum Tour Guide Series, a set of thematic history guidebooks; exhibition catalogs
Activities: Workshops; lect, 4-5 visiting lectr per year; tours
M Fairbanks Gallery, Gill Coliseum, 26th near Western, 97331. Tel 503-754-4745. *Dir* Dr Phyllis A Yes; *Asst Dir* John Rock
Open 8 AM - 5:30 PM. No admis fee. Estab 1933 to display work of contemporary American artists. One gallery space 20 x 50 ft
Income: Financed by state appropriation and grants
Exhibitions: Annual Faculty and Student Exhibition; Lee Chesney; Paul Clinton; Lukman Glasgow; Herb Lubalin; Bill Rades; Miriam Schapiro
Publications: Posters and flyers announcing shows
Activities: Lect; 5 vis lectr per year; gallery talks; exten dept serving Oregon; traveling exhibitions organized and circulated
M Memorial Union Art Gallery, Gill Coliseum, 26th near Western, 97331. Tel 503-754-2416. *Secy & Dir* George F Stevens
Open daily 8 AM - 10 PM. Estab 1928. Average Annual Attendance: 50,000. Mem: 15,000; annual meeting May
Income: $70,000
Collections: William Henry Price Memorial Collection of Oil Paintings
Publications: Calendar and exhibition pamphlets
Activities: Educ program; lect; exten dept serving the State; individual paintings lent to schools; material available to responsible galleries for fees; traveling exhibitions organized and circulated
L Library, Gill Coliseum, 26th near Western, 97331.
Collections: Color Reproductions

EUGENE

M MAUDE I KERNS ART CENTER, Henry Korn Gallery, 1910 E 15th Ave, 97403. Tel 503-345-1571. *Dir* Anne Jensch; *Pres* Nancy Hayward; *Secy* Pat Tucker
Open daily 11 AM - 5 PM. No admis fee. Estab 1955, the Center is a nonprofit educational organization dedicated to promoting quality in the Arts and Crafts through classes, exhibitions, workshops, community projects, and special events. The Center houses the Henry Korn Gallery, the Main Gallery featuring monthly shows of contemporary artists; the Mezzanine Gallery, suited to photographs, prints, drawings and smaller works of art. Average Annual Attendance: 9000. Mem: 500; dues sponsor $25 or more, family $20, couple $15, individual $10, teen-child $5; annual meeting second Mon in April
Income: $100,000 (financed by endowment, membership)
Collections: Sculpture and painting of Oregon artists
Exhibitions: (1979) Annual Christmas Sale; Buckendorf (painting); Faye Nakamura and Vicki Halper (ceramics); Feathers: The Art of Personal Style; Tom Hardy (sculpture); Local Artists Auction; Susan Lomerford (painting); Pretti (sculpture); Valley Calligraphy Guild; Brett Weston (photography)
Publications: Membership newsletter, monthly
Activities: Classes for adults and children; dramatic programs; docent training; lect open to the public and for members only on request; concerts; gallery talks; tours; competitions; the Rental-Sales Gallery, featuring an artist of the month, as well as a stock of a variety of art works

UNIVERSITY OF OREGON
M Musuem of Art, 97403. Tel 203-686-3027. *Dir* Richard C Paulin; *Designer-Preparator* Tommy L Griffin; *Supv, Visual Art Resources* Michael Whitenack; *Admin Asst* Norine M Arens; *Registrar* Barbara Zentner
Open Tues - Sun Noon - 5 PM, cl Mon and university holidays. No admis fee. Estab 1930 to promote among university students and faculty and the general public an active and continuing interest in the visual arts of both Western and Oriental cultures. Average Annual Attendance: 90,000. Mem: 425; dues $15-$250; annual meeting Apr
Income: $201,000 (financed by state appropriation and private donations)
Collections: African; Contemporary Northwest Collection; Greater Pacific Basin Collection; Oriental Art representing the cultures of China, Japan, Cambodia, Korea, Mongolia, Tibet, Russia, and American and British works executed in the traditional Oriental manner
Exhibitions: Australian Graphics; Gund Collection of Western Art; Norwegian Pathfind in Glass-Benny Motzfeldt; Oregon Folk Art
Activities: Docent training; exten dept serving Oregon and Washington; museum shop selling books, magazines, original art, reproductions, prints, slides and gift items; rental-sales gallery
M Erb Memorial Union Art Gallery, 13th & University Sts, 97403. Tel 503-686-4373. *Dir* Adell McMillan; *Prog Consultant* Frank Geltner; *Craft Center Coordr* Thomas Urban
Open Mon - Sat 7:30 AM - 11:30 PM; Sun Noon - 11:30 PM. No admis fee. Estab 1950 to provide art in various forms and programs for enrichment of university community
Income: Financed by student fees
Purchases: $100-$2000
Collections: †Pacific Northwest Art
Exhibitions: Periodic art exhibitions on portable display boards in various rooms; display in the art gallery of selections from the permanent collection
Activities: Classes for adults; craft workshops
L School of Architecture and Allied Arts Library, Lawrence Hall, 97403. Tel 503-686-3637. *Librn* Reyburn R McCready; *Librn* Alan C Miller; *Slide Cur* Carmi Weingrod
Open Mon - Thurs 8 AM - 10 PM; Fri 8 AM - 5 PM; Sat 1 - 5 PM; Sun 2 - 10 PM. Estab 1919 to provide resources for the courses, degree programs, and research of the departments in the School of Architecture and Allied Arts and related Institute for Community Art Studies and Center for Environmental Research. Circ 58,882

Income: Financed by city appropriation
Library Holdings: Vols 23,000; Per subs 250; AV—Slides 140,000; Other—Exhibition catalogs, pamphlets, photographs 45,000

JACKSONVILLE

M **SOUTHERN OREGON HISTORICAL SOCIETY,** Jacksonville Museum, 206 N Fifth St, PO Box 480, 97530. Tel 503-899-1847. *Dir* C William Burk; *Cur Coll* Donald Draisner; *Exhib Cur* Renee Bush; *Programs Dir* Ethel Ann Ackerman; *Historian-Newsletter Editor* Marjorie Edens; *Photographer* Margaret Davis; *Restoration Coordr* Ruth Preston
Open Tues - Sat 9 AM - 5 PM; Sun Noon - 5 PM; summers, Mon 9 AM - 5 PM. No admis fee. Estab 1950 to collect and exhibit materials showing the history of Southern Oregon. Included are the Peter Britt Gallery (Jackson County history and Indian artifacts); the Costume Gallery; Old Jail Museum; a touching museum for children; Pinto's Theater. The historic houses include the Cornelius C Beekman House (1876); Catholic Rectory (circa 1861); Cool-Beeckman-Armstrong House (1858). Average Annual Attendance: 90,000. Mem: 800; dues $5 and up; annual meeting June
Income: Financed by membership and county tax
Exhibitions: Annual Children's Festival; Annual Handweaving; Annual Quilts; (1978) Feminine Lingerie, 1865-1940
Publications: Newsletter, 6 times year
Activities: Handcraft workshops for children; docent training; film program; lect open to the public; sales shop selling books
L **Library,** 206 N Fifth St, PO Box 480, 97530. *Librn* Richard H Engeman
Open to public for reference only
Library Holdings: Vols 2700; Per subs 75; Other—Manuscripts, photographs, Ephemera, art on paper
Special Subjects: Historic preservation, museum techniques

KLAMATH FALLS

M **FAVELL MUSEUM OF WESTERN ART & INDIAN ARTIFACTS,** 125 W Main, PO Box 165, 97601. Tel 503-882-9996. *Pres* Gene H Favell; *VPres & Treas* Winifred L Favell; *Admin* Walter Havens; *Asst Admin* Mrs John Vest
Open Mon - Sat 9:30 AM - 5:30 PM; Sun 1 - 5:30 PM. Admis adults $2, youth 6 - 16 years $1. Estab 1972 to preserve Western heritage as represented by Indian artifacts and contemporary Western art. Gallery features contemporary western artists combined with art and artifacts displays. Average Annual Attendance: 15,000 - 20,000. Mem: Annual meeting May
Income: $200,000 - 250,000 (financed by owners)
Collections: †Contemporary Western Art; †Western Indian Artifacts: pottery, stonework, baskets, bead and quillwork, miniature firearms
Activities: Museum shop selling books, original art, reproductions, prints, slides, jewelry, artifacts

M **KLAMATH COUNTY MUSEUM,** 1451 Main St, 97601. Tel 503-882-2501, Ext 208. *Dir* Harry V Drew; *Archivist* Charles Wells
Open Tues - Sat 9 AM - 5 PM; cl Sun and Mon. No admis fee. Estab 1953 to tell the story of the Klamath Country and to preserve and exhibit related material. Average Annual Attendance: 18,000. Mem: Dues $5; monthly meetings
Income: Financed by county appropriation
Collections: Four Original Rembrandt Etchings; Indian Artifacts; Pioneer Artifacts
Publications: Museum Research Papers, every 2 years
Activities: Lect open to public; traveling exhibitions orgainzed and circulated; museum shop selling books
L **Research Library,** 1451 Main St, 97601.
Open to the public for reference by appointment
Library Holdings: Vols 12,000
Collections: Modoc Indian War Books, Documents and Manuscripts
M **Baldwin Hotel Museum Annex,** 31 Main St, 97601. Tel 503-882-2501, Ext 207.
Open Tues - Sat 10 AM - 4 PM. Small admis charge. A state and national historic landmark purchased by Klamath County in January 1978. Restoration of building began in February 1978 and it was dedicated as a museum by Oregon's Governor Robert Straub June 3, 1978. Opened to the public August 19, 1978. May be viewed by tour only

O **KLAMATH FALLS ART ASSOCIATION,** Klamath Art Gallery,* 120 Riverside Dr, PO Box 955, 97601. *Pres* Warren Kerr; *Chmn Exhib* Nina Pence
Open Mon - Sat 1 - 4 PM, Sun 2 - 5 PM, and special occasions. No admis fee. Estab 1948 to provide art training for local residents. Gallery estab 1960 to provide display and teaching space for the Association's activities. Average Annual Attendance: 5000. Mem: 200; dues $7 and higher; annual meeting Sept
Income: $7000 (financed by membership, gallery sales, tuition)
Collections: Ceramics; paintings; weaving (owned by members)
Exhibitions: Twelve annually; one membership show, one juried show, and the remainder varies
Activities: Classes in painting, drawing, ceramics, weaving; children's summer art classes; workshops; lect, visiting lectrs; annual arts festival, mid-Sept

MEDFORD

O **ROGUE VALLEY ART ASSOCIATION,** 40 S Bartlett, PO Box 763, 97501. Tel 502-772-8118. *Pres* Judy Morris; *Gallery Dir* Lucy Brown Warnick
Open Mon - Sat 10 AM - 5 PM (winter), 9 AM - 4 PM (summer); cl Sun & national holidays. No admis fee. Estab 1960 to provide the surrounding area with changing exhibits in what is going on in the world of art; Auxiliary Board initiated in 1971. Maintains the Rogue Gallery. Average Annual Attendance: 8000. Mem: 800; dues $10 - $25; annual meeting Apr
Exhibitions: New exhibit each month
Publications: Newsletter, approx 4 annually
Activities: Art education for children; adult education classes throughout year have included calligraphy, drawing and workshops in stained glass and printmaking; tours and artist lect; scholarships

MONMOUTH

M **OREGON COLLEGE OF EDUCATION GALLERIES,** 97361. Tel 503-838-1220. *Gallery Chmn* Eileen Senner; *Coordr of Art* James T Mattingly
Open Mon - Fri 8 AM - 5 PM during scheduled exhibits. No admis fee. Estab to bring contemporary art work to the community and the college for study and visual understanding. Library maintained. Average Annual Attendance: 3000-4000
Income: $1000 (financed by state appropriation)
Collections: Contemporary Northwest Visual Art Work
Activities: Lect open to the public, 3 - 5 vis lectr per year; gallery talks; tours; lending collection contains 500 lantern slides, 8000 slides
M **Fine Arts Auditorium Exhibit Area,** 97361.
Exhibitions: Exhibits generated by the Creative Arts Department Performance & Exhibitions Committee
M **Presidents Gallery,** 97361.
Exhibitions: Original Art; generated by the Visual Art Gallery Chairman; varies per academic year
M **Gallery 107,** 97361.
Exhibitions: Original Art; generated by the Creative Arts Department Performance & Exhibitions Committee

PORTLAND

M **BASSIST INSTITUTE MUSEUM,** 923 SW Taylor St, 97205. Tel 503-228-6528. *Pres* Donald H Bassist; *Secy* Ernest Buhlinger
Open 9 AM - 5 PM. No admis fee. Estab 1964 to provide practical instruction in retail merchandising, interior design, display, fashion design, advertising and promotion, fashion history and textiles. Average Annual Attendance: 200
Collections: Collection of Fashion and Costume History Books; Collection in Furniture and Interior Decoration Fields
Activities: Lect open to the public; scholarships; lending collection of 150 motion pictures; book shop

M **CONTEMPORARY CRAFTS ASSOCIATION AND GALLERY,*** 3934 SW Corbett Ave, 97201. Tel 503-223-2654. *Dir* Marlene Gabel
Open Mon - Sat 11 AM - 5 PM, Sun 1 - 4 PM. No admis fee. Estab 1938 to promote, exhibit and sell contemporary crafts. Gallery is maintained also as a consignment outlet, and holds exhibits monthly. Average Annual Attendance: 30,000. Mem: 1400; dues $5 - $100 depending on classification
Income: $114,000 (financed by membership)
Collections: †Craft objects including ceramics, glass, textiles, wood collected over a 40-year period
Exhibitions: (1978) Keith Jones (constructions); Alan Kluber (ceramics); Jane Marquis (stained glass)
Publications: Contemporary Crafts News, quarterly
Activities: Craftsmen-in-the-Schools program; lect open to the public, 5 visiting lectrs per year; gallery talks; tours; lending collection contains books, cassettes, slides; sales shop selling books, magazines, original art
L **Library,*** 3934 SW Corbett Ave, 97201. *Librn* Bea Parisi
Open to members
Library Holdings: Vols 430; Per subs 260

O **METROPOLITAN ARTS COMMISSION,*** 430 SW Morrison, 97204. Tel 503-248-4569. *Chmn* Henry Stanley; *Dir* Emily Carpenter
Open 8 AM - 5 PM. Estab 1973, to promote and encourage programs to further the development and public awareness of and interest in the visual and performing arts
Income: Financed by city and county appropriation
Publications: Newsletter, quarterly

L **MULTNOMAH COUNTY LIBRARY,** Henry Failing Art and Music Department, 801 SW Tenth Ave, 97205. Tel 503-223-7201. *Librn* James H Burghardt; *Head Art & Music Dept* Barbara J Kern
Open Mon - Thurs 9 AM - 9 PM; Fri & Sat 9 AM - 5:30 PM. Estab 1864 as a public library service to Multnomah County
Library Holdings: Vols 23,000; AV—Rec, slides; Other—Clipping files, framed reproductions

O **OREGON HISTORICAL SOCIETY,** 1230 SW Park Ave, 97205. Tel 503-222-1741. *Dir* Thomas Vaughan; *Assoc Dir* Millard McClung; *Museum Adminr* Robert Stark
Open Mon - Sat 10 AM - 4:45 PM. No admis fee. Estab 1873, incorporated 1898, to collect, preserve, exhibit and publish materials pertaining to the Oregon country. Approx 20,000 sq ft of exhibit space; Society maintains historic 1856 Bybee Howell House, Sauvie Island. Average Annual Attendance: 125,000. Mem: 7000; dues $10; annual meeting Nov
Income: Financed by endowment, membership, state appropriation
Collections: Approx 60,000 museum objects
Exhibitions: James Madison Alden, Yankee Artist of the Pacific Coast, 1854-1860; The Genius of Ivan Collins: Wagons in Miniature; Indians of the Oregon Country; Darius Kinsey, Photographer, document Northwest Logging Industry; Last View of The First North Americans: Edward Curtis photographs of North American Indians; A Sense of Proportion: Oregon architects
Publications: Oregon Historical Quarterly; books; maps; pamphlets; newsletter
Activities: Educational program for all ages; lect; field trips; films; exhibits
L **Library,*** 1230 SW Park Ave, 97205. *Chief Librn* Louis Flannery; *Managing Editor* Priscilla Knuth
Open Mon - Sat 10 AM - 5 PM
Library Holdings: Vols 60,500; Micro—Fiche, reels; AV—Cassettes, fs, lantern Slides, motion pictures, rec, slides, v-tapes; Other—Clipping files, exhibition catalogs, framed reproductions, prints, manuscripts, memorabilia, original art works, pamphlets, photographs, reproductions, sculpture, original documents
Collections: 3000 separate manuscript collections containing 15,000,000 pieces; 1,000,000 historic photographs; 10,000 maps

M **OREGON SCHOOL OF ARTS AND CRAFTS,** Hoffman Gallery, 8245 SW Barnes Rd, 97225. Tel 503-297-5544. *Executive Dir* Bridget Beattie McCarthy; *Curriculum Dir* Sharon Marcus; *Public Relations* Rojean Evans
Open Mon - Thurs 9 AM - 9 PM, Sat & Sun 9 AM - 4 PM, cl Fri. No admis fee, except for special events and classes. Estab 1906 to teach standards of quality in crafts. Average Annual Attendance: 3000. Mem: 2900; dues $10 - $1000
Income: Financed by endowment, membership, state appropriation and National Endowments of the Arts, Washington, DC
Exhibitions: Circa Northwest 1980 in each of the crafts fields; invited and juried exhibits monthly; exhibit of winners of Northwest crafts juried show
Publications: Course catalogues, quarterly; Gallery announcements, 12 per year; newsletter to members, 6 per year
Activities: Classes for adults and children; docent training; lect open to public, 10 visiting lectr per year; gallery talks; tours; competitions; book traveling exhibitions 2 per year; sales shop sells books, magazines, original art and prints

L **Library,** 8245 SW Barnes Rd, 97225. Tel 503-297-5544. *Librn* Beverly B Stafford
Open Mon - Thurs 9:30 AM - 7 PM, Fri 9:30 AM - 4 PM, Sat 11 AM - 4 PM, cl Sun. Estab 1979 to serve as a craft reference library for students and faculty and others interested in crafts
Library Holdings: Vols 800; Per subs 65; AV—Slides; Other—Pamphlets
Special Subjects: Calligraphy, Ceramics, Drawings, Metalwork, Photography, Printmaking, Stained Glass, Textiles
Activities: Interlibrary loan services available

O **PORTLAND ART ASSOCIATION,** 1219 SW Park Ave, 97225. Tel 503-226-2811. *Dir* Donald Jenkins; *Deputy Dir* Barbara Gibbs; *Art School Acting Dean* Harry Widman; *Dir Film Study Center* Robert Sitton; *Cur* William Chiego; *Assoc Cur* Rachel Rosenfield; *Cur of Prints & Drawings* Gordon Gilkey; *Cur of Ed* Pauline Eyerly; *Editor* Robert Peirce; *Development Officer* Eve Bachman; *Business Mgr* E Scott Clodfelter; *Chief of Operations* Evelyn Lamon; *Registrar* Kathryn Gates

M **Museum,** 1219 SW Park Ave, 97225.
Open Tues, Thurs, Sat & Sun 12 - 5 PM, Wed & Fri 12 - 10 PM, cl Mon. Admis adults $1, students 50¢, children under 12, senior citizens and members free. Estab 1892 to make a collection of works of art and to erect and maintain a suitable building in which the same may be studies and exhibited, and to develop and encourage the study of art. Average Annual Attendance: 180,000. Mem: 6000; dues $20 and up; annual meeting Sept
Collections: Contemporary ceramics; contemporary paintings; Gebauer Collection of Cameroon art; Gordon and Vivian Gilkey Print and Drawing Collection; Hirsch Collection of Oriental rugs; Samuel H Kress Collection of Renaissance painting and sculptures; Mary Andrews Ladd Collection of Japanese prints; William S Ladd Collection of Pre-Columblan art; Lawther Collection of Ethiopian crosses; Lewis Collection of Classical Antiquities (ancient Chinese sculptures, bronzes and ceramics); Alice B Nunn Collection of English Silver; Oriental painted screens and lacquers; Persian and Hindu Miniatures; Rasmussen Collection of Northwest Coast Indian and Eskimo arts; Roberts Collection of 19th & 20th Century Sculpture
Exhibitions: (1978) Herbert Bayer: Photographic Works; Calders Universe; Gitter Collection: Zenga and Nanga; Illuminated Manuscripts from Portland Area Collections; Jade and Other Hardstone Carvings; Frederick Littman: Themes and Variations; Ralph Eugene Meatyard; Museum Art School Thesis Projects; New Testament Narratives in Master Drawings; Paintings by Wayne Thiebaud; Sculpture by Pol Bury; Selections from the Gilkey Collection; Seventy Years of Costume; Utamaro and Hiroshige: A Survey of Japanese Prints from the James A Michener Collection; (1979) Art About Art; Artists' Postcards; Bonnie Bronson: Recent Works; Louis Bunce Retrospective; Gebauer Photographs of the Cameroon; Graphic Arts of Goya; Image of Urban Optimism; Islamic Rugs; Jasper Johns Screenprints; Max Klinger Graphics; Clarence John Laughlin; Jack Levine Retrospective; Vienna Moderne; Al Monner: Photographs of Gypsies; Museum Art School Thesis Exhibition; Turkish Treasures from the Collection of Edwin Binney, 3rd; 20th Century and Contemporary Works from the Collection
Publications: Annual report; Art Of Cameroon; Calendar, monthly; exhibition catalogs
Activities: Classes in studio art and art history; docent training; gallery talks; lect; tours; concerts; film and video programs; rental-sales gallery; museum shop

L **Museum Library,** 1219 SW Park Ave, 97225. Tel 503-226-2811, Ext 36. *Librn* Emily Evans; *Slide Librn* James H Hicks
Open Tues - Fri 9 AM - 1:30 PM & 3 - 5 PM, cl Mon; special schedules for holidays. Estab 1892 to provide a reference collection for MAS as supportive materials for the museum collection. Museum Art School, see entry under Art Schools
Income: $19,000 (financed by endowment and grants)
Purchases: $19,000
Library Holdings: Vols 11,000; Per subs 77; AV—Motion pictures, slides; Other—Exhibition catalogs, photographs

O **Northwest Film Study Center,** 1219 SW Park Ave, 97225. Tel 503-221-1156. *Dir* Robert Sitton
Estab 1972. Maintains film archives and circ film library
Exhibitions: Annual Northwest Film and Video Festival; Young Peoples Film Festival
Activities: Film screening program; courses in film and video; Filmmaker-in-the-Schools program

M **PORTLAND CENTER FOR THE VISUAL ARTS,** 117 NW Fifth Ave, 97209. Tel 503-222-7107. *VPres* Mel Katz; *Executive Dir* Mary L Beebe; *Asst Dir* Donna Milrany; *Business Mgr* Melissa Thompson; *Slide Bank Dir & Special Studies Program Dir* Jane Craford; *Co-Chairman* Robert Stoll; *Co-Chairman* Orleonok Pitkin; *Secy - Treas* Charles Banta
Open Tues - Sun 12 - 5 PM. No admis fee. Estab 1972 to bring a wide cross-section of nationally recognized contemporary art to Oregon. The gallery covers 6200 sq ft in one large space and has adjustable partitions. Average Annual Attendance: 13,200. Mem: 701; dues $6 - $240; annual meeting in fall
Income: Financed by membership, city and state appropriation, and NEA grants
Exhibitions: (1978) Laurie Anderson; Alice Aycock; John Baldessari; Louis Bunce; Norma Jean Deak; Bob Gardiner; John Gibson; Lynn Hershman; Ingram Marshall; Thara Memory; Brenda Miller; Meridith Monk; Charlemagne Palestine; Morton Subotnick; Jo Harvey Allen; Newton & Helen Harrison; Nancy Holt; Robert Irwin; Bessie Jones & Guy Carrawan; Deborah Jowitt; Meredith Monk; Sandra Nelson; Phill Niblock; Gladys Nilsson; Pat Oleszko; Michele Russo; Robert Rauschenberg; Salvatore Scarpitta; Michael Singer; Michelle Stuart; Morton Subotnick; Sam Tchakalian
Activities: Lect open to public, 24 vis lectr per yr; concerts; gallery talks; traveling exhibitions organized and circulated

L **Library,** 117 NW Fifth Ave, Portland, OR 97209. *Librn* Mary Beebe
Open to the public for reference only
Library Holdings: Vols 7; Per subs 6; Other—Exhibition catalogs

M **PORTLAND CHILDREN'S MUSEUM,** 3037 SW Second Ave, 97201. Tel 503-227-1505. *Dir* Robert G Bridgeford
Open Mon - Fri 9 AM - 5 PM; Sat 9 AM - 4 PM. Estab 1949; sponsored by Portland Bureau of Parks and Recreation. Average Annual Attendance: 65,000
Collections: Children's art; natural history, toys, dollhouses, miniatures
Activities: Classes in painting, photography, filmmaking, jewelry, graphics, pottery, calligraphy, weaving for children 4-18; lect; tours

M **PORTLAND STATE UNIVERSITY,** White Gallery,* PO Box 751, 97207. Tel 503-229-3000. *Dir* Kim Bradley
Open Mon - Fri 8 AM - 10 PM, Sat 9 AM - 7 PM. No admis fee. Estab 1970 as a student operated gallery exhibiting works by professional artists representing a wide range of media, style and geographical distribution. Gallery is basically a wide long hall in the Student Union. Mem: 350
Income: $4200 (financed by city and state appropriations, and student incidental fees)
Collections: Permanent collection contains work by local professional artists, with a few nationally recognized artists
Activities: Lect open to the public, 12 visiting lectrs per year; gallery talks; individual paintings and original objects of art lent to other schools or museums; lending collection contains original prints, paintings and sculpture

M **REED COLLEGE ART GALLERY,*** 3202 SE Woodstock Blvd, 97202. Tel 503-771-1112. *Chmn Division of Arts* Judy Massee
Open Sat & Sun Noon - 5 PM, or by appointment. No admis fee. Estab 1962 to bring to the college and the community shows of significant contemporary art not previously available in the Northwest. Many shows relate to advanced art courses at the college and to important exhibitions at the Portland Art Museum, the PCVA or other Northwest institutions. Mem: 55 Art Associates; dues $100
Income: $15,000 (financed by endowment, membership, state appropriation, individual donations and NEA grants)
Collections: †Drawings; †paintings; †pre-20th century prints; sculpture; †20th century prints
Exhibitions: (1978-79) Francoise Grossen (fiber as sculpture); Scott Sonniksen (recent paintings and drawings); Garery Winogrand (public relations)
Publications: Poster with introductory write-up on back published for each show
Activities: Lect open to public, 4-6 visiting lectrs per year; gallery talks; individual paintings and original objects of art lent to other museums only for major exhibitions; traveling exhibitions organized and circulated

L **Eric V Hauser Memorial Library,*** 97202. Tel 503-771-1112, Ext 260. *Librn* Luella Pollock
Open Mon - Fri 8 AM - 2:30 AM, Sat 8 AM - Midnight, Sun Noon - Midnight. Estab 1912 to support class work and research of Reed faculty and students
Income: Financed by endowment, student tuition and individual donations
Purchases: $155,000
Library Holdings: Vols 267,352; Per subs 1200; Micro—Fiche, reels; AV—Lantern Slides, motion pictures, rec; Other—Exhibition catalogs, framed reproductions, prints, memorabilia, original documents

M **SCHOOL OF THE ARTS AND CRAFTS SOCIETY OF PORTLAND,** Hoffman Gallery,* 8245 SW Barnes Rd, 97225. Tel 503-228-4741. *Dir* Jack Townes
Open Mon - Thurs 8 AM - 10 PM, Fri 8 AM - 4 PM, Sat 9 AM - 4 PM, Sun 11 AM - 4 PM. Estab 1906 to promote quality handcrafts. The Julia E Hoffman Gallery is a small well-designed area occupying part of the building's first floor. It presents thoughtfully planned and well installed exhibitions of work both by contemporary artists and craftsmen and by traditional, folk and primitive cultures. It aspires to exemplify the highest standards of design and workmanship, to set goals and provide stimulation of ideas for students, to elevate the capacity for judgment and appreciation in all viewers. It adheres to no bias toward the avant garde or the traditional, but seeks instead to call attention to quality, in whatever mode it comes. Main gallery is L shaped with 500 sq ft of floor space and white walls for hanging shows. Average Annual Attendance: 4000. Mem: 1200; dues $8 - $100; annual meeting May
Income: $196,000 (financed by membership, city and state appropriations and school tuitions)
Exhibitions: Kristen Anderson (enamelings); Ray Atkeson (photography); Cynthia and Edwina Bringle (pottery and weaving); Sandra Haefker (sculpture and drawings); Handmade Stones; Julia Hoffman (photography)
Publications: Catalog, quarterly; gallery announcements, monthly; descriptive brochure; newsletter
Activities: Lect open to the public; gallery talks

L **Library,*** 8245 SW Barnes Rd, 97225. *Librn* Beverly B Stafford
Library Holdings: Vols 1500; Per subs 23

L **UNIVERSITY OF PORTLAND,** Wilson W Clark Memorial Library, 5000 N Willamette Blvd, 97203. Tel 503-283-7111. *Dir* Joseph P Browne; *Reference Librn* Jane Wahl; *Technical Services Librn* Mary K Devlin; *Special Services Librn* Bro Frank Drury
Open Sun 1 - 11 PM; Mon - Thurs 8 AM - 11 PM; Fri 8 AM - 5 PM; Sat 9 AM - 4 PM. Estab 1901 to support the University curriculum. Circ 50,000. Maintains an art gallery with a rotating exhibit
Income: Financed through the University
Library Holdings: Vols 180,000; Per subs 1300; Micro—Fiche, reels; AV—Rec
Exhibitions: Ron Craig (pen & ink drawing); Joseph Corish (oils); Paul Feldhaus (graphics); Barbara Garrison (color graphics); Patricia Lambert (photographs); Annie Lenney (oils); E I Maurics (watercolors, collage); Brother David Martin (oils); Marianne Nelson (watercolors & drawings); Leonard Scheu (watercolors); Jean Schonwalter & Carol Jacobstein; Reta Soloway (mixed media); Stewart Williams (acrylics)

O WEST HILLS UNITARIAN FELLOWSHIP, 8470 SW Oleson Rd, 97223. Tel 503-246-3351. *Pres* Eric Johnson; *VPres* Kitsy Snouffer; *Office Admin* Connie Morgan; *Secy* Gloria George; *Fine Arts Chmn* Jill Prislin
Open Mon - Fri 9 AM - Noon. No admis fee. Estab 1970 to give professional artists one or two-man shows in a lovely gallery space and to expose the congregation and public to fine visual art. The entire sanctuary wall space is like a large gallery and the building is light, airy with a woodsy backdrop. Average Annual Attendance: 10,000
Income: $30,000 (financed by membership)
Collections: Paintings, wall sculptures by local artists
Exhibitions: Rex Amos (pastel collages, drawings and embossed prints); Bonnie Butler (oils and watercolors); Ellen Debenedetti (paintings); Fred Harwin & Joel Ito (medical illustrations); Laverne Krause (watercolors and drawings); Mike Lloyd (photojournalism); Claude McGraw (paintings)
Publications: Bulletin, weekly; newsletter, monthly
Activities: Classes for adults and children; dramatic programs; lect open to the public, 8 vis lectr per yr; concerts; sales shop selling books

SALEM

M SALEM ART ASSOCIATION, Bush House, and Bush Barn Art Center,* 600 Mission St SE, 97301. Tel 503-363-4714, 581-2228. *Exec Dir* Betty Jo Simmons; *Cur* Sharon Hanford
Open Bush House, Summer Tues - Sat 12 - 5 PM, Sun 2 - 5 PM, Winter Tues - Sun 2 - 5 PM, Bush Barn Tues - Sat 9:30 AM - 5 PM, Sat - Sun 1 - 5 PM. Admis Bush House adults $1, students 50¢, children 6 - 12 25¢, free Wed, Winter. No admis fee Bush Barn. Incorporated 1938, Museum opened 1953. Bush Barn Art Center opened 1965 to preserve the best of the past and encourage the arts of the present. Average Annual Attendance: 25,000. Mem: 1000; dues $10 and higher; annual meeting in May
Exhibitions: Changed monthly

M WILLAMETTE UNIVERSITY, George Putnam University Center, 900 State St, 97301. Tel 503-370-6267. *Dir* Sally Howell
Open Mon - Sun 8 AM - 11 PM. No admis fee. Estab 1970 to enrich the atmosphere of the University Center and to acquaint students, faculty and staff with various forms of art. Two separate areas are used: one area is a paneled wall; the other area is comprised of free standing art panels with surface area of approx 54 x 54 inches. Average Annual Attendance: 45,000
Income: Financed through the University
Exhibitions: China exhibit; Robert Hess; Betty LaDuke; sculptures; several exhibits from Visual Arts Resources (University of Oregon); several local artists and photographers
Activities: Lect; gallery talks

SPRINGFIELD

O EMERALD EMPIRE ARTS ASSOCIATION, 421 North A, 97477. Tel 503-726-8595. *Pres* Mrs Frank Light
Estab 1957 to advance art in community, and to build up funds for a workshop and gallery. Mem: 160; dues $5; monthly meetings third Tues
Exhibitions: Exhibitions twice a year at local shopping centers
Publications: Monthly Art League Bulletin
Activities: Classes for adults and children; 10 week classes each year plus 2-3 workshops, area served is Willamette Valley, material available to anyone; lect open to the public; gallery talks; tours; competitions; individual paintings and original objects of art lent; traveling exhibitions organized and circulated; book shop

THE DALLES

O THE DALLES ART ASSOCIATION, The Dalles Art Center, Fourth & Washington, 97058. Tel 503-296-4759. *Pres* Pat Rayburn; *VPres* Linda Pyles; *Secy* Dorothy Luthy; *Treas* Betty Sholl; *Exhibit Chmn* Ray Hotka
Open Tues - Sat 10 AM - 4 PM. No admis fee. Estab 1959 for presentation of community arts activities. Gallery maintained. Average Annual Attendance: 4500. Mem: 150; dues $10; meetings held each month on 3rd Mon
Income: Financed by dues, fund-raising events
Exhibitions: Member and guest exhibits; state services exhibits
Publications: Monthly bulletin
Activities: Classes for adults and children; summer children's program; lect open to public; competitions; individual paintings lent to schools

PENNSYLVANIA

ALLENTOWN

M ALLENTOWN ART MUSEUM, Fifth & Courts Sts, PO Box 117, 18105. Tel 215-432-4333. *Pres Board Trustees* Bernard Berman; *Dir* Richard N Gregg; *Cur* Peter F Blume; *Cur Educ* Mimi Miley; *Comptroller* Barbara Strohl; *Registrar* Patricia Delluva; *Mem Secy* Valerie Heins; *Sales Desk Mgr* Gloria Hvazda
Open Tues - Sat 10 AM - 5 PM, Sun 1 - 5 PM, cl Mon. No admis fee. Estab 1939 to acquire, protect, display and interpret the visual arts from the past and present, world wide. Building and land cover three quarters of a city block; 28,000 sq ft wing was added in 1975 to more than double the space. Average Annual Attendance: 100,000. Mem: 3600; dues benefactor $500, student $7.50
Income: $580,000 (financed by endowment, membership, city and state appropriations, and contributions)
Collections: †American 18th, 19th & 20th century paintings, sculptures and prints; Chinese porcelains; English and American silver; Samuel H Kress Memorial Collection of European paintings & sculpture, c 1350-1750 (bugiardini, Hals, de Heem, Rembrandt, Ruisdael, Steen and others); †Textile study room; Frank Lloyd

Wright period room, 1912
Exhibitions: Art for the Private Citizen in the Early Renaissance; Aspects of Ancient Greece; Beyond Nobility; Valley Collects: American Decorative Arts, 1780-1880
Publications: Calendar of events, monthly; catalogs of major exhibitions
Activities: Docent training; lect open to public; gallery talks; tours; competitions; individual paintings lent to museums; lending collection contains original art works, original prints, paintings and textiles; traveling exhibitions organized and circulated; museum shop selling books, original art, reproductions, prints, slides, cards and catalogs

L Mack Trucks Art Reference Library, Fifth $ Court Sts, 18105. *Librn* Richard N Gregg
Open to staff, volunteers and members for reference
Library Holdings: Vols 7000; Per subs 25

M MUHLENBERG COLLEGE CENTER FOR THE ARTS, 24th & Chew Sts, 18104. *Gallery Dir* Linda Weintraub; *Asst Dir* Polli Sawruk
Open daily during school term. No admis fee. Estab 1976. The building was designed by architect Philip Johnson; the focal point of its design and function is a 220 ft glass-covered galleria which bisects the structure
Collections: Contemporary art collection has recently been initiated
Exhibitions: Three exhibitions each semester

AUDUBON

M AUDUBON WILDLIFE SANCTUARY, Mill Grove, Box 25, 19407. Tel 215-666-5593. *Cur & Dir* Edward W Graham
Open daily 10 AM - 5 PM, cl Mon. No admis fee. Estab 1951 to display the major artwork of John James Audubon, artist-naturalist, who made Mill Grove his first home in America, 1804-06. This is a National Historic Site and features two original artworks by Audubon, plus examples of all his major publications. Average Annual Attendance: 25,000 - 30,000
Income: Financed by county appropriation
Collections: Birds of America (double elephant folio, 4 vols, Audubon & Havell); Birds of America (first ed Octavo, 7 vols, Audubon, Lithos by Bowen); Quadrupeds of North America (Imperial size, 2 vols, Audubon & Bachmann); Quadrupeds of North America (Octavo, 3 vols, Audubon, Lithos by Bowen)

BETHLEHEM

M ANNIE S KEMERER MUSEUM, 427 North New St, 18018. Tel 215-868-6868. *Pres* Mrs John W Leming Jr; *VPres* Mrs Peter P Prichett; *Secy* Ray R Brennen; *Dir* Deborah L Evans; *Secy* Joan Niemitz; *Secy* Susan I Adleman
Open Mon - Fri 1 - 4 PM, second and fourth Sun 2 - 4 PM. No admis fee, donation appreciated. Estab 1954 for public education, devoted to the display of antiques and historical and other objects illustrative of the growth of the museum's geographical area. Gallery on second floor of the south wing provides monthly exhibits; showcase for local, national and international artists. Average Annual Attendance: 10,000. Mem: 200; dues donated
Income: $40,000 (financed by endowment and membership)
Collections: Bohemian Glass, Early Bethlehem Oil Paintings and Prints, 18th and 19th Century Furniture, Oriental Rugs, Pennsylvania German Frackturs, Victoriana, quilts and coverlets, locally made tall case clocks, and tinware
Exhibitions: (1979-80) Birds of a Feather (mixed medium); Continuation of George Papashvily, Sculptor: A Retrospective Exhibit; Crystal Christmas; 18th and 19th Century Toys; Handmade Quilts and Coverlets; Hans Moller (paintings); Richard Redd (color collages); Stained Glass by Morgan Bockius Studios; Mary Grace Wible (watercolors); annual juried show, annual school show
Publications: Newsletter, quarterly
Activities: Docent training; lect for members only; gallery talks; tours; competitions; individual paintings and original objects of art lent to individuals and organizations; museum shop sells books, original art, reproductions, prints and handicrafts

M LEHIGH UNIVERSITY GALLERIES, Fine Arts Bldg, Chandler-Ullmann Hall, Rm 17, 18015. Tel 215-691-7000, Ext 736. *Dir Exhib & Coll* Ricardo Viera; *Asst to Dir* Judith Goldworm
Open Mon - Fri 9 AM - 10 PM, Sat 9 AM - Noon, cl Sun (DuBois Gallery). Open 9 AM - 5 PM, Sat 9 AM - Noon, Sun 2 - 5 PM (Ralph Wilson Gallery). Estab to bring diverse media and understanding to the Lehigh students and general public of the Lehigh Valley area. Collection is maintained in two galleries: DuBois Gallery has four floors of approx 250 running ft of wall hanging space per floor; Ralph Wilson Gallery has three rooms of exhibition space. Average Annual Attendance: 15,000 (per both galleries)
Income: Financed by endowment and gifts
Collections: Adler Collection of Paintings; Baker Collection of Porcelain; Berman Collection of Paintings; Driebe Collection of Paintings; Grace Collection of Paintings; Kempsmith Collection of Sculpture and Graphics; photography collection; Ralph Wilson Collection of Paintings and Graphics
Exhibitions: (1979) French Contemporary Architecture (DuBois Gallery); 800 Years of Japanese Printmaking (Ralph Wilson Gallery); Intentions and Techniques: Photography (Ralph Wilson Gallery); Jane Mitchell: Paintings (Ralph Wilson Gallery); Bruce Onobrakpeya: Nigerian Printmaker (DuBois Gallery); Pennsylvania Painters: Paul Binal, Rosalind Pace, Phil Richards, Lisa Rundel (DuBois Gallery); Herbert Simon: Sculptor (Ralph Wilson Gallery)
Publications: Calendar, twice per year; exhibition catalogs
Activities: Classes for adults; lect open to the public, 6 visiting lectrs per year; gallery talks; individual paintings and original objects of art lent to other schools and galleries

BLOOMSBURG

M BLOOMSBURG STATE COLLEGE, Haas Gallery of Art, 17815. Tel 717-389-2607. *Dir* John F Cook Jr; *Chmn Dept of Art* Dr Percival R Roberts III
Open Mon - Fri 9 AM - 5 PM. No admis fee. Estab 1966 as an educational and

cultural extension of the College's Department of Art. Gallery covers 2350 sq ft with track lighting and three dome skylights. Average Annual Attendance: 16,000
Income: Financed by city appropriation and grants
Collections: Permanent Collection
Exhibitions: Ten monthly exhibitions in a variety of media
Publications: Exhibition catalogs and brochures, monthly
Activities: Lect open to the public, 6-8 vis lectr per yr; gallery talks; tours
L **Andruss Library,** 17815. Tel 717-389-2607. *Librn* William V Ryan
Library Holdings: Vols 500,000; Per subs 200,000
Collections: Fine Arts books and prints

BOALSBURG

M **COLUMBUS CHAPEL, BOAL MANSION AND MUSEUM,** Rte 322, 16827. Tel 814-466-6210. *Dir* Mathilde Boal Lee; *Dir* Christopher G Lee; *Cur* Lillian Major
Open June - Labor Day 10 AM - 5 PM; May, Sept & Oct 2 - 5 PM. Admis adults $2.50, students $1.75, children $1.00. Estab 1952 as a nonprofit educational organization devoted to preservation of this historic homestead built in 1789. Average Annual Attendance: 3,000
Income: Financed by admissions
Collections: Chapel contains 16th & 17th century Spanish, Italian and Flemish art; furniture, china and glassware; mansion contains 18th and 19th century French, Spanish, Italian, Flemish and American art; weapons: American, French and German (1780-1920)
Activities: Sales shop selling books, slides and postcards

BRYN MAWR

L **BRYN MAWR COLLEGE,** Art and Archaeology Library, 19010. Tel 215-645-5088, 645-5087. *Head Librn* Eileen Markson; *Library Asst* Babette Bauerle
Open during academic year Mon - Thurs 9 AM - 12 PM; Fri 9 AM - 10 PM; Sat 9 AM - 5 PM; Sun 2 PM - 12 PM. Estab 1931 to serve the needs of the general college program and the undergraduate majors and graduate students through the PhD degree in both history of art and Classical and Near Eastern archeology. For reference only
Income: Financed by college funds
Library Holdings: Vols 44,000; Per subs 400
Special Subjects: Italian Renaissance, Italian Baroque, ImpressionismGreek architecture and sculpture, Near Eastern archaeology, Aegean archaeology

BUCK HILL FALLS

O **BUCK HILL ART ASSOCIATION,** PO Box 113, 18323. *Pres* Dr K Roald Bergethon; *VPres* Mrs Walter Meditz; *Secy* Mrs Thomas P Tanis; *Treas* Edward C Jenkins
Open 10 AM - 5 PM. No admis fee. Estab 1931 to further appreciation of art. Average Annual Attendance: 1850. Mem: 125
Income: $8000 (financed by endowment and membership)
Purchases: $500
Collections: Contemporary American artists
Exhibitions: (1980) Members Show in Sept
Activities: Lect open to public, 2 visiting lectr per year

CHADDS FORD

M **BRANDYWINE RIVER MUSEUM,** PO Box 141, 19317. Tel 215-388-7601. *Dir* James H Duff; *Business Mgr* Charles Burns; *Dir Public Relations* John Sheppard; *Cur Coll* Ann Barton Brown; *Cur* Joan H Gorman; *Registrar* Gene E Harris; *Coordinator Visitor Services* Cynthia Repplier; *Bookstore Mgr* Sue Coleburn
Open daily 9:30 AM - 4:30 PM, cl Christmas. Admis adults $1.75, senior citizens, students and children $1.00. Estab 1971, devoted to the preservation, documentation and interpretation of art history in the Brandywine Valley, the history of American illustration and the relationship of regional art to the natural environment. Three main galleries are housed in a renovated 1864 grist mill with contemporary additions for public services, storage, offices and bookstore. Average Annual Attendance: 175,000. Mem: 2400; dues $15 - $1000
Purchases: $33,000
Collections: †American Illustration; art of the Brandywine Valley from early and mid-19th century; regional artists of the 20th century, painting, drawing and sculpture, including a major Andrew Wyeth Collection
Exhibitions: Art in the Folk Tradition; Art of American Illustration; Beyond Necessity; Jefferson David Chalfant; George Cope; Faces of Old Kris: Santa Clause in American Art; Peter Hurd: a Retrospective; Horace Pippin
Publications: The Catalyst, quarterly; exhibition catalogs
Activities: Classes for children; dramatic programs; tours; individual paintings and original objects of art lent to other museums for exhibition purposes; traveling exhibitions organized and circulated; museum shop selling books, reproductions, slides, postcards and catalogs
L **Library,** PO Box 141, 19317. *Librn* Mary Bassett
Open daily 9 AM - 5 PM. For reference to staff and volunteers; by appointment to the public
Library Holdings: Vols 4000; Per subs 20; Other—Memorabilia
Special Subjects: The history of American illustration in books and periodicals
Collections: Howard Pyle's published work; N C Wyeth memorabilia

CHESTER

M **ALFRED O DESHONG MUSEUM,** (Formerly Deshong Memorial Art Galleries) Widener University, 11th St and Avenue of the States, 19013. *Cur* Anne Fabbri Butera
Open Mon - Fri 10 AM - 4 PM. Estab 1913
Income: Financed by endowment and University functions
Collections: 18th and 19th century Oriental art objects; 19th century European landscape and genre pictures; 20th century American paintings and sculpture

CLARION

M **CLARION STATE COLLEGE,** Hazel Sanford Gallery, 16214. Tel 814-226-2000; WATS 800-669-2000. *Chmn Gallery Committee* William T Edwards Jr; *Asst Prof* Andor P Jobb
Open Mon - Fri 9 AM - 3 PM. No admis fee. Estab 1970 for aesthic enjoyment and artistic education of students. Gallery is 66 ft long, 17ft 3 inches wide; lit by some 50 adjustable spot lights; one side of gallery is glassed in; other side is cinderblock and fitted with a walker system for displaying paintings; and a dozen free standing panels, not available for hanging. Average Annual Attendance: 300
Income: $500 (financed by state appropriation)
Collections: Original paintings, drawings and prints, purchased from selected artists who have shown at gallery
Exhibitions: Ceramics, Drawings, Paintings, John Bloomqist; Watercolor Show, Frances Burkett; Greensburg Art Club, Traveling Exhibit; IUP Students Drawing Show; Paintings David Ludwick; Clay and Fiber Show, Stuart and Karen Thompson
Publications: Monthly announcements of shows
Activities: Competitions; cash awards; individual paintings and original objects of art lent to departments on campus and other state colleges; lending collection contains original art works, original prints, paintings, photographs and sculpture

DOYLESTOWN

M **BUCKS COUNTY HISTORICAL SOCIETY MERCER MUSEUM,** Pine & Ashland Sts, 18901. Tel 215-345-0210. *Pres* William F Heefner; *Chief Cur* Lynne F Poirier
Open Tues 10 AM - 9 PM; Wed - Sat 10 AM - 5 PM; Sun 1 - 5 PM; Mar - Dec. Admis family $4.50, adults $2 and students $1. Estab 1880. Inside this poured, re-inforced concrete building, four galleries wrap around a towering central court where different hand crafts are exhibited inside small cubicles. Additional artifacts hang from ceilings, walls and railings. A six story tower on each end completes the building. Average Annual Attendance: 40,000. Mem: 2400; dues $20 and up; annual meeting Nov
Collections: Over 40,000 artifacts representing more than 40 early American crafts, their tools and finished products; large American folk art collection; the history and growth of our country as seen through the work of the human hand
Exhibitions: Continuous small changing exhibits
Publications: Journal, semi-annually; newsletter, monthly
Activities: Classes for adults and children; lect open to public, 6-7 vis lectr per year; Annual Folk Festival; museum shop selling books, magazines, reproductions and prints
L **Spruance Library,** Pine & Ashland Sts, 18901. *Librn* Terry A McNealy
Open to the public for reference only
Library Holdings: Vols 18,000; Per subs 50; Other—Manuscripts, Archives

DUNCANSVILLE

M **LEE ATKYNS STUDIO-GALLERY,** Box 120, Route 2, 16635. Tel 814-695-0186. *Dir* Lee Atkyns
Open by appointment. No admis fee. Estab 1950, original gallery was in Washington, DC; present studio gallery opened in 1975 in what was once an abandoned chapel, the old cemetery adjacent has been converted into a flower garden
Income: Financed personally
Collections: Paintings by Lee Atkyns of Liberated Lines Series, showing the derivative trends through yhe years from 1947 to the present time; Landscapes, abstractions and Music Expressionist paintings; Paintings in oils, watercolor, acrylic from around the world; Tapestry, weavings, ceramics, prints and small sculptures including primitive old New Guinea and early Egyptian works
Activities: Individual paintings lent to galleries

ERIE

O **ERIE ART CENTER,** 338 West Sixth St, 16507. Tel 814-459-5477. *Pres* Sally Lund; *VPres* Marvin Gold; *Secy* Karen Corle; *Treas* Charles Roberts; *Exec Dir* John Vanco
Open Tues - Sun 1 - 5 PM. No admis fee. Estab 1898 for the advancement of visual arts. Galleries are located in historic building. Average Annual Attendance: 12,000. Mem: Dues family $20, individual $12
Income: $100,000 (financed by membership)
Collections: Contemporary graphics, paintings, photographs, sculpture and some historical paintings and graphics
Exhibitions: Artists Commission of W.N.Y. (works on paper); Ansel Adams & Edward Weston (Photo); Patricia Bellan-Gillen & Robert Rotella (Prints & Photo); Edinboro State College Students & Faculty (Paintings & Drawings): Joyce Fernandes (Paintings); 56th Annual Spring Show; Cities USA (Photos); David Gilhooly (Ceramics); Jim Munn & Jerry Wagner (Ceramics & Mixed Media); Anne Philbin (Paintings); Take a Good Look (Paintings & Drawings)
Publications: Catalogs for exhibitions; flyers for shows, monthly
Activities: Classes for adults and children; docent training; gallery talks; tours; competitions; individual paintings and original objects of art lent to public buildings, community centers, colleges; lending collection contains original art works; traveling exhibitions organized and circulated; sales shop selling frames

L ERIE DISTRICT LIBRARY CENTER, * 3 S Perry Square, PO Box 1631, 16507.
Tel 814-452-2333. *Dir* Kenneth G Sivulich
Open, Winter Mon - Fri 9:30 AM - 9 PM, Sat 9 AM - 5:30 PM, cl Sun, Summer
Mon & Fri 9:30 AM - 9 PM, Tues, Wed & Thurs 9:30 AM - 6 PM, Sat 9 AM -
5:30 PM, cl Sun. No admis fee. Estab 1899 to provide public library services to the
community. Gallery contains original paintings, drawings, prints and reproductions
of paintings and sculpture
Income: Financed by city and state appropriations
Exhibitions: Exhibitions by local artists
Activities: Original paintings, prints, drawings and sculpture reproductions lent;
lending collection contains color reproductions and photographs

FACTORYVILLE

L KEYSTONE JUNIOR COLLEGE LIBRARY, Art Section, College Ave, 18440.
Head Libr Mary Van Nort
Open 8:30 AM - 11 PM during college sessions. Estab circa 1965 as research and
enrichment; to augment college art courses. Gallery is located in the Library
Income: $1169 (financed by college and grants)
Library Holdings: Vols 1065; Per subs 9; AV—Fs, motion pictures, slides, v-tapes;
Other—Prints, original art works, sculpture
Exhibitions: Professional exhibition series plus two juried student exhibits per year

FRANKLIN CENTER

M FRANKLIN MINT CORP MUSEUM, 19091. Tel 215-459-6348. *Dir & VPres
Collector Relations* William F Krieg; *Supvr Guest Relations* Judie Gorbey
Open Mon - Fri 9 AM - 5 PM, except holidays. No admis fee. Estab 1973 to make
available to the general public a location where the collectibles created by The
Franklin Mint can be viewed. Average Annual Attendance: 55,000
Income: Financed by Franklin Mint funding
Collections: Etchings and woodblock prints; foreign coinage - coins minted for 19
foreign governments; Heirloom furniture; medallic collections recognizing the
genius of Michelangelo, DaVinci and Rembrandt; leather bound books ornamented
in 22 kt gold; porcelain, crystal, bronze and pewter art
Activities: Gift shop selling jewelry, medals, greeting cards and collectibles

GLENSIDE

M BEAVER COLLEGE, Eugene R Fuller Gallery of Art, Church and Limekiln Pike,
19038. *Gallery Dir* Zina Goldsmith; *Chmn Dept Fine Arts* Jack Davis
Open 1 - 5 PM except school holidays. No admis fee. Estab 1969 to show
contemporary art generally. Gallery dimensions 20 x 50 ft. Average Annual
Attendance: 5000
Purchases: $500
Collections: A few prints and drawings
Exhibitions: Jack Beal, Prints, Clay, Fibre, Metal Exhibition; Faculty Exhibition;
William Larson, etc, Recent Photographs
Publications: Brochures for major exhibitions, 3 per year
Activities: Gallery talks; competitions

GREENSBURG

M WESTMORELAND COUNTY MUSEUM OF ART, 221 N Main St, 15601. Tel
412-837-1500. *Dir* Dr Paul A Chew; *Executive Secy* Regina L Narad; *Membership
Secy* Loretta Meyer; *Registrar* Jeffrey P Rouse
Open Tues - Sat 10 AM - 5 PM; Sun 1 - 5 PM, cl Mon & holidays. No admis fee.
Estab 1949 to create, establish and maintain a memorial foundation of a public,
charitable, cultural, literary and educational nature and in conjunction therewith,
to maintain a public art museum. The museum houses two large galleries and one
small gallery for changing exhibitions, two English 18th century pine-panelled
rooms, and a suite of Victorian period rooms. Average Annual Attendance: 17,600.
Mem: 859; dues $10 - $1000
Income: Financed by endowment
Collections: †American art (paintings, drawings, sculpture and decorative arts);
American and European prints; †antique toys; British drawings; Continental and
british paintings
Exhibitions: Ron Bennett: Phase I and II Photographic; Caucasian Rugs and
Carpets; Ray DeFazio; 18th & 19th century regional folk art; Kenneth Frazier,
American Impressionist; David Hanna; Julio Larraz; Jack Massey; Jim Myford;
New American Still Life; 19th & early 20th century regional painters; Polish Textile
Artists; Survey of Westmoreland County Architecture; three centuries of American
Painting; Henry Wo Yue-Kee
Publications: Calendar of events, twice a year; exhibition catalogs
Activities: Dramatic programs; lect open to public, 6 vis lectr per yr; concerts;
gallery talks; tours; individual paintings lent to museums; lending collection
contains original prints, paintings and sculpture; museum shop selling books,
original art, reproductions, slides and cards
L Art Reference Library, 221 N Main St, 15601.
Open Tues - Sat 10 AM - 5 PM; Sun 1 - 5 PM. Estab 1959 for art reference. For
reference only
Income: $3600
Purchases: $3600
Library Holdings: Vols 5900; Per subs 40; Other—Clipping files, exhibition
catalogs, pamphlets, photographs
Special Subjects: American art

GREENVILLE

M THIEL COLLEGE, Sampson Art Gallery, College Ave, 16125. Tel 412-588-7700,
Ext 265. *Dir* Alvin Dunkle; *Dir of Permanent Collection* Richard Hayes; *Student
Dir* Lori Stevenson
Sun - Fri 1 - 4 PM & 7 - 9 PM; Sat 1 - 4 PM. No admis fee. Estab 1971 to provide
students, faculty, college staff and the community with a gallery featuring a variety
of exhibitions, and give students an opportunity to show their work. Gallery has
white walls, track floodlighting system, linoleum tile floor, and one window wall.
Average Annual Attendance: 1000
Exhibitions: Oil Paintings of William Bukowski; Paintings & drawings of Mark
Mentzer; Photography & Sculpture of George Shoemaker
Activities: Lect open to the public, visiting lectr; gallery talks

HARRISBURG

O ART ASSOCIATION OF HARRISBURG, 21 N Front St, 17101. Tel
717-236-1432. *Studio Dir* Charles A Schulz
Open Mon - Fri 10 AM - 2 PM. No admis fee. Estab 1926 to act as showcase for
member artists and other area professionals; community services offered. Building
consists of 5 galleries with 4 studio areas for school classes. Mem: 300; dues $15
- $25; annual meeting May
Income: Financed by endowment and membership
Collections: Old area masters; member's work
Exhibitions: Annual juried exhibition
Publications: Exhibition announcements, 8 times per year; newsletter, 12 times per
year
Activities: Classes for adults and children; lect open to public, 4 visiting lectr per
year; competitions; monetary awards; sales shop sells original art and prints

O DOSHI CENTER FOR CONTEMPORARY ART, 1435 N Second St, 17102. Tel
717-232-3039. *Pres* Donald Winer; *VPres* L vonBarann; *Secy* Dorothy Odom;
Executive Dir Carol E Faill
Open Mon - Fri 11 AM - 4 PM, Sun 1 - 4 PM. No admis fee. Estab 1972 as a
non-profit gallery offering exposure to artists and enlightenment to the community.
Main gallery is on street level, also two smaller rooms termed the Upper Gallery.
Average Annual Attendance: 5000. Mem: 125; dues family $25, artist $20,
individual $10, board meeting second Tues every month
Income: $12,500 (financed by endowment)
Exhibitions: Group exhibits; Bruce Samuelson (painting); Russell and Georgette
Veeders (sculpture); trio exhibit: Robbert Coon (sculpture), Caroline Eden
(painter), Jo Margolis (sculpture); special craft exhibit, photography exhibit
Activities: Lect open to public, 6 visiting lectr per year; gallery talk; Maya Schock
Educational Fund awarded; sales shop sells original art, crafts (ceramics and
jewelry)

O PENNSYLVANIA DEPARTMENT OF EDUCATION, Arts in Education
Program, 8th Floor, 333 Market St, 17126. Tel 717-787-7814. *Senior Adviser* Joe
McCarthy; *Adviser* Robert Revicki; *Dir Arts in Special Education Project* Lola
Kearns; *Dir Governor's School for the Arts* Arthur Gatty
The Arts in Education Program provides leadership and consultative and evaluative
services to all Pennsylvania schools in arts program development. Infusion of arts
processes into differentiated curriculums for all students is a particular thrust. The
program offers model programs at several sites, ongoing staff development
programs, assistance in designing aesthetic learning environments and consultation
in identifying and employing regional and community resources for arts education

O PENNSYLVANIA HISTORICAL AND MUSEUM COMMISSION, William
Penn Memorial Museum and Archives Bldg, 17120. Tel 717-787-3362. *Executive
Dir* William J Wewer; *Dir Bureau of Museum* Michael J Ripton; *Dir Bureau
Archives & History* Harry E Whipkey
Estab 1945 when the State Museum, Archives, Historical Commission and
Historical Properties combined into one agency
Income: $5,000,000 for entire commission
Activities: Tours; craft and harvest days at Farm Museum
M William Penn Memorial Museum, 17120. *Dir* Ira Smith III; *Cur of Fine Arts*
Donald A Winer
Open Mon - Sat 9 AM - 5 PM; Sun 1 - 5 PM. Offices Mon - Fri 8:30 AM - 5 PM
Collections: Anthropology; archaeology; china; decorative arts; folk art; glass;
period rooms; silver; textiles Indian artifacts
Publications: Books, brochures
Activities: Classes for children; lect; tours; art competitions; exhibitions from
outer-museum loan
L Library, 17120.
Open to the public for use on premises only
Library Holdings: Vols 40,000
Special Subjects: Archaeology, Folk Art, Historical Material

HAVERFORD

O **MAIN LINE CENTER OF THE ARTS**, Old Buck Rd & Lancaster Ave, 19041. Tel 215-515-0272. *Pres* Faye Cohen; *VPres* Maria Raday; *Admin Dir* Eleanor Daitzman; *Secy* Bev Hoffsis; *Treas* Robert Bruce
Open Mon - Fri 10 AM - 12 PM & 1 - 4 PM. No admis fee. Estab 1937 to develop and encourage the fine arts. Three large, well lit galleries, completely modernized to accommodate over one hundred sculptures and paintings. Average Annual Attendance: Several thousand. Mem: 800; dues family $18, adult $15 and children $8; meetings once a month except Aug
Income: Financed by membership and fund raising
Exhibitions: Craft Show; Membership Shows; One-man and group Graphic Shows; Porcelain Show
Publications: Brochures, three times a year
Activities: Classes for adults, teens and children; dramatic programs; lect open to public and for members only, 12 vis lectr per yr; gallery talks; concerts; tours; competitions; individual paintings and original objects of art lent to libraries, schools, hospitals, etc; lending collection contains original art works, original prints and sculpture; traveling exhibitions organized and circulated

INDIANA

M **INDIANA UNIVERSITY OF PENNSYLVANIA**, Kipp Gallery, 15705. Tel 412-357-2530. *Chmn Exhib* Ned O Wert
Open Mon - Fri 9 AM - 4:30 PM; Sat & Sun by appointment to groups. No admis fee. Estab 1970 to make available a professional gallery program to Western Pennsylvania and to the university community. Versatile space with portable wall system, track lighting, secure, humidity controlled. Average Annual Attendance: 10,000
Income: Financed by Student Coop Assn
Exhibitions: Harry Hansen, Encaustic Paintings; Nate Invitational Exhibition of Metalsmithing; New Directions in Printmaking from Pratt Graphics Center; Pennsylvania Woodworkers Invitational; Solo and group shows annually
Activities: Lect open to public, 3-5 vis lectr per yr; gallery talks; tours; traveling exhibitions organized and circulated; sales shop selling original art and prints

KUTZTOWN

KUTZTOWN STATE COLLEGE
M **Sharadin Art Gallery**, 19530. Tel 215-683-4224. *Gallery Dir* Jim Chaney; *Gallery Coordr* Eldon Katter
Open Mon - Fri 10 AM - 4 PM; Sat 12 - 5 PM; Sun 2 - 5:30 PM. No admis fee. Estab 1956 to make the best of the contemporary arts available to the town and college communities
Income: Financed by city and state appropriations
Purchases: $5000
Collections: Approximately 400 works in prints, drawings and paintings
Publications: Brochure listing a gallery season's collection of shows
Activities: Lect open to the public, occassional talks; temporary and traveling faculty and student exhibitions
L **Rohrbach Library**, 19530. *College Librn* John K Amrhein
Open Mon - Thurs 7:45 AM - 11 PM; Fri 7:45 AM - 5 PM; Sat 9 AM - 5 PM; Sun 2 - 11 PM. Estab 1866. Circ 90,000
Library Holdings: Vols 270,000; Per subs 2000; Micro—Fiche, reels; AV—A-tapes, cassettes, fs, motion pictures, rec, slides; Other—Exhibition catalogs, pamphlets
Special Subjects: Art Education, Art History, Russian art

LANCASTER

M **COMMUNITY GALLERY OF LANCASTER COUNTY**, 135 N Lime St, 17602. *Pres* Helen Woolworth; *Dir* Barbara C Newcomb
Open Mon - Fri 10 AM - 4 PM; Sat & Sun 12 - 4 PM. No admis fee. Estab 1965 to present the best quality in art exhibits. Average Annual Attendance: 10,000. Mem: 600; dues, various categories; annual meeting first Sunday in April
Income: $50,000 (financed by membership, local business and county commissioners)
Exhibitions: Arthur Armstrong; David Brumbach; Friends of the Rag; Israeli Prints; Oriental Rugs; Pfannebecker Collection; Joseph Raffael
Activities: Docent training; lect; gallery talks; bus trips

O **LANCASTER COUNTY ART ASSOCIATION**, Art Center, 22 E Vine St, 17602. Tel 717-392-9258. *Pres* Arlene Fisher
Estab 1936, incorporated 1950. Mem: 320; dues $10; annual meeting second Tues in May
Collections: Currently being enlarged by purchases
Exhibitions: Monthly exhibitions; Spring and Fall member and student shows; 3 three-man shows, and others
Activities: Classes, free for Retired Citizens Association; demonstrations; lect, 6 visiting lectr per year; programs; sponsors Lancaster County day tour of fine homes and gardens annually as a project to raise funds for community projects; gallery talks; originate traveling exhibitions

M **PENNSYLVANIA FARM MUSEUM OF LANDIS VALLEY**, 2451 Kissel Hill Rd, 17601. Tel 717-569-0401. *Dir* Robert N Sieber; *Cur Crafts & Education* John B Brooks; *Cur Collections* Vernon S Gunnion
Open Tues - Sat 9 AM - 4:30 PM; Sun 12 - 4:30 PM. Admis adults $2, over 65 or under 12 free, school groups free. Estab 1925 to collect, preserve and interpret Pennsylvania rural life and culture, circa 1750 to 1900; farm implements, crafts, tools, domestic furnishings and folk art. The outdoor museum has 25 exhibit buildings, including restored 18th and 19th century structures. Average Annual Attendance: 80,000. Mem: 1000; dues $5 and up; annual meeting third Tues in Oct
Income: $645,000 (financed by state appropriation)
Purchases: $6000
Collections: Folk art including ceramics, textiles, furniture and decorative ironware
Publications: Newsletter, monthly; special exhibit catalogs

Activities: Classes for adults and children; lect open to public, 4 vis lectr per year; tradtional crafts programs; occasional loans made from permanent collections; museum shop selling books, crafts items and period reproductions
L **Library**, 2451 Kissel Hill Rd, 17601.
Open to staff, scholars, etc by appointment for reference only
Library Holdings: Vols 12,000; Per subs 25
Special Subjects: Crafts, Decorative Arts, Folk Art, Historical Material

LEWISBURG

L **BUCKNELL UNIVERSITY**, Ellen Clarke Bertrand Library, 17837. Tel 717-524-3056. *Librn* George M Jenks; *Chief Public Services* Ronald B Daniels; *Chief Technical Services* Helena G Rivoire
Open Mon - Fri 8:30 AM - 11 PM, Sat 9 AM - 5 PM, Sun 1 - 11 PM. Estab 1846 to serve students and faculty of university. Circ 131,374. Gallery contains a study collection of 20 paintings and one sculpture of the Renaissance given by the Samuel H Kress Foundation
Income: $900,000 (financed by endowment, tuition and gifts)
Purchases: $325,000
Library Holdings: Vols 395,000; Per subs 2128; Micro—Fiche, reels; AV—Cassettes, rec; Other—Prints, manuscripts, memorabilia, original art works, pamphlets

M **FETHERSTON FOUNDATION**, Packwood House Museum, 15 N Water St, 17837. Tel 717-524-0323. *Pres* Dr Irving Williams; *VPres* Dr James Turnure; *Secy* Fred Kessler; *Dir & Cur* David W Dunn; *Cur of Education* Lorraine Bauman; *Registrar* Helen Beck; *Secy & Archivist* Heather A Clewell
Open Wed - Sat 1 - 4 PM, Sun 2 - 4 PM. Admis adults $1.75, groups over 15 $1.50, senior citizens $1.25. Estab 1976 to serve the community as an educational institution. Average Annual Attendance: 5000. Mem: 169; dues family $25 individual $15
Income: Financed by endowment and membership
Collections: American Fine Arts; Paintings by Edith H K Fetherston; Fine Period Clothing ranging from 1890's to 1960's; 1800 - 1940 accessories, ceramics, furniture, glass, metalwork, textiles
Exhibitions: (1978-80) Ice Harvesting; Model Trains; Victorian Glass; Weaving; Windsor Chairs
Activities: Classes for adults and children; docent training; lect open to public, 2 visiting lectr per year; tours; competitions between area schools during Art Festival week; monetary awards; book traveling exhibitions; originate traveling exhibitions; museum shop sells books, original art, reproductions and local handcrafted items

LORETTO

M **SOUTHERN ALLEGHENIES MUSEUM OF ART**, Saint Francis College Mall, PO Box 8, 15940. *Dir* Michael M Strueber; *Admin Asst* Deborah Davis Grazier; *Community Outreach Coordr* Michael Allison
Open Wed, Thurs & Fri 10 AM - 5 PM; Sat & Sun 1:30 - 5:30 PM. No admis fee. Estab and dedicated June 1976 to facilitate interest, understanding and the appreciation of the visual arts of the past, present and future through the exhibition of our permanent as well as temporary collections. An extremely versatile main gallery, 50 x 77 ft with ten moveable cases that are 3 x 4 x 7 ft high; print gallery upstairs. Average Annual Attendance: 10,000. Mem: 100; dues variable
Income: Financed by membership, business, corporate and foundation grants
Collections: †American paintings, ceramics, drawings, prints and sculptures
Exhibitions: Invitational Contemporary Fibre Exhibition; Selections of Photo-Realist Paintings from New York City Galleries; Twenty-Five Pennsylvania Women Artists
Activities: Classes for adults; dramatic programs; lect open to the public; concerts, tours; individual paintings and original objects of art lent; lending collection contains books, original prints, paintings, sculpture and drawings
M **Museum Extension**, Central Counties Bank Building, Altoona, PA 16603.
Open Mon - Fri 9:30 AM - 4 PM. Only one of its kind in the state

MEADVILLE

M **ALLEGHENY COLLEGE**, Bowman, Megahan and Penelec Galleries, 16335. Tel 814-724-3371. *Gallery Dir* Martha A Holt
Open Tues - Fri 12:30 - 5 PM; Fri Evening 7 - 9 PM; Sat 1:30 - 5 PM; Sun 2 - 4 PM; cl Mon. No admis fee. Estab 1971 as one of the major exhibition spaces in northwest Pennsylvania; the galleries present exhibits ranging from works of contemporary artists to displays relevant to other fields of study. Galleries are housed in three spacious rooms, white walls, stone floor, 13 ft ceilings. Average Annual Attendance: 8000
Income: Financed by college funds
Collections: General David M Shoup Collection of Korean Pottery; Samuel Pees Collection of contemporary painting
Exhibitions: Art As Language: Drawings & Paintings by Language Impaired Children & Adults; Ceramics by Richard Wukick; Fiber Invitational: Carol Atleson, Sandra August, Nancy Belfer, Marsha Cisek, Drea Howenstein, Jack D Smith; Paintings by Peter Minchell; Permanent Collection, an exhibition of works from the Allegheny College permanent collection; Print Invitational, Photographs by Mark Perrott; Three Approaches: Fiber Installation by Cindy Snodgrass, Clay Installation by Wally Mason & Photography Installation by Cly Boehs; Works on or of Metal by David Edelstein, hannelore Gabriel and Catherine Raphael; Faculty Exhibition: Carl Heeschen, Martha Holt, Richard Kleeman, George Roland; Student Show by Allegheny Students
Activities: Lect open to the public; gallery talks; tours; individual paintings and original objects of art lent to local organizations
L **Lawrence Lee Pelliter Library**, 16335. *Librn* Margaret Moser
Open to students and faculty

O **MEADVILLE COUNCIL ON THE ARTS**, Meadville Market House, PO Box 337, 16335. Tel 814-336-5051. *Executive Dir* Kay Kleeman

Open Tues - Fri 10 AM - 5 PM, Sat 9 AM - Noon. No admis fee. Estab 1975 for local arts information and programming; to create community arts center. Gallery has 50 ft of wall space. Average Annual Attendance: 1000. Mem: 170; dues businesses $25 - $250, individual $10 - $50; annual meeting Jan
Income: $10,000 (financed by membership and state appropriation)
Exhibitions: Annual October Evenings Exhibition; annual county wide exhibits; local artists and crafters exhibits
Publications: Monthly calendar; monthly newsletter
Activities: Classes for adults and children; lect open to public; concerts; competitions; awards

MERION

M **BUTEN MUSEUM OF WEDGWOOD,** 246 N Bowman Ave, 19066. Tel 215-664-9069. *Pres* Mrs Harry M Buten; *Dir* David Buten; *Asst to Dir* Patricia Pelehach; *Admin Asst* Cathryne Foedisch; *Public Relations Dir* Dorothy Manou; *Assoc Dir* Mrs Samuel Laver
Open Tues - Thurs 2 - 5 PM; Sat 10 AM - 1 PM; cl Sun, Mon & Fri. Admis adults $1, senior citizens 50¢. Estab 1957 for study and exhibition of Wedgwood ceramics. Mem: 2000; dues $20; meetings first Sun of month (Sept to May)
Income: Financed by membership
Collections: Over 10,000 examples of Wedgwood ware made from 1759 to the present
Publications: Bulletin, 7 - 9 times per yr; Monographs in Wedgwood Studies, annually
Activities: Lect open to public, 5 vis lectr per yr; gallery talks; original objects of art lent to other museums and colleges; lending collection contains kodachromes and original art works; museum shop selling books and original art
L **Library,** 246 N Bowman Ave, 19066. *Librn* Mrs S Arthur Levy
Open to scholars by appointment for reference only
Library Holdings: Vols 1600
Special Subjects: English ceramics, especially Wedgwood ware

NAZARETH

M **MORAVIAN HISTORICAL SOCIETY,** Whitefield House Museum, 210 E Center St, 18064. Tel 215-759-0292. *Pres* Rev H Williams; *Cur* E B Clewell; *Secy* Mary Henry Stites
Open Tues, Fri & Sat 2 - 5 PM; 2nd & 4th Sun of each month 2 - 5 PM; other times by appointment. No admis fee; donations requested. Built in 1740 by George Whitefield, famous preacher, and bought by the Moravians in 1741 and continued in use by various segments of the church until its present occupation as a missionary home and the seat of the Moravian Historical Society which was organized on April 13, 1857 to elucidate the history of the Moravian Church in America; not however, to the exclusion of the general history of the Moravian Church; the museum houses many unique and distinctive items pertaining to early Moraviana and colonial life. Average Annual Attendance: 1500. Mem: 400; dues $3 - $100; annual meeting second Thurs in Oct
Income: Financed by endowment, membership and donation
Collections: Clothing and textiles; John Valentine Haidt Collection of Paintings; handwrought and cast bells; Indian and foreign mission artifacts; musical instruments; pottery and Stiegel glass; rare books; manuscripts
Exhibitions: Changing exhibits
Publications: Transactions, bi-annual

NEW BRIGHTON

M **MERRICK ART GALLERY,** 5th Ave & 11th St, PO Box 312, 15066. Tel 412-846-1130. *Dir & Education Dir* Kevin Lane; *Trustee* Robert S Merrick
Open Tues - Sat 10 AM - 5 PM; Sun 1 - 5 PM, cl Mon; reduced hours during summer. No admis fee. Estab 1880 to preserve and interpret the collection of paintings and other objects owned by Edward Dampster Merrick, the founder. Also to foster local art through classes and one-man shows. All galleries are on the second floors of two parallel buildings with a connecting bridge; there are three small rooms and one large one. Three rooms have clerestory monitors overhead. Mem: 360; dues $25, $15 and $10; annual meeting February
Income: Financed by endowment and membership
Collections: Most paintings date from the 19th century. American artists Emil Bott; Birge Harrison; Thomas Hill; A F King; Edward and Thomas Moran; E Poole; F K M Rehn; W T Richards; W L Sonntag; Worthington Whittredge. European artists Gustave Courbet; Hans Makart; Pierre Paul Prud'hon; Richard Westall; Franz Xavier; Winterhalter
Exhibitions: Drawings of Edward B Lee, Sr; History Through Industry, a Bicentennial Exhibit; local artist; Oriental Carpets; Panoramic Painting of the Military Career of Garibaldi, painted during the 1850's by Robert Burford Howard Worner, Watercolors of Pittsburgh
Publications: Newsletter, bimonthly
Activities: Classes for adults and children; docent training; outdoor summer art fairs; lect open to public, 1-2 vis lectr per yr; gallery talks; concerts; tours
L **Library,** 5th Ave & 11th St, 15066.
Open to any person for reference only
Special Subjects: Old and rare books

NEW CASTLE

M **HOYT INSTITUTE OF FINE ARTS,** 124 E Leasure Ave, 16105. Tel 412-658-9418. *Pres Board of Trustees* John L Wilson; *Exec Dir* William Craig McBurney
Open Tues - Sat 9 AM - 4 PM. No admis fee. Estab 1968 to encourage the development of the arts within the community. Average Annual Attendance: 27,000. Mem: 440; dues $100, $50, $30, $15, $7.50
Income: Commission on sales of arts and crafts
Collections: Local artists
Publications: Newsletter, quarterly
Activities: Classes for adults and children; dramatic programs; lect open to public; concerts; competitions; movies on arts and crafts; scholarships

NEWTOWN

M **BUCKS COUNTY COMMUNITY COLLEGE,** Hicks Art Center, Fine Arts Department, Swamp Rd, 18940. Tel 215-968-5861. *Chairperson* Bruce Katsiff
Open Mon - Fri 8 AM - 10 PM, Sat 9 AM - 5 PM. No admis fee. Estab 1970 to bring outside artists to the community. Gallery covers 960 sq ft. Average Annual Attendance: 5000
Income: Financed by city and state appropriation
Exhibitions: (1979) Chinese Paper Cutting, Cheng-Hov-Tien; 26 Philadelphia Artists; Charles Schmidt, Drawings (1980) Drawings; Fine Woodworking; Student Annual Exhibit
Activities: Lect open to the public, 8 visiting lectr per year; competitions; artmobile

NEW WILMINGTON

M **WESTMINSTER COLLEGE ART GALLERY,*** 16142. Tel 412-946-8761. *Dir* Robert Godfrey
Open Mon - Sat 10 AM - 7 PM, Sun 2 - 7 PM. No admis fee. Estab 1854 to organize and present 9 exhibitions per season, to organize traveling exhibitions, publish art catalogs of national interest, and to conduct visiting artists program. Average Annual Attendance: 15,000
Income: Over $2000 (financed by endowment)
Collections: 19th and 20th century paintings; †20th century drawings and prints
Exhibitions: Faculty, student and loan exhibitions
Publications: Catalogs; Westminster College Art Gallery, annually
Activities: Lect open to public, 4 visiting lectrs per year; gallery talks; traveling exhibitions organized and circulated

PAOLI

M **WHARTON ESHERICK MUSEUM,** Horseshoe Trail, Box 595, 19301. Tel 215-644-5822. *Pres* Ruth E Bascom; *Secy* Miriam Phillips; *Dir* Mansfield Bascom
Open Sat 10 AM - 5 PM, Sun 1 - 5 PM, by reservation only. Admis $2. Estab 1971 to keep Studio and collection intact and make them available to the public. Studio is set high on hillside overlooking the Great Valley, and is one of Wharton Esherick's monumental achievements. He worked forty years building, enlarging and altering it. Average Annual Attendance: 3000. Mem: 200; dues family $15, individual $10
Income: $10,000 (financed by membership, endowment, admissions and sales)
Collections: 200 pieces of the artist's work, including furniture, paintings, prints, sculpture in wood, stone and ceramic, utensils and woodcuts
Publications: Brochures; catalog of Studio and Collection; Drawings by Wharton Esherick
Activities: Tours; individual paintings and original objects of art lent to museums or exhibitions; museum shop sells books, reproductions, prints and slides

PHILADELPHIA

AMERICAN COLOR PRINT SOCIETY
For further information, see National and Regional Organizations

M **AMERICAN SWEDISH HISTORICAL FOUNDATIONS MUSEUM,** 1900 Pattison Ave, 19145. Tel 215-389-1776. *Pres* Claes Bothen
Open Tues - Fri 10 AM - 4 PM, Sat Noon - 4 PM, cl Sun, Mon & holidays. Admis adults $1, students 50¢. Average Annual Attendance: 10,000. Mem: 1200; dues $10 and up; annual meeting June
Collections: †History and culture of Americans of Swedish descent
Exhibitions: Temporary exhibitions of paintings, arts and crafts by Swedish and Swedish-American artists
Publications: Newsletter
Activities: Group tours by appointment: Lucia Fest, Valsborgs, massoafton; lect; slide and film shows
L **Library,** 1900 Pattison Ave, 19145.
For general reference
Library Holdings: Vols 12,500
Special Subjects: , Fredrika Bremer, John Ericsson, Jenny Lind, Rambo Research of genealogical and colonial material

M **ATHENAEUM OF PHILADELPHIA,** 219 S Sixth St, 19106. Tel 215-925-2688. *Dir* Roger W Moss Jr; *Program Coordr* Eileen Magee; *Architectural Librn* Sandra Tatman; *Circulation Librn* Ellen Batty; *Bibliographer* Keith Kamm
Open Mon - Fri 9 AM - 5 PM. No admis fee. Estab 1814 to collect, preserve and make available original sources on American cultural history, 1814-1914. The fine and decorative arts are arranged in room settings. Average Annual Attendance: 10,000. Mem: 1000; annual meeting first Mon Feb
Income: $146,258
Purchases: $15,231
Collections: †Permanent study collection of American Decorative Arts, 1810-1850; 19th and 20th century architectural books
Exhibitions: John Notman, Architect; Thomas Ustick Walter

Publications: Annotations, quarterly newsletter; Athenaeum Architectural Archive; Annual Report; Bookshelf, six per year; Monographs, three to five per year
Activities: Lect open to public, 6-10 visiting lectr per year; concerts; gallery talks; tours; sales shop selling books, prints and slides

L **Library,** 219 S Sixth St, 19106.
Open Mon - Fri 9 AM - 5 PM by appointment for reference only
Library Holdings: Vols 100,000; Per subs 75; Micro—Reels; AV—Cassettes; Other—Exhibition catalogs, prints, manuscripts, original art works, photographs, reproductions, Architectural drawings and related materials
Collections: Nineteenth century fiction and literary periodicals; trade materials relating to the building arts

M **CLIVEDEN,*** 6401 Germantown Ave, 19144. Tel 215-848-1777. *Asst Adminr* Mary Graham
Open year round 10 AM - 4 PM, cl Christmas Day. Admis adults $1.25, senior citizens 60¢, group tours by arrangement, free to National Trust members. Cliveden is a property of the National Trust for Historic Preservation. Preserved as an historic museum operated as a community preservation center, it is a National Historic Landmark. Cliveden was built in 1763-67 as the country house of Benjamin Chew, a distinguished Philadelphia lawyer and political leader. Surrounded by six acres of centuries-old trees, it has continued to be used through seven generations. Chew family furnishings include extremely important Philadelphia pieces made by such prominent cabinetmakers as Thomas Affleck, Jonathan Goste Lowe, and Daniel Wood. There is also some Penn family furniture, as well as paintings by Smibert, Wollaston, Pine and Henry. Chew papers include over 100,000 manuscript pages plus 3000 volumes and the law library of Chief Justice Benjamin Chew. Property serves as a focal point for advancement of historic preservation. It develops new relationships among cultural, community, and preservation groups, and Trust members in its area. Responds to community preservation needs by acting as a link between community and appropriate regional or headquarters offices of National Trust. Interpretive programs are provided which relate to Cliveden's particular care study in historic preservation. Special Christmas program; Members Day during National Historic Preservation Week in early May. Set of 16 in x 8 in measured drawings, taken by Historic American Building Survey, available from Cliveden's Preservation Shop

M **DREXEL UNIVERSITY ART GALLERY AND MUSEUM COLLECTION,*** Chestnut & 32nd Sts, 19104. Tel 215-895-2424. *Cur* Geraldine Peterson Staub
Open Mon - Fri by appointment, cl Sat, Sun & holidays. No admis fee. Estab 1891; Picture Gallery 1902. Randell Hall Gallery contains the John D Lankenau and the Anthony J Drexel Collections of German and French paintings of the 19th century
Collections: Ceramics; hand printed India cottons, European textiles; decorative arts of China, Europe, India and Japan

O **FAIRMOUNT PARK ART ASSOCIATION,** 256 South 16th St, 19102. *Pres* C Clark Zantzinger Jr; *VPres* Theodore T Newbold; *VPres* Henry W Sawyer III; *Executive Secy* Karel Polch
Estab 1872 for the purpose of buying sculpture which is then given to the City of Philadelphia. Mem: 350; dues $15 - $100; annual meeting April
Income: $120,000 (financed by membership and city appropriation)
Publications: Annual Report

M **FOUNDATION FOR TODAY'S ART,** Nexus Gallery, 2017 Chancellor St, 19103. Tel 215-567-3481. *Trustee* Alexandra Lerner; *Trustee* Vivian Goldstein; *Trustee* Suzanne Horuitz; *Gallery Coordr* Linda Barton
Open Tues - Sat 11:30 AM - 6 PM. No admis fee. Estab 1975 to educate the public in trend of contemporary art and performance; for artists to have opportunity to exhibit. Average Annual Attendance: 5000. Mem: 19; dues $30 per month; meeting first Mon each month
Income: Financed by endowment, membership and state appropriation
Exhibitions: (1979) A Nexus Surprise; 500 Exposition Gallery Dallas Texas; membership exhibitions, group and student shows
Activities: Classes; lect open to public, 5 or more visiting lectr per year; concerts; gallery talks; tours upon request; internship

FREE LIBRARY OF PHILADELPHIA

L **Art Department,** Logan Square, 19103. Tel 215-686-5403. *Dir Library* Keith Doms; *Head Art Dept* Miriam L Lesley
Open Mon - Wed 9 AM - 9 PM, Thurs - Fri 9 AM - 6 PM, Sat 9 AM - 5 PM, Sun 1 - 5 PM. Estab 1891, art department estab 1896, to serve the citizens of the City of Philadelphia. Circ 39,000
Income: Financed by endowment, city and state appropriations
Purchases: $30,540
Library Holdings: Vols 150,000; Per subs 193; Micro—Fiche, reels; Other—Clipping files, exhibition catalogs, memorabilia, pamphlets
Collections: 18th and 19th century architectural pattern books; Index of exhibition catalogs of The Pennsylvania Academy of the Fine Arts 1870 to date; John Frederick Lewis Collection of books on fine prints and printmaking; 368 original measured drawings of colonial Philadelphia buildings, Philadelphia Chapter, American Institute of Architects

L **Print and Picture Department,** Room 211, 19101. Tel 215-686-5405. *Head* Robert F Looney
Open 9 AM - 5 PM, cl Sun; also cl Sat June - Sept. Estab 1954 by combining the Print Department and the Picture Collection
Collections: (non-circulating) Americana (1200); Hampton L Carson Collection of Napoleonic prints (3400); †graphic arts (2000); †greeting and tradesmen's cards (27,000); †John Frederick Lewis Collection of portrait prints (211,000); †Philadelphiana (8000). (circulating) picture collection of pictures in all media and universal in subject coverage (500,000)
Exhibitions: Bendiner Collection International; Samuel Castner Collection of Philadelphia (scrapbooks, prints, drawings, photographs, clippings); Rosenthal Collection, American; prints, original drawings

L **Rare Book Department,** Third Floor, 19103. Tel 215-686-5416. *Rare Book Librn* Howell J Heaney
Open Mon - Sat 9 AM - 5 PM. Estab 1949
Collections: American Sunday-School Union Historical Collection; Alfred Bendiner Collection of 300 caricatures, prints and drawings; Early American children's books including Rosenbach Collection (1682-1836); Elisabeth Ball Collection of Horn books; †Borneman and Yoder Collection of Pennsylvania German Fraktur; Hampton L Carson Collection of legal prints; Frederick R Gardner Collection of Robert Lawson original drawings; Kate Greenaway; early American prints and engravings; Grace Clark Haskell Collection of Arthur Rackham; John Frederick Lewis Collection consisting of cuneiform tablets and seals, Babylonian and Sumerian, †Medieval and Renaissance manuscripts, and miniatures, Oriental manuscripts and miniatures (mostly Mughul, Rajput and Persian); Thornton Oakley Collection consisting of †Howard Pyle and His School, books and original drawings; †Beatrix Potter; Evan Randolph Collection consisting of angling prints from the 17th to the 20th century, and †prints of Philadelphia from 1800-1950; and †original drawings, paintings, prints and other illustrative material relating to the works of Dickens, Goldsmith and Thackeray

O **HISTORICAL SOCIETY OF PENNSYLVANIA,** 1300 Locust St, 19107. Tel 215-732-6200. *Pres* Harold D Saylor; *VPres* Thomas C Cochran; *VPres* Caroline Robbins; *VPres* Allyn R Bell; *Secy* Harold H Lewis; *Dir* James E Mooney; *Chief Manuscript* Peter J Parker; *Head Librn* John H Platt; *Asst Treas* Patricia H Bullock
Open Mon 1 - 9 PM, Tues - Fri 9 AM - 5 PM. Admis $1 to library and manuscript department; no admis fee to museum. Estab 1824 to collect and preserve records relating primarily to Pennsylvania history; also collects various artifacts and paintings of persons relevant to Pennsylvania history. Art gallery is comprised of four exhibit rooms: two contain changing exhibits from the collections; and two serve as meeting rooms and contain numerous early American paintings and furniture. Mem: 3350; dues $15; meetings four per year
Income: Financed by endowment and membership
Collections: Unmatched collection of papers, prints, paintings, furniture, household and personal effects from pre-Revolution through 1800; more than 800 paintings and miniatures by early American artists Birch, Copley, Inman, Neagle, Peale, Stuart, Sully, Wright and others; more than 14 million manuscripts
Publications: The Pennsylvania Magazine of History and Biography, quarterly
Activities: Lect for members, 4 visiting lectr per year; individual paintings and original art objects lent primarily to other museums

C **INA CORPORATION,** 1600 Arch St, PO Box 7728, 19101. Tel 215-241-4894. *Dir & Cur* Debra J Force
Lobbies open Mon - Fri 8 AM - 5 PM; Gallery by appointment. No admis fee. Organized in 1926 to preserve the company's interest in its history through the collection of marine, fire, and Americana objects. Collection displayed in Lobbies, Gallery and throughout buildings. Lobbies of 2 buildings have artifacts in cases and on mounts; Gallery has artifacts on walls and hanging on movable cabinets which are also storage units
Collections: Fire: fire marks, full-size apparatus, equipment, models, prints; INA-related: furniture, manuscripts, portraits; Marine: figureheads, paintings, ship models
Activities: Lect; tours; individual objects of art lent (about one-third of collection) throughout the United States

M **INDEPENDENCE NATIONAL HISTORICAL PARK,** 313 Walnut St, 19106. Tel 215-597-7132. *Supt* Hobart G Cawood; *Asst Supt* Bernard Goodman; *Chief Park Historian* Martin I Yoelson; *Chief Cur* John C Milley
Open daily 9 AM - 5 PM. No admis fee. Estab 1948 to preserve and protect for the American people, historical structures, properties and other resources of outstanding national significance, and associated with the Revolution and growth of the Nation. Average Annual Attendance: 3,500,000. Mem: 1600; dues $15; annual meeting May
Income: Financed by membership and federal grant
Collections: 18th century American period furnishings; decorative arts; American portraits from 1728-1830
Publications: Friends of Independence NHP Newsletter
Activities: Classes for children; docent training; lect for members; gallery talks; tours; individual paintings and original objects or art lent to qualified professional institutions; museum shop selling books, magazines, reproductions, prints, slides

L **Library,** 120 S Third St, 19106.
Open to public Mon - Fri 8 AM - 4:30 PM
Library Holdings: Vols 5500; Per subs 23; Micro—Reels; AV—Motion pictures, slides, v-tapes; Other—Pamphlets, photographs
Collections: Decorative arts of Philadelphia and Pennsylvania for the 18th century

M **LA SALLE COLLEGE ART GALLERY,** 20th & Olney Ave, 19141. Tel 215-951-1221. *Cur* Thomas Ridington; *Asst Cur* Caroline Wistar
Open Mon - Fri 11 AM - 3 PM, Sun 2 - 4 PM. No admis fee. Estab 1975 for educational purposes and to house the collection begun in 1965, also as support for the art history program and as a service to the community. Gallery has several large spaces set up to suggest various centuries and to contain paintings of the period
Income: Financed by endowment
Collections: 15th through 20th century paintings, drawings, watercolors and prints; Western art, European and American, with a few pieces of sculpture and decorative art
Exhibitions: Two special exhibitions are held each semester
Publications: Exhibition brochures
Activities: Concerts; gallery talks; tours by appointment with gallery staff

L **Library,** 20th & Olney Ave, 19141.
Open to visitors, for reference only
Collections: Books illustrated with portrait prints; portrait collection; rare Bible collection, 15th - 20th century

L **LIBRARY COMPANY OF PHILADELPHIA,** 1314 Locust St, 19107. Tel 215-516-3181. *Librn* Edwin Wolf II; *Asst Librn* Gordon Marshall; *Cur of Printed Books* Marie Korey; *Cur of Prints* Kenneth Finkel; *Chief of Reference* Phillip Lapsansky
Open Mon - Fri 9 AM - 4:45 PM. No admis fee. Estab 1731 for the purpose of scholarly research. Average Annual Attendance: 2000. Mem: 620; dues $8; annual meeting first Mon May
Income: Financed by endowment, membership, city appropriation, and federal grants
Collections: †American Printing; †Philadelphia prints, watercolors, drawings and photography; collection of Americana

Exhibitions: (1978) À Pride of Acquisition, 1953-1978
Publications: Annual Report; Occasional Miscellany, 2-4 times per year

M **MOORE COLLEGE OF ART GALLERY,** 20th & Race Sts, 19104. Tel 215-568-4515. *Gallery Dir* Helen Williams Drutt
Open Mon - Fri 9 AM - 4:30 PM. No admis fee. Estab 1831 to offer the Philadelphia community and its students the opportunity to view contemporary artwork that is usually not available locally. Gallery is housed in moderate exhibition space with flexible panels to accommodate current exhibit. Average Annual Attendance: 5000
Income: Financed by endowment
Collections: Joseph Moore Jr, Library & Artifacts
Exhibitions: (1978) Pennsylvania Quilts, One Hundred Years. (1979) Robert Arneson: Self Portraits; Ruth Duckworth and Claire Zeisler
Publications: Bulletins, irregularly; Catalogs for major exhibitions
Activities: Classes for adults and children; lect open to the public, 16 visiting lectr per year; traveling exhibitions organized and circulated

L **Library,** 20th & Race Sts, 19104. *Librn* Marjorie Bilk
Open Mon - Thurs 8 AM - 9:30 PM, Fri 8 AM - 5 PM, Sat 8:30 AM - 1 PM. Estab to serve Moore students. For reference only
Purchases: $26,000
Library Holdings: Vols 32,000; Per subs 200; AV—Slides; Other—Clipping files, exhibition catalogs

M **MUSE ART GALLERY,** 1915 Walnut St, 19103. Tel 215-963-0959. *Dir* Carol Seitchik
Open Tues - Sun 11 AM - 5 PM. No admis fee. Estab 1977, gallery provides a professional opportunity and place for qualified women artists to exhibit their work and let it speak for itself. Average Annual Attendance: 5500. Mem: 20, qualifications: highly qualified professional women artists who are juried by members; dues $300; monthly meetings first or second Sun
Income: Financed by membership, NEA grants and Pennyslvania State Council of the Arts
Publications: Bi-annual bulletins announcing catalogue, MUSE
Activities: Docent training; workshops; student interns, volunteers group; lect open to public, 6 visiting lectr per year; slide presentations; poetry readings; gallery talks; tours; competitions; lending collection contains slides; originate traveling exhibitions; original art for sale

M **MUSEUM OF THE PHILADELPHIA CIVIC CENTER,** Civic Center Blvd at 34th St, 19104. Tel 215-823-7201. *Chmn Board* Open; *Exec Dir* Open; *Asst Dir* Ronald L Barber; *Chief Cur* Robert Nobel; *Registrar* Robert Carter; *Design Dir* Zenon L Fesczak; *Cur Educ* Edward Grusheski; *Promotion & Publicity Specialist* Henry Spector
Open Tues - Sat 9 AM - 5 PM, Sun 1 - 5 PM, cl Mon and legal holidays. No admis fee. Estab 1894 to present exhibitions of contemporary local, national and international art, craft, photography and design. Average Annual Attendance: 200,000
Income: Financed by city appropriation
Collections: Latin American crafts; New Caledonian ethnographic material; Oriental and African crafts; Philippine ethnographic collection; Southeastern Siberian ethnographic collection
Exhibitions: Changing exhibitions of contemporary local, national and international art, craft, design and photography
Activities: Classes for children; lect for scheduled school class only; suitcase exhibits on foreign countries loaned to schools

M **PENNSYLVANIA ACADEMY OF THE FINE ARTS,** Broad & Cherry Sts, 19102. Tel 215-972-7600. *Dir* Richard J Boyle; *Cur* Frank H Goodyear Jr; *Admin* Harvey Gold; *Pres & Chmn of Board* Henry McNeil; *Development* Elaine Breslow; *Public Information* Susan Rappaport; *Membership* Josephine Evans; *Museum Educ* Elizabeth Kolowrat
Open Tues - Sat 10 AM - 5 PM, Sun 1 - 5 PM. Admis adults $1, children under 12 years, students, senior citizens 50¢. Estab 1805 by C W Peale, Thos Sully, Benj West, et al, to cultivate collecting, training, and development of the fine arts in America. The Academy building, opened in 1876, was restored for the American Bicentennial. Considered the masterpiece of its architect, Philadelphian Frank Furness, its style is called, alternately, polychrome picturesque and High or Gothic Victorian. It was designated a Registered National Historic Landmark in 1975. The Peale House and Morris Galleries are maintained for exhibitions of contemporary artists. Average Annual Attendance: 90,000. Mem: 3100; dues $15 and up
Income: Financed by endowment, membership, city and state appropriation, contributions and federal grants
Collections: American Contemporary Works; the collections excel in 18th and 29th century American paintings, sculpture, drawings and prints. Allston, West, the Peale family, Stuart, Sully, Rush and Neagle are represented in important works
Exhibitions: (1978) The Last Three Years; A Selection of Recent Acquisitions; The Travel Sketches of Louis I Kahn; Contemporary Drawings, Philadelphia, Part I; as well as exhibitions of works by contemporary artists, John Dowell, Martha Erlebacher, David Fertig, Eileen Goodman, Jo Hanson, Valerie Jaudon, Don Lantzy, Deryl Mackie, Edith Neff, David Pease, Phil Simkin, Dennis Will. (1979) Artist and Teacher, Faculty Exhibition; The Private Eye; Seven on the Figure: Jack Beal, William Beckman, Joan Brown, John DeAndrea, Willem de Kooning Stephen DeStaebler, Ben Kamihira; Arlene Love; Hitoshi Nakazota; Cynthia Carlson; Isaiah Zagar. (1980) Washington Allston: Man of Genius; 79th Annual Student Exhibition; Daniel Garber; James Wyeth; (Morris Galleries) Diane Burko; Ray Metzker, Sand Creatures, Photographs; Jody Pinto; Robert Younger; Barbara Zucker
Publications: Annual report; exhibition and school catalogues; In This Academy (newspaper), three times yearly
Activities: Lect; concerts; tours; traveling exhibitions organized and circulated; museum shop sells toys, calendars, catalogs, art books, posters, postcards, notecards, reproductions and slides from collections; beautifully illustrated children's books, all with a focus on American art

L **Library,** Broad & Cherry Sts, 19102. Tel 215-972-7611. *Librn* Marietta P Bushnell
Open Mon - Fri 9 AM - 4:30 PM during school term to students, and by appointment. Estab 1805, the Library serves students of painting, sculpture and print making, and is intended as a source of visual inspiration

Income: Financed by school funds
Library Holdings: Vols 5000; Per subs 30; Other—Clipping files, exhibition catalogs

L **Archives Library,** Broad & Cherry Sts, 19102. Tel 215-972-7641.
By appointment only

O **Fellowship of the Pennsylvania Academy of the Fine Arts,** The Peale House, 1811 Chestnut St, 19103. Tel 215-299-5083. *Pres* Dorothy Pere; *Secy* Lucy Glick; *Treas* L A D Montgomery
Estab 1897 to provide opportunities for creative incentive and sharing in responsibilities for the development of facilities and activities in the field of art for its members and to maintain relations with the students of the Pennsylvania Academy of the Fine Arts. Mem: 700; dues $6, nonresident $3; meetings held Sept, Oct, Feb and May
Income: Approx $3000
Collections: Paintings and sculpture
Exhibitions: Annual Fellowship Show; Student Show; Faculty Show; Franklin Drake; Eiko Fan; Charles Kalick; Stan Merz; Harry Rosin; Saul Schary; Reve Schley; Jim Victor
Activities: Classes; lect; films; individual paintings and objects of art lent

O **PHILADELPHIA ART ALLIANCE,** 251 S 18th St, 19103. Tel 215-515-4302. *Chmn of the Board* Arthur Klein; *Pres* George A D'Angelo; *VPres in Charge Art* Dr Suzanne Horvitz; *Dir* James Boatner
Open Mon - Fri 10:30 AM - 5 PM, Sat & Sun 1 - 5 PM. No admis fee. Estab 1915, a unique, educational and cultural organization catering to all the arts: music, drama, painting, sculpture, prints, design, literary arts, illustration, architecture, photography. Galleries open free to members, guests and the public. Average Annual Attendance: 100,000. Mem: Approx 2400 individuals and organizations; dues from $20; annual meeting Mar
Publications: The Art Alliance Bulletin, published 9 times a year, Oct to May; Philadelphia Art Alliance Press publishes 3 or 4 art-related volumes, annually
Activities: Restaurant for members and guests

O **PHILADELPHIA ART COMMISSION,*** 1329 City Hall Annex, 19107. Tel 215-686-4470. *Pres* F Eugene Dixon Jr; *Exec Dir* Beverly T Volk
Open 8:30 AM - 5 PM. No admis fee. Estab 1911 under Philadelphia Home Rule Charter as the Art Jury, later retitled Art Commission. An Art Ordinance passed in 1959 provides for art work in city buildings and on city owned property. The Art Commission reviews architectural designs and art work covering all media for municipal locations or other locations in which municipal funds are expended. The Art Commission's files are open to inspection by anyone since the information contained therein qualifies as public information. As indicated, the material deals solely with art proposals and architectural designs. Designs cover all buildings, major highways, and bridges. Mem: 9; between 20 and 24 meetings annually
Income: Financed by city appropriation

M **PHILADELPHIA COLLEGE OF ART GALLERY,** Broad & Spruce Sts, 19102. Tel 215-893-3100. *Pres* Thomas F Schutte; *Dean of Faculty* Nathan Knobler
Open Mon - Fri 9 AM - 5 PM. No admis fee. Estab 1876 to prepare artists and designers for careers in business, industry, education and the fine arts. Gallery's varied exhibition program serves to stimulate its own community as well as the general public. The work of younger but innovative, recognized artists is featured
Income: Financed by endowment and city and state appropriation
Exhibitions: African Masks, Variations on a Theme, selections from the collection of Prof James E Lewis; Alumni Show, Olaf Skoogfors, Metalsmither; Art-Play-Design, Anne and Patrick Poirier; The Hand Colored Photograph, Words and Images, Paul Rand
Publications: Alumni Magazine, twice yearly; catalogs accompany each gallery exhibition

L **Library,** Broad & Spruce Sts, 19102. Tel 215-893-3126. *Library Dir* Hazel Gustow; *Readers' Services Librn* Martha Hall
Open Mon - Thurs 8:15 AM - 1 PM, Fri 8:15 AM - 8 PM, Sat 9 AM - 1 PM; (shorter hours during the summer). Estab 1876 to assist the art community in general and cooperate actively with other libraries. Circ 41,000
Library Holdings: Vols 44,000; Per subs 181; Micro—Fiche, reels; AV—A-tapes, cassettes, motion pictures, rec, slides; Other—Clipping files, exhibition catalogs, pamphlets, photographs, reproductions
Special Subjects: Visual Arts, particularly contemporary

M **PHILADELPHIA COLLEGE OF TEXTILES AND SCIENCE,** Paley Design Center, 4200 Henry Ave, 19144. Tel 215-843-9700, Ext 360, 843-9715 (weekends). *Dir* Patricia Chapin O'Donnell; *Registrar* Jean Mapes; *Cur* Leanna Lee Whitman; *Gallery Coordr* Maureen Roberts
Open Mon - Sat 10 AM - 4 PM, cl holidays. Estab 1978 to provide a study collection of textiles and related materials as a design resource. Average Annual Attendance: 3000
Library Holdings: Other—Manuscripts
Special Subjects: 19th and 20th Century design
Collections: Historic and contemporary textiles 5th - 20th Centuries, International; Fabric Library, 19th and 20th Centuries, American and Western European; manuscripts, records, textile fibers, tools, and related materials
Exhibitions: Works from permanent collection; local artists and designers of international repute

M **PHILADELPHIA MARITIME MUSEUM,** 321 Chestnut St, 19106. Tel 215-925-5439. *Pres* J Welles Henderson; *Dir* Richard K Page; *Asst Dir* Howard J Taylor; *Registrar* John Groff; *Teacher* William Ward
Open Mon - Sat 9 AM - 5 PM, Sun 1 - 5 PM. No admis fee; small donation requested. Estab 1960 to preserve and interpret the maritime heritage of the Bay and River Delaware, and the Port of Philadelphia. Gallery 1, Man and the Sea, general maritime history; Gallery 2, Man under the Sea, history of underwater technology; Gallery 3, Waterway of History, history of Bay and River Delaware and Port of Philadelphia; Gallery 4, changing exhibits. Average Annual Attendance: 40,000. Mem: 900; dues $10 minimum; annual meeting May
Income: $800,000 (financed by endowment, membership and private and corporate gifts)
Purchases: $40,000
Collections: †Paintings by major American marine artists; Philadelphia Views; †17th-20th century maritime prints; small craft; sailing vessel, 177 ft Gazela

Primeiro, built 1883
Publications: Annual Report; books and catalogs, intermittently; Spindrift (newsletter), quarterly
Activities: Classes for adults and children; lect for members only, 10 visiting lectr per year; concerts; gallery talks; competitions; individual paintings and original objects of art lent to recognized non-profit museums with adequate facilities and pertinent need, six month only; lending collection contains books, kodachromes, 150 lantern slides, 10 motion pictures, 50 original art works, 900 original prints, 80 paintings, 1200 photographs, 1500 slides; museum shop selling books, magazines, reproductions, prints, postcards, models and souvenirs

L **Library,** 321 Chestnut St, 19106. *Librn* Dorothy Mueller
Open to members and scholars, for reference only
Library Holdings: Vols 5000; Per subs 20; Other—Manuscripts, rare books and maps
Special Subjects: General maritime history and technology, Lloyds Register of Ships, 1880 to present, Philadelphia and Delaware Valley history
Collections: Nautical Artifacts and Decorative Arts (navigation instruments, China trade items)

M **PHILADELPHIA MUSEUM OF ART,** 26th and Parkway, Box 7646, 19101. Tel 215-763-8100. *Pres* William P Wood; *Chmn* Henry P McIllhenny; *Dir* Jean Sutherland Boggs; *Asst Dir* Noble Smith; *Asst Dir* Laurence Snyder; *Asst Dir* Carl Colozzi; *Cur 20th Century Art* Anne d'Harnoncourt; *Cur Decorative Arts: Medieval & Renaissance* David T Dubon; *Cur American Art* Darrel Sewell; *Cur Paintings before 1900* Joseph Rishel; *Cur European Decorative Arts after 1700* Kathryn Heisinger; *Cur Far Eastern Art* Jean Gordon Lee; *Cur Emeritus Indian Art* Stella Kramrisch; *Cur Prints, Drawings & Photographs* Kneeland McNulty; *Cur Costume & Textiles* Adolph Cavallo; *Advisor Alfred Stieglitz Center* Michael Hoffman; *Conservator* Marigene Butler; *Chief Division Educ* Theodore Katz; *Registrar* Barbara Chandler; *Public Relations Mgr* Sandra Horrocks; *Mgr Museum Shop* Kathleen O'Neill; *Publicity Editor* George Marcus; *Park Houses* Charlotte Shapiro; *Vol Guides Coordr* Caroline Thierman Gladstone; *Annual Giving Coordr* Melanie Yulman
Open daily 10 AM - 5 PM. Admis adults $1.50, children, senior citizens, art students 75¢, under 5 years free. Estab 1876 as an art museum and for art education; known as Pennsylvania Museum of Art until the present name was adopted in 1938. Buildings owned by the City, opened 1928; wings 1931 and 1940; Fashion Galleries 1949, 1951 and 1953; Gallatin and Arensberg Collections 1954; Far Eastern Wing 1957; Decorative Arts Galleries 1958; Charles Patterson Van Pelt Auditorium 1959; Napalese-Tibetan Gallery 1960; New Galleries of Italian and French Renaissance Art 1960; new American Wing and Kienbusch Armor Collection. Museum contains 250 Galleries. Average Annual Attendance: 600,000. Mem: 18,000; dues family $30, individual $20; annual meeting Oct
Income: $5,906,548 (financed by endowment, membership, city and state appropriations, grants and bequests)
Purchases: $137,669
Collections: The general history of American, Eastern and European art since the beginning of the Christian era is covered. Included are: American and European period rooms; art from India; Chinese palace hall, temple and scholar's study; 18th century French work; a French Renaissance choir screen; Gothic chapel; an Indian temple; Japanese temple and teahouse; 19th and 20th century art (the Gallatin Arensburg, Tyson, White and Stern Collections); Old Masters Collection (including †Wilstach, Elkins, McFadden, and John G Johnson Collections); Romanesque cloister and facade; Sasanian units from Iran; sculpture, with an emphasis on medieval Renaissance work; The American Art Galleries contain architectural elements; Philadelphia furniture and silver; Tucker Porcelain Collection; Stiegel Glass Collection; Geesey Collection of Pennsylvania Dutch folk art; Barberini-Kress Foundation Tapestry Series (The History of Constantine the Great). The Italian and French Renaissance Art Collections (housed in the Italian and French Renaissance Art Galleries) include architectural elements, furniture bronzes and decorative arts (from the Edmund Foule and other Collections); The Nepalese-Tibetan Gallery houses the Nepalese-Tibetan Collection; the Crozier Collection (imported Persian and Chinese art
Exhibitions: Kienbusch Collection of Arms & Armor; three centuries of American Art
Publications: Bulletin, quarterly; Engagement Calendar, annually; exhibitions catalogs; newsletter, monthly
Activities: Classes for adults and children; dramatic programs; docent training; lect open to public, 20 visiting lectr per year; concerts; gallery talks; tours; exten dept serving all Philadelphia communities; artmobile; traveling exhibitions organized and circulated; museum shop selling books, magazines, original art, reproductions, prints, slides, jewelry, needlework, and postcards; junior museum

M **Rodin Museum,** 22nd & Benjamin Franklin Parkway, Box 7646, 19101.
Open Tues - Sun 10 AM - 5 PM, cl holidays. Admis by donation. Estab 1928 as an art museum of Rodin works. Rodin Museum houses one of the largest collections outside of Paris of works by the major late 19th Century French sculptor, Auguste Rodin. Average Annual Attendance: 30,000
Income: Financed through Museum
Collections: Collection includes many of the most famous subjects created by Rodin, as well as drawings, prints, letters, books and a variety of documentary material
Activities: Classes for adults and children; dramatic programs; docent training; lect open to public, 35-40 visiting lectr per year; concerts; gallery talks; tours; individual paintings and original objects of art lent to museums for exhibitions; originate traveling exhibitions; museum shop sells books, reproductions, prints, slides, jewelry, cards, glass, ceramics and memorabilia

M **Mount Pleasant,** Fairmount Park, 19101.
Open daily except Mon, cl major holidays. Admis adults 50¢, children 25¢. Built 1761, an elaborate example of 18th century building and carving; a perfect model of Georgian symmetry. Some of the finest achievements of the master craftsmen in the Philadelphia area are well preserved in the boldly ornate woodwork and Chippendale style furnishings
Collections: Contents of the house from the Museum represent the elegant way of life in Philadelphia in the 1760's

M **Cedar Grove,** Lansdowne Dr, Fairmount Park, 19101.
Open Wed - Mon 10 AM - 5 PM, cl Tues. Admis adults 50¢, children 25¢. Built in 1740's, a country farmhouse for Elizabeth Coates Paschall. The house was enlarged in the 1790's and a piazza added in the 1840's. In 1926, Lydia Thompson Morris, fifth generation owner of Cedar Grove, had the house dismantled stone by stone and moved to Fairmount Park as her gift to the city
Collections: The furniture was given with the house and reflects changes in styles through the 17th, 18th and 19th centuries

M **John Graver Johnson Collection,** Parkway & 25th St, 19101. Tel 215-763-8100, Ext 249. *Cur* Joseph J Rishel
Open daily 10 AM - 5 PM. Admis to Philadelphia Museum of Art $1.50. Upon his death in 1917, prominent Philadelphia l lawyer, John Graver Johnson left his extensive collection intact to the people of Philadelphia; since 1933 the collection has been housed in the Philadelphia Museum of Art; administration and trusteeship of the collection is maintained separately from the other collections in the museum
Collections: Early and later Italian Renaissance paintings; French 19th century paintings; northern European schools of Flanders, Holland and Germany in the 15th, 16th and 17th century
Publications: Several catalogs for various parts of the collection including Catalog of Italian Paintings and Catalog of Flemish and Dutch Paintings
Activities: Special lect and related activities; occasional lending of collection to significant exhibitions

L **John Cramer Johnson Collection Library,** Parkway & 25th St, 19101.
For reference only
Library Holdings: Vols 4500; Other—rare sales catalogues

M **Samuel S Fleisher Art Memorial,** 719 Catharine St, 19147. Tel 215-922-3456. *Chmn* Mrs Stuart F Louchheim; *Treas* George B Clothier; *Adminr* Thora E Jacobson
Open during exhibitions Mon - Fri 10 AM - 4 PM, Mon - Thurs 7 - 9:30 PM, Sat 1 - 3 PM. No admis fee. Estab 1898 as a free art school and sanctury (Museum of Religious Art). It is housed in an Italian Romanesque Revival building; Gallery is primarily used for school-related exhibitions, also for special shows of contemporary artists
Income: $160,000 (financed by endowment)
Collections: Medieval and Renaissance religious paintings and sculpture; 18th - 19th century Portuguese liturgical objects; 17th - 20th century Russian icons; 20th century paintings and prints; some sculpture
Exhibitions: Annual student, faculty, adult and childrens' exhibitions
Activities: Classes for adults and children; lect open to the public; concerts; gallery talks; original objects of art lent; traveling exhibitions organized and circulated

L **Marian Angell Boyer and Francis Boyer Library,** Philadelphia Museum of Art, PO Box 7646, 19101. Tel 215-763-8100, Ext 229. *Librn* Barbara Sevy; *Asst Librn & Archivist* Merle Chamberlain
Open Tues, Wed, Fri 10 AM - 4 PM. Estab 1876, as a research source for Museum staff, and to serve the public three days per week. For reference only
Income: $83,000
Purchases: $16,500 (plus $5,000 endowment and gifts)
Library Holdings: Vols 100,000; Per subs 500; Micro—Fiche, reels; AV—Slides; Other—Clipping files, exhibition catalogs, pamphlets
Special Subjects: Decorative Arts, Drawings, Photography, Prints, 20th century art
Collections: Art auction sale catalogs; Kienbusch collection of arms and armor; Museum archives

O **Women's Committee,** 19101. *Pres* Mrs Stanley Root
Estab 1877, incorporated 1915; takes an active interest in the Museum. Organization sponsors art sales and rental; Park Houses; volunteer guides; craft show and blind program

O **PHILADELPHIA SKETCH CLUB INC,** 235 S Camac St, 19107. Tel 215-545-9298. *Pres* Herbert E Armstrong; *VPres* Frank R Nicosia; *Secy* John V Baltadonis; *Treas* Frank R Davis
Open Wed - Sun 1 - 5PM. No admis fee. Estab 1860 for artistic practice, exhibitions, and education as well as social functions. Club owns building and maintains sky-lit gallery on the second floor; dimensions approximately 30 x 42 ft. Average Annual Attendance: 3000. Mem: 100; dues $80; monthly meeting on first Fri
Income: Financed by endowment, and membership
Collections: Forty Thomas Anshutz Portraits; J Pennell Citiscapes; deceased members collection
Exhibitions: Annual Children's Show; Annual Invitational; Annual Members Show (Guildmasters Presentation); Small Oil (117th Annual); 10 exhibitions yearly
Publications: The Portfolio, (bulletin), monthly
Activities: Classes for adults and children from Sept - June; lect open to the public, 8 visiting lectr per year; gallery talks; competitions with cash prizes, purchase awards and certificates; individual paintings and original objects of art lent on a very limited basis; lending collection contains books, original art works, original prints, paintings

L **Library,** 235 S Camac St, 19107.
Open by special permission of the Board
Library Holdings: Vols 1000

O **PLASTIC CLUB,** Art Club for Women, 247 S Comac St, 19107. Tel 215-515-9324. *Acting Pres* Mary Bolden; *VPres* Mrs George Taylor; *Secy* Isabel Stone; *Treas* Sara Sharpe; *Finance* Mrs Wallace Jones; *House Chmn* Mrs William Gibson
Open Mon 10 AM - 3 PM, Tues 10 AM - 2 PM, Wed 10 AM - 3 PM. Estab 1897 to promote wider knowledge of art and to advance its interest among artists. Art gallery maintained in small club house. Mem: 70; must qualify for membership by submitting three framed paintings or two sculptures to be juried; annual meeting first Wed May
Income: Financed by membership and money-making projects
Exhibitions: Monthly exhibitions of paintings by members
Activities: Lect open to public and members; gallery talks; competitions with cash awards and medals; individual paintings lent to hospitals and public buildings; sales shop selling books, original art and small craft items

M **PLEASE TOUCH MUSEUM,** 1910 Cherry St, 19103. Tel 215-963-0666, 567-5551. *Chmn* Carol Anne Spielma; *Vice Chmn* Richard Ferst; *Secy* Dr R M Klein; *Executive Dir* Portra Sperr; *Admin Dir* Patricia Foley; *Development Dir* Donald Smith III; *Dir Education* Carol Krause; *Cur* Lorraine Minott
Open Tues - Sat 10 AM - 4:30 PM, Sun 1:30 - 4:30 PM. Admis $1.50, children 7 years and younger $1. Estab 1976 to provide a developmentally appropriate museum for young children, their parents and teachers. Gallery spaces are small-scaled, objects are accessible; dual interpretation is being developed for use by adults and children (arts, crafts, ethnic materials and exhibits). Average Annual

Attendance: 100,000. Mem: 400; dues family $25; annual meeting second Thurs in April
Income: $160,000 (financed by membership, state appropriation, admissions, foundation and corporate support)
Purchases: $5000
Collections: †Costumes, †playthings and †toys from world wide ethnic groups
Exhibitions: Artists for Young Children; Thematic exhibits are changed semi-annually; (1979) Places; The Sky's the Limit; (1980) The Built Environment; Children of India
Publications: Newsletters, quarterly; thematic exhibition catalogs, bi-annually; follow-through materials for groups and parents
Activities: Classes for adults and children; docent training; work with area colleges and art schools; coop programs; lect open to public; workshops for teachers; tours; competitions; exten dept serves other junior museums; museum shop sells books, games, toys reflecting the museum's focus

O **PRESBYTERIAN HISTORICAL SOCIETY,** 425 Lombard St, 19147. Tel 215-627-1852. *Pres* Dr R Douglas Brackenridge; *Mgr* William B Miller; *Records Researcher* Jane Ramsay; *Treas* H Woodward McDowell; *Research Historian* Gerald W Gillette; *Catalog Librn* Barbara Roy
Open Mon - Fri 9 AM - 5 PM. No admis fee. Estab May 1852 to collect and preserve official records and memorabilia of the United Presbyterian Church, its predecessors nd affiliates. Portraits displayed in the Reading Room, Mackie Room, Board Room and hallways. Six Calder statues representing American Presbyterian personalities who played a significant role in the history of the Church are displayed outside in front of the building. Average Annual Attendance: 1200. Mem: 1250; dues $10; annual meeting first Fri Mar
Income: $226,000 (financed by membership and General Assembly)
Collections: Church plates; relics; silver and pewter communionware
Publications: Journal of Presbyterian History, quarterly
Activities: Tours
L **Library,** 425 Lombard St, 19147. *Librn* William B Miller
Open to the public for reference
Library Holdings: Vols 130,000; Per subs 800; Other—Manuscripts 3,000,000
Collections: Jackson Collection; National Council of Churches Collection; Scotch-Irish Society Archives; Shane Collection

PRINT CLUB
For further information, see National and Regional Organizations

M **THE ROSENBACH MUSEUM AND LIBRARY,** (Formerly Philip H & A S W Rosenbach Foundation Museum) 2010 DeLancey Place, 19103. Tel 215-732-1600. *Dir* Suzanne Bolan; *Asst Dir* Walter C Johnson; *Cur Arts* Arline Segal; *Cur Education* Barbara A Nashner
Open daily 11 AM - 4 PM except Mon, open to scholars 10 AM - 5 PM, cl August and national holidays. Admis adults $1.50, students 75¢, groups of 8 or more $1 per person. exhibit only 75¢. Estab 1953 as a nonprofit corporation
Collections: 18th century English antiques and silver, paintings, prints and drawings, porcelain, rugs and objets d'art; rare books and manuscripts, consisting of British and American literature, Americana, and book illustrations; 130,000 manuscripts; 30,000 books, Marianne Moore Archive
Exhibitions: (1978) Alice Returns to Wonderland: Lewis Caroll; John Bunyan and The Pilgrim's Progress; Letters of Love. (1979) Dear Julia, or The True and Revealing History of the Family Fortunes of Benjamin Franklin, Dr Rush, Jonathan Williams and the Biddles (written by themselves); Treasures of a Quarter Century. (1980) In Her Own Image; Photographers, Sculptors and Painters View Marianne Moore
Publications: A Selection from Our Shelves; Fantasy Sketches; Lewis Carroll's Photographs of Nude Children; Marianne Moore Newsletter

M **ROBERT W RYERSS LIBRARY AND MUSEUM,** Burholme Park, Central & Cottman Aves, 19111. Tel 215-745-3061. *Park Historian & Admin Supv* John McIlhenny
Open Wed - Sun 10 AM - 5 PM. No admiss fee. Estab 1910. House (Historic Register) left to City complete with contents in 1905; two period rooms; three other museum rooms with art objects - predominately Victorian. Average Annual Attendance: 20,000. Mem: 75; dues $3; meeting first Mon every month
Income: $17,000 (financed by endowment, city appropriation and trust fund)
Collections: Static collection; export china, ivory, paintings, period rooms, prints, sculpture, weapons
Activities: Tours; lending collection contains 12,000 books
L **Library,** Burholme Park, Central & Cottman Aves, Philadelphia, PA 19111. *Librn & Facility Supv* Mary L Campbell
Open Wed - Sun 10 AM - 5 PM. Estab 1910. Victoriana Collection available to scholars by appointment only
Library Holdings: Vols 20,000; Per subs 40; AV—Cassettes, fs, slides; Other—Framed reproductions, prints, memorabilia, original art works, photographs, sculpture
Collections: Victoriana

SOCIETY OF ARCHITECTURAL HISTORIANS
For further information, see National and Regional Organizations

TEMPLE UNIVERSITY
M **Tyler School of Art-Galleries,** Beech and Penrose Ave, 19126. Tel 215-224-7575. *Dean* David Pease; *Gallery Dir* Richard Cramer
Open daily 11 AM - 5 PM (while in session). No admis fee. Estab to present work in visual arts to students and the Philadelphia area. Three galleries (Elkins, Tyler, Penrose); track lighting, each gallery approximately 30 x 40 ft. Average Annual Attendance: 7000
Income: Financed by state appropriation and grants
Exhibitions: Intricate Structure: Repeated Image; Philadelphia Clay Today; Polish Glass; Graduate and Undergraduate exhibits
Publications: Posters; announcements for most exhibits; catalogs for major shows
Activities: Lectures open to the public, 4 - 10 visiting lecturers per year; concerts; gallery talks

L **Tyler School of Art Library,** Beech and Penrose Ave, 19126. Tel 215-224-7575, Ext 245. *Librn* Ivy Bayard
Open Mon - Thurs 8:30 AM - 9 PM, Fri 8:30 AM - 6 PM, Sat 9 AM - 5 PM, Sun 1 - 9 PM. Estab 1934 to provide library services to students and faculty. Circ 20,774
Income: $72,822
Purchases: $22,000
Library Holdings: Vols 18,516; Per subs 77; Micro—Fiche, reels; AV—Cassettes, v-tapes; Other—Exhibition catalogs, pamphlets

M **UNIVERSITY OF PENNSYLVANIA,** University Museum, 33rd and Spruce St, 19104. Tel 215-386-7400. *Dir* Martin Biddle; *Admin & Financial Officer* Lavon H Bair; *Keeper of Coll* Mary Elizabeth King; *Keeper of Public Services* Alan M Cook; *Cur African Ethnology* Igor Kopytoff; *Cur American Section* William R Coe; *Cur Latin American Ethnology* Ruben E Reina; *Cur North American Ethnology* Anthony F C Wallace; *Assoc Cur in charge American Historical Archaeology* Robert Schuyler; *Cur Syro-Palestinian Archaeology* Open; *Assoc Cur, Co-Dir, Egyptian Expedition* David O'Connor; *Assoc Cur European Archaeology* Bernard Wailes; *Cur Mediterranean Section* Spyros Iakovidis; *Cur Near Eastern Section* Robert H Dyson, Jr; *Cur Tablet Coll* Ake W Sjoberg; *Cur Akkadian Language & Literature* Erle Leichty; *Cur Oceanian Section* William H Davenport; *Cur Oceanian Ethnology* Ward H Goodenough; *Assoc Cur Palaeolithic Archaeology* Jacques Bordaz; *Cur Physical Anthropology* Francis E Johnston; *Cur Physical Anthropology* Solomon H Katz; *Asst Cur in Charge South and Southeast Asian Section* Chester F Gorman
Open Tues - Sat 10 AM - 5 PM, Sun 1 - 5 PM, cl Mon. Admis $1. Estab 1897 to investigate the origins and varied developments of man's cultural achievements in all times and places; to preserve and maintain collections to document these achievements, and to present to the public results of these investigations by means of permanent exhibits and temporary exhibitions. Average Annual Attendance: 100,000. Mem: 3,188; dues from junior $5 to benefactor $5,000
Income: $3,400,000 (financed by endowment, membership, state appropriation and University)
Collections: Archaeological and enthnographic displays relating to the Old and New World; the classical civilization of the Mediterranean, Egypt, Mesopotamia, Iran, India, Southeast Asia and the Far East, North, Middle and South America, Oceania; physical anthropology
Exhibitions: Changing exhibitions in the Nevil Gallery for the Blind and Sighted; permanent galleries have exhibits from each of the broad geographical areas represented in collections; temporary exhibitions composed of ethnological and archaeological specimens from the Museum's own collections and from other institutions
Publications: Expedition Magazine, quarterly
Activities: Classes for adults and children; docent training; lect open to public, 5 visiting lectrs per year; concerts; gallery talks; tours; exten dept serving Pennsylvania Commonwealth; original objects of art lent to libraries and instructional centers in the state; lending collection contains motion pictures, original art works and slides; traveling exhibitions organized and circulated; museum shop selling books, magazines, reproductions, slides, jewelry and craft items
L **John and Ada Lewis Memorial Library,** 33rd and Spruce St, 19104. *Librn* Jean Adelman
Open to staff and students of the University and the public
Library Holdings: Vols 63,000; Per subs 1500
Special Subjects: Anthropology, Archaeology
Collections: Brinton Collection
O **Institute of Contemporary Art,** 34th and Walnut St, 19104. Tel 215-243-7108. *Dir* Janet Kardon; *Cur & Admin* Matthew McClain; *Asst to Dir* Paula Marincola
Open Wed - Fri 10 AM - 5 PM, Sat & Sun Noon - 5 PM, Tues 10 AM - 7:30 PM. No admis fee. Estab 1963 to provide a continuing forum for the active presentation of advanced development in the visual arts. Two large gallery spaces devoted to exhibiting contemporary art in all media. Average Annual Attendance: 80,000. Mem: 800; dues $20, $50, $125, $500 and up
Income: Approx $300,000 (financed by endowment, membership and grants)
Exhibitions: Architecture: Seven Architects; The Decorative Impulse; Eight Abstract Painters; Joan Jonas: Stage Sets; Improbable Furniture; Made in Pennsylvania: A Selection of Amish Quilts; Material Pleasures; The Philadelphia Houston Exchange; Charles Ross: The Substance of Light; George Segal: Environments; Talismans: Masks, Tents, Vessels; Paul Thek: Processions; Urban Encounters
Publications: Annual newsletter; calendar of events; exhibition catalogs
Activities: Lect open to the public, 10-15 visiting lectrs per year; concerts; gallery talks; tours; traveling exhibitions organized and circulated; sales shop sells original art and catalogs

M **WILLET STAINED GLASS STUDIOS,** 10 East Moreland Ave, 19118. Tel 215-247-5721. *Chmn* Henry Lee Willet; *Pres* E Crosby Willet; *General Manager* William G Stewart
Open Mon - Fri 8 AM - 4:30 PM by appointment. Estab 1890 as the largest stained glass studio in the United States
Activities: Lectures; Individual paintings and original objects of art lent; lending collection contains photographs, Kodachromes and motion pictures; traveling exhibitions organized and circulated
L **Library,** 19118. *Librn* Helene H Weis
Open Mon - Fri 8 AM - 4:30 PM. Estab 1898 as a resource for staff artists. Limited use for students and the general public
Income: Financed by the company
Library Holdings: Vols 1000; Per subs 20; AV—Kodachromes; Other—Clipping files, exhibition catalogs, memorabilia, original art works, photographs
Special Subjects: Architecture, Religious Art, Stained Glass
Collections: photographs and slides of the same

M **WOODMERE ART GALLERY,** 9201 Germantown Ave, 19118. Tel 215-247-0476. *Chmn of the Board* Dr John H Wolf; *Pres* Mrs Harry G Kuch; *VPres* Dr Patricia Allison; *Secy* Mrs William S Geiger; *Treas* Wallace S Martindale Jr; *Dir* Harry A Harris
Open daily 10 AM - 5 PM, Sun 2 - 5 PM, cl holidays. No admis fee. Estab 1940; founded by Charles Knox Smith, in trust for benefit of the public. A large addition in 1965 provides additional gallery and studio space. Average Annual Attendance:

14,000. Mem: 1500; dues $10 and higher; annual meeting April

Collections: Contemporary American †paintings, †sculpture, and †graphics; European porcelains and furniture; European and American sculpture; Oriental rugs, furniture, porcelains; Smith Collection of European and American paintings

Exhibitions: 8 current exhibitions annually; prizes awarded in Members' Annual Juried and Special Exhibitions

Activities: Classes for adults and children; Philadelphia Guild of Handweavers' classes; concerts, lect, gallery tours

PITTSBURGH

M **ART INSTITUTE OF PITTSBURGH GALLERY,** 536 Penn Ave, 15222. Tel 412-263-6600. *Pres* Bradford Daggett
No admis fee. Estab 1921 as an art school and proprietary trade school

Exhibitions: Local art group shows; local artists; loan exhibitions; student and faculty members; technical art exhibits

Publications: Brochures; Catalog; School Newspaper

Activities: Scholarships available

L **Resource Center,** 526 Penn Ave, 15222. *Admin* Diana K Hunt
Open Mon - Fri 7:30 AM - 3 PM, Mon, Tues & Thurs 6 - 10 PM. Estab 1971 to supply our students with readily available reference materials. Circ Approx 2600

Purchases: $1295

Library Holdings: Vols 631; Per subs 65; AV—Cassettes, fs, rec, slides; Other—Clipping files, exhibition catalogs, framed reproductions, memorabilia, pamphlets

Special Subjects: Architecture, Art History, Commercial Art, Crafts, Fashion Arts, Graphic Arts, Inter Design, Mixed Media, Photography

O **ARTS AND CRAFTS CENTER OF PITTSBURGH,*** Mellon Park, Fifth & Shady Ave, 15232. Tel 412-361-0873. *Dir* Audrey Bethel
Open Tues - Sat 10 AM - 5 PM, Sun 2 - 5 PM. Estab 1944, incorporated 1947. Galleries maintained for monthly contemporary exhibitions, group and one-man shows. Headquarters for non-profit organizations in the creative arts consists of fifteen resident and two affiliated member groups. Average Annual Attendance: 85,000. Mem: 1600; dues resident members pay per capita according to own membership; affiliated members, group dues

Income: $225,000

Exhibitions: Artist of the Year, retrospective show honoring a Pittsburgh artist chosen by Board; Invitational one-man or group show

Publications: Class brochure 4 times a year; Center brochure

Activities: Arts and crafts classes for adults and children; workshops; rental facilities provided for outside groups for art programs

O **ASSOCIATED ARTISTS OF PITTSBURGH ARTS AND CRAFTS CENTER,** Fifth & Shady Aves, 15232. Tel 412-361-4235. *Pres* Anna Marie Sninsky; *VPres* John Seitz; *Secy* David Nowicki; *Exec Dir* Sylvia M Solof
Open Tues - Sat 10 AM - 4 PM, Sun 2 - 5 PM, cl Mon. Estab 1910 to give exposure to member artists and for education of the area in the field of art. A small art gallery is maintained. Average Annual Attendance: 25,000. Mem: 450 (must be juried into the group); dues $25

Income: Financed by membership

Exhibitions: Annual Exhibition for five weeks at Museum of Art, Carnegie Institute; one, two or group shows by members

Activities: Lect open to public

M **CARNEGIE INSTITUTE,** Museum of Art, 4400 Forbes Ave, 15213. Tel 412-622-3300. *Pres* James M Walton; *Chmn Museum of Art Committee* Richard M Scaife; *Dir* Leon A Arkus; *Cur Exhib* Paul F Binai; *Cur Film Section* William Judson; *Cur Painting & Sculpture* Herdis Bull Teilman; *Registrar* Charles W Cathey; *Admin Secy* Nancy Noyes; *Executive Secy* Helen J Goodman; *Cur Education* Anthony N Landreau
Open Tues - Sat 10 AM - 5 PM, Sun 10 AM - 6 PM, cl Mon and major holidays. Admis by suggested contribution adults $1.50, children and students 75¢, no admis fee Sat. Estab 1896, incorporated 1926. Original building 1896-1907; Scaife Gallery for permanent collection opened 1974; Heinz Galleries for special exhibitions opened 1975; Ailsa Mellon Bruce Decorative Arts Galleries opened 1975. Average Annual Attendance: 800,000. Mem: 11,500; dues $17.50 and up

Income: Financed by endowment, membership, city and state appropriation and other funds

Collections: American and European Paintings and Sculpture, especially Impressionist and Post-Impressionist; Ailsa Mellon Bruce Furniture Collection; Japanese Woodblock Prints; Oriental and Decorative Arts; antiquities, drawings, films, photographs, prints and watercolors

Exhibitions: Associated Artists of Pittsburgh; Henri Cartier-Bresson Exhibition; Constructivist Art from Cubism to the Present; Sonia Delaunay Retrospective; Neopolitan Presepe; Series of One-Man Exhibitions by Local Artists; Shakespeare, The Globe and The World; Three Rivers Art Festival; Utagawa Hiroshigi I, The 53 Stages of the Tokaido

Publications: Annual report; Carnegie Magazine, ten times per year; catalogue of permanent collection; employee newsletter; exhibition catalogs

Activities: Classes for adults and children; dramatic programs; docent training; lect open to public, 15 visiting lectr per year; concerts; gallery talks; tours; competitions; exten dept serving public schools; originate traveling exhibitions; museum shop sells books, magazines, original art, reproductions, prints, slides, textiles, jewelry, pottery, sculpture, china and postcards

L **Library,** 4400 Forbes Ave, 15213.
Open to staff and museum docents for reference only

L **CARNEGIE LIBRARY OF PITTSBURGH,** Art Room, Music and Art Department, 4400 Forbes Ave, 15213. Tel 412-622-3107. *Librn in Charge* Anne W Gordon; *Librn* A Catherine Tack; *Librn* Katherine Kepes
Open Mon, Tues, Fri & Sat 9 AM - 9 PM, Wed & Thurs 9 AM - 5:30 PM, cl Memorial Day and Labor Day. Estab 1930 to provide reference and circulating materials on all aspects of art

Income: Financed by city, state and county appropriation

Library Holdings: Vols 40,000; Per subs 60; AV—Fs, slides; Other—Clipping files, exhibition catalogs, pamphlets

Collections: Architecture; Costume

CARNEGIE-MELLON UNIVERSITY

M **Forbes Street Gallery,** 5200 Forbes Ave, 51213. Tel 412-578-2081. *Dir* Buddy Fiedler; *Asst Dir Operations* Jenny McChesney; *Asst Dir Public Relations* Susan Sloan
Open Tues & Thurs 7 - 9 PM, Wed & Sun Noon - 4 PM. Estab 1969 to offer exhibition space to students, and an opportunity to learn about gallery management through practice. Gallery is approximately 20 x 40 ft plus small back room space. Average Annual Attendance: 750

Income: $1700 (financed by university funding)

Exhibitions: Weekly student exhibitions

L **Hunt Library,** 5000 Forbes Ave, 51213. Tel 412-578-2000. *Fine Arts Librn* Helen A Lingelbach; *Dir of University Libraries* Ruth R Corrigan
Open Mon - Thurs 8 AM - Noon, Fri 8 AM - 9 PM, Sat 9 AM - 9 PM, Sun 1 - 12 PM. Estab 1912. The Fine Arts Library is a part of Hunt Library housed on the fourth floor of the main Library building

Library Holdings: Vols 26,000; Per subs 300; AV—Slides; Other—Clipping files, prints, pamphlets, photographs, reproductions

M **CHATHAM COLLEGE ART GALLERY,** Woodland Rd, 15232. Tel 412-441-8200. *Co-Dir* Shirley Stark; *Co-Dir* Jerry Caplan; *Co-Dir* Joseph Shepler
Open Tues - Sun 2 - 5 PM, Fri 7 - 9 PM. No admis fee. Estab 1960 as an art gallery in a small liberal arts college, serving both the college and community by mounting exhibitions of high quality. Gallery is 100 running ft, is located in Jennie King Mellon Library, and is fitted with track lighting. Average Annual Attendance: 1000

Activities: Lect open to the public, 2 visiting lectr per year; gallery talks

M **FRICK ART MUSEUM,** 7227 Reynolds St, 15208. Tel 412-371-7766. *Dir* Virginia E Lewis; *Exec Secy* Catherine Rudy Kiefer; *Registrar* Kathryn D Cox; *Asst Curator* Marilyn Miller Russell
Open Wed - Sat 10 AM - 5:30 PM, Sun Noon - 6 PM. No admis fee. Estab 1970 as an art museum for public enjoyment and education. Average Annual Attendance: 15,500

Income: Financed by endowment

Collections: Chinese 18th century porcelains; English and Irish 18th century silver; French 18th century period room; French 18th century furniture; †Italian, Flemish, French paintings from the early Renaissance through the 18th century; Italian and Flemish bronzes of the 15th, 16th and 17th centuries; Italian 16th to 18th century furniture; Russian 18th century silver; Sculpture, Houdon, Clodion, tapestries, French mille fleurs and Flemish 16th century

Publications: Five Lectures; The Arts in Changing Societies; Madame Jean Antoine Houdon (reprinted from the Art Bulletin); Reflections Inspired by Works of Art in the Frick Art Museum, Pittsburgh, Check List; The Treasures of Frick Art Museum

Activities: Lect open to the public, 3-5 visiting lectrs per year; 24 gallery talks; 50 tours; concerts; small working library

M **GALLERIES OF IVY SCHOOL OF PROFESSIONAL ART,** University Ave, 15214. Tel 412-323-3200. *Dir* Morris B Kirshenbaum
Open Mon - Fri 9 AM - 4 PM, Sat 9 AM - 2:30 PM. No admis fee. Estab 1961 for exhibition of fine arts, group or one person shows; student shows; applied arts (graphic design, photography, textiles, advertising art). Approx 500 running ft of wall space is comprised of hall galleries connecting two small galleries

Income: Financed by school budget

Collections: Faculty and student works

Activities: Educ dept

L **Library,** University Ave, 15214. *Librn* Tamara Caskey
Open to students and faculty for reference

M **Downtown Annex Gallery,** 927 Penn Ave, 15222.

M **PITTSBURGH HISTORY AND LANDMARKS FOUNDATION,** Old Post Office Museum, One Landmarks Square, 15212. Tel 412-322-1204. *Pres* Arthur P Ziegler; *VPres* Barbara Hoffstot; *Secy* Anne S Genter; *Chmn of Board* Charles C Arensberg; *Asst Museums & Special Projects* Patricia A Wiley; *Curatorial Asst* Gregory J Weidner
Open Tues - Fri 10 AM - 4:30 PM, Sat & Sun 1 - 4:30 PM. Admis adults $1, children 40¢. Estab 1971 to preserve our historical and architectural heritage. Museum is housed in the Old Allegheny Post Office; main gallery is in rotunda room; additional galleries in basement and on third floor; also artifacts garden court. Average Annual Attendance: 15,000. Mem: 3000; dues $12; annual meeting March

Income: $30,000 (financed by membership, private donations and private foundation grants)

Collections: Architectural artifacts from demolished buildings and sites, decorative arts, documents, fashions, furniture, industrial artifacts, paintings, prints, stained glass and toys

Exhibitions: Art Deco International; John Bower Riverboat Collection; Recent Acquisitions; Stained Glass in Pittsburgh

Activities: Classes for adults and children; restoration seminars; preservation conferences; historic district survey training; lect, 5 visiting lectr per year; concerts; gallery talks; tours; exten dept serves Allegheny County; original objects of art lent to museums in Pittsburgh area; book traveling exhibitions; museum shop sells books, magazines, reproductions, prints, slides, gift items and artifacts; Toy Museum

C **PITTSBURGH NATIONAL BANK,** Fifth Ave & Wood St, 15222. Tel 412-355-3352. *Real Estate Adminr* Robert F Lew
No admis fee. Estab 1970 to enhance offices. Collection displayed at Pittsburgh National Building

Collections: Eclectic medias and periods

Activities: Awards to local groups only; individual objects of art lent

O **PITTSBURGH PLAN FOR ART GALLERY,** 407 S Craig St, 15213. Tel 412-683-7600. *Pres* Sylvester Damianos; *VPres* James Winokur; *Secy* Margaret Engel; *Dir* Alice K Beckwith
Open Tues - Sat 10 AM - 5 PM, Sun 1 - 5 PM; cl Mon. No admis fee. Estab 1955 as a nonprofit organization under aegis of Education to Learn by Looking. Maintains an art gallery for rental and-or sale of artworks; two floors over 6000 sq

ft. Average Annual Attendance: 10,000. Mem: 567; dues public $10, artists free
Income: Financed by membership, rental and sales fees
Exhibitions: One-person and group shows every month
Activities: Lect open to public; tours; individual paintings lent; lending collection contains original art works, original prints, paintings, sculptures and slides; originate traveling exhibitions

C **ROCKWELL INTERNATIONAL CORPORATION,** 600 Grant St, 15219. *Secy* J J Christin
Annual amount of contributions and grants $288,000; supports fine and performing arts

UNIVERSITY OF PITTSBURGH
M **University Art Gallery,** 15260. Tel 412-624-4121. *Dir* David G Wilkins
Open Tues - Sat 10 AM - 4 PM, Thurs 4 - 7 PM, Sun 2 - 5 PM; cl Mon. No admis fee. Estab 1970 to provide exhibitions for the university community and the community at large and to provide students with gallery experience. Gallery comprised of 350 running ft in five areas. Average Annual Attendance: 4000
Income: Financed through the University
Collections: Drawings, paintings, prints and sculpture
Exhibitions: Architectural Studies; Architecture by Ivan Leonidov; Art Nouveau; Contemporary Latin-American Painting and Prints; Contemporary Yugoslavian Graphics; Frank J Mangano Collection; New Paintings by David Summers; Oil Sketches by F E Church; Photography by Clyde Hare; Printmaking from Ashland Oil, Ltd; Prints by Jacob Kainen; Works of Art from the University's Collections and Recent Acquisitions
Publications: Exhibition catalogs, three per year
Activities: Original objects of art lent; lending collection contains 922 original art works, 700 original prints, paintings, 100 photographs, 100 sculptures and drawings; originate traveling exhibitions
L **Henry Clay Frick Fine Arts Library,** Henry Clay Frick Fine Arts Bldg, 15260. *Librn* Elizabeth C Booth; *Reference Librn* Marsha Stevenson
Open Mon - Thurs 9 AM - 10 PM, Fri & Sat 9 AM - 5 PM, Sun 2 - 5 PM. Estab 1928 to support the teaching activities of the Departments of Fine Arts and Studio Arts. For reference only
Library Holdings: Vols 52,000; Per subs 320; Micro—Fiche, reels; AV—Slides; Other—Clipping files, exhibition catalogs, pamphlets
Special Subjects: Architecture, Art History, Graphic Arts, Sculpture, Medieval, Renaissance and Modern art
Collections: Facsimile mss

C **WESTINGHOUSE ELECTRIC CORPORATION,** Stanwix St, Westinghouse Building, 15222. Tel 412-255-3513. *In Charge Art Coll* Jon Philip Andrews
Open 8:15 AM - 5:15 PM. No admis fee. Estab 1970 to create pleasant working environment for employees. Collection displayed in headquarter building; is a working collection used by the employees
Collections: 1200 pieces: American Indian prints, tapestries and watercolors
Activities: Individual objects of art lent

POTTSTOWN

O **POTTSTOWN AREA ARTISTS' GUILD,** PO Box 512, 19464. *Pres* Bertha Trumbore; *Secy* Lorene Abel; *VPres* Open
Estab 1960 as a nonprofit organization open to all who are interested in art in its many forms. Consists of both professional and nonprofessional artists, and also many others who are interested in art. Mem: 154; dues $7
Income: Financed by membership
Exhibitions: Anvil Studio and Gallery; Ursinus College; membership show
Publications: Sketch Pad, monthly
Activities: Lect for members only; 9 visiting lectr per year; tours; competitions; traveling exhibitions organized and circulated locally

READING

M **ALBRIGHT COLLEGE,** Freedman Gallery, 13th & Exeter Sts, 19603. Tel 215-921-2381, Ext 337. *Pres* David G Ruffer; *Dean* S Shirk; *Treas* A Van Bodegraven; *Dir of Gallery* Marilyn A Zeitlin
Open Mon - Fri Noon - 4 PM, Tues evenings 6 - 9 PM, Sun 2 - 5 PM, also by appointment. No admis fee. Estab 1975 to present primarily contemporary art in a context of teaching. Gallery is 40 x 50 ft with flexible wall arrangements. Average Annual Attendance: 8000. Mem: 220; dues $20, students $5; annual meeting Feb
Income: $27,000 (financed by endowment, membership and college)
Purchases: $3000
Collections: †Contemporary Painting, Prints, Sculpture; †Vintage and Contemporary Photography
Exhibitions: (1978-79) Oriole Farb: New Portraits; George Papashvily (sculpture); Small is Beautiful; Tibetan Art from the Horch Collection; Works by Women; local artists
Publications: Neil Anderson (four-color limited edition poster); exhibition catalogues
Activities: lect open to public, 4 - 6 visiting lectr per year; gallery talks; tours; Freedman Gallery Student Award; scholarships; individual paintings and original objects of art lent to galleries and museums; lending collection contains original art works, original prints, paintings and sculpture; originate traveling exhibitions; sales desk sells catalogues, prints, t-shirts

O **BERKS ART ALLIANCE,** Wyomissing Institute of Art Bldg, Trent & Belmont St, 19610. Tel 215-376-1576. *Pres* Jack Coggins; *First VPres* Leonard Boyer; *Second VPres* Mary Ann DiSegi; *Record Secy* Joanne Stephan; *Correspondence Secy* Adele Hoadley
Estab 1941 to maintain active art center in Reading and Berks county. Mem: 150; dues $12; annual meetings 2nd Tues of odd months
Exhibitions: Three annual membership shows, plus solo or two-persons shows of a two week period each
Activities: Life or costume drawing workshop Thurs morning; open painting workshop Thurs afternoon; life drawing workshop Thurs evening; sponsors annual trip to American Watercolor Society Show in New York

M **READING PUBLIC MUSEUM AND ART GALLERY,** 500 Museum Rd, 19611. Tel 215-373-1525. *Dir* Bruce L Dietrich; *Cur Fine Arts* Jefferson A Gore
Open Mon - Fri 9 AM - 5 PM, Sat 9 AM - Noon, Sun 2 - 5 PM. No admis fee. Estab 1904 to promote knowledge, pleasure, and cultivation of the arts and sciences. Ground floor: oil painting gallery. First floor: natural and social sciences exhibits. Second floor: permanent and temporary art exhibitions. Average Annual Attendance: 100,000
Income: $500,000 (financed by government)
Collections: 19th Century Paintings; Old Masters Gallery; Pennsylvania-German Room
Exhibitions: Artists of Lancaster County; Illuminated Rock; Inner Dimensions; Victor Vasarely; Youth Art Show
Activities: Classes for children; docent training; lect open to public; concerts; tours; museum shop and sales shop sells books, reproductions, prints and slides
L **Reading Public Museum Library,** 500 Museum Rd, 19611.
Open Mon - Fri 9 AM - 4 PM
Library Holdings: Vols 12,000; Per subs 30; Other—Exhibition catalogs, prints, manuscripts, memorabilia, pamphlets, reproductions, Original documents
Collections: American Bureau of Ethnology Collection

SCRANTON

M **EVERHART MUSEUM OF NATURAL HISTORY, SCIENCE AND ART,** Nay Aug Park, 18510. Tel 717-346-7186. *Chmn Trustees* Edwin M Kosik; *Dir* James D Bowne
Open 10 AM - 5 PM; Sun 2 - 5 PM; cl Mon & holidays. No admis fee. Estab and incorporated 1908, a gift to the city from Dr Isiah F Everhart; building rebuilt 1928-29. Average Annual Attendance: 200,000. Mem: 1200; dues $5 and higher; annual meeting June
Income: $100,000 (financed by endowment and city appropriation)
Purchases: $2000
Collections: African Art; †American Folk Art; †American Indian material; European and American painting, prints and sculpture; Dorflinger Glass (1852-1921); Oceanic Art; Oriental Art
Exhibitions: Monthly exhibitions
Activities: Weekly classes in art and science for children and adults; lect series in art and science for members; outside lect; guided tours; artists-in-residence programs
L **Library,** Nay Aug Park, 18510.
For reference only
Library Holdings: Vols 8500

SHIPPENSBURG

M **SHIPPENSBURG STATE COLLEGE,** Kauffman Gallery, Prince St, 17257. Tel 717-532-1530. *Secy* Veronica Moubry; *Dir* Dr Harry D Bentz
Open Mon - Fri 9 AM - 4 PM, Tues evenings 6:30 - 9 PM. No admis fee. Estab 1972 to bring art to the college community. Average Annual Attendance: 1500
Income: $Financed by Student Association funds and college
Purchases: $1000
Activities: lect open to public, 5 visiting lectr per year; gallery talks

SWARTHMORE

L **SWARTHMORE COLLEGE,** Friends Historical Library, 18081. Tel 215-447-7496. *Dir* Dr J William Frost; *Asst Dir* Albert W Fowler; *Cur Peace Collection* Bernice B Nichols
Open Mon - Fri 8:30 AM - 4:30 PM, Sat 9 AM - Noon; cl August and Sat when college not in session. Estab 1871 to preserve and make available to the public material by and about Quakers and their concerns, records of non-sectarian peace organizations and papers of peace movement leaders. Circ 4885
Income: $113,670 (financed by endowment and college)
Purchases: $11,631
Library Holdings: Vols 38,735; Per subs 442; Micro—Reels; AV—A-tapes, cassettes, Kodachromes, lantern slides, motion pictures, rec, slides, v-tapes; Other—Clipping files, prints, manuscripts, memorabilia, original art works, pamphlets, photographs, sculpture, charts; maps; original documents; posters
Collections: Quaker paintings; Quakers as subject in art; Meeting House Picture Collection; portraits, group pictures, residence pictures, silhouettes and sketches of individual Friends; Swarthmore College pictures; Swarthmore College Peace Collection consists primarily of archival material, records of non-sectarian peace organizations in the United States and 59 foreign countries, papers of peace leaders including Jean Addams, Emily Greene Balch, Elihu Burritt, A J Muste, Wilhelm Sollmann and others; 1400 peace posters and war posters

UNIVERSITY PARK

PENNSYLVANIA STATE UNIVERSITY
M **Museum of Art,** University Park, 16802. Tel 814-865-7672. *Dir* William Hull; *Asst Dir* William D Davis; *Cur* Olga Preisner; *Registrar* Richard Porter
Open Tues - Sun Noon - 5 PM, cl Mon & legal holidays. No admis fee. Estab 1972 to promote a variety of visual experiences through a program of changing exhibitions; a window to the world for the university community. Museum is a three-story brick building with one large gallery on each floor which can be sub-divided with movable panels. Average Annual Attendance: 60,000
Income: Financed by state appropriation
Collections: American and European painting, drawings, graphics and sculpture with some emphasis on Pennsylvania artists; Oriental ceramics, painting and prints, limited material in Ancient, African and Near Eastern areas; Kehl and Nina Markley Collection of Ancient Peruvian Ceramics; Ralph C Marcove Collection of Oriental Art

Exhibitions: Chinese Paintings and Mounted Rocks; Chinese Export Porcelains from the Collection of Dr and Mrs Harold L Tonkin; 26 Contemporary Japanese Potters and French Works from the Permanent Collection; Works of Arthur B Davies from the Collection of Mr and Mrs Herbert Brill; William Dole: A Retrospective Exhibition of Collages, 1958 - 1978; French Drawings from European Collections (the former Armand Gobiet Collection); Heritage Sampler: An Introduction to the Domestic Arts and Crafts of Central Pennsylvania 1750 - 1900; The Intimate Worlds of Faust and Titolo; John F Kensett Drawings; Robert Kulicke, Painter, Designer, Craftsman; Pennsylvania Prints from the Collection of Ralph M Yeager and John C O'Connor; The Song of Roland (Art of the Heroic Era); Recent Paintings and Drawings by George Zoretich

Publications: Calendar of Events, bi-monthly

Activities: Docent training; lect open to public, 8 visiting lectr per year; concerts; gallery talks; tours; museum store sells books, magazines, original art, reproductions, prints and slides

L **Pattee Library,** Arts Library, E 405, 16802. Tel 814-865-6481. *Arts & Architecture Librn* Jean Smith; *Music Librn* Carole Franklin

Open Mon - Thurs 8 AM - Midnight, Sat 8 AM - 5 PM, Sun 1 PM - Midnight. Estab 1957 to support the academic programs of the College of Arts and Architecture and the Division of Art and Music Education; to provide information on the arts to members of the university and community. Circ 19,000

Income: Financed through University Libraries

Library Holdings: Vols 40,000; Per subs 510; Micro—Fiche; AV—Cassettes, rec; Other—Prints

Special Subjects: Medieval, Baroque and Renaissance art and architecture history, history of printmaking, illuminated manuscripts

Collections: Warren Mack Memorial Collection of original prints

WASHINGTON

M **WASHINGTON AND JEFFERSON COLLEGE,** Commons Gallery, Lincoln St, 15301. Tel 412-222-4400. *Chmn* Paul B Edwards

Open daily 9 AM - 7 PM. No admis fee. Estab 1969 for the display of circulating art shows and the college collection. The gallery is modern, well-lighted and large. Average Annual Attendance: 3000

Income: Financed by private funding

Purchases: $2000

Collections: Washington and Jefferson College Permanent Collection

Exhibitions: National Painting Show; annual slide exhibition (juried)

Publications: Catalogs

WAYNE

O **WAYNE ART CENTER,** 413 Maplewood Ave, 19087. Tel 215-688-3553. *Pres* Linda Rodgers; *VPres* Rosemary Beardsley; *VPres* Susan Hopkins; *Secy* Beth Kempf; *Treas* Bruce Gillespie

Open Mon - Fri 10 AM - 4 PM. No admis fee. Estab 1930 as a community art center. Two galleries offer rotating exhibits of work by local artists. Average Annual Attendance: 2000. Mem: 400; dues $15; annual meeting May

Income: $25,000 (financed by membership, grants, corporations and Pennsylvania Council on the Arts)

Activities: Classes for adults and children; lect for members, 6 visiting lectr per year; gallery talks; competitions

WEST CHESTER

O **CHESTER COUNTY HISTORICAL SOCIETY,** 225 N High St, 19380. Tel 215-692-4800. *Pres* Robert M Goshorn; *Secy* Dr Robert E Carlson; *Treas* H B Beale; *Exec Dir* Kurt E Brandenburg; *Cur* Ruth K Hagy; *Registrar & Conservator* Marilyn Norcini

Estab 1893 for the acquisition and preservation of property and information of historic value or interest to the people of Chester County. Average Annual Attendance: 7000. Mem: 1200; dues family $25, individual $15; annual meeting third Tues in May

Income: $124,000 (financed by endowment and membership)

Collections: Museum houses regional collections of furniture, from William & Mary through Victorian; ceramics, needlework, glassware, pewter, and textiles

Exhibitions: Chester County Clocks; Chester County Colonial Furniture and Pewter

Publications: Chester County History, occasionally; Newsletter, monthly

Activities: Docent training; lect open to public, 10 visiting lectr per year; tours; individual paintings and original objects of art lent to other museums; museum shop selling books, reproductions and prints

L **Library,** 225 N High St, 19380. Tel 215-692-4800. *Asst Librn* Kathy J Shady

Admis adults $2, students 50¢; members free. Open to the public; for reference only

Library Holdings: Vols 20,000; Per subs 110; Other—Manuscripts

WILKES-BARRE

M **WILKES COLLEGE,** Sordoni Art Gallery, 150 S River St, 18703. Tel 717-824-4651, Ext 289. *Dir* Dr William H Sterling; *Exhib Coordr* Cara Berryman

Open Mon - Fri 1 - 5 PM, Sat 10 AM - 5 PM, Sun 1 - 5 PM. No admis fee. Estab 1973 to encourage art appreciation in the Wilkes-Barre and the Northeastern Pennsylvania areas. The Gallery has one room, 30 x 40 ft, with adjustable flats used for hanging. Average Annual Attendance: 20,000. Mem: Monthly meetings

Income: Financed by memberships, foundation endowment, and Wilkes College appropriations

Collections: Nineteenth Century European Sculpture and Paintings; Traveling Mining Photography Collection

Exhibitions: Abstract Watercolors by Walter Stevens; Aluminum Modular Sculpture 1975-1979: Herbert Simon; Louis Carpenter: A Retrospective (painting); Counterpoints in Contemporary Painting: Joseph Shepler and Harry Holland; National Design Marker Competition Show (mixed media); Poster Art in Poland; Recent Paintings by Ricardo Viera; Regional Scholastic Art Awards (all media); Three American Women: Cecilia Beaux, Martha Walter and Mary Cassatt (painting, etchings, pastels); Wilkes College Art Alumni (all media)

Publications: Gallery Briefs, bimonthly

Activities: Lect; films; competitions; gallery talks; tours; bus trips; individual paintings and original objects of art lent to other universities; lending collection contains paintings and sculpture

WILLIAMSPORT

M **LYCOMING COLLEGE GALLERY,** 17701. Tel 717-326-1951. *Co-Dir* Jon Bogle; *Co-Dir* Roger Shipley

Open Mon - Thurs 8 AM - 11 PM, Fri 8 AM - 4:30 PM, Sat 10 AM - 5 PM, Sun 1 - 11 PM. No admis fee. Estab 1980 to bring quality art work to the students and faculty as well as to the interested community. The new gallery, 30 x 60 ft, is located in the College Library. Average Annual Attendance: 1000

Income: Financed by school budget

Collections: Paintings and prints of 19th and 20th century artists

Exhibitions: One-man shows of regional and area artists and alumni of the Department; traveling exhibitions

Activities: Gallery talks; tours; individual paintings lent; book traveling exhibitions; originate traveling exhibitions

YORK

O **HISTORICAL SOCIETY OF YORK COUNTY,*** 250 E Market St, 17403. Tel 717-848-1587. *Exec Dir* Douglas C Dolan; *Cur Education* Steven Young

Open Mon - Sat 9 AM - 5 PM, Sun 1 - 5 PM, Historic Houses Mon - Sat 10 AM - 4 PM, Sun 1 - 4 PM, cl New Years, Easter, Thanksgiving, Christmas. Admis adults $2.75, children $1.25, senior citizen group rates for Historic Houses. Estab 1895 to record, preserve, collect and interpret the history of York County and Pennsylvania, including music and art of the past and present. Restoration Properties: General Gates House (1751); Golden Plough Tavern (1741) and Log House (1812), 157 W Market; Bonham House (1870), 152 E Market. Average Annual Attendance: 30,000. Mem: 3500; dues $12 and higher; annual meeting in April

Income: $160,000

Collections: †Fraktur and other Pennsylvania folk art; works by Lewis Miller and other local artists; James Shettel Collection of theater and circus material

Exhibitions: Five gallery shows per year featuring living artists; two major shows on some aspect of regional and national decorative or folk arts; three to four secondary shows featuring subject areas (e.g. textiles, Fraktur, etc) from the collection

Publications: The Kentucky Rifle; Lewis Miller Sketches and Chronicles; Monthly Newsletter; Regional Aspects of American Folk Pottery

Activities: Educ program; classes for adults and children; summer internship program; guided tours; lect; concerts; gift shop

L **Library,*** 250 E Market St, 17403. *Librn* Landon C Reisinger

Open to the public, cl Sun. For reference only

Library Holdings: Vols 15,000; Other—Manuscripts, photographs

L **MARTIN MEMORIAL LIBRARY,*** 159 E Market St, 17401. Tel 717-843-3978. *Dir* Mary Catharine Weaver; *Fine Arts* Ruth Funk

Open Mon - Fri 9 AM - 9 PM, Sat 9 AM - 5 PM. No admis fee. Estab 1935

Income: $382,000

Library Holdings: Vols 129,000; Per subs 350; AV—Motion pictures, rec; Other—Pamphlets, mounted pictures

Exhibitions: Frequent exhibitions of arts, crafts, books, manuscripts, paintings

Publications: Annual Reports; Bulletin, monthly; Martin Memorial Library Historical Series; occasional bibliographies of special collections

Activities: Programs for adults and children; lect; concerts

RHODE ISLAND

BRISTOL

M BRISTOL ART MUSEUM, Wardwell St, Box 42, 02809. Tel 401-253-8800. *Pres & Chmn* Sally D Wilson; *VPres* David Habershaw; *Secy* Dory Boland; *Treas* Earl Rounds
Open May - Oct daily 1 - 5 PM, Fri evenings 7 - 9 PM. No admis fee, donations accepted. Estab 1963 for the cultural and aesthetic advantage of the community, exhibiting artists and tourists to this 300 year old salt water seaport. Building was designed in 1905 as a ballroom on the grounds of Linden Place, the old De Wolf Mansion built in 1810. Made available by owners, heirs of Samuel Pomeroy Colt. Average Annual Attendance: 6000. Mem: 350; dues $100, $25, $10, $5; executive officers and board meeting three times a year
Income: $7500 (financed by membership, donations and jury show entry fees)
Collections: An Old Gilt Coach built in France and used to transport Senator James De Wolf from Bristol to Washington, DC, in 1817
Exhibitions: (1979) Bloan - Jacobs Photos; Burnside Street Artists (historical costumes, furniture, painting, sculpture, weaving); Wayne Ensrud, Sherrill Hunnibell painters; quilts
Activities: Lect open to public, 2 - 4 visiting lectr per year; jury show; awards; original art sold by exhibiting artists

KINGSTON

O SOUTH COUNTY ART ASSOCIATION, Helme House, 1319 Kingstown Rd, 02852. Tel 401-783-2195. *Pres* Rita Lepper; *VPres* William Gilroy; *Recording Secy* Lynn Feiner; *Treas* Ann Aldrich; *Cur & Caretaker* Lynda W O'Malley
Open Tues - Sun 2 - 5 PM during exhibitions. No admis fee. Estab 1929 to promote an interest in art and to encourage artists and to support, in every way, the aesthetic interests of the community. Average Annual Attendance: Approx 350; applicants for membership must submit three paintings and be accepted by a committee; dues sustaining $15, lay member $10, artist $7.50, student $3; annual meeting Oct
Collections: No large permanent collection; paintings by early members, usually not on display
Exhibitions: Art Annual Open Show (juried with prizes totaling $250); Members Show; Regional Open Earthworks Show (juried with prizes totaling $250)
Publications: Newsletter, 3 - 4 annually
Activities: Classes for adults and children; lect for members only; competitions with awards; scholarships; original objects of art lent to other art associations; lending collection contains books, lantern slides, sculpture, original art works and slides

M UNIVERSITY OF RHODE ISLAND GALLERY, 02881. Tel 401-792-2131. *Dir Exhib* Ronald J Onorato
Open Tues - Sat Noon - 3 PM, Tues - Fri 7:30 - 9:30 PM. No admis fee. Estab 1970 to expose campus and community to contemporary and historical art. Average Annual Attendance: 5000
Income: Financed through University
Collections: Contemporary artists in various media
Exhibitions: Vito Acconci; Dale Chihuly; Pinchas Cohen Gan; Bart Parker; Mary Shaffer; Steve Wood
Publications: Catalogs, occasionally; brochures for each exhibit
Activities: Gallery talks

NEWPORT

O ART ASSOCIATION OF NEWPORT, 76 Bellevue Ave, 02840. Tel 401-847-0179.
Open Tues - Sat 10 AM - 5 PM, Sun & most holidays 2 - 5 PM; early closing in winter months; cl Mon, Christmas, New Year's Day, Thanksgiving. The Griswold House, designed by Richard Morris Hunt for John N A Griswold in 1862-1863, has been the home of the Art Association since 1916. Retaining some of the original interior decor of the era, the building is listed in the National Register of Historic Places. Cushing Memorial Gallery was built in 1920, commissioned from the firm of Delano and Aldrich, by friends and associates of artist Howard Gardiner Cushing
Exhibitions: Annual Exhibition of Contemporary American Art (juried); Annual All Media Members' Show; Annual Members' Painting Show
Activities: Art school with day and evening classes; lect for members

O NEWPORT HISTORICAL SOCIETY, 82 Touro St, 02840. Tel 401-846-0813. *Pres* William A Sherman; *VPres* Dr William Reitzel; *Secy* Patrick O'Hayes; *Exec Dir* Wilbur T Holmes
Open Tues - Fri 9:30 - 4:30 PM, Sat 9:30 AM - Noon; summer, Sat 9:30 AM - 4:30 PM, Sun 1 - 5 PM. No admis fee. Estab 1853 to collect and preserve items of historical interest pertaining to the city. Maintains an art gallery and small marine museum. Also owns and exhibits the first Seventh Day Baptist Church in America (1729); the Wanton-Lyman-Hazard House (1675), the first home to be restored in Newport; the Friends Meeting House (1699), site of the annual New England Quakers Meeting for over 200 years. Average Annual Attendance: 5000. Mem: 850; dues $15 and up; annual meeting May
Income: Financed by endowment, membership, state appropriation and other contributions
Collections: Artifacts, china, Colonial silver, dolls, glass, furniture, Newport scenes and portraits, pewter and toys
Publications: Newport History, quarterly
Activities: School programs; lect open to public, 4-6 visiting lectr per year; tours; original objects of art lent to museums
L Library, 82 Touro St, 02840. *Librn* Mrs Edmund M Wordell
Open Tues - Fri 9:30 AM - 4:30 PM, Sat 9 AM - Noon; summers, Sat 9:30 AM - 4:30 PM. Estab 1853 to provide resource materials. For reference only
Library Holdings: Vols 10,000; Per subs 30; Micro—Reels; AV—Kodachromes, slides; Other—Clipping files, prints, manuscripts, memorabilia, photographs
Special Subjects: Decorative Arts

L REDWOOD LIBRARY AND ATHENAEUM, 50 Bellevue Ave, 02840. Tel 401-847-0292. *Pres* Dr Donald B Fletcher; *Librn* Donald T Gibbs
Open Mon - Sat 10 AM - 6 PM, 10 AM - 5 PM in August. Estab 1747 as a general library. Circ 53,000. Art gallery maintained
Income: Financed by endowment and membership
Library Holdings: Vols 138,000; Per subs 100; AV—Rec
Collections: Portraits by Feke, Healy, Charles Wilson Peale, Rembrandt Peale, Stuart, Sully, and other early American painters; many paintings by Charles B King; pictures, statues
Activities: Library tours

PROVIDENCE

BROWN UNIVERSITY

M Bell Gallery, 64 College St, 02912. Tel 401-863-2421. *Dir* Nancy R Versaci
Open Mon - Fri 11 AM - 4 PM, Sat & Sun 1 - 4 PM; cl holidays. No admis fee. Estab 1971 to present exhibitions of interest to the university and community. The gallery is modern, covers 2625 sq ft, 14 ft ceilings, and has track lighting. Average Annual Attendance: 12,000
Income: Financed by endowment and university funds
Collections: Substantial collection of Modern Masters; prints dating from the 15th - 20th century
Exhibitions: (1978) After Brown - The Seventies; Walter Feldman; Ed Mayer; New Photography - RI '78; Origins of the Italian Veduta; Prints from Major Workshops; Recent Acquisitions; Richard Tuttle. (1979) Festivities; Richard Fraenkel and David Ketner; Sherron Francis and Sandi Slone; Helen and Newton Harrison; Minimal Prints; Native American Images; The New Landscape; John Walker
Activities: Lect open to public, 14 visiting lectr per year; individual paintings and original objects of art lent to museums and galleries; lending collection contains 1200 original prints, 50 paintings and 20 sculptures
M Annmary Brown Memorial Gallery, 21 Brown St, PO Box 1905, 02912. Tel 401-863-2429. *Cur* Samuel J Hough; *Research Asst* Catherine Denning
Open 9 AM - 5 PM. Estab 1907 to offer representatives of schools of European and American painting. There are three galleries which house early printed books (to 1501 AD), the art collection of the founder and his wife, and portraits of the Brown family

O PROVIDENCE ART CLUB, 11 Thomas St, 02903. Tel 401-331-1114. *Pres* Fred A Andrews Jr; *VPres* Walter Coupe; *Secy* Marilyn Fletcher; *Gallery Secy* Majory Dalenius
Open daily 10 AM - 4 PM, Sun 3 - 5 PM. No admis fee. Estab 1880 for art culture, and to provide exhibition space for artists. Gallery maintained in two rooms of an historic building built in 1790. Average Annual Attendance: 5000. Mem: 846, to qualify, artists' work must pass a board of artists; no qualifications for non-artists; dues non-artist $160, artist $100; annual meeting first Wed in June
Income: Financed by endowment and membership
Collections: Small permanent collection of paintings and sculpture
Exhibitions: Eighteen shows a season of which two-three are juried open shows
Publications: Newsletter for members
Activities: Classes for adults; lect open to members and guests, 20 visiting lectr per year; gallery talks; competitions with awards; scholarships; work in shows usually for sale

M PROVIDENCE ATHENAEUM, 251 Benefit St, 02903. Tel 401-421-6970. *Pres* Robert S Davis; *Treas* Merton P Stolz; *Secy* Roger T Clapp; *Exec Dir* Sylvia Moybayed
Open Mon - Fri 8:30 AM - 5:30 PM, Sat 9:30 AM - 5:30 PM, cl Sun. No admis fee. Estab 1753 to provide cultural services, information, rare and current materials in an historic setting. Mem: 1304; dues $47; annual meeting fourth Mon in Sept
Income: $114,988
Purchases: $15,650
Collections: Strength in the 19th century
Exhibitions: Exhibitions vary each month
Publications: The Athenaeum Bulletin, three times a year; Annual Report
Activities: Dramatic programs; film programs; lectures open to the public and some to members only; tours; festivals; original objects of art lent to bonafide institutions, libraries or societies; lending collection contains cassettes, color reproductions, motion pictures, original art works, original prints, paintings, phonorecords, and sculpture; The center sells Audobon prints in limited editions, and stationery
L Library, 251 Benefit St, 02903. *Pres* Robert S Davis; *Treas* Merton Stolz; *Secy* Robert T Clapp; *Executive Dir* Sylvia Moubayed
Open Mon - Fri 8:30 AM - 5:30 PM, Sat 9:30 AM - 5:30 PM, cl Sun. Estab 1753 to provide cultural services, information rare and current materials in a historic setting. Circ 64,550
Income: $114,000
Purchases: $15,650
Library Holdings: Vols 150,433; Per subs 125; AV—Cassettes, motion pictures, rec; Other—Clipping files, exhibition catalogs, framed reproductions, prints, manuscripts, memorabilia, original art works, pamphlets, photographs, reproductions, sculpture, posters
Special Subjects: Biography, old fiction, fiction, history
Collections: 19th century Robert Burns collection; Audobon, Old Fiction, Holder Border Bowen collection
Activities: Docent training; childrens programs; film programs; festivals; readings and lectures; tours; trips

L PROVIDENCE PUBLIC LIBRARY, Art and Music Dept, 150 Empire St, 02906. Tel 401-521-7722, Ext 235. *Head* Susan R Waddington; *Asst* Margaret Chevian; *Asst* Sarah Shaw
Open Mon - Thurs 8:30 AM - 9 PM, Fri & Sat 8:30 AM - 5:30 PM; summer hours vary. Estab 1878 to serve needs of the public. An art gallery is maintained in large exhibit hall
Income: $2,000,000 (financed by endowment, city and state appropriations and federal funds)
Purchases: $6750 (art and music books)
Library Holdings: Vols 36,000; Per subs 85; AV—Fs, rec; Other—Clipping files, framed reproductions, original art works, posters

Special Subjects: Architecture, Crafts, Jewelry, design
Collections: Nickerson Architectural Collection
Exhibitions: An Injury to One is an Injury to All (Rhode Island Labor History); Figure Drawings by Robin Wiseman and Costume Drawings by Robin Jones; Paintings by Leonard Jefferson and Photographs by Rufus Abdullah; Sources: Creative Use of the Library by Designers and Illustrators; Uncle Tom's Cabin (multi-media); Rhode Island College senior group show; the World From Above (aerial photography)

O **PROVIDENCE WATER COLOR CLUB,** 6 Thomas St, 02903. Tel 617-272-9864. *Pres* Carl U Peterson; *VPres* John DeMelim Jr; *Recording Secy* A E S Peterson; *Corresp Secy* Clara M Stewart; *Treas* Barbara P Sunman; *Asst Treas* Pearl F Ashton
Open Tues - Fri 12:30 - 3:30 PM, Sun 3 - 5 PM, during exhibitions 1 - 3 PM; cl Mon. Estab 1898. Mem: 230; dues $15; annual meeting March
Collections: Small collection of paintings and drawings by early members; prints and paintings by contemporary members
Exhibitions: Annual exhibition of members' work; Annual Christmas Exhibition; Annual Print Show; Annual Open Juried National Show; six or more one-man exhibitions per year
Activities: Lect, slide lect; demonstrations

M **RHODE ISLAND COLLEGE,** Edward M Bannister Gallery, 600 Mount Pleasant Ave, 02908. Tel 401-456-8054, 274-4900, Ext 335. *Coordr* Craig T Coonrod; *Asst* Michele Saillant
Open Mon - Fri 11 AM - 4 PM, Sun 1 - 4 PM; cl Sat. No admis fee. Estab 1977 to provide the Rhode Island community with a varied and progressive exposure to the visual arts, to offer to the college community, with its liberal arts perspective, access to top quality exhibits, artists and workshops. Gallery consists of one room, 25 x 60 ft separated by supports; a 12 ft ceiling on one side and an 8 ft ceiling on the other; a total of 55 spots and floods on tracks. Walls are a light beige with a black floor. A large bank of windows fills one end of the gallery. Average Annual Attendance: 16,000
Income: Financed by state appropriation
Collections: Groundwork is presently being laid for the establishment of a permanent collection with annual purchases and possible gifts
Exhibitions: (1979) Faculty Exhibit; Sidney Goodman (drawings); Colette Perazio-Itkin (sculpture and drawings); Rhode Island College Art Dept. (1980) Graduate Senior Exhibit; Krisjohn Horvat (sculpture and drawings); Metal and Clay Invitational; Victoriana Exhibit
Publications: Brochures, 6-8 per year; calendars, 1-2 per year
Activities: Competitions; workshops; open forums

O **RHODE ISLAND HISTORICAL SOCIETY,** 52 Power St, 02906. Tel 401-331-8575. *Dir* Albert T Klyberg; *Ed, Nathanael Green Papers* Richard K Showman; *Ed, Roger Williams Corresp* Glenn LaFantasie; *Museum Cur* Ann LeVeque; *Cur Education* Laura Roberts; *Public Relations* Kate Waterman
Admis adults $1.50, students 50¢. Estab 1822 to preserve, collect and interpret Rhode Island historical materials, including books, manuscripts, graphics, films, furniture and decorative arts. Mem: 2500; dues $15 and up; annual meeting in Jan
Income: Financed by endowment, membership and city and state appropriation
Exhibitions: Changing exhibitions on Rhode Island history and decorative arts
Publications: American Paintings in the Rhode Island Historical Society, (catalogue); The John Brown House Loan Exhibition of Rhode Island Furniture; Nathanael Green Papers; Rhode Island History, quarterly; Roger Williams Correspondence; occasional monographs; newsletter, bimonthly
Activities: Classes for adults and children; children's tours; film programs; lect open to public, 4-6 visiting lectr per year; concerts; gallery talks; tours; lending collection contains 10,000 prints for reference and copying; bookshop
M **John Brown House,** 52 Power St, 02906.
Open Tues - Sat 11 AM - 4 PM, Sun 1 - 4 PM; cl weekdays Jan & Feb except by appointment. Estab 1942, the 1786 house carefully restored and furnished with fine examples of Rhode Island heritage. Average Annual Attendance: 7000
Collections: Carrington Collection of Chinese export objects; McCrellis Collection of Antique Dolls; †Pieces by Rhode Island Cabinetmakers, some original to the house; †portraits, †china, †glass, †pewter, and †other decorative objects; Rhode Island furniture, silver, porcelain, paintings, textiles
M **Museum of Rhode Island History,** Aldrich House, 110 Benevolent St, 02906.
Open Tues - Sat 11 AM - 4 PM, Sun 1 - 4 PM. Aldrich Gardens open by appointment May - Sept on Fri 1 - 4 PM. Aldrich was acquired in 1974. Galleries for changing exhibitions on Rhode Island history
Exhibitions: The Lay of the Land
L **Library,** 121 Hope St, 02906. *Librn* Open
Open Tues - Sat 10 AM - 5 PM; June, July & Aug Mon - Fri 10 AM - 5 PM. No admis fee. Open to public. Average Annual Attendance: 9000
Collections: †1000 manuscripts dating from 17th century; †Rhode Island Imprints, 1727-1800; †Rhode Island Broadsides; †Providence Postmaster Provisional Stamps; †Rhode Island Post Office Covers; †genealogical sources, all state newspapers, maps, films, TV news films and movies, graphics, architectural drawings; 200,000 reference volumes; 20,000 photographs

M **RHODE ISLAND SCHOOL OF DESIGN,** Museum of Art, 224 Benefit St, 02903. Tel 401-331-3511, Ext 270. *Dir* Franklin Robinson; *Chmn Museum Council* Barnet Fain; *Cur Decorative Arts* Christopher Monkhouse; *Cur Education* Cora Lee Gibbs; *Museum Shop Mgr* Susan Handy; *Museum Shop Mgr* Alice Westervelt
Open Tues, Wed, Fri, Sat 10:30 AM - 5 PM, Thurs 1 - 7 PM. Admis adults $1, children 5 - 18 25¢, children under 4 free. Estab 1877 to collect and exhibit art for general education of the public. Present buildings opened in 1897, 1906 and 1926. Average Annual Attendance: 80,000. Mem: 2500
Income: Financed by endowment, membership, state and federal appropriation, private and corporate contributions
Collections: Lucy Truman Aldrich Collection of European porcelains and Oriental textiles; Ancient Oriental and ethnographic art; American painting; contemporary graphic arts; Nancy Sayles Day Collection of modern Latin American art; English watercolors; 15th through 18th century European art; 19th and 20th century French art from Romanticism through post-Cubism; Albert Pilavin Collection of 20th century American Art; Pendleton House collection of 18th century American furniture and decorative arts; Abbey Aldrich Rockefeller collection of Japanese birds and flower prints

Exhibitions: Art for Your Collection XVII; Herbert Bayer: Photographic Works; Costumes in Contaxt; Designed for Another Age: Decorative Arts from Newport mansions;Contemporary drawings form the Museums Collection; Installation 80; Richard Fleischer; Jaspar Johns: Prints 1970 - 1977; Wolf Kahn: Paintings and Pastels; Landscape-Cityscape: Photographs from the Museums Collection; Neil Maurer: Photographs
Publications: Museum Notes, annually; Calendar of Events, five per year
Activities: Classes for adults and children; dramatic programs; docent training; field trips; lectures open to the public, 15 - 20 visiting lecturers per year; gallery talks; concerts; tours; extension department serves schools in the area; lending collection contains color reproductions, original artwork and slides; traveling exhibitions organized and circulated; museum shop sells books, original art, reproductions, prints, jewelry, posters and postcards
L **Library,** 2 College St, 02903. *Librn* Jeanne Borden
Open to the public for reference
Library Holdings: Vols 55,000; Per subs 250; AV—Rec, slides; Other—Clipping files, photographs
Special Subjects: Fine Arts and Crafts

SAUNDERSTOWN

M **GILBERT STUART BIRTHPLACE,** Gilbert Stuart Rd, 02874. Tel 401-294-3001. *Cur* Mrs Kenneth W Pettigrew; *Pres* Mrs Oliver Marion
Open daily 11 AM - 5 PM; cl Fri. Admis adults $1, children under 12 50¢. Estab 1932 as a national historic landmark, the furnished birthplace of America's foremost portrait painter; the home was built 1751. Average Annual Attendance: 10,000. Mem: 180; dues $5 - $10; annual meeting June
Income: Financed by endowment, membership and grants
Activities: Guided tours of the home

WAKEFIELD

M **HERA EDUCATIONAL FOUNDATION,** Hera Gallery, Main St, Box 336, 02879. Tel 401-789-1488. *Coordr* Roberta Richman
Estab 1975 to display art work by women. Gallery has large neutral space on ground floor, 30 x 50 ft. Mem: 15, dues $24
Income: Financed by endowment, membership and grants
Publications: Catalogs, quarterly
Activities: Lect open to public, 6 visiting lectr per year; concerts; gallery talks; tours; originate traveling exhibitions

WARWICK

M **RHODE ISLAND JUNIOR COLLEGE,** Art Department Gallery, Knight Campus, 400 East Ave, 02886. Tel 401-825-1000. *Chmn* Rita C Lepper
Open Mon - Fri 8 AM - 9:30 PM. Library maintained
Exhibitions: Exhibitions are changed monthly
Activities: Lect open to public; original objects of art lent; lending collection contains 300 color reproductions, 20 filmstrips, 10,000 Kodachromes, 12 motion pictures and 200 clippings and small prints; book shop
M **Blackstone Valley Campus Art Gallery,** Louisquisset Pike, Lincoln, 02865. Tel 401-333-7154.
Open Mon - Fri 8 AM - 4 PM

O **WARWICK ARTS FOUNDATION,** City Hall, 02886. Tel 401-738-2000, Ext 197. *Pres* Joseph DesRoches; *VPres* Janet Whelan; *Secy* Laraine Palmer; *Executive Dir* Maureen Maynard
Estab 1963 to foster the arts within the city of Warwick. Mem: 200; dues individual $3; annual meeting April
Income: $5000 (financed by membership, city and state appropriation and Federal grants)
Exhibitions: Rotating Art Show in public buildings and banks in the city, using artwork of professional and nonprofessional artists in the area; Benefit Show for Geriatric Day Care Center; Member's Art Show
Publications: Warwick Arts Foundation Newsletter, monthly Sept - June
Activities: Film series; competitions; awards; scholarships

WESTERLY

L **WESTERLY PUBLIC LIBRARY,** Broad St, 02891. Tel 401-596-2877. *Dir* Ardis Holliday; *Asst Dir* Susan Collins; *Art Dir* Open
Open Mon - Thurs 9 AM - 9 PM, Fri 9 AM - 6 PM, Sat 9 AM - 5:30 PM. Estab 1892 as a memorial to soldiers of the Civil War, and to provide a library and activities center for the community. Circ 130,000. Art gallery maintained, 30 x 54 ft, 16 ft ceiling, with incandescent track lighting
Income: Financed by endowment, city and state appropriation
Purchases: $40,000
Library Holdings: Vols 115,000; Per subs 250; Micro—Reels; AV—Rec; Other—Framed reproductions, original art works
Exhibitions: Ten - twelve exhibitions scheduled per year
Activities: Lect open to public; library tours

SOUTH CAROLINA

ANDERSON

O **ANDERSON COUNTY ARTS COUNCIL,** 405 N Main St, 29621. Tel 803-224-8811. *Pres* Helen Camak; *VPres* Janet Bowen; *Secy* Fred Raetsch; *Executive Dir* Sue A Parks; *Programs Coordr* Rebecca Michaels
Open Mon - Fri 9 AM - 5 PM, Sun 2 - 5 PM. No admis fee. Estab 1972 as a non-profit institution, serving as a clearinghouse for individuals and organizations interested in the promotion of visual, literary and performing arts. Gallery rotates exhibits monthly, featuring locally, regionally and nationally known artists. Average Annual Attendance: 10,000. Mem: 550; dues $1000, $500, $100, $50, $25, $18, $10, $5; annual meeting last Tues of Sept
Income: $45,000 (financed by membership, foundations, donations, county appropriation and grants)
Publications: Calendar of events; newsletter, bi-monthly
Activities: Classes for adults and children; gallery talks; tours

CHARLESTON

M **CAROLINA ART ASSOCIATION,** Gibbes Art Gallery, 135 Meeting, 29401. Tel 803-722-2706. *Pres* Dr William H Coles; *VPres* Nancy C Smythe; *VPres* Robert W Marks; *Secy* Elfrida B Moore; *Dir* Charles L Wyrick Jr; *Adminr* Mary M Muller; *Cur Collection* Martha R Severens; *Cur Education* Paul C Figueroa; *Supv Art School* Valerie Miller; *Asst Cur Collection* Jean C Stewart
Open Tues - Sat 10 AM - 5 PM, Sun 2 - 5 PM; cl Mon and national holidays. No admis fee. Estab 1858 as an art gallery and museum. Gallery is 31,000 sq ft. Average Annual Attendance: 75,000. Mem: 3200; dues family $25, individual $15, student $5; annual meeting second Mon in Oct
Income: $200,000 (financed by endowment, membership, city and county appropriation)
Collections: Colonial and Federal Portraits; †Contemporary American Paintings and Prints; Japanese Woodblock Prints; †Miniature Portraits; Oriental Art Objects
Exhibitions: An Artist Collects: Jasper Johns; Etchings and Drypoints-Alfred Hutty; Expressions of Nature in Art; Edgefield Pottery; Impressions of Women; Constantine Manos Photos: A Greek Portfolio; Recent American Etching: Spoleto Festival USA; Alice Ravenel Huger Smith: Visions of Lowcountry; South Carolina State Arts Commission Annual Exhibition
Publications: Bulletins, quarterly; books
Activities: Classes for adults and children; docent training; lect open to public, 3 visiting lectr per year; concerts; gallery talks; tours; individual paintings and original objects of art lent; originate traveling exhibitions; sales shop sells books, original art, prints, reproductions, jewelry, and crafts
L **Library,** 135 Meeting, 29401. *Librn* Eleanor C Gaver
Open to members and scholars for reference only
Library Holdings: Vols 3000; Per subs 10

M **CHARLESTON MUSEUM,** 360 Meeting St, 29403. Tel 803-722-2996. *Pres* Arthur Wilcox; *VPres* Robert L Clement Jr; *Dir* Donald G Herold; *Cur Anthropology* Allen Liss; *Cur Decorative Arts* J Kenneth Jones; *Cur Historic Houses* Mrs Edward Webb; *Cur Natural History* Albert E Sanders; *Registrar* Jan Hiester
Open daily 9 AM - 5 PM. Admis adults $1.50, children 50¢. Estab 1773 as a museum and library to diffuse knowledge of history, decorative arts, art, natural history, anthropology and technology; also to preserve houses and monuments. It is the oldest museum in the United States. Average Annual Attendance: 225,000. Mem: 1500; dues $12.50 and up; annual meeting March
Income: $530,000 (financed by membership, city and county appropriations, admissions and sales)
Collections: Ceramics, decorative arts, furniture, glass, maps, photos, prints and textiles
Publications: Newsletter, occasionally
Activities: Courses; lect; films
L **Library,** 350 Meeting St, 29403. Tel 803-722-2996, Ext 3. *Librn* K Sharon Bennett; *Library Technician* Myrtle Brown
Open daily 9 AM - 5 PM. Estab 1773 as an educational institution, collects, preserves and uses artifacts of natural history, history, anthropology and decorative arts
Library Holdings: Vols 30,000; Per subs 100; AV—Rec; Other—Clipping files, manuscripts, pamphlets
M **Heward-Washington House,** 87 Church St, 29403.
Open daily 10 AM - 5 PM. Admis adults $2.25, students 50¢. Built 1772; home of Thomas Heyward, Jr; purchased by the Museum in 1929. Museum is furnished with Charleston-made furniture of the period; a National Historic Landmark
M **Hunley Museum,** 50 Broad St, 29403.
Open daily 10 AM - 5 PM. No admis fee. Built about 1798 as a bank, restored in 1966. Museum is in the basement; it houses a display of Charleston Civil War Naval History
M **Joseph Manigault House,** 350 Meeting St, 29403.
Open daily 10 AM - 5 PM. Admis adults $2.25, students 50¢. Built 1803 as Adam style mansion designed by Gabriel Manigault. Museum contains Charleston-made furniture of the period; a National Historic Landmark

CLEMSON

CLEMSON UNIVERSITY
M **Rudolph E Lee Gallery,** College of Architecture. 29631. Tel 803-656-3081, Ext 2-30. *Coordr Educational Media & Exhib* Tom Dimond
Open Mon - Fri 9 AM - 4:30 PM, Sun 2 - 5 PM, cl Sat. No admis fee. Estab 1956 to provide cultural and educational resources; to collect, preserve, interpret and display items of historical, educational and cultural significance. Average Annual Attendance: 20,000
Income: Financed by state appropriation
Collections: †Clemson Architectural Foundation Collection; Contemporary American Paintings and Graphics

Exhibitions: (1978-79) John Acorn, Sculpture; America's Architectural Heritage; Dianne Arbus Photographs; Anna Campbell Bliss; Bob Chance Ceramics; Courthouse Photographs; Deborah Frederick, Rainbow Nets; Hollis Holbrook Paintings; Sauna Jen, Chinese Watercolors; Harlan McClure, Watercolors; Kemp Mooney, Architect; National Sculpture-1978; Bill Owens Photographs; Paris Prize Winners; Paris Review Posters; Photography, A Representative Survey; SECCA Award Winners; State Art Collection; Three Photographers-Bravo, Winogrand, Erwitt; Three South Carolina Painters-David Freeman, Steven Gately, Danny Taylor; Joan Tweedy, Ceramics; summer art show
Publications: Exhibition Bulletin, annually; Posters on Exhibits, monthly
Activities: Lect open to public, 12-15 visiting lectr per year; gallery talks; tours; exten dept serving southeast United States; individual paintings and original objects of art lent to museums, universities; lending collection contains original prints, paintings, sculpture; originate traveling exhibitions
L **Emery A Gunnin Architectural Library,** College of Architecture, 29631. *Librn* Mrs Dillman B Sorrells
For reference only
Library Holdings: Vols 10,000; Per subs 200; AV—Slides
Collections: Rare Book Collection
M **Fort Hill,** 29631. Tel 803-656-2061. *Cur* Mrs Revelie Brannon
Open Tues - Sat 10 AM - Noon & 1 - 5:30 PM, Sun 2-6 PM, cl holidays and Christmas week. No admis fee. An historic museum located in the home of John C Calhoun
Collections: Flemish Paintings; Family Portraits; Period Rooms and Furnishings
Publications: Fort Hill, brochure
Activities: Lect; guided tours; sales shop

CLINTON

L **PRESBYTERIAN COLLEGE,** James H Thomason Library, 29325. Tel 803-833-2820. *Assoc Prof of Art* Robert Jolly
Sun - Fri 2 - 10 PM, Sat 2 - 5 PM. Estab 1974 to serve educational institution. Small gallery with monthly exhibits
Income: Financed by college
Library Holdings: Vols 110,000; Per subs 650; Micro—Cards, fiche; AV—A-tapes, cassettes, fs, rec; Other—Framed reproductions, original art works
Exhibitions: Regional artists exhibits
Activities: Lect open to public; gallery talks

COLUMBIA

M **COLUMBIA MUSEUMS OF ART AND SCIENCE,** 1112 Bull St, 29201. Tel 803-799-2810. *Chmn Museum Commission* W Croft Jennings; *Pres* Lee J Baker; *VPres* Nicholas K Moore; *Dir* Walter M Hathaway; *Asst Cur & Registrar* Beverley H Means; *Admin Asst* Sarah A Cahill; *Dept of Education* Cassandra Baker; *Controller* Fred Panasiuk; *Chief Cur* Nina Parris
Open Tues - Sat 10 AM - 5 PM, Sun 2 - 6 PM, cl Mon. No admis fee. Estab 1950 to extend and increase art understanding, to assist in the conservation of a valuable cultural heritage, and to recognize and assist contemporary art expression. Average Annual Attendance: 119,344. Mem: 2759; dues family $25 and up, single $15; annual meeting Jan
Income: $379,647 (financed by membership, city, county and state appropriation)
Collections: †Barringer Collection of Contemporary Art; Hammond Collection; Erin Kohn Collection of Dolls; Samuel H Kress Collection of Renaissance Paintings; Neuhoff Collection of English Furniture; Scotese Collection of Graphics; Seibels Collection; †European and American Paintings and Decorative Art; South Carolina Dispensary Bottles; Spanish Colonial Collection
Exhibitions: (1980) Charles Burchfield 1893-1967; 15th Annual Junior Mid-South; Guild of Handloom Weavers; Jouets Americans 1925-1975; LaBelle Epoque; Late Twentieth Century Art; New Handmade Furniture; Photographs, Steichen; Veda Reed Paintings and Drawings 1955-1980. (1981) African Furniture; American Photography: A Southern Focus; Berlin Porcelain; Bracquemond; 5000 Years of Art from the Met; Kate Freeman Clark; Nancy Graves; Mississippi River Craft Show; Palladio
Publications: Annual Report; exhibition folders and catalogs, occasionally
Activities: Docent training; lect open to public, 6 visiting lectr per year; concerts; gallery talks; tours; exten dept serving Metropolitan area; individual paintings and original objects of art lent to qualified galleries, historic houses, and approved city and state facilities; originate traveling exhibitions; museum shop sells postcards and exhibition catalogs
L **Library,** 1112 Bull St, 29201. *Librn* Beverley H Means
Open Tues - Fri 10 AM - 5 PM. Open to members and scholars for reference only
Library Holdings: Vols 5200; Per subs 15; Other—Clipping files, exhibition catalogs, pamphlets
Special Subjects: Reference relating to the permanent collection, plus general art sources
Collections: A S Salley Collection of early South Carolina exhibition catalogs and books
O **Columbia Art Association,** 1112 Bull St, 29201. *Pres* Lee J Baker; *VPres* Nicholas K Moore; *Secy* Mrs D C H Belser
Estab 1915, the association is the operating agent for the Museum
M **Columbia Science Museum,** 1519 Senate St, 29201. *Secy* Mary F Galloway; *Cur of Sciences* William Lazarus
Open Tues - Sat 10 AM - 5 PM, Sun 2 - 6 PM, cl Mon. Estab 1959 to present a coherent framework for the understanding of natural history. Average Annual Attendance: 55,364. Mem: Annual meeting last Thurs in Jan
Collections: Dr Robert Gibbes Collection of Shells; Kendall Collection of Pan American pots
Publications: Newsletter, monthly
Activities: Docent training; lectr for school groups; tours; sales shop sells books

O **GUILD OF SOUTH CAROLINA ARTISTS,** PO Box 12621, 29211. *Pres* Leo Manske; *Pres Elect* Bette Lee Coburn; *Admin Asst* Lynn Robertson Myers
Estab 1951 for the purpose of promoting the visual arts in South Carolina. Mem: 400; dues Commercial patron $50, patron $25, active $10, association $5; annual meeting Nov 1

Income: $8906
Exhibitions: Annual exhibition, juried, by members; rotates from Columbia Museum of Art, Greenville County Museum of Art, Florence Museum of Art and Gibbes Art Gallery in Charleston; host gallery receives purchase award
Publications: Brochure; newsletter; annual membership dictionary
Activities: Workshops; programs; lectures open to the public, 1 or 2 visiting lecturers per year; competitions

O **SOUTH CAROLINA ARTS COMMISSION,** 1800 Gervais St, 29201. Tel 803-758-3442. *Chmn* Charlotte Cassels; *Exec Dir* Rick George; *Deputy Dir* Scott Sanders; *Dir Support Services* Joyce Huey; *Dir Arts Development* Susie Surkamer; *Public Information* Fred Box
Open 8:30 AM - 5 PM. Estab 1967 to promote and develop the arts in South Carolina
Income: Federal, state and private sources
Collections: †State Art Collection
Exhibitions: (1978) Annual Exhibition at Columbia College
Publications: Quarterly newsletter
Activities: grafts-in-aid

C **SOUTH CAROLINA NATIONAL BANK,** 1241 Main St, PO Box 168, 29205. Tel 803-765-3756. *VPres* Virginia M Grose
Open to public. No admis fee. Estab 1971 to recognize and promote artists who have or have had a connection with South Carolina National. Collection displayed in offices throughout South Carolina
Collections: Contemporary South Carolina art
Activities: Sponsor purchase and merit awards for selected competitions in the state; individual objects of art lent to museums for display; originate traveling exhibitions, have carried-out two statewide tours from collection, work was displayed in a number of cities at museums, libraries, court houses and banks

M **UNIVERSITY OF SOUTH CAROLINA,** McKissick Museums, 29208. *Dir & Archivist* Dr Barry H Rosen; *Cur Historical Collection* George Terry; *Cur Art Gallery* Lynn Myers; *Education Museums* Dr William Savage
Open Mon - Fri 9 AM - 4 PM, Sun 1 - 5 PM, cl Sat. Estab 1976 to centralize and promote the university's museum collections for the benefit of the academic program, the community, and the state. Average Annual Attendance: 24,000
Income: Financed by state appropriation
Collections: Bernard Baruch Collection of 18th Century Silver; James F Byrnes Collection; J Harry Howard Gemstone Collection; Richard Mandell: Art Nouveau Collection
Activities: Dramatic programs; lect open to public, 5-6 visiting lectr per year; concerts; gallery talks; tours; competitions; originate traveling exhibitions; sales shop sells books and magazines
L **Slide Library,** Sloan College, Room 202, 29208. *Instructional Media Specialist* Carol Molten; *Photo Technician* John Kelley
Open Mon - Fri 8:30 AM - 5 PM. Estab as a major teaching resource for the Art Department
Library Holdings: AV—Slides 90,000

FLORENCE

M **FLORENCE MUSEUM,** * 558 Spruce St, 29501. Tel 803-662-3351. *Dir* Dr William A Burns; *Board Pres* Andrew Kampiziones; *Treas* O S Aiken; *Secy* E Cart
Open Tues - Sat 10 AM - 5 PM, Sun 2 - 5 PM, cl Mon. No admis fee. Estab 1936 as a general museum of art, natural science, and history of South Carolina, with emphasis on the region known as the Pee Dee, and to acquaint the public with fine art. Twelve galleries exhibit artwork. Mem: 400; dues $15 - $1000; annual meeting third Thurs in April
Income: $40,000 (financed by membership, county appropriation, and donations)
Collections: African, Chinese, Japanese and Korean Collections; artifacts; works of local Black artists, particularly William H Johnson; works of local and regional artists
Exhibitions: Batiks, Prints and their Makers; Bicentennial Year in SC History Hall; Charles Councell; Children's Art; Janet Dreskin-Haig paintings; Dixie Dugan; 50th Annual Art Exhibition of Florence Art Association; Flora Exotics; Steve Gately; Nell LaFaye; Papal Coins; South Carolina Guild of Artists; SC State Artists; Southern Phenomena; 24th Pee Dee Regional Art Exhibition
Activities: Classes for adults and children; docent training; puppet shows; lect open to the public, 6 visiting lectrs per year; gallery talks; tours; competitions with prizes; lending collection contains books, photographs; traveling exhibitions organized and circulated
L **Evans Research Library,** * 29501.
Open to students, for reference only
Library Holdings: Vols 2000

GREENVILLE

M **BOB JONES UNIVERSITY,** Museum and Art Gallery, 29614. Tel 803-242-5100. *Chmn of the Board* Bob Jones; *Dir* Joan C Davis; *Staff Supv* Janice Churdar; *Conservator* Barbara Votaw
Open Tues - Sun 2 - 5 PM; cl Mon, Dec 20 - 25, New Year's Day and July 4. No admis fee. Estab 1951 to show how universal is the Word of God in its appeal to human hearts in every generation; the Bowen Collection of Biblical antiquities was presented to the University by Mr and Mrs Frank Bowen in 1932; the permanent sacred art collection was made by Dr Bob Jones, Chancellor of the University, and open to the public in 1951; it is termed one of the most remarkable collections of famous religious paintings in the world. Average Annual Attendance: 29,000
Income: Financed by University and gifts
Collections: †Bob Jones University Collection of sacred art including only religious art by the Old Masters from the 13th - 19th centuries and numbering works by such artists as Benson, Botticelli, Cranach the Elder, G David, Murillo, Rembrandt, Ribera, Rubens, Solimena del Piombo, Tintoretto, Titian, Van Leyden, Veronese and Zurbaran Bowen Collection of Biblical antiquities and illustrative material from Palestine, Syria, Lebanon, Egypt and Jordan; furniture and sculpture. In 1963 Bob Jones University acquired for its War Memorial Chapel a series of important

paintings on Revealed Religion by Benjamin West. These were originally executed for King George III to be placed in his new Chapel at Windsor Castle. Because of the illness of the King, plans for the construction of the Chapel were abandoned and the completed paintings were returned to the painter. The posthumous sale of West's works in 1829 included a number of the pictures on Revealed Religion. Joseph Neeld, MP, was the successful bidder and the pictures hung in his home until 1962. At that time they were offered for sale by Christie's of London. Six were acquired for the Bob Jones University with funds provided for that purpose by an anonymous friend of the University
Publications: Catalogs; illustrated booklets
Activities: Tours for school and adult groups by appointment; individual paintings lent to other galleries in the US and abroad; sales shop selling reproductions, prints and slides
L **Mack Library,** 29614. *Libn* Dr L Gene Elliott
Open to the public
Library Holdings: Per subs 36

M **GREENVILLE COUNTY MUSEUM OF ART,** 420 College St, 29601. Tel 803-271-7570. *Executive Dir* Jack A Morris Jr; *Chief Cur* Ed Barnwell; *Dir of Education* Sylvia L Marchant; *Dir of Museum School of Art* Sharon Whitley
Open Mon - Sat 10 AM - 5 PM; Sun 1 - 5 PM. No admis fee. Estab 1958 for the collection and preservation of North American Art. Average Annual Attendance: 100,000. Mem: 1500; dues graduated schedule; annual meeting June
Income: Financed by membership and county appropriation
Collections: Limited to North American art with emphasis on Southeast. 26 works by Andrew Wyeth plus 230 preliminary studies by Wyeth from the Holly & Arthur Magill Collection on permanent loan
Exhibitions: (1978) Richard Hunt; (1979) Artists of Brandywine: Howard Pyle & his Students; Lewis W Hine: A Retrospective of the Photographer
Publications: Museum Notes, three times per yr
Activities: Classes for children & adults; workshops; lect; films; gallery talks; museum shop and cafe

C **LIBERTY LIFE INSURANCE COMPANY,** 2000 Wade Hampton Blvd, PO Box 789, 29602. Tel 803-268-8396. *Legal VPres* Glenn Hilliard
Open Mon - Thurs 8:30 AM - 5 PM, Fri 8:30 AM - 12:30 PM. Estab 1978 to collect textile art selections which are the last of their kind and show a different culture than our own. Collection displayed throughout corporate headquarters
Collections: Limited edition prints, graphics and silkscreens; textile art works from around the world
Activities: Sponsors Scholastic Art Awards Contest for high school students annually

GREENWOOD

M **MUSEUM,** 567 Phoenix St, PO Box 3131, 29646. Tel 803-229-7093. *Pres* Dr James Cheezem; *Acting Cur & Treas* J W Bolton; *Secy* Willie McLaughlin
Open Mon - Fri 9 AM - 5 PM; Sun 2 - 5 PM; cl Sat. No admis fee. Estab June 1967 for educational purposes. Average Annual Attendance: 7654. Mem: 220; dues $15; meeting Jan, March, May and Nov
Income: $7500 (financed by endowment)
Purchases: $24,000
Collections: Frank E Delano Gallery of African animal mounts and rare African works of art by the now extinct Katanga Tribe; bone, wood and ivory carvings; chinaware; crystals; glassware; limited art works; photographs

MURRELLS INLET

M **BROOKGREEN GARDENS,** 29576. Tel 803-237-4218. *Pres* Joseph Veach Noble; *First VPres* A Hyatt Mayor; *Second VPres* Marshall M Fredericks; *Dir* Gurdon L Tarbox; *Secy* Eric S Malm; *Treas* Robert R Coker
Open 9:30 AM - 4:45 PM. Admis adults $2, 6-12 years 50¢, under six free. Estab 1931 to exhibit the flora and fauna of South Carolina and to exhibit objects of art. The outdoor museum exhibits American sculpture, while smaller pieces are shown in the Small Sculpture Museum and indoor gallery. Average Annual Attendance: 160,000. Mem: 550; dues $25 - $1000; annual meeting in Oct
Income: $350,000 (financed by endowment, membership and admission)
Purchases: $27,000
Collections: †Representative collection of American sculpture, by 182 sculptors
Publications: Brookgreen Bulletin, quarterly
Activities: Competitions; museum shop selling books, reproductions and slides
L **Library,** 29576. *Libn* Gurdon L Tarbox Jr
For reference only to staff
Library Holdings: Vols 406; Per subs 72; Micro—Prints; Other—Clipping files, maps, architectural and engineering drawings and plans
Special Subjects: American sculpture

ROCK HILL

M **MUSEUM OF YORK COUNTY,** Route 4 Box 211, Mount Gallant Rd, 29730. Tel 803-366-4116. *Executive Dir* Charles W Hall; *Assoc Dir* Chris Houmes; *Secy* Sue Sanders
Open Mon - Sat 9 AM - 5 PM; Sun 1 - 5 PM. Admis 50¢ per person. Estab 1949 as a natural and physical science museum. Average Annual Attendance: 186,000
Income: Financed by county appropriation and donations
Publications: Newsletter, monthly
Activities: Classes for adults and children; dramatic programs; lect open to the public; traveling exhibitions organized and circulated; museum shop selling books, prints
L **Library,** Route 4 Box 211, Mount Gallant Rd, 29730.
Open to the public for research only

M **WINTHROP COLLEGE GALLERY OF ART,** * 701 Oakland Ave, 29733. Tel 803-323-2191. *Dir* Edmund D Lewandowski

Open Mon - Fri 8:30 AM - 5 PM, Sun 2 - 5 PM, cl Sat. No admis fee. Estab 1970 to present area viewers with a wide variety of exhibitions, local, regional and national in scope; and to provide an opportunity for regional artists to exhibit. Two galleries 40 x 80 x 20 ft and 15 x 15 x 12 ft. Average Annual Attendance: 15,000
Income: Financed by city appropriation
Collections: Limited collections
Exhibitions: Annual Textile Invitational; Foundry Art; South Carolina Architectures 1670-1970; South Carolina State Art Collection; Spring Mills Annual Traveling Exhibition; several one-person shows
Activities: Classes for adults; lect open to public; gallery talks; originate traveling exhibitions; museum shop sells original art and prints

SPARTANBURG

O **ARTS COUNCIL OF SPARTANBURG COUNTY, INC,** 385 S Spring St, 29301. Tel 803-583-2776. *Executive Dir* Georgia K Allen; *Asst Executive Dir* Mrs Danny R Hughes; *Business Mgr* William C Taylor Jr
Open Mon - Fri 9 AM - 5 PM, Sun 3 - 5 PM. No admis fee. Estab 1968 to coordinate all cultural activities in the area; to promote its member organizations; maintain an Arts Center with changing and permanent exhibitions. Average Annual Attendance: 100,000
Income: $170,000 (financed by state appropriation and private donations)
Collections: The Girl with the Red Hair by Robert Henri; twenty other paintings
Exhibitions: Changing exhibits
Publications: Spartanburg Arts, bi-monthly
Activities: Classes for adults and children; dramatic programs; docent training; arts camp for children; drama festival; lect open to public; concerts; gallery talks; tours; scholarships; exten dept serves schools in county; sales shop sells original art, prints, original pottery, jewelry, hand-printed cards and stationery
L **Library,** 385 S Spring St, 29301.
For reference
Library Holdings: Vols 50; Per subs 2
Special Subjects: Art History

M **CONVERSE COLLEGE,** Milliken Art Gallery, PO Box 29, 29301. Tel 803-585-6421, Ext 251. *Dir* Dr Henry Fagen
Open Mon - Fri 2 - 4 PM, cl Sat & Sun. No admis fee. Estab 1971 for educational purposes. A brick and glass structure of 40 x 60 ft; movable panels 4 x 6 ft for exhibition of work, 16 panels, 12 sculpture stands. Average Annual Attendance: 1500
Income: Financed by endowment
Exhibitions: Invitational exhibits of regional artists
Activities: Eight to ten traveling exhibitions each year; traveling exhibitions organized and circulated

O **SPARTANBURG COUNTY ART ASSOCIATION,*** 385 S Spring St, 29301. Tel 803-582-7616. *Dir* Mary Ward Wisnewski
Open Mon - Fri 10 AM - 5 PM, Sat 2 - 4 PM, Sun 3 - 5 PM. No admis fee. Estab 1969 to promote the works of contemporary artists in the southeastern United States. Gallery is located in the Spartanburg County Arts Center and contains both a permanent sales section and a changing exhibit area. Average Annual Attendance: 4500. Mem: 300; dues $7 - $500
Income: Financed by endowment, membership
Collections: †Contemporary Southeastern Artists
Exhibitions: (1978-1979) Marianna Hamilton of Myrtle Beach; Pierre Humbert from Paris, France; Invitational Crafts by craftspeople throughout the United States; Invitational Graphics by artists from the Southeast region; Anne Lattimore of Aiken; Jean McWhorter of Columbia; Jeanette Ritsch and Elaine Wagner of Spartanburg; South Carolina Collections from the 19th Century
Publications: Newsletter, quarterly
Activities: Classes for adults and children; docent training; lect open to the public, 2 visiting lectrs per year; gallery talks; tours; competitions; sales shop selling books, original art
L **Library,*** 385 S Spring St, 29301.
Library Holdings: Vols 150; Per subs 2
Special Subjects: Books on Art
Collections: Limited art historical volumes

SUMTER

M **SUMTER GALLERY OF ART,** 421 N Main St, PO Box 1316, 29150. Tel 803-775-0543. *Chmn Board Dir* J Eugene Matthews; *Gallery Dir* Laura E Ayers
Open Tues - Sun 3 - 6 PM. No admis fee. Estab 1970 to bring to area exhibits of works of recognized artists, to provide an outlet for local artists for showing and sale of their work, and to serve as a facility where visual art may become a part of life and education of the people, particularly children of this community. The Gallery is the 1850 home of the late Miss Elizabeth White, well-known artist of Sumter, which was deeded to the gallery in 1977 under the terms of her will. Presently using hall and four downstairs rooms. Average Annual Attendance: 8500. Mem: 460; dues commercial patron $40, patron $30, family $15, individual $10; annual meeting May
Income: $18,000 (financed by membership, earned income, personnel development grant from SC Arts Com, CETA employee)
Collections: Approximately sixty paintings, etchings and drawings of Elizabeth White given to the gallery by trustees of her estate
Exhibitions: Annual Young People's Exhibit; Individual and group exhibits of paintings, sculpture, collages, photography and crafts by recognized artists primarily from Southeast
Publications: Newsletter, monthly
Activities: Classes for adults and children; lect open to public, 8 vis lect per yr; gallery talks; competitions; awards given; sales shop selling original art and prints

SOUTH DAKOTA

ABERDEEN

M **DACOTAH PRAIRIE MUSEUM,** 21 S Main St, PO Box 395, 57401. Tel 605-229-1608. *Dir* Clark Walz; *Cur of Education* Helen Bergh; *Cur of Design & Displays* Megan Ried
Open Mon - Fri 9 AM - 5 PM, Sat & Sun 1 - 4 PM. No admis fee. Estab 1969 to preserve the heritage of the peoples of the Dakotas; to maintain and develop exhibits that educate people about the heritage of the Dakotas. Museum has two galleries devoted to art: the Lamont Gallery and the Prairie Heritage Gallery
Collections: Sioux and Arikara Indian artifacts; local and regional artists; photography
Exhibitions: Art from the Red Cloud Indian School; Thomas Hart Benton; Bronze Sculpture (local); Brown County Junior and Senior High School of Art; Jan S Dacotah Works on Paper; Dacotah Photo Documentary Show; Rockwell Kent; South Dakota National Sculpture Camp II; Grant Wood; W P A Prints
Publications: Annual Report; Dacotah Prairie Times, ten per year
Activities: Classes for adults and children; lect open to public, 3 visiting lectr per year; gallery talks; tours; individual paintings and original objects of art lent to museums, art centers and some materials to schools; museum shop sells books, magazines, original art and reproductions
L **Historical Research Center Library,** 21 S Main St, PO Box 395, 57401. Tel 605-229-1608. *Dir* Clark Walz
Open upon request for reference only
Library Holdings: Vols 5000; Per subs 7

BROOKINGS

M **SOUTH DAKOTA STATE UNIVERSITY,** South Dakota Memorial Art Center, Medary Ave at Harvey Dunn St, 57006. Tel 605-688-5423. *Dir* Joseph Stuart; *Asst Dir* Sheila Agee; *Cur of Marghab Collection* Cora Sivers; *Secy* Elaine Hietbrink
OPen Mon - Fri 8 AM - 5 PM; Sat 10 AM - 5 PM; Sun 1 - 5 PM. No admis fee. Estab 1969 as the state center for visual arts with various Programs. The facility was designed by Howard Parezo, AIA, Sioux Falls, and occupies 112 x 90 foot site. There are seven galleries and a 147 seat auditorium. Average Annual Attendance: 140,000. Mem: 3000; annual meeting in April
Income: $80,000 (financed by state appropriation, endowment, gifts and grants)
Purchases: $2500
Collections: Art of South Dakota; Harvey Dunn Paintings; Marghab Linens; Native American Art; Northwestern Art; United States Art
Exhibitions: Herbert Bayer Photographic Works; Ada Caldwell Paintings; Contemporary South Dakota Art; Drawings by Northwestern Artists; Richard Edie Ceramics; Oscar Howe Painting; Mitakuye Oyasin (Sioux Art); National Sculpture Competition Models; Northwesten Painting and Sculpture; Prints from the Guggenheim Museum; South Dakota Art Faculty Biennial V; South Dakota Biennial IV; Women Artists Today
Publications: Annual report; bulletin, quarterly; exhibition catalogues; newsletter, monthly
Activities: Docent training; lect; films; tours; competitions; traveling exhibitions; sales shop
L **Jeannette Lusk Library Collection,** Medary Ave at Harvey Dunn St, 57006.
Open to the public for lending through the main library
Library Holdings: Vols 2500; Per subs 15; AV—Slides
Special Subjects: Archives of South Dakota Art

CUSTER

M **WESTERN WOODCARVINGS,** Hwy 16, Box 747, 57730. *Mgr* Dale Schaffer; *Mgr* Gloria Schaffer
Open May 15 - Oct 1 daily 9 AM - 5 PM; June, July & Aug 8 AM - 6 PM; other times for special events. Group rates available. Estab 1966 in general area of Black Hills near the place Custer's party found gold in 1874
Collections: Niblack Collection of Woodcarvings; work of wood sculptors
Exhibitions: Temporary exhibitions of collection and current work
Activities: Lect; gallery talks; tours; competitions
L **Library,** Hwy 16, Box 747, 57730.
Collections: Books and reference material on sculpturing and woodcarving available on premises

DEADWOOD

M **DEADWOOD GULCH ART GALLERY,** Lee St, 57732. Tel 605-578-3636. *Pres* J D Sulentic; *Secy* Margaret Sulentic
Open April - Dec 9 AM - 5 PM. Estab 1967 to display and sell works of art. Gallery is operated in conjunction with a Chinese Museum Tunnel Tour, for which a charge of 50¢ per person is made
Collections: Chinese Art; paintings
Activities: Book shop

MITCHELL

O **OSCAR HOWE ART CENTER,** 119 W Third Ave, 57301. Tel 605-996-4111. *Dir* Margaret Quintal
Open Jan - March, Wed - Sat 10 AM - 5 PM; April - Dec, Mon - Sat 10 AM - 5 PM; cl holidays. No admis fee; donations accepted. Center is housed in a former Carnegie Library building constructed in 1902 and designated as a National Historic Site. **Mem:** Dues benefactor $250, sustaining $100, patron $50, sponsor $35, family $18 and individual $12.50
Collections: 19 paintings by Sioux artist and South Dakota Artist Laureate, Oscar Howe
Exhibitions: Main Gallery show changing every 6 weeks during June, July and August
Activities: Classes; workshops; tours; concerts; competitions; Garret Gift Shop sells original art work of regional artists including pottery, watercolors, weavings, oils and acrylics, books and Indian beadwork

RAPID CITY

M **DAKOTA ART GALLERY,** Dakota Artists Guild, Dahl Fine Arts Center, 713 Seventh St, 47701. Tel 605-342-2144.
Open Mon - Sat 10 AM - 5 PM. Estab 1965 as Civic Art Gallery by Dakota Artists Guild. Average Annual Attendance: 6000. **Mem:** 200; dues $15
Income: $40,000 (financed by membership and public contributions)
Exhibitions: Local exhibits and exhibits of national artists by invitation; all exhibits changed monthly
Publications: Brochure; newsletter, monthly
Activities: Classes of instruction; community art projects; lect and monthly meetings open to public; gallery tours; scholarships

M **SIOUX INDIAN MUSEUM,** Box 1504, 57709. Tel 605-348-0557. *Cur* Rena McGhan
Open June - Sept, Mon - Sat 9 AM - 5 PM, Sun 1 - 5 PM; Oct - May, Tues - Sat 10 AM - 5 PM, Sun 1 - 5 PM; cl New Year's Day, Thanksgiving, Christmas. No admis fee. Estab 1939 to promote the development of contemporary native American arts and crafts of the United States. Average Annual Attendance: 80,000
Income: Financed by federal appropriation
Collections: Contemporary native American arts and crafts of the United States; Historic works by Sioux craftsmen
Exhibitions: Contemporary Sioux Quillwork; Photographs and Poems by Sioux Children; continuing series of one-person exhibitions
Publications: One-person exhibition brochure series, monthly
Activities: Gallery talks; traveling exhibitions organized and circulated; sales shop selling books and original art

SIOUX FALLS

O **AUGUSTANA COLLEGE,** Center for Western Studies, 57197. Tel 605-336-4007. *Promotion Dir* Wayne L Petersen; *Admin Asst* Rebecca Johnson; *Pres* Sven G Froiland
Open 9 AM - 5 PM. Estab 1974 for collection and preservation of Historic Material for the promotion of South Dakota and its Western Artists. New gallery open May 1980. **Mem:** 200; dues vary
Income: Financed by endowment and membership
Collections: South Dakota Art
Exhibitions: South Dakota Artists
Publications: Sundancing at Pine Ridge and Rosebud by Thomas Mails; The Wind Blow Free by Fred Manfred; Natural History of the Black Hills, by S G Froiland
Activities: Lectures open to the public; gallery talks; awards; scholarships offered; Artmobile serving South Dakota; individual paintings and original objects of art lent; lending collection contains books, cassettes, motion pictures, nature artifacts, original art works, paintings, photographs, sculpture, slides; six to eight traveling exhibitions booked per year; traveling exhibitions organized and circulated; museum shop sells books, original art, prints and slides
L **Resource Center,** 57197.
Library Holdings: Vols 30,000
Special Subjects: Western Americana

M **CIVIC FINE ARTS ASSOCIATION MUSEUM,** 235 W Tenth St, 57102. Tel 605-336-1167. *Pres* Ward Whitwaur; *VPres* Dr W P McKenzie; *Executive Dir* Raymond Shermoe; *Office Mgr* Beverly Friedhoff; *Treas* Robert Flint; *Secy* Mrs W S Baker
Open Tues - Sat 11:30 AM - 5 PM; Sun 2 - 5 PM; cl Mon. No admis fee. Estab 1961 as a contemporary museum. Circ museum. Art gallery maintained. Average Annual Attendance: 80,000
Income: 1500; dues $15
Purchases: $70,000 (financed by endowment, membership, city appropriation and fund-raising projects)
Collections: Poster collection; regional art
Exhibitions: Arts '76; Contemporary Sioux Quilts; Drawings USA; Library of Congress-An American Album; Women Painters' Biennial
Publications: Newsletter, monthly
Activities: Classes for adults and children; lect open to the public, 2 vis lectr per yr; tours; competitions with awards; scholarships; lending collection contains 200 books; 200 books; traveling exhibitions organized and circulated; museum shop selling books, magazines, original art, prints, reproductions, pottery and imports, cards
L **Library,** 235 W Tenth St, 57102.
Open to members only

SPEARFISH

M **BLACK HILLS ART CENTER,** Little Gallery, 57783. *Dir* Joan Marie Rudell
Open Mon - Fri 8 AM - 10 PM; Sat & Sun 12 - 6 PM. Estab 1936 to encourage art expression and greater appreciation in the Black Hills area. Work of the Art Center is promoted jointly by Black Hills State College Art Department and the Student Union. Average Annual Attendance: 1500. **Mem:** 500; dues $5 and up
Exhibitions: Black Hills State College Regional Art; Graphic; Photography; local artists as well as an exchange program operating among regional colleges and universities
Activities: Classes for adults; programs held each semester; summer workshop; competitions; traveling exhibitions
L **Library,** Little Gallery, 57783.
Library Holdings: Vols 200; AV—Motion pictures; Other—Reproductions
Collections: Carnegie gift library containing 1000 prints and 150 books

VERMILLION

M **UNIVERSITY OF SOUTH DAKOTA ART GALLERIES,** W M Lee Center for the Fine Arts, 57069. Tel 605-677-5636. *Dir* John A Day
Open Mon - Fri 10 AM - 4:30 PM; Sat & Sun 1 - 5 PM. No admis fee. Estab 1965. Primary mission is educational, serving specifically the needs of the college and augmenting the university curriculum as a whole. There are two galleries. One is a changing gallery 50' x 50' located in the Fine Arts Center. The second houses the university collection of Works by Oscar Howe, a native American painter. This facility is approximately 30' x 20'. Average Annual Attendance: 15,000
Income: $12,000 (financed by state appropriation and student fee allotment
Purchases: $4000
Collections: 35 Works by Oscar Howe; variety of media by contemporary artists
Exhibitions: (1978-80) Camera Work 1903-1917; Marsden Hartley Exhibition; Native American Paintings; Vermillion 79: National Print and Drawing Exhibition; Women Artists Today: A Regional Competition; faculty and student shows
Publications: Catalogues for major exhibitions
Activities: Lect open to public; gallery talks; tours; competitions, awards given; exten dept serves 150 miles in general region; individual paintings and original objects of art lent to professional museums and galleries; book traveling exhibitions, 2 per year; originate traveling exhibitions

YANKTON

M **YANKTON COLLEGE,** Durand Art Collection, James Lloyd Library, 57078. *Cur* Prof Jerome E Gallagher
Estab 1909. Chiefly serves the Art Department. Open to students, faculty and townspeople
Collections: Some original paintings, sculpture and prints
Exhibitions: Frequently changed exhibitions
Activities: Lect for schools and clubs; loan exhibits circulated
L **James Lloyd Library,** 57078.

TENNESSEE

CHATTANOOGA

M **HOUSTON ANTIQUE MUSEUM,** 201 High St, 37403. Tel 615-267-7176. *Dir & Cur* Mary E Baker
Open Tues - Sat 10 AM - 4:30 PM; Sun 2 - 4:30 PM; cl Mon & holidays. Admis adults $1.50, children 75¢. Estab 1961, incorporated 1949, collection willed to Chattanooga by the late Anna Safley Houston. Average Annual Attendance: 10,000. **Mem:** 500; dues $100, $25, $10 & $7; annual meeting April
Collections: Early American Furniture; Rare Collection of Glass (15,000 pitchers, 600 patterns of pressed glass, all types of art glass, steins and Tiffany glass); dolls
Publications: The Fabulous Houston
Activities: Slide program for schools, clubs and churches; lect, 6 lectr per year

M **HUNTER MUSEUM OF ART,** 10 Bluff View, 37403. Tel 615-267-0968. *Dir* Cleve K Scarborough; *Cur Education* Diana W Suarez; *Coordr of Exhib* J Bradley Burns; *Admin Asst* Kay S Parish; *Registrar* Kay T Morris
Open Tues - Sat 10 AM - 4:30 PM; Sun 1 - 4:30 PM; cl Mon. No admis fee. Estab 1924, chartered in 1951, to present a visual arts program of high quality, maintain a fine collection of American art, and to carry out a vigorous educational program in the community and the schools. The permanent collection of American Art is housed in the George Thomas Hunter Mansion constructed in 1904; a contemporary addition was opened in 1975 with 50,000 sq ft of space in four major gallery areas, a classroom wing and an auditorium. Average Annual Attendance: 50,000. **Mem:** 1603; dues general $25, student and older $15
Income: $370,000
Collections: American paintings including works by Beirstadt, Bellows, Benton, Burchfield, Hassam, Henri, Marsh and others; Contemporary American Prints; Sculpture by Snelson and Sugarman
Exhibitions: American Impressionists; An American Collection; An American Inspiration (Danish Modern & Shaker Design); Andean Folk Art; Art For Public Places by Doris Leeper; Art Scene 1979 (juried); Stanley Boxer Drawings (1945 - 1975); California Landscape Painting; Christo's Wrapped Walkways; Contemporary Printmaking: Selections from the Collection of Ashland Oil, Inc; Egyptian Children's Tapestries; Eleven Photographers of the South: I Shall Save One Land Unvisited; Fabric, Fiber $ Dye; Graphicstudio (prints); Lithographs & Etchings of Philip Pearlstein; Lithographs by Albert Christ-Janer; Harvey Littleton's Glass; Log Cabin & String Quilts; Robert Nelson Drawings; New American Auto-Graphs (Photos); Arnold Newman Photographs; Nigerian Crafts: A Personal View; Paintings by Hung Hsien; Edward Penfield Posters; Photographs of Edward Weston; Rare View of American Art; Southeast Seven; John Stockdale Photographs; Tapestries from Muhelyart, Switzerland; Tennessee Watercolor Society Traveling Exhibit; Threadlines Pakistan; Brett Weston Photographs; Young Americans: Fiber-Wood-Plastic-Leather; (all 1978-79) Regional Exhibits: Gay B Alvarez-Telfair Brooke (pottery & acrylic collage); Sandra Baker-Erin Yon (watercolor & stained glass); Gerald Cannon (collage); Edward Carlos (drawings

& watercolors); Routh Cline (painting); Jim Collins (sculpture); David Craft-Stephen LeWinter (drawing & printmaking); Jack Denton (drawings, 7 paintings); Dot Gannon (watercolor); Frances Hostetler (painting); Hunter Museum Faculty; Edward Kellogg (painting & printmaking); Mary Ferris Kelly (etchings); Sherry Lusk (painting); Charles Pfitzer (graphite works); Photography Without A Camera (works from a children's workshop); Ann Poss (painting); Carol Reddick Hare (drawing); Arthur Rivituso (watercolor); Betty Robinson (painting); Sylvia Ruffner-Deborah Belvin (watercolor); Frank O Swanson-Joan Bennett (watercolor); Bettye Winter Thomas (drawing and painting); Frances Vella-Henry Henegar (calligraphy); Doyle Wolfe-Peggy Wolfe (painting and & printmaking)
Publications: Brochures and announcements; bulletin, monthly
Activities: Classes for adults and children; docent training; lect open to public, approximately 12 vis lectr per yr; gallery talks; concerts; tours; competitions; individual paintings are lent to other museums; museums; museum shops sells miscellaneous items; museum shops sells miscellaneous items
L **Reference Library,** 10 Bluff View, 37403. Tel 615-267-0968. *Cur of Education* Diana Suarez; *Librn* Keating Griffiss
Open Tues - Sat 10 AM - 4:30 PM; Sun 1 - 4:30 PM; cl Mon; open to public by appointment. Estab 1958; art gallery maintained
Library Holdings: Vols 1000; Per subs 38; Micro—Cards; AV—Cassettes, motion pictures, slides; Other—Clipping files, exhibition catalogs, prints, memorabilia, original art works, pamphlets, photographs, sculpture
Special Subjects: American Art

M **UNIVERSITY OF TENNESSEE AT CHATTANOOGA ART GALLERY,** Baldwin St, 37402. Tel 615-755-4177. *Dir* George Cress
Open Mon - Fri 9 AM - 4 PM, cl University holidays. No admis fee. Estab 1952
Collections: Graphics; paintings; students work
Activities: Gallery talks; loan program; temporary and traveling exhibitions

CLARKSVILLE

M **AUSTIN PEAY STATE UNIVERSITY,** Margaret Fort Trahern Gallery, Art Department, 37040. Tel 615-648-7236. *Chmn Dept Art* Charles T Young; *Cur* Lewis B Burton
Open Mon - Fri 9 AM - 3 PM. No admis fee. Estab 1962 as a university community service to exhibit a variety of visual media from regional professionals and university art majors
Income: Financed by university appropriations
Collections: Graphics and sculpture; primarily watercolors; regional artists
Exhibitions: Average 8-10 per year
Publications: Announcements of shows and artist biographies, monthly
Activities: Classes for adults and children; dramatic programs; lect open to the public, 20 vis lectr per yr; gallery talks; competitions; scholarships; extension department
L **Library,** 37040.
Noncirculating department library
Library Holdings: AV—Fs, Kodachromes, motion pictures, slides; Other—Reproductions

COOKEVILLE

O **CUMBERLAND ART SOCIETY,** Cookeville Art Center,* 186 S Walnut, 38501. Tel 615-526-2424. *Pres* Reba Bacon; *VPres* Sally Crain
Open Tues - Fri 1:30 - 4 PM, Sun 2 - 5 PM. No admis fee. Estab 1961 to promote arts in the community and area. A new building with adequate gallery and studio space. The gallery is carpeted and walls are finished with wallscape and track lighting. Average Annual Attendance: 3000. Mem: 100
Income: $1500 (financed by membership, city and state appropriations)
Exhibitions: Changing exhibits, monthly
Activities: Classes for children; lect open to public; exten dept

JACKSON

O **UNION UNIVERSITY ART GUILD,** Hwy 45 Bypass, 38301. Tel 901-668-1818.
Open 8 - 10 PM. No admis fee. Estab 1973 to further art as a beneficial and needed factor of life. Gallery maintained. Mem: 43; dues $2
Income: Financed by membership
Collections: Individual student collections
Activities: Dramatic programs; lect for members only; one tour per year; concerts; competitions

JOHNSON CITY

EAST TENNESSEE STATE UNIVERSITY
M **Carroll Reece Museum,** 37601. Tel 615-929-4392, 929-4283. *Dir* Harvey A Dean; *Registrar* Helen Roseberry; *Museum Secy* Virginia L Schweighauser
Open Mon - Fri 12:45 - 4:45 PM; Sat & Sun 1 - 5 PM. No admis fee. Estab 1964 to enhance the cultural and educational advantages of the university and the people of upper east Tennessee. Purpose of Friends of the Reece Museum is to acquire paintings to be a part of the permanent collection. Average Annual Attendance: 28,000. Mem: Dues benefactor $250, regular $10 - $100 and student $1
Collections: Colonel Hart Collection of Military Art; Marks Collection of Pre-Columbian Art; Music From the Past, a collection of early musical instruments; Old Master and Contemporary Prints; Reece Room, an exhibition of memorabilia of former United States Congressman from Tennessee, B Carroll Reece; John Steele Collection of Contemporary Prints; Tennessee Craftsman Collection; Tennessee Frontier Room, a reconstructed scene of frontier life in the latter part of the 18th century and early 19th century; contemporary painting; historical material
Exhibitions: Three galleries of traveling exhibitions, some rented and some organized by museum staff
Activities: Educational programs; concerts; film series; receptions; originate traveling exhibitions

M **Elizabeth Slocum Gallery,** Art Department, 37601. Tel 615-929-4292, 929-4247. *Chmn Art Dept* W Radford Thomas; *Dir Exhibitions* George Moldovan
Open daily 8 AM - 5 PM; Sat 9 - 12 AM. No admis fee. Estab to augment all the programs and areas of instruction within the Art Department and to foster interest in various modes of artistic expression in the campus at large
Collections: A small teaching collection of prints, paintings, ceramics and weaving
Publications: Catalogs; posters
Activities: Classes for adults and children; art education program; seminars and workshops; lect; scholarships and fellowships; originate traveling exhibitions
L **University Library,** Art Department, 37601.
Library Holdings: Vols 2500

KINGSPORT

O **KINGSPORT FINE ARTS CENTER,** Church Circle, 37660. Tel 615-246-9351. *Pres* C F Earnhardt; *Secy* Margy Clark; *Dir* C C Hill; *Secy* Juanita Eaton
Open weekdays 9 AM - 5 PM. No admis fee. Estab 1968 to promote and present all the arts to all the people in area; this includes performing arts, visual arts and classes. Average Annual Attendance: 26,000. Mem: 548; dues $10 - $250; annual meeting May
Income: 40,000 (financed by membership)
Publications: Newsletter, bimonthly
Activities: Classes for adults and children; dramatic programs; gallery talks; tours; concerts; competitions; traveling exhibitions

KNOXVILLE

M **DULIN GALLERY OF ART,** 3100 Kingston Pike, 37919. Tel 615-525-6101. *Pres* Mrs Steve H Apking; *VPres* Mrs John R Ruggles; *Chrm* George L Ogdin Jr; *Dir* Sutherland McColley; *Treas* R Neal Culver; *Secy* Mrs Stuart Worden
Open Tues - Fri 12 - 4 PM; Sat & Sun 1 - 5 PM, cl Mon. No admis fee. Estab 1962 as a nonprofit private corporation. The Gallery is located in the historic house designed in 1915 by John Russell Pope for H L Dulin and is listed in the National Register. Average Annual Attendance: 20,000. Mem: 1000; dues from $15 - $1000
Income: Financed by membership, contributions, foundations and state and federal grants
Collections: American Paintings; Southeast Regional Art; works from last thirteen National Print and Drawing Competitions
Exhibitions: American Folk Art; Annual National Print and Drawing Competition; Art in East Tennessee from Private Collections; Community Project; Contemporary Art from Southeast Region; Photography; Tennessee Watercolor Society; Young People's Gallery
Publications: Russell Briscoe - An American Folk Artist; calendar, bi-monthly; H L Dulin Residence; Thorne Miniature Rooms
Activities: Classes for adults and children; docent training; arts to the schools; lect open to public; tours; competitions; inner city outreach Art Van

UNIVERSITY OF TENNESSEE
M **Frank H McClung Museum,** 1327 Circle Park Dr, 37916. Tel 615-974-2144. *Dir* Dr Paul Parmalee; *Exhib Coordr* Joseph W Hopkins; *Cur Coll* Elaine A Evans
Open Mon - Fri 9 AM - 5 PM. No admis fee. Estab 1961 to collect, maintian and interpret paintings, works of art, items of natural history and historical objects with emphasis placed on the Tennessee area. A major purpose is to provide research materials for students and faculty of the university. The museum, galleries and all cultural related departments will move to a new Art and Architecture Building in Jan 1981. Average Annual Attendance: 35,000
Income: Financed by city and state appropriations
Collections: Frederick T Bonham Collection (18th - 20th Century furniture, art objects); Lewis-Kneberg Collection (Tennessee archaeology); Grace Moore Collection (memorabilia of her career 1920's - 1940's)
Activities: Lect open to public; gallery talks; tours; competitions; exten dept serves the Southwest; original objects of art lent; lending collection contains prints and photographs
M **Eleanor Dean Audigier Art Collection,** Hoskins Library, 1401 Cumberland Ave, 37916. Tel 615-974-3408.
Estab 1934. Average Annual Attendance: 5000
Income: Financed by state appropriations
Collections: The Audigier Collection contains over 800 art objects: Ancient Egyptian scarabs, shawbtis; 19th Century Cameos; Chinese, French and German porcelain; Greco-Roman jars and lamps; 19th Century copies of Italian Renaissance paintings, furniture, sculpture and silver; ivory miniatures; personal jewelry; Turkish and Arabic trays
M **Art Department Exhibition Gallery,** University of Tennessee, 921 Volunteer Blvd, 37916. Tel 615-974-6081. *Dir* Open
Exhibitions: Corporation collections, fund raising, professional and student exhibitions
O **University of Tennessee Exhibits Committee,** 305 University Center, 37916. *Dir* Marilyn Kent
Open Mon - Fri 7:30 AM - 10:30 PM, Sat 7 AM - 10 PM, Sun 1 - 8 PM. No admis fee. Estab to provide cultural arts for the students of the university. Two major galleries: Gallery Concourse has 300 running ft and Gallery II has 60 running ft for intimate shows. Average Annual Attendance: 20,000
Income: $8000 (financed by state appropriation and student activities fees)
Purchases: $1000
Collections: †Dunford Collection; †Marion Heard Collection of Crafts
Exhibitions: 20 exhibits per year - student shows and traveling shows
Activities: Lect open to public, 3 visiting lectr per year; book traveling exhibitions

MARYVILLE

C BANK OF MARYVILLE, PO Box 528, 37801. Tel 615-982-6300, Ext 326. *In Charge of Art Coll* Ruth C Fouche
Estab to provide community interest in the arts; to aid participating artists; to enhance lobby. Supports local artists and art forms or displays that lend an interest to the community
Activities: Sponsors Wildlife Artist Guy Coheleach

M MARYVILLE COLLEGE FINE ARTS CENTER GALLERY, 37801. Tel 615-982-6950. *Chmn Dept Fine Arts* Harry H Harter
Open daily except Sun
Collections: †Print Collection
Exhibitions: Paintings of local and visiting artists exhibited twice a year
Activities: Gallery programs in connection with circulating exhibitions; art movies, four times a year; Ten to twelve traveling exhibitions during college year

MEMPHIS

M BROOKS MEMORIAL ART GALLERY, Overton Park, 38112. Tel 901-726-4762. *Dir* Jay Gates; *Secy to Dir* Gail Chumley; *Cur of Collections* Deborah Emont; *Asst Cur Education* Bea Carps; *Coordr of Public Information & Special Events* Lisa Durkan; *Exhibitions Preparator* Randy Toy; *Registrar* Maurine F Newell; *Cur Education* Diana Prewitt
Open Tues - Sat 10 AM - 5 PM; Sun 1 - 5 PM; cl Mon. No admis fee. Estab 1914 by gift from Mrs Samuel H Brooks to promote interest and development in cultural arts; to present a diversity of exhibitions; to assist people in their quest for knowledge and aesthetic experiences as well as contributing to their mental health through art education. The original building was opened in 1916 with additions in 1955 and 1973. Average Annual Attendance: 129,000. Mem: Dues $25 and up; annual meeting Sept
Income: Financed by city appropriation
Collections: American Paintings and Sculpture, 18th-20th centuries; Dutch and Flemish Paintings, 16th-18th centuries; Eastern and Near-Eastern Decorative Arts Collection (Han, T'ang and Ching Dynasty Chinese); English Paintings, 17th-19th centuries; French Paintings, 16th-19th centuries; †International Collection of Paintings and Sculpture, 19th & 20th centuries; Kress Collection of Italian Paintings and Sculptures, 13th-18th centuries; Dr Louis Levy Collection of American Prints; Mid-South Collection of 20th century paintings and sculptures; glass, textile and porcelain collection
Publications: Newsletter, bimonthly
Activities: Education Department; lect open to public; concerts; gallery talks; tours; competitions; museum shop selling books, reproductions and museum replicas

L Library, Overton Park, 38112. *Librn* Letitia Proctor
Open to the public for reference only
Library Holdings: Vols 11,500

M DIXON GALLERY AND GARDENS, 4339 Park Ave, 38117. Tel 901-761-5250. *Dir* Michael Milkovich; *Cur of Education* Reba Russell; *Asst Cur* Kitty Lawrence; *Gallery Asst* Elaine Dunn
Open Tues - Sat 11 AM - 5 PM; Sun 1 - 5 PM; cl Mon. Admis adults $1, children 5-11 years, students and senior citizens 50¢. Estab 1976 to provide community with opportunity to view original works of art and to enjoy the formal and informal gardens surrounding the gallery. Ten exhibition galleries are located in the downstairs area of the house and in an addition completed in 1977. Seventeen acres of formal and informal gardens, a large camellia house and two small greenhouses are part of the premises. Average Annual Attendance: 25,000. Mem: 1050; dues patron $500, donor $100, supporting $50, family $25, individual $15 and students $5
Income: Financed by endowment
Collections: British portraits and landscapes of the 18th - 19th century; French and American Impressionists, Post-Impressionists and related schools; French, English and American sculpture of the 19th and 20th century; porcelain; Works by Pierre Bonnard, Eugene Boudin, A F Cals, Jean-Baptiste Carpeaux, Mary Cassatt, Marc Chagall, John Constable, J B C Corot, Kenyon Cox, Henri-Edmond Cross, Charles Francois Daubigny, Edgar Degas, Julien Dupre, Sir Jacob Epstein, Henri Fantin-Latour, Thomas Gainsborough, Paul Gauguin, Paul Guigou, Armand Guillaumin, Henri Joseph Harpignies, William James, Johan Jongkind, S V E Lepine, Maximilien Luce, Albert Marquet, Paul Mathey, Henri Matisse, Claude Monet, Henriette A Oberteuffer, Ludovic Piette, Camille Pissarro, Sir Henry Raeburn, Auguste Renoir, Sir Joshua Reynolds, George Romney, Henri Rouart, Paul Signac, Alfred Sisley, Allen Tucker, J M W Turner, Horatio Walker and Richard Wilson
Exhibitions: (1978) Collected in Memphis; Charles Francois Daubigny; Flowers in Art; Henri-Joseph Harpignies; Impressionists in 1877; Memphis Collects Sculpture; (1979) A Bouquet for Memphis; American Impressionists; William Chadwick 1879-1962, An American Impressionist; Lovis Corinth; Jules Dupre 1811-1889; Louise Herreshoff; Japanese Prints; Henriette Amiard Oberteuffer and George Oberteuffer; Joseph Mallord William Turner 1775-1851
Publications: Exhibition catalogues; newsletter, bi-monthly; Paintings and Sculpture, Volume One
Activities: Classes for adults; docent training; film series, lect open to the public; concerts; gallery talks; tours; individual paintings and original objects of art lent to museums and galleries; lending collection contains original paintings, prints and sculpture, porcelain, silver and antique furniture

L Library, 4339 Park Ave, 38117. Tel 901-761-5250.
Open to the public during museum hours for reference only
Library Holdings: Vols 4000; Per subs 35; AV—Slides
Collections: Antique garden statuary; English 18th and 19th century furniture and porcelain

MEMPHIS ACADEMY OF ARTS

M Frank T Tobey Gallery, Overton Park, 38112. Tel 901-726-4085. *Pres* Dr Jameson J Jones; *Dir Emeritus* Edwin C Rust
Open Mon - Sat 9 AM - 5 PM, Sun 1 - 5 PM, cl summers, Sat & Sun, school holidays. No admis fee. Estab 1936 as an adjunct educational program. The Standing Committee on Exhibitions arranges visiting shows

Collections: Jacob Marks Memorial Collection; works by college graduates
Exhibitions: Juried student shows; one and two-man faculty shows; senior exhibition; summer student show; traveling exhibitions
Publications: Exhibition catalogs
Activities: Classes for adults, children and undergraduate college students; lect; guided tours; films; competitions; book traveling exhibitions

L G Pillow Lewis Memorial Library, Overton Park, 38112. *Librn* Robert Scarlett; *Asst Librn* Bette Ray Callow
Open Mon - Fri 8 AM - 5 PM, Sat 9 AM - Noon, Mon & Wed evenings until 10 PM
Income: $8500 (financed by city and county appropriations)
Library Holdings: Vols 15,000; Per subs 104; AV—Slides 22,000; Other—Reproductions, Original prints

L MEMPHIS-SHELBY COUNTY PUBLIC LIBRARY AND INFORMATION CENTER, Department of Art, Music and Recreation, 1850 Peabody, 38104. Tel 901-528-2976; TWX 810-591-1347. *Dir* C Lamar Wallis; *Chief Main Library* Robert Smith; *Head Art, Music, Recreation Dept* Ruth Martin
Open Mon - Fri 9 AM - 9 PM, Sat 9 AM - 6 PM. Estab 1895 to serve the reference, informational, cultural and recreational needs of residents of Memphis-Shelby County. Turner-Clark Gallery exhibits promising and established local and regional artists of various media
Income: $61,000 (financed by city and state appropriation)
Purchases: $39,000
Library Holdings: Vols 26,000; Per subs 225; Micro—Fiche, reels; AV—A-tapes, cassettes, rec; Other—Clipping files, exhibition catalogs, framed reproductions, prints, pamphlets
Special Subjects: Memphis musicians and artists
Collections: Photographic collections of local photographers
Exhibitions: Guild of Handloom Weavers; Memphis Embroiderers Guild
Publications: Various brochures and bibliographies; the Met in Memphis; Crafts for the Handicapped
Activities: Library provides concerts and tours; Extension department serves more rural areas and parts of the population underserved; books traveling exhibitions

MEMPHIS STATE UNIVERSITY

M E H Little Gallery, Southern Ave, 38152. Tel 901-454-2216. *Dir Exhib* C H Allgood
Open daily 9:30 AM - 11 AM, 12 - 3:30 PM, Sun 2 - 5 PM, cl Sat. No admis fee. Estab 1968 to provide information for the general public and instruction for students. Average Annual Attendance: 12,000
Income: $13,000 (financed by state appropriation)
Collections: Neil Nokes Collection of African Masks and other artifacts; Ancient Egyptian Art from the Boston Museum of Fine Arts; collection of over 100 prints, an overview
Exhibitions: E H Little Gallery Old Cafeteria: The High School Art Teacher; Memphis State University Art Faculty; Andrew Polk, paintings, prints, drawings; Second National Clay and Paper Show; Pochoir, stenciling; Senior Problem Reviews; Patrick Schuck, prints; A University Collects; Memphis State Prints; Hall Gallery third floor, Jones Hall: Art Education, MSU Students; Interior Design, MSU Students; Kelly Brother, Roger Clayton, recent works; MSU Students, recent work; Sculpture, MSU Students; Faculty Student Gallery, third floor, Jones Hall: Memphis State Faculty and student exhibitions; Memphis City School Teachers exhibitions; Second National Clay and Paper Show
Publications: Flyers
Activities: lectures open to the public, 6 visiting lecturers per year; gallery talks; tours; competitions; book traveling exhibitions

L Art History Slide Library, Jones Hall, Room 220, 38152. *Slide Cur* Mary Alice Martin
Open Mon - Fri 8:00 AM - 4:30 PM. Estab 1967 to provide slides for Art Faculty, University Faculty, and some outside organizations. Circ 30,000
Library Holdings: Vols 100; AV—Cassettes, fs, slides; Other—Reproductions

M SOUTHWESTERN AT MEMPHIS, Jessie L Clough Art Memorial for Teaching, Clough Hall, 2000 N Parkway, 38112. Tel 901-274-1800, Ext 248. *Cur* Dr George Apperson
Collection donated by the late Miss Floy K Hanson of her fine and valuable collection of oriental objects of art to be known as the Jessie L Clough Art Memorial for Teaching in memory of her first art teacher and friend Miss Clough
Collections: Brass; copper; Japanese prints; jewelry; pottery; precious metals; textiles; woodcarvings

MURFREESBORO

M MIDDLE TENNESSEE STATE UNIVERSITY, Photographic Gallery, 18th and Jackson Sts, 37132. Tel 615-898-2491. *Cur* Harold L Baldwin
Open Mon - Fri 8 AM - 4 PM; Sat 9 AM - 5 PM; Sun 1 - 6 PM. No admis fee. Estab 1969 for the exhibition of outstanding photographers and beginners. Gallery has 42 panels lighted individually. Average Annual Attendance: 8,000 - 10,000
Income: Financed by the University
Purchases: $1800
Collections: Ansel Adams; Richard Avedon; Harold Baldwin; Hang Callahan; Geri Della Rocea de Candal; Jim Ferguson; Minor White & Others; Jim Norton; Aaron Siskind; Marianne Skogh; H H Smith; Jerry Velsman; Ed Weston by Cole; Kelly Wise
Exhibitions: Jim Bishop; Connor; Bruce Davidson; Toth; John Grady; Robert Lindenmann Jr; Jane McGinnis; Steve Mulligan; Benjamin Porter; Raymo; Redmond
Publications: Lightyear, annually
Activities: Classes for adults; exten dept serving the area; original objects of art lent to responsible organizations; lending collection contains photographs; traveling exhibitions organized and circulated

NASHVILLE

M FISK UNIVERSITY MUSEUM, 18th and Jackson Sts, 37203. Tel 615-329-8685. *Dir* Earl J Hooks; *Cur* Robert Hall; *Asst to Cur* Pearl Cresswell
Open Mon - Fri 9 AM - 12 PM & 1 - 5 PM; cl Sat & Sun; June, July & Aug. No admis fee. Estab 1949 as an education resource center for the Fisk and Nashville communities and for the promotion of the arts. Van Vechten Gallery houses the library, temporary exhibits and art offices; Library Gallery houses the permanent collection and African Art. Average Annual Attendance: 4000
Income: Financed through the University
Collections: †Afro-American Collection; Alfred Stieglitz Collection of Modern Art; †Traditional African Art Collection
Exhibitions: Alumni Exhibit; Faculty Exhibits; Wilhelmina Godfrey (textiles); William H Johnson (prints); Ben Jones (mixed media); Metropolitan Nashville Artists; Lev Mills (prints)
Publications: Fisk Art Report, yearly
Activities: Lect open to public, 3 vis lectr per yr; gallery talks; tours; individual paintings and original objects of art lent to institutions, organizations, community groups; lending collection contains original prints and paintings; traveling exhibitions organized and circulated; sales shop selling reproductions and exhibition catalogs
L Florine Stettheimer Library, 18th and Jackson Sts, 37203. *Cur* Robert Hall
Open Mon - Fri 9 AM - 12 PM & 1 - 5 PM. Estab 1949. Publications are used by students and instructors for research
Library Holdings: Vols 1100; AV—Kodachromes, motion pictures; Other—Exhibition catalogs

M GEORGE PEABODY COLLEGE FOR TEACHERS, Cohen Memorial Museum of Art,* Box 513, 37203. Tel 615-327-8178. *Dir* Michael Taylor; *Cur* Michael Samford
Open Mon - Fri 8 AM - 12 Noon, 1 - 4:30 PM, Sat & Sun 2 - 5 PM, cl college vacations. No admis fee. Galleries are used to exhibit student works, faculty works, and visiting artist's works; on occasion permanent collection exhibited. Average Annual Attendance: 3000
Income: Financed by college funds
Collections: Contemporary American painting, prints and sculpture; 18th and 19th Century European painting and sculpture; English china and silver; Kress Study Collection of Renaissance paintings; antique furniture, lace, tapestries; Algernon Sydney Sullivan Collection of 19th Century paintings
Exhibitions: Middle Tennessee High School Art Exhibit; Peabody Senior Exhibition; four graduate exhibitions; six visiting artists
Activities: Lect; book traveling exhibitions
L Library,* Box 513, 37203.
Library open to the public; slide library for student and faculty use only
Library Holdings: Vols 2000

M THE PARTHENON, Centennial Park, West End Ave, Nashville, TN. (Mailing Add: Metro Postal Service, Centennial Park Office, Nashville, TN 37201,) Tel 615-327-3413. *Dir* Wesley M Paine; *Museum Guide* Gary Pace; *Pres Board* Dr George Richardt
Open Tues - Sat 9 AM - 4:30 PM, Sun 1 - 4:30 PM, cl Mon & legal holidays. No admis fee. Estab 1897 to offer Nashville residents and tourists quality art for viewing and sale in a historical setting of significance and beauty. two large and two small galleries in the basement of the only, exact size, replica of the Parthenon in the world. Average Annual Attendance: 900,000
Collections: Cowan Collection, sixty three paintings by 19th and 20th century American artists, donated by James M Cowan; †Contemporary collection, thirty paintings purchased out of the annual Central South Exhibition
Exhibitions: Exhibitions change monthly
Activities: Co-sponsor, with Tennessee Art League of Annual Central South Exhibition, juried show with awards given; individual paintings occasionally lent; Smithsonian Institute has borrowed individual paintings from the Cowan Collection; sales shop sells books, magazines, souvenirs, prints and slides

M TENNESSEE BOTANICAL GARDENS AND FINE ARTS CENTER, INC,* Cheekwood, Cheek Rd, 37205. Tel 615-352-5310. *Exec Dir* P Duncan Callicott; *Exec Secy* Julia C Haworth
Open Tues - Sat 10 AM - 5 PM, Sun 1 - 5 PM, cl Mon. Admis adults $2, students 7-17 $1, children under 6 free. Estab 1957, the Fine Arts Center is in a Mansion; the Botanic Hall was built in 1971. Main galleries maintained for major exhibitions; Mary Cheek Hill Gallery maintained for smaller exhibitions; Nashville Artist Guild holds members shows; Permanent Collection Gallery maintained. Mem: 5000; dues $20
Income: Financed by membership and private donation
Collections: Works by American artists
Publications: Newsletter, monthly; Trees of Christmas (book)
Activities: Classes for adults and children; dramatic programs; docent training; lect open to public and members, 6-10 visiting lectrs per year; gallery talks; individual paintings and original objects of art lent to museums and corporations; lending collection contains original art works, paintings and sculpture; traveling exhibitions organized and circulated; sales shop selling books, original art, prints and film strips
L Botanic Hall Library,* Cheekwood, Cheek Rd, 37205.
Open to staff and members for reference
Library Holdings: Vols 5000; Per subs 45
Collections: Extensive snuff bottle collection

O TENNESSEE HISTORICAL SOCIETY,* 200 State Library Archives Bldg, 37219. Tel 615-741-2660. *Pres* Ward DeWitt Jr
Open Mon - Sat 8 AM - 4:30 PM, cl national holidays. No admis fee. Estab 1849. Mem: Dues life $100, active $10
Collections: Paintings, some contemporary
Exhibitions: Temporary exhibitions
Publications: History Imprints, eight times per year; Tennessee Historical Quarterly
Activities: Guided tours

M TENNESSEE STATE MUSEUM, War Memorial Building, 37219. Tel 615-741-2692. *Dir* Dr Ellsworth Brown; *Admin Asst* Dancy Jones; *Cur of Collections* Peter LaPaglia; *Chief Researcher* Dr James Kelly; *Chief of Exhibits* Charles Baker; *Cur of Education* Lois Riggins; *Coordr of Museum Information* Debby Dale Mason; *Coordr of Tennessee State Museum Association Inc* Marti Rosenberg; *Coordr of Museum Development* John Buchanan; *Cur of Military History* William Baker
Open Sun & Mon 1 - 5 PM; Tues - Sat 9 AM - 5 PM, cl Christmas, Easter, Thanksgiving, New Year's Day. No admis fee. Estab 1937 to preserve and interpret the historical artifacts of Tennessee through museum exhibits and statewide outreach and educational programs. A military history museum in the War Memorial Building depicts Tennessee's involvement in modern wars (Spanish-American to World War II). The new State Museum in the multimillion dollar Polk Cultural Complex will open on November 13, 1980 with exhibits highlighting Life in Tennessee from early man to present. An art gallery will house changing exhibits. Average Annual Attendance: 50,000
Income: Financed by state appropriation
Collections: The museum collection of objects relating to Tennessee history from pre-historic times to the present. It holds in trust the collection of the Tennessee Historical Society as well as portraits and paintings of and by prominent Tennesseans
Publications: The Mosaic; newsletter, bi-monthly; The Open Eye, three times per yr
Activities: Classes for adults and children; docent training; lect open to the public; exten dept serving statewide; museum shop selling books, Tennessee crafts, items relating to the collection

M VANDERBILT UNIVERSITY, Art Gallery, Department of Fine Arts, West End Ave at 23rd, Box 1801 B, 37235. Tel 615-322-2831. *Chmn* Prof F Hamilton Hazlehurst; *Gallery Dir* Helen D Baldwin
Open Mon - Fri 1 - 4 PM; Sat & Sun 1 - 5 PM, cl holidays and some University vacations. No admis fee. Estab collection 1956, gallery 1961, to provide exhibitions for the University and Nashville communities, and original art works for study by Vanderbilt students. The gallery is included in a building of 1880 which is on the National Register of Historic Places. Mem: 300; dues $5 - $500
Income: Financed by university resources and Art Association dues
Collections: †Vanderbilt Collection of Western, Eastern, Ancient and Modern Cultures; Harold P Stern Collection of Oriental Art; Anna C Hoyt Collection of Old Master Prints; former Peabody College Art Collection including Kress Study Collection of Italian Renaissance Paintings
Exhibitions: Selections from the Vanderbilt Art Collection including paintings by Carol Mode, Victor Huggins, prints by Hogarth, exhibitions including Airlayers, Twentieth Century American Paintings and Graphics, The British Point of View; Desired Acquisitions, and the Harold P Stern Collection of Oriental Art; Chinese Paintings by Su-chin Wen Chen; Tennessee Watercolor Society Traveling Exhibitions for 1979; Photographs of Union Stations, Nashville, by John Netherton; Works by Vanderbilt students
Activities: Art Association lect open to members only

O WATKINS INSTITUTE,* Sixth Ave at Church St, 37219. Tel 615-242-1851. *Dir* C H Sargent; *Art Dir* Anton Weiss; *Exec Secy* Dorris Stone
Open Mon - Thurs 9 AM - 9 PM, Fri 9 AM - 1:30 PM, cl Sat & Sun, Christmas, New Years, July 4, Labor Day, Thanksgiving Day. No admis fee. Estab 1885 as an adult education center for art, home economics, business education, adult evening high school, and courses of a general nature
Income: Financed by rent from business property
Collections: All-State Artist Collection (oldest collection of Tennessee art in the state); this is a purchase-award collection of oil, pastels, watercolors, graphics and sculpture; several other collections of lesser value
Exhibitions: Six or eight exhibitions per year
Publications: Art brochure; quarterly catalogue listing courses
Activities: Classes for adults and children; lect open to public, 6-8 visiting lectrs per year; competitions; individual paintings lent to schools; original objects of art lent; traveling exhibitions organized and circulated
L Library,* Sixth Ave at Church St, 37219. *Librn* Mildred Egan
Open 9 AM - 8:30 PM. Estab 1885
Library Holdings: Vols 22,000; Per subs 40; AV—Fs, lantern slides, slides, v-tapes

OAK RIDGE

O OAK RIDGE COMMUNITY ART CENTER, PO Box 105, 37830. Tel 615-482-1182. *Pres* Bill Felling; *Dir* Jewel Stallions
Open Mon - Fri 9 AM - 4 PM; Sun 2 - 4 PM. No admis fee. Estab 1952 to help fulfill the cultural needs of the community and encourage enjoyment and understanding of the arts. Mem: 700; dues family $20, individual $15
Income: $30,000 (financed by membership)
Collections: The Mary and Alden Gomez Collection
Publications: Bulletin, monthly
Activities: Classes for adults and children; lect open to public; competitions; sales shop selling books, magazines, original art prints and slides
L Library, PO Box 105, 37830. *Librn* Gen Stoughton
Open to members for reference only

SEWANEE

M UNIVERSITY OF THE SOUTH GALLERY OF FINE ARTS, Guerry Hall, 37375. Tel 615-598-5917. *Dir* Dr Edward Carlos
Open daily 2-4 PM except holidays and non-university sessions. Estab 1938; museum chambers estab 1972. Average Annual Attendance: 5000 - 6000
Collections: Period Rooms; drawings, furniture and artifacts, paintings, photography, prints, sculpture
Exhibitions: Monthly exhibitions during school year, 2 - 4 per month; changing shows
Activities: Two lect per year; tours

TEXAS

ABILENE

M ABILENE FINE ARTS MUSEUM, Box 1858, 79604. Tel 915-673-4587. *Dir* Chet Kwiecinski
Open Tues - Fri 9 AM - 5 PM; Sat & Sun 1 - 5 PM; cl Mon. No admis fee. Estab 1937 as an art and history education institution. Two galleries and gift shop, built in 1964, cover approximately 5000 sq ft. Average Annual Attendance: 25,000. Mem: 800; dues $15 and up; monthly meeting 3rd Wed
Income: $85,000 (financed by membership)
Collections: American Paintings and Prints
Exhibitions: Blaffer Foundation Show of Modern Expressionism; Goya, Disasters of War; Russell-Remington Show of Western Art; regional and national exhibits
Publications: Newsletter, monthly
Activities: Classes for adults and children; docent training; lect open to the public; gallery talks; tours; competitions; individual paintings and original objects of art lent to local civic and business organizations; lending collection contains paintings; sales shop selling original art, reproductions, prints

M MCMURRY COLLEGE, Ryan Fine Arts Center, Sayles Blvd, Box 8, 79697. Tel 915-692-4130, Ext 307. *Dept Chmn & Gallery Dir* Sherwood E Suter
Open Mon - Fri 8 AM - 5 PM, cl Sat & Sun (open some Sun 2 - 5 PM for Opening Receptions). No admis fee. Estab 1970 when building was completed. Large room overlooking larger sculpture garden. Average Annual Attendance: 2500
Income: Financed by college art budget
Collections: Artists represented include Picasso, Jack Levine, Adolph Dehn, Frelander
Exhibitions: (1978-1979) Art Faculty Show - Solo Show by John Crump; Senior Student Solo Shows; West Texas Photographic Society
Publications: Art Through the Ages (color reproductions and slides to accompany text)
Activities: Classes for adults; lect open to the public; gallery talks; competitions; individual paintings and original objects of art lent to college offices
L Jay-Rollins Library, Sayles Blvd, Box 8, 79697. *Dir* Joe Specht
Open daily 8 AM - 9 PM; Sat 10 AM - 6 PM; Sun 1 - 6 PM. Estab 1964 for student and faculty use
Purchases: $1400
Library Holdings: Micro—Cards; AV—A-tapes, cassettes, fs, motion pictures, v-tapes; Other—Memorabilia
Activities: Annual Book Sale in spring

AMARILLO

M AMARILLO ART CENTER, 2200 S Van Buren, PO Box 447, 79178. Tel 806-372-8356. *Dir* Thomas A Livesay; *Cur of Art* Jerry M Daviee; *Cur of Education* David Turner; *Bus Mgr* Emma Avara; *Dir of Development* Jackie Wilson; *Admin Asst* Karen Powers; *Sales Gallery Mgr* Pauline Jones; *Asst Sales Gallery Mgr* Ursula Muntz
Open Tues - Fri 10 AM - 5 PM; Sat & Sun 1 - 5 PM; Wed 7 - 9 PM. No admis fee. Estab 1972 for cultural enrichment and education in the visual arts. Gallery 100, 90 x 30 ft, atrium area 45 ft; Gallery 200 & 203, 90 x 32 ft, 11 ft ceiling; Gallery 305 & 307, each 32 x 28 ft, 10 ft ceiling. Average Annual Attendance: 100,000
Income: $325,000 (financed by membership and college)
Collections: American Images, a collection of Farm Security Administration (FSA) photographs; Contemporary American Drawings
Exhibitions: (1978-1979) Amarillo Competition 1979, with John Canaday as Juror; Approaches to Photography; Jewelry by Peter Carl Faberge; James A Michener Collection of American Art; Minimal Prints from the Art Gallery of Ontario; Rembrandt, Durer $ Canaletto, the Adolph Weil Jr Collection; Richardson Collection of Western Art
Publications: Annual Report; Calendar of Events, bimonthly; catalogs on exhibits; brochures, as needed
Activities: Classes for adults; lect open to the public; 10 vis lectr per year; gallery talks; tours; competitions; originate traveling exhibitions; museum shop selling books, magazines, original art, reproductions, prints
L Library, 2200 S Van Buren, PO Box 447, 79178.
For reference only
Library Holdings: Vols 5000; Per subs 14
O Amarillo Art Center Association, 2200 S Van Buren, PO Box 447, 79178. *Chmn of the Board of Trustees* Dr Merrill Winsett; *Secy* Gerry McKay; *Treas* Robert Hucker
Open Tues - Fri 10 AM - 5 PM; Sat & Sun 1 - 5 PM; Wed 7 - 9:30 PM. Estab 1972 to provide quality visual and performing arts to the Texas Panhandle. Mem: 1200; dues $50-$5000, family $25, single $15, student $5
Income: Financed by endowment, membership and Amarillo College funds
Activities: Classes for adults and children; docent training; classes in art appreciation and film appreciation; lect open to the public, 10 vis lectr per year; concerts; gallery talks; tours; individual paintings and original objects of art lent to other institutions; originate traveling exhibitions

ARLINGTON

M UNIVERSITY OF TEXAS AT ARLINGTON, University Art Gallery, Fine Arts Bldg, 76019. Tel 817-273-2891. *Dir* Max W Sullivan; *Secy-Registrar* Sherry R Dunaway
Open Mon - Fri 9 AM - 4 PM; Sun 1 - 4 PM; cl Sat and major holidays. No admis fee. Estab 1975 on completion of Fine Arts Complex. The Gallery serves the entire university; exhibitions draw on all cultures and all periods. Main and Mezzanine Galleries are air cooled, carpeted, fabric wall covered with incandescent light. Average Annual Attendance: 15,000
Income: $43,000 (financed by state appropriation and private gifts)
Collections: Very small collection mainly American and Contemporary
Exhibitions: (1978-1979) Herbert Bayer: Photographic Works; Richard Ferrier: Watercolor, Alvar Aalto, 1898-1976; Garrison Roots Sculpture; Graphic Arts of the Mexican Revolution; Japanese Ukiyo-e Prints; Old Master Paintings from the Blaffer Collection; Off Loom Weaving: Dixie Strickland's Class; Nathan Oliveira: A Survey of Monotypes, 1973-78; Pictures of a Floating World Jack Plummer: Drawings & Recent Work; Steve Rascoe Exhibition; Richard Munday of Newport: David Merrill; Judd Scott: Recent Work; Second Annual Student Competition; Serge Lifar Collection of Ballet Set & Costume Designs; Student Summer Exhibition; The Divine Presence, Asian Sculptures; UTA Art Faculty Exhibition
Activities: Undergraduate course on museum techniques; lect open to the public, 3 vis lect per year; catalogs on sale

AUSTIN

M LAGUNA GLORIA ART MUSEUM, 3809 West 25th St, PO Box 5568, 78763. Tel 512-458-8192. *Dir* Laurence Miller; *Dir Prog* Judith Sims; *Dir Admin* Bab Hatch; *Dir Development* Jo Lynn Hoffman; *Public Information* Sandra Gregor
Open Tues - Sat, 10 AM - 5 PM, Thur 10 AM - 9 PM, Sun 1 - 5 PM. No admis fee. Museum is housed in a historic Mediterranean villa situated on twenty-nine acres of ground overlooking Town Lake; three galleries downstairs, one upstairs. Laguna Gloria at First Federal, a downtown branch programming exhibitions and related events year round. Average Annual Attendance: 80,000. Mem: 1600; dues $1000 - $25; annual meeting September
Income: $525,000 (financed by City of Austin, Fiesta, Memberships, Annual Fund, grants, Art Schools, corporate donations)
Exhibitions: Changing exhibitions of 20th Century American Art, its roots and antecedents
Publications: Calendar, bi-monthly; Estate-Planning, quarterly; exhibition catalogs
Activities: Art School classes for children and adults; cultural and educational programs in conjunction with exhibitions; museum guides program; art after school; museum shop
L Library, 3809 West 25th St, PO Box 5568, 78763.
Open for reference to Art School instructors and staff

M ELIZABET NEY MUSEUM, 304 E 44th, 78751. Tel 512-454-1762. *Dir* James Fisher; *Cur* Sarah Bolz; *Cur* Terence Keane; *Cur* Martha Hughes; *Specialist* Willie Nunn
Open Tues - Fri 11 AM - 4:30 PM, Sat & Sun 2 - 4:30 PM. No admis fee. Estab 1909 for the preservation and promotion of Elizabet Ney's works, studio and historical importance through relevant educational interpretation. Eclectic limestone castle, one of few 19th century American sculpture studios to survive intact with its contents. Average Annual Attendance: 15,000
Income: $64,000 (financed by city appropriation)
Collections: Works of Elizabet Ney in the form of original plaster casts, supplemented by bronze and marble works and tools, furnishings and memorabilia
Publications: Sursum (annotated letters of Elizabet Ney)
Activities: Classes for adults and children; lect open to public, 1 vis lectr per year; concerts; gallery talks; tours; original objects of art lent to museums; museum shop selling books and stationary
L Library, 304 E 44th, 78751.
Open Tues - Fri 11 AM - 4:30 PM, Sat - Sun 2 - 4:30 PM. Estab to collect background material on subjects relevant to the Museum's history and period. For reference only
Library Holdings: Vols 300; AV—Slides; Other—Clipping files, exhibition catalogs, manuscripts, memorabilia, original art works, pamphlets, photographs, Letters
Special Subjects: 19th century sculpture

M SAINT EDWARD'S UNIVERSITY, Fine Arts Exhibit Program, 78704. Tel 512-444-2621, Ext 327.
Open Mon - Fri 8 AM - 6 PM, Sun 1 - 5 PM. No admis fee. Estab 1961 to present for the university population and general public a monthly schedule of exhibits in the visual arts, as a means of orientation toward established and current trends in art styles in terms of their historical-cultural significance and aesthetic value, through teaching exhibitions, art films, public and private collections from distributing and compiling agencies, museums, galleries and artists. Average Annual Attendance: 10,000
Income: $6000
Purchases: $400
Exhibitions: Annual and art student exhibitions
Activities: Classes; lect, one visiting lectr per year; tours; literature
L Library, Fine Arts Exhibit Program, 78704.
For reference
Library Holdings: Vols 2300

UNIVERSITY OF TEXAS AT AUSTIN

L Fine Arts Library, 23rd at Red River, 78712. Tel 512-471-4777. *Librn* Carole Cable
Open Mon - Thurs 8 AM - 10 PM; Fri 8 AM - 5 PM; Sat 10 AM - 5 PM; Sun 2 PM - 10PM. Estab 1948 to support teaching and research to the PhD level in art history, and to the master's level in art education and studio art. Circ 140,000 (1978-79)
Income: Financed by state appropriation
Library Holdings: Vols 42,000; Per subs 400; Micro—Fiche, reels; Other—Clipping files, exhibition catalogs, pamphlets, reproductions

M **University Art Museum,** 23rd and San Jacinto, 78703. Tel 512-471-7324. *Dir* Dr Eric McCready; *Chief Cur* Dr Andrea Norris
Open Mon - Sat 9 AM - 5 PM; Sun 1 - 5 PM. No admis fee. Estab 1963 to serve the student body and all departments of the university. Huntington Galleries house temporary exhibitions; Michener Galleries house the permanent collections. Average Annual Attendance: 125,000
Collections: Latin American Paintings; James and Mari Michener Collection of 20th Century American Art; C R Smith Collection of Western American Painting; other collections include prints, drawings, plaster casts
Activities: Classes for adults; project for gifted and talented children; docent training; lect open to public; concerts; gallery talks; tours; exten dept serves Austin area; individual paintings, original objects of art and children's catalogues are lent to other museums; originate traveling exhibitions to other university art museums and city museums; museum shop sells books, reproductions

BANDERA

M **FRONTIER TIMES MUSEUM,** PO Box 563, 78003. Tel 512-796-3864. *Pres* Mrs D W Hicks; *Cur & Mgr* John V Saul
Open daily 10 - 12 AM, 1 - 4:30 PM; cl Mon. Admis adults 50¢, children under 10 years 25¢ (free when accompanied by teachers). Estab 1933 to preserve records, photographs, and artifacts of the American West with emphasis on the local Texas hill country area. Average Annual Attendance: 10,000. Mem: 17; no dues; meetings 3 times a year
Income: $10,000 (financed by endowment, $4000 from F B Doane Foundation)
Collections: F B Doane Collection of Western Paintings; Louisa Gordon Collection of Antiques, including bells from around the world; J Marvin Hunter Collection of Photographs, Artifacts, Memorabilia of American West and the Texas Hill Country; Photograph Collection; many rare items
Exhibitions: Occasional one-man shows by Texas artists whose work coincides with the theme of the museum
Activities: Book shop

BEAUMONT

M **BEAUMONT ART MUSEUM,** 1111 Ninth St, 77702. Tel 713-832-3432. *Pres* Robert G Quinn; *First VPres* C Tyrell Garth; *Second VPres* Patrick E Boyt; *Dir* Kay Paris; *Secy* Nancy Neild; *Treas* Albert A Pollans; *Asst to the Dir* Georgia Baier; *Registrar* Linda Lange; *Cur of Education* Janet Krulick
Open Tues - Fri 10 AM - 5 PM, Sat & Sun 2 - 5 PM, cl Mon and holidays. No admis fee. Estab 1950 as a non-profit community owned institution chartered to serve the community-at-large through education, cultural enrichment and aesthetic enjoyment activities. The museum has 2785 sq ft of exhibition space, three galleries downstairs devoted to temporary exhibitions which change monthly, and three galleries upstairs devoted to the permanent collection. Average Annual Attendance: 44,000. Mem: 1250; dues $500 - $25; annual meeting May
Income: $225,000 (financed by endowment, membership, city and state appropriation, Kaleidoscope and grants)
Collections: Eskimo and Thai prehistoric artifacts; 19th century decorative arts; 20th century Texas and American painting, sculpture and graphics; photography
Exhibitions: Biennial Invitation Exhibition of Texas Artists; changing exhibitions monthly in painting, sculpture graphics, decorative arts and archaeology
Publications: Newsletter, bi-monthly
Activities: Classes for adults and children; in-school education program; monthly seminars for high school students; slide lectures; monthly slide lectures for 8th grade American history classes; gallery talks; tours; traveling exhibitions organized and circulated; museum shop selling books, original art, reproductions, original jewelry, pottery, handcrafted items

L **Library,** 77702. Tel 713-832-3432. *Library Cur* Bonna B Wescoat
Open to staff and docents for reference only
Library Holdings: Vols 1000; Per subs 25; AV—Slides

O **BEAUMONT ARTS COUNCIL,** 3360 Beard St, 77703. Tel 713-892-0336. *Chmn* Jeannette Doiron
Estab 1969 to foster total esthetic involvement in the community and improve communications among cultural organizations. Mem: Annual meeting in spring and fall
Activities: Sponsored forum for city election candidates to discuss their attitudes toward cultural environment

BROWNSVILLE

M **BROWNSVILLE ART LEAGUE MUSEUM,** PO Box 3404, 78520. Tel 512-542-0941.
Open Mon - Sat 9:30 AM - 4 PM, Sun 2 - 4 PM. No admis fee. Estab 1977 for the preservation of valuable collection. Mem: 125
Income: Financed by endowment
Collections: Collection of fine art, all media
Exhibitions: Arts and Crafts; International Art Show; loaned exhibitions
Publications: Brush Strokes, six per year
Activities: Classes for adults

BUCHANAN DAM

O **BUCHANAN ARTS AND CRAFTS INC,** Hwy 29, 78609. Tel 512-793-2858. *Chmn of Board* Evelyn Peters; *Pres* Dolly Barbour; *Treas* Fay Caswell; *Secy* Pearl Patterson
Open Mon - Sat 10 AM - 5 PM; Sun 1 - 5 PM. No admis fee. Estab 1963 to increase interest in our community. Building approx 1800 ft floor space. Average Annual Attendance: 4500. Mem: 57; dues $25; meeting second Tues monthly
Income: Financed by membership
Exhibitions: Aqua Festival; Blue Bonnet Trail Exhibit; Highland Lakes Arts & Crafts Trail in Oct; monthly exhibitions in Burnet First State Bank
Activities: Classes for adults; lect open to the public; sales shop selling original art

CANYON

M **PANHANDLE-PLAINS HISTORICAL SOCIETY MUSEUM,*** 2401 Fourth Ave, 79015. Tel 806-655-7194. *Dir* William C Griggs; *Asst Dir* Jack Downing
Open Mon - Sat 9 AM - 5 PM, Sun 2 - 6 PM, cl New Years Day, Thanksgiving, Christmas. No admis fee. Estab 1921 to preserve history of the region, including all phases of history, fine arts and natural sciences. Average Annual Attendance: 125,000. Mem: 1000; dues contributing $500, life $250, annual $10, student $5; annual meeting May
Collections: Over 1300 paintings by early and contemporary American painters
Exhibitions: Exhibitions normally changed monthly
Publications: Panhandle-Plains Historical Review, annually

L **Library,*** 2401 Fourth Ave, 79015. *Archivist & Librn* Claire Kuehn
Reference library
Library Holdings: Vols 10,000; Other—Photographs

COLLEGE STATION

M **TEXAS A & M UNIVERSITY,** Art Exhibits, PO Box 5718, 77844. Tel 713-845-1914. *Dir Art Exhib and Special Asst to the Pres for Development of Cultural Programs* J W Stark; *Coordr University Art Exhib* JR Arredondo Jr
Open 8 AM - 11 PM. No admis fee. Estab 1974 to bring art exhibits of state and national significance to Texas A & M University. Exhibit space is 35 ft x 200 ft by 35 ft in height; exhibits are hung on portable panels. Average Annual Attendance: 18,000
Income: Financed by endowment, University funds from bookstore profits
Collections: Paintings by Texas artists
Exhibitions: (1978) Ansel Adams: Photographs of the Southwest; Canadian Tapestries. (1979) American Abstract Expressionist Collection from Buoffer Foundation; H O Cowboy Kelly: an exhibition of paintings
Activities: Docent training; lectures open to the public; gallery talks; tours; individual paintings lent to qualified exhibitors, and publishers of books; lending collection contains original art works, paintings, sculpture

O **Memorial Student Center Arts Committee,** Memorial Student Center, PO Box 5718, 77840. Tel 713-845-1515. *Chmn* Kerri Kernan; *Gallery Chmn* Sheri Williams; *Asst Program Coordr* Bart Block; *Asst Program Coordr* Karen Penny
Open daily 8 AM - 8 PM. No admis fee. Gallery is 35 x 35 ft with movable hanging partitions and lighting; two exterior walls are glass for partial viewing after hours. Mem: 45; meetings are held each week
Income: $1765 (financed by student service fees allotment)
Exhibitions: (1979-80) Kettie Brownwill: Abstract Oil; Camera Committee Fall Photo Contest; John Carter: Recent Watercolors; Aggie Con XI; Georgia Eckhardt and Lea Lyman: Fibre Works; Five Houston Painters; Interpretations of American Housing; Salon; Technological Tools; The Works of Jesse Trevino; Triology III; juried student art contest
Publications: Exhibition borchures; gallery calendar, two per year
Activities: Lect open to public, 10 visiting lectr per year; concerts; gallery talks; competitions; cash awards and honorable mention certificates; book traveling exhibitions 3-4 per year; sells prints

COMMERCE

M **EAST TEXAS STATE UNIVERSITY,** Little Gallery, Art Department, 75428. Tel 214-468-2216. *Dir* Charles McGough
Open Mon - Fri 9 AM - 5 PM. No admis fee. Estab 1977 to house all student exhibitions; 9-month exhibition calendar of exchange and traveling shows. Gallery 55 x 69 ft
Income: Financed by state appropriation
Collections: Collection of Student Work
Activities: Lect open to the public, 30 vis lectr per year; gallery talks; tours; competitions; individual paintings and original objects of art lent to regional citizens; traveling exhibitions organized and circulated; sales shop selling original art

CORPUS CHRISTI

M **ART MUSEUM OF SOUTH TEXAS,** 1902 N Shoreline, PO Box 1010, 78403. Tel 512-884-3844. *Dir* Cathleen S Gallander; *Adminr* Linda B Walker
Open Tues - Sat 10 AM - 5 PM; Sun 1 - 5 PM. No admis fee. Estab 1960 as a non-profit organization offering a wide range of programs to the South Texas community in an effort to fulfill its stated purpose to stimulate and encourage the fullest possible understanding and appreciation of the fine arts in all forms. A large central area, the Great Hall, and a small gallery. The sky-lighted Upper Gallery on the second floor level has over 1900 sq ft of space. Average Annual Attendance: 110,000. Mem: 1268; dues $25
Income: $410,000 (financed by membership, city and state appropriations, school district)
Collections: Works on Paper (permanent drawing collection)
Exhibitions: American Paintings of the 1970's; Lester and Joan Avnet Collection of Drawings; Jerry Dantzic and the Circuit Camera; Etchings by Rembrandt and His Followers; Winslow Homer Watercolors; Photographs by Manual Alvarez Bravo; Rodin Burghers of Calais; Spain and New Spain: Mexican Colonial Art in its European Context; Target Collection of American Photography
Activities: Lect open to public, 4 vis lectr per year; gallery talks; tours; competitions; originate traveling exhibitions; museum shop selling books, magazines, hand crafted and one of a kind items

L **Library,** 1902 N Shoreline, PO Box 1010, 78403. *Asst Cur* Susie Walker Atcheson
Open Tues - Fri 10 AM - 5 PM. Estab 1972, to provide reference information for visitors to museum and docent students. For reference only
Income: $2723
Purchases: $2100
Library Holdings: Vols 2500; Per subs 13; AV—Slides; Other—Clipping files, exhibition catalogs

M **CORPUS CHRISTI STATE UNIVERSITY,** Weil Art Gallery, 6300 Ocean Dr, 78412. Tel 512-991-6810, Ext 316. *Dir* Dr William Otton
Open Mon - Fri 9 AM - 9 PM. No admis fee. Estab 1979 to provide high quality art exhibitions to the university and the public. Average Annual Attendance: 7000
Exhibitions: Mrs John Allen King Collection; Clayworks by Texans, 18 Texans; Sue Wheeler, Thesis Show; Gladys Nillson; Fred Rossiter; Goya, The Disasters of War; Indiana Print
Publications: Exhibition catalogs
Activities: Classes for adults; dramatic programs; lectures open to the public; concerts; gallery talks; scholarships; individual paintings and original objects of art lent; Artmobile; book traveling exhibitions yearly

M **DEL MAR COLLEGE,** Department of Art Gallery, Baldwin at Ayers, 78404. Tel 512-881-6216. *Chmn* Joseph A Cain
Open Mon - Fri 8 AM - 9:30 PM. No admis fee. Estab 1932 to teach art and provide exhibition showcase for college and community. Gallery consists of over 200 running feet space, plus other smaller areas
Income: Financed by city and state appropriation
Collections: Purchases from Annual National Drawings and Small Sculpture Show; art donations
Exhibitions: National Drawings and Small Sculpture Show in Apr
Activities: Originate traveling exhibitions

M **SOUTH TEXAS ARTMOBILE,** Corpus Christi State University, 6300 Ocean Dr, 78412. *College of Arts & Humanities Dir* Dr Bill Otton; *Gallery & Artmobile Cur* Patricia Fugitt
Open during school hours through school year. No admis fee. Estab 1969 to take original works of art to the people throughout South Texas who would not have the opportunity to see art of this calibre; also where there are no museums available. Average Annual Attendance: 35,000
Income: Financed by James R Dougherty Foundation
Collections: European period
Exhibitions: (1979) American Contemporary 1900 - 1980; Sculpture by Russell
Publications: Catalog of each exhibit, yearly; handbook
Activities: Dramatic programs; docent training; slide lect; lect open to public; concerts
L **Library,** Corpus Christi State Univ, 6300 Ocean Dr, 78412.
Open to Artmobile staff only
Library Holdings: Vols 30; Per subs 6

DALLAS

O **ARTISTS COALITION OF TEXAS,** 2727 Turtle Creek Blvd, Seventh Floor, PO Box 12693, 75225. Tel 214-521-1881. *Pres* Gene Amend; *VPres* Mem Cunningham; *Secy* Janet Stanger; *Adminr* Jeanine Thompson; *Editor & Publisher* J R Compton
Open Mon - Fri 8:30 AM - 5 PM. No admis fee. Estab 1977 to help support the visual arts and artists working in Texas through services and programs geared towards education and communication. Mem: 150; dues $15, student $7.50; meetings fourth Mon of each month
Income: $25,000 (financed by membership, city appropriation, individual and corporate contributions)
Publications: Texas Arts Revue, bi-monthly magazine; Texas Arts Revue Letter, monthly newsletter update
Activities: Education department provides programs and projects for the public; lectures open to the public, three visiting lecturers per year; film series on the visual arts open to the public

O **DALLAS HISTORICAL SOCIETY,** Hall of State, Fair Park, PO Box 26038, 75226. Tel 214-421-5136. *Dir* John W Crain; *Business Mgr* Jan Upton; *Cur of Coll* Kathleen Hallock; *Cur of Exhib* Ronnie Roese; *Cur of Education* Cosy McLemore; *Asst to Dir* Candace Prevost
Open Mon - Sat 9 AM - 5 PM, Sun 1 - 5. No admis fee. Estab 1922 to collect & preserve materials relative to the history of Texas and Dallas. The Hall of State is an example of Art-Deco architecture. Average Annual Attendance: 200,000. Mem: 1350; annual meeting in May
Income: Financed by membership and city appropriation
Exhibitions: Be Prepared: Scouting in America; Dallas Rediscovered; Crying for a Vision: A Rosebud Sioux Trilogy; Flora of the Pastureland; Forty Dollar Saddle: Tools & Equipment of the Texas Cowboy; Homemade and Storebought; Homespun Patterns: Southern Overshot Coverlets; Santos; Taking the Measure of the Land: Cartographic Images of the US 1769 to Present; Ten Dollar Horse; Texas Naive Art; Texas 1939: Photographs by Russell Lee; Texas Prison Rodeo; Treasure, People, Ships, & Dreams; Turquoise & Tobacco
Publications: Dallas Historical Society Report (newsletter) bimonthly; Dallas Rediscovered: A Photographic Chronicle of Urban Expansion Activities
Activities: In-class programs; docent training; summer children's workshops; tours; gift and bookstore
L **Research Center Library,** Hall of State, Fair Park, PO Box 26038, 75226. *Adminr* Sugar Glaspy
For reference only
Library Holdings: Vols 12,000; Other—Archives, pages 2,000,000
Collections: R M Hayes Photographic Collection of Texas Historic Sites; J J Johnson & C E Arnold Photographs of Turn-of-the-Century Dallas; Frank Reaugh Paintings; Allie Tennant Papers

M **DALLAS MUSEUM OF FINE ARTS,** Fair Park, PO Box 26250, 75226. Tel 214-421-4187. *Dir* Harry S Parker; *Asst Dir Admin* Eugene W Mitchell; *Cur* John Lunsford; *Acting Cur Contemporary Art* Sue Graze; *Cur Exhib* Barney Delabano
Open Tues - Sat 10 AM - 5 PM; Sun 1 - 5 PM; cl Mon. No admis fee. Estab 1903 to purchase and borrow works of art from all periods for the aesthetic enjoyment and education of the public. Fifteen galleries for permanent collection; five for temporary exhibition. Average Annual Attendance: 350,000. Mem: 4000; dues $25 - $1000; annual meeting May
Income: $2,000,000 (financed by endowment, membership and city appropriation)
Purchases: $1,000,000
Collections: †African; †American; †Contemporary; †European 18th and 19th Century; †Pre-Columbian

Exhibitions: America: The Third Century; Clader's Universe; Face of Egypt; Irish Watercolors; Edvard Munch; New Photographs and Prints; Renaissance Prints: Berlin-Hanover 1920's; Salvages and Paste-ups by Jess; Santos; Texas Painting and Sculpture Competition and Invitational; Titian and the Venetian Woodcut; Translations; Two Centuries of Black American Art
Publications: Newsletter, bimonthly; annual report
Activities: Classes for children; docent training; lect open to public, 10 vis lectr per year; concerts; gallery talks; tours; competitions; exten dept serving Dallas County; artmobile; museum shop selling books, magazines, original art, reproductions, prints and slides
L **Library,** PO Box 26250, 75226. *Librn* Donna E Rhein
For reference only
Library Holdings: Vols 15,500; Per subs 30; Other—Exhibition catalogs

L **DALLAS PUBLIC LIBRARY,** Fine Arts Division, 75201. Tel 214-748-9071. *Division Head* Kay Krochman; *Art Librn* William C Haddaway; *Theatre Librn* Robert Eason; *Music Librn* Jim Calhoun; *Recordings Librn* Donna Mendro
Open Mon - Fri 9 AM - 9 PM; Sat 9 AM - 6 PM; cl Sun. Estab 1901 to furnish the citizens of Dallas with materials and information concerning the arts. Circ 14,083
Income: $50,000
Purchases: $50,000
Library Holdings: Vols 40,000; Per subs 500; Micro—Fiche, reels; AV—A-tapes, fs, rec, slides; Other—Clipping files, exhibition catalogs, framed reproductions, prints, manuscripts, memorabilia, original art works, pamphlets, photographs, reproductions
Collections: W E Hill Collection (history of American theater); Lawrence Kelly Collection of Dallas Civic Opera Set and Costume Designs; Manuscript Archives (music); Margo Jones Theater Collection; original fine print collection; John Rosenfield Collection (art and music critic)
O **Dallas Print and Drawing Society,** 1954 Commerce St, 75201. Tel 214-748-9071. *Pres* Barbara Brown; *VPres* Kevin Vogel; *Secy* P Bush Elkin; *Treas* Mrs Charles E Naylor
Estab 1935 to study history, techniques and to collect prints and drawings. Mem: 75; annual dues $10; meeting six times per year
Income: Approx $1000 (financed by membership and income from legacy)
Purchases: $250 - $500
Activities: Lect open to the public, 5 - 6 vis lectr per year

SOUTHERN METHODIST UNIVERSITY
M **University Gallery,** 75275. Tel 214-692-2516. *Dir* William B Jordan
Open Mon - Sat 10 AM - 5 PM; Sun 1 - 5 PM. No admis fee. The exhibitions scheduled in the gallery are primarily for the purpose of study and the committee selects them according to the needs of the classes. A one-room gallery with movable walls used for changing exhibitions. Average Annual Attendance: 10,000
Income: Financed through the University
Exhibitions: (1978-1979) Contemporary Paintings from the Meadows Collection; Drawings: Matisse to Lichtenstein; Egypt Day and Night (Keith Achepohl); MFA Qualifying Exhibitions; Modern Sculpture from the Nasher Collection; Recent Paintings by James Dowell; Student Exhibition. (1979-1980) Canaletto's Venice; Cy Twombly: Paintings and Drawings; McManaway Works Twenty Years; MFA Qualifying Exhibitions; Recent Paintings by Roger Winter; Student Exhibition
L **Art Library,** 75275. *Librn* Helen Lawrence
Open to the public for reference and research
M **Meadows Museum,** 75275. *Dir* William B Jordan; *Asst Dir* Irene Martin; *Cur Educ* Nancy Berry
Open Mon - Sat 10 AM - 5 PM; Sun 1 - 5 PM. No admis fee. Estab 1965 to preserve and study the art of Spain. Average Annual Attendance: 40,000
Income: Financed by endowment
Collections: Spanish Paintings from Late Gothic to Modern including works by Juan de Borgona, Velazquez, Murillo, Zurbaran, Ribera, Goya, Miro, Juan Gris, and Picasso
Activities: docent training; lect open to public; scholarships
L **Meadows Collection Fine Arts Library,** 75275.
Open for reference to scholars
Special Subjects: Spanish art

DENTON

M **NORTH TEXAS STATE UNIVERSITY,** Art Gallery, Mulberry and Ave A, North Texas Box 5098, 76203. Tel 817-788-2398, 788-2561. *Gallery Dir* C Kenneth Havis
Open Mon - Fri Noon - 5 PM. No admis fee. Estab 1960 as a teaching gallery directed to students of North Texas State University and the Denton community. The gallery covers 193 running ft of exhibition wall space, approximately 10 ft high, which may be divided into smaller spaces by the use of semi-permanent portable walls; the floor is carpeted-terrazzo. Average Annual Attendance: 10,000
Income: $4500 (financed by state appropriation)
Purchases: $1500
Collections: Fashion Collection; †Voertman Collection (student purchases); permanent collection; †permanent student collection
Exhibitions: American Abstract Expressionist Collection of the Sarah Campbell Blaffer Foundation; Children's Art Exhibition USA; Children's International Art Exhibition; Drawings by Mark Williams; Exhibition of Crafts by Sandra Simon (ceramic); Exhibition of Design from NTSU students; Amy Freeman Lee Watercolors; Gator Tracks: Exhibition of Sculpture from the Grear Gator Group of Louisiana; Graphic Design from Dallas and Fort Worth Advertising Artists; William Harper (metals); North Texas Invitational, John Chatmas and Patricia Tillman; NTSU Art Faculty Exhibition; NTSU Studio Art Faculty Exhibition; Painting and Sculpture Exhibition for the O K Harris Gallery; Jim Pomeroy Recent Work; Cynthia Schira (fibers); Michael Simon (ceramics); Southern Watercolor Society 16 State Competitive Exhibition (juried); Voertman Awards; Voertman Awards for NTSU Art Students (juried)
Publications: Exhibition announcements
Activities: Lect open to the public, 4 - 8 vis lectr per year; tours; competitions; individual paintings and original objects of art lent to the university offices

L Art Slide Library, Art Department, 76203. *Slide Librn* Karen Olvera
Open during school term Mon - Fri 7:45 AM - 9 PM. Estab to provide art slides for instruction. For reference only
Purchases: $6000
Library Holdings: AV—Cassettes, fs, lantern Slides, motion pictures, slides, v-tapes
L Willis Library, Humanities Division, 76203. *Humanities Librn* Johnnye Louise Cope; *Asst Humanities Librn* Charles E Perry
Open Mon - Thurs 8 AM - 12 PM; Fri 8 AM - 6 PM; Sat 9 AM - 6 PM; Sun 1 - 11 PM. Estab 1903 to support the academic programs and faculty and student research
Purchases: $17,000
Library Holdings: Vols 38,100; Per subs 137; AV—Fs, motion pictures, slides; Other—Exhibition catalogs
Special Subjects: Art Education, Inter Design, African art, Medieval art, advertising, museum catalogs
Collections: Artists and Exhibitions File (for local artists); Interior Design Product File

M TEXAS WOMAN'S UNIVERSITY ART GALLERY, TWU Station, Box 22995, 76204. *Dir* Alfred E Sreen
Open Mon - Fri 8 AM - 7 PM, Sat & Sun upon request. No admis fee. Approx 2000 sq ft of exhibition area; Administration Conference Tower Building, Second Floor, Promenade University Gallery (new facility). Existing Art Galleries are currently being renovated and completion approx one year
Income: Financed by Art Department and student activities fees
Collections: Graphic Art Collection; Japanese Prints
Exhibitions: A C T Building Gallery has approx eleven exhibits per school year

EL PASO

M EL PASO MUSEUM OF ART,* 1211 Montana, 79902. Tel 915-543-3800. *Dir* Leonard P Sipiora; *Cur Educ* Patricia Davenport; *Cur History* Wanda Bell; *Cur Coll* William Rakocy; *Asst Cur Coll* Loretta Martin
Open Tues - Sat 10 AM - 5 PM, Sun 1 - 5 PM, cl Mon & national holidays. No admis fee. Estab 1960 as a cultural and educational institution. One gallery houses a permanent display of the Kress Collection; second gallery is used for monthly changing exhibits; Heritage Gallery has decorative arts from 18th, 19th and 20th centuries. Average Annual Attendance: 80,000. Mem: 1036; dues $10 - $10,000; meetings Jan, Mar, Apr, Sept, Nov
Income: Financed by membership and city appropriation
Collections: †Early American Impressionists; Kress Collection; †Mexican Colonials
Exhibitions: The American Abstract Expressionist; American Drawings 1976; Anschutz Collection of Western Paintings; The Art of Edward Borein; Bartolozzi; Reynolds Beal Show; Big Bend Photographs; A Blending of Cultures; Collection of the Sarah Campbell Blaffer Foundation; A Decade of Gifts and Acquisitions; El Paso Art Association; El Paso Designer Craftsmen; First Ladies of the White House; Folk Woodcuts, Brazil; The Glaser Collection; Arthur Heinztleman: Retrospective; The Holbein Drawings; Winslow Homer; Industry Paintings by Garrett Beneker; Ke Kaethe Kolwitz Graphics Show; McKee Foundation Collection of Western Art; Miller Collection of Retablos; Edvard Munch: Major Ra Graphics; New Glory: Part II Flags; Scholastic Art Awards; Sissom; Sun Carnival Show: American Landscapes; Tenth Anniversary Members Guild Acquisitions Retablos; Toys from Switzerland; World Print Competition
Publications: Artline (newsletter), quarterly
Activities: Classes for adults and children; dramatic programs; docent training; lect open to the public, 12 visiting lectrs per year; concerts; gallery talks; tours; competitions; individual paintings and original objects of art lent to other museums on request; museum shop selling books, original art, reproductions, prints and replicas
L Library,* 1211 Montana, 79902.
Open to the public and members for reference only
Library Holdings: Vols 500
M Cavalry Museum,* 12901 Gateway W, 79935. Tel 915-543-3828. *Cur* Wanda Bell
Open Tues - Sat 9 AM - 5 PM, Sun 1 - 5 PM, cl New Years, Memorial Day, July 4, Labor Day, Thanksgiving, Christmas. No admis fee. Estab 1974 as a tribute to the mounted rider, who played a major role in the settling of the Southwest. The collections tell the story of the Indian, the conquistador, the vaquero, the cowboy and the United States Army Cavalryman
Exhibitions: Cisneros Drawings; Image of America in Caricature and Cartoon; Moody Exhibition; Texas and Her Constitutions
M Wilderness Park Museum,* 2000 Trans Mountain Rd, 79924. Tel 915-543-3819. Estab 1977. Museum contains replica of Olla Cave and Mogollon cliff dwelling
Collections: Five dioramas depict life styles and climate changes of Paleo Indians; the hunting and gathering era and the Jueco Tanks site

M UNIVERSITY OF TEXAS AT EL PASO, Department of Art Galleries, 79968. Tel 915-747-5181. *Department Chmn* Willette M Munz
Department Studios and Galleries open Mon - Fri 8 AM - 5 PM. No admis fee. University established 1916, Department of Art established 1940
Income: Financed by city and state appropriation
Collections: Small collection of prints from old and modern Masters; †collection of student works
Exhibitions: Best of Show Exhibitions out of the Texas Fine Arts Association; annual student shows and faculty exhibitions
Publications: Exhibition catalogs
Activities: Classes for adults and children; lectures open to the public, 2 - 4 gallery talks per year; tours; Extension work is offered through the regular University Extension Service to anyone over high school age; fees vary

FORT WORTH

M AMON CARTER MUSEUM OF WESTERN ART, 3501 Camp Bowie Blvd, PO Box 2365, 76113. Tel 817-738-1933. *Pres* Ruth Carter Johnson; *Dir* Jan Keene Muhlert; *Dir Education* Dr John A Diffily; *Dir Publ & Cur History* Dr Ron Tyler; *Cur Paintings* Carol Clark; *Cur Photographic Coll* Martha Sandweiss; *Registrar*

Anne Adams
Open Tues - Sat 10 AM - 5 PM; Sun & holidays 1 - 5:30 PM; cl Mon. No admis fee. Estab 1961 for the study and documentation of westering North America through permanent collections, exhibitions and publications. Main gallery plus ten smaller galleries. Average Annual Attendance: 110,000
Income: Financed by endowment
Collections: †American and Western American Paintings and Sculpture; †Print Collection; †photographs
Exhibitions: Chromolithography: The Democratic Art; Edward Weston Photographs; Laura Gilpin Photographs; Posada; Ben Shahn, A Retrospecitve Exhibition; The Bison in Art: A Graphic Chronicle of the American Bison
Publications: Newsletter, nine per a year
Activities: Docent training; produces films and TV cassettes; lect open to public, 12 vis lectr per year; gallery talks; tours; individual paintings and original objects of art lent to museums; traveling exhibitions organized and circulated; museum shop selling books, magazines, reproductions, prints and slides
L Amon Carter Museum Library, 3501 Camp Bowie Blvd, 76113. *Librn* Nancy G Wynne
Open Mon - Fri 10 AM - 5 PM. Estab 1961. For reference only
Library Holdings: Vols 20,000; Per subs 100; Micro—Fiche, reels; Other—Clipping files, exhibition catalogs, pamphlets
Collections: Western Americana; exhibition catalogs (including the Knoedler Library on fiche)

M FORT WORTH ART MUSEUM, 1309 Montgomery, 76107. Tel 817-738-9215. *Dir* David Ryan; *Cur* Marge Goldwater; *Coordr of Education* Susan Freudenheim; *Registrar* Marcia Clark; *Dir of Installations* David Jensen
Open Tues 10 AM - 9 PM; Wed - Sat 10 AM - 5 PM; Sun 1 - 5 PM. No admis fee. Estab 1901 as a museum of 20th century art. Five large galleries on the main floor. Average Annual Attendance: 92,000. Mem: 1200; dues $1000, $100, $25; annual meeting Oct
Income: $673,816 (financed by membership, city and state appropriations, grants and acquisition trusts)
Purchases: $136,011
Collections: 20th Century Paintings, Sculpture, Drawings and Prints
Exhibitions: (1978) Ed Ruscha and Allen Ruppersburg; Light on Fort Worth; Los Angeles in the Seventies; Danny Lyon; Meredith Monk - The House; Modern American Painting & Sculpture from the Dallas Museum of Fine Arts; Photographs and Films; Selections from the Permanent Collection: 1900-1940; Stella Since 1970; The Collection of Germano Celant; The Modern Chair: Its Origins and Evolution; The Record as Artwork; The Target Collection of American Photography. (1979) Wallace Berman Retrospective; Focus: Jack Caspary; Focus: Sam Gummelt; Invisible Inc - Metrognomes Dance Residency; Focus: Cork Marcheschi; David Ross Video Residency; Focus: Laurence Scholder; Richard Smith: Recent Work 1972-77; Twyla Tharp Dance Foundation; Jackie Winsor; Focus: Nicholas Wood; selections from the permanent collection always on view
Publications: Monthly calendar
Activities: Classes for adults and children; docent training; lect open to the public, 10 - 20 vis lectr per year; competitions; traveling exhibitions organized and circulated
M Fort Worth Art Museum Library, 1309 Montgomery, 76107. *Librn* Leila Adams; *Slide Librn* Pam Edwards
Tues - Fri 10 AM - 1 PM & 2 - 5 PM. Estab 1971 as a reference library for the museum staff
Income: $3910
Purchases: $3586
Library Holdings: Vols 5000; Per subs 46; Micro—Fiche; AV—Motion pictures, rec, slides, v-tapes; Other—Clipping files, exhibition catalogs, pamphlets, photographs
Special Subjects: 20th Century Art

C THE FORT WORTH NATIONAL BANK, 500 Throckmorton St, PO Box 2050, 76101. Tel 817-338-8101. *VPres* Archie L Nance
Estab 1974 to enhance the public areas of bank lobby and building; to provide art for offices of individual bank officers. Collection displayed throughout bank building, offices and public space
Collections: Alexander Calder sculpture; more than 400 pieces of drawings, graphics, paintings, prints, sculpture and tapestries, focusing on art of the Southwest, including artists throughout the nation and abroad
Exhibitions: Public Schools Secondary Schools Art Show; Woman's Club Art Show
Activities: Tours for special groups only; sponsor two art shows annually; provide cash prizes; scholarships

L FORT WORTH PUBLIC LIBRARY, Arts Section, 300 Taylor St, 76102. Tel 817-870-7739. *Coordr of Art* Lirl Treuter; *Asst* Thomas K Threatt
Open Mon - Thurs 9 AM - 9 PM, Fri & Sat 10 AM - 6 PM, cl Sun. No admis fee. Estab 1902. Not a commercial gallery, but exhibit areas for framed and matted reproductions of paintings which are displayed
Income: Financed by appropriation
Library Holdings: AV—Rec; Other—Photographs, books, sheet music, music scores, tune cards, framed and matted reproductions of paintings, special files of clipped pictures, articles, pamphlets and programs
Collections: Hal Coffman Collection of original cartoon art; Nancy Taylor Collection of bookplate; historic picture and photograph collection autographed by various celebrities; rare books
Exhibitions: Antiques, crafts, framed and matted reproductions of paintings, prints, original photographs and original works, annual original kite exhibition in March
Publications: Bibliographies; catalogs; monthly Focus
Activities: Classes for adults; competitions; lending collection contains 280 circulating reproductions, 150 photographs, 115 albums

M KIMBELL ART MUSEUM, Will Rogers Rd W, PO Box 9440, 76107. Tel 817-332-8451. *Pres* Kay Fortson; *Dir* Open; *Chief Cur* David M Robb Jr; *Assoc Cur* Nicky Holland; *Cur* Ellen Oppenheim; *Cur* Emily Sano; *Cur* Ruth Sullivan; *Cur* Michael Mezzatesta; *Bussiness Mgr* Andrew Resnick; *Education & Public Relations Dir* Shirley Spieckerman; *Registrar* Foster Clayton; *Conservator* Perry Huston
Open Tues - Sat 10 AM - 5 PM, Sun 1 - 5 PM, cl Mon, July 4, Thanksgiving, Christmas and New Year's. No admis fee. Open to public 1972 for the collection,

preservation, research, publication and public exhibition of art of all periods.
Average Annual Attendance: 200,000
Income: Financed by endowment
Collections: Highly selective collection of European paintings, sculpture and graphic arts from Ancient to early 20th Century; African sculpture; Asian sculpture, painting and ceramics; Pre-Columbian sculpture and ceramics
Exhibitions: (1977) Chinese Ceramics; Dutch Drawings from American Collections; European Drawings from the Fitzwilliam Museum; Japanese Collections: Jazz (Henri Matisse); The Last Empire; From The Tokugawa Collection: No Robes and Masks; (1978) Louis I Kahn: Sketches for the Kimbell Art Museum; Silver for the Gods: 800 Years of Greek and Roman Silver; (1979) Chanoyu: Japanese Tea Ceremony; Chatsworth; The Devonshire Inheritance; Chinese Paintings from the Arthur M Sackler Collection; The Ideal Image: The Gupta Sculptural Tradition and its Influence; (1980) Eighteenth Century Master Drawings from the Ashmolean; The Great Bronze Age of China: An Exhibition from the People's Republic of China; Recent Acquisitions: Prints and Drawings
Publications: Catalog and Handbook of the Collection; Light is the Theme
Activities: Classes for children; docent training; lect open to public, 6 - 9 visiting lectr per year; concerts; gallery talks; tours; film series; museum shop sells books, magazines and slides

L **Library,** Will Rogers Rd W, PO Box 9440, 76107. *Librn* Ilse S Rothrock
Open Tues - Fri 10 AM - 5 PM by appointment. Estab 1967 to support museum staff, docents and research in area
Purchases: $65,000
Library Holdings: Vols 20,000; Per subs 120; Micro—Fiche, reels; AV—Motion pictures, slides; Other—Exhibition catalogs

M **TEXAS CHRISTIAN UNIVERSITY,** Student Center Gallery, Brown-Lupton Student Center, PO Box 292-80A, 76129. *Dir* Pat Crowley
Open Mon - Fri 10 AM - 4 PM; Sat & Sun Noon - 4 PM. No admis. Estab to present the best art possible to the student body; to show faculty and student work. Gallery consists of one large room, 30 x 40 ft, with additional moveable panels. Average Annual Attendance: 10,000
Income: $4800 (financed by college funds)
Exhibitions: (1979) Robert Arneson (brick series); Joe Draegert (watercolors); Robert Gordy (prints and drawings); Linda Dee Guy Recent Prints and Drawings; David Hurn (photographs); Susan Kristoferson (textiles); Mid-Term Senior Exhibition. (1980) Art of the Spirit: The Search for Spiritual Significance Made Visual; John Majerowicz: Chairs; Juried Student Exhibition; MFA Thesis Exhibition: Jan Pierce; Don Ivan Punchatz: Commercial Artist Par Excellence; Senior Exhibition; TCU Faculty Exhibition; University of Dallas Sixth National Invitational Print Exhibition
Publications: Exhibition notes, mailers and posters
Activities: Classes for adults; lect open to the public, 15 vis lectr per year; gallery talks; competitions

GAINESVILLE

L **COAKE COUNTY COLLEGE LIBRARY,** Art Department, Highway 51, PO Box 240, 76240. *Dir Library Services* Patsy Wilson
Open Mon - Thur 8 AM - 9:30 PM, Fri 8 AM - 4:30 PM, Sun 2 - 5 PM. Estab 1924 to serve the needs of the administration, faculty and students. Circ 500
Purchases: $1500
Library Holdings: Vols 1800; Per subs 10; Micro—Cards, fiche; AV—A-tapes, cassettes, fs, Kodachromes, lantern slides, motion pictures, rec, slides, v-tapes; Other—Clipping files, prints, pamphlets, reproductions

GALVESTON

L **ROSENBERG LIBRARY,** 2310 Sealy, 77550. Tel 713-763-8854. *Librn* John D Hyatt; *Cur Special Coll* Jane Kenamore; *Rare Books Librn* Robert Stevens; *Museum Cur* Lise Darst
Open Mon - Thurs 9 AM - 9 PM; Fri & Sat 9 AM - 6 PM; cl Sun and national holidays. No admis fee. Estab 1900 to provide library services to the people of Galveston, together with lectures, concerts, exhibitions. Library includes the Harris Art Gallery, The James M Lykes Maritime Gallery, The Hutchings Gallery, together with miscellaneous art and historical exhibit galleries and halls. Mem: 523; dues $5 - $100
Income: $681,212 (financed by endowment, city and state appropriation)
Purchases: $83,000
Library Holdings: Vols 438,395
Collections: †Contemporary American Graphics; †Historical Artifacts relating to Texas, 15th century to present; Lalique Crystal; 19th Century American and European Paintings and Sculptures; 19th Century Japanese Art; Photographic Reference Collection; incunabula through fine contemporary printing
Exhibitions: Approx 18 per year; numerous one-man shows
Publications: The Rosenberg Library Bulletin, irregular, semiannual
Activities: Classes for adults and children; lect; gallery talks; concerts; dramatic programs; exten dept serves Galveston County; material available to individuals and organizations; original objects of art lent; lending collection contains 18,444 color reproductions, 810 motion pictures, 310 film strips, 487 framed pictures, 17 sculptures; 1961 items lent in average year; originate traveling exhibitions

HOUSTON

O **ART LEAGUE OF HOUSTON,** 1953 Montrose Blvd, 77006. Tel 713-523-9530. *Pres* Kenneth R Duff; *VPres* Glenn A Bahm; *Secy* Lari Ehni; *Coordr* Elizabeth West
Open Mon - Fri 10 AM - 4 PM; Sat noon - 4 PM. No admis fee. Estab 1948 to promote public interest in art and the achievements of Houston area artists. Gallery maintained for monthly exhibits. Average Annual Attendance: 10,000. Mem: 850; dues single $15; annual meeting May
Income: $50,000 (financed by membership and fund-raising functions)
Exhibitions: Dimension Houston; Membership Exhibits; Student Exhibits
Publications: Newsletter, monthly; year book and membership roster, annually
Activities: Classes for adults; lect open to the public, 6 vis lectr per year; competitions with prizes

M **CONTEMPORARY ARTS MUSEUM,** 5216 Montrose, 77006. Tel 713-526-3129. *Dir* Linda L Cathcart; *Cur* Marty Mayo; *Cur Educ* Ann Bunn
Open Tues - Sat 10 AM - 5 PM; Sun Noon - 6 PM; cl Mon. Estab 1948 to promote a better understanding of contemporary art. The 15,000 sq ft building was designed by Detroit architect Gunnar Birkerts; the parallelogram shaped structure consists of two floors. The upper level houses a 3000 sq ft gallery with a ceiling height of 20 ft. The lower level houses shipping and receiving, research library, multipurpose room, staff offices and storage. Average Annual Attendance: 300,000. Mem: 2000; dues $25 and higher, students $10; annual meeting May
Income: $650,000
Collections: Damaged in the 1976 flood. †New collection of contemporary paintings, sculpture and constructions
Exhibitions: Contemporary Art in Painting, Sculpture, Drawing, Video, Dance, Theater, Poetry and Music, with an emphasis on Texas artists
Activities: Wide ranging educational program including the prototypical Art After School, a program of art classes in selected elementary schools; docent programs; special events

C **COOPER INDUSTRIES FOUNDATION,** Suite 2700, Two Houston Center, 77002. *Pres* K Grant Hutchins
Annual amount of contributions and grants $125,706; supports non-profit organizations (including the arts) located in and offering services to the communities where Cooper Industries has major plant operations
Activities: Supports some capital campaigns, general support; matching contributions of employees to qualified organizations

L **HOUSTON PUBLIC LIBRARY,** Fine Arts and Recreation Department, 500 McKinney, 77002. Tel 713-224-5441, Ext 336, 337, 338. *Head, Fine Arts & Recreation* John Harvath Jr; *First Asst* Alice Jacqmin; *AV Librn* Rebecca Hubert; *Art Librn* Nicholas McCauley; *Music Librn* Open
Open Mon - Fri 9 AM - 9 PM, Sat 9 AM - 6 PM, Sun 2 - 6 PM. Estab 1848 as a private library for the Houston Lyceum and opened to the public in 1895. Circ 80,000. Monthly exhibits, including art shows are spread throughout the Central Library Building
Income: $90,000 (financed by ednowment, city appropriation, federal and state aid (LSA & LSCA), Friends of the Library)
Purchases: $90,000
Library Holdings: Vols 80,000; Per subs 400; Micro—Fiche, reels; AV—A-tapes, cassettes, fs, Kodachromes, rec, slides; Other—Clipping files, exhibition catalogs, framed reproductions, pamphlets, reproductions, sculpture, exhibition posters, portrait file, sheet music collection, auction catalogs
Special Subjects: Decorative Arts, Oriental Art
Activities: Lect open to public; tours

MID-AMERICA COLLEGE ART ASSOCIATION
For further information, see National and Regional Organizations

M **MUSEUM OF FINE ARTS, HOUSTON,** 1001 Bissonnet, PO Box 6826, 77005. Tel 713-526-1361. *Pres* Alexander K McLanahan; *Chmn Board* Isaac Arnold; *Chief Cur* John Minor Wisdom; *Adjunct Cur* John Scott; *Assoc Cur* Katherine Howe; *Cur* Patrice Marandel; *Cur* Judith M Rooney; *Cur of Photography* Anne Tucker; *Development Officer* Margaret Skidmore
Open Tues - Sat 10 AM - 5 PM, Sun Noon - 6 PM. No admis fee. Estab 1926 as an art museum containing works from prehistoric times to the present. Average Annual Attendance: 375,000. Mem: 13,000; dues $25; annual meeting May
Collections: †African, Oceanic, Pre-Columbian and American Indian Art Objects; †American and European Graphics, Paintings and Sculpture; †European and American Decorative Arts; major Collection of Impressionist and Post-Impressionist Paintings; †Medieval and Early Christian Work; †Oriental Art; †Western Americana; †antiquities; †photography
Exhibitions: American Art 1845-1945; The American Monument, Photographs by Lee Friedlander; Anne Ryan Collages and Prints; The Armand Hammer Collection: Four Centuries of Masterpieces; Art on Paper from the Collection of The Museum of Fine Arts, Houston; Patric Henry Bruce: American Modernist; Cezanne: The Late Work; Endpapers: An Element of Design; Imperial China: Photographs 1850-1912; Italian Master Drawings 1350-1800 from The Janos Scholz Collection; Paul Mogenson: Paintings and Drawings; Photographic Crossroads: The Photo League; Mark Rothko 1903-1970; A Retrospective; A Survey of Texas Native Artists; Synchromism and American Color Abstraction; Target II: Five American Photographers; Wood in Art
Publications: Bulletin, quarterly; calendar of events, bimonthly; catalogs of exhibitions
Activities: Classes for adults and children; docent training; lect open to public, 20 visiting lectr per year; concerts; gallery talks; tours; originate traveling exhibitions; museum shop sells books, magazines, reproductions, prints, slides, postcards and others

L **Museum Library,** 1001 Bissonnet, PO Box 6826, 77005. *Librn* Linda Nelson
Open Tues - Sat 10 AM - 5 PM, Sun Noon - 6 PM. For reference only
Library Holdings: Vols 11,000; Per subs 75; Other—Clipping files, exhibition catalogs
Special Subjects: Art History, Photography

L   **Alfred C Glassell Jr School of Art Library,** 5101 Montrose, 77005. *Librn* Honey Harrison
Estab 1979 for research. Students and faculty only
Library Holdings: Vols 550; Per subs 12; AV—Slides

M   **RICE UNIVERSITY,** Institute for the Arts, Rice Museum, University at Stockton Sts, PO Box 1892, 77001. *Dir* Mrs John de Menil; *Exec Adminr* Harris Rosenstein; *Production Mgr* Jesse Lopez; *Registrar* Patricia McQueen
Open Tues - Sat 10 AM - 5 PM, Sun Noon - 6 PM. No admis fee. Estab to organize and present art exhibitions. Average Annual Attendance: 38,000
Exhibitions: (1978) Embroidery through the Ages (with the Musee des Arts Decoratifs, Paris); Leger; Visions of Courtly India. (1979) CPLY: Reflection on a Past Life; Crosscurrents: Neoclassical Drawings & Prints from the Cooper-Hewitt Museum; Day and Night: Works from the Menil Foundation Collection; Franz Kline: The Color Abstractions, 1947-1961; Michelangelo Pistoletto: Mirror-Works; The Image of the Black in Western Art
Publications: Exhibition catalogues
Activities: Docent training; lect open to public; originate traveling exhibitions
L   **Art Library,** Fondren Library, PO Box 1892, 77001. *Art Librn* Jet M Prendeville
Open Mon - Thurs 1 - 5 PM and 7 - 10 PM, Fri 1 - 5 PM, Sat 2 - 5 PM, Sun 2 - 5 PM and 7 - 10 PM
Library Holdings: Vols 32,000; Per subs 329; Other—Exhibition catalogs 6000
Special Subjects: Art History, Film, Photography

C   **TRANSCO COMPANIES INC,** 2700 S Post Oak Rd, PO Box 1396, 77001. Tel 713-871-8000, Ext 4204, 871-2313. *Admin VPres* W H Cook; *Cur* Martha Terrill
Open to public by appointment only. No admis fee. Estab 1974 to enhance atmosphere for employees. Collection displayed within office spaces and hallways; annual amount of contributions and grants $20,000; supports Museum of Fine Arts, Houston Ballet, Houston Symphony, Grand Opera, Business Committee for the Arts, Public Library, Public Television, Combined Arts Corporation Campaign
Collections: 486 original works, mostly on paper by living contemporary artists
Exhibitions: Employee's Annual Juried Competition
Activities: Competitions with awards

M   **UNIVERSITY OF HOUSTON,** Sarah Campbell Blaffer Gallery, Entrance 5 off Cullen Blvd, 4800 Calhoun, 77004. Tel 713-749-1329. *Dir* William A Robinson; *Asst Dir* Toni Beauchamp; *Exhib Coordr* William Frazier; *Registrar* Susan Smith
Open Tues - Sat 10 AM - 6 PM; Sun 1 - 6 PM; cl Mon, major holidays, Aug, and between exhibitions. Estab 1973 to present a broad spectrum of visual arts, utilizing the interdisciplinary framework of the University, to the academic community and to the rapidly increasing diverse population of greater Houston. Main gallery is 5000 sq ft, ceiling height varies from 10-25 ft; Mezzanine gallery is 1500 sq ft. Average Annual Attendance: 22,000
Income: Financed by state appropriation, University, local funds, grants, gifts
Collections: Charles & Katherine Fleetwood and Edward F Heyne Pre-Columbian Collections; Freda and Clara Radoff Mexican Print Collection; †Print Study Collection; Roy Hofheinz Tapestry Collection
Exhibitions: Pierre Alechinsky: A Print Retrospective; Ancient Roots - New Visions; Beyond the Box: Architecture of Philip Johnson and John Burgee Photographed by Richard Payne; Houston Area Juried Exhibition; Frida Kahlo; Texas Crafts; Vienna Moderne: 1898-1918; Way West: Artist-Explorers of the Frontier
Publications: Exhibition catalogues
Activities: Lect open to public; concerts; gallery talks; tours; competitions; originate traveling exhibitions; sales shop selling books

INGRAM

O   **HILL COUNTRY ARTS FOUNDATION,** Hwy 39, PO Box 176, 78025. Tel 512-367-5121. *Pres* Herbert S Long; *VPres* Andrew J Ritch; *Secy* Mrs N F Allen; *Treas* John G Benson; *Art Dir* Elizabeth VanPelt; *Theatre Dir* James H Weisman
Hours vary seasonally. No admis fee except for special events. Estab 1959 to provide a place for creative activities in the area of visual arts and performing arts; and to provide classes in arts, crafts and drama. Art Gallery is maintained for members artwork. Average Annual Attendance: 30,000. Mem: 850; dues $500 and up, $250, $100, $50, $25, $15; annual meeting second Sat Sept
Income: Financed by endowment, membership, benefit activities and donations
Exhibitions: Biannual Craft Exhibit; 8th Annual Juried Exhibit; Photography-Graphics Exhibit; Young Artists Exhibit
Publications: Newsletter, quarterly
Activities: Classes for children; dramatic programs, art workshops; competitions with awards; shop sells original art, prints, and original work by members, including crafts
L   **Alice Naylor Memorial Art Library,** Hwy 39, PO Box 176, 78025. Tel 512-367-5121.
Open to members for reference only

KINGVILLE

M   **TEXAS A AND I UNIVERSITY,** Art Gallery, Art Department, Santa Gertrudis, 78363. Tel 512-592-2619. *Chmn* R Scherpereel
Open 8 AM - Noon & 1 - 5 PM. No admis fee. Estab to exhibit art work of students, as well as visitors. Average Annual Attendance: 3000
Income: Financed by state appropriations
Exhibitions: Fifteen exhibitions a year of students, instructors, and regional artists

LONGVIEW

M   **LONGVIEW MUSEUM AND ARTS CENTER,** 102 W College, Box 562, 75606. Tel 214-753-8103. *Dir* Joan Nachbaur Rathbun; *Secy* Patricia A Sandison
Open Mon - Fri 9 AM - 5 PM; Sun 1 - 3 PM. No admis fee. Estab 1970 for the encouragement of art through a program of exhibition, education, participation of members of the community and the surrounding area. East Gallery 40 x 60 ft, large windows, overhead lights; West Gallery smaller but similar; galleries between are

rooms that were once a private home. Mem: Dues sponsor $500, sustaining $100, contributing $50, patron $40, general $35; Exec meeting monthly, Board of Trustees quarterly
Income: Financed by membership and guild projects
Collections: †Regional Artists Collection formed by purchases from Annual Invitational Exhibitions over the past 20 years
Exhibitions: (1980) Abstract Expressionists; Annual Invitational Exhibition; Citation Show of East Texas Fine Arts Association; Leonardo De Vinci: Working Models of Inventions; Nacogdoches Artists; Sarah Campbell Blaffer Foundation Invitational 1980; Ari Von Selm; 20th Annual Student Art Exhibition; monthly exhibitions
Publications: Invitational 1980 Catalogue from Blaffer Collection of Abstract Expressionists Exhibition
Activities: Classes for adults and children; docent training; day at museum with artist in residence for all 4th grade students; lect open to the public, 2 vis lectr per year; tours; competitions; individual paintings and original objects of art lent to Courthouse and church; lending collection contains film strips, original art works, original prints; paintings, photographs, sculpture, slides
L   **Library,** 102 W College, 75601. *Library Chmn* Ruth Grissette
Open Mon - Fri 9 AM - 5 PM; Sun 1 - 3 PM. Estab 1973 for the enjoyment of members and public
Library Holdings: Vols 300; Per subs 3
Collections: Photography Collection
Activities: Films and slide shows when available with exhibition

LUBBOCK

O   **LUBBOCK ART ASSOCIATION, INC,** Municipal Garden & Art Center, 4215 University Ave, 79413. Tel 806-762-6411, Ext 2724. *Pres* Peggy Benton Young; *VPres* Marcia Breedlove; *Secy* Floy Hopkins; *Treas* Jim Kimmel
Open Mon - Fri 9 AM - 5 PM, Sun 1 - 5 PM. No admis fee. Estab 1951 to promote art in Lubbock-South Plains. Located in beautiful Municipal Garden & Art Center near arboretum and is 54 x 64 ft. Average Annual Attendance: 100,000. Mem: 500; dues $8; meeting first Tues every month
Income: Financed by membership
Collections: Regional and nationally known artists; works representing professional quality in graphics, painting, sculpture and crafts
Exhibitions: Membership show, permanent collection, special one and three-person exhibitions, state level invitationals
Publications: Quarterly newsletter
Activities: Workshops for adults; lect; demonstrations; competitions; cash awards; fels; lending collection contains 1000 books; book traveling exhibitions; originate traveling exhibitions; studio art and gallery sales
L   **Library,** 4215 University Ave, 79413.
Open Mon - Fri 9 AM - 5 PM, Sun 1 - 5 PM. Estab 1960
Library Holdings: Vols 1000; Per subs 6

M   **MUSEUM OF TEXAS TECH UNIVERSITY,** Fourth St & Indiana, PO Box 4499, 79409. Tel 806-742-2442. *Dir* Leslie C Drew
Open Mon - Fri 8:30 AM - 4:30 PM; Sat & Sun 1 - 4:30 PM. No admis fee. Estab 1929 for public service, research, and teaching
Income: Financed by state appropriations, West Texas Museum Association, Ranching Heritage Association, Women's Council
Collections: Primarily contemporary Southwestern American art in all media reflecting the theme of man in(and) the dry lands of the world
Exhibitions: Twelve Acre Outdoor Museum of 30 Restructures related to the ranching industry; changing exhibitions of art, textiles and costumes; permanent exhibitions of anthropology and history
Publications: Museum Digest, quarterly; Ranch Record, quarterly; Museum Journal; occasional papers
Activities: Lect; two sales shops

MARSHALL

M   **HARRISON COUNTY HISTORICAL MUSEUM,** Old Courthouse, Peter Whetstone Square, 75670. *Pres* Dr Gwin Morris; *Dir* Inez H Hughes
Open Mon - Fri & Sun 1:30 - 5 PM; cl Sat & holidays. Admis adults $1, students 50¢, children under 6 free. Estab 1965, housed in a 1901 courthouse. Mem: Dues life $150, individual $8
Collections: Cut and Pressed Glass; 400 BC - 1977 Ceramics; Hand-painted China; Historical Material; Religious Artifacts; etchings; jewelry; paintings; porcelains; portraits
Activities: Guided tours; genealogical records researched
L   **Library,** Old Courthouse, Peter Whetstone Square, 75670.
Open to the public for reference
Library Holdings: Vols 1000; Other—Manuscripts, photographs

MCALLEN

M   **MCALLEN INTERNATIONAL MUSEUM,*** 1900 Nolana, PO Box 2495, 78501. Tel 512-682-1564. *Exec Dir* Charles McLaughlin; *Cur Coll* Vicki Stubbs
Open Tues - Sat 9 AM - 5 PM, Sun 1 - 5 PM, cl holidays. No admis fee. Estab 1969 to exhibit art, science and cultural history. Average Annual Attendance: 50,000. Mem: 350; dues $25 and up
Income: Financed by membership, city appropriation and other funds
Collections: Local, state and regional artists; †Mexican Folk Art; †original prints
Exhibitions: Continuous traveling exhibits for one to two month duration; American Bison; Pan American University Faculty Art Exhibition; Sculptures by Marie Lesher; West African folk art; Western art
Publications: Bulletins and brochures periodically; Newsletter, monthly
Activities: Classes for adults and children; docent training; art and craft demonstrations; lect open to the public, 6 visiting lectrs per year; concerts; gallery talks; tours; traveling exhibitions organized and circulated; museum shop selling books, reproductions, prints, slides, jewelry, museum related science kits

L **Library,** * 1900 Nolana, PO Box 2495, 78501.
  Open to staff, volunteers, and researchers for reference only
  Library Holdings: Vols 2000; Per subs 10; AV—Slides; Other—Photographs

MIDLAND

M **MUSEUM OF THE SOUTHWEST,** 1705 W Missouri, 79701. Tel 915-683-2882.
  Dir Joan E Hellen; *Coordr of Museum Services* Leila B Seal; *Registrar* Sandra J
  Hiller; *Exhib Preparator* Jim Chiolo; *Education Coordr* Denise Eschberger; *Secy*
  Marlene Ray; *Clerical Asst* Mai Hughes
  Open Mon - Sat 10 AM - 5 PM, Sun 2 - 5 PM. No admis fee. Incorporated 1965
  as an art and history museum with a separate planetarium providing various science
  exhibits. Average Annual Attendance: 17,000. Mem: 1200; dues couple $30; board
  meeting third Wed monthly
  Income: Financed by endowment and membership
  Collections: Art and historical materials of the Southwest; European fan collection;
  Indian art collection; Oriental furniture collection; and permanent art collection
  Exhibitions: Amodio Collection of 14-17th Century European paintings; Frank
  Armstrong (one man show); The Art and Techniques of Graphics; Ceramics: New
  Definitions; Texas Watercolor Society Circuit Show; West Texas History Exhibit;
  Winter Scenes and Western Art; Steuben Glass and Lalique Glass; 14th Annual
  Southwestern Area Art Show; Student Art Festival
  Publications: Annual Report; Museletter, bimonthly
  Activities: Docent training; arts and crafts classes; lect open to public; museum shop
L **Library,** 1705 W Missouri, 79701. *Librn* Sandra Hiller
  Library Holdings: Vols 400

NACOGDOCHES

M **STEPHEN F AUSTIN STATE UNIVERSITY,** Art Gallery, North St, 75962. Tel
  713-569-4804. *Dir* Mary McCleary
  Open Mon - Fri 9 AM - 4 PM, Sun (for special exhibits). No admis fee. Estab as
  a teaching gallery and to bring in art from outside this area for our students and
  the entire community. One large room approx 42 x 27 ft, plus storage. Average
  Annual Attendance: 5300
  Collections: Student works
  Exhibitions: (1979) Jane Allensworth, Nancy Chambers and Sandra Hu; Fall
  Faculty Show; Graduate Shows; Three Dans Show; (1980)Goya Disasters of War
  Etchings, First Edition from the Blaffer Foundation; Old Master Paintings from the
  Sarah Campbell Blaffer Foundation; James Surls, Charmaine Lock; Undergraduate
  and Graduate Shows
  Activities: lectures open to the public, six visiting lecturers per year; gallery talks;
  competitions with awards; book two traveling exhibitions per year

ODESSA

M **PRESIDENTIAL MUSEUM,** 622 N Lee, 79761. Tel 915-332-7123. *Chmn*
  Dorothy Croft; *Dir* Gary E Hacking
  Open 9 - 12 AM $ 1 - 5 PM. No admis fee. Estab 1965 to heighten appreciation
  of and respect for the responsibilities of the Office of the President; to dramatize,
  in nonpartisan manner the background, accomplishments, trials and human side of
  all presidents of the United States and of Texas. Portraits of all presidents, wives
  and vice-presidents on one canvas in oil; gallery of vice-presidents, also-rans, and
  pets of presidents, as well as wood mosaics of all presidents. Average Annual
  Attendance: 40,000. Mem: 500; dues $100 and $25; annual meeting Feb
  Income: $20,000 (financed by membership)
  Purchases: $18,500
  Collections: †Acetate brush drawings of vice-presidents; †birthplace replicas of the
  presidents; churches of the presidents; coins; †first lady dolls in inaugural gowns;
  †hand-carved caricatures of the presidents; †mothers and fathers of presidents;
  †personal items of presidents; portrait galleries of Presidents, †also-rans, †pets of
  presidents; presidents of Texas; sculptures; †signatures; †White House china; wood
  mosaics of all presidents
  Publications: Presidential Museum Newsletter, monthly
  Activities: Special programs for schools, teachers, and service groups, including
  tours and visual instruction; lect open to public
L **Library,** 622 N Lee, 79761.
  For reference only
  Library Holdings: Vols 3000; AV—A-tapes; Other—Photographs, books relating
  to the presidency

ORANGE

M **STARK MUSEUM OF ART,** 712 Green Ave, PO Box 1897, 77630. Tel
  713-883-6661. *Chmn* Nelda C Stark; *VChmn* Eunice R Benckenstein; *Secy* Clyde
  V McKee; *Cur of Collections* Sarah E Boehme; *Registrar* Anna Jean Caffey
  Open Wed - Sat 10 AM - 5 PM, Sun 1 - 5 PM. No admis fee. Estab 1978 to preserve
  and display the Stark collection of art and promote interests in subjects relative to
  the same through exhibitions, publications and educational programs. Five galleries
  and lobby exhibition area. Average Annual Attendance: 30,000
  Income: Financed by endowment
  Collections: American Indian art; Western American art; porcelain and crystal
  Exhibitions: American Birds of Dorothy Doughty; American Indian Collection;
  Steuben Glass Collection; Western Collection
  Publications: Exhibition catalogs
  Activities: Gallery talks; museum shop sells books, posters and postcards

PANHANDLE

M **CARSON COUNTY SQUARE HOUSE MUSEUM,** Fifth and Elsie Sts, Box 276,
  79068. Tel 806-537-3118. *Pres* J R Hogge; *VPres* Clarence Williams; *Secy* Edwin
  Hinshaw; *Dir* Jo Stewart Randel; *Office Mgr* Pam Herring; *Dir of Education* Mogie
  McCray; *Cur Exhib* Floyd Scott
  Open Weekdays 9 AM - 5:30 PM, Sat 1 - 5:30 PM, Sun afternoons. No admis fee.
  Estab 1965 as a general museum with art galleries, area and State and National
  historical displays; Wildlife building and displays; Historic house, listed in National
  Register of National Trust. Two enclosed security controlled art galleries. New
  gallery is being designed and will be open to the public by September 1980. Average
  Annual Attendance: 25,000
  Income: Financed by endowments, county funds and public contributions
  Collections: Paintings of area pioneers by Marlin Adams; Sculpture and bronze by
  Jim Thomas, Grant Speed and Keith Christi; Kenneth Wyatt paintings; Ben
  Carlton Mead and Harold Bugbee paintings; Indian art beadwork, water colors,
  Acoma pottery
  Exhibitions: Karl Bodmer's Maxmilian Exhibit of aquatints and sketches from
  Northern Natural Gas, Joslyn Museum in Omaha; The Big Bend, Photographs by
  Bank Longmore, Amon Carter Museum. (1980) Goya's Disasters of War, 84
  aquatints and sketches owned by the Sarah Blaffer Foundation of Houston;
  changing monthly exhibits of state artists
  Activities: Classes for adults and children; dramatic programs; docent training;
  lectures open to the public, seven visiting lecturers per year; gallery talks; tours;
  lending collection contains cassettes, film strips, lantern slides, nature artifacts,
  slides; book four traveling exhibitions per year; sales shop sells books, prints,
  reproductions

SAN ANGELO

M **ANGELO STATE UNIVERSITY,** Houston Harte University Center, Box 11027,
  76901. Tel 915-942-2062. *Dir* Wes Davis; *Progress Consultant* Janet R Sharpe;
  Chmn Art Committee Scott Steger
  Open Mon - Fri 9 AM - 4 PM, Wed 7 - 9:30 PM. No admis fee. Estab 1970 to
  provide entertainment and informal education for the students, faculty and staff.
  Gallery is maintained
  Income: $3000 (financed by city and state appropriations)
  Collections: wax drawings done by Guy Rowe for illustration of the book In Our
  Image by Houston Harte
  Exhibitions: Historical artifacts; modern drawings; photography; pottery; weaving;
  childrens, students and faculty exhibitions
  Activities: lect open to public, 2 visiting lectr per year; gallery talks; tour; concerts,
  dramatic programs; compeitions

M **SAN ANGELO ART CLUB,** Kendall Art Gallery, 119 W First St, Box 3362,
  76901. *Pres* Sarah Holland; *Secy* Arleta Massey; *Exhib Chmn* June Bratton
  Open Wed, Sat & Sun 2 - 5 PM, year round. Estab 1949 to promote the fine arts
  in San Angelo. Mem: 100; dues $15; annual meeting Aug
  Income: $8000 (financed by Memorial Endowment Fund)
  Collections: Paintings by Bryon Browne, Gladys Rockmore Davis, Xavier
  Gonzales, Iver Rose and Frederick Waugh
  Exhibitions: Monthly exhibits from area artists
  Publications: Newsletter
  Activities: Classes; special workshops

SAN ANTONIO

O **COPPINI ACADEMY OF FINE ARTS,** * 115 Melrose Place, 78212. Tel
  512-824-8502. *Pres* Dr Warren Hester; *Correspondence Secy* Margaret Jones; *Exhib
  Chmn* Erwin O Wesp
  Open Sat & Sun 2 - 5 PM or by appointment. No admis fee. Estab 1945 to foster
  a better acquaintance and understanding between artists and patrons; to encourage
  worthy accomplishment in the field of art and to serve as a means of public
  exhibition for active members works and other works of art. Upstairs gallery
  donated by founder Dr Pompeo Coppini to the academy for exhibition of works.
  Mem: 191; dues $2 - $100; annual meeting third Sun in Jan
  Income: Financed by membership
  Collections: Oil Paintings by Rolla Taylor; Sculpture by Waldine Tauch and
  Pompeo Coppini; photography collection
  Exhibitions: Different artists and exhibits from Victoria, Houston, Clifton and
  Georgetown, Texas
  Publications: Coppini News Bulletin, monthly
  Activities: Educ programs; art demonstrations; sponsors workshops; lect open to
  public; approximately 5 tours; competitions; scholarships

M **MARION KOOGLER MCNAY ART INSTITUTE,** 6000 N New Braunfels St,
  78209. Tel 512-824-5368. *Pres* Mrs Edgar Tobin; *Dir* John Palmer Leeper
  Open Tues - Sat 9AM - 5 PM, Sun 2 - 5 PM cl Mon. No admis fee. Incorporated
  1950 for the encouragement and development of modern art. Mem: 800; dues
  patrons $500, friends $100
  Income: $400,000 (financed by endowment)
  Collections: †American watercolor from Winslow Homer to present; French 19th
  century paintings including Gauguin, Cezanne, Matisse, Picasso; Lang Collection
  of 19th and 20th century French and American art; Oppenheimer Collection of
  Gothic and Medieval art; print collection
  Publications: Collection catalogs
  Activities: Concerts; films; gallery talks; lectures; tours; originates traveling
  exhibitions
L **Library,** 6000 N New Braunfels St, 78209. *Librn* Mrs John P Leeper
  Open Tues - Fri 9 AM - 5 PM to the public. Estab 1970 as an adjunct to the museum.
  For reference only
  Income: $5000 (financed by endowment and gifts)
  Purchases: $5000
  Library Holdings: Vols 9000; Per subs 20; Other—Clipping files, exhibition
  catalogs, pamphlets
  Special Subjects: Visual arts

Collections: Far Eastern art, especially Japanese woodblock prints; 19th - 20th century Western visual arts

L **OUR LADY OF THE LAKE UNIVERSITY**, Saint Florence Library, 411 Southwest 24th St, 78285. *Dir Library System* Sr Miriam Dorothy Lueb
Open daily except holidays, times vary with the needs of the students
Library Holdings: Vols 28,500; Micro—Fiche; AV—A-tapes, cassettes, fs, Kodachromes, rec, slides, v-tapes; Other—Clipping files
Special Subjects: Texana
Collections: Carnegie Reference Set, photographic set, rare book collection

O **SAN ANTONIO ART LEAGUE**, 310 W Ashby, 78212. Tel 512-732-6048. *Pres* Mrs Seth Temple; *Secy* Mrs Joe C Rust; *Executive Dir* Mrs Jack Casey; *Museum Consultant* Charles Long
Open Tues - Fri 10 AM - 4 PM, weekends 1 - 4 PM, cl Mon. No admis fee. Estab 1912 as a public art gallery for San Antonio, and for the promotion of a knowledge and interest in art by means of exhibitons. Mem: 1000; dues $10 - $100; meetings monthly Oct - May
Income: $28,000 (financed by membership and fund raising projects)
Purchases: $1500
Collections: Crafts, paintings, prints and sculpture
Exhibitions: Annual San Antonio Art League Artists exhibition; San Antonio Artist of the Year, a one-man show; permanent collection on exhibit during summer
Publications: Exhibiton catalogs; monthly calendar of events
Activities: Lect open to public; gallery talks; tours; competitions; paintings and original art objects lent; originate traveling exhibitions
L **Library**, 310 W Ashby, 78212.
For reference only
Library Holdings: Vols 350

M **SAN ANTONIO MUSEUM ASSOCIATION, INC**, 3801 Broadway, 78029. Tel 512-826-0647. *Chmn* A Baker Duncan; *Pres* Nancy B Negley; *Treas* Gordon George; *Asst Secy* Mrs Frank Valdez; *Executive Dir* Helmuth J Naumer; *Assoc Dir* Adair R Sutherland; *Dir Public Relations* Paul R Rossbach; *Business Mgr* Phil Bauman; *Sr Cur of History & Decorative Arts* Cecilia Steinfeldt; *Cur of Education* Marcia Solon; *Cur of Transportation* Joseph Zawatski; *Community Relations Coordr* Roberto Esparza; *Outreach Coordr* Pati Park; *Development Officer* Marjorie Shackelford; *Membership Secy* Sue Burkhalter
Open 9 AM - 5 PM weekdays, 10 AM - 6 PM weekends and holidays. No admis fee, voluntary contributions. Estab 1922 to further education and awareness of local and regional history, art, science and technology. Average Annual Attendance: 300,000. Mem: 1500; dues indivudal $15; monthly meeting
Income: $2,575,924 (financed by endowment, membership, city appropriation and other fund raising projects)
Purchases: $267,582
Collections: Local historical objects collection; modern and contemporary art
Exhibitions: The American Cowboy; Buildings Reborn, New Uses, Old Places; Christmas Creches; The Great American Foot; The National Gem Collection; Saltillo Sarapes; Soviet Sports Exhibition; Treasures from Chatsworth: The Devonshire Inheritance; Twentieth Century Drawings from the Whitney Museum of American Art
Publications: Calendar, monthly; books
Activities: Lect open to public, 2 - 3 visiting lectr per year; gallery talks; tours; SAMAVan for community involvement; paintings and original art objects lent; lending collection contains books; originate traveling exhibitions; shop sells books, prints, reproductions, slides and local crafts
L **Ellen S Quillin Memorial Library**, 3801 Broadway, 78029. *Librn* Linda M Hardberger; *Slide Librn* George Anne Cormier
Open 8:30 AM - 5 PM weekdays. Estab 1942 as a reference library for curators and the general public on the subjects of art, decorative art, history and natural science
Library Holdings: Vols 10,000; Per subs 50; AV—Slides; Other—Clipping files, exhibition catalogs, manuscripts, memorabilia, photographs
Special Subjects: Decorative Arts, Primitive Art, American Indian Art, American and Texan Art

L **SAN ANTONIO PUBLIC LIBRARY,*** Art, Music & Films Dept, 203 S Saint Marys St, 78202. Tel 512-223-6651, Ext 49 or 50. *Dir* Irwin Sexton; *Asst Dir* Geraldine LeFevre
Open Mon - Fri 9 AM - 9 PM, Sat 9 AM - 6 PM. Estab to provide art reference and lending materials to the residents of Bexar County. Art gallery is maintained
Income: $30,000 (financed by membership, and city appropriation)
Purchases: $30,000
Library Holdings: Micro—Reels; AV—Cassettes, fs, motion pictures, rec, slides; Other—Clipping files, pamphlets
Exhibitions: Monthly exhibit of local artists work
Activities: Lect open to the public, 2 visiting lectrs per year

O **SOUTHWEST CRAFT CENTER,*** 300 Augusta St, 78205. Tel 512-222-0926. *Dir* Betty Hutzler
Open daily 10 AM - 5 PM. Estab 1963, shop estab 1968, to keep crafts alive by giving craftsmen an outlet for their work, to educate the public in crafts by putting good crafts before them and also maintaining a school where these medias can be taught. Average Annual Attendance: 100,000. Mem: 1500 students, 35 craftsmen; dues $10 and up; annual meeting May
Income: Financed by endowment and membership
Exhibitions: Student-Faculty Show; approx twelve one-man and group craft shows
Publications: Opening Invitations; Yearbook
Activities: Classes for adults and children; crafts workshop programs with visiting artists; sales shop selling juried crafts of over 110 craftsmen
L **Library,*** 300 Augusta St, 78205. *Librn* Mrs William Larsen
Reference library contains craft books, slides and films

L **TRINITY UNIVERSITY**, Department of Art Slide Collection, 715 Stadium Dr, 78284. Tel 512-736-7216. *Cur* Jane Preddy
Library Holdings: AV—Slides 65,000

SHERMAN

M **AUSTIN COLLEGE**, Ida Green Gallery, PO Box 1149, 75090. Tel 214-892-9101, Ext 218. *Dir* C R Neidhardt
Open 9 AM - 5 PM weekdays. No admis fee. Estab 1972 to serve campus and community needs. Average Annual Attendance: 5000
Income: Financed by endowment
Collections: Prints
Exhibitions: Monthly, except summer
Activities: Lect open to public, 2 - 4 visiting lectrs per year; tours

SNYDER

M **DIAMOND M FOUNDATION MUSEUM**, Diamond M Bldg, 911 25th St PO Box 1149, Snyder, TX 79549) *Dir* T S Gilbreth
Open 9 AM - 4 PM weekdays. Estab 1950
Collections: Bronzes; Currier and Ives lithographs; jade; ivory; paintings by Korner, Remington, Wyeth and others

SUNSET

M **SUNSET TRADING POST OLD WEST MUSEUM**, Route 1, 76270. Tel 817-872-2027. *Cur* Jack N Glover
Open 8 AM - 6 PM daily. Admis adults 50¢, children free. Estab 1956
Collections: Anthropological, archaeological, historical materials; Indian artifacts; paintings; prints and drawings; sculpture
Exhibitions: Loans from permanent collections; loans from other museums
Activities: Classes for adults and children; lectures, guided tours; sales shop
L **Library**, Route 1, 76270.
Reference use only
Library Holdings: Vols 500
Collections: Indian and frontier books

TYLER

M **TYLER MUSEUM OF ART**, 1300 S Mahon Ave, 75701. Tel 214-595-1001. *Dir* Ron Gleason; *Cur of Education* Lee Hutchins; *Cur of Exhib* Michael Dillon; *Admin Asst* Carol Pianta
Open Tues - Sat 10 AM - 5 PM, Sun 1 - 5 PM. No admis fee. Estab 1971 as a museum of 19th and 20th century art. Two galleries are 40 x 60 ft with 20 ft ceilings; one gallery covers 25 x 45 ft. Average Annual Attendance: 35,000. Mem: 650; dues $25 - $2000
Income: $140,000 (financed by endowment, membership and auction)
Activities: Classes for children; docent training; lect open to public, 5 - 6 visiting lectr per year; concerts; gallery talks; tours; original art objects lent; originate traveling exhibitions; shop sells books
L **Library**, 1300 S Mahon Ave, 75701.
Open for reference only
Library Holdings: Vols 1000; Per subs 12; AV—Motion pictures

VERNON

M **RED RIVER VALLEY MUSEUM**, 2030 Cumberland, PO Box 2004, 76384. Tel 817-553-4948. *Pres* Bill Benson; *VPres* Sam Phelps; *Secy* Ann Slaugenhop; *Executive Dir* Jim Henson; *Clerical Hostess* Bettye Coffey; *Clerical Hostess* Jessie Marlow
Open daily 1 - 5 PM. No admis fee. Estab 1976 to provide for and preserve local heritage while maintaining national exhibits in the arts, history, and science programs. One gallery with one hundred linear feet of hanging space. Average Annual Attendance: 4000. Mem: 500; dues family $25, individual $15; annual meeting third Tuesday in October
Income: $15,000 (financed by membership, contributions)
Purchases: $2000
Collections: Electra Waggoner Biggs Sculpture Collection; J H Ray Indian Artifacts; Taylor Dabney mineral collection
Publications: Museum Newsletter, quarterly
Activities: Classes for children; lectures open to the public, three visiting lecturers per year; gallery talks; tours; book traveling exhibitions; museum shop selling books, art supplies; brochures; collectors items

WACO

M **ART CENTER**, 1300 College Dr, Box 5396, 76708. Tel 817-752-4371. *Dir* Paul Rogers Harris; *Cur* Gordon McConnell
Open 10 AM - 5 PM Tues - Sat, 1 - 5 PM Sun. No admis fee. Estab 1972 to provide a variety of exhibitions for appreciation, and classes for participation. Former residence of William Camerone, now renovated and contains one ' ge main gallery and a small adjacent gallery, and additional exhibition space on the second floor. Average Annual Attendance: 20,000. Mem: 900; dues $25
Income: $100,000 (financed by endowment, membership and grants)
Collections: Contemporary regional art
Exhibitions: John Chatmas: paintings; Cowboys, Indians and Settlers; Jerry Dantzic and Cirkut Camera; Doors; Fifteen from Dallas; Pedro Friedeberg; Richard Hunt sculpture; Peruvian Colonial Paintings; Gisela-Heidi Strunck: sculptures; Ten from Houston; David Traub: glassworks; Roger Winter: paintings, prints, collages; the Art Center 1979 Competition; also many regional shows
Publications: Catalogs; newsletter
Activities: Classes for adults and children; docent training; lect open to the public, 2 - 3 visiting lectr per year; gallery talks; tours; competitions; exten dept serves ethnic minorities and low socio-economic groups; originates traveling exhibitions; museum shop sells books, reproductions and gift items

L **Library,** PO Box 5396, 76708.
Open 10 AM - 5 PM Tues - Sat, 1 - 5 PM Sun. Estab 1976 as a reference source for staff, faculty and patrons of the Art Center
Income: $500
Purchases: $650
Library Holdings: Vols 250; Per subs 20; Other—Exhibition catalogs

BAYLOR UNIVERSITY

M **Baylor Art Museum,*** 76703. Tel 817-755-1011. *Dir* J B Smith; *Cur* Vernie Logan
Open daily 8 AM - 5 PM, cl Sat & Sun. Estab 1967 as a teaching arm of the university to serve the area. Gallery contains one large room with storage and preparation room. Average Annual Attendance: 500
Income: Financed through the art department
Purchases: $2000 (annually)
Collections: Graphics; local artists; prints; sculpture from Sepik River area, New Guinea
Exhibitions: Exhibitions are held in University art gallery
Activities: Lect open to public, 4 visiting lectr per year
L **Dept of Art Reference Library,*** 76703. *Librn* Vernie Logan
Library restricted to scholars and advanced students
Library Holdings: Vols 200
L **Armstrong Browning Library,*** Eighth & Speight Sts, PO Box 6336, 76706. Tel 817-755-3566. *Dir* Dr Jack W Herring; *Librn* Betty A Coley; *Admin Asst* Rita S Humphrey; *Hostess* Nancy Dobbins
Open Mon - Fri 9 AM - Noon and 2 - 4 PM, Sat 9 AM - Noon. Estab 1918 to provide a setting for the personal possessions of the Brownings and to have as complete as is possible a collection for the use of Browning scholars. Gallery is maintained.
Mem: Dues individual $20
Income: $80,000 (financed by endowment and private university)
Purchases: $12,000
Library Holdings: Vols 10,000; Per subs 25; Micro—Reels; AV—A-tapes, cassettes, fs, motion pictures, rec, slides; Other—Clipping files, prints, manuscripts, memorabilia, original art works, pamphlets, photographs, reproductions, sculpture, original documents
Special Subjects: Robert and Elizabeth Barrett Browning, Victorian Era of Literature
Collections: Hagedorn; Kress Foundation Gallery Collection of Portraits; Meynell; Pen Browning; photograph collection of prints; portraits of Robert Browning and Elizabeth Barrett Browning; portraits of donors; Shields
Publications: Armstrong Browning Library Newsletter, semiannual; Baylor Browning Interests, irregular; Browning Music 1973, music catalog; Studies in Browning and His Circle, semiannual
Activities: Lect open to the public, 2 visiting lectrs per year; concerts; tours; scholarships

M **TEXAS RANGER HALL OF FAME AND MUSEUM,** (Formerly Fort Fisher and Homer Garrison Memorial Museum) Interstate 35 West, Box 1370, 76703. Tel 817-754-1433. *Cur* Gaines de Graffenried
Open 9 AM - 5 PM daily (winter), 9 AM - 6 PM daily (summer). Admis adults $2.50, children (6 and up) $1.50, special group rates
Collections: Texas Ranger items; Western history; paintings and sculpture
Exhibitions: Temporary and traveling exhibitions
Activities: Lectures, guided tours, research on Texas Rangers; sales shop

O **YOUTH CULTURAL CENTER,** 815 Columbus Ave, 76702. Tel 817-752-9641. *Dir* Mrs George J Moen
Open 9 AM - Noon, Mon - Fri. No admis fee. Estab 1963 by the public school district and Waco City Council PTA
Collections: Decorative arts; Indian artifacts; paintings; sculpture
Activities: Special education classes; docent program; handcraft workshops; lectures; tours; films

WICHITA FALLS

M **WICHITA FALLS MUSEUM AND ART CENTER,** Two Eureka Circle, 76308. Tel 817-692-0923. *Dir* Larry Francell; *Cur of Education* Joan McClendon; *Registrar & Preparator* Jean Joubert; *Executive Secy* Anne Jones
Open Mon - Sat 8:30 AM - 4:30 PM, Sun 1 - 5 PM. No admis fee. Estab 1967 for the purpose of serving the community. Three galleries house art exhibits, science and history exhibits. Average Annual Attendance: 60,000. Mem: 1500; dues $15 - $1000; annual meeting April
Income: $170,000; (financed by endowment, membership, city appropriation and schools)
Purchases: $10,000
Collections: †American prints
Exhibitions: (1978) A History of America Through Printmaking; Selections from the Sid Richardson Collection of Western Art. (1979) Brooke Alexander, A Decade of Prints; Paperworks, an Exhibition of Texas Artists; Photography in the West; The Way I See It
Publications: Events calendar, Sept, Jan, May
Activities: Classes for adults and children; docent training; lect open to public, 2 - 5 visiting lectr per year; gallery talks; tours; lending collection has original prints; originate traveling exhibitions; shop sells books, prints, crafts and jewelry
L **Library,** Two Eureka Circle, 76308. Tel 817-692-0923. *Librn* Larry Francell
Open to public for reference only
Library Holdings: Vols 1500; Per subs 15

WIMBERLEY

M **PIONEER TOWN,** 7A Ranch Resort, Box 259, Route 1, 78676. Tel 512-847-2517. *Dir* Raymond L Czichos
Open Memorial Day - Labor Day 9 AM - 10 PM daily, rest of the year, Sat $ Sun afternoons. No admis fee. Estab 1956 as a village and art museum
Collections: Contemporary Western artists; sculpture and metalwork

UTAH

BRIGHAM CITY

M **BRIGHAM CITY MUSEUM-GALLERY,** 24 N Third W, PO Box 583, 84302. Tel 801-723-6769. *Dir* Frederick M Huchel; *Chmn* Colleen H Bradford
Open 11 AM - 7 PM Mon - Sat, cl Sun. No admis fee. Estab 1970 to promote and preserve artistic and cultural opportunities and appreciation of the history and accomplishment of local citizens, and to further promote understanding of the natural resources and wildlife of the area. Average Annual Attendance: 13,000
Income: Financed by Brigham City Corporation
Collections: Crystal and glass; 19th century clothing, artifacts and furniture
Activities: Lectures, 5 visiting lectr per year; concerts, gallery talks, competitions; Monthly rotating exhibits of art and varied collections;; shop sells souvenirs
L **John B Rentmeister Western Americana Library,** 24 N Third W, 84302.
Open for research only
Library Holdings: Vols 600; Per subs 2; Other—Clipping files, photographs, documents

CEDAR CITY

M **SOUTHERN UTAH STATE COLLEGE,** Braithwaite Fine Arts Gallery,* Old Administration Bldg, 84720. *Dir* Thomas A Leek
Open Mon - Fri 10 AM - 5 PM, Sat 1 - 6 PM, cl mid-Aug & major holidays. No admis fee. Estab 1976 to provide a quality visual arts forum for artists' work and the viewing public. The gallery has 2000 sq ft of space with 300 lineal ft of display surface; it is equipped with facilities for two and three-dimensional media with electronic security system. Average Annual Attendance: 2500. Mem: Dues annual $25
Income: Financed by city and state appropriations and private donations
Purchases: $4400
Collections: 18th, 19th & 20th century American art; currently purchasing three-dimensional media
Exhibitions: Annual Faculty Exhibition; Annual Printmaking West; Annual Student Exhibition; Annual Watercolor West; Recent Art Gifts to College; Recent Paintings: Eric Brown; Small Metals: Carl E Riggs, Jr; Utah Open
Publications: Exhibition announcements, monthly
Activities: Classes for adults; lect open to public, 4 visiting lectrs per year; gallery talks; tours; competitions; artmobile; lending collection contains kodachromes, original art works, oroginal prints, paintings, slides
L **Library,*** 351 W Center, 84720. Tel 801-586-4411. *Librn* A Thomas Challis
Open to registered students and to public, by permission
Library Holdings: Vols 125,000

FILLMORE

M **TERRITORIAL STATEHOUSE,** 50 W Capital Ave, PO Box 657, 84631. Tel 801-743-5316. *Park Supt* C Max Martin; *Cur* Andy de Haan
Open 8 AM - 7 PM June 1 - Sept 1, all other months 8 AM - 5 PM. No admis fee. Estab 1930, as a museum for pioneer relics. Restored by the state and local Daughters of Utah Pioneers; run by Utah State Division of Parks and Recreation
Income: Financed by state appropriations
Collections: Charcoal and pencil sketches; paintings; photograph prints collection; pioneer portraits in antique frames; silk screen prints
Activities: Lectures open to the public, 2 visiting lectrs per year; tours; motion pictures; gallery talks

KAYSVILLE

O **KAYSVILLE COMMUNITY ART LEAGUE,** LeConte Stewart Art Gallery, 267 S 200 E, 84037. Tel 801-376-2694. *Pres* Stephen E Whitesides
Estab 1971 to administer affairs of gallery. Small gallery near community center remodeled from historical building. Average Annual Attendance: 1000. Mem: 655; dues $2
Income: Financed by membership
Collections: Lithography, paintings and other work of LeConte Stewart
Activities: Lect open to public; gallery talks

OGDEN

O **ECCLES COMMUNITY ART CENTER,** 2580 Jefferson Ave, 84401. Tel 802-392-6935. *Pres* Pam Carlson; *VPres* Richard Glasmann; *Secy* Rebecca Gale; *Treas* Laurie Ruskin; *Dir* Sandra H Havas
Open 9 AM - 5 PM Mon - Fri, 10 AM - 4 PM Sat, cl Sun & holidays. No admis fee. Estab 1959 to serve as a pivot and focal point for community cultural activities and to promote cultural growth. Maintains an art gallery with monthly exhibits. Average Annual Attendance: 25,000. Mem: 300; dues $5 - $100; annual meeting Nov
Income: $25,000 (financed by membership, state appropriation and fund raising)
Exhibitions: B Y Andelin; Larry and Sharlene Christensen; Farrell Collett; Steven Fawson; Alan Gibby; Oliver Parson; Jackie and Ethel Paul; Norman Skancky; Harry Taylor; Utah Watercolor Society
Publications: Newsletter, bimonthly
Activities: Classes for adults and children; dramatic programs; lect open to public, 12 visiting lectr per year; concerts; competitions

PRICE

M COLLEGE OF EASTERN UTAH, Gallery East, 451 East Fourth North, 84501. Tel 801-637-2120, Ext 239 and 264. *Dir* James L Young
Open daily 8 AM - 5 PM, open Special Nights. No admis fee. Estab 1975 to provide an educational and aesthetic tool within the community. Average Annual Attendance: 5000
Income: $1600 (financed by school appropriation)
Collections: Broad collection of contemporary prints
Exhibitions: Changing exhibits
Activities: Lectures open to the public, two or three visiting lecturers per year; gallery talks; tours; competitions with awards; scholarships; traveling exhibits organized and circulated to colleges

PROVO

BRIGHAM YOUNG UNIVERSITY

M B F Larsen Gallery, Harris Fine Arts Center F-303, 84602. Tel 801-378-2881. *Dir & Preparator* J Clyff Allen; *Dir of Art Acquisitions* Wesley M Burnside; *Secy* Joleen Meibos
Open 8 AM - 10 PM. No admis fee. Estab 1963 to bring to the University students and faculty a wide range of new experiences in the visual arts. The gallery occupies large open space on the main floor of the Harris Fine Arts Center; partitions are arranged in different ways for display; there is 10,944 sq feet for hanging art. Average Annual Attendance: 150,000
Income: Financed by university
Collections: Maynard Dixon Collection; internation collection of prints; 19th and 20th century American paintings, drawings, sculture; Utah artists; J Alden Weir Collection; Western art; Mahonri Young manuscripts
Exhibitions: Monthly invitational exhibits by students and faculty, from the permanent collections and circulating exhibits
Activities: Lect open to public; competitions; paintings lent to offices on campus and church offices only; originate traveling exhibitions
L Harold B Lee Library, Harris Fine Arts Center F-303, 84602. Tel 801-378-4005. *Dir Libraries* Donald K Nelson; *Mus and Art Librn* Beth R Webb
Open 7 AM - 11 PM Mon - Sat. Estab 1875 to support the university curriculum
Income: Financed by endowment, membership and church funds
Library Holdings: Vols 29,634; Per subs 155; Micro—Fiche, reels; AV—A-tapes, cassettes, fs, motion pictures, slides; Other—Prints, memorabilia, pamphlets, photographs
Collections: George Anderson Collection of early Utah photographs; 15th and 16th century graphic art collection; C R Savage Collection; Vough indexed and mounted art print collection
Activities: Tours

SAINT GEORGE

M DIXIE COLLEGE, Southwestern Utah Art Gallery, 84770. Tel 801-673-4811, Ext 297. *Dir* Gerald Olson
Open 8 AM - 6 PM. No admis fee. Estab 1960 to serve southwestern Utah as a visual arts exhibit center. Gallery is located in Fine Arts Center. Average Annual Attendance: 8000
Income: Financed by state appropriation
Collections: Early and contemporary Utah painters
Exhibitions: Max Blaine Watercolors; Robert Day Photo Show; Dixie College Spring Invitational; Navajo Blankets: Ritter Collection; 19th Century American Posters; Roland Lee, Jerry Olson Show; Twain Tippets, One Man's Vision; Utah 79; Watercolor West
Activities: Classes for adults; dramatic programs; lect open to public, visiting lectrs; gallery talks

SALT LAKE CITY

M CHURCH OF JESUS CHRIST OF LATTER-DAY SAINTS, Information Center and Museum, Arts and Sites Division, 50 E North Temple, Temple Square, 84150. Tel 801-531-2299. *Dir* Florence S Jacobsen; *Asst Dir* Glen M Leonard; *Cur Coll* Richard G Oman; *Cur Exhib* Paul L Anderson
Open 8 AM - 4:45 PM weekdays. No admis fee. Estab 1869 to disseminate information and display historical memorabilia to the visiting public. Assists in restorations and furnishing of Church historic sites
Income: Financed by Church
Collections: Mostly 19th and 20th century Mormon art and cultural artifacts: portraits, paintings, drawings, sculpture, prints, American furniture, china, pottery, glass; Mormon quilts and handwork; decorative arts; clothing and textiles; architectural elements and hardware; Oceanic and American Indian pottery, basketry, and textiles; Pre-Columbian pottery and sculpture
Activities: Lends to museums; temporary exhibits in Church Office Building

O SALT LAKE ART CENTER, 20 S W Temple, 84101. Tel 801-328-4201. *Pres* Paul Dougan; *Treas* Charles Boynton; *Dir* Allen Stevens Dodworth; *Sales Shop Mgr* Pam McQuarrie
Open Tues - Sun 10 AM - 5 PM, Fri evenings till 9 PM. No admis fee. Estab 1931 to educate the community in the visual arts through exhibitions and classes. Center has one large gallery of 5800 sq ft; one small gallery of 1000 sq ft; sales shop and rental sales gallery 1400 sq ft. Average Annual Attendance: 15,000. Mem: 800; dues for one year family $30, individual $20; annual meeting Sept
Income: $150,000 (financed by membership, city and state appropriation, earned income and gifts)
Purchases: $10,000
Collections: †American and European prints 19th and 20th Century; †Utah artists
Exhibitions: (1980) Main Gallery: Art Center Guild Auction; Utah Painters; Upstairs Gallery: Wulf Barsch Lithographs; Hagen Haltern Drawings; Life in the Salt Lake Valley Photographs
Publications: Bulletin, bi-monthly
Activities: Classes for adults and children; workshops; lect open to public, 3 visiting

lectr per year; concerts; gallery talks; tours; competitions; originate traveling exhibitions; sales shop sells books, original art, prints, slides and local crafts

L SALT LAKE CITY PUBLIC LIBRARY, Fine Arts Department, 84111. Tel 801-363-5733, Ext 41. *Dir* J Dennis Day; *Head Fine Arts Department* Glenda Rhodes; *Coordr Atrium Gallery* Lori Arnall
Open Mon - Fri 9 AM - 9 PM, Sat 9 AM - 6 PM, Sun 1 - 5 PM winter only. Estab 1898. Maintains an art gallery with monthly exhibitions
Income: $1,599,345 (financed by endowment and city appropriation)
Library Holdings: Micro—Fiche; AV—Cassettes, fs, rec, slides; Other—Clipping files, exhibition catalogs, framed reproductions, original art works, pamphlets, reproductions
Special Subjects: Film, Contemporary art, dance
Collections: Art of Western United States; Utah Artists
Exhibitions: Mary Atwater Weaver's Guild; one-person and group shows such as Utah Watercolor Association; traveling exhibits from state-wide Museum on the Road Program
Publications: Brochures accompanying individual shows
Activities: Folk-Life Festival; concerts; gallery talks; tours; book traveling exhibitions

M UNIVERSITY OF UTAH, Utah Museum of Fine Arts, 101 Art and Architectural Center, 84112. Tel 801-322-7332. *Dir* E F Sanguinetti; *Assoc Cur of the Coll* Thomas Southam; *Gallery Supt & Preparator* William R Balken; *Asst Gallery Supt & Preparator* Terry V Rogerson; *Asst Cur Educational Services* Elinor Sue McCoy; *Registrar* Betse Davies; *Membership & Vol Coordr* Jean Mueller; *Executive Secy* Josephine Theodore
Open 10 AM - 5 PM Mon - Fri, Sat & Sun 2 - 5 PM. No admis fee. Estab 1951 as a museum of fine arts under the administration of the College of Fine Arts. Average Annual Attendance: 75,000. Mem: 400; dues family $25, single $15
Income: Financed by state appropriations
Collections: Winifred Kimball Hudnut Collection; Natacha Rambova Egyptian Collection; Marion Sharp Robinson Collection; Trower and Michael Collections of English, American and Peruvian silver; Bartlett Wicks Collection; English 17th and 18th century furniture and pictures; Egyptian antiquities; French 18th century furnishings and tapestries; graphics, contemporary works; Italian Renaissance paintings and furniture; objects from the Buddhist culture
Exhibitions: American Painting of 1850; Cities on Stone; Graphic Styles of the American Eight; Jo Hanson: Crab Orchard Cemetery; Images of Women; Indian Basket Designs of the Greater Southwest; Sol Lewitt; Masterpieces of English watercolor from the Victoria and Albert Museum; Recent work by Manuel Neri; 19th century French Prints
Publications: Biannually
Activities: Classes for adults; docent training; lect open to public, some members only; concerts; gallery talks; tours; paintings and art objects lent; originate traveling exhibitions

L Owen Library, Art and Architecture Center, 84112. *Dir* Robert S Olpin; *Librn* Elizabeth Knudson
Open 10 AM - 5 PM Mon - Fri. Estab 1978 as a reference library for art students
Library Holdings: Vols 2000; Per subs 50; AV—Cassettes, Kodachromes, slides; Other—Clipping files, exhibition catalogs, manuscripts, memorabilia, original art works, pamphlets

M UTAH DIVISION OF STATE HISTORY,* 307 W Second S, Suite 1000, Crane Bldg, 84101. Tel 801-533-5755. *Dir* Melvin T Smith
Open Mon, Wed, Fri 8 AM - 5 PM, Tues, Thurs 8 AM - 7 PM, Sat 10 AM - 2 PM. No admis fee. Estab 1897 to collect and preserve material relating to Utah's history, and publish data relating thereto; to stimulate research, maintain history library and mark and preserve historic sites. Historical organization with limited art holdings is presently housed in temporary quarters. Average Annual Attendance: 12,000. Mem: 2624; dues $7.50
Income: $680,000 (financed by state appropriation)
Collections: Archaeological and paleontological reference collections; paintings and lithographs; sculpture
Publications: Utah Historical Quarterly; Utah State Historical Society Newsletter
Activities: Lect open to the public; awards given (Distinguished Fellow, Honorary); individual paintings and original objects of art lent to State Division of Fine Arts and Art Museums
L Library,* 307 W Second S, Suite 1000, Crane Bldg, 84101.
Library Holdings: Vols 20,000; Per subs 400; Micro—Reels; Other—Pamphlets

M UTAH STATE DIVISION OF FINE ARTS, Glendenning Gallery, 617 E South Temple St, 84102. Tel 801-533-5895, Ext 5757. *Chmn* Walter G Smith; *Executive Dir* Ruth R Draper
Estab 1899 as the Utah Art Institute by Utah State Legislature to promote the fine arts in Utah. Now a division within the Department of Development Services, Utah
Income: Financed by state and federal appropriations
Collections: Paintings, watercolors and sculptures with an emphasis on WPA period
Exhibitions: Annual visual arts competition; special exhibits
Activities: Regional art shows; competitions in visual arts; originates traveling exhibitions

O UTAH TRAVEL COUNCIL, Council Hall, Capitol Hill, 84114. Tel 801-533-5681. *Dir* Alton V Frazier; *Asst Dir* Rob Nordin; *Executive Secy* Macel Thurmond; *Information Dir* Laurie MacMillan; *Publicity Dir* Alicia Bremer
Open Memorial Day - Labor Day 8:30 AM - 6 PM, rest of year 8:30 AM - 5 PM. No admis fee. Constructed in 1866 and served as seat of government for 30 years; reconstructed on Capitol Hill and presented to Utah state in 1963; contains small museum of pioneer and historic items, paintings and furniture
Publications: Brochures; two newsletters
Activities: Lending collection contains motion pictures, photographs, transparencies for public use; originate traveling exhibitions

SPRINGVILLE

M SPRINGVILLE MUSEUM OF ART, 126 E 400 South, 84663. Tel 801-489-9434.
Dir Timothy G Rose; *Secy* Rayma Allred
Open Tues 10 AM - 9 PM, Wed - Sat 10 AM - 5 PM, Sun 2 - 5 PM, cl Mon. No
admis fee. Estab 1903 for the collection and exhibition of fine arts, and as an
educational resource. One of the largest museums in the mountain west, it has nine
galleries with 15,000 sq ft of exhibit space. Average Annual Attendance: 30,000.
Mem: 300; dues family $25, individual $15
Income: $60,000 (financed by membership, city and state appropriations)
Purchases: $5000 - $10,000
Collections: †Cyrus Dallin Bronzes; American art for the first half of the 20th
century; 18th and 19th century European art; †Utah artists (especially John Hafen)
Exhibitions: Annual April Show (national invitational painting); June Quilt Show;
Utah Valley Sculptors; High Schools of Utah Show
Publications: Newsletter, quarterly
Activities: Classes for adults and children; docent training; lect open to public, 12
visiting lectr per year; concerts; tours; museum shop sells books and reproductions
L Library, 126 E 400 South, 84663.
Open to public for reference
Library Holdings: Vols 100; Per subs 10; Other—Reproductions

VERMONT

BENNINGTON

M BENNINGTON MUSEUM, W Main St, 05201. Tel 802-442-2180. *Chief Cur &
Dir* William R Best; *Cur Military & Mechanical Arts* Eugene R Kosche; *Registrar*
Ruth Levin
Open March - Nov 9 AM - 4:30 PM, summer 9 AM - 5 PM. Incorporated 1876,
building opened 1928. Local historical museum with gallery, Grandma Moses
Schoolhouse Museum. Average Annual Attendance: 80,000. Mem: 650; dues $15
and up; annual meeting spring
Income: $150,000
Collections: Bennington Pottery; Bennington Flag; American blown and pressed
glass; contemporary Vermont and European paintings and sculptures; early
American household items; dolls; furniture; Grandma Moses paintings; rare
documents
Activities: Lectures; gallery tours; gift shop
L Library, W Main St, 05201. *Librn* Charles G Bennett

BRATTLEBORO

M BRATTLEBORO MUSEUM AND ART CENTER, Old Railroad Station, Box
800, 05301. Tel 802-257-0124. *Pres* Mary Blair; *VPres* Gordon Briggs; *Secy*
Elizabeth Stafford; *Treas* Julie Rosegrant; *Admin Dir* Carol Gochenoor
Open mid-April - mid-Dec Tues - Sun 1 - 4 PM, cl Mon. No admis fee but donations
encouraged. Estab 1972 to promote and make accessible to the community the field
of art and cultural history of Brattleboro. The museum is located in a railroad
station built in 1915, now a registered historic site. Average Annual Attendance:
5500. Mem: 325; dues $10 - $100; annual meeting Jan
Income: $40,000 (financed by membership, donations, town, state and federal
appropriations)
Collections: Estey Organ Exhibit; permanent collection is being developed as of
1979
Exhibitions: Kazuini Amano, Prints and Engravings; Judith Brown and Dennis
Verswey Veld, Sculptors; Christmas: a Festival of Trees; Retrospective on Fernando
Gerassi, Painter; Pre-Historic Cave Paintings; Sculpture and Drawings of Jack
Marshall; Life in Oldtime Vermont 1910-20; Craft Professionals of Vermont;
Children's Workshop; Vermont Painters' Invitational; Southern Vermont Artists
Association Selected Paintings
Activities: Classes for adults and children; lect open to public; concerts; gallery
talks; competitions; art lending exhibit; shop sells books, magazines, original art

BROOKFIELD

M COLLEGE OF THE AMERICAS, Museum of the Americas, Rte 14, 05036. *Pres*
Earle W Newton
Estab 1971 to gather materials in support of Anglo American and
Hispanic-American studies
Income: Financed by endowment
Collections: Anglo-American 16th - 19th century paintings; English mezzotints;
Hispanic-American decorative arts; Hogarth prints and paintings; Latin American
folk art; maps of the colonies; Pre-Columbian artifacts
L Library, Rte 14, 05036.
For reference only
Collections: Anglo-American and Latin American art

BURLINGTON

M UNIVERSITY OF VERMONT, Robert Hull Fleming Museum, 05405. Tel 802-;
Telex 656-2090. *Dir* William C Lipke; *Cur* Nina Parris; *Registrar* Colleen
Montgomery; *Admin Asst & Prog Dir* Constance S Kurth; *Exhib Designer* John
Owen
Open Mon - Fri 9 AM - 5 PM, Sat & Sun 1 - 5 PM. No admis fee. Estab 1873 as
a fine arts museum for the area and a teaching facility for the University. Four
permanent galleries, three of changing exhibits. Mem: 300; dues family $20,
individual $15, student $5
Income: Financed by endowment, membership, state and university appropriations
and grants

Collections: American, ancient, medieval and Oriental art; costumes; ethnographic
collection, especially native American; prints and drawings of various periods
Exhibitions: American; Asian; Ethnographic; Medieval and Ancient
Publications: Exhibition catalog; museum calendar: The Muse
Activities: Docent training; lect open to public and members; gallery talks; tours;
originate traveling exhibitions; sales shop sells books, cards, calendars and museum
publications
L Wilbur Room, 05405.
Open to students and others for reference

FAIRLEE

M WALKER MUSEUM,* 37 Main St, PO Box 6, 05045. Tel 802-333-9572. *Dir*
Herbert Brooks Walker II; *Asst Dir* Noel Gahagan Walker
Open by appointment only. No admis fee, donations accepted. Estab 1960. Average
Annual Attendance: 1000
Collections: †American decorative arts; †American Indian art; 18th and 19th
century American paintings; †Canadian displays; †Chinese porcelains; furniture;
Iranian Bazaar; †Japanese room; †Polynesia; prints, sculpture
Exhibitions: Temporary exhibitions
Activities: Materials and items lent to libraries and schools; wagon loans by
appointment; traveling exhibitions organized and circulated
L Library,* 37 Main St, PO Box 6, 05045.
For reference only
Library Holdings: Vols 1000; AV—Kodachromes; Other—Photographs

JOHNSON

L JOHNSON STATE COLLEGE, John Dewey Library, 05656. *Dir* Paul Gallagher
Open during school semesters 9 AM - 8 PM. Estab as a vital part of Johnson's
Academic community. For reference only
Library Holdings: Micro—Cards, fiche, prints; AV—A-tapes, cassettes, fs, motion
pictures

MANCHESTER

O SOUTHERN VERMONT ART CENTER, 05254. Tel 802-362-1405. *Pres* Dr
Ilsley S Zecher; *Dir* Thomas Reilly Dibble; *Dir Public Relations* Mrs Arthur Pierce
Open June - mid-Oct daily, 10 AM - 5 PM, cl Mon. Estab 1929 to promote
education in the arts and to hold exhibitions of art in its various forms. Average
Annual Attendance: 20,000. Mem: 1100; dues layman $20 and higher, artist $15;
annual meeting in Sept
Income: $100,000 (financed by membership and sales)
Collections: Contemporary American sculptors and painters; loan collection
Exhibitions: Annual exhibitions for members; Fall Show; one-man and special
exhibitions
Publications: Annual catalog and brochures
Activities: Classes for adults in painting, drawing, graphic arts, photography,
sculpture, weaving and pottery
L Library, 05254.
Library Holdings: Vols 500

MIDDLEBURY

M MIDDLEBURY COLLEGE, Johnson Gallery, 05753. Tel 802-388-2762. *Dir*
David M Bumbeck; *Asst Dir* Glenn Andres
Open Mon - Fri Noon - 5 PM, Sat 9 AM - Noon, Sun Noon - 5 PM. No admis
fee. Estab 1968 as a teaching collection and also to sponsor exhibitions of selected
artists
Income: Financed through the college
Collections: †Drawings; †paintings; †prints; †sculpture
Exhibitions: (1979) Art of Lithography; Assemblage by Don Reichert; Photographs
by Lewis Hine and Peter Moriarty; Paintings by Rosemary Beck. (1980) Annual
Student Show; Graphic Works by Isabel Bishop; Fibre Works by Sheila Hicks,
Clare Zeisler and Daniel Griffin; Permanent Collection; Sculpture by Eric Nelson
Publications: Annual Report

M SHELDON ART MUSEUM, One Park St, 05753. Tel 802-388-2117. *Pres* Harold
M Curtiss; *Cur* Nina R Mudge
Open June 1 - Oct 15 Mon - Sat 10 AM - 5 PM, winter hours by appointment. Admis
adults $1, children 50¢. Estab 1882 for the preservation of portraits, furniture and
artifacts of Middlebury. Seventeen rooms arranged as a 19th century Vermont
home. Average Annual Attendance: 2500. Mem: 400; dues $5 and up
Collections: China; Glass; Pewter; Historical material; Portraits
Activities: Educ dept; guided tours
L Library, One Part St, 05753.
Open all year; Mon, Wed & Fri 10 AM - 5 PM, Tues and Thurs 1 -5 PM & 6 -
9 PM, cl holidays
Library Holdings: Vols 8000; Other—Manuscripts, Library has 40,000 documents;
bound copies of newspapers, manuscripts

M VERMONT STATE CRAFT CENTER AT FROG HOLLOW, Frog Hollow
Road, 05753. Tel 802-388-4871. *Chmn of Board* David Crawford; *Vice Chmn of
Board* Deborah Clifford; *Exec Dir* Judith Versweyveld; *Secy* Nancy Wright; *Treas*
Herbert Kingsland Jr
Open Mon - Sat 10 AM - 5 PM. No admis fee. Estab 1971 to provide craft
educational, informational and marketing services to school children, adults and
professionals. The building was once a working mill. Average Annual Attendance:
40,000. Mem: 350; dues $10 - $30; annual meeting Sept
Income: $175,000 (financed by membership, Federal and State grants, consignment
receipts and tuition)
Purchases: $500-$1000
Collections: †Vermont Crafts

Exhibitions: Catching the Light: glass,metal and flowery pieces for spring; Dimensions: prints and containers; Fibers and Fabrics, and Things Made by Hand for Christmas; Ice Cream, Stars, and Butterflies: Crafts for Children; Pot Pourri: a celebration of Vermont Crafts
Publications: Information services bulletin, bi-monthly
Activities: Classes for adults and children; dramatic programs; lect open to public, 3 vis lectr per yr; original objects of art lent to non-profit organizations; traveling exhibitions organized and circulated; sales shop

MONTPELIER

M **WOOD ART GALLERY,** 135 Main St, 05602. Tel 802-229-0036. *Cur* Ronald Slayton; *Asst Cur* Olivia Bravakis
Open Tues - Sat Noon - 4 PM. No admis fee. Estab 1895; set up by the late Montpelier artist Thomas Waterman Wood as a place to house and exhibit a portion of his oils and watercolors of genre paintings. Also an exhibit place for local and regional artists. The gallery has two exhibit areas; a large room 50 ft square and a small room 20 ft square; rooms are lighted with fluorescent lights. Average Annual Attendance: 4000. Mem: 300; dues $5 - $25; annual meeting Dec
Income: Financed by endowment and partial funding from city
Collections: Paintings by contemporaries DeHass, Durand, Wyant; Paintings by Thomas Waterman Wood; a collection of American artists of the 1920s & 1930s
Exhibitions: Group shows by artists and craftsmen; monthly exhibits by local and regional artists
Publications: Monograph on the Wood Collection
Activities: Lect open to public, 1-2 vis lectr per yr; gallery talks; competitions; musical performances; individual paintings lent to other galleries, museums and businesses in the area

RUTLAND

O **RUTLAND AREA ART ASSOCIATION, INC,** Chaffee Art Gallery, 16 S Main St, 05701. Tel 802-775-0356. *Chmn of Board* Katherine King Johnson; *Pres* Edward L Mach
Open Mon - Fri 10 AM - 5 PM, weekends by appointment and special events. No admis fee. Estab and incorporated 1961 and sponsored by the Rutland Area Art Association to promote and maintain an educational and cultural center in Rutland for the area artists, photographers, craftsmen and others in the art field. Average Annual Attendance: 6000. Mem: dues $10; annual meeting in Oct
Income: Financed by a small city grant, memberships and contributions
Exhibitions: Annual Members Exhibit, juried; Art-in-the-Park outdoor festival; Autumn Members Exhibit, juried; Foliage Festival: displays of photography, flower arrangements, hobby collections, special shows; one-man and invitational exhibits
Publications: Calendar of events, annually
Activities: Workshops; special events in performing arts; art lectures; musicals, craft and art demonstrations, slide shows; special fund raising events

SAINT JOHNSBURY

M **FAIRBANKS MUSEUM AND PLANETARIUM,** Main and Prospect Sts, 05819. Tel 802-748-2372. *Pres* Dr Arnold Waters; *VPres* Mrs Joseph Bamford; *Secy* Peter Crosby; *Dir* William J Brown; *Assoc Dir* Howard B Reed; *Asst Dir Museum Education* William C Vinton; *Asst Dir for Public Programs* Charles C Browne; *Registrar* Ruth Crane
Open Mon - Sat 10 AM - 4 PM, Sun 1 - 5 PM, extended Summer hours. Admis Adults $2, students and seniors $1.50, children $1.00. Estab 1889 as a center for exhibits, special exhibitions, and programs; special exhibitions and programs on science, technology, the arts and the humanities. Art gallery for special exhibitions and work of regional artists. Average Annual Attendance: 50,000. Mem: 300; dues $100, $25, $15, $10; annual meeting January
Income: $200,000 (financed by admissions income, grants, endowment, membership and city appropriation)
Collections: Hudson River School, primarily oil paintings; 19th century American and European art; Extensive natural science, history and anthropology collections
Exhibitions: Technology and Perception, the Photographic Vision of Nature; Victorian Legacies, the Fairbanks Family and their Peers; Sweedish Nature Photography
Publications: Newsletter
Activities: Classes for adults and children; lectures open to the public; concerts; gallery talks; tours; competitions; Extension department serving Northeast Vermont; artmobile; individual paintings and original objects of art lent to other accredited museums; book traveling exhibitions; museum shop sells books, magazines, original art, reproductions, prints, slides, Science kits, kites and crafts; junior museum

M **SAINT JOHNSBURY ATHENAEUM,** 30 Main St, 05819. Tel 802-748-8291. *Librn* Jean F Marcy
Open Mon - Sat 9:30 AM - 5 PM, Mon & Fri open to 8 PM. No admis fee. Estab 1873 and maintained as a 19th century gallery; given to the townspeople by Horace Fairbanks. It is the oldest art gallery still in its original form in the United States; a one-room addition to the public library building
Income: Financed by endowment and city appropriation
Collections: 19th century American landscape paintings of the Hudson River School (Bierstadt, Colman, Whittredge, Cropsey, Gifford, Hart brothers); copies of masterpieces; sculpture

SHELBURNE

M **SHELBURNE MUSEUM,** Route 7, 05482. Tel 802-985-3346. *Dir* Jody Kenney; *Comptroller* Joseph Mullen; *Registrar* Celia Y Oliver
Open 9 AM - 5 PM, mid-May - mid-Oct. Admis adults $5, children $2.50; special group and student rates. Estab 1947 as Museum of the American Spirit to collect, preserve and exhibit American fine, decorative and utilitarian arts, particular emphasis on Vermont. 35 buildings on 45 acres. Average Annual Attendance:

130,000
Income: Financed primarily by admissions and fund raising from members
Collections: American paintings, folk art, decoys, architecture, furniture, quilts and textiles, dolls, sporting art and sculpture, ceramics, tools, sleighs and carriages, toys, farm and home implements; European material: Impressionist and Old Master paintings; English furniture and architectural elements; seven period houses; Native American ethnographic artifacts; Sidewheeler Ticonderoga, railroad memorabilia including steam train, circus material and carousel animals
L **Library,** Route 7, 05482.
Open to public by appointment
Library Holdings: Vols 10,000

SPRINGFIELD

O **SPRINGFIELD ART & HISTORICAL SOCIETY,** 9 Elm St, 05156. Tel 802-885-2415. *Pres* Mrs Lawrence B Woolson; *VPres* Ronald Knapp; *Treas* Lawrence B Woolson; *Clerk* David Shuffleburg; *Dir* Mrs Fred R Herrick
Open Noon - 4:30 PM. No admis fee. Estab 1955 for the purpose of presenting history, art and classes in the arts to the community. Gallery maintained for monthly exhibits. Average Annual Attendance: 3000. Mem: 150; dues $25, $15, and $7.50; annual meeting in Sept
Income: $3500 (financed by endowment and membership)
Collections: Primitive portraits by H Bundy, Aaron D Fletcher, and Ashel Powers; Richard Lee, pewter; Bennington pottery; paintings by local artists
Exhibitions: Childrens Model Show; crafts; Christmas Show & Sale; Historical exhibits: costumes, toys, books; photography; Stuart Eldridge, paintings; Member Artists Show
Publications: Annual schedule of events and monthly notices
Activities: Classes for adults and children; lect open to the public; gallery talks; individual paintings lent; lending collection contains original art work, paintings, photographs, sculpture, slides; sales shop sells books, original art, slides
L **Library,** 9 Elm St, 05156. *Librn* Mrs Fred R Herrick
Open to the public
Library Holdings: Vols 300; Per subs 3

WAITSFIELD

M **BUNDY ART GALLERY,*** Route 100, PO Box 19, 05673. Tel 802-496-3713. *Dir* Harlow Carpenter; *Admin* Elizabeth Joslin
Open July - Aug Mon, Wed, Sat 10 AM - 5 PM, Sun 1 - 5 PM, cl national holidays & Nov. No admis fee. Estab 1962, inc 1963 to make contemporary art and an art library accessible to the public and to enhance the cultural life of surrounding communities. Average Annual Attendance: 2000
Collections: †Contemporary painting and sculpture
Exhibitions: traveling exhibitions
Activities: Concerts
L **Library,*** Route 100, PO Box 19, 05673.
Library Holdings: Vols 450; Per subs 6

VIRGINIA

ALEXANDRIA

O **NORTHERN VIRGINIA FINE ARTS ASSOCIATION,*** 201 Prince St, 22314. Tel 703-548-0035. *Pres* Prudence D Montague; *Exec Dir* Nancy F Achenbach
Open Tues - Sat 10 AM - 4 PM, Sun 1 - 4 PM, cl Mon & holidays. No admis fee. Estab 1964 to promote education, appreciation, participation and pursuit of excellence in all forms of art and crafts; to enrich the cultural life of the metropolitan area and Northern Virginia. Main gallery space on main floor, with additional area available. Average Annual Attendance: 15,000. Mem: 650; dues double $25, single $20
Exhibitions: Annual Athenaeum Christmas Exhibit; Alexandria, VA, The First 100 Years; Allen Carter-Horace Day (two man show); 9th Annual Juried Show; John Toole (1815-60): Virginia Primitive into Painter; Prayer Rugs; winners of the 8th Annual Juried Athenaeum Show: Betty Kubalak (graphics), Claire Monderer (paintings), Bob Romanowski (sculpture)
Publications: Newsletter, monthly
Activities: Gallery talks; tours; competitions with awards; sales shop selling slides

BLACKSBURG

O **BLACKSBURG REGIONAL ART ASSOCIATION,** PO Box 525, 24060. Tel 703-552-0769. *Pres* Joyce Lewis; *VPres* Yuji Kishimoto; *Secy* Mary Ann Mattus
Estab 1950, a chapter of the Virginia Museum of Fine Arts dedicated to the encouragement and the enjoyment of the arts. Mem: Dues family $7.50, individual $5
Collections: †Collection of paintings by contemporary artists who have exhibited in Blacksburg
Activities: Dramatic programs; lect open to public, 3 - 5 visiting lectr per year; concerts; competitions; originate traveling exhibitions

VIRGINIA POLYTECHNIC INSTITUTE AND STATE UNIVERSITY
M **University Art Gallery,** 20 Owens Hall, 24061. Tel 703-951-5547. *Head Art Dept* Prof John Link
Open Mon - Fri 8 AM - 5 PM, Tues & Thurs 7 - 9 PM, Sat & Sun 1 - 5 PM. No admis fee. Estab 1969; new location Sept 1975 to serve needs of Art Department as a teaching gallery as well as to meet community needs in an area where there are few large art centers and museums. Gallery is located in same building as Art Department; exhibition area is approx 30 x 30 ft. Average Annual Attendance: 800 plus student use
Income: Financed through Departments Operational Budget

Collections: Student print collection
Exhibitions: Art Alumni Exhibition; Art Faculty Exhibition; Art Student Christmas Show and Sale; Bridges: The Spans of North America; Collectors Exhibition; Crafts Invitational; Fifth Annual Invitational; Freshworks; Graduate Student Invitational; Milton Avery Prints: 1933-1955; Paperworks Exhibition; Photographic Concepts of Nova Scotia and New Brunswick by Bob Veltri; Popular Art Culture, Christiana Prints; Prints by Bill Lidh; Senior Arts Majors Exhibition; Watercolors from the Virginia Museum; Works on Paper by Jerome Neuner
Publications: Exhibition calendar; gallery announcements
Activities: Docent training to college students; lect open to the public, 3 vis lectr per yr; gallery talks; individual paintings and original objects of art lent to faculty and staff offices on campus, as well as library and continuing education center; traveling exhibitions organized and circulated

M **Squires Art Gallery**, Squires Student Center, 24061. Tel 703-951-5535. *Dir of Squires* Thomas C Lile; *Dir Arts* Thomas F Butterfield
Open Mon - Sat 8 AM - Noon, Sun 9 AM - Noon. Estab 1969 to provide interesting and informative exhibits on the local and national level for the students, faculty and the college community. Weekly meetings of students and advisors to plan shows and events. Average Annual Attendance: 50,000
Income: $3000-$5000 (financed by student activity fee and building operation)
Purchases: $300
Activities: Lect open to the public, 3 vis lectr per yr; competitions

L **Architecture Library**, Cowgill Hall, 24061. Tel 703-961-6182. *Dean* Julio M San Jose; *Librn* Robert E Stephenson
Open Mon - Thurs 8 AM - 11 PM, Fri & Sat 8 AM - 5 PM, Sun 2 - 11 PM. Estab 1928 to provide service to the College of Architecture and Urban Studies and the other divisions of the University. Circ 30,890
Income: $64,815 (financed by State Appropriation and Gifts)
Purchases: $64,815
Library Holdings: Vols 37,700; Per subs 390; Micro—Fiche, reels; AV—Cassettes, slides, v-tapes; Other—Clipping files, exhibition catalogs, pamphlets
Special Subjects: Architecture, Art Education, Building construction, urban affairs and planning
Collections: Planning file, including urban affairs and planning, (1800 books and pamphlets)

CHARLES CITY

M **SHIRLEY PLANTATION**, Route 2, Box 130, 23030. Tel 804-795-2385. *Owner* Charles Hill Carter Jr
Open daily 9 AM - 5 PM, cl Christmas Day. Admis $3. Estab 1723 to show the history of one distinguished family from colonial times to the present. Average Annual Attendance: 36,000
Income: $75,000 (maintained by admission fees)
Collections: Original portraits; silver and furniture: English and American
Activities: individual paintings and original objects of art lent occasionally for exhibitions staged by such organizations as Virginia Museum and Colonial Williamsburg; museum shop sells books, reproductions, prints and slides

M **WESTOVER**, Charles City County, 23030. *Owner* Mrs B C Fisher; *Mgr* F S Fisher
Grounds and garden open daily 9 AM - 6 PM. Admis $1; house not open. Built about 1730 by William Byrd II, Founder of Richmond, the house is considered an outstanding example of Georgian architecture in America, with steeply sloping roof, tall chimneys in pairs at both ends, the elaborate Westover doorway; three story central structure with two end wings. The path from the Caretakers House near the gate to the house is lined with tulip poplars over 100 years old; former kitchen is a separate small brick building. East of the house is the foundation of an old icehouse and a dry well with passageways leading under the house to the river. The Westover gates of delicate ironwork incorporate initials WEB; lead eagles on the gateposts, supporting fence columns topped with stone finials cut to resemble pineapples, beehives, and other symbolic designs. Long established boxwood garden with tomb of William Byrd II. Members of his family, and Captain William Perry, who died August 6, 1637, are located in old church cemetary one-fourth mile west of the house

CHARLOTTESVILLE

M **MONTICELLO**, Thomas Jefferson Memorial Foundation, PO Box 316, 22902. Tel 804-295-2657. *Cur-Dir* James A Bear Jr
Open Mar 1 - Nov 1, 8 AM - 5 PM, Nov 1 - Feb 28, 9 AM - 4:30 PM. Admis adults $3, children 6 - 11 $1, school groups 50¢. Monticello is owned and maintained by the Thomas Jefferson Memorial Foundation, a non-profit organization founded in 1923. The home of Thomas Jefferson, designed by him and built 1769-1809, contains many original furnishings and art objects

M **SECOND STREET GALLERY**, 116 N E Second St, 22901. Tel 804-977-7284. *Pres* Gail McIntosh; *VPres* Cynthia Davis; *Secy* Anneliese Henry; *Executive Dir* Marilyn Mars
Open Tues - Sat 10 AM - 4 PM, Sun 1 - 4 PM. No admis fee. Estab 1973 to exhibit and acquaint the Piedmont area with new and innovative visual art by local, state and national artists. Gallery has second story exhibition space, consisting of three rooms (largest is 25 sq ft), uncluttered and well-lit. Average Annual Attendance: 2680. Mem: 110; dues family $20, individual $15; annual meeting August
Income: $21,000 (financed by membership, state appropriation, art auction and fund-raising)
Exhibitions: 8th National Juried Exhibition of Prints, Drawings and Photography
Publications: Juried Exhibition catalogue
Activities: Lect open to public, 5 visiting lectr per year; gallery talks; tours; competitions; cash awards; sales shop sells books, original art, prints and original cards

UNIVERSITY OF VIRGINIA

M **Art Museum**, Thomas H Bayly Memorial Bldg, Rugby Rd, 22903. Tel 804-924-3592. *Cur* David B Lawall
Open Tues - Sun 1 - 5 PM, cl Mon. No admis fee. Estab 1935 to make original works of art available to students of the University and to the general public. Average

Annual Attendance: 22,000. Mem: 500
Income: Financed by membership and state appropriation
Collections: †American art; †Art from the age of Jefferson; †Asian art; †contemporary art; †20th century prints; ethnic art
Exhibitions: (1978-79)Die Brucke Paintings, drawings, prints; Conrad Felixmuller; Post Modern Man; Renewal of Classicism
Publications: Calendar, monthly; exhibition catalogs
Activities: Docent training; extensive program of tours for school children; lect open to public, 3 vis lectr per yr; individual paintings lent to other museums; museum shop sells books, original art, reproductions

L **Fiske Kimball Fine Arts Library**, Bayly Dr, 22903. Tel 804-924-7024. *Librn* Mary C Dunnigam; *Slide Librn* Kathleen Dobbins; *Bibliographer* Christie Stephenson
Open school year Mon - Fri 8 AM - 11 PM, Sat 8 AM - 6 PM, Sun 1 - 11 PM. Estab 1970; combination of existing Art and Architecture libraries to provide a Research facility providing printed and microfilm materials for the art, architecture and drama curriculum. Circ 107,344. Fifty percent of collection is noncirculating
Income: $117,000
Purchases: $117,000
Library Holdings: Vols 139,000; Per subs 237; Micro—Fiche, reels; AV—Cassettes, lantern Slides, slides; Other—Exhibition catalogs, memorabilia, photographs
Special Subjects: Archaeology, Architecture, Art History, Film, Photography, Drama, Landscape Architecture, Planning and Urban Design
Collections: Francis Benjamin Johnson Photographs of Virgina Architecture; playbills, primarily New York Theatre; Rare books
Publications: Accession list; Slide Library three times per yr
Activities: Lect; tours

DANVILLE

M **VIRGINIA MUSEUM**, Danville Museum of Fine Arts and History, 975 Main St, 24541. Tel 804-793-5644. *Pres* J William Clement; *VPres* Frances Kepachar; *Secy* Phyllis Jones; *Dir* Dr James W Jennings; *Gallery Mgr* Deborah Hundley; *Museum Shop Mgr* Martha Corr; *Social Dir* Matilda Turbiville; *Office Secy* Betty Jones
Open Tues - Fri 10 AM - 5 PM, Sun 2 - 5 PM. No admis fee. Estab 1974. Museum has two galleries: 27 x 35 ft with track lighting; two smaller galleries: 24 x 17 ft with track lighting. Average Annual Attendance: 8000. Mem: 779; annual meeting March & Sept
Income: Financed by membership and city appropriation
Collections: Lithography Collection: Thomas Hart Benton, Regionalist School, Grant Wood; Taiwan Collection: Modern scrools, porcelain and bronzes
Activities: Classes for adults and children; dramatic programs; docent training; lect open to public, 5 visiting lectr per year; concerts; gallery talks; tours; museum shop sells books, original art and reproductions

FARMVILLE

M **LONGWOOD COLLEGE**, Bedford Gallery, Pine St, 23901. Tel 804-392-9359. *Chmn of Art Dept & Dir* Barbara L Bishop
Open Mon - Fri 9 AM - Noon, 1 - 5 PM, Sat & Sun 2 - 6 PM, except college holidays. No admis fee. Estab 1970 to present educational exhibits of professional artists for students and community
Income: Financed by state appropriation
Collections: †Art Department collection; †collection of works by contemporary Virginia artists; †Thomas Sully Gallery Collection of 19th and 20th Century Art
Exhibitions: The Agrarian Series: With Other Forms and Words by Conway Thompson (sculpture, poetry); Craft Collectables V (pottery, fibers, jewelry); Four with Paper: Handmade paper works by Nancy Dahlstrom, Vera Dickerson, Katherine Liu and Joni Pienkowski; Paintings by James Wall and Jeff Davis (Scott-McKennis); Twenty Utah Artists (VMFA traveling exhibit); Virginia Fiber Artists Invitational (traveling); Susan C Waters, Nineteenth Century Itinerant Painter
Publications: Exhibition catalogues
Activities: Lect open to public; Individual paintings and original objects of art lent

FREDERICKSBURG

M **BELMONT**, Gari Melchers Memorial Gallery, Mary Washington College, 224 Washington St, 22401. Tel 703-373-3634. *Dir* Richard S Reid
Open 1 - 4 PM. Admis adults $1.50, students 50¢, group rates available. Estab 1975 to exhibit, preserve and interpret the works of art and memorabilia of the late American Artist Gari Melchers, in his former estate and studio. Studio consists of three gallery rooms, a work room, and storage rooms. Average Annual Attendance: 3500
Income: $60,000 (financed by endowment and state appropriation)
Collections: Over six hundred works of art, paintings, drawings and etchings by Gari Melchers; Over 1000 sketches and studies by Gari Melchers; Paintings and drawings by Berthe Morisot, Franz Snyders, Puvis de Chavannes, Rodin and others; Furnishings from Europe and America
Exhibitions: Murals by Gary Melchers
Activities: lectures open to the public, three visiting lecturers per year; gallery talks; tours; individual paintings lent to public institutions; book traveling exhibitions yearly; sales shop sells postcards, pamphlets, magazines and reproductions

M **JAMES MONROE LAW OFFICE - MUSEUM AND MEMORIAL LIBRARY**, 908 Charles St, 22401. Tel 703-373-8426. *Dir* Paulette Skirbunt Watson
Open daily 9 AM - 5 PM, cl Dec 24, 25, 31 & Jan 1. Admis adults $1.50, children 50¢, group rates available. Estab to keep in memory the life and service of James Monroe and of his contribution to the principles of government, to preserve his treasured possessions for present and future generations. Open to the public in 1928; owned by Commonwealth of Virginia and under the control of Mary Washington College; a National Historic Landmark
Income: Financed by gifts, grants and Commonwealth of Virginia
Collections: Louis XVI furniture purchased by the Monroes in France in 1794 and later used by them in the White House; portraits; sculpture; silver; china; jewelry
Publications: Library of James Monroe, catalog

Activities: Tours; museum shop sells books, reproductions, prints, slides and history related objects; exclusive items from local crafts people

L **Library,** 908 Charles St, 22401. *Chmn Libr Committee* Ruby Weinbrecht
Open by appointment only
Library Holdings: Vols 20,000; Other—Manuscripts, letters; documents

HAMPTON

O **HAMPTON CENTER FOR ARTS AND HUMANITIES,** 22 Wine St, 23669. Tel 804-723-1776, 723-1779. *Cultural Center Mgr* Jeanne Zeidler; *Cultural Programs Coordr* Bill Eyre; *Dir Fine Arts* James Steele; *Dir Photography* Colis Davis Jr
Open Year Round Mon - Fri 8 AM - 5 PM. No admis fee. Estab 1966 as a non-profit organization; now a division of Hampton Recreation Department
Collections: Archaeology; paintings; photography; sculpture;
Exhibitions: One person shows
Activities: Seminars and workshops in Arts and Humanities; art classes; music classes; lectures; demonstrations

M **HAMPTON INSTITUTE,** College Museum, 23668. Tel 804-727-5308. *Dir* Julia R Vodicka
Open Mon - Fri 8 AM - 5 PM, Sat & Sun by appointment. No admis fee
Income: Financed by college funds
Collections: American Indian and Oceanic Art; Contemporary Afro-American Art; Traditional African
Activities: Lect open to public; film series; individual paintings and original objects of art lent

HARRISONBURG

M **JAMES MADISON UNIVERSITY,** Sawhill Gallery, Duke Fine Arts Center, 22801. Tel 703-433-6216. *Head Arts Dept* Dr J David Diller
Open Mon - Fri 8 AM - Noon, 1 - 5 PM, 7 - 9 PM, Sat & Sun 1 - 5 PM. No admis fee. Estab 1967 to schedule changing exhibitions for the benefit of students and citizens of this area. One-room gallery of 1040 sq ft with movable panels. Average Annual Attendance: 7000 - 10,000
Income: Financed by state appropriation, and is part of operation in Art Department budget
Collections: Sawhill Collection, mainly artifacts from classical civilizations; Staples Collection of Indonesian art; †small group of modern works
Exhibitions: Annual JMU Faculty Exhibition; Annual JMU Undergraduate Student Exhibition; Art Directors Club 58th Annual Awards Show; Contemporary Work from New York Galleries; Contemporary Video Work; Exposure Time IV (National Juried Photo Competition); Fiber Arts International; Four With Paper; Lenore Tawney; 20th Century Botanical Art; Virginia High School Invitational
Activities: Competitions

LEESBURG

M **OATLANDS,** Route 2, Box 352, 22075. Tel 703-777-3174. *Exec Dir* Nicole Sours
Open April 1 - Oct 31, Mon - Sat 10 AM - 5 PM, Sun 1 -5 PM. Admis adults $2, senior adults and students $1.25, under 6 free; Christmas at Oatland November 1 - 5, special rates; group rates by arrangement; free to National Trust members. Oatlands is a Classical Revival Mansion constructed by George Carter, son of Robert (Councillor) Carter (circa 1800-06). Oatlands is a property of the National Trust for Historic Preservation operated as an historic house museum and a community preservation center. It was partially remodeled in 1827 when the front portico with hand carved Corinthian capitals was added. Confederate troops were billeted here during the Civil War. The home remained in possession of the Carters until 1897. In 1903 Mr and Mrs William Corcoran Eustis, of Washington DC, bought Oatlands. Their daughters gave the property to the National Trust for Historic Preservation; the property is protected by 261 preservation easements which help insure the estates continuing role as a center for equestrian sports and events which are produced by various groups. Average Annual Attendance: 21,100
Collections: Eustis Collection of Furniture; Greek-Revival ornaments adorn interior

LEXINGTON

WASHINGTON AND LEE UNIVERSITY
M **Gallery of DuPont Hall,*** 24450. Tel 703-463-9111, Ext 350. *Chmn Art Division* Dr Gerard Maurice Doyon; *Dir* Dr Albert C Gordon
Open Mon - Fri 8 AM - 5 PM, cl June, July & Aug. No admis fee. Estab 1929 in separate gallery, in existence since 1742, as teaching resource of the Art Department of the College of Liberal Arts. One room, 30 x 60 ft, is maintained for temporary exhibits; also maintained are offices, studios and one storeroom. Average Annual Attendance: 40,000
Income: Financed through the university
Collections: Contemporary works (students, faculty, alumni); European paintings from 17th-mid 19th centuries; Reeves Collection of Chinese Export Porcelain
Exhibitions: American Art Exhibition; annual faculty show; annual student show; Chinese Art Exhibit; French Art Exhibition; monthly exhibitions
Activities: Lect open to public, 10-20 visiting lectrs per year; gallery talks; original objects of art lent
L **McCormick Library,*** 24450. Tel 703-463-9111, Ext 403. *Librn* Maurice D Leach Jr
Open for reference to students, scholars, public; this library is part of the main University library
Library Holdings: Vols 241,227; Per subs 1224; AV—Slides
Special Subjects: American Art of 18th & 19th centuries
Collections: Rare Books, 17th - 19th centuries
M **Lee Chapel and Museum,*** 24450. Tel 703-463-9111, Ext 289. *Dir* Robert C Peniston
Open mid-Apr to mid-Oct Mon - Sat 9 AM - 5 PM, Sun 2 - 5 PM, mid-Oct to mid-Apr Mon - Sat 9 AM - 4 PM, Sun 2 - 5 PM. No admis fee. Estab 1868 as a part of the University. It is used for concerts, speeches and other events. Museum is used also to display the paintings, collections and personal items of the Washington and Lee families. The Lee Chapel is a National Historic Landmark. Average Annual Attendance: 38,000
Income: Financed through the University
Collections: Custis-Washington-Lee Art Collection; Lee archives; Lee family crypt; Lee's office; recumbent statute of General Lee by Valentine
Publications: Brochure
Activities: sales shop selling books, prints, slides, souvenirs

LORTON

M **GUNSTON HALL PLANTATION,** Gunston Rd, 22079. Tel 703-550-9220. *First Regent* Mrs Franklin W Hobbs; *Dir* Walter W Price; *Mgr* Louise L Stockdale
Open daily 9:30 AM - 5 PM, except Christmas. Admis adults $2, students (6 - 15) 50¢. Estab 1949 to acquaint the public with George Mason, Colonial patriot and his 18th Century house and gardens, covering 555 acres. Owned and operated by the Commonwealth of Virginia. Average Annual Attendance: 50,000
Income: $300,000 (financed by state appropriation and admis fee)
Collections: 18th century English and American deocrative arts, furniture and paintings; 18th and 19th century family pieces
Exhibitions: Rotating special exhibits
Activities: Docent training; tours; individual paintings and original objects of art lent to other museums; lending collection contains cassettes, film strips, motion pictures, slides; sales shop sells books, reproductions; Childrens Touch Museum located in basement
L **Library,** Gunston Rd, 22079. Tel 703-550-9220. *Librn & Archivist* Bennie Brown Jr
Open Tues - Sat 9:30 AM - 5 PM by appointment. Estab 1974 to recreate an 18th Century Virginia gentlemen's library as a research source plus acquiring a working reference collection on George Mason and the decorative arts
Income: Financed by endowment
Library Holdings: Vols 6000; Per subs 50; Micro—Fiche, reels; AV—Slides; Other —Pamphlets, photographs, original documents
Special Subjects: Decorative Arts, Mason family, Early Virginiana
Collections: Pamela C Copeland Collection; Robert Carter Collection; Mason-Mercer Collection

LYNCHBURG

O **LYNCHBURG FINE ARTS CENTER INC,** 1815 Thomson Dr, 24501. Tel 804-846-8451. *Pres* Orion A Templeton; *Adminr* Jane McKee Mundy; *Secy & Bookkeeper* Donna M Hudson; *Art Coordr* Ron Boehmer
Open Mon - Fri 9 AM - 5 PM; other hours depending upon programs. No admis fee to building; $4 for theatre and concert productions, $5 for musical play. Estab 1958 to promote interest in and appreciation and talent for art, music, dramatic literature and other fine arts. Mem: Dues; student $15, single $30, double $50; annual meeting in June
Income: Financed by membership
Exhibitions: 22 per yr
Publications: FACets, (newspaper), monthly except July
Activities: Classes for adults and children; dramatic programs; docent training; lect open to public, 2 - 3 vis lectr per yr; concerts; gallery talks; tours; competitions; exten dept serving youth; concerts for youth and theatre classics in public schools; artmobile mobile; sales shop sells original art

M **RANDOLPH-MACON WOMANS COLLEGE,** Art Gallery, 2500 Rivermont Ave, 24503. Tel 804-846-7392, Ext 362, 433. *Cur* Nancy Mowll Mathews
Open Mon - Fri 10 AM - 12 PM, 2 - 4 PM, Sun 2 - 5 PM. Estab a collection of American painting for general and specific educational use; endowment. Art gallery was built in 1952 in cooperation with the National Gallery of Art, it houses part of the permanent collection and is used for special exhibitions
Collections: Extensive collection of American paintings; European and American graphics
Exhibitions: American Folk Art and Queena Stovall. (1978) Art through 19th century Eyes
Activities: Dramatic programs; lectures; concerts; objects of art lent
L **Library,** 2500 Rivermont Ave, 24503.
Collections: Photography collection

MIDDLETOWN

M **BELLE GROVE,** PO Box 137, 22645. Tel 703-869-2028. *Pres* Mrs Lilburn Talley; *Exec Dir* Edwin W Watson
Open April - Oct Mon - Sat 10 AM - 4 PM, Sun 1 - 5 PM, Nov - March by appointment. Admis varies. Open to the public in 1967, it is preserved as an historic house and is the property of the National Trust for Historic Preservation and managed by Belle Grove, Inc, an independent local nonprofit organization. It serves as a local preservation center and resource for the interpretation of regional culture in the Shenandoah Valley. Built in 1794 for Major Isaac Hite, Jr, a Revolutionary War officer and brother-in-law of James Madison, Belle Grove was designed with the help of Thomas Jefferson. During the Battle of Cedar Creek in 1864, the house served as headquarters to General Phillip Sheridan. The property is a working farm, and Belle Grove maintains an active program of events for the visiting public
Exhibitions: Farm Craft Days in July; a traditional farm oriented craft show and demonstrations with entertainment; 18th Century Christmas Candlelight Tour; Needlework Show in May; yearly exhibits on local decorative arts
Activities: Seminars on various subjects in museum field offered through the year; gift shop open all year

MOUNT VERNON

M **MOUNT VERNON,** 22121. Tel 703-780-2000. *Regent* Mrs John H Guy Jr; *Resident Dir* John A Castellani
Open to the public every day in the year from 9 AM: entrance gate closes Mar 1 - Oct 1 at 5 PM, Oct 1 - Mar 1 at 4 PM. Admis $3. The home of George Washington purchased in 1858 from his great-grand-nephew by the Mount Vernon Ladies Association of the Union, which maintains it. The estate includes spinning house, coach house, various quarters, restored flower and kitchen gardens; also the tomb of George and Martha Washington. Average Annual Attendance: 1,000,000. Mem: Annual meeting Oct
Collections: Mansion is fully furnished with original and period furniture, silver, portraits and prints; Large collection of relics

M **POPE-LEIGHEY HOUSE,** 22121. Tel 703-557-7881. *Adminr* George M Smith; *Asst Adminr* Mrs Stancil M Smith
Open Mar - Oct, Sat & Sun 9:30 AM - 4:30 PM. Pope-Leighey is a house museum of the National Trust for Historic Preservation, located on the grounds of Woodlawn. This residence was designed in 1940 by Frank Lloyd Wright for his client, the Loren Pope Family. Built of cypress, brick and glass, the Usonian structure contains such features as a flat roof, radiant heat, indirect lighting and built in furniture, all designed by Frank Lloyd Wright, and all considered unusual for their time. Threatened by proposed construction of an interstate highway in 1964, Mrs Marjorie Folson Leighey, second owner, presented the property to the National Trust for Historic Preservation. It was then moved to the Woodlawn grounds
Publications: Brochure and paperback history of house

M **WOODLAWN PLANTATION,** 22121. Tel 703-557-7881. *Adminr* George M Smith; *Asst Adminr* Mrs Stancil M Smith
Open 9:30 AM - 4:30 PM, except Thanksgiving Day, Christmas Day, and New Years Day. Admis charge; group rates by arrangement; combination ticket (in season) with Pope-Leighey House (on grounds). Originally part of Mount Vernon. Built in 1800-05 for George Washington's daughter upon her marriage to Lawrence Lewis. It was designed with central pavilion an and flanking wings by Dr William Thornton, winner of the architectural competition for the design of the United States Capitol. A group of Quakers, a pioneer anthropologist, a playwright and Senator Oscar W Underwood of Alabama were among Woodlawns residents after the Lewises. In 1951 the foundations trustees decided that the visiting public would be better served if Woodlawn was administered by the National Trust. The mansion furnishings are largely from the Federal and early Empire periods and include Lewis family memorabilia and gifts from the Robert Woods Bliss and Colonel Garbish Collection
Exhibitions: Candlelight, Music and Champagne in July; Carols by Candelight in December; Fall Festival of Needlework, seminar in October; Needlework Exhibit each March

NEWPORT NEWS

M **MARINERS MUSEUM,** One Museum Dr, 23606. Tel 804-595-0368. *Pres* George W Passage; *Dir* William D Wilkinson; *Assoc Dir* Dr Nancy Melton; *Assoc Dir* Alene N Cofer; *Asst Dir for Coll* John O Sands
Open Mon - Sat 9 AM - 5 PM, Sun Noon - 5 PM, cl Christmas Day. Admis adults $1.50, children 6 - 16 years 75¢, children under 6 free. Estab 1930, the museum is devoted to the culture of the sea and its tributaries, its conquest by man and its influence on civilization. Museum has thirteen galleries. Average Annual Attendance: 150,000. Mem: 1000, dues family $15, individual $10, student $7.50
Collections: †Crabtree Collection of miniature ships; †thousands of marine artifacts; †over 10,000 paintings; †over 1000 ship models
Publications: The Journal, quarterly
Activities: Classes for adults and children; dramatic programs; lect open to public, 10 visiting lectr per year; gallery talks; tours; competitions; individual paintings and original objects of art lent; lending collection contains 120 motion pictures, 2000 original art works, 8000 original prints, 1000 paintings; museum shop sells books, reproductions, prints, slides, decorative items (maritime related)

L **Library,** One Museum Dr, 23606. Tel 804-595-0368. *Librn* Ardie L Kelly; *Asst to Librn* Kathryn B Braig; *Archivist* Dr Paul Hensley
Open Mon - Sat 9 AM - 5 PM. Estab 1930. For reference only
Income: Financed by endowment
Library Holdings: Vols 55,000; Per subs 188; AV—Fs, motion pictures, rec; Other —Clipping files, manuscripts, memorabilia, pamphlets, photographs, original documents

O **PENINSULA FINE ARTS CENTER,** Mariners Museum Park, PO Box 6438, 23606. Tel 804-596-8175. *Pres* David Peebles; *VPres* Mrs Ward Scull III; *Dir* Mary M Lake
Open Tues - Sat 10 AM - 4 PM, Sun 1 - 4 PM. No admis fee. Estab 1962 to bring the best art possible; to educate the people of the Virginia Peninsula; to encourage local artists. Three galleries maintained with changing exhibitions. Mem: 850; dues family (including membership) $25, individual $18; annual meeting fourth Mon in March
Income: Financed by membership
Exhibitions: Crafts Invitational; Persian Rugs; Woodblock Prints; juried shows, photography
Publications: Art class schedules; newsletter to members, quarterly; notification of special events
Activities: Classes for adults and children; lect open to public, 8 visiting lectr per year; gallery talks; competitions; cash awards and certificates of distinction; gallery shop sells books, original art and crafts

NORFOLK

M **CHRYSLER MUSEUM,** Olney Rd and Mowbray Arch, 23510. Tel 804-622-1211. *Dir* Richard J Wattenmaker; *Admin Asst* Diane Scillia; *Cur American Art* Thomas W Styron; *Cur Decorative Arts* Mark A Clark; *Cur Glass* Nancy O Merrill; *Registrar* Judith C Riley; *Dir Education* Ann Dearsley-Vernon; *Pres Board of Trustees* Walter P Chrysler Jr; *VPres Board of Trustees* Mrs Reid Spencer; *Chmn Board of Trustees* Dr Thomas L Stokes
Open Tues - Sat 10 AM - 4 PM, Sun 1 - 5 PM, cl Mon. No admis fee (donation $1). Estab 1905 as a memorial association housing a collection of tapestries and paintings donated in name of Irene Leache. Norfolk Society of Arts founded in 1917 to house collection. Funds raised in 1920s for a building which became the Norfolk Museum of Arts and Sciences. WPA money and labor completed the present Florentine Renaissance style building in 1933. New additions were added in 1960s and 1970s. Named Chrysler Museum in 1971 when deeded collections of the Chrysler Museum of Provincetown, Mass. 85,000 sq ft houses 39 galleries. Average Annual Attendance: 140,000. Mem: 3335; dues friend $100, sustaining $50, family $25, individual $15, student & senior citizen $10
Income: Financed by municipal appropriation
Collections: Anschutz Collection, paintings of the American West; Contemporary Glass, Virginia and North Carolina; 100 drawings from the Permanent Collection; regional juried shows painting and graphics shows; graphics; †Italian Renaissance & Baroque; †18th century English; †17th century English; †16th, 17th & 18th century French; †French Impressionists; †Post Impressionists; 17th century Dutch; †Flemish; †American art; †20th century art; †Greco-Roman; †Institute of Glass; †Early Renaissance; †Indian, Persian, Japanese and Chinese
Exhibitions: Alexander Calder Tapestries; The Dutch Republic in the Days of John Adams, 1775-1795; Yasuo Kauniyoshi, Paintings and graphics; Treasures from Greece
Publications: Bulletin, monthly; exhibition catalogs
Activities: Classes for adults and children; docent training; lect open to public, 20 vis lectr per yr; gallery talks; tours; competitions with cash prizes; exten dept operates three historic homes; traveling exhibitions organized and circulated; museum shop sells books, original art, reproductions, prints, slides, postcards, jewelry and toys

M **HERMITAGE FOUNDATION MUSEUM,** 7637 North Shore Road, 23505. Tel 804-423-2052. *Dir* Philip R Morrison; *Cur & Registrar* Lela M Hine; *Asst to Dir* Mary Jean Redon Levin; *Pres of Board* W P Chilton
Open daily 10 AM - 5 PM, Sun 12 - 5 PM, cl New Years Day, Thanksgiving Day, Christmas Day. Admis adults $2, children 6 - 18 50¢. Estab 1937 to disseminate information concerning arts, and maintain a collection of fine art materials. Mansion on 16-acre site houses major collections as well as two small changing exhibition galleries. Average Annual Attendance: 20,000. Mem: 375; dues $25; meeting four times per yr
Income: $110,000 (financed by endowment and membership)
Collections: English oak and teakwood woodcarvings; Major collection of decorative arts from various periods and countries; Oriental collection of Chinese bronzes and ceramic tomb figures, lacquer ware, jades and Persian rugs; Spanish and English furniture; 20th century paintings
Exhibitions: American Illustrator; Art on Paper; Isabel Bishop; Bernard Chaet (paintings); Contemporary American Graphics; Currier and Ives; Export Porcelain from a Private Collection; Freshwork (Virginia photographers); Alexandra Georges (photographs); The Photographs of Wright Morris; Henry Pitz (one man show); student exhibitions from summer workshops
Activities: Classes for adults and children; dramatic programs; docent training; lect open to public and auxiliary lect for members only, 10 - 12 vis lectr per yr; concerts; gallery talks; tours; slides for sale

L **Library,** 7637 North Shore Rd, 23505.
Open to students for reference only
Library Holdings: Vols 800; Per subs 6

O **IRENE LEACHE MEMORIAL,** c/o Mrs Charles R Dalton Jr, 556 Mowbray Arch, 23507. Tel 804-623-8189. *VPres* Mrs F N Bilisolij; *Secy* Claiborne Fitchett; *Treas* Mrs Edward Wolcott; *Art Chmn* Julia Bristow; *Lecture Chmn* Mrs Arthur Porter; *Literary Chmn* Mrs Fred Martin
Estab 1905 as a private foundation created to promote culture in Norfolk. Memorial owns object of art and helps to maintain room of early Renaissance art in the Chrysler Museum at Norfolk. Mem: Board of Dir 25, selected by election; annual meeting May
Income: $13,000 (financed by endowment)
Activities: Lect open to public; competitions; cash awards; original objects of art lent; lending collection contains paintings, sculpture, tapestries and furniture

M **MACARTHUR MEMORIAL,** One MacArthur Square, 23510. Tel 804-441-2256. *Dir* Lyman H Hammond Jr; *Archivist* Edward J Boone Jr; *Secy* Janice Stafford Dudley; *Research Asst* Roger T Crew Jr
Open Mon - Sat 10 AM - 5 PM, Sun 11 AM - 5 PM, cl Mondays November - March. No admis fee. Estab 1964 to memorialize General Douglas MacArthur. Located in the Old Court House which was rebuilt in 1962; nine galleries contain memorabilia. Average Annual Attendance: 90,000 - 100,000
Income: $255,131 (financed by city appropriation and Federal revenue sharing funds)
Collections: Objets d'art, gifts, murals, portraits, photographs, awards and personal property of General Douglas MacArthur
Activities: Individual paintings and original objects of art lent to schools, museums, and municipal agencies; sales shop created by MacArthur Memorial Foundation sells books, reproductions, prints, slides

M **MacArthur Memorial Library and Archives,** One MacArthur Square, 23510. *Archivist* Edward J Boone; *Research Asst* Roger T Crew Jr
Library Holdings: Vols 4000; Micro—Fiche, reels; AV—A-tapes, cassettes, motion pictures, rec, slides; Other—Clipping files, framed reproductions, prints, memorabilia, original art works, photographs, reproductions, sculpture, original documents
Activities: Lect open to the public, 2 -3 vis lectr per yr; tours; Scholarships offered; traveling exhibitions organized and circulated

M **NAVAL AMPHIBIOUS MUSEUM,** Naval Amphibious Base, Little Creek, 23510. Tel 804-464-7923, 464-8130. *Dir* Howard A Wallace; *Cur* A J Leake
Open Sat & Sun 1 - 5 PM, during week by appointment only. No admis fee. Estab 1970 to preserve the history of the Amphibious Force of the United States Navy. Average Annual Attendance: 30,000
Income: Financed by federal appropriation
Collections: Naval historical memorabilia, ship models, paintings, sculpture and

silver
Activities: Lect; guided tours

M **OLD DOMINION UNIVERSITY GALLERY,*** 5215 Hampton Blvd, 23508. Tel 804-489-6213. *Coordr Arts* Glen A Ray; *Art Chmn* E May Dreyer
Open Mon - Sun 1 - 5 PM. No admis fee. Estab 1972 for the exhibition of contemporary work; also established as a public forum for contemporary artists, with student exposure. Average Annual Attendance: 3000
Income: Financed by endowment and city appropriation
Exhibitions: Josef Albers; Atomic Art; Mo Leibowitz; Jerry Noe; Will Reiman; Charles Sibley
Activities: Lect open to public, 10 visiting lectrs per year; gallery talks; tours; competitions; exten dept
L **Library,*** 5215 Hampton Blvd, 23508.
Open to students and faculty; open to the public for reference

PETERSBURG

M **CENTRE HILL MANSION,** Centre Hill Court, 15 West Bank Street, 23803. Tel 804-732-8081. *Cur* Elizabeth T Lyon; *Hostess* Jane B Holt
Open Mon - Sat 9 AM - 5 PM, Sun 1 - 5 PM. Estab 1978 as a historic house museum, built in 1823. Twenty five rooms with period interiors. Average Annual Attendance: 11,000
Collections: Period furnishings of mid 19th century America
Activities: Concerts, gallery talks, tours

PORTSMOUTH

M **PORTSMOUTH MUSEUMS AND COMMUNITY ARTS CENTER,** 420 High St, Portsmouth, VA. (Mailing Add: PO Box 850, Portsmouth, VA 23705) Tel 804-393-8543, 393-8718. *Dir* Frederick S Bayersdorfer Jr; *Admin Asst* William G Shea; *Theatre Mgr* Ronn Harris; *Museum Asst* Sandi Alexander
Open Tues - Sat 11 AM - 4 PM, Sun 2 - 5 PM. No admis fee. Estab 1974 to offer a wide variety of the visual and performing arts to the citizens of Tidewater area. Average Annual Attendance: 25,000. Mem: 375; dues $12; meetings third Tues of each month
Income: $192,000 financed by city appropriation
Purchases: $3000
Collections: Contemporary drawings by American artists
Exhibitions: Antique Toys; American Drawings; Artifacts from the Sea; Black Arts Festival; Will Decoux and Hank Lewis; Quintessential Quilts; Tidewater weavers Guild; Photography; 3 person show; 4 person show
Publications: Monthly calendar; biannual catalog of American Drawings shows
Activities: Classes for adults and children; dramatic programs; lectures open to the public, six visiting lecturers per year; concerts; American drawings, biannual national drawing competition with awards

RESTON

NATIONAL ART EDUCATION ASSOCIATION
For further information, see National and Regional Organizations

NATIONAL ASSOCIATION OF SCHOOLS OF ART
For further information, see National and Regional Organizations

RICHMOND

O **AGECROFT ASSOCIATION,** Agecroft Hall, 4305 Sulgrave Rd, 23221. Tel 804-353-4241. *Pres & Dir* John C Williams; *Asst Secy Treas & Cur* William McKemie
Open Tues - Fri 10 AM - 4 PM, Sat & Sun 2 - 5 PM. Admis adults $1, students and children 50¢, group rates by prior arrangements. Estab 1968 to exhibit 15th century Tudor Manor House brought over from England in 1925-26 and rebuilt in Richmond, together with furnishings and period objects of art. It is said to be the oldest house in America though originally constructed in Lancster, England. Average Annual Attendance: 14,000
Income: $250,000 (financed by endowment and admis)
Collections: 15th and 16th Century Furniture and Objects of Art depicting the Elizabethan Life of time, when Agecroft Hall was at its pinnacle
Activities: Guided tours for classes of school children, schools and college classes; audio-visual introduction
L **Library,** Agecroft Hall, 4305 Sulgrave Rd, 23221.
Lending to universities only
Library Holdings: AV—Fs, lantern slides, slides; Other—Original art works, books

O **ASSOCIATION FOR THE PRESERVATION OF VIRGINIA ANTIQUITIES,** 2705 Park Ave, 23220. Tel 804-359-0239. *Pres* Robert H Garbee; *Exec Dir* Robert A Murdock; *Registrar* Charlotte L Duarte
Estab 1889 to acquire and preserve historic buildings, grounds and monuments in Virginia. Branches administer forty properties in Virginia. Among the properties: Jamestown Island; Walter Reed Birthplace: Gloucester; Rolfe-Warren House, Surry County; John Marshall House, Richmond, Scotchtown, Hanover County; Mary Washington House and Rising Sun Tavern, Fredericksburg; Smithfield Plantation, Blacksburg; Farmers Bank, Petersburg; Cape Henry Lighthouse, Virginia Beach. Hours and admissions vary according to location
Collections: Decorative arts; 17th - 19th century furniture, glass, ceramics, metalwork and textiles
Publications: Discovery (newsletter) quarterly
L **Library,** 2705 Park Ave, 23220.
Library Holdings: Vols 5000

C **FEDERAL RESERVE BANK OF RICHMOND,** 701 E Byrd St, 23219. Tel 804-643-1250. *Art Coordr* Charlotte Minor
Open to public by appointment only. No admis fee. Estab 1978 to provide enjoyment, education and a stimulating work environment for employees and visitors; to give encouragement and support to artists of the Fifth Federal Reserve District. Collection displayed throughout building
Collections: Primarily a regional collection, representing artists who live or who formerly lived in the Fifth Federal Reserve District
Activities: Tours

O **FEDERATED ARTS COUNCIL OF RICHMOND, INC,** 5 North Sixth St, 23219. Tel 804-643-4993. *Chmn* Adrienne G Hines; *Pres* Charles B Davis; *Exec Dir* Kathy L Dwyer
Open daily 9 AM - 5 PM. Established to promote and support the arts and to act as a unified voice for member agencies. Mem: 350; dues Active $30, Associate $15
Income: $130,000 (financed by grants, contributions, membership and city appropriation)
Publications: Monthly newsletter; Cultural Calendar of Events; PR Handbook; Membership Directory
Activities: Management seminars; downtown arts festival, lunchtime concerts; biannual art show; Outreach program to hospitals, senior centers and prisons

C **FIRST AND MERCHANTS NATIONAL BANK,** F & M Center, PO Box 27025, 23261. Tel 804-788-2148. *In Charge Art Coll* Marilyn Keppel
Certain areas open to public 9 AM - 5 PM, or by appointment with tour guides. No admis fee. Estab 1974 to support the arts, mostly Virgina artists; to enhance bank surroundings; as an investment. Collection displayed on 2nd floor (monthly exhibits); permanent collection in reception areas and offices throughout 24 floors
Collections: Contemporary works of art in different media, mostly local and Va artists, and some known artists
Activities: Tours by appointment; sponsored employee art exhibit; individual objects of art lent; Monthly exhibits by local, employee and Virginia artists; paintings on loan by local gallery

O **HAND WORK SHOP, INC,*** 7 N Sixth St, 23219. Tel 804-649-0674. *Executive Dir* Ruth T Summers; *Education Coordr* Sally Garret; *Staff* Mary Lou Deal
Open Tues - Sat 10 AM - 4:30 PM, cl Mon. No admis fee. Estab 1963 as a non-profit tax exempt organization dedicated to excellence in designer crafts; as a retail outlet. Gallery consists of three rooms selling designer crafts made in the United States only. Average Annual Attendance: 20,000. Mem: 300; dues $10 - $100
Income: $100,000 (financed by membership, state appropriation and grants)
Exhibitions: Monthly exhibitions
Publications: Newsletters, monthly
Activities: Classes for adults and children; docent training; workshops; lect open to public; competitions; sales shop sells original art, slides and crafts

L **RICHMOND PUBLIC LIBRARY,** 101 E Franklin St, 23219. Tel 804-780-4740. *Head Art & Music Department* Myra Knight; *Staff Artist* Anne Newhold Perkins
Open Mon - Fri 9 AM - 9 PM, Sat 9 AM - 5 PM, Sun 2 - 6 PM. Estab 1924 to select, collect and organize human record to meet information needs and cultural interests of citizens. For lending and reference; gallery maintained
Income: $1,652,854
Library Holdings: Vols 614,981; Per subs 1776; Micro—Fiche, reels; AV—Cassettes, rec; Other—Clipping files, exhibition catalogs, original art works, pamphlets
Exhibitions: Seventy two art exhibits during 1978-79, three new ones each month; one ongoing exhibit during 1978; Glass case displays include hand crafted jewelry; teddy bears (in celebration of his 75th birthday); miniature dolls and furniture; paper dolls created by a young woman in the early 1900s; shells; photographs; items made by children in the Visual Literacy classes in the public school; Black History items; Senior Citizen crafts; Small periodicals; Chinese rubbings and hand carved animals, boats and guns
Activities: Lectures open to the public, eight visiting lecturers per year; concerts; tours

C **UNITED VIRGINIA BANK,** 900 E Main St, 23219. Tel 804-782-5737. *In Charge Art Coll* Lucy B Turlington
Estab 1970. Collection displayed in banks and offices; separate gallery used for new exhibit each month
Purchases: $25,000
Collections: Contemporary Art
Activities: Competitions with awards

M **VALENTINE MUSEUM,** 1015 E Clay St, 23219. Tel 804-649-0711. *Dir Coll* Jean DuVal Kane; *Asst Dir* Dr Bruce King; *Admin Asst* Roberta Carew; *Cur of General Coll* Elizabeth Childs
Open Tues - Sat 10 AM - 5 PM, Sun 1:30 - 5 PM. Admis adults $2, children and students $1. Estab 1894 as a museum of the life and history of Richmond. Average Annual Attendance: 28,000. Mem: 1100; dues individual $15
Income: $203,000 (financed by endowment, membership, city and state appropriation and gifts)
Purchases: $500
Collections: Conrad Wise Chapman (oils, almost entire life works); William Ludlow Sheppard (drawings and watercolors); Edward Virginus Valentine (sculpture); outstanding collection of Southern photographs; †candlesticks, ceramics, costumes, glass, jewelry, lace, †paintings, †photographs, prints and sculpture
Exhibitions: Life and History of Richmond
Publications: Silhouette, bimonthly; Visitor, monthly
Activities: Classes for adults and children; docent training; dramatic programs; lect open to public, 2 vis lectr per year; competitions; exten dept serving city and area counties; individual paintings lent to member corporations and other museums; lending collection contains color reproduction, paintings, photographs, decorative art objects; originate traveling exhibitions; museum shop selling books, original art, reproductions, prints, slides and silver; Junior Museum
L **Library,** 1015 E Clay St, 23219. *Cur of Library Materials* E Michale Schanches Saavedra
Open to the public for reference only
Library Holdings: Vols 1000; Per subs 20; Other—Photographs 20,000

VIRGINIA COMMONWEALTH UNIVERSITY

M **Anderson Gallery,** 907 1/2 W Franklin St, 23824. Tel 804-257-1522. *Dir* Michael Walls
Open Tues & Fri 10 AM - 6 PM, Wed & Thurs 10 AM - 8 PM, Sat 11 AM - 5 PM, Sun 1 - 5 PM, cl Mon except by appointment. Estab 1930, re-opened 1970 as the showcase for the contemporary arts in Richmond; to expose the university and community to a wide variety of current artistic ideas and expressions. Gallery is situated on campus in a four-story converted mansion stable. There are six galleries with a variety of exhibition spaces. Average Annual Attendance: 20,000
Collections: †Contemporary Prints and Paintings; cross section of Prints from the 15th to 20th Century covering most periods
Exhibitions: Art of The Kuba; Five in Fiber; INDEX Series: Frances Barth, Jake Berthot, Lester Van Winkle; Three Bravura Painters of The Human Figure: William Beckman, Jillian Denby, James Valerio; Andy Warhol: selected works from the Still Life group of 1976; Joan Snyder; works by students and members of the faculty
Publications: Catalogs and brochures, periodically
Activities: Lect open to public, 6 visiting lectr per year; concerts; gallery talks; tours; competitions; individual paintings and original objects of art lent to various museums and universities; lending collection contains 100 original art works, 100 original paintings and photographs; originate traveling exhibitions
L **School of The Arts Library,** 901 W Franklin St, 23284. Tel 804-257-1683. *Dir* Joan L Muller
Open Mon - Thurs 9 AM - 8 PM, Fri 9 AM - 4:30 PM, Sat 1 - 5 PM. Estab 1926 to support the teaching program of the eleven departments of the School of the Arts
Income: Financed by state appropriation
Library Holdings: Micro—Fiche; AV—Slides 250,000; Other—Exhibition catalogs 14,000
Collections: Transparencies (2 x 2 inch) of Works of Art; exhibition catalogs, worldwide in scope, from museums and galleries

O **VIRGINIA HISTORICAL SOCIETY,*** 428 North Blvd, PO Box 7311, 23221. Tel 804-358-4901. *Dir* Edwin L Dooley Jr
Virginia House open Tues - Fri 10 AM - 4 PM, Sat & Sun 2 - 5 PM, cl Mon & national holidays; Battle Abbey open Mon - Fri 9 AM - 5 PM, Sat & Sun 2 - 5 PM. Admis Virginia House $1.50; Battle Abbey $1. Estab 1831 for collecting, preserving and making available to students and scholars research material relating to the history of Virginia. Gallery maintained housing historical portraiture and paintings. Average Annual Attendance: 18,000. Mem: Dues $15 - $500
Income: Financed by endowment and membership
L **Library,** 428 North Blvd, PO Box 7311, 23221. Tel 804-358-4901. *Librn* Howson W Cole; *Library Asst* Rebecca Perrine
Open Mon - Fri 9 AM - 5 PM, Sat & Sun 2 - 5 PM. Estab 1831 for the study of Virginia history
Income: Financed by endowment, membership, state appropriation and private donations
Library Holdings: Vols 200,000; Micro—Fiche, reels; Other—Clipping files, exhibition catalogs, prints, manuscripts, memorabilia, original art works, pamphlets, photographs, reproductions, sculpture
Publications: Bulletin, semi-annually; Virginia Magazine of History and Biography, quarterly
Activities: Lect open to public

M **VIRGINIA MUSEUM OF FINE ARTS,** Boulevard & Grove, 23221. Tel 804-770-6344. *Pres* Edwin Hyde; *Dir* Dr R Peter Mooz; *Head Communications Division* George Cruger; *Secy* Helen Dohn; *Public Relations Dir* David Griffith; *Head Graphic Design* Ray Geary; *Chief Cur* Pinkney Near; *Programs Dir* William Gaines; *Registrar* Lisa Hummel; *Artmobile Coordr* David Pittman; *Development Dir* Paul Hood; *Institute for Contemporary Art Sup v* Julia Boyd
Open Tues - Sat 11 AM - 5 PM, Sun 1 - 5 PM, cl Mon. Admis 50¢. Estab 1934; theatre opened 1955; South Wing added 1970. Participating in the museum's programs are The Fellows of Virginia Museum, who meet yearly to counsel the museum on its future plans; The Women's Council, which sponsors and originates special programs; the Collector's Circle, a group of Virginia art lovers which meets four times a year to discuss various aspects of collecting; the Corporate Patrons, state and local business firms who lend financial support to museum programs; Virginia Museum Youth Guild; and The Institute for Contemporary Art , which presents exhibitions of works by state, nationally and internationally known contemporary artists. Average Annual Attendance: 1,250,000. Mem: 16,000; dues $25 and higher; annual meeting in May
Collections: Lady Nancy Astor Collection of English China; Branch Collection of Italian Renaissance Paintings, Sculpture and Furniture; Ailsa Mellon Bruce Collection of 18th Century Furniture and Decorative Arts; Mrs Arthur Kelly Evans Collection of Pottery and Porcelain; †Arthur and Margaret Glasgow Collection of Flemish and Italian Renaissance Paintings, Sculpture and Decorative Arts; Nasli and Alice Heeramaneck Collection of Art of India, Nepal, Kashmir and Tibet; T Catesby Jones Collection of 20th Century European Paintings and Drawings; Dr and Mrs Arthur Mourot Collection of Meissen Porcelain; The John Barton Payne Collection of Paintings, Prints and Portuguese Furniture; Lillian Thomas Pratt Collection of Czarist Jewels by Peter Carl Faberge; †Adolph D and Wilkins C Williams Collection of Paintings, Tapestries, China and Silver; Archaic Chinese Bronzes; Archaic Chinese Jades; Comprehensive collections of early Greek vases (8th century to 4th century BC); Representative examples of the arts from early Egypt to the present time, including paintings, sculpture, furniture and objects d'art
Exhibitions: Virginia Artists; Virginia Designers; Virginia Architects; Virginia Photographers; Virginia Craftsmen (Biennials); 25 special exhibitions annually
Publications: Arts in Virginia, 3 times per Year; brochures; bulletins, nine per year; catalogues for special exhibitions and collections; programs
Activities: Classes for adults and children in painting, drawing, graphics, ceramics and weaving; workshops; demonstrations; lectures; concerts; drama productions; fels offered (10 - 15 per year) to Virginia artists; art mobile; originate traveling exhibitions throughout the state of Virginia

L **Library,** Boulevard & Grove, 23221. *Librn* Betty Stacy
Open Mon - Fri 9 AM - 5 PM. Estab 1934 for art history research. For reference only
Library Holdings: Vols 40,000; Per subs 100; AV—Slides; Other—Clipping files, exhibition catalogs, pamphlets

ROANOKE

O **ROANOKE FINE ARTS CENTER,** 302 23rd St, SW, 24014. Tel 703-342-8945. *Executive Dir* Peter Rippe; *Cur* Ann D Masters; *Business Mgr* Virginia B Porten; *Membership & Education Coordr* Dori B Fitzgerald; *Downtown Gallery Curator* Carol D Bivens
Open Tues - Sat 10 AM - 5 PM, Sun 1 - 5 PM. No admis fee. Estab 1951 to encourage and develop interest in the study of the arts; to provide ways and means for the purchase of works in the arts, and to exhibit fine arts and other works of art. The center is housed in an old home with extremely fine architectural detail. The main rooms have been turned into galleries. Average Annual Attendance: 10,000. Mem: 1300; dues $15 and up; annual meeting in Sept
Income: $150,000 (financed by endowment and membership)
Collections: Contemporary Art (predominately by regional artists); Classical Collection; Decorative Arts; Oriental Artifacts; Print Collection
Exhibitions: (1979) Approximately 20 changing exhibitions
Activities: Classes for adults and children; docent training; lect open to the public; gallery talks; tours; competitions; museum shop selling books, original art, prints, reproductions, handmade crafts including jewelry and children's items
L **Library,** 302 23rd St SW, 24014.
Open to the public for reference only
Library Holdings: Per subs 25

STAUNTON

M **WOODROW WILSON BIRTHPLACE FOUNDATION,** 20 N Coalter St, PO Box 24, 24401. Tel 703-885-0897. *Dir* Raymond F Pisney; *Executive Dir* Thomas H Hartig
Open daily 9 AM - 5 PM, cl Sun of Dec, Jan & Feb, Thanksgiving, Christmas and New Year's Day. Admis adults $2, senior citizens 1.50, children 6-16 $1. Estab 1938 in the 1846 Presbyterian Manse which was the birthplace of Woodrow Wilson. Mem: Dues $15 - $1000, students $7.50
Collections: Historical Material pertinent to the Wilson family; decorative arts, furniture, manuscripts, musical instruments, paintings, photographs, prints and drawings, rare books, textiles
Publications: Brochures; guides; Newsletter, semi-annually; pamphlets
Activities: Educ dept; lect; gallery talks; tours; films; loan programs; sales shop
L **Library,** 20 N Coalter St, PO Box 24, 24401. *Librn* Trudy Davis
Library Holdings: Vols 6000

STRASBURG

M **STRASBURG MUSEUM,** E King St, 22657. Tel 703-465-3175. *Pres* J J Crawford; *VPres* Mrs John F Cadden; *Secy* Carole Hunt; *Treas* Mrs Paul Hatmaker; *Resident Potter* Mrs A L Dryer
Open May to Oct, daily 10 AM - 4 PM. Admis adults $1, children 25¢. Estab 1970 to present the past of a Shenandoah Valley community and to preserve the pottery-making tradition of Strasburg. The museum is housed in the former Southern Railway Depot, which was orginally built as a steam pottery. Average Annual Attendance: 3600. Mem: 125; dues $2.50; annual meeting in March
Income: Financed by membership, admission fees and gifts
Collections: Indian Artifacts; pottery
Exhibitions: Models of Pre-Civil War Era Rooms; Models of Victorian Rooms, Country Store, Old Depot
Activities: Classes for adults and children in pottery making; museum shop selling books, original art, pottery and other local crafts

SWEET BRIAR

L **SWEET BRIAR COLLEGE,** Babcock Art Library, 24595. Tel 804-381-5451. *Librn* Henry James; *Cataloger* Patricia Wright; *Asst Librn* Jan Johnson; *Service Librn* Mary Hartman
Estab 1961, when it was separated from the Main library and Babcock Art Building was opened. There is a small gallery in the lobby and Reading Room of Babcock Fine Arts Building. For reference only
Income: Financed by college funds
Library Holdings: Vols 5500; Per subs 22; AV—Cassettes, Kodachromes, lantern Slides; Other—Prints, original art works
Exhibitions: (1979-80) Douglas Abdell (sculpture and drawings); Barbara Cornett (weaver); Nancy Blackwell and Wendell Raby (photography); Charles Forrester (sculpture); Four Washington area artists, Jo Harrop, Beth Hobby, Karen Montgomery, Linda Thern-Smith (ceramics, painting and sculpture); Will Harrington (sculptor); Robert Nelson (works on paper); Loren Oliver (painter); Trudy Paddock (paintings); Mary Jane Schroeder Oliver (paintings); Ashlin Smith and Ann Slaughter (painters); Sweet Briar College Senior Art Studio majors show; The University of Virginia Studio Art Faculty (painting, sculpture and photography): Brown Wrapper

VIRGINIA BEACH

O VIRGINIA BEACH ARTS CENTER, 1711 Arctic Ave, 23451. Tel 804-428-9294. *Admin Dir* Anthony J Radich; *Asst Dir* Linda Hale; *Bookkeeper Secy* Willie Jo Dortch; *Receptionist* Harriet Ross Smith
Open Mon - Fri 9 AM - 5 PM, Sat 11 AM - 4 PM, cl Sun. No admis fee. Exhibition space 20 x 30 ft and 140 ft in hall gallery, eight medium classrooms. Average Annual Attendance: 50,000. Mem: 1450; dues family $15, individual $12
Income: Financed by membership, grants, donations and sales
Exhibitions: Art in the Public Places Program (including sculpture competitions); Boardwalk Art Show; Handheld Print Competition; two shows monthly of local, regional and national artists, especially from Western Association of Art Museums and SITES
Publications: Newsletter, monthly
Activities: Classes, four session per year; members sponsor Printsmakers Association and Potters' Guild; workshops for members use; lect; tours; Unicorn Gift Shop

WILLIAMSBURG

M COLLEGE OF WILLIAM AND MARY, Department of Fine Arts Gallery, 23185. Tel 804-253-4385. *Chmn* Dr Miles Chappell; *Registrar* Louise Kale
Open Mon - Fri 9 AM - 4 PM. No admis fee. Art collection was started for teaching purposes and for the commemoration of the college's history, alumni and friends. Average Annual Attendance: 5000
Income: Financed by endowment, state appropriations and donations
Collections: Colonial and Contemporary American Paintings; Contemporary Sculpture by Joseph Lonas; Oriental Art
Exhibitions: American Abstract Expressionist Paintings from Walter and Jean Chrysler; Jules Kirschenbaum (paintings); Paintings by Robert Kaiser; Arthur Strauss and the German Expressionists
Publications: Catalogs and brochures
Activities: Lect open to the public

M COLONIAL WILLIAMSBURG FOUNDATION, PO Drawer C, 23185. Tel 804-229-1000. *Pres* Charles R Longsworth; *Dir Press Bureau* Randall Foskey; *Dir Public Affairs* Norman G Beatty; *Dir & Cur Coll* Graham S Hood
Open 9 AM - 5 PM, Folk Art Center noon - 6 PM. The colonial area of this 18th century capital of Virginia, encompassing 173 acres with nearly 500 homes, shops, taverns, public buildings and dependencies, has been carefully restored to its original appearance. Included are 90 acres of gardens and greens. The work was initiated by the late John D Rockefeller, Jr. There are more than 30 exhibition homes, public buildings and craft shops where guides and craftsmen in colonial costume show visitors the arts and decoration as well as the way of life of pre-Revolutionary Virginia. Included are the historic Bruton Parish Church, the Abby Aldrich Rockefeller Folk Art Center and The Courthouse of 1770. The exhibition properties include 225 furnished rooms. Average Annual Attendance: 1,000,000
Collections: 18th Century American Painting; English Pottery and Porcelains; English Silver; Collections of American and English furnishings, with frequent additions, include representative pieces, rare English pieces in the palace; exceptionally fine textiles and rugs
Exhibitions: Brush-Everard House (small well-appointed home, typical of a comfortable but not wealthy colonial); The Capitol (one of colonial America's most important buildings, scene of Patrick Henry's oration against the Stamp Act); Craft Shops (the trades and crafts of 200 years ago are carried on in 20 authentically furnished craft shops where artisans use the tools and methods of the 18th century); The Gaol (where debtors, criminals and Blackbeard's pirates were imprisoned); James Geedy House (original dwelling and workshop of a well-known colonial silversmith and businessman); Goveronr's Palace and Gardens (residence of royal governors. Outstanding English and American 18th century furnishing and extensive formal colonial gardens); Public Magazine (arsenal of the Virginia colony, now exhibiting colonial arms); Raleigh Tavern (one of the most famous taverns of colonial times, where Virginia patriots plotted Revolutionary action, and social center of the capital); Peyton Randolph House (original residence of the first president of the Continental Congress); Wetherburn's Tavern (among the most famous of the 18th century Virginia hostelries, over 200 years old); Wren Building of the College of William and Mary (the oldest academic building in British America in Continuous Use with six room open to the public and the remainder still in use for college classes and faculty offices); Wythe House (home of George Wythe, signer of Declaration of Independence and teacher of Jefferson and John Marshall)
O Information Center, PO Drawer C, 23185.
Outside the historic area this modern center houses graphic exhibits of the restoration and colonial life. Continuous showings of a full-color, vista vision film, Williamsburg: The Story of a Patriot
Publications: Books and brochures on Williamsburg and colonial life; gallery book of the Folk Art Collection
Activities: Limited grant-in-aid program for researchers; Annual events including Antiques Forum; Garden Symposium; regular performance of 18th century dramas, organ recitals and concerts; slide lectures
L Library, PO Drawer C, 23185.
Library Holdings: Vols 25,000 on American history

M ABBY ALDRICH ROCKEFELLER FOLK ART CENTER, 307 S England St, PO Drawer C, 23185. Tel 804-229-1000, Ext 2424. *Dir* Beatrix T Rumford
Open Winter, Mon - Fri noon - 6 PM, Summer, Mon - Fri noon - 9 PM. Admission by donation. Estab 1939 for research, education and the exhibition of one of the country's leading collections of American folk art of the 18th and 19th centuries. Nine galleries of American folk art, including a craft gallery. Average Annual Attendance: 150,000
Collections: Decorative usefulwares, decoys, needlework, painted furniture, paintings, sculpture and shop signs
Exhibitions: (1979) Caring for a Collection; Christmas Exhibit; Christmas Preview; Lewis Miller's Virginia Sketchbook, 1853. (1980) Back by Popular Demand; Contemporary Folk Art from the Herbert Hemphill Collection; Latest Additions; Traditions Across the Sea: Naive Paintings from England

Publications: Exhibition catalogs
Activities: Originate traveling exhibitions
L Library, 307 S England St, PO Drawer C, 23185.
Open to serious scholors of folk art for reference
Library Holdings: Vols 1500

WASHINGTON

BELLEVUE

M BELLEVUE ART MUSEUM, (Formerly Pacific Northwest Arts and Crafts Association) 10310 NE Fourth St, 98004. Tel 206-454-3322.
Open Tues - Sun noon - 5 PM, cl Mon and month of August. Sponsored by the Pacific Northwest Arts and Crafts Association. Average Annual Attendance: dues patron $500, business $50 and $100, contributor $100, family $20, individual $15, student $7.50
Collections: 20th Century American Art, especially the Pacific rim
Exhibitions: Annual Pacific Northwest Arts and Crafts Fair; Exhibitions of local, regional and national significance
Publications: Exhibition catalogs
Activities: Classes for adults and children on a credit and/or non-credit basis; credit courses offered through Western Washington University in Bellingham; art demonstrations; lect; films; concerts

BELLINGHAM

M WHATCOM MUSEUM OF HISTORY AND ART, 121 Prospect St, 98225. Tel 206-676-6981. *Dir* George Thomas; *Cur* Rod Slemmons; *Education Coordr* Richard Vanderway; *Preparator* Eric Taylor; *Registrar* Janis Olson; *Public Relations* Kathleen Green
Open Tues - Sun noon - 5 PM, cl Mon and holidays. No admis fee. Estab 1940 to collect, preserve and use, through exhibits, interpretation and research, objects of historic or artistic value, and to act as a multi-purpose cultural center for the Northwest Washington area providing presentations in all aspects of the arts. Seven galleries cover 3750 sq ft floor space and 625 linear ft wall space, plus a permanent history exhibit space. Average Annual Attendance: 80,000. Mem: 700; dues family $25, individual $15; annual meeting in February
Income: $250,000 (financed by private and public funds)
Collections: Contemporary Northwest Arts; Darius Kinsey and Wilbur Sandison Historic Photograph Collection; Northwest Native American Artifacts; Regional Historic Photographs and Artifacts
Exhibitions: (1978) Directions in Glass (area artists); Gilkey Paintings; Gonzales, 24 Years (paintings); Photography in the Northwest: 1860 - 1935; Tomkins, Paintings and Sculpture; The Warp and Weft of Islam (middle eastern rugs, carpets and bags). (1979) Annual Fibers Unlimited Textile Exhibit; Darius Kinsey Collection of Historic Photographs; The Etchings of Helen Loggie; The Meander Series (serigraphs by Mark Tobey); Whatcom County Shipbuilding
Publications: Art and Events Calendar, monthly; Exhibit catalogs; History texts
Activities: Classes for adults and programs for children; decent training; lect open to the public; concerts; gallery talks; tours; individual paintings and original objects of art lent to other museums and galleries; originate traveling exhibitions; museum shop selling books, craftwork from around the world, original art and prints
L Library, 122 Prospect St, 98225.
Open to public by appointment only. For reference only
Library Holdings: Vols 500; Per subs 10 - 15

CLARKSTON

O VALLEY ART CENTER INC, 842 Sixth St, PO Box 65, 99403. Tel 509-758-8331. *Executive Dir* Pat Rosenberger; *Co-Chmn & Secy* Veda Taylor; *Treas* Richard Schutte; *Admin Asst* Nadine Peterson
Open Mon - Fri 9 AM - 4 PM, Sun 2 - 4 PM, cl Sat. Estab 1968 to encourage and instruct in all forms of the visual arts and to promote the cause of art in the community. A portion of the Center serves as the gallery. Average Annual Attendance: 7000. Mem: 150; dues $50, $25, $10
Income: Financed by membership and class fees
Exhibitions: Annual Heritate Show; Annual Western Bronze Show; Lewis-Clark Art Association Show
Publications: newsletter, semi-annually
Activities: Classes for adults and children; lect open to the public, 5 vis lectr per year; gallery talks; tours; competitions; individual paintings lent to banks, business offices and professional people; originate traveling exhibitions; sales shop selling original art and prints, fine handcrafts and reproductions

ELLENSBURG

M CENTRAL WASHINGTON UNIVERSITY, Sara Spurgeon Gallery, 98926. Tel 509-963-2665. *Chmn Art Department* George Stillman; *Dir Art Gallery* James Sahlstrand
Open Mon - Fri 8 AM - 5 PM. No admis fee. Estab 1970 to serve as university gallery and hold community functions. The gallery is a large, single unit. Average Annual Attendance: 20,000
Income: Financed by state appropriations
Exhibitions: New Photographics (the annual competitive national exhibit of photographic work is presented each spring); several national invitation shows (group and individual) each year; student, graduate thesis and faculty exhibitions
Publications: Catalogs for all National shows
Activities: Lect open to the public; competitions

GOLDENDALE

M MARYHILL MUSEUM OF ART, Star Route 677, Box 23, 98620. Tel 509-773-4792. *Adminr* Dorothy Brokaw; *Dir Coll* Harvey Freer; *Pres Board of Dir* Muriel Jacobsen

Open daily 9 AM - 5 PM Mar 15 - Nov 15. Admis adults $1.50, senior citizens $1, students (6-18) 50¢, under six free. Estab 1923 as a museum of art. Average Annual Attendance: 65,000. Mem: 100; dues $15

Collections: American Indian Baskets; Antique and Modern Chessmen; Columbia River Basin Prehistoric Arts; European and American Paintings; 19th Century American and French Sculpture; Rodin Sculpture and Drawings; Royal Furniture designed by Marie, Queen of Romania and memorabilia; World War II costumed French Fashion Mannequins

Publications: Brochure and souvenir booklet

OLYMPIA

M STATE CAPITOL MUSEUM, 211 W 21st Ave, 98501. Tel 206-753-2580.

Open Tues - Fri 10 AM - 4 PM, Sat & Sun noon - 4 PM, cl Mon. No admis fee. Estab 1941 to interpret history of the State of Washington and of the capital city. The one-room gallery presents changing monthly shows. Average Annual Attendance: 40,000. Mem: 400; dues family $12, individual $6; annual meeting in June

Income: $100,000 (financed by city and state appropriation and local funds)

Collections: Etchings by Thomas Handforth; Winslow Homer Woodcuts; Northwest Indian serigraphs; small collection of paintings by Washington artists

Publications: Museum newsletter, monthly

Activities: Classes for adults and children; dramatic programs; docent training; lect open to the public; concerts; gallery talks; tours; individual paintings and original objects of art lent to State offices; lending collection contains original prints, paintings; originate traveling exhibitions; sales shop selling books and slides

PULLMAN

M WASHINGTON STATE UNIVERSITY, Museum of Art, 99164. Tel 509-335-1910, 335-1603. *Dir* Sanford S Shaman; *Cur* Patricia Watkinson; *Asst Cur* Ann McGuigan; *Registrar* David Whelchel; *Executive Secy* June Harbour

Open Mon - Fri 10 AM - 4 PM, Mon & Fri evenings 7 - 10 PM, Sat & Sun 1 - 5 PM. No admis fee. Estab 1974 to contribute the humanities educational purpose and goal of the university for the direct benefit of the undergraduate and graduate students. Gallery covers 5000 sq ft and is centrally located on campus. Average Annual Attendance: 35,000

Income: Financed by endowment, membership and state appropriation

Collections: Late 19th Century to present-day American Art, with particular strength in the areas of the Ash Can School and North West regional art scene

Exhibitions: (1979-80) The American Eight from permanent collection; Americans in Glass; Diverse Directions: The Fiber Arts; Drawing 1900-45, A Survey of American Works; Earthworks; Canaletto Ethcins; Form and Figure; The Fred Harvey Collection: An Indian Show; Historic Visions: Early Photography as Document; Imperial Robes from the Ch'ing Dynasty; Mel Katz: Works 1971-78; Kinsey Collection; A Partial View: Young Photographers in the Northwest; Regionalism: Northwest Artists; Richard Smith: Recent Work 1972-77; Spectrum - New Directions in Color Photography

Publications: Special Exhibition catalogs, two per year

Activities: Classes for adults; lect open to public; gallery talks; tours; exten dept serves State of Washington; individual paintings and original objects of art lent to art community of the State of Washington; lending collection contains cassettes, color reproductions, original art works; originate traveling exhibitions; museum shop sells books and magazines

RICHLAND

O ARTS COUNCIL OF THE MID-COLUMBIA REGION, PO Box 735, 99352. Tel 509-943-0524. *Pres* Louise Gustafson; *Office Coordr* Tracy DeMeyer; *Asst* Carol Miles

Open Mon - Fri 8 AM - 4:30 PM. Estab April 1968 to encourage, promote and coordinate the arts. Mem: 300; dues $25, $15, $7.50; Board meeting 3rd Thurs monthly

Income: $10,000 (financed by membership)

Publications: Calendar and Newsletter, monthly

Activities: Creative arts development; Consultant Service on grant writing; dramatic programs; lect; Talent Bank, art awards; scholarships

SEATTLE

O ALLIED ARTS OF SEATTLE, INC,* 107 S Main St, 98104. Tel 206-624-0432. *Pres* James R Uhlir; *Acting Dir* Marga Rose Hancock

Open daily 9 AM - 5 PM. No admis fee. Estab 1954 to promote and support the arts and artists of the Northwest and to help create the kind of city that will attract the kind of people who support the arts. Mem: 1000; dues $5 - $250 depending on category; annual meeting Jan

Income: $27,000 (financed by membership)

Publications: Allied Arts Newsletter, 11 times per year; calendar of cultural events, quarterly; directory of arts organizations in Puget Sound area, biannual

Activities: Co-sponsorship with Seattle Public Schools of visits by school children to artists studios; also co-sponsors an exhibition in a Seattle gallery or museum; scholarships

O AND-OR, Resources in Contemporary Arts, 1525 Tenth Ave, 98122. Tel 206-324-5400. *Librn* Claudia Clement

Open daily noon - 6 PM. Estab 1975 to provide a focused and accessible resource of information about recent activities in the contemporary arts. Exhibition space

Income: Financed by National Endowment for the Arts and locally matched funds

L Library, 1525 Tenth Ave, 98122.
For reference only
Library Holdings: Vols 800; Per subs 125; AV—V-tapes; Other—Clipping files, exhibition catalogs, original art works, pamphlets, original documents
Special Subjects: Contemporary Art
Activities: Tours available upon request; discussion groups

M CORNISH INSTITUE OF ALLIED ARTS, Cornish Gallery,* 710 E Roy St, 98102. Tel 206-323-1400. *Dir* Victor Baumgartner

Open Mon - Fri 10 AM - 5 PM, Sat 1 - 4 PM. No admis fee. Estab 1975 to support and enhance the visual arts curricula and reflect current trends in art. Gallery is 36 x 22 ft and has a lite-trak system, double door entry, 120 ft of free wall space, 10 ft ceilings, and tile floor

Income: Financed through Institute

Exhibitions: BFA Thesis Shows; Ralph Baker (paintings); Walter Cotton (prints); Faculty selected works; Albert Fisher (paintings); Tom Holland (paintings and sculpture); Robert Maki (sculpture); Frank Okada (paintings); Kathleen Rabel (prints); Robert Rauschenberg (prints, drawings); Chris Watts (drawings); Student Awards Show

Publications: Gallery mailers

Activities: Classes for adults; dramatic programs; lect open to public; gallery talks; competitions; exten dept serving adults interested in part-time study; traveling exhibitions organized and circulated

L Poncho Library,* 710 E Roy St, 98102. Tel 206-329-0901. *Librn* Ron McComb
Open to students and faculty
Library Holdings: Vols 3,500; Per subs 75; AV—Rec, slides
Special Subjects: Design, fine arts, music, dance, theatre

O' CORPORATE COUNCIL FOR THE ARTS, 421 Skinner Bldg, 98101. Tel 206-682-9270. *Pres* W J Pennington; *VPres* David E Skinner; *Secy* Christopher T Bayley; *Treas* Joseph L Silva; *Executive Dir* Robert E Gustavson; *Membership Dir* John Renforth

Open 9 AM - 5 PM. Estab 1968 as a clearinghouse for corporate contributions to the arts, to monitor budgeting of art agencies and assess ability of business to provide funding assistance. Gallery not maintained. Mem: 300; minimum contribution of $500 to qualify for membership; annual meeting first Wed in August

Income: $660,000 (financed by membership)

Publications: Annual Report; brochures; periodic membership reports

M CHARLES AND EMMA FRYE ART MUSEUM, 704 Terry Ave, PO Box 3005, 98114. Tel 206-622-9250. *Pres & Dir* Mrs W S Greathouse

Open weekdays 10 AM - 5 PM, Sun noon - 6 PM. No admis fee. Estab 1952 to display and preserve the Frye Art Collection. Three galleries cover 30 x 60 ft and four galleries cover 30 x 30 ft, plus foyer. Average Annual Attendance: 60,000

Income: Financed by endowment

Collections: Charles and Emma Frye Collection represents 13 nationalities and includes Baer, Boudin, Carlsen, Corrodi, Dahl, Diaz, Degregger, Grubner, Hoch, Jongkind, Kaulbach, Koester, Lenbach, Leibl, Liebermann, Lier, Llermitte, Manet, Gabriel Max, Monticelli, Slevogt, Soren, Stuck, Thoma, Willroider, Winterhalter, Uhde, Ziem, Zugel, Zumbusch

Exhibitions: Changing exhibitions in four galleries every two to four weeks

Publications: Frye Vues, monthly

Activities: Lect open to the public; gallery talks; tours

L Library, 704 Terry Ave, PO Box 3005, 98114.
For reference only

O KING COUNTY ARTS COMMISSION, 300 King County Administration Bldg, 98104. Tel 206-344-7580. *Chmn* Carol Duke; *Vice Chmn* Dr Morton Kroll; *Treas* Ken P Todd; *Executive Dir* Yankee Johnson; *Prog Coordr* Barbara McDonald; *Visual Arts Coordr* Jerry Allen; *Community Arts Development Coordr* Tony Wally

Open Mon - Fri 8:30 AM - 4:30 PM. No admis fee. Estab 1968 to provide cultural arts opportunities to the citizens of King County. The Arts Commission purchases and commissions many works of art for public buildings. Mem: 18; membership by appointment of County Executive; monthly meetings third Tues

Income: Approx $1,000,000 (financed by county government, including one percent for art in county construction projects)

Publications: Earthworks: Land Reclamation as Sculpture

Activities: Workshops; performances; originate traveling exhibitions

C PACIFIC NORTHWEST BELL, 1600 Bell Plaza, 98191. Tel 206-345-6349. *Staff Specialist* Joycelyn Dixon

Open Mon - Fri 8:30 AM - 5 PM. No admis fee. Estab 1977 to display the varying cultural traditions which have contributed to Pacific Northwest Art. Collection displayed throughout 32 floors of Bell Plaza

Collections: Reflects the Pacific Northwesterner's eye and shows the influence of the region (restricted to include only artists who live in Washington, Oregon and Idaho)

C RAINIER NATIONAL BANK, 1301 Fifth Ave, PO Box 3966, 98124. Tel 206-621-5547. *In Charge Art Coll* Jon W Adams

Open to public by appointment. No admis fee. Estab 1976 to support art and artists indigenous to the Northwest and Alaska. Collection displayed in main section in the corporate headquarters building

Purchases: $50,000

Collections: Oriental Porcelain Collection

Activities: Gallery talks; tours; individual objects of art lent to museums, galleries and public displays

M SEATTLE ART MUSEUM, Volunteer Park, 98112. Tel 206-447-4710. *Chmn of Board* John H Hauberg; *Pres of Board* C Bagley Wright; *Dir* Arnold H Jolles; *Asian Art Cur* Henry Trubner; *Asian Art Cur* William Jay Rathbun; *Development Officer* Dia M Dorsey; *Controller* Marilyn Davis; *Public Relations Mgr* Annie Searle

Open Mon - Fri 10 AM - 5 PM, Thurs 7 - 10 PM, Sun & holidays noon - 5 PM, cl New Year's, Memorial Day, Thanksgiving & Christmas. Estab 1906, incorporated 1917, building opened 1933; gift to the city from Mrs Eugene Fuller and Richard Eugene Fuller, for recreation, education and inspiration of its citizens. Average Annual Attendance: 300,000. Mem: 12,000; dues $18 and up

Collections: LeRoy M Backus Collection of Drawings and Paintings; Manson F

Backus Collection of Prints; Norman Davis Collection (with emphasis on classical art); Eugene Fuller Memorial Collection of Chinese Jades from Archaic through 18th Century; Eugene Fuller Memorial Collection (with special emphasis on Japan, China, India, and including Egypt, Ancient Greece and Rome, European, Near Eastern, primitive and contemporary Northwest art); Alice Heeramaneck Collection of Primitive Art; Henry and Marth Issacson Collection of 18th Century European Porcelain; H Kress Collection of 14th - 18th Century European Paintings; Thomas D Stimson Memorial Collection (with special emphasis on Far Eastern art); Extensive Chinese and Indian Collection; 18th Century Drawing Room (furnished by the National Society of Colonial Dames of American in the State of Washington); major holdings in Northwest art, including Tobey, Callahan, Graves as well as all contemporary art, especially American artists Gorky, Pollock, Warhol and Lichtenstein; selected highlights on Asian collection on permanent display (with special emphasis on on Japanese screens, paintings, sculpture and lacquers)

Publications: Annual Report; Japanese Paintings from the Sanso Collection; Johsel Namking: An Artist's View of Nature; Newsletter, 10 per year; Northwest Traditions; Song of the Brush; Museum State catalog

Activities: Docent service; film programs; double lecture course under the Museum Guild; adult art history classes; lect open to the public, 12 visiting lectr per year; tours; programs for Senior Citizens; approximately 300 Treasure Box visits yearly to King County Public Schools 5th and 6th grade classrooms and special groups; museum store sells books, gifts and jewelry

L **Library,** Volunteer Park, 98112. *Librn* Elizabeth de Fato; *Photography & Slide Librn* Jo H Nilsson
For reference only
Library Holdings: Vols 9000; AV—Slides 44,000

M **Modern Art Pavilion,** Seattle Center, 2nd N & Thomas St, 98109. Tel 206-447-4795. *Cur* Charles Cowles; *Assoc Cur* Bruce Guenther; *Mgr* Tore Hoven
Open Tues - Sun 11 AM - 6 PM, Thurs 11 AM - 8 PM, cl Mon, New Year's Day, Thanksviging, Christmas. A branch of the Seattle Art Museum in the former British Pavilion at Seattle World's Fair, remodeled through a gift from Poncho Association and a bequest from the late Richard Dwight Merrill into a year round exhibition facility, officially opened June 4, 1965. Average Annual Attendance: 108,000
Collections: 20th Century Art
Exhibitions: Permanent Collection
Activities: Docent service; Rental and Sales Gallery; museum store sells books, gifts and jewelry

C **SEATTLE-FIRST NATIONAL BANK,** 1001 Fourth Ave, 98104. Tel 206-583-5966. *Art & Design Officer* Lawney Reyes
Open 9 AM - 4 PM by appointment only. No admis fee. Estab 1968 for complementing the interiors, the appreciation of the general public, and for the support of the fine arts. Collection displayed in state of Washington and overseas; supports visual and performing arts
Purchases: $300,000
Collections: Contemporary World Class
Activities: Lect; gallery talks; tours; awards at local art exhibitions; individual objects of art lent to museums and exhibitions; book traveling exhibitions; originate traveling exhibitions to other public exhibitions spaces

L **SEATTLE PUBLIC LIBRARY,*** Art & Music Department, 1000 Fourth Ave, 98104. Tel 206-625-4952. *Librn* Ronald A Dubberly; *Art & Music Librn* Carolyn Holmquist
Open Mon - Thurs 9 AM - 9 PM, Fri & Sat 9 AM - 6 PM, cl Sun. No admis fee. Art Dept estab 1907
Income: $30,000
Library Holdings: Vols 100,000; Other—Framed reproductions, prints, photographs, reproductions, sculpture, bound periodicals, drawings, paintings

O **SEATTLE WEAVER'S GUILD,** Museum of History and Industry, 2161 East Hamlin St, 98112. Tel 206-324-1125. *Pres* Carlene Striker; *Recording Secy* Anita Peckham; *Corresp Secy* Eleanor Helliwell
Estab 1937 to further interest in hand weaving. Mem: 242; dues $10; monthly meetings except Dec, June, July & Aug
Exhibitions: Northwest Association of Handweavers biannual conference; Northwest Craftsmen's Exhibition at the Henry Gallery
Activities: Workshops throughout the year

UNIVERSITY OF WASHINGTON

M **Henry Art Gallery,** 98195. Tel 206-543-2280. *Dir* Harvey West
Open Tues - Fri 10 AM - 5 PM, Sat & Sun 1 - 5 PM, Thurs evenings 7 - 9 PM, cl Mon. Admis fee for certain exhibits only. Estab 1927 by gift of Horace C Henry. 8 galleries, 6000 sq ft of exhibition space. Average Annual Attendance: 100,000. Mem: 650; dues $10 and up
Collections: 19th Century American Landscape Painting; Contemporary West Coast Ceramics; works on paper (drawings, prints and photographs)
Exhibitions: American Impressionism; The City: The Urban Block; Edward Kienholz, Sculpture 1976-1979; 1st - 3rd Century Roman Portraits from the Getty Collection; West Coast Drawing
Publications: Exhibition catalogues; Index of Art in the Pacific Northwest series
Activities: Symposia; lect; book traveling exhibitions; originate traveling exhibitions

L **Art Library,*** 101 Art Bldg, DM 10, 98195. Tel 206-543-0648. *Librn* Marietta M Ward
Open Mon - Thurs 8 AM - 9 PM, Fri 8 AM - 5 PM, Sun 1 - 5 PM. Estab 1940 primarily to provide resources for the courses, degree and research programs of the School of Art; and serves as the Art Library for university community as a whole. Circ 63,189
Income: Financed by city appropriation
Library Holdings: Vols 24,000; Per subs 406; Other—Clipping files, exhibition catalogs, photographs, reproductions
Special Subjects: Art Education, Art History, Ceramics, Graphic Design, Industrial Design, painting
Activities: Library tours

M **Costume and Textile Study Center,*** DL-10 Univ of Washington, 98195. Tel 206-543-1739. *Cur* Virginia I Harvey; *Preparator* Krista Turnbull; *Conservator* Martha Fletcher
Open daily 1 - 5 PM. No admis fee. Estab 1958 as a center for the maintenance and

as a study collection of historic and ethnic costumes and textiles for use by students, designer craftsman and scholars. Gallery is not maintained, items are displayed for study on tables. Average Annual Attendance: 3500
Collections: Elizabeth Palmer Bayler Collection of textiles from India; Choate Collection of Lace; Eugene Garbaty Collection; Harriett Tidball Collection
Activities: Lect open to public, 2 - 3 visiting lectr per year; tours

L **Costume and Textile Study Center Library,*** DL-10 Univ of Washington, 98195. *Librn* Andrea K Bebee
Open to public for reference only
Library Holdings: Vols 2000; Per subs 20
Special Subjects: Costume Design & Construction, Embroidery, Textiles, Looms, weaving

M **Thomas Burke Memorial Washington State Museum,*** 98195. Tel 206-543-5590. *Dir* George I Quimby; *Asst Dir* Robert M Free; *Cur Ethnology & Anthropology* Dr James Nason; *Cur Northwest Coast Indian Art* Bill Holm; *Registrar* Roxana Augusztiny
Open Tues - Sat 10 AM - 4:30 PM, Thurs 10 AM - 9 PM, Sun 1 - 4:30 PM. No admis fee. Estab 1889 for research and exhibitions. Mem: Dues $10 - $5000 and up
Collections: Anthropology and natural history of the Northwest and the Pacific, specializing in Primitive Art of these regions
Activities: Museum classes; circulates study collection

SPOKANE

M **EASTERN WASHINGTON STATE HISTORICAL SOCIETY,** Cheney Cowles Memorial Museum, 2316 W First Ave, 99204. Tel 509-456-3931. *Dir* Albert H Culverwell; *Cur Art* Fred Ploeger
Open Tues - Sat 10 AM - 5 PM, Sun 2 - 5 PM, cl Mon. Estab 1916, Museum of history and art. Fine arts gallery with regular monthly art exhibitions of Pacific Norhtwest artists. Average Annual Attendance: 83,000. Mem: 1100; dues $5 per person; annual meeting usually in May
Income: Financed by membership, county, city and state appropriations
Collections: Regional history including collection of Indian arts and handicrafts; historic house of 1898 by architect Kirtland K Cutter, interior designed and decorated with period furnishings
Exhibitions: 145 exhibitions since 1967
Publications: Museum Notes, ten per year
Activities: Lect open to the public; concerts; lending collection contains 500 Kodachromes; traveling exhibitions organized and circulated; museum shop

L **Library,** 2316 W First Ave, 99204. *Librn* Elinor Kelly
For reference only
Library Holdings: Vols 4000; Other—Prints 15,000 prints and negatives, Newspaper clipping file, manuscripts for library use only, copies available upon request

M **FORT WRIGHT COLLEGE,** Art Gallery, W 4000 Randolph Rd, 99204. Tel 519-328-2970, Ext 45. *Chmn* Sr Paula M Turnbull
Open daily 9 AM - 5 PM. No admis fee. The main purpose of this gallery is for presentation of student BFA exhibitions. It is adjacent to the main art building and is of substantial size
Income: Financed through the College
Collections: Student works retained from exhibitions
Exhibitions: Student BFA shows; faculty shows; student art shows and sales
Activities: Classes for adults; dramatic programs; lect open to the public, 4 - 5 vis lectr per yr; competitions; exten department serving Yakima and Omak; museum shop

M **GONZAGA UNIVERSITY,** AD Gallery, 502 East Boone Ave, 99258. Tel 509-328-4220. *Dir* J Scott Patnode
No admis fee. Estab 1971 to service the art program and art department at Gonzaga University. One room 24 ft x 40 ft, with moveable trac lighting. Average Annual Attendance: 5000
Income: Financed by Art Department funds
Collections: Student art collection; †Contemporary and old master print collection
Exhibitions: Governor's Invitational; Photo Collage Print by Maxine Burns; Weavings by Larry Metcalf
Activities: Education department; lectures open to the public, one visiting lecturer per year

M **SPOKANE FALLS COMMUNITY COLLEGE FINE ART GALLERY,** W 3410 Fort George Wright Dr, 99204. Tel 509-456-6100. *Chmn Visual Arts Department* Jo Fyfe; *Supv Creative & Performing Arts Department* Donald Nepean; *Exhib* Jack Tworkov
Open Mon - Fri 8:30 AM - 4 PM. No admis fee. Estab 1968 to bring in fine artists and craftsmen outside the Spokane area for the benefit of students and community. Gallery is 20 x 40 ft, carpeted, airy, with windows to front and back; in center of art building. Average Annual Attendance: 5000
Collections: Glass vase, handblown; paintings
Exhibitions: Annual faculty show and student drawing, ceramics, printmaking, stained glass

L **SPOKANE PUBLIC LIBRARY,** W 906 Main St, 99201. Tel 509-838-3361. *Chairperson Board of Trustees* J Dan Schoedel; *Dir* Betty W Bender; *Asst Dir* Nancy P White
Open Mon - Thurs 9 AM - 9 PM, Fri & Sat 9 AM - 6 PM. Estab 1894 basically to meet citizens education, information, recreation and cultural lifelong learning needs through a variety of programs and facilities. Circ 1,199,661. Gallery maintained to exhibit mainly local work and changed monthly
Income: $1,825,334
Purchases: $1,675,065
Library Holdings: Vols 456,757; Per subs 1516; Micro—Fiche, reels; AV—A-tapes, cassettes, fs, lantern Slides, motion pictures, rec, slides, v-tapes; Other—Clipping files, exhibition catalogs, framed reproductions, prints, manuscripts, memorabilia, original art works, pamphlets, photographs, reproductions, sculpture, original documents
Collections: Rare books

Exhibitions: One each month in picture gallery
Activities: Classes for adults and children; dramatic programs; lect open to the public, 9 vis lectr per yr; concerts, gallery talks; tours

TACOMA

M **TACOMA ART MUSEUM,** 12th and Pacific Ave, 98402. Tel 206-272-4258. *Dir* Jon W Kowalek; *Educ Head* Gale Janes
Open Mon - Sat 10 AM - 4 PM, Sun Noon - 5 PM. No admis fee. Estab 1895 to perpetuate the finest in the visual Fine Arts. Museum features galleries for permanent collection, traveling exhibitions and a specialized Childrens Gallery. Average Annual Attendance: 150,000. Mem: 1300; annual meeting varies
Income: $200,000 (financed by endowment and membership)
Collections: †American paintings and sculpture; †American crafts (glass, ceramics, weaving, etc); †European and Asian works of Art
Exhibitions: Circulating and original exhibitions of National importance
Publications: Bulletin, monthly
Activities: Docent training; lect open to the public, 24 vis lectr per yr; gallery talks; tours; competitions; individual paintings and original objects of art lent to other professional museums; lending collection contains paintings, sculpture; museum shop sells books, original art, reproductions, prints
L **Library,** 12th and Pacific Ave, 98402. *Librn* Sally Norris
Open to the public for reference only
Library Holdings: Vols 1000; Per subs 25
Collections: Unique collection of research material on Japanese woodcut

L **TACOMA PUBLIC LIBRARY,** Handforth Gallery, 1102 Tacoma Ave S, 98402. Tel 206-572-2000. *Dir* Kevin Hegarty; *Asst Dir* Marile Creager; *Chief Librn* Gary Reese; *Dir Handforth Gallery* Clayton Kirking
Open Mon - Thurs 9 AM - 9 PM, Fri & Sat 9 AM - 6 PM. Estab 1952 to extend library services to include exhibits in all media in the Thomas S Handforth Gallery. Circ 1,237,000
Income: Financed by city appropriation
Library Holdings: Vols 594,700; Per subs 1759; Micro—Reels; AV—A-tapes, cassettes, fs, motion pictures, rec, slides; Other—Clipping files, exhibition catalogs, framed reproductions, prints, memorabilia, original art works, pamphlets, photographs
Special Subjects: Genealogy, manuscripts, Northwest Collection, photographs of local and regional subjects
Collections: Kaiser Collection; Lincoln Collection; city, county, federal and state documents
Exhibitions: Monthly changing exhibits
Publications: Administrative Bulletin, weekly
Activities: Classes for children; dramatic programs; lect open to public, 3 - 4 visiting lectr per year; originate traveling exhibitions

M **UNIVERSITY OF PUGET SOUND,** Kittredge Art Gallery, 15th and Lawrence, 98416. Tel 206-756-3356. *Dir* John McCuistion
Open Mon - Fri 10 AM - 4 PM, Sun 1 - 4 PM. No admis fee. Estab for showing of student and professional works. University operated. Average Annual Attendance: 1000
Collections: Abby Williams Hill, who painted Northwest scenes from the 1880s to the 1930s
Exhibitions: Local, community and regional art shows; faculty and student shows
Publications: Monthly show bulletins

M **WASHINGTON STATE HISTORICAL SOCIETY,** 315 N Stadium Way, 98403. Tel 206-593-2830. *Dir* Bruce LeRoy
Open Tues - Sat 9:30 AM - 4:30 PM, Sun 2 - 5 PM, cl Mon & holidays. Estab 1891. Society owns three buildings; art gallery under the direction of the Society. Average Annual Attendance: 225,000. Mem: 964; dues $7 and up; annual meeting May
Income: Financed by membership and other funding
Collections: Pre-historic relics; †Indian and Eskimo artifacts, baskets, clothing, utensils; Oriental items; †Washington-Northwest pioneer relics
Exhibitions: Exhibitions changed monthly
Publications: News Notes and sponsors Pacific Northwest Quarterly with the State University; books and pamphlets on Pacific-Northwest history
Activities: Special school tours
L **Hewitt Memorial Library,** 315 N Stadium Way, 98403. *Librn* Frank L Green; *Asst Librn* Jeanne Engerman
Open Tues - Sat 9:30 AM - 4:30 PM. Estab 1941 for research in Pacific Norhtwest history. For reference only
Income: Financed by membership, state appropriations and gifts
Library Holdings: Vols 15,000; Micro—Reels; Other—Clipping files, manuscripts, memorabilia, pamphlets, photographs
Special Subjects: Railroads, lumber, fishing, Indians, missions, labor
Collections: Asahel Curtis Photograph Collection of early Seattle
Publications: Circuit Rider, quarterly

WALLA WALLA

O **CARNEGIE CENTER OF THE ARTS,*** Elliott Square, 109 S Palouse, 99362. Tel 509-525-4270.
Open nine months Tues - Sat 11 AM - 4:30 PM, June & July Noon - 4 PM, cl Aug. No admis fee. Estab 1970 in 1905 Carnegie Library, built of Kansas brick and paneled with oak, inc 1971 as a non-profit educational organization. Mem: 750; dues from student $1 to life $1500 or more
Income: Financed by endowments, dues, contributions, art sales and rentals, and gift shop
Exhibitions: Area artists' exhibit in August; professional exhibits, changing monthly, of the work of National Northwest artists; youth gallery for display of art and craft work of school children
Activities: Art and craft classes; workshops; lect; recitals; rental-sales gallery; sales shop

WENATCHEE

M **WENATCHEE VALLEY COLLEGE,** Gallery 76, 1300 Fifth St, 98801. Tel 509-662-1213. *Pres* Tom Warren; *VPres* Marcia Van Doren; *Coordr* Ric Evans
Open Mon - Fri 1 - 4 PM, Mon and Thurs Eve 7 - 9 PM. Donation accepted. Estab 1976 to serve a rural, scattered population in North Central Washington State, which without Gallery 76, would not have access to a non-sales gallery. Non-profit community art gallery housed in Sexton Hall on Wenatchee Valley College Campus. Average Annual Attendance: 3150. Mem: 185; dues $10; annual meeting February
Income: $12,000 (financed by membership, grants, donations, fund raising events, art auction, Casino Night)
Collections: Oil Painting, Stephen Tse
Exhibitions: Bay Area Painters; The Collagraph Print: Glen Alps; Painting and Pottery: Stephen Tse; American Movie Still As Photography; The Fiftythree stages of the Tokaido: Sekino Junichiro; Women Painters of the West; New Artists Invitational; Johsel Namkung: An Artists View of Nature; Space Art from the USSR
Publications: Annual Brochure
Activities: Lectures open to the public; one or two visiting lecturers per year; gallery talks; tours; Invitational Exhibit for North Central Washington Artists; book traveling exhibitions; sales shop, located in another building, sells and rents original art

YAKIMA

O **ALLIED ARTS COUNCIL OF THE YAKIMA VALLEY,*** 5000 W Lincoln Ave, 98908. Tel 509-966-0930. *Pres* Peggy Lewis; *Exec Dir* Tom Tomlinson
Open 9 AM - 5 PM. No admis fee. Estab 1962 to encourage, promote and coordinate the practice and appreciation of the arts among the people of Yakima Valley. General gallery shows changing monthly exhibits; attic gallery rents art in addition to selling it. Mem: 600; dues $5 - $150
Income: Financed by membership
Exhibitions: Monthly exhibits by local and area artists
Publications: Artscope (arts calendar) monthly
Activities: Lect open to the public
L **Warehouse Library,*** 5000 W Lincoln Ave, 98908. Tel 509-966-0930. *Librn* Fran Marble

WEST VIRGINIA

CHARLESTON

O **SUNRISE FOUNDATION, INC,** (Formerly Charleston Art Gallery of Sunrise) 746 Myrtle Rd, 25314. Tel 304-344-8035. *Executive Dir* Dr Glenn A Long; *Cur Fine Arts* Nancy Beers; *Business Mgr* Mary Ann Steed
Open Tues - Sat 10 AM - 5 PM, Sun 2 - 5 PM, summer Tues - Sat 10 AM - 4 PM, cl national holidays. No admis fee. Estab 1960. Sunrise is located on a 16 acre estate containing two restored mansions housing a children's museum, planetarium, live animal fair and botanical center. The Art Gallery is situated in a Georgian style mansion known as Torquilstone. Mem: 1600; dues organizational $25, family $25, individual $15; annual meeting mid-April
Income: $300,000 (financed by endowment, membership, city and state appropriation)
Collections: Botany; Living Mammals, Reptiles and Amphibians of the Appalachian Region; Native American, African and Oceanic Artifacts; Natural History specimens in Geology, Mineralogy 19th and 20th Century American Decorative Arts, Graphics, Paintings and Sculpture
Exhibitions: Numerous exhibitions held throughout the year
Activities: Classes for adults and children; dramatic programs; docent training; hobby workshops; sponsors Art in School program for local schools; lect open to public, 12 visiting lectr per year; concerts; gallery talks; guided tours; competitions; recitals; arts festivals; garden clinics; book traveling exhibitions; originate traveling exhibitions; museum shop sells books, original art, reproductions and prints
L **Library,** 746 Myrtle Rd, 25314.
Tues - Sat 10 AM - 5 PM, Sun 2 - 5 PM, summer hours: Tues - Sat 10 - 4 PM, cl holidays. Reference library with books and periodicals related to Museum collections; inter-library loan
Library Holdings: Vols 3000; Per subs 20; AV—Slides; Other—Exhibition catalogs

HUNTINGTON

M **HUNTINGTON GALLERIES,** Park Hills, 25701. Tel 304-529-2701. *Dir* Roberta Shinn Emerson; *Adminr* James C Lawhorn; *Cur Collections* G Eason Eige; *Cur Exhib* Louise Polan; *Cur Education* David M Veater; *Development Officer* James F Weidman; *Registrar* Isabelle Umpleby; *Program Coordr* Gay Jackson; *Comptroller* Cynthia Riggs
Open Tues - Sat 10 AM - 4 PM, Sun 1 - 5 PM, cl Mon. No admis fee. Estab 1952 to own, operate and maintain an art museum for the collection of paintings, prints, bronzes, porcelains and all kinds of art and utility objects; to permit the study of arts and crafts and to foster an interest in the arts. Three building complex on 52-acre site includes ten galleries, two sculpture courts, seven studio workshops, a 10,000 volume capacity library, 300 seat auditorium, two and one-half miles of nature trails, (one marked with braille signs for the visually handicapped), an observatory with Celestron-14 telescope and an amphitheatre. Average Annual Attendance: 75,000. Mem: Membership dues vary; annual meeting June
Income: Financed by endowment, membership, city, state and county appropriations
Collections: American and European paintings and prints; American decorative arts; Georgian silver; firearms; historical and contemporary glass; Turkish prayer rugs

Exhibitions: Exhibition 280 (annual competitive exhibition); Selections from the Olga Hirshhorn Collection; New American Glass: Focus West Virginia (annual); New Deal for Art; Survival: Life and Art of the Alaskan Eskimo; Twenty-Five at the Huntington Galleries
Publications: Bulletin, bi-monthly; catalogues for exhibitions
Activities: Classes and workshops for adults and children; docent training; public lectures; concerts; theatre productions; gallery talks; tours; individual paintings and original objects of art lent to museums; traveling exhibitions organized and circulated; museum shop sells books, original art, reproductions, prints and crafts; Junior Art Museum
L **Library**, Park Hills, 25701. *Librn* Elizabeth Bostwick
Open to the public for reference only
Library Holdings: Vols 3500

MORGANTOWN

WEST VIRGINIA UNIVERSITY
M **Galleries A and B**, Evansdale Campus, 26506. Tel 304-314-2140. *Dean* Gilvert Trythall; *Chmn Art Department* Urban Couch; *Cur CAC Galleries* John D Clarkson
Open 10 AM - 5 PM. Estab 1968 primarily as teaching galleries for students and for the pleasure of students, public and campus community. Two galleries, 22 x 42 ft, flexible arrangements, approximately 600 running ft. Average Annual Attendance: 6000
Income: Financed by state appropriation and the Claude Benedum Foundation
Collections: Drawings; paintings; prints
Exhibitions: Graduate Thesis Exhibits of ceramics, paintings, and prints produced by candidates for the degree of Fine Arts in the Division of Art; Contemporary Photography of Carlton Perilla; Adrian Ryan, Watercolorist; Lecturer at Goldsmith College School of Art, London University and at the Cambridge College of Art; Undergraduate exhibits of ceramics, drawings, prints, paintings, designs and sculptures; Norfolk, Virginia Invitational National Potters Teachers Exhibit
Activities: Classes for children; dramatic programs; lect open to the public, 4 vis lectr per yr; concerts; gallery talks; individual paintings and original objects of art lent; lending collection contains 80 filmstrips, 6000 Kodachromes, 500 lantern slides, 6 motion pictures, 500 original art works, 300 original prints, 150 paintings, 7000 slides; traveling exhibitions organized and circulated
L **Galleries A and B Library**, Evansdale Campus, 26506.
Library Holdings: Vols 5000; Per subs 36
M **Creative Arts Center and Gallery**, Evansdale Campus, 26506. Tel 304-293-0111. *Cur Art and Dir Acquisition* John D Clarkson
Open Mon - Fri 1 - 4 PM, cl National holidays. No admis fee. Estab 1867
Collections: Costumes; music; paintings; theatre
Activities: Lectures; gallery talks; tours; concerts; drama; competitions; temporary traveling exhibitions
L **Creative Arts Center Library**, Evansdale Campus, 26506. *Librn* Mrs Thomas Canning
Library Holdings: Vols 10,000; Other—Music scores; records

PARKERSBURG

O **PARKERSBURG ART CENTER**, 220 Eighth Street, PO Box 131, 26101. Tel 304-485-3859. *Program Dir* Barbara Bays; *Educ Coordr* Karen Wilson; *Dir* P Joseph Mullins
Open Tues - Fri 10 AM - 4 PM, Sat & Sun 1 - 4 PM. No admis fee. Estab 1938 for the operation and maintenance of an art center and museum facility for the appreciation and enjoyment of art, both visual and decorative, as well as art history, crafts, and other related educational or cultural activities. Main gallery 43 x 27 ft and upper gallery 38 x 27 ft, completely carpeted, airconditioned and climate controlled. Average Annual Attendance: 10,000. Mem: 600; dues individual $15, family $25, sustaining $75, corporate or patron $125; annual meeting June
Income: $116,000 (financed by endowment, membership and state appropriation)
Collections: Advice of Dreams (oil by Beveridge Moore); Patrick Henry Land Grant Document; The Hinge (watercolor by Rudolph Ohrning; Parmenides (sculpture by Beverly Pepper)
Exhibitions: Archeological Find of the Ohio Valley Area; Han Hoffman;Dan Whitlach; New Handmade Furniture (From American Crafts Museum); West Virginia Artists George Snyder; Victor Vasarely
Publications: Calendar of events, bimonthly; annual report
Activities: Classes for adults and children; docent training; workshops; lectures open to public, 4 vis lectr per yr; concerts; gallery talks; competitions
L **Library**, 220 Eighth St, 26101.
Open to the public
Library Holdings: Vols 500; Per subs 5

ROMNEY

L **HAMPSHIRE COUNTY PUBLIC LIBRARY**, Main St, 26757. Tel 304-822-3185. *Pres* Carol Winland; *Secy* Mary Pugh; *Librn* Brenda Riffle
Open Mon - Sat 10 AM - 5 PM. No admis fee. Estab 1942. Display cases changed every month. Average Annual Attendance: 25,000
Income: $31,680
Purchases: $31,680
Library Holdings: Vols 17,975; Per subs 12; Micro—Reels; AV—A-tapes, cassettes, fs, motion pictures, v-tapes; Other—Prints, manuscripts, pamphlets, photographs
Exhibitions: Children's art; private collections of rocks, antiques, displays of items of other countries; various local artists collection; weaving
Activities: Classes for adults and children; dramatic programs; concerts

WHEELING

M **OGLEBAY INSTITUTE**, Stifel Fine Arts Center, 1330 National Rd, 26003. Tel 304-242-7700. *Executive Dir* Stanley H Coulling; *Dir Creative Arts Department* Mary E Fish
Open Mon - Fri 9:30 AM - 5 PM, Sun 12:30 - 5 PM, evenings by appointment. No

admis fee. Estab 1978 for education and participation in the visual and performing arts. Gallery has central hallways, 1st and 2nd floors; small exhibits gallery, 2nd floor. Average Annual Attendance: 28,000
Exhibitions: (1979-80) Crosscurrents 1980; Expressions and Impressions (Five Contemporary Belgians organized by the Belgian Embassy); Group Invitational; Pictures of a Floating World; Upper Ohio Valley Art Show
Publications: Activity and exhibition brochures; Oglebay Institute Activities, seasonal
Activities: Classes for adults and children; workshops; lect open to public, 4 visiting lectr per year; gallery talks; tours; films; forums; competitions; cash prizes and merit awards; exten dept; sales shop sells original art, prints, original handcrafted pottery, jewelry, stitchery and woodworking

M **OGLEBAY INSTITUTE MANSION MUSEUM**, Oglebay Park, 26003. Tel 304-242-7272. *Cur* Gary E Baker; *Executive Dir* S H Coulling; *Museum Dir* John A Artzberger
Open Mon - Sat 9:30 AM - 5 PM; Sun & holidays 1:30 - 5 PM; cl Thanksgiving, December 24, 25, 30 and Jan 1. Admis adults $2, senior citizen $1.50, student $1, children 12 and under free; group rates of 25 or more $1.50. Estab and incorporated 1930 to promote educational, cultural and recreational activities in Wheeling Tri-State area. Building and grounds are the property of the city; an exhibition wing adjoins the main house. Average Annual Attendance: 30,000. Mem: Approximately 1000; dues $10 and up
Collections: †Early china; †early glass made in Wheeling and the Midwest; period rooms; †pewter
Exhibitions: Current exhibits of art and other allied subjects change monthly
Activities: Antique seminars, twice per yr; antique classes; gallery talks
L **Library**, Oglebay Park, 26003.
Highly specialized on the early history of the area
Library Holdings: Micro—Prints; Other—documents and maps
O **Oglebay Institute Mansion Museum Committee**, Oglebay Park, 26003. *Chmn* Mrs R C Miller; *Vice Chmn* R C Haylett Jr; *Secy* Mrs R E Di Bartolomeo

WISCONSIN

BELOIT

M **BELOIT COLLEGE**, Theodore Lyman Wright Art Center, 53511. Tel 608-365-3391. *Dir & Cur* Marylou S Williams; *Registrar* Carol Simon
Open Mon - Fri 9 AM - 5 PM; Sat 11 AM - 5 PM; Sun 1 - 5 PM. No admis fee. Estab 1893; Wright Art Center built 1930 to house the collection for the enrichment of the college and community through exhibition of permanent collection and traveling and temporary regional art exhibitions of cultural and aesthetic value. A Georgian building architecturally styled after The Fogg Museum in Cambridge, Mass. Three galleries on main floor, on a large center court; Art Department shares other floors in which two student galleries are included. Average Annual Attendance: 10,000 - 20,000. Mem: Dues $15
Collections: European and American (paintings, sculpture and decorative arts); Fisher Memorial of Greek Casts; Graphics, emphasis on German Expressionist and contemporary works; Gurley Collection of Korean pottery, Japanese sword guard, Chinese snuff bottles and jades; Morse Collection of Paintings and Other Art Objects; †Neese Fund Collection of Contemporary Art; Oriental; Pitkin Collection of Oriental Art; Prints by Durer, Rembrandt, Whistler and others; †Ross Collection of Graphics; sculpture of various periods
Exhibitions: Beloit and Vicinity Exhibition (juried); Bruce Cornelius; Clay and Fiber Biennial Invitational; Colt on Paper by John Colt; Looking at Prints Series - Master Graphics; Paintings and Prints by Gabor Peterdi; Photography by Michael Simon and James Auer; Sculpture and Paintings by John and Diane Baisley; Works on Paper; student and faculty exhibitions
Publications: Exhibition catalogs
Activities: Classes for children; dramatic programs; docent training; lect open to public, 12 vis lectr per yr; gallery talks; tours; competitions; individual paintings lent to faculty offices and students; traveling exhibitions organized and circulated
L **Morse Library**, c/o Wright Art Center, 53511. *Dir & Librn* Vail Deale; *Asst Librn* Ruth Williams; *Asst Librn* Julie Van Valen
Open daily 8 AM - 10 PM during school term only. Estab 1846 for undergraduates, faculty and researchers
Income: $200,000
Purchases: $45,000
Library Holdings: Vols 230,000; Per subs 990; Micro—Fiche, reels, prints; AV—Fs, Kodachromes, lantern slides, rec, slides, v-tapes; Other—Clipping files, exhibition catalogs, framed reproductions, prints, manuscripts, memorabilia, original art works, pamphlets, photographs, reproductions, sculpture
Special Subjects: Furniture, Sculpture, Oriental Ceramics, Oceanic, Modern American
Collections: Modern prints in all media, drawings, paintings and sculpture
O **Friends of the Wright Art Center**, 53511.
Mem: 200; dues $5 and up; holds annual meeting

GREEN BAY

M **NEVILLE PUBLIC MUSEUM,*** 129 S Jefferson St, 54301. Tel 414-497-3767. *Cur Art* James W Kreiter; *Assoc Cur* Mary Schauer
Open Mon - Sat 9 AM - 5 PM, Sun 2 - 5 PM. No admis fee. Estab 1915 as Green Bay Public Museum; names changed 1926. Average Annual Attendance: 100,000. Mem: 350; dues family $10, individual $5; annual meeting in the spring
Income: Financed by city and county appropriation
Collections: David Belasco Collection of Victoriana antique furniture, †china, †glass, †silver, fans, lace, costumes and †accessories; †contemporary and historical paintings; †drawings; Neville family portraits; †prints and sculpture
Exhibitions: Local art clubs exhibit annually; Northeastern Wisconsin Art Show annually with cash awards; rotating monthly exhibits

Publications: Annual Report
Activities: Classes for adults and children; lect open to the public, 4 visiting lectrs per year; gallery talks; competitions; individual paintings and original objects of art lent to municipal offices; traveling exhibitions organized and circulated; sales shop selling reproductions and educational items
L **Library,*** 129 S Jefferson St, 54301.
Open to the public for reference

KENOSHA

M **KENOSHA PUBLIC MUSEUM,** 5608 Tenth Ave, 53140. Tel 414-656-6026. *Dir* Stephen H Schwartz; *Cur Education* Paula Touhey; *Cur Exhibitions* Keven Williams
Open Mon - Fri 9 AM - Noon & 1 - 5 PM; Sat 9 AM - Noon; Sun 1 - 4 PM. No admis fee. Estab 1936 to promote interest in general natural history and regional art. The gallery has 8000 sq ft of permanent exhibition space and 1000 sq ft for temporary exhibits. Average Annual Attendance: 40,000. Mem: 250; dues $10; annual meeting April
Income: $127,000 (financed by city appropriation)
Purchases: $1200
Collections: Historic Winconsin pottery; Oriental decorative arts; regional artists; regional natural history; worldwide ethnology
Exhibitions: Yousouf Karsh: People Who Make Our World; Roses
Publications: Newsletter, monthly
Activities: Classes for adults and children; lect open to public, 10 vis lectr per yr; gallery talks; tours; competitions; lending collection contains cassettes, color reproductions, film strips, framed reproductions, motion pictures, nature artifacts and slides; museum shop selling original art
L **Library,** 5608 Tenth Ave, 53140.
Open to public for reference only
Library Holdings: Vols 2000; Per subs 20
Special Subjects: Natural history

KOHLER

C **KOHLER COMPANY,** 44 Kohler Memorial Dr, 53044. Tel 414-457-4441. *Dir Public Affairs* Jim Stiner
Estab 1973. Collection displayed in Kohler Company general office
Collections: Original ceramic art pieces, some of which were created in Kohler Company Pottery
Activities: Individual objects of art lent

LA CROSSE

M **VITERBO COLLEGE ART GALLERY,*** 815 S Ninth St, 54601. Tel 608-784-0040. *Dir* Sr Carlene Unser
Open Mon - Fri 8 AM - 5 PM. Estab 1964 to exhibit arts and crafts which will be a valuable supplement to courses offered. Gallery is located in the center of the Art Department; 100 running feet; soft walls; good light
Income: $2000 (financed by school appropriation)
Purchases: $500
Collections: Mrs Lynn Miller Collection of contemporary United States primitives; Peter Whitebird Collection of WPA project painting
Activities: Classes for adults; dramatic programs; lect open to public; gallery talks
L **Zoeller Fine Arts Library,** S Ninth St, 54601. *Librn* Sr Rosella Namer
Open 8 AM - 9:30 PM for students of Viterbo College. Estab 1971 to service the Music-Art-Theatre Arts Departments
Library Holdings: Vols 1326; Per subs 30; AV—Cassettes

MADISON

M **EDGEWOOD COLLEGE,** DeRicci Gallery, 855 Woodrow, 53711. Tel 618-257-4861. *Pres* Sr Alice O'Rourke; *Art Department Chmn* Sr M Stephanie Stauder
Open 9 AM - 5 PM Mon - Fri. Estab 1965 to serve local artists, and provide educational opportunity for students. Large room; carpeted walls. Average Annual Attendance: 5000
Collections: Edgewood College Collection
Exhibitions: Old Bergen Art Guild; Local Artists

M **MADISON ART CENTER,** 211 State St, 53703. Tel 608-257-0158. *Dir* Joseph E Wilfer; *Cur* Janet Ela; *Asst Cur* Marian Kane; *Office Mgr* Michael Paggie; *Admin Asst* Julie Griffin; *Membership Secy* Gayle Mulliner; *Gallery Shop Mgr* Nancy Ivey; *Receptionist* Barbara Scherz
Open Tues - Sun. No admis fee. Estab 1901. Average Annual Attendance: 90,000. Mem: 1500; dues $10 and up
Income: $100,000
Purchases: $10,000
Collections: Emphasis on Contemporary Americans; large print and drawing collection (Japanese, European, Mexican and American); paintings; sculpture
Exhibitions: 8-10 major shows usually organized by the staff; occasional loan or rented exhibitions; smaller shows include one-person shows, print exhibitions, photographic exhibitions, group shows and theme exhibitions
Publications: Catalogs; posters and announcements usually accompany each exhibition
Activities: Docent program; workshops for adults and children; lect and demonstrations; bus tours; weekly film series; gallery talks; art fair; loan program to public schools
L **Library,** 53703.
Open for research only
Library Holdings: AV—Slides; Other—Exhibition catalogs

L **MADISON PUBLIC LIBRARY,** 201 West Mifflin St, 53703. Tel 608-266-6311. *Dir* Bernard Schwab
Open 8:30 AM - 9 PM Mon - Fri, 9 AM - 5:30 PM Sat. Estab 1875 to serve the people of Madison. Circ 1,800,000. Gallery maintained; an unsupervised area used primarily by local artists
Purchases: $450,000
Library Holdings: Vols 500,000; Per subs 1480; Micro—Fiche, reels; AV—A-tapes, cassettes, fs, motion pictures, rec, v-tapes; Other—Clipping files, exhibition catalogs, pamphlets
Activities: Lectures open to the public, eight visiting lecturers per year; concerts; gallery tours; traveling exhibitions organized and circulated to other libraries in the service area

M **STATE HISTORICAL SOCIETY OF WISCONSIN,** 816 State St, 53706. Tel 608-262-3266. *Dir* Richard A Erney; *Assoc Dir* Don W Wilson; *Asst Dir* William H Applegate; *Dir Museum* Thurman O Fox; *Dir Research* William F Thompson; *Cur Decorative Arts* Anne Woodhouse; *Cur of Textiles* Joan Severa
Open Mon - Fri 8 AM - 10 PM, Sat 8 AM - 4 PM, Sun Noon - 4 PM, cl holidays. No admis fee. Estab 1846, museum added 1854; organized to promote a wider appreciation of the American heritage, with particular emphasis on the collection, advancement and dissemination of knowledge of the history of Wisconsin and of the Middle West. Average Annual Attendance: 487,000. Mem: 7000; dues $15 and up
Income: Financed by state appropriation, earnings, gifts and federal grants
Collections: Historical Material; Iconographic Collection; china, coins, dolls, furniture, paintings, prints, photographs and slides
Exhibitions: Frequent special exhibitions; four annual gallery changes
Activities: Founders Day; regional meetings of local historians; films; materials lent to other museums; originate traveling exhibitions
L **Library,** 816 State St, 53706. *Librn* Peter Draz
Library Holdings: Vols 205,214; Other—Pamphlets 409,337, government pulpblications 297,632, microforms 561,435
Collections: Newspaper Collection of more than 35,000 volumes
L **Archives,** 816 State St, 53706. *Archivist* F Gerald Ham
Library Holdings: AV—Motion pictures; Other—Prints, photographs, Original documents, maps

UNIVERSITY OF WISCONSIN

M **Memorial Union Gallery,** 800 Langdon St, 53706. Tel 608-262-2214. *Dir & Secy* Ted Crabb; *Art Coordr* Jan Marshall Fox
Open 10 AM - 8 PM. No admis fee. Estab 1907 to provide a cultural program for the members of the university community. Owns two fireproof buildings with four galleries and maintains Union South at 227 N Randall Ave. Average Annual Attendance: 193,000. Mem: 46,500 faculty, alumni and townspeople, plus 38,000 students; dues $30; annual meeting May
Purchases: $1500
Collections: Oil and watercolor paintings, prints and sculptures, mostly by contemporary American artists
Activities: Informal classes in arts and crafts; films; gallery talks; loan collection availble on rental to students and members
M **Elvehjem Art Center,** 800 University Ave, 53706. Tel 608-263-2246. *Dir* Eric S McCready; *Asst Dir* David S Berreth; *Cur Coll* Carlton E Overland; *Registrar* Lisa C Calden; *Cur Education* Anne Lambert; *Coordr* Doreen Holmgren
Open Mon - Sat 9 AM - 4:45 PM, Sun 11 AM - 4:45 PM; cl holidays. No admis fee. Estab 1962, building opened 1970 to display, preserve and build a general art collection of high quality for the study and enjoyment of students, community and state. Three levels, 12 galleries covering 25,000 sq ft of exhibition space. Average Annual Attendance: 100,000. Mem: 2500; dues $7.50 - $250
Income: Financed by endowment, membership, state appropriation and private sources
Purchases: Vary according to income
Collections: Ancient Egyptian and Greek pottery, sculpture, glass and coins; 18th, 19th and 20th century American painting, sculpture and furniture; 18th, 19th, and 20th century Russian paintings and icons; Indian sculpture and miniatures; Medieval painting and sculpture; Renaissance painting and sculpture, 17th - 20th century European painting, sculpture, furniture and decorative arts; 16th - 20th century prints
Exhibitions: Twelve to fourteen temporary exhibitions per year in all media from varied periods of art history
Publications: Annual bulletin; calendar, quarterly; special exhibition catalogs
Activities: Classes for children; docent training; lect open to the public, 10-15 vis lectr per yr; concerts; gallery talks; tours; individual paintings lent to qualified art museums and galleries for special exhibitions; traveling exhibitions organized and circulated; museum shop selling reproductions, gift items, catalogs, posters, exhibition related articles
M **Art Department Gallery,** 6241 Humanities, 455 N Park Street, 53706. Tel 608-262-1660. *Chmn* Prof Richard Lazzaro
Open hours varied. No admis fee. Estab 1968 for MA and MFA exhibitions. Average Annual Attendance: 10,000
Income: Financed by state appropriation
Exhibitions: Graduate student exhibitions
L **Kohler Art Library,** 800 University Ave, 53706. Tel 608-263-2256. *Dir* William Bunce; *Reference Librn* K Louise Henning
Open Mon - Fri 8 AM - 4:45 PM & 7 - 9:45 PM; Sat & Sun 1 - 4:45 PM. Estab 1970 to support the teaching and research needs of the Art History Department and the Elvehjem Art Center. Circ 43,000
Library Holdings: Vols 80,000; Per subs 388; Micro—Fiche, reels; AV—Slides; Other—Exhibition catalogs, pamphlets
Special Subjects: Architecture, Decorative Arts
Activities: Tours

MANITOWOC

M **RAHR-WEST MUSEUM AND CIVIC CENTER,** Park St at N Eighth, 54220. Tel 414-684-4181. *Board Chmn* Tom Musial; *Dir* Gary Whitbeck; *Museum Asst* Richard Quick

Open Tues - Fri 9 AM - 4 PM; Sat & Sun 1 - 4 PM; cl Mon. No admis fee. Estab 1950 as an art center to serve the city of Manitowoc. Transitional gallery in new wing built 1975; period rooms in Victorian Rahr Mansion built c 1891; a Registered Historic home. Average Annual Attendance: 5000. Mem: 237; dues $3 - $500; annual meeting held in Feb

Income: $73,000 (financed by membership and city appropriation)

Collections: 19th and 20th Century American Paintings and Prints; Schuette Woodland Indian Artifacts; Schwartz Collection of Chinese Ivories; contemporary art glass

Exhibitions: Monthly changing exhibitions

Activities: Classes for adults and children; docent training; lect open to the public, 4-5 vis lectr per yr; gallery talks; tours; traveling exhibitions organized and circulated

L **Library,** Park St at N Eighth, 54220.
Open to the public for reference only
Library Holdings: Vols 1500; Per subs 6
Special Subjects: Art reference

MENOMONIE

M **UNIVERSITY OF WISCONSIN-STOUT,** Gallery 209, 54751. Tel 715-232-1428. *Cur* Eddie Wong
Open Mon - Fri 9 AM - 5 PM. No admis fee. Estab 1966 to serve university and local community with exhibits of art. A single room gallery; cloth walls and track lighting. Average Annual Attendance: 9500. Mem: Financed by state appropriation
Collections: African Art; paintings including works by Warrington Colescott, Roy Deforest, Walter Quirt, George Rovalt and Raphael Sover; drawings; prints; sculpture
Exhibitions: Changing exhibits
Activities: Classes for children; lect, 2-3 vis lectr per yr; gallery talks

MILWAUKEE

M **ALVERNO COLLEGE GALLERY,** 3401 S 39th St, 53215. Tel 414-671-5400. *Dir* Julie Holmquist
Open Tues - Fri 1 - 3 PM, Sun appointment only, cl non-school days. Estab for the aesthetic enrichment of community and the aesthetic education of students

M **CARDINAL STRITCH COLLEGE,** Studio San Damiano, 6801 N Yates Rd, 53217. Tel 414-352-5400. *Head Department* Sr Mary Tomasita
Open daily 9 AM - 5 PM. No admis fee. Estab 1947 to encourage creative art in each individual
Income: Financed by endowment, city and state appropriations and tuition
Collections: Folk Crafts; paintings
Exhibitions: Acquisitions from distant lands, children's art, professor's works, senior graduating exhibitions, approx 5 student's work, well-known area artists
Publications: CSC News, monthly
Activities: Classes for adults and children; dramatic programs; lect open to public, 20 visiting lectr per year; competitions; concerts; scholarships; individual paintings and original objects of art lent; originate traveling exhibitions; book shop
L **Library,** Studio San Damiano, 6801 N Yates Rd, 53217.
Library Holdings: Vols 200; Other—Photographs

M **CONCORDIA COLLEGE,** Fine Arts Galleries, 3201 West Highland, 53208. Tel 414-344-3400. *Pres* John Bunck; *Academic Dean* Ronald Berg; *Cur* William L Chandler
Open Sun Tues, Wed, Thurs 1 - 4 PM, Tues 7 - 9 PM. No admis fee. Estab 1972 to exhibit work of area and national artists as an educational arm of the college. Galleries are found in a turn of the century Milwaukee mansion; they occupy the first floor, former living quarters for a delightful and homey gallery space. Average Annual Attendance: 1000
Income: Financed through college budget
Collections: Russian bronzes and paintings; Graphics include Roualt, Altman and local artists
Exhibitions: Exhibits annually featuring local artists, student exhibit, etc

C **THE MARINE CORPORATION,** 111 E Wisconsin, PO Box 481, 53201. Tel 414-765-2423. *In Charge Art Coll* Mary Louise Roozen
Estab to encourage Wisconsin art and artists; to enhance the environment of Marine personnel. Collection displayed in offices, conference rooms and corridors of headquarters of bank holding company
Purchases: $7000
Collections: Acrylics, batik, bronze sculpture, lithographs, oils, wall sculpture, watercolors by Wisconsin artists
Activities: Invitational competitions in 1965, Wisconsin Renaissance in 1976; cash and purchase awards sponsored for college university and community art exchange; individual ojbects of art lent

M **MARQUETTE UNIVERSITY,** Marquette Fine Art Collection, 134 Coughlin Hall, 53233. Tel 414-224-7290. *Dir* Curtis L Carter; *Cur Asst* Mary Ladish
Open daily 8 AM - 10 PM. No admis fee. Estab 1950 to house the University's permanent collection of art, sponsor fine arts activities and to exhibit traveling and special art exhibits
Income: Financed through the university
Collections: 17th - 20th century paintings and prints, sculpture and decorative art
Exhibitions: Art and Industry; Barbara Morgan Photography; Karl Priebe Retrospective; Romanian Contemporary Paintings; From a Grain of Sand: The Marquette University Art Collection Builds
Publications: Catalogs of Exhibitions
Activities: Lectures; tours; objects of art lent

M **MILWAUKEE AREA TECHNICAL COLLEGE,** Kronquist Craft Gallery, 1015 N Sixth St, 53203. Tel 414-278-6600. *Gallery Dir* John Strachota
Open daily. No admis fee. Estab 1961 to stimulate appreciation for fine metalwork. Gallery is 30 x 40 ft located on sixth floor of central building; glass display cases house permanent collection, spotlit walls for artwork, carpeted lounge area.

Average Annual Attendance: 2500
Collections: Sculpture, bronze castings and other metalcraft by Emil F Kronquist; sterling hollowware, flatware and jewelry by Danish Silversmiths, Jensen, Rhode and Anderson
Exhibitions: Continous graphic and applied art student and faculty showings

M **MILWAUKEE ART CENTER,** 750 N Lincoln Memorial Dr, 53202. Tel 414-271-9508. *Pres Board Trustees* Sheldon B Lubar; *Dir* Gerald Nordland; *Assoc Dir* I Michael Danoff; *Cur Education & Acting Cur Decorative Arts* Barbara M Brown; *Asst Cur Decorative Arts & Praire Archives* Cheryl Robertson; *Asst Cur* Verna Curtis; *Public Relations* Ann Abshier; *Registrar* Thomas Beckman
Open Tue, Wed, Fri & Sat 10 AM - 5 PM, Thurs Noon - 9 PM, Sun 1 - 6 PM. Admis adults $1, students & sr citizens 50¢, children under 12 with adult free. Estab 1888 to create an environment for the arts that will serve the people of the greater Milwaukee community. Large, airy, flexible galleries, including a sculpture court and outdoor display areas. Fine arts and decorative arts are mixed to create an overview of a period, especially in the fine American Wings; small galleries provided for specific or unique collections. Average Annual Attendance: 150,000. Mem: 3800; dues family $25, individual $20; annual meeting May
Income: Financed by endowment, membership, county and state appropriations and fund drive
Collections: 19th and 20th Century American and European Art, including the Bradley and Layton Collections: The American Ash Can School and German Expressionism are emphasized; All media from Ancient Egypt to Modern America; The Flagg Tanning Corporation Collection of Hairtian Art; a study collection of Midwest Architecture - The Prairie Archives; The von Schleinitz collection of 19th Century German Painting, Mettlach Steins, and Meissen Porcelain
Exhibitions: The Afro-American Tradition in Decorative Arts; The American Indian and The American Flag; American 1976, Collecting The Masters; 19th Century Art by the American People; The Bible through Dutch Eyes; Jerome Krause and Thomas Uttech: Visions from the North Woods; Cork Marcheschi and Eric Schwartz; Masters Prints from the permanent collection; Max Ernst Tapestries; The Art of Ludwig Meidner; Naive Art in Yugoslavia; Six Decades: The News in Picture; (1979) German Expressionist Art: Robert Gore Rifkind Collection; The Great American Foot Color; Reinstallation of the European Galleries; Spectrum of Recent Photography-Immergence
Publications: Exhibitions and program brochure, tri-yearly; numbers calendar, bi-monthly
Activities: Classes for adults and children; docent training; lect open to public, 5 visiting lectr per year; concerts; gallery talks; tours; competitions; originate traveling exhibitions; museum shop sells books, magazines, original art, reproductions, slides and cards
L **Library,** 750 N Lincoln Memorial Dr, 53202. *Librn* Betty Karow
For reference Tues & Thurs 10 AM - 4 PM
Library Holdings: Vols 15,000; Per subs 31; Other—Vertical files, 27 drawers
Special Subjects: 19th Century German painting
Collections: Prairie Archives material (architecture and decorative arts of the Frank Lloyd Wright period) gift of Jacobson; von Schleinitz bequest of material on Meissen porcelain and 19th Century German painting

L **MILWAUKEE PUBLIC LIBRARY,** Art and Music Department, 814 West Wisconsin Ave, 53233. Tel 414-278-3000. *City Librn* Henry E Bates; *Supv Central Services* Kirk L Pressing; *Coordr Fine Arts* June M Edlhauser
Open Mon - Thurs, 8:30 AM - 9 PM, Fri & Sat 8:30 AM - 5:30 PM, Sun 1 - 5 PM. No admis fee. Estab 1897. Circ 56,000
Income: $37,268 (financed by budgeted funds and endowments)
Library Holdings: Vols 138,712; Micro—Fiche, reels; AV—Cassettes, fs, motion pictures, rec, slides, v-tapes; Other—Clipping files, exhibition catalogs, framed reproductions, prints, manuscripts, memorabilia, original art works, pamphlets, photographs, reproductions, sculpture, original documents
Special Subjects: Architecture, Art History, Coins & Medals, Costume Design & Construction, Crafts, Decorative Arts, Landscape Architecture, Photography, , City planning, philately
Publications: Auction and exhibition catalogs; Milwaukee Reader, weekly

M **MILWAUKEE PUBLIC MUSEUM,** 800 Wells St, 53233. Tel 414-278-2700. *Dir* Dr Kenneth Starr; *Cur of History* Dr Rudolph Dornemann; *Cur Oriental, Classical and Decorative Art* John Luedtke; *Cur European Folk Art* Dr Lazar Brkich; *Cur Anthropology* Dr Nancy Lurie; *Art Dir* Edward Green; *Asst Art Dir* Robert Frankowiak
Open daily 9 AM - 5 PM; cl holidays. Admis Milwaukee County residents adults $1, children 25¢, Mon no admis fee; non-Milwaukee County residents adults $2, children 75¢. Estab 1882 to assemble, preserve, meaningfully organize, carry on research and promote interest in materials relevant to the fields of natural science, anthropology and human history; to use materials in exhibits and in organized education programs to educate, enlighten and provide pleasurable experiences for the public. Four floors of exhibits includes a decorative arts gallery and special exhibits hall. Average Annual Attendance: 500,000. Mem: 3,000; dues Enrichment Club $60, family $25, individual $15, student $10
Income: $4,500,000 (financed by county appropriations)
Collections: American Indian Artifacts; I A Dinerstein Art Collection; Carl Netzow Collection of Antique Jewelry; Nunnemacher Gun Collection; Pre-Columbian Art
Publications: Lore, quarterly
Activities: Classes for adults and children; dramatic programs; docent training; films; demonstrations; lectr open to the public, 10 - 12 vis lectr per yr; tours; museum shop selling books, reproductions, prints, slides, jewelry, ethnic and crafts; junior museum
L **Library,** 800 Wells St, 53233. *Librn* Judith Turner
Open to public for reference only
Library Holdings: Vols 80,765; Per subs 850; Micro—Reels; Other—maps
Special Subjects: Antropology, Architecture, Decorative Arts, Ethnology

L **MILWAUKEE SCHOOL OF THE ARTS,** Library, 207 North Milwaukee St, Fifth Floor, 53202. *Librn* Malanie Herriges
Open Mon and Fri 8:30 AM - 5 PM, Tues, Wed and Thurs 8:30 AM - 8:30 PM. Estab 1976 as an Art and Design Library for the art school
Income: $5000

Purchases: $5000
Library Holdings: Vols 10,000; Per subs 35; AV—Kodachromes, slides; Other—Clipping files, exhibition catalogs, memorabilia, pamphlets, reproductions
Special Subjects: Art and Design

M MOUNT MARY COLLEGE, Tower Gallery, 2900 Menomonee River Parkway, 53222. Tel 414-258-4810. *Chmn* Sr M Regina Collins
Open Mon - Fri 8 AM - 4:30 PM, Sat & Sun 1 - 4 PM. No admis fee. Estab 1940 to provide both students and local community with exposure to art experiences and to provide artists, both estab professionals and aspirants with a showplace for their work
Income: Financed by private funds
Collections: Antique furniture, 16th Century and Victorian period; contemporary print collection; watercolors by Wisconsin artists
Exhibitions: Six exhibitions a year

UNIVERSITY OF WISCONSIN
M School of Fine Arts Galleries, 2400 E Kenwood Blvd, 53211. Tel 414-963-4946. *Dir* John Lloyd Taylor
Open Mon - Fri 10 AM - 4 PM; Wed 10 AM - 9 PM; Sun 1 - 4 PM; cl Sat & holidays. No admis fee. Estab 1967 to function as university museum
Income: Financed by state appropriation
Collections: †Large graphic collection, primarily 20th century; 19th and 20th century painting, sculpture, drawings and photography; Oriental art
Exhibitions: Permanent, temporary & traveling exhibitions; faculty, student & MFA shows
Publications: Catalogs
Activities: Lect; gallery talks; concerts; inter-museum loans
M Department of Art History Gallery, Mitchell Hall, 53201. Tel 414-963-4060. *Cur of Collections* Mark Chepp
Open Mon, Tues, Thurs & Fri 1 - 4 PM; Wed 6 - 9 PM. No admis fee. Estab 1964 to support gallery-museum for an academic department. Average Annual Attendance: 7500
Collections: Collection of Greek & Russian icons and liturgical objects; collection of prints, paintings and drawings from Renaissance to modern
Exhibitions: African Art from local collections; American Graphics of 1930's; Architecture of W R MacDonald; Japanese Woodcuts
Publications: Annual schedule of temporary exhibitions
Activities: Lect open to public, 1 vis lectr per yr; gallery talks; tours; individual paintings are lent to other galleries and museum; lending collection contains original art works and prints, paintings; book traveling exhibitions, 3 times per yr
M Union Art Gallery, 2200 E Kenwood Blvd, 53211. Tel 414-963-6310. *Gallery Mgr* Mary Zane Allen
Open Mon & Fri 10 AM - 5 PM; Tues & Thurs 10 AM - 8 PM. No admis fee. Estab 1971 to provide space for student art, primarily undergraduate, to be shown in group exhibits established by peer selection and apart from faculty selection
Income: Supported through student segregated fees
Exhibitions: Annual exhibit of alumni work; undergraduate and graduate student exhibits
Activities: Lect; gallery talks; competitions

O WISCONSIN PAINTERS AND SCULPTORS, INC, c/o Tom Uttech, 2582 N Cramer, 53211. Tel 414-964-3349. *VPres* Quido Brink; *Secy* Claudia Gorecki; *Treas* Muriel Mennen
Estab 1900 to promote and develop Wisconsin art. Mem: 150; dues $8 and up; annual meeting Nov
Exhibitions: Bi-annual exhibitions in April
Activities: Active program of exhibitions and lect in cooperation with the Art Center and allied groups in the state

NEENAH

M BERGSTROM ART CENTER AND MUSEUM, 165 N Park Ave, 54956. Tel 414-722-4808. *Dir* Alex Vance; *Cur* Geraldine Casper; *Secy* Kathy Smits
Open Wed - Fri 12 - 4:30 PM; Sat & Sun 1 - 4:30PM; June - Aug Tues 1 - 5 PM. No admis fee. Estab 1959 to provide cultural and educational benefits to the public. Average Annual Attendance: 29,000. Mem: 40; annual meeting Dec
Income: $70,000 (financed by endowment, state and county appropriations and gifts)
Collections: Evangeline Bergstrom Collection of Antique and Modern Glass Paperweights; †Ernst Mahler Collection of Germanic Glass; †Wisconsin and Midwestern Paintings; sculpture
Exhibitions: Monthly exhibitions in varied media
Publications: Museum Quarterly
Activities: Classes for adults and children; docent training; lect open to public, 6 vis lectr per yr; concerts; gallery talks; tours; exten dept serving an area of 50 mile radius; individual paintings and original objects of art lent to museums; museum shop selling books, original art, prints, ceramics, paperweights and needlework
L Library, 165 N Park Ave, 54956.
Open to the public for reference only
Library Holdings: Vols 2000; Per subs 10
Special Subjects: Art History, Glass

OSHKOSH

M OSHKOSH PUBLIC MUSEUM, 1331 Algoma Blvd, 54901. Tel 414-424-0452. *Pres of Board* James Cartwright; *Dir & Cur Art* John H Kuony; *Asst Dir & Cur Anthropology* Robert J Hruska; *Registrar* Brenda Hauber; *Cataloger* Lynn Hoffmann
Open Tues - Sat 9 AM - 5 PM; Sun 1 - 5 PM; cl Mon. No admis fee. Estab 1924 to collect and exhibit historical, Indian and natural history material relating to the area and fine and decorative arts. Museum housed in city owned mansion near University campus. Average Annual Attendance: 85,000
Income: Financed by city appropriation
Collections: †American artists and 18th century English portraits; †Indian artifacts; †pressed glass

Exhibitions: Monthly changing exhibits
Activities: Classes for adults and children; art school; lect; art fair; sales shop
L Library, 1331 Algoma Blvd, 54901. *Archivist* Kitty A Hobson
Open Tues 9 AM - 5 PM; Sun 1 - 5 PM. Estab 1923. Research for museum exhibits and general public. For reference only
Library Holdings: Vols 10,000; Per subs 30; Other—Clipping files, exhibition catalogs, pamphlets, photographs
Special Subjects: Wisconsin, Upper Midwest
Activities: Classes; lect

O PAINE ART CENTER AND ARBORETUM, 1410 Algoma St, PO Box 1097, 54901. Tel 414-235-4530. *Dir* Ralph A Bufano; *Cur Horticulture* Mark Streufert; *Dir Public Relations* Jean Peters; *Arboretum Mgr* Allen Singstock; *Cur Education* Connie Dempsey; *Cur Education* Marti Nurton; *Gift Shop Mgr* Lee Kester; *Cur Collections* Janet Rothe
Open Tues, Thurs, Sat & Sun 1 - 4:30 PM; from Memorial Day to Labor Day open Tues - Sun 1 - 4:30 PM; cl Mon and national holidays. Admis $1. Estab 1948 as a non-profit corporation to serve the needs of the upper midwest by showing fine and decorative arts and horticulture. Average Annual Attendance: 90,000. Mem: 600; dues $20
Income: Financed by endowment, membership and donations
Collections: American Glass; Chinese Collection; Decorative Arts; Icons; 19th Century English and French Paintings; Period Rooms; Oriental Rugs; Arburetum contains displays of native and exotic trees, shrubs and Herbacious plants
Exhibitions: American Antique Furniture; Antique Toys 1875-1950; Contemporary Polish Posters; English Brass Rubbings European Masters in Portraiture; Icons from Orthodox Church Museum of Finland; Retrospective: John McCrady
Publications: Catalogues; Helen Farnsworth Mears; newsletter, quarterly
Activities: Classes for adults; dramatic programs; docent training; lect open to public, 2 vis lectr per yr; concerts; gallery talks; tours; competitions; individual paintings and original objects of art lent to other museums and institutions; lending collection contains cassettes, original art works, original prints, paintings, photographs, sculptures and slides; traveling exhibitions organized and circulated; sales shop selling books, magazines, original art, reproductions and jewelry
L Art Reference Library, 1410 Algoma St, 54901.
Open Mon - Fri 8 AM - 5 PM upon request. Estab primarily for staff use as an art reference but also open to public. For reference only
Library Holdings: Vols 850; Per subs 30; Other—Exhibition catalogs
Special Subjects: Architecture, Decorative Arts, English furniture

M UNIVERSITY OF WISCONSIN, Allen Priebe Gallery, Arts and Communications Center, Corners of Elmwood & Woodland, 54901. Tel 414-424-0147. *Dir* David Hodge; *Asst to Dir* Jill Harycki
Open Mon - Fri 10 AM - 3 PM, Mon - Thurs 7 - 9PM, Sat & Sun 1 - 4 PM. No admis fee. Estab 1971 for the purpose of offering exhibits which appeal to a wide range of people. Gallery is 60 x 40 with additional wall space added with partitions, a skylight along back ceiling. Average Annual Attendance: 15,000
Income: Financed by student allocated monies
Purchases: $1500
Collections: Works Progress Administration Collection; †prints and drawings
Exhibitions: Art Teachers of Wisconsin
Activities: Classes for adults and children; lectures open to the public, 2 - 4 visiting lecturers per year; gallery talks; tours; competitions with awards; individual paintings and original objects of art lent to University staff, and area museums

PLATTEVILLE

M UNIVERSITY OF WISCONSIN, Harry Nohr Art Gallery, 53818. Tel 608-342-1398. *Dir* Richard Field
Open Mon - Sat 11 AM - 4 PM, Sun Noon - 4 PM. No admis fee. Estab 1978. Average Annual Attendance: 6000
Income: Financed by state appropriation
Purchases: $2000
Exhibitions: Seven State Annual 2-D
Activities: Lect open to public, 2 visiting lectr per year; competitions; purchase awards; book traveling exhibitions 5 per year

RACINE

O RACINE ART ASSOCIATION, 2519 Northwestern Ave, 53404. Tel 414-636-9177. *Pres of Board* Gerald P Ptacek; *VPres of Board* Richard J Carbonneau; *Treas of Board* Earl W Hammill; *Secy of Board* Edna M Olson; *Art Project Dir* Bruce Pepich; *Secy* Mildren Shields; *Education* Sylvester Jerry
Estab 1941 to foster and aid the establishment and development of public art galleries and museums, programs of education and training in the fine arts, and to develop public appreciation and enjoyment of the fine arts. Maintains an art gallery with six galleries. Mem: 400; dues $10 and up; annual meeting May
Income: $70,000 - $75,000 (financed by membership and fund raising)
Publications: Newsletter, quarterly
M Charles A Wustum Museum of Fine Arts, WI 53404. Tel 414-636-9177. *Art Dir* Bruce Pepich; *Cur Exhib* William Blaesing
Open Sun - Sat 1 - 5 PM & Mon & Thurs 5 - 9 PM. No admis fee. Estab 1940 to serve as cultural center for greater Racine community. There are five galleries in old (1856) residence converted for exhibition purposes. Average Annual Attendance: 40,000
Income: $150,000 (financed by endowment, city and county appropriations, private gifts and programs)
Purchases: $500 - $1000
Collections: Contemporary Wisconsin Watercolors; WPA Project paintings and prints
Exhibitions: Gladys Nilsson: Works on Paper; Studio Potters; Totems, Icons and Environments; Watercolor Wisconsin; Wisconsin Sculpture '79
Activities: Classes for adults and children; lect open to public, 3-6 vis lectr per yr; concerts; gallery talks; tours; competitions; exten dept serving Racine County; individual paintings and original objects of art lent to other institutions; lending

collection contains original art works, original prints; traveling exhibitions organized and circulated; museum shop selling original art

L **Wustum Art Library,** 53404.
Open Sun - Sat 1 - 5 PM & Mon & Thurs 5 - 9 PM. Estab 1941 to provide museum visitors and students with exposure to art history and instructional books. For reference only
Income: $75,000
Purchases: $75,000
Library Holdings: Vols 600; Per subs 11

RIPON

M **RIPON COLLEGE ART GALLERY,** Harwood Union Bldg, 54971. Tel 414-748-8110. *Dir* E M Breithaupt
Open Mon - Fri 9 AM - 4 PM. No admis fee. Estab 1965 to provide student body with changing exhibits. Average Annual Attendance: 4000
Collections: Paintings, print, sculpture, multi-media
Activities: Individual paintings lent to schools

RIVER FALLS

M **UNIVERSITY OF WISCONSIN,** Gallery 101, Cascade St, 54022. Tel 715-425-7803. *Gallery Dir* Michael Padgett
Open Mon - Fri 9 AM - 5 PM & 7 - 9 PM; Sat & Sun 1 - 5 PM. No admis fee. Estab 1973 to exhibit artists of regional and national prominence and for educational purposes. Maintains one gallery. Average Annual Attendance: 80,000
Income: $5000 (financed by state appropriation and student activities funds)
Collections: †National and International Artists; †Regional Artists; WPA Artists
Exhibitions: Area High School Exhibit; American Coverlets; Art Faculty Exhibit; Fine Arts Festival Prints and Drawings; Greater Christian Carnival; Paterick Dedication Exhibit; Senior Exhibit; Student Juried Exhibit; Student Photography Exhibit; Theme Exhibit; Kurt Wild; Womans Invitational WARM Gallery Members
Activities: Lect open to public; gallery talks

SHEBOYGAN

O **JOHN MICHAEL KOHLER ARTS CENTER,** 608 New York Ave, 53081. Tel 414-458-6144. *Dir* Ruth Kohler
Open Sun - Sat 12 - 5 PM, Mon 7 - 9 PM; cl national holidays. No admis fee. Estab 1967 to provide aesthetic and educational opportunities in the creative, visual and performing arts. Contains five exhibition galleries, theatre, four studio-classrooms, library, sales gallery. Average Annual Attendance: 110,000. Mem: 900; dues contributing membership categories $35 - $500 plus, family $22, individual $18, student $9
Collections: Contemporary American Crafts; European and American Decorative Arts; Kuehne Collection of Prehistoric Wisconsin Indian Artifacts; contemporary prints
Exhibitions: Major emphasis on 18 temporary exhibitions
Publications: Annual report; exhibition catalogues; newsletter, bimonthly
Activities: Classes for adults and children; summer theatre; lect; demonstrations; film series; concerts; tours; sales gallery
L **Library,** 608 New York Ave, 53081.
Contains art books and periodicals

WAUSAU

M **LEIGH YAWKEY WOODSON ART MUSEUM, INC,** 700 North 12th St, Franklin and Twelfth Sts, 54401. Tel 715-845-7010. *Pres* W F McCormick; *VPres* Alice Forester; *Secy* Helen Scholfield; *Dir* David J Wagner; *Cur* Thomas S Schleif; *Office Mgr* Marcia M Theel
Tues - Fri 9 Am - 5 PM, Sat & Sun 1 - 5 PM. No admis fee. Estab 1973 for acquisition of a creditable permanent collection of decorative art; program of changing exhibits; art education. 5455 net square feet of exhibition space; galleries on both first and second floors; parquet and carpeted floors; 377 running feet in galleries. Average Annual Attendance: 30,000. Mem: 100; dues $225
Income: $150,000 (financed by membership and private foundation)
Purchases: $20,000
Collections: †Decorative arts of porcelain highlighted by a complete collection of Dorothy Doughty porcelain birds and historical period pieces of Royal Worcester; †20th century art glass featuring Victorian glass baskets, Art Noveau and Art Deco; †wildlife theme paintings and wood sculptures with birds as the main subject
Exhibitions: African Artists in America; Americans in Glass; Chinese Decorative Art of the Ch'ing Dynasty; Photographs by Henri Cartier-Bresson; Louis M Eilshemius; Japanese Prints; Pre-Columbian Art; Student Art Exhibition; Third Annual Bird Art Exhibition
Publications: Exhibition catalogs and brochures
Activities: Docent training; docent visits to lectures and exhibitions at other museums; lectures open to the public, four visiting lecturers per year; gallery talks; tours; competitions for participation in exhibitions; certificates of merit and art supply gift certificates to Student Art Exhibition participants and winners; Scholarships; individual paintings and original objects of art lent to recognized museums and art centers; lending collection contains cassettes, motion pictures, and slides; book eight traveling exhibitions per year; traveling exhibitions organized and circulated to Western Association of Art Museums; National Collection of Fine Arts; Midwest Museums and art centers; historical societies
L **Leigh Yawkey Woodson Art Library,** 54401.
Open by appointment. Estab 1976. For reference only
Income: $1500
Purchases: $1500
Library Holdings: Vols 500; Per subs 20; AV—Cassettes, motion pictures, slides; Other—Clipping files, exhibition catalogs, pamphlets

WEST BEND

M **WEST BEND GALLERY OF FINE ARTS,** 300 S Sixth Ave, PO Box 426, 53095. Tel 414-334-9638. *Pres* Joan Pick; *Executive Dir* E G Kocher; *Executive Secy* F J Derer
Open Wed - Sun 1 - 4:30 PM; cl Mon & Tues. No admis fee. Estab 1961 to encourage the varied art interests of the community. The large colonial style building contains eight gallery exhibit rooms and three basement art classrooms. Average Annual Attendance: 5500. Mem: 450; annual meeting Feb
Income: Financed by endowment, membership and donations
Purchases: $2000
Collections: Carl von Marr Collection; †current Wisconsin art
Exhibitions: Monthly exhibitions; annual show
Publications: Bulletin, monthly
Activities: Classes for adults and children; lect open to public, 8 vis lectr per yr; gallery talks; tours; competitions; individual paintings lent to business organizations; lending collection contains books and paintings
L **Library,** 300 S Sixth Ave, 53095.
Open to members only
Library Holdings: Vols 300; Per subs 4

WYOMING

BIG HORN

M **BRADFORD BRINTON MEMORIAL RANCH MUSEUM,** State Rd 335, PO Box 23, 82833. Tel 307-672-3173. *Dir* James Taylor Forrest; *Asst Dir* Dan Nelson; *Asst Dir* Osea Nelson
Open May 15 - Labor Day daily 9 AM - 5 PM. No admis fee. Estab 1961 to show a typical well-to-do ranch of the area of northern Wyoming as established in the late 19th century. Two galleries and house museum are maintained. Average Annual Attendance: 13,000
Income: $100,000 (financed by endowment)
Collections: Plains Indians Artifacts; Western American Art by Frederic Remington and Charles M Russell; American art and a few pieces of European art, largely of the 19th and 20th century; china; furniture; silver
Exhibitions: American Quilts; Art of Bill Gallings
Publications: Monographs on artists in the collection from time to time
Activities: Sales shop selling books, original art, reproductions, prints and slides
L **Library,** State Rd 335, 82833.
Open to staff and to the public by appointment
Library Holdings: Vols 1200

CASPER

M **NICOLAYSEN ART MUSEUM,** (Formerly Central Wyoming Museum of Art) 104 Rancho Rd, 82601. Tel 307-235-3347. *Chmn Board* Jan Larimer; *Vice Chmn* Norma Howard; *Secy* Mary Velous; *Dir* Jody L Lillen
Open Tues - Sun 11:30 AM - 4:30 PM. No admis fee. Estab 1967 to exhibit nationwide traveling exhibits and educate through Museum Art classes and workshops. One main exhibition area 2500 - 3000 sq ft. Average Annual Attendance: 12,000. Mem: Annual meeting first Friday in September
Income: $40,234 (financed by membership, Wyoming Council for the Arts, contributions)
Collections: Matesse prints (lithographs); Joseph Mugnaini Intaglio print; Montana Naegel, watercolor; Stephen Naegel, watercolor; Russian Sculpture
Publications: Newsletter; brochures
Activities: Classes for adults and children; lectures open to the public; tours; lending collection contains original art works, original prints, paintings, sculpture; museum sales shop sells original art, reproductions, and regional artwork

CHEYENNE

O **WYOMING COUNCIL ON THE ARTS,** 122 W 25th St, State of Wyoming, 82002. *Chmn* Peter Hassrick; *VChmn* Donna Dickson; *Executive Dir* John Buhler; *Dir of Programs* David J Fraher; *Artists in Residence Coordr* Steven P Smith; *Information Officer* Laurie Kutchins
Open Mon - Fri 8 AM - 5 PM. Estab 1967 to encourage the study and presentation of all the arts; develop interest and participation in the arts; to raise standards of local art groups. The Council grants funds to local groups for various activities. Mem: 10, membership appointed by the Governor; meeting quarterly
Income: $380,000 (financed by federal grants and state appropriation)
Publications: Artist in Residence brochure, annually; Calendar; Wyoming Council on the Arts Newsletter, bi-monthly
Activities: Artists in Residence provides visual artists, craftsmen, poets-writers, musicians, dancers, filmmakers and actors-actresses in residence for schools and communities

M **WYOMING STATE ART GALLERY,** Barrett Building, 82002. Tel 307-777-7519. *Dir Wyoming State Archives, Museums and Historical Department* Vincent P Foley
Open Mon - Fri 8 AM - 5 PM; Sat 9 AM - 5 PM. No admis fee. Estab 1969 to collect, preserve and to exhibit the work of Wyoming and Western artists. Average Annual Attendance: 50,000
Income: Financed by state appropriation
Collections: Works by Wyoming and Western artists

CODY

O **BUFFALO BILL MEMORIAL ASSOCIATION,** PO Box 1000, 82414. Tel 307-587-4771. *Chmn* Mrs Henry H R Coe; *Secy* Melvin C McGee; *Dir* Peter H

Hassrick; *Executive Secy* Joyce Mayer; *Cur Plains Indian Museum* George P Horse Capture; *Cur Winchester Museum* Richard Rattenbury; *Cur Buffalo Bill Museum* Richard I Frost

Open daily Sept - May 8 AM - 5 PM; June - Aug 7 AM - 10 PM. Admis varies; group rates. Estab 1917 to preserve and exhibit art, artifacts and memorabilia of the Old West; to operate Buffalo Bill Museum, Plains Indian Museum, Whitney Gallery of Western Art and Winchester Firearms Museum

Income: $150,000 (financed by admissions and private funds)

M **Whitney Gallery of Western Art,** PO Box 1000, 82414.
   Collections: Catlin, Bierstadt, Miller, Remington, Russell and all documentary artists of the Old West
   Exhibitions: Annual exhibition of prominent contemporary Western artists; loan exhibitions
   Activities: Gallery talks; sales shop selling books, prints, Indian artifacts and postcards

L **Gallery Library,** PO Box 1000, 82414.
   Open to the public for reference only
   Library Holdings: Vols 2000; Other—Photographs

O **CODY COUNTRY ART LEAGUE,*** 836 Sheridan Ave, 82414. Tel 307-587-3597. *Pres* Mrs George W Tresler; *Dir* Mrs Gordon Way
   Open Noon - 8 PM. No admis fee. Estab 1964 for promotion of artistic endeavor among local and area artists; also established for exhibits, displays and sales. Average Annual Attendance: 15,000. Mem: 115; dues $10; annual meeting Dec
   Income: $18,365 (financed by endowment, membership, grants from Wyoming Council on the Arts, yearly auction, and sponsors)
   Purchases: $18,064
   Collections: One work each by Nicholas Eggenhoffer and Robert Myers
   Exhibitions: Western States Art Exhibit ($500 purchase award and over $1000 in other prizes); one-man shows
   Activities: Classes for adults and children; dramatic programs; films; workshops; lect open to public, 2-3 visiting lectrs per year; competitions

DUBOIS

O **WIND RIVER VALLEY ARTISTS GUILD,** Box 26, 82513. *Pres* Fred S Finley Jr; *VPres* John Murdock; *Secy* Margaret Mabbott
   Estab 1948 to promote art and interest in art and to hold an annual exhibit of Art Works. Mem: 186; dues $5
   Income: Financed by membership and patrons
   Collections: †Fremont County Library Collection; WRVAG Permanent Collection
   Exhibitions: Annual National Art Exhibit
   Publications: Newsletter, 6 times a year
   Activities: Workshops; competitions with cash awards

LARAMIE

M **UNIVERSITY OF WYOMING,** Art Museum, Fine Arts Building, 19th St and Willett St, 82071. Tel 307-766-2374. *Dir* James T Forrest; *Cur Collections* Jerry A Berger; *Cur Exhib* William A Little Jr
   Open Sun - Fri 1:30 - 5 PM during spring and fall semester; Sun - Fri 1 - 4:30 PM during summer sessions; cl holidays. Estab 1968 to serve as an art resource center for faculty, students and the general public; the museum serves as a training ground for students interested in museums as a profession. Exhibition space consists of two galleries totaling 5625 sq ft; work room, receiving room, storage vault, offices and outdoor sculpture court. Average Annual Attendance: 12,000. Mem: 300; dues $10 and up
   Income: $75,000 (financed by state appropriation and friends organization)
   Purchases: $2500
   Collections: 19th and 20th century European paintings, graphics and sculpture; 19th century American paintings, graphics and sculpture; 20th century American †paintings, †graphics and †sculpture
   Exhibitions: Special exhibits from the permanent collections as well as traveling exhibitions on a regular basis during the fall and spring semesters; faculty shows; student shows
   Publications: Annual report; exhibition catalogs
   Activities: Lect open to the public, 6 vis lectr per yr; gallery talks; tours; individual paintings and original objects of art lent to other museums; lending collection contains 2000 original art works, 1100 original prints and 900 paintings; originates traveling exhibitions

RIVERTON

M **CENTRAL WYOMING COLLEGE,** Dobler Room, Box 1520, 82501. Tel 307-856-9291. *Cultural Affairs Coordr* John Metzke
   Open Mon - Fri 8 AM - 5 PM. No admis fee. Estab 1966 to allow local artists and students to display works and to make traveling exhibitions available to the general public. The Dobler Room is a reading room. Average Annual Attendance: 500
   Activities: Classes for adults and children; dramatic programs; lectures open to the public, four visiting lecturers per year; concerts; gallery talks; student art contests; scholarships; lending collection contains books, cassettes, film strips and slides; book four traveling exhibitions per year

L **Central Wyoming College Library,** Box 1520, 82501. *Librn* Tom Humphrey
   Open Mon - Fri 8 AM - 5 PM, 7 - 10 PM, Sun 2 - 6 PM. Established 1966. For lending and reference
   Library Holdings: Vols 1300; Per subs 18; Micro—Fiche; AV—Cassettes, fs, slides; Other—Exhibition catalogs, original art works, sculpture

ROCK SPRINGS

O **SWEETWATER COMMUNITY FINE ARTS CENTER,** 400 C St, 82901. Tel 307-382-4599. *Dir* Allen L Keeney; *Secy* Diane V Beckwith; *Finance Officer* Mary Kornitnik
   Open Mon - Fri 1 - 5 PM & 6:30 - 8:30 PM; Sat 2 - 5 PM; cl Sun. No admis fee. Estab 1966 to house permanent art collection and hold various exhibits during the year; Halseth Gallery houses permanent art collection. Average Annual Attendance: Approx 5000
   Income: Financed by endowment, city appropriation and county funds
   Collections: †Rock Springs High School permanent collection
   Exhibitions: Monthly
   Publications: Calendar of events, two or three a year
   Activities: Classes for adults; dramatic programs; concerts; competitions

PACIFIC ISLANDS

PAGO PAGO, AMERICAN SAMOA

M **JEAN P HAYDON MUSEUM,** PO Box 1540, 96799. Tel 809-633-4347. *Chmn Board of Trustees* Palauni Tuiasosopo; *Executive Dir* Enosa Pili; *Cur* Fa'ailoilo Lauvao
   Open Mon - Fri 10 AM - 4 PM, Sat 10 AM - Noon. No admis fee. Estab 1971 for preservation of Samoan culture, history and custom. New extension of the museum is an Art Gallery displaying local artists work and student arts
   Income: Financed by city or state appropriations and grants from NEA
   Collections: Natural Sciences; Polynesian Artifacts; Samoan Village Life; US Navy History

L **Library,** PO Box 1540, 96799.
   Reference library
   Library Holdings: AV—Slides; Other—Photographs, 16 mm films
   Collections: Photograph Collection

PUERTO RICO

PONCE

M **MUSEO DE ARTE DE PONCE,** Ponce Art Museum, The Luis Ferre Foundation. (Mailing Add: Avenida de las Americas, PO Box 1492, Ponce, PR 00731) *Dir* Dr Rene Taylor; *Asst to Dir* Haydee Venegas; *Conservator* Anton Konrad
   Open Mon & Wed - Fri 10 AM - Noon and 1 - 4 PM, Sun 10 AM - 5 PM, cl Tues. Admis adult $1, children 50¢. Estab to exhibit a representative collection of European paintings and sculpture; Puerto Rican art. Seven hexagonal galleries on upper floor; three rectangular galleries on lower floor. Mem: 600; dues $15
   Income: Financed by endowment and membership
   Collections: African, Latin American, Pre-Columbian and Puerto Rican Santos Art; 19th Century art, contemporary art, 14th - 18th Century paintings and sculpture
   Exhibitions: (1978-79) Retrospective of Puerto Rican Artist Lorenzo Homar; Modern Tapestries by Luis Cienfuegos
   Activities: Lect open to public, 2 - 3 visiting lectr per year; concerts; tours; individual paintings and original objects of art lent to other museums; museum shop sells books, original art, reproductions, prints, slides and plaster copies of Pre-Columbian artifacts

L **Library,** Avenida de las Americas, PO Box 1492, 00731. *Librn* Ana Zayas
   Open for reference
   Library Holdings: Vols 4000; Per subs 4

RIO PIEDRAS

M **UNIVERSITY OF PUERTO RICO,** Museum of Archaeology, History and Art,* 00931. Tel 809-764-0000. *Dir* Dr Arturo V Davila; *Cur Archaeology* Luis A Chanlatte; *Cur Art* Pedro J Gispert
   Open Mon - Fri 9 AM - 9 PM, Sat & Sun 8 AM - 3:30 PM, cl national holidays. No admis fee. Estab 1940
   Collections: Archaeology; Puerto Rican paintings of the past and present; sculpture
   Exhibitions: Temporary exhibitions from the collection and from museum loans
   Activities: Lect; guided tours; concerts

SAN JUAN

M **ATENEO PUERTORRIQUENO,*** Ponce de Leon, Stop One, 00902. Tel 809-725-1265. *Pres Board Trusts* O'Siris Delgado
   Open Mon - Fri 9 AM - 9 PM, Sat 9 AM - 5 PM, cl Sun & holidays. No admis fee. Estab 1876. Mem: Dues $12
   Collections: Decorative arts; drawings; historical material; prints; Puerto Rican paintings; sculpture
   Exhibitions: Temporary exhibitions
   Publications: Annual catalogs; reports
   Activities: Lect; gallery talks; guided tours; films; concerts; dance recitals; competitions; dramas; book shop

L **Library,*** Ponce de Leon, Stop One, 00902. *Librn* Delia Lourido
   Library Holdings: Vols 12,000

M INSTITUTE OF PUERTO RICAN CULTURE, Museo de Bellas Artes, Museum of Fine Arts. (Mailing Add: Calle del Santo Cristo de la Salud 253, San Juan, PR 00915) Tel 809-723-2320. *Executive Dir* Luis M Rodirquez Morales; *Dir Program Fine Arts* Maria E Somoza; *Adminr* Raul Joglar
Open 9 AM - 5 PM. No admis fee. Estab 1977 for the exhibition of paintings and sculptures of Puerto Rican artists in a chronological way from 18th - 20th Centuries
Income: Financed by state appropriation
Collections: Campeche-Oller Hall - religious and profane paintings of these two painters; 1900 Hall - exhibition of paintings of the period by Oscar Colon Delgado, Ramon Frade and Miguel Pou; Primitive Paintings Hall - works of Manuel Hernandez; documental and folklorical painting of the history of Puerto Rico; contemporary artists
Exhibitions: Works from permanent collection
Activities: Lect open to public; gallery talks; tours; exten dept; individual paintings and original objects of art lent to educational and cultural organizations and government offices; lending collection contains original art works, original prints, paintings; originate traveling exhibitions

O INSTITUTO DE CULTURA PUERTORRIQUENA, Institute of Puerto Rican Culture,* 98 AV Norzagaray, 00901. Tel 809-724-0700. *Exec Dir* Luis M Rodriquez Morales
Open Mon - Sun 8 AM - Noon & 1 - 5 PM. No admis fee. Estab 1955 to stimulate, promote, divulge and enrich Puerto Rico's cultural and historical heritage. The Institute has created 16 museums around the island and has five more in preparation, including museums of historical collections, art museums and archaeological museums
Income: Financed by endowment, and state appropriation
Collections: Puerto Rican art, archaeology and historical collections
Publications: Revista del Instituto de Cultura Puertorriquena, quarterly
Activities: Educ dept; lect open to public; gallery talks; concerts; tours; competitions; exten dept serving cultural centers around the Island; artmobile; individual paintings and original objects of art lent to Government agencies, universities and cultural centers; lending collection contains motion pictures, original art works, original prints, paintings, photographs; traveling exhibitions organized and circulated; sales shop selling books, records and craft items; junior museum
L General Library of Puerto Rico,* Avenida Ponce de Leon 500, 00905. *Librn* Miguel A Nieves
Open for reference to public, investigators and students
Collections: Pre-Columbian Archaeological Collection

M LA CASA DEL LIBRO, House of Books, Calle del Cristo 255, 00901. Tel 809-723-0354. *Pres* Rafael Fabregas; *VPres* Max Goldman; *Treas* Miguel A Ferrer; *Dir* David Jackson McWilliams
Open Mon - Fri 11 AM - 5 PM, Sat 2 - 5 PM. No admis fee. Estab 1955 as a museum-library devoted to the history and arts of the book and related graphic arts. Average Annual Attendance: 14,000. Mem: 350; dues $10 and up
Income: $26,000 (financed by membership and state appropriation)
Collections: Bibliography of graphic arts; binding; book illustration; calligraphy; early printing, especially 15th and 16th Century Spanish; modern fine printing; papermaking
Exhibitions: Gallery has displays on the first floor relating to printing and other arts of the book, such as: Bookplates, The Boundaries of the World, Concrete Poetry, Editions of the Quixote, Fifteen Years of Posters at La Casa del Libro, The Illustrated Book in Puerto Rico, Objetivos de Julio Plaza, Original Art Work for the Emperor's New Clothes, Por los Caminos del Dia, Printing of Music in Books, Spanish Incunables
Activities: Classes for adults; visits from school groups; students of library science and workers in graphic arts; material available, no fees; lect open to public; gallery talks; original objects of printing arts, material must be used on premises; originate traveling exhibitions; book shop
L Library, Calle del Cristo 255, 00901.
5000 items

SANTURCE

M MUSEO HISTORICO DE PUERTO RICO INC, 1396 Giorgetti St, 00909. Tel 809-725-4426. *Pres* Rosa G Coll Vidal; *VPres* Josefina Villafine; *Secy* Alba Raquel
Open 8:30 AM - 11:30 AM and 1 PM - 3 PM. Admis 50¢ and 25¢. Estab 1969 to study Puerto Rican art, culture and history. Twenty three rooms. Average Annual Attendance: 2000. Mem: Annual dues $100
Income: $10,000 (financed by state appropriation)
Collections: Puerto Rican painters
Exhibitions: Permanent exhibitions
Activities: Classes for children; docent training; lectures open to the public; gallery talks; tours; original objects of art lent to the government and to other museums

National and Regional Organizations In Canada

O **ASSOCIATION OF CANADIAN INDUSTRIAL DESIGNERS, ONTARIO,** 55 University Ave, Suite 600, Toronto, ON M5J 2H7. Tel 416-862-1799. *Admin Secy* Audrey Shaw
Estab 1948 to promote and foster a high standard of design in industrial products as a service to the public, the manufacturing industries, and the national culture and economy. Mem: 87; dues $125; annual meeting Jan

O **CANADIAN CONFERENCE OF THE ARTS,** 141 Laurier Ave W, Suite 707, Ottawa, ON K1P 5J3. Tel 613-238-3561. *National Dir* John Hobday; *Treas* Russell Disney; *Secy* John A Paterson
Estab 1945 to encourage and to advance the role of the arts and culture in Canada's national life, and to serve the interests of Canadian artists and the Canadian public. Mem: 1150; dues individuals $20, organizations based on budget: annual meeting May
Income: Financed by membership and grants
Publications: Arts Bulletin; Handbook Series: Who We Are, Who's Who, Who Does What, Who's Got the Money, updated annually
Activities: Awards Diplome d'Honneur to persons who have contributed outstanding service to the arts in Canada

O **CANADIAN CRAFTS COUNCIL,** Conseil Canadien de l'Artisanat, 16-46 Elgin St, Ottawa, ON K1P 5K6. Tel 613-235-8200. *Exec Dir* Peter H Weinrich; *Pres* Ann Mortimer; *VPres* Joan Chalmers; *Secy* Anthony Ibbotson
Open Mon - Fri 9 AM - 5 PM. Estab 1974 to encourage the highest quality Canadian crafts and improve standards of craftsmen through education and information. Mem: 25,000; dues individuals $20; annual meeting Oct
Income: $100,000 - $250,000 (financed by membership and federal appropriation)
Collections: †Massey Foundation Collection of Contemporary Canadian Crafts
Exhibitions: Canadian Cultural Centre, Paris and Other European Centres; Artisan '78; traveling exhibition
Publications: Artisan, bimonthly
Activities: Originate traveling exhibitions
L **Library,** 16-46 Elgin St, K1P 5K6.
Open to the public for reference only
Library Holdings: Vols 700; Per subs 40; AV—A-tapes, v-tapes; Other—Exhibition catalogs, pamphlets
Special Subjects: Crafts

O **CANADIAN MUSEUMS ASSOCIATION,** Association des Musees Canadiens, 331 Cooper St, Suite 400, Ottawa, ON K2P 0G5. Tel 613-233-5653. *Pres* Dr George MacBeath; *VPres* Dr George Lammers; *Secy* Pierre Lachapelle; *Executive Dir* R Lynn Ogden; *Head Training & Standards* Mary-Lou Brown
Estab 1947 to advance public museum services in Canada, to promote the welfare and better administration of museums, and to foster a continuing improvement in the qualifications and practices of museum professions. Mem: 1800; dues $25 - $500; annual meeting first week of June
Income: Financed by membership, and government grants
Publications: Gazette, quarterly; Museogramme, monthly
Activities: Correspondence course in basic museology; bursary program; travel grants; book sales
L **Library,** 331 Cooper St, Suite 400, K2P 0G5. *Library Technician* Micheline M Boucher
Open for reference only
Library Holdings: Vols 1300; Per subs 108
Special Subjects: Museology

O **CANADIAN SOCIETY FOR EDUCATION THROUGH ART,*** Faculty of Education, University of Regina, Regina, SK S4S 0A2. Tel 306-584-4546. *Pres* John M Emerson; *Secy General* Dr Les Groome
Estab 1954 to promote art education in Canada. Average Annual Attendance: 300. Mem: 1000; dues professional $20, affiliate $2; annual meeting Oct
Income: Financed by membership
Publications: Journal; Newsletter, quarterly; Research Bulletin
Activities: Workshops; research; annual conference; scholarships

O **CANADIAN SOCIETY OF PAINTERS IN WATERCOLOUR,** c/o Julius Griffith, 102 Hillsdale Ave W, Toronto, ON M5P 2G3. *Pres* Julius Griffith; *Secy* Aimee Millin
Exhibitions: (1980) 55th Annual Exhibition

O **MARITIME ART ASSOCIATION,** c/o Allan Rankin, PO Box 1378, Summerside, PE C1N 4K2. *Pres* Allan Rankin; *Treas* Frank M Gillard
Estab 1934 to coordinate work of art societies in New Brunswick, Newfoundland, Nova Scotia and Prince Edward Island. Mem: 13 societies paying corporate dues of $25; annual meeting May.
Member Organizations: Conseil Acadien de Cooperation Culturele, Moncton, NB; Fredericton Art Club, NB; Fredericton Society of Artists, NB; Moncton Art Society Inc, NB; St Andrews Music, Art and Drama Club, NB; Woodstock Art Club, NB; Art Society of Newfoundland and Labrador, St John's, NF; Acadia University Art Gallery, Wolfville, NS; Contemporary Art Society, Halifax, NS; Dartmouth Heritage Museum, NS; Town of Amherst, NS; Western Counties Regional Library, Yarmouth, NS; Yarmouth Art Society, NS; plus individual members
Activities: Lect tours; lending collection contains lantern slides; regional and traveling exhibitions organized

O **PRINTING AND DRAWING COUNCIL OF CANADA,*** c/o Visual Arts Ontario, 417 Queen's Quay W, Toronto, ON M5V 1A2.
Estab 1977, following merger of the Society of Canadian Painter-Etchers and Engravers and the Canadian Society of Graphic Arts. Maintains three print cabinets in Royal Ontario Museum, Toronto; Public Library and Museum, London, Ontario; University of Toronto
Exhibitions: Annual exhibition in March
Activities: Administers G A Reid Silver Memorial Award, Nicholas Hornyansky Memorial Award; maintains Archives and Prints of 3-4 purchase awards per year; originate traveling exhibitions

O **PROFESSIONAL ART DEALERS ASSOCIATION OF CANADA,** 65 Queen St W, Suite 1800, Toronto, ON M5H 2M5. Tel 416-868-1540. *Pres* John K Robertson; *Admin VPres* Aaron M Milrad; *VPres* Avrom Isaacs; *Secy* Albert White
Estab 1966 to further art in Canada. Mem: 48, members must have five years in operation plus approved reputation, general exhibitions, financial integrity; dues $200; annual meeting May
Income: Financed by membership and appraisal fees
Publications: General information brochure
Activities: Scholarships

O **ROYAL ARCHITECTURAL INSTITUTE OF CANADA,** 151 Slater St, Suite 1104, Ottawa, ON K1P 5H3. Tel 613-232-7165. *Pres* Gilbert R Beatson; *Pres-Elect* David Hambleton; *Executive VPres* Robbin Elliott
Open 9 AM - 5 PM. Estab 1908 to promote a knowledge and appreciation of architecture and of the architectural profession in Canada and to represent the interests of Canadian architects
Publications: RAIC Directory, annually
L **Library,** 151 Slater St, Suite 1104, K1P 5H3.
Special Subjects: Architecture, building and construction

O **ROYAL CANADIAN ACADEMY OF ARTS,** 601-11 Yorkville Ave, Toronto, ON M4W 1L3. Tel 416-922-5535. *Pres* John C Parkin; *VPres* David Blackwood; *Executive Dir* Rebecca Sisler
Estab 1880 to better the visual arts field in Canada through exhibitions. Mem: 550; membership open to visual artists concerned with excellence in their own medium; dues $50; annual meeting late Nov
Income: Non-profit association financed by membership
Exhibitions: Special exhibitions of the History of the Royal Canadian Academy 1880-1980
Publications: History of the Royal Canadian Academy 1880-1980; Newsletter
Activities: Originate traveling exhibitions

O **SCULPTOR'S SOCIETY OF CANADA,*** c/o Visual Arts Ontario, 417 Queen's Quay W, Toronto, ON M5V 1A2. Tel 416-366-1607. *Pres* Irene Blogg; *Secy* Betty Moss
Estab 1928 to promote the art of sculpture; to present exhibitions (some to travel internationally); to educate the public about sculpture. Mem: 107, qualifications: professional sculptor; dues $25; meetings once a month
Income: $10,000 (financed by membership, provincial appropriation and sales commission)
Activities: Workshops; lect open to public

O **SOCIETY OF CANADIAN ARTISTS,** c/o Visual Arts Ontario, 417 Queen's Way W, Toronto, ON M5V 1A2.
Estab in 1957 as the Society of Cooperative Artists and operated the first cooperative gallery in Toronto. In 1967 the name was changed to the Society of Canadian Artists and the gallery moved to larger premises. In 1968 the members elected to give up the gallery and concentrate on organizing group art shows for members in galleries across Canada. Mem: 120, membership by jury, open to artists throughout Canada
Income: Financed by membership, and local grants
Exhibitions: (1978) Royal Bank Plaza, Toronto; Muttart Gallery, Calgary. (1979) Birmingham Festival of the Arts, Alabama; Merton Gallery, Toronto. (1980) Tour to Northern Ontario Galleries; Merton Gallery, Toronto
Publications: Two Decades, members' biographical catalog
Activities: Audioslide presentations; sponsorship of art conferences; promotion of Canadian artists; originate traveling exhibitions

O **UNIVERSITIES ART ASSOCIATION OF CANADA,** 4700 Keele St, York Univ, Dept of Visual Arts, Downsview, ON M3J 1P3. Tel 416-667-3498. *Pres* Eric Cameron; *Secy & Treas* Joyce Zemans

Estab to offer forum for meeting and discussion of common issues and goals amongst university art programs in Canada. Mem: 300; qualifications for mem, a faculty member of a university or college of art in Canada; dues $20; annual meeting Spring

Income: Financed by federal and provincial appropriation

Publications: RACAR (Revue d'artes canadienne), twice annually; University Art Association Journal, quarterly

Museums, Libraries and Associations In Canada

ALBERTA

BANFF

M **BANFF CENTRE,** Walter Phillips Gallery,* PO Box 1020, T0L 0C0. Tel 403-762-3391. *Cur* Barry Morrison; *Asst Cur* Lorne Falk
Open daily 1 - 5 PM. No admis fee. Estab 1977 to serve the community and students of the visual arts department at the Banff Centre, School of Fine Arts. Gallery is 15.24 x 21.34 m with 60.96 m of running space. Average Annual Attendance: 15,000
Income: Financed by provincial and public funding
Collections: Contemporary works; Group of Seven; Walter J Phillips Collection
Exhibitions: Banff Centre Faculty Exhibition; Dennis Burton; Lee Freelander; Southwest Indian Art; Tatsuzo Shimaoka
Activities: Lect open to public; individual paintings and original objects of art lent
L **Library,*** PO Box 1020, T0L 0C0. *Librn* Betty Macaulay

M **PETER AND CATHARINE WHYTE FOUNDATION,** Peter Whyte Gallery, 111 Bear St, Box 160, T0L 0C0. Tel 403-762-2291. *Pres* Cliff White; *Adminr & Head Archivist* E J Hart
No admis fee. Estab 1968 to preserve and collect materials of importance in the Canadian Rocky Mountain regions; to exhibit, publish and make material available for research, study and appreciation. Total exhibit space: 224 running ft, 1504 sq ft. Average Annual Attendance: 75,000
Income: Financed by endowment, state appropriation, federal and provincial special activities grants
Purchases: $1500
Collections: Canadian Artists, particularly Western Canadian, such as Belmore Browne, Illingworth Kerr, Walter Phillips, Sandy Spencer, Takao Tanabe, Catharine Whyte, Peter Whyte
Exhibitions: Approximately 47 per year: local, regional and national interest; ceramics, paintings, photographs, sculpture, textiles both historic and contemporary. One gallery contains works from the permanent collection at all times and changing
Publications: The Cairn, quarterly
Activities: Lect open to public, 10 visiting lectr per year; concerts; gallery talks; tours; individual paintings and original objects of art lent to accredited art galleries and museums; lending collection contains 2000 original art works, 500 original prints, 2000 paintings, 100 sculptures; book traveling exhibitions; originate traveling exhibitions; sales shop sells books, reproductions, note cards (all items sold pertain to the Foundation only)
L **Peter Whyte Gallery Library,** 111 Bear St, PO Box 160, T0L 0C0. *Librn* Mary Andrews
Open Tues & Sat 10 AM - 5 PM, Wed - Fri 1 - 9 PM, Sun 1 - 5 PM. For reference only
Library Holdings: Vols 563; Other—Clipping files, exhibition catalogs

CALGARY

M **ALBERTA COLLEGE OF ART GALLERY,** 1301 - 16th Ave NW, T2M 0L4. Tel 403-284-8661. *Head* Ken Sturdy; *Adminr* Robert Douglas; *Academic Supv* Richard Halliday; *Sr Cur* Valerie Greenfield
Open Mon - Fri Noon - 8 PM, Sat 2 - 5 PM, cl Sun & holidays. No admis fee. Estab 1958 as an academic-didactic function plus general visual art exhibition service to public. Two galleries: 450 sq meters of floor space; 131 meters running wall space; full atmospheric and security controls
Collections: Permanent collection of ceramics, graphics, paintings, photography, student honors work
Exhibitions: Local, provincial, national and international National Gallery of Canada; Western Association of Art Museums, North American public and commercial gallery offerings; monthly catalogues
Publications: Exhibition catalogs
Activities: Lect open to public, 20 visiting lectr per year; book traveling exhibitions
L **Library,** 1301 - 16th Ave NW, T2M 0L4. *Library Supv* Mike Parkinson; *Slide Librn* Joan Cuddy
Open Mon - Thurs 8 AM - 10 PM, Fri 8 AM - 4:45 PM, Sat 10 AM - 5 PM. Estab 1972 to support college academic and studio programs. Circ 45,000
Purchases: $25,000
Library Holdings: Vols 550; Per subs 70; AV—Cassettes, fs, lantern slides, motion pictures, slides, v-tapes; Other—Clipping files, exhibition catalogs, pamphlets, reproductions
Collections: Art History and Studio (40,000 slides)

O **ALBERTA SOCIETY OF ARTISTS,** Alberta College of Art,* 1301 17th Ave, Room S545, T2M 0L4. Tel 403-289-6641. *Pres* Barbara Roe Hicklin
Estab 1931 as an association of professional artists designed to foster and promote the development of visual and plastic fine arts primarily within the province. Mem:

Approx 100; dues $15; annual meeting May
Publications: Highlights (newsletter), bimonthly

O **CALGARY ARTISTS SOCIETY,** c/o James Jones, 1024 First Ave NW, T3E 1A5. Tel 403-283-0605. *Pres* James Jones; *Secy* Alice Christenson; *Treas* Lynn Wheadon
Estab 1965 to foster and improve standard of art of members and community. Mem: 40; dues $15; monthly meeting first Thurs
Income: $1000 (financed by membership)
Collections: Muttart Gallery Mount Royal College, Group Exhibitions Juried Show, bi-annual
Activities: Lect for members only; gallery talks; competitions; monthly cirtique of current work of members

M **GLENBOW MUSEUM,** Nine Ave & First St SE, T2G 0P3. Tel 403-264-8300. *Chmn of Board* Jane Edwards; *Controller & Corporate Secy* C S Tomsik; *Dir* Duncan F Cameron; *Chief Cur* H A Dempsey; *Cur of Art* Jeffrey Spalding; *Cur of Cultural History* Ron Getty; *Cur of Ethnology* Julia Harrison; *Head Extension & Education* Joyce Gibson; *Mgr Museum Shop* Martha Bailey; *Head Security* L Lockhart
Open daily 11 AM - 9 PM. Admis adult $1, student & sr citizen 50¢, children under 12 with adult free. Estab 1966 for art, books, documents, Indian and archaeological specimens and pioneer artifacts that lead to the preservation and better understanding of the history of Western Canada. Museum has three exhibition floors; 100,000 sq ft of exhibition space. Average Annual Attendance: 160,000. Mem: 23,000; dues family $15, individual $10, sr citizen & student $5
Income: $4,500,000 (financed by endowment, provincial and federal appropriation)
Purchases: $100,000
Collections: †Art: Representative collections of Canadian historical and contemporary art, Indian and Inuit. Large collection of natural history illustration and works of art on paper; †Ethnology: Large collection of material relating to Plains Indians; representative holdings from Africa, Australia, Oceania, Central and South America, Inuit and Northwest Coast; †Library and Archives: Western Canadian historical books, manuscripts and photographs
Exhibitions: (1978) Picasso; (1979) Carl Andre; The Henry Birks Collection of Canadian Silver; Max Ernst: From the Collection of Mr and Mrs Jimmy Ernst; 20th Century European Painting and Sculpture from the Envoy and Latner Family Collection; (1980) Aspects of Canadian Painting
Publications: Charles Livingston Bull; David Bucan: Modern Fashions; calendar of events, bi-monthly; Chautauqua in Canada; Max Ernst; Silversmithing in Canadian History
Activities: Classes for children; docent training; lect open to public, 20 - 25 visiting lectr per year; concerts; gallery talks; tours; guided tours for adults and children; exten dept; artmobile; individual paintings and original objects of art lent to public museums and galleries; lending collection contains 10,000 original prints, 10,000 paintings, 3000 sculpture and 5000 drawings; book traveling exhibitions 25 per year; originate traveling exhibitions; museum shop sells books, magazines, reproductions, slides, gifts, posters and postcards; Luxton Museum, Baniff, Alberta
L **Library,** Ninth Ave & First St SE, T2G 0P3. *Library & Archives* Len Gottselig
Open for reference
Library Holdings: Vols 30,000; Per subs 300

M **MUTTART GALLERY ASSOCIATES,** 1221 Second St SW, T2R 0W5. Tel 403-266-2764. *Pres* Frank Stewart; *VPres* Don Ray; *Secy* Marianne Norris; *Treas* Dennis A Anderson; *Dir & Cur* Daniel Deyell; *Secy* Eva Tym
Open Tues - Fri 10 AM - 9 PM, Sat & Sun 1:30 - 5 PM. No admis fee. Estab 1978 to exhibit the works of amateur and emerging professional artists and to provide artists information for the Calgary community. Top floor of the restored Memorial Park Library (old Carnegie Library). Average Annual Attendance: 10,000. Mem: 600; annual meeting June
Income: $80,000 (financed by membership, city and state appropriation, private donations and corporate funds)
Exhibitions: (1979) Alberta Handicraft Guild; Alberta Porcelain Artists; Allard; Muschi Aziz; Bazalgette Junior High Photographs; John Beresford; Margaret Bergman; Murray Blanc; The Bow Valley Group; Boychuk; Bragg Creek Artisans; Calgary Community Painters; Calgary Public School, Graphics; Calgary Separate School Board; Calgary Sketch Club; Gordon Christopher; Chris Cran; Paul de Groot; Andre Dube; Foothills Camera Club; Jackie Forrie; Rosemarie Gall; Ruth Garson; Brian Grandbois; The Group; Helen Hadala; Edgar Harrison; Myrna Harvie; Robert Hirano; Matilde Ho; Dennis Hrubzna; Johnson; Pat Jones; Stefa Kvietys; Judith Lamb; Robert Manders; Tony Mascardelli; Cynthia McKenzie; Santo Mignosa; Kennedy O'Brien; Julia Oko; Jan Paulus-Maly; Elaine Rathie; Eva Roberts; Diedre Russell; Robin Sales; Anneke Schoemaker; Sercombe; Barrie Smylie; Strakowski; Vella Strand; Joan Sundeen; Helen Suska; Swain; Doug Swalling; Ruth Tepson; Crane Thomas; Josephine Weidel; Witting-Robinson; Women's Art; Young; (1980) Kevin Baer; Lee Byng; Calgary Artists Society; Calgary Public Schools; Calgary Sketch Club; Ceramics; Ceramics in Calgary; Edgar; Michelle Gallant; The Group; Kevin Kanashiro; Ron Kanashiro; Grant Leier; Life Drawing Workshop; McAvity; Robert McInnis; Gordon Milne; Meg Nicks; Faye Nutting; Pike; Pope; Deib Russhfield; Nancy Tice

Publications: Annual Report (One and One Third); Visual Arts Information Project
Activities: Classes for adults; literary readings; lect open to public, 10 visiting lectr per year; gallery talks; tours; competitions; book traveling exhibitions three per year

M UNIVERSITY OF CALGARY, The Nickle Arts Museum, Office of the Art Curator, 2500 University Drive NW, T2N 1N4. Tel 403-284-7234. *Facility Adminr* John Heywood; *Cur of Numismatics* C H Orton; *Cur of Art* Open
Open Tues - Fri 10 AM - 5 PM, Wed evenings 7 - 10 PM, Sat & Sun 1 - 5 PM, cl Mon and holidays. No admis fee. In 1970 an Alberta pioneer, Mr Samuel C Nickle, gave the University a gift of one million dollars and the museum was opened in 1979. His son, Carl O Nickle, presented the University with an immensely valuable collection of some 10,000 ancient coins, covering over 1500 years of human history which is housed in the Numismatics department of the museum. Museum houses the permanent collection; exhibitions are presented on a continuous basis in the gallery on the main floor (15,000 sq ft) with a smaller numismatic gallery attached. The smaller Teaching Gallery on the second floor (1500 sq ft) is used for smaller exhibits, lectures, films and seminars. Average Annual Attendance: 3000
Income: Financed by state appropriation
Purchases: $12,000
Collections: Roloff Beny - A Visual Odyssey; ceramics; paintings; photography; sculpture; Western Canadian Art consisting of prints, photography, oils, sculpture and watercolors
Exhibitions: Local, national and international exhibitions are presented on a continuous basis
Activities: Docent training; seminars; lect open to public; gallery talks; films; individual paintings and original objects of art lent to offices on campus; originate traveling exhibitions

EDMONTON

O ALBERTA ART FOUNDATION, 11th Floor, CN Tower, 10004 104th Ave, T5J 0K5. Tel 403-482-6820, 427-2031. *Chmn* Giuseppe Albi; *Secy* W H Kaasa; *Coordr* W Tin Ng
Estab 1972 to collect and to exhibit art works pertinent to the Province of Alberta
Income: Financed by the Province of Alberta
Collections: Alberta Art Foundation Collection
Exhibitions: (1978) Alberta Art Foundation (exhibition to commemorate the eleven Commonwealt Games in Edmonton); Alberta Art (exhibition on tour in Japan); 33 Alberta Artists; Maximum 200; Silk 'n' Earth; Women Artists in Alberta
Publications: Annual Report; Exhibition catalogues; Newsletter, semi-annually
Activities: Acquisition of art works by Alberta artists; exhibition program in and outside Canada

DEPARTMENT OF CULTURE, GOVERNMENT OF THE PROVINCE OF ALBERTA
O Cultural Development Division, CN Tower, 10158 103rd St, T5J 0K5. Tel 403-427-2553. *Dir Visual Arts* Leslie F Graff
Open Mon - Fri 8:15 AM - 4:30 PM. No admis fee. Estab to provide assistance to the Province of Alberta in the development of the visual arts and crafts. Small, informal gallery approx 400 sq ft created for the purpose of training community personnel in the handling of exhibitions. Average Annual Attendance: 150,000 - 200,000
Income: Financed by provincial appropriations
Exhibitions: Provincial Paintings and Sculpture
Publications: Various technical journals, articles of history and others, 10 - 15 per year
Activities: Leadership training for instructors who work with adults and-or children; serves entire province; material available to residents of Alberta; course fees only; lect open to public; competitions; scholarships; individual paintings and original objects of art lent; lending collection contains 150 Kodachrome slides and photographs
L Cultural Development Division Library, CN Tower, 10158 103rd St, T5J 0K5. Reference library
Library Holdings: Vols 500
M Provincial Museum of Alberta, 12845 102nd Ave, T5N 0M6. Tel 403-452-2150. *Art Dir* Eric C Waterton; *Extension Supv* Charles Williams; *Display Supv* Gordon E Johnston
Open winter Mon - Sat 9 AM - 5 PM, Sun 11 AM - 9 PM, summer 9 AM - 9 PM daily. No admis fee. Estab 1967 to preserve and interpret the human and natural histories of the province of Alberta. Four major areas divided equally into human and natural history under broad themes of settlement history, anthropology, natural history habitat groups and natural history interpretive displays. Average Annual Attendance: 43,000
Income: $1,600,000
Purchases: $20,000
Collections: Archaeological; †Ethnographical; Fine and Decorative Arts; †Folk Life; †Geology; †Historical; †Palaeontology
Exhibitions: Approx 20 feature exhibits
Publications: Museum Notes; occasional papers; occasional series; Publication Series
Activities: Classes for adults and children; lect open to public; competitions; exten dept serving province of Alberta; Museumobiles; individual artifacts lent; originate traveling exhibitions; sales shop sells books
L Provincial Archives of Alberta, 12845 102nd Ave, T5N 0M6. *Provincial Archivist* A D Ridge; *Asst Provincial Archivist* W B Speirs; *Sr Archivist* J E Dryden; *Historical Resources Librn* J Toon
Open Mon - Fri 9 AM - 4:30 PM. Estab 1967 to identify, evaluate, acquire, preserve, arrange and describe and subsequently make available for public research, reference and display those diversified primary and secondary sources that document and relate to the overall history and development of Alberta. Maintains an art gallery for major exhibitions of archival sources and historical themes
Income: Financed by provincial appropriation
Purchases: $39,000
Library Holdings: Vols 17,000; Per subs 180; Micro—Fiche, reels; AV—A-tapes, cassettes, motion pictures, rec, slides; Other—Clipping files, prints, manuscripts, original art works, pamphlets, photographs, Original documents
Special Subjects: Ethno-cultural groups and activities, genealogy, immigration and

land settlement, local histories, religious archives
Exhibitions: Documentary Heritage; several small displays each year highlighting recent accessions

M EDMONTON ART GALLERY,* 2 Sir Winston Churchill Square, T5J 2C1. Tel 403-429-6781. *Dir* T Fenton; *Canada Art* Christopher Varley; *Exten Cur* Maggie Callahan
Open Mon - Sat 10:15 AM - 5 PM, Tues & Fri 10:15 AM - 10 PM, Sun 1:15 - 5 PM, cl New Years, Christmas. No admis fee. Estab 1923 to collect and exhibit paintings, sculptures, photographs and other works of visual art and to teach art appreciation. Gallery covers 63,000 sq ft; exhibition area 20,000 sq ft. Average Annual Attendance: 200,000. Mem: 1300; dues $20
Income: $800,000 (financed by membership, city appropriation, state appropriation and federal grants)
Purchases: $119,000
Collections: †Contemporary Canadian art; †Contemporary & Historical photography; †Contemporary International art; †Historical Canadian art; Historical European and American Art
Exhibitions: 35 in-house exhibitions and 26 extension shows
Publications: Edmonton Art Gallery Bulletin, 6 copies per year
Activities: Classes for adults and children; docent training; workshops; lect open to the public, 6 visiting lectrs per year; concerts; gallery talks; tours; exten dept serving Alberta and British Columbia interior; individual paintings and original objects of art lent to smaller galleries in area, and other large galleries; traveling exhibitions organized and circulated; sales shop selling books, magazines, original art, reproductions, craft items; junior museum maintained
L Library,* 2 Sir Winston Churchill Square, T5J 2C1. *Librn* Luella Oeste
Open to the public
Library Holdings: Vols 2500; Per subs 22
Special Subjects: Architecture, Art Education

M UKRAINIAN MUSEUM OF CANADA, 10611 - 110 Ave, T5H 1H7. Tel 403-483-5932. *Pres* N Seniw
Open by appointment, July & Aug Sun 2 - 5 PM. No admis fee. Estab 1941
Collections: Drawings, historical material, national costumes, paintings, prints, sculpture and textiles
Activities: TV and radio programs; study clubs; lect; guided tours; films; loan service
L Library, 10611 - 110 Ave, T5H 1H7. Tel 403-483-6851. *Librn* Mrs O Lukomsky
Library Holdings: Vols 2500; Other—Manuscripts
Special Subjects: Ukrainian arts and crafts, general culture

M UNIVERSITY OF ALBERTA, Ring House Gallery, T6G 2E2. Tel 403-432-5834, 432-5818. *Cur* Helen Collinson; *Registrar* Susan Heth; *Departmental Secy* Audrey Bell; *Exhib Coordr* Darrell Colyer
Open Mon, Tues, Wed & Fri 11 AM - 4 PM, Thurs 11 AM - 9 PM, Sun 2 - 5 PM. No admis fee. Estab 1964 to display items from the University's permanent collection and from traveling exhibitions from outside sources. Gallery is located in former residence of the University President, which has been converted to an art gallery; three exhibition areas on first floor; two on second; space totals 350 running ft. Average Annual Attendance: 4000
Income: Financed by state appropriation and university funds
Collections: Antiquities, ethnographic material, furniture, graphics, paintings, sculpture and textile
Activities: Competitions; book traveling exhibitions; originate traveling exhibitions
L Library, T6G 2E2.
For reference to staff
Library Holdings: Vols 500
Special Subjects: Conservation techniques, contemporary Canadian art, museum management

LETHBRIDGE

O ALLIED ARTS COUNCIL OF LETHBRIDGE, Bowman Arts Center,* Ninth St & Fifth Ave S, T1J 0V2. Tel 403-327-2813. *Pres* Terry Morris
Open Mon - Fri 10 AM - 11 PM. No admis fee. Estab 1958 to encourage and foster cultural activities in Lethbridge, to provide facilities for such cultural activities, and to promote the work of Alberta and Western Canadian artists. Average Annual Attendance: 1500. Mem: 300; dues $15; annual meeting Feb
Income: $39,000 (financed by membership and city appropriation)
Exhibitions: Local exhibitions: Children's art, fabric makers, painters, potters; one-man shows: Paintings, photography, prints, sculpture, silversmithing; provincial government traveling exhibits
Publications: Calendar of Arts, weekly
Activities: Classes for adults and children; dramatic programs; concerts; competitions; scholarships; traveling exhibitions organized and circulated; sales shop selling original art

M UNIVERSITY OF LETHBRIDGE ART GALLERY,* 4401 University Dr, T1K 3M4. Tel 403-379-2691. *Chmn Art Dept* L E Weaver; *Gallery Dir* B J McCarroll
Open Mon - Fri 8:30 AM - 4:30 PM, Sun 1 - 4 PM. No admis fee. Estab 1968 for public service and the teaching mechanism
Income: Financed by city and state appropriations
Collections: Some professional prints and drawings; student work
Exhibitions: Local and regional shows in addition to those traveling exhibitions by the National Gallery, The Winnipeg Gallery and the Western Association of Art Museums, approx ten shows per year
Activities: Lect open to the public; gallery talks; tours; individual paintings and original objects of art lent; lending collection contains Kodachromes and motion pictures

MEDICINE HAT

L MEDICINE HAT PUBLIC LIBRARY, 414 First St SE, T1A 0A8. Tel 403-527-5551. *Chief Librn* R M Block
Open Mon - Fri 9 AM - 9 PM. No admis fee. Estab 1914 to provide display area for traveling and local art shows
Library Holdings: Vols 2000; Micro—Reels 175
Activities: Dramatic programs; lect open to public, 10 vis lectr per year; concerts

MUNDARE

O BASILIAN FATHERS, Box 379, T0B 3H0. Tel 403-764-3860. *Dir* Damien Welesehuk
Open May - Oct, Mon - Sat 10 AM - 6 PM. Donations accepted. Estab 1951
Collections: Ukrainian Folk Art, Arts and Crafts; Historical Church Books
L Library, Box 379, T0B 3H0.
Library Holdings: Vols 650

BRITISH COLUMBIA

BURNABY

M BURNABY ART GALLERY, 6344 Gilpin St, V5G 2J3. Tel 604-291-9441. *Pres Board of Trustees* E Eakins; *Dir* Jack N Hardman; *Gallery Asst* Elisa Anstis; *Educator* Judith O'Keeffe; *Chief Preparator* Brent Beattie
Open Mon, Tues, Thurs, Fri 10 AM - 5 PM, Wed 10 AM - 9 PM, weekends & holidays Noon - 5 PM. No admis fee. Estab 1967 to present continually changing exhibitions of the prints, paintings, sculpture, ceramic, fabric and other arts of local and other Canadian artists both contemporary and historic. Gallery is situated in a house built in 1909 surrounded by the 25 acres of Century Park. Average Annual Attendance: 45,000. Mem: 500; dues sponsor $100, group $25, family $15, single $10, student $5; annual meeting May
Income: Financed by endowment, membership, city and state appropriation and federal grants
Collections: Collection of Canadian Prints from the earliest to those by Contemporary Artists
Exhibitions: Biennial Prints Exhibition; juried exhibitions
Publications: Catalogues and brochures to accompany exhibitions; Paper BAG, quarterly members bulletin
Activities: Classes for adults and children; docent training; lect open to public, 20 vis lectr per year; gallery talks; tours; competitions, sponsors juried exhibitions, offers biennial prints exhibition purchase awards; exten dept; book traveling exhibitions once or twice per year; originate traveling exhibitions; museum shop sells books, magazines, original art, reproductions, prints, crafts and pottery by local and other artists

M SIMON FRASER UNIVERSITY, Simon Fraser Gallery, Centre for the Arts, Academic Quadrangle 3004, V5A 1S6. Tel 604-291-4266. *Dir* James Warren Felter; *Gallery Asst* Catherine Johnston
Open Mon 1:30 - 4 PM and 5 - 8 PM, Tues - Fri 10 AM - 1 PM and 2 - 4 PM, cl Sat & Sun. No admis fee. Estab 1971 to collect, conserve and display original works of art, principally contemporary Canadian. Gallery is 150 to 310 running ft, 1200 sq ft. Permanent works are installed throughout the university campus. Average Annual Attendance: 1200
Income: Financed by public university appropriations, government grants and corporate donations
Purchases: $9000
Collections: Simon Fraser Collection, including contemporary and Invit art; international graphics
Exhibitions: 1978: Arctic Images - Graphics by Cape Dorset Artists with Photographs by Tessa MacIntosh; Feliciano Bejar; Contemporary Canadian Images from Simon Fraser Collection; Cook and the Mapping of the North Pacific; Ho Chao Hwa (Chinese brush paintings); J Frederic McCulloch (works on paper); New Testament Narratives in Master Drawings Selected from Collections of E B Crocker Art Gallery; Process and Transformation - Eleven American Photographers; Recent Acquisitions - Selections from Simon Fraser Collection; Jack Wise - A Decade of Work; Women in Art - Ten B.C. Artists; Wordsand by Richard Kostelanetz; Works in Progress - Sculpture by Mark Anderson. 1979: Art of Lithography; Drawings by Jack Weldon Humphrey; Graficas - Contemporary Latin American Prints from Collection of Carton y Papel de Mexico; Herbert Bayer (photography); Images of the Inuit from Simon Fraser Collection; Inner Eye of Chen Chi-Kwan; Jasper Johns (screenprints); Native Canadian Graphics from Simon Fraser Collection; Szeto, Kei and Nigel (Chinese painting)
Publications: Bi-annual Report, every 2 yrs
Activities: international exten dept; artmobile; individual paintings and original objects of art lent; lending collection contains 700 original art works, 600 original prints, paintings and sculpture; book traveling exhibitions; originate traveling exhibitions
L Library, Centre for the Arts, Academic Quadrangle 3004, V5A 1S6.
Reference library
Library Holdings: AV—Slides; Other—Clipping files

O WESTERN CANADA ART ASSOCIATION INC, c/o Centre for the Arts, Simon Fraser University, V5A 1S6. Tel 604-291-4266. *Chmn* James Warren Felter; *Secy & Treas* Allan McKay
Estab 1970 to promote high standard of excellence and uniform methods in the care and presentation of works of art; to assist developing visual art centres in Western Canada; to encourage cooperation among members, and between members and other gallery and museum associations. Mem: 47 organizations; dues active $20, associate $10, individual subscribing $5
Income: Financed by membership
Publications: WCAA Newsletter, 6 - 8 per year

Activities: Training committee, organization and presentation of gallery training workshops
L Library, c/o Centre for the Arts, Simon Fraser University, V5A 1S6.
For members only

CHILLIWACK

O CHILLIWACK ARTS COUNCIL,* (Formerly Community Arts Council of Chilliwack) Box 53, V2P 6H7. Tel 604-792-2069. *Pres* Murray Mackie; *VPres* Clint Hames; *Secy & Coordr* Susan Hohby
Open 9 AM - 4 PM. Estab 1960 as Arts Council, Arts Centre estab 1972 to encourage all forms of art in the community. Mem: 200; dues organizational $5, individual $3; annual meeting June
Income: Financed by endowment and membership
Collections: 26 Salish Weavings
Exhibitions: Local artists' exhibitions, including oils, pottery, prints, weavings, wood carving and other fabric arts
Publications: Arts Council Newsletter, 8 per year
Activities: Classes for adults and children; dramatic programs; concerts; scholarships

COQUITLAM

O PLACE DES ARTS, 166 King Edward St, V3K 4T2. Tel 604-526-2891. *Dir* Lenore Peyton
Open Mon - Thurs 9 AM - 10 PM, Fri 9 AM - Noon, Sat 9 AM - 4 PM. No admis fee. Estab Sept 1, 1972 as a cultural, community crafts and resource center, an art school and gallery. Average Annual Attendance: 3000
Income: Financed by municipal and fine arts council program funds
Exhibitions: Bi-weekly shows of artists and craftsmen throughout the year
Publications: Program (12 weeks), every three months
Activities: Special Educ Dept serving retarded young adults, school children, senior citizens and women's groups; satellite courses within the school of the district on request; classes for adults and children; dramatic programs; lect open to public; concerts; gallery talks; scholarships

DAWSON CREEK

M SOUTH PEACE ART SOCIETY, Dawson Creek Museum Art Gallery, 10100 13th St, V1G 4H8. Tel 604-782-2601. *Pres* G Humphrey; *VPres* Hilde Bittman; *Secy* M Poole; *Treas* Lois Roberts
Open 9 AM - Noon and 1 - 5 PM. Admis family $1, individual 35¢. Estab 1961 to promote art appreciation in community. Museum and Art Gallery combined and adjacent to Tourist Information Office. Average Annual Attendance: 28,000. Mem: 30; dues $3; annual meeting third Thurs of March
Income: Financed by membership, city appropriation and commissions on sales
Exhibitions: Approximately 15 - 18 per year, local and traveling
Activities: Classes for adults and children; lect open to public, 3 - 4 visiting lectr per year; paintings lent to members; lending collection contains color reproductions and slides; book traveling exhibitions

KELOWNA

M KELOWNA CENTENNIAL MUSEUM AND NATIONAL EXHIBIT CENTRE, 470 Queensway Ave, V1Y 6S7. Tel 604-763-2451. *Pres* C W Knowles; *Secy* Sadie Conrad; *Dir & Cur* Ursula Surtees; *Museum Educator* Leslie Hopton; *Display Coordr* Wayne Wilson
Open summer Mon - Sat 10 AM - 5 PM, Sun 2 - 5 PM, winter Tues - Sat 10 AM - 5 PM. No admis fee. Estab 1935 as a community museum, a national exhibit center where traveling exhibits are received and circulated. Gallery maintained for local art exhibits and small traveling exhibits. Mem: Annual meeting March
Income: Financed by membership, city and state appropriation
Exhibitions: National and provincial exhibition on archaeological items, conservation, festive beads, lighting, multi-culture items and stern wheeler travel; many private exhibitions including coins, pottery, silver and weapons
Publications: A Short History of Early Fruit Ranching Kelowna; Lak-La-Hai-Ee Volume III Fishing; Sunshine and Butterflies
Activities: Classes for adults and children; lect open to public; individual items lent to schools; lending collection contains 2000 lantern slides; book traveling exhibitions; originate traveling exhibitions
L Library, 470 Queensway Ave, V1Y 6S7.
Library Holdings: Other—Photographs
Collections: Photograph Collection

NELSON

M KOOTENAY SCHOOL OF ART AND GALLERY, David Thompson University Centre, V1L 1C8. Tel 604-352-2241. *Gallery Curator & Dir* E H Undergill
Open 10 AM - Noon, 1 - ? PM. No admis fee. Estab 1962. Gallery is 50 x 50 ft with 96 running ft, 296 running ft with optional partitions; fluorescent lighting and adjustable floodlamps; office and two storage rooms. Average Annual Attendance: 9580
Income: Financed by provincial appropriation
Collections: Permanent collection consists of graduate student examples in painting, drawing, sculpture, ceramics and applied design
Exhibitions: ...And the Rains Came; Animatoon; Art History; How Now; Inuit Games and Contest (printmaking); KSA Graduation Exhibition of Graphic Arts and Fine Arts; Painting and Sculpture; Photography; Small Delights and Greater Mysteries; Student Prints - Osaka Alberta; Watercolors; What Happened at Emma Lake; Young Artists of the Prairies; applied design, ceramics, faculty exhibition, painting, printmaking
Publications: Calendar, yearly; exhibition catalogs
Activities: Classes for adults and children; docent training; lect open to public, 12 vis lectr per year; gallery talks; tours; scholarships and fels; exten dept; individual paintings and original objects of art lent to educational institutions; lending collection contains cassettes, film strips, motion pictures, original art works, original prints, paintings, phonorecords and 25,000 slides; book traveling exhibition; originate traveling exhibitions

PRINCE GEORGE

M PRINCE GEORGE ART GALLERY, 2820 15th Ave, V2M 1T1. Tel 604-563-6447, 563-9484. *Pres* Audrey Thompson; *Treas* Gloria Gunther; *Coordr* Mark Lightfoot; *Asst Coordr* Rosalind Burnell
Open Tues - Sat 10 AM - 5 PM, Wed 7 - 9 PM. No admis fee. Estab 1970 to foster development of arts and crafts in the community; to foster and promote artists. Gallery is wood frame building, 5849 sq ft including two 1200 sq ft galleries, with track-lighting and carpet. Average Annual Attendance: 14,000. Mem: 323; dues $10; annual meeting June
Income: $33,550 (financed by membership, city and provincial appropriations and grants)
Collections: Individual paintings and original art
Publications: Newsletter, monthly
Activities: Classes for children; docent training; lect open to public, 8 vis lectr per year; gallery talks; tours for schoolchildren; competitions; exten dept serving northern British Columbia; individual paintings and original objects of art rented to members; lending collection contains books, original art works, paintings; originate traveling exhibitions; sales shop sells original paintings, drawings, pottery, handicrafts, prints, cards, art books and catalogues and Opus frames
L Library, 2820 15th Ave, V2M 1T1. *Librn* Fran Evans
Open to members for reference only
Library Holdings: Vols 20; Per subs 13; AV—Cassettes, slides; Other—Original art works

PRINCE RUPERT

M MUSEUM OF NORTHERN BRITISH COLUMBIA, Prince Rupert Museum Art Gallery, McBride St & First Ave, PO Box 669, V8J 3S1. Tel 604-624-3207. *Pres Board of Dir* J H Jefferies; *VPres Board of Dir* P Purdy; *Adminr* R Denman; *Cur* M J Patterson
Open Sept - April Mon - Sat 9 AM - 4 PM, May - Aug 9 AM - 9 PM. No admis fee. Estab 1924, new building opened 1958, to collect, maintain and display the history of the north coast, particularly of the Prince Rupert area. One main hall has two small side galleries, and a third gallery is the Museum art Gallery, which is shaped to resemble a native long house. Average Annual Attendance: 90,000. Mem: 140; dues $1; annual meeting May
Income: $47,000 (financed by municipality and province)
Collections: †Contemporary North Coast Indian Art; †Historical Collections; †Native Indian Collections; Natural History; †Photographs
Exhibitions: A continually changing display program; Fine Arts Exhibitions from large Galleries; local artists shows
Activities: Classes for adults and children; lect open to public, 5 vis lectr per year; concerts; gallery talks; tours; competitions
L Library, McBride St and First Ave, v8J 3S1.
Small reference library for staff
Library Holdings: Vols 100; Per subs 3; Other—Some archival materials

RICHMOND

O RICHMOND ARTS CENTRE, 7671 Minoru Gate, V6Y 1R8. Tel 604-278-1755. *Cultural Coordr* Kathryn MacLean; *Museum Archives Coordr* William Anderson
Open Mon - Fri 10 AM - 5 PM and 7 - 9 PM, Sat 10 AM - 4 PM, Sun 1 - 4 PM. No admis fee. Estab 1967. Maintains gallery. Average Annual Attendance: 36,000
Income: Financed by city appropriation
Collections: Oil paintings, ink and wash, pencil and ink sketches of local or related importance; Photograph Collection of 200 prints
Exhibitions: Change every two weeks
Publications: Newsletter, monthly
Activities: Classes for adults and children; dramatic programs, junior museum
L Library, 7671 Minoru Gate, V6Y 1R8.
Reference Library
Library Holdings: Vols 60; Other—AV - Taped interviews on local history, summarized and indexed 600 hours

SURREY

M SURREY ART GALLERY, Surrey Centennial Arts Centre, 13750 88th Ave, V3W 3L1. Tel 604-596-7461. *Dir & Cur* Open; *Cur* Rosa Ho; *Asst Cur* Gordon Rice; *Education & Events Coordr* Ingrid Kolt
Open Mon - Fri 9 AM - 4:30 PM, Tues & Thurs evenings 7 - 9:30 PM, Sat & Sun 1 - 5 PM. No admis fee. Estab 1975. Average Annual Attendance: 32,000
Income: $150,000 (financed by city and state appropriation, special private foundations grants, and federal grants per project application)
Purchases: $2000 - $3000
Collections: Contemporary Canadian Art, mostly works on paper
Exhibitions: (1978) Art of the Woodland Indian; Max Bates - Secrets of the Grand Hotel; Nora Blank - Wall Environmentals Piece; Karen Chapnik - Fibre Hangings; Contemporary Indian Art; Otto Dix and Erich Heckel; Chris Harris - Paintings; Lithographs of Apollo II Launch; 19th Century Posters, Talouse Letrec, Bonnard, Cheret; Setsuko Piroche - Paintings and Soft Sculpture; Robert Rauschenberg - Stoned Moon; Diego Rivera - Drawings and Prints; Abani Sen - 1925-1975 Watercolours; Tempra Drawings from Bengal, India; Transparency Show - Group Show; Bob Van der Mey - Recent works and paintings. (1979) Lorne Beug: Works on paper from the past ten years; Brazilian and Watanabe Woodcuts; Creative Flight; Eskimo Art From Private Collections; Henry Hinton Photographs; Dorothea Lange; Amy Mukai; Segments I: Art Work and Mail Art by L Guderna; Surrey Collects; Three Painters: George Fertig, Maurice Spira, Birnie Wren; Worlds in Clay; Young Contemporaries 1978. (1980) Animatoon; Suzy Berstein; Joe Farfard - Recent Sculpture; Sherry Grauer - So Far; Haitian Paintings; Impressionist Prints; Photography B C; Rick Robinson; Share Corsault-Lyse Lemieux: Working in Two Spaces; Severino Trinca; Nelson Yuen
Publications: Exhibition catalogues; What's On, (newsletter) On
Activities: Classes for children; dramatic programs; docent training; lect open to public, 6 visiting lectr per year; concerts; gallery talks; tours; exten dept serves local community; lending collection contains cassettes and film strips; book traveling exhibitions 2 or 3 per year
L Library, Surrey Centennial Arts Centre, 13750 88th Ave, V3W 3L1.
Estab 1975, reference for staff and docents only
Purchases: $300
Library Holdings: Vols 50; Per subs 15; Micro—Cards; AV—Slides; Other—Clipping files, exhibition catalogs

VANCOUVER

M ARTISTS GALLERY, 555 Hamilton St, V6B 2R1. Tel 604-687-1345. *Dir* Paul Bolding; *Asst* Olga Froehlich
Open Tues - Fri 10 AM - 5 PM. No admis fee. Estab 1971 as an exhibition space for BC artists; as a non-profit gallery for the City of Vancouver Art Collection and Loan program. The Gallery has a medium sized exhibition area with space at the back for storage collection and framing area. Average Annual Attendance: 8000
Income: Financed by Federal Government, Agency consulting fees, and Federal Tax Exemption status under the name of the Greater Vancouver Artists Gallery Society
Collections: †City of Vancouver Art Collection
Exhibitions: Local BC artists; special exhibitions of recent acquisitions of artists on grant
L Art Library Service, 555 Hamilton St, V6B 2R1. *Dir* Paul Bolding; *Asst Dir & Cur* Olga Froehlich
Open Tues - Fri 10 AM - 5 PM. Estab 1971 for public enhancement, the Gallery provides this service to non-profit organizations for free, commercial agencies pay a fee. Circ 3000
Income: $45,000
Library Holdings: Micro—Cards; AV—Slides; Other—Clipping files, prints, original art works, pamphlets, photographs, sculpture
Collections: City of Vancouvers Public Collection

O COMMUNITY ARTS COUNCIL OF VANCOUVER, 315 W Cordova St, V6B 1E5. Tel 604-683-4358. *Pres* John Springer; *VPres* Bob Sanderson; *Honorary Secy* William Grant; *Honorary Treas* Kenneth Cross; *Executive Dir* Ann MacDonald; *Secy* Joanna Cram; *Recording Secy* Tania Murenko
Open 10 AM - 4 PM. No admis fee. Estab 1946 as a society dedicated to the support of arts, with a wide range of interest in the arts; to promote standards in all art fields including civic arts; also serves as a liaison centre. Small gallery-office shows works of emerging artists who have not exhibited before. Mem: 700; dues groups $20, individual $10; annual meeting Sept
Income: Financed by membership, donations and British Columbia Cultural Fund
Exhibitions: Approx 12 shows per year
Publications: Newsletter, 10 issues per year

O CRAFTSMEN'S ASSOCIATION OF BRITISH COLUMBIA, 801-207 W Hastings St, V6B 1H7. Tel 604-681-9613. *Pres* Peggy Achofield; *Executive Dir* Gail Rogers
Open Mon - Fri 10 AM - 4 PM. No admis fee. Estab 1972 to promote and encourage the finest quality of craft work in the province. Mem: 550; dues $15 per year; annual meeting April
Income: Financed by endowment and membership
Exhibitions: Annual juried exhibition Made by Hand, all media
Publications: Craft Contacts, monthly
Activities: Specific workshops; lect; competitions; awards
L Library, 801-207 W Hastings St, V6B 1H7. *Librn* Jean Plummer
Library Holdings: Vols 55; Per subs 4

L EMILY CARR COLLEGE OF ART LIBRARY, 249 Dunsmuir St, V6B 1X2. Tel 604-681-9525. *Head Librn* Ken Chamberlain; *Library Asst* Liselotte Boenden
Open Mon - Fri 9 AM - 6 PM. Estab 1942
Library Holdings: Vols 5000; Per subs 110; Other—Clipping files, exhibition catalogs
Collections: Albers, Interaction of Color

UNIVERSITY OF BRITISH COLUMBIA

M Fine Arts Gallery, Main Library Bldg, V6T 1W5. Tel 604-228-2759, 228-4381. *Cur* Glenn Allison; *Asst Cur* Megan Doran
Open winter Tues - Sat 10:30 AM - 5 PM, summer Mon - Fri 10 AM - 4:30 PM. No admis fee. Estab 1958, the exhibitions are organized from numerous sources and thus the gallery is able to bring to the university the widest variety of material representative of the principal trends in art, past and present. Gallery covers 27,000 sq ft. Average Annual Attendance: 15,000
Income: $15,000 (financed by departmental funds)
Exhibitions: (1978) Faney Basketey 1895-1935; Degikup: Washoe; Headspace: An Exhibition in Celebration of Hats and Headgear; Liz Magor (documentary); Joey Morgan; Sophie Pemberton 1869-1959; Walter J Phillips: Works on Paper; selections from Corporate Collections; Graduating Class; from the University Collections
Publications: Catalog, annually
Activities: Lect open to public, 2 vis lectr per year; gallery talks; originate traveling exhibitions; original art pieces by exhibiting artists available for sale

L Fine Arts Division Library, 1956 Main Mall, V6T 1Y3. Tel 604-228-2720. *Head Librn* Melva J Dwyer; *Reference Librn* Diana Kraetschmer; *Reference Librn* Peggy Wroblewski
Open Mon - Thurs 8 AM - 11 PM, Fri 8 AM - 6 PM, Sat 9 AM - 5 PM, Sun 1 - 9 PM. Estab 1948 to serve students and faculty in all courses related to fine arts, architecture and planning
Library Holdings: Micro—Fiche, reels, prints; Other—Clipping files, exhibition catalogs, pamphlets, photographs, reproductions, dial iconographic index
Special Subjects: Architecture and planning (emphasized in clipping files), Canadian art
Publications: Fine Arts Masters Theses, updated annually; List of Canadian Artists' Files - 1977, updated 1978; Start Heres (short introductory bibliographies), produced as needed; Theses Related To Planning, updated annually
Activities: Classes for adults and children; workshops; lect open to public; awards; scholarships; exten dept; book traveling exhibitions

M Museum of Anthropology, 6393 NW Marine Dr, V6T 1W5. Tel 604-228-6774. *Dir* M M Ames; *Curatorial Asst* Inge Ruus; *Cur of Ethnology* Marjorie Halpin; *Cur of Ethnology & Public Programming* Madeline Bronsdon Rowan; *Extension Cur* Hindy Ratner; *Admin Officer* Ria Rowe; *Archivist* Audrey Shane; *Designer* Bill McLennan; *Technician* Len McFarlane; *Visual Designer* Herb Watson

M VANCOUVER ART GALLERY, 1145 W Georgia St, V6E 3H2. Tel 604-682-5621. *Pres* Sheldon Cherry; *VPres* Margaret Pitts; *VPres* Geoffrey Massey; *Secy* Maxine Shaw; *Dir* Luke Rombout; *Cur* Jo-Anne Birnie-Danzker; *Cur* Ann Pollock; *Cur* Lorna Farrell-Ward; *Education* Ann Morrison; *Information Department* Dorothy Metcalfe; *Vanguard Ed* Russell Keziere; *Registrar* Scott Watson
Open Tues, Thurs - Sat 10 AM - 5 PM, Wed 10 AM - 10 PM, Sun 1 - 5 PM, cl Mon. No admis fee. Estab 1931 to inform, to collect and to preserve. Maintains slide library. Average Annual Attendance: 250,000. Mem: 2287; dues family $20, individual $15, Senior citizens and students $5; annual meeting last week of March
Income: Financed by local, provincial and federal government grants
Collections: Emily Carr Collection; Canadian Painting, Sculpture and Graphics; 17th - 20th Century European Paintings; Contemporary American Painting and Graphics
Exhibitions: Bewilderness: The Origins of Paradise by Glenn Lewis; Bill Featherston; The Fell Collection; Muntadas Personal - Public Information; Jerry Pethick: The Eskimo - Krieghoff Proximity Device, A Cultural Osmosis; Leslie Poole: Confessions; Richard Turner; (1980) Vito Acconci; Another Dimension II; Architectural Concept For A New National Gallery; British and European Paintings from the Permanent Collection, 1660 - 1900; Eric Cameron - Noel Harding: Two Audio-Visual Constructs; Emily Carr; Contemporary Works from the Permanent Collection; Don Druick; Duchamp Readymades; R Fish; Formats; Vera Frenkel; Adolph Gottlieb: Pictographs; H x W x D: Sculpture from the Permanent Collection; Richard Hamilton Graphics; Handmade Paper: Extending the Process; Image of Man in Canadian Painting; Inuit Works from the Permanent Collection; Donald Judd; Alex Katz; Chris Knudsen, Suzy Lake, Robert Walker; Landscape Reflections; Darcy Lange; MIA Westerlund: Recent Work - Sculpture and Drawing; Montreal Tapes: Video as a Community or Political Tool; N E Thing Co Ltd, Another Two Projects; National Gallery; Olympic Posters; Toni Onley: A Retrospective Exhibition; Painter as Photographer by David Octavius Hill, Auguste Salzmann and Charles Negre; Pottery by Wayne Ngan; Helen Pitt Graduate Awards; Robert Rauschenberg: Works from Captiva; Jack Shadbolt: Seven Years; 13 Cameras; Vancouver Video Works; Vancouver Women's Video and Film Festival; Various Video; Video Portraits; Vittorio's Vittorios
Publications: Vanguard, ten times a year; exhibition catalogs
Activities: Docent training; lect open to public; gallery talks; tours; exten dept serving Province of British Columbia; individual paintings and original objects of art lent to museums who comply only with security and climate control standards; lending collection contains 20,000 slides; book traveling exhibitions; originate traveling exhibitions; museum shop sells books, handicrafts, magazines, original art, reproductions, prints and slides

L Library, 1145 W Georgia St, V6E 3H2. *Librn* Jean Martin
Open Tues - Sat 10 AM - Noon and 1 - 4 PM, cl Sun & Mon. Estab to serve staff, docents, students and the public. For reference only
Library Holdings: Vols 7492; Per subs 115; Other—Clipping files, exhibition catalogs, pamphlets
Special Subjects: Fine arts specializing in Canadian and contemporary art

L VANCOUVER CITY ARCHIVES AND LIBRARY, 1150 Chestnut St, V6J 3J9. Tel 604-736-8561. *Dir* Sue M Baptie; *Deputy Dir* John R Chang; *Chief Cur* Mrs Sheelagh Draper; *Cur Coll* Paul Yee
Open Mon - Fri 9:30 AM - 5:30 PM, other times by appointment, cl weekends and legal holidays. No admis fee. Estab 1933
Income: Financed by city appropriation
Collections: Charts, civic records, drawings, manuscripts, maps, paintings, photographs and prints

Exhibitions: Temporary exhibitions
Activities: Classes for adults and children; docent training; lect; tours

VERNON

M VERNON ART ASSOCIATION, Topham Brown Gallery, 3009 - 32 Ave, PO Box 433, V1T 6M3. Tel 604-545-3173. *Pres* Rick Thorburn; *VPres* Dorothy Gower; *Secy* Marie Hill; *Treas* Larry Hill; *Public Relations* Lee Kowalski; *Cur* Jude Clarke
Open Mon - Sat 10 AM - 1 PM and 2 - 5 PM. No admis fee. Estab 1967 to display exhibits by local artists, Valley Jury Shows, and other significant shows by well known artists. Gallery professionally designed measuring approx 34 x 34 sq ft. Average Annual Attendance: 20,000. Mem: 150; dues family $8, individual $5; annual meeting first Mon of March
Income: $3000 (financed by membership, city appropriation and grants)
Collections: Permanent collection consists of ceramics, paintings, prints, sculpture and serigraphs
Exhibitions: 25 exhibits annually; Okanagan Valley Jury Show; shows change every two weeks
Publications: Art Quarterly
Activities: Classes for adults and children; docent training; supports the Vernon Resident Artists League; lect for members only; tours; competitions; fels; individual paintings and original objects of art lent to Chamber of Commerce, City Hall Vernon; originate traveling exhibitions

VICTORIA

M ART GALLERY OF GREATER VICTORIA, 1040 Moss St, V8V 4P1. Tel 604-384-4101. *Pres* Dr Burton O Kurth; *Dir* Roger H Boulet; *Cur of Contemporary Art* Ian Thom; *Cur Decorative Art* Margaret Bell
Open Mon, Tues, Wed, Fri, Sat 10 AM - 5 PM, Thurs 10 AM - 9 PM, Sun 1 - 5 PM, cl Mon in winter. Admis adults 50¢, children $25, children free. Estab 1949. Six modern galleries adjoin 19th Century Spencer Mansion-Japanese Garden. Average Annual Attendance: 52,500. Mem: 2000; dues family $20, individual $15
Income: $470,000 (financed by membership, city, federal and state appropriation)
Collections: Chinese, Indian, Persian and Tibetan Art; Contemporary Canadian, American and European; European Painting and Decorative Arts from 16th - 19th Centuries; Japanese Art from Kamakura to Contemporary; Primitive Arts
Exhibitions: (1980) Emily Carr; David Milne Watercolors; Nanga Paintings from Permanent Collection
Publications: Arts Victoria, six times a year
Activities: Docent training; lect open to public; concerts; gallery talks; tours; exten dept serves Vancouver Island; individual paintings and original objects of art lent to museums and local public buildings; lending collection contains works from permanent collection; book traveling exhibitions, 20 - 25 per year; originate traveling exhibitions; museum shops sells books, crafts, jewelry, magazines, original art, reproductions, prints, textiles

L Library, 1040 Moss St, V8V 4P1. *Asst Dir* Robert Amos
Open Mon - Fri 10 AM - 5 PM. Estab 1951. only for staff and public
Income: $1000
Purchases: $1000
Library Holdings: Vols 4000; Per subs 20; Other—Clipping files, exhibition catalogs, pamphlets
Special Subjects: Oriental Art, Canadian Art
Activities: Used book sale

M OPEN SPACE GALLERY, Secession Gallery of Photography, 510 Fort St, PO Box 5207, Station B, V8R 6N4. Tel 604-383-8833. *Cur* Tom Gore
Open Tues - Fri 10 AM - 5 PM, Sat Noon - 5 PM. No admis fee. Estab 1975 for the encouragement and promotion of photography as a fine art and of those photographers, particularly in Western Canada, who are engaged in making photographs as art. Gallery has 3000 sq ft, 220 running ft with full light grid controlled to level for works of art on paper. Average Annual Attendance: 10,000. Mem: 220; dues $10
Income: $110,000 (financed by federal and provincial appropriations)
Exhibitions: Marian Bancroft; Colour Cast; Contemporary Young British Photographers; Don Corman: Photographs; Robert Doisneau; Robert Frank; Art Grice; Mattie Gunterman; Richard Holden; Tom Knott; Polaroid Collaboratory; Tim Porter; Recent Seattle Photographs; Michael Semak; Ken Straiton
Publications: B C Photos 1978, Photos 1979; Secession Excerpts from the Literature of Photography, periodic
Activities: Classes for adults; lect open to public, 5 vis lectr per year; gallery talks; competitions

L Open Space Photographic Library, 510 Fort St, V8R 6N4.
Open daily 11 AM - 5 PM. Estab 1975. Reference library
Library Holdings: Vols 200; Per subs 10; AV—V-tapes; Other—Exhibition catalogs
Special Subjects: Contemporary Canadian photography

L PROVINCIAL ARCHIVES OF BRITISH COLUMBIA, 655 Belleville St, V8V 1X4. Tel 604-387-3621. *Provincial Archivist* John A Bovey; *Head, Paintings, Drawings and Prints* J Mossop
Open Mon - Fri 9 AM - 5 PM. Estab 1893 to collect and preserve all records relating to the historical development of British Columbia. Maintains a gallery for exhibiting archival materials, and a small gallery for exhibiting paintings by Emily Carr
Income: Financed by provincial appropriation
Library Holdings: Vols 51,000; Per subs 300; Micro—Reels; AV—A-tapes; Other—Clipping files, exhibition catalogs, manuscripts, original art works, pamphlets, photographs, original documents
Special Subjects: British Columbia history
Publications: Sound Heritage, quarterly

M UNIVERSITY OF VICTORIA, Maltwood Art Museum and Gallery, Ring Rd, PO Box 1700, V8W 2Y2. Tel 604-477-6911, Ext 6169; Telex 049-7222. *Dir & Cur* Martin Segger; *Pres* Dr H Petch; *VPres* T Matthews; *Chmn of Board* Dr F Fischer; *Secy-Registrar* B Jackson
Open Mon - Fri 10 AM - 4 PM. No admis fee. Estab 1968 to collect, preserve and exhibit the decorative arts. Gallery has 3000 sq ft of environmentally controlled exhibition space. Average Annual Attendance: 150,000

Income: $100,000 (financed by endowment and state appropriation)
Purchases: $25,000
Collections: †Maltwood Collection of Decorative Art; †Contemporary Art
Exhibitions: Permanent Collections, continuing and rotating
Activities: Lect open to public, 3 visiting lectr per year; gallery talks; tours; individual paintings lent to offices and public spaces on campus; lending collection contains 500 original prints, 300 paintings and sculpture; book traveling exhibitions 5 per year; originate traveling exhibitions

WEST VANCOUVER

O **WEST VANCOUVER VISUAL ARTS SOCIETY,** c/o Norma Sorensen, 993 Sinclair, V7W 3W1. Tel 604-922-1450. *Pres* Norma Sorensen; *VPres* Val Brouwer; *Secy* Myrtle Mayall; *Treas* Mrs W D M Patterson
Estab 1968, incorporated as a nonprofit society 1970, to provide a greater opportunity for people in the community to participate in the enjoyment of the visual arts; special emphasis has been directed toward exhibitions of high quality. Mem: 35, dues $2; annual meeting Sept
Income: Financed by membership, provincial and municipal government grants and private foundations
Exhibitions: (1978) Under Thirty; (1979) Prints and Sculpture 1979

MANITOBA

BRANDON

O **BRANDON ALLIED ARTS COUNCIL,*** 1036 Louise Ave, R7A 0Y1. Tel 204-727-1036. *Dir* K Marlow
Open Mon - Sat 9 AM - 5 PM, Sun 2 - 5 PM. No admis fee. Estab 1960 to promote and foster cultural activities in Western Manitoba. Average Annual Attendance: 2400. Mem: 700; dues $6 - $20; annual meeting May
Income: $45,000 (financed by membership, city and provincial appropriations, federal grants)
Exhibitions: Changing monthly exhibitions of Western Manitoba and nationally known artists
Publications: Bulletin, every 2 months
Activities: Classes for adults and children; lect open to public, 2 visiting lectrs per year; gallery talks; tours; competitions; individual paintings and original objects of art lent to members; lending collection contains original art works, original prints, paintings, weavings
L **Brandon Allied Arts Center Library,*** 1036 Louise Ave, R7A 0Y1. *Librn* Joyce Holland
Open to members
Library Holdings: Vols 2000

CHURCHILL

M **ESKIMO MUSEUM,** 230 La Verendrye, Box 10, R0B 0E0. Tel 204-675-2252. *Dir* Omer Robidoux; *Cur* Bro Jacques Volant; *Asst Cur* Lorraine Brandson
Open Mon - Sat 9 AM - Noon and 1 - 5 PM, Sun 1 - 4 PM. No admis fee. Estab 1944 to depict the Eskimo way of life through the display of artifacts. Museum has large single display room. Average Annual Attendance: 10,000
Income: $30,000 (administered and funded by the Roman Catholic Episcopal Corporation of Churchill Hudson Bay)
Collections: †Contemporary Inuit carvings; ethnographic collections; prehistoric artifacts; wildlife specimens
Publications: The Churchill Eskimo Museum by Jeannine Veisse
Activities: Films and slide shows for school groups upon request; tours upon request; original objects of art lent to special exhibits and galleries; sales shop sells books, magazines, and original art
L **Library,** 230 La Verendrye, Box 10, R0B 0E0.
Estab mainly for Arctic Canada material
Purchases: $200
Library Holdings: Vols 450; Other—Clipping files, exhibition catalogs, photographs
Special Subjects: European exploration of Arctic Canada

DAUPHIN

O **DAUPHIN ALLIED ARTS CENTRE,** 104 First Ave NW, R7N 1S1. *Admin* Emily Kutcher
Open 1 - 5 PM. No admis fee. Estab 1973 as an amalgamation of the arts in Dauphin for a united voice. Small gallery exhibiting works of local artists, changing monthly. Average Annual Attendance: 20,000. Mem: 50; dues $5; annual meeting Jan
Income: $30,000 (financed by rental fees)
Exhibitions: Art Show; Pottery Show
Publications: Newsletter, monthly
Activities: Classes for adults and children; dramatic programs; insturction in all crafts; lect open to public, 5 visiting lectr per year; gallery talks; competitions; awards; scholarships; lending collection contains 100 film strips; originate traveling exhibitions; original art for sale
L **Library,** 104 First Ave NW, R7N 1S1.
Open to public
Library Holdings: Vols 200

PORTAGE LA PRAIRIE

O **PORTAGE AND DISTRICT ARTS COUNCIL,*** PO Box 215, R1N 3B5. Tel 204-239-6029. *Pres* Mrs Nell Owens
Estab 1976 as a coordinating body of local arts groups

WINNIPEG

O **CANADIAN ARTISTS' REPRESENTATION,** 44-221 McDermott Ave, R3B 0S2. Tel 204-943-5948. *National Representative* Bill Lobchuk; *Vice-Representative* Gary Greenwood; *Vice-Representative* Dale Amundson; *Secy* L F Shiels
Estab 1971 as an association of professional artists practicing in the visual arts. It acts on behalf of these artists to deal with all aspects and issues in the profession and to solve problems by a collective and democratic mode of action. Average Annual Attendance: 1000 (open to practicing professional artists); dues $12 - $25; annual meeting May
Income: Financed by endowment and membership
Publications: CARFAC News, quarterly
Activities: Lect open to public

O **MANITOBA ASSOCIATION OF ARCHITECTS,** 710-177 Lombard Ave, R3B 0W9. Tel 204-942-7767. *Pres* J McFeetors; *Executive Secy* H C Peters
Established 1906: Provincial Architectural Registration Board and professional governing body. Mem: 300; dues $200; annual meeting Jan
Activities: The Manitoba Association of Architects has established a joint lectureship fund with the School of Architecture at the University of Manitoba, and has established a practice of bringing three or more outstanding lecturers to Winnipeg each year for university and public lectures. The Association has a yearly donation of $600 in prizes awarded to students pursuing the course at the School of Architecture

M **MANITOBA HISTORICAL SOCIETY,** Dalnavert - MacDonald House Museum, 61 Carlton St, R3C 1N7. Tel 204-943-2835. *VPres* B Thompson; *Secy* A Mulder; *Chmn Management Committee* Dr W S Martin; *Pres Manitoba Historicas Society* A L Crossin; *Cur* Tim Worth
Open summer 10 AM - 6 PM, winter Noon - 5 PM. Admis adults $1.50, senior citizens and students $1, children 50¢. Estab 1975 to preserve and display the way of life of the 1895 upper class family. Average Annual Attendance: 8000
Income: $40,000 (financed by membership, city and state appropriation and private donation)
Collections: Home furnishings of the 1895 period: clothing, decorative arts material, furniture, household items, paintings and original family memorabilia
Activities: Lect open to public, 6 visiting lectr per year; tours; competitions; museum shop sells books and tourist items

O **MANITOBA SOCIETY OF ARTISTS,** c/o Ellen B Cringan, 82 Cordova St, R3N 0Z8. Tel 204-489-4417. *Pres* Hans Osted; *Secy* Barbara Cook-Endres; *Treas* Eleanor Golfman
Estab 1970 to further the work of the artist at the local and community levels. Mem: 60; dues $10; annual meeting Oct
Income: Financed by memberbership and commission on sales
Activities: Educ aspects include teaching by members in rural areas and artist-in-residence work in public schools; workshops; lect open to public; gallery talks; tours; competitions; scholarships; individual paintings and original objects of art lent; originate traveling exhibitions

L **PROVINCIAL ARCHIVES OF MANITOBA,** 200 Vaughan St, R3C 1T5. *Archivist* John A Bovey
Open Mon - Fri 10 AM - 5 PM, cl holidays. No admis fee. Estab 1952
Income: Financed by provincial appropriation through the Minister of Cultural Affairs and Historical Resources

M **UNIVERSITY OF MANITOBA GALLERY III,*** School of Art, R3T 2N2. Tel 204-474-9367. *Dir Exhib* Daniel Mato
Open May 1 - Sept 1 Mon - Fri 8:30 AM - 4:30 PM, Sept 16 - April 30 Mon, Thurs, Fri 9 AM - 5 PM, Sat 9 AM - Noon. No admis fee. Estab 1946. Gallery III estab 1965 to provide exhibitions for students and faculty on the university campus; exhibitions also open to the public. Average Annual Attendance: 20,000
Collections: †Contemporary Canadian and American painting, prints and sculpture
Exhibitions: Exhibitions from Museum of Modern Art, American Federation of Arts, Smithsonian Institution, National Gallery of Canada and others; annual exhibitions by the students of the School of Art
Activities: Discussion groups; workshops; lect; gallery talks
M **Faculty of Architecture Exhibition Centre,*** Architecture Bldg, R3T 2N2. *Dir of Exhib* Donald Ellis
Open Mon - Fri 9 AM - 10:30 PM, Sat 9 AM - 5 PM. Estab 1959 with the opening of the new Faculty of Architecture Building to provide architectural and related exhibitions for students and faculty on the University campus and particularly for architecture students. Exhibitions also open to the public. Average Annual Attendance: 15,000
Exhibitions: Exhibitions from National Gallery of Canada, Smithsonian Institution, American Federation of Arts, Museum of Modern Art and from other private and public sources; annual exhibitions by the students in the Faculty of Architecture
Activities: Lect; gallery talks; symposia

M **WINNIPEG ART GALLERY,** 300 Memorial Blvd, R3C 1V1. Tel 204-786-6641. *Admin Officer* James Bristow; *Head of Education Department* Jane Christiani; *Head Design Department* Glenn Tinley; *Chief Cur* Nancy Dillow; *Dir* Roger L Selby; *Pres* Arthur V Mauro; *VPres* J Kassenaar
Open Tues - Sat 11 AM - 5 PM; Sun Noon - 5 PM; cl Mon. No admis fee. Estab 1912, incorporated 1963. Rebuilt and relocated 1968, opened 1971, to present a diversified, quality level porgram of art in all media, representing various cultures, past and present. Educational function to surrounding community; to act as a major art resource for Canadian prairies. Average Annual Attendance: 250,000. Mem: 3000; dues $7.50 and up; annual meeting June
Income: $1,750,000 (financed by endowment, membership, city and state appropriation)
Purchases: $125,000
Collections: †Canadian Art; †Eskimoa Art; graphics, paintings, sculpture and other media
Exhibitions: American Painting 1955 - 1976; The Coming and Going of the Shaman; French and German Porcelain; Frontiers of Our Dreams: Quebec Painting in the 40's and 50's; Lionel Lemoine Fitzgerald; Gambling on the Future; Los

Mayas; Dennis Oppenheim Retrospective; Picasso; Drawings of Christiane Studies in Connoisseurship; A Terrible Beauty, The Art of Canada at War; Winnipeg Perspective
Publications: Calendar of Events, monthly; exhibition catalogues
Activities: Classes for adults and children; docent training; lect open to public, 20 - 30 visiting lectr per year; concerts; gallery talks; tours; exten dept serves Manitoba and Internationally; individual paintings and original objects of art lent to centres and museums; lending collection contains 10,500 books and 10,000 slides; book traveling exhibitions; originate traveling exhibitions; sales shop sells books, gift items, prints, reproductions and slides

L **Clara Lander Library,** 300 Memorial Blvd, R3C 1V1. *Chief Librn* David William Rozniatowski; *Library Asst* Tammy Bridges
Open Tues - Fri 11 AM - 4 PM. Estab 1954 to serve as a source of informational and general interest materials for members and staff of the Winnipeg Art Gallery and to art history students. Circ 1500
Income: Financed by membership, city and provincial appropriations
Purchases: $100,000
Library Holdings: Vols 11,000; Per subs 47; Other—Clipping files, exhibition catalogs, prints, manuscripts, memorabilia, pamphlets, photographs, reproductions, original documents
Special Subjects: Eskimo Art, Canadian Art
Collections: Archival material pertaining to Winnipeg Art Gallery; Rare Books on Canadian and European Art

O **WINNIPEG SKETCH CLUB,*** 434 Assiniboine Ave, R3C 0Y1. Tel 204-943-4772. *Pres* Bernice Sutton
Estab 1914 to provide a ground where members may meet for the purpose of advancing their studies by means of sketch meetings and for the encouragement of work done independently. Open to members only. Mem: 90; dues $10; annual meeting first week in Feb
Income: Financed by membership
Collections: Archives collection of work by past and present members
Exhibitions: Annual juried exhibition in Manitoba Archive Building; exhibits at the Assiniboine Park Conservatory; many local shows

L **Library,*** 434 Assiniboine Ave, R3C 0Y1. *Librn* Muriel King
Open to members only

NEW BRUNSWICK

CAMPBELLTON

M **GALERIE RESTIGOUCHE GALLERY,** 39 Andrew St, PO Box 674, E3N 3H1. Tel 506-753-5750. *Dir & Cur* Paul Soucy; *Secy-Accountant* Carole Laflamme; *Preparator* Leopold Thibeault
Open Mon - Fri 9 AM - 5 PM, Tues - Thurs evenings 7 - 9 PM, Sat 2 - 5 PM. No admis fee. Estab 1975 for exhibitions and activities. Building has 4800 sq ft; the Exhibition Hall is 1500 sq ft, small gallery 400 sq ft; 230 running feet. Average Annual Attendance: 10,000 - 15,000. Mem: 185; dues $10
Income: $55,000 (financed by federal, provincial, and city appropriations, by Art Society and by private donations)
Exhibitions: (1979-81) Couleurs d'Acadie; color photography traveling exhibition illustrating the phenomenon of brightly painted houses along the Acadian areas of the Atlantic provinces
Publications: Exhibitions catalogues; Restigouche Gallery brochure
Activities: Classes for adults and children; art and craft workshops; lect open to public, 10 visiting lectr per year; concerts; gallery talks; tours; traveling exhibitions exten service; originate traveling exhibitions

FEDERICTON

M **NEW BRUNSWICK CRAFT SCHOOL AND CENTRE GALLERY,** PO Box 6000, E3B 5H1. Tel 506-453-2305. *Dir of Crafts* George Fry
Open Mon - Fri 8:30 AM - 4:30 PM. Estab 1947 as a training school for professional craftspeople. Small gallery, craft related shows monthly. Average Annual Attendance: 1800
Income: Financed by provincial government
Collections: New Brunswick Permanent Craft Collection
Exhibitions: Glass from private collections; Elizabeth Gurrier: Stitchery and Soft Sculpture; Freeman Patterson: Photography; student and staff projects; juried shows
Publications: Exposition Metiers d'Art Acadien; Provincial Craft Directory
Activities: Classes for adults; lect open to public, 12 visiting lectr per year; original objects of art lent; originate traveling exhibitions

L **Library,** PO Box 6000, E3B 5H1.
A very small but growing library which is primarily for students

FREDERICTON

M **BEAVERBROOK ART GALLERY,** 703 Queen St, PO Box 605, E3B 5A6. Tel 506-455-6551. *Cur* Ian G Lumsden; *Asst Cur* Paul A Hachey
Open winter Sept 4 - May 31 Tues - Sat 10 AM - 5 PM, Sun Noon - 5 PM, summer June 1 - Sept 3 Tues - Sat 10 AM - 7 PM, Sun Noon - 7 PM, cl Mon. Admis adults 50¢, students and members free; also booked tours. Estab 1959 to foster and promote the study and the public enjoyment and appreciation of the arts. Three major galleries upstairs: British, Canadian, and High galleries; Exhibition, Pillow Porcelain Room and Foyer gallery downstairs. Average Annual Attendance: 40,000. Mem: 556; dues couple $7.50, single $5
Income: $210,000 (financed by endowment, and private foundation)
Purchases: $25,000
Collections: British Drawings, Paintings, Prints and Sculpture, 16th Century to Contemporary; 18th and 19th Century British Porcelain; Canadian Drawings,

Paintings and Prints, early 19th Century to Contemporary
Exhibitions: Monthly traveling exhibitions shown, primarily in the area of Canadian Art
Publications: Exhibition catalogs; Quarterly announcing gallery's program
Activities: Lect open to the public, 3 - 4 visiting lectr per year; concerts; gallery talks; tours; exten dept serving New Brunswick as well as the rest of Canada; individual paintings lent to recognized art galleries and museums which operate as educational institutions; lending collection contains 1246 original art works, sculpture; book traveling exhibitions; originate traveling exhibitions; sales shop sells books, magazines, reproductions, exhibition catalogs, Christmas cards, postcards and hasty-notes

L **Library,** 703 Queen St, E3B 5A6.
Open to gallery personnel only, for reference

M **FREDERICTON NATIONAL EXHIBITION CENTRE,** Queen St, PO Box 6000, E3B 5H1. Tel 506-453-3747. *Exhib Dir* Robert M Guthrie
Open summer Mon - Thurs & Sat 10 AM - 5 PM, Fri 10 AM - 9 PM, Sun 1 - 4 PM. No admis fee. Estab 1976. Gallery deals with traveling exhibitions only. Average Annual Attendance: 18,000
Income: Financed by federal and provincial appropriation
Activities: Classes for adults and children; lect open to public, 10 visiting lectr per year; concerts; gallery talks; tours; book traveling exhibitions 10 - 12 per year

M **UNIVERSITY OF NEW BRUNSWICK ART CENTRE,** University Ave, PO Box 4400, E3B 5A3. Tel 506-453-4623; Telex 014-46202. *Dir* Bruno Bobak; *Cur* Marjory Donaldson
Open Mon - Fri 10 AM - 5 PM, Sun 2 - 4 PM, cl Sat. No admis fee. Estab 1941 to broaden the experience of the university students and serve the city and province. Two galleries, each with approx 100 running ft of wall space; display case. Average Annual Attendance: 23,000
Income: Financed by university and from province
Purchases: $6000
Collections: Chiefly New Brunswick Artists; some Canadian (chiefly printmakers)
Publications: Catalogues
Activities: Classes for adults and children; lect open to public, 2 visiting lectr per year; gallery talks; tours; individual paintings and original objects of art lent to public but secure areas on this campus and the university campus in Saint John, and reproductions to students; lending collection contains 200 framed reporductions, 100 original prints, 300 paintings, photographs and sculpture; book traveling exhibitions 4 per year; originate traveling exhibitions

MONCTON

M **GALLERIE D'ART DE L'UNIVERSITE DE MONCTON,** E1A 3E9. Tel 506-858-4081, 858-4082. *Dir* Jean Daigle; *Cur* Marc Pitre; *Secy* Marguerite Fournier
Open daily 1 - 4:30 PM, Wed 7 - 9 PM, Sat - Sun 2 - 4 PM. Estab 1965 to offer outstanding shows to the university students and to the public. Gallery of approx 2700 sq ft exhibition area, will open in new building Clement Cormier in Fall 1980. Average Annual Attendance: 8000
Income: $15,000 (financed through university)
Collections: Artists represented in permanent collection: Bruno Bobak; Alex Colville; Francis Coutellier; Tom Forrestall; Georges Goguen; Hurtubise; Hilda Lavoie; Fernand Leduc; Rita Letendre; Toni Onley; Claude Roussel; Romeo Savoie; Pavel Skalnik; Gordon Smith
Exhibitions: Marie-Reine Chiasson-Ulmer; Francis Coutellier; Claude Gauvin; Jean-Marie Martin; Andre Michel; Peter Powning; Roger Savage; Gruppe Sieben German Artists; Pavel Skalnik; Survival Atlantic Style; Claude Theriault
Activities: Lect open to public, 5 visiting lectr per year; gallery talks; tours; individual paintings and original objects of art lent to University staff; lending collection contains original art works, original prints, paintings, photographs, sculpture; originate traveling exhibitions

L **Champlain Library,** E1A 3E9. *Librn* A Levesque
Open to students and public
Library Holdings: Vols 250,000

SACKVILLE

M **MOUNT ALLISON UNIVERSITY,** Owens Art Gallery, York St, E0A 3C0. Tel 506-536-2040. *Dir* T Keilor Bentley
Open Mon - Fri 10 AM - 5 PM, Thurs evenings 7 - 10 PM, Sat & Sun 2 - 5 PM, cl school holidays. No admis fee. Estab 1893, rebuilt 1972. Building includes five gallery areas; lecture hall; reading room
Collections: Broad collection of graphics, paintings, sculpture; parts of collection on display throughout the campus
Activities: Classes for adults and children; lect; gallery talks; guided tours; films; concerts; dance recitals; competitions; art rental service; book traveling exhibitions

SAINT ANDREWS

O **SUNBURY SHORES ARTS AND NATURE CENTRE, INC,** 139 Water St, PO Box 100, E0G 2X0. Tel 506-529-3386. *Pres* Irene Scarratt; *Dir* Henrik Kreiberg; *Executive Secy* Paddy Paul
Open weekdays 9 AM - Noon and 1 - 4:30 PM. No admis fee. Estab 1906, incorporated 1910, to function as a link for, and harmonize views of scientists, artists and industrialists. Gallery maintained, 200 running ft, fire and burglar protection, security during hours, controllable lighting and street frontage. Average Annual Attendance: 3000. Mem: 450; dues family $10, individual $5; annual meeting Sept
Income: Financed by endowment, membership and grants
Publications: Brochure, summer annually; Sunbury Notes, quarterly
Activities: Lect open to public, 10 - 15 visiting lectr per year; gallery talks; scholarships

L **Library,** 139 Water St, PO Box 100, E0G 2X0.
Open to public
Library Holdings: Vols 250; Per subs 10

SAINT JOHN

O **ARCHITECTS ASSOCIATION OF NEW BRUNSWICK,** c/o Freda M Large,
PO Box 910, Rothesay, E0G 2W0. *Executive Secy* Freda M Large
Incorporated 1933. Mem: 54; dues $250; annual meeting Feb

M **NEW BRUNSWICK MUSEUM,** 277 Douglas Ave, E2K 1E5. Tel 506-693-1196.
Dir David Ross; *Cur Art* Robert Percival; *Cur Canadian History* Gregg Finley
Open Winter 2 - 5 PM, summer 10 AM - 9 PM. Admis adults $1, children 25¢,
senior citizens free. Estab 1842 to collect, conserve, exhibit and interpret the Human
and Natural history of New Brunswick in relation to itself and to the outside world.
Six major galleries for permanent exhibits, three galleries for changing temporary
exhibits. Average Annual Attendance: 60,000. Mem: 600; dues $15; annual meeting
June
Income: $900,000 (financed by membership. federal and provincial appropriations)
Purchases: $5000
Collections: New Brunswick and Maritime artists
Publications: The Beacon, six per year; Journal of the New Brunswick Museum,
yearly
Activities: Classes for children; docent training; gallery talks; extension department
serving New Brunswick; individual paintings and original objects of art lent to
museums and galleries; traveling exhibitions organized and circulated; sales shop
selling books and gifts
L **Library,** 277 Douglas Ave, E2K 1E5. *Librn* Carol Rosevear
Open to the public for reference only
Library Holdings: Vols 30,000; Per subs 60

NEWFOUNDLAND

SAINT JOHN'S

M **MEMORIAL UNIVERSITY NEWFOUNDLAND,** Art Gallery, Arts and
Culture Centre, Elizabeth Ave, A1C 5S7. Tel 709-753-1200, Ext 2211. *Cur* Edythe
Goodridge; *Coordr of Operations* Edward Cadigan; *Coordr of Exhibitions* Patricia
Grattan; *Secy* Gwendyln Kerri
Open Tues - Sun Noon - 10 PM, cl Mon. No admis fee. Estab 1963 to display
contemporary Canadian art; to promote contemporary Newfoundland work; to
reflect the cultural history of the province. Three galleries with 130 running ft each.
Average Annual Attendance: 70,000
Income: Financed through the university and federal funding
Collections: Canadian Art of the 1960's and 1970's
Exhibitions: Contemporary Canadian and Newfoundland Folk Art
Activities: Classes for adults and children; dramatic programs; workshops; lect open
to public; concerts; gallery talks; tours; exten dept serves the province; artmobile;
individual paintings and original objects of art lent to other institutions; lending
collection contains books, catalogues and 1500 slides; book traveling exhibitions 20
per year; originate traveling exhibitions; sales shop sells original prints, works on
paper, original art and prints
L **Library,** Arts and Culture Centre, A1C 5S7.
Open to artists, docents and members

M **NEWFOUNDLAND MUSEUM,** Duckworth St, A1C 1E3. Tel 709-737-2460. *Dir*
Martin Bowe; *Asst Dir* David Mills; *Cur Coll* Victoria Dickenson; *Information
Officer* Linda Dale
No admis fee. Estab 1878 as the Athenaeum for the preservation of Provincial
Heritage. The Newfoundland Museum now houses collections and exhibitions
reflecting the 7000 year history of Newfoundland and Labrador
Income: Financed by federal and provincial appropriations
Collections: Beothuk, Thule, Maritime Archaic, pre-Dorset, Dorset, Naskapi,
Montagnais and Micmac artifacts; history material; maps; naval and military; 19th
Century Newfoundland domestic artifacts
L **Library,** Duckworth St, A1C 1E3.
Open to researchers for reference
Special Subjects: Military history
Collections: Mercury Series of National Museums in Archaeology, Ethnology,
Restoration; National Historic Parks and Sites Reports

NOVA SCOTIA

DARTMOUTH

M **DARTMOUTH HERITAGE MUSEUM,** Wyse Rd, B3A 1L9. *Dir* G S Gosley;
Secy Mrs R Gargan; *Asst Art* John Tate
Open summer 9 AM - 9 PM, winter 1 - 5 PM. No admis fee. Estab 1968 to collect
and preserve the story of the City of Dartmouth. Average Annual Attendance:
44,000. Mem: Annual meeting June
Income: Financed by city appropriation
Collections: †Nova Scotia Glass; aircraft models; †artifacts (local history); †works
of art
Activities: Classes for adults and children; tours of school classes

HALIFAX

M **ART GALLERY OF NOVA SCOTIA,** 6152 Coburg Rd, PO Box 2262, B3J 3C8.
Tel 902-424-7542. *Pres Board of Dir* Kent Sweeney; *VPres* Jack Craig; *Secy & Cur*
Bernard Riordon; *Asst Cur* Patrick Laurette; *Acting Registrar* Judy Dietz;
Education Officer Alice Hoskins; *Traveling Exhib Officer* Deborag Young
Open Mon, Wed, Fri, Sat 10 AM - 5:30 PM, Tues & Thurs 10 AM - 9 PM, Sun
Noon - 5 PM. No admis fee. Estab 1975 to replace the Nova Scotia Museum of
Fine Arts; dedicated to the collection, preservation, display and interpretation of
art. Three galleries: Main, Mezzanine and Permanent Collection. Average Annual
Attendance: 40,000. Mem: 500; dues family $10, individual $5, student $2; annual
meeting April
Income: $215,000 (financed by membership, province and federal agencies)
Purchases: $38,000
Collections: †Nova Scotia Folk Art; †Nova Scotian, Canadian Collection (both
historical and contemporary); drawings, paintings, prints and sculpture
Exhibitions: (1978) Claude Breeze; Sandra Brownlee; Emily Carr; Coalface 1900;
Designer Craftsmen 1978; Sydney Drum; Sorel Etrog; Robert Field; Scott Goudie;
Suzanne Guite; Toni Onley; Pratt-Gaucher Prints; Hu Shien Peasant Paintings; Joe
Sleep; Michael Thompson; Norman Yates; selections of works from the permanent
collection; (1979) Anneke Betlem; Leighton Davis; Designer Craftsmen 1979; Ed
Falkenberg; Tom Forrestall; Frances and Michael Morris; French Folk Art;
Gionvanni Battista Piranesi; Graham Metson - Rugby Drawings; Sandy MacIntoch
- Contributing Factors; selections from The McAlpine Collection; New Scottish
Painting; Don Pentz; Felicity Redgrave; Roger Savage; Scottish Painting Canada;
Karl Spital; Visual Record; Young Contemporaries; Young Quebec Abstract
Artists
Activities: ocent training; lect open to public, 12 visiting lectr per year; concerts;
gallery talks; children's art competitions; scholarships; exten dept serves
Canada; artmobile; individual paintings and original objects of art lent to Province
and Government House; lending collection contains original art works; originate
traveling exhibitions; museum and sales shop sells books, magazines, original art,
prints and crafts and also rental service

M **DALHOUSIE UNIVERSITY,** Art Gallery, 6101 University Ave, B3H 3J5. Tel
902-424-2403. *Dir* Linda J Milrod
Open Tues - Fri 11 AM - 5 PM and 7 - 10 PM, Sat & Sun 1 - 5 PM, cl Mon. No
admis fee. Dalhousei Art Gallery is located in the Dalhousie Arts Centre and open
to university community and local area. Average Annual Attendance: 20,000
Income: Financed by university supplemented by government grants
Collections: †Canadian drawings
Publications: Exhibition publications; information bulletin, quarterly
Activities: Docent training; lect open to public, 12 visiting lectr per year; concerts;
gallery talks; guided tours; individual paintings and original objects of art lent to
galleries in Canada; book traveling exhibitions; originate traveling exhibitions; sells
exhibition catalogues, current Canadian art magazines

O **EYE LEVEL GALLERY,*** Marble Bldg, 1672 Barrington St, B3J 2A2. Tel
902-425-6412. *Pres* Roger Savage; *Coordr* Susan Beaver
Open Mon - Sat Noon - 5 PM. No admis fee. Estab 1973 as an artist cooperative
gallery to provide exhibition opportunities for contemporary regional artists.
Gallery consists of three rooms, located on second floor. Mem: 57; dues $5; monthly
meetings last Thurs
Income: Financed by endowment and membership
Collections: Slide collection of Nova Scotia artists
Publications: Eye Level Newsletter, monthly
Activities: Classes for adults; demonstrations; dramatic programs; lect open to the
public; gallery talks; tours; competitions; original objects of art lent; traveling
exhibitions organized and circulated

M **MOUNT SAINT VINCENT UNIVERSITY ART GALLERY,** B3M 2J6. Tel
902-443-4450, Ext 160. *Dir Art Gallery* Mary Sparling; *Exhib Officer* Peter Latta;
Accessionist & Secy Debbie Cameron
Open Mon - Fri 9 AM - 5 PM, Sat, Sun & holidays Noon - 5 PM. No admis fee.
Estab 1970 and operating throughout the year with continuously-changing
exhibitions of local, regional, national and international origin in the area of fine
arts and crafts. Gallery situated on the main floor and mezzanine. Average Annual
Attendance: 16,000
Income: Financed by university funds
Collections: The Art Gallery is custodian of a collection of Pictures, Ceramics and
Pottery of the late Alice Egan Hagen of Mahone Bay, noted Nova Scotia potter and
ceramist, which is on permanent display in Rosaria Hall. It also has a growing
permanent collection
Exhibitions: (1978) Canadian Political Cartoons; Canadians; Fiber Landscape by
Karen Casselman; Changing Prospects: Views of America on Paper; Contemporary
Micmac Fibre Hangings; The Eskasoni Micmac Community, Photo Silkscreens by
Susan McEachern; Folksong in Fabric; Paintings by Graham Fowler; The
Landscape Art of Quebec; Paper Tigers; The Graphic Work of Odilon Redon;
Religious Art; Roses, Hunt Institute of Botanical Documentation; Six in Clay
(Nova Scotia potters); Drawings by Sally Spector; The Graphic Work of Felix
Vallotton; Views of Childhood including Drawings of Agnes Nanogak; Fifth
Annual University Community Art, Craft, Baking, Hobby and Talent Show;
current work, faculty; (1979) Contemporary Deewatin Wallhangings; Drawings
from Papua, New Guinea; Pennant Rocks: Variations on a Theme - Pastel
Drawings by Christine Ross-Hooper; Photography by George Steeves; Wood
Works - Woodcut Prints by Doris Larson; (1980) Fibre Metal Clay; A Retrospective
of Prints by Edward Porter; Seaform Variations - Sculpture by Ken Guild; Sixth
Annual University Community Art, Craft, Baking, Hobby and Talent Show
Publications: Gallery News; catalogs
Activities: Classes for adults and children; lect open to public, 12 visiting lectr per
year; concerts; gallery talks; tours; competitions; individual paintings and original
objects of art lent to other galleries; lending collection contains cassettes; originate
traveling exhibitions

O **NOVA SCOTIA ASSOCIATION OF ARCHITECTS,*** Suite 630, 5991 Spring
Garden Rd, B3H 1Y6. Tel 902-423-7607. *Exec Secy* Kae Worsley
Estab 1932. Mem: 116; annual meeting Feb

M NOVA SCOTIA COLLEGE OF ART AND DESIGN, Anna Leonowens Gallery,* 5163 Duke St, B3J 3J6. Tel 902-422-7381. *Pres* Garry Neill Kennedy; *Dean* James Daives; *Dir* Robert MacKeeman
Open daily. Estab for educational purposes. One small and one large gallery
Income: Financed by city and state appropriations and tuition
Exhibitions: 30-40 exhibitions per year
Publications: Ten books; one periodical
Activities: Exten dept has courses throughout the province
L Library, 5163 Duke St, B3J 3J6. Tel 902-422-7381. *Dir* John Murchie; *Asst Dir* Mary Snyder
Open Mon - Fri 8:30 AM - 11 PM, Sat 9 AM - 6 PM, Sun 1 - 11 PM. Circ 24,000
Income: $180,000 (financed by state appropriation and student fees)
Purchases: $50,000
Library Holdings: Vols 18,000; Per subs 350; Micro—Fiche, reels; AV—A-tapes, cassettes, fs, rec, slides, v-tapes; Other—Exhibition catalogs, pamphlets
Special Subjects: Contemporary art
L PUBLIC ARCHIVES OF NOVA SCOTIA, Cobury Rd, B3K 5K5. Tel 902-423-7040. *Provincial Archivist* Hugh A Taylor; *Assoc Archivist* Dr Phyllis R Blakely
Open Mon - Fri 8:30 AM - 10 PM, Sat 9 AM - 6 PM, Sun 1 - 10 PM. Estab 1931 to preserve Nova Scotian heritage. Maintains art gallery of portraits and historical paintings
Income: Financed by provincial appropriations
Library Holdings: Vols 40,000; Micro—Fiche, reels; AV—Slides; Other—Clipping files, manuscripts, memorabilia, original art works, pamphlets, photographs, original documents
Publications: Numerous special publications

YARMOUTH

M YARMOUTH COUNTY HISTORICAL SOCIETY MUSEUM, 22 Collins St, B5A 3L8. Tel 902-742-5539. *Pres* Christopher Allworth; *VPres* Charles Allen; *Secy* Frances Goridey; *Cur* Eric Ruff
Open May - June 14 & Oct 10 AM - Noon and 2 - 5 PM, June 15 - Sept 9 AM - 5 PM, July Wed, Thurs & Fri evenings 7 - 9 PM, Sun 1 - 5 PM, Nov - April 2 - 5 PM, cl Mon. Admis adults 50¢, students 25¢, children 10¢. Estab 1958 to display artifacts and paintings relating to Yarmouth's past. Located in former Congregational Church built in 1893. Average Annual Attendance: 14,000. Mem: 330; dues $5; annual meeting second Fri in Jan
Income: $25,000 (financed by state appropriation)
Purchases: $500
Collections: Historial Collection; Paintings of Yarmouthians; Collection of Ship Portraits of Yarmouth Vessels and Vessels Commanded by Yarmouthians
Activities: Lect open to public, 12 visiting lectr per year; concerts; gallery talks; tours; museum shop sells books

ONTARIO

ALMONTE

M R TAIT MCKENZIE MEMORIAL MUSEUM, Mill of Kintail, RR 1, K0A 1A0. Tel 613-256-3610. *Cur & Adminr* Dianna Carlisle
Open May - Oct Wed - Mon 10 AM - 6 PM, cl Tues, July and Aug open daily. Admis 50¢. Estab 1952 as a private museum, publicly owned since 1973 by Mississippi Valley Conservation Authority as a memorial to Dr R Tait McKenzie, Canadian sculptor, physical educator, surgeon and humanitarian. Average Annual Attendance: 9000
Income: Financed by provincial government grant
Collections: 70 Original Athletic, Memorial and Monumental Sculptures, nearly all in plaster; 600 Pioneer Artifacts, mostly collected by Dr McKenzie
Exhibitions: Athletic Sculpture Plaque exhibited in connection with Olympiad in Montreal 1976
Activities: Educ programs for adults and children; film shows; lect open to public; nature walks; sales shop sells medal reproductions

BARRIE

L GEORGIAN COLLEGE OF APPLIED ARTS AND TECHNOLOGY, Georgian Learning Resources Centre, One Georgian College Dr, L4M 3X9. Tel 705-728-1951; Telex 068-75713. *Mgr Learning Resources* P Hull; *Librn Barrie Campus* J McNeice
Open Mon - Thurs 8 AM - 9 PM, Fri 8 AM - 6 PM, Sat 10 AM - 3 PM. Estab 1968 to support instructional program at college. Circ 100,000
Income: $5000
Purchases: $5000
Library Holdings: Vols 3000; Per subs 30; Micro—Cards, fiche, reels; AV—A-tapes, cassettes, fs, motion pictures, rec, slides, v-tapes; Other—Clipping files
Special Subjects: Crafts, Inter Design
Exhibitions: (1978-79) student work
Activities: Lect open to public; student competitions with awards; scholarships

BELLEVILLE

M HASTINGS COUNTY MUSEUM, 257 Bridge St E, K8N 1P4. Tel 613-962-2329. *Cur* Mrs M E Simonds; *Exhib Designer* Connie Potts; *Education* Claire Lakins
Open summer Tues - Sun 10 AM - 4:30 PM, winter Tues - Sun 1 - 4:30 PM. Admis $1. Estab 1973. Historic House with art gallery dedicated to local artist Manley McDonald. Average Annual Attendance: 7000
Income: Financed by city and state appropriation
Exhibitions: (1979) Permanent Collection of Manley McDonald Originals and Beverley McDonald Originals; artists, photographers
Activities: Classes for children; gallery talks; tours; lending collection contains nature artifacts and slides; museum shop sells books and magazines

BRAMALEA

L CITY OF BRAMPTON PUBLIC LIBRARY AND ART GALLERY, 250 Central Park Dr, Bramalea, ON. (Mailing Add: 65 Queen St E, Brampton, ON L6W 3L6) Tel 416-453-2444. *Dir* Judith Ruan
Open Tues - Fri 10 AM - 9 PM, Sat 10 AM - 5 PM, Sun 1 - 5 PM. No admis fee. Estab 1972 to encourage an interest in and knowledge of the arts through exhibits and related activities. Gallery is 2950 sq ft, 250 running ft and walls are stretch fabric over wood. Average Annual Attendance: 80,000
Income: $48,897 (financed by city and state appropriation)
Collections: Small permanent collection
Activities: Classes for children; dramatic programs; lect open to public; concerts; gallery talks

BRAMPTON

M REGION OF PEEL MUSEUM AND ART GALLERY, 3 Wellington St E, L6W 1Y1. Tel 416-451-9051. *Dir* William D Barber; *Asst to Dir* Lynne Clifford
Open daily 1:30 - 4:30 PM. Admis adults 75¢, sr citizens and students 50¢, members free. Estab 1968. Average Annual Attendance: 10,000. Mem: 300; dues family $8, individual $5; annual meeting last Tues in Jan
Collections: Permanent art collection of Peel Artists: Artifacts of Peel 1850 to present
Exhibitions: 7 exhibits per year, all mediums: Annual Open Juried Show; Regional Artists
Activities: Children's workshops; lect

BRANTFORD

M ART GALLERY OF BRANT, INC, 76 Dalhousie St, PO Box 1747, N3T 5V7. Tel 519-753-7581. *Dir* Richard Pottruff; *Chmn* H J Meiritt; *Secy* Edie Mountjoy
Open Tues - Fri 9 AM - 5 PM, Sat 10 AM - 5 PM, cl Sun & Mon. No admis fee. Estab 1971 as a non-profit public art gallery serving the citizens of Brantford and Brant County. Store-front gallery; one main gallery room. Average Annual Attendance: 20,000. Mem: 375; dues sustaining $25, family $10, individual $7, student and senior citizens $2; annual meeting Sept
Income: Financed by membership, city and provincial appropriations and local foundations
Collections: †Original Prints and Drawings by Contemporary Canadian Artists; Original Prints by European and American Artists; Works of Historical Nature by local area Artist Robert Whale
Publications: Annual report; Calendar of Events, quarterly; catalogues for exhibitions throughout the year
Activities: Classes for adults and children; docent training; film series; lect open to public, 8 visiting lectr per year; gallery talks; competitions; individual paintings and original objects of art lent to galleries and businesses; originate traveling exhibitions
L Library, 76 Dalhousie St, N3T 5V7.
Open to public for reference
Library Holdings: Vols 35

M BRANT COUNTY MUSEUM,* 57 Charlotte St, N3T 2W6. Tel 519-752-2483. *Pres* D Alan Young; *Dir* William R Robbins; *Cur* Dr Irmgard Jamnik
Open Nov 1 - Apr 30 Mon - Fri 9 AM - 5 PM, Sat 1 - 4 PM, May 1 - Oct 31 Mon - Fri 9 AM - 5 PM, Sat & Sun 1 - 4 PM. Admis adults 75¢, students 50¢, children 25¢, under 6 accompanied by parent, free. Estab 1908. Mem: Dues annual $25; individual $5
Income: Financed by county appropriation
Collections: Early Indian history; historical figures; portraits and paintings
Publications: Annual brochure
L Library,* 57 Charlotte St, N3T 2W6.
Library Holdings: Vols 500
Collections: First editions of history and archaeology; old Bibles available for research on premises under supervision of curator; rare books

O GLENHYRST ARTS COUNCIL OF BRANTFORD INC, 20 Ava Rd, N3T 5G9. Tel 519-756-5932. *Pres* Dale Simpson; *Adminr* Elsie Kerrigan
Open Tues - Fri 2 - 8 PM, Sat & Sun 2 - 6 PM, cl Mon. No admis fee. Estab 1957. Arts centre occupies 11 room house left to the city by the late E L Cockshutt, maintained by the city. Average Annual Attendance: 20,000
Income: Financed by membership and fund-raising events
Collections: †Small permanent collection
Exhibitions: Held on regular basis
Publications: Newsletter, monthly
Activities: Classes for adults and children; lect open to public, visiting lectr; competitions
L Library, 20 Ava Rd, N3T 5G9.
Small reference library

CAMBRIDGE

L CAMBRIDGE PUBLIC LIBRARY AND ARTS CENTRE, 20 Grand Ave N, N1S 2K6. Tel 519-621-0460. *Chief Librn* Norman Hebblethwaite; *Programs Coordr* Eric Dewdney
Open Mon - Thurs 9:30 AM - 8:30 PM, Fri & Sat 9:30 AM - 5:30 PM. No admis fee. Estab 1969. Gallery on second floor mezzanine with 2000 sq ft, 250 linear ft. Average Annual Attendance: 25,000
Income: $70,000 (financed by provincial appropriation, federal and private)
Collections: Regional Artists
Publications: Bi-monthly newsletter
Activities: Classes for adults and children; lect open to public, 10 visiting lectr per year; concerts; gallery talks; tours; competitions; awards; individual paintings and original objects of art lent; book traveling exhibitions five per year; originate traveling exhibitions

CHATHAM

O THAMES ARTS CENTRE, 75 William St N, N7M 4L4. Tel 519-354-8338. *Dir* David K McNeil; *Gallery Education Coordr* Tim Child
Open Tues - Sun 1 - 5 PM. No admis fee. Estab 1963 to operate as a regional arts centre, to advance knowledge and appreciation of, and to encourage, stimulate and promote interest in the study of culture and the visual and performing arts. Gallery maintained; designated National Exhibition Centre for the presentation of visual art works and museum related works, to the public of this country. Average Annual Attendance: 19,000. Mem: 600; dues family $18, single $10; annual meeting June
Income: Financed by membership, city and state appropriation, and National Museum Grants
Exhibitions: (1978-79) Artists' Invitational; Henri Carter-Bresson Photographs; Collins, Pachter and Tinkl (artists); Faculty of Craft and Design at Saint Clair College; Hundertwasser - 25 Years; Japanese Canadian Centennial Exhibition; Leonard Jubenville - Recent Work; London Regional Art Gallery Collection; The Magical Machines of Rowland Emett; John Mars - Painting and Works on Paper; McMichael Canadian Collection from Kleinburg; More than Meets the Eye - microphotography at the Royal Ontario Museum; Recent Work by Fred McSherry; From Muo Into Immortality - Ceramics; Ontario Society of Artists Exhibition; The Queen's Silver Anniversary Exhibition; William Tilland - Photographer; Barbara C Whitson - Watercolors
Publications: Bi-monthly bulletin
Activities: Classes for adults and children; dramatic programs; docent training; workshops; theatre series; lect open to the public; concerts; gallery talks; tours; films; lending collection contains 1500 slides

DOWNSVIEW

UNIVERSITIES ART ASSOCIATION OF CANADA
For further information, see National and Regional Organizations

M YORK UNIVERSITY ART GALLERY, 4700 Keele St, Ross Bldg N145, M3T 1P3. Tel 416-667-3427. *Cur of Art* Michael Greenwood; *Cur Asst* Shelagh Keeley; *Asst* Louise Greenwood; *Secy* Maxine Burns
Open Mon - Fri 10 AM - 4:30 PM. No admis fee. Estab to maintain a program of exhibitions covering a broad spectrum of the visual arts and artifacts of mankind from diverse cultures. Gallery is 2115 sq ft, exhibition space only 1200 sq ft, program space only 420 sq ft and support space only 485 sq ft. Average Annual Attendance: 18,000
Income: Financed by university
Collections: Approx 750 works including ethnographical items and artifacts, approx 550 of the works are by Canadian artists
Exhibitions: (1978) George Grosz (1893-1959); Historic Canadian Silver from The Henry Birks Collection; Hungarian Folk Art from the 18th - 20th Century; Ukiyo-e Glimpses into the Floating World
Publications: Illustrated catalogue of the Historic Canadian Silver Show from the Henry Birks Collection
Activities: School groups from the community visit and are given talks and film showings; lect open to public, 5 visiting lectr per year; concerts; gallery talks; individual paintings and original objects of art lent for major shows or retrospectives to other members of the University and faculty for their offices; originate traveling exhibitions
L York University Library, 4700 Keele St, M2T 1P3.
Library Holdings: Vols 16,235; AV—A-tapes, cassettes, fs, Kodachromes, lantern Slides, motion pictures, rec, slides, v-tapes; Other—Clipping files, exhibition catalogs, manuscripts
Collections: Bazin Library; Rare Books Library
L Fine Arts Slide Library, 4700 Keele St, M3T 1P3.
Library Holdings: AV—Slides 145,000

GANANOQUE

M GANANOQUE HISTORICAL MUSEUM, 10 King St, E, PO Box 158, K7G 2T8. Tel 613-382-4663. *Pres* Derrol Simpson; *Secy* Lorna Whyte; *Cur* Evelyn Symons
Open Mon - Sat Noon - 5 PM. Admis adults 50¢, children under 12 10¢. Estab 1964 to house many local artifacts. Average Annual Attendance: 3500
Collections: China Collection; Military and Indian Artifacts; Victorian Dining Room, Parlour and Bedroom; glass; portraits and photographs pertaining to local history
Activities: book traveling exhibitions

GUELPH

M MACDONALD STEWARD ART CENTRE, 358 Gordon St, PO Box 330, N1G 2W1. Tel 519-824-4120, Ext 3158. *Chmn* Charles C Ferguson; *VChmn* Dr F Hamilton; *Secy* Mrs V Myers; *Dir* Judith Nasby; *Asst Cur* Lynn Barbeau; *Gallery Technician* Rob Freeman
Open Tues - Fri 11 AM - 5 PM, Sat 10 AM - 5 PM, Thurs 7 - 9 PM. Estab 1978 to collect and exhibit works of art; maintain and operate a gallery; and related facilities for this purpose fulfilling a public role in city and county. 30,000 sq ft building comprising galleries, lecture room, studio, meeting rooms, resource centre, gift shop and rental service. Restored and renovated in 1980. Average Annual Attendance: 40,000. Mem: 200; dues family $25, individual $15, student $5; annual meeting Sept-Oct
Income: Financed by endowment, membership, city and state appropriation and federal grants
Collections: Some Decorative Arts; †Historical and Contemporary Canadian Art; †Historical and Contemporary International Prints; †Inuit Collection
Exhibitions: (1979-80) Artwheels - All about Kids; Aspects of Printmaking; Ed Bartram: 12 Years (retrospective of prints); Harry Callaghan-City (urban photography); Robert Field 1769-1819; Mark Grenville and Ian McKay (paintings and drawings); International Year of the Child (photographs); The Klamer Family Collection of Inuit Art; 100 Years of the Poster in Canada; Plants in Art Through The Centuries; Miho Sawada 1974-1979; Seven Prairie Painters; Survival Atlantic Style; Youth Art; changing exhibits including Chinese Scrolls by Dr Kingscote; Fine Art Faculty; Student Jury Show
Publications: Catalogue of permanent collection of University of Guelph; exhibition catalogues; Newsletter
Activities: Classes for children; artist-in residence programs; workshops; lect open to public; visiting lectr; concerts; gallery talks; tours; films; performances; competitions; awards; exten dept serves Wellington County; artmobile; individual paintings and original objects of art lent to institutions and public galleries; art rental to gallery members; lending collection contains original art works, original prints, paintings, photographs, sculpture and slides; book traveling exhibitions seven per year; originate traveling exhibitions; sales shop sells books, magazines, reproductions, slides, pottery, textiles, jewelry and catalogues

HAMILTON

M ART GALLERY OF HAMILTON, 123 King St W, L8P 4S8. Tel 416-527-6610. *Dir* Glen E Cumming; *Cur* Andrew J Oko; *Asst to Dir* Ted Pietrzak; *Education & Extension Officer* Sheila Greenspan; *Community Relations* Keith Courtney; *Preparator* Dan Thorburn; *Registrar* Margaret Haupt
Open Tues - Sat 10 AM - 5 PM, Thurs evenings 7 - 9 PM, Sun 1 - 5 PM. No Admis fee. Estab Jan 1914 to develop and maintain a centre for the study and enjoyment of the visual arts; new gallery opened Oct 1977. Building is 76,000 sq ft, 24,000 sq ft of exhibition space. Average Annual Attendance: 100,000. Mem: 3395; dues family $25, single $15; annual meeting last Thurs in May
Income: $1,006,500 (financed by endowment, membership, city and provincial appropriation and federal grants)
Purchases: $100,000
Collections: The complete Graphics of Karel Appel; principally Canadian Fine Arts, but also American, British and other European
Exhibitions: (1979) Antique, Noamdic and Village Rugs of the Near East; Milton Avery: Paintings; Robert Bateman; Robin C H Bell: Sculpture; Therese Bolliger: Drawings and Constructions; Ron Bolt: The Inner Ocean; Armando Brasini: Roma Imperiale; Walter Carsen Gifts to Hamilton; Certain Traditions: Recent British and Canadian Art; Contemporary Art of Senegal; Paul Dempsey: Recent Works; Selections from The Dofasco Collection; Ecanada Art Pottery; Ton Forrestall: A Retrospective; Conrad Furey: Paintings and Soft Sculpture; Kieter Hastenteufel: Recent Works; Teresa Hitch; Hungarian Folk Art; Robert Mason: Recent Work; Tibor Nyilasi: The Figurative Image; The Order of the Broom; Dora de Pedery-Hunt: Sculpture; The Price Collection of Eastern Canadian Folk Art; Otto Rogers: New Paintings and Sculpture 1977-78; E Robert Ross: Wilderness Spirit; The Jack Sher Collection; John Street: New Works on Paper; Steven Toth: Drawings and Paintings; Susana Wald and Ludwig Zeller: By Four Hands; The Woodcuts of Naoko Masubara; annual juried show
Publications: Art Gallery of Hamilton Calendar, monthly
Activities: Classes for adults and children; docent training; lect open to public, 18 visiting lectr per year; concerts; gallery talks; tours; exten dept; individual paintings and original objects of art lent to other galleries and museums; lending collection contains 1751 original prints, 1361 paintings, 135 sculpture, 461 drawings; originate traveling exhibitions; museum shop sells books, magazines and reproductions
L Muriel Isabel Bostwich Library, 123 King St W, L8P 4S8. *Registrar* Margaret Haupt
Open to gallery members and researchers for reference
Library Holdings: Vols 3000; Per subs 14
Special Subjects: Good references on Canadian art history and large holding of exhibition catalogues relating to this field

M DUNDURN CASTLE, Dundurn Park, York Blvd, L8R 3H1. Tel 416-551-5313. *Managing Dir* Tharten Lewis; *Asst Dir* Mary Alix Groneau
Open mid-June to Labor Day daily 11 AM - 4 PM, evening appointments for groups of 25 or more, Labor Day to mid-June booked tours mornings and evenings, open to public 1 - 4 PM, cl Christmas and New Year's Day, children must be accompanied by adults. Dundurn, the home of Sir Allan Napier MacNab; Hamilton's Centennial Project was the restoration of this historic house; built in 1832-35, it was tenured by MacNab until his death in 1862. The terminal date of the furnishings is 1855. Approximately 37 rooms are shown; three-room on-site museums. Average Annual Attendance: 90,000
Income: Financed by City of Hamilton, owner and operator
Activities: Seminars; demonstrations

M MCMASTER UNIVERSITY ART GALLERY, 1280 Main St W, L8S 4M2. Tel 416-525-9140, Ext 4685. *Secy* Mrs S Waxman; *Dir* Prof George Wallace; *Cur* David G Taylor
Open Mon - Thurs 10 AM - 5 PM, Thurs evenings 7 - 9 PM, Sun 1 - 5 PM. No admis fee. Estab 1967 to provide the university and public with historical and

contemporary art from Canada and other countries. Two galleries 2285 sq ft and 540 sq ft; incandescent lighting throughout; display casses; sculpture stands. Average Annual Attendance: 7000

Income: $3300 (financed by university and private endowment)

Purchases: $10,000

Collections: †American and Canadian Art; European paintings, prints and drawings; †German Expressionist Prints

Exhibitions: (1978-79) German Art at the Turn of the Century; 18th Century Japanese Theatrical Prints; 100 Years of the Poster in Canada; 18th Century Portraiture; Georges Ronault Prints including Miserere and Pere Ubn series

Activities: Classroom facilities; lect open to public; concerts; gallery talks; individual paintings and original objects of art lent to National Gallery of Canada, Art Gallery of Ontario; University of Minnesota Art Gallery

L **Library,** McMaster University, 1280 Main St W, L8S 4M2.
Open Mon - Thurs 10 AM - 5 PM, Thurs evenings 7 - 9 PM, Sun 1 - 5 PM. Houses reference materials on art gallery management, exhibition and sales catalogues
Library Holdings: Vols 100; Other—Exhibition catalogs

JORDAN

M **JORDAN HISTORICAL MUSEUM OF THE TWENTY,** Vintage House, Main St, L0R 1S0. Tel 416-562-5242. *Dir* H L Crowfoot
Open May - Oct daily Noon - 6 PM. No admis fee. Estab 1953 to preserve the material and folklore of the area known as The Twenty Mile Creek vicinity. Average Annual Attendance: 20,000. Mem: 820; annual meeting Dec
Income: $14,500
Collections: Archives, china, furniture, glass, historical material and textiles
Activities: Special displays as requested by the community; Pioneer Day first Sat after Canadian Thanksgiving Holiday

KINGSTON

M **QUEEN'S UNIVERSITY,** Agnes Etherington Art Centre, K7L 3N6. Tel 613-547-6551. *Dir* Robert F Swain; *Cur* Dorothy Farr; *Assoc Cur* William Muysson; *Educational Officer* Catherine Bull
Open Tues - Sat 10 AM - 5 PM, Tues and Thurs evenings 7 - 9 PM, Sun 1 - 5 PM. No admis fee. Estab 1957 to provide the services of a public art gallery and museum for the community and region. Gallery has approximately 8000 sq ft of space, in four separate areas, showing a balanced program of exhibitions of the contemporary and historical, of national, international and regional art. Average Annual Attendance: 30,000. Mem: 850; dues $5 - $100; annual meeting May
Income: $425,000 (financed by endowment, city and state appropriation, University and Canada Council funds)
Purchases: $35,000
Collections: †Canadian Paintings, Prints, Sculpture, Historical and Contemporary; †European Graphics; Ethnological Collection; Old Master Paintings
Exhibitions: About 30 exhibitions mounted each year, William Brymner; Daniel Fowler of Amherst Island; George Heriot Painter of the Canadas; Inuit Art of the 1970's (all mounted in 1978-79)
Publications: Bulletin, bimonthly; exhibition publications and catalogues; studies
Activities: Classes for adults and children; docent training for school groups; studio classes; lect open to public, 10 visiting lectr per year; concerts; gallery talks; tours; individual paintings lent by Gallery Association Art Rental to private individuals and businesses; lending collection contains original prints and paintings; originate traveling exhibitions
L **Library,** K7L 3L6.
Open to students, researchers and the public for reference only
Library Holdings: Per subs 4; Other—Exhibition catalogs, reference books
Collections: Archival records on a few Canadian artists where special study has been undertaken: Andre Bieler; Daniel Fowler; George Heriot; Goodridge Roberts; William Sawyer; George Harlow White

KITCHENER

M **KITCHENER-WATERLOO ART GALLERY,** The Centre in the Square, 101 Queen Street N, N2G 3H1. Tel 519-745-6671. *Pres Board of Dir* Ann Gawman; *First VPres* J M Carty; *Secy* G Eastman; *Treas* J Bowman; *Cur* Bradley Blain; *Education Officer* Paul Blain
Average Annual Attendance: 30,000. Mem: 700; dues business $50, family $20, individual $15, senior cityizens and students $5
Income: Financed by membership, city, municipal, provincial and federal funds
L **Eleanor Calvert Memorial Library,** 43 Benton St, N2G 3H1. *Librn* Nancy E Francis
Estab 1972 for art reference
Library Holdings: Vols 1300; Per subs 3; AV—Slides, v-tapes; Other—Clipping files, exhibition catalogs, photographs
Special Subjects: Canadian artists biographical material

KLEINBURG

M **MCMICHAEL CANADIAN COLLECTION,** L0J 1C0. Tel 416-893-1121. *Dir* Dr Robert McMichael; *Chmn Board Turstees* J Allyn Taylor; *Vice Chmn Board Trustees* Warren E Jones
Open Tues - Sun Noon - 5:30 PM, school tours Mon - Fri mornings, by appointment. No admis fee. Estab 1965 to give better understanding of Canadian art to people of all ages. Average Annual Attendance: 281,000.
Income: Operations financed by the Government of Ontario
Collections: Canadian Group of Seven and their contemporaries: Emily Carr, David Milne, Tom Thomson, etc; Canadian Eskimo and Indian Art
Publications: Annual art calendar; The Group of Seven and Tom Thomson (book); The McMichael Canadian Collection (book)
Activities: Ext dept serves Ontario; individual paintings and original objects of art loaned; museum shop sells books, reproductions and prints

L **Library,** L0J 1C0. *Librn & Archivist* Linda Barr
Library Holdings: AV—Cassettes, fs, motion pictures, slides; Other—Clipping files, exhibition catalogs, prints, manuscripts, memorabilia, original art works, pamphlets, photographs, reproductions, Mainly archival material
Special Subjects: Inuit, West Coast Indian, Woodland Indian

LONDON

M **LONDON REGIONAL ART GALLERY,** 421 Ridout St N, N6A 5H4. Tel 519-672-4580. *Dir* William C Forsey; *Asst Dir & Cur* Paddy O'Brien; *Coordr Education Services* Antony Jeffery; *Registrar* Barry Fair; *Coordr Gallery Services & Mem Secy* Jan Delaney; *Communications Officer* Hetty Ventura Aaron
Open Tues, Fri & Sat 10 AM - 6 PM, Wed & Thurs 10 AM - 9 PM, Sun Noon - 6 PM. Admis adults $1, senior citizens & students 50¢. Estab 1976. Seven exhibiting spaces, totalling 22,000 sq ft. New Gallery opening May 3, 1980; architecture by Raymond Moriyama. Mem: 3300; dues $25, senior citizens and students $10; annual meeting in the Fall
Income: Financed by membership, city and province appropriation and federally funded
Collections: Permanent Collection stresses regional and local artists, who have become internationally and nationally recognized such as Jack Chambers, Greg Curnoe, Paul Kane and Paul Peel
Exhibitions: Works of art - international, national and regional; programmes of milti-media nature, including performing arts
Publications: Exhibition catalogues
Activities: Classes for children; docent training; lect open to public, some for members only; concerts; gallery talks; tours; exten dept serves the Region; individual paintings and original objects of art lent; book traveling exhibitions; originate traveling exhibitions; museum shop sells books, jewelry magazines, original art, prints and reproductions

M **UNIVERSITY OF WESTERN ONTARIO,** McIntosh Art Gallery, 1151 Richmond St, N6A 3K7. Tel 519-679-3181, 679-6027. *University Art Cur* Marucie Stubbs; *Exhib Coordr* Arlene Kennedy; *Secy* Margaret Allen
Open Sept - April Mon - Fri Noon - 5 PM, Sat & Sun 2 - 5 PM, Wed & Thurs evenings 7 - 9 PM, May - Aug Mon - Fri Noon - 4 PM, Sun 2 - 5 PM, cl Sat. No admis fee. Estab 1942. Three galleries with a total of 2960 sq ft. Average Annual Attendance: 12,000. Mem: 91
Income: Financed by endowment, membership, provincial appropriation, special grants and University funds
Purchases: $2000
Collections: Canadian Art
Exhibitions: Aspects of Canadian Printmaking; Barbara Astman (photographs); Bikkers-Appel; Brahma and Buddha; Connections: Krizan, McAulay and Wright (paintings and drawings); Conservation of University of Western Ontario Collection; Reflections of an Age: 19th Century British Art; Steel: The Engineer and the Sculptor; Visual Arts Faculty Show
Publications: Bulletin, bimonthly; catalogues for exhibition
Activities: Lect open to public, 4 - 6 visiting lectr per year; concerts; gallery talks; tours; individual paintings and original objects lent to galleries; originate traveling exhibitions
L **Library,** 1151 Richmond St, N6A 3K7.
Open to gallery staff and museology students
Library Holdings: Vols 250; Per subs 3

MISSISSAUGA

L **MISSISSAUGA LIBRARY SYSTEM,** 110 Dundas St W, L5B 1H3. Tel 416-279-7002. *Chief Librn* Noel Ryan; *Gallery Mgr* Ona Alisauskas
Hours vary according to branch. No admis fee. Outlet for local artists at branch galleries; present more widely recognised artists at Central and Burwhamthorp Galleries. Total of nine galleries in system, 100 running ft, often multi-purpose rooms
Collections: Permanent Collection of 100 Paintings and Prints by Canadian Artists, emphasis on prints (all framed)
Exhibitions: Annual Juried Art Show Open
Publications: Artifacts, monthly brochure; Link News Tabloid Format, every other month; Monthly Branch Brochure
Activities: Lect open to public; competitions with cash prizes; lending collection contains books and 50 motion pictures; book traveling exhibitions; originate traveling exhibitions
L **Central Library, Art Division,** 110 Dundas St W, Mississauga, ON L5B 1H3. *Personnel* Albert Spratt
Open Mon - Fri Noon - 9 PM, Sat 9 AM - 5 PM, Sun 1 - 5 PM. Deposit library for Central Ontario Regional Library System
Library Holdings: Vols 22,700; Per subs 29; AV—Cassettes, fs, lantern Slides, motion pictures, slides, v-tapes; Other—Clipping files, exhibition catalogs, framed reproductions, prints, original art works, pamphlets
Special Subjects: Canadian prints

L **SHERIDAN COLLEGE SCHOOL OF APPLIED ARTS AND TECHNOLOGY,** School of Crafts and Design Library, 1460 S Sheridan Way, L5H 1Z7. Tel 416-274-3685. *Head Librn* Cathy Zuraw; *Library Technician* Madeleine LaPointe
Estab 1970 to accommodate students on campus
Income: Financed by college
Purchases: $7000
Library Holdings: Vols 5200; Per subs 85; AV—Cassettes, fs, slides, v-tapes; Other—Clipping files, exhibition catalogs
Special Subjects: Architecture, Ceramics, Metalwork, Sculpture, Textiles, Design, glass-blowing, wood
Activities: Classes for adults

NIAGARA FALLS

M **OAK HALL,** Portage Rd, c/o The Niagara Parks Commission, Box 150, L2E 6T2. Tel 416-356-2241. *Cur* L Burns
Open daily mid-June - Labor Day 11 AM - 7 PM. Admis adults 75¢, children 12 and under free. Estab 1959, the restored home of the late Sir Harry Oakes
Income: Financed by Niagara Parks Commission, a self-sustaining provincial agency
Collections: Early Niagara Prints and Oils on display in gallery
Publications: Historical Niagara Frontier Revisited, annual promotional brochure

OAKVILLE

M **OAKVILLE CENTENNIAL-GAIRLOCH GALLERIES,** 120 Navy St, L6J 2Z4. Tel 416-844-4402. *Chmn* G G Mills; *VChmn* R Mahler; *Dir* Margot Fisher-Page; *Asst Dir* Ian Paterson; *Education Officer* Dianne Bos
Centennial open Mon - Fri 10 AM - 9 PM, Sat 10 AM - 5 PM, Sun 1 - 5 PM; Gairloch, located at 1306 Lakeshore Rd E, open Tue - Sun 1 - 5 PM, July - Aug Tue - Sun 1 - 8 PM. Estab Centennial 1967, Garloch 1972, to exhibit and to educate historical and contemporary visual arts. Centennial is the larger, more central gallery; Gairloch is a smaller, estate house-gallery in park setting. The two galleries now have been renamed as one organization - The Oakville Centennial-Gairloch Galleries. Average Annual Attendance: 31,000. Mem: 400
Income: $130,000 (financed by city and state appropriation)
Purchases: $3000
Collections: Contemporary Canadian Painting, Drawing and Prints; Keene Collection of Posters; North American Native Indian Art and Artifacts
Exhibitions: (1979) Centennial: Clay and Cloth (pottery, stitchery and children's clay work); Dieter Hastenteufel (multi-media exhibition of drawings, paintings, sculpture and constructions); Michael Hitchcox - Watercolours; Stan Molak - Steel Sculpture; Norval Morrisseau (paintings and prints); The Oakville Group; Out of the Woods (wood design); School Art (prints, drawings, paintings and sculpture); Seven Prairie Artists; Alice Waywell - Solitudes (recent paintings); The Words of the God, Egyptian Hieroglyphs (drawings based on nature, symbolizing an object, place, idea or sound); Gairloch: Contemporary Fibre Statements (large scale fibre works of seven Ontario artists); Live with Art; Robert Marchessault and Theresa Cullen (pastels, watercolours, weavings); Mostly Metal; Ontario Society of Artists Print Show; Sheridan College School of Visual Arts Faculty Exhibition; Year of the Child - Photographs
Activities: Classes for adults and children; docent training, volunteer committee; lect open to public, 12 - 15 visiting lectr per year; gallery talks; tours; competitions; individual paintings and original objects of art lent to qualified and controlled art galleries and museums in Canada; lending collection contains 100 original art works; originate traveling exhibitions; sales shop sells books, original art, reproductions, prints and locally produced pottery etc
L **Gairloch Gallery Library,** 1306 Lakeshore Rd E, L6J 1L6.
Open Tue - Sun 1 - 5 PM, July & August 1 - 8 PM. Estab 1979, primarily art magazines from 1967-79 dealing with contemporary art. Reference library
Library Holdings: AV—Slides, v-tapes; Other—Magazines
Special Subjects: Contemporary Canadian Art

M **TARAS H SCHEVCHENKO MUSEUM AND MEMORIAL PARK FOUNDATION,** 1363 Dundas St W, L6J 4Z2. Tel 416-827-2651. *Pres & Cur* Peter Prokop; *Secy* Stanley Dobrowolsky
Open July & Aug Sun Noon - 5 PM, and by appointment. Admis by voluntary donation. Estab 1952, a 16.5 acre park, complete with monument and museum opened as a symbol of the unity and brother of Ukrainian Canadians with Canadians of all national origins. Toronto Office: 42 Roncesvalles Ave, Toronto M6R 2K3; Tel: 416-535-1063
Income: Financed by donations
Collections: Reproductions and copies in oil and watercolor of Taras H Schevchenko's own paintings and sketches, also paintings done by other artists and authors representing some aspects of T H Shevchenko's life. Display and handicrafts - ceramics from Ukraine, handicrafts made by Ukrainian Canadians and exhibits of Ukranian pioneer life in Western Canada

L **SHERIDAN COLLEGE OF APPLIED ARTS AND TECHNOLOGY,** Visual Arts Library, 1430 Trafalgar Rd, L6H 2L1. Tel 416-823-9730. *Chief Librn* Cathy Zuraw; *Library Technician* Jacqueline Payne
Open daily 9 AM - 5 PM. Estab 1970 to serve the students and faculty of the School of Visual Arts
Library Holdings: Vols 3500; Per subs 68
Special Subjects: Art History, Photography, animation

OSHAWA

M **THE ROBERT MCLAUGHLIN GALLERY,** Civic Centre, L1H 3Z3. Tel 416-576-3000. *Dir* Joan Murray; *Asst to Dir* Lucia Raczkowski; *Asst Cur & Registrar* Jennifer Watson; *Asst Cur & Registrar* Allan Walkinshaw; *Education & Extension* Marg Jackson; *Publicity & Public Relations* Bernice Bradt
Open Mon - Fri 10 AM - 6 PM, Tues evenings 7 - 9 PM, Sat Noon - 5 PM, Sun 2 - 5 PM. No admis fee. Estab Feb 1967 as The Art Gallery of Oshawa, in May 1969 as the Robert McLaughlin Gallery. Main Gallery 28 x 46 x 15 ft; North Gallery 24 x 31 x 10 ft; South Gallery 18 x 27 x 10 ft, with foyer and Director's office. Average Annual Attendance: 27,000. Mem: 600; dues family $15, single $10, student $2.50; annual meeting Feb
Income: Financed by endowment, membership and city appropriation
Collections: Canadian 19th and 20th Century Drawings, Paintings, Prints and Sculpture; Major Collection of Works by Painters Eleven
Exhibitions: (1978) A Terrible Beauty: The Art of Canada at War; (1979) Canadian Treasures (Permanent Collection); Christmas: Another Dimension; Fourteen Artists of Durham Region; Painters Eleven in Retrospect; Gordon Rayner Retrospective; 'Twas ever Thus (Folk Art); Windows and Doorways: Susan Scott, Denise Therrien, Victoria Walker
Publications: Annual Report; Bulletin, monthly; Calendar of Events, annually, Exhibition catalogs

Activities: Classes for adults and children; docent training; lect open to public, 10 visiting lectr per year; concerts; gallery talks; tours; competitions; exten dept; individual paintings and original objects of art lent to schools, institutions and industries; lending collection contains 100 cassettes, 300 color reproductions, framed reproductions, 90 original art works, 20 original prints, 50 paintings, photographs, 4500 slides; originate traveling exhibitions; sales shop sells books, original art and local crafts
L **Library,** Civic Centre, L1H 3Z3. *Librn* Patricia Claxton-Oldfield
Open to gallery members
Library Holdings: Vols 3500
Special Subjects: Research of Painters Eleven and 19th and 20th Century works

OTTAWA

M **CANADIANA SPORT ART COLLECTION,** 333 River Rd, K1L 8B9.
Estab 1970 to provide a vehicle through which recognition could be passed on to the many fine amateur athletes of Canada, by Canadian artists
Exhibitions: Jack Bush: The Pass (painting); Ken Danby - Skates (and other watercolors); Paintings from Prudential Insurance Company of America's collection; Great Moments in Canadian Sport; Louis Phillipe Hebert (bronze sculpture); McKenzie Bronze Sculptures: Athlete, Boxer, The Competitor, The Relay, Sprinter, Supple Juggler; Allan de la Plante (photographs); Siggy Puchta Bronze Sculptures: Decisive Moment, Karate Player and Touchdown; Joe Rosenthal's Struggle with Time (bronze sculpture); Hanni Rothschild: Hockey Player, Ball Game (ceramics); Alan Sapp: Playing Hockey (painting); Esther Wertheimer: The Olympics (metal sculpture); William Winter's Street Hockey

CANADIAN CONFERENCE OF THE ARTS
For further information, see National Organizations in Canada

CANADIAN CRAFTS COUNCIL
For further information, see National Organizations in Canada

CANADIAN MUSEUMS ASSOCIATION
For further information, see National Organizations in Canada

M **NATIONAL FILM BOARD OF CANADA,** Still Photography Division, Photo Gallery, 150 Kent St, Tunney's Pasture, K1A 0N1. Tel 613-922-5258. *Executive Producer* Maureen Cumbers; *Producer* Martha Hanna; *Producer* Martha Langford; *Producer* Pierre Dessureault
Open daily noon - 6 PM, cl major holidays. No admis fee. Estab 1939 to initiate and promote the production and distribution of still photographs designed to interpret Canada to Canadians and to other nations. Gallery is 6463 sq ft of exhibition space. Average Annual Attendance: 21,000
Income: Financed by federal government agency
Collections: Collection of works by Contemporary Canadian Photographers
Exhibitions: Barbara Astman; Garry Berteig; Robert Bourdeau; Tim Clark; Alain Desvergnes; Jennifer Dickson; Robert Frank; Michel Gaboury; Normand Gregoire; Clara Gutsche; David Heath; David Hlynsky; Thaddeus Holownia; Michel Lambeth; James Lisitza; Dan Milek; Tim Porter; Randy Saharuni; Michael Schreier; Separate From The World: Meetings with Doukhobor-Canadians in British Columbia; 13 Cameras Vancouver; Vecu - I Have Lived; Robert Walker
Publications: An Experiment in Photographic Imagery; A Review of Contemporary Photography in Canada; A Time To Dream; B C Almanac; Between Friends; Robert Bourdeau; Call Them Canadians; Canada; Canada-A Year of The Land; Earth Visions; The Female Eye; Tom Gibson; Gregoire Portfolio; If This Is The Time; The Many Worlds of Lutz Dille; Other Places; Photography Canada 1967; Seeds of the Spacefields; Separate from the World, Meetings with Doukhobot Canadians in British Columbus by Robert Minden; Stones of History; Michael Torosian
Activities: Gallery talks on request; originate traveling exhibitions, across Canada and outside the country under the auspices of the Department of External Affairs

M **NATIONAL GALLERY OF CANADA,** Lorne Bldg, Elgin & Slater Sts, K1A 0M8. Tel 613-992-4636. *Dir* Dr Hsio-Yen Shih; *Asst Dir Public Programs* Michael Bell; *Asst Dir Coll & Research* Brydon Smith; *Asst Dir Finance & Admin* Michael Carroll; *Chief Department of Exhib* Richard Graburn; *Chief Information Services* Janine Smiter; *Head Publications & Communications* Peter Smith; *Cur Post Confederation Canadian Art* Charles Hill; *Cur Drawings* Mary Cazort; *Cur Prints* Douglas Druick; *Research Cur Canadian Art* Jean-Rene Ostiguy; *Research Cur European Art* Myron Laskin Jr; *Acting Head Restoration & Conservation Lab* Ursus Dix; *Registrar* Andre Fronton
Open Tues - Sat 10 AM - 5 PM, Sun & holidays 10 AM - 5 PM, cl Christmas Day, Mon Oct - April. No admis fee. Founded 1880 under the patronage of the Governor-General, the Marquess of Lorne, and his wife the Princess Louise; first incorporated 1913 and charged with the development and care of the National Collections and the promotion of art in Canada. Since 1968, the gallery has been part of the National Museums of Canada, reporting to a Board of Trustees estab for the Corporation. The Gallery is housed (since 1960) in the Lorne Building with 8 floors devoted to exhibition space, auditorium, workshops, offices, laboratories and cafeteria. Average Annual Attendance: 300,000
Collections: Canadian decorative arts, painting and sculpture from 17th - 20th Century; contemporary American Art; Diploma works of the Royal Canadian Academy of the Arts; European decorative arts, painting and sculpture from 14th - 20th Century; Far Eastern Art; photography; prints and drawings of the principal schools. Among the principal acquisitions 1977-79, were American painting and sculpture, including Andre (Pile), Calder (Jacaranda), Newman (The Way I); Canadian works by Brymner, Carr-Harris, Max Dean, Edson, FitzGerald, Fraser, Goodwin, Jacobi, Bill Jones, Lyman, Magor, Massey, Peel, D and R Rabinowitch, Snow; European painting and sculpture, including Jan Both (Landscape with Hunters), Annibale Carracci (Vision of St Francis), Courbet (Still-Life), A Cuyp (A Herd of Cows with Herdsmen and a Rider), Philippe de Champaigne (Crucifixion), Jean-Germain Drouais (The Shepherd Paris), Baron Gros (Bacchus and Ariadne), Klee (Angst), Jean-Francois Millet (The Pig Slaughter), Murillo (Portrait of a Vacalier), Preti (The Feast of Absalom), Theodore Rousseau (The Old Park at St Cloud); prints and drawings by Cezanne, Degas, Fragonard, M Gandolfi, Kandinsky, Le Prince, A Milani, Pissaro, Rembrandt, Redon

Exhibitions: Exhibitions from abroad, permanent collections, private and public sources are organized and circulated in Canada and abroad

Publications: Annual Bulletin (incorporating Annual Review, with current acquisition lists); Canadian Artists; catalogues of permanent collections (beginning Nov 1980); Documents in the History of Canadian Art; exhibition-related books and catalogues; Masterpieces in the National Gallery of Canada; National Gallery of Canada Journal

Activities: Lect; films; gallery talks; guided tours at Gallery and lect tours throughout Canada; rents transparencies and colour separations and sells slides, catalogues and black and white prints, through sub-section Reproduction Rights and Sales; originate traveling exhibitions; specialized art bookstore with reproductions, postcards, etc

L **Library,** Lorne Building, Elgin & Slater Sts, K1A 0M8. *Acting Chief Librn* J Hunter; *Reference Librn* M Vilcins; *Art Documentalist* S Hasbury
Open Mon - Fri 10 AM - 6 PM. Estab 1918 to support the research and information requirements of gallery personnel; to make its collections of resource materials in the fine arts available to Canadian libraries and scholars; to serve as a source of information about Canadian art and art activities in Canada
Library Holdings: Vols 67,000; Per subs 976; Micro—Fiche, reels; AV—Rec; Other—Clipping files, exhibition catalogs, pamphlets
Special Subjects: Canadian art, post-medieval Western art with special emphasis on drawings, painting, prints, photography and sculpture
Collections: Art Documentation; Canadiana; Conservation of Art; prints, drawings and photography
Publications: Artists in Canada; Files in National Gallery Library; Files of Fiche: Canadian Art Microdocuments; Serials Currently Received, annually
Activities: Library tours

M **NATIONAL MUSEUM OF MAN,** Victoria Memorial Museum Bldg, Metcalfe and McLeod Sts, K1A 0M8. *Dir* W E Taylor Jr; *Asst Dir Pub Prog* Frank Corcoran; *Asst Dir Admin* W J Kozar; *Chief Archaeological Survey of Canada* Dr R Marois; *Chief Canadian Ethnology Service* A McFadyen Clark; *Chief Canadian Centre for Folk Culture Studies* Pierre Crepeau; *Chief History Division* Dr F Thorpe; *Chief Cur Canadian War Museum* L Murray; *Acting Chief Education & Cultural Affairs Div* Rhoda Barrett; *Acting Chief Nat Prog Div* Sylvie Morel-Hall; *Senior Scientist Canadian Centre for Folk Culture Studies* Dr Carmen Roy; *Senior Archaeologist* Dr George MacDonald
Victoria Memorial Museum Building open Tues - Sun 10 AM - 6 PM, summer Sun - Sat 10 AM - 6 PM. Canadian War Museum open Sun - Sat 9 AM - 5 PM. No admis fee. Estab 1968 as one of four components of the National Museums of Canada; to trace the development of Man from prehistoric times to the present, particularly Canadian development. The Victoria Memorial Museum Building, located at Metcalfe and McLeod Streets, houses on the first floor the development of early man and the technology of Canada's indigenous peoples and archaeological method of recovering such past; on the second floor an overview of the Plains Indians and Iroquois; on the third floor an overview of the West Coast Indians; on the fourth floor Canadian history to present and tracing the contribution made by ethnic peoples in Canada. The Canadian War Museum, located at 330 Sussex Drive, displays historical material relating to the military history of Canada and of other countries. 1980 marks the centennial of the Canadian War Museum. Average Annual Attendance: Victoria Memorial Museum Building 450,000; Canadian War Museum 390,000
Income: $8,000,000
Purchases: $320,000
Collections: Archaeological Collection; Ethnological Collection; Folk Culture Collections; Historical Collection; War Collection
Exhibitions: A Common Valour; A Deadly Grandeur; A Terrible Beauty; Arctic Images; The Art of the Gunmaker; Asia Calling; Charles Comfort: The War Years; Contemporary Canadian Indian Art; Gift of the Raven: Canadian Northwest Coast Indian Art; The Hammer's Art: Blacksmiths and Tinsmiths at Work; The Inuit Print; Land of the Maple Leaf-Home of the Beaver; The Last Best West; The Search for Early Man in Canada; Shamans and Spirits: Myths and Medical Symbolims in Eskimo Art; Toys; What's It
Publications: Several series of publications and periodicals, 500 titles published in-house in last six years
Activities: Classes for adults and children; dramatic programs; docent training; lect open to the public, several vis lectr per year; extension department; original artifacts and individual artifacts lent to museums and other institutions meeting specifications regarding security, environment, etc; originate traveling exhibitions; museum shop selling books, reproductions, magazines, prints, museum kits, multi-media packages on topics relevant to the disciplines of the Museum

M **NATIONAL MUSEUMS OF CANADA,** Esplanade Laurier, 300 Laurier W, K1A 0M8. Tel 613-995-9832. *Secy General* Ian Christie Clark
The beginnings of the National Gallery of Canada are associated with the founding of the Royal Canadian Academy of Arts in 1880. The purposes of the Corporation are to demonstrate the products of nature and the works of man, with special but not exclusive reference to Canada, so as to promote interest therin throughout Canada and to disseminate knowledge thereof. Until 1907 the National Gallery was under the direct control of a minister of the Crown but in that year, an Advisory Arts Council, consisting of three persons outside government, was appointed to administer grants to the National Gallery. In 1913 the National Gallery was incorporated by Act of Parliament and placed under the administration of a board of trustees appointed by the Governor General in Council.
Since 1960, the National Gallery has occupied the Lorne Building in Ottawa. The National Museum of Man and the National Museum of Natural Sciences evolved from the collections of the Geological Survey of Canada in the nineteenth century. The collections were transferred to the newly built Victoria Memorial Museum Building in 1911. The National Museum of Canada was formally established in 1927. In 1957 this Museum was divided into two branches: Human History and Natural History, with an additional branch, Science and Technology, being established in 1966
In April 1968 a new act amalgamated these three branches, together with the National Gallery of Canada, under the aegis of one corporation known as the National Museums of Canada. The individual museums of The National Museums of Canada are located in Ottawa. Average Annual Attendance: Exceeds two and one-half million for all museums
Activities: Conducted tours; talks and lectures; film and theatre presentations;

boutiques sells prints, books, bulletins, recordings, models, artifacts, postcards and slides

M **National Gallery of Canada,** Lorne Building, Elgin & Slater Sts, K1A 0M8. Tel 613-992-4636. *Dir* Dr Hsio-Yen Shih
M **National Museum of Man,** Metcalfe & McLeod Sts, K1A 0M8. Tel 613-992-3497. *Dir* Dr W E Taylor Jr
M **Canadian War Museum,** 330 Sussex Dr, K1A 0M8. Tel 613-992-2774. *Cur* L F Murray
M **National Museum of Natural Sciences,** Metcalfe and McCleod Sts, K1A 0M8. Tel 613-996-3102. *Dir* Dr Louis Lemieux
M **National Museum of Science and Technology,** 1867 Saint Laurent Blvd, K1A 0M8. Tel 613-998-4566.
M **National Aeronautical Collection,** Rockcliffe Air Force Base, K1A 0M8. Tel 613-993-2010.
L **Library,** 2086 Walkley Rd, K1A 0M8. *Chief Librn* Valerie Monkhouse
Open Mon - Fri 9 AM - 4:30 PM. Estab 1945 to serve the staff of the Corporation of the National Museums of Canada and other workers in subject areas related to the disciplines of the Museums. To staff of the Corporation; other users may use collection for reference purposes or borrow through interlibrary loan
Income: Financed by the government
Purchases: $178,500
Library Holdings: Vols 128,000; Per subs 1322; Micro—Fiche, reels; Other—Exhibition catalogs, manuscripts, pamphlets
Special Subjects: Antropology, Archaeology, Folk Art, Conservation of art objects and restoration
Collections: Anderson Collection (mammalogy); C M Sternberg Reprint Collection (palaeontology); Human Relations Area Files (anthropology)
Publications: Monthly list of accessions to the library

L **OTTAWA PUBLIC LIBRARY,** 120 Metcalfe St, K1P 5M2. Tel 613-236-0301. *Dir* Gilles Frappier; *Asst Dir* Jean de Temple; *Admin Officer* Wilfred Blain
Open Mon - Thurs 10 AM - 9 PM, Fri 10 AM - 6 PM, Sat 9:30 AM - 5 PM. Estab 1906 to serve the community as a centre for general and reliable information; to select, preserve and administer books and related materials in organized collections; to provide opportunity for citizens of all ages to educate themselves continuously. Circ 2,153,068
Income: $4,849,423 (financed by city and provincial appropriations, fees and fines)
Purchases: $561,678
Library Holdings: Vols 609,314; Per subs 777; Micro—Fiche, reels; AV—Cassettes, fs; Other—Clipping files, pamphlets
Collections: Foreign Languages Collection (over 35 languages); Local History Collection (Ottawa Room - maps, books, phamphlets about Ottawa and region, plus books by local authors, city directories)
Exhibitions: Monthly exhibits highlighting local artists, craftsmen, photographers and collectors
Publications: Booklists; bulletin, monthly; film catalogs, brochures
Activities: Lect open to public; library tours

PUBLIC ARCHIVES OF CANADA
L **Public Archives Library,*** 395 Wellington St, K1A 0N3. Tel 613-992-2669. *Dominion Archivist* Dr W I Smith; *Chief Librn* Normand St Pierr
Open daily 9 AM - 9 PM. Estab 1872 to acquire and preserve significant Canadian archival material in all media relating to all aspects of Canadian life and to the development of the country, and to provide suitable research services and facilities to make this documentation available to the public
Income: Financed by federal appropriation
Library Holdings: Vols 1000
Exhibitions: French-Canadian Historian: Francois Xavier Garneau; Illustrated Children's Books; Toronto Photographer: F W Micklethwaite
Publications: Catalog of publications available on request
M **Laurier House,*** 335 Laurier Ave E, K1N 6R4. Tel 613-992-8142. *Cur* Valerie Proctor
Open Tues - Sat 10 AM - 5 PM, Sun 2 - 5 PM, April 1 - Nov 15 Mon - Sat 8 AM - 5 PM, Sun 1 - 5 PM. No admis fee. Estab 1951. This is a historic house and former residence of two Prime Ministers, Sir Wilfrid Laurier and the Rt Honorable William Lyon Mackenzie King, and contains furniture and memorabilia belonging to a third Prime Minister, Lester Pearson. The house is primarily furnished in the style of its last occupant, the Rt Honorable William Lyon Mackenzie King, with space given to the Laurier Collection. In 1974 the Lester Pearson study was installed. Average Annual Attendance: 25,000
Income: Financed by endowment and federal government
Exhibitions: A Child's Best Friend (a doll display); Our Shared Responsibility (a photographic exhibit on the care and handling of artifacts)

ROYAL ARCHITECTURAL INSTITUTE OF CANADA
For further information, see National Organizations in Canada

OWEN SOUND

M **TOM THOMSON MEMORIAL GALLERY AND MUSEUM OF FINE ART,** 840 First Ave W, Box 312, N4K 5P5. Tel 519-376-1932.
Admis 50¢, students, sr citizens and members free. Estab 1967 to collect and display paintings by Tom Thomson, a native son of Canadas foremost landscape artist; to educate the public. Two galleries: paintings by Tom Thomson on permanent display; changing exhibitions in both galleries. Average Annual Attendance: 10,000. Mem: 395; dues family $15, individual $10
Income: Financed by city appropriation and provincial grants
Collections: Tom Thomson; 19th Century artists; †contemporary Canadian artists; Group of Seven
Publications: Bulletin, ten per year
Activities: Classes for children; docent training; lect open to public; gallery talks; tours; films; competitions; museum shop sells books, reproductions, prints and postcards
L **Library,** 840 First Ave W, Box 312, N4K 5P5.
Open for reference
Library Holdings: Vols 500; Per subs 300; Other—Exhibition catalogs
Collections: Files on Tom Thomson

PARRY SOUND

L PARRY SOUND PUBLIC LIBRARY, 29Mary St, P2A 1E3. Tel 705-746-9601. *Librn* Laurine Tremaine; *Asst* Louise Armitage-Besman
Open Mon - Fri 10 AM - 9 PM, Sat 10 AM - 5 PM. Estab 1889 to promote education, leisure interests and cultural enrichment for the community. Circ 52,000
Income: $68,000 (financed by endowment, membership, city and provincial grants, miscellaneous sources)
Purchases: $20,000
Library Holdings: Vols 25,300; Per subs 140; AV—Cassettes, rec; Other—Clipping files, pamphlets

PETERBOROUGH

M ART GALLERY OF PETERBOROUGH, 2 Crescent St, K9J 2G1. Tel 705-743-9179. *Board Pres* Bruno Morawetz; *VPres* Margaret Fleming; *Secy* Maralin Munro; *Dir* Illi-Maria Tamplin; *Education Officer* Marilyn Bondar; *Secy* Sally Wright
Open Tues - Sun 1 - 5 PM, Thurs 1 - 9 PM. No admis fee. Estab 1973. Gallery situated along a lake and in a park; new extension added and completed June 1979. Average Annual Attendance: 14,000. Mem: 1000; dues sustaining $25, family $6, individual $5, student $2; annual meeting June
Income: $100,000 (financed by membership and city appropriation)
Collections: European and Canadian Works of Art
Exhibitions: Contemporary and Traditional Art; Provincial Artists; selections from permanent collection, traveling exhibitions
Publications: Catalogues on some exhibitions; Bulletin of Events, monthly; pamphlets on artists in exhibitions
Activities: Classes for adults and children; dramatic programs; docent training; workshops; art program to public schools; lect open to public, 10 visiting lectr per year; concerts; gallery talks; tours; films; exten dept serves local area; individual paintings and original objects of art lent; lending collection contains 70 original art works; book traveling exhibitions six per year; originate traveling exhibitions; sales shop sells books, cards, craft items, magazines and original art

SAINT CATHARINES

O RODMAN HALL ARTS CENTRE, 109 St Paul Crescent, L2S 1M3. Tel 416-684-2925. *Pres* A Hansen; *VPres* Dr A Taliano; *Secy* A Pattemore; *Dir* A Peter Harris; *Executive Secy* Susan Dickinson; *Cur of Education* Barbara Todd; *Chief Custodian* Charles Verworn
Open Tues, Thurs, Fri 9 AM - 5 PM, Wed 9 AM - 5 PM & 7 - 10 PM, Sat & Sun 1 - 5 PM, cl Mon. No admis fee. Estab 1960, art gallery, cultural centre and visual arts exhibitions. Four galleries in an 1853, 1960 and 1975 addition. 1975 - A1 - National Museums of Canada. Average Annual Attendance: 32,000. Mem: 850, dues $15, $10, $5; annual meeting Sept
Income: $143,700 (financed by membership, city, state and national appropriation)
Purchases: $5000
Collections: American Graphics and Drawings; †Canadian Drawings, †Paintings, †Sculpture and †Watercolours; International Graphics and Drawings
Exhibitions: Karel Appel; Five Artists; General Motors Employees Art Show; J Gould Retrospective; Graphex 7; Graphics; Hungarian Folk Art; Imperial Oil Collects; Ozias Leduc; John Mieczinkowski Sculpture and Drawing; Painters Eleven; William Perehudoff; W J Philips; Nadine Powers Sculpture and Drawing; Gordon Rayner Retrospective; St Catharines Art Association; Sickert: The Graphic Work; Anne Tremain Sculpture; jury show, permanent collection and student art shows
Publications: Catalogue - Lord and Lady Head Watercolours; monthly calendar
Activities: Classes for adults and children; dramatic programs; docent training; lect open to public, 8 visiting lectr per year; concerts; gallery talks; tours; jury show competitions; jury and public awards given for best three works in exhibition; exten dept serves city of St Catharines; individual paintings and original objects of art lent to schools and gallery at City Hall; lending collection contains 10 original art works and 200 original prints; book traveling exhibitions, 16 per year; originate traveling exhibitions; sales shop sells books, crafts, magazines, paper things, prints, reproductions and weaving
L Library, 109 St Paul Crescent, L2S 1M3.
Open Tues - Fri 9 AM - 5 PM. Estab 1960. Reference library
Income: $3000
Purchases: $1000
Library Holdings: Vols 1000; Per subs 300; Micro—Prints; AV—Lantern Slides, slides; Other—Clipping files, exhibition catalogs, memorabilia, pamphlets, photographs, reproductions

SARNIA

L SARNIA PUBLIC LIBRARY AND ART GALLERY, 124 Christina St S, N7T 2M6. Tel 519-337-3291; Telex 064-76116. *Dir* R T Bradley; *Chmn* L V Langan
Open Mon - Fri 9 AM - 9 PM, Sat 9 AM - 5:30 PM, Sun Oct - May 2 - 5 PM. No admis fee. Estab 1961, a collection of Canadian paintings instituted in 1919 and administered by the Women's Conservation Art Association of Sarnia. The Collection was turned over to the Sarnia Library Board in 1956 and additions are being made from time to time. Average Annual Attendance: 33,300
Collections: Canadian Paintings; Eskimo Carvings; a Collection of Old Photographs of Sarnia and Lambton County; sculpture
Exhibitions: Twelve to fifteen shows a year, either traveling from other galleries or initiated by the Sarnia Art Gallery
Activities: Children's art classes in July and August; workshops; lect; book traveling exhibitions

SIMCOE

M EVA BROOK DONLY MUSEUM, 109 Norfolk St S, N3Y 2W3. Tel 519-426-1583. *Managing Dir* Kenneth S McArthur; *Cur* William Yeager
Open Wed - Sun 1:30 - 5 PM, other times by appointment. Admis tours $5 per 35, 10¢ each additional person, $3 per year mem, children free with adult, adult 50¢, student 25¢, children under 12 free. Estab 1946 to display and aid research in the history of Norfolk County. Average Annual Attendance: 2800. Mem: dues family $7, individual $5
Income: Financed by endowment, membership, city and provincial appropriation
Collections: Large Collection of important Early Documents and Newspapers, 370 Paintings of Historic Norfolk by W E Cantelon; Display of Artifacts of the 19th Century Norfolk County; Historical Material
Exhibitions: Concerned mainly with focusing new light on some aspects of the permanent collection
L Library, 109 Norfolk St S, N3Y 2W3.
Reference and a photograph collection for display

O LYNNWOOD ARTS CENTRE, 21 Lynnwood Ave, PO Box 67, N3Y 4Y1. Tel 519-428-0540. *Pres* Tom Wardlaw; *VPres* Hugh Lorriman; *Secy & Office Mgr* Gail Hill; *Dir* Ellen McIntosh; *Education Coordr* Julie Stone; *Gallery Asst* Susan O'Heron
Open Tues - Fri 10 AM - 5 PM, Sat & Sun 1 - 5 PM. No admis fee. Estab 1973 to provide a focal point for the visual arts in the community. Built in 1851 - Greek Revival Architecture; orange brick with ionic columns; and is a National Historic Site. Average Annual Attendance: 20,000. Mem: 800; dues family $10, individual $7; annual meeting March
Income: $100,000 (financed by membership, patrons - private and commerical, Ministry of Culture and Recreation, Town of Simcoe, Regional Municipality of Haldimand-Norfolk)
Collections: †Contemporary Canadian Art; Early Canadian Quilts and Mats
Exhibitions: (1979) Blown Glass - Donald Black; Contemporary Fibre Statements; Blair Drawson and Joe Rosenblatt; Electric Art; Fabric Art - Annette Francoise; Fibre and Metal Sculpture - Jeanine Lodge; Figures and Portraits of the 30's and 40's; Fraktur Art; Peter Harris - Ten Years 1965-75; In Search of Azure Dragons; Out of the Woods; Photographs by Jack MacAulay; Gery Puley Watercolours - 1968-78; Three New Artists: Elizabeth Barrett, Daphne Harker, Rosemary Sloot; juried art exhibitions; school art Book Illustrations by Margaret Atwood
Publications: Monthly Newsletter
Activities: Classes for adults and children; dramatic programs; docent training; lect open to public, 15 lectr per year; concerts; gallery talks; tours; seminars; juried art exhibitions (every two years) with purchase awards; individual paintings and original objects of art lent to members; book traveling exhibitions; originate traveling exhibitions; museum shop sells books, hand-crafted items, original art, prints and reproductions

STRATFORD

M GALLERY STRATFORD, 54 Romeo St N, N5A 4S9. *Dir* Paul Bennett; *Pres Bd of Trustees* Bruce Swerdfager
Open Sept - May Sun, Tues - Fri 1 - 5 PM, Sat 10 AM - 5 PM; Summer Hours June - Sept Tues - Sun 10 AM - 8 PM, Mon 10 AM - 5 PM; business hours Weekdays 9:30 AM - 5 PM. Admis $1, children under 12 free. Estab 1967 as a non-profit permanent establishment open to the public and administered in the public interest for the purpose of studying, interpreting, assembling and exhibiting to the public. Average Annual Attendance: 50,000. Mem: 600; annual meeting March
Income: $200,000 (financed by membership, city appropriation and federal grant)
Collections: Works of art on paper
Exhibitions: Changing exhibits, monthly geared to create interest for visitors to Stratfor Shakespearean Festival
Publications: Catalogs; calendar of events
Activities: Classes for adults and children; docent training; lectures open to the public, 4 visiting lecturers each year; concerts; gallery talks; tours; competitions; extension department serving art in the schools; traveling exhibitions organized and circulated; sales shop sells books, prints, slides and crafts
L Library, 54 Romeo St, N5A 4S9.
Open for reference only
Library Holdings: Vols 500; Per subs 12

SUDBURY

LAURENTIAN UNIVERSITY

M Museum and Arts Centre, c/o Department Cultural Affairs, Laurentian University, P3E 2C6. Tel 705-675-1151, Ext 400, 401. *Dir* Pamela Krueger; *Education & Extension Officer* Shirley Anne
Open Tues & Fri Noon - 9 PM, Wed, Thurs, Sat & Sun Noon - 5 PM, cl Mon mornings by appointment. No admis fee. Estab 1968 to present a continuous program of exhibitions, concerts and events for the people of Sudbury and the district. Gallery has two floors of space: 124 running ft in one and 131 running ft in the second gallery. Average Annual Attendance: 20,000. Mem: 300; dues family $10, single $5; annual meeting June
Income: Financed by endowment, membership, city and state appropriation, government and local organizations
Collections: Canadian Collection dating from the late 1800's and early 1900's to Contemporary. The Group of Seven, Eskimo Sculptures and Prints as well as works of Historical Canadian Artists comprise the collection; †Indian works from Northern Ontario
Exhibitions: (1978) A Graphic Extravaganza from The Suburbs of The Mind; David Blake - Hill Study; Canadian Paintings in the Collection of the University of Toronto; Collins-Pachter-Tinkl (examples of humorous expression in their work); Eskimo Prints and Sculptures; William Kurelek - A Prarie Boy's Summer; Latvian Celebration; Soren Madsen (prints and drawings); Northern Ontario Art Association Celebration; Old-Fashioned Christmas; Recent Acquisitions - including the Heritage Quilt and two watercolours by Ivan Wheale: Dired Creek and Sumac; Roseisle, Manitoba - Photographs by Cal Bailey; Ukrainian Exhibition;

White Water on the Road to Nickel City; (1979) Lynn Donoghue (paintings and drawings); Norart (first annual exhibition open to all artists living and working in Northern Ontario); Sculpture in Canada; Sculpture Ybes Trudeau; 10th Annual Secondary School Art Exhibition
Publications: Communique, every six weeks
Activities: Docent training; lect open to public, 10 visiting lectr per year; concerts; gallery talks; tours; lending collection contains 40 framed reproductions, 400 original art works and 4000 slides; museum shop sells magazines, catalogues, postcards, posters and prints
L **Library,** c/o Department Cultural Affairs, Laurentian University, P3E 2C6.
Open daily 9 - 4:30 PM. Estab 1977 for reference
Library Holdings: Vols 1000; Per subs 10; Micro—Cards; AV—Lantern Slides, slides 3000; Other—Exhibition catalogs, framed reproductions, pamphlets
M **Art Gallery,** 11th Floor Library Tower, Department Cultural Affairs, Laurentian University, P3E 2C6. *Dir* Pamela Krueger; *Education & Extension Officer* Shirley Anne
Samll gallery space located at the University, accommodating small exhibitions, usually reproductions
Exhibitions: (1978) Henri Cartier-Bresson: Photographs; Hagan: The Mind and the Hand; Indian Rock Paintings; Les Levine - Landscapes; More Than Meets the Eye; prints and paintings from the permanent collection. (1979) Prints by Contemporary Canadian Artists

TORONTO

M **ART GALLERY OF ONTARIO,** 317 Dundas St W, M5T 1G4. Tel 416-977-0414.
Dir W J Withrow; *Chief Cur* Dr Roald Nasgaard; *Chief of Admin* Herb Grant; *Controller* Timothy Hopcraft; *Head Exten Services* Penny-Lynn Grosman; *Head Education Services* James Williamson; *Mgr Physical Plant* Jack Beckett; *Mgr Public Affairs* Alex MacDonald
Open Tues, Fri, Sat & Sun 11 AM - 5:30 PM, Wed & Thurs 11 AM - 9 PM, cl Mon. Admis adults $2, students and children 75¢, members, Ontario Privilege Card holders and accompanied children under 12 free, Thurs evenings free to everyone. Estab 1900 to cultivate and advance the cause of the visual arts in Ontario; to conduct programmes of education in the origin, development, appreciation and techniques of the visual arts; to collect and exhibit works of art and displays and to maintain and operate a gallery and related facilities as required for this purpose; to stimulate the interest of the public in matters undertaken by the Gallery. Average Annual Attendance: 1,129,949. Mem: 42,000; dues supporting $75, family $35, individual $20, catalogue subscriber $35 extra; annual meeting June
Income: Financed by membership, provincial, city and federal appropriations and earned income
Purchases: $927,648
Collections: American and European Art (16th Century to present); Canadian Historical and Contemporary Art; Henry Moore Sculpture Centre
Exhibitions: 1979 Coming Out: Six Generations of Women; Louis de Niverville Retrospective; Egyptomania; Daniel Fowler of Amherst Island 1810-1894; Charles Gagnon; The Grange Through the Eyes of the Artist; Selections from the Klamer Family Gift of Inuit Art; Lionel LeMoine FitzGerald (1890-1965) - The Development of An Artist; Matisse: Prints and Illustrated Books; The Henry Moore Sculpture Centre Collection; One Man's Vision: The Graphic Work of Odilon Redon; The Other 19th Century: Paintings and Sculpture in the Collection of Mr and Mrs Joseph M Tanenbaum; Our Own Country Canada; Nina Raginsky; Recent Acquisitions of Master Prints from the 15th - 20th Centuries; Selected Impressions; Travels with Pen, Pencil and Ink: John Henry Hinton Photographs - China: 1894-1918; Treasures of Tutankahmun; Jackie Winsor
Publications: The Gallery, ten times per year
Activities: Art classes for adults and children; dramatic programs; docent training; lectures open to public; concerts; gallery talks; films; scholarships; exten dept organizes traveling exhibitions, circulated throughout the Province, Canada and United States; individual paintings and original objects of art loaned; originate traveling exhibitions; sales shop sells books, magazines, reproductions, prints, slides and jewelry; art rental shop for members to rent original works of art
L **Edward P Taylor Reference Library,** 317 Dundas St W, M5T 1G4. *Librn* Sybille Pantazzi; *Library Coordr* Lee Kimball; *Research Asst* Larry Pfaff; *Library Technician* Carol Frymer
Open Tues, Wed & Fri 10 AM - 5 PM, Thurs 10 AM - 9 PM. Estab 1933 to collect printed material for the documentation and interpretation of the works of art in the Gallery's collection and to provide the staff with the necessary source material for the compilation of exhibition catalogues and other publications and for the preparation of lectures
Library Holdings: Vols 25,000; Per subs 70; Other—Clipping files, exhibition catalogs, manuscripts, pamphlets, photographs, reproductions, original documents
Special Subjects: Canadian, American and European Art from the Renaissance to the present, concentrating mainly on drawing, engraving, painting and sculpture
Collections: Canadian Illustrated Books; Alan Garrow Collection of British Illustrated Books and Wood Engravings of the 1860's Canadian Book-Plates; International Guide Books; Robert D McIntosh Collection of Books on Sepulchral Monuments
Publications: Selected Acquisitions List, quarterly
L **Edward P Taylor Audio-Visual Centre,** 317 Dundas St W, M5T 1G4. *Head* Cathy Goldsmith
Library Holdings: Micro—Reels 250; AV—Cassettes 160, slides 50,000, v-tapes 60; Other—Circulating collection

O **ART METROPOLE,** 217 Richmond St W, M5V 1W2. Tel 416-362-1685. *Pres* Ronald C Gabe; *VPres* Margaret Gale; *Secy & Treas* A A Bronson; *Dir Film & Video* Martha Fleming; *Publications Dir* David Buchan; *Archivist* Tim Guest
Open Mon - Sat Noon - 6 PM. No admis fee. Estab 1974 as a nonprofit agency to collect, promote, publish and distribute work by international artists in non-traditional formats; basically books, periodicals, recordings, film and videotapes
Special Subjects: Books by artists, performance by artists, video by artists
Collections: Ongoing collection of Books by Artists
Publications: Catalog of available stock, semi-annually
Activities: Lect; lending collection contains 250 video-tape titles by 35 artists and

research archive of information on contemporary art; originate traveling exhibitions; sales shop sells books, magazine and original art
L **Library,** 217 Richmond St W, M5V 1W2. *Archivist* Tim Guest
Open Tues - Sat Noon - 6 PM. Estab 1974 to document work by artist internationally working in non-conventional and multiple media. For reference only
Library Holdings: AV—A-tapes, motion pictures, rec, v-tapes; Other—Exhibition catalogs, prints, manuscripts, memorabilia, original art works, pamphlets, photographs
Collections: Books, vidio and performances by artists

O **ARTS AND LETTERS CLUB OF TORONTO,** 14 Elm St, M5G 1G7. *Pres* John A Morrow; *Secy* William Osler
Estab 1908. Mem: 450; annual meeting May
Collections: Club Collection - art by members and others; Hertiage Collection - art by members now deceased
L **Library,** 14 Elm St, M5G 1G7.
Open to club members and researchers for reference
Library Holdings: Vols 2000
Special Subjects: Architecture, Sculpture, Theatre Arts, Literature, music, paintings

ASSOCIATION OF CANADIAN INDUSTRIAL DESIGNERS, ONTARIO
For further information, see National and Regional Organizations

CANADIAN SOCIETY OF PAINTERS IN WATERCOLOUR
For further information, see National and Regional Organizations

O **CULTURAL INITIATIVE,** (Formerly Centre for Experimental Art and Communication) 124 Liscar St, M5H 3H1. Tel 416-593-4111. *Pres & Art Dir* Amerigo Marras; *VPres* Suber Corley; *Secy* John Faichney; *Video Officer* Saul Goldman; *Film Officer* Ross McLaren; *Publicity* Bruce Eves; *Admin* Lily Chiro
Open Mon - Sat 11 AM - 5 PM, 8 - 10 PM. No admis fee. Estab 1973 to provide the production, presentation and dissemination of radical and marginal art. Average Annual Attendance: 15,000
Income: $160,000 (financed by endowment, city and provincial appropriation)
Exhibitions: Behavious workshops; Contextual Art seminars; Participation at Documenta 6; Polemics
Publications: Strike, bimonthly
Activities: Classes for adults and children; theoretical and technical classes; lectures open to the public, 12 visiting lecturers per year; concerts; grants to individual artists residing in Ontario; extension department serving foreign countries chiefly; traveling exhibitions organized and circulated
L **Library,** 124 Liscar St, M5H 3H1. *Art Librn* John Faichney
Open to scholars and students for reference
Library Holdings: Vols 4000; Per subs 200; AV—A-tapes, motion pictures, v-tapes
Special Subjects: , Performance arts, sociological art, language art
Collections: European videotapes
L **Cultural Initiative Archives,** 124 Lisgar St *Librn* John Faichney
Estab 1974 for reference only. Not open to the public
Library Holdings: Vols 5000; AV—A-tapes, cassettes, fs, Kodachromes, rec, slides, v-tapes; Other—Clipping files, exhibition catalogs, framed reproductions, prints, manuscripts, original art works, pamphlets, photographs, reproductions
Special Subjects: , Political Art Materials
Activities: Seminars; discussions

O **LYCEUM CLUB AND WOMEN'S ART ASSOCIATION OF CANADA,** 23 Prince Arthur Ave, M5R 1B2. Tel 416-922-2060. *Pres* Mrs G H Rawson; *Recording Secy* Mrs H Macknight
Open Mon - Fri 8:30 AM - 2:30 PM, cl Sat & Sun. Estab 1885, branches in Ontario in Hamilton, Owen Sound, St Thomas and Peterborough. Mem: 250; annual meeting April
Activities: Special exhibitions; drawing, painting; study groups; awards Founder's memorial scholarships to art students annually; scholarships given to Ontario College of Art, Royal Conservatory of Music, National Ballet
L **Library,** 12 Prince Arthur Ave, M5R 1B2.
Library Holdings: Vols 500
Special Subjects: Extensive Canadiana

METROPOLITAN TORONTO LIBRARY BOARD
L **Fine Art Department,** 789 Yonge St, M4W 2G8. Tel 416-928-5214. *Head Fine Art Department* Alan Suddon
Open Mon - Fri 9 AM - 9 PM, Sat 9 AM - 5 PM, Sun Oct 15 - April 30 1:30 - 5 PM. Estab 1959 for public reference
Income: Financed by city appropriation
Library Holdings: Vols 36,066; Per subs 390; Micro—Fiche, reels; AV—A-tapes, cassettes, rec, slides; Other—Clipping files, exhibition catalogs, memorabilia
Special Subjects: Costume Design & Construction, Decorative Arts, fine arts, printing and printing design
Collections: Postcards, scenic and greeting; Printed Ephemera; Private Presses with emphasis on Canadian
L **Baldwin Room (Canadian History Department),** 789 Yonge St, M4W 2G8. Tel 416-928-5275. *Head Canadian History Department* Edith G Firth
Open Mon - Fri 9 AM - 9 PM, Sat 9 AM - 5 PM, Sun Oct 15 - April 30 1:30 - 5 PM. Estab 1960 to house rare Canadiana and to support Canadian historical research
Library Holdings: Other—Prints, original art works, photographs
Collections: J Ross Robertson Collection - 4400 paintings, prints and photographs; Toronto and Early Canada Collection - 60,000 paintings, prints and photographs

O **ONTARIO ASSOCIATION OF ARCHITECTS,*** 50 Park Rd, M4W 2N5. Tel 416-929-0623. *Exec Dir* Brian Parks
Estab 1890. Mem: 140
Exhibitions: Sponsors exhibition of new building materials and techniques
Activities: Awards and annual cash prizes through School of Architecture, University of Toronto, and Ryerson Institute of Technology, Ontario College of Art, University of Waterloo, and Carleton University

O ONTARIO ASSOCIATION OF ART GALLERIES, 38 Charles St E, M4Y 1T3. Tel 416-920-8378. *Pres* Robert Swain; *VPres* Pamela Krueger; *Executive Dir* Rory O'Donal; *Programs Coordr* Pamela Cribb-Carsley; *Admin Asst* Charlene Morgan; *Special Projects Officer* Diane Sage; *Admin Asst* Janice Bishop
Open 9 AM - 5 PM. Estab 1968 to encourage cooperation among member galleries and museums; to encourage cooperation between Ontario Asn of Art Galleries and the Arts Council and all similar agencies involved in the cause of the visual arts; to assist the development of visual arts centres in the Province of Ontario; to promote high standards of excellence and uniform methods in the care and presentation of art; to serve as an advisory body in matters of professional interest in the Province of Ontario. Gallery not maintained. Mem: 82; dues full member .15 of total revenue, business $250, affiliate $75, individual $10; annual meeting June
Income: Financed by membership, Ontario Arts Council, Ministry of Culture and Recreation and National Museums
Publications: Magazine, seasonal; Newsart, bi-monthly
Activities: Training seminars under gallery development and professional development committees; job referral assistance; counseling to professional and galleries
L Resource Centre, 38 Charles St E, M4Y 1T3. *Admin Asst* Charlene Morgan
Open 9 AM - 5 PM. Estab to provide information to estab and growing galleries pertinent to existance. Reference library
Income: $100
Library Holdings: Vols 300; Per subs 10; Other—Exhibition catalogs, framed reproductions, prints, manuscripts, memorabilia, original art works, pamphlets, photographs, reproductions
Special Subjects: Taxation and litagation pertaining to visual arts

M ONTARIO COLLEGE OF ART, Gallery 76,* 100 McCaul St, M5T 1W1. Tel 416-366-4977, Ext 62. *Pres* Dr Paul D Fleck
Open Mon - Fri 10 AM - 5 PM, Sat & Sun Noon - 5 PM. Estab 1970 for faculty and student exhibitions and to exhibit outside work to benefit the college. Average Annual Attendance: 15,000
Income: Financed by College
Collections: Small print collection
Publications: Invitations; small scale catalogs
Activities: Dramatic programs; Concerts; competitions; individual paintings and original objects of art lent; traveling exhibitions organized and circulated
**L Library,* 100 McCaul St, M5T 1W1.
Library Holdings: AV—Slides
**L Library, Audio-Visual Centre,* 100 McCaul St, M5T 1W1. Tel 416-362-5311, Ext 54 and 55. *Dir* Ian Carr-Harris
Open Mon - Thurs 9 AM - 9:30 PM, Fri 9 AM - 5 PM, Sat 1 - 4 PM. Estab to support the curriculum. Circ 10,000
Income: Financed through the College
Purchases: $50,000
Library Holdings: Vols 16,000; Per subs 350; Micro—Fiche, reels; AV—A-tapes, cassettes, fs, Kodachromes, lantern slides, motion pictures, rec, slides, v-tapes; Other—Clipping files, exhibition catalogs, pamphlets, picture file
Special Subjects: Art Education, Inter Design
Collections: Alan Fleming Collection; Robert Holmes Collection

O ONTARIO CRAFTS COUNCIL, 346 Dundas St W, M5T 1G5. Tel 416-366-3551. *Pres* Bill Hodge; *VPres* Sue Willoughby; *Admin Dir* Joan Hyland; *Field Coordr* Stephen Dryden; *Coordr Craft Resource Centre* Irene Bolliger
Open Tues - Sat 10 AM - 5:30 PM. No admis fee. Estab 1976 to foster crafts and craftsmen in Ontario. Maintains an art gallery. Average Annual Attendance: 12,000. Mem: 3200; dues $15; annual meeting May
Income: Financed by membership and provincial appropriation, and guild shop
Collections: †Canadian Contemporary Crafts
Exhibitions: Ontario Crafts Regional Juried Exhibition; various changing exhibits
Publications: Craftsman (magazine); Craftnews (newsletter)
Activities: Tours; competitions; originate traveling exhibitions; sales shop sells original art, prints, reproductions and handcrafted Canadian items
L Craft Resource Centre, 346 Dundas St W, M5T 1G5. *Librn Coordr* Irene Bolliger; *Asst Coordr* Sandra Dunn
Open Tues - Fri Noon - 5 PM. Estab 1976. Clearinghouse for craft and craft related information. For reference only
Library Holdings: Vols 500; Per subs 150; AV—A-tapes, slides, v-tapes; Other—Clipping files, exhibition catalogs, manuscripts, memorabilia, pamphlets, photographs, Portfolios of craftsmen, archives
Special Subjects: Enamels, Glass, Metalwork, Pottery, Fibre, wood
Publications: Craft information: Directory of Suppliers of Craft Materials; Directory of Craft Organizations in Canada; Ontario Craft Directory
Activities: Outreach program; slide rental

O ONTARIO SOCIETY OF ARTISTS,* 417 Queen's Quay W, M5V 1A2. Tel 416-366-1607. *Pres* Ian Trowell; *Secy* Nomi Cameron
Estab 1872 for the encouragement of original art in Ontario. Mem: 110; annual meeting March
Exhibitions: Annual exhibition in Spring open to all Canadian artists; juried exhibition with awards; annual small picture exhibition
Activities: Competitions with awards; traveling exhibitions organized and circulated

PRINTING AND DRAWING COUNCIL OF CANADA
For further information, see National and Regional Organizations

PROFESSIONAL ART DEALERS ASSOCIATION OF CANADA
For further information, see National Organizations in Canada

C ROTHMANS OF PALL MALL CANADA LIMITED, 75 Dufflaw Rd, M6A 2W4. Tel 406-789-7711. *Dir Rothmans Art Program* Alan R Hanlon
Open to public. No admis fee. Estab 1967. Collection displayed at head office
Collections: Contemporary Canadian Art from last decade
Activities: Awards for Toronto Outdoor Art Exhibition each year; individual objects of art lent to traveling or special exhibitions; originate traveling exhibitions to all major public galleries in Canada

ROYAL CANADIAN ACADEMY OF ARTS
For further information, see National and Regional Organizations

M ROYAL ONTARIO MUSEUM, Canadiana Gallery, 14 Queen's Park Cres W. (Mailing Add: 100 Queen's Park, Toronto, ON M5S 2C6,) Tel 416-978-6738. *Pres & Cur* D B Webster; *VPres & Asst Cur* Mrs M Allodi; *Secy* K Haslan; *Dir* Dr J E Cruise; *Cur Asst* Mrs H dePencier; *Cur Asst* J Holmes
Open Mon - Sat 10 AM - 5 PM, Sun 1 - 5 PM. No admis fee. Estab 1951 to collect, exhibit and publish material on Canadian historical paintings and Canadian decorative arts. Museum has three galleries: first gallery has six rooms showing English Colonial, French, Maritime, Ontario and German-Ontario furniture, also silver, glass, woodenware; second gallery has ceramics, toys, weathervanes, religious carving, early 19th Century Quebec panelled room; third is a picture gallery for changing exhibitions. Average Annual Attendance: 35,000
Collections: Canadian 18th and 19th Century Decorative Arts - ceramics, coins and medals books, †furniture, †glass, guns, silver, woodenware; 16th - 18th exploration; †portraits of Canadians and military and administrative people connected with Canada; 18th and 19th Century topographic and historical Canadian views; 19th Century travels
Exhibitions: (1980) Printmaking in Canada; Views and Portraits to 1850, exhibition and catalogues
Publications: M Allodi Canadian Watercolours and Drawings, 2 Volumes 1974; The William Eby Pottery, Congestogo, Ontario, 1855 - 1970; D B Webster Brantford Pottery
Activities: Classes for children; lect; gallery talks; exten dept serves Ontario; original objects of art lent to institutions

M ROYAL ONTARIO MUSEUM, 100 Queen's Park, M5S 2C6. Tel 416-978-3690. *Chmn Board of Trustees* Sydney M Hermant; *Secy Board of Trustees* Frank Dunbar; *Dir* Dr James E Cruise; *Assoc Dir* Barbara Stephen; *Asst Dir Admin & Facilities* C Gordon G Bristowe; *Asst Dir Education & Communication* R McCartney Samples; *Head, Programmes & Public Relations* David Young
Estab 1914 and includes 20 curatorial departments in the fields of art, archaeology and the natural sciences. The Royal Ontario Museum is currently undergoing a major programme of renovation and expansion and will reopen in the late spring of 1982. Average Annual Attendance: 900,000. Mem: 7400; dues individual $25
Income: $10,498,134 (financed by federal grants, provincial grants, museum income, memberships, bequests, grants and donations)
Exhibitions: Austria Presents Hundertwasser to the Continents; Ladders to Heaven: Our Judeo-Christian Heritage; Peasant Paintings from Hu County, Shensi Province, China
Publications: Numerous academic publications; Gallery Guides; exhibition catalogs; Publications in Print
Activities: Classes for adults and children; throughout the school year, pre-booked classes receive lessons in the Museum. Unconducted classes can also be arranged with the Museum at a cost of 50¢ per student; lect open to public with visiting lectr, special lect for members only; concerts; gallery talks; tours; competitions; extend dept serves Ontario; artmobile; individual paintings and original objects of art lent to museums and galleries; originate traveling exhibitions; museum shop sells books, magazines, reproductions, prints and slides
L Library, 100 Queen's Park, M5S 2C6. *Librn* E R Wilburn
Estab 1960 for curatorial research
Library Holdings: Vols 75,000; Micro—Fiche
Special Subjects: Decorative Arts, Textiles

L RYERSON POLYTECHNICAL INSTITUTE LIBRARY, 50 Gould St, M5B 1E8. Tel 416-595-5398. *Dean Applied Arts* A M Gifford; *Dean Arts* T W Grior; *Dir* John North
Open during term Mon - Thurs 8:30 AM - 10:30 PM, Fri 8:30 AM - 5 PM, Sat 9 AM - 5 PM. Estab 1948 to meet the needs of the students. Circ 185,000
Income: Financed by provincial appropriation
Purchases: $252,700
Library Holdings: Vols 225,000; Per subs 1800; Micro—Fiche, reels, prints; AV—A-tapes, cassettes, fs, motion pictures, rec, slides, v-tapes
Special Subjects: Architecture, Fashion Arts, Graphic Arts, Inter Design, Photography, Television arts
Collections: Architecture; History of Art
Activities: Classes for adults and children; dramatic programs; lect open to public; concerts; scholarships; exten dept
L Architecture Library, 50 Gould St, M5B 1E8. Tel 416-595-5161. *Librn* Chung S Kim
Open 9 AM - 8:30 PM. Estab 1969 to provide information for architectural students and instructors. Circ 33,600
Library Holdings: Vols 16,000; Per subs 120; Micro—Fiche; AV—A-tapes, cassettes, slides, v-tapes; Other—Clipping files
Special Subjects: Architecture, Landscape Architecture

SCULPTOR'S SOCIETY OF CANADA
For further information, see National and Regional Organizations

SOCIETY OF CANADIAN ARTISTS
For further information, see National Organizations in Canada

UNIVERSITY OF TORONTO
M Hart House, 7 Hart House Circle, M5S 1A1. Tel 416-978-2453, 978-2436. *Warden* Richard Alway; *Dir* Judith Schwartz
Open Mon 11 AM - 9 PM, Tues - Sat 11 AM - 5 PM, Sun 2 - 5 PM. No admis fee. Estab 1919 to promote young Canadian artists, as well as present a historical outlook on Canadian art. House has modern setting and total wall space of 147 running ft; outdoor quadrangle is available for summer sculpture shows. Average Annual Attendance: 12,000. Mem: 2000; dues $40
Income: Financed by membership
Purchases: $50,000
Collections: †Canadian Art (historical and contemporary)
Exhibitions: (1979) Therese Bolliger (drawings and screens); Johnny Canuck (ten Toronto cartoonists); Nancy de Boni (oil, pen and ink); Lorraine Gogan (terragrams); Elaine Schuman Krueger (handmade paperscapes); Angeline Kyba (paintings); Heather Moore (watercolour paintings); Miho Sawada (acrylic

paintings); Sir Edmund and Lady Head (watercolours); Linda White (acrylic paintings); Paul Worldman (paintings); (1980) City Life (young Quebec representational artists); Rada Greg (naive paintings); Hart House Camera Club - 58th Annual Salon; Clarissa Inglis (sculpture); Katja Jacobs (paintings and screens); Reimi Kobayashi (tapestries); Korean Canadian Arts Exhibition (juried show); selections from permanent collection

Publications: The Hart House Collection of Canadian Paintings by Jeremy Adamson

Activities: Classes for adults; docent training; lect for members only, 8 visiting lectr per year; concerts; gallery talks; tours; individual paintings and original objects of art lent; originate traveling exhibitions

L **Fine Arts Library,*** Smith Hall, Room 6032B, 100 St George St, M5S 1A1. Tel 416-978-3290. *Chief Librn* R Blackburn; *Librn* A Retfalvi
Open Mon - Fri 10 AM - 5 PM. Estab 1936 for reference only
Income: Financed by state appropriation and Department of Fine Arts
Library Holdings: Vols 13,869; Other—Exhibition catalogs, framed reproductions, photographs, reproductions
Special Subjects: Archaeology, Art History
Collections: Catalog materials including temporary, permanent, dealer and auction catalogs; photographic archives in various field of Western art
Publications: Canadian Illustrated News (Montreal): Index to Illustrations, quarterly

O **VISUAL ARTS ONTARIO,** 417 Queen's Quay W, M5V 1A7. Tel 416-366-1607. *Chmn Board* Alan Bakes; *VChmn Board* John Lindsay; *Secy* A Meredith Barry; *Treas* Lyman Henderson; *Exec Dir* William J S Boyle; *Exec Asst* Janni de Savoye; *Communications Officer* Gail J Habst; *Secy* Laura Lerand
Open 9 AM - 5 PM. Estab 1974 to further the awareness and appreciation of the visual arts. Mem: 4500; dues mem organizations $250, affiliates $50, individual $10
Income: $250,000 (financed by membership, provincial appropriation, and private donations)
Collections: Archival Material from several major professional art societies
Exhibitions: Traveling exhibits of member organizations
Publications: Artcards; Artviews, bimonthly; The Index of Ontario Artists, biannually; The Visual Arts Handbook, biannually
Activities: Workshops for professional artists; art rental program designed for government offices and corporations called The Bare Facts; originate traveling exhibitions

L **Library,** 417 Queen's Quay W, M5V 1A7.
Resource library open to public for reference
Library Holdings: Other—Archival material and current art periodicals
Special Subjects: Archives for Society of Canadian Painters-Etchers and Engravers, Canadian Society of Graphic Art, Canadian Society of Painters in Watercolour, Ontario Society for Education Through Art, Ontario Society of Artists, Sculptors Society of Canada, Society of Canadian Artists

WATERLOO

UNIVERSITY OF WATERLOO

M **Arts Centre Gallery,** N2L 3G1. Tel 519-884-4281. *Adminr* Marlene Bryan; *Installations Officer & Designer* Peter McLay
Open Mon - Fri 9 AM - 4 PM, Sun 2 - 5 PM, cl Sun June - Aug. No admis fee. Estab 1962
Collections: Contemporary Canadian Art

L **Dana Porter Arts Library,** University Ave, N2L 3G1. Tel 519-885-1211, Ext 2282; Telex 069-5259. *University Librn* Murray Shepherd; *Special Coll Librn* Susan Bellingham; *Reference and Coll Development Librn - Fine Arts and Architecture* Jo Beglo
Open Mon - Fri 8 AM - 12 AM, Sat 9 AM - 12 AM, Sun 1 PM - 12 AM. Estab 1958 to provide access to information appropriate to the needs of the academic community
Library Holdings: Vols 653,000; Per subs 5500; Micro—Cards, fiche, reels; AV—Fs, motion pictures, rec; Other—Clipping files, exhibition catalogs
Collections: The Dance Collection (monographs, periodicals and pamphlets from 1535 to date relating to the history of dance-ballet)
Publications: Library publishes four bibliographic series: Aids, Bibliography, Focus, Research Guide, irregularly
Activities: Undergraduate curriculum in art history and studio

WINDSOR

M **ART GALLERY OF WINDSOR,** 445 Riverside Dr W, N9A 6T8. Tel 519-258-7111. *Pres* Mrs W G Curry; *VPres* Ron Pfaff; *Secy* Mrs Mignon Briggs; *Dir* Dr Kenneth Saltmarche; *Business Mgr* Ken Ferguson; *Cur* Ted Fraser; *Education Cur* Megan Bice; *Publications* Pat Morris; *Registrar* Betty Wilkinson
Open Tues, Thurs, Fri, Sat 10 AM - 5 PM, Wed 10 AM - 10 PM, Sun 1 - 5 PM, cl Mon. No admis fee. Estab 1943 for collection and exhibition of works of art, primarily Canadian, for the study and enjoyment of the Windsor-Detroit area. Gallery contains 56,000 sq ft of space on three floors; it is environmentally-controlled and highly fire resistant; outdoor sculpture terrace. Average Annual Attendance: 120,000. Mem: 1700; dues patron $50, family $25, single $15, out-of-town $10, student $7.50; annual meeting mid-March
Income: $500,000 (financed by membership, city and provincial appropriation and federal grants
Collections: †Primarily Canadian Drawings, Paintings, Prints and Sculpture 18th Century to present; †Inuit Prints and Sculpture; non-Canadian Paintings and Sculpture; decorative arts
Exhibitions: Approximately 35 exhibitions a year, besides installation of permanent collection, of mostly Canadian Historic and Contemporary Sculpture, Painting and Graphics
Publications: Projections monthly bulletin and catalogues for exhibitions organized by this gallery, six times a year
Activities: Summer Arts Club classes for children; docent training; occasional workshops for adults and children; lect open to public, 20 visiting lectr per year; concerts; tours; exten dept serves Essex County; individual paintings and original objects of art lent; book traveling exhibitions approximately 20 per year; originate

traveling exhibitions; museum shop sells Canadian handicrafts, original art, reproductions and prints; Children's Gallery

L **Reference Library,** 445 Riverside Dr W, N9A 6T8. *Librn & Registrar* Betty F Wilkinson
Open Tues, Thurs, Fri Sat 10 AM - 5 PM, Wed 10 AM - 10 PM, Sun 1 - 5 PM, cl Mon. Estab 1966. Reference for staff, members and public
Income: $1000
Purchases: $1000
Library Holdings: Vols 300; Per subs 12; Other—Clipping files, exhibition catalogs, Catalogs and museum bulletins

WOODSTOCK

M **WOODSTOCK ART GALLERY,** Woodstock Public Library, 445 Hunter St, N4S 4G7. Tel 519-539-6761. *Chief Librn* Carolyn Croke; *Cur* J T Henderson
Open Mon - Thurs Noon - 8 PM, Tues Noon - 9 PM, Fri & Sat Noon - 5 PM, cl Sun. No admis fee. Estab 1966 to bring art to the public. Two galleries, 210 ft wall space, 1823 sq ft. Average Annual Attendance: 15,000. Mem: 275; dues family $7.50, individual $5
Income: $48,000 (financed by membership, city and state appropriation, Ontario Arts Council and Ministry of Culture and Recreation)
Collections: Small collection of Canadian Art, concentrating on Florence Carlyle
Exhibitions: (1978-79) Bervoets; Bowman; Bozak; Hassan; Hunsberger; Ari Jansen; John Mars; McMillan; O'Henly; Devona Paquette; Quebec Silver; Ted Roi; Sarazin; Tingley; David Wright; Zarski; juried show; permanent collection; photography; school art
Publications: Monthly newsletter
Activities: Classes for children; docent training; lect open to public, 4 visiting lectr per year; concerts; gallery talks; tours; individual paintings are lent to residents of Oxford County and business firms; lending collection contains 100 paintings; book traveling exhibitions 1 - 3 per year

PRINCE EDWARD ISLAND

CHARLOTTETOWN

M **CONFEDERATION CENTRE ART GALLERY AND MUSEUM,** PO Box 848, C1A 7L9. Tel 902-892-2464. *Chmn* Robert MacLeod; *Dir* Dr Moncrieff Williamson; *Executive Dir* William J Hancox; *Personal Asst & Secy* Janet MacGregor; *Cur* Mark Holton; *Registrar* Judy MacDonald
Open Tues - Sat 10 AM - 5 PM, Sun 2 - 5 PM, cl Mon. No admis fee. Estab 1964 as a national collection devoted to Canadian art and fine crafts. Average Annual Attendance: 100,000. Mem: 600, family $12, individual $5
Income: Financed by federal, provincial, city and the private sector
Collections: †Canadian Art early and contemporary; †Canadian Fine Crafts; Robert Harris Paintings and Drawings
Exhibitions: An average of thirty exhibitions a year from own and circulation collections; special exhibitions each July and August to coincide with summer festival
Activities: Classes for adults and children; dramatic programs; contemporary dance; lect open to public; tours; concerts; exten dept serving province; lending collection contains paintings, 7000 Kodachromes, 12 motion pictures, 50 film strips, slides; originate traveling exhibitions; junior museum

L **Library,** PO Box 848, C1A 7L9.
Open for reference
Library Holdings: Vols 1547; Other—Photographs

SUMMERSIDE

MARITIME ART ASSOCIATION
For further information, see National Organizations in Canada

WEST ROYALTY

L **HOLLAND COLLEGE,** School of Visual Arts Library, Burns Ave, C1A 7N8. Tel 902-894-5104. *Dir* Henry Purdy
Open Mon - Fri 9 AM - 5 PM and 6:30 - 8:30 PM, Sat & Sun 10 AM - 6 PM
Library Holdings: Vols 2000; Per subs 35

QUEBEC

CAHUGHNAWAGA

M **MUSEE KATERI TEKAKWITHA,** Mission Saint Francois Xavier, CP 70, J0L 1B0. Tel 514-632-6030. *Dir* Paul-Emile Beaudoin
Open daily 9 AM - Noon and 1 - 5 PM. No admis fee. Estab as a mission in 1667
Collections: Archives, Canadian church silver, historic chapel, old paintings
Publications: Kateri

CHICOUTIMI

O **LA SOCIETE DES ARTS DE CHICOUTIMI,*** 272 du Seminaire, PO Box 230, G7H 1Z5. Tel 418-549-3618.
Open Mon - Sat 1:30 - 5 PM & 7 - 10 PM. No admis fee. Estab 1963. Mem: Dues adults $10, students $3
Income: Financed by city appropriation and membership
Collections: Ceramics, graphics, paintings, sculpture
Publications: Monthly Journal
Activities: Gallery talks; films; traveling exhibitions organized and circulated

DORVAL

O **DORVAL CULTURAL CENTRE,** 1401 Lakeshore Dr, H9S 2E5. Tel 514-636-6000. *Coordr* Danyelle Brodeur; *Animator* Linda Burdayron
Open 2 - 9 PM. No admis fee. Estab 1967 to promote culture and art. Maintains an art gallery
Income: Financed by city appropriation
Exhibitions: All Visual and Expression Arts
Publications: Leisuregram
Activities: Classes for adults and children; dramatic programs; lect open to public; gallery talks; tours

JOLIETTE

M **MUSEE D'ART DE JOLIETTE,** 145 Wilfrid-Corbeil St, PO Box 132, J6E 3Z3. Tel 514-756-0311. *VPres* Me Serge Joyal; *Secy* Raymond C Lapierre; *Dir* Jacques Toupin; *Animator* Carmen DeLorme; *Technician* Paul Coutu; *Technician* Fernand Laurin; *Secy* Elyse Houle; *Guide* Gerard Brisson
Open Tues & Thurs 2 - 5 PM and 7 - 9:30 PM, Sat & Sun 2 - 5 PM. Admis adults $1, students 25¢. Estab 1961 for educational purposes; preservation of the collections; save local patrimony. Gallery Six - Contemporary Gallery, temporary exhibitions; Sacred Art Gallery; Medieval Gallery; Canadian Gallery; Permanent Collection. Average Annual Attendance: 15,000. Mem: 125; dues $5; annual meeting March
Income: $79,000 (financed by endowment and provincial government grants)
Purchases: $7000
Collections: American Art; Amerindian Art; †Canadian Art; Costumes 1850-1920; European Art; Pre-Columbian Art; Sacred Art of Quebec; furniture, painting and sculpture
Exhibitions: Mostly Contemporary Art (18 per year); Modern Art; Traditional Art; traveling exhibitions
Publications: Catalog and pamphlet entitled Le Musee d'Art de Joliette
Activities: Classes for adults and children; dramatic programs; lect open to public, 500 visiting lectr per year; concerts; gallery talks; tours; films; book traveling exhibitions 2 or 3 per year; originate traveling exhibitions in Joliette area; sales shop books, magazines, postcards and reproductions
L **Library,** 145 Wilfrid-Corbeil St, J6E 3Z3. *Animator* Carmen Delorme; *Secy* Elyse Houle
Estab 1976. Open on reservation only for art reference
Purchases: $200-$250
Library Holdings: Vols 1000; AV—Slides; Other—Exhibition catalogs, photographs, sculpture
Special Subjects: History of art, well-known artists
Collections: Art Journal; Great Masters; History of Painting; Larousse Mensuel

JONQUIERE

M **INSTITUT DES ARTS AU SAGUENAY,** National Exhibition Center, Mont Jacob, Box 605, G7X 7W4. *Pres* Celine Gagnon; *VPres* Helene St-Gelais; *Secy* Michel Levesque; *Admin Dir* Pierre Houle; *Animator* Jean-Guy Theriault
Open daily 2 - 5 PM and 7 - 10 PM. No admis fee. Estab 1979 to democratize and make art accessible. Average Annual Attendance: 20,000. Mem: 220; dues $10; annual meeting First of Sept
Income: $130,000 (financed by membership, city and state appropriation)
Exhibitions: (1979-80) Abstraction Lyrique en Europe; Artistes Americains Contemporains; Adrienne Bouchard; Le Collectionneur de Meubles Anciens; Concours d'Expression Artistique Regional; Club de Photo J A K; Jean Dallaire; Rodolphe Duquay; Exposition d'Odette Ducasse; Jean-Daniel Gagnon; Heritage d'Hier et de Demain; Denis Langolois; Metiers d'Art Ontario-Quebec; 10 Metres Cubes; Photographies d'Enfants par Tanuma; Que'est-ce Donc; Recontre de 2 types; Revolution Automatiste; Sculpteurs Regionaux; Tendances de la Sculpture Quebecoise de 1960 a 1970; (1981) L'Art du Connaissaur; Courtepointe Quebecoise; Marc Demers; Iapisserie Quebecoise; Richard Langevin; Ginette Lefebvre; Raymond-Guy Simard
Activities: Lect; concerts; gallery talks; tours

MONTREAL

C **ALCAN SMELTERS AND CHEMICALS LIMITED,** 1, Place Ville Marie, PO Box 6090, H3C 3H2. Tel 514-877-3042. *Chief Admin Officer* W A Redman
Estab 1979 to enhance the offices in which they are installed and enrich the lives of those who work there. Collection displayed in reception areas and private offices
Purchases: $80,000
Collections: Contemporary Canadian Art
Activities: Lect; individual objects of art lent for special exhibits upon request

C **BENSON & HEDGES (CANADA) INC,** 1010 Lagauchetiere St W, H3B 2P4. Tel 514-878-3471. *Dir of Corporate Affairs* Cynthia Heide
Estab to assist arts in different areas of the Country. Annual amount of contributions and grants $30,000
Activities: Sponsors exhibitions, including an Eskimo Art Exhibition

O **SAIDYE BRONFMAN CENTRE,** 5170 Cote Ste Catherine Rd, H3W 1M7. Tel 514-739-2301. *Executive Dir* Nahum Ravel; *Dir Continuing Education* Harvey Golden; *Dir Fine Arts School* Alina Michaely; *Dir Institute* Eva Epstein; *Cur* Peter Thomas Krausz
Open Mon - Thurs 9 AM - 9 PM, Fri 9 AM - 3:30 PM, Sun 10 AM - 4 PM, cl Sat. No admis fee. Estab 1967 as a non-profit cultural centre for the promotion and dissemination of the arts. Centre located in building given by Phyllis Lambert and her mother, Saidye Bronfman; 3000 sq ft gallery. Average Annual Attendance: 90,000
Income: Financed by membership
Exhibitions: Three major exhibitions per year from traveling exhibitions, student exhibitions
Publications: Exhibition catalogs
Activities: Educ dept, courses in visual and fine arts; performing arts; general studies and Jewish studies; lect open to public, 3 visiting lectr per year; concerts; 10 gallery talks; scholarships

M **CHATEAU DE RAMEZAY,** Antiquarian and Numismatic Society of Montreal, 280 Notre-Dame E, H2Y 1C5. Tel 514-861-7182. *Dir* Jacques Poulin
Open Tues - Sun 10 AM - 4 PM, cl Mon. Admis adults $1, students 50¢. Estab 1895 in residence (1705) of Claude de Ramezay, governor of Montreal. Average Annual Attendance: 40,000. Mem: Dues life $500, individual $10
Collections: Early Canadian Portraits; Indian Collection; furniture, handicrafts and woodcarving
L **Library,** 280 Notre-Dame E, H2Y 1C5.
Library Holdings: Vols 2200
Special Subjects: Canadian history

M **CONCORDIA UNIVERSITY,** Sir George Williams Art Galleries, 1455 de Maisonneuve Blvd, H3G 1M8. Tel 514-879-5917. *Dir* Edwy F Cooke; *Cur* Donald F Andrus; *Registrar* Patrick Landsley
Open Mon - Fri 11 AM - 9 PM, Sat 11 AM - 5 PM. No admis fee. Estab 1962 to display in a scholarly fashion the University collection; provide a venue for a variety of significant touring exhibitions chosen from within the region and across Canada, all with the idea of providing an interesting cultural milieu both for the university and public alike. Three galleries, 4000 sq ft with 521 running ft, located in mezzanine area. Average Annual Attendance: 66,000
Income: Financed by university funds
Collections: Small Collection of Indigenous Arts of Africa, Meso-America and New Guinea; Modern and Contemporary Canadian Art
Exhibitions: Advanced Drawing by Fine Arts Students; Eva Brandi: Sculptures; Grahma Cantieni: Drawings; Edwy Cooke: Recent Watercolors, A Retrospective Exhibition; Paterson Ewen: Recent Paintings; Roger Fry Artist and Critic; Pnina Gagnon: On the Human Body; Ann Kipling: Drawings ; Ann McCall: Prints; Sue Real: Drawings; Michael Thompson: Paintings; Ukiyo-E: Glimpses into the Floating World; Ron Webber: Photography; Norman Yates: Drawings and Paintings; Annual Fine Arts Student Exhibition; Exhibition of Works from the Permanent Collection; Graduate Students in Fine Arts, Fall and Spring Exhibitions; Members of the Faculty of the Fine Arts Collection; selections from the Concordia University Collection of Art
Activities: Lect open to public, 3 visiting lectr per year; originate traveling exhibitions; book store

O **FEDERATION DES QUEBECOISE DES SERVICES SOCIO-CULTURELS,*** (Formerly Federation des Centres Culturels de la Province de Quebec) 3100 rue Saint-Donat, H2E 2Z7. Tel 514-374-4700. *Pres* Pierre Babin; *Admin Secy* Eva Tetreault
Open daily. No admis fee. Estab 1967. Mem: Dues institutional $50, individual $25
Income: Financed by state appropriation
Collections: Graphics, paintings, sculpture and theatre
Exhibitions: Temporary, traveling and selected from collections exhibitions
Activities: Lect; gallery talks; concerts; films; dance recitals; dramas; hobby workshops; competitions; lending program to museums
L **Library,*** 3100 rue Saint-Donat, H2E 2Z7. Tel 514-354-0320.
Library Holdings: Vols 5000; Other—Manuscripts

O **GUILDE CANADIANNE DES MIETIERS D'ART, QUEBEC,** Canadian Guild of Crafts, Quebec, 2025 Peel St, H3A 1T6. Tel 514-849-6091. *Managing Dir* Virginia J Watt
Mem: Dues $25 and up; annual meeting April
Collections: Permanent collection of Eskimo and Indian Arts and Crafts
Exhibitions: Works by professional craftsmen and artists from Canada; group and one-man shows
L **Library,** 2025 Peel St, H3A 1T6.
Reference

O **LA SOCIETE DES DECORATEURS-ENSEMBLIERS DU QUEBEC,** Interior Decorators' Society of Quebec, Studio G, 451 St Sulpice St, H2Y 2V9. Tel 514-288-9046. *Pres* Benoit Diechome; *First VPres* Claude Thiebeige; *Second VPres* Pauline Dupie; *Secy* Margueite Seruey; *Treas* Michel Degio
Open 9 AM - 5 PM. Estab 1935 as a nonprofit professional association. Mem: 437; dues $125
Income: $30,000 (financed by membership)
Exhibitions: Traveling exhibitions in the Province of Quebec
Publications: Journal magazine, monthly; News Bulletin, 10 issues per year
Activities: Education Committee to improve the level of teaching in interior design; lect for members only; book traveling exhibitions

MCGILL UNIVERSITY

M **McCord Museum,** 690 Sherbrooke St W, H3A 1E9. Tel 514-392-4778. *Chief Cur* David Bellman; *Cur Photography* Stanley Triggs; *Cur Costume* Jacqueline Beaudoin-Ross; *Exhib Coordr* Craig Laberge; *Registrar* Conrad Graham
Open Wed - Sun 11 AM - 5 PM, cl Mon & Tues. No admis fee. Estab 1919 as a museum of Canadian Ethnology and Social History. Average Annual Attendance: 35,000
Income: $500,000 (financed by endowment, federal and provincial government and university
Collections: †Canadian ethnology; †decorative arts; †documentary photography;

†documentary prints, drawings, paintings - historical; †historical costume
Exhibitions: Approximately ten temporary exhibitions annually; semi-permanent thematic displays
Publications: Exhibition catalogs and monographs; Guides to collections for children
Activities: Lect; exten dept; individual paintings and original objects of art lent to international museum - art gallery exhibitions; book traveling exhibitions 3 per year; originate traveling exhibitions

L **Blackader-Lauterman Library of Architecture and Arts,** 3459 McTavish St, H3A 1Y1. Tel 514-392-5211. *Librn* Mrs E Doelle; *Sr Library Asst* Mrs M Berger
Open winter 9 AM - 9 PM, summer 9 AM - 6 PM. Estab 1922 to establish a special collection of architectural material. Circ 68,000
Library Holdings: Vols 45,000; Per subs 247; Other—Exhibition catalogs, pamphlets, photographs

M **MONTREAL MUSEUM OF FINE ARTS,*** 3400 Ave du Musee, H3G 1K3. Tel 514-285-1600. *Dir* Jean Trudel; *Chief Conservator* Robin Ashton; *Cur Decorative Arts* Robert Little; *Assoc Cur Dept Prints and Drawings* Dr Micheline Moisan; *Research Cur* Dr Myra Nan Rosemfeld; *Cur Contemporary Canadian Art* Normand Theriault; *Registrar* Elaine Tolmatch
Open Tues - Sun 11 AM - 5 PM, cl Mon. Admis adults $1, children under 12 50¢. Estab 1860 as an Art Association for the exhibition of paintings; museum estab 1916. Average Annual Attendance: 275,000. Mem: 11,000; dues $20 and up; annual meeting Sept
Income: Financed by endowment, membership and provincial appropriation
Collections: Collection of African Art by Fr Gagnon; Chinese, Near Eastern, Peruvian, Inuit primitive art; Saidye and Samuel Bronfman Collection of Contemporary Canadian art; European decorative arts; French, Spanish, Dutch, British, Canadian and other schools; Japanese incense boxes; The Parker Lace Collection; Harry T Norton Collection of ancient glass; Lucile Pillow Collection of porcelain; decorative arts, painting, sculpture from 3000 BC to the present
Exhibitions: Art in Quebec in the Wake of the Conquest; Gold of the Gods; Hundertwasser; Japanese Incense Boxes rediscovered; Leningrad; Master paintings from The Hermitage and the State Russian Museum; Guido Molinari Retrospective; Alfred Stevens
Publications: Collage (a calendar of events)
Activities: Docent training; lect open to public; concerts; gallery talks; tours; exten dept serving Quebec and other provinces; individual paintings and original objects of art lent to art galleries and cultural centers; museum shop selling books, original art, reproductions, prints and slides

L **Library,*** 3400 Ave du Musee, H3G 1K3. *Librn* Juanita Toupin
Open for reference to students, scholars, teachers, researchers
Library Holdings: Vols 49,710; Per subs 500; Other—Clipping files, exhibition catalogs, art sales catalogs
Collections: Canadiana; costumes

M **MUSEE D'ART CONTEMPORAIN,** Cite du Havre, H3C 3R4. Tel 514-873-2878. *Dir* Louise Letocha; *Admin Asst* Hector Thisdlae; *Dir of Exhib* Claude Gosselin; *Dir of Traveling Exhib* Anne-Marie Sioui
Open Tues - Sat 10 AM - 6 PM, Thurs 10 AM - 10 PM, cl Mon. No admis fee. Estab 1964. Conservation and information about contemporary art are the most important aspects of the museum; also to present contemporary artists to the general public. Building is a medium-sized two-story art museum and with an exhibition area of 2200 sq meters divided in four galleries and a foyer. Average Annual Attendance: 80,000
Income: $1,200,000 (financed by provincial grants)
Purchases: $200,000
Collections: Contemporary Art - †Canadian, International and †Quebecois: drawings, engravings, paintings, photographs and sculptures
Exhibitions: Jocelyne Alloucherie (dessins et sculptures); Pierre Ayot (oeuvres graphiques et installations, 1979); Dessin Et Surrealisme Au Quebec (une exposition du Service des expositions itinerantes); Pnina Gagnon (dessins); Yves Gaucher (serie Jericho 1978); Pierre Gaudard (photographies - Les Prisons); Gravure Du Quebec (Bilan 1970-80); Hommage A Kokoschka (plus de 100 oeuvres graphiques de la collection du Comte Bethusy-Huc d'Autriche); Fernand Leduc (les microchromies 1970-80); Nouvelles Formes De Realisme; Gabor Szilasi (photographies recentes); Gabor Szilasi (photographies - Les Prisons); William Vazan
Publications: Atelier, quarterly; catalogs of exhibitions
Activities: Lect open to public, 15 visiting lectr per year; concerts; gallery talks; tours; competitions; exten dept serving Quebec province; originate traveling exhibitions; sales shop sells books, magazines, reproductions, prints and slides

L **Bibliotheque,** Cite du Havre, H3C 3R4. *Librn* Isabelle Montplaisir
Open Tues - Fri 10 AM - 5 PM, Sat & Sun Noon - 6 PM, except summer. Estab 1967. For reference only
Income: Financed by Quebec Government
Purchases: $14,000
Library Holdings: Vols 4631; Per subs 128; Micro—Fiche, reels; AV—A-tapes, slides, v-tapes; Other—Clipping files 2000, exhibition catalogs 6146, manuscripts, photographs
Special Subjects: Contemporary art
Collections: Archives of Paul-Emile Borduas (Painter 1905-1960); about 12,500 items including writings, correspondence, exhibition catalogs, etc

M **MUSEE DE L'EGLISE NOTRE-DAME,** 430 St Sulfice St, H2Y 2V5. Tel 514-842-2925. *Pastor & Dir* Fernand Lecavalier
Estab 1937 as an historical and religious museum. Due to the arson of Dec, 1978, the Musee de l'Eglise Notre-Dame de Montreal will be closed for 1980 and 1981
Collections: Old Greek and Roman Coins; Documents, Furniture, Manuscripts, Religious Ornaments, Statues and Volumes pertaining to the History of Canada; medals, paintings and silverware

O **ORDER OF ARCHITECTS OF QUEBEC,** 1825 Dorchester Blvd W, H3H 1R4. Tel 514-937-6168. *Pres* Patrick Blouin; *Secy* Antoine Ghattas
Open 9 AM - 5 PM. Estab 1890. Mem: 1550; dues $350; annual meeting May
Publications: Bulletin; Register

M **PAVILION OF HUMOUR,** Man and His World, H3C 1A0. Tel 514-872-6079. *Dir* Robert LaPalme; *Asst Cur* Serge Jongue; *Secy* Jocelyne Gagne; *Cur* Andre Carpentier
Open June 21 - Labor Day 10 AM - 8:30 PM. Estab 1968 to show graphic humor from over 60 countries, plus humorous sculptures borrowed from all over. Pavilion of Humour is part of Man and His World. Average Annual Attendance: 300,000
Income: $300,000 (financed by endowment and city and state appropriations)
Collections: Collection of American Editorial Cartoons from 1867 to present; Collection of Panel Cartoons from 1860 to present; Drawings from Pulitzer Prize Winners; Drawings from Reuben Award Winners; Drawings on International Salon of Cartoons Winners; Strip Cartoons
Publications: Catalogs for Cartoonist of the Year Exhibition and International Salon of Cartoons
Activities: Competitions; original books and money are awarded to winners in a junior cartoon exhibition; objects of art lent; material available to universities and museums; originate traveling exhibitions

L **Library,** H3C 1A0.
Reference
Library Holdings: Vols 2744

M **SAINT JOSEPH'S ORATORY,** 3800 Queen Mary Ch, H3V 1H6. Tel 514-733-8211. *Dir* Marcel Lalonde; *Artistic Cur* Paul LeDuc
Open daily 10 AM - 5 PM. Admis adults 50¢, children 25¢, special group rates. Shrine founded 1904, estab 1953 as art museum. St Joseph's Oratory is also a Montreal landmark, the highest point in this city (856 ft above sea level), a piece of art - architecture - with a history, style, etc of its own
Collections: Ancient and Contemporary Art
Exhibitions: (1979) Complete Series of 58 Engravings titled Miserere and Guerre by well-known French Artist Georges Rouault (1877-1958); (1980) Sculpture in Taille Directe (direct carving as opposed to modeling) by French and Canadian Sculptors Henri Charlier (1883-1975), Fernand Py (1887-1949) and Sylvia Daoust (comtemporary)
Activities: Concerts; films

L **Library,** 3800 Queen Mary Ch, H3V 1H6.
Open to public for use on the premises, and for inter-library loan
Library Holdings: Vols 80,000; Micro—Reels; Other—Photographs

M **SOCIETY OF THE MONTREAL MILITARY AND MARITIME MUSEUM,** Saint Helen's Island Museum, The Old Fort, St Helen's Island, PO Box 1024 Station A, H3C 2W9. Tel 514-861-6738. *Mgr* Bruce D Bolton; *Mgr* Guy P E Duchesneau; *Cur* Guy Vandeboncoeur
Open summer daily 10 AM - 5 PM, cl Mon, Sept - April. Admis mid-June to Labour Day adults 50¢, children and groups 25¢. Estab 1955 to exhibit artifacts relating to Canada's colonial history, with emphasis on military and maritime themes. Located in an old British Arsenal, built between 1820-24; galleries cover theme chronologically and by collection. Average Annual Attendance: 100,000. Mem: 100; dues $2; annual meeting May
Income: $650,000 (financed by endowment, membership, city and state appropriation, federal funds and donations)
Collections: Arms and Ammunition; Kitchen and Fireplace, dating from 16th Century; prints
Publications: The 4-M's Society Newsletter, irregularly
Activities: Lect open to public and some to members only, 10 visiting lectr per year; museum shop sells books, reproductions, prints and slides

L **MacDonald-Steward Library,** The Old Fort, St Helen's Island, H3C 2W9. *Librn* Elizabeth F Hale
Average Annual Attendance: Open to researchers and members for reference
Library Holdings: Vols 6000; Per subs 50

L **UNIVERSITE DE MONTREAL,** Bibliotheque d'Amenagement, 5620 Darlington #1004, CP 6128, H3C 3J7. Tel 514-343-6009, 343-7177. *Chef de Bibliotheque* Jacqueline Pelletier
Estab 1964
Purchases: $38,000
Library Holdings: Vols 25,000; Per subs 545; AV—Slides; Other—Clipping files
Special Subjects: Architecture, Constructions, Design
Collections: Rare Books

PERCE

O **LE CENTRE D'ART DE PERCE,** G0C 2L0. *Dir* Josee Tommi
Open July - Aug 10 AM - 10 PM. No admis fee. Estab 1955 to promote art in all its forms. Gallery of contemporary arts and crafts. Average Annual Attendance: 15,000
Income: $10,000 (financed by endowment)
Collections: Permanent collections of Alberto Tommi's late paintings
Publications: Le Centre d'Art de Perce, annually
Activities: Classes for children; dramatic programs; concerts; cinema

POINTE CLAIRE

O **POINTE CLAIRE CULTURAL CENTRE,** Stewart Hall, 176 Lakeshore Rd, H9S 4G7. Tel 514-695-3312, 695-3317. *Chmn Stewart Hall* Henry Bolker; *Admin* Jeanette Lamarche; *Art Gallery Dir* Helen Judkins; *Cultural Dir* Ruth Aversperg
Open Mon & Wed 7:30 - 9:30 PM, Tues & Fri 2:30 - 4:30 PM, Sat 2 - 5 PM. No admis fee. Estab 1963. Gallery is 25 x 80 ft. Average Annual Attendance: 10,000.
Mem: Policy and Planning Board meets ten times per year
Income: $460,000 (financed by endowment and city appropriation)
Exhibitions: Approximately ten per year, local, provincial, national and international contest
Publications: Bulletins; schedules of classes, study series, social events, approximately 30 per year
Activities: Classes for adults and children; dramatic programs; resident workshops in pottery, weaving and photography; lect open to public, 10 visiting lectr per year; concerts; gallery talks; tours; individual paintings lent; lending collection contains framed reproductions, original prints and paintings; sells framed reproductions for young people and adults in Art Lending Service

QUEBEC

M **L'UNIVERSITE LAVAL,** Ecole des Arts Visuels de L'Universite Laval,* Pavillon de la Faculte des Arts, Cite Universitaire, G1K 7P4. Tel 418-656-3703. *Dir* Pierre Larochelle
Open Mon - Fri 10 AM - 10 PM, cl holidays. No admis fee. Estab 1921
Collections: Art color slides, decorative arts, graphics, paintings, sculpture
Exhibitions: Temporary and traveling exhibitions, changing monthly
Activities: Traveling exhibitions organized and circulated
L **Library,*** Pavillon de la Faculte des Arts, G1K 7P4.
Open to the public for use on the premises; original prints and works of art available for study
Library Holdings: Vols 25,000

M **MUSEE DES AUGUSTINES DE L'HOTEL DIEU OF QUEBEC,** 32 rue Charlevoix, G1R 3R9. Tel 418-692-2492. *Supvr* Sr Jeanne Roy; *Conservator* Sr Claire Gagnon
Open daily 9 - 11 AM & 2 - 5 PM, Sun 2 - 5 PM, other times by appointment, cl carnival time. No admis fee. Estab 1639 in the Monastere des Augustines (1695)
Collections: Archives, medical history, paintings, sculpture
L **Library,** 32 rue Charlevoix, G1R 3R9.
Religious and medical books available for research upon special request
Library Holdings: Vols 2000

M **MUSEE DU QUEBEC,** Parc des Champs de Bataille, G1S 1C8. Tel 418-643-2150. *Dir* Lise Nantais-Picher; *Conservator Ancient Art* Claude Thibault; *Conservator Contemporary Art* Michel Martin; *Conservator & Ethnographer* Paul Carpentier; *Educatives Services* Guy Mercier; *Conservator Drawing* Guy Paradis
Open daily 9 AM - 5 PM, Sun & holidays 1 - 5 PM. Estab 1933 under Government of Province of Quebec. Branch Museums, Hotel Chevalier, 5 Champlain St: Old French Canadian Homestead
Purchases: $60,000
Collections: †Furniture by Quebec Artists and Carvers from the 17th Century to present; †paintings; sculpture
Exhibitions: Rotating exhibitions
L **Bibliotheque des Art,** Parc des Champs de Bataille, G1S 1C8. *Chief Librn* F Lafortune; *Asst* Diane Aubry; *Asst* Luce Gariepy; *Asst* Philippe Trefry
Open 9 AM - 5 PM. Estab 1933
Income: $150,000 (financed by city appropriation)
Purchases: $35,000
Library Holdings: Vols 20,000; Per subs 325; Micro—Fiche, reels; AV—A-tapes, cassettes, lantern Slides, motion pictures, rec, slides, v-tapes; Other—Clipping files, exhibition catalogs, pamphlets, photographs
Special Subjects: Ethnology, Art

M **MUSEE DU SEMINAIRE DE QUEBEC,** 6 Rue de l'Universite, CP 460, G1R 4R7. Tel 418-692-3981. *Conservateur* Jean-Marie Thivierge; *Conservateur-Adjoint* Jean-Pierre Pare
Open 10 AM - 4 PM. Admis 50¢. Estab 1874. Average Annual Attendance: 10,000
Income: Financed by state appropriation and university funding
Collections: Chinese Artwork; coins, furniture, gold, paintings, stamps

RIMOUSKI

M **LE MUSEE REGIONAL DE RIMOUSKI,** 35 W St Germain, G5L 4B4. Tel 418-724-2272. *Dir Museum* Diane Paquin; *Pres Board Dir & Pres Executive Committee* Jean-Guy Cote
Open summer daily 10 AM - 10 PM, winter Wed - Sun 1:30 - 9:30 PM. No admis fee. Estab 1972 for the diffusion of Fine arts, painting, sculpture and tapestry; to present local, national and international exhibitions and organize itinerant exhibitions. An old church, built in 1823, now historical monument, completely restored inside, beautiful frame of wood, three floors of exhibitions. Average Annual Attendance: 60,000. Mem: 500; annual meeting May
Income: $135,000 (financed by membership, city, provincial and federal appropriations, annual subscription campaign)
Collections: Canadain Art, Paintings, Sculpture and Silversmithing; European Paintings
Exhibitions: L'Art du Vitrail; Artisanat 1978; Edward Curtis; Dessins et Surrealisme au Quebec; Une Famille au Musee: Famille Jomphe; Peinture d'Email de Jacqueline de Champlain; Philatelistes et Numismates; le Quebec au Jour le Jour de Lida Moser; la Revolution Automatiste; la Semaine Multiculturelle; Un Village au Musee: Trois-Pistoles
Activities: Lect open to public; concerts; originate traveling exhibitions; sales shop sells reproductions, prints and slides

L **Library,** 35 W St Germain, G5L 4B4.
Open to public for reference
Library Holdings: Vols 1500; Per subs 40; AV—Slides 8000; Other—Documents 600

SAINT-LAURENT

M **MUSEE D'ART DE SAINT-LAURENT,** 615 Blvd Sainte-Croix, H4L 3X7. Tel 514-747-7367. *Pres* Mrs L Ethier; *VPres* G Lavallee; *Secy* Mrs L Aubin; *Dir & Cur* Gerard Lavallee; *Exhib* Andre Jerome; *Research* Danielle Legentil
Open Sun & Tues - Fri 11 AM - 5 PM. No admis fee. Estab 1962 to didactic exhibitions of Traditional Arts and Crafts of Quebec. Gallery situated in a Gothic chapel of the Victorian period, built in 1867 in Montreal and moved in Saint-Laurent in 1930. Besides its permanent collection, the Museum presents periodical modern art exhibitions
Collections: European and African Prehistoric Stones; Indian Artifacts: artifacts, ceramics, costumes, prehistoric stones; Traditional and Folk Art of French Canada from 17th - 19th Century: artifacts, ceramics, furniture, metalworks, sculpture, silver, textiles, tools, wood-carving
Exhibitions: (1979) Periodical Exhibitions: Batiks, Children Paintings and Drawings, Contemporary American Painters, Lithographs, Old and Modern Weathercock, Old Pewters, Puppets Exhibition, Sunday Painters, photographs, wood-carving, works of art classes students
Publications: Album: Images Taillees du Quebec; monthly calendar
Activities: Lect open to public; concerts; gallery talks; tours

SAINTE ANNE DE BEAUPRE

M **PERES REDEMPTORISTES,** 10018 Avenue Royale, G0A 3C0. Tel 418-827-3781. *Pres* S Baillargeon
Open daily 10 AM - 5 PM, June - Oct. Admis adults $1, children 50¢. Estab 1960. Average Annual Attendance: 50,000.
Income: Financed by private funds
Collections: Ex Votos Paintings; Sculptures of Lorus John

SHAWINIGAN

O **CENTRE CULTUREL DE SHAWINIGAN,*** 2100 rue Dessaules, CP 48, Station B, G9N 6V3. Tel 819-539-4822 or 539-5333. *Dir* Henry J Blanchard; *Asst Dir* Jean-Luc Houde
Open daily 2 - 5 PM, 7 - 9 PM. No admis fee. Estab 1967. Gallery is maintained. Average Annual Attendance: 100,000
Income: Financed by city appropriation
Activities: Classes for adults and children; dramatic programs; concerts; lending collection contains original art works, original prints, paintings, sculpture, slides; sales shop selling original art

SHERBROOKE

M **UNIVERSITY OF SHERBROOKE CULTURAL CENTER,** Art Gallery, J1K 2R1. Tel 819-565-5446. *Art Dir* Graham Cantieni; *Promotions* Johanne Brouillet
Open Mon - Fri 12:30 - 5 PM, Mon - Thurs evenings 7 - 9:30 PM, Sun 2 - 5 PM. No admis fee. Estab 1964 to introduce public to the best art work being done in Canada and to place this work in an historical (European) and geographical (American) context. Gallery has three exhibition areas totalling 10,000 sq ft on university campus and serves the community. Average Annual Attendance: 18,000
Income: $150,000 (financed by city and state appropriation and university funds)
Collections: Contemporary Quebec Graphics and Paintings
Exhibitions: (1979) Approx 40 exhibitions including Metiers d'Art des Cantons de l'Est (crafts); Concours d'Estampe et de Dessin Quebecois (prints and drawings); Concours d'Art Graphique Quebecois-Sherbrooke 1977 (prints and drawings); (1980) Arts Visuels des Cantons de l'Est; l'Art des Cantons de l'Est 1800-1950
Publications: Bulletin, monthly
Activities: Classes for adults and children; lect open to public, 20 visiting lectr per year; gallery talks; tours; competitions; cash awards; lending collection contains books, cassettes, color reproductions, Kodachromes, original prints, paintings, photographs, sculpture, slides and videos; book traveling exhibitions 3 per year; originate traveling exhibitions

TROIS RIVIERES

O **CENTRE CULTUREL DE TROIS RIVIERES,** 1425 Place de l'Hotel de Ville, G9A 4S7. Tel 418-374-3521, Ext 216. *Dir* Francois Lahaye
Open 9 AM - Noon, 1:30 - 5 PM and 7 - 10 PM. Estab 1967
Income: Financed by city appropriation
Activities: Classes for adults and children; dramatic programs

VAUDREUIL

M **MUSEE HISTORIQUE DE VAUDREUIL,** Vaudreuil Historial Museum, 431 Blvd Roche, CP 121, J7V 2N3. Tel 514-455-1092. *Pres* Lucien Theriault; *VPres* Fernande Letourneau; *Secy* Pierre Edmond; *Dir* David Aird; *Mgr* Andree Boileau
Open Wed - Sun 2 - 8 PM. Admis adults $1, children 25¢. Estab 1953, non-profit organization subsidized by the Direction des Musees et Centres d'Exposition of the Ministere des Affaires culturelles du Quebec. The collection consists of artefacts and artists production that have and still illustrate the traditional way of life in the counties of Vaudreuil and Soulanges, the surroundings and the Province of Quebec. Museum has four rooms for permanent collection and one for temporary and traveling exhibitions. A documentation centre is open for searchers ans students and an animator will receive groups on reservation for a commented tour. Average Annual Attendance: 10,000. Mem: 100; dues $5; annual meeting May 26
Income: Financed by endowment

Collections: Edison Gramophone 1915; Antique Pottery; Historic Documents and Material; Farming; furniture, paintings, portraits, sculpture and woodworking
Exhibitions: Ten local artists' exhibits; les Instruments d'Eclairage; les Moules and le Moulage Domestique
Publications: Musee de Vaudreuil Catalog (selectif); Vaudreuil Soulanges, Western Gateway of Quebec
Activities: Classes for children; concerts; original objects of art lent; book shop
L Library, 431 Blvd Roche, J7V 2N3.
Reference only
Library Holdings: Other—Photographs

SASKATCHEWAN

LLOYDMINSTER

O LLOYDMINSTER BARR COLONY MUSEUM COMMITTEE, c/o City Hall, 5011 49th Ave, S9V 0T8. Tel 403-825-6184, 825-3726. *Chmn* Richard Larsen; *Secy* Blaire L Bowsfield; *Cur* Mrs D Barradell
Open May 1 to Sept 30 9 AM - 9 PM. Admis adults 75¢, students 50¢, children 15¢. Estab 1965 to promote an interest in the history of our city. Mem: 5; dues donations
Income: Financed by donations
Collections: Antique Museum; Fuch's Wildlife; Imhoff Paintings

MOOSE JAW

M MOOSE JAW ART MUSEUM AND NATIONAL EXHIBITION CENTRE, Crescent Park, S6H 0X6. Tel 306-692-4471. *Dir* Gerald Jessop; *Adminr Asst to Dir* Joan Goodnough; *Caretaker & Watchman* Gordon Ambrose
Open summer Noon - 5 PM and 7 - 9 PM, cl Mon, winter Tues Noon - 5 PM and 7 - 9 PM, Wed 2 - 5 PM, Thurs & Fri 2 - 5 PM and 7 - 10 PM, Sat & Sun 1 - 5 PM, cl Mon. No admis fee. Estab 1966 for preservation, education, collection and exhibitions. Museum is 150 running ft; Gallery I is 120 running ft; Gallery II is 90 running ft; walls are burlap, smoke retardant. Average Annual Attendance: 16,000. Mem: 167; dues $5
Income: $95,000 (financed by city, state and national appropriation)
Collections: †Canadian Traditional and Contemporary; Local and District Historical Artifacts 3000; Sioux and Cree Beadwork, Native Weapons and Tools
Activities: Classes for children; docent training; lect open to public, 6 visiting lectr per year; gallery talks; tours; individual paintings and original objects of art lent; lending collection contains 14 cassettes, 200 paintings, 400 slides; book traveling exhibitions 20 per year; originate traveling exhibitions

PRINCE ALBERT

L JOHN M CUELENAERE LIBRARY, Grace Campbell Gallery, 125 12th St E, S6V 1B7. Tel 306-763-8496. *Head Librn* Eleanor Acorn
Open Mon - Fri Noon - 8:30 PM, Sat 9 AM - 5 PM. No admis fee. Estab 1973. Gallery is 100 linear ft
Income: Financed by city appropriation
Library Holdings: Vols 65,000; Per subs 210; AV—Cassettes, rec

REGINA

CANADIAN SOCIETY FOR EDUCATION THROUGH ART
For further information, see National and Regional Organizations

M LEGISLATIVE BUILDING ART GALLERY, 2405 Legislative Dr, S4S 0B3. Tel 306-565-5357.
Open daily winter 9 AM - 5 PM, summer 9 AM - 9 PM. Estab 1912. Average Annual Attendance: 30,000
Income: Financed by provincial government and donations
Collections: Pencil Sketchings by Howard Hatton; famous collection of Indian Paintings by Edmund Morris; pictures of Former Premiers, Cabinets, Lieutenant-Governors of Province
Activities: Classes for adults; guided tours

M REGINA PUBLIC LIBRARY, Dunlot Art Gallery, 2311 12th Ave, S4P 0N3. Tel 306-569-7576. *Dir & Cur* W P Morgan; *Asst Cur* Gary Essar; *Cur Asst* Elise Stoesser; *Asst Cur* Pamela Perry
Open Mon - Fri 9:30 AM - 9 PM, Sat 9:30 AM - 6 PM, Sun 1:30 - 5 PM, cl holidays. No admis fee. Estab 1947. Also operating: Glen Elm Branch Gallery, Connanght Branch Exhibits and Sherwood Village Branch Gallery. Average Annual Attendance: 80,000
Income: Financed by city appropriation
Collections: Small permanent collection of paintings and drawings
Exhibitions: About 45 per year; local, regional, provincial, national and international art, artists, and themes in all media, both as loan exhibitions and self-organized
Activities: Programming of all types; gallery talks; tours; originate traveling exhibitions

O SASKATCHEWAN ARTS BOARD,* 200 Lakeshore Dr, S4S 0A4. Tel 206-565-4056. *Executive Dir* Vern Bell
Open 8:30 AM - 5 PM, summer 8:30 AM - 4:30 PM. Estab 1948 as an autonomous agency for promotion and development of the arts in Saskatchewan; Board is composed of 7 - 15 appointed, unpaid members, whose major concern at the present time is the support and development of professionals and professional standards within the province
Income: Financed by annual provincial government grant
Collections: †Permanent collection containing over 600 works by Saskatchewan

artists and artisans only, dating from 1950 to present; part of collection hangs in the Saskatchewan Centre of the Arts, Regina
Publications: Annual Report; brochures for Saskatchewan School of the Arts classes; services and programs brochure
Activities: Programs include individual and group assistance grants; workshop assistance; aid for exhibitions; community assistance for the performing arts; script reading service; play-script duplication subsidy; community artists program; consultative services; operates Saskatchewan School of the Arts at Echo Valley Centre, summer classes for young people and fall and spring classes for adults are offered in a wide variety of crafts, visual and performing arts

L SASKATCHEWAN PHOTOGRAPHIC ART DIVISION, Photographic Art Library, Legislative Bldg Room 3, S4S 0B3. Tel 306-565-6298. *Library Technician* Dorothy Redlin
Open 8:30 - Noon and 1:15 - 5 PM. Estab to supply photographs to government departments and to public
Income: Financed by provincial government
Library Holdings: AV—Slides; Other—Photographs
Collections: Photographs of Saskatchewan

C SASKATCHEWAN POWER CORPORATION, Gallery on the Roof, 2025 Victoria Ave, S4P 0S1. Tel 306-525-7359. *Secy* Pauline Boesser; *Graphics Supv* R Bourassa; *Commerical Artist* E Styba
Open Mon - Fri 9 AM - 9 PM, Sun & holidays 2 - 9 PM. No admis fee. Estab 1963 to give local artists and art groups exposure. Gallery approx 100 ft of wall space adjoining the observation deck that overlooks the city. Average Annual Attendance: 100,000
Exhibitions: Changing monthly
Publications: Exhibition brochures

M UNIVERSITY OF REGINA, Norman Mackenzie Art Gallery, College and Scarth Sts, S4S 0A2. Tel 306-352-5801. *Acting Dir* Carol Phillips; *Community Program Head* Shirley Bracewell; *Business Mgr* Joy Paull; *Public Relations* Bess Jillings; *Art Education Officer* Brenda Parres; *Community Program Officer* R Roycroft; *Community Program Officer* K Forrest; *Resource Centre* P Roulston
Open Mon - Fri Noon - 5 PM, Sat & Sun 1 - 5 PM, Wed & Thurs evenings 7 - 10 PM. No admis fee. Estab 1954 to preserve and expand the collection left to the gallery by Norman Mackenzie and to offer traveling exhibitions to the city of Regina; to offer works of art to rural areas through the Community Programme. There are five discreet galleries totalling approx 750 running ft of exhibition space. Average Annual Attendance: 50,000
Income: $500,000 (financed by city and state appropriation, federal and private funds)
Collections: Contemporary Canadian Work; Contemporary Saskatchewan Work; 19th and Early 20th Century Works on Paper; a part of the collection is Early 20th Century Replicas of Eastern and Oriental Artifacts and Art
Exhibitions: Changing exhibitions from the permanent collection and traveling exhibitions
Publications: Exhibition catalogues; staff publications of a professional nature; Tabloid, six times a year
Activities: Docent training; community programme of touring exhib in Saskatchewan; interpretive programs; lect open to public, 8 - 10 visiting lectr per year; concerts; gallery talks; tours; films; exten dept serves entire province; originate traveling exhibitions nation-wide; cards and catalogues sold at front desk
L Norman Mackenzie Art Gallery Resource Centre, S4S 0A2. *Librn* Pat Roulston
Open Mon - Fri Noon - 5 PM, Sat & Sun 1 - 5 PM, Wed & Thurs 7 - 10 PM. Estab 1970 to offer the community a resource for art information, both historical and current. For reference only
Library Holdings: Vols 1000; Per subs 32; AV—Slides; Other—Clipping files, exhibition catalogs, original art works, pamphlets, sculpture
Special Subjects: Canadian art
Collections: Regional press clippings from 1925
L Fine Arts Library, College Ave, S4S 0A2. *Librn* L Eley
Open Mon - Thurs 8:30 AM - 5 PM and 6:30 - 9:30 PM, Fri & Sat 9 AM - 5 PM. Estab 1969 to service the students of music, drama and the visual arts
Purchases: $13,593
Library Holdings: Vols 21,500; Per subs 75; AV—Rec
L Slide Library, Visual Arts Department, S4S 0A2.
Estab for the instruction of art history
Library Holdings: AV—Slides 45,000

SASKATOON

L NUTANA COLLEGIATE INSTITUTE, Memorial Library and Art Gallery, 411 22th St E, S7N 0E9. Tel 304-653-1677. *Principal* Ron Perkins; *VPrincipal* Jim Beeke; *Librn* Philip Listoe
Open daily 8 AM - 4 PM, summer 9 AM - 5 PM. No admis fee. Estab 1919 to promote an appreciation for art; a memorial to students who lost their lives in the two world wars. Maintains an art gallery of Paintings by Canadian Artists (55 paintings plus wood cuts)
Library Holdings: Vols 12,000; Per subs 100; Micro—Reels; AV—A-tapes, cassettes, fs, Kodachromes, motion pictures, rec, slides, v-tapes; Other—Clipping files, exhibition catalogs, original art works, pamphlets

M PHOTOGRAPHERS GALLERY, 236 Second Ave S, S7K 1K9. Tel 306-244-8018. *Dir* Patrick Close; *Asst Dir* Open
Open daily Noon - 5 PM. No admis fee. Estab 1970, incorporated 1973 to encourage the development of photography as a creative visual art. Main gallery is 500 sq ft, and workshop gallery is 250 sq ft. Average Annual Attendance: 6000. Mem: 40; dues $60 - $80; annual meeting second Sun in May
Income: $75,000 (financed by membership, state appropriation and federal grants)
Collections: Permanent Collection of Contemporary Photographs (emphasizes Canadian work)
Publications: Members monthly newsletter
Activities: Classes for adults and children; lect open to public, 10 visiting lectr per year; concerts; gallery talks; tours; competitions; extension department; original objects of art lent; book traveling exhibitions; originate traveling exhibitions

L Library, 236 Second Ave S, S7K 1K9.
Open daily Noon - 5 PM. Estab 1970. Reference
Purchases: $2000
Library Holdings: Vols 1500; Per subs 10; AV—A-tapes, cassettes, slides; Other—Clipping files, exhibition catalogs, manuscripts, pamphlets, reproductions

O SASKATCHEWAN ASSOCIATION OF ARCHITECTS, LM1 Phoenix House, 226 20th St E, S7K 0A6. *Pres* Roger James Walls; *Secy & Treas* Ian Innes
Estab 1911. Mem: 95; dues $275; annual meeting Feb
Activities: Book prize given to architectural technology student at Saskatchewan Technical Institute, Moose Jaw (4 twice a year); scholarships

M SASKATOON GALLERY AND CONSERVATORY CORPORATION, 950 Spadina Crescent E, PO Box 569, S7K 3L6. Tel 306-664-9610. *Pres* F Alexson; *VPres* M F Mitchell; *Secy* Mrs L Whelan; *Dir & Cur* Allan MacKay; *Asst Cur* G Moppett; *Extension Officer* M Gibson; *Business Mgr* R Moldenhauer
Open daily 10 AM - 10 PM. No admis fee. Estab 1964 to exhibit, preserve, collect, works of art; to encourage the development of the visual arts in Saskatoon; to provide the opportunity for citizens to enjoy, understand and to gain a greater appreciation of the fine arts. Maintains an art gallery. Average Annual Attendance: 225,000
Income: $658,000 (financed by city and federal appropriations)
Purchases: $22,000
Collections: Regional, National and International Art
Exhibitions: (1978) As I See It; Selections from the Canada Council Art Bank; Current Directions; The Edmonton Art Gallery; Five from California; Images of the Buffalo; Harald Mante; Realists from the Permanent Collection; (1979) Douglas Bentham: recent works; Four Directions; Images, A Celebration; Images of the Prairie; New Faces; Frank Nulf, Charles Ringness, recent work 1978-79; The Private Eye; Selections from the Saskatchewan Arts Board; The Silver Image, A History of Photography 1839-1970; Brian Wood, photographic works
Publications: Exhibition catalogues; Folio, monthly
Activities: Lect open to public; concerts; gallery talks; tours; exten dept serves Western Canadian Provinces; originate traveling exhibitions; sales shop sells books, magazines, original art, prints, reproductions and gift items

L Library, 950 Spadina Crescent E, PO Box 569, S7K 3L6. *Librn* Joan Steel
Open to public for reference
Library Holdings: Vols 5000; Per subs 40; AV—Rec, slides; Other—Photographs, Pamphlet files
Special Subjects: Canadian art, Saskatchewan art

M UNIVERSITY OF SASKATCHEWAN, Gordon Snelgrove Art Gallery, S7N 0W0. Tel 306-343-4528. *Gallery Supv* Robert Christie
Open Mon, Wed & Fir 10 AM - 4 PM, Sun, Tues & Thurs 2 - 5 PM and 6 - 9 PM. No admis fee. Estab approx 1960 for the education of students and local public. Gallery covers approx 3000 sq ft of floor space, 300 running ft of wall space. Average Annual Attendance: 5000
Income: $11,000 (financed by provincial and federal government appropriations and university funds)
Exhibitions: Constantly changing exhibitions of art works; internationally organized and traveling shows
Publications: Show announcements, every three weeks
Activities: originate traveling exhibitions on a limited basis

ARGENTINA

BUENOS AIRES

M CENTRO DE ARTE Y COMMUNICACION, Center of Art and Communication, Elpidio Gonzalez 4070. Tel 566-8046, 566-8066. *Pres* Jorge Glusberg; *VPres* Leonardo Glusberg; *Secy* Amelia Montes; *Dir Architectural Department* Carlos A Sallaberry; *Cur E05* Cur; *Video Coordr* Renato Santucci; *Sound Coordr* Rafael H Antonacci; *Music Department* Martin Muller; *Courses & Conferences* Enrique Dimant; *Architecture Coordr* Diego Forero; *Industrial Design* Ricardo Blanco
Open 11 AM - 9 PM, cl Sun. Estab 1969 to introduce in Argentina, on a pedagogycal level, the most important events of experimental and avantgarde art from international art centers and also present the Latin American circuit from the artistical activities. Gallery consists of three floors, each 16 m x 20 m documentation center consists of two floors each 18 m x 30 m and two departments for the School of High Studies of CAYC. The Center holds exhibitions of objects, paintings, engravings; also courses and conferences on art, architecture and music. Average Annual Attendance: 20,000. Mem: 150
Income: Financed by membership
Collections: Catalogs and bulletings on every art exhibition and seminary held by the Center in Argentina and abroad; 150 motion pictures on art, architecture, †music; photograph collection of 7000 †prints; collection of 5000 slides; 400 video-tapes
Exhibitions: The Art of Performance (Palazzo Grassi, Venice); Art Systems in Israel; John Baldessri, Douglas Davis (USA); Rene Berger (Switzerland); Oriol Bohigas (Spain); CAYC at XV Sao Paulo Biennial; CAYC Group (Argentina); Arch Pablo Carlodalatri (Italy); Contemporary Venezuelan Art; Arch Felix Candela (Spain); Ricardo Cristobal (Spain); Drawings from Peru; XIV Sao Paulo Biennial; Fifty Works of Artists from Paris; Fifty Years with Photography (International exhibition); I International Meeting of Architectural Critics (Joan Miro Foundation, Barcelona); Fred Forest (France); Image and Words (traveling exhibition); Interdisciplinary Encounter on Body Art (Centre Georges Pompidou (Paris); Richard Kriesche (Austria); Udo Kultermann (USA); David Lamelas (Argentina); Gerald Minkoff; Marta Minujin (Argentina); Daniel Giralt Miracle (Spain); Robert Mizrahi (France); Muriel Olesen (Switzerland); Andrzej Partum (Poland); The Post-Figuration; Thirty Years in North American Art; Decio Tozzi (Brazil); Regina Vater (Brazil); Dorothy Walker (Ireland)
Publications: Breviaries on Criticism, monthly; catalogs for shows and activities in the country and abroad, 30 per year; Theory and Criticism magazine, 3 per year
Activities: Educ dept; lect open to public, 550 visiting lectr per year; gallery talks; competitions; cash, medals and steel cubes awards; individual paintings and original objects of art lent to other local and abroad museums and art centers; lending collection contains 6895 books, 450 cassettes, 350 color reproductions, 5000 lantern slides, 150 motion pictures, 200 original art works, 300 original prints, 150 paintings, 7000 photographs, 75 sculptures, catalogs; artmobile; originate traveling exhibitions
L Library, Viamonte 452. *Librn* Lidia Rabinovich
Library Holdings: Vols 4500; Other—Bulletins
Special Subjects: Industrial Design, Research in architecture, sociology of art

M ESCUELA SUPERIOR DE BELLAS ARTES ERNESTO DE LA CARCOVA, National Superior School of Fine Arts Ernesto de la Carcova,* Sculpture Museum, Avda Costanera Sur Esq Brasil. *Rector & Prof* Jorge E Lezama; *Regent & Prof* Jorge Guillermo Luna Ercilla; *Secy* Nelida Maria Luisa Guido
Open Mon - Fri 9 AM - 3 PM. No admis fee. Estab for the exhibition of didactical elements of the school. Gallery consists of two large rooms. Average Annual Attendance: 21,900
Income: Financed by school and state appropriation
Collections: Reproductions of world sculpture through the ages: Egyptian, Gothic, Greek, Renaissance, Roman, Romanic, including Michelangelo's David and Moses
L Enrique Prince Library, Avda Costanera Sur Esq Brasil. *Librn* Elsa Rosenthal de Sosa
Open to all fine arts students for reference only
Library Holdings: Vols 4500; Other—Prints, magazines, plates
Special Subjects: Drawings, Etchings & Engravings, Sculpture, Painting, set-designing

M MUSEO NACIONAL DE ARTE DECORATIVO, National Museum of Decorative Art,* Av del Libertador 1902. Tel 83 09 14. *Dir* Dr Federico Aldao
Estab 1937
Collections: European and South American works; furniture, sculptures and tapestries
Publications: Exhibition catalogs; guides
Activities: Lect; concerts

M MUSEO NACIONAL DE BELLAS ARTES, National Museum of Fine Arts,* Avda Libextador 1473. Tel 83-8814. *Dir* Samuel F Oliver; *Conservator* Samuel Paz
Open Wed - Mon 3 - 7 PM. Estab 1895
Collections: Argentine and American paintings; European paintings 16th - 20th Centuries; sculpture
Activities: Lect; concerts; films; modern pavilion for special exhibitions
L Biblioteca Publica de Arte, Avda Libertador Gen San Martin 1473. Tel 826-0714. *Chief Librn* Raquel Edelman
Open 9 AM - 12:30 PM and 2:30 - 7 PM
Income: Financed by endowment and Estatal Nacional
Purchases: $500
Library Holdings: Vols 30,000; Per subs 170; Other—Exhibition catalogs, pamphlets

ROSARIO

M MUSEO MUNICIPAL DE BELLAS ARTES JUAN B CASTAGNINO, Municipal Museum of Fine Arts,* Br Orono Av Pellegrini. Tel 27310. *Dir* Horacio E Correas
Open Wed - Sat 4 - 7 PM, Sun & holidays 10 AM - Noon and 4 - 7 PM. No admis fee. Estab 1920; present building inaugurated 1937. Average Annual Attendance: 100,000
Income: Financed by appropriation
Collections: American and European paintings and sculpture from 16th Century to contemporary, includes works by Jose de Ribera, Goya, El Greco, Valdes Leal and Titian; complete collection of Argentine art from 19th Century to present
Publications: Exhibition catalogs
Activities: Dramatic programs; concerts; competitions

AUSTRALIA

ADELAIDE

M ART GALLERY OF SOUTH AUSTRALIA, North Terrace. Tel 08-223-8911. *Dir* David Thomas; *Deputy Dir* Ronald Appleyard; *Cur Decorative Arts* Dick Richards; *Cur Presentations* Ian Maidment; *Cur Art Education* Don Hein
Open Mon - Sat 10 AM - 5 PM, Wed 10 AM - 9 PM, Sun 1:30 - 5 PM. No amdis fee. Estab 1881 for the public display of works of art including paintings, sculpture, prints, etc, and items of historical interest relating to the exploration and colonization of the State of South Australia. Gallery is a stone, brick, concrete and steel structure; Elder Wing 19th Century neo-classical style, opened 1900; Melrose wing 20th Century Art Deco style, opened 1936; three-story north wing opened 1962. Average Annual Attendance: 366,563
Income: $680,000 (financed by state appropriation, bequests and gifts)
Purchases: $160,000
Collections: Representative selection of Australian and European paintings and sculpture; large collection of ceramics, drawings, glass, prints and silver; extensive South Australian Historical Collection; South East Asian ceramics; coins, furniture and medals
Exhibitions: American Figure Drawing; Diane Arbus; Jean Arp; The Artist's Medium; Australian Realist Painters; British Artist's Prints; The Chinese Exhibition; William Delafield Cook; Engravings and Etchings by Durer and Rembrandt; Form and Freedom; David Hockney Prints; Master·Drawings from the Albertina, Vienna; Rundle Mall Sculpture Maquettes; South Australia Illustrated
Publications: Annual Bulletin and Report; catalogues to major exhibitions
Activities: Classes for children; docent training; lect open to public; exten dept; artmobile; individual paintings and original objects of art lent to schools and organizations; sales shop sells books, magazines, original art, reproductions and slides
L Library, North Terrace.
Open for reference to staff and students
Library Holdings: Vols 6000; Per subs 120; Other—Catalogues 20,000
Special Subjects: Visual arts

BRISBANE

M QUEENSLAND ART GALLERY, Fifth Floor, MIM Bldg, 160 Anne St. Tel 292138. *Dir* Raoul Mellish; *Asst Dir* Robert Cunningham
Open Mon - Sat 10 AM - 5 PM, Sun 2 - 5 PM, cl Christmas, Good Friday & Anzac Day. Estab 1895
Collections: Predominantly Australian Art, Paintings and Drawings; European Paintings and Sculpture, including works by leading Impressionists
Exhibitions: L J Harvey Memorial Exhibit; Annual Trustees Exhibit; continuous

exhibition program from the permanent collection, loan exhibitions from overseas
Activities: Educ program for school, tertiary and adult audiences; classes for children; lect; competitions; awards
L **Library,** Sixth Floor, MIM Bldg, 160 Ann St. *Librn* Richard Yeates
Estab 1974. Special library for the use of professional officers only
Income: $10,000
Purchases: $10,000
Library Holdings: Vols 3850; Micro—Fiche, reels; AV—A-tapes, cassettes, rec, slides; Other—Exhibition catalogs, framed reproductions, pamphlets
Special Subjects: Australian art

HOBART

M **TASMANIAN MUSEUM AND ART GALLERY,** 5 Argyle St, GPO Box 1164M. Tel 002-232696. *Dir* D R Gregg; *Cur Art* Carl Andrew; *Art Conservator* Romek Pachucki; *Art Education Officer* Open
Open 10 AM - 5 PM. No admis fee. Estab 1829 as a state museum and art gallery with emphasis on Tasmanian material and relevant material from other places. Gallery has a display area of 2755 sq meters. Average Annual Attendance: 115,000
Income: Financed by state appropriation
Collections: †Australian Contemporary Art; †British 18th and 19th Century Watercolours; †Tasmanian 19th Century Paintings; †photography
Exhibitions: Art Acquisitions 1977-79; Australian Colonial Portraits; Australian Crafts; Australian Etchings; Anthony Caro Table Sculptures; Creatures; John Glover; Walter Burley Griffin; David Hockney Photographs; Lion Rugs; Navajo Blankets; Oenpelli Paintings on Bark; Rodin and his Contemporaries; Vasarely, his Predecessors and Contemporaries
Publications: Annual Report; catalogues and handbooks
Activities: Classes for adults and children; lect open to public; concerts; gallery talks; exten dept serves Tasmania; individual paintings and original objects of art lent to other galleries; artmobile; originate traveling exhibitions; sales shop sells books, reproductions and slides
L **Library,** 5 Argyle St, GPO Box 1164M. *Librn* Janet Middleton
Open for reference to public upon application
Library Holdings: Vols 5000; Per subs 50
Special Subjects: Australia and Tasmania

MELBOURNE

M **NATIONAL GALLERY OF VICTORIA,** 180 St Kilda Rd. Tel 03-62-7411. *Dir* Eric Rowlison; *Asst Dir* Sonia Dean; *Deputy Dir* Kenneth Hood; *Secy* R P Nolan
Open Tues - Sun 10 AM - 5 PM, Wed 10 AM - 9 PM, cl Mon. Admis 50¢ (with concessions to pensioners and families). Estab 1861 as a public art gallery; present gallery opened in 1968. Gallery is a large blue-stone building built around three rectangular courtyards with galleries on three floors and service areas below. Average Annual Attendance: 750,000. Mem: 8000; dues family $18, individual $12
Income: Financed by state appropriation
Purchases: $200,000
Collections: †Asian Art; †Australian Art; †Tribal Art; †antiquities, †ceramics, †costumes, †glass, †metalwork, †old master and modern drawings, paintings, prints and sculpture, †textiles, †woodwork
Exhibitions: Continuous program of temporary exhibitions
Publications: Art Bulletin of Victoria, annually; catalogues and handbooks to collections
Activities: Classes for children; docent training; lect open to public, 3 visiting lectr per year; original objects of art lent to state and local government department and offices; originate traveling exhibitions; museum shop sells books, reproductions and slides
L **Library,** 180 St Kilda Rd. *Librn* Patricia Forster
Open Tues, Wed & Thurs 1:30 - 4:30 PM. Estab 1968 to support the work of the gallery in acquisition, research and publication. For reference only
Income: $30,000
Library Holdings: Vols 21,000; Per subs 250
Special Subjects: Decorative Arts, Fine art
Collections: European Painting, Prints and Drawings; ceramics and glass

PERTH

M **ART GALLERY OF WESTERN AUSTRALIA,** Administration Centre, 47 James St. Tel 328-7233. *Dir* W F Ellis; *Deputy Dir* L Klepac; *Cur Crafts* R Bell; *Cur Painting & Asst Cur Historical Coll* Mrs B Chapman
Open Mon - Sat 10 AM - 5 PM, Thurs evenings 6 - 9 PM, Sun 1 - 5 PM. Gallery opened as part of Museum and Library 1895; became an autonomous body 1959; new building completed 1979. Building incorporates ethnic gallery; prints and drawings gallery and study room; two permanent collection galleries; two traveling exhibition galleries; decorative arts and crafts gallery; conservation laboratories; 300 seat auditorium; 160 seat restaurant and separate administration centre, library and theatrette. Average Annual Attendance: 120,000
Income: $2,836,000 (financed by state appropriation and acquisitions)
Collections: Antique and Modern Silver; Australian Aboriginal Artefacts; bronzes, ceramics, glass and pottery, gold and furniture, oils, prints and drawings, sculptures, watercolours
Exhibitions: America and Europe - A Century of Modern Masters from the Thyssen Collection; Jean Arp; Bourdelle Sculpture and Drawings; The Colonial Eye - Early Western Australian Art; Contemporary Australian Art; 1978 Contemporary Survey and Drawings; Sir Russell Drysdale; El Dorado Columbian Gold; Geneois of a Gallery Parts I and II (The Australian National Gallery); John Glover Survey; Hans Heysen: Centenary Retrospective; Leicester Gallery Collection of Sickert Etchings; Jon Molvig Retrospective; Morandi Etchings; Navajo Blankets; Oenpelli Paintings on Bark (Australian Aboriginal); Paintings acquired through the Great Australian Paintings Appeal; 1979 and 1980 Perth Survey of Drawings; Rodin and his Contemporaries; Walter Richard Sickert; Ten Western Australian Printmakers; Treasures of London's Goldsmiths; Western Australia Young Artists Award 1978
Activities: Tours; educational and holiday activities; book traveling exhibitions

L **Library,** 47 James St. *Librn* Alyson Hogg
Open Mon - Fri 9 AM - 5 PM by appointment. Estab 1895 to provide reference service to professional staff and members of the public
Income: $10,000
Purchases: $10,000
Library Holdings: Vols 5000; Per subs 58; Micro—Cards, fiche, reels, prints; AV —A-tapes, cassettes, fs, Kodachromes, lantern slides, motion pictures, rec, slides, v-tapes; Other—Clipping files, exhibition catalogs, pamphlets
Special Subjects: Australian art history, contemporary biographical files (Australia and Western Australia)
Collections: Australian Art History

SYDNEY

M **ART GALLERY OF NEW SOUTH WALES,*** Art Gallery Rd, Domain. Tel 02-211-2100. *Dir* Edmund Carson
Open Mon - Sat 10 AM - 5 PM, Sun Noon - 5 PM, cl Christmas Day & Good Friday. Estab 1874 as the state art museum. In 1972 the Art Gallery reopened after being closed for remodeling. Average Annual Attendance: 300,000
Collections: Australian Aboriginal, including notable burial posts and bark paintings; Australian Art; Contemporary Tapestries, Lurcat and Matisse; Decorative Arts - British pewter 17th - 18th Centuries; English porcelain 18th Century and Victorian; European painting and sculpture: Albers, Bonnard, Boudin, Madox Brown, Burne-Jones, Constable, Corot, Danby, Davie, Etty, Fantin-Latour, Fildes, John Gibson, Gore, Hayden, Hepworth, Hogarth, Leger, Leighton, Morris Louis, Monet, Moore, Nash, Ben Nicholson, Pasmore, R E Pine, Pissarro, Poynter, Reynolds, Sickert, Stomer, Strozzi, Sutherland, Tiepolo, Turner, Van Bijlert, Van Bloemen, Wilson, Zadkine; Japanese Ceramics and Woodcuts; Melanesian; Oriental Art - Chinese bronzes and ceramics; Persian ceramics; Persian and Indian miniatures; Primitive Art; Prints and Drawings - a good systematic collection, including Callot, Canaletto, Constable, Durer, Goya, Mantegna, Matisse, Meryon, Munch, Picasso, Piranesi, Rembrandt, Turner, Whistler; Thai sculpture; Tibetan, Japanese and Chinese paintings
Exhibitions: Recent Australian art; Australian art the 1870's; British Painting 1600-1800; The Chinese Exhibition; John Constable; The Heritage of American Art; Hirshfield-Mack and Lyonel Feinger; Paul Klee; Ladies in Landscapes; Modern Masters: Manet to Matisse; 17th Century Pastoral Holland; Two Masters of the Weimar Bauhaus; Victorian Olympians; Victorian Social Conscience
Publications: Art Gallery Annual; special exhibition catalogs
Activities: Docent training; lect open to public; films; gallery talks; tours; originate traveling exhibitions; book shop

M **MUSEUM OF APPLIED ARTS AND SCIENCES,** 659-695 Harris St, Broadway. Tel 02-211-3911. *Pres* John Hurley; *Dir* L G Sharp; *Cur Arts* J P Wade
Open daily 10 AM - 5 PM, Sun 2 - 5 PM, cl Good Friday & Christmas Day. No admis fee. Estab 1880 to display and offer scholarships in the applied arts and sciences. Administered by Board of Seven Trustees. Average Annual Attendance: 230,000
Income: Financed by endowment and state appropriation
Collections: Asian Arts; †Ceramics, costume, glass, ivory, metalwork, numismatics, ship models and textiles
Publications: Annual report; bulletins; guides; leaflets
Activities: Educ dept conducts teaching sessions; exten dept serves area schools; photograph collection lent on approval of director; book shop
L **Library,*** 659-695 Harris St, Broadway.
For reference only
Library Holdings: Vols 14,000

TASMANIA

M **QUEEN VICTORIA MUSEUM AND ART GALLERY,** Wellington St Launceston. Tel 003-31 6777. *Dir* C B Tassell; *Cur Fine Art* P F McIntyre; *Cur Exhib* D R Barratt
Open Mon - Sat 10 AM - 5 PM, Sun 2 - 5 PM. No admis fee. Estab 1891 as headquarters of a professionally conducted complex of art galleries, theatres, museums and educational services conducted mainly as a city authority but extending over half the state. Average Annual Attendance: 90,000
Income: $210,000 (financed by city and state appropriation)
Purchases: $3000
Collections: Colonial Period (1803 - 1900); †contemporary work, visual art collections, relating to Australia
Publications: Records of the Queen Victoria Museum, 4 per year
Activities: Dramatic programs; lect open to public, 10 visiting lectr per year; gallery talks; tours; concerts; competitions; exten dept serves area of 13,000 sq miles; individual paintings and original objects of art lent to trailside museums; originate traveling exhibitions
L **Library,** Wellington St Launceston.
Reference library
Library Holdings: Vols 8000
Collections: Photographs Collection of 750 prints

AUSTRIA

LINZ

M **WOLFGANG-GURLITT-MUSEUM,** Neue Galerie der Stadt Linz, Blütenstrabe 15. Tel 0732-340 55. *Dir* Peter Baum
Open Mon, Tues, Wed & Fri 10 AM - 6 PM, Thurs 10 AM - 10 PM, Sat 10 AM - 1 PM, cl Sun and holidays. Admis adults $10, groups, students and pupils $5. Estab 1947. Average Annual Attendance: 25,000
Collections: 19th and 20th Century paintings, drawings, sculptures and prints;

about 550 paintings and small sculptures; 2600 graphics
Exhibitions: About 12 changing exhibitions per year
Publications: Catalogs, six per year
Activities: Classes for children; 12 visiting lectr per year; tours; museum shop sells prints and catalogs
L **Library,** Blütenstrabe 15.
Open Mon & Thurs 10 AM - Noon and 2 - 5 PM
Library Holdings: Vols 9000
Collections: Kubin Collection

SALZBURG

M **SALTZBURGER MUSEUM CAROLINO AUGUSTEUM,** Salzburg Museum,*
Museumsplatz 6, Postfach 525. Tel 43 1 45, 41 1 37. *Dir Ethnology, History of Civilization, Arts and Crafts* Dr Freidrike Prodinger; *Cur Art History* Dr Albin Rohmoser; *Cur Ethnology* Dr Kurt Conrad; *Cur Prehistory* Fritz Moosleitner; *Cur Theatrical Sciences & Public Relations* Dr Volker Kutschera; *Cur Restoration* Annemarie Fiebich-Ripke; *Admin* Otto Rainer
Open daily 9 AM - 5 PM. Estab 1834. Average Annual Attendance: 400,000
Income: $1,600,000 Austrian schillings (financed by city appropriation)
Purchases: $500,000 Austrian schillings
Collections: Baroque 19th Century, modern art, coins, furniture, historical chambers, medieval art, prints and drawings, Prehistoric and Roman archaeology
Exhibitions: Frequent special changing exhibitions at the Salzburg Museum and at the Museum Pavilion
Publications: Catalogs on major exhibitions; Jahresschrift, annually; postcards; posters; Schriftenreihe; slides
Activities: Symposia on important changing exhibitions; gallery talks; demonstrations; concerts; tours; lending services to other exhibitors; sales shop sells books; production of silent and sound pictures on Austrian national customs, local theatre history and on research work on toys
L **Library,*** Museumsplatz 6, Postfach 525.
Open Mon - Fri 9 AM - Noon
Library Holdings: Vols 55,000; Other—Technical literature, local archives
M **Volkskundemuseum,*** Museum of Folklore. (Mailing Add: Monatsschlosschen, near Castle of Hellbrunn)
Open April - Oct daily 10 AM - 6 PM. Estab 1924
Collections: Folklife: costumes, faience, furniture, imigration, miniature farmhouses and perchten-masks
M **Burgmuseum,*** Castle of Hohensalzburg. (Mailing Add: Museumsplatz 6, Postfach 525)
Open daily 9 AM - 5 PM,. Estab 1959
Collections: Arms and armor; flags; guilds furniture; wrought iron

VIENNA

M **GEMALDEGALERIE DER AKADEMIE DER BILDENDEN KUNSTE IN WIEN,** Art Gallery of the Academy of Fine Arts, Schillerplatz 3. Tel 0222 57 95 16. *Dir* Dr Heribert R Hutter; *Asst* Dr Renate Trnek; *Head Conservator* Peter Halbgebauer
Open Tues, Thurs & Fri 10 AM - 2 PM, Wed 10 AM - 1 PM and 3 - 6 PM, Sat & Sun 9 AM - 1 PM, cl Mon. Estab 1822 to house the collections of Count Anton Lamberg-Sprinzenstein who, at his death in 1822, willed his collections to serve as teaching materials and examples for the students of the Academy of Art. Average Annual Attendance: 14,000
Income: Financed by state appropriation
Collections: Prince Liechtenstein; Paintings of the 12th - 18th Centuries - Hieronymus Bosch, Hans Baldung Grien; 17th Century Dutch (Rembrandt, Ruisdael, van Goyen, Jan Both and others); Flemish, (Rubens, Jordaens, van Dyck), Guardi, Magnasco, Tiepolo, W von Wurzbach
Exhibitions: Annual exhibition from the permanent collection
Publications: Bildhefte der Akademie, annually
M **Kupferstichkabinett der Akademie der Bildenden Kunste,** Print and Drawing Collection of the Academy of Fine Arts, Schillerplatz 3. *Dir* Dr Albert Massiczek
Open Mon - Fri 10 AM - Noon and 2 - 4 PM after notification, time-to-time expositions Mon - Sat 9 AM - Noon. Estab 1773. Average Annual Attendance: 14,000
Collections: Drawings and Prints of the 15th - 20th Centuries, especially German, Italian, Netherland; Gothic Architectural Drawings, Durer, Rembrandt, Nazarenes, Daffinger (watercolors of flowers), Thomas Ender, Rudolf von Alt. More than 28,000 drawings, 29,000 prints, and 21,000 photographs

M **GRAPHISCHE SAMMLUNG ALBERTINA,** Albertina Graphic Art Collection, Augustinerstrasse 1. Tel 52-4232, 5769. *Dir* Dr Walter Koschatzky
Study Room open Mon - Thurs 1 - 4 PM, cl during July & Aug, Exhibition Mon, Tues & Thurs 10 AM - 4 PM, Wed 10 AM - 6 PM, Fri 10 AM - 2 PM, Sat & Sun 10 AM - 1 PM. Estab 1796. Average Annual Attendance: 80,000
Collections: Drawings (44,000), watercolors and prints of all schools 14th - 20th centuries; sketchbooks, miniatures and posters. This is one of the largest (1,800,000) and best Print Collections in Europe
Exhibitions: Vienna Graphic Biennial Exhibition
L **Library,** Augustinerstrasse 1.
Library Holdings: Vols 45,000

M **KUNSTHISTORISCHES MUSEUM,** Museum of Fine Arts, 1 Burgring 5. *Dir* Dr Friderike Klauner
Open Tues - Fri 9 AM - 3 PM and 7 - 9 PM, Sat & Sun 9 AM - 1 PM, cl Mon. Estab 1891
Collections: Schloss Ambras Collection; Egyptian and Oriental Collections; antiques, ceramics, historical carriages and costumes, jewelry, old music instruments, paintings, tapestries, weapons
Exhibitions: Funde aus Agypten; Portraitgalerie zur Geschichte Osterreichs 1400 - 1800; Ephesos Museum

L **Library,** 1 Burgring 5.
Library Holdings: Vols 70,000; Other—Prints 50,000
Collections: Photograph Collection

M **MUSEUM MODERNER KUNST,** Museum of Modern Art, Schweizergarten. *Dir* Dr Dieter Ronte; *Asst Dir* Detlev Kreidl
Palais Liechtenstein, Fürstengasse 1, Vienna 1090; Tel 34 12 59, 34 63 06; open 10 AM - 6 PM, cl Tues. Museum des 20 Jahrhunderts (Museum of the 20th Century), Schweizergarten, Vienna 1030; open 10 AM - 6 PM, cl Wed. Palais Liechtenstein estab 1979; Museum des 20 Jahrhunderts estab 1962
Income: Financed by state appropriation
Collections: Works of the 20th Century: Archipenko, Arp, Barlach, Beckman, Boeckl, Bonnard, Delaunay, Ernst, Gleizes, Hofer, Hoflehner, Jawlensky, Kandinsky, Kirchner, Klee, Kokoschka, Laurens, Leger, Marc, Matisse, Miro, Moore, Munch, Nolde, Picasso, Rodin, Rosso, Wotruba and others
Publications: Books; catalogs
Activities: Classes for adults; dramatic programs; lect open to public; concerts; originate traveling exhibitions
L **Library,** Schweizergarten.
Collections: Photograph Collection

M **OSTERREICHISCHE GALERIE,** Austrian Gallery, Prinz Eugen-Str 27, Postfach 134. Tel 72 64 21, 72 43 58. *Dir* Dr Hans Aurenhammer; *Cur* Dr Hubert Adolph
Open Tues - Thurs & Sat 10 AM - 4 PM, Fri 10 AM - 1 PM, Sun 9 AM - Noon, cl Mon. Estab 1903 for the collection, exhibition and publication of Austrian art (excepting drawings, watercolors, prints and arts and craft) from the Middle Ages until the present. Average Annual Attendance: 160,000
Income: Financed by state appropriation
Collections: Austrian Gallery of 19th and 20th Century Art; Museum of Austrian Baroque Art; Museum of Austrian Medieval Art
Exhibitions: Gerhard Gutruf; Gustav Hessing; Osterreichische Barockmaler aus der Nationalgalerie Prag; Arnulf Rainer; Rudolf Ribarz; Philipp Otto Runge und Caspar David Friedrich; Slowenische Impressionisten; F Zadrazil
Publications: Mitteilungen, annually
L **Library,** Prinz Eugen-Str 27, Postfach 134.
Reference, not open to public
Library Holdings: Vols 4000; Other—Photographs

M **ÖSTERREICHISCHES MUSEUM FÜR ANGEWANDTE KUNST,** Stubenrign 5. Tel 72 56 96, 72 56 97, 72 68 39.
Open Tues, Wed & Fri 10 AM - 4 PM, Sat 10 AM - 6 PM, Sun 10 AM - 1 PM. Admis adult ÖS 10, children ÖS 5. Estab 1864. Average Annual Attendance: 150,000
Income: Financed by state appropriation
Purchases: $100,000
Collections: Ceramics, glass, metal, oriental tapestry, porcelain, textile
Exhibitions: Design aus Schweden, Die unbekannte Sammlung, Oswald Haerdtl, Hundertwasser-Tapisserien, Jerusalem, Rudolf Kalvache und H Mailler-Lesigang, Hugo F Kirsch, Anton Kling, Barockes Kupfer aus Herrengrund, Koloman Moser, Miniature Textiles, Wladimir Narbutt-Lieven, Organische Bauformen, Fritz Riedl, Heinrich Sussmann
Activities: Educ Dept; lect open to public, 5000 visiting lectr per year; four concerts; ten gallery talks; tours; exten dept; museum shop sells books, reproductions and slides

BELGIUM

ANTWERP

L **BIBLIOTHEEK NATIONAAL HOGER INSTITUUT VOOR BOUWKUNST EN STEDEBOUW,** Mutsaertstraat 31. *Prof* Dr Guido Persoons
Open 9 AM - 1 PM and 2 - 6 PM. Estab 1811 to specialize in architecture, town planning and design; as the Library of the National Higher Institute and Royal Academy of Fine Arts
Library Holdings: Vols 40,000; Per subs 175; AV—Lantern Slides, slides; Other—Exhibition catalogs, prints, manuscripts, photographs, Archives of the Saint-Luc's Guild Antwerp (1382)

M **INTERNATIONAAL CULTUREEL CENTRUM,** International Cultural Centre, Meir 50. Tel 031-31-91-81, 31-91-82. *Dir* Florent Bex; *Asst* Glenn Van Looy
Open daily 10 AM - 5 PM. No admis fee. Estab 1970 to organize exhibitions of contemporary art. Average Annual Attendance: 150,000
Income: Financed by state appropriation
Exhibitions: Architecten van Buenos Aires; Walter Beckers; Biënnale van de Kritiek; Laurens Bisscheroux; Bernadette Bour; Bouwen door de eeuwen heen in Vlaanderen; Robert Bruyninckx; France Calone; Pieter De Bruyne; Paul Den Hollander; Carlo De Roover; Willy De Sauter; Yves De Smet; Dimensies van onze stedelijke omgeving; Keith Eliott; Karl Goffin; Greop Creatieve Energie; Harry Gruyaert; Jano; 11 jaar fotografie S I S A; Kunst met papier als arbeid - Arbeid met Papier als Kunst; Marie-Jo Lafontaine; Jonier Marin; Maurizio Nannucci; Daniël Peralta; Personal Worlds; Michelangelo Pistoletto; poëzie Extra: Kompas op Kotte; Kinderen van Overal: hoe even ze; Wijs op Weg
Publications: Exhibition catalogues
Activities: Lect open to public, 19 per year; concerts; performances, video shows; films (evenings); middays of poetry; conferences about architecture and contemporary art; originate traveling exhibitions; sales shop sells books and prints
L **Library,** Meir 50. *Librn* Dany Smet
Open 10 AM - 5 PM. Estab 1970
Library Holdings: Vols 6000; Per subs 152; Micro—Fiche; AV—A-tapes, fs, Kodachromes, slides, v-tapes; Other—Clipping files, exhibition catalogs, photographs, reproductions
Special Subjects: Architecture, Theatre Arts, Contemporary art, Literature, poetry

M KONINKLIJK MUSEUM VOOR SCHONE KUNSTEN, Royal Museum of Fine Arts, Leopold de Waelplein. Tel 38 78 01-09, 38 58 75. *Dir & Cur* Dr G Gepts
No admis fee. Estab 1810. Average Annual Attendance: 105,000
Collections: Five Centuries of Flemish Painting: Jordaens, Memling, Metsijs, Rubens, Van Dyck, Van Eyck, Van der Weyden; Masterpieces (4000); Survey of Western Painting: Fouquet, Hals, Simone Martini, Ruysdaels, Titiaan, Van Goyen; important works of De Braekeleer, Ensor, Leys, Permeke, Smits and Wouters
Exhibitions: Special shows according to year's program
Publications: Jaarboek van het Koninklijk Museum voor Schone Kunsten, Antwerpen, annually; catalogs
Activities: Visiting lect; gallery talks; junior museum
L Library, Leopold de Waelplein.
Library Holdings: Vols 40,000

M MUSEUM MAYER VAN DEN BERGH, Lange Gasthuisstraat 19. Tel 031-324237. *Dir* F Baudouin; *Cur* Hans M J Nieuwdorp
Open 10 AM - 5 PM, cl Mon. No admis fee. Estab 1904 for the preservation of the former private collection of Sir Fritz Mayer van den Bergh. House built in Flemish 16th-Century style; nine rooms; modern extension (1974), three rooms. Average Annual Attendance: 40,000
Income: Financed by city appropriation
Collections: Antique pottery and sculpture; applied arts; ceramics and porcelain; decorative arts, ivories and illuminated manuscripts of the Middle Ages; European painting 13th - 18th Century, expecially Flemish 15th - 16th Century; Flemish sculpture 14th - 16th Century; furniture; numismatics; painted windows; prints; textiles
Publications: Catalog
Activities: Sales shop selling reproductions, slides and illustrated catalogs
L Library, Lange Gasthuisstraat 19.
Open to scholars for reference only
Library Holdings: Vols 2000
Collections: Sale catalogs 1875-1901

M MUSEUM PLANTIN-MORETUS, Plantin-Moretus Museum, Vrijdagmarkt 22. Tel 00-32-37-330688, 322455. *Dir* Dr L Voet; *Asst Dir* F de Nave
Open daily 10 AM - 5 PM. Estab 1876: 16th and 17th Century Printing Plant and Patrician's House
Income: Financed by city appropriation
Collections: Designs, moulds, printing presses, punches and matrices, wood blocks and copper plates
L Library, Vrijdagmarkt 22.
Library Holdings: Vols 30,000
Collections: Incunabula (including Gutenberg Bible); Old Antwerp Impressions; E Verhaeren Collection; old bookbindings; 16th - 17th Century manuscripts

M MUSEUM SMIDT VAN GELDER, Smidt van Gelder Museum, Belgielei 91. Tel 03-39 06 52, 39 10 90. *Chief Asst* Maria Snoeckx
Open Tues - Sun 10 AM - 5 PM, cl Mon. Estab 1949 as a private collection and given to the city by Knight Pieter Smidt van Gelder
Income: Financed by city appropriation
Collections: Museum arranged as an 18th Century artistic living house with 18th Century French furniture and paintings, Dutch paintings from the 17th, 18th and 19th Centuries, tapestries and most important: 18th Century Chinese and European porcelains
L Library, Belgielei 91.
For reference
Library Holdings: Vols 600; Other—Prints 1000, photographs

M OPENLUCHTMUSEUM VOOR BEELDHOUWKUNST, MIDDELHEIM, Open Air Museum for Sculpture Middelheim, Middelheimlaan 61. Tel 031-27 15 34. *Cur* F Baudouin; *Asst Cur* M R Bentein
Open daily 10 AM - Sunset. No admis fee, except during biennials. Estab 1950 to exhibit contemporary sculpture, starting with Rodin, and up to the present; make a collection for the biennials; a beautiful park; small sculpture in a pavilion. Average Annual Attendance: 125,000
Income: Financed by city appropriation
Collections: Contemporary sculpture, medals, drawings and graphics by sculptors
Exhibitions: (1979) 15th Biennial for Sculpture; Scandinavian sculpture
Publications: Collection and exhibition catalogues
Activities: Educ dept; lect; gallery talks; tours; sales desk sells reproductions and catalogues
L Lode Craeybeck Documentation Center, Middelheimlaan 61.
Open daily 10 AM - 4 PM. Estab 1950, since 1976 was renamed to collect all possible information on contemporary sculpture and environmental art
Income: Financed by city appropriation
Library Holdings: Vols 32,500; Per subs 40; AV—Slides; Other—Exhibition catalogs, photographs
Publications: Catalogue of the Library; General works, 1980, Part II

M RUBENIANUM, Belgielei 91. Tel 031-39 10 90. *Keeper Art Historical Museum* Frans Baudouin; *Asst Keeper* Nora de Poorter
Open Mon - Fri 8:30 AM - 4:30 PM. Estab 1950 as the art-historical department and documentation center of the city, concerning Rubens, and Flemish art of the 16th and 17th Centuries. Its first aim is the publication of the Corpus Rubenianum Ludwig Burchard
Income: Financed by city appropriation
Collections: Library and documentation of the Nationaal Centrum voor de Plastische Kunsten van de 16de en de 17de Eeuw are incorporated
Publications: Corpus Rubenianum Ludwig Burchard (an illustrated Catalogue Raisonne of the work of P P Rubens in 26 parts, based on material of Dr Ludwig Burchard)

M STEDELIJK PRENTENKABINET, Municipal Gallery of Graphic Arts, Vrijdagmarkt 23. Tel 031-322455. *Dir* Dr L Voet; *Asst Dir* F de Nave
Open Mon - Fri 10 AM - 4 PM. No admis fee. Estab 1936 for research work on Flemish graphic art
Income: Financed by city appropriation
Collections: Antwerp iconographic collection; Modern drawings: J Ensor, F

Jespers, H Leys, W Vaes, Rik Wouters; Modern engravings: Cantre, Ensor, Masereel, J Minne, W Vaes; Old drawings: Jordaens, E and A Quellin, Rubens, Schut, Van Dyck; Old engravings: Galle, Goltzius, Hogenbergh, W Hollar, Jegher, Wiericx, etc
L Library, Vrijdagmarkt 23.
Library Holdings: Vols 9000; Other—Prints 15,000, photographs

BRUGES

M STEDELYKE MUSEA, City Museums, Dyver, 12. Tel 33 99 11. *Dir* Dr A Janssens de Bisthoven; *Cur* Dr V Vermeersch
Open Mar - Sept daily 9:30 AM - Noon and 2 - 6 PM, Oct - Feb 10 AM - Noon and 2 - 5 PM. Admis 40 francs, groups 20 francs, students 10 francs. Estab in 18th Century. Consists of four museums: Groeningemuseum, Gruuthusemuseum, Arentshuis and Museum voor Volkskunde. Average Annual Attendance: 300,000
Income: Financed by city appropriation
Collections: Arentshuis - paintings, porcelain, furniture of the 18th and 19th Century; Groeningemuseum - Flemish paintings and modern art; Gruuthusemuseum - furniture, numismatics, sculpture, tapestries, textile art; Museum voor Volkskunde - Folklore
Activities: Classes for adults and children; lect open to public, 4 visiting lectr per year; individual paintings and original objects of art lent to other museums; sales shop sells books, reproductions, prints and slides
L Library, Dyver, 12.
Library Holdings: Vols 8000; Per subs 450

BRUSSELS

M MUSEES ROYAUX D'ART ET D'HISTOIRE, Royal Museums of Art and History, 10 Parc du Cinquantenaire. Tel 733 96 10. *Cur* Rene de Roo
Open 9:30 AM - 12:30 PM and 1:30 - 5 PM, cl Mon. Estab 1835
Collections: †American archaeology; Belgium, Egyptian, Far Eastern, Greek, Oriental, Roman and classical art; Medieval, Renaissance and Modern Art - ceramics, furniture, glass, lace, silver, tapestries, textiles, silver; †ethnography; †folklore
Publications: Bulletin, annually
Activities: Lect organized by Educ Service on subjects relating to collections, 50 Dutch and French visiting lectr per year; gallery talks; tours
L Library, 10 Parc du Cinquantenaire.
Open Mon - Fri 9:30 AM - Noon and 5 - 6 PM. Estab 1835
Library Holdings: Vols 100,000; Per subs 2000

M MUSEES ROYAUX DES BEAUX-ARTS DE BELGIQUE, Royal Museums of Fine Arts of Belgium, rue du Musee 9. Tel 02-513 96 30. *Dir* Philippe Roberts-Jones; *Cur Ancient Art* Henri Pauwels; *Cur Modern Art* Francine-Claire Legrand
Estab 1830
Collections: Medieval, Renaissance and Modern Paintings, Drawings and Sculpture
Exhibitions: (1978) Alechinsky a l'Imprimerie; Creativite dans l'Art Bresilien Contemporain; Lismonde Retrospective; Mural Art USA; Willem Paerels 1878-1962; Surrealism from the Collection of the Museum of Modern Art, New York; (1979) Fleurs, la Nature et l'Image; Portaels et ses Eleves; Tendances de l'Art Actuel en Yougoslavie
Publications: Bulletin
M Musse d'Art Ancien, rue de la Regence 3.
Collections: Paintings, drawings and sculpture of the 19th - 20th Century
Exhibitions: Temporary exhibitions
M Musee Constantin Meunier, rue de l'Abbaye 59.
Collections: Paintings, Drawings and Sculptures by Constantin Meunier; the Artist's house and studio
M Musee Wiertz, rue Vautier 62.
Collections: Paintings of Antoine Wiertz
L Bibliotheque, rue du Musee 5.
Estab 1909
Library Holdings: Vols 100,000; Per subs 400; Micro—Cards, fiche, reels, prints; AV—A-tapes, cassettes, fs, Kodachromes, lantern slides, motion pictures, rec, v-tapes; Other—Framed reproductions, prints, manuscripts, memorabilia, original art works, pamphlets

L ROYAL ACADEMY OF FINE ARTS, Bibliotheque Artistique, 144, rue du Midi. *Librn* Monique Deleu; *Asst Librn* Simone Crepin
Open Mon, Tues, Thurs & Fri 9 AM - 5 PM, Wed 9 AM - Noon and 6 - 9 PM, Sat 9 AM - Noon. Estab 1883
Purchases: 200,000 F
Library Holdings: Vols 17,000; Per subs 53; Other—Exhibition catalogs, prints, memorabilia, original art works, photographs, rare books
Collections: Photos du Comite du Vieux Bruxelles; Releves de la Societe Centrale d'Architecture; Releves du Prix Carsoel - Releves de la mission du Ministrer des Sciences et des Arts; Region de l'Yser 1914-18

GHENT

M MUSEUM VOOR SCHONE KUNSTEN, Citadelpark. Tel 091-22 1703. *Cur* Paul Eeckhout; *Asst* Robert Hoozee; *Asst* Monique Van Roose
Open 9 AM - Noon and 2 - 5 PM. Estab 1904. Average Annual Attendance: 60,000
Income: Financed by city appropriation
Purchases: F 2,000,000
Collections: †European Art - drawings, paintings, prints, sculpture, mainly national art; small collection of icons, tapestry
Exhibitions: (1978) Bateau-Lavoir; (1979) Veertig Kunstenaars Rond Karel Van de Woestone 1878-1929
Activities: Lect open to public, 4 - 6 visiting lectr per year; concerts; guided tours upon request; individual paintings and original objects of art lent to museums and official institutions; museum shop sells reproductions, slides and catalogues of exhibitions

L **Bibliotheek,** Citadelpark.
Open 9 AM - Noon and 2 - 5 PM. Estab for ducoments and books relating to museum collection
Library Holdings: Per subs 20; Other—Exhibition catalogs, photographs

LIEGE

M **MUSEES D'ARCHEOLOGIE ET D'ARTS DECORATIFS,** Liege Museums of Archeology and Decorative Arts, 13 Quai de Maastricht. *Dir* Joseph Philippe; *Asst Cur* Marie-Claire Gueury
Open 10 AM - 12:30 PM and 2 - 5 PM, Sun & holidays 10 AM - 4 PM. Ansembourg Museum estab 1905; Curtis Museum in 1909; Glass Museum 1959
Income: Financed by city and state appropriations
Collections: Musee Ansembourg - 18th Century Decorative Arts of Liege, housed in a mansion of the same period; Musee Curtius - archeology; decorative arts from prehistory to 18th Century; Musee du Verre - history and art of glass
Exhibitions: Collection of International Glass; Nouvelle Presentation des Collections Internationales du Verre
Publications: Annales of the Association; Bulletin de l'Association Internationale pour l'Histoire du Verre, 2 - 3 per year
Activities: Lect open to public, 45 visiting lectr per year; gallery talks; museum shop sells books and slides
L **Libraries,** 13 Quai de Maastricht.
Open for reference
Library Holdings: Per subs 550

VERVIERS

M **MUSEES COMMUNAUX BEAUX-ARTS ET ARCHEOLOGIE,** Community Museum of Fine Arts and Archaeology, Beaux Arts-rue Renier 17. Tel 087-331695. *Cur* V Bronowski
Open Mon - Thurs & Sat 9 AM - Noon and 2 - 5 PM, Sun 10 AM - 1 PM and 3 - 6 PM. No admis fee. Estab 1884
Income: Financed by appropriation
Collections: Ancient and modern painting and sculpture, ceramics, folk arts, furniture, graphic arts, regional archaeology, Roman antiquities
Exhibitions: Eight exhibitions of fine arts and archaeology per year
Publications: Guide books
Activities: Classes for children

BOLIVIA

LA PAZ

M **MUSEO NACIONAL DE ARQUEOLOGIA,** National Museum,* Calle Tihuanacu 93, Casilla oficial 64. Tel 29624. *Dir* Gregorio Cordero Miranda; *Asst Dir* Olga Joffre Chavez; *Secy* Victor Vera; *Cur Archaeology* Federico Dietz de Medina
Estab 1846, reinaugurated 1960. Average Annual Attendance: 9500
Collections: Anthropology, archaeology, Colonial Art, ethnology, Folklore, Lake Titicaca District Exhibitions, Traditional Native Arts and Crafts
Publications: Anales de Museo, Centenario del Museo 1940
L **Library,*** Calle Tihuanacu 93, Casilla oficial 64.
Library Holdings: Vols 3000

BRAZIL

OURO PRETO

M **MUSEU DA INCONFIDENCIA,** History of Democratic Ideals and Culture in Minas Gerais, Praca Tiradentes, 139. Tel 332. *Dir* Rui Mourao
Open Noon - 5:30 PM. Estab 1938, inaugurated 1944 to honor the first movement towards Brazil's independence, the Inconfidencia Mineira, which took place in Ouro Preto, then the capitol of Minas Gerais; to explain how this movement and its ideals first appeared; to show a general view of the cultural development of Minas Gerais to the public through the collections. Museum belongs to the Federal Government and is an organ of the Ministry for Education's Department for the Preservation of the National Historic and Artistic Property. Average Annual Attendance: 150,000
Income: Expenditures are paid directly by the Federal Treasury
Collections: Objects related to the 1789 Revolutionaries of Minas Gerais (the Inconfidentes); †furniture, painting, sacred arts, silver, †wood carvings
Exhibitions: Tombs containing the remains of the Inconfidentes who died exiled in different regions of Africa; Original Drawings, Documents and Wood Carvings by Antonio Francisco Lisboa, the Little Cripple, who is Brazil's most important artist, sculptor and architect
L **Library,** Praca Tiradentes, 139.
Library Holdings: Vols 2200; Per subs 1600
Special Subjects: Brazil's history and history of art, with emphasis on Minas Gerais problems
Collections: Latin American, Portuguese and Spanish Arts and History

RIO DE JANEIRO

M **MUSEU DE ARTE MODERNA,** Museum of Modern Art,* Av Beira Mar, Box 44, ZC-39. Tel 231-1871. *Executive Dir* Helosia Aleixo Lustosa
Open Noon - 7 PM. Admis 80¢. Estab 1948 to document the evolution of the Contemporary Fine Arts. Museum of Modern Art is an outstanding architectural project by Alfonso Eduardo Reidy. It consists of a connected three-story building of two blocks; one for temporary exhibitions and collections, and the other for the administration, courses, library, experimental displays and film collection. Average Annual Attendance: 33,000. Mem: 2000
Income: Financed by endowment and state appropriation
Collections: Large portion of collection destroyed by fire in 1978
Publications: Bulletin, monthly
Activities: Classes for adults and children; lect open to public, 20 visiting lectr per year; concerts; gallery talks; sales shop sells books, magazines, original art, reproductions and prints
L **Library,*** Av Beira Mar. *Head Librn* Dr Alicia Dantas Leite; *Librn* Germana Maria Camarao Costa
Open daily 2 - 7 PM for reference. Estab 1968 to enable the public to consult documentaries related to the Arts in general
Library Holdings: Vols 9000; Per subs 300
Special Subjects: Contemporary and modern art
Publications: Library Bulletin, annually

M **MUSEU NACIONAL DE BELAS ARTES,** National Museum of Fine Arts, Ave Rio Branco 199. *Dir & Prof* Edson Motta; *Chief Technical Department* Pedro Martins Caldas Xexeo
Open Tues - Fri 12:30 - 6:30 PM. No admis fee. First floor of gallery has temporary exhibition room; second floor has Brazilian art of the 19th and 20th Century; on the third floor is the foreign gallery. Average Annual Attendance: 30,000
Income: Financed by state appropriation
Collections: 19th and †20th Century Brazilian art, works by outstanding painters; †Foreign collections - works by Dutch, English, French, German, Italian, Portuguese and Spanish masters; Masterpieces of Foreign Collection: Dutch School - Eight Brazilian Landscapes by Frans Post; French School - 20 Paintings by Eugene Boudin; Ventania (Storm) by Alfred Sisley; Italian School: Portrait of the Cardinal Amadei by Giovanni Battista Gaulli, Baciccia; Sao Caetano (circa 1730) by Giambattista Tiepolo. Graphic Art Department: Prints and drawings by Annibale Carracci, Chagall, Daumier, Durer, Toulouse Lautrec, Picasso, Guido Reni, Renoir, Tiepolo, etc
Exhibitions: (1978-79) 44 Exhibitions
Publications: Artistas de Juiz de Fora; Aspectos da Paisagem Brasileira, 1816-1916; Museum Anthologies: The Renaissance (1978); The Romanticism (1980); Museu Nacional de Belas Artes, first volume of the National Foundation of Arts Collection: Brazilian Museums
Activities: Classes for adults; docent training; lect open to public; concerts; gallery talks
L **Library,** Ave Rio Branco 199. *Chief Librn* Vera Monteiro Pereira
Open 1:30 - 6:30 PM. Estab 1937 as a reference library
Income: Financed by state appropriation
Library Holdings: Vols 6000; Other—Exhibition catalogs, pamphlets

SAO PAULO

M **MUSEU DE ARTE DE SAO PAULO,** Sao Paulo Art Museum, Ave Paulista 1578. *Dir* D M Bardi
Open 2 - 6 PM. Founded 1947
Collections: Representative works by Portinari and Laser Segall; †ancient and modern paintings and sculptures: American, 19th - 20th Centuries; Brazilian, 17th - 20th Centuries; British, 18th - 20th Centuries; Dutch, Flemish and German, 15th - 20th Centuries; French, 16th - 20th Centuries; Italian, 13th - 20th Centuries; Spanish and Portuguese, 16th - 19th Centuries
Exhibitions: Printing and photography exhibitions
Activities: Art history school
L **Library,** Av Paulista 1578. *Librn* Claudia Marino Semeraro
Open 2 - 6 PM. Estab 1948
Library Holdings: Vols 25,000; Micro—Cards, fiche; AV—Kodachromes, slides; · Other—Prints, original art works, pamphlets, photographs, reproductions

CHILE

SANTIAGO

M **MUSEO DE ARTE POPULAR AMERICANO,** Art of the American Peoples Museum,* Casilla 10-D, Univ of Chile. Tel 2 01 28. *Dir* Patricio Court del Pedregal
Open Tues - Sat 10 AM - 5:30 PM, Sun 3 - 6 PM. No admis fee. Estab 1944 for the study and exposure to popular American art. Museum has three rooms with showcasses and panels for exhibitions
Collections: Araucarian silver; Popular Art of the American Peoples
Exhibitions: Arte Popular Chileno; Arte Popular Rumano; Artesania Popular Mexicana; Arte y Artesanias de China Popular; Pesebres, retablos e imagineria religiosa; Tejidos indigenas y populares de America
Publications: Exhibition catalogs, annually
Activities: Lect; exten dept serves the faculty of fine arts; originate traveling exhibitions
L **Library,*** Casilla 10-D, Univ of Chile.
For reference
Library Holdings: Vols 3500; Other—Photographs

M **MUSEO NACIONAL DE BELLAS ARTES,** National Museum of Fine Arts, Parque Forestan s/n, Casilla 3209. *Cur* Nena Ossa
Open Tues - Sat 10 AM - 6 PM, Sun 10 AM - 2 PM. Admis $9, students $5. Estab

1880 to show the Chilean collection of fine arts (painting and sculpture). 20 permanent exhibition galleries; 3 temporary exhibition galleries; one gallery for audio-visual exhibits and an auditorium for conferences and concerts. Average Annual Attendance: 66,730. Mem: 11
Income: $6,000,000
Collections: Baroque, Chilean and Spanish Paintings; sculpture
Exhibitions: Four contemporary exhibitions from abroad; 15 contemporary and retrospective national exhibitions
Publications: Exhibition and general catalog
Activities: Classes for children; docent training; lect open to public; competitions; individual paintings and original objects of art lent to government institutions
L **Library,** Parque Forestal s/n, Casilla 3209. *Librn* Doralisa Duarte Pinto
Open Tues - Fri 10 AM - 6 PM. Estab 1973 as reference to students and public
Income: $120,000
Purchases: $120,000
Library Holdings: Vols 1500; Per subs 3; Other—Exhibition catalogs, framed reproductions, prints
Special Subjects: Chilean and Latin American art, histories of museums and fine arts, monographies of universal artists
Collections: Clipping-files of the Chilean Artists and museum exhibitions
Publications: Exhibition catalogs

REPUBLIC OF CHINA

TAIPEI

M **NATIONAL PALACE MUSEUM,** Shih-Lin, Wai Shuang Hsi, 111. Tel 881-2021 4. *Dir* Dr Chiang Fu-tsung; *Deputy Dir & Cur Department Antiquities* Li Lin-ts'an; *Deputy Dir & Cur Department Calligraphy & Painting* Chiang Chao-shen; *Cur Department Rare Books & Documents* Peter Chang
Open daily 9 AM - 5 PM. Admis NT$15. Estab 1925 in Peiping, re-opened in present building 1965, to serve as a center of Chinese art; to conserve, research and exhibit the former Imperial collections assembled over the previous thousand years. Average Annual Attendance: 1,500,000
Income: Financed by state appropriation
Collections: Bronzes, calligraphy, carved lacquer, Ch'ing dynasty court and governmental documents, embroidery, enamelware, jades, miniature crafts, oracle bones, painting, porcelain, pottery, rare and old books, tapestry, writing implements
Publications: Bulletin, bi-monthly; National Palace Museum Quarterly; Newsletter, monthly
Activities: Programs for school children; lect open to public; originate traveling exhibitions; sales shop sells books, reproductions, prints and slides
L **Library,** Shih-Lin, Wai Shuang Hsi, 111. *Head Librn* Wang Ching-hung
Open Mon - Fri 9 AM - 5 PM, Sat 9 AM - Noon. Estab 1965 to complement the collection of cultural properites. Open for reference to researchers and students
Income: $18,000
Purchases: $15,000
Library Holdings: Vols 180,000; Per subs 380; Micro—Fiche, reels; Other—Exhibition catalogs, manuscripts, pamphlets
Special Subjects: Art History, Asian art, sinology
Collections: Palace memorials of the Ch'ing dynasty and other Ch'ing dynasty archival materials; Rare Books Collection, 153,222 volumes, including more than 70 wood-block editions printed during the Sung dynasty

COLOMBIA

BOGOTA

M **COLOMBIAN INSTITUTE OF CULTURE,** Museum of Colonial Art, Carrera 6 No 9-77. Tel 241 6017. *Dir* Francisco Gil Tovar
Open Tues - Sat 9 AM - 7 PM, Sun & holidays 10 AM - 5 PM. Admis adults 5 pesos, children 2 pesos. Estab 1942 to promote culture. Museum is a dependency of the national cultural directorate and reflects through the 17th Century mansion that it occupies, and the works of art that it conserves, that period in which the nation formed part of the Spanish Empire. Average Annual Attendance: 32,000
Income: Financed by state appropriation
Collections: Large collection of Paintings and Drawings of Gregorio Vasquez Ceballos (1638-1711); native master Figueroa and Joaquin Gutierrez; Gilded Trunks of the 17th Century; painting, drawings, decorative carving, furniture and silver relating to aesthetics and life in New Granada between 1550 and 1820
Exhibitions: Artistic Fusion: Angels and Devils in the Colony; Birth and Infancy of Jesus in Colonial Art; Drawings of Gregorio Vasquez Ceballos; Didactic Synthesis of Art of New Granada; Images of Colombia; Little Pictures in Big Frames; Religious Colonial Art; one-person exhibitions dedicated to authors, schools, themes
Publications: Monthly bulletin
Activities: Classes for adults and children; docent training; artmobile

CYPRUS

NICOSIA

M **CYPRUS MUSEUM,** Museum St. Tel 40-2189. *Cur* Open; *Asst Cur* Open
Open daily 8 AM - 5:30 PM, Sun 10 AM - 1 PM. Admis 150 mils. Estab 1909 to collect, preserve and exhibit antiquities dating from the Neolithic period (sixth millenium BC) to Graeco-Roman times (4th century AD). Average Annual Attendance: 34,493
Income: $5000 (financed by state appropriation)
Purchases: $5000
Collections: Bronze Cauldron from Salamis; middle and late Bronze-age Geometric, Archaic, Classical, Hellenistic and Graeco-Roman Pottery; Mycenaean Vases; Neolithic stone tools and vessels; Sculpture including the Fine Arsos Head, the Aphrodite of Soli, and the Bronze Statue of Septimus Sevarus; Silver Trays from Lambousa; Terra Cotta Figurines from Ayia Irini; bronzes, coins, early bronze-age pottery, glass, jewelry, lamps, sanctuary and ploughing models, and other minor works of art
L **Library,** Museum St. *Librn* Lygia Ieromonachou
Open to public for reference
Library Holdings: Vols 11,000; Per subs 10
Special Subjects: Cypriot, Greek, Roman and Near Eastern archaeology

CZECHOSLOVAKIA

BRATISLAVA

M **SLOVENSKA NARODNA GALERIA,** Slovak National Gallery,* Razusovo nabrezie 2. Tel 301 93, 300 37, 300 94. *Dir* Dr Stefan Mruskovic; *Chief Department Slovak & European Art to 19th Century* Dr Karol Vaculik; *Chief Department Contemporary Art* Dr Silvia Ileckova; *Chief Department Graphic Art* Dr Eva Trojanova; *Chief Department Nonprofessional Art* Dr Katarina Schreiberova
Open 10 AM - 6 PM. Estab 1948 as the leading national art institution. The main exhibition halls in Bratislava under reconstruction since 1972; at present all the collections concentrated in the castle of the central Slovakian city of Zvolen and in the castle of the locality of Cerveny Kamen. The permanent installation of paintings and graphics by one of the leading artists of the the Slovak modern art, Ludovit Fulla, in the city of Ruzomberok
Collections: Applied Arts (1400); European and Slovak painting (4500), Dutch, Flemish and Italian; graphics and drawings (17,000); Institic Art (700); sculpture (1700)
Exhibitions: Biennale of Illustrations Bratislava, an exhibition of children's books illustrations; International exhibitions organized by Slovak National Gallery; Triennale of Insitic (Naive) Art Exhibition, extended to include all forms of nonprofessional art; permanent collection, specialized exhibitions
Publications: Selected material from each symposium
Activities: National and international symposiums and seminars; competitions; awards; originate traveling exhibitions
L **Library,*** Razusovo nabrezie 2.
Library Holdings: Vols 40,000

BRNO

M **MORAVSKA GALERIE V BRNE,** Moravian Gallery at Brno, Husova ulice 14, 66 226. Tel 20 151, 24 809. *Art Historian & Dir* Jiri Hlusicka
Open daily 10 AM - 6 PM, cl Mon. Admis 4, 2, 1, Czech crowns. Estab 1817 as a regional gallery of fine arts; collects all-world art; specializing in Moravian Art
Income: Financed by state appropriation
Collections: †Applied Art Collection - ceramics, furniture, glass, graphic design, jewelry, photography, textiles; †Fine Art Collection - graphic art, painting, sculpture since 14th Century to present; Oriental Art Collection; (over 100,000 pieces in collections)
Exhibitions: Biennael of Czechoslovak Contemporary Photography; Biennale of Graphic Design; Cut Glass Triennale; and other exhibitions from own collections or lent exhibitions
Publications: Bulletin of Moravian Gallery, 3 per year; catalogs; Museology Papers, 4 per year
Activities: Classes for adults; lect open to public; gallery talks; tours; concerts; exten dept serves south Moravia; original objects of art lent for exhibitions only; originate traveling exhibitions
L **Library,** Husova ulice 14, 66 226. *Librn* Marie Dohnalova
Open Mon - Fri 10 AM - 6 PM. Estab 1873, specializing in art literature
Income: Financed by state appropriation
Library Holdings: Vols 66,190; Per subs 150
Collections: Rare Moravian Prints; 20th Century bookbindings; old prints
Exhibitions: Art Noveau Textile; Czech Modern Pictures - New Acquisitions; Czech Sculpture 20th Century; Glass and Medals by Jiri Harcuba; Posters by Alphens Mucha; Illustrations by Jaroslav Serych

LITOMERICE

M **SEVEROCESKA GALERIE VYTVARNEHO UMENI,** North Bohemian Gallery of Fine Arts,* Michalska 7. Tel 23 38. *Dir* Berta Velesikova
Open Mon - Fri 10 AM - Noon and 2 - 5 PM, Sat & Sun 10 AM - 5 PM. Admis adults 2 Kes, students 1 Kes. Estab 1958 as a collection of 13th - 20th Century North Bohemian paintings and sculptures
Income: Financed by city and state appropriations
Collections: †Art of the 19th Century; Baroque Art of the 17th - 18th Centuries; contemporary art; Gothic Art of the 13th - 16th Centuries; special collections of naive paintings and sculpture; Renaissance paintings and sculptures of the 15th -

16th Centuries

Exhibitions: Approximately 10 mutual exhibitions yearly: Art Protis, tapestry; Dutch Paintings of the 17th Century; Naive Art; North-Bohemian County in the works of the painters and graphic artists

Activities: Classes for children; lect open to public, 8 visiting lectr per year; gallery talks; tours; concerts; exten dept serves North Bohemian county; individual paintings and original objects of art lent; lending collection contains books, color reproductions, lantern slides, slides, original prints, photographs and sculpture; originate traveling exhibitions

L **Library,*** Michalska 7.
Library Holdings: Vols 9000

PRAGUE

M **NARODNI GALERIE V PRAGUE,** National Gallery of Prague, Hradcanske Namesti 15, 1 Hradcany. Tel 35 24 41-3, 53 44 57-8. *Pres* Dr Jiri Kotalik; *Deputy Dir & Chief Graphic Art Coll* Dr Libuse Jandova; *Chief Ancient Art Coll* Dr Jiri Masin; *Chief Modern Art Coll* Dr Vaclav Prochazka; *Chief Oriental Art Coll* Dr Lubor Hajek; *Deputy Dir* Vladimir Benes

Open daily 10 AM - 6 PM, cl Mon. Admis 2 crowns. Estab 1796 as picture gallery of the Society of Patriotic Friends of Art; 1901 estab Gallery of Modern Art; 1945 both collections united in the National Gallery; to collect and expertly safeguard the collections of Czech and world paintings, sculpture and graphic art works. Average Annual Attendance: 800,000

Income: Financed by state appropriation

Collections: Czech Sculpture of the 19th and 20th Century; French and European Art of the 19th and 20th Century; Old Czech Art; Old European Art; graphic art, modern art

Exhibitions: (1978) Art and Postmark; Baroque Painting of the National Gallery Collection (Vienna, Austria); Frantisek Bilek; British Watercolors and Drawings; Manuscripts, Paintings and Sculptures of the Charles IV Period; Fritz Cremer; Czech and Slovak Art 20th Century; Czech Drawing 19th and 20th Century; Adolf Kaspar; Vaclav Hollar Graphic Art; Josef Lada; 100 Old European Drawings; Petrus Paulus Rubens; Serbian Neolit-Memorials; Thracian Art; 300 Years Painting in (Dresden DDR); (1979) Mikolas Ales; Antique Art of the CSSR Collections; Josef Capek; Contemporary Spanish Art; Czech Gotic Art (Yugoslavia); Czechoslovak Graphic Art (Lisbon); Georg Flegel Still Lifes; French Art of the Middleages; Otto Gutfreund (Edinborouhg, London); Renato Guttuso; Hungarian Revolutionary Graphic Art; Josef Maratka; Masterpieces of the 16th and 17th Century of the NG Collection; Modern India Art; Eugen Nevan; Prague Castle during the Last Centuries; Drawings of the Rudolph II Period; Russian Folk Wood-carving and Painting; Stanislav Sucharda; To the Anniversary of AVU Foundation; Jiri Trnka (d'Annecy France); Jan Zrzavy

Activities: Classes for adults and children; lect open to public, 20 visiting lectr per year; individual paintings and original objects of art lent to galleries and museums in Czech and abroad; originate traveling exhibitions; sales shop sells reproductions and slides

L **Library,** Hradcanske Namesti 15, 1 Hradcany. *Head of the Service* Dr Marcala Vanyslova
Estab 1796
Library Holdings: Vols 40,000; Per subs 170; Micro—Cards, fiche, reels, prints; AV—A-tapes, Kodachromes, lantern Slides, slides; Other—Exhibition catalogs, prints, manuscripts, memorabilia, photographs, reproductions
Collections: Picture Postcards Collections

M **STATNI ZIDOVSKE MUZEUM,** State Jewish Museum, 110 01 Jachymova 3. Tel 633-74-76. *Dir* Dr Miroslav Jaros; *Deputy Dir* Dr V Sadek; *Chief of Department Expositions* Dr A Frankova

Open Sun - Fri 9 AM - 5 PM, cl Sat. Admis adults 5 Kcs, students 3 Kcs. Estab 1950 to inform the public about the history of Jews in Bohemia and Moravia; Jewish Cemetery of the 15th - 18th Centuries and the old-new synagogue of the 13th century. Average Annual Attendance: 700,000

Collections: Historical Archival Materials of Bohemian and Moravian Jewish Religious Communities; Library of Ancient Books with a collection of Hebrew Manuscripts; children's drawings and works of painters from the concentration camp Terezin; silver liturgical objects; textiles from Synagogues of historic interest

Publications: Judaica Bohemiae, bi-annually

L **Library,** 110 01 Jachymova 3.
Library Holdings: Vols 80,000

DENMARK

AALBORG

M **NORDJYLLANDS KUNSTMUSEUM,** Art Museum of Northern Jutland,* Kong Christians Alle 50. Tel 13 80 88. *Dir* L Rostrup Boyesen

Open Tues - Sun 10 AM - 5 PM, cl Mon. Admis 5 DKr. Estab 1972 as an art gallery. Average Annual Attendance: 100,000

Income: Financed by city and state appropriation

Purchases: 150,000 DKr

Collections: Collection of graphics, painting and sculpture from this Century, Danish and international. Main museum for the Cobra movement

Exhibitions: Approx 75 exhibitions per year

Publications: Bulletin, monthly

Activities: Classes for adults and children; lect open to public, 5 visiting lectr per year; concerts; gallery talks; originate traveling exhibitions; museum shop sells magazines, original art, reproductions and prints

L **Library,*** Kong Christians Alle 50.
Open for reference
Library Holdings: Vols 40,000; Per subs 50

AARHUS

M **AARHUS KUNSTMUSEUM,** Aarhus Art Museum, Vennelystparken. Tel 06-135255. *Dir* Kristian Jakobsen

Open 10 AM - 5 PM, cl Mon. Estab 1859. Average Annual Attendance: 70,000

Income: Financed by endowment, state and city appropriation

Collections: Danish Art - painting, sculpture, graphic arts, 1750 to present; European Art, mostly recent graphics; some outstanding works from the 19th and 20th Century, photograph collection

Exhibitions: About 15 per year

Activities: Lect; films; concerts

L **Library,** Vennelystparken.
Open for research

CHARLOTTENLUND

M **ORDRUPGAARD COLLECTION,** Vilvordevej 110. Tel 01 641183. *Dir* Hanne Finsen

Open May - Sept daily 1 - 5 PM, Wed evenings 7 - 10 PM, cl Mon, Oct - April Sat & Sun 1 - 5 PM. Admis 5 Danish crowns

Collections: Wilhelm Hansen Collection; Paintings by Cezanne, Corot, Courbet, Degas, Delacroix, Degas, Gauguin, Manet, Pissarro, Renoir, Sisley, and other French and Danish artists from the 19th Century and the beginning of the 20th Century

COPENHAGEN

M **DET DANSKE KUNSTINDUSTRIMUSEUM,** Museum of Decorative Art, Bredgade 68. Tel 14 94 52. *Pres* Jorgen Trolle; *Dir* Erik Lassen; *Keeper* Vibeke Woldbye; *Keeper* Jorg Jorgen Schou-Christensen

Open daily 1 - 4 PM, Sept - May Tues 1 - 9 PM, cl Mon. Estab 1894

Collections: Chinese and Japanese Art and Handicrafts; European Decorative Art from the Middle Ages to present - bookbindings, carpets and tapestries, furniture, jewelry, porcelain and pottery, silverware and textiles

Exhibitions: Approximately 20 per year

Publications: Kunstindustrimuseets Virksomhed

Activities: Lect, 2 - 3 visiting lectr per year

L **Library,** Bredgade 68. *Librn* Eva Steinaa
Open Tues - Fri 10 AM - 4 PM, Sept - May Tues 10 AM - 9 PM
Library Holdings: Vols 50,000
Collections: Photograph Collection

L **DET KONGELIGE DANSKE KUNSTAKADEMI BIBLIOTEK,** 1 Kongens Nytoru. *Dir* Hakon Lund

Open Sept - May Mon - Fri 10 AM - 5:30 PM, Sat 10 AM - 2 PM, June Mon - Fri 10 AM - 5:30 PM, July & Aug Mon - Fri 1 - 5 PM. Estab 1755 for art (painting, sculpture, architecture) and art history

Income: $400,000

Purchases: $60,000

Library Holdings: Vols 90,000; Per subs 278; Micro—Fiche, reels; AV—Rec, slides; Other—Clipping files, exhibition catalogs, prints, manuscripts, original art works, pamphlets, photographs, reproductions, sculpture, architectural drawings 100,000, architectural models

M **KOBENHAVNS BYMUSEUM,** Copenhagen City Museum,* Vesterbrogade 59. Tel 01 210772. *Cur* Steffen Linvald; *Asst Cur* John Erichsen

Open Tues - Sun 10 AM - 4 PM, Tues evenings 7 - 9 PM, cl Mon. Admis adults 1 kr, children 50 ore. Estab 1901 to record the history and development of Copenhagen from 1167 to present

Income: Financed by city appropriation

Collections: Photographs 1850 to present; topographical drawings, paintings and prints

Exhibitions: John Christensen, drawings and paintings from Norrebro; Copenhagen Slum; Prince and Horse - J F J Saly's equestrian monument of Frederik V 1753-74

Publications: Kobenhavns Bymuseum, yearly

Activities: Concerts

M **NATIONALMUSEET,** National Museum, Prinsens Palae, Frederiksholms Kanal 12. Tel 01-13 44 11. *Dir* Dr P V Glob; *Keeper Danish Prehistoric Coll* Mogens Orsnes; *Keeper Danish Prehistoric Coll* Harald Langberg; *Keeper Danish Folk Museum* H Rasmussen; *Keeper Ethnographic Coll* Dr Torben Monberg; *Keeper Coll Classical Antiquities* Dr M L Buhl; *Keeper Royal Coll of Coins & Medals* Otto Morkholm; *Keeper Open-air Museum at Sorgenfri* P Michelsen
Estab 1807. Consists of ten divisions

M **NY CARLSBERG GLYPTOTHEK,** Carlsberg Gallery, Dantes Plads. *Dir* L Johonsen; *Cur French & Danish Art* H E Norregaard Nielsen; *Cur Greek & Roman Art* J Christiansen; *Cur Greek & Roman Art* M Moltesen

Open summer daily 10 AM - 4 PM, winter Tues - Fri Noon - 3 PM, Sun 10 AM - 4 PM, cl Mon all year. Admis 5 kroner, Wed & Sun free. Estab 1897. Average Annual Attendance: 155,000

Collections: †Danish and †French Paintings and Sculptures from 19th Century; †Egyptian, †Etruscan, †Greek and †Roman Sculpture

L **Library,** Dantes Plads.
Reference library
Library Holdings: Vols 35,000

STATENS MUSEUM FOR KUNST

M **Department of Painting and Sculpture,** Solvgade 1307. Tel 01 11 21 26. *Dir*; *Chief Cur* Bente Skovgaard; *Cur* Hanne Westergaard; *Cur* Olaf Koester; *Asst* Marianne Brons; *Acting for Chief Restorer* Henrik Bjerre; *Restorer* Lone Bogh

Open 10 AM - 5 PM, Wed 10 AM - 8 PM, cl Mon. No admis fee. Estab 1896 to collect, conserve, examine and publish Danish painting and sculpture and foreign (mostly west-European) painting and sculpture. Average Annual Attendance: 200,000

Income: Financed by endowment and state appropriation

Purchases: $750,000
Collections: †Old, Modern and Contemporary Danish Art; †Old and Modern French Art; †Old Dutch, Flemish and Italian Art (mostly painting); †Scandinavian Art
Exhibitions: (1979) Children's Drawings; Kalejdoskop 1979; Arthur Köpcke; Salut for Bournonville; Sigurd Swane
Publications: Kunstmuseets Arsskrift (the Royal Museum of Fine Arts Yearbook)
Activities: Lect open to public; concerts; gallery talks; tours; individual paintings and original objects of art lent to other museums and collections; lending collection contains 200 phonorecords; sales shop sells prints, slides, catalogs and posters

L **Department of Painting and Sculpture Library,** Solvgade 1307. *Cur* Dr Harald P Olsen
Reference library open to public
Library Holdings: Vols 50,000; Per subs 150; Other—Exhibition and auction catalogs, documentary newspaper clippings

M **Den Kongelige Kobberstiksamling,** Department of Prints and Drawings, Solvgade DK-1307. Tel 01 11 21 26. *Keeper* Erik Fischer; *Asst Keeper* Jan Garff; *Asst Keeper* Jan Würtz Frandsen
Open 10 AM - 3 PM, Wed 10 AM - 6 PM, cl Mon. No admis fee. Estab 1835 to collect, conserve, examine and publish prints and drawings
Income: $1800
Collections: N A Abildgaard (drawings); Povl Christensen, one-man show; Danish Drawings of All Times; Greenlandic Prints and Drawings from Older Times; Palle Nielsen - Orfeus Under Way; Posada (prints); 10 Years Acquisitions, 1969-79, (prints and drawings); Three Young Danish Draughtsmen: Birthe Kronkvist, Karin Birgitte Lund and Erling Jorgensen; one-man show
Publications: Exhibition catalogs
Activities: Sales shop sells prints, slides, catalogs and posters

L **Department of Prints and Drawings Library,** Solvgade, DK-1307. *Librn* Marianne Rorup
Reference library
Library Holdings: Vols 38,841; Per subs 47
Special Subjects: Art on paper
Collections: W Gernsheim's Corpus Photographicum of Drawings; 20th Century Illustrated Books, mainly French with original prints
Publications: Catalogs of auctions and exhibitions

M **THORVALDSEN MUSEUM,** Porthusgade 2, 1213 K. Tel 01 121532. *Mayor* Bent Nebelong; *Dir* Dr Dyveke Helsted; *Cur* Dr Bjarne Jornaes; *Cur Archaeology* Dr Torben Melander; *Cur Education* Dr Eva Henschen
Open May - Sept daily 10 AM - 4 PM, Oct - April 10 AM - 3 PM, cl Tues during winter months. No admis fee. Opened to public 1848 as a museum for the works of the sculptor Bertel Thorvaldsen (1770-1844) and for his collections. Museum was built from 1839 - 1848 by the young architect, M G Bindesboll, whom Thorvaldsen had chosen and who created a very untraditional building. He used strong colours, both in the ochre yellow facades, decorated by the painter Jorgen Sonne with a frieze depicting Thorvaldsen's return to Copenhagen in 1838, and in the interior where changing wall colors, ceilings with polychrome Pompeian motifs, and tesselated terracotta floors form the background to Thorvaldsen's white marbel sculptures. Average Annual Attendance: 70,000
Income: 4,000,000 DKr (financed by city appropriation)
Collections: Greek, Etruscan and Roman bronzes, gems, marbles and vases; 19th Century European Paintings and Drawings; Sculpture and Drawings by Thorvaldsen
Exhibitions: (1978-79) N A Abildgaard; John Flaxman - Mythology and Industry
Publications: Bulletin
Activities: Educ dept; didactic activities for children; lect open to public, 5 - 10 visiting lectr per year; concerts; tours in English, German and Danish; individual paintings and original objects of art lent to museums; museum shop sells books, reproductions, prints, slides catalogues, posters and copies in Parian ware

L **Bibliotek,** Porthusgade 2, 1213 K.
Open May - Sept 10 AM - 4 PM, Oct - April 10 AM - 3 PM. Reference library for students
Library Holdings: Vols 5000; AV—Slides; Other—Exhibition catalogs, framed reproductions, manuscripts, pamphlets, photographs
Special Subjects: Neoclassical and Romantic art

HUMLEBAEK

M **LOUISIANA MUSEUM OF MODERN ART,** Gammel Strandvej 13. Tel 03-190719. *Dir* Knud W Jensen; *Dir* Borge Hansen; *Cur* Hugo Arne Buch; *Cur* Hans Erik Wallin
Open 10 AM - 5 PM. Admis 10 Danish kroner. Estab 1958 to introduce new trends in modern art from all over the world to a Danish public. Average Annual Attendance: 300,000. Mem: 20,000; dues firms 300 Danish kroner, couples 115 Danish kroner, individual 93 Danish kroner
Income: Financed by endowment, membership, city and state appropriation
Collections: Modern Art from 1950, including Sculpture—Arp, Max Bill, Calder, Cesar, Max Ernst, Gabo, Giacometti, Ipousteguy, Kienholz, Laurens, Henry Moore, Richier, Sekine, Tinguely. Painting—Albers, Alechinsky, Bacon, Corneille, Dine, Dubuffet, Fontana, Sam Francis, Herbin, Hundertwasser, Jorn, Kelly, Klein, Lichtenstein, Louis, Morley, Noldand, Tapies, Warhol
Exhibitions: (1978-80) Art from Mesopotamia; Soto and Hantai; Mark Boyle; Children are a People; Crex Collection; Sekine and Lee U Fan; Sam Francis; Günther Grass Etchings; Kienholz; McCrory Collection (constructivists); Christo Running Fence; Outsiders; Pompeji AD 79; Surrealists from Moma, NY; Warhol
Publications: Louisiana Klubben, 4 per year; Louisiana Revy, 3 per Year
Activities: Concerts; theater; performances; sales shop sells books, magazines, reproductions, prints and slides

ECUADOR

QUITO

M **NATIONAL MUSEUM OF COLONIAL ART OF THE CASA DE LA CULTURA EDUCATORIANA,** Calles Cuenca y Mejia 915. Tel 212-297. *Dir* Carlos Rodriquez
Open Tues - Sun 10 AM - 1 PM and 3 - 6 PM, cl Mon. Admis 5 sucres. Founded 1914 the museum is of authentic colonial style, dating from the 17th Century. Its first owner was Marquis of Villacis; its last owner was Dr Angel Saenz, who sold the building to the government of Dr Carlos Arroyo del Rie. The building was restored by the Ministry of Public Works, under the direction of the painter Nicolas Delgade, who was its director in 1944. Museum has two floors, first floor contains works from the 19th century; second floor, halls and galleries contain works from the 17th and 18th Centuries. Average Annual Attendance: 2400. Mem: 10; dues 454,800 sucres
Income: 33,000 sucres (financed by state appropriation)
Collections: Collections date from the 18th Century
Publications: Museum guide
Activities: Individual paintings and original objects of art lent to Ministries and institutions; museum shop sells slides

EGYPT

ALEXANDRIA

M **GRECO-ROMAN MUSEUM,** Museum St. *Dir* Yousseff El Ghiriani
Estab 1892. Average Annual Attendance: 88,000
Income: 18,000 Egyptian pounds
Collections: Exhibits from the Coptic, Greek and Roman eras
Publications: Annual Report

L **Library,** Museum St. *Librn* Lalla Halim Nessim; *Librn* Nadia Sayed Sidky; *Librn* Samira Hanafy Mahmoud
Open 9 AM - 1:30 PM. Estab 1892 for university and archeological studies
Library Holdings: Vols 12,000; Other—Exhibition catalogs, prints, manuscripts, memorabilia, original art works, pamphlets, photographs, reproductions, sculpture
Special Subjects: Archeological and historical books on Greek Roman Epocs in Alexandria
Collections: Filologia Numismatica; Journal Expedition; Omar Tosson: A Gift from the Egyptian Prince

CAIRO

M **COPTIC MUSEUM,** Masr Ateeka. *Dir* Mounir Basta
Open daily & holidays 9 AM - 4 PM. Estab 1910
Collections: Architecture, bone, ebony, frescos, glass, icons, ivory, manuscripts, metalwork, pottery, sculpture, textiles, woodcarvings
Publications: Catalogs for some of the manuscripts; guides; one vol work covering the principal churches of Cairo

L **Library,** Masr Ateeka.
Library Holdings: Vols 7000

M **EGYPTIAN MUSEUM,** Sh Selim Hassan. *Dir General of Museum* Dr Dia Abou-Ghazi; *Dir* Mohammed A Mohsen; *First Sub-Dir* Dr Moh Saleh; *Sub-Dir* Mrs Saniyeh Abd el Saniyeh Abd el Aal; *Sub-Dir* Mrs Mahasen Nassar; *First Cur* Abd el-Hadi el Nhaff
Open daily 9 AM - 4 PM, Fri 9 - 11:30 AM and 1:30 - 4 PM. Admis PT 100. Estab 1858, present building 1902. The ground floor contains objects arranged chronologically according to ancient Etyptian history; the first floor is arranged according to categories. Average Annual Attendance: 50,000
Income: $1,000,000 (financed by state appropriation)
Collections: Ancient Egyptian Art - Pahraonic Period, Hellenistic and Roman Periods; Complete sets of Jewelry, Papyrus and Coins from tombs - Hemaka tomb, Tutankhamen, Yuya and Thuya
Exhibitions: The Egyptian Museum in 1955-75
Publications: Catalogue General du Musee; sets on excavations
Activities: Classes for children; dramatic programs; docent training; lect open to public; originate traveling exhibitions; museum shop sells books, magazines, original art, reproductions, prints and slides

L **Library,** Sh Mariette Pacha. *Dir* Dr Dia Abou-Ghazi
Open daily 9:30 AM - 1:30 PM, Fri 9 - 11 AM, cl Mon. Estab 1858 as a reference library to serve the staff of the antiquities service and those studying ancient civilizations
Income: $12,500 (financed by state appropriation)
Library Holdings: Vols 35,800; Per subs 100
Special Subjects: Ancient civilizations up to the Middle Ages
Publications: Annales du Service des Antiquites, annually, supplements; Catalogue de la Bibliotheque

ENGLAND

BATH

M **AMERICAN MUSEUM IN BRITAIN,** Claverton Manor. *Dir & Cur* Ian McCallum; *Deputy Dir* John Huitson
Open April - Oct Tues - Sun 2 - 5 PM, cl Mon. Admis adults L1.20, senior citizens

and children L1, grounds only 40p. Estab 1961 to fulfill a desire to increase Anglo-American understanding and to interpret the history and arts of the United States. Museum has 18 period furnished rooms from 17th - 19th Centuries, and a folk art gallery. Average Annual Attendance: 97,000
Publications: America in Britain, 3 per year
Activities: Classes for children; lect open to public, 20 visiting lectr per year; concerts; gallery talks; tours; individual paintings and original objects of art lent to The John Judkyn Memorial; originate traveling exhibitions; museum shop sells books and slides
L **Library,** Claverton Manor. *Librn* Margaret Irwin
Open for reference to students

BIRMINGHAM

M **BIRMINGHAM MUSEUMS AND ART GALLERY,** Chamberlain Square. Tel 021 235-2834. *Dir* Dennis Farr; *Asst Dir* J J Henderson; *Dir Science Museum* P Robinson; *Keeper Applied Art* Glennys Wild; *Keeper Archaeology* John Ruffle; *Keeper Conservation* G S Learmonth; *Keeper Fine Art* Richard Lockett; *Keeper Natural History* Dr Brian Abell Seddon; *Publications Mgr* J T Jones; *Museum Education Officer* A Meredith
Open Mon - Sat 10 AM - 5:30 PM, Sun 2 - 5:30 PM. No admis fee. Estab 1867 to display collections to the public. Museum has 13 picture galleries; 30 galleries for archaeology and natural history, applied arts; administers 6 branch museums: Museum of Science and Industry, Aston Hall, Blakestery Hall, Sasehole Mill, Webley Castle, Nature Centre. Average Annual Attendance: 650,000. Mem: 1000; dues L 3
Income: L 684,000 (financed by city and state appropriation)
Purchases: L 15,000
Collections: Branch Museums Collections; applied arts - †ceramics, costume, silver, textiles; †paintings and drawings from 15th Century to present including important collection of Pre-Raphaelite Works
Exhibitions: (1980) 16 temporary exhibitions, including: Drawings from Polish Museums; English Watercolours and Drawings - The J Leslie Wright Bequest; Ingres Drawings; William Morris; Pre-Raphaelite Drawings
Publications: Gallery Diary - a monthly list of events
Activities: Classes for adults and children; lect open to public, 20 visiting lectr per year; concerts; gallery talks; tours; individual paintings and original objects of art lent to museums and galleries; book traveling exhibitions; originate traveling exhibitions; museum shop sells books, magazines, original art, reproductions, prints, slides

BRIGHTON

M **ROYAL PAVILION, ART GALLERY AND MUSEUMS,** Church St. Tel 273-603005. *Dir* John Morley
Open daily Oct - June 10 AM - 5 PM, July - Oct 10 AM - 7:30 PM. Admis adults L1 - L1.50, children 40 - 55p. Built in its present form in 1822 as the seaside palace of the Prince Regent. Average Annual Attendance: 400,000
Income: Financed by Brighton Borough Council
Collections: Magnificent interiors in Chinese, with regency furniture and works of art of the period
Publications: Illustrated Guide Book
M **Art Gallery and Museum,** Church St.
Open Tues - Sat 10 AM - 5:45 PM, Sun 2 - 5 PM, cl Mon. No admis fee. Museum built in 1808, opened in 1873; gallery estab 1851. Average Annual Attendance: 200,000
Collections: The Willett Collection of Ceramics; archaeology, English watercolours, ethnology, ethnography, important collection of art nouveau and art deco, old master paintings
Activities: Classes for adults; lect open to public, gallery talks; tours; museum shop sells books, magazines, reproductions, prints and slides
M **Grange Art Gallery and Museum,** The Green. *Keeper* M Waller
Open Thurs - Sat & Mon, Tues 10 AM - 5 PM, Sun 2 - 5 PM, cl Good Friday, Christmas and Boxing Day. No admis fee. Estab 1954 as a branch museum and art gallery administered by Brighton Borough Council
Income: Financed by Brighton Borough Council
Collections: Books, Illustrations and Letters of Rudyard Kipling; †selection of toys from National Toy Museum Collection; Sussex Room - local history
Publications: Guide to Kipling Room
Activities: museum shop
M **Thomas-Stanford Museum, Preston Manor,** Preston Park BN1 6SD. Tel 273-552101.
Open Wed - Sat 10 AM - 5 PM, Sun 2 - 5 PM, cl Good Friday, Chirstmas and Boxing Day. Admis adults 50p, senior citizens 45p, children 30p. Estab 1933. The Georgian and Edwardian house, the home of the Stanford family, was given to Brighton Corporation on the understanding that the fine furniture, paintings, etc, would be displayed in their period settings as they were in the donor's lifetime. Furnished country house with small collections of fine silver, paintings, books, glass and Chinese porcelain Dogs of Fo. Average Annual Attendance: 13,000
Income: Financed by Brighton Borough Council
Collections: The MacQuoid Bequest of Fine Furniture, Paintings and Silver; Original 16th Century Spanish Leather wall hangings; books relating to Sussex and archival material; ceramics, furniture (16th - 19th Centuries), glass, paintings, silver
Exhibitions: Children and Food; Toys of War - A Pacifist's Approach
Publications: Preston Manor Guide
L **Preston Manor Library**
Open for reference to students upon application to Keeper
Library Holdings: Vols 500
Special Subjects: Archives relating to Sussex, books about Sussex or written by men born in Sussex, books by John Selden
Collections: John Selden Collection

BRISTOL

M **CITY ART GALLERY,** Queen's Rd. Tel 272 299971. *Dir* A D P Wilson; *Cur Applied Art* E C Witt; *Asst Cur Applied Art* K Walton; *Cur Fine Art* F W Greenacre; *Cur Oriental Art* P Hardie; *Conservator Prints & Watercolors* B Boyd
Open Mon - Sat 10 AM - 5 PM. Estab 1905
Income: Financed by city appropriation
Collections: †Bristol porcelain and glass; †English pottery, porcelain, silver, glass, furniture; †Paintings, drawings, sculpture, British and Continental 13th - 20th Century; †Schiller Collection of Oriental ceramics, glass and metalwork
Exhibitions: Circulating exhibitions from Arts Council and others
Publications: Abstracts, quarterly; exhibition catalogs and guides
Activities: Lect open to public; concerts; book traveling exhibitions
M **Red Lodge,** Park Row. Tel 272 299771.
A 16th Century mansion, panelled interiors and period furnishings
M **Georgian House,** Park St, Clifton. Tel 272 299771.
Open 10 AM - 5 PM, cl Sun. No admis fee. Estab 1937, a period house (18th Century) exhibiting paintings and decorative arts from the collection of the City art Gallery, based on the date 1790, but including some earlier examples. Average Annual Attendance: 31,000
Income: Financed by city appropriation
Collections: Bristol-made Furniture and Porcelain; Pastels by James Sharples; 18th Century furniture and paintings, works of art made in Bristol
Activities: Sales shop sells books and postcards

CAMBRIDGE

M **UNIVERSITY OF CAMBRIDGE,** Fitzwilliam Museum, Trumpington St. *Dir* A M Jaffe; *Keeper Coins & Medals* G Pollard; *Keeper Antiquities* R Nicholls; *Keeper Applied Arts* R Crighton; *Keeper Manuscripts & Printed Books* P Woudhuysen; *Keeper Paintings & Drawings* D Robinson; *Keeper Prints* E Chamberlain; *Keeper Admin* J Huskinson
Open Tues - Sat 10 AM - 5 PM, Sun 2:15 - 5 PM. Estab 1816 to collect, research and exhibit works of art. Average Annual Attendance: 190,000
Income: Financed by University
Collections: European ceramics; Oriental works of art; antiquities, arms and armour, coins, drawings, furniture, illuminated manuscripts, manuscripts, paintings, prints, sculpture, textiles
Exhibitions: Changing exhibitions
Publications: Annual Report; catalogues of permanent collection and exhibitions
Activities: Lect open to public; concerts; gallery talks; tours; original objects of art lent to museums; museum shop sells books, reproductions, prints and slides
L **Department of Manuscripts and Printed Books,** Trumpington St. *Librn* P Woudhuysen
Estab 1816 to collect illuminated manuscripts, historical manuscripts and rare books. Open for reference by appointment only
Income: Financed by University
Library Holdings: Vols 140,000; Per subs 250; Micro—Reels; Other—Exhibition catalogs, manuscripts, memorabilia, original art works, pamphlets, photographs, original documents
Collections: Illuminated manuscripts, incunabula, letters, literary manuscripts, manuscript music, private press books, rare books of all periods
Exhibitions: The Art of the Book: Morris and After

CUMBRIA

M **ABBOT HALL ART GALLERY,** Kendal. Tel 0539 22464. *Pres* P F Scott; *VPres* R S Boumphrey; *Secy* G C Whitwham; *Dir* M E Burkett; *Deputy Dir* V A J Slowe; *Cur* J Anstee; *Gallery Secy* J Harvey
Open Mon - Fri 10:30 AM - 5:30 PM, Sat & Sun 2 - 5 PM. Admis adults 35p, retired people 20p, children 10p. Estab 1962. Built by Carr of York in 1759; ground floor has 18th Century furnished rooms, paintings by Romney, Ruskin, Turner, porcelain, silver and glass; upper floor has modern galleries for changing exhibitions. Average Annual Attendance: 35,873. Mem: 950; dues life L75, individuals L3
Income: Financed by endowment, membership, city and county appropriations, Arts Council Grant, local authorities
Purchases: L2000
Collections: †18th Century paintings and furniture; †18th Century porcelain and glass; †Sculpture by Hans Arp, Barbara Hepworth; †work by contemporary artists including Ben Nicholson, Kurt Schwitters
Exhibitions: (1978-79) The Art of the Feltmaker; The Barbers of Winster; The Cooper Family; L S Lowry: Paintings and Drawings
Publications: Pamphlets on some aspects of collections and exhibitions; quarterly magazine
Activities: Educ dept for school visits; classes for adults and children; lect open to public, 10 visiting lectr per year; gallery talks; tours; individual paintings, original objects of art lent to local colleges, universities, hotels, galleries, exhibitions, firms, and private individuals; lending collection contains framed reproductions, Kodachromes, 200 motion pictures, nature artifacts, 200 original art works, original prints, paintings, photographs, sculpture and slides; originate traveling exhibitions; museum shop sells books, magazines, original art from exhibitions, reproductions, prints, slides; craft shop sells items produced by local craftsmen
L **Library,** Kendal.
Open 10:30 AM - 5:30 PM. Estab 1963. For research by staff; researchers on application
Library Holdings: Vols 1000; Per subs 5; Other—Clipping files, exhibition catalogs, pamphlets, photographs

DEVON

L DARTINGTON COLLEGE OF ARTS, Library and Resources Centre, Totnes. *Librn* Timothy B Giles; *Asst Librn* Elizabeth J Grove; *Asst Librn* Rosemary B Burn
Open Term Mon - Fri 9:30 AM - 10 PM, Sat & Sun 1:30 - 6:30 PM, vacation Mon - Fri 9:30 AM - 5 PM. Estab 1974 to serve the needs of the courses in art & design, theatre and music run by the college
Library Holdings: Vols 30,000; Per subs 100; Micro—Reels; AV—A-tapes, cassettes, motion pictures, rec, slides, v-tapes; Other—Original art works
Special Subjects: Crafts, Film, Photography, Theatre Arts, Art and design (especially 20th Century), music (including ethnic and folk), music therapy
Collections: Collection associated with the Arts and the Handicapped; Dartington Collection of ethnic and folk artefacts, with emphasis on textiles, some musical instruments; The Dartington Hall Trust collection of paintings including some by Rabindranath Tagore and Mark Tobey
Exhibitions: 6 per year on material in the Dartington Collection and loans

DONCASTER

M DONCASTER MUSEUM AND ART GALLERY, Chequer Rd. Tel 0302-62095, 60814.
Open daily 10 AM - 5 PM, Sun 2 - 5 PM. No admis fee. Estab 1908. Average Annual Attendance: 100,000
Income: Financed by city appropriation
Purchases: $40,000
Collections: †European painting, ceramics and †glass, silver and jewelry
Exhibitions: Masterpieces of European Art; monthly changing exhibitions on art and historical topics
Publications: List available on application, books and postcards
Activities: Classes for children; lect, 10 visiting lect per year; concerts; gallery talks; original objects of art lent to museums and galleries; museum shop sells books and reproductions

EXETER

O UNIVERSITY OF EXETER, American Arts Documentation Centre, Queens Building. Tel 0392-77911, Ext 431. *Dir* Dr Mick Gidley; *Secy* Angela Day
Estab 1970 to provide information by correspondence on the literary, visual and other arts of the United States, including the publication of study aids and the circulation of exhibitions
Exhibitions: Traveling exhibitions: American Photographs of the Late 1960's; Indian Photographs by Edward S Curtis
Publications: American Arts Pamphlet Series
Activities: Originate traveling exhibitions

HANLEY

M STOKE-ON-DISTRICT COUNCIL, City Museum and Art Gallery, Broad St. Tel 29611, Ext 2258. *Dir* A R Mountford; *Town Clerk* S W Titchener; *Design & Display Officer* Mrs R S Hurt; *Keeper of Archaeology* S J Greaves; *Keeper of Ceramics* M R Parkinson; *Keeper of Decorative Art* Mrs S A Bradbury; *Keeper of Fine Art* P F Vigurs; *Keeper of Natural History* G Halfpenny; *Keeper of Social History* J H Kelly
Open Mon - Sat 10:30 AM - 5 PM, Wed 10:30 AM - 8 PM. No admis fee. Estab 1846 to collect and conserve ceramics, natural history, social history and archaeological material relating to the County of Staffordshire. One of the major provincial Museums in the United Kingdom - the first to be built since World War II; closed for past four years to facilitate building program
Collections: One of the finest collections of English Ceramics in the world, pre-eminent in Staffordshire ware
Publications: Annual Report of the City of Stoke-on-Trent Museum Archaeological Society; Journal of Ceramic History
Activities: Lect open to public, one visiting lectr per year; gallery talks; tours; museum shop sells books, prints, slides, postcards, greeting cards, keyrings, badges, posters, notelets and mugs

LEEDS

M LEEDS ART GALLERIES, Temple Newsam House. Tel 0532 647321, 641358. *Dir* Robert Rowe; *Principal Keeper* Christopher Gilbedt
Admis Temple Newsam House & Lotherton Hall 50p, Art Gallery no admis fee. Estab 1888 for local authority art gallery. Temple Newsam House and Lotherton Hall of Leeds Art Galleries are County House Museums of Decorative Art; the Art Gallery displays Fine Art. Average Annual Attendance: 200,000
Purchases: $100,000
Collections: Art Gallery - †Old Masters and modern paintings, †prints, †sculpture and †watercolours; Temple Newsam - †County House ceramics, †paintings, †silver, †tapestries circa 1500 - 1800; Lutherton Hall - †19th Century Decorative Arts, †contemporary fashion, †modern crafts, †Oriental ceramics
Publications: Leeds Arts Calendar, bi-monthly
Activities: Classes for adults and children; docent training; university teaching; lect open to public, one lectr per year; concerts; gallery talks; tours; competitions of pottery and textile design; awards; individual paintings, original objects of art and print lent to galleries; lending collection contains color reproductions, 300 original prints, paintings; museum shop sells books, original art, reproductions, prints and slides

LEICESTER

M LEICESTERSHIRE MUSEUMS, ART GALLERIES AND RECORDS SERVICE, Leicestershire Museum and Art Gallery, 96 New Walk. Tel 0533-554100. *Dir of Museums and Art Galleries* Patrick J Boylan; *Asst Dir Arts* N A Pegden; *Keeper of Decorative Arts* P M Inder; *Keeper of Fine Art* Mrs R M Paisey
Open Mon - Sat 10 AM - 5:30 PM, Sun 2 - 5:30 PM. No admis fee. Estab 1846 as regional museum and art gallery. Original building 1836; extended 1876-1930; reconstructed and modernized internally, including installation of full air conditioning 1975-1979. Average Annual Attendance: 150,000
Income: $1,300,000 (financed by city appropriation)
Purchases: $67,000
Collections: Major special collections include †British Art, †German Impressionism and Expressionism (largest public collection in Britain); European Art from Renaissance to present; Oriental Decorative Arts; †contemporary art
Exhibitions: German Expressionism; Great Victorian Pictures: Their Paths to Fame; Rodrigo Moynihan Restrospective; various one-man shows by contemporary British artists
Publications: Catalogues of special collections; Leicestershire Museums Record, annually
Activities: Classes for adults and children; holiday activities; concerts; Honorary Associate award for distinguished voluntary service to Museums; museum shop sells books, reproductions, prints and slides
L Library, 96 New Walk.
Open Mon - Sat 10 AM - 5:30 PM, Sun 2 - 5:30 PM. Estab 1880 for staff research and public reference
Purchases: $15,000
Library Holdings: Vols 10,000; Per subs 80; AV—Kodachromes, lantern Slides, slides, v-tapes; Other—Clipping files, exhibition catalogs, prints, pamphlets, photographs, reproductions

LINCOLN

M LINCOLNSHIRE MUSEUMS, USHER GALLERY, Lindum Rd. Tel 522 27980. *Dir* Antony J H Gunstone; *Keeper of Art* Richard H Wood
Open Mon - Sat 10 AM - 5:30 PM, Sun 2:30 - 5 PM. No admis fee. Estab 1927 to house the collection of decorative art material formed by a local jeweller James Ward Usher. Average Annual Attendance: 70,000
Collections: Topographical Paintings of Lincolnshire; James Ward Usher Collection; Watercolour by Peter de Wint; ceramics, coins, glass, silver
Exhibitions: Sally Beaumont (paintings and drawings); Peter Brannan (paintings and drawings); Michael Carlo (prints); Cinzano Glass Collection; John Gray (paintings and drawings); Max and Jill Marschner (prints and tapestries); Regional Fine Art Exhibition; Russian Graphic Art
Activities: Individual paintings and original objects of art lent to subscribers; Friends of Lincoln Libraries, Museums and Art Gallery

LIVERPOOL

M WALKER ART GALLERY, Merseyside County Council, William Brown St. Tel 051-227-5234. *Dir* Timothy J Stevens; *Keeper British Art* Mary G Bennett; *Keeper Foreign Art* Edward S Morris; *Admin Officer* M J Lindop; *Education Officer* F J Milner
Open Mon - Fri 10 AM - 5 PM, Sun 2 - 5 PM. Estab 1871 for the conservation and display of the permanent collection; and for organization of loan exhibitions. Gallery is comprised of some 17 display galleries, restoration studio, office accommodation, education room and workshop. Average Annual Attendance: 200,000
Income: Financed by state appropriation
Purchases: $509,360
Collections: European drawings, painting, prints, sculpture, watercolors 1300 - present, including notable collections of Italian and Netherlandish painting 1300 - 1600, 19th Century British painting
Exhibitions: (1979-80) John Moores and Peter Moores
Publications: Annual report and bulletin
Activities: Classes for children; lect open to public, 2 visiting lectr per year; gallery talks; tours; originate traveling exhibitions; museum shop sells books, magazines, reproductions, prints and slides
L Library, William Brown St.
Reference library open to public by appointment
Library Holdings: Vols 10,000

LONDON

L BRITISH LIBRARY, Reference Division, Great Russell St. Tel 01-636 1544. *Chmn British Library Board* Fred Dainton; *Chief Executive* H T Hookway; *Dir General Reference Division* A Wilson
Galleries open Mon - Sat 10 AM - 5 PM, Sun 2:30 - 6 PM, Reading Room open Mon, Fri & Sat 9 AM - 5 PM, Tues - Thurs 9 AM - 9 PM. Admis for research to the Public Reading Rooms is by ticket. Estab 1795 as the British Museum Library; name changed 1973; the organization's purpose is to make its 10 million books and manuscripts available to readers in the reading rooms; to have photographic and other services available; and to run exhibitions. Library maintains four galleries of printed books and manuscripts. Average Annual Attendance: 550,000
Income: $28,000,000
Library Holdings: Vols 10,000,000; Other—charters and rolls 85,000, detached seals and casts of seals 18,000, Egyptian papyri 3100, Greek and Latin papyri 3100, Oriental manuscripts 37,100 vols, Western manuscripts 81,600 vols
Publications: The British Library Journal, six monthly; exhibition catalogue; numerous catalogues and books
Activities: Lect open to public; tours; book shop

M BRITISH MUSEUM, Great Russell St. *Dir* D M Wilson
Open Mon - Sat 10 AM - 5 PM and 2:30 - 6 PM. No admis fee. Estab 1753. It is the national museum of archaeology and antiquity, showing the works of man from all over the world from pre-history to comparatively modern times. Average Annual Attendance: 4,000,000
Collections: Egyptian, Greek and Roman Prehistoric and Romano-British, Western Asiatic; coins and medals; prints and drawings; Oriental ethnography
Exhibitions: (1980) American Prints 1879-1979; Asante: Kingdom of Gold; The Ancient Olympic Games; African Textiles; Kiln Sites of Ancient China The Vikings; changing exhibitions

Publications: Exhibition programme available upon request
Activities: Lect open to public; films; gallery talks

M **COURTAULD INSTITUTE GALLERIES,** Woburn Square. Tel 580 1015. *Dir* Peter Lasko; *Cur Coll* Philip Troutman; *Asst to Cur* Suzanne Alexander; *Academic Asst* William Bradford
Open Mon - Sat 10 AM - 5 PM, Sun 2 - 5 PM. No admis fee. Estab 1958. Galleries are a department of the Courtauld Institute of Art, London University. They have on permanent exhibition the collections of the Courtauld Institute and provide temporary exhibitions. One floor with natural overhead lighting; paintings not glazed; the collections arranged chronologically. Average Annual Attendance: 110,000
Income: Financed through London University
Collections: Samuel Courtauld Collection of French Impressionist and Post-Impressionist Paintings (Cezanne, Degas, Gauguin, Manet, Monet, Pissarro, Renoir, Seurat, Sisley, Toulouse-Lautrec, Van Gogh); The Roger Fry Collection of French and English, Early 20th Century; The Gambier-Parry Collection of Old Master Paintings and other works of art (mainly Italian Primitives, 14th and 15th Century, Fra Angelico, Bernardo Daddi, Lorenzo Monaco, verrocchi); The Lord Lee of Fareham Collection of European Old Master Paintings (Botticelli, Cranach, Rubens, Simon Martni, Veronese, to Gainsborough and Goya)
Exhibitions: Bulgarian Icons; Drawings by Guercino and the Baroque Masters; Dutch Drawings from the Witt Collection, II - other than landscape; English Landscape Watercolours, The Graphic Work of Felix Vallotton; Otto Gutfreund: Sculptures and Drawings; Augustus John: Composition Studies; Spanish Drawings from the Witt Collection; Watercolours from the Witt Collection; Watercolours, Drawings and Engravings from the Courtauld Collection
Activities: Lect open to public; gallery talks; tours; individual paintings and original objects of art lent to other museums; museum shop sells books, magazines, reproductions, prints, slides and catalogues of exhibitions

M **DULWICH PICTURE GALLERY,** College Rd.
Admis 2. Estab to display the Dulwich College Art Collection for public benefit; representative of many of the most famous schools and painters of 17th Century Europe, with additional works from 18th Century English, French and Venetian masters. Average Annual Attendance: 18,000
Collections: Alleyn; Bourgeois; Cartwright; Linley; Fairfax Murray; collections from 1626 onwards, gallery 1815
Activities: Sales shop sells books, reproductions, prints and slides

M **NATIONAL GALLERY,** Trafalgar Square. Tel 01-839-2231. *Dir* Michael Levey; *Keeper* Allan Braham; *Scientific Adviser* Garry Thomson; *Chief Restorer* Martin Wylo; *Public Manager* Gordon Booth
Open Mon - Sat 10 AM - 6 PM, Sun 2 - 6 PM. No admis fee. Estab 1824 to house the national permanent collection of Western European painting (circa 1300 to circa 1900). Main floor galleries have 46 exhibition rooms and the lower floor galleries, 10 exhibition rooms. Average Annual Attendance: 2,500,000
Income: Financed by state appropriation and trust funds
Purchases: $1,730,000
Collections: Principal schools, British, Dutch, Early Netherlandish, French, German, Italian; Western European Painting circa 1300 to circa 1900
Exhibitions: Art in 17th Century Holland; Late Gothic Art from Cologne; Painting in Focus Series; many smaller exhibitions
Publications: National Gallery News, monthly
Activities: Classes for adults and children; lect open to public; gallery talks; museum shop sells books, magazines, reproductions, prints, slides, photographs and postcards

M **NATIONAL PORTRAIT GALLERY,** St Martin's Place. Tel Britain 01-930-1552. *Dir* John Hayes; *Deputy Dir* Richard Ormond; *Asst Keeper* John Kerslake; *Asst Keeper* Colin Ford; *Asst Keeper* Robin Gibson; *Education Officer* Angela Cox; *Admins* Roger Aylward; *Archive & Library* Sarah Wimbush; *Archive & Library* Elspeth Evans; *Display* Caroline Brown; *Ed* Mary Pettman; *Education* Eilean Hooper-Greenhill; *Exhib* Jacquie Meredith; *Photographs* Terence Pepper; *Press & Public Relations* Jean Liddiard; *Publications* Roger Sheppard; *Registrar* Kai Kin Yung
Open Mon - Fri 10 AM - 5 PM, Sat 10 AM - 6 PM, Sun 2 - 6 PM. No admis fee. Estab 1856 for collection of likenesses of famous British men and women; to increase space for growing collection. Archive to move to annexe at Carlton House Terrace SW1 in near future. Average Annual Attendance: 450,000
Income: Financed by government funds
Collections: National Collection of portraits from Tudor times to present, including sculpture and photographs; †caricatures, †drawings, †miniatures, †photographs; †printings, †sculpture, †watercolours
Exhibitions: The Great British: Photographs by Arnold Newman; Sir Thomas Lawrence 1769-1830 Paintings and Drawings; People in Camera: The History of Photography 1839-1914; John Singer Sargent and The Edwardian Age
Publications: Catalogues of whole collection; guides to gallery; annual report
Activities: Classes for adults and children; play activities for children; lect open to public, visiting lectr; gallery talks; competitions in conjunction with BBC television program, portrait competition for children; individual paintings and original objects of art lent to museums and galleries; book traveling exhibitions; originate traveling exhibitions; museum shop sells books, reproductions, prints and slides

L **Library,** St Martin's Place. *Asst Keeper Archive & Library* Malcolm Rogers
Estab 1856. Open by appointment only for reference
Library Holdings: Vols 35,000; Micro—Reels; AV—Slides; Other—Clipping files, exhibition catalogs, prints, manuscripts, pamphlets, photographs, reproductions

M **QUEEN'S GALLERY,** Buckingham & St James's Palace, Lord Chamberlain's Office. Tel 930-3007. *Registrar* M E Bishop
Open Tues - Sat 11 AM - 5 PM, Sun 2 - 5 PM, cl Mon except open on bank holidays, entrance on Buckingham Palace Rd. Admis adults 60p, children, students with vaid card, senior citizens 25p. Small gallery where items in the Royal Collection are put on view

M **ROYAL COLLEGE OF ART GALLERY,** Kensington Gore. Tel 01-584-5020. *Rector & VProvost* Richard Guyatt; *Pro-Provost* Cob Sterhan; *Treas* John Crittall; *Registrar* Brian Cooper; *Bursar* Russell Brown
Open 10 AM - 6 PM. No admis fee. Estab 1837, received Royal Charter 1967, for higher education in Art and Design. Various exhibition areas used mainly for students' work
Income: Financed through College
Exhibitions: Annaul Degree Shows; students' works from various departments including ceramics, graphic art, industrial design, painting, photography, sculpture, textiles
Activities: Lect open to public, one visiting lectr per year

L **College Library,** Kensington Gore. *Librn* Hans Brill Ma
Estab 1953 to provide adequate background of reading materials for all college courses and projects; to meet the educational and professional needs of staff and students
Library Holdings: Vols 30,000

M **SOUTH LONDON ART GALLERY,** Peckham Rd. *Deputy Cur* P W Taylor; *Keeper* K Sharpe; *Cur* K A Doughty
Open daily 10 AM - 6 PM, Sun 3 - 6 PM. No admis fee. Estab 1891 as a public gallery for the benefit of the inhabitants of the London Borough of Southwark. Sustained war damage 1941, re-opened 1949 partially restored. A large Victorian exhibition gallery with a glass roof and which is completely lit by daylight. There is approx 221 ft of single line hanging space. Average Annual Attendance: 20,000
Income: $65,000 (financed by city appropriation)
Purchases: $8000
Collections: Contemporary British art; †20th Century original prints; paintings of the Victorian period; †topographical paintings and drawings of local subjects
Exhibitions: African Sculpture from private collections in London; Drawing towards Painting: Samuel Scott (circa 1702-1772); A H Gerrard (retrospective of sculpture, drawings and paintings); A Londoner's London: Grace Golden ARCA 55 Years - a retrospective exhibition; Denys Wells (1881-1973) a retrospective of paintings and drawings
Activities: Classes for children; lect open to public; gallery talks

M **TATE GALLERY,** Millbank. Tel 821 1313, Recorded Information 821 7128. *Dir* Alan Bowness
Open Mon - Sat 10 AM - 6 PM, Sun 2 - 6 PM, cl New Year's Day, Good Friday, May Day Holiday, Christmas Eve, Christmas Day and Boxing Day. Estab 1897 by Sir Henry Tate. Average Annual Attendance: 1,000,000
Collections: Works of Blake, Hogarth, Turner and the Pre-Raphaelites; British painting from the 16th Century to present; modern foreign painting from Impressionism onward; modern sculpture (5500 works in collections and 4000 prints)
Exhibitions: Special exhibitions held regularly throughout year
Publications: Photography and publication of coloured prints and transparencies, photographs, postcards, books and catalogs
Activities: Lect open to public

M **VICTORIA AND ALBERT MUSEUM,** Cromwell Rd. Tel 589 6371. *Dir* Dr Roy Stong; *Keeper Architecture & Sculpture* A Radcliffe; *Keeper Ceramics* J V G Mallet; *Keeper Conservation* Dr J Ashley-Smith; *Keeper Far Eastern Department* J G Ayers; *Keeper Furniture* P K Thornton; *Keeper Indian Art* R Skelton; *Keeper Metalwork* C Blair; *Keeper Museum Services* J Physick; *Keeper Paintings, Prints, Drawings & Photographs* C Kauffman; *Keeper Textiles* D King
Open Mon - Thurs 10 AM - 5:50 PM, Sun 2:30 - 5:50 PM, cl Good Friday, Christmas Day, Christmas Eve, Boxing Day, New Year's Day, May Day Bank Holiday. Estab 1852. Average Annual Attendance: 2,000,000
Collections: †Collections of fine and applied arts of all Countries, periods and styles, including Oriental Art. European collections are mostly post-Classical, architectural details, †art of the book, bronzes, calligraphs, †carpets, †ceramics, †clocks, costumes, †cutlery, †drawings, †embroideries, †enamels, engravings, †fabrics, †furniture, glass, gold and silversmiths' work, ironwork, ivories, †jewelry, lace, lithographs, manuscripts, †metalwork, miniatures, †musical insturments, oil paintings, †posters, †pottery and procelain, †prints, †sculpture, †stained glass, tapestries, †theatre art, vestments, watches, †watercolors, †woodwork
Exhibitions: (1979) The Art of Hollywood - 50 Years of Art Direction; The Doulton Story; Fans from the Past; The Garden; Eileen Gray Designer 1879-1976; Ingres: Drawings from the Musee Ingres at Mortauban and Omen Collections; Masterpieces of Cutlery and the Art of Eating; The Open and Closed Book (contemporary book arts); Treasures of the Print Room; Vienna in the Age of Schubert: The Biedermeiw Interior 1815-1848; The Way We Live Now: Design for Interiors 1950 to present

L **National Art Library,** Cromwell Rd. *Keeper* R W Lightbown
Open Mon - Thurs 10 AM - 5:50 PM, Sat 10 AM - 12:50 PM and 2 - 5:50 PM. Estab 1837 as art historical research for public and museum staff. For reference only
Library Holdings: Vols 750,000; Per subs 1500; Micro—Fiche, reels; Other—Exhibition catalogs, framed reproductions, manuscripts, pamphlets
Special Subjects: Costume Design & Construction, Art of the book, fine and applied arts of all countries and periods, heraldry, Oriential books
Collections: Clements Collection; Dyce and Forster Collection; Piot Collection

M **WALLACE COLLECTION,** Hertford House, Manchester Square. Tel 01-935-0687, 8. *Dir* J A S Ingamells; *Asst to Dir* P Hughes; *Asst to Dir* R J Savill
Open Mon - Sat 10 AM - 5 PM, Sun 2 - 5 PM. No admis fee. Estab 1897, opened as a national museum 1900, to display as appropriately as possible Lady Wallace's great bequest to the nation in the London house of the founders of the collection, the large private mansion of the Marquesses of Hertford and Sir Richard Wallace
Income: Financed by state appropriation, and administered through Trustees
Collections: European and Oriental Arms and Armour; French Furniture; Sevres Porcelain; paintings and works of art of all European schools, especially the French in the 18th Century; goldsmiths' work, miniatures, sculpture
Publications: Booklets, catalogues, guides on the collections
Activities: Sales shop sells catalogues, guides, booklets, prints, slides and postcards

L **Library,** Hertford House, Manchester Square.
Not open to public, and based on the collection

M **WELLINGTON MUSEUM,** Apsley House, 149 Piccadilly. Tel 0904-23839. *Officer in Charge* H V T Percival
Open Mon - Sat 10 AM - 5 PM, Sun 2:30 - 5 PM. No admis fee. Estab 1952 to

display the art collection and personal relics of the first Duke of Wellington (1769-1852) in his town house. House was built 1771-78 from designs by Robert Adam, extensively altered 1828-30 by Benjamin Dean Wyatt. Average Annual Attendance: 100,000

Income: Financed by state appropriation and administered by Victoria and Albert Museum

Collections: Furniture, medals, military orders, paintings, sculpture, services of porcelain, silver plate, snuff boxes, swords, and other personal relics of the first Duke of Wellington

Exhibitions: Permanent exhibition of Political caricatures

Activities: Lect open to public, 12 visiting lectr per year; gallery talks; tours; individual paintings and original objects of art lent to museums and art galleries; sales shop sells books, reproductions and slides

O **WORSHIPFUL COMPANY OF GOLDSMITHS,** Goldsmiths' Hall, Foster Lane. Tel 01-606-8971. *Clerk* Peter Jenkins; *Art Dir* Graham Hughes

Open 10 AM - 5 PM strictly by appointment and usually for people associated with the craft. No admis fee. In existence by 1100, royal charter in 1327, as a guild for craftsmen of gold and silver and as a centre of London hallmarking

Income: Financed by self

Collections: †Antique plate, †Modern silver, jewelry and medals

Exhibitions: Extensive exhibitions of the four collections both in the United Kingdom and abroad

Publications: The Review, annually

Activities: Hallmarking gold, silver and platinum wares; technical advisory service for the trade; artist-craftsmen and students; placing graduate apprentices; lect open to public, once a month; competitions; scholarships; lending collection contains motion pictures, 35mm color slides and photographs

L **Library,** Goldsmiths' Hall, Foster Lane.

Library Holdings: Vols 6000; Other—35mm color slides

MANCHESTER

M **MANCHESTER CITY ART GALLERIES,** Mosley St. *Dir* T P P Clifford; *Keeper Conservation* B Cardy; *Keeper Costume* Jane Tozer; *Keeper Decorative Arts* Open; *Keeper Fine Arts* J B Treuherz; *Keeper Military Coll* P R Russell-Jones

Open Mon - Sat 10 AM - 6 PM, Sun 2:30 - 6 PM. No admis fee. Estab 1882 to educate and entertain the public. City Art Gallery in centre of city and 6 branch galleries in Greater Manchester. Average Annual Attendance: 350,000

Income: Financed by city appropriation

Purchases: $100,000

Collections: †British Art 17th Century; †English costume, †enamels, †silver; †Thomas Greg Collection of English Pottery; Old Master and Dutch 17th Century Painting; †Pre-Raphaelite Painting; †Royal Lancastrian Pottery; †Tylecote Collection of Glass

Exhibitions: Gainsborough in the North West; Victorian High Renaissance; decorative art, furniture and sculpture

Activities: Classes for children; lect open to public; concerts; gallery talks; tours; exten dept serves schools and colleges in Northwest England; artmobile; individual paintings and original objects of art lent to educational institutions; lending collection framed reproductions, 860 original art works, 500 original prints, paintings and sculpture

M **UNIVERSITY OF MANCHESTER,** Whitworth Art Gallery, Whitworth Park. *Dir* C R Dodwell; *Principal Keeper* Francis W Hawcroft; *Asst Keeper Art* Robert Hopper; *Asst Keeper Prints* Michael Clarke; *Keeper of Textiles* Joan Allgrove; *Gallery Services Officer* Sarah Beare; *Exhibitions Officer* Robin Vousden

Open Mon - Sat 10 AM - 5 PM, Thurs 10 AM - 9 PM. No admis fee. Estab 1889 to collect, display and preserve works of art and to arrange special exhibitions. Built in 1890's and extension completed 1908; interior modernized 1960's. In addition to galleries for displaying permanent collections, there are two exhibition galleries, a lecture hall, print room, textile study room and library. Average Annual Attendance: 72,000. Mem: 1000; dues L4

Income: Financed by university and grant towards special exhibitions from the Greater Manchester Council

Purchases: $10,000

Collections: †British drawings and watercolors; †contemporary British paintings and sculpture; †Old Master and modern prints; †textiles, †wallpapers

Exhibitions: William Blake; Historic Hungarian Costume from Budapest; Paintings from Paris; Giovanni Battista Piranesi; Treasures from Chatsworth

Publications: Annual Report, yearly

Activities: Lect open to public, 6 visiting lectr per year; competitions; exten dept serves Greater Manchester County; individual paintings and original objects of art lent to art galleries and museums; lending collection contains framed reproductions, prints, slides, original prints, paintings and photographs; originate traveling exhibitions; sales shop sells reproductions, prints and slides

L **Library,** Whitworth Park.

Open for reference to students and scholars by appointment

Library Holdings: Other—Exhibition catalogues; monographs on art and artist in collection, on textiles, wallpapers and prints

NEWCASTLE UPON TYNE

M **TYNE AND WEAR COUNTY COUNCIL MUSEUMS,** Laing Art Gallery and Museum, Higham Place. Tel 0632 27734. *Dir of County Museums* J M A Thompson; *Cur Lains Art Gallery* Open; *Keeper of Applied Art* Lois Jones; *Keeper of Fine Art* Andrew Greg; *Asst Keeper of Applied Art* Open; *Asst Keeper of Fine Art* Gill Hedley; *Asst Keeper of Costume* Louise Hamer

Open Mon, Wed, Fri & Sat 10 AM - 6 PM, Tues & Thurs 10 AM - 8 PM, Sun 2:30 - 5:30 PM. No admis fee. Estab 1904 to collect and display British fine and applied arts, mount exhibitions, hold lectures, and to encourage art appreciation. Four large picture galleries for British painting; two small new galleries for watercolours etc; silver, glass, pewter and ceramics galleries on second floor. Average Annual Attendance: 100,000

Income: Financed by county appropriation

Collections: †British oil paintings circa 1750-1979; †British prints and watercolours; †British (especially local) ceramics, costume, glass, pewter, silver, etc, of all periods

Exhibitions: (1978) Thomas Berrick; Drawings from the Constauld Institute; Enamel Signs; Federation of Northern Art Societies; John Hilliard; (1979) Comic Books; Graphics of Max Ernst; Lains 75th Anniversary Exhibition; National Exhibition of Children's Art; Newcastle Society of Arts; Printmaking Works; The Shipley Bequest; Sir Joseph Swan Centenary; (1980) The British Art Show

Publications: Exhibition and collection catalogues

Activities: Classes for adults and children; dramatic programs; lect open to public, 6 visiting lectr per year; concerts; gallery talks; tours; picture lending scheme lends 200 framed reproductions, 200 original prints and paintings from its own collection; book traveling exhibitions 3 or 4 per year; originate traveling exhibitions; museum shop sells books, magazines, original art, reproductions, prints, slides and postcards

OXFORD

M **MUSEUM OF MODERN ART OXFORD,** 30 Pembroke St. Tel 0865 722733. *Pres* Lord Bullock; *Chmn Council of Management* David Pears; *Dir of Museum* David Elliott; *Asst Dir* John Hoole; *Education & Information Officer* Christine Newton

Open Tues - Sat 10 AM - 5 PM, Sun 2 - 5 PM, cl Mon. No admis fee. Estab 1966 to show changing exhibitions of contemporary art; lectures, seminars, performances and other events. Average Annual Attendance: 70,230. Mem: 300; dues L4, student members L2

Income: Financed by membership, county and state appropriation

Exhibitions: (1978-79) Education Events; Kandinsky; Richard Lay Na; Jackson Pollock; Alexande Rodchenko; Aaron Siskind

Publications: Exhibition catalogues

Activities: Classes for adults and children; dramatic programs; docent training; workshops; lect open to public, 20 - 30 visiting lectr per year; gallery talks; tours; slide talks; exten dept; individual prints and original objects of art lent to schools; lending collection contains slides; museum shop sells reproductions, postcards, Rodchenks slides

M **OXFORD UNIVERSITY,** Ashmolean Museum of Art and Archaeology, Beaumont St. *Dir* D T Piper; *Secy* R B Winter; *Public Officer* R I H Charlton; *Keeper Department Antiquities* H J Case; *Keeper Depart Eastern Art* J C Harle; *Keeper Heberden Coin Room* C M Kraay; *Keeper Western Art* K J Garlick; *Cur Cast Gallery* J Boardman

Open Mon - Sat 10 AM - 4 PM, Sun 2 - 4 PM. No admis fee. Estab 1683. Average Annual Attendance: 200,000

Income: Financed through university

Collections: British, European, Egyptian, Mediterranean and Near Eastern Archaeology; Chinese Bronzes; Chinese and Japanese porcelain, painting and lacquer; Dutch, English, Flemish, French and Italian Oil Paintings; English Silver; European Ceramics; Hope Collection of Engraved Portraits; Indian sculpture and painting; Islamic pottery and metalwork; Old Master and modern drawings, watercolors and prints; Tibetan Art; casts from the antique, coins and medals of all countries and periods, miniatures, sculpture and bronzes

Publications: Annual Report

Activities: Lect open to public; museum shop sells books, reproductions, prints, slides and replicas

L **Library,** Beaumont St.

Open for reference to university staff and students

PLYMOUTH

M PLYMOUTH CITY MUSEUM AND ART GALLERY, Drake Circus. Tel 0752-68000, Ext 4378. *Sr Keeper - Keeper of Conservation* James Manning; *Keeper of Art* M V Attrill; *Asst Keeper of Art* I W O'Riordan; *Keeper of Archaeology* C Gaskell Brown; *Archaeological Asst* W H Scutt; *Keeper of National History* D Curry
Open Mon - Thurs & Sat 10 AM - 6 PM, Fri 10 AM - 8 PM, Sun 3 - 5 PM. No admis fee. Estab 1899 to provide for the instruction and enjoyment of the citizens of Plymouth and of visitors; comprehensive collections of high quality in the fine and decorative arts, archaeology and natural history, with specialization in regional aspects in all subjects. Main museum and art gallery building was erected in 1910 and contained 2 large exhibition galleries, 2 smaller galleries were added in 1938; 1 large and 1 small gallery were added in 1976. Mem: 240; dues L3 and up
Income: L185,770 (financed by city appropriation)
Purchases: L3000
Collections: The Clarendon Loan Collection of Portraits of 16th and 17th Century English worthies; Collection of Cookworthy's Plymouth and Bristol Porcelain; The Cottonian Collection of Old Master and English bronzes, drawings, paintings, prints and engravings, early printed books and manuscripts including medieval books of hours (2), watercolours; Dorothy Doughty Royal Worcester Porcelain Figures; The Eddystone Lighthouse Slat being outstanding; English, Continental and Oriental Ceramics; general collections of paintings and drawings with Stanhope Forbes, James Northcote, William Payne, Samuel Prout, Joshua Reynolds and contemporary artists; Silver with special reference to Plymouth Hallmarked Pieces
Exhibitions: (1979) Artists of the Newlyn School (1880-1900); (1980) Algernon Newton; Drake 4000
Activities: Classes for adults and children; dramatic programs; docent training; lect open to public, 6 visiting lectr per year; gallery talks; concerts; tours

SHEFFIELD

M SHEFFIELD CITY ART GALLERIES, Surrey St. Tel 742-734781, 2. *Dir* H F Constantine; *Deputy Dir* J Spalding; *Keeper Mappin Art Gallery* James Hamilton
Sheffield City Art Galleries maintains two galleries to present a broad spectrum of art of the highest quality to the public of Sheffield and its environs
M Graves Art Gallery, Surrey St.
Open Mon - Sat 10 AM - 8 PM, Sun 2 - 5 PM. No admis fee. Estab 1934. Gallery situated in the centre of the city. Average Annual Attendance: 250,000
M Mappin Art Gallery, Weston Park S10 2TP.
Open Mon - Sat 10 AM - 5 PM, Sun 2 - 5 PM. No admis fee. Estab 1887. Gallery is a neo-classical building with three 19th Century galleries, and five 20th Century galleries. Average Annual Attendance: 180,000
Income: Financed by city appropriation
Collections: English portraits and watercolours; French painting; Modern British Art; Old Masters (Italian, Dutch and Spanish); Oriental Art including the Grice Collection of Chinese Ivories; Victorian Art (including Pre-Raphaelites); 18th and 19th Century Oil Landscapes; contemporary graphics, painting and sculpture
Exhibitions: Art into Landscape; Micael Ayrton; Beyond Light: Liliane Lijn and Bill Culbert; Bill Brandt; H Gaudier Brzeska; Victor Burgin; Edward Burra; The Burrell Collection; Carpets of Central Persia; Constable, Drawings and Watercolours; Drawings from the Courtauld Collection; Erte, Fashion and Theatre Design; 500 Years of English Printmaking, William Caxton; French Paintings from the Courtauld Collection; Roger Fry Portraits; German Naive Paintings; Arshile Gorky (paintings and drawings); David Hockney (photographs); Howard Hodgkin; Bernard Leach (pottery); Live-In Architecture; Malevich and the Russian Suprematists; New York in the Thirties, Berenice Abbott; Peruvian Ground Drawings; Photography in Switzerland 1840 to present; The Quashqa'i of Iran; Robert Rauschenberg; Norman Shaw (architectural drawings); Jack Smith; John Swanson (graphics); William Tucker; Christopher Wood
Activities: Classes for adults and children; lect open to public; concerts; gallery talks; tours; competitions; exten dept serves the city; individual paintings and original objects of art lent to schools, colleges, community centres, private individuals; lending collection contains color reproductions; framed reproductions, original art works, original prints, paintings, photographs, sculpture, slides; originate traveling exhibitions; sales shop sells books, magazines, reproductions, prints and slides

SOUTHAMPTON

M SOUTHAMPTON ART GALLERY AND MUSEUM SERVICE, Commercial Rd. (Mailing Add: Civic Centre, Southampton SO9 4XF) Tel 0703-23855, Ext 464, 465. *Cur* Anthony J Howarth; *Keeper of Art* Elizabeth Ogborn; *Keeper of Education* Helen Luckett
Open Tues - Sat 11 AM - 5:45 PM, Sun 2 - 5 PM. Estab 1951, gallery 1939, for reference works on fine art, particularly relevant to Southampton's Collection. Gallery maintained for British and European art from Trecento to 20th Century
Income: L200,000 (financed by city appropriation)
Library Holdings: Vols 1000; Per subs 14; AV—Kodachromes, lantern Slides, slides; Other—Clipping files, exhibition catalogs, prints, original art works, photographs
Collections: Arthur Jeffres Collection of Paintings
Exhibitions: Historical and modern art exhibitions
Publications: Exhibition and collections catalogues; events program
Activities: Classes for adults and children; lect open to public; concerts; gallery talks; tours; book traveling exhibitions 10 - 12 per year; originate traveling exhibitions

SOUTHPORT

M SEFTON METROPOLITAN BOROUGH, Atlinson Art Gallery, Lord St. Tel 71 33133, Ext 129. *Librn & Arts Services Officer* R E Marston; *Keeper of Fine Art* A W Moore
Open Mon, Tues, Wed & Fri 10 AM - 5 PM, Thurs & Sat 10 AM - 1 PM. No admis fee. Estab 1878 for the presentation of temporary art exhibitions and selections from the permanent collection. Eight roomed gallery on first floor level above library.

Average Annual Attendance: 60,000
Collections: †British Art - local, contemporary and historic; British 18th, 19th and 20th Century Oils; Chinese ceramics; 18th Century English glass; Roman coins; drawings, prints, sculpture and watercolours
Exhibitions: (1978) Centenary Exhibition of Victorian Oils; (1979) The Literal Landscape (Victorian Oils)
Activities: Lect open to public; concerts; gallery talks; tours; competitions with children's art and open art (local); individual paintings and original objects of art lent to Town Hall; book traveling exhibitions 4 per year; sales shop sells postcards
L Atkinson Library, Lord St. *Librn* R Livesey
Open Mon, Tues, Wed & Fri 10 AM - 5 PM, Thurs & Sat 10 AM - 1 PM. Estab 1878

WOLVERHAMPTON

M CENTRAL ART GALLERY, Lichfield St. *Cur* David Rodgers; *Keeper Art* Brendan Flynn; *Keeper Applied Art* Yvonne Jones; *Keeper of Local History* Peter Neeld
Open Mon - Sat 10 AM - 6 PM. No admis fee. Estab 1884 as an art gallery and museum. Victorian classical - three galleries on ground floor; four galleries on first floor. Average Annual Attendance: 100,000. Mem: 300; dues L2
Income: L139,000 (financed by city appropriation)
Purchases: L4000
Collections: †Contemporary British and American Art; †18th Century British paintings; 19th and 20th Century British paintings and watercolors; Oriental Applied Art and Weapons
Exhibitions: Liliane Lijn (drawings and sculpture); Modern Craft Pottery; Victorian Rural Life
Activities: Lect open to public; concerts; gallery talks; tours; individual paintings and original objects of art lent to corporation departments; lending collection contains 60 original art works; originate traveling exhbitions; sales shop sells original art, prints and catalogs
L Library, Lichfield St.
Reference library open to staff and others by appointment
Library Holdings: Vols 600; Per subs 4; Other—Sales catalogs

YORK

M YORK CITY ART GALLERY, Exhibition Square. Tel 0904-13839. *Cur* Richard Green; *Art Asst* Tessa Sidey
Admis 20p. Estab 1879 and provides a permanent collection of works of art and local topography, together with exhibitions, lectures, an art library and other supporting activities and services for the citizens of, and visitors to, York. Built to the designs of Edward Taylor for the Yorkshire Fine Art and Industrial Exhibition of 1879, the gallery has a facade in Italian Renaissance style; entrance hall; two galleries on ground floor; staircase leading to upstairs gallery, exhibition room, projected print room and education room. Average Annual Attendance: 70,000. Mem: 250; dues L2; annual meeting March
Income: Financed by city appropriation
Purchases: $2000
Collections: †British and European paintings from 1350 to present, including the Lycett Green Collection of Old Masters; Modern Stoneware Pottery; †paintings and drawings by York artists, notably William Etty; †watercolors, drawings and prints, mostly local topography
Exhibitions: (1980) Townes in Yorkshire
Publications: Preview (bulletin), 3 per year
Activities: Classes for adults and children; lect open to public, 6 visiting lectr per year; concerts; gallery talks; tours; competitions; museum shop sells reproductions, slides, catalogs of collections, exhibition catalogs and postcards
L Library, Exhibition Square.
Reference library
Library Holdings: Vols 7000; Per subs 10
Special Subjects: European post-medieval art - drawings, paintings, prints, sculpture and watercolors, particularly of the British school

ETHIOPIA

ADDIS ABABA

M UNIVERSITY OF ADDIS ABABA, Museum of the Institute of Ethiopian Studies,* Entoto St, PO Box 1176. Tel 110844, Ext 352. *Dir* Dr Richard Pankurst; *Museum Cur* Dr Girma Kidane
Open Mon - Fri 8:30 AM - 12:30 PM and 2:30 - 5:30 PM, Sat & Sun 8:30 AM - 12:30 PM. Admis 50¢, students free. Estab 1963 to develop and operate an ethnographic museum, including household artifacts, clothes, musical instruments, traditional paintings, and church paraphernalia. Average Annual Attendance: 25,000
Purchases: $10,000
Collections: 1350 Crosses, the oldest circa 11th - 12th Centuries; 6000 pieces in ethnological collections; 395 paintings, the oldest circa 15th Century
Exhibitions: France, Nigeria, USSR
Publications: Albums and catalogs
Activities: Classes for children; dramatic programs; docent training; lect open to public; individual paintings and original objects of art lent to museums or galleries of other countries; sales shop sells books, magazines, reproductions, prints and slides
L Library,* Entoto St, PO Box 1176.
Small reference library
Library Holdings: Other—Color slides 1200, negatives in photograph collection 7000

FINLAND

HELSINKI

M **SUOMEN KANSALLISMUSEO,** National Museum of Finland, Mannerheimintie, PO Box 913. Tel 40251. *Dir* Osmo Vuoristo
Open Sept - April Tues - Sat 11 AM - 3 PM, Tues evenings 6 - 9 PM, Sun 11 AM - 4 PM, cl Mon. Estab 1884 as a research institute and museum. Museum is a branch of the National Board of Antiquities and Historical Monuments. In 1893 the Historical-Ethnographical Museum of the Helsinki University, the collections of the Finnish Archeological Society and the Ethnographical Museum of the Finnish Undergraduates Corporation were united under the name of the State Historical Museum and later as the National Museum. In 1916 the first departments were opened to the public. The Open-Air Museum at Seurasaari (Folison) and the museums at Suomenlinna (Sveaborg) are branches of the National Museum
Collections: Ethnographical Department with Finnish, Finno-Ugrian and Comparative Ethnographical Collections; Finnish Historical Department with a Collection of Coins and Medals; Prehistoric Department with Finnish and Comparative Collections
L **National Board of Antiquities and Historical Monuments Library,** Mannerheimintie, PO Box 913. *Librn* Kerttu Itkonen; *Librn* Tua Zilliacus
Open Mon - Fri 8 AM - 4:15 PM; cl Sat & Sun. Estab 1875 to serve as a research library and as a special public library for archaeology, ethnology and the history of art
Library Holdings: Vols 100,000; Per subs 2000; Other—Includes the Finnish Archaeological Society
Special Subjects: Archaeology, Art History, Ethnology, European art industry

TURKU

M **TURUN TAIDEMUSEO,** Turku Art Museum, Puolalanpuisto 20100. Tel 921-330954, 921-330960. *Pres* Leif B Sourander; *VPres* Osmo Laine; *Dir* Erik Bergh
Open Mon - Fri 10 AM - 4 PM, Thurs evenings 6 - 9 PM, Sun 10 AM - 6 PM. Admis adults 5 mk, students & children 1 mk. Estab Turku Art Association 1891, Turku Art Museum 1904. Average Annual Attendance: 70,000. Mem: 1092, permanent mem 400; dues 20 mk
Income: Financed by city and state appropriation
Collections: 19th and 20th Century Finnish art, drawings, paintings, prints and sculpture; 19th and 20th Centuries international print collection
Exhibitions: Continuing program of changing exhibitions
Activities: Turku Art School, (oldest in Finland), estab 1830; lect open to public; gallery talks; tours; original objects of art lent
L **Library,** Puolalanpuisto 20100.
For reference
Library Holdings: Other—Photographs 2000, posters

FRANCE

ANGERS

M **MUSEE DES BEAUX-ARTS,** Museum of Fine Arts, 10 rue du Musee. *Conservator* Viviane Huchard; *Asst Conservator* Catherine Lagrue
Open 10 AM - Noon and 2 - 6 PM, cl Tues in winter. Admis 1F, students free. Built 1493-95 by Olivier Barrault. Museum houses the collection of the marquis de Livois and other statesmen; also the works of sculptor David d'Angers (1788-1839)
Income: Financed by city appropriation
Collections: Belgian, Dutch, Italian and Spanish painters of the 17th and 18th Centuries; French Painters of the 17th and 18th Centuries - Boucher, Chardin, Fragonard, Greuze, Lancret, Pater, de Troy; French Painters of the 19th Century - Delacroix, Gerard, Gericult, Ingres; works of David d'Angers - busts, bas-relief, medallions, statues and statuettes; contemporary French artists; paintings - Primitive Art of various schools

AVIGNON

M **MUSEE DU PETIT PALAIS,** Place du Palais des Papes. *Chief Cur* Georges de Loye; *Conservator* Elisabeth Mognetti
Cl Tues. Estab 1976. Museum in the old 14th and 15th Century Archibishop's Palace
Collections: Italian paintings covering the period from 14th - 16th Century; Medieval Sculpture from Avignon from 12th - 15th Century; Paintings of the Avignon School of 14th - 15th Centuries
L **Centre International de Documentation et de Recherche,** Place du Palais des Papes. *Dir* Marie-Claude Leonelli; *Conservator* Mrs Claude Cordier
Open Mon, Tues, Wed & Fri 9 AM - Noon and 2 - 6 PM. Estab 1979 for Italian and Provence's paintings from 14th and 15th Centuries
Income: $17,500
Purchases: 15,000
Library Holdings: Vols 600; Per subs 27; Other—Exhibition catalogs, photographs
Collections: Main Collection of Sienese Paintings' Photographs

DIJON

M **MUSEE DES BEAUX-ARTS DE DIJON,** Museum of Fine Arts, Place de la Sainte-Chapelle. *Staff* M Georgel
Open 9 AM - Noon and 2 - 6 PM
Collections: Furniture, objects of art, paintings and sculpture
Publications: Bulletin de la Societe des Amis des Musee de Dijon

FONTAINEBLEAU

M **MUSEE NATIONAL DU CHATEAU DE FONTAINEBLEAU,** National Museum of Fontainebleau, Tel 422 27 40. *Cur* Jean-Pierre Samoyault; *Cur* B Chevallier
Open 10 AM - Noon and 2 - 6 PM, Oct - March 2 - 5 PM. No admis fee. Estab in the 12th Century
Income: Financed by state appropriation
Collections: 16th - 19th Century paintings, furniture and interiors
Activities: Book shop
L **Library**
Library Holdings: Other—Photographs

LILLE

M **MUSEE DES BEAUX-ARTS DE LILLE,** Museum of Fine Arts, Place de la Republique. *Conservator* Herve Oursel; *Asst* Annie Scottez
Open daily 10 AM - 12:30 PM and 2 - 5 PM, cl Tues and holidays. Admis 3F
Income: Financed by city appropriation
Collections: Western European Art from 15th - 20th Centuries - ceramics, coins, medals, objects of art and sculptures
Exhibitions: Dessins Parisiens des 19e et 20e Siecles; Vic Gentils; Peinture Flamande au Temps de Rubens dans les Musees du Nord de la France; Sculptures Romanes el-Golhiquer du Nord de la France
Activities: Classes for adults and children; originate traveling exhibitions; museum shop sells books, reproductions and slides

LYON

M **MUSEE DES BEAUS-ARTS, PALAIS SAINT PIERRE,** Museum of Fine Arts, 20 Place des Terreaux. Tel 28-07-66. *Chief Cur* Madeleine Rocher-Jauneau
Open daily 10 AM - Noon and 2 - 6 PM. No admis fee. Estab in the 17th Century in the Monastery of the Nuns of St Pierre as a museum of painting, sculpture and objects of art
Collections: Ancient, Medieval and Modern sculpture; Egyptian, Greek and Roman antiquities; French Art since the Middle Ages; French, Hispano-Moorish, Italian and Oriental Ceramics; Gothic and Renaissance Art; Islamic Art; Modern Art and Murals by Purvis de Chavannes; Painting of the Lyonnaise School since the 17th Century; Paintings of the French, Flemish, Dutch, Italian and Spanish Schools; coins, drawings, furniture, local painters and prints
Publications: Bulletin des Musees et Monuments Lyonnais, quarterly; illustrated guides
Activities: Lect for high school and college students; book shop

ORLEANS

M **MUSEE DES BEAUX-ARTS,** Museum of Fine Arts, 1 Place de la Republique. Tel 38 53 39 22. *Cur-Dir* David OJalvo
Open April - Sept 10 AM - Noon and 2 - 6 PM, Oct - Mar 10 AM - Noon and 2 - 5 PM. Admis 2F. Estab 1825
Collections: Baugin; Boucher; Deruet (les quatre elements); French Paintings of the 16th - 20th Centuries; Fragonard; Foreign Schools of the 16th - 18th Centuries; Gauguin; La Hyre; Le Nain; Pastels of the 18th Century; group of Portraits by Corregio, Perronneau, Velasquez, etc; Hubert Robert; Sculpture of the 16th - 20th Centuries; Vouet; Watteau
Exhibitions: Aligny; Alexandre Antigna; Dessins Francais du 16e au 18e S; Raoul Dufy; Gaudier-Brzeska; Les Ponts d'Orleans; Vingt-cinq ans d'Acquisitions

PARIS

L **ECOLE NLE SUPERIEURE DES BEAUX-ARTS,** La Bibliotheque, 17, quai Malaquais. *Conservateur* Annie Jacques
Open 9:30 AM - 5 PM
Library Holdings: Vols 110,000; Per subs 150; Other—Exhibition catalogs, prints, manuscripts, original art works, photographs, sculpture

M **INSTITUT DE FRANCE,** Musee Conde, Chantilly. Tel 15 4 457 0362. *Asst to Museum* Amelie Lefebure; *Conservator of Coll* Raymond Cazelles
Open 10:30 AM - 5 PM. Admis 7 F. Estab 1897
Collections: Ceramics, manuscripts, mobiles and paintings
Publications: Bulletin du Musee Conde
L **Bibliotheque du Musee Conde,** Chateau de Chantilly.
Open Tues - Fri 11 AM - 5 PM. Estab 1897
Library Holdings: Vols 70,000; Per subs 100

M **MUSEE COGNACQ-JAY,** Cognacq-Jay Museum, 25 Boulevard des Capucines. Tel 742 3471. *Dir* Therese Burollet
Open 10 AM - 5:30 PM, cl Mon. Estab 1928
Income: Financed by city appropriation
Collections: Art of silversmiths; Drawings by Fragonard, Watteau; 18th Century works of art; Paintings of Boucher, Fragonard, Tiepolo; Quentin de la Tour Pastels; Sculpture by Lemoyne, Clodion, Falconet, Houdon; miniatures

M **MUSEE D'ART MODERNE DE LA VILLE DE PARIS,** 11 Ave du President Wilson. Tel 723-61-27. *Secy* Suzanne de Coninck; *Dir* Suzanne Page; *Conservator in Chief* Bernadette Contensou; *Dir Musee Enfants* Catherine Huber
Open 10 AM - 5:45 PM, Wed evenings until 8:30 PM. Admis 6 F. Estab 1937
Income: Financed by city appropriation
Collections: All the Art Movements from 1900
Exhibitions: Abstraction-Creation Chieze, Domoto, Froerdlaender, Zorres Garcia, Honegger, Laweats du Festival de Cagnes, Miro, Montanier, Orozes, Savin
Publications: Exhibition catalogues
Activities: Classes for children; lect open to public, lect on private exhibitions and permanent collections from 1900; concerts; fels; exten dept; individual paintings and

original objects of art lent to museums in France and outwards; lending collection contains cassettes, film strips, motion picutres and nature artifacts; book traveling exhibitions; museum shop sells books, magazines, reproductions, prints and slides
L **Library,** 11 Ave du President Wilson.
Open 10 AM - 5 PM. Estab Jan 1980 to lend books and catalogues to students
Library Holdings: Micro—Cards, prints

M **MUSEE DE CLUNY,** Cluny Museum,* 6 Place Paul Painleve (V). Tel 325-6200. *Dir* Francis Salet
Open daily 10 AM - 12:45 PM and 2 - 5 PM, cl Tues
Collections: †Enamels, furniture, ivories, sculptures and tapestries of the Middle Ages

M **MUSEE DU JEU DE PAUME,** Gallery of Impressionists, Place de la Concorde. Tel 260 12 07. *Chief Cur* Michel Laclotte
Open Wed - Mon 9:45 AM - 5:15 PM, cl Tues. Admis 5 F, Sun 2.50 F. The Gallery, the original orangerie of the Palais de Tuileries, was estab 1862; remodeled in 1954 and again in 1969
Collections: Impressionists
Publications: Catalog of the Musee du Jeu de Paume
Activities: Museum shop sells books, reproductions and slides

M **MUSEE DU LOUVRE,** Louvre Museum, Palais du Louvre, Place du Carrousel. Tel 260 39 26. *Dir* M Andre Chabaud; *Cur Drawings* Maurice Serullaz; *Cur Egyptian Antiquities* Christian Desroches Noblecourt; *Cur Greek & Roman Antiquities* Francois Villard; *Cur Objects d'Art* M de Groër; *Cur Orangerie & Jeu de Paume Galleries* Helene Adhemar; *Cur Oriental Antiquities* Pierre Amiet; *Cur Paintings* Michel Laclotte; *Cur Sculptures* M Jean Rene Gaborit
Open daily 9:45 AM - 5:15 PM, cl Tues & holidays. Estab 1793. The collections are divided into six departments and offer a panorama of the arts of all periods.
Average Annual Attendance: 3,000,000
Collections: Islamic Art; The Edmond de Rothschild Collection; antiquities, decorative arts, drawings, paintings, sculpture
L **Library,** Palais du Louvre, Place du Carrousel.
Library Holdings: Vols 100,000

M **MUSEE DU PETIT PALAIS,** Municipal Museum, Champs-Elysees. Tel 265-99-21, 265-12-73. *Chief Cur* Adeline Cacan
Open Wed - Sun 10 AM - 6 PM, cl Mon & Tues. Estab 1902
Collections: Chinese collections; drawings and paintings of the 17th, 18th and 19th Centuries; Egyptian, Etruscan and Greek antiquities; furniture, porcelains, tapestries of Sevres and Saxe; objets d'art Art Nouvian and of the the Middle Ages and Renaissance; Roman bronzes, ceramics and coins
Exhibitions: Various changing exhibitions
L **Library,*** Champs-Elysees.
Library Holdings: Vols 10,000; Other—Prints 7000

M **MUSEE MARMOTTAN,** 2 rue Louis Boilly. Tel 224 07 02. *Keeper of Art* M Yves Brayer
Open 10 AM - 6 PM, cl Mon. Admis 10,00 FF. Estab for Impressionist art
Collections: Marmottan; Michel Monet; Donop de Monchy
Exhibitions: (1978) Forain; (1979) Musee de l'Or de Bogota; National Museum of Wales; temporary exhibitions
Publications: Collection and exhibition catalogues
Activities: Lending collection contains books, color reproductions, lantern slides and slides; museum shop sells books, prints and slides

M **MUSEE NATIONAL D'ART MODERNE,** Centre National d'Art et de Culture Georges Pompidou, Cedex 04.
Open daily until 10 PM. No admis fee. Estab 1976, opened Jan 1977. Building has transparent walls; wide open doors; outdoor escalators. Center houses the museum; an industrial design center; a public library for contemporary writing; institute of music research; theatre for showing old films; a tree-covered mall for modern music, drama, poetry readings, ballets and other entertainment
Collections: †Twentieth century movements in painting and sculpture including: Abstraction, Avant-Garde, Cubism, Expressionism, Fauvism, Futurism, Hyperrealism, Pop Art
Exhibitions: The inaugural exhibitions were works by Marcel Duchamp; changing exhibitions
Activities: Classes; lect; gallery talks; tours; concerts of 20th Century music

M **MUSEE NATIONAL DES MONUMENTS FRANCAIS,** National Museum of French Sculpture and Murals, Palais de Chaillot, Place du Tracadero. Tel 727 97 27, 727 35 74. *Cur* Philippe Chapu; *Keeper* Francois Hilaize; *Keeper* Christian de Merindol
Open Wed - Mon 9:45 AM - 12:30 PM and 2 - 5 PM, cl Tues. Estab 1882
Collections: Full scale casts of the principal French Monuments and Sculpture from the beginning of Christianity to the 19th Century; full scale reproductions of Medieval Murals
Publications: Guides
L **Library,** Palais de Chaillot, Place du Tracadero.
Open Wed - Mon 10 AM - Noon and 2 - 5 PM, cl Tues. Open to students of the Louvre and archeologists
Library Holdings: Vols 10,000; Other—Photographs 200,000, copies of medieval murals 2000
Special Subjects: Roman Antiquities, Art History
Collections: Photograph collection of prints 20,000

UNION CENTRALE DES ARTS DECORATIFS
M **Musee des Arts Decoratifs,** Museum of Decorative Arts, 107 rue de Rivoli. Tel 260 32 14. *Pres* Robert Bordaz; *Secy* Pierre Meilhac; *Chief Cur* Francois Mathey; *Cur* Yvonne Brunhammer; *Cur* Gerard Mabille; *Cur* Marie Noele de Gary; *Cur* Nadine Gasc; *Cur* Odile Nouvel
Open Wed - Sat 10 AM - Noon and 2 - 5 PM; National Information and Documentation Craft Center open 12:30 - 5:30 PM, cl Tues & Sun. Admis 6F. Estab 1863 to adapt beauty to industry. Gallery maintained for exhibition of decorative art, architecture and art. Average Annual Attendance: 80,000. Mem: 2500; dues 75 F; one annual meeting

Income: Financed by city and state appropriations and membership
Collections: Dubuffet bequest; Home Decor of the French Middle Ages; Oriental Art; †paper paints, tapestry, †textiles
Activities: Lect with guided tours; films; original objects of art lent; originate traveling exhibitions
L **Bibliotheque des Arts Decoratifs,** Library of Decorative Arts, 107 rue de Rivoli. *Chief Conservator* Genevieve Picon; *Conservator* Genevieve Bonte; *Conservator* Josiane Sartre
Open Tues - Sat 10 AM - 5:30 PM, Mon 1:45 - 5:30 PM. Estab 1864 to adapt beauty to industry. Reference library
Library Holdings: Vols 100,000; Per subs 300
Collections: Iconographique Maciet
M **Musee de l'Affiche,** 18 rue de Paradis, Paris 75010. *Chief Conservator* Genevieve Picon; *Conservator* Alan Weill
Open Noon - 6 PM, cl Tues. Admis 6 F. Museum opened in 1978
Library Holdings: Other—Old and contemporary French and foreign posters 60,000
Activities: book traveling exhibitions in Paris and abroad

REIMS

M **MUSEE SAINT-DENIS,** 8 rue Chanzy. Tel 47 28 44. *Conservator* F Pomarede; *Asst Conservator* J P Bonnal
Open 10 AM - Noon and 2 - 6 PM. No admis fee. Estab 1795 as a museum of art, archeology and local history
Income: Financed by city appropriation
Collections: †25 Paintings by Corot; †10 Designs by Cranach; †French Paintings of the 19th Century; †Paintings on Canvas of the 15th - 16th Centuries; 17th - 18th Century paintings; ceramics
Activities: Expositions, classes and service for scholars
L **Library,** 8 rue Chanzy.
Library Holdings: Vols 2000
Collections: Photograph collection of prints 1000

RENNES

M **MUSEE DES BEAUX-ARTS,** 20, quai Emile Zola. Tel 16 - 99 30 83 87. *Cur* Nicole Barbier; *Asst Cur* Sylvie Blottiere; *Asst Cur* Patrick Ramade
Open 10 AM - Noon and 2 - 6 PM. Admis 3 FF. Estab 1801 for conservation, exhibition and increasing of the collections. Average Annual Attendance: 18,000
Income: 206,000 FF (financed by city appropriation)
Purchases: 100,000 FF
Collections: Egyptian, Greek and Roman archeology; †drawings, †paintings and †sculptures from 15th - 20th Century
Exhibitions: (1978) l'Art Manieriste; l'Ecole de Pont-Aven dans les Collections Publiques et Privees de Bretagne; (1979) Theodore Caruelle d'Aligny; Dessins d'Architecture; Retrospective Henri Hayden; Jean Le Moal; Maquettes et projets de vitraux; (1980) Miniatures indiennes
Publications: Dessins de la Collection du President Robien; exhibition catalogues; Intailles et Camees de la Collection du President de Robien; Le Dossier d'Un Tableau: Saint Luc Peignant la Vierge de Martin Van Heemskerck; Peintures de la Collection Robien
Activities: Classes for children; second Thurs every month from 2 - 8 PM special animation; concerts; gallery talks; fellowships; originate traveling exhibitions; sales shop sells books, magazines, reproductions, prints and slides

STRASBOURG

M **MUSEE DE L'OEUVRE NOTRE DAME,** Cathedral Museum, 3 Place du Chateau. Tel 32 06 39. *Conservation* Hans Zumstein; *Conservation* Marie-Josee Nohlen
Open April - Sept daily 10 AM - Noon and 2 - 6 PM, cl Good Friday & May 1st, Oct - March daily 2 - 6 PM, cl Tues, Nov 1st, Dec 25th & Jan 1st. Admis 3 F, half-price for groups of 25
Collections: 15th Century Rooms - Alsatian paintings, sculptures, stained glass. Gothic Rooms - originals of the 13th Century Sculptures from the Cathedral; Drawings of the Cathedral, 13th - 15th Centuries; meeting room of the Lodge of Stonemasons and Stonecutters (1580). Houses dating from 14th, 16th and 17th Centuries. Renaissance Rooms - graphic arts and illustration of books produced at Strasbourg from 1500 - 1600; paintings, drawings by Hans Baldung Grien; rooms devoted to Renaissance furniture and sculpture; still-life room; development of gold and silverware in Strasbourg from 15th - 19th Century. Romanesque Rooms - sculptures of the 11th and 12th Centuries; stained glass windows from Strasbourg's former Romanesque Cathedral. Rooms of Medieval Archaeology. Glass Collection
Publications: Collections catalogs

M **MUSEE DES BEAUX-ARTS,** Museum of Fine Arts, Chateau des Rohan, 2 Place du Chateau. Tel 32-48-95. *Conservation* Jean Faviere
Open daily April - Sept 10 AM - Noon and 2 - 6 PM, cl Good Fri and May 1st, Oct - March 2 - 6 PM, cl Tues, Nov 1st, Dec 25th and Jan 1st. Admis 4 F, half-price for groups of 25. Museum occupies two floors of the Rohan Castel, which also contains the Archaeological Museum, the Museum of Decorative Arts, the Print Department and the Library
Collections: Paintings of the chief European Schools, 14th - 19th Century, from Giotto to modern times; works by Boucher, Chardin, Corot, Corregio, De Hoogh, El Greco, Fragonard, Goya, Guardi, Filippino Lippi, Lucas of Leyden, Marmion, Memling, Rubens, Tassel, Tiepolo, Tintoretto, Valentin, Van Dyck, van Heemskerk, Veronese, Vouet, Watteau, Zurbaran

TOULOUSE

M **MUSEE DES AUGUSTINS,** Museum of Augustins,* 2 ter rue Alsace-Lorraine. Tel 23 11 44. *Cur* Denis Milhau
Open daily 10 AM - Noon and 2 - 6 PM, cl Tues. Admis 1 F. Estab 1795. Museum

housed in the former Augustine convent of which parts date from the 14th and 15th Centuries; maintains gallery

Income: Financed by city and state appropriations

Collections: Gothic, Modern and Romanesque Sculpture of Languedoc; paintings of the 16th - 20th Centuries, Flemish, French, Italian and Spanish

Activities: Classes for children; lect open to public, 200 visiting lectr per year; exten dept serves schools; originate traveling exhibitions

L **Library,*** 2 ter rue Alsace-Lorraine.

For reference

Library Holdings: Vols 4000; Other—Prints in photograph collection 1000

TOURS

M **MUSEE DES BEAUX-ARTS,** Museum of Fine Arts, 18 Place Francais Sicard. Tel 05 68 73. *Chief Conservator* Mrs M N Pinot de Villechenon; *Asst Conservator* S Guillot de Suduiraut; *Asst Conservator* C Legrand

Open Nov - Feb 9 AM - Noon and 2 - 5 PM, cl Tues, March - Oct 9 AM - Noon and 2 - 6 PM, cl Jan 1, May 1, July 14, Nov 1 & 11, Dec 25. Admis 5 F. Estab 1793 as a museum of the French Revlution; installed into the Palais of the Archbishop in 1910

Income: Financed by municipal appropriation

Collections: Ancient and Modern Tapestries; Furniture: Chollot, Demoulin; French School of 18th Century: Boucher, Lancret, Largilliere, Peronneau; Italian Paintings of 13th to 16th Century: Mantegna, primitives; 17th Century Paintings; Rembrandt, Rubens, Van Goyen; 19th Century Paintings: Boulanger, Cazin, Chasseriau, Degas, Delacroix, Monet; Sculptures: Bourdelle, Houdon, Lemoyne

Exhibitions: (1978-79) Aristide Caillaud; Art russe non officiel; Collection de Collectionneurs; Jeanne d'Arc et sa legende; L'Atelier Nadar; Ponts de Tours; Touraine neo-gothique

Activities: Educ dept; films

VERSAILLES

M **MUSEE NATIONAL DU CHATEAU DE VERSAILLES,** National Museum of the Chateau of Versailles, Palais de Versailles. Tel 950 58 32. *Cur* Gerald van der Kemp; *Cur* Pierre Lemoine

Open 10 AM - 5 PM. Admis 7 F. Estab 1837 for the conservation and display of the Royal Apartments and the collections they contain

Collections: Furniture, paintings and objects of art contained in the Royal Apartments; paintings of the 16th - 19th Centuries contained in the History Museum of France

Activities: Bureau of Cultural Affairs organizes visiting conferences for the purpose of educating scholars; lect open to public; original objects of art lent

L **Library,** Palais de Versailles.

Reference only

FEDERAL REPUBLIC OF GERMANY

AACHEN

M **SUERMONDT-LUDWIG-MUSEUM DER STADT AACHEN,** Wilehlmstrasse 18. Tel 0241-472580. *Dir* Dr Ernst-Gunther Grimme; *Cur* Martin Mayer; *Cur* Hella Lorenz

Open Tues - Fri 10 AM - 5 PM, Sat & Sun 10 AM - 1 PM. No admis fee. Estab 1880 to present a general view of European art from the Classical Period to the present. Average Annual Attendance: 70,000. Mem: 1600; dues DM 10

Income: Financed by city appropriation

Collections: Paintings from the Middle Ages to the Baroque; portraits from Middle Ages to present; sculpture from the Roman to Baroque; graphic art (ceramics, textiles)

Exhibitions: Eight rotating exhibitions; sculpture exhibition

Publications: Aachener Kunstblatter

Activities: Classes for adults and children; lect open to public; gallery talks; tours; original objects of art lent; museum shop sells books, magazines and reproductions

L **Library,** Wilhelmstrasse 18. *Librn* Renate Puvogel

Library Holdings: Vols 15,000; Per subs 8

BERLIN

M **STAATLICHE MUSEEN PREUSSISCHER KULTURBESITZ,** State Museums, Foundation for Prussian Cultural Treasures, Stauffenbergstrasse 41. Tel 2666. *Dir* Dr Stephan Waetzoldt

Museums in Dahlem open Tues - Sun 9 AM - 5 PM, cl Mon; Museums in Charlottenburg open Sat - Thurs 9 AM - 5 PM, cl Fri; Nationalgalerie open Mon Noon - 8 PM, Tues - Sun 9 AM - 5 PM, cl Fri; Plaster Cast House open Mon - Fri 9 AM - 4 PM. Estab 1830. Average Annual Attendance: 2,000,000

—**Picture Gallery.** *Dir* Dr Henning Bock

Collections: Paintings from 13th - 18th Centuries, Old Dutch, Old German, Italian, Netherlands and French works, including Durer and 26 paintings by Rembrandt

—**Department of Sculpture.** *Dir* Dr Peter Bloch

Collections: †Late antiquity to classicism, among others Donatello, Riemenschneider

—**Department of Prints and Drawings.** *Dir* Dr Fedja Anzelewsky

Collections: †300,000 drawings, prints and illustrated books of all epochs of European Art; greatest collection of Durer drawings, Bruegel and Rembrandt

—**Museum of Ethnology.** *Dir* Dr Kurt Krieger

Collections: †300,000 items of different cultures; Africa, East Asia (China, Tibet), Europe and North America; Ancient America, ceramics, gold; Department of Oceania, houses, masks, ships; South Asia, masks, string puppets

Activities: Junior Museum; Museum for the Blind

—**Museum of Indian Art.** *Dir* Dr Herbert Härtel

Collections: †Central Asiatic Frescoes of the early middle ages from Turfan and Indian sculpture

—**Museum of Far Eastern Art.** *Dir* Dr Beatrix von Rague

Collections: Paintings and ceramics of China and Japan

—**Museum of Islamic Art and Antiquities.** *Dir* Dr Klaus Brisch

Collections: †Book design, ceramics, ebony, glass, metal, stucco and tapestry from Near East, North Africa and Spain

—**Museum of German Ethnology.** *Dir* Dr Theodor Kohlmann

Collections: Folklore objects from German speaking population in Europe, beginning in the 17th Century

—**Museums Library.** *Dir* Dr Frauke Steenbock

—**Department for Museology.** *Dir* Dr Andreas Grote

—**Education Department.** *Dir* Dr Janni Mueller-Hauck

—**Egyptian Antiquities.**

Collections: †All periods; bust of Queen Nofretete; sculptures from Tel el Amarna

—**Greek and Roman Antiquities.** *Dir* Dr Wolf-D Heilmeyer

Collections: †Bronzes, gold jewelry, marble sculptures and vases up to the Byzantine period; Hildesheimer Silberfund (silvertrove)

—**Museum of Pre-history and Proto-history.** *Dir* Dr Adriaan von Mueller

Collections: †Objects found by excavation and in settlements in Europe and Asia from Old Stone Age to the height of the Middle Ages

—**Museum of Arts and Crafts.** *Dir* Dr Franz-Adrian Dreier

Collections: †Objects from the Middle Ages to the 20th Century; Welfenschatz

—**Art Library and Lipperheide Costume Library.** *Dir* Dr Ekhart Berckenhagen Estab 1867

Collections: 25,000 drawings of architecture and design; prints and rare books; 160,000 volumes of history of art and costume

—**Nationalgalerie.** *Dir* Dr Dieter Honisch

Collections: C D Friedrich, Menzel, French and German impressionists; †paintings, sculptures and drawings 19th and 20th Centuries

Exhibitions: Modern exhibitions

—**Rathgen-Research-Laboratory.** *Dir* Dr Josef Riederer

—**Kunstbibliothek,** Jebensstr 2, 1000, Berlin 12. *Dir* Prof Ekhart Berckenhagen Open Mon Wed Thurs 9 AM - 9 PM, Tues & Fri 9 AM - 8 PM, Sat 9 AM - 1 PM. Estab 1867

Library Holdings: Vols 160,000; Other—Exhibition catalogs, prints, original art works, photographs

Special Subjects: Prints and drawings of history of architecture and design

Collections: Posters, covers, examples of objects of applied graphic art

BONN

M **RHEINISCHES LANDESMUSEUM BONN,** Rhineland Museum, Colmantstrasse 14-16. Tel 0228-63 21 58. *Dir* Dr Christoph B Rüger; *Department Dir* Dr Walter Janssen

Open Tues - Fri 9 AM - 5 PM, Wed 9 AM - 9 PM, Sat & Sun 10 AM - 6 PM. Admis DM 1, children to 18 and groups .50. Estab 1820, and in 1873 as Rhineland Regional Museum for the purpose of collecting and showing Rhineland history and art from prehistoric times to present. Average Annual Attendance: 150,000

Income: Financed by Landschaftsverband Rheinland

Collections: Art from the Middle Ages until today; Frankish period; medieval archaeology; prehistoric times; Roman period; coins

Exhibitions: Viarel Appel; E Atget; Ausgrabungen in Rheinlang 1977 and 1978; Samuel Bak; H Daumier; Die Nabatäer - Ein Uönigreich in der Wüste; Die Numider-Reiter und Konige Nöordl der Sahara; Otto Freundlich; Hutton; Meislerwerke Deutscher und Russischer Malerei aus Sowjet Museen; Clarkson Stanfield; V Stevending; Hommage a Teriade; A Paul Weber

Publications: Bonner Jahrbucher, annual; Das Rhein; Landesmuseum Bonn, research series

Activities: Classes for children; lect open to public; concerts; gallery talks; tours; museum shop sells books, reproductions and slides

L **Library,** Colmantstrasse 14-16. *Librn* Johannes Seifert

Open Mon - Fri 8 AM - 12:30 PM and 1 - 4 PM, Tues & Thurs evenings until 5:30 PM. Estab 1841 originally as Library of the Verein von Altertumsfreunden still a part of the museum's library. Reference only

Income: DM 45,000 (financed by membership and Landschaftsverband Rheinland)

Library Holdings: Vols 70,000; Per subs 500

M **STADTISHCES KUNSTMUSEUM BONN,** Art Museum of the City of Bonn, Rathausgasse 7. Tel 773686, 772440. *Dir* Dr Dicrk Stemmler; *Asst* Dr Irene Klimschmidt; *Public Relations* Dr Elhe Brathe

Open daily 10 AM - 5 PM, Thurs 10 AM - 9 PM, cl Mon. Average Annual Attendance: 90,000

Income: Financed by city appropriation

Collections: Art of the 20th Century, especially August Macke and the Rhenish expressionists; German Art since 1945; graphic arts

Exhibitions: Handzeichnungen-International - der 60-er und 70-er-Jahre aus dem; Heinrich Nauen zum 100. Geburtstag; 30 Jahre Kunst in der Bundesrepublik - Ausgewählte Graphik aus dem Städtisches Kunstmuseums Bonn; 30 Jahre Kunst in der Bundesrepublik - die Sammlung des Städtischen Kunstmuseums Bonn; August Macke und die Rheinischen Expressionisten; Neuerwerbungen des Städtischen Kunstmuseums 1979; Tingting Bilong Mi - Zeitgenössische Kunst aus Papua-Neuguinea; Arnulf Rainer - das Bisherige Oeuvre in Allen Perioden und Werkgruppen; Franz Erhard Walther - das Frühwerk vor dem ersten Werksatz, 1958-1963

Publications: Bestandskataloge: August Macke und die Rheinischen Expressionisten; 1949-1975 25 Jahre Kuns in der Bundesrepublik

Activities: Concerts; originate traveling exhibitions; sales shop sells reproductions, prints, slides and catalogs

L **Library,** Rathausgasse 7.

Library Holdings: Vols 5000; Per subs 20

Special Subjects: Contemporary art

BREMEN

M KUNSTHALLE BREMEN, Bremen Art Gallery, Am Wall 207. Tel 32 47 85. *Dir* Dr Gunter Busch; *Cur* Dr Jurgen Schultze; *Asst Cur* Dr Annemarie Winther; *Asst Cur* Dr Gerhard Gerkens
Open Tues - Sun 10 AM - 4 PM, Tues & Fri evenings 7 - 9 PM, cl Mon. Admis DM .50, for special exhibitions DM 3. Estab 1823. Gallery houses European art since the Middle Ages. Mem: 3313; dues DM 15 and up; annual meeting
Collections: Coins and medals up to the end of the 19th Century; 18th and 19th Century Japanese drawings and prints; European paintings, Middle Ages to modern, especially French and German Art of the 19th Century (drawings, sculpture and prints); 17th - 20th Century plastic collections
Publications: Exhibition catalogs; Katalog der Gemalde des 19 and 20 Jahrhunderts in der Kunsthalle Bremen; Katalog der Medaillen und Plaketter des 19 und 20 Jahrhunderts in der Kunsthalle Bremen; Meisterwerke der Kunsthalle Bremen; Schriften zu Kunstwerken der Kunsthalle Bremen
Activities: Classes for adults; lect open to public, 15-18 visiting lectr per year; gallery talks; scholarships; objects of art lent; originate traveling exhibitions
L Library, Am Wall 207.
Reference library
Library Holdings: Vols 40,000; Micro—Prints 400; Other—Photographs 4600

BRUNSWICK

M HERZOG ANTON ULRICH-MUSEUM, Medieval Section: Burg Dankwarderode, Museumstrasse 1, Braunschweig D-33. Tel 0531 1551, 0531 1552. *Dir* Ruediger Klessman; *Chief Cur* Dr Bodo Hedergott; *Cur* Dr Christian von Heusinger; *Asst* Dr Sabine Jacob; *Asst* Dr Johanna Lessmann
Open Tues - Sun 10 AM - 4 PM, Wed 10 AM - 8 PM; Medieval Section open Tues - Sun 10 AM - 4 PM, cl Mon. Estab 1754. Average Annual Attendance: 100,000
Income: Financed by state appropriation
Collections: Chinese Lacquers; Egyptian, Greek and Roman Antiquities; †European paintings of the 15th - 18th Centuries; †European Renaissance and Baroque Decorative Art, including bronzes, clocks, French 16th Century enamels, furniture, glass, Italian majolica, ivory and wood carvings, laces, porcelain, waxes; illustrated books; Medieval Art; †prints and drawings from the 15th Century to present
Exhibitions: (1978) Die Sprache der Bilder; Gemalde im Licht der Naturwissenschaft; 15 Jahre Staatliche Hochschule für Bildende Künste. (1979) Expressionistische Tendenzen der polnischen Graphik; Graphik des 20. Jahrhunderts - Erwerbungen der letzten Jahre; Jan Lievens-ein Maler im Schatten Rembrandts
Publications: Catalogs; guides
Activities: Lect; concerts
L Library, Museumstr 1, Braunschweug D-33. *Librn* Eleanore Westermeyer
Open Mon - Fri 10 AM - 12:30 PM and 1:30 - 4 PM, Wed 10 AM - 12:30 PM and 1:30 - 6:30 PM. For reference
Purchases: DM 5000
Library Holdings: Vols 40,000; Per subs 90; AV—Slides; Other—Exhibition catalogs, prints, manuscripts, photographs, reproductions, postcards

COLOGNE

MUSEEN DER STADT KÖLN
M Kunstgewerbemuseum der Stadt Köln, Eigelsteintorburg. Tel 0221-2213860. *Dir* Prof Brigitte Klesse; *Vice-Dir* Dr Gisela Reineking von Bock; *Staff* Dr Rüdiger Joppien; *Staff* Dr Gerhard Dietrich
Open daily 10 AM - 5 PM. Admis 1 DM. Estab 1888 for European applied arts and design from the Middle Ages to present: collecting, presentation, preservation and scientific documentation. Average Annual Attendance: 20,000
Income: Financed by state appropriation
Collections: †Ceramics, †Design 20th Century, †furniture, †glass, †textiles
Exhibitions: (1979) Various exhibitions of old and contemporary decorative arts and design: Design in Austria, Denmark, Germany; Amber; Glass; Industrial Design; private donations
Publications: Bulletin der Museen der Stadt Köln, monthly; Wallraf-Richartz-Jahrbuch, annually
Activities: Classes for adults and children; gallery talks; originate traveling exhibitions; Unterricht im Museum, Kunstgewerbemuseum, Overstolzenhaus, Rheingasse 8 D-5000 Köln 1
M Wallraf-Richartz-Museum, Museum Ludwig,* An der Rechtschule. Tel 221-23-72. *General Dir* Dr Gerhard Bott; *Cur Engravings* Dr Hella Robels; *Cur Engravings* Dr Dieter Ronte; *Cur Modern Art* Dr Kurt Locher; *Cur Modern Art* Dr Evelyn Weiss; *Cur Modern Art* Dr Rainer Budde
Open daily 10 AM - 5 PM, Tues & Thurs 10 AM - 8 PM. Admis adults 1 DM, groups, students and children .50 DM. Estab 1824. Mem: 1750
Collections: Museum Ludwig: Painting and sculpture from 1900 to present, especially Expressionism and contemporary art. Wallraf-Richartz-Museum: Painting from 13th Century to 1900, especially old Cologne painting and Netherlandish painting; 19th Century sculpture
Exhibitions: Lovis Corinth; Peter Paul Rubens; Bertel Thorvaldsen
Publications: Bulletin; yearbook
Activities: Classes for adults and children; docent training; originate traveling exhibitions; museum shop sells books and prints
L Wallraf-Richartz-Museum Bibliothek,* An der Rechtschule. *Librn* Dr Albert Schug
Reference library
Library Holdings: Vols 120,000; Per subs 730
M Römisch-Germanisches Museum,* Roncallinplatz. Tel 221-45-90, 221-44-38. *Dir* Dr Hugo Borger
Open Schatzkammer in der Alten Wache (Treasures in the Old Guardhouse) daily 10 AM - 5 PM, Thurs 10 AM - 10 PM; Dionysos-Mosaik daily 10 AM - 8 PM, Tues & Fri 7 - 10 PM; Prätorium daily 10 AM - 5 PM. Estab 1946
Collections: †Early and pre-historic discoveries; †gold ornaments of the era of migrating tribes; †Roman excavations; glass and industrial arts
Activities: Lect open to public; gallery talks; tours; discussions; seminars

L Romisch-Germanisches Museum Bibliothek,* Roncalliplatz.
Library Holdings: Vols 8000
M Rautenstrach-Joest-Museum,* Ubierring 45. Tel 31-10-65, 31-10-66. *Dir* Dr Axel von Gagern
Open Sun - Wed 10 AM - 5 PM, Thurs - Sat 10 AM - 8 PM. Estab 1906
Collections: †Culture and art of the non-European peoples
Activities: Lect open to public; gallery talks; tours; films; seminars
L Rautenstrach-Joest-Museum Bibliothek,* Ubierring 45. *Dir* Dr Axel von Gagern
Library Holdings: Vols 20,000
M Kölnisches Stadtmuseum im Zeughaus,* Cologne City Museum, Zeughaustrasse 1. Tel 221-23-52-221-23-52. *Dir* Hugo Borger
Open daily 10 AM - 5 PM, Thurs evenings until 10 PM. Estab 1888
Collections: †Graphic Arts of Cologne and the Rhineland; †national development and history; †photograph collection of the Rhineland (145,000 prints); †trade and industrial arts of Cologne religious and rural art and culture
Activities: Lect open to public; gallery talks; tours; seminars
L Kölnisches Stadtmuseum Bibliothek,* Zeughaustrasse 1.
Library Holdings: Vols 12,000
M Kunstgewerbemuseum,* Arts and Crafts Museum, Overstolzenhaus, Rheingasse 8-12. Tel 221-9521. *Dir* Dr Brigitte Klesse; *Chief Cur Gisela Reinking/Von Gisela-Reineking/von Bock* f Cu; *Cur* Dr Carl-Wolfgang Schumann; *Asst Cur* Dr Rudiger Joppien
Open daily 10 AM - 5 PM. Admis adults DM 4, students DM .50. Estab 1889 to propagate interest in the applied and decorative arts. Approx 600 sq meters in the permanent exhibition rooms at the Overstolzenhaus, a medieval house of the 13th Century. Since the old museum was bombed during the war, no adequate gallery has been estab - permanent home is planned for 1985. Average Annual Attendance: 35,000. Mem: 200
Income: Financed by city appropriation
Collections: European applied arts from the Middle Ages to present, some holdings in Islamic arts
Exhibitions: Bader, Duft und Seife; Weisses Gold und Bunte Seide; Walter Gropius, Bauten und Projekte; Emil Lettre - Andreas Mortiz; Sammlung Giorgio Silzer, Berlin; Siftung Elisabeth Treskow, Schmuck aus 3000 Jahren; Piet Zwart - ein niederlandischer Designer; Dei-gner; Kommunaler Wohnbau, Wien 1923-1934; textile objects
Publications: Bulletin
Activities: Sales shop sells books, reproductions and slides
L Kunst und Museumsbibliothek, Kattenbug 18 (Verwaltung), Lesesaal (An der Rechtschule). *Librn* Dr Albert Schug
Open daily 10 AM - 5 PM, Sat & Sun 10 AM - 8 PM
Purchases: $150,000
Library Holdings: Vols 145,000
M Museum für Ostasiatische Kunst,* Museum of East Asian Art. (Mailing Add: Universitatstrasse 100, 5000, Hahnentorburg, Rudolfplatz,) Tel 221-38-63. *Dir* Dr Roger Goepper
Open Mon - Thurs & Sat & Sun 10 AM - 5 PM, Fri 10 AM - 8 PM. Admis DM 1. Estab 1913. Average Annual Attendance: 15,000
Collections: Art of China, Korea and Japan, especially Buddhist Art from Japan; Chinese bronzes; Japanese lacquers; Korean ceramics
Exhibitions: Chinese Art from the Collection of Gustav VI, King of Sweden; Masterworks from China, Japan and Korea
Publications: Catalog
Activities: Classes for adults and children; museum shop sells books, reproductions, prints and slides
L Museum für Ostasiatische Kunst Bibliothek,* Universitatstrasse 100, 5000, Hahnentorburg, Rudolfplatz. *Librn* Dr Ji Hyun Whang
Open Mon - Thurs 10 AM - 5 PM, Fri 10 AM - 12:30 PM
Library Holdings: Vols 7000; Per subs 35
Special Subjects: The arts of Korea, China and Japan
M Schnutgen-Museum,* Cacilienstrasse 19. Tel 221-23-20, 221-23-11. *Dir* Dr Anton Legner
Open daily 10 AM - 5 PM, Wed evenings 7 - 10 PM. Estab 1906
Collections: †Religious Art, early Middle Ages to Baroque
L Schnutgen Museum Bibliothek, Cacilienstrasse 19.
Library Holdings: Vols 8000
M Kunsthalle,* Cologne Art Gallery. (Mailing Add: Joset-Haubrich-Hof 1,) Tel 221-23-35. *Dir* Helmut R Leppier
Open daily 10 AM - 10 PM, Sat & Sun 10 AM - 8 PM. Estab 1967 for showing special exhibitions. Average Annual Attendance: 170,000

DUSSELDORF

M KONSERVATOR DER KUNSTDENKMALER,* von Nordrhein - Westfalen, Volkinger Str 49. Tel 4000 303 53 53. *Dir* Dr Paul Memmesheimer; *Cur* Dr Volkmar Essers
Open Tues - Sun 10 AM - 5 PM, Wed 10 AM - 8 PM, cl Mon. Admis DM 1. Estab 1961 as a 20th Century art collection. Gallery is an 18th Century castle. Average Annual Attendance: 50,000
Income: Financed by state appropriation
Collections: Paintings of the 20th Century starting from Fauvism, Expressionism and Cubism, it represents the main streams of contemporary art
Exhibitions: American painting since 1950; Paul Klee; Picasso
Activities: Classes for adults and children; lect open to public, 96 visiting lectr per year; tours
L Library,* von Nordrhein - Westfalen, Volkinger Str 49. *Librn* Gudrun Harms; *Asst to Librn* Helga Obschruff
Estab 1962 for the needs of the scientific staff members, will be opened to public in 1982. Maintains an art gallery
Income: Financed by city appropriation
Library Holdings: Vols 39,500; Per subs 32; Other—Exhibition catalogs, original art works
Special Subjects: Art of the 20th Century

L STAATLICHE KUNSTAKODEMIE DUSSELDORF - BIBLIOTHEK, Eiskellerstr 1. *Librn* Helmut Kleinenbroich
Open 9 AM - 4 PM. Estab 1777 as academic library for training and research

Purchases: $30,000
Library Holdings: Vols 60,000; Per subs 100; AV—Lantern Slides, slides; Other—Exhibition catalogs, framed reproductions, prints, manuscripts, original art works, photographs, reproductions, sculpture, German newspaper clippings
Special Subjects: Fine art
Collections: Archive on the Academy's actions

M **STÄDTISCHE KUNSTHALLE,** City Art Gallery, Grabbeplatz 4, Postfach 1120. Tel 36 57 83. *Dir* Jürgen Harten; *Executive Secy* Renata Sharp
Open Tues - Thurs 10 AM - 6 PM, Fri - Sun 10 AM - 8 PM, cl Mon. Admis DM 2, students DM .50. Estab 1967
Income: Financed by city and state appropriations
Publications: Exhibition catalogs
Activities: Dramatic programs; concerts

FRANKFURT

M **LIEBIEGHAUS, MUSEUM ALTER PLASTIK,** Museum of Sculpture, Schaumainkai 71. Tel 611-63 89 07. *Dir* Dr Herbert Beck; *Staff* Dr Peter C Bol; *Staff* Dr Bernhard Decker
Open Tues - Sun 10 AM - 5 PM, Wed 10 AM - 8 PM, cl Mon. Estab 1906-07 to exhibit sculpture. Average Annual Attendance: 60,000. Mem: 1300
Income: Financed by city appropriation
Collections: Sculpture from Ancient Times to the Middle Ages
Exhibitions: Altarkunst des Barock; Ariadne; Die Nabataer - Eine Arabische Kultur der Antike; Elfenbeinarbeiten aus der Sammlung Hupsh; Kunst um 1400 am Mittelrehein - Ein Teil der Wirklichkeit; Olympia - Eine Archaologische Grabung; Shulpturen - qarten 1929
Activities: Classes for adults and children; docent training; lect open to public, 3000 visiting lectr per year; original objects of art lent to different institutions; museum shop sells books, prints and slides
L **Library,** Schaumainkai 71.
Library Holdings: Vols 10,000; Per subs 50

M **MUSEUM FUR KUNSTANDWERK,** Museum of Arts and Crafts, Schaumainkai 15. Tel 212 4037. *Dir* Annaliese Ohm; *Cur* Dr Margrit Bauer
Open daily 1 - 5 PM, Wed 1 - 8 PM, cl Mon. No admis fee. Estab 1877 for decorative arts from the Middle Ages to the 20th Century, and Asiatic art. Average Annual Attendance, 47,000
Income: Financed by city appropriation
Purchases: $20,000
Collections: Bronzes, ceramics, furniture, glass, iron work, manuscripts, pewter, silverwork, textiles
L **Library,** Schaumainkai 15.
Reference only
Library Holdings: Vols 10,000; Micro—Prints 2000; Other—Photographs

M **STADELSCHES KUNSTINSTITUT,** Staedel Art Institute, Durerstrasse 2. *Dir* Dr Klaus Gallwitz; *Cur* Dr Paul Eich; *Cur* Dr Lutz S Malke; *Cur* Dr Margret Stuffman; *Cur* Dr Hans-Joachim Ziemke
Open Tues - Sun 10 AM - 5 PM, Wed 10 AM - 8 PM. Admis DM 2, Sun free. Estab 1816 to gather and to exhibit works of art for the public. Large building with 20 large rooms and 40 small rooms for paintings; an auditorium; department of prints and drawings; library; workshops and store-rooms. Average Annual Attendance: 150,000
Income: Financed by endowment, city and state appropriations
Purchases: DM 500,000
Collections: European schools from the 14th - 20th Centuries; 19th and 20th Centuries romantics, French Impressionists and modern paintings, drawings, prints; Old Masters; Dutch and Flemish - Hals, Jordaens, Rembrandt, Rubens, Vermeer; Early Netherland - Master of Flemalle, Bosch, Bouts, van der Goes, van der Weyden, van Eyck; German - Altdorfer, Durer, Holbein; Italian - Fra Angelico, Bellini, Botticelli, Pontormo, Tiepolo
Exhibitions: Dada in Europe; French Drawings from the Art Institute of Chicago; The Nazarenes; George Rickey; Russian Painting from 1890 - 1917
Publications: Stadel-Jahrbuch, bi-annually
Activities: Lect and exhibitions for members; concerts; gallery talks; tours; museum shop sells books, reproductions and slides
L **Bibliothek,** Duererstr 2. *Librn* Dr Marlinde Reinold; *Exchange Librn* Dr Sophie Bauer
Open Tues - Sat 10 AM - 5 PM. Estab 1816 for reference
Library Holdings: Vols 40,000; Per subs 92; Other—Clipping files 100,000, exhibition catalogs
Special Subjects: Auction catalogues since 18th Century

HAMBURG

M **HAMBURGER KUNSTHALLE,** Hamburg Art Museum, Glockengiesserwall 2. Tel 24 82 51. *Dr Werner/Hofmann*
Open Tues, Thurs - Sun 10 AM - 5 PM, Wed 10 AM - 7 PM, cl Mon. Admis DM 1. Estab 1869. Average Annual Attendance: 200,000
Collections: Ancient Coins; Masterworks of Painting from 14th Century to present, including Arp, Beckmann, Bertram, Boucher, Cranach, Dubuffet, Francke, Friedrich, Graubner, Hockney, Jones, Kandinsky, Klee, Kokoschka, Leger, Liebermann, Calude Lorrain, Manet, Menzel, Munch, Nolde, Olitzki, Picasso, Rembrandt, Runge, Tiepolo; Medals from 15th - 20th Centuries; Prints and Drawings from 14th - 20th Centuries; recent schools of Western Art for paintings and sculptures; Sculpture of 19th and 20th Centuries, including Arp, Barlach, Calder, Caro, Carpeaux, Giacometti, Grase, Hildebrand, Kolbe, Lehmbruck, Luginbuhl, Maillol, Marini, Moore, Nachi, Paolozzi, Man Ray, Rickey, Rodin, Schadow, Segal, Uhlmann
Exhibitions: Das Bild des Künstlers; Courbet und Deutschland; Leonardo da Vinci - Anatomische Zeichnungen; Honre Daumier - Bildwitz und Zeitkritik; John Flaxman - Mythologie und Industrie; Goya - Das Zeitalter der Revolutionen; Im Lebenstraum gefangen; Italienische Zeichnungen aus der Stiftung Ratjen; Jens Lausen: Der Bruch; Kasimir Malewitsch; Das Profilierungskarussell; Klaus Rinke;

Runge in seiner Zeit; Russische Malerei zur Zeit Gogols; Bernard Schultze: Zerbrochene Verstecke; Aby Warburg
Publications: Catalogs of permanent collection and exhibitions; series; special issues; Zur Sache
Activities: Lect open to public, 10 visiting lectr per year
L **Bibliothek der Hamburger Kunsthalle,** Glockengiesserwall 2. *Librn* Annette Stewner; *Librn* Ruth Latzel; *Librn Asst* Ursula Kabelac
Open Tues - Sat 10 AM - 5 PM, Wed 10 AM - 7 PM, cl Sun & Mon. Estab 1869 as reference, especially for staff members
Purchases: $43,000
Library Holdings: Vols 80,000; Per subs 262; AV—Fs, lantern Slides, slides, v-tapes; Other—Exhibition catalogs, prints, manuscripts, memorabilia, original art works, pamphlets, photographs, reproductions, sculpture
Special Subjects: 19th Century
Collections: Catalogues of auctions, collections and exhibitions

HANNOVER

M **KESTNER-MUSEUM,** Trammplatz 3. Tel 1 68 21 20, 1 68 21 27 30. *Dir* Dr Peter Munro; *Cur* Dr Helga Hilschenz; *Asst Cur* Dr Margildis Schulter
Open Tues, Wed & Fri 10 AM - 4 PM, Sat & Sun 10 AM - 6 PM, cl Mon & Thurs. No admis fee. Estab 1889
Income: Financed by city appropriation
Collections: Ancient, medieval and modern coins and medals; Egyptian, Greek, Etruscan and Roman art objects and medieval art; handicrafts, illuminated manuscripts and incunabula of the 15th - 20th centuries
Publications: Exhibition catalogues
Activities: Lect open to public; concerts
L **Library,** Trammplatz 3.
Library Holdings: Vols 30,000

KARLSHRUHE

M **STAATLICHE KUNSTHALLE,** State Art Gallery, Hans Thoma Str 2-4. Tel 071-135355. *Dir* Dr Horst Vey; *Deputy Dir* Dr Werner Zimmermann; *Dir Education* Dr Anneliese Reuter; *Dir Engraving* Dr Johann Eckart von Borries
Open Tues - Sun 10 AM - 1 PM and 2 - 5 PM, cl Mon. No admis fee. Estab 1803 for collecting and exhibiting
Income: Financed by state appropriation
Collections: 15th - 20th Century German Painting and Graphics; 16th - 20th Century Dutch, Flemish and French Paintings and Graphics
Exhibitions: Changing exhibitions
Publications: Yearbook
Activities: Classes for adults and children; docent training; lect open to public, 500 visiting lectr per year; gallery talks; competitions; junior museum
L **Library,** Hans Thoma Str 2-4. Tel 0721 1353358. *Librn* Sabine Schwermer
Open for reference Tues, Wed & Thurs 10 AM - Noon and 2 - 4 PM
Income: Financed by state appropriation
Purchases: $40,000
Library Holdings: Vols 110,000; Per subs 405; Other—Clipping files, exhibition catalogs, prints, memorabilia, original art works, pamphlets, photographs
Collections: Art periodicals, art sales catalogues, exhibition catalogues

MUNICH

O **BAYERISCHEN STAATSGEMALDESAMMLUNGEN,** Bavarian State Galleries of Art, 2 Meiserstr 10. Tel 089 55911. *Dir* Dr E Steingraber; *Cur 19th Century Art* Dr Eberhard Ruhmer; *Cur 19th Century Art* Dr Clinstof Heilmann; *Cur 20th Century Art* Dr Wolf-Dieter Dube; *Cur 20th Century Art* Dr Carla Schulz-Hoffmann; *Cur Flemish Paintings* Dr Rüdiger an der Heiderr; *Cur French Paintings* Dr J G Prinz von Hohenzollern; *Cur Italian Paintings* Dr Rolf Kultzen; *Cur Netherlandish Paintings* Dr Peter Eikemeier; *Cur Old German Paintings* Dr Gisela Goldberg; *Cur German Baroque Paintings* Dr Christian Lenz; *Dir Restoration Department* Dr Hubert Falkner von Sonnenburg; *Restoration Department* Dr Frank Preusser; *Restoration Department* Bruno Heimberg; *Restoration Department* Johann Koller
This organization administers art galleries of the Bavarian State. It has a laboratory for conservation and scientific research of paintings. Average Annual Attendance: 450,000
Income: Financed by state appropriation
Publications: Annual report
M **Alte Pinakothek,** Old Picture Gallery, Barerstr 27. Tel 089 286105.
Open Tues - Sun 9 AM - 4:30 PM, Tues & Thurs 7 - 9 PM, cl Mon. Estab 1836; founded upon the collections of the Bavarian Princes (since 1520)
Collections: European Old Masters
M **Staatsgalerie Moderne-Kunst,** State Gallery of Modern Art, Prinzregentenstr 1. Tel 089 292710.
Open Tues - Sun 9 AM - 4:30 PM, Thurs 7 - 9 PM, cl Mon
Collections: 20th Century Art - European paintings and sculpture
M **Schackgalerie,** Prinzregentenstr 9.
Open daily 9 AM - 4:30 PM, cl Tues
Collections: Late Romantic German Art
M **Neue Pinakothek,** Barrerstr 20.
Collections: European paintings and sculpture of the 19th Century

M **BAYERISCHES NATIONALMUSEUM,** Bavarian National Museum, Prinzregentenstrasse 2. Tel 2168-1. *General Dir* L Kriss-Rettenbeck; *Cur Ceramics and Glass* Dr R Rueckert; *Cur Clocks* Dr K Maurice; *Cur Conservation* J Haag; *Cur Folk Art* Dr I Bauer; *Cur Folk Art* Dr N Gockerell; *Cur Furniture* Dr G Himmelheber; *Cur Sculpture & Paintings* Dr A Schaedler; *Cur Sculpture & Paintings* Dr P Volk; *Cur Textiles* Dr S Durian-Ress
Open April - Sept Tues - Fri 9:30 AM - 4:30 PM, Oct - Mar 9 AM - 4:30 PM, Sat & Sun 10 AM - 4:30 PM. Estab 1855. Branch museum: Meissener Porzelan-Sammlung, Stiftung Ernst Schneider, Schloss Lustheim bei Schleissheim. Open Apr - Oct Tues - Fri 10 AM - 12:30 PM, and 1:30 - 5 PM, Nov - Mar 10

AM - 12:30 PM and 1:30 - 4 PM
Collections: European Art from 900 - 1850, decorative arts, paintings, sculpture; Meissen Porcelain; bronze, ceramics, clocks, folk art, furniture, glass, ivory, metalwork, stained glass, tapestries
Publications: Bildfuehrer; Forschungshefte; Muenchner Jahrbuch der Bildenden Kunst, annually
Activities: Lect open to public, 50 visiting lectr per year; book shop
L **Library,** Prinzregentenstrasse 2.
Library Holdings: Vols 55,000

M **MUISKA-MUSEUM,** Metzstrsse 31. Tel 089-453280. *Pres* Gisela von Frankenberg; *Chmn* Ike Neumann; *Art-Cur in Charge of Serigraphed Reproductions* Uli Binegger
Open Fri, Sat & Sun 4 - 8 PM. No admis fee. Estab 1977 for the translation of art from all times and races with the help of the Afro-American artist Lawrence Compton Kolawole's Motion-Art and its 24 ground-motives into informations, concerning all scientific faculties. Museum is divided in 5 sections: changing shows and library; synoptic world-formula; music-room; research-center; gallery for Kolawole's Motion-art, and Africa-Archiv in all sections
Income: Financed by membership and private donations
Collections: Gisela von Frankenberg's Collection of †Kowlawole's Motion-Art, consisting of paintings, sculptures, drawings and big-size photographs of antique art; plus a self-developed Sun-Computer of universal signs as key
Exhibitions: Permanent exhibition called 25,000 Years Knowledge as Art; combining antique art back to rock-carving with modern art; (1979) Pharao-Symbolics, decoded; (1980) American-Indian symbols, decoded; Germanic Symbols, decoded; Goddess Europe and The Double-Ax, decoded
Publications: Quarterly bulletin
Activities: Lending collection contains color reproductions and slides; museum shop sells original art, prints and catalogs
L **LIbrary,** Metzstrasse 31. *Librn* Gisela von Frankenberg
Reference library and information-system
Library Holdings: Vols 200
Special Subjects: Ancient Egypt, Africa, esterics and the manuscripts of the 3 vols Nommo-Logie written by Gisela von Frankenberg, as fundament for new science and research-center Muiska Workshops

M **STAATLICHE GRAPHISCHE SAMMLUNG,** National Graphic Collection, Meiserstr 10. Tel 089 5591-341. *Dir* Dr Dieter Kuhrmann; *National Cur* Dr Annegrit Schmitt; *Cur* Dr Gisela Schelfler; *Cur* Dr Richard Harprath; *Cur* Dr Konrad Renger
Open Mon - Fri 9 AM - 1 PM and 2 - 4:30 PM. Estab 1758 for the collection of prints and drawings of Western European and American masters. Average Annual Attendance: 13,000
Income: Financed by state appropriation
Collections: American, English, French, German, Italian and Netherlandish prints and drawings
Exhibitions: Ankäufe 1974-1978; Peter Candid, Zeichnungen; Graphik der Niederlande 1508-1617; Jasper Jones, Working Proofs; Vermächtnis Kruss, Graphik des Expressionismus; Giovanni Battista Piranesi, Zeichnungen und Druckgraphik; Karl Rössing, Linolschnitte; Von Dillis Bis Piloty
Publications: Exhibition catalogs
Activities: Lect open to public; original objects of art lent to other print rooms; originate traveling exhibitions
L **Library,** Meiserstr 10. *Librn* Liselotte Becher
Library Holdings: Vols 25,000; Per subs 20; Other—Exhibition catalogues of graphics
Special Subjects: Illustrated books

M **STAATLICHE SAMMLUNG AEGYPTISCHER KUNST,** State Collection of Egyptian Art, Residenz, Hofgartenstr, Meiserstr 10. Tel 089 55 91 350. *Dir* Dr Dietrich Wildung
Open 9:30 AM - 4 PM, Tues 7 - 9 PM, cl Mon. Admis DM 1.50. Estab 1970 to collect and preserve Egyptian art from prehistory to Coptic period. Average Annual Attendance: 40,000. Mem: 900; dues DM 75; annual meeting June
Income: Financed by state appropriation
Purchases: DM 55,000
Exhibitions: Götter - Pharaonen Egyptian Art from Cairo and Alexandria; Von Troja bis Amarna; Blumen der Wuste; Tutanchamun
Publications: Studien zur altaegyptischen Kultur, 2 vols per year
Activities: Lect open to public, 2 - 3 visiting lectr per year; original objects of art lent to museums; lending collection contains original prints, photographs, sculpture and slides

M **STADTISCHE GALLERIE IM LANBACHHAUS,** Lenbach House City Gallery, Luisenstrasse 33. Tel 52 1041-43. *Dir* Dr Armin Zweite; *Cur* Dr Helmut Friedel; *Cur* Dr Rosel Bollek; *Archivist* Dr Felena Hahl
Open daily 9 AM - 4:30 PM, cl Mon. Admis 1.50 DM, students .50 DM. Estab 1925 to collect objects of art produced in Munich and Bavaria, mainly paintings and sculpture. Average Annual Attendance: 100,000
Collections: Art Nouveau; †The Blue Rider and Kandinsky and Klee; †Paintings of the 19th century (Munich school); Kirbin Archives; Neue Sachlichkeit; Franz von Lenbach, his paintings and private collection of art objects; †contemporary art, prints and drawings, 19th and 20th Centuries

NUREMBERG

L **BIBLIOTHEK DER AKADEMIE DER BILDENDEN KÜNSTE IN NÜRNBERG,** Bingstr 60.
Estab 1662
Library Holdings: Vols 12,000; Per subs 20; Other—Exhibition catalogs

M **GERMANISCHES NATIONAL MUSEUM,** Germanic National Museum, Kornmarkt 1. Tel 20 39 71. *Chief Dir* Dr Arno Schönberger
Open Tues - Sun 9 AM - 4 PM, Thurs evenings 8 - 9:30 PM. Admis DM 2. Estab 1852. Average Annual Attendance: 220,000. Mem: 9000; dues DM 25
Collections: Ancient historical objects, archives, coins, furniture, graphics,

instruments, musical instruments, paintings, sculpture, textiles, toys, weapons
Activities: Lect; gallery talks; tours; concerts
L **Bibliothek,** Kartäusergrasse 1, Nürnberg D-8500. *Dir* Dr Elisabeth Rücker; *Asst* Dr Eduard Isphording; *Asst* Dr Ursula Mende
Open Tues 9 AM - 5 PM, Wed & Thurs 9 AM - 8 PM, Fri 9 AM - 4 PM, cl Sat, Sun & Mon. Estab 1852 as special library for public with reading room
Library Holdings: Vols 420,000; Per subs 1400; Micro—Fiche; Other—Exhibition catalogs, prints, manuscripts, original art works, pamphlets, photographs
Special Subjects: History of culture and civilization in German speaking areas of the middle of Europe
Collections: History of Art; Historical Periodicals from the 19th Century to present; History of Musical Instruments; 3000 prints of the 16th Century manuscripts; Volkskunde 1000 incunables

STUTTGART

M **STAATSGALERIE STUTTGART,** Konrad-Adenauer-Strasse 32. Tel 0711-212-5108. *Dir* Prof P Beye; *Dir* Dr G Ewald; *Dir Department of Prints & Drawings* Dr G Thiem; *Cur Prints & Drawings 15th - 18th Century* Dr H Geissler; *Cur Prints & Drawings 19th - 20th Century* Dr V Gauss; *Cur 19th Century* Dr V Holst; *Cur 20th Century* Dr K Frank V Maut; *Cur 20th Century* Dr G Tuboden; *Cur Nederlandish Painting* Dr R Klapproth
Open 10 AM - 5 PM, Tues & Thurs 10 AM - 8 PM, cl Mon. No admis fee. Estab 1843 for collection of European Art 14th - 20th Century; main section for International Art of the 20th Century. Average Annual Attendance: 170,000
Collections: †European Art 14th - 20th Century; †International Art of the 20th Century
Publications: Exhibition catalogs
Activities: Tours 16 per month; sales shop sells catalogs, reproductions, prints and slides
L **Bibliothek,** Konrad-Adenauer-Strasse 32.
Open only for art historians, mainly for staff members
Library Holdings: Vols 40,000; Per subs 50

GHANA

ACCRA

M **GHANA NATIONAL MUSEUM,*** Barnes Rd, PO Box 3343. Tel 021-21633, 021-21635. *Dir* Prof R B Nunoo; *Asst Dir* K A Myles; *Archaeology Keeper* E K Agorsah; *Admin Secy* J D Amissah-Arthur
Open daily 8 AM - 6 PM, cl Mon. Admis 10 pesewas. Estab 1957 as a teaching museum at Achimota and Legon, University of Ghana. Gallery is circular in shape with masonite floor which accommodates both archaeological art and ethnographic materials. Average Annual Attendance: 206,702
Income: Financed by state appropriation
Collections: Archaeology: Materials showing the sequence culture in the whole of Africa, also materials obtained from sites in Ghana, such as Ahinsan, Asebu, Beifikrom, Dawu, Efutu, Twifu Hemang, indicating Stone and Iron Ages; Art: Contemporary Ghanaian graphics, metal products, painting and sculpture; Ethnographic: Materials on Chieftaincy and other traditional institutions, festivals, rites, traditional occupations
Exhibitions: Asafo Companies; Kobina Bucknor (paintings); Ekow Bentil, Quao and Company (paintings and sculpture); Ewe Textiles; Museums in Education; Vittorio Quintavalle (paintings)
Publications: Annual Museum Lectures; Elmina Castle; Christiansborg; Museum Handbook
Activities: Classes for adults and children; lect open to public, 6 visiting lectr per year; gallery talks; tours; exten dept serves Ghana; museum shop sells books
L **Library,*** Barnes Rd, PO Box 3343. *Librn* Ramsay F K Abaze
Open for reference to staff, visiting researchers and students
Library Holdings: Vols 3000; Per subs 30
Special Subjects: Archaeology, African art and history
Collections: African Archaeology and Studies

GREECE

ATHENS

M **BENAKI MUSEUM,** 1, odos Koumbari. Tel 3612694, 3611617. *Chmn* Lambros Eftaxias; *Dir* Dr Angleos Delivorrias; *Cur Photographic Archives Department* Emilia Yeroulanou
Open Nov - May 8:30 AM - 2 PM, June - Oct 8:30 AM - 2 PM and 4:30 - 7:30 PM. Admis 50 drachmas, students 20 drachmas, Sun free. Estab 1931, the house of Emmanuel Benakis was donated to the State by his children and was transformed into a museum by Anthony Benakis in order to house his private collections. Gallery consists of - Greek-Roman Antiquities Department; Byzantine and Post-Byzantine Department; Greek Popular Department; Greek Historical Relics Department; Historical Archives Department; Photographic Archives Department; Eastern Art Department. Average Annual Attendance: 136,921. Mem: 630; dues 400 drachmas
Income: $2,500,000 drachmas (financed by admission fees, endowment and state appropriation)
Collections: Ancient Greek Art, chiefly jewelry; Byzantine and post-Byzantine Art, Icons and minor crafts; Collections of Islamic Art and Chinese Porcelain; Greek Popular Art and Historical Relics; Greek Historical Archives
Exhibitions: (1978) Ancient Greek Art, N P; Goulandris Collection; (1979) Domenicos Theotokopoules El Greco; Traditional Greek Jewellery
Publications: Catalogs and guides

Activities: Lect for members only; original objects of art lent to other museums; originate traveling exhibitions; museum shop sells books, reproductions, prints, slides, jewelry and postcards

L **Library,** 1, odos Koumbari. *Librn* Mrs Pitsa Tsakona
Open 8:30 AM - 2 PM. Estab 1931, the collection of the library assists the study and research of the exhibits of the museum and other related objects
Library Holdings: Vols 18,000; Per subs 51; Other—2 Incunabula, rare books
Collections: 250 Volumes of valuable and Rare Books; 2000 watercolours, engravings and sketches

M **BYZANTINE MUSEUM,** Vassilissis Sofias Ave 22. Tel 711-027. *Dir Ephore of Byzantine Antiquities* Paul Lazaridis
Open winter 9 AM - 4:30 PM, summer 7:30 AM - 7:30 PM. Estab 1931
Collections: Byzantine icons, ceramics, marbles, metalwork; Post-Byzantine icons, ceramics, marbles, metalwork; Icons enlarged by the Loverdos Collection
Activities: Lect; individual paintings and original objects of art lent; book traveling exhibitions; originate traveling exhibitions; sales shop sells books, reproductions, prints and slides

M **NATIONAL PINAKOTHIKI AND ALEXANDER SOUTZOS MUSEUM,** 50, av Vass Constantinoulos. Tel 711-010. *Dir* Dr Dimitrious Papastamos; *Restorer* Mrs Evdoxia Carayanni
Open Tues - Sat 9 AM - 4 PM, Sun 10 AM - 2 PM, cl Mon. Admis 20 drachmas. Estab 1900 as a picture gallery for Greek painting, sculpture and prints from the 17th - 20th Century; European painting and prints from the 14th - 20th Century. Museum consists of two main parts, the first houses temporary exhibitions while the permanent collections are displayed in the second. Average Annual Attendance: 160,000. Mem: 115; dues 200 drachmas; annual meeting Aug
Income: Financed by endowment and state appropriation
Collections: Engravings, including Dürer, Goya, Rembrandt; 14th - 20th Century European painting, including Caravaggio, El Greco, Jordaens, Mondrian, Picasso, Poussin and Tiepolo; 17th - 20th Century Greek engravings, paintings and sculpture; impressionist, post-impressionist and contemporary drawings
Exhibitions: Recent British Art; Contemporary Bulgarian Paintings; Contemporary Yugoslavian Art; Fifteen Finnish Artists; French Medieval Sculpture; 19th and 20th Century Hungarian Prints; Graphics by Oskar Kokoschka; Panorama of French Art 1960-1975; Retrospective Exhibitions of A Asteriadis, G Busianis, A Diamantis, D Diamantopoulos, A Kontopoulos, S Papaloukas, V Semertzidis, D Yoldassis
Publications: Catalogs of all exhibitions and studies on aspects of contemporary art
Activities: Classes for children; lect open to concerts; gallery talks; tours; exten dept; individual paintings lent; sales shop sells books, magazines and prints

L **Library,** 50, av Vass.
Open to students and scholars for reference only
Library Holdings: Vols 2500

HONG KONG

EDINBURGH PLACE

M **HONG KONG MUSEUM OF ART,** City Hall. Tel 5-224127. *Cur* L C S Tam
Open Sun & public holidays 1 - 6 PM, weekdays 10 AM - 6 PM, cl Thurs. No admis fee. Estab 1962 to provide through the museum's collections, displays and specialized staff, an education centre for all residents of Hong Kong. Average Annual Attendance: 300,000
Income: HK$ 50,000 (financed by Hong Kong taxpayers)
Purchases: HK$ 360,000
Collections: Chinese Antiquities including comprehension collection of Chinese Pottery from the Neolithic to the Q'ing (Ch'ing) Period, and other minor arts such as cloissone, lacquer, bronze and enamelled wares; Chinese Paintings with a specialization of Cantonese artists, Historical Collection of paintings, prints and drawings of Hong Kong, Macau and China; local and contemporary art
Exhibitions: Children's Art; Chinese Bamboo Carving; Contemporary French Prints; Contemporary Japanese Paintings; Pictures of the Floating World and Exhibitions on Contemporary Hong Kong Artists; Snuff Bottle of the Ch'ing Dynasty
Publications: Exhibition catalogs and books; free newsletter, monthly; reproductions and postcards
Activities: Guided tours for schools; competitions

HUNGARY

BUDAPEST

M **MAGYAR NEMZETI GALERIA,** Hungarian National Gallery, Budavari Palota, 1250 Budapest, PO Box 31. Tel 160-100. *Dir General* Dr G E Pogany; *Deputy Dir General* Dr Balint Szege; *Deputy Dir General* Mrs Gyöngyi Eri; *Scientific Secy* Eva Penzes
Open Tues - Sun 10 AM - 6 PM, cl Mon. Admis 3 F, children free & Sat free. Estab 1957 for the collection, conservation and exhibition of works of Hungarian plastic arts. Average Annual Attendance: 710,000
Income: Financed by state appropriation
Purchases: 1,790,000 F
Collections: †Ancient Hungarian Art, †Contemporary Hungarian Collection, †Hungarian graphic art, †Modern Hungarian paintings and †Sculpture; †Medal cabinet; †Naive Art
Publications: Bulletin Annales; catalogs; exhibition catalogs
Activities: Classes for children; dramatic programs; docent training; lect open to public; concerts; gallery talks; tours; competitions; individual paintings and original

objects of art lent to museums and exhibition halls; originate traveling exhibitions; sales shop sells reproductions

L **Library,** Budapest 1250, Budavari Palota Pf 31. *Librn* Eva Rozsa
Open Mon - Fri 9 AM - 4 PM. Estab 1957 for special literature
Income: Financed by state appropriation
Library Holdings: Vols 40,000; Per subs 103
Special Subjects: Fine Arts

M **SZEPMUVESZET MUSEUM,** Museum of Fine Arts, Dozsa Gyorgy ut 41. Tel 429-759. *Dir-General* Dr Klara Garas; *Deputy Dir* Dr T Szentlekey; *Head Egyptian Antiquities* Dr V Wessetsky; *Head Egyptian Antiquities* Edit Varga; *Head Greek & Roman Antiquities* Dr J Gy Szilagyi; *Head Modern Art* Brigitta Cifka; *Head Old Pictures* Dr M H Takacs; *Head Old Pictures* Zsuzsanna Urbach; *Head Old Sculpture* Dr E Eszlary; *Head Prints & Drawings* Terez Gerszi
Open Tues - Sun 10 AM - 6 PM, cl Mon. Admis 3 florins, students and schools free. Estab 1906 to collect works of art within the spheres of classic archaeology and European art history, 13th - 20th Century. Average Annual Attendance: 400,000. Mem: 500; annual meeting 4 per year
Income: Financed by state appropriation
Collections: †Egyptian, Greek and Roman Antiquities; †modern paintings and sculpture, 19th - 20th Century; †old pictures, 13th - 18th Century; old sculpture, 4th - 18th Century; †prints and drawings, 14th - 20th Century
Publications: Bulletin, semi-annually; catalogs
Activities: Educ dept; educ program for adults; free university; classes for adults and children; lect open to public; gallery talks; guided tours for schools and groups; original objects of art lent; originate traveling exhibitions

L **Library,** Dozsa Gyorgy ut 41. *Head Art Historian* Eszter Gabor
Open Mon, Wed & Fri 1 - 8 PM, Tues, Thurs & Sat 9 AM - 1 PM, cl Sun and holidyas. Founded in 1896, opened to public in 1906, to aid research work in the field of classic archaeology and European art history
Library Holdings: Vols 80,000; Per subs 1200
Special Subjects: Classic archaeology, European art history
Collections: Literature dealing with Egyptian, Greek and Roman Antiquities, European sculpture, paintings, prints and drawings

ICELAND

REYKJAVIK

M **LISTASAFN EINARS JONSSONAR,** National Einar Jonsson Gallery, Eiriksgata, PO Box 1051. Tel 1-37-97. *Dir* Olafur Kvaran; *Chmn* Jon Auduns
Open May - Aug Tues - Sun 1:30 - 4 PM, winter Sun & Wed 1:30 - 4 PM. Admis 100 Icel Krones. Estab 1923. Museum contains almost all works of the sculptor Einar Jonsson (1974-1954) donated by him to the Icelandic State
Income: Financed by state appropriation

M **THJODMINJASAFN,** National Museum of Iceland, Sudurgata, PO Box 1439. Tel 1-67-79, 1-32-64. *Dir* Filkand Thor Magnusson; *Cur* Prudmundur Olafsson; *Cur Textiles* Elsa E Gudjonsson; *Cur* Halldor J Jonsson; *Cur* Arni Bjornsson; *Cur* Thorkell Grimsson
Open Sept - May Sun, Tues, Thurs & Sat 1:30 - 4 PM, June - Aug daily 1:30 - 4 PM. No admis fee. Estab 1863 for archaeology, ethnology and folklore. Average Annual Attendance: 40,000
Income: $4000 (financed by state appropriation)
Collections: Archaeological and ethnological artifacts, Icelandic antiquities, portraits, numismatics
Publications: Arbok (yearbook), published by the Archaeological Society

INDIA

BARODA

M **MUSEUM AND PICTURE GALLERY,** Sayaji Park. Tel 64-605, 63-609. *Dir* Dr S K Bhowmik; *Keeper Art & Archaeological Sections* Shri M N Gandhi; *Keeper Gandhi, Art and Architecture* R K Shri
Open Mon, Tues, Wed and Fri 9:30 AM - 5 PM, Thurs 10 AM - 5 PM. Museum estab 1894; Picture Gallery estab 1920. Average Annual Attendance: 600,000
Collections: Ancient, Medieval and Modern Indian Art; Asiatic and Egyptian collections; Coins; European, Greek and Roman civilizations and art; European paintings; Indian archaeology, prehistoric and historic; Modern paintings; Natural History and Ethnological Collection
Exhibitions: Four exhibitions per year
Publications: Bulletin, annually; thematic monograph
Activities: Lect, 5 visiting lectr per year; films; children's section

CALCUTTA

M **INDIAN MUSEUM,** 27 Jawaharlal Nehru Rd. Tel 23-98-55. *Dir* Dr Sunil C Ray
Open winter AM - 4:30 PM, summer 10 AM - 5 PM. Estab 1814 through the efforts and collections of the Asiatic Society of Bengal which had been founded in 1784. Average Annual Attendance: 9,000,000. Mem: Being under a Board of Trustees and subsidized by the Union Government of India, the Board meets 4 times a year; annual general meeting third week of March
Income: Rs 34,000,000 (financed by Grant-in-aid from Union Government)
Purchases: Rs 1,000,000

Collections: Bronzes and bronze figures, ceramic, coins, copper and stone implements of prehistoric and proto-historic origin, crystal, gold and silver ornaments, ivory, jade, metalware, miniature paintings, papiermache, steatite objects, stone sculptures, stucco figures, terracotta objects, textiles, woodcarvings, tribal and regional objects including sets of cultural objects represented by garments, headdress, ornaments, weapons, utensils, etc
Exhibitions: Mobil-exhibitions on Indian History and Archaeology by 28 diorama cases kept in Museo-lens, and rotating exhibitions
Activities: Educ film-shows under students programme; special gallery class for children and primary students; exten dept; loan-kit service for the school students; book traveling exhibitions
L **Library,** 27 Jawaharlal Nenru Rd.
Library Holdings: Vols 8800; Per subs 6500; Other—Rest area maps, reprints, and other publications

NEW DELHI

M **LALIT KALA AKADEMI,** National Academy of Art,* Rabindra Bhavan, Ferozeshan Rd. Tel 387241. *Chmn* Karl J Khandalavala
Open 10 AM - 5 PM. Estab 1954 by the Government of India as an autonomous body of artists, critics, art historians and state representatives, variously elected and partly nominated. The Academy is a Central State Organization to evolve a program to further the cause of art and artists through publications, exhibitions, artists' camps, survey, seminars, and a major triennial of world art held in New Delhi
Income: Financed by state appropriation
Collections: Permanent collection of graphics, paintings and sculpture
Publications: Two journals - Lalit Kala (ancient), Lalit Kala Contemporary, bi-annually; monographs; large multicolor reproductions; portfolios; scholarly publications; treatises
Activities: Artists workshop with well-equipped studios for painters, sculptors, ceramists and printmakers
L **Library,*** Rabindra Bhavan, Ferozeshan Rd.
Open 10 AM - 5 PM for scholars, students and artists
Library Holdings: Other—Archival material of catalogs, photographs and slides

M **NATIONAL GALLERY OF MODERN ART,** Jaipur House, Dr Zakir Husain Rd. Tel 38-2835, 38-4560, 38-4640. *Dir* Dr L P Sihare; *Restorer* Sukanta Basu; *Deputy Keeper Art Coll* S K Sahni; *Deputy Keeper Education* Dr Anis Farooqi; *Sr Guide Lecture* Vacant; *Guide Lecture* R N Batham; *Sr Technical Asst* Chintamani Vgas; *Technical Asst* B K Pant; *Photographer* P K Ray
Open weekdays 10 AM - 5 PM, cl Mon. No admis fee. Inaugurated 1954 to develop a representative collection of Indian and international modern art, essentially painting, sculpture, graphics, photography, industrial design and architecture recovering a span of more than 100 years and put them on view to the public. Museum has a very intensive special exhibition, educational and publication programme
Income: Financed by the Government of India, Union Ministry of Education, Social Welfare and Culture, under whom it is functioning as a subordinate office
Collections: Indian contemporary paintings, sculptures and graphics. These are displayed in a chronological order as far as possible so as to give a bird's eye view of the evolution of modern Indian Art since 1857
Publications: Colour reproductions; expressionist; folders; Handbook of Bengal School; Handbook of Painting and Graphics; Handbook of Sculptures; monographs; picture postcards; selections from the Collection of the National Gallery of Modern Art
Activities: Short term art appreciation seminars for students and teachers organized; gallery talks at 11 AM and 3 PM daily by guide lectrs; conducted tours on prior appointment; Mobile Exhibition Bus; art objects lent only under special circumstances; lending collection contains 3000 Kodachrome slides; originate traveling exhibitions
L **Reference Library,** Jaipur House, Dr Zakir Husain Rd. *Librn* Mrs Geeta Ray
Open 10 AM - 5 PM, cl Mon. Estab 1954 for reference purposes and research in contemporary Indian and international art
Income: Financed by Central Government
Purchases: Rs 40,000
Library Holdings: Vols 6000; Per subs 30
Special Subjects: Architecture, Graphic Arts, Industrial Design, Photography, Sculpture, painting

M **NATIONAL MUSEUM OF INDIA,** Janpath 11. Tel 38-5441, 38-5444. *Dir* N R Bannerjee
Open 10 AM - 5 PM, cl Mon. Estab 1949. Average Annual Attendance: 200,000
Collections: †Arabic, Indian, Persian, Sanskrit Language Manuscripts 10,000; Central Asian Antiquities and Murals; Museum Conservation Laboratory; Pre-Columbian and Western Art Collection 800; Prehistory Indus Valley Culture; †arms, bronzes, †coins 40,000, †decorative arts, †technology, †Miniatures and drawings 14,000, mural paintings, †sculptures (stone and terra cottas) from 3rd Century BC to 18th Century
Exhibitions: Four - five per year
Publications: Annual Bulletin; special publications on art and archaeology
Activities: Cultural programs; educational movies related to archaeology, monuments, art; lect open to public, 10 - 20 visiting lectr per year; guided tours
L **Library,** Janpath 11. *Sr Librn* Bal Krishan
Open 10 AM - 5 PM
Purchases: 50,000
Library Holdings: Vols 28,000; Per subs 100; AV—Slides; Other—Clipping files, exhibition catalogs, photographs, reproductions
Collections: T Desika Chari; Verrier Elwin Collection; Nasli and Alice Heeramanechk Collection

IRELAND

DUBLIN

M **HUGH LANE MUNICIPAL GALLERY OF MODERN ART,** Charlemont House, Parnell Square. Tel 01-741903. *Cur* Ethna Waldron; *Clerical Officer* Patricia Flavin
Open Tues - Sat 10 AM - 6 PM, Sun 11 AM - 2 PM, cl Mon. Estab 1908; in present premises since 1933. The house is an 18th Century town house, once the home of Lord Charlemont. The collection of paintings owes its inception largely to the generosity and public spirit of Sir Hugh Lane. Average Annual Attendance: 45,000
Income: Financed by city appropriation
Purchases: L30,000
Collections: Works of Irish artist Jack B Yeats; 19th Century French works; works by contemporary painters
Exhibitions: Temporary exhibitions are held monthly
Activities: Lect open to public; concerts; gallery talks; tours; individual paintings and original objects of art lent to government offices and libraries; lending collection contains original art works, original prints and paintings

M **NATIONAL GALLERY OF IRELAND,** Merrion Square W. Tel 01 767571. *Dir* James White; *Asst Dir* Michael Wynne; *Restorer Paper* Maighread McParland; *Restorer Painting* Andrew O'Connor; *Education Officer* N O'Sullivan; *Registrar* Eibhlin McCarthy; *Cur* R Keaveney; *Cataloguer* J Hutchinson
Open Mon - Sat 10 AM - 6 PM, Sun 2 - 5 PM, Thurs 10 AM - 9 PM. No admis fee. Estab 1854 to show all aspects of Western painting. Gallery consists of 42 rooms containing 2000 works of art. Average Annual Attendance: 557,345
Income: Financed by government endowment
Collections: †American, British, Dutch, Flemish, French, German, Greek, Italian, Irish, Russian, and Spanish Art
Exhibitions: Frequent temporary exhibitions
Publications: Catalogs
Activities: Classes for adults and children; treasure hunts for children, to identify and explain pictures; lect open to public; concerts; gallery talks; tours; individual paintings and original objects of art lent to museums and art galleries; sales shop sells books, reproductions, prints and slides
L **Art Reference Library,** Merrion Square W. *Librn* Ann Stewart
Open Mon - Fri 10 AM - 5:15 PM. Estab 1968 as art reference library for public use and staff research
Library Holdings: Vols 20,000; Per subs 160; AV—Slides; Other—Clipping files, exhibition catalogs, prints, manuscripts, memorabilia, original art works, pamphlets, photographs, reproductions, posters
Special Subjects: Gallery collections, Irish art
Collections: Photographs, sales and exhibition catalogues

M **NATIONAL MUSEUM OF IRELAND,** Kildare St. Tel 76 55 21. *Dir* A B O Riordain; *Keeper Antiquities* M F Ryan; *Keeper Art* John Teahan; *Keeper Folklife* John C O'Sullivan; *Keeper Natural History Division* Dr C O'Riordan
Open Tues - Sat 10 AM - 5 PM, Sun 2 - 5 PM, cl Mon. Estab 1731 by Royal Dublin Society. Average Annual Attendance: 173,000
Collections: †Art and Industrial Division, †Irish Antiquities Division, Irish Folklife Division, †Natural History Division
Publications: Occasional guides to collections and specialist catalogs of particular collections
L **Library,** Kildare St.
Library Holdings: Vols 10,000

RATHKEALE

L **IRISH INTERNATIONAL ARTS CENTRE,** Castle Matrix Library, *Librn* Denise Economos
Open July & Aug Mon - Fri 2 - 5 PM. Estab 1970 as student reference library
Purchases: $3500
Library Holdings: Vols 12,000; AV—Fs, Kodachromes; Other—Prints, manuscripts, memorabilia, original art works, pamphlets
Special Subjects: Printmaking, Irish history, mythology
Collections: Original Prints of the great masters from Dürer and Rembrandt to modern times
Exhibitions: Original prints and manuscripts

ISRAEL

BEIT-SHAN

M **MUNICIPALITY OF BEIT-SHAN,** Municipal Beit-Shan-Museum, PO Box I. Tel 065-86221. *Dir* Eizenberg Arie; *Archaeology in Beit-Shan* Nehemia Zuri
Open 8 AM - 3:30 PM, Fri 8 AM - 12:30 PM. Admis tours 25 IL, adults 15 IL, children 7 IL. Estab 1949-50 for showing the history and place of Beit-Shan from 700 years before Christ until 1800. Built in a historical mosque
Income: Financed by city appropriation; Municipality and department of education and department of education in Jerusalem
Collections: Ceramic archaeological items, mosaic floors, statues, showing boxes
Activities: Lect and explanations open to public

HAIFA

M **MUSEUM OF ANCIENT ART,*** 26 Shabbetai Levy St. *Dir* Dr J Elgavish; *Archaeologist* Mrs M Banai
Open Mon 10 AM - 5 PM, Sat 10 AM - 1 PM. Estab 1948 for Ancient art of the Mediterranean basin, till the Islamic conquest 632 AD

Collections: Ancient Haifa; Ancient coins from Israel; Antiquities from the excavations of Shikmona from the 18th Century BC until 7th Century AD; Biblical, Cypriote and Greek pottery; Coptic Textiles; Egyptian collection; Jewish and provincial coins; objects from the sea of Haifa; oil lamps from Israel; Roman glass from Israel; Roman portraits from Fayum; Roman portrait paintings from Egypt
Publications: Catalogues, reports on the excavations of Shikmona
Activities: Lect open to public; gallery talks; tours
L **Library,** 26 Shabbetai Levy St. *Librn* Mrs E Pizanti

M **MUSEUM OF JAPANESE ART,** 89, Hanassi Ave. Tel 04 - 83554. *Dir* Eli Lancman; *Secy* Channa Ben-David; *Research Asst* Pnina Eden
Open Mon - Thurs 10 AM - 1PM and 4 - 7 PM, Sat 10 AM - 2 PM. Admis 25 Ag, Sat free. Estab 1958 to preserve and display Japanese art. One exhibition hall divided into permanent display and changeable exhibitions. Average Annual Attendance: 40,000
Income: Financed by city appropriation
Purchases: $10,000
Exhibitions: (1978-79) Art in Monochrome-Paintings and Drawings; Big Art in Small Size; Ghosts and Demons in Japanese Art; Ikebana-Flower Exhibition; Japanese Paintings and Drawings in the Genere Tradition; Modern Japanese Prints; Tea Taste in Japanese Art; Utagawa Kuniyoshi-Prints and Drawings; Years of Transition-Japanese Prints and Paintings
Publications: Bilingual exhibition catalogues
Activities: Educ Dept on Japanese Culture; lect open to public; concerts; original objects of art lent to museums; sales shop sells reproductions, posters, photographs and postcards
L **Library of the Japanese Museum,** 89, Hanassi Ave.
Open daily 10 AM - 1 PM. Estab 1960 to serve the public on research work on Japanese art and cultural
Purchases: $15,000
Library Holdings: Vols 1500; Micro—Cards, fiche, prints; Other—Clipping files, exhibition catalogs, framed reproductions, manuscripts, reproductions

M **MUSEUM OF MODERN ART,** 26 Shabtai Levi St. Tel 04-52 32 55. *Dir* Gabriel Tadmor; *Cur* Judith Shen-Dar; *Cur* Ioana Nicolau
Open Sun - Thurs 10 AM - 5 PM, Sat 10 AM - 1 PM, cl Fri. Estab 1951. Average Annual Attendance: 10,500
Collections: Special collection of paintings by the late M Shemi Hall. †Israel paintings, sculpture, drawings and prints; †Modern American, French, German and English paintings; reproductions; †Posters
Exhibitions: Special bi-annual shows, Young Israeli Artis' Show, in honor of the late Dr Schiff
Activities: Weekdays films; lect and student lect; gallery talks; Sat lect for tourists in English; competitions; awards; lending collection contains reproductions and slides for schools
L **Library,** 26 Shabtai Levi St.
8000 items with emphasis on modern art

JERUSALEM

M **ISRAEL MUSEUM,** Hakirya, PO Box 1299. Tel 02-636231. *Dir General* Yoram Ravin; *Dir of Public Affairs* Meir Meyer; *Chief Cur Arts* Dr Martin Weyl; *Chief Cur Bronfman Archaeological Museum* Dr Yaakov Meshorer; *Cur Youth Wing* Ayala Gordon
Open Sun, Mon, Wed, Thurs AM - 5 PM, Fri & Sat 10 AM - 2 PM, Tues 4 - 10 PM. Admis adults IL 15, students IL 5, under 18 IL 3. Estab 1965 as a comprehensive museum. Average Annual Attendance: 800,000. Mem: 5800; dues family IL 300, individual IL 180; annual meeting April or May
Income: Financed by endowment, membership, city and state appropriation
Collections: Ancient Glass; Archaeological Wing; 18th Century English Dining Room; 18th Century French Period Room; 18th Century Venetian Room; Judaica; Pre-Columbian; Billy Rose Art Garden; Shrine of the Book (housing the Dead Sea Scrolls); Youth Wing; ethnography, impressionist and post-impressionist, old masters
Exhibitions: (1979-80) Ancient Glass; Arts in Palestine in the 19th Century; Chiaroscuro: The Beginning of Color Woodcut; Lou Dorfsman and 25 Years of CBS Design; Egyptian Children Paint Peace; Sam Francis: Paintings 1976-78; The Ladejinsky Collection of Asian Art; The Maremont Collection of Pre-Columbian Art: The Human Image; New Buildings in Old Environments; Pins Collection: Chinese and Japanese Paintings and Prints; Studies in Connoisseurship: Chinese Paintings from the Arthur M Sackler Collection; Turner and the Bible
Publications: Exhibition catalogs; Israel Museum News, annually; program, monthly
Activities: Classes for adults and children; dramatic programs; docent training; lect open to public; concerts; gallery talks; tours; competitions; originate traveling exhibitions; museum shop sells books, reproductions, prints, slides and postcards; Youth Wing
L **Library for Art and Archaeology,** Hakirya, PO Box 1299. *Chief Librn* Yaffa Szereszewski; *Librn* Naama Marom; *Librn* Elisheva Rechtman; *Librn* Carmela Teichman
Open Sun, Mon, Wed, Thurs 10 AM - 2 PM, Tues 4 - 8 PM. Estab 1965 for use of staff, students, teachers and general public
Income: Financed by endowment
Library Holdings: Vols 55,000; Per subs 200; Other—Clipping files, exhibition catalogs

TEL-AVIV

M **HAARETZ MUSEUM,** University St, Ramat Aviv, PO Box 17068. Tel 03-415244-248. *Dir General Haaretz Museum* J Caleff; *Secy Haartz Museum* Mrs S Navot; *Dir Institute for Promotion Art & Science* Dr E Landau; *Public Relations Officer in Charge Activities & Members Organization* Miss P Unger; *Dir Theater Museum* Y Gabay
Open 9 AM - 4 PM, Fri 9 AM - 1 PM, Sat 10 AM - 2 PM. Admis $1, Sat free. Founded in 1952, opened to public 1959, originally founded as a pavilion-style museum of the east Mediterranean, aiming to familiarize the public, especially the

youth, with the rich cultural heritage of this cradle region of humanity. Museums that were added are: Man and His Work Museum; Open-Air Museum; Teaching, Research, Documentation and Instruction Center for the History of Work Implements; Theater Museum with a collection of historical data concerning the Jewish theater in the last hundred years; the Independence Hall with an adjacent museum. Average Annual Attendance: 600,000. Mem: Dues 300 lira
Income: Financed by city and state appropriation and contributions
Purchases: $5000
Collections: †Ancient Glass; Historical Documents of Tel Aviv-Yafo; †Jewish Costumes; †Jewish Ritual and Secular Art objects; †ceramics, †coins, prehistoric finds, †scientific and technical apparatus, traditional work tools and methods
Exhibitions: (1978-80) Antiquities of Tel-Aviv Yajo Museum - 2 exhibitions; Ceramics Museum - 6 exhibitions; Ethnography and Folklore Museum - 9 exhibitions; Glass Museum - 4 exhibitions; Lasky Planetarium - 1 exhibition; Nechushtan Pavilion - 1 exhibition; Numismatic Museum - 4 exhibitions; Tel-Aviv Yajo Historic Museum - 4 exhibitions; Theater Museum - 3 exhibitions
Publications: Yearbook, bi-annually
Activities: Classes for children; dramatic programs; docent training; lect open to public, 25 visiting lectr per year; gallery talks; tours; museum shop sells books, reproductions and slides
L **Central Library,** University St, Ramat Aviv, PO Box 17068. *Librn* Ernest Heinemann; *Asst Librn* Mariam Kumpan
Sun - Thurs 9 AM - 4 PM, Fri 9 AM - 1 PM. Estab 1958, mainly intended as reference library for museum staff, also serves the general public and students
Income: Financed by city appropriation
Purchases: $3000
Library Holdings: Vols 7000; Per subs 37
Special Subjects: Ceramics, Coins & Medals, Alphabet, ancient glass, Bible, Greco-Roman and Near East archaeology, history

M **TEL AVIV MUSEUM,** 25-27 Shaul Hamelech Blvd. Tel 257361. *Dir & Chief Cur* Marc Scheps; *Admin Dir* Avner Idan; *Cur* Mira Friedman; *European & American Art* Nehama Guralnik; *Israeli Art* Sara Breitberg; *Graphics* Edna Moshenson
Open Sun - Thurs 10 AM - 10 PM, Sat 10 AM - 2 PM and 4 - 7 PM. Helena Rubinstein Pavilion estab 1959; New Building estab 1971. A Graphics Study Room holds the museum's collection of 15,000 prints and drawings
Collections: Abstract Expressionism and Abstract Art in America—Albers, Baziotes, Frankenthaler, Louis, Noland, Pollock, Pousette d'Art; Comprehensive Collection of Jewish Art including Maurycy Gottlieb, Jozef Israels; Cubism—Archipenko, Gris, Leger, Picasso; Dada and Surrealism—Arp, Dali, de Chirico, Ernst, Janco, Masson, Matta, Miro, Picabia, Tanguy; European and American Modern Art—Impressionism and Post-Impressionism including Corot, Degas, Ensor, Monet, Pissarro, Renoir, Signac; Expressionism—Heckel, Kokoschka, Nolde, Pechstein, Rouault, Schmidt-Rottluff; Fauvism—Derain, Dufy, Matisse, Vlaminck; 19th and 20th Century Sculpture including Bourdelle, Caro, Cesar, Degas, Epstein, Lipchitz, Moore, Rodin, Zadkine; Old Masters: Works of English, Italian, French, Dutch Schools 16th - 18th Century; School of Paris—Chagall, Friesz, Kisling, Modigliani, Pascin, Soutine, Utirllo
Exhibitions: (1978) Art of The Sixties: Europe and America (Ludwig Museum, Cologne); Constructivism in the 20th Century (McCrory Collection); Eric Mendelshohn: Drawings of an Architect; major one-man and group exhibitions of Israeli art (Artist - Society - Artist, Benny Efrat, Pinhas Cohen-Gan, Moshe Kupferman, Raffi Lavie)
Activities: Classes and workshops for adults and children; lect; gallery talks; theatre; art films; cinema; concerts
M **Helena Rubinstein Pavilion,** 6 Tarsat St. Tel 287196.
Open Sun - Thurs 9 AM - 2 PM, Tues 9 AM - 2 PM and 4 - 7 PM, Sat 10 AM - 2 PM
L **Library,** 6 Tarsat St.
Helena Rubinstein Art Library at the New Building has a collection of volumes 30,000 (books and periodicals) covering most fields of art

ITALY

FLORENCE

M **GALLERIA DEGLI UFFIZI,** Uffizi Gallery, Piazzale degli Iffizi. Tel 21-83-41, 45. *Dir* Prof Luciano Beryi
Estab 16th Century
Collections: Finest collection of Florentine Renaissance painting in the world. Antique statues, famous drawing collection, miniatures, tapestries, unique and complete collection of artists' self-portraits, ranging from the 16th - 20th Century, which was begun in the 17th Century by Cardinale Leopoldo de' Medici, and continued by his successors

M **GALLERIA PALATINA,** Palatine Gallery, Palazzo Pitti, Piazza Pitti, 1. Tel 26 06 95, 27 03 23. *Dir* Dr Marco Chiarini
Open Tues - Sat 9 AM - 2 PM, Sun & holidays 9 AM - 1 PM, cl Mon. Admis 200 Lire, holidays 100 Lire, Sun free. Estab 17th Century. Ufficio Ducmentazione Pitti. Dir Dr Marilena Moseo; Secy Juallerto Carrci. Contains news about History of the Palace, exhibitions, collections; catalog of exhibitions; audio-visual materials
Income: Supported by government appropriation
Collections: Paintings from 15th - 18th Centuries, Andrea del Sarto, Raffaello, Tiziano
M **Museo degli Argenti,** Palazzo Pitti, Piazza Pitti, 1. *Dir* Dr Kirsten Aschengreen Piacenti
Collections: Amber jewels, enamels, gold, ivories, silver and tapestries from the 15th - 18th Centuries
M **Museo delle Porcellane,** Palazzo Pitti, Piazza Pitti, 1.
M **Appartamenti Monumentali,** Palazzo Pitti, Piazza Pitti, 1.
Collections: Furniture and tapestries of the 18th and 19th Centuries

M **Galleria d'Arte Moderna,** Palazzo Pitti, Piazza Pitti, 1. Tel 28 70 96. *Dir* Dr Sandra Pinto
Open daily 9 AM - 2 PM, cl Mon. Admis 1.50 Lire. Estab 1924 as a show of the permanent collections of Italian art of the 19th and early 20th centuries existing in Florence
Income: Financed by state and city appropriations
Collections: Italian, mainly Tuscan Art of the 19th and 20th Century; photography collection
Publications: Catalog of exhibitions
Activities: Lect

M **MUSEO DI S MARCO,** Piazzo S Marco. Tel 055-210741. *Dir* Dr Giorgio Bonsanti
Open Tues - Sat 9 AM - 4 PM, Sun 9 AM - 1 PM, cl Mon. Admis 1000 lire. Average Annual Attendance: 150,000
Collections: Fro Angelico frescoes and panels; 16th Century paintings; 15th Century frescoes; illuminated manuscripts 13th - 16th Century
Exhibitions: Late Gothic through Renaissance in Florence

L **ROSARY COLLEGE,** Aquinas Library, Via Boccaccio 123. *Dir* Paolina Candelari
Open 10 AM - 6 PM. Library used by students of fine arts to prepare their examinations and their theses and term papers
Library Holdings: Vols 4500; Per subs 24; Micro—Cards; AV—Slides

GENOA

M **GALLERIA DI PALAZZO BIANCO,** White Palace Gallery,* via Garibaldi II. Tel 010-28 26 41. *Dir* Dr Arch Vincenzo Oddi
Open Tues - Sat 9:30 - 11:45 AM and 2:30 - 5:45 PM, Sun 9:30 - 11:45 AM, cl Mon, legal and religious holidays. Estab 1892
Collections: Paintings by Genoese and Flemish Masters and other schools, sculpture and tapestries

LUCCA

M **MUSEO NAZIONALE DI VILLA GUINIGI,** National Museum of Villa Guinigi, via della Quarquonia. Tel 460-33. *Dir* Dr Clara Barrachini
Open summer 9:30 AM - 1 PM and 3 - 6 PM, winter 9:30 AM - 2 PM, cl Mon. Estab 1968 for documentation of arts and crafts in Lucca through the Centuries (from prehistory to approximately 1850)
Collections: Ancient textiles; Gothic, Neoclassical, Romanesque and Renaissance sculpture; Medieval Goldsmiths' Art; Old Master paintings, 12th - 18th Century; Roman and late Roman sculptures and Mosaics; wooden inlays and sculptures

M **PINACOTECA NAZIONALE,** National Picture Gallery, piazza Napoleone. Tel 0583 55570. *Dir* Dr Clara Baracchini
Open 8 AM - 2 PM, Sun 9 AM - 1 PM, cl Mon. Admis 1 L. Estab 1875 for exhibition of Lucchese works of art. Average Annual Attendance: 30,000
Income: Financed by appropriations
Collections: Paintings from churches and palaces of the city and territory, also from the Medici family and the Tuscan, Venetian, French and Flemish Schools; photographs

MANTUA

M **GALLERIA E MUSEO DEL PALAZZO DUCALE,** Gallery and Museum of the Palazzo Ducale, Piazza Sordello. Tel 369167, 320568. *Dir* Dr Ilaria Toesca Bertelli
Open Tues - Sat 9 AM - 2 PM, Sun 9 AM - 1 PM. Admis L 150. Estab as a monument to the Gonsaga family who lived here for centuries. Gallery contains capital works of art, including Mantegna frescoes, Castello and Pisanello murals. Average Annual Attendance: 70,000
Collections: Classical Antiquities and Sculpture; Egyptian Antiquities; Medieval, Renaissance and Baroque Sculpture; Numismatic Collection; Prehistorical Relics from Mantuan Territory
Publications: Catalog, fully illustrated
L **Library,** Piazza Sordello.
Reference only, closed to public
Library Holdings: Vols 2000; Other—Photographs 17,000

MILAN

M **CIVICA GALLERIA D'ARTE MODERNA,** Via Palestro 16. Tel 02-702819. *Dir* M Garberi; *Cojservator* M T Fiorio
Open 9:30 AM - Noon and 2:30 - 5:30 PM, cl Tues. No admis fee. Estab 1920. Modern Art Gallery 29 rooms; Ouiseo Oeariuo Mariui (6 rooms); Collezione Gram (6 rooms). Average Annual Attendance: 166,303
Income: Financed by city appropriation
Collections: Collezione Gram; Museo Marino Marini; paintings, sculptures from the beginning 19th Century to present including Appiani, Ballo, Boccioni, Carro, Hayes, Legantini, Medaids, Pelizza de VoCpesis, Olorandi, Rosso
Exhibitions: (1979) Il Novecento nelle collezioni civiche; Letteratura e arte: miti del '900; Umberto Boccioni: i disegni nelle Civiche collezioni di Milano
Publications: Exhibitions catalogues
Activities: Lect open to public; gallery talks; tours; museum shop sells books, magazines, reproductions, prints and slides

M **MUSEO D'ARTE ANTICA,** Museum of Ancient Art, Castello Sforzesco. *Dir* Dr Mercedes Garberi
Open 9:30 AM - 12:30 PM and 2:30 - 5:30 PM, cl Mon. No admis fee. Estab 1879
Income: Financed by city appropriation
Collections: Paintings including works by Bellini, Brauianbino, Foppa, Guiadi, Lippi, Lotto, Mantegna, Tiepolo, Tintoretto and others; sculpture from early Middle Ages to 16th Century mostly concerning Lombard Art, including Masterpieces like Michelangelo's Pieta-Rondanini; ancient and contemporary

drawings, with a very important group of Boccioni works
Exhibitions: Fonti dells Prospelti va - sale delle asse castello Sforzesco (1977-78)
L **Museum of Ancient Art Library,** Castello Sforzesco.
Library Holdings: Vols 41,000
M **Civiche Raccolte de Arte Applicata,** Collection of Minor Arts, Piazza Castello, Milan 21022. Tel 02 803071. *Dir* Dr Clelia Alberici
Open 9:30 AM - 12:30 PM and 2:30 - 5:30 PM, cl Mon. No admis fee. Estab to serve the public. Galleries are in the castle. Average Annual Attendance: 500,000
Income: Financed by city appropriation
Collections: Armor, bronzes, ceramics, coins, costumes, ironworks, ivories, mobiles, musical insturments, porcelains, sculpture, textiles
Exhibitions: Costumes
Publications: Rassegna di studi e di notizie, annually
Activities: Exten dept serves the Modern Art Gallery; original objects of art lent to other museums; museum shop sells books
M **Racolta delle Stampe Achille Bertarelli,** Bertarelli Collection of Engravings, Castello Sforzesco. *Dir* Dr Clelia Alberici
Open 9 AM - Noon and 2:30 - 5 PM, cl Sat & Sun
Special Subjects: Etchings & Engravings
Exhibitions: Incisioni di Pietro Testa; Stampe Popolari Lombarde dell'800
L **Bertarelli Collection Library,** Castello Sforzesco.
Library Holdings: Vols 30,000; Other—Exhibition catalogs, Engravings 600,000
M **Raccolte Archaeologiche e Numismatiche,** Collection of Archeology and Coins, Castello Sforzesco & Corse Magenta 15. *Dir* Dr Ermanno Arslan
Open 9:30 AM - 12:30 PM and 2:30 - 5:30 PM
Collections: Castello Sforzesco: Ancient Egyptian, antique and modern coins, prehistoric and later; Corso Magenta: Etruscan, Greek and Roman Collections
Activities: Lect open to public; sales shop sells catalogs and postcards
L **Archeology and Coin Library,** Castello Sforzesco & Corse Magenta 15.
Library Holdings: Vols 4423
Special Subjects: Antiuqe coins, coins
M **Museo di Milano,** Museum of Milan, Vedi Sant'Andrea 6. *Dir* Dr Ermanno Arslan
Open 9:30 AM - 12:30 PM and 2:30 - 5:30 PM, cl Mon
Collections: Paintings of Milan subjects of the 19th Century

M **MUSEO POLDI PEZZOLI,** Poldi Pezzoli Museum,* via A Manzoni 12. Tel 02-79-48-89. *Dir* Dr Alessandra Mottola Molfino
Open daily & holidays 9:30 AM - 12:30 PM and 2:30 - 5:30 PM, Thurs evenings 9 - 11 PM, cl Mon, New Year's, Easter, May 1, Aug 15, Nov 1 & Christmas. Admis L 500. Estab 1881. Mem: 600; assembly of mem of Associazione Amici del Poldi Pezzoli
Collections: Paintings, Italian and Foreign from 14th - 18th Centuries; antique weapons and armor, archaeology, bronzes, carpets, clocks and watches, furniture, glasses, glass windows, gold, Islamic objects, jewels, pottery
Publications: Catalogs of exhibitions and of the museum collections; brief guide to the museum
Activities: Classes for adults; educ section for children; lect open to public, 130 visiting lectr per year; scholarships
L **Library,*** via A Manzoni 12.
For reference
Library Holdings: Vols 3000; Other—Prints 2047, photographs

M **PINACOTECA AMBROSIANA,** Ambrosian Picture Gallery, Piazza Pio XI, 2. Tel 02-800146. *Dir* Dr Angelo Paredi
Open daily 9:30 AM - 5 PM, cl Sat. Admis Lire 500, Sun free. Estab 1618. Average Annual Attendance: 35,000
Collections: Botticelli, Caravaggio, Leonardo, Raphael, Titian

M **PINACOTECA DI BRERA,** Brera Picture Gallery,* via Brera 28. Tel 02-800985, 808387, 862634. *Dir* Dr Carlo Bertelli
Open Tues - Sat 9 AM - 2 PM, Sun & holidays 9 AM - 1 PM, cl Mon. Admis L 200. Average Annual Attendance: 100,000
Collections: Drawings and paintings of the 14th - 20th Centuries
Activities: The Pinacoteca, in collaboration with the Friends of Brera and Museums of Milan, sponsors special courses which are open to public. In these courses the more important works in the Pinacoteca collection are explained in eight lessons

MODENA

M **GALLERIA, MUSEO E MEDAGLIERE ESLENSE,** Este Gallery and Museum,* Palazzo dei Musei, Piazza S Agostino 109. Tel 22-21-45. *Dir* Dr Giorgio Bonsanti
Open Tues - Sat 9 AM - 2 PM, Sun 9 AM - 1 PM, cl Mon. Admis L 150. Museum has one vestibule; two corridors; four large rooms. Average Annual Attendance: 4000
Income: Financed by state appropriation
Collections: Bronzes, coins, drawings, medals, minor arts, paintings, prints and sculptures, most from the Este family
L **Biblioteca della Soprintendenza,*** Superintendent's Library. (Mailing Add: Palazzo dei Musei, Pizza S Agostino 109,) *Librn* Dr Mazzino Fossi
Library Holdings: Vols 5000; Per subs 26

NAPLES

M **MUSEO DE CAPODIMONTE,** Mount Capodi Museum, Reggia di Capodimonte Tel 081-7410881. *Dir* Dr Raffaello Causa; *Asst Supt* Dr Vitaliano Tiberia; *Asst Supt* Dr Ciro Florillo; *Asst Supt* Dr Umberto Chianese; *Dir Museo Villa Pignatelli* Salvatore Abita; *Supv & Dir Drawings & Prints* Dr Rossana Muzii; *Supv & Dir Museo S Martino* Teodore Fittipaldi; *Supv & Dir Museo Villa Floridiana* Dr Nicola Spinosa
Open Mon - Sat 9 AM - 2 PM, Sun & holidays 9 AM - 1 PM, cl Mon. Admis 150 lira. Estab 1956. Average Annual Attendance: 220,000
Income: Financed by state appropriation
Collections: Armour from 15th - 19th Centuries; drawings and prints of 15th - 19th Century; bronzes and medals from the Renaissance; furniture 18th and 19th Centuries; Italian and foreign paintings from 13th - 19th Centuries, porcelains; Italian Majolica; ivory and objects of minor art; Murano glass; tapestries from 16th

- 18th Centuries
Activities: Lect open to public, 36 visiting lectr per year; concerts; gallery talks; tours; exten dept serves the area; artmobile; originate traveling exhibitions; museum shop
L **Library,** Reggia di Capodimonte. *Librn* Vega de Martini
Open for reference
Library Holdings: Vols 8600

M **MUSEO NAZIONALE DI SAN MARTINO,** National Museum, Piazzele San Martino. Tel 37-70-05. *Dir* Dr Teodore Fittipaldi
Estab 18th Century
Collections: Works of art from Farnese, Borgia and Noia Collections, and works recovered from excavations in Southern Italy, particularly in Pompeii and Herculaneum. A foremost collection of ancient bronzes, wall paintings and mosaics; 17th Century pictures and paintings, 13th - 17th Century sculpture, majolicas and porcelains; section of modern prints, paintings and engravings
Exhibitions: (1978-79) Mostra delle Sculpture lignee di Pietro e Giovanni Alemanni dal presepe della Chiesa di S Giovanni a Carbonara di Napoli; (1979-80) Mostra sulla Civilta del '700 a Napoli 1734 - 1799 - Sculture e Presepi enl '700 a Napoli
L **Biblioteca,** Largo San Martino 5.
Estab 1870
Library Holdings: Vols 3000; Per subs 100; Other—Exhibition catalogs, prints, manuscripts, memorabilia, pamphlets, photographs, reproductions

PADUA

M **MUSEO CIVICO DI PADUA,** Municipal Museum, Piazza del Santo. Tel 2-31-06, 2-27-13. *Dir* Prof Giovanni Gorini
Open 9:30 AM - 1:30 PM
Income: Financed by city appropriations
Collections: Archaeological Museum; Art Gallery - Bronzes, ceramics, industrial arts, painting, sculpture; Bottacin Museum - Greco-Roman, Italian, Paduan, Venetian, Napoleonic coins and medals; Gallery of Pictures; Lapidary Collection
Publications: Bollettino del Museo Civico di Padua, semi-annual
L **Biblioteca,** Piazza del Santo. *Librn* Dr Mirella Blason
Open 9 AM - 1:30 PM. Estab 1825 for history of archeology and art of Padua and Veneto
Income: $30,000
Purchases: $5000
Library Holdings: Vols 350,000; Per subs 300; AV—Kodachromes, slides; Other—Exhibition catalogs, prints, manuscripts, memorabilia, original art works, pamphlets, photographs, reproductions, sculpture

PERUGIA

M **GALLERIA NAZIONALE DELL'UMBRIA,** Umbrian National Gallery,* Corso Vannucci Palazzo, dei Prior. Tel 075 233 85, 207 12. *Dir* Dr Francesco Santi
Open 9 AM - 2 PM. Admis L 150. Estab 1863 for documentation of the arts (painting, sculpture and jewels) in Umbria from the 13th - 18th Century. Average Annual Attendance: 45,000
Income: Financed by state appropriation
Collections: Furniture of the Renaissance; Jewels (Umbria-Siena) 13th and 14th Centuries; paintings from the Umbrian School from the 13th - 18th Centuries; 13th, 14th and 15th Century sculpture
Exhibitions: Annual shows (lasting a week), on the restoration of art works in cooperation with two churches and museums in the region of Umbria
Publications: Catalog of Romanesque and Gothic works; F Santi, Itinerary of the Gallerie Nazionale dell'Umbria (bried guide)
L **Library,** Corso Vannucci Palazzo, dei Priori.
For specialized study only
Library Holdings: Vols 3995; Other—Photographs

PISA

M **MUSEO NAZIONALE DI SAN MATTEO,** Saint Matteo National Museum,* Lungarno Mediceo, piazzetta San Matteo. Tel 050 237-50. *Dir* Dr Antonino Caleca
Open summer 9:30 AM - 4 PM, winter 9:30 AM - 2 PM, cl Mon. Admis L 100. Estab 1846 for documentation of art in Pisa throughout the Centuries
Income: Financed by appropriation
Collections: Italian and Roman coins and medals; Marble and Wooden sculpture 10th - 18th Century; Medieval illuminated manuscripts; Old Master paintings 11th - 18th Centuries; Renaissance tapestries
Activities: Concerts

ROME

L **AMERICAN ACADEMY IN ROME LIBRARY,** Via Angelo Masina 5. *Dir of Library* Dr Rogers Scudder; *Librn* Lucilla Marino
Estab 1885. Open for research to fellows, Academy residents and guests and members of the Academy Advisory Council
Purchases: $60,000
Library Holdings: Vols 86,000; Micro—Fiche; AV—Slides; Other—Clipping files, exhibition catalogs, manuscripts, memorabilia, original art works, photographs
Special Subjects: Art History, Classical art and archaeology, musicology
Collections: Oliver Strunk Collection (musicology); Fototeca (photographs of archaeological sites in Italy, eastern Mediterranian and North Africa); rare books and manuscripts (general Renaissance art and architecture)
Activities: Lectures

M **GALLERIA BORGHESE,** Borghese Gallery,* Villa Borghese. Tel 85-85-77. *Dir* Sara Staccioli; *Second Dir* Luciana Ferrara
Open 9 AM - 2 PM, holidays 9 AM - 1 PM, cl Mon. Estab 1616
Collections: Baroque and Classical sculptures - G Bernini, Canova; paintings by

Caravaggio, Antonello da Messina, Andrea del Sarto, Lorenzo di Credi, Domenichino, Dosso Dossi, Raffaello, Tiziano, Veronese

M **GALLERIA DORIA PAMPHILJ,** Dorian Gallery, Piazza del Collegio Romano l/a. *Dir* Dr Eduard A Safarik
Collections: Paintings by Caravaggio, Carracci, Correggio, Filippo Lippi, Lorrain, del Piombo, Titian, Velazquez

M **GALLERIA NAZIONALE D'ARTE ANTICA - PALAZZO BARBERINI,** National Gallery in Barberini Palace, Via Quattro Fontane 13, 00. Tel 06-4750184. *Dir* Dr Giuseppina Magnanimi
Open Tues - Sat 9 AM - 2 PM, Sun 12:30 - 2 PM, cl Mon. Gallery is in Palazzo Barberini, built of Roman baroque art (Maderno, Bernini, Borromini, Pietro da Cortona). Average Annual Attendance: 25,000
Income: Financed by state appropriation
Collections: Barberini 1952, Cervinara 1962, Chigi 1918, Corsini 1883, Dusmet 1943, Hertz 1915, Monte de Pieta 1895, Torlonia 1892; Italian and Flemish Paintings from 12th - 18th Century
Exhibitions: Pictures of the public collections: Barberini, Cervinara, Chigi, Corsini, Dusmet, Torlonia - complete exhibition from 12th - 18th Century
Activities: Educ dept; gallery talks; tours
M **Galleria Nazionale d'Arte Antica - Palazzo Corsini,** National Gallery in Corsini Palace, Via della Lungara 10, 00. Tel 06-6542323. *Dir* Dr Giuseppina Magnanimi
Open by appointment from 10 AM - 1 PM. Estab for historic Corsini collection. Average Annual Attendance: 5000
Collections: Corsini

M **INSTITUTO NAZIONALE PER LA GRAFICA,** Via Della Lungara, 230. *Dir* M Catelli Isola; *Asst* Simonetta Prosperi Rodino; *Asst* Giulia Fusconi
Open 9 AM - 1 PM. No admis fee
Collections: Drawings, engravings
Publications: Grafica, Grafica (periodical)
Activities: Lending collection books; sells exhibition catalogues during exhibitions

M **MUSEI CAPITOLINI,** Museum of Sculpture, Piazza del Campidoglio 1471. Tel 67 97 034, 67 82 862. *Staff* E La Rocca; *Staff* E Tittoni Monti
Open daily 9 AM - 2 PM, Tues & Thurs evenings 5 - 8 PM, Sat evenings 8:30 - 11 PM, cl Mon. Average Annual Attendance: 250,000
Collections: †Ancient sculptures 3500, †bronzes, †paintings, pottery, †tapestry and other works of art

M **MUSEO NAZIONALE ROMANO,** National Museum of Rome,* piazza delle Finanze 1. Tel 06 46-05-30, 46-08-56. *Dir* Dr A La Regina
Open Mon - Fri 9 AM - 2 PM, holidays 9 AM - 1 PM. Estab 1889
Income: Financed by city and state appropriation
Collections: Archaelogical collection; glass; Greek Hellenistic and Roman bronzes and sculpture; numismatics; pictures and mosaics
Activities: Educ dept

SASSARI

M **MUSEO NAZIONALE G A SANNA,** G A Sanna National Museum, via Roma 64. Tel 27-22-03. *Dir* F Nicosia
Open 9 AM - 2 PM. Admis L 100, no admiss fee Settimana dei Musei exhibition. Estab 1930; enlargement and reorganization in line with didactic standards and modern esthetics. Finnaced by state appropriation
Collections: Archeological Collections, Picture Gallery with Medieval and Modern Art; Collection of Sardinian Ethnography; sculptures
Exhibitions: Museum weeks
Activities: Visiting students; lect open to public with special permission, 300 visiting lectr per year
L **Library,** via Roma 64. *Dir* Dr F Nilone
Open 9 AM - 1 PM, cl Mon. Estab 1958
Library Holdings: Vols 3000; AV—Slides 3000; Other—Photographs 10,000

TRIESTE

M **CIVICO MUSEO REVOLTELLA-GALLERIA D'ARTE MODERNA,** Revoltella Civic Museum-Gallery of Modern Art, Via Armando Diaz 27. Tel 040 750546, 68562. *Dir* Dr Giulio Montenero
Open daily 9 AM - 1 PM, cl Mon. Estab 1872 to maintain the buildings inherited by the foundation in their original decor; increase the number of pictures, sculptures and graphic arts. The temporary exhibits are prepared in the communal hall of art at the Constanzi Palace in Trieste. Average Annual Attendance: 18,400
Collections: Graphic arts, pictures and sculptures by artists from the region of Friuli-Venezia Giulia, Italian artists and some European artists
Exhibitions: Mostra postuma di Romeo Daneo; Mostra di Gianni Brumatti; Mostra postuma di Piero Lucano; Imogen Cunningham: 75 anni di fotografia; Tina Modotti: la vita e l'opera fotografica; La Scuola di Wagner: idee, premi, concorsi; Documenta a Kassel; Mostra di Renato Daneo
Activities: Lect open to public
L **Library,** Via Armando Diza 27.
Library Holdings: Vols 4000; Other—Prints 5000, photographs

TURIN

M **ARMERIA REALE,** Piazza Castello 191. (Mailing Add: Soprintendenza per i Beni Artistici e Storici, Via Accademia delle Scienze 5, Turin 10123,) *Pres* Giovanni Romano; *Staff Member* Claudio Bertolotto; *Staff Member* Giorgio Dondi e Marisa Cartesegna; *Staff Member* Domenica D'Ambrosio
Open Tues - Sat 9 AM - 2 PM, Sun 9 AM - 1 PM. Admis L 100. Section I, Rotonda; Section II, Galleria Beaumont; Section III, Medagliere. Average Annual Attendance: 54,799
Income: L 376,850 (financed by state appropriation and admission fees)
Collections: Archaeological Arms; Arms and Armours from 13th - 18th Century;

Arms of the 19th and 20th Century; Oriental Arms; Collection of the last Savoia: Carlo Alberto, Vittorio Emanuele II and III, Umberto I
Publications: L'Armeria Reale riordinate, Torino 1977
Activities: Tours; exten dept; original objects of art lent to public institutions

M **GALLERIA SABAUDA,** Soprintendenza per i Beni Artistici e Storici, Via Accademia delle Scienze 5. Tel 011-542 888. *Pres* Giovanni Romano; *Dir* Giovanna Galante Garrone; *Staff Member* Michela Di Macco; *Staff Member* Carla Enric Spantigari; *Staff Member* Claudio Bertolotto
Open Tues - Sat 9 AM - 2 PM, Sun 9 AM - 1 PM. Admis L 150. Gallery occupies the second floor of building (sections containing the Italiam masters I, Piedmontese masters, offices); and third floor (Italian Masters II, Flemish and French painters, Collection Gualino). Average Annual Attendance: 27,095
Income: L 887,550 (financed by state appropriation and admission fees)
Collections: G Ceruti portraits; Aimone Ducc painting; †Flemish Masters; French Masters; Collection Gualino; Italian Masters I until the 16th Century; †Italian Masters II, including 16th Century Venitian painters, until the 18th Century; †Piedmontese Masters; tapestry
Exhibitions: Ciacomo Jaquerio e il gotico internazionaie; Exhibition in Palazzo Madama, Turin 1979; exhibitions from temporary and permanent collections
Publications: Collection and exhibition catalogues
Activities: Tours; exten dept serves Piedmont; individual and original objects of art lent to institutions
L **Biblioteca,** Via Accademi delle Scienze 5. *Librn* Paola Lojacono Astrua
Open only at request 9 AM - 2 PM. Estab to help research in history of art, especially concerning Piedmontese subjects
Income: L 1,000,000
Purchases: L 1,000,000
Library Holdings: Micro—Prints; Other—Exhibition catalogs, prints, manuscripts, photographs
Special Subjects: Piedmontese documentary literature
Collections: Namuscripts of the 18th and 19th Centuries; prints of different periods

M **MUSEO CIVICO DI TORINO,** Municipal Museum, via Magenta 31. Tel 516-416, 54.18.2. *Dir* Dr Anna Serena Fava; *Cur Antique Art Collection* Dr Silvana Pettenati; *Cur Modern Art Collection* Dr Rosanna Maggio Serra
Open 9 AM - 8 PM, cl Mon. Admis L 200 free on holidays
Income: Financed by city and state appropriations
Collections: Antique and modern art from 4th - 20th Centuries; coins, paintings; sculpture
Publications: Catalogs for temporary shows and for each section of the museum
Activities: Lect open to public; original objects of art lent; lending collection contains 27,200 photographs; originate traveling exhibitions
L **Library,*** via Magenta 31.
Library Holdings: Vols 32,894

VATICAN CITY

M **MONUMENTI MUSEI E GALLERIE PONTIFICIE,** Vatican Museums and Galleries, Tel 06 698 3332. *Dir General* Prof Carlo Pietrangeli; *Secy-Treas* Walter Persegati; *Cur for Classical Art (Greek & Roman Sculpture)* Georg Daltrop; *Cur for Ethnographical Coll* Giuseppe Penkowski; *Cur Etruscan Antiquities (Etruscan Museum)* Francesco Roncalli; *Cur for Medieval & Modern Art* Fabrizio Mancinelli; *Cur for Oriental Antiquities (Egyptian Museum)* Gianfranco Nolli; *Asst Cur for Modern Religious Art Coll* Mario Ferazza
Open 9 AM - 2 PM, July - Sept 9 AM - 5 PM. Admis 2000 & 1000 lire for holders of International Student Card. Estab circa 1510; organized as a museum in the years 1770-75. Average Annual Attendance: 1,500,000
Income: Financed by state appropriation
Exhibitions: (1979) Close-up of a Masterpiece: The Transfiguration by Raphael; exhibition of autographs and manuscripts, 400 world-wide known personalities
Publications: Bollettino Dei Musei Vaticani, yearly
Activities: Educ dept; lect and occasional tours; sales shop sells books, reproductions, prints, slides and cassettes
M **Museo Pio Clementino**
Founded by Clement XIV and Pius VI in 1772
M **Museo Chiaramonti and Braccio Nuovo,**
Founded by Pius VII in 1810 and 1822
M **Museo Gregoriano-Profano**
Founded by Gregory XVI in 1844. Formerly located at Lateran Palace
Collections: Greek and Roman sculpture and antiquities
M **Museo Gregoriano Etrusco**
Founded by Gregory XVI in 1837
Collections: Greek, Roman and Etruscan antiquities
M **Museo Gregoriano Egizio**
Founded by Gregory XVI in 1839
Collections: Egyptian antiquities, mummies
M **Museo Pio-Cristiano**
Founded by Pius IX in 1854. Formerly located at the Lateran Palace
Collections: Early Christian Art
M **Medieval and Modern Art**
Chapel of Nicholas V painted by Beato Angelico 1448-1450; Sistine Chapel built by Sixtus IV 1475-1483, and frescoed by several masters of 15th Century, and by Michelangelo 1508-1512 and 1535-1541; Borgia Apartment with frescoes by Pinturicchio 1492-1495, and others; Loggia and Stanze painted by Raphael 1508-1520; Gallery of the Tapestries with works of 16th and 17th Centuries; Pinacoteca Vaticana, founded by Pius XI in 1932, with painting, frescoes, tapestries of Byzantine, Medieval and Modern periods
M **Museo Missionario Ethnologico**
Founded by Pius XI in 1926-27. Formerly at the Lateran Palace
Collections: Ethnological Collection
M **Collection of Modern Religious Art**
Inaugurated by Paul VI in 1973
M **Museo Sacro, Museo Profano, Salone Sistino,** Vatican Library.
Collections: Ceramics, frescoes, illuminated books, ivories, old fabrics, tapestries

JAPAN

KURASHIKI

M **OHARA BIJITSUKAN,** Ohara Museum of Art,* 1-1-15 Chuo. Tel 0864-22-0005. *Cur* Shin-ichiro Foujita
Open April - Oct 9 AM - 5 PM, Nov - Mar 9 AM - 4 PM. Admis 100 yen, students 50 yen. Estab 1930 to exhibit and collect the fine arts
Collections: Ancient Egyptian, Persian and Turkish ceramics and sculpture; Modern American and European paintings and sculpture; Modern Japanese oil paintings, pottery, sculpture and textiles
Activities: Lect open to public; gallery talks; book shop

KYOTO

M **KYOTO KOKURITSU KINDAI BIJUTSUKAN,** National Museum of Modern Art, Kyoto, Enshoji-cho, Okazaki, Sakyo-ku. *Dir* Michiaki Kawakita; *Chief Cur* Tadao Ogura; *Cur* Takeo Uchiyama; *Cur* Shigeki Fukunaga
Open 10 AM - 5 PM. Admis adults 200 Yen, students 60 Yen, children 40 Yen. Estab 1963 for exhibitions and research of modern art, in particular trends in contemporary art, modern handi-crafts and artists who have been active in Kyoto. Museum is reinforced concrete with total area of 2050 sq meters, and has two stories and a basement. Exhibition halls on the first and second floors have 684 sq meters each. Average Annual Attendance: 300,000. Mem: 900; dues 2000 Yen
Income: Financed by state appropriation
Collections: Kawakatsu Collection which consists of 25 pieces of Pottery by Kanjiro Kawai; ceramic works by artists abroad, †contemporary print works in Japan and Japanese artists who are active abroad, †contemporary sculptures, †handicrafts works by contemporary artists, †paintings by the artists who have been active in Kyoto mainly
Exhibitions: Crafts in Japan since 1927; Fifty Contemporary Artists of the World; Great Masters of French Painting from the Museum of Fine Arts, Boston; Hayami Gyoshu; Ryusei Kishida; Oskar Kokoschka; Peruvian Textile of Pre-Colombian Period; Posters of Europe, from origine to today; Scandinavian Crafts; Three Unique Sumi-e Painters; Sotaro Yasui, Recent Acquisitions; Saeki Yuzo
Publications: Miru, monthly
Activities: Originate traveling exhibitions

NARA-SHI

M **NARA KOKURITSU HAKUBUTSUKAN,** Nara National Museum, 50 Noborioji-cho. Tel 0742-22-7771. *Chief Cur* Shin-ya Inagaki
Open 9 AM - 4:30 PM, cl Mon. Admis adults 200 Yen, children 60 Yen. Estab 1895 specifically for display of Buddhist Art
Collections: Art objects of Buddhist Art, mainly of Japan, including applied arts and archaeological relics, calligraphs, paintings, sculptures, 6th - 14th Century
Exhibitions: Shoso-in Treasures; annual spring exhibitions of special themes of Buddhist Art, permanent exhibition

TOKYO

M **BRIDGESTONE BIJUTSUKAN,** Bridgestone Museum of Art,* 10-1, 1-chome, Kyobashi Chuo-ku. Tel 563-0241. *Pres* Shojiro Ishibashi; *Executive Dir* Yasuo Kamon; *Chief Cur* Takatsugu Rolujo; *Cur* Norio Shimada
Open 10 AM - 5:30 PM, cl Mon. Admis 100 yen. Estab 1952 for permanent display of Ishibashi Collection. Museum has five exhibit rooms and lobby. Average Annual Attendance: 100,000
Income: Financed by endowment
Collections: Foreign bronze wares, glass wares and pottery from Ancient times to Early Modern times; Foreign original prints from 17th Century to present; Foreign paintings, mainly Impressionism and after; Foreign sculptures from Ancient time to present; Japanese Western style paintings late 19th Century to present
Publications: Annual Report; catalogs in English, French and Japanese; illustrated catalogs in English and Japanese
Activities: Educ dept; lect open to public, 44 visiting lectr per year
L **Library,*** 10-1, 1-chome, Kyobashi Chuo-ku.
For reference
Library Holdings: Vols 2200; Other—Photographs

M **NATIONAL MUSEUM OF WESTERN ART,** Kokuritsu Seiyo Bijutsukan, Ueno Park, Taito-ku. Tel 03-828-5131. *Dir* Tadashi Uchiyama; *Chief Cur* Hideo Tomiyama; *Cur* Haruki Yaegashi
Open 9:30 AM - 5 PM, cl Mon, Dec 28 - Jan 4. Admis 200 Yen. Estab 1959 to display French paintings and sculptures of the Matsukata Collection (Impressionists and Rodin), and to build up a collection of European art for display in order to show to Japanese public the tradition of European art and its historical development. Main building designed by Le Corbusier (1959), and new wing designed by Kunio Maekawa (1979). Average Annual Attendance: 550,000
Income: Financed by state appropriations
Purchases: $650,000
Collections: Many works of European Art from the 14th - 20th Century; Matsukata Collection contains 300 paintings, 63 sculptures, including 12 Monet, 3 Renoir and 53 Rodin; Old Master Paintings, including Cranach, Barna da Siena, El Greco, Magnasco, Patinir, Rubens, Tintoretto, Joos van Cleve, Van der Weyden
Exhibitions: Boston Museum Exhibition - Human Figures in Fine Art; European Landscape Painting; European Master Drawings of Six Centuries from the Collection of the Fogg Art Museum
Publications: Annual Bulletin of the National Museum of Western Art; Catalogue of Paintings; Masterpieces of the National Museum of Western Art
Activities: Lect open to public

L **Library,** Ueno Park, Taito-ku.
For scholars and students of the History of Arts only

M **NIHON MINGEI KAN,** Japanese Folk Art Museum,* 861 Kamaba Meguro-ku. Tel 4-3-33. *Cur* S Hamada
Collections: 20,000 objects of Folk-craft Art from all parts of the world

M **TOKYO KOKURITSU KINDAI BUJUTSUKAN,** National Museum of Modern Art, Tokyo, 3 Kitanomaru Koen, Chiyoda-ku 102. Tel 03 214 2561, 214 2565. *Dir* Kenji Adachi; *Deputy Dir* Kazuo Anazawa; *Chief Cur Fine Art Department & Cur Sculpture* Yoshikazu Iwaskai; *Chief Cur Project and Reference Materials Department* Tamon Miki; *Cur Education & Public Relations* Masahiro Koike; *Cur Painting* Toru Asano; *Cur Planning & International Exchange* Yashushi Takizawa; *Cur Prints & Drawing* Hisae Fujii; *Admin Chief* Kensuke Koiwa
Open Tues - Sun 10 AM - 5 PM, cl Mon and New Year Holidays. Admis adult 200 Yen. Estab 1952, new building completed 1969, as a place to show permanent and special exhibitions, mainly modern and contemporary Japanese art; and to introduce world art trends. First floor houses temporary exhibitions; second to fourth floors galleries and permanent collections. Average Annual Attendance: 299,408. Mem: 1000; dues 2500 Yen
Income: Financed by state appropriation
Collections: 19 Calligraphies, 114 drawings, 605 Japanese-style paintings, 861 oil paintings, 1135 prints, 219 sculptures, 65 watercolours
Exhibitions: Commemorative Exhibition for Opening of the Crafts Gallery: Masterpieces of Contemporary Japanese Crafts; Robert and Sonia Delaunay; The 11th International Biennial Exhibition of Prints in Tokyo; Enamelled Porcelain of Modern Japan; Fiber Works - American and Japanese; Casper David Friedrich und sein Kreis; Ryusei Kishida; Lacquer Art of Modern Japan; L'Affiche; Marino Marini; Gonroku Matsuda; Bridget Riley; Saito Yoshishige; Scandinavian Crafts; Yuzo Seaki
Publications: Annual report; monthly bulletin; exhibition catalogues

M **National Film Center,** 7-6, 3-chome, Kyobashi, Chuo-ku 104. Tel 03 561 0823. *Chief Film Center* Sadamu Maruo
Open 12:30 - 8 PM, film shows at 3 PM & 6:15 PM. Admis adult 200 Yen. Estab 1952. Film Center uses old museum building. Average Annual Attendance: 78,290
Collections: 158 Animation films; 2749 documentary and news reels; 1164 feature films

M **Crafts Gallery,** 1 Kitanomaru Koen, Chiyoda-ku 102. Tel 03 211-7781. *Chief Crafts Gallery* Nobuhiko Sugihara; *Cur Ceramics* Mitsuhiko Hasebe
Open Tues - Sun 10 AM - 5 PM, cl Mon and New Year Holidays. Admis 200 Yen. Estab 1977. Average Annual Attendance: 33,365
Collections: 178 Ceramics; 198 dyeing and weaving; 96 lacquer ware; 50 metal works

M **TOKYO-TO BIJUTSUKAN,** Tokyo Metropolitan Art Museum,* Ueno Park 8, Daito-ku. Tel 03-823-6921. *Dir* Kazuaki Kudo
Open Tues - Sun 9 AM - 4:30 PM, cl Mon & Dec 29 - Jan 3. Estab 1925, new building opened Sept 1976. Museum contains gallery; auditorium; library; studios; provides rental galleries. Average Annual Attendance: 1,320,000
Collections: †Contemporary crafts, paintings and sculptures
Exhibitions: Museum originates three or four major exhibitions per year; 160 art groups exhibitions per year at rental galleries
Publications: Catalog of special exhibitions; News of Museum, monthly
Activities: Painting class; lect with visiting lectr; films
L **Library,*** Ueno Park 8, Daito-ku.
Library Holdings: Vols 7000; Per subs 70

WAKAYAMA

M **KOYASAN REIHOKAN,** Museum of Buddhist Art,* Koyasan, Koyacho, Ito-gun. *Cur* Chikyo Yamamoko
Open 8 AM - 5 PM. Admis 200 yen. Estab 1921 to keep the treasures handed down in Koyasan. Museums is one of the centers of Japanese Buddhism
Collections: More than 25,000 pieces of calligraphy, images, manuscripts, paintings, sculptures and sutras, some of them registered National Treasures and important cultural properites

REPUBLIC OF KOREA

SEOUL

M **NATIONAL MUSEUM OF KOREA,** Kyong Bok Palace, 1 Sejongro, Chongro-ku. Tel 72-9295. *Dir-General* Sunu Choi; *Dir Kyongju Museum* Han Byongsam; *Dir Puyo Museum* Kunkil Gee; *Chief Cur* Yagmo Chong; *Cur in Charge of Archaeology* Ingu Kang; *Cur in Charge of Registrar* Nanyong Lee
Open 9 AM - 6 PM. Admis adults 150 won, children 70 won. Estab 1915. Average Annual Attendance: 538,000. Mem: 800
Income: Financed by governmental appropriation
Collections: Bronze wares, Buddhist sculptures, calligraphy, ceramics, paintings and pottery (historical and artistic materials)
Exhibitions: 5000 Years of Korean Arts; special exhibition of Cultural Relics found off Sinan Coast; special exhibition of Paintings selected from National Museum Collections
Publications: Misul Charyo, bi-annually; Museum News, monthly
Activities: Classes for adults; lect for members only; originate traveling exhibitions; museum shop sells books and reproductions
L **Library,** Kyong Bok Palace, 1 Sejongro, Chongro-ku. *Librn* Chol Sunu
Open 9 AM - 5 PM. Estab 1972 to research archaeological art science and to educate and enlighten the public and students
Purchases: $4000
Library Holdings: Vols 12,000; Per subs 1000; Other—Clipping files, exhibition

catalogs, original art works, pamphlets, sculpture
Special Subjects: Archaeology, Art History
Activities: 3600

LEBANON

BEIRUT

M **AMERICAN UNIVERSITY OF BEIRUT,** Archaeological Museum, Tel 340740, Ext 2523. *Dir* Dr Leila Badre; *Secy* Lamia Awad
Open Mon - Fri 10 AM - Noon and 1 - 3 PM, Sat 10 AM - Noon. No admis fee. Estab 1868 to house a teaching and study collection. Museum has two galleries containing 51 show cases; the exhibits are arranged in chronological sequence, dating from the Palaeolithic to the Islamic periods. Average Annual Attendance: 3000
Income: $1000 (financed by endowment)
Purchases: $1000
Collections: †Bronze and Iron Age Near Eastern Pottery Collections; †bronze figurines, weapons and implements of the Bronze Age Near East; Graeco-Roman imports of pottery from Near East sites; Palaeolithic-Neolithic Flint Collection; Palmyrene Funerary Sculpture; Phoenician Glass Collection; Pottery Collection of Islamic periods; substantial coin collection
Publications: Berytus Archaeological Studies, annually
Activities: Classes for adults; extension courses in archaeology; gallery talks; tours; museum shop sells books and photographs
L **Library,** Beirut. *Librn* J Khoury
Library Holdings: Vols 45,000
Special Subjects: Near Eastern archaeology

M **MUSEE NATIONAL,** National Museum of Lebanon,* rue de Damas. Tel 401-00-440. *Dir & Chief Cur* Emir Maurice Chehab
Open winter 9 AM - Noon and 2 - 5 PM, summer 9 AM - Noon and 3 - 6 PM. Estab 1920
Collections: Anthropological sarcophagi of the Greco-Persian period; Byzantine Mosaics; ceramics and wainscoting of the Arabic period; Dr C Ford Collection of 25 sarcophagi of the Greek and Hellenistic epoch; goblets, mosaics, relief and sarcophagi of the Greco-Roman period; jewelry and statues of the Phoenician period; jewelry in gold of the Arabic, Byzantine and Roman periods; monies in gold, silver and bronze of the Arabic, Byzantine, Helenistic, Phoenician and Roman periods; objects and statues of the Prehistoric period; sarcophagus of Ahiram 13th Century BC, depicting the prototype of the whole modern alphabet
Publications: Bulletin du Musee de Beyrouth, annually; Etudes et Documents d'Archeologie (Publications des fouilles enterprises au Liban); texts and historical documents

MALTA

VALLETTA

M **NATIONAL MUSEUM OF FINE ARTS,** South St. Tel 20756. *Dir* Marius J Zerafa
Open summer 8:30 AM - 1:30 PM, winter 8:30 AM - 1 PM and 2 - 4 PM. Admis 15¢. Estab 1905. Average Annual Attendance: 500,000
Income: Financed by government
Collections: European Art from 14th Century to modern times; collection of works by Mattia Preti; collection of historical objects and coins connected with the Nights of Malta
Exhibitions: Maltese and Foreign Works of Art, every other week
Publications: Museum reports
Activities: Lect; tours; scholarships
L **Library,** South St.
Library Holdings: Vols 3000
Collections: Manuscripts collection

MEXICO

CHOLULA

M **UNIVERSIDAD DE LAS AMERICAS,** Galeria de Arte,* Department of Graphic Arts and Design, PO Box 100, Santa Catarina Martir. Tel 47-06-55, Ext 127, 128. *Chairperson* Pamela M de Artasanchez
Open 8 AM - 5 PM. No admis fee. Estab 1969 to promote cultural and artistic events for the benefit of the university community. One-man gallery located in the Library Building of the campus at the university. Average Annual Attendance: 3000
Activities: Classes for adults; lect open to public; tours; exten dept; artmobile; lending collection contains color reproductions, framed reproductions, motion pictures and 15,000 slides
L **Library,** PO Box 100, Santa Catarina Martir. *Dir* Jare Watts; *Asst to Dir* Gullermo Rivero; *Asst to Dir* Mrs Eniro Name
Open 8 AM - 9 PM. Estab 1970 for service to university departments. Circ 17,000
Income: $300,000
Library Holdings: Vols 128,000; Per subs 1500; Micro—Cards, fiche, reels, prints; AV—A-tapes, cassettes, fs, Kodachromes, motion pictures, rec, slides, v-tapes;

Other—Clipping files, exhibition catalogs, prints, manuscripts, memorabilia, original art works, pamphlets, photographs, reproductions
Special Subjects: Aglonial manuscripts, Colonial History of Mexico
Collections: Herra Carrillo, Eddy, Ibanet, Jose M Saramiento Collections

GUADALAJARA

M **MUSEO DEL ESTADO DE TALISEO,** National Museum,*
Founded 1700 as a seminary
Collections: Archaeological discoveries; Early Mexican objects; Folk Art and costumes

MEXICO CITY

M **MUSEO DE ARTE MODERNO,** Museum of Modern Art,* Chapultepec Paseo de la Reforma, y Gandhi, 5. Tel 553 63 13. *Dir* Fernando Gamboa
Open Tues - Sun 11 AM - 7 PM. Estab 1964. Average Annual Attendance: 600,000
Income: Financed by state appropriation from the National Institute of Fine Arts
Collections: Contemporary Art 1950-1973; First Six Decades of 20th Century Mexican Painting; Jose Maria Velasco - Academic Bridge to 20th Century Mexican Painting; International Works; Mexican and foreign
Exhibitions: Mexican and International exhibitions of Modern Art
Publications: Artes Visuales, tri-annual magazine; exhibition catalogs
Activities: Films; lect and round table discussions; guided tours

M **MUSEO DE SAN CARLOS,** Museum of San Carlos, Puente de Alvarado 50. Tel 903-535-1256. *Dir* Graciela Reyes Retana; *Cur* Aurea Ruiz de Gurza; *Cur Museography* Pilar de la Fuente de Irezabal
Open Tues - Sun 10 AM - 5 PM, cl Mon. No admis fee. Estab 1968 to act as a cultural organism in the community; to allow the public to see and understand European painting from 14th - 19th Centuries; to establish a bond between the styles produced in Europe and our national art. Average Annual Attendance: 150,000
Income: Financed by state appropriation
Collections: English, Flemish, French, German, Hungarian, Italian, Polish, Netherlandish and Spanish Paintings from 14th - 19th Centuries; 19th Century Mexican Sculpture
Exhibitions: Permanent European Collection; several temporary exhibitions of Baroque, Gothic, Renaissance and 19th Century Art
Publications: Catalogs of exhibitions, bi-monthly
Activities: Classes for adults and children; lect open to public, 10 visiting lectr per year; concerts; gallery talks; individual paintings and original works of art lent to other museums; originate traveling exhibitions; museum shop sells books
L **Biblioteca,** Puente de Alvarada 50. *Librn* Aurea Ruiz de Gurza; *Asst* Elizabeth Jimenez
Estab 1968 for a reference in art subjects
Library Holdings: Vols 3000; Per subs 15; Other—Exhibition catalogs, prints, pamphlets
Special Subjects: European art

M **MUSEO NACIONAL DE ANTROPOLOGIA,** National Museum of Anthropology, Ave Paseo de la Reforma y Gandhi S/N. Tel 553-62-66. *Dir Fisico* Arturo Romano Pacheco; *Head Anthropological Department* Noemi Castille; *Head Education Department* Maria Eugenia Sanchez Bueno; *Head Ethnographical Department* Teresa Sepulveda; *Head Museographical Department* Prof Mario Vasquez; *Head Promotion Department* Gabriela Guzman; *Head Public Relations* Margarita A de Laris
Open Tues - Sat 9 AM - 7 PM, Sun 10 AM - 6 PM. Admis 15 pesos, Sun 10 pesos, children under 13 free. Estab 1964 for educational purposes. 12 Archaeological Halls, dealing with Prehispanic cultures; 11 Halls dealing with actual Indian groups; Orientation Room - Audio-visual light and sound. Average Annual Attendance: 1,500,000
Income: Financed by state appropriation
Collections: Archaeological and ethnographical
Exhibitions: Cinemateca Paquetes a Prestamo Fototeca; Exposicion Temporal Los Codices de Mexico
Activities: Classes for adults and children; docent training; lect open to public; tours; original objects of art lent; originate traveling exhibitions; museum shop sells books, magazines, reproductions, prints, slides and popular art
L **Library,** Ave Paseo de la Reforma y Gandhi S/N. *Librn* Yolanda Mercader
Reference library
Library Holdings: Vols 250,000; AV—Fs; Other—Maps
Collections: Codeces

M **MUSEO NACIONAL DE ARTES E INDUSTRIAS POPULARES,** National Museum of Crafts and Popular Industries, Av Juarez No 44. Tel 510-34-04, 521-66-79. *Dir* Teresa Pomar
Museum Halls open Tues - Sat 10 AM - 6 PM; Store open Mon - Sat 10 AM - 6 PM. Estab 1951 for exhibit and sale of traditional Mexican crafts. Museum supports five regional museums of crafts: Museo Regional de la Ceramica at Tlaquepaque, Jalisco; Museo Regional de Arte Popular de la Huatape ra at Uruapan, Michoacan; Museo de la Laca at Chiapa de Corzo, Chiapas; Museo Regional del Noroeste and Museo de Artes Populares Nacionales at Hermosillo, Sonora
Collections: Major permanent collections of Mexican popular arts and crafts with emphasis on native pottery, textiles and lacquer
Exhibitions: Permanent exhibit at the Museum of Mexico City and the regional Museums
Publications: Books: Ceramica Popular Mexicana; Booklets: a serie of 8 Cuadernos de Trabajo (these are relating to popular arts and exhibitions)
Activities: Operates provincial museums of arts and crafts, contests, conferences; celebration with a special exhibition in Mexico City Museum of All Saint's Day, Carnival Day, Holy Week and Christmas

M **MUSEO NACIONAL DE HISTORIA,** National Hisotrical Museum, Castillo de Chapultepec. *Dir* Felipe Lacouture
Estab 1825, moved to Chapultepec Castle and opened 1944. Museum attached to the National Institute of Anthropology and History
Collections: The History of Mexico from the Spanish Conquest to the 1917 Constitution, through collections of ceramics, costumes, documents, European and Oriental China, flags and banners, furniture, jewelry, personal objects, murals by the Mexican painters Gonzalez Camarena, O'Gorman, Clemente Orozco and Siqueiros, paintings, silverware, uniforms. The Alcazar shows apartments of some of the 19th Century governors of the country
Publications: Catalogs: El Escudo Nacional 1978; Historia de un Bosque 1979

MONTERREY

M **MUSEO REGIONAL DE NUEVO LEON,** Regional Museum of Nuevo Leon, Obispo Verger, Cerro del Obispado, Apdo Postal 566 Suc C. *Dir* Felipe J Garcia Campuzano; *Cur* Israel Cavazos Gza
Open Tues - Sat 10 AM - 1 PM and 3 - 6 PM, Sun 10 AM - 5 PM, cl Mon. No admis fee. Estab 1956 to extend cultural interests. Average Annual Attendance: 40,000. Mem: 13
Income: Financed by state appropriation
Collections: Permanent collection
L **Library,** Obispo Verger, Cerro del Obispado, Apdo Postal 566 Suc C.
Library Holdings: Vols 70
Collections: Guias de Zonas Arquelogicas y Monumentos Prehispanicos

PUEBLA

M **MUSEO DE ARTEJOSE LUIS BELLO Y GONZALES,** Museum of Art, Ave 3, Poniente 302. Tel 41-94-75. *Dir* Alicia Torres de Araujo; *Secy* Isabel Navarro Lima
Open 10 AM - 5 PM. Admis $5. Estab 1944 to diffuse art. Museum was house of Mariano Bello y Acedo; rooms are decorated with floors carpeted, stuccos and French-style curtains; there are 14 rooms. Average Annual Attendance: 25,000
Income: $125,000 (financed by state appropriation and admissions)
Collections: Agustin Arrieta; Chinese Porcelain; European and Mexican Furniture with Marquetry; European Porcelain; Puebla's Ceramic (Talavera) lace; bronzes, calamine, coopers, crystal, enamels, engraving, forged irons, ivories, miniatures, pictures, religious ornaments, sculptures, watches
Exhibitions: (1979) Casa de la cultura of this city paintings by Agustin Arrieta, Juan Cordero, Manuel Serrano, Mexican painters
Publications: Pamphlets
Activities: Classes for adults and children; lect for members only, 50 visiting lect per year; concerts; gallery talks; tours; lending collection contains color reproductions, photographs, motion pictures, film strips 5000 catalogs, postcards; museum shop
L **Library,** Ave 3, Poniente 302.
Open to members only
Library Holdings: Vols 1028; Per subs 3
Special Subjects: Books of art
Collections: Mexican History

SAN MIGUEL DE ALLENDE

L **INSTITUTO ALLENDE LIBRARY,** Instituto Allende. *Librn* Marne Martin
Open Mon - Fri 9:30 AM - 6 PM, Sat 9 AM - Noon. Estab for collecting Fine Arts volumes, bilingual Spanish - English
Library Holdings: Vols 4000; Per subs 14

NETHERLANDS

ALKMAAR

M **STEDELIJK MUSEUM ALKMAAR,** Alkmaar Municipal Museum, Doelenstraat 3. *Dir* K J Kriek
Open 10 AM - Noon and 2 - 5 PM, cl Sat. Estab 1861 to encourage interest in the history of Alkmaar and art
Income: Financed by city appropriation
Collections: Archaeological items, dolls and other toys, modern sculpture, paintings, silver, tiles
Exhibitions: Arthoteek; Dirk Bakker; Gerrit Brinkman; Doorwerken; Simon Erb; A K V Grafici; Cor en Kees Hak; Jan Deckwitz en Otto Heuvelink; Piet Lont; Gouden Naald; Overtoom; Potjeslatijn; Theo Ros; Tour-in; Bob van der Born; Geologische Vereniging
Activities: Individual paintings and original objects of art lent to public offices and other museums

AMSTERDAM

M MUSEUM HET REMBRANDTHUIS, Rembrandthouse Museum, Jodenbreestraat 4-6, 1011 NK. Tel 020-24 94 86. *Cur* Eva Ornstein-van Slooten; *Asst Cur* Cecile van Oosterwijk
Open Mon - Sat 10 AM - 5 PM, Sun & holidays 1 - 5 PM. Admis adults f1.50, groups (minimum 15) f1.00, children f0.50. Estab 1906 to maintain the house Rembrandt lived in from 1639-1660 and show his works - in this instance prints and drawings. 17th Century interior furnished with contemporary furniture. Average Annual Attendance: 100,000. Mem: 1000; dues f10.00
Income: Financed by endowment, earned income and state appropriation
Collections: Almost complete collection of Rembrandt's Etchings; 8 Drawings by Rembrandt; †drawings by Rembrandt's pupils; paintings by Rembrandt's pupils and teachers
Exhibitions: Wenzel Hollar (Prints and drawings); Rembrandt and Rubens (prints)
Publications: Kroniek van het Rembrandthuis, bi-annually
Activities: Sales shop sells books, reproductions, prints and slides
L Library, Jodenbreestraat 4-6, 1011 NK.
Open to public for reference by request
Special Subjects: Dutch artists, Rembrandt's etchings

M RIJKSMUSEUM, State Museum, Stadhouderskade 42. (Mailing Add: Hobbemastraat 21, PO Box 50673, Amsterdam 1007 DD,) *Dir General* Dr S H Levie; *Secy General* R van Eijle; *Dir Decorative Art* Dr A L den Blaauwen; *Dir Department Paintings* Dr P J J van Thiel; *Dir Printroom* Dr J W'Niemeijer; *Head Department Asiatic Art* Dr K W Lim; *Head Department Dutch History* Dr W H Vroom
Open daily 10 AM - 5 PM, Sun 1 - 5 PM. Admis Dfl 3, Wed free. Estab 1808 as a National Gallery of Art. The actual building was completed in 1883 and contains 250 rooms open to public. Average Annual Attendance: 1,300,000
Income: Financed by state appropriation
Collections: †Asiatic Art; †Dutch History; †Dutch Paintings 15th - 19th Centuries; †prints and drawings from all parts of the world, †sculpture and applied art
Exhibitions: The Age of Harunobu (Japanese woodcuts); Dutch Silver 1580-1830; Early Venetian Paintings; Indian Miniatures; Het Vaderlandsch Gevoel (19th Century paintings)
Publications: Bulletin, quarterly
Activities: Classes for adults and children; individual paintings and original objects of art lent to other galleries and museums; museum shop sells books, reproductions, prints and slides
L Library, Hobbemastraat 21, PO Box 50673. Tel 020-732121. *Librn* Mrs E van der Vossen-Delbruck; *Asst Librn* Y Grose
Open Mon - Wed, Fri & Sat 10 AM - 5 PM, cl Thurs & Sun. Estab 1885 as a reference library
Income: Financed by state appropriation
Library Holdings: Vols 50,000; Per subs 400; Other—Exhibition catalogs
Special Subjects: Art History
Collections: Auction catalogs; museum and exhibition catalogs

M RIJKSMUSEUM VINCENT VAN GOGH, Vincent Van Gogh State Museum, Paulus Potterstraat 7 1071 CX. Tel 020-764881. *Dir* Dr J van der Wolk; *Dir General* Dr S H Levie; *Cur* Dr H·van Crimpen; *Cur* Mrs L Couvee-Jampoller
Open Mon - Sat 10 AM - 5 PM, Sun & holidays 1 - 5 PM. Admis Hfl 3. Estab 1973 to house the family collection of Vincent van Gogh. Average Annual Attendance: 500,000
Income: Financed by state appropriation
Collections: Drawings and Paintings by Vincent van Gogh and contemporaries; Prints and Letters by Vincent van Gogh
Exhibitions: (1978) Japanese Prints collected by Vincent van Gogh; Frits Klein; Dirkjan Ribbeling; Marius Richters; John Peter Russell; (1979) Dutch Painting from the Century of van Gogh; Monticelli; World Press Photo
Activities: Workshop; sales shop sells books, reproductions, prints and slides
L Library, Paulus Potterstraat 7 1071 CX. *Librn* Sophie Pabst
Open Mon - Fri 10 AM - 12:30 PM and 2 - 5 PM. Estab 1973 as a documentation center on van Gogh; reference for public and scientific investigators
Income: f 16,000
Library Holdings: Vols 9000; Per subs 40; Micro—Fiche, prints; AV—Motion pictures, rec, slides; Other—Clipping files, exhibition catalogs, prints, manuscripts, photographs, reproductions
Special Subjects: Life and work of Vincent van Gogh and his time
Collections: Theo van Gogh Collection; Tralbaut Archive

M STEDLIJK MUSEUM-AMSTERDAM, Municipal Museum, Paulus Potterstraat 13, PO Box 5082 1007 AB. Tel 020-73 21 66. *Dir* E L L de Wilde; *Deputy Dir* J van Loenen Martinet; *Deputy Managing Dir* W H Brabander; *Head Department Applied Art* W Bertheux; *Head Communication Department* T van Grootheest; *Head Department Painting & Sculpture* R M Dippel; *Head Department Prints & Drawings* A J Petersen; *Research Cur* J M Joosten
Open Mon - Sat 9:30 AM - 5 PM, Sun 1 - 5 PM. Admis adult 2DFL, children under 16 1DL, group rates. Estab 1895, new wing opened 1954. Average Annual Attendance: 319,000
Collections: Applied Art and Design - especially bibliophile editions, ceramics, furniture (Rietveld), glass, photography, posters, textiles, typography; Cezanne; Chagall; Dutch Art 1850 to present; European and American tendencies after 1960 (Colorfield Painting, Conceptual Art, Pop Art, Nouveau Realisme, Zero); European Expressionism; International Paintings and Sculptures dating from 1850 to present; Monet; Paintings by Cobra-group, Dubuffet, Malevich, Matisse, Mondrian; Printroom - drawings, graphic art, especially Werkman, Cobra; van Gogh Collection
Exhibitions: Approximately 30 group exhibitions and one-person shows dedicated to art tendencies since 1960
Activities: Guided tours for school children (10-13); concerts of contemporary music; films; information desk; reproduction dept - posters, reproductions, postcards, books, catalogs for sale; subscriptions and season-tickets; restaurant with terrace

L Library, Paulus Potterstraat 13, PO Box 5082 1007 AB.
Open Mon - Fri 1 - 5 PM, Sat 9:30 AM - 5 PM
Library Holdings: Vols 18,000; Per subs 150; Other—Exhibition catalogs 70,000
Special Subjects: Modern art 1850 to present

ARNHEM

M GEMEENTEMUSEUM ARNHEM, Municipal Museum of Arnhem, Utrechtseweg 87, 6812 AA. Tel 085-431841. *Dir* P L A Janssen; *Cur* J R de Groot; *Cur* C van Kooten; *Cur* R Neerincx; *Cur* R Borman
Open Mon - Sat 10 AM - 5 PM, Sun & holidays 11 AM - 5 PM. No admis fee. Estab 1852. Building was built in 1873-75; remodeled in 1912 and used as a museum; a new wing was added in 1956; it has a panoramic view of the river Rhine. Average Annual Attendance: 100,000
Income: Financed by city appropriation
Collections: Chinese Porcelain 15th - 18th Centuries; Delftware; Dutch Painting 17th - 20th Century (new realism); drawings and prints of the 18th - 20th Centuries; Provincial Archaeology and History; Silverware of the 18th - 19th Centuries; Tin Dutch 15th - 19th Centuries; Topographical and Historical Maps of the Province of Gelderland; bronze, copper
Publications: Information leaflets
Activities: Educ dept; docent training; lect open to public; gallery talks; museum shop sells books, original art, reproductions, prints and slides
L Library, Utrechtseweg 87, 6812 AA.
Open for reference upon request
Library Holdings: Vols 2500; Per subs 10; Other—Catalogs 5000

DELFT

M STEDELIJK MUSEUM HET PRINSENHOF, Het Prinsenhof State Museum, St Agathaplein 1. Tel 015-13111, Ext 2336, 2339. *Dir* Dr R A Leeuw; *Cur* Dr I Spaander; *Public Relations* B Singeling
Open daily 10 AM - 5 PM, Sun & holidays 1 - 5 PM. Estab 1947 as a museum for fine arts of Delft and Holland and for the history of William the Silent and the 80-year war. Museum began as the Museum Historische Zaal in 1833; became City Museum and Archives 1906. Gallery, DeVolle Maan for contemporary art, mainly Delft artists
Income: Financed by city and state appropriation
Collections: Delft silver, Delftica, tapestries and †ware; Dutch Art of the 15th, 16th, 17th and 18th Centuries; Collection of Paintings of Orange-Nassau family, especially William the Silent and the 80-year war
Exhibitions: Antique Fair, The City of Delft until 1572; Bijbels and Burgers; Contour; DPG Humbert de Superville; Icons; Antoni van Leeuwenhoek; Water Als Vijand; Water Als Vriend; Zwitserland Project
Publications: Museum Information, quarterly
Activities: Classes for children; concerts; original objects of art lent; museum shop sells books, prints and slides
L Library, St Agathaplein 1.
Reference only
Library Holdings: Vols 3800; Other—Photographs

EINDHOVEN

M MUNICIPAL VAN ABBEMUSEUM, Eindhoven Municipal Museum, Bilderdijklaan 10, PO Box 235, 5600 AE. Tel 040-448555, Ext 2199. *Dir* R H Fuchs; *Cur* J Bremer; *Cur* J Debbaut; *Cur* M Suren
Open Mon - Sat 10 AM - 5 PM, Sun & holidays 1 - 5 PM. Admis adults Dfl 1, children Dfl 0.50. Estab 1936 as a museum of the art of the 20th century; city property
Income: Financed by membership and city appropriation
Collections: Collection ranges from Cubism to the latest trends in art (conceptual art, etc); concept art, Lissitzky Collection, Postpainterly Abstraction, neoconstructivism, specialities
Exhibitions: Armando, Baselitz, Brusselmans, Denmark, Yves De Smet, Braco Dimitrijevic, Jan Gregoor, Hans Haacke, Rebecca Horn, Douglas Huebler, Joan Jonas, Donald Judd, Anselm Kiefer, Bernd Lohaus, Richard Long, Jan Maaskant, Alexander Rodchenko, Katharina Sieverding, Gerhard von Graevenitz
Publications: Artistbooks; exhibition catalogs; information bulletins
Activities: Lect open to public; tours; originate traveling exhibitions; sales shop sells books, magazines, reproductions
L Library, Bilderdijklaan 10, PO Box 235, 5600 AE. *Librn* Aloys van den Berk
Reference library
Library Holdings: Vols 10,000; Other—Exhibition catalogs 25,000, magazines 6000

GRONINGEN

M GRONINGEN MUSEUM VOOR STAD EN LAND, Groningen Museum, Praediniussingel 59. Tel 17 29 29. *Dir* Dr F Haks; *Adjunct-Dir & Cur Paintings & Drawings* P I M Vries; *Cur Archaeology* Dr J W Boersma; *Cur Medieval & Later History* Dr E A J Boiten; *Cur Oriental Ceramics* C J A Jörg; *Scientific Asst* Peter Hofstede; *Scientific Asst Silver* J H Leopold
Open 10 AM - 5 PM, cl Mon. Admis fl 0.50, Sun free. Estab 1894. Average Annual Attendance: 36,500
Income: Financed by state appropriation
Collections: Paintings and drawings form the 16th - 20th Century, mainly Dutch, including Hofstede de Groot Collection, 17th Century and Veendorp Collection, second-half 19th Century; European Ceramics; Oriental Ceramics; local archaeology and history; silver
Exhibitions: Principally modern art
Publications: Annual Report
Activities: Concerts; performances especially in the field of visual art; objects of art lent

L **Library,** Praediniussingel 59. *Librn* Peter Hofstede
Open to public upon request
Purchases: $7500
Library Holdings: Vols 1000; Per subs 30; Micro—Reels; AV—Cassettes, rec, slides, v-tapes; Other—Exhibition catalogs, original art works
Collections: Asiatic Pottery

HAARLEM

M **FRANS HALSMUSEUM,** Frans Hals Museum, Groot Heiligland 62. *Dir* D H Couvee; *Cur Ancient Art* Dr P Biesboer; *Asst Ancient Art* W Zetteler; *Cur Modern Art* Dr M Hoogendonk; *Education Department* Dr G F Walberg; *Asst Education Department* C Brinkgreve; *Asst Education Department* E Wouthuyzen
Open daily 10 AM - 5 PM, Sun & holidays 1 - 5 PM. Admis adult & groups Dfl 1.75, children Dfl 0.75, Nov - Feb free. Estab 1862 to show permanent collection of ancient and modern art; temporary exhibitions; socio-cultural exhibitions - oriented on local and regional developments. Average Annual Attendance: 160,000
Income: Financed by city appropriation
Collections: Dutch Art of the 20th Century; Group Portraits by Frans Hals; Still Lifes Portraits and Landscapes of the Haarlem School from 16th - 19th Century; doll's house, old pharmacy, period rooms, silver
Exhibitions: Modern and old art, socio-cultural exhibitions
Activities: Educ dept; originate traveling exhibitions; sales shop sells books, reproductions and slides

M **TEYLERS MUSEUM,** Spaarne 16. (Mailing Add: Damstraat 21, Haarlem 2011 HA,) Tel 023-32 01 97. *Board of Trustees* H E Stenfert Kroese; *Board of Trustees* C W D Vrijland; *Board of Trustees* L van Nouhuys; *Board of Trustees* H D de Vues Robbi; *Cur Coins & Medals* Prof H E van Gelder; *Cur Minerals & Fossils* Dr J H C Walenkamp; *Cur Physics* Prof J Kistemaker; *Deputy Cur Art Coll* J H van Borssum Buisman
Open March - Sept Tues - Sat 10 AM - 5 PM, first Sun of month 1 - 5 PM, Oct - Feb Tues - Sat 10 AM - 4 PM, first Sun of month 1 - 4 PM. Admis adults Dfl 2, children Dfl 0.75. Estab 1778 to promote art and science. The oldest part of the museum dates from 1780; a new wing was added in 1880, 7 rooms. Average Annual Attendance: 24,000. Mem: 300
Income: Financed by Foundation
Collections: Drawings 16th - 19th Century Dutch, Italian and French School; 19th Century Dutch Paintings; cabinet of coins and medals, historical physical instruments, minerals and fossils
Activities: Lect open to public, 5 visiting lectr per year; concerts; tours; original objects of art; sales shop sells books, reproductions and slides
L **Library,** Damstraat 21. *Librn* J G de Bruijn
Estab 1778 for the promotion of science
Library Holdings: Vols 120,000; Per subs 1200

HERTOGENBOSCH

M **NOORD-BRABANTS MUSEUM,** Bethaniestraat 4. Tel 073-13 87 12. *Dir* Dr M M A van Boven; *Cur* Dr T Graas; *Cur* Dr M Trappeniers
Open Mon - Fri 10 AM - 5 PM, Sat & Sun 1 - 5 PM. No admis fee. Estab 1925 to study and display art and history of the province of Noord-Brabant. Building is a late-gothic church of 1470 circa; the ground floor houses the permanent exhibition of local history and paintings; the upper floor has changing exhibitions. Average Annual Attendance: 38,000
Income: $230,000 (financed by membership, city appropriation and sales)
Collections: All collections have an emphasis on local history: archaeology, arts and crafts 1500-1800, coins and medals, painting and sculpture 1500-1900, religious art
Exhibitions: Jan Bogaerts, 1878-1962; Dorpen in Brabant; Kees Maks, 1876-1967; Niel Steenbergen 40 jaar Beeldhouwer; Het Beleg van Den Bosch in 1629; Het onstaan van de Neogothiek in Brabant; Winter Landscapes Dutch School 15th and 17th Centuries
Activities: Exten dept serves Noord-Brabant; individual paintings and original objects of art lent; originate traveling exhibitions; sales shop sells books and reproductions

HOORN

M **WESTFRIES MUSEUM,*** Huis Verloren, Kerkstraat 10. Tel 15 97. *Dir* W A Braasem; *Archaeology Department* Mrs T Y v-d Walle; *Sr Research Asst* H W Saaltink; *Admin* Mrs W N Mallekote
Open April - Oct daily 10 AM - 5 PM, Sun Noon - 5 PM, Oct - April daily 10 AM - Noon and 2 - 5 PM, Sun in Oct & March 2 - 5 PM. Admis families of more than three persons f2.50, adult f.1, children f0.50. Estab 1880, building dates from 1632. Average Annual Attendance: 40,000
Income: f.350,000 (financed by appropriations)
Purchases: f.20,000
Collections: Collections from the Westfrisian Area and Town Culture of Old Trading-Town Hoorn; †16th - 19th Century Paintings; 17th and 18th Interiors with Fine Fittings; 20th Century Painting; †business, †china, costumes, †glass, †navigation, †objects of folk art, †objects of trade, †silverware
Publications: Annual Report
Activities: Concerts; original objects of art lent

LEERDAM

M **NATIONAAL GLASMUSEUM,** Lingedijk 28. Tel 4-7102. *Pres* J Colporaal; *Secy* J I H de Bluyne
Open 10 AM - 5 PM, Sun 1 - 5 PM, cl Sat & Sun Nov - April. Admis $1.50. Estab 1953 to collect modern and ancient glass. Average Annual Attendance: 14,000
Income: $36,000 (financed by endowment, city and state appropriation and admission fees)
Collections: Antique, machine-made and packaging glass; handmade serial glass; unique pieces

Exhibitions: Young Glass; free glass of young artists; permanent collection exhibition
Activities: Classes for adults and children; docent training
L **Library,** Lingedijk 28.
Open 10 AM - 5 PM, Sun 1 - 5 PM, cl Sat & Sun Nov - April
Library Holdings: Vols 100

LEEUWARDEN

M **FRIES MUSEUM,** Turfmarkt 24. Tel 05100 - 23001. *Dir* Dr C Boschma; *VDir* Dr J A Bosmans; *Cur Archaeology & Prints & Drawings* Dr G Elzinga; *Cur Textiles* S Wille Engelsma; *Educational Officer* H Kingmans
Open 10 AM - 5 PM, Sun 1 - 5 PM. Admis adult F 1.50, sr citizens over 65 and children under 18 F 1. Estab 1881 for preservation of Frisian art and culture from the earliest times. Average Annual Attendance: 50,000
Income: Financed by province and state appropriation
Collections: †Archaeology, †ceramics, †costumes, †Folk Art, †historical items, †painting, †prints and drawings, †sculpture, †silver, †textiles
Exhibitions: (1978-79) Art from Friesland, made in recent past and present (temporary shows); Equestrian Portraits; Jan Hofman; Jopie Huisman; Auke Komter; A W Kort; Jan Mankes; Johan Miedema; Joh Mulders; Provincial Collections; L P Roodbaard; Willem van Althuis; Ids Wiersma
Publications: De Vrije Fries, yearly; Fries Museum Bulletin, 4 per year
Activities: Classes for adults and children; docent training; originate traveling exhibitions; museum shop sells books, magazines, reproductions, prints and slides

LEIDEN

M **STEDELIJK MUSEUM DE LAKENHAL,** Leyden Municipal Museum, Oude Singel 28-32. Tel 071 144044. *Dir* M L Wurfbain; *Adminr* J M van Leeuwen; *Cur History* I W L Moerman; *Cur Modern Art* D Wintgens; *Head Education Department* S M Blokhuis
Open Mon - Sat 10 AM - 5 PM, Sun & holidays 1 - 5 PM. Admis adults 1.50 guilders, children .75 guilders. Estab 1874 to preserve paintings, sculpture, arts and crafts from Leyden and surroundings, and to present these to the public in their historical context. Building dates back to 1640 with extensions in 1890 for paintings, and in 1918 for arts and crafts, and exhibitions. Average Annual Attendance: 35,000. Mem: 550; dues 15 guilders
Income: $900,000 (financed by city appropriation)
Purchases: $24,000
Collections: †Paintings (Lucas van Leyden, Rembrandt, Steen, van Goyen, and others - 2000 items); †sculpture (medieval, 17th - 20th Century); arms, ceramics, furniture, glass, period rooms, pewter, †silver, tiles
Exhibitions: Eight per year. Geschildert tot Leyden anno 1626 et al; Lucas van Leyden et al; Leids Zilver et al
Publications: Bulletins, quarterly; catalogs, 6 - 8 times per year
Activities: Docent training; lect open to public; concerts; tours; individual paintings and original objects of art lent to institutions; museum shop sells books, magazines, reproductions, slides and catalogs
L **Library,** Oude Singel 28-32. *Librn* P M Couwenbergh
Open Mon - Sat 10 AM - 12:30 PM, Mon & Wed 2 - 5 PM. Estab 1978 to offer staff and visitors information on Leyden, the Lakenhal Museum and western European art
Income: Financed through museum
Purchases: $2000
Library Holdings: Vols 7000; Per subs 70; AV—Slides; Other—Clipping files, exhibition catalogs, photographs, reproductions
Special Subjects: Art and culture of the Netherlands

NIJMEGEN

M **NIJMEEGS MUSEUM COMMANDERIE VAN SAINT JAN,** Franse Plaats 3. Tel 80-229193. *Dir* Dr G T M Lemmens; *Cur Modern Art* J van der Grinten; *Education Department* D van Golberdinge
Open Mon - Sat 10 AM - 5 PM, Sun 1 - 5 PM. No admis fee. Estab 1974. Average Annual Attendance: 45,000
Income: $1,000,000 (financed by city appropriation)
Purchases: $100,000
Collections: Art and history of Nijmegen and region: Middle Ages - 20th Century; modern international art
Exhibitions: 15 - 30 exhibitions per year
Publications: Exhibition catalogues, 8 - 10 per year
Activities: Classes for children; docent training; lect open to public; concerts; exten dept serves schools; lending collection contains lantern slides and slides; museum shop sells books and reproductions
L **Library,** Franse Plaats 3.
Estab circa 1950. Not open to public
Purchases: $6000
Library Holdings: Vols 7000; Per subs 90; Other—Exhibition catalogs, photographs

OTTERLO

M **RYKSMUSEUM KROLLER-MULLER,** Kroller-Muller State Museum, National Park de Hoge Veluwe. Tel 08382-241. *Dir* Dr R W D Oxenaar; *Deputy Dir* Dr E Joosten; *Secy* M A Geerlings; *Cur* Dr P H Hefting; *Cur* Dr A van der Woud
No admis fee (Admis to National Park). Estab 1938. Average Annual Attendance: 400,000
Income: Financed by state appropriation
Collections: Van Gogh Collection (278 works); 19th and 20th Century Art - drawings, paintings, sculptures, sculpture garden, sculptor drawings
Publications: Museum Journal, 6 times per year
Activities: Individual paintings and original objects of art lent to museums and galleries; originate traveling exhibitions; museum shop sells books, reproductions, prints, slides and catalogs
L **Library,** National Park de Hoge Veluwe
Open for reference to students

ROTTERDAM

M **MUSEUM BOYMANS-VAN BEUNINGEN,** Mathenesserlaan 18-20, PO Box 2277. Tel 36 05 00. *Dir* Dr W A L Beeren
Open Mon - Sat 10 AM - 5 PM, Sun 11 AM - 5 PM. Estab 1847
Collections: Heronimus Bosch's The Prodigal Son; Pieter Breughel's The Tower of Babel; Italian and French Paintings from the 15th - 19th Centuries and contemporary paintings and objects; Rembrandt's Portrait of Rembrandt's Son Titus; 21 Paintings by Rubens; Hubert and Jan van Eyck's The Three Marys at the Open Sepulchre; Paintings of the Netherlands from the brothers van Eyck to Vincent van Gogh; works by Salvador Dali, Jim Dine, Kandinsky, Oscar Kokoschka, Franz Marc, Rene Margritte, Andy Warhol, and others; ceramics, furniture, glass, lace, old and modern drawings and graphic art, pewter, silver
L **Library,** Mathenesserlaan 18, PO Box 2277.
Open Mon - Fri 10 AM - 5 PM. Estab 1935 as reference library for staff and public
Purchases: $25,000
Library Holdings: Vols 100,000; Micro—Cards, fiche, reels, prints

THE HAGUE

M **HAAGS GEMEENTEMUSEUM,** Municipal Museum of The Hague, Stadhouderslaan 41, 2517 HV, PO Box 72, 2501 CB. Tel 070-51 41 81. *Dir* Dr T van Velzen; *Deputy Dir & Head Educative Department* Dr H Overduin; *Head Department of Decorative Arts* Dr A Westers; *Head History Department* Dr W M van der Mast; *Head Modern Art Department* Open; *Head Music Department* Dr C C J von Gleich; *Head Prints Departments* Dr C H A Broos
Open weekdays 10 AM - 5 PM, Sun & holidays 1 - 5 PM, Wed 8 - 10 PM. No admis fee, except special fees for temporary exhibitions and reduced fees for groups. Estab 1883. Present museum was built by the well-known architect Dr H P Berlage in 1935; extension for temporary exhibitions since 1962. Average Annual Attendance: 291,276. Mem: 1400 (Society of Friends of the Municipal Museum of The Hague); dues F 30, member of family F 15
Collections: Ancient Decorative Arts Collection includes Chinese pottery and porcelain, Delft pottery, Islamic pottery, Italian and Spanish majolica; Ancient Indonesian Art; Art of the Ancient World: Coptic textiles, Greek pottery, terracottas; Dutch Artists: Jongkind, van Gogh, Weissenbruch; Dutch Colonial Furniture; Dutch Period Rooms 1680-1780; Egyptian, Roman, Islamic, Venetian and Dutch glass; German Expressionists: living Dutch artists, Escher, Heyboer, Mondiran, Werkman; Hague procelain 1776-1784; Hague silver 17th - 19th Century; Modern Art Collection includes decorative arts, paintings and sculpture of the 19th and 20th Century; objects in Bronze and Dutch pewter; largest collection of works (257) by Piet Mondrian, van Doesburg and other members of the Stijl group; recent trends: Karel Appel, Constant, Visser and Westerik; Foreign artists, notably: Bonington, Monet, Redon; Expressionist: Kirchner, Kokoschka, Lissitsky, Picasso; Paintings by Bacon, Kitaj, Vasarely; Sculptures by Arp, Lipchitz, Moore. Printroom: large Collection of prints and drawings of Dutch and Foreign Masters of the 19th and 20th Century, notably: Bresdin, Toulouse Lautrec, Redon
Publications: General and specific publications related to each department. Ancient Decorative Arts: catalog of Chinese Ceramics (1976); catalogs of Dutch glass (1962) and Hague silver (1962); guides to the collections of European and Islamic Decorative Arts; many picture books concerning the various collections (also in English). Modern Art: Catalog of paintings (1962) and sculptures (1972); Mondrian (1974). Music Department: Catalogs of the music library I and II (1969, 1973); catalog of wind instruments, volume I (1970); large number of microfiches; selection of old European instruments; picture books
Activities: Museum lessons for children; courses for adults and children; children's workshop (only children of visitors); explicatory slide shows and film programs; Winter Programs (Sept - May); lect; concerts; music projects; gallery talks; special exhibits for students (high-schools); museum shop sells exhibition catalogues, books, postcards, slides and reproductions
M **Museum Bredius,** Prinsegracht 6, PO Box 72, 2501 CB. Tel 63 16 03. *Dir* T van Velzen
Open weekdays 10 AM - 5 PM, Sun & holidays 1 - 5 PM, Wed 8 - 10 PM. Admis f 0.25. The well-known art-historian, Dr A Bredius, donated his collection and private 17th century house in 1946, to the municipality of The Hague, on loan since 1923. Average Annual Attendance: 5716
Collections: Drawings by Breughel, Rembrandt, van Goyen; paintings by Rembrandt, Ruisdael, Seghers, Steen, Terborch; furniture, glass, porcelain, silver
Publications: Catalog (paintings and drawings); Museum Bredius (1980)
L **Art Library,** *Asst* F Blijenburg; *Asst* W Notenboom
Estab 1935 as a reference library for the museum staff and public
Income: $23,000
Purchases: $13,500
Library Holdings: Vols 45,000; Per subs 70; Other—Exhibition catalogs

M **KONINKLIJK KABINET VAN SCHILDERIJEN,** Royal Picture Gallery, Korte Vijverberg 8. Tel 46 92 44. *Dir* H R Hoetink; *Asst* F J Duparc

Open weekdays 10 AM - 5 PM, Sun 11 AM - 5 PM. Building erected 1633; museum estab 1816
Collections: Paintings of the Dutch and Flemish Masters of the 15th, 16th, 17th and 18th Centuries
Publications: Catalogue Dutch landscape paintings (1980); general illustrated catalogue (1977); Rembrandt in the Mauritshuis (1978); Johan Maurits van Nassau-Siegen, a Humanist Prince in Europe and Brazil (1979)

NEW ZEALAND

AUCKLAND

M **AUCKLAND CITY ART GALLERY,** Kitchener St, PO Box 5449. Tel 792 020. *Head of Department* Grant Kirby; *Sr Cur* Andrew Bogle; *Cur of New Zealand Paintings and Sculpture* Alexa Johnston; *Registrar* Erick Young; *Art Research Consultant, Ed* Ron Brownson; *Conservator* Katharine Woodgate-Jones; *Exhibitions Designer* Ross Ritchie; *Security Officer* Laurie Teixeira
Open Mon - Thurs 10 AM - 4:30 PM, Fri 10 AM - 8:30 PM, Sat & Sun 1 - 5:30 PM. Estab 1887 as a general purpose gallery of the fine arts with collections for exhibition and study and facilities for the organization and receipt of touring exhibitions (New Zealand and International); provides art services to general public, schools and university and support to New Zealand artists. Gallery has seven exhibition areas with full facilities devoted to permanent and special exhibitions. Average Annual Attendance: 135,000
Income: $680,000 (financed by endowment, membership, city and state appropriation)
Purchases: $40,000
Collections: †American and Australian Paintings; †general collection of European paintings and sculpture from 12th Century on; †historical and contemporary European prints and drawings; †historical and contemporary New Zealand painting, sculpture and prints; †International and New Zealand Photography
Publications: Catalogs; posters; prints
Activities: Outreach Program
L **Art Research Library,** Kitchener St, PO Box 5449. *Art Research Consultant* Ron Bronnon
Open by appointment. Estab to collect, sponsor and record art information both International and New Zealand
Purchases: $8000
Library Holdings: Vols 15,000; Per subs 50; AV—A-tapes, cassettes, motion pictures, rec, v-tapes; Other—Clipping files, exhibition catalogs, manuscripts, memorabilia, original art works, pamphlets, photographs, reproductions
Collections: Archives of the Auckland City Art Gallery; Archives of New Zealand Art

L **UNIVERSITY OF AUCKLAND,** Fine Arts Library, School of Fine Arts, 20 Whitaker Place. *Librn* Valerie Richards
Open during Term Mon - Thurs 8:45 AM - 8 PM, Fri 8:45 AM - 5:30 PM, vacation Mon - Fri 9 AM - 4:30 PM. Estab 1961 to provide research materials for faculty and students of Fine Arts and Art History Department. Circ 25,000
Purchases: $NZ21,000
Library Holdings: Vols 25,000; Per subs 320; Micro—Fiche, reels; AV—Cassettes, fs, rec, slides, v-tapes; Other—Clipping files, exhibition catalogs, prints, memorabilia, original art works, pamphlets, photographs, reproductions, sculpture, artists supplies
Special Subjects: New Zealand art
Collections: Quoin Club Collection

DUNEDIN

M **DUNEDIN PUBLIC ART GALLERY,** Logan Park, PO Box 566. *Dir* Leslie Charles Lloyd; *Asst Dir* Frank Holdsworth Dickinson; *Secy* Harold Joffre Tyrie
Open Mon - Fri 10 AM - 4:30 PM, Sat, Sun & holidays 2 - 5 PM. No admis fee. Estab 1925 for the exhibition of picutre collection, furniture and porcelain. Gallery was built in 1925 and consists of twelve exhibition rooms, plus a conservation laboratory and a training centre. Average Annual Attendance: 27,000. Mem: 711; dues $3.88; annual meeting May
Income: Financed by endowment, membership, city appropriation
Purchases: $8000
Collections: †Major collection in Australian, English, Italian and New Zealand paintings
Exhibitions: Approximately 32 changing exhibitions per year
Publications: Art Gallery News and Views
Activities: Career training for conservation; lect open to public; concerts; gallery talks; tours; exten dept serves provinces in South Island; originate traveling exhibitions; sales shop sells reproductions and prints
L **Library,** Logan Park.
Estab 1930. For reference only by special request
Library Holdings: Vols 2700; Per subs 8; AV—Slides; Other—Clipping files, exhibition catalogs, framed reproductions, prints, original art works, pamphlets, photographs, reproductions, sculpture

INVERCARGILL

M **ANDERSON PARK ART GALLERY,*** Myross Bush Rd, Waikiwi, PO Box 755. *Pres* K A Ballinger; *Secy* Mrs J Taylor; *Treas* Mrs P Green; *Dir* J Husband
Open Tues - Thurs, Sat & Sun 2 - 4:30 PM, cl Mon, Fri & Christmas Day. No admis fee, except for special exhibitions 30¢. Estab 1951 for the collection of contemporary works of art. Gallery is the former home of the late Sir Robert Anderson; was offered to Invercargill City Council for use as a public park and gallery. It is set in ten acres of garden and fifty acres of native bush on the outskirts of the city. Mem: 120; dues family $5, individual $3; committee meets monthly
Income: $6000 (financed by endowment, membership and city appropriation)
Purchases: $550
Collections: Contemporary New Zealand Art
Activities: Lect open to public

NAPIER

M **HAWKES BAY ART GALLERY AND MUSEUM,** Herschel St, PO Box 429. Tel 57781. *Acting Dir* R B McGregor
Open Mon - Fri 10:30 AM - 4:30 PM, Sat, Sun & holidays 1 - 4:30 PM. Admis family $1, adult 50¢, children 20¢. Estab 1856 as a regional museum. Holt Gallery contains Maori artifacts; Bestall Gallery, fine arts; Malden Gallery, itinerant exhibitions; also Historical Research Library. Average Annual Attendance: 45,000. Mem: 1700; dues $5; annual meeting May
Income: $68,000 (financed by endowment, membership and city appropriations)
Purchases: $6000
Collections: †Antiques; Maori artifacts; †New Zealand painting and sculpture
Exhibitions: Local craftwork and paintings; touring exhibitions of New Zealand and overseas art, crafts, historical material and sculpture
Publications: Newsletter, quarterly
Activities: Classes for children; concerts; objects of art lent to museums; lending collection contains film strips, cassettes, lantern slides, motion pictures, original art works, original prints, 250 paintings, 5500 photographs, sculpture, maps and 1000 plans; book traveling exhibitions
L **Library,** Herschel St, PO Box 429.
For reference
Library Holdings: Vols 8000; Other—Photographs, maps
Special Subjects: Hawkes Bay History

WANGANUI

M **SARJEANT GALLERY,** Queens Park, Box 637. Tel 57052. *Dir* W H Milbank; *Registrar* Jill Studd; *Technician* Denis Rainforth; *Education Officer* Paul Johnson
Open Mon Noon - 4:30 PM, Tues - Fri 10 AM - 4:30 PM, Sat, Sun & holidays 1 - 4:30 PM. No admis fee. Estab 1917 to collect and exhibit works of art for the information and interest of the general public. Gallery is built on the Greek cross principle with a sculpture court in the centre. The Front Gallery exhibits 18th, 19th & 20th Century international works; the West Wing, New Zealand paintings; the East Wing and Back Gallery are devoted to touring and local exhibitions. Average Annual Attendance: 30,000
Income: Financed by endowment and city appropriation
Collections: European works; †local works; †New Zealand collection of paintings; photographic works (based around Denton Collection); †sculpture and applied arts
Exhibitions: (1978-79) Billy Apple: Toward the Centre; Diane Arbus; Don Driver; Augustus John; Owen Merton (watercolours); Sculpture at Mildura; Tsutsumu: The Art of Japanese Package; Vasarely and His Contemporaries
Activities: Originate traveling exhibitions
L **Library,** Queens Park, Box 637.
Open for reference to public and staff
Library Holdings: Other—Not catalogued
Special Subjects: New Zealand art, British Victoriana

WELLINGTON

M **NATIONAL ART GALLERY OF NEW ZEALAND,** Buckle St. Tel 859 703. *Dir* L H Bieringa; *Cur Paintings & Sculpture* I A Hunter; *Cur Prints & Drawings* Anne Kirker; *Registrar* Kate Martin; *Education Officer* Moira Johnson; *Exhib Officer* Louise Upston
Open daily 10 AM - 4:45 PM. Estab 1936 to house National Collection of art works; archival preservation; acquisition of good representative works of art to augment collection; educative centre in art for New Zealand. Average Annual Attendance: 200,000
Income: NZ$300,000 (financed by government appropriation)
Purchases: NZ$40,000
Collections: Australian, British, European and New Zealand Art; Sir Harold Beauchamp Collection of early English drawings, illustrations and watercolors; Sir John Illott Collection of graphics; Nan Kivell Collection of British original prints; Monrad Collection of early European graphics; National Collection of New Zealand drawings; small collection of Old Master drawings; Archdeacon Smythe Collection; †John Weeks Collection; Harold Wright Collection of graphics
Publications: Educational newsletter, monthly; educational audio-visual material; exhibition catalogs and supplementary material; gallery calendar, three monthly
Activities: Weekend public programs; art educ programs at primary, secondary and adult levels; in-service courses; holiday art programs; docent training; Women's Art Archive; programs relating to exhibitions; weekend lect and performances; films; originate traveling exhibitions
L **Library,** Buckle St.
For reference
Library Holdings: Vols 2000

NORWAY

BERGEN

M **VESTLANDSKE KUNSTINDUSTRIMUSEUM,** Western Norway Museum of Applied Art, Nordal Brunsgate 9. Tel 05-21 51 08. *Chmn of the Board* Ole Hauge; *Museum Dir* Peter M Anker; *Cur* Mrs Thale Riisön
Open May - Aug weekdays 10 AM - 3 PM, Sun Noon - 3 PM, off season every day except Mon, Noon - 3 PM. Estab 1887 to encourage Norwegian industry and crafts as regards tastefulness and appropriate work, and to try to develop the taste of the general public in a similar way. Average Annual Attendance: 25,000. Mem: 400; approx four meetings a year in connection with lectures, opening of temporary exhibitions
Collections: Antique Bergen Silver; Chinese Arts from the Renaissance to modern times; contemporary Norwegian and European ceramics; The General Munthe Collection of Chinese Art; †collections of old European arts and crafts; The Anna B and William H Singer Collection of art and antiquities; furniture, glass, metalwork, textiles
Publications: Exhibition catalogs; Vestlandske Kunstindustrimuseums Arbok (yearbook every 3 - 5 years)
Activities: Receives classes from the primary school level upwards, also students from art colleges and from the University Department of Art History, for teaching and lectures given by the staff; certain courses are also arranged in cooperation with various popular educational organizations; lect open to public and few for members only, 2 - 3 visiting lectr per year; concerts; gallery talks; tours; scholarships; lending collection contains photographs, Kodachromes (5x5 cm), slides (8x8 cm)
L **Library,** Nordal Brunsgate 9. *Librn* Marit Kolltveit
Open Mon - Fri 10 AM - 3 PM. Estab 1887 to encourage Norwegian arts and crafts as regards tastefulness and appropriate work. Also a library-museum of general art history
Library Holdings: Vols 15,000; Per subs 150; AV—Slides; Other—Clipping files, exhibition catalogs, framed reproductions, manuscripts, pamphlets, photographs, booklets 4000, posters
Special Subjects: Art History, Costume Design & Construction, Crafts, Furniture, Silver, Textiles, Norwegian arts and crafts

LILLEHAMMER

M **LILLEHAMMER BYS MALERISAMLING,** Lillehammer Art Museum, Kirkegaten 69. Tel 062 51944. *Chief Executive* Ole Ronning Johannesen
Open Mon - Sat 10 AM - 3 PM, Sun Noon - 4 PM. Admis NKr 2. Estab 1927 to give exhibitions of art. Average Annual Attendance: 15,000
Income: Financed by city appropriation
Collections: Norwegian paintings, sculpture and graphic art from 19th and 20th Centuries
Exhibitions: Ten exhibitions of contemporary Norwegian Art
Publications: A yearbook
Activities: Lect open to public, 16 visiting lectr per year; concerts; gallery talks; tours
L **Library,** Kirkegaten 69.
Reference library for staff
Library Holdings: Vols 1000

OSLO

M **CITY OF OSLO ART COLLECTION,** Munch Museum, Toyengaten 53. (Mailing Add: PO Box 2812, Kampen 5, Oslo) *Dir* Alf Boe; *Chief Cur* Arne Eggum; *Cur* Gerd Woll; *Museum Lectr* Marit Lande Pedersen
Open Tues - Sat 10 AM - 8 PM, Sun Noon - 8 PM, cl Mon. No admis fee. Estab 1963 to take care of the bequest of Edvard Munch to the City of Oslo, and to show selected items of the collections. Museum covers 1150 sq meters of exhibition area, including a concert hall which is also used for changing exhibitions. Museum also contains a library, offices, storerooms, and a technical department. Average Annual Attendance: 217,355
Income: Financed by city appropriation
Collections: Paintings, Prints and Drawings of Edvard Munch; works by the Sculptor Gustav Vigeland (Nobelsgt 32); contemporary paintings (donated by Rolf E Stenersen); decorations, monuments and sculptures belonging to the city of Oslo
Exhibitions: The works of Edvard Munch; changing exhibitions
Activities: Classes for adults and children; lect open to public; concerts; gallery talks
L **Library,** PO Box 2812, Kampen 5. *Librn* Frida Tank
Open to museum staff and researchers for reference
Library Holdings: Vols 12,300; Per subs 24; Other—Clipping file concerning Edvard Munch 1895 to present
Special Subjects: Books and articles concerning Munch, modern art
Collections: Munch's own library

M **KUNSTINDUSTRIMUSEET I OSLO,** Oslo Museum of Applied Art, St Olavs Gate 1. Tel 02-203578. *Pres* Hans Höegh; *Dir* Lauritz Opstad; *Cur* Inger Marie Kvaal Lie; *Cur* Aase Bay Sjövold; *Cur* Albert Steen; *Conservator Textiles* Kari Fostervoll
Open Tues - Sun 11 AM - 3 PM, Jan 15 - May 1 & Sept 15 - Dec 1 Tues & Thurs evenings 7 - 9 PM, cl Mon. No admis fee. Estab 1876 to further the aesthetic value of the products of artisans and promote the understanding for these values among the public. Gallery has six stories, exhibitions are in four: ground floor - changing exhibitions, mainly modern; first floor - Old Norwegian collections from the Middle Ages until 1850; second floor - collections from abroad 1600-1850; third floor - modern Scandinavian applied art, textiles and costumes. Average Annual Attendance: 60,000
Income: $450,000 (financed by city and state appropriation)
Purchases: $40,000
Collections: †Ceramics, †furniture, †glass, †silver, †textiles, old and modern
Exhibitions: Approximately 12 per year, plus traveling exhibitions
Publications: Catalogs; monographies; Yearbook

Activities: Classes for adults; lect open to public, 4 visiting lectr per year; concerts; gallery talks; tours; lending collection contains 30,000 books, 2500 slides; book traveling exhibitions; originate traveling exhibitions; sales shop sells books, prints and slides

L **Library,** St Olavs Gate 1. Tel 02-20 14 07. *Head Librn* Ase Markussen; *Librn* Lise Halvorsen; *Librn* Astrid Skjerven
Open Mon - Sat 11 AM - 3 PM. Estab 1876 to supply the museum in its research into the fields of applied art, arts and crafts; also an institutional research library
Income: $5000 (financed by city appropriation)
Library Holdings: Vols 31,000; Per subs 150; Other—Exhibition catalogs
Publications: Bibliographies covering the publications of the museum

M **NASJONALGALLERIET,** National Gallery, Universitetsgaten 13. Tel 20 04 04. *Dir* Knut Berg; *Keeper Paintings* Magne Malmanger; *Keeper Prints & Drawings* Sidsel Helliesen; *Keeper Sculpture* Oscar Thue; *Chief Restorer* Leif Plahter
Open Mon - Fri 10 AM - 4 PM, Sat 10 AM - 3 PM, Sun Noon - 3 PM, Wed & Thurs evenings 6 - 8 PM. Estab 1837 as the principal art gallery in Norway
Collections: European paintings with examples of modern French, Danish and Swedish Art; small collection of Greek and Roman sculpture; †Norwegian painting and sculpture; casts, icons, prints and drawings
L **Library,** Universitetsgaten 13. *Librn* Anne Lise Rabben
Library Holdings: Vols 25,000
Collections: Exhibition catalogs and slides

M **NORSK FOLKEMUSEUM,** Norwegian Folk Museum, Bygdöy. Tel 55 80 90. *Dir* Halvard Björkvik
Open summer 10 AM - 6 PM, Sun Noon - 6 PM, winter 11 AM - 4 PM, Sun Noon - 3 PM. Admis 8 Kr. Estab 1894. Average Annual Attendance: 300,000
Income: Financed by state appropriation
Collections: The Lappish section provides an insight into the ancient culture of the Lapps. †The Open Air Museum totals about 170 old buildings, all original. Among them are the Stave Church from Hallingdal; farmsteads from different districts of the country; single buildings of particular interest; The Old Town - 17th, 18th and 19th Century town houses. †Urban Collections - Norwegian town interiors from the Renaissance to the present; Henrik Ibsen's study; the first Parliament Hall of Norway (1814); post-Renaissance costumes; †other collections include peasant art and furniture; post-medieval church art; woven tapestries; tools and techniques of old Norwegian farming; toys and dolls; modern primitive musical instruments
Publications: Annual yearbook (By og Bygd)
L **Norsk Folkemuseums Bibliotek,** Museumsveien 10. *Librn* Randi Foss
Open 9 AM - 3 PM. Estab 1894 to serve staff of the museum; open to public for reference
Library Holdings: Vols 35,000; Per subs 450; AV—Slides; Other—Manuscripts, photographs
Special Subjects: , Costume and textile history, European cultural anthropology

M **NORSK SJÖFARTSMUSEUM,** Norwegian Maritime Museum, Bygodöynes 2. Tel 55 63 95. *Dir* SVen Molaug; *Cur* Bard Kolltveit
Exhibition Halls open April 15 - Sept 10 AM - 8 PM, Oct - April 14 10:30 AM - 4 PM, Tues & 10:30 AM - 8 PM, Sun 10:30 AM - 5 PM. Estab 1914, museum opened 1974, to collect and exhibit items illustrating Norwegian maritime civilization. Average Annual Attendance: 105,000. Mem: 500; annual meeting May
Collections: The Polarship Gjoa; archives pertaining to maritime history; instruments, paintings, photographs of ships, ship models, tools and other items pertaining to maritime collections; special exhibitions of small crafts
Publications: Arsberetning, annually; Norsk Sjofartsmuseum
Activities: Instruction of school classes; underwater escavations; courses in rope-work, seamanship, etc; training ship, Svanen, (one-week expeditions during the summer); semi-weekly meetings during the winter for divers; lect; souvenir shop
L **Library,** Bygodöynesveien 37. *Librn* Else Marie Thorstvedt
Open May 15 - Sept 15 8:30 AM - 3 PM, Sat 8:30 AM - 1 PM, Sept 16 - May 14 8:30 AM - 4 PM, Sat 8:30 AM - 1 PM. Estab 1914 for maritime literature
Purchases: $5600
Library Holdings: Vols 20,000; Per subs 200; AV—Kodachromes, motion pictures, rec, slides; Other—Clipping files, exhibition catalogs, framed reproductions, prints, manuscripts, memorabilia, original art works, pamphlets, photographs, reproductions, maps
Special Subjects: Maritime history

L **STATENS KUNSTAKADEMI BIBLIOTEKET,** Uranienborgsvn 2. *Librn* Tamiko Kauakami Nielsen
Open 10 AM - 4 PM
Library Holdings: Vols 3300; Per subs 10; AV—Slides; Other—Exhibition catalogs
Special Subjects: Drawings, Graphic Arts, American Painting, Sculpture, painting

M **UNIVERSITETETS SAMLING AV NORDISKE OLDSAKER,** University Museum of National Antiquities, Frederiksgate 2. Tel 416300. *Dir* Dr Sverre Marstrander; *Head Early Iron Age Department* Wencke Slomann; *Head Medieval Age Department* Martin Blindheim; *Head Stone & Bronze Age Department* Irmelin Martens; *Head Viking Age Department* Charlotte Blindheim
Open summer 11 AM - 3 PM, winter Noon - 3 PM; Viking Ship Museum open Nov - March 11 AM - 3 PM, April & Oct 11 AM - 4 PM, May - Aug 10 AM - 6 PM, Sept 11 AM - 5 PM. Estab 1829 for the exhibition of finds from the prehistoric periods, medieval church art and objects from medieval towns. The Viking ship finds with magnificent grave goods in the Viking Ship Museum at Bygdöy (branch museum); responsibility for archaeological finds and for the preservation of prehistoric monuments in the southeastern and southern part of Norway; educational and research institution (Scandinavian archaeology) of the University of Oslo
Income: Financed by state appropriation
Purchases: $400,000
Collections: Church Art and profane objects from the Medieval Age; material from the Norwegian Stone, Bronze and Iron Age
Publications: Guides; Skrifter, proceedings; Universitetets Oldsaksamlings Arbok, yearbook
Activities: Lect in Scandinavian archaeology; special lect open to public

L **Library,** Frederiksgate 2.
Library Holdings: Vols 30,000; Other—Photograph prints 30,000

PAKISTAN

KARACHI

M **NATIONAL MUSEUM OF PAKISTAN,*** Burns Garden. Tel 5-51-08. *Supt of Museum* Taswir Husain Hamidi
Open 10 AM - 5 PM, cl Fri. Admis adults 50 paisa, children 25 paisa, students free. Estab 1950 to collect, preserve, study and exhibit the records of the cultural history of the country; to promote a learned insight into the personality of its people; to promote research work to create understanding among the masses for the appreciation of their cultural heritage and sense of preservation for the relics of their rich past. Average Annual Attendance: 100,000
Income: 30,000 rupees
Collections: Specimen of calligraphy, large collection of coins and miniature paintings spreading from 6th Century BC to 19th Century AD; ethnological material from the various regions of Pakistan; gold jewelry from Taxila; Gradhara sculptures in stone, stucco and terra-cotta; Hindu sculptures in stone; Islamic period glass, pottery, scientific instruments and carpets; manuscripts, largely of Muslim period; Prehistoric and Protohistoric period material from the Indus Valley sites
Publications: Brochures; catalogs; guide books
Activities: Classes for children; lect open to public; gallery talks; originate traveling exhibitions; sales shop sells books and reproductions

LAHORE

M **LAHORE MUSEUM,** Shahrah-E-Quaid-E-Azam. *Chmn* B A Kureshi; *Dir* Dr Saifur Rahman Dar; *Keeper Coins & Medals* Mrs Tahira A Beg; *Keeper Muslim Period Coll* F M Anjum Rehmani; *Display Officer* Mrs Nusrat Ali; *Public Relations Officer* Mrs Zarina Khurshid
Open summer 9 AM - 5 PM, winter 8:30 AM - 4:30 PM. Admis adults 50 paisas, students and children 25 paisas, delegations and students tours free. Estab 1890 to educate and preserve national heritage
Purchases: $70,000
Collections: Coins Room; Ethnological I, II and III - Fabrics and Clay Models; Fagir; Gandhara; Hindu; Islamic; Jain Temple; Pakistan movement; Sadequain's Paintings; arms, calligraphy and miscellaneous, contemporary paintings, miniature paintings, pre-historic and proto-historic, stamps and medals
Exhibitions: (1978-79) Calligraphy; Kharoshiti Inscriptions; Manuscripts on Khat-E-Bahar; Miniature Paintings: Regan and Ragarri; Muslim Press; Punch Marked Coins
Publications: A brief guide to Lahore Museum; Karoshiti Priemer
Activities: Special classes are organized; lect open to public, 12 visiting lectr per year; tours; study circle meeting held the 15th of every month; exten dept; lending collection contains 25,000 books; museum shop sells books, magazines, original art, reproductions, prints, slides, postcards, plaster casts precious and semi-precious stones; Bahamalpur Museum, Central Library Rd, Bahamalpur
L **Library,** Shahrah-E-Quaid-E-Azam. *Librn* Muhammad Asghar; *Librn Asst* Muhammad Ghal; *Librn Clerk* Bashir Ahmerd
Open summer 7:30 AM - 2:30 PM, winter 8:30 AM - 6 PM. Estab 1908 for research and to supplement education objects and exhibits
Purchases: $2000
Library Holdings: Vols 25,000; Per subs 30; Other—Exhibition catalogs, prints, manuscripts, pamphlets, photographs
Special Subjects: Antropology, Archaeology, Art History, Culture and civilization-specially of sub-continent, museology, fine arts

PESHAWAR

M **PESHAWAR MUSEUM,*** Grand Trunk Rd. *Dir* Prof Fidaullah Sehrai; *Cur* S M Jaffar
Estab 1907. Maintains an art gallery
Collections: Architectural pieces and minor antiquities; mainly sculptures of the Grandhara School containing images of Buddha, Bodhisattvas, Buddhist deities, reliefs illustrating the life of the Buddha and Jataka stories
Publications: Guides and handbooks

RAWALPINDI

M **ART GALLERY SOCIETY OF CONTEMPORARY ART,** Rawalpindi Gallery of Modern Art,* 25 Civil Lines. Tel 6 27 27. *Executive Dir* Zubeida Agha
Open 9:30 AM - 1 PM and 3 - 5:30 PM. No admis fee. Estab 1961 to provide a show window to the artists; to help sell their work; to introduce the young and upcoming artists; maintain a high standard for the exhibitions. Average Annual Attendance: 4000. Mem: restricted; dues $2.50; meeting first week of June and second week of Oct
Income: Financed by membership and grant-in-aid
Collections: Thirty-three paintings by top Pakistani and Foreign artists; permanent collection is not on view due to lack of space
Exhibitions: 45 Art Exhibitions including three Anniversary Shows; Zebeida Agha; Shakir Ali; American Prints; British Graphics; Children's Paintings; A R Chughtai; Colin David; French Graphics; German Paintings; Ahmed Parvez; Persian Miniatures; Turkish artists; 25th Anniversary of Pakistan Day and RCD paintings
Activities: Lect open to public; tours; films; original objects of art lent; originate traveling exhibitions

TAXILA

M ARCHAEOLOGICAL MUSEUM,* Rawalpindi, Taxila District. *Custodian* A A Farooq
Open winter 9 AM - 4 PM, summer 9 - Noon and 2 - 6 PM. Estab 1928. Museum is member of Museums Association of Pakistan. Average Annual Attendance: 40,000
Collections: Antiquities from Taxila Sites ranging from 7th Century BC to 5th Century AD; gold and silver ornaments; pottery; sculptures of stone and stucco of Ganhara and Indo-Afghan School
Exhibitions: Temporary exhibitions on special occasions
Activities: Lect on the archaeology of Pakistan with special reference to Taxila are arranged for the college and university students
L Library,* Rawalpindi, Taxila District.
Library Holdings: Vols 1450

PERU

LIMA

M MUSEO DE ARTE, Museum of Art,* Paseo Colon 125. Tel 32 62 42. *Dir* Dr Alberto Santibanez Salcedo
Open Thurs - Sun 10 AM - Noon and 3 - 7 PM. Admis 30¢, students free, Sun morning free. Estab 1960 for permanent exhibits of Peruvian art from the different historical periods. Museum has six galleries. Average Annual Attendance: 200,000
Income: $4600 (financed by membership and government appropriation)
Collections: Colonial Painting; Pre-Inca and Inca Collections; Republic Paintings; carvings, ceramics, furniture, metals, modern paintings, religious art, sculpture, textiles
Exhibitions: Temporary exhibitions changing monthly
Publications: Catalogs; guides
Activities: Classes for children and students; lect open to public, 12 visiting lectr per year; gallery talks; tours in English and Spanish weekly; competitions; lending collection contains Kodachromes, reproductions, photographs and slides; originate traveling exhibitions; book shop
L Library,* Paseo Colon 125.
For reference
Library Holdings: Vols 1000

M MUSEO NACIONAL DE LA CULTURA PERUANA, National Museum of Peruvian Culture, Avenida Alfonso Ugarte 650, Apdo 3048. Tel 23 58 92. *Pres* Dr Luis E Valcarcel; *Dir* Dr Rosalia Avalos de Matos
Estab 1946
Collections: Ethnography of Amazonic Tribes; ethnology, folklore, popular art

PHILIPPINES

MANILA

M LOPEZ MEMORIAL MUSEUM, 10 Lancaster Ave. Tel 80-16-29, 80-51-96. *Pres* Oscar M Lopez; *Dir* Celso G Cabrera
Open Tues - Sat 7:30 AM - Noon and 1 - 4:30 PM, Sun 9 AM - 1 PM, Mon and holidays by appointment only. Admis adult P2, group of 20 college students P1. Estab 1960 by Don Eugenio Lopez to honor his parents; to house his private collection; to serve scholars and students. Average Annual Attendance: 6000
Income: Financed by endowment
Collections: De Muluccis Insulis by Maximilianus Transylvanus (1954); rare Philippine imprints from early 17th Century: Laureano Atlas, Juan Correa, Nicolas de la Cruz Bagay, Raymundo Magysa, Pinpin and other printers; 13,000 Filipiniana titles; 14th - 15th Century Artifacts recovered in the Calatagan burial sites, consists chiefly of a few Annamese and Siamese pieces, beads, Filipino earthenwares and porcelain of Chinese origin; Luna and Hidalgo paintings; Relacion de las Islas Filipinas by Jesuit Pedro Chiroino (1604); 90 priceless letters of Rizal to his mother and sisters; †Spanish and early American period - albums of pictures, maps, microfilms, old periodicals and woodcuts; Travel Literature by Gemelli Careri, Dampier, Hakluyt, La Perouse, Linschoten, Navarrete, Purchas and others
Publications: A Guide to Luna and HIdalgo Paintings; R M Taylor, The Philippine Insurrection Against the United States, 5 volumes
Activities: sales shop sells reproductions and slides
L Library, 10 Lancaster Ave. *Chief Librn* Mrs Zenaida D Cipriano
Library Holdings: Vols 13,000; Per subs 10; Micro—Fiche, reels, prints; Other—Clipping files, framed reproductions, manuscripts, memorabilia, original art works, pamphlets, photographs, reproductions

M UNIVERSITY OF SANTO TOMAS, Santo Tomas Museum,* Calle Espana. Tel 47-22-31, Ext 269.
Open 9 AM - Noon and 2 - 5 PM. No admis fee. Estab 1848 as a museum to house collections started in 1682. Museum started as an aid to medicine and pharmacy classes, developed into a repository of natural history specimens, and Philippine culture items; completed by art gallery. The Main Hall is divided into sections - natural history, ethnology, archaeology and art. Average Annual Attendance: 40,000
Income: Financed through the university
Purchases: $6000
Collections: Archeology, cultural and historical items; †Chinese trade pottery; †coins; †ethnology of the Philippines; †medals; †Philippine art; †shells; †stamps
Activities: Individual paintings and original art objects lent to museums and exhibitions

L Library,* Calle Espana. *Chief Librn* Juana L Abello; *Librn* Javier Arrazola
Open to public by appointment
Library Holdings: Vols 260,000; Per subs 3000
Collections: Large collection of rare books

POLAND

CRACOW

L CENTRAL LIBRARY OF THE ACADEMY OF FINE ARTS, ul Smilensk 9. *Dir* Anna Pankowicz
Open Sept - June 9 AM - 7 PM, cl July - Aug. Estab 1868. For reference
Library Holdings: Vols 72,299; Per subs 126; AV—Slides; Other—Exhibition catalogs, prints, manuscripts, original art works, photographs, reproductions
Special Subjects: Industrial Design, Fine arts, conservation
Collections: 44,250 Photographs, posters, prints

M MUZEUM NARODOWE W KRAKOWIE, National Museum in Cracow, ul Manifestu Lipcowego 12. Tel 227-33, 227-63. *Dir* Tadeusz Chruscick; *Ancient Coins* Dr Stefan Skowronek; *Arms & Armour* Dr Irena Grabowski; *Arms & Armour, Near Eastern Minor Arts* Dr Zdzislaw Zygulski; *Documents* Dr Yadwiga Bezwinska; *European Painting of the 15th - 17th Centuries* Dr Marek Rostworowski; *Far Eastern Art* Dr Zofia Alber; *Greek & Roman Art* Koystyna Moczulska; *Icons* Janina Klosinska; *Italian Painting* Yenusz Waiek; *Manuscripts* Dr Adam Homecki; *Deputy Dir Polish Art of 16th - 18th Centuries* Dr Franziszek Stolot; *Polish Coins* Dr Janusz Reyman; *Polish Costumes & Textiles* Dr Maria Taszycka; *Polish Iconography* Dr Jerzy Banach; *Polish Illuminated Manuscripts* Dr Barbara Miodonska; *Polish Painting & Sculpture of the 14th - 18th Centuries* Dr Maria Kopff
Estab 1879 for historic and artistic collections of Polish and foreign art and objects of culture. Average Annual Attendance: 337,000. Mem: Association of Museum Friends
Collections: National Museum in Cracow consists of several departments with various collections. The Director and Administration seat is in the Palace of E Hutten Czapski. The Emeryk Hutten Czapski Department, ul Manifestu Lipcowego 12 - graphics 120,000, numismatic collections 250,000, old books 45,000. Department of Textiles, ul Smolensk 9. Szolayski House, pl Szczepanski 9 - department of arms and armour, Far Eastern Art, icons. Gallery of Polish painting and sculpture of the 16th - 18th Centuries, Gallery of Polish painting and sculpture of the 19th - 20th Centuries. Czartoryski Collection
Exhibitions: 1 - 2 temporary exhibitions per month
Publications: Rozprawy i Sprawozdania Muzeum Narodowego w Krakowe, annually; various catalogs, guides and monographs
Activities: Classes for children; films on art; lect for schools; concerts; guided tours; book traveling exhibitions
L Biblioteka, 30-062 Krakow, Al 3-go Maja 1. *Mgr* Marta Knapikowa; *Mgr* Sylwig Liszkowa; *Mgr* Irena Kowalska
Open daily 8 AM - 3 PM. Estab 1945 for collecting books on the history of art, useful in elaboration of museum exhibits
Library Holdings: Vols 37,000; Per subs 36; Other—Exhibition catalogs
L Czartoryski Library and Archives, ui Sw Marka 17.
For reference
Library Holdings: Vols 208,000; Other—Documents 13,300, illuminated codices, incunabula
M Galeria Polskiego Malarstwa i Rzezby od 14 do 18 wieku, Gallery of Polish Painting and Sculpture of the 14th - 18th Centuries. (Mailing Add: pl Szczepanski 9, Kamienica Szolayskich) Tel 270-12.
Open daily 10 AM - 4 PM, Mon Noon - 6 PM, Sun 10 AM - 4 PM, cl Tues and days after holidays. Admis zl 6
Collections: Very valuable and exquisite collection of Polish painting and sculpture, mostly of Cracow School, from the 14th - 18th Century, among them the famous sculpture Madonna of Kruzlowa (circa 1400)
M Galeria Polskiego i Rzezby Malarstwa w XIX, Gallery of Polish Painting and Sculpture of the 19th Century, Rynek Glowny, Sukiennice. Tel 211-66.
Open daily 10 AM - 4 PM, Thurs Noon - 6 PM, Sun 10 AM - 4 PM, cl Tues and days after holidays. Admis zl 6
Collections: Famous collection of Polish paintings and sculpture which formed a foundation of the National Museum in Cracow; The Historical Compositions by Matejko; The Nero's Torches by Siemiradszki; The Prussian Homage, among others
M Galeria Sztuki Polskiej Wieku XX, Gallery of Polish Art of the 20th Century, Al Trzeciego Maja 1. Tel 333-77, 335-26.
Open daily 10 AM - 4 PM, Wed Noon - 6 PM, Sun 10 AM - 4 PM, cl Mon and days after holidays. Admis zl 6
Collections: Very outstanding collection of Polish painting and sculpture from the Modern Art Movement (Mloda Polska) until the present, with a large representation of the artists of Cracow
M Zbiory Czartoryskich, Czartoryski Collection, ul Pijarska 15. Tel 255-66.
Open daily 10 AM - 4 PM, Thurs Noon - 6 PM, Sun 9 AM - 3 PM, cl Wed and days after holidays. Admis zl 4
Collections: Painting gallery (Leonardo da Vinci, Lady with an Ermine; Rembrandt Landscape); arms and armour, decorative and Oriental Art; Egyptian, Greek and Roman Art; Polish national relics
M Dom Jana Matejki, House of Jan Matejko, ul Florianska 41. Tel 259-26.
Open daily 10 AM - 4 PM, Fri Noon - 6 PM, Sun 9 AM - 3 PM, cl Mon and days after holidays. Admis zl 6. Biographic museum of Jan Matejko, the outstanding Polish painter of the second half of the 19th Century, who with his great historical compositions, largerly contributed to the national culture and consciousness

M PANSTWOWE ZBIORY SZTUKI NA WAWELU, Wawel State Collections of Art, Wawel 5. *Dir* Dr Jerzy Szablowski; *Deputy Dir* Stanislaw Cischkiewicz; *Deputy Dir* Stefan Zajac
Open 9 AM - 5 PM. Admis zl 10. Began in 1882 as innitiation of the collection, estab 1920 as museum for research works of archaeology, history of art and history

connected with the monuments situated on the Wawel Hill and in the Wawel Museum; restoration of the works of art; educational works; organization of permanent and temporary exhibitions

Income: Financed by government appropriation

Collections: Italian Renaissance Furniture; King Sigismund Augustus 16th Century Collection of Flemish Tapestries; Oriental carpets and tents; †Polish, Western-European and Oriental weapons; Royal Treasury; †Western-European and Oriental pottery; Western European painting; banners, crown jewels, gold objects, historical relics

Exhibitions: Court Art of Vas Adnasty in Poland (together with the Staatens Historiska Museum in Stockholm); 60 Years of The Wawel Museum 1918-1978; Thousand years of Art in Poland (two exhibitions in Paris and in London organized together with the National Museum of Cracow); Thousand years of Polish-Hungarian Relations (together with the National Museum of Budapest)

Publications: Biblioteka Wawelska; Studai do Dziejow Wawelu; Zrodla do Dziejow Wawelu

Activities: Special courses for staff members; classes for adults and children; lect open to public; concerts; competitions

L **Library,** Wawel 5.
Reference library
Library Holdings: Vols 8906; Per subs 1836
Activities: No permanent lending collection but any print supplied on request

LODZ

M **MUZEUM SZTUKI,** Wieckowskiego 36. Tel 397-90. *Dir* Ryszard Stanislawski; *Cur* Teresa Kmiecinska-Kaczmarek; *Restorer* Maria Potemska; *Cur* Urszula Czartoryska; *Cur* Janina Ladnowska
Open Tues Noon - 7 PM, Wed 10 AM - 5 PM, Thurs 11 AM - 7 PM, Fri & Sat 10 AM - 5 PM, Sun & holidays 10 AM - 4 PM. Admis 6 Zl. Estab 1930
Collections: Paintings of Karol Hiller, Wladyslaw Strzeminski; sculptures of Katarzyna Kobro
Exhibitions: Actual Trends of Japanese Art; British Avantgarde Films; Karol Broniatowski (sculptures); S I Witkiewicz (photographs 1885-1939); Lothar Wolleh (photographs)

WARSAW

M **MUZEUM NARODOWE,** National Museum, Al Jerozolimski 3. Tel 21 10 31. *Dir* Dr Stanislaw Lorentz; *VDir* Dr Kazimierz Michalowski; *VDir* Dr Andrzej Rottermund; *Head of Education Department* M Plominska
Open Tues 10 AM - 8 PM, Thurs Noon - 6 PM, Sun & holidays 10 AM - 5 PM, other days 10 AM - 4 PM, cl Mon. Admis adults zl 7, children zl 5, Thurs free. Estab 1862. Branch museums: Palaces in Warsaw-Wilanow, Lazienki, Krolikarnia, Posters Museum; and outside Warsaw - Nieborow and museum in Lowicz. Average Annual Attendance: 300,000
Income: Financed by state appropriation
Collections: †Antiquities; †European and Polish Art from the 15th Century to present; †Medieval Art; †decorative art, drawings, paintings, prints and sculpture
Exhibitions: Temporary art exhibitions; Polish and Foreign
Publications: Bulletin du Musee National de Varsovie, quarterly; exhibition catalogs; Rocznik Muzeum Narodowego w Warszawie (Annual of the National Museum in Warsaw)
Activities: Educ dept service to the visitors at the national museums, action of the popularization of art, cycles of popular talks and discussions; lect open to public; films; concerts; competitions; Club of Young Friends of the Museum; original objects of art lent; lending collection contains 106,000 photograph negatives, 8000 slides; originate traveling exhibitions; book shop
L **Library,** Al Jerozolimskie 3. *Chief Librn* Mrs Zofia Wisniowska
Open Mon - Fri 9 AM - 3:30 PM, Sat 9 AM - Noon. Estab 1916 for museum staff
Library Holdings: Vols 90,000; Per subs 261; Other—Exhibition catalogs, prints
Special Subjects: Archaeology, Decorative Arts, Graphic Arts, Sculpture, Museology, painting

WROCLAW

M **MINISTRY OF CULTURE AND ART,** Museum of Architecture in Wroclaw, Bernardynska nr 5. Tel 871-336 75. *Dir* Prof Olgierd Czerner; *Mgr* Malgorzata Szelepin; *Mgr* Zofia Gunaris
Open summer Wed, Thurs & Fri 11 AM - 4 PM, Tues & Sat Noon - 7 PM, Sun 11 AM - 6 PM, winter Tues - Fri 11 AM - 3 PM, Sat & Sun 11 AM - 6 PM. Estab 1965 for collecting the exponents documenting the development of the architecture in past and present. Museum has three galleries: Romanic Architecture, Gothic Architecture and Art connected with Architecture. Average Annual Attendance: 30,000
Income: Financed by city and state appropriation
Collections: Elements of architecture, drawings, graphics, memorials of architects, objects of artistic craftsmanship, pictures, projects, sketches
Exhibitions: Internationale Triennale of Drawings; The projects for artistic children playes places; Polish Architecture 1918-1978; Secession - architecture designs
Publications: Exhibition catalogues; guide in Germany Museum Für Architektur
Activities: Classes for adults and children; lect open to public; concerts; gallery talks; tours; lending collection contains slides; originate traveling exhibitions; museum shop sells books, reproductions and slides

M **MUZEUM NARODOWE WE WROCLAWIU,** National Museum,* Place Powstancow Warszawy 5, 50-153. Tel 3 88 39. *Dir* Dr Leszek Itman
Open Tues & Wed 10 AM - 4 PM, Fri 10 AM - 2 PM, Sat 11 AM - 5 PM, Sun 11 AM - 6 PM, summer Thurs Noon - 7 PM, winter Thurs 10 AM - 4 PM, cl Mon. No admis fee. Estab 1948 for collecting, conservation, scientific research, education and the organization of cultural activities. In 1970 became National Museum; departments are Etnographical Museum, the Bolkow Castle and the Cistercian Abbey - Lubiaz. Average Annual Attendance: 70,000
Income: Financed by appropriations
Collections: †Contemporary art, ceramics, glass, painting and sculpture;

†Decorative Hunters Arms 16th - 18th Centuries; †Medieval Art 14th - 16th Centuries; †Polish painting 18th - 20th Centuries; Silesian Art 16th - 18th Centuries; Silesian stone carvings 12th - 16th Centuries
Publications: Catalogs; guides; Roczniki Sztuki Saskiej, annually
Activities: Classes for children and adults; cinema programs; dramatic programs; lect open to public; competitions; shows; exten dept; book shop
L **Library,*** Place Powstancow Warszawy 5, 50-153.
For reference
Library Holdings: Vols 70,000; Other—Photographs

PORTUGAL

LISBON

M **MUSEU NACIONAL DE ARTE ANTIGA,** National Museum of Ancient Art,* Rua das Janelas Verdes. Tel 664151, 672725. *Dir* Maria Alice Beaumont
Open Tues - Sun 10 AM - 5 PM, Thurs & Sat 10 AM - 7 PM, cl Mon & holidays. Admis free Sat & Sun. Estab 1884. Alvor Palace houses European art and Oriental carpets; the New Building (1939) houses Portuguese and Oriental art. Average Annual Attendance: 50,000. Mem: 500
Income: Financed by state appropriation
Collections: Foreign Art - ceramic, goldsmith art, painting and sculpture; Oriental Art of Portuguese influence; Ornamental Art - ceramics, furniture, goldsmith art and textiles; Persian carpets; Portuguese Art - paintings from the 15th - 19th Centuries; sculpture 13th - 18th Centuries
Exhibitions: English Medieval Alabasters, drawings from the collection of Albettina's Gallery (facsimile); French Portraits 1610-1789; Illuminated Manuscript 16th Century; The Nativity (Portuguese paintings, engravings and sculptures); Oriental Art Namban
Publications: Bulletin
Activities: Classes for adults and children; docent training; lect open to public; concerts; gallery talks; museum shop sells books, slides and postcards
L **Library,*** Rua das Janelas Verdes, 2.
Library Holdings: Vols 16,500; Per subs 30
Collections: Capela das Albertas 16th - 17th Centuries; colored glazed tiles 14th - 20th Centuries; Convento da Madre de Deus; Gulbenkian donation; Patino Room late 18th Century French designed Boiseries, furniture, savonierie carpet

M **MUSEU NATIONAL DE ARTE CONTEMPORANEA,** National Museum of Contemporary Art,* Rua Serpa Pinto 6. Tel 36 80 28. *Dir* Maria de Lourdes Bartolo
Founded 1911
Collections: Contemporary painting and sculpture

OPORTO

M **MUSEU NACIONAL DE SOARES DOS REIS,** National Museum of Soares Dos Reis,* Palacio dos Carrancas, Rua de D Manuel II. Tel 27110. *Dir* Maria Emilia Amaral Teixeira; *Cur* Maria Clementina Quaresma; *Cur* Maria Teresa Viana; *Cur* Catarina Maria Castro
Open 10 AM - Noon and 2 - 5 PM, cl Mon. Admis free Sat & Sun. Estab 1833 for maintaining the collections of the museum. The ground floor of the gallery has religious art and pottery; first floor has modern painting and temporary exhibition; second floor has decorative arts. Average Annual Attendance: 50,000
Income: Financed by state appropriation
Collections: Furniture, glass, goldsmith, jewelry, old and †modern paintings, porcelain, pottery, sculpture
Publications: Museu, bi-annually
Activities: Classes for children; dramatic programs; lect open to public; concerts; gallery talks; tours for schools; sales shop sells catalogs and slides
L **Library,*** Palacio dos Carrancas, Rua de D Manuel II.
For reference only
Library Holdings: Vols 8800
Special Subjects: Art History

ROMANIA

CLUJ-NAPOCA

M **MUZEUL DE ARTA CLUJ-NAPOCA,** Museum of Art, Piata Libertatii 30. Tel 951-26952, 951-26953. *Pres Scientific Council* Dr Virgil Vatasiano; *Dir* Alexandra Rus
Open Mon & Thurs 11 AM - 7 PM. Estab 1951
Income: Financed by state appropriation
Collections: Decorative arts; European and Romanian Art, including graphics, paintings and sculpture of the 15th - 20th Centuries
Publications: Exhibition catalogs, semi-annually
Activities: Classes for adults and children; dramatic programs; concerts; individual paintings and original objects of art lent to schools; originate traveling exhibitions; book shop; junior museum
L **Library,** Piata Libertatii 30.
Library Holdings: Vols 3000; Other—Photographs 2000, Romanian books of art and catalogs of art

SCOTLAND

DUNDEE

M **DUNDEE MUSEUMS AND ART GALLERY,** Albert Square. Tel 0382-25492. *Dir* James D Boyd; *Deputy Dir* Adam B Ritchie; *Keeper Antiquities* C A Zealand; *Keeper Art* Open; *Keeper Natural History* Richard K Brinklow
Open Mon - Sat 10 AM - 5:30 PM. No admis fee. Estab 1873 to provide the town of Dundee and surrounding area with a public service, by conserving, storing, displaying and publicizing the museum collection of art, natural history and antiquity. Four large Victorian galleries and one gallery specially designed to hang watercolors, prints and drawings. Mem: 100; annual meeting May
Income: Financed by city appropriation
Collections: 18th, 19th and 20th Century Scottish and English paintings; 17th Century Venetian and Flemish works; varied selection of watercolors and prints from the 18th - 20th Century
Publications: Showcase, quarterly
Activities: Classes for adults and children; lect open to public, 3 visiting lectr per year; concerts; 10 gallery talks; 10 - 15 tours; exten dept; individual paintings and original objects of art lent to public institutions in Dundee; originate traveling exhibitions; museum shop sells books, magazines, original art, reproductions, prints, slides and postcards

EDINBURGH

L **EDINBURGH COLLEGE OF ART LIBRARY,** Lauriston Place. *Sr Librn* Glenn Craig
Open Mon - Thurs 9 AM - 8:30 PM, Fri 9 AM - 5 PM. Estab 1907 to service the teaching program of the college and provide material for research
Income: $100,000
Purchases: $100,000
Library Holdings: Vols 36,000; Per subs 310; Micro—Fiche, reels; AV—A-tapes, cassettes, Kodachromes, lantern slides, slides, v-tapes; Other—Clipping files, exhibition catalogs, framed reproductions, prints, pamphlets, photographs, reproductions, maps, trade literature
Special Subjects: Architecture, Crafts, Drawings, Sculpture, Design, painting, town and country planning

NATIONAL GALLERIES OF SCOTLAND

M **National Gallery of Scotland,** The Mound EH2 2EL. *Dir* Colin Thompson; *Keeper National Gallery of Scotland* Hugh Macandrew; *Keeper of Prints & Drawings* Keith Andrews
Open Mon - Sat 10 AM - 5 PM, Sun 2 - 5 PM. No admis fee. Estab 1850 to house the national collections of paintings, sculpture and the graphic arts from the 14th Century to the present. Neo-classical building by William Playfair with modern extension opened 1978. Average Annual Attendance: 338,000
Income: Financed by national government
Collections: Drawings, paintings, prints and sculpture, 14th - 19th Centuries
Exhibitions: (1978) The Discovery of Scotland; (1979) Degas 1879. The Department of Prints and Drawings has regular exhibitions from its own holdings
Publications: Annual Report; bulletin, quarterly
Activities: Educ dept; lect open to public, 4 visiting lectr per year; gallery talks; competitions; sales shop sells books, magazines, prints and slides
M **Scottish National Gallery of Modern Art,** The Royal Botanic Garden, Edinburgh EH3 5LR. *Keeper* Douglas Hall
Open Mon - Sat 10 AM - 6 PM, Sun 2 - 6 PM. No admis fee. Gallery temporarily (since 1960) in large 18th Century mansion in Royal Botanic Garden; will move into a converted early 19th Century school building before 1982
Collections: 20th Century graphic art, painting and sculpture
Exhibitions: America, America; The Edward James Collection
M **Scottish National Portrait Gallery,** 1 Queen St, Edinburgh EH2 1JD. *Keeper* Robin Hutchison
Open Mon - Sat 10 AM - 5 PM, Sun 2 - 5 PM. No admis fee. Estab 1889 to collect and exhibit portraits of the principal figures in Scottish history. A neo-Gothic building shared with National Museum of Antiquities
Collections: Portraits of Scottish men and women prominent in all fields of human endeavor
Exhibitions: (1978) Van Dyck in Check Trousers; (1979) Women in Scotland 1660-1780

M **ROYAL SCOTTISH MUSEUM,** Chambers St. Tel 031 225 7534. *Dir* Dr Norman Tebble; *Keeper Department of Art & Archaeology* Revel Oddy; *Keeper Department of Natural History* Dr A S Clarke; *Keeper Department of Geology* Dr C D Waterston; *Keeper Department of Technology* J D Storer
Open Mon - Sat 10 AM - 5 PM, Sun 2 - 5 PM, cl Dec 25, Jan 1 - 4. No admis fee. Estab 1854 to acquire and exhibit to the public, specimens (decorative arts of the works, archaeology and ethnography); to conserve the national collections; to make its study collections available to research workers; to provide temporary exhibitions in addition to permanent displays. Average Annual Attendance: 600,000
Income: Financed by government
Collections: Collections of the Decorative Arts of the World
Exhibitions: Children's Christmas Art Various changing exhibitions
Publications: Brochures; Triennial report of the Royal Scottish Museum
Activities: Educ dept provides a wide range of education-activities formal and informal, for adults, students, young people and children; classes for adults and children; lect with visiting lectr; gallery talks; films; a Society of Friends of the Royal Scottish Museum; competitions; museum shop sells slides, museum publications, postcards and posters
L **Library,** * Chambers St. *Librn* D C F Smith
Open for reference to Royal Scottish Museum staff and research workers

GLASGOW

M **GLASGOW MUSEUMS AND ART GALLERIES,** Kelvingrove Art Gallery and Museum, Argyll St. Tel 041 334 1134. *Dir* Alasdair A Auld; *Deputy Dir* Anthony S E Browning; *Keeper of Archaeology, History & Ethnography* David W Phillipson; *Keeper of Burrell Collection* Richard Marks; *Keeper of Decorative Art* Brian J R Blench; *Keeper of Fine Art* Anne Donald; *Keeper of Natural History* Charles E Palmar; *Keeper of Technology* Open; *Education Officer, Schools Museums Service* Louise G Annand
Open Mon - Fri 10 AM - 5 PM, Sun 2 - 5 PM
Collections: Archaeology; British and Scottish Art (especially the Scottish Colourists); Decorative Art Collection of ceramics, glass, jewelry, silver (especially Scottish); Ethnography; Fine Art Collection representing the Dutch, Flemish, French and Italian Schools; History; Natural History
Exhibitions: Approximately 15 per year
Publications: Calendar of Events, quarterly; Scottish Art Review, bi-annually
Activities: Classes for adults and children; intra-mural teaching; classes are brought from schools and other establishments to the museum; lect programme; films
M **Haggs Castle,** 100 Saint Andrews Dr, Glasgow G41 4RB. Tel 041 427 2725. Museum for children with displays showing the history of the castle
Activities: Workshops
M **Museum of Transport,** 25 Albert Dr, Glasgow G41 2PE. Tel 041 423 8000. Museum illustrating the history of transport by land and sea
Collections: History of Transport by Land and Sea: bicycles, buses, horse-drawn vehicles, motor cars, steam locomotives and trams; outstanding collection of model railway system and ship models
M **People's Palace,** Glasgow Green, Glasgow G40 1AT. Tel 041 554 0223. Museum of Glasgow history. Palace situated in the oldest public park in the city, Glasgow Green, with adjoining Winter Gardens housing exotic plants
M **Pollok House,** Pollok Park, Glasgow G43 1AT. Tel 041 632 0274.
M **Adam House,**
Built circa 1752 with later additions. House interior in rococo style
Collections: British furniture 1750-1820; English and Spanish glass; important Stirling Maxwell collection of Spanish paintings
M **Saint Enoch Exhibition Centre,** St Enoch Square, Glasgow C1. Tel 041 221 5264. Opened in Sept 1979 as a gallery for temporary exhibitions
Exhibitions: Contemporary decorative and fine arts
L **Library,** Argyll St, Glasgow G3 8AG.
For reference
Library Holdings: Vols 12,500
O **Glasgow Art Gallery and Museums Associations,** Argyll St, Glasgow G3 8AG. Founded in 1944 for the cultivation and advancement of interest in the various activities, artistic, educational and scientific, promoted by the museums. Average Annual Attendance: 3000
Activities: Lect; films; tours in and around Glasgow; cultural holidays in the United Kingdom and overseas; events for younger people

REPUBLIC OF SINGAPORE

SINGAPORE

M **NATIONAL MUSEUM ART GALLERY,** Stamford Rd. Tel 326077, 321281. *Dir* Christopher Hooi; *Cur of Art* Weng Yang Choy; *Asst Cur* Seok Chee Eng
Open 10:30 AM - 7 PM. No admis fee. Estab 1976 as a museum of ethnology history and art of Singapore and Southeast Asia. Gallery has 9 exhibition rooms, storage room and a Theatrette which seats 80 people. National Museum Art Gallery is a component of the National Museum (estab 1849); occupies its existing site at Stamford Road from 1887. Average Annual Attendance: 340,000
Income: S$15,000 (financed by city appropriation)
Purchases: S$40,000
Collections: Paintings and sculptures by artists of Singapore and Southeast Asia
Exhibitions: Belgian Contemporary Art; Chinese Blue and White Porcelain; Indian Jewelry from India; Singapore Art 78
Publications: Exhibition catalogues; The Heritage journal, bi-annually
Activities: Classes for adults and children; dramatic programs; docent training; creative workshops; lect open to public, 20 visiting lectr per year; concerts; gallery talks; tours; sponsors competitions held in The Young People's Gallery; awards; fels for personnel of museums in ASEAN countries; individual paintings and original objects of art lent to schools and institutions; lending collection contains books, color reproductions, nature artifacts, original art works, paintings, photographs and slides; sales shop sells books, magazines, reproductions, greeting cards and postcards
L **Library,** Stamford Rd. *Librn* Mrs Gek Eng Seah
Open 8:30 AM - 5 PM. Estab 1849 for departmental use; supply of library material relevant to the activities of the department and to the public for reference
Income: $7000
Library Holdings: Vols 12,000; Per subs 9; AV—Lantern Slides, motion pictures, slides; Other—Clipping files, exhibition catalogs, prints, manuscripts, original art works, pamphlets, photographs, reproductions, sculpture
Special Subjects: Ethnology, History
Collections: Art, Ethnology and History Journals

REPUBLIC OF SOUTH AFRICA

CAPE PROVINCE

M **MICHAELIS COLLECTION,** * Old Town House, Greenmarket Square. Tel 048 43 40 15. *Dir* W H Gravett
Open 10 AM - 5:30 PM. Admis 10¢. Estab 1917 to house collection of 16th and

17th Century Dutch and Flemish masters donated to the nation by Sir Max Michaelis. Average Annual Attendance: 30,000
Income: $30,000
Purchases: $3000
Collections: †Dutch and Flemish graphic art and paintings of the 16th - 18th Centuries
Publications: Annual Reports; general and special catalogs
Activities: Classes for adults and children; dramatic programs; lect; concerts

M **SOUTH AFRICAN NATIONAL GALLERY,** Government Ave, PO Box 2420. *Dir* Dr Raymund H van Niekerk; *Asst Dir* Open; *Conservation* Edgar C L Bosman; *Education Department* Pat Kaplan; *Paintings & Sculpture* Lynn McClelland
Open Mon 1 - 5 PM, Tues - Sat 10 AM - 5:30 PM, Sun 10 AM - 5 PM. Admis 20¢, Wed & Sat free. Estab 1871, incorporated 1895, present building 1931. Gallery is a single-story building of 15 galleries. Average Annual Attendance: 90,000. Mem: 600; dues life $75, corporate, Society of Friends of the Gallery $50, family $10, individual $7
Income: $29,400 (financed by state appropriation)
Purchases: $40,000
Collections: South African Art 19th and 20th Century and European Art 15th - 20th Century, including drawings, paintings, prints, sculptures and watercolours
Exhibitions: (1978-79) The Animal in Art; The Art of The Printmaker; Cape Town Biennial; Ceramic Sculpture (Touch Gallery); Contemporary British Bookbinding; German Expressionist Prints; Katrine Harries Retrospective; May Hillhouse Retrospective; Movement in Structured Space; South African Colour Photography; South African Printmakers; Maud Sumner Retrospective; Turner Watercolours; Victorian Paintings
Publications: Agenda, monthly bulletin; exhibition catalogues; information sheet
Activities: Educ dept; children's workshops; training programs for volunteer guide; lect open to public; gallery talks; concerts; film shows; tours; participat exhibitions for sighted and blind; individual paintings and original objects of art lent to other institutions; lending collection contains 3000 slides; originate traveling exhibitions; sales shop sells reproductions, slides, catalogues and postcards
L **Library,** Government Ave, PO Box 2420. *Librn* Josephine Minicki
Open Mon - Fri 7:45 AM - 3:45 PM. Reference and research library for staff and public
Income: $6000 (financed by city appropriation)
Library Holdings: Vols 6480; Per subs 173; Other—Clipping files, exhibition catalogs, pamphlets
Special Subjects: Handicapped, particularly the blind, restoration, South African art and architecture

DURBAN

M **DURBAN ART GALLERY,** City Hall, Smith St, PO Box 4085. *Cur* E S J Addleson; *Art Technician* D Smith; *Education Officer* J Trembath
Open Mon, Tues, Thurs - Sat 9:30 AM - 5 PM, Wed 9:30 AM - 2 PM, Sun 2:30 - 5 PM. No admis fee. Estab 1892 to provide exhibitions of contemporary art for the benefit of the public and the city's cultural program. Gallery is housed in the City Hall, which is a fine Victorian building in the neo-Baroque style. Average Annual Attendance: 200,000
Income: Financed by city appropriation
Purchases: $10,000
Collections: †Chinese ceramics; †Dutch and Flemish 17th Century; †French 19th Century; †Sevres ceramics; †South African; †Victorian; †contemporary art
Exhibitions: Walter Battiss; Contemporary British Bookbinding; Fashion Plates by Sonia Delaunay; The Japanese Color Print; Jean Lurcat; Paul Nash (photographs); Paolozzi
Activities: Classes for children; lect open to public, 2 visiting lectr per year; concerts; gallery talks; tours

JOHANNESBURG

M **JOHANNESBURG ART GALLERY,** Joubert Park. Tel 725-3130. *Dir* Mrs P A Senior; *Asst Dir* Mrs R Keene
Open Tues - Sun 10 AM - 5 PM, during Dec & Jan Sun & Wed evenings 7 - 9 PM, cl Mon. No admis fee. Estab 1915 as a modern art museum reflecting international and local movements and trends. Gallery designed and built by the English architect Edwin Lutyens (pseudo neo-classic). Average Annual Attendance: 90,000
Income: Financed by city appropriation
Collections: Approximately 2500 prints from Durer to present; 17th Century Dutch; 19th Century French; 19th Century English; South African; international modern art; small collection of ceramics and textiles
Exhibitions: The Animal in Art; Art of The Space Age; William Blake; German Expressionist - Prints; Constance Stuart Larrabee; Modern British Bookbinders; Isaac Witkin
Publications: Catalog list; history of gallery
Activities: Classes for adults and children; docent training; working with art teachers; plays; poetry readings; lect open to public, 8 visiting lectr per year; concerts; gallery talks; tours; competitions; museum shop sells books, reproductions, slides, postcards, photographs and greeting cards
L **Library,** Joubert Park.
Open to staff and docents, or by appointment, for reference
Library Holdings: Vols 5000; Per subs 22
Special Subjects: Reference works to the collection

KIMBERLEY

M **WILLIAM HUMPHREYS ART GALLERY,** Civic Centre, PO Box 885. Tel 0531-28031. *Cur* Mrs R J Holloway
Open Mon - Sat 10 AM - 1 PM and 2:30 - 5:30 PM, Sun 2:30 - 5:30 PM. Admis adults 10¢, children 5¢, only on weekends and public holidays. Estab 1952. Average Annual Attendance: 25,000. Mem: 325; dues $2
Income: $59,000 (financed by central government)
Collections: Representative collection of Dutch, English, Flemish and French Old

Masters; †collection of South African works of art
Exhibitions: Approximately 10 temporary exhibitions per year
Activities: Lect open to public, 2 visiting lectr per year; concerts; individual paintings and original objects of art lent to other museums in the Republic of South Africa
L **Library,** Civic Centre, PO Box 885. *Dir* Mrs R J Holloway
Reference only
Library Holdings: Vols 362; Per subs 3

PIETERMARITZBURG

M **TATHAM ART GALLERY,*** 2nd Floor City Hall, Commerical Rd, PO Box 321. Tel 27031, Ext 127. *Cur* Lorna Ferguson
Open Mon - Fri 10 AM - 5 PM. No admis fee. Estab 1903. The top floor of City Hall was made available to house the municipal art collection, it is divided into two main galleries: painting and sculpture, and graphics. Average Annual Attendance: 5000. Mem: 100; dues R1000; annual meeting June
Income: Financed by city appropriation
Purchases: $20,000
Collections: †19th and 20th Century English and French paintings and sculpture; †19th and 20th Century English graphics; †modern European graphics; †South African painting and sculpture 1920-1940; the Whitwell bequest
Publications: Exhibition catalogs; newsletter, quarterly
Activities: Lect open to public, 2 visiting lectr per year; concerts; gallery talks; tours; competitions; individual paintings and original objects of art lent to accredited art institutions; originate traveling exhibitions

PORT ELIZABETH

M **KING GEORGE VI ART GALLERY,** One Park Dr. Tel 041-28589. *Dir* Clayton S Holliday; *Asst Prof Officer* Julian Gous; *Secy* Betty Ann Young
Open Mon - Sat 10 AM - 5 PM, Sun 2:30 - 5:30 PM, public holidays 10:30 AM - 12:30 PM and 2:30 - 5:30 PM. Estab 1957 for the development of permanent collections; to provide a centre for art for Port Elizabeth and Hinterland. There are two buildings flanking entrance to St George's Park with the Main Hall consisting of three galleries; Arts Hall consists of a major hall and sunken gallery. Average Annual Attendance: 25,000
Income: Financed by city appropriation
Collections: †English painting; †international graphics; Oriental ceramics and miniatures; †South African Art
Exhibitions: The Animal in Art; Blake; Hommage A Lurcat; Japanese Prints
Publications: Newsletter
Activities: Lect open to public; quarterly concerts by Musica Rara Society; occasional lunch hour films; guided tours; 500 framed reproductions lent to registered borrowers; sales shop sells reproductions, original graphics, postcards, etc
L **Library,** One Park Dr.
Open to students for reference
Library Holdings: Vols 1500; Per subs 5; Other—Exhibition catalogs
Special Subjects: English and South African painting

PRETORIA

M **PRETORIA ART MUSEUM,** Arcadia Park, Transvaal. Tel 444271. *Dir* Dr A J Werth; *Asst Dir* Katinka Kempff; *Professional Asst* D Crafford; *Professional Asst* A Seyffert
Open Tues - Sat 10 AM - 5 PM, Wed 7:30 - 10 PM, Sun 1 - 6 PM. No admis fee. Estab 1963 to collect and exhibit South African art and European art (mainly graphics). Museum is a modern building in park-like surroundings; four main galleries and one small gallery; plus a sculpture entrance hall. Average Annual Attendance: 60,000. Mem: 600; dues R5
Income: Financed by city appropriation
Purchases: R 30,000
Collections: †American and European graphics, mostly 20th Century; 17th Century Dutch Art; 19th and 20th Century South African
Exhibitions: Average eight exhibitions annually on work by South African Artists; Walter W Battiss Retrospective; International Tapestries; Constance Stuart Photograph Exhibition
Publications: Bulletin, quarterly
Activities: Lect open to public, 3 visiting lectr per year; concerts; gallery talks; tours; competitions; individual paintings lent to museums; originate traveling exhibitions; museum shop
L **Library,** Arcadia Park, Transvaal.
For reference
Library Holdings: Vols 2000; Per subs 20; Other—Prints, photographs, newspaper clippings

SPAIN

BARCELONA

M **MUSEO DE ARTE CATALUNA,** Museum of Ancient Art,* Parque de Montjuich Palacio Nacional. Tel 2-23-18 24. *Cur* M Carmen Farie Sanpera
Estab 1934
Collections: Baroque and Renaissance paintings; Catalan Gothic and Romanesque paintings and sculpture
Activities: Scholarships

M **MUSEO DE ARTE MODERNO,** Museum of Modern Art, Palacio de la Ciudadela. Tel 319 57 30. *Dir* Juan Barbeta Antones; *Cur* Eloisa Sendra; *Cur* Cristina Mendoza
Open 9:30 AM - 7:15 PM, cl Mon. Estab 1946

Collections: Modern Art
Exhibitions: Commemorative expositions
Publications: Exhibition catalogs
Activities: Scholarships
L Library, Palau de la Ciutadella. *Dir* Rosa Granes; *Librn* Margarida Massaguer; *Librn* Carmen Sobrevila; *Librn* Neus Pons; *Librn* Frances Font
Open to public 9:30 AM - 1:30 PM & 4:30 - 7:30 PM. Estab 1945 to attend technical staff of museums, art students and specialists. For reference only
Income: $500,000
Library Holdings: Vols 54,400; Per subs 531; Other—Exhibition catalogs

BILBAO

M MUSEO DE BELLAS ARTES, Museum of Fine Arts, Parque de Dona Casilda de Iturriza. *Pres* D Patricio de la Sota MacMahon; *Secy* D Manuel Llano Gorrostiza; *Dir* D Javier de Bengoechea Niebla
Open 10 AM - 1:30 PM and 4 - 6:30 PM, varies in seasons. No admis fee. Estab 1908, modern section 1924, to exhibit art works
Income: 25,000,000 Pts (financed by city appropriation)
Collections: †Basque modern and contemporary art; Classical Gothic, Renaissance and Romanesque Art; †general contemporary art; 12th Century Romantic Art; Traditional Spanish 12th Century Art
Exhibitions: Anthological, non-commerical exhibits
Activities: Lect open to public, 5 visiting lectr per year; gallery talks; tours
L Library, Parque de Dona Casilda de Iturriza.
Reference only
Library Holdings: Vols 1000; Other—Photographs

MADRID

M MUSEO CERRALBO, Ventura Rodriguez 17. Tel 2-47-36-46. *Dir of Found of the Museum* Dr Consuelo Sanz-Pastor y Fernandez de Pierola
Open 9 AM - 2 PM, cl Thurs. Admis 50 pesetas, except students. Estab 1924. Foundation was bequeathed to Spain by its founder Enrique de Aguilera y Gamboa, 17th Marquis of Cerralbo. His palace, which is now the museum, was built in 1886
Collections: 15th - 19th Centuries paintings, arts and crafts, coins and medals, drawings and prints
Publications: Catalogue of Drawings; Cerralbo Museum; Guide of the Cerralbo Museum; Museums and Collections of Spain
Activities: Lect open to public; concerts; gallery talks; tours; sales shop sells books and slides
L Library, Ventura Rodriguez 17.
Library Holdings: Vols 11,549; Per subs 7
Special Subjects: Archaeology, Art History, Coins & Medals

M MUSEO DEL PRADO, National Museum of Paintings and Sculpture,* Calle de Felipe IV. Tel 468 09 50.
Open 10 AM - 5 PM or 6 PM according to season. Estab 1819
Collections: Ancient and Renaissance sculptures; Paintings from 14th - 19th Century; sections of 19th and 20th Century in the Cason of Buen Retiro; drawing, jewels and medals
Publications: Catalogs
Activities: Weekly public lect
L Library,* Calle de Felipe IV.
Library Holdings: Vols 10,000

M MUSEO ROMANTICO, Museum of the Romantic Epoch, San Mateo 13. Tel 448-10-45, 448-10-71. *Dir* Maria Elena Gomez-Moreno; *Cur* Manuel Casamar; *Secy* Raul Diez
Open 10 AM - 6 PM, Sun 10 AM - 2 PM, cl Mon. Estab 1924. Average Annual Attendance: 10,000
Collections: †Books, †decorations, †furniture and †paintings of the Spanish Romantic period
Activities: Lect; concerts; exhibitions
L Library, San Mateo 13. *Librn* Manuel Llanes
Library Holdings: Other—Lithographs
Special Subjects: Art of the Romantic period, literature, history
Collections: 5000 engravings collection

TOLEDO

M CASA Y MUSEO DEL GRECO, El Greco's House and Museum,* Calle de Samuel Levi. Tel 22 40 46. *Dir* Maria Elena Gomez-Moreno
Open 10 AM - 2 PM and 3 - 6 PM, summer 10 AM - 7 PM. Admis 15 pesetas. Estab 1910. Average Annual Attendance: 250,000
Income: Supported by the Fundaciones Vega-Inclan
Collections: Furniture, objects of the period, paintings of El Greco, including the series of Christ and the Apostles; other paintings of various periods, 15th - 18th Century
Publications: Catalogo de las Picturas de la Casa y Museo del Greco, 1968

SRI LANKA

COLOMBO

M COLOMBO NATIONAL MUSEUM, Albert Crescent, PO Box 854. Tel 94767. *Dir* Dr P de Silva; *Cur Anthropology* P Endegama
Open Mon - Thurs & Sun 9 AM - 5 PM. Admis adults 25¢, children 10¢, students in groups and clergy free. Estab 1877 for cultural, scientific and educational purposes. Average Annual Attendance: 380,000
Income: $3820 (financed by state appropriation)

Collections: Antiquities of Sri Lanka; rare books and palm leaf manuscripts of Sri Lanka
Exhibitions: Photographic exhibition of Monuments and Antiquities of several non-aligned countries; several temporary exhibitions by Embassies of the Peoples Republic of China, USSR and France
Publications: Spolia Zeylanica
Activities: Classes for children; lect open to public, 15 visiting lectr per year; sales shop sells books and prints
L Library, Albert Crescent, PO Box 854. *Librn* C I Karunanayake
Open for research and reference
Library Holdings: Vols 500,000; Per subs 4133; Other—Manuscripts 3570
Special Subjects: Archaeology, Architecture

SWEDEN

GOTHENBURG

M GÖTEBORG KONSTMUSEUM, Gothenburg Art Gallery, Götaplatsen 412 56. Tel 031-189537. *Dir* Karl-Gustaf Heden; *Cur Exhib Department* Hakan Wettre; *Cur Modern Department* Nils Ryndel; *Cur Old Masters Department* Björn Fredlund; *Asst Cur Deposit* Lena Boethius; *Asst Cur Graphics & Drawings* Küllike Montgomery
Open Sept - April Tues - Fri Noon - 3 PM, Sat & Sun 11 AM - 5 PM, Wed 5 - 9 PM, May - Aug daily 11 AM - 4 PM. Admis adults Sw Cr 2, children Sw Cr 1. Estab 1861; main building inaugurated in 1925; new wing in 1968. Average Annual Attendance: 150,000
Income: Financed by city appropriation
Purchases: S 40,000
Collections: French Art 1800-1945; Old Masters, especially Dutch and Flemish 17th Century; Scandinavian Art, 17th Century to present; contemporary art (international collection of prints and drawings); collections include drawings, prints and watercolours circa 45,000, paintings 2400, sculptures 550
Exhibitions: Approximately 25 exhibitions per year
Publications: Exhibitions catalogs
Activities: Classes for children; lect open to public, 10 visiting lectr per year; concerts; gallery talks; tours; exten dept; individual paintings and original objects of art lent to museums, galleries and libraries; sales shop sells books, reproductions, prints, slides and postcards
L Library, Götaplatsen 412 56. Tel 031-206861.
Library Holdings: Vols 20,000; Per subs 110; AV—A-tapes, lantern Slides, motion pictures, slides, v-tapes; Other—Clipping files, exhibition catalogs, reproductions

M ROHSSKA KONSTSLOJDMUSEET, Rohss Museum of Arts and Crafts, 37-39 Vasgatan. Tel 031-188930. *Dir* Jan Brunius; *Cur Coll* Thomas Baagoe; *Cur Exhib* Karin Aasma; *Asst Cur* Gunnel Kernell; *Asst Cur Textiles* Marianne Erikson; *Education Officer* Anne Pettersson
Open Mon - Fri Noon - 3 PM, Sat & Sun 10 AM - 5 PM. Estab 1916 to collect and exhibit all kinds of craftsmanship and industrial design - old and new. Average Annual Attendance: 75,000
Income: Financed by city appropriation
Collections: The Falk Simon Bequest of Old Silver; †bookbindings, †ceramics, †furniture, †glass, metalworks, †textile
Exhibitions: 25 exhibitions per year, mostly concerning modern domestic culture
Publications: Yearbook, every 3 years
Activities: Educ dept; classes for children; lect open to public; concerts; gallery talks; tours; originate traveling exhibitions; sales shop sells books, magazines and postcards
L Library, 37-39 Vasgatan. *Librn* Thomas Baagoe
Open to specialists and researchers
Library Holdings: Vols 28,000; Per subs 18

MARIEFRED

M SVENSKA STATENS PORTRAHSAMLING, Swedish State Portrait Gallery, Gripsholm Castle, Mariefred S-150-30. (Mailing Add: Nationalmuseum, Box 161 76, Stockholm S-103 24,) Tel 01 59-10194. *Cur* Ulf G Johnsson; *Asst Keeper* Lars Sjoeberg
Open May 15 - Aug daily 10 AM - 5 PM, hours reduced during winter. Admis Sw cr 4.50. Estab circa 1550. Gallery administrated by Nationalmuseum, Stockholm
Collections: Portraits, mainly Swedish, from 15th Century to modern times, approximately 3500 items
Activities: Authorized guides May - Aug for school and visitors

STOCKHOLM

M KUNGL MYNTKABINETTET STATENS MUSEUM FÖR MYNT MEDALJ OCH PENNINGHISTORIA, Royal Coin Cabinet, National Museum of Monetary History, Storgatan 41, PO Box 5405. Tel 08-63 07 70. *Keeper* Ulla Westermark; *Deputy Keeper* Lars O Lagerqvist; *Asst Keeper* Tamas Sarkany; *Asst Keeper* Ernst Nathorst-Böös
Open Mon - Fri 11 AM - 4PM, Sat & Sun Noon - 5 PM. Admis 3 Sw cr. Estab circa 1572, since 1975 a museum of monetary history and medals. Museum was a department of the Museum of National Antiquities 1849-1975; four exhibition rooms. Average Annual Attendance: 22,000
Income: Financed by state appropriation
Collections: Bank notes (40,000), coins (400,000), medals (35,000). The collections range over the entire world and all periods
Exhibitions: Beautiful Books about Old Coins; Byzantium and Scandinavia; Coin Import and Imitations; Greek Coins - traveling exhibition; Helgeandsholmen; Modern Hungarian Medals; Money and Banking in Canada; Numismatic News from the Excavations in 1978; Örebro and Helgö; Primitive Money
Publications: Numismatica Stockholmiensis (annual report)
L Numismatic Section, Storgatan 41, PO Box 5405. *Librn* Jannis Ambatsis
Library Holdings: Vols 35,000
Special Subjects: Coins & Medals

M NATIONALMUSEUM, Box 16 176. Tel 24 42 00. *Dir* Per Bjurström; *Head Applied Arts* D Widman; *Head Art Education Department* N G Hökby; *Head Painting & Sculpture Department* P Grate; *Head Prints & Drawings Dept* B Magnusson; *Head Royal Castles Coll* Ulf G Johnsson; *Head Department of Long-term Loans & Traveling Exhib* M Winqvist
Open daily 10 AM - 4 PM, Tues 10 AM - 9 PM. Estab 1792
Collections: Arts and crafts, drawings, icons, miniatures, †paintings, prints and sculpture. Administers the State collections of paintings and sculptures in the royal castles and Gustaf III's antikmuseum (The Collection of Antiquities of Gustaf III) in the Royal Palace of Stockholm; collections of 20th Century paintings and sculptures, housed in Moderna museet (The Museum of Modern Art). Collections of ancient Far Eastern Art in Ostasiatiska museet (Museum of Far Eastern Art)
Publications: Annual Report; Bulletin; catalogs; Yearbook
L Library, Blasieholmskajen, Box 161 76. *Head Librn* Yvonne Frendel; *Assoc Librn* Margit Hoffman; *First Library Asst* Margareta Rosvall; *Asst for Clippings* Marie Opolzer Herrington
Open 10 AM - 3:30 PM. Estab 1919 as a service for the National Museum
Income: 991,000 Skr
Purchases: $15,000
Library Holdings: Vols 240,000; Per subs 600; Micro—Cards; AV—Lantern Slides; Other—Clipping files 635,000, exhibition catalogs, manuscripts, pamphlets
Special Subjects: Decorative Arts, Paintings, sculpture in ancient and modern art
Collections: Exhibition catalogues, Oeuvre catalogues
M Moderna Museet, Museum of Modern Art. (Mailing Add: Skeppsholmen, Box 16382,) Tel 08-24 42 00. *Acting Dir* Olle Granath; *Chief Cur* Björn Springfeldt; *Cur* Nina Öhman
Open daily 11 AM - 9 PM. Admis 5 Kdr. Estab 1958 to collect and preserve Swedish and international art of the 1900's to present; have exhibitions of the most recent movements in art. Three main halls, two galleries (along one of the main halls), studyroom, cinema with smaller filmroom, bookshop and restaurant with garden open during spring and summer season. Average Annual Attendance: 200,000. Mem: 1500; dues 175 Skr, 135 or 60 Skr; meetings ten per year
Income: $1,014,000 Skr (financed by state appropriation and admission fees)
Purchases: $757,000 Skr
Collections: †International and Swedish Art from the 20th Century; †paintings and †sculptures
Exhibitions: (1978) Thousand and One Picture, photographs from all over the world; (1979) Öyvind Fahlström; La Biennale di Venezia, The Nordic Contribution from Denmark, Norway, Finland, Island and Sweden; Who's World Is It, Germany during the Weimarrepublic
Publications: Exhibition catalogues
Activities: Workshop for adults and children; lect open to public, 25 - 40 visiting lectr per year; concerts; tours; individual paintings and original objects of art lent to museums; lending collection contains 3500 original art works and paintings; museum shop sells books, magazines, posters and postcards

M NORDISKA MUSEET, Scandinavian Museum, Djurgarden. Tel 63 08-63. *Chmn The Institute of Ethnology* Mats Rehnberg; *Dir* Dr Sune Zachrisson; *Head Administration Department* Greger Oxhammar; *Keeper Conservations Department* Ulf Hamilton; *Keeper Domestic Life Department* Dr Elisabet Hidemark; *Keeper Education, Public Relations and Library Department* Skans Torsten Nilsson; *Keeper Field Research & Archives* Dr Matyas Szabo; *Keeper Industrial & Social History Department* Jonas Berg; *Keeper Textiles & Costume* Ingrid Bergman
Open Tues - Fri 10 AM - 4 PM, Sat & Sun Noon - 5 PM, cl Mon. Estab 1873 to further the knowledge of the culture and history of the Swedish people through scientific research and through popular teaching and instructing. Average Annual Attendance: 200,000
Collections: †Costumes, †Folk Art, †handcrafts, †period furnishings; approximately one million exhibits
Exhibitions: Permanent exhibitions giving a survey representative of the field of action of the museum, with about four temporary exhibitions per year
Publications: Books on ethnology and history of art; catalogs of collections; Yearbook
Activities: Collaboration with educ organizations; guided visits and prize competitions for school children; 2 - 3 lect series per year
L Library, Djurgarden. *Librn-in-Chief* Dr Jan Öjvind Swahn
Open 10 AM - Noon and 1 - 3 PM. Estab 1884 to collect literature on ethnology and folk art
Income: Financed by state appropriation
Purchases: $23,000
Library Holdings: Vols 120,000; Per subs 300
Special Subjects: Swedish (Scandinavian) ethnology and culture history
Collections: The John Bottiger Collection of literature on arts and crafts; The Viktor Rydberg Library; The August Strindberg Library

Publications: Bibliografiska meddelanden fran Nordiska Museets bibliotek, quarterly

M OSTASIATISKA MUSEET, Museum of Far Eastern Antiquities, Skeppsholmen, PO Box 163 81. Tel 08 244200. *Dir* Bo Gyllensvard; *Cur* Jan Wirgin; *Cur* Per-Olow Leijon
Open Tues Noon - 9 PM, Wed - Sun Noon - 4 PM, cl Mon. Admis 5 Sw cr. Estab 1963 to display in permanent and temporary exhibitions Art and Handicraft from the Far East, primarily from China, India, Korea and Japan from ancient times to present. Six galleries solely devoted to Chinese art; one gallery for Indian art; and one for the arts of Korea and Japan. Average Annual Attendance: 50,000. Mem: 600; dues 75 Sw cr
Income: Financed by city appropriation
Purchases: $8000
Collections: Approximately 110,000 objects in the permanent collection including Chinese Art from Neolithic times to present, Buddhist sculpture, bronzes, painting and porcelain, Stone-age pottery; Indian, Japanese and Korean Art
Exhibitions: The Bequest of Axel and Nora Lungren - Chinese Ceramics, Bronzes and Paintings; Paintings by Asian Children; Childrens Drawings from China; China Yesterday, Today and Tomorrow, The Modernization of China, Posters; From the Chinese Collection of King Gustaf Vi Adolf; Geishas and Samurais - Japanese Wood Block Prints; Minhwapainting from Corea, Corean Folk Art Colour Prints; The Sacred Angkor of Campuchea, Photographs by Gun Kessle; Shooting Orioles - Painting by Ma Yüan; Suiboku - Ink Paintings by Hozan Matsumoto
Publications: Bulletin, annually
Activities: Classes for adults and children; docent training; lect open to public, 600 visiting lectr per year; gallery talks; tours; originate traveling exhibitions; museum shop sells books, magazines, reproductions and prints
L Library, Skeppsholmen, Box 163 81. *Librn* Margareta Martens
Open for reference to scholars

M STATENS HISTORISKA MUSEUM, Museum of National Antiquities, Storgatan 41, PO Box 5405. *Dir* Olov Isaksson; *Head Education Department* Maj Odelberg; *Head Exhib Department* Eric Sorling; *Keeper of Museum Department* Bjorn Ambrosiani
Open Mon - Fri 11 AM - 4 PM, Sat & Sun Noon - 5 PM. Admis 3 Sw cr. Estab 1855 to protect and illustrate old culture. Average Annual Attendance: 200,000
Income: Financed by state appropriation
Collections: Prehistory, medieval art, wooden sculpture, gold and silver treasures up to 16th Century
Exhibitions: Boatgraves
Publications: Annual report; catalogues; History in pocket size; Historical News, quarterly
Activities: Classes for adults and children; lect open to public, 25 visiting lectr per year; concerts; tours; originate traveling exhibitions; museum shop sells books, reproductions, prints and slides
L Library of Royal Academy of Letters, History and Antiquities, Storgatan 41, PO Box 5405. *Head Librn* Anders Hedvall
Library Holdings: Vols 150,000; Per subs 2100; Other—Prints and drawings 1000
Special Subjects: Archaeology, Coins & Medals, Medieval history of art, preservation of cultural monuments

SWITZERLAND

BASEL

M MUSEUM FÜR VÖLKERKUNDE UND SCHWEIZERISCHES MUSEUM FÜR VOLKSKUNDE BASEL, Museum of Ethnological Collections and Folklore, Augustinergasse 2-Münsterplatz 20, PO Box 1048. Tel 061 25 82 82. *Dir* Dr Gerhard Baer; *Cur Africa & Textiles* Dr Renee Boser; *Cur America* Dr Annemarie Foote; *Cur East Asia* Dr Marie-Louise Nabholz; *Cur Education Department* Dr Brigitta Hauser; *Cur Europe* Dr Theo Gantner; *Cur Indonesia* Dr Urs Ramseyer; *Cur Oceania* Dr Christian Kaufmann; *Cur Prehistory & India* Dr Susanne Haas
Schweizerisches Museum für Volkskunde open Tues - Sun 10 AM - Noon and 2 - 5 PM. No admis fee Wed afternoon and weekends. Estab 1893. Museum für Völkerkunde closed until 1981. Average Annual Attendance: 80,000
Collections: Africa, America, Asia, Melanesia, Polynesia, Switzerland; collection of textiles
Exhibitions: Permanent and special exhibitions
L Library, Augustinergasse 2-Münsterplatz 20, PO Box 1048. *Librn* Elisabeth Idris
Open Mon - Fri 8:45 - 11:45 AM and 2 - 5 PM
Library Holdings: Vols 30,000

M OFFENTLICHE KUNSTSAMMLUNG-KUNSTMUSEUM BASEL, Museum of Fine Arts, St Albangraben 16. Tel 22 08 28. *Dir* Dr Franz Meyer; *Secy* Verena Trueb; *Cur 19th & 20th Century Paintings* Dr Christian Geelhaar; *Cur Paintings* Dr Paul-Henry Boerlin; *Cur Prints & Drawings* Dr Dieter Koepplin
Open June - Sept 10 AM - 5 PM, Oct - May 10 AM - Noon and 2 - 5 PM, cl Mon. Estab as private collection about 1550; founded as public collection 1662; new building 1936. Average Annual Attendance: 220,000
Collections: American painting since 1945; †16th and 17th Century Dutch paintings; †15th and 16th Century paintings, including Konrad Witz, Grünewald, Holbein and others; †19th and 20th Century paintings from Corot to present; prints and drawings from Upper Rhine, German and Swiss Masters; sculptures by Rodin and 20th Century artists
Exhibitions: Regular exhibitions from the collections of prints and drawings
L Library, St Albangraben 16. *Librn* Nikolaus Meier
Library Holdings: Vols 100,000

BERNE

M KUNSTMUSEUM BERN, Museum of Fine Arts Berne, Hodlerstrasse 12. Tel 22-09-44. *Dir* Dr Hugo Wagner; *Cur* Dr Sandor Kuthy; *Cur* Dr Jürgen Glaesemer
Open 10 AM - Noon and 2 - 5 PM, Tues 8 - 10 PM, cl Mon mornings. Estab 1879; enlarged 1936. Average Annual Attendance: 45,000
Collections: Dutch and contemporary artists; †French and other European Masters of the 19th and 20th Centuries; †Italian Masters; collection of †Paul Klee works of 2600 items; †Niklaus Manuel; †Foundation Hermann and Margrit Rupf, important Cubist collection; †Swiss Baroque Masters; †Swiss 19th and 20th Century Masters; 20,000 drawings and engravings; illustrations
Exhibitions: Temporary exhibitions
Publications: Berner Kunstmitteilungen, 8 per year; catalogs of collections and temporary exhibitions
L Library, Hodlerstrasse 12.
Library Holdings: Vols 30,000

CHUR

M BÜNDNER KUNSTMUSEUM CHUR, The Grisons Museum of Art, (Formerly Bünder Art Museum) Postplatz. Tel 22 17 63. *Dir* Hans Hartmann; *Secy* A K Ott
Open daily 10 AM - Noon and 2 - 5 PM, first and third Fri evenings 7:30 - 10 PM, cl Mon. Admis to permanent exhibit SFr 1, special show SFr 3 - 4. Estab 1900 for support of local art, Swiss art and modern art
Income: Financed by endowment, membership, city and state appropriation
Collections: Augusto, Alberto Giacometti, Giovanni, Angelika Kauffmann, E L Kirchner, Plastic Art, 19th and 20th Centuries, Swiss painting
Publications: Exhibition catalogs
Activities: Dramatic programs; concerts; competitions; originate traveling exhibitions; book shop
L Library, Postplatz.
For reference use only

GENEVA

M MUSEE D'ART ET D'HISTOIRE, Museum of Art and History, 5 Promenade du Pin. Tel 022-29 60 33. *Cur* Rainer M Mason
Open during meetings and temporary exhibitions. No admis fee. Estab 18th Century for collection, research and information. Museum has three exhibition rooms. Average Annual Attendance: 20,000
Income: Financed by city appropriation
Purchases: $40,000
Collections: Dutch, French, German, Italian, Spanish and Swiss prints of the 15th - 19th Centuries; Japanese prints of the 18th and 19th Centuries; prints of the 20th Century from all countries
Exhibitions: Genevieve Asse; Diables et Diableries (15th Century engravings); Dieux et Heros (16th Century engravings); Fritz Glarner; Donald Judd; Willem de Kooning; Kuniyoshi; Denise Mennet; Hernandez Pijuan; Martin Schongauer; Kurt Seligmann; Timbres et Tampons d'Artistes; Jean Tinguely (dessins et gravures pour les sculptures); Vallotton; Bram van Velde
Publications: Exhibition catalogs
Activities: Classes for adults and children; lect open to public; prints and original objects of art lent to museums; lending collection contains 200,000 original prints, 2000 photographs; originate traveling exhibitions; museum shop
L Bibliotheque d'Art et d'Archeologie, Library of Art and Archaeology, 5 Promenade du Pin. *Cur* Jean-Pierre Dubouloz
Open Mon - Fri 9 AM - 7 PM, Sat 9 AM - Noon and 2 - 5 PM, cl Sun. Estab 1952 for scientific research
Income: Financed by city appropriation
Purchases: $100,000
Library Holdings: Vols 100,000; Per subs 1200; Micro—Fiche; AV—Slides; Other —Exhibition catalogs, reproductions

M MUSEE D'ART MODERNE, Modern Art Museum, Petit Palais, 2 Terrasse Saint-Victor. *Pres & Founder* M Oscar Ghez
Open daily 10 AM - Noon and 2 - 6 PM, cl Mon mornings. Estab 1968 for cultural purposes; the new Orangerie du Petit Palais inaugurated in 1979. The Petit Palais is an elegant Second Empire home converted into a unique museum. There are six floors of paintings, sculptures, and drawings which comprise part of the collection of Oscar Ghez and form an exhibit. Average Annual Attendance: 30,000. Mem: 1500; dues Fr 50
Income: Financed by endowment
Collections: Covers the period 1880-1930, includes Expressionists, Fauves, Impressionists, Nabis, Naifs, Pointillists, Post-Impressionists and Primitives of the 20th Century
Exhibitions: From Renoir to Kisling and Picasso (Oscar Ghez Collection); Steinlen (retrospective)
L SCHOOL OF FINE ARTS LIBRARY, 9, bd Helvetique. Tel 022-29 05 10. *Librn* Brigitte Oggier
Open Mon - Fri 8 AM - Noon. Estab 1976 for reference to teachers and students of the school
Library Holdings: Vols 5000; AV—Lantern Slides, slides, v-tapes; Other— Exhibition catalogs, framed reproductions, prints, memorabilia, original art works, photographs, reproductions, sculpture

LA CHAUX DE FONDS

M MUSEE DES BEAUX-ARTS ET SOCIETE DES AMIS DES ARTS, Museum of Fine Arts, 33 Rue des Musees. Tel 039 22 12 50. *Pres* M Andre Sandoz; *Dir & Cur* Paul Seylaz
Open daily 10 AM - Noon and 2 - 5 PM, cl Mon. No admis fee, escept for special exhibits. Estab 1864 for the enrichment of the permanent collection and the organization of exhibitions, chiefly modern art. Gallery has 10 rooms on 2 floors and a hall for exhibition space, constructed in 1926. Mem: 500; dues SFr 25
Income: Financed by membership and city appropriation
Collections: Works of local artists as Leopold Robert a le Corbusier and contemporaries; Swiss works of the 19th and 20th Centuries; contemporary art including English, French, German, Italian, Japanese and Polish
Exhibitions: (1978) Pasmore; Makowski; Rozanes; 55th Biennale Cantonale-Ung-no-Lee (catalogues); (1979) Hetey; Konok; Sartoris; Woog; (1980) Arnal; Novoa; Sanchez; 56th Biennale Cantonale
Publications: Exhibition catalogs

SAINT GALLEN

M HISTORISCHES MUSEUM, Historical Museum, Musemstrasse 50. *Dir* Open; *Conservator* Rudolf Hanhart; *Technical Asst* Max Winiger
Open June - Sept Tues - Sun 10 AM - Noon and 2 - 4 PM, cl Mon, Oct - May Tues - Sat 2 - 4 PM, Sun 10 AM - Noon and 2 - 4 PM. No admis fee. Estab 1921. Average Annual Attendance: 16,000
Income: Financed by city appropriation
Collections: Burgundian Standards of 1476; costumes, ethnology, furniture, glass and glass painting, graphics, period rooms, pewter, porcelain, textiles, weapons
Exhibitions: Changing exhibitions
Publications: Museumsbrief

SCHAFFHAUSEN

M MUSEUM ZU ALLERHEILIGEN, All Saints' Museum, Klosterplatz. *Dir* Dr Max Freivogel
Open April - Oct 9 AM - Noon and 1:30 - 5 PM, Nov - Mar 10 AM - Noon and 1:30 - 4:30 PM. No admis fee. Estab 1938 to encourage interest and skill in art. Average Annual Attendance: 70,000
Collections: Industrial art; 19th Century; Prehistoric; Roman
Exhibitions: Die Staufer; Zwischen Improvisation und Fuge
Activities: Originate traveling exhibitions

SOLOTHURN

M KUNSTMUSEUM SOLOTHURN, Solothurn Art Museum, Werkhofstrasse 30. *Conservator* Andre Kamber
Closed in 1980 for construction. Estab to house a collection of Swiss art. Average Annual Attendance: 24,000
Income: Financed by city appropriation
Purchases: SFr 30,000
Collections: Large collection of Frank Buschser and Otto Grölicher; Holbein d J: Solothurner Madonna 1522; Meister des Paradiesgärtleins: Madonna in den Erdbeeren, um 1425; 20th Century Swiss Art; Cuno Amiet, B Luginbuhl, Alois Carigiet, Franz Eggenschwiler, Max Gubler, Ferdinand Hodler, Schang Hutter, Rolf Iseli, Bernhard Luthi, Manuboules, Otto Morach, Robert Muller, Meret Oppenehim, Dieter Roth, Heinz Schwarz, Rolf Spinnler, Spoerri, Hans Stocker, J Tinguely, Andre Thomkins, Valloton, Karl Walser, Oscar Wiggli
Exhibitions: Martin Disteli; Karl Gerstner; Jakob Tuggener - a pioneer of Swiss photography
Publications: Exhibition catalogs

WINTERTHUR

M KUNSTMUSEUM, Art Museum, Museumstrasse 52. Tel 84 51 62. *Cur* Dr Rudolf Koella
Open 10 AM - Noon and 2 - 5 PM, cl Mon mornings. Estab 1866. Administered by Museum Association. Average Annual Attendance: 12,000. Mem: 960
Collections: Portraits by Anton Graff; French, German and Italian painting and sculpture of the 19th and 20th Centuries; Swiss painting and sculpture since 1700; drawings and prints
Exhibitions: Annual show of local artists; tri-annual show of artists from Canton of Zurich; two to three exhibitions per year of contemporary Swiss and International Art; retrospective exhibits
Publications: Collection and exhibition catalogs
Activities: Two lect per year, generally on contemporary art
L Library, Museumstrasse 52.
Library Holdings: Vols 4000

ZURICH

M KUNSTHAUS ZURICH, Museum of Fine Arts, Heimplatz 1, Box 8024. Tel 01 32 67 65. *Dir* Dr F Baumanu; *Asst Dir* Dr E Billeter; *Asst Dir Business Admin* M Marti
Open Mon 2 - 5 PM, Tues - Fri 10 AM - 9 PM, Sat & Sun 10 AM - 5 PM. Admis SFr 5 and SFr 2. Estab 1910 as an official Zurich Museum of Fine Arts. Gallery includes space for the permanent collection and changing exhibitions; a graphic arts room; a photo gallery; and a foyer for exhibitions. Average Annual Attendance:

300,000. Mem: 6000; dues adults SFr 50, juniors SFr 10
Income: Financed by membership, city and state appropriation
Collections: Alberto Giacometti-Foundation; medieval and modern sculptures; paintings 15th - 20th Centuries, mainly 19th and 20th
Activities: Classes for children; concerts; original objects of art lent; originate traveling exhibitions; museum shop sells books, original art, reproductions, prints and slides
L **Library,** Heimplatz 1, Box 8024. *VDir Graphic Coll & Library* Dr U Perucchi
Open to members of Zurcher Kunstgesellschaft, students and professors
Library Holdings: Vols 40,000; Per subs 90; Other—Exhibition catalogs, manuscripts, annual reports, auction catalogs, museum bulletins
Special Subjects: Fine arts - paintings, prints, sculpture, especially 19th and 20th Century

M **MUSEUM RIETBERG ZURICH,** Gablerstrasse 14 & 15. Tel 202 45 28. *Dir* Dr Eberhard Fischer; *Cur East Asia* Dr Helmut Brinker
Main Building (Villa Wesendonck) open Tues - Sun 10 AM - 5 PM, Wed evenings 8 - 10 PM, cl Mon. No admis fee. Estab 1952 as a museum of non-western art. Entrance room houses ancient Oriental art; one room Pre-Columbian art; four rooms Indian and Southeast Asian art; six rooms East Asian art; three rooms African art; one room of Oceanic art. Average Annual Attendance: 40,000. Mem: 550; dues SFr 50 and up
Income: Financed by city appropriation
Purchases: $50,000
Collections: †African Art; †Chinese Painting; Baron von der Heydt Collection; †Japanese Sculpture
Publications: Exhibition catalogs
Activities: Lect open to public, 10 visiting lectr per year; concerts; originate traveling exhibitions; sales shop sells books, reproductions, prints, slides and postcards
L **Library,** Gablerstrasse 14 & 15.
Open by appointment for reference
Library Holdings: Vols 6000
Collections: Baron von der Heydt; Library of Prof Osvald Siren and others
M **Museum Rietberg,** Zurich am Hirschengraben 20, Zurich CH-8001. Tel 47 96 52.
Open Tues - Fri 2 - 7 PM, Sat & Sun 2 - 5 PM, Thurs evenings 7 - 9 PM, cl Mon. Estab 1974
Exhibitions: Special temporary exhibitions on non-European art

M **SCHWEIZERISCHES LANDESMUSEUM,** Swiss National Museum, Museumstrasse 2, PO Box 2760. Tel 01-221 10 10. *Dir* Dr Hugo Schneider; *VDir* Dr Jenny Schneider
Open Mon 2 - 5 PM, Tues - Sun 10 AM - Noon and 2 - 5 PM, cl holidays. No admis fee. Estab 1898 to serve as a basis for scientific research. Museum houses the largest collections relating to the cultural history of Switzerland; permanent and changing exhibitions on display give a comprehensive survey of Swiss culture from pre-historic times to present. Average Annual Attendance: 330,000
Income: Financed by state appropriation
Purchases: SFr 400,000
Collections: Ancient crafts and trades, banners, ceramics, clocks and watches, coins, costumes, excavations, farming implements, furniture, glassware, goldsmith's art, interiors, jewelry, medals, military items, musical instruments, nonferrous metals, paintings, prints and drawings, pewter, prehistory and ancient history, stained glass, statuary, textiles, uniforms, weapons
Exhibitions: Permanent and changing exhibitions
Publications: Annual report: Zeitschrift für schweizerische Archaeologie und Kunstgeschichte, quarterly
Activities: Educ dept; docent training; lect open to public, 3200 visiting lectr per year; gallery talks; tours; sales shop sells books and slides
L **Library,** Museumstrasse 2, PO Box 2760. *Librn* Helen Merz
Open Mon - Fri 8 AM - Noon and 2 - 5 PM. Estab 1898
Library Holdings: Vols 70,000; Per subs 900; Other—Exhibition catalogs
Special Subjects: Coins & Medals, Handicrafts, Folklore, military, prehistory

SYRIA

DAMASCUS

M **NATIONAL MUSEUM OF DAMASCUS,** Reda Saeed St. *General Dir* Dr Afif Bahnassi; *Cur* Adman Joundi
Open winter 8 AM - 1 PM and 2 - 4 PM, summer 9 AM - 1 PM and 4 - 9 PM. Estab 1919. The Directorate-General of Antiquities is located here (which all museums in Syria depend upon), to preserve and conserve Syrian Antiquities and to supervise the archaeological museums and the excavations
Collections: Ancient, Byzantine, Greek, Islamic, Modern, Oriental, Prehistoric and Roman Art
Publications: Annales Archeologiques Arabes Syrienne, yearly
L **Library,** Reda Saeed St. *Librn* Rihab Daoud
Library Holdings: Vols 15,000

TUNISIA

LE BARDO

M **MUSEE NATIONAL DU BARDO,** Bardo National Museum, Tel 261-002. *Dir* Ennaifer Mongi
Open 9:30 AM - 4:30 PM. Estab 1888
Income: Financed by government appropriation
Collections: Medieval and modern art, modern Islamic art; Greek and Roman

antiquities; Roman mosaics
Publications: Antiquites Africa, articles and documents (National Institute of Archeology is the publisher)
Activities: Guides for student and official tours; book traveling exhibitions
L **Library,**
Library Holdings: Other—Photographs

TURKEY

ISTANBUL

M **ISTANBUL ARKEOLOJI MÜZELERI,** Archaeological Museums of Istanbul, Sultanahmet. Tel 279069, 279070. *Dir* Aykut Özet; *Asst Dir* Yücel Erten; *Asst Dir* Ismail H Köse; *Cur Cuneiform Tablet Coll* Fatma Yildiz; *Cur Cuneiform Tablet Coll* Veysel Donbaz; *Cur Department of Greek & Roman Antiquities* Nusin Asgari; *Cur Islamic Coins* Teoman Cankilioglu; *Cur Laboratory Restoration* Nejet Özatay; *Cur Laboratory Preservation* Behcet Erdal; *Cur Laboratory Preservation* Revza Özil; *Cur Museum of Ancient Orient* Edibe Uzunoglu; *Cur Photography* Turhan Birgili; *Cur Non-Islamic Coins* Nekriman Olcay
Open Tues - Sun 9:30 AM - 5 PM, cl Mon. Estab 1846 to show to the public the richness of antiquities of the country. Average Annual Attendance: 160,000. Mem: 120; dues $6; annual meeting April
Income: $50,000 (financed by state appropriation)
Collections: Architectural pieces, coins and cuneiform tablets from 6000 BC - 1500 AD, glass, inscriptions, metal, portraits, sarcophagi, statues
Exhibitions: Changing exhibitions from permanent collection
Publications: Annual of the Archaeological Museums of Istanbul
Activities: Lect for members, 4 visiting lectr per year; concerts; sales shop sells reproductions, prints and slides
L **Library,** Sultanahmet. *Librn* Havva Kivircik
Open daily 9:30 AM - 4:30 PM. Estab 1912 as a resource to members and universities
Library Holdings: Vols 50,000; Micro—Cards, fiche, prints; Other—Clipping files, exhibition catalogs, prints, manuscripts, memorabilia, original art works, pamphlets, photographs
Special Subjects: Archaeology, Art History, Coins & Medals, Cuneiform studies, history
Collections: Sakir and Cevat Pasa
Exhibitions: New books

M **TOPKAPI SARAY MUSEUM,** Sultanahmed. Tel 28 3546-47. *Dir* Sabahattin Batur; *Asst Dir* M Pazi
Open daily 9:30 AM - 5 PM, cl Tues. Admis adult 80 TL, children half-price. Estab 1924 to offer exhibitions of art
Income: Financed by state appropriation
Collections: Chinese and Japanese porcelains; miniatures and portraits of Sultans; Alay Kiosk exhibit of Kenan Ozbel; Sami Ozgiritli's collection of furniture; Sultan's costumes; Turkish embroideries; calligraphy, clocks and watches, holy relics, rugs, throne room, tiled kiosk
L **Library of Manuscripts,** Sultanahmed. *Librn* Filiz Cagman
Open 9 AM - 12:30 PM and 1 - 4:30 PM, cl Sat & Sun. Estab 1924 to researchers for reference
Library Holdings: Vols 20,000; Other—Turkish and Persian manuscripts

M **TURK VE ISLAM ESERLERI MUZESI,** Museum of Turkish and Islamic Art,* Süleymaniye, 6 Sifahane St. Tel 22 1888. *Dir* Can Kerametli
Open daily 10 AM - 5 PM, cl Mon. Estab 1914
Collections: Books with miniatures and illumination; fermans and monograms of the Sultans, and other monuments of Islamic Art; metalwork and ceramics; old Korans; the oldest Turkish carpets; sculpture in stone and stucco; wood carvings

URUGUAY

MONTEVIDEO

M **MUSEO NACIONAL DE ARTES PLASTICAS,** National Museum of Fine Arts,* Tomas Giribaldi 2283, Parque Rodo. Tel 43 800. *Dir* Angel Kalenberg
Open winter 2 - 6 PM, summer 6 - 10 PM, cl Mon. No admis fee. Estab 1911. Average Annual Attendance: 300,000
Income: Financed by government appropriation
Collections: Rafael Barradas, Juan Manuel Blanes, Jose Cuneo, Alfredo de Simone, Pedro Figari, Torres Garcia, Carlos Gonzalez, Carlos Federico Saez; 4217 ceramics, drawings, engravings, paintings and sculptures
Publications: Exhibition catalogs, quarterly
Activities: Lect open to public, 6 visiting lectr per year; gallery talks; tours; concerts; competitions; exten dept serves museums; original objects of art lent; originate traveling exhibitions
L **Library,*** Tomas Giribaldi 2283, Paruqe Rodo.
For reference
Library Holdings: Vols 4500

USSR

MOSCOW

M **STATE MUSEUM OF ORIENTAL ART,** ul Obukha, 16. *Dir* Dr H Popov; *Art Secy* Mrs N Sichova
Open 11 AM - 7 PM, cl Mon. Admis adult 30 copecks, pupils and students 10 copecks, museum staff, artists, students of Art institutions free. Estab 1918 for gathering, keeping, studying and popularizing works of art of the countries and peoples of the East. Average Annual Attendance: 150,000
Income: Financed by state appropriation
Collections: Art of the Republics of Soviet Orient; Chinese Art; Monuments of Art of Japan, India, Vietnam, Korea, Mongolia, Iran and other countries of the East
Exhibitions: Applied Art of Bur a; Collection of Miniature Paintings from National Museum in Delhi; The East and the Russian Art; Fine Arts of Afghanistan and Yemen; Indian Applied Art; Traditions and the Present in the Art of the Soviet Orient
Publications: Collected articles on problems of art and culture of the countries and peoples of Orient
Activities: Classes for children; lect open to public, 8 visiting lectr per year; exten dept serves various organizations; artmobile; individual paintings and original objects of art lent to state museums and exhibitions; originate traveling exhibitions; museum shop sells books, magazines, reproductions, prints and slides

TALLINN

L **LIBRARY OF THE ESTONIAN STATE ART INSTITUTE,** Tartu maantee 1. *Head of Library* E Mutt
Open 10 AM - 5 PM, cl Sat & Sun. Estab to provide students and teaching staff with special art literature
Income: Financed by state appropriation
Library Holdings: Vols 29,000; Other—Exhibition catalogs, manuscripts, reproductions 13,250
Collections: Books designed by graphic art students

VENEZUELA

CARACAS

M **MUSEO DE BELLAS ARTES,** Museum of Fine Arts,* Parque Sucre, Los Caobos 105. Tel 54 37 92. *Dir* Miguel G Arroyo; *Secy* Prisca Dale de Moleiro; *Conservation Department* Carlos Duarte; *Cur Prints & Drawings* Gerd Leufert; *Asst to Cur* Alvaro Sotillo
Open daily 9 AM - Noon and 3 - 5:30 PM, cl Mon. Estab 1938. Average Annual Attendance: 200,000
Collections: Chinese and European porcelain; Egyptian Art; European painting; Latin American paintings and sculpture, including primitives; Pre-Columbian Art; Venezuelan painting from the end of the 19th Century to the present; drawings and prints
Exhibitions: Approximately 24 per year
Activities: Classes for children; 12 lect per year; gallery talks
L **Library,*** Parque Sucre, Los Caobos, 105.
Library Holdings: Vols 3100; Other—Catalogs, magazines

WALES

CARDIFF

M **NATIONAL MUSEUM OF WALES,** Cathays Park. Tel 0222-397951. *Pres* William Crawshay; *VPres* W A Twiston-Davies; *Treas* H Morrey Salmon; *Secy* D W Dykes; *Dir* Douglas A Bassett; *Keeper of Art* P Cannon-Brookes
Open 10 AM - 5 PM. No admis fee. Museum received its Charter of Incorporation by King Edward VII in 1907, and officially opened by King George V in 1927. Museum is to record the story of Wales from earliest times in the displays and collections of the departments of archaeology, art, botany, geology, industry and zoology. Nine other branches are throughout Wales of which two are art galleries; Turner House became a branch in 1921, and Graham and Kathleen Sutherland Foundation opened in 1976. The supreme governing body is the Court of Governors. Average Annual Attendance: 300,000
Income: Financed by British Government Treasury Grant
Collections: Davis Collection includes British paintings and drawings; French Art of the 19th Century including Renoir's La Parisienne (1874), and major works by Bonnard, Cezanne, Corot, Daumier, Manet, Millet, Monet, Pisarro, van Gogh; Old Masters, including the History of Aaneas, The Four Rubens Tapestry Cartoons, and works by Batoni, Canaletto, Cima, Constable, Gaulli, Guercino, Turner, Richard Wilson; De Winton Collection in continental porcelain; Jackson Collection of silver, containing many rarities (in the National Museum), and the Mostyn Ewer and Dish (Bruges circa 1540); Nance Collection specializes in pottery and porcelain of Swansea and Nantgarw; Pyke Thompson Collection includes ceramics, enamels, prints and watercolours by great artists of the early 19th Century - Colman, Cox, De Wint, Girtin, Turner, and later artists including Holman Hunt and Rossetti
Exhibitions: Over 50 temporary exhibitions annually
Activities: Lect open to public; gallery talks; concerts; individual paintings and original objects of art lent to galleries and museums; book shop

L **Library,** Cathays Park.
Open for reference by arrangement
Library Holdings: Vols 100,000

NEWPORT

M **NEWPORT MUSEUM AND ART GALLERY,** John Frost Square. Tel 0633-840064. *Cur & Keeper of Antiquities* Cefni Barnett; *Deputy Cur* Bruce Campbell; *Keeper of Art* Roger Cucksey; *Keeper of Natural Sciences & Social & Industrial History* Walter Lucas; *Schools Service Officer* Leslie James
Open Mon - Fri 10 AM - 5:30 PM, Sat 9:30 AM - 4 PM. No admis fee. Estab 1887 to preserve and to present the heritage of the county of Gwent. Average Annual Attendance: 150,000
Income: $380,000 (financed by city appropriation)
Purchases: $23,000
Collections: Art Gallery: †ceramics and other applied art objects; †early English watercolours; †oil paintings by British artists; †prints and drawings. Museum: geology; local archaeology (especially Roman); natural and social history
Exhibitions: Approximately 12 per year, and frequent visiting exhibitions
Activities: Classes for children; lect open to public, 6 visiting lectr per year; gallery talks; tours; organized visits to museum and places of various interests; loan scheme to schools and galleries for specific exhibitions; sales shop sells books, reproductions, prints and postcards

SAINT FAGANS

M **WELSH FOLK MUSEUM,** near Cardiff. Tel Cardiff 569441. *Cur* T M Owen; *Keeper Family and Rural Life* E Scourfield; *Keeper Oral Coll* Vincent H Phillips
Open Mon - Sat 10 AM - 5 PM, Sun 2:30 - 5 PM, cl Christmas Day, Boxing Day, May Holiday and New Year's Day. Admis adults 10p, children 5p. Estab 1947 to illustrate the old way of life in Wales with collections and activities. It comprises an open air museum, including the Elizabethan mansion of St Fagan's Castle, the rooms are furnished in period style, its gardens and grounds, and an adjoining area of eighty acres of woodland. Buildings from all parts of Wales are re-erected there, craftsmen may be seen practicing their crafts, and the study of folk-life is exhibited in a new museum block. Average Annual Attendance: 280,000

YUGOSLAVIA

BELGRADE

M **MUSEUM OF MODERN ART,*** USCE SAVE BB. Tel 011-326-544. *Dir* Miodrag B Protic; *Chief Cur* Draga Panic; *Head of Documentation* Marija Pusic
Open Fri - Wed 10 AM - 7 PM, cl Thurs. Admis 10,000 dinars. Estab 1959 to collect and exhibit works of Yugoslav art since 1900. Gallery houses the permanent display and has room for temporary exhibitions. Average Annual Attendance: 100,000
Income: Financed by city appropriation and the Republic of Serbia
Collections: †Drawings, †foreign collection of prints, †new media, †painting, †prints, †sculpture and †tapestry
Exhibitions: American Painting 1846-1976; Art in Belgium from the end of the 18th Century; Danish Design; Der Blaue Reiter; Yanis Gaitis; German Expressionism (Die Bruckle) prints; International Exhibition of Plastic Arts
Publications: Exhibition catalogs
Activities: Classes for adults and children; lect open to public, 7 visiting lect per year; gallery talks; tours; exten dept serves the area; originate traveling exhibitions; museum shop sells reproductions, slides and catalogs
L **Library,*** USCE SAVE BB. *Librn* Olga Caric
Library Holdings: Vols 2500; Per subs 36; Other—Catalogs 10,350

LJUBLJANA

M **MODERNA GALERIJA,** Modern Art Gallery,* Tomsiceva 14. Tel 061 21-709. *Dir* Zoran Krzisnik; *Cur Museum Coll* Melita Stele-Mozina; *Cur Documentation* Ljerka Menase; *Cur Exhib* Majda Jerman
Open Tues - Sun 10 AM - 6 PM, cl Mon. Admis adults 5 Din, students 3 Din, groups 2 Din. Estab 1948 to collect contemporary works of art in Slovenia; permanent collections of Slovene art; to mount exhibitions. Average Annual Attendance: 10,000
Income: Financed by city and state appropriations
Collections: †Slovene painting; †sculpture and graphic art from 1900 to present
Exhibitions: Fantasy in Graphic Art from 16th Century to present; International Exhibition of Graphic Art in Ljubljana; New British Art; Retrospective exhibitions of Slovene artists - Dusan Dzamonja, Oskar Kokoschka, Miha Males, France Mihelic and Matej Sternen
Publications: Exhibition catalogs
Activities: Classes for adults and children; lect open to public, 12 visiting lectr per year; concerts; gallery talks; tours; originate traveling exhibitions
L **Library,*** Tomsiceva 14.
Library Holdings: Vols 17,206; Per subs 93

M **NARODNA GALERIJA,** National Art Gallery, Prezihova ulica 1-pp 432. Tel 21-765, 21-249. *Dir* Dr Anica Cevc; *Asst* Dr Ksenija Rozman; *Asst* Polonca Vrhunc
Open Tues - Sat 10 AM - 6 PM, Sun 10 AM - 1 PM, cl Mon. Admis adults N din 8, students and groups N din 3. Estab 1918 for the presentation of Slovenian art from the 13th Century to the beginning of the 20th Century. Average Annual Attendance: 40,000
Income: Financed by city and state appropriations
Collections: Copies of medieval frescoes; Foreign Masters from the 14th Century to the beginning of the 20th Century; Slovenian sculptures and paintings from the 13th to the beginning of the 20th Century
Exhibitions: (1978) Od Corota do Bonnarda (From Corot to Bonnard); Holandija

17.stoletja v oceh svojih umetnikov (Holland of the 17th Century seen by her painters); Cesko in slovasko slikarstvo med vojnama (Szech and Slovakian painting between Two Wars); (1979) Ceska gotska um etnost (Bohemian Gothic Art); Podobe otrok v preteklosti (Children portraits in the past); Barvna grafika Nemske demokraticne republike (Coloured graphic art from the German Democratic Republic); Ivana Kobilca: 1862-1926

Publications: Exhibition catalogs

Activities: Lect open to public; concerts; tours; original objects of art lent to museums; originate traveling exhibitions; museum shop sells reproductions and catalogs

L **Library,** Prezihova ulica 1-pp 432.
Open for reference
Library Holdings: Vols 13,040; AV—Slides; Other—Bibliographic files concerning Slovenian art photonegatives

ZAGREB

M **GALERIJE GRADA ZAGREBA,** City Art Galleries,* Katarinin trg 2. Tel 041 424 490. *Dir* Dr Boris Kelemen
Open 11 AM - 1 PM and 5 - 8 PM. Admis 3 Din. Estab 1961. Average Annual Attendance: 20,000
Income: Financed by endowment
Collections: Photograph collection
Publications: Bit International, Spot (photography journal); catalogs
Activities: Original objects of art lent; originate traveling exhibitions; book shop

M **Galerija Suvremene Umjetnosti,*** Gallery of Contemporary Art. (Mailing Add: Katarinin trg 2, PO Box 233) Tel 041 443 227. *Chief Cur* Bozo Bek; *Cur* Marijan Susovski; *Cur* Davor Maticevic
Open 11 AM - 1 PM and 5 - 8 PM. Admis 5 Din. Estab 1955, gallery collects and exhibits contemporary art; organizes exhibitions of avant-garde Yugoslavian artists and artists from abroad; promotes experimental and new trends as well as new media in art. Average Annual Attendance: 20,000
Income: Financed by city appropriation
Collections: †Conceptual works, †film, †graphics, †objects of art, †paintings, †sculpture and †video
Exhibitions: Bucan; Confrontations; De Lale; Dobrovi; German Expressionism; Gorgona; Graphics from Portugal; Photography as Art; Gudac; Ivekovic; Martinis; Photography from San Francisco; Polish Photography; III World Exhibition of Photography; Ulay; Video meeting; Young Yugoslav Cineasts
Publications: Documents; Spot, quarterly
Activities: Lect open to public, 10 visiting lectr per year; concerts; gallery talks; tours; individual paintings and original objects of art lent to organizations and institutions; originate traveling exhibitions; museum shop sells books, magazines, original art, prints and slides

L **Gallery of Contemporary Art Library,*** Katarinin trg 2, PO Box 233. *Librn* Marijan Susovski
Library Holdings: Vols 5000; Per subs 20

M **Galerija Primitivne Umjetnosti,*** Cirilometodska 3. (Mailing Add: Gallery of Primitive Art, Katarinin trg 2) Tel 041 443 294. *Chief Cur* Dr Boris Kelemen; *Cur* Tomislav Sola
Open 11 AM - 1 PM and 5 - 8 PM. Admis 5 Din, groups 3 Din. Estab 1952 to gather, keep and exhibit naive art of Yugoslavia and foreign countries. Gallery consists of six exhibit rooms, 197 sq meters, 1195 running meters
Income: Financed by city and state appropriation
Collections: Approximately 700 works of Yugoslav and foreign naive artists
Activities: Lect open to public; originate traveling exhibitions; sales shop sells original art, reproductions and prints

M **Atelje Mestrovic,*** Studio Mestrovic, Mletacka 8. Tel 041 445 075. *Chief Cur* Vesna Barbic
Estab 1959 to house the collection of sculpture of Ivan Mestrovie
Income: Financed by endowment

M **Galerija Benko Horvat,*** Collection Benko Horvat, Rokov perivoj 4. Tel 041-424-490. *Chief Cur* Radoslav Putar
Estab 1948
Income: Financed by endowment
Collections: Drawings, prints and paintings of the 15th - 19th Centuries

M **Centar za Fotografija, Film i Televiziju,** Centre for Photography, Film and Television, Rokov perivoj 4. *Cur* Prof Dimitrije Basicevic

M **STROSSMAYEROVA GALERIJA STARIH MAJSTORA JUGOSLAVENSKE AKADEMIJE ZNANOSTI I UMJETNOSTI,** Strossmayer's Gallery of Old Masters of the Yugoslavia Academy of Sciences and Arts, Zrinjski trg 11. Tel 441-849. *Pres* Dr Jakov Sirotkovic; *Dir* Prof Vinko Zlamalik; *Cur* Prof Ljerka Gasparovic
Open Tues 5 - 7 PM, Wed & Fri 10 AM - Noon, Thurs & Sun 10 AM - 1 PM. Admis 5 & 10 dinar. Estab 1884 for the preservation, exhibition and explanation of Old Masters
Income: Financed by city and state appropriations
Collections: Paintings and sculpture with emphasis on 15th - 16th Century Austrian painting, 16th - 18th Century Dutch and Flemish School, 18th - 20th Century French School, 16th Century German Art, Italian School from Renaissance to 18th Century

L **Library,** Zrinjski trg 11.
Open for reference
Library Holdings: Vols 13,000

ZIMBAHWE RHODESIA

SALISBURY

M **NATIONAL GALLERY OF ZIMBABWE RHODESIA,** PO Box 8155, Causeway. Tel 2 05 41. *Acting Dir* C M Till
Open Tues - Sun 9 AM - 5 PM, cl Mon. Estab 1957
Collections: African traditional and local contemporary sculpture and paintings; ancient and modern European paintings and sculpture; tapestries
Exhibitions: Annual exhibition of Rhodesian artists; large loan collections exhibited
Activities: African sculpture workshop functioning since 1961; Friends of the Gallery organization; lect; films

L **Thomas Meikle Library,** PO Box 8155, Causeway. *Librn-Tutor* M J McDermott
Open Tues - Fri 9 AM - 5 PM. Estab 1957 to provide an art reference for the country
Library Holdings: Vols 2000; Per subs 20; AV—Cassettes, motion pictures, slides; Other—Clipping files, exhibition catalogs
Special Subjects: African art

II ART SCHOOLS

Arrangement and Abbreviations

Art Schools in the U.S.

Art Schools in Canada

Major Art Schools Abroad

ARRANGEMENT AND ABBREVIATIONS
KEY TO ART SCHOOLS

ARRANGEMENT OF DATA

Name and address of institution; telephone number, including area code.

Name and title of the head of the school or department; names and titles of primary art faculty.

Date school or department was established.

Control of institution (denominational, private, public).

Number of classes held during the day and evening.

Entrance requirements.

Degrees granted and number of years required for graduation.

Scholarships and fellowships offered.

Number of studio courses, lecture courses, lab courses, and graduate courses offered.

Enrollment for day and evening classes and for majors and nonmajors.

Tuition and statement of campus residence availability.

Adult hobby and children's classes offered.

Summer school enrollment, tuition, duration, and courses.

ABBREVIATIONS AND SYMBOLS

Acad — Academic
Admis — Admission
AM — Morning
Approx — Approximate, Approximately
Assoc — Associate
Asst — Assistant
Ave — Avenue
Blvd — Boulevard
Bro — Brother
c — circa
Cert — Certificate
Chmn — Chairman
Cl — Closed
Col — College
Coordr — Coordinator
Cr — Credit
D — Day
Den — Denominational
Dept — Department
Dipl — Diploma
Dir — Director
Div — Division
Dorm — Dormitory
Dr — Doctor, Drive
E — East, Evening
Educ — Education

Enrl — Enrollment
Ent Req — Entrance Requirements
Estab — Established
Exam — Examination
Fel(s) — Fellowship(s)
FT — Full Time Instructor
GC — Graduate Course
Gen — General
Grad — Graduate
Hr — Hour
HS — High School
Hwy — Highway
Incl — Including
Instr — Instructor
Jr — Junior
Lab C — Laboratory Course
LC — Lecture Course
Lect — Lecture(s)
Lectr — Lecturer
M — Men
Maj — Major in Art
N — North
Nonres — Nonresident
PM — Afternoon
Pres — President
Prin — Principal

Prof — Professor
Prog — Program
PT — Part Time Instructor
Pts — Points
Pub — Public
Pvt — Private
Qtr — Quarter
Rd — Road
Reg — Registration
Req — Requirements
Res — Residence, Resident
S — South
SC — Studio Course
Schol — Scholarship
Sem — Semester
Sr — Senior, Sister
St — Street
Tui — Tuition
TV — Television
Undergrad — Undergraduate
Univ — University
W — West, Women
Wk — Week
Yr — Year(s)

*No response to questionnaire
† Denotes subject field is offered as major

Art Schools In The United States

ALABAMA

ATHENS

ATHENS STATE COLLEGE, Art Department, Beaty St, 35611. Tel 205-232-1802, Ext 203. Instrs FT 1
Estab 1832; D & E; ent req HS dipl; degrees BA and BS 2 yr; schol; SC 26, LC 6; enrl D 951, E 590, maj 15
Courses: Art Education, Ceramics, Commercial Art, Costume Design & Construction, Drawing, Graphic Arts, Handicrafts, History of Art & Archaeology, Painting, Photography, Sculpture, Teacher Training, Theatre Arts
Summer School: Term of 25 wks beginning June

AUBURN

AUBURN UNIVERSITY, Department of Art,* School of Architecture and Fine Arts, 36830. Tel 205-826-4000. *Dean* E K McPheeters; *Head* C Hiers
Estab 1928; pub; D; ent req HS dipl, ACT, SAT; degrees BFA 4 yr, MFA 2 yr; SC 48, LC 9, GC 19; enrl 300
Courses: Drawing, Illustration, Painting, Printmaking, Sculpture
Adult Hobby Classes: Courses—Drawing, Painting

BIRMINGHAM

BIRMINGHAM-SOUTHERN COLLEGE, Art Department,* 800 Eighth Ave W, 35204. Tel 205-328-5250. *Chmn* William Hubbard Baxter, Jr
Estab 1946; den; D; ent req HS dipl, ACT, SAT scores, C average; degrees AB, BS, BFA, BM and BME 4 yr; financial aid awarded, some leadership scholarships available on variable basis; SC 22, LC 8, interim term courses of 4 or 8 wk, 4 req of each student in 4 yr period; enrl 500, maj 50
Tuition: Res—$2,550 per yr
Courses: Art Education, Drawing, Graphic Arts, Graphic Design, History of Art & Archaeology, Painting, Sculpture
Children's Classes: Enrl approx 20. Laboratory for training teachers
Summer School: 8 wk beginning June 11 and Aug 10. Courses—Advanced Painting, Art and Music, Graphics, Painting and Drawing, Problems in Composition, Sculpture

SAMFORD UNIVERSITY, Art Department, 800 Lakeshore Dr, 35209. Tel 205-870-2840, 870-2849. *Chmn* Dr Lowell C Vann. Instrs FT 3, PT 1
Estab 1841; pvt; D; ent req HS dipl, ent exam, ACT, SAT; degrees BA and BSEduc 4 yrs; SC 24, LC 4, GC 1
Tuition: $68 per sem hr plus fees
Courses: Advertising Design, Art Education, Ceramics, Commercial Art, Costume Design & Construction, Drawing, Graphic Arts, Graphic Design, Handicrafts, History of Art & Archaeology, Interior Design, Painting, Photography, Sculpture, Stage Design, Teacher Training, Theatre Arts
Adult Hobby Classes: Enrl 40. Courses—Ceramics, Drawing, Painting
Summer School: Tui $68 per sem hr for term of 5 wks beginning June 7. Courses—regular semester courses on rotating basis

UNIVERSITY OF ALABAMA IN BIRMINGHAM, Department of Art, University College, Building 3, 35294. Tel 205-934-4941. *Chmn Dept* John M Schnorrenberg, PhD; *Assoc Prof* John Dillon, MFA; *Assoc Prof* Edith Frohock, MFA; *Asst Prof* James Alexander, MFA; *Asst Prof* Sonja Rieger, MFA; *Asst Prof* Howard Risatti, PhD; *Asst Prof* Richard Urban, MFA. Instrs FT 8, PT 4
Estab 1966, dept estab 1974; pub; D & E; ent req HS dipl, ACT, SAT; degrees BA; SC 24, LC 27, GC 10; enrl D 234, E 108, maj 130, grad 2
Tuition: Res—undergrad $756 per yr, $252 per term, $33 per hr, grad $750 per yr, $250 per term, $39 per hr; nonres—double res rate
Courses: Aesthetics, †Art History, Ceramics, Drawing, †Graphic Design, †Painting, Photography, †Printmaking, †Sculpture, Teacher Training, Theatre Arts
Adult Hobby Classes: Enrl 150; tui $35-$50. Courses—Basic Art, Calligraphy, Portraiture, Stained Glass
Children's Classes: Enrl 40; tui $15. Courses—Art for Mothers and Children, Basic Drawing, Sculpting with Wire and Paper Mache
Summer School: Enrl 173; tui as above for term of 11 wks beginning June 9. Courses—range over all fields and are about one half regular offerings

BREWTON

JEFFERSON DAVIS STATE JUNIOR COLLEGE, Art Department, Alco Dr, 36426. Tel 205-867-4832. *Instructor* Larry Manning; *Instructor* John B Spicer
Estab 1965; pub; D & E; ent req HS dipl or equiv; degrees AA and AS 2 yr; SC 10, LC 1; enrl D 700, E 332, maj 25
Tuition: 100 per quarter; no campus res
Courses: Ceramics, Drawing, Handicrafts, Painting, Photography, Basic Design, Introduction to Art
Summer School: Enrl 200. Courses—Ceramics, Drawing, Introduction to Art

DECATUR

JOHN C CALHOUN STATE COMMUNITY COLLEGE, Art Department, Hwy 31 North, PO Box 2216, 35602. Tel 205-353-3102. *Head Dept* Arthur Bond, MA; *Instr* Helen C Austin, MEd; *Instr* Richard Green, MFA; *Vis Prof* Ruth Holt, MEd
Estab 1963, dept estab 1963; pub; D & E; ent req HS dipl, GED; degrees AS and AAS 2 yrs; scholarships; SC 46, LC 8; enrl D 80, E 22, non-maj 29, maj 70, others 3
Tuition: $300 per yr, $100 quarterly
Courses: Advertising Design, †Art Education, Art History, Ceramics, Commercial Art, Drawing, †Film, †Graphic Arts, †Graphic Design, Illustration, Lettering, Museum Staff Training, Painting, †Photography, Printmaking, Sculpture, Video
Summer School: Courses are selected from regular course offerings

FLORENCE

UNIVERSITY OF NORTH ALABAMA, Department of Art,* Wesleyan Ave, 35630. Tel 205-766-4100, Ext 334. *Head Dept* Duane L Phillips, MFA; *Asst Prof* Albert Charles Hausmann, MFA; *Asst Prof* Fred Owen Hensley, MFA; *Asst Prof* Myrt W Hubbuch, MA; *Asst Prof* Thomas E Mims, MFA; *Asst Prof* Lawman F Palmer, MEd; *Instr* Jacqueline Simone Innes, MA; *Instr* Elizabeth Walter, MA
Estab 1872, dept estab approx 1930; pub; D; ent req HS dipl, or GED, ACT; degrees BS and BA 4 yr, MA 30 sem hr; SC 46, LC 6; enrl D 675, non-maj 475, maj 200, grad 20
Tuition: Res—undergrad $290 per sem, $30 per hr; campus res—room and board $1040
Courses: Art Education, Art History, Calligraphy, Ceramics, Collage, †Commercial Art, Drafting, Drawing, Handicrafts, Illustration, Lettering, Painting, †Photography, Printmaking, Sculpture, Teacher Training
Summer School: Tui $145 for term of 8 wks beginning June 4. Courses—lect and studio areas

HUNTSVILLE

ALABAMA A & M UNIVERSITY, Art Education Department,* 35762. Tel 205-859-7354. *Head Dept* Clifton Pearson, EdD; *Asst Prof* Robert Adams, MA; *Asst Prof* Jimmie Dawkins, MFA
Estab 1875, dept estab 1966; pub; D & E; ent req HS dipl; degrees BS(Art Educ); SC 18, LC 3; enrl non-maj 430, maj 35, grad 10
Tuition: Res—undergrad $205 per sem; nonres—undergrad $345 per sem; campus res $496
Courses: †Art Education, Art History, Ceramics, Drawing, Handicrafts, Painting, Printmaking, Sculpture, Teacher Training, Fibers
Summer School: Courses—Various specialized workshops and art education offerings

UNIVERSITY OF ALABAMA IN HUNTSVILLE, Department of Art, 4701 University Dr, PO Box 1247, 35807. Tel 205-895-6114. *Chmn Dept* Jeffrey J Bayer, MFA; *Assoc Prof* John P Dempsey, MA; *Assoc Prof* Richard C Pope, MFA; *Asst Prof* John A Sarn, PhD; *Instructor* Rosemarie T Bernardi, MFA
Estab 1969 (as independent, autonomous campus), dept estab 1965; pub; D & E; ent req HS dipl, ACT; degrees BA; schol; SC 46, LC 14; enrl D 150
Tuition: Res—undergrad $256 (8-13 hrs), $32 per hr; campus res—pvt room $68 month
Courses: Advertising Design, †Art Education, †Art History, Calligraphy, Collage, †Commercial Art, Drafting, Drawing, Film, Graphic Arts, Illustration, Industrial Design, Interior Design, Lettering, Mixed Media, Painting, Photography, †Printmaking, †Sculpture
Adult Hobby Classes: Courses—Calligraphy, Watercolor, other miscellaneous workshops offered through Division of Continuing Education
Summer School: Dir, Jeffrey J Bayer. Tui $256 for 8-13 hrs for term of 10 wk beginning mid-June. Courses—vary from summer to summer, part of the 46 studio classes and some art history offered

JACKSONVILLE

JACKSONVILLE STATE UNIVERSITY, Art Department, Pelham, 36265. Tel 205-435-9820, Ext 293. *Head* Dr Emilie E Burn, EdD; *Assoc Prof* Oakley N Holmes, MFA; *Asst Prof* Stephen Griffi..., MFA; *Asst Prof* Rhonda Roebuck, MFA
Estab 1883; pub; D & E; ent req HS dipl, ACT; degrees BS and BA 4 yr; SC 22, LC 8, GC 4; enrl D 7000, E 24, non-maj 60, maj 80, grad 11, others 15
Tuition: Res—undergrad $300 per semester, $26 per cr hr; grad $325 per semester, $33 per cr hr; Campus Res—room & board $900 per yr
Courses: Art Education, Art History, Ceramics, Commercial Art, Drawing, Handicrafts, Jewelry, Painting, Photography, Printmaking, Sculpture, Teacher Training

LIVINGSTON

LIVINGSTON UNIVERSITY, Division of Fine Arts,* 35470. Tel 205-652-9661. *Chmn* Dennis P Kudlawiec
Estab 1835; pub; degrees BA, BS, BMus, MEd, MSc; scholarships; enrl 1800
Tuition: Res—undergrad $165 per quarter; campus res—room and board $342 to $366
Courses: Art Education, Art History, Ceramics, Display, Drawing, Graphic Arts, Industrial Design, Painting, Art Appreciation, Art for the Teacher, Crafts, Design, Mechanical Drawing, Metal Work, Woodworking

MARION

JUDSON COLLEGE, Division of Fine Arts,* 36756. Tel 205-683-6161. *Chmn* Laurence Brasey Campbell
Estab 1838; den, W; D & E; ent req HS grad, adequate HS grades and ACT scores; degrees BA 3-4 yr; scholarships, loans, grants; SC 23, LC 6; enrl 450
Tuition: Res—undergrad $1760 per yr; campus res available
Courses: Commercial Art, Drawing, Painting, Crafts, Design, Watercolor, Special Courses
Adult Hobby Classes: Enrl 5. Courses—Studio Drawing, Painting
Children's Classes: Enrl 15. Courses—Studio Drawing

MOBILE

SPRING HILL COLLEGE, Fine Arts Department, 36609. Tel 205-460-2371. *Chmn* Daniel A Creagan, MA; *Instructor* Thomas Loehr, MFA; *Instructor* Barbara Patten, MFA
Estab 1830, dept estab 1965; den; D & E; ent req HS dipl, ACT, CEEB, SAT; degrees BA; SC 6, LC 1; enrl D 40, non-maj 35, maj 5
Tuition: Undergrad $1450 per sem; campus res—room & board $820 per sem
Courses: Art Education, Art History, †Ceramics, Drawing, Film, Graphic Design, †Painting, Photography, †Textile Design, Video

UNIVERSITY OF SOUTH ALABAMA, Department of Art, 307 University Blvd, 36688. Tel 205-460-6335. *Chmn* James E Kennedy, MAT; *Prof* John H Cleverdon, MA; *Prof* James E Conlon, MA; *Prof* Lee M Hoffman, MFA; *Assoc Prof* Lloyd L Patten, MS; *Assoc Prof* Linda Schele, MFA; *Asst Prof* Robert J Bantens, PhD; *Asst Prof* Philippe Oszuscik, PhD
Estab 1963, dept estab 1964; pub; D & E; ent req HS dipl, ACT; degrees BA, BFA and BA(Art History) 4 yrs; SC 32, LC 25; enrl maj & 150
Tuition: Res—undergrad $17 per cr hr; campus residency available
Courses: Advertising Design, Aesthetics, Architecture, Art Education, Art History, Ceramics, Commercial Art, Drawing, Graphic Arts, Painting, Photography, Printmaking, Sculpture
Summer School: Chmn, James E Kennedy. Tui $17 per cr hr. Courses—Drawing, Painting, Three-Dimensional Design

MONTEVALLO

UNIVERSITY OF MONTEVALLO, College of Fine Arts,* Art Department, 35115. Tel 205-665-2521, Ext 224. *Dean* John Stewart; *Chmn* L Frank McCoy
Estab 1896; pub; D & E; ent req ACT; degrees BA, BS and BFA 4 yr; scholarships, Work Study; SC 35, LC 10, GC 7; enrl Maj 80, others 2800
Tuition: Res—undergrad & grad $1548-$1782 per session (includes room and board); nonres—additional $210 per session
Courses: Advertising Design, Art Education, Art History, Ceramics, Handicrafts, Painting, Photography, Printmaking, Sculpture
Summer School: Enrl 1000; two 5 wk sessions beginning June 5 and July 5

MONTGOMERY

AUBURN UNIVERSITY AT MONTGOMERY, Art Department, 36109. Tel 205-279-9110, Ext 376. *Head Dept* Joseph Schwarz, PhD; *Asst Prof* Philip Coley, MFA; *Asst Prof* Richard Mills, MFA; *Adjunct Instructor* Reynolds Brown, MA; *Adjunct Instr* Russell Everett, MFA; *Adjunct Instr* Nita Whetstone, MFA. Instrs FT 4, PT 3
Estab 1972; pub; D & E; ent req HS dipl; degrees BA; SC 18, LC 5, GC 4; enrl D 400, nonmaj 200, maj 60
Tuition: Res—undergrad $555 yr; campus residence available
Courses: Art Education, Art History, Ceramics, Drawing, Graphic Arts, Painting, Photography, Sculpture
Adult Hobby Classes: Courses—Ceramics, Painting
Summer School: Head, Joseph Schwarz. Tui $185. Courses—same as above

HUNTINGDON COLLEGE, Dept of Visual and Performing Arts,* 1500 E Fairview Ave, 36106. Tel 205-265-0511, Ext 55. *Chmn* Jeanne Shaffer
Estab 1973; E; enrl 119
Courses: Drafting, Painting, Photography, Sculpture, Architectural Rendering, Creative Thinking, Graphics,
Adult Hobby Classes: Courses—non-credit offered through continuous educational programs

TROY

TROY STATE UNIVERSITY, Department of Art, 36081. Tel 205-566-3000, Ext 278. *Dean School of Fine Arts* Dr John M Long; *Head Dept* Dr R C Paxson; *Dept Chmn* 10. Instrs FT 7
Estab 1957; pub; ent req HS grad, ent exam; degrees BA and BS(Arts & Sciences) BA, BS and MS; schol and fel; SC 23, LC 11
Courses: †Art History, Commercial Art, Drawing, Graphic Arts, Handicrafts, Jewelry, Lettering, Painting, Photography, Silversmithing, Teacher Training, Museology, Pottery

TUSCALOOSA

STILLMAN COLLEGE, Stillman Art Gallery and Art Department, 3601 15th St, PO Box 1430, 35403. Tel 205-752-2548, Ext 64 or 28. *Coordr of Art* Brenda C Lispcome, MS; *Asst Prof* Raymond L Guffin, MFA
Estab 1876, dept estab 1959; pvt den; D; ent req HS dipl, ent exam; SC 8, LC 2; enrl D 73, non-maj 73
Tuition: $550 per yr; campus res—room & board $2973 per yr
Courses: Advertising Design, Art Education, Art History, Ceramics, Commercial Art, Drawing, Mixed Media, Painting, Sculpture, Afro-American Art
Summer School: Dir, Dr George E Jones. Courses—Art Education, Painting

TUSKEGEE INSTITUTE

TUSKEGEE INSTITUTE, Art Department, College of Arts and Sciences, 36088. *Dept Chmn* Elaine Thomas. Instrs FT 5
Estab 1881; pvt; degrees 4 yr
Courses: Art Education, Art History, Handicrafts, Textile Design, Applied Art, Art Appreciation, Design, Mural Techniques, Weaving

UNIVERSITY

UNIVERSITY OF ALABAMA, Art Department, Box F, 35486. Tel 205-348-5967. *Chmn Dept* Angelo Granata, MFA
Estab 1831, dept estab 1919; pub; D & E; ent req HS dipl, ACT; degrees BA and BFA 4 yr, MFA 2 yr, MA 1 yr; schol; SC 43, LC 12, GC 18; enrl D 950, maj 240, grad 17
Tuition: Res—undergrad & grad $333.75; nonres—undergrad & grad $706.25; campus res available
Courses: Art Education, Art History, Graphic Design, Painting, Photography, Printmaking, Sculpture, Ceramics-Glass, Drawing and Design
Summer School: Dir, Angelo Granata. Enrl 300; two 5 wk terms beginning June. Courses—same as above

ALASKA

ANCHORAGE

UNIVERSITY OF ALASKA AT ANCHORAGE, Department of Art, College of Arts and Sciences, 2533 Providence Ave, 99504. Tel 907-263-1800. *Chmn* Keith Appel. Instrs FT 4, PT 5
Pub; D & E; ent req open enrl; degrees AA in art, BA in art, BFA 4 yr; schol; SC 22, LC 3-5; enrl 800
Courses: Art Education, Ceramics, Drawing, Graphic Arts, History of Art & Archaeology, Jewelry, Painting, Photography, Sculpture, Stage Design, Teacher Training, Theatre Arts, Metalcraft, Weaving
Adult Hobby Classes: Same as regular prog
Summer School: Term of 13 wk beginning May. Courses—Ceramics, Drawing, Painting

FAIRBANKS

UNIVERSITY OF ALASKA, Department of Art,* Fine Arts Complex, 99701. Tel 907-479-7530. *Dept Head & Prof* Ronald Senungetuk
Estab 1963; pub; D & E; ent req HS dipl; degrees BA 4 yr; scholarships; SC 28, LC 4; enrl D 293, E 50, maj 45
Tuition: Res—$160 per sem; nonres—undergrad $300 per sem, grad—$240 per sem
Courses: Ceramics, Drawing, Graphic Arts, History of Art & Archaeology, Jewelry, Lettering, Painting, Sculpture, Textile Design
Adult Hobby Classes: Enrl 30; tui $90 per 3 cr hr. Courses—Crafts, Drawing, Painting, under the direction of the community college
Children's Classes: Enrl 40; tui $45 per 8 wk on Sat. Courses—Ceramics, Drawing & Painting, Sculpture, under the direction of the community college
Summer School: Dean, Donald R Theophilus. Tui $63 per studio course plus lab fee $20 for term of 3 or 6 wk. Courses—Drawing, Painting, Printmaking, Sculpture, Watercolor

ARIZONA

DOUGLAS

COCHISE COLLEGE, Art Department, 85607. Tel 602-364-7943. *Head Dept* Dr Don Johnson; *Prof* Albert Kogel, MFA; *Prof* Ray Levra, MFA; *Prof* Manny Martinez, MFA; *Vis Prof* Dr Robert Massey, fresco - 1978; *Vis Prof* Ken Ferguson, ceramics - 1979. Instrs PT 11

Estab 1965, department estab 1965; pub; D & E; ent req HS dipl, GED; degrees AA; scholarships; SC 12, LC 2; enrl D 280, E 225, maj 20

Tuition: Res—undergrad $100 per sem; non-res undergrad $650 per sem; lab fees $10 each art class; campus res—room & board $600 per sem

Courses: Advertising Design, Architecture, Art Education, Art History, Calligraphy, Ceramics, Collage, Commercial Art, Constructions, Costume Design & Construction, Display, Drafting, Drawing, Fashion Arts, Goldsmithing, Graphic Arts, Graphic Design, Handicrafts, History of Art & Archaeology, Illustration, Jewelry, Lettering, Mixed Media, Occupational Therapy, Painting, Photography, Printmaking, Sculpture, Silversmithing, Teacher Training

Adult Hobby Classes: Painting

FLAGSTAFF

NORTHERN ARIZONA UNIVERSITY, Art Department, 86001. Tel 602-523-4612. *Head* Dr R Piotrowski, EdD; *Instructor* Richard Beasley, MFA; *Instructor* Dr Donald Bendel, EdD; *Instructor* Ellery Gibson, MS; *Instructor* Burce Horn, MFA; *Instructor* M Webster, MFA; *Instructor* W Williams, MFA; *Vis Prof* Kent Ibsen, glass - spring workshop

Estab 1899; pub; D & E; ent req HS dipl, ACT; degrees BFA and BS 4 yr, MA 1-2 yr; schol; SC 56, LC 19, GC 8-10; enrl D 400, E 100, non-maj 250, maj 350, grad 20

Tuition: Res—undergrad & grad $400 yr, $200 per sem; nonres nonres—undergrad & grad $1400 yr, $700 per sem; campus res available

Courses: Advertising Design, Art Education, Calligraphy, Ceramics, Commercial Art, Conceptual Art, Constructions, Goldsmithing, Graphic Arts, Graphic Design, History of Art & Archaeology, Illustration, Jewelry, Lettering, Mixed Media, Museum Staff Training, Painting, Photography, Printmaking, Sculpture, Silversmithing, Teacher Training, Textile Design

Adult Hobby Classes: Courses—Most of the above studio areas

Children's Classes: Sat morning art classes 6-15 yr

Summer School: Dir, R Piotrowski. Courses—Art History; Ceramics; Glass; Graphics; Paintings; Sculpture; Weaving

MESA

MESA COMMUNITY COLLEGE, Department of Art, 85201. Tel 602-833-1261, Ext 270. *Chmn Dept Art* Jim Garrison, MA; *Instructor* Gene Corno, MA; *Instructor* Marlan Miller, MA; *Instructor* Woodward Payne, MA; *Instructor* Darlene Swaim, MFA; *Instructor* Ned Tuhey, MA; *Instructor* Bill Voss, MA

Estab 1965; pub; D & E; ent req HS dipl or GED; degrees AA 2 yrs; schol; SC 8, LC 5; enrl D 646, E 394

Tuition: Res—$50 (10 hrs or more), $30 (9 or less); nonres—out of state $870 (10 hrs or more), $75 (7-9 hrs), $20 (1-6 hrs), out of county $615 (10 hrs or more), $55 (7-9 hrs), $20 (1-6 hrs); no campus res

Courses: Advertising Design, Art History, Commercial Art, Drawing, Graphic Design, Handicrafts, History of Art & Archaeology, Jewelry, Lettering, Painting, Sculpture

PHOENIX

GRAND CANYON COLLEGE, Art Department, 3300 W Camelback Rd, 85061. Tel 602-249-3300, Ext 227. *Chmn* James E Nelson, MAT; *Instructor* Cary Adkins, MFA; *Instructor* Penny McElhaney, BFA

Estab 1951; den; D & E; ent req HS dipl; degrees BA and BS; scholarships; SC 23, LC 10; enrl D 175, E 75, non-maj 75, maj 40

Tuition: Res—undergrad $1664 per yr, $832 per sem, $61 per hr; nonres—undergrad $2958 per yr, $1479 per sem, $61 per hr; campus residency available

Courses: Aesthetics, †Art History, Ceramics, Drawing, Jewelry, Mixed Media, Painting, Printmaking, Sculpture, Teacher Training

PHOENIX COLLEGE, Department of Art and Photography, 1202 W Thomas Rd, 85013. Tel 602-264-2492, Ext 470. *Chmn* Doug Brooks. Instrs FT 7, PT 22

Estab 1948; pub; ent req HS dipl; degrees AA 2 yrs; schol; Res—$50 per sem

Courses: Ceramics, Commercial Art, Drawing, Handicrafts, Interior Design, Painting, Photography, Sculpture, Art Appreciation, Basic Design, Mexican Arts & Crafts, Oil Painting, Watercolor

PRESCOTT

YAVAPAI COLLEGE, Art Department, 86301. Tel 602-445-7300. *Chmn* Glen L Peterson, EdD; *Instructor* Edward V Branson, MA; *Instructor* Elaine W Farrar, MA; *Instructor* Vincent N Kelly, MA; *Instructor* Richard B Marcusen, MFA

Estab 1966, dept estab 1969; pub; D & E; ent req HS dipl; degrees AA 2 yr; schol; SC 50, LC 50; enrl D 1650, E 1563

Tuition: Res—undergrad $84 per sem, 1 cr hr $21, 2-6 cr hrs $42, 7-11 cr hrs $7 per cr hr; nonres—undergrad 1-6 cr hrs $2, 7-11 cr hrs $79 per cr hr, 12 or more cr hrs $950; campus res $230, board $395 per sem

Courses: Advertising Design, Art History, Ceramics, Commercial Art, Drafting, Drawing, Sculpture, Glass, Handicrafts (batik, crafts, dyeing, macrame, spinning, stitchery, weaving, wood), Indian art survey, Stained Glass, Watercolor, Welded Metal

Adult Hobby Classes: Enrl open; tui per course. Courses offered through Retirement College

Children's Classes: Enrl open; tui $15 per course. Courses—Ceramics, Drawing, Painting

Summer School: Dir, Donald D Hiserodt. Enrl open; tui $12 per sem hr for term of 6 wks beginning June 4. Courses—Ceramics, Drawing, Jewelry, Painting, Photography, Printmaking

TEMPE

ARIZONA STATE UNIVERSITY
—Department of Art, 85281. Tel 602-965-3468. *Dean College of Fine Arts* Jules Heller, PhD; *Chmn* Leonard Lehrer, MFA

Estab 1885; pub; D & E; ent req HS dipl, ACT; degrees BA and BFA 4 yrs, MFA 3 yrs, MA 2 yrs, EdD 3 yrs; SC 80, LC 74, GC 84; enrl D 38,000, maj 1200, grad 150

Tuition: Res—undergrad $275 per sem, grad $303 per sem; nonres—undergrad $1050 per sem, grad $1155 per sem; campus res—room & board $1300

Courses: Art Education, Art History, Ceramics, Drawing, Graphic Design, Illustration, Intermedia, Jewelry, Painting, Photography, Printmaking, Sculpture, Art Criticism, Fibers, Papermaking, Watercolor, Wood Art

Summer School: Chmn, Leonard Lehrer. Tui $30 per sem hr for two 5 week sessions June through August. Courses—same as regular session

—College of Architecture, 85281. Tel 602-965-3216. *Dean* Hugh Burgess, MS(Archit); *Chmn Archit* James W Scalise, MArchit; *Chmn Design Sciences* Vaughn P Adams, PhD; *Chmn Planning* Bernard M Boyle, PhD

Estab 1885, dept estab 1949; pub; D & E; ent req HS dipl, SAT; degrees BArchit 5 yrs, BS(Design) 4 yrs, MEP 2 yrs; enrl non-maj 650, maj 280, grad 40

Tuition: Res—undergrad $275 per sem, grad $303 per sem; nonres—undergrad $1050 per sem, grad $1155 per sem; PT $30-$33 per hr; campus res—room & board $600 per yr without meals

Courses: Advertising Design, †Architecture, Drafting, Drawing, Film, Graphic Arts, Graphic Design, †Industrial Design, †Interior Design, †Landscape Architecture, Lettering, Mixed Media, Photography, Restoration & Conservation, Video, Architectural History

Summer School: Courses—pre-professional courses primarily in Design, Graphics, History, Sketching and Rendering

THATCHER

EASTERN ARIZONA COLLEGE, 85552. Tel 602-428-1133, Ext 47. *Head* Justin Fairbanks, MFA; *Instructor* David Meyer, BFA. Instrs PT 9

Estab 1888, dept estab 1946; pub; D & E; ent req HS dipl or GED; degrees AA 2 yrs; scholarships; SC 25, LC 3; enrl D 105, E 202, maj 12

Tuition: Res—undergrad $170 per yr, $85 per sem, $29 PT, $19 per hr; nonres—undergrad $1956 per yr, $978 per sem, $196 per month; campus res—room & board $1374 per yr, $687 per sem

Courses: Advertising Design, Art History, Ceramics, Commercial Art, Drafting, Drawing, Handicrafts, Illustration, Jewelry, Lettering, Painting, Photography, Sculpture, Silversmithing, Lapidary, Weaving

TUCSON

TUCSON MUSEUM OF ART SCHOOL, 179 N Main Ave, 85705. Tel 602-622-1327. *Dir* David Jones. Instrs PT 21

Estab 1924; pvt; D & E; ent req none; schol; SC 42, LC 2; enrl D & E 1139

Tuition: Varies per course; no campus res

Courses: Ceramics, Drawing, Painting, Photography, Printmaking, Sculpture, Textile Design, Papermaking, Stained Glass

Children's Classes: Courses—Ceramics, Drawing, Painting, Photography, Primary art

Summer School: Enrl 300

UNIVERSITY OF ARIZONA, Department of Art, College of Fine Arts, 85721. Tel 602-884-1251. *Dept Head* Howard Conant, EdD; *Coordr Painting & Drawing* Robert W McMillan, PhD; *Coordr Three-Dimentional Areas* Michael Croft, MFA; *Coordr Photography* Harold Jones, MFA; *Coordr Art History* Robert M Quinn, PhD; *Coordr Art Educ* Jean C Rush, PhD; *Coordr Graphic Design* Margaret Doogan, MA; *Coordr Printmaking* Lynn Schroeder, MFA

Estab 1891, dept estab 1927; pub; D; ent req HS dipl, ACT; degrees BFA(Studio), BFA(Art Educ) and BA(Art History) 4 yrs, MFA(Studio) and MA(Art History or Art Educ) 2-3 yrs; scholarships; SC 30, LC 21, GC 32; enrl D 3094, maj 570, grad 75

Tuition: Res—undergrad $275 per sem, grad $303 per sem; nonres—undergrad $775 tui plus $275 reg per sem, grad $853 tui plus $303 reg per sem; campus res—room & board $300 per sem

Courses: Art Education, Art History, Ceramics, Drawing, Graphic Arts, Painting, Photography, Printmaking, Sculpture, Silversmithing, Fibers, Metalwork, Wood Design

Summer School: Two sessions offered. Request catalog (available in April) by writing to: Summer Session Office, University of Arizona, Tucson, AZ 85721

ARKANSAS

ARKADELPHIA

QUACHITA BAPTIST UNIVERSITY, Department of Art,* School of Arts and Sciences, 410 Ouachita St, 71923. Tel 501-246-4531, Ext 196. *Chmn* Phares Raybon, MA; *Primary Faculty* Betty Berry, MSE
Estab 1886, dept estab 1934; den; D; ent req HS dipl, ACT; degrees BA, BSE, BS and BME 4 yr, MSE and MME 1 yr; scholarship; SC 11, LC 2
Tuition: Res—$860 per sem, under 8 hrs $50 per sem hr; nonres—18 hrs and over, $50 per sem hr
Courses: †Advertising Design, Aesthetics, †Art Education, Art History, Ceramics, Commercial Art, Costume Design & Construction, Graphic Arts, Handicrafts, History of Art & Archaeology, Illustration, Interior Design, Lettering, Painting, Photography, Sculpture, Teacher Training, †Theatre Arts, Macrame, Tole, Weaving
Summer School: Dir, Mike Arrington. Enrl 550; tui $40 sem hr; two terms of 5 wks beginning June 5

CLARKSVILLE

COLLEGE OF THE OZARKS, Department of Art, Ward and College St, 72830. Tel 501-754-3431. *Head Dept* Lyle Ward, MFA
Estab 1836, dept estab 1952; den; D; ent req HS dipl, ACT; degrees BA and BS 4 yr; schol; SC 9, LC 2; enrl D 83, nonmaj 8, maj 17
Tuition: Res & nonres—undergrad $1110 yr; campus res—room & board $1095
Courses: Art Education, Art History, Ceramics, Drawing, Painting, Art Appreciation
Summer School: Dir, Lyle Ward. Workshop in Art Education and Painting

COLLEGE CITY

SOUTHERN BAPTIST COLLEGE, Dept of Art,* 72476. Tel 501-886-6741. *Chmn* Jerry Gibbons, MS
Den; D & E; scholarships
Tuition: Res—$1350 per yr; campus residence available
Courses: Art Education, Ceramics, Conceptual Art, Drawing, Graphic Design, Painting, Theatre Arts
Summer School: Dir, Dr Jerrol Swain. Tui $560 for 12-16 hrs, $37.50 for less than 12 hrs, $32.50 for each additional hr over 16 hrs

CONWAY

UNIVERSITY OF CENTRAL ARKANSAS, Art Department, 72032. Tel 501-329-2931, Ext 224. *Head Dept* Dr Jerry D Poole. Instrs FT 6
Estab 1908; pub; ent req HS dipl; degrees 4 yr; SC 14, LC 4
Tuition: Campus residence available
Courses: Art History, Ceramics, Commercial Art, Drawing, Handicrafts, Illustration, Lettering, Painting, Printmaking, Sculpture, Teacher Training, Advanced Design, Art Appreciation, Color & Design,
Summer School: Courses offered

FAYETTEVILLE

UNIVERSITY OF ARKANSAS, Art Department, FA 116, 72701. Tel 501-575-5202. *Chmn Dept* Neppie Conner, MA; *Prof* Lothar Krueger, MS; *Assoc Prof* Subrata Lahiri, MFA; *Assoc Prof* Thomas D Turpin, MFA; *Asst Prof* Edward C Bernstein, MFA; *Asst Prof* Walter D Curtis, MFA; *Asst Prof* Dominic Ricciotti, PhD; *Asst Prof* Robert F Ross, MFA; *Asst Prof* John W Smith, EdD
Estab 1871; pub; D & E; ent req HS dipl, ent exam, GED; degrees MFA 2 1 2 yrs and BA 4 yrs; scholarships; SC 34, LC 16, GC 20; enrl D 13,500, non-maj 650, maj 200, grad 20
Tuition: Res—undergrad and grad $600 per yr, $300 per sem, $30 per cr hr; nonres —undergrad and grad $1230 per yr, $615 per sem, $62 per cr hr; registration and tui fees waived for students 60 yrs or older; campus res—room & board $1300-$1410
Courses: Art Education, Art History, Calligraphy, Ceramics, Constructions, Drawing, Graphic Arts, Jewelry, Painting, Photography, Printmaking, Sculpture
Adult Hobby Classes: Ceramics, Painting, Sculpture
Summer School: Courses offered

HARRISON

NORTH ARKANSAS COMMUNITY COLLEGE, Art Department, Pioneer Ridge, 72601. Tel 501-743-3000, Ext 48. *Prof* Coleman Wheeler, MEd
Estab 1974, dept estab 1975; pub; D & E; ent req HS dipl; degrees AA 2 yrs; SC 7, LC 1; enrl in art dept D 80, E 30-40, non-maj 45, maj 35
Tuition: Res $11 per cr hr, non-res $13 per cr hr
Courses: Advertising Design, Aesthetics, Architecture, Art Education, Art History, Calligraphy, Ceramics, Collage, Commercial Art, Constructions, Costume Design & Construction, Display, Drafting, Drawing, Fashion Arts, Film, Graphic Arts, Graphic Design, Handicrafts, History of Art & Archaeology, Illustration, Intermedia, Interior Design, Jewelry, Landscape Architecture, Lettering, Mixed Media, Occupational Therapy, Painting, Photography, Printmaking, Sculpture, Stage Design, Teacher Training, Textile Design, Theatre Arts, Video
Adult Hobby Classes: Various courses offered each sem through Continuing Education Program
Summer School: Enrl 20-30; tui $30-$35 for term of 6-8 wks beginning June 1. Courses —open; Art Workshop on Buffalo National River

HELENA

PHILLIPS COUNTY COMMUNITY COLLEGE, Department of English and Fine Arts,* Box 785, 72342. Tel 501-338-6474. *Chmn* Sally Nelson
Estab 1966; pub; D & E; ent req HS dipl, ent exam, GED; degrees AA and AAS 2 yr; scholarships; SC 8, LC 1; enrl 55
Tuition: Res—$280 per yr; nonres—$520 per yr
Courses: Ceramics, Drafting, Drawing, History of Art & Archaeology, Painting
Summer School: Tui same. 5 wk term beginning May 28

LITTLE ROCK

ARKANSAS ARTS CENTER, Mac Arthur Park, PO Box 2137, 72203. Tel 501-372-4000. *Exec Dir* Townsend Wolfe; *Dir of Educ* Anne Michael Pappas, MA; *Dir of Theatre* Bradley Anderson, BA; *Instructor* Manolo Agullo; *Instructor* David Anhalt, BS; *Instructor* Rosemary Fisher, Dipl; *Instructor* Antonio Mesa; *Instructor* B J Moses, BA; *Instructor* Susan Purvis, BA; *Instructor* Cathryn Rounsavall, MFA; *Instructor* Fred Wilson, MA. Instrs FT 4, PT 27
Estab 1960, dept estab 1965; pub; D & E; ent req open to anyone age 3 through adult; schol; SC 62, LC 3; enrl D 350, E 300 children & adults
Tuition: 12 wk course for adults $60, 12 wk course for children $33, dance classes $25 per month
Courses: Art History, Calligraphy, Drawing, Jewelry, Painting, Photography, Printmaking, Sculpture, Theatre Arts, Acting, Ballet, Creative Drama, Disco, Enameling, Glassblowing, Jazz, Movement, Pottery, Stage Lighting, Stained Glass, Woodworking, Yoga
Summer School: Dir Educ, Anne Michael Pappas. Tui for 8 wk term $42 for adults, $25 for children, dance classes $25 per month. Courses—same as regular session

PHILANDER SMITH COLLEGE, Department of Art,* 812 W 13th St, 72203. Tel 501-375-9845. *Chmn* Ralph L Odom
Estab 1952; pvt; degrees BA 4 yr (in cooperation with the Arkansas Arts Center); scholarships; SC 12, LC 4; enrl 600, maj 5, others 35
Tuition: $475 for 36 weeks
Courses: Art History, Drawing, Painting, Printmaking, Sculpture, Afro-American Art History, Art Appreciation, Arts & Crafts, Basic Design
Summer School: Dir, Dr Crawford Mims

UNIVERSITY OF ARKANSAS AT LITTLE ROCK, Department of Art, 32nd and University Sts, 72204. Tel 501-565-7531, Ext 323. Instrs FT 10, PT 5
Estab 1928; pub; D & E; ent req HS grad; degrees BA 4 yr, MA(studio), MA(art history); schol; SC, LC; enrl 5000
Courses: Art Education, Art History, Commercial Art, Drawing, Handicrafts, Painting, Printmaking, Sculpture, Design, Pottery

MAGNOLIA

SOUTHERN ARKANSAS UNIVERSITY, Department of Fine Arts,* Magnolia Branch, Jackson & Southern University, 71753. Tel 501-234-5120. *Chmn* Robert G Campbell; *Asst Prof* Fred Henry, MFA; *Asst Prof* Dianne O'Hern, MA
Estab 1909; pub; D & E; ent req HS dipl; degrees BA and BSE 4 yr; scholarships; SC 18, LC 4; enrl D 240, non-maj 190, maj 50
Tuition: Res—undergrad $470 per yr; nonres—undergrad $740 per yr
Courses: Art Education, Art History, Ceramics, Drawing, Graphic Arts, Painting, Printmaking, Sculpture, Architecture

PINE BLUFF

SOUTHEAST ARKANSAS ARTS AND SCIENCE CENTER, Little Firehouse Studio,* Civic Center, 200 E Eighth, 71601. Tel 501-536-3375. *Dir* Joseph L Kagle
Estab 1966; pvt; D & E; No degrees granted; SC 14, LC 1; enrl D 200, E 250
Tuition: $15-$75 per course; no campus res
Courses: Art Education, Art History, Ceramics, Drawing, Graphic Arts, Jewelry, Painting, Photography, Printmaking, Theatre Arts, Raku Pottery
Children's Classes: Enrl 15; tui $15 per course. Courses—Crafts, ·Drawing, Mixed Media, Painting, Pottery, Weaving. Special workshops with guest artists

RUSSELLVILLE

ARKANSAS TECH UNIVERSITY, Department of Art, 72801. Tel 501-968-0244. *Head Dept* Ed Wilwers, MFA; *Asst Prof* Gary Barnes, MA; *Asst Prof* Ron Reynolds, MS; *Instructor* Lance Eggleston
Estab 1909; pub; D & E; ent req HS dipl; degrees BA and BFA 4 yr; schol; SC 28, LC 5, GC 1; enrl D 200, nonmaj 130, maj 75
Tuition: Res—undergrad $245 per sem, $21 per cr hr, grad $25 per cr hr; nonres nonres —undergrad $420 per sem, $36 per cr hr, grad $42.50 per cr hr; no campus res
Courses: Advertising Design, Aesthetics, Architecture, Art Education, Art History, Ceramics, Commercial Art, Conceptual Art, Display, Drafting, Drawing, Graphic Arts, Graphic Design, Illustration, Industrial Design, Lettering, Painting, Printmaking, Teacher Training, Packaging Design
Summer School: Head Dept, Ed Wilwers. Enrl 30-50; tui res—$90, nonres—$155; term of 6 wk beginning June 5 and July 10. Courses—Art Education, Art History, Design, Drawing, Painting

SEARCY

HARDING UNIVERSITY, Department of Art, Box 938, 72143. Tel 501-268-6161, Ext 426. *Chmn Dept* Don D Robinson, MA; *Prof* Elizabeth Mason, MA; *Assoc Prof* Faye Doran, EdD; *Asst Prof* Paul Pitt, MA; *Instructor* Stanley Green, BSE; *Instructor* John Keller, MA; *Instructor* James La Rue, MEd
Estab 1924; pvt; D; ent req HS dipl, ACT; degrees BA and BS 4 yrs, MEd 5-6 yrs; schol; SC 27, LC 9, GC 7; enrl D 90, non-maj 15, maj 90
Tuition: $65 per sem hr; campus res—room & board $3600 per yr
Courses: Advertising Design, Aesthetics, Art Education, Art History, Ceramics, Commercial Art, Constructions, Drafting, Drawing, Goldsmithing, Graphic Arts, Graphic Design, Handicrafts, History of Art & Archaeology, Illustration, Jewelry, Lettering, Mixed Media, Painting, Printmaking, Sculpture, Silversmithing
Summer School: Dir, Dr Jimmy Carr. Enrl 700; tui $65 per sem hr for 10 wk term beginning June 9. Courses—vary depending upon the demand, usually Art History, Ceramics, Drawing, Painting, Watercolor

SILOAM SPRINGS

JOHN BROWN UNIVERSITY, Art Department, 72761. Tel 501-524-3131. *Head Dept* Doris I Brookhart, MFA; *Instructor* Darrell Hill, BFA
Estab 1919; pvt; D; ent req HS grad; SC 9, LC 3
Tuition: $2100 yr, $1050 per sem, $90 per sem hr; campus res—room & board $1500
Courses: Art Education, Art History, Commercial Art, Drawing, Illustration, Painting, Teacher Training, Design and Color, Crafts (copper tooling, enameling, jewelry, macrame, mosaic, pottery, weaving)

STATE UNIVERSITY

ARKANSAS STATE UNIVERSITY, Department of Art, Drawer AAAA, 72467. Tel 501-972-3050. *Chmn Dept* Karl Richards, PhD; *Prof* Evan Lindquist, MFA; *Assoc Prof* T R Baker, DEd; *Assoc Prof* R E Mitchell, MFA; *Asst Prof* Tom Chaffee, MFA; *Asst Prof* Donn Hedman, MFA; *Asst Prof* Charlott Jones, PhD; *Asst Prof* John Keech, MFA. Instrs FT 14
Estab 1909, dept estab 1938; pub; D & E; ent req HS dipl; degrees BFA, BSE and BS 4 yrs, MA; scholarships; SC 33, LC 10, GC 4; enrl D 800, E 100, non-maj 800, maj 180, grad 3
Tuition: Res—$300 per sem, $25 per sem hr; nonres—$475 per sem, $40 per sem hr; campus res—room & board $820 per yr
Courses: †Advertising Design, Aesthetics, †Art Education, Art History, Calligraphy, †Ceramics, †Commercial Art, Constructions, Drawing, †Graphic Arts, †Graphic Design, History of Art & Archaeology, †Illustration, †Jewelry, Lettering, †Painting, †Printmaking, †Sculpture, †Silversmithing, Stage Design, †Teacher Training, Theatre Arts
Adult Hobby Classes: Enrl 100; tui $30 per sem hr. Courses—Ceramics, Jewelry, Painting, Printmaking
Summer School: Tui res $140, nonres $210 for term of 5 wks beginning June 5 and July 10. Courses—Art Appreciation, Art Education, Art History, Commercial Art, Drawing, Painting, Selected Studio Courses, Watercolor

CALIFORNIA

APTOS

CABRILLO COLLEGE, Visual Arts Division, 6500 Sequel Dr, 95003. Tel 408-425-6464. *Chmn* David J McGuire. Instrs FT 12, PT 8
Estab 1959; pub; D & E; ent req HS dipl; degrees AA 2 yr; SC 46, LC 7
Courses: Ceramics, Drawing, Graphic Arts, Graphic Design, Handicrafts, History of Art & Archaeology, Jewelry, Painting, Photography, Sculpture, Textile Design
Summer School: Courses offered

ARCATA

HUMBOLDT STATE UNIVERSITY, Art Department,* 95521. Tel 707-826-3625. *Chmn* R E Dickerson
Estab 1913; pub; D & E; degrees BA 4 yr, BA with credential 5 yr; scholarships; SC 35, LC 11, GC 11
Tuition: Res—$1800 per yr; campus residence available
Courses: Ceramics, Graphic Design, Jewelry, Painting, Photography, Printmaking, Sculpture, Teacher Training, Design, Metalsmithing
Children's Classes: Enrl 10, art 12
Summer School: Enrl 800; tui $25 per unit, 6 wk term beginning June 22

AZUSA

AZUSA PACIFIC COLLEGE, Art Dept, Alosta at Citrus Ave, 91702. Tel 213-969-3434. *Chmn Dept* Robert Bullock, MA
Estab 1915, dept estab 1974; den; D & E; ent req HS dipl, state test; degrees BA(Art) 4 yrs; scholarships; SC 21, LC 3; enrl E 80, non-maj 120, maj 22
Tuition: $1400 per sem; campus res—room & board $4500
Courses: Advertising Design, †Art Education, Art History, †Ceramics, Drawing, Graphic Arts, Illustration, †Painting, Printmaking, Teacher Training

CITRUS COMMUNITY COLLEGE, Art Department, 18824 Foothill Blvd, 91702. Tel 213-335-0521. *Art Dept Chmn* Robert Hallett, MA; *Instr* Robert Bullock, MA; *Instr* Adney Gass, MA; *Instr* Robert Jenkins, MA; *Instr* Carolyn Ramos, MA
Estab 1915; pub; D & E; ent req HS dipl; degrees AA and AS 2 yrs; scholarships; SC 26, LC 7; enrl D 400, E 175, non-maj 400, maj 175
Tuition: Res $60 per yr, non-res $600 per yr

Courses: Advertising Design, Art History, Calligraphy, Ceramics, Collage, Commercial Art, Drawing, Graphic Arts, History of Art & Archaeology, Interior Design, Jewelry, Lettering, Mixed Media, Painting, Photography, Printmaking
Children's Classes: Ceramics, Painting
Summer School: Dir, Robert Hallet. Enrl 150; tui $20 for term of 6 wks beginning June 20. Courses—Art History, Ceramics, Drawing, Painting

BAKERSFIELD

BAKERSFIELD COLLEGE, Art Department,* 1801 Panorama Dr, 93305. Tel 805-395-4011. *Chmn* Albert Naso
Estab 1913; pub; D & E; ent req ent exam, open door policy; degrees AA 2 yr; SC 16, LC 4; enrl D 6000, maj 150-200
Tuition: None
Courses: Architecture, Ceramics, Commercial Art, Drafting, Drawing, Graphic Arts, History of Art & Archaeology, Illustration, Jewelry, Lettering, Painting, Photography, Sculpture, Stage Design, Theatre Arts, Glassblowing
Adult Hobby Classes: Enrl 100-150. Courses—Ceramics, Painting
Summer School: Dir, Ron McMasters. For term of 6 wks beginning June. Courses—Ceramics, Design, Drawing, Figure Drawing, Photography

BELMONT

COLLEGE OF NOTRE DAME, Department of Art, 1400 Ralston Ave, 94002. Tel 415-593-1601. *Chmn* Robert David Ramsey. Instrs FT 2, PT 6
Estab 1951; den; D & E; ent req HS dipl, ent exam; degrees BA 3 1 2-4 yrs, BFA, MAT; scholarships; SC 18, LC 12; enrl D 200, E 70, maj 50
Courses: Art Education, Ceramics, Drawing, History of Art & Archaeology, Interior Design, Painting, Photography, Sculpture, Anatomical Drawing, Color, Composition, Etching, Gallery Techniques, Lithography, Silk Screen, Two and Three-Dimensional Design, Weaving
Summer School: Dir, Mr Gary Murdough. Upper division courses as in regular program plus special art education workshops; 6 wk term

BERKELEY

UNIVERSITY OF CALIFORNIA, BERKELEY, Department of Art,* College of Letters and Science, 238 Kroeber Hall, 94720. Tel 415-642-2582, Art Dept. *Assoc Prof* Jerrold Ballaine, MFA
Estab 1868; pub; D; ent req undergrad ent req same as for ent to Univ; degrees BA, MA, MFA, BA, MA, PhD (History of Art); scholarships; SC approx 20, LC approx 60
Tuition: Res—undergrad $243.50 per quarter, grad $263.50 per quarter; nonres—undergrad $1043.50 per quarter, grad $1063.50 per quarter; campus res available
Courses: Art History, Ceramics, Drawing, Painting, Printmaking, Sculpture

CARMEL

CARMEL ART INSTITUTE, Monte Verde and Ocean Ave, PO Box 9, 93921. Tel 408-624-9951. *Pres* John Cunningham
Estab 1938, inc 1955; pvt; D; degrees Certificate of Completion, 4 yr course for Fine Arts, objective painter; enrl D 20
Tuition: $125 per month
Courses: Aesthetics, Painting, Anatomy, Design, Etching, Lithography
Summer School: Dir, John Cunningham. Enrl 20; tui $200 for 6 wks

CARSON

CALIFORNIA STATE UNIVERSITY, DOMINGUEZ HILLS, School of Humanities & Fine Arts,* 1000 E Victoria St, 90747. Tel 213-515-3300. *Chmn* S Glen White
Estab 1965; pub; D & E; ent req upper one-third of HS class; degrees BA 4 yr; SC 35, LC 25; enrl maj 130
Tuition: Res—undergrad 1-6 units, $40 per qt, grad $50 per qt; nonres—undergrad 15 units or less $40 per unit, grad 15 units or more $600, max charge per academic yr $1800; no campus res
Courses: Aesthetics, Drawing, History of Art & Archaeology, Painting, Sculpture, Teacher Training, Design, Graphics

CHICO

CALIFORNIA STATE UNIVERSITY, CHICO, Art Dept, 95929. Tel 916-895-5331, 895-5218. *Chmn* Richard Hornaday
Estab 1887; pvt; D & E; ent req ent exam and test scores; degrees BA 4 yr, MA 1 1 2 yr minimum; SC 39, LC 29, GC 29; enrl nonmaj & maj 1704, grad 59
Tuition: Res—$85.50 per sem for less than 6 cr hrs, $100.50 per sem for over 6 cr hrs; nonres—same as resident plus $52.50 additional fee for each sem unit up to 15 units, $787.50 for 15 units or more
Courses: Aesthetics, Art History, †Ceramics, †Drawing, †Painting, †Printmaking, †Sculpture, †Teacher Training, Glass, Weaving
Summer School: Chmn, Richard Hornaday. Courses—same as above

CLAREMONT

PITZER COLLEGE, Department of Art,* 1050 N Mills Ave, 91711. Tel 714-621-8129. *Prof Art* C H Hertel
Estab 1964; pvt; D; ent req HS dipl, various criteria, apply Dir of Admis; degrees BA 4 yr; scholarships; SC 8, LC 6; enrl Sept-June maj 19, grad 10 (Claremont Grad School)
Tuition: Res—$7110 (including campus res)
Courses: Aesthetics, Ceramics, Drawing, Graphic Arts, History of Art & Archaeology, Painting, Photography, Sculpture, Environments, Weaving

POMONA COLLEGE, Art Department, College & E Bonita Ave, 91711. Tel 714-626-6594, Ext 2221. *Chmn Dept* Gerald M Ackerman, PhD; *Prof* Carl Benjamin, MFA; *Prof* Charles Daugherty, MFA; *Prof* Norman Hines, MFA; *Assoc Prof* David Steadman, PhD; *Asst Prof* Rita Dibert, MFA; *Asst Prof* Judson Emerick, PhD
Estab 1889; pvt; D; ent req HS dipl; degrees BA 4 yrs; schol; SC 15, LC 25; enrl D 330 maj 30
Tuition: Res—undergrad $2500 per sem, $3500 with room & board
Courses: †Art History, †Ceramics, †Drawing, Graphic Design, Sculpture

SCRIPPS COLLEGE, Art Department, Lang Art Bldg, Ninth at Columbia, 91711. Tel 714-621-8000, Ext 2973. *Chmn Dept* Alan Blizzard, PhD; *Prof* Aldo Casanova, PhD; *Prof* Paul Darrow, MFA; *Prof* James Fuller, MA; *Prof* Paul Soldner, MFA; *Assoc Prof* Neda Al-Hilali, MFA
Estab 1928, dept estab 1933; pub; D; ent req HS dipl; degrees BA; schol; enrl D 580, non-maj 480, maj 100
Tuition: Res—$6200 yr
Courses: Architecture, Art History, Ceramics, Drawing, Film, History of Art & Archaeology, Painting, Photography, Printmaking, Sculpture, Fabrics, Watercolor

COLUMBIA

COLUMBIA JUNIOR COLLEGE, Department of Physical Creative & Performing Arts,* PO Box 1849, 95310. Tel 209-532-3141. *Chmn Dept* David Purdy, MA
Estab 1968; pub; D & E; ent req HS dipl or over 18 yrs old; degrees AA 2 yrs; SC 50, LC 4; enrl D 100, E 75, non-maj 90, maj 10
Tuition: None; no campus res
Courses: Art History, Calligraphy, Ceramics, Costume Design & Construction, Drawing, Jewelry, Lettering, Painting, Photography, Printmaking, Sculpture, Silversmithing
Summer School: Dir, C H Palmer. Courses—Ceramics, Watercolor

COMPTON

COMPTON COMMUNITY COLLEGE, Art Department, 1111 E Artesia Blvd, 90221. Tel 213-635-8081, Ext 283. *Assoc Prof* Van E Slater. Instrs FT 1, PT 5
Estab 1929; pub; D & E; ent req HS dipl, 21 yrs of age; degrees AA 2 yr; schol; SC 16, LC 6; enrl D 3500, E 2000, maj 18
Courses: Advertising Design, Drafting, Drawing, Handicrafts, History of Art & Archaeology, Lettering, Painting, Photography, Theatre Arts, Afro-American Art, Art Appreciation, Showcard Writing
Summer School: Courses—Art Appreciation

CORONA DEL MAR

BRANDT PAINTING WORKSHOPS, 405 Goldenrod Ave, 92625. Tel 714-675-0093. *Co-Dir* Rex Brandt, BA; *Co-Dir* Joan Irving
Estab 1946; pvt; D; ent req grad degree in art or equivalent; schol; SC 3; enrl D 145
Tuition: 11 day session $175; no campus res. Summer school only
Courses: Painting

CORONADO

CORONADO SCHOOL OF FINE ARTS, 176 C Ave, PO Box 156, 92118. *Dir* Monty Lewis. Instrs FT D 2, E 1, PT 6
Estab 1944; pvt; degrees dipl 3-4 yr; SC, LC; enrl D 50, E 25
Tuition: 143 per 4 wks, PT $93 per 4 wks. Approved for veterans and foreign students
Courses: Advertising Design, Art History, Commercial Art, Graphic Arts, Illustration, Painting, Sculpture, Fine Arts, Mural Decoration
Children's Classes: Enrl 15; tui $25 for Sat morning classes
Summer School: Dir, Monty Lewis. Enrl 75; tui $143 per 4 wk; Watercolor Seminar $85 per 4 wk, $143 per 8 wk

COSTA MESA

ORANGE COAST COLLEGE, Division of Fine Arts,* 2701 Fairview, 92626. Tel 714-556-5629 (Fine Arts Dept). *Chmn Dept* Edward R Baker
Estab 1946; pub; D & E; ent req ent exam; degrees AA 2 yr; scholarships; SC 288, LC 52; enrl D 1500, E 1400, maj 2397
Tuition: None; no campus res
Courses: Advertising Design, Architecture, Art Education, Ceramics, Commercial Art, Display, Drafting, Basic Exhibition Design, Weaving Fibers
Adult Hobby Classes: Courses—Furniture refinishing
Summer School: Eight wk session. Courses—same as regular session

CUPERTINO

DE ANZA COLLEGE, Art Department, Fine Arts Division, 21250 Stevens Creek Blvd, 95014. Tel 408-996-4832. *Dean of Fine Arts* William W F Cleveland; *Instructor* Gerald Eknoian; *Instructor* Gaylord Forbes; *Instructor* Joyce Hendry; *Instructor* Sal Pecoraro; *Instructor* Lillian Quirke; *Instructor* Lee Tacang; *Instructor* Charles Walker
Estab 1967, dept estab 1967; pub; D & E; ent req 18 yrs of age; degrees AA 2 yrs; scholarships
Courses: Aesthetics, Art History, Calligraphy, Ceramics, Costume Design & Construction, Drafting, Drawing, Film, Graphic Arts, Graphic Design, Handicrafts, Interior Design, Jewelry, Lettering, Painting, Photography, Printmaking, Sculpture, Silversmithing, Stage Design, Textile Design, Theatre Arts, Video, Dye, Spinning, Weaving, Wood
Adult Hobby Classes: Tui $10 per class. Courses—Bronze Casting, Calligraphy, Museum Tours, Quilting
Summer School: Dean, William W F Cleveland. Courses—Drawing, Jewelry, Painting, Printmaking, Textile Class

CYPRESS

CYPRESS COLLEGE, Fine Arts Division, 9200 Valley View St, 90630. Tel 714-826-2220, Ext 142. *Chairperson* Lester Johnson, MA
Estab 1966; pub; D & E; ent req HS dipl; degrees AA 2 yrs; enrl D 12,100
Tuition: 47.50 per unit; no campus res
Courses: Advertising Design, Art History, Ceramics, Costume Design & Construction, Drawing, Film, History of Art & Archaeology, Jewelry, Painting, Printmaking, Sculpture, Stage Design, Textile Design, Theatre Arts
Adult Hobby Classes: Adults may take any classes offered both day and extended; also offer adult education classes
Summer School: Extended Day Coordinator, Dr Bonnie Fouste

DAVIS

UNIVERSITY OF CALIFORNIA, DAVIS, Art Department, College of Letters and Science, 95616. Tel 916-752-0105. *Head Dept* Richard D Cramer. Instrs FT 17
Estab 1952; pub; D; degrees BA 4 yrs, MA, MFA; scholarships; SC 28, LC 35; enrl maj 130, others 1000
Tuition: Res $229; nonres $635 per quarter
Courses: Architecture, Art History, Ceramics, Drawing, Film, Graphic Arts, Painting, Photography, Sculpture

EL CAJON

GROSSMONT COLLEGE, Art Department, Div of Fine Arts, 8800 Grossmont College Dr, 92020. Tel 714-465-1700. Instrs FT 11
Estab 1961; pub; D & E; ent req none; degrees AA; schol; SC 22, LC 1; enrl total 1000
Tuition: None; no campus res
Courses: Ceramics, Drawing, Painting, Photography, Sculpture, Art History, Composition, Primitive Art
Summer School: Courses—Ceramics, Drawing, Photography

EUREKA

COLLEGE OF THE REDWOODS, Art Department, 95501. Tel 707-443-8411. Instrs FT 5 PT 8
Estab 1964; pub; D & E; ent req HS grad; degrees AA 2 yrs; scholarships; SC 15, LC 3 per quarter; enrl 8330, maj 160
Courses: Ceramics, Commercial Art, Drafting, Drawing, Graphic Arts, History of Art & Archaeology, Jewelry, Lettering, Painting, Photography, Sculpture, Art Fundamentals, Fabrics
Summer School: Tui free. Courses to be announced

FRESNO

CALIFORNIA STATE UNIVERSITY, FRESNO, Art Department, Maple & Shaw Aves, 93740. Tel 209-487-2516. *Chmn* Joyce Aiken, MA; *Prof* Terry Allen; *Prof* Charles Gaines; *Prof* Roger Bolomey, MA; *Prof* Frank Laury, MA; *Prof* Norman Lockwood, MFA; *Prof* Mary Maughelli, MA; *Prof* Bill Minschey, MFA; *Prof* Michael Opper, PhD; *Prof* Gayle Smalley, MFA; *Assoc Prof* Larry Anderson, MA; *Assoc Prof* Richard Delaney, MA; *Assoc Prof* Tom McDougall, MA; *Asst Prof* Susan Herman, MA; *Asst Prof* Gina Strumwasser, PhD
Estab 1911, dept estab 1915; pub; D; ent req HS dipl, SAT or ACT; degrees BA 4 yrs, MA 2 yrs; schol; SC 45, LC 9, GC 4; enrl 1000
Tuition: Res—undergrad and grad $109; non-res nonres—undergrad $900; campus residence available
Courses: Art Education, Art History, Calligraphy, Ceramics, Drawing, Film, Goldsmithing, Graphic Design, Handicrafts, Jewelry, Museum Staff Training, Painting, Photography, Printmaking, Sculpture, Silversmithing, Teacher Training, Textile Design
Adult Hobby Classes: Tui $35 unit. Courses—various
Summer School: Tui $35 unit for term of 6 wks beginning June 15. Courses—various, mainly Ceramics

FRESNO CITY COLLEGE, Art Department, 1101 E University Ave, 93741. Tel 209-442-4600. *Dean* Franz Weinschenk, MA; *Chmn* Leon H Osborne, MA; *Instr* Dean C Draper, MA; *Instr* Rodney Krueger, MA; *Instr* Kenneth Owens, MA; *Instr* Kent Steadman, MFA; *Instr* Walter Witt, MFA; *Instr* Kathy Wosika, MA
Estab 1910, dept estab 1955; pub; D & E; ent req none, open door policy; degrees AA 2 yrs; SC 13, LC 3; enrl D 705, E 340
Tuition: $6 membership fee per sem (6 units or more); nonres $685 per sem (16 units or more)
Courses: Art History, Ceramics, Drawing, Handicrafts, Painting, Printmaking, Sculpture, Art Appreciation
Summer School: Dean, Franz Weinschenk. Enrl 200; tui res free, non-res $46 per unit for term of 6 wks beginning June. Courses—all art courses

FULLERTON

CALIFORNIA STATE UNIVERSITY, FULLERTON, Art Department, 92634. Tel 714-773-3471. *Dean Sch Arts* Jerry Samuelson, MA; *Chmn Dept* Don Lagerberg, MA
Estab 1957, dept estab 1959; pub; D & E; ent req HS dipl, SAT or ACT; degrees BA 4 yrs, MA 1 yr; SC 62, LC 27, GC 12; enrl grad 95, undergrad 733
Tuition: Res—undergrad & grad $93 for 0-6 units, $108 for 7 or more units; nonres—undergrad & grad $60 per units plus $93 or $108; no campus res
Courses: Art Education, Art History, Ceramics, Display, Drawing, Goldsmithing, Graphic Arts, Graphic Design, Illustration, Jewelry, Lettering, Museum Staff Training, Painting, Photography, Printmaking, Sculpture, Silversmithing, Teacher Training, Textile Design, Weaving, Woodworking

FULLERTON COLLEGE, Fine Arts and Art Department,* 321 E Chapman Ave, 92634. Tel 714-871-8000. *Chmn* Kenneth W Helvey
Estab 1913; pub; D & E; ent req HS dipl, ent exam; degrees AA 2 yr; scholarships
Tuition: Nonres—undergrad $710.50; no campus res
Courses: Advertising Design, Aesthetics, Architecture, Art Education, Ceramics, Commercial Art, Costume Design & Construction, Drafting, Drawing, Fashion Arts, Graphic Arts, Graphic Design, Handicrafts, History of Art & Archaeology, Illustration, Industrial Design, Jewelry, Landscape Architecture, Lettering, Painting, Photography, Sculpture, Stage Design, Teacher Training, Textile Design, Theatre Arts

GILROY

GAVILAN COLLEGE, Art Department, 5055 Santa Therese Blvd, 95020. *Chmn Humanities Div* Kent Child. Instrs FT 2, PT 6
Estab 1919; pub; D & E; ent req HS dipl or 18 yrs of age; degrees AA 2 yrs; SC 15, LC 2; enrl D 150, E 75, maj 30
Tuition: None to res; no campus res
Courses: Ceramics, Drafting, Drawing, Graphic Arts, Jewelry, Painting, Photography, Sculpture, Teacher Training, Theatre Arts, History of Art & Architecture
Summer School: Courses—Ceramics, Drawing, Painting

GLENDALE

GLENDALE COLLEGE, Department of Fine Arts, 1500 N Verdugo Rd, 91208. Tel 213-240-1000. *Chmn Dept* Robert Belknap, MA; *Prof* Robert W Brown, MA; *Prof* Leonard de Grassi, MA; *Prof* Louis Gross, MA; *Prof* Emil Miller, MA; *Prof* Martin Mondrus, MA; *Prof* Robert E Thomsen, MA; *Asst Prof* Andrew Georgias, MA
Estab 1927; pub; D & E; ent req HS dipl, ent exam; degrees AA 2 yrs; SC 25, LC 7; enrl D 4100, E 3900, nonmaj 800, maj 200
Tuition: None
Courses: Advertising Design, Architecture, Art History, Ceramics, Commercial Art, Drafting, Drawing, Film, Graphic Arts, Graphic Design, History of Art & Archaeology, Jewelry, Lettering, Painting, Photography, Printmaking, Sculpture, Stage Design, Theatre Arts
Summer School: Dir, Dr Charles Wheelock. Term of 8 wk beginning end of June. Courses—Art History, Photography

HAYWARD

CALIFORNIA STATE UNIVERSITY, HAYWARD, Art Department,* 25800 Carlos Bee Blvd, 94542. Tel 415-881-3111. *Chmn* Alan Shepp
Estab 1960; pub; D & E; ent req HS dipl, ent exam, ACT; degrees BA 4 yr; scholarships; SC 30, LC 12; enrl 9000
Tuition: Res—undergrad $197 per yr; nonres—undergrad $1710 per yr
Courses: Aesthetics, Architecture, Art History, Ceramics, Drawing, Lettering, Museum Staff Training, Painting, Photography, Printmaking, Sculpture

CHABOT COLLEGE, Humanities Division, 25555 Hesperian Blvd, 94545. Tel 415-782-3000, Ext 287. *Chmn* Dr Clyde Allen. Instrs FT 240, PT 400
Estab 1961; pub; D & E; ent req HS dipl; degrees AA 2 yr; schol; SC 27, LC 5
Tuition: None to res; nonres—$24.49 per quarter unit, 15 units or more, $367.35 per yr; no campus res
Courses: Advertising Design, Art Education, Ceramics, Commercial Art, Costume Design & Construction, Drafting, Drawing, History of Art & Archaeology, Illustration, Lettering, Painting, Sculpture, Stage Design, Theatre Arts, Cartooning
Summer School: Term of 6 wks. Courses—Art History, Drawing, Introduction to Art, Sculpture

HUNTINGTON BEACH

GOLDEN WEST COLLEGE, Arts, Humanities and Social Sciences Institute, 15744 Golden West St, 92647. Tel 714-892-7711, Ext 405 and 406. *Acad Dean* William Shawl, EdD; *Instructor* R Alderett, MFA; *Instructor* R Camp, MFA; *Instructor* H Clemans, MA; *Instructor* B Conley, MA; *Instructor* P Donaldson, MFA; *Instructor* D Ebert, MA; *Instructor* J Heard, MA; *Instructor* R Huber, MA; *Instructor* A Jackson, MA; *Instructor* C Mitchell, MA; *Instructor* K Mortenson, MFA; *Instructor* R Schiffner, MA; *Instructor* P Sopocko, MA; *Instructor* N Tornheim, MA; *Instructor* H Warner, MA. Instrs PT 17
Estab 1966; pub; D & E; ent req HS dipl; degrees AA 2 yrs; SC 12, LC 6; enrl D 11,800, E 8700
Tuition: Nonres—undergrad $53 per unit
Courses: †Advertising Design, Art History, Calligraphy, Ceramics, Costume Design & Construction, Display, Drafting, Drawing, Illustration, Interior Design, Jewelry, Lettering, Mixed Media, Painting, Photography, Printmaking, Sculpture, Silversmithing, Stage Design, Textile Design, Theatre Arts, Video
Summer School: Classes offered

IDYLLWILD

UNIVERSITY OF SOUTHERN CALIFORNIA, IDYLLWILD CAMPUS, Idyllwild School of Music and the Arts, PO Box 38, 92349. Tel 714-659-2171. *Chmn Painting & Drawing Workshops* Francoise Gilot; *Instructor* Maria Martinez; *Instructor* Joseph Mugnaini; *Instructor* Susan Peterson; *Instructor* Fritz Scholder; *Instructor* Sueo Serisawa; *Instructor* Charlene Weisberg
Estab 1950; pvt; Idyllwild School of Music and the Arts is a 10 wk summer program beginning in mid-June with courses in the arts for all ages; degrees not granted by the Idyllwild Campus, university credits earned through USC-LA Campus; documentation

provided to high schools for credit; schol
Tuition: Ranges from $120-140 wk; campus res available
Courses: Ceramics, Painting, Sculpture, Etching, Stained Glass
Adult Hobby Classes: Enrl open; tui $165 wk. Courses—Hopi Silversmithing, Navajo Two Grey Hills Weaving, Sandpainting, Tewa Pottery
Children's Classes: Enrl open; tui $70 - $75 per wk, $35 for half day program. Day and residential Children's Arts Program; also Youth Ceramics

IRVINE

UNIVERSITY OF CALIFORNIA, IRVINE, Studio Art Department,* School of Fine Arts, 92717. Tel 714-833-6648. *Dean* Clayton Garrison; *Chmn* Melinda Wortz
Estab 1965; pub; D; ent req HS dipl; degrees BA(Studio Art) 4 yr, MFA(Art); scholarships; SC 24, LC 2, GC 4
Tuition: Nonres—$800 per quarter, $1200 per sem, $67 per unit less than 12 units
Courses: Ceramics, Costume Design & Construction, Drawing, Film, History of Art & Archaeology, Painting, Sculpture, Stage Design, Theatre Arts

KENTFIELD

COLLEGE OF MARIN, Department of Art, 94904. Tel 415-485-9480. *Chmn Dept* Martin C Stoelzel, MFA; *Instructor* Rick Hall, MFA; *Instructor* Thano Johnson, MA; *Instructor* Deborah Loft, MA; *Instructor* Glen Miller, MA; *Instructor* Timo Pajunen, MFA; *Instructor* Alton Raible, MFA; *Instructor* Nancy Soper, MA; *Instructor* Gilbert Wheat, MA; *Instructor* Allan Widenhofer, MA; *Instructor* Betty Wilson, MA; *Instructor* Tom Johnson, MA
Estab 1926; pub; D & E; ent req HS dipl, ent exam; degrees AA, AS 2 yrs; SC 48, LC 8; enrl D 5000
Tuition: Res—only tui is for lab fees for some classes; nonres nonres—$840 per sem, $56 per unit; no campus res
Courses: Advertising Design, Architecture, Art History, Ceramics, Drawing, Interior Design, Jewelry, Museum Staff Training, Painting, Photography, Printmaking, Sculpture, Textile Design, History of Art & Architecture
Adult Hobby Classes: Courses—Calligraphy, Drawing, Illustration, Jewelry, Printing
Children's Classes: College for Kids (varied)
Summer School: Dir, Jared Sharon. Course—Ceramics, Color, Drawing, Painting, Textile Arts

LAGUNA BEACH

LAGUNA BEACH SCHOOL OF ART, 2222 Laguna Canyon Rd, 92651. Tel 714-494-1520. *Admin Dir* Ruth Osgood Salyer
Estab 1962; pvt; D & E; ent req HS dipl or desire to learn at any age beyond high school; degrees BFA 4 yrs, cert of completion 3 yrs; schol; SC 20, LC 1
Tuition: Res—$85 each 6 hr class per quarter
Courses: Art History, Ceramics, Collage, Drawing, Graphic Arts, Graphic Design, Jewelry, Mixed Media, Painting, Photography, Printmaking, Sculpture, Silversmithing
Children's Classes: Enrl 15; tui $25 per quarter. A 2 hr class on Sat

LA JOLLA

UNIVERSITY OF CALIFORNIA, SAN DIEGO, Visual Arts Department, B-027, 92093. Tel 714-452-2860. *Dept Chmn* David Antin; *Prof* Harold Cohen; *Prof* Manny Farber; *Prof* Newton Harrison; *Prof* Madlyn Kahr; *Prof* Allan Kaprow; *Prof* Italo Scanga; *Assoc Prof* Eleanor Antin; *Assoc Prof* Standish Lawder; *Assoc Prof* Sheldon Nodelman; *Assoc Prof* Moira Roth; *Lectr* Jehanne Teilhet
Estab 1967; pub; D & E; ent req HS dipl; degrees BA(Studio Art, Art History Criticism, & Communications Visual Arts) 4 yrs, MFA(Studio or Art Criticism) 2-3 yrs; scholarships; SC 55, LC 30, GC 15; enrl D 3600, maj 250, grad 40
Tuition: Res—undergrad $246 per quarter, grad $260 per quarter; nonres—undergrad $1046 per quarter, grad $1060 per quarter; campus res—$732 per quarter (3 quarters per yr)
Courses: Art History, Collage, Conceptual Art, Drawing, Film, Intermedia, Mixed Media, Painting, Photography, Sculpture, Video, Art Criticism Film Criticism

LA MIRADA

BIOLA COLLEGE, Art Department, 13800 Biola Ave, 90639. Tel 213-944-0351. *Chmn Dept* Jack Schwarz, DMA; *Assoc Prof* Grant Logan, MFA; *Assoc Prof* Frank Zamora, MFA
Estab 1908, dept estab 1971; pvt; D & E; ent req HS dipl, SAT or ACT; degrees BA 4 yrs; scholarships; SC 17, LC 4; enrl D 57, maj 57
Tuition: $2766 per yr, $1383 per sem, PT $116; campus res—room & board $1674 per yr
Courses: †Advertising Design, Art History, Ceramics, Drawing, Graphic Arts, History of Art & Archaeology, Lettering, Painting, Sculpture

LANCASTER

ANTELOPE VALLEY COLLEGE, 3041 W Ave K, 93534. Tel 805-943-3241. *Dean* Jennings Brown, MS
Estab 1929; pub; D & E; degrees AA 2 yrs
Tuition: Nonres—undergrad $1170 yr; no campus res

LA VERNE

UNIVERSITY OF LA VERNE,* (Formerly La Verne College) Division of Humanities, 1950 Third St, 91750. Tel 714-593-3511. *Chmn* John Gingrich

Estab 1899; pvt; D & E; ent req HS dipl; degrees BA(Art) 4 yrs; scholarships; SC 12, LC 4; enrl D 125, E 60, maj 6
Tuition: $1335 per sem; campus res—room and board $635 per sem
Courses: Ceramics, Drawing, History of Art & Archaeology, Painting, Photography, Sculpture, Theatre Arts, Batik, Quilt & Patch Work, Stained Glass
Summer School: Terms of 3 and 4 wks

LONG BEACH

CALIFORNIA STATE UNIVERSITY AT LONG BEACH, Art Department, 1250 Bellflower Blvd, 90840. Tel 213-498-4376. *Chmn* Howard G Hitchcock. Instrs FT 52, PT 38
Estab 1949; pub; ent req HS grad, ent exam; degrees BA, BFA 4 yrs, MA, MFA; SC 164, LC 26, GC 23; enrl 2000
Tuition: Res—$206 per yr; nonres—$1710 per yr; campus res $1575-$1800 per yr
Courses: Art Education, Art History, Ceramics, Display, Drawing, Graphic Arts, Handicrafts, Illustration, Industrial Design, Interior Design, Jewelry, Painting, Printmaking, Sculpture, Textile Design, General Art, Metalsmithing
Summer School: Dean, Dr Roderick Peck. Tui $39 per unit for one 6 wk session beginning June 22

LONG BEACH CITY COLLEGE, Department of Art, 4901 E Carson St, 90808. Tel 213-420-4319. *Head Dept Art* Ted Baird, MA; *Instructor* Joseph Hooten, MA; *Instructor* Marcia Lewis, MA; *Instructor* Robert McMenomy, MA; *Instructor* Richard Keyes, MA; *Instructor* James Simpson, MA
Pub; D & E; ent req HS dipl, ent exam; degrees AA and cert 2 yrs; SC 13, LC 2; enrl D 400, E 200, non-maj 450, maj 150
Tuition: None
Courses: Advertising Design, Art History, Ceramics, Collage, Commercial Art, Drawing, Film, Handicrafts, History of Art & Archaeology, Illustration, Jewelry, Lettering, Mixed Media, Painting, Photography, Printmaking, Sculpture, Stage Design, Theatre Arts, Video, Stained Glass, Weaving
Adult Hobby Classes: Enrl 800; tui none. Courses—Crafts, Drawing, Painting
Summer School: Tui none. Courses—same as above

LOS ANGELES

ART IN ARCHITECTURE - JOSEPH YOUNG, 1434 S Spaulding Ave, 90019. Tel 213-933-1194, 656-2286. *Dir* Joseph L Young, BA
Estab 1955; pvt; D; ent req HS dipl, ent exam; schol; SC 4, LC 4, GC 4; enrl D 6, E 7, non-maj 2, maj 8, grad 3
Tuition: $900 for annual nine month program
Courses: Architecture, Art History, Conceptual Art, Drawing, Mixed Media, Painting, Sculpture

CALIFORNIA STATE UNIVERSITY, LOS ANGELES, Art Department, 5151 State University Dr, 90032. Tel 213-224-3521. *Chmn* T W Little, MA; *Assoc Chmn* Charles Borman, MA
Estab 1947; pub; D & E; ent req HS dipl, ent exam; degrees BA(Art) 4 yrs, MA(Art) 1 yr; SC 85, LC 12, GC 9; enrl D 2500 (Art), non-maj 45, maj 55, grad 180 (per quarter)
Tuition: Res—undergrad and grad $70 per quarter; nonres—undergrad and grad $38 per hr; no campus res
Courses: Advertising Design, Art Education, Art History, Ceramics, Drawing, Graphic Arts, Graphic Design, Illustration, Interior Design, Jewelry, Lettering, Painting, Printmaking, Sculpture, Teacher Training, Textile Design, Costume Design, Design Theory, Enameling, Exhibition Design, Fashion Illustration, Textiles, Weaving
Summer School: Same as any academic quarter

EL CAMINO COLLEGE, Division of Fine Arts, 16007 Crenshaw Blvd, 90506. Tel 213-532-3670, Ext 526. *Dean Div* Lewis E Hiigel, EdD. Instrs FT 19, PT 21
Estab 1947; pub; D & E; ent req HS dipl; degrees AA 2 yrs; schol; SC 46, LC 6; enrl D 2650, E 1380, non-maj 3319, maj 711
Tuition: None; no campus res
Courses: Advertising Design, Architecture, Art History, Calligraphy, Ceramics, Costume Design & Construction, Display, †Advertising Design, Architecture, Art History, Calligraphy, Ceramics, Costume Design & Construction, Display, Stage Design, Textile Design, Theatre Arts
Children's Classes: Courses—Exploration of Children's Art
Summer School: Enrl limited; tui none for term of 6 wks, beginning June 19. Courses —Art Appreciation, Ceramics, Freehand Drawing

HOLLYWOOD ART CENTER SCHOOL, 2025-2027 N Highland Ave, 90028. Tel 213-851-1103.
Estab 1912; pvt; D & E; ent req HS dipl, submission of art work; degrees 3 yr cert; SC 6; enrl D 40, E 12
Courses: Advertising Design, Art History, Ceramics, Commercial Art, Costume Design & Construction, Display, Drafting, Drawing, Fashion Arts, Graphic Arts, Graphic Design, Illustration, Industrial Design, Interior Design, Lettering, Painting, Sculpture, Textile Design, Cartooning, Fabric Design, Furniture

LOS ANGELES CITY COLLEGE, Department of Art, 855 N Vermont Ave, 90029. Tel 213-663-9141, Ext 240. *Chmn* Kazuo Higa, MA; *Prof* Russell Cangialosi, PhD; *Prof* Clyde Kelly, MA; *Assoc Prof* Raoul De Sota, MA; *Assoc Prof* Olga Kooyman, MA; *Asst Prof* Dennis Ellmore, MA; *Asst Prof* Gloria Bohanon, MA; *Asst Prof* Phyllis Muldavin, MA; *Asst Prof* Lee Whitten, MA. Instrs PT 11
Estab 1929; pub; D & E; ent req HS dipl and over 18 yrs of age; degrees AA 2 yr; schol; SC 48, LC 8; enrl D 450, E 150, non-maj approx 2 3, maj approx 1 3
Tuition: None, $6.50 student fee but not required
Courses: †Advertising Design, Aesthetics, Architecture, †Art History, Ceramics, †Commercial Art, Display, Handicrafts, †History of Art & Archaeology, Lettering, †Painting, Printmaking, Sculpture
Adult Hobby Classes: Enrl 2090; tui approx $20 per class of 8 wks
Children's Classes: Tui approx $20 per class for 8 wks

Summer School: Chmn, Kazuo Higa. Enrl 250; tui none, term of 6 wks beginning mid-June. Courses—basic courses only

LOYOLA MARYMOUNT UNIVERSITY, Department of Art,* College of Fine and Communication Arts, Loyola Blvd & W 80th St, 90045. Tel 213-642-3128. ; *Assoc Prof Art & Chmn Dept* Genevieve Underwood, MFA; *Assoc Prof* Regina Buchholz, PhD; *Asst Prof* Teresa Munoz, MA; *Asst Prof* Rudolf Fleck, MA; *Asst Prof* Katherine Harper Lorenzana, PhD; *Asst Prof* Susan Barnes Robinson, PhD
Estab as Marymount Col in 1940, merged with Loyola Univ 1968; pvt; D; ent req HS dipl; degrees BA 4 yrs; scholarships; SC 37, LC 21
Tuition: Res—undergrad $3000; campus res room & board
Courses: Advertising Design, †Art Education, †Art History, Ceramics, Display, Drawing, Film, Jewelry, Lettering, Mixed Media, Painting, Photography, Printmaking, Sculpture, Silversmithing, Stage Design, Theatre Arts, †Studio Arts
Summer School: Dean Continuing Educ & Summer Session, Dr Leon Levitt

MOUNT SAINT MARY'S COLLEGE, Art Department, 12001 Chalon Rd, 90049. Tel 213-476-2237, Ext 250. *Chmn* Jake Gilson, MFA; *Assoc Prof* Jim Murray, MA; *Assoc Prof* Norman Schwab, MA; *Asst Prof* Leonard Esbensen, MFA; *Instr* Michael Davis, print & design - 1979-80
Estab 1925; den; D & E; ent req HS dipl; degrees BA and BFA 4 yrs; scholarships; enrl D 60, non-maj 31, maj 29
Tuition: $2700 per yr; campus res—room & board $1490 per yr
Courses: Aesthetics, Art Education, †Art History, Calligraphy, †Ceramics, Collage, Commercial Art, Conceptual Art, Constructions, †Drawing, Film, †Graphic Arts, †Graphic Design, History of Art & Archaeology, Illustration, †Intermedia, Lettering, †Mixed Media, Museum Staff Training, †Painting, †Photography, †Printmaking, †Sculpture, †Textile Design, Video
Summer School: Dir, Dr Catherine Grant. Enrl 30-50; tui $300 per unit. Courses— Ceramics, Drawing, History, Painting, Printmaking

OCCIDENTAL COLLEGE, Art Department, 1600 Campus Rd, 90041. Tel 213-259-2749. *Chmn* Constance M Perkins. Instrs FT 5, PT 3
Estab 1887; pvt; D; ent req HS dipl, col transcript, SAT, recommendations; degrees BA 4 yr; schol & grants according to need; SC 19, LC 25, GC 5; enrl maj 50, others 300
Tuition: $1584; campus res—room & board $625-700 per term
Courses: Art Education, Art History, Drawing, Painting, Sculpture, Graphics, Theory & Criticism
Summer School: Enrl 25. Courses—Art Education, Art History, Ceramics

OTIS ART INSTITUTE OF PARSONS SCHOOL OF DESIGN, 2401 Wilshire Blvd, 90057. Tel 213-387-5288. *Dean* Neil Hoffman
Estab 1918; pvt(see also Parsons School of Design, New York, New York); degrees BFA 4 yrs, MFA 2 yrs; scholarships; SC 52, LC 16, GC 24; enrl D 330, E 78, maj 102, grad 98, others 208
Tuition: $2940 per yr, $1470 per sem, $85 per cr; no campus res
Courses: Art History, Ceramics, Drawing, Illustration, Intermedia, Interior Design, Painting, Printmaking, Sculpture, Communication Design, Environmental Design, Fashion Design
Adult Hobby Classes: AA degree offered through Continuing Education. Enrl 1500; tui $85 per cr. Courses—Advertising Design, Environmental Design, Fashion Design, Graphic Design, Illustration, Interior Design

UNIVERSITY OF CALIFORNIA, LOS ANGELES, Department of Art,* College of Fine Arts, 405 Hilgard Ave, 90024. Tel 213-825-3281. *Chmn* R Brown
Estab 1919; degrees AB 4 yr, MA, MFA, PhD, teaching assistantships; enrl maj 700
Courses: Art History, Costume Design & Construction, Drawing, Graphic Design, Industrial Design, Painting, Photography, Printmaking, Sculpture, Textile Design, Video, Ceramics Design, Glass Design, New Forms & Concepts

UNIVERSITY OF SOUTHERN CALIFORNIA, School of Fine Arts, Watt Hall 103, University Park, 90007. Tel 213-741-2788. *Dean* Stephen E Ostrow, PhD; *Asst Prof* Patricia Berger; *Asst Prof* K Patricia Erhart, PhD; *Asst Prof* Rebecca Gowen, PhD; *Asst Prof* Susan Larsen, PhD; *Vis Prof* Jiri Frel, PhD; *Prof* Pratapaditya Pal, PhD
Estab 1887, dept estab 1979; pvt; D & E; ent req HS dipl, SAT, GRE; degrees BA and BFA 4 yrs, MFA 2-3 yrs, MA 2 yrs, MA with Museum Studies Option 3 yrs, PhD 4 yrs minimum; scholarships; SC 78, LC 11, GC 23; enrl non-maj 600, maj 300, grad 33
Tuition: $154 per unit; campus res available
Courses: Art Education, Art History, Ceramics, Conceptual Art, Drawing, History of Art & Archaeology, Intermedia, Mixed Media, Museum Staff Training, Painting, Photography, Printmaking, Sculpture, Teacher Training
Adult Hobby Classes: Tui $154 per unit
Summer School: Tui $154 per unit

WOODBURY UNIVERSITY, Professional Arts Division, 1027 Wilshire Blvd, 90017. *Chmn Div* Rosalie Utterbach, MA; *Chmn Dept Commercial Art* Marguerite Hossler, MLA; *Chmn Dept Fashion Design* Betty Bixenman, BS; *Chmn Dept Interior Design* Toby Merman
Estab 1884; pvt; D & E; ent req HS dipl; degrees BS 3-4 yrs, MBS 2 yrs; SC 56, LC 18; enrl 1341
Tuition: Campus residency available
Courses: Advertising Design, Aesthetics, Art History, Calligraphy, †Commercial Art, Constructions, Costume Design & Construction, Display, Drawing, †Fashion Arts, Film, Graphic Arts, Graphic Design, History of Art & Archaeology, Illustration, †Interior Design, Lettering, Photography, Textile Design
Summer School: Regular session

MALIBU

PEPPERDINE UNIVERSITY, Humanities-Fine Arts Division, 24255 Pacific Coast Hwy, 90265. *Chmn* James E Smythe. Instrs FT 3, PT 2
Estab 1937; pvt; D; degrees BA (grad 8 trimesters, with credential 10 trimesters); schol; LC 5, workshop 23; enrl maj 35, others 135
Tuition: 143 per unit; campus res—semiprofessional, room and board per trimester $1085
Courses: Teacher Training, Fine Arts, Studio Art
Summer School: Tui $143 sem unit

MARYSVILLE

YUBA COLLEGE, Fine Arts Division,* 2088 N Beale Rd, 95901. Tel 916-742-7351. *Division Head* Ann Rusk
Estab 1927; pub; D & E; ent req HS grad or 18 yrs of age; degrees AA 2 yr; scholarships; SC 23, LC 2; enrl total 1437, maj 493
Tuition: Nonres—$420 per yr, foreign (Visa) $200 per yr; campus res $1200 per yr
Courses: Advertising Design, Aesthetics, Art Education, Ceramics, Drafting, Drawing, Graphic Arts, Lettering, Painting, Photography, Sculpture, Stage Design, Theatre Arts
Summer School: Dean & Assoc Dean Community Educ, Rex McDougal. Term of 6 wks beginning mid-June. Courses—Full Curriculum, plus Home Decorative Arts, Lapidary, Navajo Silversmithing, Non-Loom Weaving

MENDOCINO

MENDOCINO ART CENTER, INC, 45200 Little Lake St, PO Box 765, 95460. Tel 707-937-5818. *Executive Dir* Karen A Kesler, MFA; *Dir Textile Arts* Lolli Jacobsen, MFA
Estab 1959, inc 1974; pvt; D & E; ent req mutual interview, textile arts 3 yr program; SC 24, LC 6; enrl D 18, maj 18
Tuition: $1800
Courses: Art Education, Art History, Calligraphy, Ceramics, Collage, Conceptual Art, Constructions, Display, Drawing, Graphic Arts, Painting, Photography, Sculpture, Textile Design, Silkscreen
Summer School: Tui $50 per each one week workshop offered between June 23 and Aug 22. Courses—over 50 week long classes in all media

MODESTO

MODESTO JUNIOR COLLEGE, Arts Humanities and Speech Division, College Ave, 95355. Tel 209-526-2000, Ext 270. *Chairperson Div* Lloyd E Faukner, MA; *Instructor* Paul J Corrigan, MA; *Instructor* Robert G Gauvreau, MFA; *Instructor* Terry L Hartman, MA; *Instructor* Walter F Lab, MAA; *Instructor* Daniel W Petersen, MA; *Instructor* Jerry M Reilly, MFA; *Instructor* Joseph G Remsing, MA. Instrs FT 259, PT 385
Estab 1921, div estab 1964; pub; D & E; ent req grad of accredited high school, minor with California High School Proficiency Cert and parental permission, 11th and 12th graders with principal's permission, persons 18 or older who are able to profit from the instruction; degrees AA and AS 2 yrs; schol; enrl 16,024 total
Tuition: Res—$4 health fee; nonres—$42 per sem unit to maximum of $631 per sem plus health fee; no campus res
Courses: Advertising Design, Architecture, Art History, Ceramics, Display, Drafting, Drawing, Film, Jewelry, Lettering, Painting, Photography, Printmaking, Sculpture, Silversmithing, Theatre Arts, Enameling, Lapidary
Adult Hobby Classes: Courses—Arts & Crafts, Lapidary
Summer School: Dir, Dr Julius C Manrique. Tui $2 health fee. Courses—a wide variety offered

MONTEREY

MONTEREY PENINSULA COLLEGE, Art Department, Div of Creative Arts, 980 Fremont St, 93940. Tel 408-649-1150. *Chairperson Div Creative Arts* Jo L Hysong, MA; *Chairperson Dept Art* Richard N Janick, MA; *Instructor* Richard Bibler, MA; *Instructor* Pat Boles, BA; *Instructor* Alex Gonzales, MFA; *Instructor* Skip Kadish, MA; *Instructor* Larry Kappen, MA; *Instructor* Peter Pilat, MA; *Instructor* Joe Tanous, MA
Estab 1947; pub; D & E; ent req HS dipl, 18 yrs or older; degrees AA and AS 2 yrs; schol; SC 17, LC 8; enrl D 1343, E 623, maj 160
Tuition: None to res; nonres—$28 per unit; no campus res
Courses: Architecture, Art History, Ceramics, Drawing, Jewelry, Lettering, Mixed Media, Painting, Photography, Sculpture, Silversmithing, Textile Design, Commercial Graphics
Summer School: Dir, Joel Hysong. Term of 6 wks beginning June. Courses—same as above

MONTEREY PARK

EAST LOS ANGELES COLLEGE, Art Department, 1301 E Brooklyn Ave, 91754. Tel 213-265-8650. Instrs FT 8, PT 10
Estab 1949; pub; D & E; degrees AA 2 yr; SC 35, LC 10; enrl D 350, E 310, maj 660
Courses: Advertising Design, Art History, Ceramics, Display, Drawing, Graphic Design, Handicrafts, Illustration, Interior Design, Jewelry, Lettering, Painting, Printmaking, Sculpture, Textile Design, Art Fundamentals, Design, Fashion Design, Life Drawing
Children's Classes: Enrl 60. Courses—Ceramics, Direct Printing Methods, Drawing, Painting

NORTHRIDGE

CALIFORNIA STATE UNIVERSITY, NORTHRIDGE, Department of Art-Two Dimensional Media, 18111 Nordhoff St, 91330. Tel 213-885-2348. *Dept Chmn* Art Weiss, MFA
Estab 1956; pub; D & E; ent req HS dipl, GRE, SAT; degrees BA 4-5 yrs, MA; SC 13, GC 5; enrl D & E 2231, grad 101
Courses: †Advertising Design, Calligraphy, †Drawing, †Graphic Arts, †Graphic Design, Illustration, Lettering, †Painting, †Photography, †Printmaking, Airbrush, Animation, Typography, Packaging Graphics, Reproduction Graphics
Summer School: Dir, Art Weiss. Tui $39 per unit for 8 wks beginning June 26. Courses—Advertising Graphics, Airbrush, Beginning Design, Drawing, Illustration, Packaging, Painting, Photography, Reprographics
—**Art History Department**, 18111 Nordhoff St, 91324. Tel 213-885-2192. *Chmn* Dolores M Yonker, PhD
Estab 1958, dept estab 1971; pub; D & E; ent req HS dipl, SAT, subject to GPA; degrees BA(Art) 4 yrs, MA(Art History) 5 yrs; SC 1, LC 30, grad 10; enrl grad 50, undergrad 850
Tuition: $72 per sem, $57 PT, plus $60 per unit
Courses: Aesthetics, †Art History, Display, History of Art & Archaeology, Museum Staff Training, Restoration & Conservation
Adult Hobby Classes: Tui $33 per lecture unit. Courses—available through Continuing Educ Extension Prog
Summer School: Tui $33-$60 for term of 6 wks beginning June. Courses—survey courses only

NORWALK

CERRITOS COLLEGE, Art Department,* 11110 Alondra Blvd, 90650. Tel 213-860-2451. *Chmn* Allan Boodnick
Estab 1956; pub; D & E; ent req HS dipl or 18 yrs of age; degrees AA 2 yrs; scholarships; SC 36, LC 6
Tuition: Res—None; nonres—$32 per unit
Courses: Aesthetics, Architecture, Ceramics, Commercial Art, Display, Drawing, Graphic Arts, Graphic Design, Handicrafts, History of Art & Archaeology, Jewelry, Lettering, Museum Staff Training, Painting, Photography, Sculpture, Theatre Arts

OAKLAND

CALIFORNIA COLLEGE OF ARTS AND CRAFTS, 5212 Broadway, 94618. Tel 415-653-8118. *Pres* Harry X Ford, MA; *Instructor* Andry Addkison; *Instructor* Skip Benson; *Instructor* Dr Ruth Boyer; *Instructor* Sydney Carson; *Instructor* Harry Critchfield; *Instructor* Viola Frey; *Instructor* Charles Gill; *Instructor* Robert Harper; *Instructor* David Heintz; *Instructor* Dennis Leon; *Instructor* Philip Linhares; *Instructor* Marvin Lipofsky; *Instructor* Vincent Perez; *Instructor* Dr Trude Piatkowski; *Instructor* Steve Reott; *Instructor* Florence Resnikoff; *Instructor* Dr Piroja Shroff; *Instructor* Mary Snowden; *Instructor* Dean Snyder; *Instructor* Hugh Wiley; *Instructor* Dr Michael Wright
Estab 1907; pvt; D & E; ent req HS dipl, SAT or ACT requested not required, C grade-point average, 1 sem of lab science; degrees 3 yr cert, BFA 4 yrs, MFA 1 1 2 yrs, MAEd 2 yrs; scholarships; SC 24, LC 58, GC 5; enrl D 1101, non-maj 132, maj 906, grad 63, exten school 266
Tuition: Per trimester $1895; campus residency available
Courses: Advertising Design, Aesthetics, Art History, Calligraphy, †Ceramics, Conceptual Art, Drafting, †Drawing, Film, Goldsmithing, Graphic Arts, †Graphic Design, Handicrafts, †Illustration, †Interior Design, †Jewelry, Lettering, Mixed Media, †Painting, †Photography, Printmaking, †Sculpture, Silversmithing, Teacher Training, Textile Design, †Video, †Environmental Design, †Ethnic Studies, †Fine Arts, †General Design, †Glass, †Textiles, TV, Wood
Adult Hobby Classes: Enrl 266; tui $85-$135. Courses—Art Therapy, Artists' Business, Design, Drawing, Film & TV, Graphic Design, Jewelry, Painting, Papermaking, Photography, Printmaking, Sculpture, Textiles
Children's Classes: Enrl 52; tui $40 per class. Courses—Ceramics, Crafts, Drawing, Printmaking
Summer School: Dir, Ken Davids. Enrl 262 per session; tui $135 per unit for term of 5 wks beginning mid May, June, July. Courses—Full range

HOLY NAMES COLLEGE, Art Department, 3500 Mountain Blvd, 94619. Tel 415-436-0111. Instrs FT 2, PT 5
Estab 1917; pvt; D & E; ent req HS dipl; degrees BA and BFA 4 yrs; schol; SC 24, LC 4
Courses: Art History, Calligraphy, Ceramics, Drawing, Jewelry, Painting, Photography, Printmaking, Sculpture, Bookbinding, Gallery Techniques, Stained Glass, Weaving

LANEY COLLEGE, Art Department, 900 Falcon St, 94607. *Chmn* Bill Snyder. Instrs FT 8, PT 7
Estab 1962; pub; D & E; ent req HS dipl; degrees AA 2 yrs; SC 52, LC 8; enrl D 1600, E 600
Courses: Advertising Design, Ceramics, Commercial Art, Drawing, Graphic Arts, Graphic Design, Handicrafts, History of Art & Archaeology, Illustration, Interior Design, Lettering, Painting, Photography, Sculpture, Architectural Design, Cartooning, Fashion Design, Figure Drawing, Painting Materials & Techniques

MILLS COLLEGE, Art Department,* 5000 MacArthur Blvd, PO Box 9975, 94613. Tel 415-632-2700. *Prof Art & Chmn Dept* Ralph S DuCasse, MFA; *Prof* Robert A Dhaemers, MFA; *Visiting Lucie Stern Prof* Ron Nagle, MFA; *Lectr* Carol Molly Prier, MFA; *Lectr* Joanne Leonard, BA; *Lectr* Ralph Reed, MFA; *Lectr* William Wu, MA; *Assoc Prof* Wanda Corn, PhD; *Asst Prof* Joanne Bernstein, PhD
Estab 1852; pvt; D; ent req HS dipl, SAT, Advanced Placement Exam; degrees BA 4 yrs, MFA 2 yrs; scholarships; SC 23, LC 22, GC 20; enrl grad 16-20
Tuition: Res—undergrad $5550 yr, grad $1500 yr, $750 per sem, $250 per course, $125 per half course; nonres—undergrad $3512 yr, other $170 course to audit; campus res—room & board $1990 per yr
Courses: Aesthetics, †Art History, Ceramics, Collage, Constructions, Costume Design & Construction, Drawing, Film, Illustration, Intermedia, Mixed Media, Museum Staff Training, Painting, Photography, Printmaking, Sculpture, Stage Design, Theatre Arts, Video, Practice of Art
Children's Classes: Course—Ceramics

OCEANSIDE

MIRACOSTA COLLEGE, Creative Arts Department,* 1 Barnard Dr, 92054. Tel 714-757-2121. *Chmn* Howard Ganz, MA
Estab 1934; pub; D & E; ent req HS dipl, GED test, probationary student; degrees AA and AS normally 2 yrs; scholarships; SC 12, LC 4; enrl maj 200
Tuition: Res—no fee; nonres—$1272 per yr; no campus res
Courses: Aesthetics, Art History, Ceramics, Drafting, Drawing, Film, Graphic Arts, Handicrafts, Interior Design, Jewelry, Painting, Photography, Printmaking, Sculpture, Stage Design, Theatre Arts, Design workshop in crafts, Design workshop in fibers

ORANGE

CHAPMAN COLLEGE, Art Department, 333 N Glassell, 92666. Tel 714-997-6729. *Chairperson* Richard Turner, MFA; *Instr* William Boaz, MA; *Instr* Brett Price, MFA; *Instr* Jane Sinclair, MFA; *Instr* Bruce Williams, MFA
Estab 1918, branch estab 1954; den; D & E; ent req HS dipl, ACT, SAT or CLEP; scholarships; SC 20, LC 15; enrl D 245, non-maj 200, maj 35
Tuition: $120 per unit; campus res—room $800-$1300 & board $940-$1100
Courses: Advertising Design, Art Education, Art History, Ceramics, Drawing, Film, Graphic Arts, History of Art & Archaeology, Illustration, Painting, Photography, Printmaking, Sculpture, Stage Design, Teacher Training, Theatre Arts, Video
Children's Classes: Tui $10 per class. Courses—workshops in connection with art education classes

OROVILLE

BUTTE COMMUNITY COLLEGE, Humanities Division (III), Route 1, Box 183A, 95965. Tel 916-895-2544. *Div Chairperson* Joseph Rich, MA; *Coordr* Albert J Walsh Jr, MA; *Ceramic Coordr* Idie Payne MA; *Prof* Jeffrey Nelson, MA; *Prof* John R Wilson, MA; *Vis Prof* Sal Casa, commercial art; *Vis Prof* Ruben Heredia, commercial art
Estab 1968; pub; D & E; ent req HS dipl or 18 yrs or older; degrees AA 2 yrs; schol; SC 21, LC 4; enrl D 3100, E 4000
Tuition: 5-$9 per cr hr; no campus res
Courses: Ceramics, Commercial Art, Costume Design & Construction, Drafting, Fashion Arts, Photography, Video
Adult Hobby Classes: Courses—Macrame, Stained Glass
Summer School: Dir, Ken Lucas. Tui $5-$9 per cr hr

PALM DESERT

COLLEGE OF THE DESERT, Art Department, 43-500 Monterey Ave, 92260. Tel 714-346-8041. Instrs FT 4, PT 12
Estab 1962; pub; D & E; ent req HS dipl, ent exam; degrees AA 2 yrs; schol; SC 10, LC 3; enrl D 150, E 150, maj 15
Tuition: None; no campus res
Courses: Art History, Ceramics, Drawing, Handicrafts, Photography, Printmaking, Sculpture, Advertising Art, Introduction to Art

PASADENA

ART CENTER COLLEGE OF DESIGN, 1700 Lida St, 91103. Tel 213-577-1700, Ext 264. *Pres* Don Kubly, BA; *VPres* Joseph R Henry; *Acting Communication Design Chmn* George Gaw; *Fine Arts Dept Chmn* Laurence Drieband, MFA; *Film Dept Chmn* Jim Jordan, BA; *Photography Dept Chmn* Charles Potts, BPA; *Industrial Design Chmn* Keith Teter, BS
Estab 1930; pvt; D & E; ent req HS dipl, ACT, SAT if no col background, portfolio required, at least 12 samples of work in proposed maj; degrees BFA 4 yrs, MFA additional 48 units plus master's project & thesis; scholarships; SC 168, LC 82, GC 22; enrl D 1000, E 200, non-maj 200, maj 1000, grad 20
Tuition: Res—$1625 for 15 wk sem (trimester); no campus res
Courses: †Advertising Design, Art History, Display, Drawing, †Film, †Graphic Design, †Illustration, †Industrial Design, Lettering, Painting, †Photography, , †Advertising Illustration, †Environmental Design, †Fashion Illustration, †Graphic Packaging, †Product Design, †Transportation Design

PASADENA CITY COLLEGE, Art Department, 1570 E Colorado St, 91106. Tel 213-578-7238. *Chmn Dept* David J Schnabel; *Area Chmn Design* John Caldwell, MA; *Area Chmn Studio Art* Ben Sakaguchi, MA; *Area Chmn Photography* Michael Mims, MA; *Area Chmn Art History* Dick Cassady, MA; *Area Chmn Art History* Vern Wells, MA; *Area Chairperson Apparel Arts* Lily Heftman, MA; *Area Chmn Crafts* John Dickenhof, MA; *Area Chmn Ceramics* Phil Cornelius, MA
Estab 1902, dept estab 1916; pub; D & E; ent req HS dipl; degrees AA 2 yrs; SC 50; enrl D 2000, E 1200, non-maj 3200, maj 400
Courses: Advertising Design, Architecture, Art History, Ceramics, Commercial Art, Costume Design & Construction, Display, Drafting, Drawing, Fashion Arts, Film, Graphic Arts, Graphic Design, Handicrafts, History of Art & Archaeology, Illustration, Interior Design, Jewelry, Lettering, Museum Staff Training, Painting, Photography, Printmaking, Sculpture, Silversmithing, Stage Design, Textile Design, Video
Summer School: Dir, John Dickenhof. Courses—complete program

POMONA

CALIFORNIA STATE POLYTECHNIC UNIVERSITY, POMONA, Art Department, School of Arts, 3801 Temple Blvd, 91768. Tel 714-598-4567. *Chmn* Yoram Makow, MA; *Prof* Diane Divelbess, MFA; *Prof* Walter Glaser, MFA; *Assoc Prof* Charles Fredrick, MFA; *Assoc Prof* Maren Henderson, MA; *Assoc Prof* Stanley Wilson, MFA; *Lectr* Jerry Alexander, MFA; *Lectr* Shelly Marcus, MA; *Lectr* Barbara Thomason, MFA
Estab 1966; pub; D & E; ent req HS dipl, plus testing; degrees BA 4 yrs; SC 66, LC 15; enrl D approx 300, E approx 50, non-maj 470, maj 175
Tuition: Res—undergrad (commuting) $153 quarterly, (living in dorms) $603 quarterly; campus res $1809 yr
Courses: Advertising Design, Aesthetics, Art Education, Art History, Calligraphy, Ceramics, Collage, Commercial Art, Constructions, Display, Drafting, Drawing, Graphic Arts, Graphic Design, Handicrafts, History of Art & Archaeology, Illustration, Jewelry, Lettering, Mixed Media, Museum Staff Training, Painting, Printmaking, Sculpture, Silversmithing, Teacher Training, Textile Design, Batik, Enameling, Woodworking
Summer School: Regular 10 wk quarter

PORTERVILLE

PORTERVILLE COMMUNITY COLLEGE, Department of Fine Arts, 900 S Main St, 93257. Tel 209-781-3130, Ext 66. *Chmn Dept* Florence S Offutt, MA; *Prof* Tom Howell, MA; *Assoc Prof* Phil Simons, MA; *Vis Prof* Peter Flint, jewelry. Instrs FT 50, PT 80
Estab 1927; pub; D & E; ent req HS dipl or over 18 yrs of age; degrees AA and AS 2 yrs; SC 18, LC 3; enrl D 300, E 78, non-maj 320, maj 58
Tuition: Res—none; nonres—$43 per unit; no campus res
Courses: Art History, Ceramics, Drawing, Goldsmithing, Handicrafts, Jewelry, Painting, Photography, Sculpture, Silversmithing, Textile Design, Theatre Arts, Weaving
Adult Hobby Classes: Courses—Jewelry, Weaving
Summer School: Dir, Nero Pruitt. Enrl 700; tui $43 per unit for term of 6 wks beginning June 13. Courses—Ceramics, Jewelry, Weaving

REDDING

SHASTA COLLEGE, Art Department, Fine Arts Division, 1605 Old Oregon Trail, 96001. Tel 916-241-3523, Ext 361. *Dir Div Fine Arts* Judith Knowles, MA
Estab 1950; pub; D & E; ent req HS dipl; degrees AA 2 yr
Courses: Art History, Ceramics, Commercial Art, Drawing, Film, Jewelry, Painting, Photography, Printmaking, Sculpture

REDLANDS

UNIVERSITY OF REDLANDS, Department of Art,* Division of Fine and Performing Arts, 1200 W Colton Ave, 92373. Tel 714-793-2121. *Dean Division* Wayne R Bohrnstedt; *Chmn Dept* John P Brownfield
Estab 1909; pvt; D & E; ent req HS grad, ent exam; degrees BA and BS 4 yr, MA, ME, MAT; scholarships and fels; SC 18, LC 12; enrl 1500
Tuition: $4470 per yr; campus res available
Courses: Art History, Ceramics, Drawing, Graphic Arts, Jewelry, Painting, Sculpture, Teacher Training, Ethnic Art
Summer School: Tui $42.50 per unit, three terms (two for 5 wks and one for 3 wks), June 1-19, June 22-July 24 and July 23-Aug 28

RIVERSIDE

LOMA LINDA UNIVERSITY, LA SIERRA CAMPUS, Art Department,* 92515. Tel 714-785-2170. *Chmn Prof* Roger Churches, MFA; *Prof* Alan Collins; *Asst Prof* Susan Davis
Estab 1905; den; D & E; ent req HS dipl, SAT; degrees BA, BS 4 yrs; SC 29, LC 8, GC 1; enrl D 2354
Tuition: Campus Res—$1095 per quarter; cam res—$530 per quarter available
Courses: Aesthetics, Art History, Calligraphy, †Ceramics, Commercial Art, †Drawing, Graphic Arts, †Graphic Design, Handicrafts, History of Art & Archaeology, Illustration, Lettering, Occupational Therapy, †Painting, †Photography, †Printmaking, †Sculpture, Stained Glass

RIVERSIDE CITY COLLEGE, Department of Art,* Fine Arts Division, 4800 Magnolia Ave, 92506. Tel 714-684-3240. *Head Dept* Richard Stover
Estab 1917; pub; D & E; ent req HS dipl or over 18 yrs of age; degrees AA 2 yrs; SC 20, LC 3; enrl D 910, E 175
Tuition: Res—free; nonres—$930 per yr; no campus res
Courses: Advertising Design, Art Education, Ceramics, Commercial Art, Drawing, Graphic Arts, Graphic Design, History of Art & Archaeology, Illustration, Jewelry, Lettering, Painting, Sculpture, Teacher Training
Summer School: Dir, Leo B Kraus. Enrl 225; term of 6 wks beginning June 21. Courses—Art for Elementary Teachers, Art History, Ceramics, Drawing, Painting, Sculpture

UNIVERSITY OF CALIFORNIA, RIVERSIDE
—Art History Department, 92521. Tel 714-787-4627. *Chmn* Richard G Carrott, PhD; *Prof* Dericksen M Brinkerhoff, PhD; *Assoc Prof* Francoise Forster-Hahn, PhD; *Assoc Prof* Thomas O Pelzel, PhD
Estab 1954; pub; D; ent req HS dipl, res grad-point average 3.1, nonres grade-point average 3.4; degrees BA 4 yrs, MA 2 yrs; LC 18; enrl maj 20, grad 10
Tuition: Res—undergrad $246 per quarter, grad $258 per quarter; nonres—$800 per quarter; campus res—room & board $535 per quarter
Courses: Art History
—Program in Art, 92521. Tel 714-787-4634. *Head Dept* William T Bradshaw, MA; *Prof* James S Strombotne, MFA; *Asst Prof* Joe M Deal, MFA; *Lectr* Steven J Cahill, MFA; *Lectr* Kenda North, MFA; *Lectr* Gordon L Thorpe, MA

Estab 1954; pub; D; ent req HS dipl; degrees BA 4 yrs; SC 14, LC 2; enrl maj 60
Tuition: Res—undergrad $246 per quarter; nonres—undergrad $1046 per quarter; campus residence available
Courses: Drawing, Graphic Design, Painting, Photography

ROCKLIN

SIERRA COLLEGE, Art Department,* Humanities Division, 5000 Rocklin Rd, 95677. Tel 916-624-3333. *Chmn Division* Loren Orr, MA; *Instr* Jim Adamson, MA; *Instr* Fritz Blodgett, MA; *Instr* John Hamilton, MA; *Instr* Bob Ridley, MA
Estab 1914; pub; D & E; ent req English Placement Test; degrees AA and AS; SC 18, LC 4; enrl D & E approx 9000
Tuition: Campus res available
Courses: Art Education, Art History, Ceramics, Collage, Conceptual Art, Costume Design & Construction, Drafting, Drawing, Film, Goldsmithing, History of Art & Archaeology, Jewelry, Painting, Photography, Printmaking, Sculpture, Silversmithing, Stage Design, Theatre Arts, Video
Adult Hobby Classes: Courses—Weaving, Woodcarving

ROHNERT PARK

CALIFORNIA STATE COLLEGE, SONOMA, Department of Art, 1801 E Cotati Ave, 94928. Tel 707-664-2151. *Chairperson* William Morehouse, MA; *Chairperson* Dr Susan Moulton, PhD; *Prof* Dr Leland Gralapp, PhD; *Assoc Prof* Shane Weare; *Asst Prof* Marsha Bailey, MFA; *Asst Prof* J DeFeo, MFA; *Asst Prof* Susan McKillop, PhD; *Asst Prof* Don Potts, MA; *Instructor* John Doane, MFA
Estab 1965; pub; D & E; ent req HS dipl, SAT; degrees BA 4 yr; SC 42, LC 15, GC 1; enrl D 1300, E 40, Non-maj 200, maj 350, grad 20
Tuition: Res—undergrad $85 per sem, $65 part-time; nonres—undergrad per yr, $52 per unit; campus res - res—room & board $1800 per yr
Courses: Aesthetics, Architecture, Art Education, Art History, Ceramics, Collage, Conceptual Art, Constructions, Costume Design & Construction, Drawing, Film, Graphic Arts, History of Art & Archaeology, Intermedia, Mixed Media, Museum Staff Training, Occupational Therapy, Painting, Photography, Printmaking, Sculpture, Teacher Training, Theatre Arts, Video, Papermaking, Women in Art
Summer School: Dir, Dr Stuart Cooney. Tui $42 per unit for term beginning early June. Courses—all types

SONOMA STATE UNIVERSITY, Art Department, 1801 East Cotati Ave, 94928. Tel 707-664-2151, 664-2364. *Dept Chairperson* William Morehouse, PhD equivalent; *Dir Sonoma Film Institute* Peter Scarlet; *Prof* Kathryn Armstrong, MA & MFA; *Prof* Leland Gralapp, PhD; *Prof* Susan McKillop, PhD; *Prof* Susan Moulton, PhD; *Prof* Shane Weare, ARCA
Estab 1961, dept estab 1961; pub; D & E; ent req HS dipl, SAT, eligibility req must be met; degrees BA and BS; SC 38, LC 17; enrl D 5000
Tuition: Res $97 per sem, non-res $97 per sem plus $60 per unit; campus residence available
Courses: Art Education, Art History, Ceramics, Collage, Conceptual Art, Constructions, Display, Drawing, Film, History of Art & Archaeology, Jewelry, Mixed Media, Painting, Photography, Printmaking, Sculpture, Teacher Training, Video
Adult Hobby Classes: Various classes offered through Extended Education
Summer School: Courses—Various classes offered through Extended Education

SACRAMENTO

AMERICAN RIVER COLLEGE, Department of Art,* 4700 College Oak Dr, 95841. Tel 916-484-8011. *Chmn* James S Kaneko, MA; *Instr* Phyllis Y Robbins, MA; *Instr* Joe Patitucci, BA; *Instr* Jean A Pratt, MA; *Instr* Gary L Pruner, MA; *Instr* John H Kaneko, MA; *Instr* Tom J Brozovich, MA
Estab 1954; pub; D & E; ent req HS dipl; degrees AA 2 yrs or more; scholarships; SC 50, LC 12; enrl D 10,000, E 10,000, non-maj 5000, maj 5000
Tuition: Nonres—$600 per sem or $40 per unit
Courses: Advertising Design, Art Education, Art History, Calligraphy, Ceramics, Commercial Art, Conceptual Art, Constructions, Costume Design & Construction, Display, Drawing, Fashion Arts, Film, Graphic Arts, Graphic Design, Handicrafts, History of Art & Archaeology, Interior Design, Jewelry, Lettering, Mixed Media, Painting, Photography, Printmaking, Sculpture, Silversmithing, Teacher Training, Textile Design, Theatre Arts
Summer School: Dean, Anne Stewart. Tui none. Courses—same as above

CALIFORNIA STATE UNIVERSITY, SACRAMENTO, Department of Art, 6000 J St, 95819. Tel 916-454-6166. *Chmn* P Hitchcock. Instrs FT 30
Estab 1950; pub; D; ent req HS dipl, ent exam; degrees BA 4 yr, MA; schol; SC 40, LC 18, GC 12; enrl major 606
Courses: Art Education, Art History, Ceramics, Drawing, Handicrafts, Jewelry, Painting, Printmaking, Sculpture, Cinematography
Summer School: Enrl 225; 1 wk pre-session, 6 wks

SACRAMENTO CITY COLLEGE, Art Department, 3835 Freeport Blvd, 95822. Tel 916-449-7551. *Subject Area Rep* George A Esquibel, MA; *Instructor* Al Byrd, MFA; *Instructor* David Curry, MA; *Instructor* Gregory Kondos, MA; *Instructor* Laureen Landau, MFA; *Instructor* Patricia Tool McHugh, MA; *Instructor* Willard Melton, MFA; *Instructor* Larry Welden, MAEd
Estab 1927, dept estab 1929; pub; D & E; ent req HS dipl; degrees AA 2 yr; SC 17, LC 9; enrl D 880, E 389
Tuition: None; no campus res
Courses: Art Education, Art History, Ceramics, Commercial Art, Costume Design & Construction, Drafting, Drawing, Film, Painting, Photography, Printmaking, Sculpture, Stage Design, Theatre Arts, Video
Summer School: Dir, George A Esquibel. Courses—Art History, Design, Drawing, Oil-Acrylic, Watercolor

SALINAS

HARTNELL COLLEGE, Art and Photography Departments, 156 Homestead Ave, 93901. Tel 408-758-8211. *Chmn* Robert Lee. Instrs FT 3, PT 3
Estab 1922; pub; D & E; ent req HS dipl; degrees AA 2 yr; SC 14, LC 3; enrl D 350 E 160, major 30
Tuition: None; no campus res
Courses: Architecture, Ceramics, Commercial Art, Drafting, Drawing, Graphic Arts, History of Art & Archaeology, Jewelry, Painting, Photography, Sculpture, Stage Design, Theatre Arts, Video, Foundry, Gallery Management, Glassblowing, Metalsmithing, Stained Glass
Summer School: Enrl 150; tui free; begins approx June 15. Courses—Art Appreciation, Ceramics, Drawing, Film Making, Photography

SAN BERNARDINO

CALIFORNIA STATE COLLEGE AT SAN BERNARDINO, Fine Arts Department, 5500 State College Parkway, 92407. Tel 714-887-7459. *Chmn Dept* Julius Kaplan, PhD; *Instructor* Leo Doyle, MFA; *Instructor* Roger Lintault, MFA; *Instructor* Jose Moran, MFA; *Instructor* Bill Warehall, MFA; *Instructor* Don Woodford, MFA
Estab 1965; pub; D & E; ent req HS dipl, SAT; degrees BA 4 yrs; schol; enrl D 4000, maj 125
Tuition: Res—undergrad $48 per 15 units; nonres nonres—undergrad per unit; campus res—room & board $1450 yr
Courses: Advertising Design, Art Education, Art History, Ceramics, Drawing, Jewelry, Painting, Printmaking, Sculpture, Textile Design, Furniture Design, Glassblowing

SAN BERNARDINO VALLEY COLLEGE, Art Department, 701 S Mount Vernon Ave, 92403. Tel 714-888-6511. *Head Dept* David Lawrence. Instrs FT 224, PT 510
Estab 1926; pub; D & E; ent req HS dipl or 18 yrs of age; degrees AA and AS 2 yrs; schol; enrl D 750, E 400, maj 230
Tuition: Res—none; nonres—$1110 per yr; no campus res
Courses: Advertising Design, Architecture, Art Education, Art History, Ceramics, Drafting, Drawing, Film, Jewelry, Landscape Architecture, Lettering, Painting, Photography, Sculpture, Theatre Arts, Artistic Weaving, Glass Blowing, Life Drawing
Summer School: No tui

SAN DIEGO

SAN DIEGO MESA COLLEGE, Art Department, 7250 Mesa College Drive, 92111. Tel 714-279-2300, Ext 239. *Chairperson* Ross Stockwell, MA; *Instructor* Barbara Blackmun, PhD; *Instructor* John Courad, PhD; *Instructor* Albert J Lewis, MA; *Instructor* Hiroshi Miyazaki, MA; *Instructor* Malcolm Nichols, MA; *Instr* Anita Waehrer, MA
Estab 1964; pub; D & E; ent req HS dipl or age 18; degrees AA 2 yrs; schol; SC 29, LC 7; enrl in col D 10,000, E 10,000, maj 300
Tuition: Res—none; nonres—$38 per unit; no campus res
Courses: †Architecture, †Art History, †Ceramics, Drafting, †Drawing, Jewelry, Lettering, †Painting, Photography, Sculpture, Crafts, Fibers
Summer School: Tui $38 per unit. Courses—all basic, varied advanced

SAN DIEGO STATE UNIVERSITY, Department of Art, 92182. Tel 714-265-6800. *Chmn* Fredrick Orth, MFA; *Grad Coordr* Robert Berg, MFA
Estab 1897; pub; D & E; ent req HS dipl; degrees BA 4 yrs, MA; schol; SC 140, LC 35, GC 30; enrl maj 1021
Tuition: Campus res—room & board
Courses: Advertising Design, Aesthetics, Architecture, Art Education, †Art History, †Ceramics, Commercial Art, Conceptual Art, Costume Design & Construction, Drawing, Fashion Arts, Goldsmithing, Graphic Arts, †Graphic Design, Handicrafts, History of Art & Archaeology, Intermedia, †Interior Design, †Jewelry, Lettering, Mixed Media, †Painting, †Printmaking, †Sculpture, Silversmithing, Teacher Training, †Textile Design, †Enameling, †Environmental Design, †Furniture Design Gallery Design, Weaving

UNITED STATES INTERNATIONAL UNIVERSITY, School of Performing and Visual Arts,* 10455 Pomerado Rd, 92131. Tel 714-271-4300, Ext 271. *Dean School* Netter Worthington
Estab 1966; pvt; D; ent req HS dipl, interview, portfolio, letters of recommendation; degrees BA (Advertising, Costume, Set Design, Painting & Drawing or Teaching), BFA 4 yrs; scholarships; SC 27, LC 4; enrl D 300
Tuition: $1080 per qt, $72 per unit; campus res available
Courses: Advertising Design, Art Education, Ceramics, Commercial Art, Costume Design & Construction, Drafting, Drawing, Fashion Arts, Graphic Arts, Graphic Design, History of Art & Archaeology, Illustration, Painting, Sculpture, Stage Design, Teacher Training, Theatre Arts
Summer School: Dir, Netter Worthington. Tui $60 per unit for term of 8 wks beginning June 14. Courses—Drawing, Introduction to Visual Thinking, Painting

UNIVERSITY OF SAN DIEGO, Art Department, 92110. Tel 714-291-6480. *Chmn* Therese Truitt Whitcomb. Instrs FT 3, PT 3
Estab 1952; pvt; D & E; ent req HS dipl, SAT; degrees BA 4 yrs; schol; SC 19, LC 7; enrl univ 2300, maj 50
Tuition: 105 per unit; campus res—room and board $700-$1000 per sem
Courses: Art History, Ceramics, Drawing, Painting, Photography, Printmaking, Sculpture, Art in Elementary Education, Design, Enameling, Exhibition Design, Weaving
Summer School: Tui $105 per unit for terms of 3 wk, 6 wk beginning June 1; 4 courses offered

SAN FRANCISCO

ACADEMY OF ART COLLEGE, 625 Sutter St, 94102. Tel 415-673-4200. *Pres* Richard A Stephens, MFA; *Dir Advertising/Graphic Design* Michael Dattel, BFA; *Dir Illustration* Barbara Bradley, BFA; *Dir Fine Art* Michael Woods, MFA; *Dir*

Photography Paul Raedeke. Instrs FT 20, PT 40
Estab 1929; pvt; D & E; ent req HS dipl; degrees BFA 4 yrs, MFA 2 yrs; scholarships;
SC 100, LC 50; enrl D 1050, E 150, grad 20
Tuition: Res—undergrad $2720 per yr, $1360 per sem, $95 per unit, grad $2240 per
yr, $1120 per sem, $110 per unit; campus res available
Courses: Advertising Design, Aesthetics, Art Education, Art History, Calligraphy,
Ceramics, Collage, Commercial Art, Conceptual Art, Display, †Drawing, †Fashion
Arts, Film, Goldsmithing, †Graphic Arts, †Graphic Design, Handicrafts,
†Illustration, Jewelry, Lettering, †Painting, †Photography, †Printmaking, †Sculpture,
Theatre Arts
Adult Hobby Classes: Enrl 75; tui $95 per unit. Courses—Basic Painting, Ceramics,
Portrait Painting, Pottery
Summer School: VPres, Donald A Haight. Tui $640 for term of 6 wks beginning June
23. Courses—Commercial and Fine Art

CITY COLLEGE OF SAN FRANCISCO, Art Department, 50 Phelan Ave, 94112.
Tel 415-239-3156. *Chairperson* Jesse Hover, MA; *Coordr Fine Arts* Richard Rodrigues,
MA; *Coordr Professional Art* Arthur Irwin, MA
Estab 1935; pub; D & E; degrees AA 2 yrs; SC 45, LC 10; enrl col D 15,000, E 11,000
Tuition: None
Courses: Art History, Ceramics, Drawing, Graphic Arts, Graphic Design, Illustration,
Industrial Design, Jewelry, Lettering, Painting, Sculpture, Basic Design, Metal Arts
Summer School: Courses—same as regular yr

DE YOUNG MUSEUM ART SCHOOL,* Golden Gate Park, 94118. Tel
415-555-2887. *Cur in Charge* Elsa Cameron; *Chmn Drawing & Painting* Jerry Concha;
Chmn Photography John Friedman; *Chmn Textiles* Patricia Hickman; *Chmn Metal
Arts* Janet Tyne; *Chmn Ceramics* Tad Sekino; *Chmn Art History* Tom Gates; *Chmn
Children's Classes* Eileen Lew
Estab 1966; pub; D & E; scholarships; SC 96, LC 7; enrl D 750, E 1750
Courses: Art History, Calligraphy, Ceramics, Costume Design & Construction,
Drawing, Goldsmithing, Graphic Arts, Jewelry, Mixed Media, Museum Staff Training,
Painting, Photography, Printmaking, Sculpture, Silversmithing, Teacher Training,
Textile Design, Video
Adult Hobby Classes: Same as regular session
Children's Classes: Courses—Mixed Media

MUSEUM MANAGEMENT INSTITUTE, 270 Sutter St, 94108. Tel 415-392-9222.
Western Assoc of Art Museums Exec Dir Lynn Jorgenson; *Western Assoc of Art
Museums Professional Training Coordr* Patricia McDonnell; *Institute Dir* Robert
Simerly, EdD; *Co-Dir* Malcom Arth, PhD; *Co-Dir* Craig C Black, PhD; *Co-Dir* Harold
K Skramstad Jr, PhD; *Co-Dir* Steven E Weil, LLB; *Institute Advisor* Milton R Stern
Estab 1979; pvt; 4 wk seminar developed by Western Assoc of Art Museums; ent req
middle to upper management museum staff; degrees cert of completion; scholarships
Tuition: $1200 per session; campus res—room & board $500 per session
Courses: Museum Staff Training

SAN FRANCISCO ART INSTITUTE, Admissions Office, 800 Chestnut St, 94133.
Tel 415-771-7020. *Chmn Filmmaking Dept* Don Lloyd; *Chmn Painting Dept* Carlos
Villa; *Chmn Printamking Dept* Gordon Kluge; *Chmn Photography Dept* Reagan Louie;
Chmn Sculpture Dept Richard Berger
Estab 1871; pvt; D & E; ent req HS dipl or GED; degrees BFA 4 yrs, MFA 2 yrs; schol;
SC 80, LC 22, GC 11; enrl non-maj 89, maj 660, grad 95
Tuition: $3540 per yr, $1770 per sem, $510 per course; no campus res
Courses: Art History, Ceramics, Drawing, †Film, †Painting, †Photography,
†Printmaking, †Sculpture, Video
Summer School: Tui $510 for term of 6 wks beginning June 2 and July 14. Courses
—above areas

SAN FRANCISCO STATE UNIVERSITY, Art Department, 1600 Holloway, 94132.
Tel 415-469-2176. *Chmn* Margery Livingston, BA; *Assoc Chmn* Wesley Chamberlin,
MA. Instrs FT 28, PT 8-15
Estab 1899; pub; D; ent req HS dipl; degrees BA 4 yrs, MA 2 yrs; SC 80, LC 20, GC
15; enrl D 450, maj 450, grad 80
Tuition: Res—undergrad & grad $103; nonres—undergrad $855; campus
residence available
Courses: Art Education, Art History, Ceramics, Conceptual Art, Drawing, Graphic
Arts, Jewelry, Painting, Photography, Printmaking, Sculpture, Textile Design,
Conceptual Design
Summer School: Not regular session. Self-supporting classes in Ceramics, Photography
and Printmaking

RUDOLPH SCHAEFFER SCHOOL OF DESIGN, 2255 Mariposa St, 94110. Tel
415-863-0715. *Dir* Rudolph Schaeffer; *Instructor* John Carden Campbell; *Instructor*
Wayne Davis; *Instructor* Welland Lathrop; *Instructor* John Neil Parker; *Instructor* Juk
San; *Visiting Prof* Evans Ecke, art history - school yr
Estab 1926; pvt; D & E; degrees dipl 3 yr prog; schol; SC all, LC 3; enrl D 100, E 40,
grad 22
Tuition: Res—undergrad $2950 yr; no campus res
Courses: Drafting, Drawing, Interior Design
Summer School: Enrl 25; tui $425 for term of 6 wks beginning June. Courses—
Architectural Graphics, Color

SAN JACINTO

MOUNT SAN JACINTO COLLEGE, Art Department, 21400 Hwy 79, 92383. Tel
714-654-7321. *Instr* John Christenson, MFA; *Instr* Margo Cooper, BA; *Instr* Max
DeMoss, MFA; *Instr* Dana Hogan, MFA; *Instr* David Weirich, BA
Estab 1964; pub; D & E; ent req HS dipl; degrees AA and AS; SC 8, LC 2; enrl D 250,
E 420, non-maj 400, maj 50
Tuition: $13
Courses: Art History, Ceramics, History of Art & Archaeology, †Interior Design,
†Jewelry, †Painting, Printmaking, †Sculpture, Silversmithing, †Theatre Arts

SAN JOSE

SAN JOSE CITY COLLEGE, School of Fine Arts,* 2100 Moorpark Ave, 95128. Tel
408-298-2181. *Dir Instr* Edwin L Stover, PhD; *Instr* Luis Gutierrez, MFA; *Instr*
Ramon E Oeschger, MA; *Instr* Steve Salisian, MA; *Instr* Luraine Tansey, MA; *Instr*
James M Wayne, MA; *Instr* Joseph Zirker, MFA
Estab 1921; pub; D & E; ent req HS dipl or 18 yrs of age or older; degrees AA 2 yrs;
SC 7, LC 2; enrl D 65
Tuition: Nonres—$52 per unit; no campus res
Courses: Art History, Ceramics, Commercial Art, Drawing, Jewelry, Painting,
Printmaking, Theatre Arts

SAN JOSE STATE UNIVERSITY, Art Department, 125 S Seventh St, 95192. Tel
408-277-2641. *Chmn* Kathleen Cohen, PhD; *Art Educ Coordr* Jose Colchado, EdD;
Art History Coordr Bruce Radde, PhD; *Ceramics Coordr* David Middlebrook, MFA;
Crafts Coordr David Castleberry, MFA; *Design Coordr* Michael Shenon, BFA; *Painting
& Drawing Coordr* Albert Barela, MA; *Printmaking & Photography Coordr* Stephen
French, MFA; *Vis Prof* Donald Blumberg, photography
Estab 1857, dept estab 1911; pub; D & E; ent req ACT and grade point average, SAT;
degrees BA(Art), BA(Art History) 4 yrs, BS(Graphic Design), BS(Industrial Design),
BS(Interior Design) and BFA 4 yrs, MA 1 yr, MFA 2 yrs; SC 90, LC 28, GC 25;
enrl D 4529, maj 1223, grad 94
Tuition: Res $105 per sem, $90 general fee; non-res $1575 per sem, $53 per hr
Courses: Architecture, †Art Education, †Art History, †Ceramics, Drawing, †Graphic
Arts, †Graphic Design, †Handicrafts, History of Art & Archaeology, Illustration,
†Industrial Design, Intermedia, †Interior Design, Jewelry, Lettering, Mixed Media,
Museum Staff Training, †Painting, Photography, †Printmaking, †Sculpture,
Silversmithing, Teacher Training, Textile Design
Summer School: Dean Continuing Educ, Ralph C Bohn. Tui $40 lecture, $50 activity
for three summer sessions of 3, 3 and 6 wks; 3 wk January session. Courses—vary
according to professors available and projected demand

SAN LUIS OBISPO

CALIFORNIA POLYTECHNIC STATE UNIVERSITY AT SAN LUIS OBISPO,
Art Department, 93407. Tel 805-546-2324, 546-2325, 546-2350. *Head Dept* Thomas V
Johnston, DA; *Prof* Bernard Duseck, MA; *Prof* Helen Kelley, MS; *Prof* Bernice
Loughran, EdD; *Prof* Robert Reynolds, MA; *Assoc Prof* Donald Bjorkman, MFA;
Assoc Prof Robert Howell, MA; *Assoc Prof* Pierre Rademaker, MFA; *Assoc Prof* Henry
Wessels, MFA; *Asst Prof* Clarissa Hewitt, MFA. Instrs FT 14
Estab 1901, dept estab 1969; pub; D & E; ent req HS dipl, portfolio review; degrees
BS(Applied Art & Design) 4 yrs; SC 40, LC 12; enrl D 1000, E 100, non-maj 1100,
maj 200
Tuition: Res—undergrad $300 yr; non-res—undergrad $1380; campus res—room &
board $560 yr
Courses: Advertising Design, Art History, Ceramics, Drawing, Graphic Arts, Graphic
Design, Jewelry, Lettering, Painting, Photography, Printmaking, Sculpture,
Silversmithing
Summer School: Summer quarter prog is limited in course offerings

CUESTA COLLEGE, Art Department, PO Box J, 93406. Tel 805-544-2943, Ext 267.
Chmn Fine Arts Div Chester Amyx, MA; *Instructor* Rupert Deese, MFA; *Instructor*
Barry Frantz, MA; *Instructor* Robert Pelfrey, MA
Estab 1964; pub; D & E; ent req HS dipl or Calif HS Proficiency Exam; degrees AA
and AS; schol; enrl in col D 3200, E 3082
Courses: Art History, Ceramics, Display, Drawing, Graphic Design, Jewelry, Painting,
Printmaking, Sculpture, Stage Design, Theatre Arts, Video, Camera Art
Summer School: Chmn Div Fine Arts, Chester Amyx

SAN MATEO

COLLEGE OF SAN MATEO, Fine Arts Division, 1700 W Hillsdale Blvd, 94402. Tel
415-574-6288. *Div Dir* Leo N Bardes
Pub; D & E; ent req HS dipl
Tuition: None; no campus res
Courses: Architecture, Art History, Ceramics, Commercial Art, Drafting, Drawing,
Film, History of Art & Archaeology, Interior Design, Lettering, Painting,
Photography, Printmaking, Sculpture, Theatre Arts, Stained Glass

SAN PABLO

CONTRA COSTA COLLEGE, Department of Art, 2600 Mission Bell Dr, 94806. Tel
415-235-7800. *Dept Head* Robert McLean, MA; *Instructor* Paul Pernish, MFA;
Instructor Patrick Tidd, MA
Estab 1950; pub; D & E; ent req HS dipl or 18 yrs old; degrees Cert of Achievement
1 yr, AA and AS 2 yrs; SC 10, LC 16; enrl D 468, E 200
Tuition: Res—undergrad none; non-res—undergrad $41 per sem unit, maximum $1230
per acad sem; no campus res
Courses: Art History, Ceramics, Graphic Arts, Painting, Photography, Sculpture
Summer School: Assoc Dean Continuing Educ, William Vega. Enrl 50; tui free for term
of 8 wks beginning June 26. Courses—Art, Art Appreciation

SANTA ANA

SANTA ANA COLLEGE, Art Department, 17th and Bristol, 92706. Tel 714-835-3000. *Dean Acad Affairs* Richard Sneed, PhD; *Dept Chmn* Sharon Ford, MA; *Instructor* Patrick Crabb, MA; *Instructor* Estelle Friedman, MFA; *Instructor* George E Geyer, MA; *Instructor* Mayde Herberg, MA; *Instructor* Gene L Isaacson, MFA; *Instructor* Michael Johnson, MA; *Instructor* Frank Molner, MA
Estab 1915, dept estab 1960; pub; D & E; ent req HS dipl; degrees AA 2 yrs; schol; SC 21, LC 5; enrl D 280, E 160, maj 57
Tuition: Charged for out of state students only; no campus res
Courses: Advertising Design, Architecture, Art History, Ceramics, Commercial Art, Display, Drawing, Film, Graphic Arts, Graphic Design, Handicrafts, Interior Design, Jewelry, Museum Staff Training, Painting, Photography, Printmaking, Sculpture
Adult Hobby Classes: Batik and Dyeing Process, Stained Glass
Summer School: Dir, Dean Lee Ford. Enrl 3000; tui free for term of 8 wks beginning late June. Courses—Ceramics, Design, Drawing, Painting

SANTA BARBARA

UNIVERSITY OF CALIFORNIA, SANTA BARBARA, Art Department, 93106. Tel 805-961-3138. *Chmn Dept* Larry M Ayres, PhD
Estab 1868, dept estab 1950; pub; D; ent req HS dipl; degrees BA 4 yrs, MFA 2 yrs, MA 2 yrs, PhD 7 yrs; schol; SC 32, LC 17, GC 7; enrl D 431, grad 60
Courses: Art Education, Art History, Ceramics, Collage, Drawing, Printmaking, Sculpture

SANTA CLARA

UNIVERSITY OF SANTA CLARA, Fine Arts Department, Alameda & Bellomy, 95053. Tel 408-984-4008. *Chmn* Gerald P Sullivan; *Asst Prof* Dr Brigid S Barton, PhD; *Asst Prof* Kristi Hager, MFA; *Asst Prof* Samuel R Hernandez, MFA; *Asst Prof* Keith Walker, MFA; *Lectr* Joanne Thompson, PhD
Estab 1850, dept estab 1972; pvt; D; ent req HS dipl; degrees BA(Fine Arts); SC 9, LC 14; enrl D 244, non-maj 216, maj 28
Tuition: $1181 per quarter; campus res—room & board $682 per quarter
Courses: †Art History, Ceramics, Drawing, Film, Museum Staff Training, Painting, Photography, Printmaking, Sculpture, Introduction to Studio Art, Life Drawing

SANTA CRUZ

UNIVERSITY OF CALIFORNIA AT SANTA CRUZ, Art Board of Studies,* Performing Arts Bldg, 95064. Tel 408-429-2272. *Chmn* Douglas McClellan
Pub; D; ent req HS dipl; degrees BA 4 yrs; SC per quarter 11, LC per quarter 3; enrl D approx 7000, maj 90
Tuition: Res—undergrad $795 per yr; nonres—undergrad $3195 per yr
Courses: Aesthetics, Ceramics, Drawing, Graphic Arts, History of Art & Archaeology, Painting, Photography, Sculpture, Stage Design, Theatre Arts

SANTA MARIA

ALLAN HANCOCK COLLEGE, Fine Arts Department, 800 South College Drive, 93454. *Head* George Muro. Instrs FT 11, PT 7
Estab 1920; pub; D & E; ent req HS dipl, over 18 and educable; degrees AA 2 yrs; SC 24, LC 4; enrl D 800, E 220, maj 115
Courses: Art History, Ceramics, Drawing, Film, Graphic Design, Handicrafts, Jewelry, Lettering, Painting, Photography, Sculpture, Theatre Arts, Art Appreciation, Design, Life Drawing, Silk Screen
Adult Hobby Classes: Tui varied; classes offered upon need
Summer School: Enrl 230; term of 6 - 8 wks beginning June. Courses—Ceramics, Crafts, Drawing, Opera Workshop, Repertory Theatre, Watercolor

SANTA MONICA

RUSTIC CANYON ARTS AND CRAFTS CENTER, Los Angeles City Dept of Recreation and Parks, 601 Latimer Rd, 90402. Tel 213-454-9872, 454-5734. *Dir* Rosanne Mangio. Instrs PT 14
Estab 1963; pub; D & E; ent req none, classes for adults and children, 8 wk sessions; degrees none; SC 38
Courses: Ceramics, Drawing, Jewelry, Painting, Sculpture, Copper Enameling

SANTA ROSA

SANTA ROSA JUNIOR COLLEGE, Art Department, 1501 Mendocino Ave, 95401. Tel 707-527-4259. *Chmn Dept* Elizabeth Quandt, MFA; *Prof* Will Collier, MFA; *Prof* Sarah Gill, PhD; *Prof* Max Hein, MFA; *Prof* Maurice Lapp, MA; *Prof* James M Rosen, MFA; *Prof* John Watrous, MFA; *Prof* Jean Yates, MA; *Vis Prof* Alan Gussow; *Vis Prof* Nathan Olivera; *Vis Prof* Louis Siegriest; *Vis Prof* Terry St John; *Vis Prof* Wayne Thieband
Estab 1918, dept estab 1935; pub; D & E; ent req HS dipl; degrees AA 2 yrs; schol; SC 40, LC 8; enrl D approx 200, E approx 400, non-maj 100, maj 100
Tuition: Res—undergrad none; nonres—undergrad $510 per sem, $34 per unit; campus res available
Courses: Advertising Design, Art History, Calligraphy, Ceramics, Commercial Art, Conceptual Art, Display, Drawing, Graphic Design, Handicrafts, Intermedia, Interior Design, Jewelry, Lettering, Mixed Media, Museum Staff Training, Painting, Photography, Printmaking, Sculpture, Textile Design, Ceramic Sculpture, Fiber Arts
Summer School: Chmn Dept, Elizabeth Quandt. Term of 6 wks beginning June 20. Courses—Art History, Ceramics, Design, Drawing, Jewelry, Painting, Printmaking, Sculpture

SARATOGA

WEST VALLEY COLLEGE, Art Department, 14000 Fruitvale Ave, 95070. Tel 408-867-2200. *Chmn* Moises Roizen. Instrs FT 11, PT 37
Estab 1964; pub; D & E; ent req HS dipl or 18 yrs of age; degrees 8, 2 yrs; SC 51, LC 12; enrl D 1260, E 801
Tuition: Res fee under $10; no campus res
Courses: Aesthetics, Ceramics, Commercial Art, Costume Design & Construction, Drawing, Graphic Arts, History of Art & Archaeology, Jewelry, Lettering, Museum Staff Training, Painting, Sculpture, Stage Design, Theatre Arts, Design, Furniture Design, Occupational Work Experience, Metal Casting, Stained Glass, Weaving
Adult Hobby Classes: Tui varies. Courses—many classes offered by Community Services Dept
Summer School: Tui under $10 for term of 6 wks beginning mid-June. Courses—Ceramics, Design, Drawing, Jewelry, Sculpture

SIMI VALLEY

GISELA DAWLEY ART STUDIO, 4848 Seminole Circle, 93063. Tel 805-526-7125. *Owner* Gisela Dawley, MF
Estab 1964; pvt; D & E; children and adults; SC 3, LC 1; enrl D 60, E 20
Tuition: 3.50 per hr; no campus res
Courses: Art History, Drawing, Painting
Adult Hobby Classes: Enrl 30; tui $3.50 per hr. Courses—Drawing, Painting, Watercolor
Children's Classes: Enrl 60; tui $3.50 per hr. Courses—Drawing, Painting, Watercolor

SOUTH LAKE TAHOE

LAKE TAHOE COMMUNITY COLLEGE, Art Department, PO Box 14445, 95702. Tel 916-541-4660, Ext 45. *Chmn Art Dept* David Foster, MA
Estab 1975; pub; D & E; ent req HS dipl; degrees AA 2 yrs; schol; SC 22, LC 6; enrl D 375, E 150, non-maj 300, maj 75
Tuition: $2 per quarter
Courses: Art History, Ceramics, Drawing, Graphic Arts, Painting, Printmaking, Sculpture, Color, Design
Summer School: Art Media Workshop, Landscape Drawing, Landscape Painting, Primitive Pottery

STANFORD

STANFORD UNIVERSITY, Department of Art, Cummings Art Building, 94305. Tel 415-497-3404. *Chmn Dept Art* Lorenz Eitner, PhD. Instrs FT 18, PT 1
Estab 1891; pvt; D; ent req HS dipl; degrees BA 4 yrs, MA 1 yr, MFA 2 yrs, PhD 5 yrs; schol; SC 38, LC 55, GC 19 (seminars); enrl 2850, maj 120, grad 35
Tuition: $5595 per yr; campus res—room and board $2350 per yr
Courses: Art Education, †Art History, †Drawing, †Graphic Design, †Painting, †Photography, †Printmaking, †Sculpture, †Textile Design
Summer School: Dir, Lorenz Eitner. Enrl 300; term of 8 wks beginning mid-June

STOCKTON

SAN JOAQUIN DELTA COLLEGE, Art Department,* 5151 Pacific Ave, 95207. Tel 209-478-2011. *Chmn* Rowland Cheney
Estab 1935; pub; D & E; ent req HS dipl; degrees AA 2 yrs; scholarships; SC 12, LC 2; enrl D 7000, E 6000, Maj 100
Tuition: Nonres—$1530 per yr; no campus res
Courses: Ceramics, Drafting, Drawing, Graphic Arts, History of Art & Archaeology, Jewelry, Lettering, Painting, Photography, Sculpture, Stage Design, Theatre Arts
Adult Hobby Classes: Enrl 25 per class; tui $6 per class. Courses—Ceramics, Drawing, Jewelry, Painting

UNIVERSITY OF THE PACIFIC, Department of Art, 3600 Pacific Ave, 95211. Tel 209-946-2242. *Chmn* Larry Walker. Instrs FT 8
Estab 1851; pvt; ent req HS grad with 20 sem grades of recommending quality earned in the 10th, 11th and 12th years in traditional subjects, twelve of these grades must be in acad subj; degrees 4 yr undergrad art programs (4-1-4 calendar prog); 42 (4 unit) courses available over 4 yrs, Independent Study; enrl maj 40-45
Tuition: $4831 per yr, $202 per unit (6 1 2 - 11 1 2 units), $158 per unit (1 2 - 6 units); campus res—$2106
Courses: Art Education, Art History, Ceramics, Commercial Art, Drawing, Painting, Photography, Sculpture, Design
Summer School: Two 5 wk sessions

SUISUN CITY

SOLANO COMMUNITY COLLEGE, Department of Fine & Applied Art,* Suisun Valley Rd, PO Box 246, 94585. Tel 707-864-7000. *Chmn Fine & Applied Art* Carol Bishop; *Instr* Dorothy Herger
Estab 1945; pub; D & E; ent req HS dipl; degrees AA 2 yrs; SC 16, LC 5; enrl D 215, E 60
Tuition: Nonres—$47.65 per unit; no campus res
Courses: Art History, Ceramics, Commercial Art, Drawing, Jewelry, Lettering, Painting, Printmaking, Sculpture, Form & Composition, Fundamentals of Art, Stained Glass Window Making, Survey of Modern Art
Summer School: Dean Summer Session, William Cochran. Courses—Art Appreciation, Art Workshop

TAFT

TAFT COLLEGE, Division of Performing Arts, 29 Emmons Park Dr, 93268. Tel 805-765-4191. *Chmn Div* Jack Mettier, MA; *Instr* John Christensen, MA; *Instr* Karen Kuckreja, MA; *Instr* Konrad McMillan, MA
Estab 1922; pub; D & E; ent req HS grad or 18 yrs old; degrees AA 2 yrs; scholarships; SC 67, LC 6; enrl 1500 total
Courses: Architecture, †Art History, Ceramics, Commercial Art, Conceptual Art, †Drafting, Drawing, Fashion Arts, Graphic Arts, Graphic Design, Handicrafts, †History of Art & Archaeology, Illustration, Interior Design, Jewelry, Painting, †Photography, Sculpture, Silversmithing, Textile Design, †Theatre Arts
Adult Hobby Classes: Ceramics
Summer School: Dean, Mr Don Zumbro. Term of 6-8 wks. Courses—vary

THOUSAND OAKS

CALIFORNIA LUTHERAN COLLEGE, Art Department, 60 Olson Rd, 91360. Tel 805-492-2411, Ext 367. *Chmn Dept* B M A Weber, MFA; *Assoc Prof* John Solem, MA; *Asst Prof* Jerry Slattum, BA; *Instructor* Jim Hugunin, MA; *Lectr* Mrs K Neprud, BA
Estab 1961; pvt; D & E; ent req HS dipl, SAT or ACT, portfolio suggested; degrees BA 4 yr; MA(Educ) 1 - 2 yr; scholarships; SC 12, LC 7; enrl D 110, non-maj 46, maj 64
Tuition: Res—undergrad $4600 per yr, $3000 per sem, $95 PT; campus res—room & board $1600 per year
Courses: Advertising Design, Art Education, Art History, Calligraphy, Ceramics, Collage, Commercial Art, Costume Design & Construction, Drawing, Fashion Arts, Graphic Arts, Graphic Design, History of Art & Archaeology, Illustration, Mixed Media, Painting, Photography, Printmaking, Sculpture, Stage Design, Teacher Training, Theatre Arts
Summer School: Dir, James Jackson. Tui $75 per unit for term June-July, July-Aug. Courses—Design, Drawing, Pottery, Sculpture

TUJUNGA

MCGROARTY CULTURAL ART CENTER, 7570 McGroarty Terrace, 91040. Tel 213-352-5285. *Dir* Evaline V Carrie, MA. Instrs FT 4
Estab 1953; pub; D & E; scholarships; SC 20, LC 1; enrl D 250, E 100
Tuition: Fees for adults $10-$23 per 10 wk session; fees for children and teens $8-$10 per 10 wk session
Courses: Aesthetics, Art Education, Art History, Calligraphy, Ceramics, Collage, Costume Design & Construction, Drawing, Goldsmithing, Graphic Arts, Handicrafts, Jewelry, Mixed Media, Painting, Textile Design

TURLOCK

CALIFORNIA STATE COLLEGE, STANISLAUS, Art Department, 800 Monte Vista Ave, 95380. Tel 209-633-2431. *Chmn Dept* Winston McGee, MA; *Prof* Martin Camarata, MA; *Prof* Ralf Parton, MA; *Prof* James Piskoti, MFA; *Vis Lectr* Hope B Werness, PhD; *Vis Lectr* Robert Chiarito
Estab 1963, dept estab 1967; pub; D & E; ent req HS dipl; degrees BA 4 yrs; Printmaking Cert Prog, Special Masters Degree Prog; scholarships; SC 27, LC 6, GC 4; enrl D 400, E 50, non-maj 350, maj 100, grad 12
Tuition: Res—undergrad & grad $190 yr, $83.50 per sem, $59.50 PT, $23 winter term; nonres—undergrad & grad are same as res plus $52.50 per unit, $766 for 13 units; no additional fees for students taking more than 13 units; campus residence available
Courses: Art History, Ceramics, Drawing, Film, Graphic Arts, History of Art & Archaeology, Painting, Photography, Printmaking, Sculpture, Teacher Training, Theatre Arts, Gallery Management
Children's Classes: Enrl 40; tui $25 per 10 wks. Courses—Drawing, Painting
Summer School: Chmn, Winston McGee. Enrl 50. Courses—Ceramics

VALENCIA

CALIFORNIA INSTITUTE OF THE ARTS, School of Art, 24700 McBean Pkwy, 91355. Tel 805-255-1050. *Pres* Robert Fitzpatrick; *Dean* Eric Martin. Instrs FT 10
Estab 1970; pvt; ent req portfolio, health cert; degrees BFA 4 yrs, MFA; scholarships; enrl D 130 first yr, 150 in 1973
Tuition: Campus res available
Courses: Drawing, Graphic Arts, Painting, Photography, Sculpture, Video, Post Studio, Visual Information

COLLEGE OF THE CANYONS, Art Department, 26455 Rockwell Canyon Rd, 91355. Tel 805-259-7800, Ext 308. *Head Dept* Joanne Julian, MFA
Estab 1970, dept estab 1974; pub; D & E; ent req must be 18 yrs of age; degrees AA and AS 2 yrs; SC 11, LC 4; enrl D 300, E 300, maj 50
Courses: Advertising Design, Art History, Ceramics, Drafting, Drawing, Painting, Photography, Printmaking, Sculpture
Adult Hobby Classes: Tui $10 plus lab fees usually another $10 per sem

VENICE

VENICE PAINTING, DRAWING AND SCULPTURE STUDIO, INC, 346 Sunset Ave, 90291. Tel 213-399-9653. *Chmn Painting Dept* Jan Saether; *Chmn Sculpture Dept* Martine Olga Vaugel; *Teacher* Bonnie Helmer, BA; *Teacher* Jonathan Hirschfeld
Estab 1976; pvt; D & E; ent req portfolio; degrees none; SC 22; enrl D 50, E 50
Tuition: $55-$70 monthly; no campus res
Courses: Drawing, Painting, Sculpture
Children's Classes: Tui $55 per month. Courses—Painting
Summer School: Dir, Martine Olga Vaugel. Courses—same as regular offerings

VENTURA

VENTURA COLLEGE, Fine Arts Division, 4667 Telegraph Rd, 93003. Tel 805-642-3211, Ext 229. Instrs FT 13, PT 15
Estab 1925; pub; D & E; ent req HS dipl or 18 yrs of age; degrees AA and AS; scholarships; SC 50, LC 15; enrl D 500, E 500, maj 300
Tuition: None to res; no campus residence
Courses: Advertising Design, Art Education, Ceramics, Commercial Art, Display, Drawing, Fashion Arts, Graphic Arts, Graphic Design, Handicrafts, History of Art & Archaeology, Illustration, Jewelry, Painting, Photography, Sculpture, Stage Design, Textile Design, Fiber Design
Summer School: Assoc Dean, Eric Nicolet. Many of the regular session courses are offered

VICTORVILLE

VICTOR VALLEY COLLEGE, Art Department, 18422 Bear Valley Rd, 92392. Tel 714-245-4271. *Chmn Dept* Gene Kleinsmith, MFA; *Instr* Molly Haines Kohlschreiber, MFA; *Instr* Ruth Rutledge, AA; *Ceramics Technician* Brent Taylor, BA; *Vis Prof* Rudy Autio, ceramics - 1979; *Vis Prof* Warren McKenzie, ceramics - 1981; *Vis Prof* Don Reitz, ceramics - 1978; *Vis Prof* Paul Soldner, ceramics - 1977; *Vis Prof* Bill Warehall, ceramics - 1980
Estab 1961, dept estab 1971; pub; D & E; ent req HS dipl; degrees AA 2 yrs; scholarships; SC 20, LC 5; enrl D 125, E 125, non-maj 200, maj 50
Courses: Advertising Design, Aesthetics, Art History, Calligraphy, Ceramics, Commercial Art, Conceptual Art, Drawing, Graphic Arts, Graphic Design, History of Art & Archaeology, Interior Design, Painting, Photography, Printmaking, Sculpture
Summer School: Chmn Dept, Gene Kleinsmith. Enrl 50; term beginning June 15. Courses—Art History, Ceramics

VISALIA

COLLEGE OF THE SEQUOIAS, Art Department, Fine Arts Division, Mooney Blvd, 93277. Tel 209-733-2050. *Chmn* George C Pappas, MA; *Instructor* Ralph Homan, MA; *Instructor* Gene Maddox, MA; *Instructor* Alfred Pietroforte, MA; *Instructor* Barbara Strong, MA; *Instructor* Robert Marcellus, MA
Estab 1925, dept estab 1940; pub; D & E; ent req HS dipl, must be 18 yr of age; degrees AA 2 yr; scholarships; SC 12, LC 4; enrl D 60, E37, maj 10
Tuition: None; no campus res
Courses: Aesthetics, Art Education, Art History, Ceramics, Commercial Art, Drawing, Film, Graphic Arts, History of Art & Archaeology, Lettering, Museum Staff Training, Painting, Printmaking, Sculpture, Stage Design, Theatre Arts
Adult Hobby Classes: Ceramics, China Painting, Jewelry, Stained Glass
Summer School: Dir, George C Pappas. Courses—Drawing, Painting, Stained Glass

WALNUT

MOUNT SAN ANTONIO COLLEGE, Art Department, 1100 N Grand Ave, 91789. Tel 714-594-5611, Ext 319. *Chmn* Ronald B Ownbey. Instrs FT 14, PT 3
Estab 1945; pub; D & E; ent req over 18 yrs of age; degrees AA and AS 2 yrs; SC 24, LC 5; enrl D 2254, E 852, maj 500
Tuition: None to res; no campus residence
Courses: Advertising Design, Ceramics, Commercial Art, Drafting, Drawing, Graphic Arts, Art History, Illustration, Lettering, Painting, Photography, Printmaking, Sculpture, Theatre Arts, Fibers, Life Drawing, Metals & Enamels, Watercolor, Woodworking
Summer School: Enrl art 50; term of 6 wks beginning June 16. Courses—Ceramics, Drawing

WEED

COLLEGE OF THE SISKIYOUS, Art Department, 800 College Ave, 96094. Tel 916-938-4463, Ext 239. *Head Dept* Barry R Barnes, MA
Estab 1957; pub; D & E; ent req HS dipl; degrees AA 2 yrs; scholarships; SC 15, LC 2; enrl D 1200, maj 20
Tuition: None to res; no campus residence available
Courses: Art History, Ceramics, Collage, Constructions, Drafting, Drawing, Graphic Arts, History of Art & Archaeology, Painting, Photography, Printmaking, Sculpture

WHITTIER

RIO HONDO COLLEGE, Fine Arts Department, 3600 Workman Mill Rd, 90608. Tel 213-692-0921, Ext 361. *Chmn Dept* John R Jacobs, MA. Instrs FT 21, PT 16
Estab 1962; pub; D & E; ent req HS dipl; degrees AA 2 yrs; SC 18, LC 3; enrl D & E 2546, non-maj 1000, maj 200
Tuition: None; no campus residence
Courses: Advertising Design, Art History, Ceramics, Commercial Art, Costume Design & Construction, Display, Drawing, Film, Graphic Arts, History of Art & Archaeology, Illustration, Jewelry, Lettering, Painting, Photography, Printmaking, Sculpture, Stage Design, Theatre Arts, Video
Summer School: Enrl approx 200; tui free for term of 6 wks beginning June 20

WHITTIER COLLEGE, Department of Art, Stauffer Art Center, 90608. Tel 213-693-0771, Ext 309. *Chmn* Robert W Speier. Instrs FT 2, PT 2
Estab 1901; pvt; D & E; ent req HS dipl, accept credit by exam CLEP, CEEBA; degrees BA 4 yrs; scholarships and fels; SC 12, LC 12; enrl 552-560 per sem
Tuition: $3800 per yr, FT $115 per unit, PT $130 per unit, audit $65 per unit, grad $115 per unit; campus res $1740
Courses: Art Education, Ceramics, Drawing, Graphic Arts, History of Art & Archaeology, Painting, Adult and children's classes for special students; tui $5
Summer School: Enrl 25; July 7-July 31, Aug 4-Aug 29

WILMINGTON

LOS ANGELES HARBOR COLLEGE, Art Department,* 1111 Figueroa Place, 90744. Tel 213-518-1000. *Humanities & Fine Arts Chmn* Robert H Billings, MA; *Asst Prof* Nancy E Webber, MFA; *Prof* Jarmila Havlena, MFA; *Asst Prof* Jon L Grider, MA; *Assoc Prof* Frank P Matranga, MA
Estab 1949; pub; D & E; ent req HS dipl; degrees AA 2 yrs; SC 48, LC 11; enrl D 6500, E 2500
Tuition: Nonres—$810 per yr
Courses: Advertising Design, Architecture, Art History, Ceramics, Commercial Art, Costume Design & Construction, Drawing, Fashion Arts, Graphic Design, Handicrafts, History of Art & Archaeology, Jewelry, Lettering, Painting, Photography, Printmaking, Sculpture, Silversmithing, Stage Design, Theatre Arts, Video
Summer School: Art Dept Chmn, John Cassone. Courses—Art Fundamentals, Art History

WOODLAND HILLS

PIERCE COLLEGE, Art Department,* 6201 Winnetka, 91371. Tel 213-347-0551. *Art Dept Chmn* Howell Pinkston, MA; *Prof* Alfred Van Auker, MFA; *Assoc Prof* Roberta Barrager, MFA; *Asst Prof* Alfred Carrillo, MFA; *Assoc Prof* John W Corbeil, MA; *Asst Prof* James Crandall, MA; *Assoc Prof* John deKramer, BE; *Prof* Garo Gazurian, MA; *Prof* Milton Hirschl, MFA; *Prof* Eli Karpel, MA; *Prof* Walter Smith, MFA; *Asst A* Nancy Snooks, MA; *Instr* Paul C Nordberg, AA
Estab 1947, dept estab 1956; pub; D & E; ent req HS dipl 18 yrs and over; degrees AA 60 units; scholarships; SC 35, LC 3; enrl D & E 23,000
Tuition: $44 per unit; no campus res
Courses: †Advertising Design, †Architecture, Art Education, †Art History, Ceramics, Commercial Art, †Constructions, Display, †Drafting, Drawing, Film, Graphic Arts, Graphic Design, History of Art & Archaeology, †Illustration, †Industrial Design, Interior Design, Jewelry, †Landscape Architecture, Lettering, Painting, †Photography, Printmaking, †Restoration & Conservation, Sculpture, Stage Design, Theatre Arts, Video
Summer School: Dir, Barry S Haskell

COLORADO

BLACK HAWK

BLACKHAWK MOUNTAIN SCHOOL OF ART, Box 258, 251 Main St, 80422. Tel 303-582-5235. *Executive Dir* Michael J Reardon; *Instr* Ken Bowman, BFA; *Instr* Jordan Krimstein, BFA; *Instr* Robert Lockart, MFA; *Instr* Seymour Rosofsky, MFA
Estab 1963; pub; D & E, summers only; ent req letter of recommendation and a personal contract; degrees none; SC 6, LC 3; enrl D 25-35
Tuition: $950 for term beginning June 21 through Aug 2; campus res—room & board included in total cost
Courses: Ceramics, Drawing, Film, Graphic Arts, Mixed Media, Painting, Photography, Printmaking, Sculpture

BOULDER

UNIVERSITY OF COLORADO, Sibell-Wolle Fine Arts Bldg N196A, Campus Box 318, 80309. Tel 303-492-6504. *Chmn* Jerry W Kunkel. Instrs FT 44
Estab 1861; pub; D & E; ent req HS dipl; degrees BA or BFA(Art, Art History and Studio Arts) 4 yrs, MA(Art Educ and Art Hist) 3-5 yrs, MFA(Studio Arts) 2-3 yrs; schol; SC 55, LC 53, GC 67; enrl D 2000, E 150, non-maj 400, maj 399, grad 84, others 100
Tuition: Res—undergrad $346 per sem plus $100 fees; grad $363 per sem for 10-18 hrs plus $100 fees; non-res—undergrad $1525 per sem plus $100 fees; grad $1594 per sem plus $100 fees; campus res—room & board $795 per sem, $1590 per yr
Courses: †Art Education, †Art History, †Ceramics, †Drawing, Film, †Jewelry, †Painting, †Printmaking, †Sculpture, Teacher Training, Video, Watermedia
Children's Classes: Enrl 15-30; tui $20 per sem, Sat mornings
Summer School: Enrl 20-25 per course; tui $335 for term of 5 wks beginning first wk in June. Courses—Art History, Basic Drawing, Basic Painting, Basic Sculpture, Beginning Photography, Painting, Watermedia

COLORADO SPRINGS

COLORADO COLLEGE, Department of Art, 80903. Tel 303-473-2233, Ext 510. *Chmn* Bernard Arnest; *Prof* James Trissel, MFA; *Assoc Prof* Mary Chenoweth, MFA; *Asst Prof* Gale Murray, PhD; *Asst Prof* Carl Reed, MFA; *Instructor* Ruth Kolarik, PhD; *Instructor* Donald Paoletta, MA
Estab 1874; pvt; D; ent req HS dipl or equivalent and selection by admissions committee; degrees BA and MAT 4 yr; schol; SC 20, LC 20; maj 40
Tuition: Res—undergrad $4200 per yr; campus res—room and board $1600
Courses: Art Education, Art History, Drawing, Graphic Design, Painting, Photography, Printmaking, Sculpture, Three-dimensional Design
Summer School: Dean, Gilbert R Johns. Tui $215 per unit for term of 8 wks beginning June 19. Courses—Architecture, Art Education, Photography

DENVER

COLORADO INSTITUTE OF ART, 200 E Ninth Ave, 80203. Tel 303-837-0825. *Pres* John T Barclay; *Dir of Educ* James Graft
Estab 1952; pvt; D & E; ent req HS dipl; degrees dipl 2 yr; schol; SC all; enrl D 725, E 200 non-maj 200, maj 725
Tuition: Res—undergrad $750 per quarter; non-res—undergrad $750 per quarter; photography $825; campus res $2500
Courses: †Advertising Design, Commercial Art, Drawing, †Fashion Arts, Graphic

Design, Illustration, †Interior Design, Lettering, Mixed Media, Painting, †Photography
Adult Hobby Classes: Tui $100 per 36 hrs. Courses—Drawing and Painting, Interior Decorating, Photography
Children's Classes: Tui $15 per 16 hrs; advanced placement is available

COLORADO WOMEN'S COLLEGE, Department of Art,* Montview Blvd & Quebec, 80220. Tel 303-394-6012. *Chmn* Maynard Whitney; *Assoc Prof* Elizabeth Schoeberlein; *Asst Prof* Suzanne Martin; *Instr* Bernie Marek; *Vis Prof* Joyce Eakins, painting
Estab 1898; pvt; D; ent req HS dipl; degrees BA 4 yr, BFA 5 yr; scholarships; SC 30, LC 15; enrl D 158, maj 45
Tuition: Res—undergrad $115 per cr hr; campus res—room and board $2000
Courses: †Art Education, †Art History, Ceramics, Conceptual Art, Drawing, Jewelry, †Mixed Media, Painting, Photography, Printmaking, Sculpture, Stage Design, Teacher Training, Textile Design, Theatre Arts
Summer School: Dir, James Polt. Enrl 15 per class; tui $115 per cr hr for term of 3 wks beginning May and July. Courses—Jewelry, Painting, Photography, Primitive Pottery, Printmaking

LORETTO HEIGHTS COLLEGE, Department of Art, 3001 S Federal Blvd, 80236. Tel 303-922-4011. *Prog Dir* Max Di Julio. Instrs FT 2, PT 3
Estab 1880; pvt; D & E; ent req HS dipl, ent exam; degrees BA, BS and BFA 4 yrs; SC 8, LC 4
Tuition: $3150 per yr; campus res $4900
Courses: Art Education, Ceramics, Drawing, Graphic Arts, History of Art & Archaeology, Jewelry, Lettering, Painting, Sculpture, Weaving
Summer School: Courses—Ceramics, Glass, Jewelry, Printmaking, Weaving

METROPOLITAN STATE COLLEGE, Art Department, 1006 11th St, 80204. Tel 303-629-3090. *Chmn* J Thomas Logan, MFA; *Prof* Howard Brown, MFA; *Prof* Charles Hayes, MFA; *Prof* Rodger Lang, MFA; *Prof* Robert Mangold, MFA; *Prof* Robert Strohmeier, MFA; *Asst Prof* Gene Eidy, MFA; *Asst Prof* Sally Everett, MFA; *Asst Prof* Barbara Houghton, MFA; *Asst Prof* Jean Schiff, MFA; *Asst Prof* Craig Smith, PhD; *Asst Prof* Francis Sprout, MFA
Estab 1963, dept estab 1963; pub; D & E; ent req HS dipl or GED; degrees BA 4 yrs; SC 52, LC 8; enrl D 650, E 325, maj 465
Tuition: Res $275 per sem, non-res $1000 per sem
Courses: Advertising Design, Art Education, Art History, Ceramics, Commercial Art, Drawing, Graphic Arts, Graphic Design, Industrial Design, Jewelry, Painting, Photography, Printmaking, Sculpture, Silversmithing, Design in Wood, Product Design
Summer School: Same as regular session

ROCKY MOUNTAIN SCHOOL OF ART, 1441 Ogden St, 80218. Tel 303-832-1557. Instrs FT 10
Estab 1963; pvt; D & E; ent req portfolio; degrees 2 yr cert; scholarships; enrl D 100, E 25
Tuition: $525 per quarter; no campus res
Courses: Advertising Design, Art History, Commercial Art, Drawing, Fashion Arts, Graphic Design, Illustration, Lettering, Painting

UNIVERSITY OF COLORADO AT DENVER, Department of Fine Arts, 1100 14th St, Box 103, 80202. Tel 303-629-2626. *Chmn* Ludwik Turzanski, MFA; *Prof* Charles L Moone, MFA; *Assoc Prof* Jose Arguelles, PhD; *Assoc Prof* John R Fudge, MFA; *Assoc Prof* Gerald C Johnson, MFA; *Assoc Prof* Ernest O Porps, MFA; *Visiting Instructor* Jane Comstock, art history
Estab 1876, dept estab 1955; pub; D & E; ent req HS dipl, ACT or SAT, previous academic ability and accomplishment; degrees BA and BFA 4 yrs; schol; SC 21, LC 13, GC 11; enrl maj 114
Tuition: Res—undergrad & grad $261 per sem, $23 per cr hr; non-res—undergrad & grad $1146 per sem, $77 per cr hr; no campus res available
Courses: Art History, †Drawing, Film, †Painting, †Photography, †Printmaking, †Sculpture
Adult Hobby Classes: Tui $2 - $40 per class. Courses—Drawing, Glass Etching, Needlework, Painting, Rug Braiding, Sketching, Spinning, Stained Glass, Wood Inlay
Summer School: Dir, Ludwik Turzanski. Tui same as regular sem, term of 10 wk beginning June 12. Courses—Art History, Studio Workshops

UNIVERSITY OF DENVER, School of Art, 2121 E Asbury, 80208. Tel 303-753-2846. *Dir* Mel Strawn, MFA
Estab 1880; pvt; D; ent req HS dipl; degrees BA and BFA 4 yrs, MFA 2 yrs, MA 4 quarters; honors program; scholarships; SC 44, LC 33, GC 50; enrl D 450, non-maj 170-200, maj 176, grad 40
Tuition: $4170 per yr, $1390 per sem, $107 per quarter hr; campus residency available
Courses: Advertising Design, †Art Education, †Art History, †Ceramics, Commercial Art, †Drawing, Film, Graphic Arts, Graphic Design, Handicrafts, Jewelry, Lettering, †Museum Staff Training, †Painting, †Photography, †Printmaking, †Sculpture, Fabric Dyeing, †Graphic Communications Design, Off-loom Weaving
Adult Hobby Classes: Enrl 25; tui $35-$60 per course. Courses—Ceramics, Drawing, Jewelry, Painting, Photography, Printmaking
Summer School: Dir, Mel Strawn. Enrl 100; tui $107 per quarter hr for sem of 8 wks beginning June 16. Courses—Art History, Ceramics, Photography and Design, Workshop-Seminar in conjunction with Aspen Design Conference

FORT COLLINS

COLORADO STATE UNIVERSITY, Department of Art, 80523. Tel 303-491-6774. *Chmn* Peter A Jacobs, EdD; *Asst Chmn* William Imel; *Asst Chmn* Leroy Twarogowski; *MFA Coordr* Dave Dietemann; *Coordr Teacher Cert* Perry Ragouzis; *Prof* John Curfman, MS; *Prof* Richard DeVore, MFA; *Prof* Nilda C Getty, MFA; *Prof* John Sorbie, MSA Ed. Instrs FT 30, PT 5
Estab 1870, dept estab 1956; pub; D; ent req HS dipl, portfolio if by transfer; degrees BA(Art History & Art Education) and BFA 4 yr, MFA 70 hrs; SC 55, LC 13, GC 5; enrl D 547, non-maj 860, maj 547, grad 13
Tuition: Res—undergrad $795 per yr, $397 per sem, $20 per cr up to 8 cr; grad $825 per yr, $412 per sem; non-res—undergrad $2849 per yr, $1424 per sem; grad $2970 per yr, $1485 per sem; campus residence available $2528
Courses: †Advertising Design, †Art Education, †Art History, †Ceramics, †Commercial Art, †Drawing, Goldsmithing, †Graphic Design, †Illustration, †Interior Design, †Jewelry, †Painting, †Printmaking, †Sculpture, †Silversmithing, †Textile Design, Photography, †Fibers
Summer School: 4 wk and 8 wk sessions beginning May 19 and June 16

GOLDEN

FOOTHILLS ART CENTER, INC, 809 15th St, 80401. Tel 303-279-3922. *Exec Dir* Marian J Metsopoulos, MA. Instrs PT 10
Estab 1968; pvt; D & E (winter and spring); ent req none
Tuition: $20-$54 for 6-10 wk class
Courses: Calligraphy, Drawing, Jewelry, Painting, Printmaking, Pottery, Watercolor
Adult Hobby Classes: Enrl limited; tui $15-$20 for 8-10 wk class. Courses—Pottery, Printmaking
Summer School: Exec Dir, Marian J Metsopoulos. Workshops for adults and classes for children beginning in June

GRAND JUNCTION

MESA COLLEGE, Art Department,* 81501. Tel 303-248-1020. *Chmn* Donald E Meyers, MA; *Asst Prof* Larry D Runner, MFA; *Asst Prof* Douglas T DeVinny, MFA
Estab 1925; pub; D & E; ent req HS dipl, GED; degrees AA, BA (Visual & Performing Arts) 4 yrs; scholarships; SC 23, LC 5; enrl D 538, E 103
Tuition: Res—undergrad $423 per yr, $211.50 per sem; nonres—undergrad $1695 per yr, $847.50 per sem; campus res—room and board $1920 per yr
Courses: Aesthetics, Art Education, Art History, Ceramics, Collage, Conceptual Art, Constructions, Drafting, Drawing, Graphic Arts, Jewelry, Mixed Media, Painting, Photography, Printmaking, Sculpture, Silversmithing, Stage Design, Theatre Arts

GREELEY

UNIVERSITY OF NORTHERN COLORADO, Department of Fine Arts,* 80639. Tel 303-351-1890. *Chmn* Richard Munson; *Assoc Prof* Robert B Turner, PhD; *Prof* Herb Schumacher, EdD; *Asst Prof* Hyun Shin, EdD; *Assoc Prof* Frederick Myers, MFA; *Assoc Prof* David Haas, MA; *Assoc Prof* William Cordiner, MA; *Instr* Susan Hoover; *Asst Prof* Betty Johnson
Estab 1889; pub; D & E; ent req HS dipl; degrees BA
Tuition: Res—undergrad and grad $20 per 9 cr hrs or less, $192 per 10-18 cr hrs; nonres —undergrad and grad $80-$84 per 9 cr hrs or less, $803-$840 per 10-18 cr hrs; campus res room and board $500-$535 per quarter
Courses: Art Education, Art History, Ceramics, Drawing, Graphic Arts, Intermedia, Jewelry, Painting, Printmaking, Sculpture, Teacher Training, Video
Summer School: Courses—Comparative Arts Program in Florence, Italy, Study of the Indian Arts of Mesa Verde, Mesa Verde workshop and on campus courses, Workshops in Weaving & Ceramics in Steamboat Springs, Colorado

GUNNISON

WESTERN STATE COLLEGE OF COLORADO, Department of Art, 81230. Tel 303-943-3083. Instrs FT 7, PT 1
Estab 1911; pub; D & E; ent req HS dipl, special exam; degrees 4 yr; SC 29, LC 7, GC 8; enrl 850
Courses: Art Education, Calligraphy, Ceramics, Drawing, Jewelry, Painting, Printmaking, Sculpture, Design, Indian Art, Introduction to Art, Studio Art, Weaving
Summer School: Dir, Dr Edwin H Randall. 2, 4 and 8 wk courses

LA JUNTA

OTERO JUNIOR COLLEGE, Art Department,* 81050. Tel 303-384-8721. *Head Dept* Kenneth Brandon
Estab 1941; pub; D & E; ent req HS grad; degrees AA and AAS 2 yr; scholarships; SC 12, LC 3; enrl 776
Tuition: Res—$339 for 12-18 hrs; nonres—$389; campus res—room and board $1209-$1284
Courses: Art History, Ceramics, Drawing, Painting, Creative Design, Metal Sculpture, Watercolor

PUEBLO

UNIVERSITY OF SOUTHERN COLORADO, BELMONT CAMPUS, Department of Art, 2200 Bonforte Blvd, 81005. Tel 303-549-2817. *Chmn* Edward R Sajbel, MA; *Prof* Jo Ann Brassill, MFA; *Prof* Lewis Tilley, MFA; *Assoc Prof* Robert Hench, MA; *Assoc Prof* Dr Mildred Montverde, PhD; *Asst Prof* Carl Jensen, MFA; *Asst Prof* Robert Wands, MA; *Instructor* Nick Latka, MFA
Estab 1933; pub; D & E; ent req HS dipl, GED, Open Door Policy; degrees BA and BS 4 yrs; schol; SC 66, LC 19, GC 2; enrl D 700, E 50, non-maj 150, maj 600
Tuition: Res—undergrad $350 18 hr sem; non-res—undergrad $1237 18 hr sem; campus residency available
Courses: Advertising Design, Art History, Ceramics, Collage, Commercial Art, Drawing, Film, Graphic Design, Illustration, Jewelry, Museum Staff Training, Painting, Photography, Printmaking, Sculpture, Silversmithing, Teacher Training
Summer School: Courses—Art Education, Art History, Ceramics, Introduction to Art, Painting

STERLING

NORTHEASTERN JUNIOR COLLEGE, Department of Art, 80751. Tel 303-522-6600, Ext 671. *Head Dept* Peter L Youngers, MFA; *Instructor* Larry Presteich, MA
Estab 1941; pub; D & E; ent req HS dipl, GED; degrees AA 2 yr; schol; SC 16, LC 2; enrl D 103, E 23, non-maj 73, maj 30, others 23
Tuition: Res—in county $8 cr hr, out county $80 quarter, $16 cr hr; non-res—$330 quarter, $28 cr hr; all students $70 college fee and $34 Associated Student fee; campus res—$450 per quarter
Courses: Art Education, Art History, Ceramics, Display, Drawing, Handicrafts, Lettering, Mixed Media, Painting, Printmaking, Sculpture, Teacher Training
Adult Hobby Classes: Enrl 100; tui $8 per cr hr. Courses—Basic Crafts, Ceramics, Drawing, Macrame, Painting, Stained Glass
Summer School: Dir, Dick Gritz. Courses—vary each yr

VAIL

COLORADO MOUNTAIN COLLEGE, Summervail Workshop for Art & Critical Studies, PO Box 1114, 81657. Tel 303-827-5703. *Dir* Randy Milhoan, BFA
Estab 1971 for summers only; enrl 1500 per summer
Tuition: (in-state) $14 per cr hr; (out-state) $48 per cr hr
Courses: Ceramics, Drawing, Jewelry, Painting, Photography, Printmaking, Sculpture, Blacksmithing, Fibers & Surface Design, Flat & Hot Glass, Metalsmithing, Watercolor, Woodworking

CONNECTICUT

BRIDGEPORT

HOUSATONIC COMMUNITY COLLEGE, Art Department,* 510 Barnum Ave, 06680. Tel 203-579-6440. *Chmn* Burt Chernow, MA
Estab 1967, dept estab 1968; pub; D & E; ent req HS dipl; degrees AA 2 yr; SC 15, LC 5; enrl maj 100
Tuition: Res—$200 per yr; nonres—$850 per yr
Courses: Art Education, Art History, Ceramics, Collage, Constructions, Drafting, Drawing, Film, History of Art & Archaeology, Mixed Media, Painting, Photography, Sculpture, Teacher Training
Adult Hobby Classes: Varied
Summer School: Dir, Dr Joseph Shive. Courses—Same as regular session

SACRED HEART UNIVERSITY, Department of Fine Arts, PO Box 6460, 06606. Tel 203-374-9441, Ext 210. *Chmn* Virginia F Zic, MFA. Instrs 10
Estab 1963, dept estab 1977; pvt; D & E; ent req HS dipl; degrees BA 4 yrs; SC 10, LC 3; enrl D 200, E 50, non-maj 185, maj 40
Tuition: $1225 per sem; no campus res
Courses: Art History, †Drawing, Graphic Design, †Illustration, †Painting, Design
Summer School: Term of 5 wks beginning June and July

UNIVERSITY OF BRIDGEPORT, Art Department, College of Fine Arts, University and Iranistan Ave, 06602. Tel 203-576-4436. *Chmn* Peter E Schier, MS; *Prof* Eileen Lord, PhD; *Prof* August Madrigal, MA; *Prof* Robert Morris, MFA; *Assoc Prof* Arthur Nager, MFA; *Assoc Prof* Paul Vazquez, MFA
Estab 1927, dept estab 1947; pvt; D & E; ent req portfolio for BFA candidates only, college boards; degrees certificate 1 yr, AA 2 yr, BA, BS and BFA 4 yr, MS 1 yr; schol; SC 38, LC 24, GC 15; enrl D 1150, E 200, non-maj 1070, maj 260, GS 22
Tuition: Res—undergrad $1980 per sem, grad $108 per cr hr; non-res—undergrad $103 per cr hr, grad $108 per cr hr; campus residence available
Courses: †Advertising Design, †Art Education, †Art History, Calligraphy, †Ceramics, Commercial Art, Drafting, Drawing, †Film, Graphic Arts, †Graphic Design, Handicrafts, Illustration, †Industrial Design, Jewelry, Lettering, †Painting, †Photography, †Printmaking, †Sculpture, Silversmithing, Stage Design, Teacher Training, Textile Design, †Theatre Arts, Video, †Art Therapy, †Pre-Architecture, Weaving
Adult Hobby Classes: Enrl open; tui $75 per course. Courses—most crafts
Summer School: Chmn, Peter E Schier. Tui $103 per hr for term of 5 wks beginning May or June. Courses—Art History, Color, Crafts, Design, Drawing, Graphic Design, Painting, Photography

DANBURY

WESTERN CONNECTICUT STATE COLLEGE,* 180 White St, 06810. Tel 203-797-4336. *Instr* Walter Boelke, MFA; *Instr* David Holzman, BA
Estab 1800; pub; D & E; ent req HS dipl; degrees BA (graphic communications) 4 yr; scholarships; SC 30, LC 3-6, GC 5; enrl D 25
Tuition: Res—undergrad $540 per yr, $32 per cr hr, grad $40 per cr hr; nonres—undergrad $1530 per yr; campus res—room and board $1250
Courses: Advertising Design, Aesthetics, Architecture, Art Education, Art History, Ceramics, Commercial Art, Drawing, Film, Graphic Arts, Graphic Design, Handicrafts, History of Art & Archaeology, Illustration, Jewelry, Lettering, Mixed Media, Painting, Photography, Printmaking, Sculpture, Silversmithing, Teacher Training, Theatre Arts, Video, Cloth as an art form
Summer School: Dir, Dr Jack Rudner. Courses—same as regular session

FARMINGTON

TUNXIS COMMUNITY COLLEGE, Graphic Design & Applied Arts Dept, Junction Route 6 & 177, 06032. Tel 203-677-7701. *Acad Exec Dean* Dr Henry Steeger; *Graphic Design Coordr* Anna Lafferty, MFA & MAEd; *Fine Arts Coordr* George Fitch, MFA
Estab 1970, dept estab 1973; pub; D & E; ent req HS dipl; degrees AS; SC 15, LC 4; enrl non-maj 40, maj 90
Tuition: $250 per yr; $125 per sem, $9 per cr; no campus res
Courses: Advertising Design, Art Education, Art History, Commercial Art, Conceptual Art, Drawing, †Graphic Arts, History of Art & Archaeology, Illustration, Lettering, Painting, Photography
Adult Hobby Classes: Tui $9 per cr. Courses—Design, Drawing, Painting, Watercolor
Summer School: Dir Community Services, Dr Kyle. Courses—Drawing, Painting

GREENWICH

PROPERSI GALLERIES AND SCHOOL OF ART INC, 44 W Putnam Ave, 06830. Tel 203-869-4430. *Dir* August Propersi; *Instructor* William Fraccio; *Instructor* Jacques Maloubier
Estab 1958; pvt; D & E; ent req HS dipl, portfolio; degrees dipl, 3 yrs; schol; SC 7, LC 2; enrl D 45, E 45, non-maj 27, maj 63
Tuition: $2034 per yr; no campus res
Courses: Advertising Design, Commercial Art, Conceptual Art, Drawing, Fashion Arts, Graphic Design, Illustration, Lettering, Mixed Media, Painting, Communications, Fashion Illustration, Fine Arts Career, Studio Skills
Adult Hobby Classes: Enrl 10; tui $258 per sem. Courses—Oils, Painting, Watercolor
Children's Classes: Enrl 15; tui $157 per sem. Courses—Art History, Drawing, Painting
Summer School: Dir, August Propersi. Tui $384 for term of 7 wks beginning July 5. Courses—same as above

HAMDEN

PAIER SCHOOL OF ART, INC, 6 Prospect Court, 06511. Tel 203-777-7319. *Pres* Edward T Paier. Instrs PT 17
Estab 1946; pvt; D & E; ent req HS grad, presentation of portfolio, transcript of records, recommendation; degrees BFA (in cooperation with Albertus Magnus College); SC 10, LC 6 GC 1; enrl D 385, E 150
Tuition: $3795 per yr
Courses: Graphic Arts, Illustration, Interior Design, Photography, Fine Arts
Summer School: Dir E T Paier. Enrl 150; term of 6 wk beginning July. Courses—part-time and unit subjects available

HARTFORD

TRINITY COLLEGE, Department of Fine Arts, Summit St, 06106. Tel 203-527-3151. *Chmn* Michael R T Mahoney, PhD; *Dir Studio Arts Prog* George Chaplin, MFA; *Prof* Thomas P Baird, MFA; *Asst Prof* Mardges Bacon, PhD; *Asst Prof* Alden R Gordon, PhD; *Artist-in-Residence* Mary Kenealy, MFA; *Artist-in-Residence* Steve Wood, MFA
Estab 1823, dept estab 1939; pvt; D; ent req HS dipl; degrees MA; scholarships; SC 20, LC 22; enrl D 400, non-maj 350, major 50
Tuition: Res—undergrad $4600 per yr; campus res room $980, board $990
Courses: Aesthetics, Architecture, †Art History, Drawing, Painting, Printmaking, †Theatre Arts, †Studio Arts

MANCHESTER

MANCHESTER COMMUNITY COLLEGE, Fine Arts Department, Bidwell St, PO Box 1046, 06040. Tel 203-646-4900. *Dept Chmn* Robert F Manning, MAEd; *Asst Prof* John E Stevens, MFA; *Asst Prof* Suzanne Howes Stevens, MAEd. Instrs FT 5
Estab 1963, dept estab 1968; pub; D & E; ent req HS dipl, portfolio for visual fine arts prog; degrees AA and AS 2 yrs; enrl D & E 300, non-maj 240, maj 60
Tuition: Res $354 per yr, $177 per sem; non-res $1054 per yr, $527 per sem
Courses: Art History, Calligraphy, Ceramics, Drawing, Film, Lettering, Painting, Photography, Printmaking, Sculpture, Basic Design, History of Film, Sign Painting

MIDDLETOWN

WESLEYAN UNIVERSITY, Art Department, Center for the Arts, Wesleyan Station, 06457. Tel 203-347-9411. *Chmn* John Risley, MFA; *Prof* John Frazer, MFA; *Prof* John Martin; *Assoc Prof* John T Paoletti, PhD; *Assoc Prof* David Schorr, MFA; *Asst Prof* Clark Maines, PhD; *Asst Prof* J Seeley, MFA
Estab 1831, dept estab 1928; pvt; D; ent req HS dipl, SAT; degrees BA 4 yrs; SC 30, LC 25; enrl in school D 2686, maj 95, grad 15
Tuition: Res—undergrad & grad $5200 per yr, $520 per course; non-res—undergrad $650 per course; grad $520 per course, $285 night student; campus res available
Courses: Architecture, Art Education, Calligraphy, Ceramics, Conceptual Art, Constructions, Costume Design & Construction, Drawing, Graphic Arts, Graphic Design, History of Art & Archaeology, Industrial Design, Jewelry, Mixed Media, Painting, Photography, Printmaking, Sculpture, Silversmithing, Stage Design, Teacher Training, Video, Film History, Film Production, History of Prints, Printroom Methods & Techniques
Summer School: Dir, James L Steffensen, Jr. Enrl 576; tui $520 for term of 8 wks beginning July 5. Courses—grad courses in all areas

NEW BRITAIN

CENTRAL CONNECTICUT STATE COLLEGE, Department of Art, 1615 Stanley St, 06050. Tel 203-827-7326. *Chmn Dept* Walter J LaVoy, DEd. Instrs FT 16, PT 21
Estab 1849; pub; D & E; ent req HS dipl, screening required for admission to dept; degrees BA, BA(Graphic Design) and BS(Art Educ) 4 yrs; SC 36, LC 8, GC 20; enrl D 200, E 150, non-maj 1000, maj 200, grad 500
Courses: Advertising Design, Art Education, Art History, Ceramics, Costume Design & Construction, Display, Drafting, Drawing, Graphic Arts, Handicrafts, Jewelry, Lettering, Painting, Photography, Printmaking, Sculpture, Silversmithing, Stage Design, Teacher Training, Theatre Arts, Video, Ceramic Sculpture, Color Theory, Fibre Sculpture, Serigraphy (Silk Screen), Stained Glass, Weaving
Children's Classes: Enrl 6-17 yr olds; tui $6. Courses—vary
Summer School: Dean Exten Col, R Tupper. Tui $35 per cr hr for term of 5 wks beginning July 5. Courses—varied and comprehensive

NEW CANAAN

SILVERMINE GUILD SCHOOL OF THE ARTS, 1037 Silvermine Rd, 06840. Tel 203-866-0411. *Dir* Robert Franco
Estab 1949; pvt; D & E; ent req none; degrees none; SC 60, LC 1; enrl 560
Tuition: No campus res
Courses: Advertising Design, Calligraphy, Ceramics, Collage, Commercial Art, Conceptual Art, Drawing, Graphic Arts, Handicrafts, Illustration, Jewelry, Mixed Media, Painting, Photography, Printmaking, Sculpture, Air Brush Painting, Chinese Landscape Painting, Design, Weaving
Children's Classes: Courses—Acting Studio, Art Workshops
Summer School: Dir, Robert Franco. 8 wk prog. Courses—same as above

NEW HAVEN

ALBERTUS MAGNUS COLLEGE, Art Department, 700 Prospect St, 06511. Tel 203-777-6631. *Chmn* Sr Thoma Swanson, MFA; *Prof* Denise Buckley, MFA; *Prof* Juliana D'Amato, PhD; *Prof* Mark; *Instructor* Beverly Chieffo, MA; *Instructor* Joan Killion, MFA
Estab 1925, dept estab 1970; pvt; D & E; ent req HS dipl, SAT, CEEB; degrees BA, BFA 8 sem; schol; SC 20, LC 9; enrl D 120, non-maj 60, maj 40
Tuition: Res—undergrad $5000 per yr, part-time $98 per cr; nonres—undergrad $2950 per yr; campus res—room & board $1850 per yr
Courses: Aesthetics, Art Education, Art History, Ceramics, Collage, Drawing, Graphic Arts, History of Art & Archaeology, Lettering, Mixed Media, Painting, Photography, Printmaking, Sculpture, Stage Design, Teacher Training, Art Therapy, Papermaking, Weaving
Summer School: Dir, Sister Jane McDermott. Courses—vary

SOUTHERN CONNECTICUT STATE COLLEGE, Department of Art, 501 Crescent St, 06515. Tel 203-397-4279. *Dept Head* Elizabeth Turner Hall, MFA. Instrs FT 21, PT 8
Estab 1893; pub; D & E; ent req HS dipl, SAT; degrees BS, MS(Art Educ), BA(Art History) and BA, BS(Studio Art) 4 yrs; SC 40, LC 18, GC 20; enrl D 400, GS 400
Tuition: Res—$500 yr, $32 per cr hr; non-res—$1400 yr, $40 per cr hr; campus residence available
Courses: Art Education, Art History, Ceramics, Drawing, Graphic Design, Illustration, Jewelry, Painting, Photography, Printmaking, Sculpture, Eastern Art Histories, Glassblowing, Graphic Processes, Metalsmithing, Weaving
Summer School: Dir, George Cole. Two terms of 5 wks beginning May 30 and July 5

YALE UNIVERSITY
—School of Art, 180 York St, 06520. Tel 203-436-0308. *Dean* Andrew Forge; *Dir* Howard S Weaver, BA; *Prof* William Bailey, MFA; *Prof* Alvin Eisenman, MA; *Prof* Todd Papageorge, BA; *Prof* Gabor Peterdi, MA; *Assoc Prof* David vonSchlegell
Estab 1868; pvt; D; ent req HS dipl, BA or BFA, portfolio; degrees MFA 2 yrs; scholarships; GC 95
Tuition: $5100 per yr
Courses: Drawing, Graphic Design, Painting, Photography, Printmaking, Sculpture
—Department of the History of Art, Box 2009, 56 High St, 06520. Tel 203-436-8853. *Dir Undergrad Studies* David J Cast; *Chmn* Walter Cahn; *Admin Asst* Nancy A Walchli. Instrs FT 27, PT 2
Estab 1940; pvt; D; ent req for grad prog—BA and foreign language; degrees BA, MA, PhD; scholarships, fels and assistantships
Courses: Art History, Museum Staff Training
—School of Architecture, 06520. Tel 203-436-0550. *Dean* Cesar Pelli
Estab 1869; pvt; ent req Bachelor's degree, grad record exam; degrees MArchit 3 yrs, MEnviron Design 2 yrs; enrl 142 maximum

NEW LONDON

CONNECTICUT COLLEGE
—**Department of Art,** Mohegan Ave, 06320. Tel 203-442-5391. *Chmn* Peter Leibert; *Prof* Richard Lukosius; *Prof* David Smalley; *Prof* William McCabe; *Assoc Prof* Barkley L Hendricks; *Assoc Prof* Maureen McCabe; *Asst Prof* Robert Straight; *Asst Prof* Vicky Tomayko
Estab 1911; pvt; D; ent req HS dipl, ent exam; degrees BA 4 yrs; scholarships; SC 20, LC 34
Tuition: $5240 per yr; campus res—room & board $1900
Courses: Many offered in a variety of areas
Summer School: Dir, Peter Leibert. Courses—Ceramics, Drawing, Painting, Photography, Printmaking, Sculpture
—**Department of Art History,** 06320. Tel 203-447-1911. *Chmn* Charles Price, PhD; *Prof* John H B Knowlton, PhD; *Prof* Edgar Mayhew, PhD; *Assoc Prof* Nancy Rash Fabbri, PhD; *Asst Prof* Richard Chafee, MA; *Asst Prof* Barbara B Zabel, PhD
Estab 1911, dept estab 1972; pvt; D & E; ent req HS dipl, SAT; degrees BA 4 yrs
Tuition: $5240 per yr; campus res—room $1900 per yr
Courses: Art History

NORWICH

NORWICH ART SCHOOL, Norwich Free Academy, Art Dept, 108 Crescent St, 06360. Tel 203-887-2505. *Head Dept* Frank T Novack, MFA; *Instructor* Caroline T Battisto, AFA; *Instructor* Daniel C Charron, BS; *Instructor* Dennis H Driscoll, BFA; *Instructor* John R Fix, MAT; *Instructor* Theodora S Goberis; *Instructor* Melody A Leary, MS; *Instructor* Janet M Mol, BFA; *Instructor* Mary-Anne Hall, MA; *Instructor* Johanna D Vacca, MA
Estab 1890; pvt; D & E; ent req HS dipl and submission of portfolio for one year Basic Art Program post high school; Fine Arts Program available to high school students beginning 10th grade and special program for advanced students in all studio or art history courses to prepare portfolio for further art college education; SC 18, LC 3; enrl D 685, E 120, fine arts maj 150
Tuition: Res—$1400 yr, $700 per sem plus supplies; no campus res
Courses: Art History, Ceramics, Drawing, Fashion Arts, Handicrafts, Painting, Photography, Printmaking, Sculpture, Silversmithing, Textile Design, Design, Drawing & Composition, Macrame, Poster & Layout, Weaving
Adult Hobby Classes: Enrl 75; tui $40 for 15 wk session. Courses—Ceramics, Drawing, Jewelry & Metalsmithing, Painting
Children's Classes: Enrl 121; tui $40 for 24 wk session. Courses—Collage, Design, Drawing, Murals, Painting, Pottery
Summer School: Dir, Frank T Novack. Enrl 15-18 per class; tui $65 for term of 6 wk beginning first wk of July. Courses—Drawing and Painting, General Art

STORRS

UNIVERSITY OF CONNECTICUT, Art Department, 06268. Tel 203-429-3930. *Head Dept* Richard Thornton. Instrs FT 30, PT 6
Estab 1882, dept estab 1950; pub; D; ent req HS dipl; degrees BA(Art History), BFA(Studio) 4 yrs; SC 32, LC 20; enrl D 1500, maj 270
Tuition: Res—undergrad $270, nonres—undergrad $615; campus residency available
Courses: Advertising Design, Architecture, †Art History, †Ceramics, Drawing, †Graphic Arts, †Painting, †Photography, †Printmaking, †Sculpture
Summer School: Tui $45 per cr hr; three week workshops beginning May 19. Courses—Drawing, Graphic Design, Lithography, Painting, Sculpture

VOLUNTOWN

FOSTER CADDELL'S ART SCHOOL, Rt 49, RFD 1, 06384. Tel 201-376-9583. *Head Dept* Foster Caddell
Estab 1958; D & E; enrl D 75, E 50
Tuition: $350 per course; no campus res
Courses: Drawing, Painting, †Teacher Training, Pastel
Summer School: Tui $150 per wk. Courses—Painting Demonstrations and Lecture; Summer Workshops and Seminars

WEST HARTFORD

HARTFORD ART SCHOOL OF THE UNIVERSITY OF HARTFORD, 200 Bloomfield Ave, 06117. Tel 203-243-4391, 243-4398. *Dean* Edwin E Stein, PhD; *Asst to the Dean* Steven Keller, MA; *Prof* Wolfgang Behl; *Prof* Rudolph Zallinger, MFA; *Prof* Paul Zimmerman, MFA; *Assoc Prof* Robert Cumming, MFA; *Assoc Prof* Lloyd Glasson, MFA; *Assoc Prof* Gary Hogan, MS; *Assoc Prof* Christopher Horton, MAT; *Assoc Prof* Peter McLean, MFA; *Asst Prof* Gilles Giuntini, MFA; *Asst Prof* Nancy Hoffman, MFA; *Asst Prof* Doris Kinsella, BA; *Asst Prof* Maria Kurcbart, MFA and MAT; *Asst Prof* Frederick Wessel, MFA; *Instructor* Mary Frey, MFA; *Instructor* Jack Goldstein, MFA; *Instructor* Walter Hall, MFA
Estab 1877; pvt; D & E; ent req HS dipl, SAT, solution of Hartford Art School's Preliminary Art Problems; degrees BFA and BFA(Art Ed) 4 yr, MFA and MA Ed 2 yr; schol; SC 70, LC 5, GC 32; enrl D 300, E 200, non-maj 125, maj 300, grad 75
Tuition: Undergrad $3800 yr, $1900 per sem, $90 per cr hr; $80 evening; campus res—room and board $1733
Courses: Advertising Design, Art Education, Ceramics, Conceptual Art, Drawing, Film, Illustration, Intermedia, Painting, Photography, Printmaking, Sculpture, Video, Performance
Summer School: Tui same for term of 4-6 wks beginning July

SAINT JOSEPH COLLEGE, Department of Fine Arts, 1678 Asylum Ave, 06117. Tel 203-232-4571. Instrs FT 2, PT 1
Estab 1932; pvt; W; D & E; ent req HS dipl, CEEB; degrees BA, BS and MA 4 yr; schol; SC 5, LC 7; enrl D 104
Tuition: $3100 yr; campus res $1850
Courses: Art Education, Drawing, †Art History, Graphic Arts, Painting, Batik, Enameling, Mosaic, Creative Crafts, Fundamental of Design, Pre-Art Therapy

WEST HAVEN

UNIVERSITY OF NEW HAVEN, Department of Fine Arts, School of Arts & Sciences, 300 Orange Ave, 06516. Tel 203-934-6321, Ext 258. *Chmn* Jean Henry, PhD; *Prof* Elizabeth Moffitt, MA; *Assoc Prof* Edward Maffeo, PhD; *Asst Prof* Joan Gardner, MFA. Instrs FT 4, PT 12
Estab 1927, dept estab 1972; pvt; D & E; ent req HS dipl; degrees BA & BS 4 yrs, AS 2 yrs; SC 30, LC 5; enrl D 350, E 110
Tuition: Res—undergrad $4277 yr, $2139 per sem; nonres—undergrad $2642 yr, $1321 per sem, $60 per cr hr; campus res $1580
Courses: †Advertising Design, Art History, Calligraphy, Ceramics, Collage, Commercial Art, Constructions, Drawing, Fashion Arts, Graphic Arts, Graphic Design, History of Art & Archaeology, Illustration, Interior Design, Lettering, Mixed Media, Painting, Photography, Printmaking, Sculpture, Textile Design, Dimensional Design, Film Animation, Interaction of Color, Weaving
Summer School: June 12th - July 20th. Courses—Ceramics, Drawing, History of Art, Painting, Photography, Sculpture

WILLIMANTIC

EASTERN CONNECTICUT STATE COLLEGE, Art Department, Windham St, 06226. Tel 203-456-2331, Ext 507. *Chmn* Julian Akus. Instrs FT 3, PT 4
Estab 1881; pub; D & E; ent req HS dipl; degrees BA(Fine Arts) & BS(Art) 4 yrs; scholarships; enrl D 300, E 75, maj 40
Tuition: $450 per yr plus $250 fee; campus res $870
Courses: Art History, Ceramics, Drawing, Graphic Arts, Interior Design, Jewelry, Painting, Sculpture, Textile Design, Enameling, Weaving
Summer School: Dir, Owen Peagler. Courses—Art & Craft Workshop

DELAWARE

DOVER

DELAWARE STATE COLLEGE, Department of Art and Art Education, 19901. Instrs FT 4
Estab 1960; pub; D & E; ent req HS dipl or GED, SAT or ACT; degrees BA(Art Educ) & BS(Art) 4 yrs; scholarships; SC 13, LC 9; enrl over 60 maj
Courses: Advertising Design, Aesthetics, Art Education, Ceramics, Commercial Art, Drawing, Handicrafts, History of Art & Archaeology, Interior Design, Jewelry, Lettering, Painting, Photography, Printmaking, Sculpture, Teacher Training, Design, Fibers, Independent Study

NEWARK

UNIVERSITY OF DELAWARE, Department of Art, 19711. *Chmn* Daniel K Teis, PhD; *Coordr Art Educ* Norman Sasowsky, EdD; *Coordr Sculpture* Joe Moss, MA; *Coordr Photography* John Weiss, MFA; *Coordr Ceramics* Victor Spinski, MFA; *Coordr Printmaking* Rosemary Hooper, MFA; *Coordr Jewelry* Anne Graham, MFA; *Coordr Drawing & Painting* Steven Tanis, MFA; *Coordr Foundations* Larry Holmes, MFA; *Coordr Design* George Nocito, MFA; *Coordr Fibers* Vera Kaminsky, MFA; *Coordr Graphic Design* Ray Nichols, MFA
Estab 1833; pub; D & E; ent req portfolio, BFA prog and graphic design prog (both sophomore yr); degrees BA, BS and BFA 4 yrs, MFA 2 yrs, MA 1 yr; SC 62, LC 2, GC 12, non-maj 600, maj 400, grad 30
Tuition: Res—undergrad $940 yr, grad $52 per cr hr; nonres—undergrad $2200, grad $122 per cr hr; campus res—room & board $1644, nonres room & board $1744
Courses: †Art Education, †Ceramics, †Drawing, †Graphic Design, †Handicrafts, †Jewelry, †Painting, †Photography, †Printmaking, †Sculpture, Design, Fibers

REHOBOTH BEACH

REHOBOTH ART LEAGUE, INC, PO Box 84, 19971. Tel 302-227-8408. *Head Dept* Mary L Pearce; *Instructor* Nanette Cunliffe; *Instructor* Marion Farquharson; *Instructor* Richard Harrison; *Instructor* Betty Hessemer, MA; *Instructor* James Drake Iams, BA; *Instructor* Debra Jahnigan; *Instructor* Dorothy H Lewis; *Instructor* John I Lewis, MA; *Instructor* Howard S Schroeder, BA
Estab 1938; pvt; D; ent req interest in art; SC 7; enrl D 400, others 400
Tuition: $45-$55 depending on class; no campus res
Courses: Ceramics, Drawing, Graphic Arts, Painting, Printmaking
Adult Hobby Classes: Tui $45. Courses—Ceramics, Drawing, Painting, Printmaking, Weaving
Children's Classes: Tui $20-$70. Courses—Art forms
Summer School: Dir, Mary L Pearce

DISTRICT OF COLUMBIA

WASHINGTON

AMERICAN UNIVERSITY, Department of Art, Massachusetts & Nebraska Aves NW, 20016. Tel 202-686-2114. *Chmn Dept* Robert D'Arista; *Prof* Mary D Garrard, PhD; *Prof* Helene M Herzbrun; *Prof* Ben L Summerford; *Assoc Prof* Norma Broude, PhD; *Assoc Prof* Stephen Pace; *Assoc Prof* Lucinao J Penay, MA; *Asst Prof* Michael Graham, MFA
Estab 1893, dept estab 1945; pvt; D & E; ent req HS dipl; degrees BA, BFA(Studio Art), BA(Design), BA(Art History) & BS(Art Educ) 4 yrs, MA(Art History) 18 months, MFA(Painting, Sculpture, Printmaking) 2 yrs; scholarships; SC 19, LC 14;

GC 26; enrl D & E 1520, maj 191, grad 65
Tuition: $1845 per sem, $123-$129 per cr hr; campus residence available
Courses: Advertising Design, Art Education, Ceramics, Drawing, Graphic Arts, Graphic Design, History of Art & Archaeology, Illustration, Lettering, Painting, Printmaking, Sculpture
Summer School: Dir, Ben L Summerford. Tui $123-$129 per cr hr. Courses—Design, Studio & Art History

CATHOLIC UNIVERSITY OF AMERICA
—Department of Architecture & Planning, 20064. Tel 202-635-5000. *Chmn Undergrad Studies* Forrest Wilson, PhD; *Asst Chmn Undergrad Studies* James O'Hear III, MArchit; *Chmn Grad Studies* Peter Blake; *Prof* Seymour Auerbach, MArchit; *Prof* John Dundin, BArchit; *Prof* Joseph Miller, BArchit; *Prof* W Dodd Ramberg, BArchit; *Assoc Prof* Julius S Levine, MCP; *Assoc Prof* Peter Lizon, PhD; *Assoc Prof* George T Marcou, MArchit; *Assoc Prof* Theodore Naos, MArchit; *Assoc Prof* John V Yanik, MArchit; *Adjunct Assoc Prof* Philip L Brach, PhD; *Adjunct Assoc Prof* Louis W Johnson; *Adjunct Assoc Prof* Armando M Lago, PhD; *Asst Prof* J Ronald Kabriel, MArchit; *Asst Prof* Judith Meaney, MCRP; *Asst Prof* Steven F Sachs, BArchit; *Instr* R O'Konski; *Instr* Raymund Sluzas, MArchit; *Instr* Thomas Walton, MArchit
Estab 1887, dept estab 1930; den; D & E; ent req HS dipl and SAT for undergrad, BS or BA in Archit or equivalent plus GPA of 2.5 in undergrad studies for grad; degrees BS(Archit) 4 yrs, MArchit and MArchit(Urban Design) 2 yrs, PhDArchit; SC 6, LC 12 per sem, GC 39 per sem; enrl D 260, maj 260, grad 80
Tuition: Undergrad—$3750 per yr, PT (10 hrs or less) $140 per hr; grad—$3950 per yr, PT (7 hrs or less) $140 per sem hr; campus res—room $370-$525 per sem, bd $435-$550 per sem
Courses: †Architecture, Drafting, Photography, History and Theory of Architecture
Adult Hobby Classes: Session of 8 wks. Courses—Photography
Children's Classes: Session of 2 wks. Courses—Experiences in Architecture
Summer School: Dir, John McDermott. Enrl 150; term of 5-7 wks beginning mid-May. Courses—Design Studio, History of Architecture, Mechanical Equipment Planning, Structures, Theory of Architecture
—Department of Art, 20064. *Chmn* Thomas P Rooney, MFA; *Assoc Prof* John R Winslow, MFA
Estab 1930; den; D & E; ent req HS dipl and SAT for undergrad, BA-BFA, MAT, GRE for grad; degrees BA 4 yrs, MFA 2 yrs; scholarships; SC 17, LC 9, GC 20; enrl D 48, maj 38, grad 10
Tuition: Res undergrad—$3450 per yr, $1725 per sem, $130 per cr hr; grad—$3950 per yr, $1970 per sem, $140 per cr hr; campus res—room and board $370-$525 per sem
Courses: Art Education, Art History, Ceramics, Drawing, History of Art & Archaeology, Jewelry, Painting, Printmaking, Sculpture
Summer School: Chmn, Thomas P Rooney. Tui $300 for term of 8 wks beginning June. Courses—Drawing, Jewelry, Painting, Special Independent Courses

CORCORAN SCHOOL OF ART, 17th St & New York Ave NW, 20006. Tel 202-638-3211. *Dean* Peter G Thomas, MA; *Chmn Foundation & Second Year* Rona Slade, ADT; *Chmn Third Year* Robert Stackhouse, MA; *Chmn Fourth Year* Blaine Larson, MA; *Chmn Visual Communications* Sam Holvey, MA; *Chmn Complementary Studies* Andrew Hudson, BA; *Chmn Drawing & Design* A Brockie Stevenson; *Chmn Ceramics* William Lombardo, MFA; *Chmn Printmaking* Jack Perlmutter; *Chmn Sculpture* Berthold Schmutzhart; *Chmn Photography* Frank DiPerna Jr, MA
Estab 1890; pvt; D & E; ent req HS dipl, portfolio and interview for degree-diploma candidates; degrees BFA 4 yrs; scholarships; SC 20, LC 7; enrl D 650, E 250, non-maj 725, major 175, others 650
Tuition: $2600 per yr, $1300 per sem $275 per 3 cr hr course; no campus res
Courses: †Aesthetics, †Ceramics, †Commercial Art, †Drawing, †Film, †Graphic Arts, †Graphic Design, †Illustration, †Painting, †Photography, †Printmaking, †Sculpture, History of Photography, Typography, Watercolor
Children's Classes: Tui $140 per sem. Saturday. Ages 11-14. Courses—Ceramics, Drawing, Painting, Printmaking, Sculpture, Watercolor. Ages 15-18 College Prep Workshop
Summer School: Dean, Peter G Thomas. Adult—Tui $250 for 5-6 wks beginning June 21. Courses—Drawing, Painting, Photography, Printmaking, Sculpture, Visual Communications, Watercolor. High School (15-18)—Tui $125 for term of 4 wks beginning June 26. Pre-College Workshop, Portfolio Prep. Courses—Ceramics, Drawing, Painting, Printmaking. Junior High (11-14)—Tui $125 for 4 wks beginning June 26. Summer Session in Maine in Photography & Fine Arts. Adult tui $590 (including room and board)

GEORGETOWN UNIVERSITY, Department of Fine Arts, 20057. Tel 202-625-4085. *Chmn* Carra Ferguson, PhD; *Prof* Clifford Chieffo, MA; *Prof* Donn Murphy, PhD; *Assoc Prof* Daniel Brush, MFA; *Asst Prof* Kent Ahrens, PhD; *Asst Prof* Eugene M Geinzer, MFA; *Instructor* Paul McCarren
Estab 1789, dept estab 1960; pvt; D; ent req HS dipl; degrees BA 4 yrs; SC 8, LC 6; enrl D 600 (includes non-maj), maj 25 per year
Tuition: $3240 yr, $108 per cr hr; campus residence available
Courses: Aesthetics, †Art History, †Drawing, Graphic Arts, †Painting, †Sculpture, Stage Design, Theatre Arts, Music History
Summer School: Contact Gerald Sullivan, Georgetown University, Washington, DC 20057

GEORGE WASHINGTON UNIVERSITY, Department of Art,* 2000 G St, NW, 20052. Tel 202-676-6086. *Chmn* Lilien F Robinson, PhD; *Asst Prof* Jeffrey C Anderson, PhD; *Asst Prof* Constance C Costigan, MFA; *Asst Prof* H I Gates, MFA; *Asst Prof* Fuller O Griffith, MFA; *Prof* Francis S Gruber, PhD; *Asst Prof* D Michael Hitchcock, PhD; *Asst Prof* Jerry L Lake, MFA; *Prof* William A MacDonald, PhD
Estab 1821, dept estab 1893; pvt; D & E; ent req HS dipl, ent exam; degrees BA 4 yr, MA 2-2 1 2 yr, MFA 2 yr; scholarships; SC 103, LC 74, GC 68; enrl D 1500, maj 190, GS 196
Tuition: Res—$3301 per yr; campus res—room and board $1690-$2020
Courses: Advertising Design, Architecture, †Art History, †Ceramics, Display, †Drawing, Film, †Graphic Arts, †Graphic Design, History of Art & Archaeology, Illustration, Interior Design, Jewelry, Lettering, Mixed Media, †Museum Staff Training, †Painting, †Photography, †Printmaking, †Sculpture, Typography, Visual Communication
Summer School: Dean, William F Long. Tui $105 per hr for term of 3 separate terms beginning May 15

HOWARD UNIVERSITY, Department of Art, College of Fine Arts, Sixth St & Fairmount St NW, 20001. Tel 202-636-7047. *Dean* Thomas J Flagg; *Chmn* Starmanda Bullock. Instrs FT 16
Estab 1921; pvt; D & E; degrees BFA, MA(History of Art and Art Educ) and MFA 2 yrs; scholarships and fels; enrl 200, others 450
Tuition: $783 per sem; campus residency available
Courses: Art Education, Art History, Ceramics, Painting, Photography, Printmaking, Sculpture, Design

MOUNT VERNON COLLEGE, Art Department, 2100 Foxhall Rd NW, 20007. Tel 202-331-3416, 331-3495. *Asst Prof* James Burford, MFA; *Instr* James M Carder, PhD; *Instr* Richard Howard, MFA; *Instr* Slaithong Schmutzhart, BA
Estab 1875; pvt; D & E; degrees AA and BA; scholarships; SC 16
Tuition: $3300 per yr, $114 per cr hr; campus res—room & board $2500 per yr
Courses: Advertising Design, Architecture, Art History, Ceramics, Commercial Art, Display, Drafting, Drawing, Fashion Arts, Film, Graphic Arts, Graphic Design, History of Art & Archaeology, Interior Design, Landscape Architecture, Museum Staff Training, Painting, Photography, Printmaking, Restoration & Conservation, Sculpture, Stage Design, Teacher Training, Theatre Arts, Video

TRINITY COLLEGE, Department of Fine Arts, 20017. Tel 202-244-2272, 244-2273, 224-2275. *Head Dept* Dr Liliana Gramberg; *Instructor* Barbara Wolanin; *Lectr* Suzanne Eagerman; *Lectr* Larry Harden; *Lectr* Kristen Hoffman; *Lectr* Judith Pratt; *Lectr* M E Armstrong
Estab 1897; den; D & E; ent req HS dipl, SAT or ACT, recommendation; degrees BA & BS 4 yrs, MAT & MBA 2 yrs; scholarships; SC 8, LC 2-3; enrl D 120, maj 25
Tuition: $3400 per yr, $1700 per sem, $106 per cr hr; campus res—room & board $2050
Courses: Aesthetics, Calligraphy, Drawing, Graphic Arts, Graphic Design, History of Art & Archaeology, Lettering, †Painting, Photography, Printmaking, Sculpture, Textile Design, Design, Documentary Photography, Photojournalism, Techniques of Etching
Summer School: Dir, Dr J Van Dien. Courses vary

UNIVERSITY OF THE DISTRICT OF COLUMBIA, Art Department, 916 G Street NW, 20001. Tel 202-727-2662. *Head Dept* Charles A Young, MA; *Prof* Mavera Morgan, PhD; *Prof* Meredith Rode, MFA; *Assoc Prof* Manon Cleary, MFA; *Assoc Prof* David Lanier, MFA; *Assoc Prof* Frederick Ropko, PhD; *Asst Prof* Yvonne Carter, MFA; *Asst Prof* Zeki Findkoglu, MFA; *Asst Prof* Walter Lattimore, BFA; *Asst Prof* George Smith, MS; *Asst Prof* William Taylor, Cert; *Asst Prof* Paula Weaver, MS; *Asst Prof* Rufus Wells, BFA; *Asst Instr* Rodney Donahue, BA
Estab 1969, dept estab 1969; pub; D & E; ent req HS dipl, GED; degrees AA(Advertising Design) 2 yrs, BA(Studio Art) and BA(Art Educ) 4 yrs; SC 65, LC 21; enrl D 708, E 30 percent, non-maj 505, maj 203
Tuition: Res—undergrad $135 per yr, $68 per sem, $6 per sem hr; nonres—undergrad $48 per sem hr; no campus res
Courses: †Advertising Design, †Art Education, Art History, †Calligraphy, †Ceramics, Commercial Art, Conceptual Art, Drawing, Film, †Graphic Arts, †Graphic Design, Handicrafts, Illustration, Interior Design, Lettering, Mixed Media, Museum Staff Training, †Painting, Photography, †Printmaking, †Sculpture, †Teacher Training, Textile Design, Design, Museum Techniques
Summer School: Chmn Art Dept, C A Young. Courses—Art History, Basic Drawing, Life Drawing, Photography, Silkscreen Printing

FLORIDA

BOCA RATON

FLORIDA ATLANTIC UNIVERSITY, Art Department, 33431. Tel 305-395-5100, Ext 2573. *Chairperson* Sydney Tal-Mason. Instrs FT 7, PT 1
Estab 1964; pub; D & E; ent req AA; degrees BFA and BA 2 yrs; SC 37, LC 14, GC 1; enrl D 1600, maj 150, grad 8, special students 7
Tuition: Res $17 per cr hr; nonres $52 per cr hr; campus res $190 per quarter
Courses: Aesthetics, Art Education, Art History, Ceramics, Commercial Art, Costume Design & Construction, Drawing, Graphic Arts, Handicrafts, Jewelry, Lettering, Museum Staff Training, Painting, Photography, Sculpture, Stage Design, Teacher Training, Theatre Arts, Applied Art, History of Architecture, Weaving

BRADENTON

MANATEE JUNIOR COLLEGE, Department of Art, PO Box 1849, 33506. Tel 813-755-1511, Ext 251, 254. *Chmn* Cortez Francis, MA; *Prof* Edward Camp, MFA; *Prof* James McMahon, MFA; *Prof* Priscilla Stewart, MA; *Prof* Cynthia Taylor, MA. Instrs FT 4, PT 1
Estab 1958; pub; D & E; ent req HS dipl, SAT; degrees AA & AS 2 yrs; scholarships; SC 9, LC 5, GC 6; enrl D 700, E 361, maj 75
Tuition: Res—undergrad $15 per cr hr; nonres—undergrad $30 per cr hr
Courses: Art History, Ceramics, Drawing, Handicrafts, Interior Design, Lettering, Painting, Photography, Printmaking, Sculpture, Art Appreciation, Dimensional Design, Color Fundamentals, Figure Drawing, Weaving
Adult Hobby Classes: Enrl approx 200; average tuition $20 per class. Courses—Abstract Painting & Expression, Antiques, Batik, Calligraphy, Color Theory, Drawing, Fabric Painting, Flower Arranging, Frame Making, Interior Design, Introduction to Art & Creativity, Life Study, Oil Painting, Photography, Portraiture Painting, Sumie, Tole Painting, Watercolor
Summer School: Dir, Stephen Korcheck; tui $15 per cr for term of 6 wks

CLEARWATER

FLORIDA GULF COAST ART CENTER, INC,* 222 Ponce de Leon Blvd, 33516. Tel 813-584-8634. *Managing Dir* Judith B Powers
Estab 1949; pvt; D & E; enrl D 315
Courses: Ceramics, Drafting, Drawing, Handicrafts, History of Art & Archaeology, Jewelry, Painting, Photography, Sculpture, Creative Writing, Crewel, Weaving, Wood Carving
Children's Classes: Tui $30 per 10 wks. Courses—Art Sampler grades 1-3, Art Youth grades 4-6, Young Adult General Drawing & Painting grades 6, 7, 8

CORAL GABLES

UNIVERSITY OF MIAMI, Department of Art, PO Box 248106, 33124. Tel 305-284-2542. *Chmn* William E Betsch, PhD; *Instructor* R W Downs, MFA; *Instructor* Christine Federighi, MFA; *Instructor* Edward Ghannam, MFA; *Instructor* Eugene Massin, MFA; *Instructor* Andrew Morgan, MFA; *Instructor* Marilyn Schmitt, PhD; *Instructor* Ken Uyemura, MFA; *Instructor* Bill Ward, MFA; *Instructor* Gerald G Winter, MFA; *Instructor* Marcilene Wittmer, PhD; *Instructor* Peter Zorn, MFA
Estab 1925, dept estab 1960; pvt; D & E; ent req HS dipl, SAT; degrees BA and BFA 4 yrs; scholarships; SC 81, LC 15, GC 25; enrl D 1300, non-maj 1000, maj 300, grad 25
Tuition: Res & nonres—undergrad $3900 per yr, $1970 per sem, $130 per cr hr
Courses: †Advertising Design, †Art History, †Ceramics, Commercial Art, †Drawing, †Graphic Arts, †Graphic Design, Handicrafts, Illustration, Painting, Photography, Printmaking, Sculpture, Weaving

DE LAND

STETSON UNIVERSITY, Art Department, 32720. Tel 904-734-4121, Ext 248. *Head Dept* Fred Messersmith. Instrs FT 2, PT 1
Estab 1880; den; ent req col boards; degrees 4 yr; scholarships; SC 5, LC 5; enrl 200
Tuition: $3065
Courses: Art Education, Art History, Ceramics, Commercial Art, Drawing, Graphic Arts, Painting, Photography, Sculpture, Design

DUNEDIN

DUNEDIN FINE ARTS AND CULTURAL CENTER, 1143 Michigan Blvd, 33528. Tel 813-734-5371. *Dir* Deborah K Eckstein, BA; *Instructor* Bede Clark; *Instructor* Frank Federico; *Instructor* Charles Hines; *Instructor* Charles Holder; *Instructor* Jim Nordmeyer; *Instructor* Dave Pierson; *Instructor* Lois Rector; *Instructor* Jeanne Taylor; *Instructor* Canning Young; *Instructor* Harry Zimmerman
Estab 1975; pub; D & E and weekends; scholarships; SC 20-25, LC 5-10; enrl approx 900
Tuition: Members $25-$45; nonmembers $28-$48; no campus res
Courses: Aesthetics, Art History, Ceramics, Collage, Drawing, Handicrafts, Landscape Architecture, Painting, Photography, Printmaking, Sculpture, Textile Design, Theatre Arts, Antiques, Arts for Handicapped, Batik, Etching, Performing Arts, Weaving, Scrimshaw
Children's Classes: Tui $15-$25 per quarter. Courses—Fine Arts, Drama
Summer School: Dir, Deborah K Eckstein; enrl approx 250; tui $15-$45 for two 5 wk sessions beginning June. Courses—Visual Arts

FORT LAUDERDALE

ART INSTITUTE OF FORT LAUDERDALE, 3000 E Las Olas Blvd, 33316. Tel 305-463-3000. *Pres* Mark Wheeler, BA; *Dir Admissions* Robert S Peterson, BBA; *Dir Education* Frank Raia, MA; *Dir Advertising Design* Nevin Meinhardt, BS; *Dir Photography* Dennis Harkins, MA; *Dir Fashion* Jack Rose, BA; *Dir Interior Design* Bill Kobrynich, AA; *Curriculum Chmn Fashion Illustration* Joh Miele; *Asst Chmn Advertising Design* Judith Damm
Estab 1968; pvt; D & E; ent req HS dipl; degrees AS(technology); scholarships; enrl D 1100, E 130, non-maj 10, maj 1100
Tuition: Varies with major campus res available, rates vary with dorm
Courses: †Advertising Design, Art History, †Commercial Art, Conceptual Art, Display, Drafting, Drawing, †Fashion Arts, Graphic Arts, Graphic Design, Illustration, †Interior Design, Lettering, Mixed Media, Painting, †Photography, Video, †Fashion Illustration, †Fashion Merchandising
Adult Hobby Classes: Tui $85 for 10 wks. Courses—Airbrush, Basic Photography, Color Photography, Creative Photography, Drawing, Graphics, Human Figure, Interior Decorating, Painting, Photography, Photo Retouching
Children's Classes: Tui $100 for 4 wks during the summer
Summer School: Same as regular semester

FORT LAUDERDALE MUSEUM OF THE ARTS, Art School,* 426 E Las Olas Blvd, 33301. Tel 305-463-5184. *Dir* George S Bolge
Estab 1959; pvt; GC 2; enrl 20, 3 terms per yr
Children's Classes: Courses—Art Appreciation, Painting, Photography, Sculpture, Slab Pottery, Watercolor, Weaving

FORT MYERS

EDISON COMMUNITY COLLEGE, Department of Fine & Performing Arts, College Parkway, 33907. Instrs FT 1, PT 3
Estab 1962; pub; D & E; ent req HS dipl; degrees AA & AS 2 yrs; scholarships
Tuition: Res—$14 per cr hr; non-res—$29 per cr hr
Courses: Art History, Ceramics, Commercial Art, Drawing, Jewelry, Painting, Printmaking, Sculpture, Design
Adult Hobby Classes: Enrl 20. Courses—any non-cr activity of interest for which a teacher is available

GAINESVILLE

UNIVERSITY OF FLORIDA, Department of Art, 302C, APA Complex, 32611. Tel 904-392-0211. *Chmn* Robert H Westin, PhD; *Prof* Eugene E Grissom, MFA; *Prof* Kenneth A Kerslake, MFA; *Prof* Geoffrey J Naylor, MFA; *Prof* Jack C Nichelson, MFA; *Prof* Robert C Skelley, MFA; *Prof* Phillip A Ward, MFA; *Prof* Hiram D Williams, MEd; *Graduate Research Prof* Jerry N Uelsmann, MFA; *Assoc Prof* Don E Murray, MFA; *Assoc Prof* John A O'Connor, MFA; *Assoc Prof* Evon Streetman, MFA; *Assoc Prof* John L Ward, MFA. Instrs FT 21
Estab 1925; pub; D & E; ent req HS dipl, SAT, ACT, TOEFL, SCAT or AA degree (transfers must have 2.0 average) GRE; degrees BAA and BFA 4 yrs, MFA 2 yrs; scholarships; SC 40, LC 26, GC 11; enrl maj 200 upper div, grad 16
Tuition: Res—undergrad $15-$22 per cr hr, grad $17-$24 per cr hr; nonres—undergrad $38-$62 per cr hr, grad $52-$64 per cr hr; campus res $570 per yr without air conditioning, $735 per yr with air conditioning
Courses: †Art Education, †Art History, †Ceramics, †Drawing, †Graphic Design, Jewelry, Lettering, †Painting, †Photography, †Printmaking, †Sculpture

HOLLYWOOD

SOUTH FLORIDA ART INSTITUTE OF HOLLYWOOD,* 1301 S Ocean Dr, 33019. Tel 305-923-6490. *Dir* Elwin Porter
Estab 1958; pvt; D & E; ent req portfolio; degrees cert fine arts and cert graphic art 2 and 4 yrs; scholarships; SC 30, LC 2, GC 2; enrl D 230, E 20
Tuition: $900 per yr, $500 per sem, $125 per month; no campus res
Courses: Advertising Design, Ceramics, Commercial Art, Drawing, Graphic Design, Jewelry, Painting, Photography, Printmaking, Sculpture
Children's Classes: Enrl 30; tui $20 per 10 wks. Courses—Mixed Media
Summer School: Dir, Elwin Porter. Tui $450 for term of 15 wks beginning May 15. Courses—Ceramics, Design, Drawing, Painting, Photography, Printmaking, Sculpture

JACKSONVILLE

FLORIDA JUNIOR COLLEGE AT JACKSONVILLE, SOUTH CAMPUS, Art Department, 11901 Beach Blvd, 32216. Tel 904-646-2150. *Chmn Div Fine Arts & Humanities* Dr Duane D Dumbleton. Instrs FT 6
Estab 1966; pub; D & E; ent req HS dipl; degrees AA & AS 2 yrs; scholarships; SC 14, LC 6; enrl D 150, E 75
Tuition: Res—$13 per cr hr; nonres—$26 per cr hr; no campus res
Courses: Ceramics, Drawing, Graphic Design, Handicrafts, History of Art & Archaeology, Painting, Photography, Sculpture, Batik, Blockprinting, Glaze Techniques, Leathercraft, Macrame, Weaving
Adult Hobby Classes: Enrl 75-80; for term of 6 wks beginning June. Courses—Art Appreciation, Crafts, Drawing, Painting, Photography

JACKSONVILLE UNIVERSITY, Department of Art,* College of Fine Arts, 2800 University Blvd N, 32211. Tel 904-744-3950. *Dean* Frances Bartlett Kinnie
Estab 1932; pvt; D & E; ent req HS dipl, ent exam; degrees BFA (studio art, art history) and BA Ed 4 yr; SC 29, LC 16; enrl D 403, maj 80
Tuition: $2050 per yr

LAKE CITY

LAKE CITY COMMUNITY COLLEGE, Art Department, 32055. Tel 904-752-1822, Ext 256. Instrs FT 1, PT 2
Estab 1962; pub; D & E; ent req HS dipl; degrees AA 2 yrs; SC 9, LC 2; enrl D 160, maj 10
Courses: Ceramics, Drawing, Handicrafts, Jewelry, Painting, Sculpture, Composition, Weaving

LAKELAND

FLORIDA SOUTHERN COLLEGE, Art Department, 33802. Tel 813-683-5521, Ext 431, 244. *Coordr Dept* Dr Donna M Stoddard; *Assoc Prof* Downing Barnitz, MFA; *Assoc Prof* Banton S Doak, EdS; *Instructor* Gale L Doak, MA; *Instructor* Beth M Ford, MA
Estab 1885; den; D; ent req HS dipl; degrees AB & BS 128 hr; scholarships; SC 20, LC 6, maj 34
Tuition: Res—undergrad $4597 yr, $2298 per sem, $65 per cr hr; nonres—undergrad $2747 yr, $1373.50 per sem; campus res room and board $1850
Courses: Architecture, Art Education, Art History, Ceramics, Drawing, Graphic Arts, Handicrafts, Jewelry, Lettering, Painting, Photography, Sculpture, Silversmithing, Teacher Training, Theatre Arts, Ancient & Medieval Art, Art in Contemporary Living, Design (19th & 20th century art), Instrumental Drawing, Renaissance & Baroque Art
Adult Hobby Classes: Tui $25 per 6 wk. Courses—Graphics, Interior Design, Oil Painting
Summer School: Dean, David Mobberley. Tui $60 per cr hr for 2 terms of 4 wks beginning June and July

LAKE WORTH

PALM BEACH JUNIOR COLLEGE, Department of Art,* 4200 South Congress Ave, 33461. Tel 305-439-8149. *Chmn* Dr James B Miles
Estab 1935; pub; D & E; ent req HS dipl or over 25; degrees AA and AS 2 yr; SC 20, LC 5; enrl D 3400, E 3200, maj 200
Courses: Advertising Design, Ceramics, Commercial Art, Drawing, Graphic Arts, Graphic Design, Handicrafts, History of Art & Archaeology, Interior Design, Jewelry, Lettering, Painting, Photography, Sculpture, Architectural Drawing, Basic Design, Enameling, Typography
Adult Hobby Classes: Courses—Floral Design, Jewelry, Picture Frame Making, Weaving
Summer School: Courses—Art Appreciation, Design, Drawing, History of Art, Photography

MARIANNA

CHIPOLA JUNIOR COLLEGE, Art Department,* 32446. Tel 904-526-2761.
Division Dir Lawrence B Nelson
Estab 1954; pub; D & E; ent req HS dipl; degrees AA 2 yr; scholarships; SC 14, LC
2; enrl D 60
Courses: Ceramics, Drafting, Drawing, History of Art & Archaeology, Industrial
Design, Jewelry, Painting, Sculpture, Stage Design, Theatre Arts
Summer School: Term of 2-6 wks summer session

MELBOURNE

ELIOT MCMURROUGH SCHOOL OF ART, 909 E Newhaven Ave, Suite 201-204,
32901. Tel 305-723-8876. *Pres* Margaret Sheppard; *Exec Secy* Nancy L Crawford;
Faculty Dir Betty Clifton. Instrs FT 1, PT 4
Estab 1954; ent req HS dipl or ability to meet school requirements
Courses: Art Education, Drawing, Painting, Sculpture, Basic Forms, Color,
Composition, Design, Perspective, Tools and Uses, Watercolor

MIAMI

FLORIDA INTERNATIONAL UNIVERSITY, Visual Arts Department, Tamiami
Trail, 33199. Tel 305-552-2897. *Chairperson* Francis Wyroba, MFA; *Assoc Prof*
William J Burke; *Assoc Prof* James M Couper; *Assoc Prof* Ellen Jacobs; *Asst Prof* R F
Buckley; *Asst Prof* Richard Duncan; *Asst Prof* Barbara Forbes; *Asst Prof* William
Maguire
Estab 1972, dept estab 1972; pub; D & E; ent req 2 yrs of university work; degrees BFA,
BS(Art Educ) and MS(Art Educ); scholarships; SC 20, LC 12, GC 18; enrl D 320, E
100, non-maj 225, maj 175, grad 20
Tuition: Res—undergrad $750 per yr, grad $945 per yr; non-res—undergrad $2835 per
yr, grad $3000 per yr; no campus res
Courses: Art Education, Art History, Ceramics, Drawing, Goldsmithing, Jewelry,
Painting, Photography, Printmaking, Sculpture, Silversmithing, Teacher Training
Summer School: Dir, Francis Wyroba. Enrl 160; tui $250 for term of 10 wks beginning
June 24

INTERNATIONAL FINE ARTS COLLEGE, 1737 N Bayshore Dr, 33132. Tel
305-373-4684. *Chmn* Gregory Hoffman; *Instr* Darcy Gottlieb, MA; *Instr* Diane
Schulner, MA
Estab 1965, dept estab 1966; pvt; D; ent req HS dipl; degrees AA; SC 6; enrl D 180,
maj 180
Tuition: $5385 per yr; campus res—apartment $1725 per yr
Courses: Art History, Costume Design & Construction, Display, Drawing, Fashion
Arts, History of Art & Archaeology, Illustration, Interior Design, Painting

MIAMI-DADE COMMUNITY COLLEGE CAMPUSES, Art Department,* 11011
SW 104 St, 33176. Tel 305-596-1281. *Chmn Dept* Margaret M Pelton, MS
Estab 1960, dept estab 1967; pub; D & E; ent req open door; degrees AA and AS 2
yr; scholarships; SC 14, LC 4; enrl E 300, non-maj 150, maj 150
Courses: Architecture, Art Education, Art History, Ceramics, Commercial Art,
Costume Design & Construction, Drafting, Drawing, Fashion Arts, Graphic Arts,
Graphic Design, Illustration, Interior Design, Jewelry, Landscape Architecture,
Museum Staff Training, Painting, Photography, Printmaking, Sculpture, Stage Design,
Theatre Arts
Adult Hobby Classes: Tui $10-$15. Courses—by demand
Summer School: Tui $15 per cr hr for term of 6 wks beginning June

MIAMI SHORES

BARRY COLLEGE, Department of Art, 11300 NE Second Ave, 33161. Tel
305-758-3392. Instrs FT 4, PT 3
Estab 1940; pvt; D & E; ent req HS dipl, portfolio for BFA; degrees BA, BFA,
BA(Educ) 4 yrs; scholarships; SC 8, LC 2; enrl D 300, E 60, maj 40
Tuition: $1200 per sem; campus res $600 per sem
Courses: Advertising Design, Art Education, Ceramics, Commercial Art, Costume
Design & Construction, Drawing, Fashion Arts, Graphic Arts, Graphic Design,
History of Art & Archaeology, Illustration, Jewelry, Painting, Photography, Sculpture,
Stage Design, Teacher Training, Textile Design, Theatre Arts

NICEVILLE

OKALOOSA-WALTON JUNIOR COLLEGE, Dept of Fine & Performing Arts, 100
College Blvd, 32578. Tel 904-678-5111. *Head Dept* Dr James Durham, EdD; *Instr*
Arnold Hart, MEd; *Instr* David Owens, MFA
Estab 1964, dept estab 1964; pub; D & E; ent req HS dipl; degrees AA 2 yrs;
scholarships; SC 26, LC 3; enrl D 2000, E 1000, maj 80
Tuition: $14 per hr; campus residence available
Courses: Architecture, Art History, Ceramics, Costume Design & Construction,
Drafting, Drawing, Graphic Arts, Graphic Design, Handicrafts, History of Art &
Archaeology, Interior Design, Jewelry, Painting, Photography, Printmaking,
Sculpture, Silversmithing, Stage Design, Teacher Training, Theatre Arts, Weaving
Adult Hobby Classes: Enrl 15 per class; tui $4 per course. Courses—Antiques, Interior
Decorating, Painting, Photography, Pottery, Vase Painting, others as needed
Summer School: Dir, Dr James Durham. Term of 6 or 12 wks beginning May 2 and
June 18. Courses—same as regular sessions

OCALA

CENTRAL FLORIDA COMMUNITY COLLEGE, Humanities Department,* 3001
SW College Rd, 32670. Tel 904-237-2111. *Chmn Dept* Charles Adams, MA
Estab 1957; pub; D & E; ent req HS dipl; degrees AA and AS 2 yr; SC 5, LC 1; enrl
2015, non-maj 85, maj 15
Tuition: Res—$12 per cr hr; nonres—$27 per cr hr
Courses: Art History, Ceramics, Drawing, Painting, Printmaking

ORLANDO

VALENCIA COMMUNITY COLLEGE, Art Department, 1800 S Kirkman Rd, PO
Box 3028, 32802. Tel 305-299-5000, Ext 258 & 259. *Dept Chmn* Qurentia P Throm,
MA; *Instructor* Richard W Blackney, MA; *Instr* Nancy Jay, MA
Estab 1967, dept estab 1974; pub; D & E; ent req HS dipl; degrees AA and AS 2 yrs;
scholarships; SC 16, LC 5; enrl D 6858
Tuition: Res $15 per hr, non-res $30 per hr
Courses: Art History, Ceramics, Drawing, History of Art & Archaeology, Painting,
Photography, Printmaking, Sculpture
Summer School: Same as for regular academic yr

PALATKA

FLORIDA SCHOOL OF THE ARTS, Visual Arts, 5001 Saint John Ave, 32077. Tel
904-328-1571. *Dean* David R Humphrey, PhD; *Coordr Fine Art* Gene Roberds, MFA;
Coordr Graphic Design Steven Lebeck, MA; *Dir Galleries* Stephen Berern, MFA
Estab 1974, dept estab 1974; pub; D; ent req recommendation, review, interview;
degrees AA 2 yrs, AS 2 1 2 yrs; scholarships; SC 35, LC 10; enrl D 85, maj 85
Tuition: Res $13 per hr, non-res $25 per hr; no campus res
Courses: Advertising Design, Art History, Ceramics, Commercial Art, Display,
Drafting, Drawing, Graphic Arts, †Graphic Design, Illustration, Intermedia,
Lettering, Mixed Media, Museum Staff Training, †Painting, Photography,
†Printmaking, †Stage Design, †Theatre Arts

PANAMA CITY

GULF COAST COMMUNITY COLLEGE, Division of Fine Arts, 5230 W Highway
98, 32401. Tel 904-769-1551. *Chmn* Norman J Hair, MM; *Assoc Prof* Sharron Barnes,
MA; *Assoc Prof* Roland L Hockett, MS; *Assoc Prof* Louise L Lewis, MA
Estab 1957; pub; D & E; ent req HS dipl; degrees AA 2 yrs; SC 5, LC 2; enrl D 300,
E 70, non-maj 330, maj 40
Tuition: Res—undergrad $13 per cr hr; nonres—undergrad $15 per cr hr
Courses: Advertising Design, Art History, Ceramics, Commercial Art, Drawing,
Graphic Arts, Graphic Design, Illustration, Lettering, Photography, Printmaking
Adult Hobby Classes: Courses—Macrame, Painting

PENSACOLA

PENSACOLA JUNIOR COLLEGE, Department of Visual Arts, 1000 College Blvd,
32504. Tel 904-476-5410, Ext 268. *Head Dept* Carl F Duke. Instrs FT 11, PT 5
Estab 1948; pub; D & E; ent req HS dipl; degrees AS & AA 2 yrs; scholarships; enrl
maj 100
Tuition: Res—$14 per cr hr; nonres—$28 per cr hr; no campus res
Courses: Art History, Ceramics, Drawing, Graphic Arts, Illustration, Painting,
Photography, Printmaking, Sculpture, Design, Pottery
Summer School: Dept Head, Carl F Duke. Courses offered

UNIVERSITY OF WEST FLORIDA, Department of Art, College of Arts & Sciences,
32504. *Chmn* Robert L Armstrong, PhD; *Prof* John T Carey, PhD; *Assoc Prof* Henry
J Heuler, MFA; *Assoc Prof* Robert B Marshman, MFA; *Assoc Prof* William A Silhan,
EdD; *Asst Prof* Judith A Heuler, MFA; *Asst Prof* Duncan E Stewart, MFA
Estab 1967; pub; D & E; ent req students usually have AA degree when they enter;
degrees BA 2 yr; SC 20, LC 10; non-maj 40, maj 80
Tuition: Res—undergrad $16.50 per quarter hr, grad $22 per quarter hr; nonres—
undergrad $51.50 per quarter hr, grad $62 per quarter hr; campus res—room and board
$375
Courses: †Art Education, †Art History, Ceramics, Commercial Art, Drawing, Graphic
Arts, Jewelry, Lettering, Painting, Photography, Printmaking, Sculpture,
Silversmithing, Teacher Training, †Studio Art
Adult Hobby Classes: Tui $15 per course. Courses—Leisure Class Series
Summer School: Same as above

SAINT AUGUSTINE

FLAGLER COLLEGE, Visual Arts Department,* King St, 32084. Tel 904-829-6481.
Chmn Tom Rahner; *Asst Prof* Enzo Torcoletti, MFA; *Instr* Don Martin, MFA
Estab 1968; pvt; D & E; ent req HS dipl; degrees BA 4 yr; scholarships; SC 29, LC
7; enrl D 50, maj 45
Tuition: Res—$3350 per yr; campus res available
Courses: Art Education, Art History, Drawing, Graphic Design, Jewelry, Mixed
Media, Painting, Photography, Printmaking, Sculpture, Silversmithing, †Teacher
Training, †Theatre Arts
Summer School: Dir, Dr Drew Dillon. Tui $60 per hr for term of 4 or 6 wks beginning
May. Courses—Ceramics, Creative Photography, Landscape Drawing

SAINT PETERSBURG

SAINT PETERSBURG JUNIOR COLLEGE, Department of Humanities,* 6605 Fifth Ave N, 33733. Tel 813-381-0681.
Estab 1927; pub; D & E; ent req HS dipl; degrees AA and AS 2 yr; scholarships; SC 13, LC 3; enrl D 7031, E 2478
Tuition: Full-time students pay matriculation and tuition fee $13 per cr hr; nonres—$28 per cr hr; no campus res
Courses: Advertising Design, Aesthetics, Ceramics, Drafting, Drawing, Graphic Arts, History of Art & Archaeology, Painting, Photography, Sculpture, Stage Design, Theatre Arts, Design I & II, Survey in Crafts
Summer School: Courses—Same as regular session

SARASOTA

FRIENDS OF THE ARTS AND SCIENCES, HILTON LEECH STUDIO, 4433 Riverwood, 33581. Tel 813-924-5770. *Consultant Special Projects* Katherine L Rowland; *Instructor* James H (Pete) Carmichael; *Instructor* Emily Holmes; *Instructor* Robert Pelham; *Instructor* Elden Rowland
Estab 1946, dept estab 1963; pvt; SC 16; enrl D 200, E 10
Tuition: Varies from $40 to $75 per workshop; no campus res
Courses: Drawing, Painting, Photography

NEW COLLEGE OF THE UNIVERSITY OF SOUTH FLORIDA, Fine Arts Department, Humanities Division, 5700 N Tamiami Trail, 33580. Tel 813-355-1151. Instrs FT 4
Estab 1963; pvt; D; ent req ent exam, SAT; degrees BA(Fine Arts) 3 yrs; SC 6, LC 5; enrl D 150-200, maj 15
Courses: Aesthetics, Art History, Ceramics, Drawing, Painting, Printmaking, Sculpture, Color Theory, Design, Life Drawing, Stained Glass

RINGLING SCHOOL OF ART, 33580. Tel 813-355-5259. *Pres* Robert E Perkins, MA, LHD; *Dir Admissions* Lisa Redling, MA. Instrs 28
Estab 1931; pvt; ent req HS dipl or equivalency, portfolio; degrees 3-year certificate, BFA, 4 yrs; enrl 465
Tuition: $2100; campus res—room & board $1570
Courses: Advertising Design, Art History, †Graphic Design, Illustration, †Interior Design, Lettering, Painting, Photography, Sculpture, †Fine Arts, Space Planning

TALLAHASSEE

FLORIDA A&M UNIVERSITY, Department of Visual Arts & Humanities,* 32307. Tel 904-599-3000. *Chmn* H L Williams, EdD
Estab 1887; pub; D & E; ent req HS dipl, ent exam; degrees BS and BA 4 yr; enrl D 5887, non-maj 5800, maj 87
Tuition: Res—undergrad $225-$248 for 15 hrs per quarter, grad $330 for 15 hrs per quarter; nonres—undergrad $570-$773 for 15 hrs per quarter, grad $930 for 15 hrs per quarter
Courses: Art Education, Art History, Ceramics, Drawing, Handicrafts, History of Art & Archaeology, Lettering, Painting, Printmaking, Sculpture, Teacher Training, Textile Design
Summer School: Enrl 125; tui same as regular session for term of 9 and 7 wks beginning June. Courses—Ceramics, Design, Drawing, Arts, Textile Design, Wood, Metal & Plastics

FLORIDA STATE UNIVERSITY
—Art Department,* 236 Fine Arts Bldg, 32306. Tel 904-444-6474. *Assoc Chairperson Studio Art* Francis W Kenniston; *Assoc Chairperson Art History* Patricia Rose
Estab 1857, dept estab 1911; pub; D & E; ent req HS dipl, C average and upper 40 percent of graduating class, SAT; degrees BA, BFA, MFA, MA, PhD; scholarships; SC 36, LC 46, GC 34; enrl maj 329, grad 40
Tuition: Res—undergrad $700 per yr, $15 per hr lower level, $17 upper level, grad $1035 per yr, $22 per hr non-thesis, $24 per hr grad thesis and dissertation; nonres—undergrad $23 per hr lower level, $35 per hr upper level, grad $40 per hr; campus res—room & board $1720 per yr
Courses: Advertising Design, Art Education, †Art History, Commercial Art, Conceptual Art, Constructions, Drawing, Fashion Arts, Film, Graphic Arts, Graphic Design, History of Art & Archaeology, Illustration, Interior Design, Lettering, Museum Staff Training, Painting, Photography, Printmaking, Sculpture, †Studio Art
Summer School: Tui in-state $9 per hr lower level, $11 per hr upper level; out-of-state $32 per hr lower level, $46 per hr upper level for term of 8 wks beginning June
—Art Education Craft Design,* 123 Education Bldg, 32306. Tel 904-644-5473, 644-5474. *Chairperson* Virginia M Brouch
Estab 1857, dept estab 1948; pub; D & E; ent req HS dipl, slide review for crafts design; degrees BA 4 yrs, MA 1 yr, EdD and PhD 3 yrs, Advan MAE 2 yrs; scholarships; SC 27, LC 34, GC 29; enrl D 250, E 60, non-maj 60, maj 190, grad 25, other 10
Tuition: Res—undergrad $51 per hr lower level, $17 per hr upper level, grad $22 per hr non-thesis, $24 per hr thesis or dissertation; nonres—undergrad $38 per hr lower level, $52 per hr upper level, grad $62 per hr no thesis, $64 per hr thesis or dissertation; campus res—$3275-$3452 depending on class and residence
Courses: †Art Education, Ceramics, Jewelry, Textile Design, Woods Synthetics, †Craft Design
Summer School: Same as regular session

LEMOYNE ART CENTER, 32301. Tel 904-222-8800. *Dir* Nancy J McIntyre. Instrs Teaching staff consists of professional artists in the community, and varies from term to term
Estab 1964; pvt; D & E; scholarships
Tuition: $400 per yr, 4 quarters
Courses: Art Education, †Art History, Ceramics, Drafting, Drawing, Graphic Arts, Graphic Design, †Painting, Photography, †Printmaking, †Sculpture
Adult Hobby Classes: Enrl 10-14; tui $35 per 8 wk course. Courses—Ceramics, Drawing, Painting, Photography, Printmaking
Children's Classes: Tui $25 per 8 wk course. Courses—Cartooning, Ceramics, Drawing, Painting, Puppetry

TALLAHASSEE COMMUNITY COLLEGE, Art Department, 32304. Tel 904-576-5181. *Chmn Art Prog* Ruth Dryden Deshaies, MA
Estab 1966; pub; D & E; ent req HS dipl; degrees AA 2 yrs; SC 8, LC 2; enrl D 130, E 40
Tuition: $11 per sem hr
Courses: Art History, Drawing, Painting, Photography, Color Theory, Design

TAMPA

UNIVERSITY OF SOUTH FLORIDA, Art Department, College of Fine Arts, 4202 Fowler Ave, 33620. Tel 813-974-2360. *Chmn* George Pappas. Instrs FT D 20
Estab 1956; pub; ent req HS grad, 14 units cert by HS, ent exam; degrees BA(Art) minimum 180 quarter hrs and MFA 72 quarter hrs
Tuition: Res—undergrad $15 per cr hr, grad $22 per cr hr; nonres—undergrad $38 per cr hr, grad $62 per cr hr
Courses: Art History, Ceramics, Drawing, Graphic Arts, Painting, Photography, Sculpture, Cinematography
Summer School: One to four equal yearly quarters

UNIVERSITY OF TAMPA, Department of Art, Fine Arts Division, 401 W Kennedy Blvd, 33606. Tel 813-253-8861. *Dir* Dorothy Cowden. Instrs FT 5
Estab 1930; pvt; D & E; degrees 4 yrs; SC 17, LC 8
Courses: Art Education, Art History, Ceramics, Drawing, Painting, Photography, Printmaking, Sculpture, Design

WINTER HAVEN

POLK COMMUNITY COLLEGE, Division of Communications and Fine Arts, 33880. *Dir* Dion K Brown, EdS; *Prof* Gary Baker, MFA; *Prof* Jane Jaskevich, MEd; *Prof* Bob Morrisey, MFA
Estab 1964; pub; D & E; ent req HS dipl; degrees AA & AS 2 yrs; scholarships; SC 10, LC 1; enrl D 175, E 50
Tuition: Res—undergrad $13 per cr hr; nonres—undergrad $27 per cr hr; no campus res
Courses: Advertising Design, Art History, Ceramics, Drafting, Drawing, Film, Graphic Arts, Interior Design, Painting, Photography, Sculpture, Video
Adult Hobby Classes: Enrl 60; tui $1 per class hr. Courses—Calligraphy, Ceramics, Christmas Crafts, Interior Design, Jewelry

WINTER PARK

ROLLINS COLLEGE, Department of Art, Main Campus,* 32789. Tel 305-646-2000. *Chmn* Ronald Larned
Estab 1885; pvt; D & E; degrees 4 yrs; scholarships; SC 11, LC 10; enrl D & E 250
Tuition: Res—$4,990
Courses: Aesthetics, Art History, Drawing, Painting, Sculpture, Art History Survey, Design, Humanities Foundation, Principles of Art

GEORGIA

ATHENS

UNIVERSITY OF GEORGIA, FRANKLIN COLLEGE OF ARTS AND SCIENCES, Division of Fine Arts, 30602. Tel 404-542-1511. *Dean* William J Payne; *Head Dept* Francis A Ruzicka
Opened 1801, chartered 1875; degrees BA, BFA, MA, MFA, EdS, EdD, PhD; scholarships, fels and grad assistantships
Tuition: Res—$251 per quarter; nonres—$601 per quarter; campus residence available
—Department of Art, 30602. Instrs FT 53, PT 2
Estab 1932; SC 76, LC 43, GC 91; enrl undergrad maj 750, grad 80, others 1200
Courses: Art Education, Art History, Ceramics, Drawing, Graphic Design, Interior Design, Jewelry, Painting, Printmaking, Sculpture, Fabric Design, Metal Work, Photographic Design
Summer School: Dir, Francis A Ruzicka. Term of 8 wks, prog of 10 wks in Cortona, Italy. Courses—most studio and lecture areas

ATLANTA

ATLANTA AREA TECHNICAL SCHOOL, Department of Commercial Art, 1560 Stewart Ave SW, 30310. Tel 404-758-9451. *Head Dept* Don M Ballentine
Estab 1967; pub; D & E; ent req HS dipl, ent exam; degrees AA in conjunction with The Atlanta Jr Col; SC 13; enrl D 25, E 25
Tuition: $27 per quarter plus testing fees
Courses: Advertising Design, Commercial Art, Graphic Arts, Photography, Video, Print Production Art

ATLANTA COLLEGE OF ART, 1280 Peachtree St NE, 30309. Tel 404-892-3600. *Pres* William J Voos, MFA; *Academic Dean* Anthony J Greco, MFA; *Dean of Students* Guthrie Foster; *Foundation Chmn* Corrinne Colarusso; *Video Chmn* Ben Davis; *Academic Chmn* Barbara DeConcini; *Painting Chmn* Tom Francis; *Drawing Chmn* Richard Hill; *Sculpture Chmn* Curtis Patterson; *Printmaking Chmn* Keith Rasmussen; *Visual Communication Chmn* William Reusswig; *Photography Chmn* Robert Stewart; *Instructor* Santo Bruno, MFA; *Instructor* Neill Clark, PhD; *Instructor* Scott Gilliam, MFA; *Instructor* Fred Gregory, MFA; *Instructor* William Nolan, MFA; *Instructor* Norman Wagner, MS
Estab 1928; pvt; D & E; ent req HS dipl, ent exam, SAT, portfolio of art work; degrees BFA 4 yrs; scholarships; SC 96, LC 48; enrl D 272, E 350, non-maj 350, maj 272
Tuition: $2950 yr; no campus res
Courses: Art Education, Constructions, Drawing, Graphic Arts, Graphic Design, Illustration, Intermedia, Lettering, Mixed Media, Painting, Photography,

Printmaking, Sculpture, Video
Children's Classes: Enrl 80; tui $50 for 12 wks. Courses—Crafts, Drawing, Painting, Printmaking, Sculpture. Young Artists-in-Residence High School Summer Program—Enrl 75, tui $350 for 5 wk term, housing available
Summer School: Dir, Katherine Gregory. Enrl 400; tui $85 for term of 8 wks. Courses—Studio Arts

CLARK COLLEGE, Department of Art, 240 Chestnut St SW, 30314. Tel 404-681-3080, Ext 346. *Chmn Dept* Dr Emmanuel V Asihene, PhD
Estab 1869, dept estab 1964; pvt; D; ent req HS dipl; degrees BA(Art) and BA(Art Educ) 4 yrs, Honors Program; SC 8, LC 8; enrl D 300, non-maj 242, maj 32
Tuition: Res—undergrad $3940 yr; non-res—undergrad $2080 yr; campus res—$1450
Courses: Art Education, Art History, Drawing, Painting, Photography, Printmaking, Sculpture, Design

EMORY UNIVERSITY, Art History Department, 30322. Tel 404-329-6282. *Chmn* John Howett, PhD; *Prof* William R Crelly, PhD; *Prof* Thomas W Lyman, PhD; *Assoc Prof* Clark V Poling, PhD; *Asst Prof* Dorinda Evans, PhD; *Vis Prof* Robert Scranton, PhD, archaeology; *Vis Asst Prof* Irina Andreescu, PhD; *Affiliate* William Archie Brown, MFA; *Affiliate* Mollie Michala, MFA; *Affiliate* Margaret Mott, *Affiliate* Eycke Strickland
Estab 1847; pvt; D; ent req HS dipl, ent exam, SAT; degrees MA(Art History) and PhD through Institute of Liberal Arts; scholarships; SC 4, LC 29, GC 18; enrl non-maj 600, maj 20, grad 27
Tuition: $4095 per yr; campus residency available
Courses: Art History, Ceramics, Drawing, Film, Handicrafts, History of Art & Archaeology, Photography, Video, Weaving
Summer School: Dir, Dean Thigpen. Enrl 15; tui $1600-$1800 for term of 6 wks beginning June 15. Courses—Seminars in Europe (variable) 10 cr hrs

GEORGIA INSTITUTE OF TECHNOLOGY, College of Architecture, 225 North Avenue NW, 30332. Tel 404-894-3880. *Dean* William L Fash, MA; *Assoc Prof* Neill W Connah, MFA; *Asst Prof* Albert H Smith, MFA; *Instructor* Jessica P McLean, MFA; *Lectr* Joe de Cassares Reshower, Cert; *Lectr* Joan Templer
Estab 1885, dept estab 1908; pub; D; ent req HS dipl, CEEB; degrees BS(Architecture), BS(Industrial Design) and BS(Building Construction) 4 yr, M Architecture and MCP 2 yr; schol; SC 41; enrl D 904, maj 904, grad 165
Tuition: Res—undergrad and grad $676.50 yr, $225.50 per quarter; non-res—undergrad and grad $1843.50 yr, $614.50 per quarter; campus res—room and board $1225
Courses: Architecture, Industrial Design, Building Construction, City Planning
Summer School: Tui same. Courses—vary

GEORGIA STATE UNIVERSITY, 33 Gilmer St SE, 30303. Tel 404-658-2257. *Head Dept* Joseph S Perrin. Instrs FT 38, PT 4
Estab 1914; pub; ent req HS dipl, ent exam, college board, interview; degrees BVA, AB(Art) and BA(Art History) 4 yrs, MA(Art History); schol; SC 80, LC 17; enrl maj 300, others 20
Courses: Advertising Design, Art History, Ceramics, Drawing, Graphic Arts, Handicrafts, Illustration, Interior Design, Jewelry, Lettering, Painting, Sculpture, Teacher Training, Textile Design, Metalwork, Weaving
Summer School: Enrl 450; term of 9 wks beginning June

AUGUSTA

AUGUSTA COLLEGE, Department of Fine Arts,* 2500 Walton Way, 30904. Tel 404-828-2054. *Head Dept* Eloy Fominaya, PhD; *Assoc Prof* Nathan Bindler, MA; *Asst Prof* Jack King, MFA; *Asst Prof* Eugenia Comer, MFA; *Asst Prof* Richard Frank, MFA; *Asst Prof* Cecilia Voelker, PhD
Estab 1925, dept estab 1965; pub; D & E; ent req HS dipl, SAT; degrees MA 5 yr, BA and BFA 4 yrs and AA 2 yr; scholarships; SC 46, LC 4, GC 1; enrl D 150, E 30, non-maj 10, maj 140, GS 5
Tuition: Res—undergrad $145 per quarter, $12 per quarter hr; nonres—undergrad $238 per quarter, $32 per quarter hr; no campus res
Courses: Advertising Design, Art Education, Art History, Ceramics, Commercial Art, Constructions, Drafting, Drawing, Fashion Arts, Graphic Arts, Graphic Design, Handicrafts, Illustration, Lettering, Mixed Media, Painting, Printmaking, Sculpture, Teacher Training
Adult Hobby Classes: Enrl 25; tui $30 per 10 sessions. Courses—Painting

CARROLLTON

WEST GEORGIA COLLEGE, Art Department, 30017. Tel 404-834-1235. *Chmn* Bruce Bobick
Estab 1975; pub; D; ent req HS dipl, ent exam; degrees AB(Studio, Art Educ) 4 yr; schol; SC 24, LC 10, GC 1; enrl maj 124
Tuition: $536 per yr, PT $12 per quarter hr; non-res—$238 per quarter, PT $20 per quarter hr; campus res—$140 to $165 per quarter
Courses: Art Education, Art History, Ceramics, Graphic Arts, Graphic Design, Painting, Photography, Sculpture, Teacher Training, Textile Design, Art Appreciation, Weaving
Summer School: Courses—Art Education, Art History, Ceramics, Drawing, Graphics, Painting

CLEVELAND

TRUETT-McCONNELL COLLEGE, Fine Arts Department,* 30528. Tel 404-865-4422. *Head Fine Arts* David George
Estab 1946; den; D & E; ent req HS dipl, SAT; degrees AA and AS 2 yr; SC 10, LC 2; enrl D 700, non-maj 15
Tuition: Res—$900 per yr; nonres—$1300 per yr
Courses: Aesthetics, Art History, Ceramics, Drawing, Graphic Design, Handicrafts, Painting, Sculpture, Three Dimensional Design
Children's Classes: Enrl 21; tui $20. Courses—Children's Art

COCHRAN

MIDDLE GEORGIA COLLEGE (JUNIOR COLLEGE UNIT OF THE UNIVERSITY OF GEORGIA), Department of Art, 31014. Tel 912-934-6221, Ext 288. Instrs FT 2
Pub; D & E; ent req HS dipl, GED; degrees AA 2 yr; SC 6; enrl D 270, E 45
Tuition: $112 per quarter; campus res—$190 to $265 per quarter; board (5 day) $225, (7 day) $235 per quarter
Courses: Art Education, Commercial Art, Drawing, Handicrafts, Lettering, Painting
Summer School: Dir, Robert R Nason. Enrl 30; term of 10 wk beginning approx June. Courses—as above

COLUMBUS

COLUMBUS COLLEGE, Department of Art, Algonquin Dr, 31907. Tel 404-568-2047. *Chmn* John H Anderson
Estab 1949; pub; D & E; ent req HS dipl, ent exam; degrees BS (Art Educ), BA (Art) and MEd (Art Educ) 4 yr; scholarships; SC 29, LC 7, GC 14; enrl D 300, E 50, maj 130, grad 20
Tuition: Res—$145 for 12 or more quarter hr; nonres—$483; no campus res
Courses: Art Education, Ceramics, Costume Design & Construction, Drawing, Graphic Arts, History of Art & Archaeology, Illustration, Jewelry, Painting, Photography, Macrame, Weaving
Adult Hobby Classes: Enrl 60. Courses—various subjects
Children's Classes: Enrl 60. Courses—various subjects
Summer School: Enrl 200; term of one quarter. Courses—Art History, Studio

DALTON

DALTON JUNIOR COLLEGE, Division of Humanities, PO Box 2168, 30720. *Chmn* Dr Thomas A Wilkerson, EdD; *Instructor* W Joseph Helseth, MFA; *Instructor* Ronald O McBride, MS
Estab 1967, dept estab 1974; pub; D & E; ent req HS dipl and SAT; degrees AA 2 yr; SC 3, LC 3; enrl D 300, E 60, non-maj 200, maj 30
Tuition: Res—undergrad $116 per quarter; non-res—undergrad $158 per quarter
Courses: Art History, Drawing, History of Art & Archaeology, Painting, Design, Introduction to the Visual Arts

DECATUR

AGNES SCOTT COLLEGE, Department of Art,* East College Ave, 30030. Tel 404-373-2571. *Chmn* Marie Huper Pepe, PhD; *Assoc Prof* Robert F Westervelt, PhD; *Assoc Prof* Leland Steven, MFA; *Instr* Terry McGehee, MFA
Estab 1889; pvt; D; degrees BA 4 yr; scholarships; SC 13, LC 15; enrl non-maj 200, maj 23
Tuition: Res—undergrad $1950 yr; nonres—undergrad $4450 yr
Courses: Aesthetics, Architecture, Art Education, Art History, Ceramics, Drawing, Graphic Arts, History of Art & Archaeology, Painting, Printmaking

FORSYTH

TIFT COLLEGE, Department of Art, 31029. Tel 912-994-6689. *Assoc Prof* Alan Parker, MFA
Estab 1849, dept estab 1976; den; D - W, E & off campus - M & W; D & E; ent req HS dipl, SAT; degrees BA and BS 4 yr; SC 6, LC 3; enrl D 5, non-maj 50, maj 10, others 1
Tuition: Res—undergrad $1455 yr; non-res—undergrad $2835 yr; campus res—room and board $1440
Courses: Art History, Drawing, Illustration, Painting, Photography, Printmaking, Teacher Training, Advertising, Art Survey, Design

GAINESVILLE

BRENAU COLLEGE, Art Department, 30501. Tel 404-534-6299, Ext 6245. *Dir* Bill Gingles, MUA; *Asst Prof* Sherry Churn; *Instructor* Susan Harlan, MFA; *Instructor* Page Harvey, MFA; *Instructor* Mary Jane Taylor, MAEd
Estab 1878; pvt; D & E; ent req HS dipl; degrees BA & BS 4 yrs; Schol; enrl maj 45
Tuition: $4250 yr (includes room and board), $43 per cr hr for non-res students
Courses: Advertising Design, †Art Education, Art History, Calligraphy, Ceramics, †Commercial Art, Drawing, Graphic Design, †Handicrafts, History of Art & Archaeology, †Interior Design, Jewelry, Lettering, Painting, Photography, Printmaking, Sculpture, Textile Design, Silkscreen

LA GRANGE

LA GRANGE COLLEGE, Art Department, 30240. Tel 404-882-2911, Ext 491. *Head Dept* John D Lawrence. Instrs FT 3, PT 1
Estab 1831; pvt; D & E; ent req HS dipl, ent exam; degrees BA 4 yr; schol; SC 11, LC 2; enrl maj 40
Tuition: $2562 per yr, incl room and board
Courses: Art Education, Art History, Ceramics, Commercial Art, Drawing, Painting, Photography, Printmaking, Sculpture, Textile Design, Art History Survey, Batik, Weaving

MACON

MERCER UNIVERSITY, Art Department, 1400 Coleman Ave, 31207. Tel 912-745-6811, Ext 232. *Chmn* Marshall Daugherty. Instrs FT 4
Estab 1945; den; D; ent req HS dipl; degrees BA 4 yr; SC 9, LC 7, GC 2; enrl maj 15
Tuition: $3006 per yr; campus res—room and board $1497
Courses: Art Education, Art History, Ceramics, Drawing, Graphic Arts, Sculpture

Summer School: Dir, JoAnna Watson. 2 terms, 5 wks each beginning June. Courses—Ceramics, Crafts, Drawing, Painting, Photography, Sculpture

WESLEYAN COLLEGE, Art Department, Forsyth Rd, 31201. Tel 912-477-1110. *Head of Dept* Joel Plum, MFA; *Asst Prof* Antony Rice, MFA; *Instructor* Elizabeth Bailey, MFA; *Instructor* Zdzislaw Sikora, MFA
Estab 1836; den; D & E; ent req HS dipl, SAT, GPA; degrees BFA 4 yrs; schol; SC 38, LC 10; enrl D 159, non-maj 13, maj 45, others 12
Tuition: $2970 per yr, $50 per course; $4560 per yr incl room & board
Courses: †Advertising Design, Aesthetics, Art History, †Art Education, Calligraphy, †Ceramics, †Commercial Art, Printmaking, Graphic Arts, †Graphic Design, History of Art & Archaeology, Illustration, Jewelry, Lettering, †Painting, Photography, †Printmaking, †Sculpture, Stage Design, Teacher Training, Textile Design, Theatre Arts
Summer School: Dir, Dr Thomas Boyd. Courses—Art Appreciation, Cartooning, Ceramics, Graphic Design, Illustration, Printmaking, Watercolour

MOUNT BERRY

BERRY COLLEGE, Art Department, 30149. *Chmn* T J Mew, PhD; *Asst Prof* Jere Lykins, MEd; *Asst Prof* Tom Pitts, MA
Estab 1902, dept estab 1942; pvt; D & E; ent req HS dipl, SAT, CEEB, ACT; degrees BA, BS 4 yrs; scholarships; SC 24, LC 9; enrl D 122, non-maj 38, maj 84, others 7
Tuition: Res—undergrad $3150 yr; nonres—undergrad $3630 yr; campus residency available
Courses: Aesthetics, Art Education, Art History, Calligraphy, †Ceramics, Collage, Conceptual Art, Constructions, Drawing, Film, Graphic Arts, Handicrafts, †History of Art & Archaeology, Intermedia, Mixed Media, †Painting, Photography, Printmaking, Sculpture, Teacher Training, Video, Ecological Art, Weaving
Summer School: Dir, Dr T J Mew

MOUNT VERNON

BREWTON-PARKER COLLEGE, Visual Arts, Hwy 280, 30445. Tel 912-583-2241, Ext 44. *Visual Arts Dir* Janet Gilmore-Bryan, MA & MFA; *Vis Prof* Pamela Burnley, film & video; *Vis Prof* John Groth, ink & watercolor
Estab 1906, dept re-estab 1976; pvt, den; D & E; ent req HS dipl; degrees AA(Visual Arts) 2 yrs; SC 10, LC 4; enrl in dept D 19, non-maj 4, maj 15
Tuition: $1500 per yr, $490 per quarter, $30 per hr; campus res—room $225 per quarter & board $185 per quarter
Courses: Art History, Drawing, Film, Graphic Arts, Graphic Design, Illustration, Intermedia, Mixed Media, Painting, Photography, Printmaking, Sculpture, Art Media & Theory

ROME

SHORTER COLLEGE, Art Department, Shorter Ave, 30161. Tel 404-291-2121. *Head Dept* Jane M McCord, MFA; *Asst Prof* George Hayes, MFA
Estab 1873, dept estab 1900; den; D; ent req HS dipl; degrees AB(Art) and BS(Art Ed) 4 yr; schol; SC 5; enrl D 140, non-maj 115, maj 25
Tuition: Boarding students $3500 per yr, non-boarding students $2150 per yr
Courses: †Art Education, Art History, Ceramics, Commercial Art, Drawing, Handicrafts, Painting, Teacher Training, Textile Design, Enameling

SAVANNAH

SAVANNAH STATE COLLEGE, Department of Fine Arts, State College Branch, 31404. Tel 912-356-2208. *Acting Head Dept* Dr O F Becker, PhD; *Asst Prof* William Anderson, MFA; *Asst Prof* Farnese Lumpkin, MA; *Asst Prof* John Mach, MA
Estab 1880s, dept estab 1950s; pub; D; ent req HS dipl; degrees BS(Art Educ); SC 13, LC 3
Tuition: Res $540, non-res $238; campus residence available
Courses: Art History
Summer School: Dir, Dr O F Becker. Enrl 60; tui $180. Courses—on demand

STATESBORO

GEORGIA SOUTHERN COLLEGE, Department of Art, 30458. *Head Dept* Stephen Bayless, EdD; *Assoc Prof* Bronislaw Bak, MFA; *Assoc Prof* Henry Iler, MFA; *Assoc Prof* Joseph Olson Jr, EdD; *Asst Prof* Kenneth Guill, MA; *Asst Prof* Bernard Solomon, MFA; *Asst Prof* Thomas Steadman, MFA; *Instructor* David Posner, MFA; *Instructor* Tom Raab, MFA
Pub; D & E; ent req HS dipl; degrees AB and BSEd 4 yr
Tuition: Res—undergrad $145 per quarter; non-res—undergrad $383 per quarter; campus res—room and board $885
Courses: Art Education, Art History, Ceramics, Commercial Art, Constructions, Drawing, Graphic Arts, Graphic Design, Lettering, Mixed Media, Painting, Photography, Printmaking, Sculpture, Teacher Training, Textile Design
Adult Hobby Classes: Enrl 40; tui $35 per 10 wks. Courses—Painting, Photography
Children's Classes: Offered in Laboratory School

VALDOSTA

VALDOSTA STATE COLLEGE, Department of Art, Patterson St, 31601. Tel 912-247-3319, 247-3330. *Head Dept* Irene Dodd. Instrs FT 8
Estab 1911; pub; D; ent req SAT; degrees AB, BFA and BFA(Art Ed) 4 yr; SC 25, LC 10, GC 9; enrl 400, maj 90, total 4500
Tuition: Res—$182 or more per quarter, $12 per hr; non-res—$420 less than 12 hrs, $32 per hr; plus other fees
Courses: Advertising Design, Art Education, Art History, Ceramics, Commercial Art, Drawing, Graphic Arts, Graphic Design, Illustration, Painting, Photography, Sculpture, Teacher Training, Museum Tour, Weaving
Children's Classes: Crafts, Drawing, Sculpture, Watercolor
Summer School: Head Dept, Irene Dodd

YOUNG HARRIS

YOUNG HARRIS COLLEGE, Department of Art, 30582. Tel 404-379-2161. *Chmn* Richard Aunspaugh; *Instructor* Vee Brown. Instrs FT 2
Estab 1886; den; D; ent req HS dipl; degrees AFA 2 yr; schol; SC 6, LC 4; enrl D 540, maj 48
Tuition: $900 per yr, PT $407; campus res—$1245
Courses: Drawing, History of Art & Archaeology, Painting, Sculpture, Design
Children's Classes: Enrl 20; tui non; 4 wks in summer
Summer School: Enrl 18; tui none; 6 wk term. Courses—Painting

HAWAII

HONOLULU

HONOLULU ACADEMY OF ARTS, Studio Program, 900 Beretania St, 96814. Tel 808-538-3693. *Cur* Joseph Feher; *Instructor* James Koga; *Instructor* Yuk-Wong Li. Instrs FT 3, PT 1
Estab 1946; pvt; ent req 16 yrs of age with talent
Tuition: $225 half day, $450 full day per sem
Courses: Drawing, Painting, Printmaking, Etching, Lithography
Summer School: Tui $100 for 6 wk half days. Courses—Drawing, Painting, Printmaking

HONOLULU COMMUNITY COLLEGE, Department of Art, Department of Commercial Art, Department of Graphic Art,* 874 Dillingham Blvd, 96817. Tel 808-845-9211.
Pub; D & E; ent req 18 yrs of age, eng & math requirements, motivation, interest in learning, willingness to work; degrees AS 2 yr; SC 20, LC 2; enrl D 150 majors
Tuition: Res—undergrad $40 per sem, $80 per yr; nonres—undergrad $450 per sem, $900 per yr
Courses: †Advertising Design, Commercial Art, Drafting, Drawing, Film, †Graphic Arts, †Graphic Design, †Illustration, Lettering, Painting, †Photography, Textile Design, Video

KAPIOLANI COMMUNITY COLLEGE, Diamond Head Campus,* 4303 Diamond Head Rd, 96816. Tel 808-735-3511. Instrs FT 1, PT 3
Estab 1965; pub; D & E; ent req ent exam; degrees AA and AS 1-2 yr; scholarships; SC 6, LC 7; enrl D 3800, E 500
Tuition: No campus res
Courses: Art History, Ceramics, Drawing, Jewelry, Painting, Textile Design, Art Appreciation, Light and Color, Macrame, Perception, Visual Arts
Adult Hobby Classes: Enrl 25 per class; tui depends on amount of units. Courses—Ceramics and Macrame, Drawing and Painting, Jewelry, Textile Design
Summer School: Enrl 700; tui depends on amount of units taken for term of 6 wks. Courses—vary each summer

UNIVERSITY OF HAWAII AT MANOA, Department of Art, 2535 The Mall, 96822. Tel 808-948-8251. *Chmn* John Wisnosky, MFA. Instrs FT 30, PT 30
Estab 1907; pub; D & E; ent req HS dipl or GED and SAT or ACT; degrees BA(Art History), BA(Studio) and BFA 4 yr; schol; SC 64, LC 34; enrl maj 600, grad 60
Tuition: Res—undergrad $225 per sem, $19 per cr hr; grad $275 sem, $23 per cr hr; non-res—undergrad $562 per sem, $48 per cr hr; grad $687 per sem, $58 per cr hr; plus fees; campus res available
Courses: Art History, Ceramics, Drawing, Graphic Arts, Graphic Design, Painting, Photography, Printmaking, Sculpture, Textile Design, Fiber
Adult Hobby Classes: Evenings only. Courses—Chinese Brush Painting, Drawing, Painting
Summer School: Head, Dean Robert. Tui res $20 per cr hr, non-res $30 per cr hr, plus fees. Courses—Art History (Western and Pacific), Ceramics, Drawing, Design, Painting, Printmaking, Sculpture

KAHULUI

MAUI COMMUNITY COLLEGE, Art Program, 310 Kaahumanu Ave, 96732. Instrs FT 1, PT 3
Estab 1967; pub; D & E; ent req ent exam; degrees AS 2 yr; schol; SC 8, LC 2; enrl D 300, E 100
Courses: Advertising Design, Architecture, Ceramics, Display, Drafting, Drawing, Graphic Arts, Graphic Design, History of Art & Archaeology, Jewelry, Painting, Photography, Sculpture, Textile Design, Batik, Copper Enameling, History of Architecture, Welding, Weaving
Adult Hobby Classes: Enrl 60; tui $10-$30. Courses—Batik, Jewelry, Silk Screen
Summer School: Enrl 40; term of 6 wk beginning June. Courses—Introduction to the Visual Arts

LIHUE

KAUAI COMMUNITY COLLEGE, Department of Art, RR 1, Box 216, 96766. Tel 808-245-8311. Instrs FT 2, PT 1
Estab 1965; pub; D & E; ent req HS dipl; degrees AA and AS 2 yr; schol; SC 6, LC 2; enrl D 965, E 468
Courses: Ceramics, Drafting, Drawing, Graphic Arts, History of Art & Archaeology, Painting, Photography, Oriental Brush Painting, Watercolor
Summer School: Term of 6 wk beginning June and July. Courses—Ceramics, Photography

PEARL CITY

LEEWARD COMMUNITY COLLEGE, Arts and Humanities Division, 96-045 Ala Ike, 96782. Tel 808-455-0350. *Head Div* Douglas Kaya; *Instructor* Allyn Bromley, MFA; *Instructor* Kay M Davidson, MFA; *Instructor* Richard Hayashida, MFA; *Instructor* Barbara Saromines, MFA
Estab 1968; pub; D & E; ent req over 18 yrs of age; degrees AA and AS 2 yrs; schol; SC 11, LC 3; enrl D 400, E 100
Tuition: Res—undergrad $45 per sem, $3.50 per cr hr; non-res—undergrad $455 per sem, $38 per cr hr; no campus res
Courses: Art History, Ceramics, Costume Design & Construction, Drawing, Graphic Arts, Painting, Photography, Printmaking, Sculpture, Theatre Arts, Aspects of Asian Art, Two Dimensional Design, Three Dimensional Design
Summer School: Enrl 100; tui $60 per term of 7 wks beginning June 12th. Courses—vary

IDAHO

BOISE

BOISE STATE UNIVERSITY, Art Department,* 1910 University Blvd, 83725. Tel 208-385-1011. *Chmn* Louis A Peck
Estab 1932; pub; D & E; ent req HS dipl; degrees BA, BFA, BA (Educ), BFA (Educ), BA (Advertising Design) and BFA (Advertising Design) 4 yr; scholarships; SC 51, LC 8, GC 4; enrl D 2539, maj 441, GS 14
Tuition: Res—$227 per sem; nonres—$827 per sem
Courses: Advertising Design, Art Education, Ceramics, Commercial Art, Drawing, Graphic Arts, Graphic Design, History of Art & Archaeology, Illustration, Jewelry, Lettering, Painting, Photography, Sculpture, Teacher Training, Textile Design, Metal

LEWISTON

LEWIS-CLARK STATE COLLEGE, Art Department, 83501. Tel 208-746-2341. *Discipline Coordr* Robert Almquist, MFA; *Instructor* Brian L Sprague, MFA. Instrs FT 2
Estab 1893; pub; D & E; ent req HS dipl or GED, ACT; degrees BA and BS 4 yrs; schol; SC 20, LC 2; enrl D 126, E 16, maj 9
Tuition: Res—undergrad $370 per yr; non-res—undergrad $1420 per yr; PT (up to 7 cr) $15 per cr; campus res—room and board $1530 double room, $1730 single room
Courses: Art Education, Art History, Ceramics, Drawing, Graphic Arts, History of Art & Archaeology, Painting, Printmaking, Sculpture, Stage Design, Teacher Training, Theatre Arts, Video, Composition, Independent Study, Watercolor

MOSCOW

UNIVERSITY OF IDAHO, Department of Art and Architecture,* 83843. Tel 208-885-6111. *Head Dept* Paul Blanton; *Chmn* George T Wray, MFA; *Prof* George Roberts, MS; *Assoc Prof* David Moreland, MFA; *Assoc Prof* Frank Cronk, MFA; *Prof* Nelson Curtis, MFA; *Asst Prof* David Giese, MFA; *Asst Prof* Lynn Haagensen, MFA; *Asst Prof* Jim Engelhardt, BA
Estab 1923; pub; D & E; ent req HS dipl; degrees BA and BFA 4 yr, MFA 2 yr minimum, MA 1 yr; scholarships; SC 30, LC 6, GC 8; enrl D 450 (Art and Architecture), non-maj 345 (Architecture), maj 105 (Art), GS 18 (Art)
Tuition: Res—undergrad $440 per yr; nonres—undergrad $1640 per yr; campus res available
Courses: Advertising Design, †Architecture, †Art Education, †Ceramics, †Commercial Art, Drawing, Graphic Arts, Graphic Design, Illustration, †Interior Design, †Jewelry, Landscape Architecture, †Painting, Photography, †Printmaking, †Sculpture

NAMPA

NORTHWEST NAZARENE COLLEGE, Art Department, Holly at Dewey, 83651. Tel 208-467-8412. Instrs FT 3
Den; D & E; ent req HS dipl; degrees AA and AB 4 yrs; schol; SC 12, LC 5; enrl D 200, E 40, maj 24
Courses: Advertising Design, Art Education, Ceramics, Commercial Art, Drafting, Drawing, Graphic Arts, History of Art & Archaeology, Illustration, Lettering, Painting, Sculpture, Teacher Training, Crafts for Teachers
Adult Hobby Classes: Crafts
Summer School: Courses—Art Education

POCATELLO

IDAHO STATE UNIVERSITY, Department of Art,* 741 South Seventh Ave, PO Box 8004, 83209. Tel 208-236-0211. *Chmn* Dennis Snyder
Estab 1901; pub; D & E; ent req HS dipl, GED, ACT; degrees BA, BFA and MFA 4 yr; SC 32, LC 6, GS 22; enrl maj 75, GS 15, total 500
Tuition: Res—$205 per sem, $420 per yr; nonres—$630 per sem, $1420 per yr; campus res $1260 per yr
Courses: Art Education, Art History, Ceramics, Drawing, Painting, Printmaking, Sculpture, Design, Metals, Weaving
Summer School: 4 wk and 8 wk sessions

REXBURG

RICKS COLLEGE, Department of Art, 83440. Tel 208-356-2339. *Head Dept* Richard Bird, MFA; *Instructor* Arlo Coles, MFA; *Instructor* Brent Gehring, MFA; *Instructor* Leon Parson, BFA; *Instructor* Robert Powell, MFA; *Instructor* Robert Worrell, MA
Estab 1888; pvt; D & E; ent req HS dipl; degrees AAS, AAdv Design and AFA 2 yrs; schol; SC 23, LC 1; enrl D 123, maj 123
Tuition: $460 per sem LDS members; $637 non-LDS members; campus residency available
Courses: †Advertising Design, Art Education, Art History, Ceramics, †Commercial Art, Drawing, Graphic Design, History of Art & Archaeology, Illustration, Interior Design, Lettering, Painting, Sculpture, Teacher Training
Summer School: Tui $460

SUN VALLEY

SUN VALLEY CENTER FOR THE ARTS & HUMANITIES, Department of Fine Art, PO Box 656, 83353. Tel 208-622-9371. *Head Dept* David Griffith, PhD; *Dir* D W Wharton, MFA; *Dir Photography* Ellen Manchester, MFA; *Artist in Res* Jim Ronberg, MFA; *Instr* Mark C Klett, MFA; *Vis Prof* Connor Everts, printmaking; *Vis Prof* John Pfhal, photography
Estab 1970, dept estab 1977; den; D & E; ent req portfolio; scholarships; SC 25, LC 5, GC 5; enrl D 20, E 15, grad 5
Tuition: $1375 per yr, $700 per sem, $150 monthly, $60 PT, $8 per hr; campus res—room $800 per yr
Courses: Aesthetics, Art Education, Art History, Ceramics, Conceptual Art, Drawing, Fashion Arts, Film, Graphic Arts, Illustration, Mixed Media, Museum Staff Training, Painting, Photography, Printmaking, Restoration & Conservation, Theatre Arts, Video
Adult Hobby Classes: Enrl 10-25; tui $35 per term. Courses—Glassblowing, Metalsmithing, Self-Motification, Woodworking
Children's Classes: Enrl 15-30; tui $25 per term. Courses—Ceramics, Graphics, Mixed Media, Photography
Summer School: Enrl 50; tui $650 for term of 8 wks beginning June 18. Courses—all of the above

TWIN FALLS

COLLEGE OF SOUTHERN IDAHO, Art Department, PO Box 1238, 83301. Tel 208-733-9554, Ext 260. *Chmn* Lavar Steel, MS; *Assoc Prof* Michael Green, MFA; *Assoc Prof* Wes Wada
Estab 1965; pub; D & E; ent req HS dipl, ACT; degrees dipl or AA; schol; SC 26, LC 2; enrl D 3000, E 2000, non-maj 50, maj 45
Tuition: Res—undergrad $200 per yr, $100 per sem, $10 per sem hr; non-res—undergrad $600 per yr, $300 per sem, $30 per cr hr; campus res room and board
Courses: Art History, Ceramics, Drawing, Handicrafts, Jewelry, Lettering, Mixed Media, Painting, Photography, Sculpture, Silversmithing, Theatre Arts, Acrylic Painting, Design, Weaving, Watercolor
Adult Hobby Classes: Enrl 15 per class; tui $30 per sem. Courses—Jewelry, Photography, Pottery, Weaving
Children's Classes: Enrl 15 per class; tui $20 per 10 wks. Courses—Drawing, Painting, Puppets
Summer School: Tui $44 per class beginning June 5th. Courses—Ceramics, Drawing, Painting, Photography

ILLINOIS

AURORA

AURORA COLLEGE, Art Department, 347 S Gladstone Ave, 60507. Tel 312-892-6431. *Head Dept* John L Rogers, MFA; *Instr* Jay Constantine, MFA; *Instr* Brent Wall, MFA
Estab 1893, dept estab 1979; pvt; D & E; ent req HS dipl; degrees BA 4 yrs; SC 12, LC 5; enrl D 80, E 40, non-maj 120, maj 1
Tuition: $3000 per yr, $900-$1050 per trimester; campus res $1785 per yr
Courses: Advertising Design, Aesthetics, †Art Education, †Art History, Collage, Costume Design & Construction, †Drawing, Graphic Design, History of Art & Archaeology, Intermedia, †Painting, †Printmaking, Sculpture, Stage Design, †Teacher Training, †Theatre Arts
Summer School: Tui $300 for term of 6 wks. Courses—Design, Drawing or Painting

BELLEVILLE

BELLEVILLE AREA COLLEGE, Art Department,* 2500 Carlyle Rd, 62221. Tel 618-239-2700. *Chmn Art Dept* Wayne L Shaw, MFA
Estab 1948; pub; D & E; ent req HS dipl; degrees AA and AS 2 yrs; scholarships; SC 36, LC 9; enrl D 4000, E 3500, maj 200
Tuition: Res—undergrad $390 per yr; nonres—undergrad $1035-$1500 per yr; no campus res
Courses: Advertising Design, Art Education, Art History, Ceramics, Commercial Art, Drawing, History of Art & Archaeology, Jewelry, Painting, Photography, Sculpture, Theatre Arts
Adult Hobby Classes: Enrl 175; tui $9 per hr. Courses—Ceramics, Design, Drawing, Jewelry, Photography
Summer School: Dir, Wayne Shaw. Enrl 175; tui $9 per sem hr for term of 8 wks beginning June 5. Courses—Art History, Ceramics, Drawing, Jewelry, Photography

BLOOMINGTON

ILLINOIS WESLEYAN UNIVERSITY, School of Art, 61701. Tel 309-556-3077. *Dir* Miles Bair, MA; *Instructor* Fred Brian, MFA; *Instructor* Anna Holcombe, MFA; *Instructor* Ed McCollough, MA; *Instructor* Ben Paskus, PhD; *Instructor* Kevin Strandberg, MFA
Estab 1855, school estab 1946; pvt; D; ent req HS dipl, SAT or ACT; degrees BA, BFA and BFA with Teaching Cert 4 yrs; enrl non-maj 150, maj 75
Courses: Art Education, Art History, Ceramics, Conceptual Art, Drawing, Film, Graphic Arts, History of Art & Archaeology, Painting, Photography, Printmaking, Sculpture, Teacher Training
Summer School: Enrl 15; tui $400 for term of 3 wks. Courses—Papermaking, Photography, Printmaking

CARBONDALE

SOUTHERN ILLINOIS UNIVERSITY, School of Art, 62902. Tel 618-453-2571. *Dir* Benjamin T Miller, MA; *Undergrad Admissions* Patricia C Beene; *Chmn of Metals* Brent Kington, MFA; *Chmn Sculpture* Thomas Walsh, MFA; *Chmn Two-Dimensional Design* Robert Paulson, MFA; *Chmn Art Educ* Roy Abrahamson, PhD; *Chmn Art History* George Mavigliano, MA; *Printmaker-Drawer* Herbert Fink, MFA
Estab 1874; pub; D & E; ent req HS dipl, upper 50 percent of class, ACT; degrees BA and BS 4 yrs, MFA 2 yrs; scholarships; SC 100, LC 24, GS 28; enrl D 1304, E 338, non-maj 672, maj 500, grad 70, others 400
Tuition: Res—undergrad and grad $429 per sem, $24 per cr hr; nonres—undergrad and grad $1003 per sem, $72 per cr hr; campus res available
Courses: †Advertising Design, Aesthetics, †Architecture, †Art Education, †Art History, †Ceramics, Collage, †Commercial Art, Conceptual Art, Constructions, †Costume Design & Construction, †Drafting, †Drawing, Fashion Arts, Film, Goldsmithing, Graphic Arts, Graphic Design, †History of Art & Archaeology, Illustration, Industrial Design, †Jewelry, Lettering, Mixed Media, Museum Staff Training, †Painting, Photography, †Printmaking, †Sculpture, †Silversmithing, Stage Design, †Teacher Training, Textile Design, Art for Elementary Education, †Blacksmithing, Fibers, †Foundry, †Glassblowing, †Weaving
Adult Hobby Classes: Enrl 40; tui $10-$15 per sem. Courses—Ceramics, Drawing, Fibers, Jewelry
Children's Classes: Enrl 40; tui $10 per class. Courses—vary per sem
Summer School: Enrl 500; tui $22 per hr for term of 8 wks beginning June. Courses—selection from regular courses plus workshops in Art Therapy, Blacksmithing, Foundry, and High School Art Workshop
—Department of Design, 62902. *Chmn* Wayne L St John. Instrs 10
Estab 1956; pub; ent req students transferring from another university cannot receive credit for design courses but will be evaluated on the basis of his or her work; degrees BA 4 yrs, MS 2 yrs; enrl maj 120
Courses: Basic Design, Product-Shelter Design, Visual Design

CARLINVILLE

BLACKBURN COLLEGE, Department of Art, 62626. Tel 217-854-3231. *Chmn* James M Clark. Instrs FT 2, PT 2
Estab 1949; pvt; D & E; ent req HS grad; degrees BA 4 yrs; scholarships; SC 14, LC 7; enrl maj 40
Tuition: $2040 per yr; campus res $380
Courses: Art History, Ceramics, Drawing, Painting, Printmaking, Teacher Training, Theatre Arts

CHAMPAIGN

UNIVERSITY OF ILLINOIS, URBANA-CHAMPAIGN, College of Fine and Applied Arts, 61820. Tel 217-333-1661. *Dean* Jack H McKenzie. Instrs FT 260, PT 150
Estab 1931; pub; D; ent req HS grad, ent exam; degrees bachelors 4 yrs, masters, doctors; scholarships, fels and assistantships; enrl undergrad $2881, grad 730
Adult Hobby Classes: Scheduled through University Extension
Children's Classes: Sat; summer youth classes
Summer School: courses offered
—Department of Art and Design, 143 Art and Design Bldg, Fourth and Peabody Dr, 61820. Tel 217-333-0855. *Head Dept* Eugene C Wicks, MFA; *In Charge Art Educ* George W Hardiman, EdD; *In Charge Art History* Jerrold Ziff, PhD; *In Charge Graphic Design* Raymond Perlman, MFA; *In Charge Industrial Design* Edward J Zagorski, MFA; *In Charge Undergrad Painting* Glenn R Bradshaw, MFA; *In Charge Grad Painting* M Douglas Hilson, MFA; *In Charge Photography* Luther Smith, BA; *In Charge Sculpture* Frank Gallo, MFA
Estab 1867, dept estab 1877; pub; D & E; ent req HS dipl, ACT, SAT, CLEP; degrees BFA 4 yrs, MA 1 yr, MFA 2 yrs, EdD and PhD 5 yrs; scholarships; SC 119, LC 72, GC 77; enrl maj 563, grad 106, others 15
Tuition: Res—undergrad $814 per yr, $407 per sem, PT $292 per sem, grad $844 per

yr, $422 per sem; PT $302 per sem; nonres—undergrad $1986 per yr, $993 per sem, PT $692 per sem, grad $2076 per yr, $1038 per sem, PT $722 per sem; campus res—room & board $1628 per sem
Courses: †Art Education, †Art History, †Ceramics, Drawing, Film, †Graphic Design, †History of Art & Archaeology, †Industrial Design, Jewelry, Museum Staff Training, †Painting, †Photography, †Printmaking, †Sculpture, Silversmithing, Teacher Training, †Cinematography
Children's Classes: Enrl 220; tui $16 per sem. Courses—Creative Arts for Children
Summer School: Dir, Eugene C Wicks. Courses—foundation and lower division courses with some limited offerings and independent study at upper division and graduate levels

CHARLESTON

EASTERN ILLINOIS UNIVERSITY, Art Department, FAA 216, 61920. Tel 217-581-3410. *Dept Chmn* James K Johnson, MFA; *Prof* Carl Emmerich, DEd; *Prof* Bill Heyduck, DEd; *Prof* June Krutza, PhD; *Prof* Carl Shull, DEd; *Prof* Walter Sorge, DEd; *Prof* Lynn Trank, DEd; *Prof* Ben Watkins, PhD; *Assoc Prof* Suzan Braun, MFA; *Assoc Prof* Garret DeRuiter, MFA; *Assoc Prof* Cary Knoop, MFA; *Assoc Prof* Al Moldroski, MA; *Assoc Prof* Carl Wilen, MFA; *Asst Prof* Paul Bodine, MA; *Asst Prof* Rod Buffington, MA; *Asst Prof* Hannah Eads, MSE; *Asst Prof* Paul McDowell, MFA; *Asst Prof* Jerry McRoberts, PhD; *Instructor* Janina Darling, PhD; *Instructor* Melinda Hegarty, MA; *Instructor* Terry Roller, MFA. Instrs FT 23, PT 6
Estab 1895, dept estab 1930; pub; D & E; ent req HS dipl, grad - MAT or GRE; degrees BA 4 yrs, MA 1 yr, Specialist Educ 2 yrs; scholarships; enrl 1750, non-maj 1500, maj 250, grad 20
Tuition: Res—undergrad $790 per yr, $395 per sem, $33 per hr; grad $583 per yr, $269 per sem, $33 per hr; nonres—undergrad $1906 per yr, $953 per sem, $83 per hr; grad $1346 per yr, $673 per sem, $83 per hr
Courses: Art Education, Art History, Ceramics, Drawing, Painting, Printmaking, Sculpture, Silversmithing, Design, Visual Communications, Watercolor, Weaving
Summer School: Dept Chmn, James K Johnson, MFA; intersession 3 weeks, one 5 wk session, one 8 wk session. Tui res—undergrad $225, $33 per hr, grad $269, $33 per hr; nonres—undergrad $627, $78 per hr, grad $673, $83 per hr. Courses—same as Fall and Spring semesters

CHICAGO

AMERICAN ACADEMY OF ART, 220 S State St, 60604. Tel 312-939-3883. *Dir* Irving Shapiro. Instrs FT 18, PT 8
Estab 1923; pvt; D & E; ent req HS dipl, portfolio; degrees AA 2-3 yrs; scholarships; SC 10; enrl D 350, E 600
Tuition: $2600 per yr; no campus res
Courses: Advertising Design, Commercial Art, Drawing, Graphic Arts, Graphic Design, Illustration, Lettering, Painting, Photography, Cartooning
Summer School: Dir, Irving Shapiro. Enrl 300 FT, 500 PT; tui $370 for term of 8 wks beginning June 26. Courses—general

CITY COLLEGES OF CHICAGO, Central Administration Offices, 180 N Michigan Ave, 60601. Tel 312-269-8000.
Pub; D & E; ent req HS dipl, ACT; degrees AA, AAS and dipl 2 yrs; scholarships
Tuition: Res—$15 per cr hr per sem; out-of-city $25 per cr hr, out-of-state $44 per cr hr; lab fees vary; no campus res
—Daley College, Art and Architecture Dept, 7400 S Pulaski Rd, 60652. Tel 312-735-3000.
Estab 1960; enrl 4700
Courses: Art Education, Ceramics, Drafting, Drawing, Graphic Arts, Graphic Design, History of Art & Archaeology, Illustration, Painting, Photography, Sculpture, Weaving
—Kennedy-King College, Art and Humanities Dept, 6800 S Wentworth Ave, 60621. Tel 312-962-3200.
Estab 1935; enrl 9010
Courses: Art Education, Drafting, Drawing, History of Art & Archaeology, Industrial Design, Painting, Photography, Theatre Arts, Radio-TV
—Loop College, Art and Humanities Dept, 64 E Lake St, 60601. Tel 312-269-8000.
Estab 1962; enrl 5000
Courses: Art Education, Drafting, Drawing, History of Art & Archaeology, Industrial Design, Painting, Theatre Arts
—Malcolm X College, Art and Humanities Dept, 1900 W Van Buren St, 60612. Tel 312-942-3000.
Estab 1911; enrl 5000
Courses: Art Education, Art History, Ceramics, Drafting, Drawing, Industrial Design, Painting, Sculpture, Theatre Arts, Radio-TV
—Olive-Harvey College, Art and Humanities Dept, 10001 S Woodlawn Ave, 60628. Tel 312-568-3700.
Estab 1957; enrl 4700
Courses: Art Education, Drafting, Drawing, History of Art & Archaeology, Industrial Design, Painting, Theatre Arts
—Truman College, Art and Humanities Dept, 1145 W Wilson Ave, 60640. Tel 312-878-1700.
Estab 1956; enrl 3800
Courses: Art Education, Ceramics, Drafting, Drawing, History of Art & Archaeology, Industrial Design, Painting, Photography, Theatre Arts
—Wright College, Art and Humanities Dept, 3400 N Austin Ave, 60634. Tel 312-777-7900. Instrs FT 5
Estab 1934; pub; D & E; ent req HS dipl; degrees AA 2 yrs; SC 15, LC 5; enrl D 3000, E 2500
Courses: Advertising Design, Architecture, Ceramics, Commercial Art, Drafting, Drawing, Graphic Design, History of Art & Archaeology, Lettering, Painting, Sculpture, Theatre Arts
Adult Hobby Classes: Enrl 30 per class; tui $3 for 8 sessions. Courses—Interior Design, Oil Painting, Watercolor
Summer School: Term of 8 wks beginning July 2. Courses—Figure Drawing, Painting

COLUMBIA COLLEGE, Art Department, 600 S Michigan Ave, 60605. Tel 312-663-1600. *Chairperson Art & Photography Depts* John Mulvany, MFA; *Coordr Graphics* Marlene Lipinski, MFA; *Coordr Interior Design* Tony Patano, BFA; *Coordr Fine Arts* Phyllis Bramson, MFA; *Coordr Crafts* Tom Taylor, BFA; *Coordr Two-Dimensional Design* Owen McHugh, MFA
Estab 1893; pvt; D & E; ent req HS dipl; degrees BA 4 yrs; scholarships; SC 43, LC 17
Tuition: Nonres—undergrad $1250 per sem, $87 per cr hr; no campus res
Courses: †Advertising Design, Architecture, Art Education, Art History, Calligraphy, Ceramics, Commercial Art, Costume Design & Construction, Drafting, Drawing, Fashion Arts, †Film, Goldsmithing, †Graphic Arts, †Graphic Design, Handicrafts, Illustration, †Interior Design, Jewelry, Mixed Media, Museum Staff Training, Painting, †Photography, Printmaking, Sculpture, Silversmithing, Stage Design, Textile Design, †Theatre Arts, †Video, Silk Screen, Typography, Weaving
Summer School: Dir, John Mulvany

CONTEMPORARY ART WORKSHOP, 542 W Grant Place, 60614. Tel 312-525-9624. *Dir* John W Kearney, BA; *Admin Dir* Lynn Kearney; *Sculpture* Paul Zakoian, MA
Estab 1950; pvt; D & E; ent req studio artists must submit slides; degrees none; apprentice prog
Tuition: $80 for 10 wks
Courses: Painting, Sculpture
Adult Hobby Classes: Tui $80 for 10 wks. Courses—Sculpture
Summer School: Summer courses—Painting, Sculpture, Theatre

DEPAUL UNIVERSITY, Department of Art, School of Liberal Arts and Sciences, 2323 N Seminary, 60614. Tel 312-321-8194. *Chmn Dept* Sally Kitt Chappell, PhD; *Assoc Prof* William Conger, MFA; *Assoc Prof* Robert Donley, MFA; *Asst Prof* Stephen Luecking, MFA; *Asst Prof* Simone Zurawski, PhD
Estab 1897, dept estab 1965; pvt; D; ent req HS dipl, SAT or ACT; degrees BA(Art) 4 yrs; SC 20, LC 12; enrl D 30 art maj
Tuition: All tuition fees are subject to change, contact admissions office for current fees; campus residency available
Courses: Art Education, Art History, Drawing, Painting, Photography, Printmaking, Sculpture, Teacher Training, Design
Summer School: Dir, Sally Kitt Chappell

FELICIAN COLLEGE, Art Department, 3800 W Peterson Ave, 60659. Tel 312-539-1919. *Art Dir* Mary Lauriane, MFA; *Lectr* Joan Kalk, MA
Estab 1953; pvt; D & E; ent req HS dipl; degrees AA 2 yrs; enrl D 26, E 25
Tuition: $1400 per yr, $700 per sem
Courses: Art Education, Art History, Drawing, Mixed Media, Painting
Summer School: Dir, Mary Lauriane. Tui $90 for term of 15 wks beginning June 17. Courses—Creative Art, Methods in Teaching Art

HARRINGTON INSTITUTE OF INTERIOR DESIGN, 410 S Michigan, 60605. Tel 312-939-4975. *Dean* Robert C Marks
Estab 1931; pvt; D & E; ent req HS dipl, interview; degrees Associate Degree 3 yr; enrl D 228, E 220
Tuition: $2850 per yr, $1425 per sem; campus res—room & board $2100
Courses: Interior Design

ILLINOIS INSTITUTE OF TECHNOLOGY
—College of Architecture, Planning and Design, Department of Architecture, * Crown Hall Bldg, 3300 S Federal St, 60616. Tel 312-567-3262. *Acting Chmn Archit* David C Sharpe; *Planning Chmn* Paul Thomas
Estab 1895 as Armour Institute, consolidated with Lewis Institute of Arts and Sciences 1940; pvt; degrees BArchit, MSArchit, MSCity and Regional Planning 5 yrs; enrl 200
Tuition: $1845 per sem; foreign $6500 per yr
Courses: Architecture
Summer School: Term June 15 through August 8
—Institute of Design, * 3360 S State St, 60616. Tel 312-567-3250, Ext 3250. *Chmn* Dietmar R Winker; *Chmn Design* John Grimes. Instrs FT 17, PT 2
Estab 1937; pvt; D & E; ent req CEEB exam; degrees BS(Design) 4 yrs, MS(Visual Educ, Visual Design, Product Design, Photography); scholarships; enrl D 275, E 115
Tuition: Res—undergrad and grad $1845 per sem; foreign $6500 per yr
Summer School: Dir, Jack Weiss; Grad Art Educ Prog. Term June 15 through Aug 8

INSTITUTE OF LETTERING AND DESIGN, 202 S State St, Box A-3380, 60604. Tel 312-341-1300. *Dir* Sidney Borden
Estab 1948; pvt; D & E; ent req HS dipl, waived if student is interviewed; enrl D 49, E 30
Tuition: $2000 per sem, $265 monthly, $95 for 12 sessions
Courses: Advertising Design, Calligraphy, Commercial Art, Graphic Arts, Graphic Design, Lettering, Photography, Sign Painting, Photolithography

LOYOLA UNIVERSITY OF CHICAGO, Fine Arts Department, 820 N Michigan Ave, 60611. *Acting Chmn Fine Arts Dept* Mary S Lawton, PhD; *Prof* Margaret Dagenais, MAE; *Prof* Jean Unsworth, MFA; *Assoc Prof* Ralph Arnold, MFA; *Assoc Prof* Juliet Rago, MFA; *Asst Prof* Ralph Schaller, MFA; *Asst Prof* Justine Wantz, MFA. Instrs PT 20
Estab 1870, dept estab 1970; den; D & E; degrees BA & BS 4 yrs; SC 25, LC 17
Tuition: $2790 per yr, $1395 per sem; $75 per hr; campus res—room & board $895-$985 per sem
Courses: Art Education, Art History, Calligraphy, Ceramics, Commercial Art, Drawing, Goldsmithing, Graphic Arts, Jewelry, Painting, Photography, Printmaking, Sculpture, Medical Illustration
Summer School: Dir, Phyllis Gallagher. Courses—Art Appreciation, Art History, Commercial Art, Ceramics, Drawing, Painting, Photography

NORTHEASTERN ILLINOIS UNIVERSITY, Art Department, St Louis at Bryn Mawr Ave, 60625. Tel 312-583-4050, Ext 580, 581. *Chmn* Russell Roller
Estab 1869; pub; D & E; ent req HS dipl, GED, upper half high school class or higher ACT; degrees BA 4 yrs; scholarships; SC 44, LC 22; enrl total 10,200, maj 175, grad 1583, others 798
Courses: Art Education, Art History, Ceramics, Drawing, Graphic Arts, Handicrafts,

Industrial Design, Jewelry, Lettering, Painting, Photography, Printmaking, Sculpture, Teacher Training, Metal Enameling

NORTH PARK COLLEGE, Art Department, 5125 N Spaulding, 60625. Tel 312-583-2700, Ext 385. *Chmn Dept* Neale Murray, MA; *Prof* Gayle Bradley-Johnson, MA; *Prof* Lenore Pressman, MA; *Prof* Lars Sponberg; *Prof* Gordon Stromberg
Estab 1957; den; D & E; ent req HS dipl; degrees BA 4 yrs; scholarships; SC 18, LC 5; enrl D 40
Tuition: Res—undergrad $3900 per yr; nonres—undergrad $5750; campus res available
Courses: Advertising Design, Aesthetics, Art Education, Art History, Calligraphy, Ceramics, Commercial Art, Drawing, Illustration, Painting, Photography, Printmaking, Sculpture, Teacher Training
Adult Hobby Classes: Tui $35 per term. Courses—Calligraphy, Painting
Summer School: Enrl 25; tui $200 course for term of 8 wks beginning June 12. Courses—Ceramics, Drawing, Painting, Sculpture

RAY-VOGUE SCHOOL OF DESIGN, 750 N Michigan Ave, 60611. Tel 312-280-3500. *Dir* Wade Ray; *Dept Head* Karen Amirsoltani; *Dept Head* Bernie Dennett; *Dept Head* John Goehlich; *Dept Head* Norman Mier; *Dept Head* Robert Miller; *Dept Head* Jeanne Radysh
Estab 1916; pvt; D & E; ent req HS dipl, portfolio review; degrees dipl 1 or 2 yr courses; SC 7; enrl D 350, E 125
Tuition: $2440 per yr, $1220 per sem; no campus res
Courses: Advertising Design, Commercial Art, Display, Fashion Arts, Graphic Design, Illustration, Interior Design, Photography, Fashion Merchandising
Adult Hobby Classes: Enrl 85; tui $120 for 20 eve. Courses—Dress Design, Photography
Summer School: Dir, Wade Ray. Enrl 190; tui $490 for 10 wks beginning June 23. Courses—Commercial Art, Dress Design, Fashion Illustration, Interior Design, Photography

SCHOOL OF THE ART INSTITUTE OF CHICAGO, Jackson Blvd at Columbus Dr, 60603. Tel 312-443-3700. *Dir* Donald J Irving; *Chmn Grad Div* Karen Savage; *Chmn Undergrad Div* Paul Ashley. Instrs FT 75, PT 20
Estab 1866; pvt; ent req portfolio; degrees BFA 4 yrs, MFA; SC 103, LC 22; enrl FT 950, PT 700
Tuition: $95 per cr hr
Courses: Aesthetics, Art History, Art Education, Drawing, Fashion Arts, Film, Display, Photography, Printmaking, Sculpture, Video, Design & Communication, Fiber-Clay-Fabric, Generative Systems, Sound & Music
Summer School: Dir, Donald J Irving; Admis, Lynn Tomko. Enrl 500; term of 4 full days for 8 wks

UNIVERSITY OF CHICAGO, Department of Art History & Committee on Art & Design, 5540 S Greenwood, 60637. Tel 312-753-1234. *Chmn* Charles E Cohen, PhD; *Dir Committee* Thomas Map; *Prof* Pramod Chandra, PhD; *Prof* Francis H Dowley, PhD; *Prof* Reinhold Heller; *Prof* Edward Maser, PhD; *Prof* Earl Rosenthal, PhD; *Prof* Harrie Vanderstrappen, PhD; *Assoc Prof* Linda Seidel, PhD; *Asst Prof* Ronald Cohen, MFA; *Asst Prof* Robert Melson
Estab 1892; pvt; D; ent req through college of admissions; degrees BA 4 yrs, MA 1 yr, PhD 4-6 yrs; scholarships; SC, LC and GC vary; enrl maj 11, grad 104, others 3
Tuition: Undergrad $1365 per quarter (4 courses); grad $1785 per quarter (3 courses); campus res—$1300 per yr
Courses: Aesthetics, Architecture, †Art History, Ceramics, Collage, Conceptual Art, Drawing, Film, Graphic Arts, Graphic Design, †History of Art & Archaeology, Mixed Media, Museum Staff Training, Painting, Photography, Printmaking, Sculpture, Video
Summer School: Enrl varies; tui $300 for term of 10 wks beginning June. Courses—vary

UNIVERSITY OF ILLINOIS AT CHICAGO CIRCLE, College of Architecture, Art & Urban Sciences, PO Box 4348, 60680. Tel 312-996-3351, Art & Design 996-3337. *Dean* Richard R Whitaker Jr; *Dir School Architecture* Michael Gelick; *Dir School Art & Design* Morris Barazani; *Chmn Dept Hist of Architecture & Art* David Sokol. Instrs FT 80, PT 28
Estab 1946; pub; D; ent req 3 units of English plus 13 additional units, rank in top one-half of HS class for beginning freshman, transfer students 3.25 grad point average; degrees BA(Design), BA(Studio Arts), BA(Art Educ), BA(History of Archit and Art) and BArchit 4 yrs, MFA(Studio Art or Design) 2 yrs, MArchit 5 yrs; scholarships; SC 79, LC 10, GC 3; enrl D 579, non-maj 325, maj 579, grad 17
Tuition: Res—undergrad $885 yr, grad $930 yr; nonres—undergrad $2151, grad $2286; no campus res
Courses: †Art Education, Ceramics, Drawing, Film, †Industrial Design, †Painting, †Photography, †Printmaking, †Sculpture, Video, †Communications Design, †Comprehensive Design, †Studio Arts
Children's Classes: Enrl 50; tui $5. Courses—Saturday school in connection with art education classes
Summer School: Dir, Morris Barazani. Enrl 30% of regular term; tui res—undergrad $229, nonres—undergrad $547 for term of 8 wks beginning June

UNIVERSITY OF ILLINOIS AT THE MEDICAL CENTER, Dept of Biocommunication Arts-Medical Art, Room 211, 1919 W Taylor St, 60612. Tel 312-996-7337. *Head* Emil W Hospodar, BA; *Assoc Prof* Robert Parshall, BS; *Assoc Prof* William Schwarz, BS; *Assoc Prof* Alfred Teoli, MFA; *Asst Prof* Alice Katz, MEd
Estab 1963, dept estab 1967; pub; D; ent req HS dipl, also same as College of Fine & Applied Arts, Champaign; degrees BS 4 yrs

CHICAGO HEIGHTS

PRAIRIE STATE COLLEGE, Art Department, 197th & Halsted, 60411. Tel 312-756-3110. *Chmn* Dr Albert Piarowski. Instrs FT 3, PT 14
Estab 1958; pub; D & E; ent req HS dipl, ACT; degrees AA 2 yrs; SC 24, LC 6; enrl dept 300, maj 200
Tuition: $17.50 per cr hr, out of district $35 per cr hr, out of state $55 per cr hr
Courses: Advertising Design, Art History, Drawing, Illustration, Interior Design, Painting, Photography, Sculpture, Design, Life Drawing, Materials Workshop, Production Processes
Summer School: Dir, Dr Albert Piarowski. Tui $14 per cr hr for term of 8 wks. Courses —Art History, Design, Drawing, Materials Workshop, Painting, Photography

DECATUR

MILLIKIN UNIVERSITY, Art Dept, 1184 W Main St, 62522. Tel 217-424-6227. *Chmn Art Dept* Marvin L Klaven, MA. Instrs FT 3, PT 1
Estab 1901, dept estab 1904; pvt; D & E; ent req HS dipl, ACT; degrees BA & BFA 4 yrs; scholarships; SC 47, LC 3; enrl D 1500, non-maj 25, maj 40
Tuition: $3300 per yr; campus res—room & board $1425 yr
Courses: Art Education, Art History, Ceramics, Commercial Art, Drawing, Graphic Arts, History of Art & Archaeology, Jewelry, Mixed Media, Painting, Printmaking, Sculpture, Theatre Arts, Art Management, Art Therapy
Summer School: Dir Special Prog, William Lewis. Enrl 25; tui $100 cr hr for term of 7 wks beginning June 13. Courses—Studio Painting, Drawing & Printmaking

DE KALB

NORTHERN ILLINOIS UNIVERSITY, Department of Art, College of Visual and Performing Arts, 60115. Tel 815-753-1473. *Chmn Dept Art* Robert L Even, PhD; *Asst Chairperson Dept* Helen Merritt, MFA; *Grad Coordr* Carl Hayano, MAE; *Area Coordr* Elisabeth Bond, MSEd; *Area Coordr* Robert Bornhuetter, MFA; *Area Coordr* William Brown, EdD; *Area Coordr* Eleanor Caldwell, EdD; *Area Coordr* J Dimitri Liakos
Estab 1895; pub; D & E; ent req HS dipl; degrees BA, BFA, BSEd 4 yrs, MA, MSEd 2 yrs, MFA 3 yrs, EdD 3 yrs; scholarships; SC 140, LC 606, GC 70; enrl D 5000, maj 1200, grad 215
Tuition: Res—$2885 per yr; nonres—$3982 per yr; campus residency available
Courses: †Art Education, †Art History, †Ceramics, Commercial Art, Display, Drafting, Drawing, Film, Graphic Arts, Graphic Design, History of Art & Archaeology, Illustration, Intermedia, Interior Design, †Jewelry, Lettering, Mixed Media, Museum Staff Training, Painting, Photography, †Printmaking, †Sculpture, Silversmithing, Stage Design, Teacher Training, Textile Design, Theatre Arts, Video, Art Therapy, Visual Communication
Summer School: Dir, Robert L Even. Tui res $185, nonres $459. Courses—vary

EAST PEORIA

ILLINOIS CENTRAL COLLEGE, Art and Humanities Department, 61635. Tel 309-694-5113, 694-5114. *Chmn* Ronald Holohan, MA; *Instr* Lyle Anderson; *Instr* Lee Benz; *Instr* Wayne Forbes; *Instr* Fred Hentchel, MFA; *Instr* Robert Majeske; *Instr* Marlene Miller
Estab 1967, dept estab 1967; pub; D & E; ent req HS dipl; degrees Associate in Arts and Science 2 yrs, Associate in Applied Science; SC 27, LC 3; enrl D 800, E 400, maj 272
Tuition: $12 per sem hr; no campus res
Courses: Advertising Design, †Architecture, Art Education, Art History, Ceramics, †Commercial Art, Drafting, Drawing, Film, †Graphic Arts, †Graphic Design, Handicrafts, Illustration, Interior Design, Jewelry, Lettering, Painting, Photography, Printmaking, Sculpture, Textile Design, Color, Design
Adult Hobby Classes: Tui $12 per sem hr. Courses—Antiques, Crafts, Drawing, Flower Arranging, Interior Decorating, Oil Painting, Stained Glass
Summer School: Chmn, Ronald Holohan. Tui $12 per sem hr. Courses—Basic Drawing, Ceramics, Color & Design, Figure Drawing, Jewelry, Photography, Sculpture

EDWARDSVILLE

SOUTHERN ILLINOIS UNIVERSITY AT EDWARDSVILLE, Department of Art and Design, 62026. Tel 618-692-3071. *Chmn Dept* Don F Davis, MA; *Asst Chmn Dept* Dr Pamela Decoteau, PhD; *Head Art History* John A Richardson, EdD; *Head Printmaking* Robert R Malone, MFA; *Head Drawing* Robert I Katz, MFA; *Head Painting* Michael J Smith, MFA; *Head Sculpture* Thomas D Gipe, MFA; *Head Fiber & Fabric* Judith A Millis, MFA; *Head Ceramic* Paul A Dresang, MFA
Estab 1869, dept estab 1959; pub; D & E; ent req HS dipl, ACT, portfolio req for BFA and MFA; degrees BA, BS and BFA 4 yrs, MFA 3 yrs, MS 2 yrs; scholarships; SC 65, LC 26, GC 45; enrl D 325, E 75, maj 200, grad 50
Tuition: Res—undergrad & grad $789 per yr, $263 per quarter, $104 for 5 hrs, $188 for 6-11 hrs, $263 for 12 hrs or more; nonres—undergrad & grad $1923 per yr, $641 per quarter, $230 for 5 hrs, $439 for 6-11 hrs, $641 for 12 hrs or more; campus res available
Courses: Aesthetics, Art Education, Art History, Ceramics, Drawing, Film, Graphic Design, History of Art & Archaeology, Jewelry, Mixed Media, Painting, Photography, Printmaking, Sculpture, Silversmithing, Teacher Training, Textile Design
Summer School: Chmn, Don F Davis. Term of 8 weeks beginning June 16. Courses —full curriculum

ELGIN

JUDSON COLLEGE, Division of Fine Arts, 1151 N State, 60120. Tel 312-695-2500. *Chmn* Clarence Young, MFA; *Vis Instr* Ruth Hopkins, MA
Pvt; D; ent req HS dipl, ent exam, ACT; degrees BA 4 yrs; scholarships; SC 15, LC 10; enrl D 500
Tuition: $1320 per sem; campus res—room & board $1720 per yr
Courses: Aesthetics, Art Education, Art History, Ceramics, Drawing, Graphic Arts, Graphic Design, History of Art & Archaeology, Painting, Printmaking, Stage Design, Teacher Training, Textile Design, Theatre Arts

ELMHURST

ELMHURST COLLEGE, Art Department,* 190 Prospect, 60126. Tel 312-279-4100. *Chairperson Art Dept* Sandra Jorgensen, MFA; *Assoc Prof* John Weber, MFA; *Asst Prof* Carole R Brown, MFA; *Instr* Richard Paulsen, MFA
Estab 1871; den; D & E; ent req HS dipl, ACT or SAT; degrees BS, BA and BM 4 yrs; scholarships; SC 13, LC 8; enrl D 1550, E 1100, maj 32
Tuition: $4910 per yr including room and board, $3220 per yr without room and board
Courses: Architecture, Art Education, Art History, Collage, Conceptual Art, Constructions, Drawing
Summer School: Enrl 1000; tui $272 course for term of 8 wks beginning June 14. Courses—Regular Curriculum

EVANSTON

NORTHWESTERN UNIVERSITY, EVANSTON
—Department of Art, 60201. Tel 312-492-7346. *Chmn Dept* J Wesley Burnham. Instrs FT 5, PT 3
Estab 1924; pvt; degrees AB 4 yrs, MFA; scholarships and fels; SC 15, LC 8, GC 5; enrl 300-500
Tuition: $1805 each quarter
Courses: Practice of Art, Teaching of Art
—Department of Art History, 1859 Sheridan Rd, 60201. Tel 312-492-3230. *Chmn Dept* Carl W Condit, PhD; *Prof* James Breckenridge, PhD; *Assoc Prof* Betty Iverson Monroe, PhD; *Asst Prof* Frederick Levine, PhD; *Asst Prof* Olan A Rand Jr, PhD; *Asst Prof* Leland M Roth, PhD; *Asst Prof* Thomas L Sloan, PhD
Estab 1851; pvt; D; ent req HS dipl, SAT or ACT; degrees BA 4 yrs, MA 1 yr, PhD 3 yrs; scholarships; LC 36, GC 15; enrl maj 29, grad 15
Tuition: Undergrad $4620 per yr, $1540 per quarter; grad $4290 per yr, $1430 per quarter; PT $550 per course; campus res available
Courses: Architecture, †Art History

FREEPORT

HIGHLAND COMMUNITY COLLEGE, RFD 2, Pearl City Rd, 61032. Tel 815-235-6121. *Instructor* Jody Schultz. Instrs FT 1, PT 5
Estab 1962; pub; D & E; ent req HS dipl, ent exam; degrees AS, AA, ABA, AAS 2 yrs; scholarships; SC 6, LC 1; enrl 126
Courses: Art History, Drawing, Graphic Design, Painting, Printmaking, Art Materials & Processes, Design, Introduction to Art, Pottery
Adult Hobby Classes: Enrl 278. Courses—Basic Drawing, Oil, Charcoal, Printmaking, Sculpture, Pottery, Handweaving & Related Crafts, Rosemaking, Macrame, Needlepoint
Children's Classes: Occasional summer workshops for high school and elementary school students
Summer School: One course offered each year

GLEN ELLYN

COLLEGE OF DUPAGE, Humanities Div, Lambert Rd at 22nd St, 60137. Tel 312-858-2800. *Instructor* Patricia Kurriger, PhD; *Instructor* Adam Ertas, MFA; *Instructor* Pamela B Lowrie, MS-MA; *Instructor* Richard Lund, MFA; *Instructor* Willard Smith, MS; *Instructor* John A Wantz, MA
Estab 1966; pub; D & E; ent req completion of application; degrees AA(Art) & AAS(Interior Design, Fashion Design, Commercial Art) 2 yrs; SC 24, LC 5
Tuition: $12.50 per cr hr; no campus res
Courses: Aesthetics, Architecture, Art History, Ceramics, Commercial Art, Costume Design & Construction, Drafting, Drawing, Fashion Arts, Graphic Arts, Illustration, Interior Design, Jewelry, Landscape Architecture, Painting, Photography, Printmaking, Sculpture, Textile Design, Theatre Arts
Children's Classes: Courses—Ceramics
Summer School: Tui $12.50 per hr for term of 3, 5 or 10 wks. Courses vary

NAGUIB SCHOOL OF SCULPTURE, INC, One S 101 Rt 53, 60137. Tel 312-858-7797. *Dir* Mustafa Naguib
Estab 1973; pvt nonprofit corp; D & E; ent req HS dipl or over 18 yrs; degrees cert for 3 yr cert prog; enrl D 10, E 15, maj 10, others 15
Tuition: $1200 per sem of 12 wks, PT $17 per 3 hr session; campus res—room & board approx $640
Courses: Drawing, Sculpture
Adult Hobby Classes: Tui $17 per 3 hr class. Courses—Life Drawing, Sculpture
Children's Classes: Tui $15 per 3 hr class. Courses—Sculpture
Summer School: Dir, Mustafa Naguib. Tui $600 for term of 6 wks. 30 Day Technology of Sculpture Workshop $500. Bronze Casting Workshop $700 for 5 wks

GODFREY

LEWIS AND CLARK COMMUNITY COLLEGE, Art Dept, 5800 Godfrey Rd, 62035. Tel 618-466-3411, Ext 279. *Chmn Div Communications & Humanities* Edna Hollis. Instrs FT 2, PT 3
Estab 1970, formerly Monticello College; pub; D & E; ent req HS dipl, ent exam, open door policy; degrees AA 2 yrs; scholarships; SC 13, LC 2; enrl D 1800, E 600, maj 40
Tuition: $14 per sem hr; no campus res
Courses: Art History, Ceramics, Drafting, Drawing, Handicrafts, Painting, Sculpture, Basic Design, Weaving
    Adult Hobby Classes: Enrl 30; tui variable. Courses—Antiques, Interior Design, Introduction to Drawing & Painting
    Summer School: Enrl 15; pre-summer 4 wk session painting on location 4 hrs daily; $42 for 3 sem cr hrs for term of 8 wks beginning mid-June

GRAYSLAKE

COLLEGE OF LAKE COUNTY, Art Department, 19351 W Washington St, 60030. Tel 312-223-6601, Ext 377. *Chmn* Russ Hamm, MA; *Instr* Reginald Coleman, MFA; *Instr* Nancy Cook, MA; *Instr* Tony Holmes, MFA; *Instr* Ed Kanwischer, MFA; *Instr* Dan Ziembo, MFA
Estab 1969, dept estab 1969; pub; D & E; ent req HS dipl, SAT; degrees AA and AS 2 yrs; SC 22, LC 5; enrl D 250, E 250, non-maj 500, maj 100
Tuition: Res $15 per sem; non-res $46 per sem; out-of-state $68 per sem; no campus res
Courses: Art Education, Art History, Ceramics, Costume Design & Construction, Drafting, Drawing, Fashion Arts, Landscape Architecture, Mixed Media, Painting, Photography, Printmaking, Sculpture, Stage Design, Theatre Arts
    Adult Hobby Classes: Advertising, Ceramics, Drawing, Lettering, Mixed Media, Portrait, Stained Glass
    Summer School: Dir, Russ Hamm. Courses—same as above

GREENVILLE

GREENVILLE COLLEGE, Dept of Art, 62246. Tel 618-664-1840, Ext 311. *Chmn* Donald Parker Hallmark, PhD; *Assoc Prof* Kenneth G Ryden, MFA; *Asst Prof* C Lane Raiser, MFA; *Instructor* Anna Raiser, BS
Estab 1892, dept estab 1965; pvt; D & E; ent req HS dipl; degrees BA 4 yrs, BS 4 1 2 yrs; SC 16, LC 4; enrl D 135, non-maj 105, maj 30
Tuition: $3350 yr, $1675 per sem, $106 per cr hr; campus res—room & board $1400 yr
Courses: †Art Education, Art History, Calligraphy, †Ceramics, †Drawing, †Graphic Arts, †Graphic Design, Handicrafts, History of Art & Archaeology, Lettering, †Painting, Photography, †Sculpture, †Teacher Training
    Summer School: Registrar, Norman Swanson. Tui $424 or $848 for term of 8 wks beginning June. Courses—Introduction to Fine Arts

JACKSONVILLE

MACMURRAY COLLEGE, Art Department,* 447 East College, 62650. Tel 217-245-6151. *Chmn Dept* Howard F Sidman
Estab 1846; den; degrees 4 yr degrees; SC 29, LC 6
Tuition: Res—$3160 per yr
Courses: Advertising Design, Ceramics, Costume Design & Construction, Drawing, Industrial Design, Interior Design, Painting, Teacher Training, Textile Design

JOLIET

COLLEGE OF ST FRANCIS, Art Department,* Division of Humanities and Fine Arts, 500 Wilcox, 60435. Tel 815-740-3400. *Chmn Div* Marjorie Marion
Estab 1950; pvt; D & E; ent req HS dipl, ent exam; degrees BS, BA (Art or Art Educ) 4 yrs; SC 19, LC 6; enrl D 150, E 20, maj 70
Tuition: $1080 per yr; campus res $695 per yr
Courses: Aesthetics, Architecture, Art Education, Ceramics, Drawing, Graphic Arts, History of Art & Archaeology, Jewelry, Lettering, Painting, Sculpture, Teacher Training, Textile Design, Enameling
    Children's Classes: Enrl 20 (limit); tui $80 for 16 wk lessons, 2 hrs Sat AM. Courses—Art in variety of media
    Summer School: Tui $105 for term of 6 wks beginning June. Courses—Art, Calligraphy, Ceramics

JOLIET JUNIOR COLLEGE, Art Dept, 1216 Houbolt Ave, 60436. Tel 815-729-9020, Ext 297. *Chmn Dept* William Fabrycki, MA; *Instructor* James Dugdale, MA; *Instructor* Sharlene Kassiday; *Instructor* Sue Latocha, MA; *Instructor* Joe Milosevich, MFA
Estab 1901, dept estab 1920; pub; D & E; ent req HS dipl, ent exam; degrees AA 2 yrs; scholarships; SC 15, LC 4; enrl D 10,000, maj 120
Tuition: $13 per sem cr for res of Ill Dist 525; from $33.10 to $54.62 per sem cr for res outside Ill Dist 525; no campus res
Courses: Art Education, Art History, Ceramics, Drawing, History of Art & Archaeology, Interior Design, Jewelry, Painting, Silversmithing, Two & Three Dimensional Design
    Summer School: Dir, William Fabrycki. Courses—Same as winter school

KANKAKEE

OLIVET NAZARENE COLLEGE, Dept of Art, 60901. Tel 815-939-5229. *Chmn Dept* Harvey A Collins, MFA; *Instructor* J Paul Thompson, MA
Estab 1907, dept estab 1953; den; D & E; ent req HS dipl; degrees BS & BA 4 yrs, MEd & MTheol 2 yrs; scholarships; SC 14, LC 4; enrl D 100, non-maj 80, maj 21
Tuition: $1940 per yr, $970 per sem, $81 per sem hr; campus res—room & board
Courses: †Art Education, Art History, †Ceramics, Drawing, Film, Graphic Arts, Graphic Design, History of Art & Archaeology, Lettering, †Painting, Photography, Printmaking, Sculpture, Teacher Training, Textile Design
    Summer School: Dir, Harvey A Collins. Tui $60 per hr for term of 5 wks beginning June 26. Courses—Ceramics, Introduction to Fine Arts, Painting

LAKE FOREST

BARAT COLLEGE, Dept of Art, 700 E Westleigh Rd, 60045. Tel 312-234-3000, Ext 353. *Chmn Dept* Sharon Wells Kouris. Instrs FT 6, PT 4
Estab 1858; den; W; D; ent req HS dipl, ent exam; degrees BA & BFA 4 yrs; scholarships; SC 32, LC 16; enrl maj 58
Courses: Ceramics, Drawing, History of Art & Archaeology, Illustration, Painting, Photography, Printmaking, Sculpture, Theatre Arts, Fibers, Three Dimensional Design, Weaving
    Summer School: Courses—Ceramics, Fibers, History of Art, Painting, Photography, Two Dimensional Design

LAKE FOREST COLLEGE, Dept of Art, Sheridan Rd, 60045. Tel 312-234-3100, Ext 324. *Chmn Dept* Alex F Mitchell, MA; *Prof* Michael Croydon, ARCA; *Prof* Franz Schulze, MFA; *Instructor* Laura McKeon, MA; *Lectr* Michael Burke, BA; *Lectr* Ramona Mitchell, Staatsexamen; *Lectr* Robert Orr, BA
Estab 1857; pvt; D & E; ent req HS dipl, SAT, CEEB or ACT; degrees BA 4 yrs; scholarships; SC 8, LC 21; enrl D 1050 (sch total), maj 38
Tuition: Res—undergrad $6507 per yr, $3349.50-$3157.50 per sem; nonres—undergrad $4725 per yr, $2417.50-$2307.50 per sem; $577 per course; campus res—room & board $1700 per yr, $1892 with fees
Courses: Aesthetics, Architecture, Art Education, Art History, Drawing, Film, Graphic Arts, History of Art & Archaeology, Painting, Photography, Sculpture, Teacher Training
    Summer School: Chmn, Alex F Mitchell. Courses—Photography

MACOMB

WESTERN ILLINOIS UNIVERSITY, Dept of Art, 61455. Tel 309-298-1549. *Chmn Dept* Daniel L Kuruna, DEd. Instrs Visiting artists in various media
Estab 1900, dept estab 1968; pub; D & E; ent req HS dipl; degrees BA 4 yrs, MA 2 yrs; scholarships; SC 40, LC 30, GC 50; enrl maj 200
Tuition: Res—undergrad $377.25 per sem, grad $363.75 per sem; nonres—undergrad $935.25 per sem, grad $903.75 per sem; $12 per sem hrs over 18 res; $36 per sem hrs over 18 nonres; campus residence available
Courses: Advertising Design, †Art Education, Art History, †Ceramics, †Commercial Art, Conceptual Art, Costume Design & Construction, Drafting, †Drawing, Fashion Arts, †Graphic Design, †Handicrafts, Illustration, Interior Design, †Jewelry, †Painting, †Printmaking, †Sculpture, Stage Design, Foundry Casting, Metal Working, Weaving
    Children's Classes: Dir, R Law, EdD. High School Summer Arts Prog

MOLINE

BLACK HAWK COLLEGE, Art Dept, 6600 34th Ave, 61265. Tel 309-796-1311, Ext 232. *Chmn Dept* Joseph F Ramsauer, MFA; *Assoc Prof* William Hannan; *Assoc Prof* Philip Johnson, MS; *Assoc Prof* Jan Rorem, MFA
Estab 1962; pub; D & E; ent req HS dipl; degrees AA 2 yrs; SC 15, LC 3; enrl D 500, E 450, non-maj 450, maj 200
Tuition: Res—undergrad $21.25 per cr hr; nonres—undergrad $69.75 per cr hr; outside dist res undergrad $45.50 per cr hr; no campus res
Courses: Advertising Design, Art History, Calligraphy, Ceramics, Drawing, Film, Graphic Design, Jewelry, Lettering, Painting, Photography, Printmaking, Sculpture, Art Appreciation
    Summer School: Chmn, Joseph E Ramsauer. Enrl 20; tui $21.25 per cr hr for term of 6 wks beginning June 15. Courses—Art Appreciation, Ceramics, Photography

MONMOUTH

MONMOUTH COLLEGE, Dept of Art, Art Center, N Ninth St, 61462. Tel 309-457-2341. *Chmn Dept* George L Waltershausen. Instrs FT 2, PT 1
College estab 1853; pvt; D; ent req 15 units incl English, history, social science, foreign language, mathematics & science, SAT or ACT; degrees BA; scholarships, grants; SC 16, LC 4
Courses: Art History, Drawing, Film, Painting, Photography, Printmaking, Sculpture, Advanced Special Topics, Contemporary Art, Independent Study, Secondary Art Methods, Senior Art Seminar, Studio A & B

NORMAL

ILLINOIS STATE UNIVERSITY, Art Dept, Center for the Visual Arts, 61761. Tel 309-438-5621. *Chmn Art Dept* Fred V Mills, EdD. Instrs FT 50; 6 vis profs per sem Estab 1857; pub; D & E; ent req HS dipl; degrees BA & BS 4 yrs, BFA 5 yrs, MA, MS, MFA, EdD; scholarships; SC 50, LC 35, GC 40; enrl D 5000, E 300, non-maj 1972, maj 3076, grad 452
Tuition: Res—undergrad & grad $548 per yr, $274 per sem, $18 per hr; nonres—undergrad $1644 per yr, $822 per sem, $45 per hr, grad $1064 per yr, $532 per sem
Courses: †Advertising Design, †Art Education, †Ceramics, Commercial Art, Constructions, Display, †Drawing, Film, †Goldsmithing, †Graphic Arts, †Graphic Design, †History of Art & Archaeology, Illustration, †Jewelry, Lettering, Mixed Media, Museum Staff Training, Occupational Therapy, †Painting, †Photography, Teacher Training, †Textile Design
Summer School: Tui res $149.75, nonres $266.25 for term of 8 wks beginning June 20

PEORIA

BRADLEY UNIVERSITY, Art Dept, 61625. Tel 309-676-7611, Ext 496, 497, 498. *Dir* Walter Thompson. Instrs FT 9
Pvt; ent req HS grad; degrees AB, BS, BFA 4 yrs, MA, MFA; scholarships; enrl maj 91, others 400
Tuition: $1640 per sem
Courses: Art History, Ceramics, Drawing, Film, Graphic Design, Jewelry, Painting, Photography, Printmaking, Sculpture, Art Metal

QUINCY

QUINCY COLLEGE, Dept of Art, 62301. Tel 217-222-8020. *Chmn* Thomas Brown. Instrs FT 3
Estab 1860, dept estab 1953; ent req HS grad, ACT or SAT ent exam; degrees BA, BS & BFA 4 yrs; SC 21, LC 13; enrl maj 35, total enrl 1715, E 150
Tuition: $1400 per sem; campus res $265-$330 per sem
Courses: Aesthetics, Art History, Ceramics, Commercial Art, Drawing, Film, Jewelry, Mixed Media, Painting, Photography, Printmaking, Sculpture, Art Seminars, Modern Art, Non-Western Art, Two & Three Dimensional Design, Watercolor, Weaving
Summer School: Dir, Thomas Brown. Tui $60 per sem hr for 8 wks beginning June 9 or 4 wks beginning June 5 or July 7. Summer Seminar in Europe: Optional junior year abroad

RIVER GROVE

TRITON COLLEGE, School of University Transfer Studies, 2000 Fifth Ave, 60171. Tel 312-456-0300, Ext 467. Instrs FT 5, PT 6
Estab 1965; pub; D & E; ent req HS dipl, some adult students are admitted without HS dipl, but with test scores indicating promise; degrees AA 2 yrs; SC 17, LC 3; enrl D 650, E 150, maj 138, adults and non-cr courses
Tuition: No campus res
Courses: Advertising Design, Art Education, Ceramics, Commercial Art, Drawing, Graphic Arts, Graphic Design, History of Art & Archaeology, Illustration, Lettering, Painting, Printmaking, Sculpture, Theatre Arts, Recreational Arts & Crafts
Adult Hobby Classes: Enrl 550; tui $11 per hr. Courses—Candle Making, Continuing Education Classes, Crafts, Drawing, Ceramics, Jewelry, Quilting, Painting, Plastics, Stained Glass, Sculpture, Theatre Arts
Summer School: Term of 8 wks beginning June. Courses—Most of above courses are offered

ROCKFORD

ROCKFORD COLLEGE, Department of Fine Arts,* Clark Arts Center, 5050 E State St, 61101. Tel 815-226-4000. *Chmn Dept Fine Arts* Philip Dedrick, MA; *Dir Gallery* Hon Ching Lee, MFA; *Prof* Andrew Langoussis, MFA; *Prof* Robert McCauley, MFA; *Prof* Judith Moonelio, MFA
Estab 1847, dept estab 1848; pvt; D & E; ent req HS dipl, SAT or ACT; degrees BA, BFA and BS 4 yrs, MAT and MLS 2 yrs; scholarships; SC 20, LC 3-4; enrl D 600, E 600, non-maj 24, maj 16
Tuition: $1500 per sem; campus res—room and board $1310 yr
Courses: Aesthetics, †Art History, †Ceramics, Costume Design & Construction, †Drawing, Graphic Arts, Handicrafts, †History of Art & Archaeology, Painting, Printmaking, †Sculpture, Stage Design, Teacher Training, Textile Design, Papermaking
Summer School: Dir, Dr Curtis Moore. Tui $42 per cr hr. Courses—Art History, Fine Arts (Studio), Stage Design

ROCK VALLEY COLLEGE, Dept of Art, 3301 N Mulford Rd, 61101. Tel 815-226-3721. *Chmn* R David Gustafson, MS; *Instructor* Suzanne Kaufman, MA; *Instructor* Lester Salberg, MFA. Instrs FT 2, PT 1
Estab 1964, dept estab 1965; pub; D & E; degrees AA, AS & AAS 2 yrs; SC 10, LC 4; enrl D 158, non-maj 70, maj 27
Tuition: $15 per cr hr; no campus res
Courses: Art Education, Art History, Commercial Art, Drawing, Painting, Printmaking, Color Theory, Design
Adult Hobby Classes: Enrl 40; tui $16-$19 per course. Courses—Ceramics, Drawing, Painting, Weaving
Summer School: Enrl 27; tui $15 per cr hr for term of 8 wks beginning June 6. Courses—Design, Drawing, Painting

ROCK ISLAND

AUGUSTANA COLLEGE, Art Department, 61201. Tel 309-794-7000. *Chmn Dept* Alvin Ben Jasper. Instrs FT 3, PT 5
Estab 1860; den; D & E; ent req HS grad plus exam; degrees 4 yr degree; scholarships & fels; SC 8, LC 9, LabC 3; enrl 2000
Tuition: $870 per quarter
Courses: Art History, Ceramics, Drawing, Handicrafts, Jewelry, Painting, Photography, Printmaking, Sculpture, Design, Elementary School Art Methods, Fabric Introduction to Visual Arts, Secondary School Art Methods
Children's Classes: Sat

SPRINGFIELD

SANGAMON STATE UNIVERSITY, Creative Arts Program, Shepherd Rd, 62708. Tel 217-786-6786. *Asst Prof* Bob Dixon, MFA & MS; *Asst Prof* Margaret Rossiter, MFA
Estab 1969, dept estab 1974; pub; D & E; ent req 2 yrs col educ; degrees BA(Creative Arts) 2 yrs; scholarships; SC 24, LC 10
Tuition: Res $324 per sem, $23 per hr PT; non-res undergrad $872 per sem, $69 per hr PT; no campus res
Courses: Advertising Design, Aesthetics, †Art History, †Ceramics, Constructions, Drawing, †Painting, Photography, †Printmaking, †Sculpture, Theatre Arts, Video

SPRINGFIELD COLLEGE IN ILLINOIS, Dept of Art, 1500 N Fifth, 62702. Tel 217-525-1420. *Head Dept* Regina Marie Fronmuller, MA; *Instructor* Marian Buck Hoopes, BA; *Instructor* John Seiz, MA
Estab 1929, dept estab 1968; pvt; D & E; ent req HS dipl, ACT; degrees AA 2 yrs; SC 12, LC 4; enrl D 27, E 6, non-maj 11, maj 16
Tuition: Res—undergrad $1600 per yr, $1025 per sem; nonres—undergrad $1950 per yr, $1150 per sem; private room $500 per sem
Courses: Art History, Ceramics, Drawing, Mixed Media, Painting, Photography, Printmaking, Sculpture, Two & Three Dimensional Design, Weaving
Adult Hobby Classes: Courses—Pottery, Weaving
Children's Classes: Enrl 20; tui $30 for 2 wks in summer. Courses—Art for Children 6-9 yrs, 10-14 yrs
Summer School: Dir, Regina Marie Fronmuller. Term of 6 wks beginning June 2 & July 14. Courses—Ceramics, Photographic Serigraphy

SUGAR GROVE

WAUBONSEE COMMUNITY COLLEGE,* Creative Arts Division, Route 47 at Haster Rd, 60554. Tel 312-466-4811. *Chairperson* Carol J Viola, Cert of Advanced Standing
Estab 1967; pub; D & E; ent req HS dipl, open door policy for adults without HS dipl; degrees AA, AS and AAS 2 yrs; scholarships; SC 8, LC 3; enrl D approx 275, E approx 200, maj 25
Tuition: Res—$13 per hr; nonres—$67 per hr; no campus res
Courses: Art Education, Art History, Ceramics, Drawing, Jewelry, Painting, Teacher Training, Theatre Arts, Video
Adult Hobby Classes: Enrl 175; tui $13 per sem hr. Courses—Ceramics, Drawing, Jewelry, Painting, Stained Glass
Summer School: Asst Dean Instrs, Carol J Viola. Tui $13 for term of 8 wks beginning June 6. Courses—Per regular session

WHEATON

WHEATON COLLEGE, Dept of Art, 501 E Seminary, 60187. Tel 312-682-5050. *Admin Dir* Dr Harold Best. Instrs FT 4, PT 2
Estab 1861; pvt; D & E; ent req HS dipl; degrees BA 4 yrs; scholarships; SC 20, LC 5; enrl 2981, maj 20
Tuition: $1042 per quarter; campus res $308 per quarter
Courses: Advertising Design, Aesthetics, Art Education, Ceramics, Drawing, Graphic Arts, Graphic Design, History of Art & Archaeology, Painting, Photography, Sculpture, Teacher Training

WINNETKA

NORTH SHORE ART LEAGUE, 620 Lincoln, 60093. Tel 312-446-2870. *Pres* Lois Verb
Estab 1924; pvt; D & E; scholarships to Chicago Art Inst grad; SC 28; enrl D 310, E 84
Tuition: 16 wks, 3 hrs a session; no campus res
Courses: Drawing, Graphic Arts, Graphic Design, Jewelry, Painting, Photography, Sculpture, Critique, Pottery, Stichery, Woodcut

INDIANA

ANDERSON

ANDERSON COLLEGE, Art Dept, 1100 E Fifth & College, 46011. Tel 317-644-0951, Ext 458. *Chmn* Raymond A Freer, MFA; *Prof* Martha Beakley, MA; *Prof* Donald Weisflog, MFA. Instrs PT 5
Estab 1928; pvt; D & E; ent req HS dipl, ent exam plus recommendation; degrees BA 4 yrs; scholarships; SC 30, LC 3; enrl non-maj 15, maj 60
Tuition: $3720 per yr, $1860 per sem; campus res—room $500 yr
Courses: Advertising Design, Art Education, Art History, Ceramics, Commercial Art, Drawing, Graphic Arts, Graphic Design, History of Art & Archaeology, Illustration, Jewelry, Lettering, Museum Staff Training, Painting, Photography, Printmaking, Sculpture, Stage Design, Teacher Training, Air Brush & Watercolor Painting
Summer School: Dir, Robert Smith. Tui $87 per cr hr

BLOOMINGTON

INDIANA UNIVERSITY, BLOOMINGTON, Department of Fine Arts,* 47401. Tel 812-332-0211. *Chmn* Thomas F Coleman
Estab 1911; pub; D; ent req admis to the Univ; degrees AB, BFA, BS 4 yrs, MA, MFA, MAT, PhD; scholarships; SC 55, LC 100, GC 110; enrl maj undergrad 430, grad 135 (65 Art History, 70 Studio), others 5600
Tuition: Res—$810 per yr; nonres—$1980 per yr; campus res available
Courses: Art History, Ceramics, Drawing, Graphic Design, Jewelry, Painting, Photography, Printed Textiles, Woven Textiles
Summer School: Tui res $27 per cr hr; nonres—$66 per cr hr

CRAWFORDSVILLE

WABASH COLLEGE, Art Department, 47933. Tel 317-362-1400, Ext 386. *Chmn* Gregory Huebner, MFA; *Asst Prof* Lee Sido, MFA
Estab 1832, dept estab 1950; pvt; D; ent req HS dipl, SAT; degrees BA 4 yrs; SC 19, LC 6; enrl D 80, non-maj 80
Tuition: $3765 per yr, $1882 per sem; campus res—room & board $1715
Courses: Aesthetics, Art History, Ceramics, Display, Drawing, Graphic Arts, History of Art & Archaeology, Painting, Photography, Printmaking, Sculpture

EVANSVILLE

INDIANA STATE UNIVERSITY, EVANSVILLE, Art Department,* 8600 University Blvd, 47712. Tel 812-864-8600. Instrs FT 5, PT 1
Estab 1969; pub; D & E; ent req HS dipl; degrees BS (Art Educ), BA (Art) 4 yrs; scholarships; SC 27, LC 4; enrl D 150, E 30, maj 90
Tuition: Res—$735 per yr; nonres—$1470 per yr
Courses: Aesthetics, Art Education, Ceramics, Commercial Art, Drafting, Drawing, History of Art & Archaeology, Jewelry, Painting, Photography, Sculpture, Teacher Training, Furniture Design, Stained Glass
Adult Hobby Classes: Enrl 25. Courses—Silkscreen

UNIVERSITY OF EVANSVILLE, Art Dept, PO Box 329, 47702. Tel 812-479-2043. *Chmn Dept* Leslie Miley Jr, MFA; *Assoc Prof* Nanene Engle, MAT; *Assoc Prof* Howard Oagley, MA; *Asst Prof* Dr Leslye Bloom, PhD; *Asst Prof* William Richmond, MFA; *Lectr* John Begley, MFA; *Lectr* Theresa Callahan, MFA
Estab 1854; pvt; D & E; ent req HS dipl; degrees BA(Educ), BS(Art), BFA 4 yrs, MA 1 yr; scholarships; SC 22, LC 11, GC 11; enrl D 800, E 400, maj 72, grad 21
Tuition: Campus res available
Courses: Aesthetics, Art Education, Art History, Ceramics, Drawing, History of Art & Archaeology, Jewelry, Lettering, Painting, Printmaking, Sculpture, Teacher Training, Art Therapy

FORT WAYNE

INDIANA UNIVERSITY-PURDUE UNIVERSITY, Department of Fine Arts, 1026 W Berry St, 46804. Tel 219-482-5121. *Chmn Dept* Russell L Oettel, MFA; *Prof* Noel Dusendschon, MFA; *Assoc Prof* Clyde Burt, MFA; *Assoc Prof* Hector Garcia, MFA; *Assoc Prof* Donald Kruse, BS; *Assoc Prof* Leslie Motz, MFA; *Instr* Stanley Lee, PhD
Estab 1920, dept estab 1976; pub; D & E; degrees AB and BFA 4 yrs; scholarships; SC 96, LC 5; enrl non-maj 85, maj 167, others 10
Tuition: Res—$35 per cr hr; nonres—$63 per cr hr; no campus res
Courses: †Advertising Design, Art History, †Ceramics, †Drawing, Film, †Graphic Arts, Graphic Design, †History of Art & Archaeology, Illustration, †Jewelry, †Painting, Photography, †Printmaking, †Sculpture, Silversmithing, Weaving
Children's Classes: Enrl 150; tui $35 for 10 wks. Courses—Ceramics, Painting, Sculpture
Summer School: Chmn, Russell L Oettel. Tui $35 per cr hr beginning May 22. Courses—Ceramics, Painting

SAINT FRANCIS COLLEGE, Art Department, 2701 Spring St, 46808. Tel 219-432-3551, Ext 236. *Head Dept* Maurice A Papier, MS & MA; *Assoc Prof* Sufi Ahmad, MFA; *Asst Prof* Rick Cartwright, MFA
Estab 1890; den; D & E; ent req HS dipl, class rank in HS, SAT; degrees AA(Commercial Art) 2 yrs, BA and BS(Art or Art Educ) 4 yrs, MA(Art Educ) 1 yr; scholarships; SC 22, LC 6, GC 14; enrl D 90, maj 80
Tuition: Undergrad $58 per sem hr, grad $62 per sem hr; campus res—room & board $1500 yr
Courses: Advertising Design, †Art Education, Art History, Calligraphy, Ceramics, †Commercial Art, Display, Drawing, Fashion Arts, Graphic Arts, Graphic Design, Illustration, Interior Design, Jewelry, Lettering, Painting, Photography, Printmaking, Sculpture, †Teacher Training
Children's Classes: Enrl 80; tui $30 per sem. Courses—Art
Summer School: 3 wk session begins June, 5 wk session begins July. Courses—Art

---

History, Ceramics, Commercial Art, Drawing, Painting, Photography, Sculpture, Weaving

FRANKLIN

FRANKLIN COLLEGE, Art Department, 46131. Tel 317-736-8441. *Chmn Dept* Luigi Crispino. Instrs FT 1, PT 1
Estab 1834; den; D; ent req HS grad; degrees BA 4 yrs; SC 9, LC 4; enrl 700
Tuition: $4980 per yr includes room & board
Courses: Art Education, Ceramics, Drawing, Painting, Sculpture, Basic Design, Print Shop

GOSHEN

GOSHEN COLLEGE, Art Department, 1600 S Main St, 46526. Tel 219-533-3161, Ext 354. *Chmn* Abner Hershberger, MFA; *Asst Prof* Judy Wenig-Horswell, MFA
Estab 1950; den; D & E; ent req HS dipl, top half of class; degrees AB(Art) and AB(Art) with Indiana Teaching Cert; scholarships; enrl D 145, E 25, non-maj 60, maj 40
Tuition: $2735 per yr, $1235 per trimester, $110 per hr; campus res—room & board $1260 yr
Courses: Aesthetics, Art Education, Art History, Ceramics, Drawing, Graphic Design, Jewelry, Painting, Photography, Printmaking, Sculpture, Teacher Training, Textile Design
Children's Classes: Enrl 20; tui $28 per 10 sessions. Courses—Art, Drawing, Printmaking and others
Summer School: Acad Dean, John Lapp. Tui $265 for term of 3 1 2 wks beginning end of Apr, ending in late July. Courses—New York Art Study; Florence, Italy Tour

GREENCASTLE

DEPAUW UNIVERSITY, Art Department, 46135. Tel 317-653-9721. *Chmn* William Meehan, MFA; *Prof* Ray H French, MFA; *Asst Prof* David Herrold, MFA; *Asst Prof* Robert Kingsley, MFA
Estab 1837; pvt den; D; ent req HS dipl, upper half of high school graduating class; degrees BA & BM 4 yrs, MAEd, MAT; SC 14, LC 9, GC 18; enrl D 300, E 20 (Art Dept), non-maj 25%, maj 75%, grad 20
Tuition: 2061 per sem; campus res—room & board $900 per sem
Courses: Advertising Design, Art Education, Art History, Ceramics, Commercial Art, Drawing, Graphic Arts, History of Art & Archaeology, Illustration, Jewelry, Painting, Photography, Printmaking, Sculpture, Stage Design, Teacher Training, Theatre Arts

HAMMOND

PURDUE UNIVERSITY CALUMET CAMPUS, Department of Creative Arts, 46323. Tel 219-844-0520, Ext 422. *Head Dept Art* Edwin Cohen, PhD; *Instructor* Mary Geimer, MA; *Instructor* Barbara Meeker, MA; *Instructor* John Mohamed, MA; *Instructor* Andrew Smock, MA
Estab 1946; pub; D & E; ent req HS dipl; scholarships; SC 1-4, LC 1-2, GC 1
Tuition: Res—undergrad $26 per sem, grad $34 per sem; non-res—undergrad $58 per sem, grad $69 per sem; no campus res
Courses: Architecture, Art Education, Ceramics, Drawing, Film, Painting, Teacher Training, Theatre Arts, Video, Watercolor

HANOVER

HANOVER COLLEGE, Department of Art, 47243. Tel 812-866-2151. *Chmn* James W Shaffstall, MFA; *Assoc Prof* Robert Rosenthal, PhD; *Assoc Prof* Lee Schroeder, MS; *Asst Prof* John Z Thomas, MFA
Estab 1827, dept estab 1967; pvt; D; ent req HS dipl; degrees BS and BA 4 yrs; schol; SC 16, LC 4; enrl D 960
Tuition: $2415 per yr; campus res—room & board $1320 per yr
Courses: Advertising Design, Aesthetics, Art Education, Art History, Ceramics, Collage, Commercial Art, Constructions, Drawing, Film, Graphic Arts, Graphic Design, Jewelry, Painting, Photography, Printmaking, Sculpture, Stage Design, Teacher Training, Textile Design, Theatre Arts, Video

INDIANAPOLIS

HERRON SCHOOL OF ART, Indiana University-Purdue University, Indianapolis, 1701 N Pennsylvania St, 46202. Tel 317-923-3651. *Dean* Arthur Weber; *Chmn Commercial Art & Design* Henry Aguet, MFA; *Chmn Art Educ* William Detmers, PhD; *Chmn Printmaking* Robert Eagerton, BA; *Chmn Sculpture* Gary Freeman, MFA; *Chmn Found Prog* Aaron Law, MFA; *Chmn Painting* Richard Nickolson, MFA; *Chmn Art History* Samuel Roberson, PhD
Estab 1902; pub; D & E; ent req portfolio; degrees BFA and BAE 4 yrs, MAE 5 yrs; scholarships; SC 112, LC 16, GC 20; enrl D 385, non-maj 300, grad 20
Tuition: Res—undergrad $26 per cr hr, grad $40 per cr hr; nonres—undergrad $59 per cr hr; grad $96 per cr hr; no campus res
Courses: Advertising Design, Art Education, Art History, Ceramics, Commercial Art, Constructions, Drawing, Graphic Arts, Graphic Design, History of Art & Archaeology, Illustration, Mixed Media, Painting, Photography, Sculpture, Teacher Training, Video, Furniture Design
Summer School: Enrl 151; tui $26 per cr hr, two 6 wk sessions available. Courses—Art Education, Art History, Design, Drawing, Painting, Photography, Sculpture, Three-Dimensional Design

INDIANA CENTRAL UNIVERSITY, Fine Arts Department, 1400 E Hanna Ave, 46227. Tel 317-788-3253. *Chmn Dept* Gerald G Boyce, MFA; *Assoc Prof* Earl Snellenberger, MFA; *Asst Prof* Dee Schaad, MFA
Estab 1902; den; D & E; ent req HS dipl, SAT, upper half of HS class; degrees BA and BS 4 yrs; scholarships; SC 24, LC 7, GC 7; enrl D 360, E 150, maj 36, grad 60

Tuition: Commuter $2230 per yr; campus res—room & board $3500 per yr
Courses: Aesthetics, Architecture, †Art Education, Art History, Ceramics, Commercial Art, Drawing, Graphic Arts, History of Art & Archaeology, Jewelry, Lettering, Painting, Photography, Printmaking, Sculpture, Silversmithing, Textile Design

MARIAN COLLEGE, Art Department,* 3200 Cold Spring Rd, 46222. Tel 317-924-3291. *Coordr* Sr Mary de Paul Schweitzer, MEd; *Instr* Sr Dolorita Carper, MEd; *Instr* Peggy Lovett, MA; *Instr* George Neal, MA; *Instr* Patric O'Keeffe, Cert; *Instr* Elli Siskind, BA; *Instr* Karen Wolf, MA
Estab 1851, dept estab 1938; den; D & E; ent req HS dipl, SAT; degrees AA 2 yrs, BA and BS 4 yrs; scholarships; SC 21, LC 6; enrl D 36, E 16, non-maj 20, maj 11
Tuition: Res—undergrad $2080 per yr; nonres—undergrad $2080 per yr; campus res —room and board $1280 per yr
Courses: Art Education, Art History, Ceramics, Costume Design & Construction, Drawing, Graphic Arts, Handicrafts, Interior Design, Painting, Sculpture, Stage Design, Teacher Training, Theatre Arts, Art therapy
Adult Hobby Classes: Enrl 15; tui $38 per sem hr. Courses—Arts & Crafts

MARION

MARION COLLEGE, Art Department, 4201 S Washington, 46952. Tel 317-674-6901. *Head Dept* Ardelia Williams, MA; *Instr* Bruce Campbell, BSEd; *Vis Prof* Ed Breen, photography; *Vis Prof* Dan Jordan, ceramics
Estab 1890, dept estab 1969; den; D & E; ent req HS dipl; degrees BS(Art Educ); SC 20, LC 4; enrl D 35, non-maj 5, maj 30
Tuition: Res $4316 per yr; non-res $2810 per yr; campus res available
Courses: †Art Education, Art History, Ceramics, Commercial Art, Drawing, Graphic Arts, Graphic Design, Jewelry, Painting, Photography, Sculpture, Silversmithing, †Teacher Training, Batik, Fibers, Weaving

MUNCIE

BALL STATE UNIVERSITY, Art Department, 2000 University Ave, 47306. Tel 317-285-5638. *Head Art Dept* Ned H Griner, DEd; *Vis Prof* Manfred Maier, design - 1979. Instrs FT 26
Estab 1918; pub; D & E; ent req HS dipl; degrees BS & BFA 4 yrs, MA 1 yr, DEd 2 yrs or more; SC 28, LC 21, GC 40; enrl non-maj 633, maj 600, grad 30
Tuition: Res—undergrad $280 per quarter, grad $300 per quarter; non-res—undergrad $600 per quarter, grad $645 per quarter; campus residency available
Courses: Advertising Design, Aesthetics, †Art Education, Art History, Ceramics, †Drawing, †Interior Design, Jewelry, †Painting, †Photography, †Printmaking, †Sculpture, †Silversmithing, †Textile Design, †Visual Communications, Typography
Adult Hobby Classes: Enrl 20; tui $35 per person. Courses—Painting, Textile Design
Children's Classes: Enrl 75; tui $5 per child. Courses—General Art Activities
Summer School: Enrl 7000; tui $180 for term of 5 wks beginning June. Courses—Art Education, Art History, Studio

NEW ALBANY

INDIANA UNIVERSITY SOUTHEAST, Fine Arts Department, Grantline Rd, 47150. Tel 812-945-2731, Ext 343. *Chmn Dept* Jonas A Howard, MA; *Asst Prof* John R Guenthler, MFA; *Asst Prof* Brian H Jones, MFA; *Asst Prof* Susan M Matthias, MFA
Estab 1945, dept estab 1966; pub; D & E; ent req HS dipl; degrees BA 4 yrs; SC 25, LC 2; enrl D 130, E 35, non-maj 85, maj 45
Tuition: Res—undergrad $26 per hr, grad $34 per hr; nonres—undergrad $59 per hr, grad $70 per hr; no campus res
Courses: Art Education, Art History, Ceramics, Drawing, Painting, Printmaking, Teacher Training, Textile Design, Theatre Arts
Adult Hobby Classes: Enrl 35; tui $25 per sem. Courses—Crafts, Watercolor
Summer School: Enrl 50; term of two 6 wk sessions beginning May 15 and July 5. Courses—same as above

NORTH MANCHESTER

MANCHESTER COLLEGE, Art Department,* College Ave, 46962. Tel 219-982-2141. *Head Dept* James R C Adams, MFA; *Prof* Max I Allen, MFA; *Asst Prof* Stephen Batzka, BA
Estab 1889; den; D & E; ent req HS dipl; degrees AA 2 yrs, BA and BS 4 yrs; scholarships; SC 15, LC 3; enrl D 45, maj 15
Tuition: Res—undergrad $4270 per yr, including room and board
Courses: Advertising Design, Art Education, Art History, Ceramics, Drawing, Film, Graphic Arts, Handicrafts, History of Art & Archaeology, Lettering, Mixed Media, Museum Staff Training, Painting, Photography, Printmaking, Sculpture, Teacher Training, Textile Design

NOTRE DAME

SAINT MARY'S COLLEGE, Department of Art,* 46556. Tel 219-232-3031. *Chmn* H James Paradise
Estab 1855; pvt, W; D & E; ent req CEEB, standing, recommendations, others; degrees BA and BFA 3 1 2-5 yrs; scholarships, fels; SC 21, LC 10; enrl maj 117, others 418
Tuition: Res—$1775 full time per sem, $140 per sem hr - part time; campus res—room $350-$580 per sem, board $465 per sem
Courses: Art Education, Ceramics, Drawing, Jewelry, Painting, Photography, Printmaking, Sculpture, Design, Photo Silkscreen, Weaving. Rome Program: Courses —Art History, Design, Drawing

UNIVERSITY OF NOTRE DAME, Department of Art, 46556. Tel 219-283-7602. *Chmn* James F Flanigan. Instrs FT 9, PT 2
Estab 1855; pvt; D; ent req upper third HS class, ent exam; degrees AB, BFA 4 yrs, MA, MFA; fels; SC 38, LC 8, GC 20; enrl maj 100

Tuition: $4000 per yr; campus res available
Courses: Advertising Design, Art History, Ceramics, Drawing, Industrial Design, Painting, Photography, Printmaking, Sculpture, Fibre, Pottery
Summer School: Chmn, James F Flanigan. Enrl 50. Courses—Ceramics, Printmaking, 10 courses in Studio and Art History (chiefly for high school art teachers working on advanced degrees), Women Artists in Residence

OAKLAND CITY

OAKLAND CITY COLLEGE, Division of Fine Arts, 47660. Tel 812-749-4781, Ext 53. *Chmn Dept* Marie M McCord. Instrs FT 4, PT 1
Estab 1961; den; D & E; ent req HS dipl, SAT; degrees AA 2 yrs, BA and BS 4 yrs; scholarships; SC 10, LC 5; enrl maj 35
Courses: Advertising Design, Art Education, Ceramics, Drawing, History of Art & Archaeology, Lettering, Painting, Sculpture, Teacher Training, Macrame, Pottery, Weaving
Summer School: Two 5 wk terms. Courses—Painting, Pottery, plus others

RICHMOND

EARLHAM COLLEGE, Art Department, National Rd W, 47374. Tel 317-962-6561, Ext 410. *Chmn Dept* Garret Boone, MFA; *Asst Prof* Peter Barnett, PhD; *Artist-in-Res* Mitsuo Kakutani
Estab 1847; den; D; ent req HS dipl; degrees BA 4 yrs; scholarships; SC 10, LC 7; enrl maj 10
Tuition: $4300 per yr, $450 per course; campus res—room & board $1800
Courses: Aesthetics, Art History, Ceramics, Drawing, Film, Graphic Arts, Graphic Design, Lettering, Mixed Media, Museum Staff Training, Painting, Photography, Printmaking, Sculpture, Stage Design, Theatre Arts, Video

SAINT MARY-OF-THE-WOODS

SAINT MARY-OF-THE-WOODS COLLEGE, Art Department,* 47876. Tel 812-535-4141. *Chmn* Sr Cynthia Ann Crestreet
Estab 1840; den; D; ent req HS dipl, SAT or ACT; degrees AS 2 yrs, BA and BS 4 yrs; scholarships; SC 15, LC 4; enrl maj 15
Tuition: $2700 per yr; campus res available
Courses: †Art Education, Art History, Ceramics, Drawing, Intermedia, Painting, Photography, Printmaking, Teacher Training

SAINT MEINRAD

SAINT MEINRAD COLLEGE, Department of Art,* 47577. Tel 812-357-6611. *Chmn* Columba Kelly
Estab 1854; pvt; D & E; ent req admis and reg in the school; SC 3, LC 3; enrl D 36, E 30
Tuition: $1595 per yr
Courses: Advertising Design, Aesthetics, Ceramics, Drawing, Graphic Design, History of Art & Archaeology, Painting, Theatre Arts
Adult Hobby Classes: Enrl 30. Courses—Ceramics, Painting

SOUTH BEND

INDIANA UNIVERSITY AT SOUTH BEND, Fine Arts Department, 1700 Mishawaka Ave, 46615. Tel 219-237-4278. *Chmn* Harold Zisla, AM; *Assoc Prof* Anthony Droege, MFA; *Assoc Prof* Harold Langland, MFA; *Asst Prof* Alan Larkin, MFA; *Adjunct Lectr* Marie Remington, MFA
Estab 1964; pub; D & E; ent req HS dipl; degrees BA(Fine Arts) 4 yrs; SC 18, LC 6; enrl non-maj 300, maj 80
Tuition: Res—undergrad $26 cr hr, grad $34 cr hr; nonres—undergrad $59 cr hr, grad $70 cr hr
Courses: Art Education, Art History, Drawing, Graphic Design, Painting, Printmaking, Sculpture
Summer School: Chmn, Harold Zisla. Tui same as regular session; two 6 wk summer sessions. Courses—Art Appreciation, Drawing, Painting

TERRE HAUTE

INDIANA STATE UNIVERSITY
—**Art Department,** 47809. Tel 812-232-6311, Ext 2222. *Chmn* Jack Stewart, MA. Instrs FT 20, PT 7
Estab 1870; pub; D & E; ent req HS dipl; degrees BS and BFA 4 yrs, MS, MA and MFA 2 yrs; SC 67, LC 47, GC 65; enrl D 2350, E 250, maj 275, grad 30
Tuition: Res—undergrad & grad $28 per cr hr; nonres—undergrad & grad $59 per cr hr; campus res—room and board $375 for halls, except Lincoln Guard which is $391
Courses: Art Education, Art History, Ceramics, Commercial Art, Drawing, Goldsmithing, Graphic Design, Jewelry, Mixed Media, Painting, Photography, Printmaking, Sculpture, Silversmithing, Woodworking & Furniture Design
Summer School: Dir, Dr Harriett Darrow. Tui res $28, nonres $56 for term of two 5 wks beginning June. Courses—same as above
—**Department of Humanities,** Terre Haute, IN 47809. Tel 812-232-6311. *Acting Chairperson* David Johnson; *Prof* Harriet Caplow, PhD; *Prof* Roslyn Erbes, PhD; *Asst Prof* Charles Mayer, PhD
Dept estab 1964; pub; D & E; degrees BA(Art History) 4 yrs, MA in Humanities with Art History concentration 1 1 2-2 yrs; scholarships; LC 12, GC 12; enrl in dept D 1250, E 50, maj 10, grad 10
Courses: Architecture, Art History
Summer School: Dean, Harriet Darrow

UPLAND

TAYLOR UNIVERSITY, Art Department, 46989. Tel 317-998-2751, Ext 322. *Chmn* Ray E Bullock, EdD; *Prof* Craig Moore, MFA; *Instructor* Kathy Hermann
Estab 1846, dept estab 1968; pvt; D & E; ent req HS dipl, SAT, recommendations; degrees BA and BS 4 yrs; SC 12, LC 7; enrl D 175, E 16, non-maj 125, maj 50
Tuition: Res—$3046 per yr; campus res—room & board $1604 per yr
Courses: Advertising Design, Aesthetics, †Art Education, Art History, Calligraphy, Ceramics, Collage, Drawing, Graphic Arts, †Jewelry, Lettering, Mixed Media, Painting, Photography, Printmaking, Sculpture, Silversmithing, Stage Design, †Teacher Training
Children's Classes: Enrl 40; tui free. Courses—Design, Drawing, Jewelry, Painting, Pottery
Summer School: Dir, Dr Ray E Bullock. Courses—Photography, Survey of Fine Arts

VINCENNES

VINCENNES UNIVERSITY, Art Department, 1002 N First St, 47591. Tel 812-882-3350. *Coordr* James G Gorman, MFA; *Asst Prof* Amy Delap Jendrzejewski, MFA; *Asst Prof* Jim Pearson, MFA; *Instructor* Andrew Jepdrzejewski, MFA; *Instructor* Don Mullis
Estab 1801; pub; D & E; ent req HS dipl or GED; degrees AA and AS 2 yrs; scholarships; SC 17, LC 4; enrl maj 32
Tuition: Res—undergrad $650 per yr, $325 per sem, $21 per hr; nonres—undergrad $1150 per yr, $575 per sem, $37 per hr; campus res—room & board $1180 per yr
Courses: Advertising Design, Art History, Ceramics, Commercial Art, Drawing, Graphic Arts, Handicrafts, Lettering, Painting, Photography, Printmaking, Sculpture, Textile Design, Design
Summer School: Dir, James G Gorman. Enrl 15-20; tui $21 per hr for term of 5 wks beginning May 30 and July 5. Courses—Ceramics, Drawing, Painting, Photography, Printmaking

WEST LAFAYETTE

PURDUE UNIVERSITY, LAFAYETTE, Department of Creative Arts, Art & Design Section, School of Humanities, 47907. Tel 317-494-8702. *Head Dept* R G Beelke; *Chmn Dept* R B Reed. Instrs FT 33
Estab 1925; pub; D & E; ent req BA 4 yrs, MA; scholarships; SC 50, LC 22, GC 22; enrl maj 394, others 1746
Tuition: Nonres $1337, campus res $1730 additional
Courses: Art History, Ceramics, Film, Graphic Arts, Industrial Design, Interior Design, Jewelry, Painting, Photography, Sculpture, Teacher Training, Video, Visual Design, Weaving

WINONA LAKE

GRACE COLLEGE, Department of Art, 46590. Tel 219-267-8191, Ext 156. *Head Dept* Jean L Coverstone, MA; *Asst Prof* Art Davis, MA
Estab 1952, dept estab 1971; pvt; D & E; ent req HS dipl, SAT; degrees 4 yr Art Major, 4 yr Art Educ Major, and 2 yr cert; SC 12, LC 3; enrl maj 30, non-maj 80
Tuition: $65 per hr; campus res available
Courses: Art Education, Art History, Ceramics, Drawing, Graphic Design, Handicrafts, Painting, Photography, Printmaking, Sculpture, Teacher Training
Adult Hobby Classes: Enrl 12; tui $70 per hr. Courses—Survey of Crafts
Summer School: Dir, Jean L Coverstone. Tui $70 per hr for term of 4 wks. Courses—Drawing II, Photography

IOWA

AMES

IOWA STATE UNIVERSITY, Department of Design,* 215 Mackay Hall, 50011. Tel 515-294-4111. *Chmn Dept* Jon Sontag, PhD; *Coordr Drawing & Painting* Elizabeth Miller, MFA; *Coordr Interior Design* Jane Navin, MA; *Coordr Crafts* Terry Tow, MA; *Coordr Advertising Design* Ronald Fenimore, MA; *Coordr Art Educ* Dennis Dake, MA; *Coordr Design* Nancy Polster, MA
Estab 1858, dept estab 1920; pub; D & E; ent req HS dipl; degrees BA (Advertising Design, Art Educ, Craft Design & Interior Design); SC 45, LC 15, GC 6; enrl non-maj 1500, maj 815, grad 20
Tuition: Res—undergrad $272 per quarter; nonres—undergrad $627 per quarter; campus res available
Courses: †Advertising Design, †Art Education, Art History, Calligraphy, Ceramics, Drawing, Fashion Arts, Goldsmithing, Graphic Design, Weaving, Wood Design
Summer School: Dir, Dr Jon Sontag. Tui $136 res; $314 nonres, for term of 5 wks beginning June 7. Courses—Advertising Design, Art Education, Calligraphy, Ceramics, Drawing, Interior Design, Painting

BOONE

DES MOINES AREA COMMUNITY COLLEGE, Art Department,* 1125 Hancock Dr, 50036. Tel 515-432-7203. *Head Dept* Jo Myers, MA
Estab 1927, dept estab 1970; pub; D & E; ent req HS dipl; degrees AA 2 yrs; SC 3, LC 2; enrl D 100, E 60
Tuition: Res—undergrad $600 per yr, $150 per quarter, $15 per cr hr; nonres—undergrad $1200 per yr, $300 per quarter, $30 per cr hr; campus res available
Courses: Art History, Painting, Stage Design, Teacher Training, Theatre Arts, Life Drawing

CEDAR FALLS

UNIVERSITY OF NORTHERN IOWA, Department of Art, Col of Humanities and Fine Arts, 50613. Tel 319-273-2077. *Head Dept* Joseph M Ruffo, MFA; *Prof* David Delafield, EdD; *Prof* Don Finegan, MFA; *Prof* Ken Gogel, MA; *Prof* Harry Guillaume, EdD; *Prof* Ken Lash, MA; *Prof* John Page, MFA; *Assoc Prof* Reed Estabrook, MFA; *Assoc Prof* Edwin Harris, MA; *Assoc Prof* Shirley Haupt, MFA; *Asst Prof* Hale Anderson, MFA; *Asst Prof* Steve Bigler, MFA; *Asst Prof* Allan Brookes, PhD; *Asst Prof* Barbara Cassino, MFA; *Asst Prof* Felipe Echeverria, MFA; *Asst Prof* Allan Shickman, MA; *Asst Prof* Vera Jo Siddens, MA; *Instructor* Carol Scharff, MA; *Instructor,* Christine Streed
Estab 1876, dept estab 1945; pub; D & E; ent req HS dipl, ACT; degrees BA and BFA 4 yrs, MA 1 yr; scholarships; SC 30, LC 10, GC 10; enrl D 350, E 30, non-maj 150, maj 350, grad 15
Tuition: Res—undergrad $774 per yr, $387 per sem, grad $818 per yr, $409 per sem; nonres—undergrad $1460 per yr, $730 per sem, grad $1680 per yr, $840 per sem; campus res—room and board $1350 per yr
Courses: Art Education, Art History, Ceramics, Commercial Art, Drawing, Film, Graphic Arts, Graphic Design, Illustration, Jewelry, Painting, Photography, Printmaking, Sculpture, Silversmithing, Teacher Training
Summer School: Head Dept, Jospeh M Ruffo. Enrl 3538; tui $195 for term of 8 wks beginning June 9. Courses—same curriculum as acad yr, but limited

CEDAR RAPIDS

COE COLLEGE, Department of Art, 52402. Tel 319-398-1669. *Chmn* Charles Stroh, MFA; *Prof* Robert L Kocher, MA; *Asst Prof* John Beckelman, MFA; *Instructor* David Goodwin, MFA; *Lectr* Will Valk; *Lectr* Steve Whitney; *Gallery Dir* Shirley Donaldson, BA
Estab 1851; pvt; D & E; ent req HS dipl, SAT, ACT or portfolio; degrees BA 4 yr; scholarships; SC 15, LC 8; enrl D 1200
Tuition: Campus res—room & board $4600 per yr
Courses: Art Education, Art History, Ceramics, Drawing, Illustration, Painting, Photography, Printmaking, Sculpture, Textile Design, Theatre Arts
Summer School: Chmn Dept, Charles Stroh. Enrl average 80; tui $290 per course for term of 5 wks beginning in June and mid-July. Courses—American Art History, Ceramics, Drawing, Painting, Photography

KIRKWOOD COMMUNITY COLLEGE, Department of Fine Arts, 6301 Kirkwood Blvd SW, 52406. Tel 319-398-5534. *Head Dept* Doreen Maronde, MS; *Instructor* Doug Hall, MFA; *Instructor* Ray Mullen, MFA; *Instructor* John Puffer, MFA
Estab 1966; pub; D & E; ent req HS dipl; degrees AA 2 yr; SC 18, LC 6; enrl D 150, E 50
Tuition: $14.35 per cr hr; no campus res
Courses: Art History, Ceramics, Drafting, Drawing, Fashion Arts, Graphic Arts, Lettering, Occupational Therapy, Painting, Photography, Printmaking, Sculpture
Summer School: Tui $14.35 per cr hr. Courses—Art Appreciation, Ceramics, Drawing, Painting

MOUNT MERCY COLLEGE, Art Department, 1330 Elmhurst Dr NE, 52402. Tel 319-363-8213, Ext 256. *Chmn Dept* Charles Barth, MS; *Asst Prof* Jane Gilmor, MFA; *Instructor* Robert Naujoks
Estab 1928, dept estab 1960; pvt; D & E; ent req HS dipl, ACT; degrees BA 4 yr; SC 20, LC 6; enrl D 150, E 35, non-maj 150, maj 35
Tuition: $2830 per yr, $1415 per sem, $195 per course; campus res—room & board $945
Courses: †Art Education, Art History, Drawing, Painting, Photography, Printmaking, Sculpture, Textile Design
Summer School: Dir, Robert Lesniak. Courses—Introduction to Art, Watercolor

CENTERVILLE

INDIAN HILLS COMMUNITY COLLEGE, Department of Art, N First St, 52544. Tel 515-856-2143, Ext 27. *Head Dept* Richard H Dutton, MA; *Instructor* S Scott Sittner, MS
Estab 1932, dept estab 1967; pub; D & E; ent req HS dipl or equal, open door; degrees AA 2 yr; scholarships; SC 10; enrl D 70, E 30, non-maj 50, maj 16
Tuition: Res—$480 per yr; nonres—$720 per yr
Courses: Art History, Ceramics, Drawing, Painting, Sculpture, Art Appreciation, Arts & Crafts, Design, Watercolor
Adult Hobby Classes: Enrl 22; tui $38 for 12 wks. Courses—Painting
Summer School: Dir, Dick Sharp. Courses—Art Appreciation, Design, European Art Tours, Painting

CLINTON

MOUNT SAINT CLARE COLLEGE, Art Department, 400 N Bluff, 52732. Tel 319-242-4023. *Head Dept* Shirley Bahnsen, MAT; *Instructor* Joan Richeson, MA
Estab 1928, dept estab 1940; den; D & E; ent req HS dipl; degrees AA 2 yr; scholarships; SC 5, LC 1; enrl non-maj 65, maj 14
Tuition: $600 per sem; campus res—room & board $1300 per yr
Courses: Calligraphy, Ceramics, Drawing, Painting, Art Appreciation, Color & Design
Summer School: Courses—Art Appreciation, Calligraphy, Painting

CRESTON

SOUTHWESTERN COMMUNITY COLLEGE, Art Department,* 1501 W Townline Rd, 50801. Tel 515-782-7081. *Dir Arts & Science* Richard Engleson, MA; *Instr Art* P Terry Gieber, MA; *Instr Art* Mary Ellen Kimball, BA
Estab 1966; pub; D & E; ent req HS dipl; degrees AA 2 yrs; SC 6, LC 3; enrl D 550, E 200, non-maj 40, maj 15, others 15
Tuition: Res—$220 per yr; nonres—$330 per yr; no campus res
Courses: Art Education, Art History, Ceramics, Drawing, Painting, Teacher Training, Design
Adult Hobby Classes: Enrl 10-30; tui $30 per sem. Courses—Per regular session

DAVENPORT

MARYCREST COLLEGE, Art Department,* 1607 W 12th St, 52804. Tel 319-326-9512. *Chmn* Dr Laurence Conner
Estab 1939; den; D & E; ent req HS dipl; degrees BA 3-4 yrs, MA; scholarships; SC 35, LC 15, GC 13; enrl D 446, E 129, maj 68, grad 56
Tuition: Res—$2250 per yr
Courses: Advertising Design, Aesthetics, Art Education, Ceramics, Commercial Art, Costume Design & Construction, Drafting, Drawing, Fashion Arts, Graphic Arts, Graphic Design, History of Art & Archaeology, Illustration, Jewelry, Lettering, Museum Staff Training, Painting, Photography, Sculpture, Stage Design, Teacher Training, Theatre Arts
Summer School: Dir, Dr R Schwieso. Courses—Independent Study, Painting, Readings

SAINT AMBROSE COLLEGE, Art Department,* 518 W Locust St, 52803. Tel 319-324-1681. *Chmn Dept* Thomas F Chouteau
Estab 1892; den; D & E; ent req HS dipl; degrees BA 4 yrs; scholarships; SC 17, LC 12; enrl D 450, E 40, maj 55
Tuition: Res—undergrad $2460 per yr; campus res available
Courses: Advertising Design, Art Education, Calligraphy, Ceramics, Commercial Art, Drafting, Drawing, Graphic Arts, Graphic Design, History of Art & Archaeology, Illustration, Lettering, Painting, Photography, Sculpture, Teacher Training

DECORAH

LUTHER COLLEGE, Art Department, 52101. Tel 319-387-1110. *Head Dept* Douglas Eckheart. Instrs FT 4, PT 3
Estab 1861; den; D; ent req HS dipl or ent exam; degrees BA 4 yr; scholarships; SC 13, LC 5; enrl D 160
Tuition: $4900 includes room & board
Courses: Aesthetics, Art Education, Ceramics, Drawing, Graphic Arts, History of Art & Archaeology, Lettering, Painting, Printmaking, Stage Design, Teacher Training, Theatre Arts, Weaving
Summer School: Courses—Drawing, Painting

DES MOINES

DRAKE UNIVERSITY, Art Department, 25th & University Ave, 50311. Tel 515-271-2863. *Chairperson Dept* Condon Kuhl, MFA; *Prof* Richard Black, MSAE; *Prof* Lee Ferber, MFA; *Prof* Stanley Hess, MFA; *Prof* John Hicks, EdD; *Prof* Jules Kirschenbaum. Instrs FT 17, PT 2
Estab 1881; pvt; D & E; ent req 2 pt average in HS or previous col; degrees BFA 4 yrs, MFA 2 yrs, MAE and MAT 1 yr; scholarships; SC 64, LC 15, GC 33; enrl D 275, maj 275, grad 15
Tuition: $4060 per yr; campus res—room $910-$1150 per yr, board $1020 per yr
Courses: †Advertising Design, Aesthetics, †Art Education, †Ceramics, †Commercial Art, Constructions, Costume Design & Construction, †Drawing, Film, †Goldsmithing, †Graphic Arts, †Graphic Design, Handicrafts, History of Art & Archaeology, Illustration, †Interior Design, Sculpture, †Silversmithing, Stage Design, Teacher Training, Textile Design, †Theatre Arts, Video, Photography, †Printmaking, †Sculpture, †Silversmithing, Stage Design, Teacher Training, Textile Design, †Theatre Arts, Video, Creative Arts Therapy
Summer School: Dir, Lewis Hainlin. Courses—Art Education, Art History, Ceramics, Drawing, Jewelry, Painting, Sculpture

DUBUQUE

CLARKE COLLEGE, Department of Art,* 1550 Clarke Dr, 52001. Tel 319-588-6300. *Chmn* Joan Lingen
Estab 1843; den; D & E; ent req HS grad, 16 units and Col Ent Board; degrees BA (Art) 4 yrs; SC 15, LC 4; enrl maj 50, others 200
Tuition: $2500 per yr
Courses: Art History, Ceramics, Drawing, Jewelry, Lettering, Painting, Printmaking, Sculpture, Teacher Training, Adult Continuing Educ Program: D & E
Summer School: Enrl art 50; three 3 wk sessions

FOREST CITY

WALDORF COLLEGE, Art Department, 50436. *Chmn Dept* John Nellermoe. Instrs FT 1, PT 1
Estab 1903; den; D; ent req HS dipl, ACT or SAT; degrees AA, AC and AAS 2 yr; scholarships; SC 4; enrl D 80, maj 15
Tuition: $1297 per yr; campus res $746
Courses: Art History, Ceramics, Drafting, Drawing, Painting, Woodcrafts

FORT DODGE

IOWA CENTRAL COMMUNITY COLLEGE, Department of Art, 330 Ave M, 50501. *Assoc Prof* Robert J Halm, MFA; *Instructor* Raymond R Atwood, MA
Pub; D & E; ent req HS dipl; degrees AA 2 yr; SC 4, LC 2; enrl D 120, E 15, non-maj 117, maj 18
Tuition: Res—$220 per sem, $19 per hr; nonres—$330 per sem, $27.75 per hr; campus res—room & board $1210 per yr
Courses: Art History, Painting, Studio Art

GRINNELL

GRINNELL COLLEGE, Department of Art,* 1202 Park St, 50112. Tel 515-236-7545. *Chmn Dept* William W Wolf III, PhD; *Prof* Richard Cervene, MFA; *Prof* A Richard Turner, PhD; *Prof* Louis G Zirkle, MFA; *Asst Prof* Robert H McKibbin, MFA; *Asst Prof* Merle Waller Zirkle, MFA
Estab 1846, dept estab 1930; pvt; D; ent req HS dipl, SAT or ACT; degrees BA 4 yrs; scholarships; SC 9, LC 9; enrl D 150, non-maj 125, maj 25
Tuition: Res—undergrad $5670 per yr; campus res—room and board
Courses: Aesthetics, Art Education, Art History, Ceramics, Conceptual Art, Constructions, Drawing, Graphic Arts, Handicrafts, History of Art & Archaeology, Jewelry, Painting, Printmaking, Sculpture, Silversmithing, Loom & off-loom weaving

INDIANOLA

SIMPSON COLLEGE, Art Department,* 50125. Tel 515-961-6251. *Chairperson Dept* Gaile Gallatin, MA
Estab 1860, dept estab 1965; pvt; D & E; ent req HS dipl, ACT or SAT; degrees BA and BM 4 yrs; scholarships; SC 3, LC 3; enrl D 67, maj 6
Tuition: Res—undergrad $3,565 per yr; campus res—room $585 and board $730
Courses: Art Education, Art History, Ceramics, Drawing, History of Art & Archaeology, Jewelry, Mixed Media, Painting, Photography, Printmaking, Silversmithing, Stage Design, Teacher Training, Textile Design, Theatre Arts, Video, Fibers, Macrame, Weaving

IOWA CITY

UNIVERSITY OF IOWA, School of Art and Art History, N Riverside Dr, 52242. Tel 319-353-4550. *Dir* Wallace J Tomasini, PhD. Instrs FT 36, PT 1
Estab 1847, school estab 1911; pub; D & E; ent req HS dipl, ACT or SAT, upper half rank in HS; degrees BA and BFA 4 yr, MA 1 1 2 yr, MFA 2 yr, PhD 5 yr; scholarships; SC 60, LC 55, GC 55; enrl D 590 maj 400, grad 190
Tuition: Res—undergrad $415 per sem, grad $475 per sem; nonres—undergrad $945 per sem, grad $1000 per sem; campus res—room and board $1515 per yr
Courses: Aesthetics, †Art Education, †Art History, †Ceramics, †Drawing, †Graphic Design, †Industrial Design, †Intermedia, †Interior Design, †Jewelry, Lettering, †Painting, †Photography, †Printmaking, †Sculpture, Teacher Training, Video, †Multimedia
Summer School: Dir, Wallace J Tomasini. Enrl undergrad 160, grad 135; tui res undergrad $415, grad $475; nonres undergrad $945, grad $1000 for term of 8 wks, beginning June 9. Courses—Full range of art education, art history and studio courses

IOWA FALLS

ELLSWORTH COMMUNITY COLLEGE, Department of Fine Arts, 1100 College Ave, 50126. Tel 515-648-4611. *Chmn* Steve Kramer, MA; *Instr* Robert Myers, MA
Estab 1890, dept estab 1890; pub; D & E; ent req HS dipl, ACT; degrees AA 2 yrs; SC 10, LC 1; enrl in dept D 20-25
Tuition: Res $440 per yr; non-res undergrad $880; campus res—room & board $1390
Courses: †Advertising Design, Art Education, Art History, Calligraphy, Ceramics, Commercial Art, Conceptual Art, Drawing, Handicrafts, Illustration, Lettering, Mixed Media, Painting, Photography, Sculpture, Teacher Training, Theatre Arts, Weaving
Adult Hobby Classes: Enrl 12; tui $15 per 20 hrs. Courses—Pottery
Summer School: Dir, Dr Thomas Seymour. Term of 8 wks beginning June. Courses —Art Appreciation, Studio

LAMONI

GRACELAND COLLEGE, Art Department, College Ave, 50140. Tel 515-784-3311. *Head Dept* Les Wight, MFA; *Assoc Prof* Mel L Clark, MFA; *Asst Prof* Dan Keegan, MFA
Estab 1895, dept estab 1961; pvt den; D; ent req HS dipl; degrees BA and BS 4 yrs; scholarships; SC 30, LC 10; enrl D 180, maj 52, others 4
Tuition: Campus residence available
Courses: Advertising Design, †Art Education, Art History, Ceramics, Commercial Art, Constructions, Drawing, Graphic Arts, History of Art & Archaeology, Intermedia, Lettering, Painting, Photography, Printmaking, Sculpture, Teacher Training
Summer School: Dir, Dr Velma Ruch

LEMARS

WESTMAR COLLEGE, Art Department, 51031. Tel 712-546-7081, Ext 231. *Head Dept* Gary R Bowling. Instrs FT 1, PT 2
Estab 1890; pvt; D; ent req ACT, SAT or PSAT; degrees BA, BMEd and BAS 4 yr; enrl 700, maj 22
Courses: Art Education, Art History, Ceramics, Commercial Art, Drawing, Graphic Arts, Handicrafts, Painting, Sculpture, Art Philosophy & Criticism, Business World of Art, Design, Foundations of Art, Synthetic Media & Color, Watercolor
Adult Hobby Classes: JANUS Continuing Education for Retired Persons

MASON CITY

NORTH IOWA AREA COMMUNITY COLLEGE, Department of Art, 500 College Dr, 50401. Tel 515-423-1264, Ext 242. Instrs FT 1
Estab 1964; pub; D & E; ent req HS dipl; degrees AA 2 yr; scholarships; SC 4, LC 2; enrl D 198, E 25, maj 30
Courses: Art Education, Art History, Ceramics, Drawing, Painting, Basic Design
Adult Hobby Classes: Enrl 30. Courses—Crafts, Painting
Summer School: Term of 5 wks beginning early June. Courses—Art Essentials, Painting

MOUNT PLEASANT

IOWA WESLEYAN COLLEGE, Art Department,* 601 North Main, 52641. Tel 319-385-8021. *Head Dept* Theodore Rasmussen
Estab 1842; den; degrees 4 yr degrees; scholarships; SC 10, LC 4; enrl maj 32
Tuition: Res—$2910 per yr
Courses: Art Education, Art History, Ceramics, Drawing, Graphic Arts, Painting, Sculpture, Introduction to Art, Secondary Art, Special Problems, Twentieth Century Art History

MOUNT VERNON

CORNELL COLLEGE, Art Department, Armstrong Hall, Fine Arts, 52314. Tel 319-895-8811, Ext 128. *Head Dept* Hank Lifson. Instrs FT 3
Estab 1853; den; D; ent req HS dipl; degrees BA, BSS and BPhil 4 yr; scholarships; SC 30, LC 3; enrl 900
Tuition: $2600 per yr
Courses: Art History, Ceramics, Conceptual Art, Drawing, Jewelry, Painting, Sculpture, Batik, Design, Metal & Fiber Design, Weaving

ORANGE CITY

NORTHWESTERN COLLEGE, Art Department, 51041. Tel 712-737-4904. *Chmn Dept* John Kaericher, MFA; *Asst Prof* Rein Van Derhill, MFA
Estab 1882, dept estab 1965; den; D & E; ent req HS dipl; degrees BA 4 yr; scholarships; SC 25, LC 3-4; enrl D 200, non-maj 175, maj 23-25
Tuition: Campus residency available
Courses: †Art Education, Art History, Ceramics, Drawing, Graphic Arts, †Graphic Design, Mixed Media, Printmaking, Sculpture, Stage Design, †Art Therapy

OSKALOOSA

WILLIAM PENN COLLEGE, Art Department, 52577. Tel 515-673-8311. *Chairperson* Linda Eliason, MA; *Assoc Prof* Henry E Grafke Jr, MS; *Assoc Prof* Pearl Wormhoundt, MA
Estab 1876; pvt; D & E; ent req HS dipl, ACT, PSAT or SAT; degrees BA; scholarships; SC 5, LC 5; enrl D 120
Tuition: Res and nonres undergrad $2800 per yr, $1400 per sem, $90 per hr; campus res—room $260 per sem, board $395 per sem
Courses: Art Education, Ceramics, Costume Design & Construction, Drafting, Drawing, History of Art & Archaeology, Industrial Design, Interior Design, Teacher Training
Adult Hobby Classes: Enrl 20; tui $90 per hr. Courses—Crafts
Summer School: Acad Dean, Howard Reitz. Enrl 200; tui $90 for term of 5 wks beginning June 2 and July 3. Courses—Ceramics, Elementary Art Education

OTTUMWA

INDIAN HILLS COMMUNITY COLLEGE, OTTUMWA HEIGHTS CAMPUS, Dept of Art, Grandview at Elm, 52501. Tel 515-682-4551. *Dept Head* Richard Dutton; *Dir of Arts & Sciences* David Harris
Estab 1925; pvt; D & E; ent req HS dipl, GED, ACT or SAT; degrees AA, AAS and AAA 2 yrs; scholarships; SC 3, LC 2; enrl D 73, E 5
Tuition: In-state $160 per quarter; out-of-state $240 (res acquired after 90 days)
Courses: Ceramics, Drawing, History of Art & Archaeology, Painting

PELLA

CENTRAL COLLEGE, Art Department,* 812 University, 50219. Tel 515-628-4151. *Head Dept* Lawrence Mills, PhD; *Assoc Prof* Joline De Jong, MA; *Assoc Prof* John Vruwink, MFA
Estab 1853; pvt; D & E; ent req HS dipl, ACT; degrees BA 4 yrs; scholarships; SC 20, LC 6; enrl D 180, non-maj 140, maj 40
Tuition: Res—undergrad $3264 per yr; campus res—room and board $1296 per yr
Courses: Aesthetics, Art Education, Art History, Ceramics, Drawing, Film, History of Art & Archaeology, Interior Design, Jewelry, Lettering, Painting, Photography, Silversmithing, Teacher Training, Theatre Arts
Children's Classes: Enrl 40; part of Elementary School Art Program

SIOUX CITY

BRIAR CLIFF COLLEGE, Art Department, 3303 Rebecca St, 57038. Tel 712-279-5321, Ext 452. *Chairperson* William J Welu, MFA; *Instructor* Mary Ann Lonergan, MA
Estab 1930; den; D & E; ent req HS dipl, ACT; degrees BA and BS 4 yr; scholarships; SC 7, LC 7; enrl D 250, non-maj 150, maj 30
Tuition: $800 per trimester, $80 per hr; campus res—room & board $1200 per yr
Courses: Art Education, Art History, Drawing, Teacher Training, Art 1, 2, 3 & 4 (major studio areas & independent study), Critical Seminar, Design
Summer School: Tui $65 per term of 6 wks beginning June 12. Courses—Art Appreciation, Ceramics, Contemporary Art, Drawing, Elementary Art Education, Independent Studio Courses

MORNINGSIDE COLLEGE, Art Department,* 1501 Morningside Ave, 51106. Tel 712-277-5821. . Instrs FT 2
Pvt; D & E; ent req HS dipl; degrees BA and BS (Art Educ) 4 yrs; SC 17, LC 4; enrl D 161, maj 35
Tuition: $2654 per yr; campus res—$990 per yr
Courses: Art Education, Ceramics, Drawing, Painting, Photography, Sculpture, Teacher Training, Textile Design
Summer School: Tui $30 per hr for two 5 wk sessions, beginning June 8 and July 15. Courses—Art Education, Art History, Ceramics

SIOUX CITY ART CENTER, 513 Nebraska St, 51101. *Asst Dir* Tom Butler; *Educ Coordr* Dianne Mumm; *Instructor* Gary Bowling, MA; *Instructor* Marvel Cox, BA; *Instructor* John Gordon, MFA; *Instructor* Peggy Parris, BA; *Instructor* Ernest Ricehill, BA; *Instructor* David Wost, BFA
Estab 1938; pvt; D & E; SC 14-20, LC 1-2; enrl D 100, E 400
Tuition: None
Courses: Art Education, Art History, Ceramics, Drawing, Interior Design, Jewelry, Mixed Media, Painting, Photography, Printmaking, Sculpture, Silversmithing, Teacher Training

KANSAS

ATCHISON

BENEDICTINE COLLEGE, Art Department, 66002. Tel 913-367-6110. *Chmn* Sr Helen Buening, MFA; *Prof* Dennis McCarthy, MFA
Estab 1971; den; D; ent req HS dipl, ent exam; SC 15, LC 3; enrl D 145, non-maj 123, maj 22
Tuition: Campus res—room and board $3800
Courses: Art Education, Art History, Calligraphy, Ceramics, Drawing, Graphic Arts, Interior Design, Jewelry, Painting, Photography, Printmaking, Sculpture, Stage Design, Teacher Training, Textile Design, Theatre Arts

BALDWIN CITY

BAKER UNIVERSITY, Department of Art,* 606 Eighth St, 66006. Tel 913-594-6451. *Chmn* Walter J Bailey
Estab 1858; pvt; D; ent req HS dipl, provision made for entrance without HS dipl by interview and committee action; degrees AB (Art) 4 yrs; scholarships; SC 11, LC 3; enrl D 105, maj 28
Tuition: $2350 per yr; campus res—room and board $2160 per yr
Courses: Art Education, Ceramics, Drawing, Graphic Arts, History of Art & Archaeology, Painting, Sculpture, Teacher Training, Textile Design

COFFEYVILLE

COFFEYVILLE COMMUNITY JUNIOR COLLEGE, Art Department, 67337. Tel 316-251-7700, Ext 47. *Head Dept* Douglas Keller, MA
Estab 1923, dept estab 1969; pub; D & E; ent req HS dipl; degrees AA; scholarships; SC 8, LC 2; enrl D 75, E 60, non-maj 25, maj 110
Tuition: Res—undergrad approx $375 per yr (includes $41.50 fees); nonres—undergrad $33.50 per cr hr (includes $41.50 fees); campus res $1100
Courses: Art History, Ceramics, Drawing, Handicrafts, Painting, Photography, Printmaking, Sculpture
Adult Hobby Classes: Crafts

COLBY

COLBY COMMUNITY COLLEGE, Visual Arts Department,* 1255 South Range, 67701. Tel 913-462-3984. *Head Dept* Kenneth Eugene Mitchell, MA; *Instr* Ronald I Bruner, MA; *Instr* Vicki L Mitchell, BA
Estab 1965, dept estab 1966; pub; D & E; ent req HS dipl; degrees AA 2 yrs; scholarships; SC 18, LC 8; enrl D 141, E 210, maj 18
Tuition: Res—undergrad $460 per yr; nonres—undergrad $1510 per yr; campus res—room and board $1260 per yr
Courses: Art Education, Art History, Calligraphy, Ceramics, Commercial Art, Costume Design & Construction, Drafting, Drawing, Fashion Arts, Graphic Arts, Graphic Design, Handicrafts, History of Art & Archaeology, Interior Design, Jewelry, Lettering, Painting, Photography, Sculpture, Stage Design, Teacher Training, Theatre Arts, Color Structure and Design, Figure Drawing: Advanced, Problems in Drawing, Problems in Painting, Watercolor I & II
Adult Hobby Classes: Enrl 10-20; tui $15 per hr
Summer School: Enrl 5-20; tui $15 per cr hr for term of 4 wks beginning June 1. Courses—Drawing, Jewelry, Watercolor

EL DORADO

BUTLER COUNTY COMMUNITY COLLEGE, Art Department,* Route 1, PO Box 888, 67042. Tel 316-321-5083. *Chmn* Robert H Chism, MA; *Instr* Lynn B Havel, MFA; *Instr* Peter Johnson, MFA
Estab 1927, dept estab 1964; pub; D & E; ent req HS dipl, ACT, EED; degrees AA 2 yr; scholarships; SC 13, LC 1; enrl D 168, E 57
Tuition: Res—$280 per yr; nonres—$800 per yr
Courses: Art History, Ceramics, Drawing, Interior Design, Painting, Printmaking, Silversmithing

EMPORIA

EMPORIA STATE UNIVERSITY, Department of Art, 66801. Tel 316-343-1200, Ext 246. *Chmn* Donald Perry, MFA
Estab 1863, dept estab early 1900's; pub; D & E; ent req HS dipl, HS seniors may enroll in regular classes; degrees BFA and BSEd 4 yr; scholarships; SC 42, LC 15, GC 30; enrl D 700, E 25, maj 200, grad 45
Tuition: Res—undergrad and grad $274 per sem; nonres—undergrad and grad $574 per sem; campus res—room & board $1326
Courses: Art Education, Art History, Ceramics, Commercial Art, Costume Design & Construction, Display, Drafting, Drawing, Fashion Arts, Goldsmithing, Graphic Arts, Handicrafts, History of Art & Archaeology, Illustration, Interior Design, Jewelry, Mixed Media, Painting, Photography, Printmaking, Sculpture, Silversmithing, Stage Design, Teacher Training, Textile Design, Theatre Arts, Art Therapy, Weaving
Summer School: Tui res $13.25 per hr, nonres $40 per hr for term beginning June 5th. Courses—most of the regular classes

HAYS

FORT HAYS STATE UNIVERSITY, Department of Art, 67601. Tel 913-628-4247. *Chmn* John C Thorns Jr, MFA; *Prof* Jim Hinkhouse, MFA; *Prof* Kathleen Kuchar; *Prof* Darrell McGinnis, MA; *Assoc Prof* Dale Ficken, MA; *Assoc Prof* Eugene Harwick, MFA; *Assoc Prof* Joanne Harwick, MFA; *Assoc Prof* Frank Nichols, MFA; *Assoc Prof* Zoran Stevanov, MFA; *Instructor* Ellen Schiferl, ABD
Estab 1902, dept estab 1930; pub; D & E; ent req HS dipl; degrees BA and BFA 4 yrs, AA and MA 2 yrs, MFA 2-3 yrs; scholarships; SC 59, LC 19, GC 29; enrl D 945, E 43, non-maj 785, maj 182, grad 25, others 7
Tuition: Res—undergrad and grad $21 per cr hr; nonres—undergrad and grad $42 per cr hr; other various incidental fees; campus res—room & board $628 and up
Courses: †Advertising Design, †Art Education, †Art History, Calligraphy, †Ceramics, †Collage, †Commercial Art, †Conceptual Art, †Constructions, †Drawing, Goldsmithing, †Graphic Arts, †Graphic Design, †Handicrafts, †History of Art & Archaeology, †Illustration, Intermedia, †Interior Design, †Jewelry, Lettering, †Mixed Media, †Painting, †Photography, †Printmaking, †Sculpture, †Silversmithing, Stage Design, †Teacher Training, †Textile Design, Theatre Arts, Video, †Art Therapy
Summer School: Enrl 300; tui $21 per cr hr for term of 8 wks beginning June 2. Courses —Studio Courses & Workshops

HESSTON

HESSTON COLLEGE, 67062. Tel 316-327-4221, Ext 240. *Head Dept* John Blosser, MA
Estab 1915; den; D & E; ent req HS dipl; degrees AA 2 yr; SC 9, SC 1; enrl non-maj 50, maj 5
Tuition: Campus residency available
Courses: Art History, Ceramics, Drafting, Drawing, Painting, Photography, Sculpture, Design

HUTCHINSON

HUTCHINSON COMMUNITY JUNIOR COLLEGE, Art Department,* 1300 N Plum St, 67501. Tel 316-663-5781. *Chmn* Dave Blackim, MA; *Prof* Dennis Chegwidden, MFA; *Prof* Jane Dronberger, MA; *Prof* Roy Swanson, BFA
Estab 1928; pub; D & E; ent req HS dipl; degrees AA 2 yrs; scholarships; SC 17, LC 4; enrl D 215, E 41, non-maj 180, maj 29
Tuition: Res—$10 per cr hr; nonres—$500 per sem; campus res—room and board $1060 per yr
Courses: †Art Education, †Art History, †Ceramics, †Drawing, †Graphic Design, †History of Art & Archaeology, †Jewelry, †Painting, †Printmaking, †Sculpture, †Silversmithing, †Theatre Arts
Summer School: Tui $9 per course

INDEPENDENCE

INDEPENDENCE COMMUNITY JUNIOR COLLEGE, Fine Arts Department, College Ave & Brookside Dr, 67301. Tel 316-331-4100. *Pres* Dr Richard Taylor; *Instructor* Leonard E Wood, MA
Pub; D & E; ent req HS dipl; degrees AA; scholarships; SC 8; enrl D 60, E 10, non-maj 64, maj 6
Tuition: No campus res
Courses: Ceramics, Drawing, Painting, Photography, Sculpture, Silversmithing, Stage Design, Art for Elementary Schools, Design, Introduction to Art

IOLA

ALLEN COUNTY COMMUNITY COLLEGE, Art Department, 66749. Tel 316-365-5116. *Dept Head* Joseph F Caron, EdD
Estab 1965; pub; D & E; ent req HS dipl or GED; degrees AA 2 yr; scholarships; SC 5, LC 2; enrl D 400, E 435, non-maj 40, maj 6
Tuition: Res—undergrad $335 per yr; nonres—undergrad $1095 per yr; campus residence available
Courses: Art History, Ceramics, Commercial Art, Drawing, Handicrafts, Painting, Photography, Printmaking, Sculpture, Art Appreciation, Art Fundamentals, Design (2nd and 3rd dimensional)
Summer School: Tui $8 per cr hr. Courses—all courses

LAWRENCE

HASKELL INDIAN JUNIOR COLLEGE, Art Department, 66044. Tel 913-841-2000. *Instr* Jean S Allen, MFA; *Instr* Clinton J Leon, MS
Estab 1884, dept estab 1970; pub; D; ent req HS dipl or GED, at least 1 4 Indian, Eskimo or Aleut and receive agency approval; degrees AA and AAS 2 yrs; SC 14, LC

1; enrl in dept D, non-maj 40, maj 10
Tuition: Campus residence available
Courses: Art Education, Ceramics, Drawing, Jewelry, Painting, Textile Design, Theatre Arts, Art Appreciation, Design, Dyeing, Printing, Watercolor, Weaving

UNIVERSITY OF KANSAS, School of Fine Arts, 66044. Tel 913-864-4401. *Dean* J Moeser
Pub; degrees BFA, BAE, BS, MFA 4-5 yrs; scholarships and fels; Freshman Common Curriculum (required for all new freshmen), Advisor-Lee Mann; enrl 250
—**Department of Visual Communications,** 66044. *Chmn* Phillip Blackhurst. Instrs PT 5
Estab 1885; SC 50, GC 25; enrl maj 150
Courses: Art History, Painting, Printmaking, Sculpture, Theatre Arts
—**Department of Design,** 66044. *Chmn* Richard Branham. Instrs FT 24, PT 12
Estab 1921; SC 83, LC 32, GC 26; enrl maj 250, grad 40
Courses: Ceramics, Industrial Design, Interior Design, Jewelry, Silversmithing, Textile Design, Design, Weaving
—**Kress Foundation Department of Art History,** Spencer Museum of Art, 66045. Tel 913-864-4713. *Chairperson* Jeanne Stump, PhD; *Grad Advisor* Stephen Addiss, PhD; *Prof* Chu-tsing Li, PhD; *Prof* Marilyn Stokstad, PhD; *Assoc Prof* James L Connelly, PhD; *Assoc Prof* Edmund Eglinski, PhD; *Assoc Prof* Charles Eldredge, PhD; *Asst Prof* Douglas Hyland, PhD; *Instr* Thomas Southall, MA; *Lectr* Ralph T Coe; *Lectr* Laurence Sickman; *Lectr* Ross Taggart; *Lectr* Marc Wilson
Estab 1866, dept estab 1953; pub; D & E; ent req HS dipl; degrees BA, BGS, MFA, MA, PhD; scholarships; LC 30, GC 10; enrl D 900, E 40, maj 50, grad 55
Tuition: Campus res available
Courses: Art History, History of Art & Archaeology, Chinese and Japanese Art, North American Art, Western European Art
Summer School: Chairperson, Prof Jeanne Stump. Courses—Introductory courses in Western and Eastern Art, Summer Institute in Great Britain
—**Department of Visual Arts Education,** 109 Bailey Hall, 66044. Tel 913-864-3167. *Chmn Dept* Philip H Rueschhoff, EdD; *Assoc Prof* Marguerite Baumgartel, EdD; *Instr* Dixie Glenn, MA
Estab 1865, dept estab 1969; pub; D & E; ent req HS dipl, ent exam; degrees BAE 4 yrs, MA 1-6 yrs, EdD and PhD 3-6 yrs; scholarships; GC 12; enrl D 535, maj 123, grad 123, others 289
Tuition: Res—$358 per sem, $31 per cr hr; nonres—$853 per sem, $64 per cr hr; campus res available
Courses: Visual Arts Education
Summer School: Term of 8 wks beginning June

LEAVENWORTH

SAINT MARY COLLEGE, Art Department, 66048. Tel 913-682-5151. *Head Dept* Sr M Rebecca Conner, MA; *Instructor* Sr Carmen Echevarria, MA
Estab 1923; pvt; D & E; ent req HS dipl; degrees BA, BS, BM and BME 4 yr; scholarships; SC 25, LC 5; enrl non-maj 80, maj 10
Tuition: $2050 per yr; PT $70 per cr hr; campus res—room & board $1400
Courses: Art Education, Art History, Calligraphy, Ceramics, Commercial Art, Drawing, Graphic Arts, Handicrafts, History of Art & Archaeology, Interior Design, Jewelry, Lettering, Mixed Media, Painting, Photography, Printmaking, Sculpture, Teacher Training, Textile Design, Stitchery, Weaving
Children's Classes: Enrl 30; tui $200 per 2 wks. Courses—Crafts Camp; Painting (Saturday)
Summer School: Tui $240 for term of 3 wks. Courses—variable 3 wk workshop

LIBERAL

SEWARD COUNTY COMMUNITY COLLEGE, Art Department,* North Hwy 83, Box 1137, 67901. Tel 316-624-1951. *Head Art Dept* Steve Heckman, MFA; *Instr* Robert Carder, MA
Estab 1969; pub; D & E; ent req HS dipl; degrees AA 2 yrs; scholarships; SC 13, LC 6; enrl D 650, E 350
Tuition: Res—$360 per yr; nonres—$1120 per yr; campus res—room and board $1210 per yr
Courses: Art Education, Art History, Ceramics, Costume Design & Construction, Drawing, History of Art & Archaeology, Painting, Photography, Sculpture, Stage Design
Summer School: Dir, Steve Heckman. Tui $12 per cr hr for term of 6 wks beginning June 4. Courses—Varied and subject to change

LINDSBORG

BETHANY COLLEGE, Box 111, 67456. Tel 913-227-3311, Ext 146. *Head Art Dept* Baniel Mason, MFA; *Assoc Prof* Ray Kahmeyer, MA; *Asst Prof* Nicholas Hill; *Asst Prof* Don Osborne, MFA
Den; D; ent req HS dipl; degrees BA 3-4 yr; scholarships; SC 19, LC 3; enrl D 195, non-maj 200, maj 50
Tuition: $3700 per yr, $225 per course; campus residency available
Courses: †Art Education, Art History, Ceramics, Drawing, Painting, Photography, Printmaking, Sculpture, Studio Concentration
Summer School: Acad Dean, Dr Alan Steinbach

MANHATTAN

KANSAS STATE UNIVERSITY
—**Art Department,** Art Bldg, 66506. Tel 913-532-6605. *Head Dept* Jerrold Maddox, MFA; *Prof* Angelo Garzio, MFA; *Prof* Oscar V Larmer, MFA; *Assoc Prof* James C Munee; *Assoc Prof* Elliott Pujol, MFA; *Assoc Prof* Rex Replogle, MFA; *Assoc Prof* John Vogt, MFA; *Assoc Prof* Gary Woodward, MFA
Estab 1863, dept estab 1965; pub; D & E; ent req HS dipl; degrees BS(Art Educ) jointly with Col Educ, BA and BFA 4 yrs, MA 2 yrs; scholarships; SC 45, LC 19, GC 7; enrl D 1940, E 60, non-maj 1800, maj 200, grad 15

Tuition: Res—$348 per sem; nonres—$843 per sem; campus res available
Courses: Art Education, Art History, Ceramics, Drawing, Graphic Design, Jewelry, Lettering, Painting, Printmaking, Sculpture, Theatre Arts
Summer School: Dir, Jerrold Maddox. Enrl 150; tui res $24 per cr hr, nonres $57 per cr hr for term of 4 to 8 wks beginning June 5. Courses—most of above, varies from summer to summer
—College of Architecture and Design, 66506. Instrs FT 53
Estab 1904; degrees BArch, BInterior Archit and BLandscape Archit 5 yrs, MArchit, MLandscape Archit, MRegional and Community Planning; enrl approx 1150
Courses: †Architecture, †Landscape Architecture, †Interior Architecture, †Regional and Community Planning
Summer School: Dean, Bernd Foerster. 8 wks from June 4

MCPHERSON

MCPHERSON COLLEGE, Art Department, 1600 E Euclid, 67460. Tel 316-241-0731, Ext 18. Chmn Mary Ann Robinson, MA
Estab 1887; den; D & E; ent req HS dipl, ACT; degrees AB 4 yr; scholarships; SC 14, LC 5; enrl D 150, maj 10, others 140
Tuition: Res—undergrad $2500 per yr, $75 per cr hr; campus res—room and board $1400
Courses: †Art Education, Art History, Ceramics, Drawing, †Interior Design, Lettering, Museum Staff Training, Teacher Training, Textile Design
Summer School: Dir, Dr Dayton Rothrock. Term of 10 wks beginning end of May, Courses—Varied Liberal Arts

NORTH NEWTON

BETHEL COLLEGE, Dept of Art, 67117. Tel 316-283-2500. Chmn Robert W Regier, MFA; Assoc Prof Paul Friesen, MA; Asst Prof Miguel Almanza, MA
Estab 1888, dept estab 1959; den; D; ent req HS, ACT; degrees BA(Art) 4 yrs; scholarships; SC 11, LC 3; enrl D 240, non-maj 215, maj 25
Tuition: $2400 per yr, $1200 per sem, $90 per hr; campus res—room & board $1500 per yr
Courses: Advertising Design, Art Education, Art History, Ceramics, Drafting, Drawing, Graphic Arts, Graphic Design, Painting, Photography, Printmaking, Sculpture, Teacher Training, Batik, Weaving
Adult Hobby Classes: Enrl 15; tui $5 per 2 hr session. Courses—Ceramics

OTTAWA

OTTAWA UNIVERSITY, Department of Art,* Tenth & Cedar Sts, 66067. Tel 913-242-5200. Dir Pal T Wright. Instrs FT 2, PT 1
Estab 1865; pvt; D; ent req HS grad, SAT, ACT; degrees BA 4 yrs; scholarships; SC 16, LC 5; enrl D 35, maj 5
Tuition: Res—$2280 per yr
Courses: Art Education, Ceramics, Drawing, Fashion Arts, Graphic Arts, Graphic Design, History of Art & Archaeology, Painting, Photography, Sculpture

OVERLAND PARK

JOHNSON COUNTY COMMUNITY COLLEGE, Communications-Arts Division, Col Blvd at Quivira Rd, 66210. Tel 913-888-8500, Ext 550. Dir James M Williams, MA; Coordr Commercial Art Prog Dorothy Wadsworth, MFA; Instructor Stuart Belas, BA; Instructor Judy Brazil, BA; Instructor Ron Hicks, MS; Instructor Jean Howard, EEd; Instructor Karen Schory, MFA; Instructor Thomas Tarnowski, MFA
Estab 1969; pub; D & E; ent req HS dipl or equivalent; degrees AA 2 yr; SC 30, LC 4; enrl D 200, E 100
Tuition: Res $14.50 per cr hr; nonres $36.50 per cr hr; no campus res
Courses: Art Education, Art History, Ceramics, Commercial Art, Illustration, Lettering, Painting, Photography, Printmaking, Sculpture, Silversmithing, Design (2-dimensional, 3-dimensional & color), Layout, Preparation of Portfolio, Silkscreen, Weaving, Visual Communications, Visual Technology
Summer School: Enrl 100; tui $14.50 per cr hr for term of 8 wks beginning June 5

PITTSBURG

PITTSBURG STATE UNIVERSITY, Art Department, (Formerly Kansas State College) 1701 S Broadway St, 66762. Acting Chairperson Robert Blunk Jr, MS; Prof Harry E Krug, MS; Assoc Prof Alex Barde, MS; Assoc Prof Robert Russell, MFA; Assoc Prof Marjorie Schick, MFA; Assoc Prof Laurence Wooster, MA
Estab 1903, dept estab 1921; pub; D & E; ent req HS dipl; degrees BFA and BSEd 4 yr, MS 36 hr; SC 48, LC 12, GC 14; enrl D 600, E 50, non-maj 400, maj 200, grad 30
Tuition: Res—undergrad and grad $255 per sem, $13.50 per sem hr; nonres—undergrad and grad $555 per sem, $36.50 per sem hr; campus res—room and board $1296 per yr
Courses: †Art Education, Art History, †Ceramics, †Drawing, Film, †Jewelry, †Painting, Teacher Training, †Sculpture, †Silversmithing, †Teacher Training, †Art Therapy
Summer School: Enrl 200; tui res $16.50 per cr hr, nonres $36.50 per cr hr for term of 8 wks beginning June 5th. Courses—as above

PRATT

PRATT COMMUNITY COLLEGE, Art Department,* Highway 61, 67124. Tel 316-672-5641. Chmn Gene Wineland, MA
D & E; ent req HS dipl; degrees AA and AS; scholarships; SC 12, LC 1
Tuition: Res—$215 per sem; nonres—$1000 per yr
Courses: Art History, Commercial Art, Display, Drawing, Graphic Design, Interior Design, Jewelry

SALINA

KANSAS WESLEYAN UNIVERSITY, Art Department,* Santa Fe & Clafin St, 67401. Tel 913-827-5541. Head Dept George F Chlebak
Estab 1886; den; degrees AB 4 yr; scholarships; SC 8, LC 3; enrl maj 15, others 500 for two sem
Tuition: Res—$2476 per yr; campus res available
Courses: Art History, Drawing, Painting, Design
Summer School: Enrl 125; for term of 8 wks beginning June

STERLING

STERLING COLLEGE, Art Department, 540 E Main, 67579. Tel 316-278-3609, Ext 245. Head Dept Gordon Zahradnik, MFA
Estab 1876; den; D & E; ent req HS dipl; degrees AB and BS; scholarships; SC 16, LC 2; enrl D 556
Tuition: Campus residency available
Courses: Advertising Design, Art Education, Art History, Calligraphy, Ceramics, Collage, Commercial Art, Costume Design & Construction, Drawing, Graphic Arts, Graphic Design, Handicrafts, Interior Design, Jewelry, Lettering, Painting, Photography, Printmaking, Textile Design, Theatre Arts, Copper Enameling, Fibers
Adult Hobby Classes: Enrl 25; tui $20. Courses—all areas
Children's Classes: Courses—Art Education

TOPEKA

WASHBURN UNIVERSITY OF TOPEKA, Department of Art, Mulvane Art Center, 17th and Jewell Sts, 66621. Tel 913-235-5341. Head Dept R J Hunt. Instrs FT 4
Estab 1900; pub; ent req HS dipl; degrees AB and BFA 4 yr; SC 11, LC 5; enrl maj 60, others 280
Courses: Art History, Ceramics, Drawing, Jewelry, Painting, Sculpture, Art Appreciation, Design, Metalcraft
Adult Hobby Classes: Tui $22 for twelve 3 hr sessions
Children's Classes: Tui $18 for twelve 1 1 2 hr sessions

WICHITA

FRIENDS UNIVERSITY, Art Department, 2100 University Ave, 67213. Tel 316-363-9131, Ext 315. Head Dept Dee M Connett, MA; Instructor Judy Dove, MFA; Instructor Don Filby, MA; Instructor Glynice Mathews, MFA; Instructor Michael Oliver, MFA
Estab 1898; den; D & E; ent req HS dipl; degrees BA and BS 4 yr; scholarships; SC 18, LC 4; enrl D 329, E 37
Tuition: Res—undergrad $2250 per yr or $1125 per sem, 1-6 hrs $60 per cr hr, 7-11 hrs $75 per cr hr; nonres—undergrad $2295 per yr, $1147.50 per sem; campus res—room & board $1205 per yr, $602.50 per sem
Courses: Art Education, Art History, Calligraphy, Ceramics, Commercial Art, Drawing, Graphic Arts, Graphic Design, Jewelry, Painting, Photography, Printmaking, Sculpture, Silversmithing, Teacher Training
Adult Hobby Classes: Courses—Drawing, Jewelry, Painting
Summer School: Tui $68 per cr hr for term of 6 wks beginning June 5th

SCHOOL OF THE WICHITA ART ASSOCIATION, 9112 E Central, 67206. Tel 316-686-6687. Dir John R Rouse. Instrs 20
Estab 1923; pvt; D & E; scholarships; enrl 300
Courses: Art History, Ceramics, Commercial Art, Drawing, Fashion Arts, Painting, Photography, Printmaking, Silversmithing, Enameling, Pottery, Weaving
Summer School: 6 wk June-July

WICHITA STATE UNIVERSITY, Division of Art, College of Fine Arts, 67208. Tel 316-689-3555. Asst Dean Robert M Kiskadden; Grad Coordr Ron Christ, MFA; Chmn Art Educ Mary Sue Foster, MA; Chmn Art History Mira P Merriman, PhD; Chmn Graphic Design Clark Britton, MAA; Chmn Studio Arts Richard St John, MFA
Estab 1895, dept estab 1901; pub; D & E; ent req HS dipl; degrees BAE and BFA 4 yr, MFA 2 yr, MA 1 yr; scholarships; enrl D 1149, E 194, non-maj 78, maj 285, grad 51, others 2
Tuition: Res—undergrad and grad $24 per cr hr per 15 hrs or more; nonres—undergrad and grad $57 per cr hr per 15 hrs or more; no campus res
Courses: †Art Education, †Art History, †Ceramics, Drawing, †Graphic Design, Illustration, Photography, †Printmaking, †Sculpture, Teacher Training
Summer School: Tui as above for term of 8 wks beginning June 5th

WINFIELD

SOUTHWESTERN COLLEGE, 67156. Prof Warren D Brown, MA; Adjunct Prof William Boulware, MA
Estab 1885; pvt & den; D & E; ent req HS dipl; degrees BA 4 yr; scholarships; SC 12, LC 4

KENTUCKY

ANCHORAGE

LOUISVILLE SCHOOL OF ART, 100 Park Rd, 40223. Tel 502-245-8836. *Dir* Bruce Yenawine, MA; *Assoc Dir* Diana Arcadipone, MFA; *Instructor* Peter David Bodnar III, MFA; *Instructor* Mary Ann Currier; *Instructor* Lida Gordon, MFA; *Instructor* Garry Kaulitz, MFA; *Instructor* David Keator, MFA; *Instructor* Skip Koebbeman, MFA; *Instructor* Margaret Meloy, MA; *Instructor* Les Nash, PhD; *Instructor* Phil Wakeman, MA; *Instructor* Nadene Wegner, MFA
Estab 1909; pvt; D & E; ent req HS dipl, HS transcripts, transfer transcripts, application form & fee, portfolio, interview; degrees BFA 4 yr; scholarships; SC 25, LC 4; enrl 153, non-maj 67, maj 86
Tuition: $875 per yr, $75 per cr hr; no campus res
Courses: Art History, Ceramics, Drawing, Jewelry, Painting, Photography, Printmaking, Sculpture, Textile Design, Color, Design, Metalsmithing
Adult Hobby Classes: Enrl 74 PT; tui $75 per cr. Courses—Ceramics, Drawing, Life Drawing, Metal, Painting, Prints, Sculpture, Textiles
Summer School: Tui $80 for term of 4 wks beginning June. Courses—Glassblowing, Metal, Painting, Papermaking, Photography, Prints, Textiles

BARBOURVILLE

UNION COLLEGE, Art Department,* College St, 40906. Tel 606-546-4151. *Head Dept* Elizabeth Burke
Den; D & E; ent req HS dipl; degrees BA, BS and MA (Educ) 4 yr
Courses: Art Education, Art History, Drawing, Painting, Teacher Training, Theatre Arts, Art Appreciation, Art Fundamentals, Recreational Arts and Crafts

BEREA

BEREA COLLEGE, Art Department, 40404. Tel 606-986-9341, Ext 292, 293 & 294. *Chmn* Lester F Pross, MA; *Prof* Dorothy Tredennick, MA; *Assoc Prof* Neil DiTeresa, AM; *Assoc Prof* Walter Hyleck, MFA; *Assoc Prof* Sally Wilkerson, MFA; *Instructor* Christopher Pierce, MFA; *Instructor* William Morningstar, MFA; *Instructor* Resident Potter
Estab 1855, dept estab 1936; pvt; D; ent req HS dipl (preference given to students from Southern Appalachian region); degrees BA 4 yr; scholarships; SC 14, LC 8; enrl D 324, maj 54
Tuition: None; campus res—room and board $1468
Courses: Art Education, Art History, Ceramics, Drawing, Painting, Printmaking, Sculpture, Teacher Training, Textile Design

BOWLING GREEN

WESTERN KENTUCKY UNIVERSITY, Art Department, Ivan Wilson Center for Fine Arts, Room 441, 42101. Tel 502-745-3940. *Head Dept* Dr Joseph W Gluhman. Instrs FT 14, PT 1
Pub; D; ent req HS dipl; degrees BA and BFA 4 yrs, MA(Art Educ); SC 46, LC 19; enrl maj 200
Tuition: $260 per sem; nonres—$670; campus res $245-$255 per sem
Courses: Art Education, Art History, Ceramics, Drawing, Graphic Design, Painting, Photography, Printmaking, Sculpture, Design, Weaving
Summer School: Tui $189, nonres $477 for term of 5 1 2 wks beginning May 27. Courses—Art Education, Art History, Ceramics, Design, Drawing, Painting

CAMPBELLSVILLE

CAMPBELLSVILLE COLLEGE, Fine Arts Division, 42718. Tel 502-465-8158. *Div Head* Larry W Reed; *Asst Prof* Ted Barnes, MFA; *Instructor* Tommy Clark, MFA; *Adjunct Instr* Debbie Barnes
Estab 1906, dept estab 1967; den; D & E; ent req HS dipl, ACT; degrees BA, BS, BS(Med Tech), BM and BChM 4 yr, AA, AS and ASSW 2 yr; scholarships; SC 28, LC 5; enrl D 35, E 10, non-maj 12, maj 22, others 8 minors
Tuition: $930 for regular term
Courses: Advertising Design, Architecture, Art Education, Art History, Ceramics, Commercial Art, Conceptual Art, Display, Drafting, Drawing, Graphic Arts, Graphic Design, Handicrafts, Jewelry, Painting, Photography, Printmaking, Sculpture, Silversmithing, Stage Design, Teacher Training, Theatre Arts
Summer School: Tui $480 for term of 8 wks beginning June 9, 1980. Courses—Art Education, Art Appreciation, Drawing, Painting

DANVILLE

CENTRE COLLEGE OF KENTUCKY, Art Department, 40422. Tel 606-236-5211. *Chmn* Tom Gaines. Instrs FT 4
Estab 1819; pvt; degrees 4 yrs; SC, LC; enrl D 750-800
Courses: Art History, Ceramics, Commercial Art, Drawing, Painting, Printmaking, Sculpture, Design
Adult Hobby Classes: Ceramics, Drawing, Painting

FORT MITCHELL

THOMAS MORE COLLEGE, Art Department, PO Box 85, 41017. Tel 606-341-5800. *Chmn* Sr M de Deo, MFA; *Prof* Darrell Brothers, MFA
Estab 1921; pvt; D & E; ent req HS dipl; degrees BA, BES, BS, AA and AES; SC 9, LC 4; enrl D 12, E 5, maj 17
Tuition: $53 per sem hr; campus res—room and board $1560
Courses: Aesthetics, Art Education, Art History, Ceramics, Drawing, Painting, Photography, Sculpture, Teacher Training, Theatre Arts, Arts Management

GEORGETOWN

GEORGETOWN COLLEGE, Art Department, Fine Arts Division, 40324. Tel 502-863-8351. *Chmn* Charles James McCormick. Instrs FT 2
Estab 1829; den; D; ent req HS transcript, ACT; degrees BA 4 yrs; scholarships and grants; SC 14, LC 6; enrl 1150
Tuition: Res—$1045 per term; nonres—$1095 per term; 4-1-4 curriculum; Jan interterm
Courses: Art History, Ceramics, Graphic Arts, Painting, Photography, Sculpture, Art Appreciation, Art Careers, Art Survey, Public School Art, Secondary Art, Three-Dimensional Design, Travel Classes, Two-Dimensional Design
Summer School: Three 3 wk modules of one course each. Courses—Art Education, Art Humanities, Studio Classes

HIGHLAND HEIGHTS

NORTHERN KENTUCKY UNIVERSITY, Fine Arts Department, 41076. Tel 606-292-5420. *Chmn* Don Kelm. Instrs FT 10, PT 3
Estab 1968; pub; D & E; ent req HS grad, ACT scores; degrees BA(Art Educ), BA(Art History), BFA, BFA(Graphic Design); SC 31, LC 10
Tuition: Res—$210 per sem, PT $18 per cr hr; nonres—$475 per sem, PT $40 per cr hr
Courses: Art Education, Art History, Ceramics, Drawing, Graphic Design, Painting, Photography, Printmaking, Sculpture

LEXINGTON

TRANSYLVANIA UNIVERSITY, Studio Arts Department,* 300 N Broadway, 40508. Tel 606-233-8159. *Chmn* Gary Anderson, DMus; *Instr* Louise Calvin, MA; *Instr* Dan Selter, MA
Estab 1780; pvt; D & E; ent req HS dipl; degrees BA and BS; scholarships; SC 20, LC 3; enrl D 105, E 14, maj 18
Tuition: Res—$3600 per yr 1979-1980; campus res—room and board $1690
Courses: Art Education, Art History, Ceramics, Costume Design & Construction, Drafting, Drawing, History of Art & Archaeology, Mixed Media, Painting, Sculpture, Stage Design, Teacher Training, Theatre Arts

UNIVERSITY OF KENTUCKY, Department of Art, College of Fine Arts, 40506. Tel 606-258-9000, Ext 2452 & 2453. *Dean* J Robert Wills Jr; *Chmn* Leonard L Hunter III. Instrs FT 20, PT 1
Estab 1918; pub; degrees BA, BFA, MA and MFA 4 yr; scholarships and grad assistantships; SC 23, LC 19, GC 6; enrl maj 200, others 800
Tuition: Res $275, nonres $750; campus residency available
Courses: Art Education, Art History, Ceramics, Drawing, Painting, Photography, Printmaking, Sculpture, Textile Design
Summer School: Enrl 200; tui res $154, nonres $400 for 8 wks beginning June. Courses—Art Education, Drawing, History of Art, Painting

LOUISVILLE

JEFFERSON COMMUNITY COLLEGE, Fine Arts, First & Broadway, PO Box 1036, 40201. Tel 502-584-0181, Ext 289. *Coordr Fine Arts* P J Krantz; *Assoc Prof* R M Crask; *Asst Prof* Ann Hemdahl-Owen. Instrs PT 5
Estab 1964; pub; D & E; ent req HS dipl; degrees AFA, AAA and Assoc in Photography 2 yrs; scholarships; SC 11, LC 6; enrl D 4774, E 4172
Tuition: $195 per sem, $17 per hr
Courses: †Advertising Design, Aesthetics, Art Education, Art History, †Commercial Art, Display, Drawing, Graphic Arts, Graphic Design, History of Art & Archaeology, Mixed Media, Painting, †Photography, Sculpture, †Theatre Arts
Summer School: Dir, Dr Ronald Horvath. Courses—Drawing, Photography

UNIVERSITY OF LOUISVILLE, Allen R Hite Art Institute, Department of Fine Arts, Belknap Campus, 40208. Tel 502-588-6794. *Dir* Donald P Anderson, MFA; *Prof* Henry J Chodkowski, MFA; *Prof* E Thomas Marsh, MAT. Instrs FT 14, PT 6
Estab 1846, dept estab 1935; pub; D & E; ent req HS dipl, CEEB; degrees BA 4 yr, MA 1 to 2 yrs; scholarships; SC 35, LC 71, GC 26; enrl D 1000, E 90, non-maj 800, maj 264, grad 29
Tuition: Res—undergrad $570 per yr, $285 per sem, $24 per hr, grad $648 per yr, $324 per sem, $27 per hr; nonres—undergrad $2000 per yr, $1000 per sem, $84 per hr, grad $1992 per yr, $996 per sem, $83 per hr; campus res—room & board $1380
Courses: Art Education, Art History, †Ceramics, Drawing, †Graphic Design, Handicrafts, †History of Art & Archaeology, †Painting, †Photography, †Printmaking, †Sculpture, Teacher Training, Textile Design
Summer School: Tui res $24 pr hr, nonres $84 per hr for term of 5 wks, beginning early June. Courses—3 or 4 of above courses

MIDWAY

MIDWAY COLLEGE, Art Department, Stephens St, 40347. Tel 606-846-4423, Ext 27. *Chmn* Virginia Hutton. Instrs FT 1
Den; D, W; ent req HS dipl, ACT; degrees 2 yr; scholarships; SC 7, LC 3; enrl 55
Courses: Art Education, Ceramics, Drawing, Painting, Sculpture, Textile Design, Basic Design, Historical Furniture

MOREHEAD

MOREHEAD STATE UNIVERSITY, Art Department,* Claypool-Young Art Bldg, UPO Box 714, 40351. Tel 606-783-2221. *Head Dept* Dr Bill R Booth, PhD; *Assoc Prof* Douglas Adams, MA; *Assoc Prof* Roder H Jones, EdD; *Assoc Prof* Maurice Strider, MA; *Instr* Louise A T Booth, MA; *Asst Prof* Franz Altschuler, BFA; *Asst Prof* Gene J Pyle, AB; *Asst Prof* Joe D Sartor, MA; *Asst Prof* Donald B Young, MA; *Prof* Jose A Maortua, MFA
Estab 1922; pub; D & E; ent req HS dipl, ACT; degrees BA 4 yr, MA l yr; scholarships; SC 40, LC 16, GC 28; enrl D 900, E 20, non-maj 800, maj 180, GS 55, others 145
Tuition: Res—undergrad $240 per sem, grad $275 per sem; nonres—undergrad $600 per sem, grad $700 per sem; other part-time res—undergrad $20, grad $31; nonres—$50, grad $78; campus res—room and board $300
Courses: Advertising Design, †Art Education, Art History, Calligraphy, Ceramics, †Commercial Art, †Drawing, Fashion Arts, †Graphic Arts, †Graphic Design, Handicrafts, History of Art & Archaeology, Illustration, Lettering, †Painting, Photography, Printmaking, Sculpture, †Teacher Training, Weaving
Adult Hobby Classes: Courses—Ceramics, Crafts, Oil Painting, Watercolor painting, Weaving
Summer School: Courses—same as above on demand

MURRAY

MURRAY STATE UNIVERSITY, Art Department, College of Creative Expression, 42071. Tel 502-762-3784. *Chmn* Robert W Head, MFA; *Instructor* Karen W Boyd, MFA; *Instructor* Harry Furches, MFA; *Instructor* Richard Jackson, MFA; *Instructor* Michael Johnson, MFA; *Instructor* William Lew, PhD; *Instructor* Dale Leys, MFA; *Instructor* Luke Oas, MFA; *Instructor* Joe Rigsby, BFA; *Instructor* Fred Shepard, MFA; *Instructor* Jerry Speight, MA; *Instructor* Jim Stickler, MFA; *Instructor* Mary Jane Timmerman, MFA; *Instructor* Vernon Town, MFA; *Instructor* Melody Weiler, MFA; *Instructor* Jim White, MFA
Estab 1925, dept estab 1931; pub; D & E; ent req HS dipl from accredited Kentucky HS, out of state must rank in the upper half of their HS and/or ACT test score of 22 or above; degrees BA, BS and BFA 4 yr, MAEd, MACT and MA(Studio) approx 1 1 2 yrs; scholarships; SC 104, LC 44, GS 29; enrl D 700, E 50, non-maj 114, maj 290, grad 8
Tuition: Res—undergrad $520 per yr, $260 per sem, $20 per hr, grad $590 per yr, $295 per sem, $31 per hr; nonres—undergrad $1340 per yr, $670 per sem, $54 per hr, grad $1440 per yr, $720 per sem, $78 per hr; campus res—room and board $940
Courses: Advertising Design, †Art Education, Art History, †Ceramics, Commercial Art, †Drawing, †Graphic Design, History of Art & Archaeology, †Jewelry, †Painting, †Photography, †Printmaking, †Sculpture, Silversmithing, Teacher Training, Textile Design, †Design Materials, Weaving
Children's Classes: Enrl 25; tui $410 for 6 wks. Courses—Sat workshop for grades 1-9, various media used; special program for advanced students; summer workshop for HS students (they stay on campus, $89 per wk)
Summer School: Enrl 100; tui res—undergrad $240 per sem, $20 per hr, grad $279 per sem, $31 per hr; nonres—undergrad $648 per sem, $54 per hr, grad $702 per sem, $78 per hr for two 4 wk terms beginning June 2 and July 7

OWENSBORO

BRESCIA COLLEGE, Art Department,* 120 W Seventh St, 42301. Tel 502-685-3131. *Chmn* James D White
Estab 1950; den; D & E; ent req HS dipl, ent exam, ACT, GED; degrees AA, BA, BS and BM (Music & Music Educ) 4 yr; scholarships; SC 22, LC 10; enrl D 400, E 360, maj 50
Tuition: Res—$1800 per yr
Courses: Advertising Design, Aesthetics, Architecture, Art Education, Art History, Ceramics, Drafting, Drawing, Graphic Arts, Lettering, Painting, Photography, Teacher Training, Textile Design, Three-Dimensional Design
Summer School: Enrl 50; tui for term of 6 wk beginning June. Courses—Ceramics, Drawing, Photography

KENTUCKY WESLEYAN COLLEGE, Department of Fine Arts,* 3000 Frederica St, 42301. Tel 502-926-3111. *Chmn* Jerome Redfearn
Dept estab 1950; den; degrees BA 4 yr; scholarships; SC 11, LC 4; enrl maj 40
Tuition: Res—$2340 per yr; campus res available
Courses: Advertising Design, Art History, Ceramics, Commercial Art, Drawing, Graphic Arts, Illustration, Jewelry, Painting, Sculpture, Teacher Training, Art Appreciation, Arts and Crafts, Design, Watercolor
Summer School: Enrl 60. Courses—Art for the Elementary Schools, Art Survey

PIKEVILLE

PIKEVILLE COLLEGE, Fine Arts Dept, 41501. Tel 606-432-9200. *Chmn* Dr Dianna Duffin, PhD; *Prof* Josiah L M Baird, PhD; *Asst Prof* Janice B Ford, MS
Estab 1889; pvt den; D & E; ent req SAT, ACT; degrees BA and BS 4 yrs; SC 16, LC 5
Tuition: $975 per sem, $75 per hr; campus res $625 per yr
Courses: †Art Education, Art History, Ceramics, Drawing, History of Art & Archaeology, Painting, Printmaking, Sculpture, †Teacher Training
Summer School: Tui $75 per hr. Courses—vary

PIPPA PASSES

ALICE LLOYD COLLEGE, Art Department, 41844. *Chmn* Golden Glen Hale. Instrs FT 1, PT 1
Estab 1922; pvt; D & E; ent req HS dipl, ent exam; degrees AA and CA 2 yr; scholarships; SC 6, LC 1; enrl maj 5
Courses: Drawing, Painting, Photography, Sculpture
Adult Hobby Classes: Enrl 40; tui free. Courses—Ceramics

PRESTONSBURG

PRESTONSBURG COMMUNITY COLLEGE, Art Department, 41653. Tel 606-886-3863. *Chmn* Tom J Whitaker, MA
Estab 1964, dept estab 1964; pub; D & E; ent req 18 yrs of age; degrees Associate; SC 5, LC 4; enrl D 400, E 200, maj 126
Tuition: Res—undergrad $195 per sem; no campus res
Courses: Art Education, Art History, Drawing, Painting, Photography, Sculpture

RICHMOND

EASTERN KENTUCKY UNIVERSITY, Art Department,* Lancaster Ave, 40475. Tel 606-622-2046. *Chmn* Daniel N Shindelbower
Estab 1910; pub; D; ent req HS grad; degrees BA, BFA and MA Educ 4 yrs; SC 30, LC 6, GC 6
Tuition: Res—$500 per yr; nonres—$1270 per yr
Courses: Painting, Sculpture, Drawing Media, Figure Drawing, Figure Painting, Graphics II, Greek & Roman Art, Metal Casting, Synthetic Media, Senior Exhibition, Twentieth Century Painting
Summer School: Tui; campus res available beginning June

WILLIAMSBURG

CUMBERLAND COLLEGE, Department of Art,* 615 Main St, College Station Box 523, 40769. Tel 606-549-2082. *Head Dept* Russell A Parker
Estab 1959; den; D & E; ent req HS dipl, special approval may be granted for admission; degrees BA and BS 4 yr; scholarships; SC 26, LC 12; enrl D 720, E 90, maj 38
Tuition: Res—$746 per sem; campus res—room and board $562
Courses: Aesthetics, Art Education, Ceramics, Drawing, Graphic Arts, Handicrafts, History of Art & Archaeology, Jewelry, Lettering, Museum Staff Training, Painting, Sculpture, Teacher Training, Basketry, Batik, Enameling, Weaving
Summer School: Enrl 110; term of 5 wks beginning June. Courses—Art Appreciation, Art History, Two and Three Dimensional Studio

WILMORE

ASBURY COLLEGE, Art Dept, 40390. Tel 606-858-3511. *Div Head* Dr Gilbert Roller
Estab 1892; pvt; D & E; ent req HS dipl; degrees AB & BS 4 yr; scholarships; SC 30, LC 6; enrl D 1250, maj 65, others 250
Tuition: $500 per quarter; campus res—room & board $1000
Courses: Aesthetics, Art Education, Art History, Ceramics, Drawing, Handicrafts, Lettering, Mixed Media, Painting, Photography, Printmaking, Sculpture, Teacher Training, Batik, Weaving
Summer School: Enrl 12 each for term of 4 - 8 wks beginning June 9th. Courses—Crafts, Drawing, Painting

LOUISIANA

BATON ROUGE

LOUISIANA STATE UNIVERSITY, Department of Fine Arts,* 70803. Tel 504-388-3202. *Head Dept* Dr Walter E Rutkowski, Ded; *Assoc Prof* Gerald Bower, MFA; *Assoc Prof* Marchita Mauck, PhD; *Prof* Jim Burke, MFA; *Prof* Tom Cavanaugh, MFA; *Prof* Sid Garrett, MFA; *Prof* Paul Dufour, MFA
Estab 1874, dept estab 1935; pub; D & E; ent req HS dipl, ACT scores; degrees BFA 4 yr, MFA 2 additional yrs; scholarships; SC 90, LC 40, GC 40
Tuition: Res—undergrad and grad $277 per sem; nonres—undergrad $742 per sem, grad $527 per sem; campus res—room and board $235-$464 per sem
Courses: Advertising Design, Aesthetics, Art Education, Art History, Ceramics, Commercial Art, Conceptual Art, Constructions, Drafting, Drawing, Film, Goldsmithing, Graphic Arts, Graphic Design, History of Art & Archaeology, Illustration, Interior Design, Jewelry, Landscape Architecture, Lettering, Mixed Media, Painting, Photography, Printmaking, Sculpture, Silversmithing, Teacher Training
Summer School: Tui $122 for term of 9 wks beginning June 5. Courses—per regular session

SOUTHERN UNIVERSITY A & M COLLEGE, Division of Architecture, Southern University Branch PO, 70813. Tel 504-771-3015. *Acting Dir* Henry L Thurman, MA
Estab 1956; pub; D & E; ent req HS dipl; degrees BA 5 yrs; SC 7, GC 12; enrl D 130, non-maj 7, maj 123
Tuition: Res—undergrad $1434 per sem, grad $1059 per sem; non-res undergrad $225 per sem, grad $235
Courses: Architecture, Art Education
Summer School: Dir, Henry L Thurman. Tui $117 for term of 8 wks beginning June. Courses—vary according to student need

HAMMOND

SOUTHEASTERN LOUISIANA UNIVERSITY, Dept of Visual Arts, 70402. *Head Dept* Ronald M Zaccari, EdD; *Prof* Hymel G Falgoust, MA; *Assoc Prof* Barbara Tardo, MA; *Assoc Prof* Barbara Walker, PhD; *Asst Prof* C Roy Blackwood, MFA; *Asst Prof* Ronald Kennedy, MFA; *Instructor* Gail Hood, MFA; *Instructor* Carol Leake, MFA
Estab 1925; pub; D & E; ent req HS dipl, ACT; degrees BA(Educ) & BA(Humanities) 4 yrs; SC 25, LC 4, GC 2; enrl D 109, E 75, maj 109
Courses: Aesthetics, Art Education, Art History, Ceramics, Drawing, Goldsmithing, Graphic Arts, Jewelry, Painting, Photography, Printmaking, Sculpture, Teacher Training

LAFAYETTE

UNIVERSITY OF SOUTHWESTERN LOUISIANA, School of Art & Architecture, 70504. Tel 318-264-6224. *Dir* Michel Pillet. Instrs FT 31, PT 5
Estab 1900; pub; degrees BArchit & BFA 4-5 yrs; enrl univ 14,500
Courses: Advertising Design, Architecture, Art Education, Ceramics, Photography, Choreographic Design, Fine Arts, Interior Architecture

LAKE CHARLES

MCNEESE STATE UNIVERSITY, Department of Visual Arts,* Ryan St, 70609. Tel 318-477-2520. *Head Dept* Nowell A Daste, MA; *Assoc Prof* Grace Ramke, MFA; *Asst Prof* Constance Davis, MFA; *Asst Prof* James A Hooper Jr, MA; *Asst Prof* William Iles, MFA
Estab 1950, dept estab 1953; pub; D & E; ent req HS dipl; degrees BA (Art Educ) and BA (Studio Arts) 4 yrs; scholarships; SC 24, LC 4, GC 1; enrl D 85, E 15, non-maj 215, maj 85
Tuition: Res—$449; campus res—room and board $1120
Courses: Advertising Design, Architecture, Art Education, Art History, Drafting, Drawing, Handicrafts, Painting, Printmaking, Sculpture, Teacher Training, Survey crafts course
Adult Hobby Classes: Enrl 15; tui $75 per sem. Courses—Drawing and Composition, Painting
Summer School: Courses—per regular session

MONROE

NORTHEAST LOUISIANA UNIVERSITY, Department of Art,* College of Liberal Arts, 71209. Tel 318-342-3110. *Head Dept* Edward E Schutz, EdD; *Prof* James B Edwards, PhD; *Assoc Prof* Robert G Ward, MFA; *Asst Prof* Brian R Fassett, MA; *Asst Prof* Richard E Hayes, MFA; *Asst Prof* Gary L Ratcliff, MFA; *Asst Prof* Jean F Taylor, MA; *Asst Prof* Jo Ella Williams, MA
Estab 1931, dept estab 1956; pub; D & E; ent req HS dipl; degrees BA and BFA 4 yrs, MEd; SC 28, LC 4, GC 9; enrl non-maj 300, maj 150, GS 3
Tuition: Res—$80-$206; nonres—$80-$521; campus res available
Courses: Advertising Design, Aesthetics, Art Education, Art History, Ceramics, Drawing, Graphic Arts, Handicrafts, Jewelry, Lettering, Painting, Photography, Printmaking, Sculpture, Teacher Training, Fiber Art, Weaving
Summer School: Tui res—$44-$70; nonres—$44-$175. Courses—per regular session

NATCHITOCHES

NORTHWESTERN STATE UNIVERSITY OF LOUISIANA, Dept of Art, 71457. Tel 318-357-4544. *Head Dept* Billy J Bryant, DEd; *Prof* Grady Harper, PhD; *Prof* Rivers C Murphy, MFA; *Assoc Prof* Charles V Coke, MA; *Assoc Prof* Robert Rector, MFA; *Assoc Prof* Mary C Roberts, DEd; *Assoc Prof* James C Thorn, MFA
Estab 1885; pub; D & E; degrees BA & BS 4 yrs, MA 2 yrs, special prog for advanced students MA in Art; SC 67, LC 17, GC 36; enrl maj 93, grad 9
Courses: †Advertising Design, †Art Education, Art History, Ceramics, Collage, Commercial Art, Drawing, Fashion Arts, Graphic Arts, Graphic Design, Illustration, †Interior Design, Lettering, Mixed Media, Painting, Photography, Printmaking, Sculpture, Teacher Training, Stained Glass, Stringed Instrument Construction
Adult Hobby Classes: Courses—Drawing, Painting

NEW ORLEANS

DELGADO COLLEGE, Department of Fine Arts,* (Formerly Delgado Junior College) 615 City Park Ave, 70119. Tel 504-483-4114.
Dept estab 1967; pub; D & E; ent req HS dipl, 18 yr old; degrees AA and AS 2 yrs; scholarships; SC 12-20, LC 12-20; enrl D 150, E 65, maj 60
Tuition: Res—$340; nonres—$970; no campus res
Courses: Drawing, History of Art & Archaeology, Painting, Art Appreciation

JOHN MCCRADY ART SCHOOL OF NEW ORLEANS,* 910 Bourbon St, 70016. Tel 504-529-5628.
Estab 1942; pvt; D & E; ent req HS dipl, ent exam, examples or color slides of work; degrees none; scholarships; SC 4
Courses: Advertising Design, Commercial Art, Drawing, Fashion Arts, Graphic Design, History of Art & Archaeology, Illustration, Lettering, Painting, Textile Design
Adult Hobby Classes: Courses—Painting (various mediums and techniques)
Children's Classes: Courses—all subjects
Summer School: Dir, Mary B McCrady. Term June and July

LOYOLA UNIVERSITY OF NEW ORLEANS, Department of Visual Arts,* 6363 Saint Charles Ave, 70118. Tel 504-865-2780. *Chmn* Bro Gebhard Frohlich
Den; D & E; ent req HS dipl, ent exam; degrees BA Visual Arts 4 yrs; scholarships; SC 9, LC 3; enrl D 150, E 45, maj 28
Tuition: $2100 per yr
Courses: Ceramics, Drawing, Painting, Sculpture, Teacher Training
Summer School: Chmn, Walter S Maestri IV. Enrl 40; term of 6 wks beginning in June. Courses—Drawing, Painting, Sculpture

NEW ORLEANS ART INSTITUTE,* 2926 Canal St, 70119. Tel 504-822-1453. *Dir* Walter A Labiche
Estab 1970; pvt; D & E; ent req HS equivalent; degrees dipl; enrl D 22, E 22
Tuition: $93.50
Courses: Advertising Design, Calligraphy, Commercial Art, Fashion Arts, Graphic Arts, Graphic Design, Illustration, Lettering, Mixed Media, Painting, Air Brush, Isometrics, Photography Retouching, Technical Illustration

SOUTHERN UNIVERSITY IN NEW ORLEANS, Art Dept, 6400 Press Dr, 70126. Tel 504-282-4401, Ext 267. *Head Dept* Dr Jack Jordan; *Asst Prof* Roscoe Reddix, MA; *Asst Prof* Sara Dickenson, MA; *Asst Prof* Rodney Ferguson, MFA
Estab 1951, dept estab 1960; pub; D & E; ent req HS dipl; BA 4 yrs; enrl D 21, E 26,

non-maj 700, maj 47
Courses: Art Education, Art History, Ceramics, Commercial Art, Drawing, Fashion Arts, Graphic Arts, Handicrafts, Painting, Photography, Printmaking, Sculpture, Teacher Training, Design

TULANE UNIVERSITY
—School of Architecture, 70018. Tel 504-865-6472. *Dean* William K Turner. Instrs FT 19, PT 4
School estab 1907; pvt; degrees BArchit 3 yrs and 5 yrs, MArchit 1 yr; enrl 320
Courses: †Architecture
—Newcomb College, Art Department, 1229 Broadway, 70118. Tel 504-865-4631. *Chmn* John Clemmer; *Prof* Norman Boothby, MFA; *Prof* Jessie Poesch, PhD; *Prof* Donald Robertson, PhD; *Prof* James Steg, MFA; *Prof* Jules Struppeck, MA; *Prof* Pat Trivigno, MA; *Vis Prof* Lucy Lippard, history-criticism - 1979; *Vis Prof* Peter Voulkos, ceramics - 1978
Estab 1886; pvt; D & E; ent req HS dipl, CEEB, interview, review of work by chairman and or faculty (optional); degrees BA and BFA 4 yrs, MA, MFA and MAT 2 yrs; scholarships; SC 33, LC 25, GC 29; enrl D 817 per sem, E 37 per sem
Tuition: Campus res available
Courses: †Art Education, †Art History, †Ceramics, †Drawing, †History of Art & Archaeology, †Painting, †Photography, †Printmaking, †Sculpture, Glass
Adult Hobby Classes: Courses—Ceramics, Drawing, Painting, Photography, Printmaking, Sculpture
Summer School: Acting Dean, Wayne S Woody. Courses—Art History, Ceramics, Drawing, Glass, Painting, Sculpture

UNIVERSITY OF NEW ORLEANS, Dept of Fine Arts, 70122. Tel 504-283-0493. *Chmn* Richard A Johnson, MFA; *Prof* William Thomas Young, EdD; *Prof* Howard Jones, MFA; *Assoc Prof* Doyle Gertjejansen, MFA; *Assoc Prof* Calvin Harlan, MFA; *Assoc Prof* Peggy McDowell, MA; *Assoc Prof* Jim Richard, MFA; *Assoc Prof* George Rowan, MFA; *Asst Prof* Carolyn K Lewis, PhD; *Asst Prof* John P Smith, MA
Estab 1958, dept estab 1968; pub; D & E; ent req HS dipl; degrees BA 4 yrs, MFA 2 yrs; SC 16, LC 11, GC 3; enrl D 14,000 (university), non-maj 1000, maj 150, grad 14
Tuition: Res—undergrad $524 yr, $262 per sem, $103-$222 PT, grad $524 per yr, $262 per sem, $121-$222 PT; nonres—undergrad $727 per sem, $280-$631 PT, grad $512 per sem, $221-$422 PT; campus residence available
Courses: Art Education, †Art History, Drawing, †Graphic Arts, †Painting, Photography, †Printmaking, †Sculpture
Summer School: Tui $139 for term of 6 wks beginning June. Courses—Art History, Art Structure, Drawing, Graphics, Painting

XAVIER UNIVERSITY OF LOUISIANA, Department of Fine Arts,* Palmetto and Pine St, 70125. Tel 504-486-7411. *Chmn* John T Scott, MFA; *Prof Emeritus* Numa Rousseve, MA; *Prof* Claudine McKay, MFA; *Asst Prof* Lloyd Bennett, MFA; *Asst Prof* Charles Graves, MFA; *Instr* Diane Lehder, MA; *Instr* Martin Payton, MFA
Estab 1926, dept estab 1935; den; D & E; ent req HS dipl, SAT or ACT, health cert, C average at least; degrees BA, BFA, BS and MA; scholarships; SC 48, LC 10; enrl D 50, E 12, non-maj 10, maj 52
Tuition: Res—undergrad $1700 per yr, $50 per sem, $75 per cr hr, res—room and board $1260
Courses: †Advertising Design, Aesthetics, †Art Education, Art History, Calligraphy, †Ceramics, Collage, Constructions, †Drawing, Film, †Graphic Arts, †Graphic Design, Handicrafts, Jewelry, Lettering, Mixed Media, †Painting, Photography, †Printmaking, †Sculpture, Stage Design, Teacher Training, Textile Design, Theatre Arts, Video
Adult Hobby Classes: Courses—Creative Crafts

PINEVILLE

LOUISIANA COLLEGE, Dept of Art, 71360. Tel 318-487-7262. *Chmn* John T Suddith; *Assoc Prof* Charles Jeffress
Den; ent req HS grad; degrees BA & BS 4 yrs, 48 hrs of art req plus 78 hrs acad for degree; LC, Lab C; enrl maj 35
Courses: Art Education, Studio Arts

RUSTON

LOUISIANA TECH UNIVERSITY, School of Art & Architecture, PO Box 6277 Tech Station, 71270. Tel 318-257-3909. *Dir* Joseph W Strother. Instrs FT 19, PT 6
Estab 1904; pub; D; ent req HS dipl; degrees BA, BFA, MA & MFA 4 yrs, BArchit 5 yrs; SC 98, LC 8, GC 87; enrl maj 652, others 538
Tuition: $116.50 per quarter
Courses: †Architecture, Ceramics, Drawing, Graphic Design, Interior Design, Painting, Photography, Printmaking, Sculpture
Summer School: Summer program in Rome

SHREVEPORT

CENTENARY COLLEGE OF LOUISIANA, Department of Art, Centenary Blvd, 71104. Tel 318-869-5261. *Chmn Dept* Willard Cooper, MFA; *Adjunct Prof* Elizabeth Friedenberg, MA; *Lectr* David Middleton, MEd; *Lectr* B Lee Sutton, BID
Estab 1825, dept estab 1935; den; D & E; ent req HS dipl, SAT or ACT; degrees BA 4 yrs; scholarships; SC 22, LC 8; enrl D 125 per sem
Tuition: $2200 per yr, $95 per hr; campus res—room & board $1520 per yr
Courses: Aesthetics, Art Education, Art History, Ceramics, Drafting, Drawing, Graphic Arts, Handicrafts, †Painting, Printmaking, Sculpture, Teacher Training, Weaving
Adult Hobby Classes: Enrl 550 (for people over 60); no tui. Courses—Studio Art & Appreciation
Summer School: Dir, Willard Cooper. Tui $48 per hr for term of 8 wks beginning June 8. Courses—Art Education, Art History, Drawing, Painting

THIBODAUX

NICHOLLS STATE UNIVERSITY, Dept of Art, PO Box 2025, 70301. *Head Dept* Dr Armando Garzon-Blanco, PhD; *Asst Prof* Lula Ameen, MED; *Instructor* Rob Carpenter; *Instructor* Michael Howes, MFA. Instrs FT 5
Estab 1948; pub; D & E; ent req HS dipl, ACT; degrees BA 4 yrs; SC 73, LC 6; enrl D 100, non-maj 20, maj 80, others 20
Tuition: Res—undergrad $215 per sem; nonres—undergrad $530 per sem; campus res room $270, board $300
Courses: †Advertising Design, Art Education, Art History, †Ceramics, Commercial Art, Conceptual Art, †Drawing, Graphic Arts, Graphic Design, Illustration, Mixed Media, †Painting, Photography, †Printmaking, †Sculpture, Teacher Training, Applied Design, Rendering, Water Media
Summer School: Enrl 3000; tui res—$110, nonres—$170, room $135, board $170; term of 9 wks beginning June 6th. Courses—Advertising Design, Art Education, Art History, Ceramics, Painting, Photography, Printmaking, Sculpture

MAINE

AUGUSTA

UNIVERSITY OF MAINE AT AUGUSTA, Division of Arts and Humanities, University Heights, 04330. Tel 207-622-7131. *Chmn Div* Charles D Danforth, MM; *Prof* Joshua Nadel, MFA; *Prof* Rhoda Oakley, MA; *Prof* Philip Paratore, MFA; *Prof* Michael Woods, MFA
Estab 1965, dept estab 1970; pub; D & E; ent req HS dipl; degrees AA 2 yrs; SC 20, LC 8; enrl D 50, E 40, non-maj 40, maj 50
Tuition: Res—$770 per yr, $30 per cr hr; non-res—$2612 per yr, $97 per cr hr
Courses: Advertising Design, Aesthetics, Art History, Ceramics, Drawing, Graphic Arts, Mixed Media, Painting, Photography, Printmaking, Sculpture, Video
Adult Hobby Classes: Enrl 50; tui $50 per 10 wk class. Courses—Furniture Refinishing, Pottery
Summer School: Asst Dean Acad Affairs, Tom Abbott. Enrl 30-50; tui $30 per cr hr for term of 7 wks beginning last wk in June. Courses—Art History, Drawing, Painting

BRUNSWICK

BOWDOIN COLLEGE, Art Department, Visual Art Center, 04011. Tel 207-725-8731, Ext 697 & 695. *Chmn* Larry Lutchmansingh, PhD; *Dir Visual Arts Prog* Gerald Haggerty; *Instr* Philip C Beam, PhD; *Instr* James Harley, MA; *Instr* John McKee, MA; *Instr* Jeffrey Muller, PhD; *Instr* Joseph Nicoletti, MFA
Estab 1794; pvt; D & E; ent req HS dipl; degrees BA 4 yrs; scholarships; SC 15, LC 18; enrl D 655, maj 47
Tuition: $5100 per yr, campus res—room & board $2000
Courses: †Art History, †Painting

DEER ISLE

HAYSTACK MOUNTAIN SCHOOL OF CRAFTS, 04627. Tel 207-348-6946. *Dir* Howard M Evans. Instrs FT 28
Estab 1951; pvt; D, Summer school; ent req HS dipl; enrl D 75
Tuition: $80 per wk plus shop fees
Courses: Ceramics, Graphic Arts, Photography, Fabric, Glassblowing, Metalsmithing, Stained Glass, Woodworking, Weaving

GORHAM

UNIVERSITY OF SOUTHERN MAINE, Art Dept, College Ave, 04038. Tel 207-780-5460. *Chmn* Michael G Moore, MFA; *Assoc Prof* Jeanna Bearce, MFA E03; *Assoc Prof* Duncan Hewitt, MFA; *Assoc Prof* Juris Ubans, MFA
Estab 1878, dept estab 1956; pub; D & E; ent req HS dipl, portfolio; degrees BFA, BA & BS 4 yrs; SC 9, LC 2; enrl maj 120
Tuition: Res—undergrad $820 per yr, $410 per sem, $30 per cr hr; nonres—undergrad $2625 per yr, $97 per cr hr; campus residence available
Courses: Aesthetics, †Art Education, Art History, †Ceramics, †Drawing, Museum Staff Training, †Painting, †Photography, †Printmaking, †Sculpture, Teacher Training, †Textile Design, Two & Three Dimensional Design
Summer School: Dir, William Mortensen, CED. Tui $30 per cr hr. Courses—Art History, Ceramics, Design, Drawing, Photography, Painting

KENNEBUNKPORT

ROGER DEERING SCHOOL OF OUTDOOR PAINTING,* Ocean Ave, 04046. Tel 207-967-2273. *Dir* Roger Deering; *Registrar & Secy* Winifred Deering
Estab 1940; pvt; D; enrl 15 for each course
Summer School: Term of 5 wks beginning June through July. Courses—Demonstrations, Lectures, Marine and Landscape Oil and Watercolor, Outdoor Painting Classes

LEWISTON

BATES COLLEGE, Art Dept, Liberal Arts College, 04240. Tel 207-783-3941. *Chmn* Donald Lent. Instrs FT 3, PT 1
Estab 1864, dept estab 1964; pvt; D; degrees BA 4 yr; SC 9, LC 13; enrl 1200 total
Courses: Art History, Ceramics, Drawing, Painting, Printmaking

ORONO

UNIVERSITY OF MAINE, Art Department, 04469. Tel 207-581-7691. *Chmn* Michael H Lewis, MFA; *Prof* Vincent A Hartgen, MFA; *Assoc Prof* Barbara Cushing, MFA; *Assoc Prof* David O Decker, MA; *Assoc Prof* Ronald Ghiz, MFA; *Asst Prof* David Ebitz, PhD; *Asst Prof* C Regina Kelley, MFA; *Asst Prof* Mary Ann Stankiewicz, PhD
Estab 1862, dept estab 1946; pub; D & E; ent req HS dipl, 3 CEEB tests; degrees BA and BS 4 yrs; SC 24, LC 24; enrl D 135, maj 135
Tuition: Res—undergrad $895 per yr, $448 per sem; nonres—undergrad $2688 per yr, $1344 per sem; campus res—room & board $1855 per yr
Courses: †Art Education, Art History, †Drawing, †Painting, Printmaking, †Sculpture, Teacher Training
Summer School: Dir, Edward W Hackett. Tui $30 per cr hr. Courses—Basic Drawing, Basic Painting, Fundamentals of Painting, Principles of Art, Problems in Art, Teaching of Art

PORTLAND

PORTLAND SCHOOL OF ART, 04101. Tel 207-775-3052. *Dir* William C Collins, MFA; *Instructor* Richard A Butz, MFA; *Instructor* Edwin P Douglas, MFA; *Instructor* John Eide, MFA; *Instructor* Allan R Gardner; *Instructor* Joseph Guertin, BFA; *Instructor* Ernest T Thompson; *Instructor* John T Ventimiglia, MFA; *Visiting Prof* Harold Schremmer, silver & light metals
Estab 1882; pvt; D & E; ent req HS dipl, portfolio; degrees BFA 4 yr (under Maine law, an academically advanced high school senior may take the freshman yr at Portland School of Art for both HS and Portland School of Art credit); SC 37, LC 9; enrl D 230, E 200, maj 193, others 140 PT
Tuition: $2750 per yr, student activity fee $10 per sem, non-maj lab fees $15-$30 per sem, maj lab fees $15-$50 per sem; no campus res
Courses: Art History, †Ceramics, Drawing, †Graphic Design, History of Art & Archaeology, †Jewelry, †Painting, †Photography, †Printmaking, †Sculpture, †Silversmithing
Adult Hobby Classes: Enrl 200; tui $75 per course plus lab fee $10-$15. Courses—Ceramics, Design, Drawing, Photography, Printmaking
Children's Classes: Enrl 140; tui $75 per class. Courses—Ceramics, Drawing, Photography, Sculpture, Silversmithing
Summer School: Enrl 81; tui $75 per cr for term of 8 wks beginning June 23, 1979. Courses—Art History, Ceramics, Drawing, English, Graphic Design, Jewelry & Silversmithing, Painting, Photography, Printmaking, Sculpture, Two & Three Dimensional Design, Watercolor

SKOWHEGAN

SKOWHEGAN SCHOOL OF PAINTING AND SCULPTURE, Box 449, Skowhegan, ME. (Mailing Add: Winter Office, 329 E 68th St, New York, NY 10021) Tel 207-474-9345; 212-861-9270. *VPres* Roy Leaf. Instrs Six each summer; 7 visiting artists
Estab 1946; pvt summer school for independent work; ent req presentation of slide portfolio; degrees credits recognized for transfer, no degrees; enrl 65
Tuition: Summer only $2200 includes room & board (residency required)
Courses: Drawing, Painting, Sculpture, Fresco Technique

WATERVILLE

COLBY COLLEGE, Art Dept, 04901. Tel 207-873-1131, Ext 215. *Chmn Dept* James M Carpenter, PhD; *Prof* William B Miller, PhD; *Assoc Prof* Harriett Matthews, MFA; *Asst Prof* Barbara Kassel, MFA; *Asst Prof* Margaret Miller, BA
Estab 1813, dept estab 1944; pvt; D & E; ent req HS dipl; degrees BA 4 yrs; scholarships; SC 12, LC 17; enrl D 350, non-maj 305, maj 45
Tuition: $4300 per yr; campus res available
Courses: History of Art & Archaeology, Painting, Sculpture

MARYLAND

BALTIMORE

COLLEGE OF NOTRE DAME OF MARYLAND, Art Dept, 4701 N Charles St, 21210. Tel 301-435-0100. *Chmn* Ruth Nagle Watkins, MEd; *Prof* Mary John Bersch, MFA; *Assoc Prof* Virginia Adams, MFA; *Assoc Prof* Gladys Goldstein, BA
Pvt den; D & E; ent req HS dipl, SAT; degrees BA 4 yrs; scholarships; SC 16, LC 8; enrl D 285, non-maj 250, maj 35
Tuition: Res—undergrad $4100 yr, $2050 per sem; nonres—undergrad $2800 per yr, $1400 per sem; campus res—room & board $1700. Adult Classes—$65 per cr
Courses: Advertising Design, Aesthetics, Art History, Ceramics, Collage, Commercial Art, Drawing, Film, Graphic Arts, Graphic Design, Handicrafts, History of Art & Archaeology, Interior Design, Painting, Photography, Printmaking, Sculpture, Stage Design, Teacher Training
Summer School: Dir, Mary Lu McNeal. Tui $65 per cr. Courses—Advanced Painting

COMMUNITY COLLEGE OF BALTIMORE, Dept of Fine & Applied Arts, 2901 Liberty Heights Ave, 21215. Tel 301-396-7980. *Chmn* Bennard B Perlman, MA; *Prof* Nelson Adlin, MA; *Prof* Allyn O Harris, MFA; *Assoc Prof* David Bahr, MFA; *Assoc Prof* Carlton Leverette, MFA; *Assoc Prof* Frieda Sohn, BA; *Instructor* Carroll Frey, BFA; *Instructor* Sally Monteferrante, MEd. Instrs FT 8, PT 11
Estab 1947; pub; D & E; ent req HS equivalency, ent exam; degrees AA 2 yrs; scholarships; SC 17, LC 2; enrl D & E 9400, non-maj 400, maj 190
Tuition: City res—$360 per yr, $180 per sem, $18 per cr hr; state res—$720 per yr, $360 per sem, $36 per cr hr; nonres—$1080 per yr, $540 per sem; no campus res
Courses: Advertising Design, †Art Education, Art History, Ceramics, †Commercial

Art, Drawing, Graphic Arts, Graphic Design, History of Art & Archaeology, Interior Design, Jewelry, Lettering, †Painting, †Photography, Printmaking, Sculpture, Textile Design, Fashion Design
Summer School: Tui same as above per cr hr for term of 5 wks beginning June

COPPIN STATE COLLEGE, Art Dept, 2500 W North Ave, 21218. Tel 301-448-5925, 448-5929. *Dept Coordr* Luke A Shaw. Instrs FT 1, PT 2
Degrees BA, BS & MA; scholarships; SC 6, LC 7; enrl D 350, E 45
Courses: Advertising Design, Art Education, Art History, Calligraphy, Ceramics, Collage, Drawing, Film, Graphic Design, Lettering, Painting, Photography, Printmaking, Sculpture, Teacher Training, Theatre Arts

JOHNS HOPKINS UNIVERSITY
—**Department of the History of Art,** Charles and 34th Sts, 21218. Tel 301-338-7117. *Chmn* Herbert L Kessler. Instrs FT 7, PT 2
Estab 1947; pvt; D & E; degrees 4 yrs; scholarships; LC; enrl 10-30 in advanced courses, 200 in introductory courses
Tuition: $4700 per yr; campus res available
Courses: Art History
—**School of Medicine, Department of Art as Applied to Medicine,** 725 N Wolfe St, 21205. Tel 301-955-3213. *Dir Dept* Ranice W Crosby, MLA; *Asst Prof* Gary P Lees, MS; *Asst Prof* Leon Schlossberg; *Instr* Howard C Bartner, MA; *Instr* Elizabeth Blumenthal; *Instr* J Lindsey Burch; *Instr* Marjorie Gregerman, BA; *Instr* Timothy Hengst, MA
Univ estab 1876, School Medicine estab 1893, dept estab 1911; pvt; D; ent req Baccalaureate degree; degrees MA 2 yrs; scholarships; SC, LC 5, GC 14; enrl 14, grad 13, special 1
Tuition: $4050 per yr; campus res—room & board $1164 per yr
Courses: Display, Drawing, Graphic Design, Illustration, Intermedia, Mixed Media, Painting, Photography, Sculpture, Video

MARYLAND INSTITUTE, College of Art, 1300 W Mt Royal Ave, 21217. Tel 301-669-9200. *Pres* Fred Lazarus IV. Instrs FT 49, PT 46
Estab 1826; pvt; D & E; ent req HS grad, exam; degrees BFA and MFA 4 yrs; scholarships; enrl D 1107, E 554, Sat 280
Tuition: $3750 per yr; campus res—$2500
Courses: Ceramics, Drawing, Graphic Design, Handicrafts, Illustration, Interior Design, Painting, Photography, Printmaking, Sculpture, Teacher Training, Foundation
Summer School: Dir Continuing Studies, Barbara Miller. Enrl 850; tui $3000 per yr for Continuing Studies
—**Hoffberger School of Painting,** 21217. *Artist-in-Res* Grace Hartigan
Fel awarded annually for study at the grad level; enrl limited to 20
—**Rinehart School of Sculpture,** 21217. *Sculptor-in-Res* Norman Carlberg
—**Mount Royal School of Painting,** 21217. *Artist-in-Res* Babe Shapiro
MFA programs

MORGAN STATE UNIVERSITY, Department of Art,* Hillen Road at Coldspring Lane, 21239. Tel 301-444-3333. *Chmn* Oliver Patrick Scott, MA; *Prof* James S Lewis, MFA; *Assoc Prof* James E Jones, MFA; *Assoc Prof* Patrick F McQuire, MFA; *Asst Prof* Suzanne Daniel, MA; *Asst Prof* Kenneth L Royster, MFAE; *Asst Prof* Samuel L Green, MA; *Instr* Thelma Hill, BS
Estab 1867, dept estab 1950; pub; D & E; ent req HS dipl; degrees BA (Art) and BS (Art Educ) 4 yr, MA (Art History & Museology) and MA (Art Studio) 2 yr; scholarships; SC 28, LC 11, GC 17; enrl D 340, E 50, non-maj 250, maj 140, GS 11
Tuition: Res—undergrad $830 per yr, $415 per sem, grad $38 per cr hr; nonres—undergrad $1750 per yr, $865 per sem; campus res—room and board $1721
Courses: Aesthetics, †Architecture, †Art Education, †Art History, Ceramics, Costume Design & Construction, Drafting, Drawing, Film, Graphic Design, Handicrafts, Interior Design, Jewelry, †Landscape Architecture, Lettering, Mixed Media, Museum Staff Training, †Painting, †Photography, Printmaking, †Sculpture, †Stage Design, Teacher Training, Textile Design, Theatre Arts, Video, Art Appreciation, Weaving
Children's Classes: Enrl 20; tui $10 per sem. Courses—Painting, Printmaking, Sculpture
Summer School: Dir, Dr Beryl W Williams. Tui $35 per cr hr for term of 6 wks beginning June and July. Courses—Art Appreciation, Art Education, Basic Design, Photography

SCHULER SCHOOL OF FINE ARTS,* 5 E Lafayette Ave, 21202. Tel 301-685-3568. *Dir* Hans C Schuler
Estab 1959; pvt; D & E; degrees 4 yrs; SC 9, GC 3; enrl D 50, E 30, grad 2
Tuition: $1200 per yr, part-time students pay by schedule for sem
Courses: Drawing, Graphic Arts, Painting, Sculpture
Children's Classes: Tui $165-$225 (summer - ages 14 and over)
Summer School: Dir, Hans C Schuler. Enrl 30; tui $180 for term of 6 wks beginning June, $270 for 6 hrs. Courses—Drawing, Oil Painting, Sculpture, Watercolor

TOWSON STATE UNIVERSITY, Dept of Art, 21204. Tel 301-321-2808. *James W/Flood* . Instrs FT 24, PT 12
Estab 1866; pub; D & E; ent req HS grad; degrees BA, BS & MEd(Art Educ) 4 yr
Courses: Art Education, Art History, Ceramics, Drawing, Graphic Arts, Jewelry, Painting, Sculpture, Textile Design, Enameling, Weaving, Wood & Metal
Summer School: Enrl 450; two 5 wk sessions

BEL AIR

HARFORD COMMUNITY COLLEGE, Humanities Div, 401 Thomas Run Rd, 21014. Tel 301-879-8920. *Assoc Dean* Homer Morris. Instrs FT 4, PT 5
Estab 1957; pub; D & E; ent req HS dipl; degrees AA 2 yrs; scholarships; SC 17, LC 4; enrl FT 1000, PT 1000
Tuition: No campus res
Courses: Ceramics, Drawing, Graphic Arts, History of Art & Archaeology, Interior Design, Painting, Photography, Sculpture, Architectural Drawing, Design

BOWIE

BOWIE STATE COLLEGE, Department of Fine and Performing Arts, Jericho Park Rd, 20715. Tel 301-464-3000. *Chairperson Dept* Dr H D Flowers II; *Instr* Isaac Creek; *Instr* Connie Devito, MA; *Instr* Clark Mester Jr, MFA; *Instr* Lyn Ostrov, MFA; *Instr* Robert Ward, MFA; *Instr* Amos White, MFA
Estab 1865, dept estab 1968; pub; D; ent req HS dipl; degrees BA (Art) and BS (Art Educ); SC 7, LC 3; enrl D 1600, E 350, non-maj 180, maj 45
Tuition: Res—undergrad $830 per yr, grad $45 per cr hr; nonres—undergrad $1730 per yr; campus res available
Courses: Art Education, Art History, Ceramics, Collage, Drawing, Graphic Arts, Mixed Media, Painting, Photography, Printmaking, Sculpture, Teacher Training
Summer School: Dir, Dr Ida Brandon. Courses—Ceramics, Media Workshop

CATONSVILLE

CATONSVILLE COMMUNITY COLLEGE, Art & Applied Art Dept, 21228. *Chmn Art* William Zwingle; *Chmn Applied Arts & Design* Stuart M Singer
Estab 1957; pub; D & E; ent req HS dipl; degrees cert & AA 2 yrs; scholarships; SC 26, LC 6; enrl D 600, E 400, non-maj 200, maj 300, applied arts maj 350
Tuition: $20 per cr
Courses: †Advertising Design, Aesthetics, Architecture, Art Education, Art History, Ceramics, Commercial Art, Drafting, Drawing, Film, †Graphic Arts, Graphic Design, History of Art & Archaeology, Illustration, Interior Design, Lettering, Painting, †Photography, Sculpture, Theatre Arts, Video, History of Photography, Typography
Summer School: Same as above

UNIVERSITY OF MARYLAND BALTIMORE COUNTY, Visual Arts Department, 5401 Wilkens Ave, 21228. Tel 301-455-2150. *Chmn* LeRoy Morais, MFA; *Prof* Stan VanDerBeek; *Assoc Prof* Patrick Canavan; *Assoc Prof* James Fasanelli; *Assoc Prof* Jaromir Stephany; *Assoc Prof* Fred Stern; *Asst Prof* Harvey Kirstel; *Vis Asst Prof* Bill Schmidt, studio - 1979-80
Estab 1966, dept estab 1966; pub; D & E; ent req HS dipl, SAT; degrees BA 4 yrs; SC 27, LC 12, GC 4; enrl in dept D 485, non-maj 375, maj 110
Tuition: Res—undergrad $410 per sem, grad $55 per hr; nonres—undergrad $1175 per sem, grad $100 per hr; campus res—room & board $785 per yr
Courses: Advertising Design, Aesthetics, †Art History, Calligraphy, Ceramics, Collage, Commercial Art, Conceptual Art, †Drawing, †Film, †Graphic Arts, †Graphic Design, †History of Art & Archaeology, Intermedia, Lettering, Mixed Media, †Painting, †Photography, Printmaking, †Video

COLLEGE PARK

UNIVERSITY OF MARYLAND, Art Dept, Art-Sociology Bldg, 20742. Tel 301-454-3431. *Chmn* David C Driskell. Instrs FT 40, PT 3
Estab 1944; pub; D; ent req 3.0 grad average; degrees BA, MA, MFA, PhD 4 yrs; SC 39, LC 37, GC 22; enrl 3200 per sem, maj 600, grad 100
Tuition: Res—undergrad $842 yr, grad $50 per cr hr; nonres—undergrad $2562 yr, grad $95 per cr hr
Courses: Art Education, Art History, Drawing, Museum Staff Training, Painting, Printmaking, Sculpture, Design
Summer School: Tui $41 per cr hr for term of 6 wks beginning mid-May through June, second session July through mid-August. Courses as above

CUMBERLAND

ALLEGANY COMMUNITY COLLEGE,* Willow Brook Rd, PO Box 870, 21502. Tel 301-724-7700. *Head Dept* Jerry L Post
Estab 1966; pub; D & E; ent req HS dipl; degrees AA 2 yrs; scholarship; SC 6, LC 1; enrl Enrl D 30, E 9
Tuition: No campus res
Courses: Ceramics, Drawing, Painting, Theatre Arts, Survey of Art History, Two & Three Dimensional Design
Summer School: Term of 6 wks beginning July. Courses—Painting, Two Dimensional Design

EMMITSBURG

MOUNT SAINT MARY'S COLLEGE, Fine Arts Department,* 21727. Tel 301-447-6122. *Chmn* Lewis McAllister, MA; *Prof* John Lyle, MA; *Prof* Dorothea Barrick O'Toole, MFA
Estab 1808; pvt; D & E; ent req HS dipl, SAT; degrees BA and BS 4 yrs, MFA 2 yrs; scholarships; SC 9, LC 10; enrl D 1200, maj 12
Tuition: $2500 per yr, $1250 per sem; campus res available
Courses: Art History, Drawing, Painting, Sculpture, Theatre Arts

FREDERICK

HOOD COLLEGE, Department of Art, 21701. Tel 301-663-3131. *Chairperson* Alexander Russo, DA; *Assoc Prof* Elaine Gates, MFA; *Assoc Prof* Mary Ellen Randolph, MA; *Instr* Judith Lyons, MFA; *Instr* William Bucher, MFA; *Lectr* Anne Derbes, PhD
Estab 1893; pvt; W; D; ent req HS dipl; degrees BA 4 yrs; SC 18, LC 16; enrl D 700, maj 60
Tuition: Res—undergrad $5500 per yr; nonres—undergrad $3800 per yr; campus res—room & board $2000
Courses: Advertising Design, Aesthetics, Art Education, Art History, Calligraphy, Ceramics, Collage, Commercial Art, Costume Design & Construction, Display, Photography, Printmaking, Sculpture, Teacher Training, Textile Design, Theatre Arts, Video, Art Therapy, Visual Communications
Summer School: Chairperson Dept Educ, Dr Charles Tressler. Tui by course for term of 6 wks, June - Aug. Courses—Internships and Independent Studies, Photography, Watercolor and Sketching, Woodcut

FROSTBURG

FROSTBURG STATE COLLEGE, Department of Art & Art Education,* East College Ave, 21532. Tel 301-689-4000. *Head Dept* George Kramers
Estab 1898; pub; D; ent req HS dipl; degrees BA (Art, Art Educ), BS and MEd (Art Educ) 4 yrs; SC 25, LC 5; enrl D 230, maj 150, GS 13
Tuition: Res—$310 per sem; nonres—$760 per sem; campus res—room and board $1330-$1502 per yr
Courses: Advertising Design, Art Education, Art History, Ceramics, Drawing, Graphic Design, Jewelry, Painting, Photography, Printmaking, Sculpture, Teacher Training, Textile Design, Two & Three Dimensional Design
Children's Classes: Tui $5. Sat school program
Summer School: Tui $25 per cr hr for term of 4 wks beginning May

LARGO

PRINCE GEORGE'S COMMUNITY COLLEGE, Art Department,* Humanities Division, 301 Largo Rd, 20870. Tel 301-336-6000, Ext 324. *Chmn* Jerry Parsons, MFA; *Assoc Prof* Doyle Eskew, MFA; *Assoc Prof* Cecile C Huff, MFA; *Assoc Prof* Gerald King, MFA; *Assoc Prof* John Krumrein, MFA; *Assoc Prof* Joseph Mayer, MFA
Estab 1958, dept estab 1967; pub; D & E; ent req HS dipl, CGP test; degrees AA; scholarships; SC 18, LC 2; enrl D 220, E 140, maj 11
Tuition: Res—In County $17.50 per hr, In State $41 per hr; nonres—$71 per hr; no campus res
Courses: Advertising Design, Art History, Ceramics, Drawing, Illustration, Jewelry, Lettering, Painting, Printmaking, Sculpture

SAINT MARY'S CITY

SAINT MARY'S COLLEGE OF MARYLAND, Arts & Letters Div, 20686. Tel 301-994-1600, Ext 387. *Chmn* Michael Glaser, PhD; *Assoc Prof* Jonathan Ingersoll, MS; *Assoc Prof* William Thomas Rowe, MFA; *Asst Prof* Joseph B Ross, MA; *Asst Prof* Norma Strickland; *Instructor* Sandra L Underwood, MA
Estab 1964; pub; D & E; ent req HS dipl, SAT scores; degrees BA & BS 4 yrs; scholarships; SC 14, LC 16; enrl D 155, E 43, non-maj 128, maj 70
Tuition: Res—undergrad $600 per yr; nonres—undergrad $1500 per yr; campus res—room & board $1135
Courses: Art Education, Art History, Ceramics, Drawing, Graphic Arts, Handicrafts, Jewelry, Museum Staff Training, Painting, Photography, Printmaking, Sculpture, Stage Design, Theatre Arts
Summer School: Dir, Dr John Rushbrook. Enrl 7-15; tui $30 per cr for term of 6 wks

SALISBURY

SALISBURY STATE COLLEGE, Art Dept, College & Camden Ave, 21801. Tel 301-546-3261, Ext 417. *Chmn* Kent N Kimmel, MA; *Asst Prof* James L Burgess, MA; *Asst Prof* Nancy L Lytwyn, MS; *Asst Prof* Marie A Tator, MA; *Instructor* John R Cleary, MFA; *Instructor* Ursula M Ehrhardt, MA
Estab 1925, dept estab 1970; pub; D & E; ent req HS dipl, SAT verbal & math; degrees BA, BS & BSW 4 yrs, MA & MEd 1 yr; SC 26, LC 7, GC 1; enrl non-maj 400, maj 70, grad 2
Tuition: Res—undergrad $705 per yr, $352.50 per sem, $25 per cr hr, other $20 reg-col ctr; nonres—undergrad $1605 per yr, $802.50 per sem, $35 per cr hr, other $20 reg-col ctr, grad $48 per cr hr, $20 reg-col ctr; campus res—room and board $1300
Courses: Aesthetics, †Art Education, †Ceramics, †Commercial Art, Costume Design & Construction, Drawing, Film, †Graphic Design, †Handicrafts, †History of Art & Archaeology, Museum Staff Training, †Painting, †Photography, †Printmaking, †Sculpture, Stage Design, †Teacher Training, †European Field Study, †Independent Study, †Principles of Color
Summer School: Dir, Dr Harold Schaeffer. Courses—Various art education and studio courses

SILVER SPRING

MARYLAND COLLEGE OF ART AND DESIGN, 10500 Georgia Ave, 20902. Tel 301-649-4454. *Pres* Terrence J Coffman; *Academic Dean* Beatrice Rivas Sanchez; *Instructor* Christopher Bartlett, MFA; *Instructor* Oscar Chelimsky, BA; *Instructor* Ursula Gill; *Instructor* Lewis Hawkins, MFA; *Instructor* Jack Hammond, MEd; *Instructor* Jeannette Heiberger, AA; *Instructor* Charles Mendez, BA; *Instructor* Ellen Vincent, MFA
Estab 1955; pvt; D & E; ent req HS dipl, portfolio interview; degrees AA 2 yrs; scholarships; SC 30, LC 12; enrl D 125, E 50, non-maj 135, maj 40
Tuition: $2700 per yr, $900 per quarter, $72 per cr hr; no campus res
Courses: Advertising Design, Art History, Ceramics, †Commercial Art, †Drawing, Graphic Arts, Graphic Design, Illustration, †Painting, Photography, Printmaking, Sculpture
Children's Classes: Enrl 12, tui $50 per course. Courses—Drawing, Painting
Summer School: Dir, Terrence J Coffman. Tui same as above. Courses—Same as regular quarters

TOWSON

GOUCHER COLLEGE, Art Department,* 1021 Dulaney Valley Rd, 21204. Tel 301-825-3300. *Chmn* Lincoln F Johnson, Jr
Estab 1885; pvt; D; ent req HS dipl, SAT achievement tests (CEEB), American College Testing Program; degrees MA 4 yrs, MA (Dance Movement Therapy) 2 yrs; scholarships; SC 38, LC 18; enrl D 970, non-maj 558, maj (art) 29
Tuition: $4050 per yr; campus res available
Courses: Aesthetics, Art History, Ceramics, Constructions, Costume Design & Construction, Drawing, Film, Graphic Design, Handicrafts, History of Art & Archaeology, Museum Staff Training, Painting, Photography, Printmaking, Restoration & Conservation, Sculpture, Stage Design, Teacher Training, Theatre Arts
Summer School: Dir, Fontaine M Belford. Enrl 160; tui $50 per cr hr for term of 4 wks beginning June 12 and July 10. Courses—(Art) Dance, Fibers Workshop, Nature Drawing Workshop, Photography, Pottery Workshop, Theatre

WESTMINSTER

WESTERN MARYLAND COLLEGE, Art Dept, 21157. Tel 301-848-7000, Ext 241. *Head Dept* Wasyl Palijczuk. Instrs FT 3, PT 1
Estab 1867; independent; D & E; ent req HS dipl, ent exam, SAT; degrees BA, BS & MEd 4 yrs; SC 15, LC 12, GC 6; enrl D 1113, maj 35-50, grad 13
Tuition: $3475 per yr; campus res $1550
Courses: Aesthetics, Art Education, Ceramics, Drawing, History of Art & Archaeology, Illustration, Jewelry, Lettering, Painting, Photography, Printmaking, Sculpture, Teacher Training, Design, Watercolor
Children's Classes: Enrl over 120 Sat AM conducted by col students
Summer School: Two 5 wk terms beginning June 21. Courses—Ceramics, Painting, Printmaking, Sculpture, Weaving

MASSACHUSETTS

AMHERST

AMHERST COLLEGE, Dept of Fine Arts, Mead Art Bldg, 01002. Tel 413-542-2365. *Chmn Dept* Robert Sweeney. Instrs FT 7
Estab 1822; pvt; D; ent req HS dipl; degrees BA 4 yrs; scholarships; SC 15, LC 15
Tuition: Approx $4550 per yr; campus res approx $1854
Courses: Aesthetics, Art History, Drawing, Display, Film, Anatomy, Serigraphy

UNIVERSITY OF MASSACHUSETTS, AMHERST
—**College of Arts and Sciences,** Department of Art, 01002. Tel 413-545-1902. *Chmn Dept* George Wardlaw. Instrs FT 41
Dept estab 1958; pub; ent req HS grad, portfolio required, 15 units HS, ent exam; degrees BA(Studio, Art History) and BFA (Studio, Interior Design, Art Educ) 4 yrs, MA(Art History), MFA(Ceramics, Painting, Printmaking, Sculpture), MS(Interior Design), MAT; SC 40, LC 19, GC 20; enrl maj undergrad 450, grad 80
Courses: Art Education, Art History, Ceramics, Drawing, Graphic Design, Interior Design, Painting, Photography, Printmaking, Sculpture, Teacher Training, Computer Graphics, Glassblowing, Light Workshop, Three-Dimensional Design, Two-Dimensional Design
—**Art History Prog,** 317 Bartlett Hall, 01003. Tel 413-545-3595. *Dir* Craig Harbison, PhD; *Prof* Jack Benson, PhD; *Prof* Iris Cheney, PhD; *Prof* Paul Norton, PhD; *Prof* Mark Roskill, PhD; *Assoc Prof* Walter B Denny, PhD; *Asst Prof* Kristine Edmondson-Haney, PhD; *Asst Prof* Martha Hoppin, PhD; *Asst Prof* Anne Mochon, PhD
Estab 1947, prog estab 1958; pub; D & E; ent req HS dipl and transcript, SAT; degrees BA(Art History) 4 yrs, MA(Art History) 2 yrs; scholarships; LC 36, GC 8; enrl D 1400, non-maj 600, maj 55, grad 35
Tuition: Res—undergrad $525 per yr, grad $40 per hr; nonres—undergrad $2150 per yr, grad $108 per hr; campus res—room & board $1700 per yr
Courses: Aesthetics, Architecture, †Art History, History of Art & Archaeology, Museum Staff Training
Summer School: Enrl 15 per course. Tui $30 per cr and $42 service fee for term of 6 wks beginning June 2 and July 14. Courses—American Art and Modern Art
—**College of Food and Natural Resources,** Dept Landscape Archit and Regional Planning, Landscape Archit Prog, 01003. Tel 413-545-2255. *Head* E Bruce MacDougall, PhD; *Dir MLA Prog* Nicholas Dines, MLA
Estab 1903; pub; D; ent req Bachelor's degree, grad rec, exams, portfolio; degrees MLA 3 yrs; SC 6, LC 5; enrl 35
Tuition: Res—$335 per sem, $35 per cr hr; nonres—$775 per sem, $78 per cr hr; campus res—room & board $4000 per yr
Courses: Drafting, Drawing, Landscape Architecture

AUBURNDALE

LASELL JUNIOR COLLEGE, Art Department,* 1844 Commonwealth Ave, 02166. Tel 617-243-2000. *Head* Leonie S Bennett
Estab 1851; pvt; W; D & E; ent req HS dipl, ent exam in some depts, portfolio in art dept; degrees AA and AS 2 yrs; scholarships
Tuition: Res—undergrad $2900 per yr
Courses: Advertising Design, Aesthetics, Ceramics, Drawing, History of Art & Archaeology, Jewelry, Painting, Photography, Art for Child Study, Design & Color, Three-Dimensional Design

BEVERLY

ENDICOTT COLLEGE, Art Dept, 376 Hale St, 01915. Tel 617-927-0585. *Head Dept* J David Broudo, EdM
Estab 1939; pvt; W; D; ent req HS dipl; degrees AA & AS 2 yrs; scholarships; enrl 205,

non-maj 13, maj 192
Tuition: Res—$4900 per yr (incl tuition, room & board); nonres—$3000 per yr
Courses: Advertising Design, Art History, Ceramics, †Commercial Art, †Costume Design & Construction, Drafting, Drawing, Fashion Arts, Graphic Arts, Illustration, †Interior Design, Jewelry, Painting, †Photography, Printmaking, Sculpture, Silversmithing, Weaving

MONTSERRAT SCHOOL OF VISUAL ART, Dunham Rd, Box 62, 01915. Tel 617-922-8222. *Dir* Joseph Jeswald; *Instr* Oliver Balf; *Instr* Ethan Berry; *Instr* Thorpe Feidt; *Instr* George Gabin; *Instr* Roger Martin; *Instr* Barbara Moody; *Instr* Paul Scott; *Instr* Kenton Sharp; *Instr* Peter Spellman; *Instr* Dennis Sweeney
Estab 1970; pvt; D & E; ent req personal interview and portfolio review; degrees 4 yr dipl granted; scholarships; SC 43, LC 3; enrl D 100, E 200
Tuition: $1650 per yr, $825 per sem, $275 per yr per course; no campus res
Courses: Advertising Design, Art History, Collage, Commercial Art, Drawing, Graphic Arts, Graphic Design, Illustration, Jewelry, Mixed Media, Painting, Photography, Printmaking, Sculpture, Silversmithing
Adult Hobby Classes: Enrl 120; tui $70 per 8 wks. Courses—same as above
Children's Classes: Enrl 40; tui $50 per 4 wks during summer. Courses—Drawing, Painting
Summer School: Dir, Joseph Jeswald. Enrl 220; tui $40-$70 for term of 8 wks beginning June 30. Courses—same as regular session

BOSTON

ART INSTITUTE OF BOSTON, 700 Beacon St, 02215. Tel 617-262-1223. *Pres* William H Willis Jr, MFA; *Chmn Design Dept* Sue Morrison, MFA; *Chmn Fine Arts Dept* John Bageris, MFA; *Chmn Photography Dept* Bruce Kinch, MFA; *Chmn Found Dept* Nathan Goldstein, MFA; *Chmn Acad Studies* Robert Simon, MFA
Estab 1912; pvt; D & E; ent req HS dipl, portfolio and interview; degrees (with Northeastern University) BS(Art) and BFA yrs vary; scholarships; SC 80, LC 20; enrl D 400, E 150
Tuition: Res—$2200 per yr, $1100 per sem
Courses: †Advertising Design, Art History, Calligraphy, †Ceramics, Collage, †Commercial Art, Drawing, Film, Graphic Arts, †Graphic Design, History of Art & Archaeology, †Illustration, Interior Design, Lettering, Mixed Media, †Painting, †Photography, †Printmaking, †Sculpture
Adult Hobby Classes: Enrl 200; tui $65 per cr. Courses—Continuing education offers most of the above typically 2-3 cr each
Summer School: Dir, Barbara J Apel. Enrl 150; tui $65 per cr for term of 8 wks beginning July 15. Courses—Most of above

BOSTON CENTER FOR ADULT EDUCATION, 5 Commonwealth Ave, 02116. Tel 617-267-4430. *Exec Dir* Harriet McLean; *Instr* Alexander Farquharson, Dipl; *Instructor* Shirley Pransky, Dipl; *Instructor* Tom Shooter, Dipl; *Instructor* Ellen Stutman, MFA
Estab 1933; pvt; D & E; ent req open to all over 18; scholarships; SC 26, LC 2; enrl D 2300, E 11,218
Tuition: $44 for art or craft studio course; $41 for lecture course; no campus res
Courses: Advertising Design, Art History, Calligraphy, Ceramics, Display, Drawing, Graphic Design, Handicrafts, History of Art & Archaeology, Lettering, Painting, Photography, Printmaking, Sculpture, Theatre Arts
Summer School: Same as winter program

BOSTON STATE COLLEGE, Art Department, 625 Huntington Ave, 02115. Tel 617-731-3300, Ext 405. *Chairperson* Ronald Polito, EdD; *Prof* Constantine Arvanites, MFA; *Prof* Robert Bertolli, EdD; *Prof* John V Cody, EdM; *Prof* Robert DiGiovanni, MFA; *Prof* Truman Egleston, MFA; *Prof* Joseph Fiorello, AM; *Prof* Walter Fox Tree, MA; *Prof* Gretchen D Lipchitz, MA; *Prof* Carolyn St Pierre, MA, JD; *Prof* Vincent J Tringale, MEd; *Prof* Clifford S Wrigley, MEd
Estab 1852; pub; D & E; ent req HS dipl, SAT, student descriptive questionnaire; degrees BA, BS and BSN 4 yrs, MA, MS; SC 20, LC 14, GC 17; enrl D 869, E 229
Tuition: Res—undergrad $250 per sem, $20 per cr; nonres—undergrad $625 per sem, $53 per cr; no campus res
Courses: Advertising Design, Art Education, Art History, Ceramics, Collage, Commercial Art, Conceptual Art, Drawing, Film, Graphic Arts, Handicrafts, History of Art & Archaeology, Jewelry, Mixed Media, Painting, Photography, Sculpture, Teacher Training, Video
Summer School: Dir, William T Morrissey. Tui $75 res, $96 nonres for one 3 credit course beginning June

BOSTON UNIVERSITY, School of Visual Arts, 855 Commonwealth Ave, 02215. Tel 617-353-3371. *Dir* Edward F Leary, EdM; *Prof* David Aronson; *Prof* Philip Guston; *Prof* Nancy Smith; *Prof* Harold Tovish; *Prof* James Weeks; *Assoc Prof* Ben Day
Estab 1869, school estab 1954; pvt; D; ent req HS dipl, portfolio and SAT or ACT; degrees BFA 4 yrs, MFA 2 yrs; scholarships; SC 38, LC 12, GC 15; enrl 385, non-maj 200, maj 100, grad 85
Tuition: $4720 per yr, $148 per cr; campus res—room & board $2280 per yr
Courses: †Art Education, Drawing, †Graphic Design, Jewelry, †Painting, Photography, Printmaking, †Sculpture, Teacher Training, †Studio Teaching (grad level), Typographic Design
Adult Hobby Classes: Enrl 25; tui free. Courses—High School Drawing Class
Summer School: Dir, Edward F Leary. Tui $88 per cr for term of 6 wks beginning May 23 and July 5. Courses—Art Education, Drawing, Painting, Sculpture

BUTERA SCHOOL OF ART, 111 Beacon St, 02116. Tel 617-536-4623. *Dir* Joseph L Butera, MFA; *Head Commercial Art* Hal Trafford; *Head Sign Painting* Stan Morrisson
Estab 1932; pvt; D & E; ent req HS dipl, portfolio; degrees 2 yr and 3 yr dipl progs; enrl D 100, E 60
Tuition: $2000-$2150 per yr; independent dormitories available
Courses: Advertising Design, Art Education, Art History, Calligraphy, Commercial Art, Drawing, Fashion Arts, Graphic Arts, Graphic Design, Illustration, Lettering, Painting, Sign Painting

CHAMBERLAYNE JUNIOR COLLEGE, Department of Graphic and Applied Arts, 128 Commonwealth Ave, 02116. Tel 617-536-4500. *Chmn Dept* Herbert T Anderson; *Prof* Henry A Tate, PhD; *Instructor* L B Bibly, MA; *Instructor* Patricia Bjorklund, B Architecture; *Instructor* Don Robert Brown, M Architecture; *Instructor* Dwight Carter, BFA; *Instructor* Sara Gidard, AAS; *Instructor* Thomas Lemon, BS; *Instructor* Phyllis Magri, BS; *Instructor* Gladys Maynard; *Instructor* Joanne M Vascovitch, BFA; *Instructor* Kathleen Vilk, BFA; *Instructor* Maria Vitagliano, MFA; *Instructor* Stephanie Warburg, MA
Estab 1892, dept estab 1952; pvt; D & E; ent req HS dipl; degrees AAS 2 yrs, Interior Design 3 yrs; SC 23, LC 11; enrl D 253, E 38, maj 253
Tuition: 235 per one 3 cr course; campus res—room & board $2175
Courses: Architecture, Art History, Ceramics, †Commercial Art, Conceptual Art, †Costume Design & Construction, Drafting, Drawing, Fashion Arts, †Graphic Arts, †Illustration, †Interior Design, Jewelry, Painting, Sculpture, Textile Design, †Landscape Architecture
Summer School: Dir, Francis X Cronin. Tui $235 per each 3 cr course for term of 12 wks beginning June 1. Courses—same as regular academic yr

EMMANUEL COLLEGE, Art Department, 400 The Fenway, 02115. Tel 617-277-9340, Ext 204. *Chairperson Dept* Theresa Monaco, MFA; *Prof* Ellen Marie Glavin, PhD; *Asst Prof* Michael Jacques, MFA; *Instructor* David Kowal, Cand PhD; *Instructor* Patricia M Lyster, BA, Master Weaver; *Instructor* C David Thomas, MFA; *Instructor* Jean Thomas, MA
Estab 1919, dept estab 1960; pvt; D & E; ent req HS dipl, SAT, 3 achievements, portfolio; degrees BA 4 yrs, BFA 4-5 yrs; scholarships; SC 41, LC 14, GC 9; enrl D 300, E 50, non-maj 200, maj 100, grad 15
Tuition: $90 per cr hr; $70 per cr hr for students without BA; campus res—room & board $1305 per yr
Courses: Aesthetics, Art Education, †Ceramics, Commercial Art, Drawing, Graphic Arts, Graphic Design, Handicrafts, History of Art & Archaeology, Illustration, Mixed Media, Occupational Therapy, †Painting, Photography, †Printmaking, Sculpture, Teacher Training, Textile Design, Art Therapy, †Fiber Arts
Adult Hobby Classes: Tui $25-$35. Courses—Drawing, Fibers, Printmaking, Sculpture
Summer School: Dean, Catherine Theresa Rice. Enrl 100; tui $85 per cr hr for term of 1 wk beginning July for 2 wks. Courses—Art Therapy, Fibers, Printmaking, Sculpture

MASSACHUSETTS COLLEGE OF ART,* 364 Brookline Ave, 02215. Tel 617-731-2340. *Pres* John F Nolan, MS; *Academy Dean* Donald R Lettis, MFA; *Chmn Fine Arts-2D* George B Nick, MFA; *Chmn Fine Arts-3D* Dan Dailey, MFA; *Chmn Design* William J Hannon, BFA; *Chmn Art Educ* Diana Korzenik, DEd; *Chmn Media* Johanna Gill, PhD; *Chmn Critical Studies* Athanasios Bouloukos, PhD
Estab 1873; pub; D & E; ent req HS dipl, SAT and Portfolio; degrees BFA 4 yrs, MFA 2 yrs, MSAE 1 yr; SC 400, LC 250, GC 50; enrl D 1094, E 1900, maj 1058, grad 90, others 1800
Tuition: Res—$500 per yr; nonres—$1250 per yr; no campus res
Courses: Advertising Design, Aesthetics, Architecture, Art Education, Art History, Calligraphy, Ceramics, Commercial Art, Conceptual Art, Constructions, Costume Design & Construction, Display, Drafting, Drawing, Fashion Arts, Film, Goldsmithing, Graphic Arts, Graphic Design, History of Art & Archaeology, Illustration, Industrial Design, Intermedia, Interior Design, Jewelry, Landscape Architecture, Lettering, Mixed Media, Painting, Photography, Printmaking, Sculpture, Silversmithing, Stage Design, Teacher Training, Textile Design, Theatre Arts, Video, Glassblowing, Stained Glass
Adult Hobby Classes: Tui $25 per cr hr. Courses—All areas
Children's Classes: Enrl 750; tui $10. Courses—All areas
Summer School: Dir Continuing Educ, Dr Dorothy Simpson. Enrl 900; tui $25 per cr hr. Courses—all areas

NEW ENGLAND SCHOOL OF ART AND DESIGN, 28 Newbury St, 02116. Tel 617-536-0383. *Pres* Christy R Rufo; *VPres* W M Davis; *Chmn Dept of Graphic Design* Wendell Arsenault; *Chmn Dept of Interior Design* Robert Stickles; *Chmn Fine Arts* William Maynard; *Chmn Fashion Illustration* Frank Raneo
Estab 1923; pvt; D & E; ent req HS dipl, portfolio; degrees 3 yr dipl; enrl D 200, E 160, maj 200
Tuition: $1950 per yr, $975 per sem, $100 per cr for PT; no campus res
Courses: †Advertising Design, Art History, Calligraphy, Commercial Art, Drafting, Drawing, †Fashion Arts, Film, Graphic Arts, †Graphic Design, Illustration, Industrial Design, †Interior Design, Lettering, Painting, Photography, Printmaking, †Fine Arts, Landscape Architecture
Summer School: Dir of Admis, W M David. Enrl approx 200; tui $115 per cr for term beginning early June. Courses—those above

SCHOOL OF FASHION DESIGN,* 136 Newbury St, 02116. Tel 617-536-9343. *Head Art Dept* Isabelle Torroelia, Baccalaureat; *Art Instr* Rita Berkowitz, BA; *Art Instr* Kathy Fay, BS-Dipl
Estab 1934; pvt; D & E; ent req HS dipl; degrees no degrees, 2 yr cert or 3 yr dipl; scholarships; enrl D approx 90, E approx 150
Tuition: Res—$1800 per yr; no campus res
Courses: Costume Design & Construction, Drawing, Fashion Arts, Illustration, Photography, Textile Design, Theatre Arts
Summer School: Instr, Rita Berkowitz. Tui $160 for term of 5 wks beginning July 10. Courses—Fashion Sketching, Life Drawing

SCHOOL OF THE MUSEUM OF FINE ARTS, 230 The Fenway, 02115. Tel 617-267-9300. *Dean* Bruce K MacDonald, PhD
Estab 1876; pvt; D & E; ent req HS dipl, HS and col transcripts, portfolio; degrees BFA 4 yrs, BFA plus BA or BS 5 yrs, BSEd 5 yrs, MFA 2 yrs (all degrees in affiliation with Tufts University); scholarships; SC 139, LC 16; enrl D 609, E 310, grad 12, others 25
Tuition: Dipl $3300 per yr; BFA $3720 per yr; MFA $5050 first yr, none second yr; E $195 per course; no campus res
Courses: Art Education, Ceramics, Drawing, Film, Goldsmithing, Graphic Design, Intermedia, Jewelry, Painting, Photography, Printmaking, Sculpture, Silversmithing, Video, Stained Glass
Summer School: Enrl 10 per class minimum; tui $260 for term of 6 wks beginning last wk in June

VESPER GEORGE SCHOOL OF ART, * 44 St Botolph St, 02116. Tel 617-267-2045. *Dir* Fletcher Adams
Estab 1924; pvt; degrees 3 yrs; scholarships
Courses: Illustration, Interior Design, Advertising Art, Design, Fashion Illustration, Fine Arts
Children's Classes: Sat

BRADFORD

BRADFORD COLLEGE, Art Department, 320 S Main St, 01830. Tel 617-372-7161. *Chmn* Richard Newman, MFA; *Asst Prof* Kathy Hoffman, PhD; *Asst Prof* Ellen Longsworth, MA; *Asst Prof* Marc Mannheimer, MFA; *Asst Prof* David Powell, BFA; *Asst Prof* Kay Rosenberg, MFA; *Asst Prof* Jan Watson, MA
Estab 1803; pvt; D & E; ent req HS dipl; degrees AA 2 yrs, BA(Creative Arts) 4 yrs; scholarships; SC 20, LC 12; enrl D 300
Tuition: Res $6300 per yr, non-res $3800; campus res—room $2250 per yr, $4050 tui
Courses: Aesthetics, Art History, Ceramics, Collage, Constructions, Drawing, Film, History of Art & Archaeology, Jewelry, Painting, Photography, Printmaking, Sculpture, Silversmithing, Stage Design, Textile Design, Theatre Arts, Weaving

BRIDGEWATER

BRIDGEWATER STATE COLLEGE, Art Department, School and Summer Sts, 02324. Tel 617-697-8321, Ext 249 & 486. *Chmn* Stephen Smalley, EdD; *Assoc Prof* John Droege, MFA; *Assoc Prof* John Heller, MFA; *Asst Prof* Joan Hausrath, MFA; *Asst Prof* William Kendall, MFA; *Asst Prof* Arnold Klukas, PhD; *Asst Prof* Dorothy Pulsifer, MA
Estab 1840, dept estab 1840; pub; D & E; ent req HS dipl, SAT; degrees BA 4 yrs; SC 35, LC 10, GC 35; enrl D 500, E 100, non-maj 440, maj 150, grad 10
Tuition: $25 per cr; campus residence available
Courses: †Art Education, Art History, Ceramics, Drawing, Goldsmithing, Graphic Arts, History of Art & Archaeology, Jewelry, Painting, Printmaking, Sculpture, Silversmithing, Stage Design, Textile Design, Theatre Arts, Weaving

BROCKTON

BROCKTON ART CENTER, Art Workshops,* Oak St, 02401. Tel 617-588-6000. *Dir* Marilyn F Hoffman
Estab 1970; pvt; D & E; ent req HS dipl; degrees through Massachusetts College of Art; scholarships; SC 30, LC 2, GS 10; enrl D 400, E 300, non-maj 30, grad 20, other 650
Tuition: $50-$60 per course for 10 wk term, additional $10 per cr hr for credit; no campus res
Courses: Art Education, Art History, Calligraphy, Ceramics, Collage, Drawing, Film, Graphic Arts, Graphic Design, Handicrafts, Illustration, Jewelry, Mixed Media, Museum Staff Training, Painting, Printmaking, Sculpture, Teacher Training, Textile Design, Theatre Arts, Cartooning, Weaving
Children's Classes: Term of 10 wks. Courses—Drawing, Painting, Printmaking, Sculpture
Summer School: Dir, Beverly Edwards. Enrl 150-200; tui $50-$55 for term of 5 wks beginning July 10. Courses—Same as regular session

CAMBRIDGE

HARVARD UNIVERSITY
—**Department of Fine Arts,** Fogg Museum, 02138. Tel 617-495-2377. *Chmn Dept* Oleg Grabar. Instrs FT 23
Estab 1874; pvt, M (Radcliffe Col for W); degrees 4 yrs; scholarships and fels; LC 26 incl GC 12; enrl undergrad Harvard 53, Radcliffe 49, grad Harvard (incl W) 80
Courses: Art History
—**Department of Visual and Environmental Studies,** 19 Prescott St, 02138. Tel 617-495-3251. *Chmn Dept* Louis Bakanowsky, MA; *Prof* Alfred Guzzetti, PhD; *Prof* Dimitri Hadzi, MA; *Prof* Eduard F Sekler, PhD; *Prof* Albert Szabo, MArchit; *Sr Lectr* Robert Gardner, MA; *Sr Lectr* Flora Natapoff, MA; *Sr Lectr* Paul Rotterdam, PhD
Estab 1972; pvt; D; ent req HS dipl, SAT, achievements; degrees BA 4 yrs; scholarships; SC 48, LC 20; enrl 1610, non-maj 1300, maj 110, grad 200
Courses: Architecture, Drawing, Film, Graphic Design, Painting, Photography, Printmaking, Sculpture, Environmental Design, Film Theory
—**Graduate School of Design, Departments of Architecture, City and Regional Planning, Landscape Archit and Urban Design Prog,** Gund Hall, 02138. Tel 617-495-2951. *Dean* Gerald M McCue. Instrs FT and PT 40
Degrees AB, SB, BLA, BCP or BArchit or equivalent; scholarships and fels; enrl 240
Courses: Architecture, Landscape Architecture, City and Regional Planning, Urban Design

MASSACHUSETTS INSTITUTE OF TECHNOLOGY
—**School of Architecture and Planning,** Dept of Archit & Urban Studies & Planning, 77 Massachusetts Ave, 02139. Tel 617-253-4401. *Dean* William L Porter; *Head Dept Architecture* N John Habraken; *Head Dept Urban Studies and Planning* Lawrence Susskind. Instrs FT 55, PT 50
Estab 1865; pvt; degrees SB(Art and Design), SB(Urban Studies), MArchit, AS(Advanced Studies), MCP, PhD(City Planning), PhD(Archit, Art Environmental Studies) 2, 4 and 6 yrs; SC, LC, GC; enrl 544
—**Center for Advanced Visual Studies,** 40 Massachusetts Ave, W11, 02139. Tel 617-253-4415. *Dir* Otto Piene
Estab 1967; pvt; D & E; ent req none for MS degree; degrees MS 2 yrs; SC 9, LC 1, GC 5; enrl D & E 250, non-maj 240, grad 6, other 5
Tuition: Same as Institute
Courses: Architecture, Art History, Film, Graphic Arts, Graphic Design, Mixed Media, Photography, Printmaking, Video, History of Architecture

CHICOPEE

COLLEGE OF OUR LADY OF THE ELMS, Department of Art, 291 Springfield St, 01013. Tel 413-598-8351, Ext 55. *Chmn Dept* Theresa Amiot; *Assoc* James McDowell; *Assoc* Arthur Moses
Estab 1928, dept estab 1950; pvt; D & E; ent req HS dipl, Col Ent Exam (Verbal and Math); degrees BA 4 yrs; scholarships; SC 14, LC 6; enrl D 120, non-maj 100, maj 20
Tuition: Res—$4800 per yr; nonres—$3000 per yr
Courses: Art Education, Art History, Calligraphy, Ceramics, Drawing, Jewelry, Painting, Printmaking, Sculpture

DOVER

CHARLES RIVER CREATIVE ARTS PROGRAM, 56 Centre St, 02030. Tel 617-785-0068, 785-1260. *Dir* Priscilla B Dewey
Estab 1969; pvt summer school; D; ent req none
Courses: Ceramics, Costume Design & Construction, Drawing, Film, Mixed Media, Painting, Photography, Printmaking, Silversmithing, Stage Design, Theatre Arts, Video

FRAMINGHAM

DANFORTH MUSEUM SCHOOL, 123 Union Ave, 01701. Tel 617-872-0858, 620-0050. *Owner* Lee Daley; *School Administrator* Marcia Rosenberg; *Instr* Gaetano Alibrandi, MA; *Instr* Judith Bookbinder, MA; *Instr* James Eng, MFA; *Instr* Johanna Erickson, MA; *Instr* Saralee Erwin, BFA; *Instr* Nan Feldman, BFA; *Instr* Dudty Fletcher, MA; *Instr* Gillian Frazier, BS; *Instr* Louis Gippetti, MFA; *Instr* Anna Linderholm, BFA; *Instr* Eleanor Mahoney; *Instr* Mary Mead, BFA; *Instr* Rose Shechet Miller, Dipl; *Instr* Ron Morris, BA; *Instr* Ludmila McKannay; *Instr* E Linda Poras, BA; *Instr* Cheryl Sapino, BFA; *Instr* Richard Sauer, MFA; *Instr* Marc Vachon, Dipl; *Instr* Patricia Walker, MA; *Instr* Mathidle Wood, MEd
Pub; ent req none; scholarships
Tuition: Varies per course; museum members receive a tuition reduction
Courses: Art History, Calligraphy, Ceramics, Drawing, Fashion Arts, Graphic Arts, Illustration, Painting, Photography, Printmaking, Sculpture, Stained Glass, Weaving
Children's Classes: Tui varies per course. Courses—Ceramics, Drawing, Painting

FRAMINGHAM STATE COLLEGE, Art Department, State St, 01701. Tel 617-620-1220. *Chmn* Leah Lipton; *Prof* Stephen Durkee, MS; *Instr* Dr Brucia Witthoft, PhD; *Asst Prof* Fred Fiandaca, MA; *Asst Prof* Gene Sullivan, MFA
Estab 1839, dept estab 1920; pub; D & E; ent req HS dipl, portfolio review; degrees BA 4 yrs; scholarships; SC 20, LC 10, GC 10; enrl D 3000, E 2500, maj 124
Tuition: Res $500 per yr, non-res $800; campus res—room & board $1500 per yr
Courses: Art History, Studio
Summer School: Dir, Dr Joseph Palladino. Tui $170 per course for term of 8 wks. Courses—Art History, Studio

FRANKLIN

DEAN JUNIOR COLLEGE, Visual and Performing Arts Department, 99 Main St, 02038. Tel 617-528-9100. *Chairperson Dept* Lawry Reid, MFA; *Dir Art Therapy* Phyllis Cohen, MA; *Prof* John Locke, MA; *Assoc Prof* John Fulgoni, MA; *Assoc Prof* Stanley Sobocinski, EdM; *Asst Prof* Richard Dean, MFA; *Asst Prof* Myron Schmidt, MA; *Instructor* Theodore P Casher, MM
Estab 1865, dept estab 1960; pvt; D & E; ent req HS dipl; degrees AA, AS 2 yrs; scholarships; SC 12, LC 4; enrl D 220, E 30, non-maj 180, maj 40
Tuition: $3395 per yr; campus res—room & board $1880 per yr; $5410 total cost
Courses: Art Therapy, Fashion Merchandising, Theatre Arts, Visual Arts, including Art History, Color, Drawing, Graphics, Painting, Photography, Three Dimensional Design

GREAT BARRINGTON

SIMON'S ROCK OF BARD COLLEGE, Studio Arts Department, Fine Arts Division, Alford Rd, 01230. Tel 413-528-0771. *Chairperson Studio Arts Dept* William Jackson, MFA; *Instructor* Arthur Hillman, MFA; *Instructor* Jeffrey Zamek, MFA
Estab 1966; pvt; D & E; ent req personal interview; degrees AA 2-3 yrs, BA 4 yrs; scholarships; SC 14, LC 4
Tuition: $4400 per yr, room & board $1775
Courses: Aesthetics, Art History, Ceramics, Drawing, Graphic Design, Jewelry, Painting, Photography, Printmaking, Sculpture, Artist and the Book, Introduction to the Arts

GREENFIELD

GREENFIELD COMMUNITY COLLEGE, Art Department, 10 College Dr, 01301. Tel 413-774-3131. *Head Art Dept* T Budge Hyde, MFA; *Instructor* John Bross, MFA; *Instructor* Peter Dudley, MFA; *Instructor* Pamela Sacher, MA; *Instructor* Margaret Stein, MFA; *Instructor* Tom Young, MFA; *Art Historian* Joan Rising, MFA
Estab 1962; pub; D & E; ent req HS dipl; degrees AA, AS 2 yrs; scholarships; SC 16; enrl in school D 1400, E 400, maj 110
Tuition: Res—$300 per yr, $175 per sem; nonres—$900 per yr, $441 per sem
Courses: Advertising Design, Art History, Commercial Art, Constructions, Display, Drawing, Graphic Arts, Graphic Design, History of Art & Archaeology, Illustration, Painting, Photography, Printmaking
Summer School: Dir, T Budge Hyde, MFA. Tui $20 per hr for term of 6 wks beginning June. Courses—Art History, Drawing, Painting, Photography

HOLYOKE

HOLYOKE COMMUNITY COLLEGE, Department of Art, 303 Homestead Ave, 01040. Tel 413-538-7000. *Chmn* Gerhard M Wioko
Estab 1946; pub; D & E; ent req HS dipl, portfolio; degrees AA 2 yrs; scholarships; SC 7, LC 4; enrl D 115, E 20, maj 50
Tuition: Res—$300 per yr; nonres—$600 per yr
Courses: Art Education, Drawing, Graphic Arts, Graphic Design, History of Art & Archaeology, Painting, Photography
Summer School: Dir, William Murphy. Courses—Per regular session, on demand

LONGMEADOW

BAY PATH JUNIOR COLLEGE, Department of Art, 588 Longmeadow St, 01106. Tel 413-567-0621. Instrs FT 2, PT 10
Estab 1947; pvt, W; D & E; ent req HS dipl; degrees AFA 2 yr; scholarships; SC 18, LC 2; enrl D 475, E 200, maj 40
Courses: Ceramics, Drawing, Graphic Arts, Handicrafts, History of Art & Archaeology, Painting, Photography, Sculpture, Foundation Art
Adult Hobby Classes: Tui varies; evenings. Courses—12 studio subjects; lecture series, twice annually

LOWELL

UNIVERSITY OF LOWELL, Department of Art, One University Ave, 01854. Tel 617-452-5000, Ext 2455. *Chairperson Dept* Fred Faudie, MFA; *Assoc Prof* Leo Panas, EdM; *Assoc Prof* Carlton Plummer, MFA; *Asst Prof* Liana Cheney, PhD; *Asst Prof* Robert Griffith, MFA; *Instructor* Michael Costello, MFA
Estab 1975 (merger of Lowell State College and Lowell Technological Institute); pub; D & E; ent req HS dipl, SAT; degrees BA(Art), BFA 4 yrs; SC 24, LC 11; enrl D 1200, E 25, non-maj 450, maj 150
Tuition: Res—undergrad $525 per yr, $263 per sem; nonres—undergrad $1300 per yr, $650 per sem; campus res—room & board $1500 per yr
Courses: Art History, Art Therapy, Studio Art
Adult Hobby Classes: Enrl 10-15 per course; tui approx $44 per course. Courses—Ceramics, Drawing, Jewelry, Painting, Photography, Quilt Making, Stained Glass, Watercolor, Wood Sculpture
Summer School: Dir, Ernest James. Courses—Appreciation of the Visual Arts, Photography

MEDFORD

TUFTS UNIVERSITY, Fine Arts Department, 11 Talbot Ave, 02155. Tel 617-628-5000, Ext 396. *Chmn Fine Arts Dept* Madeline H Caviness, PhD; *Assoc Prof* Ivan Galantic, PhD; *Asst Prof* Pamela Allara, PhD; *Asst Prof* Margaret Floyd, PhD; *Asst Prof* Anne van Buren, PhD; *Asst Prof* Barbara White, PhD; *Lectr* Elizabeth Swinton; *Vis Lectr* Bruce MacDonald, Dean of the Museum of Fine Arts; *Vis Lectr* William Young
Pvt; D; ent req HS dipl; degrees BA, BS, BEd, BFA, MA, MFA
Tuition: $5050 per yr; campus res—room & board $1370 per yr
Courses: Ceramics, Drawing, Graphic Arts, History of Art & Archaeology, Jewelry, Occupational Therapy, Painting, Photography, Sculpture

NEW BEDFORD

SWAIN SCHOOL OF DESIGN, 19 Hawthorn St, 02740. Tel 617-997-7831. *Pres* James R Davies, PhD; *Chmn Design* Meg Sherman, BA; *Chmn Liberal Arts* Leo Kelley, MS; *Chmn Painting* David Smith, MFA; *Chmn Printmaking* John Osborne, MFA; *Chmn Sculpture* Russell Daly, MFA
Estab 1881; pvt; D; ent req HS dipl, portfolio; degrees BFA 4 yr; Scholarships; SC 16, LC 16; enrl D 170, maj 210
Tuition: $2700 per yr, $1350 per sem, $90 per cr; no campus res
Courses: Art History, Drawing, Graphic Design, History of Art & Archaeology, Painting, Photography, Printmaking, Sculpture

NORTHAMPTON

SMITH COLLEGE, Art Department, 01063. Tel 413-584-2700. *Chairperson Art Dept* Helen Searing, PhD; *Prof* Elliot Melville Offner, MFA; *Assoc Prof* Peter Garland, MArch; *Asst Prof* Peter Johnson, MFA; *Asst Prof* Gary Niswonger, MFA; *Instructor* A Lee Burns, MFA; *Instructor* Pamela Endacott, MFA; *Instructor* Susan Heideman, MFA. Instrs FT 19, PT 6
Estab 1875, dept estab 1877; pvt, W; D; ent req HS dipl, col board exam; degrees BA 4 yrs; scholarships; SC 24, LC 34; enrl maj 170
Tuition: $6600 per yr incl room & board
Courses: Aesthetics, Architecture, Art Education, Art History, Calligraphy, Constructions, Costume Design & Construction, Drafting, Drawing, Graphic Arts, Graphic Design, History of Art & Archaeology, Intermedia, Landscape Architecture, Mixed Media, Museum Staff Training, Painting, Photography, Printmaking, Sculpture, Stage Design

NORTH DARTMOUTH

SOUTHEASTERN MASSACHUSETTS UNIVERSITY, College of Visual and Performing Arts, Old Westport Rd, 02747. Tel 617-997-9321, Ext 301, 302. *Dean Col* Dietmar R Winkler; *Chairperson Music Dept* Eleanor Carlson, DMA; *Chairperson Art Educ* Peter London, EdD; *Chairperson Fine Art* Willoughby Elliott, MFA; *Chairperson Design* Margot Neugebauer, MFA; *Chairperson Art History* Thomas Puryear, PhD; *Coordr Gallery* Robert E Barry, MAT. Instrs FT 28, PT 12
Estab 1895, col estab 1948; pub; D & E; ent req HS dipl, SAT, portfolio; degrees BFA and BA 4 yr, MFA and MAE 2-5 yrs; SC 75, LC 41, GC 7; enrl D 450
Tuition: Res—undergrad & grad $679 per yr; nonres—undergrad & grad $2486 per yr; campus res—room & board $2466 per yr
Courses: Advertising Design, Aesthetics, Art Education, Art History, Calligraphy, Ceramics, Collage, Commercial Art, Conceptual Art, Display, Drafting, Drawing, Film, Goldsmithing, Graphic Arts, Graphic Design, History of Art & Archaeology, Illustration, Intermedia, Jewelry, Lettering, Mixed Media, Occupational Therapy, Painting, Photography, Printmaking, Sculpture, Silversmithing, Stage Design, Teacher Training, Textile Design, Theatre Arts, Video
Summer School: Dean, Dr Robert E Piper

NORTON

WHEATON COLLEGE, Art Department, 02766. Tel 617-285-7722. *Chmn Dept* Vaino Kola. Instrs FT 6, PT 4
Estab 1834; pvt, W; degrees AB 4 yr; scholarships; SC 6, LC 18; enrl 1143
Tuition: $7300 incl room and board
Courses: Art History, Painting, Photography, Printmaking, Sculpture, Two and Three Dimensional Design

PAXTON

ANNA MARIA COLLEGE, Department of Art, Sunset Lane, 01612. Tel 617-757-4586. *Chmn Dept* David T Green. Instrs FT 3
Estab 1948; pvt; D & E; ent req HS dipl, ent exam; degrees 4 yr; scholarships; SC 15, LC 12; enrl D 190, E 144, maj 56
Courses: Advertising Design, Aesthetics, Art Education, Art History, Ceramics, Drawing, Handicrafts, Lettering, Occupational Therapy, Painting, Photography, Sculpture, Teacher Training, Enameling, Macrame, Modeling, Rug Design, Silk Screen, Stitchery, Weaving
Summer School: Dir, Edward Goldstein. Two sessions beginning May. Courses—Crafts for the Retarded, Lettering, Oil Painting, Watercolor Techniques

PITTSFIELD

BERKSHIRE COMMUNITY COLLEGE, Department of Fine Arts and Visual Communication,* West St, 01201. Tel 413-499-4660. *Chmn Dept* Nancy Delaiti, MA; *Prof* Robert M Boland, MFA; *Asst Prof* Julio Granda, MFA; *Instr* Benigna Chilla, MFA; *Instr* Philip Lief, MFA
Estab 1960, dept estab 1961; pub; D & E; ent req HS dipl, studio art testing, portfolio; degrees AA 2 yrs; scholarships; SC 16, LC 4; enrl D 72, E 75, non-maj 12, maj 72
Tuition: Res—$150 per sem; nonres—$441 per sem; no campus res
Courses: Advertising Design, Art History, Calligraphy, Commercial Art, Constructions, Costume Design & Construction, Drawing, Graphic Arts, Graphic Design, Mixed Media, Painting, Photography, Printmaking, Stage Design, Theatre Arts
Summer School: Division of Continuing Educ. Enrl 75; tui $66 per course for term of 7 wks beginning June. Courses—Design, Drawing, Painting, Photography

PROVINCETOWN

CAPE SCHOOL OF ART, Conwell St, 02657. Tel 617-487-0703. *Dir* Henry Hensche
Estab 1930; pvt summer school; D; ent req none
Tuition: $150 for 2 months, July-August
Courses: Art History, Drawing, Painting

SALEM

SALEM STATE COLLEGE, Art Department,* 352 LaFayette St, 01970. Tel 617-745-0556. *Chmn Dept* N E Wagman Jr, ME(Art); *Prof* Elissa Ananian, MAT; *Prof* Thomas Leary, MFA; *Prof* Ingrida Mangulis; *Prof* Stephen Panosian, MEd; *Prof* Mark Roudzens, MFA; *Prof* Vito Sammarjano, MEd; *Prof* Arthur Smith, MEd
Estab 1854; pub; D & E; ent req HS dipl; degrees BA 4 yrs, internships; scholarships; SC 19, LC 8, GC 5; enrl maj 102
Tuition: Res—$645 per yr; nonres—$1465 per yr; campus res available
Courses: Art Education, Art History, Ceramics, Drawing, Film, Graphic Arts, History of Art & Archaeology, Jewelry, Painting, Photography, Printmaking, Sculpture, Silversmithing, Stage Design, Teacher Training

SOUTH HADLEY

MOUNT HOLYOKE COLLEGE, Art Department, College St, 01075. Tel 413-538-2000. *Chmn* Martha Leeb Hadzi, PhD; *Prof* Leonard De Longa, MFA; *Prof* Jean C Harris, PhD; *Assoc Prof* John L Varriano, PhD; *Asst Prof* Joan Esch, PhD; *Asst Prof* Marion G Miller, MFA; *Asst Prof* E James Mundy, PhD; *Asst Prof* Barry W Seace, MFA; *Asst Prof* Paul J Staiti, PhD; *Lectr* Marilyn M Rhie, PhD; *Visiting Artist* Garth Evans, Dipl FA
Estab 1858; pvt, W; D & E; ent req SAT, college boards; degrees BA; scholarships; SC 13, LC 32; enrl D 227, maj 227
Tuition: $4550 per yr; campus res—room & board $2270; $6820 total
Courses: †Art History, Graphic Arts, †History of Art & Archaeology, Museum Staff Training, †Painting, Photography, †Printmaking, †Sculpture

SPRINGFIELD

SPRINGFIELD COLLEGE, Department of Visual and Performing Arts, 263 Alden St, 01109. Tel 413-787-2332. *Chmn Dept* William Blizard, MA; *Asst Prof* Sam Annino, MFA; *Asst Prof* Richard Robishaw, MFA; *Adjunct Prof* Emil Schnorr, MA; *Instructor* Lynn Cox, MFA; *Instructor* Gwen Gugell, MFA; *Instructor* Lila Kane, MA; *Instructor* Ed Thomas, MA; *Instructor* Harriett Wallis, MA
Estab 1885, dept estab 1971; pvt; D & E; ent req HS dipl, SAT, portfolio; degrees BA, BS 4 yr; schol; SC 30, LC 6; enrl D 335, E 10, non-maj 300, maj 35
Tuition: $3000 per yr, $89 per hr; campus res—room and board $1683; $4683 total
Courses: Advertising Design, Art History, Ceramics, Collage, Conceptual Art, Constructions, Drawing, Graphic Arts, Illustration, Intermedia, Mixed Media, †Museum Staff Training, Occupational Therapy, †Painting, Photography, †Printmaking, Restoration & Conservation, †Sculpture, Stage Design, Theatre Arts, Video, †Art Therapy, †Creative Arts Therapy, †Environmental Design
Summer School: Dir, David Wuerthele. Enrl 1000; tui $89 per hr for term of 3 or 6 wks beginning May 30. Courses—Ceramics, Drawing, Painting, Photography, Sculpture

STOCKBRIDGE

BEAUPRE, A Creative and Performing Arts Center, 01262. *Dir* Mrs Stanley North. Instrs FT 2
Estab 1944; pvt; W; summer boarding and day school, term of 7 wks beginning June 27; ent req none; degrees offers a major in art for girls 9-17
Courses: Ceramics, Drawing, Lettering, Painting, Macrame, Mobiles, Stitchery, Tie Dyeing

TRURO

TRURO CENTER FOR THE ARTS AT CASTLE HILL, INC, Castle Rd, Box 756, 02666. Tel 617-349-3714. *Dir* Daniel Ranalli; *Instructor* Alan Dugan; *Instructor* Xavier Gonzalez; *Instructor* Elloyd Hanson; *Instructor* Bruce Hoadley, PhD; *Instructor* Sidney Simon; *Instructor* John Wallace, MFA. Instrs over 45 other nationally known instructors
Estab 1972; pvt summer school; D & E; ent req none; degrees none, credits granted through Massachusetts College of Art; SC 50, LC 3, GC 30; enrl 3400
Tuition: $60 for one wk; no campus res
Courses: Ceramics, Drawing, Painting, Sculpture, Bronze Foundry, Cartooning, Fresco Painting, Weaving

WALTHAM

BRANDEIS UNIVERSITY, Department of Fine Arts, 02254. Tel 617-647-2555. *Chmn* Gerald S Bernstein. Instrs FT 11, PT 1
Estab 1948; pvt; D; ent req HS dipl, college board ent exam; degrees BS 4 yr; scholarships; SC 10, LC 28; enrl 2800
Tuition: $5075; campus res available
Courses: Art History, Drawing, Graphic Arts, Painting, Sculpture, Design

WELLESLEY

WELLESLEY COLLEGE, Art Department, 02181. Tel 617-235-0320, Ext 306. *Chmn* Anne de Clapp; *Prof* Lilian Armstrong, PhD; *Prof* Peter J Fergusson, PhD; *Prof* James F O'Gorman, PhD; *Prof* James W Rayen, MFA; *Prof* Richard W Wallace, PhD; *Assoc Prof* Eugenia P Janis, PhD; *Assoc Prof* Miranda C Marvin, PhD; *Asst Prof* Nan B Freeman, PhD; *Asst Prof* Bunny Harvey, MFA
Estab 1875, dept estab 1897; pvt; D; ent req HS dipl; degrees BA; SC 15, LC 49; enrl D 2117
Tuition: 4650 per yr; campus res—room & board $2450
Courses: †Art History, Drawing, Film, Graphic Arts, Painting, Photography, Printmaking

WEST BARNSTABLE

CAPE COD COMMUNITY COLLEGE, Art Dept, Humanities Division, 02668. Tel 617-362-2131. *Coordr Art* Robert McDonald, MFA; *Prof* Barbara Hawley, MA; *Prof* Douglas Mitchell, MFA
Estab 1963, dept estab 1973; pub; D & E; ent req HS dipl; degrees AA and AS 2 yrs; SC 14, LC 7; enrl in school D 1650, E 3000, maj 40
Tuition: Res $300 per yr, non-res $882 per yr
Courses: Architecture, Art History, Commercial Art, Drafting, Drawing, Film, Graphic Design, Illustration, Mixed Media, Painting, Sculpture, Stage Design, Theatre Arts, Video
Adult Hobby Classes: Calligraphy, Interior Design, Photography, Stained Glass, Toy Making
Summer School: Dean Continuing Educ, Peter Birkel. Tui $75 for term of 8 wks beginning June. Courses—Drawing, Graphic Design, Painting, Sculpture, Watercolor

WESTFIELD

WESTFIELD STATE COLLEGE, Art Department,* Western Ave, 01085. Tel 413-568-3311, Ext 256. *Chmn Dept* Arno Maris, MFA
Estab 1972; pub; D & E; ent req HS dipl; degrees BA (Fine Arts) 4 yrs
Tuition: Res—$500 per yr; nonres—$1200 per yr; campus res—room $680-$950 per yr, board $500 per yr; student fees $115 per yr
Courses: Advertising Design, Art Education, Art History, Ceramics, Commercial Art, Drawing, Graphic Arts, Illustration, Lettering, Mixed Media, †Painting, Printmaking, Sculpture, Teacher Training

WESTON

REGIS COLLEGE, Department of Art, 235 Wellesley St, 02193. Tel 617-893-1820. *Chmn of Dept* Marie de Sales Dinneen, PhD; *Prof* Louisella Walters, MFA; *Painter* Aileen Callahan, MFA; *Painter* Judy Goldsmith Baron, MFA; *Ceramist* Mary Deweerd Edick, AB; *Lectr* Phyllis London, MA; *Art Therapist* Patricia Hanify Boardman, MA
Estab 1927, dept estab 1944; den; D & E; ent req HS dipl, SAT, various tests; degrees AB 4 yr; scholarships; SC 12, LC 12; enrl D 250, non-maj 200, maj 50
Tuition: $2990 per yr; campus res—room & board $1990 per yr
Courses: Aesthetics, Art Education, Art History, Ceramics, Drawing, Graphic Arts, Handicrafts, History of Art & Archaeology, Painting, Printmaking, †Sculpture, Art Therapy, Collograph, Enameling, Etching, Silk Screen, Stained Glass, Weaving, Woodcut

WILLIAMSTOWN

WILLIAMS COLLEGE, Department of Art, 01267. Tel 413-597-2377. *Chmn Dept* Eugene J Johnson, PhD; *Vis Prof* Robert Sterling Clark, history of art. Instrs FT 9, PT 13
Estab 1793, dept estab 1903; pvt; D; ent req HS dipl; degrees BA 4 yrs, MA(History of Art) 2 yrs; scholarships; SC 14, LC 40, GC 10; enrl 1338, maj 62, grad 20
Tuition: $4500 per yr; campus res—room & board $2100 per yr
Courses: Architecture, Art History, Drawing, History of Art & Archaeology, Painting, Photography, Printmaking, Sculpture

WORCESTER

ASSUMPTION COLLEGE, Department of Fine Arts and Music, 500 Salisbury St, 01609. Tel 617-752-5615, Ext 259. *Chmn* Keith Daniel; *Prof* Richard Richards, MA; *Asst Prof* Richard E Lamoureux, PhD; *Asst Prof* J Michael Russom, MFA
Estab 1904, dept estab 1976; den; D & E; ent req HS dipl; degrees BA 4 yr, MAT, MA, Cert Advanced Grad Study; scholarships; enrl D 600, E 25, grad 25
Tuition: $3300 per yr, $137.50 per hr; campus res—room & board $1785 per yr; total $5085 per yr
Courses: Aesthetics, Architecture, Art Education, Art History, Drawing, Graphic Arts, History of Art & Archaeology, Painting, Printmaking, Theatre Arts
Summer School: Dir, Dr Marjorie Nickel. Tui $65 per cr hr

CLARK UNIVERSITY, Art Program, Dept of Visual & Performing Arts, 950 Main St, 01610. Tel 617-793-7561. *Chmn Art Prog & Dept Visual & Performing Arts* Donald W Krueger, MFA; *Assoc Prof* Samuel P Cowardin III, PhD; *Asst Prof* Bonnie Lee Grad, PhD
Estab 1887; pvt; D & E; ent req HS dipl, portfolio, CEEB, achievement tests; degrees BA 4 yr, BFA 4 1 2 yr; scholarships; SC 27, LC 12; enrl D 500, non-maj 454, maj 36, others 10
Tuition: $4650 per yr; campus res—room & board $1855 per yr
Courses: Advertising Design, Aesthetics, Art Education, Art History, Ceramics, Collage, Commercial Art, Drawing, Film, Graphic Arts, Graphic Design, History of Art & Archaeology, Illustration, Painting, Photography, Printmaking, Sculpture, Stage Design, Teacher Training, Theatre Arts, Video

COLLEGE OF THE HOLY CROSS, Department of Fine Arts, 01610. Tel 617-793-2237. *Chmn* Joan N Italiano, MFA; *Assoc Prof* John P Reboli, PhD; *Asst Prof* James P Monson, MFA; *Asst Prof* Terri Priest, MFA; *Asst Prof* Virginia C Raguin, PhD; *Asst Prof* Joseph S Scannell, MA; *Visiting Lectr* Anthony Kurneta, art history - 1979-1980; *Visiting Lectr* Gerard Quigley, painting - 1979-1980
Estab 1843, dept estab 1954; pvt; D; ent req HS dipl, SAT, ATS; degrees BA 4 yr; SC 12, LC 15; enrl D 485, maj 40
Tuition: Res—undergrad $6100 per yr; nonres—undergrad $4200; campus residence available
Courses: Aesthetics, Architecture, †Art History, Ceramics, Drawing, Graphic Arts, Graphic Design, History of Art & Archaeology, Museum Staff Training, Painting, Printmaking, Sculpture, Stage Design, Theatre Arts

SCHOOL OF THE WORCESTER ART MUSEUM, 55 Salisbury St, 01608. Tel 617-799-4406, Ext 66. *Dean* Sante Graziani, MFA
Estab 1896; pvt; D; ent req HS dipl; degrees none, cert awarded after completion of 3 yr prog; scholarships; SC 21, LC 2; enrl 115
Tuition: $2195 per yr, $1080 per sem; no campus res
Courses: Advertising Design, Art History, Commercial Art, Drawing, Graphic Arts, Graphic Design, Illustration, Painting, Photography, Printmaking, Sculpture

WORCESTER CRAFT CENTER, 25 Sagamore Rd, 01605. Tel 617-753-8183. *Exec Dir* Cyrus D Lipsitt, BFA; *Educ Coordr* John I Russell, MFA
Estab 1856; pvt; D & E; ent req portfolio review for professional prog, no req for adult educ; scholarships; SC 33, LC varies; enrl D & E 280, non-maj 30, maj 12
Tuition: $850 per sem; adult educ $60-$75 per sem; no campus res
Courses: Calligraphy, †Ceramics, †Goldsmithing, †Jewelry, †Photography, Restoration & Conservation, †Silversmithing
Adult Hobby Classes: Ceramics, Enamel, Furniture Refinishing, Photography, Quilting, Stained Glass, Weaving, Wood Working
Children's Classes: Tui $50 per 2 wks. Courses—General Crafts
Summer School: Exec Dir, Cyrus D Lipsitt

WORCESTER STATE COLLEGE, Art Department, 486 Chandler, 01602. Tel 617-752-7700. *Chairperson* Sandra Kocher, MA; *Prof* Doris Carter, EdD; *Prof* Ellen Kosmer, PhD; *Asst Prof* Jacqueline Casale, MA; *Asst Prof* Mary Dolphin, EdM; *Asst Prof* Michel Merle, MA & MFA
Estab 1874; pub; D & E; ent req HS dipl, col board exams, completion of systems application form; degrees BA and BS 4 yrs; SC 18, LC 9; enrl D & E 725
Tuition: Res $600 per yr, $300 per sem; non-res $2100 per yr, $1050 per sem; campus res—room $1000 per yr and board $318 per yr

Courses: Art Education, Art History, Collage, Drafting, Drawing, Graphic Design, Handicrafts, Intermedia, Mixed Media, Painting, Printmaking, Sculpture, Environmental Design, History of Urban Form
Summer School: Usually 5-8 courses and workshops

MICHIGAN

ADRIAN

ADRIAN COLLEGE, Art Department, 110 S Madison, 49221. Tel 517-265-5161, Ext 246. *Chmn Art Dept* Michael Cassino, MFA; *Assoc Prof* Norman Knutson, MFA; *Instructor* Pauleve Benio, MFA; *Vis Prof* Doramae O'Kelley, art history - 1978-79
Estab 1859, dept estab 1962; den; D & E; ent req HS dipl; degrees BA, BA with teaching cert and BFA 4 yrs; scholarships; SC 27, LC 6; enrl in dept D 250, E 50, non-maj 200, maj 30
Tuition: $1680 per sem, $80 per sem hr; $640 per yr for room, $920 per yr for board
Courses: Art Education, Art History, †Ceramics, Drawing, †Painting, Photography, †Printmaking, Silversmithing, Fibers, Two & Three-Dimensional Design, Weaving

SIENA HEIGHTS COLLEGE, Art Department, 1247 Siena Heights Dr, 49221. Tel 517-263-0731, Ext 272. *Chairperson Dept* Jeannine Klemm, EdD; *Instr* Joseph Bergman, MFA; *Instr* Sr Barbara Cervenka, MFA; *Instr* Lois DeMots, MFA; *Instr* Sr Jean Agnes Klemm, PhD; *Instr* Dave LaBarge; *Instr* David Van Horn, MFA; *Instr* Tom Venner, MFA; *Instr* John Wittershiem
Estab 1919; pvt; D & E; ent req HS dipl; degrees AFA 2 yrs, BFA and BA 4 yrs; SC 56; enrl D 200, maj 96, grad 3
Tuition: Undergrad $84 per cr hr, grad $89 per cr hr; campus res—room & board $1350 per yr
Courses: Advertising Design, Aesthetics, Art Education, Art History, Calligraphy, Ceramics, Costume Design & Construction, Drawing, Fashion Arts, Goldsmithing, Graphic Arts, Jewelry, Painting, Photography, Printmaking, Sculpture, Silversmithing, Stage Design, Teacher Training, Textile Design, Theatre Arts, Fibers
Summer School: Dir, Jeannine Klemm. Tui $84 per cr hr, June 30-July 17. Courses —Ceramics, Graphics, Metalsmithing, Photography, Traveling Course, Watercolor

ALBION

ALBION COLLEGE, Department of Visual Arts, 49224. Tel 517-629-5511, Ext 246. *Chmn Dept Visual Arts* Frank Machek, MFA; *Prof* Richard Leach, MFA; *Instructor* Richard Brunkus, MFA; *Instructor* Craig Hoernschemeyer, MFA; *Instructor* Peter Kaniaris, MFA
Estab 1835; den; D & E; ent req HS dipl; degrees BA and BFA 4 yrs; SC 32, LC 8; enrl in col D 1672
Tuition: $1864 per sem; campus res—room & board $900 per sem
Courses: Art History, Ceramics, Drawing, Film, Painting, Photography, Printmaking, Sculpture, Stage Design, Teacher Training, Theatre Arts
Summer School: Acad Dean, Dr Neil Thorburn. Tui $70 per sem hr for term of 7 wks beginning May 15

ALLENDALE

GRAND VALLEY STATE COLLEGES, Art Department, College Landing, 49401. Tel 616-895-6611, Ext 486. *Chairperson Dept* Chester Alkema, MFA; *Prof* Donald A Kerr, MFA; *Prof* Beverly Seley, MFA; *Asst Prof* Gray Sweeney, PhD; *Asst Prof* Takeshi Takahara, MFA
Estab 1960; pub; D & E; ent req HS dipl or equivalent, ent exam; degrees BA(Art History), BS(Studio) and BFA 4 yrs; SC 15, LC 12, GC 1; enrl D 80, E 40
Tuition: Res—undergrad $907 per yr, $20 per hr, grad $1170 per yr, $26 per hr; nonres —undergrad $2000 per yr, $45 per hr, grad $2600 per yr, $58 per hr; campus res— room & board $2600 per yr
Courses: Advertising Design, Aesthetics, Art Education, Art History, Ceramics, Drawing, Goldsmithing, Graphic Arts, Jewelry, Occupational Therapy, Painting, Photography, Printmaking, Sculpture, Silversmithing, Teacher Training
Summer School: Courses—Introduction to Art, Introduction to Studio, Workshops

ALMA

ALMA COLLEGE, Department of Art and Design, 614 W Superior, 48801. Tel 517-463-2141, Ext 323 & 405. *Chmn* Kent Kirby, MFA; *Assoc Prof* Jeffrey Havill; *Assoc Prof* Edward Jacomo
Estab 1886; pvt; D & E; degrees BA, BFA; scholarships; SC 10, LC 3; enrl D 200, maj 15
Tuition: Res—$3716; campus res—room and board $1740
Courses: Art Education, Art History, Ceramics, Drawing, Film, Graphic Design, History of Art & Archaeology, Jewelry, Museum Staff Training, Painting, Photography, Printmaking, Sculpture, Teacher Training, Textile Design

ANN ARBOR

UNIVERSITY OF MICHIGAN, ANN ARBOR
School of Art, 2000 Bonisteel Blvd, 48109. Tel 313-764-0397. *Dean School* George V Bayliss, MFA
Estab 1817, school estab 1974; pub; D & E; ent req HS dipl, portfolio exam; degrees BFA 4 yrs, MA 1 yr, MFA 2 yrs, MS(Med Illustration) 2 1 2 yrs; scholarships; SC 50, LC 6, GC 12; enrl D 430, E 25, non-maj 100, maj 430, grad 35, special students 6
Tuition: Res—undergrad $606 per sem, grad $934 per sem; nonres—undergrad $1824 per sem, grad $2044 per sem; campus res available
Courses: Advertising Design, Art Education, Ceramics, Drawing, Film, Graphic Design, Illustration, Industrial Design, Interior Design, Jewelry, Lettering, Mixed Media, Painting, Photography, Printmaking, Sculpture, Silversmithing, Textile Design, Video

Summer School: Dean, George V Bayliss. Enrl varies; tui res $303, nonres $912 for term of spring or summer, spring May 1 to June 30, summer July 1 to Aug 30. Courses —vary from year to year
—Department of History of Art, 48109. Tel 313-764-5400. Instrs FT 11
Dept estab 1910; pub; degrees BA, MA, PhD; scholarships and fels; enrl maj 100, grad 75
Courses: Art History, Museology

BATTLE CREEK

KELLOGG COMMUNITY COLLEGE, Arts Department, 49016. Instrs FT 3, PT 9
Estab 1962; pub; D & E; ent req none; degrees AA 2-4 yr; scholarships; enrl D 2200, E 2000, maj 50
Courses: Advertising Design, Architecture, Art Education, Art History, Ceramics, Commercial Art, Costume Design & Construction, Drafting, Drawing, Graphic Arts, Graphic Design, Illustration, Industrial Design, Jewelry, Lettering, Painting, Photography, Sculpture, Stage Design, Teacher Training, Theatre Arts
Adult Hobby Classes: Courses—all areas
Summer School: Courses—Basic Art & Appreciation

BENTON HARBOR

LAKE MICHIGAN COLLEGE, Department of Art,* 2755 E Napier Ave, 49022. Tel 616-927-3571. *Asst Prof* Ken Schaber, MA
Estab 1943; pub; D & E; ent req open door policy; degrees AA 2 yrs; scholarships; SC 10, LC 5; enrl 3577 total
Tuition: Res—$16 per sem hr; nonres—$22 per sem hr; no campus res
Courses: Art Education, Art History, Ceramics, Drawing, Jewelry, Painting, Printmaking, Sculpture

BERRIEN SPRINGS

ANDREWS UNIVERSITY, 49104. Tel 616-471-7771. *Chmn* Greg Constantine. Instrs FT 4
Estab 1952; den; D & E; ent req HS grad; degrees BS(Art Educ), BA 4 yrs, MAT; SC 18, LC 5; enrl 130, maj 35
Tuition: Tuition, room & board $2025 per quarter
Courses: Advertising Design, Art Education, Ceramics, Drawing, Painting, Photography, Printmaking, Sculpture, Design, European Study

BIRMINGHAM

BIRMINGHAM-BLOOMFIELD ART ASSOCIATION, 1516 S Cranbrook Rd, 48009. Tel 313-644-0866. *Exec Dir* Kenneth R Gross, MFA
Estab 1956; pub; D & E; scholarships; SC 90-100, LC 4; enrl 3000 total
Tuition: No campus residence
Courses: Aesthetics, Art History, Calligraphy, Ceramics, Collage, Commercial Art, Drawing, Goldsmithing, Graphic Arts, Graphic Design, Handicrafts, Illustration, Intermedia, Jewelry, Mixed Media, Painting, Sculpture, Silversmithing, Textile Design, Design, Surface Design
Children's Classes: Courses—Crafts, Drawing, Glass, Metals, Painting, Pottery, Sketching
Summer School: Same program on abbreviated basis

BLOOMFIELD HILLS

CRANBROOK ACADEMY OF ART, 500 Lone Pine Rd, 48013. Tel 313-645-3300. *Pres* Roy Slade; *Assoc Head Design Dept* Katherine McCoy; *Assoc Head Design Dept* Michael McCoy, MA; *Head Fiber Dept* Gerhardt Knodel, MA; *Head Graphics Dept* Connor Everts, BA; *Head Metalsmithing Dept* Richard C Thomas, MFA; *Head Painting Dept* George Ortman; *Head Photography Dept* Carl Toth, MFA; *Head Ceramics Dept* Jun Kaneko, MFA; *Head Architecture Dept* Daniel Libeskind, MA; *Head Sculpture Dept* Michael D Hall, MFA
Estab 1932; pvt; D; ent req portfolio; degrees MFA & MArchit 2 yrs; scholarships; enrl 150
Tuition: $3000 per yr; campus res—room & board $2000
Courses: Architecture, Ceramics, Graphic Arts, Painting, Photography, Sculpture, Design, Fiber, Metalsmithing

DEARBORN

HENRY FORD COMMUNITY COLLEGE, Art Dept, 5101 Evergreen Rd, 48121. Tel 313-271-2750, Ext 295. *Chmn Dept* Robert J Ferguson. Instrs FT 6, PT 19
Estab 1938; pub; D & E; ent req HS dipl; degrees AA 2 yrs; scholarships; SC 25, LC 9; enrl D 3500, E 7500, maj 600
Tuition: Res—$13 per cr hr; nonres—$22 per cr hr, plus lab fees; drive in campus
Courses: Advertising Design, Art Education, Ceramics, Commercial Art, Drafting, Drawing, Graphic Arts, History of Art & Archaeology, †Interior Design, Jewelry, Painting, Photography, Sculpture, Teacher Training, Textile Design, Weaving
Summer School: Dir, Robert J Ferguson. Tui $10 per cr hr, nonres $15. Courses—Art Appreciation, Art History, Ceramics, Directed Study, Drawing, Black & White Photography, Two-Dimensional Design

DETROIT

CENTER FOR CREATIVE STUDIES COLLEGE OF ART AND DESIGN, 245 E Kirby, 48202. Tel 313-872-3118. *Pres* Jerome L Grove; *Chmn Advertising Design* Powell Tripp; *Chmn Industrial Design* F Del Coates; *Chmn Photography* Robert Vigiletti; *Chmn Fine Arts* Jay Holland; *Chmn Crafts* Michael Vizzini; *Chmn General Studies* Harry Smallenberg
Estab 1926; pvt; D & E; ent req HS dipl & portfolio; degrees BFA 4 yrs; scholarships; enrl D 650, E 200, others 300

Tuition: $2900 yr, $1450 per sem
Courses: †Advertising Design, Aesthetics, Art History, Calligraphy, Ceramics, Drawing, Graphic Arts, Illustration, †Industrial Design, †Jewelry, Lettering, †Painting, †Photography, †Printmaking, Sculpture, Textile Design, †Glass
Adult Hobby Classes: Tui varies with class. Courses—Most of the above
Summer School: Dean, Arthur Greenblatt. Enrl 250; tui $595 for term of 8 wks beginning June 16. Courses—Advertising Design, Crafts, Fine Arts, Photography

MARYGROVE COLLEGE, Dept of Art & Art History, 8425 W McNichols Rd, 48221. Tel 313-862-8000. *Chmn Dept* Sr Edith Kenny; *Assoc Prof* Rose E Desloover; *Assoc Prof* Sr John Louise Leahy, DEd; *Assoc Prof* Helen Sherman, PhD; *Assoc Prof* David Vandegrift, MFA
Estab 1910; pvt; D & E; ent req interview with portfolio; degrees BA & BFA 4 yrs; SC 37, LC 20, GC 5; enrl D 150, E 25, non-maj 60, maj 50, grad 5
Tuition: Undergrad $86 per cr hr; grad $86 per cr hr; campus residence available
Courses: Advertising Design, Aesthetics, Art Education, Art History, †Ceramics, Collage, Commercial Art, Conceptual Art, Constructions, †Drawing, †Graphic Arts, Graphic Design, †History of Art & Archaeology, Lettering, Mixed Media, †Painting, Photography, †Printmaking, †Teacher Training
Adult Hobby Classes: Enrl 65; tui $35-$90 per course. Courses—Drawing, Painting, Photography
Children's Classes: Enrl 100; tui $20-$50 per course. Courses—Ceramics, Painting, Photography
Summer School: Dean Continuing Educ, Philip J Rosen, PhD. Enrl 40, tui $86 per cr hr for term of two 6 wk terms. Courses—Basic courses, graduate and undergraduate

WAYNE STATE UNIVERSITY, Department of Art and Art History, College of Liberal Arts, 450 W Kirby St, 48202. Tel 313-577-2424. *Chmn* Lee Anne Miller, MFA. Instrs FT 35, PT 35
Tuition: Res—undergrad $404 for 12 cr hrs, grad $331 for 8 cr hrs; nonres—undergrad $826, grad $991 for 8 cr hrs

EAST LANSING

MICHIGAN STATE UNIVERSITY, Dept of Art, College of Arts & Letters, 113 Kresge Art Center, 48828. Tel 517-355-7610. *Chmn Dept* Roger L Funk. Instrs FT 38, PT 2
Estab 1855; pub; D & E; ent req HS dipl; degrees BA & BFA 4 yrs, MA 1 yr, MFA 2 yrs; scholarships; SC 76, LC 49, GC 88; enrl D 2000, non-maj 1000, maj 550, grad 70
Tuition: Res—undergrad $24.50-$27 per cr hr, grad $32.50 per cr hr; nonres—undergrad $55-$57 per cr hr, grad $63 per cr hr; campus res—room & board $566.25
Courses: †Advertising Design, †Art Education, †Art History, †Ceramics, †Commercial Art, †Drawing, †Film, †Goldsmithing, †Graphic Arts, †Graphic Design, †History of Art & Archaeology, †Industrial Design, †Jewelry, †Painting, †Photography, †Printmaking, †Sculpture, †Silversmithing, †Teacher Training
Adult Hobby Classes: Tui $30-$40 per class, these meet once per wk. Courses—Drawing, Jewelry, Painting, Photography, Sculpture
Children's Classes: Saturday Art Program $10 per quarter. Courses—Fabrics & Fibers, Drawing, Painting, Photography, Printmaking, Two & Three Dimensional Media
Summer School: See Leland, Michigan

FLINT

CHARLES STEWART MOTT COMMUNITY COLLEGE, Fine Arts Division, 1401 E Court St, 48503. Tel 313-762-0443. *Chmn Dept* Samuel E Morello, MFA; *Instructor* Dorothy Bates, MA; *Instructor* Thomas Bomnert, MFA; *Instructor* Robert Caskey, MFA; *Instructor* Thomas Nuzum, MFA; *Instructor* William O'Malley, MAe; *Instructor* Douglas Warner, MSDes; *Instructor* Barbara White, MFA
Estab 1923; pub; D & E; ent req HS dipl or 19 yrs old; degrees AA 2 yrs; scholarships; enrl D & E 250, maj 250
Tuition: Dist res—$20 per cr hr; state res—$27 per cr hr; nonres—$39 per cr hr; no campus res
Courses: Art Education, Art History, Ceramics, Drafting, Drawing, Film, Jewelry, Painting, Photography, Printmaking, Sculpture, Stage Design, Teacher Training, Theatre Arts, Video
Summer School: Chmn, Samuel E Morello. Tui same as above; 8 wk sessions, first May 15-July 1, second July 1-Aug 15. Courses—vary

GRAND RAPIDS

AQUINAS COLLEGE, Art Department, 1607 Robinson Rd SE, 49502. Tel 614-459-8281. *Chmn Dept* Ronald Watson, MFA; *Assoc Prof* Larry Blovits, MFA; *Assoc Prof* James Karsina, MFA; *Asst Prof* Diane Shaffer, MFA
Estab 1940, dept estab 1965; pvt; D & E; ent req HS dipl; degrees BA and BFA 4 yrs; scholarships; SC 28, LC 9; enrl D 250, non-maj 210, maj 40
Tuition: $3174 per yr; campus res—room & board $1700 per yr
Courses: Art Education, Art History, †Drawing, †Painting, †Printmaking, †Sculpture, Teacher Training, Basic Design

CALVIN COLLEGE, Art Dept, 49506. Tel 616-949-4000, Ext 326. *Chmn Dept* Chris Stoffel Overvoorde, MFA; *Assoc Prof* Edgar G Boeve, MSD; *Assoc Prof* Carl J Huisman, MFA; *Assoc Prof* Robert A Jensen, MFA; *Asst Prof* Helen Bonzelaar, MA; *Instructor* James Kuiper, MFA; *Instructor* Ronald Pederson, MFA; *Instructor* Brenda Van Halsema, MA; *Instructor* Timothy Van Laar, MFA
Estab 1876, dept estab 1965; den; D & E; ent req HS dipl, SAT or ACT; degrees BA(Art), BA(Art Educ) & BFA(Art) 4 yrs, MAT; scholarships; SC 16, LC 4, GC 5; enrl maj 130, grad 4, others 4
Tuition: $1460 per sem, $375 per class; campus res—room & board $1500 per yr
Courses: Aesthetics, Architecture, †Art Education, †Art History, Ceramics, Collage, Conceptual Art, Drawing, Film, Graphic Arts, Jewelry, Painting, Photography, Printmaking, Sculpture, †Teacher Training, Art Therapy
Summer School: Chmn Art Dept, Chris Stoffel Overvoorde. Enrl varies; tui $350 for term of 3 wks beginning May. Courses vary

GRAND RAPIDS JUNIOR COLLEGE, Art Dept, 143 Bostwock NE, 49502. Tel 616-456-4572. *Chmn* Glenn T Raymond. Instrs FT 6, PT 4
Estab c 1920; pub; D & E; ent req HS dipl or ent exam; degrees AA 2 yrs; scholarships; SC 17, LC 2; enrl D 250, E 75, maj 60
Tuition: $700 per yr; no campus res
Courses: Art Education, Ceramics, Drafting, Drawing, Graphic Arts, Graphic Design, History of Art & Archaeology, Jewelry, Painting, Printmaking, Sculpture, Teacher Training, Fiber & Fabric Art, Watercolor
Summer School: Term of 8 wks beginning June. Courses—Art History & Appreciation, Drawing, Teacher Training

KENDALL SCHOOL OF DESIGN, 1110 College NE, 49503. Tel 616-451-2787. *Dir* Phyllis I Danielson, PhD; *Chmn Foundation* Connie Phillips, BA; *Chmn Visual Communications* Ron Riksen, BA; *Chmn Interiors* Erli Gronberg, BA. Instrs FT 17, PT 25
Estab 1928; pvt; D; ent req HS dipl, ACT, SAT, portfolio; degrees 3 yr cert, AFA, BFA 4 yrs; scholarships; SC 64, LC 9; enrl D 400, non-maj 55, others 20
Tuition: $70 per cr hr
Courses: Advertising Design, Architecture, Art History, Commercial Art, Drawing, Graphic Arts, Graphic Design, Illustration, Interior Design, Lettering, Painting, Textile Design, Environmental Design, Furniture Design
Children's Classes: Courses—Design, Drawing, Painting
Summer School: Full semester, May - July; same program as regular session

HANCOCK

SUOMI COLLEGE, Fine Arts Department, Quincy St, 49930. Tel 906-482-5300. *Chairperson Dept* Rob Roy, BA; *Instr* Jon Brookhouse, MA; *Instr* Elizabeth Leifer, MA; *Instr* Carol Salo, BA
Estab 1896, dept estab 1974; pvt; D & E; ent req HS dipl, open door policy; degrees AA 2 yrs; SC 5; enrl D 24, E 30, non-maj 18, maj 12
Tuition: $4000 per yr, $2000 per sem; campus residence available
Courses: Ceramics, Drawing, Graphic Arts, Painting, Photography, Printmaking

HILLSDALE

HILLSDALE COLLEGE, Art Dept, 49242. Tel 517-437-7341, Ext 288. *Acting Dir* Samuel Knecht, MFA; *Asst Prof* Brian Curtis, MFA
Estab 1844; pvt; ent req HS dipl, SAT; degrees BA, BS & BLS 4 yrs; SC 12, LC 5; enrl D 1000, non-maj 150, maj 10
Tuition: $3690 per yr, $1845 per sem; campus residence available
Courses: Art Education, Art History, Ceramics, Drawing, Painting, Printmaking, Sculpture, Teacher Training
Summer School: Dir, Dr Jerome Fallon. Courses vary

HOLLAND

ART SCHOOL OF THE CRAFTS GUILD, 0-380 S 168th Ave, 49423. Tel 616-399-4885. *Dir* Alleene Lowery Fisher
Estab Detroit 1927, Holland 1948; pvt; enrl limited to 10
Tuition: $300 per month yr round
Courses: Drawing, Painting, Design, Home Study (Oil Painting Fundamentals, Still Life, Portraiture, Landscape—$300 each course)

HOPE COLLEGE, Art Department,* 49423. Tel 616-392-5111. ; *Asst Prof* Bruce McCombs, MFA; *Assoc Prof* Delbert Michel, MFA; *Prof* Robert Vickers, MA
Estab 1866, dept estab 1962; den; D & E; ent req HS dipl, CEEB-SAT or ACT; degrees BA and BM 4 yrs; scholarships; SC 18, LC 12; enrl D 185, E 61, non-maj 228, maj 18
Tuition: Res—$5050 per yr; campus res —room and board $1590 per yr
Courses: Architecture, Art Education, Art History, Ceramics, Drawing, History of Art & Archaeology, Painting, Photography, Printmaking, Sculpture, Teacher Training, Silkscreen, Two-Dimensional & Three-Dimensional Design
Summer School: Dir, Dr Donald Williams. Tui $55 per cr hr. Courses—Vary from year to year

INTERLOCHEN

INTERLOCHEN ARTS ACADEMY, Dept of Visual Art, 49643. Tel 616-276-9221, Ext 272. *Chairperson Dept* Lary Lien, MFA; *Instructor* James Alley, MFA; *Instructor* Wayne Brill, BS; *Instructor* John Church, MFA; *Instructor* Lina Dean, BFA; *Instructor* Jean Parsons, MFA
Pvt; D; ent req portfolio, HS dipl; scholarships; enrl 70, non-maj 40, maj 30
Tuition: $5450 per yr, includes room and board
Courses: Ceramics, Drawing, Painting, Photography, Printmaking, Sculpture, Foundation Design, Metalsmithing, Weaving
Summer School: National Music Camp

IRONWOOD

GOGEBIC COMMUNITY COLLEGE, Art Department, Jackson Rd & Greenbush St, 49938. Tel 906-932-4231. *Asst Prof* James A Wing, MA
Estab 1932; pub; D & E; ent req HS dipl or equivalent; degrees AA 2 yrs; scholarships; SC 14, LC 3; enrl D 37, E 32, non-maj 65, maj 4
Tuition: Res $403 per yr, non-res $589; out-of-state res $775; average additional expenses $400; campus res—room $720 per yr
Courses: Advertising Design, Architecture, Art History, Calligraphy, Ceramics, †Commercial Art, Drafting, Drawing, †Graphic Arts, Jewelry, Painting, Photography, Sculpture
Summer School: Dean Acad Prog, Andrew Angwin. Courses—Ceramics, Ceramic Sculpture, Drawing, Painting, Raku

KALAMAZOO

KALAMAZOO COLLEGE, Art Department,* 1200 Academy St, 49007. Tel 616-383-8400. *Chmn Dept* Bernard S Palchick, MFA; *Instr* Marcia J Wood, MFA; *Instr* Billie Fischer, PhD
Estab 1833, dept estab approx 1940; pvt; D; ent req HS dipl, SAT, ACT, class rank; degrees BA 4 yrs; scholarships; SC 14, LC 10; enrl (school) 1500, non-maj 350 (dept), maj 38, others 5
Tuition: $3657 per yr; campus res available
Courses: Art Education, †Art History, †Ceramics, Drawing, †Painting, †Printmaking, †Sculpture

KALAMAZOO INSTITUTE OF ARTS, Genevieve & Donald Gilmore Art Center, 314 S Park St, 49007. Tel 616-349-7775. *Educ Coordr* William Tye, BFA; *Head Ceramics Dept* Thomas Kendall, MA; *Head Photography Dept* Gary Cialdella, MA; *Head Painting Dept* Marcia Blaustein, MAT
Estab 1924; pvt; D & E; SC 29; enrl D 798, E 726
Tuition: $33-$75 depending upon class; no campus res
Courses: Ceramics, Drawing, Jewelry, Painting, Photography, Sculpture, Weaving
Children's Classes: Tui varies. Courses—Ceramics, Drawing, Painting, Printmaking
Summer School: Educ Coordr, William Tye. Visiting professionals teach 1 & 2 wk workshops in various media. Courses—Same as fall and spring

KALAMAZOO VALLEY COMMUNITY COLLEGE, Department of Art,* 6767 W O, 49009. Tel 616-372-5000. *Head Dept* Drew Krouse, MFA; *Instr* Arleigh Smyavois, MA
Estab 1968; pub; E; ent req HS dipl or over 19 yrs old; degrees AA and AS; SC 12; enrl D & E 500
Courses: Ceramics, Drafting, Drawing, Graphic Arts, Graphic Design, Jewelry, Painting, Photography, Sculpture, Textile Design, Two-Dimensional Design

WESTERN MICHIGAN UNIVERSITY, Department of Art, 49008. Tel 616-383-1858. *Chairperson Dept* John Carney, MFA; *Prof* Joe Delvca, MFA; *Prof* Charles E Meyer, PhD; *Prof* Paul Robbert, MFA; *Assoc Prof* Andy Argyropoulos, MFA; *Assoc Prof* Joe Frattallone, PhD; *Assoc Prof* Curtis Rhodes, MFA. Instrs FT 25
Estab 1904, dept estab 1939; pub; D & E; ent req HS dipl, ACT; degrees BA and BFA 4 yrs, MA 1 yr, MFA 2 yrs; scholarships; SC 60, LC 9, GC 8; enrl non-maj 200, maj 550, grad 20
Tuition: Res—undergrad $27 per cr hr, grad $35 per cr hr; nonres—undergrad $62 per cr hr, grad $78 per cr hr; campus res—room & board $1540 per yr
Courses: Aesthetics, †Art Education, †Art History, †Ceramics, Commercial Art, Conceptual Art, Constructions, Drawing, †Graphic Design, History of Art & Archaeology, †Intermedia, †Jewelry, Mixed Media, †Painting, †Photography, †Printmaking, †Sculpture, Silversmithing, †Teacher Training, †Textile Design, Video
Summer School: Chairperson Dept, John Carney. Enrl 100; tui same per hr as acad yr for two 8 wk terms beginning May and July. Courses—same as above
—Art History Division, W Michigan Ave, 49008. Tel 616-383-1625. *Chmn* Robert P Johnston, MA; *Prof* Charles E Meyer, PhD; *Assoc Prof* Elizabeth Dull, PhD; *Instr* Sebastian Buffa, MA
Div estab 1903; pub; D & E; degrees BA, BS and BFA 4 yrs; scholarships; LC 15, GC 2; enrl D 380, E 50, non-maj 415, maj 15
Courses: †History of Art & Archaeology, History of Photography
Summer School: Chmn Art Dept, John Carney. Enrl 50 (art history); tui same as regular rates per sem hr. Courses—various History of Art courses

LANSING

LANSING COMMUNITY COLLEGE, Performing & Creative Arts Dept, 419 N Capital Ave, PO Box 40010, 48901. Tel 517-373-7460. *Prog Dir Art* Harry A Worst
Estab 1957, dept estab 1967; pub; D & E; ent req HS dipl; degrees AA 2 yrs; scholarships; SC 60, LC 15; enrl D 758, E 506, non-maj 460, maj 504, others 300
Tuition: Res—$11 per cr hr; nonres—$17 per cr hr; out-of-state—$27 per cr hr; no campus res
Courses: †Ceramics, †Commercial Art, †Drawing, †Illustration, †Interior Design, †Jewelry, †Painting, Printmaking

LELAND

LEELANAU SUMMER ART SCHOOL, 49654.
Estab 1939; (Sponsored by Michigan State University Art Dept)
Tuition: $28 per term hr

LIVONIA

MADONNA COLLEGE, Art Dept, 36600 Schoolcraft Rd, 48150. Tel 313-591-1200, Ext 8. *Chairperson Art Dept* Sr M Angeline, PhD; *Instructor* Anthony Balogh, MA; *Instructor* Margaret Collins; *Instructor* Loretta Hubley, MA; *Instructor* Lula Simakas, MA
Estab 1947; pvt; D & E; ent req HS dipl, portfolio; degrees AA 2 yrs, AB 4 yrs; SC 17, LC 3; enrl D 43, E 22, maj 17
Tuition: $42 per cr hr; campus residence available
Courses: Advertising Design, Art History, Calligraphy, Ceramics, Commercial Art, Drawing, Jewelry, Lettering, Mixed Media, Painting, Photography, Printmaking, Sculpture, Teacher Training
Adult Hobby Classes: Enrl 65; tui $40 per 10 wks. Courses—Calligraphy, Jewelry & Lapidary, Painting
Summer School: Dir, Sr M Angeline. Tui $42 per sem hr for term beginning May 1. Courses—Art for the Elementary Teacher, Printmaking, Watercolor & Acrylics. Also a non-cr course in calligraphy offered; tui $40

SCHOOLCRAFT COLLEGE, Department of Art,* 18600 Haggerty Rd, 48151. Tel 313-591-6400. *Chairperson Dept Art* Robert Dufort, MFA; *Instr* James R Black, MFA; *Instr* Cecilia Kelley, MA; *Instr* Lincoln Lao, MFA
Estab 1964; pub; D & E; ent req ent exam; degrees AA 2 yrs; SC 13, LC 4; enrl D 200,

E 60, maj 48
Tuition: Res—In District $510 per yr, In State $825 per yr; nonres—$1215 per yr; no campus res
Courses: Art Education, Art History, Ceramics, Costume Design & Construction, Drawing, Film, Graphic Arts, History of Art & Archaeology, Jewelry, Painting, Photography, Printmaking, Sculpture
Adult Hobby Classes: Courses—Acrylic Painting, Macrame, Stained Glass

MARQUETTE

NORTHERN MICHIGAN UNIVERSITY, Dept of Art & Design, 49855. Tel 906-227-2194. *Head Dept* Michael J Cinelli; *Prof* John V Rauch; *Prof* Marvin Zehnder; *Assoc Prof* Thomas Cappuccio; *Assoc Prof* John D Hubbard; *Assoc Prof* James Quirk; *Asst Prof* Diane D Kordich; *Asst Prof* William C Leete; *Asst Prof* Natalie Paul; *Asst Prof* Dennis Staffne
Estab 1899, dept estab 1964; pub; D & E; ent req HS dipl, ACT; degrees BS, BFA, BA 4 yrs, MAE; scholarships; SC 30, LC 20, GC 18
Tuition: Res—undergrad $29.50 per cr hr, grad $38.50 per cr hr; nonres—undergrad $66 per cr hr, grad $66 per cr hr; campus res—room & board $1750 per yr
Courses: Art Education, Art History, Ceramics, Drawing, Film, Graphic Design, Industrial Design, Jewelry, Painting, Photography, Printmaking, Sculpture, Environmental, Furniture & Package Design, Metalworking, Weaving, Woodworking

MIDLAND

MIDLAND CENTER FOR THE ARTS, 1801 W St Andrews, 48640. Tel 517-631-3250. *Acting Dir Midland Art Council* Ann Boehm, BS; *Studio Coordr* Rae Cooker. Instrs FT 15
Estab 1971; pvt; D & E; SC 12-20, LC 2; enrl D & E 100
Tuition: $35-$55 per sem; no campus res
Courses: Calligraphy, Ceramics, Mixed Media, Painting, Photography, Printmaking, Sculpture, Design, Metalsmithing, Papermaking, Stained Glass, Weaving
Children's Classes: Enrl 50; tui $25-$30 per sem

MOUNT PLEASANT

CENTRAL MICHIGAN UNIVERSITY, Dept of Art, 48859. Tel 517-774-3025. *Chmn Dept* Richard M Graham, MFA. Instrs FT 19, PT 4
Estab 1892; pub; D & E; ent req HS dipl; degrees BA, BFA & AB 4 yrs, MA; SC 50, LC 9; enrl for univ 16,000
Tuition: Res—undergrad $24 per cr hr, grad $32 per cr hr; nonres—undergrad $62 per cr hr, grad $71 per cr hr; campus res—room & board $2365 per yr
Courses: Aesthetics, Art Education, Art History, Ceramics, Collage, Commercial Art, Conceptual Art, Constructions, Drawing, Film, Goldsmithing, Graphic Arts, Intermedia, Jewelry, Lettering, Mixed Media, Painting, Photography, Printmaking, Sculpture, Silversmithing
Summer School: Dir, Dr Dan Millar

MUSKEGON

MUSKEGON COMMUNITY COLLEGE, Dept of Creative & Performing Arts, 221 S Quarterline, 49443. Tel 616-773-9131, Ext 324. *Chairperson Dept* Blair Morrissey; *Instructor* Lee Collet, MFA; *Instructor* Ken Foster, MFA; *Instructor* John Walson, MS; *Instructor* Robert Sheardy, MA
Estab 1926; pub; D & E; ent req HS dipl; degrees AA 2 yrs; scholarships; SC 18, LC 6; enrl D 280, E 60
Tuition: Res—$15 per cr hr; nonres—$21 per cr hr; no campus res
Courses: Art Education, Art History, Ceramics, Costume Design & Construction, Drawing, Film, Interior Design, Painting, Printmaking, Sculpture, Stage Design, Teacher Training, Theatre Arts
Adult Hobby Classes: Tui $15 or $21 per hr. Courses—Ceramics, Interior Design, Painting
Summer School: Chairperson Dept, Blair Morrissey. Tui $15 per cr hr for term of 7 wks beginning July 5. Courses—Ceramics

OLIVET

OLIVET COLLEGE, Art Dept, 49076. Tel 616-749-7661. *Chmn* Donald Rowe, MFA; *Assoc Prof* H James Hay, MFA; *Asst Prof* Carolyn Loeb, MA
Estab 1844, dept estab 1870; pvt; D & E; ent req HS dipl; degrees BS and BM 4 yrs, MA 1 yr; scholarships; SC 17, LC 8, GC 10; enrl D 610, non-maj 50, maj 20, grad 2
Tuition: $3390 per yr, part-time $110 per hr; campus res—room & board $1700 per yr
Courses: Art History, Drawing, Graphic Arts, Painting, Printmaking, Sculpture, Design, Metalwork

PONTIAC

PONTIAC ART CENTER,* 47 Williams St, 48053. Tel 313-333-7849. *Exec Dir* Ian R Lyons, MA; *Instr* James Gilbert, MFA; *Instr* Carol Goodale, BA; *Instr* Lorraine McCarty, MFA; *Instr* Sybil Oshinsky, MFA; *Instr* Eve Szilagyi, BA; *Instr* James Zimmerman, MFA
Estab 1964; pub; D & E; ent req open enrollment; scholarships; SC 15; enrl 200
Tuition: Varies; no campus res
Courses: Ceramics, Drawing, Jewelry, Painting, Photography, Sculpture, Metalsmithing, Watercolor, Weaving
Children's Classes: Tui $25 per class. Courses—Drawing, Painting, Sculpture
Summer School: Exec Dir, Ian R Lyons. Term of 10 wks beginning June. Courses—Drawing, Jewelry, Metalsmithing, Painting, Photography, Sculpture, Weaving

PORT HURON

SAINT CLAIR COUNTY COMMUNITY COLLEGE, Fine Arts Department,* 323 Erie St, 48060. Tel 313-984-3881. *Chmn Fine Arts* James Voss
Estab 1923; pub; D & E; ent req HS dipl, ent exam; degrees AA and AAS 2 yrs; scholarships; SC 30, LC 5; enrl D 60
Tuition: Res—$428 per yr; nonres—$792 per yr
Courses: Advertising Design, Art Education, Ceramics, Commercial Art, Display, Drawing, Graphic Arts, Graphic Design, History of Art & Archaeology, Illustration, Lettering, Painting, Photography, Sculpture, Theatre Arts

ROCHESTER

OAKLAND UNIVERSITY, Dept of Art & Art History, 48063. Tel 313-377-3375. *Chmn Dept* John B Cameron, PhD; *Prof* Carl F Barnes Jr, PhD; *Assoc Prof* John Beardman, MFA & MA; *Asst Prof* C Franklin Sayre, PhD; *Asst Prof* Charlotte Stokes, PhD; *Visiting Instr* Janice C Schimmelman; *Lectr* Lisa Brantigan, MA; *Lectr* Judith Toth, MFA; *Lectr* Paul Webster, MFA
Estab 1957, dept estab 1960; pub; D & E; ent req HS dipl; degrees BA 4 yrs; scholarships; SC 3, LC 9
Tuition: Res—undergrad on campus $25.25 per cr hr, off-campus $32.50 per cr hr; nonres—undergrad $67 per cr hr, grad on campus $38.50 per cr hr, off-campus $43 per cr hr; campus res—room & board $860 fall & winter sems, $459 spring & summer sems
Courses: Art History, History of Art & Archaeology, Studio Art

SAUGATUCK

OXBOW SUMMER ART WORKSHOPS, 49453. Tel 616-857-5811. *Workshop Dir* Gordon J Dorn; *Instructor* Lennart Anderson; *Instructor* Steve Britko; *Instructor* Howard Clark; *Instructor* Kathryn Clark; *Instructor* Harold Gregor; *Instructor* Philip Hanson; *Instructor* Jack Leman; *Instructor* Roland Poska; *Instructor* Chris Ramberg; *Instructor* Charlotte Rollman-Shay; *Instructor* Ed Rollman-Shay; *Instructor* Jane Wengler
Estab 1910; pvt; D & E; ent req over 18 yrs, slides must be submitted; degrees credit toward graduation recognized by most schools; scholarships; enrl 55 per session, 3 sessions per summer
Tuition: $475 for 3 wk session, incl room & board
Courses: Ceramics, Collage, Conceptual Art, Drawing, Graphic Arts, Intermedia, Mixed Media, Painting, Photography, Printmaking, Sculpture, Theatre Arts, Papermaking

SCOTTVILLE

WEST SHORE COMMUNITY COLLEGE, Div of Humanities & Fine Arts, 3000 N Stiles Rd, 49454. Tel 616-845-6211. *Head Dept* Leo Teholiz, MA; *Prof* Joseph Jarkowski, MA; *Instr* Mrs Pat Monton, Cert. Instrs PT 3
Pub; D & E; ent req HS dipl; degrees AA 2 yrs; scholarships; SC 18, LC 10; enrl non-maj 273, maj 10
Tuition: Res—$180 per quarter, $12 per cr hr; nonres—$360 per quarter, $24 per cr hr; no campus res
Courses: Art History, Calligraphy, Ceramics, Drafting, Drawing, Graphic Design, Lettering, Mixed Media, Painting, Photography, Printmaking, Sculpture, Stage Design, Teacher Training, Theatre Arts
Adult Hobby Classes: Enrl approx 15-20 per class, directed by Community Services. Classes—Art workshops, Crafts, Photography
Children's Classes: Enrl approx 15; conducted by Community Services
Summer School: Dir, Leo Teholiz. Enrl 20-24; tui $5 per non-cr class, $12 per cr hr for term of 8 wks beginning mid-June. Summer Art Workshop (Outdoor Off-Campus Classes). Courses—Clay Modeling, Pottery

SPRING ARBOR

SPRING ARBOR COLLEGE, Art Department, 49283. Tel 517-750-1200. *Dir* Bill Bippes, MFA; *Prof* Rhoda Knisley, MA; *Prof* Paul Wolber, MA; *Instr* Edie Rosenfeld, MFA
Estab 1873, dept estab 1971; pvt den; D & E; ent req HS dipl; degrees AA(Commercial) 2 yrs, BA 4 yrs; scholarships; SC 17, LC 6; enrl D 200, E 20, non-maj 20, maj 32
Tuition: $3100 per yr, $1550 per sem, $65 per hr; campus res—room & board $1450 per yr
Courses: †Advertising Design, Commercial Art, †Drawing, †Graphic Arts, †Illustration, †Painting, †Printmaking, †Sculpture, †Teacher Training
Children's Classes: Summer programs. Enrl 15-20; tui $25
Summer School: Dir, Dr Charles Campbell. Courses—Crafts, Drawing

TRAVERSE CITY

NORTHWESTERN MICHIGAN COLLEGE, Art Dept, 1701 E Front St, 49684. Tel 616-946-5650, Ext 525. *Chmn Dept* Paul Welch, MA; *Instr* Norman Averill, MA; *Instructor* Robert Bach; *Instructor* Stephen Ballance, MA; *Instructor* Jack Ozegovic, MFA; *Instructor* Jill Thompson
Estab 1951, dept estab 1957; pub; D & E; ent req HS dipl; degrees AA 2 yrs; scholarships; SC 40, LC 4; enrl non-maj 400, maj 75
Tuition: 11.50 per cr hr per term In-Dist, $19 per cr hr per term In-Serv Area, $21 per cr hr per term In-State, $23 per cr hr per term Out-of-State; campus res room & board
Courses: Advertising Design, Art Education, Art History, Ceramics, Commercial Art, Drafting, Drawing, Film, Goldsmithing, Graphic Arts, Graphic Design, Illustration, Industrial Design, Jewelry, Lettering, Painting, Photography, Printmaking, Sculpture, Silversmithing, Textile Design
Summer School: Dir, Paul Welch. Tui same as regular session

UNIVERSITY CENTER

DELTA COLLEGE, Art Department,* Humanities Division, 48710. Tel 517-686-0400. *Chmn Dept* Charles A Breed, MA; *Asst Prof* Larry Butcher, MA; *Asst Prof* Larry Oughton, MFA; *Assoc Prof* John McCormick, MFA; *Assoc Prof* Russell Thayer, MA; *Lectr* Linda Menger, MA
Estab 1960; pub; D & E; ent req open door policy; degrees AA 2 yrs; scholarships; SC 21, LC 5; enrl D 550, E 100, maj 190
Tuition: Res—In District $496 per yr, Out of District $883 per yr; nonres—$1193 per yr; campus res—room and board $775 per sem
Courses: Art Education, Art History, Ceramics, Commercial Art, Drawing, Graphic Design, Interior Design, Painting, Photography, Printmaking, Sculpture

SAGINAW VALLEY STATE COLLEGE, Dept of Art & Design, Pierce Rd, 48710. *Chmn Dept* Barron Hirsch, MFA; *Prof* Matthew Zivich, MFA; *Instructor* Paul Davis, MA; *Instructor* Curtis Leece, BFA; *Instructor* Gayle Leece, BFA; *Instructor* Martha Yeatman, BA
Estab 1960, dept estab 1968; pub; D & E; ent req HS dipl; degrees BA(Art) 4 yrs or less; scholarships; SC approx 20, LC approx 15; enrl D 200, E 50, maj 37
Tuition: $22 per cr hr; campus residence available
Courses: Advertising Design, Aesthetics, Art Education, Art History, Collage, Commercial Art, Conceptual Art, Graphic Arts, Graphic Design, Handicrafts, History of Art & Archaeology, Illustration, Intermedia, Painting, Photography, Printmaking, Sculpture, Teacher Training, Textile Design
Summer School: Courses vary

WARREN

MACOMB COUNTY COMMUNITY COLLEGE, Art Department,* Division of Humanities, 14500 Twelve Mile Rd, 48093. Tel 313-779-7000. *Prof* David Barr, MA; *Prof* Al Herbert, MA; *Prof* James Johnston, MA; *Prof* James Pallas, MFA
Estab 1960, dept estab 1965; pub; D & E; ent req HS dipl, ent exam; degrees AA 2 yrs; scholarships; SC 14, LC 6
Tuition: Res—In County $15 per hr, In State $28 per hr; nonres—$38 per hr
Courses: Advertising Design, Architecture, Ceramics, Commercial Art, Costume Design & Construction, Display, Drafting, Drawing, Graphic Arts, Graphic Design, Handicrafts, History of Art & Archaeology, Illustration, Industrial Design, Jewelry, Painting, Photography, Sculpture, Watercolor

YPSILANTI

EASTERN MICHIGAN UNIVERSITY, Dept of Art, 48197. Tel 313-487-1268. *Head Dept* John E Van Haren, MS
Estab 1849, dept estab 1901; pub; D & E; ent req HS dipl; degrees BA, BS & BA(Art Educ) 4 yrs, MA(Art Educ), MA(Studio) & MFA 2 yrs; scholarships; SC 55, LC 18; enrl undergrad maj 580, non-maj 800, grad 220
Tuition: Res—undergrad $24.50 per cr hr, grad $37 per cr hr; nonres—undergrad $60 per cr hr, grad $90 per cr hr; campus res—room & board $1600 per yr
Courses: Advertising Design, †Art Education, Art History, Ceramics, Commercial Art, Conceptual Art, Drawing, Goldsmithing, Graphic Arts, Graphic Design, History of Art & Archaeology, Illustration, Intermedia, Jewelry, Lettering, Mixed Media, †Museum Staff Training, Painting, Photography, Printmaking, Sculpture, Silversmithing, †Stage Design
Summer School: Head Dept, John E Van Haren, MS. Term of 6 wks beginning June 23

MINNESOTA

BEMIDJI

BEMIDJI STATE UNIVERSITY, Art Department, 56601. Tel 218-755-3939. *Chmn* Sally James, BFA; *Prof* Eugene Dalzotto, MFA; *Prof* A Keith Malmquist, MFA; *Assoc Prof* Marlin Kaul, MFA; *Assoc Prof* William Kelly, MFA; *Instructor* Larry Stene, MFA; *Instructor* Rimas T VisGirda, MFA
Estab 1918; pub; D & E; ent req HS dipl, ACT, SAT, PSAT, or SCAT; degrees BA, BS(Teaching) and BS(Tech Illustration, Commercial Design) 4 yrs; SC 54, LC 17, GC individual study
Tuition: Res—undergrad $11 per quarter hr, grad $14 per quarter hr; nonres—undergrad $23 per quarter hr, grad $25 per quarter hr; campus residency available
Courses: †Art Education, Art History, Ceramics, †Commercial Art, Conceptual Art, Drafting, Drawing, Film, Graphic Arts, Graphic Design, Handicrafts, History of Art & Archaeology, Illustration, Industrial Design, Jewelry, Lettering, Painting, Photography, Printmaking, Sculpture, Silversmithing, Teacher Training, Textile Design, Theatre Arts, Video, Basketry, Batik, Beading, Leaded Glass, Macrame, Needlepoint, Quilting, Spinning, Stitchery, Trapunto, Weaving
Children's Classes: Enrl 20; tui free. Courses—Art, preschool classes offered each fall
Summer School: Dir, William Sellon. Tui as above for term of two 5 wk sessions beginning June. Courses—most of regular courses plus special summer session only courses

COLLEGEVILLE

ST JOHN'S UNIVERSITY, Art Department, 56321. *Head Dept* Hugh Witzmann, MFA; *Assoc Prof* Bela Petheo, MFA; *Asst Prof* Jim Hendershot, MFA; *Instructor* Bro Alan Reed, MFA
Estab 1856; pvt; D; ent req HS dipl; degrees BA, BS; scholarships; SC 33, LC 10
Tuition: $3195 per yr; campus res—room & board $500-$800
Courses: Aesthetics, Art Education, Art History, Ceramics, Drawing, Graphic Arts, Jewelry, Mixed Media, Painting, Photography, Printmaking, Sculpture, Teacher Training

DULUTH

UNIVERSITY OF MINNESOTA, DULUTH, Art Dept, 55812. Tel 218-726-8224. *James H/Brutger, MA* ; *Prof* William G Boyce, MEd; *Prof* Rudolph I Schauer, MS; *Prof* Arthur E Smith, EdD; *Assoc Prof* Leif Brush, MFA; *Assoc Prof* Thomas L Kerrigan, MFA; *Assoc Prof* Philip K Meany, MFA; *Asst Prof* Joseph W Boudreau, MFA; *Asst Prof* Alyce B Coker, MFA; *Asst Prof* Edna J Garte, PhD; *Asst Prof* Thomas F Hedin, PhD; *Visiting Prof* Peter Collingwood, Fibers
Pub; D & E; ent req HS dipl; degrees BFA, BA 4 yrs, MA; scholarships; SC 30, LC 6, GC 10; enrl D 200, E 50, maj 200, grad 12
Tuition: Averages $20 per cr hr; campus residence available
Courses: Advertising Design, Art Education, Art History, Calligraphy, Ceramics, Commercial Art, Constructions, Drawing, Film, Graphic Arts, Graphic Design, History of Art & Archaeology, Jewelry, Lettering, Mixed Media, Museum Staff Training, Painting, Photography, Printmaking, Sculpture, Silversmithing, Teacher Training, Textile Design, Fibers
Adult Hobby Classes: Courses—Ceramics, Photography, Stained Glass
Summer School: Dir, Terry Anderson. Courses—Art Education, Art Today, Drawing, Museum Practice, Fibers (Weaving), Painting, Photography

ELY

VERMILION COMMUNITY COLLEGE, Art Department,* 1900 East Camp St, 55731. Tel 218-365-3256. *Dept Head* Dan Wood, MAE
Estab 1922, dept estab 1964; pub; D & E; ent req HS dipl; degrees AA 2 yr; SC 13, LC 5; enrl D 27, E 38, non-maj 55, maj 10
Tuition: Res—undergrad $550 per yr; nonres—undergrad $1100 per yr
Courses: Aesthetics, Ceramics, Display, Drafting, Drawing, History of Art & Archaeology, Lettering, Painting, Photography, Printmaking, Sculpture
Adult Hobby Classes: Tui $10 per class. Courses—Ceramics, Stained Glass
Children's Classes: Tui $10 per class. Courses—Crafts, Drawing, Painting
Summer School: Dir, Ray Kenney. Enrl 20; tui $56 for term of 2 wks beginning June 19 and July 5. Courses—Photography: Applications in the Arts and Portraits and Darkroom Techniques

FERGUS FALLS

LUTHERAN BRETHREN SCHOOLS, 56537. Tel 218-739-3371, 739-3372, 739-3373. *Head Dept* Joel Lunde, BA
Estab 1900; den; D & E; ent req HS dipl, questionnaire; SC 1, LC 1; enrl enrl D 65, E 20
Tuition: $525 per sem; campus res—room & board $530 per sem
Courses: Ceramics, Drawing, Painting

GRAND MARAIS

GRAND MARAIS ART COLONY, 55604. Tel 218-387-1541. *Head Dept* Birney M Quick, MFA; *Instructor* Byron Bradley, MFA; *Instructor* Harvey Turner, MFA
Estab 1947; pvt; D & E; ent req course open; scholarships; SC 4; enrl D 125
Tuition: $400 per sem
Courses: Drawing, Painting, Printmaking, Sculpture
Adult Hobby Classes: Courses—Drawing, Painting, Sculpture
Children's Classes: Sat School
Summer School: Same as above

MANKATO

BETHANY LUTHERAN COLLEGE, Art Department, 56001. Tel 507-625-2977. *Head of Dept* Karen Reit
Estab 1927, dept estab 1960; den; D; ent req HS dipl, ACT; degrees AA 2 yr, dipl; scholarships; SC 2, LC 2; enrl D 36, non-maj 26, maj 10
Tuition: $1150 per sem, $85 per cr hr; campus res—room and board $785 per sem
Courses: Advertising Design, Art History, Ceramics, Drawing, Interior Design, Painting, Art Structure

MANKATO STATE UNIVERSITY, Art Department, 56001. Tel 507-389-6413. *Chmn* John E Spurgin, MFA. Instrs FT 16
Estab 1868, dept estab 1938; pub; D & E; ent req HS dipl; degrees BA, BFA and BS 4 yr, MA and MS 1-1 1 2 yr; SC 42, LC 28, GC 54; enrl D 3000 (total), E 500, non-maj 1000, maj 225, grad 50
Tuition: Res—undergrad $512 per yr, $11 per quarter hr, grad $615 per yr, $14 per quarter hr; nonres—undergrad $1016 per yr, $21 per quarter hr, grad $951 per yr, $27 per quarter hr
Courses: Advertising Design, Art Education, Art History, Calligraphy, Ceramics, Commercial Art, Drawing, Graphic Arts, Graphic Design, Illustration, Jewelry, Lettering, Painting, Photography, Printmaking, Sculpture
Summer School: Tui same as above

MINNEAPOLIS

ART INSTRUCTION SCHOOLS, 500 S 4th St, 55415. Tel 612-339-8721. *Dir* A Conrad, EdD; *Assoc Dir* Don Jardine, PhD
Estab 1914; pvt
Courses: Fundamentals of Art and Specialized Art

AUGSBURG COLLEGE, Art Department, 731 21st Ave W, 55454. *Chmn* Philip Thompson. Instrs FT 2, PT 5
Estab 1869, dept estab 1960; den; D & E; ent req HS dipl; degrees BA 4 yrs; scholarships; SC 15, LC 4; enrl D 200, maj 42, others 1700
Tuition: $3100 per yr; campus res—room & board $1500
Courses: Aesthetics, Art Education, Ceramics, Drawing, Graphic Design, Handicrafts, History of Art & Archaeology, Jewelry, Lettering, Museum Staff Training, Painting,

Photography, Sculpture, Stage Design, Teacher Training, Theatre Arts, Weaving
Summer School: Enrl 250; term of six or four wks beginning end of May

MINNEAPOLIS COLLEGE OF ART AND DESIGN, 133 E 25th St, 55404. Tel 612-870-3346. *Pres* Jerome H Hausman, PhD; *Acting Chmn Fine Arts* Kinji Akagawa, MFA; *Chmn Design* Patrick Whitney, MFA; *Basic Studies* Gerald Allan, MA; *Liberal Arts* Frank Dreisbach, MA; *Vis Prof* Michele Amateau, painting sculpture - 1980; *Vis Prof* Dee Axelrod, 1980. Instrs FT 42, PT 8
Estab 1886; pvt; D & E; ent req HS dipl or GED; degrees BFA 4 yr; scholarships; SC 78, LC 23; enrl D 650, E 480
Tuition: res & nonres—undergrad $2920 per yr, $1423 per sem, part-time $120 per cr; campus res—room $800 per yr
Courses: Art History, Calligraphy, Drawing, Fashion Arts, Film, Graphic Arts, Illustration, Painting, Photography, Printmaking, Sculpture, Video, Critical Studies, Design Theory and Methods, Liberal Arts, Packaging and Product Design
Children's Classes: Courses offered
Summer School: Dir of Extension Prog, Ellen Meyer. Courses—Drawing, Graphic Design, History of Art and Design, Liberal Arts, Painting, Papermaking, Photography, Printmaking, Sculpture, Video

NORTH HENNEPIN COMMUNITY COLLEGE, Art Department,* 7411 85th Ave N, 55445. Tel 612-425-4541. *Head Dept* Frank Schreiber
Estab 1964; pub; D & E; ent req HS dipl. ent exam; degrees AA 2 yr; scholarships; SC 15, LC 4; enrl D 500, E 100, maj 200, others 100
Tuition: In-state $12 per hr; out-of-state $24 per hr
Courses: Advertising Design, Aesthetics, Architecture, Commercial Art, Display, Drawing, Graphic Arts, Graphic Design, History of Art & Archaeology, Illustration, Lettering, Occupational Therapy, Painting, Photography, Stage Design, Theatre Arts, Audiovisual, Contemporary Arts
Adult Hobby Classes: Enrl 30-100. Courses—Painting, Photography, Video
Summer School: Dir, Don Durand. Enrl 700; term of 5 wks beginning June. Courses—Costume, Drawing, Introduction to Arts, Theatre

UNIVERSITY OF MINNESOTA, MINNEAPOLIS
—School of Architecture and Landscape Architecture, Institute of Technology, 110 Architecture Bldg, 55455. Tel 612-373-2198. *Head* Ralph E Rapson. Instrs FT 12, PT 25
Estab 1912; pub; D & E; ent req completion of recommended first yr col work, selective admis; degrees BArchit, BLandscape Archit, BEnviron Design, MArchit, MLandscape Archit 4-6 yrs; scholarships and fels; SC 20, LC 25, GC 15
—Art History, 27 Pleasant St SE, 108 Jones Hall, 55455. Tel 612-373-3057. *Chmn* Frederick M Asher; *Prof* Norman W Canedy, PhD; *Prof* Frederick A Cooper, PhD; *Prof* Sheila J McNally, PhD; *Prof* Marion J Nelson, PhD; *Prof* Carl D Sheppard, PhD; *Prof* Sidney Simon, PhD; *Prof* Melvin Waldfogel, PhD; *Assoc Prof* Karal Ann Marling, PhD; *Assoc Prof* Robert Poor, PhD; *Assoc Prof* M Alison Stones, PhD; *Asst Prof* Frederick T Smith, PhD; *Asst Prof* John Steyaert, PhD; *Asst Prof* Michael Stoughton, PhD
Pub; D & E; ent req HS dipl, ent exam, GRE required for grad school; degrees BA 4 yrs, MA 2 yrs; scholarships; LC 28, GC 59; enrl D 1200 per quarter, E 300 per quarter, maj 80, grad 105
Tuition: Res—undergrad $254 per quarter, grad $29 per cr hr; nonres—undergrad $724 per quarter, grad $80 per cr hr; campus res available
Courses: †Art History, History of Art & Archaeology, Museum Staff Training
—Department of Studio Art, 216 21st Ave S, Minneapolis, MN. (Mailing Add: 208 Art Bldg, West Bank, 55455) Tel 612-373-3663. *Chmn Dept* Herman Rowan, MFA
Estab 1851, fine arts estab 1939; pub; D & E; ent req HS dipl, PSAT, ACT; degrees BA and BFA 4 yrs, MFA 2-3 yrs; scholarships; SC 39, LC 7; enrl D 1630, E approx 1000, maj 537, grad 53
Tuition: Res—$310 per quarter, $29 per cr hr; nonres—$724 per quarter, $80 per cr hr; extension $17-$29 per cr hr; campus res—$1300 per yr
Courses: Advertising Design, †Ceramics, Commercial Art, †Drawing, †Film, Illustration, †Painting, †Photography, †Printmaking, †Sculpture, †Glassworking
Summer School: Dir, Willard Thompson. Tui $15 per cr hr for term of 5 wks beginning June 12 and July 17. Courses—Ceramics, Drawing, Film, Glassworking, Painting, Photography, Printmaking, Sculpture

MOORHEAD

CONCORDIA COLLEGE, Art Department,* 920 S Eighth, 56560. Tel 218-299-4000. *Chmn* Barbara Glasrud, MA; *Prof* Dean B Bowman, MFA; *Prof* Elizabeth Strand, MFA; *Asst Prof* Paul F Allen, MFA; *Asst Prof* Orland J Rourke, MA
Estab 1891; pvt; D; ent req HS dipl, character references; degrees BA and BM 4 yrs, independent studio work, work-study prog and special studies; scholarships; SC 10, LC 5; enrl D 150, maj 40, total 2600
Tuition: $2995 per yr, $490 per course, student association dues $35; campus res—room $520 & board $625
Courses: Art Education, Art History, Ceramics, Drawing, History of Art & Archaeology, Mixed Media, Painting, Printmaking, Sculpture, Teacher Training, Design
Summer School: Dir, Donald Dale. Enrl 40; tui $295 for term of 4 wks beginning May 15 and June 12. Courses—Art History, Art History Travel Seminar, Drawing, Painting, Printmaking

MOORHEAD STATE UNIVERSITY, Department of Art, 56560. Tel 218-236-2151. *Chmn* P R Szeitz, MFA; *Prof* Lyle Laske, MFA; *Prof* John Youngquist, MFA; *Assoc Prof* Dr Virginia Barsch, PhD; *Assoc Prof* Dr John Boyd Holland, PhD; *Assoc Prof* Donald B McRaven Jr, MFA; *Assoc Prof* P J Mousseau, MFA; *Assoc Prof* Timothy Ray; *Assoc Prof* Marcel C Stratton, MA
Estab 1887; pub; D & E; ent req HS dipl; degrees BA, BS 4 yr, BFA 5 yr, MS additional 1 1 4 yr; scholarships; SC 47, LC 20, GC 11; enrl D 4520, maj 175, grad 2
Tuition: Res—undergrad $10 per cr hr, grad $13 per cr hr; nonres—undergrad $21 per cr hr, grad $27 per cr hr; campus res—room & board $1158 per yr
Courses: Advertising Design, Aesthetics, Art Education, Art History, Ceramics, Collage, Conceptual Art, Constructions, Display, Drawing, Graphic Arts, Graphic Design, History of Art & Archaeology, Illustration, Jewelry, Mixed Media, Painting, Photography, Printmaking, Sculpture, Stage Design, Teacher Training, Theatre Arts,

Video
Summer School: Tui per cr hr for term of 5 wks beginning June. Courses—Basic Drawing, Ceramics, Elements of Art Design, Graphic Design, Painting, Photography, Printmaking

MORRIS

UNIVERSITY OF MINNESOTA, MORRIS, Humanities Department,* 56267. Tel 612-589-4501. *Chmn* W D Spring; *Coordr* Lois Hodgell, MFA; *Coordr* Frederick Peterson, PhD
Estab 1960, dept estab 1963; pub; D; ent req top 50% in HS, ACT or PSAT; degrees BA 4 yrs; scholarships; SC 16, LC 8; enrl D 195, non-maj 150, maj 45
Tuition: Res—undergrad $271 per quarter; nonres—undergrad $772 per quarter; campus res—room and board $475
Courses: Aesthetics, Art Education, †Art History, Ceramics, Drawing, Graphic Arts, Painting, Photography, Printmaking, Sculpture, Teacher Training, †Studio Art

NORTHFIELD

CARLETON COLLEGE, Department of Art History,* 55057. Tel 507-663-4000. *Chmn* R I Jacobson
Estab 1921; pvt; degrees 4 yr; scholarships; SC 14, LC 15; enrl maj 30, others 550
Tuition: $5277, campus res
Courses: Art History, General Art

ST OLAF COLLEGE, Art Department, 55057. Tel 507-663-3248. *Chmn* Arch Leeam, MA; *Prof* John Maakestad, MFA; *Prof* Edward Sovik; *Assoc Prof* Reidar Dittman, PhD; *Assoc Prof* Dorothy Divers, MFA; *Asst Prof* Wendell Arneson; *Asst Prof* Malcolm Gimse, MFA
Estab 1875, dept estab 1932; den; D & E; ent req HS dipl, SAT; degrees BA 4 yr; scholarships
Tuition: Campus residency available
Courses: Aesthetics, Architecture, †Art Education, †Art History, Calligraphy, Ceramics, Commercial Art, Drafting, Drawing, Film, Graphic Arts, Graphic Design, History of Art & Archaeology, Interior Design, Lettering, Painting, Photography, Printmaking, Sculpture, Stage Design, Teacher Training, Theatre Arts
Summer School: Dir, Lydia Quanbeck. Courses—Production Art, 20th Century Art

ROCHESTER

ROCHESTER COMMUNITY COLLEGE, Art Department, 55901. Tel 507-285-7236. *Instr* Robert Clausen, MFA; *Instr* Terry Dennis, MFA; *Instr* Pat Kraemer, BA; *Instr* Flo Sandon, MA
Estab 1920s; pub; D & E; ent req state req; degrees AA; SC 17, LC 4; enrl D & E 2500, maj 35
Tuition: Res $30 per cr; non-res $60 except in reciprocal states
Courses: Advertising Design, Art History, Ceramics, Drawing, Handicrafts, Jewelry, Painting, Photography, Printmaking, Sculpture, Stage Design, Fibers, Studio, Watercolor
Adult Hobby Classes: Tui variable. Courses—Embroidery, Stained Glass, Wood Carving, others on less regular basis
Summer School: Art workshops are offered for at least one session each summer

SAINT CLOUD

SAINT CLOUD STATE UNIVERSITY, Department of Art, 56301. Tel 612-255-4283. *Chmn* Dr James Roy. Instrs FT 15, PT 4
Pub; D & E; ent req HS dipl; degrees BA, BFA, BS MA(Studio Art) and MS 4 yrs; SC 65, LC 15, GC 20; enrl maj 400, grad 60
Tuition: Res—undergrad $12 per hr, grad $16 per hr; nonres—undergrad $25 per hr, grad $31 per hr
Courses: Advertising Design, Aesthetics, Art Education, Ceramics, Commercial Art, Display, Drawing, Graphic Arts, Graphic Design, History of Art & Archaeology, Illustration, Jewelry, Lettering, Museum Staff Training, Painting, Photography, Sculpture, Teacher Training, Textile Design, Glass Blowing, Weaving

SAINT JOSEPH

COLLEGE OF SAINT BENEDICT, Art Department, 56374. Tel 612-363-5785. *Dean of Fine Art* S Firmin Escher, MM; *Chmn* Stan Shafer, MFA; *Instructor* Sr Johanna Becker, PhD; *Instructor* Don Bruno, MFA; *Instructor* Sr Thomas Carey, BFA; *Instructor* Sr Dennis Frandrup, MFA; *Instructor* Gordon Goetemann, MFA; *Instructor* Sr Baulu Kuan, MA
Estab 1913; pvt; D & E; ent req HS dipl, SAT PSAT, ACT; degrees BA(Art Educ), BA(Art) and BA(Art History) 4 yr, internships and open studio; scholarships; SC 28, LC 15; enrl D 1500, maj 80
Tuition: $3375 per year; campus res—room and board $525-$600 per year
Courses: †Art Education, †Art History, Calligraphy, †Ceramics, †Commercial Art, Conceptual Art, Constructions, Costume Design & Construction, Drawing, †Graphic Arts, †Graphic Design, Jewelry, Mixed Media, †Painting, †Photography, †Printmaking, †Sculpture
Children's Classes: Enrl 30; tui $25 per term. Courses—mixed and various media

SAINT PAUL

BETHEL COLLEGE, Department of Art, 3900 Bethel Dr, 55112. Tel 612-614-6400, Ext 6263 & 6366. *Chmn* David Johnson; *Prof* Eugene Johnson, MFA; *Assoc Prof* Dale R Johnson; *Assoc Prof* Stewart Luchman; *Assoc Prof* George Robinson, BFA
Estab 1871; den; D & E; ent req HS dipl, SAT, ACT, PSAT or NMSQT, evidence of a standard of faith and practice that is compatible with Bethel lifestyle; degrees BA(Art Educ) and BA(Studio Arts) 4 yr; scholarships; SC 20, LC 12; enrl non-maj 100, maj 100

Tuition: $1495 per sem; campus res—room ($350) and board ($325)
Courses: Art Education, Art History, Ceramics, Drawing, Graphic Design, Painting, Printmaking, Sculpture, , Three Dimensional Design, Two Dimensional Design, Visual Awareness
Summer School: Dir, Tricia Brownlee. Tui $250 per each course taken for cr, $55 for each course taken without cr; summer housing $18 per wk; food service available; terms begin May 23, June 20th and an extended term from June 19 to Aug 11. Courses—Art, Music, Theatre Arts

COLLEGE OF SAINT CATHERINE, Visual Arts Department, 2004 Randolph, 55105. Tel 612-698-5571, Ext 6635. *Chmn* Peter Lupori. Instrs FT 4, PT 6
Pvt; W; D; ent req HS dipl; degrees BA(Art) 4 yr; scholarships
Courses: Art Education, Art History, Calligraphy, Ceramics, Drawing, Graphic Arts, Graphic Design, Jewelry, Lettering, Painting, Photography, Sculpture
Summer School: Summer high school workshop

COLLEGE OF SAINT THOMAS, Department of Art, 2115 Summit Ave, 55108. Tel 612-647-5789. *Chmn* Eileen Michels, PhD; *Adjunct Instr* Mary Swanson, MFA & MA
Estab 1885, dept estab 1978; den; D & E; ent req HS dipl; degrees BA 4 yrs; scholarships; SC 25, LC 8; enrl D 2847, E 275, maj 40
Tuition: $1280 per sem, $80 audit; campus res—room $275-$375 per sem and board $375 per sem
Courses: Art Education, †Art History, Calligraphy, Ceramics, Drawing, Graphic Arts, Graphic Design, Jewelry, Painting, Photography, Printmaking, Sculpture, Teacher Training
Adult Hobby Classes: Enrl 15-20 per class; tui $25-$30. Courses—vary
Summer School: Dir, Dr James Byrne. Courses—Introduction to Art History

CONCORDIA COLLEGE, Art Department, Fine Arts Division, Hamline - Marshall, 55104. Tel 612-641-8494. *Chmn Div* Fred Brauer, MA; *Chmn Art Dept* Robert E Rickels, MA; *Assoc Prof* Ben Marxhansen, MA; *Instr* John Mueller, MA
Estab 1897, dept estab 1967; den; D & E; ent req HS dipl; degrees BS and BA 4 yrs; scholarships; SC 14, LC 3; enrl D 84, E 20, others 35
Tuition: $2160 per yr; campus res—room & board $1215 per yr
Courses: Aesthetics, Art Education, Art History, Ceramics, Drawing, Jewelry, Painting, Photography, Printmaking, Sculpture, Teacher Training, Theatre Arts
Summer School: Dean of Faculty, David Schmiel. Courses—Art Educ Methods, Art Fundamentals

HAMLINE UNIVERSITY, Art Department, 55104. Tel 612-641-2230, Ext 2296. *Head Dept* Dr Frederick D Leach, PhD; *Prof* James Conaway, MFA; *Prof* Leonardo Lasansky, MFA; *Prof* Michael Price, MFA; *Instructor* Clifford Garten, MFA
Estab 1854; pvt; D & E; ent req HS dipl; degrees BA 4 yrs; scholarships; SC 13, LC 13; enrl non-maj 70, maj 35
Tuition: $3400 per yr; campus res—room & board $700 per yr
Courses: Art Education, Art History, Ceramics, Drawing, History of Art & Archaeology, Museum Staff Training, Painting, Photography, Printmaking, Sculpture
Summer School: Dean, Jack Johnson

MACALESTER COLLEGE, Department of Art,* 1600 Grand Ave, 55105. Tel 612-647-6221. *Head Dept* Anthony Caponi
Estab 1946; den; D; degrees 4 yr; scholarships; SC 9, LC 8; enrl 20
Tuition: Average yr $4210; campus residence available
Courses: Aesthetics, Art History, Ceramics, Drawing, Graphic Arts, Painting, Sculpture, American Art, Design, Modern and Oriental Art, Primitive Art, Principals, Processes and Application, Senior Seminar
Summer School: Dir, W Harley Henry. Two 4 wk sessions June and July

MINNESOTA MUSEUM OF ART, ART SCHOOL, Education Division, 30 E Tenth St, 55101. Tel 612-227-7613. *Dir* Nell McClure
Estab 1926; pub; D & E; SC 12
Courses: Drawing, Painting, Photography, Pottery, Watercolor
Adult Hobby Classes: Tui $48 for 8 wks
Children's Classes: Tui $30 for 3 wks

SCHOOL OF THE ASSOCIATED ARTS, 344 Summit Ave, 55102. Tel 612-224-3416. *Dir* Virginia Rahja, MFA; *Dean* Ronald Swenson, MFA; *Instructor* Jerry Lefevre, MFA; *Instructor* John Lenertz, BFA; *Instructor* Philip Ogle, MFA
Estab 1924; pvt; D; ent req HS dipl; degrees BFA 4 yr; scholarships; SC 30, LC 8; enrl D 95, maj 95
Tuition: $2700 per yr; campus res—room & board $3488
Courses: Advertising Design, Art History, †Commercial Art, †Drawing, †Graphic Design, Illustration, Lettering, †Painting, Photography, Sculpture, Mass Communications, Production, TV Productions

UNIVERSITY OF MINNESOTA, Department of Design, 1985 Buford Ave, Saint Paul, MN. (Mailing Add: 240 McNeal Hall, Saint Paul, MN 55108) Tel 612-373-1032. *Head Dept* Gertrude Esteros, PhD; *Prof* Marian Bagley, MA; *Prof* Eugene Larkin, MA; *Assoc Prof* Richard Abell, MA; *Assoc Prof* Homa Amir-Fazli, MA; *Assoc Prof* Ann Erickson, MA; *Assoc Prof* Virginia Nagle, BA; *Assoc Prof* Joseph Ordos, MA; *Asst Prof* Timothy Blade, PhD; *Asst Prof* Charlene Burningham, MA; *Asst Prof* Delores Ginthner, MA; *Instructor* Evelyn Franklin, MA
Pub; D & E; ent req HS dipl; degrees BS, MS and PhD 4 yr, evening extension 2 yr cert; SC 31, LC 15, GC 33; enrl D 1012 (winter quarter 78), non-maj 265, maj 747, grad 39, others 21 adult specials
Tuition: Res—undergrad $320 per quarter, $27 per cr hr, grad $34 per cr hr with appointment; nonres—undergrad $880 per quarter, grad $34 per cr hr with appointment, $94 per cr hr without appointment
Courses: Art History, Calligraphy, †Costume Design & Construction, Drawing, Goldsmithing, Handicrafts, †Interior Design, Jewelry, †Silversmithing, Textile Design, Costume History, Decorative Arts, Housing, Weaving Off-Loom
Summer School: Tui $15 per cr. Courses—Color and Design, Introduction to Design, Materials, Three Dimensional Design Process, Visual Presentation

SAINT PETER

GUSTAVUS ADOLPHUS COLLEGE, Art Department, Schaefer Fine Arts Center, 56082. Tel 507-931-4300, Ext 462. *Chmn* Gene D Buckley. Instrs FT 5 PT 1
Estab 1876; den; D; ent req HS grad, ent exam; degrees BA 4 yr; scholarships; SC 27; enrl 2300 total, 750 art, maj 50
Tuition: $4300 per yr (comprehensive fee); PT $375 per course
Courses: Art Education, Art History, Ceramics, Costume Design & Construction, Drawing, Film, Jewelry, Painting, Photography, Printmaking, Sculpture, Stage Design, Teacher Training, Textile Design, Theatre Arts, Basic Design, Bronze Casting, Weaving
Summer School: Enrl approx 50; two 4 wk terms from June to July and July to Aug. Courses—Ceramics, Painting, Photography, Printmaking

WILLMAR

WILLMAR COMMUNITY COLLEGE, * 56201. Tel 612-235-2131. *Head Dept* Robert Mattson. Instrs FT 1, PT 1
Estab 1962-63; pub; D & E; ent req HS dipl; degrees AA, AS and AAA 2 yrs; SC 8, LC 3; enrl D 50, maj 15
Tuition: Res—undergrad $12 per cr
Courses: Art Education, Ceramics, Display, Drawing, Graphic Arts, Graphic Design, History of Art & Archaeology, Painting, Teacher Training, Introduction to Studio Practices, Structure
Adult Hobby Classes: Courses—Design, Etching, History of Art, Painting

WINONA

COLLEGE OF SAINT TERESA, Art Department, 55987. Tel 507-454-2930. *Head Dept* Anna Poulos, MFA; *Prof* Earl F Potvin, MFA; *Assoc Prof* Sr Clairvaux McFarland, MA; *Asst Prof* Mary Matthews, MA - ATR
Estab 1904, dept estab 1964; pvt; D; ent req HS dipl, SAT; degrees BA 4 yrs; scholarships; SC 28, LC 10; enrl D 450, non-maj 10, maj 40
Tuition: Res and nonres—undergrad $3057 per yr, $1019 per sem, $345 per course; campus res available
Courses: Advertising Design, Aesthetics, †Art Education, Art History, Ceramics, Commercial Art, Drawing, †Graphic Arts, Handicrafts, Jewelry, Mixed Media, Painting, Printmaking, Sculpture, Silversmithing, †Teacher Training, Textile Design, Art Therapy

SAINT MARY'S COLLEGE, Art Department, Terrace Heights, 55987. Tel 507-452-4430. *Head Dept* Karen Kryzsko, MFA; *Assoc Prof* Helen Galloway, PhD; *Asst Prof* Margaret Mear, MFA; *Asst Prof* Roderick Robertson, MFA
Estab 1912, dept estab 1970; den; D; ent req HS dipl; degrees BA 4 yrs; SC 20, LC 6; enrl in school D 1240
Tuition: $2976 per yr; campus res—room & board $1540 per yr
Courses: Aesthetics, Art History, Ceramics, Drawing, Graphic Design, Handicrafts, Jewelry, Painting, Photography, Printmaking, Sculpture, Batik, Copper, Enameling, Macrame

WINONA STATE UNIVERSITY, Art Department,* Johnson and Sanborn Sts, 55987. Tel 507-457-2110. *Head Dept* Charles F Evans, MFA; *Prof* Virginia H Vint, EdD; *Asst Prof* Wallace N Johnson, PhD; *Asst Prof* Raymond R Kiihne, MFA; *Asst Prof* Wilfred McKenzie, MFA; *Instr* Judy Schlawin, MS
Estab 1860; pub; D & E; degrees BA and BS
Tuition: Res—undergrad $10 per cr hr, grad $13 per cr hr; nonres—undergrad $20 per cr hr, grad $25 per cr hr; plus student fees; campus res $437 per yr single occupancy
Courses: Art Education, Art History, Ceramics, Commercial Art, Drawing, Graphic Arts, Interior Design, Jewelry, Lettering, Painting, Printmaking, Sculpture

MISSISSIPPI

BLUE MOUNTAIN

BLUE MOUNTAIN COLLEGE, Art Department, 38610. Tel 601-685-5711, Ext 62. *Chmn Dept* William Dowdy, MA
Estab 1873, dept estab 1875; den; D & E; ent req HS dipl; degrees BA and BS(Educ) 4 yr; scholarships; SC 16, LC 2; enrl D 28, E 12, non-maj 20, maj 8, others 12
Tuition: $1260 per yr, $42 per sem hr; campus res—room & board $1170 per yr
Courses: Art Education, Art History, Commercial Art, †Drawing, †Painting
Adult Hobby Classes: Enrl 12; tui $42 per sem hr. Courses—Drawing, Painting
Summer School: Dir, William Dowdy. Enrl 20, tui $42 per sem hr for term of 10 wks beginning June 5 and July 10

BOONEVILLE

NORTHEAST MISSISSIPPI JUNIOR COLLEGE, Art Department, 38829. *Chmn* Barbara B Curlee. Instrs FT 2
Estab 1948; pub; D & E; ent req HS dipl, ent exam; degrees 2 yr Associate degrees in art educ, fine arts and interior design; scholarships; SC 5, LC 3; enrl D 1800, maj 30
Courses: Aesthetics, Art Education, Art History, Ceramics, Drafting, Drawing, Painting, Teacher Training, Theatre Arts, Design

CLEVELAND

DELTA STATE UNIVERSITY, Department of Art, Box D02, 38733. Tel 601-843-2151. *Chmn* Malcolm M Norwood, MA; *Assoc Prof* Sam Glenn Britt, MFA; *Assoc Prof* Carolyn Rea Stone, PhD; *Asst Prof* Lallah M Perry, MEd; *Asst Prof* Floyd D Shaman, MA; *Asst Prof* Terry Kay Simmons, MA; *Asst Prof* Robert Jerry Walden, MFA; *Instructor* Mary Jane Baird, ASID; *Instructor* William Carey Lester Jr, MFA; *Instructor* Mary Anne Ross, BFA
Estab 1924; pub; D & E; ent req HS dipl; degrees BA, BFA and BSE 4 yr, MEd(Art Educ) 1 yr; scholarships; SC 42, LC 10, GC 30; enrl maj 110
Tuition: Res—undergrad & grad $1546 per yr, $776 per sem; nonres—undergrad & grad $2346 per yr, $1176 per sem
Courses: Advertising Design, Aesthetics, Art Education, Art History, Calligraphy, Ceramics, Commercial Art, Costume Design & Construction, Drawing, Fashion Arts, Graphic Arts, Graphic Design, Handicrafts, Illustration, Interior Design, Lettering, Mixed Media, Painting, Printmaking, Sculpture, Teacher Training, Textile Design, Clay, Fibers
Children's Classes: Enrl 15 per class; tui $25 per sem. Two classes ages 6-8 and 9-12
Summer School: Tui $318 per term, June 2 - July 3 or July 7 - August 8. Courses—Art for Elementary, Ceramics, Drawing, Internship in Commercial Design, Introduction to Art, Painting, Sculpture

CLINTON

MISSISSIPPI COLLEGE, Art Department, 39056. Tel 601-924-5131. *Head Dept* Dr Samuel M Gore. Instrs FT 3, PT 4
Estab 1825, dept estab 1950; den; HS grad; ent req BA, BE(Art) and ME(Art) 4 yr, Freshman Art merit; scholarships and student assistantships; SC 22, LC 3; enrl maj 80, others 300
Tuition: $825 per sem; campus res—room & board $1497 per sem
Courses: Art Education, Art History, Ceramics, Commercial Art, Drawing, Interior Design, Painting, Sculpture, Foundry Casting
Summer School: Courses—Art Appreciation, Art Education, Basic Design, Ceramics, Painting, Sculpture

COLUMBUS

MISSISSIPPI UNIVERSITY FOR WOMEN, Art Department, 1100 Fifth Ave S, PO Box W-70 MUW, 39701. Tel 601-328-4881. *Chmn* Charles E Ambrose, MA; *Prof* Mary Evelyn Stringer, PhD; *Prof* Eugenia Summer, MA; *Assoc Prof* Elizabeth J Dice, MDes, MA; *Assoc Prof* Lawrence Feeny, MFA; *Assoc Prof* David Frank, MFA; *Assoc Prof* Thomas Nawrocki, MFA; *Asst Prof* Alan Thurlow, MA; *Instructor* Frances Hardy, MA; *Instructor* Beverly Kissinger, MFA; *Instructor* Margaret Nagy, MFA; *Instructor* Paul Olsen, MFA
Estab 1884; pub; D & E; ent req HS dipl, ACT, SAT; degrees BA, BS and BFA 4 yrs, MFA 2 yrs; scholarships; SC 44, LC 11, GC 43; enrl D 379, E 45, non-maj 379, maj 200
Tuition: Res—undergrad and grad $574 per yr, $287 per sem, $23 per hr; nonres—undergrad and grad $1324 per yr, $662 per sem, $31 per hr; campus res—room & board $1054
Courses: †Advertising Design, †Art Education, Art History, Calligraphy, †Ceramics, Collage, †Commercial Art, Conceptual Art, Interior Design, Jewelry, Lettering, Mixed Media, †Painting, Photography, †Printmaking, †Sculpture, †Illustration, †Interior Design, Jewelry, Lettering, Mixed Media, †Painting, Photography, †Printmaking, †Sculpture, Silversmithing, Stage Design, Teacher Training, Textile Design, †Theatre Arts, †Video, Glassblowing, Metalcrafts, Weaving
Adult Hobby Classes: Enrl 45; tui $23 per hr. Courses—Calligraphy, Ceramics, Drawing, Interior Decorating, Painting
Summer School: Tui $23 per hr for term of 5 wks beginning June 2. Courses—vary according to demand

DECATUR

EAST CENTRAL JUNIOR COLLEGE, Art Department, Box 27, 39327. Tel 601-635-2121. *Head Dept* J Bruce Guraedy, MEd
Estab 1928, dept estab 1965; pub; D & E; ent req HS dipl, GED; degrees AA and AS 2 yrs; SC 10, LC 4; enrl in dept D 120, E 52, non-maj 58, maj 10
Tuition: Res—$320 per yr, $160 per sem; non-res—$720 per yr, $360 per sem; campus residence available
Courses: Art Education, Art History, Ceramics, Drafting, Drawing, Fashion Arts, Industrial Design, Painting, Sculpture, Teacher Training, Theatre Arts
Adult Hobby Classes: Enrl 48; tui $23 per sem
Children's Classes: Pvt lessons available
Summer School: Acad Dean, Dr B J Tucker. Enrl 200-300; tui $15 per sem hr for term of 10 wks. Courses—vary according to student demand

ELLISVILLE

JONES COUNTY JUNIOR COLLEGE, Art Department,* Court St, 39437. Tel 601-477-9311. *Chmn* Milfred Valentine
Estab 1927; pub; D; ent req HS dipl; degrees AA 2 yrs; scholarships; SC 12, LC 4; enrl D 100, E 12, maj 15, others 12
Tuition: In-state $180; out-of-state $570
Courses: Advertising Design, Architecture, Art Education, Ceramics, Commercial Art, Display, Drafting, Drawing, Graphic Arts, History of Art & Archaeology, Lettering, Painting
Adult Hobby Classes: Enrl 20. Courses—Painting
Summer School: Dir, B F Ogletree. Term of 4 wks beginning June. Courses—same as regular session

HATTIESBURG

UNIVERSITY OF SOUTHERN MISSISSIPPI, Department of Art, College of Fine Arts, 39401. Tel 601-266-7281. *Chmn* Dr Jeff R Bowman, EdD. Instrs FT 10, PT 4
Estab 1910; pub; D & E; ent req HS dipl, qualifications; degrees BA, BFA, MAE, MFA; scholarships; SC 64, LC 41, GC 34; enrl non-maj 35, maj 185, grad 18
Tuition: Campus residency available
Courses: Aesthetics, †Art Education, Art History, Ceramics, †Commercial Art, Display, †Drawing, Goldsmithing, Graphic Arts, Graphic Design, Handicrafts, Illustration, Jewelry, Lettering, †Painting, Printmaking, †Sculpture, Silversmithing, Teacher Training, Textile Design, Weaving
Adult Hobby Classes: Ceramics, Drawing, Painting
Children's Classes: Arts & Crafts, Drawing, Painting
Summer School: Courses—as above

WILLIAM CAREY COLLEGE, Art Department, 39401. Tel 601-582-5051, Ext 237. *Chmn* Lucile Parker, MFA; *Asst Chmn* Patrice Box-Pope, MFA
Estab 1906, dept estab 1889; den; D & E; ent req HS dipl, qualifications; degrees BA, BS, BM, MM and MEd 4 yr; scholarships; enrl D 75, E 25, non-maj 86, maj 14
Tuition: Res—undergrad $2400 per yr (incl boarding); nonres—undergrad $1400 per yr
Courses: Advertising Design, Art Education, Art History, Ceramics, Drawing, Graphic Arts, Graphic Design, Lettering, Painting, Photography, Printmaking
Adult Hobby Classes: Drawing, Painting

JACKSON

BELHAVEN COLLEGE, Art Department, 1500 Peachtree, 39202. Tel 601-355-6893. *Chmn* Jon Whittington, MA
Estab 1883, dept estab 1889; den; D & E; ent req HS dipl; degrees BA; scholarships; LC 3; enrl D 650, E 200, maj 30
Courses: Art History, Drawing, Graphic Arts, Painting, Photography, Printmaking
Summer School: Dir, Dr Dewey Buckley

JACKSON STATE UNIVERSITY, Department of Art,* Lynch at Dalton St, 39207. Tel 601-968-2040. *Chmn* Grace Hampton
Estab 1949; pub; D; ent req HS dipl; degrees BS(maj in Art) 4 yrs; scholarships; SC 16, LC 7, GC 1; enrl D 486, maj 112
Tuition: Res—$620 per yr; nonres—$1420 per yr; campus res available
Courses: Advertising Design, Art Education, Ceramics, Costume Design & Construction, Drawing, Graphic Arts, History of Art & Archaeology, Jewelry, Painting, Stage Design, Teacher Training, Leather, Weaving
Adult Hobby Classes: Enrl 80; Athenian Art Club activities
Summer School: Dir, Dr Wilbert Greenfield. Courses—same as regular session

LORMAN

ALCORN STATE UNIVERSITY, Department of Fine Arts,* 39096. Tel 601-877-3711. *Chmn* Joyce Bolden, PhD; *Asst Prof* Constance Alford, MFA; *Asst Prof* Henry Sumpter, MFA
Estab 1871, dept estab 1973; pub; D & E; ent req HS dipl, ACT; SC 9, LC 3
Tuition: In-state $628 per yr; out-of-state $1428
Courses: Art Education, Art History, Ceramics, Drawing, Handicrafts, Painting
Adult Hobby Classes: Enrl 20. Courses—Drawing, Painting
Summer School: Enrl 25 for term of 10 wks beginning May 28. Courses—Art Education, Fine Arts

MISSISSIPPI STATE

MISSISSIPPI STATE UNIVERSITY, Art Department, PO Box 5182, 39762. Tel 601-325-4522. *Prof* Authur Leonard Farley, MA; *Assoc Prof* Kenneth Clifford, MFA; *Assoc Prof* Larry Jan Webber, BFA; *Asst Prof* Jack Bartlett, MFA; *Asst Prof* Michael Dorsey, MFA; *Asst Prof* DeAnna Douglas, MFA; *Asst Prof* Paul Grootkerk, PhD; *Asst Prof* Robie Scucchi, MFA
Estab 1879, dept estab 1971; pub; D; ent req HS dipl; degrees BA 4 yrs; SC 23, LC 6; enrl D 750, non-maj 650, maj 100
Tuition: Campus res—room & board $205-$250 per yr
Courses: †Art Education, Art History, Ceramics, †Commercial Art, Drawing, †Painting, Photography, Printmaking
Summer School: Head Dept, A L Farley. Courses—Art History, Design, Drawing

MOORHEAD

MISSISSIPPI DELTA JUNIOR COLLEGE, Department of Fine Arts,* 38761. Tel 601-246-5311. *Chmn* Joe Abrams; *Coordr* Jean Abrams
Estab 1926; pub; D & E; ent req HS dipl, ent exam; degrees AA and AS(Commercial Art) 2 yrs; SC 11, LC 2; enrl D 68, E 29, maj 28
Tuition: $280 average per yr
Courses: Advertising Design, Ceramics, Commercial Art, Drawing, Graphic Arts, Painting, Art Appreciation
Adult Hobby Classes: Enrl 29. Courses—Ceramics, Painting

POPLARVILLE

PEARL RIVER JUNIOR COLLEGE, Fine Arts Department,* Station A, 39470. *Chmn Dept* Ray Patten
Estab 1921; pub; D; ent req HS dipl; enrl D 20, non-maj 20
Tuition: Out-of-state $150 per yr; in-state $200 per yr; campus residence available
Courses: Art Education, Drafting, Photography

RAYMOND

HINDS JUNIOR COLLEGE, Department of Art, 39154. Tel 601-857-5261, Ext 302. *Chmn* Bob A Dunaway. Instrs FT 4
Estab 1917; pub; D & E; ent req ent exam; degrees AA 2 yr; SC 5, LC 2; enrl D 400, E 75, maj 60
Courses: Advertising Design, Ceramics, Commercial Art, Display, Drawing, Graphic Design, Interior Design, Lettering, Painting, Political Cartooning, Sign Writing
Summer School: Term of 5 wks beginning June. Courses—Art Appreciation, Ceramics, Drawing, Introduction to Watercolors

SCOOBA

EAST MISSISSIPPI JUNIOR COLLEGE, Art Department, Box 176, 39358. Tel 601-476-5669. *Chmn* Terry Cherry, MA
Estab 1927; pub; D; ent req HS dipl, ACT; degrees AA 2 yr; scholarships; SC 5, LC 1; enrl D 650 total, non-maj 7, maj 9
Tuition: Res—undergrad $1060 per yr, $530 per sem; nonres—undergrad $1460 per yr, $730 per sem; campus res—room and board $760
Courses: Advertising Design, Commercial Art, Drawing, Painting, Photography, Printmaking

TOUGALOO

TOUGALOO COLLEGE, Art Department,* 39174. Tel 601-956-4941. *Chmn Dept* Ronald Schnell, MFA; *Asst Prof* Bruce O'Hara, MFA; *Adjunct Prof* Anne O'Hara
Estab 1869, dept estab 1968; pvt; D; ent req HS dipl; degrees BA and BS 4 yrs; scholarships; SC 14, LC 4; enrl D 800, non-maj 420, maj 28
Tuition: Res—undergrad average $1686 per yr
Courses: Art Education, Art History, Commercial Art, Drawing, Graphic Arts, History of Art & Archaeology, Painting, Photography, Printmaking, Sculpture, Photo Journalism

UNIVERSITY

UNIVERSITY OF MISSISSIPPI, Department of Art, 38677. Tel 601-232-7193. *Chmn* Margaret Gorove, MFA; *Prof* Robert L Tettleton, MEd; *Assoc Prof* Charles M Gross, MFA; *Assoc Prof* James Quinn, PhD; *Assoc Prof* John L Winters, MFA; *Asst Prof* Jere H Allen, MFA; *Asst Prof* William S Conrad, MFA; *Asst Prof* Tom Dewey II, PhD; *Asst Prof* Randall Harris, EdD; *Asst Prof* Roger H Wood, MFA; *Instructor* Mark W Ackley, MFA. Instrs FT 10, PT 5
Dept estab 1949; pub; D; ent req HS dipl; degrees BA and BFA 4 yr, MFA 2 yr and MA 1 yr; scholarships; SC 73, LC 36, GC 46; enrl D 612, non-maj 250, maj 130, grad 15
Tuition: Res—undergrad $440 per sem, $31 per cr hr, grad $352 per sem, $33 per cr hr; nonres—undergrad $865 per sem $66 per cr hr, grad $739 per sem, $76 per cr hr; campus res—room $230
Courses: Advertising Design, Aesthetics, †Art Education, †Art History, †Ceramics, Collage, Commercial Art, Conceptual Art, Drawing, Graphic Arts, †Graphic Design, Illustration, Interior Design, Jewelry, †Painting, †Printmaking, †Sculpture, Watercolor
Summer School: Dr, C E Noves. Two 6 wk sessions beginning June. Courses—Art Education, Art History, Ceramics, Design, Drawing, Painting, Printmaking, Sculpture

UTICA

UTICA JUNIOR COLLEGE, Humanities Division, 39175. Tel 601-885-6062. *Div Head* Dr Bobby Cooper, EdD; *Instructor* Michael McCarty, MFA
Estab 1903, dept estab 1976-77; pub; D & E; ent req HS dipl; degrees AA 2 yr; SC 9, LC 1; enrl in col 600, non-maj 30, maj 2

MISSOURI

CANTON

CULVER-STOCKTON COLLEGE, Division of Fine Arts,* 63435. Tel 314-288-5221. *Head Div* Dr A Wesley Tower
Estab 1853; pvt; D; ent req HS dipl, ACT or Col Board Ent Exam; degrees BA(Visual Arts), BS(Art Educ) and BS(Arts Management) 4 yrs; scholarships; SC 16, LC 6; enrl 844, maj 30
Tuition: $2730 per yr; campus res—room & board $1630
Courses: Aesthetics, Art Education, Ceramics, Costume Design & Construction, Drawing, Film, Graphic Arts, History of Art & Archaeology, Illustration, Jewelry, Museum Staff Training, Painting, Photography, Sculpture, Stage Design, Teacher Training, Theatre Arts
Summer School: Reg, Olga Bays. Tui $560 for 5 wks, $1120 for 10 wks. Courses—Art Appreciation, Art Education, Ceramics

CAPE GIRARDEAU

SOUTHEAST MISSOURI STATE UNIVERSITY, Department of Art, Normal Ave, 63701. Tel 314-651-2143. *Chairperson Dept Art* Bill Needle
Estab 1873, dept estab 1920; pub; D & E; ent req HS dipl; degrees BS, BS(Educ) and BA 4 yrs, MAT; scholarships; SC 28, LC 10, GC 18; enrl D 1300
Tuition: Res—$165 per sem; nonres—$415 per sem; campus res— $1150 for 7 day meal ticket, $1090 for 5 day meal ticket
Courses: Advertising Design, Art Education, Art History, Ceramics, Commercial Art, Drawing, Handicrafts, History of Art & Archaeology, Illustration, Jewelry, Lettering, Painting, Photography, Printmaking, Sculpture, Silversmithing, Teacher Training
Summer School: Chairperson Dept Art, Bill Needle. Enrl 164 undergrad, 60 grad; tui $135 for res, $350 for nonres

CLAYTON

FONTBONNE COLLEGE, Department of Art, 6800 Wydown Blvd, 63119. Tel 314-862-3456, Ext 296. *Chmn Dept* Rudolph E Torrini, MFA; *Dir Grad Prog* Henry Knickmeyer, MFA; *Assoc Prof* Kenneth Stout, MFA; *Asst Prof* Catherine Connor, MFA; *Asst Prof* David Hollowell, MFA; *Instructor* Frank Ferrario; *Instructor* Anne Martin; *Instructor* Gail Soliwoda
Estab 1923; den; D & E; ent req HS dipl; degrees BA and BFA 4 yr, MFA 2 yr; scholarships; SC 11, LC 2; enrl in dept D 60, maj 49, grad 8, others 3 special
Tuition: $2880 per yr, $1440 per sem, $105 per hr; campus res—room & board $740 to $850
Courses: Art Education, Art History, Ceramics, Drawing, Interior Design, Painting, Photography, Printmaking, Sculpture
Children's Classes: Enrl 25; tui $100 for 5 wks. Courses—Drawing, Design, Sculpture & Ceramics (junior and senior high level)
Summer School: Courses—Ceramics, Drawing, Painting, Photography, Sculpture

COLUMBIA

COLUMBIA COLLEGE, Art Department, Christian College Ave, 65216. Tel 314-449-0531. *Chmn Art Dept* Ben Cameron. Instrs FT 8, PT 3
Estab 1851; den; D; ent req HS dipl or equivalent, ACT or SAT, also accept transfer students; degrees AA 2 yrs, BA and BFA 4 yrs; scholarships; SC 30, LC 4; enrl maj 130
Tuition: $2900 per yr, activity fee $70; campus res $1700
Courses: Advertising Design, Architecture, Art Education, Ceramics, Commercial Art, Costume Design & Construction, Display, Drawing, Fashion Arts, Graphic Design, History of Art & Archaeology, Illustration, Jewelry, Lettering, Painting, Photography, Sculpture, Stage Design, Teacher Training, Textile Design, Theatre Arts

STEPHENS COLLEGE, Art Department, 65215. Tel 314-442-2211, Ext 302. *Head Dept* Gardiner R McCauley, MA; *Instructor* Bruno Andrade, MFA; *Instructor* Louise Luthi, MFA; *Instructor* Ralph Komives, MFA; *Instructor* Nancy P McCauley, MA; *Instructor* Rosalind Moulton, MFA; *Instructor* Nicholas Peckham, MArch; *Instructor* Peter Salter, MFA
Estab 1833, dept estab 1850; pvt; D & E; ent req SAT or ACT, recommendations, interview; degrees BA 3-4 yrs, BFA 3 1 2-4 yrs; scholarships; SC 25, LC 6; enrl D 950, maj 125, others 10
Tuition: $5675 per yr; Stephens Col without Walls $265 per course; campus res—room & board incl in tui
Courses: Advertising Design, Aesthetics, Architecture, †Art Education, †Art History, †Ceramics, Commercial Art, Costume Design & Construction, Drafting, Drawing, †Fashion Arts, †Film, Graphic Arts, †Graphic Design, Illustration, †Interior Design, Museum Staff Training, Occupational Therapy, †Painting, †Photography, †Printmaking, †Sculpture, †Stage Design, Teacher Training, †Theatre Arts, †Video
Children's Classes: Tui $700 per yr; Stephens Child Study Center, grades K-3, preschool; includes special creative arts emphasis
Summer School: Dir, Bobbie Burk. Tui $1225 for term of 7 wks beginning May 17. Courses—Ceramics Sculpture, Color, Drawing & Painting, Graphic Design

UNIVERSITY OF MISSOURI
—Art Department, A 126 Fine Arts, 65201. Tel 314-882-3555. *Chmn Dept* Don Bartlett, MFA
Estab 1901, dept estab 1912; pub; D & E; ent req HS dipl; degrees BA, BS(Art Educ) MA, MA(Educ), MEd, DEd, PhD and Educ Specialist; SC 76, LC 1, GC 53; enrl non-maj 1600 per sem, maj 250, grad 25
Tuition: Res—undergrad $384 per sem, grad $420 per sem; nonres—undergrad $1104 per sem, grad $1212 per sem; campus res—room & board $1460 per yr
Courses: Advertising Design, Art Education, Calligraphy, Ceramics, Drawing, Graphic Design, Illustration, Jewelry, Lettering, Painting, Photography, Printmaking, Sculpture, Textile Design
Summer School: Dir, Brooke B Cameron. Enrl 175, tui $161 for term of 8 wks beginning June 12. Courses—Art Education, Ceramics, Design, Drawing, Jewelry, Printmaking, Sculpture, Watercolor
—Art History and Archaeology Department, 109 Pickard Hall, 65211. Tel 314-882-6711. *Chmn* William R Biers, PhD; *Prof* Osmund Overby, PhD; *Prof* Homer Thomas, PhD; *Assoc Prof* Edward Baumann, PhD; *Assoc Prof* Norman Land, PhD; *Assoc Prof* David Soren, PhD; *Assoc Prof* Vera B Townsend, PhD; *Vis Prof* Theodore Reff, 1980
Estab 1839, dept estab 1915; pub; D; ent req HS dipl, SAT, GRE for grad students; degrees BA 4 yrs, MA 2-3 yrs, PhD 4 yrs; scholarships; LC 32, GC 16; enrl D 1071
Tuition: Res—grad $33 per course; nonres—grad $1400; campus res available
Courses: †Art History, Film, History of Art & Archaeology, Museum Staff Training, Sculpture

FERGUSON

SAINT LOUIS COMMUNITY COLLEGE AT FLORISSANT VALLEY, Department of Art, 3400 Pershall Rd, 63135. Tel 314-595-4365. *Chairperson Dept* Sue Eisler, MFA; *Prof* Robert Bay, MA; *Prof* Richard Buckman, MFA; *Prof* Edward Menges, MFA; *Prof* Frank Stanton, MFA; *Assoc Prof* George Bartko, MFA; *Assoc Prof* Charles J Jones, MFA; *Asst Prof* Larry Kozuszek, MFA; *Asst Prof* Kim Mosley, MFA; *Asst Prof* John Ortbals, MFA; *Instructor* Kermit Ruyle, BA
Estab 1962; pub; D & E; ent req HS dipl, ent exam; degrees AA, AAS 2 yr; SC 36, LC 4; enrl maj 70
Tuition: Res—$19 per cr hr; nonres—$27 per cr hr; no campus res
Courses: †Advertising Design, Art History, Ceramics, Commercial Art, Drawing, Graphic Arts, History of Art & Archaeology, Illustration, Lettering, Painting, Photography, Printmaking, Sculpture, Technical Illustration
Summer School: Dir, Sue Eisler. Enrl 270; tui $19 per cr hr for term of 8 wks beginning June 9. Courses—Design, Drawing, Figure Drawing, Lettering, Painting

FULTON

WILLIAM WOODS-WESTMINSTER COLLEGES, Art Department, William Woods College, 65251. Tel 314-642-2251, Ext 323. *Chmn Div Fine Arts & Head Art Dept* George E Tutt, MA; *Asst Prof* Paul Clervi, MA; *Asst Prof* Francis Sporer, MA; *Instructor* Joanne Berneche, BFA; *Instructor* Rodney Casebier, MA; *Instructor* Nick Clapp, MFA; *Instructor* Suzanne Sayre, BA; *Instructor* Phyllis Strawn, MA; *Emeritus Prof* George Latta, MFA
Estab 1870; pvt; D; ent req HS dipl, SAT or ACT; degrees BA, BS and BFA 4 yr; scholarships; SC 54, LC 6; enrl maj 71
Tuition: Res—$5600 per yr (incl room and board); nonres—$3905 per yr; campus res —room and board $1695
Courses: Aesthetics, Art Education, Art History, Ceramics, Collage, Commercial Art, Costume Design & Construction, Drawing, Handicrafts, History of Art & Archaeology, Illustration, Interior Design, Jewelry, Occupational Therapy, Painting, Photography, Printmaking, Sculpture, Silversmithing, Stage Design, Teacher Training, Theatre Arts, Art Therapy, Weaving

JEFFERSON CITY

LINCOLN UNIVERSITY, Art Department, Lafayette at Dunklin St, 65101. Instrs FT 2, PT 1
Estab 1927; pub; degrees BS(Art) and BS(Art Educ) 4 yr; enrl maj 35, others 100
Tuition: Res—$200 plus $15 per sem hr for over 15 hrs; nonres—$400 plus $25 per sem hr over 15 hrs; campus res—room and board $570 to $585 per sem
Courses: Teacher Training, Applied Art

JOPLIN

MISSOURI SOUTHERN STATE COLLEGE, Dept of Art, Newman & Duquesne Rds, 64801. Tel 417-624-8100, Ext 263. *Dir Dept* Darral A Dishman
Estab 1937; pub; D & E; ent req HS dipl; degrees BA & BSE 4 yrs; scholarships; SC 22, LC 3; enrl D 425, E 83, non-maj 360, maj 105, others 10 (over sixty)
Tuition: Res—$175 for 8 cr hrs or more, $17 per cr hr; nonres—$370 for 8 cr hrs or more, $27 per cr hr
Courses: Art Education, Art History, Ceramics, Commercial Art, Drawing, Handicrafts, Jewelry, Painting, Photography, Printmaking, Sculpture, Teacher Training, Metal Casting
Adult Hobby Classes: Enrl approx 30; tui $1 per hr. Courses—Photography, Tole, plus others. Offered by Continuing Educ Div
Summer School: Dir Art, Darral A Dishman. Enrl 15-20 per workshop; tui res $17 per cr hr, nonres $27 per cr hr for term of 2 wks beginning June. Courses—Arts & Crafts, Drawing, Jewelry, Pottery, Printmaking, Watercolor, and others

KANSAS CITY

AVILA COLLEGE, Art Department,* 11901 Wornall Rd, 64145. Tel 816-942-8400. *Chmn* William J Louis; *Prof* Sr Margaret Reinhart, MA; *Asst Prof* Sr Colette Doering, MA; *Instr* Martha Crow, MFA; *Instr* Jan Norman, MAE; *Instr* Joel Vogt, MA; *Instr* Carol Zastoupil, MFA
Estab 1963; den; D & E; ent req HS dipl, SAT and PSAT; degrees BA 4 yrs; scholarships; SC 35, LC 4; enrl D 140, E 20, non-maj 120, maj 40
Tuition: $1225 per yr; D $70 per cr hr, E $50 per cr hr
Courses: Art Education, Art History, Calligraphy, Ceramics, Drawing, Lettering, Mixed Media, Occupational Therapy, Painting, Photography, Printmaking, Sculpture, Teacher Training, Textile Design

KANSAS CITY ART INSTITUTE, 4415 Warwick Blvd, 64111. Tel 816-561-4852. *Pres* John W Lottes, BFA; *Chmn Crafts* Kenneth Ferguson, MFA; *Chmn Design* Victor Papanek; *Chmn Painting & Printmaking* Wilbur Niewald, MFA; *Chmn Photography* Lloyd Schnell, BFA; *Chmn Sculpture* Dale Eldred, MFA; *Chmn Found* Steven Whitacre, MFA; *Chmn Liberal Arts* George Burris, MA
Estab 1885; D & E; ent req HS dipl, portfolio interview; degrees BFA 4 yrs; scholarships; SC 9 maj areas, LC 104 liberal arts; enrl D 592, E 200, non-maj 200, maj 592
Tuition: $3580 per yr, $1790 per sem, $118 per cr hr; campus res—room & board $850 per yr (double occupancy)
Courses: Advertising Design, Art History, Ceramics, Commercial Art, Display, Drawing, Film, Graphic Arts, †Graphic Design, History of Art & Archaeology, Illustration, Industrial Design, Interior Design, Landscape Architecture, Mixed Media, †Painting, †Photography, †Printmaking, †Sculpture, Textile Design, Video
Adult Hobby Classes: Enrl 200; tui $118 per cr hr. Courses—Ceramics, Fiber, Painting, Printmaking, Photography
Children's Classes: High school only; tui $75 per sem. Courses—Ceramics, Drawing, Painting, Photography
Summer School: Summer Studio Workshops. Tui $600 for term of 6 wks beginning

June 19. Courses—Ceramics, Design, Fiber, Painting, Photography, Printmaking, Sculpture

MAPLE WOODS COMMUNITY COLLEGE, Dept of Art & Art History, 2601 NE Barry Rd, 64156. Tel 816-436-6500, Ext 79. *Head Dept* Helen Mary Turner, MSecEd. Instrs PT 7
Estab 1969; pub; D & E; ent req HS dipl or GED; degrees AA 2 yrs; scholarships; SC 12, LC 2; enrl D 100, E & Sat 50
Tuition: Res—$142-$274 per sem, $12-$23 per cr hr; nonres state—$586 per sem, $49 per cr hr; no campus res
Courses: Art History, Ceramics, Commercial Art, Drawing, Painting, Photography, Printmaking, Sculpture, Art Fundamentals, Stained Glass
Adult Hobby Classes: Enrl 30; tui same as above. Courses—Stained Glass
Children's Classes: Enrl 30; tui $30 for 6 wks
Summer School: Dir, Helen Mary Turner. Tui same as above for 8 wks beginning June 1. Courses—Batik, Ceramics, Silver, Painting

UNIVERSITY OF MISSOURI-KANSAS CITY, Dept of Art & Art History, 5100 Rockhill Rd, 64110. Tel 816-276-1501. *Chmn* Burton L Dunbar. Instrs FT 13, PT 2
Estab 1933; pub; D & E; ent req contact Admis Office; enrl maj 210
Tuition: $300 per sem; nonres—$600
Courses: Art History, Drawing, Graphic Design, Painting, Printmaking, Sculpture
Summer School: 1 term. For information contact Admis Office

KIRKSVILLE

NORTHEAST MISSOURI STATE UNIVERSITY, Art Department, Division of Fine Arts, 63501. Tel 816-665-5121, Ext 7196. *Head Div Fine Arts* Dean Dale Jorgenson; *Gallery Dir* Linda Emmerman; *Prof* Mary Belle Martin, EdD; *Prof* William Unger, MA; *Assoc Prof* Helen Babbitt, MFA; *Assoc Prof* Kent McAlexander, MFA; *Asst Prof* Ed McEndarfer, MFA; *Asst Prof* William Murray, MA; *Asst Prof* James Pauls, MFA; *Instructor* Robert Jones, MFA
Estab 1867; pub; D & E; ent req HS dipl, portfolio; degrees BSE(Art Educ) and BA(Commercial, Studio) 4 yrs, MA(Art Educ) 5 yrs; scholarships; SC 27, LC 8, GC 8; enrl D 220, non-maj 45, maj 175, grad 12
Tuition: $150 per sem, $20-$40 per cr hr; campus residency available
Courses: Advertising Design, Aesthetics, †Art Education, Art History, Ceramics, †Commercial Art, Constructions, Drawing, †Graphic Arts, Graphic Design, Handicrafts, Illustration, Lettering, Museum Staff Training, †Painting, Photography, †Printmaking, †Sculpture, †Teacher Training, Textile Design, Macrame
Adult Hobby Classes: Enrl 35; tui free. Courses—Art Appreciation for Sr Citizens
Summer School: Enrl 80-100; tui $15 per hr for term of two 5 wk sessions beginning June & July

LIBERTY

WILLIAM JEWELL COLLEGE, Art Dept, College Hill, 64068. Tel 816-781-3806. *Chmn* David B Johnson, MFA; *Prof* Lyn Walker, MA; *Instructor* Robert McNeely, McNeely, BFA; *Instructor* Phil Masun, BFA
Estab 1849, dept estab 1966; pvt (cooperates with the Missouri Baptist Convention); D & E; degrees BA & BS 4 yrs; enrl D 120 (art dept), E 35-40, maj 20
Tuition: $3700 (incl room & board)
Courses: Art Education, Art History, Calligraphy, Ceramics, Drawing, Jewelry, Painting, Photography, Printmaking
Children's Classes: Enrl 10
Summer School: Courses vary

MARYVILLE

NORTHWEST MISSOURI STATE UNIVERSITY, Dept of Art, 64468. Tel 816-582-7141, Ext 1314. *Chmn Dept* Lee Hageman, MFA; *Assoc Prof* Donald Robertson, MA; *Assoc Prof* Robert Sunkel, MFA; *Assoc Prof* Philip VanVoorst, MFA; *Asst Prof* Kenneth Nelsen, MFA; *Asst Prof* Russell Schmaljohn, MS; *Asst Prof* Norman Weil, MFA; *Instructor* Philip Laker, MA
Estab 1905, dept estab 1915; pub; D & E; ent req HS dipl; degrees BFA, BSE & BA 4 yrs; scholarships; SC 74, LC 19; enrl D 450, E 50, non-maj 350, maj 150
Tuition: Res—$210 per sem, $24 per hr; nonres—$420 per sem, $46 per hr; campus res $210 (room only)
Courses: †Art Education, Art History, Ceramics, Drawing, Goldsmithing, Jewelry, Painting, Photography, Printmaking, Sculpture, Silversmithing, Teacher Training, Fibers, Pewtersmithing
Summer School: Chmn Dept Art, Lee Hageman. Two wk short courses varying from summer to summer; cost is hourly rate listed above. Courses—Photography, Watercolor, Weaving

NEOSHO

CROWDER COLLEGE, Dept of Art, 64850. Tel 417-451-3223. *Instructor* Richard Boyt. Instrs FT 1, PT 7
Estab 1964; Pub; D & E; ent req HS grad or equivalent; degrees AA & AAS 2 yrs; scholarships; enrl D 1000, E 300, maj 15, others 100
Courses: Art History, Ceramics, Commercial Art, Drawing, Jewelry, Painting, Photography, Sculpture, Design, Foundry, Introduction to Visual Arts, Quilting, Weaving
Summer School: Dean of Col, J Cavanough. Term of 8 wks beginning in June. Courses —Varied academic courses

NEVADA

COTTEY COLLEGE, Fine Arts Div, 64772. Tel 417-667-8181. *Dean of Col* Earl M Tinsley. Instrs FT 3
Estab 1884; pvt; W; D; ent req HS grad, AC Board; degrees AA 2 yrs; SC 15, LC 4; enrl maj 12-15, total 369
Courses: Art History, Ceramics, Drawing, Graphic Arts, Handicrafts, Jewelry, Painting, Photography, Printmaking, Design, Metals, Weaving

POINT LOOKOUT

SCHOOL OF THE OZARKS, Department of Art, 65726. Tel 417-334-6411, Ext 255. *Chmn* Kenneth F Burchett, PhD; *Assoc Prof* Donald Barr, MA; *Assoc Prof* Janie Brewster, MS; *Asst Prof* Jayme Burchett, MFA; *Asst Prof* Cletus Johnson, MA
Estab 1906, dept estab 1962; pvt; D & E; ent req HS dipl, ACT; degrees BA 4 yrs; scholarships; SC 22, LC 4; enrl D 200, E 25, non-maj 150, maj 75
Tuition: No fees are charged; each student works 960 hrs in on-campus employment
Courses: †Advertising Design, †Art Education, Art History, Ceramics, †Drawing, Handicrafts, †Painting, †Printmaking, †Sculpture, †Teacher Training, †Textile Design, Color, Fibers, Glass
Adult Hobby Classes: Drawing, Stained Glass

SAINT CHARLES

LINDENWOOD COLLEGES, Art Dept, 63301. Tel 314-723-7152, Ext 241. *Chmn Dept* W Dean Eckert. Instrs FT 5, PT 4
Estab 1827; pvt; D & E; ent req HS dipl, ent exam; degrees BA, BS, BFA 4 yrs, MA; scholarships; SC 42, LC 24; enrl D 200, E 100, maj 45, continuing educ 25
Tuition: $2950 per yr
Courses: Art Education, Ceramics, Drawing, History of Art & Archaeology, Museum Staff Training, Painting, Photography, Printmaking, Sculpture, Teacher Training

SAINT JOSEPH

MISSOURI WESTERN STATE COLLEGE, Art Department, Downs Dr, 64507. Tel 816-271-4200, Ext 422. *Chmn Dept* Dr William Eickhorst, EdD; *Assoc Prof* John Hughes, MFA; *Asst Prof* Jim Estes, MFA; *Asst Prof* Jean Harmon, MFA; *Asst Prof* Jane Nelson, MFA
Estab 1969; pub; D & E; ent req HS dipl, GED, ACT; degrees BS(Art Educ) and BA 4 yrs; scholarships; SC 25, LC 8; enrl D 355, E 100, non-maj 120, maj 70
Tuition: Res—$442 per yr, $221 per sem, $29 per cr hr; nonres—$820 per yr, $410 per sem, $50 per cr hr; campus res—room & board $1016 per yr
Courses: Art Education, Art History, Ceramics, Drawing, Jewelry, Mixed Media, Painting, Photography, Printmaking, Sculpture, Art Appreciation, Design, Tools and Techniques
Summer School: Chmn, Art Dept, Dr William Eickhorst. Tui res $118 for 5 or more cr hrs, nonres $223 for 5 or more cr hrs; term of 8 wks beginning May 30. Courses —Art Education, Ceramics, Introduction to Art, Photomedia, Printmaking, Woodworking

SAINT LOUIS

FONTBONNE COLLEGE, Art Department, 6800 Wydown Blvd, 63105. Tel 314-862-3456, Ext 296. *Chmn Dept* Rudolph E Torrini, MFA; *Dir Grad Prog* Henry Knickmeyer, MFA; *Assoc Prof* David Hollowell, MFA; *Assoc Prof* Kenneth Stout, MFA; *Asst Prof* Catherine Connor, MFA; *Instr* Frank Ferrario, BFA
Estab 1923; pvt; D & E; ent req HS dipl, portfolio; degrees BA and BFA 4 yrs, MA 1 yr, MFA 2 yrs; scholarships; SC 10, LC 2, GC 6; enrl non-maj 10, maj 46, grad 12, others 5
Tuition: Undergrad $400 per yr, $200 per sem; grad $240 per yr, $120 per sem; $20-$25 fee charged per 3 hr course; campus res—room & board $1480 per yr
Courses: Aesthetics, Art Education, Art History, †Ceramics, Drawing, Interior Design, Mixed Media, †Painting, Photography, Printmaking, †Sculpture
Summer School: Dir, Rudolph E Torrini. Tui undergrad $55 per cr hr, grad $90 per cr hr. Courses—Ceramics, Drawing, Painting, Photography, Sculpture

MARYVILLE COLLEGE, Art Department, 13550 Conway Rd, 63141. Tel 314-576-9300, Ext 283. *Prof* Rodney M Winfield; *Assoc Prof* Charles F Jamieson, MFA; *Assoc Prof* Virginia O'Meara, MA; *Instr* Jerene Au; *Instr* Robert Lewis; *Instr* Clay Pursell; *Instr* Nancy Rice, MFA; *Instr* Corine Schleif; *Instr* Steven Teczar; *Instr* Roy Zinarch
Estab 1872, dept estab 1961; pvt; D & E; ent req HS dipl, ACT or SAT; degrees BA and BFA 4 yrs; scholarships; SC 74, LC 6; enrl D 150, E 30, non-maj 60, maj 90
Tuition: $2850 per yr, $1425 per sem, $95 per cr hr; campus res—room & board $1750 per yr
Courses: Art History, Calligraphy, †Ceramics, Drafting, Drawing, Graphic Arts, Graphic Design, †Interior Design, Jewelry, †Painting, Photography, †Printmaking, †Sculpture

NOTRE DAME COLLEGE, Art Department,* 320 E Ripa Ave, 63125. Tel 314-544-0455, Ext 36. *Dir* Sr Angelee Fuchs
Estab 1954; pvt; D & E; ent req HS dipl, ACT; degrees Teacher Cert, BA 3-4 yrs; scholarships; SC 23, LC 6; enrl D 25, maj 25
Adult Hobby Classes: Courses—Ceramics, Crafts, Fabric Design
Summer School: Dir, Sr Angelee Fuchs. Courses—Crafts, Painting

SAINT LOUIS COMMUNITY COLLEGE AT FOREST PARK, Dept of Art, 5600 Oakland, 63110. Tel 314-644-9351. *Chmn Dept* Mary L Fifield, MFA; *Assoc Prof* Leon Anderson, MFA; *Assoc Prof* James Hogan, BA; *Asst Prof* Bruce Pasley, MFA. Instrs PT 12
Estab 1962, dept estab 1963; pub; D & E; ent req HS dipl; degrees AA & AAS 2 yrs; scholarships; SC 36, LC 6; enrl D 100, E 100, non-maj 75, maj 75
Tuition: $600 per yr, $300 per sem, $18 per cr hr; no campus res
Courses: Advertising Design, Art History, Ceramics, †Commercial Art, Drawing,

Graphic Design, Illustration, Lettering, Painting, Photography, Printmaking, Color, Design
Summer School: Dir, Mary L Fifield. Enrl 100; tui $18 per cr hr. Courses—Same as those above

SAINT LOUIS COMMUNITY COLLEGE AT MERAMEC, Art Dept, 11333 Big Bend Blvd, 63122. Tel 314-966-7632. *Chmn Dept* F Robert Allen; *Instructor* Fred R Allen, MFA; *Instructor* Garth Bell, AM; *Instructor* David Durham, BFA; *Instructor* John Ferguson; *Instructor* Ruth Hensler, MFA; *Instructor* Peter Hoell, BFA; *Instructor* John Nagel, BA; *Instructor* Patrick Shuck, MFA; *Instructor* Mary Sprague, AM; *Instructor* Ronald Thomas, MFA; *Instructor* Sam Wayne, MA; *Instructor* Yvette Woods, BFA
Estab 1964; D & E; ent req HS dipl; degrees AA 2 yrs; scholarships; SC 15, LC 2
Tuition: $18.50 per cr hr; no campus res
Courses: Advertising Design, Art History, Ceramics, Commercial Art, Drawing, Illustration, Interior Design, Painting, Photography, Printmaking, Sculpture
Summer School: Chmn Dept, F Robert Allen. Tui $18.50 per cr hr for term of 9 wks beginning June 4. Courses—Art History, Art Appreciation, Ceramics, Drawing, Design, Photography, Sculpture

UNIVERSITY OF MISSOURI-SAINT LOUIS, Art Dept, 8001 Natural Bridge, 63121. Tel 314-453-5975. *Chairperson Dept* Sylvia Solochek Walters, MFA; *Assoc Prof* Michael D Taylor, PhD; *Asst Prof* Janet Berlo; *Asst Prof* Mark Pascale; *Asst Prof* Thomas Pickrel; *Asst Prof* James Smith, MFA; *Asst Prof* Mary Wilson, PhD
Estab 1963; pub; D & E; ent req HS dipl; degrees BA(Art Hist), BFA; SC 10, LC 20; enrl maj 80
Tuition: $360 per sem; no campus res
Courses: Art Education, Art History, Ceramics, Drawing, Graphic Design, History of Art & Archaeology, Painting, Printmaking
Summer School: Courses—Abstract Painting & Drawing, Drawing the Landscape, Introduction to Art & to Painting, Primitive Art

WASHINGTON UNIVERSITY
—School of Fine Arts, Lindell and Skinker, 63130. Tel 314-889-6500. *Dean School* Roger DesRosiers, MFA; *Asst Dean School* Kim Strommen, MFA; *Chairperson Three-Dimensional Dept* James Sterritt, MFA; *Chairperson Two-Dimensional Dept* Peter Marcus, MFA; *Chairperson Design Dept* Richard Brunell, BFA
Estab 1853; pvt; D; ent req HS dipl, SAT or ACT, portfolio; degrees BFA 4 yrs, MFA 2 yrs; scholarships; SC 62, LC 10, GC 31; enrl 390, non-maj 5, maj 325, grad 60
Tuition: $5350 per yr, $2675 per sem, $225 per cr hr; campus res—room & board $2780 per yr
Courses: †Advertising Design, Aesthetics, Architecture, Art Education, Art History, Calligraphy, †Ceramics, Commercial Art, †Conceptual Art, Costume Design & Construction, Drawing, †Fashion Arts, Goldsmithing, Graphic Arts, †Graphic Design, History of Art & Archaeology, †Illustration, Intermedia, †Jewelry, Lettering, Mixed Media, †Painting, †Photography, †Printmaking, †Sculpture, †Silversmithing, Teacher Training, Textile Design, Theatre Arts, Video
Children's Classes: Sat and summer classes for High School students
Summer School: Asst Prof, Kim Strommen. Courses—Drawing, Graphic Communications, Metalsmithing, Painting, Printmaking, Sculpture
—School of Architecture, Box 1079, 63130. Tel 314-889-6200. *Dean School* C Michaelides, MArchit
Estab 1910; pvt; D; degrees BA(Archit) 4 yrs, MArchit and Urban Design 1-2 yrs, MArch 2-4 yrs; scholarships; SC 28, LC 58, GC 42; enrl 330, maj 190, grad 140
Tuition: $4300 per yr; campus res—room & board tui varies
Courses: †Architecture
Summer School: Dir, Michael Nelson. Tui varies. Courses—Advanced Architectural Design, Fundamentals of Design, Independent Study, Structural Principles

SPRINGFIELD

DRURY COLLEGE, Art, Art History & Architecture Dept, 65802. Tel 417-865-8731, Ext 239. *Chmn Dept* John H Simmons. Instrs FT 2, PT 7
Estab 1873; den; degrees 4 yrs; scholarships; SC 12, LC 5; enrl 200
Courses: Architecture, Teacher Training

SOUTHWEST MISSOURI STATE UNIVERSITY, Dept of Art, 901 S National, 65802. Tel 417-836-5110. *Head Dept* Norman Annis. Instrs FT 25, PT 5
Estab 1901; D & E; ent req HS dipl, ent exam; degrees BFA, BS(Educ, Educ Comprehensive) & BA 4 yrs; scholarships; SC 31, LC 14; enrl maj 405, others 2000, total 13,118
Tuition: Res—$200; nonres—$450; campus res $470 or $510 per sem
Courses: Art Education, Art History, Ceramics, Drawing, Graphic Design, Jewelry, Painting, Photography, Printmaking, Sculpture, Silversmithing, Teacher Training, Fibers, Lithography, Bronze Casting
Summer School: Dir, Dean Russell Keeling. Enr 3500; special workshops available during summer session; tui $20 per cr hr for 4, 5 & 8 wk sessions. Courses—Selected from above curriculum

UNION

EAST CENTRAL JUNIOR COLLEGE, Art Dept, PO Box 529, 63084. Tel 314-583-5193. *Head Dept* Larry Pogue. Instrs FT 1, PT 6
Estab 1968; pub; D & E; ent req HS dipl, ent exam; degrees AA & AAS 2 yrs; scholarships; SC 8, LC 8; enrl D 370, E 120, maj 37
Tuition: $132 per sem
Courses: Art Education, Drawing, Handicrafts, Painting, Photography, Printmaking, Sculpture, Art Appreciation, Design, Watercolor

WARRENSBURG

CENTRAL MISSOURI STATE UNIVERSITY, Art Department, 64093. Tel 816-429-4480. *Head Dept* Richard A Luehrman, PhD; *Prof* Edwin C Ellis, MFA; *Assoc Prof* Richard D Monson, MFA; *Asst Prof* John R Haydu, MFA; *Asst Prof* Margaret Peterson, MFA; *Asst Prof* Harold M Reynolds, EdD; *Asst Prof* George Sample, MSEd; *Instructor* Reza Ahmadi, MA; *Instructor* Raeford W Lewis, MA; *Instructor* Stephen Phillips, MFA; *Instructor* Anna L Spiro, MA
Estab 1871; pub; D & E; ent req HS dipl, Missouri School & Col Ability Test, ACT; degrees BA, BSE, and BFA 4 yrs, MSE & MA 1 yr; scholarships; SC 40, LC 14, GC 7; enrl D 272, maj 272
Tuition: Res—$135 per quarter; nonres—$335 per quarter; campus res—room & board $375
Courses: Art Education, Art History, Calligraphy, Commercial Art, Drawing, Graphic Arts, Illustration, Interior Design, Painting, Printmaking, Sculpture, Teacher Training
Summer School: Head Dept, Richard A Luehrman. Term of 8 wks beginning first wk in June. Courses—Ceramics, Drawing, Grad Studio Courses, Painting

WEBSTER GROVES

WEBSTER COLLEGE, Art Dept, 470 E Lockwood Blvd, 63119. Tel 314-968-0500, Ext 460. *Chairperson Dept* Kathleen J Regier, PhD; *Assoc Prof* Jack Canepa, MA; *Assoc Prof* Leon Hicks, MFA; *Assoc Prof* Sr Gabriel Mary Hoare, MA; *Assoc Prof* Thomas Lang, MFA; *Assoc Prof* Phil Sultz, BFA; *Asst Prof* Michael Beresford, MFA; *Asst Prof* Susan Hacker, MFA; *Instructor* Paul Hrusovsky, MA; *Lectr* Jan Sultz, MFA
Estab 1915; dept estab 1946; pvt; D & E; ent req HS dipl, SAT or ACT; degrees BA & BFA 4 yrs; scholarships; SC 60, LC 15; enrl 424, non-maj 318, maj 100
Tuition: $3050 per yr, $95 per cr hr; campus res—room & board $1460 per yr
Courses: †Art Education, †Art History, †Ceramics, Collage, Conceptual Art, †Drawing, Film, †Painting, †Photography, †Printmaking, †Sculpture, Teacher Training, Papermaking
Summer School: Undergrad Dean, Charles Madden. Tui $95 per cr hr for term of 6 or 8 wks beginning June 19. Courses vary each summer

MONTANA

BILLINGS

EASTERN MONTANA COLLEGE, Art Dept, 1500 N 30th St, 59101. Tel 406-657-2324, 657-2323. *Head* Alan K Newberg. Instrs FT 7, PT 8
Estab 1927; pub; ent req HS dipl; degrees AA 2 yrs, BS(Educ), BA(Lib Arts) 4 yrs, MS(Art Educ)
Tuition: Res—$173 per quarter; nonres—$509 per quarter
Courses: Art History, Ceramics, Commercial Art, Drawing, Graphic Arts, Jewelry, Lettering, Painting, Photography, Sculpture, Crafts, Design, Fibers, Metalwork
Summer School: Usually 6 courses with emphasis on courses for teachers

ROCKY MOUNTAIN COLLEGE, Art Dept, 1511 Poly Dr, 59102. Tel 406-245-6151, Ext 263. *Chmn Dept* Robert Morrison, MA; *Assoc Prof* Kathleen Joyce, PhD
Estab 1878; dept estab 1957; pvt; D; ent req HS dipl, ACT; degrees BA & BS 4 yrs; scholarships; SC 12, LC 5; enrl 112, non-maj 40, maj 30, others 5
Tuition: $1990 per yr, $995 per sem, $85 per sem hr; campus res—room & board $1385 per yr
Courses: Art Education, Art History, Ceramics, Drawing, Graphic Arts, Graphic Design, Illustration, Painting, Photography, Printmaking, Sculpture, Stage Design, Teacher Training
Adult Hobby Classes: Enrl 100; tui $20 for 5 wks. Courses—Crafts, Painting, Picture Framing

BOZEMAN

MONTANA STATE UNIVERSITY
—School of Art, Haynes Hall, 59717. Tel 406-994-4501. *Dir School* John Catterall, MFA
Estab 1893; pub; D; ent req HS dipl; degrees BA 4 yrs, MFA 2 yrs; SC 38, LC 19, GC 13; enrl maj 300, grad 19
Tuition: Res—$558 per yr; nonres—$1925 per yr; campus res available
Courses: †Architecture, Art Education, Art History, Ceramics, †Drafting, Drawing, †Film, Graphic Arts, Graphic Design, Interior Design, Jewelry, Lettering, Painting, †Photography, Printmaking, Sculpture, Silversmithing, Teacher Training, †Theatre Arts, †Video
Summer School: Dir, Dr Rex Dayl. Courses—vary each summer according to demand
—School of Architecture, Creative Arts Complex, 59717. Tel 406-994-4255. *Dir School* Robert C Utzinger. Instrs FT 14, PT 1
Pub; degrees BArchit 5 yrs; LabC 15, LC 14; enrl maj 300
Tuition: Res—$558 for 3 quarters; nonres—$1368; campus res—room & board $1371 for 3 quarters
Courses: Architecture

DILLON

WESTERN MONTANA COLLEGE, Art Dept, 710 S Atlantic, 59725. Tel 406-683-7312. *Chmn Dept* Don Walters. Instrs FT 3
Estab 1897; pub; D & E; ent req HS dipl; degrees BS 4 yrs, MA; scholarships; SC 15, LC 6, GC 21
Courses: Art Education, Art History, Ceramics, Commercial Art, Drawing, Graphic Arts, Handicrafts, Jewelry, Lettering, Painting, Photography, Sculpture, Design, Glass Blowing, Stained Glass, Weaving
Summer School: Chmn Dept, Don Walters. Term of 4 & 9 wks beginning June. Courses—Same as regular year

GREAT FALLS

COLLEGE OF GREAT FALLS, Dept of Art, 1301 20th St S, 59405. Tel 406-452-9584. *Dean of Studies* Dr Charles M Hepburn; *Head Dept* Jack N Franjevic. Instrs FT 2, PT 2
Estab 1933; den; D & E; degrees 4 yrs; SC, Lab C, LC; enrl approx 1250
Courses: Art Education, Ceramics, Drawing, Handicrafts, Jewelry, Painting, Photography, Printmaking, Sculpture, Silversmithing, Textile Design, Design
Summer School: Dir, Richard Gretch; 6 wks

HAVRE

NORTHERN MONTANA COLLEGE, Department of Art,* 611 16th St, 59501. Tel 406-265-7821. *Chmn* John P Varrum
Estab 1929; pub; D & E; ent req HS dipl; degrees AA 2 yrs, BS(Educ) and BA 4 yrs, MSc(Educ); scholarships; SC 15, LC 5, GC 9; enrl D 425, grad 7
Tuition: In-state $461; out-of-state $1469
Courses: Art Education, Ceramics, Commercial Art, Drafting, Drawing, Graphic Arts, Painting, Sculpture, Teacher Training
Children's Classes: Enrl 60; tui $1 enrl fee. Courses—Ceramics, Drawing, Painting, Sculpture
Summer School: Dir, Dr Lee Spuhler. Enrl 700 col, 47 art classes; term of 8 wks. Courses—Art Appreciation, Art Education, Ceramics, Sculpture

MILES CITY

MILES COMMUNITY COLLEGE, Dept of Fine Arts & Humanities, 2715 Dickinson St, 59301. Tel 406-232-3031. *Head Dept* Sydney R Sonneborn, MA; *Instructor* Fred McKee, MFA
Estab 1937, dept estab 1967; pub; D & E; ent req HS dipl, ACT; degrees AA 2 yrs, cert; scholarships; SC 17, LC 1; enrl D 36, E 23, non-maj 55, maj 4
Tuition: Res—$302.50 per yr; nonres—$722.50 per yr; no campus res
Courses: Advertising Design, Ceramics, Drawing, Jewelry, Painting, Photography, Stage Design, Teacher Training, Theatre Arts
Adult Hobby Classes: Enrl minimum of 8; tui $30 per 3 cr course. Courses—Ceramics, Jewelry Making, Macrame, Painting, Photography

MISSOULA

UNIVERSITY OF MONTANA, Dept of Art, 59812. Tel 406-243-4181. *Chmn Dept* Ken D Little, MFA; *Prof* Rudy Autio, MFA; *Prof* Bruce Walter Barton, MA; *Prof* Don Bunse, MFA; *Prof* James Dew, MA; *Assoc Prof* Stephen Connell, MA; *Assoc Prof* Richard Reinholtz, MEd; *Asst Prof* Julie F Codell, PhD; *Asst Prof* Lynda Ross, MFA; *Asst Prof* Mary Warner, MA
Pub; D & E; ent req HS dipl; degrees BA & BFA 4 yrs, MA & MFA 2 yrs; SC 28, LC 20, GC 10; enrl D 850, E 30
Tuition: Res—$204.50 per quarter (12-18 cr hrs); nonres—$660.50 per quarter (12-18 cr hrs)
Courses: Aesthetics, Art Education, Art History, Ceramics, Drawing, Handicrafts, History of Art & Archaeology, Jewelry, Lettering, Painting, Photography, Printmaking, Sculpture, Silversmithing
Summer School: Chmn, Ken D Little. Term of 4 wks. Courses vary due to availability of funds and instructors; normally art education, ceramics, painting, photography

NEBRASKA

CHADRON

CHADRON STATE COLLEGE, Div of Fine Arts, Tenth & Main Sts, 69337. Tel 308-432-4451, Ext 317. *Chmn Div* Harry E Holmberg, EdD; *Prof* Noel Gray, EdD; *Asst Prof* John Dillon, MFA; *Instr* Paul Pfrehm, MFA
Estab 1911, div estab 1935; pub; D & E; ent req HS dipl; degrees BSE & BA 4 yrs; scholarships; SC 20, LC 4, GC 2; enrl D 195, non-maj 155, maj 40
Tuition: Res—$15.50 per hr; nonres—$27.50 per hr; campus res—room & board $400
Courses: Aesthetics, Art Education, Art History, Ceramics, Commercial Art, Drafting, Drawing, Graphic Arts, Jewelry, Lettering, Painting, Sculpture, Teacher Training, Theatre Arts, Glass Blowing, Weaving
Adult Hobby Classes: Tui $10 per hr. Courses vary on demand
Summer School: Dir, Harry E Holmberg. Tui same as above. Courses—Usually 4 to 6 courses on semi-rotation basis

COLUMBUS

PLATTE TECHNICAL COMMUNITY COLLEGE, Creative and Social Cluster, Mason Rd, 68601. Tel 402-564-7132. *Head Dept* Richard Abraham, MA; *Instr* Roger Augspurger, PhD
Estab 1969, dept estab 1971; pub; D & E; ent req HS dipl; degrees AA 2 yrs; scholarships; SC 8, LC 1; enrl D 100, E 20, non-maj 77, maj 43
Tuition: Res $594 per yr, $297 per sem, $17 per hr; no campus res
Courses: Advertising Design, Aesthetics, Art History, Ceramics, Commercial Art, Drafting, Drawing, Graphic Arts, Graphic Design, Handicrafts, History of Art & Archaeology, Interior Design, Mixed Media, Painting, Photography, Printmaking, Stage Design, Textile Design, Theatre Arts
Summer School: Dir, Richard D Abraham. Enrl 40; tui $17 per hr for term of 6 wks beginning June. Courses—Drawing, Painting

CRETE

DOANE COLLEGE, Dept of Art, 68333. Tel 402-826-2161, Ext 273. *Head Dept* Richard Terrell, MFA; *Instructor* Michael Hershey, MFA
Estab 1872, dept estab 1958; pvt; D; ent req HS dipl; degrees BA 4 yrs; scholarships; SC 6, LC 5; enrl 150, non-maj 140, maj 10
Tuition: $2335 per yr; campus res—room and board $1130 per yr
Courses: Art Education, Art History, Ceramics, Drawing, Film, Graphic Design, Jewelry, Painting, Printmaking, Sculpture, Stage Design

HASTINGS

HASTINGS COLLEGE, Art Dept, 68901. Tel 402-463-2402. *Chmn Dept* Gary E Coulter. Instrs FT 3
Estab 1925; den; ent req HS grad; degrees BA 4 yrs; scholarships; SC 16, LC 5; enrl maj 50, others 350
Tuition: $2400; campus res—room & board $1350
Courses: Art Education, Art History, Ceramics, Drawing, Painting, Printmaking, Sculpture, Composition
Summer School: Acad Dean, Dr A L Langvardt. Enrl 25; tui $175 per unit for 6 wks beginning June

KEARNEY

KEARNEY STATE COLLEGE, Dept of Art, 68847. Tel 308-236-4221. *Chmn Dept* Jack Karraker, MFA; *Prof* Keith Lowry, MFA; *Prof* Larry D Peterson, EdD; *Prof* Raymond W Schultze, MFA; *Prof* Gary E Zaruba, EdD; *Assoc Prof* John N Dinsmore, EdD; *Asst Prof* Jerry Austin, MFA; *Asst Prof* Elmer Holzrichter, MA; *Asst Prof* Mary Lierley, MA; *Asst Prof* James M May, MA; *Asst Prof* Martin Wnuk, MFA. Instrs PT 7
Estab 1903; pub; D & E; ent req HS dipl, SAT or ACT recommended; degrees BFA, BA, BA(Educ) 4 yrs, MA(Educ-Art); scholarships; SC 23, LC 10, GC 16; enrl D 970, E 30, non-maj 800, maj 212, grad 25
Tuition: Res—$18 per cr hr; nonres—$32 per cr hr; campus res—$551 per yr
Courses: Aesthetics, †Art Education, †Art History, †Ceramics, Commercial Art, †Drawing, †Painting, Photography, †Printmaking, †Sculpture, †Teacher Training, †Textile Design, Color Theory, Design, Glass Blowing, Weaving
Summer School: Second summer session 8 wks; tui $18 per cr hr. Courses—Basic art curriculum

LINCOLN

NEBRASKA WESLEYAN UNIVERSITY, Art Dept, 50th & St Paul, 68504. Tel 402-466-2371. *Head Dept* Betty Wallace, MFA; *Asst Prof* Brent Funderburk; *Vis Prof* Nadine McHenry; *Vis Prof* Ron Geibert; *Vis Prof* Chad Keel; *Vis Prof* Dan Peragine; *Vis Prof* Jeanne James
Estab 1888, dept estab 1890; pvt; D & E; ent req HS dipl, ent exam; degrees AA 2 yrs, BA & BS 4 yrs; scholarships; SC 22, LC 4; enrl non-maj 300, maj 30
Tuition: $1250 per sem
Courses: Advertising Design, Art Education, Art History, Ceramics, Commercial Art, Drawing, History of Art & Archaeology, Jewelry, Museum Staff Training, Painting, Photography, Printmaking, Sculpture, Silversmithing, Design

UNIVERSITY OF NEBRASKA-LINCOLN, Department of Art, 207 Nelle Cochrane Woods Hall, 68588. Tel 402-472-2631. *Chmn Dept* Dan F Howard, MFA; *VChmn Dept* Howard Collins, PhD; *Chmn Graduate Committee* Douglas Ross, MFA; *Chief Acad Advisor* Peter Worth, ARCA. Instrs FT 20, PT 19
Estab 1869, dept estab 1912; pub; D & E; ent req HS dipl; degrees BA, BFA and BFA(Educ) 4 yrs, MFA 3 yrs; scholarships; SC 71, LC 27, GC 45; enrl D 1950, E 175, non-maj 600, maj 525, grad 25
Tuition: Res—$360 per sem for 15 hrs, $24 per cr hr; nonres—$975 per sem for 15 sem hrs, $65 per cr hr; campus res—room & board $1775 per yr (single), $1425 (double)
Courses: Advertising Design, †Art Education, †Art History, †Ceramics, Commercial Art, †Drawing, Film, †Graphic Design, Handicrafts, Illustration, Lettering, Mixed Media, †Painting, †Photography, †Printmaking, †Sculpture, Teacher Training, Two & Three-Dimensional Design, Weaving
Summer School: Dir, Alan Seagren. Enrl 250; two 5 wk sessions beginning June and Aug. Courses—Art History, Ceramics, Design, Drawing, Painting, Printmaking, Special Problems & Topics

NORFOLK

NORTHEAST TECHNICAL COMMUNITY COLLEGE, Dept of Art, 801 E Benjamin Ave, 68701. Tel 402-371-2020, Ext 245. *Chmn Dept* Mary Ann Clark, MFA; *Instructor* Trish Stevenson, BA; *Instructor* Dan Craig, AS
Estab 1928; pub; D & E; ent req HS dipl; degrees AA 2 yrs; scholarships; SC 5, LC 5; enrl D 150, E 50, non-maj 100, maj 50
Tuition: Res—$187.50 per sem, $12.50 per cr hr; nonres—$300 per sem, $20 per cr hr; campus res—room & board $1100 per yr
Courses: Art Education, Art History, Drawing, Graphic Design, Painting, Photography
Summer School: Chmn Dept, Mary Ann Clark. Tui same as regular yr. Courses—Photography

OMAHA

COLLEGE OF SAINT MARY, Art Department,* 1901 S 72nd St, 68124. Tel 402-393-8800. *Chmn Dept* Tom Schlosser
Estab 1923; pvt, W; D & E; ent req HS dipl; degrees BA and BS 4 yrs; scholarships; SC 11, LC 5; enrl D 278, maj 18, special 2
Tuition: $88 per cr hr; campus res—room & board $56 per wk, $650 per sem
Courses: Aesthetics, Art Education, Ceramics, Drawing, Graphic Arts, History of Art & Archaeology, Jewelry, Lettering, Painting, Photography, Printmaking, Sculpture, Teacher Training, Design

CREIGHTON UNIVERSITY, Fine and Performing Arts Department,* 2500 California St, 68178. Tel 402-449-2509. *Chmn Dept* Donald A Doll; *Instr* Bob Bosco, MFA; *Instr* Suzanne Dieckman, PhD; *Instr* Alan Garfield, MA; *Instr* Bill Hutson, MA; *Instr* Lee Lubbers, PhD; *Instr* Joellen Meglin, MFA; *Instr* Valerie Roche, ARAD; *Instr* John Thein, MFA; *Artist-in-Res* Joseph Brown, theatre & poetry - 1977-78
Estab 1878, dept estab 1966; den; D & E; ent req HS dipl, regular col admis exam; degrees BA and BFA 4 yrs; scholarships; SC 87, LC 16; enrl 888, non-maj 850, maj 38, cert prog 24
Tuition: $3020 average per yr; campus res available
Courses: Advertising Design, Aesthetics, Art Education, Art History, Ceramics, Collage, Costume Design & Construction, Drawing, History of Art & Archaeology, Painting, Photography, Printmaking, Sculpture, Teacher Training, Theatre Arts, Design, Intaglio, Lithography, Pottery, Studio Fundamentals
Adult Hobby Classes: Enrl variable; tui $2 per class. Courses—Life Drawing
Summer School: Dir, Donald A Doll. Enrl 60; tui $63 per cr hr for term of 5 wks beginning June 12. Courses—Ceramics, Collage, Drawing, Etching, Figure Modeling for Sculpture, Painting, Sculpture, Watercolor

UNIVERSITY OF NEBRASKA AT OMAHA, Dept of Art, 60th & Dodge Sts, 68182. Tel 402-554-2420. *Chmn Dept* Dr J V Blackwell; *Prof* Peter Hill, MFA; *Prof* Thomas H Majeski, MFA; *Prof* Sidney Buchanan, MA; *Assoc Prof* Larry Bradshaw, MFA & MA; *Assoc Prof* Henry Serenco, MFA; *Asst Prof* Dr Donald B Doe; *Asst Prof* Dr Dorothy Habel; *Asst Prof* Dr J Stephen Lahr; *Asst Prof* Gary Day, MFA. Instrs PT 2
Estab 1908, dept estab 1910; pub; D & E; ent req HS dipl; degrees BA & BFA 4 yrs; scholarships; SC 32, LC 22, GC 10; enrl D 550, E 100
Tuition: Res—undergrad $24 per cr hr, grad $24 per cr hr; nonres—undergrad $65 per cr hr, grad $65 per cr hr; no campus res
Courses: Aesthetics, Architecture, †Art Education, Art History, Ceramics, Collage, Constructions, †Drawing, †History of Art & Archaeology, Jewelry, †Painting, †Printmaking, †Sculpture, Silversmithing
Summer School: Chmn Dept, J V Blackwell. Tui same as above for term of 5 wks. Courses vary

SCOTTSBLUFF

NEBRASKA WESTERN COLLEGE, Div of Language & Arts, 1601 E 27th St NE, 69361. Tel 308-635-3603, Ext 260. *Chairperson Div* Helen Burnstad, MA; *Instructor* Roy D Doerfler, MA
Estab 1926; pub; D & E; ent req HS dipl; degrees AA & AS 2 yrs; scholarships; SC 8, LC 3; enrl D 60, E 150, non-maj 50, maj 10
Tuition: Res—$210 per sem, $14 per cr hr; nonres—$315 per sem, $21 per cr hr; campus res room & board
Courses: Art Education, Art History, Drawing, Painting, Photography, Theatre Arts
Adult Hobby Classes: Enrl 150; tui $15 per course. Courses—Carving, Drawing, Macrame, Pottery, Sculpture, Stained Glass, Watercolor & Oil Painting, Weaving

SEWARD

CONCORDIA COLLEGE, Art Department, 800 N Columbia, 68434. Tel 402-643-3651. *Head Dept* William R Wolfram, MFA; *Prof* Donald Dynneson, MFA; *Prof* Renhold P Marxhausen, MFA; *Prof* Richard Wiegmann, MFA
Estab 1894; den; D & E; ent req HS dipl; degrees BS, BA 4 yr; scholarships; SC 8, LC 4; enrl non-maj 30, maj 40
Tuition: $2246 per yr, $50 per cr hr; campus res—room $320, board $380
Courses: Art Education, Art History, Ceramics, Drawing, Handicrafts, History of Art & Archaeology, Painting, Photography, Sculpture, Teacher Training
Summer School: Dir, Dr Orville Walz. Tui $40 per cr hr for term of 2 1 2 wks beginning June 6. Courses—Fundamentals of Art

WAYNE

WAYNE STATE COLLEGE, Art Department, 68787. Tel 402-375-2200, Ext 235. *Div Chmn* Cornell Runestad. Instrs FT 4
Estab 1910; pub; ent req HS grad; degrees BA, BFA; scholarships; SC 21, LC 8; enrl maj 65, others 700, total 2200
Tuition: Res—$18 per cr hr; nonres—$32 per cr hr
Courses: Art History, Ceramics, Drafting, Drawing, Graphic Arts, Handicrafts, Jewelry, Painting, Sculpture, Teacher Training, Design, Watercolor
Summer School: Pres, Lyle Seymour. Two sessions, Apr 28-June 15, June 16-Aug 4

NEVADA

LAS VEGAS

UNIVERSITY OF NEVADA, LAS VEGAS, Department of Art,* 4505 Maryland Parkway, 89154. Tel 702-739-3011. *Chmn Dept* Thomas J Holder, MFA; *Prof* Rita Deanin Abbey, MFA; *Assoc Prof* Michael L McCollum, MFA; *Asst Prof* Robert E Brown, MFA; *Asst Prof* David J Lurie, MFA; *Asst Prof* Nils W Ramstedt Jr, PhD; *Instr* Claudia L King, MA
Estab 1955; pub; D & E; ent req HS dipl, ACT; degrees BA and BFA 4 yrs; scholarships; SC 32, LC 18; enrl all courses 551, maj 95
Tuition: Out-of-state $750 per sem, $24 per hr; campus res—room & board $770-$804 per sem
Courses: Art History, Ceramics, Conceptual Art, Drawing, Film, Intermedia, Painting, Photography, Printmaking, Sculpture
Summer School: Dir, Paul Aizley, Tui $23 per cr hr for 5 wks beginning June 12 and July 17. Courses—vary with each session

RENO

UNIVERSITY OF NEVADA, RENO, Art Department, 89557. Tel 702-784-6682. *Chmn Dept* Robert J Morrison. Instrs FT 10
Estab 1940; pub; ent req HS grad and 16 units; degrees BA 4 yr; scholarship; SC 20, LC 6, GC 5; enrl maj 120, others 800
Courses: Art Education, Art History, Ceramics, Drawing, Painting, Photography, Printmaking, Sculpture
Summer School: Courses offered

NEW HAMPSHIRE

CONCORD

SAINT PAUL'S SCHOOL, Art Department, Art Center in Hargate, 325 Pleasant St, 03301. Tel 603-225-3341, Ext 58. *Head Dept* Thomas R Barrett. Instrs FT 4
Estab 1967; pvt, independent secondary boarding school; D; ent req HS dipl; SC 8, LC 1; enrl all students boarding (496,227 registrations)
Courses: Aesthetics, Architecture, Art History, Ceramics, Drawing, Graphic Arts, Painting, Photography, Sculpture, Woodworking
Summer School: Dir, Alan N Hall. Term of 6 wks beginning last wk in June. Courses—Advanced Studies Program, Introduction to Creative Arts

DURHAM

UNIVERSITY OF NEW HAMPSHIRE, Department of the Arts, Paul Creative Arts Center, 03824. Tel 603-862-2190. *Chmn* Arthur Balderacchi, MFA; *Prof* Sigmund Abeles, MFA; *Prof* John Hatch, MFA; *Prof* John Laurent, MFA; *Prof* Melvin Zabarsky, MFA; *Assoc Prof* Conley Harris, MFA
Estab 1928, dept estab 1941; pub; D & E; ent req HS dipl, portfolio; degrees BA, BFA and BA(Art History) 4 yrs, MAT 5 yrs; scholarships; SC 60, LC 20; enrl non-maj 1000, maj 175, grad 5
Tuition: Campus res available
Courses: Architecture, Art Education, Art History, Ceramics, Drawing, History of Art & Archaeology, Jewelry, Landscape Architecture, Museum Staff Training, Occupational Therapy, Painting, Photography, Printmaking, Sculpture, Silversmithing, Stage Design, Teacher Training, Textile Design, Theatre Arts, Video
Summer School: Dir, Paul DuBois. Courses—varied

HANOVER

DARTMOUTH COLLEGE, Department of Art, 03755. Tel 603-646-2306. *Acting Chmn* Fred Berthold. Instrs FT 11, PT 3
Estab 1906; pvt; degrees AB 4 yr; scholarship and fel; SC 16, LC 26; enrl in col 4000, maj 46
Tuition: Incl campus res fee, $1790 per term; operating 4 terms on yr-round basis
Courses: Architecture, Drawing, Graphic Arts, Painting, Photography, African & Afro-American Arts, Design, Three-Dimensional Design

MANCHESTER

MANCHESTER INSTITUTE OF ARTS AND SCIENCES, 148 Concord St, 03104. Tel 603-623-0313. *Exec Dir* Angelo Randazzo; *Program Coordr* Marc Normand; *Educational Coordr* Pamela Riel; *Registrar* Linda Lord. Instrs PT 30
Estab 1898; pvt; credit and adult educ courses; ent req none; SC 16; enrl 1000
Courses: Calligraphy, Ceramics, Drawing, Graphic Design, Jewelry, Painting, Photography, Silversmithing, Pewtersmithing, Stained Glass, Weaving

NOTRE DAME COLLEGE, Art Department, 2321 Elm St, 03104. Tel 603-669-4298. *Prof* Frank Oehlschlaeger, MFA; *Assoc Prof* Sr Liliosa Shea, MFA; *Asst Prof* Armand Szainer; *Asst Prof* Harry Umen, MFA; *Instructor* William Dobe; *Lectr* John Bowers; *Lectr* Fred Dobrowolski, MFA; *Lectr* Charles Lemay, AB; *Lectr* Gloria Martin, MFA; *Lectr* Annette Mitchell, MFA; *Lectr* Jean Nelson, AB. Instrs 2Estab 1950, dept estab 1965
Pvt; D & E; ent req HS dipl; degrees BA(Fine Arts), BA(Commercial Art & Art Educ) 4 yr; scholarship; SC 20, LC 6; enrl non-maj 28, maj 120
Tuition: Undergrad $2500 yr, $1250 sem, $150 PT, grad $180 PT; campus res—room and board $1600 yr
Courses: Advertising Design, †Art Education, Art History, Calligraphy, Ceramics, †Commercial Art, Display, Drafting, Drawing, Graphic Arts, Graphic Design, Handicrafts, Illustration, Lettering, Painting, Printmaking, Sculpture, Teacher Training, Art Therapy, Visual Arts

SAINT ANSELM'S COLLEGE, Department of Fine Arts, 03102. Tel 603-669-1030, Ext 256. *Chmn* Joseph E Scannell. Instrs FT 2
Estab 1889; pvt; D & E; ent req HS dipl, relative standing, SAT, interview; degrees BA 4 yr; SC 2, LC 9; enrl 1500
Courses: Art History, Photography, Studio
Summer School: Courses—History of American Art Seminar, Still Photography

NASHUA

ARTS AND SCIENCE CENTER, 14 Court St, 03060. Tel 603-882-1506. Instrs PT 35-40
Estab 1958; pub; D & E; ent req none; degrees none, noncredited; SC, LC
Tuition: No campus res
Courses: Ceramics, Drawing, Jewelry, Painting, Photography, Sculpture, Theatre Arts, Enameling, Macrame, Weaving
Adult Hobby Classes: Tui varied. Courses—Hand-Built Pottery, Stained Glass
Children's Classes: Tui varied. Courses—Drawing, Jewelry, Painting, Pottery, Preschool Art, Puppet Making, Sculpture
Summer School: Tui varied; 5 wk terms from June to July

RIVIER COLLEGE, Art Department,* 410 S Main St, 03060. Tel 603-888-1311. *Chmn Dept* Sr Marie Couture, MA; *Instr* Michael Brodeur, MFA; *Instr* Sr Theresa Couture, MA; *Instr* Lynne Johnson, MFA; *Instr* Jafar Shoja, MFA
Estab 1933, dept estab 1940; pub; D & E; ent req HS dipl, SAT, certain HS equivalencies, preliminary evidence of artistic ability; degrees AA and AS 2 yrs, BA, BS and BFA 4 yrs; scholarships; SC 47, LC 8; enrl D 221, E 57, non-maj 12, maj 266
Tuition: Res—undergrad $2400 per yr, E $60 per hr, grad $80 per hr; fee for sem studio course; campus residence available
Courses: Advertising Design, Aesthetics, †Art Education, Art History, Calligraphy, †Ceramics, Commercial Art, Conceptual Art, Constructions, Display, Drawing, Fashion Arts, Film, Graphic Arts, †Graphic Design, Handicrafts, Illustration, Interior Design, Jewelry, Lettering, Mixed Media, †Painting, Photography, Printmaking, †Sculpture, Teacher Training, Textile Design, Art Therapy, Film Graphics, Loom Weaving, Stitchery
Summer School: Dir Summer Session, Sr Eunice Fluet. Enrl 15; tui $325 for term of 3 wks beginning July 10. Pre-college Art Program—a non-credit prog meeting 9 - 12 AM and 1 - 4 PM 5 days a wk with specific purpose of helping art school aspirants to prepare portfolios for use in application process

NEW LONDON

COLBY-SAWYER COLLEGE, Art Department, 03257. Tel 603-526-2010, Ext 229. *Chairperson* Donald Campbell, MFA; *Instr* John Bott, MFA; *Instr* Loretta Barnett, MFA; *Instr* Martha Andrea, MFA; *Instr* Lou Thompson, MA. Instrs FT 5
Estab 1928; pvt; W; D; degrees BA & BFA 4 yr; scholarship; SC 9, LC 7; enrl 250
Tuition: res—undergrad $5975 per yr, $2990 per sem; nonres—undergrad $4032 per yr, $2016 per sem; campus res available
Courses: Ceramics, Commercial Art, Drawing, Painting, Photography, Printmaking, Sculpture, Design, Watercolor

PETERBOROUGH

SHARON ARTS CENTER, RFD 2, Box 361, 03458. Tel 603-924-7256. *Dir* Alan Erdossy. Instrs PT 10
Estab 1947; pvt; D & E; ent req none; scholarship; SC 20; classes yr round
Courses: Calligraphy, Ceramics, Drawing, Fashion Arts, Graphic Arts, Jewelry, Lettering, Painting, Photography, Textile Design, Batik, Patchwork & Applique, Pottery, Stained Glass, T'ai Chi Ch'uan, Weaving
Children's Classes: Pottery, Pre-School Expression

PLYMOUTH

PLYMOUTH STATE COLLEGE, Art Department, 03264. Tel 603-536-1550, Ext 201. *Head Dept* Christopher Kressy. Instrs FT 9
Estab 1871; pub; D & E; ent req HS grad, references, health record, transcript, SAT, CEEB, ACT; degrees BS and BA 4 yrs; scholarships; SC 17, LC 8; enrl D 3000, maj 170
Tuition: Res—$800; nonres—$2500; campus res $1535 double, $1635 single
Courses: Art Education, Art History, Ceramics, Drawing, Painting, Photography, Printmaking, Sculpture, Design
Summer School: Dir, Dr Julian Shlager. Tui in-state undergrad $40, grad $50; out-of-state undergrad $60, grad $80 per cr hr for term of 6 wks. Courses—varied

RINDGE

FRANKLIN PIERCE COLLEGE, Art Department, 03461. Tel 603-899-5111.
Estab 1962; pvt; D & E; ent req HS dipl; degrees BA(Creative and Performing Arts) 4 yrs; scholarships; SC 20, LC 2
Tuition: $3600; campus res—room & board $1800
Courses: Art History, Ceramics, Drawing, Graphic Arts, Jewelry, Painting, Photography, Sculpture, Stage Design, Glassblowing, Metalcraft, Primitive Woodworking, Stained Glass
Summer School: Dir, Marjorie Zerbel

NEW JERSEY

BLACKWOOD

CAMDEN COUNTY COLLEGE, Department of Art,* PO Box 200, 08012. Tel 609-227-7200. *Chmn Dept* William Marlin, EdD; *Asst Prof* Joseph Conroy, MFA; *Asst Prof* Lawrence Delliho, MA
Estab 1966; ent req HS dipl or equivalent; degrees AA 2 yrs; SC 12, LC 10; enrl 100
Tuition: In-county $400; out-of-county $500; out-of-state $1560
Courses: Art History, Calligraphy, Drawing, Lettering, Painting, Sculpture, Art Therapy, Design

CALDWELL

CALDWELL COLLEGE, Art Department, 07006. Tel 201-228-4424. *Chmn Dept* Mary Costantini. Instrs FT 3, PT 6
Estab 1964; pvt; W; D; ent req HS grad, ent exam, art portfolio; degrees BA 3-4 yr, BFA 4-5 yr; scholarship; SC 24, LC 12; enrl maj 67, dept 80
Courses: Advertising Design, Aesthetics, Art Education, Ceramics, Commercial Art, Drawing, Graphic Arts, Handicrafts, History of Art & Archaeology, Jewelry, Lettering, Painting, Photography, Sculpture, Teacher Training, Batik, Chip Carving, Enameling, Leather Carving, Metal Workshop, Weaving
Summer School: Dir, Sr Mary Daniel. Three terms of 3 wks each beginning June. Courses—Crafts, Drawing, Painting, Sculpture

CAMDEN

RUTGERS UNIVERSITY, CAMDEN, Art Department, Camden College of Arts and Sciences, 311 N Fifth St, 08102. Tel 609-757-6244. *Chmn* William Hoffman. Instrs FT 5, PT 8
Pub; D; ent req HS dipl, must qualify for regular col admis, portfolio; degrees BA(Art) 4 yrs; SC 24, LC 13; enrl D 450, maj 75
Courses: Aesthetics, Calligraphy, Ceramics, Drawing, Graphic Arts, Graphic Design, History of Art & Archaeology, Painting, Photography, Printmaking, Sculpture, Anatomical Drawing, Bronze Casting, Environmental Design, Etching, Gallery Operations, Lithography, Serigraphy, Typography

CONVENT STATION

COLLEGE OF SAINT ELIZABETH, Art Department,* 07961. Tel 201-539-1600. *Chmn Dept* Sr Ann Haarer
Estab 1899, dept 1956; den; W; D & E; ent req HS dipl, ent exam; degrees BA 4 yrs; scholarships; SC 17, LC 4; enrl D 250, maj 27
Tuition: $2790 average per yr; campus residence available
Courses: Art Education, Ceramics, Drafting, Drawing, Graphic Arts, Handicrafts, History of Art & Archaeology, Interior Design, Jewelry, Lettering, Painting, Sculpture, Teacher Training, Color and Design, Leather Work, Sand Casting, Stitchery
Summer School: Dir, Sr Mary Kathleen. Tui $67 per cr for PT students. Courses—Art Education, Painting

DOVER

COUNTY COLLEGE OF MORRIS, Art Department,* Route 10, Center Grove Rd, 07801. Tel 201-361-5000. *Chmn* Carl J Raw
Estab 1970; pub; D & E; ent req HS dipl; degrees AA(Humanities Art) 2 yrs; SC 15, LC 3; enrl maj 263
Tuition: In-county $450 per yr; in-state $1076 per yr; out-of-state $1726 per yr
Courses: Advertising Design, Ceramics, Drawing, History of Art & Archaeology, Painting, Photography, Sculpture

JOE KUBERT SCHOOL OF CARTOON AND GRAPHIC ART INC, 45 Lehigh St, 07801. Tel 201-361-1327. *Pres* Joe Kubert; *Instr* John Belfi; *Instr* Phillip Blaisdell; *Instr* Hy Eisman; *Instr* Irwin Hasen; *Instr* Milton Neil; *Vis Lectr* Sergio Aragones, cartoons; *Vis Lectr* Frank Thorne, cartoons

Estab 1976; pvt; D & E; ent req HS dipl, interview, portfolio; degrees 3 yr dipl; SC all, LC all; enrl D 60, E 25
Tuition: $2850 per yr; PT $600; campus res—room $850 per yr
Courses: Advertising Design, Commercial Art, Graphic Arts, Cartoon Graphics
Adult Hobby Classes: Enrl 25, tui $300 per sem or $48 per month. Courses—Basic and Advanced Paste-Ups and Mechanicals, Saturday Cartoon Sketch Class
Children's Classes: Enrl 25; tui $48 per month. Courses—Saturday Cartoon Sketch Class

FLEMINGTON

GRAZIANO STUDIOS OF FINE ARTS INC, Summer Art Workshop, RD 3, 1413 Highland Ave, Box 672, 07060. Tel 201-755-1442. *Dir* Florence Mercolino Graziano, PhD
Estab 1968, workshop estab 1974; pvt; E (no D except during summer); ent req individual basis acceptance; enrl 10-15
Tuition: $125 per wk beginning July 11; no campus res
Courses: Drawing, Graphic Arts, Mixed Media, Printmaking, Model Painting, Portraiture, Watercolor

GLASSBORO

GLASSBORO STATE COLLEGE, Department of Art,* Route 322, 08028. Tel 609-445-7081. *Chmn Dept* George Neff
EStab 1925; pub; D & E; ent req HS dipl, ent exam, portfolio and SAT; degrees BA 4 yrs, MA; enrl D 6100, E 5000, maj 300, grad 100
Tuition: In-state $660 per yr, $22 per cr; out-of-state $1320 per yr, $44 per cr
Courses: Aesthetics, Art Education, Ceramics, Drawing, Graphic Arts, Handicrafts, History of Art & Archaeology, Jewelry, Lettering, Painting, Photography, Sculpture, Stage Design, Teacher Training, Textile Design, Theatre Arts, Batik, Enameling

HACKETTSTOWN

CENTENARY COLLEGE, Art Department, Fine Arts Division, 07840. Tel 201-852-1400. Instrs FT 4, PT 3
Estab 1874; pvt; W; degrees AA(Fine & Applied Arts), AA(Fashion Illustration), AA(Interior Design) and BFA(Art & Design); SC 11, LC 2; enrl maj 70, others 367, total 678

JERSEY CITY

JERSEY CITY STATE COLLEGE, Art Department, 2039 Kennedy Blvd, 07305. Tel 201-547-3214, Ext 3241 or 3242. *Chairperson* Dr Jean C Lane, EdD; *Prof* Dr Elaine Foster, EdD; *Prof* Harold Lemmerman, EdD; *Prof* Anneke Prins Simons, PhD; *Prof* Dr Raymond Walker, EdD; *Assoc Prof* Dr Esther Barrish, EdD; *Assoc Prof* Charles Boyens, MFA; *Assoc Prof* Dr Robert Russell, EdD; *Asst Prof* Dr Eleanor Campolli, EdD; *Asst Prof* Dorothy Harris, MFA; *Asst Prof* Benjamin Jones, MA; *Asst Prof* Marguarite LaBelle, MA; *Asst Prof* Doris Muller, MA; *Asst Prof* Charles Plosky, MFA; *Asst Prof* Herbert Rosenberg, MFA; *Asst Prof* Raymond Statlander, MFA; *Asst Prof* Sr Joan Steans, MFA; *Asst Prof* William White, MFA; *Instructor* Mary Campbell, MA. Instrs PT 12
Estab 1927, dept estab 1961; pub; D & E; ent req HS dipl or equivalent; degrees BA 128 sem hrs, MA; SC 61, LC 19, GC 31; enrl D 250, E 60, GS 60
Tuition: Res—undergrad $22 per cr, grad $45 per cr; nonresident—undergrad $44 per cr, grad $65 per cr; campus residence available
Courses: Advertising Design, Aesthetics, Art Education, Art History, Ceramics, Collage, †Commercial Art, Constructions, Display, Drawing, Film, Goldsmithing, Graphic Arts, Graphic Design, History of Art & Archaeology, Illustration, Interior Design, Jewelry, Lettering, Mixed Media, Museum Staff Training, Painting, Photography, Printmaking, Sculpture, Silversmithing, Stage Design, Teacher Training, Textile Design
Summer School: Dir, Dr Jean C Lane. Tui $22 per sem hr for two terms beginning May 27 and June 23. Courses—Air Brush & Other Rendering Techniques, Art & Society, Ceramics, Contemporary Art, Cultural Resources, Drawing & Composition, Gothic to Modern, Painting, Photography, Two-Dimensional Design

SAINT PETER'S COLLEGE, Fine Arts Department, 2641 Kennedy Blvd, 07306. Tel 201-333-4400, Ext 330. *Chmn* Oscar G Magnan
Estab 1963; den; D & E; ent req HS dipl; degrees BA, BA in Cursu Classico, BS 4 yrs; scholarships; SC 4, LC 13; enrl D 650, E 250, maj 20
Tuition: $93 per cr hr; no campus res
Courses: Art History, Drawing, Film, Painting, Sculpture
Summer School: Two 5 wk sessions. Courses—Drawing, Film History, Introduction to Visual Arts, Painting, Visual Arts in America

LAKEWOOD

GEORGIAN COURT COLLEGE, Department of Art, Lakewood Ave, 08701. Tel 201-364-2200, Ext 48. *Head Dept* Sr M Christina Geis, MFA; *Assoc Prof* Douglas L McIlvain, MA; *Asst Prof* Sr M Phyllis Breimayer, MA; *Lectr* Sayed Aboyoussef, MA; *Lectr* Vincent Hart; *Lectr* Carol Reilly, PhD; *Lectr* Geraldine Velasquez, MA
Estab 1908, dept estab 1924; pvt; D; ent req HS dipl, col board scores, portfolio; degrees BA 4 yr; scholarships; SC 18, LC 11; enrl in dept 220, non-maj 170, maj 50
Tuition: Tui undergrad $2500, $75 per cr; campus res—room & board 7 day $1600, 5 day $1450
Courses: Advertising Design, Art Education, Art History, Ceramics, Commercial Art, Drafting, Drawing, Fashion Arts, Handicrafts, History of Art & Archaeology, Illustration, Jewelry, Painting, Photography, Printmaking, Sculpture, Teacher Training, Art Therapy, Basic Design, Weaving
Summer School: Enrl 30; tui $75 for term of 6 wks beginning June 23. Courses—Ceramics, Painting, Sculpture, Textile Design

RALYN ART CENTER, 316 Main St, 08701. Tel 201-363-7500. *Dir* Ralph F Salisbury. Instrs PT 4
Estab 1964; pub; D & E; ent req none; degrees none; enrl approx 50
Courses: Drawing, Acrylics, Oils, Pastels, Watercolors

LAWRENCEVILLE

RIDER COLLEGE, Department of Fine Arts,* 2083 Lawrenceville, 08648. Tel 609-896-0800. *Chmn* Larry Capo. Instrs FT 3
Estab 1966; pvt; D & E; ent req HS dipl; degrees BA(Fine Arts) 4 yrs; SC 9, LC 4; enrl D 3500, E 5169, maj 100
Tuition: $2950 per yr; campus res—room & board $1542 per yr
Courses: Ceramics, Costume Design & Construction, Drawing, Graphic Arts, Graphic Design, History of Art & Archaeology, Painting, Sculpture, Stage Design

LAYTON

PETERS VALLEY CRAFT CENTER, Star Rte, 07851. Tel 201-948-5200. *Exec Dir* Philip C Homes; *Asst Dir* Patricia A Demby; *Instructor* Suzanne Adams; *Instructor* Colin Butler; *Instructor* Thom Collins; *Instructor* Wendy Holmes; *Instructor* Robert Meadow; *Instructor* Bob Natalini; *Instructor* Tom Neugebauer; *Instructor* Dick Sextone; *Instructor* Casdiss Ann Cole; *Instructor* Sandy Noyes; *Instructor* Katsuyuki Sakazume; *Instructor* Rinny Staber. Instrs 12
Estab 1970; pvt; D, internship - fall, winter, spring; weekend workshops - fall, spring; ent req previous craft experience for some courses; degrees none; college credit available; enrl 375
Tuition: Internship tui & room $1100-$1350 per term; campus res—room & board $80-$85 weekly
Courses: Ceramics, Goldsmithing, Jewelry, Mixed Media, Photography, Silversmithing, Blacksmithing, Fabric Printing, Paper Making, Weaving, Woodworking
Summer School: Tui $80 weekly for regular workshop program

MADISON

DREW UNIVERSITY, Art Department, College of Liberal Arts, Main Ave, 07940. Tel 201-377-3000, Ext 330. *Chmn Dept* Martyvonne Dehoney, EdD; *Asst Prof* Sara Henry, PhD; *Instr* Livio Sagonic, MFA; *Vis Prof* Robert Reid, watercolor; *Vis Assoc Prof* Sally Roberts, PhD; *Vis Instr* David Rohn, MFA
Estab 1928; pvt; D & E; ent req HS dipl; degrees BA 4 yrs; scholarships; SC 17, LC 10; enrl D 275, E 12, maj 42, minors 4
Tuition: Res—undergrad $1700 per sem; tui is less for Continuing Educ prog
Courses: Aesthetics, Architecture, †Art History, Ceramics, Drawing, History of Art & Archaeology, Painting, Photography, Printmaking, Sculpture
Summer School: Dir, Robert K Ackerman. Tui $255 per 3 cr hr course for term of 3 1 2 wks beginning June. Courses—Art Appreciation, Studios

MONTCLAIR

MONTCLAIR ART MUSEUM, Art School, 3 S Mountain Ave, PO Box X, 07042. Tel 201-746-5555. *Dir* Robert J Kpenig; *Registrar* Patricia P Barnes; *Instructor* Herbert Beerman; *Instructor* Tim Gaydos; *Instructor* Edwin Havas; *Instructor* Frances McQuillan; *Instructor* Diana Naspo; *Instructor* Florence Noa; *Instructor* Paul Ortlip; *Instructor* Meryl Taradash; *Children's Instructor* Leone Otis; *Children's Instructor* Nancy Smith
Art school estab 1924; pvt; D & E; ent req desire to study art; degrees none; scholarships; SC 17; enrl D 150 per term, E 50 per term
Tuition: Young people $40 for 12 sessions; adults $75 for 12 sessions
Courses: Aesthetics, Art Education, Collage, Constructions, Drawing, Mixed Media, Painting, Printmaking, Sculpture, Portraiture, Watercolor

MONTCLAIR STATE COLLEGE, Fine Arts Department, School of Fine & Performing Arts, 07043. Tel 201-893-4308. *Dean* Dr Donald Mintz; *Chmn* William McCreath. Instrs FT 26, PT 8
Estab 1908; pub; ent req HS grad and exam, interview, portfolio; degrees BFA 4 yr, MA; scholarship; SC 35, LC 18; enrl maj 100, grad maj 175
Courses: Art Education, Art History, Ceramics, Drawing, Film, Jewelry, Painting, Photography, Printmaking, Sculpture, Textile Design, Theatre Arts, Metalwork, TV as Art

NEWARK

NEWARK SCHOOL OF FINE AND INDUSTRIAL ART, 550 High St, 07102. *Dir* Edward John Stevens Jr. Instrs D PT 42, E PT 28
Estab 1882; pub; enrl D 300, E 300
Courses: Advertising Design, Ceramics, Fashion Arts, Illustration, Industrial Design, Interior Design, Painting, Sculpture, Textile Design, Fine Arts

RUTGERS UNIVERSITY, NEWARK, Art Department, Newark Col of Arts & Sciences, 392 High St, Bradley Hall, 07102. *Chmn Dept* Judith K Brodsky. Instrs FT 5, PT 5
Pub; D; ent req HS dipl, or as specified by col and univ; degrees BA 4 yr; scholarship; enrl D 486, maj 50
Courses: Art Education, Ceramics, Drawing, Graphic Design, History of Art & Archaeology, Illustration, Museum Staff Training, Painting, Photography, Printmaking, Sculpture, Weaving
Summer School: Courses offered vary from year to year

NEW BRUNSWICK

RUTGERS, THE STATE UNIVERSITY OF NEW JERSEY
—**Cook College, Department of Landscape Architecture,** Blake Hall, 08903. Tel 201-932-9317. *Chmn* Roy H DeBoer

Courses: Landscape Architecture
—Douglass College, Walters Hall, 08903. Tel 201-932-9856. *Chmn* Peter Stroud, MFA. Instrs FT 15, PT 12
Estab 1918; pub, W; D; ent req HS dipl; degrees BS(Studio, Educ, Art History) 4 yrs; scholarships; SC 28, LC 27; enrl 1000, maj 150
Courses: Art Education, Art History, Ceramics, Drawing, Film, Graphic Arts, Mixed Media, Painting, Photography, Video, Design, Environmental Art
—Livingston College, Lucy Stone Hall, 08903. Tel 201-932-4160. *Chmn* Melvin Edwards. Instrs FT 15, PT 8
Estab 1969; pub; D; ent req HS dipl; degrees BA(Studio, Educ, Art History) 4 yrs; scholarships; SC 37, LC 16; enrl 1000, maj 190
Courses: Art Education, Art History, Ceramics, Commercial Art, Drawing, Film, Graphic Arts, Handicrafts, Photography, Video, Design, Environmental Art, Glassblowing, Performance, Weaving
—Mason Gross School of the Arts, Graduate Program in Visual Arts, 358 George St, 08903. Tel 201-932-9078. *Dean* John Bettenbender, MFA; *Chmn Visual Arts* Larry Rosing, MAT; *Chmn Grad Prog* Markel Bruce Berger, MA & MFA; *Prof* Leon Golub, MFA; *Prof* John Lake Goodyear, MDes; *Prof* Daniel Newman, BA; *Prof* Bille Pickard-Pritchard, PhD; *Assoc Prof* Gary Kuehn, MFA; *Assoc Prof* Peter Stroud, MFA
Estab 1766, school estab 1976; pub; D; ent req HS dipl, BFA or equivalent, portfolio; degrees MFA 2 yrs; scholarships; SC 26, LC 10, GC 37; enrl 60, grad 60
Tuition: Res—grad $592 per sem; nonres—grad $852 per sem; campus res—$900 per yr
Courses: Ceramics, Conceptual Art, Drawing, Film, Intermedia, Mixed Media, Painting, Photography, Printmaking, Sculpture, Video
—Rutgers College, Voorhees Hall, 08903. Tel 201-932-7041. *Chmn* Matthew Baigell. Instrs FT 12, PT 15
Estab 1766; pub; D; ent req HS dipl; degrees BA(Studio, Educ, Art History) 4 yrs; scholarships; SC 32, LC 33; enrl 1000, maj 125
Tuition: Res—$300 per term; nonres-$600 per term
Courses: Art Education, Art History, Drawing, Film, Graphic Arts, Painting, Photography, Video, Art and the Computer, Foundry Metal, New Materials and Techniques Design
—Graduate Program in Art History, Voorhees Hall, Hamilton St, 08903. Tel 201-932-7041. *Dir Prog* Elizabeth Parker McLachlan, PhD; *Prof* Matthew Baigell, PhD; *Prof* Olga Berendsen, PhD; *Prof* Jack J Spector, PhD; *Prof* James H Stubblebine, PhD; *Assoc Prof* John F Kenfield, PhD; *Asst Prof* Joan Marter, PhD; *Asst Prof* Tod Marder, PhD; *Asst Prof* Sarah Wilk, PhD
Estab 1766, grad prog estab 1971; pub; D; ent req BA; degrees MA 2 yrs, PhD 4 yrs; scholarships; grad courses 15; enrl grad students 80
Tuition: Res—grad $50 per cr; nonres—grad $72 per cr plus student fee; campus res—room $890 per yr maximum & board $425
Courses: †Art History

NUTLEY

NUTLEY ART CENTER,* 200 Chestnut St, 07110. Tel 201-661-2280. *Dir* Vivian Noyes Fikus
Estab 1969; pvt; D & E; ent req none; degrees none; scholarships; SC 6; enrl D 40, E 25
Tuition: Adults $33-$35 per term (7 sessions); children $21-$28 per term (7 sessions)
Courses: Commercial Art, Drawing, Graphic Arts, Graphic Design, Handicrafts, Illustration, Lettering, Mixed Media, Painting, Printmaking, Sculpture, Teacher Training, Macrame, Portraiture, Puppetry
Summer School: Tui $25 for term of 4 wks beginning July and Aug. Courses—Crafts, Drawing, Painting, Portraiture, Sculpture

OCEAN CITY

OCEAN CITY SCHOOL OF ART, 409 Wesley Ave, 08226. Tel 609-399-7628 or 399-6111, Ext 280. *Executive Dir* Frances J Taylor; *Head Teaching Staff* Lorraine Watson; *Instructor* Pamela Altemose, BFA; *Instructor* Lance Balderson, BA; *Instructor* Chris Damico, BA; *Instructor* Schyular Dawson, BAEd; *Instructor* Cynthia Dougherty, BAEd; *Instructor* Kathleen Fell, BS; *Instructor* Wayne Goodman, BFA; *Instructor* Scott Griswold; *Instructor* Lucinda Hathaway, MFA; *Instructor* William Hopkins; *Instructor* Judith Kohn, BA; *Instructor* Sandra Miller, BMAEd; *Instructor* Dorothy Pere; *Instructor* Attilio Sinagra, BFA
Estab 1974; pvt; D & E; ent req none; degrees 3 yr cert; scholarship; SC 14, LC 1; enrl D 1, E 8
Tuition: $480 per yr, $160 per sem
Courses: Art History, Ceramics, Drawing, Mixed Media, Painting, Photography, Sculpture, Chinese Brush, Portrait, Sumi, Watercolor
Summer School: Executive Dir, Frances J Taylor. Courses—Same classes offered during summer plus workshops and demonstrations

PATERSON

PASSAIC COUNTY COMMUNITY COLLEGE, Division of Humanities, College Blvd, 07509. Tel 201-279-5000. *Chairperson Div* Aidea J Kenny, EdD; *Prof* Phyllis Saunders, MA
Estab 1969, dept estab 1969; pub; D & E; ent req HS dipl, New Jersey basic skills exam; degrees AA 2 yrs; SC 4, LC 3; enrl D 100, E 25
Tuition: $20 per cr
Courses: Advertising Design, Aesthetics, Art History, Drawing

PRINCETON

PRINCETON UNIVERSITY
—Department of Art and Archaeology, 104 McCormick Hall, 08540. Tel 609-452-3780. *Chmn Dept* John Shearman, PhD; *Chmn Prog Chinese and Japanese Art and Archaeology* Wen Fong, PhD; *Chmn Prog in Classical Archaeology* T Leslie Shear Jr, PhD; *Prof* David Coffin, PhD; *Prof* Sam Hunter, MFA; *Prof* Robert Koch, PhD;

Prof John Martin, PhD; *Prof* John Plummer, PhD
Estab 1746; pvt; degrees AB, MFA, PhD; scholarships; LC 14, GC 9; enrl 761, maj 35, grad 50
Tuition: Res—undergrad $5585 per yr, grad $5685 per yr; campus res—room & board $2220 per yr; total budget per yr $8721
Courses: Art History, History of Art & Archaeology, Visual Arts
—School of Architecture and Urban Planning, Architecture Bldg, 08540. *Dean* Robert L Geddes. Instrs FT 20
Estab 1919; pvt; D; ent req high; degrees AB, 4 yrs, MArchit, MArchit and Urban Planning, PhD(Archit), PhD(Urban Planning); scholarships and fels; SC 6, LC 13, GC 6, seminars 17; enrl undergrad 120, grad 50

RIDGEWOOD

RIDGEWOOD SCHOOL OF ART AND DESIGN, 83 Chestnut St, 07450. Tel 201-444-7100. *Dir* Robert Crawford
Estab 1961; pvt; D & E; ent req HS dipl; SC 35, LC 2; enrl D 150, E 50
Tuition: $2000 per yr; no campus res
Courses: Advertising Design, Art History, Ceramics, Commercial Art, Drawing, Fashion Arts, Graphic Design, Illustration, Lettering, Painting, Photography, Printmaking, Sculpture

SOUTH ORANGE

SETON HALL UNIVERSITY, Department of Art and Music, South Orange Ave, 07079. Tel 201-762-9000. *Chmn* Petra T D Chu, PhD; *Prof* Louis de Crenascol, LDD; *Prof* Julius Zsako, PhD; *Asst Prof* William K Burns, MA; *Asst Prof* Edwin Havas; *Asst Prof* Barbara Kaufman, MA; *Asst Prof* Anthony Triano. Instrs FT 10, PT 9
Estab dept 1968; pvt; D & E; degrees BA 4 yr; SC 8
Courses: Architecture, Art History, Commercial Art, Drawing, Illustration, Mixed Media, Painting, Sculpture, Music Art

TOMS RIVER

OCEAN COUNTY COLLEGE, Humanities Department, Hooper Ave, 08753. Tel 201-255-4000, Ext 333 or 255-1131. *Chmn Dept* Dr James Doran, EdD; *Coordr Fine and Performing Arts* Robert L Huber, MA; *Prof* Tom Funk, MFA; *Prof* William Schoenfeld, MA; *Prof* Howard Unger, EdD
Estab 1964, dept estab 1964; pub; D & E; ent req HS dipl; degrees AA in Liberal Arts with concentration in Fine Art & AAS(Visual Communication Technology) 2 yrs; SC 19, LC 3; enrl D 1500, E 1500, maj 67
Tuition: Res—undergrad $500 per yr, $250 per sem, PT $17; non-res—undergrad $1000 per yr, $500 per sem, PT $34; no campus res
Courses: Advertising Design, Aesthetics, Art History, Calligraphy, Ceramics, †Commercial Art, Conceptual Art, Costume Design & Construction, †Drawing, Film, Graphic Arts, Graphic Design, Handicrafts, Lettering, Painting, Photography, Printmaking, Sculpture, Stage Design, †Theatre Arts
Summer School: Dir, Dr James Doran. Enrl 9; tui $51 for term of 6 wks beginning June. Courses—Arts and Humanities, Basic Drawing, Ceramics, Crafts

TRENTON

TRENTON STATE COLLEGE, Art Department, Pennington Rd, 08625. Tel 609-771-2652. *Chmn Dept* Norval C Kern, EdD; *Prof* Henry Ahrens, EdD; *Prof* Howard Goldstein, EdD; *Prof* Joseph Shannon, EdD; *Asst Prof* Ruth Breil, MA; *Asst Prof* Wendell Brooks, MFA; *Asst Prof* George Chapman, MFA; *Asst Prof* Christina Craig, MA; *Asst Prof* Sylvia Honig, MAATR; *Assoc Prof* Ilse Johnson, MFA; *Asst Prof* Charles Kumnick, MFA; *Asst Prof* Mark Lehman, MFA; *Asst Prof* Hiroshi Murata, MFA; *Asst Prof* Wilbur Pendley, MFA; *Asst Prof* William Phelan, MFA; *Asst Prof* Bruce Rigby, MFA; *Asst Prof* Louis Ross, MA; *Asst Prof* Marcia Taylor, MAATR. Instrs FT 16, PT 12
Estab 1855; pub; D & E; ent req HS dipl; degrees BA 4 yr; scholarship; SC approx 40, LC 10, GC 11; enrl non-maj 300, maj 450
Courses: †Advertising Design, †Art Education, Art History, Calligraphy, Ceramics, Drawing, Fashion Arts, Graphic Arts, Illustration, †Interior Design, Jewelry, Lettering, Painting, Photography, Printmaking, Silversmithing, †Art Therapy

UNION

KEAN COLLEGE OF NEW JERSEY, Fine Arts Department, Morris Ave, 07083. Tel 201-527-2307. *Chmn Fine Arts Dept* Robert B Coon, EdD; *Coordr Interior Design* H Bernard Lipscomb III, MA; *Coordr Art Educ* Pearl Greenbert, EdD; *Coordr Visual Commun* W Martin Holloway, MFA; *Coordr Specialized Studio* Leonard Pierro, MA; *Coordr Art History* Virginia Stotz, MA. Instrs FT 31
Estab 1855; pub; D & E; ent req HS dipl, portfolio interview for art maj; degrees BA 4 yrs; scholarships; SC 58, LC 37, GC 24; enrl FT 383, PT 236, maj 656, grad 37
Tuition: Res—$704 per yr, $352 per sem; nonres—$1408 per yr, $704 per sem; campus res—room & board $1549 per yr
Courses: Advertising Design, Aesthetics, †Art Education, †Art History, Ceramics, †Commercial Art, Display, Drafting, Drawing, Film, Graphic Arts, Graphic Design, Illustration, †Interior Design, Jewelry, Lettering, Museum Staff Training, Occupational Therapy, Painting, Photography, Printmaking, Sculpture, Textile Design, Furniture Making
Summer School: Asst Dir, Mrs Madsen. Tui $25 per cr for term of 6 wks beginning June 26. Courses—Art History, Art in Education, Ceramics, Drawing, Introduction to Art, Introduction to Interior Design, Jewelry, Life Drawing, Painting, Printmaking, Sculpture, Watercolor

WAYNE

WILLIAM PATERSON COLLEGE, Art Department, Div of Fine and Performing Arts, 300 Pompton Rd, 07470. Tel 201-881-2402. *Chairman* Alan H Lazarus H Lazarvi. Instrs FT 24, PT 8
Dept estab 1958; pub; degrees BA 4 yr; SC 9, LC 9; enrl maj 420, grad 105, E non-maj 170
Courses: Ceramics, Drawing, Graphic Arts, Graphic Design, Jewelry, Painting, Photography, Sculpture, Teacher Training, Textile Design, Theatre Arts, Enameling, Furniture Design, Gallery Workshop & Design, Lapidary, Metal
Summer School: Term of 6 wks beginning June

WEST LONG BRANCH

MONMOUTH COLLEGE, Department of Art, Norwood & Cedar Aves, 07764. Tel 201-222-6600, Ext 346. *Chmn Dept* Arie van Everdingen, MFA; *Assoc Prof* Vincent DiMattio, MFA; *Assoc Prof* Alfred Provencher, MA; *Assoc Prof* Martin Ryan, MA; *Asst Prof* Carolyn Bloomer, MA; *Asst Prof* Edward Jankowski, MFA; *Instructor* Hedy daCosta-Nunes, MA
Estab 1933; pvt; D & E; ent req HS dipl, portfolio for transfer students; degrees BA(Art), BFA and BA(Art Educ) 4 yr; scholarship; SC 25, LC 8; enrl in dept D 108, E 6, non-maj 80, maj 108, audits 6
Tuition: $3480 per yr, $740 per sem, $105 per cr hr; campus res—room and board $900
Courses: †Art Education, Art History, †Ceramics, Drawing, Goldsmithing, Graphic Arts, Handicrafts, History of Art & Archaeology, †Painting, Photography, Printmaking, †Sculpture, Silversmithing, Teacher Training, Appreciation of Art, Macrame, Papermaking
Summer School: Dean, Kenneth C Streibig. Enrl approx 80; tui $89 per cr hr for 3 or 6 wk courses beginning June 2. Courses—Art Appreciation, Ceramics, Independent Study, Painting, Sculpture

NEW MEXICO

ABIQIUI

AMERICAN STAINED GLASS INSTITUTE, Ghost Ranch Conference Center, Abiqiui, NM. (Mailing Add: PO 4605, Santa Fe, NM 87501,) Tel 505-982-9981. *Head Dept* Maurice Loriaux, PhD; *Dir Abstract Design* Dr Frank Relemen, PhD; *Art Prof Adminr* Karen Wisdon, MA; *Crafts Dept Dir* Robert Bailey, PhD
Estab 1971; D & E; ent req advanced proficiency in stained glass construction; degrees Award of Merit in Stained Glass Art (2 seminars), Maitre d'art Vitrail (4 seminars); partial scholarships; SC 4, LC 3, GC 1; enrl all seminars are limited to 16 delegates
Tuition: $630 per 2 wk seminar includes room & board
Courses: Advertising Design, Graphic Arts, History of Art & Archaeology, Interior Design, Stained Glass

ALBUQUERQUE

AMERICAN CLASSICAL COLLEGE, 614 Indian School Rd NW, 87102. Tel 505-843-7749. *Dir* Dr C M Flumiani. Instrs FT 2
Estab 1970; pvt; D; ent req ent exam; degrees none; scholarship
Tuition: FT $100 mo
Courses: Advertising Design, Aesthetics, Art Education, Commercial Art, Drawing, History of Art & Archaeology, Painting, Sculpture

SOUTHWESTERN SCHOOL OF ART, 1504 B Wyoming NE, 87112. Tel 505-299-0316. *Dir* Ted C Hogsett, BS; *Asst Dir* Doug Dean; *Instructor* Lita Chavez; *Instructor* Tina Fuentes, MA; *Instructor* Jean Hawley
Estab 1974; pvt; D & E; degrees cert; SC 7, LC 8; enrl D 20, E 46
Tuition: Adults $35 per 8 week session, children $25 per 8 week session; no campus res
Courses: Art History, Drawing, Painting, Printmaking

UNIVERSITY OF ALBUQUERQUE, Art Department, Saint Joseph Place NW, 87140. Tel 505-831-1111. *Dept Head* Ed Vega, MFA; *Instr* Russell Adams, MFA; *Instr* Betty Colbert, MA; *Instr* Dick Knapp, MFA; *Instr* Jo Ann Main, MA; *Instr* Mie Shu Ou, MFA; *Instr* Peggy Walden, MA
Estab 1920; den; D & E; ent req HS dipl; degrees AA(Advertising Art) 2 yrs, BA and BFA 4 yrs; scholarships; SC 30, LC 12; enrl maj 40
Tuition: Res and non-res $83 per cr hr; campus residence available
Courses: †Advertising Design, Art Education, Art History, Ceramics, Commercial Art, Costume Design & Construction, †Drawing, Fashion Arts, Graphic Arts, Graphic Design, Illustration, Industrial Design, Jewelry, Lettering, †Painting, †Photography, Printmaking, Sculpture, Silversmithing, Stage Design
Summer School: Dean, Jack Kranston. Tui $83 per cr hr for term of 5 wks beginning May 26-June 30. Courses—Bronze Casting, Ceramics, Drawing, Watercolor

UNIVERSITY OF NEW MEXICO
—**College of Fine Arts,** 87131. Tel 505-277-2111. *Dean Col* Donald C McRae, MA
Estab 1935; pub
—**Department of Art,** 87131. Tel 505-277-5861. *Chmn* Wayne R Lazorik, MFA
Estab 1889; pub; D & E; ent req HS dipl; degrees BA and BFA 4 yrs, MA 2 yrs, MFA 3 yrs, PhD 3 yrs; scholarships; SC 190, LC 43, GC 73; enrl E 511, non-maj 133, maj 243, grad 150
Tuition: Res—undergrad $624 per yr, $312 per sem, grad $596 per yr, $298 per sem; nonres—undergrad $1872 per yr, $936 per sem, grad $1844 per yr, $922 per sem; campus res—$1625 per yr, $838 for fall sem, $763 for spring sem
Courses: Aesthetics, Architecture, Art Education, Art History, Ceramics, Costume Design & Construction, Drafting, Drawing, Film, Graphic Arts, Graphic Design, History of Art & Archaeology, Jewelry, Landscape Architecture, Mixed Media, Museum Staff Training, Painting, Photography, Printmaking, Sculpture, Stage Design,

Teacher Training, Theatre Arts, Video
Children's Classes: Offered through Art Educ Dept
Summer School: Tui res—$26 per cr hr, nonres—$78 per cr hr for term of 8 wks beginning June 16. Courses—same as regular session but limited
—**Tamarind Institute,** 108 Cornell Ave SE, 87131. Tel 505-277-3901. *Dir* Clinton Adams; *Tech Dir* John Sommers, Tamarind Master Printer; *Studio Mgr* Stephen Britko
Degrees 2 yr prog leading to cert as Tamarind Master Printer
Tuition: Res—$22-$24; nonres—$63-$72
Courses: Lithography

HOBBS

NEW MEXICO JUNIOR COLLEGE, Art Department, Lovington Hwy, 88240. Tel 505-392-6526. *Chmn* Joe Walker, MA; *Prof* Terry Bumpass, MFA
Estab 1965, dept estab 1965; pub; D & E; ent req HS dipl, GED or special approval; degrees AA 2 yrs; scholarships; SC 5, LC 1; enrl D 75, E 25, non-maj 95, maj 5
Tuition: Res—undergrad $144 per yr, $72 per sem; nonres—undergrad $216 per yr, $108 per sem; no campus res
Courses: Ceramics, Drawing, Goldsmithing, Interior Design, Jewelry, Painting, Photography, Printmaking
Summer School: Div Chmn, Joe Walker. Enrl 30; tui $36 for term of 8 wks beginning June 10. Courses—Ceramics, Printmaking

LAS CRUCES

NEW MEXICO STATE UNIVERSITY, Art Dept, College of Arts & Sciences, Box 3572, 88003. Tel 505-646-1705. *Head Dept* Christiane L Joost-Gaugier, PhD; *Prof* Ken Barrick, MA; *Prof* William Charland, MFA; *Prof* Spencer Fidler, MFA; *Prof* Trinidad Lopez, MA; *Prof* W C Miles, MFA; *Prof* John Moffitt, PhD; *Prof* Lee Richards, EdD; *Prof* Richard Wickstrom, MFA; *Prof* Peter Voris, MFA; *Vis Prof* John Torreano, Spring Sem
Estab 1975; pub; D & E; ent req HS dipl; degrees BA, BFA & BS(Art Educ) 4 yrs, MA(Studio), MA(Art Hist) & MS(Art Educ) 2 yrs; SC 52, LC 25, GC 53; enrl maj 100, grad 24
Tuition: Res—$644 per yr, $322 per sem; nonres—$1888 per yr, $944 per sem
Courses: Architecture, Art Education, Art History, Ceramics, Conceptual Art, Drawing, Graphic Arts, Handicrafts, History of Art & Archaeology, Jewelry, Museum Staff Training, Painting, Photography, Printmaking, Sculpture, Design, Metal Arts, Weaving
Summer School: Tui $105 for term of 6 wks. Courses—Art Appreciation, Ceramics, Drawing, Painting, Sculpture

LAS VEGAS

NEW MEXICO HIGHLANDS UNIVERSITY, Dept of Fine Arts, 87701. Tel 505-425-7111, Ext 359. *Chmn Dept* Dr Loren E Wise, DMA; *Prof* Harry M Leippe, MA; *Prof* Helen Thompson, MFA; *Asst Prof* Carolyn Powers, MA; *Asst Prof* Nancy Rosnow, MFA
Estab 1898; pub; D & E; ent req HS dipl, ACT, Early Admis Prog, GED; degrees BA 4 yrs, MA 1 yr; scholarships; SC 24, LC 8, GC 12; enrl non-maj 55, maj 51, grad 4
Tuition: Res—$199.20 per sem, $398.40 per yr; nonres—$641.40 per sem; campus residence available
Courses: Art Education, Art History, Calligraphy, Ceramics, Constructions, Drawing, Graphic Arts, Jewelry, Lettering, Painting, Photography, Printmaking, Sculpture, Silversmithing, Stage Design, Teacher Training, Theatre Arts
Adult Hobby Classes: Courses—Ceramics, Painting, Weaving
Summer School: Dean, John Pacheco. Tui same as above. Courses—Mainly studio plus core curriculum, depending upon staffing

PORTALES

EASTERN NEW MEXICO UNIVERSITY, Department of Art & Education, 88130. Tel 505-562-2652. *Chmn Dept* Chris Gikas, MFA; *Prof* Vern Acker, MFA; *Prof* Charles Wiley, PhD; *Assoc Prof* Dale Hamlett, MA
Estab 1932; pub; D & E; ent req HS dipl, GED, ACT; degrees AA 2 yrs, BS, BA & BFA 4 yrs; scholarships; SC 44, LC 6, GC 25; enrl D 550, E 220, maj 105, grad 20
Tuition: Res—$768.80 per yr, $284.40 per sem, $23.70 per cr hr; nonres—$1453.70 per yr, $726.60 per sem, $60.55 per cr hr; campus res—room & board $540 per yr
Courses: †Advertising Design, Art Education, Art History, Calligraphy, †Ceramics, †Commercial Art, Drafting, †Drawing, †Graphic Arts, Graphic Design, History of Art & Archaeology, Illustration, †Jewelry, Lettering, †Painting, Photography, †Sculpture, Silversmithing, †Teacher Training, Theatre Arts, Video
Summer School: Chmn, Chris Gikas. Tui res—$23.70 per cr hr; nonres—$60.55 per cr hr for term of 8 wks beginning June 4. Courses—Ceramics, Commercial Art, Crafts, Drawing, Lettering, Photography

RUIDOSO

CARRIZO ART AND CRAFT WORKSHOPS, Carrizo Canyon Rd, PO Drawer A, 88345. Tel 505-257-2375. *Dir* Hilma Greggerson Collier, MS. Instrs PT 20
Estab 1956; pvt; D; ent req art interest; SC 19; enrl 300 summer school
Tuition: $90 to $165 for 2 wk workshop; campus res—room & board $140-$270 for 2 wks
Courses: Calligraphy, Goldsmithing, Jewelry, Mixed Media, Painting, Sculpture, Silversmithing, Stained Glass
Adult Hobby Classes: Tui $125 for 2 wks. Courses—Stained Glass

SANTA FE

BARNA POTTERY, Village Tesuque, Village of Tesuque, 87574. Tel 505-982-8232. *Dir* Iris Barna. Instrs FT 2, PT 4
Estab 1960; pvt; D & E; ent req HS dipl; SC 3

Tuition: No campus res
Courses: Aesthetics, Ceramics, Display, History of Art & Archaeology, Sculpture, Needle Work

COLLEGE OF SANTA FE, Visual Arts Dept, Saint Michael's Dr, 87501. Tel 505-982-6011. *Instructor* Marie Askan, MA; *Instructor* Ronald Berger, MFA; *Instructor* Douglas Coffin, MFA; *Instructor* Meridel Rubenstein, MFA
Estab 1947, dept estab 1974; pvt; D & E; ent req HS dipl or GED; degrees BA(Visual Arts); scholarships; SC 26, LC 20; enrl D 200, E 50, non-maj 50, maj 164, others 20 (sr citizens)
Tuition: $73 per sem hr plus general fees; campus res—room & board $1800 per yr
Courses: †Art Education, †Art History, Ceramics, Drawing, Goldsmithing, Handicrafts, Jewelry, Painting, Photography, Printmaking, Sculpture, Silversmithing, Pottery, †Studio Arts
Summer School: Dir, Winona Garmhausen. Enrl 60; tui $73 per sem hr for term of 4 or 8 wks beginning May 15. Courses—Art History, Drawing, Jewelry, Outdoor Sketching, Painting, Photography, Printmaking, Pottery

INSTITUTE OF AMERICAN INDIAN ARTS, Cerrillos Rd, 87501. Tel 505-988-6281. *Dir* Charles A Dailey
Estab 1962; pvt; D; ent req HS dipl; degrees AA (Fine Arts) 2 yrs; SC 18, LC 11; enrl 263
Courses: Advertising Design, Ceramics, Commercial Art, Costume Design & Construction, Drawing, Fashion Arts, Graphic Arts, Graphic Design, Handicrafts, History of Art & Archaeology, Jewelry, Lettering, Museum Staff Training, Painting, Sculpture, Traditional Indian Techniques, Two & Three-Dimensional Design

SANTA FE WORKSHOPS OF CONTEMPORARY ART, Box 1344, 87501. Tel 505-983-5573. *Adv Dir* Geraldine Price
Estab 1959, Santa Fe 1971; pvt; D; ent req age 18 or over; scholarships; enrl limited
Tuition: $500 each 8 wks
Courses: Drawing, Painting, Art Therapy

SILVER CITY

WESTERN NEW MEXICO UNIVERSITY, Dept of Fine Art, Art Div, 88061. Tel 505-538-6517. *Chmn Dept* Robert Omick; *Prof* Ed Dunn, MFA; *Prof* Cecil Howard, MFA; *Prof* Polly Hughes, MA; *Prof* Dorothy McCray, MFA; *Prof* Claude Smith, MFA; *Prof* Mona Tanzola
Pub; D & E; ent req HS dipl; degrees BA, 4yrs; SC 10, LC 7; enrl D 200, non-maj 160, maj 40
Tuition: Campus residence available
Courses: Aesthetics, Art Education, Art History, †Ceramics, Collage, Constructions, Drawing, Graphic Design, History of Art & Archaeology, †Jewelry, Mixed Media, †Painting, †Printmaking, †Sculpture, Silversmithing, Teacher Training, Textile Design
Adult Hobby Classes: Courses—Ceramics, Lapidary, Silversmithing, Stained Glass
Summer School: Dir Summer Sessions, Dorothy Blalock. Courses—Art Appreciation, Ceramics, Drawing, Painting

NEW YORK

ALBANY

COLLEGE OF SAINT ROSE, Division of Art,* 432 Western Ave, 12203. Tel 518-454-5111. *Chmn* Patricia Clahassey, EdD; *Instr* Karene Faul, MFA; *Instr* Leonard LaRoux, MFA; *Instr* Paul Mauren, MFA; *Instr* Edward McCartan, MA; *Instr* Margaret M O'Donnell, MA
Estab 1920, dept estab 1970; pvt; D & E; ent req HS dipl, SAT or ACT, rank in top 2 5 of class; degrees BS (Art) and BS (Art Educ) 4 yrs, MS in Art Educ; scholarships; SC 21, LC 7, GC 8; enrl non-maj 200, maj 111, GS 14
Tuition: Res—undergrad $1250 per sem; campus res—room and board $800 per sem
Courses: Advertising Design, Aesthetics, †Art Education, Art History, Calligraphy, Ceramics, †Drawing, Graphic Arts, Handicrafts, Illustration, Jewelry, †Painting, Photography, †Printmaking, Sculpture, Teacher Training, Fibers, Weaving
Adult Hobby Classes: Enrl 20; tui $57.50 per cr hr. Courses—Some continuing education courses each semester

JUNIOR COLLEGE OF ALBANY, Fine Arts Division, 12208. Tel 518-445-1711. *Chairwoman* Willie Marlowe; *Instructor* Don Bessette, MA; *Instructor* Jesse Collins, MFA; *Instructor* Ruth Funk, MA; *Instructor* Timothy Martin, MFA; *Instructor* William Schade, MFA; *Instructor* Leo Bouchard; *Instructor* William Claus, MA
Estab 1957, dept estab 1970; pvt; D & E; ent req HS dipl, references, records, SAT; degrees AA, AS and AAS 2 yrs; scholarships; SC 43, LC 16 (Art); enrl D 900 (total), 156 (art), E 823 (total)
Tuition: $1200 per yr
Courses: Advertising Design, Art Education, Art History, Ceramics, Commercial Art, Drawing, Graphic Arts, Graphic Design, Handicrafts, Illustration, Interior Design, Jewelry, Mixed Media, Painting, Photography, Printmaking, Sculpture, Theatre Arts, Serigraphy, Special Education, State Design
Summer School: Dir, Robert Pennock. Courses—vary

STATE UNIVERSITY OF NEW YORK AT ALBANY, Art Department, 1400 Washington Ave, 12222. Tel 518-457-8487. *Chmn Dept* Richard Callner, MAFA; *Prof* Dennis Byng, MS; *Prof* Edward Cowley, MA; *Prof* Mojimir Frinta, PhD; *Prof* Thom O'Connor, MFA; *Prof* Richard Stankiejica; *Prof* William Wilson, MFA; *Assoc Prof* Robert CArtmell, MFA; *Assoc Prof* Mark Greenwold; *Assoc Prof* Arthur Lennig; *Asst Prof* Phyllis Galembo; *Asst Prof* Alex Markhoff
Estab 1848; pub; D & E; ent req HS dipl and portfolio; degrees BA (36 hr major), 4 yrs, BA (60 hr maj), 4 yrs; MA (30 hr maj), 1 1 2 yrs; scholarships; SC 43, LC 20, GC 33; enrl D 750, E 400, non-maj 600, maj 150, grad 45

Tuition: Res—Undergrad $3100-$3250 yr, $25 cr, $1800-$2000 for commuter, grad $4700 per sem, $58.50 hr; Nonres—Undergrad $3650-$3850 yr, $40 cr hr, grad $900 per sem, $75 hr; campus residence room and board $740 per yr
Courses: Aesthetics, Art History, Calligraphy, Collage, Constructions, †Drafting, History of Art & Archaeology, Intermedia, Mixed Media, †Painting, †Photography, †Printmaking, †Sculpture, Theatre Arts, Plastics
Adult Hobby Classes: Courses in all studio areas
Summer School: Asst Dean Grad Studies, Paul Saimond. Enrl 350; term of 3 - 6 wks beginning July 1

ALFRED

NEW YORK STATE COLLEGE OF CERAMICS AT ALFRED UNIVERSITY, Division of Art & Design, 14802. Tel 607-871-2442. *Head Dept* Tony Hepburn. Instrs FT 20
Estab 1900; degrees BFA and MFA 4 yrs; enrl maj undergrad 250, grad 25, others 250. Two yrs of foundation study and two yrs of upper level study
Tuition: Res—Undergrad $1285, grad $1685; non-res—undergrad $1885, grad $2085; campus res—room & board $1765-$1965
Courses: Art Education, Ceramics, Painting, Photography, Printmaking, Sculpture, Design, Glass
Summer School: Dean, Lewis Butler

AMHERST

DAEMEN COLLEGE, Art Department, 14226. Tel 716-839-3600, Ext 241. *Chmn Dept* Dennis W Barraclough, MFA; *Prof* Sr M Jeanne File, PhD; *Prof* James K Y Kuo, MA; *Assoc Prof* James A Allen, MFA; *Assoc Prof* Margaret Bain, EdD; *Assoc Prof* Carol Townsend, MFA; *Asst Prof* David Kulik, MFA; *Asst Prof* Bruce Marzahn, MFA; *Asst Prof* Elizabeth Simon, MFA
Estab 1947; pvt; D & E; ent req HS dipl, art portfolio; degrees BFA(Ceramics, Graphic Design, Painting, Printmaking, Sculpture), BS(Art) and BS(Art Educ) 4 yrs; SC 55; enrl D 1400, non-maj 1100, maj 100
Tuition: Res—Undergrad $2087.50 per sem, $82 per cr hr; Nonres—Undergrad $1337.50 per sem, $82 per cr hr; campus res—room and board $1500
Courses: Advertising Design, Aesthetics, Art Education, Art History, Calligraphy, Ceramics, Commercial Art, Drawing, Graphic Arts, Graphic Design, Handicrafts, Museum Staff Training, Painting, Photography, Printmaking, Sculpture, Silversmithing, Teacher Training, Theatre Arts
Summer School: Dir, Terry Brancato

ANNANDALE-ON-HUDSON

BARD COLLEGE, Division of Art, Music, Drama, 12504. Tel 914-758-6822. *Art Chmn* William Driver
Estab 1865; pvt; degrees BA 4 yrs; scholarships; enrl 600
Courses: Drawing, Painting, Printmaking, Sculpture, Stage Design, Criticism & History of Art, Woodcut

AURORA

WELLS COLLEGE, Department of Art & Art History,* 13026. Tel 315-364-3011. *Division Chmn* Nancy Wynn, MA
Estab 1868; pvt; W; D; ent req HS dipl, credit by examination programs; degrees BA 4 yrs; SC 19, LC 20; enrl D 500(total), non-maj 122, maj 18
Tuition: Res—undergrad $6,500 per yr; campus res available
Courses: Aesthetics, †Art History, Ceramics, †Drawing, Film, †History of Art & Archaeology, †Painting, Photography, Printmaking, Teacher Training, †Theatre Arts

BAYSIDE

QUEENSBOROUGH COMMUNITY COLLEGE, Department of Art and Design, 11364. Tel 212-631-6395. *Chmn* Dr Lola B Gellman, PhD; *Assoc Prof* Priva Gross, PhM; *Assoc Prof* John Hawkins, MFA; *Assoc Prof* Paul Tschinkel, MFA; *Asst Prof* Robert Rogers; *Asst Prof* Kenneth Walpuck, PhD; *Asst Prof* Heinz Wipfler, MA
Estab 1958, dept estab 1968; pub; D & E; ent req HS dipl, placement exams; degrees AA, AS and AAS; scholarships; SC 21, LC 14; enrl D 9000, E 4000
Tuition: Res—undergrad $388 per sem, $35 per cr; nonres—undergrad $713 per sem, $55 per cr; no campus res
Courses: Advertising Design, Art History, Ceramics, Drawing, Painting, Photography, Printmaking, Sculpture, Video, Color Theory, Design
Adult Hobby Classes: Enrl 15; tui $40-$60 per course. Courses—Antiques, Calligraphy, Interior Design, Jewelry, Photography, Stained Glass
Children's Classes: Ceramics
Summer School: Tui $35 per cr for term of 7 wks beginning mid-June. Courses—Ceramics, Drawing, Photography, Watercolor

BEDFORD HILLS

GOETZ ART SCHOOL, 535 Bedford Center Rd, 10507. Tel 914-234-9417. *Dir* Richard V Goetz; *Instructor* Edith Goetz
Estab 1946; pvt; D & E; SC 6, LC 2; enrl D 70, E50
Tuition: Monthly; no campus residence
Courses: Aesthetics, Drawing, Mixed Media, Painting, Painting (figure, landscape, portrait, still life)
Summer School: Enrl 50-70; tui $75 per wk for term of 4 wks beginning June 1

BINGHAMTON

ROBERSON CENTER FOR THE ARTS AND SCIENCES, 30 Front St, 13905. Tel 607-772-0660. *Dir* Duane P Truex
D & E

Tuition: Fees vary per instruction
Courses: Drawing, Jewelry, Mixed Media, Painting, Photography, Sculpture, Theatre Arts, Art Experience, Crafts, Pottery, Silk Screen, Weaving
Children's Classes: Tui varies per class. Courses—Craft Workshops, Jewelry, Painting & Drawing, Pottery, Sculpture

STATE UNIVERSITY OF NEW YORK AT BINGHAMTON, Department of Art History,* Vestal Parkway East, 13901. Tel 607-798-2000. *Chmn Dept* Stanley Ferber, PhD
Estab 1950; pub; D; ent req HS dipl, Regents Scholarship, ACT or SAT; degrees BA 4 yrs, MA 1-2 yrs, PhD varies; scholarships; SC 18, LC 32, GC 63; enrl 679, non-maj 400, maj 82, grad 45
Tuition: Res—undergrad $750-$900 per sem, grad $1400 per sem; nonres—undergrad $1200-$1500, grad $1800; campus res—room and board $1500 per yr
Courses: Advertising Design, Architecture, †Art History, Collage, Conceptual Art, Constructions, Drawing, Photography, †Printmaking, †Sculpture

BROCKPORT

STATE UNIVERSITY OF NEW YORK COLLEGE AT BROCKPORT, Department of Art, Fine Arts Bldg, 14220. Tel 716-395-2209. *Chmn* Roger J Adams. Instrs FT 15
Pub; D; ent req HS dipl, ent exam; degrees BA & BS 4 yrs; scholarships; SC 23, LC 29(Art History); enrl 8188, maj 200, grad 2000
Courses: Ceramics, Drawing, History of Art & Archaeology, Jewelry, Painting, Photography, Printmaking, Sculpture

BRONX

HERBERT H LEHMAN COLLEGE, Art Department, 2 Van Cortlandt Ave E. (Mailing Add: Bronx, NY 10468) Tel 212-960-8256. *Chmn* William McGee, MAT; *Prof* Ursula Meyer, MA; *Prof* Richard Ziemann, MFA; *Assoc Prof* Arwin Bose; *Assoc Prof* Theo Stavropoulos, BFA; *Asst Prof* George Corbin, PhD; *Asst Prof* Salvatore Romano
Dept estab 1968; pub; D & E; ent req HS dipl, ent exam; degrees BA & BFA 4 yrs, MA, MFA & MA 2 yrs; SC 18, LC 29, GC 31; enrl non-maj 100, major 75, grad 25
Tuition: Res—undergrad $462.50 per sem, $35 & $40 per cr, grad $750 per sem, $75 per cr; non-res—undergrad $712.50 per sem, $55 per cr, grad $1000 per sem, $95 per cr; no campus res available
Courses: , Two & Three Dimentional Design, Relativity of Color
Summer School: Dean, Chester Robinson. Enrl 45; tui $35 & $40 per cr for 6 wk term beginning June 30. Courses—Art History, Painting

MANHATTAN COLLEGE, School of Arts and Sciences, Manhattan College Parkway, 10471. Tel 212-548-1400. *Chmn Fine Arts Dept* George L McGeary, EdD; *Asst Prof* John F Omelia, PhD; *Adjunct Prof* Philip Dowd, PhD; *Adjunct Lectr* Cornelia Danielson, MA
Estab 1853; pvt den; D & E; ent req HS dipl; degrees BA 4 yrs; scholarships; LC 8; enrl D approx 3000
Tuition: Res—undergrad $5000 per yr, $2500 per sem, $90 per cr, grad $90 per cr; nonres—undergrad $3100 per yr, $1550 per sem, $90 per cr, grad $90 per cr; campus res—room & board $1820 per yr
Courses: Aesthetics, Art Education, Art History, Ceramics, Drawing, Film, Graphic Arts, Graphic Design, History of Art & Archaeology, Painting, Photography, Printmaking, Sculpture, Video
Summer School: Dean General Studies, Toni C Chambers. Enrl varies; tui $90 per cr for term of 4 wks beginning May 15. Courses—vary

BRONXVILLE

CONCORDIA COLLEGE,* 171 White Plains Rd, 10708. Tel 914-337-9300. *Chmn* James Brauer
Estab 1881; pvt; D; ent req HS dipl, SAT or ACT; degrees BA and BS 4 yrs; scholarships; SC 4, LC 2
Tuition: $2150 per yr; campus res—room and board $1250
Courses: Art Education, Art History, Ceramics, Drawing, Handicrafts, History of Art & Archaeology, Painting, Photography, Sculpture, Teacher Training
Adult Hobby Classes: Courses—Painting

SARAH LAWRENCE COLLEGE, Department of Art, 10708. Tel 914-337-0700, Ext 394. *Head Dept* M Zakin. Instrs FT 2, PT 7
Estab 1928; pvt; D; ent req HS dipl; degrees AB 4 yrs; scholarships; SC 10; enrl 170
Courses: Ceramics, Drawing, Graphic Arts, Painting, Art History, Photography, Sculpture, Theatre Arts
Summer School: Center for Continuing Education

BROOKLYN

BROOKLYN MUSEUM ART SCHOOL, 188 Eastern Parkway, 11238. Tel 212-638-4486. *Dir* David O'Lenick; *Registrar* Marjorie Stephens. Instrs FT 2, PT 8
Estab 1898; pub; D & E; scholarships; enrl approx 900
Courses: Drawing, Painting, Printmaking, Sculpture, Etching
Children's Classes: Enrl 75, July-August. Courses—Drawing, Printmaking, Sculpture
Summer School: Courses—Drawing, Graphics, Painting, Sculpture

KINGSBOROUGH COMMUNITY COLLEGE, Department of Art, 2001 Oriental Blvd, 11235. Tel 212-394-5718. *Chmn* Thomas I Nonn, PhD; *Prof* Frederic Thursz, MFA; *Assoc Prof* Jack Bolen, MFA; *Assoc Prof* Peter Hanssen, MFA; *Assoc Prof* Michael Sherker, EdD; *Asst Prof* Anthony Martin, MFA
Estab 1965, dept estab 1972; pub; D & E; ent req HS dipl; degrees AS 2 yrs; SC 10, LC 8; enrl maj 135
Tuition: $675 per yr; no campus res
Courses: Art History, Ceramics, Drawing, Graphic Arts, Graphic Design, History of Art & Archaeology, Intermedia, Mixed Media, Painting, Printmaking, Sculpture,

Theatre Arts
Summer School: Courses—Art

LONG ISLAND UNIVERSITY, Brooklyn Center Art Department, 385 Flatbush Ave Extension, 11201. Tel 212-834-6060. *Dir* Cynthia Dantzic. Instrs FT 2, PT 3-4
Pvt; D & E; ent req HS dipl, ent exam; degrees BA & BS 4 yrs; scholarships; SC 5, LC 3
Tuition: $107 per cr
Courses: Art History, Calligraphy, Drawing, Painting, Printmaking, Sculpture, History of the Motion Picture, Media Arts, Pottery, Visual Experience
Summer School: Tui $107 per cr for term of two 6 wk sessions beginning June and July. Courses—Drawing, History of Art, Painting

NEW YORK CITY COMMUNITY COLLEGE OF THE CITY UNIVERSITY OF NEW YORK, Department of Art and Advertising Design, 300 Jay St, 71210. Tel 212-643-8378. *Chairperson* Benjamin Einhorn, MA; *Prof* John Koos, MA; *Assoc Prof* Alan Damon, MFA; *Assoc Prof* Dorothy Hayes, BS; *Assoc Prof* Richard Karwosia, MA; *Assoc Prof* Seymour Pearlstein; *Assoc Prof* Marilyn Schaeffer, MA & MFA
Estab 1949, dept estab 1949; pub; D & E; ent req HS dipl; degrees AAS 2 yrs; SC 16, LC 3; enrl D 350, E 125
Tuition: Nonres—undergrad $450 per sem, $35 per cr; no campus res
Courses: Advertising Design, Commercial Art, Drawing, Graphic Design, Illustration, Lettering, Painting, Printmaking, Packaging, Paste-ups, Type Spacing
Summer School: Chairperson, Benjamin Einhorn. Courses—Design, Lettering, Life Drawing, Paste-ups

PRATT INSTITUTE
—School of Art and Design,* 215 Ryerson St, 11205. Tel 212-636-3600, 636-3619. *Dean* Bruce Sharpe; *Assoc Dean* Andrew Phelan
Pub; enrl 4400
Tuition: Res—undergrad $112 per cr, grad $128 per cr
Courses: Art Education, Art History, Ceramics, Drawing, Fashion Arts, Film, Industrial Design, Interior Design, Painting, Photography, Printmaking, Sculpture, Theatre Arts, Communication Design, Environmental Design
—School of Architecture,* 11205. Tel 212-636-3405. *Dir* Constantine Karalis
Degrees BS and BProf Studies 4 yrs, BArch 5 yrs, MArch 1 yr, MS(Urban Design) 1 yr, MS(Planning) 2 yrs, BArch MS(Urban Design) and BArch MS(Planning) 6 yrs
Tuition: Res—undergrad $112 per cr, grad $128 per cr
Courses: Architecture, Art History, Landscape Architecture, Design, History of Architecture, Materials, Structures

BUFFALO

STATE UNIVERSITY OF NEW YORK COLLEGE AT BUFFALO, Fine Arts Department, 1300 Elmwood Ave, 14222. Tel 716-862-6014. *Chmn* Francis R Kowsky, PhD
Estab 1875, dept estab 1961; pub; D & E; ent req HS dipl; degrees BA(Art), BA(Art History) & BFA 4 yrs; SC 34, LC 17, GC 6; enrl maj 250 (art)
Tuition: Res—undergrad lower division $375 per sem, $25 per cr hr, upper division $450 per sem, $30 per cr hr; nonres—undergrad lower division $600 per sem, $40 per cr hr, upper division $750 per sem, $50 per cr hr; campus res available double $375 per sem, single $562.50 per sem
Courses: Drawing, Graphic Arts, History of Art & Archaeology, Museum Staff Training, Painting, Photography, Printmaking, Sculpture

STATE UNIVERSITY OF NEW YORK, UNIVERSITY CENTER AT BUFFALO, Department of Art and Art History,* 3435 Main St, 14214. Tel 716-831-9000. *Chmn* Willard R Harris
Estab 1894; pub; D & E; ent req HS dipl, portfolio, acceptance by univ; degrees BA and BFA 4 yrs, MFA 2 yrs, MAH 1 yr; scholarships, fellowships; SC, LC, GC; enrl D 260, E 150, grad 60
Courses: Art Education, Art History, Drawing, Painting, Photography, Sculpture, Design, Intaglio, Lithography, Serigraphy, Visual Communications
Summer School: Dir, James H Blackhurst. Courses—Design Workshops, Drawing, Painting, Photo & Film Workshops, Printmaking Workshops, Sculpture

VILLA MARIA COLLEGE OF BUFFALO, Art Department, 240 Pine Ridge Rd, 14225. Tel 716-896-0700, Ext 324. *Chmn* James W Jipson, MFA; *Assoc Prof* Katherine Verney, MA; *Instructor* Richard Ancona, BA; *Instructor* Andy Topolski, MFA; *Instructor* Carol Wells; *Lectr* Irene Adamski; *Lectr* Bary Biantoo, BA; *Lectr* Brian Duffy, MFA; *Lectr* Lee Mitchell, BFA
Estab 1961; pvt; D & E; ent req HS dipl of equivalency; degrees AA, AAS & AS 2 yrs; scholarships; SC 27, LC 3; enrl D 450, E 100, maj 170
Tuition: $1650 per yr, $825 per sem, $60 per cr hr; no campus residence
Courses: Advertising Design, Art History, Ceramics, Commercial Art, Drafting, Drawing, Graphic Arts, †Graphic Design, †Interior Design, Lettering, Painting, †Photography, Printmaking, Sculpture, Textile Design
Adult Hobby Classes: Courses—Arts & Crafts, drawing, painting, photography, quilting
Summer School: Enrl 10 - 20; tui $180 per cr, $60 per non-cr for term of 6 wks beginning June 28. Courses—a variety of interest courses, including drawing, painting and photography

CANANDAIGUA

COMMUNITY COLLEGE OF THE FINGER LAKES, Visual & Performing Arts Department,* Lincoln Hill Campus, 14424. *Chmn* Thomas F Insalaco, MFA; *Prof* Wayne Williams, MFA; *Instr* John Fox, MFA
Estab 1966; pub; D & E; ent req HS dipl; degrees AA 2 yrs; SC 14, LC 2; enrl D 60, non-maj 700, maj 50
Tuition: Res—undergrad $78 per cr hr; nonres—undergrad $156 per cr hr; no campus res
Courses: Advertising Design, Art History, Ceramics, Commercial Art, Drawing, Graphic Arts, Graphic Design, Illustration, Painting, Photography, Printmaking, Sculpture, Stage Design, Theatre Arts
Summer School: Courses—Per regular session

CANTON

SAINT LAURENCE UNIVERSITY, Department of Fine Arts, 13617. Tel 315-379-5180. *Chmn* J Michael Lowe, MFA; *Prof* Harlan H Holladay, PhD; *Assoc Prof* Roger Bailey, MFA; *Assoc Prof* Guy Berard, MFA; *Asst Prof* Elizabeth Baldewiez, PhD; *Asst Prof* Paul D Schweizer, PhD
Estab 1856; pvt; D; ent req HS dipl; degrees BA; SC 16, LC 13; enrl maj 40
Tuition: $4405 per yr; campus res—room & board $1780
Courses: Art History, Ceramics, Drawing, Painting, Photography, Printmaking, Sculpture, Teacher Training
Summer School: Dir, P J Angelo

CAZENOVIA

CAZENOVIA COLLEGE, Art Program, 13035. Tel 315-655-3466, Ext 246. *Dir* John Aistars, MFA; *Instructor* Pam Chapklin, MFA; *Instructor* Jeff Pike, MFA; *Instructor* Josef Ritter, BFA
Estab 1824; pvt; D & E; ent req HS dipl; degrees AA, AS & AAS 2 yrs; scholarships; SC 18, LC 2
Tuition: Res $3670 per yr, $100 per cr hr; campus res—room & board $1985
Courses: , Illustration, Interior Design, Landscape Architecture, Lettering, Painting, Photography, Printmaking, Basic Design, Figure Drawing, Typography

CHAUTAUQUA

CHAUTAUQUA INSTITUTION, Box 28, 14722. Tel 716-357-4411, 357-5635, Ext 232, 233, 234. *Head Painting & Drawing* Revington Arthur; *Head Ceramics* James Achuff; *Head Sculpture* H Richard Duhme Jr; *Head Photography* George Gambsky; *Head Weaving* Ruth Holroyd
Estab 1874; pub; D (summers only); scholarships; SC 26, LC 7; enrl D 500
Tuition: Varies depending on course enrollment. Catalog sent on request
Courses: Calligraphy, Ceramics, Drawing, Handicrafts, Interior Design, Jewelry, Painting, Photography, Sculpture, Handicrafts (batik, macrame, needlepoint, quilting, weaving), Porcelain, Paper Sculpture, Stained Glass

CLAYTON

**THOUSAND ISLANDS MUSEUM CRAFT SCHOOL,* 401 Riverside Dr, Old Town Hall, 13624. Tel 315-686-5794. *Admin* Richard V Palmer; *Asst Admin* Joseph Perrucio. Instrs PT 20
Estab 1964; D & E; ent req an interest in arts and crafts; degrees no degrees but transfer credit; scholarships; SC 21; enrl D 210, E 10
Tuition: $95 plus $20 registration fee for each wk course
Courses: Ceramics, Jewelry, Acrylic Painting, Advanced EA, Bird Carving, Ceramics, China Painting, Decoy Carving, Quilt Making
Summer School: July 3 - August 25. Courses—Country Painting, Creative Stitchery, Enameling, Loom Techniques, Pattern Weaving, Pottery, Reverse Painting on Glass, Rug Hooking, Watercolor Painting, Weaving

CLINTON

HAMILTON COLLEGE, Art Department, 13323. Tel 315-859-7468. *Chmn* Robert Bruce Muirhead, MFA; *Assoc Prof* Rand Carter, PhD; *Assoc Prof* William Salzillo, MFA; *Asst Prof* Steve Liebman, MFA; *Asst Prof* Ralph Lieberman, PhD; *Asst Prof* Robert Palusky, MFA; *Instr* Deborah Pokinski, MA
Pvt; D; ent req HS dipl, SAT; degrees AB; enrl non-maj 850, maj 50
Tuition: Res—undergrad $5000 per yr; campus res $1800
Courses: Aesthetics, Art History, Ceramics, Drawing, Graphic Design, History of Art & Archaeology, Painting, Photography, Printmaking, Sculpture, Stage Design, Theatre Arts

COBLESKILL

STATE UNIVERSITY OF NEW YORK, Art and Technical College, 12043. Tel 518-234-5325. *Head Dept* H D South III, MFA
Estab 1950; pub; D & E; ent req HS dipl; degrees AA and AS 2 yrs; SC 2, LC 2; enrl D 95
Tuition: Res—undergrad $375 per sem, $28 per cr; nonres—undergrad $600 per sem; campus res—room & board $758 per yr
Courses: Art Education, Art History, Drawing, History of Art & Archaeology, Painting, Sculpture, Teacher Training, Theatre Arts
Adult Hobby Classes: Enrl 4000 per yr; tui $9 per course. Courses—large variety of mini-courses

CORNING

CORNING COMMUNITY COLLEGE, Division of Humanities, 14830. Tel 607-962-9238. *Chmn* John M Runyon, MFA; *Assoc Prof* Charles R Ringsmuth, MFA; *Asst Prof* Margaret Brill, MA; *Asst Prof* Horst Werk, MFA. Instrs FT 3 PT 1
Estab 1958, dept estab 1963; pub; D & E; ent req HS dipl, SAT; degrees AA, AS, AAS 2 yrs; SC 8, LC 6
Courses: Art History, Ceramics, Drawing, Handicrafts, Jewelry, Painting, Silversmithing, Two & Three Dimensional Design
Summer School: Dir, Nan Lanning

CORTLAND

STATE UNIVERSITY OF NEW YORK COLLEGE AT CORTLAND, Art Department, 13045. Tel 607-753-4316. *Chmn* David L Simon, PhD; *Prof* Steven Barbash, MFA; *Prof* Gerald DiGiusto, BFA; *Prof* John Jessiman, MFA; *Prof* Barbara Kuhlman, MA; *Assoc Prof* George Atcheson, MFA; *Assoc Prof* George Dugan, MFA; *Assoc Prof* James Thorpe, MFA; *Assoc Prof* Frederick Zimmerman, PhD; *Asst Prof* David Craven, PhD; *Asst Prof* J Catherine Gibian, MFA; *Asst Prof* Bard Prentiss, MFA
Estab 1868, dept estab 1948; pub; D & E; ent req HS dipl, all college admissions standards based on high school average or scores from SAT, ACTP or Regent's tests; degrees BA 4 yrs; scholarships; SC 40, LC 10; enrl D 5300 (total), 1200 (art), maj 80
Tuition: Res—undergrad $750 freshman and sophomore, $900 junior and senior; nonres—undergrad $1200 freshman and sophomore, $1500 junior and senior; other college fee & activity assessment $95; campus res—$750 (room) and $664 (board)
Courses: Aesthetics, Art Education, Art History, Ceramics, Drawing, Film, Goldsmithing, Graphic Arts, Handicrafts, History of Art & Archaeology, Jewelry, Painting, Photography, Printmaking, Sculpture, Silversmithing, Textile Design, Design, Enameling, Metalwork, Weaving
Summer School: Dir, William Lowe. Enrl approx 40; term of 6 wks beginning June 26. Courses—Art History, Studio

ELMIRA

ELMIRA COLLEGE, Art Department, 14901. Tel 607-734-3911, Ext 354. *Instructor* Peter Chamberlain, MFA; *Instructor* Douglas Holtgrewe, MFA; *Instructor* William Lee, MFA; *Instructor* Joann Smith, MFA
Estab 1855; pvt; D & E; ent req HS dipl; degrees AA, AS, BA, BS and MEduc; scholarships; SC 26, LC 15, GC 8; enrl D 250, E 125, maj 35, grad 6
Tuition: $3420 per yr; campus res—room & board $5030
Courses: Architecture, Art Education, Art History, Ceramics, Costume Design & Construction, Drawing, Graphic Arts, History of Art & Archaeology, Jewelry, Painting, Photography, Printmaking, Sculpture, Silversmithing, Stage Design, Teacher Training, Theatre Arts

FOREST HILLS

CATAN-ROSE INSTITUTE OF ART,* 72-72 112th St, 11375. Tel 212-263-1962. *Dir* Richard Catan-Rose
Estab 1943; pvt; D & E; ent req HS grad, no ent req for adult or children's classes; degrees Assoc Cert 2 yrs, Cert 4 yrs; scholarships
Courses: Advertising Design, Architecture, Art History, Calligraphy, Drawing, Fashion Arts, Film, Illustration, Industrial Design, Interior Design, Lettering, Painting, Photography, Printmaking, Sculpture, Stage Design, Textile Design, Applied Art, Basic Art, Cartooning, Crafts, Fine Arts & Design, Weaving
Summer School: 7 and 11 wks. Foundation courses—Advertising, Fine Arts, Graphic Arts, Indoor and Outdoor, Interiors

FREDONIA

STATE UNIVERSITY COLLEGE, Department of Art, 14063. Tel 716-673-3537. *Chmn* John Hughson, MFA; *Prof* Marvin Bjurlin, MFA; *Prof* Emmitt Christian, MFA; *Prof* William Proweller, PhD; *Prof* Daniel Reiff, PhD; *Assoc Prof* Paul Bowers; *Assoc Prof* Carole Harrison, MFA; *Asst Prof* Mary Lee Lunde, MA; *Instructor* Bob Booth, MFA; *Prof Emeritus* Lawrence Urbschett, MFA; *Asst Gallery Dir* Nancy Weekly, BA
Estab 1867, dept estab 1948; pub; D & E; ent req HS dipl, GRE, SAT, portfolio review; degrees BA 4 yrs; scholarships; SC 30, LC 18, GC 4; enrl D 650, E 70, non-maj 610, major 110
Tuition: Res—undergrad $1400 per yr; non-res—undergrad $1800 per yr; campus res—room $800, board $720
Courses: †Art History, †Ceramics, †Commercial Art, †Drawing, †Graphic Arts, †Graphic Design, Illustration, Intermedia, Lettering, Mixed Media, †Painting, Photography, †Printmaking, †Sculpture, Video

GARDEN CITY

ADELPHI UNIVERSITY, Department of Art and Art History, 11530. Tel 516-294-8700, Ext 7387. *Chmn* Yvonne Korshak; *Prof* Grace Cantone, MA; *Prof* Milton Goldstein, MA; *Prof* W P Jennerjahn, MFA; *Assoc Prof* Madeleine Lane, MA; *Assoc Prof* Richard Vaux, MFA; *Asst Prof* Harvey Weiss, MA; *Vis Asst Prof* Jon Palmer, sculpture - 1980. Instrs FT 8, PT 15
Estab 1896; pvt; D & E; ent req HS dipl; portfolio recommended for undergrad admission, required for grad; degrees BA 4 yrs, MA 1 1 2 yrs; scholarships; SC 40, LC 20, GC 20; enrl D 700, E 100, maj 70, grad 60
Tuition: Undergrad $118 per cr; grad $130 per cr; campus res—room & board $1400 per yr
Courses: Advertising Design, Aesthetics, †Art Education, †Art History, Calligraphy, Ceramics, Collage, †Commercial Art, Constructions, Costume Design & Construction, Display, Drafting, Drawing, Fashion Arts, Film, Goldsmithing, Graphic Arts, Graphic Design, Handicrafts, Enameling, Jewelry, Macrame, Oriental Brush Painting, Stained Glass, Weaving
Summer School: Dir, Deith Donnelly. Tui same as regular session; two 5 wk summer terms. Courses—Art Therapy, Creative Crafts, Drawing, Painting, Photography

NASSAU COMMUNITY COLLEGE, Art Department,* Stewart Ave, 11530. Tel 516-742-0600, Ext 258. *Chmn* Dr Stella Russell, PhD; *Prof* Jack Fink, MA; *Prof* Russell Housman, PhD; *Prof* Stanley Kaplan, MA; *Prof* Helen Muller, MA; *Assoc Prof* Salli Zimmerman, MA; *Asst Prof* Leon Frankston, EDD; *Asst Prof* Charles Reina, MA; *Asst Prof* Helen Sisserson, MA; *Asst Prof* Robert Tawn, MA
Estab 1959, dept estab 1960; pub; D & E; ent req HS dipl; degrees AA, AS and AAS 2 yrs; scholarships; SC 22, LC 5; enrl D 1213, E 712, non-maj 900-1000, maj 300
Tuition: No campus res
Courses: Advertising Design, Art History, Ceramics, Costume Design & Construction, Drafting, Drawing, Fashion Arts, Graphic Design, History of Art & Archaeology, Painting, Photography, Printmaking, Sculpture, Arts and Crafts (including macrame, jewelry, wood, paper, leather)
Summer School: Dir, Henry Kean. Two 5 wk terms. Courses—By popular demand

GENESEO

STATE UNIVERSITY OF NEW YORK COLLEGE AT GENESEO, Department of Art, College of Arts & Science, 14454. Tel 716-245-5415. Instrs FT 10, PT 4
Estab 1871; pub; D & E; ent req HS dipl, ent exam; degrees BA(Art) 3-4 yrs; SC 35, LC 7; enrl D 1000, E 1150, maj 140
Courses: Art Education, Art History, Ceramics, Drawing, Graphic Arts, Jewelry, Museum Staff Training, Painting, Photography, Sculpture, Textile Design, Photolithography Wood Design
Summer School: Courses vary

GENEVA

HOBART & WILLIAM SMITH COLLEGES, Art Department,* Houghton House, 14456. Tel 315-789-5500. *Chmn Dept* Lois Drewer
Estab approx 1800; pvt; D; ent req HS dipl, ent exam; degrees BA and BS 4 yrs; scholarships; SC 15, LC 8; enrl D 1600
Tuition: Res—$4,730 per yr; campus res available
Courses: Aesthetics, Architecture, Drawing, Graphic Arts, History of Art & Archaeology, Painting, Photography, Sculpture, Theatre Arts

GREENVALE

SCHOOL OF THE ARTS, C W POST CENTER OF LONG ISLAND UNIVERSITY, Art Department, 11548. Tel 516-299-2464. *Dean* Julian Mates, PhD; *Chmn* Arnold Simonoff; *Prof* Stanley Brodsky, EdD; *Prof* Lynn Croton; *Prof* Donald Dwyer; *Prof* Rose Krebs; *Prof* Arthur Leipzig; *Prof* James Lewicki; *Prof* Dr Joyce Rosa; *Prof* Arthur Silver, BArchit; *Prof* Stephen Soreff; *Prof* Harold Stevens; *Prof* Jack Stuck; *Prof* Alfred Van Loen; *Prof* Vincent Wright; *Assoc Prof* Donald Yaloe, MFA; *Assoc Prof* Robert Yasada, MFA; *Assoc Prof* Jerome Zimmerman, MFA
Dept estab 1957; pvt; D & E; ent req HS dipl, portfolio; degrees BA(Art Educ), BA(Art Hist) and BA(Studio) and BFA 4 yrs, MA(Photography), MA(Studio), MS(Art Educ) and MFA(Art or Design) 2 yrs; scholarships; SC 70, LC 15, GC 40; enrl D 2000, E 450, non-maj 2000, maj 250, grad 150, others 50
Tuition: Undergrad $105 per cr hr, grad $114 per cr hr; campus residency available
Courses: †Advertising Design, Aesthetics, †Art Education, †Art History, Ceramics, Collage, Commercial Art, Conceptual Art, Constructions, Drawing, Film, Graphic Arts, Graphic Design, Handicrafts, Illustration, Intermedia, Jewelry, Lettering, Mixed Media, Painting, Photography, Printmaking, Sculpture, Stage Design, Teacher Training, Theatre Arts, Video, Enameling, †Fine Arts, Weaving
Summer School: Dir, Arnold Simonoff. Tui undergrad $105 per cr, grad $114 per cr for 3 summer sessions from May 19 to June 20, June 23 to July 25 and July 28 to August 29

HAMILTON

COLGATE UNIVERSITY, Department of Fine Arts, 13346. Tel 315-824-1000, Ext 633. *Chmn* Eric Van Schaack, PhD; *Prof* Jim Loveless, MFA; *Assoc Prof* Edward Bryant, MA; *Asst Prof* Miriam Bloom, MFA; *Asst Prof* Kathryn Horste, PhD; *Instructor* Tamara Bryant, MFA; *Instructor* Patrick Clancy, MFA; *Instructor* Marion Faller, MFA; *Instructor* Barbara Houze, MFA
Estab 1819, dept estab 1905; pvt; D; ent req HS dipl, CEEB or ACT; degrees BA 4 yrs; scholarships; SC 15, LC 26; enrl D 650, maj 50
Tuition: $4800 per yr; campus res—room and board $1900
Courses: Drawing, Film, Graphic Arts, Painting, Photography, Printmaking, Sculpture, Video

HEMPSTEAD

HOFSTRA UNIVERSITY
—Department of Fine Arts, 11550. Tel 516-560-3231. *Chmn* James J Gaboda. Instrs FT 14, PT 3
Estab 1935; pvt; D & E; ent req good secondary school record, coll ent board exam; degrees BA and BS(Art Educ) 4 yrs; scholarships; SC 32, LC 1, GC 3
Tuition: $1700 per sem, PT $114 per cr hr
Courses: Drawing, Handicrafts, Painting, Photography, Sculpture, Applied Design, Color and Design, Etching, Figure Drawing, Graphic Expression, Metalsmithing, Pottery, Three-Dimensional Design, Two-Dimensional Representation, Woodcut
—Department of Art History, 11550. Tel 516-560-3528, 560-3529. *Chmn* Dr Robert Myron, PhD; *Assoc Prof* George Cohen, PhD; *Assoc Prof* Sam Toperoff, MA; *Asst Prof* Yonia Fain, MA
Estab 1935, dept estab 1972; pvt; D & E; ent req HS dipl; degrees BA 4 yrs, MA 1-2 yrs; scholarships; LC 20, GC 16; enrl D 1610, maj 40, grad 35
Tuition: Campus res available
Courses: Advertising Design, Art Education, Art History, Ceramics, Commercial Art, Drawing, Graphic Arts, History of Art & Archaeology, Painting, Sculpture, Appraisal of Art and Antiques
Summer School: Dir, Dr Harold Yuker. Courses—Art History, Fine Arts

HERKIMER

HERKIMER COUNTY COMMUNITY COLLEGE, Humanities Division, 13350. Tel 315-866-0300, Ext 51. *Assoc Prof* Guido Correro, MA; *Instructor* James Bruce Schwabach, MFA
Estab 1966; pub; D & E; ent req HS dipl, SAT or ACT; degrees AA, AS & AAS 2 yrs; SC 8, LC 4; enrl D 329 (total), maj 16
Tuition: Res—undergrad $275 per sem, $23 per cr hr; nonres—undergrad $550 per sem, grad $46 per cr hr; no campus res
Courses: Art History, Drawing, Film, Museum Staff Training, Painting, Photography, Theatre Arts, Video
Adult Hobby Classes: Tui varies. Courses—Jewelry Making, Studio in Painting
Children's Classes: Courses—Workshop in Television
Summer School: Courses—vary depending on the year

HIGHLAND FALLS

LADYCLIFF COLLEGE, Art Department, 10928. Tel 914-446-4747. *Chmn* Adrienne Pregno, MA; *Asst Prof* Don Gray, MA; *Asst Prof* Roselaine Perkis, MA; *Lectr* John E Davis, BA; *Lectr* Ellen Gannon; *Lectr* Roy Hyrkin, MA
Estab 1933; pvt; D & E; ent req HS dipl, HS record; degrees BA and BS 4 yrs, field experience in Art Therapy, Crafts, Museum Work to upperclassmen in good academic standing; scholarships; SC 55, LC 10; enrl D 50, E 20, non-maj 25, maj 30
Tuition: $80 per cr hr; campus res available
Courses: Advertising Design, Architecture, †Art Education, Art History, Ceramics, Commercial Art, Conceptual Art, Drafting, Drawing, †Graphic Arts, Graphic Design, †Handicrafts, History of Art & Archaeology, Jewelry, Lettering, Mixed Media, †Museum Staff Training, Painting, Photography, Printmaking, Sculpture, Teacher Training, Art Therapy, Enameling, Fiber, Metal Working, Pottery, Weaving
Children's Classes: Enrl 30 per sem; tui $20-$35 per 8 classes. Courses—Crafts, Drawing, Macrame, Papier Mache, Working with Clay
Summer School: Dir, Joanne Adler. Enrl 20; tui $80 per cr for term of 4-6 wks beginning May 22. Courses—Cloisonne Enameling, Crafts, Drawing, Jewelry, Metal Working, Painting, Photography, Pottery, Printing, Weaving

HOUGHTON

HOUGHTON COLLEGE, Art Department,* 14744. Tel 716-567-2211. *Head Art Dept* James D Mellick
Estab 1883; den; D & E; scholarship; SC 8, LC 6
Tuition: $2790 per yr; campus res available
Courses: Art Education, Art History, Ceramics, Collage, Drawing, Graphic Arts, Graphic Design, History of Art & Archaeology, Painting, Printmaking
Summer School: Chmn, William T Allen. Tui $234 for term of 3 wks beginning June and July

ITHACA

CORNELL UNIVERSITY
—Department of Art, College of Architecture, Art and Planning, 14853. Tel 607-256-3558. *Dean Col* Kermit C Parsons; *Chmn Dept* Stanley Bowman, MFA; *Prof* Victor Colby, MFA; *Prof* Jason Seley, BA; *Prof* Arnold Singer; *Prof* Jack L Squier, MFA; *Assoc Prof* Zevi Blum, BArchit; *Assoc Prof* Steve Poleskie, BS; *Assoc Prof* James Valerio, MFA; *Asst Prof* Eleanore Mikus, MA
Estab 1868, dept estab 1921; pvt; D; ent req HS dipl, portfolio interview, HS transcript, SAT; degrees BFA 4 yrs, MFA 2 yrs; scholarships; SC 25, LC 1, GC 4; enrl maj 100, grad 13, special students 2
Tuition: $5256 per yr, campus res
Courses: Aesthetics, Drawing, †Painting, †Photography, †Printmaking, †Sculpture
Summer School: Dir, Arnold Singer. Term of 3 wks beginning June 27. Courses—Drawing, Painting, Photography, Printmaking, Sculpture
—Department of the History of Art, College of Arts and Sciences, 35 Goldwin Smith Hall, 14853. Tel 607-256-4905. *Chmn* Robert G Calkins, PhD; *Prof* Theodore M Brown, PhD; *Prof* Creighton E Gilbert, PhD; *Prof* H Peter Kahn, MFA; *Prof* Thomas W Leavitt, PhD; *Prof* Stanley J O'Connor, PhD; *Prof* Albert S Roe, PhD; *Prof* Martie W Young, PhD; *Assoc Prof* Esther G Dotson, PhD; *Assoc Prof* Andrew Ramage, PhD; *Asst Prof* Jacqueline V Falkenheim, PhD; *Asst Prof* Robert C Hobbs, PhD; *Asst Prof* Nancy C Neaher, African art - 1980; *Asst Prof* Srisakra Vallibhatama, SE Asian art - 1980
Estab 1939; pvt; D; ent req HS dipl, SAT, grad admission requires GRE; degrees BA 4 yrs, MA 3 yrs, PhD 4-6 yrs; scholarships; LC 64, GC 12; enrl D 1300, maj 30, grad 15, others 5
Tuition: $5256 per yr, $2628 per sem, $100-125 per cr hr; campus res—room and board $2250 per yr
Courses: Architecture, Art History, Calligraphy, †History of Art & Archaeology, Museum Staff Training, Archaeology, Art Criticism, Techniques and Materials
Summer School: Dir, Robert D MacDougall. Tui $100 per cr hr. Courses—introductory
—New York State College of Human Ecology, Dept of Design and Environmental Analysis, 14853. Tel 607-256-2168. *Chmn Dept* Rose Steidl. Instrs FT 23

ITHACA COLLEGE, Art Department, Danby Road, 14850. Tel 607-274-3011, Ext 3330. *Dean* Tom Longin; *Chmn* Harry McCue, MFA; *Prof* Salvatore Grippi; *Prof* Robert Richenburg; *Asst Prof* Gary Wojcik, MFA; *Vis Prof* David Smyth, MFA
Estab 1892, dept estab 1968; pvt; D & E; ent req HS dipl, SAT scores, review of portfolio; degrees BA and BFA 4 yrs; SC 10; enrl non-maj 200, maj 40
Tuition: $6200 per yr; campus residency available
Courses: Art History, Calligraphy, Conceptual Art, Constructions, Drawing, Film, Intermedia, Mixed Media, Occupational Therapy, Painting, Photography, Printmaking, Sculpture, Stage Design, Theatre Arts, Video

JAMAICA

SAINT JOHN'S UNIVERSITY, Department of Fine Arts,* Grand Central & Utopia Parkways, 11439. Tel 212-969-8000. *Chmn* Claude Ponsat
Pvt; D; ent req HS dipl, ent exam, portfolio review; degrees BFA and BS 4 yrs; scholarships; SC 24, LC 9; enrl D 1300, maj 100
Tuition: Res—$2880 per yr
Courses: Advertising Design, Ceramics, Display, Drawing, Graphic Arts, Graphic Design, Handicrafts, Jewelry, Museum Staff Training, Photography, Sculpture, Teacher Training, Saturday Scholarship Program
Summer School: Dir, Dr Mahdesian

YORK COLLEGE OF THE CITY UNIVERSITY OF NEW YORK, Fine and Performing Arts, 150-91 87th Rd, 11451. Tel 212-969-4062. *Chmn* Arthur Anderson, MFA; *Instr* Elena Borstein, MFA; *Instr* Ernest Garthwaite, MA; *Instr* Jane Schuyler, PhD; *Instr* Phillips Simkin, MFA
Estab 1968; dept estab 1968; pub; D & E; ent req HS dipl; degrees BA 4 yrs; enrl D 200, E 50, non-maj 205, maj 45
Tuition: Nonres—undergrad $30 per cr, max $450 per sem; no campus res
Courses: Art Education, Art History, Commercial Art, Constructions, Drawing, Film, Graphic Arts, Painting, Photography, Printmaking, Sculpture, Theatre Arts, Video
Summer School: Dean, Wallace Schoenberg. Enrl $20 per course; tui $30 per cr for term of 4-5 wks beginning late June. Courses—Art History, Drawing, Painting

JAMESTOWN

JAMESTOWN COMMUNITY COLLEGE, Art Department, 14701. *Chmn* William Disbro, MA; *Asst Prof* John Hiester, MA; *Coordr Artisan Center* Gregory Comstock; *Asst Instructor* E Terry Lorenc. Instrs PT 5
Estab 1950, dept estab 1970; pub; D & E; ent req open; degrees AA 60 cr hrs; scholarships; SC 11, LC 1; enrl D 310, E 254
Tuition: Res—undergrad $350 per sem, $23.50 per cr hr; nonres—undergrad $700 per sem, $47 per cr hr
Courses: Calligraphy, Ceramics, Drawing, Film, Painting, Photography, Printmaking, Sculpture, Stage Design, Theatre Arts, Video, Design, Fine Woodworking, Survey of Visual Arts, Wood Sculpture
Summer School: Enrl 25; tui $60 for term of 6 wks beginning last wk of June. Courses—Ceramics, Photography

LAKE PLACID

LAKE PLACID SCHOOL OF ART,* Center for Music, Drama and Art, Faranack Ave, 12946. Tel 518-523-2591. *Dir* Brian Gormley, MA; *Chmn Ceramics Dept* John R Thompson, MA; *Chmn Painting Dept* Harry Bartnick, MFA; *Chmn Photography Dept* Helmmo Kindermann, MFA; *Chmn Printmaking Dept* James J Catalano, MFA; *Instr* Martin Anderson, MFA; *Instr* Colette Stemple, MFA
Estab 1972; pvt; D & E; ent req HS dipl, portfolio; degrees dipl 2 yrs; scholarships; SC 25, LC 2; enrl D 35, E 75, maj 35
Tuition: campus res available
Courses: Art History, †Ceramics, †Drawing, †Painting, †Photography, †Printmaking, Sculpture
Adult Hobby Classes: Enrl 75; tui $45 per 6 wks. Courses—Batik, Calligraphy, Ceramics, Drawing, Framing, Painting, Photography, Printmaking, Silversmithing, Studio Skills
Children's Classes: Courses—Creative Arts (gallery, music, theater, visual arts), Mixed Media
Summer School: Enrl 60; tui $250 for term of 6 wks beginning June. Courses—Ceramics, Drawing, Painting, Photography, Printmaking. Intensive visiting artist workshops in all departments

LARCHMONT

ADAMY'S PLASTICS & MOLD-MAKING WORKSHOPS, 10538. Tel 914-834-6276. *Dir* George E Adamy, MFA. Instrs FT 1, PT 1
Estab 1968; pvt; D & E; SC 13, LC 2, GC 13; enrl D 20, E 30
Tuition: From $25 for 3 hr open-ended sessions to $225 for 10 sessions advanced courses. Individual arrangements for special projects or commissions, and for lectures and demonstrations of other schools, museums, art organizations; no campus res
Courses: Collage, Constructions, Museum Staff Training, Painting, Printmaking, Sculpture, Teacher Training, Bonded Bronze & other Metals, Fiberglass Lay-up, Mold-Making, Plastics, Syntactic and Expandable Foam
Adult Hobby Classes: As above

LOCH SHELDRAKE

SULLIVAN COUNTY COMMUNITY COLLEGE, Div of Commercial Art and Photography, Leroy Rd, 12759. Tel 914-434-5750, Ext 215. *Chmn* Joe Hopkins, MFA; *Assoc Prof* L Jack Agnew, MEd; *Asst Prof* Earl Wertheim, BS; *Instructor* Thomas Ambrosino, BPS; *Instructional Asst* Bernie Kroop
Estab 1962, dept estab 1965; pub; D & E; ent req HS dipl or equivalent; degrees AS & AAS 2 yrs; SC 24; enrl D 160, maj 160
Tuition: Res—undergrad $375 per sem, $31 per cr; non-res—undergrad $750 per sem, $62 per cr
Courses: Advertising Design, Art History, Calligraphy, †Commercial Art, Conceptual Art, Display, Drawing, Film, Graphic Arts, Graphic Design, Illustration, Lettering, Mixed Media, †Photography, Video
Summer School: Assoc Dean of Faculty for Community Services, Allan Dampman

MALDEN BRIDGE

MALDEN BRIDGE SCHOOL OF ART, 12115. Tel 518-766-3666. *Dir* Betty Warren; *Instructor* John Lancaster; *Instructor* Michael Lancaster. Instrs FT 2, PT 5
Estab 1965; pvt; D; ent req students who are seriously interested in developing their skills and knowledge; scholarships; SC 6; enrl D 55
Tuition: undergrad $500 per 6 wk summer session, $350 per month; nonres—undergrad $375 per 6 wk session, $275 per month, $225 PT; room available
Courses: Ceramics, Drawing, Painting, Sculpture

MIDDLETOWN

ORANGE COUNTY COMMUNITY COLLEGE, Art Department, 115 South St, 10940. Tel 914-343-1121. *Chmn Dept* Leonard R Wallace, MFA; *Instr* Patrick Kennedy, BFA; *Instr* Ivan R Miseho, Dipl; *Instr* Claude Seward, MFA
Estab 1950, dept estab 1950; pub; D & E; ent req HS dipl; degrees AA 2 yrs; SC 10, LC 4; enrl D 135, maj 135
Tuition: Res—undergrad $450 per sem; non-res undergrad $900 per sem; no campus res
Courses: Art History, Ceramics, Drawing, Painting, Photography, Sculpture, Color, Design

NEW PALTZ

STATE UNIVERSITY OF NEW YORK COLLEGE AT NEW PALTZ
—Studio Art Department, 12561. *Chmn* Michael Zadro. Instrs 25
Pub; degrees BFA, BA, BS and MFA; enrl total 8000
Courses: Ceramics, Goldsmithing, Painting, Photography, Printmaking, Sculpture, Silversmithing, Wood Design
—Art Education Department, 12561. *Chmn* Susan Wisherd. Instrs 5
Degrees BS(Art Educ) and MS(Art Educ)
Summer School: Dir, Robert Davidson. 8 wk sem

NEW ROCHELLE

COLLEGE OF NEW ROCHELLE, Art Department, School of Arts and Sciences, 10801. Tel 914-632-5300. *Head Dept* Sr Theresa Eppridge, MFA; *Instr* Douglas Craft, MFA; *Instr* Dr Charles Daly, EdD; *Instr* Irene Kutsky, MFA; *Instr* Dr William Maxwell, EdD; *Instr* Mary Jane Robertshaw, MFA; *Instr* Anne Terhune
Estab 1904, dept estab 1929; pvt; D; ent req HS dipl, SAT recommended, college preparatory program in high school; degrees BA, BFA and BS 4 yrs; scholarships; SC 52, LC 14, GC 21; enrl D 340, non-maj 35, maj 207, grad 98
Tuition: $3200 per yr; campus res—room and board $2320
Courses: Advertising Design, Aesthetics, †Art Education, †Art History, Ceramics, Drafting, Drawing, Fashion Arts, Film, Graphic Arts, Illustration, Interior Design, Jewelry, Mixed Media, Painting, Photography, Printmaking, Sculpture, Teacher Training, Textile Design, Theatre Arts, Video, †Applied Design, Art Psychology, †Studio Arts, Two and Three-Dimensional Design, Weaving
Summer School: Dir, Steven Sweeney. Enrl 300; tui $80 per cr for two terms of 5 wks beginning June. Courses—Advertising Design Layout, Applied Design Independent Study, Art of North America, Ceramics, Ceramic Sculpture, Creative Watercolor, Creative Workshop in Mixed Media, Designing Educational Media, Drawing, Drawing and Composition, Enameling, Figure and Portrait Painting, Fine Arts, Independent Study, History of Medieval Art, Jewelry, Loomless Weaving, Photography, Relief Process, Sculpture, Thesis Project Art Education, Weaving

NEW YORK

ABINGDON SQUARE PAINTERS, INC, 242 W 14th St, 10014. Tel 212-243-7343. *Dir* Harriet Fitzgerald; *Pres* Jeanne Morrow. Instrs 2
Estab 1948; pvt; D; ent req must show serious intentions; enrl limited to 15

ARTIST STUDIO CENTERS, INC, 1651 Third Ave, 10028. Tel 212-348-3102. *Head Dept* James E Youngman
Estab 1956; pvt; ent req D & E
Tuition: $1620 per yr, $14 per class
Courses: Drawing, Painting, Sculpture
Adult Hobby Classes: Tui $40 per month. Courses—Painting, Sculpture

ART STUDENTS LEAGUE OF NEW YORK, 215 W 47th St, 10019. Tel 212-247-4510. *Exec Dir* Stewart Klonis. Instrs FT 53
Estab 1875; pvt; ent req none; schol; LC; enrl D 1200, E 600, Sat 450 (adults and children)
Courses: Calligraphy, Graphic Arts, Illustration, Painting, Sculpture, Textile Design
Summer School: Enrl 750, beginning June

BERNARD M BARUCH COLLEGE OF THE CITY UNIVERSITY OF NEW YORK, Art Department, 46 E 26th St, New York, NY. (Mailing Add: 17 Lexington Ave, Box 281, New York, NY 10010) Tel 212-725-3240. *Chmn* Richard Wengenroth, MA; *Prof* Vigeo Saule, MA; *Assoc Prof* Pamela Sheingorn, PhD; *Asst Prof* Virginia Smith, MFA; *Asst Prof* Elsbeth Woody, MA; *Vis Asst Prof* K Porter Aichele, art history - 1978-79
Estab 1968, dept estab 1968; pub; D & E; ent req HS dipl; degrees BA, BBA and BSEd 4 yrs, MBA 5 yrs, PhD; SC 26, LC 16; enrl D 2000, E 500, maj 40
Tuition: Res—undergrad $750 per sem, $55 per cr; nonres—undergrad $1000 per sem, $95 per cr; no campus res
Courses: Advertising Design, Art Education, Art History, Ceramics, Constructions, Drawing, Graphic Arts, Graphic Design, History of Art & Archaeology, Industrial Design, Lettering, Painting, Photography, Printmaking, Sculpture
Summer School: Dir, Katherine Crum. Courses—Art History Survey, Ceramics, Crafts, Drawing, Painting, Photography

CHILDREN'S AID SOCIETY, Visual Arts Center, 209 Sullivan St, 10012. Tel 212-254-3075. *Dir* Allen M Hart
Estab 1853, dept estab 1968; D & E; SC 7; enrl D 200, E 175
Tuition: Adults $60 per sem; children $32-$42 per sem; no campus res
Courses: Aesthetics, Art Education, Art History, Ceramics, Collage, Constructions, Drawing, Handicrafts, Jewelry, Mixed Media, Painting, Photography, Silversmithing, Teacher Training, Cabinet Making, Enameling, Pottery, Puppet Making
Adult Hobby Classes: Tui $60 per sem. Courses—Cabinetmaking, Ceramics, Drawing, Enameling, Painting, Photography, Pottery
Children's Classes: $32-$42 per sem. Courses—Dance, Drawing, Enameling, Mixed Media, Painting, Photography, Puppet Making, Woodwork

CITY COLLEGE OF THE CITY OF NEW YORK, Art Department, 138th and Convent Ave, Eisner Bldg, 10031. Tel 212-690-4201, 690-4202. *Chmn* Jack Rothenberg, PhD; *Prof* Madeleine Gekiere, Matura Gymnasium; *Prof* Irving Kaufman, MFA; *Prof* Stanley Wyatt, MA; *Assoc Prof* Joan Price, EdD; *Assoc Prof* Gabrielle Roos, MFA; *Assoc Prof* Anne Shaver-Crandell, PhD
Estab 1847, dept estab 1933; pub; D & E; ent req HS dipl; degrees BA 4 yrs, MA(Art History, Museum Studies or Art Educ) 2 yrs, MFA 2 yrs; scholarships; SC 45, LC 30, GC 39; enrl D 1350, E 135, maj 150, grad 65
Tuition: Res—undergrad $463 per yr, grad $75 per cr, $750 maximum; nonres—undergrad $713 per yr, PT $55 per cr, grad $95 per cr, $1000 maximum; no campus res
Courses: Advertising Design, †Art Education, †Art History, Calligraphy, Ceramics, Commercial Art, Drawing, †Graphic Arts, Graphic Design, Handicrafts, †History of Art & Archaeology, Illustration, Intermedia, Interior Design, Jewelry, Lettering, Mixed Media, Museum Staff Training, †Painting, †Photography, †Printmaking, †Sculpture, †Teacher Training
Summer School: Dir, Stanley Wyatt. Tui same for term of 7 1 2 wks beginning June. Courses—Art Education, Art History, Studio

CITY UNIVERSITY OF NEW YORK, PhD Program in Art History, Grad School & University Center, 33 West 42nd St, 10036. Tel 212-790-4451. *Chmn Exec Committee* William H Gerdts, PhD; *Prof* Marcia E Allentuck, PhD; *Prof* Eugene C Goossen, PhD; *Prof* Diane Kelder, PhD; *Prof* Rosalind Krauss, PhD; *Prof* Robert Pincus-Witten, PhD; *Prof* John Rewald, PhD; *Res Prof* Milton W Brown, PhD; *Assoc Prof* Jack Flam, PhD; *Assoc Prof* Mona Hadler, PhD; *Assoc Prof* Rose-Carol Long, PhD; *Assoc Prof* H Barbara Weinberg, PhD; *Asst Prof* Eugene A Santomasso, PhD; *Vis Prof* Linda Nochlin-Pommer, 19th century realism and women artists - 1975-76; *Vis Prof* Gail Levin, early 20th century American painting - 1979
Estab 1961, prog estab 1971; pub; D; ent req BA or MA in Art History; degrees PhD; scholarships; LC 6, GC 6; enrl D 95, grad 95
Tuition: Res—$125; nonres—$170; no campus res
Courses: †Art History

CLAYWORKS, Pottery Department, 332 E Ninth St, 10003. Tel 212-677-8311. *Instructor* Susan Claflin; *Instructor* Alix Leff; *Instructor* Darby Ortolano; *Instructor* Helaine Sorgen
Estab 1973; pvt; D & E; ent req none; SC 3; enrl D 5, E 10
Tuition: $120 sem, $45 month
Courses: Ceramics
Adult Hobby Classes: Enrl 5; tui $120 per 12 wks. Courses—Pottery (wheel and handbuilding)
Children's Classes: Enrl 5; tui $55 per 6 wks. Courses—Pottery (wheel and handbuilding) 5-10 and 10-14 yr age groups
Summer School: Courses—vary according to student demand and interest

COLUMBIA UNIVERSITY
—School of Architecture and Planning,* Avery Hall, Broadway & 116th St, 10027. Tel 212-280-2783. *Dean* James Stewart Polshek. Instrs FT 29, PT 50
Estab 1881; pvt; ent req Bachelor's degree in appropriate area of study; degrees MArchit 3 yrs, MSArchit & Urban Design 1 yr, MSPlanning 2 yrs, MSArchit Tech 1 yr, MSHistoric Prevention 2 yrs; scholarships and fels; enrl 350
Tuition: $3560-$4110 per yr; campus res available
Courses: Architecture, Architectural Technology, Architecture and Urban Design, Health Services Planning and Design, Historic Preservation, Urban Planning
—Department of Art History and Archaeology,* 815 Schermerhorn Bldg, 10027. *Chmn* David Rosand; *Dir Grad Studies* James H Beck
Pvt
Tuition: $2560 per term
—Columbia College,* 10027.
Pvt, M; degrees BA 4 yrs
Tuition: $2560 per yr (FT 15 or more cr); $170 (PT under 15 cr)
Courses: See listing under Graduate Dept
—Graduate Department,* 614 Schermerhorn Bldg, 10027. *Chmn* Alfred Frazer
Pvt; degrees MA 2 yrs, MPhil 4 yrs, PhD 7 yrs; scholarships and fels
Tuition: $2560 per yr (FT 15 or more cr); $170 (PT under 15 cr)
Courses: Art and Archaeology of South Eastern Asia, Asian Art and Archaeology, Classical Art and Archaeology, History of Western Art, Near Eastern Art and Archaeology, Primitive and Pre-Columbian Art and Archaeology
—Division of Painting and Sculpture,* 305 Dodge Hall, 116th St & Broadway, 10027. *Chmn Div* Leon Goldin, MFA; *Prof* Andre Racz, BA; *Asst Prof* Jean Linder, MFA; *Asst Prof* David Lund, BA; *Asst Prof* Sahl Swarz, BA; *Lectr* Tony Harrison, BA
Estab 1754, div estab 1945; pvt; D & E; ent req BA in conjunction with School of General Studies, slide folio for MFA; degrees MFA 2 yrs; scholarships; SC 22, LC 1, GC 5; enrl non-maj 250, maj 5, grad 30
Tuition: $160 per cr; campus res available
Courses: Drawing, Painting, Printmaking, Sculpture
Summer School: Dir Summer Session, Peter D Shamonsey. Enrl 10-15; tui $119 per cr for term of 6 wks beginning May. Courses—Drawing, Painting
—Barnard College,* Dept of Art History, 606 W 120th St, 10027. Tel 212-280-2014. *Dept Art History* Barbara Novak
Estab 1923; pvt, W; degrees 4 yrs; scholarships; enrl maj 29, total 1930
Tuition: $4785 per yr; campus res available
Courses: Art History, Painting

—Department of Art and Education,* Teachers College, 525-W 120th St, 10027. Tel 212-678-3000. *Dean* Harold J Noah
Estab 1888; pvt; ent req Bachelor's degree; degrees MA, MEduc, PhD; scholarships and fels; GC; enrl 225
Tuition: $147 per cr
Courses: Graphic Arts, Handicrafts, Painting, Sculpture, Art Appreciation, Design, Teacher Education
Summer School: Two 6 wk sessions beginning early June; tui $129 per cr

COOPER UNION SCHOOL OF ART, Cooper Square, 10003. Tel 212-254-6300, Ext 286, 287, 288. *Dean* George Sadek, MFA
Estab 1859; pvt; D & E; ent req HS dipl, ent exam; degrees BFA 4 yr; schol
Tuition: No tuition

CRAFT STUDENTS LEAGUE OF THE YWCA, 610 Lexington Ave, 10022. Tel 212-755-4500, Ext 59. *Dir* Margaret-ann Murphy, MA. Instrs PT 65
Dept estab 1932; D & E; SC 50; enrl E 3500
Courses: Calligraphy, Ceramics, Drawing, Handicrafts, Jewelry, Painting, Sculpture, Art Appreciation, Basketry, Bookbinding, Enameling, Lapidary, Macrame, Metalsmithing, Silk Screen, Stained Glass, Watercolor, Weaving
Adult Hobby Classes: Tui $68-$152 per sem of 12 wks. Courses—Decoupage, Picture Framing, Woodworking
Summer School: same as above

FASHION INSTITUTE OF TECHNOLOGY, Art & Design Division, 10001. Tel 212-760-7700. *Acting Dean* Hilde W Jaffe, BA; *Chmn Interior Design* Stanley Barrows, BA; *Chmn Fashion Design* B Zamkoff, BFA; *Chmn Advertising Design* T Giaccone, BFA; *Chmn Fine Arts* F Shapiro, BFA; *Chmn Illustration* Elinore Brandon, BA; *Chmn Photography* H Berg, AAS; *Chmn Display Design* H Christie, AAS; *Chmn Textile Design* Lorraine Har; *Chmn Jewelry Design* M Strump, AAS
Estab 1951; pub; D & E; ent req HS dipl, ent exam; degrees AAS 2 yr, BFA 4 yr; schol; SC 317, LC 26; enrl D 3468, E 7004
Tuition: Res—undergrad $450 per sem; non-res—undergrad $900 per sem; campus res —room and board $2050 per yr
Courses: †Advertising Design, Aesthetics, Art History, Calligraphy, †Costume Design & Construction, †Display, Drafting, Drawing, Fashion Arts, †Goldsmithing, Graphic Arts, Graphic Design, History of Art & Archaeology, Illustration, †Interior Design, †Jewelry, Lettering, Mixed Media, †Painting, †Photography, †Printmaking, Restoration & Conservation, †Sculpture, †Silversmithing, Stage Design, †Textile Design, Theatre Arts, Video
Summer School: Dean, Richard Meagher. Enrl 2900; tui $48 to $96 per course for term of 3, 5 and 7 wks beginning June. Courses—as above

HARRIET FEBLAND ART WORKSHOP, 245 E 63rd St, Suite 408, 10021. Tel 212-759-2215. *Dir* Harriet FeBland; *Instructor* Manuel Barradas; *Instructor* Bernard Kassoy; *Instructor* Hortense Kassoy
Estab 1962; pvt; D & E; ent req Review of previous work, paintings or sculpture; schol; SC 6, LC 1, GC 4; enrl D 115, E 35, grad 115, others 35
Tuition: Tui varies from $140-$170 per 15 wk class, $65 for 5 wk lect and critiques
Courses: Collage, Constructions, Drawing, Painting, Sculpture, Wood Carving

FORDHAM UNIVERSITY,* Arts Division, 60th St & Columbus Ave, 10023. Tel 212-841-5210. *Division Chmn* David Davis
Estab 1968; pvt; D & E; ent req HS dipl; degrees BA 4 yrs; scholarships; SC 18, LC 25; enrl D 900, E 1750, maj 56
Tuition: $1550 per sem; campus res available
Courses: Aesthetics, Costume Design & Construction, Drawing, Graphic Arts, History of Art & Archaeology, Painting, Photography, Sculpture, Stage Design, Teacher Training, Theatre Arts, New Media and Concepts
Summer School: Dir, Dr Levak. Four terms per summer for 5 wks each

GERMAIN SCHOOL OF PHOTOGRAPHY,* 225 Broadway, 10007. Tel 212-964-4550. *Dir* Elaine Kaye Willenson; *Registrar* Thomas J Reynolds. Instrs FT 10, PT 30
Estab 1947; pvt; D & E; ent req HS dipl; degrees 1 yr cert; scholarships
Tuition: $2500 for a full time day session of 600 hrs
Summer School: Courses—variety of short courses at our main school in New York and branch school in Kingston, Jamaica, WI

GREENWICH HOUSE POTTERY, School of Ceramics, 16 Jones St, 10014. Tel 212-242-4106. *Dir* Jane Hartsook, MFA. Instrs 17
Estab 1902, dept estab 1948; pvt; D & E; ent req none; degrees none; schol; SC 32; enrl D 200, E 94
Tuition: $100 per sem; no campus res
Courses: Ceramics, Sculpture, Glazing Chemistry
Children's Classes: Enrl 94; tui $40 and $50 per sem
Summer School: Tui $100 per term of 6 wks June 5 to July 14th. Courses—advanced classes in Ceramics; special seminars; workshop seminars

HENRY STREET SETTLEMENT ARTS FOR LIVING CENTER,* 466 Grand St, 10002. Tel 212-766-9334. *Dir* Renata Karlin, PhD
Estab 1895; pvt; D; ent req None; scholarships; SC 18; enrl D 60, E 60
Tuition: $25-$65 per course
Courses: Advertising Design, Art Education, Calligraphy, Ceramics, Commercial Art, Drawing, Film, Graphic Arts, Graphic Design, Jewelry, Mixed Media, Painting, Photography, Printmaking, Sculpture, Textile Design, Video
Children's Classes: Courses—Leather Crafts, Pottery, Tie Dye

HUNTER COLLEGE, Art Department,* 695 Park Ave, 10021. Tel 212-860-1131. *Chmn Art Dept* Sanford Wurmfeld
Estab 1890, dept estab 1935; pub; D & E; ent req HS dipl; degrees BA and BFA 4 yrs; SC 20-25, LC 10, GC 14-20; enrl D 250 (including evening), maj 250, GS 250
Tuition: Res—$750-$900 per yr; nonres—$1650 per yr; no campus res
Courses: Art Education, Art History, Ceramics, Conceptual Art, Costume Design & Construction, Drafting, Drawing, Graphic Arts, Graphic Design, History of Art & Archaeology, Lettering, Mixed Media, Painting, Photography, Printmaking, Sculpture, Teacher Training, Textile Design

THE JEWELRY INSTITUTE, Metro New York Academy, 305 Seventh Ave, 10001. Tel 212-691-1080. *Dir* Meryl Greenberg. Instrs FT 2, PT 7
Estab 1979; pvt; ent req 18 yrs of age, good manual dexterity and vision; degrees none, Cert of Completion
Tuition: Varies according to course content and length; no campus res
Courses: Silversmithing, Casting, Jewelry Design, Jewelry Repair, Model Making, Rubber Mold Making, Stone and Diamond Setting, Wax Model Making and Carving

JOHN JAY COLLEGE OF CRIMINAL JUSTICE, Department of Art, Music and Philosophy, 10019. Tel 212-489-3557. *Head Dept* Robert P Montgomery, ThD; *Prof* Marlene Park, PhD; *Prof* Laurie Schneider, PhD; *Assoc Prof* John Dobbs, BFA; *Assoc Prof* Helen Ramsaran, MFA; *Lectr* John Russell, BFA. Instrs FT 6, PT 4
Estab 1964, dept estab 1971; pub; D & E; ent req HS dipl; degrees BA and BS 4 yr; SC 5, LC 6; enrl D 180, E 180
Tuition: Res—undergrad $462 per sem, $35 per cr (lower division), $40 per cr (upper division); non-res—undergrad $712 per sem, $55 per cr; no campus res
Courses: Art History, Drawing, Film, Painting, Photography, Sculpture

MAYER SCHOOL OF FASHION DESIGN, Art Department,* 64 W 36th St, 10018. Tel 212-563-3636. *Dir* Herbert Mayer
Estab 1931; pvt; D & E; ent req ent exam; degrees 9 month Cert in Designing, Patternmaking, Draping, Fashion Drawing, Dressmaking, Grading; SC 11; enrl D 110, E 350
Courses: Drawing, Fashion Arts, Dressmaking, Fashion Design, Fashion Draping, Patternmaking

NATIONAL ACADEMY OF DESIGN, 1083 Fifth Ave, 10028. Tel 212-369-4880. *Dir* John H Dobkin
D & E; SC 6
Courses: Drawing, Graphic Arts, Painting, Sculpture

NATIONAL ACADEMY SCHOOL OF FINE ARTS, 5 E 89th St, 10028. Tel 212-369-4880. *Dir* John Dobkin. Instrs 21
Estab 1826; pvt; D & E; ent req none; schol; SC 12; enrl 220
Courses: Drawing, Graphic Arts, Painting, Sculpture, Composition-Portraiture, Life Sketch Class, Watercolor
Summer School: May and August

NEW YORK INSTITUTE OF PHOTOGRAPHY, 880 Third Ave, 10022. Tel 212-255-5150.
Estab 1910; D & E; ent req admission any Monday; approved by New York State; approved for Veterans; individualized instruction, home study course; enrl 500
Courses: Commercial Art, Photography, Airbrush Technique, Motion Picture Production, Oil Coloring, Portrait Retouching

NEW YORK SCHOOL OF INTERIOR DESIGN, 155 E 56th St, 10022. Tel 212-753-5365. *Pres* Arthur Satz, MFA; *Academic Dean* Kerwin E Kettler, MS; *Administrative Dean* Nancy di Benedetto; *Instructor* Robert Murray, BFA
Estab 1916; pvt; D & E; ent req HS dipl, portfolio and interview; degrees 3 yr design program, AAS, BFA; schol; SC 25, LC 8; enrl D 700, E 300, non-maj 865, maj 135
Tuition: 2650 per yr, $1325 per sem, $85 per cr; no campus res
Courses: Architecture, Art History, Drafting, Drawing, Graphic Design, Interior Design, Photography
Summer School: Enrl 200; tui $85 per cr for term of 6 wks beginning July 7th. Courses —variety of lecture and studio courses

NEW YORK STUDIO SCHOOL OF DRAWING, PAINTING AND SCULPTURE, 8 West Eighth St, 10011. Tel 212-673-6466. *Dean* Mercedes Matter, BA; *Assoc Dean* William Wright, BA
Estab 1964; pvt; D; ent req HS dipl, portfolio of recent work; scholarships; SC 13, LC 2; enrl D 80, grad 40
Tuition: $1350 per sem; campus res available in summer only
Courses: Art History, Drawing, Painting, Sculpture
Adult Hobby Classes: Enrl 20; tui $125 per 12 wks. Courses—Drawing
Summer School: Dir, William Wright. Enrl 60-80; tui $800 for term of 8 wks beginning June 19th. Courses—Art History, Drawing, Painting, Sculpture

NEW YORK UNIVERSITY, Institute of Fine Arts, 1 E 78th St, 10021. Tel 212-988-5550. *Chmn* A Richard Turner
Pvt; D & E; scholarships and fels; enrl grad 400
Courses: History of Art & Archaeology, Museum Staff Training, Conservation and Technology of Works of Art
—Department of Art Education & Div of Creative Arts, School of Education, 239 Greene St, Rm 735, 10003. Tel 212-598-3481. *Chmn* Dr Angdola Churchill. Instrs FT 10, PT 15
Pvt; D & E; ent req col board ent exam, 85 HS average, portfolio, interview; degrees BS, EdD, MA and PhD; scholarships and fels; undergrad SC 26, LC 13, grad SC 11, LC 15; enrl maj undergrad 115, grad 130
Courses: Aesthetics, Art History, Drawing, Graphic Arts, Handicrafts, Painting, Printmaking, Sculpture, Teacher Training, Art Therapy, Costume History and Design, Design, Lithography

PACE UNIVERSITY, Art and Music Department,* Pace Plaza, 10038. Tel 212-285-3000. *Chmn* Peter Fingesten
Estab 1950; pvt; D & E; ent req HS dipl, ent exam; degrees 4 yr, no art major; SC 4, LC 20; enrl D 200, E 150, 700-800 per yr art only
Tuition: PT $80 per cr hr; campus res available
Courses: Architecture, Ceramics, Drawing, Graphic Design, History of Art & Archaeology, Painting, Sculpture, Silversmithing, Leather, Macrame
Summer School: Three summer sessions. Courses—Art and Architecture Design

PARSONS SCHOOL OF DESIGN, 66 Fifth Ave, 11215. Tel 212-741-8910. *Dean* David C Levy, PhD
Estab 1896; pvt (see also Otis Art Institute of Parsons School of Design, Los Angeles, California); D & E; ent req HS dipl, portfolio review; degrees AAS, BFA and MFA 2 yr; scholarships; SC 200, LC 400, GC 25; enrl D 1450, E 2000, GS 25, others 40
Tuition: $4000 per yr, $125 per cr; campus res—room & board $2300
Courses: †Advertising Design, Aesthetics, Architecture, †Art Education, Art History,

Calligraphy, †Ceramics, †Commercial Art, Conceptual Art, †Graphic Design, †Handicrafts, History of Art & Archaeology, †Illustration, †Industrial Design, †Interior Design, †Jewelry, Landscape Architecture, Sculpture, †Silversmithing, †Teacher Training, †Textile Design, †Environmental Design, Weaving
Adult Hobby Classes: Enrl 1500; tui $125 per course. Courses—varied
Summer School: Dir, Bill Barrett. Enrl 500; tui $300 for term of 4 wks, beginning July 1. Courses—same as regular session

PELS SCHOOL OF ART, Dept of Commercial Art, 2109 Broadway at 73rd St, 10023. Tel 212-873-4283. *Dir* Albert Pels, DFA; *Dean* Richard Beltran, BA; *Instructor* Peter English, BFA; *Instructor* Paul Fortenberry, MA; *Instructor* Robert Frank, BFA
Estab 1945; pvt; D & E; ent req 2 yrs HS, portfolio; degrees cert of completion 2 yr; schol; SC 6; enrl D 150, E 30, maj all
Tuition: 1750 per yr, $175 per month, PT $95-175, $1.75 per hr; no campus res
Courses: †Advertising Design, Calligraphy, †Commercial Art, Drawing, Graphic Arts, Graphic Design, †Illustration, Interior Design, Lettering, Painting, Textile Design, Layouts, Mechanicals, †Paste-ups
Children's Classes: Courses—Drawing, Painting
Summer School: Enrl 80; tui $225 for term of 8 wks

PRATT-PHOENIX SCHOOL OF DESIGN, Associate Degree Department, 160 Lexington Ave, 10016. Tel 212-685-2973. *Chairperson* Rose Wasserman
Estab 1892; pvt; D; ent req HS dipl, portfolio, interview; degrees Assoc 2 yrs; scholarships
Tuition: $112 per cr, no campus res
Courses: Advertising Design, Art History, Calligraphy, Fashion Arts, Illustration, Textile Design, Batik, Typography, Weaving

SCHOOL OF VISUAL ARTS, 209 E 23rd St, 10010. Tel 212-679-7350, Div Continuing Educ 683-0600. *Chmn* Silas H Rhodes; *Pres* David Rhodes; *Coordr Acad Advancement* Stephen Pite
Estab 1947; pvt; ent req HS transcript, portfolio review, interview; degrees BFA, provisional teachers' cert (K-12) in Art Educ; scholarships; enrl FT 2200, PT 3000
Tuition: $3100 plus fees per yr
Courses: Advertising Design, Drawing, Film, Graphic Design, Illustration, Lettering, Painting, Photography, Sculpture, Textile Design, Video, Airbrush, Typographic Design, Journalistic Art

SCULPTURE CENTER, 167 E 69th St, 10021. Tel 212-737-9870. *Dir* Mary Stiles
Estab 1933; pvt; D & E; ent req no ent req; degrees no degrees; scholarships
Courses: Sculpture
Adult Hobby Classes: Sculpture

TOBE-COBURN SCHOOL FOR FASHION CAREERS, LTD, 851 Madison Ave, 10021. Tel 212-879-4644. *Pres* Avon Lees Jr. Instrs FT 9, PT 15
Estab 1927; pvt; D; degrees AA(Occupational Studies); partial schol; 2 yr course for HS grad, 1 yr course for those with 2 or more yr col, classroom study alternates with periods of work in stores or projects in fashion field; enrl 200
Courses: Display, Fashion Arts, Fabrics

TRAPHAGEN SCHOOL OF FASHION, 257 Park Ave S, 10010. Tel 212-673-0300. *Dir* Wanda Wdowka; *Chmn Design Dept* Marion Roller, BA; *Chmn Fashion Illustration* Elsbeth Edwards; *Chmn Interior Design & Dec* Jean Pierre Pique, BA; *Instructor* Elena Braithewaite, BA; *Instructor* Gabrielle Jean-Bart, BA; *Instructor* Harold Silverman, BA
Estab 1923; pub; D & E; ent req HS dipl, personal interview; degrees cert 2 yr, co-op BA prog with NY Institute of Technology issuing degrees; schol; enrl D 300 max, E 150
Tuition: $2465 per yr, $1233 per sem; no campus res
Courses: Costume Design & Construction, Fashion Arts, Interior Design, Lettering
Summer School: Enrol 15 per class; tue $350 per term of 6 wk. Courses—Draping, Dressmaking, Fashion Art, Interior Design, Patternmaking, Samplemaking

UMBERTO ROMANO SCHOOL OF CREATIVE ART, 162 E 83rd St, 10028. Tel 212-288-9621. *Dir* Umberto Romano
Estab 1933; pvt; D
Courses: Drawing, Graphic Arts, Painting, Sculpture

OAKDALE

DOWLING COLLEGE, Department of Art,* Idle Hour Blvd, 11769. Tel 516-589-6100, Ext 246. *Div Coordr* Carlo Lombardi
Pvt; D & E; ent req HS dipl; degrees BA (Visual Art & Speech, Drama), BS and BBA 4 yrs; scholarships; enrl D 1100, E 500
Tuition: Res—$86 per cr hr; campus res—$900 room
Courses: Advertising Design, Aesthetics, Architecture, Art Education, Ceramics, Commercial Art, Drafting, Drawing, Graphic Arts, Graphic Design, Handicrafts, History of Art & Archaeology, Painting, Photography, Sculpture, Silversmithing, Stage Design, Teacher Training, Theatre Arts
Adult Hobby Classes: Courses—Composition, Drawing, Painting

OLD WESTBURY

NEW YORK INSTITUTE OF TECHNOLOGY, Fine Arts Department, Wheatley Rd, 11568. Tel 516-686-7543. *Chmn* John Murray, MFA; *Prof* Frances Lassiter, PhD; *Assoc Prof* Marvin Horowitz, MFA; *Assoc Prof* Valdes Kubris, MFA; *Assoc Prof* Shirley Marein, MFA; *Adjunct Assoc Prof* Phoebe Helman, MFA; *Adjunct Assoc Prof* Roger Williams, MFA; *Asst Prof* Janet de Cecilia, MA; *Asst Prof* Thomas Martin, MFA; *Adjunct Instructor* Domenic Alfano; *Adjunct Instructor* Anthony Clementi, MA; *Adjunct Instructor* Janet Cohen, MA; *Adjunct Instructor* Cynthia Gallagher, MFA; *Adjunct Instructor* Robert Parao, BFA; *Master Printer* Roni Henning; *Photographer in Res* Neil Scholl
Estab 1910, dept estab 1963; pvt; D; ent req HS dipl, portfolio review; degrees BFA 4 yr; schol; SC 11, LC 85; enrl D 427, non-maj 100, maj 327
Tuition: $1560 per yr, $80 per cr; no campus res
Courses: Art History, Calligraphy, Drawing, †Graphic Arts, Graphic Design,

Illustration, †Interior Design, Lettering, †Painting, Photography, †Printmaking, †Sculpture, Stage Design, †Teacher Training, Textile Design, Computer Animation
Summer School: Tui $80 per cr for term of 8 wks. Courses—Drawing, Interior Design, Painting, Sculpture

STATE UNIVERSITY OF NEW YORK COLLEGE AT OLD WESTBURY, Communicative & Creative Arts Department, Box 210, 11568. Tel 516-876-3000, 876-3056.
Estab 1968, Dept estab 1969; pub; D & E; ent req HS dipl, skills proficiency exam, GED, special exception - inquire through admissions; degrees BA(Communicative & Creative Arts) 4 yr; SC 10, LC 10; enrl D & E 277
Tuition: Res—lower division $375 per sem, $25 per cr hr, upper division $450 per sem, $30 per cr hr; non-res—lower division $600 per sem, $40 per cr hr, upper division $750 per sem, $50 per cr hr; campus res—room and board $1500 per yr
Courses: Art History, Ceramics, Conceptual Art, Drawing, Graphic Arts, Intermedia, Mixed Media, Painting, Photography, Printmaking, Sculpture
Summer School: Dir, Marc Bomse

ONEONTA

HARTWICK COLLEGE, Art Department, 13820. Tel 607-432-4200, Ext 520. *Prof* Roberta Griffith, MFA. Instrs FT 5, PT 8
Estab 1927; pvt; D; ent req HS dipl; enrl 930, non-maj 930, maj 65
Tuition: $4100 per yr; campus res $1750
Courses: Art Education, Art History, Ceramics, Drawing, Handicrafts, Jewelry, Painting, Photography, Printmaking, Sculpture, Silversmithing, Teacher Training, Video, Fiber, Papermaking, Weaving

STATE UNIVERSITY OF NEW YORK COLLEGE AT ONEONTA, Department of Art,* 13820. Tel 607-431-3500. *Chmn* James Mullen, MA
Estab 1889; pub; D & E; ent req HS dipl, regents scholarship exam, SAT and ACT; degrees BA (Studio Art, Art History) 4 yrs, Col at Oneonta offers programs leading to MA (Museum History, Folk Art, Conservation & Restoration of Works of Art) in conjunction with the New York State Historical Association at Cooperstown, NY 13326 (Dr Bruce R Buckley, SUNY Dir); SC 31, LC 22; enrl D 660, E 35, maj 123, approx 25-30 at Cooperstown Center
Tuition: Res—undergrad $750-$900, grad $1400-$1800; nonres—$1200-$1500; campus res—room and board $1231
Courses: Ceramics, Drawing, Graphic Arts, History of Art & Archaeology, Jewelry, Museum Staff Training, Painting, Photography, Sculpture, Stage Design, Textile Design, Theatre Arts
Adult Hobby Classes: Offered only on a subscription basis at normal tuition rates through the Office of Continuing Education
Children's Classes: Dir, Dr Robert Porter. Enrl varies between 20-40 per yr. Offered only through the Upper Catskill Study Council
Summer School: Dir, Dr Robert Nichols. Tui same as in regular session for two 6 wk terms beginning June and July. Courses—Art Criticism, Art History, Studio Courses (depending on demand)

OSWEGO

STATE UNIVERSITY OF NEW YORK COLLEGE AT OSWEGO, Art Department, 13126. Tel 315-341-2111. *Chmn* T C Eckersley, MFA. Instrs FT 18
Estab 1861; pub; D & E; ent req HS dipl, SAT or NYS regents scholarship exam; degrees BA 4 yr, MA 2yr; SC 31, LC 9; enrl maj 200, grad 5
Tuition: Res—undergrad lower division $375 per sem, upper division $450 per sem; non-res—undergrad lower division $600 per sem, upper division $750 per sem; campus res—room $750 and board $600 per year
Courses: Graphic Arts, Graphic Design, Jewelry, Museum Staff Training, Painting, Photography, Printmaking, Sculpture, Silversmithing, Aesthetics, Art History, Ceramics, Drawing, Environmental Painting
Adult Hobby Classes: Tui $25 per person. Courses—Glass Media, Painting
Summer School: Dir, Lewis C Popham III. Tui NYS res $25.85 lower division per cr hr, $30.85 upper division per cr hr

PLEASANTVILLE

PACE UNIVERSITY, Department of Art & Design, 10603. Tel 914-769-3200. *Chmn* Brenda Bettinson; *Prof* John Mulgrew, MA; *Instructor* Beth Treadway, MA. Instrs 7
Estab 1906, dept estab 1978; pvt; D & E; ent req HS dipl, SAT scores, review by admissions committee and dept interview; degrees BS(Fine Arts) 4 yrs; scholarships
Tuition: Campus residency available
Courses: Art History, Ceramics, Drawing, Graphic Arts, Graphic Design, Illustration, Interior Design, Painting, Photography, Printmaking, Sculpture, Scientific and Medical Illustration, Typography

POTSDAM

STATE UNIVERSITY OF NEW YORK COLLEGE AT POTSDAM, Department of Fine Arts, 13676. Tel 315-268-5040. *Chmn* Mark H Sandler, PhD; *Prof* John Riordan, PhD; *Prof* Arthur Sennett, MFA; *Prof* James Sutter, MFA; *Assoc Prof* George Green, MFA; *Assoc Prof* Joseph Hildreth, MFA; *Assoc Prof* Steven Sumner, MFA; *Asst Prof* James Czainuki, PhD; *Instructor* Mary Barnes, MFA; *Gallery Dir* Kendall Taylor, PhD
Estab 1948; pub; D & E; ent req HS dipl, SAT, portfolio review recommended; degrees BA 4 yrs, special prog Empire State studio sem in New York City, study in London (Jr yr)
Tuition: Res—undergrad lower div $750 per yr, $375 per sem, $25 per cr hr, upper div $900 per yr, $450 per sem, $30 per cr hr; nonres—undergrad lower div $1200 per yr, $600 per sem, $40 per cr hr, upper div $1500 per yr, $750 per sem, $50 per cr hr; no grad students; campus res—$750 room & $676 (10 meals per wk)
Courses: Art Education, †Art History, †Ceramics, Drawing, Goldsmithing, †Graphic Arts, Jewelry, †Painting, †Photography, †Printmaking, †Sculpture, Silversmithing, Teacher Training
Summer School: Dir, Jill Ellsworth. Enrl max 25 per class; term of 3-6 wks. Courses—Masterpieces of World Art, Photo Workshop, Pottery Workshop

POUGHKEEPSIE

DUTCHESS COMMUNITY COLLEGE, Department of Visual Arts,* 1 Pendell Rd, 12601. Tel 914-471-4500, Ext 339. *Head Dept* William M Brown
Estab 1957; pub; D & E; ent req HS dipl; degrees AAS (Commercial Art); scholarships; SC 24, LC 22; enrl D 660, E 340, maj 100
Courses: Ceramics, Commercial Art, Drawing, Graphic Arts, History of Art & Archaeology, Illustration, Jewelry, Lettering, Painting, Photography, Sculpture, Textile Design, Glass, Leather, Metal, Plastic, Weaving, Wood

VASSER COLLEGE, Art Department, 12601. Tel 914-452-7000, Ext 2642. Instrs FT 13, PT 4
Estab 1861; pvt; D; ent req HS grad, ent exam; degrees BA(Art History) 4 yr; schol; SC 8, LC; enrl maj 90, others 2400
Tuition: $4525 per yr; campus res $2125
Courses: Architecture, Art History, Drafting, Drawing, Painting, Sculpture

PURCHASE

MANHATTANVILLE COLLEGE, Art Department, 10577. Tel 914-946-9600. *Head Dept* Louis Trakis; *Prof* John Ross, BFA; *Assoc Prof* Mathew Broner, MFA
Estab 1841; pvt; D & E; ent req HS dipl, portfolio, interview; degrees BA and BFA 4 yrs, MAT 1 yr, special prog MATA (Masters of Art in Teaching Art); scholarships; SC 25, LC 10, GC 7; enrl D 180, non-maj 90, maj 90, grad 10
Tuition: Res—undergrad $6465 per yr, $3233 per sem, grad $420 to $460 per course per sem; nonres—undergrad $4250 per yr, $2125 per sem; other application fee $20; campus res available
Courses: Advertising Design, Art Education, Art History, Calligraphy, Ceramics, Collage, Commercial Art, Constructions, Drawing, Film, Graphic Arts, Graphic Design, History of Art & Archaeology, Lettering, Mixed Media, Painting, Photography, Printmaking, Sculpture, Teacher Training, Theatre Arts, Book Design, Design, Metal Sculpture
Summer School: Dir, Mary Thompson. Courses—Art History, Ceramics, Drawing, Painting, Photography, Sculpture

STATE UNIVERSITY OF NEW YORK COLLEGE AT PURCHASE
—Division of Visual Arts,* School of the Arts, 10577. Tel 914-253-5000. *Dean* Robert H Gray
Estab 1966; pub
Tuition: Res—undergrad $750 per yr, grad $900 per yr; nonres—undergrad $1200 per yr, grad $1500 per yr; campus res—room $750-$840 per yr, board $748-$778 per yr
Courses: Aesthetics, Architecture, Art Education, Drafting, Drawing, Graphic Arts, Graphic Design, History of Art & Archaeology, Industrial Design, Landscape Architecture, Painting, Photography, Sculpture, Stage Design, Theatre Arts
—Department of Art History, 10577. Tel 914-253-5025. *Chmn* Shirley N Blum, PhD; *Assoc Prof* Eric Carlson, PhD; *Assoc Prof* Irving Sandler, PhD; *Asst Prof* Eleanor Saunders, PhD
Estab 1971, dept estab 1977; pub; D & E; ent req HS dipl, essay on application, grades, test scores; degrees BA and BALA 4 yrs; scholarships; enrl total 2000, maj 25
Tuition: Res—undergrad $750 per yr; nonres—undergrad $1200 per yr; campus res—room & board $1500 per yr
Courses: Art History

RIVERDALE

COLLEGE OF MOUNT SAINT VINCENT, Fine Arts Department, West 263rd St and Riverdale Ave, 10471. Tel 212-549-8000. *Acting Chmn* Karen Gunderson; *Assoc Prof* Richard Barnet, MA; *Assoc Prof* Larry Fuschman, MFA; *Assoc Prof* Enrico Giordano, MS; *Assoc Prof* Susan Kay, MA; *Assoc Prof* Sr Christine Murphy, MFA
Estab 1911; pvt; D & E; ent req HS dipl and SAT; degrees BA, BS and BS(Art Educ) 4 yrs; scholarships; SC 22, LC 10; enrl D 950, E 50
Tuition: $3400 per yr; campus res—room & board $2100 per yr
Courses: Aesthetics, †Art Education, Art History, †Ceramics, †Drawing, Film, Graphic Arts, Mixed Media, †Painting, Design
Summer School: Dir Continuing Education, Dr Marjorie Connelly. Tui $80 per cr. Courses—vary each summer

ROCHESTER

NAZARETH COLLEGE OF ROCHESTER, Art Department, 14610. Tel 716-586-2525, Ext 259. *Head Dept* Sr Magdalen LaRow, MFA; *Assoc Prof* Margaret Crawford, MFA; *Assoc Prof* Mary Jane Edwards, MFA; *Asst Prof* Samuel Hudson, MFA; *Asst Prof* Ron Netsky, MFA; *Instructor* Lynn Duggan, MFA; *Instructor* Susan

Rowley, MST; *Lectr* Roger Adams, PhD; *Lectr* Richard Margolis, MFA
Estab 1926, dept estab 1936; pvt; D & E; ent req HS dipl; degrees BA and BS 4 yrs; scholarships; SC 40, LC 15, GC 6; enrl D 180, E 74, non-maj 50, maj 200, grad 48
Tuition: Undergrad $1550 per sem, $84 per cr hr; nonres—grad $96 per cr hr; campus res—room & board $1800 per yr
Courses: †Art Education, †Art History, Ceramics, Drawing, Goldsmithing, Jewelry, Painting, Photography, Printmaking, Sculpture, Silversmithing, Textile Design
Summer School: Dir, Elaine Hayden. Enrl 60; tui $84-$96 per cr hr for term of 6 wks beginning July 5th. Courses—grad and undergrad

ROCHESTER INSTITUTE OF TECHNOLOGY
—**College of Fine and Applied Arts,** One Lomb Memorial Dr, 14623. Tel 716-475-2646. *Dean College* Dr Robert H Johnston; *Assoc Dean College* Peter Giopulos
—**School of Art and Design,** 14623. *Dir* Peter Giopulos; *Fine Arts* Philip W Bornarth; *Environmental Design* Craig J McArt; *Foundation Studies* Robert Cole; *Communication Design* James VerHague. Instrs FT 40, PT 14
Estab 1829; pvt; ent req HS grad, ent exam, portfolio; degrees AAS, BFA, MFA, MST, 4-5 yrs; enrl 400
Tuition: $3495; campus res available
Courses: Art Education, Painting, Printmaking, Communication Design, Environmental Design, Medical Illustration
—**School of American Craftsmen,** 14623. *Dir* Dr Robert H Johnston; *Crafts* Gary Griffin. Instrs FT 10
Estab 1946; pvt; ent req HS grad, ent exam, portfolio; degrees AAS, BFA, MFA, MST 4-5 yrs; enrl 150
Tuition: $3495; campus res available
Courses: Ceramics, Jewelry, Textile Design, Ceramic Sculpture, Furniture Design, Glass, Metalcrafts, Weaving, Woodworking
Summer School: Two 5 wk terms
—**College of Graphic Arts and Photography,** 14623. *Dean* Lothar K Engelmann, PhD; *Assoc Dean* John L Kronenberg, BS
The College includes School of Photographic Arts and Sciences, School of Printing, and Graphic Arts Research Center

UNIVERSITY OF ROCHESTER, Department of Fine Arts, Morey Hall, 424, 14627. Tel 716-275-4284. *Chmn* Archibald M Miller. Instrs FT 13, PT 8
Estab 1902; degrees 4 yrs; scholarships; SC 25, LC 25; enrl Maj 45, others 900
Tuition: $4050 per yr
Courses: Art History, Painting, Photography, Sculpture

ROSLYN

HABER SCHOOL OF SCULPTURE, 1170 Old Northern Blvd, 11576. Tel 516-484-9322. *Dir* Mortimer N Haber
Estab 1965; pvt; D & E; ent req based on availability of openings; degrees none; SC 5, LC integrated into prog; enrl D 60, E 13
Courses: Sculpture, Stone Carving
Summer School: Enrl 39-48; term of 8 wks beginning July. Courses—same as regular session

SANBORN

NIAGARA COUNTY COMMUNITY COLLEGE, Fine Arts Div, 3111 Saunders Settlement Rd, 14303. Tel 716-731-3271, Ext 158. *Chmn* Donald R Harter. Instrs FT 6, PT 6
Estab 1965; pub; D & E; ent req HS dipl; degrees AS(Fine Arts) 2 yrs; SC 12, LC 4; enrl D 400, E 120, maj 140
Courses: Art Education, Drawing, Fashion Arts, Graphic Design, History of Art & Archaeology, Illustration, Interior Design, Painting, Photography, Printmaking, Sculpture
Summer School: Dir, Judith Shipengrover. Enrl 30; term of 6-7 wks beginning June. Courses—Same as regular yr

SARATOGA SPRINGS

SKIDMORE COLLEGE, Department of Art, 12866. Tel 518-584-5000. *Chmn* Peter B Baruzzi. Instrs FT 20
Estab 1911; pvt; ent req HS grad, 16 cr, ent exam, portfolio; degrees BA and BS 4 yrs; scholarships; SC 32, LC 18; enrl maj 350, 2000 total
Tuition: $5030 per yr; dormitory room and board $2370 per yr or apartment $1525 per yr
Courses: Art Education, Art History, Drawing, Film, Graphic Design, Jewelry, Lettering, Painting, Photography, Printmaking, Sculpture, Design, Enameling, Pottery, Screen Printing, Weaving
Summer School: Dir, Regis Brodie. Enrl 194 for two 6 wk sessions. Courses—Advanced Studio & Independent Study, Art History, Ceramics, Drawing, Etching, Film Making, Jewelry, Lettering, Painting, Photography, Sculpture, Two-Dimensional Design, Watercolor, Weaving

YADDO, Box 395, 12866. *Pres* Newman E Wait Jr; *Exec Dir* Curtis Hornack
Yaddo is a working retreat for writers, composers, and visual artists. The country estate of the late Mr & Mrs Spencer Trask was estab 1926 and opened to all who have achieved some measure of professional accomplishment. Applications must be received by Feb 1; work must be shown to an admission committee; invitations are issued by April 15 for periods up to 2 months; room board and studio space for limited number; no cash grants; enrl limited number

SCHENECTADY

UNION COLLEGE, Department of the Arts, Union St, 12308. Tel 518-370-6201. *Chmn* Hugh Allen Wilson. Instrs FT 8
Estab 1795; pvt; D; ent req HS dipl, ent exam; degrees BA with emphasis in music, art or drama 4 yr; schol; SC 14, LC 4; enrl maj 52
Tuition: $5000 per yr
Courses: Drawing, Graphic Arts, Graphic Design, Painting, Photography, Sculpture, Stage Design, Theatre Arts

SEA CLIFF

STEVENSON ACADEMY OF TRADITIONAL PAINTING, 11579. Tel 516-676-6611. *Head Dept* Harold Ransom Stevenson; *Asst Instr* Alma Gallanos. Instrs FT 2
Estab 1960; pvt; E; ent req interview; SC 3, LC 5; enrl 95
Tuition: $100 per 10 wk sem, one evening per wk; $500 per 10 wk sem, five evenings per wk; no campus res
Courses: Drawing, Illustration, Painting, Artistic Anatomy, Basic Form
Summer School: Enrl 57; tui $80-$230 per term of 8 wks beginning June 1. Courses —Artistic Anatomy, Drawing, Painting

SENECA FALLS

EISENHOWER COLLEGE,* Humanities Division, 13148. Tel 315-568-7475. *Chmn* Sandra Saari, PhD; *Prof* Edmund Demers, PhD; *Asst Prof* Susan Sauvageau, MFA; *Asst Prof* Peter Slusarski, MA
Estab 1965, dept estab 1968; pvt; D; ent req HS dipl, SAT, CEEB or ACT; degrees BA 4 yrs; scholarships; SC 14, LC 15; enrl D 80-90, non-maj 400, maj 15
Tuition: Res—$3700 per yr; campus res available
Courses: Art History, Calligraphy, Ceramics, Drawing, Graphic Arts, Painting, Sculpture

SOUTHAMPTON

SOUTHAMPTON COLLEGE OF LONG ISLAND UNIVERSITY, Fine Arts Division, 11968. Tel 516-283-4000. *Assoc Dean* Donald L Wyckoff, PhD; *Prof* Colonius Davis, PhD; *Prof* Robert Shaughnessy, PhD; *Prof* Robert Skinner, PhD; *Prof* Marie Wynn, MFA; *Assoc Prof* Constance Evans, MFA; *Assoc Prof* Yosh Higa, MGA; *Assoc Prof* Robert Munford
Estab 1963; pvt; D & E; ent req HS dipl and portfolio review; degrees BFA, BA(Art Educ), BA(Fine Arts), 4 yrs, MA Educ; schol; SC 36, LC 17, GC 11; enrl D 398, E 20, non-maj 100, maj 280, grad 20, others 18
Tuition: $1715 sem; campus res—room and board $1045 sem
Courses: †Advertising Design, †Art Education, †Art History, Calligraphy, †Ceramics, Collage, †Commercial Art, Constructions, Drafting, Drawing, Graphic Arts, Handicrafts, History of Art & Archaeology, Illustration, †Jewelry, Lettering, Museum Staff Training, †Painting, †Photography, †Printmaking, †Sculpture, Silversmithing, Stage Design, †Teacher Training, Textile Design, Theatre Arts, Art Therapy, Basketry, Enameling, Weaving
Adult Hobby Classes: Courses—Drawing, Painting, Photography, Various Crafts
Children's Classes: 8 wk summer children's prog
Summer School: Dir, Donald L Wyckoff. Tui $133 per cr hr for term of 3 wks beginning July. Courses—various

SPARKHILL

SAINT THOMAS AQUINAS COLLEGE, Art Department,* Route 340, 10976. Tel 914-359-9500. *Chmn* Carl Rattner, MFA; *Instr* Roger Howrigan, MFA; *Instr* Sr Adele Myers, MFA; *Instr* Sr Elizabeth Slenker, MFA
Estab 1952, dept estab 1969; pvt; D & E; ent req HS dipl; degrees BA and BS 4 yrs; scholarships; SC 20, LC 10; enrl D 1100, maj 50
Tuition: Res—$1900 per yr; campus res available
Courses: Advertising Design, Art Education, Art History, Calligraphy, Ceramics, Commercial Art, Drawing, Handicrafts, Jewelry, Painting, Photography, Printmaking, Sculpture, Teacher Training, Textile Design, Theatre Arts, Video
Summer School: Dir, Dr Joseph Keane. Tui $180 for 3 cr course. Courses—Varies 6-9 art courses including Ceramics, Painting, Photography

STATEN ISLAND

STATEN ISLAND INSTITUTE OF ARTS AND SCIENCES, Staten Island Museum,* 75 Stuyvesant Place, 10301. Tel 212-727-1135. *Cur* Freda Esterly
Estab 1881; pvt (with added support from New York City); degrees no degrees
Courses: Drawing, Handicrafts, History of Art & Archaeology, Painting
Adult Hobby Classes: Late afternoon and evening
Children's Classes: During the day

WAGNER COLLEGE, Department of Art,* 631 Howard Ave, 10301. Tel 212-390-3000. *Chmn* William Levitt Jr
Estab 1948; den; D & E; ent req HS grad; degrees BA (Art or Art Educ) 4 yrs; scholarships; SC 20, LC 6; enrl maj 130, others 2500
Tuition: Res—undergrad $3480 per yr (based on 12 to 18 cr per sem); campus res—room and board $1650 per yr
Courses: Art Education, Art History, Ceramics, Drawing, Film, Mixed Media, Painting, Photography, Printmaking, Sculpture, Black Art History, Crafts Design, Experiments, Three Dimensional Design, Two Dimensional Design
Summer School: Two sessions of 4 wks. Special 2 wk course (3 cr). Courses—Exploring Art in New York

STONE RIDGE

ULSTER COUNTY COMMUNITY COLLEGE, Department of Visual Arts,* 12484. Tel 914-687-7621, Ext 76. *Head Dept* Allan Cohen, MFA; *Asst Prof* John A Locke III, MFA; *Instr* Joyce Veldhuis, MFA
Estab 1963; pub; D & E; ent req HS dipl, SAT; degrees AA 2 yrs; SC 17, LC 6; enrl D 250, E 100, non-maj 305, maj 45
Tuition: Res—undergrad $750 per yr; nonres—undergrad $1500 per yr; no campus res
Courses: Advertising Design, Aesthetics, Art History, Drawing, Fashion Arts, Painting, Photography, Theatre Arts, Life Drawing & Anatomy, Three Dimensional Design, Two Dimensional Design
Summer School: Enrl 75; $27 per cr for term of 6-8 wks beginning June. Courses— Drawing, Painting

STONY BROOK

STATE UNIVERSITY OF NEW YORK AT STONY BROOK, Art Department, 11794. Tel 516-246-7070. *Chmn* Donald B Kuspit, PhD; *Prof* Jacques Guilmain, PhD; *Prof* George Koras; *Prof* Lawrence Alloway; *Assoc Prof* Howardena Pindell, MFA; *Assoc Prof* Nina Mallory, PhD; *Assoc Prof* Mel Pekarsky, MA
Estab 1957; pub; D; ent req HS dipl, SAT; degrees BA(Art History) and BA(Studio Art) 4 yr; SC 33, LC 39; enrl D 1072
Tuition: Res—undergrad lower division $750 per yr, $375 per sem, $25 per cr hr, upper division $900 per yr, $450 per sem, $30 per cr hr; grad $1400 per yr, $700 per sem, $58.50 per cr hr; non-res—undergrad lower division $1200 per yr, $600 per sem, $40 per cr hr, upper division $1500 per yr, $750 per sem, $50 per cr hr; grad $1800 per yr, $900 per sem, $75 per cr hr; campus res—room and board $750 per yr
Courses: Architecture, †Art History, Ceramics, Costume Design & Construction, Drawing, Graphic Arts, Painting, Photography, Printmaking, Sculpture, Stage Design, †Theatre Arts, 2-D Design, 3-D Design
Summer School: Dir, Sally Springer. Tui res—undergrad lower division $25 per cr hr, upper division $30 per cr hr; grad $58.50 per cr hr; non-res—undergrad lower division $40 per cr hr, upper division $50 per cr hr; grad $75 per cr hr for term of 5 1 2 wks June 2 - July 9 and July 10 - Aug 15. Courses—vary

SUFFERN

ROCKLAND COMMUNITY COLLEGE, Art Department,* 145 College Rd, 10901. Tel 914-356-4650, Ext 285. *Chmn* J P Murphy
Estab 1965; pub; D & E; ent req open; degrees AAS 2 yrs; SC plus apprenticeships; enrl D 900, E 300, maj 200
Tuition: No campus res
Courses: Advertising Design, Art History, Drawing, Graphic Arts, Graphic Design, Lettering, Painting, Photography, Sculpture, Art Appreciation, Art Therapy, Color Production, Electric Art
Adult Hobby Classes: Tui depends on enrl. Courses—varied
Children's Classes: Courses—Overseas programs
Summer School: Courses—Art History, Drawing, Graphic Techniques, Painting, Sculpture

SYRACUSE

LE MOYNE COLLEGE, Art Department, Le Moyne Heights, 13214. Tel 315-446-2882. *Dir* Jacqueline Belfort-Chalat, member Royal Acad, DK; *Adjunct Asst Prof* Joel Gaines, BFA; *Adjunct Asst Prof* Charles Wollowitz, MFA; *Adjunct Instr* Charles Aho, MA
Pvt; D; ent req HS dipl, SAT or ACT; degrees BS and BA 4 yrs; SC 4, LC 1; enrl non-maj 300
Tuition: Res—undergrad $4740 per yr, $2370 per sem, $105 per hr; non-res— undergrad $3040 per yr, $1520 per sem, $105 per hr; campus residence available
Courses: Art History, Drawing, Graphic Arts, Painting, Sculpture
Summer School: Dir, James F Welter

SYRACUSE UNIVERSITY
—**College of Visual and Performing Arts,** School of Art, 200 Crouse College, 13210. Tel 315-423-2611. *Dean* August L Freundlich, PhD; *Dir* Joseph Scala, MFA; *Chmn* Michael Andres, PhD; *Chmn* Arthur Pulas, MFA; *Chmn* John Sellers; *Chmn* John Oren Tlicker; *Chmn* Sylvia Wyckoff, MFA; *Acting Chmn* Charles Dibble; *Acting Chmn* Rodger Mack. Instrs FT 62, PT 15
Estab 1873; pvt; D & E; ent req HS dipl, portfolio review; degrees BID 5 yrs, BFA 4 yrs, MFA, MID and MS 2 yrs; scholarships; SC 200, LC 25, GC 50; enrl D 1097, E 250, maj 1200, grad 190
Tuition: Campus res available
Courses: Advertising Design, Aesthetics, Art Education, Art History, Ceramics, Commercial Art, Conceptual Art, Constructions, Costume Design & Construction, Drawing, Fashion Arts, Film, Goldsmithing, Graphic Arts, Graphic Design, Handicrafts, Illustration, Industrial Design, Intermedia, Interior Design, Jewelry, Mixed Media, Museum Staff Training, Painting, Photography, Printmaking, Sculpture, Silversmithing, Stage Design, Teacher Training, Textile Design, Theatre Arts, Video, Editorial Design, Selected Studies, Weaving
Children's Classes: Courses—General Art
Summer School: Enrl 100. Courses—Ceramics, Drawing, Film, Freshman's Core Prog, Painting, Sculpture, Textile Arts, Visual Communications
—**Department of Art History,** 441 Hall of Languages, 13210. Tel 315-423-4184. *Chmn* David Tatham, PhD; *Prof* Alison Luchs, PhD; *Instr* Meredith Lillich, PhD; *Instr* Ellen Oppler, PhD; *Instr* Sidney Thomas, PhD; *Vis Prof* Rab Hatfield, art history - 1979-80
Estab 1870, dept estab 1946; pvt; D & E; ent req HS dipl, SAT; degrees BA 4 yrs, MA 1-2 yrs, PhD 3-6 yrs; scholarships; LC 25, GC 12; enrl non-maj 750, maj 50, grad 20
Tuition: Res—undergrad $4500 per yr, $2250 per sem, grad $150 per cr; campus res available
Courses: †History of Art & Archaeology

TARRYTOWN

MARYMOUNT COLLEGE, Art Department, 10591. Tel 914-631-3200. *Chmn* Bianca Haglich, MA; *Prof* John Lochtefeld, MFA; *Assoc Prof* John Hull; *Assoc Prof* Robert J Lee; *Asst Prof* Jane Henle, PhD; *Asst Prof* Marilyn Picard
Estab 1918; pvt; D & E; ent req HS dipl, CEEB; degrees BA and BS 4 yrs; schol; SC 42, LC 15; enrl D 285, E 25, maj 32
Tuition: Res—undergrad $6020 per yr; non-res—undergrad $3530 per yr; PT student $111 per hr; campus res—room board $2490 per yr
Courses: Advertising Design, Art Education, Art History, Ceramics, Costume Design & Construction, Drawing, Fashion Arts, Film, Handicrafts, Illustration, Interior Design, Jewelry, Mixed Media, Painting, Photography, Printmaking, Sculpture, Stage Design, Teacher Training, Textile Design, Theatre Arts, Stitchery, Weaving
Summer School: Dir, Margaret Ellen Flannelly. Tui $67 per cr. Courses—American Architecture, Mixed Media (Art, Vision and Form), Raku - Japanese Ceramics

TROY

EMMA WILLARD SCHOOL ARTS DIVISION, Pawling Avenue, 12180. Tel 518-274-4440, Ext 482. *Div Chmn* Pat Peterson, MA; *Chmn Art Dept* Chris Leith, BFA; *Chmn Music Dept* Russell F Locke, MA; *Instructor* Elaine Mara; *Instructor* Ron Skorton; *Instructor* Cornelia Thayer; *Instructor* Mark Van Wormer, BA; *Instructor* Christine Zimmerman, MA
Estab 1814, dept estab 1969; pvt; D & E; schol
Tuition: $6400 including room and board; day student $3025 per yr
Courses: Art History, Ceramics, Drawing, Jewelry, Photography, Theatre Arts, Advanced Studio Art, Dance, Music, Spinning and Natural Dyeing, Visual Arts Foundation, Weaving

RENSSELAER POLYTECHNIC INSTITUTE
—**School of Architecture,** 12181. Tel 518-270-6460. *Dean* Patrick J Quinn. Instrs FT 17, PT 7
EStab 1929; pvt; D; degrees BArchit, BS, MArchit and MS 4-5 yrs; scholarships; enrl 230
Tuition: $4790 per yr; campus res
Courses: Architecture, Building Science
—**Department of Art,** School of Humanities and Social Science, 12181. *Chmn* Ernest F Livingstone
Courses: Ceramics, Drawing, Painting, Sculpture, Color and Design

RUSSELL SAGE COLLEGE, Visual and Performing Arts Department,* 203 Second St, 12180. Tel 518-270-2000. *Chmn* Marjorie Semerad
Pvt, W; ent req HS grad; degrees fine arts and divisional maj in Music, Art and Drama 4 yrs; enrl 20-40 per class
Tuition: Res—undergrad $3600 per yr full time, $120 per cr part time, $115 per cr part time grad; campus res—room and board $2090 per yr

UTICA

MOHAWK VALLEY COMMUNITY COLLEGE, Advertising Design and Production, 1101 Sherman Dr, 13510. Tel 315-792-5446. *Pres* George H Robertson, PhD; *Head Dept* Milton Richards, PhD; *Asst Prof* Henry Godlewski; *Asst Prof* James O'Looney; *Instructor* Robert Duffek, BA; *Instructor* Karen Faryniak, BFA; *Instructor* Cheryl Fogarty, BFA; *Instructor* James Mannino, BS; *Instructor* Babette Martino, MFA; *Instructor* Kenneth Murphy, BA. Instrs FT 9, PT 2
Estab 1947, dept estab 1955; pub; D & E; ent req HS dipl; degrees AAS 2 yrs; SC 18 (over 2 yr period), LC 6 (over 2 yr period); enrl D 260, E varies, maj 260
Tuition: $750 per yr; campus residency available
Courses: †Advertising Design, †Drawing, †Graphic Arts, Photography
Adult Hobby Classes: Tui varies per quarter. Courses—Air Brush, Painting, Photography, Sketching, Watercolor

MUNSON-WILLIAMS-PROCTOR INSTITUTE, School of Art, 310 Genesee St, 13502. Tel 315-797-000. *Dir* John R Manning; *Dir Emer* William C Palmer. Instrs FT 12, PT 10
Estab 1941; pvt; degrees AS and BA; enrl adults 650, HS students 75, children 700 (350 summer, 350 winter)
Courses: Ceramics, Drawing, Graphic Arts, Painting, Photography, Sculpture, Dance, Enameling, Introduction to Visual Arts, Metal Arts, Pottery
Summer School: Courses—four morning classes per wk for 4 wks, classes on Tues & Thurs afternoon or E for 4 wks

UTICA COLLEGE OF SYRACUSE UNIVERSITY, Division of Humanities, Burrstone Rd, 13502. Tel 315-792-3057. *Chairperson Div* John Cormican, PhD; *Coordr Div* Edween Ham, PhD; *Dir Munson-Williams-Proctor School of Art* John Manning, BFA; *Instr* Vincent Clemente, MFA; *Instr* Francis Fiorentino, MFA; *Instr* John Loy, MFA; *Instr* Marjorie Salzillo, MFA; *Vis Prof* Ralph Goings, paint - 1978; *Vis Prof* Fred Mitchell, paint - 1978
Estab 1946, school of art estab 1973; pvt; D; degrees BA(Fine Arts) 4 yrs; SC 20, LC 7; enrl school of Art D 94, Utica College maj 14
Tuition: Res and nonres $3735; campus res—room & board $1810
Courses: Art History, †Ceramics, Drafting, Drawing, Film, Graphic Arts, Occupational Therapy, †Painting, Photography, †Sculpture, Stage Design, Theatre Arts, Video, Design

WATERTOWN

JEFFERSON COMMUNITY COLLEGE, Art Department, PO Box 473, 13601. Tel 315-782-5250. *Pres* John T Henderson; *Prof* Klaus Ebeling. Instrs FT 1
Estab 1963; pub; D & E; degrees 2 yr; SC 2, LC 1; enrl 850 (total)
Courses: Art History, Photography, Sculpture, Art Appreciation, Film Appreciation, Snow Sculpture, Two-Dimensional Studio

WHITE PLAINS

PACE UNIVERSITY, WHITE PLAINS, Division of Arts and Letters, 78 N Broadway, 10603. Tel 914-682-7070. *Chmn* Carol B Gartner. Instrs PT 2
Pvt; D & E; ent req HS dipl; SC 4, LC 4
Courses: Art Education, Drawing, Graphic Arts, History of Art & Archaeology, Painting, Photography, Stage Design, Theatre Arts
Summer School: Dir, Sister M Berchmanns Coyle. Courses—Painting

WESTCHESTER ART WORKSHOP, County Center, 10607. Tel 914-682-2481. *Dir* Paul E Lohner, MA
Estab 1926; pub; D & E; ent req no special req; degrees none; SC 60 per sem, 3 sem per yr; enrl D 450, E 250, others 700 (no credits given for courses)
Tuition: $63 per 3 hr, $42 per 2 hr; two 14 wk sem and one 7 wk sem; no campus res
Courses: Calligraphy, Ceramics, Drawing, Interior Design, Jewelry, Painting, Photography, Printmaking, Sculpture, Silversmithing
Children's Classes: Courses—Ceramics, Handicrafts, Jewelry, Painting
Summer School: Enrl 700; tui same for term of 7 wks beginning June 26th. Courses —same

YONKERS

ELIZABETH SETON COLLEGE, Art Department, 10701. Tel 914-969-4000. *Chmn* Sr Margaret Beaudette, MFA; *Assoc Prof* Sr Regina Kraft, MFA; *Instructor* Robin Landa
Estab 1960; pvt; D, E & weekends; ent req HS dipl; degrees AS, AAS and AOS; schol; SC 15, LC 3; enrl D 30, E 20, maj 25
Tuition: Res—undergrad $3800 per yr; non-res—undergrad $2200 per yr; campus res —room and board $1600 per yr
Courses: Advertising Design, Art History, Calligraphy, Ceramics, Drawing, Fashion Arts, Film, Interior Design, Jewelry, Lettering, Painting, Printmaking, Sculpture
Adult Hobby Classes: Enrl 60. Courses—Calligraphy, Chinese Painting, Etching, Frame Making, Painting

NORTH CAROLINA

ASHEVILLE

UNIVERSITY OF NORTH CAROLINA AT ASHEVILLE, Dept of Art & Music, University Heights, 28804. Tel 704-258-0200. *Prof* S Tucker Cooke, MFA; *Instructor* Tony Bradley, MFA; *Instructor* Elma Johnson, MFA; *Instructor* Jos Vandermeer, MFA
Estab 1927, dept estab 1965; pub; D & E; ent req HS dipl, ent exam; degrees BA 4-5 yrs; scholarships; SC 20, LC 5; enrl D 1280, E 300, non-maj 50, maj 40
Tuition: Res—undergrad $460 yr, $230 sem, $17 PT; nonres—undergrad $1115 yr, $90 PT; campus residence available
Courses: Art Education, Art History, Ceramics, Commercial Art, Costume Design & Construction, Drawing, Graphic Arts, Intermedia, Jewelry, Mixed Media, Painting, Photography, Printmaking, Sculpture, Stage Design, Theatre Arts
Summer School: Dir, S Tucker Cooke. Courses vary

BELMONT

SACRED HEART COLLEGE, Department of Art,* Main St, 28012. Tel 704-825-5146. *Chmn* Sr M Theophane Field, MFA
Estab 1935, dept estab 1966; pvt & den; D; ent req HS dipl, ent exam; degrees BA and BS 4 yrs, AA 2 yrs; SC 30, LC 3; enrl maj 27, others 50
Tuition: Res—undergrad $2960 per yr, $55 per sem hr; nonres—undergrad $1610 per yr; campus res available
Courses: Graphic Arts, Graphic Design, Jewelry, Mixed Media, Painting, Photography, Printmaking

BOONE

APPALACHIAN STATE UNIVERSITY, Department of Art,* 28608. Tel 704-262-2000. *Chmn* Noyer C Long
Estab 1960; pub; D; ent req HS dipl, ent exam; degrees BA and BS (commercial design, art educ, studio art) 4 yrs; scholarships; SC 38, LC 10, GC 12; enrl D 1000, maj 236, grad 5
Tuition: Res—undergrad $294.75, grad $302.25; nonres—undergrad $1154.75, grad $1162.25
Courses: Art Education, Ceramics, Commercial Art, Drawing, Graphic Arts, Graphic Design, Handicrafts, History of Art & Archaeology, Jewelry, Lettering, Painting, Photography, Sculpture, Teacher Training, Art Appreciation, Fabric Design
Summer School: Dir, L F Edwards. Enrl 300; term of 2, 4 & 6 wks beginning May-Aug. Courses—per regular session

BREVARD

BREVARD COLLEGE, Div of Fine Arts, 28712. Tel 704-883-8292. *Chmn* Dr John D Upchurch; *Assoc Prof* Timothy G Murray, MACA; *Instructor* Cheryl Harrison
Estab 1853; den; D & E; ent req HS dipl; degrees AFA 2 yrs; scholarships; SC 12, LC 2
Tuition: Res—undergrad $2600 per yr; nonres—undergrad $3200 per yr
Courses: Art History, Ceramics, Drawing, Film, Graphic Arts, Graphic Design, Painting, Photography, Printmaking, Theatre Arts
Summer School: Courses vary

CHAPEL HILL

UNIVERSITY OF NORTH CAROLINA AT CHAPEL HILL, Art Department, 104 Ackland Art Center 003A, 27514. Tel 919-933-2015. *Chmn* Jay Richard Judson, PhD; *Asst Chmn Studio Art* Richard Kinnaird, MFA; *Asst Chmn Undergrad Study* Mike Cindric, MFA; *Asst Chmn Grad Study* Arthur S Marks, PhD; *Prof* Robert Barnard, MFA; *Prof* Jaroslav Folda, PhD; *Prof* Robert Howard, MA; *Prof* Frances Huemer, PhD; *Prof* J Richard Judson, PhD; *Prof* Marvin Saltzman, MFA; *Assoc Prof* Richard Shiff, PhD; *Vis Lectr* Ronald Kraver, printmaking - 1979-1980; *Vis Lectr* Jenifer Neils, Greek and Roman art - 1979-1980; *Vis Lectr* Lauren Weingarden, modern art history - 1979-1980
Estab 1793, dept estab 1943; pub; D; ent req HS dipl, SAT; degrees BA, BS and BFA 4 yrs, MFA and MA(Art History) 2 yrs, PhD(Art History) to 8 yrs; scholarships; SC 15, LC 15, GC 10; enrl D 200 undergrad, 65 grad
Tuition: Res—undergrad $288 per sem, grad $286 per sem; nonres—undergrad $1143 per sem, grad $1141; campus res available
Courses: Art History, Ceramics, Drawing, Painting, Printmaking, Sculpture
Summer School: Chmn, Arthur S Marks. Term of 5 wks beginning May 19. Courses —various art history and studio courses

CHARLOTTE

QUEENS COLLEGE, Art Dept, 1900 Selwyn Ave, 28207. Tel 704-332-7121. *Head* Ben Pfingstag. Instrs FT 3, PT 1
Estab 1857; den, W; degrees granted; scholarships; SC 19, LC 7
Courses: Art History, Ceramics, Commercial Art

UNIVERSITY OF NORTH CAROLINA-CHARLOTTE, Creative Arts Dept, UNCC Station, 28223. Tel 704-597-2471. *Chmn* Joseph R Spence, DEd; *Prof* Eric Anderson, MFA; *Prof* Ronald Booth, PhD; *Assoc Prof* Clyde Appleton, PhD; *Assoc Prof* William Dailey, PhD; *Assoc prof* Robert Gehner, MM; *Assoc Prof* Robert Glazer, MEd; *Assoc Prof* Esther Hill, MA; *Assoc Prof* Michael Kampen, PhD; *Assoc Prof* Roderick MacKillop, MFA; *Assoc Prof* William Rackley, MA; *Assoc Prof* Roland Ree, PhD; *Assoc Prof* Gerda Zimmermann; *Asst Prof* Jack Beasley, MA; *Asst Prof* Edwina Bringle; *Asst Prof* Donald Byrum, MFA; *Asst Prof* Robert Crogahn, BA; *Asst Prof* Jane Dillard, MEd; *Asst Prof* Jan Loyd, MFA; *Asst Prof* Patricia McLaney, MA; *Asst Prof* Michael Mosley, MM; *Asst Prof* Pamela Sofras, MEd; *Asst Prof* Martha Strawn, MFA; *Asst Prof* Joan Tweedy, MFA; *Asst Prof* Thomas Turner, MM; *Instructor* Richard Kennedy, MM; *Lectr* Constance Welsh, BFA
Estab 1965, dept estab 1971; pub; D & E; ent req HS dipl, SAT, Col Boards; degrees BCA 4 yrs; SC 25, LC 3; enrl D 670, non-maj 500, maj 185
Tuition: Res—undergrad $268 per sem; nonres—undergrad $1134 per sem; campus residence available
Courses: Art Education, Ceramics, Costume Design & Construction, Drawing, Graphic Arts, Jewelry, Painting, Photography, Printmaking, Sculpture, Silversmithing, Stage Design, Fibers, Metalsmithing, Performing Arts, Weaving

CONCORD

BARBER-SCOTIA COLLEGE, Art Department, 28025. Tel 704-786-5171. *Prof* Grady Garfield Miles, MA
Estab 1867; pvt den; D & E; ent req HS dipl, contact admissions office for other req; degrees BA and BS; SC 10, LC 5; enrl non-maj 100, maj 1
Courses: Aesthetics, Art Education, Art History, Ceramics, Collage, Commercial Art, Constructions, Display, Drawing, Film, Graphic Arts, Graphic Design, Handicrafts, History of Art & Archaeology, Illustration, Intermedia, Interior Design, Lettering, Mixed Media, Occupational Therapy, Painting, Photography, Printmaking, Sculpture, Teacher Training, African Art, Afro-American Art

CULLOWHEE

WESTERN CAROLINA UNIVERSITY, Dept of Art, Belk Bldg, 28723. Tel 704-293-7210. *Head Dept* Evan R Firestone, PhD; *Assoc Prof* Lee P Budahl, PhD; *Assoc Prof* Perry Kelly, EdD; *Assoc Prof* James E Smith, MFA; *Asst Prof* William C Buchanan, MFA; *Asst Prof* Joan F Byrd, MFA; *Asst Prof* William R Lidh, MFA; *Asst Prof* Theodore P Matus, MFA; *Asst Prof* David Nichols, MFA; *Asst Prof* F Duane Oliver, MA; *Instructor* Judith Duffey, PhD; *Instructor* Wade Hobgood, MFA
Estab 1889, dept estab 1968; pub; D & E; ent req HS dipl, SAT & C average in HS; degrees BFA, BA & BSE 4 yrs, art honors studio; SC 36, LC 12; enrl non-maj 1200 per sem, maj 150
Tuition: Res—undergrad and grad $310 per yr, $155 per sem; nonres—undergrad and grad $2048 per yr, $1024 per sem; campus res—room & board $1090 per yr
Courses: Art Education, Art History, Ceramics, Commercial Art, Drawing, Graphic Design, Handicrafts, Illustration, Jewelry, Lettering, Painting, Photography, Printmaking, Sculpture, Teacher Training, Glass Blowing
Summer School: Dir, Dr Jerry Rice. Tui $14 per sem hr for summer beginning June 19. Courses—Glassblowing, Introductory Studio Courses, Workshops in Primitive Pottery, Wheel Throwing & Techniques

DALLAS

GASTON COLLEGE, Art Department,* New Dallas Highway, 28034. Tel 704-922-3136. *Head* Franklin U Creech
Estab 1965; pub; D & E; ent req HS dipl; degrees AA and AFA 2 yrs; SC 22, LC 3; enrl D 140, E 50, maj 50
Courses: Art Education, Ceramics, Drawing, Graphic Arts, Handicrafts, History of Art & Archaeology, Jewelry, Painting, Sculpture, Stage Design, Theatre Arts
Adult Hobby Classes: Courses—Ceramics, Jewelry, Macrame, Weaving
Summer School: Dir, Franklin U Creech. Enrl 20; term of 11 wks beginning June. Courses—Design, Drawing, Painting, Pottery, Sculpture

DAVIDSON

DAVIDSON COLLEGE, Art Dept, Main St, 28036. Tel 704-892-2000. *Chmn* Herb Jackson, MFA; *Asst Prof* Melinda K Lesher, PhD; *Asst Prof* Larry L Ligo, PhD; *Instructor* Russell Warren, MFA
Estab 1837, dept estab 1950; pvt & den; D; ent req Col Boards, HS transcripts; degrees BA & BS 4 yrs; scholarships; SC 12, LC 9; enrl non-maj 300, maj 6
Tuition: $5000 per yr (comprehensive fee); campus res—room & board fee included in tuition
Courses: Aesthetics, Art History, Collage, Conceptual Art, Drawing, Graphic Design, History of Art & Archaeology, Painting, Printmaking, Theatre Arts

DURHAM

DUKE UNIVERSITY, Department of Art, 112 East Duke Bldg, 27708. *Chmn Dept* John R Spencer, PhD; *Assoc Prof* W K Stars, MA; *Asst Prof* Ann Epstein, PhD; *Asst Prof* Rona Goffen, PhD; *Asst Prof* Duncan Kinkead, PhD; *Asst Prof* Vernon Pratt, MFA; *Instr* Frank Smullin, MFA
Pvt; D; ent req HS dipl & ent exam; degrees MA 4 yrs; SC 7, LC 30, GC 10; enrl D 496, non-maj 467, maj 29
Tuition: Campus residency available
Courses: Art Education, Art History, Ceramics, Conceptual Art, Drawing, Painting, Photography, Printmaking, Sculpture

NORTH CAROLINA CENTRAL UNIVERSITY, Art Dept, Fayetteville St, 27707. Tel 919-683-6391, 683-6062. *Chmn* Lana T Henderson, PhD; *Prof* Melvin Carver, MPD; *Prof* Mohinder Gill, EdD; *Prof* Caryle Johnson, MFA; *Prof* Robert Kennedy, MFA; *Prof* Isabell Levitt, MFA; *Prof* Norman Pendergraft, MA; *Prof* Mercedes Thompson, MA
Estab 1910, dept estab 1944; pub; D & E; ent req HS dipl, SAT; degrees in Art Educ, Visual Communications & Studio Art 4 yrs; SC 30, LC 11; enrl D 120, E 30, non-maj 1678, maj 120
Tuition: Res—undergrad $421.50 yr; nonres—undergrad $1800 yr; campus res $2041.50-$2854.50 per yr
Courses: †Advertising Design, †Art Education, Art History, Ceramics, Commercial Art, Drawing, Graphic Arts, Handicrafts, Illustration, Jewelry, Lettering, Painting, Printmaking, Sculpture, Teacher Training
Summer School: Dir, Dr W Maynor. Tui $225 for term of 9 wks. Courses—Art Appreciation, Crafts, Design, Drawing, Painting

ELIZABETH CITY

ELIZABETH CITY STATE UNIVERSITY, Department of Art,* Parkview Dr, 27909. Tel 919-335-0551. *Chmn* Dr Vincent J de Gregorio, PhD; *Assoc Prof* Dr Mohinder S Gill, EDD; *Instr* Eugene O'Neal, MFA; *Instr* Dan M Pearce, MED
Estab 1891, dept 1961; pub; D & E; ent req HS dipl, portfolio; degrees BS 4 yrs; SC 27, LC 18, advance courses in Studio and History of Art; enrl D 1650, E 455, non-maj 1500, maj 55
Tuition: Res—undergrad $340 per yr; nonres—grad $1082 per yr; campus residence available
Courses: Art Education, Art History, Ceramics, Drawing, Graphic Arts, Handicrafts, History of Art & Archaeology, Lettering, Mixed Media, Painting, Printmaking, Sculpture, Teacher Training
Summer School: Dir, Edyth B Cole. Enrl 950; tui $45 per credit for term of 4 1 2 wks beginning May. Courses—same as regular session

FAYETTEVILLE

FAYETTEVILLE STATE UNIVERSITY,* 1200 Murchison Rd, 28301. Tel 919-486-1111. *Chmn* Harvey C Jenkins
Estab 1877; pub; D & E; ent req HS dipl, ent exam; enrl D 60, E 20
Tuition: Res—undergrad $1648 yr; nonres—undergrad $3074 per yr
Courses: Advertising Design, Aesthetics, Art Education, Ceramics, Drawing, Graphic Arts, Handicrafts, History of Art & Archaeology, Lettering, Painting, Photography, Sculpture, Leather Craft, Weaving
Summer School: Dir, Dr Ronald Smith. Courses—Art in Childhood Education, Arts & Crafts, Drawing, Photography, Survey of Art

METHODIST COLLEGE, Art Dept, Raleigh Rd, 28301. Tel 919-488-7110, Ext 257. Instrs FT 2, PT 1
Estab 1960; den; D & E; ent req HS dipl, SAT; degrees BA & BS 4 yrs; scholarships; SC 6, LC 4; enrl D 650, maj 22
Tuition: $1800 yr; campus res—room & board $1490
Courses: Art Education, Art History, Drawing, Graphic Arts, Handicrafts, Painting, Photography, Sculpture, Weaving
Summer School: 3 terms, 3 wk early session, 5 wk main session, 6 wk directed study. Courses—Art Appreciation, Painting, Sculpture, others as needed

GOLDSBORO

GOLDSBORO ART CENTER, 901A E Ash St, 27530. Tel 919-736-3335. *Instructor* Gloria Hasselbach, BA; *Instructor* Jim Morgan, BFA; *Instructor* Sara Paddison, BFA. Instrs PT 14
Estab 1971; pub; D & E; scholarships; SC 25; enrl D 150, E 60, others 210
Tuition: $5 for adults, $18 for children per quarter
Courses: Calligraphy, Drawing, Handicrafts, Painting, Printmaking
Adult Hobby Classes: Enrl 180 per quarter; tui $5 per quarter. Courses—Calligraphy, Drawing, Interior Design, Painting, Pottery, Printmaking, Watercolor, Woodcarving
Children's Classes: Enrl 30 per quarter; tui $18 per quarter. Courses—Discovering Art, Drawing, Painting, Pottery

GREENSBORO

GREENSBORO COLLEGE, Department of Art, 815 W Market St, 27420. Tel 919-272-7102. *Chmn Dept* Robert Kowski, MFA; *Asst Prof* Jerry Bontrager, MFA
Estab 1838; pvt den; D; ent req HS dipl; degrees BFA and BA 4 yrs; scholarships; SC 15, LC 4; enrl D 50, non-maj 30, maj 20
Tuition: Res and nonres undergrad $2250 per yr; campus res—room & board $1390 per yr
Courses: †Art Education, Art History, Ceramics, Drawing, †Painting, †Sculpture
Summer School: Greensboro Regional Consortium Dir, Dr William Lanier. Tui $75 per hr for term of 5 wks beginning May 12. Courses—Art Appreciation, Art History, Ceramics, others

NORTH CAROLINA AGRICULTURAL AND TECHNICAL STATE UNIVERSITY, Art Department,* 312 N Dudley St, 27411. Tel 919-379-7500. *Chmn* LeRoy F Holmns. Instrs FT 4, PT 1
Estab 1930; pub; SC 29, LC 7; enrl maj 150
Courses: Art Education, Art History, Ceramics, Commercial Art, Drawing, Graphic Arts, Handicrafts, Painting, Art Design, Three-Dimensional Design, Two-Dimensional Design
Summer School: 6 wk and 2 wk sessions

UNIVERSITY OF NORTH CAROLINA AT GREENSBORO, Art Dept, 27412. Tel 919-379-5248. *Head* Dr Joan Gregory, EdD; *Prof* Peter Agostini; *Prof* Gilbert Carpenter; *Assoc Prof* Walter Barker, MFA; *Assoc Prof* Carl Goldstein, PhD; *Asst Prof* Jo Alice Leeds, PhD; *Asst Prof* Roberta Rice, PhD. Instrs FT 22, PT 4
Dept estab 1935; pub; ent req HS grad, ent exam; degrees BA, BFA, MEd & MFA 4 yrs; SC 22, LC 6, GC 8; enrl D 1000, non-maj 750, maj 250, grad 60
Tuition: Res—undergrad $364 per yr; non-res—undergrad $2082 per yr; campus res—room & board $1300-$1700 per yr
Courses: Art History, Ceramics, Drawing, Graphic Arts, Lettering, Painting, Photography, Printmaking, Sculpture, Teacher Training, Fibers
Summer School: Dir, Dr Jean Eason. Enrl 225; beginning May - June and July - Aug. Courses—Art History, Drawing, Etching, Fibers, Jewelry, Moldmaking-Metal Casting, Painting, Photography, Picture Composition, Sculpture, Watercolor

GREENVILLE

EAST CAROLINA UNIVERSITY, School of Art, 27834. Tel 919-758-6665. *Dean* Dr Richard H Laing; *Chmn Drawing & Painting* ; *Chmn Sculpture* Robert S Edmiston, MFA; *Chmn Art Educ* William H Holley, EdD; *Chmn Printmaking* Donald R Sexauer, MA; *Chmn Ceramics* Charles F Chamberlain, MFA; *Chmn Design* Sara Edmiston, MA; *Chmn Communication Arts* Arthur Robert Rasch, MA; *Chmn Interior Design* Melvin S Stanforth, MFA; *Chmn Art History* Frances P Daugherty, PhD. Instrs FT 36, PT 12
Estab 1946; pub; ent req HS dipl, 15 units, Col Board Exam; degrees AB, BS, BFA, MA & MFA 4 yrs; SC 131, LC 29, GC 112; enrl maj 736
Tuition: Res—$141; nonres—$965; campus residence available
Courses: Art Education, Art History, Ceramics, Interior Design, Painting, Printmaking, Sculpture, Communication Arts, Design
Summer School: Dir, Dr Susan McDaniel; Art Dir, Dr Richard H Laing. Enrl 13,800 for 10 wks beginning June

HICKORY

LENOIR RHYNE COLLEGE, Department of Art, 28601. Tel 704-328-1741. *Head Dept* Dr Marion Love, PhD; *Asst Prof* Margaret Berry, MA; *Asst Prof* Douglas Burton, MA
Estab 1892, dept estab 1976; den; D & E; ent req HS dipl; degrees AB and BS 4 yrs; scholarships; SC 5; enrl D 1200, E 350
Tuition: Res—undergrad $2672 per yr; campus res—room & board $1282 per yr
Courses: Aesthetics, Art Education, Art History, Ceramics, Drawing, History of Art & Archaeology, Painting, Sculpture
Summer School: Dir, Dr Robert Spuller. Enrl 900; tui $42 per sem hr for 2-5 wk terms beginning June. Courses—Art Appreciation, Art Educ

HIGH POINT

HIGH POINT COLLEGE, Fine Arts Department,* Montlieu Ave, 27262. Tel 919-885-5101. *Chmn* Dr James Elson
Estab 1924, dept estab 1956; pvt den; D & E; ent req HS dipl, SAT; degrees AB and BS 4 yrs; scholarships; SC 16, LC 6; enrl non-maj 400, maj 35
Tuition: Res—undergrad $2600 per yr, $1300 per sem; nonres—undergrad $1450 per yr, $725 per sem; campus residence available
Courses: Advertising Design, Aesthetics, Art Education, Art History, Ceramics, Costume Design & Construction, Drawing, Film, History of Art & Archaeology, Museum Staff Training, Painting, Printmaking, Sculpture, Stage Design, Teacher Training, Theatre Arts
Summer School: Dean, David Cole. Courses—general college courses

JAMESTOWN

GUILFORD TECHNICAL INSTITUTE, Commercial Art Dept, PO Box 309, 27260. Tel 919-454-1126, Ext 224. *Head* Norman D Faircloth, MEd Art; *Instructor* Ralph E Calhoun, MEd Art; *Instructor* Frederick N Jones, BFA; *Instructor* Robert B Mahan, MA; *Instructor* F Eugene Stafford, BFA; *Instructor* N Jeanne Ward, AAS
Estab 1964; pub; D & E; ent req HS dipl, English & math placement; degrees AAS 2 yrs; scholarships; SC 20, LC 4; enrl D 70, E 60
Tuition: Res—undergrad $3.25 hr up to $45.50 per quarter; nonres—undergrad $16.50 hr up to $204.50 per quarter; no campus res available
Courses: Advertising Design, Art History, †Commercial Art, Drafting, Drawing, Graphic Arts, Illustration, Lettering, Painting, Photography, Video
Adult Hobby Classes: Tui $5 per quarter. Courses—Variety of subjects

LAURINBURG

SAINT ANDREWS PRESBYTERIAN COLLEGE, Art Program, 28352. Tel 919-276-3652, Ext 315. Instrs FT 2
Estab 1960; den; D; ent req HS dipl, SAT, 2.6 grade point average, 12 academic units; degrees BA, MS & BM 4 yrs or 32 courses; scholarships; SC 14, LC 2; enrl D 852, maj 15-20
Courses: Aesthetics, Art Education, Art History, Drawing, Painting, Sculpture, Stage Design
Summer School: Studio courses offered

LEXINGTON

DAVIDSON COUNTY COMMUNITY COLLEGE, Language-Fine Arts Dept, Old Greensboro Rd, PO Box 1287, 27292. Tel 704-249-8186, Ext 247. *Chmn* Antoinette Wike, MA; *Instructor* Camille Lawrence, MA; *Instructor* Katherine Montgomery, MFA. Instrs FT 2, PT 3
Estab 1963, dept estab 1966; pub; D & E; ent req HS dipl; degrees AFA & AA 2 yrs; scholarships; SC 14, LC 4; enrl D 100. E 30, non-maj 195, maj 35
Tuition: Res—undergrad $39 per quarter; no campus res available
Courses: Art Education, Art History, Ceramics, Drafting, Handicrafts, Painting, Printmaking, Sculpture, Design, Independent Studio
Adult Hobby Classes: Courses—Variety taught through continuing education

MARS HILL

MARS HILL COLLEGE, 28754. *Chmn* Joe Chris Robertson, MFA; *Prof* Stephen Wing, MA; *Assoc Prof* Gordon Mahy, MFA
Estab 1856, dept estab 1932; pvt and den; D & E; ent req HS dipl, ent exam; degrees BA 4 yrs; scholarships; SC 9, LC 6; enrl D 130, non-maj 88, maj 42
Tuition: Undergrad $3300 yr, $1650 per sem incl room & board
Courses: Advertising Design, Aesthetics, †Art Education, †Art History, Ceramics, †Graphic Arts, †Painting, Photography, Printmaking, Sculpture, Teacher Training, Theatre Arts
Summer School: Dir of Admissions, Dr John Hough. Enrl 400; tui $450 for term of 6 wks beginning May 31. Courses—Aesthetics, Art Education, Photography, Pottery

MISENHEIMER

PFEIFFER COLLEGE, Art Program, 28109. Tel 704-463-7343. *Dir* James Haymaker. Instrs FT 1
Estab 1965; den; D; ent req HS dipl; scholarships; SC 4, LC 4; enrl D 100
Tuition: $2345 yr; other fees $385; campus res $1450
Courses: Art Education, Art History, Ceramics, Drawing, Painting, Sculpture

MOUNT OLIVE

MOUNT OLIVE COLLEGE, Department of Art,* Breazeale Ave, 28365. Tel 919-658-2502.
Estab 1951; den; D & E; degrees AA and AS; scholarships; SC 5, LC 3
Tuition: Res—undergrad $2650 per yr; campus residence available
Courses: Art History, Ceramics, Drawing, Painting, Art Appreciation, Color and Design, Three-Dimensional Design

MURFREESBORO

CHOWAN COLLEGE, Division of Art, Jones Dr, 27855. Tel 919-398-4101, Ext 267. *Head Div* David W Parker, MFA; *Prof* Rinda M Metz, MFA; *Prof* Stanley A Mitchell, MA
Estab 1848, dept estab 1970; den; D; ent req HS dipl, SAT recommended; degrees AA 2 yrs; scholarships; SC 10, LC 2; enrl D 90, maj 60
Tuition: Res—undergrad $3250 per yr includes room & board, $1625 per sem includes room & board; non-res—undergrad $3400 per yr includes room & board, $1700 per sem includes room & board; commuter $1595 per yr, $798 per sem
Courses: Advertising Design, Art History, Ceramics, †Commercial Art, Drafting, Drawing, Graphic Arts, Illustration, Lettering, Painting, Printmaking
Summer School: Dean, Dr Franklin B Lowe. Enrl approx 20; tui $50 per sem hr for term of 5 wks beginning June 9. Courses—Art Appreciation and Studio by demand

PEMBROKE

PEMBROKE STATE UNIVERSITY, Art Dept, Box 64, 28372. Tel 919-521-4214, Ext 216. *Chmn Dept* Paul VanZandt. Instrs FT 4, PT 1
Estab 1941; pub; ent req CEEB scores, HS record, scholastic standing in HS grad class, recommendation of HS guidance counselor & principal; degrees BA & BS 4 yrs; SC 30, LC 12; enrl maj 60
Courses: Art Education, Art History, Ceramics, Commercial Art, Drawing, Graphic Arts, Handicrafts, Jewelry, Painting, Photography, Sculpture, Design
Summer School: Variety of courses

PENLAND

PENLAND SCHOOL OF CRAFTS,* Penland Rd, 28765. Tel 704-765-2359. *Dir* William J Brown, MFA
Estab 1929; pvt; D (summer only); ent req age 18, special fall and spring sessions require portfolio and resume; degrees none granted but credit may be obtained through agreement with East Tennessee State Univ; scholarships; SC 10-20; enrl D approx 100
Tuition: $70 per wk for term of 2-3 wks; campus res—room & board $80 per wk
Courses: Ceramics, Handicrafts, Jewelry, Painting, Photography, Printmaking, Sculpture, Silversmithing, Textile Design

RALEIGH

MEREDITH COLLEGE, Art Department,* 27611. Tel 919-833-6461. *Chmn* Leonard White
Estab 1898; den, W; D & E; ent req HS dipl; degrees AB 4 yrs; scholarships; SC 15, LC 5; enrl D 250, E 40, maj 50, others 10
Tuition: $2100 per yr; campus res—room & board $1100 per yr
Courses: Art Education, Art History, Ceramics, Commercial Art, Costume Design & Construction, Drawing, Graphic Arts, Graphic Design, Painting, Photography, Sculpture
Adult Hobby Classes: Courses—Art History, Painting, Sculpture
Summer School: Dir, John Hiott. Courses—vary

NORTH CAROLINA STATE UNIVERSITY AT RALEIGH, School of Design, 27650. Tel 919-737-2201. *Dean* Claude E McKinney; *Dir Landscape Architecture* Arthur L Sullivan; *Dir Architecture* Martin Harms; *Dir Product Design Prog* Vincent M Foote; *Dir Design Fundamentals* Charles Joyner. Instrs FT 4, PT 3
Estab 1948; pub; ent req col board, ent exam; degrees BEnvDesign (in Architecture, Landscape Architecture, Product Design & Visual Design Option), MArch, MLandscape Arch, MUrb Design, MProduct Design 4-6 yrs; enrl Architecture 266, Landscape Architecture 77, Product Design 123
Tuition: Res—$582; nonres—$2294

PEACE COLLEGE, Art Department, 15 E Peace St, 27604. Tel 919-832-2881. *Head Dept* Linda Fitz-Simons, BA; *Instr* Pamela Lehnert, MA
Estab 1857; pvt; D; ent req HS dipl, SAT; degrees AA and AFA 2 yrs; SC 8, LC 2; enrl D 500
Tuition: Res and nonres $1830 per yr; campus res—room & board plus tui $3400-$3500 per yr
Courses: Art Education, Art History, Ceramics, Drawing, Fashion Arts, Graphic Design, History of Art & Archaeology, Painting, Sculpture, Theatre Arts

SAINT MARY'S COLLEGE,* 900 Hillsborough St, 27611. Tel 919-828-2521. *Chmn Dept* Margaret Click Williams, MFA; *Instr* Betty Adams, MAT
Estab 1842; pvt den; D; ent req HS dipl, SAT or PSAT; degrees AA; scholarships; SC 11, LC 2; enrl D 150
Tuition: Res—undergrad $2375 per yr, grad $4295 per yr; campus residence available
Courses: Art History, Ceramics, Drawing, Graphic Arts, Painting, Printmaking, Stage Design, Theatre Arts
Summer School: Dean of the College, Robert J Miller. Enrl varies; tui $200 for term of 3-5 wks beginning May or June. Courses—vary

STATESVILLE

MITCHELL COMMUNITY COLLEGE, Visual Art Dept, E Broad St, 28677. Tel 704-873-2201, Ext 202. *Acting Chmn* Donald Everett Moore, MA. Instrs FT 2, PT 8
Estab 1852, dept estab 1974; pub; D & E; ent req HS dipl, HS transcripts, Placement Test; degrees AA & AFA 2 yrs; scholarships; SC 12-15, LC 5; enrl D 85, E 25, non-maj 100, maj 30-35
Tuition: Nonres—undergrad $150 yr, $50 per sem, $8 per course part-time; no campus res available
Courses: Art History, †Ceramics, Collage, Drawing, Graphic Arts, Handicrafts, Intermedia, Jewelry, Mixed Media, †Painting, Photography, Printmaking, †Sculpture
Adult Hobby Classes: Tui $8 per 10 wks. Courses—Continuing education courses in art & crafts available
Summer School: Acting Chmn, Donald Everett Moore. Enrl 50; tui $50 for term of 10 wks beginning June 6. Courses—Varies, but same as courses listed above

SYLVA

SOUTHWESTERN TECHNICAL COLLEGE, Commercial Art & Advertising Design Dept, Webster Rd, PO Box 67, 28779. Tel 704-586-4091, Ext 233. *Head Dept* Bob Clark, MS; *Instructor* Karen Greenebaum, BFA. Instrs FT 2, PT 3
Estab 1964, dept estab 1967; pub; D; ent req HS dipl; degrees AAS; scholarships; SC 19, LC 14; enrl D 40, maj 40
Tuition: Res—undergrad $39 quarterly; nonres—undergrad $198 quarterly; no campus res
Courses: †Advertising Design, Art History, Calligraphy, †Commercial Art, Display, Drafting, Drawing, Fashion Arts, Graphic Arts, Graphic Design, Illustration, Lettering, Painting, Photography
Adult Hobby Classes: Enrl 30; tui $3.25 per quarter hr. Courses—Painting

WILKESBORO

WILKES COMMUNITY COLLEGE, Arts and Science Division, Drawer 120, 28697. Tel 919-667-7136, Ext 51 or 52. *Dir* Joseph R Austell, MS IE; *Instr* Sherrie Dancy, MS; *Instr* Ken Nelson, MS
Estab 1965, dept estab 1967; pub; D & E; ent req HS dipl; degrees AA, AFA; scholarships; SC 2, LC 2; enrl D 1600, E 800
Tuition: $39 per quarter; no campus res
Courses: Art History, Costume Design & Construction, Drafting, Drawing, Painting, †Theatre Arts
Summer School: Dir, Joseph D Austell

WILMINGTON

UNIVERSITY OF NORTH CAROLINA AT WILMINGTON, Art Department,*
PO Box 3725, 28406. Tel 919-791-4330. *Chmn* James K McGowan; *Asst Prof* Ann
Louise Conner, MA; *Asst Prof* Ralph Michael Goins, MA; *Instr* Bertram F Bradshaw,
MA; *Lectr* Christie R Pattison, MA
Estab 1789, dept estab 1952; pub; D & E; ent req HS dipl, ent exam; degrees BCA 4
yrs; scholarships
Tuition: Res $235; nonres $1113; campus res—room & board $675-$700
Courses: Art Education, Art History, Drawing, History of Art & Archaeology,
Jewelry, Mixed Media, Painting, Printmaking
Adult Hobby Classes: Courses—Drawing, Painting
Summer School: Two sessions. Courses—varied

WILSON

ATLANTIC CHRISTIAN COLLEGE, Art Dept, 27893. Tel 919-237-3161. *Chmn*
Edward Brown, MFA; *Assoc Prof* Norbert Irving, MFA; *Asst Prof* Thomas Marshall,
MA; *Asst Prof* Chris Wilson, MFA
Estab 1903, dept estab 1950; pvt; D & E; ent req HS dipl, ent exam; degrees BS, BA
& BFA 4 yrs; SC 13, LC 8; enrl D 68, E 5, non-maj 68, others 8 (PT)
Tuition: Undergrad $1510 yr, $755 per sem; campus res—room & board $950 yr
Courses: Advertising Design, Art Education, Art History, Ceramics, Commercial Art,
Display, Drawing, Graphic Arts, Graphic Design, Handicrafts, History of Art &
Archaeology, Illustration, Museum Staff Training, Painting, Photography,
Printmaking, Sculpture, Teacher Training, Textile Design, Theatre Arts
Adult Hobby Classes: Tui $75 audit per term. Courses—any adult can audit any studio
class
Summer School: Dir, Edward Brown. Enrl varies; tui $150 per course for term of 5
wks beginning May 29-June 30 & July 4-Aug 10. Courses—Art Survey, Art Education
Lab, Drawing

WINGATE

WINGATE COLLEGE, Division of Fine Arts,* 28174. Tel 704-233-4061. *Chmn Div*
Ronald Bentic
Estab 1896, dept estab 1958; den; D & E; ent req HS grad; degrees AA and AS 2 yr;
scholarships; enrl D 608, E 50
Tuition: $1690 average per yr, campus residency available
Courses: Art History, Ceramics, Drafting, Film, Handicrafts, Painting, Photography,
Art Appreciation, Composition, Gallery Tours, Introduction to Fine Arts, Sketching
Children's Classes: Art courses
Summer School: Pres, Dr Thomas E Corts. Term of 5 wks beginning first wk in June.
Courses—all regular class work available if demand warrants

WINSTON-SALEM

ARTS AND CRAFTS ASSOCIATION, INC, 610 Coliseum Dr, 27106. Tel
919-723-7395. *Pres* Al Rufty; *Dir* Randy Williams
Estab 1953
Courses: Photography, Clay, Fiber
Adult Hobby Classes: Classes on all levels of skill offered in art and craft areas;
professional level short-term workshops offered 3 times per yr
Children's Classes: Offered on Sat mornings
Summer School: Invitational Summer Art Honors Prog for junior-senior high students

SALEM COLLEGE, Art Department,* 27108. Tel 919-721-2683. *Assoc Prof* William
Mangum
Den, W; D; ent req HS Dipl; degrees BA 4 yrs; scholarships; enrl D 642, maj 44
Tuition: Res—$5000 per yr, includes room and board
Courses: Art Education, Art History, Ceramics, Drawing, Graphic Arts, Painting,
Sculpture

WAKE FOREST UNIVERSITY, Department of Art, Box 7232, 27109. Tel
919-761-5310, 761-5303 and 761-5302. *Chmn* Dr Robert Knott, PhD; *Assoc Prof*
Margaret Supplee Smith; *Asst Prof* Brian Legakis, PhD; *Asst Prof* Russell Sale; *Lectr*
Marvin S Coats, MFA; *Instr* Gary A Cook, MFA; *Instr* Andrew Polk III, MFA;
Gallery Dir Victor Faccinto
Estab 1834, dept estab 1968; pvt; D; ent req HS dipl, SAT; degrees BA 4 yrs;
scholarships; SC 14, LC 28; enrl D 250, non-maj 200, maj 50
Tuition: Res—undergrad $3970 yr, $1985 per sem, $85 per cr, grad $2750 yr, $90 per
cr; nonres—undergrad $2750 yr, $85 per cr; campus res—room & board $1220 (no
dormitory facilities are available on campus for grad students)
Courses: Aesthetics, Architecture, Art History, Drawing, Graphic Arts, Graphic
Design, History of Art & Archaeology, Painting, Printmaking, Sculpture
Summer School: Dir, Percival Perry. Enrl 25; tui $35 per cr, grad $45 per hr for term
of two 5 wk sessions beginning May 22 & June 26. Courses—Design, Drawing, Painting

WINSTON-SALEM STATE UNIVERSITY, Art Department, 27102. Tel
919-761-2090. *Chmn* Hayward L Ourbre, MFA; *Assoc Prof* Roland S Watts, MFA;
Asst Prof Mitzi Shewhake, MFA; *Asst Prof* Teresa Unseld, EdD
Estab, 1892, dept estab 1970; pub; D & E; ent req HS Dipl; degrees BA 4 yr; SC 10,
LC 7; enrl D 65, nonmaj 65
Tuition: Campus residence available
Courses: Art Education, Art History, Drawing, Graphic Arts, Painting, Sculpture

NORTH DAKOTA

DICKINSON

DICKINSON STATE COLLEGE, Department of Art, Div of Fine Arts and
Humanities, 58601. Tel 701-227-2312. *Chmn* Frank C Pearson, PhD; *Prof* Dennis
Edward Navrat, MFA; *Assoc Prof* Donald L Duda, MA; *Assoc Prof* Clinton A
Sheffield, MA
Estab 1918, dept estab 1959; pub; D & E; ent req HS dipl, out-of-state, ACT, minimum
score 18 or upper-half of class; degrees AA 2 yr, BA, BS and BCS 4 yr; scholarship;
SC 36, LC 8; enrl D approx 150 per quarter, non-maj 130, maj 20
Tuition: Res—undergrad $486 yr, $162 per quarter, $14 per quarter hr, $17 extension
per quarter hr; nonres—undergrad $1047 yr, $349 per quarter, $29 per quarter hr, $17
extension per quarter hr; campus res—room & board $1000 yr
Courses: Advertising Design, †Art Education, Art History, †Ceramics, Costume
Design & Construction, Display, Drawing, Goldsmithing, Graphic Design,
Handicrafts, Intermedia, Interior Design, †Jewelry, Lettering, †Painting,
Photography, †Printmaking, †Sculpture, Silversmithing, Stage Design, Teacher
Training, †Theatre Arts, Color, Enameling, Foundry, Leather, Mosaic, Plastics,
Serigraphy
Adult Hobby Classes: Above classes available for credit or audit
Summer School: VPres for Academic Affairs, Dr Paul Larsen. Enrl approx 200; tui
same as above for term of 2, 4 wks beginning June 2. Courses—Basic Art, Photography,
Watercolor, other division offerings

GRAND FORKS

UNIVERSITY OF NORTH DAKOTA, Visual Arts Department, College of Fine Art,
58202. Tel 701-777-2257. *Chmn* Ronald Schaefer. Instrs D FT 10
Estab 1883; pub; degrees BFA, BA, BSEd, MFA; SC 30, LC 4, GC 14; enrl maj 120,
others 1000
Tuition: Campus residency available
Courses: Art History, Ceramics, Drawing, Graphic Arts, Jewelry, Painting,
Printmaking, Sculpture, Teacher Training, Design, Fibers
Summer School: Chmn, Ronald Schaefer

JAMESTOWN

JAMESTOWN COLLEGE, Art Department, 58401. Tel 701-253-2517. *Chmn* Robert
Carter. Instrs FT 1, PT 2
Pvt; D; ent req HS dipl; degrees BA and BS 4 yr, directed study and individual study
in advanced studio areas, private studios; scholarship; SC 13, LC 4; enrl 146, maj 14
Tuition: $2800 campus res—room & board $1375
Courses: Art Education, Art History, Ceramics, Drawing, Painting, Photography,
Printmaking, Two-Dimensional Design
Summer School: Dir, Dr Andersen. Term of 6 wks beginning June

MINOT

MINOT ART GALLERY, Art School,* ND State Fairgrounds, PO Box 325, 58701.
Tel 701-838-4445.
Estab 1970; pub; D & E
Courses: Art History, Ceramics, Drawing, Graphic Design, Lettering, Painting,
Printmaking, Sculpture, Textile Design, Framing, Matting

MINOT STATE COLLEGE, Division of Fine Arts, 58701. Tel 701-857-3108. *Chmn*
C R Schwieger. Instrs FT 3, PT 2
Estab 1913; pub; degrees BA and BS 4 yr; SC 30; enrl per quarter 300, maj 75
Tuition: Res $190; nonres $376; campus residency available
Courses: Advertising Design, Art History, Ceramics, Drawing, Graphic Arts,
Handicrafts, Jewelry, Painting, Photography, Sculpture, Design, Silk Screen, Weaving

VALLEY CITY

VALLEY CITY STATE COLLEGE, Art Department, 58072. Tel 701-845-7561.
Chairperson David Behlke, MFA. Instrs FT 2
Estab 1890, dept estab 1921; pub; D & E; ent req HS dipl, ACT; degrees AA 2yr, BS
and BA 4 yr; scholarship; SC 20, LC 3; enrl D 1000, E 200, non-maj 120, maj 30
Tuition: Res—undergrad $472 per yr, $157 per quarter, $13 per cr; nonres—undergrad
$1033 per yr, $344 per quarter, $29 per cr; campus res—room and board $1095 per
yr
Courses: Art Education, Art History, Ceramics, Commercial Art, Drawing, Painting,
Printmaking, Sculpture, Teacher Training
Adult Hobby Classes: Enrl 10-15; tui $16 per quarter. Courses—Drawing, Watercolor

WAHPETON

NORTH DAKOTA STATE SCHOOL OF SCIENCE, Department of Art, Sixth St
N, 58075. Tel 701-671-2231. *Dir* Mary Sand, BA
Estab 1903, dept estab 1970; pub; D & E
Courses: Art Education, Drawing, Graphic Design, Handicrafts, Lettering,
Occupational Therapy, Painting
Adult Hobby Classes: Enrl 15; tui $30. Courses—Calligraphy, Drawing, Painting
Summer School: Dir, Mary Sand. 2 wk term, 3 hrs per day. Courses—Teacher's Art
Workshop

OHIO

ADA

OHIO NORTHERN UNIVERSITY, Department of Art,* 500 S Main St, 45810. Tel 419-634-9921. *Chmn* Thomas L Gordon
Pvt; D; ent req HS dipl, ent exam; degrees BA and BFA 4 yrs; scholarships; SC 30, LC 8; enrl maj 30
Tuition: $3186 per yr
Courses: Aesthetics, Art Education, Ceramics, Costume Design & Construction, Drawing, Graphic Arts, History of Art & Archaeology, Jewelry, Lettering, Painting, Sculpture, Stage Design, Teacher Training, Theatre Arts

AKRON

UNIVERSITY OF AKRON, Department of Art, 44325. Tel 216-375-7010. *Dept Head* Thomas Morin, MFA
Estab 1926; pub; D & E; ent req HS dipl; degrees AA 2 yr, BA, BS and BFA 4 yr; scholarship; SC 25, LC 7, GC 8; enrl D 943, E 129, non-maj 429, maj 538
Tuition: Res—undergrad $930 yr, grad $24 per credit; nonres—undergrad $3366 yr, grad $24 per cr; campus residency available
Courses: †Advertising Design, †Art History, †Ceramics, Commercial Art, †Drawing, †Goldsmithing, †Graphic Design, Handicrafts, Illustration, †Jewelry, †Painting, †Photography, †Printmaking, †Sculpture, †Silversmithing, Textile Design, Weaving
Summer School: Dir, Dr Carrino. Tui by credit for term of 6 wks. Courses—all of the above

ALLIANCE

MOUNT UNION COLLEGE, Department of Art, 44601. Tel 216-821-5320. *Chmn* James Hopper, MFA; *Asst Prof* Joel Collins, MFA
Estab 1846; pvt; D; ent req HS dipl, SAT; degrees BA; scholarships; SC 27, LC 6; enrl D 150, non-maj 125, maj 25
Tuition: Res—undergrad $5000 per yr; campus residence available
Courses: Aesthetics, Art Education, Art History, Drawing, Lettering, Painting, Printmaking, Sculpture, Teacher Training

ASHLAND

ASHLAND COLLEGE, Art Department, College Ave, 44805. Tel 419-289-4005. *Chmn* Albert W Goad. Instrs FT 4
Estab 1878; den; D & E; ent req HS dipl; degrees BA, BS 4 yr; scholarship; enrl D 1460, maj 32, minors 12
Tuition: $3722 per yr; campus res—$1630 per yr
Courses: Art Education, Art History, Ceramics, Drawing, Graphic Arts, Graphic Design, Handicrafts, Painting, Photography, Sculpture, Stage Design, Teacher Training, Theatre Arts, Available through affiliation with the Art Institute of Pittsburgh: Fashion Design, Interior Design, Photography Multi-media, Visual Communication

ATHENS

OHIO UNIVERSITY, School of Art, College of Fine Arts, 45701. Tel 614-594-5667, 594-5668. *Dean* Henry H Lin; *Assoc Dean* James H Conover; *Dir* Erik Forrest. Instrs FT 27, PT 24
Estab 1936; pub; D & E; ent req secondary school dipl, portfolio; degrees BFA, MA and MFA 4-5 yr; scholarships and fel; SC 88, LC 30, LGC 29, SGC 50; enrl maj 573, others 1718
Courses: Art Education, Art History, Ceramics, Drawing, Graphic Design, Illustration, Painting, Photography, Printmaking, Sculpture, Fibers, Glass
Summer School: Two 5 wk sessions June-July and July-August; 18 quarter hr maximum per session; SC, LC, GC

BEREA

BALDWIN-WALLACE COLLEGE, Department of Art,* 95 E Bagley Rd, 44017. Tel 216-826-2900. *Chmn Div* Harold D Cole; *Head Dept* Dean Drahos
Estab 1845; den; D & E; degrees AB 4 yrs; SC 23, LC 12; enrl 1900, maj 65
Tuition: $3712 per yr; campus residence available
Courses: Art Education, Art History, Ceramics, Drawing, Handicrafts, Painting, Photography, Printmaking, Sculpture, Design and Color
Summer School: Tui $51 per cr hr

BETHANY

BETHANY NAZARENE COLLEGE, Art Department,* 6729 NW 39th Expressway, 73008. Tel 405-789-6400. *Head Dept* Nila West Murrow; *Assoc Prof* Melvin Unruh
Estab 1920; den; D & E; ent req HS dipl, ACT; SC 13, LC 7; enrl D 51, E 6, non-maj 38, maj 13
Tuition: $42 per hr; campus residence available
Courses: Aesthetics, Art Education, Art History, Ceramics, Commercial Art, Drawing, Handicrafts, Painting, Sculpture, †Teacher Training, Macrame, Quilting

BOWLING GREEN

BOWLING GREEN STATE UNIVERSITY, School of Art, Fine Arts Bldg, 43403. Tel 419-372-2787. *Dir* Maurice J Sevigny, PhD; *Asst Dir* Phillip Wigg, MFA; *Chmn Grad Studies* Robert Mazur, MFS; *Chmn Design Studies* Carl Hall, MFA; *Chmn Three-Dimensional and Crafts Studies* Kathy Hagan, MFA; *Chmn Two-Dimensional Studies* David Cayton; *Chmn Art Educ* Mary Mabry, MFA; *Chmn Art History* Dr Willard Misfeldt
Estab 1910, dept estab 1946; pub; D & E; ent req ACT (undergrad), GRE (grad); degrees BA, BS & BFA 4 yr, MA 1 yr, MFA 2 yr; scholarships and fels; SC 53, LC 14, GC 33; enrl D 2460, E 150, non-maj 995, maj 629, grad 33, others 40
Tuition: Undergrad—res $362 per quarter, housing $292 per quarter, meal plan $205 per quarter, non-res fee $455 per quarter; grad—$46 per cr hr, FT $460 per quarter, non-res $429 additional per quarter
Courses: Advertising Design, †Art Education, †Art History, Calligraphy, †Ceramics, Collage, Commercial Art, Conceptual Art, Constructions, Display, †Drawing, Goldsmithing, †Graphic Arts, †Graphic Design, Handicrafts, Illustration, †Jewelry, Lettering, Mixed Media, †Painting, Photography, †Printmaking, †Sculpture, Silversmithing, †Teacher Training, †Environmental Design, Fibers, Glass Working, Weaving
Summer School: Dir, Dr Maurice Sevigny. Courses—Art History, Drawing, Jewelry, Photography, Printmaking, Sculpture, Various Special Workshops

CANTON

CANTON ART INSTUTUTE, 1001 Market Ave North, 44702. Tel 216-453-7666. *Dir* Joseph R Hertzi; *Assoc Dir* Manuel J Albacete; *Administrative Asst* Bebo Adams; *Registrar* Thelma Dittmar; *Administrative Secy* Verna R Blyer
Pub; D & E; SC 28; enrl D 322, E 984, others 1306
Courses: Ceramics, Drawing, Mixed Media, Painting, Photography, Sculpture, Textile Design

MALONE COLLEGE, Department of Art,* Division of Fine Arts, 515 25th St NW, 44709. Tel 216-489-0800. *Chmn Div* Donald R Murray
Estab 1956; den; D & E; ent req HS dipl, ent exam; degrees BA and BS(Educ) 4 yrs; scholarships; SC 20, LC 2; enrl D 75, maj 30
Tuition: $2883 per yr; campus residence available
Courses: Advertising Design, Art Education, Ceramics, Drawing, Graphic Arts, Graphic Design, History of Art & Archaeology, Jewelry, Lettering, Painting, Photography, Sculpture, Teacher Training, Textile Design, Leather
Summer School: Enrl 850; tui $76 cr for term of 5 wks beginning June 15 and July 15. Courses—Art Education, Music and Art in the Western World

CINCINNATI

ART ACADEMY OF CINCINNATI, Eden Park, 45202. Tel 513-721-5205. *Dir* Roger Williams, MFA; *Instructor* Anthony Batchelor, dipl; *Instructor* Walter Driesbach, dipl; *Instructor* April Foster, MFA; *Instructor* Gary Gaffney, MFA; *Instructor* Stewart Goldman, BFA; *Instructor* Laurence W Goodridge, MFA; *Instructor* Diana Holmes, MEd; *Instructor* Calvin Kowal, MS; *Instructor* Barron Krody, dipl; *Instructor* Larry May, MFA; *Instructor* Anne Miotke, MFA; *Instructor* Diane Smith, MA; *Instructor* William Sontag, BS; *Instructor* Jane T Stanton, MA; *Instructor* Julio Zumeta, MFA
Estab 1887; pvt; D & E; ent req HS grad; degrees cert, BS collaboration with Univ of Cincinnati, BFA offered at the academy, 4-5 yr; scholarships; enrl 195
Tuition: $2340 per yr, $65 per cr hr; plus other fees
Courses: Art History, Drawing, Graphic Arts, Graphic Design, Illustration, Painting, Photography, Printmaking, Sculpture, Communication Design
Summer School: Supvr, Roger Williams. Enrl 64; tui $65 per cr hr for term of 6 wks beginning June 16

CENTRAL ACADEMY OF COMMERCIAL ART, 2326 Upland Pl, 45206. Tel 513-961-2484. *Pres* Mrs Jackson Grey Storey; *Dean of Educ* Michael C McGuire; *Instructor* Samuel B McGuire; *Instructor* Robert A Trau; *Instructor* Barbara J Toennis
Tuition: $2000 yr, $1000 per sem
Courses: Advertising Design, Calligraphy, Commercial Art, Drawing, Fashion Arts, Illustration, Lettering, Painting, Color Composition, Finished Art, Keyline, Layout, Letterhead, Life Class Mediums, Logotype, Magic Marker, Mediums, Package Design, Perspective, TV Storyboard, others

CINCINNATI ART MUSEUM, Education Department, Eden Park, 45202. Tel 513-721-5204, Ext 70, 71. *Cur* Kenneth R Trapp, MA
Estab 1881; pvt; D & E; ent req must be museum member; scholarships; SC 3; enrl D 150, E 60-80
Courses: Museum Staff Training
Adult Hobby Classes: Enrl 60-80; tui $10 per adult
Children's Classes: Enrl 130; tui $10 for members, $20 non-members. Courses—Children's Workshops, Creative Movement, Drawing

EDGECLIFF COLLEGE, Department of Art, 2220 Victory Pwy, 45206. Tel 513-961-3770. *Chairperson Dept* Ann Beiersdorfer, RSM
Pvt; degrees BFA and BA(Fine Arts, Handicrafts, Art Certification, Art Therapy and History of Art); scholarships

GABLE ADVERTISING ART SCHOOL, Division of Advertising Design School, Inc, 1216 E McMillan, 45206. Tel 513-861-6421. *Dir* Ronald L French; *Instructor* Teresa Dave, BS. Instrs FT 2
Estab 1958; pvt; D & E; ent req HS dipl, personal interview with portfolio; degrees Cert of Completion 2 yrs (day), 3 yrs (night); enrl D 30, E 15
Tuition: Day - 22 months (average) $150 per month, $50 registration; night - 33 months (average) $55 per month, $20 registration; no campus res
Courses: Advertising Design, Commercial Art, Fashion Arts, Graphic Design, Illustration, Lettering, Painting

OHIO VISUAL ART INSTITUTE, 124 E Seventh St, 45202. Tel 513-241-4338. *Dir* James E Price; *Instructor* John Cunningham; *Instructor* Nikki Howard; *Instructor* Tom Hubbard; *Instructor* Richard Laubenstein; *Instructor* Skip Marten; *Instructor* Jim

Slouffman; *Instructor* Kelly Towe; *Instructor* Bob Wilson. Instrs FT 4, PT 5
Estab 1947; pvt; D & E; ent req HS dipl, review of portfolio; enrl D 100, E 25
Tuition: Undergrad $2400; no campus res
Courses: Advertising Design, Art History, Commercial Art, Drawing, Film, Graphic Arts, Graphic Design, Illustration, Industrial Design, Interior Design, Photography, Business Art

UNIVERSITY OF CINCINNATI, College of Design, Architecture and Art, 45221. Tel 513-475-4934. *Dean* Bertram Berenson. Instrs FT 77, PT 30
Estab 1922; pub; full-time programs; also cooperative programs whereby students spend alternate periods in classroom and in establishments in his chosen profession; degrees B Architecture, B Urban Planning, BS(Design - with major in fashion design, graphic design, industrial design and interior design), BFA, BFA(Art Educ), BA(Art History), 4 yr, MFA, 2 yr, MFA(Art Educ), MA(Art History), MS(Architecture), 1 yr, MCP, EdD; enrl 1800
Tuition: Res—$960 per yr FT; nonres—$2280 per yr
Children's Classes: Sat classes available

XAVIER UNIVERSITY, Fine Arts Department, 1500 Dana Ave, 45207. Tel 513-745-3107. *Head Dept* Jerome Pryor, EDD; *Instr* Constatine Soriano, MA
Dept estab 1974; pvt; D & E; ent req HS dipl, SAT, PSAT; SC 8, LC 8; enrl D 120, E 30
Tuition: Res and nonres—undergrad $1400 per sem; campus res—room $350 per sem & board $415 per sem
Courses: Art History, Drawing, Film, History of Art & Archaeology, Mixed Media, Painting, Theatre Arts

CLEVELAND

CASE WESTERN RESERVE UNIVERSITY, Department of Art,* Wickenden Building, 44106. Tel 216-368-2000. *Chmn* D Harvey Buchanan, PhD; *Prof* Henry S Robinson, PhD; *Assoc Prof* Edward J Olszewski, PhD; *Assoc Prof* Anita Rogoff, MS; *Asst Prof* Inabelle Levin, PhD; *Asst Prof* Carol Nathanson, PhD; *Vis Prof* John Cooney, BA
Estab 1875; pvt; D; ent req HS transcript, SAT or ACT, TOEFL for foreign students; degrees BA, BS, MA, MS and PhD; scholarships; SC 24, LC 55, GC 73; enrl D 644, grad 75
Tuition: $3900 per yr; campus res available
Courses: †Art Education, †Art History, Ceramics, Drawing, Film, Handicrafts, †History of Art & Archaeology, Jewelry, Museum Staff Training, Painting, Photography, Textile Design, Enameling
Summer School: An occasional introductory course in Art History

CLEVELAND INSTITUTE OF ART, 11141 E Blvd, 44106. Tel 216-421-4322. *Pres* Joseph McCullough, MFA; *Instr* Jerome Aidlin; *Instr* Sandra August; *Instr* Carroll Cassill; *Instr* Marco DeMarco; *Instr* Robert Palmer; *Instr* Viktor Schreckengost; *Instr* Julian Stanczak; *Vis Prof* Laurence Barker; *Instr* Robert Jergens; *Instr* Lawrence Krause; *Instr* James Mazurkewicz; *Instr* Mary Ellen McDermott; *Instr* Francis Meyers; *Instr* Raphael Poritsky; *Instr* Judith Salomon; *Instr* Brent Young
Estab 1882; pvt; D & E; ent req HS dipl and transcript, portfolio; degrees BFA 5 yrs, BS (educ with Case Western Reserve Univ) 4 yrs; scholarships; SC 90, LC 38; enrl D 529, E 193, nonmaj 246, maj 283, others 21
Tuition: Undergrad $3180 per year; campus res—room and board $1970
Courses: Aesthetics, Art Education, Art History, Calligraphy, †Ceramics, †Drawing, Film, †Graphic Arts, †Illustration, †Industrial Design, †Jewelry, †Painting, †Photography, †Printmaking, †Sculpture, †Silversmithing, †Textile Design, †Enameling, †Glass, †Medical Illustration, †Weaving
Adult Hobby Classes: Enrl 185; tui $35 per session. Courses—Art Basics, Ceramic Sculpture, Crafts, Design, Drawing, Painting, Printmaking, Photography
Summer School: Dean of Faculty, Robert Weitzel. Enrl 120; tui $312 for term of 6 wks beginning June. Courses—Ceramics, Design, Drawing, Jewelry and Metalsmithing, Photography, Printmaking, Sculpture, Watercolor

CLEVELAND STATE UNIVERSITY, Art Department, 2307 Chester Ave, Cleveland, OH. (Mailing Add: 1938 E 24th St, Cleveland, OH 44115,) Tel 216-687-2090, 687-2089. *Chmn* Jan van der Meulen, PhD; *Assoc Prof* Betty Copeland, PhD; *Assoc Prof* Thomas E Donaldson, PhD; *Assoc Prof* Henry Drewal, PhD; *Assoc Prof* June E Hargrove, PhD; *Assoc Prof* Marvin H Jones, MA; *Assoc Prof* Gene Kangas, MFA; *Assoc Prof* Walter C Leedy Jr, PhD; *Assoc Prof* Richard D Schneider, MA; *Assoc Prof* Thomas C Silver, MFA; *Asst Prof* Kenneth Nevadomi, MFA
Dept estab 1972; pub; D & E; ent req HS dipl; degrees BA 4 yr; scholarships; SC 26, LC 32
Courses: Art Education, Art History, Ceramics, Drawing, Painting, Photography, Printmaking, Sculpture, Fiber Arts, Glass, Introduction to Art and Design, Studio Practices

COOPER SCHOOL OF ART, 2341 Carnegie Ave, 44115. Tel 216-241-1486. Instrs FT & PT 32
Estab 1936; pvt; ent req HS grad, art portfolio and personal interview; degrees 3 yr prog, 6 sem to complete dipl; scholarships; SC; enrl 250
Courses: Advertising Design, Art History, Drawing, Fashion Arts, Film, Graphic Design, Illustration, Painting, Photography, Printmaking, Design, Portrait, Silkscreen, Typography, Watercolor
Summer School: 3 sessions starting in June

CUYAHOGA COMMUNITY COLLEGE, Department of Art, 2900 Community College Ave, 44115. Tel 216-241-5966. *Department Head* Evelyn Boyd, MA; *Assoc Prof* David Haberman, MFA; *Assoc Prof* Richard Karberg, MA; *Instr* Betty Drake, MFA
Estab 1963; pub; D & E; ent req HS dipl; degrees AA; scholarships; SC 15, LC 4; enrl D 150, E 80, maj 50
Tuition: $10 per hr, $110 per quarter; no campus res
Courses: Art Education, Art History, Calligraphy, Ceramics, Graphic Design, Occupational Therapy, Painting, Photography, Printmaking, Sculpture, Stage Design, Teacher Training, Theatre Arts, Video
Summer School: Courses—various

COLUMBUS

COLUMBUS COLLEGE OF ART AND DESIGN, 47 N Washington Ave, 43215. Tel 614-224-9101. *Pres* Joseph V Canzani; *Dean* Mary T Kinney. Instrs 68
Estab 1879; pvt; approved for Veterans; D & E; ent req HS grad, art portfolio; degrees BFA 4 yr; scholarships
Courses: Advertising Design, Fashion Arts, Graphic Arts, Illustration, Industrial Design, Interior Design, Painting, Sculpture, Fine Arts, Packaging Design, Retail Advertising

OHIO DOMINICAN COLLEGE, Art Department,* 1216 Sunbury Rd, 43219. Tel 614-253-2741. *Chmn Dept* Juris Kakis, MA; *Assoc Prof* Melvyn J Rozen, MFA
Estab 1911; den; D & E; ent req HS dipl; degrees BA 4 yrs, also secondary educ cert or special training cert, K-12; scholarships; SC and LC 709 per sem; enrl D 139, E 105, maj 17
Tuition: $2480 per yr; campus res available
Courses: Art Education, Art History, Ceramics, Drawing, Film, Graphic Arts, Painting, Photography, Printmaking, Sculpture, Teacher Training, Textile Design, Theatre Arts, Video
Summer School: Dir, Joe Stotski. Tui $90 per cr hr for term of 7 wks beginning June

OHIO STATE UNIVERSITY
—School of Architecture, 190 W 17th Ave, 43210. *Dir* Masao Kinoshita, AIA AIP & ASLA. Instrs FT 32, PT 19
Estab 1899; pub; degrees BSArchit, BSLand Archit, MArchit, MLA, MCP 4-6 yrs; enrl Archit 303, Landscape Archit 248, City and Regional Planning 161
Courses: Architecture, Landscape Architecture, City and Regional Planning
—College of the Arts, 305 Mershon Auditorium, 30 W 15th Ave, 43210. Tel 614-422-5171. *Dean Col* Andrew J Broekema, PhD
Univ estab 1870, col estab 1968; pub; D & E; ent req HS dipl; degrees BA, BAEd, BFA, BS and BSID 4 yrs, MA, MFA, PhD; scholarships; SC 106, LC 192, GC 208; enrl D 3678, E varies, non-maj 2598, maj 998, grad 164
Tuition: Res—undergrad $1005 per yr, $335 per quarter, grad $1275 per yr, $425 per quarter; nonres—undergrad $2280 per yr, $760 per quarter, grad $2550 per yr, $850 per quarter; campus res—room & board $1725 per yr
Courses: †Art Education, †Art History, †Ceramics, †Costume Design & Construction, †Drawing, Graphic Arts, Graphic Design, †Handicrafts, †History of Art & Archaeology, Illustration, †Industrial Design, †Interior Design, Mixed Media, †Painting, Printmaking, †Sculpture, †Stage Design, †Teacher Training, Textile Design, †Theatre Arts, Graphics of Communication, Weaving
Adult Hobby Classes: Enrl 450 per quarter; tui $9 per quarter; Saturday School. Courses—art experiences in all media for local adults
Children's Classes: Enrl 450 per quarter; tui $9 per quarter; Saturday School. Courses—art experiences in all media for local children
Summer School: Same as regular session
—Department of Art, 43210. *Chmn Dept* Robert Stull, MA. Instrs FT 36, PT 34
Degrees BA, BFA, MA, MFA; SC 56, LC 6, GC 30
Courses: Ceramics, Drawing, Graphic Arts, Painting, Sculpture, Fine Arts
—Department of Art Education, Hopkins Hall 340, 43210. Tel 614-422-7183. *Chmn Dept* Kenneth A Marantz, EdD; *Prof* Arthur Efland, PhD; *Assoc Prof* Robert Arnold; *Asst Prof* Rogena Degse, PhD; *Assoc Prof* Donald Duncan, MFA; *Assoc Prof* Nancy MacGregor, PhD; *Assoc Prof* Ross Norris; *Asst Prof* Charles Wieder, MA
Estab 1907; pub; D & E; ent req HS dipl; degrees BAEd, MA, PhD; scholarships; SC 6, LC 10, GC 16; enrl maj 95, grad 83
Courses: †Art Education, Film, Goldsmithing, Graphic Arts, Handicrafts, †Jewelry, Mixed Media, Silversmithing, †Teacher Training, Art Appreciation, Art Criticism, Bookmaking, Photo Criticism
—Department of Industrial Design. *Chmn Dept* Charles A Wallschlaeger, MFA. Instrs FT 11, PT 4
Degrees BSID, MA; SC 29, LC 1, GC 15
Courses: Product Design, Space and Enclosure Design, Visual Communication Design
—Department of the History of Art, 100 Hayes Hall, 108 N Oval Mall, 43210. Tel 614-422-7481. *Chmn Dept* Howard Crane, PhD; *Prof* Franklin Ludden, PhD; *Assoc Prof* Mathew Herban, PhD; *Assoc Prof* Susan Huntington, PhD; *Assoc Prof* Francis Richardson, PhD; *Asst Prof* Barbara Groseclose, PhD; *Asst Prof* James Morganstern, PhD; *Vis Prof* Charlotte Douglas, Russian Art - 1978-80; *Vis Prof* John Hallam, Northern Baroque and 18th century art - 1979-80
Estab 1871, dept estab 1968; pub; D & E; ent req HS dipl; degrees BA, BFA 4 yrs, MA 2 yrs, PhD 4-6 yrs; scholarships; LC 53, GC 34; enrl D 832, E 100, non-maj 800, maj 60, grad 72
Tuition: Res—undergrad $335 per quarter, grad $425 per quarter, PT (less than 9 hrs) $53 per cr hr; nonres—undergrad $760 per quarter, grad $850 per quarter, PT $88 per cr hr; campus res—room & board undergrad $636 per quarter, $417 per quarter without meals; grad $128 per month
Courses: †Art History, History of Art & Archaeology
Summer School: Chmn, Howard Crane. Enrl 250; tui same as regular session for term of 10 wks beginning June. Courses—vary each yr

CUYAHOGA FALLS

CUYAHOGA VALLEY ART CENTER, 1886 Front St, 44221. Tel 216-928-8092. *Pres* Pat Selby; *Instr* Eugene Bell; *Instr* Jane Boyd; *Instr* Jean Deemer; *Instr* Dino Massaroni; *Instr* John Smolko; *Instr* Frank Susi
Estab 1942; pvt; D & E; ent req none, interest in art; degrees none; SC 23; enrl 200
Tuition: $65 for 10 wks; no campus res
Courses: Calligraphy, Ceramics, Collage, Drawing, Painting, Textile Design, Acrylic Painting, Oil Painting, Watercolor
Children's Classes: Tui $35 per 10 wks. Courses—Ceramics, Painting
Summer School: Courses—same as regular session

STUDIOS OF JACK RICHARD CREATIVE SCHOOL OF DESIGN, 2250 Front St, 44221. Tel 216-929-1575. *Dir* Jack Richard. Instrs FT 3
Estab 1960; pvt; D & E; scholarships; SC 4, LC 10; enrl D 50-60, E 50-60
Courses: Aesthetics, Art Education, Drawing, Illustration, Occupational Therapy, Painting, Photography, Sculpture, Color, Design, Portrait
Adult Hobby Classes: Enrl 100-120 per session; tui $10 per class. Courses—Drawing,

Painting

Summer School: Dir, Jack Richard. Tui $80 for term of 8 wks beginning June. Courses—Design, Drawing, Painting

DAYTON

SINCLAIR COMMUNITY COLLEGE, Department of Art,* 444 W Third St, 45402. Tel 513-226-2500. *Chmn* John Polston
Estab 1973; pub; D & E; ent req HS dipl, ent exam; degrees AA 2 yrs
Tuition: In-county $450; in-state $675; out-of-state $900; no campus res
Courses: Advertising Design, Ceramics, Commercial Art, Drawing, Painting, Sculpture, Theatre Arts

UNIVERSITY OF DAYTON, Fine Arts Division, 300 College Park, 45469. Tel 513-229-3237. *Head Dept* Dr Bernard E Plogman, DEd; *Assoc Prof* A Jos Barrish, MA; *Assoc Prof* Louis Weber, MA; *Asst Prof* Joann Fiehler, MA; *Asst Prof* Gordon Richardson, MFA; *Asst Prof* Mary Zahner, MA; *Instr* Terry Hitt, BA; *Instr* Thomas Strohmaier, MFA
Estab 1850; pvt; D & E; ent req HS dipl; degrees BFA, BFA(Commercial Design), BFA(Crafts), BFA(Teaching) and BA 4 yrs; SC 15, LC 8; enrl D 225, E 75-100, non-maj 100, maj 200
Tuition: Res and nonres—undergrad $1300 per yr, $70 per cr hr; campus res—room & board $400
Courses: Advertising Design, †Art Education, Art History, Calligraphy, Ceramics, Collage, †Commercial Art, Drawing, Graphic Arts, Graphic Design, Illustration, Jewelry, Lettering, Mixed Media, †Painting, †Photography, †Printmaking, †Sculpture, Silversmithing, Teacher Training
Children's Classes: Enrl 12-15; tui $20 per 8 wks. Courses—Crafts, Drawing, Painting; special program offered for advanced high school seniors
Summer School: Dir, Dr Bernard E Plogman. Enrl 20-30; tui $50 per cr hr for term of 6 wks beginning May 7. Courses—Crafts, Design, Drawing, Painting

WRIGHT STATE UNIVERSITY, Art Department, Colonel Glenn Hwy, 45435. Tel 513-837-2896. *Acting Chairer* Thomas Macaulay, MFA; *Prof* Eugene Cantelupe, PhD; *Assoc Prof* Ernest Koerlin, MFA; *Associate Prof* Raymond Must, MA; *Assoc Prof* Carol Nathanson, PhD; *Adjunct Assoc* Robert Bingenheimer, BA; *Adjunct Assoc* David Givler, BAE; *Adjunct Assoc* Michael Jones, MFA; *Asst Prof* George Creamer, MFA; *Asst Prof* Peter D'Agostino, MA; *Asst Prof* Martha Dunkelman, PhD; *Asst Prof* Katherine Fishman, MFA; *Asst Prof* Kimmerly Kiser, MFA; *Asst Prof* David Leach, MFA; *Asst Prof* Nancy Rexroth, MFA
Estab 1964; dept estab 1965; pub; D & E; ent req HS dipl; degrees BA(Studio Art), BA(Art History), BFA 4 yr; scholarships; SC 67, LC 16, GC 8; enrl D 516, E 43, non-maj 80, maj 103
Tuition: Res—undergrad $330 per quarter; nonres—undergrad $660 per quarter; campus res—double room $343 per quarter, two bedroom apartment $375 per quarter, light food service $190 per quarter, heavy food service $250 per quarter
Courses: Art History, Drawing, Film, Painting, Photography, Printmaking, Sculpture, Video, Foundations, Gallery Management, Museology, Visual Communication
Summer School: Two 10 wk terms. Courses—Art History, Drawing, Foundations, Painting, Photography, Printmaking, Sculpture

DELAWARE

OHIO WESLEYAN UNIVERSITY, Fine Arts Department,* S Sandusky St, 43015. Tel 614-369-4431. *Chmn* Justin Kronewetter, MFA; *Prof* Everett Haycock, MA; *Prof* Jarvis Stewart, PhD; *Assoc Prof* Marty Kalb, MFA; *Asst Prof* Betty Heald, MFA; *Asst Prof* Amanda Jaffe, MFA
Estab 1841; dept estab 1864; pvt; D & E; ent req HS dipl, SAT or ACT; degrees BA and BFA 4 yrs; enrl D 1200, non-maj 1075, maj 125
Tuition: Res $4315 per yr; campus res—room & board $1840 per yr
Courses: Aesthetics, Art Education, Art History, Ceramics, Commercial Art, Drafting, Drawing, Film, Interior Design, Jewelry, Painting, Photography, Printmaking, Sculpture, Teacher Training, Textile Design, Theatre Arts
Children's Classes: Enrl 55; tui $5 per 5 wks. Courses—various media
Summer School: A limited selection of regular course offerings plus a special six week traveling seminar to the American southwest

FINDLAY

FINDLAY COLLEGE, Art Department, 1000 N Main St, 45840. Tel 419-422-8313, Ext 277. *Assoc Prof* Doug Salveson, MFA
Estab 1882; pub; D & E; ent req HS dipl; degrees AA 2 yr, BA and BS 4 yr; scholarships; SC 21, LC 4; enrl maj 30
Tuition: Undergrad $1620 per sem, $108 per sem hr; campus res—room & board $1478 per yr
Courses: Advertising Design, Aesthetics, Art Education, Art History, Ceramics, Collage, Drawing, Graphic Design, History of Art & Archaeology, Illustration, Lettering, Painting, Photography, Printmaking, Sculpture, Teacher Training, Theatre Arts
Adult Hobby Classes: Enrl 10-20; tui $50 per sem. Courses—Ceramics
Summer School: Dir, Thom Lowther

GAMBIER

KENYON COLLEGE, Art Department, 43022. Tel 614-427-2244. *Chmn* Eugene J Dwyer, PhD; *Prof* Joseph Slate, BFA; *Assoc Prof* Martin Garhart, MFA; *Asst Prof* Barry Gunderson, MFA; *Asst Prof* Gregory P Spaid, MFA; *Instr* Theresa Schupbach, MFA; *Vis Prof* Joyce Parr, MFA
Estab 1824; dept estab 1965; pvt; D; ent req HS dipl; degrees BA and BFA; scholarships; SC 15, LC 10; enrl D 450, non-maj 250, maj 60
Tuition: Res—undergrad $5700 yr; campus residency available
Courses: Art History, Drawing, History of Art & Archaeology, Painting, Photography, Printmaking, Sculpture

GRANVILLE

DENISON UNIVERSITY, Department of Art, Box M, 43023. Tel 614-587-0810. *Chmn Dept* Michael Jung, MFA; *Prof* George Bogdanovitch, MFA; *Prof* Eric E Hirshler, PhD; *Asst Prof* Chris Bunge, MFA; *Asst Prof* Paul Cardile, PhD; *Asst Prof* Kate Dolan, MFA; *Asst Prof* Richard Wheeler, MFA; *Vis Prof* Terry Bailey, Oriental art - fall term
Estab 1831, dept estab 1931; pvt; D; ent req HS; degrees BA, BFA, BS 4 yr; scholarships; SC 24, LC 16; enrl D 800, maj 65, double maj 35
Tuition: Res—undergrad $4350 per yr; campus res—room & board $1730 per yr
Courses: Aesthetics, Architecture, †Art History, †Ceramics, Conceptual Art, Constructions, Costume Design & Construction, Drawing, †Film, Graphic Arts, Graphic Design, History of Art & Archaeology, Mixed Media, Museum Staff Training, †Painting, Photography, †Printmaking, Restoration & Conservation, †Sculpture, Stage Design, †Theatre Arts

HIRAM

HIRAM COLLEGE, Art Department, Dean St, 44234. Tel 216-569-3211, Ext 243 & 244. *Chmn* George S Schroeder; *Prof* Paul A Rochford, MA; *Assoc Prof* Dennis Kievets, MA; *Instructor* Bruce Bowers, MFA; *Instructor* Susan Schroeder, BS. Instrs FT 3, PT 2
Estab 1850; pvt; D; ent req HS dipl; degrees AB 4 yr; scholarships; SC 20, LC 14; enrl D 400
Tuition: $4037 per yr; campus res—room $661 per yr & board $714 per yr
Courses: Aesthetics, Art Education, †Art History, Ceramics, Drawing, Handicrafts, Lettering, †Painting, †Photography, Printmaking, Sculpture, Teacher Training, Textile Design, Dyeing, Spinning, Weaving
Summer School: Dir, George S Schroeder. Enrl 180. Courses—vary

HURON

BOWLING GREEN STATE UNIVERSITY, Art Department, Firelands Col, Div of Humanities, 901 Rye Beach Rd, 44839. Tel 419-433-5560. *Chmn Art Dept* Julius T Kosan, MFA. Instrs FT 1, PT 3
Estab 1907, col estab 1966; pub; D & E; ent req HS dipl, SAT; degrees AA 2 yr; scholarships; SC 12, LC 3; enrl D 1200
Tuition: $921 per yr, $306 per quarter, $31 per cr hr; no campus res
Courses: Art Education, Art History, Drawing, History of Art & Archaeology, Painting, Photography, Teacher Training, Theatre Arts, Enameling
Summer School: Tui $31 per cr hr for term of 5 wks beginning June 18. Courses—Art Education, Studio Courses

KENT

KENT STATE UNIVERSITY, School of Art, Col of Fine & Professional Art, 44242. Tel 216-672-2192. *Dir* Stuart Schar, PhD; *Div Coordr Design* J Charles Walker, MFA; *Div Coordr Painting* Robert Culley, MFA; *Div Coordr Art History* Ben Bassham, PhD; *Div Coordr Art Educ* Thompson Lehnert, MA; *Div Coordr Crafts* Jack Smith, MA; *Grad Coordr* Richard Myers, MA. Instrs FT 43, PT 6
Estab 1910; pub; D & E; ent req HS dipl, ACT; degrees BFA, BA, BS 4 yrs, MA 1-2 yrs, MFA 2-3 yrs; scholarships; SC 105, LC 35, GC 50; enrl non-maj 450, maj 830, grad 120
Tuition: Res—undergrad $502 per sem, grad $607 per sem; nonres—undergrad $1102 per sem, grad $1207 per sem, $100 per sem hr; campus res—room & board $1500-$1700
Courses: †Art Education, †Art History, Calligraphy, †Ceramics, †Drawing, †Film, Goldsmithing, †Graphic Design, †Illustration, †Industrial Design, †Jewelry, Lettering, Mixed Media, Museum Staff Training, †Painting, †Printmaking, †Sculpture, Silversmithing, Teacher Training, Textile Design, Arts Therapy
Adult Hobby Classes: Enrl 50; tui $25 per class. Courses—Ceramics, Drawing, Fiber, Painting
Children's Classes: Enrl 20; tui $5 per class. Courses—Art for Elementary School Students
Summer School: Dir, Dr Stuart Schar. Enrl 300-400; tui undergrad $259 and grad $297 for term of 5 wks beginning June 16 and July 21. Courses—Art Education, Art History, Crafts, Drawing, Graphic Design, Painting, Printmaking, Sculpture

MARIETTA

MARIETTA COLLEGE, Art Department, 45750. Tel 614-373-4643. *Chmn* M Jeanne Tasse. Instrs FT 4, PT 1
Estab 1835; pvt; degrees AB, BFA 4 yr; grants in aid and student loans; SC 20, LC 7; enrl maj 75, total col 1600
Courses: Calligraphy, Ceramics, Costume Design & Construction, Drawing, Graphic Arts, Painting, Sculpture, Teacher Training, Theatre Arts, Television

MOUNT SAINT JOSEPH

COLLEGE OF MOUNT SAINT JOSEPH, Art Department, Delhi and Neeb Roads, 45051. Tel 513-244-4309. *Chmn* John Nartker, MFA; *Asst Prof* Sharon Kesterson Bollen, MA; *Assoc Prof* Betty Brothers, MAT; *Assoc Prof* Daniel Mader, MA
Estab 1920; den; D & E; ent req HS dipl, national testing scores; degrees AA 2 yr, BA and BFA 4 yr; scholarships; SC 35, LC 4; enrl D 80, non-maj 35, maj 80
Tuition: Res—undergrad $2664 per yr; campus res—room & board $860 per sem
Courses: †Art Education, Art History, †Ceramics, †Drawing, Graphic Design, Handicrafts, †Interior Design, †Jewelry, Lettering, †Painting, †Photography, †Printmaking, †Sculpture, †Silversmithing, Batik, Enameling, Pre-Art Therapy

MOUNT VERNON

MOUNT VERNON NAZARENE COLLEGE, Art Department, Martinsburg Rd, 43050. Tel 614-397-1244. *Chmn* Kenneth Shaffer, MA; *Instr* James Hendrickx, MFA; *Vis Prof* Bert Goodman, graphic communication
Estab 1968, dept estab 1970; den; D & E; ent req HS dipl and grad of upper 2 3, ACT; degrees AAS, BA; SC 19, LC 3; enrl D 1024, non-maj 1000, maj 24
Tuition: Res and nonres—undergrad $2000 per yr, $83 per hr; campus res $3522
Courses: Aesthetics, Art History, Ceramics, Commercial Art, Drafting, Drawing, Handicrafts, Interior Design, Painting, Printmaking, Sculpture

NEW CONCORD

MUSKINGUM COLLEGE, Art Department, 43762. Tel 614-826-8101. *Chmn* Richard Probert. Instrs FT 2
Estab 1837; pvt; D; ent req HS dipl, ent exam, specific school standards; degrees BA and BS 4 yr; scholarships; SC 13, LC 6; enrl D 300, maj 15
Tuition: $3850, residence $1545, fees $135
Courses: Aesthetics, Art Education, Ceramics, Commercial Art, Drawing, Graphic Arts, History of Art & Archaeology, Jewelry, Museum Staff Training, Painting, Sculpture, Teacher Training, Theatre Arts, Art Therapy

OBERLIN

OBERLIN COLLEGE, Department of Art, 44074. Tel 216-775-8181. *Chmn* Forbes Whiteside, MFA; *Prof* Paul B Arnold, MFA; *Prof* Richard Spear, PhD; *Assoc Prof* John Pearson, MFA; *Assoc Prof* Athena Tacha, D Univ Paris; *Asst Prof* William Hood, PhD; *Asst Prof* Susan Kane, PhD; *Asst Prof* Kathleen Nicholson, PhD; *Instructor* Marsha Weidner; *Instructor* Diane Bouillette
Estab 1833, dept estab 1917; pvt; D; ent req HS dipl, SAT; degrees BA 4 yr, MA 2 yr; scholarships; SC 28, LC 38, advanced undergrad and grad courses 13; enrl D approx 1200, non-maj 500, maj 100, grad 5
Tuition: Undergrad and grad $4725 yr; campus res—room and board $2000
Courses: Art History, Drawing, History of Art & Archaeology, Painting, Printmaking, Sculpture

OXFORD

MIAMI UNIVERSITY, Art Department,* School of Fine Arts, 208 Heistand Hall, 45056. Tel 513-529-6010. *Dean School Fine Arts* Charles L Spohn; *Chmn Dept* Robert B Butler, MFA; *Prof* Peter Dahoda, MFA; *Prof* Judith P George, MFA; *Prof* John Michael, DEd; *Prof* Harold R Truax, DEd; *Prof* Robert Wolfe Jr, MFA; *Assoc Prof* Joseph L Cox III, MFA; *Assoc Prof* Crossan H Curry, MFA; *Assoc Prof* Willis H Davis, MA; *Assoc Prof* Thomas J Gilmore, MA; *Assoc Prof* James C Kaufman; *Assoc Prof* W Alex McKibben, MFA; *Assoc Prof* Jerry W Morris; *Assoc Prof* Sandra P Packard; *Assoc Prof* Edward L Talbott, MFA; *Assoc Prof* Helen V Worrall, MFA; *Asst Prof* Lon L Beck, MFA; *Asst Prof* Philip M Joseph, MFA; *Asst Prof* E James Killy, MFA; *Asst Prof* Edward K Montgomery, MFA; *Asst Prof* M Ellen Patton, MFA; *Asst Prof* Barry A Rosenberg, MFA; *Asst Prof* Michael H Stuckhardt, DEd; *Asst Prof* Gary Wheeler, MFA; *Sr Instr* Jane E Toadvine, MA; *Instr* Marior Cooley, MA; *Lectr* Carlos de Azevedo, MA
Estab 1809, dept estab 1929; pub; D & E; ent req HS dipl, class rank, ACT or SAT; degrees BFA and BS(Art) 4 yrs, MFA 2 yrs, MA(Art or Art Educ) and Med(Art Educ) 1 yr; scholarships; SC 49, LC 35, GC 20; enrl D 2309, non-maj 1890, maj 419, grad 32
Tuition: Res—undergrad $625 per sem, grad $700 per sem; nonres $700 per sem; campus res available
Courses: †Advertising Design, Architecture, †Art Education, Art History, Calligraphy, †Ceramics, Collage, Commercial Art, Display, †Drawing, Graphic Arts, †Graphic Design, History of Art & Archaeology, Illustration, †Jewelry, Lettering, Museum Staff Training, †Painting, Photography, †Printmaking, †Sculpture, †Silversmithing, †Teacher Training, †Textile Design, Stitchery, Weaving
Children's Classes: Enrl 70; tui $5 per sem. Courses—General Art
Summer School: Dir, Peter Dahoda. Tui $68 per wk, no credit; undergrad for credit $68; grad $80 for credit; nonres $98 per wk; campus res—room & board 1-5 days $9 single, $6 double, 6-10 days $8 single, $6 double, 11 or more days $8 single, $5 double. Courses—varied workshops

PAINESVILLE

LAKE ERIE COLLEGE-GARFIELD SENIOR COLLEGE, Art Department, 44077. Tel 216-352-3361, Ext 413 and 429. *Instr Coordr* Stephen J Wilcox. Instrs FT 3, PT 4
Estab 1856; pvt; ent req col board exam; degrees BA and BFA 4 yrs; SC 20, LC 7; enrl 800 total
Courses: Art Education, Art History, Ceramics, Painting, Sculpture, Design, Introductory Art

SPRINGFIELD

SPRINGFIELD ART CENTER, 107 Cliff Park Rd, 45501. Tel 513-325-4673. *Dir* Patricia D'Arcy Catron. Instrs PT 20
Estab 1951; pvt; D & E; scholarships; D 600
Tuition: No campus res
Courses: Ceramics, Drawing, Jewelry, Painting, Photography, Sculpture
Adult Hobby Classes: Tui $45 per quarter. Courses—Batik, Gourmet Cooking, Weaving
Children's Classes: Tui $25 per quarter. Courses—Art Experiences, Drawing, Pottery and Sculpture

WITTENBERG UNIVERSITY, Art Department, Crabill Art Center, 818 N Fountain Ave, 45501. Tel 513-327-6311. *Chmn* John O Schlump, MA; *Assoc Prof* Don Dunifon,

MFA; *Assoc Prof* George Ramsay, MFA; *Asst Prof* Richard Hagelberger, MFA; *Asst Prof* Jack Mann, MA; *Asst Prof* Jack Osbun, MFA
Estab 1842; pvt den; D & E; ent req HS dipl, class rank, transcript, SAT or ACT test results, recommendations and if possible, a personal interview; degrees AB and BFA 4 yr; scholarships; SC 30, LC 17; enrl D 350, non-maj 270, maj 80
Tuition: Nonres—undergrad $3987 yr; campus res—room & board $1785 yr
Courses: Advertising Design, Aesthetics, †Art Education, †Art History, †Ceramics, †Commercial Art, Drawing, †Graphic Arts, Graphic Design, History of Art & Archaeology, †Illustration, Industrial Design, Interior Design, Jewelry, †Painting, Photography, †Printmaking, †Sculpture, †Teacher Training
Summer School: Assoc Provost, Dr Joseph O'Connor. Enrl 400; tui $250 for term of 7 wks beginning June 14. Courses—Art in the Elementary School, Fundamental of Art, Painting

SYLVANIA

LOURDES COLLEGE, Art Department, 6832 Convent Blvd, 43560. Tel 419-882-2016. *Instr* Sr Helen Chmura, MFA; *Instr* Agneta Ganzel, MA
Estab 1958; pvt, den; D & E; ent req HS dipl, ACT or SAT; degrees AA 2 yrs; SC 18, LC 4; enrl D 40, E 26, non-maj 56, maj 10
Tuition: Nonres—undergrad $1200 per yr, $600 per sem, $40 per hr; no campus res available
Courses: Aesthetics, Art History, Calligraphy, Ceramics, Collage, Drawing, Graphic Arts, Handicrafts, History of Art & Archaeology, Lettering, Mixed Media, Occupational Therapy, Painting, Printmaking, Sculpture, Teacher Training, Copper Enameling, Weaving
Adult Hobby Classes: Tui $40 per hr. Courses—Calligraphy, Ceramics, Copper Enameling, Painting, Weaving
Children's Classes: Enrl 30; tui $40 for ten Saturday classes. Courses—Ceramics, Drawing, Painting
Summer School: Dir, Jane Mary Sorosiak. Tui $40 per hr for term of 2 wks beginning June 25. Courses—Ceramics, Silk Screen Printing, Watercolor, Weaving

TIFFIN

HEIDELBERG COLLEGE, Department of Art,* 44883. Tel 419-448-2000.
Estab 1850; pvt; D; ent req HS dipl, each applicant's qualifications are considered individually; degrees AB 4 yrs, independent study, honors work available; scholarships; SC 22, LC 9; enrl 200, maj 24
Tuition: $3390 per yr; campus res available
Courses: Advertising Design, Aesthetics, Art Education, Ceramics, Commercial Art, Display, Drawing, Graphic Arts, Graphic Design, History of Art & Archaeology, Illustration, Jewelry, Lettering, Museum Staff Training, Painting, Sculpture, Stage Design, Teacher Training, Textile Design, Chip Carving, Copper Enameling, Metal Tooling, Mosaic
Summer School: Dir, Dr Roy M Bacon. Term of 6 wks beginning June. Courses—Materials and Methods in Teaching, Practical Arts

TOLEDO

TOLEDO MUSEUM OF ART, School of Design, Box 1013, 43697. Tel 419-255-8000. *Asst Dir* Charles F Gunther. Instrs FT 13, PT 5
Estab 1919; pvt; D & E; degrees in cooperation with Univ of Toledo 4 yr; scholarships
Courses: Art History, Ceramics, Drawing, Painting, Printmaking, Sculpture, Design, Glass, Metalsmithing
Adult Hobby Classes: Enrl 1000 per quarter
Children's Classes: Enrl 1800 per quarter. Free classes for children on Sat in art and music

UNIVERSITY OF TOLEDO, Department of Art, Art Education and Art History, 43606. Tel 419-537-2696. *Dir Art Educ* Charles F Gunther
Ent req HS dipl; degrees BA, BA(Art History), BFA, MA(Art Educ); Same as regular session
Courses: Advertising Design, Art History, Ceramics, Drawing, Painting, Printmaking, Sculpture, Design, Glass, Metals

TROY

HOBART SCHOOL OF WELDING TECHNOLOGY, Trade Square East, 45373. Tel 513-339-6011, Ext 4300. *Vis Prof* K Milonadis, sculpture
Estab 1930, dept estab 1966; pvt; D & E; degrees none, cert; SC 15, LC 90
Tuition: $360 for 3 wks; sleeping rooms available in homes in Troy, Ohio, average $30 per wk per person
Courses: Sculpture
Adult Hobby Classes: Enrl 20; tui $360 per person. Courses—Welding for Artists

WESTERVILLE

OTTERBEIN COLLEGE, Department of Visual Arts,* 43081. Tel 614-882-3000. *Chmn* Earl Hassenpflug
Pvt; ent req HS dipl; degrees BA 4 yrs; scholarships; SC 11, LC 4; enrl D 1400, maj 32
Courses: Architecture, Art Education, Ceramics, Drawing, Graphic Design, Handicrafts, History of Art & Archaeology, Painting, Photography, Sculpture, Stage Design, Teacher Training, Theatre Arts, Art Psychotherapy, Bronze Casting, Macrame

WILBERFORCE

CENTRAL STATE UNIVERSITY, Department of Art, 45384. Tel 513-376-6610. *Chmn* Willis Bing Davis. Instrs FT 5

Estab 1856; D; ent req HS dipl; degrees BA and BS 4 yr; SC 20, LC 8; enrl D 175, maj 45, others 130
Courses: Advertising Design, Art Education, Art History, Ceramics, Drawing, Graphic Arts, Lettering, Painting, Sculpture, Teacher Training
Summer School: Chmn, Willis Bing Davis. Enrl maj 30, others 200; term of 12 wks beginning June 16, two sessions. Courses—Art for the Elementary Teacher, Art History, Black Artists, Ceramics, Introduction to Art, Painting, Sculpture

WILBERFORCE UNIVERSITY, Art Department,* 45384. Tel 513-376-2911. *Head Dept* Edward G Hill, MA; *Instr* James Padgett, MFA; *Instr* Richard Wheatley, BA
Estab 1856, dept estab 1973; pvt; D; ent req HS dipl; degrees BA, BS and BS(Educ) 4 yrs; SC 22, LC 5; enrl D 26, maj 26
Tuition: $2230 per yr
Courses: Advertising Design, Art Education, Art History, Ceramics, Commercial Art, Drawing, Fashion Arts, Handicrafts, History of Art & Archaeology, Painting, Photography, Printmaking, Sculpture, Teacher Training

WILLOUGHBY

SCHOOL OF FINE ARTS, Visual Arts Department, 38660 Mentor Ave, 44094. Tel 216-951-7500. *Dir* James Savage, BM; *Visual Arts Coordr & Gallery Dir* Doris Foster, BFA
Estab 1957; pvt; D & E; scholarships; SC 24; enrl D 252, E 240
Tuition: $45-$70 per sem; no campus res
Courses: Ceramics, Drawing, Intermedia, Mixed Media, Painting, Photography, Stage Design, Theatre Arts
Adult Hobby Classes: Tui $65-$70 per sem. Courses—Ceramics, Drawing, Painting, Photography
Children's Classes: Tui $45 per sem. Courses—Ceramics, Ceramic Sculpture, Drawing, Painting, Photography
Summer School: Dir, James Savage. Tui $35-$80 for term of 6 wks beginning June 16. Courses—same as above

WOOSTER

COLLEGE OF WOOSTER, Department of Art, University St, 44691. Tel 216-264-1234, Ext 388; WATS 800-321-9885 or 9888. *Chmn* Donald MacKenzie, PhD; *Prof* Arnold Lewis, PhD; *Prof* Thalia Gouma-Peterson, PhD; *Asst Prof* George Olson, MFA; *Instructor* Mary Breckenridge, MA; *Instructor* Becky Seeman, MFA
Estab 1866; pvt; D & E; ent req HS dipl; degrees BA 4 yr; SC 13, LC 19; enrl D 1000, maj 40
Tuition: $5670 per yr (board & room included)
Courses: Architecture, Art Education, Art History, Ceramics, Constructions, Drawing, Graphic Arts, History of Art & Archaeology, Painting, Photography, Printmaking, Sculpture, Teacher Training, Theatre Arts
Adult Hobby Classes: Available through student activities board. Enrl 12-20; tui varies
Children's Classes: Available through Community Art Center. Enrl 10-20; tui varies
Summer School: Dir, Dr Raymond McCall

YELLOW SPRINGS

ANTIOCH COLLEGE, Department of Art,* 45387. Tel 513-767-7331, Ext 464. *Chmn* Allan L Jones, MFA; *Assoc Prof* James W Jordan, MFA; *Assoc Prof* John P Ritterskamp, MFA; *Assoc Prof* Karen Shirley, MFA; *Asst Prof* Janis Crystal Lipzin, MFA; *Instr* Nancy Rexroth, MFA
Estab 1853; pvt; D & E; ent req HS dipl; degrees BA and BFA 5 yrs; SC 48, LC 10; enrl D 665 per quarter, non-maj 100, maj 50
Tuition: $4500 per yr
Courses: Aesthetics, Art Education, †Art History, †Ceramics, Conceptual Art, Constructions, Drafting, †Drawing, †Film, †Graphic Arts, †Painting, †Photography, †Printmaking, †Sculpture

YOUNGSTOWN

YOUNGSTOWN STATE UNIVERSITY, Art Department,* 410 Wick Ave, 44555. Tel 216-742-3624. *Chmn Dept* William R McGraw; *Prof* Jon Naberezny, MA; *Assoc Prof* Joseph Babisch, MA; *Assoc Prof* Alfred Bright, MA; *Assoc Prof* Elaine Juhasz, MEd; *Assoc Prof* James Lepore, MFA; *Assoc Prof* James Lucas, MFA; *Assoc Prof* Russell Maddick, MFA; *Assoc Prof* Richard Mitchell, MFA; *Assoc Prof* Michael Walusis, MFA; *Assoc Prof* Louis Zona, DA; *Asst Prof* Jaroslav Ryska, PhD; *Asst Prof* R Ulrich, MA; *Instr* Dan Fantauzzi, MFA; *Instr* Michael Moseley, MFA
Estab 1908, dept estab 1952; pub; D & E; ent req HS dipl; degrees AB, BFA and BS 4 yrs; SC 44, LC 26, GC 8; enrl D & E 1250, maj 300, grad 15
Tuition: Res $795 per yr; nonres $1455 per yr
Courses: †Art Education, †Art History, Ceramics, †Commercial Art, Drawing, Graphic Arts, †Graphic Design, Illustration, Interior Design, Jewelry, Lettering, Museum Staff Training, †Painting, Photography, †Printmaking, †Sculpture, Teacher Training
Adult Hobby Classes: Tui $35 per 8 wks. Courses—Calligraphy, Ceramics, Drawing, Painting, Photography, Weaving
Summer School: Dir, Jon Naberezny. Tui same as above for term of 5 1 2 wks beginning June and July. Courses—same as above

OKLAHOMA

ADA

EAST CENTRAL UNIVERSITY, Art Department, 74820. Tel 405-332-8000, Ext 353. *Chmn* Dee J Lafon, MFA; *Instructor* Robert Sieg, MFA; *Instructor* Grant Thorp, MFA; *Vis Prof* Marc Etier, MFA
EStab 1909; pub; D & E; ent req HS dipl, ATC; degrees BA and BA(Educ) 4 yr, MEd 33 hrs, post graduate work, public service program; scholarships; SC 22, LC 10, GC 8; enrl D 222, E 105, non-maj 103, maj 80, grad 3, others 36
Tuition: Res—1000-2000 level courses $12, 3000-4000 level courses $13, 5000 level courses $15; nonres—1000-2000 level courses $31, 3000-4000 level courses $34, 5000 level courses $39
Courses: †Art Education, Art History, †Ceramics, Conceptual Art, †Drawing, Film, Graphic Arts, Jewelry, Mixed Media, †Painting, Photography, †Printmaking, †Sculpture, Silversmithing, †Teacher Training, Wood Design
Adult Hobby Classes: Enrl 25 average; tui $30. Courses—Drawing, Painting, Silk Screen
Summer School: Dir, Dr Stephenson. Courses—Ceramics, Drawing, Painting, Printmaking

ALVA

NORTHWESTERN OKLAHOMA STATE UNIVERSITY, Art Department, 73717. Tel 405-327-1700, Ext 243. *Chmn* Don Bellah, BFA
Estab 1897; pub; D; ent req HS dipl; degrees BA(Art), BA(Educ) and standard cert 4 yr, grad study for master of teaching degree 18 grad hrs available; SC 28, LC 6, GC 3; enrl D 50-80, non-maj 50, maj 30, grad 3
Tuition: Res—undergrad lower division $13 hourly, upper division $14 hourly, grad $15 hourly; nonres—undergrad lower division $31 hourly, upper division $35 hourly, grad $40; other correspondence and extension $17; campus res—room and board $960 per yr
Courses: Advertising Design, †Art Education, Art History, Ceramics, Commercial Art, Drawing, Graphic Arts, History of Art & Archaeology, Painting, Printmaking, Sculpture, Textile Design
Summer School: Enrl 40; tui same as above for term of 5 wks beginning May 28. Courses—vary each summer

CHICKASHA

UNIVERSITY OF SCIENCE AND ARTS OF OKLAHOMA, Arts Department, 73018. Tel 405-224-3140, Ext 301. Instrs FT 3, PT 3
Estab 1909; pub; D; degrees 124 hr req for grad; SC 26, LC 3; enrl maj 57, others 180
Courses: Art History, Ceramics, Commercial Art, Drawing, Graphic Arts, Handicrafts, Jewelry, Painting, Sculpture, Teacher Training, Design, Pottery & Modeling, Watercolor
Summer School: Courses offered

CLAREMORE

CLAREMORE COLLEGE, Art Department,* College Hill, 74017. Tel 918-341-7510. *Dir* Fred R Warford, EdD; *Instr* Sam Hildebrand, BFA; *Instr* Rowe Lee-Mills, BA; *Instr* Grace McCoy, MFA
Estab 1971; pub; D & E; ent req HS dipl, ACT; degrees AA and AS 2 yr; scholarships; SC 22, LC 3; enrl D 126, E 60, non-maj 146, maj 40
Tuition: Res $400 per yr; nonres $850 per yr; campus res available
Courses: Art History, Ceramics, Drawing, Graphic Arts, Lettering, Painting, Photography, Printmaking, Sculpture
Adult Hobby Classes: Tui $20 per 8 wk course. Courses—Landscape, Portrait Painting
Children's Classes: Tui $10 per hr. Courses—Children's Art
Summer School: Tui $10 per hr for term of 8 wks beginning June 5th. Courses—Advanced Ceramics, Art Appreciation, Drawing, Painting

DURANT

SOUTHEASTERN OKLAHOMA STATE COLLEGE, Art Department,* 74701. Tel 405-924-0121.
Estab 1909; pub; ent req HS dipl, col exam; degrees BA, BS and MEduc 4-5 yrs; enrl 330
Tuition: Res$13 per cr hr; nonres $32 per cr hr
Courses: Art History, Ceramics, Handicrafts, Painting, Applied Design, Design, Modeling (Clay), Perspective Drawing, Pictorial Composition, Watercolor

EDMOND

CENTRAL STATE UNIVERSITY, Art Department,* 100 North University Dr, 73034. Tel 405-341-2980. *Chmn* Kathryn Alcorn
Estab 1890; pub; D & E; ent req HS dipl, health exams, IQ test, scholarship tests; degrees BA, BS and MEduc 3-4 yrs; scholarships; enrl maj 280, grad 20, dept 1168, school 10,000
Tuition: Res—undergrad $356 per yr; nonres—undergrad $949 per yr
Courses: Advertising Design, Art Education, Art History, Ceramics, Commercial Art, Jewelry, Painting, Sculpture, Teacher Training, Art Appreciation, Art in America, Arts & Crafts, Design, Etching & Lithography, Figure Drawing, Metal Design, Modeling, Perspective & Composition, Puppetry & Related Arts, Studio Art, Watercolor, Weaving

ENID

PHILLIPS UNIVERSITY, Department of Art,* University Place, 73701. Tel 405-237-4433. *Chmn* Donald F Heath; *Assoc Prof* Jim Bray, MA; *Assoc Prof* Paul Denny Jr, MFA; *Asst Prof* Susan Appel, MA; *Instr* Elbert Wheeler, MA; *Instr* Meme Wheeler, BAE
Estab 1907, dept estab 1909; den; D & E; ent req HS dipl; degrees MBA and ME 5 yrs, BA, BS and BFA 4 yrs; scholarships; SC 20, LC 6; enrl D 45, E 18, non-maj 20, maj 25, others 18
Tuition: Res & nonres—undergrad $65 per hr; campus res—room and board $3000
Courses: Advertising Design, Art Education, Art History, Ceramics, Commercial Art, Constructions, Drawing, Goldsmithing, Graphic Arts, Graphic Design, Handicrafts, History of Art & Archaeology, Jewelry, Lettering, Painting, Sculpture, Silversmithing, Teacher Training
Adult Hobby Classes: Enrl 18; tui $50 per course. Courses—Ceramics, Jewelry
Summer School: Enrl 15; tui $50 for term of one cr hr. Courses—varies

LANGSTON

LANGSTON UNIVERSITY, Art Department, General Delivery, 73050. Tel 405-466-2231. *Chmn* Wallace Owens, MFA; *Asst Prof* Juanita Cotton, MA; *Instructor* Edwin Helm, MA
Estab 1897, dept estab 1928; pub; D & E; ent req HS dipl; degrees BA(Art Educ) and BA(Arts & Science); enrl D 51, non-maj 20, maj 31
Tuition: Res—undergrad $370, nonres-undergrad $405; campus res—room & board $950 per yr
Courses: Art Education, Art History, Ceramics, Commercial Art, Drawing, Graphic Arts, History of Art & Archaeology, Jewelry, Lettering, Mixed Media, Painting, Photography, Printmaking, Sculpture, Silversmithing, Teacher Training, Theatre Arts
Summer School: Tui $96 for term of 8 wks beginning June 5th. Courses—Drawing, Painting, Public School Art

LAWTON

CAMERON UNIVERSITY, Art Department,* 2800 Gore Blvd, 73505. Tel 405-248-2200. *Chmn* Jack Bryant
Estab 1970; pub; D & E; ent req HS dipl; degrees BA 4 yrs; scholarships; SC 22, LC 5; enrl D 417, E 90, maj 60
Tuition: $13-$34 per sem hr; campus res—room and board $643 per sem
Courses: Art Education, Ceramics, Drawing, Graphic Arts, Graphic Design, History of Art & Archaeology, Jewelry, Painting, Sculpture
Summer School: Courses—Art Education, Ceramics, Graphics, Jewelry, Painting

MIAMI

NORTHEASTERN OKLAHOMA A & M COLLEGE, Art Department, 74354. Tel 918-542-8441, Ext 263. *Chmn* Nick Calcagno, PhD. Instrs FT 2, PT 1
Estab 1919; pub; D & E; ent req HS dipl; degrees AA 2 yr; scholarships; SC 11, LC 1
Tuition: Res $10 per hr; nonres $25 per cr hr; campus residency available
Courses: Art Education, Calligraphy, Costume Design & Construction, Drafting, Drawing, History of Art & Archaeology, Lettering, Mixed Media, Painting, Sculpture, Stage Design, Theatre Arts

NORMAN

UNIVERSITY OF OKLAHOMA, School of Art,* 73019. Tel 405-352-0311. *Dir* Joe F Hobbs
Estab 1911; pub; degrees BFA, M (Art Educ) and MFA 4 yrs; scholarships; SC 27, LC 22, GC 12; enrl maj 350, others 1200
Tuition: Res—undergrad $538 per yr; nonres—undergrad $1460
Courses: Advertising Design, Art Education, Art History, Ceramics, Drawing, Film, Graphic Arts, Painting, Sculpture, Metal Design, Product Design

OKLAHOMA CITY

OKLAHOMA CITY UNIVERSITY, Art Department, 73106. Tel 405-521-5014. *Chmn* Brunel D Faris. Instrs FT 2, PT
Estab 1904; den; D & E; degrees 4 yr; scholarships; LC 2; enrl maj 50
Tuition: $3400 per yr includes books, fee estimates, meals & room
Courses: Advertising Design, Art History, Ceramics, Drawing, Graphic Arts, Jewelry, Painting, Sculpture, Teacher Training, Design, Watercolor
Summer School: Dir, Jack Davis. Enrl 300; tui $65 per cr hr for two 6 wk sessions June to July, July to August

OKMULGEE

OKLAHOMA STATE UNIVERSITY, School of Technical Training, 4th and Mission, 74447. Tel 918-756-6211. *Head Dept* Carlisle J Waugh, BS; *Instructor* Gary Borchert, BA; *Instructor* Paul A Gresham, MFA; *Instructor* Larry Rose; *Instructor* H Allen Shaw Jr, BFA; *Instructor* Bill Welch, BS. Instrs FT 5, PT 1
Estab 1948, dept estab 1970; pub; D & E; ent req HS dipl or 17 1 2 yrs of age; degrees 2 yr dipl, degree granting technical school, 2 yr associate degree; scholarships; SC 12, LC 1; enrl D 130, E 18
Tuition: Res—undergrad $735 per yr, $245 per trimester; nonres—undergrad $444 per trimester; campus res $1100 per yr
Courses: Advertising Design, Art Education, Commercial Art, Drafting, Drawing, Graphic Arts, Graphic Design, Illustration, Jewelry, Landscape Architecture, Lettering, Photography
Summer School: Tui same as above per trimester beginning June 1st to last of Sept

SHAWNEE

SAINT GREGORYS JUNIOR COLLEGE, Department of Art, 1900 MacArthur, 74801. Tel 405-273-9870. *Head Humanities* Patric McCoal, MA; *Prof* Shirlie Bowers, BFA
Estab 1898, dept estab 1960; den; D & E; ent req HS dipl, ACT or SAT; degrees AA 2 yrs; SC 6; enrl B 325
Tuition: Res and nonres—undergrad $1400 per yr, $700 per sem, PT $47 per hr; campus res—room & board $1440 per yr
Courses: Art History, Ceramics, Commercial Art, Drawing, Mixed Media, Sculpture
Adult Hobby Classes: Courses—Ceramics, Drawing, Sculpture

STILLWATER

OKLAHOMA STATE UNIVERSITY, Art Department, Gardiner Hall, 74074. Tel 405-624-6016. *Chmn* Herbert Gottfried, PhD
Estab 1890, dept estab 1928; pub; D & E; ent req HS dipl; degrees BA, BA(Art Educ), BFA, 4 yr; SC 20, LC 4; enrl D 850, E 60, non-maj 810, maj 100
Tuition: Res—undergrad hr; campus res—room and board $1218
Courses: Art History, Ceramics, Drawing, Graphic Design, Jewelry, Lettering, Painting, Printmaking, Sculpture
Summer School: Dir, Herbert Gottfried. Tui same as fall and spring

TAHLEQUAH

NORTHEASTERN OKLAHOMA STATE UNIVERSITY, 74464. Tel 918-456-5511, Ext 405. *Chmn* Dr Tom Cottrill, EdD; *Instructor* Jerry Choate, MFA; *Instructor* R C Coones, MFA; *Instructor* Dr Kathleen Schmidt, EdD
Estab 1889; pub; D & E; ent req HS dipl; degrees BA and BA(Educ) 4 yr; scholarships; enrl non-maj 50, maj 30, grad 10
Tuition: Campus residency available
Courses: Art Education, Art History, Ceramics, Commercial Art, Costume Design & Construction, Drafting, Drawing, Graphic Arts, Jewelry, Lettering, Painting, Photography, Printmaking, Sculpture, Silversmithing, Stage Design, Teacher Training, Theatre Arts
Adult Hobby Classes: Courses— Indian Art, Silversmithing
Summer School: Regular summer session

TULSA

ORAL ROBERTS UNIVERSITY, Fine Arts Department, 7777 S Lewis, 74171. Tel 918-492-6161, Ext 2144. *Head Dept* Dr Leon Kroeker, Doctorate; *Assoc Prof* Sue B Montgomery, MFA; *Assoc Prof* Dr Eileen Straton, Doctorate; *Instr* Charles Ramsay Sr, BS; *Vis Prof* Paul Davidson, commercial art; *Vis Prof* Dorothea Heit, photography; *Vis Prof* Susan Henderson, commercial art; *Vis Prof* Bob Howie, commercial art; *Vis Prof* Carol Kiper, printmaking; *Vis Prof* Stan Weir, commercial & studio art; *Vis Prof* Don Wilson, photography
Estab 1965; pvt; D & E; ent req HS dipl, SAT; degrees BA(Art Educ), BA(Commercial Art) and BA(Studio Art) 4 yrs; scholarships; SC 22, LC 3; enrl D 65, non-maj 40, maj 65, others 10
Tuition: Res and nonres—undergrad $80 per hr; campus res—room & board $1440 per sem
Courses: †Advertising Design, †Art Education, †Ceramics, †Commercial Art, Constructions, Costume Design & Construction, Drawing, Fashion Arts, Film, Graphic Arts, Graphic Design, Handicrafts, History of Art & Archaeology, Illustration, Intermedia, Interior Design, Lettering, Mixed Media, Painting, Photography, Printmaking, †Sculpture, †Teacher Training, Video

TULSA JUNIOR COLLEGE, Art Department, 909 S Boston, 74119. Tel 918-587-6561. *Instr* William Derrevere, MA; *Instr* Nota Johnson, MA. Instrs PT 8
Estab 1970; pub; D & E; ent req HS dipl; degrees AA 2 yrs; scholarships; SC 16, LC 7; enrl non-maj 40, maj 160
Tuition: Campus residency available
Courses: Art History, Drawing, Goldsmithing, Jewelry, Painting, Printmaking, Silversmithing, , Three-Dimensional Design
Adult Hobby Classes: Special prog of art courses and crafts courses

UNIVERSITY OF TULSA, Department of Art,* 600 S College Ave, 74104. Tel 918-939-6351. *Head Dept* Bradley E Place
Estab 1898; pvt; degrees BA, BS, BFA, MA, MFA and MTA 4 yrs; scholarships; SC 20, LC 13, GC 22; enrl maj 160, others 400
Tuition: Res—$1900 per yr; campus res available
Courses: Advertising Design, Ceramics, Drawing, Graphic Arts, Handicrafts, Industrial Design, Painting, Technical Illustration
Summer School: Dir, Bradley E Place. Enrl 150; two sessions June and July

WEATHERFORD

SOUTHWESTERN OKLAHOMA STATE UNIVERSITY, Art Department, 73096. Tel 405-772-6611, Ext 5000. *Chmn* James A Terrell; *Asst Prof* Montee Hoke; *Asst Prof* R Park Lang; *Asst Prof* LeRoy Schultz; *Instructor* George Calvert; *Instructor* Marge Donley; *Instructor* Pat Lazelle
Estab 1901, dept estab 1941; pub; D & E; ent req HS dipl; degrees BA(Art), BA(Art Educ) and BA(Commercial Art) 4 yr; SC 35, LC 8, GC 43; enrl D 5000
Tuition: Varies; campus residency available
Courses: Advertising Design, Art Education, Art History, Ceramics, Commercial Art, Drawing, Graphic Arts, Graphic Design, Illustration, Jewelry, Lettering, Mixed Media, Painting, Sculpture, Teacher Training
Summer School: Courses—Ceramics, Drawing, Elements of Art, Fundamentals of Art, Introduction to Clay, Jewelry, Metal I & II, Painting

OREGON

ALBANY

LINN BENTON COMMUNITY COLLEGE, Art Department,* 6500 SW Pacific Blvd, 97321. Tel 503-928-2361. *Chmn Humanities Div* Kenneth D Cheney
Estab 1968; pub; D & E; ent req open entry; degrees AA, AS and AGS 2 yrs; SC 14, LC 2; enrl D 2000, E 4000
Tuition: Res—$333 per yr
Courses: Advertising Design, Aesthetics, Ceramics, Commercial Art, Display, Drafting, Drawing, Graphic Arts, Graphic Design, Handicrafts, History of Art & Archaeology, Illustration, Jewelry, Lettering, Painting, Photography, Sculpture, Architecture, Textile Design, Theatre Arts, Stitchery, Weaving
Adult Hobby Classes: Courses—Painting, Tole Painting, Watercolor

ASHLAND

OREGON COLLEGE OF ART, 30 S First St, 97520. Tel 503-482-0113. *Pres* Dr Richard K Walsh. Instrs FT 2, PT 5
Estab 1971; pvt; D; ent req HS dipl, portfolio; degrees Bachelor of Professional Arts or cr transfer for AA or BA at adjacent Southern Oregon State Col 4 yrs; scholarships; SC 24, LC 5; enrl D 40
Courses: Advertising Design, Commercial Art, Drawing, Fashion Arts, Graphic Arts, Graphic Design, Illustration, Lettering, Painting

SOUTHERN OREGON STATE COLLEGE, Department of Art,* 1250 Siskiyou Blvd, 97520. Tel 503-482-6386. *Chmn Dept Art* Wesley G Chapman, PhD
Estab 1926; pub; D & E; ent req HS dipl; degrees BA or BS(Art Educ), BA or BS(Art) 4 yrs; scholarships; SC 48, LC 11, GC 1; enrl D 120, E 30, non-maj 100, maj 75
Tuition: Res—undergrad $699 per yr; nonres—undergrad $1968 per yr; campus res available
Courses: Advertising Design, Art Education, †Art History, Calligraphy, †Ceramics, Commercial Art, †Drawing, Graphic Design, †Handicrafts, Illustration, †Jewelry, Lettering, †Painting, Photography, †Printmaking, †Sculpture, †Teacher Training, Watercolor, †Weaving

BEND

CENTRAL OREGON COMMUNITY COLLEGE, Department of Art, College Way, 97701. *Assoc Prof* Douglas Campbell Smith, MA; *Assoc Prof* Tom Temple, MA
Estab 1949; pub; D & E; ent req HS dipl; degrees AA, AS, Cert; scholarships; enrl in col D 1500, E 2000
Tuition: In-district $132 per yr, out-of-district $205 per yr, out-of-state $630 per yr; campus res—room & board $1305
Courses: Calligraphy, Ceramics, Drawing, Painting, Photography, Printmaking, Stage Design, Theatre Arts
Summer School: Dir, Forrest Daniel. Enrl 450; term of 8 wks beginning June 17; additional workshop formats

COOS BAY

COOS ART MUSEUM, 515 Market Ave, 97420. Tel 503-267-3901. *Educ Dir* Jo Reid. Instrs PT 8
Estab 1966; pvt; D & E; SC 7; enrl D 15, E 100
Courses: Calligraphy, Display, Drawing, Jewelry, Lettering, Painting, Sculpture, Children's Craft & Stitchery, Spinning, Stitchery, Weaving
Adult Hobby Classes: Enrl 100; tui for 10 wks, non-mem $23, mem $20
Children's Classes: Enrl 40
Summer School: Dir, Jane Farrell. Tui same as above. Courses—Children's Craft, Drawing & Painting

SOUTHWESTERN OREGON COMMUNITY COLLEGE, Visual Arts Department, Empire Lakes, 97420. Tel 503-888-3234. *Div Chmn* Nathan Douthit, PhD; *Assoc Prof* Howard A Hall, MFA; *Asst Prof* Carol Vernon, MA
Estab 1962, dept estab 1964; pub; D & E; degrees AA 2 yrs; scholarships; SC 11, LC 1; enrl D 420, E 300, non-maj 250, maj 170
Tuition: Res—undergrad $140 per quarter; nonres—undergrad $280 per quarter; no campus res
Courses: Art Education, Art History, Calligraphy, Ceramics, Commercial Art, Drawing, Graphic Design, Painting, Photography, Printmaking, Sculpture, Theatre Arts, Video
Adult Hobby Classes: Tui $150 per quarter. Courses—Art Appreciation, Ceramics, Painting, Tole Painting, Wood Carving
Children's Classes: Only as occasional workshops
Summer School: Dean Instruction, John Rulifson. Tui varies. Courses—Ceramics, Painting and Composition, Watercolor

CORVALLIS

OREGON STATE UNIVERSITY
—Department of Art, Fairbanks Hall, 97331. Tel 503-754-4745. *Chmn Dept* Berkley W Chappell. Instrs FT 20, PT 2
Estab 1908; pub; D & E; ent req HS grad; degrees BA, BS and BFA 4 yrs; scholarships; SC 40, LC 15; enrl 1400, maj 250
Tuition: Res—$262 per quarter; nonres—$878 per quarter term
Courses: Art Education, Art History, Ceramics, Graphic Design, Illustration, Jewelry, Painting, Photography, Printmaking, Sculpture
Summer School: Tui undergrad $191, grad $286 for term of 8-11 wks. Courses—same as regular session
—Department of Architecture and Landscape Architecture, AG Hall, 97331. Tel 503-754-2606. *Chmn Dept* John R Stewart. Instrs FT 9
Archit estab 1947, Landscape Archit estab 1908, combined dept 1971; pub; D & E; ent req HS dipl; degrees BS and BA 4 yrs; SC 36, LC 12; enrl non-maj 200, maj 150
Tuition: Res—undergrad $738 per yr, grad $1164 per yr; nonres—undergrad $1311 per yr, grad $2487 per yr; campus res available
Courses: Architecture, Drafting, Drawing, Interior Design, Landscape Architecture, Architectural Design and Drawing, Architectural Design Studios, Construction and Materials, Graphics and Delineation, History and Theory, Housing and Architectural Philosophy, Influence of Man on his Physical Environments, Landscape Design Studios, Landscape Design and Theory, Maintenance and Construction, Plant Materials and Composition

EUGENE

LANE COMMUNITY COLLEGE, Art and Applied Design Department,* 4000 E 30th Ave, 97405. Tel 503-747-4501, Ext 306. *Chmn Dept* Roger Cornell McAlister, MFA; *Instr* Bill Blix, MFA; *Instr* Bruce Dean, MFA; *Instr* Harold Hoy, MFA; *Instr* Craig Spilman, MFA; *Instr* Alda Vinson, MA; *Instr* Dan White, MFA
Estab 1964, dept estab 1967; pub; D & E; ent req HS dipl; degrees AA, AS 2 yrs; SC 42, LC 4; enrl D 300, E 75, non-maj 240, maj 60
Tuition: Res—In County $396 per yr, In State $792 per yr; nonres—$1650 per yr; no campus res
Courses: Art History, Ceramics, Drafting, Drawing, Goldsmithing, Graphic Arts, Jewelry, Painting, Photography, Printmaking, Sculpture, Silversmithing, Metal Casting
Summer School: Dir, Roger Cornell McAlister. Tui $11 per cr hr. Courses—Drawing, Painting, Sculpture

MAUDE KERNS ART CENTER SCHOOL, 1910 E 15th Ave, 97403. Tel 503-345-1571. *Dir* Anne Jensch
Estab 1955; pvt; D & E; scholarships; SC 45; enrl D & E 450
Tuition: $38-$45 per class per quarter
Courses: Calligraphy, Ceramics, Graphic Arts, Handicrafts, Jewelry, Painting, Photography, Stitchery
Adult Hobby Classes: Enrl 420. Courses—Per regular session
Children's Classes: Enrl 50; tui $20. Courses—Ceramics, Drawing
Summer School: Courses varied

UNIVERSITY OF OREGON, Department of Fine & Applied Arts,* School of Architecture and Allied Arts, 97403. Tel 503-686-3610. *Dept Head* David G Foster Pub; D; degrees BA, BS 4 yrs, BFA 5 yrs, MFA 2 yrs minimum after BFA or equivalent; scholarships; enrl D 1500, non-maj 367, maj 926, others 231
Tuition: Res—undergrad $789 per yr, grad $1206 per yr; nonres—undergrad $2637 per yr, grad $1530 per yr; campus res—room and board $1400 per yr
Courses: Calligraphy, Ceramics, Drafting, Drawing, Goldsmithing, Graphic Design, Jewelry, Painting, Photography, Printmaking, Sculpture, Silversmithing, Video
Summer School: Dir, C W Schminke. Tui $252 for term of 8 wks beginning June

FOREST GROVE

PACIFIC UNIVERSITY IN OREGON, Department of Fine Arts, Division of Humanities, 2043 College Way, 97116. Tel 503-357-6151. *Chmn Div* Miles Shishido; *Asst Prof* Gary V Mueller, MS & MFA; *Asst Prof* Jan G Shield, MFA
Estab 1849; D & E; ent req HS dipl, SAT or ACT, counselor recommendation, transcript of acad work; degrees BA, MA(Teaching); scholarships
Tuition: $860 per 7 wk term, PT $430; campus res—room $125-$175 & board $215-$225 per term
Courses: Art History, Ceramics, Drawing, Graphic Design, Jewelry, Painting, Printmaking, Sculpture, Stained Glass
Summer School: Dir, John L Parker

LA GRANDE

EASTERN OREGON STATE COLLEGE, Division of Humanities and Fine Arts, Eighth and K Sts, 97850. Tel 503-963-2171. *Chmn* John L Cobb; *Assoc Prof Art* Ian Gatley, MA; *Assoc Prof Art* Thomas Morandi, MFA; *Asst Prof Art* Robin Alexander, PhD; *Asst Prof Art* Thomas Dimond, MFA
Estab 1929; pub; D & E; ent req HS dipl; degrees BA & BS in Art, BA & BS in Secondary Educ with Endorsement in Art, BA & BS in Elementary Educ with Specialization in Art 4 yrs; SC 32, LC 8, GC 2
Tuition: Res—$732 per yr; campus res available
Courses: Aesthetics, †Art Education, Art History, Calligraphy, Ceramics, Drawing, Lettering, Painting, Photography, Printmaking, Sculpture, Stage Design, Teacher Training, Textile Design, Theatre Arts, Glassblowing
Summer School: Dir, Dr Richard Hiatt. Term of 4-8 wks. Courses—Two or three a summer, beginning level

MCMINNVILLE

LINFIELD COLLEGE, Art Department, 97128. Tel 503-472-4121, Ext 274. *Chmn Dept* Steven Karatzas, MFA; *Prof* Helen Alford; *Prof* Patricia Fields, MFA
Estab 1849, dept estab 1964; pvt; D; ent req HS dipl; degrees BA 4 yr, ME 2 yr; scholarships; SC 16, LC 2; enrl non-maj 150, maj 20
Tuition: $1400 per sem, $55 per hr; campus res—room and board $1450 per yr
Courses: Advertising Design, Art Education, Art History, Calligraphy, Ceramics, Commercial Art, Constructions, Costume Design & Construction, Drawing, Film, Graphic Arts, Graphic Design, Interior Design, Lettering, Mixed Media, Painting, Photography, Printmaking, Sculpture, Stage Design, Teacher Training, Textile Design, Theatre Arts, Video
Summer School: Tui $430 for 5 sem hrs; block of 5 wks

MONMOUTH

OREGON COLLEGE OF EDUCATION, Creative Arts Department, Visual Arts, 97361. Tel 503-838-1220, Ext 340. *Art Coordr* James T Mattingly. Instrs FT 10, PT 2
Estab 1856; pub; D & E; degrees BA and BS 4 yr; SC 63, LC 17, GC 6; enrl total 3500
Tuition: Res—undergrad $684; nonres—undergrad $1953
Courses: Art Education, Art History, Ceramics, Drawing, Handicrafts, Jewelry, Lettering, Mixed Media, Painting, Photography, Printmaking, Sculpture, Textile Design, Design, Individual Studies, The Art Idea: Visual Thinking, Visual Learning & Communication, Watercolor, Weaving
Summer School: Tui res—undergrad $281 for 12-21 hrs, grad $426 for 9-16 hrs. Courses—as above

PORTLAND

JUDSON BAPTIST COLLEGE, Department of Fine Arts,* 9201 NE Fremont St, 97220. Tel 503-252-5563. *Head Dept* David S Johnson, MFA; *Instr* Janet Otter, BA
Estab 1956, dept estab 1964; den; D & E; ent req HS dipl, CEEB, references; degrees AA and AS 2 yrs; scholarships; SC 5, LC 2; enrl D 66, E 15, non-maj 60-65, maj 12-15
Tuition: Res—$3390 per yr; nonres—$2070 per yr: campus res—room and board $1320
Courses: Advertising Design, Art History, Calligraphy, Drawing, Painting, Art Appreciation, Basic Design

LEWIS AND CLARK COLLEGE, Department of Art, 0615 SW Palatine Hill Rd, 97219. Tel 503-244-6161, Ext 305. *Chmn of Dept* Stewart Buettner; *Prof* Ken Shores, MFA; *Assoc Prof* Norman Paasche; *Asst Prof* Phyllis A Yes; *Lectr* Judith Fawkes; *Lectr* Jack Portland; *Lectr* Bruce West
Dept estab 1946; pvt; D; ent req HS dipl; degrees BS and BA 4 yr; scholarships; SC 10, LC 2
Courses: Art History, Calligraphy, Ceramics, Drawing, Graphic Arts, History of Art & Archaeology, Painting, Printmaking, Sculpture, Weaving
Summer School: Dir, Sid Eiders

OREGON SCHOOL OF ARTS AND CRAFTS, (Formerly School of the Arts and Crafts Society) 8245 SW Barnes Rd, 97225. Tel 503-297-5544. *Dir* Bridget Beattie McCarthy. Instrs PT 40
Estab 1906; pvt; D & E; ent req none; degrees none; college credit available on request through affiliate university; scholarships; SC and LC 50; enrl D 225-250, E 200-225
Tuition: All courses cost $90 per ten wk period; classes vary in laboratory fees; no campus res
Courses: Calligraphy, Ceramics, Drawing, Jewelry, Photography, Printmaking, Silversmithing, Textile Design, Design, Flat Glass, Weaving, Woodworking

PORTLAND ART MUSEUM, Museum Art School, 1219 SW Park Ave, 97205. Tel 503-226-4391. *Acting Dean* Harry Widman, MFA; *Instructor* George Cummings; *Instructor* William Grand; *Instructor* Manuel Izquierdo; *Instructor* George Johanson; *Instructor* Edward Malin; *Instructor* Jack McLarty; *Instructor* Jack Myers. Instrs FT 14, PT 29
Estab 1909; pvt; D & E; ent req HS dipl, home drawing test; degrees BFA 4 yr; scholarships; SC 17, LC 7; enrl D FT 146, PT 50, E 248
Tuition: $2300 per yr, $1150 per sem; no campus res
Courses: Advertising Design, Art History, Calligraphy, Ceramics, Commercial Art, Drawing, Fashion Arts, Graphic Arts, Graphic Design, Illustration, Lettering, Painting, Photography, Printmaking, Sculpture
Adult Hobby Classes: Enrl 248; tui $88 per sem. Courses—Calligraphy, Ceramics, Graphic Design, Life Drawing, Painting, Printmaking
Children's Classes: Enrl 120; tui $70 per sem. Courses—General Art
Summer School: Acting Dean, Harry Widman. Tui $80 for 6 wks beginning June 19

PORTLAND COMMUNITY COLLEGE, Department of Fine Arts, 12000 SW 49th, 97219. Tel 503-244-6111. *Dept Chmn* Eugene Barrett, MA; *Instr* Owen Chamberlain, MFA; *Instr* Mary Coffee, MA; *Instr* Richard Helzer, MFA; *Instr* Robert Hughitt, MFA; *Instr* Richard Loleama, MFA; *Instr* Charles Ransom, MFA; *Instr* Allison Renwick, MFA; *Instr* James Schuld, MA; *Instr* Jacqueline Svaren, MA; *Instr* Russell Svaren, MFA; *Instr* Kenneth Weeks, MFA; *Instr* Sharon Bronzan, MS
Estab 1961, dept estab 1963; pub; D & E; ent req none; degrees AA 2 yrs; SC 40, LC 5; enrl D 864, E 282
Tuition: Res—undergrad $398 per yr, $133 per sem, PT (1-8 cr hrs) $15 per hr; nonres—undergrad $756 per yr, $252 per sem, PT $28 per hr; no campus res
Courses: Advertising Design, Aesthetics, †Architecture, Art Education, †Art History, Calligraphy, Ceramics, Collage, †Drawing, Fashion Arts, Graphic Arts, Graphic Design, Illustration, Industrial Design, Jewelry, Landscape Architecture, Lettering, Painting, Photography, Sculpture, Silversmithing, Stage Design, Video
Adult Hobby Classes: Tui varies per quarter. Courses—various
Summer School: Dept Chmn, Eugene Barrett. Enrl 400; tui $133 for term of 8 wks beginning June. Courses—same as regular session

PORTLAND STATE UNIVERSITY, Department of Art and Architecture, PO Box 751, 97207. Tel 503-229-3515. *Head Dept* Leonard B Kimbrell, PhD; *Prof* Byron Gardner, Cert; *Prof* Jean Glazer, MA; *Prof* Raymond Grimm, MA; *Prof* James L Hansen, Dipl; *Prof* Frederick H Heidel, MFA; *Prof* James Hibbard, MFA; *Prof* Robert Kasal, MA; *Prof* Melvin Katz, Cert; *Prof* Robert Morton, MA; *Prof* Louis Ocepek, MA
Estab 1955; pub; D & E; ent req HS dipl; degrees BS and BA(Art) 4 yr, MST, MAT(Art) 1 yr, MFA(Painting, Ceramics, Sculpture) 2 yr; scholarships; enrl E 2000, non-maj 1300, maj 600, grad 30, others 70
Tuition: Res—undergrad $179 per term, grad $311 per term; nonres—undergrad $710 per term; campus residency available
Courses: Architecture, Art History, †Ceramics, †Drawing, †Graphic Design, †Painting, Printmaking, †Sculpture, Textile Design, Design, Metalsmithing
Summer School: Enrl 4-500; term of 8-12 wks beginning June 28. Courses—vary. Two centers, one in Portland and one at Cannon Beach: The Haystack Program

REED COLLEGE, Department of Art, 97202. Tel 503-771-1112. *Chmn Dept* Scott T Sonniksen. Instrs FT 4, PT 1
Estab 1911; pvt; D; degrees BA 3-5 yr; scholarships; SC 7, LC 5; enrl D 1150, E 15

Tuition: $4920 per yr; student body fee $70 per yr; campus res—room & board $1820 per yr
Courses: Aesthetics, Calligraphy, Drawing, History of Art & Archaeology, Painting, Sculpture, Experimental Media, Paleography

ROSEBURG

UMPQUA COMMUNITY COLLEGE, Art Department, PO Box 967, 97470. Tel 503-672-5571, Ext 32. *Coordr* Joel Lynn Boyce Jr, MFA; *Instructor* Ed Beardsley, MFA; *Instructor* Robert Bell, MFA; *Instructor* Gary Courter, MFA; *Instructor* Didier Mau Jean, MFA; *Instructor* Marie Rasmussen, MS
Estab 1964; pub; D & E; ent req HS dipl; degrees AA 2 yr; scholarships; SC 5, LC 2; enrl D 190, E 90, maj 18
Tuition: $145 per 10 wk term; no campus res
Courses: Art History, Calligraphy, Ceramics, Drawing, Painting, Photography, Printmaking, Sculpture, Theatre Arts, Jewelry, Art Appreciation, Basic Design, Lapidary, Music Arts, Weaving
Adult Hobby Classes: Courses—Ceramics, Drawing, Painting, Photography

SALEM

CHEMEKETA COMMUNITY COLLEGE, Department of Humanities & Social Science, 4000 Lancaster Dr NE, PO Box 14007, 97309. Tel 503-399-5000. *Dir* Thomas Gill, MFA; *Instructor* Robert Bibler, MFA; *Instructor* Lee Jacobson, MFA
Estab 1969, dept estab 1975; pub; D & E; ent req none; degrees AA 2 yr; scholarships; SC 9, LC 3; enrl D 125, E 75
Tuition: Res—$15 per cr hr, $150 quarterly; nonres—$20-$50 per cr hr, $195-$485 quarterly; no campus res
Courses: Art History, Calligraphy, Ceramics, Drafting, Drawing, Film, Painting, Photography, Printmaking, Theatre Arts
Adult Hobby Classes: Enrl 150-200; tui 75¢ per contact hr
Summer School: Dir, Thomas Gill. Term of 8 wks

PENNSYLVANIA

ALLENTOWN

CEDAR CREST COLLEGE, Art Department, 18104. Tel 215-437-4471. *Chmn Dept* Ryland W Greene. Instrs FT 3, PT 2
Estab 1867; pvt; D & E; ent req HS dipl, CEEB; degrees BA, BS, Interdisciplinary Fine Arts Maj (art, theatre, music, dance, creative writing), 4 yr; scholarships; SC 11, LC 4; enrl 750
Courses: Aesthetics, Art Education, Art History, Ceramics, Drawing, Jewelry, Painting, Sculpture, Theatre Arts, Comparative Study of Art, Metal Forming
Summer School: Courses—Ceramics, Jewelry-Metalsmithing

BETHLEHEM

LEHIGH UNIVERSITY, Department of Art and Architecture, Chandler-Ullmann Hall, Bldg 17, 18015. Tel 215-861-3610. *Chmn Dept* Nicholas Adams, PhD; *Prof* Richard J Redd, MFA; *Assoc Prof* Carlos J Alvare, MArchit; *Assoc Prof* Ricardo Viera, MFA; *Asst Prof* Gary M Burnley, MFA; *Asst Prof* Paul Felder, MSArchit. Instrs PT 1
Estab 1925; pvt; D & E; ent req HS dipl, SAT, CEEB; degrees BA 4 yrs; SC 22, LC 16; enrl D & E 700
Tuition: $4550 per yr, $2275 per sem; campus residency available
Courses: †Architecture, †Art History, Drawing, Mixed Media, Painting, Photography, Printmaking, †General Art
Summer School: Dir, Dr Norman Sam. Courses—Teacher Training

MORAVIAN COLLEGE, Department of Art, South Campus, 18018. Tel 215-865-0741. *Chmn Dept* Rudy S Ackerman, DEd; *Assoc Prof* Daniel Tereshko, MFA; *Asst Prof* Charlene Engel, PhD; *Instr* Jamie Musselman, MA; *Instructor* Kevin Raines, MFA; *Photographer-in-Residence* Judy Ross, MA; *Ceramist-in-Residence* Renzo Faggioli, Master Craftsman
Estab 1807, dept estab 1963; pvt; D & E; ent req HS dipl; degrees BA and BS 4 yrs; SC 15, LC 8; enrl D 350, E 15, non-maj 1200, maj 50
Tuition: $5000 per yr
Courses: †Art History, †Ceramics, †Drawing, Film, Jewelry, †Painting, †Photography, Printmaking, Sculpture, Silversmithing, Textile Design
Summer School: Tui $250 for term of 6 wks. Courses—same as during regular terms

NORTHAMPTON COUNTY AREA COMMUNITY COLLEGE, Art Department, 3835 Green Pond Rd, 18017. Tel 215-865-5351. *Prog Coordr* Gerald Rowan
Estab 1967; pub; D & E; ent req HS dipl, portfolio; degrees AAS(Advertising), cert in photography; scholarships; SC 12, LC 8; enrl D 100, E 350
Courses: Advertising Design, Architecture, Art History, Ceramics, Commercial Art, Drafting, Drawing, Fashion Arts, Graphic Arts, Graphic Design, Handicrafts, History of Art & Archaeology, Illustration, Interior Design, Lettering, Painting, Photography, Printmaking, Sculpture, Pottery

BLOOMSBURG

BLOOMSBURG STATE COLLEGE, Department of Art, Blakeless Center for the Humanities, 17815. *Chmn Dept* Percival R Roberts III, EdD; *Asst Prof* Robert Koslosky, MA; *Assoc Prof* Stewart Nagel, MFA; *Assoc Prof* Barbara J Strohman, MFA; *Assoc Prof* Kenneth T Wilson, MA; *Asst Prof* Karl Beamer, MFA; *Asst Prof* Gary F Clark, MA; *Asst Prof* John Cook, MA; *Asst Prof* Charles Thomas Walter, PhD
Estab 1839, dept estab 1940; pub; D & E; ent req HS dipl; degrees BA(Art Studio) and BA(Art History) 4 yrs, MA(Art Studio); scholarships; SC 7, LC 12; enrl D 1800, E 200, maj 75
Tuition: Res—$475 per sem; nonres—$750 per sem; campus residency available
Courses: Aesthetics, Art Education, Art History, Ceramics, Drawing, Goldsmithing, Handicrafts, History of Art & Archaeology, Jewelry, Museum Staff Training, Painting, Printmaking, Sculpture, Silversmithing, Stage Design, Textile Design, Theatre Arts, General Design, Weaving
Children's Classes: Enrl 25; tui $10 per sem; Sat classes for children
Summer School: Dean, Richard O Wolfe. Enrl 200-300; tui $39 per cr hr. Courses—vary

BRYN MAWR

BRYN MAWR COLLEGE, Department of the History of Art, 19010. Tel 215-645-5333, 645-5334. *Chmn Dept* Charles Dempsey. Instrs FT 6, PT 1
Estab 1913; pvt, W (men in grad school); degrees BA 4 yr, MA, PhD; scholarships and fel; LC 10, GC 8; enrl maj 20, grad 30, others 150
Tuition: $4650, campus res $2300
Courses: Art History

HARCUM JUNIOR COLLEGE, Department of Fine Arts, 19010. Tel 215-525-4100, Ext 215. *Chmn Dept* Martin Zipin. Instrs FT 1, PT 5
Estab 1915; pvt, W; D & E; ent req HS dipl; degrees AA 2 yr; scholarships; SC 7, LC 1; enrl D 40, E 8, maj 10
Courses: Commercial Art, Drawing, Fashion Arts, Graphic Design, History of Art & Archaeology, Lettering, Painting, Sculpture

CALIFORNIA

CALIFORNIA STATE COLLEGE, Department of Art, 15419. Tel 412-938-4000. *Pres* Dr John P Watkins, PhD; *Chmn* Raymond E Dunlevy, MEd; *Asst Prof* Gale H Boak, MAE; *Asst Prof* Richard H Grinstead II, MAE & MFA; *Asst Prof* Leslie A Parkinson, MEd; *Asst Prof* Philip Schaltenbrand, MEd
Estab 1852, dept estab 1968; pub; D & E; ent req SAT; degrees BA 4 yrs; SC 20, LC 5; enrl maj 64
Tuition: Res—undergrad $950 per yr, $475 per sem, PT $39 per cr; nonres—undergrad $1780 per yr, $890 per sem, PT $71 per cr; campus res—room & board $1060
Courses: Advertising Design, Architecture, Art History, Calligraphy, Ceramics, Drafting, Drawing, Graphic Arts, Graphic Design, Industrial Design, Intermedia, Jewelry, Painting, Photography, Printmaking, Sculpture, Teacher Training
Adult Hobby Classes: Enrl 25 per class; tui $20 per class. Courses—Pottery, Stained Glass
Summer School: Chmn, Raymond E Dunlevy. Tui $39 per cr for term of 5 or 10 wks beginning June

CARLISLE

DICKINSON COLLEGE, Fine Arts Department,* High St, 17013. Tel 717-243-5121. *Chmn Fine Arts Dept* Dennis Akin, MFA; *Asst Prof* Caroline Bruzelius, PhD; *Asst Prof* Sharon Latchaw Hirsch, PhD; *Asst Prof* Morris Perinchief; *Assoc Prof* Harry Krebs
Estab 1773, dept estab 1940; pvt; D; ent req HS dipl, SAT; degrees BA and BS 4 yrs; SC 7, LC 11; enrl 250, non-maj 185, maj 65
Tuition: Res—undergrad $6345 per yr; campus res available
Courses: †Art History, Ceramics, Drawing, Film, †Mixed Media, Painting, Photography, Printmaking, Sculpture
Summer School: Dir, Peggy Garrett. Tui $295 per course for term of 5 1 2 wks beginning May. Courses—per regular session

CHELTENHAM

CHELTENHAM ART CENTRE, 439 Ashbourne Rd, 19012. Tel 215-379-4660. *Pres* Marsha Moss
Estab 1940; enrl 3600
Courses: Drawing, Jewelry, Mixed Media, Painting, Photography, Sculpture, Pottery, Stained Glass, Theatre Glass

CHEYNEY

CHEYNEY STATE COLLEGE, Department of Art,* 19319. Tel 215-399-6880. *Chmn Dept* Samuel L Curtis
Estab 1937; pub; D & E; ent req HS dipl, ent exam; degrees BA 4 yrs; scholarships; SC 16, LC 4
Tuition: Res—$890; nonres—$1580
Courses: Aesthetics, Ceramics, Drawing, Graphic Arts, Handicrafts, History of Art & Archaeology, Painting, Sculpture, Art Therapy

CLARION

CLARION STATE COLLEGE, Department of Art, 16214. Tel 814-226-6000, Ext 379. *Chmn* Robert D Hobbs, EdD; *Prof* Francis C Baptist, EdD; *Assoc Prof* Alfred B Charley, MFA; *Assoc Prof* William T Edwards Jr, EdD; *Assoc Prof* William E Grosch, MEd; *Assoc Prof* Eugene A Seelye, MA; *Asst Prof* Cathie Joslyn; *Asst Prof* Andor S P-Jobb, MFA
Estab 1867; pub; D & E; ent req HS dipl; degrees BA(Art); SC 4, LC 21, GC 1; enrl D & E 925 per sem, maj 25
Tuition: Campus residency available
Courses: Art Education, Art History, Ceramics, Drawing, Graphic Arts, Graphic Design, Handicrafts, Jewelry, Painting, Sculpture, Three-Dimensional Design
Adult Hobby Classes: Continuing Education. Tui $35-$50 for 12 wk course. Courses—Applique & Quilting, Ceramics, Drawing, Patchwork
Summer School: Dir, Dr Charles Schontz

CRESSON

MOUNT ALOYSIUS JUNIOR COLLEGE, Art Department, Rte 22, 16630. Tel 814-886-4131, Ext 40. *Assoc Prof* Sr Maria J D'Angelo, RSM. Instrs FT 4
Estab 1939; den; D & E; ent req HS dipl, SAT, ACT, health record, art portfolio and interview; degrees AA 2 yr; scholarships; SC 10, LC 12; enrl D 153, E 8, maj 23
Tuition: $83 per cr; campus res—room and board $1650 per yr
Courses: Advertising Design, Art Education, Art History, Calligraphy, Ceramics, Commercial Art, Display, Drawing, Graphic Design, Lettering, Occupational Therapy, Painting, Photography, Printmaking, Sculpture, Teacher Training, Two & Three-Dimensional Design

DALLAS

COLLEGE MISERICORDIA, Art Department, 18612. Tel 717-675-2181, Ext 234. *Chmn Dept* Ralph G Kaleshefski, MA; *Asst Prof* Martha Rochester Kaleshefski, MFA; *Asst Prof* Sr Flora Mulhearn, MA; *Asst Prof* Sr Elaine Tulanowski, MA
Estab 1924, dept estab 1965; pvt; D & E; ent req HS dipl; degrees AAS, BA, BS, BM; scholarships; SC 35, LC 10; enrl D 40, non-maj 25, maj 40, others 4 extension
Tuition: $2630 per yr; campus residency available
Courses: Aesthetics, †Art Education, Art History, Calligraphy, Ceramics, Drawing, Painting, Photography, Printmaking, Sculpture, Teacher Training, Theatre Arts
Summer School: Dir, Sr Mary Glennon. Courses—vary

EASTON

LAFAYETTE COLLEGE, Department of Art, 18042. Tel 215-253-6281, Ext 328. *Acting Dept Head* David S Crocket
Estab 1827; pvt; D & E; ent req HS dipl, ent exam, selective admis; degrees BS and AB 4 yr; scholarships; SC 8, LC 12; enrl D 300, E 250, maj 4
Courses: Art History, Drawing, Painting, Printmaking, Sculpture, History of Architecture, Two & Three-Dimensional Design

EDINBORO

EDINBORO STATE COLLEGE, Art Department, 16444. Tel 814-732-2406. *Chmn Art Dept* George R Shoemaker; *Chmn Two-Dimensional Area* Ian Short, MFA; *Chmn Three-Dimensional Area* Jerry Valley, MFA; *Chmn Crafts* Donna Nicholas, MFA; *Chmn Art History* Barthwell Farmer, MA; *Chmn Art Educ* Dorn Howlett, MA; *Dir Galleries* Mary Jane Kidd, MFA; *Cur Coll* L Rosenfeld, MA. Instrs FT 43
Estab 1857; pub; D & E; ent req HS dipl, SAT; degrees BSEd, BFA and BA 4 yrs, MEd 1 yr, MFA 2 yrs; scholarships; SC 86, LC 30, GC 20; enrl D 850 art maj, non-maj 6000, grad 25
Tuition: Res—undergrad $1854 per yr, $425 per sem, grad $475 per sem, $51 per cr hr; nonres—undergrad $2604 per yr, $800 per sem, grad $890 per sem, $75 per cr hr; campus residency available
Courses: Aesthetics, Art Education, Art History, Ceramics, Conceptual Art, Drawing, Film, Graphic Design, Illustration, Jewelry, Lettering, Mixed Media, Painting, Photography, Printmaking, Sculpture, Silversmithing, Teacher Training, Textile Design, Communications Graphics, Weaving
Summer School: Dir, Dr George R Shoemaker. Courses—Drawing, Jewelry, Painting, Printmaking, Sculpture, Textile Design, Weaving

ERIE

MERCYHURST COLLEGE, Department of Art, 501 E 38th St, 16501. Tel 814-864-0681. *Acting Dir* Daniel Burke, MEd; *Prof* Joseph Pizzat, EdD; *Assoc Prof* Edward Higgins, MS; *Assoc Prof* Ernest Mauthe, MA. Instrs PT 4
Estab 1926, dept estab 1950; pvt; D & E; ent req HS dipl, col boards, portfolio review; degrees BA 4 yr; scholarships; SC 45, LC 12; enrl D 100, E 30, maj 100
Tuition: $2975 per yr; campus res—room and board $1530 per yr
Courses: Advertising Design, Art Education, Art History, Ceramics, Commercial Art, Drawing, Jewelry, Painting, Photography, Printmaking, Sculpture, Art Appreciation, Art Foundations, Art Therapy, Child Art, Contemporary Art Theories, Creative Arts for Adolescents and Children, Creativity, Fabrics, Fibers, Independent Study, Individualized Studio, Senior Seminar, Teaching Internship, Television Internship
Adult Hobby Classes: 6-8 wks. Courses—Crafts, Drawing, Painting
Summer School: Dir, Daniel Burke. Tui $300 per course for term 0f 5-6 wks beginning June July. Courses—vary

FACTORYVILLE

KEYSTONE JUNIOR COLLEGE, Art Department, College Avenue, Factoryville, PA. (Mailing Add: LaPlume, PA 18440) Tel 717-945-5141. *Chmn Fine Arts* Karl O Neuroth, MEd; *Instr* William Tersteeg, MFA; *Instr* Clifton A Prokop, MFA
Estab 1868, dept estab 1965; pvt; D & weekends; ent req HS dipl, SAT; degrees AA 2 yrs; scholarships; SC 15, LC 2; enrl D 155, weekenders 15, non-maj 100, maj 55
Tuition: Res—$2650 per yr; campus res—room & board $1630
Courses: Art History, Ceramics, Drawing, Painting, Photography, Printmaking, Sculpture, Life Drawing, Three-Dimensional Design, Two-Dimensional Design
Summer School: Dean of College, William Messner. Enrl limited to 18; tui $70 per cr for term of 5 wks beginning June. Courses—Photography

GETTYSBURG

GETTYSBURG COLLEGE, Department of Art,* 17325. Tel 717-334-3131, Ext 243. *Chmn* Ingolf J Qually, MFA; *Asst Prof* Alan Paulson; *Instr* Marsha Munie; *Instr* Carol Small
Estab 1832, dept estab 1956; pvt; D; ent req HS dipl, ent exam; degrees BA 4 yrs; scholarships; SC 10, LC 15; enrl D 300
Tuition: Res—$4260 per yr; campus res—room $870, board $780
Courses: Aesthetics, †Art History, †Drawing, †Painting, †Printmaking, †Sculpture, Basic Design, Figure Drawing

GLENSIDE

BEAVER COLLEGE, Department of Fine Arts, Easton & Church Rds, 19038. Tel 215-884-3500. *Asst Prof* Bonnie Hayes, MA, ABD; *Asst Prof* Ron Kalla, MEd; *Asst Prof* Dennis Kuronen, MFA; *Asst Prof* Ann Williams, MFA. Instrs PT 7
Estab 1853; pvt; D & E; ent req HS dipl, SAT, ACT, optional portfolio review; degrees BA and BFA 4 yrs, MA(Educ) 1 yr; scholarships; SC 43, LC 14; enrl in col D FT 639, PT 133, non-maj in dept 20, maj in dept 126
Tuition: $3950 per yr, $1975 per sem, $494 per 4 cr course; campus res-room & board $1900
Courses: Advertising Design, Aesthetics, †Art Education, †Art History, †Ceramics, Commercial Art, Drawing, †Graphic Design, Illustration, †Interior Design, †Jewelry, †Painting, Photography, †Printmaking, Teacher Training, Weaving
Summer School: Chmn, Jack Davis. Enrl approx 200; tui $70 per cr hr for term of 7 wks beginning June 8. Courses—Painting, Printmaking

GREENSBURG

SETON HILL COLLEGE, Department of Art, 15601. Tel 412-834-2200, Ext 388. *Chmn Dept* Stuart R Thompson, PhD; *Instructor* Laura Bench, MFA; *Instructor* Raymond DeFazio, MEd; *Instructor* Josefa Filkosky, MFA; *Instructor* Mary Janice Grindle, BA; *Instructor* Rosalie O'Hara, ML
Estab 1918, dept estab 1950; den; D & E; ent req HS dipl, review portfolio; degrees BFA 4 yr; SC 20, LC 6; enrl D 70, non-maj 50, maj 20
Tuition: $2740 per yr; campus res—room and board $1484 per yr
Courses: Aesthetics, †Art Education, †Calligraphy, †Ceramics, Costume Design & Construction, †Drawing, Fashion Arts, †Film, Goldsmithing, Handicrafts, †Jewelry, Lettering, †Painting, †Photography, †Printmaking, †Sculpture, Silversmithing, Stage Design, Teacher Training, Textile Design, Theatre Arts, Fabrics
Summer School: Dir Continuing Educ, Jan Orris. Courses—Clay, Fabrics, Metalsmithing, Photography, Raku

GREENVILLE

THIEL COLLEGE, Department of Art, College Ave, 16125. Tel 412-588-7700, Ext 265. *Chmn Dept* Alvin S Dunkle, MA; *Assoc Prof* Richard L Hayes, MA; *Instr* William S Bukowski
Estab 1866, dept estab 1965; pvt; D & E; ent req HS dipl, interviews; degrees BA 4 yrs; scholarships; SC 15, LC 11; enrl D 275, non-maj 200, maj 75
Tuition: Res—$2105 per yr; nonres—$1425 per yr, $96 per cr hr; Jan interim term $487; campus res—room & board $1380 per yr
Courses: Art History, Ceramics, Drawing, Graphic Arts, Jewelry, Painting, Printmaking, Sculpture, Stage Design, Theatre Arts, Design
Summer School: Asst Acad Dean, Richard Houpt. Tui $288 per course for term of 4 wks beginning June 3. Courses—Art History, Extended Studies, Painting

HARRISBURG

HARRISBURG AREA COMMUNITY COLLEGE, Division of Communication and the Arts, 3300 Cameron Street Rd, 17110. Tel 717-236-9533. *Chairperson* Paul Hurley, MA; *Assoc Prof* Robert Wicks, MA; *Asst Prof* Edith Socolow, MA; *Vis Prof* Lawrence von Barann; *Vis Prof* Daniel Fitch
Estab 1964; pub; D & E; ent req HS dipl; degrees AA 2 yrs; SC 15, LC 5; enrl D 400, E 100, maj 50
Tuition: Res—undergrad $560 per yr, $280 per sem, $24 per hr of cr; nonres—undergrad $1680 per yr, $840 per sem, $71 per hr of cr; out-of-state $1120 per yr, $560 per sem, $47 per hr of cr; no campus res
Courses: Art History, Ceramics, Commercial Art, Drafting, Drawing, Film, Graphic Arts, Handicrafts, Jewelry, Painting, Photography, Printmaking, Sculpture, Stage Design, Theatre Arts
Adult Hobby Classes: Courses—Calligraphy, Drawing, Painting
Summer School: Dir, Paul Hurley. Courses—vary

HAVERFORD

HAVERFORD COLLEGE, Fine Arts Department,* 19041. Tel 215-649-9600. *Chmn Dept* Charles Stageman
Estab 1833, dept estab 1969; pvt; D, M; ent req HS dipl, programs in cooperation with Bryn Mawr College, Fine Arts Department; degrees BA 4 yrs; scholarships; enrl maj 15
Tuition: Res—$4880 per yr; campus res available
Courses: Drawing, Graphic Arts, History of Art & Archaeology, Painting, Photography, Sculpture

MAINLINE CENTER OF THE ARTS, Old Buck Rd & Lancaster Ave, 19041. Tel 215-LA5-0272. *Admin Dir* Eleanor Daitzman; *Instructor* Angie Arlen, BFA; *Instructor* Tom Ewing, BFA; *Instructor* Robert Finch, BFA; *Instructor* George Gansworth, BFA; *Instructor* Cyril Gardner, BFA; *Instructor* Gerald Kolpan, BFA; *Instructor* Richard Leiberman, BFA; *Instructor* Itzhaic Sankowsky, MA
Estab 1937; pvt; D & E; ent req must be member of the Arts Center; SC 45; enrl D 300, E 250
Tuition: $25 to $70 for 8-15 wks; no campus res
Courses: Art History, Calligraphy, Ceramics, Collage, Commercial Art, Conceptual Art, Constructions, Drawing, Film, Goldsmithing, Graphic Arts, Graphic Design, Handicrafts, Illustration, Jewelry, Lettering, Mixed Media, Painting, Photography, Printmaking, Sculpture, Silversmithing, Theatre Arts, Basketry, Batik, Cartoon & Caricature, China Painting, Decorative Arts, Tie-dyeing, Weaving
Children's Classes: Enrl 150; tui $40 for 15 wks. Courses—General Arts, Pottery
Summer School: Admin Dir, Eleanor Daitzman. Tui varies, classes begin June 12 and June 19. Courses—same as above

HUNTINGDON

JUNIATA COLLEGE, Department of Art, Moore St, 16652. Tel 814-643-4310. *Chmn Dept* Alex McBride. Instrs FT 1, PT 1
Estab 1876; pvt; D; ent req HS dipl; degrees BA 4 yrs; scholarships; SC 12, LC 3; enrl 300, maj 10
Tuition: $5995 inclusive, campus res
Courses: Aesthetics, Ceramics, Drawing, Graphic Arts, History of Art & Archaeology, Painting, Photography, Teacher Training, Theatre Arts
Summer School: Dir, Dr James J Lakso. Courses—Art History, Ceramics, Studio Art

INDIANA

INDIANA UNIVERSITY OF PENNSYLVANIA, Department of Art and Art Education, Sprowls Hall, 15705. Tel 412-357-2530. *Chairperson* Joanne P Lovette, DA; *Instructor* Dr B Balsiger, PhD; *Instructor* Thomas Dongilla, MEd; *Instructor* Dr F Ross, DA; *Instructor* Dr H Russell, DA; *Instructor* Dr R C Seelhorst, EdD; *Instructor* Dr R J Vislosky, EdD
Estab 1875, dept estab 1875; pub; D & E; ent req HS dipl, SAT, portfolio review; degrees BS(Art Educ), BA(Humanities with Art Concentration), BFA 4 yr, MEd, MA 2 yr; scholarships; SC 26, LC 21, GC 30; enrl D 315, non-maj 850, maj 315, grad 50
Tuition: Res—undergrad $900 per yr, grad $1750 per yr; nonres—undergrad $1700 per yr, grad $1750 per yr; campus res—room & board $1200 per yr
Courses: Aesthetics, †Art Education, Art History, Ceramics, Collage, Conceptual Art, Constructions, Drawing, Goldsmithing, Graphic Arts, Graphic Design, Jewelry, Lettering, Mixed Media, Museum Staff Training, Painting, Printmaking, Restoration & Conservation, Sculpture, Silversmithing, Teacher Training, Textile Design, Art Therapy
Children's Classes: Enrl 40-50; tui $10 per 8 wks. Courses—all studio areas
Summer School: Enrl 150; tui $250 for term of 6 wks

LANCASTER

FRANKLIN AND MARSHALL COLLEGE, Art Department, 17604. Tel 717-291-4199. *Chmn Dept* James Peterson; *Asst Prof* Linda Cunningham, MFA; *Adjunct Prof* Diana Galis, PhD
Estab 1966; pvt; D & E; ent req HS dipl, SAT; degrees BA and BS 4 yr; scholarships; SC 10, LC 20; enrl in col D 2011, E 605
Tuition: Res—$5695 per yr; nonres—$4130 per yr
Courses: Architecture, Art History, Drawing, History of Art & Archaeology, Painting, Printmaking, Sculpture, Basic Design
Summer School: Dir, Russ Burke. Tui $300 for course, two 5 wk sessions beginning June 7. Courses—Architecture, Drawing, Painting, Sculpture

LEWISBURG

BUCKNELL UNIVERSITY, Department of Art, 17837. Tel 717-524-1307. *Head Dept* Gerald Eager, PhD; *Instr* Neil Anderson, MFA; *Instr* Joan Curran, MFA; *Instr* William Lasansky, MFA; *Instr* James Turner, PhD
Estab 1846; pvt; D; ent req HS dipl; degrees BA 4 yrs; scholarships; SC 19, LC 20, GC 30; enrl D 500, non-maj 450, maj 50, grad 2
Tuition: $5000 per yr; campus residency available
Courses: Art History, Drawing, Graphic Arts, History of Art & Archaeology, Painting, Printmaking, Sculpture
Summer School: Dir Summer Session, Hugh McKeegan. Enrl 50; tui $200 per course for term of 3 or 6 wks beginning June 5. Courses—Lectures, Studio

MANSFIELD

MANSFIELD STATE COLLEGE, Art Department, School of Fine and Applied Arts, 16933. Tel 717-662-4092. *Chmn Dept* Jay D Kain, PhD; *Prof* Steve Bencetie, DEd; *Prof* Jim Cecere, DEd; *Assoc Prof* Ernest Frombach, MEd; *Asst Prof* Tom Loomis, MA; *Asst Prof* Sam Thomas, MEd; *Asst Prof* Dale Witherow, MFA; *Asst Prof* Stan Zujkowski, MS
Estab 1857; pub; D; ent req HS dipl, SAT, portfolio and optional interview; degrees BA(Studio Art), BA(Art History) and BSE(Art Educ) 4 yr, MEd(Art Educ); SC 26, LC 18; enrl D 700, maj 90
Tuition: Res—$950 per yr, $475 per sem; nonres—$1780 per yr, $890 per sem; campus residency available
Courses: Aesthetics, Art Education, Art History, Ceramics, Drawing, Handicrafts, Jewelry, Painting, Photography, Printmaking, Sculpture, Silversmithing, Teacher Training, Textile Design
Children's Classes: Tui $10 per sem for Sat classes
Summer School: Dir, Dr Jay D Kain. Term of 3-6 wks beginning June 9. Courses—Drawing, Fibers, Graduate Courses, Pottery, Sculpture, Stained Glass, Studio Courses

MEADVILLE

ALLEGHENY COLLEGE, Art Department, 16335. Tel 814-724-3371. *Head Dept* Richard Kleeman, MFA; *Prof* Carl F Heeschen, MA; *Prof* George Roland, MFA; *Instructor* Sharon Dale, PhD; *Gallery Dir* Martha Holt, MFA
Estab 1815, dept estab 1930; pvt; D; ent req HS dipl, ent exam; degrees BA and BS 4 yr; scholarships; SC 17, LC 7; enrl 450, maj 15
Tuition: $3885 per yr, $1295 per term; campus res—room and board $1470 per yr
Courses: Art History, Ceramics, Drawing, Graphic Arts, Lettering, Painting, Photography, Printmaking, Sculpture

MEDIA

DELAWARE COUNTY COMMUNITY COLLEGE, Communications and Humanities House, Route 252 & Media Line Rd, 19063. Tel 215-353-5400. *Assoc Dean Instruction* Dr Jerry R Smith, EdD; *Assoc Prof* John Botkin, MFA; *Assoc Prof* Alf Suendsen, MFA; *Adjunct Instr* Irving Kline, EdM; *Adjunct Instr* Faith Smith, MFA
Estab 1967; pub; D & E; degrees AS, AA and AAS 2 yrs
Tuition: Res—undergrad $265 per sem, $22 per cr; nonres—undergrad $795 per sem, $66 per cr; no campus res
Courses: Art Education, Art History, Drawing, Graphic Design, Painting, Printmaking, Theatre Arts
Adult Hobby Classes: Enrl varies; tui varies. Courses—Calligraphy, Crafts, Drawing, Graphic Design, Interior Design, Needlepoint, Photography, Stained Glass, Sketching, Woodcarving
Summer School: Tui res $22 per cr hr, nonres $66 per cr hr for term of 6 wks. Courses—Drawing, Painting

MERCERSBURG

MERCERSBURG ACADEMY, Department of Fine Arts,* 17236. Tel 717-328-2151. *Chmn Dept* William C Fowle
Estab 1972; pvt; D; ent req ent exam req, secondary school granting HS dipl; scholarships; SC 4, LC 3; enrl 100
Courses: Ceramics, Drawing, Graphic Arts, Graphic Design, Handicrafts, History of Art & Archaeology, Painting, Photography, Sculpture, Stage Design, Textile Design, Theatre Arts, Pottery, Weaving

MIDDLETOWN

PENNSYLVANIA STATE UNIVERSITY, CAPITOL CAMPUS, Department of Humanities, 17057. Tel 717-783-6189. *Prof* Irwin Richman, PhD; *Asst Prof* Elenor Ebersole, EdD; *Instructor* Troy Thomas, MFA & MA. Instrs PT 10
Estab 1965; pub; D & E; ent req 2 yrs of col or CLEP; degrees BHumanities 2 yrs, MHumanities 1 1 2 - 2 yrs; scholarships; SC 7, LC 15; enrl D & E 60, grad 40
Tuition: Res—$1440 per yr; nonres—$2982 per yr; campus res—room & board $1665 per yr
Courses: Aesthetics, Architecture, Art Education, Art History, Ceramics, History of Art & Archaeology, Mixed Media, Painting, Photography, Sculpture, Theatre Arts, Video

MILLERSVILLE

MILLERSVILLE STATE COLLEGE, Art Department, 17064. Tel 717-872-5411, Ext 253. *Dir* R Gordon Wise, EdD; *Instructor* Dom Fanani, EdD; *Instructor* John Ground, MFA; *Instructor* Ike Hay, MFA; *Instructor* Robert Hustrad, MFA; *Instructor* Robert Lowing, MFA; *Instructor* Robert Lyon, MEd; *Instructor* Robert A Nelson, PhD; *Instructor* Jane Reinhard, MEd; *Instructor* Sheba Sharrow, MFA; *Instructor* Ronald Sykes, EdD
Estab 1855, dept estab 1965; pub; D & E; ent req HS dipl; degrees BS(Art Educ) and BA(Art) 4 yr, MEd(Art Educ) 1 yr; SC 65, LC 10, GC 64; enrl maj 285, grad 20
Tuition: Res—undergrad $1000 per yr, $500 per sem, $35 per cr hr, grad $45 per cr hr; nonres—undergrad $1600 per yr, $900 per sem, $60 per cr hr, grad $65 per cr hr; campus res—room and board $975 per yr
Courses: Art Education, Art History, Calligraphy, Ceramics, Drawing, Film, Graphic Arts, Illustration, Jewelry, Lettering, Painting, Photography, Printmaking, Sculpture, Silversmithing, Teacher Training
Summer School: Dir, Gordon Wise. Enrl 300; tui $200 for term of 5 wks, two sessions beginning June and July. Courses—all studio

MONROEVILLE

COMMUNITY COLLEGE OF ALLEGHENY COUNTY, BOYCE CAMPUS, Art Department, Beatty Rd, 15146. Tel 412-327-1327. *Assoc Prof* Bruno Sorento, MFA; *Asst Prof* Jeanne Connors, MEd
Pub; D & E; ent req HS dipl; degrees AS 2 yrs; SC 13, LC 1; enrl D 200, E 40, non-maj 140, maj 60
Tuition: Nonres—undergrad $600 per yr, $300 per sem; PT $25 per cr; no campus res
Courses: Architecture, Art History, Ceramics, Collage, Constructions, Drawing, Graphic Arts, Mixed Media, Painting, Photography, Printmaking, Sculpture
Adult Hobby Classes: Courses—Calligraphy, Drawing, Painting, Photography
Children's Classes: Enr varies. Tui $17 per course. Courses—Drawing, Painting
Summer School: Tui $25 per cr. Courses vary

MOUNTAINHOME

DREISBACH ART GALLERY, Rte 191, 18342. *Owner* C I Dreisbach. Instrs FT 1
Estab 1958; pvt; D (summers only); ent req none; enrl 200
Tuition: $8 per day
Courses: Painting

NEW KENSINGTON

PENNSYLVANIA STATE UNIVERSITY AT NEW KENSINGTON, 3550 Seventh St, 15068. *Dir* Robert Arbuckle. Instrs FT 1
Estab 1968; pub; D; ent req col boards; degrees 2 yr (option for 4 yr at main campus at University Park); scholarships; SC 3-4, LC 1 per sem
Tuition: No campus res
Courses: Art Education, Art History, Ceramics, Drawing, Painting, Theatre Arts, Design, Watercolor

NEWTON

BUCKS COUNTY COMMUNITY COLLEGE, Fine Arts Department, Swamp Rd, 18940. Tel 215-968-5861, Ext 236. *Chairperson Dept* Bruce Katsiff, MFA; *Instructor* Jon Alley; *Instructor* Selma Bortner; *Instructor* Robert Dodge; *Instructor* Frank Dominguez; *Instructor* Jack Gevins; *Instructor* Alan Goldstein; *Instructor* Nancy Hellebrand; *Instructor* Catherine Jansen; *Instructor* Paul Keene; *Instructor* Diane Lindenheim; *Instructor* Marlene Miller; *Instructor* Stephen Ripper; *Instructor* Charlotte Schatz; *Instructor* Helen Weisz
Estab 1965; pub; D & E; ent req HS dipl; degrees AA; enrl D & E 9200 (school)
Courses: Art History, Ceramics, Drawing, Graphic Design, Jewelry, Painting, Photography, Printmaking, Sculpture, Design, Glass, Woodworking

NEW WILMINGTON

WESTMINSTER COLLEGE, Art Department, 16142. Tel 412-946-8761, Ext 366. *Head Dept* Nelson E Oestreich. Instrs 3
Estab 1852; den; D; degrees BS and BA(Fine Arts, Educ) 4 yrs; enrl maj 50, total 1500
Tuition: $3940 incl campus res

PHILADELPHIA

ANTONELLI SCHOOL OF PHOTOGRAPHY, 1210 Race St, PO Box 1767, 19105. Tel 215-563-8558. *Pres* Joseph B Thompson; *VPres* Harry W Hollingsworth; *Instructor* James Donato, MBA; *Instructor* Robert D Golding, BFA; *Instructor* Patricia Guidos, BS; *Instructor* Cathy Palermo, BS; *Instructor* Gilbert H Weiss, BS
Estab 1938; pvt; D & E; ent req HS dipl; enrl D 200, E 75
Tuition: No campus res
Courses: Professional Photography

ART INSTITUTE OF PHILADELPHIA, 1818 Cherry St, 19103. Tel 215-567-7080. *Pres* Philip Trachtman, BFA; *Coordr Interior Design* Charles Agnew, BA; *Coordr Commercial Art* Charles Ellis. Instrs 4
Estab 1966; pvt; D; ent req HS dipl, portfolio; degrees AST 2 yr; SC 30, LC 8; enrl 300
Tuition: $2250 per yr, $750 per quarter; no campus res
Courses: Advertising Design, Art History, †Commercial Art, Conceptual Art, Drafting, Drawing, †Fashion Arts, Graphic Arts, Graphic Design, †Illustration, †Interior Design, Lettering, †Mixed Media, Painting, †Photography, Printmaking
Summer School: Dir, Philip Trachtman. Courses—as above

DREXEL UNIVERSITY, Department of Design, Nesbitt Col, Nesbitt Hall, 33rd & Market Sts, 19104. Tel 215-895-2390. *Dean* Marjorie E Rankin; *Head Dept* Mary Epstein. Instrs FT 13, PT 20
Estab 1891; pvt; ent req col board exam; degrees BS 4 yr, MS and cooperative plan; scholarships; SC 39, LC 9; enrl undergrad 480, grad 45
Courses: Fashion Arts, Interior Design, Design & Merchandising
Summer School: Dean, Marjorie E Rankin. Enrl 159; term of 6 or 12 wks

SAMUEL S FLEISHER ART MEMORIAL, 715-721 Catharine St, 19147. Tel 215-922-3456. *Administrator* Thora E Jacobson; *Instructor* Filomena Dellaripa; *Instructor* Mac Fisher; *Instructor* Frank Gasparro; *Instructor* Tom Gaughan; *Instructor* Martin Jackson
Estab 1898; administered by the Philadelphia Museum of Art; pvt; E; ent req none; degrees none; LC 1; enrl E 2000
Courses: Ceramics, Drawing, Painting, Photography, Printmaking, Sculpture
Adult Hobby Classes: Enrl 2000
Children's Classes: Enrl 500; no tui. Courses—Drawing, Painting, Sculpture
Summer School: Courses—Ceramics, Drawing, Landscape Painting, Painting, Photography, Printmaking, Sculpture, Welding

HUSSIAN SCHOOL OF ART, INC, Commercial Art Department, 1300 Arch St, 19107. Tel 215-563-5726. *Pres* Ronald Dove. Instrs FT 4, PT 22
Estab 1946; pvt; D; ent req HS dipl, portfolio interview; degrees AST; enrl 225
Tuition: No campus res
Courses: Advertising Design, Commercial Art, Drawing, Graphic Arts, Graphic Design, History of Art & Archaeology, Illustration, Lettering, Painting, Photography

LA SALLE COLLEGE, Department of Fine Arts, 20th St & Olney Ave, 19141. Tel 215-951-1000. *Chmn Dept Fine Arts* George K Diehl, PhD; *Asst Prof* James Hanes; *Asst Prof* Thomas Ridington, MFA; *Lectr* Herman Gundersheimer, PhD; *Lectr* James Lang, MFA
Estab 1865, dept estab 1972; den; D & E; ent req HS dipl; degrees BA 4 yr; SC 2; enrl D 15, maj 15
Tuition: Res—$3500 per yr; nonres—$2730 per yr; campus residency available
Courses: Art History, Painting, Printmaking

L'ATELIER, THE SCULPTURE WORKSHOP, 1604 Locust St, 19103. Tel 215-735-2800. *Dir* Sheila S Greenberg, BA; *Instr* Joseph J Greenberg, BFA & BE
Estab 1977; pvt; D & E; ent req none; degrees none; SC 6; enrl D 50, E 20
Tuition: $160 for 12 wk sem; no campus res
Courses: Sculpture
Adult Hobby Classes: Courses—Carving, Casting, Clay Modelling, Mold Making

MOORE COLLEGE OF ART, 20th & The Parkway, 19103. Tel 215-568-4515. *Pres* Herbert Burgart, DEd; *Chmn Advertising Design* Adelaide Faralli, Dipl; *Chmn Art Educ* Janette Banks, MFA; *Chmn Ceramic Design* Jack Thompson, MFA; *Chmn Fashion Design* Theo Young, MFA; *Chmn Fashion Illustration* Mildred Ivins, Dipl; *Chmn Art History* Lewis Greenberg, MFA; *Chmn Illustration* Beth Krush, Dipl; *Chmn Interior Design* John Strite, BArchitecture; *Chmn Painting* Harold Jacobs, MFA; *Chmn Photography* Judy Steinhauser, MFA; *Chmn Printmaking* Charles Fahlen, MFA; *Chmn Printmaking* William Walton; *Chmn Sculpture & Metalsmithing* Gerald Crimmins, MFA; *Chmn Sculpture & Metalsmithing* Richard Posniak, MFA; *Chmn Textile Design* Deborah Warner, MFA
Estab 1844; pvt; D; ent req HS dipl, portfolio, SAT; degrees BS and BFA 4 yr; enrl in col D 475, E 70, non-maj 75, maj 475
Tuition: Res—$5500 per yr; nonres—$3700 per yr; PT students $120 per cr; campus res—room & board $1800 per yr
Courses: †Advertising Design, †Art Education, †Art History, †Ceramics, Drawing, †Fashion Arts, Goldsmithing, History of Art & Archaeology, †Illustration, †Interior Design, †Jewelry, Lettering, Mixed Media, †Painting, †Photography, †Printmaking, †Sculpture, Silversmithing, Stage Design, Teacher Training, †Textile Design, Theatre Arts, †Fashion Design, †Fashion Illustration
Children's Classes: Enrl 202; tui $50 per sem. Courses—General Art
Summer School: Dean, Hilda Schoenwetter. Term usually 4-6 wks

PENNSYLVANIA ACADEMY OF THE FINE ARTS, Broad & Cherry Sts, 19102. Tel 215-972-7624. *Dean* Ephraim Weinberg, MAE. Instrs FT 31
Estab 1805; pvt; D & E; ent req HS dipl, portfolio; degrees BFA coordinated program with Univ of Pennsylvania or Philadelphia Col Art, 5 yr; scholarships; SC 11, LC 3; enrl D 400, E 150
Tuition: $1620 per yr, $810 per sem; campus res $980 per yr (women only)
Courses: Art History, Drawing, Painting, Printmaking, Sculpture
Summer School: Registrar, Tish Byrne. Enrl 175; tui $75-$263 for term of 4-6 wks beginning June 13. Courses—Life, Portrait, Still Life & Landscape Painting & Drawing

PHILADELPHIA COLLEGE OF ART, Broad & Spruce Sts, 19102. Tel 215-893-3100. *Pres* Thomas F Schutte, PhD; *Dean Faculty* Nathan Knobler, MA; *Assoc Dean Liberal Arts* Patricia Cruser, MA; *Co-Chairperson Crafts* Richard H Reinhardt, BA; *Co-Chairperson Crafts* Petras Vaskys, Dipl; *Chairperson Educ* Arlene Gostin, MA; *Chairperson Environmental Design* Benjamin Martin, MArchit; *Chairperson Graphic Design* William Longhauser, MFA; *Co-Chairperson Graphic Design* Hans Allemann, MFA equiv; *Co-Chairperson Illustration* Robert Stein, MFA; *Co-Chairperson Illustration* Stephen Tarantal, MFA; *Chairperson Industrial Design* Noel Mayo; *Co-Chairperson Painting & Drawing* Cynthia Carlson, MFA; *Co-Chairperson Painting & Drawing* Gerald Nichols, MFA; *Chairperson Photography & Film* Ronald Walker, MFA; *Chairperson Printmaking* Michael Lasuchin, MFA; *Chairperson Sculpture* Walter Erlebacher, MID
Estab 1876; pvt; D & E; ent req HS dipl, portfolio, SAT; degrees BFA 4 yrs, MA 5 yrs; scholarships; SC 339, LC 74, GC 5; enrl D 1160, E 720, grad 11
Tuition: $4323 per yr, $131 per cr; campus res—room & board $1964 per yr
Courses: Advertising Design, Art Education, Art History, Calligraphy, Ceramics, Drafting, Drawing, Film, Graphic Arts, Graphic Design, Illustration, Industrial Design, Intermedia, Interior Design, Jewelry, Landscape Architecture, Mixed Media, Painting, Photography, Printmaking, Sculpture, Silversmithing, Teacher Training, Textile Design, Art Therapy, Glassblowing, Woodworking
Adult Hobby Classes: Saturday non-cr courses through Educ Dept. Courses—Ceramics, Drawing, Figure Drawing, Jewelry, Painting, Photography, Printmaking, Sculpture
Children's Classes: Enrl 350; tui $65 per sem. Courses—Ceramics, Design, Drawing, Jewelry, Painting, Photography and Film, Printmaking
Summer School: Dir, Robert Stein. Enrl 225; tui $325 plus additional $75 for weekend trips; term of 5 wks beginning June 26. Courses—Pre-College Program

PHILADELPHIA COLLEGE OF TEXTILES AND SCIENCE, School of Textiles, School House Lane & Henry Ave, 19144. Tel 215-843-9700. *Pres* Donald B Partridge
Estab 1884; pvt; degrees BS 4 yrs; scholarships; enrl D 1600, E 1100
Tuition: $1600
Courses: Drawing, Apparel Design, Apparel Management, Basic Design, Chemistry & Dyeing, Fabric Design, Fashion Textile Retailing, Knitted Design, Print Design, Textile Engineering, Textile Quality Control & Testing, Weaving Design
Summer School: Dir, Peter Mills

PHILADELPHIA COMMUNITY COLLEGE, Department of Fine Arts, 34 S 11th St, 19107. Tel 215-972-7210. *Dir Div Humanities* William Baker, MA; *Assoc Prof* Wallace Peters, MA; *Assoc Prof* Valerie Seligsohn, MFA; *Asst Prof* Diane Burko, MFA; *Asst Prof* Robert Paige, MFA; *Instructor* Kyung Lee, MFA
Estab 1967; pub; D & E; ent req HS dipl, portfolio; degrees AA 2 yr; SC 10, LC 6; enrl D 80 art maj

Tuition: $500 per yr; no campus res
Courses: Art History, Ceramics, Drawing, Graphic Design, Painting, Photography, Design, Transfer Foundation Program

SAINT JOSEPH'S COLLEGE, Fine Arts Program, 54th & City Ave, 19131. Tel 215-879-7604. *Dir of Prog* Dennis W Weeks, MFA; *Lectr* Betsy Anderson, MA; *Lectr* Danny Baker, BA; *Lectr* Lynn Denton, MFA; *Lectr* Dennis McNally, MA; *Lectr* Peg Schofield, MFA; *Lectr* Don Scioli, BA; *Lectr* Robert Wilde, PhD
Estab 1851, prog estab 1975; den; D & E; ent req HS dipl; SC 15, LC 4; enrl D 150, E 30
Tuition: Res—$4500 per yr; nonres—$2200 per yr; campus residency available
Courses: Aesthetics, Art Education, Art History, Ceramics, Drawing, Film, Painting, Photography, Printmaking, Stage Design, Theatre Arts

STUDIO SCHOOL OF ART AND DESIGN, 1424 Spruce St, 19102. Tel 215-735-0908. *Dir* Janet R Goodfriend, Dipl; *Asst Dir* John Koomar; *Instr* Robert Harmon; *Instr* Nicholas Leslie; *Instr* Larry Palmer; *Instr* Philip Taylor; *Instr* Andrew Theis; *Instr* Millard Warren; *Instr* Preston Williamson
Estab 1959; pvt; D; ent req HS dipl, interview, portfolio; SC 8, LC 4; enrl 41
Tuition: Res—$1250 per yr, $625 per sem, $131.60 monthly; no campus res
Courses: †Advertising Design, Art History, †Commercial Art, Drawing, †Graphic Arts, †Graphic Design, †Illustration, Lettering, Mixed Media, Painting, Photography, Three-Dimensional Design, Two-Dimensional Design

TEMPLE UNIVERSITY, Art Department, Humanities Bldg, Rm 311, 12th & Berks Sts, 19122. Tel 215-787-7191. *Chmn* Neil Kosh, MFA; *Assoc Prof* Rochele Toner, MFA; *Assoc Prof* John Wade, MFA; *Asst Prof* Anthony Gorny, MFA; *Asst Prof* Marilyn Holsing, MFA; *Asst Prof* Larry Spaid, MFA; *Instr* Richard Bottwin, MFA; *Instr* Neill Slaughter, MFA; *Instr* Stephen Weitz, MFA
Dept estab 1965; pub; D & E; ent req HS dipl, SAT; degrees BA granted by College of Liberal Arts; SC 40; enrl D 500, E 20, maj 58
Tuition: Res—undergrad $1810 per yr, $905 per sem, $62 per sem hr, grad $1968 per yr, $984 per sem, $84 per sem hr; nonres—undergrad $3374 per yr, $1687 per sem, $90 per sem hr, grad $112 per sem hr; campus res—room & board $2000
Courses: Drawing, History of Art & Archaeology, Mixed Media, Painting, Photography, Printmaking, Sculpture, Fiber Structure

TRACEY-WARNER SCHOOL,* 401 N Broad St, 19108. Tel 215-574-0402. *Pres* Lewis H Warner; *Instr* Louise Boyce
Estab 1956; pvt; D; ent req HS dipl; degrees AA 2 yrs, dipl or cert; enrl D 125
Tuition: $990 per sem; no campus res
Courses: Advertising Design, Art Education, Art History, †Costume Design & Construction, Fashion Arts, Handicrafts, †Illustration, Jewelry, Textile Design, †Draping Design, Pattern Drafting, Pattern Grading

TYLER SCHOOL OF ART OF TEMPLE UNIVERSITY, Beech & Penrose Aves, 19126. Tel 215-224-7575. *Dean* David Pease. Instrs FT 58, PT 6
Estab 1935; pub; D & E; ent req HS grad, SAT, portfolio; degrees BFA 4 yr, MFA, MEd (2 yrs work in all arts required before specializing); grad assistance and scholarships; enrl D 650, E 250
Courses: Art Education, Art History, Ceramics, Drawing, Film, Graphic Design, Painting, Photography, Printmaking, Sculpture, Metalsmithing, Typography, Weaving
Summer School: Acting Asst Dean, James Slayman. Courses—Art History, Ceramics, Drawing, Metalsmithing, Painting, Photography, Printmaking, Sculpture, Watercolor, Weaving

UNIVERSITY OF PENNSYLVANIA, Graduate School of Fine Arts, 19104. Tel 215-243-8321. *Dean* Lee G Copeland, MArchit & MCP
Estab 1874; pvt; ent req ent exam; scholarships and fels; GC
Tuition: Grad $5545 per yr; campus res available
—Department of Architecture, 19104. *Chmn* Peter McCleary; *Chmn Grad Group* G Holmes Perkins. Instrs FT 7, PT 25
Degrees MArchit, PhD; LC 10, GC 9; enrl 160
Courses: Architectural Design and Construction
—Department of City and Regional Planning, 19174. Instrs FT 11, PT 8
Degrees MCP, PhD; LC 21, GC 4; enrl 100
—Department of Landscape Architecture and Regional Planning, 19104. *Chmn* Ian L McHarg. Instrs FT 8, PT 5
Degrees MLA, MRP; LC 7, Design Courses 4; enrl 60
—Department of Fine Arts, 19104. *Chmn* Robert Engman; *Chmn* Neil G Welliver. Instrs FT 7, PT 4
Degrees BFA, MFA; SC 21, LC 5, GC; enrl 60
Courses: Graphic Arts, Painting, Sculpture

PITTSBURGH

ART INSTITUTE OF PITTSBURGH, 526 Penn Ave, 15222. Tel 412-263-6600. *Pres* Bradford Daggett
Estab 1921; pvt; ent req HS grad; degrees AA 2 yrs, dipl; enrl D 1700, E 150
Courses: Interior Design, Photography, Airbrush Technique, Fashion Illustration, Photography-Audiovisual-Multimedia Visual Communications
—Commercial Art Prep School, 15222.
Children's Classes: Teenage summer classes, six wks 1 2 day; Saturday teenage classes
Summer School: Term of 4 wks. Free 2 wk art instructors workshop

CARLOW COLLEGE, Art Department, 333 Fifth Ave, 15213. Tel 412-578-6000, 578-6033. *Chmn Dept* Richard Devlin. Instrs FT 2, PT 3
Estab 1945; den; D & E; ent req HS dipl and transcript, col boards; degrees in Art, Art Educ, Art Therapy Preparation 4 yrs; scholarships; SC 17, LC 6; enrl 200, maj 42
Courses: Aesthetics, Art Education, Ceramics, Drawing, Graphic Arts, History of Art & Archaeology, Jewelry, Lettering, Painting, Photography, Sculpture, Teacher Training, Theatre Arts, Art & Psychology, Art Therapy, Batik, Metalcraft, Weaving
Summer School: Acad Dean, Sr Elizabeth McMillan. Enrl approx 40; two summer sessions 4 wks each. Courses—Art Fundamentals, Ceramics

CARNEGIE-MELLON UNIVERSITY, College of Fine Arts, 5000 Forbes Ave, 15213. Tel 412-578-2000, Ext 2354. *Dean* Akram Midani
Estab 1905; pvt; ent req col board ent exam plus auditions or portfolio; degrees 4-5 yr; scholarships and fels
Tuition: $4100; campus res available
Summer School: Term of 6 wks. Courses—includes some pre-college courses
—Department of Architecture, 15213. *Head* Louis Sauer. Instrs FT 23, PT 5
Degrees MArchit first and second degree, PhD in conjunction with School of Urban and Public Affairs; enrl 206
Courses: Architecture
—Department of Design, 15213. *Head* Joseph Ballay. Instrs FT 11, PT 6
Degrees MFA(Design); enrl 162
Courses: Graphic Design, Illustration, Industrial Design, Design Theory, Interior Environments
—Department of Art, 15213. *Head* Orvill Winsand. Instrs FT 22, PT 3
Degrees MFA, DA; enrl 235
Courses: Art Education, Handicrafts, Painting, Printmaking, Sculpture
—Department of Drama, 15213. *Head* Walter Eysselinck. Instrs FT 24, PT 1
Degrees MFA, PhD; enrl 223
Courses: Stage Design

CHATHAM COLLEGE, Department of Art, Woodland Rd, 15232. Tel 412-441-8200. *Chmn* Shirley Stark. Instrs FT 3, PT 1
Estab 1869; pvt, W; ent req HS grad; degrees BA 4 yrs; SC 17, LC 7
Tuition: $5250 incl res fees
Courses: Art History, Ceramics, Drawing, Graphic Arts, Painting, Photography, Sculpture, Design, Independent Study

IVY SCHOOL OF PROFESSIONAL ART, Downtown Annex, 927 Penn Ave, 15214. Tel 413-323-3200. *Dean* Philip Mendlow, MFA; *Instructor* Jon Crawford, Dipl; *Instructor* Kenneth Dunlap, MFA; *Instructor* Harry Edelman, BFA; *Instructor* Andre Fazekas, PhD Equivalent; *Instructor* Joseph Fiedler, BFA; *Instructor* Carol Klein; *Instructor* Chris Lambl, MFA; *Instructor* Harold Neal; *Instructor* Jerry Nichols, Dipl; *Instructor* Walter Quader, Dipl; *Instructor* Norman Rice, BA; *Instructor* Penny Rode, BFA; *Instructor* Frank Sparrow, Dipl; *Instructor* Jozef Stachura; *Instructor* Abe Weiner, BFA; *Instructor* Milton Weiss; *Instructor* Greg Yost, Dipl
Estab 1960; pvt; D; ent req HS dipl, portfolio, letters of recommendations; degrees AST 2 yr; enrl 300
Tuition: $715 per quarter; campus res available to women
Courses: †Advertising Design, Art History, Calligraphy, Collage, †Commercial Art, Display, Drawing, Fashion Arts, Film, †Graphic Design, †Illustration, Intermedia, Interior Design, Lettering, Mixed Media, †Painting, †Photography, Printmaking, †Sculpture, Stage Design, Textile Design, Video, †Design & Art Direction, †Environmental Design, Exhibition Design, †Retail & Fashion

LA ROCHE COLLEGE, Division of Graphic Arts & Design, 9000 Babcock Blvd, 15237. Tel 412-931-9333. *Chairperson* Harvey R Levenson, MS; *Instructor* Wendy Bockwith, MArchitecture; *Instructor* Grant Dinsmorg, MFA; *Instructor* Sally McCoy, MA; *Instructor* Martha Shepler, MFA; *Instructor* Mack Taylor, BFA. Instrs PT 15
Estab 1963, dept estab 1965; pvt; D & E; ent req HS dipl; degrees BA and BS 4 yr; SC 25, LC 15; enrl D & E 200, non-maj 20, maj 180
Tuition: $4200 per yr; campus res—room & board $2200 per yr
Courses: Advertising Design, Aesthetics, Art History, Calligraphy, Ceramics, Commercial Art, Display, Fashion Arts, †Graphic Arts, †Graphic Design, Illustration, Industrial Design, Interior Design, Lettering, Painting, Photography, Sculpture, Platemaking, Presswork—Lithography, Reproduction Processes, Typesetting
Summer School: Dir, Betsey Devon. Tui $70 cr

UNIVERSITY OF PITTSBURGH
—Henry Clay Frick Fine Arts Department, 15260. Tel 412-624-4121. *Chmn* John Williams, PhD; *Prof* Donald Gordon, PhD; *Prof* John Haskins, PhD; *Prof* M F Hearn, PhD; *Prof* Aaron Sheon, PhD; *Prof* David Summers, PhD; *Assoc Prof* Kathy Linduff, PhD; *Assoc Prof* David Wilkins, PhD; *Asst Prof* Anne Weis, PhD; *Vis Prof* Ilene Forsyth, art history - 1980; *Vis Prof* Edward Fry, art history - 1980
Estab 1787, dept estab 1927; pvt; D & E; ent req HS dipl, BA, GRE for grad work; degrees BA 4 yrs, MA 2 yrs, PhD; scholarships; LC 35, GC 20; enrl D 600, E 200, grad 30
Tuition: Grad $860 per term, PT $72 per cr
Courses: †Art History
—Department of Studio Arts, 15260. Tel 412-624-4118. *Chmn* Virgil D Cantini. Instrs FT 8
Estab 1968; pvt; D; degrees undergrad maj in Studio Arts; LC 34; enrl 1500
Courses: Graphic Arts, Painting, Sculpture

RADNOR

CABRINI COLLEGE, Department of Fine Arts, Eagle & King of Prussia Rds, 19087. Tel 215-687-2100, Ext 53. *Chmn Dept* Adeline Bethany. Instrs FT 1, PT 1
Estab 1957; den; D & E; ent req HS dipl, satisfactory average and rank in secondary school class, SAT, recommendations; degrees BA, BS and BSEd 4 yr, no art major; scholarships; SC 11, LC 4
Courses: Art Education, Ceramics, Drawing, History of Art & Archaeology, Painting, Teacher Training, Design & Composition
Summer School: Dir, Dr Frank Saul. Term of 6 wks beginning May and July. Courses—vary according to demand

READING

ALBRIGHT COLLEGE, Department of Art, 13th & Exeter Sts, 19604. Tel 215-921-2381. *Head Dept* Thomas C Watcke, MFA; *Assoc Prof* Barbara M Fahy, PhD; *Assoc Prof* Harry G Koursaros, MA; *Asst Prof* Marilyn A Zietlen
Estab 1856, dept estab 1964; ent req HS dipl, SAT; degrees BA 4 yrs; SC 14, LC 7; enrl D 322, E 41, non-maj 340, maj 8, others 15
Tuition: Res and nonres—undergrad $3740 per yr; campus res—room & board $1570 per yr
Courses: †Art History, Ceramics, Constructions, Drafting, Drawing, Fashion Arts, Film, Graphic Arts, History of Art & Archaeology, Interior Design, Mixed Media, †Painting, Photography, Printmaking, †Sculpture, Theatre Arts
Summer School: Chairperson Art Dept, Thomas Watcke. Enrl 35; term of 4 wks beginning June. Courses—Drawing, Photography

ROSEMONT

ROSEMONT COLLEGE, Division of the Arts, 19010. Tel 215-527-0200. *Chmn Div* Patricia M Nugent. Instrs FT 3, PT 19
Estab 1925; pvt, W (exchange with Villanova Univ); D; ent req HS dipl, ent exam; degrees BA(Studio Art, Art History) and BFA(Studio Art) 4 yr; scholarships; SC 6, LC 3; enrl total col 705, art 300, grad approx 15
Tuition: $2875; campus res $1725
Courses: Aesthetics, Art Education, Ceramics, Drawing, Graphic Arts, History of Art & Archaeology, Painting, Photography, Sculpture, Teacher Training, Theatre Arts, Fibres, Watercolor

SCRANTON

INTERNATIONAL CORRESPONDENCE SCHOOLS, School of Interior Design, Oak St, 18515. Tel 717-342-7701, Ext 254. *VPres Educ* Robert G Donovan; *Dir* Elaine G Thomas, BS. Instrs FT 2
Estab 1890, School of Interior Design estab 1969; pvt; ent req HS dipl; enrl 1800
Courses: Elements of Interior Design, Interior Decoration & Design, Principles of Interior Design, Room Decor

MARYWOOD COLLEGE, Art Department, 2300 Adams Ave, 18509. Tel 717-343-6521, Ext 339. *Chairperson Dept* Sr Cor Immaculatium. Instrs FT 5, PT 4
Estab 1926; pvt; D & E; ent req HS dipl, portfolio and interview; degrees BA in fine arts, advertising art, interior desing, BS(Art Educ) 4 yr, MA(Studio Art), MA(Art Educ), MA(Art Therapy); scholarships; SC 28, LC 7, GC 12; enrl maj 150, grad 31
Courses: Advertising Design, Art Education, Art History, Calligraphy, Ceramics, Drawing, Fashion Arts, Graphic Arts, Illustration, Interior Design, Jewelry, Mixed Media, Painting, Photography, Printmaking, Sculpture, Textile Design, Theatre Arts, Art Therapy, Contemporary Learning Theories, Fabrics, Metalcraft, Serigraphy, Tapestry, Weaving
Summer School: 6 wk term beginning in June. Courses—both graduate and undergraduate levels

SHIPPENSBURG

SHIPPENSBURG STATE COLLEGE, Art Department, Prince St, 17257. Tel 717-532-1530. *Chmn Art Dept* Harry D Bentz, EdD; *Instructor* Betsy Farmer, PhD; *Instructor* William Hynes, MEd; *Instructor* Harry Kirk, MEd; *Instructor* George Waricher, MEd
Estab 1871, dept estab 1920; pub; D & E; ent req HS dipl; degrees BA(Art), BS(Elementary Educ); scholarships; SC 13, LC 4; enrl D 400, E 100, non-maj 600, grad 15, others 20 continuing educ
Tuition: Res—$475 per sem; nonres—$890 per sem; PT $39-$71 per cr hr; campus res—room and board $602 per sem
Courses: Art History, Ceramics, Drawing, Graphic Arts, Handicrafts, Lettering, Painting, Printmaking, Sculpture, Teacher Training, Textile Design
Adult Hobby Classes: Enrl 25; tui $15 per course. Courses—Basic Watercolor, Ceramics
Summer School: Dir, Dr Harry D Bentz. Tui $39 per cr hr for term of 3-5 wks beginning May 27. Courses—Arts & Crafts, Introduction to Art, Ceramics, Creative Experiences in Art

SLIPPERY ROCK

SLIPPERY ROCK STATE COLLEGE, Department of Art, 16057. Tel 412-794-7271. *Chmn Dept* Glen Brunken. Instrs FT 9
Pub; D & E; ent req HS dipl; degrees BA(Art), BFA(Art) 4 yr; SC 27, LC 3; enrl maj 70
Tuition: $1000 per yr; campus res $1008 per yr
Courses: Art Education, Ceramics, Drawing, History of Art & Archaeology, Painting, Photography, Printmaking, Sculpture, Textile Design, Metalsmithing
Summer School: Tui $33 per cr hr

SWARTHMORE

SWARTHMORE COLLEGE, Department of Art, 19081. Tel 215-447-7116. *Chairperson Dept Art* T Kaori Kitao, PhD; *Assoc Prof* Kit-Yin Tieng Snyder, MFA; *Asst Prof* Michael Cothren; *Asst Prof* Constance Cain Hungerford, PhD; *Asst Prof* Alison Kettering, PhD; *Asst Prof* Michael Knutson, MFA; *Instr* Brian A Meunier, MFA
Estab 1864, dept estab 1925; pvt; D; ent req HS dipl, SAT, CEEB; degrees BA 4 yrs; scholarships; SC 14, LC 33; enrl non-maj 500, maj 25
Tuition: $4700 per yr; campus res—room & board $2040 per yr
Courses: Art History, Ceramics, Drawing, Painting, Photography, Printmaking, Sculpture, History of Architecture, History of Cinema, Urban History

UNIONTOWN

PENNSYLVANIA STATE UNIVERSITY, FAYETTE CAMPUS, Department of Art, Col of Arts & Architecture, Hwy 119 N, 15401. Tel 412-437-2801, Ext 29. *Chmn Dept* Zeljko Kujundzic, MFA; *Asst Prof* Gloria De Paolis, MA; *Asst Prof* D Drost; *Asst Prof* V Romanek, PhD
Estab 1968; pub; D & E; ent req HS dipl
Tuition: $427 per 10 wk term
Courses: Architecture, Art History, Ceramics, Drafting, Drawing, Painting, Sculpture, Teacher Training

UNIVERSITY PARK

PENNSYLVANIA STATE UNIVERSITY, UNIVERSITY PARK
—**College of Arts and Architecture,** 111 Arts Building, 16802. Tel 814-865-2591. *Dean* Walter H Walters, PhD; *Head Dept Archit* Raniero Corbelletti, MS; *Acting Dir School Visual Arts* Harlan Hoffa, DEd; *Head Dept Art History* Hellmut Hager, Dr Phil; *Head Dept Landscape Archit* David Young, MLA; *Head Dept Theatre and Film* Douglas Cook, MA
Estab 1855, col estab 1963; pub; D & E; ent req HS dipl and GPA, SAT; degrees BA, BS and BFA 4 yrs, Bachelor of Archit and Bachelor of Landscape Archit 5 yrs, MS, MA, MArchit, MFA, MEd, DEd, PhD; scholarships; SC 282, LC 99, GC 104; enrl D 23,798, maj 1320, grad 171
Tuition: Res—undergrad $1485 per yr, $495 per term, $62 per cr, grad $1581 per yr, $527 per term, $66 per cr; nonres—undergrad $2982 per yr, $994 per term, $125 per cr, grad $3150 per yr, $1050 per term, $131 per cr; campus res—room & board $1665
Courses: Aesthetics, †Architecture, †Art Education, †Art History, Ceramics, Constructions, Costume Design & Construction, Drafting, Drawing, †Film, Graphic Arts, Graphic Design, History of Art & Archaeology, Jewelry, †Landscape Architecture, Mixed Media, Painting, Photography, Printmaking, Restoration & Conservation, Sculpture, Silversmithing, Stage Design, †Teacher Training, †Theatre Arts, Video
Adult Hobby Classes: Tui varies. Courses—informal, vary with demand
Children's Classes: Enrl 200-250; tui $10 per term. Courses—Ceramics, Drawing, Fibers, Jewelry, Painting, Photography, Printmaking, Sculpture
Summer School: Courses—same as regular session, but limited; summer band clinic
—**Department of Art History,** 229 Arts II Bldg, 16802. Tel 814-865-6326. *Dept Chmn* Dr Hellmut Hager, PhD; *Evan Pugh Prof* Eugenio Battisti, PhD; *Prof* Anthony Cutler, PhD; *Prof* Roland E Fleischer, PhD; *Prof* George L Mauner, PhD; *Assoc Prof* Dawson Kiang, PhD; *Assoc Prof* Jeanne Chenault Porter, PhD; *Vis Asst Prof* Dr Wilma Stern, art history
Estab 1855, dept estab 1963; pub; D & E; ent req HS dipl; degrees BA 4 yrs, MA 2-3 yrs, PhD approx 4 yrs; scholarships; LC 53, GC 39; enrl D 75, maj 30, grad 25, others 20
Tuition: Res—undergrad $456 per term, grad $484 per term; nonres—undergrad $916 per term, grad $944 per term; campus res—room & board $522
Courses: Aesthetics, Art History, History of Art & Archaeology, Restoration & Conservation

VILLANOVA

VILLANOVA UNIVERSITY, Department of Art and Art History, 19085. Tel 215-527-2100, Ext 238. *Prof* George Radan
Estab 1842, dept estab 1971; pvt; D & E; ent req HS dipl, SAT; degrees BFA 4 yrs; courses taught in conjunction with Rosemont College; SC 25, LC 6; enrl D 35, maj 35
Tuition: Res—undergrad $3500 per yr; campus res—room & board $2200 per yr
Courses: Aesthetics, Art Education, Art History, Ceramics, Drawing, Film, Graphic Arts, Graphic Design, History of Art & Archaeology, Painting, Photography, Printmaking, Restoration & Conservation, Sculpture, Stage Design, Theatre Arts, Watercolor
Summer School: Courses—Art History

WASHINGTON

WASHINGTON AND JEFFERSON COLLEGE, Art Department, S Lincoln St, 15301. Tel 412-222-4400. *Chmn Art Dept* Paul B Edwards, MA; *Prof* Hugh H Taylor, MA; *Instructor* Patricia Maloney, MFA
Estab 1787, dept estab 1959; pvt; D & E; ent req HS dipl, SAT, achievement tests; degrees BA 4 yr, MA; scholarships; SC 14, LC 8; enrl D 162, E 18, non-maj 139, maj 23, others 15
Tuition: $4055 per yr; campus res—room & board $813 per yr
Courses: Art History, Ceramics, Drawing, Graphic Arts, Painting, Printmaking, Restoration & Conservation, Sculpture
Adult Hobby Classes: Tui $60 for 8 wks
Summer School: Dir, Dr William W Leake. Tui $75 per cr hr for term of 4 wks beginning June 13. Courses—full range

WAYNE

WAYNE ART CENTER, 413 Maplewood Ave, 19087. Tel 215-688-3553. *Pres* Linda Rodgers; *Instructor* Joanne Cleveland; *Instructor* Robert Cox; *Instructor* David Day; *Instructor* Toni Famolari; *Instructor* Art Forster; *Instructor* Paul Gorka; *Instructor* Roy La Plante; *Instructor* Edward Lis; *Instructor* Dan Miller; *Instructor* Mary Richardson Miller; *Instructor* Holly Silverthorne; *Instructor* Will Ursprung; *Instructor* Rita Wissink
Estab 1930; pvt; D & E; ent req none; free program for senior citizens; SC 15; enrl D 130, E 50, others 40
Courses: Drawing, Jewelry, Mixed Media, Painting, Photography, Printmaking, Sculpture
Adult Hobby Classes: Tui $65 for 14 wk sem, yearly dues $15. Courses—as above
Children's Classes: Tui $35 for 10 wk sem, yearly dues $6. Courses—Drawing, Painting, Sculpture
Summer School: Pres, Linda Rodgers. Tui $35 for 6 wks beginning June. Courses—same as above plus Landscape Painting

WAYNESBURG

WAYNESBURG COLLEGE, Department of Fine Arts, 15370. Tel 412-627-8191. *Acting Chmn* Susan Howsare, MFA; *Asst Prof* Daniel Morris, MA; *Instr* Stephen Fischer, MA
Estab 1849, dept estab 1971; pvt; D & E; ent req HS dipl; degrees BA(Fine Arts) and BA(Visual Arts) 4 yrs; scholarships; SC 25, LC 6; enrl D 131, E 3, maj 17
Tuition: Res—undergrad $4990 per yr; nonres—undergrad $3460 per yr; campus residence available
Courses: Aesthetics, Art Education, Art History, Ceramics, Drawing, Lettering, Museum Staff Training, Painting, Photography, Printmaking, Sculpture, Theatre Arts, Design
Summer School: Acting Dept Chmn, Susan Howsare. Tui $270 for term of 5 wks beginning June 2 and July 7

WILKES-BARRE

WILKES COLLEGE, Department of Art, S River St, 18703. Tel 717-824-4651, Ext 486, 480 & 368. *Chmn* William H Sterling, PhD; *Prof* Chester Colson, MS; *Assoc Prof* Berenice D'Vorzon, MA; *Assoc Prof* Richard Fuller, MA; *Assoc Prof* Herbert Simon, MA; *Asst Prof* Allan Maxwell, MFA
Estab 1947; pvt; D & E; ent req HS dipl, SAT; degrees BA 4 yr; scholarships; SC 18, LC 6; enrl D 115, E 40, non-maj 80, maj 55
Tuition: Undergrad $3250 per yr, $1625 per sem, $110 per cr hr; campus res—room & board $1700
Courses: Advertising Design, Aesthetics, Art Education, Art History, Ceramics, Drawing, Handicrafts, Jewelry, Painting, Photography, Printmaking, Sculpture, Stage Design, Teacher Training, Theatre Arts, Batik, Fiber Design, Weaving
Summer School: Dir, John Meyers. Enrl variable; tui $75 per cr hr for term of 5-8 wks beginning June 8. Courses—variable

WILLIAMSPORT

LYCOMING COLLEGE, Art Department, 17701. Tel 717-326-1951, Ext 260. *Chmn Dept* Roger Douglas Shipley, MFA; *Asst Prof* Jon Robert Bogle, MFA; *Instructor* Diane M Lesko, MA; *Instructor* Terry Wild, BFA
Estab 1812; pvt; D & E; ent req HS dipl, ACT or SAT; degrees BA 4 yr; scholarships; SC 20, LC 7; enrl D 620, E 80, non-maj 668, maj 32
Tuition: $3300 per yr; campus res—room & board $1600 per yr
Courses: Advertising Design, Art History, Ceramics, Drawing, Graphic Arts, History of Art & Archaeology, †Painting, Photography, †Printmaking, †Sculpture
Summer School: Chmn Dept, Roger Douglas Shipley. Enrl 10; tui $569 room & board for term of 6 wks beginning June 5. Courses—Painting, Photography, Printmaking. Mini-Term: Tui room & board $459. Courses—Art History, Color Theory, Photography, Silkscreen Printing

WILLIAMSPORT AREA COMMUNITY COLLEGE, Department of Engineering and Design, 1005 W Third St, 17701. Tel 717-326-3761. *Dir Dept* Dr Paul L McQuay; *Prof* Dale Straub, MEd; *Assoc Prof* Chalmer Van Horn, BS; *Asst Prof* Lloyd Cotner; *Asst Prof* William Ealer, BS & BArchitecture; *Asst Prof* Dale Metzker; *Asst Prof* Patrick Murphy, BS; *Instructor* Joseph Mark, BArchitecture; *Instructor* Harold Newton; *Instructor* Fred Schaefer Jr; *Instructor* Jackie Welliver, CET
Estab 1965; pub; D & E; ent req HS dipl, placement test; degrees AA 2 yr; scholarships; enrl D 2903, E 2909
Tuition: No campus res
Courses: Advertising Design, Architecture, Calligraphy, Commercial Art, Constructions, Drafting, Drawing, Graphic Arts, Illustration, Landscape Architecture, Lettering, Restoration & Conservation
Summer School: Coordr, Thomas E Vargo

YORK

YORK ACADEMY OF ARTS, 625 E Philadelphia St, 17403. Tel 717-848-1447. *Educ Dir* Florian Suitak, MA
Estab 1952; pvt; D; ent req HS dipl, portfolio; enrl 270
Tuition: $1647 per yr, $549 per trimester, $55 per class; no campus res
Courses: Advertising Design, Art History, Calligraphy, †Commercial Art, Display, Drawing, Film, Graphic Arts, Graphic Design, Illustration, †Interior Design, Lettering, Painting, Photography, Printmaking, Textile Design, †Fine Arts, Television Art
Adult Hobby Classes: Enrl 100; tui $55 for 12 wks. Courses—Art for Beginners, Introduction to Commercial Art, Painting, Photography, Portraiture, Stained Glass
Children's Classes: Enrl 100; tui $35 for 10 wks. Courses—Drawing & Painting
Summer School: Enrl 50; term of 4 wks beginning June 14. Courses—Drawing & Painting Workshop $78, Oil Painters Workshop $120

YORK COLLEGE OF PENNSYLVANIA, Department of Humanities and Fine Arts, Country Club Rd, 17405. Tel 717-846-7788. *Chmn* Heinz L Hosch, MA; *Instr* Otto H Tomasch, MA; *Asst Prof* Siham A Osman, PhD
Estab 1941; D & E; ent req HS dipl, SAT or ACT; degrees BA 4 yrs and AA 2 yrs; SC 17, LC 7
Tuition: Res—undergrad $999 per sem; campus res—room and board $696 per sem
Courses: Art Education, Art History, Commercial Art, Drawing, Painting, Photography, Sculpture
Adult Hobby Classes: Enrl 40; tui $51 per cr hr. Courses—per regular session
Summer School: Dir, Thomas Michalski. Enrl 15; tui $51 per cr hr for term of three weeks beginning May 19 and two 5 week sessions beginning June and July

RHODE ISLAND

BRISTOL

ROGER WILLIAMS COLLEGE, Art Department, Old Ferry Road, 02809. Tel 401-255-1000. *Coordr* Carol J Hathaway, MA; *Instructor* James Cathers, MFA; *Instructor* Richard Carbotti; *Instructor* Michele McRoberts; *Instructor* Thomas Russell; *Instructor* Charlotte Spencer, MA
Estab 1948, dept estab 1967; pvt; D & E; ent req HS dipl; degrees BFA 4 yr, AA 2 yr, apprenticeship and senior teaching; SC 18, LC 8; enrl D 1800, E 1500, maj 42
Tuition: Res $3048 per yr; campus res—room & board $2076 per yr
Courses: Aesthetics, Architecture, Art Education, Art History, Ceramics, Costume Design & Construction, Drafting, Drawing, Film, Graphic Arts, Handicrafts, History of Art & Archaeology, Museum Staff Training, Painting, Photography, Printmaking, Restoration & Conservation, Sculpture, Stage Design, Teacher Training, Theatre Arts, Leather, Macrame, Two and Three Dimensional Design, Weaving
Summer School: Dean, Edwin Wilde. Courses—Ceramics, Design, Drawing, Painting, Weaving

KINGSTON

UNIVERSITY OF RHODE ISLAND, Department of Art, Fine Arts Center, 02881. Tel 401-792-2131, 792-5821. *Chairperson* Richard Fraenkel, MFA; *Prof* William Klenk, PhD; *Prof* William Leete, MFA; *Prof* Bart Parker, MFA; *Prof* Robert H Rohm, MFA; *Assoc Prof* Richard Calabro, MFA; *Assoc Prof* David Ketner, PhD; *Asst Prof* Christopher Cordes, MFA & TMP; *Asst Prof* Wendy Holmes, PhD; *Asst Prof* Natalie Kampen, PhD; *Asst Prof* Marjorie Keller, MFA; *Asst Prof* Ronald J Onorato, PhD; *Asst Prof* Gary Richman, MFA; *Asst Prof* Wendy Roworth, PhD. Instrs FT 14, PT 3
Estab 1892; pub; D & E; ent req same as required for Col of Arts & Sciences; degrees BA(Studio), BA(Art History) and BFA(Art Studio) 4 yrs; scholarships; SC 21, studio seminars 24, LC 23; enrl D 900, E30, non-maj 725, maj 175, others 10-20
Tuition: In-state—undergrad $2785 per yr, $1392 per sem, $397 per month, $974 PT, $42 per cr hr; out-of-state—undergrad $4595 per yr, $2297 per sem, $656 per month, $2288 PT, $104 per cr hr; campus res
Courses: Art History, Drawing, Film, Graphic Design, Painting, Photography, Printmaking, Sculpture
Summer School: Chairperson Dept Art, Richard Fraenkel. Enrl 45-50; tui $44 per undergrad cr for term of 5 wks beginning June 16. Courses—Art History, Design, Drawing, Painting, Photography

NEWPORT

SALVE REGINA THE NEWPORT COLLEGE, Art Department, Ochre Point Ave, 02840. Tel 401-847-6650, Ext 217. *Head Dept* Sr Arlene Woods, RSM, MFA; *Instructor* David Jorgensen, MFA; *Instructor* Sr Michaeline Lewnadowski, MFA
Estab 1947; den; D & E; ent req HS dipl, ent exam; degrees BA 4 yr; SC 28, LC 8; enrl D 95 (dept), non-maj 95, maj 12
Tuition: Res—undergrad $2400 per sem, $90 per sem hr, $45 per cr (night), grad $90 per cr; nonres—undergrad $1470 per sem, $90 per cr (day), $45 per cr (night), grad $90 per cr; campus res—room & board $930 per sem
Courses: Aesthetics, Art Education, Art History, Calligraphy, Ceramics, Drawing, Painting, Photography, Printmaking, Teacher Training

SCHOOL OF THE ART ASSOCIATION OF NEWPORT, 76 Bellevue Ave, 02840. Tel 401-847-0179. *Administrator* Susan Bowen
Estab 1913; D & E; ent req none; degrees none; col cr given through Roger Williams Col; scholarships; SC 14, LC 3; enrl D 200 (total)
Tuition: $65 per course per 12 wk sem; classes meet 3 hr per wk
Courses: Drawing, Painting, Photography, Printmaking, Sculpture, Etching, Pastels, Pottery
Children's Classes: Enrl 100; tui $45-52 per course per sem. Courses—Drawing, Cultural Trips, Multi-media, Photography, Printing, Printmaking, Watercolor
Summer School: Tui prorated to above scale for term of 4 wks; classes meet twice a wk. Courses—as above

PROVIDENCE

BROWN UNIVERSITY, Department of Art,* 02912. Tel 401-863-2421. *Chmn* Kermit S Champa, PhD
Pvt; D; degrees BA 4 yrs, MA & PhD in Art History; SC 8-10, LC 10-14, GC 10-12; enrl maj 70, GS 45
Tuition: Res—undergrad $7140 per yr, $3570 per sem, $632 per unit, grad depends on boarding arrangements; nonres—undergrad & grad $5050 per yr; campus res available
Courses: Art History, Drawing, History of Art & Archaeology, Painting, Printmaking, Sculpture
Summer School: Dir, John L McLaughry

THE JEWELRY INSTITUTE, New England Academy, 40 Sims Ave, 02909. Tel 401-351-0700. *Temporary Managing Dir* Harold Howland Jr. Instrs PT 15
Estab 1976; pvt
Tuition: No campus res
Courses: Casting, Electroplating, Epoxy, Jewelry, Modelmaking, Mold Making for White Metal, Polishing, Stone Setting, Tool Making, Wax Carving

PROVIDENCE COLLEGE, Department of Fine Arts, River Ave & Eaton St, 02918. Tel 401-865-2401, 865-1000. *Chmn* Richard N Elkington, MFA; *Prof* Lawrence M Hunt, OP, PhD; *Instructor* James Baker, MFA; *Instructor* Adrian G Dabash, OP, MFA; *Instructor* Suzanne H D'Avanzo, MA; *Instructor* Jon DiCicco, MFAEd; *Instructor* Alice H Hauck, MA; *Instructor* Nancy E Garner, MA; *Instructor* Richard A McAlister, OP, MFA
Estab 1917, dept estab 1969; pvt; D & E; ent req HS dipl, portfolio needed for transfer students; degrees BA 4 yr; SC 49, LC 8; enrl D 464, E 250, non-maj 399, maj 65
Tuition: Res & nonres—undergrad $3342 per yr, grad $165 per course; campus res—

room & board $2310 per yr
Courses: Architecture, †Art Education, †Art History, Calligraphy, †Ceramics, Drafting, †Drawing, Handicrafts, Lettering, †Painting, †Photography, †Printmaking, †Sculpture, Stage Design, Teacher Training, Watercolor
Summer School: Dir, James M Murphy, OP. Tui $111 for term of 6 wks beginning mid-June through July. Courses—Art History, Calligraphy, Ceramics, Drawing, Painting, Photography, Printmaking, Soft and Hard Crafts. A summer program is offered at Pietrasanta, Italy: Dir, Richard A McAlister, OP, MFA. Courses—Art History, Languages, Literature, Religious Studies, Studio

RHODE ISLAND COLLEGE, Art Department, 02908. Tel 401-456-8054. *Chmn* Harriet E Brisson, MFA; *Prof* John DeMelim, MFA; *Prof* Angelo V Rosati, MA; *Prof* Donald C Smith, AM; *Prof* Ronald M Steinberg, PhD; *Prof* Lawrence F Sykes, MS; *Assoc Prof* David M Hysell, PhD; *Assoc Prof* Richard A Kenyon, MS; *Assoc Prof* Pauline Ladd, MFA; *Assoc Prof* Curtis K LaFollette, MFA; *Assoc Prof* Enrico Pinardi, MFA; *Asst Prof* Samuel B Ames, MFA; *Asst Prof* Krisjohn O Horvat, MFA; *Asst Prof* Mary Ball Howkins, PhD; *Asst Prof* Betty E Ohlin, MA; *Instructor* Roberta Houllahan, MFA
Estab 1854, dept estab 1969; pub; D & E; ent req HS dipl, CEEB and SAT; degrees BA(Art History), BA(Studio) and BS(Art Educ) 4 yr, MAT 1 yr; SC 31, LC 10, GC 5; enrl D 443, E approx 50, non-maj approx 228, maj 188, grad 30
Tuition: Res—$585 plus fees $145, grad $41 per cr; nonres $1888 plus fees $145, grad $61 per cr; campus res—room & board $1800-$2256
Courses: Aesthetics, Art Education, Art History, Ceramics, Drawing, Film, Graphic Design, †Painting, †Photography, †Printmaking, †Sculpture, Teacher Training, Fiber, Metal
Children's Classes: Enrl 165; tui $75 per 20 wks. Courses—Ceramics, Drawing, Life Drawing, Painting, Printmaking
Summer School: Dir, Richard A Kenyon. Enrl approx 150; tui $35 per cr, nonres $46 per cr for term of 6 wks beginning June 26th. Courses—Ceramics, Drawing, Fiber, Painting, Photography

RHODE ISLAND SCHOOL OF DESIGN, 2 College St, 02903. Tel 401-331-3507. *Pres* Lee Hall; *Dean Archit Div* Friedrich St Florian, MS; *Dean Fine Arts and Design Div* Gilbert Franklin, BFA; *Acting Chmn Fine Arts Div* Roland J Belhumeur, MFA; *Chmn Grad Studies Div* David B Manzella, EdD; *Chmn Design Div* Thomas Ockerse, MFA; *Acting Chmn Freshman Foundation Division* John Udvardy, MFA; *Head Art History* Dirk Bach, MA; *Head Photography* Albert P Beaver; *Head Glass* Dale Chihuly, MFA; *Head Spec Studies* Morton Fink, MFA; *Head Industrial Design* Mark S Harrison, MFA; *Head Apparel Design* Lorraine Howes; *Head Sculpture* Richards Jarden, BFA; *Acting Head Film* Robert Jungels, MA; *Head Archit Dept* Rodolfo Machado, MA; *Head Textile Design* Alice Marcoux; *Acting Head Jewelry & Light Metal* Louis Mueller; *Head Jewelry and Light Metals* John A Prip, Dipl; *Head Ceramics* Jacquelin Rice, MFA; *Head Illustration* Thomas Sgouros, BFA; *Acting Head Textile Design* Maria Tulokas, MAE & MFA
Estab 1877; pvt; endowed; ent req HS grad; degrees BARch, BID, BFA, BLandscape Arch, MA(Art Educ), MAT, MFA and MID 4-5 yrs; scholarships, grants-in-aid to res, student loans, fels; enrl D 1353, E 650
Tuition: $4550 per yr plus fees; campus res—room & board $1960; approved housing
Courses: Architecture, Ceramics, Film, Graphic Design, Illustration, Industrial Design, Jewelry, †Landscape Architecture, Painting, Photography, Printmaking, Sculpture, Teacher Training, Textile Design, Apparel Design, Glass, Interior Architecture, Metalsmithing, Television Studies, Wood & Furniture Design

WARWICK

RHODE ISLAND JUNIOR COLLEGE, Department of Art, 400 East Ave, 02886. Tel 401-825-2267. *Chmn* Rita C Lepper. Instrs FT 10, PT 2
Estab 1964; pub; D & E; ent req HS dipl, ent exam, equivalency exam; degrees AA, AS and AAS 2 yr; scholarships; SC 16, LC 3, seminar 1; enrl D 4600
Courses: Ceramics, Commercial Art, Drafting, Drawing, Graphic Arts, Graphic Design, Handicrafts, History of Art & Archaeology, Interior Design, Painting, Photography, Sculpture

SOUTH CAROLINA

AIKEN

UNIVERSITY OF SOUTH CAROLINA AT AIKEN,* 171 University Parkway, 29801. Tel 803-648-6851. *Head Dept* Jane Winer, MFA
Estab 1961, dept estab 1970; pub; D & E; ent req HS dipl, GED, SAT; SC 15, LC 5; enrl D 100, E 50, non-maj 80, maj 20
Tuition: Res—undergrad $810 per yr, $27 per sem hr, grad $1020 per yr, $34 per sem hr; nonres—undergrad $1950 per yr, $65 per sem hr, grad $2550 per yr, $85 per sem hr; no campus res
Courses: Advertising Design, Art Education, Art History, Ceramics, Commercial Art, Conceptual Art, Drawing, History of Art & Archaeology, Illustration, Painting, Photography, Printmaking, Stage Design, Theatre Arts
Summer School: Tui varies; 2 terms - 11 wks. Courses—varies

CHARLESTON

BAPTIST COLLEGE AT CHARLESTON, Department of Art,* Hwy 78 at I-26, 29411. Tel 803-797-4177. *Chmn* Joseph Ward
Estab 1960; den; D & E; ent req GED or HS dipl; degrees BA and BS 4 yrs; scholarships; SC 14, LC 2; enrl D 80, E 71, maj 15
Tuition: $1200 per sem full time, $600 per sem 8-9 hrs; campus res—room and board $875 per sem
Courses: Art Education, Ceramics, Drawing, Graphic Arts, History of Art & Archaeology, Painting, Sculpture, Teacher Training, Theatre Arts, Batik, Papier Mache, Weaving

Summer School: Enrl 1500; tui $35 per sem hr; campus res—room and board $240 per sem; two 5 wk sessions beginning June. Courses—same as regular session

COLLEGE OF CHARLESTON, Fine Arts Department,* 66 George St, 29401. Tel 803-792-5600. *Chmn* David W Maves
Estab 1966; pub; D & E; ent req HS dipl; degrees BA(Fine Arts) 4 yrs; SC 36, LC 24
Tuition: Res—$750 per yr; nonres—$1650 per yr
Courses: Aesthetics, Architecture, Costume Design & Construction, Drawing, Graphic Arts, History of Art & Archaeology, Painting, Sculpture, Stage Design, Theatre Arts

GIBBES ART GALLERY SCHOOL, 135 Meeting St, 29401. Tel 803-577-7275. *Dir* Valerie Miller. Instrs PT 20
Estab 1969; pub; D & E; ent req none; scholarships; SC 18; enrl D 150, E 150
Tuition: $55 per course, materials fee $10
Courses: Calligraphy, Drawing, Graphic Design, Handicrafts, Interior Design, Photography, Printmaking, Pottery, Weaving
Children's Classes: Enrl 15 per course; tui $30 per course per sem. Courses—Mixed Media (ages 4-7)
Summer School: Dir, Valerie Miller. Courses—same as regular session

CLEMSON

CLEMSON UNIVERSITY, Department of History & Visual Studies,* College of Architecture, Lee Hall, 29631. Tel 803-656-3311. *Head Dept* John Thomson Acorn
Estab 1967; pub; D; ent req available on request; degrees MFA 60 hrs; GC 24, SC 40, LC 29 (undergrad courses for service to pre-architecture and other Univ requirements): enrl approx 1500 annually, grad maj 10
Tuition: Res—$425 per sem; nonres—$900 per sem; campus res—room $265-$310 per sem, board $300-$355 per sem
Courses: Architecture, Art History, Ceramics, Drawing, Graphic Design, Painting, Photography, Printmaking, Sculpture

CLINTON

PRESBYTERIAN COLLEGE, Fine Arts Department, 29325. Tel 803-833-2820, Ext 296. *Head* Robert Jolly, MFA
Estab 1880, Dept estab 1960; den; D & E; ent req HS dipl with C average, SAT; degrees BA 4 yr; scholarships; SC 8, LC 5; enrl D 200, non-maj 190, maj 10
Tuition: $3060; campus res—room & board $1640
Courses: †Art Education, Art History, Drawing, †Painting, Printmaking, Sculpture
Summer School: Dean, Dr Don King. Enrl 150; tui $75 per cr hr for term of 5 wks beginning June 5. Courses—Art Appreciation, Painting

COLUMBIA

BENEDICT COLLEGE, Visual Art Studies,* Taylor and Harden Sts, 29204. Tel 803-256-4220. *Dir Visual Arts* David Johnson Sr
Estab 1870; pvt; D; ent req HS dipl; degrees BA(Teaching of Art) and general art major 4 yrs; scholarships; SC 11, LC 6
Tuition: $2000 per yr; campus res—room and board $1400 per yr
Courses: Art Education, Ceramics, Drawing, Graphic Arts, Graphic Design, Handicrafts, History of Art & Archaeology, Lettering, Painting, Photography, Sculpture, Teacher Training
Summer School: Term of two 5 wk sessions beginning June. Courses—Art Appreciation and others

RICHLAND ART WORKSHOP OF THE COLUMBIA MUSEUM OF ART, 1112 Bull St, 29201. Tel 803-799-2810. *Supervisor* Jean McWhorter. Instrs PT 4
Estab 1950 (operates as service of the Columbia Museum of Art); D & E; ent req none; classes for youths and adults
Courses: Drawing, Painting

UNIVERSITY OF SOUTH CAROLINA, Department of Art, Sloan College, 29208. Tel 803-777-4236. *Chmn* John Oneil, PhD; *Chmn Studio* Harry Hansen, MFA; *Chmn Art Educ* Truman Teed, EdD; *Chmn Art History* John Bryan, PhD; *Artist in Res* Philip Mullen, PhD; *Instr* Howard Woody, MA; *Instr* Annie Quinsac, PhD; *Vis Prof* Lewis Jones, painting - 1980
Estab 1801, dept estab 1924; pub; D & E; ent req HS dipl; degrees BA, BFA and BS 4 yrs, MA and MAT 5 yrs, MFA 6 yrs; scholarships; SC 89, LC 57, GC 73; enrl D 1620, E 174, non-maj 1000, maj 620, grad 82
Tuition: Res—undergrad $740 per yr, $370 per sem, PT $30 per cr, grad $980 per yr, $490 per sem; nonres—undergrad $1700 per yr, $850 per sem, PT $70 per cr, grad $980 per yr, $490 per sem; campus res—room $620 & board $900 per yr
Courses: †Advertising Design, †Art Education, †Art History, Calligraphy, †Ceramics, Collage, †Commercial Art, Conceptual Art, †Drawing, Film, Goldsmithing, †Graphic Arts, †Graphic Design, Handicrafts, †History of Art & Archaeology, Illustration, †Interior Design, Jewelry, Lettering, Mixed Media, Museum Staff Training, †Painting, Photography, †Printmaking, Restoration & Conservation, †Sculpture, Silversmithing, †Teacher Training, †Textile Design, Video
Adult Hobby Classes: Tui $30 per cr. Courses—Ceramics, Painting, Printmaking, Sculpture
Children's Classes: Enrl 60; tui $20 per sem. Courses—Crafts, Drawing, Painting
Summer School: Dir, John Oneil. Enrl 400; tui res $30 per cr, nonres $70 per cr for term of 5 wks. Courses—same as regular session

DUE WEST

ERSKINE COLLEGE, Department of Art, 29639. Tel 803-379-8887. *Head Dept* James M Meaders, MFA
EStab 1839; den; D; degrees none; SC 3, LC 1; enrl 60-80 per sem
Courses: Drawing, Painting, Art Appreciation, Art for Teachers, K-6, Color & Design, Studio
Summer School: Courses—Art Appreciation, Art for Teachers, K-6

GAFFNEY

LIMESTONE COLLEGE, Art Department,* Division of Fine Arts, 29340. Tel 803-489-7151. *Chmn* Robert B Welch
Estab 1845; pvt; D & E; ent req HS dipl, ent exam; degrees BS(Educ, Studio) 4 yrs; scholarships; SC 19, LC 9; enrl D 112, maj 42, others 3
Tuition: Res—$1335 per sem; campus res—room and board $765-$815 per sem
Courses: Aesthetics, Art Education, Ceramics, Drawing, History of Art & Archaeology, Jewelry, Painting, Printmaking, Sculpture, Teacher Training, Theatre Arts, Silk-Screen, Wood-Block
Summer School: Dir, Dr Nelson. Tui $70 per cr hr; campus res—room and board $200 per term. Term of 6 wks beginning June. Courses—Art Appreciation, Ceramics, Drawing, Painting

GREENVILLE

BOB JONES UNIVERSITY, School of Fine Arts, 29614. Tel 803-242-5011, Ext 239. *Dean* Dwight Gustafson, DMus; *Chmn* Emery Bopp, MFA; *Instructor* David Appleman, MA; *Instructor* Kathy Bell, MA; *Instructor* Carl Blair, MFA; *Instructor* James Brooks, BA; *Instructor* Lorrainne Edwards, MA; *Instructor* Darrel Koons, MA; *Instructor* Harrell Whittington, MA
Estab 1927, dept estab 1945; pvt; D; ent req HS dipl, letters of recommendation; degrees BA & BS 4 yrs, MA 1-2 yrs; SC 29, LC 12, GC 10; enrl D 235, non-maj 108, GS 5
Tuition: $1296 per yr, $648 per sem; campus res—room & board $1827
Courses: Advertising Design, Aesthetics, Art Education, Art History, Calligraphy, Ceramics, Collage, Commercial Art, Conceptual Art, †Costume Design & Construction, Drawing, Film, Graphic Arts, Graphic Design, Handicrafts, History of Art & Archaeology, Illustration, Lettering, Painting, †Photography, Printmaking, Restoration & Conservation, Sculpture, †Stage Design, Teacher Training, Theatre Arts, Elective courses available from the Division of Cinema and the Dept of Dramatic Production

FURMAN UNIVERSITY, Department of Art, 29613. Tel 803-294-2074. *Chmn* Richard Olof Sorensen, PhD; *Prof* Thomas E Flowers, MFA; *Prof* Glen E Howerton, MA
Estab 1826; pvt den; D & E; ent req HS dipl, SAT; degrees BA 4 yr; scholarships; SC 19, LC 7; enrl D 80, non-maj 40, maj 40
Tuition: $3008 per yr; campus res—room & board $1888
Courses: Advertising Design, Aesthetics, Art Education, Art History, Calligraphy, Ceramics, Drawing, Graphic Design, Handicrafts, History of Art & Archaeology, Lettering, Museum Staff Training, Painting, Printmaking, Sculpture, Teacher Training, Book Arts, Watercolor
Adult Hobby Classes: Enrl 500 per term in all courses including art; tui $15-$50 per term. Courses—A variety of changing evening classes
Summer School: Dir, Hazel Harris. Enrl 500; tui $500 for term of 6 wks beginning June 9, $250 for term of 4 wks beginning June 21. Courses—Art Educ for the Elementary Teacher, Drawing Workshop, Painting Workshop

GREENVILLE COUNTY MUSEUM OF ART, Museum School of Art, 420 College St, 29601. Tel 803-271-7570. *Dir* Sharon H Whitley. Instrs FT 1, PT 31
Estab 1960; pub; D & E; degrees AAA and AFA 2-3 yr; scholarships; SC 12, LC 2, GC 6; enrl D 250, E 170
Courses: Advertising Design, Art History, Drawing, Film, Handicrafts, Painting, Photography, Printmaking, Sculpture, Video, Museology, Philosophy of Art, Pottery, Weaving
Children's Classes: Enrl 15 per course, ages 4-12. Courses—Mixed-media
Summer School: Enrl approx 300 per sem; 8 wk term. Courses—same as regular sem

GREENWOOD

LANDER COLLEGE, Dept of Fine Arts, 29646. Tel 803-229-8231. *Coordr Visual Arts* Robert Harold Poe. Instrs FT 3, PT 2
Estab 1872; pub; D & E; ent req HS dipl; degrees BA(Art) 4 yrs; scholarships; SC 25, LC 5; enrl D 235, E 60, maj 45
Tuition: 700 per yr; nonres $1300 per yr; campus res $1300-$1500
Courses: Advertising Design, Aesthetics, Art Education, Ceramics, Commercial Art, Drawing, Graphic Arts, Graphic Design, History of Art & Archaeology, Illustration, Painting, Photography, Sculpture, Teacher Training

HARTSVILLE

COKER COLLEGE, Art Department, 29550. Tel 803-332-1381, Ext 417. *Head Dept* R Nickey Brumbaugh. Instrs FT 3
Estab 1908; pvt; D & E; ent req HS dipl, ent exam; degrees AB and BS 4 yrs; scholarships; SC 29, LC 8; enrl 300, art maj 20
Tuition: $2655 per yr; campus res—room & board $1441 per yr
Courses: Art Education, Art History, Ceramics, Commercial Art, Drawing, Graphic Arts, Handicrafts, Painting, Photography, Sculpture
Summer School: Term of 5 wks. Courses—Art Appreciation, Art Education

NEWBERRY

NEWBERRY COLLEGE, Department of Art,* College St, 29108. Tel 803-276-5010. *Head Dept* Kenneth David Brown, MA; *Instr* Cathy Cherry Crowell, MA
Estab 1856, dept estab 1973; den; D & E; ent req HS dipl, SAT; degrees AB(Art) 4 yrs, two courses in independent study, financial aid available; SC 35, LC 2; enrl D 114, non-maj 106, maj 9
Tuition: Res—$2900 per yr; campus res—room $515-$590, board $835
Courses: Art History, Ceramics, Costume Design & Construction, †Drawing, Mixed Media, †Painting, †Printmaking, Sculpture, Stage Design, Theatre Arts
Summer School: Term two 5 wk sessions. Courses—Crafts, Drawing, Painting

ORANGEBURG

SOUTH CAROLINA STATE COLLEGE, Art Program, 29115. Tel 803-536-7174. *Dir* Leo F Twiggs, EdD; *Assoc Prof* Henry G Michaux, EdD; *Asst Prof* James L McFadden, MA; *Instructor* Terry J Hunter, MFA
Dept estab 1972; D & E; ent req HS dipl; degrees BA & BS 4 yrs, MA & MS approx 2 yrs; SC 15, LC 7; enrl D 73, nonmaj 8, maj 73
Tuition: Res $300 per sem, nonres $650 per sem; campus residence available
Courses: Art Education
Summer School: Dir, Dr A S Belcher. Tui $34 per cr hr. Courses—Art Appreciation, Arts & Crafts for Children

ROCK HILL

WINTHROP COLLEGE, Department of Art, 29733. Tel 803-323-2126. *Chmn* Edmund D Lewandowski, Dipl; *Assoc Prof* David Freeman, MFA; *Assoc Prof* Mary Mintich, MFA; *Asst Prof* Jean McFarland, MFA; *Asst Prof* Lary Pierce, MA; *Asst Prof* Rex Stambaugh, MFA
Estab 1886; pub; D & E; ent req HS dipl, SAT, CEEB; degrees BA and BVA 4 yrs; SC 42, LC 10; enrl in college D 4983, non-maj 360, maj 147, grad 6
Tuition: Res—undergrad $620 per yr, $310 per sem, grad $605 ; nonres—undergrad $1280 per yr, $640 per sem, grad $605; campus residence available
Courses: †Advertising Design, Art Education, Art History, Calligraphy, †Ceramics, Collage, †Commercial Art, Conceptual Art, †Drawing, Fashion Arts, †Graphic Arts, †Graphic Design, Handicrafts, †Illustration, Interior Design, Jewelry, Lettering, Mixed Media, †Painting, †Photography, †Printmaking, †Sculpture, Silversmithing, Teacher Training, Textile Design
Summer School: Dir, Edmund D Lewandowski. Enrl 60. Courses—Art Appreciation, Creative Art for Children, Design, Drawing, Graphic Design, Painting

SPARTANBURG

ART ASSOCIATION SCHOOL, 385 S Spring St, 29301. Tel 803-583-1399. *Educ Chmn* Maurice Johnson
Estab 1970; D & E; ent req none; SC 25; enrl D 200, E 300
Tuition: $35-$50 for 10 wks
Courses: Ceramics, Drawing, Graphic Arts, Handicrafts, Mixed Media, Painting, Printmaking, Commercial Art, Life Drawing, Portraiture, Weaving
Adult Hobby Classes: Courses offered
Children's Classes: Courses offered

CONVERSE COLLEGE, Art Dept, PO Box 20, 29301. Tel 803-585-6421, Ext 251, 331. *Chmn Dept* Henry Fagen Jr, EdD; *Instructor* Mayo MacBoggs, MFA; *Instructor* Judy Voss Jones, MFA; *Instructor* Melba LeGrande Long, MFA
Col estab 1889; pvt; D; ent req HS dipl, SAT, CEEB, ACT, Advanced placement in Art & Art History; degrees BA & BFA 4 yrs; SC 40, LC 17; enrl D 290, non-maj 240, maj 50, others 12
Tuition: Undergrad—$3500 per yr; campus res—room & board $1800 per yr
Courses: Art Education, †Art History, Ceramics, †Drawing, Film, Interior Design, Museum Staff Training, †Painting, Photography, †Printmaking, †Sculpture, Teacher Training

SOUTH DAKOTA

ABERDEEN

NORTHERN STATE COLLEGE, Art Dept, 57401. Tel 605-622-2514. *Chmn* Jim Gibson, MFA; *Assoc Prof* Mark Shekore, MFA; *Asst Prof* Lynn Carlsgaard, MA; *Asst Prof* Bill Hoar, MA; *Asst Prof* James Lauver, MS; *Asst Prof* Mark McGinnis, MFA. Estab 1901, dept estab 1920
Pub; D & E; ent req HS dipl; degrees AA 2 yrs, BA, BS, BSEd 4 yrs; scholarships; SC 40, LC 14, GC 6; enrl D 385, non-maj 300, maj 85
Tuition: Res—undergrad $18.50 per cr, grad $29.25 per cr; nonres—undergrad $39.55 per cr, grad $53.55 per cr; campus res—room $270.75 per sem
Courses: Advertising Design, Aesthetics, †Art Education, †Ceramics, †Commercial Art, †Drawing, Goldsmithing, Handicrafts, History of Art & Archaeology, Illustration, Interior Design, Jewelry, Mixed Media, †Painting, Photography, †Printmaking, †Sculpture, Silversmithing, †Teacher Training, Textile Design
Adult Hobby Classes: Enrl 30; tui $18.50 per cr
Summer School: Dir, Jim Gibson. Enrl 35; tui $18.50 per cr for term of 4 wks beginning June 9

BROOKINGS

SOUTH DAKOTA STATE UNIVERSITY, Art Dept, Solberg Hall, 57007. Tel 605-688-4103. *Acting Head Dept* Richard Edie, MFA; *Prof* Frederick W Bunce, PhD; *Assoc Prof* Alice Berry, MA; *Assoc Prof* Helen Morgan, MAE; *Assoc Prof* Melvin Spinar, MFA; *Asst Prof* Dennis Guastella, MFA; *Asst Prof* Gerald Kruse, MFA; *Asst Prof* Chris Martens, MFA
Estab 1881; pub; D & E; ent req HS dipl, ent ACT; degrees BA & BS 126 sem cr; SC 28, LC 8
Courses: Art Education, Calligraphy, Ceramics, Commercial Art, Drawing, Graphic Arts, Graphic Design, History of Art & Archaeology, Intermedia, Lettering, Museum Staff Training, Painting, Printmaking, Sculpture, Textile Design, Design, Watercolor, Weaving

HURON

HURON COLLEGE, Art Department,* 57350. Tel 605-352-8721.
Pub; D; ent req HS dipl, ent exam; degrees BA and BS 4 yrs; scholarships; SC 9, LC 2; enrl D 580
Tuition: Res—$2175 per yr
Courses: Art Education, Drawing, Graphic Arts, Graphic Design, History of Art & Archaeology, Painting, Photography, Sculpture, Teacher Training
Summer School: Courses—Drawing Techniques, Three Dimensional Design

MADISON

DAKOTA STATE COLLEGE, Division of Fine and Applied Art, 57042. Tel 605-256-3551, Ext 219. Instrs FT 1, PT 1
Estab 1881; pub; D; ent req HS dipl, ACT; degrees BS 4 yrs; scholarships; SC 16, LC 5; enrl D 120, maj 20
Courses: Art Education, Art History, Ceramics, Drawing, Jewelry, Painting, Sculpture, Teacher Training
Summer School: Term of 8 wks beginning June

SIOUX FALLS

AUGUSTANA COLLEGE, Art Department,* 57102. Tel 605-336-0770. *Head Dept* John Carlander
Estab 1860; den; D & E; ent req HS dipl, ent exam; degrees BA and MAE 4 yrs; scholarships; SC 14, LC 3; enrl total 1861
Tuition: Res—$3650 per yr; campus res—room and board $1345 per yr
Courses: Art Education, Art History, Ceramics, Drawing, Painting, Sculpture, Etching, Lithography
Summer School: Dir, Dr Arthur Olsen. Term of 8 wks beginning June. Courses—Arts, Crafts, Drawing

SIOUX FALLS COLLEGE, Department of Art,* Division of Fine Arts, 1501 S Prairie St, 57101. Tel 605-331-5000. *Chmn* Jay Olson
Estab 1883; pub; degrees BA with maj in Art or Art Educ 4 yrs; scholarships; SC, LC; enrl 1000
Tuition: $2400 per yr; campus res—room $580-$730 per yr, board $810 per yr
Courses: Art Education, Art History, Drawing, Handicrafts, Painting, Design & Illustration
Summer School: Terms one 3 wk session, two 4 wk sessions. Courses—Crafts, Design, Drawing, Education

SPEARFISH

BLACK HILLS STATE COLLEGE, Art Department, 57783. Tel 605-642-6272. *Chmn* Dr Victor Weidensee; *Dept Head* Richard DuBois. Instrs FT 5
Estab 1883; pub; D; ent req HS dipl, transcripts, ACT, physical exam; degrees BA 4 yrs; scholarships; SC 15, LC 4; enrl maj 50
Tuition: $19 per sem hr; non-res $40 per sem hr; campus res $1815
Courses: Art Education, Calligraphy, Ceramics, Commercial Art, Drafting, Drawing, Painting, Photography, Sculpture
Summer School: Courses—Art in our Lives, Ceramics, Drawing, Painting, School Arts & Crafts

SPRINGFIELD

UNIVERSITY OF SOUTH DAKOTA, SPRINGFIELD,* 57062. Tel 605-369-2201. *Head Dept* Ed Gettinger
Estab 1881; pub; D; ent req HS dipl; degrees AA, AS and AAS 2 yrs; scholarships; SC 12, LC 2; enrl D 70, maj 14, grad 70
Tuition: Res—$692; nonres—$1316
Courses: Ceramics, Drawing, Graphic Design, Lettering, Painting, Sculpture, Technical Illustration
Adult Hobby Classes: Enrl 15. Courses—Ceramics, Painting
Summer School: Enrl 20; term of 5 wks beginning June. Courses—Art Appreciation, Design, Drawing, Independent Study, Painting

VERMILLION

UNIVERSITY OF SOUTH DAKOTA, Dept of Art, 57069. Tel 605-677-5636. *Dean* Wayne Knutson, PhD; *Chmn Dept* John A Day, MFA; *Prof* Robert Aldern, BFA; *Assoc Prof* Kenneth Grizzell, MFA; *Assoc Prof* Daniel Packard, MFA; *Asst Prof* John Risseeuw, MFA; *Assoc Prof* William Wold, MA; *Asst Prof* Wu Chien Lem, MFA; *Asst Prof* Lloyd Menard, MFA; *Asst Prof* Martin Wanserski, MFA; *Instructor* Cecelia Condit, MFA
Estab 1862, dept estab 1931; pub; D & E; ent req HS dipl, ACT; degrees BFA, BS, BFA with Teacher Cert; scholarships; SC 32, LC 9, GC 9; enrl non-maj 50, maj 100, grad 10
Tuition: Res—undergrad $19.50 per cr hr, grad $30.75 per cr hr; nonres—undergrad $44.55 per cr hr, grad $58.55 per cr hr; campus res—room & board $1200
Courses: Aesthetics, †Art Education, Calligraphy, Ceramics, Drawing, Graphic Arts, Graphic Design, History of Art & Archaeology, Museum Staff Training, Painting, Photography, Printmaking, Sculpture, Weaving
Summer School: Chmn, John A Day. Tui $21 per cr hr for term of 8 wks beginning June

YANKTON

MOUNT MARTY COLLEGE, Art Dept, 57078. Tel 605-668-1011, 668-1574. *Asst Prof* Michael Gontesky, MFA; *Instructor & Res Artist* Sr Leonarda Longen, MFA; *Lectr* Sr Kathleen Courtney, MA
Estab 1936; den; D; ent req HS dipl; degrees BA 4 yrs; scholarships; SC 17, LC 5;

9 enrl
Tuition: $1200 per sem; campus res—room $290 per sem, board $420 per sem
Courses: †Advertising Design, †Art Education, Art History, Calligraphy, Ceramics, †Commercial Art, Drawing, Film, Graphic Arts, Handicrafts, †Painting, †Photography, †Printmaking, †Sculpture
Summer School: Dir, Sr Jacqueline Ernster. Tui $70 per cr hr for term of 4 wks beginning June and July

YANKTON COLLEGE, Dept of Art, 57078. Tel 605-665-3661. *Head Dept* Jerome Gallagher. Instrs PT 3
Estab 1881; pvt, den; ent req HS grad; degrees 4 yr; scholarships
Tuition: $2850 per term; PT $75 per cr hr; room & board $1340 per term
Courses: Art Education, Art History, Ceramics, Drawing, Jewelry, Painting, Photography, Sculpture, Art Appreciation, Foundations, Philosophy of Art, Weaving

TENNESSEE

ATHENS

TENNESSEE WESLEYAN COLLEGE, Department of Art,* PO Box 40, 37303. Tel 615-745-5872. *Chmn* Robert Jolly
Estab 1857, dept estab 1966; den; D & E; ent req HS dipl; degrees BA and BS 4 yrs; SC 7, LC 5; enrl total 500, maj 10
Tuition: $1440 per yr; campus res—room and board $1320
Courses: Art Education, Art History, Drawing, Painting, Sculpture, Design

CHATTANOOGA

UNIVERSITY OF TENNESSEE AT CHATTANOOGA, Department of Art,* 615 McCallie Ave, 37401. Tel 615-755-4178. *Head* George Cress, MFA; *Prof* Jim Collins, MFA; *Asst Prof* Stephen S LeWinter, MA; *Asst Prof* E Alan White, MFA
Estab 1928; pub; D & E; ent req HS dipl, ACT or SAT, health exam; degrees BA and BS 4 yrs; SC 11, LC 13, GC 1; enrl D 420, E 80, non-maj 500, maj 130, grad 6, others 14
Tuition: Res—undergrad $273 per sem, grad $292 per sem; nonres—undergrad $773 per sem, grad $792 per sem; campus res—room and board $260-$350 per sem
Courses: Art Education, Art History, Ceramics, Commercial Art, Drawing, Graphic Design, Painting, Printmaking, Sculpture
Adult Hobby Classes: Tui $60 for 6 wks. Courses—Stained Glass
Summer School: Tui $292 for 5 wk term

CLARKSVILLE

AUSTIN PEAY STATE UNIVERSITY, Dept of Art, College St, 37040. Tel 615-648-7011. *Chmn Dept* Charles T Young, EdD; *Instructor* Olen Bryant, MFA; *Instructor* Lewis Burton, MA; *Instructor* Algar Dole, MFA; *Instructor* T Max Hochstetler, MFA; *Instructor* Larry Hortenburg, MFA; *Instructor* Andrew Ladis, PhD; *Instructor* Marilyn Zimmermann
Estab 1927, dept estab 1930; pub; D & E; ent req HS dipl; degrees AA 2 yrs, BFA, BA & BS 4 yrs; GC 3; enrl D 615, E 75, non-maj 475, maj 140
Tuition: Res—$500 per yr; nonres $1425 per yr; campus res—room & board $1375 per yr
Courses: Advertising Design, Art Education, Art History, Calligraphy, Ceramics, Commercial Art, Drafting, Drawing, Graphic Arts, Graphic Design, Handicrafts, History of Art & Archaeology, Illustration, Lettering, Mixed Media, Painting, Photography, Printmaking, Sculpture, Stage Design, Teacher Training, Textile Design, Theatre Arts
Adult Hobby Classes: Courses—Crafts, Italic Handwriting, Painting
Summer School: Chmn Dept Art, Charles T Young. Enrl 125; tui $150 for term of 6 wks beginning June 14. Courses—Art Appreciation, Art Education, Painting

CLEVELAND

CLEVELAND STATE COMMUNITY COLLEGE, Department of Art, Adkisson Dr, 37311. *Dept Coordr* Jere L Chumley, MA; *Instr* Cathy Smith-Robison, MS
Estab 1967; pub; D & E; ent req HS dipl or GED; degrees AA and AS 2 yrs; SC 6, LC 5; enrl D 107, E 28, non-maj 76, maj 59
Tuition: Res—$270 per yr, $90 per quarter, $8 per quarter hr; nonres—$1002 per yr, $334 per quarter, $28 per quarter hr; no campus res
Courses: Art Education, Art History, Ceramics, Commercial Art, Drawing, Handicrafts, Painting, Printmaking, Sculpture, Art Appreciation, Design, Weaving
Adult Hobby Classes: Enrl 35; tui $10-$25 per course. Courses—Ceramics, Macrame and Painting offered through Community Serv Div
Summer School: Dir, Jere L Chumley. Enrl approx 12 per class; tui $90 per quarter, $8 per quarter hr for two 5 wk sessions beginning June 10. Courses—Art Appreciation, Arts & Crafts, Ceramics, Painting, Weaving

COLLEGEDALE

SOUTHERN MISSIONARY COLLEGE, Art Department,* 37315. Tel 615-396-2111.
Estab 1969; den; D & E; ent req HS dipl, ent exam; degrees BA(Art) and BA(Art Educ) 4 yrs; LC 3; enrl maj 34
Tuition: $2880 per yr
Courses: Advertising Design, Art Education, Art History, Ceramics, Drawing, Graphic Arts, Graphic Design, Handicrafts, History of Art & Archaeology, Industrial Design, Landscape Architecture, Painting, Photography, Sculpture, Teacher Training, Textile Design

COLUMBIA

COLUMBIA STATE COMMUNITY COLLEGE, Dept of Art, 38401. Tel 615-388-0120. *Head Dept* Fred Behrens, MFA
Estab 1966; pub; D & E; ent req open door institution; degrees AA & AS 2 yrs; scholarships; SC 17, LC 4; enrl D 230, non-maj 215, maj 12-15
Tuition: $252 per yr, $33 per hr; no campus res
Courses: †Art Education, Ceramics, Drawing, Film, History of Art & Archaeology, Painting, Photography, Printmaking, †Art Studio
Summer School: Dir, Fred Behrens. Enrl 30-40; tui $84 for term of 5 wks beginning June. Courses—Art Appreciation & School Art

FRANKLIN

HARRIS SCHOOL OF ART, INC,* 1109 Battlewood St, Battlewood Estates, 37064. Tel 615-790-0407.
Estab 1932; pvt; D; ent req HS dipl; degrees 2, 3 and 4 yr cert in advertising art; SC, LC; enrl 75
Courses: Advertising Layout, Advertising and Fiction Illustration, Airbrush Rendering, Artistic Anatomy, Composition and Design, Figure Drawing and Painting, Head Drawing and Painting, Lettering and Typography, Lithography, Mechanical Art and Paste-Up, Perspective Drawing, Photoengraving, Printing Processes, Still Life Painting

GATLINBURG

ARROWMONT SCHOOL OF ARTS AND CRAFTS, Parkway, Box 567, 37738. Tel 615-436-5860. *Dir* Sandra J Blain
Estab 1945; pvt; D & E (operate mostly in summer with special programs for fall, winter & spring); ent req HS dipl; degrees none granted, though credit is offered for courses through the Univ of Tennessee, Knoxville & other similar institutions; scholarships; SC 44-50, GC 30; enrl D 1000
Tuition: $80 per wk, 1 or 2 wk sessions; campus res—room & board $85-$105 per wk
Courses: Ceramics, Drawing, Graphic Arts, Jewelry, Painting, Photography, Textile Design, Bookbinding, Leather, Papermaking, Stained Glass

GREENEVILLE

TUSCULUM COLLEGE, Fine Arts Department,* Division of Creative Arts & Humanities, Box 48, 37743. Tel 615-639-2861. *Chmn Creative Arts* Clement Allison
Estab 1794; den; D; ent req HS dipl; degrees BA and BS 4 yrs; scholarships; SC 25, LC 3; enrl D 445, maj 18
Tuition: $1920 per yr; campus res—room and board $1491
Courses: Art Education, Ceramics, Drawing, History of Art & Archaeology, Painting, Printmaking, Sculpture, Glassblowing, Life Drawing, Two & Three-Dimensional Design
Adult Hobby Classes: Enrl 14. Courses—Painting

HARROGATE

LINCOLN MEMORIAL UNIVERSITY, Department of Fine Arts, Box 670, 37752. Tel 615-869-3611. *Chmn* Robert Brown, EdD; *Instr* Alex Buckland, MFA; *Instr* Richard Cary, MFA
Estab 1897, dept estab 1974; pvt; D & E; ent req HS dipl; degrees BA 4 yrs; SC 30, LC 3; enrl D 120, E 75, non-maj 97, maj 98
Tuition: Res—undergrad $45 per hr; campus residency available
Courses: Aesthetics, †Art Education, Art History, †Ceramics, †Commercial Art, †Drawing, Film, Goldsmithing, Graphic Arts, †Jewelry, Lettering, Museum Staff Training, †Painting, †Photography, †Sculpture, Silversmithing, †Teacher Training, †Textile Design, †Theatre Arts, Weaving

JACKSON

LAMBUTH COLLEGE, Department of Art, 38301. Tel 901-427-6743. *Chmn Dept* Joanna H Ross, MFA; *Dir Interior Design* Lawrence Ray, MA
Estab 1843, dept estab 1950; den; D & E; ent req HS dipl; degrees BA and BS 4 yrs; SC 21, LC 10
Tuition: Res—undergrad $1400 per sem; nonres—undergrad $1000 per sem; campus res—room & board $2000 per yr
Courses: Advertising Design, Aesthetics, Architecture, †Art Education, †Art History, †Commercial Art, Drawing, Fashion Arts, Graphic Design, †History of Art & Archaeology, †Interior Design, †Painting, Photography, †Printmaking, †Sculpture, Stage Design, Teacher Training, Theatre Arts, Stained Glass

UNION UNIVERSITY, Department of Art, Hwy 45 Bypass, Union University Box 2078, 38301. Tel 901-668-1818. *Chmn Dept Art* Grove Robinson, MFA; *Assoc Prof* Meredith Luck, MFA; *Assoc Prof* Patricia Pinson, PhD; *Instr* Elizabeth Emison, BA
Estab 1824, dept estab 1958; den; D & E; ent req HS dipl, ACT; degrees BA and BS 4 yrs; scholarships; SC 20, LC 5; enrl D 200, E 40, maj 28
Tuition: $45-$65 per sem hr; campus res—room & board $466 per sem
Courses: Advertising Design, Art Education, Art History, †Ceramics, Commercial Art, Drawing, Handicrafts, Jewelry, Lettering, †Painting, Photography, Printmaking, Sculpture, Silversmithing, Teacher Training, Art Appreciation
Summer School: Dir, Grove Robinson. Enrl 50; tui $65 per hr for term of 5 wks beginning June and July

JEFFERSON CITY

CARSON-NEWMAN COLLEGE, Art Dept, 37760. Tel 615-475-9061, Ext 242.
Chmn Dept R Earl Cleveland. Instrs FT 3
Col estab 1851; den; D & E; ent req HS dipl; degrees BA(Art) 4 yrs; scholarships; SC 26, LC 7; enrl maj 36
Tuition: $1700 per yr, studio fees $5-$25; campus res $1350
Courses: Aesthetics, Art Education, Art History, Ceramics, Drawing, Handicrafts, Lettering, Painting, Photography, Stage Design, Teacher Training, Theatre Arts
Summer School: Chmn, R Earl Cleveland. Courses—Art Appreciation, Teacher Workshops; Travel Study in Europe

JOHNSON CITY

EAST TENNESSEE STATE UNIVERSITY, Fine Arts Dept, Box 23740A, 37601. Tel 615-929-4247. *Chmn Dept* William Radford Thomas, PhD; *Prof* John Pav, PhD; *Assoc Prof* Gerald Edmundson, MA; *Assoc Prof* David Logan, PhD; *Assoc Prof* James Mills, PhD; *Assoc Prof* George Moldovan, MA; *Assoc Prof* John Steele, MA; *Asst Prof* Charles Thompson, MFA; *Instructor* Vickie Bourek, MFA; *Instructor* Spencer Crawford, MFA; *Instructor* Teresa Lonier, MFA
Estab 1909, dept estab 1949; pub; D & E; ent req HS dipl, ACT or SAT; degrees BA, BS & BFA 4 yrs, MA, MFA; scholarships; SC 102, LC 30, GC 46; enrl D approx 1400
Tuition: Res—undergrad $14 per quarter hr, $154 per quarter, grad $16 per quarter hr, $167 per quarter; nonres—undergrad $26 per quarter hr, $312 per quarter; campus res—room & board approx $550 per quarter
Courses: †Art Education, †Art History, †Ceramics, †Drawing, Goldsmithing, †Graphic Design, †Jewelry, Lettering, †Painting, †Photography, Printmaking, †Sculpture, Silversmithing, Enameling, Weaving
Summer School: Dir, Dr William Radford Thomas. Tui $154 for term of 4 wks beginning June 13 and July 17. Courses—Same as above

KNOXVILLE

UNIVERSITY OF TENNESSEE, KNOXVILLE
—Department of Art, 927 Volunteer Blvd, 37916. Tel 615-974-3408. *Head Dept Art* Donald F Kurka, PhD. Instrs FT 31
Estab 1794, dept estab 1951; pub; D & E; ent req HS dipl; degrees BA and BFA 4 yrs, MFA 3 yrs; scholarships; SC 51, LC 23, GC 50; enrl D 1500, E 250, non-maj 300, maj 350, grad 25
Tuition: Res—undergrad $16 per quarter hr, grad $22 per quarter hr; nonres—undergrad $38 per quarter hr, $52 per quarter hr; campus res—room and board $1300 per yr
Courses: †Advertising Design, †Art History, †Ceramics, †Commercial Art, †Constructions, †Drawing, Film, Graphic Arts, Graphic Design, Jewelry, Lettering, †Painting, †Printmaking, †Sculpture, †Fiber-Fabric
Summer School: Prof, William Kennedy. Enrl 400; term of 2 sessions beginning June and Aug. Courses—same as above
—Interior Design Department, 13th and Cumberland Ave, 37916. Tel 615-974-2360. *Head Dept* Robbie G Blakemore, PhD. Instrs FT 4
Estab 1794, dept estab 1936; pub; D & E; ent req HS dipl; degrees BS 4 yrs; SC 44, LC 5, GC 55; enrl maj 394, grad 73
Tuition: Res—undergrad $150 per quarter, grad $160 per quarter; nonres—undergrad and grad $460 per quarter; prog and serv fee $15
Courses: Aesthetics, Display, Drafting, Interior Design, Mixed Media

MARYVILLE

MARYVILLE COLLEGE, Division of Fine Arts, Art Section, 37801. Tel 615-982-9132. *Head* Thelma Roper Bianco. Instrs FT 2, PT 1
Estab 1937; den; degrees 4 yr; scholarships; SC 10, LC 5
Courses: Art Education, Art History, Ceramics, Drawing, Jewelry, Painting, Photography, Printmaking, Enameling, Fabric Design, Visual Theory & Design, Weaving
Children's Classes: Art Education, Crafts

MEMPHIS

MEMPHIS ACADEMY OF ARTS, Overton Park, 38112. Tel 901-726-4085. *Pres* Jameson M Jones, PhD; *Dean* Phillip S Morris, MFA. Instrs FT 17, PT 10
Estab 1936; pvt; D & E; ent req HS dipl; degrees BFA & cert 4 yrs; scholarships; enrl D 240, E 300
Tuition: $950 per sem; no campus res
Courses: Advertising Design, Aesthetics, Art History, Calligraphy, Ceramics, Commercial Art, Drawing, Illustration, Jewelry, Lettering, Painting, Photography, Printmaking, Sculpture, Silversmithing, Textile Design, Enameling
Adult Hobby Classes: Enrl 200; term of 16 wks. Courses—Drawing, Metal Arts, Painting, Photography, Pottery, Sculpture, Watercolor
Children's Classes: Enrl 250; tui $60 for 25 wks. Courses—Drawing, Jewelry, Painting, Photography, Pottery, Sculpture
Summer School: Enrl 500; tui $80 per cr hr for term of 6 wks beginning early June. Courses—Drawing, Metal Arts, Painting, Photography, Printing & Dyeing, Sculpture, Watercolor

MEMPHIS STATE UNIVERSITY, Dept of Art, 38152. Tel 901-454-2216. *Chmn Dept* Lawrence F Edwards, MFA
Estab 1912; pub; D & E; ent req HS dipl, SAT; degrees BA & BFA 4 yrs, MA & MAT 1 yr, MFA 2 yrs; SC 100, LC 40, GC 30; enrl D 2200, maj 400, grad 80
Tuition: Campus residence available
Courses: Advertising Design, Art Education, Art History, Ceramics, Commercial Art, Display, Drawing, Graphic Design, History of Art & Archaeology, Illustration, Intermedia, Interior Design, Jewelry, Lettering, Museum Staff Training, Painting, Photography, Printmaking, Sculpture, Teacher Training, Textile Design
Summer School: Dir, Lawrence F Edwards

SOUTHWESTERN AT MEMPHIS, Dept of Art, 2000 N Parkway, 38112. Tel 901-180-0321. *Chmn Dept* Lawrence K Anthony, MFA; *Asst Prof* George Apperson, PhD; *Asst Prof* Peter Bowman, MFA; *Asst Prof* Murray Riss, MFA; *Asst Prof* Anne Robbins, MA; *Instructor* Rosemary Dougherty, BFA; *Instructor* William Womack, BFA; *Lectr* John Whitlock, PhD
Estab 1848, dept estab 1940; pvt; D & E; ent req SAT or ACT, 13 acad credits, 16 overall; degrees BA 4 yrs; SC 17, LC 12; enrl D 250, non-maj 240, maj 10
Tuition: $3400 per yr; campus res—room & board $1620 per yr
Courses: Aesthetics, Architecture, Art History, Calligraphy, Drawing, Film, History of Art & Archaeology, Museum Staff Training, Painting, Photography, Printmaking, Sculpture, Textile Design, Theatre Arts
Summer School: Dir, Dr John Streety. Tui $65 per cr hr for term of 4 or 6 wks beginning June 5 & July 3. Courses—Art History, Painting

MURFREESBORO

MIDDLE TENNESSEE STATE UNIVERSITY, Art Dept, Box 25, 37132. Tel 615-898-2455. *Chmn Art Dept* Lon Nuell, EdD; *Prof* David LeDoux, MFA; *Assoc Prof* James S Gibson, MFA; *Assoc Prof* Howard Gold, PhD; *Assoc Prof* Klaus Kallenberger; *Asst Prof* Raymond Allen, MFA; *Asst Prof* David Bigelow, MFA; *Asst Prof* Oliver Fancher, MFA; *Asst Prof* Charles Jansen, EdS; *Asst Prof* Janet Higgins, MFA; *Asst Prof* Bobby Louise Rowe, PhD; *Asst Prof* Phillip Vander Weg, MFA
Estab 1911, dept estab 1952; pub; D & E; ent req HS dipl; degrees BS(Art Educ), BA & BFA 4 yrs; scholarships; SC 62, LC 10, GC 35; enrl non-maj 900, maj 200, grad 5
Tuition: Res—undergrad $221 per sem, grad $241 per sem; nonres—undergrad $689 per sem, grad $709 per sem; campus res—room & board $198 per sem
Courses: †Advertising Design, †Art Education, †Ceramics, †Commercial Art, Drawing, Goldsmithing, †Jewelry, †Painting, †Printmaking, †Sculpture, †Silversmithing, Textile Design
Children's Classes: Creative Art Clinic for Children; enrl 45; tui $25 per term
Summer School: Chmn Art Dept, Dr Lon Nuell. Enrl 200; tui $468 for term of 10 wks beginning June 6. Courses—Art Education, General Studio

NASHVILLE

FISK UNIVERSITY, Art Dept, PO Box 2, 37203. Tel 615-329-8685. *Chmn Dept* Earl Hooks, MA; *Cur* Robert Hall, MA; *Prof* Phillip Mason, MFA; *Assoc Prof* Stephanie Pogue, MFA
Estab 1867, dept estab 1937; pvt; D; ent req HS dipl, SAT; degrees BS & BA 4 yrs; SC 10, LC 3; enrl 120, non-maj 90, maj 30
Tuition: $2890 per yr; campus residence available
Courses: Aesthetics, Art History, Ceramics, Drawing, Painting, Photography, Printmaking, Sculpture

GEORGE PEABODY COLLEGE FOR TEACHERS, Art Faculty Department,* 21st Ave S, 37203. Tel 615-327-8121. *Chmn* Michael L Taylor, MFA; *Assoc Prof* Robert E Pletcher, EdD; *Assoc Prof* Michael Samford, MFA; *Prof* John M Frase, MFA; *Asst Prof* Alan Vaughan, MA
Estab 1875, dept estab 1914; pvt; D & E; ent req HS dipl, SAT; degrees BS 4 yrs, BSMS 5 yrs, MS 2 yrs; scholarships; SC 14, LC 5, GC 15; enrl D approx 2000, non-maj 700, maj 50, grad 10
Tuition: Res—undergrad $2700 per yr, $1350 per sem, $60 per sem hr, grad $3200 per yr, $1600 per sem, $70 per sem hr; campus res available
Courses: Aesthetics, Art Education, Art History, Calligraphy, Ceramics, Collage, Conceptual Art, Constructions, Drawing, Film, Goldsmithing, Graphic Arts, Graphic Design, Intermedia, Jewelry, Landscape Architecture, Mixed Media, Painting, Printmaking, Sculpture, Silversmithing, Teacher Training
Summer School: Chmn, Michael L Taylor. Ten wk regular sessions

TENNESSEE BOTANICAL GARDENS AND FINE ARTS CENTER, Cheekwood, 37205. Tel 615-356-3306. *Exec Dir* P Duncan Callicott; *Dir Fine Arts Ctr* Kevin Grogan; *Dir Educ* Trond Sandvik
Estab 1960; pvt; D & E; SC 10-15, LC 5-10
Courses: Ceramics, Collage, Commercial Art, Drawing, Graphic Arts, Handicrafts, Jewelry, Painting, Printmaking, Sculpture, Textile Design
Children's Classes: Courses—Art History, Drawing, Jewelry, Painting, Sculpture, Watercolor

VANDERBILT UNIVERSITY, Dept of Fine Arts, West End Ave at 23rd St, Box 1801 Station B, 37235. Tel 615-322-2831. *Chmn Dept* F Hamilton Hazlehurst, PhD; *Prof* Thomas B Brumbaugh, PhD; *Assoc Prof* Robert A Baldwin, MFA; *Assoc Prof* Donald Evans, MFA; *Assoc Prof* Christine Hasenmueller, PhD; *Assoc Prof* Milan Mihal, PhD; *Assoc Prof* Robert L Mode, PhD; *Assoc Prof* Ljubica D Popovich, PhD; *Mellon Asst Prof* Barbara B Walsh, PhD
Estab 1873, dept estab 1944; pvt; D; ent req HS dipl, ent exam; degrees BA 4 yrs, MA(Art Hist) 1-2 yrs; scholarships; SC 8, LC 35, GC 30; enrl non-maj 2000, maj 75, grad 5
Tuition: $4260 per yr, $2130 per sem, $177 per sem hr; campus res—room & board $2140 per yr
Courses: †Art History, Drawing, Film, Painting, Photography, Multimedia Design
Summer School: Dean, Robert Donaldson. Tui $92 per sem hr for two 4 wk terms beginning June 6. Courses vary

WATKINS INSTITUTE, School for Adults, 601 Church, 37219. Tel 615-242-1851. Instrs PT 7
Estab 1913; pvt; D & E; ent req noncredit adult educ program, must be 17 yrs of age or older; SC 4, LC 1; enrl D 125, E 200
Courses: Art Education, Art History, Commercial Art, Drawing, Painting, Photography, Sculpture, Art Essentials, Landscape Painting

SEWANEE

UNIVERSITY OF THE SOUTH, Dept of Fine Arts, Carnegie Hall, 37375. Tel 615-598-5931, Ext 256, 223. *Chmn Dept* Dr Edward Carlos, PhD; *Prof* Warren Jacobson, MFA; *Prof* Ron Jones, MFA; *Prof* William Wadley, MA
Pvt, den; D; degrees BS & BA, MDivinity; scholarships; SC 20, LC 20; enrl D 250, non-maj 225, maj 30
Tuition: $2035; campus res—room $345, board $380
Courses: Aesthetics, Art Education, Conceptual Art, Costume Design & Construction, Drawing, Film, Graphic Arts, History of Art & Archaeology, Mixed Media, Painting, Photography, Printmaking, Sculpture, Stage Design, Teacher Training, Theatre Arts
Children's Classes: Enrl 30-60; tui $15 per 6 wk session. Art classes in conjunction with art education classes
Summer School: Dir, Dr William Cocke. Enrl 150 for term of 6 wks beginning June. Courses—Regular university curriculum

TEXAS

ABILENE

ABILENE CHRISTIAN UNIVERSITY, Art Dept, 79699. Tel 915-677-1911, Ext 2085. *Head Dept* Norman Whitefield. Instrs FT 5, PT 3
Estab 1906; den; D & E; ent req upper 3 4 HS grad class or at 15 standard score ACT composite; degrees BA, BFA & BS(Educ) 4 yrs; SC 29, LC 8; enrl maj 79
Courses: Art History, Commercial Art, Drawing, Painting, Sculpture, Teacher Training, Design, Pottery
Summer School: 5 wks beginning June

HARDIN-SIMMONS UNIVERSITY, Art Dept, Hickory at Ambler St, Box 837 Univ Station, 79698. Tel 915-677-7281. *Chmn* Ira M Taylor, MFA; *Instructor* Martha Kiel, MEd; *Instructor* Claude B Salley, MFA; *Instructor* Jo Dean Salley, MA
Univ estab 1891; den; D & E; ent req HS dipl, SAT, ACT; degrees BFA, BEd & BA 4 yrs; SC 27, LC 5; enrl D 130, E 25, non-maj 65, maj 65
Tuition: $55 per cr hr; campus res—room and board $610-$635
Courses: †Art Education, Art History, Ceramics, †Painting, Printmaking, Sculpture, Stage Design, †Teacher Training, †Theatre Arts
Summer School: Dir, Ira M Taylor. Enrl 50; tui $55 per cr hr for term of 15 wks beginning June 2. Courses vary

MCMURRY COLLEGE, Art Dept, Box 8 McMurry Station, 79697. Tel 915-692-4130, Ext 307. *Head Dept* Sherwood E Suter, MFA; *Asst Prof* Robert Howell, MFA; *Lectr* J Robert Miller, BS
Estab 1923; pvt; D & E; ent req HS dipl; degrees BA, BFA & BS 4 yrs; scholarships; SC 19, LC 1; enrl D 80, E 8, non-maj 50, maj 27
Tuition: Res—undergrad $3370 per yr, $1685 per sem (incl room & board), $58 per sem hr; nonres—same as resident fees
Courses: Art Education, Art History, Ceramics, Drawing, Jewelry, Lettering, Painting, Printmaking, Teacher Training, Design
Summer School: Dir, Dr Paul Jungmeyer. Enrl 25; tui $58 per sem hr for term of 6 wks beginning June into first wk of July. Courses—Ceramics, Design, Painting

ALPINE

SUL ROSS STATE UNIVERSITY, Department of Art,* Division of Fine Arts, 79830. Tel 915-837-3461. *Head Dept* Miriam A Lowrance, MA; *Prof* Roy E Dodson, EdD; *Asst Prof* Charles R Hext, MFA
Estab 1920, dept estab 1922; pub; D & E; ent req HS dipl, ACT or SAT; degrees BA and BFA 4 yrs, MA(Ed in Art) 1 1 2 yrs; scholarships; SC 21, LC 3, GC 19; enrl D 183, E 32, non-maj 170, maj 45-60, GS 32
Tuition: Res—$58-$156 per sem; nonres—$58-$912 per sem; campus res—room and board $730-$925
Courses: Advertising Design, Aesthetics, †Art Education, Art History, Ceramics, Commercial Art, Drawing, Graphic Arts, Handicrafts, History of Art & Archaeology, Illustration, Jewelry, Mixed Media, Painting, Photography, Printmaking, Sculpture, Silversmithing, Teacher Training, Textile Design, Fibers, Weaving
Adult Hobby Classes: Enrl 75; tui $20 per 3-4 wk session. Courses—Ceramics, China Painting, Drawing, Jewelry, Macrame, Painting
Summer School: Tui res—$33-$72; nonres—$48-$396 for a term of 6 wks. Courses—Art Education, Ceramics, Crafts, Fibers, Jewelry, Painting, Sculpture

ALVIN

ALVIN COMMUNITY COLLEGE, Art Dept, 77511. Tel 713-331-6111. *Chmn* Ziya Sever, MA
Estab 1949; D & E; ent req HS dipl; degrees AA 2 yrs
Tuition: Res—$84 per sem, $40 PT; nonres—$250 per sem, $125 PT; no campus res
Courses: Ceramics, Commercial Art, Drawing, Graphic Design, Painting, Art Appreciation, Watercolor
Summer School: Enrl 20; for term of 12 wks beginning May 31. Courses—Art Appreciation, Design, Drawing, Watercolor

AMARILLO

AMARILLO COLLEGE, Art Dept, 2200 S Washington, PO Box 447, 79178. Tel 806-376-5111, Ext 397. *Chmn* Denny Fraze, MFA; *Asst Prof* David Cale, MFA; *Instructor* Tom Glover, MFA
Estab 1926; pub; D & E; ent req HS dipl, CEEB; degrees AA 2 yrs; scholarships; SC 18, LC 2; enrl D 142, E 60
Tuition: Res—undergrad $125 per sem; nonres—undergrad $200 per sem; no campus res

Courses: Art History, Ceramics, Drawing, Jewelry, Painting, Printmaking, Sculpture, Design, Watercolor

TEXAS STATE TECHNICAL INSTITUTE, Department of Commercial Art, PO Box 11016, 79111. Tel 806-335-2316. *Prog Chmn* Robert O Bayle; *Asst Chmn* Lloyd Cook, BSOE; *Instr* James S Cost, MA
Estab 1970; pub; D; ent req HS dipl, GED; degrees AAA 2 yrs; scholarships; SC 32, LC 2; enrl D 42, non-maj 1, maj 42
Tuition: Res—undergrad $87 per sem, $5 per hr; nonres—undergrad $267 per sem, $24 per hr; campus residence available
Courses: Advertising Design, Calligraphy, †Commercial Art, Display, Drafting, Graphic Arts, Graphic Design, Illustration, Lettering, Mixed Media, Painting, Photography, Video, Air Brush, Corporate Design, Delineation, Screen Printing, Sign Painting, Television Art
Summer School: Same as regular session

ARLINGTON

UNIVERSITY OF TEXAS AT ARLINGTON, Dept of Art, 144 Fine Arts Bldg, 76019. *Chmn* Vincent J Bruno, PhD
Estab 1895, dept estab 1933; pub; D & E; ent req HS dipl; degrees BFA 4 yrs; SC 60, LC 7
Courses: †Advertising Design, †Art Education, †Art History, †Ceramics, †Commercial Art, Drawing, †Fashion Arts, †Film, †Goldsmithing, †Jewelry, †Painting, †Photography, †Printmaking, †Sculpture, †Silversmithing, Art Therapy, Metalsmithing, Papermaking

AUSTIN

AUSTIN COMMUNITY COLLEGE, Dept of Commercial Art & Fine Arts, 12th & Rio Grande, 78701. Tel 512-476-6381, Ext 16. *Head Dept* Luis Guerra, MFA. Instrs FT 12
Estab 1974; pub; D & E; ent req HS dipl or GED; AA 2 yrs; special problems course which allows students to specialize or get college credit for free-lancing with live job situations; enrl 250 per sem
Tuition: Res—undergrad $10 per cr hr; nonres—undergrad $30 per cr hr; other adult continuing education non-cr courses $1 per hr
Courses: Advertising Design, Art History, Calligraphy, Ceramics, Commercial Art, Drafting, Drawing, Fashion Arts, Film, Graphic Arts, Graphic Design, Illustration, Lettering, Mixed Media, Painting, Photography, Printmaking, Sculpture, Stage Design, Theatre Arts, Video, Design, Intaglio, Production Art, Printing & Design, Sign Painting, Silkscreen Printing, Typography
Adult Hobby Classes: Tui $1 per hr. Courses—Calligraphy, Drawing, Handicrafts, Macrame, Painting, Photography, Pottery, Stained Glass, Weaving, Woodworking
Summer School: Enrl 250; tui $10 per cr hr for term of 11 wks beginning June 5th. Courses vary

CONCORDIA LUTHERAN COLLEGE, Department of Fine Arts,* 3400 North Interregional Highway, 78705. *Chmn* Harold Rutz
Estab 1925; den; D; ent req HS dipl; degrees AA 2 yrs; scholarships; SC 1, LC 1; enrl D 350
Tuition: $1500 per yr; campus res available
Courses: Drawing, Painting, Art Fundamentals

UNIVERSITY OF TEXAS
—School of Architecture, University Station, PO Box 7908, 78712. Tel 512-471-1922. *Dean* Harold Box. Instrs FT 20, PT 10
Estab 1910; pub; ent req 16 cr incl 3.5 math, 1 science; degrees 5-6 yrs; enrl 387
Tuition: Res—$50 per sem; nonres—$40 per sem hr
Courses: †Architecture
—Department of Art, College of Fine Arts, University Station, 78712. *Dean* Peter M Garvie. Instrs FT 49, PT 4
Estab 1938; degrees 4 yr; SC 78, LC 21; enrl maj 1000, others 1162
Tuition: Res—$50 per sem; nonres—$40 per sem hr
Courses: Art History, Ceramics, Commercial Art, Drawing, Graphic Arts, Handicrafts, Illustration, Painting, Sculpture, Teacher Training, Criticism of Art, Design, Pictorial Composition
Summer School: Two 6 wk terms

UNIVERSITY OF TEXAS - AUSTIN, Art Department, Art Bldg, 23rd & San Jacinto, 78712. Tel 512-471-3365. *Chmn* Kenneth Prescott, PhD; *Undergrad Advisor* J Ulbricht, PhD; *Grad Advisor* M P Taylor, MFA
Estab 1880, dept estab 1938; pub; D; ent req HS dipl, SAT, GRE; degrees BFA and BA 4 yrs, MA 1 yr, MFA 2 yrs, PhD 2 yrs; scholarships; enrl D 850, non-maj 900, maj 850, grad 86
Tuition: Res—undergrad $469 per yr, grad $310 per yr; nonres—undergrad $1549 per yr, grad $930 per yr; campus res—room & board $1825 per yr
Courses: Advertising Design, †Art Education, †Art History, Ceramics, Drawing, Graphic Arts, Graphic Design, Handicrafts, Illustration, Jewelry, Painting, Photography, Printmaking, Sculpture, Silversmithing, Teacher Training, Textile Design, †Studio, Watercolor
Summer School: Dept Chmn, Kenneth Prescott

BEAUMONT

LAMAR UNIVERSITY, Art Department, PO Box 10027, 77710. Tel 713-838-7427. *Head Dept* Robert C Rogan, DEd; *Prof* J Robert Madden, MFA; *Prof* Jerry Newman, MFA; *Prof* Robert O'Neili, MFA; *Instructor* Philip Fitzpatrick, MFA; *Instructor* Meredith M Jack, MFA; *Instructor* Lynn Lokensgard, MA; *Instructor* John F Sommerfeld; *Adjunct Instructor* Steve Crain
Estab 1923, dept estab 1951; pub; D & E; ent req HS dipl; degrees BA and BS 4 yr; scholarships; SC 50, LC 10; ent D 589, E 45, non-maj 160, maj 200
Tuition: Res—undergrad $89 for 3 sem hrs; nonres—undergrad $239 for 3 sem hrs; campus residency available
Courses: Advertising Design, †Art Education, Art History, Ceramics, †Commercial Art, Drawing, Fashion Arts, Film, Graphic Arts, †Graphic Design, Handicrafts, History of Art & Archaeology, Illustration, Jewelry, †Painting, Photography, Printmaking, Sculpture, Weaving
Children's Classes: Enrl 77; tui $13 per 2 wks. Courses—Children's Workshop
Summer School: Tui $56 per 3 cr hrs for term of 6 wks beginning May 30th

BELTON

UNIVERSITY OF MARY HARDIN-BAYLOR, Department of Fine Arts,* 76513. Tel 817-939-5811. *Chmn* George Stansbury
Estab 1845; den; D & E; ent req upper half of HS grad class; degrees BA, BFA and BS 4 yrs; scholarships; SC 6, LC 1 and one independent learning course per sem
Courses: Art Education, Art History, Ceramics, Drawing, Graphic Arts, Jewelry, Painting, Design
Summer School: Dir, Ted L Austin. Sem of 5 wks, from 1 to 4 cr hrs. Courses—Crafts, Independent Learning

BIG SPRING

HOWARD COLLEGE, Art Department,* Division of Fine Arts, Birdwell Lane, 79720. Tel 915-267-6311. *Chmn* Kathleen Weber, MEd; *Instr* Susan King, MA; *Instr* David Norvella, BFA
Estab 1948, dept estab 1972; pub; D & E; ent req HS dipl, ACT; degrees AA; scholarships; SC 5, LC 1; enrl D 70, E 20, non-maj 60, maj 10
Tuition: Res—undergrad $4 per hr; nonres—undergrad $20 per hr; campus res available
Courses: Advertising Design, Art Education, Art History, Ceramics, Drawing, Handicrafts, History of Art & Archaeology, Illustration, Interior Design, Lettering, Teacher Training, Textile Design
Adult Hobby Classes: Enrl 150; tui $12 per 6 wks. Courses— Needlepoint, Pottery, Quilting, Stained Glass
Children's Classes: Enrl 20, tui $15 for 6 wk session. Courses—General Art

BORGER

FRANK PHILLIPS COLLEGE, Art Department, Fine Arts Division, Box 5118, 79007. Tel 806-274-5311. *Chmn Div* R K Palmer, MA
Estab 1948; pub; D & E; ent req HS dipl, GED or transfer from another college; degrees AA, AS and AAS 2 yrs; scholarships; SC 14, LC 3; enrl D 60, E 10, non-maj 20, maj 40
Tuition: Res—undergrad $150 per sem; nonres—undergrad $200 per sem; campus res —room & board $520 per yr
Courses: Advertising Design, Art Education, Art History, Calligraphy, Ceramics, Commercial Art, Drawing, Graphic Arts, Painting, Photography, Sculpture, Design, Pottery
Adult Hobby Classes: Enrl varies; tui varies. Courses—Calligraphy, Ceramics, Drawing, Painting, Photography, others on demand
Summer School: Dir, R K Palmer. Courses—Painting, others on demand

BROWNSVILLE

TEXAS SOUTHMOST COLLEGE, Fine Arts Department,* 83 Fort Brown, 78520. Tel 512-541-1241. *Chmn* Jean Serafy
Estab 1973; pub; D & E; ent req HS dipl; degrees AA(Fine Arts) 2-3 yrs; scholarships; SC 10, LC 10; enrl D 300, E 100
Tuition: Res—undergrad In District $256, In State $308; nonres—undergrad $1118
Courses: Art Education, Ceramics, Drawing, Graphic Design, History of Art & Archaeology, Painting, Sculpture, Design I and II
Adult Hobby Classes: Courses—Ceramics, Drawing
Summer School: Term of 16 wks. Courses—Art Appreciation

BROWNWOOD

HOWARD PAYNE UNIVERSITY, Department of Art,* School of Fine and Applied Arts, Howard Payne Station, 76801. Tel 915-646-2502. *Dean* Charles A Stewart
Estab 1889; den; D & E; ent req HS dipl, ent exam; degrees BA, BFA(Studio or Art Educ) and BS 4-5 yrs; SC 18, LC 12; enrl D 200, E 69, maj 3
Tuition: $42 per sem hr; campus res available
Courses: Advertising Design, Aesthetics, Art Education, Ceramics, Commercial Art, Drawing, History of Art & Archaeology, Painting, Photography, Sculpture, Teacher Training, Metalcrafts
Adult Hobby Classes: Enrl 30; tui $35 per course. Courses—Metalcrafts, Painting, Weaving
Summer School: Enrl 75; tui term of 6 wks beginning June. Courses—Art Education, Crafts, Painting

CANYON

WEST TEXAS STATE UNIVERSITY, Art Department, 79016. Tel 806-656-2291. *Head Dept* Steven L Mayes, MFA; *Asst Prof* Margie Adkins, MFA; *Asst Prof* David Rindlisbacher, MFA; *Assoc Prof* Darold Smith, MFA; *Instructor* Margaret Campbell, MEd; *Instructor* Hunter Ingalls; *Instructor* Bill Shires; *Instructor* O W Tarter
Estab 1910; pub; D & E; ent req HS dipl; degrees BA, BS, BFA and MA; scholarships; SC 70, LC 23, GC 50; enrl maj 120, grad 23
Tuition: Res $64 per sem, $50 PT; nonres $640 per sem, $360 PT; foreign students $640 per sem. There are additional fees all students must pay; campus res $1000
Courses: Advertising Design, Aesthetics, Art Education, Art History, Ceramics, Commercial Art, Drawing, Goldsmithing, Graphic Arts, Graphic Design, Handicrafts, History of Art & Archaeology, Illustration, Jewelry, Painting, Printmaking, Sculpture, Silversmithing, Teacher Training, Textile Design, Macrame, Rugs
Summer School: Courses—as above

COLLEGE STATION

TEXAS A & M UNIVERSITY, College of Architecture and Environmental Design, 77843. *Dean* Raymond D Reed. Instrs FT 55
Estab 1905; pub; D; ent req SAT; CEEB, Achievement, HS average; degrees BEnviron Design, BS(Landscape Arch), DEnviron Design, MArch, M Landscape, M Planning 4 yr; enrl maj Arch 820, total 1500
Tuition: Res $4 per sem cr hr; nonres $40 per sem cr hr; fees approx $652

COMMERCE

EAST TEXAS STATE UNIVERSITY, Department of Art,* 75428. Tel 214-882-5208. *Head Dept* Charles E McGough, MA; *Chmn Painting* Karl Umlauf, MFA; *Chmn Ceramics* James Watral, MFA; *Chmn Graphics* Lee Baxter Davis, MFA
Pub; D & E; ent req HS dipl, ACT or SAT; degrees BA, BS and BFA 4 yrs, MFA 2 yrs, MA and MS 1 1 2 yrs. There is a special program called the Post Masters-MFA which is worked out on an individual basis; scholarships; SC 64, LC 29, GC 19; enrl maj 300, GS 34
Tuition: campus res available
Courses: †Advertising Design, Aesthetics, †Art Education, Art History, †Ceramics, Collage, †Commercial Art, Conceptual Art, Constructions, Costume Design & Construction, Drafting, †Drawing, Fashion Arts, Film, †Graphic Arts, †Graphic Design, History of Art & Archaeology, †Illustration, Industrial Design, Intermedia, Interior Design, †Printmaking, †Sculpture, Silversmithing, Stage Design, †Teacher Training, Theatre Arts, Video, Jewelry, Lettering, Mixed Media, Painting, Photography, †Watercolor
Adult Hobby Classes: Enrl 15; tui $77 per sem. Courses—Bonzai, Ceramics, Drawing, Painting, Watercolor
Summer School: Enrl 15; tui res—$37-$187; nonres—$52-$727, for a term of 2 to 6 wks beginning June. Courses—Art Education, Ceramics, Design, Drawing, Graphics, Hobby Styled Courses, Painting

CORPUS CHRISTI

DEL MAR COLLEGE, Department of Art, Ayers at Baldwin, 78404. Tel 512-881-6216. *Chmn* Joseph A Cain, MA; *Assoc Prof* Ronald Dee Sullivan, MA; *Asst Prof* W E Lambert, MFA; *Asst Prof* Jan R Ward, MA; *Instructor* Rodrigo Benavides, BFA; *Instructor* Baxter Coffee, MFA; *Instructor* Pat Fisk, BFA; *Instructor* John Freeman, MFA; *Instructor* June McKinley, BFA
Estab 1941, dept estab 1965; pub; D & E; ent req HS dipl, SAT score or any accepted test including GED; degrees AA 2 yr in studio, art educ and art history; scholarships; SC 21, LC 3; enrl D 500, E 100, non-maj 400, maj 126
Tuition: Res $4 per sem hr, $25 minimum; nonres—$5 per sem hr, $60 maximum; foreign students $14 per sem hr, $200 minimum; plus other fees; no campus res
Courses: Advertising Design, Aesthetics, Architecture, Art Education, Art History, Collage, Commercial Art, Display, Drawing, Graphic Arts, Graphic Design, Handicrafts, History of Art & Archaeology, Lettering, Painting, Photography, Printmaking, Sculpture, Teacher Training, Textile Design, Theatre Arts, Handweaving
Adult Hobby Classes: Tui varies according to classes. Courses—as above
Summer School: Chmn, Joseph A Cain, MA. Tui same. Courses—as above

CORSICANA

NAVARRO COLLEGE, Art Department, Box 1170, 75110. Tel 214-874-6501. *Dir* Margaret Hicks. Instrs FT 1, PT 1
Estab 1946; pub; D & E; ent req HS dipl, ent exam, special permission; degrees AA, AS, A Gen Educ and A Appl Sci 60 sem hr; scholarships; SC 11, LC 1; enrl D 50, maj 15
Courses: Advertising Design, Commercial Art, Drawing, Illustration, Lettering, Painting, Photography
Adult Hobby Classes: Enrl 20. Courses—Painting

DALLAS

DALLAS BAPTIST COLLEGE, Department of Art, 7007 W Kiest, PO Box 21206, 75211. Tel 214-331-8311. *Asst Prof* Dawna Hamm Walsh, MA & MFA; *Instr* Ernie Bush, MA; *Instr* Jack Hamm, BFA; *Instr* Thomas L Iverson, MA
Estab 1965; pvt den; D & E; ent req HS dipl; degrees BA and BS 4 yrs, Bachelor of Career Arts 2-4 yrs; scholarships; enrl D 75, E 25, non-maj 75, maj 25
Tuition: Res and nonres—undergrad $60 per sem hr; campus residence available
Courses: Art Education, Art History, Ceramics, Drawing, Graphic Design, History of Art & Archaeology, Jewelry, Painting, Photography, Sculpture, Teacher Training, Theatre Arts
Adult Hobby Classes: Courses—Batik, Candle Making, Macrame, Raku
Children's Classes: Enrl 30; tui $10 per 2 wks. Courses—Arts for Summer
Summer School: Dir, Dawna Hamm Walsh. Courses—Ceramics, Pottery

SOUTHERN METHODIST UNIVERSITY, Division of Art and Art History, 75275. Tel 214-692-2489. *Chmn* Larry Scholder, MA; *Chmn* Mary Vernon, MA; *Dir of Meadows Museum* William B Jordan, PhD
Estab 1911, Meadows School of Arts estab 1964; pvt; D & E; ent req selective admission; degrees BFA(Art), BFA(Art History), BA(Art History) 4 yr, MFA(Art) 2 yr, MA(Art History) 2 yr; scholarships; enrl maj 165, grad 37
Tuition: $1730 per sem, $145 per cr hr, $230 fee per sem; campus res—room & board $2200
Courses: Architecture, †Art Education, †Art History, †Ceramics, Drawing, †History of Art & Archaeology, Museum Staff Training, †Painting, †Photography, †Printmaking, †Sculpture
Children's Classes: Enrl 75-100; tui $45-$65 per class. Courses—Bronze Sculpture, Exploring Techniques and Materials, Drawing, Painting, Printmaking, Puppets
Summer School: Tui $390 per course for term of 5 wks beginning June 2. Selected courses in art and art history

DENISON

GRAYSON COUNTY COLLEGE, Art Department, 6101 Hwy 691, 25020. Tel 214-465-6030. *Head Dept* Mary Lois O'Neal, MEd
Estab 1965; pub; D & E; ent req HS dipl; degrees AA 2 yrs; scholarships; LC 3; enrl D 63, E 35
Courses: Art Education, Art History, Ceramics, Drawing, Graphic Design, Painting, Photography, Appreciation, Watercolor
Adult Hobby Classes: Courses—Ceramics, Crafts, Drawing, Painting
Summer School: Dir, Mary Lois O'Neal. Courses—Drawing, Painting, Watercolor

DENTON

NORTH TEXAS STATE UNIVERSITY, Art Department, PO Box 5098, 76203. Tel 817-788-2071, 788-2398 or 788-2561. *Head Dept* D Jack Davis, PhD; *Grad Studies Coordr* Margaret O Lucas, DEd; *Undergrad Coordr* Henry Swartz, MFA; *Interior Design Coordr* Ira Shuemaker, MFA; *Advertising Design Coordr* Mack Vaughan, EdD; *Printmaking Coordr* Donald Scaggs, MA; *Photography Coordr* Marianne Gellman, MA & MFA; *Painting & Drawing Coordr* Henry Whiddon, MFA; *Sculpture Coordr* Richard Davis, MA; *Art History Coordr* Larry Gleeson, PhD; *Fashion Design Coordr* Alberta Marzan, MA; *Crafts Coordr* Roger Thomason, MFA; *Vis Prof* David Dowe, video technology
Estab 1897, dept estab 1901; pub; D & E; ent req HS dipl, SAT, GRE, portfolio for MFA, letters of recommendation for PhD; degrees BFA 4 yrs, MFA, MA, PhD; scholarships; SC 92, LC 54, GC 83; enrl non-maj 230, maj 932, grad 78, others 15
Tuition: Res—undergrad and grad $4 per sem hr, minimum of $50 plus fees; nonres —undergrad and grad $40 per sem hr, minimum of $40 plus fees; international $200 per sem hr; campus res—room & board $813-$961 per sem
Courses: †Advertising Design, Aesthetics, †Art Education, †Art History, †Ceramics, Commercial Art, Conceptual Art, †Costume Design & Construction, Drafting, †Drawing, Fashion Arts, Graphic Arts, Graphic Design, †Handicrafts, †Interior Design, †Jewelry, Museum Staff Training, †Painting, †Photography, Printmaking, Restoration & Conservation, †Sculpture, Silversmithing, Teacher Training, Textile Design, Video, Weaving
Adult Hobby Classes: Tui determined by class. Courses—Mini-classes in arts and craft related areas
Children's Classes: Courses—Mini-classes in arts and crafts related areas; special prog for advanced students
Summer School: Dir, D Jack Davis. Enrl approx 275 per session; tui $4 per sem hr for term of 6 wks; 2 summer sessions. Courses—all studio and lecture courses as needed

TEXAS WOMAN'S UNIVERSITY, Department of Art, Box 22995, TWU Station, 76204. Tel 817-382-8923. *Chmn* J Brough Miller, MFA; *Prof* Warren V Casey, MA; *Prof* Dr John Rios, MFA; *Assoc Prof* Winifred S Williams, MS; *Asst Prof* A E Green, MFA; *Asst Prof* Shirlee Shaver, BA; *Instructor* William E Meek, BFA; *Instructor* Mark S Smith, MFA; *Instructor* Linda Stuckenbruck-Smith, MFA
Estab 1901; pub; D & E; ent req HS dipl, MA and MFA portfolio review required; degrees BA, BS and BFA 4 yrs, MA 1 yr, MFA 2 yrs; scholarships; SC 21, LC 34, GC 17; enrl D 297, E 79, non-maj 214, maj 161, grad 76, others 300 undergrad
Tuition: Res $4 per sem hr, $50 minimum; nonres $40 per sem hr, campus res $470-$1000 for room only, meal plan available at extra charge
Courses: Advertising Design, Art Education, Art History, Ceramics, Commercial Art, Constructions, Costume Design & Construction, Drafting, Drawing, Fashion Arts, Graphic Arts, Graphic Design, Illustration, Interior Design, Jewelry, Painting, Photography, Printmaking, Sculpture, Textile Design, Community Service Courses, Fibers, Metalsmithing
Summer School: Enrl 112; tui same as above for term of 6 wks beginning June 7. Courses—as above

EDINBURG

PAN AMERICAN UNIVERSITY, Art Department, 78539. Tel 512-381-3141. *Head Dept* Dr Nancy Moyer Prince, PhD; *Chmn Art Educ* Dr Norman Browne, EdD; *Chmn Painting* E E Nichols, MFA; *Chmn Printmaking* Philip Field, MFA; *Chmn Ceramics* Richard Hyslin, MA; *Chmn Metals* Jerry Bailey, MFA; *Chmn Advertising Design* James Humphrey, MA; *Chmn Art History* Sandra Swenson, MA
Estab 1927, dept estab 1972; pub; D & E; ent req open, immunization; degrees BA and BFA 4 yrs; scholarships; SC 43, LC 14; enrl D 1200, E 150, non-maj 650, maj 209
Tuition: Res—$56-$167 (depending on number of hrs); nonres—$46-$887; foreign $206-$367; campus res—room & board $1000
Courses: †Advertising Design, †Art Education, Art History, †Ceramics, Drawing, Graphic Arts, Graphic Design, Illustration, †Jewelry, Lettering, †Painting, Photography, †Printmaking, †Sculpture, †Silversmithing
Summer School: Enrl 23 per class; tui $31-$78 for term of 5 wks beginning June 2 and July 9. Courses—Art Appreciation, Beginning Painting, Ceramics, Design, Drawing, Elementary Art Educ, Metals, Photography, Sculpture

EL PASO

UNIVERSITY OF TEXAS AT EL PASO, Department of Art, 79968. Tel 915-747-5181. *Head Dept* Willette M Munz. Instrs FT 10
Estab 1939; pub; D & E; degrees BA 4 yrs and BFA 5 yrs; scholarships; SC 24, LC 7, GC 7; enrl 750
Courses: Art Education, Art History, Ceramics, Drawing, Graphic Arts, Jewelry, Painting, Sculpture, Silversmithing, Design, Modeling
Adult Hobby Classes: Tui varies from class to class. Courses—offered through Extension Division
Summer School: Two terms, June to July and July to August

FORT WORTH

TEXAS CHRISTIAN UNIVERSITY, Art Department, School of Fine Arts, 76129. *Dean* George T Tade; *Chmn* Anthony Jones. Instrs FT 10, PT 9
Estab 1909; pvt; degrees BA, BFA, BSEd, MFA and MA (American Studies & Museum Training) undergrad 4 yr, grad 2 yr minimum; scholarships and grad fels; SC 35, LC 10, GC; enrl maj 150, others 450
Tuition: $80 per sem hr; campus residence available
Courses: Art Education, Art History, Ceramics, Commercial Art, Drawing, Graphic Arts, Painting, Sculpture, Design, Metals
Summer School: Courses offered

TEXAS WESLEYAN COLLEGE, Department of Art,* PO Box 3277, 76105. Tel 817-534-0251. *Dean* Donald W Bellah
Den; D & E; ent req HS dipl; degrees BA 4 yrs; scholarships; SC, LC
Tuition: Res—full time $900 per sem, part time $60 per sem hr; campus res—room and board $250 per sem
Courses: Art Education, Ceramics, Drawing, History of Art & Archaeology, Painting, Printmaking, Teacher Training
Summer School: Tui $175 for term of 5 wks beginning in June; campus res—room $90 per session. Courses—Basic Art

GAINESVILLE

COOKE COUNTY COLLEGE, Fine Arts Dept, Hwy 51, PO Box 240, 76240. Tel 817-668-7731. *Chairperson Dept* Vera Speece, MA
Estab 1924; pub; D & E; ent req HS dipl, SAT or ACT, individual approval; degrees AA and AFA 2 yrs; scholarships; SC 14, LC 1; enrl D 50
Tuition: Res—undergrad $98 per sem; nonres—undergrad $210 per sem; Texas res $126 per sem; campus res $200 per sem
Courses: Art Education, Ceramics, Drafting, Drawing, Graphic Design, Painting, Photography, Sculpture, Teacher Training, Textile Design, Weaving
Adult Hobby Classes: Courses—Drawing, Macrame, Painting

GEORGETOWN

SOUTHWESTERN UNIVERSITY, Art Department, 78626. Tel 512-863-6511. *Chmn* Mark Lesly Smith, MA; *Assoc Prof* Clande L Kennard, MA; *Asst Prof* Guss Farmer, MFA; *Instr* Mary Visser, MFA
Estab 1840, dept estab 1940; pvt; D; ent req HS dipl, SAT, portfolio; degrees BA and BFA 4 yrs; scholarships; SC 28, LC 9; enrl D 160, maj 35
Tuition: Res—undergrad $3800 per yr, $85 per hr; nonres—undergrad $2400 per yr, $85 per hr; campus residence available
Courses: Art History, Ceramics, Commercial Art, Conceptual Art, Constructions, Drawing, Graphic Design, Illustration, Mixed Media, Painting, Photography, Printmaking, Sculpture
Summer School: Courses—various

HOUSTON

ART INSTITUTE OF HOUSTON, 821 Chelsea, 77002. Tel 713-523-2564. *Head Dept* Ellen Chadick, Cert; *Instructor* Susan Johnson, BFA. Instrs FT 6, PT 5
Estab 1964; pvt; D & E; ent req HS transcripts and graduation or GED, interview; financial aid programs; enrl D 170, E 50
Tuition: $695 per quarter; no campus res
Courses: Advertising Design, Interior Design, Fashion Illustration

HOUSTON BAPTIST COLLEGE, Department of Art,* 7502 Fondren Rd, 77074. Tel 713-774-7661. *Dean* Gary M Horton
Estab 1963; den; D & E; ent req HS dipl, ent exam; degrees BA $ BS; scholarships; SC 7, LC 9; enrl D 1300, maj 35
Tuition: $778 per sem; campus res—room and board $547 sem
Courses: Art Education, Ceramics, Drawing, Graphic Arts, History of Art & Archaeology, Painting, Sculpture, Teacher Training

MUSEUM OF FINE ARTS, Alfred C Glassell Junior School of Art, 5101 Montrose, PO Box 6826, 77005. Tel 713-529-7659. *Dir* Kenneth R Jewesson, MFA; *Dean Junior School* Norma R Ory, BFA; *Art Historian* David Brauer, MFA equivalent; *Instr* William Dennard, MFA; *Instr* Suzanne Manns, BFA; *Instr* Arthur Turner, MFA; *Instr* Robert Weimerskirch, MFA equivalent; *Instr* Casey Williams, MFA; *Instr* Ben Woitena, MFA; *Instr* Dick Wray; *Instr* Sandra Parmer Zilker, MFA
Estab 1926; pvt; D & E; ent req HS dipl preferred; degrees 3 yr cert; scholarships; SC 52, LC 6; enrl D 314, E 300, maj 501, Junior School 256
Tuition: $506 FT, $135 each SC, $90 each Art History; no campus res
Courses: Art History, †Ceramics, Drawing, Handicrafts, History of Art & Archaeology, †Jewelry, †Painting, Photography, †Printmaking, †Sculpture, Papermaking, Visual Fundamentals
Adult Hobby Classes: Enrl 613; tui $135 each SC
Children's Classes: Enrl 256; tui $65 per sem (4-12 yrs), $93 per sem (13-18 yrs). Courses—General curriculum incl Clay Sculpture, Design, Drawing, Painting and special classes for advanced teenagers
Summer School: School Dir, Kenneth r Jewesson; Junior School Dean, Norma R Ory.

Enrl 194 adult, 349 Junior School; tui $100 (adult) for term of 6 wks and $40 (junior) for term of 4 wks beginning June 9. Courses—same as regular session except Art History

RICE UNIVERSITY, Department of Art and Art History, PO Box 1892, 77001. Tel 713-527-4815. *Chmn* C A Boterf, MFA; *Prof* Katherine T Brown, MFA; *Prof* William A Camfield, PhD; *Prof* Neil Havens, MA; *Prof* John O'Neil, MFA; *Prof* David G Parsons, MS; *Prof* Philip Oliver Smith, PhD; *Prof* Geoffrey Winningham, MFA; *Asst Prof* Basilios Poulos, MFA; *Asst Prof* John F Scott, PhD; *Asst Prof* Walter M Widrig, PhD; *Asst Prof* Dadi Wirz, Cert; *Lectr* Brian Huberman; *Vis Asst Prof* Enrique Zanartu, Cert; *Vis Lectr* Peter T Brown, MFA; *Vis Lectr* Bertrand Davezac, PhD; *Vis Lectr* Thomas McEvilley, PhD
Estab 1912, dept estab 1966-67; pvt; D; ent req HS dipl, CEEB, evaluations of HS counselors and teachers, interview; degrees BA 4 yrs, BFA 5 yrs for additional studio work; scholarships; SC 27, LC 31, GC (BFA) 7; enrl D 125, non-maj 75, maj 50, grad 2 (BFA)
Tuition: $2700 and $140 fees per yr, $1350 and $70 fees per sem, grad $2700 for first six sem; PT $125 per hr and $50 registration fees; campus res—room & board $2190
Courses: Art History, Constructions, Drawing, Film, History of Art & Archaeology, Painting, Photography, Printmaking, Sculpture, Theatre Arts, Video
Adult Hobby Classes: Tui $300 per class. Courses—Photography

SAN JACINTO COLLEGE NORTH, Art Department, 77015. Tel 713-458-4050. *Chmn* Al Clinkinbeard, MFA; *Instructor* Lydia Bodnar-Balahutrak, MFA
Estab 1972; pub; D & E; ent req HS dipl; degrees AA 2 yrs; scholarships; SC 16, LC 1; enrl D 93, E 35, non-maj 20, maj 40
Tuition: Res—undergrad $96 per yr, $48 per 12 hrs, $25 for 6 hrs; nonres—undergrad $400 per yr, $200 per sem, $120 for 6 hrs; no campus res
Courses: †Advertising Design, Calligraphy, Commercial Art, Drawing, Fashion Arts, Graphic Arts, Graphic Design, Illustration, Interior Design, Lettering, Painting, Photography, Sculpture, Textile Design
Adult Hobby Classes: Enrl 15; tui $49 per 60 hrs. Courses—Oil Painting
Children's Classes: Enrl 15, tui $35 per 2 wks. Courses—Awareness Workshop

TEXAS SOUTHERN UNIVERSITY, Department of Art,* 3201 Wheeler Ave, 77004. Tel 713-527-7011. *Head Dept* Dr John T Biggers
Estab 1949; pub; D & E; ent req HS dipl; degrees BFA and B(Art Educ) 5 yrs; scholarships; SC 31, LC 12, GC 4; enrl maj 85, other 100
Tuition: Res—$358; nonres—$1438
Courses: Advertising Design, Aesthetics, Art Education, Ceramics, Commercial Art, Drawing, Graphic Arts, Graphic Design, History of Art & Archaeology, Lettering, Painting, Sculpture, Teacher Training, Textile Design, Weaving
Summer School: Dir, Joseph Jones, Jr. Enrl 100; for a term of 6 wks beginning June. Courses—Art Appreciation in Educational Program, Advanced crafts for Teachers, Basic Art for Elementary Teachers, Exhibition: Mural Painting in School, Problems in Art Education, Problems in Secondary Art Education, Research Projects

UNIVERSITY OF HOUSTON, Department of Art, 77004. Tel 713-749-2601. *Chmn* George R Bunker, BA. Instrs FT 27, PT 18
Estab 1927; pub; D & E; ent req HS dipl, SAT; degrees BA(Art History) and BFA 4 yrs, MFA 2 yrs; scholarships; enrl D 1500, E 200
Tuition: Res $4 per cr hr, minimum of $50 plus fees; campus residency available
Courses: Advertising Design, Art Education, †Art History, Calligraphy, Ceramics, Commercial Art, Drafting, †Drawing, Goldsmithing, †Graphic Design, History of Art & Archaeology, Illustration, †Interior Design, †Jewelry, Lettering, Museum Staff Training, †Painting, Photography, †Printmaking, †Sculpture, Silversmithing, Video

UNIVERSITY OF SAINT THOMAS, Art Department, 3812 Montrose Blvd, 77030. Tel 713-524-3719, Ext 317 or 318. *Acting Chmn* Nancy L Jircik, MA; *Assoc Prof* Jack Boynton, MA; *Assoc Prof* Early Staky, MA; *Asst Prof* Hannah Stewart, MA
Den; D & E; ent req HS dipl; degrees BA 4 yrs; SC 15, LC 7; enrl E 30, maj 44
Tuition: $85 per sem; campus residence available
Courses: Art History, Ceramics, Commercial Art, Drawing, Film, Graphic Arts, History of Art & Archaeology, Painting, Photography, Printmaking, Sculpture, Video
Summer School: Chmn Art Dept, Mancy Jircik. Enrl 30; tui $240 for term of 6 wks beginning June 1. Courses—Ceramics, Drawing, Painting, Photography

HUNTSVILLE

SAM HOUSTON STATE UNIVERSITY, Art Department, 77341. Tel 713-295-6211, Ext 1315. *Dept Head* Darryl Patrick, PhD; *Prof* Gene M Eastman, MFA; *Prof* L Gaddis Geeslin, MFA; *Prof* Gene E Jackson, MFA; *Prof* Stanley E Lea, MFA; *Prof* Charles A Pebworth, MA; *Assoc Prof* Harry J Ahysen, MFA; *Assoc Prof* Evelyn E Anderson, MFA; *Assoc Prof* William J Breitenbach, MFA; *Asst Prof* Jimmy H Barker, MFA; *Asst Prof* Kenneth L Zonker, MA; *Temporary Instructor* Ida Harless; *Vis Prof* Ben Peterman, ceramics - 1981
EStab 1879, dept estab 1936; pub; D; ent req HS dipl, ACT or SAT; degrees BA, BFA 4 yrs, MFA 2 yrs; SC 37, LC 9, GC 12; enrl D 844, non-maj 150, maj 237, grad 12
Tuition: Res—$64 per 16 hrs; nonres—$640 per 16 hrs; campus res—room & board $616 per yr
Courses: †Advertising Design, †Art Education, Art History, †Ceramics, †Drawing, †Handicrafts, Illustration, †Painting, †Printmaking, †Sculpture, Fibers
Summer School: Chmn, Darryl Patrick. Enrl varies; tui $50 per term of 6 wks beginning May 30th and July 6. Courses—Art Educ, Art History, Ceramics, Crafts, Drawing, Painting, Printmaking

HURST

TARRANT COUNTY JUNIOR COLLEGE, NORTHEAST CAMPUS, 76053. Tel 817-281-7860. *Chmn* Arnold Leondar, MA; *Assoc Prof* Richard Hlad, MA; *Asst Prof* Martha Gordon, MFA; *Instructor* Roger Tufts, MEd
Estab 1967, dept estab 1968; pub; D & E; ent req HS dipl, GED, admission by individual approval; degrees AA and AAS 2 yrs; SC 19, LC 3; enrl D 250, E 200, non-maj 200, maj 250
Tuition: Res—$4 per hr, minimum $25 per sem; nonres—of county $3 per sem hr added to res fee, others $40 per sem hr, aliens $40 per sem hr with $200 minimum fee; no campus res
Courses: Advertising Design, Art Education, Art History, Ceramics, Collage, Constructions, Drawing, Jewelry, Mixed Media, Painting, Photography, Printmaking, Sculpture, Silversmithing
Adult Hobby Classes: Enrl 20; for 8 wks. Courses—Drawing, Oil-Acrylic, Printmaking, Tole Painting
Children's Classes: Enrl 20; 8 wks. Courses—Drawing, Painting
Summer School: Enrl 20; tui as above for term of 6 wks beginning May 19. Courses—Art Education, Ceramics, Design, Drawing, Painting, Photography

INGRAM

HILL COUNTRY ARTS FOUNDATION, Box 176, 78025. Tel 512-367-5121. *Art Dir* Elizabeth Vanfelt. Instrs PT 20
Estab 1959; pub; D; ent req none; degrees none; scholarships; enrl 440
Courses: Ceramics, Drawing, Painting, Photography, Art Fundamentals for Young People; Watercolor
Children's Classes: Two one wk classes. Courses—Clay, Textiles

KILGORE

KILGORE COLLEGE, Department Art and Art Education, Fine Arts, 1100 Broadway, 75662. Tel 214-984-8531. *Chmn Art Dept* Gary Q Frields, MFA; *Instr* Donald Churchill, MEd; *Instr* Jeanne E Velde, MA
Estab 1935; D & E; ent req HS dipl; degrees AA and AFA 2 yrs; scholarships; SC 7, LC 3; enrl D 75, E 25, non-maj 25, maj 50
Tuition: Res—undergrad $4 per hr; nonres—undergrad $20 per hr; alien $14 per hr; campus res—room $250 per sem and board $375 per sem
Courses: †Advertising Design, †Art Education, Art History, †Commercial Art, Costume Design & Construction, †Drawing, †Fashion Arts, Graphic Arts, Graphic Design, History of Art & Archaeology, Lettering, Mixed Media, Painting, Photography, Sculpture, Theatre Arts

KINGSVILLE

TEXAS A & I UNIVERSITY, Art Department, Box 157, 78363. Tel 512-595-2619. *Chmn* Dr Richard Scherpereel; *Assoc Prof* William Renfrow; *Assoc Prof* Maurice Schmidt; *Instructor* Mark Anderson; *Instructor* Ralph Magruder; *Instructor* Gilbert Munoz
Estab 1925, dept estab 1930; pub; D & E; ent req HS dipl; degrees BFA and BA 4 yr; SC 21, LC 5, GC 2; enrl D 700, non-maj 300, maj 400, art maj 150, grad 20
Tuition: Res—undergrad $250 per sem, grad $300 per sem; nonres—undergrad $900 per sem, grad $1000; campus residency available
Courses: Advertising Design, Art Education, Art History, Ceramics, Collage, Drawing, Graphic Arts, Intermedia, Lettering, Painting, Printmaking, Sculpture, Teacher Training
Summer School: Courses—full schedule

LAKE JACKSON

BRAZOSPORT COLLEGE, Art Department, 500 College Dr, 77566. *Assoc Prof* Lynn Hayes, MFA; *Instr* Bruce Good, MA
Estab 1968; pub; D & E; ent req HS dipl or GED; degrees AA 2 yrs; scholarships; SC 10, LC 3; enrl D 50
Tuition: Res—undergrad $100 for 12-15 hrs; no campus res
Courses: Art History, Ceramics, Drawing, History of Art & Archaeology, Mixed Media, Painting, Sculpture, Stage Design, Theatre Arts, Art Appreciation
Adult Hobby Classes: Courses—Ceramics, Painting, Weaving

LEVELLAND

SOUTH PLAINS COLLEGE, Fine Arts Department, College Ave, 79336. Tel 806-894-9611, Ext 281. *Chmn* Don Stroud. Instrs FT 3
Estab 1958; pub; D & E; ent req HS dipl; degrees AA 2 yrs; SC 1, LC 5; enrl D 250, E 206, maj 182
Tuition: In-dist $4 per sem hr; out-of-dist $4 per sem hr; out-of-state $20 per sem hr; foreign $14 per sem hr
Courses: Advertising Design, Art History, Ceramics, Commercial Art, Drafting, Drawing, Graphic Arts, Graphic Design, Lettering, Painting, Photography, Sculpture, Teacher Training
Adult Hobby Classes: Enrl varies; tui same as above. Courses—China Painting, Flower Arranging, Gift Wrapping, Oil Painting, Photography, Tole Painting

LUBBOCK

TEXAS TECH UNIVERSITY, Department of Art, 79409. Tel 806-742-3825. *Chmn* James Broderick, MA; *Asst Chmn* Paul Hanna, MFA; *Prof* Frank Cheatham, MFA; *Prof* Don Durland, MA; *Prof* Verne Funk, MFA; *Prof* Hugh Gibbons, MA; *Prof* Reid Hastie, PhD; *Prof* Jim Howze, MS; *Prof* Clarence Kincaid, DED; *Prof* Lynwood Kreneck, MFA; *Prof* Bill Lockhart, DED; *Prof* Terry Morrow, MS; *Prof* Francis Stephen, MFA; *Assoc Prof* Eugene Alesch, PhD; *Assoc Prof* Bill Bagley, MFA; *Assoc Prof* Peggy Bright, MA; *Assoc Prof* Ken Dixon, MFA; *Assoc Prof* Edna Glenn, MA; *Assoc Prof* H V Greer, MA; *Assoc Prof* Olive Jensen, PhD; *Assoc Prof* Marvin Moon, PhD; *Assoc Prof* John Queen, MFA; *Assoc Prof* Donna Read, MS; *Assoc Prof* Nancy Reed, PhD; *Assoc Prof* Betty Street, MS; *Asst Prof* Laura Farias, MFA; *Asst Prof* James Hanna, MA; *Asst Prof* Alex Karther, BArchit; *Asst Prof* Marty Robins, BPA; *Asst Prof* Sara Waters, MFA; *Vis Asst Prof* Alan Crockett; *Vis Asst Prof* France Whitehead
Estab 1925, dept estab 1967; pub; D & E; ent req HS dipl, SAT or ACT test; degrees BA, BFA, and BSE 4 yr, MAE 36 hrs, MFA 60 hrs minimum, PhD 54 hrs beyond MA minimum; scholarships; SC 80 undergrad, 23 grad, LC 27 undergrad, 17 grad, GC 46; enrl D 1459 non-maj 700, maj 750, Grad 43
Tuition: Variable for res and nonres; campus residence available
Courses: Art Education, Art History, Ceramics, Drawing, Film, Graphic Design, Illustration, Interior Design, Jewelry, Lettering, Mixed Media, Painting, Photography, Printmaking, Sculpture, Textile Design, Video, Design Communication, Enameling, Metals, Weaving
Summer School: Same as academic yr

MARSHALL

WILEY COLLEGE, Department of Fine Arts,* Roseborough Springs Rd, 75670. Tel 214-938-8341. *Head Dept* R Ronald O'Neal
Estab 1873; den; D & E; ent req HS dipl; degrees no art major; scholarships; SC 16, LC 2; enrl D 56
Tuition: $50 per hr, plus special fees; campus res—$500-$794 per yr
Courses: Advertising Design, Art Education, Art History, Ceramics, Commercial Art, Drawing, Fashion Arts, Graphic Design, Painting, Teacher Training, Theatre Arts, Decoupage, Enameling
Summer School: Dir, Dr David R Houston. Tui $50 per hr for term of 8 wks beginning June. Courses—as required

MIDLAND

MIDLAND COLLEGE, Art Department, 79701. Tel 915-684-7851. *Chmn* Stan Jacobs, MFA; *Instructor* Sara Gilstrap, MA; *Instructor* Warren Taylor, MFA
Estab 1972; pub; D & E; ent req HS dipl; degrees AA and AAA 2 yrs; scholarships; SC 28, LC 4; enrl D 70, E 80, non-maj 125, maj 25
Tuition: Res—undergrad $48 per 12 hrs plus $36 fee; nonres—undergrad $200 per 12 hrs plus $36 fee; no campus res
Courses: †Advertising Design, Aesthetics, Art Education, Art History, †Ceramics, Collage, †Commercial Art, Constructions, Drafting, †Drawing, Fashion Arts, Film, Graphic Arts, Graphic Design, Handicrafts, Illustration, Interior Design, †Jewelry, Lettering, Mixed Media, †Painting, †Photography, †Printmaking, †Sculpture, Silversmithing, Stage Design, Teacher Training
Adult Hobby Classes: Tui $20 per 6 wks. Courses—Drawing, Painting
Summer School: Same as regular term

NACOGDOCHES

STEPHEN F AUSTIN STATE UNIVERSITY, Art Department, Box 3001, 75962. Tel 713-569-4804. *Chmn* Jon D Wink, MFA
Estab 1923; pub; D & E; ent req HS dipl, ACT score 18; degrees BFA 4 yrs, MFA 2 yrs, MA 1 yr; SC 28, LC 11, GC 11; enrl D 461, non-maj 270, maj 216, grad 30
Tuition: Res—undergrad $160 for 15 hr, grad $50 per 12 hr; nonres—undergrad $600 per 15 hr, grad $480 per 12 hr; campus residence available
Courses: Advertising Design, Art Education, Art History, Ceramics, Commercial Art, Drawing, Graphic Arts, Graphic Design, Illustration, Jewelry, Lettering, Mixed Media, Painting, Printmaking, Sculpture, Cinematography

ODESSA

UNIVERSITY OF TEXAS OF PERMIAN BASIN, Art Discipline, 79762. Tel 915-367-2133. *Chmn* Stanley Marcus, EdD; *Asst Prof* Pam Price, MFA; *Lectr* Sonya Haynie
Estab 1972; pub; D; ent req Associate degree or 60 college credits; degrees BA 2 yr (we are an upper level institution); scholarships; SC 45, LC 10; enrl non-maj 10, maj 30
Tuition: Campus residency available
Courses: Ceramics, Commercial Art, Painting, Printmaking, Sculpture
Summer School: Courses—varied

PARIS

PARIS JUNIOR COLLEGE, Art Department, 2400 Clarksville St, 75460. Tel 214-785-7661, Ext 131. *Instr* Michael F Boles, MFA; *Instr* Johnye Robertson, BA
Estab 1924; pub; D & E; ent req none; degrees AA 2 yrs; scholarships; SC 7, LC 1; enrl D 110, E 32, non-maj 90, maj 12, others 24
Tuition: Res—undergrad $160 for 15 hrs; nonres—undergrad $295 for 15 hrs; campus res—room and board $1350 per yr
Courses: Art Education, †Ceramics, †Drawing, †Painting, †Photography, †Sculpture, Art Appreciation, Design

PASADENA

SAN JACINTO COLLEGE, Art Department, 77505. Tel 713-476-1830. *Chmn* Charles R Brown, MAE; *Instructor* William C Balusek, MFA; *Instructor* Sandi Marks, AA; *Instructor* Douglass Sweet, MFA
Estab 1961; pub; D & E; ent req HS dipl, GED or individual approval; degrees AA and AS 2 yrs; SC 5, LC 1; enrl D 230, E 45, non-maj 120, maj 155
Tuition: Res—$60 per sem; nonres—$135 per sem; no campus res
Courses: Advertising Design, Calligraphy, Commercial Art, Drafting, Drawing, Graphic Arts, Graphic Design, Interior Design, Lettering, Painting, Photography, Sculpture, Theatre Arts
Summer School: Enrl 25; tui $25 for term of 6 wks beginning June 5th. Courses—Design, Painting Workshop

PLAINVIEW

WAYLAND BAPTIST COLLEGE, Department of Art & Music,* Division of Fine Arts, Box 54, 1900 W Seventh, 79072. Tel 806-296-5521. *Chmn* Dr Robert E Bicknell
Den; D & E; ent req HS dipl, ent exam; degrees BA and BS 4 yrs; scholarships; SC 15, LC 2; enrl D 81, E 24, maj 10
Tuition: $45 per sem hr
Courses: Aesthetics, Art Education, Ceramics, Drawing, Graphic Arts, Graphic Design, History of Art & Archaeology, Illustration, Jewelry, Lettering, Museum Staff Training, Painting, Photography, Sculpture, Teacher Training
Summer School: Courses—vary each term

ROCKPORT

SIMON MICHAEL SCHOOL OF FINE ARTS, 510 E King, PO Box 1283, 78382. Tel 512-729-6233. *Head Dept* Simon Michael. Instrs FT 1
Estab 1947; pvt; D; ent req none; degrees none; enrl D 200, others professionals and beginners
Courses: Architecture, Drawing, Landscape Architecture, Mixed Media, Painting, Sculpture
Summer School: Enrl varies; tui varies for each 1 wk workshop. Courses—Travel Art Workshop

SAN ANGELO

ANGELO STATE UNIVERSITY, Art and Music Department, ASU Station, 76901. *Coordr* Dr Robert Prestiano; *Chmn Art and Music* Dr Charles Robison, PhD
Estab 1963, dept estab 1976; pub; D & E; ent req HS dipl; degrees BA(Art) and BA(Art) and Teaching Certification; SC 13, LC 8; enrl D 400 (art), E 50, non-maj 320, maj 80
Tuition: Res—$60 per sem hr; nonres $50 per sem hr; campus res—room and board $750 per sem
Courses: Architecture, Art Education, Art History, Ceramics, Commercial Art, Drawing, Graphic Arts, Painting, Printmaking, Sculpture, Stage Design, Creative Design, History of Contemporary Art, History of Italian Renaissance, Greek and Roman Art, Itaglio Processes
Summer School: Tui as above for term of 17 wks beginning June 10. Courses—Art History, Introduction to Art, Studio Courses incl Design and Drawing

SAN ANTONIO

INCARNATE WORD COLLEGE, Humanities and Fine Arts, 4301 Broadway, 78201. Tel 512-828-1261, Ext 234. *Chmn* B C O'Halloran, PhD; *Asst Prof* Eloise Stoker, MA; *Instr* Sr Martha Ann Kirk, MA; *Lectr* Nancy Pawel, BS
Estab 1881, dept estab 1964; den; D; ent req HS dipl, ent exam; degrees BA 4 yrs; scholarships; SC 14, LC 9; enrl D 195, non-maj 120, maj 75
Tuition: Undergrad $70 per hr, grad $75 per hr; campus res—room & board $976-$1836
Courses: Art Education, Art History, Ceramics, Drawing, History of Art & Archaeology, Mixed Media, Museum Staff Training, Painting, Printmaking, Sculpture, Teacher Training

OUR LADY OF THE LAKE UNIVERSITY, Department of Art, Fine Arts Division, 78285. Tel 512-434-5711. *Dir* Richard Slocum, MA; *Prof* Sr M Tharsilla Fuchs, MA; *Asst Prof* Sr Jule Adele Espey, PhD; *Asst Prof* Sr Dorcas Mladenka, MA. Instrs FT 1, PT 2
Estab 1911, dept estab 1920; den; D & E; ent req HS dipl, completion of GED tests, 35 on each test or average of 45 on tests; degrees BA(Art); scholarships; SC 12, LC 3; enrl non-maj 145, maj 21
Tuition: Undergrad $60 per sem hr cr; grad $65-$74 per hr cr; English as a foreign language program $560 per sem, campus res—room & board $275-$425
Courses: Art Education, Art History, Drawing, Painting, Photography, Printmaking, Cinema, Design, Practicum in Art, Problems
Adult Hobby Classes: Enrl varies; tui varies. Courses—vary

ST MARY'S UNIVERSITY OF SAN ANTONIO, Department of Fine Arts, 78284. Tel 512-436-3737. *Dir* Margaret Ivy. Instrs FT 6, PT 3
Estab 1852; pvt; D & E; ent req HS dipl or GED, ent exam; degrees BA 4-5 yrs; scholarships; SC 10, LC 20; enrl D 60, maj 58
Tuition: $60 per sem hr, $15 lab fee per course; campus res—room & board $340-$640 per sem
Courses: Aesthetics, Art Education, Ceramics, Drafting, Drawing, Film, Graphic Design, History of Art & Archaeology, Lettering, Painting, Photography, Sculpture, Teacher Training, Theatre Arts
Adult Hobby Classes: Enrl 75-100; tui $25. Courses—vary
Summer School: Courses—vary

SAN ANTONIO ART INSTITUTE, 6000 N New Braunfels, PO Box 6092, 78209. Tel 512-824-0531. *Exec Dir* Jack A Rodgers, MA; *Acad Dir* George Parrino, MFA; *Instr* Carl Embrey, MFA; *Instr* Reginald M Rowe, MFA
D & E; ent req none; scholarships
Tuition: $110 per sem; no campus res
Courses: Art History, Calligraphy, Ceramics, Collage, Drawing, Painting, Photography, Printmaking, Sculpture, Life Drawing, Three-Dimensional Design, Tutorial Critique
Adult Hobby Classes: Tui $54 per 12 wks for ages 6-10 yrs
Summer School: Regular courses offered

SAN ANTONIO COLLEGE, Art Department, 1300 San Pedro Ave, 78284. Tel 512-734-7311, Ext 2894. *Chmn* Mel Casas. Instrs FT 11, PT 10
Estab 1955; pub; D & E; ent req HS dipl, ent exam; degrees AA and AS 2 yrs; SC 32, LC 3; enrl D 1000-1300, E 250-450
Tuition: $14 per sem hr res; no campus res
Courses: Advertising Design, Architecture, Art Education, Display, Drawing, History of Art & Archaeology, Illustration, Industrial Design, Jewelry, Lettering, Painting, Photography, Sculpture

TRINITY UNIVERSITY, Department of Art, 715 Stadium Dr, 78284. Tel 512-736-7216. *Chmn* Department of Art; *Prof* William A Bristow, MFA; *Prof* Glenn N Patton, PhD; *Prof* Elizabeth Ridenhower, MA; *Assoc Prof* Philip J Evett; *Assoc Prof* Jim Stoker, MA; *Assoc Prof* Robert E Tiemann, MFA; *Instructor* Letha E McIntire, MA & MPh
Estab 1869; pvt; D & E; ent req HS dipl, CEEB, SAT, 3 achievement tests; degrees BA 4 yrs; SC 39, LC 20; enrl D 144, E 30, non-maj 50, maj 90
Tuition: $3109 per yr; campus res—room & board $1565 per yr
Courses: Art Education, Commercial Art, Drawing, Graphic Arts, History of Art & Archaeology, Interior Design, Painting, Photography, Printmaking, Sculpture, Stage Design, Theatre Arts, Video
Adult Hobby Classes: Courses offered by Department of Continuing Educ
Summer School: Dir, Dept of Continuing Educ. Tui $114 per hr. Courses—vary

UNIVERSITY OF TEXAS AT SAN ANTONIO, Division of Art and Design, FM 1604, 78285. Tel 512-691-4352. *Div Dir* Ronald Binks, MFA; *Prof* Charles Field, MFA; *Prof* Jacinto Quirarte, PhD; *Assoc Prof* Stephen Reynolds, MFA; *Assoc Prof* Judith Sobre, PhD; *Asst Prof* Stephen Daly, MFA; *Asst Prof* Alvin Martin, PhD; *Asst Prof* Robert Mullen, PhD; *Asst Prof* Felipe Reyes, MFA; *Vis Prof* Sharon Gold, painting - 1979-80; *Vis Prof* Paul Rotterdam, painting; *Vis Prof* Alan Weinstein, printmaking
Pub; D & E; ent req HS dipl, ACT, grad, GRE; degrees BFA 4 yrs, MFA 2 yrs; scholarships; SC 31, GC 17; enrl maj 200, grad 35
Tuition: $50 per sem (12 hrs or under); no campus res
Summer School: Tui $25 per sem. Courses—Art History, Ceramics, Drawing, Painting, Photography, Printmaking, Sculpture

SAN MARCOS

PALOMAR COLLEGE, Art Department, 1140 W Mission Rd, 92069. Tel 714-744-1150, Ext 345. *Chmn* James T Saw, MA; *Assoc Prof* Harry E Bliss, MFA; *Assoc Prof* George D Durrant, MA; *Assoc Prof* James C Hulbert, BPA; *Assoc Prof* Frank Jones, MFA; *Assoc Prof* Anthony J Lugo, MA; *Assoc Prof* Berry C Reed, MFA; *Assoc Prof* Val G Sanders, MA; *Assoc Prof* Donna Tryon Sakakeeny, MA; *Assoc Prof* Rita A White, MA
Estab 1950; pub; D & E; ent req ent exam; degrees AA 2 yr; schol; SC 31, LC 4; enrl D 775, E 200
Tuition: None; no campus res
Courses: Art History, †Ceramics, Collage, †Commercial Art, †Drawing, Graphic Arts, Graphic Design, Handicrafts, Illustration, †Jewelry, Lettering, †Painting, †Printmaking, Sculpture, †Silversmithing, Glassblowing, Life Drawing, Stained Glass, 2-D and 3-D Design
Summer School: Courses—basic courses except commercial art and graphic design

SOUTHWEST TEXAS STATE UNIVERSITY, Department of Art, 78666. Tel 512-245-2611. *Dean* Ralph Harrel; *Chmn* Brian G Row, MFA
Estab 1903, dept estab 1916; pub; D & E; ent req HS dipl, ACT score minimum of 15; degrees BS(Secondary Educ), BS(Educ all-level) and BFA(Commercial & Studio) 4 yrs; scholarships; SC 31, LC 7, GC 6; enrl D 1800, E 150, non-maj 1338, maj 465, grad 27
Tuition: Res $50 per hr; nonres $40 per hr; campus res—room & board $563 per sem
Courses: Advertising Design, Art Education, Art History, Ceramics, †Commercial Art, Conceptual Art, †Drawing, Graphic Arts, Graphic Design, Illustration, †Jewelry, Lettering, Mixed Media, †Painting, †Printmaking, †Sculpture, Teacher Training, †Textile Design, Video
Summer School: Chmn, Brain G Row. Tui $25 for 6 hrs for term of 6 wks beginning June 5th. Courses—as above

SEGUIN

TEXAS LUTHERAN COLLEGE, Department of Visual Arts, 78155. Tel 512-379-4161, Ext 58. *Chmn* Harold W Hill. Instrs FT 2
Estab 1961; den; D; ent req HS dipl; degrees BA(Art) 4 yrs; SC 18, LC 3; enrl 1000, maj 30
Tuition: Campus residency available
Courses: Advertising Design, Art Education, Art History, Ceramics, Drawing, Painting, Printmaking, Sculpture, Teacher Training, Design, Introduction to Visual Arts, Watercolor

SHERMAN

AUSTIN COLLEGE, Art Department, 75090. Tel 214-892-9101, Ext 251. *Chmn* Carl R Neidhardt, PhD; *Asst Prof* Judy Miller, MFA; *Instructor* Joseph Havel, MFA
Estab 1848; pvt; D; ent req ent exam plus acceptance by admission committee; degrees BA 4 yrs, MA 5 yrs; scholarships; SC 9, LC 5, GC 8; enrl D 340, maj 60, grad 5
Tuition: $3300 per yr, $1650 per sem, $410 per course; campus res—room & board $1642
Courses: Art Education, Art History, Ceramics, Drawing, Graphic Design, Painting, Photography, Printmaking
Summer School: Tui undergrad $330 per course, grad $360 per course for term of 7 wks beginning June 2, 1980. Courses—Ceramics, Introduction to Art, Photography

TEMPLE

TEMPLE JUNIOR COLLEGE, Art Department, 2600 S First, 76501. Tel 817-773-9961. *Chmn* Michael Donahue, MFA; *Prof* Laura Reinowski, MFA; *Vis Prof* Candace Knapp, sculpture - 1980
Estab 1926; pub; D & E; ent req HS dipl, ACT or SAT; degrees AA 2 yrs; SC 4, LC 2; enrl D 50, E 10, non-maj 63, maj 7
Tuition: Res—undergrad $4 per sem hr ($25 min); campus residence available
Courses: Art Education, Drawing, Graphic Design, Painting, Printmaking, Sculpture
Adult Hobby Classes: Enrl 15 per class; tui $19 per 8 sessions. Courses—Arts & Crafts, Calligraphy, Drawing

TEXARKANA

TEXARKANA COMMUNITY COLLEGE, Art Department,* 2500 N Robinson Rd, 75501. Tel 214-838-4541. *Chmn* William Caver; *Prof* Ralph Caver, MFA; *Assoc Prof* Mary Lone, MA
Estab 1927; D & E; ent req HS dipl; scholarships
Tuition: Res—$322 per yr, in district $115 per yr; nonres—$267 per yr; no campus res
Courses: Art Education, Ceramics, Drafting, Drawing, History of Art & Archaeology, Painting, Sculpture, Teacher Training, Weaving
Adult Hobby Classes: Enrl 30, tui $38 per term. Courses—Ceramics
Summer School: Tui $50 for term of 6 wks beginning May. Courses—Art Education, Ceramics, Design, Drawing, Painting

TYLER

UNIVERSITY OF TEXAS AT TYLER, Department of Art, (Formerly Texas Eastern University) 3900 University Blvd, 75701. Tel 214-566-1471, Ext 289. *Chmn* William B Stephens, EdD; *Assoc Prof* Kenneth Casstevens, EdD; *Asst Prof* Donald Van Horn, MFA
Estab 1973; pub; D & E; ent req AA degree or 60 hrs of college study; degrees BA and BFA; scholarships; SC 28, LC 6, GC 11
Tuition: Res—$173 per sem; nonres—$323 per sem
Courses: Aesthetics, Art Education, Art History, Ceramics, Drawing, Graphic Arts, Graphic Design, History of Art & Archaeology, Interior Design, Mixed Media, Painting, Photography, Printmaking, Sculpture, Stage Design, Teacher Training
Summer School: Tui res $76, nonres $151. Courses—vary

VICTORIA

VICTORIA COLLEGE, 2200 Red River, 77901. *Head Dept* Larry Shook, MA; *Vis Prof* Nancy Bandy
Estab 1925; pub; D & E; ent req HS dipl; SC 9, LC 3; enrl D 100, E 40, non-maj 40, maj 100
Tuition: Res—$100 per sem; nonres—$200 per sem; no campus res
Courses: Art Education, Art History, Commercial Art, Display, Drafting, Drawing, Graphic Design, Printmaking, Sculpture, Teacher Training
Summer School: Courses—as above

WACO

BAYLOR UNIVERSITY, Department of Fine Arts, 76703. Tel 817-755-1867. *Chmn* Harold C Simmons, PhD; *Crafts* Paul Kemp, MFA; *Painting* John McClanahan, MFA; *Printmaking* Berry Klingman, MFA; *Communication Design* Charles Isoline, MA; *Ceramics* Hilda S Smith; *Art History* William M Jensen, PhD
Estab 1845, dept estab 1870; den; D & E; ent req HS dipl, ent exam, ACT tests; degrees AB, BS(Art Educ) and BFA 4 yrs; scholarships; SC 60, LC 26, GC 12; enrl D 500, E 30, non-maj 200, maj 350, grad 2
Tuition: $2100 per yr, $70 per sem hr; campus res—room & board $1680
Courses: †Art Education, †Art History, †Ceramics, Drawing, Graphic Arts, Handicrafts, †Painting, Photography, Sculpture, †Art Therapy, †Communication Design, Two and Three-Dimensional Design
Summer School: Dean, William Cooper. Enrl 75; tui $70 per cr hr for term of 6 wks beginning May 26 & July 5. Courses—Art Education, Art History, Ceramics, Communication Design, Crafts, Painting

MCLENNAN COMMUNITY COLLEGE, Fine Arts Department,* 1400 College, 76708. Tel 817-756-6551. *Chmn* William R Haskett
Estab 1965; pub; D & E; ent req HS dipl; degrees AA 2 yrs; SC 8, LC 3; enrl D 35, non-maj 10, maj 25
Tuition: Res—$230 per yr; nonres—$660 per yr; no campus res
Courses: Art History, Drawing, Painting, Sculpture, Art Appreciation, Color, Design
Adult Hobby Classes: Tui depends on the class. Courses—Ceramics, Drawing, Jewelry, Painting, Sculpture, Stained Glass
Summer School: Tui $60. Courses—Design, Drawing

WEATHERFORD

WEATHERFORD COLLEGE, Department of Humanities and Art, Park Ave, 76086. Tel 817-594-5471, Ext 32. *Head Dept of Art* Myrlan Coleman, MA; *Instructor* Donna Miller, BA
Estab 1856, dept estab 1959; pub; D & E; ent req HS dipl; degrees AA; SC 10, LC 4; enrl D 58, non-maj 30, maj 16, others 12
Tuition: Res—undergrad $4 per sem hr, grad $14 per sem hr, minimum $200; nonres—undergrad $17 per sem hr, maximum $200; campus residency available
Courses: Advertising Design, Aesthetics, Art Education, Art History, Ceramics, Commercial Art, Constructions, Drawing, Graphic Arts, History of Art & Archaeology, Illustration, Intermedia, Mixed Media, Painting
Summer School: Term May 24 and July 10

WHARTON

WHARTON COUNTY JUNIOR COLLEGE, Art Department, 77488. Tel 713-532-4560, Ext 52. *Chmn* Bruce F Turner, PhD; *Instructor* Morna Nation, MFA
Pub; D & E; ent req HS dipl, GED; degrees 2 yrs; SC 8, LC 2; enrl D 90, E 15
Tuition: Campus residency available
Courses: Art Education, Art History, Ceramics, Drawing, History of Art & Archaeology, Painting, Sculpture, Teacher Training

WICHITA FALLS

MIDWESTERN STATE UNIVERSITY, Department of Art, 76308. Tel 817-692-6611. *Chmn* Thomas G Crossnoe, MA; *Prof* Richard M Ash III, MFA; *Assoc Prof* Larry H Davis, MFA; *Asst Prof* Donald Harter, MFA; *Instructor* Fred Burton, MFA
Estab 1926; pub; D & E; ent req HS dipl, ACT, SAT; degrees BA, BFA and BSE 4 yrs; SC 20-30, LC 406; enrl D 300 per sem, E 30-50 per sem, non-maj 60, maj 125, others 10
Tuition: Res—$176 per sem based on 15 hr load; nonres $716 based on 15 hr load; campus res—room & board $480
Courses: †Advertising Design, †Art Education, Art History, †Ceramics, †Commercial Art, Drawing, †Goldsmithing, †Graphic Arts, †Graphic Design, Handicrafts, †Jewelry, †Painting, †Photography, †Printmaking, †Sculpture, †Silversmithing, Fibers
Summer School: Enrl 100-150; tui $70 for 6 hrs for term of 6 wks beginning June 1. Courses—same as full yr with minor variations

UTAH

CEDAR CITY

SOUTHERN UTAH STATE COLLEGE, Department of Art, 84720. Tel 801-586-9481. *Chmn* Glen Dale Anderson. Instrs FT 4, PT 2
Estab 1897; pub; D & E; ent req HS dipl ent exam; degrees BA and BS 4 yrs; scholarships; SC 29, LC 6; enrl D 300, E 80, maj 60, minors 45
Tuition: Res—$188 per quarter; nonres—$448 per quarter; campus res—room & board approx $400 per quarter
Courses: Advertising Design, Art Education, Ceramics, Commercial Art, Drawing, Graphic Arts, Graphic Design, History of Art & Archaeology, Illustration, Lettering, Painting, Sculpture, Teacher Training
Summer School: (Special Program) Tui $120 for term of 8 wks beginning June. Courses—Art History, Ceramics, Drawing, Painting

LOGAN

UTAH STATE UNIVERSITY
—Department of Landscape Architecture, * 84322. Tel 801-752-4100, Ext 7346. *Head* Richard Toth
—Department of Art, * 84322. Tel 801-752-4100, Ext 7538. *Head* Dr Ray W Hellberg, PhD; *Prof* Jon Anderson, MFA; *Prof* Ralph T Clark, MFA; *Prof* Larry Elsner, MFA; *Prof* Harrison Groutage, MFA; *Prof* Moishe Smith, MFA; *Assoc Prof* Adrian VanSuchtelen, MFA; *Asst Prof* Tetsuo Kusama, MFA
Estab 1890; D & E; ent req HS dipl, HS transcript, ACT; degrees BS, BA, BFA, MFA and MA; scholarships; enrl D 340, maj 340, grad 24
Tuition: Res—$559 per yr; nonres—$1690 per yr; campus res available
Courses: †Advertising Design, †Art Education, †Ceramics, †Drawing, †Illustration, †Painting, †Photography, †Printmaking, †Sculpture, †Textile Design
Summer School: Head, Dr Ray W Hellberg. Courses—Ceramics, Ceramic Handbuilding, Ceramic Wheelthrow, Design, Drawing, Individual Projects, Landscape Painting, Metalsmithing, Painting, Photography, Printmaking Studio, Sculpture, Watercolor

OGDEN

WEBER STATE COLLEGE, Art Department 2001, 84408. Tel 801-626-6762. *Chmn* Richard J Van Wagoner, MFA; *Prof* Arthur R Adelmann, MFA; *Prof* Dale W Bryner, MFA; *Prof* Charles M Groberg, MFA; *Prof* James R McBeth, MFA; *Assoc Prof* David N Cox, MFA; *Assoc Prof* Fred Rabe, MA; *Assoc Prof* Doyle Strong, BA; *Asst Prof* Susan Makov, MFA; *Asst Prof* Barbara Schulman, MFA
Estab 1933, dept estab 1937; pub; D & E; ent req HS dipl, ACT; degrees BA, BS 4 yrs; scholarships; SC 66, LC 17; enrl D 2464, E 694, non-maj 700, maj 251
Tuition: Res—undergrad $196 per quarter; nonres—undergrad $466 per quarter; campus res—room & board $1450 per yr or apartment $450
Courses: Advertising Design, †Art Education, Art History, Ceramics, †Commercial Art, Drawing, Film, Goldsmithing, †Graphic Arts, †Graphic Design, †Illustration, Jewelry, Lettering, Painting, †Photography, Printmaking, Sculpture, Silversmithing, Teacher Training, Textile Design
Summer School: Dir, Richard J Van Wagoner. Tui $196 for term of 8 wks beginning June 19

PROVO

BRIGHAM YOUNG UNIVERSITY, Department of Art and Design, C-502 HFAC, 84602. Tel 801-374-1211, Ext 4266. *Chmn* Robert L Marshal, MFA. Instrs FT 27
Estab 1875, dept estab 1893; den; D & E; ent req HS dipl or ACT; degrees BA and BFA 4 yrs, MFA 2 yrs and MA 1 1 2 yrs; scholarships; SC 61, LC 19, GC 20; enrl D 6545, E 1563, maj 550, grad 30
Tuition: Undergrad $1455 per yr, $485 per sem, PT $50 per cr hr, grad $1620 per yr, $785 per sem, PT $55 per cr hr; nonchurchmember—undergrad $2130 per yr, $710 per sem, PT $75 per cr hr, grad $2355 per yr, $785 per sem, PT $82 per cr hr; campus res—room & board $2200
Courses: Art Education, †Art History, †Ceramics, †Drawing, †Graphic Design, †Handicrafts, †Illustration, †Industrial Design, †Jewelry, Lettering, †Painting, †Printmaking, †Sculpture, †Teacher Training, Fibers, Metals, Wood

SAINT GEORGE

DIXIE COLLEGE, Art Department, 84770. Tel 801-673-4811, Ext 297. *Head Dept* Gerald Olson, MS; *Instructor* Glen Blakely, MFA; *Instructor* Roland Lee, BA
Estab 1911; pub; D & E; ent req HS dipl, ACT; degrees AA and AS 2 yrs; scholarships; SC 24, LC 7, GC 1; enrl D 400, maj 30
Tuition: Res—undergrad $147 per quarter; nonres—undergrad $297 per quarter; campus res—$100-$140 per quarter
Courses: Advertising Design, Art Education, Art History, Ceramics, Commercial Art, Costume Design & Construction, Drafting, Drawing, Film, Illustration, Interior Design, Painting, Photography, Printmaking, Sculpture, Teacher Training, Textile Design, Theatre Arts, Video, Life Drawing, Portrait Drawing, Three Dimensional Design
Adult Hobby Classes: Enrl 20; tui $50 per quarter. Courses—Ceramics, Oil Painting, Wood Carving
Summer School: Courses—Basic Design, Basic Drawing, Oil Painting

SALT LAKE CITY

UNIVERSITY OF UTAH, Art Department, AAC 161, 84112. Tel 801-581-8678. *Chairperson* Robert S Olpin, PhD; *Prof* Dorothy Bearnson, MA; *Prof* Angelo Caravaglia, TC; *Prof* Paul Davis, MFA; *Prof* Alvin Gittins, BA; *Prof* Frank Anthony Smith, MFA; *Prof* V Douglas Snow, MFA; *Prof* Lennox Tierney; *Prof* Edward Maryon, MFA; *Assoc Prof* Richard Johnston, MFA; *Assoc Prof* Robert Kleinschmidt, MFA; *Asst Prof* Raymond Morales, BA; *Asst Prof* Sheila Muller, MA; *Asst Prof* Brian Patrick, MFA; *Asst Prof* David Pendell, MFA; *Asst Prof* Nathan Winters, PhD; *Emeritus Prof* George S Dibble, MA
Estab 1850, dept estab 1888; pub; D & E; ent req HS dipl; degrees BA and BFA 4 yrs, MA and MFA 2 yrs; scholarships; SC 79, LC 57, GC 27; enrl D 3624, E 465, non-maj 1347, maj 350, grad 10
Tuition: Res $231 (16-20 hrs) per quarter; non-res $606 (16-20 hrs) per quarter; campus res available
Courses: Advertising Design, Art Education, †Art History, †Ceramics, Commercial Art, Drawing, Film, Goldsmithing, Graphic Arts, †Graphic Design, †Handicrafts, Illustration, Jewelry, †Painting, Photography, †Printmaking, †Sculpture, †Silversmithing, Teacher Training, Fibers
Summer School: Dir, Robert S Olpin. Tui same as above for 6 wks beginning June 24-Aug 15, plus summer workshops June 9-20 and Aug 18-Sept 26. Courses—Art History, Ceramics, Drawing, Fibers, Life Drawing, Painting, Photography, Sculpture, Small Metals & Jewelry

UTAH TECHNICAL COLLEGE AT SALT LAKE, Commercial Art Department, 4600 S Redwood Rd, 84107. Tel 801-967-4111. *Dean* James Schnirel, MA; *Instr* Ralph Huddlestone, BA; *Instr* Grant M Hulet, MA; *Instr* I Douglas Jordan, BA; *Instr* Joseph Lema, BA; *Instr* Allen Reinhold, MA; *Instr* Lois Snyder, MA; *Instr* Fred Van Duke, BA
Pub; D & E; ent req HS dipl or equivalent, aptitude test; degrees AAS; scholarships; SC 44, LC 7; enrl D 123, E 10, non-maj 81, maj 42
Tuition: Res—undergrad $145 per quarter; nonres—undergrad $379 per quarter; no campus res
Courses: Advertising Design, Aesthetics, Art Education, Art History, †Commercial Art, Display, Drafting, Drawing, Fashion Arts, Graphic Arts, †Graphic Design, †Illustration, †Lettering, Photography
Summer School: Dean, James Schnirel. Enrl 30; tui $145 for term of 10 wks beginning June. Courses—Aesthetics, Drawing, Lettering, Media and Techniques

WESTMINSTER COLLEGE, Department of Art, 1840 S 13th East, 84105. Tel 801-484-7651, Ext 66. *Acting Chmn* Philip A Day Jr. Instrs FT 2, PT 5
Estab 1875; pvt; D; ent req HS dipl, ent exam acceptable, HS grade point average; degrees BA and BS 4 yrs; scholarships; SC 25, LC 2; enrl D 900-1000, maj 25
Tuition: $2400 per yr, campus res $783

Courses: Art Education, Art History, Ceramics, Drawing, Jewelry, Painting, Photography, Sculpture, Teacher Training, Weaving

VERMONT

BENNINGTON

BENNINGTON COLLEGE, 05201. Tel 802-442-5401. *Pres* Joseph S Murphy. Instrs FT 65
Estab 1932; pvt; degrees AB and MA 4 yrs; scholarships
Courses: Architecture, Art History, Ceramics, Drawing, Graphic Arts, Painting, Photography, Sculpture

BURLINGTON

UNIVERSITY OF VERMONT, Department of Art, College of Arts & Sciences, 05405. Tel 802-655-2014. *Chairperson* Barbara M Zucker. Instrs 16
Pub; D & E; degrees BA and BS 4 yrs; enrl 650
Courses: Art Education, Art History, Ceramics, Drawing, Painting, Photography, Printmaking, Sculpture, Design, Fine Metals
Summer School: Dir, John Bushey. 8 wks beginning May to Aug

CASTLETON

CASTLETON STATE COLLEGE, Art Department, 05735. Tel 802-468-5611. *Head Dept* Charles R Anderson, BFA; *Asst Prof* Warren Kimble, BFA; *Instructor* Rita Bernatowicz, MFA; *Instructor* William Ramage, MFA; *Instructor* Susan Smith, MFA
Estab 1787; Pub; D & E; ent req HS dipl, ACT, SAT, CEEB; degrees BA and BS 4 yrs, A SBA 2 yrs (business with art concentration); SC 31, LC 3, GC varies; enrl D 1400, E 1000, non-maj 300, maj 79, grad 5
Tuition: Res—undergrad & grad $970 per yr, $485 per sem, $40 per cr; nonres—undergrad & grad $2550 per yr, $1275 per sem, $106 per cr; campus res—room & board $1826
Courses: Advertising Design, Art Education, Art History, Calligraphy, Commercial Art, Costume Design & Construction, Drawing, Graphic Arts, Graphic Design, Handicrafts, Illustration, Lettering, Painting, Photography, Printmaking, Sculpture, Teacher Training, Theatre Arts, Color Design, Professional Studio Arts, Typography
Summer School: Dir, Dr Walter Reuling. Courses—Crafts, Drawing, Painting, Photography, Watercolor

JOHNSON

JOHNSON STATE COLLEGE, Art Department, 05656. Tel 802-635-2356. *Dept Chmn* Judith L Ott, MA; *Prof* Walter Dyck, MFA; *Assoc Prof* Peter Heller, BFA; *Asst Prof* Jon Batdorff, MFA; *Instr* Steven Howell, MFA; *Lectr* Peter Moriarty, MFA; *Lectr* Kathleen O'Hara, MFA; *Vis Prof* Emmett Gowin, photography - 1979; *Vis Prof* Carol Parker, sculpture - 1979
Estab 1828; pub; D & E; ent req HS dipl; degrees BA and BFA 4 yrs, K-12 teaching cert; SC 45, LC 8; enrl D 300, non-maj 225, maj 67
Tuition: Res—undergrad and grad $970 per yr, $485 per sem; nonres—undergrad and grad $2550 per yr, $1275 per sem; campus res—room & board $903 per yr
Courses: Art Education, Art History, Ceramics, Collage, Conceptual Art, Constructions, Drawing, Film, Graphic Arts, Mixed Media, Occupational Therapy, Painting, Photography, Printmaking, Sculpture, Stage Design, Teacher Training, Theatre Arts
Children's Classes: Gifted and talented prog for high school students
Summer School: Enrl 40; tui res—$40 per cr hr, nonres—$55 per cr hr for term of 6 wks beginning June. Courses—Mixed Media, Painting, Performance Art, Sculpture, Theatre

MIDDLEBURY

MIDDLEBURY COLLEGE, Department of Art, Johnson Building, 05753. Tel 802-388-2762. *Chmn* Glenn M Andres. Instrs FT 7
Estab 1942; pvt; D; ent req exam and cert; degrees AB; SC 5, LC 22; enrl maj 60, others 500 per term
Tuition: $6300 per yr includes campus res
Courses: Art History, Drawing, Painting, Printmaking, Sculpture, Design

MONTPELIER

VERMONT COLLEGE OF NORWICH UNIVERSITY, Philosophy, Religion and Fine Arts Department, College St, 05602. Tel 802-229-0522, Ext 28. *Chmn* Dr Edward Suftin, PhD; *Assoc Prof* Harald Krauth, PhD; *Asst Prof* Earl Fechter, MFA; *Asst Prof* Dean Perkins, PhD; *Asst Prof* Brian Webb, PhD
Pvt; D & E; ent req HS dipl; degrees AA; enrl D 65 (studio art), E 8, non-maj 126
Tuition: Campus residency available
Courses: Art Education, Art History, Drawing, Painting, Photography, Printmaking, Design

POULTNEY

GREEN MOUNTAIN COLLEGE, Department of Art,* 05764. Tel 802-287-9313. *Chmn* J Agard
Estab 1834; pvt, W; degrees AA 2 yrs; SC 8, LC 3; enrl maj 63
Tuition: $3700 per yr
Courses: Advertising Design, Display, Drawing, Lettering, Painting

STOWE

WRIGHT SCHOOL OF ART, 05672. Tel 802-253-4305. *Dir* Stanley Marc Wright. Instrs FT 2
Estab 1949; SC 5, LC 4; enrl 50
Tuition: $40 per wk
Children's Classes: Four Sat AM $5 per lesson, June to Sept. Courses—Drawing, Painting

VIRGINIA

ANNANDALE

NORTHERN VIRGINIA COMMUNITY COLLEGE, Art Department, 8333 Little River Turnpike, 22003. Tel 703-323-3115. *Chmn Humanities Div* Dr Eltse B Carter
Pub; D & E; ent req open admis; degrees AA(Fine Arts), AA(Art Educ) and AA(Art History) 2 yrs; scholarships; enrl D 589, E 200
Tuition: Res—undergrad $100 per quarter, $9 per cr; nonres—undergrad $335 per quarter, $28 per cr; no campus res
Courses: Aesthetics, †Art Education, †Art History, Drafting, Drawing, Graphic Design, Interior Design, Painting, Printmaking, Sculpture, Stage Design, Theatre Arts, Fine Arts
Summer School: Chmn Humanities Div, Dr Eltse B Carter. Tui same as regular session; 2 five wk D sessions and 1 ten wk E session during Summer. Courses—varied, incl study abroad

ARLINGTON

MARYMOUNT COLLEGE OF VIRGINIA, Arts & Sciences Division,* Old Dominion & N Glebe Rd, 22207. Tel 703-524-2500. *Chmn* Robert Draghi, PhD; *Asst Prof* Marie Gabrielle Berg, MFA
Estab 1950; pvt; D & E; ent req HS dipl, SAT results, letter of recommendation; degrees BA 3 yrs, AA 2 yrs; SC 14, LC 20
Tuition: $2750 per yr; campus res—room and board $1750 per yr
Courses: Art Education, †Art History, Ceramics, †Commercial Art, Costume Design & Construction, Display, Drawing, Fashion Arts, Graphic Arts, Graphic Design, †History of Art & Archaeology, †Interior Design, Painting, Sculpture, Textile Design, †Theatre Arts
Adult Hobby Classes: Courses—any course in fine arts
Summer School: Dir, James J Kelly. Tui $1375 per summer sem, for term of 5 wks beginning May

BLACKBURG

VIRGINIA TECH, Department of Art, 24061. Tel 703-961-5547. *Head Dept* John Link. Instrs FT 12, PT 3
Estab 1969; pub; degrees BA 4 yrs; SC 25, LC 12
Tuition: $800
Courses: Art Education, Art History, Ceramics, Drawing, Graphic Design, Painting, Printmaking, Sculpture, Design, Metals, Watercolor
Summer School: Head Dept, John Link. Tui proportional to acad yr for two 8 wk terms beginning May and July. Courses—same as above

BRISTOL

SULLINS COLLEGE, Art Department,* 24201. Tel 703-466-3833. *Chmn* Guy H Benson
Estab 1870; pvt, W; D; ent req HS grad; degrees AFA 2 yrs; scholarships; SC 12, LC 1; enrl maj 30, others 15
Courses: Ceramics, History of Art & Archaeology, Interior Design, Jewelry, Photography, Sculpture, Stage Design, Advanced Painting, Beginning Design, Beginning Drawing & Painting, Independent Studio Study, Weaving

VIRGINIA INTERMONT COLLEGE, Fine Arts Department,* Moore St, 24201. Tel 703-669-6101. *Chmn* Stephen J Hamilton, MFA; *Instr* David Braun, MFA; *Instr* Marvin Tadlock, MFA
Estab 1884; den; D & E; ent req HS dipl, review of work; degrees BA(Art) and BA(Art Educ) 4 yrs, AA 2 yrs; scholarships; SC 15, LC 4; enrl D 35, non-maj 110
Tuition: $2475 per yr; campus res available
Courses: †Advertising Design, †Art Education, Art History, Calligraphy, †Ceramics, Collage, †Commercial Art, Costume Design & Construction, Drawing, Fashion Arts, Film, Graphic Arts, Graphic Design, Illustration, Lettering, Mixed Media, Painting, Photography, Printmaking, Sculpture, Teacher Training

BUENA VISTA

SOUTHERN SEMINARY JUNIOR COLLEGE, 24416. Tel 703-261-6181. *Chmn* Leroy U Rudasill Jr, MA
Estab 1867; pvt; D; ent req HS dipl, SAT or ACT; degrees AA, AS and AFA 2 yrs; SC 10, LC 5; enrl D 185, non-maj 175, maj 10
Tuition: Res—undergrad $4900 per yr; nonres—undergrad $3100 per yr
Courses: Art Education, Art History, Ceramics, Display, Drawing, Graphic Arts, Handicrafts, Interior Design, Jewelry, Painting, Photography, Printmaking, Sculpture, Macrame

CHARLOTTESVILLE

UNIVERSITY OF VIRGINIA, McIntire Department of Art, Fayerweather Hall, 22903. Tel 804-924-3057, 924-3541. *Chmn* Malcolm Bell, PhD. Instrs FT 20
Estab 1819, dept estab 1951; pub; D; ent req HS dipl; degrees BA(Studio and Art History), MA(Art History) and PhD(Art History); SC 21, LC 21, GC 14; enrl D 1175, maj 100, grad 27 res, 18 non-res
Tuition: Res—undergrad $916 per yr, $458 per sem, grad $974 per yr, $487 per sem; nonres—undergrad $2161 per yr, $1081 per sem, grad $2159 per yr, $1080 per sem; campus residency available
Courses: Art Education, Drawing, Graphic Arts, Graphic Design, Painting, Photography, Printmaking, Sculpture, Design, Watercolor
Summer School: Dir, Alton L Taylor. Enrl varies; tui res $32 per sem hr, nonres $64 per sem hr for term of June 11 to Aug 7. Courses—Art History, Drawing

DANVILLE

AVERETT COLLEGE, Art Department,* 24541. Tel 804-793-7811. *Coordr* Maud F Gatewood, MA; *Assoc Prof* Robert Marsh, MFA; *Instr* Richard Gantt, MFA; *Instr* Diane Kendrick, MFA
Estab 1859, dept estab 1930; pvt; D & E; ent req HS dipl; degrees AB; scholarships; SC 13, LC 5; enrl D 1000, non-maj 250, maj 25
Tuition: $60 per cr hr; campus res—room and board $3900 per yr
Courses: Advertising Design, Art Education, Art History, Ceramics, Commercial Art, Drawing, Fashion Arts, History of Art & Archaeology, Illustration, Jewelry, Lettering, Painting, Printmaking, Sculpture, Teacher Training, Textile Design
Summer School: Two 4 wk sessions

FAIRFAX

GEORGE MASON UNIVERSITY, Department of Fine and Performing Arts, 22030. Tel 703-691-7950. *Chmn* Anita Taylor, PhD; *Assoc Prof* E Walter Kravitz, MFA; *Asst Prof* A Castro, MFA; *Asst Prof* Sheila Ffolliott; *Asst Prof* Carol C Mattusch, PhD; *Asst Prof* P B North, PhD; *Asst Prof* N W Ward, MFA. Instrs FT 6, PT 2
Estab 1948, dept estab 1966; pub; D & E; ent req HS dipl, SAT or CEEB; degrees BA; SC 16, LC 15; enrl non-maj 200, maj 96
Tuition: Res $402 per sem; nonres $762 per sem; campus residency available
Courses: Art Education, †Art History, Drafting, Drawing, Film, Graphic Arts, History of Art & Archaeology, Painting, Printmaking, Sculpture, Stage Design, Theatre Arts, †Studio Art
Summer School: Courses—Art Appreciation, Studio Arts

FARMVILLE

LONGWOOD COLLEGE, Department of Art, Pine St, 23901. Tel 804-392-9359. *Chmn* Barbara L Bishop, MFA; *Prof* Charlotte Schrader-Hooker, PhD; *Assoc Prof* Elisabeth L Flynn, PhD; *Assoc Prof* Homer L Springer Jr, MAEd; *Asst Prof* Mark S Baldridge, MFA; *Asst Prof* Mary Virginia Mitchell, MEd; *Asst Prof* Conway Betty Thompson, MFA; *Instructor* Randall W Edmonson, MFA
Estab 1839, dept estab 1932; pub; D & E; ent req HS dipl; degrees BA(Art Educ), BS(Art Educ) 4 yrs, BFA(Studio, Art History) 4 yrs; scholarships; SC 59, LC 15; enrl non-maj 450 per sem, maj 95 per sem
Tuition: Undergrad $1026 in-state, $1526 out-of-state, $90 per 3 cr course; campus res—room & board and tui $2596 in-state, $3096 out-of-state
Courses: Advertising Design, †Art Education, †Art History, †Ceramics, Display, †Drawing, Film, Goldsmithing, Illustration, Jewelry, Lettering, Museum Staff Training, †Painting, Photography, †Printmaking, †Sculpture, †Teacher Training, Basic Design, Fibers, Three Dimensional Design
Summer School: Art Dept Chmn, Barbara L Bishop. Tui varies. Courses—vary, primarily craft studios and workshops

FREDERICKSBURG

MARY WASHINGTON COLLEGE, Art Department, 22401. Tel 703-373-7250. *Chmn* Barbara Meyer, PhD; *Prof* Paul C Muick, PhD; *Prof* Cornelia Oliver, PhD; *Assoc Prof* Teruo Hara, MFA; *Assoc Prof* John Lamph, MFA; *Asst Prof* Joseph DiBella, MFA; *Instr* Joseph Dreiss, MA
Estab 1904; pub; D & E; ent req HS dipl, ent exam; degrees BA and BS 4 yrs; scholarships; SC 18, LC 20; enrl maj 50
Tuition: Campus residency available
Courses: Art Education, Ceramics, Commercial Art, Costume Design & Construction, Drawing, Graphic Arts, History of Art & Archaeology, Painting, Photography, Printmaking, Sculpture, Stage Design, Theatre Arts, Historic Preservation

HAMPTON

HAMPTON INSTITUTE, Art Department, 23368. Tel 804-727-5416, Ext 406. Instrs FT 7, PT 2
Estab 1869; pvt; D; ent req HS grad; degrees BA, BS, BFA and MA(Art Educ, Fine Arts) 4 yrs; scholarships; SC 22, LC 7, GC 9; enrl maj 69, others 300, grad 5
Tuition: Campus residency available
Courses: Art History, Ceramics, Commercial Art, Jewelry, Painting, Photography, Teacher Training, Design, Egg Tempera, Metalwork
Summer School: Courses—Advanced Workshop in Ceramics, Art Educ Methods, Art Methods for the Elementary School, Basic Design, Ceramics, Commercial Art, Design, Drawing and Composition, Graphics, Metalwork & Jewelry, Painting, Understanding the Arts

HARRISONBURG

JAMES MADISON UNIVERSITY, Department of Art,* School of Fine Arts & Communications, 22801. Tel 703-433-6228. *Head Dept* J David Diller, PhD; *Prof* Martha B Caldwell, PhD; *Prof* Jerry L Coulter, MFA; *Prof* Crystal Theodore, EdD; *Assoc Prof* Kenneth J Beer, MA; *Asst Prof* Kathleen Arthur, PhD; *Asst Prof* Rebecca Hawkins, MFA; *Asst Prof* Philip James, EdD
Estab 1908; pub; D & E; ent req HS dipl, graduates must submit portfolio, undergrads selected largely on academic merit; degrees BA(Art History), BS and BFA(Studio) 4 yrs, MA 1 1 2 to 2 yrs; scholarships; SC 31, LC 21, GC 22; enrl D & E 1254, maj 175, GS 13
Tuition: Res—undergrad $440 per sem; nonres—undergrad $715 per sem; campus res—room and board $828 per sem
Courses: Advertising Design, Aesthetics, Art Education, Art History, Ceramics, Drafting, Drawing, Goldsmithing, Industrial Design, Jewelry, Interior Design, Museum Staff Training, Painting, Photography, Printmaking, Sculpture, Silversmithing, Teacher Training, Textile Design
Summer School: Dir, Dr Elizabeth Finlayson. Tui Res—undergrad $16 per cr hr, grad $30 per cr hr; nonres—undergrad $33 per cr hr, grad $47 per cr hr for term of 8 wks beginning June. Courses—Art Appreciation, Art Criticism (grad level), Art Education, Ceramics (undergrad level), Drawing, Graphics & Painting, Painting, Photography, Printmaking, Sculpture

HOLLINS

HOLLINS COLLEGE, Art Department, 24020. Tel 703-362-6521. *Chmn* William G White, MFA; *Prof* Ann Laidlaw, PhD; *Prof* Lewis Thompson, MFA; *Assoc Prof* Nancy Dahlstrom, MFA; *Assoc Prof* W L Whitwell, MFA; *Asst Prof* Joan Diamond, PhD
Estab 1842; pvt; D; ent req HS dipl; degrees BA 4 yrs; scholarships; SC 13; enrl D 380, maj 55
Tuition: $4400 per yr; campus res—room & board $1900 per yr
Courses: Aesthetics, †Art History, Drawing, †History of Art & Archaeology, Museum Staff Training, †Painting, †Photography, †Printmaking, †Sculpture, †Teacher Training

LEXINGTON

WASHINGTON AND LEE UNIVERSITY, Department of Fine Arts, 24450. Tel 703-463-9111, Ext 190, 351. *Head Dept* Dr Gerard Maurice Doyon, PhD; *Head Dept* Dr Pamela H Simpson, PhD; *Prof* I-Hsiung Ju, MA; *Prof* Isabel McIlvain, MFA; *Prof* Marid Pellicciaro, MA; *Prof* Dr Herman W Taylor Jr, PhD
Estab 1742, dept estab 1920; pvt; D; ent req HS dipl, SAT, 3 CEEB, one English CEEB plus essay on skills in English, English composition test; entrance requirements most rigorous in English; required of all, including art majors and all others deemed necessary in individual cases; degrees BA 4 yrs; scholarships; SC 14, LC 26; enrl D 1200 (in col) non-maj 200, maj 14
Tuition: $3500 per yr; campus res—room & board and tui average cost $5000 per yr
Courses: †Art Education, Drawing, History of Art & Archaeology, Museum Staff Training, Painting, Printmaking, Sculpture, Stage Design, Theatre Arts, Study Art Abroad—Taiwan, Greece, France

LYNCHBURG

CENTRAL VIRGINIA COMMUNITY COLLEGE, Division of Humanities, Wards Road South, 24502. Tel 804-239-0321. *Chmn Div* Dr Wayne H Wiley, PhD; *Assoc Prof* John Black, MA; *Asst Prof* Roger Elliott, MFA; *Asst Prof* Lee Greever, BA; *Instr Asst* Cloyde W Wiley, BA
Estab 1966; pub; D & E; ent req HS dipl, GED or 18 yrs old, open admis policy; degrees AA, AS and AAS 2 yrs; SC 20, LC 3; enrl D 52, non-maj 12, maj 40
Tuition: Nonres—undergrad $100 per quarter, $9 per hr; no campus res
Courses: Advertising Design, Art History, Calligraphy, Ceramics, †Commercial Art, Conceptual Art, Drafting, Drawing, Graphic Arts, †Graphic Design, †Illustration, Lettering, Painting, †Photography, Printmaking
Adult Hobby Classes: Enrl varies; tui $25-30 per quarter. Courses—Decorating, Photography
Summer School: Enrl varies; tui $9 per hr for term of 10 wks beginning June

LYNCHBURG COLLEGE, Art Department, 24501. Tel 804-845-9071, Ext 295. *Chmn* W Donald Evans; *Asst Prof* Virginia Irby Davis, MEd; *Asst Prof* Thelma L Twery, MEd; *Asst Prof* Charles E Worsham, MA
Estab 1903, dept estab 1948; pvt; D & E; ent req HS dipl; degrees BA and BS 4 yrs; SC 26, LC 16, GC 2; enrl D 400, E 50, non-maj 410, maj 40
Tuition: Res—undergrad $4050 per yr; nonres—undergrad $2600; campus residency available
Courses: Aesthetics, Architecture, Art Education, Art History, Ceramics, Drawing, Film, Graphic Arts, Graphic Design, Handicrafts, History of Art & Archaeology, Occupational Therapy, Painting, Photography, Printmaking, Sculpture, Teacher Training, Theatre Arts
Summer School: Courses—Art Education, Art History and Appreciation, Crafts, Photography

RANDOLPH-MACON WOMAN'S COLLEGE, Department of Art, 24503. Tel 804-846-7392, Ext 430. *Chmn* Robert S Fuller. Instrs FT 3-4
Estab 1891; pvt; W; D; degrees BA 4 yrs; scholarships; SC 18, LC 15; enrl maj 35, others 305
Tuition: $6500 incl room & board
Courses: Architecture, Art History, Ceramics, Drawing, Film, Painting, Printmaking, Sculpture, American Art, Art Survey, Design

MCLEAN

MCLEAN ARTS CENTER, Art Department, 1437 Emerson Ave, 22101. Tel 703-790-0861, 365-3048. *Head Dept* John Bryans
Estab 1955; pvt; D & E; SC 1; enrl D 37, E 6
Tuition: Adults $65 for ten lessons; children $40 for ten lessons
Courses: Drawing, Painting
Adult Hobby Classes: Enrl 28; tui $65 per 10 lessons. Courses—Drawing, Painting (emphasis on watercolor)
Children's Classes: Enrl 15; tui $40 per 10 lessons. Courses—Drawing, Painting

NEWPORT NEWS

CHRISTOPHER NEWPORT COLLEGE, Fine and Performing Arts, 50 Shoe Lane, 23606. Tel 804-599-7073. *Head Dept* Stuart Van Orden, PhD; *Prof* David Alexick, PhD; *Prof* B Anglin, MA; *Prof* James Hines, PhD; *Prof* Bruno Koch, PhD; *Prof* Jon Petruchyk, MFA; *Prof* Skelly Warren, MFA
Estab 1974; pub; D & E; ent req HS dipl, admis committee approval; degrees BA and BS 4 yrs; SC 19, LC 4; enrl D 250, E 60, non-maj 200, maj 100
Tuition: Res—undergrad $450 per sem, nonres—undergrad $600 per sem; no campus res
Courses: Aesthetics, Art Education, Art History, Calligraphy, Ceramics, Collage, Commercial Art, Costume Design & Construction, Drawing, Graphic Arts, History of Art & Archaeology, Illustration, Lettering, Mixed Media, Painting, Photography, Printmaking, Sculpture, Stage Design, Theatre Arts
Adult Hobby Classes: Courses—Glass, Jewelry, Silver
Summer School: Dir, Dr Barry Woods. Enrl 25; tui $300. Courses—Ceramics, Drawing, Painting

NORFOLK

NORFOLK STATE COLLEGE, Fine Arts Department, 23504. Tel 804-623-8844. *Head Dept* Rod A Taylor, PhD
Estab 1935; pub; D & E; ent req HS dipl; degrees BA(Art Educ), BA(Fine Arts) and BA(Graphic Design) 4 yrs, MA and MFA in Visual Studies; SC 50, LC 7; enrl D 355, E 18, non-maj 200, maj 155
Tuition: $300 per sem, $25 per hr, grad $356 per sem, $31 per hr; campus res—room & board $701
Courses: Advertising Design, †Art Education, Art History, Calligraphy, Ceramics, Collage, Commercial Art, Drawing, †Graphic Arts, Graphic Design, Handicrafts, History of Art & Archaeology, Jewelry, Lettering, Mixed Media, †Painting, Photography, Printmaking, Sculpture, Teacher Training
Adult Hobby Classes: Enrl 30. Courses—Ceramics, Crafts
Children's Classes: Enrl 45; tui none. Courses—all areas, at AM
Summer School: Courses—Ceramics, Crafts, Graphics, Painting, Photography, Sculpture

OLD DOMINION UNIVERSITY, Art Department,* 23508. Tel 804-440-4047. *Chmn Art History* Evelyn G Dreyer
Pub; D & E; ent req HS dipl, SAT; degrees BA(Art History), BA(Studio), BS(Art Educ) and BFA 4 yrs; scholarships; SC 43, LC 12, GC 6; enrl D 250, E 86, maj 233, GS 2
Tuition: Res—$744; nonres—$1344; campus res available
Courses: †Art Education, Art History, Ceramics, Drawing, Goldsmithing, Graphic Arts, Graphic Design, Handicrafts, History of Art & Archaeology, Painting, Photography, Printmaking, Sculpture, Silversmithing, Teacher Training, Textile Design, Color, Fibers, Three D Design, Two D Design
Adult Hobby Classes: Courses—Bounty Rainbow Program (selection and costs varied)
Children's Classes: Courses—Bounty Rainbow Program (selection and costs varied)
Summer School: Courses—Art History, Studio

VIRGINIA WESLEYAN COLLEGE, Art Department of the Humanities Division,* Wesleyan Dr, 23502. Tel 804-461-3232. *Head Dept* Barclay Sheaks, BFA; *Asst Prof* Neil Britton, MFA; *Instr* Myrna Andursky, MA; *Instr* F D Cossitt, MFA; *Instr* Charles Flynn, MFA
Pvt, den; D & E; ent req HS dipl, SAT; degrees BA(Liberal Arts) 4 yrs; scholarships; SC 21, LC 8; enrl E 20
Tuition: $2935 per yr; campus res available
Courses: Art Education, Art History, Ceramics, Collage, Conceptual Art, Constructions, Drawing, Graphic Arts, Handicrafts, Jewelry, Mixed Media, Painting, Printmaking, Sculpture, Teacher Training, Fabric Enrichment, Weaving

PETERSBURG

RICHARD BLAND COLLEGE, Art Department,* Rte 1, Box 77A, 23803. Tel 804-732-0111. *Pres* Clarence Maze Jr, PhD; *Asst Prof* Susan G Brown, BFA
Estab 1960, dept estab 1963; pub; D & E; ent req HS dipl, SAT, recommendation of HS counselor; degrees AA(Fine Arts) 2 yrs; SC 3, LC 3; enrl D 73
Tuition: Res—undergrad $480 per yr, $240 per sem; nonres—undergrad $810 per yr, $405 per sem; no campus res
Courses: Art History, Drawing, Painting, Sculpture, Art Appreciation, Basic Design
Adult Hobby Classes: Courses—Interior Design, Yoga
Children's Classes: Enrl approx 20; tui $22 per hr. Courses—Art for Children, Children's Gymnastics
Summer School: Dir, John B McNeer. Enrl approx 300; tui $22 per hr for term of 6 wks beginning June 7th. Courses—varied

VIRGINIA STATE COLLEGE, Fine Arts Department, 23803. Tel 804-520-6328. *Head Dept* Dr A D Macklin, EdD; *Asst Prof* Michael Gilliatt, EdD; *Asst Prof* Eugene Vango, MFA; *Asst Prof* Doris Woodson, MFA; *Instructor* Charles Flynn, MA
Estab 1882, dept estab 1935; pub; D & E; ent req HS dipl; degrees BS, BFA(Art Educ) and BFA(Commercial Art and Design) 4 yrs; SC 16, LC 6, GC 2; enrl D 400, E 60, non-maj 302, maj 98
Tuition: Res—undergrad and grad $738 per yr; nonres—undergrad and grad $1500 per

yr; campus res—room & board $764
Courses: Advertising Design, Aesthetics, Art Education, Ceramics, Drawing, History of Art & Archaeology, Jewelry, Lettering, Painting, Printmaking, Sculpture
Adult Hobby Classes: Enrl 20; tui $105 per course. Courses—Batik, Ceramics, Jewelry, Macrame, Painting, Printmaking
Summer School: Dir, Dr Alvin Hall. Enrl 20; tui $35 per cr for term of 6 wks, beginning June 19. Courses—Basic Art, Ceramics, Crafts, Jewelry

PORTSMOUTH

TIDEWATER COMMUNITY COLLEGE, Art Department, St Route 135, 23703. Tel 804-484-2121. *Art Coordr* Harriette C F Laskin, MEd; *Instr* William G Stobo Jr, BFA
Estab 1968; pub; D & E; ent req HS dipl; degrees AA(Fine Arts), AAA(Media Arts) 2 yrs; SC 12, LC 3; enrl D 120, E 180, non-maj 190, maj 110
Tuition: In-state $300, out-of-state $900; no campus res
Courses: †Advertising Design, Art History, Ceramics, Drawing, Illustration, Lettering, Painting, Photography, Printmaking
Adult Hobby Classes: Offered through Continuing Educ Div
Children's Classes: Offered through Continuing Educ Div
Summer School: Art Coordr, H Laskin. Enrl 15 per course; tui $100 for term of 10 wks beginning June. Courses—Art History, Ceramics, Design, Drawing, Painting, Photography

RADFORD

RADFORD UNIVERSITY, Art Department, PO Box 5791, 24142. Tel 703-731-5475. *Chmn* Dr G Lynn Gordon, DEd; *Prof* Dr Paul W Frets, DA; *Prof* Dr Noel G Lawson, PhD; *Asst Prof* Jerry H Krebs, MFA; *Asst Prof* Pam F Lawson, MFA; *Asst Prof* Dr Heliede Salam, PhD; *Asst Prof* Dr Fred Thayed, DEd; *Instructor* Ed LeShock; *Instructor* Felicia Lewandowski; *Instructor* Paul Munson
Estab 1910, dept estab 1936; pub; D & E; ent req HS dipl, SAT; degrees BA, BS (non-teaching) and BS (teaching) 4 yrs, MS 1 yr; scholarships; SC 52, LC 12, GC 26; enrl D 191, E 18, non-maj 978, maj 191, grad 28, others 15
Tuition: Res—$2574 per yr, $858 per quarter, $25 per quarter hr; nonres—$867 per yr, $289 per quarter, $25 per quarter; out-of-state $3174 per yr, $1058 per quarter, $42 per quarter hr; campus residency available
Courses: Advertising Design, Architecture, †Art Education, †Art History, Calligraphy, Ceramics, Commercial Art, Drawing, Goldsmithing, Graphic Arts, Graphic Design, Handicrafts, History of Art & Archaeology, Illustration, Jewelry, Lettering, Painting, Photography, Printmaking, Sculpture, Silversmithing, Teacher Training, Textile Design, Enameling, Raku, Weaving
Summer School: Enrl 421; tui as above. Courses—all labs plus Art Appreciation, Art Education

RICHMOND

UNIVERSITY OF RICHMOND, Department of Art,* 23173. Tel 804-285-6000. *Chmn* Charles W Johnson Jr, PhD; *Assoc Prof* Demetrios Mavroudis, EdD; *Asst Prof* Jeanne Begien Campbell; *Instr* Anne P Frederick, MA; *Instr* Harvey McWilliams, MFA
Pvt; D & E; ent req HS dipl, CEEB; degrees BA and BS 4 yrs; SC 29, LC 15
Tuition: Res—$3410 per yr
Courses: Art Education, Art History, Ceramics, Drawing, Graphic Arts, Graphic Design, Handicrafts, History of Art & Archaeology, Painting, Printmaking, Sculpture
Summer School: Dir, Dr Max Graeber

VIRGINIA COMMONWEALTH UNIVERSITY, School of the Arts, 325 N Harrison St, 23284. Tel 804-257-1700. *Dean* Murry N DePillars. Instrs FT 141, PT 24
Estab 1838; pub; D & E; ent req portfolio; degrees BFA, BM and BME 4 yrs, MA, MFA, MAE, MM and MME 2 yrs; scholarships, fels and grad assistantships; enrl 2025 (art), 19,000 (total)
Tuition: Res—undergrad and grad $745; non-res—undergrad and grad $1490; art fees approx $40 each sem
Courses: Art Education, Art History, Ceramics, Fashion Arts, Interior Design, Jewelry, Painting, Photography, Printmaking, Sculpture, Theatre Arts, Communication Arts & Design, Fabric Design, Furniture Design
Children's Classes: Summer school offerings

ROANOKE

VIRGINIA WESTERN COMMUNITY COLLEGE, Commercial Art, Fine Art & Photography, 3095 Colonial Ave SW, PO Box 4195, 24015. Tel 703-982-7200. *Head Dept* Dr Clarence C Mays, PhD; *Instr* Vera M Dickerson, MFA; *Instr* Margaret G Ferris, MFA; *Instr* Rudolf Hofheinz, MS; *Instr* Thomas Porter, MS
Pub; D & E; ent req HS dipl; degrees AA 2 yrs; SC 11, LC 2
Courses: Advertising Design, Art History, †Commercial Art, Drawing, Graphic Arts, Graphic Design, Illustration, Lettering, Painting, Photography, Printmaking
Adult Hobby Classes: Courses—Oil Painting, Stained Glass, Watercolor

SALEM

ROANOKE COLLEGE, Art Department, Olin Hall, High St, 24153. Tel 703-389-2351, Ext 359 or 260. *Chairperson Fine Arts* Dr Karen Adams, PhD; *Assoc Prof* John Brust, MFA; *Asst Prof* Scott Hardwig, MFA; *Adjunct Prof* Lorna Reichel, MFA
Estab 1842; dept estab 1930; den; D; ent req HS dipl, SAT or ACT, 16 academic credits —4 English, 2 social studies, 2 foreign language, 3 math, 2 science; degrees BA 4 yrs; SC 16, LC 8; enrl D 130, non-maj 120, maj 10
Tuition: Campus residence available
Courses: Advertising Design, Art Education, Art History, Ceramics, Commercial Art, Costume Design & Construction, Drawing, Graphic Arts, Graphic Design, Painting, Photography, Printmaking, Sculpture, Stage Design, Theatre Arts
Adult Hobby Classes: Enrl 25; tui $35 per sem. Courses—Painting, Watercolor
Children's Classes: Courses—Ceramics and Textile Arts offered in summer
Summer School: Dir, Dr Harry Poindexter. Courses—Photography

STAUNTON

MARY BALDWIN COLLEGE, Department of Art, Frederick and New Streets, 24401. Tel 703-885-0811, Ext 394. *Head Dept* Ulysse Desportes, Dr Univ of Paris; *Assoc Prof* Mary Tuck Echols, PhD; *Asst Prof* Leslee N Corpier, MA & MS; *Asst Prof* William Frazier, MA; *Asst Prof* Cynthia Harris, MA & ATR; *Instructor* Jim Hanger, BFA
Estab 1842; pvt; D & E; ent req HS dipl; degrees BA 4 yrs; scholarships; SC 16, LC 18; enrl D 173, E 32, non-maj 172, maj 33, others 4 non-credit
Tuition: Res—undergrad $5120 per yr, $2560 per sem; nonres—undergrad $3520 per yr, $2760 per sem; campus res—room & board $1600
Courses: Advertising Design, Aesthetics, Art Education, Art History, Ceramics, Collage, Commercial Art, Conceptual Art, Constructions, Costume Design & Construction, Display, Drawing, Film, Graphic Arts, Graphic Design, Handicrafts, History of Art & Archaeology, Illustration, Interior Design, Lettering, Mixed Media, Museum Staff Training, Painting, Photography, Printmaking, Sculpture, Stage Design, Teacher Training, Theatre Arts, Video, Art for the Exceptional Child, Art Therapy, Fabric Arts, Historical Preservation, Weaving

SWEET BRIAR

SWEET BRIAR COLLEGE, Art History Department, 24595. Tel 804-381-5451. *Chmn Dept* Aileen H Laing, PhD; *Chmn Studio Art* Loren Oliver, MFA; *Assoc Prof* Raymond Twiddy, MFA; *Asst Prof* Susan Bandes, PhD; *Asst Prof* Diane D Moran, PhD
Estab 1901, dept estab 1930; pvt; D & E; ent req HS dipl, col boards; degrees BA 4 yrs; SC 17, LC 16; enrl D 200 per term, maj 20
Tuition: $6100 incl room and board
Courses: Architecture, †Art History, Ceramics, Drawing, Graphic Arts, History of Art & Archaeology, Mixed Media, Painting, Photography, Printmaking, Sculpture, Teacher Training, †Theatre Arts, Decorative Arts, †Studio Art

WILLIAMSBURG

COLLEGE OF WILLIAM AND MARY, Department of Fine Arts,* 23185. Tel 804-253-4000. *Chmn* Miles Chappell, PhD; *Prof* Carl Roseberg, MFA; *Assoc Prof* Henry Coleman, MA; *Assoc Prof* Paul Helfrich, MFA; *Assoc Prof* J D Kornwold, PhD; *Asst Prof* W D Barnes, MFA; *Asst Prof* Marlene Jack, MFA; *Instr* W D Houghland, AIA
Estab 1693, dept estab 1936; pub; D; ent req HS dipl; degrees BA 4 yrs; SC 20, LC 22; enrl D 5000, non-maj 693, maj 64
Tuition: Res—$1076 per yr; nonres—$2524 per yr; campus res available
Courses: †Architecture, †Art History, Ceramics, Drawing, Graphic Arts, Painting, Sculpture
Summer School: Dir, Paul Clem. Courses—Art History, Design, Painting, Sculpture

WISE

CLINCH VALLEY COLLEGE OF THE UNIVERSITY OF VIRGINIA, Humanities Department,* 24293. Tel 703-328-2431. *Chmn* J Glenn Blackburn, PhD; *Assoc Prof* Betty J Gilliam, MFA
Estab 1954, dept estab 1968; pub; D & E; ent req HS dipl, SAT or ACT; degrees baccalaureate (BA and BS) 4 yrs; scholarships; SC 9, LC 4
Tuition: Res—undergrad $630 per yr; nonres—undergrad $880 per yr
Courses: Art Education, Art History, Ceramics, Costume Design & Construction, Drafting, Drawing, Film, History of Art & Archaeology, Painting, Photography, Sculpture, Stage Design, †Teacher Training, Theatre Arts
Adult Hobby Classes: Tui $21 per hr. Courses—Christmas wrapping, Flower arranging
Summer School: Dir, Dr George E Culbertson. Tui $23 per sem hr for two terms of five wks beginning June and July

WASHINGTON

BELLEVUE

BELLEVUE COMMUNITY COLLEGE, Division of Creative Arts,* 3000 Landerholm Circle, SE, 98007. Tel 206-641-2111. *Division Chmn* Dale L Gleason
Estab 1966; pub; D & E; ent req no ent req; degrees AA 2 yrs; SC 15, LC 5; enrl 300, maj 60
Tuition: Res—undergrad $303 per yr; nonres—undergrad $1185 per yr; no campus res
Courses: Drawing, Graphic Design, History of Art & Archaeology, Painting, Photography, Sculpture, Textile Design
Adult Hobby Classes: Enrl 600. Courses—Ceramics, Design, Drawing, Jewelry, Painting, Photography, Sculpture

BELLINGHAM

WESTERN WASHINGTON UNIVERSITY, Art Department, College of Fine and Performing Arts, 89225. Tel 206-676-3660, 676-3661. *Chmn* Thomas Schlotterback, PhD. Instrs FT 15, PT 6
Estab 1899; pub; D & E; ent req HS dipl, ent exam; degrees BA, BA(Educ), BFA and MEd 4 yrs; enrl D 1500
Tuition: Res—undergrad $206, grad $228 quarterly; non-res—undergrad $661, grad $752 quarterly; SE Asian Veterans $162 per quarter; campus res—room & board approx $515 per quarter
Summer School: Tui $197 for term of 9 wks. Terms of 3 wks, 6 wks and regular sessions, full-time students

BREMERTON

OLYMPIC COLLEGE, Art Department, 98310. Tel 206-478-4511, Ext 4866. *Chmn* Polly N Zanetta, MA; *Instructor* Jack W Crouse, MA; *Instructor* Kenneth V Crow, MA; *Instructor* LaDeane V Tate, MA; *Instructor* Mel R Wallis, MA
Estab 1946; pub; D & E; ent req HS dipl; degrees AA, AS and ATA 2 yrs; scholarships; LC 3; enrl D 125, E 75
Tuition: Res—undergrad $102 per quarter, $11 per cr; nonres—undergrad $396 per quarter, $40 per cr; no campus res
Courses: Art History, Calligraphy, Ceramics, Drawing, Jewelry, Painting, Photography, Printmaking, Sculpture
Adult Hobby Classes: Courses— Painting, Stained Glass

CHENEY

EASTERN WASHINGTON UNIVERSITY, Department of Art,* 99004. Tel 509-359-2493. *Chmn* Gregory W Hawkins, PhD
Estab 1886; pub; D; ent req appropriate evidence of ability to succeed academically; degrees BA, BEd and BFA 4 yrs, MA and MEd 1 to 2 yrs; scholarships; SC 58, LC 21, GC 18; enrl D 600, non-maj 200, maj 200, GS 20
Tuition: Res—undergrad $618 per yr, $21 part-time, grad $684 per yr, $23 part-time; nonres—undergrad $1983 per yr, grad $2256 per yr; campus res—room and board $1245
Courses: Aesthetics, †Art Education, †Art History, †Ceramics, †Conceptual Art, Drawing, Film, Illustration, Intermedia, †Jewelry, Museum Staff Training, †Painting, †Photography, †Printmaking, †Sculpture, †Silversmithing, †Teacher Training, †Textile Design, Video

ELLENSBURG

CENTRAL WASHINGTON UNIVERSITY, Department of Art, 98926. Tel 509-963-2665. *Chmn* George Stillman. Instrs FT 15
Estab 1891; pub; D; ent req GPA 2; degrees BA, MA and MFA 4-5 yrs; enrl maj 300, others 4500
Tuition: FT $206 10 hrs or more, PT $21 per quarter hr; campus residency available
Courses: Art Education, Art History, Commercial Art, Drawing, Handicrafts, Jewelry, Painting, Photography, Printmaking, Sculpture, Design, Pottery
Summer School: Courses offered

LONGVIEW

LOWER COLUMBIA COLLEGE, 1600 Maple, 98632. Tel 206-577-2300. *Instructor* Arthur Miller, MA; *Instructor* Rosemary Powelson, MFA
Estab 1934; pub; D & E; ent req HS dipl; degrees AAS 2 yrs; scholarships; SC 36, LC 8; enrl D 128, E 81
Tuition: Res—undergrad $306 per yr, $10 per hr; nonres—undergrad $1188 per yr, $40 per hr; no campus res
Courses: Art History, Calligraphy, Ceramics, Drawing, Graphic Arts, Mixed Media, Painting, Printmaking, Sculpture, Design, Exhibit Technique
Adult Hobby Classes: Enrl 40; tui $31 per quarter. Courses—Recreational Painting

MOSES LAKE

BIG BEND COMMUNITY COLLEGE, Art Department, 98857. Tel 509-762-5351. *Chmn* Stephen Tse, MFA
Estab 1962; pub; D & E; ent req HS dipl; degrees AA 2 yrs; SC 8, LC 1; enrl D 325, E 60, maj 10-15
Tuition: Res—undergrad $249 per yr, $83 per quarter, $8 PT; nonres—undergrad $681 per yr, $227 per quarter, $23 PT; campus residency available
Courses: Art History, Ceramics, Drawing, Graphic Arts, Lettering, Painting, Basic Design
Summer School: Dir, Mike Lang. Tui $8 per cr hr for term of 6 wks. Courses—Ceramics, Drawing, Painting

MOUNT VERNON

SKAGIT VALLEY COLLEGE, Department of Art, 2405 College Way, 98273. Tel 206-424-1031. *Chmn* Orville K Chatti. Instrs FT 2, PT 6
Estab 1926; pub; D & E; ent req open; degrees AA 2 yrs; scholarships; SC 32, LC 1; enrl D 2500, E 3500
Courses: Ceramics, Drawing, Handicrafts, Jewelry, Painting, Photography, Art Appreciation, Design, Stained Glass

PULLMAN

WASHINGTON STATE UNIVERSITY, Fine Arts Department,* 99164. Tel 509-335-3564. *Chmn* Ross Coates, PhD; *Prof* Gaylen C Hansen, MFA; *Prof* Keith Monaghan, MA; *Assoc Prof* Robert Helm, MFA; *Assoc Prof* Fran Ho, MFA; *Assoc Prof* Arthur Okazaki, MA; *Asst Prof* Jo Hockenhull, MA; *Asst Prof* Patrick Siler, MA
Estab 1890, dept estab 1925; pub; D & E; ent req HS dipl; degrees BA(Fine Arts) 4 yrs, MFA 2 yrs; scholarships; SC 29, LC 13, GC 25; enrl D 1593, E 131, maj 220, GS 25
Tuition: Res—undergrad $686 per yr, grad $770 per yr; nonres—undergrad $2394 per yr, grad $2736 per yr; campus res—room and board $1620 per yr
Courses: Advertising Design, Art History, Calligraphy, Ceramics, Drawing, Graphic Design, Illustration, Jewelry, Lettering, Museum Staff Training, Painting, Photography, Printmaking, Sculpture
Summer School: Enrl varies; tui $27 per cr hr for term of four 2 wk workshops beginning June. Courses—varies

SEATTLE

BURNLEY SCHOOL OF PROFESSIONAL ART, INC, 905 East Pine St, 98122. Tel 206-322-0596. *Dir* Jess D Cauthorn; *Instructor* William Cumming; *Instructor* Fred Griffin, BFA; *Instructor* Gail Merrick; *Instructor* Gary Nelson; *Instructor* Marilyn Nordell, BFA; *Instructor* James Scott, BFA
Estab 1946; pvt; D; ent req HS dipl, portfolio approval; degrees prof dipl; SC 2; enrl D 150
Tuition: $1500 per yr; no campus res
Courses: Advertising Design, Commercial Art, Fashion Arts, Film, Graphic Arts, Graphic Design, Illustration, Lettering, Video
Summer School: Enrl 60; tui $600 per term of 12 wks beginning May 15

CORNISH INSTITUTE, 710 East Roy, 98102. Tel 206-323-1400. *Pres* Melvin Strauss; *Chmn Fine Arts* Chris Watts; *Chmn Design* Vernon Trevellyan. Instrs FT 14, PT 80
Estab 1914; pvt; D & E; ent req HS dipl, portfolio review, fine arts, design, personal interview; degrees BAA and BFA 4 yrs; scholarships; SC 57, LC 6; enrl non-maj 156 PT, maj 245 FT
Tuition: $80 per cr; no campus res
Courses: Advertising Design, Aesthetics, Art History, †Ceramics, Commercial Art, Conceptual Art, Drafting, Drawing, Graphic Arts, †Graphic Design, Illustration, Industrial Design, †Interior Design, Lettering, †Painting, Photography, †Printmaking, †Sculpture, Theatre Arts
Adult Hobby Classes: Enrl 249; tui $75 per cr, $60 non-cr. Courses—Design, Fine Arts
Summer School: Tui $75 per cr for term of 8 wks beginning June 16th. Courses—Design, Fine Arts, Theatre

FACTORY OF VISUAL ART, 4649 Sunnyside N, 98103. Tel 206-632-8177. *Dir* Mickey Gustin; *Instructor* Carolyn Cavalier, MFA; *Instructor* Dwight Coburn, MFA; *Instructor* Charles Draney, MFA; *Instructor* Margaret Ford, MFA; *Instructor* Karen Guzak, BFA; *Instructor* Timothy Hall, BFA; *Instructor* Joanne Hammer, MFA; *Instructor* James Hirschfield, MFA; *Instructor* Deborah Horrell, MFA; *Instructor* Lynne Leinhardt, MA; *Instructor* Steve McClelland, MFA; *Instructor* Mike Saito, MFA; *Instructor* Steve Soltar, MFA; *Instructor* Peggy Vanbianchi, MFA
Estab 1968; pvt; D & E; ent req open; degrees cert 2 yr minimum; scholarships; SC 54, LC 1; enrl D & E 350 per sem
Tuition: $212 per sem for 6 hr crs; no campus res
Courses: Art History, Calligraphy, Ceramics, Drawing, Goldsmithing, Jewelry, Mixed Media, Painting, Photography, Printmaking, Sculpture, Silversmithing, Textile Design, Bookbinding, Dye Processes, Enameling, Papermaking, Photographic Silk Screen, Printing, Spinning, Stained Glass, Weaving
Children's Classes: Enrl 45 per sem; tui $2 per hr. Courses—Bookbinding, Ceramics, Drawing, Jewelry, Painting, Textiles, Weaving
Summer School: Tui as above for term of 12 wks beginning May 19. Courses—Short workshops with local and visiting artists

NORTH SEATTLE COMMUNITY COLLEGE, Art Department, Humanities Division, 9300 Burke Ave N, 98103. Tel 206-634-4513. *Acting Chmn Dept* John Constantine, MFA; *Instructor* Elroy Christenson, MFA; *Instructor* David J Harris, MFA
Estab 1970; pub; D & E; ent req HS dipl; degrees AA 2 yrs; SC 27, LC 7; enrl D 150, E 65
Tuition: Res—$100 per quarter; nonres—$250 per quarter; no campus res
Courses: Art History, Calligraphy, Drawing, History of Art & Archaeology, Interior Design, Jewelry, Painting, Photography, Printmaking, Sculpture
Adult Hobby Classes: Drawing, Painting
Summer School: Tui $100 for term of 8 wks beginning June 20. Courses—Drawing, Introduction to Art

SEATTLE CENTRAL COMMUNITY COLLEGE, Division of Humanities,* 1718 Broadway, 98122. Tel 206-587-3877. *Chmn* John Doty
Estab 1970; pub; D & E; ent req HS dipl, ent exam; degrees AA 2 yrs; scholarships; SC 15, LC 5; enrl D 70, E 50
Tuition: Res—undergrad $96 per yr; nonres—undergrad $390 per yr; no campus res
Courses: Art History, Painting, Sculpture

SHORELINE COMMUNITY COLLEGE, Humanities Division, 98133. Tel 206-546-4741. *Chmn* Denzil Walters; *Prof* John Kirk, MFA; *Prof* Mike Larson, BA; *Prof* Denis Ostermeyer, MFA; *Prof* Chris Simons, MFA
Estab 1964; pub; D & E; ent req HS dipl, col ent exam; degrees AA and AFA; SC 9, LC Art History Survey; enrl D 5500
Tuition: Res—undergrad $100 per quarter, $10 per quarter hr; non-res—undergrad $394 per quarter, $39 per quarter hr; no campus res
Courses: †Advertising Design, Art History, Ceramics, †Commercial Art, Drawing, Illustration, Lettering, Painting, Photography, Sculpture, Stage Design, Teacher Training, Theatre Arts
Summer School: Term of 4 wks June 23-July 22. Courses—Ceramics, Design, Drawing, Photography

UNIVERSITY OF WASHINGTON, School of Art, DM-10, 98195. Tel 206-543-0970. *Dir* Richard Arnold
Estab 1878; pub; D & E; ent req must meet university admission req; degrees BFA 5 yrs, BA 4 yrs, MA, PhD and MFA; scholarships; SC 113, LC 84, GC 30; enrl D & E 3662, maj 1054, grad 109
Tuition: Res—undergrad $220, grad $247; nonres—undergrad $798, grad $912; campus res—room & board $1713-$1822 for double
Courses: Advertising Design, †Art Education, †Art History, †Ceramics, Drawing, Film, †Graphic Design, Handicrafts, Industrial Design, †Interior Design, Jewelry, †Painting, Photography, †Printmaking, †Sculpture, Silversmithing, Teacher Training, †Textile Design, Video, Bookbinding, †Fabric Surface Design, †General Art, Leather, †Metal Design, †Paper

SPOKANE

FORT WRIGHT COLLEGE OF THE HOLY NAMES, School of Art, W 4000 Randolph Rd, 99204. Tel 509-328-2970, Ext 55. *Chmn* Paula Turnbull, MFA; *Assoc Prof* Charles Palmer, MFA; *Instructor* Terry Buckendorf, MFA; *Instructor* Maury Cain; *Instructor* Henry Hawkins Lyman Jr, MFA; *Instructor* Micahel Moore
Estab 1889; pvt; D & E; ent req none; degrees BA 4 yrs and BFA; scholarships; SC 13, LC 7; enrl D 460 (total), maj 28
Tuition: $2335 per yr; campus res—room & board $1550 plus activity fee
Courses: Ceramics, Drawing, Goldsmithing, Jewelry, Painting, Printmaking, Sculpture, Silversmithing, Textile Design

GONZAGA UNIVERSITY, Department of Art, School of Arts and Sciences, Boone Ave, 99258. *Chmn* J Scott Patnode. Instrs FT 3, PT 3
Estab 1962; pvt; D & E; ent req HS dipl; degrees BA 4 yrs, grad cert in art; SC 20, LC 5, GC 12; enrl D 250 incl maj 50, grad 8, others 80
Tuition: $1600 per sem; campus res $900
Courses: Art Education, Ceramics, Drawing, History of Art & Archaeology, Painting, Printmaking, Sculpture, Teacher Training
Summer School: Dir, Bud Hazel. Term of 6 wks beginning June. Courses—Ceramics, Drawing, Painting, Printmaking, 29th Century Art History

SPOKANE FALLS COMMUNITY COLLEGE, Creative & Performing Arts,* 99204. Tel 509-456-6100. *Chmn* Donald Nepean; *Dept Chmn* Jo Fyfe; *Dept Chmn* Jac Rogers
Estab 1963; pub; D & E; ent req HS dipl, GED; degrees AAA 3 yrs, and AA 2 yrs; scholarships; SC 41, LC 5; enrl D 600, E 200
Tuition: Res—$104 per quarter; nonres—$403 per quarter; no campus res
Courses: Advertising Design, Architecture, Art History, Calligraphy, Ceramics, †Commercial Art, Display, Drawing, Illustration, Interior Design, Jewelry, Lettering, Mixed Media, Painting, †Photography, Printmaking, Sculpture, Batik, Intro to Art, Package Design, Vol Design, Weaving
Summer School: Dir, Lowell Jacobs. Courses—Batik, Ceramics, Color & Design, Faceting, Interior Design, Lettering, Oil Painting, Watercolor, Weaving

WHITWORTH COLLEGE, Art Department,* Hawthorne Rd, 99251. Tel 509-466-1000. *Coordr* Pauline Haas, MFA; *Assoc Prof* Walter Grosvenor, MAT; *Assoc Prof* J Russell Larson, MEd
Pvt; D & E; ent req HS dipl; degrees BA and BS 4 yrs, MA, MAT & MEd 2 yrs; scholarships; SC 18, LC 3
Tuition: Res—undergrad $3575 per yr; campus res—room and board $1650 per yr
Courses: Art Education, Art History, Ceramics, Drawing, Handicrafts, Jewelry, Lettering, Painting, Photography, Printmaking, Sculpture, Batik, Textile Arts
Summer School: Dir, Alvin Quall. Courses—Art Ed Methods, Ceramics, Painting, Photography, Textile Arts

TACOMA

FORT STEILACOOM COMMUNITY COLLEGE, Fine Arts Department, 9401 Far West Dr, 98499. Tel 206-964-6717. *Chmn* Hal Buckner, MFA. Instrs FT 3, PT 4
Estab 1966, dept estab 1972; pub; D & E; ent req ent exam; degrees AA 2 yrs; SC 20, LC 5; enrl D 350
Tuition: $88 per term; no campus res
Courses: Art Education, Ceramics, Drafting, Drawing, Fashion Arts, Film, Interior Design, Painting, Photography, Printmaking, Sculpture, Stage Design, Theatre Arts
Summer School: Courses—Ceramics, Drawing, Painting. Tour in Europe July 16-Aug 10, 1980

PACIFIC LUTHERAN UNIVERSITY, Department of Art,* 98447. Tel 206-531-6900. *Chmn* Walt Tomsic, MFA; *Prof* George R Elwell, MFA; *Prof* David Keyew, MFA; *Prof* Lars Kittleson, MFA; *Prof* George Roskos, MFA; *Prof* Ernst Schwidder, MFA
Estab 1890, dept estab 1971; den; D & E; ent req HS dipl, Washington Pre-College Test or ACT; degrees BA, BAEd and BFA 4 yrs; scholarships; SC 20, LC 12; enrl D 1000, E 50, maj 50
Tuition: $75 per hr; campus res—room and board $1300
Courses: †Advertising Design, Architecture, †Art Education, †Art History, Ceramics, †Commercial Art, †Drawing, †Film, †Graphic Arts, †Graphic Design, Handicrafts, History of Art & Archaeology, Illustration, Jewelry, Mixed Media, †Painting, †Photography, †Printmaking, †Sculpture, †Teacher Training, Textile Design, Fibers
Summer School: Dir, Dr Richard Moe. Enrl 100, tui $54 per sem hr for term of 4 wks, 2 terms beginning mid June and mid July. Courses—Bronze Casting Workshop, Color Slide Workshop, Landscape Painting Workshop, Plato to Pop (art history and theory), Watercolor Workshop

TACOMA COMMUNITY COLLEGE, Art Department, 5900 12th St, 98465. Tel 206-756-5070. *Art Dept Chmn* Frank Dippolito, MFA; *Instr* Carlton Ball, MFA; *Instr* Paul Clee, MA; *Instr* Paul Michaels, MFA; *Instr* Richard Rhea, MFA; *Instr* Donald Tracey, MFA
Estab 1965; pub; D & E; degrees AAS and Associate in Liberal Arts 2 yrs; scholarships; SC 35, LC 1; enrl D & E 1500
Tuition: Res—undergrad $102 per quarter, PT $10 per cr hr; nonres—undergrad $396 per quarter, PT $40 per cr hr; no campus res

Courses: Calligraphy, Ceramics, Costume Design & Construction, Drafting, Drawing, Film, Graphic Design, Handicrafts, Jewelry, Lettering, Painting, Photography, Printmaking, Sculpture, Stage Design

UNIVERSITY OF PUGET SOUND, Art Department, 1500 N Warner St, 98416. Tel 206-756-3356. *Chmn* John McCuistion. Instrs FT 7, PT 3
Estab 1935; den; D & E; ent req HS grad; degrees BA and MFA 4 yrs; SC 41, LC 11, GC 23, undergrad 177
Tuition: $3780 per yr, $1890 per sem; campus res—room and board $1770
Courses: Art History, Ceramics, Drawing, Painting, Printmaking, Sculpture, Teacher Training, Oriental Art, Studio Design, Watercolor
Summer School: 9 wks beginning June

VANCOUVER

CLARK COLLEGE, Art Department, 1800 E McLaughlin Blvd, 98663. Tel 206-694-6521. *Dept Coordr* Richard J Stensrude, MAT; *Instr* Roger Baker, MFA; *Instr* Warren Dunn, MFA; *Instr* Joan Henson, MFA
Estab 1933, dept estab 1947; pub; D & E; ent req open door; degrees Assoc of Arts and Science, Assoc of Applied Science, and Assoc of General Studies 2 yrs; scholarships; SC 87, LC 3; enrl D 300, E 400
Tuition: Res and nonres—undergrad $10 per cr (1-6 hrs), $40 per cr (7-9 hrs); campus residence available
Courses: Art History, Calligraphy, Ceramics, Drafting, Drawing, Fashion Arts, Graphic Arts, Graphic Design, Handicrafts, History of Art & Archaeology, Illustration, Interior Design, Jewelry, Lettering, Painting, Photography, Printmaking, Sculpture, Stage Design, Theatre Arts, Video
Adult Hobby Classes: Enrl 80; tui $10 per cr. Courses—Stained Glass
Children's Classes: Courses—Ceramics, Drawing, Photography, Watercolor
Summer School: Tui $10 per cr hr for term of 8 wks. Courses—most regular offerings

WALLA WALLA

WHITMAN COLLEGE, Art Department,* 345 Boyer Ave, 99362. Tel 509-527-5111. *Chmn* Paul E Dewey
Pvt; D; ent req HS dipl, ent exam; degrees BA 4 yrs; SC 15, LC 8; enrl D 225, maj 10
Tuition: Res—undergrad $1743 per sem; campus res—room and board $750-$940 per sem
Courses: Aesthetics, Art Education, Ceramics, Drawing, History of Art & Archaeology, Painting, Sculpture, Stage Design

WENATCHEE

WENATCHEE VALLEY COLLEGE, Art Department, 1300 Fifth St, 98801. Tel 509-662-1651. *Chmn Div of Humanities* Daryl Dietrich, MA; *Instructor* Ruth Allan, MFA; *Instructor* Robert Graves, MFA
Estab 1939; pub; D & E; ent req HS dipl, open door policy; degrees AA 2 yrs; scholarships; LC 4; enrl D 550, E 200, maj 45
Tuition: Res—undergrad $306 per yr, $102 per quarter, $10 per cr hr; nonres—undergrad $1188 per yr, $396 per quarter; campus residency available
Courses: Art History, Ceramics, Collage, Drafting, Drawing, Graphic Arts, Interior Design, Jewelry, Lettering, Painting, Printmaking, Sculpture, Silversmithing
Summer School: Dir, Dr Jim Flint

WEST VIRGINIA

ATHENS

CONCORD COLLEGE, Art Department,* 24712. Tel 304-384-3115. *Head Dept* Maynard R Coiner, MFA; *Assoc Prof* Gerald C Arrington, MFA; *Asst Prof* Sheila M Chipley, EdD
Estab 1872, dept estab 1925; pub; D & E; ent req HS dipl; degrees BA and BS 4 yrs; scholarships; SC 32, LC 3; enrl non-maj 200, maj 60, D 60
Tuition: Res—$182 per sem; campus res—room and board $967 per sem; nonres—$652 per sem; campus res—room and board $1437 per sem
Courses: †Advertising Design, †Art Education, Art History, Calligraphy, Ceramics, Collage, †Commercial Art, Constructions, Drawing, Graphic Arts, Graphic Design, Handicrafts, History of Art & Archaeology, Illustration, Jewelry, Lettering, Printmaking, Sculpture, Teacher Training
Summer School: Tui $80 for term of 5 wks beginning June. Courses—varied

BETHANY

BETHANY COLLEGE, Art Department,* 26032. Tel 304-829-7000. *Chmn* Walter L Kornowski, MFA; *Asst Prof* Wesley Wagner; *Lectr* Robert Nicoll
Estab 1840, dept estab 1958; den; D; ent req HS dipl; degrees BA and BS 4 yrs; scholarships; SC 27, LC 7; enrl D 136, non-maj 106, maj 30
Tuition: Res—undergrad $4900 per yr, $2450 per sem, $132 per hr; nonres—undergrad $3420 per yr, $1710 per sem, $50 per hr, grad $107 per hr over 16 hrs; campus res—room and board $1260
Courses: †Advertising Design, †Art Education, Art History, Calligraphy, Ceramics, †Commercial Art, Drawing, Graphic Design, Illustration, Jewelry, Lettering, Mixed Media, Painting, Photography, Printmaking, Sculpture, †Teacher Training
Summer School: Dir, Joseph M Kurey. Tui $50 per hr for two 5 wk summer terms and an 11 wk independent study period. Courses—Independent Studies, Seminars, Tutorials

BLUEFIELD

BLUEFIELD STATE COLLEGE, Art Department, 24701. Tel 304-325-7102. *Chmn Dept* Allen A Jonas, MFA; *Instr* Janet Littlejohn, MA
Estab 1895; pub; D & E; ent req HS dipl, 18 yrs old; degrees BA, BS, BS(Educ) and BS(Engineering Technology) 4 yrs; scholarships; SC 14, LC 4; enrl D 125, E 40, non-maj 150, maj 10, others 5
Courses: †Art Education, Art History, Ceramics, Drawing, Painting, Photography, Printmaking, Sculpture, Teacher Training
Adult Hobby Classes: Courses—Drawing, Painting, Photography, Silk-screen
Children's Classes: Enrl 10-15; tui $10 per session. Courses—general art; special program for advanced students
Summer School: Enrl 15-20; term of 5 wks beginning June July. Courses—Art Educ & Appreciation (workshops on occasion)

BUCKHANNON

WEST VIRGINIA WESLEYAN COLLEGE, Department of Fine Arts, College Avenue, 26201. Tel 304-473-8049. *Chmn* Ralph B Cook, PhD; *Assoc Prof* William B Oldaker, MA; *Assoc Prof* Michael Thiedeman, MFA; *Assoc Prof* Stephen D Tinelli, MA
Estab 1890; den; D & E; ent req HS dipl, ent exam; degrees BA and MA(Teaching); SC 12, LC 6; enrl non-maj 100, maj 40, grad 3
Tuition: $2700 per yr, $1350 per sem, $100 per hr; campus res—room & board $1600
Courses: Art Education, Art History, Ceramics, Drawing, Graphic Arts, Graphic Design, History of Art & Archaeology, Jewelry, Painting, Photography, Printmaking, Sculpture, Teacher Training, Theatre Arts
Summer School: Dir, Dr Kenneth Welliver. Courses—Art Education, Art History, Studio Arts

CHARLESTON

UNIVERSITY OF CHARLESTON, Art Department, (Formerly Morris Harvey College) 2300 MacCorkles Ave SE, 25304. Tel 304-346-9471. *Coordr* Henry C Keeling. Instrs FT 2, PT 3
Estab 1888; pvt; D & E; ent req usual col req; degrees 4 yr; enrl maj 35, others 150
Tuition: $60 per sem hr
Courses: Art Education, Art History, Ceramics, Painting, Printmaking, Sculpture, Advanced Studio, Art Appreciation, Color Theory, Design
Summer School: Tui $60 per sem hr for sessions of 3 wks beginning May 26, June 16, July 7, July 28

ELKINS

DAVIS AND ELKINS COLLEGE, Department of Art, 26241. Tel 304-636-1900, Ext 254. *Chmn* Jesse F Reed; *Div of Arts* Robert C Weber. Instrs FT 1, PT 3
Den; D; ent req HS dipl; degrees BA 4 yrs; scholarships; SC 15, LC 5; enrl maj 12
Tuition: $3175 per yr; campus res $1600
Courses: Art Education, Art History, Ceramics, Drawing, Graphic Arts, Painting, Sculpture, Teacher Training
Adult Hobby Classes: Enrl 90
Summer School: 2, 4 and 6 wk terms beginning July. Courses—Basketry, Caning, Pottery, Weaving, plus special summer workshop in mountain crafts

FAIRMONT

FAIRMONT STATE COLLEGE, Art Department, 26554. Tel 304-367-4000. *Chairperson* Dr Leta Carson; *Instructor* James Brooks, MFA; *Instructor* John Clovis, MFA; *Instructor* Dr Stephen Smigocki, PhD; *Instructor* Barry Snyder, MFA
Pub; D & E; ent req HS dipl; degrees BA(Art Educ) and BS(Graphics, Fine Arts) 4 yrs; scholarships; enrl D maj 35, non-maj 15
Tuition: Res—undergrad $149 per sem, $16 per cr hr; nonres—undergrad $599 per sem, $54 per cr hr; campus residency available
Courses: Advertising Design, †Art Education, Art History, Ceramics, Commercial Art, Drawing, Graphic Arts, Painting, Photography, Printmaking, Sculpture, Watercolor
Children's Classes: Enrl 60; tui $15 per student. Courses—offered E and summer

GLENVILLE

GLENVILLE STATE COLLEGE, Department of Art, High St, 26351. Tel 304-462-7361, Ext 243 & 244. *Prof* Gary Gillespie, PhD; *Prof* Charles C Scott, MFA; *Asst Prof* James W Rogers, MFA; *Instructor* George D Harper, MA
Estab 1872, dept estab 1952; pub; D & E; ent req HS dipl; degrees AB 4 yrs, AA 2 yrs; scholarships; SC 25, LC 3; enrl D 128, E 55, non-maj 25, maj 60
Tuition: Res—undergrad $330 per yr, $165 per sem; nonres—undergrad $1270 per yr, $635 per sem; campus residency available
Courses: Art Education, Art History, †Ceramics, Drawing, Graphic Arts, Jewelry, Lettering, †Painting, Photography, Printmaking, Sculpture, Textile Design, Weaving

HUNTINGTON

MARSHALL UNIVERSITY, Department of Art, 16th St and Third Ave, 25701. Tel 304-696-6760.
Estab 1903; pub; ent req HS grad; degrees BFA and MA in art educ and studio 4 yrs; enrl maj incl grad 275
Tuition: Res—$188 per sem; nonres—$683; campus residency available
Courses: Art Education, Art History, Ceramics, Drawing, Graphic Arts, Painting, Sculpture, Design
Summer School: Tui $68 for 6 sem hrs, non-res $306 for two 5 wk terms

INSTITUTE

WEST VIRGINIA STATE COLLEGE, Art Department,* 25112. Tel 304-766-3000. *Chmn* Cubert Smith
D & E; ent req HS dipl; degrees AB(Art) and BSEd(Art) 4 yrs; scholarships; SC 26, LC 11
Tuition: Res—$125 per sem; nonres—$635 per sem; campus res available
Courses: Art Education, Ceramics, Commercial Art, Drawing, Graphic Arts, History of Art & Archaeology, Jewelry, Painting, Photography, Sculpture, Stage Design, Teacher Training, Textile Design, Theatre Arts
Children's Classes: Tui $10 for 10 wk course
Summer School: Enrl 50; tui nonres $58 for two 5 wk terms. Courses—flexible

MONTGOMERY

WEST VIRGINIA INSTITUTE OF TECHNOLOGY, Creative Arts Department, 25136. Tel 304-442-3257. *Head Dept* Arthur Ray Pierce
Estab 1896; pub; ent req HS grad; degrees AS, BA and BS 2-4 yrs; scholarships; enrl 3500 (total)
Courses: Ceramics, Painting, Art Appreciation, Design

MORGANTOWN

WEST VIRGINIA UNIVERSITY, Division of Art, Creative Arts Center, 26506. Tel 304-293-3140. *Chmn* Urban Couch, MFA; *Prof* Robert Anderson, MFA; *Prof* Peter Charles, MFA; *Prof* John Clarkson, MA; *Prof* Michael Dupree, MFA; *Prof* David Faber, MFA; *Prof* Ben Freedman, MA; *Prof* Clifford Harvey, BFA; *Prof* Tom Nakashima, MFA; *Prof* Margaret Rajam, PhD; *Prof* Bernie Schultz, MA; *Prof* Eve Sinail, MFA; *Prof* William Thomas, PhD; *Prof* Stephen Lawson, MFA
Estab 1867, dept estab 1950; pub; D & E; ent req HS dipl; degrees BA(Art Educ) and BFA 4 yrs, MA(Art) and MFA(Art) 2-4 yrs; grad degrees; enrl D 250, maj 250, grad 50
Tuition: Res—undergrad $230 per sem, grad $245; nonres—undergrad $740 per sem, grad $765; campus residency available
Courses: †Art Education, Art History, †Ceramics, Drawing, †Graphic Design, †Painting, †Printmaking, †Sculpture, Basic Design

PARKERSBURG

PARKERSBURG COMMUNITY COLLEGE, Art Department, Route 5 Box 167-A, 26101. Tel 304-424-8000. *Chmn* Ed Pitner, MA; *Instr* Henry Aglio, MFA; *Instr* Linda Cundiff, MFA; *Vis Prof* V C Dibble, pottery - 1979
Estab 1961, dept estab 1973; pub; D & E; ent req HS dipl plus diagnostic tests in reading, math and English; degrees AA 2 yrs; scholarships; SC 25, LC 5; enrl D 60, E 80, non-maj 125, maj 8
Tuition: Res—undergrad $284 per yr, $142 for 12 hrs or over, $12 per hr; nonres—undergrad $1224 per yr, $612 for 12 hrs or over, $51 per hr; no campus res
Courses: Aesthetics, Art History, Ceramics, Costume Design & Construction, Drafting, Drawing, Graphic Arts, Jewelry, Lettering, Painting, Photography, Printmaking, Sculpture, Stage Design
Summer School: Enrl 19; tui $36 for term of 8 wks beginning June. Courses—Ceramics, Drawing, Painting

SALEM

SALEM COLLEGE, Art Department, 26426. Tel 304-782-5336. *Chmn* Harold Reed
Estab 1880; pvt; D & E; ent req HS dipl; degrees AA 2 yrs, BA 4 yrs; scholarships
Courses: †Art Education, Ceramics, Commercial Art, Drawing, Graphic Arts, Handicrafts, Jewelry, Painting, Photography, Printmaking, Sculpture, †Teacher Training

SHEPHERDSTOWN

SHEPHERD COLLEGE, Art Department, 25443. Tel 304-876-2511, Ext 294. *Chmn* Dr R L Jones. Instrs FT 5, PT 5
Estab 1872; pub; D; ent req HS dipl; degrees AA and AS, BA, BA(Educ) and BS 4 yrs; SC 16, LC 7; enrl maj 80
Tuition: $366 per yr; campus res $1787 per yr
Courses: Art Education, Art History, Ceramics, Commercial Art, Drawing, Graphic Arts, Handicrafts, Jewelry, Lettering, Painting, Photography, Printmaking, Sculpture, Teacher Training, Aesthetic Criticism, Applied Design, Art Therapy, Design
Summer School: Dir, Dr George Cordon. Tui $71 for two 5 wk sessions beginning June. Courses—offered on demand

WEST LIBERTY

WEST LIBERTY STATE COLLEGE, Art Department, 26074. Tel 304-336-8019. *Chmn* Bernie K Peace, MFA; *Prof* Ernest D Comiskey, MFA; *Assoc Prof* Karen Rychlewski, MFA; *Asst Prof* R Paul Padgett, MA; *Instructor* Daniel J Cowen, MA
Estab 1836; pub; D & E; ent req HS dipl, score of 14 on ACT test or upper three fourths of HS class; degrees BA and BS 4 yrs; scholarships; SC 40, LC 5; enrl D 855, E 140, non-maj 900, maj 90, others 12
Tuition: Res—undergrad $370 per yr, $185 per sem, approx $20 per cr hr; nonres—undergrad $1310 per yr, $655 per sem, approx $78 per cr hr; campus residency available
Courses: Advertising Design, Art Education, Art History, Ceramics, Collage, †Commercial Art, Display, Drawing, Film, Graphic Arts, Graphic Design, Handicrafts, History of Art & Archaeology, Illustration, Jewelry, Lettering, Mixed Media, Painting, Photography, Printmaking, Sculpture, Stage Design, †Teacher Training, Theatre Arts
Summer School: Dir, Alfred R de Jaager. Tui res $16 per sem hr, nonres $52 per sem hr. Courses—Art Education, Drawing, Painting, Special Education

WISCONSIN

APPLETON

LAWRENCE UNIVERSITY, Department of Art, 54911. Tel 414-739-3681. *Chmn* Arthur Thrall. Instrs FT 3
Estab 1847; ent req HS performance, CEEB scores, recommendation; degrees BA 4 yrs; SC 8, LC 17
Tuition: $6180 includes room and board per 3 term yr
Courses: Art Education, Art History, Ceramics, Drawing, Painting, Photography, Printmaking, Sculpture, Composition, Design, Metalwork

BELOIT

BELOIT COLLEGE, Department of Art, 53511. Tel 608-365-3391, Ext 677 and 678. *Head Dept* Jarrett W Strawn. Instrs FT 4, PT 1
Estab 1847; pvt; D & E; ent req top third of class, 3 yrs foreign language, 4 yrs English, SAT or ACT score encouraged but not required; degrees BA, BS & MAT 4 yrs; SC 14, LC 10; enrl maj 30, gen col enrl 900
Tuition: $3300 for two terms; campus res—room & board $1280 for two terms
Courses: Architecture, Art History, Ceramics, Drawing, Graphic Arts, Museum Staff Training, Painting, Photography, Sculpture, American Art, Design, Far Eastern Art
Children's Classes: Enrl 20; both terms $5-$10
Summer School: Summer study by special arrangement

DE PERE

SAINT NORBERT COLLEGE, Art Department, 54115. *Head Dept* X G Colevechio. Instrs FT 4
Estab 1898; pvt den; D; ent req HS dipl, ent exam; degrees BA 4 yrs; scholarships; SC 19, LC 5; enrl D 60, maj 60
Tuition: $2950 per yr; campus res $1194-$1584 includes room & board
Courses: Aesthetics, Art Education, Art History, Ceramics, Drawing, Film, Graphic Arts, Graphic Design, Jewelry, Painting, Photography, Sculpture, Teacher Training
Summer School: Dir, John Giovannini. Terms of 3 or 5 wks beginning June. Courses—Art Education, Ceramics, Drawing, History of Art, Painting, Sculpture

EAU CLAIRE

UNIVERSITY OF WISCONSIN-EAU CLAIRE, Department of Art, Park and Garfield Aves, 54701. Tel 715-836-3277. *Chmn* Charles Campbell. Instrs FT 16, PT 1
Estab 1916; pub; D & E; ent req HS dipl, ent exam; degrees BA and BFA 4 yrs; scholarships; SC 31, LC 12; enrl maj 260
Tuition: Res $838 per yr, nonres $2860 per yr
Courses: Advertising Design, Art Education, Art History, Ceramics, Drawing, Painting, Printmaking, Sculpture, Fibers, Metalsmithing
Adult Hobby Classes: Ceramics, Painting
Summer School: Two 4 wk sessions beginning June 16 and July 14. Courses—Art Appreciation, Art Education, Art History, Drawing, Painting, Pottery, Watercolor

FOND DU LAC

MARIAN COLLEGE, Art Department, 45 S National Ave, Fond Du Lac, WI. (Mailing Add: 475 Gillett St, Fond Du Lac, WI 54935) Tel 414-921-3900, Ext 254. *Coordr* Sr Mary Neff, MA; *Chmn Arts & Letters* Henry L Lindborg; *Prof* Julienne Rompf; *Instr* Sr Jean Brenner, MA
Estab 1936; pvt; E; ent req HS dipl, ACT or SAT; degrees BA and BA(Art Educ) 4 yrs; scholarships; SC 20, LC 12; enrl D 107, E 35, maj 6
Tuition: $1750 per yr, $875 per sem; campus residency available
Courses: Art Education, †Fine Arts
Children's Classes: In Relationship with Art Education

GREEN BAY

UNIVERSITY OF WISCONSIN-GREEN BAY, Visual Arts Discipline, Col of Creative Communication, 54302. *Head Dept* Robert Pum. Instrs FT 7, PT 4
EStab 1970; pub; D & E; ent req HS dipl, ent exam; degrees BA and BS 4 yrs; SC 29, LC 3; enrl D 5500
Courses: Aesthetics, Art Education, Ceramics, Drawing, Graphic Arts, Jewelry, Painting, Photography, Printmaking, Sculpture, Stage Design, Teacher Training, Textile Design, Theatre Arts, Styles
Summer School: Courses—vary

KENOSHA

UNIVERSITY OF WISCONSIN-PARKSIDE, Art Discipline, Fine Arts Division, 53140. Tel 414-553-2457. *Chmn* Rollin Jansky, MS; *Assoc Prof* John Satre Murphy, MFA; *Asst Prof* Dennis Bayuzick, MFA; *Asst Prof* Douglas DeVinny, MFA; *Asst Prof* David V Holmes, MFA
Estab 1965; pub; D & E; ent req HS dipl; degrees BA and BS 4 yrs; SC 25, LC 6
Tuition: Res—undergrad $247 per sem, $35 per hr; nonres—undergrad $895 per sem, $107 per hr; no campus res
Courses: Aesthetics, Art Education, Art History, Ceramics, Drawing, Film, Jewelry, Painting, Printmaking, Sculpture, Teacher Training, Textile Design, Life Modeling
Summer School: Tui $34 res, $101 nonres for term of 8 wks beginning mid June. Courses—vary from summer to summer

LA CROSSE

UNIVERSITY OF WISCONSIN-LA CROSSE, Art Department,* 1725 State St, 54601. Tel 608-785-8230. *Chmn* Leonard R Stach
Estab 1905; pub; D & E; ent req HS dipl; degrees BA and BS 4 yrs; scholarships; SC 25, LC 5; enrl (univ) 7600
Tuition: Res—undergrad $420 per sem; nonres—undergrad $950 per sem
Courses: Art Education, Ceramics, Drawing, Graphic Arts, History of Art & Archaeology, Jewelry, Painting, Sculpture, Theatre Arts

VITERBO COLLEGE, Art Department, 815 S Ninth, 54601. Tel 608-784-0040. *Chmn* Sr Carlene Unser, MA; *Assoc Prof* Tim Crane, MFA; *Asst Prof* Jim Knipe, MFA; *Instructor* Diane Crane; *Instructor* Jan Knipe, MFA; *Artist in Res* William Bailey; *Artist in Res* Gabriel Laderman; *Artist in Res* Jerry Liebling; *Artist in Res* Walter Nottingham; *Artist in Res* Marty Tucker; *Artist in Res* Murray Weiss
Estab 1890; pvt; D & E; degrees BA and BAEd 4 yrs; SC 10-12, LC 6; enrl D 55, maj 55
Tuition: $1990 per yr; campus res—room & board $1285
Courses: Advertising Design, †Art Education, Art History, Ceramics, Commercial Art, Costume Design & Construction, Drawing, Graphic Arts, Illustration, Painting, Photography, Printmaking, Sculpture, Teacher Training, Theatre Arts, Fibers, Weaving
Summer School: Tui $40 per sem hr. Courses—summer catalog sent on request

WESTERN WISCONSIN TECHNICAL INSTITUTE, Graphics Division, Sixth & Vine Sts, 54601. Tel 608-785-9178. *Chmn* Torval E Hendrickson, MA; *Instr* Valerie Burman, MFA; *Instr* Boyd DeGeest, BS; *Instr* Rich Knox, MS; *Instr* Alan Kraning, MFA; *Instr* Henry Michaels, MA; *Instr* John Syverson, BA
Estab 1911, dept estab 1964; pub; D & E; ent req HS dipl or GED; degrees AAS 2 yrs; scholarships; SC & LC 16; enrl D 130, E 145, non-maj 132, maj 143
Tuition: Res—undergrad $442 per yr, $6 per cr; nonres—undergrad $1 per hr; campus residence available
Courses: Advertising Design, †Commercial Art, Display, Drafting, Drawing, Film, †Graphic Arts, Graphic Design, Illustration, Intermedia, Lettering, Mixed Media, Painting, Photography, Stage Design, Video
Adult Hobby Classes: Enrl 264; tui $9 per cr. Courses—Color Photo Printing, Home Movie Making, Painting, Photography
Summer School: Dir, T E Hendrickson. Courses—varied

MADISON

EDGEWOOD COLLEGE, Art Department, 855 Woodrow St, 53711. Tel 608-257-4861, Ext 207. *Chmn* Sr M Stephanie Stauder; *Prof* Sr Alice O'Rourke, PhD; *Instructor* Sr Ruella Bouchonville; *Instructor* Sr Elizabeth Devine; *Instructor* Sr M Teresita Kelly
Estab 1941; den; D & E; ent req HS dipl, SAT; degrees BA or BS 4 yrs; institutional grants based on financial needs; SC 20, LC 4; enrl D & E 500 (total), non-maj 70, maj 20
Tuition: $2600 campus residency available
Courses: Art Education, Art History, Ceramics, Drawing, Graphic Arts, Graphic Design, Lettering, Painting, Photography, Printmaking, Sculpture, Teacher Training
Summer School: Dir, Dr Joseph Schmiedicki. Tui $93 per cr. Courses—varied

MADISON AREA TECHNICAL COLLEGE, Communication Arts,* 211 N Carroll St, 53703. Tel 608-266-5002. *Chmn* Charles M Haycock, MA; *Instr* Bruce Ellinger, BS; *Instr* William Feeny, MA; *Instr* John Fritsch, MFA; *Instr* Joann Hayes, BS; *Instr* Owen Kampen, BS; *Instr* Roberta Meyer, MFA; *Instr* Don Trudell, MFA
Estab 1911; pub; D & E; ent req HS dipl; degrees AA 2 yrs commercial art-layout-design; scholarships; SC 45, LC 12; enrl D 5300, E 23,000 (part-time)
Tuition: Res—$27 per cr, $9 per cr (in district); nonres—$58 per cr; no campus res
Courses: Advertising Design, Aesthetics, Architecture, Art History, Calligraphy, Ceramics, †Commercial Art, Conceptual Art, Display, †Drafting, Drawing, Fashion Arts, Film, Goldsmithing, Occupational Therapy, Painting
Adult Hobby Classes: Enrl 1000. Courses—same as regular session
Summer School: Tui $7.60 per cr for 6 wks. Courses—selected art

UNIVERSITY OF WISCONSIN, MADISON
—Department of Art, School of Educ, 6241 Humanities Bldg, 455 N Park, 53706. Tel 608-262-1660. *Chmn* Victor Kord. Instrs FT 40, PT 18
Estab 1911; pub; degrees BS(Art, Art Educ), BFA, MA(Art, Art Educ), MFA, PhD(Art Educ); scholarships and fels; SC 47, LC 2, GC 19; enrl maj 850
Courses: Art Education, Ceramics, Drawing, Painting, Photography, Sculpture, Art Metal, Design, Etching, Glassblowing, Lithography, Photo-Offset, Relief Printing, Serigraphy, Stage Design and Lighting, Typography, Watercolor, Woodworking
—Department of Art, College of Letters and Science, 800 University Ave, 53706. Tel 608-263-2340. *Chmn Dept* Jane C Hutchison, PhD; *Prof* Robert Beetem, PhD; *Prof* James Dennis, PhD; *Prof* Frank Horlbeck, PhD; *Assoc Prof* Warren Moon, PhD; *Asst Prof* Barbara Buenger; *Asst Prof* Gail Geiger; *Asst Prof* Narciso Menocal, PhD
Estab 1848, dept estab 1925; pub; D; ent req HS dipl; degrees BA 4 yrs, MA 1 yr, PhD 3 yrs; scholarships; LC 37, GC 4; enrl 2372, maj 61, grad 24
Tuition: Res—undergrad $439 per sem, $37 per cr, grad $619 per sem, $77 per cr; nonres—undergrad $1588 per sem, $132 per cr, grad $1936 per sem, $242 per cr; campus res—room & board $1635 per yr
Courses: Architecture, †Art History, Lettering, Graphic Production Technique, Print Illustration
Summer School: Chmn, Jane C Hutchison. Term of 8 wks beginning June 19. Courses—American Painting, Ancient and Medieval Art, Netherlandish Painting of the 17th Century, Renaissance to Modern Art, Roman Art
—School of Family Resources and Consumer Sciences, Environ, Textiles, and Design Prog Area, 1300 Linden Dr, 53706. Tel 608-262-3190, 262-2651. *Prog Coordr* Emma M Jordre, MS; *Prof* Robert P Bartholomew, MFA; *Prof* Agatha A Norton, MS; *Prof* Mary Roach-Higgins, MA; *Prof* Mary G Stieglitz, PhD; *Prof* Manfred Wentz, MA; *Assoc Prof* Jane Graff, MA; *Assoc Prof* Patricia K Mansfield, MS; *Asst Prof* Virginia T Boyd, PhD; *Asst Prof* Marion Brown; *Asst Prof* James Buesing, MA; *Asst Prof* Joyce O Marquess, MFA; *Asst Prof* Betty Wass
D & E; ent req HS dipl; degrees BS 4 yrs, MS 2 yrs; scholarships; SC 23, LC 3, GC

300; enrl D 862-978, E 53, grad 25
Tuition: Res—undergrad $439 per sem, $37 per cr, grad $619 per sem, $77 per cr; nonres—undergrad $1588 per sem, $132 per cr, grad $1936 per sem, $242 per cr; campus res—room & board $1635 per yr
Courses: Costume Design & Construction, Handicrafts, Interior Design, Textile Design, Apparel Design, Retailing, Textile Science, Textiles and Clothing, Weaving
Summer School: Tui $30-$112 per cr hr for term of several lengths. Courses—Designing for the Elderly, Experimental Textile Design, Human Factors in Design, Interior Design, Physiology of Textiles and Clothing, Visual Representation for Designers, Weaving

MANITOWOC

SILVER LAKE COLLEGE, Art Department, 2406 S Alverno Rd, 54220. Tel 414-684-6691. *Assoc Prof* Sr Andree Du Charme, MA; *Asst Prof* Sr Susan Farmer, MFA; *Instr* Sr Mariella Eroman, MFA
Estab 1936, dept estab 1959; pvt; D & E; ent req HS dipl, ACT or SAT; degrees AA(Commercial Art) 2 yrs, BS or BA(Studio Art) and BS or BA(Art Educ) 4 yrs; SC 21, LC 6; enrl D 50, E 10, non-maj 25, maj 25
Tuition: Res and nonres—undergrad $2600 per yr, $1300 per sem
Courses: Aesthetics, †Art Education, Art History, Calligraphy, Ceramics, †Commercial Art, Drawing, Film, Graphic Arts, Graphic Design, Handicrafts, Jewelry, Lettering, Mixed Media, Painting, Photography, Printmaking, Sculpture, Teacher Training, Textile Design
Children's Classes: Enrl 40; tui $2 per wk. Courses—Clay, Drawing, Fibers, Photography, Sculpture
Summer School: Dir, Sr Martina. Term of 6 wks beginning June 22. Courses—Art Metal, Children's Classes, Elementary Art Education

MARINETTE

UNIVERSITY OF WISCONSIN CENTER, Marinette County, Bay Shore Rd, 54143. Tel 715-735-7477. *Head Dept* James La Malfa, MFA
Estab 1850, dept estab 1946; pub; D & E; ent req HS dipl; degrees AA 2 yrs; scholarships
Tuition: Res—undergrad $380 per sem; nonres—undergrad $1390 per sem; campus res—room & board $630
Courses: Art History, Ceramics, Drawing, Painting, Photography, Printmaking, Sculpture, Survey of Art, Watercolor
Summer School: Dir, William A Schmidtke. Tui $25 per cr for term of 6 wks beginning June 12. Courses—Beginning and advanced photography plus courses in other disciplines

MEDFORD

UNIVERSITY OF WISCONSIN CENTER-MEDFORD, Art Department, 625 Donald St, 54451. Tel 715-748-3600. *Dir* Michael D Elvestrom, MA & MFA
Estab 1973, dept estab 1973; pub; D & E; ent req HS dipl; degrees AS and AA 2 yrs; scholarships; enrl 175-200 total
Tuition: Res—undergrad $380 per sem, $32 per cr; nonres—undergrad $1390 per sem, $116 per cr; no campus res
Courses: Art Education, Art History, Ceramics, Collage, Commercial Art, Constructions, Drawing, Graphic Arts, Graphic Design, Handicrafts, History of Art & Archaeology, Lettering, Mixed Media, Painting, Photography, Printmaking, Sculpture, Silversmithing, Theatre Arts, Leather, Metal, Weaving
Adult Hobby Classes: Enrl varies; Over 62 years of age (audit free of charge). Courses—Crafts, Painting

MENOMONIE

UNIVERSITY OF WISCONSIN-STOUT, Art Department, 54751. Tel 715-232-1141. *Head Dept* James McCormick, MFA; *Prof* Orazio Fumagalli, PhD; *Prof* Todd Boppel, MFA; *Assoc Prof* Doug Cumming, MFA; *Assoc Prof* John Perri, MFA; *Assoc Prof* William Schulman, ABD; *Assoc Prof* Charles Wimmer, MFA
Estab 1893, dept estab 1965; pub; E; ent req HS dipl; degrees BA(Art) and BS(Art Educ) 4 yrs, emphasis interior or industrial design 4 yrs; SC 60, LC 6; enrl D 24, non-maj 400, maj 275
Tuition: Res—undergrad $363 per sem, $30 per cr hr, grad $425 per sem, $589 per cr hr; nonres—undergrad $866 per sem, grad $849 per sem; campus res—room & board $705 per yr
Courses: Aesthetics, †Art Education, Art History, Ceramics, Conceptual Art, Constructions, Display, Drawing, Fashion Arts, Goldsmithing, Graphic Arts, Graphic Design, History of Art & Archaeology, Illustration, †Industrial Design, Jewelry, Mixed Media, Painting, Printmaking, Sculpture, Silversmithing, †Teacher Training
Children's Classes: Courses—Sat classes in Art (Media changes and Drama)
Summer School: Enrl varies with class; tui res $144, nonres $432 for term of 8 wks beginning June 9 through August 1. Courses—Drawing, Fundamentals of Design, Painting, Sculpture

MILWAUKEE

ALVERNO COLLEGE, Art Department,* 3401 S 39 St, 53215. Tel 414-671-5400. *Chmn Arts & Humanities Div* Christine Trimberger
Estab 1948; pvt; W only in degree program; D & E; ent req GPA, class rank and ACT or SAT; degrees BA 4 yrs (or 128 cr); scholarships; SC 20, LC 5; enrl D 200, E 50, maj 35
Tuition: $2350 per yr; campus res—room and board $1100 per yr
Courses: Art Education, Ceramics, Drawing, Handicrafts, History of Art & Archaeology, Painting, Printmaking, Sculpture, Stage Design, Teacher Training, Enameling (Cloisonne), General Crafts, Introduction to Visual Art, Metal Working, Weaving
Summer School: Term June to August. Courses—Art Education, Studio Art

CARDINAL STRITCH COLLEGE, Art Department, 53217. Tel 414-352-5400, Ext 331. *Head Dept* Sr M Thomasita Fessler, DFA; *Prof* Irene Kilmurry, MS; *Assoc Prof* Claudia M Gorecki, MS; *Assoc Prof* John Tryba, MAE; *Instructor* Sr Madonna Balestrieri, MA; *Instructor* Mildred Tryba, BA; *Lectr* Carroll Brown; *Lectr* Paul Calhoun; *Lectr* Joanne Cubbs; *Lectr* Marilyn Drucker; *Lectr* David Hackett; *Lectr* Marianne Rodwell, BS
Estab 1937; den; D & E; ent req HS dipl, ent exam; degrees BA and BFA 4 yrs, AA 2 yrs; scholarships; SC 29, LC 17; enrl maj 98
Tuition: Undergrad $1100 per sem, $60 per cr hr (1-6 hrs), $85 per cr hr, $7 and up per hr; grad $70 per cr hr (1-6 hr), $90 per cr hr, $7 and up per hr; campus res—room & board $1120-$1270 per yr
Courses: Aesthetics, Art Education, Art History, Calligraphy, Ceramics, Commercial Art, Constructions, Costume Design & Construction, Drawing, Handicrafts, Illustration, Jewelry, Lettering, Mixed Media, Painting, Photography, Printmaking, Sculpture, Textile Design, Design, Typography, Weaving
Adult Hobby Classes: Batik, Enameling, Interior Design, Mixed Media, Painting, Photography, Sign Painting, Weaving
Children's Classes: Tui $35 per child. Courses—traditional media plus various crafts
Summer School: Term of 6 wks beginning June 19th. Courses—Composition, Drawing, Sculpture, Summer Foreign Tour (possible col cr)

CONCORDIA COLLEGE, Art Department, 53208. Tel 414-344-3400. *Chmn* William L Chandler, MS
Estab 1881, dept estab 1971; den; D & E; ent req HS dipl; degrees AA 2 yrs; SC 6, LC 1; enrl non-maj 100, maj 5
Tuition: $1100 per sem, $80 per hr; campus res—room & board $790-$905 per sem
Courses: Art History, Drawing, Handicrafts, Painting, Sculpture, Design
Summer School: Terms of 5 wks. Courses—Drawing & Painting (outdoors)

MILWAUKEE AREA TECHNICAL COLLEGE, Graphic & Applied Arts Div, 53203. Tel 414-278-6432. *Head Dept* Harold A Milbrath, MFA; *Instructor* Howard Austin, BA; *Instructor* William Bonifay, BS; *Instructor* Mary Anna Brooks, MFA; *Instructor* William Crandall, MA; *Instructor* Leland Felber, BS; *Instructor* Geraldine Geischer, MA; *Instructor* Chris Hansen, BFA; *Instructor* Hans Krommenhoek, MFA; *Instructor* Jos Niesl; *Instructor* J Strachota, MS
Estab 1912, dept estab 1958; pub; D & E; ent req HS dipl; degrees AA 2 yrs; financial aid; enrl D 240, E 150
Tuition: $400 per yr, $200 per sem; tui and fees approx $12 per cr; no campus res
Courses: †Advertising Design, Calligraphy, Ceramics, †Commercial Art, Display, Drawing, Film, Graphic Design, Illustration, Jewelry, Lettering, Photography, Silversmithing
Adult Hobby Classes: Tui $12 per cr

MILWAUKEE SCHOOL OF THE ARTS, 207 N Milwaukee St, 53202. Tel 414-276-7889. *Dir* Jack H White, BFA; *Chmn Foundations Dept* Polly Ewens, MFA; *Chmn Fine Arts Dept* C W Peckenpaugh, BFA; *Chmn Design Dept* Mark Koerner, BFA. Instrs FT 10, PT 15
Estab 1974; pvt; D & E; ent req HS dipl, portfolio, letter of intent; degrees BFA and MSA 4 yrs; scholarships; enrl D 212, E 85, non-maj 85, maj 212
Tuition: $1600 per yr, $800 per sem, PT proportionate; no campus res
Courses: †Advertising Design, Art History, †Drawing, †Illustration, †Industrial Design, †Interior Design, †Painting, Photography, †Printmaking, †Sculpture
Adult Hobby Classes: Enrl 85; tui $125 per course. Courses—Advertising, Art History, Drawing, Illustration, Painting, Printmaking, Sculpture

MOUNT MARY COLLEGE, Art Department,* 2900 N Menomonee River Parkway, 53222. Tel 414-258-4810. *Chmn* Sr Regine Collins, MA; *Prof* Sr M Remy Revor, MFA; *Assoc Prof* Sr M Rosemarita Heubner, MFA; *Asst Prof* Suzanne Harker, MA; *Asst Prof* Joseph Rozman, MFA; *Instr* Sr M Angelee Fuchs, MA; *Instr* Deirdre Lee Kozlowski, MS
Estab 1913, dept estab 1929; den; D & E; ent req HS dipl; degrees BA 4 yrs; scholarships; SC 22, LC 12; enrl D 200, E 30, non-maj 50, maj 150
Tuition: $1375 per yr (includes board), $950 per sem, $80 per cr; campus res available
Courses: Art Education, Art History, Calligraphy, Ceramics, Costume Design & Construction, Drafting, Drawing, Fashion Arts, Film, Goldsmithing, Graphic Arts, Handicrafts, Illustration, Interior Design, Jewelry, Occupational Therapy, Painting, Photography, Printmaking, Sculpture, Silversmithing, Stage Design, Teacher Training, Textile Design, Art Therapy, Enameling, Fiber Arts, Weaving
Summer School: Dir, Sister Ellen Lorenz. Enrl 120; tui $65 per cr for term of 6 wks beginning June. Courses—Art Therapy, Ceramics, Design, Drawing, Environmental Design, Fiber Arts, Photography, Watercolor

UNIVERSITY OF WISCONSIN-MILWAUKEE, Department of Art, School of Fine Arts, 53201. Tel 414-963-4200. *Dean* Robert W Corrigan. Instrs FT 36, PT 6
Degrees BS(Art), BS(Art Educ), BFA(Art), BFA with teachers cert, MA(Art), MS(Art Educ), MFA(Art), MFA with teachers cert; enrl maj 860
Courses: Art Education, Ceramics, Drawing, Painting, Photography, Printmaking, Sculpture, Design, Fibers, Metals, Visual Communication

OSHKOSH

UNIVERSITY OF WISCONSIN-OSHKOSH, Department of Art, 54901. Tel 414-424-2222. *Chmn* Dr Franklin R Utech. Instrs FT 24
Estab 1871; pub; D & E; ent req HS dipl; degrees BA, BAE and BS(Art) 4 yrs, BFA 82 cr; scholarships for grad students; SC 56, LC 14, GC 31; enrl D 10,500, E 2500, maj 300, grad 15, minors 50
Tuition: Res—undergrad $415 per sem, PT $35 per cr, grad $503 per sem, PT $56 per cr; non-res—undergrad $1425 per sem, PT $119 per cr, grad $1499 per sem, PT $167 per cr; campus residency available
Courses: Advertising Design, Art Education, Art History, Ceramics, Commercial Art, Drawing, Graphic Arts, Jewelry, Lettering, Painting, Photography, Sculpture, Teacher Training, Textile Design, Museology, Woodcraft

PLATTEVILLE

UNIVERSITY OF WISCONSIN-PLATTEVILLE, Department of Fine Art,* Art Bldg 212B, 53818. Tel 608-342-1781. *Chmn* Roger Gottschalk
Estab 1866; pub; D & E; ent req HS dipl, ent exam; degrees BA and BS 4 yrs; SC 30, LC 5, GC 3; enrl maj 105
Tuition: Res—undergrad $796 per yr, grad $894 per yr; nonres—undergrad $2646 per yr, grad $2656 per yr
Courses: Aesthetics, Architecture, Art Education, Ceramics, Drafting, Drawing, Graphic Arts, History of Art & Archaeology, Industrial Design, Jewelry, Painting, Photography, Sculpture, Stage Design, Teacher Training, Theatre Arts
Summer School: Dir, Harold Hutchinson. Enrl 2200; term of 8 wks beginning June. Courses—same as regular session

RIPON

RIPON COLLEGE, Art Department, 54971. Tel 414-748-8110. *Chmn* Dr Erwin Breithaupt. Instrs FT 3
Estab 1851; pvt; D; ent req grad from accredited secondary school, SAT or ACT is recommended, but not required; degrees AB 4 yrs; scholarships and financial aid; SC 13, LC 8; enrl maj 20
Tuition: $5526 comprehensive fee
Courses: Art History, Drawing, Mixed Media, Painting, Printmaking, Design

RIVER FALLS

UNIVERSITY OF WISCONSIN-RIVER FALLS, Art Department, 54022. Tel 715-425-3266. *Chmn* Dr John Buschen; *Prof* William Ammerman, MFA; *Prof* Mary Barrett, MFA; *Prof* Walter Nottingham, MFA; *Prof* Kurt Wild, MFA; *Assoc Prof* Pat Clark, MFA; *Asst Prof* Douglas Johnson, MFA; *Asst Prof* Don Miller, MFA; *Asst Prof* Terrance Schubert, MFA; *Instructor* James Engebretson, MFA
Estab 1874, dept estab 1958; pub; D; ent req HS dipl; degrees BA, BS(Educ), BFA and BS(Liberal Arts) 4 yrs; scholarships; SC 26, LC 18, GC 3; enrl non-maj 250, maj 191
Tuition: Res—undergrad $240 per quarter; nonres—undergrad $780 per quarter; campus residency available
Courses: Aesthetics, †Art Education, Art History, Ceramics, Costume Design & Construction, Drawing, Film, Graphic Design, History of Art & Archaeology, Jewelry, Painting, Photography, Printmaking, Sculpture, Silversmithing, Stage Design, Textile Design, Glass, Weaving
Summer School: Term of 8 wks beginning June 16 to Aug 8. Courses—Art Education, Clay, Drawing, Fiber, Glass, Graphics, Introduction to Art, Sculpture, Silkscreen & Lith, Watercolor

STEVENS POINT

UNIVERSITY OF WISCONSIN-STEVENS POINT, Department of Art, Col of Fine Arts, 2100 Main St, 54481. Tel 715-346-2669. *Head Dept* Henry M Runke, MFA; *Prof* Colleen Garvey, MFA; *Prof* Norman Keats, MFA; *Prof* Herbert Sandmann, MFA; *Prof* Richard Schneider, MFA; *Assoc Prof* Daniel Fabiano, MFA; *Assoc Prof* Gail Fountain, MFA; *Assoc Prof* Gary Hagen, MFA; *Assoc Prof* David L Smith, PhD; *Asst Prof* Robert Boyce; *Asst Prof* Mark Brueggeman, MFA; *Asst Prof* Wayne Halverson, MA; *Asst Prof* Stephen Hankin
Estab 1894; pub; D & E; ent req HS dipl; degrees BA(Fine Arts), BS(Art Educ) and BS(Fine Arts); enrl D 866, non-maj 666, maj 200
Tuition: Campus residency available
Courses: Architecture, †Art Education, Art History, Ceramics, Drawing, Goldsmithing, Graphic Arts, Graphic Design, Handicrafts, Jewelry, Lettering, Painting, Printmaking, Sculpture, Silversmithing, Teacher Training, Textile Design, Glass, Leather, Wood
Children's Classes: Art Workshop
Summer School: Dir, O E Radke. Term of 8 wks beginning June 9. Courses—Ceramics, Design, Drawing, Foundry Workshop, Layout & Lettering, Sculpture. Art Workshop: Aug 3-15 at Pigeon Lake, 2 credits

SUPERIOR

UNIVERSITY OF WISCONSIN-SUPERIOR, Department of Art, 54880. Tel 715-392-8101, Ext 368. *Chmn* Mel Olsen, MFA; *Assoc Prof* James Grittner, MFA; *Assoc Prof* William Morgan, MFA; *Asst Prof* John Freeman, MFA; *Asst Prof* Leonard Petersen, MFA; *Asst Prof* Marjorie Whitsitt, PhD; *Asst Prof* W Pope Wright, MFA; *Instructor* Anthony Pfeiffer, MFA; *Lectr* Marlene Nordstrom, MA; *Lectr* Patricia Spencer, MA
Estab 1896, dept estab 1930; pub; D & E; ent req HS dipl; degrees BS, BS(Art Therapy) and BFA 4 yrs, BFA with cert 5 yrs, MA 5-6 yrs; scholarships; enrl D 250, E 100-125, non-maj 100, maj 150, grad 30
Tuition: Res—undergrad $245 per sem, grad $295; nonres—undergrad $825 per sem, grad $860 per sem; campus residency available
Courses: Advertising Design, †Art Education, †Art History, †Ceramics, Collage, Commercial Art, Conceptual Art, †Costume Design & Construction, Drawing, †Film, †Graphic Arts, †Handicrafts, †Jewelry, Mixed Media, †Occupational Therapy, †Painting, †Photography, †Printmaking, †Sculpture, †Silversmithing, †Stage Design, †Teacher Training, †Textile Design, Theatre Arts, Video, Batik
Adult Hobby Classes: Tui $40 per quarter. Courses—Batik, Blacksmithing, Photography, Rosemaling, Spinning, Stained Glass
Summer School: Tui varies for term of 8 wks beginning June 12th. Courses—All studios plus noncredit ethnic and folk arts institute

WAUKESHA

CARROLL COLLEGE, Art Department, 53186. Tel 414-547-1211, Ext 191. *Chairperson* Marceil Pultorak, MA; *Prof* C Willis Guthrie, MA; *Asst Prof* Philip Krejcarek, MFA; *Lectr* Kathe Kurz, BA; *Lectr* Thomas Selle, MFA; *Vis Prof* Peggy Farrell, graphics; *Vis Prof* Eric Talerice, photography
Estab 1846; pvt; D & E; ent req HS dipl, SAT or ACT; degrees BA; scholarships; SC 21, LC 4; enrl D 1100, E 350
Tuition: Res and nonres—undergrad $3964 per yr; campus res—room & board $1370 per yr
Courses: Art Education, Art History, Calligraphy, Ceramics, Commercial Art, Drawing, History of Art & Archaeology, Jewelry, Painting, Photography, Printmaking, Sculpture, Stage Design, Teacher Training, Textile Design, Theatre Arts, Video, Weaving
Adult Hobby Classes: Enrl 10 per session. Courses—Book Binding, Photographing your Own Art Work
Children's Classes: New program
Summer School: Dir, Dr Gary Stevens. Enrl varies; tui $200 for term of 6 wks. Courses —Drawing, Graphics, Photography

WHITEWATER

UNIVERSITY OF WISCONSIN-WHITEWATER, Department of Art, College of the Arts, 53190. Tel 414-472-1324. *Dean* Raymond E Light. Instrs FT 18
Estab 1868; pub; D & E; ent req HS dipl; degrees BA and BS(Art, Art Educ, Art History), BFA 4 yrs; SC 41, LC 18; enrl D 270, maj 270
Tuition: $701 per yr; campus residency $1322
Courses: Advertising Design, Aesthetics, Art Education, Art History, Ceramics, Commercial Art, Drawing, Film, Graphic Arts, Graphic Design, Illustration, Jewelry, Painting, Photography, Sculpture, Teacher Training, Textile Design, Weaving
Summer School: Tui $50 per cr for term of 8 wks beginning June

WYOMING

CASPER

CASPER COLLEGE, 125 College Dr, 82601. Tel 307-268-2110. *Acting Head* James L Gaither, MEd; *Instructor* Ed Gothberg, MFA; *Instructor* Carolyn J Grimes, MFA; *Instructor* Lynn Munns, MFA; *Instructor* Wilhelm Ossa, MFA
Pub; D & E; ent req HS dipl; degrees AA 2 yrs; scholarships; LC 2; enrl D 3870
Tuition: Res—undergrad $149 per sem; nonres—undergrad $455 per sem; campus res —room & board $640-$690
Courses: Advertising Design, Aesthetics, Art History, Ceramics, Collage, †Commercial Art, Drafting, Drawing, †Handicrafts, Illustration, Jewelry, †Painting, Photography, †Sculpture, Silversmithing, Textile Design, Theatre Arts, Video

CHEYENNE

LARAMIE COUNTY COMMUNITY COLLEGE, Division of Humanities, 82001. Tel 307-634-5853, Ext 132. *Div Chmn* Thomas Neal, MA; *Instructor* Betsy LaRowe, MA; *Instructor* Carolyn Palmer, MA; *Instructor* Barry Pendley, MA; *Instructor* Walter O Sills, MA; *Instructor* Maida Wedell, MA; *Instructor* Peter Piper, BA
Estab 1969; pub; D & E; ent req HS dipl; degrees AA; scholarships; SC 19, LC 3; enrl D 80, E 180, non-maj 150, maj 10
Tuition: Res—undergrad $300 per yr, $150 per sem, $13 per hr; nonres—undergrad $600 per yr, $300 per sem, $13 per hr; no campus res
Courses: Art History, Ceramics, Drafting, Drawing, Graphic Arts, Graphic Design, Jewelry, Painting, Photography, Sculpture, Silversmithing, Stage Design, Theatre Arts, Watercolor, Welded Sculpture
Adult Hobby Classes: Tui $13 per cr hr. Courses—all of the above
Summer School: Tui $13 per cr hr for term of 8 wks beginning May 26. Courses— Ceramics, Drawing, Jewelry, Painting, Watercolor

LARAMIE

UNIVERSITY OF WYOMING, Art Department, PO Box 3138, University Station, 82071. Tel 307-766-3371. *Head Dept* Carl Niederer, BS; *Prof* Joseph Deaderickm, MFA; *Prof* Richard Evans, MA; *Prof* Victor Flach, MFA; *Prof* James T Forrest, MS; *Assoc Prof* F David Reif, MFA; *Asst Prof* Jean O Schaefer, PhD; *Asst Prof* John Van Alstine, MFA. Instrs FT 8, PT 2
Estab 1886, dept estab 1946; pub; D; ent req HS dipl; degrees BA, BS and BFA 4 yrs, MFA 3 yrs, MA and MAT 2 yrs; scholarships; SC 23, LC 6, GC 13; enrl D 120, non-maj 600, maj 120 grad 21
Tuition: Res—$434 per yr, nonres—$1720 per yr; campus res—room & board $972 per yr
Courses: Advertising Design, Art History, Ceramics, Commercial Art, Drawing, Graphic Arts, Graphic Design, Lettering, Painting, Printmaking, Sculpture
Adult Hobby Classes: Ceramics, Stained Glass (through extension service)
Summer School: Tui $120-$325 for term of 8 wks beginning June 5

POWELL

NORTHWEST COMMUNITY COLLEGE, 82435. Tel 307-764-6507. *Head Dept* Ken Fulton, MA; *Asst Prof* John Banks, MA; *Instructor* John Rawlings, MFA
Estab 1946, dept estab 1952; pub; D & E; ent req HS dipl, nonres ACT; degrees AA 2 yrs; scholarships; SC 12, LC 4; enrl D 130, E 222, non-maj 317, maj 35
Tuition: Res—undergrad $130 per sem, $11 per cr; nonres—undergrad $350 per sem, $33 per cr; campus res—room & board $1171
Courses: Advertising Design, †Art Education, Ceramics, †Commercial Art, Drawing, †Graphic Arts, Handicrafts, †Jewelry, Lettering, †Painting, †Photography, †Printmaking, Sculpture, Silversmithing, Leather, Weaving
Adult Hobby Classes: Basic Painting, Ceramics, Drawing, Tole, Watercolor

RIVERTON

CENTRAL WYOMING COLLEGE, Art Center, 82501. Tel 307-856-9291. *Head Dept* Willis R Patterson, MFA; *Instructor* Jerry Antolik, MA; *Instructor* Press Stephens, MA; *Instructor* Sallie Wesaw, MFA
Estab 1966; pub; D & E; ent req HS dipl, GED; degrees AA 2 yrs; scholarships; SC 20, LC 2; enrl D 300, E 500, non-maj 50, maj 15, others 20
Tuition: $225 per yr, $113 per sem, $11 per hr; special workshop fees variable; campus res—room & board $1138
Courses: Ceramics, Constructions, Drafting, Drawing, Handicrafts, Jewelry, Mixed Media, Painting, Photography, Printmaking, Sculpture, Silversmithing, Stage Design, Textile Design, Lapidary, Stained Glass, Weaving
Adult Hobby Classes: Tui $10 per hr. Courses—Figure Drawing, Macrame, Tole Painting, Pottery, Stained Glass
Children's Classes: Tui variable. Courses—Crafts, Drawing, Music, Painting, Pottery, Sculpture, Theatre
Summer School: Dir, Dr Don Jeanroy. Enrl 150; tui varies; term varies. Courses— special workshops as scheduled plus pottery and painting

ROCK SPRINGS

WESTERN WYOMING COLLEGE, Art Department, 82901. Tel 307-382-2121, Ext 152. *Head Dept* Gary Grubb. Instrs FT 2, PT 4
Estab 1959; pub; D & E; ent req HS dipl; degrees AA 2 yrs; scholarships; SC 12, LC 1; enrl D 125, E 40, maj 20
Courses: Ceramics, Drawing, Handicrafts, History of Art & Archaeology, Painting, Photography, Sculpture, Theatre Arts
Adult Hobby Classes: Enrl 100. Courses—Crafts, Drawing, Painting, Pottery

SHERIDAN

SHERIDAN COLLEGE, Art Department, 82801. Tel 307-674-4421. *Chmn* Richard Martinsen. Instrs 2
Estab 1951; pub; D & E; ent req HS grad; degrees AA, AS and AAS 2 yrs; enrl maj 10
Courses: Ceramics, Drawing, Graphic Arts, Painting, Sculpture, Art Appreciation, Design, Etching, Pottery, Silk Screen
Adult Hobby Classes: Noncredit

TORRINGTON

EASTERN WYOMING COLLEGE, Art Department, 3200 West C St, 82240. Tel 307-532-7111, Ext 241. *Head Dept* Sue Milner. Instrs FT 1, PT 2
Estab 1948; pub; D & E; ent req varied; degrees AA and AAS 2 yrs; scholarships; SC 3, LC 1; enrl D 60, E 50, maj 2
Courses: Ceramics, Drawing, Graphic Arts, History of Art & Archaeology, Painting, Photography, Sculpture
Children's Classes: Enrl 50; 8 wks in summer. Courses—general subjects
Summer School: Enrl 18; term of 8 wks noncredit. Courses—Outdoor Sketching

PUERTO RICO

MAYAGUEZ

UNIVERSITY OF PUERTO RICO, MAYAGUEZ, Department of Humanities, 00708. Tel 809-832-4040, Ext 3156 & 3170. *Assoc Dir* Dr Luis E Baco. Instrs FT 7
Estab 1970; pub; D; ent req HS dipl; degrees BA(Art Theory) and BA(Plastic Arts) 4 yrs; SC 67, LC 8; enrl 345, maj 86
Courses: Seminar in Romanesque Art

PONCE

CATHOLIC UNIVERSITY OF PUERTO RICO, Department of History & Fine Arts,* 00731. Tel 809-844-4150. *Head Dept* Julio Micheli, MFA; *Prof* Ana Basso Bruno, MFA; *Prof* Mahir Laracuente, MM; *Prof* Adrian N Ramirez, MA; *Prof* Hufty E Rawson, BFA
Estab 1948, dept estab 1964; den; D; ent req HS dipl; degrees BA 4 yrs; scholarships; SC 22, LC 4; enrl D 50 maj
Tuition: $40 per cr hr; campus res available
Courses: Advertising Design, Aesthetics, Art Education, Art History, †Ceramics, Conceptual Art, Constructions, Drawing, Graphic Design, †Painting, †Printmaking, †Sculpture

RIO PIEDRAS

UNIVERSITY OF PUERTO RICO, Department of Fine Arts, Ponce de Leon Ave, Rio Piedras, PR. (Mailing Add: 21847 Rio Piedras, Rio Piedras, PR 00931) *Head Dept* Enrique Garcia Gutierrez, PhD; *Instructor* John Balossi, MA; *Instructor* Juan Jose Barragan Banda, PhD; *Instructor* Magdalana Ferdinandy, PhD; *Instructor* Jose Buscaglia Guillermety, MA; *Instructor* Susana Herrero, MA; *Instructor* Federico Berreda Y Monge, PhD
Estab 1902, dept estab 1950; pub; D; ent req HS dipl; degrees BA 4 yrs; scholarships; enrl D 200, maj 45
Tuition: $75; campus residence available
Courses: Aesthetics, Architecture, Art History, Conceptual Art, Graphic Arts, History of Art & Archaeology, Mixed Media, Painting, Printmaking, Sculpture, Video

SAN GERMAN

INTER AMERICAN UNIVERSITY OF PUERTO RICO, Department of Performing Arts,* 00753. Tel 809-892-1095. *Chmn* Robert M Fitzmaurice, PhD; *Assoc Chmn* Noemi Ruiz, MFA; *Assoc Prof* V Jaime Asencio hijo, MA; *Assoc Prof* Genoveva Comas, MS; *Asst Prof* Jaime Carrero, MA; *Instr* Raul Acero, MFA; *Instr* Gloria de Duncan, MA; *Instr* Carmen Vazquez de Guy, MA; *Instr* Joyce Anne Wlodarczyk, MFA
Estab 1912, dept estab 1947; pvt; D; ent req HS dipl, college board, presentation of portfolio; degrees BA 4 yrs; scholarships; SC 20, LC 12; enrl D 135, maj 135
Tuition: Res—undergrad $40 per cr, grad $60 per cr; campus res available
Courses: Art Education, Art History, Calligraphy, Ceramics, Drawing, Graphic Arts, Handicrafts, Painting, Photography, Experimental Design in Native Media, Leather, Macrame, Metals
Adult Hobby Classes: Enrl 15; tui $45 per course. Courses—Photography, Pottery
Summer School: Courses—Art Appreciation, Basic & Advanced Photography

SAN JUAN

INSTITUTE OF PUERTO RICAN CULTURE, Escuela de Artes Plasticas, School of Fine Arts, El Morro Grounds, San Juan, PR. (Mailing Add: Institute of Puerto Rican Culture, Box 4184, San Juan, PR 00905) Tel 809-725-1522. *Dir Fine Arts* Maria E Somoza; *Dir of School* Felix Rodriguez Baez; *Prof* Myanda Baez; *Prof* Tomas Batista; *Prof* Maria Socorro Cruz, PhD; *Prof* Arturo Davila, PhD; *Prof* Victoria Espinoso, PhD; *Prof* Rafael Lopez Del Compo; *Prof* Antonio Marforell
Estab 1971; pub; D; ent req HS dipl, ent exam; degrees BA 4 yrs; scholarships; SC 38, LC 12, GC 10; enrl D 160
Tuition: None
Courses: Aesthetics, Art Education, Art History, Calligraphy, †Ceramics, Drawing, †Graphic Arts, History of Art & Archaeology, †Painting, Photography, Printmaking, †Sculpture, Teacher Training
Summer School: Courses—Basic Drawing, Painting, Sculpture

VIRGIN ISLANDS

CHRISTANSTED SAINT CROIX

ST CROIX SCHOOL OF THE ARTS, INC, PO Box 1086, 00820. Tel 809-772-3767. *Dir* Dorothy F Raedler. Instrs PT 12
Estab 1970; pvt; D; ent req recommendation; scholarships; SC 27; enrl D 203
Courses: Ceramics, Drawing, Jewelry, Painting, Sculpture, Theatre Arts, Macrame, Needle Crafts, Silk Screen

Art Schools In Canada

ALBERTA

BANFF

BANFF CENTRE SCHOOL OF FINE ARTS, PO Box 1020, T0L 0C0. *Dir Banff Centre* Dr D S R Leighton; *Manager School Fine Arts* Neil Armstrong; *Art Dept Head* Takao Tanabe; *Ceramics Dept Head* Les Manning; *Fibre Dept Coordr* Pat Askren; *Photography Dept Head* Hubert Hohn. Instrs 37
Estab 1933 for summer study, winter cycle prog began 1979; ent req resume, slides of work, post-secondary art training at a university or art school and or professional experience in field; scholarships; enrl winter 60, summer 275, other disciplines 1000

CALGARY

ALBERTA COLLEGE OF ART, Southern Alberta Institute of Technology, 1301 16th Ave NW, T2M 0L4. Tel 403-284-8651. *Head Alberta Col Art* Kenneth G Sturdy, DLC, DA; *Acad Supervisor* R Halliday, BFA; *Administrator* R Douglas, Bachelor of Communication; *Prog Coordr* Kenneth Craig, BA; *Prog Coordr* K Dickerson; *Prog Coordr* Walter Drohan, RCA; *Prog Coordr* Richard Edwards, NCC & ATC; *Prog Coordr; Prog Coordr* C Milejszo, Dipl; *Prog Coordr* F Palmer, RCA; *Prog Coordr* S Parker, MA
Estab 1926; pub; D & E; ent req HS dipl, admis test; degrees 4 yr dipl; scholarships; SC approx 250, LC 14, GC 7; enrl D 600, E 500, non-maj 210, maj 321, others 58
Tuition: $300 per yr
Courses: Aesthetics, Art History, Calligraphy, Ceramics, Collage, Conceptual Art, Constructions, Costume Design & Construction, Display, Drawing, Film, Goldsmithing, Graphic Arts, Graphic Design, Handicrafts, Illustration, Intermedia, Jewelry, Lettering, Mixed Media, Painting, Photography, Printmaking, Sculpture, Silversmithing, Theatre Arts, Creative Movement & Visual Design, Metals
Adult Hobby Classes: Enrl 500; tui varies per course. Courses—Ceramics, Design, Drawing, Jewelry, Media Extension, Painting, Portraiture, Printmaking, Sculpture, Showcard Lettering, Stained Glass, Textiles, Watercolor
Children's Classes: Enrl 140; tui $35 for 20 wks. Courses—Advanced Painting for Teenagers, Ceramics, Mixed Media, Painting, Puppetry, Sculpture

MOUNT ROYAL COLLEGE, 4825 Richard Rd SW, T3E 6K6. *Chmn* Richard V Peterson. Instrs FT 6, PT 8
Estab 1910; pub; D & E; ent req HS dipl; degrees 1-2 yr dipl; scholarships; SC 12, LC 17
Tuition: $14 per cr hr
Courses: Ceramics, Display, Drafting, Drawing, Graphic Arts, Graphic Design, History of Art & Archaeology, Lettering, Painting, Photography, Sculpture, Stage Design

UNIVERSITY OF CALGARY, Department of Art, 2920 24th Ave NW, T2N 1N4. Tel 403-284-5252. *Head* Dr L Cromwell. Instrs FT 28, PT 7
Estab 1965; pub; D & E; ent req HS dipl; degrees BA(Art History), BFA, MFA in ceramics, drawing, painting, photography, printmaking, sculpture; SC 25, LC 10, GC 12; enrl D 167, E 58, all maj
Tuition: $280 half yr, $560 per yr
Courses: Art Education, Art History, Ceramics, Graphic Arts, Graphic Design, Painting, Photography, Sculpture
Summer School: Dir, L Cromwell. Two terms of 6 wks, May-July. Courses—Art History, Ceramics, Design, Drawing, Graphics, Painting

EDMONTON

UNIVERSITY OF ALBERTA, Department of Art and Design, 112 St & 88 Ave, T6G 2C9. Tel 403-432-3261. *Chmn* Douglas Haynes, Dipl
Estab 1908, dept estab 1946; pub; D & E; ent req HS dipl, portfolio; degrees BFA 4 yrs, MA & MVA 2 yrs; SC 51, LC 42, grad 23; enrl D 151, grad 15-20
Tuition: Res—undergrad $250 per yr, grad $625 per yr; nonres—grad $210 per course; campus res available
Courses: †Art History, †Graphic Design, †Industrial Design, †Painting, †Printmaking, †Sculpture
Summer School: Dir, Mr Carswell

LETHBRIDGE

UNIVERSITY OF LETHBRIDGE, Department of Art, 4401 University Dr, T1K 3M4. Tel 403-329-2691. *Assoc Dean Div Fine Arts* Larry E Weaver, MFA; *Dept Chmn* Herbert A Hicks; *Assoc Prof* Charles Crane, MA; *Assoc Prof* Pauline McGeorge, MFA; *Asst Prof* Carl Granzow, MFA; *Asst Prof* Bill McCarroll, MFA
Estab 1967; pub; D & E; ent req HS dipl; degrees BA and BFA 4 yrs; scholarships; SC 26, LC 9
Courses: †Art Education, Art History, †Ceramics, Conceptual Art, Constructions, Drawing, History of Art & Archaeology, Mixed Media, †Painting, Photography, †Printmaking, †Sculpture, Theatre Arts, Video

RED DEER

RED DEER COLLEGE, Department of Art and Design, T4N 5H5. Tel 403-346-3376. *Coordr Art and Design* Jim Westergard. Instrs FT 5, PT 2
Estab 1973; pub; D & E; ent req HS dipl, portfolio; degrees dipl, BFA 2 yrs; enrl max 40 first yr students, 12 second yr
Tuition: Res $310; nonres $460
Courses: Art History, Ceramics, Commercial Art, Drawing, Painting, Photography, Printmaking, Sculpture, Fundamentals of Visual Communication

BRITISH COLUMBIA

NELSON

SELKIRK COLLEGE, Kootenay School of Art Division, David Thompson University Centre, 820 Tenth St, V1L 3C7. *Dir* D O MacGregor, BFA; *Chief Instr* M R Levitt, BFA; *Chief Instr* E H Undergill, MA; *Instr* A Bain, MFA; *Instr* A Farrell, BFA; *Instr* S Kresta, Dipl; *Instr* G Mackie, Dipl; *Instr* S Stevenson, BA & BEd; *Instr* M Zmur, Dipl
Estab 1960; pub; D & E; ent req HS dipl, portfolio; degrees none, 2 yr dipl, 3 yr grad dipl, 8 month graphic design; enrl D 165, E 40, maj 35
Tuition: Res $125 per sem
Courses: Advertising Design, Art Education, Art History, †Ceramics, Collage, Commercial Art, Conceptual Art, Constructions, Display, Drawing, Graphic Arts, †Graphic Design, Handicrafts, Illustration, Jewelry, Lettering, Museum Staff Training, †Painting, Photography, †Printmaking, †Sculpture, Silversmithing, †Applied Design

VANCOUVER

EMILY CARR COLLEGE OF ART, 249 Dunsmuir St, V6B 1X2. Tel 604-681-9525. *Prin* Robin C Mayor; *Dean* Tom Hudson; *Dir Student Services* Thomas W Kowall
Estab 1925; pub; D & E; ent req HS dipl plus presentation of folio of art work; degrees 4 yr dipl; SC 20, LC 8; enrl 500, maj 300, grad 9
Tuition: $470 per yr; grad $225 per sem; no campus res
Courses: Advertising Design, Art History, Ceramics, Commercial Art, Conceptual Art, Drawing, Film, Graphic Design, History of Art & Archaeology, Illustration, Lettering, Mixed Media, Painting, Photography, Printmaking, Sculpture, Video, Animation, Interdisciplinary Studies

UNIVERSITY OF BRITISH COLUMBIA
—**Department of Fine Arts,** 2075 Wesbrook Mall, V6T 1W5. Tel 604-228-5650. *Acting Head* George Knox, PhD; *Prof* Roy Kiyooka; *Prof* Alan Sawyer, PhD; *Prof* Geoffrey Smedley, DFA; *Assoc Prof* James O Caswell, PhD; *Assoc Prof* W Herbert Gilbert, BA; *Assoc Prof* Mary Morehart, PhD; *Assoc Prof* Debra Pincus, PhD; *Asst Prof* Penelope Brownell, PhD; *Asst Prof* Marvin Cohodas, PhD; *Asst Prof* Wendy Dobereiner, MA; *Asst Prof* Rhodri Windsor Liscombe, PhD; *Asst Prof* Moritaka Matsumoto, PhD; *Asst Prof* Barbara Z Sungur, MFA
—**School of Architecture,** V6T 1W5. Tel 604-228-2779. *Dir* Douglas Shadbolt. Instrs FT 11
Estab 1946; pub; degrees BArch, MArch, 3 yrs
Tuition: $716 per session
Courses: Architecture

VANCOUVER COMMUNITY COLLEGE, LANGARA CAMPUS, Department of Fine Arts,* 100 W 49th Ave, V5Y 2Z6. Tel 604-324-5511. *Chmn Dept* Barry Holmes, Dipl Art; *Instr* Catherine Broderick, MFA; *Instr* Gordon Caruso, Dipl Art; *Instr* Gerald Formosa, Dipl Art; *Instr* Don Hutchinson, Dipl Art; *Instr* Michael Minot, Nat Dipl; *Instr* Barbara Shelly, MA

Estab 1970; pub; D & E; ent req HS dipl, portfolio; degrees 2 yr Fine Arts Dipl; scholarships; SC 7, LC 1; enrl D 120
Tuition: $125-$150 per sem, plus $5 material fees per each $25; no campus res
Courses: Art History, Ceramics, Drawing, Painting, Printmaking, Sculpture, Design, Fabric Arts
Adult Hobby Classes: Enrl 15 per class; tui $25 per sem. Courses—Ceramics, Design, Drawing, Fabric Arts

VICTORIA

UNIVERSITY OF VICTORIA
—**Department of Visual Arts,** PO Box 1700, V8W 2Y2. Tel 604-477-6911. *Chmn* George Tiessen, MFA; *Prof* John Dobereiner, MFA; *Prof* Donald Harvey, ATD & RCA; *Assoc Prof* Pat Martin Bates, RCA; *Assoc Prof* Roland Brener, Post Dipl AD; *Asst Prof* Ruth Beer, MVA; *Instr* Gwen Curry, MVA
Estab 1963; pub; D; ent req HS dipl; degrees BA and BFA 4 yrs, MFA 2 yrs; enrl 210, non-maj 18, maj 16
Tuition: Campus res available
Courses: Drawing, †Painting, Photography, †Printmaking, †Sculpture
Summer School: Courses—Drawing, Painting, Photography, Printmaking
—**Department of History in Art,** V8W 2Y2. *Chmn* Alan Gowans, MA; *Prof* Siri Gunasinghe, Doctorate; *Assoc Prof* S Anthony Welch, PhD; *Assoc Prof* Charles R Wicke, PhD; *Asst Prof* P Richard Stanley-Baker, MFA; *Lectr* Terry Guernsey, MA; *Lectr* Martin J Segger, BA; *Lectr* Mario Luna, MA; *Lectr* G Edward MacFarlane, BA; *Lectr* Barrie McLean
Degrees BA(Art History), MA(Art History); LC 34, grad 10

MANITOBA

WINNIPEG

UNIVERSITY OF MANITOBA
—**School of Art,** R3T 2N2. Tel 204-474-9303. *Dir* Alfred E Hammer, MFA; *Chmn Drawing* Alex Bruning, MA; *Chmn Painting* Don Reichert, BFA; *Chmn Ceramics* Robert W Archambeau, MFA; *Chmn Sculpture* Gordon Reeve, MFA; *Chmn Photography* David McMillan, MFA; *Chmn Graphic Design* Norman Schmidt, BFA; *Chmn Printmaking* Arnold Saper, MFA; *Chmn Art History* Marilyn Baker, PhD; *Chmn Foundations* Richard Williams, MFA
Estab 1950; pub; D; ent req HS dipl and portfolio; degrees BFA 3 yrs, BFA Honors 4 yrs, Dipl in Art 4 yrs; SC 35, LC 16; enrl D 350
Tuition: Varies per yr; campus res available
Courses: †Art History, †Ceramics, †Drawing, †Graphic Arts, †Graphic Design, †Painting, †Photography, †Printmaking, †Sculpture
Summer School: Dir, Alfred E Hammer. Term of 6 wks. Courses—Ceramics, Drawing
—**Faculty of Architecture,** R3T 2N2. Tel 204-474-9286. *Dean* H E Thompson; *Assoc Dean* J W Graham; *Asst Dean* Peter E Forster; *Head Environmental Studies* Rory Ionseca; *Head Dept Archit* R A Forrester; *Head Landscape Archit* Alexander Rattray; *Head Dept Interior Design* George Fuller; *Head Dept City Planning* Kent Gerecke
Estab 1913; pub; ent req Senior matriculation or Bachelor for particular subject; degrees Interior Design 4 yrs, Archit, Landscape Archit and City Planning 6 yrs; scholarships; enrl Environmental Studies 235, Archit 120, Interior Design 280, City Planning 66, Landscape 41
Courses: Architecture, Interior Design, Landscape Architecture, City Planning, Environmental Studies

NEW BRUNSWICK

EDMUNDSTON

COLLEGE SAINT-LOUIS-MAILLET, Department of Visual Arts, E3V 2S8. Tel 506-735-8804. *Prof* Yvette Bisson; *Prof* Lise Bourque, MFA; *Prof* Jaques Martin, BFA; *Prof* George Widiez; *Vis Prof* Roland Breucker, painting & theatrical sets
Estab 1946, dept estab 1968; pub; D & E; ent req HS dipl; degrees BA(Fine Arts) 4 yrs; scholarships; SC 12, LC 1; enrl D 20, E 11, non-maj 25, maj 6
Tuition: $620 per yr; campus res—room & board $475 per yr
Courses: Art History, Ceramics, Drawing, Painting, Sculpture
Children's Classes: Enrl 60; tui $20 per sem. Courses—Painting

FREDERICTON

NEW BRUNSWICK CRAFT SCHOOL AND CENTRE, PO Box 6000, E3B 5H1. Tel 506-453-2305. *Dir* George F Fry
Estab 1946; pub; D; ent req HS dipl, questionnaire and interview; degrees 3 yr dipl; enrl 50 plus PT
Tuition: New Brunswick students $300 plus materials; others $500 plus materials; no campus res
Courses: Art History, †Ceramics, Drawing, †Jewelry, Photography, †Silversmithing, †Textile Design, Weaving, Wood
Summer School: Enrl 1500; tui $5 for 1 day beginning July through Aug. Courses—Crafts

UNIVERSITY OF NEW BRUNSWICK, Art Education Section,* Faculty of Education, PO Box 4400, E3B 5A3. Tel 506-453-4995. *Head* Thomas R Smith
Tuition: Res—$660 per yr; nonres—$740 per yr
Courses: Art and Child Development, Art Education for Elementary Teachers, Pottery and Clay Sculpture

MONCTON

UNIVERSITE DE MONCTON, Department of Visual Arts, E1A 3E9. Tel 506-855-2070. Instrs FT 3
Estab 1967; pub; D & E; ent req HS dipl; degrees BA(Fine Arts) 4 yrs; SC 7, LC 3; enrl D 80, E 40, grad 10
Courses: Aesthetics, Art Education, Ceramics, Drawing, Graphic Arts, Graphic Design, History of Art & Archaeology, Painting, Photography, Printmaking, Sculpture, Teacher Training

SACKVILLE

MOUNT ALLISON UNIVERSITY, Fine Arts Department, E0A 3C0. Tel 506-536-2040, Ext 492. *Head Dept* Virgil Hammock, MFA; *Prof* E B Pulford, BFA; *Prof* David Silverberg, BA; *Assoc Prof* John Asimakos; *Assoc Prof* M J A Crooker, MA; *Assoc Prof* Thomas Henderson, MFA; *Lectr* Thaddeus Holownia; *Lectr* Dwight Siegner, MFA
Estab 1858; pub; D & E; ent req HS dipl; degrees BFA 4 yrs; SC 17, LC 5; enrl 80
Tuition: Campus residence available
Courses: Art History, Drawing, Intermedia, †Painting, †Photography, †Printmaking, †Sculpture
Summer School: Courses—Adult Workshop, Art Criticism, High School Workshop, Photography, Painting, Sculpture

NOVA SCOTIA

HALIFAX

NOVA SCOTIA COLLEGE OF ART AND DESIGN, 5163 Duke St, B3J 3J6. Tel 902-422-7381. *Pres* Garry Neill Kennedy, MFA; *Chmn Design Div* Frank Fox, ARCA; *Chmn Craft Div* Ian Austen, BD; *Chmn Studio Div* Terence Johnson, MFA; *Chmn Art Educ Div* Harold Pearse, MA; *Chmn Art History Div* Dennis Young, BA
Estab 1887; pvt; D & E; ent req HS dipl, portfolio or project; degrees BFA, BD(Environmental Planning or Common Design) and BA(Art Educ) 4 yrs, MFA and MA(Art Educ) 2 yrs; SC 67, LC 31, GC 8 each sem; enrl D 433, E 188, grad 17
Tuition: $475 per sem; Visa students $1700; no campus res
Courses: Art Education, Art History, Ceramics, Conceptual Art, Constructions, Drawing, Goldsmithing, Graphic Arts, Graphic Design, History of Art & Archaeology, Jewelry, Mixed Media, Painting, Photography, Printmaking, Sculpture, Silversmithing, Teacher Training, Textile Design, Video, Weaving
Adult Hobby Classes: Tui $10-$80 per sem. Courses—Ceramics, Drawing, Fabrics, Jewelry, Painting, Photography, Spinning & Dyeing
Children's Classes: Tui Free. Courses—Art
Summer School: Dean, Alan Barkley. Tui $375 ($850 Visa students) for term of 13 wks beginning May 15

NOVA SCOTIA TECHNICAL COLLEGE, Faculty of Architecture, Spring Garden Rd, PO Box 1000, B3J 2X4. *Dean* Peter Manning, PhD; *Prof* O Biskaps, MArchit; *Prof* J Philip McAleer, PhD; *Assoc Prof* H Stubsjoen, MScArchit; *Asst Prof* L W Richards, MArchit
Estab 1911, faculty estab 1961; pvt; D; ent req previous 2 yrs at univ; degrees BArchit 4 yrs, MArchit 1 yr minimum; scholarships; SC many, LC many, GC several; enrl approx 200, maj 200, grad 2
Courses: Art Education, Art History, Constructions, Drafting, Photography

ONTARIO

DOWNSVIEW

YORK UNIVERSITY, Department of Visual Arts, Fine Arts Bldg, 4700 Keele St, M3J 1P3. *Chairperson* Joyce Zemans. Instrs FT 28, PT 13
Estab 1969; pub; D & E; ent req HS dipl, interview and portfolio evaluation; degrees BA(Hons) 4 yrs; SC 26, LC 17; enrl D over 400, maj 400, others approx 120
Courses: Drawing, Graphic Arts, Graphic Design, History of Art & Archaeology, Painting, Photography, Sculpture

GUELPH

UNIVERSITY OF GUELPH, Fine Art Department,* Gordon St, N1G 2W1. Tel 519-824-4120, Ext 2413. *Chmn Dept* Thomas Tritschler, PhD
Estab 1966; pub; D; ent req HS dipl; degrees BA 3 yrs, BA(Hons) 4 yrs; SC 24, LC 27; enrl 959, maj 225
Tuition: Res—undergrad $250 per sem, grad $342 per sem; nonres—undergrad $650 per sem, grad $750 per sem; campus res available
Courses: Drawing, History of Art & Archaeology, Painting, Printmaking, Sculpture

HAMILTON

MCMASTER UNIVERSITY, Department of Art and Art History, 1280 Main St W, L8S 4L8. Tel 416-522-9140. *Chmn Dept* G Wallace. Instrs FT 11
Estab 1934; degrees BA(Studio and Art History), Hons BA(Studio and Art History) 3-4 yrs; SC 12, LC 29; enrl 85
Tuition: Campus res available
Courses: †Art History, †Studio Art Program

KINGSTON

QUEEN'S UNIVERSITY, Department of Art, K7L 3N6. Tel 613-547-6172. *Head Dept* Kathleen Morand. Instrs FT 18, PT 5
Estab 1932; pub; D & E; ent req Grade XIII; degrees BA 3 yrs, BA(Hons) and BAE 4 yrs, MA(Conservation), MA(Art History); SC 16, LC 25
Tuition: University admission and fees apply; campus residence available
Courses: Art History, Drawing, Painting, Printmaking, Sculpture, Design
Summer School: Courses offered

LONDON

UNIVERSITY OF WESTERN ONTARIO, Department of Visual Arts, N6A 5K7. Tel 519-679-2440. *Chmn* J L Barrio-Garay. Instrs FT 12, PT 2
Estab 1967; pub; D & E; ent req HS dipl, portfolio and or interview; degrees BA 3 yrs, BA(Hons) and BFA 4 yrs; SC 11, LC 15; enrl maj 160
Tuition: $783
Courses: Drawing, History of Art & Archaeology, Museum Staff Training, Painting, Photography, Printmaking, Sculpture
Summer School: Enrl limited; term of 6 wks beginning July. Courses—Visual Arts

OTTAWA

CARLETON UNIVERSITY, Department of Art History, Colonel By Dr, K1S 5B6. Tel 613-231-2700. *Chmn* Dr D A Goodreau. Instrs FT 5, PT 3
Estab 1964; D & E; ent req HS dipl; degrees BA 6 Hons 3-4 yrs; scholarships; SC 2, LC 25, GC 3; enrl D over 700, maj 135
Courses: Art Education, History of Art & Archaeology, Museum Staff Training
Adult Hobby Classes: Courses—Ceramics, Drawing, Painting
Summer School: Chmn, Dr D A Goodreau. Courses—Art History

REXDALE

HUMBER COLLEGE OF APPLIED ARTS AND TECHNOLOGY, Creative and Communication Arts Division,* Humber College Blvd, PO Box 1900, M9W 5L7. Tel 416-676-1200. *Dean* Jack Ross
Estab 1967; pub; D & E; ent req HS dipl, mature student status, one yr of employment plus 19 yrs of age; degrees none, 2 & 3 yr dipl courses; SC 300, LC 75, GC 6; enrl grad 50, PT 25
Tuition: $290 per yr
Courses: Advertising Design, Architecture, Ceramics, Commercial Art, Display, Drafting, Drawing, Film, Graphic Arts, Graphic Design, Handicrafts, History of Art & Archaeology, Illustration, Industrial Design, Interior Design, Jewelry, Landscape Architecture, Lettering, Painting, Photography, Printmaking, Sculpture, Stage Design, Theatre Arts, Batik, Furniture Design, Macrame, Packaging Design, Printmaking, Studio Methods, TV Production, Typography, Weaving, Wood Crafts
Adult Hobby Classes: Enrl 210. Courses—Crochet Batik; beginning classes in most of regular courses
Children's Classes: Enrl 87. Courses—Beginning Arts and Crafts, Painting
Summer School: Dean Creative Arts, Jack Ross. Term of 10-16 wks beginning May and June. Courses—Beginning and advanced classes in most of regular courses

SOUTHAMPTON

SOUTHAMPTON ART SCHOOL, 20 Albert St, N0H 1T0. *Dir* Edna Johnson; *Instr* Herbert Ariss; *Instr* Corbett Gray; *Instr* A Daniel Logan
Estab 1958 as a summer school; pub; D, July and Aug
Tuition: Adults $80 per wk; students (14-18) $60 per wk; children (10-13) $20 per wk, half days only; no campus res
Courses: Art Education, Drawing, Mixed Media, Painting, Photography

THUNDER BAY

LAKEHEAD UNIVERSITY, Department of Fine Art, Oliver Rd, P7B 5E1. Tel 807-345-2121. *Dir* Oliver Tiura, MFA
Estab 1965, dept estab 1976; pub; D & E; ent req HS dipl, portfolio; degrees BA(Visual Arts) 4 yrs
Tuition: Res—undergrad $750 per yr, PT $165 per course, grad $790 first yr, $310 second yr; nonres—undergrad $1500 per yr, $300 per course, grad $650 per term; campus res—room & board $1821-$1919
Courses: Art History, Ceramics, Drawing, History of Art & Archaeology, Painting, Photography, Teacher Training, Theatre Arts
Adult Hobby Classes: Non-credit courses vary from session to session

TORONTO

GEORGE BROWN COLLEGE OF APPLIED ARTS AND TECHNOLOGY, Box 1015, Station B, M5T 2T9. Tel 416-967-1212. *Chmn* E K Walker. Instrs FT 11, PT 9
Estab 1970; D & E; ent req HS grade 12 dipl, entr exam; degrees 3 yr dipl; enrl D 300, E 800
Courses: Advertising Design, Calligraphy, Commercial Art, Drawing, Graphic Design, Illustration, Painting, Air Brush Techniques, Cartooning, Marker Rendering Techniques, Photo Retouching, Soapstone Carving, Watercolor

ONTARIO COLLEGE OF ART, 100 McCaul St, M5T 1W1. Tel 416-977-5311. *Pres* Paul D Fleck, PhD; *Registrar* Joan Brabant; *Business Adminr* Owen Wilson; *Dir of Information Services* Ruth Hammond, APR; *Placement Officer* Esther Levin; *Financial Aid Officer* Mary Hofstetter; *Chmn Dept Found Studies* David Hall-Humpherson, AOCA; *Chmn Dept Commun & Design* Beresford Mitchell, AOCA; *Chmn Dept Design* Joan Burt, BArchit, MRAIC; *Chmn Dept Exp Art* Gustav Weisman; *Chmn Dept Fine Art* John Newman, AOCA, RCA, PDCC, CSPWC; *Chmn Dept Photo & Elec Arts* Richard Hill, PhilM; *Chmn Dept Lib Arts Studies* Thomas Gordon, MA; *Chmn Dept Technol Studies* Michael Harmes; *Coordr Gen Studies Prog* William Poole; *Sr Adv* Mary Egan Haines, BID, AXA
Estab 1876; pub; D & E; ent req HS dipl, interview; degrees Assoc, 4 yr dipl; scholarships; SC approx 450; enrl D 1235, E 1270, grad 35
Tuition: $610 per yr; $85 per course; yearly fees for applicants outside Canada $1500; no campus res
Courses: Advertising Design, Aesthetics, Art History, Ceramics, Collage, Commercial Art, Conceptual Art, Costume Design & Construction, Display, Drawing, Fashion Arts, Film, Goldsmithing, Graphic Arts, Graphic Design, History of Art & Archaeology, Illustration, Industrial Design, Interior Design, Jewelry, Mixed Media, Painting, Photography, Printmaking, Sculpture, Silversmithing, Stage Design, Textile Design, Theatre Arts, Video, Animation, Batik, Color, Corporate Design, Design Management, Editorial Design, Environmental Design, Glass Coloring and Forming, Holography, Light, Materials and Processes, Metal Work, Multimedia Printing, Packaging, Plastics, Product Design, Systems Design, Typography, Woodworking
Children's Classes: Enrl 30; tui $15 per course. Courses—Design Explorations (a Sat course for secondary school students)
Summer School: Asst Registr PT Studies, Helen Thibodeau. Enrl 700; tui $100 per course for term of 3 wks every day or 15 wks 2 evenings per wk, beginning May. Courses—Art History, Ceramics, Color, Drawing, Environmental Design, Graphics, Painting, Printmaking, Textiles, Watercolor

THREE SCHOOLS, 296 Brunswick Ave, M5S 2M7. Tel 416-920-8370. *Pres* John Sime
—**New School of Art,** M5S 2M7. *Dir* Iain Sinclair. Instrs PT 20
Estab 1965; pvt; D; ent req interview, 1-4 yrs in contemporary visual arts; degrees none; enrl 100
Tuition: $650 first yr, $450 second yr, $300 third yr
—**Artists Workshop,** M5S 2M7. *Dir* Barbara Wood. Instrs PT 100
Estab 1951; D & E; ent req none; enrl 2500
Tuition: Varies per course
Courses: Ceramics, Drawing, Film, Graphic Design, Illustration, Painting, Photography, Printmaking, Sculpture, Textile Design, Theatre Arts, Stained Glass, Hand Bookbinding
Children's Classes: Tui varies per course. Courses—Ceramics, Drawing, Painting, Sculpture

TORONTO ART THERAPY INSTITUTE, 216 St Clair Ave W, M4V 1R2. Tel 416-921-4374. *Head Dept* Martin Fischer, Doctorate of Psychology; *Senior Art Therapist* Gilda S Grossman, MSW; *Chmn Educ Committee* Morton Manilla, PhD; *Lectr* Guiliana Katz, PhD
Estab 1968; D & E; degrees Dipl, BA and MA through affiliation with other US colleges
Adult Hobby Classes: Enrl 6-12; tui $25 per session. Courses—workshops
Children's Classes: Enrl 6-12; tui $20 per session. Courses—workshops

TORONTO SCHOOL OF ART, 225 Brunswick Ave, M5S 2M6. Tel 416-921-3986. *Dir* Barbara Barrett, BA; *Instr* Alison Brannen; *Instr* Patricia Clemes; *Instr* Patricia Fairhead; *Instr* Frances Gage; *Instr* Elizabeth Griffin; *Instr* Nancy Hazelgrove; *Instr* Loris Lesynski; *Instr* Larry Middlestadt; *Instr* Dianne Pugen; *Instr* Ethel Rosenfield; *Instr* Joan van Damme
Estab 1969; pvt; D & E; ent req none; scholarships; enrl D & E 200
Tuition: $600 per yr, $300 per sem, $73 for 12 wks; no campus res
Courses: Drawing, Graphic Arts, Illustration, Mixed Media, Painting, Photography, Printmaking, Sculpture

UNIVERSITY OF TORONTO
—**Department of Fine Art,** Sidney Smith Hall, M5S 1A1. Tel 416-978-6272. *Chmn* H K Lücke. Instrs FT 15, PT 5
Estab 1934; pub; degrees 3-4 yrs; LC, GC
Tuition: Campus res available
Courses: Art History
—**School of Architecture,** 230 College St, M5S 1A1. Tel 416-928-2573. *Dir* Blanche Lemco van Ginkel, MCP; *Assoc Prof* John Hall, OSA CSGA
Estab 1948; pub; D; ent req HS dipl, portfolio of work and interview; degrees BArchit 5 yrs, MArchit 1 yr for Studio (minimum 2 yrs for research); SC 5, LC 33, GC 11; enrl 299, non-maj 6, maj 293, grad 13
Tuition: Res—undergrad $750 per yr, grad $956 per yr; nonres—undergrad $1606 per yr, grad $1950 per yr; campus res available
Courses: Architecture, Drawing, Photography
—**Department of Landscape Architecture,** 230 College St, M5S 1A1. Tel 416-978-3103. *Chmn* William Rock Jr, MLA; *Prof* Richard Strong, MLA; *Assoc Prof* Jerry Englar, MLA; *Assoc Prof* Ed Fife, MLA; *Asst Prof* James Belisle, MArchit & MLA; *Vis Asst Prof* Larry Diamond, MLA; *Vis Lectr* David McWhirter, BLA
Estab 1827, dept estab 1965; pub; D; ent req grad 13 dipl; degrees BLA 4 yrs; scholarships; enrl 140, non-maj 6, maj 140
Tuition: Nonres—undergrad $950; campus res available
Courses: Aesthetics, Architecture, Art History, Constructions, Drafting, Drawing, Film, Graphic Arts, Landscape Architecture, Landscape Architecture Technology, Landscape Planning, Planting Design

WATERLOO

UNIVERSITY OF WATERLOO, Fine Arts Department,* 200 University Ave W, N2L 3G1. Tel 519-885-4280. *Dean* R K Banks; *Chmn Dept* A M Urquhart, BFA; *Prof* Virgil Burnett, MA; *Assoc Prof* Don MacKay, MFA; *Assoc Prof* Nancy-Lou Patterson, BA; *Asst Prof* Art Green, BFA; *Asst Prof* Basia Irland, MFA; *Asst Prof* Eve Kliman, PhD; *Asst Prof* Jan Uhde, PhD
Estab 1958, dept estab 1968; pub; D & E; ent req HS dipl; degrees BA 3 yrs, BA(Hons) 4 yrs; SC 32, LC 27; enrl maj 75
Tuition: $783 per yr; campus res available
Courses: Art History, Calligraphy, Ceramics, Drawing, Film, Illustration, Painting, Photography, Printmaking, Sculpture

WINDSOR

UNIVERSITY OF WINDSOR, School of Visual Arts, Huron Church Rd at College, N9B 3P4. Tel 519-253-4232, Ext 359. *Dir* Antonio P Doctor. Instrs FT 11, PT 9
Estab 1960; pub; D & E; ent req HS dipl grade 13, adult; degrees BA, BA(Hons) and BFA 3-4 yrs, MFA 2 yrs; scholarships; SC 22, LC 18; enrl D 140, E approx 120, maj 190, others 15
Tuition: $808
Courses: Art History, Drawing, Painting, Printmaking, Sculpture
Summer School: Dir, Antonio P Doctor. Enrl 118; tui $150 per course for term of 6 wks beginning July. Courses—Art Fundamentals, Art History Survey, Basic Drawing, Beginning Painting, Ceramics, Intermediate Drawing, Printmaking, Sculpture. European Summer Prog: Dir Antonio P Doctor. Enrl 20; tui $150 per course; students must take 2 courses, 6 wks beginning July-Aug. Courses—Independent Studio Work in Drawing and Painting, Intermediate Drawing, Painting

PRINCE EDWARD ISLAND

CHARLOTTETOWN

HOLLAND COLLEGE, School of Visual Arts, Burns Ave, West Royalty, C1A 7N8. Tel 902-894-5104. *Dir* Henry Purdy
Estab 1977; enrl D 100
Courses: Commercial Art, Photography, Fabric Art, Leather, Pottery, Weaving, Wood
Adult Hobby Classes: Enrl 265
Summer School: Courses offered

QUEBEC

MONTREAL

CONCORDIA UNIVERSITY - SIR GEORGE WILLIAMS CAMPUS, Faculty of Fine Arts, (Formerly Loyola of Montreal) 1395 Dorchester Blvd W, H3G 2M5. Tel 514-879-4055. *Dean Faculty* A Pinsky; *Dir Div Visual Arts* R Parker
Estab 1936, faculty estab 1975; D & E; ent req HS dipl, CEGEP Dipl Province of Quebec; degrees BFA 3-4 yrs, MA(Art Educ) 1 yr, MFA 2 yrs, PhD(Art Educ) 2 yrs; enrl D 1170, E 950
Courses: Advertising Design, Art Education, Art History, Ceramics, Costume Design & Construction, Display, Drawing, Film, Graphic Design, Handicrafts, History of Art & Archaeology, Illustration, Lettering, Mixed Media, Painting, Photography, Printmaking, Sculpture, Stage Design, Teacher Training, Theatre Arts, Video
Children's Classes: Courses offered

CONCORDIA UNIVERSITY, SIR GEORGE WILLIAMS CAMPUS, Department of Fine Arts,* 1435 Drummond St, H3G 1M8. Tel 514-879-4132. *Dean Faculty Fine Arts* Alfred Pinsky
D & E; ent req 5 yr res req for full and part-time students; degrees BFA, BA, post-BFA Dipl in Art Educ, 1 yr full-time leading to teaching cert, MA(Art Educ) 1 yr, MFA (Studio or Art History) 2 yrs
Courses: Art Education, Art History, Film, Graphic Arts, Graphic Design, Handicrafts, Painting, Photography, Sculpture, Theatre Arts, Design

MCGILL UNIVERSITY
—**Department of Art History,** 853 Sherbrooke West, H3A 2T6. Tel 514-392-4977. *Chmn* R Bertos, PhD; *Prof* G Galavaris, PhD; *Prof* W O Judkins, PhD; *Assoc Prof* R Bergmann, PhD; *Assoc Prof* T Glen, PhD; *Lectr* R Langstadt
Pvt; D; ent req HS dipl or CEGEP Dipl; degrees BA 3 yrs, MA 2 yrs, PhD 2 yrs; teaching assistantships; SC 2, LC 7, GC 4, seminars 2
Tuition: Varies; campus res available
Courses: Drawing, †History of Art & Archaeology, Painting
—**School of Architecture,** 3484 University St, H3A 2T6. *Dir* Derek Drummond. Instrs FT 10, PT 9
Estab 1896; ent req ent exam; degrees BArchit 6 yrs; fels; SC 12, LC 7
Courses: Art History, Drawing, Architectural Design, History of Architecture

MONTREAL MUSEUM OF FINE ARTS, School of Art and Design,* 3430 Ave du Musee, H3G 2C7. *Dean* Richard S Halliday; *Chief Educ Officer* Helene Lamarche-Ouellet
Estab 1940; pvt; D & E; ent req HS grad, portfolio; degrees Dipl in Visual Arts, Animation Design and Interior Design 3 yrs; enrl 450
Children's Classes: Art classes offered Saturdays

UNIVERSITE DE MONTREAL, Department of Art History, 3150 Jean-Brillant, CP 6128, Succursale A, H3C 3J7. Tel 514-343-6182. *Prof* Nicole Dubreuil-Blondin, Doctorate
Dept estab 1961; pvt; D & E; ent req HS dipl; degrees BA; SC 20, LC 70, GC 10; enrl D 270, non-maj 113, maj 106, grad 80, others 151
Tuition: Res and nonres—grad $550 per yr; campus res available
Courses: Aesthetics, Architecture, Art History, Conceptual Art, Drawing, Film, History of Art & Archaeology, Museum Staff Training, Painting, Photography, Printmaking, Sculpture, Stage Design, Video

UNIVERSITE DU QUEBEC A MONTREAL, FAMILLE DES ARTS, Pavillon des Arts, 1199 Rue Bleury, H3C 3P8. Tel 514-282-7001.
Estab 1969; ent req 2 yrs after HS; degrees Baccalaureat specialise 3 yrs; programs in Environmental Design, Graphic Design, History of Art, Plastic Art(engraving, sculpture, painting), Plastic Art Teaching
Courses: Aesthetics, Drawing, Painting, Teacher Training, Architectural Drafting, Ceramic Sculpture, Design, Etching and Engraving, Fresco, Graphic Techniques, Modeling, Mural Painting, Perspective, Stone and Wood Carving

QUEBEC

UNIVERSITE LAVAL CITE UNIVERSITAIRE, School of Visual Arts,* Faculte des Arts, G1K 7P4. Tel 418-656-2131. *Dir Visual Arts* Bernard Jasmin; *Faculty Dean of Arts* Jean Charles Blouin
Estab 1970; pub; D; ent req 2 yrs col; degrees Baccalaure(Arts Plastiques or Communication Graphique) 3 yrs plus 1 yr for teaching cert; enrl 300
Tuition: Res—undergrad $534-$684 per yr, $20 per quarter
Courses: Drawing, Film, Graphic Arts, Graphic Design, Illustration, Painting, Photography, Sculpture, Engraving, Lithography, Silk Screen, Stained Glass, Tapestry

TROIS RIVIERES

UNIVERSITY OF QUEBEC, TROIS RIVIERES, Fine Arts Section,* 3351 boul des Forges, PO Box 500, G9A 5H7. Tel 817-379-1740. *Dir* Christian Demers
Estab 1969; pub; D & E; ent req ent exam or DEC; degrees specialized baccalaureat in fine arts 3 yrs; SC 12, LC 8, GC 28; enrl D 150, E 100
Tuition: $250 per session; no campus res
Courses: Aesthetics, Art Education, Ceramics, Drafting, Drawing, Graphic Arts, History of Art & Archaeology, Painting, Sculpture, Art Administration, Basic Design, Glass, Weaving
Adult Hobby Classes: Enrl 100. Courses—Painting, Weaving
Summer School: Dir, Henri-Georges St-Louis. Tui $50 per course of 3 wks

SASKATCHEWAN

REGINA

UNIVERSITY OF REGINA
—**Department of Visual Arts,** S4S 0A2. Tel 306-584-4872. *Head* R V J Gomez. Instrs FT 11
Pub; ent req HS grad; degrees 2 yr cert, BA 3 yrs, BFA 4 yrs, MFA 2 yrs; enrl 350
Tuition: $314 per sem
Courses: Art History, Drawing, Film, Graphic Arts, Painting, Sculpture, Pottery
—**Department of Art Education,** Faculty of Education, S4S 0A2. Tel 306-584-4546. Instrs FT 3, PT 1
Estab 1965; pub; D & E; ent req HS dipl, matriculation or degree for maj in art; degrees BEd, BA, MEd 5 yrs; scholarships; LC 6; enrl D 160, E 20, maj 10
Courses: Aesthetics, Art Education
Children's Classes: Sat
Summer School: Exten Courses, H Kindred; Dean Educ, Dr Toombs. Term of 3 to 6 wks beginning May

SASKATOON

UNIVERSITY OF SASKATCHEWAN, SASKATOON CAMPUS, Department of Art, S7N 0W0. *Head* Stan Day. Instrs FT 14, PT 2
Estab 1936; pub; D; ent req HS grad; degrees BA 3 yrs, BAHons(Art History) and BFA 4 yrs, MA(Studio Art) 2 yrs grad prog, BEd(Art) available from Col Educ; scholarships; SC, LC, GC; enrl approx 850, BFA prog 130, grad 5
Tuition: $120 per class; 5 classes per acad yr, 1 class during intersession and 1 class during summer school
Courses: Art Education, Art History, Drawing, Painting, Photography, Printmaking, Sculpture, Pottery, Survey Studio
Summer School: Emma Lake Campus and Saskatoon Campus. Courses—vary per yr

Major Art Schools Abroad

ARGENTINA

BUENOS AIRES

ESCUELA NACIONAL DE BELLAS ARTES MANUEL BELGRANO, National School of Fine Arts Manuel Belgrano,* Venceslao Villafane 1342. *Dir* Maria L San Martin
Estab 1799; pub; D & E; ent req ent exam, 3 yrs secondary school; degrees Maestro Nacional de Artes Visuales 4 yrs; SC 13; enrl D 476, E 276
Courses: Art Education, Art History, Drawing, Painting, Sculpture, Composition System and Analysis of Works, Engraving

ESCUELA SUPERIOR DE BELLAS ARTES DE LA NACION ERNESTO DE LA CARCOVA, National Superior School of Fine Arts Ernesto de la Carcova,* Avenda Costanera Sur esquina Brasil. Tel 31-5144, 31-4419. *Rector* Mario Vanarelli; *Secy* Ines B Meseguer
Estab 1923; pub; D; ent req ent exam, first and second fine arts schools dipl; degrees Superior Prof granted in the chosen subject, 4 yrs; SC 4, LC 2; enrl 85
Tuition: None
Courses: Aesthetics, Ceramics, Costume Design & Construction, Drawing, Graphic Arts, Graphic Design, History of Art & Archaeology, Illustration, Lettering, Painting, Sculpture, Stage Design, Teacher Training

AUSTRALIA

DARLINGHURST

NATIONAL ART SCHOOL, Department of Technical Education,* NSW Forbes St. Tel 310266. *Head* Mollie Douglas; *Head Div Fine Arts* Peter Laverty; *Head Div Design* Philip Hickie
Estab 1918; pub; D & E; ent req ent exam, higher school cert; degrees ASTC(Associateship of Sydney Technical College) 5 yrs; scholarships; enrl FT 939, PT 3064, day and evening
Courses: Ceramics, Commercial Art, Costume Design & Construction, Graphic Design, Illustration, Industrial Design, Interior Design, Painting, Sculpture
Adult Hobby Classes: Courses—Ceramics, Drawing, Painting, Sculpture
Children's Classes: Various subjects

MELBOURNE

VICTORIAN COLLEGE OF THE ARTS, School of Art,* (Formerly National Gallery of Victoria Art School) 234 St Kilda Rd. Tel 62-5061. *Dir* Lenton Parr; *Dean School Art* William Kelly
Estab 1973; pub; D; degrees dipl arts 3 yrs, grad dipl fine art 2 yrs; enrl dipl 68, grad dipl 12
Tuition: None
Courses: Painting, Printmaking, Sculpture

AUSTRIA

SALZBURG

INTERNATIONAL SUMMER ACADEMY OF FINE ARTS, Kaigasse 2, PO Box 18. *Pres* Herman Stuppäck
Pub; D
Tuition: $314 for 5 wks beginning July 21
Courses: Architecture, Goldsmithing, Painting, Photography, Sculpture, Stage Design, Bronze Casting, Creation of Artistic Form, Lithography

VIENNA

HOCHSCHULE FÜR ANGEWANDTE KUNST IN WIEN, University of Applied Art in Vienna, Stubenring 3. Tel 0222-72 21 91. *Rector* Oswald Oberhuber. Instrs FT 110, PT 40
Estab 1868; pub; D; degrees dipl(MA) 4-5 yrs; enrl 800
Courses: Art Education, Art History, Calligraphy, Ceramics, Drawing, Illustration, Jewelry, Lettering, Painting, Printmaking, Sculpture, Teacher Training, Art Appreciation, Bookbinding, Cartooning, Design, Enameling, Fashion Illustration, History of Interiors, Metalcraft, Mosaics, Pictorial Composition, Pottery, Weaving

BELGIUM

ANTWERP

NATIONAAL HOGER INSTITUUT VOOR BOUWKUNST EN STEDEBOUW, National Higher Institute of Architecture and Town Planning), Mutsaertstraat 31. Tel 32 41 61. *Dir* J De Mol. Instrs 17
Estab 1663; pub; ent req HS dipl; degrees Town Planning 3 yrs, Conservation of Monuments 3 yrs, Interior Architecture 4 yrs, Product-Design 5 yrs, Architectural Degree 5 yrs

BRUSSELS

ACADEMIE ROYALE DES BEAUX-ARTS, Royal Academy of Fine Arts, Brussels, 144 ru du Midi. Tel 512-73-23, 512-85-50. *Prof* Maurice Leroy. Instrs 59
Founded 1711; D & E; degrees 4 yr after secondary level; scholarships
Courses: Advertising Design, Aesthetics, Art History, Drawing, Graphic Arts, Interior Design, Painting, Sculpture, Decorative Arts, Engraving, History of Architecture, History of Costume, Plastic Arts
—**Institute Superieur d'Architecture Victor Horta,** 144 rue du Midi B-1000. *Dir* Richard Vandendaele. Instrs 80
Founded 1711; degrees 5 yr after secondary level
Courses: Architecture

ECOLE DES ARTS ET METIERS D'ETTERBEEK,* 70, rue General Tombeur. Tel 33-75-99. *Dir* J Ado Baltus
Estab 1919; pub; E; ent req none for first yr, then exam req to go on; degrees cert after 4 yrs, dipl after 2 more yrs; SC 25, LC 1
Courses: Advertising Design, Ceramics, Display, Drafting, Drawing, Graphic Arts, History of Art & Archaeology, Illustration, Jewelry, Lettering, Painting, Photography, Sculpture, Cabinet Construction, Enamel, Pottery, Tapestry and Weaving, Wrought Iron

ECOLE NATIONALE SUPERIEURE DES ARTS VISUELS, Higher School of Visual Arts, 21 abbaye de la Cambre. *Dir* Joseph Noiret. Instrs FT 24
Estab 1926; degrees 4-5 yrs; scholarships; enrl 300
Courses: Film, Industrial Design, Decorative Arts, Experimental Animation

BULGARIA

SOFIA

NIKOLAJ PAVLOVIC HIGHER INSTITUTE OF FINE ARTS,* rue Sipka 1. Tel 88-17-01. *Rektor* Sekul Krumor
Founded 1896, reorganized as an Institute 1954; enrl 427 students

REPUBLIC OF CHINA

TAIPEI

NATIONAL TAIWAN ACADEMY OF ARTS, 59 Ta-Kwan Rd, Sec I, Pan-chiao Park. Tel 220. *Pres* T L Chang. Instrs FT 82, PT 168
Estab 1955; pub; D & E; ent req HS dipl, ent exam; degrees 3-5 yrs; scholarships open to Chinese
Courses: Art Education, Ceramics, Commercial Art, Drawing, Film, Graphic Arts, Industrial Design, Photography, Printmaking, Sculpture, Theatre Arts, Chinese, Fine Arts, Printing, Radio and Television, Western Arts

COLOMBIA

BOGOTA

UNIVERSIDAD JAVERIANA, Javeriana University Faculty of Architecture and Design, Carrera 7. Tel 2455102 or 2458983. *Acad Dean* Pedro P Polo Verano, BA(Archit); *Head Archit* Juan Ferroni, BA(Archit); *Head Industrial Design* Romulo Polo, BA(Industrial Design); *Head Advertising Art* Fabio Puerta, BA; *Head Archit Drafting* Jorge Ulloa, BA(Archit); *Head Means of Expression* Ramon Munoz, BA(Archit); *Head History* Jaime Salcedo, BA(Archit); *Head Urban Studies* Jorge Londono, MS(Town Planning); *Head Construction* Alfonso Delgado, BA(Archit)
Estab 1623, faculty estab 1951; den; D; ent req HS dipl, ent exam, personal interview; degrees Technician in Advertising Art or Architectural Drafting 3 yrs, BArchit and BA(Industrial Design) 5 yrs; SC 1 per sem, LC 5 per sem; enrl 830, maj 830
Tuition: $650 per sem; no campus res
Courses: †Advertising Design, †Architecture, Art History, Calligraphy, Commercial Art, Constructions, †Drafting, Drawing, Graphic Arts, History of Art & Archaeology, †Industrial Design, Lettering, Photography, Restoration & Conservation, History of Architecture, Semiology, Structure, Town Planning

CZECHOSLOVAKIA

PRAGUE

VYSOKA SKOLA UMELECKOPRUMYSLOVA, Academy of Applied Arts,* nam Krasnoarmejcu 80. *Rector* Jan Simota
Founded 1885; enrl 310

PRAHA

AKADEMIE VYTVARNYCH UMENI, Academy of Fine Arts, U Akademie 4. *Rector* Milos Axman
Founded 1799; 16 members

DENMARK

AARHUS

SCHOOL OF ARCHITECTURE IN AARHUS,* Norreport 20. Tel 06-13-08-22. *Rector* Nils-Ole Lund
Estab 1965; pub; D; ent req HS dipl; degrees cand archit 6 yrs; enrl 1000
Courses: †Architecture, †Industrial Design, †Interior Design, †Landscape Architecture, †Restoration & Conservation, Furniture, Garden Architecture, †Physical and Economic Planning, †Town Planning, †Town Renewal

COPENHAGEN

DEN GRAFISKI HOJSKOLE, Graphic College of Denmark, Glentevej 67. *Dir* Leif Monies
Courses: Drafting, Graphic Arts, Layout, Reproduction Techniques

DET KONGELIGE DANSKE KUNSTAKADEMI, The Royal Danish Academy of Fine Arts, Kongens Nytorv 1, 1050 K. *Dir School Archit* Tobias Faber; *Dir School Painting, Sculpture and Graphic Arts* Helge Bertram
Estab 1754; ent req independent work for approval; foreigners admitted as temporary students, not admitted as beginners but may take part in voluntary instruction at School of Painting and Sculpture and join advanced classes at School of Archit; degrees cert 5 yrs
Courses: Architecture, Painting, Sculpture

ENGLAND

BIRMINGHAM

CITY OF BIRMINGHAM POLYTECHNIC,* Art and Design Centre, Perry Barr. Tel 021 356-6911 6911. *Head Dept Art* T Scott; *Head Dept History of Art and Complementary Studies* P J Barlow; *Head Dept Fashion and Textiles* D Tomlinson
Pub; ent req vary according to course; degrees grad 4-5 yrs
Courses: Architecture, Art Education, Art History, Ceramics, Fashion Arts, Graphic Design, Industrial Design, Interior Design, Jewelry, Painting, Photography, Printmaking, Sculpture, Silversmithing, Complementary Studies, Furniture, Textiles, Theatre Design, Three-Dimensional Design, Town Planning

BRIGHTON

BRIGHTON POLYTECHNIC, Faculty of Art and Design, Grand Parade. Tel 0273-604141. *Dean Faculty* R Plummer, ARCA; *Head Dept Art History* R Haynes, MPhil; *Head Dept Combined Arts* P D Rose, ATD; *Head Dept Fashion and Textiles* J Miles; *Head Dept Fine Art* G Irwin; *Head Dept Three-Dimensional Design* J Crook; *Head Dept Visual Communication* J V Lord
Estab 1970; pub; D & E; ent req 18 yrs of age by Oct 1 and completion of foundation course in art and design or equivalent qualification; degrees 3-4 yrs; enrl D & E PT 1006, FT 110, grad 439
Courses: Ceramics, Fashion Arts, Graphic Design, Interior Design, Textile Design, Expressive Arts, Fine Art, Metal, Plastics, Wood
Adult Hobby Classes: Available
Summer School: First week in August. Courses—Bookbinding, Photography

LEICESTER

LEICESTER POLYTECHNIC, Faculty of Art and Design, The Newark, PO Box 143. Tel 0533-551551. *Asst Dir* D V Clarke, ARCA & FSIA; *Head School Expressive Arts* Noel Witts, BA(Hons); *Head School Fashion and Textile Design* Peter Morgan, DesRCA; *Head School Fine Art* John Hoskin; *Head School Graphics* Jerzy Karo, FSIAD & ADD; *Head School Industrial Design* A W Hodge, DesRCA & MSIAD
Estab 1969; degrees BA(Hons), MA
Courses: †Industrial Design, †Interior Design, †Jewelry, †Painting, †Sculpture, †Textile Design, Three-Dimensional Design

LONDON

CENTRAL SCHOOL OF ART AND DESIGN, Southampton Row. Tel 01-405-1825. *Prin* T H Pannell, DesRCA & FSIAD & ATI. Instrs FT 45, PT 250
Estab 1896; ent req submission of work; degrees BA(Hons), MA; enrl 530 FT
Courses: Ceramics, Graphic Design, Industrial Design, Jewelry, Painting, Printmaking, Sculpture, Textile Design, Theatre Arts

CHELSEA SCHOOL OF ART,* Manresa Rd. Tel 01-352-4846. *Principal* Frederick Brill
Estab 1895; ent req acad qualifications, ent exam, submission of work, interview; degrees dipl, cert 3-4 yrs; enrl 250
Courses: Art History, Graphic Arts, Painting, Sculpture, Printed Surface Design

CITY AND GUILDS OF LONDON ART SCHOOL, 122-4 Kennington Park Rd. *Principal* Roger de Grey, RA. Instrs 37
Estab 1879; D & E; degrees 2 yr cert, 3 yr dipl
Courses: Graphic Arts, Lettering, Painting, Printmaking, Sculpture, Decorative Arts, Gilding, Restoration of Wood and Stone, Wood Carving

HEATHERLEY SCHOOL OF FINE ART, OW Ashburnham School, Upcerne Rd. *Principal* John Walton, RP & DFA
Estab 1845
Courses: Drawing, Painting, Printmaking, Sculpture, Foundation, Pre-Foundation

ROYAL ACADEMY SCHOOLS, ROYAL ACADEMY OF ARTS, Burlington House, Piccadilly. Tel 01-734-9052, Sch Ext 40. *Keeper* Peter Greenham, CBE & BA & RA; *Cur* Walter Woodington, RP & RBA
Estab 1768; pvt; D; ent req under 25 yrs of age, though exceptions are sometimes made; degrees Royal Acad Schs Postgrad Dipl, Royal Acad Schs Dipl Advanced Studies and Royal Acad Schs Dipl, 3 yrs
Tuition: L650-L750 per yr; no campus res
Courses: Painting, Printmaking, Sculpture

ROYAL COLLEGE OF ART, Kensington Gore. Tel 01-584-5020. *Rector* Richard Guyatt, CBE & FSIAD. Instrs FT 38, PT 79
Estab 1837; pub; D; ent req ent exam; degrees 2-3 yr postgrad degrees, MA(RCA), MDes(RCA), PhD(RCA); enrl 600
Courses: Ceramics, Fashion Arts, Graphic Arts, Graphic Design, Illustration, Industrial Design, Jewelry, Painting, Photography, Printmaking, Sculpture, Silversmithing, Textile Design, Automotive Design, Design Education, Design Management, Design Research, Environmental Design, Environmental Media, Furniture Design, General Studies, Glass

SAINT MARTINS SCHOOL OF ART, 107-111 Charing Cross Rd. Tel 01-437-0058. *Principal* Ian Simpson, ARCA; *VPrincipal* Frank Halt, FLA; *Head Painting & Sculpture* Albert Herbert, ARCA; *Head Fashion Design* Lydia Kemeny, ARCA; *Head Graphic Design* Gordon Ransom, ARCA; *Head Complementary Studies* Simon Pugh, MA; *Head Found Studies* Ken Bale, ARCA
Estab 1854; pub; D & E; ent req HS dipl, ent exam, portfolio; degrees BA(Hons) in Fine Art and Graphic Design 3 yrs, BA(Hons) in Fashion Textiles Design 3-4 yrs, MA(Fashion Design) 1 yr; SC 12, GC 1; enrl D 650, E 580, grad 10
Tuition: L3300 per yr; Found Studies L1890 per yr; no campus res
Courses: †Advertising Design, Art History, †Commercial Art, Conceptual Art,

†Constructions, †Costume Design & Construction, Drawing, †Fashion Arts, †Film, †Graphic Arts, †Graphic Design, †Illustration, †Painting, †Photography, †Printmaking, †Sculpture, †Textile Design, Video

SLADE SCHOOL OF FINE ART,* University College London, Gower St. *Dir* Lawrence Gowing
Degrees BA(Fine Arts) 4 yrs, higher dipl in Fine Arts 2 yrs, dipl in Film Studies 2 yrs, MPhil or PhD(Fine Art or Film Studies); enrl 180
Courses: Drawing, Film, Painting, Sculpture, Engraving, Etching, Lithography, Silk-Screen Printing, Theatre Design

MANCHESTER

MANCHESTER POLYTECHNIC, Faculty of Art and Design, Cavendish St, All Saints. Tel 061-228 6171. *Dir* Alex Smith, PhD; *Dean Faculty* D Wain-Hobson, ARCA; *Head Dept Visual Studies* G W Hoverstadt, ATD; *Head Dept Communication Arts & Design* A L J Connolly, ATD Assoc SIAD; *Head Dept Environmental Design* M H Darke, DiplArch & FRIBA; *Head Dept Fine Art* D C Hensler, NDD & DFA; *Head Dept Printing Technol* P R Fletcher, MIOP & MSIAD; *Head Dept Textiles-Fashion* A Levy, DesRCA & FSIAD
Estab 1838, faculty estab 1970; pub; D & E; ent req high potential creative ability in art and design, 18 yrs of age, completion of full-time foundation course; degrees BA(Hons) in Graphic Design, Fine Art, Interior Design, Industrial Design, Wood-Metal-Ceramics, Embroidery, Fashion, Printed-Woven Textiles, Landscape Design and Design for Learning 3 yrs, BA(Hons) in Architecture 4 yrs, MA in Graphic Design, Fine Art and Textiles-Fashion 1 yr, MA in Interior Design and Industrial Design 2 yrs, Dipl in Landscape Archit and Foundation course 1 yr, Dipl in Archit and Photolithography 2 yrs, Dipl in Theatre and Printing 3 yrs; enrl approx 1600
Tuition: BA courses—home students L595 per yr, overseas students L940 per yr; MA courses—home students L890 per yr, overseas students L1230 per yr
Courses: Architecture, Ceramics, Fashion Arts, Film, Graphic Design, Illustration, Industrial Design, Interior Design, Jewelry, Landscape Architecture, Painting, Photography, Printmaking, Sculpture, Silversmithing, Textile Design, Foundation Course in Art and Design, Printing Technology

NOTTINGHAM

TRENT POLYTECHNIC, School of Art and Design, Burton Street. Tel 0602-48248. *Dir* R Hedley. Instrs FT 72, PT 60
Estab 1843 (Govt School of Design); pvt; ent req exam GCE on O and A levels or equivalent; degrees BA(Hons) 3-4 yrs
Courses: Fashion Arts, Graphic Arts, Interior Design, Photography, Textile Design, Theatre Arts, Fine Art, Furniture Design, Knitwear Design, Textiles Technology

FRANCE

AIX-EN-PROVENCE

INSTITUTE FOR AMERICAN UNIVERSITIES, Fine Arts in Aix, Avignon and Canterbury, 27 Place de l'Universite. Tel 42-23 39 35. *Pres* Herbert Maza, Doctorate; *Lectr* Geoffrey Rubins, Doctorate; *Lectr* Elena Colin, MA. Instrs PT 7
Estab 1957, fine arts estab 1960; pvt; D; ent req HS dipl; degrees cert granted; scholarships; SC 5, LC 2; enrl 35, non-maj 30, maj 5
Tuition: $2580 per yr, $1440 per sem, $90 per cr hr; campus res—room & board $1900 per yr
Courses: †Art History, †Drawing, History of Art & Archaeology, †Painting, Printmaking, †Sculpture, Theatre Arts, Engraving, Iron Work, Stained Glass
Summer School: Dir Art in Provence, Elena Colin. Enrl 12; tui $745 for term of 6 wks beginning June 16. Courses—Studio Painting, Printmaking and Drawing in Avignon

FONTAINEBLEAU

AMERICAN SCHOOL OF ART, PALACE OF FONTAINEBLEAU, Tel 422-25-39. *Pres* Francois Valery; *Fine Arts Dir* M Tournon-Branley
Ent req two photographs, resume, transcript, letters of reference; scholarship; enrl 40; must apply before May 15th at the Ecoles d'Art Americaines, 47 Fifth Ave, New York, NY 10003 (Tel: 212-348-2297)
Tuition: $1800 per summer session of 2 months, includes room & board and study trips
Courses: Architecture, Art History, Drawing, Painting, Sculpture, Theatre Arts

LOCOSTE

SARAH LAWRENCE COLLEGE, Village des Arts en France du Sarah Lawrence College, (Mailing Add: Foreign Studies Office, Bronxville, NY 10708), 10708. Tel 90-75-82-07. *Dir* Bernard Pfriem; *Instructor* Evert Lindfors; *Instructor* Yasuo Mizui; *Instructor* Crystal Woodward, MA. Instrs FT 10
Col estab 1928, art prog estab in France 1970; pvt; D & E; summer June 25 to Aug 5, fall sem Sept 5 to Dec 15; ent req HS dipl, recommendations, open to all qualified students and graduates of all institutions; SC 5, LC 2; enrl summer 60, fall 30
Tuition: 3350 for fall sem; $1600 for summer session
Courses: Art History, Drawing, Painting, Photography, Printmaking, Sculpture

PARIS

AMERICAN CENTER FOR STUDENTS AND ARTISTS, 261, Boulevard Rapail. Estab 1931 as a center for instruction and performance; recognized by both French and US governments; enrl 4375

ECOLE DU LOUVRE, School of the Louvre,* 34 Quai du Louvre. Tel 488-59-40. *Dir* Emmanuel Jacquin de Margerie. Instrs 41
Estab 1881; degrees for postgrads 3 yrs; LC

ECOLE NATIONALE SUPERIEURE DES ARTS DECORATIES, National College of Decorative Arts,* 31 rue d'Ulm. Tel 326-90-61. *Dir* Jacques Adnet; *Dir* Michel Toureiere
Estab 1766 as the Royal School of Design; ent req ent exam, entrants must be 17-25 yrs old, previous training; degrees 4 yr dipl
Courses: Advertising Design, Graphic Arts, Interior Design, Jewelry, Sculpture, Stage Design, Textile Design, Decorative Art, Design for Modern Industry, Metalwork, Mural Painting

ECOLE NATIONALE SUPERIEURE DES BEAUX-ARTS, National College of Fine Arts, 17, Quai Malaquais, 6e. Instrs 75
Founded 1648; enrl 2200
Courses: Drawing, Painting, Sculpture, Engraving

PARIS AMERICAN ACADEMY, 9 rue des Ursulines. *Chmn Dept* Gregg Conway; *Head Fashion Dept* Samuel Elert
Estab 1966; pvt; D & E; ent req none
Courses: Art History, Ceramics, Drawing, Painting, Photography, Sculpture, Etching, Serigraphy
Summer School: July-Aug. Courses—same as regular session. Fashion Workshops: June-Sept-Jan

UNIVERSITE DE PARIS I A LA SORBONNE, INSTITUT D'ART ET D'ARCHEOLOGIE,* 3 rue Michelet. Tel 326-94-14. *Dir* J Deshayes
Ent req exam, BA, BS, Dipl Classical Literature; degrees BA or Dipl Doctorates in Archaeology 2 yrs; enrl 300

STRASBOURG

SCHILLER COLLEGE, EUROPE UNIVERSITY, Art Department, 161 rue Melanie. *Chmn* Erik Koch; *Instr* Martin Griffiths; *Instr* Pierre Kuentz. Instrs FT 2, PT 2
Estab 1963, dept estab 1974; pvt; D & E; ent req HS dipl, BFA or equivalent plus submission of portfolio for grad students; degrees BFA 4 yrs, MFA 2 yrs; scholarships; SC 24, LC 18, GC 20; enrl maj undergrad 10, grad 6
Tuition: Res—undergrad and grad $6800 per yr, $3400 per sem, PT $125 per cr; nonres—undergrad and grad $3800 per yr, $1900 per sem; campus res—room and board $3000 (included in the figures for resident)
Courses: Advertising Design, †Art History, Drawing, Painting, Sculpture, Theatre Arts

FEDERAL REPUBLIC OF GERMANY

BERLIN

HOCHSCHULE DER KÜNSTE BERLIN, Berlin College of Art,* (Formerly Staatliche Hochschule Für Bildende Künste Berlin) Hardenbergstrasse 33. Tel 31 03 31. *Dir* Konrad Sage
Estab 1696; pub; D & E; ent req HS dipl, ent exam; degrees Dipl, Ing, architecture only
Courses: Advertising Design, Architecture, Art Education, Ceramics, Commercial Art, Costume Design & Construction, Drawing, Fashion Arts, Graphic Arts, Graphic Design, Illustration, Industrial Design, Landscape Architecture, Lettering, Painting, Sculpture, Stage Design, Textile Design

DUSSELDORF

STAATLICHE KUNSTAKADEMIE, DUSSELDORF, Hochschule für Bildende Künste, Eiskellerstrasse 1. Tel 329334. *Dir* Norbert Kricke. Instrs FT 37, PT 8
Estab 1773; pub; ent req exam, submission of portfolio, degrees 4 yrs, cert; scholarships & fels; enrl (summer terms) 650
Courses: Architecture, Art Education, Film, Graphic Arts, Painting, Sculpture, Stage Design

HAMBURG

HOCHSCHULE FÜR BILDENDE KÜNSTE, College of Fine Arts,* D 2000 Hamburg 76, Lerchenfeld 2. Tel 22811. *Pres* Dr Carl D Vogel
Courses: Architecture, Art Education, Art History, Ceramics, Drawing, Film, Graphic Arts, Industrial Design, Painting, Photography, Sculpture, Textile Design, Video, Furniture Design, Metalwork, Topography, Weaving

HEIDELBERG

SCHILLER COLLEGE-EUROPE, Fine Arts Department,* 6900 Heidelberg, Friedrich-Ebert-Anlage 4. Tel 06221-12046. *Acad Dean* J G Eggert
Estab 1964; Study Centers in Heidelberg, London, Madrid, Paris and Strasbourg; pvt; D & E; ent req HS dipl; degrees AA, ABA, BA, BM, BBA, BFA, MA, MM, MFA; enrl 650 students from 45 various countries
Courses: Art History, Ceramics, Drawing, Painting, Printmaking, Sculpture, Stage Design, Theatre Arts, Academic-Year-Abroad and Interim Programs
Summer School: Enrl 160; 6 wk prog beginning end of June

KARLSRUHE

STAATLICHE AKADEMIE DER BILDENDEN KÜNSTE, State Academy of Fine Arts,* Reinhold-Frank-Strasse 81-83. Tel 84-30-38. *Rector* Klaus Arnold
Founded 1854

MUNICH

AKADEMIE DER BILDENDEN KÜNSTE, Academy of Fine Arts, Akademiestrasse 2. Tel 39 40 57. *Pres* Schneider Wessling. Instrs FT 16, PT 4
Estab 1770, re-estab 1808, merged with Academy of Fine Arts 1946; Studies limited to 10 sem; degrees dipl; scholarships for foreigners, scholarships of German Academy's Exchange Prog and Bavarian State Dept of Educ
Courses: Graphic Arts, Interior Design, Jewelry, Painting, Sculpture, Stage Design

NUREMBERG

AKADEMIE DER BILDENDEN KÜNSTE IN NÜRNBERG, Academy of Fine Arts in Nuremberg, Bingstrasse 60. Tel 0911-40 50 61. *Prof* Günther Voglsamer
Estab 1662; pub; D; ent req HS dipl; degrees Dipl; SC 12; enrl 256
Courses: Advertising Design, Art Education, Drawing, Goldsmithing, Graphic Arts, Graphic Design, Illustration, Interior Design, Jewelry, Painting, Printmaking, Sculpture, Silversmithing, Textiles

STUTTGART

STAATLICHE AKADEMIE DER BILDENDEN KÜNSTE, State Academy of Fine Arts,* Am Weissenhof 1. Tel 25-10-51. *Rector* Dr Wolfgang Kermer
Estab 1869; pub; D; ent req Abitur for Art Educ, practical experience in applied arts, ent exam for all classes; degrees dipl in art educ; SC, LC, GC; enrl approx 900
Courses: Art Education, Art History, Ceramics, Graphic Arts, Interior Design, Painting, Sculpture, Stage Design, Textile Design, , Furniture Design, Product Design

GREECE

PAROS CYCLADES

AEGEAN SCHOOL OF FINE ARTS, Tel Aspisia Sarris 0284-21737. *Dir* Brett Taylor, MFA; *Instr* Elizabeth Carson, BA; *Instr* Nick Louca, British equivalent MFA; *Instr* Judy Sofranko, MFA; *Instr* Gail Wetzel, BS; *Vis Prof* Michael Beer, photography - 1979
Estab 1966; pvt; D & E; ent req sincere interest in exploring the arts; scholarships; SC 10, LC 5-10, GC 10; enrl maj 28, grad 2
Tuition: $480 for first eight wks, $40 for each week thereafter
Courses: †Art History, Collage, †Drawing, †Film, Graphic Arts, †Mixed Media, †Painting, †Photography, †Printmaking, †Sculpture
Summer School: Dir, Brett Taylor. Courses—same as regular session

INDIA

BARODA

MAHARAJA SAYAJIRAO UNIVERSITY OF BARODA, Faculty of Fine Arts,* University Rd, Pushpa-Baug. Tel 645-10. *Dean Faculty Fine Arts* Dr Ratan Parimoo
Estab 1949
Courses: Advertising Design, Art History, Painting, Photography, Sculpture, Lithography, Woodcrafts

IRELAND

DUBLIN

NATIONAL COLLEGE OF ART AND DESIGN, Kildare St, 2. Tel 682911. *Acting Dir* Domhnall O'Marchadha; *Deputy Dir* David Sherlock; *Head Educ* J Bullows, NDD & Cert Ed; *Head Design* M J Ozmin, MSc & Dip Des Tech & MSDI; *Head Fine Art* C Bruce, ARCA; *Head History of Art* J Turpin, PhD; *Head Pre-Dipl Studies* Myra Maguire, ANCA; *Registrar* M Gibbons, BA & HDipEd. Instrs FT 52 PT 90
Estab 1746; pub; ent req HS dipl, ent exam; degrees Assoc of National Col of Art & Design (ANCAD) 4 yrs; scholarships to Irish Citizens; enrl FT 450
Courses: Advertising Design, Aesthetics, Art Education, Art History, Ceramics, Costume Design & Construction, Display, Drafting, Drawing, Fashion Arts, Graphic Arts, Graphic Design, Handicrafts, History of Art & Archaeology, Illustration, Industrial Design, Jewelry, Lettering, Painting, Photography, Sculpture, Stage Design, Teacher Training, Textile Design, Visual Communications
Adult Hobby Classes: Enrl 300. Courses—same as above

RATHKEALE

IRISH INTERNATIONAL ARTS CENTRE, Castle Matrix, *Dir* Sean O'Driscoll, Fine Arts Dipl; *Instr* Carol Blodau, Fine Arts Dipl; *Instr* Dietrich Blodau, Fine Arts Dipl; *Instr* Peter Holloway, Fine Arts Dipl; *Vis Prof* Dr Ömür Bakirer, glassmaking
Estab 1970; pvt; D; ent req basic arts training; degrees 2 yr cert; scholarships; SC 4, LC 2; enrl D 20
Tuition: Campus res available each 2 weeks during summer
Courses: Calligraphy, Drawing, Graphic Arts, History of Art & Archaeology, Painting, †Printmaking, †Glassmaking
Summer School: Dir, Sean O'Driscoll. Enrl 20; tui $150 for term of 2 wks beginning July

ISRAEL

YEROHAM

RAMAT HANEGEV COLLEGE,
Ent req HS dipl; degrees 1 yr and 1 sem work-study programs taught in English for North American students of art, art education, architecture, design, and environmental studies. Major emphasis on new art derived from a Jewish structure of consciousness and ecological design and architecture for desert environments. Courses are generally accepted for credit by American colleges, universities and art schools; scholarships and fels; enrl 130
Tuition: $750 per sem; room & board available
Courses: Ceramics, Painting, Art and Culture, Desert Ecology, Education, Environmental Design, Hebrew Language, Jewish Studies

ITALY

BOLOGNA

ACCADEMIA DI BELLE ARTI E LICEO ARTISTICO, Academy of Fine Arts,* via Belle Arti 54. Tel 237-961. *Prof* Umberto Mastroianni

FLORENCE

ACCADEMIA DI BELLE ARTI E LICEO ARTISTICO, * via Ricasoli 66. *Dir* Luigi Biagi
Founded 1801

FORTMAN STUDIOS FLORENCE, Via Fiesolana 34 r. Tel 055-21 80 40. *Pres* Leo Forte, BFA; *Prog Coordr* Clara Carboni, Italian Degree in Design; *Prof* Richard W Boardman, BFA; *Prof* Amanda George, BA; *Prof* George Soppelsa, BFA; *Prof* Stefania Talini, Dipl; *Prof* Michael Zacceria, PhD; *Vis Prof* Walter Curini, photography; *Vis Prof* Yvonne Di Palma, sculpture
Estab 1977; pvt; D & E; ent req HS dipl, portfolio; degrees 2 yr dipl; scholarships; SC 14, LC 4; enrl D 23, E 13, non-maj 19, maj 11, others 6 PT
Tuition: $320 per course per sem; no campus res
Courses: Art History, †Drawing, Graphic Design, History of Art & Archaeology, Jewelry, Mixed Media, †Painting, †Photography, †Printmaking, †Sculpture, Textile Design

ROSARY COLLEGE, Graduate School of Fine Arts at Schifanoia Villa, via Boccaccio, 123. Tel 055-576-297. *Dean* Sr Mary Ewens. Instrs PT 20
EStab 1948; pvt; affiliated with Rosary College in River Forest, Ill; D; ent req BFA or BA; degrees MA and MFA 1-3 yrs; scholarships; enrl 40
Tuition: $2000 per sem, $165 per cr hr
Courses: Art History, Painting, Printmaking, Sculpture
Summer School: Tui $400. Courses—Art History (with lectures by top Renaissance scholars), Renaissance Architecture in Florence

STUDIO ART CENTERS INTERNATIONAL, 40 via de' Ginori. Tel (055) 26-39-48. *Dir* Jules Maidoff, MA; *Instr* Piero Colacicchi, Dipl Sculpture; *Instr* Claudio B Curri; *Instr* Tamio Fujimura, MFA; *Instr* Kathleen Knipple, MFA; *Instr* Margherita Licht, PhD; *Instr* Martino Maringoni; *Instr* Dennis Olsen, MA; *Instr* Leonardo Passeri; *Vis Artist* Luca Alinari; *Vis Artist* Renato Bittoni; *Vis Artist* Vanni Bramante; *Vis Artist* Bruno Canova; *Vis Artist* Dino Carini; *Vis Artist* Giuliano Ghelli; *Vis Artist* Dino Pasquali; *Vis Artist* Livio Orazio Valentini
Initiated by Drake Univ 1969, incorporated 1976; academically affiliated with Univ of Connecticut and Fashion & Art Institute of Dallas, Texas as well as other school progs; ent req above freshman level of college and in good acad standing (at least 2.0 based on 4.0 scale); non-college students above the age of 18; degrees fully accredited progs, with credits readily transferable to other schools; scholarships; enrl limited to 40
Tuition: Campus res available
Courses: Art History, Ceramics, Drawing, Graphic Arts, Jewelry, Painting, Photography, Printmaking, Restoration & Conservation, Sculpture, Fabric Design, Fine Arts, Metalwork & Enameling, Serigraphy, Weaving
Summer School: A special 3 wk summer session

MILAN

ACCADEMIA DI BELLE ARTI DI BRERA, Academy of Fine Arts of Brera,* Palazzo di Brera, via Brera 28. Tel 871-379. *Pres* Dr A de Michelli
Estab 1776; ent req submission of work; degrees 4 yr dipl; enrl approx 255
Courses: Painting, Sculpture, Decoration

NAPLES

ACCADEMIE DE BELLE ARTI E LICEO ARTISTICO, Academy of Fine Arts,*
via Bellini 36. *Dir* Constanza Lorenzetti
Founded 1838

PERUGIA

ACCADEMIA DI BELLE ARTI, Academy of Fine Arts, Piazza San Francesco 5.
Pres Ing Mario Serra; *Dir* P Frenguelli; *Dir* Giorgio Ascani Nuvolo; *Dir* Rag Albertina
Possanzini; *Coordr* G F Bissietta
D & E; degrees cert
Courses: Architecture, Art History, Painting, Sculpture, Stage Design, Decoration,
History of Theatre, Theory of Art
Summer School: Courses—Art, Art History, Art Tours, Bronze Casting, Ceramics,
Engraving, Fresco, Landscape Marble and Stone Work, Painting, Restoration,
Sculpture

RAVENNA

ACCADEMIA DE BELLE ARTI RAVENNA ITALIA, Academy of Fine Arts,*
Loggetta Lombardesca, Via Roma 13. Tel 23935 30178. *Dir* Raffaele De Grada
Pub; D; ent req exam; degrees Specializzazione Mosaico 4 yrs; SC 4, LC 4
Tuition: Free for foreigners; no campus res
Courses: Mosaics

ROME

ACCADEMIA DE BELLE ARTIE LICEO ARTISTICO, Academy of Fine Arts,*
via Ripetta 222. Tel 688-834, 688-861. *Dir* Dr Bottino Vencenza
Founded 1470, licensed 1873 and 1924; ent req none except with degree, 21 yrs of age;
degrees 4 yr dipl; SC, LC; enrl 1975
Courses: Architecture, Art History, Interior Design, Painting, Sculpture, Artistic
Anatomy, Decoration, Engraving, History of Costumes (Popular and Folk), History
of Movies and Theatre, Ornamental Modeling, Scene Painting, Scenery Technique,
School of Modeling, School of the Nude in Art, Techniques of Art with Marble
Adult Hobby Classes: Courses offered

AMERICAN ACADEMY IN ROME, Via Angelo Masina 5. *Dir* John H D'Arms
Estab 1894; The American Academy of Rome is not a school; it offers no courses of
instruction and maintains no teaching staff; it is simply a place where the Rome Prize
Fellows (in architecture, landscape architecture, painting, sculpture, classics, post
classical studies, art history) work and live. Information about these fellowships must
be obtained from Secretary, American Academy in Rome, 41 E 65th St, New York,
NY 10021; ent req Rome Prize Competition

BRITISH SCHOOL AT ROME, Via Gramsci 61. *Dir* David Whitehouse, PhD;
Chmn Faculty Painting Frederick Brill; *Chmn Faculty Sculpture* Paul de Monchaux;
Chmn Faculty Printmaking Alistair Grant
Estab 1911; pvt; Postgrad Inst with facilities for artists; school provides working and
living accommodations for its scholars; ent req by competition; scholarships restricted
to British and commonwealth subjects

INSTITUTO CENTRALE DEL RESTAURO, Central Institute for the Restoration
of Works of Art,* Piazza San Francesco di Paola 9. Tel 4751142, 4751143, 4751144,
4751145. *Dir* Dr Giovanni Urbani
Estab 1939; pub; D & E; ent req secondary school dipl (license) or equivalent; degrees
dipl to conduct or practice restoration 3 yrs; SC 7; enrl 24 students, 24 brokers
Tuition: None
Courses: Art Education, Chemistry, History of Antique, Law Governing Antique and
Fine Arts, Medieval and Modern Art, Natural Science, Physics, Techniques of
Restoration

TEMPLE ABROAD OF TEMPLE UNIVERSITY, Lungotevere Arnaldo da Brescia
15. Tel 06-360-2583. *Dir* Don Lantzy, MFA; *Assoc Prof* Larry Spaid, MFA; *Vis Instr*
Nona Hershey, MFA
EStab 1966; D & E; ent req HS dipl; SC 12, LC 12, GC 4; enrl D 112, E 20, maj 103,
grad 9, others 20
Tuition: Res—undergrad $905 per sem, grad $984 per sem; nonres—undergrad $1687
per sem, grad $1744 per sem; campus res—room & board $1300 per sem
Courses: Art History, Drawing, †Graphic Design, †History of Art & Archaeology,
†Painting, †Printmaking, †Sculpture

VALDOTTAVO

STUDIO CAMNITZER, Summer Graphic Workshop in Italy, Melchiade 1, Prov de
Lucca. Tel 0583-835781. *Head* Luis Camnitzer
Estab 1971, workshop estab 1971; pvt; D & E; ent req committment to work in art
(contact: 124 Susquehanna Ave, Great Neck, NY 10021); SC 1; enrl D 12 per course
Tuition: Res—$600 per month; campus res—room $150 per session
Courses: Photography, Printmaking, Multiplate Color Etching, Photo Etching
Summer School: Same as regular session

VENICE

ACCADEMIA DI BELLE ARTI E LICEO ARTISTICO, Academy of Fine Arts,*
Dorsoduro 1050. *Pres* Conte Ing Alessandro Passi
Founded 1750

JAPAN

KANAZAWA CITY

KANAZAWA BIJUTSU KOGEI DAIGAKU, Kanazawa Municipal College of Fine
and Industrial Arts,* 11-1, Kodachino 5-chome, 920. Tel 62-35-32. *Pres* Mamoru
Osawa
Estab 1950; pub; D; ent req HS dipl, ent exam; degrees MFA, 4 yrs; scholarships; SC
40, LC 86; enrl D 530, maj 20, grad 530, others 20
Courses: Advertising Design, Aesthetics, Art Education, Ceramics, Commercial Art,
Drafting, Drawing, Graphic Arts, Graphic Design, Handicrafts, History of Art &
Archaeology, Illustration, Industrial Design, Lettering, Museum Staff Training,
Painting, Photography, Sculpture, Teacher Training, Textile Design
Adult Hobby Classes: Enrl 150; no tui. Courses—Sat lectures for citizens on various
topics of arts and crafts
Summer School: Courses—offered

KYOTO

KYOTO CITY UNIVERSITY OF FINE ARTS, School of Art,* 50, Hiyoshi-cho,
Imakumano, Higashiyama-ku. Tel 561-71-41. *Dir* Takeshi Umehara; *Head Dept*
Ryuken Sawa
Estab 1880; ent req exam for HS grad, 2 yrs schooling for postgrad; degrees 4 yrs; enrl
125
Courses: Sculpture, Textile Design, Design, Japanese Painting, Lacquer, Oil Painting,
Pottery

MEXICO

CHOLULA

UNIVERSITY OF THE AMERICAS, Graphic Arts and Design Dept, Santa
Catarina Martir. Tel 47 06 55, Ext 127 and 128. *Chmn* Pamela Maquard de
Artasanchez; *Instr* Gabriel Alatriste; *Instr* Jose Chavez Huacuja; *Instr* Arq Ignacio
Cabral Perez; *Instr* Jose Lazcarro Toquero; *Instr* Sandra B de Vazquez. Instrs FT 5,
PT 5
EStab 1947; pvt; D & E; ent req HS dipl; degrees BFA(Graphic Arts and Interior
Design) 4 1 2 yrs; enrl approx 250 per sem
Courses: Advertising Design, Art History, Drawing, Illustration, Interior Design,
Painting, Photography, Black and White, Etching and Engraving, Lithography, Silk
Screen
Summer School: Courses—Ceramics, Mexican Art History, Weaving

GUADALAJARA

UNIVERSIDAD DE GUADALAJARA, Cursos de Verano Cursos de Invierno, Apdo
Postal 1-2543, Belen 120. *Dir* Jorge Martinez Lopez. Instrs FT 13
Cursos de Verano estab 1947, Cursos de Invierno estab 1972; pub; D; degrees none;
SC 10, LC 3, GC 8
Courses: Ceramics, Drawing, Handicrafts, History of Art & Archaeology, Painting,
Sculpture

MEXICO CITY

ESCUELA NACIONAL DE ARTES PLASTICAS, National School of Plastic Arts,*
Calle Academia 22. Tel 522-06-30, 522-06-44. *Master Plastic Arts* Roberto Garibay Sida
Founded 1781; enrl 750
Courses: Commercial Art, Drawing, Painting, Sculpture, Engraving

SAN MIGUEL DE ALLENDE

INSTITUTO ALLENDE, Allende Institute, Tel 465-201 90. *Pres* Stirling Dickinson;
Admin Dir Nell Fernandez; *Dean Fine Arts and Crafts* James Pinto; *Admis Officer*
William Parker; *Head Grad Studies* Fred Samuelson. Instrs FT 40
Estab 1938; pvt, inc with the Univ Guanajuato; ent req HS grad; degrees BA, BFA,
MA, MFA; scholarships; enrl approx 1500 per yr
Tuition: $490 per quarter, $40 per cr
Courses: Aesthetics, Art History, Ceramics, Drawing, Graphic Arts, Jewelry, Painting,
Photography, Sculpture, Textile Design, Design Theory, Enameling, Etching, Fabric
Design, Lithography, Stitchery, Weaving, Woodblock
Adult Hobby Classes: Tui $170 for 4 wks, $135 for 3 wks, $100 for 2 wks. Courses—
as above, non-cr, all seasons
Summer School: Dir, Stirling Dickinson. Term of 10 wks beginning June

NETHERLANDS

AMSTERDAM

GERRIT RIETVELD ACADEMIE, * Fred Roeskestraat 96, 1076 ED. Tel
020-720406/731869. *Dir* Simon H den Hartog
Estab 1924; pub; D & E; ent req HS dl, review of portfolio; degrees 5 yr dipl granted;
enrl D 500, E 380
Tuition: Depends on income of parents, maximum $220 per yr; no campus res
Courses: †Advertising Design, Art History, †Ceramics, Costume Design &

Construction, †Drawing, †Fashion Arts, †Graphic Arts, †Graphic Design, †Illustration, †Industrial Design, †Interior Design, †Jewelry, Lettering, †Painting, †Photography, †Printmaking, †Sculpture, †Silversmithing, †Teacher Training, †Textile Design, †Theatre Arts, Video, †Animation, †Glass Design

RIJKSAKADEMIE VAN BEELDENDE KUNSTEN, State Academy of Fine Arts,*
Stadhouderskade 86. Tel 79-78-11. *Dir* Dr N R A Vroom
Courses: Art History, Fine Arts, Scenography, Visual Communication

ROTTERDAM

ACADEMIE VAN BEELDENDE KUNSTEN, Academy of Fine Arts,* G J de
Jonghweg 4. Tel 3110-366244, Ext 31. *Dir* Klaas de Jong
Estab 1773; pub; D & E; ent req HS dipl; SC 6
Courses: Advertising Design, Art History, Ceramics, Collage, Commercial Art,
Conceptual Art, Constructions, Costume Design & Construction, Display, Drawing,
Fashion Arts, Film, Graphic Arts, Graphic Design, Illustration, Interior Design,
Lettering, Mixed Media, Painting, Photography, Printmaking, Sculpture, Teacher
Training, Video

THE HAGUE

KONINKLIJKE ACADEMIE VAN BEELDENDE KUNSTEN, Royal Academy of
Fine Arts,* Prinsessegracht 4. Tel 070-643835. *Dir* J J Beljon
Estab 1682; D & E; ent req HS dipl; LC 6
Tuition: 150 Dutch guilders; no campus res
Courses: Advertising Design, Costume Design & Construction, Drawing, Fashion
Arts, Graphic Arts, Graphic Design, Illustration, Industrial Design, Interior Design,
Painting, Sculpture, Textile Design, Environmental Design

STICHTING DE VRIJE ACADEMIE VOOR BEELDENDE KUNSTEN,
Foundation The Free Academy for Fine Arts, De Vrye Academie Psychopolis, De
Gheynstraat 129, PO Box 61390. Tel 070-638968. *Dir* George Lampe. Instrs PT approx
50
EStab 1947, resorting under the Ministry of Culture and the Municipality of the Hague;
ent req none; degrees none
Courses: Advertising Design, Aesthetics, Ceramics, Conceptual Art, Constructions,
Drawing, Fashion Arts, Film, Graphic Arts, Graphic Design, Handicrafts, Illustration,
Jewelry, Painting, Photography, Printmaking, Sculpture, Textile Design, Video, Art
Appreciation, Audio Visuals, Etching, Forging, General Design, Glass, Leather Work,
Lithography, Silk Screen, Soldering, Welding

NEW ZEALAND

AUCKLAND

UNIVERSITY OF AUCKLAND, School of Fine Arts, 20 Whitaker Place, Private
Bag. *Prof* J D Saunders, DipFA(Hons); *Prof* Paul J Beadle, MFIM(Hon)
Estab 1881, school estab 1950; pub; D; ent req univ ent; degrees BFA 4 yrs, MFA 2
yrs
Tuition: On application (varies)
Courses: Advertising Design, Aesthetics, Art History, Commercial Art, Conceptual
Art, Drawing, Graphic Arts, Graphic Design, Handicrafts, Industrial Design,
Intermedia, Jewelry, Lettering, Mixed Media, Painting, Photography, Printmaking,
Sculpture, Silversmithing, Video, Fiber
Summer School: Organized by Continuing Educ Dept. Courses—Photography,
Printmaking (others from time to time)

NORWAY

OSLO

STATENS KUNSTAKADEMI, State Art Academy, Uranienborgvien 2. *Rector*
Knuse Rose; *Adminr* Aina Helgesen. Instrs FT 5, PT 6
EStab 1909; ent req exam; degrees 4 yr
Tuition: None
Courses: Drawing, Graphic Arts, Painting, Sculpture, Modeling

POLAND

CRACOW

AKADEMIA SZTUK PIEKNYCH, Academy of Fine Arts, Plac Matekji. Tel 2-60-81.
Rector Marian Konieczny
Courses: Advertising Design, Graphic Arts, Industrial Design, Interior Design,
Painting, Restoration & Conservation, Sculpture, Textile Design, Posters,
Scenography, Town Planning

LODZ

PANSTWOWA WYZSZA SZKOLA SZTUK PLASTYCZNYCH, Higher School of
Art and Design, 121 Wojska Polskiego St. Tel 728-88. *Rector* Wiestaw Garbolinski;
Vice Rector Jerzy Derkowski; *Vice Rector* Benon Liberski; *Head Dept Painting &
Graphic Arts* Krystyn Zielinski; *Head Dept Industrial Design* Andrzej Nawrot
Estab 1946; pub; D; ent req HS dipl, ent exam; degrees MA 5 yrs; enrl D 60
Tuition: Campus res available
Courses: Art History, Drawing, Fashion Arts, Goldsmithing, Graphic Arts, Graphic
Design, Industrial Design, Jewelry, Painting, Photography, Printmaking, Sculpture,
Silversmithing, Textile Design

WARSAW

AKADEMIA SZTUK PIEKNYCH, Academy of Fine Arts, Krakowskie
Przedmiescie 5.
Courses: Graphic Arts, Industrial Design, Interior Design, Painting, Restoration &
Conservation, Sculpture, Textile Design, Theatre Set Design

PORTUGAL

LISBON

ESCOLA SUPERIOR DE BELAS ARTES, School of Fine Arts, Largo da Biblioteca
Publica.
Estab 1836

SCOTLAND

EDINBURGH

EDINBURGH COLLEGE OF ART, Lauriston Place. Tel 031-229 9311. *Acting
Principal* Gavin T N Ross, DA & MArchit & RIBA & ARIAS
Estab 1907
Courses: Architecture, Drawing, Handicrafts, Painting, Sculpture, Design, Planning

REPUBLIC OF SOUTH AFRICA

PORT ELIZABETH

PORT ELIZABETH TECHNIKON, Department of Art and Design of the Port,
Private Bag X6011. *Head Dept* G H H Nesbit. Instrs FT 25, PT 3
Estab 1882; pub; D; ent req HS dipl; degrees National Dipl (Art, Design, Photo) 3 yrs,
Higher National Dipl 4 yrs; enrl 175
Tuition: Campus res available
Courses: Advertising Design, Art Education, Art History, Ceramics, Commercial Art,
Costume Design & Construction, Drawing, Fashion Arts, Graphic Arts, Graphic
Design, Illustration, Lettering, Painting, Photography, Printmaking, Sculpture,
Teacher Training, Textile Design, Animation

SPAIN

MADRID

ESCUELA DE ARTES DECORATIVAS, School of Decorative Arts,* 5 Heroes del
10 de Agosto. Tel 2 26-67-74. *Head Dept* Jose Luis Mercado Segoviano
Pvt; D & E; ent req HS dipl; degrees Interior Decoration and Technology; scholarships;
SC 3, LC 4; enrl major and grad students
Tuition: No campus res
Courses: Advertising Design, Art Education, Art History, Drawing, Interior Design
Adult Hobby Classes: Tui $35 per month. Courses—Interior Decoration and
Technology
Children's Classes: Tui $35 per month. Courses—Drawing, Painting

ESCUELA NACIONAL DE ARTES GRAFICAS, Madrid School of Graphic Arts,*
Calle Jesus Maestro, 3. Tel 234-51-26. *Dir* Don Jose Perez Calin
Estab 1911; degrees 3 yr; enrl 223
Courses: Graphic Arts

SEVILLE

**ESCUELA SUPERIOR DE BELLAS ARTES DE SANTA ISABEL DE HUNGRIA
DE SEVILLE,** Seville School of Fine Arts,* Calle Gonzalo Bilbao 7-13. *Dir* Dr
Antonio Sancho Corbacho
Founded 1940; enrl 106
Courses: Fine Arts

VALENCIA

ESCUELA SUPERIOR DE BELLAS ARTES DE SAN CARLOS, Valencia School of Fine Arts,* Calle del Museo 2. *Dir* Felipe Maria Garin Orlitz de Taranco
Estab 1765, affiliated with the Univ of Valencia; degrees 5 yrs; scholarships; enrl 300
Summer School: 8 wks from July to Sept

SWEDEN

GOTHENBURG

UNIVERSITY OF GOTHENBURG, School of Crafts and Design, Kristinelundsgatan 6-8. Tel 16 05 17 or 20 87 65. *In charge* Neils-Henry Monk
Ent req artistic talent proved in ent exams, a good knowledge of one Scandinavian language is desirable; degrees 4 yr
Courses: Crafts(Textiles, Ceramics, Metals), Environmental Design (Interior Design, Furniture Design), Information Design (Advertising and Graphic Design), Product Design (Hard Industrial Design & Soft Industrial Design)

STOCKHOLM

KUNGL KONSTHOGSKOLAN, College of Fine Arts in Stockholm, Fredsgatan 12, Box 16 317. *Dir* Sven Ljungberg. Instrs FT 19
Estab 1735; affiliated until 1979 with the Royal Swedign Academy of Fine Arts; ent req 17 yrs, submit works; degrees 5 yrs, archit 1 yr
Tuition: No campus res
Courses: Architecture, Drawing, Graphic Arts, Painting, Sculpture

SWITZERLAND

GENEVA

ECOLES D'ART DE GENEVE, Geneva Schools of Art,
—**Ecole Superieure D'Art Visuel,** Higher School of Visual Arts, 9, bd Helvetique. Tel 29-05-10.

Founded 1748; ent req HS grad, ent exam; degrees dipl
Courses: Painting, Sculpture, Audiovisual Expression, Design, Engraving, Modeling, Perspective
—**Ecole des Arts Decoratifs,** School of Decorative Arts, 15, Bd James-Fazy. Tel 31-37-57. *Head* M Claude Malinjod
Founded 1876; ent req HS grad, ent exam; degrees cert
Courses: Ceramics, Graphic Arts, Industrial Design, Interior Design, Jewelry, Enameling

LAUSANNE

LAUSANNE COLLEGE OF ART AND DESIGN, Ave Elysee 4. Tel 021 27 75 23. *Principal* Jacques Monnier-Raball, Lic es Lett; *Dean* Leon Prebandier; *Head Fine Arts* Hansjörg Gisiger; *Head General Artistic Studies* Janos Urban; *Head Graphic Design Dept* Werner Jeker; *Head Industrial Design Dept* Claude Dupraz
Estab 1821; pub; D; ent req HS dipl; degrees 5 yr dipl granted; SC 27, LC 15, GC 42
Tuition: 557.50 FrS; no campus res
Courses: Advertising Design, Aesthetics, Art Education, Calligraphy, Commercial Art, Conceptual Art, Constructions, Display, Drafting, Drawing, Film, Graphic Arts, Graphic Design, History of Art & Archaeology, Illustration, Industrial Design, Intermedia, Lettering, Mixed Media, Painting, Photography, Printmaking, Sculpture, Teacher Training, Video, Semiology

USSR

TALLINN

EESTI NSV RIIKLIK KUNSTIINSTITUUT, Tartu Maantee 1. *Rector* J Vares; *Asst Rector* P Tarvas; *Dean* A Mölder; *Dean* H Parmas. Instrs FT 95, PT 14
Estab 1914; ent req secondary educ, preliminary training in art; degrees 5-6 yrs; scholarships; SC, LC
Courses: Architecture, Ceramics, Fashion Arts, Graphic Arts, Interior Design, Painting, Sculpture, Textile Design, Design, Glass, Leather, Metalwork, Scene Decoration
Children's Classes: Courses offered

III ART INFORMATION

State Arts Councils

**Directors and Supervisors of Art Education
in School Systems**

Art Magazines

**Newspapers Carrying Art Notes
and Their Critics**

Scholarships and Fellowships

Open Exhibitions

Traveling Exhibition Booking Agencies

State Arts Councils

This Directory of State Arts Councils was compiled by the American Council for the Arts, 570 Seventh Avenue, New York, N.Y. 10018. Permission to include the listing in the AMERICAN ART DIRECTORY is gratefully acknowledged by the Editors.

NATIONAL ENDOWMENT FOR THE ARTS REGIONAL REPRESENTATIVES

Great Lakes

Bert Masor
4200 Marine DR
Chicago, IL 60613
312-525-6748 or 782-7858
(IL, IN, MI, OH, WI)

Mid-Atlantic

Eduardo Garcia
113 Valley Road
Neptun, New Jersey 07753
201-774-2714
(DE, MD, NJ, PA)

Mid-South

Gerald Ness
2130 P ST NW Apt 422
Washington, DC 20037
202-293-9042
(DC, KY, NC, SC, TN, VA, WV)

New England

Rudy Nashan
30 Savoy St
Providence, RI 02906
401-274-4754
(CT, ME, MA, NH, RI, VT)

North Plains

Joanne D. Soper
3510 Lindenwood
Souix City, IA 51104
712-258-2014
(IA, MN, NE, ND)

Northwest

Terry Melton
728 Rural Avenue S
Salem, OR 97302
503-581-5264
(AK, ID, MT, OR, WA)

Pacific

Dale Kobler
PO Box 15187
San Francisco, CA 94115
415-863-3906
(AS, CA, CM, GU, HI, NV)

South Plains

Frances Poteet
601 E Austin #1410
Alamo, TX 78516
512-787-6756
(AR, KS, MO, OK, TX)

Southwest

Bill Jamison
PO Box 1804
Santa Fe, NM 87501
505-982-2041
(AZ, CO, NM, UT, WY)

GULF

Vacant
(AL, GA, FL, LA, MS)

New York-Caribbean

John Wessel
110 West 15th Street
New York, NY 10011
212-989-6347
(NY, PR, VI)

REGIONAL ORGANIZATIONS

Affiliated State Arts Agencies of the Upper Midwest

David Haugland, Executive Director
430 Oak Grove St. (402)
Minneapolis MN 55403
612-871-6392
(IA, MN, ND, SD, WI)

The Arts Exchange, Inc.

Clint Baer, Jr., Director
Phenix Hall
40 N Main St
Concord, NH 03301
603-228-1624
(ME, NH, UT)

Consortium of Pacific Arts and Culture

Ira Perman, Director
Arts Alaska, Inc.
619 Warehouse Ave #216
Anchorage, AK 99501
907-272-3429
(AK, AS, CA, CM, GU, HI)

Great Lakes Arts Alliance

Lara Mulholland, Director
630 S 3rd St
Columbus, OH 43206
614-221-4322
(IL, IN, MI, OH)

Mid-American Arts Alliance

Henry Moran, Director
20 W. 9th St. (550)
Kansas City MO 64105
816-421-1388
(AR, KS, MO, NE, OK)

New England Foundation for the Arts, Inc.

Thomas Wolf, Director
8 Francis Ave
Cambridge, MA 02138
617-492-2914
(CT, ME, MA, NH, RI, UT)

Southern Arts Federation

225 Peachtree St #712
Atlanta, GA 30303
404-577-7244
(AL, GA, FL, KY, LA, MS, NC, SC, TN, VA)

Western States Arts Foundation

428 E 11th Ave
Denver CO 80203
303-832-7979
(AZ, CO, ID, MT, NV, NM, OR, UT, WA, WY)

STATE ART AGENCIES

Alabama State Council on the Arts and Humanities

Mr. Aubrey D. Green, Chairman
PO Drawer G
York, AL 36952

M.J. Zakrzewski, Executive Director
114 N Hull St
Montgomery, AL 36130
205-832-6758

Alaska State Council on the Arts

Mrs. Jean Mackin, Chariman
1114 Nenana
Fairbanks, AK 99701

Ronald L. Evans, Executive Director
619 Warehouse Ave #220
Anchorage, AK 99501
907-279-1558

Arizona Commission on the Arts and Humanities

Dino De Concini, Chairman
100 W. Washington, Suite #1550
Phoenix, AZ 85003

Mrs. Louise Tester, Executive Director
6330 N 7th St
Phoenix, AZ 85014
602-255-5882

Arkansas Arts Council

Mrs. Theodosia Nolan, Chairman
900 N Madison St
El Dorado, AR 71730

Carolyn Staley, Executive Director
Continental Bldg, #500
Main & Markham Sts
Little Rock, AR 72201
501-371-2539

California Arts Council

Harold Keith, Chairman
1014 Laurel Lane
Beverly Hills, CA 90210

Bill Cook, Executive Director
2022 J St
Sacramento, CA 95814
916-445-1530

Colorado Council on the Arts and Humanities

Robert B. Yegge, Chairman
121 Lafayette St
Denver, CO 80218

Ed Harrison, Acting Director
Grant-Humphreys Mansion
770 Pennsylvania St
Denver, CO 80203
303-839-2617 or 2618

Connecticut Commission on the Arts

Mrs. June Goodman, Chairman
1 Lakeside Rd
Danbury, CT 06810

Anthony S. Keller, Executive Director
340 Capitol Ave
Hartford, CT 06106
203-566-4770

Delaware State Arts Council

John E. (Gene) Derrickson, Chairman
406 Harvey Rd
Claymont, DE 19703

Don Shulman, Executive Director
State Office Bldg
820 N French St
Wilmington, DE 19801
302-571-3540

D.C. Commission on the Arts And Humanities

Peggy Cooper, Chairman
2900 45th St NW #216
Washington, DC 20016

Mildred Bautista, Executive Director
1012 14th St #1200
Washington, DC 20005
202-724-5613

Fine Arts Council of Florida

Mrs. Peggy Hurst, Chairman
12811 Griffing Blvd
N Miami, FL 33161

Rebecca Kushner, Executive Director
Div. of Cultural Affairs
Dept. of State, The Capitol
Tallahassee, FL 32304
904-487-2980

Georgia Council for the Arts and Humanities

Mrs. Isabelle Watkins, Chairman
3920 Club Dr NE
Atlanta, GA 30319

Frank Ratka, Executive Director
1627 Peachtree St., N.E.
Suite 210
Atlanta, Georgia 30309
404-656-3967

Hawaii State Foundation on Culture and the Arts

Beatrice Los Banos Ranis, Chairman
44-215 Mikiola Dr
Kaneohe, HI 96744

Alfred Preis, Executive Director
250 S King St #310
Honolulu, HI 96813
808-548-4145

Idaho Commission on the Arts

Kellie Cosho, Chairman
531 Warm Springs Ave
Boise, ID 83702

Carl J. Petrick, Executive Director
c/o Statehouse Mail
Boise, ID 83720
208-384-2119

Illinois Arts Council

William M. DuVall, Chairman
Director, Public Affairs
Borg Warner Corp.
200 S. Michigan Ave
Chicago, IL 60604

Clark Mitze, Executive Director
111 N Wabash Ave #700
Chicago, IL 60602
312-793-6750

Indiana Arts Commission

Franklin D. Schurz, Jr., Chairman
Editor, South Bend Tribune
225 West Colfax Ave.
South Bend, IN 46626

Janet Harris, Executive Director
Union Title Bldg #614
155 E. Market St
Indianapolis, IN 46204
317-232-1268

Iowa State Arts Council

Don Singer, Chairman
320 Lillian Lane
Waterloo, Iowa 50701

Kansas Arts Commission

John Reed, Executive Director
112 W 6th St
Topeka, KS 66603

Kentucky Arts Commission

Albert Smith, Chairman
The Logan Leader
Russellville, KY 42276

Ms. Nash Cox, Executive Director
302 Wilkinson St
Frankfort, KY 40601
502-564-3757

Louisiana State Arts Council

Mrs. Peg Towers, Chairman
9677 W Tampa Dr
Baton Rouge, LA 70815

Al Head, Executive Director
Div. of the Arts
PO Box 44247
Baton Rouge, LA 70801
504-342-6467

Maine State Commission on the Arts and Humanities

Eaton Tarbell, Chairman
Eaton Tarbell Assoc.
1 Merchant Plaza
Bangor, ME 04401

Alden C. (Denny) Wilson, Executive Director
State House
Augusta, ME 04330
207-289-2724

Maryland Arts Council

James L. Burgess, Chairman
1208 Camden Ave
Salisbury, MD 21801

Kenneth Kahn, Executive Director
15 W Mulberry
Baltimore, MD 21201
301-685-6740

Massachusetts Council on the Arts and Humanities

Vernon R. Alden, Chairman
MA Business Development Council
600 Atlantic Ave
Boston, MA 02106

Anne Hawley, Executive Director
1 Ashburton Pl
Boston, MA 02108
617-727-3668

Michigan Council for the Arts

Walter R. Boris, Chairman
Exec. VP of Finance
Consumer Power Co
212 W Michigan Ave
Jackson, MI 49201

E. Ray Scott, Executive Director
1200 6th Ave
Executive Plaza
Detroit, MI 48226
313-256-3735

Minnesota State Arts Board

Stephen Keating, Chairman
Honeywell, Inc.
2701 4th Ave S
Minneapolis, MN 55408

John Ondov, Executive Director
2500 Park Avenue
Minneapolis, MN 55404
612-341-7170
1-800-652-9747

Mississippi Arts Commission

Mrs. W.A. Middleton, Chairman
216 Fairgrounds
Winona, MS 38967

Lida Rogers, Executive Director
301 N Lamar St
PO Box 1341
Jackson, MS 39205
601-354-7336

Missouri State Council on the Arts

Mrs. Rosalyn Kling, Chairman
802 Bluesprings Ln.
St. Louis, MO 63181

Mary DeHahn, Executive Director
706 Chestnut St.
St. Louis, MO 63101

Montana Arts Council

Mrs. Maxine Blackmer, Chairman
635 Hastings
Missoula, MT 59801

David E. Nelson, Executive Director
1280 South Third St. W.
Missoula, MT 59801
406-543-8286

Nebraska Arts Council

Wallace A. Richardson, Chairman
1000 NBC Center
Lincoln, NE 68508

Robin Tryloff, Executive Director
8448 W. Center Rd.
Omaha, NE 68124
402-554-2122

Nevada State Council on the Arts

Chico Alvarez, Chairman
P.O. Box 7467
Las Vegas, NV 89101

Jacqueline Belmont, Executive Director
4600 Kietzke #134 Bldg D
Reno, NV 89502
702-784-6231 or 6232

New Hampshire Commission on the Arts

Barbara J. Dunfey, Chairman
35 Wentworth Rd
Portsmouth, NH 03801

John G. Coe, Executive Director
Phenix Hall
40 N Main St
Concord, NH 03301
603-271-2789

New Jersey State Council on the Arts

Henry Kulkman, Chairman
9 Homestead Dr
Millville, NJ 08332

Eileen Lawton, Executive Director
109 W State St
Trenton, NJ 08608
609-292-6130

New Mexico Arts Division

Prof. Edward P. Vega, Chairman
2913 Indiana NE
Albuquerque, NM 87110

Bernard Blas Lopez, Executive Director
113 Lincoln
Santa Fe, NM 87503
505-827-2061

New York State Council on the Arts

Mrs. Moss (Kitty) Hart, Chairman
80 Centre St
New York, NY 10013

Theodore Striggles, Executive Director
80 Centre St
New York, NY 10013
212-488-5222

North Carolina Arts Council

Martin H. Lancaster, Chairman
PO Box 916
Goldsboro, NC 27530

Mary Regan, Executive Director
NC Dept. Of Cultural Resources
407 N Person St
Raleigh, NC 27611
919-733-7897—Programs
919-733-2821—Administration

North Dakota Council on the Arts

John Hove, Chairman
Dept. of English
ND State University
Fargo, ND 58102

Glenn Scott, Executive Director
309D Minard Hall
ND State University
Fargo, ND 58102
701-237-7674

Ohio Arts Council

John Henle, Chairman
5704 Olentangy Blvd
Worthington, OH 43085

Wayne Lawson, Executive Director
50 W Broad St #3600
Columbus, OH 43215
614-466-2613

Oklahoma Arts and Humanities Council

Martin Hagerstrand, Chairman
PO Box 515
Tahlequah, OK 74464

Ben DiSalvo, Executive Director
Jim Thorpe Bldg
2101 N Lincoln Blvd
Oklahoma City, OK 73105
405-521-2931

Oregon Arts Commission

Peter Koehler, Chairman
c/o Evans Products
1121 SW Salmon St
Portland, OR 97205

Peter Hero, Executive Director
835 Summer St NE
Salem, OR 97301
503-378-3625

Commonwealth of Pennsylvania Council on the Arts

Dr. Edward Arian, Chairman
116 Boulder Rd
Plymouth Meeting, PA 19462

Peter Carnahan, Acting Director
3 Shore Dr Office Center
2001 N Front St
Harrisburg, PA 17102
717-787-6883

Rhode Island State Council on the Arts

Donald J. Aldrich, Chairman
RI Hospital Trust Natl. Bank
1 Hospital Trust Plaza
Providence, RI 02903

Robin Berry, Executive Director
334 Westminster Mall
Providence, RI 02903
401-277-3880

South Carolina Arts Commission

Charlotte N. Cassels, Chairman
P.O. Box 2167
Aiken, SC 29801

Rick George, Executive Director
1800 Gervais St
Columbia, SC 29201
803-758-3442

South Dakota State Fine Arts Council

Lynn Friefeld, Chairman
Box 26
Brookings, SD 57006

Mrs. Charlotte Carver, Executive Director
108 W 11th St
Sioux Falls, SD 57102
605-339-6646

Tennessee Arts Commission

Robert L. Huffman, Chairman
35 Oakmont Pl
Jackson, TN 38301

Arthur L. Keeble, Executive Director
222 Capitol Hill Bldg
Nashville, TN 37219
615-741-1701

Texas Commission on the Arts and Humanities

Arnold Swartz, Chairman
PO Box 2101
San Antonio, TX 78297

Allan Longacre, Executive Director
PO Box 13406
Capitol Sta
Austin, TX 78711
512-475-6593

Utah Arts Council

Walter G. Smith, Chairman
Arizona Ranch and Metals Co.
1518 Walker Bank Buildings
Salt Lake City, UT 84111

Ruth Draper, Executive Director
617 E S Temple St
Salt Lake City, UT 84102
801-533-5895

Vermont Council on the Arts

Dorothy Olson, Chairman
Box 801
Brattleboro, VT 05301

Ellen McCulloch-Lovell, Executive Director
136 State St
Montpelier, VT 05602
802-828-3291

Virginia Commission for the Arts

Norman Willcox, Chairman
PO Box 3000
Norfolk, VA 23514

Jerry Haynie, Executive Director
400 E Grace St 1st floor
Richmond, VA 23219
804-786-4492

Washington State Arts Commission

Mary Dunton, Chairman
Ft Wright
W 4000 Randolph Rd
Spokane, WA 99204

James. L. Haseltine, Executive Director
9th & Columbia Bldg
Mail Stop FU-12
Olympia, WA 98504
206-753-3860

**West Virginia Department of Culture and History,
Arts and Humanities Division**

Dr. Ronald L. Jones, Jr., Chairman
Box 389, Willowdale
Shepherdstown, WV 25443

James B. Andrews, Executive Director
WV Dept of Culture & History
Capitol Complex
Charleston, WV 25305
304-348-0240

Wisconsin Arts Board

Richard Wagner, Chairman
Dept. of Facilities' Management
Room 160
1 West Wilson Street
Madison, WI 53702

Jerrold Rouby, Executive Director
123 W Washington Ave
Madison, WI 53702
608-266-0190

Wyoming Council on the Arts

Peter Hassrick, Chairman
Dir., Buffalo Bill Hist Ctr
Box 1020
Cody, WY 82414

John Buhler, Executive Director
122 W 25th St
Cheyenne, WY 82002
307-777-7742

American Samoa Arts Council

Palauni M. Tuiasosopo, Chairman
Office of the Governor
Pago Pago, AS 96799

Mr. Enosa Pili, Executive Director
PO Box 1540
Office of the Governor
Pago Pago, AS 96799
633-4347

Insular Arts Council of Guam

Marilyn Abalos, Chairman
4 Chichirica
Dededo, GU 96912

S.M. Callista Camacho, Executive Director
PO Box 20567
Main Facility, GU 96921
477-7413 or 9845

Commonwealth of the Northern Mariana Islands

Linda Whitney, Chairman
DC Office #700
1016 16th St NW
Washington, DC 20006

Dennis Vander Tuig, Executive Director
Dept/Community & Cult Affairs
Saipan, CM 96950

Institute of Puerto Rican Culture

Carlos Sanz, Chairman
Apartado Postal 4184
San Juan, PR 00905

Luis M. Rodriguez Morales, Executive Director
Apartado Postal 4184
San Juan, PR 00905
809-723-2115

Virgin Islands Council on the Arts

Mrs. Rita L. Forbes, Chairman
PO Box 217
Christiansted, St Croix, VI 00820

Stephen J. Bostic, Executive Director
Caravelle Arcade
Christiansted, St Croix, VI 00820
809-773-3075

Directors and Supervisors of Art Education in School Systems

Compiled from a survey made by the National Art Education Association under the direction of Dr. John J. Mahlman, Executive Director. An asterisk (*) indicates no specific supervisor - supervision being handled by general supervisor listed.

ALABAMA

Dr. John B. Hall
Visual Arts Specialist
State Department of Education
111 Coliseum Boulevard
Montgomery, Alabama 36109
205-279-9245

ALASKA

Vacant

ARIZONA

Mr. Raymond G. Van Diest
Fine Arts Specialist
Arizona Department of Education
1535 W. Jefferson Street
Phoenix, Arizona 85007
602-255-5233

ARKANSAS

Ms. Brenda Turner
Specialist, Art Education
Department of Education
Capitol Mall
Little Rock, Arkansas 72201
501-371-2525 or 501-371-2526

CALIFORNIA

Dr. Louis P. Nash, Consultant
Arts and Humanities Education
California State Department of Education
721 Capitol Mall
Sacramento, California 95814
916-322-4015

COLORADO

Mr. Ken Bolin
Mr. Don Green
Supervisors of Art
1115 North El Paso Street
Colorado Springs, Colorado 80903
303-635-6681 or 303-635-6682

CONNECTICUT

Dr. Robert J. Saunders
Art Education Consultant
State Department of Education
P. O. Box 2219
Hartford, Connecticut 06115
203-566-5223

DELAWARE

Mr. James R. Gervan
State Supervisor of Art and Music
Department of Public Instruction
Townsend Building
P. O. Box 1402
Dover, Delaware 19901
302-678-4887

DISTRICT OF COLUMBIA

Mrs. Georgia Jessup Luck
Acting Supervising Director of Art
Watkins School
12th and E Streets, S.E.
Washington, D. C. 20003
202-724-4984 (art office)
202-724-4173 (emergency only)

FLORIDA

Mr. Neil Mooney, Art Consultant
Miles Johnson Building
Suite 108
State Department of Education
Tallahassee, Florida 32304
904-488-5694

GEORGIA

Ms. Ruth Gassett
Consultant, Art Education
Education Annex
156 Trinity Street, S.W.
Atlanta, Georgia 30303
404-656-2414

HAWAII

Mr. Stanley Yamamoto
Program Specialist
Art Education
1270 Queen Emma Street
Room 1201
Honolulu, Hawaii 96804
808-548-3284

IDAHO

Mr. Bert A. Burda
Fine Arts Representative
Len B. Jordan Office Building
State Department of Education
Boise, Idaho 83720
208-334-2281

ILLINOIS

Vacant

INDIANA

Mr. Barry Patrick, Art Consultant
Division of Curriculum
State Department of Education
Room 229

State House
Indianapolis, Indiana 46204
317-927-0111

IOWA

Dr. Laura Magee
Consultant, Arts Education
Curriculum Division
Department of Public Instruction
Grimes State Office Building
Des Moines, Iowa 50319
515-281-3160

KANSAS

*

Mr. George R. Neaderhiser
Education Program Specialist
State Department of Education
120 East 10th Avenue
Topeka, Kansas 66612

KENTUCKY

Mrs. Ruth West, Program Manager
Division of Program Development
Kentucky Department of Education
Frankfort, Kentucky 40601
502-564-2672

LOUISIANA

Mrs. Myrtle Kerr
State Supervisor of Art & Humanities
P. O. Box 44064
Baton Rouge, Louisiana 70804
504-342-3393

MAINE

Mr. Virgilio Mori, Arts Coordinator
State of Maine
Department of Educational and Cultural Services
Augusta, Maine 04333
207-289-2033

MARYLAND

Vacant

MASSACHUSETTS

Ms. Patricia Mazza
Arts in Education Specialist
State Department of Education
31 St. James Avenue, Room 539
Boston, Massachusetts 02116

MICHIGAN

Dr. Barbara Carlisle
Fine Arts Specialist
Michigan Department of Education
Box 30008
Lansing, Michigan 48909
517-373-1484

MINNESOTA

Ms. Mary Honetschager
Arts Education Consultant
Minnesota Department of Education
Capitol Square Building
St. Paul, Minnesota 55101
612-433-3795 (home)

MISSISSIPPI

Ms. Sandra Nicola
Art Education Consultant

Mississippi State Dept. of Education
P. O. Box 711
Jackson, Mississippi 39205
601-354-6876

MISSOURI

*

Dr. Richard L. King, Coordinator
Curriculum Unit
Missouri Department of Elementary and Secondary Education
P. O. Box 480
Jefferson City, Missouri 65102
314-751-2625

MONTANA

Mrs. Kay Burkhardt, Consultant
Arts in Education Program
Music, Visual Arts, Drama, Dance
Office of Public Instruction
State Capitol, Room #106
Helena, Montana 59601
406-449-3116

NEBRASKA

*

Mr. Stan Carlson, Administrator
School Management & Curriculum
Department of Education
301 Centennial Mall
Lincoln, Nebraska 68501
402-471-2444

NEVADA

Mr. Tom Summers
Consultant in Humanities
Nevada Department of Education
Capitol Complex
Carson City, Nevada 89710

NEW HAMPSHIRE

Mr. John Michael Gray
Consultant, Arts Education
Department of Education
64 North Main Street
Concord, New Hampshire 03301
603-271-2402

NEW JERSEY

Ms. Susan M. Brainerd
Arts Education Coordinator
New Jersey Department of Education
Division of School Programs
225 W. State Street
Trenton, New Jersey 08625
609-292-1544

NEW MEXICO

Ms. Vicki Breen
Director of Visual Arts
New Mexico State Dept. of Education
Education Building
Santa Fe, New Mexico 87503

NEW YORK

Mr. E. Andrew Mills
Mr. Jim Gilligan
Mr. Robert Reals
State Department of Education
Room 681, EBA
Albany, New York 12234
518-474-8779

NORTH CAROLINA

Mr. Doc McCulloch
State Art Supervisor
Division of Cultural Arts

State Dept. of Public Instruction
Raleigh, North Carolina 27611
919-733-7467

NORTH DAKOTA

Mr. Roger Kolsrud, Coordinator
Fine Arts & Music
Dept. of Public Instruction
Capitol Building
Bismarck, North Dakota 58505
701-224-2269

OHIO

Mr. Jerry Tollifson, Supervisor
Art Education, Dept. of Education
Ohio Departments Building
Room 815, 65 South Front Street
Columbus, Ohio 43215
614-466-2761

OKLAHOMA

Ms. Peggy Long, Administrator
Arts-in-Education Program
State Department of Education
2500 N. Lincoln
Oklahoma City, Oklahoma 73105
405-521-3361

OREGON

*

Dr. Delmer Aebischer
Basic Education Section
State Department of Education
942 Lancaster Drive, N.E.
Salem, Oregon 97310

PENNSYLVANIA

Mr. Clyde M. McGeary, Chief
Division of General Education
Bureau of Curriculum Services
Department of Education
Box 911
Harrisburg, Pennsylvania 17126
717-783-6746

RHODE ISLAND

Vacant

SOUTH CAROLINA

Dr. Thomas Hatfield
Supervisor of Art
South Carolina Dept. of Education
705 Rutledge Building
Columbia, South Carolina 29201
803-758-2652

SOUTH DAKOTA

*

Dr. Joyce Levin
Director of Curriculum
Division of Elementary and Secondary Education
Kneip Building·
Pierre, South Dakota 57501
605-773-3782

TENNESSEE

Mr. Beasley Overbey
Arts Specialist
Department of Education
State of Tennessee
805½ Nashville Highway
Columbia, Tennessee 38401

TEXAS

Mr. Phil Manning
Program Director, Fine Arts
Texas Education Agency
201 East 11th Street
Austin, Texas 78701

UTAH

Dr. Charles B. Stubbs
State Specialist in Art Education
250 E. 5th South
Salt Lake City, Utah 84111
801-533-5965 (office)
801-943-7313 (home)

VERMONT

*

Mr. Donn McCafferty
Chief of Secondary Education
Department of Education
Montpelier, Vermont 05602
802-828-3111

VIRGINIA

Mrs. Shirlee C. Loomer
Supervisor of Art Education
Box 6Q
Richmond, Virginia 23216
804-786-3057 or 804-786-2610

WASHINGTON

*

Mr. Gary P. Reul, Supervisor
Student Learning Objectives
Arts Education
Superintendent of Public Instruction
Old Capitol Building, FG-11
Olympia, Washington 98504
206-753-7389

WEST VIRGINIA

Mr. Richard W. Layman
West Virginia Dept. of Education
Capitol Complex, B-318
Charleston, West Virginia 25305
703-774-4212

WISCONSIN

Mr. Earl Collins
Supervisor - Art Education
Coordinator - Statewide Arts and Humanities
Wisconsin Dept. of Public Instruction
126 Langdon Street
Madison, Wisconsin 53702
608-266-3395

WYOMING

Vacant

GUAM

Mr. Adriano Pangelinan
Assistant Professor of Art
University of Guam
Fine Arts, P. O. Box EK
Agana, Guam 96910

PUERTO RICO

Mr. Rafael Caraballo, Director
Visual Arts Program
Commonwealth of Puerto Rico
Department of Education
Hato Rey, Puerto Rico 00118
809-754-1060 or 809-754-1065

VIRGIN ISLANDS

Mr. Douglas Covey
Supervisor of Art
Department of Education
P. O. Box 1
Christiansted, St. Croix
Virgin Islands 00820

SCHOOL SYSTEMS OF 500,000 & OVER IN POPULATION

Phoenix Union High School District

Mrs. Dorothy Johnson Bergamo
Chairman
Department of Performing Arts
Trevor G. Browne High School
7402 W. Catalina Drive
Phoenix, AZ 85033

Long Beach Unified School District

Sherry E. Swan
Art Consultant
Art Education
701 Locust Avenue
Long Beach, CA 90813

Los Angeles Unified School District

Pauline D. James
Instructional Specialist, Art
Instructional Planning Div. A-327
Administrative Offices
450 N. Grand
Los Angeles, CA 90015

San Diego Unified School District

Dr. Leven C. Leatherbury
Curriculum Specialist
Art Education
San Diego Unified School Dist.
4100 Normal Street
San Diego, CA 92103

San Francisco Unified School District

Herbert R. Simon
Director of Creative Art
135 Van Ness Avenue
San Francisco, CA 94102

Dade County Public Schools

Charles M. King
Art Supervisor
1410 Northeast Second Avenue
Miami, FL 33132

Lee County Public Schools

Mrs. Margaret A. Bare
Coordinator of Fine Arts
School Annex
3308 Canal Street
Fort Myers, FL 33902

De Kalb County Schools

Mrs. Sara Jo Sirmans
Supervisor of Art
2860 Guinevere Drive, N.E.
Atlanta, GA 30345

Chicago Public Schools

Helen M. Joyner
Art Consultant
228 North LaSalle Street
Chicago. IL 60601

Indianapolis Public Schools

Ted A. Moore
Supervisor of Art
120 East Walnut Street Rm 403
Indianapolis, IN 46204

Davenport Community School District

Lars H. Souder
Coordinator of Art Education
1001 Harrison
Davenport, IA 52803

Des Moines Independent Community School District

Ruth Mobberly
Art Education Supervisor
1800 Grand Avenue
Des Moines, IA 50307

Baltimore City Public Schools

Richard L. Micherdzinski
Director of Art
Oliver & Eden Streets
Baltimore, MD 21213

Prince George's County Public Schools

Dr. Leroy Gaskin
Supervisor of Art, K-12
Instructional Services Center
Upper Marlboro, MD 20870

Boston Public Schools

Miss Elizabeth H. Gilligan
Director of Fine Arts
26 Court Street
Boston, MA 02108

Benton Harbor Public Schools

Mr. Charles Murray
Art Department Chairman
870 Colfax Avenue
Benton Harbor, MI 49022

Detroit Public Schools

James Jennings
Supervisor
Department of Art Education
842 Schools Center
5057 Woodward
Detroit, MI 48202

Flint Board of Education

Maurice D. Frost
Coordinator of Fine Arts
942 East Sixth Street
Flint, MI 48503

Wayne Community School District

Miss Suan Price
Coordinator of Visual Arts
and Physical Education
3712 Williams Street
Wanye, MI 48184

Osseo Senior High School District

Eugene Waldowski
Art Teacher
317 Second Avenue, N.W.
Osseo, MN 55369

Kansas City Public Schools

Leonard Pryor
District Coordinator
Fine and Performing Arts
Room 808
1211 McGee Street
Kansas, MO 64106

Raytown Consolidated School District 2

Miss Jean Harrison
Art Coordinator
Kindergarten—12
Raytown C-Z Schools
100500 East 60th Terrace
Raytown, MO 64133

St. Louis Public Schools

Dr. Marie L. Larin
Supervisor of Art
5329 Columbia Avenue
St. Louis, MO 63139

Buffalo Public Schools

Dr. Thomas A. Jambrow
Supervisor of Art
Buffalo Public Schools
Room 709C - City Hall
Buffalo, NY 14202

Rochester City School District

Burt A. Towne
Director of Arts & Humanities
13 Fitzhugh Street S.
Rochester, NY 14614

Cincinnati Public Schools

Donald P. Sowell
Instructional Consultant
Art Education
230 East Ninth Street
Cincinnati, OH 45202

Columbus Public Schools

Mrs. Kay McGill
Director of Fine & Performing Arts
270 East State Street
Columbus, OH 43215

Toledo Board of Education

Miss Beverly Domalski
Director of Art
Toledo Public Schools
Manhattan & Elm
Toledo, OH 43608

Willoughby-Eastlake City Schools

Mrs. Uarda Overbaugh
Art Consultant
Willoughby-Eastlake City Schools
Royalview Elementary School
31500 Royalview Drive
Willowick, OH 44094

The School District of Philadelphia

Harry Bonelli
Director of Art Education
Board of Education
21 and Parkway
Philadelphia, PA 19103

Austin Independent School District

Sherilyn Howze
Art Coordinator
Austin Ind. School District
6100 Guadalupe
Austin, TX 78752

Houston Independent School District

Annette Wagisbach
Dir. of Art Education
Houston Ind. School District
3830 Richmond Avenue
Houston, TX 77027

Federal Way School District 210

Scott Pepper
Art Consultant
31455 28th Avenue South
Federal Way, WA 98002

Seattle School District 1

Mr. Henry W. Petterson
Art Specialist
815 Fourth Avenue N.
Seattle, WA 98107

SCHOOL SYSTEMS OF 100,000 TO 499,999

Jefferson County Board of Education

Mr. DeLeon Fancher
Assistant Art Supervisor
1009 North 21 St.
Birmingham, AL 35203

Gadsden City Schools

Mrs. Ma Lou Smith
Art Specialist
P.O. Box 184
Gadsden, AL 35902

Opelika Public Schools

Roslyn B. Stern
Art Consultant
P.O. Box 311
Opelika, AL 36801

Tuscaloosa City Schools

Mrs. Ronna Lasser
Art Teacher - Coordinator, Elementary
1100 21st Street E.
Tuscaloosa, AL 35041

Anchorage School District

Dr. Ruth Keitz
Art Coordinator
2503 Blueberry
Anchorage, AK 99503

Mesa Public Schools

Dr. Edna Gilbert
Arts Director
Mesa Public Schools
14 West Second Avenue
Mesa, AZ 85202

Phoenix Elementary District 1

Miss Betty Lou Richards
Art Director
125 East Lincoln
Phoenix, AZ 85004

Prescott Elementary Schools

Ella F. Fisher
Supervisor of Art Education
Prescott Elementary Schools
146 South Granite St.
Prescott, AZ 86301

Tucson Elementary Schools

Sunnyside School District 12
Rubina F. Gallo
Los Ninos Elementary School
Elementary Art Consultant
470 West Valencia Road
Tucson, AZ 85704

Tucson Public Schools District 1

Dr. Nik Krevitsky
Director of Art & Educational Materials Center
Thomas L. Lee Instructional Resource Center
2025 E. Winsett St.
Tucson, AZ 85712

Alameda Unified School District

Miss Olivia Krause
Supervisor of Art Educatin
400 Grand St.
Alameda, CA 94501

Alhambra City Schools

Mrs. Ann Wollen
Art Consultant
15 West Alhambra Rd.
Alhambra, CA 91801

Alum Rock Union Elementary School District

Leroy G. Wiens
Coordinator of Fine Arts
Alum Rock Elem. School Dist.
2930 Gay Avenue
San Jose, CA 95127

Bakersfield City School District

Mrs. Mary K. Mueller
Consultant
Art Education
Education Center
1300 Baker Street
Bakersfield, CA 93305

Baldwin Park Unified School District

Kathryn McIlreath
Art Specialist
Baldwin Park USD
3699 North Holly Avenue
Baldwin Park, CA 91706

Berkeley Unified School District

Philip St. Martin
Chairman
Art, Industry and Design
Berkeley High School
Berkeley, CA 94709

Burbank Unified School District

Harold R. Bucklin
Coordinator of Elementary Ed.
245 East Magnolia Blvd.
Burbank, CA 91504

Campbell Elementary School District

Mrs. Marcia Wells
Art Consultant
155 North Third Street
Campbell, CA 95008

Campbell Union High School District

Ross C. Deniston
Art Supervisor
Camden High School
2075 Camden Avenue
San Jose, CA 95124

Compton City School District

Kenneth Gregg
Staff Teacher Art
Mrs. Billie Jackson
Staff Teacher Art
Compton Unified School Dist.
604 South Tamarind Avenue
Compton, CA 90220

Kenneth R. Gregg
Staff Teacher, Art
Area Instructional Svs.
1623 E. 118th Street
Los Angeles, CA 90059

Compton Union High School District

Leonard F. Fisher
District Curriculum Assistant
Art
417 West Alondar Blvd.
Compton, CA 90220

Danville Unified School District

Arthur H. Dougherty
Fine Arts Coordinator
599 Old Orchard Drive
Danville, CA 94526

Escondido Union High School District

Rex Hamilton
Fine Arts Specialist
Fifth and Maple
Escondido, CA 92025

Fresno City Unified School District

Mr. Ralph E. Gomas
Art Coordinator
Education Center Tulare M
3132 East Fairmont
Fresno, CA 93721

Fullerton Elementary School District

Mrs. Gelsomina Barton
Fine Arts Coordinator
1401 West Valencia Drive
Fullerton, CA 92633

Garden Grove Unified School District

Bernard M. Jones, Jr.
Art Specialist
10331 Stanford Avenue
Garden Grove, CA 92640

Glendale Unified School District

Mrs. Audrey A. Welch
Arts Coordinator
223 North Jackson St.
Glendale, CA 91206

Hudson School District

Mrs. Lona Hoffman
Consultant
15959 East Gale Avenue
La Puente, CA 91745

La Mesa-Spring Valley School District

Jean A. Shour
Art Coordinator
4750 Date Avenue
La Mesa, CA 92041

Montebello Unified School District

Mrs. Jewel Bishop Starkey
Consultant, Art
123 South Montebello Blvd.
Montebello, CA 90640

Monroe Valley Unified School District

Dr. Robert Banister
District Art Supervisor
13911 Perris Boulevard
Sunnymead, CA 92388

Mt. Diablo Unified School District

Mr. James E. Snowden
Curriculum Specialist in Art
    and Industrial Education
1936 Carlotta Drive
Concord, CA 94519

Newport-Mesa Unified School District

Jenean Romberg
Newport-Mesa School Dist.
1601 Sixteenth St.
Newport Beach, CA 92660

Novato Unified School District

Lee Hilton
Curriculum Specialist, Art
1015 Seventh St.
Novato, CA 94947

Oakland Unified School District

Stanley H. Cohen
Art Specialist
1025 Second Avenue
Oakland, CA 94606

Ocean View School District

Mrs. Rose Clark
Resource Teacher, Art
7972 Warner Avenue
Huntington Beach, CA 92647

Palo Alto Unified School District

Mrs. Kathryn M. Alexander
Art Consultant
25 Churchill Avenue
Palo Alto, CA 94306

Pasadena City Unified School District

Norman E. Schmidt
Director of Program/Art Ed.
351 South Hudson
Pasadena, CA 91109

Pasadena Secondary School District

Sr. Alberta Curran
St. Andrew High School
42 Chestnut St.
Pasadena, CA 91103

San Jose Unified School District

Mr. William Shelley
Supervisor of Art Ed.
1605 Park Avenue
San Jose, CA 95126

San Lorenzo Unified School District

Thomas R. Phillips
Music & Fine Arts Coordinator
15510 Usher St.
San Lorenzo, CA 94580

San Mateo City School District

Richard Sperisen, Coordinator
Art Educ./School Design
San Mateo Co. Ofc. of Educ.
333 Main Street
Redwood, CA 94063

Santa Barbara High School District

Janice Y. Lorber
Art Department
700 E. Anapamu St.
Santa Barbara, CA 93103

Santa Clara Unified School District

Miss Janet E. Tellefsen
Coordinator of Childrens Art
P.O. Box 397
Santa Clara, CA 95052

Santa Monica Unified School District

Richard Wagnon
Supervisor of Music & Art
Joan F. Vaupen
Art Teacher, Curriculum Asst.
Art Office, Santa Monica Bd. Ed.
1723 Fourth Street
Santa Monica, CA 90401

San Mateo Union High School District

Gregg MacGibbon
Art Curriculum Council Chairman
Crestmoor High School
300 Piedmont Avenue
San Bruno, CA 94066

Sweetwater Union High School District

Mr. Frank Buzga
District Art Committee Chrmn.
Sweetwater Union H. S. Dist.
1130 Fifth Avenue
Chula Vista, CA 92011

Ventura Unified School District

Howard Quam
Coordinator Instructional
    Media Services
120 East Santa Clara
Ventura, CA 93001

School District 12, Adams County

Dr. Norma Goecke
Music & Art Subject Specialty
11285 Highline Drive
Denver, CO 80233

Aurora Public Schools

Richard D. Schafer
Art Consultant
Aurora Public Schools
1085 Peoria Street
Aurora, CO 80011

Arapahoe County School District 6

Dr. Judy Rogers
Consultant in Art Ed., K-12
6558 South Acoma St.
Littleton, CO 80120

Boulder Valley Public School District

Buck Owens
Art Resource
P.O. Box 9011
Boulder, CO 80302

Colorado Springs Public Schools, District 11

Robert Simpich
Director
Art Education
1115 North El Paso St.
Colorado Springs, CO 80903

Jefferson County School District R-1

Larry T. Schultz
Coordinator of Art
809 Quail St.
Lakewood, CO 80215

Poudre School District R-1

Miss Sylvia B. Maxey
Art Coordinator
Poudra School District R-1
2407 La Porte St.
Fort Collins, CO 80521

Bristol Public Schools

Mrs. Barbara J. Grasso
Art Department Head
Board of Education
129 Church Street
Bristol, CT 06010

East Hartford Board of Education

Richard A. Sterner
Supervisor/Fine and Performing Arts
110 Long Hill Drive
East Hartford, CT 06108

Fairfield School System

Mr. Peter Clarke
Art Coordinator
c/o Andrew Warde High School
Fairfield, CT 06430

Greenwich Board of Education

Harold L. Krevolin
Coordinator Art/Music
290 Greenwich Avenue
Greenwich, CT 06830

Hartford Public Schools

Paul J. Dilworth
Coordinator
Department of the Arts
249 High Street
Hartford, CT 06103

Meriden Public Schools

Thomas F. Potter
Supervisor of Art
Board of Education
22 Liberty St.
Meriden, CT 06450

Milford Public Schools

Frank J. Vespi
Department Head
Elemetnary Art Dept.
Ellis Hill Annex, Bldg. 3
Milford, CT 06460

New Canaan Public Schools

Mrs. Bernice D. Hall
Chairman Art K-12
New Cannaan, CT 06849

New Haven Public Schools

Margaret F. Ring
Supervisor of Art
765 Elm St.
New Haven, CT 06511

Norwalk Public Schools

Dr. Donald Rogers
Art Dept. Head
Board of Education Offices
105 Main St.
Norwalk, CT 06852

Stamford Public Schools

John C. Nerreau
Coordinator of Art
Hoyt School
1500 High Ridge Road
Stamford, CT 06903

Newark School District

Harley S. Hastings
Supervisor of Music & Art
Newark School District
83 East Main St.
Newark, DE 19711

Wilmington Public Schools

Robert C. Moore
Supervisor of Art Ed.
Newcastle County School Dist.
3606 Concord Pike
Wilmington, DE 19803

Broward County School Sytem

Mrs. Jeanette McArthur
Director of Art Ed.
1320 W.W. Fourth St.
P.O. Box 8369
Fort Lauderdale, FL 33312

Duval County School Board

William H. Dodd
Supervisor of Art Ed.
1701 Davis St.
Jacksonville, FL 32209

Escambia County School Board

Miss Mary Jo Burgess
Supervisor of Art
5502 Lillian Highway
Pensacola, FL 32506

Hillsborough County Board of Public Instruction

Dorothy Kennedy
Supervisor Art & Humanities
Instructional Svs. Center
707 East Columbus Dr.
Tampa, FL 33602

Lee County Public Schools

Mrs. Margaret A. Bare
Coordinator of Fine Arts
School Annex
3308 Canal St.
Fort Myers, FL 33902

Manatee County School System

Mrs. Eleanor H. Paul
Acting Art Supervisor
5886 17th St., West
Bradenton, FL 33507

Okaloosa County School System

Collis V. Porter
Art Supervisor
120 Lowery Place
Fort Walton Beach, FL 32548

Palm Beach County Public Schools

Mrs. Jo D. Kowalchuk
Asst. Principal in Curriculum
Atlantic High School
2501 Seacrest Blvd.
Delray, FL 33444

Panama City Public Schools

Art Davis
Art Coordinator
Bay County Schools
1855 Liddon Road
Panama City, FL 32401

Polk County School Board

Joe P. Mitchell
Coordinator of Art Instruction
P.O. Box 391
Bartow, FL 33830

St. Lucie County School Board

Mr. Harold Supank
2909 Delaware Avenue
Fort Pierce, FL 33450

Sarasota County School Board

Mary Francis MacDonald
Supervisor of Art Ed.
2418 Hatton St.
Sarasota, FL 33577

Volusia County Board of Public Instruction

Mrs. Dorothy Johnson
Art Supervisor
P.O. Box 1910
Daytona Beach, FL 32015

Atlanta Public Schools

David Walker
Coordinator
Arts & Humanities Center
1280 Peachtree St., N.E.
Atlanta, GA 30309

Callaway Educational Association

Carolyn Ann Page
Art Director
Dallis St.
LaGrange, GA 30240

Clark County School District

Jane D. Deason
Visual Art Supervisor
Box 1708
Athens, GA 30601

Clayton County Board of Education

Mrs. Martha Ellen Stilwell
Curriculum Coordinator,
   Art, Music
120 Smith St.
Jonesboro, GA 30236

Eastman Public Schools

Earl W. Woodward
Art Supervisor, Title III
Cultural Enrichment Project
Eastman, GA 31023

Fulton County School District

Miss Emory Rose Wood
Director of Art Education
786 Cleveland Avenue, S.W.
Atlanta, GA 30315

Macon Public Schools

Miss J. Elizabeth McElroy
Art Supervisor, Area 4
Hunt School
990 Shurling Drive
Macon, GA 31201

Peach City Schools

Mrs. Jean D. Pervis
Art Consultant
Fort Valley High School
Knox Valley, GA 31031

Walton County Public Schools

Mrs. Perry Nelle Darby
Art Consultant
Walton City Board of Ed.
Monroe, GA 30655

Kamehameha Schools

Mrs. Frances Pickens
Art Instructor
Senior High School Division
Bernice Pauahi Bishop Estate
Kapalama Heights
Honolulu, HI 96817

Independent School District of Boise City

Robert Wand
Supervisor of Art
1207 Fort Street
Boise, ID 83702

Arlington Township High School District 214

Edward Fischer
District Coordinator of Arts, Music & Student Teaching
Township High School Dist. 214
799 West Kensington Rd.
Mount Prospect, IL 60056

Cicero Elementary District 99

Emil R. Proska
Art Coordinator
5110 West 24th
Cicero, IL 60650

Champaign County Schools

Mrs. Josephine W. Payne
Elementary Art Consultant
   Champaign Unit 4
2035 South New St.
Champaign, IL 61820

Danville Community Consolidated School District 118

William B. Handley
Director of Fine Arts
516 North Jackson St.
Danville, IL 61832

Elgin Public Schools, District U-46

Mrs. Corinne Loeh
Director of Art Education
4 South Gifford St.
Elgin, IL 60120

District 65 Schools, Evanston

Tom Harris
Director of Fine Arts
1314 Ridge Avenue
Evanton, IL 60201

Moline Public Schools

Karl Haytcher
Coordinator of Art
1619 Eleventh Avenue
Moline, IL 61265

Oak Park Elementary Schools

Floyd Freerksen
970 Madison
Oak Park, IL 60302

District 15 Schools, Palatine

Mrs. Josephine L. Heyden
Art Chairperson
789 North Inverway
Palatine, IL 60067

Rockford Public Schools

Paul Pullin
Supervisor of Art
201 South Madison St.
Rockford, IL 61101

Rock Island Public Schools

Richard T. Klatt
Director of Art
1400 25th Avenue
Rock Island, IL 61201

Waukegan Unit School District 60

Martha D. Wasylik
Director of Art Education K-12
Unit School District 60
Lincoln Center
1201 North Sheridan Road
Waukegan, IL 60085

Anderson Public Schools

Doris Noel
Supervisor of Art
528 West 11th Street
Anderson, IN 46016

Bartholomew Consolidated School Corporation

Karl McCan
Supervisor of Art Education
Senior High School
Columbus, IN 47201

Bedford Public Schools

Jim Blyeth
Chairman
North Lawrence Art Dept.
2222 West Eighth St.
Bedford, IN 47421

Evansville-Vanderburgh School Corporation

Harry C. Friley
Supervisor of Art Education
Evansville-Vand School Corp.
1 South East Ninth Street
Evansville, IN 47708

Fort Wayne Community Schools

Mr. Gene P. Porter
Consultant for Art
1230 South Clinton St.
Fort Wayne, IN 46802

Gary Public Schools

Mr. Arnold K. Williams
Supervisor of Art
Gary Community Schools
620 East 10th Place
Gary, IN 46402

Hammond Public Schools

Robert Lee Fischer
Art Instructor
524 173rd St.
Hammond, IN 46320

Kokomo-Center Township Consolidated School Corporation

James Osborne
Coordinator of Art Education
100 West Lincoln Road
Kokomo, IN 46901

Marion Community Schools

George Kind
Art Coordinator
Marion High School
716 West 26th St.
Marion, IN 46952

Michigan City Area Schools

Mrs. Kay Behrndt
Director of Art
609 Lafayette St.
Michigan City, IN 46360

Muncie Community Schools

Virginia Schoeff
Art Consultant
Administration Building
600 N. Mulberry St.
Muncie, IN 47305

New Castle Community Schools

Mrs. Shirley A. Liby
Director of Art & Media
Media Center
522 Elliott Avenue
New Castle, IN 47362

Richmond Community Schools

Edward L. Loar
Coordinator of Art Education
Administration Bldg.
300 Whitewater Blvd.
Richmond, IN 47374

South Bend Community School Corporation

Kenneth Geoffroy
Coordinator of Fine Arts
635 South Main St.
South Bend, IN 46623

Vigo County School Corporation

Mrs. Harriet McCullough
Elementary School Art Supervisor
961 Lafayette Avenue
Terre Haute, IN 47804

Metropolitan School District of Washington Township

Max I. Briggs
Chairman, Art Dept.
North Central High School
1801 East 86th St.
Indianapolis, IN 46240

Cedar Rapids Community School District

Archie E. Bauman
Project Leader for Art Ed.
346 Second Ave., S.W.

Sioux City Community School District

Robert J. Patnaud
Division Head
Art Department
1221 Pierce Street
Sioux City, IA 51105

Unified School District 500, Kansas City

E. Eileen Hughes
Director of Art
2019 Tauromee
Kansas City, KS 66102

Shawnee Mission Public School District 512

Peter Perdaris
Supervisor of Art
7235 Antioch Road
Shawnee Mission, KS 66204

Unified School District 501, Shawnee County

Donna D. Pauler Held
Instructional Specialist
Art (K-12)
Supervisor of Art
624 W. 24th
Topeka, KS 66611

Unified School District Wichita, 259

William W. King
Director of Art Education
640 North Emporia
Wichita, KS 67214

Jefferson County Public Schools

Norma E. Brown
Art Specialist
Brown Education Center
Jefferson County Public Schs.
Louisville, KY 40202

Caddo Parish School System

Mrs. Zelphia B. Layton
Supervisor of Related Arts Education
1961 Midway
P.O. Box 3700
Shreveport, LA 71108

Calcasieu Parish School System

Brad Daigle
Supervisor
Music and Art
1732 Kirkman Street
Lake Charles, LA 70601

New Orleans Public Schools

Shirley Trusty Corey
Supervisor of Cultural Resources
4100 Touro Street
New Orleans, LA 70122

Ouachita Parish School System

Henry Camp
Fine Arts Coordinator
P.O. Box 1642
Monroe, LA 71201

Allegany County Public Schools

Harry R. Mandel
Supervisor of Art Ed.
108 Washington St.
Cumberland, MD 21502

Anne Arundel County Public Schools

Mary E. Wellham
Coordinator of Art
Board of Education
2644 Riva Road
Annapolis, MD 21401

Baltimore County Public School

James B. Laubheimer
Coordinator of Art
John L. Crossin
Supervisor of Art
Patricia A. Agee
Art Specialist
Bd. of Ed. of Baltimore Co.
Towson, MD 21204

Carroll County Public School System

Dr. Warren W. Shelley
Supervisor of Music & Art
Carroll Co. Board of Ed.
55 North Court St.
Westminster, MD 21157

Charles County Board of Education

Ann S. Richardson
Supervisor of Art
La Plata, MD 20646

Frederick County Public Schools

Carroll H. Kehne, Jr.
Curriculum Specialist - Art Ed.
Frederick Co. Bd. of Education
115 East Church St.
Frederick, MD 21701

Howard County Public Schools

H. Eugene Miller
Supervisor
Art and Music
Howard County Board of Ed.
Clarksville, MD 21029

Montgomery County Public Schools

Emil Hrebenach
Coordinator Secondary Art
850 Hungerford Drive
Rockville, MD 20850

Washington County Public Schools

Mr. Clyde H. Roberts
Supervisor of Art
Box 730
Hagerstown, MD 21740

Bourue Public Schools

Jeremiah M. Lyon
Art Director
Bourue High School
Bourue, MA 02532

Brockton Public Schools

Pasquale F. Morano
Dept. Head of Fine Arts
43 Crescent Street
Brockton, MA 02403

Cambridge School Department

Rita W. Ritterbush
Director of Art
1700 Cambridge Street
Cambridge, MA 02138

Fall River Public Schools

Edmond St. Laurent
Director of Fine Arts
417 Rock Street
Fall River, MA 02720

Framingham Public Schools

Neal Cotton
Director of Art
50 Lawrence Street
Framingham, MA 01701

Braintree Public Schools

Ms. Joanna B. Sundberg
Supervisor of Art
Braintree Public Schools
128 Town Street
Braintree, MA 02184

Greenfield Public Schools

Mary Kay Hoffman, Dir.
Arts Council of Franklin Co.
P.O. Box 364
Greenfield, MA 01302

Lexington Public Schools

Paul A. Ciano
Coordinator of the Visual Arts
Education Dept. K-12
Lexington Public Schools
Lexington, MA 02173

Lowell Public Schools

Thomas McGuire
Director of Art
Lowell Public Schools
Lowell, MA 01853

Lynn Public Schools

Marjorie Clancy
Art Department
42 Franklin Street
Lynn, MA 01902

Medford Public Schools

Frances Fanning
Art Director
25 Hall Avenue
Medford, MA 02155

New Bedford Public Schools

Raymond G. Bisaillon
Art Education Director
County St. Administration Bldg.
455 County St.
New Bedford, MA 02740

Newton Public Schools

Dr. Al Hurwitz, Coordinator
Visual & Related Arts
100 Walnut St.
Newtonville, MA 02160

Pittsfield Public Schools

Mrs. Winifred Bell
Art Coordinator, K-12
Pittsfield Public Schools
P.O. Box 1187
Pittsfield, MA 01201

Barnsville Public Schools

Deborah A. Barrows
Elementary Art Specialist
Box 424
Centerville, MA 02632

Quincy Public Schools

Richard D. Ramsdell
Coordinator
Art & Humanities Dept.
Quincy Public Schools
70 Coddington Street
Quincy, MA 02169

Somerville Public Schools

Charles Khirallah
Director of Art
City Hall Annex
Somerville, MA 02143

Springfield Public Schools

Robert L. Drummond
Director, Fine & Industrial Arts
195 State St.
Springfield, MA 01103

Weymouth Public Schools

Philip S. Dolan
Crafts & Design Instructor
Weymouth South High School
360 Pleasant Street
South Weymouth, MA 02190

Waltham School Department

Paul D. Shea
Art Director
Waltham Public Schools
Waltham, MA 02154

Worcester Public Schools

Marilyn Goodman
Acting Director of Art
Worcester Public Schools
31 Elizabeth Street
Worcester, MA 01605

Ann Arbor Public Schools

Mrs. Ruth L. Beatty
Coordinator of Art
Public School Administration Bldg.
2555 South State
Ann Arbor, MI 48104

Battle Creek Public Schools

Max D. Misner
Art Consultant
Willard Library Bldg.
Battle Creek, MI 49016

Bay City Public Schools

Jane D. Miller
Coordinator
Bay City Public Schools
Bay City, MI 48706

Benton Harbor Public Schools

Charles Murray
Art Department Chairman
870 Colfax Avenue
Benton Harbor, MI 49022

Dearborn Public Schools

Donald Boughner
Art Resource Teacher
4824 Lois Avenue
Dearborn, MI 48126

East Detroit Public Schools

Donald Olesklewicz
Chairman, Art Dept.
East Detroit Public Schools
15550 Couzens
East Detroit, MI 48201

Farmington Public Schools

Mrs. Beverly L. Ellis
Chairman
Elementary Arts Consultant
Farmington Public Schools
32500 Shiawassee
Farmington, MI 48204

Garden City Public Schools

Donald L. Beatty
Deputy Superintendent
Garden City Public Schools
1333 Radcliff Street
Garden City, MI 48135

Grand Rapids Public Schools

Mrs. Vee Matusko
Supervisor of Art
Grand Rapids Public Schools
143 Bostwick, N.E.
Grand Rapids, MI 49502

Kalamazoo Public Schools

Doris M. Miller
Consultant for Elementary Art
Kalamazoo Public Schools
1220 Howard Street
Kalamazoo, MI 49001

Lansing School District

Peggy King
Director of Art Instruction
Lansing School District
3426 South Cedar Street
Lansing, MI 48910

Midland Public Schools

James Hopfensperger
Coordinator of Art
Midland Public Schools
600 E. Carpenter Street
Midland, MI 48640

City of Pontiac School District

Otha Whitcomb
Art Specialist
Franklin Elementary School
661 Franklin Road
Pontiac, MI 48513

Portage Public Schools

Al Kushner
Chairman
Art Department
Portage Public Schools
Portage, MI 49081

Port Huron Area School District

Sally Westrick Gregg
Director
Art Education
509 Stanton Street
Port Huron, MI 48060

Roseville Public Schools

Ms. Paula Rollet
Chairperson
Art Department
Secondary Schools
Brablec High School
Roseville, MI 48066

Saginaw City School District

Richard A. Foulds
Supervisor
Art Education
550 Millard Street
Saginaw, MI 48607

Anoka-Hennepin Independence School District 11

Jean Thurston
Art Coordinator
Educational Service Center
1129 Hanson Boulevard
Anoka, MN 55303

Independent School District 709, Duluth

Sheldon Johnson
Supervisor of Art
Board of Education Bldg.
Lake Avenue & Second Street
Duluth, MN 55802

Minneapolis Public Schools

Dr. Eugenia M. Oole
Consultant in Art
807 North East Broadway
Minneapolis, MN 55413

Independent School District 281, Robbinsdale Area

Marilyn Fetter
Elementary Art Coordinator
4148 Winnetka Avenue, North
Minneapolis, MN 55427

Osseo Senior High School District

Eugene Waldowski
Art Teacher
317 Second Avenue, N.W.
Osseo, MN 55369

Rochester, District 535

Kenneth Bauman
Elementary Art Consultant
463 Northern Heights Dr., NE
Rochester, MN 55901

St. Louis Park Public Schools

Robert Anderson
Department Chairman
Art Education
6425 West 33rd Street
St. Louis Park, MN 55426

Independent School District 621, Mouns View

Ellsworth E. Erickson
District Art Coordinator
Art Research, Resource Ctr.
3555 North Victoria
St. Paul, MN 55172

Independent School District 625, St. Paul

Stephen Conger
Supervisor of Art
Independent School Dist. 625
Saint Paul Public Schools
360 Colborne
St. Paul, MN 55102

Independent School District 624, White Bear Lake

Franklin J. Zeller
Art Coordinator
Bellaire Elementary School
White Bear Lake, MN 55110

Jackson Public Schools

Mary Dell Burford
Supervisor of Art
Elementary Schools
1593 West Capital Street
Jackson, MS 39203

Berkeley Public Schools

Arthur B. Kennon
Elementary Art Coordinator
6001 Berkeley Drive
Berkeley, MO 63134

Ferguson-Florissant School District

Mrs. Alice P. Ulbright
Coordinator of Art Education
655 January Avenue
Ferguson, MO 63135

Independence School District

Louis H. Braley
Art Consultant
1231 South Windsor
Independence, MO 64055

Parkway School District

Jerrel L. Swingle
Art Coordinator
Parkway School District
455 North Woods Mill Road
Chesterfield, MO 63017

Kirkwood Public Schools

Mrs. Chris Murphy
Art Instructor K-5
230 Quan Avenue
Kirkwood, MO 63122

North Kansas City

Katherine Smith
Elementary Art Supervisor
2000 North East 46th Street
Kansas City, MO 64116

School District of St. Joseph

Marie Corcoran
Art Consultant
School District of St. Joseph
Tenth and Felix Streets
St. Joseph, MO 64501

Ritenour Consolidated School District

Mrs. Verneta Sevier
District Art Coordinator
Ritenour Consolidated Sch. Dist.
2420 Woodson Road
St. Louis County, MO 63114

School District of Springfield R 12

Bill Stockstill
Coordinator of Art
Secondary Schools
Parkview High School
516 West Meadows
Springfield, MO 65804

School District 2, Billings

Archie Elliot
Director of Art Education
101-Tenth Street West
Billings, MT 59102

School District 1, Great Falls

James D. Poor
Supervisor of Art
P.O. Box 2428
Great Falls, MT 59403

Lincoln Public Schools

Roger Dean Van Deventer
Art Consultant K-12
Public School Administration Bldg.
P.O. Box 82889
Lincoln, NE 68501

Omaha Public Schools

Gerald Pabst
Supervisor
3902 Davenport Street
Omaha NE 68131

Ralston Public Schools

Mrs. Judith C. Pittack
Elementary Art Supervisor
79th and Seymour
Ralston, NE 68127

Manchester School Union 37

Leonard R. Armstrong
Director of Art
88 Lowell Street
Manchester, NH 03104

Cherry Hill Public Schools

Yvonne L. Bieberbach
Art Coordinator
1155 Marklress Road
Cherry Hill, NJ 08034

Clifton Public Schools

Richard Ebert
Dir. of Music, Art & Elementary Education
Clifton Public Schools
745 Clifton Avenue
Clifton, NJ 07013

East Orange Public School System

Bernice E. Magnie
Director of Art
21 Winans Street
East Orange, NJ 07107

Elizabeth Public Schools

Eddie Smith
Board of Education
500 North Broad Street
Elizabeth, NJ 07202

Public Schools of Jersey City

Claire J. Warlikowski
Acting Supervisor of Art
30 Montgomery Street
Jersey City, NJ 07306

Middletown Township Public Schools

Wayne Ehlers
Middletown Township Public Schools
59 Tindall Road
Middletown, NJ 07748

Newark Public Schools

Dr. Ruth K. Assarsson
Director of Art Education
Department of Art Education
15 State Street
Newark, NJ 07102

Paterson Board of Education

Edward B. Epstein
Supervisor of Fine Arts
Board of Education
33 Church Street, B-4
Paterson, NJ 07505

Summit Public Schools

Arthur E. DeBrito
Chair, Art Department K-12
Summit Public Schools
Summit, NJ 07901

Trenton Public Schools

John T. Cunningham
Director of Fine Arts
Board of Education
Nine South Stockton Street
Trenton, NJ 08611

Wayne Public Schools

Gayle Jones Reed
Art Coordinator
50 Nellis Drive
Wayne, NJ 07470

Las Vegas City Schools

Mrs. Marjorie A. Phillips
Phil Leger
Robertson High School
Las Vegas, NM 87701

Albany Public Schools

Margaret M. Smith
Director of Art Education
Albany Board of Education
Academy Park
Albany, NY 12207

Binghamton City School District

Ann Greiner
Chairman Art Department
31 Main Street
Binghamton, NY 13905

Brentwood Public Schools

Manuel R. Vega, Coordinator
Art and Administrative Asst.
Brentwood Public Schools
Administration Building
Third Avenue and Fourth St.
Brentwood, NY 11717

Union Free School District 10

Mr. Sidney Cumins
District Art Consultant
80 Hauppauge Road
Commack, NY 11725

Connetquot City School District 7

Eugene Lissandrello
Related Arts Chairman
Connetquot High School
780 Ocean Avenue
Bohemia, NY 11716

East Meadow Public Schools

Phyllis B. Nelson
Director of Art Education
Curriculum Center
Meadowbrook Elementary School
East Meadow, NY 11554

City School District of Elmira

Mervin Slotnick
Director of Art
Administration Building
951 Hoffman Street
Elmira, NY 14905

Farmingdale Public Schools

Roger Hartford
Dept. Chairman/Coordinator
Farmingdale Senior High School
Lincoln Street
Farmingdale, NY 11735

Kenmore-Town of Tonawanda Public Schools

Robert Freeland
Art Supervisor K-12
1500 Colvin Boulevard
Kenmore, NY 14223

Levittown Union Free School District

Casimir Cetnarowski
Supervisor of Art
Board of Education Offices
North Village Green
Levittown, NY 11756

Lindenhurst Public Schools

Mrs. Barbara Payne
Elementary Art Coordinator K-6
E. W. Bower School
Montauk Highway
Lindenhurst, NY 11757

Massapequa Public Schools

Morris Brewer
Coordinating Chairman, Art
Administrative Wing
Massapequa High School
4925 Merrick Road
Massapequa, NY 11758

Mount Vernon Public Schools

Dr. C. Andrew Randall
Supervisor of Music and Art
Education Center
165 North Columbus Avenue
Mt. Vernon, NY 10553

Community School District of New Rochelle

Mortimer H. Slotnick
Arts and Humanities Consultant
515 North Avenue
New Rochelle, NY 10801

New York City Public Schools

George Kaye
Acting Director of Art
Board of Education
131 Livingston Street
Brooklyn, NY 11201

School District of Niagara Falls

Donald Banks
Supervisor of Fine Arts
607 Walnut Avenue
Niagara Falls, NY 14301

Oceanside Union Free School District

Paul C. Olivia
Director of Art Education
145 Merle Avenue
Oceanside, NY 11572

Central School District 4, Plainview-Old Bethpage

Charles Burge
Art Coordinator
John F. Kennedy High School
Plainview, NY 11803

Rome City School District

Guy Nasci
Director of Art
108 E. Garden Street
Rome, NY 13440

Schenectady Public Schools

Edwin G. Weinheimer
Supervisor of Art
108 Brandywine Avenue
Schenectady, NY 12307

Sewanhaka Central District 2

Michael A. Russo
Art Coordinator
Floral Park Art Department
210 Locust Street
Floral Park
Long Island, NY 11001

Smithtown Public Schools

Richard Mello
Art Coordinator
Smithtown Central School Dist. 1
St. James
Long Island, NY 11780

Three Village Central School District 1

Edward T. Goebel
Director of Art
Three Village Central School District 1
Nicoll Road
Setauket, NY 11733

Wappingers Central School District

Barbara H. Janoff
Director of Art Education
Wappingers Central School Dist.
John Jay High School
Route 52
Hopewell Junction, NY 12533

White Plains Public Schools

John Ruddley
Westchester Co. Supervisor of Art
Dept. of Parks & Recreation
148 Martine Avenue
White Plains, NY 10601

Yonkers Public Schools

Mrs. Ellen Kruger
Supervisor of Art
Board of Education
Yonkers, NY 10701

Charlotte-Mecklenburg Schools

Mrs. Elizabeth Mack
Acting Director
P.O. Box 149
Charlotte, NC 28201

Durham City Schools

Jessie D. Kearney
Director of Art
P.O. Box 2246
Durham, NC 27702

Greensboro Public Schools

Elizabeth H. Bell
Director of ESAA
712 N. Eugene St./Drawer V
Greensboro, NC 27402

Fort Bragg Schools

Miss Claudia J. Sailor
Art Coordinator
Fort Bragg Dependents Schools
Drawer A
Fort Bragg, NC 28307

Wake County Public School System

Rose Melvin
Supervisor of Visual Arts
1600 Fayetteville Road
Raleigh, NC 27603

Wayne County Schools

Joyce Thigpen
Supervisor of Cultural Arts
Wayne County Schools
301 N. Herman St. Bx GG
Goldsboro, NC 27530

Winston-Salem/Forsyth County Schools

Antony Swider
Coordinator of Art Education
P.O. Box 2513
Winston-Salem, NC 27102

Fargo Public Schools

Vince Lindstrom
Cultural Resources Center
Creative Arts Studio
1430 Seventh St. South
Fargo, ND 58102

Akron Public Schools

Brian B. Heard
Director of Art Education
70 North Broadway
Akron, OH 44308

Berea City Schools

Charles Armstrong
Art Supervisor
390 Fair Street
Berea, OH 44017

Cleveland Public Schools

Ronald N. Day
Directing Supervisor of Art
1380 East Sixth St.
Cleveland, OH 44114

Cuyahoga Falls City Schools

Ronald Simon
Head, Art Department
c/o Falls High School
2300 Fourth Street
Cayahoga Falls, OH 44221

Dayton Public Schools

Armand Martino
Supervisor of Art
Dayton Board of Education
Service Building
4280 North Western Ave.
Dayton, OH 45427

Findlay Public Schools

Alexander Baluch
Coordinator of Fine Arts
1001 Blanchard Avenue
Findlay, OH 45840

Kettering City School District

Robert Thygerson
Supervisor, Music & Fine Arts
Kettering City School District
3490 Fair Hills Avenue
Kettering, OH 45429

Lima City School District

Joan Hebden
Director of Art
515 South Calumet Avenue
Lima, OH 45804

Mansfield City Schools

Lois Beveridge
Art Resource Teacher
145 West Park Blvd.
Mansfield, OH 44902

Mentor Public Schools

Ted Keller
Supervisor of Art
Mentor High School
6477 Center Street
Mentor, OH 44060

Parma City Schools

Wanda Ullman
Coordinator of Art
6726 Ridge Road
Parma, OH 44129

Warren City Schools

James G. Friend
Supervising Teacher of Art
1360 Autumn Drive, N.W.
Warren, OH 44458

Washington Local Schools

Ms. Marti Bremer
Department Chair
5201 Douglas Road
Toledo, OH 43613

Youngstown City Schools

Andrew Nadzam
Supervisor of Art
20 West Wood St.
Youngstown, OH 44503

Enid Public Schools, Independent 57

Eldon Ames
Consultant
1405 Suggett
Enid, OK 73701

Tulsa Public Schools

Mrs. Bobbie Jean Brophy
Supervisor of Art
3027 South New Haven
Tulsa, OK 74145

Beaverton School District 48

Omer Gosnell
Productions Specialist
Curriculum Specialist
P.O. Box 200
Beaverton, OR 97005

Bend Public School District 1

Richard G. Dedlow
Art Specialist
Administrative School Dist. 1
1 South West Broadway
Bend, OR 97701

Eugene Public Schools, District 4J

Mrs. Freda Young
Art Education Coordinator
200 North Monroe
Eugene, OR 97402

David Douglas School District

Joseph B. Kleven
Supervisor of Art
2900 South East 122nd Avenue
Portland, OR 97236

Portland Public Schools

Roberta J. Caughlan
Project Manager
Eco-Aesthetics Continuum
Portland Public Schools
7700 S.E. Reed College Place
c/o Dunway School
Portland, OR 97202

Salem Public Schools, District 24J

Don Walton
Art Resource Teacher
P.O. Box 87
Salem, OR 97308

Abington School District

Louis S. Mohollen
Supervisor of Art
Abington School District
1841 Susquehanna
Abington, PA 19001

Allentown Public Schols

W. Valgnee Routch
Fine Arts Coordinator
31 South Penn St.
Allentown, PA 18105

Altoona Area School District

Calvin E. Folk
Supervisor of Art
1415 Seventh Avenue
Altoona, PA 16603

Armstrong School District

Charles Milton Hanna
Department Chairman
Fourth and Tenth
Ford City, PA 16226

Bristol Township Public Schools

Joseph Pavone
Supervisor of Art
63 Manor Circle
Bristol, PA 19007

Chambersburg Area School District

Mrs. Joyce S. Wyatt
Elementary Art Dept. Chrmn.
511 South Sixth St.
Chambersburg, PA 17201

Chester Upland School District

Maureen M. Roberts
Director of Fine Arts
Chester Upland School District
18th and Melrose
Chester, PA 19013

Erie School District

Paul G. Grack
Coordinator of Fine Arts
1511 Peach St.
Erie, PA 16501

Harrisburg City School District

Ray P. Firestone
Associate Director, Art Ed.
1201 North Sixth St.
Harrisburg, PA 17102

Hazelton Area School District

Albert Sarkas
Supervisor of Art
Hazelton Area School District
Church & Walnut Streets
Hazelton, PA 18201

Greater Johnstown School District

Sara Jane Stewart
Supervisor of Art
Chestnut Building
501-509 Chestnut St.
Johnstown, PA 15906

School District of Lancaster

Albert B. Minnich
Director of Art and Industrial Arts
225 West Orange St.
Lancaster, PA 17604

New Castle Public Schools

Jesse W. Badger
Director of Art Education
Administration Bldg.
Corner of North & East Sts.
New Castle, PA 16101

Pennsbury School District

Karl C. Schantz
Art Teacher
Quarry Hill School
Pennsbury School District
Fallsington, PA 19054

Pittsburgh Public Schools

Ruth M. Ebken
Director of Art
Board of Public Education
341 South Bellefield Avenue
Pittsburgh, PA 15213

Reading School District

Earl A. McLane
Director of Art
Administration Bldg.
Eighth & Washington Sts.
Reading, PA 19601

Scranton Public Schools

Terrence Gallagher
Supervisor of Art
425 North Washington Ave.
Scranton, PA 18503

Upper Darby School District

Judson G. Snyder
District Art Supervisor
Upper Darby, PA 19084

Warren County School District

James Hill
Elementary Art Supervisor
Market Street Elementary Sch.
Market and Second Sts.
Warren, PA 16365

West Chester Area School District

Dr. Richard Ciganko
Art Supervisor
Henderson Senior High School
Lincoln & Montgomery Avenue
West Chester, PA 19308

West Shore School District

Mrs. Eleanor P. Stanton
Coordinator of Art
1833 Bridge St.
New Cumberland, PA 17070

Williamsport Area School District

Dr. June E. Baskin
Supervisor of Art
Transeau Educational Center
845 Park Avenue
Williamsport, PA 17701

Pawtucket School Department

Mrs. Veronica M. Farrell
Art Director
Administration Bldg.
Park Place
Pawtucket, RI 02860

Providence School System

Mrs. Catherine W. Hill
Supervisor of Art
50 Washington Street
Providence, RI 02903

Warwick School Department

Dorothy Desmond
Department Head
Elementary Art
Box 507 Conimicut Station
34 Warwick Lake Avenue
Warwick, RI 02889

Charleston County School District

Hans A. Pawley
Director of Fine Arts
Charleston Co. School District
3 Chisolm Street
Charleston, SC 29401

Darlington County

June McCauley
Art Supervisor
St. John's High School
Darlington, SC 29532

Florence School District 1

Mrs. Barbara W. Terry
Coordinator
109 West Pine Street
Florence, SC 29501

Greenville County School District

Robert Strother
Art Consultant
Box 2848, 301 Camperdown Way
Greenville, SC 29602

Greenwood School District 50

Mrs. Ray Young
Art Supervisor
P.O. Box 248
Greenwood, SC 29646

Spartanburg County School District 7

Betty Jane Bramlett
Art Coordinator
Spartanburg City Schools
P.O. Box 970
Spartanburg, SC 29304

Rapid City Public Schools

Diana M. Tollefson
Bureau of Indian Affairs
Cheyenne-Eagle Butte High Sch.
Eagle Butte, SD 57625

Chattanooga Public Schools

C. E. Blevins
Resource Teacher
3100 Rossville Blvd.
Chattanooga, TN 37407

Knoxville City Schools

Mrs. Billie Connatser
Supervisor of Art
101 East Fifth Avenue
Knoxville, TN 37917

Knox County Board of Education

Mrs. VaLera Lewis
Supervisor of Art
Box 2188
420 Maine Avenue
City-County Building
Knoxville, TN 37902

Metropolitan Nashville Davidson County Public Schools

James D. Hughes
Supervisor
Art Education
2601 Bransford Avenue
Nashville, TN 37204

Abilene Public Schools

Scott Darr
Art Consultant
Abilene Ind. School District
P.O. Box 981
Abilene, TX 79604

El Paso Independent School District

Jeanne Weitz
Art Consultant
Department of Fine Arts
223/Arizona
El Paso, TX 79930

Edgewood Independent School District

Mrs. Isabel DeLaGarza
Art Supervisor
5358 West Commerce Street
San Antonio, TX 78237

Fort Worth Independent School District

Ted C. Couch
Program Director
Art Education
3210 West Lancaster St.
Fort Worth, TX 76107

Galveston Independent School District

Mignon Weisinger
Art Supervisor
Secondary Schools
Ball High Schools
4115 Avenue O
Galveston, TX 77558

Goose Creek Consolidated Independent School District

Tommy F. Seale
Director of Music
Arts and Crafts
P.O. Box 30
Baytown, TX 77520

Killeen Independent School District

Hazel Watson
Assistant Superintendent for Instruction
P.O. Box 967
Killeen, TX 76541

Midland Independent School District

Bill R. Cormack
Coordinator of Fine Arts
702 North "N"
Midland, TX 79701

North East Independent School District

Maxine Allert
Consultant
Art Education
10333 Broadway
San Antonio, TX 78286

Pasadena Independent School District

Katherine Reid
Supervisor of Art
3010 Bayshore Drive
Pasadena, TX 77502

Amarillo Independent School District

Betty Jo Foster
Amarillo Ind. School District
Director of Art Education
910 West Eighth Avenue
Amarillo, TX 79101

Richardson Independent School District

Karen Tindel
Secondary Art Supervisor
Richardson Schools
400 S. Greenville Avenue
Richardson, TX 75081

San Angelo Independent School District

Mrs. Velma Jo Whitfield
Art Supervisor
100 North Magdalen St.
San Angelo, TX 76901

Spring Branch Independent School District

Mrs. Altharetta Yeargin
Art Coordinator
Spring Branch Ind. School Dist.
955 Campbell Road
Houston, TX 77024

Wichita Falls Independent School District

Walter Ehlert
Supervisor of Art
Wichita Falls Public Schools
1104 Broad St. P.O. Box 2570
Wichita Falls, TX 76307

Davis County School District

Ivan Cornia
Art Supervisor
David County School District
Farmington, UT 84025

Granite School District

Delbert W. Smedley
Supervisor
Art Education
340 East 3545 South
Salt Lake City, UT 84115

Jordan School District

David R. Roberts
Art Consultant
Jordan School District
9361 South 400 East
Sandy, UT 84070

Ogden City School District

Norman L. Skanchy
Principal
Horace Mann School
1300 Ninth Street
Ogden, UT 84404

Salt Lake City Board of Education

Russell E. Bjorklund
Specialist in Art
440 East First South
Salt Lake City, UT 84111

Barre City Schools

Helen D. Cate
Art Supervisor
Barre City Schools
Barre City, VT 15641

Alexandria City Public Schools

Joseph J. Adgate
Coordinator, Art, K-12
418 South Washington St.
Alexandria, VA 22313

Chesapeake Public Schools

Mrs. Edith G. Franklin
Supervisor of Art Education
School Administration Bldg.
P.O. Box 15204
Chesapeake, VA 23320

Fairfax County Public Schools

Dr. Beverly A. Heinle
Art Curriculum Specialist
10700 Page Avenue
Fairfax, VA 22030

Hampton City Schools

Leroy Hubbard
Supervisor of Art
Thomas Street School Board Annex
1300 Thomas Street
Hampton, VA 23369

Arlington County Public Schools

Dr. Richard G. Wiggin
Supervisor of Art
1426 North Quincy Street
Arlington, VA 22207

Henrico County Public Schools

W. Randolph Cheatham
Coordinator of Art
P.O. Box 40
Highland Springs, VA 23075

Newport News Public Schools

Lee Montgomery
Acting Supervisor of Art
12465 Warwick Blvd.
Newport News, VA 23606

Norfolk City Schools

Kay White Baker
Director
School Administration Bldg.
800 East City Hall Avenue
Norfolk, VA 23510

Pittsylvania County Schools

Jeffrey R. Guenther
Supervisor of Art
Pittsylvania County Schools
Chatham, VA 24531

Portsmouth Public Schools

Mr. John Backley
Supervisor Fine Arts
Portsmouth Public Schools
253 Constitution Avenue
Portsmouth, VA 23704

Gary DiVeechia
Supervisor Fine Arts
Portsmouth Public Schools
253 Constitution Avenue
Portsmouth, VA 23704

Richmond City Public Schools

Dale Nelson
Supervisor of Elementary Arts
Richmond Public Schools
301 North Ninth Street
Richmond, VA 23219

Roanoke City Public Schools

Mrs. Leslie Willett
Art Supervisor
P.O. Box 13145
Roanoke, VA 24031

Bellevue Public Schools

Lewis G. McCord
Coordinator of Art Education
310 - 102nd
Educational Service Center
Bellevue, WA 98004

Clover Park School District 400

James D. Blanchard
Supervisor of Art
5214 Steilacoom Blvd., S.W.
Lakewood Center, WA 98499

Edmonds School District 15

Jerry Conrad
Consultant Teacher in Art
3800 - 196th St., S.W.
Lynnwood, WA 98036

Everett School District 2

Patrick Maher
Supervisor of Industrial & Fine Arts
Educational Service Center
4730 Colby
Everett, WA 98203

Highline School District 401

Marie Dunstan
Art Coordinator
Highline School District 401
15675 Ambaum Blvd., S.W.
Seattle, WA 98166

Kent School District 415

Dr. Jim Barchek
12033 South East 256th
Coordinator of Art
508 North Central Avenue
Kent, WA 98031

Lake Washington School District 414

Chester Potuzak
Coordinator of Fine/Performing Arts
410 First Street
Kirkland, WA 98033

Renton School District 403

Hal Chambers
Art Resource Teacher
1525 North Fourth Street
Renton, WA 98055

Spokane Public Schools

Mrs. Shirley A. Tupper
Coordinator of General Programs
West 825 Trent Avenue
Spokane, WA 99201

Tacoma Public Schools

Lois V. Best, Coordinator
Fine Arts
Tacoma Public Schools
P.O. Box 1357
Tacoma, WA 98401

Vancouver School District 37

Adair Hilligoss, Supervisor
Creative Arts Department
Vancouver School Dist. #37
605 North Devine Road
Vancouver, WA 98661

Yakima School District 7

Richard S. Williams
Director of Art Education
Company Seven
501 South Seventh Street
Yakima, WA 98901

Cabell County Public Schools

Libby K. Caligan
Director of Art
620 - 20th Street
Huntington, WV 25709

Kanawha County Schools

Ruby Stanfield
Consultant of Art K-12
200 Elizabeth Street
Charleston, WV 25311

Marion County Board of Education

Mrs. Sara Adams
Supervisor of Art
200 Gaston Avenue
Fairmont, WV 26554

Monongalia County Schools

Wayne L. Miller
Art Consultant
Monongalia County Schools
48 Edgewood St. - Annex I
Morgantown, WV 26505

Appleton Public Schools

Matt V. Kahnke
Art Coordinator K-12
Harold Carlson
Secondary Art Coordinator
120 East Harris Street
Appleton, WI 54911

Kenosha Unified School District 1

Sam P. Christy
Coordinator of Art
4001 - 60th Street
Kenosha, WI 53140

Madison Metropolitan School District

Frank C. Lindl
Fine Arts Coordinator
545 West Dayton Street
Madison, WI 53703

Milwaukee Public Schools

Dr. Kent Anderson
Curriculum Specialist
Art
P.O. Drawer 10K
Milwaukee, WI 53201

Racine Unified Schools

Dr. Helen F. Patton
Director of Art Education K-12
2220 Northwestern Avenue
Racine, WI 53404

Sheboygan Area School District

Allen Hanson
Art Supervisor
830 Virginia Avenue
Sheboygan, WI 53081

Waukesha City Schools Joint District 1

Roland Schrupp
K-12, Art Learning Specialist
222 Maple Avenue
Waukesha, WI 53186

School District of West Allis-West Milwaukee

Kenneth B. Cottingham
Supervisor
9333 West Lincoln Avenue
West Allis, WI 53227

Laramie County School District 1

Margaret L. Albert
2810 House Avenue
Cheyenne, WY 82001

Guam Department of Education

Adriano B. Pangelinan
Assistant Professor of Art
University of Guam
Fine Arts
P.O. Box Ek
Agana, GUAM 96910

Art Magazines

A for Annuals; M for Monthlies; W for Weeklies; Q for Quarterlies

African Arts (Q)—John Povey, Ed; African Studies Center, University of California, 405 Hilgard Ave, Los Angeles, CA 90024. Yearly 16.00

Afterimage (M)—Nathan Lyons, Ed; Visual Studies Workshop Inc, 31 Prince St, Rochester, NY 14607. Yearly 15.00

American Art & Antiques (Bi-M)—Mary Jean Madigan, Ed; 1515 Broadway, New York, NY 10036. Yearly 18.00

American Art Journal (Bi-A)—Jane Van N. Turano, Ed; Kennedy Galleries, 40 W. 57th St, Fifth Floor, New York, NY 10019. Quarterly 25.00

American Artist (M)—M. Stephen Doherty, Ed; Marlene Schiller, Mg. Ed; 1515 Broadway, New York, NY 10036. Yearly 17.00

American Art Review* (Bi-M)—Thomas R. Kellaway, Ed. & Publ; Box 689, Old Lyme, CT 06371. Yearly 22.00

American Arts (Bi-M)—William Keens, Ed; 570 7th Ave, New York, NY 10018. Yearly 15.00

American Craft (Bi-M)—Pat Dandignac, Ed; 22 West 55th St, New York, NY 10019. Yearly 25.00

American Indian Art Magazine (Q)—Mary G. Hamilton, Ed; American Indian Art Inc, 7333 E. Monterey Way, #5, Scottsdale, AZ 85251. Yearly 14.00

American Journal of Archaeology* (Q)—Jerome J. Pollitt, Ed; Archaeological Institute of America, 260 W. Broadway, New York, NY 10013. Yearly 20.00

Antiques Magazine* (M)—Wendell Garrett, Ed; 551 Fifth Ave, New York, NY 10017. Yearly 24.00

Appollo Magazine (M)—Denys Sutton, Ed; 22 Davies St, London, W. 1, England. Yearly 48.00

Archaeology* (Bi-M)—Phyllis Pollak Katz, Ed; Archaeological Institute of America, 260 W. Broadway, New York, NY 10013. Yearly 15.00

Architectural Record (M)—Walter F. Wagner, Jr, Ed; 1220 Avenue of the Americas, New York, NY 10020. Yearly 23.00

ARLIS/NA Newsletter (M)—Pamela Jeffcott Parry, Ed; 143 Bowling Green Pl, Iowa City, IA 52240. Membership

Art & the Law (Q)—Judith N. Stein, Ed; Volunteer Lawyers for the Arts, 36 W. 44th St, New York, NY 10036. Yearly 15.00

Art Bulletin (Q)—Creighton Gilbert, Ed; 16 East 52nd St, New York, NY 10022. Membership

Artcraft (Bi-M)—Beverly A. Hutton, Ed; Commerce Bldg, Suite 313, 324 Datura St, West Palm Beach, FL 33401. Yearly 16.00

Art Direction (M)—Don Barron, Ed; 19 West 44th St, New York, NY 10036. Yearly 14.00

Art Education (M)—John J. Mahlmann, Ed; National Art Education Association, 1916 Association Dr, Reston, VA 22091. Yearly 15.00

Artforum (M)—Ingrid Sischy, Ed; 667 Madison Avenue, New York, NY 10021. Yearly 28.00

The ART Gallery Magazine (Bi-M)—William C. Bendig, Publisher and Ed; Ivoryton, CT 06442. Single 5.00 Yearly 25.00

Art in America (M)—Elizabeth C. Baker, Ed; 850 Third Ave, New York, NY 10022. Yearly 24.95

Art Index* (Q)—David J. Patten, Ed; The H.W. Wilson Co, 950 University Ave, New York, NY 10452. Subscription on service basis

Art International (Bi-M)—James Fitzsimmons, Ed. & Publ; Via Maraini 17-A, Lugano, Switzerland. Yearly 65.00

Art Journal (Q)—Rose R. Weil, Managing Ed; 16 East 52nd St, New York, NY 10022. Yearly 12.00

Artmagazine (Q)—Pat Fleisher, Ed; 234 Eglinton Avenue East #408, Toronto, Ont. M4P 1K5 Yearly 15.00

Art Material Trade News (M)—Jo Yanow, Ed; (National Art Material Trade Asn), Syndicate Magazines Inc, 6 East 43rd St, New York, NY 10017. Yearly 18.00

Art News* (M Sept-May, Q June-Aug)—Milton Esterow, Ed; 122 E. 42nd St, New York, NY 10017. Yearly 20.00

Art Quarterly (Q)—Jerrold Lanes, Ed; Art Studies, Inc, c/o Metropolitan Museum of Art, Fifth Ave & 82nd St, New York, NY 10028. Yearly 25.00

Arts Atlantic (Q)—Richard Field, Ed; Confederation Centre Art Gallery and Museum, PO Box 848, Charlottetown, PE C1A 7L9, Canada. Yearly 7.50

Artscanada (Bi-M)—Anne Brodzky, Ed; 3 Church St, Toronto, Ontario, M5E 1M2. Yearly 25.00

Arts Magazine (10 Issues)—Richard Martin, Ed; 23 East 26th St, New York, NY 10010. Yearly 28.50

Arts West (Bi-M)—PO Box 8243, Station F, Calgary, AB T2J 2V4, Canada. Yearly 15.00

Artviews (Bi-M)—417 Queens Quay, Suite G100, Toronto, ON M5V 1A2, Canada. Yearly 10.00

Art Voices/South (Bi-M)—Beverly A. Hutton, Ed; Commerce Bldg, Suite 313, 324 Datura St, West Palm Beach, FL 33401. Yearly 16.00

Artweek (Weekly Sept-May, Bi-M June-Aug)—Cecile N. McCann, Ed; 1305 Franklin St, Oakland, CA 94612. Yearly 15.00 Individual; 18.00 Institutions

Black Art (Q)—Val Spaulding, Ed; 137-55 Southgate St, Jamaica, NY 11413. Yearly 10.00

CA Magazine (Bi-M)—Richard S. Coyne, Ed; 410 Sherman Ave, (P.O. Box 10300), Palo Alto, CA 94303. Single 5.00; Subscription 30.00

Canada Crafts (Bi-M)—380 Wellington St W, Toronto, ON M5V 1E3, Canada. Yearly 10.00

Ceramics Monthly (M)—Spencer Davis, Ed; Professional Publications, Inc, Box 12448, Columbus, OH 43212. Yearly 12.00

Connoisseur, The (M)—William Allan, Ed; National Magazine House, 72 Broadwick Street, London, England. 60.00

Contemporary American Painting and Sculpture (Bi-A)—Allen S. Weller, Ed; University of Illinois Press, Box 5081, Station A, Champaign, IL 61820.

Contemporary Art-Southeast (4/yr)—Julia Ann Fenton, Ed; Box 7873, Station C, Atlanta, GA 30309. Yearly 8.00

Design Quarterly* (Q)—Mildred Friedman, Ed; Walker Art Center, Vineland Place, Minneapolis, MN 55403. Yearly 6.00

Fine Print (Q)—Sandra Kirshenbaum, Publisher; 2107 Van Ness Ave, San Francisco, CA 94109. Yearly 15.00

Gazette des Beaux-Arts (10 Issues)—Daniel Wildenstein, Dir; Imprimerie Louis-Jean, 05002 Gap Cedex, France. Yearly 300 F

Glass Studio (Bi-M)—Fred Abrams, Ed; 408 SW Second Ave, Portland OR 97204. Yearly 6.00

Goodfellow Review of Crafts (Bi-M)—Sarah Satterlee, Ed; Box 4520, Berkeley, CA 94704. Yearly 4.00

Graphis Annual (A)—Walter Herdeg, Ed; Hastings House, Publs., 10 East 40th St, New York, NY 10016. Sngle 49.50

HIGH Performance (Q)—Linda Frye Burnham, Ed; 240 S. Broadway, Fifth Floor, Los Angeles, CA 90012. Yearly 8.00

Hispanic American Arts (Bi-M)—Eduardo Darino, Ed; Box 5173, Grand Central Station, New York, NY 10017. Yearly 8.00

Illustrator Magazine (Bi-A)—Don L. Jardine, Ed; 500 South Fourth St, Minneapolis, MN 55415. Two year subscription (4 issues) 4.00

Illustrators Annual: The Annual of American Illustration (A-Spring)—Gerald McConnell, Ed; Published for Society of Illustrators by Hastings House, Publishers, 10 E. 40th St, New York, NY 10016. Yearly 35.00

Industrial Design (6 Issues)—George T. Finley, Ed; 717 Fifth Ave, New York, NY 10022. Yearly 24.00

Interior Design (M)—Sherman R. Emery, Ed; 850 3rd Ave, New York, NY 10022. Yearly 27.00

Journal of Aesthetics & Art Criticism (Q)—John Fisher, Ed; Temple University, Department of Philosophy, Philadelphia, PA 19122. Membership 15.00; Institutions 20.00

Journal of Canadian Art History (Semi-A)—Concordia University, Sir George Williams Campus, 1455 de Maisonneuve Blvd W, Montreal, PQ H3G 1M8, Canada. Yearly 10.00

Leonardo: Art Science and Technology (Q)—Frank J. Malina, Ed; Pergamon Press, Inc. Journals Dept., Maxwell House, Fairview Park, Elmsford, NY 10523 (and Headington Hill Hall, Oxford OX3 0BW, England). Yearly 99.00

Marsyas (Bi-A)—Bonnie Yochelson & Laurel Bradley, Eds; Institute of Fine Arts, New York University, 1 E. 78th St, New York, NY 10021. Single 10.00

Master Drawings (Q)—Felice Stempfle, Ed; Master Drawings Association Inc, 33 E. 36th St, New York, NY 10016. Yearly 20.00

Metropolitan Museum of Art Bulletin (Q)—Joan Holt, Ed; Fifth Ave at 82nd St, New York, NY 10028. Yearly 11.50

Museum News* (Bi-M)—Ellen C. Hicks, Ed; American Association of Museums, 1055 Thomas Jefferson St, NW, Washington, DC 20007. Yearly 12.00

National Sculpture Review (Q)—Theodora Morgan, Managing Ed; 15 East 26th St, New York, NY 10010. (Non-members 7.00)

New Art Examiner (10/yr)—Jane Addams Allen, Ed; Chicago New Art Association, 230 E. Ohio St, Chicago, IL 60611. Yearly 10.00

Old-Time New England (Q)—Abbott Lowell Cummings, Ed; The Society for the Preservation of New England Antiquities, 141 Cambridge St, Boston, MA 02114. Single (current) 2.50, (back) 3.50

Opus International* (Bi-M)—Editions Georges Fall, 15 Rue Paul Fort, Paris (75014) France. Yearly 18 F

Ornament (Q)—Robert K. Liu, Ed; 1221 S. LaCienega, Los Angeles, CA 90035. Yearly 14.00

Penrose Annual (A)—Hastings House, Publishers; 10 E. 40th St, New York, NY 10016. Price varies

Photographis: International Annual of Advertising & Editorial Photography (A)—Walter Herdeg, Ed; Hastings House, Publs, 10 E. 40th St, New York, NY 10016. Single 49.50

Pictures on Exhibit (Bi-M)—Charles Z. Offin, Ed; 30 E. 60th St, New York, NY 10022. Yearly 6.00

Praxis* (3/yr)—Ronald Reimers, Ed; Box 207, Galeta, CA 93017. Yearly 9.00 Individual; 16.00 Institutions

Print, American Graphic Design Magazine (Bi-M)—Martin Fox, Ed; 355 Lexington Ave, New York, NY 10017. Yearly 23.00

Progressive Architecture (M)—John Morris Dixon, Ed; 600 Summer St, Stamford, CT 06904. Yearly 12.00

Pro: The Voice of the Cartooning World* (M)—Arnold L. Wagner, Ed. & Publ; 1130 N. Cottage, Salem, OR 97301. Yearly 10.00

Push Pin Graphic (Bi-M)—Seymour Chwast, Ed; 207 E. 32nd St, New York, NY 10016. Yearly 15.00

Royal Society of Arts Journal (M)—J.S. Skidmore, Ed; 6 John Adam St, Adelphi, London W.C. 2, N6EZ England. Yearly 22L

School Arts Magazine (M Sept-May)—David Baker, Ed; 50 Portland St, Worcester, MA 01608. Yearly 12.00

Society of Architectural Historians Journal* (Q)—Christian F. Otto, Ed; 1700 Walnut St, Room 716, Philadelphia, PA 19103. Membership

Southwest Art (M)—Susan Hallsten McGarry, Ed; P.O. Box 13037, Houston, TX 77019. Yearly 20.00

Southwestern Art* (Q)—Craig Cornelius & Bab Halberg, Eds; Box 1763, Austin, TX 78767. Yearly 20.00

Stained Glass* (Q)—Dr. Norman L. Temme, Ed; 1125 Wilmington Ave, St. Louis, MO 63111. Yearly 10.00

Structure* (Irreg)—Joost Baljeu, Ed; Wittenborn & Co, 1018 Madison Ave, New York, NY 10021.   Yearly 2.75

Studio International* (6/yr)—Richard Cork, Ed; Studio International Publications Ltd, 14 W. Central St, London WC1A 1JH, England. Yearly 30.00 Students: 34.00 Individuals

Technology & Conservation of Art, Architecture, & Antiquities (Q)—S. E. Shur, Ed; One Emerson Pl, Boston, MA 02114.   Yearly 8.00

Today's Art (M)—L. D. Solomon & J. T. Schwartz, Publishers; Syndicate Magazines Inc, 6 E. 43rd St, New York, NY 10017.   Yearly 6.00

Umbrella (Bi-M)—Judith A. Hoffberg, Ed; Umbrella Associates, Box 3692, Glendale, CA 91201.   Yearly 12.50

Visual Dialog (Q)—Roberta J. Loach, Ed; 1380 Country Club Dr, Los Altos, CA 94022.   Yearly 12.00

Washington International Arts Letter (10 Issues)—Daniel Millsaps, Ed. & Publ; P.O. Box 9005, Washington, DC 20003.   Yearly 19.50 Individual; 38.00 Institutions

Working Craftsman (Q)—Marilyn Heise, Ed; 1290 Sherman Rd, Box 42, Northbrook, IL 60062.   Yearly 9.00

Newspapers Carrying Art Notes and Their Critics

ALABAMA

Birmingham News—Tom Harper
Birmingham Post-Herald—Caroline Wingate
Fayette County Broadcaster, Fayette—Jack Black
Gadsden Times—M.D. Garmon
The Huntsville Times—Alan Moore

ALASKA

Anchorage Times—Nancy Cain Schmidt
Daily News, Anchorage—Molly B. Jones

ARIZONA

Arizona Daily Star, Tucson—Samuel Hundley
Arizona Republic, Phoenix—John Wallace
Mesa Tribune—Dorothy Jensen
The Phoenix Gazette—Marlan Miller
Prescott Courier—Ruth Kennedy
Scottsdale Daily Progress—Barbara Perlman
Tempe Daily News—Howard Redding
Tucson Citizen—Joel Rochon

ARKANSAS

The Arkansas Democrat, Little Rock—Eric E. Harrison
Arkansas Gazette, Little Rock—Bill Lewis
Paragould Daily Press—Mark Lashley

CALIFORNIA

The Anaheim Bulletin—Doris Ortiz
Bakersfield California—Camille Gavin
Berkeley Daily Gazette—William Haigwood
Contra Costa Times, Walnut Creek—Carol Fowler
Daily Pilot, Costa Mesa—Yolanda Marmalude
Davis Enterprise—Del McColm
Fresno Bee—David Hale
Fullerton News Tribune—Holly Bridges
The Hanford Sentinel—Ruth J. Gomes
Independent Press-Telegram, Long Beach—Pat DeLuna
La Habra-Brea Daily Star Progress—Barbara Corbin Giasone
La Jolla Light—Edith Gay Knapp
Los Angeles Daily Racing Form—Pierre Bellocq
Los Angeles Herald Examiner—Gene Cannoy
Los Angeles Times—William Wilson
Los Gatos Times-Observer—Iver Davidson
Modesto Bee—Kathie Newton
Monterey Peninsula Herald—Irene Iagorio
Napa Register—Bernice Dunn
The Oakland Tribune—Charles Shere
Orange County Register—Roger Lewis
Pacific Sun, Mill Valley—Tom Cervenak
Palo Alto Times—Paul Emerson
Pasdena Star News—Larry Palmer
Redlands Daily Facts—Nelda Stuck
The Richmond Independent—William Haigwood
Riverside Press—T. E. Foreman
Sacramento Bee—Al Kay
Sacramento Union—Richard Simon
San Bernardino Sun-Telegram—Ray Cooklis
San Clemente Daily Sun Post—Art Grupe
San Diego Evening Tribune—Jan Jennings

San Diego Union—Robert Fassett
San Francisco Chronicle—Allan Temko
San Jose Mercury-News—Dorothy Burkhart
San Mateo Times—Mary Helen McAllister
San Pedro News-Pilot—Lanny Williams
Santa Barbara News-Press—Richard Ames
Santa Monica Evening Outlook—Betje Howell
Santa Rosa Press Democrat—Sophia Jensen
Stockton Record—Vince Perrin
Turlock Daily Journal—Carl Baggese
Ventura County Star-Free Press—Rita Moran

COLORADO

Boulder Daily Camera—Larry Caldwell
Colorado Springs Gazette Telegraph—Linda Navarro
Colorado Springs Sun—Larry Haise
Denver Post—James Mills
Pueblo Chieftain—Tim Acosta
Pueblo Star Journal—Tim Acosta
Rocky Mountain News, Denver—Irene Clurman

CONNECTICUT

The Bridgeport Post & Sunday Post—Betty Tyler
Danbury News-Times—Jean Buoy
The Greenwich Time—Dorothy Friedman
The Hartford Courant—Malcohn Johnson
Manchester Evening Herald—June Tompkins
Middletown Press—Kim Smith
The New Britain Herald—Judith W. Brown
New Canaan Advertiser—Don Souden
New Haven Register—Don Rabin
New London Day—Roger Montgomery
New Milford Times—Joe Foster
Waterbury American (Republican, Sunday Republican)—
    Terri Rousseau
Westport News—Jeanne Davis

DELAWARE

The Morning News, Wilmington—Otto Dekom
Wilmington Evening Journal—Ruth Jillya Kaplan
Wilmington Sunday News Journal—Edith De Shazo

DISTRICT OF COLUMBIA

Washington Post—Paul Richard
The Washington Star—Benjamin Forgey

FLORIDA

Clearwater Sun—Vaughn Hughes
Fort Lauderdale News—Shubert Jonas & Roger Hulbert
Gainesville Sun—Diane Chun
Jacksonville Journal—Elihu Edelson
The Ledger, Lakeland—Jeff Kline
The Miami Herald—Griffin Smith
Miami News—Bernie Oelze
Orlando Sentinel Star—Francis Martin, Jr.
Palatka Daily News—Ruth Elibeck
Palm Beach Daily News, West Palm Beach—Millie Wolff
Playground Daily News, Fort Walton Beach—Peggy May
The St. Augustine Record—Anne L. Carling

St. Petersburg Independent—Charles Benbow
St. Petersburg Times—Charles Benbow
Sarasota Herald-Tribune—Pat Buck
Sarasota Journal—Pat Buck
Stuart News—Edward Hallicy
Sun Coast Gondolier & Times—Dorothy E. Lippstreuer
The Tampa Times—Robert L. Martin
Tampa Tribune—Josephine Milano Rodriquez

GEORGIA

Albany Herald—Louise O. Whiting
Athens Banner-Herald—Masie Underwood
Athens Daily News—Masie Underwood
The Atlanta Journal & Constitution, Mount Berry—Clyde Burnett
Augusta Chronicle & Augusta Herald—L. K. Claussen
Columbus Enquirer—Angelo Franco
Macon Telegraph—Catherine Lee
Roswell North Fulton Today—Caffilene Allen
Savannah News & Press—Marshall L. Reed

HAWAII

The Honolulu Advertiser—Ray Higuchi
The Maui News—Henry Louis Ullman
The Star Bulletin, Honolulu—Ray Higuchi

IDAHO

The Idaho State Journal, Pocatello—Paul Beebe
The Idaho Stateman, Boise—Julie T. Monroe
Lewiston Morning Tribune—Ladd Hamilton
Times-News, Twin Falls—Charles Kogod

ILLINOIS

Chicago Daily News—Franz Schulze
Chicago Reader—Joanna Frueh
The Chicago Sun-Times—Ray W. Kopriva
Chicago Tribune—Alan G. Artner
Clinton Daily Journal—David J. Zubke
Daily Courier-News—Leroy S. Clemens
Daily Sun & Hearld, Arlington Heights—Patricia D. Adam
Dectur Herald & Review—Mike O'Connor
DeKalb Daily Chronicle—Eleanor Sussex
Galesburg Register-Mail—Robert Harrison
The Herald Whig, Quincy—Kit Cherry
Illinois Times, Springfield—Susan Mogerman & Ginny Farrar
Joliet Herald-News—Lorrie Gawla
Joliette Journal—Yves Desy
Moline Daily Dispatch—William McElwain
Monmouth Daily Review Atlas—Ron Jensen
Pantagraph, Bloomington—Tony Holloway
The Pioneer Press, Wilmette—Suzanne Weiss
Rockford Morning Star—David Zimmerman
Rockford Register-Republic—David Zimmerman
Schaumburg Times—Russ Swan
The Sunday Register-Star, Rockford—David Zimmerman
Vedette, Illinois State University, Normal—Jeffrey F. Kraft

INDIANA

Anderson Herald—Holly Miller
The Brown County Democrat, Nashville—Bruce Gregory Temple
Elkhart Truth—Bettie East
Evansville Courier—Jeanne Suhrheinrich
Evansville Press—John Smith
Gary Post-Tribune—John Forwalter
Indianapolis News—Marion Simon Garmel
Indianapolis Star—Donn Fry
Journal-Gazette, Fort Wayne—Roxanne T. Mueller
Lafayette Journal & Courier—Kathy Matter
Lafayette Leader—Martha DePoy
LaPorte Herald-Argus—Maxine Ford
Muncie Evening Press—Robert Loy
The Muncie Star—Nancy Millard
New Harmony Times—Georgi Japuiss
News-Sentinel, Fort Wayne—Connie Trexler
South Bend Tribune—Johnathon J. White

IOWA

The Ames Daily Tribune—John Epperheimer
Cedar Falls Record—Gary Oyloe
Cedar Rapids Gazette—Mary Westphalen

The Charles City Press—D. Overby
Des Moines Register—Nicholas G. Baldwin
The Fort Dodge Messenger—Lois Johnson
Iowa City Press Citizen—Starla Smith
Marshalltown Times-Republican—Lois Jacobs
The Sioux City Journal—Jane Hunwardsen
Slidell Daily Times—Larry Baudot
Waterloo Courier—Phyllis Singer

KANSAS

The Daily Reporter, Independence—Georgia High
The Hutchinson News—Dorothy Melland
Lawrence Daily Journal—Sarah Iles Johnston & Lynn Bretz
Russell Daily News—Pauline Sturgeon
Topeka Capital-Journal—Peggy Greene
The Wichita Eagle-Beacon—Bob Curtright

KENTUCKY

Berea Citizen—Lea M. Schultz
Louisville Courier-Journal—Sarah Lansdell
Messenger-Inquirer, Owensboro—Ann Whittinghill

LOUISIANA

Alexandria Town Talk—Phyllis Price
News-Star & World, Monroe—Suzanne Thomas
The Morning Advocate, Baton Rouge—Anne K. Price
The Shreveport Journal—Ron Rice
The Shreveport Times—Joe Leydon
The State Times, Baton Rouge—Roger Green
States-Item, New Orleans—Alberta Collier
The Times Picayune, New Orleans—Alberta Collier

MAINE

Bangor Daily News—Robert H. Newall
Maine Sunday Telegram, Portland—Robert S. Niss
Portland Evening Express—Robert S. Niss
Portland Press Herald—Robert S. Niss
Waterville Morning Sentinel—Ann McGowan

MARYLAND

The Annapolis Evening Capital—Eric Smith
Baltimore News-American—Richard Curtis
Baltimore Sun—Edward McKee
Daily & Sunday Times, Salisbury—Dick Fleming
Hagerstown Daily Mail—Harry Warner
Hagerstown Morning Herald—Harry Warner

MASSACHUSETTS

Amherst Record—Randall Current
The Berkshire Courier, Great Barrington—Stephen Fay
The Berkshire Eagle, Pittsfield—Winifred B. Bell
The Boston Globe—Robert Taylor
Boston Herald American—Michael Kellelea
The Boston Phoenix—Kenneth Baker
Brockton Enterprise-Times—Dorothy Dale
The Christian Science Monitor, Boston—Diana Loercher & Theodore F. Wolf
Framingham South Middlesex News—Diane Satterfield
Holyoke Transcript-Telegram—Walter Merkel
The Lowell Sun—Ann Schecter
Medford Daily Mercury—Charlotte B. Berman
New Bedford Standard-Times—Rosalina Mello
Quincy Patriot Ledger—Milly Potter
The Real Paper, Cambridge—David Rosenbaum
Salem Evening News—Peggy Shehan
The Sentinel & Enterprise, Fitchburg—Robert Buckley
The Worcester Gazette—Peter Donker
The Worcester Telegram—Gerald E. Goggins

MICHIGAN

Alpena News—Betty Werth
Bay City Times—Gay McGee
Benton Harbor Herald-Palladium—Arlys Derrick
Birmingham Eccentric—Corinee Abatt
Cheboygan Daily Tribune—Terese Lindsay
Detroit Free Press—Dick Mayer
Enquirer and News, Battle Creek—Nancy Crawley
The Flint Journal—James E. Harvey

Kalamazoo Gazette—Verne Berry
Grand Rapids Press—Bernice Winslow Mancewicz
Jackson Citizen Patriot—Barbara Tidyman
Lansing State Journal—Mike Hughes
Macomb Daily, Mount Clemens—Robert Russell
Muskegon Chronicle—Susan E. Harrison
The Oakland Press—Kenn Jones
The Saginaw News—Janet I. Martineau

MINNESOTA

Duluth Herald & News Tribune—Jack Tyllia
Mankato Free Press—Robert Girouard
Minneapolis Star—Kent Gardner
Minneapolis Tribune—Robert Lundegaard
Owatonna People's Press—Jan Mittlestadt
Rochester Post-Bulletin—Pauline Walle
St. Paul Dispatch—David Hawley
St. Paul Pioneer Press—David Hawley
Winona Daily News—Lucy Eckberg

MISSISSIPPI

Biloxi South Mississippi Sun—Jerry Kinser
Clarion Ledger, Jackson—Tracy Roberts
Columbus Commercial Dispatch—Rachel Eide
Jackson Daily News—O. C. McDavid
Meridian Star—Homer Cook

MISSOURI

Columbia Missourian—Kathy Casteel
Excelsior Springs Daily Standard—Sheila Woods
Independence Examiner—Charles Burke
The Kansas City Star—Donald Hoffman
St. Joseph Gazette—Richard Allison
St. Joseph News-Press—Richard Allison
St. Louis Globe-Democrat—Rose Marie Schoenhoeffer
St. Louis Post-Dispatch—Bob Duffy
Southeast Missourian, Cape Girardeau—Judith Ann Crow
Springfield Daily News—Bill Tatum
Springfield Leader & Press—Bill Tatum
Times, Kansas City—Donald Hoffman

MONTANA

Anaconda Leader—Sally Campbell
Billings Gazette—Kathryn Wright
Bozeman Chronicle—Florence Trout
The Daily Inter Lake, Kalispell—Marlin Hanson
Missoula Missoulian—Gay Svee
The Montana Standard, Butte—Andrea McCormick

NEBRASKA

Lincoln Journal—Helen J. Haggie
Lincoln News—George D. Aiken
Omaha World-Herald—Peg Jones

NEVADA

Las Vegas Review-Journal—Denise Magnell
Las Vegas Sun—Steve Lesnick
Reno Evening Gazette & Nevada State Journal—Mark Crawford

NEW HAMPSHIRE

Keene Sentinel—Pat Haley
The Nashua Telegraph—Marilyn Solomon
The New Hampshire Times, Concord—Richard Wright

NEW JERSEY

Daily Journal, Elizabeth—Mary Epperson
Daily Record, Morristown—Marion Filler
The Daily Sunday Register, Red Bank—Hildegarde Fontaine
Homes News, New Brunswick—Doris E. Brown
Newark Star-Ledger—Eileen Watkins
Paterson Evening News—Tom Lyles
Princeton Packet (Time Off)—Ellen Kolton-Walton
The Record, Hackensack—David Spengler & Deborah Jerome
Summit Herald—Anne Cooper

Toms River Ocean County Times Observer—Gloria Barone
Vineland Times Journal—Del Brandt
Willingboro Burlington County Times—Lou Gaul
Woodbury Gloucester County Times—Roger Filardo

NEW MEXICO

The Albuquerque Journal—William Lea Hoffman
The Albuquerque Tribune—Keith Raether
Gallup Independent—Luri Owen
The New Mexican, Santa Fe—Anne Hillerman
The Taos News—Robin McKinney

NEW YORK

Albany Times Union—Fred Lebrun
Binghamton Sun Bulletin—Gene Grey
Buffalo Courier-Express—Richard Huntington
The Buffalo Evening News—Anthony Bannon
The Chatham Courier—Carole Atman & Judy Sutherland
The Daily Freeman, Kingston—Carol Guensberg
East Hampton Star—Phyllis Braff
Elmira Star-Gazette—Salle Crooks
Elmira Sunday Telegram—Salle Crooks
Goshen Independent Republican—Eugene Wright
Hamilton County News, Speculator—George List, Jr.
Jamestown Post-Journal—Patricia M. Parker
The Knickerbocker News, Albany—James R. Gray
Middletown Times Herald-Record—Maybelle Mann
Nassau Star, Long Beach—Irene Harris
The New York Times—Hilton Kramer
News, New York—C. Walker
Niagara Gazette, Niagara Falls—Rita Truschel
Nyack Journal-News—John Cornell
Oneonta Star—Jessie Nichols
Port Chester Daily Item—Sydney Stanton
The Post-Standard, Syracuse—Eileen C. Levy
Poughkeepsie Journal—Jeffrey Borak
The Press, Binghamton—Gene Grey
Register-Star, Hudson—Chris Martin
Rochester Democrat & Chronicle—Herman Auch
Saratogian, Saratoga Springs—Candace H. Wait
Schenectady Gazette—Peg Churchill
Staten Island Advance—Elaine Boies
Syracuse Herald American—Herbert Redell
Times Record, Troy—Doug deLisle
The Times-Union, Rochester—Herman Auch
Valley News, Elizabethtown—Mary B. Allen
The Village Voice, New York—Carrie Rickey & Kay Larson
The Villager, New York—Eileen Blair

NORTH CAROLINA

Asheville Citizen-Times—Richard VanKleeck
The Chapel Hill Newspaper—Charles Horton
The Charlotte News—Mary Estes
Charlotte Observer—Michael Edwin Kampen
The Daily Reflector, Greenville—Jerry S. Raynor
The Durham Morning Herald—Jim Baie, Blue Greenberg & R. C. Smith
The Durham Sun—Susan Wenzel
Greensboro Daily News—Patricia Krebs
The Greensboro Record—Abe D. Jones, Jr.
The News and Observer, Raleigh—Johanna Seltz
The Sun-Journal, New Bern—Eugene X. Bryan
Winston-Salem Journal & Sentinel—Jim Stanley

NORTH DAKOTA

The Forum, Fargo—Sylvia Paine
Times Record, Valley City—Dick Plum
Williston Herald—Corky Kaiser

OHIO

Akron Beacon Journal—Clyde Morris
Cincinnati Enquirer—Owen Findsen
Cincinnati Post—Ellen Brown
Cleveland Plain Dealer—Helen Borsick
Cleveland Press—Dick Wootten
Columbus Citizen-Journal—Babette Sirak
Columbus Dispatch—Sara Carroll
Dayton Daily News—Betty Dietz Krebs
Dayton Journal Herald—Walt McCaslin
Lorain Journal—Howard Gollop

Mansfield News Journal—Linda Martz
News-Herald, Willoughby—Mary Ellen Klar
North Canton Sun—Vernon Sell
Painesville Telegraph—James Baron
The Times Recorder, Zanesville—David Shinn
The Toledo Blade—Boris Nelson
Youngstown Vindicator—Clyde Singer

OKLAHOMA

Bartlesville Examiner Enterprise—Jim Wood
The Daily Oklahoman, Oklahoma City—Joy Donovan
Lawton Constitution—L. R. Thompson
Morning Press, Lawton—L. R. Thompson
Muskogee Daily Phoenix & Times Democrat—Joan Morrison
Norman Transcript—Delaine Dannelley
Oklahoma City Times—Joy Donovan
The Oklahoma Journal, Oklahoma City—Joy Donovan
Stillwater News-Press—Pat Webster
The Tulsa Tribune—Gary Jack Willis
The Tulsa World—David MacKenzie

OREGON

Capital Journal, Salem—Sue Bristow
Corvallis Gazette-Times—Lori Varosh
Eugene Register-Guard—Brian Lanker
The Oregon Journal, Portland—Andy Rocchia
Portland Oregonian—Beth Fagan
Willamette Week—Paul Sutinen
World, Coos Bay—Linda Meierjurgen

PENNSYLVANIA

Allentown Call-Chronicle—Albert Hofammann
Altoona Mirror—Don Baker
Beaver County Times—Ed Montini
Bethlehem Globe-Times—Alan Janesch
Chestnut Hill Local—Marguerite Stork
The Daily Intelligencer, Doylestown—Donald P. Davis
Erie Morning News—William Rogosky
Erie Times-News—William Rogosky
The Evening Chronicle, Allentown—Albert Hofammann
The Evening Phoenix—Joseph F. Rudick
Harrisburg Patriot-News—Connie M. Blackwell
Kutztown Patriot—Ade-Rolfe Floreen
Levittown Bucks County Courier Times—Dennis Moore
Lock Haven Express—Charles R. Ryan
Monessan Valley Independent—Emma Jean Lelik
News-Tribune, Beaver Falls—Susan Schild
Norristown Times Herald—Thomas J. McIntyre
Philadelphia Evening & Sunday Bulletin—Nessa R. Forman
Philadelphia Inquirer—Victoria Donahoe
The Pittsburgh Post-Gazette—Donald Miller
Pittsburgh Press—Nat Youngblood
Primos Delaware County Daily Times—Gerry Oliver
Reading Eagle—Donald Deihm
Reading Times—Debora A. Tkac
The Scranton Times—Victor Alfano
The Scranton Tribune—Mrs. Gene Brislin
Today's Post, King of Prussia—Valerie Newitt
Union County Journal-Lewisburg—John C. P. Boylan

RHODE ISLAND

Newport Daily News—Robert E. Reimer, III
The Providence Sunday Journal (Providence Journal, Evening Bulletin)—Ed Sozanski
Warwick Beacon—Donald Fowler
The Westerly Sun—Charles W. Utter

SOUTH CAROLINA

Columbia Record—Martha Beaver
Georgetown Times—Cathy McConnell
Greenville News, Greenville—Sharon G. Todd
The Greenville Piedmont—Jan Rogers
Index-Journal, Greenwood—Bo Emerson
The State, Columbia—Martha Beaver

SOUTH DAKOTA

Rapid City Journal—Sally Farrar
Sioux Falls Argus-Leader—Marchall Fine
Vermillion Plain Talk—Ed Anderson
Yankton Press & Dakotan—Jane Trumble

TENNESSEE

Chattanooga News-Free Press—Samuel A. Hunter
Chattanooga Times—Wes Hasden
The Commercial Appeal, Memphis—Donald LaBadie
Johnson City Press Chronicle—Roger Hendrix
Kingsport Times-News—Tony Kiss
Knoxville News-Sentinel—Frank Jordan
The Leaf-Chronicle, Clarksville—Max Moss
Nashville Banner—Julie Pursell
The Nashville Tennessean—Clara Hieronymus
The Oak Ridger, Oak Ridge—Jonell Schmitt

TEXAS

Abilene Reporter-News—Chris Wienandt
Amarillo Daily News—Bette Thompson
Amarillo Globe-Times—Bette Thompson
Amarillo Sunday News-Globe—Bette Thompson
Caller-Times, Corpus Christi—Maurice Schmidt
Courier Times-Morning Telegraph—Sam Nash
Dallas Morning News—Janet Kutner
Dallas Times Herald—Bill Marvel
El Paso Herald Post—Betty Pierce
The El PasoTimes—Edna Gundersen
Fort Worth Star-Telegram—Carol Nuckols
Garland Daily News—Sue Watkins
The Houston Chronicle—Ann Holmes
The Houston Post—Mimi Crossley
Hurst Mid-Cities Daily News—Wanda Adams
Kerrville Daily Times—Kit West
Longview Morning Journal & Longview Daily News—Rebecca Pflugfelder
The Lubbock Avalanche-Journal—William D. Kerns
The Odessa American—Alice Berthelsen
Plainview Herald—Myrna Smith
Port Arthur News—Mark Stansbury
San Angelo Standard Times—Renee Kientz
San Antonio Express & News—Ben King
The San Antonio Light—Glenn Tucker
Temple Daily Telegram—Kay Webb
Texarkana Gazette—Steve Morgan
Wichita Falls Times & Record News—Martha B. Steimel

UTAH

The Deseret News, Salt Lake City—Charles Nickerson
Logan Herald Journal—Edith Morgan
Provo Daily Herald—Renee Nelson
Salt Lake Tribune, Salt Lake City—Helen Forsberg
Springville Herald—Pat Conover

VERMONT

The Bennington Banner—Dennis Redmond
The Burlington Free Press—D. F. Burcae
The Sunday Rutland Herald, Barre—Steven J. Wallach
Sunday Times Argus, Barre—Steven J. Wallach

VIRGINIA

The Alexandria Gazette—Cathy Perkins
Charlottesville Daily Progress—Bill Sublette
The Ledger-Star, Norfolk—Teresa Annas
Lynchburg News—Mrs. Cecil Mullan
The Richmond News Leader—Roy Proctor
Richmond Times-Dispatch—Robert Merritt
The Roanoak Times—Sandra Kelly
The Times-Herald, Newport News—Joe West
Virginia Gazette, Williamsburg—W. C. O'Donovan
The Virginian-Pilot, Norfolk—Art Jones
World News, Roanoke—Sandra Kelly

WASHINGTON

The Goldendale Sentinel—Robert D. Smith
Seattle Post-Intelligencer—Dick Kirsten
The Seattle Times—Deloris Tarzan

The Spokane Community Press—Randall S. Barton
Spokesman-Review, Spokane—O. J. Parsons
The Spokane Daily Chronicle—Sue English
Tacoma News Tribune—Myron L. Thompson
Vancouver Columbian—Victoria Salter
Wenatchee Daily World—David Kraft
Yakima Herald-Republic—Carol Hilton

WEST VIRGINIA

The Advertiser, Huntington—Estelle Belanger
Bluefield Daily Telegraph—June Grubb
The Charleston Daily Mail—George Armstrong
The Charleston Gazette—Terry Wimmer
The Huntington Herald Dispatch—Estelle Belanger

WISCONSIN

Capital Times, Madison—Marie Pulvermacher
Green Bay Press-Gazette—Warren Gerds
Kenosha News—Elaine Edwards
The Mulwaukee Journal—James M. Auer
The Milwaukee Sentinel—Dean Jensen
Northwestern, Oskosh—Judy Russell
The Post Crescent, Appleton—Tom Richards
Racine Journal Times—Karen Tancill
Wausau Daily Herald—Barbara Lundquist
Wisconsin State Journal, Madison—Donald K. Davies

WYOMING

Wyoming Eagle, Cheyenne—Dick Moody

CANADA

ALBERTA

Calgary Albertan—Ruth Ann Mackinnon
Calgary Herald—Al Rach
The Edmonton Journal—Catherine Carson
Medicine Hat News—Paul Bilodeau

BRITISH COLUMBIA

Columbian, New Westminster—Margherita Leech

Vancouver Province—Art Perry
Vancouver Sun—E. Smith
Victoria Colonist—Jim Gibson
Victoria Daily Times—Audrey Johnson

MANITOBA

Winnipeg Free Press—Peter Kuch
Winnipeg Tribune—Jan Kamienski

NEW BRUNSWICK

Saint John Telegraph-Journal—Helmer Biermann

ONTARIO

Guelph Mercury—Dave Carter
The Globe & Mail, Toronto—Kay Kritzwiser
Kitchener-Waterloo Record—Trish Wilson
The London Free Press—J. A. Bembridge
Niagara Falls Review—Don Mullan
Ottawa Citizen—Kathleen Walker
The Ottawa Journal—Susan Scott
Ottawa Le Droit—Murray Maltais
St. Catharines Standard—Linda Crabtree
The Spectator, Hamilton—Grace Inglis
Toronto Star—Keith Branscombe
Toronto Sun—Andy Donato
Woodstock Sentinel Review—R. Spence

QUEBEC

Montreal Gazette—Virginia Nixon
Montreal La Presse—Jean Claude Dussault
Montreal Le Devoir—Jean Royer
Montreal Le Dimanche Matin—Claude Lavergne
Montreal Matin—Denis Tremblay
The Montreal Star—Doris Giller
Quebec City Le Soleil—Paul Roux
Sherbrooke La Tribune—Pierre Francoeur

SASKATCHEWAN

Regina Leader Post—Denise Ball
Saskatoon Star-Phonix—Ned Powers

Scholarships and Fellowships

OFFERED BY	AMOUNT	OPEN TO	DURATION	WHEN OFFERED
Abilene Fine Arts Museum, Oscar Rose Park, Box 1858, Abilene, TX 79605	$500	Art students of Taylor County		Annually
Alaska Artists' Guild, Ltd, PO Box 1888, Anchorage, AK 99510	$500	Senior high school students for continuing education in art field	One time	Annually in April
Alaska Association for the Arts, PO Box 2786, Fairbanks, AK 99707	$200 minimum	High school or college students residing in Alaska	One year	Annually
Alberta College of Art, Southern Alberta Institute of Technology, 1301 16th Ave NW, Calgary, AB T2M OL4, Canada	$5000 (total)	Students registered in A.C.A. programmes	One year	Annually
Alberta, Dept. of Culture, Government of the Province of Alberta,* Cultural Development Div., CN Tower, 10004 104th Ave. Edmonton, AB, Canada T5J OK5	$100-$750, (total) $15,000	Residents of Alberts	One year	Annually
Alice Lloyd College, Pippa Passes, KY 41844	Variable	Local Students	One or two years	Annually
Allied Artists of America, 15 Gramercy Park So. New York, NY 10003	$200	Rotating scholarship for any student attending that year's specified art school	One year	Annually
Lyman Allyn Museum, 625 Williams St, New London, CT 06320	$55 for children's classes	Needy children	One year	Annually
Amarillo Art Center, Box 447, Amarillo, TX 79178	Variable	Primarily to disabled or deprived children and young adults	Each semester	
American Academy and Institute of Arts and Letters, 633 W. 155th St, New York, NY 10032	5 awards of $4000 each	Painters, sculptors, graphic artists (cannot be applied for)		Annually
American Academy, 41 E 56th St, New York, NY 10021	$7444 plus residency	Citizens of the US	One year	Annually, Deadline: Nov 15
American Academy of Art, 220 State St, Chicago, IL 60604	$6000	High school seniors	One or more school semesters	Annually
American Antiquarian Society, 185 Salisbury St, Worcester, MA 01609	Up to $1666 per month (NEH Fellowships)	Qualified scholars in American history and culture to 1877	Six months-one year	Annually
	Up to $1800 (Daniels Fellowships)	Qualified scholars in American history and culture to 1877	One to three months	Annually
	Up to $1250 (Boni Fellowship)	Qualified scholar working in general field of early American bibliography or printing and publishing history	One to two months	Annually
American Numismatic Society, Broadway at 155th St, New York, NY 10032	$3500 Fellowship	Graduate student	One year	Annually
	(12) $900 grants	Graduate students and junior members of faculty	June 10-Aug 9	Annually
American Oriental Society, Secretary, 329 Sterling Memorial Library, Yale Station, New Haven, CT 06520	The American Oriental Society Fellowship Award for the Study of Chinese Painting—$5000	Students who have completed 3 years of Chinese language study at a recognized university, or the equivilant, and all the requirements for a PhD in Chinese painting studies, except for travel, the written dissertation and its defense	One year	July 1st to June 30th
	Louise Wallace Hackney Fellowship for the Study of Chinese Art—$5000	Post-Doctoral and Doctoral students who are U.S. citizens	One year	July 1st to June 30th
American Scandinavian Foundation, Exchange Division, 127 E 73rd St, New York, NY 10021	$500-$5000	Applicants with an undergraduate degree (unrestricted fields) for Denmark, Finland, Iceland, Norway and Sweden	Up to one year	Annually

OFFERED BY	AMOUNT	OPEN TO	DURATION	WHEN OFFERED
American Watercolor Society, 14 E 90th St, New York, NY 10028	Variable	Art schools and colleges for further award to outstanding students of water-color painting	One year	Annually
Arizona Commission on the Arts, 6330 N Seventh St, Phoenix, AZ 85014	Visual Artists-Sculpture (3) $4000	Residents of Arizona, over 18; students are not eligible	One year	Annually
	Literature-Fiction/Poetry (2) $2500	Same as above	One year	Annually
	Composers (1) $3000	Same as above	One year	Annually
Arizona State University, Dept of Art, Tempe, AZ 85281	$1500-$4000, also tuition waivers	Qualified graduate students—admitted students in the graduate program. Qualified minority students encouraged to apply	Semester or academic year	Annually, semi-annually
Arkansas Arts Center, MacArthur Park, Little Rock, AR 72203	Varies as to class	Qualified applicant	By semesters	
Arkansas State University,* Fine Arts Center, Dept of Art, State University, AR 72467	$460, full tuition scholarship, 6 awarded annually	1st and 2nd semester freshmen	One year	Annually
Arrowmont School of Arts and Crafts,* Parkway, Box 567, Gatlinburg, TN 37738	Varies from $250 to full tuition internships	Everyone	One to five weeks	Annually
Art Association of Richmond, McGuire Memorial Hall, 350 Whitewater Blvd, Richmond, IN 47374	$450	Richmond high school senior studying art	One year	Annually
Art Center College of Design, 1700 Lida St, Pasadena, CA 91103	$1625 or $813	Third term students	Continuous	Each semester
Art Gallery of Ontario,* 317 Dundas St W, Toronto, ON M5T 1G4, Canada	Varied subsidized grants. Gallery pays 85%	Secondary school students	One year—25 week course	Annually
Art Institute of Boston, 700 Beacon St, Boston, MA 02215	$50 to $1125	Accepted or enrolled students at the Art Institute	One-three years	Annually
Art Institute of Ft Lauderdale, 3000 E Las Olas Blvd, Ft Lauderdale, FL 33316	Varies as to art major—$33,670 total	Graduating high school seniors	Two years	Annually
Arts and Science Center, 14 Court St, Nashua, NH 03060	For education classes at the Center (4 semesters)	Qualified applicants	Ten weeks	Quarterly
Arts Club of Washington, 2017 Eye St, NW, Washington, DC 20006	$600	Students at local universities or colleges only	One year	Annually
Arts Council of Spartanburg County, Inc, 385 South Spring St, Spartanburg, SC 29301	Varies	Resident of Spartanburg County	One year	As decided by Board of Governors
Art Students League of New York, 215 W 57th St, New York, NY 10019	Tuition $5000 Traveling Scholarships (2)	League students	One year	Annually
Atlanta College of Art,* 1280 Peachtree St NE, Atlanta, GA 30309	Varies	Serious art students	Term	Annually
Atlantic Christian College, Art Department, Wilson, NC 27893	Determined by Art Faculty	All art students	Determined by Art Faculty	Anytime during the year
Ball State University, 2000 University Ave, Muncie, IN 47306	$3000 graduate assistantship academic year (tuition waived)		One year (renewable)	Annually
	$3450 doctoral fellowship academic year (tuition waived) $490 summer session		One year (renewable)	Annually
Bassist Institute, 923 SW Taylor St, Portland, OR 97205	$2000	Students	One and two years	Annually
Beloit College, Department of Art, Beloit, WI 53511	Variable	Qualified students	One year (renewable)	Bi-annually
Berry College,* Art Department, Mt Berry, GA 30149	Varies	Freshman art majors	One year	Semi-annually
Birmingham-Bloomfield Art Association, 1516 S Cranbrook Rd, Birmingham, MI 48009	Full, dependent upon course cost	Local high school art students	Per term	Per term (variable)
Blue Mountain College,* Dept of Art, Blue Mountain, MS 38610	$135	Art majors	One year	Annually
Bob Jones University, School of Fine Arts, Wade Hampton Blvd, Greenville, SC 29614	$70 to $170 per month	Undergraduate students with demonstrated financial need and satisfactory school record	One semester (renewable)	Semi-annually
Boston Architectural Center, 320 Newbury St, Boston, MA 02115	Variable	Qualified students registered in B. Arch. Program		Annually
Bradley University,* Peoria, IL 61625	Undergraduate $2600; 8 graduate assistantships of $1200 each	Any student in or entering the art program	One year (renewable)	Annually

OFFERED BY	AMOUNT	OPEN TO	DURATION	WHEN OFFERED
W Braun Co, Wolf and Mary Braun Fund, 260 Fifth Ave, New York, NY 10001	US Savings Bonds	All credited schools in the US and Canada		Annually
Brigham Young University, Harris Fine Arts Center, Provo, UT 84602	Tuition	Qualified freshmen applicants, transfer students and continuing students	One year	Annually
British Government, *Marshall Scholarships. Apply: British Consulate-General, San Francisco, 120 Montgomery St, San Francisco, CA 94104 Closing date for applications Oct 22.	(30) in the order of $1750 a year. In certain circumstances a marriage allowance is also payable	US citizens. Available to college or university graduates under 26 years of age for study of any subject leading to the award of a British University degree. Candidates may apply either in region in which they live or where they received at least two years of college training.	Two years (with possibility of extension for a third year).	Annually
Brockton Art Museum, Museum School, Oak St, Brockton, MA 02401	$60	Needy children and senior citizens	Per term	Per term
Brooklyn Museum Art School, 188 Eastern Pkwy, Brooklyn, NY 11238	(20) Max Beckmann Memorial Scholarships covering tuition and registration fees	College art majors and professional art school students completing their undergraduate studies	One year	Deadline: Apr 30
	(5) Robert Smithson Memorial Scholarships covering tuition and registration fees	College art majors and professional art school students completing their undergraduate studies	One year	Deadline: Apr 30
Bucknell University, Dept of Art, Lewisburg, PA 17837	$2000 plus tuition	Registered graduate students	One year, renewable	Annually
Burnley School of Professional Art, Inc, 905 E Pine St, Seattle, WA 98122	Semester tuition	Students who have completed one semester in School. Financial need is not considered.	Can be won as many times as student is enrolled in school	Fall/Spring semesters
Caldwell College,* Art Department, Caldwell, NJ 07006	$500-$2100	Academically qualified	One year	Renewable annually
	Grants: $100 and up	Economically qualified	One year	Renewable annually
California College of Arts and Crafts, 5212 Broadway, Oakland, CA 94618	Variable. Scholarships, loans, grants	Grants, loans, employment open to all students. Merit scholarships open to continuing students who have attended for two or more consecutive semesters and are currently enrolled	One year	Annually
California Institute of the Arts/School of Art and Design, 24700 McBean Pkwy, Valencia, CA 91355	Varies	Everyone	One year	Annually
California State University, Chico, Art Department, Chico, CA 95929	$500	Art students	One year	Annually
California State University, Hayward,* Art Dept, Hayward, CA 94542	Variable ($100-$300 annually)	Any art student	One year	
Campbellsville College,* Fine Arts Div, Campbellsville, KY 42718	Varies	All applicants who can show proficiency	Four years (renewable)	Semi-annually
Cardinal Stritch College,* Art Dept, 6801 N Yates Rd, Milwaukee, WI 53217	(2) $200 (Total of $400)	Art Concentrators of present undergraduate students of freshmen, sophomore, and junior status	One year (may apply a second year)	Annually
Carolina Art Association Gibbes Art Gallery, 135 Meeting St, Charleston, SC 29401	$10 to $100	Art Students	Per session	Several times a year
	Work-study Scholarships—part or full tuition			
Carrizo Art & Craft Workshops, Drawer A, Ruidoso, NM 88345	Tuition plus meals and lodging	Young adults	Two weeks	August
The Catholic University of America, Dept of Art, Office of Financial Aid, Michigan Ave, Washington DC 20064	Half tuition	All applicants		Annually
Catholic University of Puerto Rico, Department of History and Fine Arts, Ponce, PR 00731	Full tuition (one only)	Low income freshmen with art talent	Four years	Biennially or every four years
Cazenovia College, Cazenovia, NY 13035	$100-$1000	Advertising Design majors	Academic year (renewable)	Annually
	$100-$1000	Art majors	Academic year (renewable)	Annually
	$100-1000	Interior Design majors	Academic year (renewable)	Annually
Centenary College of Louisiana, Department of Art, Centenary Blvd, Shreveport, LA 71104	Varied from full tuition to nominal amounts	Outstanding students	One year	Annually
Center Line Arts, 3 W 18th St, New York, NY 10011	To be determined	Anyone	One year	Annually and semi-annually
Central Wyoming College, Art Center, Riverton, WY 82501	Tuition and fees	Anyone with artistic potential regardless of age, race, or sex	One year	Annually and by semester
Chabot College,* Humanities Division, 25555 Hesperian Blvd, Hayward, CA 94545	$100 annually from California Art Society	Fine arts majors	One year	Annually

OFFERED BY	AMOUNT	OPEN TO	DURATION	WHEN OFFERED
Chadron State College, Division of Fine arts, Chadron, NE 69337	Up to full in-state tuition for first year; $100 each semester for subsequent years	No restrictions		Annually
Charles River Creative Arts Program, 56 Centre St, Dover, MA 02030		Those needing financial aid (local)		Annually to boys and girls 8-15
Charles Stewart Mott Community College, Fine Arts Division, 1401 E Court St, Flint, MI 48503	Up to $450	Current art students		Annually
Chautauqua Institution Summer School, Box 28, Chautauqua, NY 14722	$2000	Any non-professionals	One summer	Annually
Cheyenne Artist Guild Inc, 1010 E 16th St, Cheyenne, WY 82001	$200	Senior high school students of Cheyenne only	One year	Annually
	$200 plus small amount toward the purchase of tools; Kurz Andrews Scholarship	Senior high school students of Cheyenne only	One year	Annually
Chicago Public School Art Society, Art Institute of Chicago, Michigan Ave at Adams St, Chicago, IL 60603	$95	Children who are involved in Society's Art Form program	Per semester	Semi-annually
Claremore Junior College, Art Department, College Hill, Claremore, OK 74017	$150	Art majors	Academic year	Every semester
	$300	Senior portfolio winner of Young Talent in Oklahoma	Academic year	Annually
Cleveland Institute of Art,* 11141 East Boulevard, Cleveland, OH 44106	$1000 per student	Qualified students	One year	Annually
Cleveland State University, Department of Art, Euclid Ave at E 24th St, Cleveland, OH 44115	Tuition (part or full)	Incoming high school students, transfer students, and continuing full time studio art majors based on merit	One year	Annually
Coe College, Art Galleries, 1221 First Ave NE, Cedar Rapids, IA 52402	Variable—Minimum of $1500 awarded	Incoming freshmen students	One to four years	Annually
Colby Community College, Art Department, 1255 S Range, Colby, KS 67701	$100 up to full tuition and fees	Any applicant, juried portfolio	Two years	Annually
Colby-Sawyer College, New London, NH 03257	Approx $600	Entering and upperclass students	One year	Annually
College of Art and Design, Center for Creative Studies, 245 E Kirby St, Detroit, MI 48202	Varies	Current students and high school seniors	One year	Annually
College of Mt Saint Joseph, Art Department, Mount Saint Joseph, OH 45051	One year $2624	High school graduates. Special scholastic scholarship	One year	Annually
College of New Rochelle,* School of Arts & Sciences, New Rochelle, NY 10801	Variable, depending on need	Incoming freshman with portfolio	Four years renewable	Annually
College of St. Catherine,* Visual Arts Dept, 2004 Randolph, St Paul, MN 55105	Variable	Art majors	One year	Annually
College of Saint Mary,* 1901 S 72nd St, Omaha, NE 68124	$1000 per year	High school graduates	Four years	Annually
College of the Ozarks, Art Department, Johnson St, Clarksville, AR 72830	$300	Art majors	One year (renewable)	Annually
The College of the School of the Ozarks, Department of Art, Point Lookout, MO 65616	Full tuition, room and board work-study scholarships	All applicants, preference to need, academic standing, and geographic location	Four years, or until degree completion	Each semester
Colorado Women's College,* Montview Blvd & Quebec, Denver, CO 80220	$500	Art students	One year, renewable annually	Annually
Columbia College, Eighth and Rogers, Columbia, MO 65201	Up to $1000 plus work study	Students showing talent and/or need	One year	Annually
Columbia University, School of the Arts, 615 Dodge, New York, NY 10027	Variable	All registered students in competition		Annually
Columbus College, Art Department, Columbus, GA 31907	Varies	Entering and undergraduate art majors	3 quarters	Annually, Spring quarter for the coming Fall
Compton Community College,* Art Department, 1111 E Artesia Blvd, Compton, CA 90221	$200-$300	Art majors	One year	Annually
Concordia College, Art Department, Moorehead, MN 56560	Up to $1500	Entering freshmen and upper classmen	One year	Annually

OFFERED BY	AMOUNT	OPEN TO	DURATION	WHEN OFFERED
Cooper School of Art, 2341 Carnegie Ave SW, Cleveland, OH 44115	Full and partial tuition total $12,000	High school seniors	One year (renewable)	Annually
Coppini Academy of Fine Arts,* 115 Melrose Pl, San Antonio, TX 78212	Senior $400 Junior $100-$250	Ages 21-30 Ages 16-20		Annually Annually
Corcoran School of Art, 17th & New York Ave NW, Washington, DC 10006	William Wilson Corcoran Scholarship	Students from area high schools	Summer course	Annually in Apr
	Rohsheim Memorial Award	Outstanding first year students	One semester	Annually in May
	Kenneth Stubbs Memorial Award	Outstanding drawing students	One semester	Annually in May
	Mary Lay Thom Sculpture Prize	Outstanding sculpture students	One semester	Annually in May
	Eugene Weisz Memorial Scholarship	Outstanding painting students	One semester	Annually in May
	Sarah Pickens Roberts Memorial Award	Student whose work is judged most promising	One semester	Annually in May
	Cash prizes in Final Annual Graduation Exhibition	Prize-winning students		Annually in May
	Corcoran School of Art Scholarships	Outstanding students enrolled in the Degree or Diploma program	One academic year	Annually in May
Cornell College, Mt. Vernon, IA 52314	$3400	Selected on recommendation of Art Dept. Also based on need		Annually
	Minimum stipend of $500 (this is an honorary stipend—more is available depending on need)	Selected on recommendation of Art Dept. Also based on need	Four years if student remains art major	Annually to freshman
Cornish Institute of Allied Arts,* 710 E Roy, Seattle, WA 98102	Variable amounts, tuition scholarships	Registered full-time students	One year	Annually
Cottey College, Nevada, MO 64772	$600	Students interested in art who are attending Cottey College	One year (renewable)	Annually
Cranbrook Academy of Art, Bloomfield Hills, MI 48013	$75,000 annually	Students enrolled in Architecture, Ceramics, Design, Fiber, Metalsmithing, Painting, Photography, Printmaking, and Sculpture at Cranbrook Academy of Art	One year	Annually
Creighton University,* Fine Arts dept, 2500 California St, Omaha, NE 68178	$250	Alternates between visual and performing arts major		Annually
C W Post Center of Long Island University, Art Department, Northern Blvd, Greenvale, NY 11548	$2000 plus tuition	Graduate assistants	Two years	Semi-annually
Davidson County Art Guild, 218 W Center St, Lexington, NC 27292	$125	Davidson County art student (or outside Davidson County if no one inside qualifies)	One year (renewable)	Annually
Dayton Art Institute,* Forest & Riverview Aves, PO Box 941, Dayton, OH 45401	$2000-$3000 (total)	Qualified students		Semi-annually
Dean Junior College,* Visual and Performing Arts Department, 99 Main St, Franklin, MA 02038	Variable	Full-time students	One year	Annually
Delaware Art Museum, 2301 Kentmere Pkwy, Wilmington, DE 19806	$15 per term	Public school pupils	One year	Semi-annually
Delta State University, Art Department, Box D-2, Cleveland, MS 38733	Smith-Patterson Award ($100)	Senior art students with 3.5 or above average and high attainment in studio work		Annually
	Maxine Boggan Holcome Scholarship ($100)	Junior art education major with scholarship and accomplishment in studio work		Annually
	Malcolm Norwood Scholarship ($300)	Entering freshman student who is an art major at DSU and shows outstanding art work in the annual Crosstie Festival		Annually
Detroit Artists' Market, 1452 Randolph St, Detroit, MI 48226	$1000	Any qualified student who is attending the specific school whose turn it is to receive the scholarship; given on rotating basis to Center for Creative Studies, Wayne State University and Cranbrook Academy of Art	One year	Annually
Dickinson State College, Department of Art, Dickinson, ND 58601	$500 TMI Systems Design Corporation Scholarship	Any art or business student	One year	Annually
	$100 Tom Niemitalo Memorial Art Scholarship	Any art major or minor	One year	Annually
	$100 DSC Alumni Foundation Scholarships	Freshmen	One Year	Annually

OFFERED BY	AMOUNT	OPEN TO	DURATION	WHEN OFFERED
Douglas Art Association Little Gallery, 300 11th St, Box 256, Douglas, AZ 85607	$200	Local students	One year	Annually
Drake University, Des Moines, IA 50311	$50-$300 (total of $18,000)	Art majors	One year (renewable)	Annually
Dumbarton Oaks Research Library and Collections, 1703 32nd St NW, Washington, DC 20007	Variable	Graduate students and post-doctoral scholars of Byzantine studies and History of Landscape Architecture	One year	Annually
Dundas Valley School of Art, 21 Ogilvie St, Dundas, ON L9H 2S1, Canada	$500 (2)	Full time and Foundation students	One year	Annually
Dunedin Fine Arts & Cultural Center, 1143 Michigan Blvd, Dunedin, FL 33528	Variable	Students sixth grade and above with sincere interest and/or talent and financial need; some collegiate assistance available	5, 8 and 10 weeks depending upon length of class	Year round, per quarter
Dutchess Community College,* Dept of Visual Arts, 1 Pendell Rd, Poughkeepsie, NY 12601	$250	Second-year students	One year	Annually
East Central Junior College,* Art Department, Box 529, Union, MO 63084	$110	Students	One year	Annually
Eastern Arizona College, Church St, Thatcher, AZ 85552	Tuition (resident)	Anyone	One year (renewable)	Annually
East Mississippi Junior College,* Art Department, Box 176, Scooba, MS 39358	Determined on merit basis	All students in art major curriculum	One year	Annually
East Tennessee State University, Carroll Reece Museum, Johnson City, TN 37601	$2000	High school seniors and college students	One year	Annually
Edgecliff College,* Art Dept, 2220 Victory Pkwy, Cincinnati, OH 45206	$1760	Graduating high school seniors	Four years	Annually
Edinboro State College,* Dept of Art, Edinboro, PA 16444	$3000	Fine arts students	One year (renewable)	Annually
El Camino College, Division of Fine Arts, 16007 Crenshaw Blvd, Via Torrance, CA 90506	$300 per year	Junior standing and transfer to an accredited school for more art training	One year	Annually
	$100 per year	Continuing Art Major	One year	Annually
	$100 per year	Continuing Printmaking Major	One year	Annually
Essex Institute, 132 Essex St, Salem, MA 01970	Fellowships arranged through Boston University American Studies Program	Graduate students in American studies	One year	Annually
Fairmont State College,* Dept of Art, Fairmont, WV 26554	$300 per year	Qualified by portfolio submission	Four years	Annually
Fashion Institute of Technology, 227 W 27th St, New York, NY 10001	Variable	All students who qualify	Renewable	Annually
Harriet FeBland Art Workshop, 245 E 63rd St (408), New York, NY 10021	Tuition for one semester	Winners of the FeBland Group Annual Exhibition Scholarship Award	Semester	Annually
Findlay College, Art Department, 1000 N Main St, Findlay, OH 45840	Variable	All students	One year (renewable)	Annually
Fletcher Farm Craft School, Ludlow, VT 05149	(4) $50 and (2) $100	Vermont Teachers of Arts & Crafts	Two or four weeks	Annually
Flint Institute of Arts, DeWaters Art Center, 1120 E Kearsley St, Flint, MI 48503	Partial	Gifted children	One semester	
	Full & Partial	Financial & Merit; Children & Adults	Term	Prior to each term
Florida Gulf Coast Art Center, 222 Ponce de Leon Blvd, Belleair, FL 33516	$100 per term	Adult members/children (membership not required)	Quarter (10 weeks)	
Florida State University,* School of Visual Arts, Art Dept, Tallahassee, FL 32306	Assistantships $1500-$2800 Fellowships $4200-$5000	Graduate students in art Graduate students in art history	One year One year	Annually Annually
Fort Hays State University, Hays, KS 67601	$15,000	Graduate students and art students	One year	Annually
Fort Wright College of the Holy Names, Department of Art, W 4000 Randolph Rd, Spokane, WA 99204	(2) $600; (2) $300; (3) $200	Students admitted to the FWC School of Art	One year (renewable)	Annually, Apr 20 of each year
Franklin and Marshall College,* Art Dept, Lancaster, PA 17604	Variable	Students with pronounced talent		Annually
Friends University,* Art Department, 2100 University Ave, Wichita, KS 67213	$300 per year	All art majors	One to four years	

OFFERED BY	AMOUNT	OPEN TO	DURATION	WHEN OFFERED
Furman University,* Art Dept, Greenville, SC 29613	Mattie Hipp Cunningham Scholarship $1350	Art major selected by the faculty of Art Department	One year (can be repeated in unusual circumstances)	Once every third year
The Gallery/Stratford, 54 Romeo St, Stratford, ON N5A 4S9, Canada	$200	Graduating high school students for further art education in Perth County	One year	Annually
Georgetown College, Georgetown, KY 40324	$250-$450 plus financial aid on a need basis	All graduates of accredited secondary schools. A portfolio is required for an art grant but not for admission to the program	As long as academic progress is being made	Semi-annually
The Alfred C Glassell, Jr School of Art Museum of Fine Arts, 5101 Montrose, Houston, TX 77005	Variable	Students, on basis of portfolio	One year	Annually
Grand Canyon College, Art Department, 3300 W Camelback Rd, PO Box 11097, Phoenix, AZ 85061	Up to 50%	Majors accepted into degree program	One year (renewable)	Annually
Grants for Graduate Study Abroad. Write: Study Abroad Programs, Institute of International Education, 809 United Nations Plaza, New York, NY 10017		Note: People in the arts may apply for any of these awards (Fulbright-Hays and Foreign Governments, ITT International Fellowships, Lusk Memorial Fellowships, Kade Memorial Fellowships), but they must be affiliated with an educational institute abroad while pursuing their studies.		One academic year
Greater Fall River Art Association,* 80 Belmont St, Fall River, MA 02720	$100	Students entering Art Department of Southeastern Massachusetts University	One year	Annually
The Elizabeth Greenshields Foundation, 1814 Sherbrooke St SW, Montreal, PQ H3H 1E4, Canada	Various (40)	Nationals of any country for study in any country in painting and sculpture	One year	No closing date
Greenwich House Pottery, A School of Ceramics, 16 Jones St, New York, NY 10014	Tuition	Adults and children with talent	One semester (renewable)	Semi-annually
John Simon Guggenheim Memorial Foundation, 90 Park Ave, New York, NY 10016	Adjusted to needs of fellows	Citizens or permanent residents of U.S., Canada, other American states, Caribbean, Phillippines, and French, Dutch, and British possessions in Western Hemisphere, normally 30 to 50 years of age	One year	Annually
Solomon R Guggenheim Museum, 1071 Fifth Ave, New York, NY 10028	Summer Volunteer Program		Summer	Annually
	Rebay Fellowships $1000	Graduate students (U.S. preferred)	10 weeks	Spring, Fall and Summer terms
Harding University, Department of Art, Box 938, Searcy, AR 72143	$125	Art majors	One semester	Each semester
Harford Community College,* Humanities Division, 401 Thomas Run Rd, Bel Air, MD 21014	$50	Student matriculating in an art program	One year	Annually
Hastings College, Art Department, Hastings, NE 68901	$200-$500	All art majors	Four years	Annually
Herron School of Art,* Indiana University-Purdue University at Indianapolis, 1701 N Pennsylvania St, Indianapolis, IN 46202	Scholarships, total per year $10,000. Also various financial aid available through Indiana University	Any student	One year	Annually
Historic Deerfield, Inc, Box 231, Deerfield, MA 01342	Full, partial, and tuition Fellowships	Men and women of undergraduate status	June 16-Aug 16	Annually
Honolulu Academy of Arts, Studio Program, 900 S Beretania St, Honolulu, HI 96814	$1000	Students, 16 years or older, who have successfully completed first year study may apply for scholarship	Two years	Annually
Hope College, Art Department, Rusk Bldg, Holland, MI 49423	$1600 total shared between four separate scholarships	Art majors	One year	Annually
Howard University Department of Art, College of Fine Arts, Sixth and Fairmont Sts NW, Washington, DC 20001	Up to $2000	Students	One year	Annually
Henry E. Huntington Library and Art Gallery, San Marino, CA 91108	$600 per month	Scholars (not to candidates for advanced degrees)	One to five months	Annually. Applications received Oct. 1-Dec. 31 for awards beginning the following June
	NEH Fellowships up to $1667 per month	Same as above	Six to twelve months	
Incorporated E A Abbey Scholarships for Mural Painting in the USA, 1083 Fifth Ave, New York NY 10028	$6000 scholarship for study in mural painting in US and abroad	US citizens not more than 35 years of age	One year	Biennially
Indiana State University, Department of Art, Terre Haute, IN 47809	$2100	MFA, MS, MA	One year	Annually
	Tuition free	BFA Freshmen	Four years	Annually
	$2000 travel grant	BFA Juniors and Seniors	One summer	Annually

OFFERED BY	AMOUNT	OPEN TO	DURATION	WHEN OFFERED
Indiana University Museum, Student Bldg 209, Bloomington, IN 47405	$2281 per academic year	Students who have previously worked as work-study employee in the Museum	Academic year (renewable)	Academic year
Indian Hills Community College,* Ottumwa Heights Campus, Dept. of Art, Grandview at Elm, Ottumwa, IA 52501	$300	Full-time students in art, drama, and/or music	One year, renewable second year	Annually
Institute of Puerto Rican Culture, Apartado 4184, San Juan, PR 00905	Variable	Artists, writers, and scholars	One year	Annually
InterAmerican University, San German, PR 00753	Variable	All with talent		Annually, semi-annually
Interlochen Arts Academy, Interlochen, MI 49463	Up to $2800	Anyone, based on need and merit	One year	Annually
International Museum of Photography at George Eastman House,* 900 East Ave, Rochester, NY 14607	$7200 (3)	Post-masters degree	One year	Annually
Ivy School of Professional Art, University Ave, Pittsburgh, PA 15214	$5720 (tuition)	11th & 12th grade participants in the Ivy sponsored national art competition, "Teachers' Choice!" who qualify by winning an award of excellence	One year, renewable for the second year if the holder maintains a 3.4 average each quarter of the first year	Annually
	$5720	Applicants who are recommended by any high school or college art teacher or art professional for consideration	One year	Annually
	Tuition	High school students who attend Ivy's short and specialized programs presented on Saturdays and Summers	One year	Annually
	$715	Art teachers	Quarter	Quaterly
James Madison University,* School of Fine Arts and Communication, Dept of Art, Harrisonburg, VA 22801	$2400-$3000	Graduate students in the Dept of Art	One year	Annually
Jamestown College, Art Department, Jamestown, ND 58401	$500	Entering freshmen art majors	One year (renewable to total of $2000)	Annually
John C Calhoun State Community College, Box 2216, Hwy 31 North, Decatur, AL 35602	Full tuition (2); sponsored by the Decatur Art Guild	Art majors and visual communication majors	Each quarter	Quarterly
Junior College of Albany, Dept of Fine Arts, 74 New Scotland Ave, Albany, NY 12208	Tuition for one semester at the American School in Paris. (Bocour Award)	Professional art students who are JCA Fine Arts majors and have completed their freshman year. (Apply to Willie Marlowe, Chairwoman, 140 New Scotland Ave, New Albany, NY 12208)	One semester	Fall semester
Kansas City Art Institute,* 4415 Warwick Blvd, Kansas City, MO 64111	Varies	Demonstrated need	One year	Annually
Kansas State University, Department of Art, Manhattan, KS 66506	$3600 Teaching Assistantships	Students working for MFA degree	Nine months	Annually
	Variable scholarship awards	Freshmen-senior undergraduates	One year	Annually
Kappa Pi International Honorary Art Fraternity, Box 7843 Midfield, Birmingham, AL 35228	$500	Student members only	One year	Annually
Kearney State College, School of Fine Arts & Humanities, Art Department, Kearney, NE 68847	$200 tuition waiver	Entering freshmen	One year	Annually
Kent State University, School of Art, New Art Bldg, Kent, OH 44242	(22) $3150	Graduate assistants	One year	Annually, Mar-Sept
	(15) Ranging from full tuition and fees to partial remissions	Students	One year	Annually, Fall semester, Spring semester
Lafayette Art Center,* 101 S Ninth St, Lafayette, IN 47901	Up to $500	Eligible students, low income and merit	One semester (24 sessions)	Semi-annually
Lahaina Arts Society, 649 Wharf St, Lahaina, HI 96761	$1000 per year	High school seniors	One year	Annually
Lake Michigan College, Art Department, 2755 E Napier Ave, Benton Harbor, MI 49022	Full tuition (three per year)	College district residents	Two years	Deadline: Mar 15
Lake Placid School of Art, Center for Music, Drama and Art, Saranac Ave, Lake Placid, NY 12946	Tuition waiver (work-study)	Full-time students who show financial need (Annual summer scholarships offered to Union of Independent Colleges of Art students)	One year	Annually
Lindenwood Colleges, Art Department, St Charles, MO 63301	$500-$3000	Art majors	One year	Annually
Loch Haven Art Center, Inc, 2416 N Mills Ave, Orlando, FL 32803	Varies (class tuition)	Qualified Applicants	Eight-week classes	Each quarter

OFFERED BY	AMOUNT	OPEN TO	DURATION	WHEN OFFERED
Los Angeles County Museum of Art, 5905 Wilshire Blvd, Los Angeles, CA 90036	Modern and Contemporary Art Council New Talent Award $3000	Two local artists under 36	One year	Annually
Louisville School of Art,* 100 Park Rd, Anchorage, KY 40223	$5250 (annual total)	Students doing quality work	One semester	Semi-annually
Lourdes College, 6832 Convent Blvd, Sylvania, OH 43560	$1200	Academically qualified high school seniors	One year	Annually
Loyola Marymount University, 7101 W 80th St, Los Angeles, CA 90045	Related to financial status	Financially deprived	One semester	Semi-annually
MacDowell Colony, Inc, Peterborough, NH 03458 (applications obtainable: The MacDowell Colony, Inc, 680 Park Ave, New York, NY 10021)	Resident fellowships to professional writers, painters, sculptors, film-makers, printmakers, and composers provide board, room, use of studio for maximum of three months. A token charge of $10 per diem is waived in cases of need	Nationals of any country	One to two months (summer); One to three months (winter)	
Madonna College, Art Department, 36600 Schoolcraft Rd, Livonia, MI 48150	Robert Svoboda Scholarship $500	Student interested in art or journalism	One year	Annually
Malden Bridge Art School,* Malden Bridge, NY 12115	(2)full tuition(1) $100	Anyone	One year	Annually
Manatee Junior College, Department of Art, 26th St W, Bradenton, FL 33505	Full tuition (4)	Students majoring in art; preference given to Fla residents; sophomore	One year	Annually
Manitoba Association of Architects, Winnipeg, MB R3B 0W9, Canada	$300	Architecture students enrolled at the University of Manitoba only	One year	Annually
McMurry College, Art Department, Sayles Blvd & S 14th St, Abilene, TX 79697	$2000	Art students who show special ability	One year	Annually
McNeese State University, Department of Visual Arts, 4000 Ryan St, Lake Charles, LA 70609	$200 (A. L. Kushner Scholarship)	Sophomore majors and up	One year (renewable)	
McPherson College, Art Department, 1600 E. Euclid, McPherson, KS 67460	$300 to $1000 per year	Entering students who plan to major in art	One year (renewable if student does satisfactory work to total of $1600)	Annually
Mankato State University, Art Department, Mankato, MN 56001	$300	Outstanding undergraduate, based upon performance academically and creatively	Unlimited	Annually
Maple Woods Community College, Art & Art History Department, 2601 NE Barry Rd, Kansas City, MO 646156	Varies	All students	One semester	Annually
Marion Art Center,* 80 Pleasant, Marion, MA 02738	$250	High school seniors	One year	Annually
Maryland College of Art & Design, 10500 Georgia Ave, Silver Spring, MD 20902	Limited half scholarships for first year	Freshman Foundation students	One year	Annually, Aug/Sept
Marymount College, Tarrytown, NY 10591	$350 per year	Any incoming freshman; portfolio required	One year (renewable for four years)	Annually
The Memphis Academy of Arts, Overton Park, Memphis, TN 38112	$50,000 (total)	High school graduates and college transfers	One year	Annually
Mercyhurst College,* Dept of Art, 501 E 38th St, Erie, PA 16501	Open	All freshmen art or art education applicants	One year, renewable	Annually
Merrick Art Gallery, Fifth Ave & 11th St, New Brighton, PA 15066	$50	New Brighton high school art students		Annually
Mesa College,* Grand Junction, CO 81501	Tuition scholarships (4)	One each class	Continuous with annual review	Annually
Mesa Community College, Dept of Art, 1833 W Southern Ave, Mesa, AZ 85202	Six at $100 cash; three at $50 activity	Area students	One year or semester	Annually
Metropolitan Museum & Art Centers, Attn: Juanita May, Dir of Schools, 1212 Anastasia Ave, Coral Gables, FL 33134	Approx $100 per year	Children		
Metropolitan Museum of Art, The Main Bldg, Fifth Ave at 82nd St, New York, NY 10028	Variable	Scholars researching art historical fields relating to Metropolitan Museum of Art collections	One year	Deadline Jan 13 Awards letters sent on Mar 1
Midland College,* Dept of Art, Midland, TX 79701	Full tuition and fees	Full time student (12hrs) art major, at least 6 credits per semester	One semester continuing for one additional semester	Semi-annually
	$100 per semester	Any student in art	One semester	Semi-annually

OFFERED BY	AMOUNT	OPEN TO	DURATION	WHEN OFFERED
Midway Studios, University of Chicago, 6016 S Ingleside, Chicago, IL 60637	Partial tuition awards	Outstanding entering graduate students	Awarded & renewed annually	Deadline: Jan 15
Miles Community College, Art Department, 2715 Dickinson St, Miles City, MT 59301	$180	Drama and visual art students	One year	Annually
Millikin University Art Department, 1184 W Main, Decatur, IL 62522	$500-$1000	Qualified students	Four years	Annually
Mills College,* Art Department, 5000 MacArthur Blvd, P.O. Box 9975, Oakland, CA 94613	Alumnae grants (covers tuition) & Assistantships	Mills graduate students		Annually
	Eleanor Crum Award in Ceramics	Graduating MFA's		Annually
	Catherine Morgan Trefethen Award	Graduating students		Annually
	Aurelia Henry Reinhardt Faculty Purse	Graduating seniors for further study		Annually
Milwaukee School of the Arts,* 207 N Milwaukee St, Milwaukee, WI 53202	Varying amounts	Full-time students of MSA attending one or more semesters-based on merit and performance	Split over 2 semesters	Annually
Minot Art Association, Minot Art Gallery, Box 325, Minot, ND 58701	$200 to attend the International Art Camp at Peace Gardens, ND	High school students (2)	One week	Annually
Mississippi University for Women, Columbus, MS 39701	$100-$300	Undergraduates	One year	Annually
	Student Assistantship $1000	Graduates	One year (renewable)	Annually
	Tuition Fellowships	Graduates	One year (renewable)	Annually
Missouri Southern State College, Art Department, Newman & Duquesne Rds, Joplin, MO 64801	$250 (2) $200 (3)	Top quality students with art skills and financial needs	One year	Annually
Missouri Western State College, Art Department, 4525 Downs Dr, St Joseph, MO 64507	Varies	Any qualifying student majoring in art	By semester	By semester
Mitchell Community College, Art Department, E Broad St, Statesville, NC 28677	(2) Full tuition	Full time students-one high school (competition and recommendation); one sophomore already enrolled	One year	Annually
Montana State University, School of Art, Bozeman, MT 59715	$3600	Graduate students	10 months	Annually-April
Montclair Art Museum,* Art School, 3 S Mountain Ave, PO Box X, Montclair, NJ 07042	Tuition	Adults or children	One year	Upon request
Montclair State College, School of Fine and Performing Arts, Upper Montclair, NJ 07043	$3000	Qualified graduate students	One year	Annually
Monterey Peninsula Museum of Art, 559 Pacific St, Monterey, CA 93940	$500 per semester (3)	Local college students	One semester with a possible renewal	Semi-annually
Mount Aloysius Junior College,* Art Dept, Rte 22, Cresson, PA 16630	$300-$500	Anyone eligible for entry with art portfolio and interview	Two years	Annually
Mount Marty College,* Art Dept, 1100 W Fifth, Yankton, SD 57078	Up to $500	Especially talented students		Annually
Mount Saint Clare College, Art Department, 400 N Bluff, Clinton, IA 52732	$300, other financial aid available, total awards	Incoming freshmen and students already enrolled	One year; renewable if work merits it	Annually
Mount Wachusett Community College, Art Department, Teaching Faculty Association (TFA), Gardner, MA 01440	Approx $100	Art majors in transfer	One year	Annually
Mulvane Art Center, Washburn University, Topeka, KS 66621	$3000	Qualified students	One year plus	Annually
Municipal Art Society of Baltimore City, c/o Mr. Beverley C. Compton, Jr,* 135 E Baltimore St, Baltimore, MD 21202	Traveling scholarship	Senior students of the Graduate School, Maryland Institute, Baltimore	One year	Annually
Murray State University, Art Department, 15th St, Murray KY 42071	$100 to $250 (one to five given)	Incoming freshmen		Annually
	$200 (Clara M Eagle Scholarship)	Freshmen, sophomores or juniors majoring in art at Murray State University		Annually
Museum Art School,* 1219 SW Park St, Portland, OR 97205	$18,000	Entering students	One school year	Annually

OFFERED BY	AMOUNT	OPEN TO	DURATION	WHEN OFFERED
Museum of Early Southern Decorative Arts Summer Institute, 924 S Main St, Winston-Salem, NC 27108	Fellowship for tuition	Graduate students in history, art history, preservation, museum studies; museum personnel	June 29-July 5	Annually
Muskegon Community College,* Dept of Creative & Performing Arts, 221 S Quarterline Rd, Muskegon, MI 49443	$200	Any art student		Each semester
National Collection of Fine Arts, Smithsonian Institution, Washington, DC 20560	$9000 plus $1000 for travel	Advanced students in art history. Deadline: Jan 15	Sept 3-July 31	Deadline Jan 15
	Limited stipend	College seniors graduate students, in art history and studio art	9 weeks, commence in June	Deadline Feb 15
National Endowment for the Arts, 2401 E St NW, Washington, DC 20506	Artists' Fellowships-$10,000; the panel will recommend a limited number of $3000 fellowships for emerging artists	Artists of exceptional talent; generally, visual artists must be working professionals	One year	Annually; deadline Oct 15
	Photographers' Fellowships-$10,000; the panel will recommend a limited number of $3000 fellowships for emerging artists	Photographers of exceptional talent; generally, visual artists must be working professionals	One year	Annually; deadline Apr 15
	Craftsmens' Fellowships-$10,000; a limited number of $3000 fellowships may be recommended by the panel	Professional craftsmen of exceptional talent and demonstrated ability	One year	Annually; deadline Dec 19
National Gallery of Art, c/o Dr. Douglas Lewis, Constitution Ave at Sixth St NW, Washington, DC 20565	David E. Finley Fellowship	Ph.D. candidates	Two years plus eight months at the National Gallery	Annually (deadline Dec 31)
	Samuel H. Kress Fellowships (2)	Ph.D. candidates	One academic year	Annually (deadline Dec 31)
	Chester Dale Fellowships (4)	Ph.D. candidates	One academic year	Annually (deadline Dec 31)
	Robert H. and Clarice Smith Fellowship	Ph.D. candidates or holders	One academic year	Annually (deadline Dec 31)
Nazareth College of Rochester, Art Department, 4245 East Ave, Rochester, NY 14610	Variable	Qualified high school graduates, ie, B+ average, total score of 1200 CEEB, and/or impressive art portfolio	One year (renewable)	Annually
New Harmony Gallery of Contemporary Art, Main St, New Harmony, IN 47631	Varied according to term of residency, usually $250 per week	Visual artists interested in living and working in New Harmony, for a short-term residency	Two-four weeks	Quarterly, flexible as funding available
New Mexico Highland University,* Dept of Fine Arts, Las Vegas, NM 87701	Up to $325 for academic year	All undergraduates	One academic year	Annually
	$2160 plus three quarters of full tuition, graduate assistantship	Graduate students only	One academic year	Annually
New Mexico State University, Art Department, Box 3572, Las Cruces, NM 88003	$2000-$4000 (graduate assistantships)	Graduate students	One-two years	Annually
New York Institute of Technology,* Fine Arts Dept, Wheatley Rd, Old Westbury, NY 11568	$2200	High school seniors	One year, renewable	Annually
New York School of Interior Design, 155 E 56th St, New York, NY 10022	$1275 maximum per term	Design students; preference given to second and third year students	One semester (renewable)	Annually (deadline May 1)
New York Studio School of Drawing, Painting & Sculpture,* 8 W Eighth St, New York, NY 10011	$25,000	Students enrolled for one year who qualify on the basis of need by semester	By semester	Each semester
Northeastern A&M College,* Art Dept, Miami, OK 74354	Three usually given	Art majors	One year	Annually
Northeastern Illinois University, Art Department, St Louis at Bryn Mawr Ave, Chicago, IL 60625	$476 (2 terms)	Board of Governers Talent Scholarships available to gifted art students	Two terms	Annually
Northeastern Oklahoma State University, Division of Arts & Letters, Tahlequah, OK 74464	Up to 15 hours general tuition (3)	Undergraduates	One semester, subject to continuation	
Northeast Missouri State University, Division of Fine Arts, Kirksville, MO 63501	Varying amounts	High school seniors; other awards available to junior college graduates	One year (renewable)	Annually
Northern Illinois University, Department of Art, DeKalb, IL 60115	Jack Arends Scholarship-about $500	Art majors with 3.0 overall grade point average, one year residence at NIU, portfolio, and 3 recommendations (2 from NIU Art Department)	One year	Annually
	James P. Bates Memorial Scholarship-about $500	Rotated among majors in the various areas of the Art Department	One year	Annually
	Richard Keefer Scholarship-about $500	Art majors-rotated among four areas-Art History and Art Education; Drawing, Painting & Printmaking; Crafts; Design & Photography	One year	Annually

OFFERED BY	AMOUNT	OPEN TO	DURATION	WHEN OFFERED
	John X. Koznarek Memorial Scholarship-about $250	Accepted or enrolled majors in studio art. Portfolio and three recommendations	One year	Annually
	Cora B. Miner Scholarship-about $400	Preferably to student from DeKalb County with interest in realistic art	One year, renewable for four years	Annually
Northern Michigan University,* c/o Prof Cinelli, Marquette, MI 49855	$500	Sophomore art and design majors who have been majors in NMU art dept at least one semester	One year	Annually
Northern Montana College,* Department of Art, 611 16th St, Havre, MT 59501	$100	An art major or minor who has demonstrated high art ability and who is in need of financial aid	No limit established	Annually
North Park College, Fine Arts Division, 5125 N Spaulding, Chicago, IL 60625	$300	Sophomore art majors	One year	Annually
	$500	Junior art majors	One year	Annually
	Lydia Poole Award-amount varies	Any art major	One year	Every two years
North Shore Art League,* 620 Lincoln, Winnetka, IL 60093	$1500	Art Institute of Chicago students	One year	Annually
Northwestern College, Art Department, Orange City, IA 51041	$100	Art majors upon acceptance of portfolio	One year	Annually
Northwest Nazarene College,* Art Department, Holly at Dewey, Nampa, ID 83651	Variable	Fine arts majors	One year	Annually
Norton Gallery & School of Art,* 1451 S Olive Ave, West Palm Beach, FL 33401	$300	High school graduate art students of South Florida	One year	For the Norton Gallery and School of Art
Oakland City College, Oakland City, IN 47660	Variable	Outstanding ability shown in art (competitive)	One year (renewable)	Annually
	$1200	Entering freshmen	One year (renewable)	Annually
Oakland Museum,* 1000 Oak St, Oakland, CA 94607	$1000	California artists	One year	Annually
Oberlin College, Department of Art, Oberlin, OH 44074	$3450 plus tuition remission (3 graduate assistantships)	Graduates with BA degrees who qualify	One year (renewable)	Annually
	Kress Art History Fellowship of up to $3500, plus tuition remission (1 or 2)	Graduates with BA degrees who qualify	One year (renewable)	Annually
Occidental College, Art Department, 1600 Campus Rd, Los Angeles, CA 90041	Open	Art majors who can demonstrate financial need	Renewable for four years	Annually
Ocean City School of Art-Ocean City Cultural Arts Center, 409 Wesley Ave, Ocean City, NJ 08226	$50	Members and students of the Art Center	One semester	Each semester
Ohio State University, Department of History of Art, 100 Hayes Hall, Columbus, OH 43210	$2970 for first year students, to $4158 for sixth year students	Students who demonstrate accomplishment and evidence of potential excellence in teaching, scholarship and/or research in History of Art	Up to 22 quarters	Annually
Ohio State University, Graduate School, Department of Art Education, Columbus, OH 43210	$4800 plus tuition	All MA and PhD candidates (special minority fellowships are also awarded)	One calendar year	Annually, deadline Feb
Ohio University School of Art,* College of Fine Arts, Athens, OH 45701	Tuition scholarship assistantships	Undergraduate students Graduates	One year (renewable)	Annually
Oklahoma Art Center, 3113 General Pershing Blvd, Fair Park, Oklahoma City, OK 73107	Part tuition		Term (6-8 weeks)	Term
Oklahoma City University, NW 23rd at N Blackwelder, Oklahoma City, OK 73106	$2500 (Mrs Iva B Kelley Art Scholarship)	Oklahoma residents (5 years) junior standing, 57 hours, art majors	One-two years	Annually
Old Dominion University,* Norfolk, VA 23508	$500	All art students	One year	Annually
Ontario College of Art,* 100 McCaul St, Toronto, ON M5T 1W1, Canada	Variable	Students only	One year	Annually
Oregon School of Arts and Crafts, 8245 SW Barnes Rd, Portland, OR 97225	Work exchange scholarships for school tuition	Students in financial need	Per term	Per term-deadline for application, one week prior to each term
Oregon College of Art, 30 S First St, Ashland, OR 97520	$200-$600	High school and college transfer students-based on competitive art work	Academic year	Annually
Otis Art Institute of Parsons School of Design,* 2401 Wilshire Blvd, Los Angeles, CA 90057	Variable	Students enrolled at Otis in the BFA or MFA degree programs	Academic year	Annually

OFFERED BY	AMOUNT	OPEN TO	DURATION	WHEN OFFERED
Our Lady of the Lake University, 411 SW 24th St, San Antonio, TX 78285	Variable	Majors in art	Variable	Annually
Palomar College,* San Marcos, CA 92069	$75 Lake San Marcos Art League Award	Returning sophomore majoring in art		June
	$50 Catherine Ann (Tim) Sawday Memorial Scholarship	Deserving student majoring in art or science		June
	$100 San Dieguito Art Guild Scholarship	Graduate planning to pursue a career in painting		June
	$300 Fallbrook Art Association	Art major continuing on to a 4-year accredited art school		June
	$150 Showcase of the Arts-Evelyn Surface Memorial	Two awards-one for art student returning to Palomar and one for a graduating art student going on to a 4-year institution		June
Palos Verdes Art Center and Museum, 5504 W Crestridge Rd, Rancho Palos Verdes, CA 90274	Class fees	High school students in Palos Verdes	One semester	
Pan American University, Department of Art, Edinburg, TX 78539	$100 tuition scholarship (12 hours per semester for 2 semesters)	Art majors with 2.5 average (4.00 system), 30 hours completed study	One year	Annually
Parsons School of Design, 65 Fifth Ave, New York, NY 10011	$250,000	All financially eligible, matriculated students in the BFA and MFA programs	Academic year	Annually, apply by Mar 1
Pasadena City College, Art Department, 1570 E Colorado Blvd, Pasadena, CA 91106	$1000 (2)	All our students majoring in art		Annually
Albert Pels School of Art, Inc, 2109 Broadway, New York, NY 10023	$1750 per year	High school seniors	One year (renewable)	Annually
	$1750 per year	Enrolled student working scholarship	One year	Annually
Pennsylvania Academy of the Fine Arts,* Broad & Cherry Sts, Philadelphia, PA 19102	Scholastic Magazine Art Award (1) 1 year tuition	High school seniors	One year	Annually
	Full and half tuition scholarships	2nd, 3rd & 4th year Academy students	One year	Annually
	Cresson European Travel Scholarship and tuition-$3300	3rd, 4th year Academy students	Three months	Annually
	Schiedt & Ware Travel Scholarship-$2000	3rd, 4th year Academy students	Three months	Annually
Peoria Art Guild, 1831 N Knoxville Ave, Peoria, IL 61603	$18-$30	Students who would benefit from artistic instruction, but who would be otherwise unable to afford art classes	8-10 weeks	4 times each year
Place des Arts, 166 King Edward St, Coquitlam, BC V3K 4T2, Canada	Up to $400 through the Coquitlam Fine Arts Council	Any artist living within the area	One year	Annually
The Ponca City Art Association,* Box 1394, 819 E Central, Ponca City, OK 74601	$50 (2)	Outstanding art student	One year	Annually
The Pontiac Art Center,* 47 Williams St, Pontiac, MI 48053	$20 and $50 (tuition for children and adults)	All	Ten-week terms	All-year
Pratt Graphics Center, extension of Pratt Institute, 160 Lexington Ave, New York, NY 10016	Tuition up to a period of one year	Talented artists; the Margaret Lowengrund Scholarship Fund and the Albert Christ-Janer Memorial Scholarship Fund are for American citizens; the Ingram-Merrill Scholarship Fund is for foreign nationals.	Up to one year	Sept through July
Presbyterian College,* Fine Arts Dept, Clinton, SC 29325	$200	All art students	One year	Annually
Princeton Art Association, Rosedale Rd, Princeton, NJ 08540	Varies-approx $50	Students interested in art with financial need	Eight weeks	Four times a year
Providence Art Club,* II Thomas St, Providence, RI 02903	Tuition and fees (3)	Rhode Island School of Design students	One year	Annually
Rensselaer County Historical Society, 59 Second St, Troy NY 12180	$1000 funded by NYSCA summer museum intern program	Seniors with art history, history majors & some museum training	Ten weeks	Annually, if funded
Congressman Fred Richmond, 1707 Longworth House Office Bldg, Washington, DC 20515	$100 a week stipend for internship	Graduate students in arts administration or related programs		Annually (3)
Ricks College, Department of Art, Rexburg, ID 83440	$200 to full tuition	Art majors	One year	
Rocky Mountain School of Art, 1441 Ogden St, Denver CO 80218	$500 quarterly (Job Scholarship only)	8 students every 2 years	Two years	

OFFERED BY	AMOUNT	OPEN TO	DURATION	WHEN OFFERED
Rogue Valley Art Association, PO Box 763, Medford, OR 97501	$200	Students	Summer classes	Annually
Rosary College, Director of Foreign Studies, River Forest, IL 60305	$500-$1000 each (15) $1000-$2000	Nationals of US for study in Florence, Italy, for study in painting, sculpture, printmaking, art history and art conservation at Rosary College Graduate School of Fine Arts, Villa Schifanoia, to men and women qualified for graduate study in fine arts who hold BA or equivilent and have knowledge of Italian	One-two years	
Roswell Museum and Art Center, 11th & Main Sts, Roswell, NM 88201	Grant provides home, studio, maintenance, materials, and stipend. Stipend varies according to size of family	Painters, sculptors, printmakers, and ceramicists	Grant period can vary-usually 6-12 months	Information supplied upon request, please specify media
Royal Architectural Institute of Canada, Suite 1104, 151 Slater St, Ottawa, ON K1P 5H3, Canada	Andre Francou Scholarship $2000	Graduate students of the School of Architecture at the University of Montreal		Annually
	Ernest Wilby Memorial Scholarship $500	A student entering a year before the final year of the main architectural course at a Canadian School of Architecture who shows definite promise and talent in his work and who requires financial assistance		Annually
St. Louis Community College at Forest Park,* Art Dept, 5600 Oakland Ave, St Louis, MO 63110	Varies	Art students	One semester	Annually
St. Thomas Aquinas College,* Art Dept, Rte 340, Sparkill, NY 10976	Variable	All eligible applicants	One year	Semi-annually
Salmagundi Club, 47 Fifth Ave, New York, NY 10003	Scholarship Membership prorated over four-year period	Qualified applicants, artists under 30 years of age, three examples of work to be submitted for approval by committee	Four years	
Sam Houston State University, Art Department, Huntsville, TX 77340	Approx $3399 (teaching fellowship)	Art majors with BFA or equivalent, with 60 or more hours in art	One year (renewable)	Annually
San Bernardino Art Association, Inc,* 1640 E Highland, San Bernardino, CA 92404	$400	High school art seniors		Annually
San Diego State University,* Department of Art, San Diego, CA 92182	$500-$1000	Upper division students	One year, renewable for up to three years	Annually
San Francisco Art Institute, 800 Chestnut St, San Francisco, CA 91433	Tuition scholarships	Undergraduate and graduate students with demonstrated financial need	Academic year	March for coming academic year
San Jacinto College North,* Dept of Art, Houston, TX 77015	Varies upon need (North Shore Area Art League Scholarship)	Any full-time student	Fall and Spring	Annually
Santa Cruz Art League, Inc, 526 Broadway, Santa Cruz, CA 95060	$500	Students in Santa Cruz County		Annually in May
Santa Rosa Junior College,* Department of Art, 1501 Mendocino Ave, Santa Rosa, CA 95401	$500	Art students	One semester or one year	
Scholastic Awards, Scholastic Magazines, Inc. 50 W 44th St, New York, NY 10036	Variable	High school seniors only; talented in art or photography; qualify by portfolio and high school record	One year	Annually
School Art League of New York City,* 131 Livingston St, Brooklyn NY 11201	$100,000 annually	High school students	One year (to be continued at the discretion of the granting institutions)	Annually
School for Creative Movement in the Arts, 265 W 87th St, New York, NY 10024	Maximum of 25% off per term-$40-$50 (term costs $150-$210)	Children only from 2¼ to 17 years based on financial need and interest	One or two terms	Semi-annually
School of American Research, PO Box 2188, Santa Fe, NM 87501	$5500	Doctoral and postdoctoral scholars; limited to 4 scholars per year	11 months	Annually
School of Fine Arts, 38660 Mentor Ave, Willoughby, OH 44094	Tuition	Talent plus need	One year	Annually
School of the Art Institute of Chicago, Columbus Dr at Jackson Blvd, Chicago, IL 60603	Variable	Full-time degree students in need	One year	Annually
School of the Associated Arts, 344 Summit Ave, St Paul, MN 55102	Variable	Advanced students	One year	Annually
School of the Museum of Fine Arts,* 230 The Fenway, Boston, MA 02115	$150 to $2000 per year	All diploma or degree matriculating students determined eligible by CCS/ACT needs analysis	Academic year	Annually
	$40,000 awarded in varying amounts (approx 15 annually)	Graduates of the School of the Museum of Fine Arts	Flexible (average one year)	Annually

OFFERED BY	AMOUNT	OPEN TO	DURATION	WHEN OFFERED
School of the Wichita Art Association, 9112 E Central, Wichita, KS 67206. Awarded through public school system and various service organizations	$2000	Art students of the Wichita area	One year	Annually
School of the Worcester Art Museum, 55 Salisbury St, Worcester, MA 01608	Up to full tuition depending on financial need	Matriculating students at the School of the Worcester Art Museum only; accepted applicants will be considered upon receipt of tuition deposit	One academic year	Annually (deadline Apr 1)
Selkirk College, Kootenay School of Art Division, David Thompson University Centre, 820-10th St, Nelson, BC V1L 3C7, Canada	Variable	Students of Kootenay School of Art	One year	Annually
Shasta College, Art Department, Old Oregon Trail, Redding, CA 96001	Various	Art students		
Skowhegan School of Painting and Sculpture, 329 E 68th St, New York, NY 10021	10 full scholarships $1950 each	Qualified U.S. art students 18 years of age and over	Nine weeks July and August	Annually
	35 partial scholarships	Qualified U.S. art students 18 years of age and over	Nine weeks July and August	Annually
Smithsonian Institution, Office of Fellowships & Grants, Washington, DC 20560	Minimum of $14,000	Post-doctoral scholars in American art history, Oriental art history	Six months to one year	Deadline Jan 15
	Minimum of $8000	Doctoral candidates in American art history, Oriental art history	Six months to one year	Deadline Jan 15
Society of Architectural Historians, 1700 Walnut St, Suite 716, Philadelphia, PA 19103	One or two given to participate in annual tour	Outstanding students engaged in graduate work in architecture, architectural history, city planning or urban history, landscape history or landscape design and current member of the Society of Architectural Historians		Annually (usually)
	Alice Davis Hitchcock Book Award			Annually
	Founders' Award			Annually
Southampton College of Long Island University, Art Department, Southampton, NY 11968	$1000	Students	Four years	Annually
South Carolina Arts Commission, 1800 Gervais St, Columbia, SC 29201	$130,000 in grant funds annually	Arts organization and artists	One year	Quarterly
	$15,000 Fellowship Funds	Resident artists-visual arts, crafts, creative writing, film/video, music composition	One year	Annually, deadline: Feb 1
	$2500 Awards	Resident choreographers		Annually, deadline: Feb 1
South Dakota State University, Memorial Art Center, Medary Ave at Harvey Dunn St, Brookings, SD 57006	$200	Art students at University	One year	Annually
Southeastern Center for Contemporary Art, 2721 Robinhood Rd, Winston-Salem, NC 27106	$2000	Southeastern artists	For their use	Every two years
Southern Baptist College, Humanities-Art Department, College City, AR 72476	$200	High school seniors and others seeking admittance, by portfolio	One semester (renewable)	Semi-annually
	Variable	Most outstanding art student		Annually
Southern Baptist College, Walnut Ridge, AR 72476	Variable	Most outstanding art student annually		Annually
Southern Illinois University at Edwardsville, Department of Art and Design, School of Fine Arts and Communications, Edwardsville, IL 62026	Stipend and tuition waiver	Graduate students accepted for admission		Annually
Southern Oregon State College,* Art Department, 1250 Siskiyou Blvd, Ashland, OR 97520	$300	Art major	One year	Annually
Southern Utah State College,* Department of Art, Cedar City, UT 84720	Tuition and supplies	Residents of Utah and nonresidents	One year	Annually and quarterly
	$256	Sophomores, juniors and seniors	Two years	Annually
South Florida Art Institute of Hollywood, 1301 S Ocean Dr, Hollywood, FL 33019	$8000 yearly	Elementary, senior and junior high school graduates	One, two and four years	Annually
Southwest Missouri State University,* Department of Art, 901 S National, Springfield, MO 65802	$240	Art majors and graduating seniors of Southwest Missouri State University	One year	Annually

OFFERED BY	AMOUNT	OPEN TO	DURATION	WHEN OFFERED
Springfield Art Center, 107 Cliff Park Rd, Springfield, OH 45501	$25-$100	Children, some adults, by semester	Ten weeks	Each semester
Springfield College, 263 Alden St, Springfield, MA 01109	Variable	Qualified students based on financial need	One year	Annually
State University Center, Department of Art and Art History, Binghamton, NY 13901	Variable graduate assistantships and teaching assistantships in art history	Incoming and resident graduate students in art history	To a maximum of 4 years, renewable yearly	Annually, April
Stephens College,* Art Department, Columbia, MO 65201	$500-$2000	Varies—contact admissions office for information and details		
Sterling College, Sterling, KS 67579	$500	Any art students	One year	Annually
Sul Ross State University,* Art Dept, Alpine, TX 79830	$300	Entering art major	One year	Annually
Summervail Workshop for Art & Critical Studies, PO Box 1114, Vail, CO 81657	$14 per credit hour in-state; $48 per credit hour out-state	Any interested student	One, two and three week workshops and special Symposia	Annually
Sunbury Sjhores Arts and Nature Centre, Inc, 139 Water St, PO Box 100, St Andrews, NB EOG 2X0, Canada	Approx $500 each; all costs covered	New Brunswick residents ages 15-23 inclusive	Two or three weeks varying with art course	Annually, for July and Aug. Submit application by Mar 31
Swain School of Design, 19 Hawthorn, New Bedford, MA 02740	$200-$500	All students	One year	Annually
Syracuse University, Joe and Emily Lowe Art Gallery, Sims Hall, Syracuse, NY 13210	Teaching assistantships, fellowships	Museology and art students	One year	Annually
Tarrant County Junior College, Northeast Campus, Department of Art, 828 Harwood Rd, Hurst, TX 76053	$50 tuition award (3)	Art students at freshman-sophomore levels	One semester	Semi-annually
Texarkana College, Art Department, Texarkana, TX 75501	$100	Art majors	One year	Annually
Texas Southern University,* Department of Art, 3201 Wheeler Ave, Houston, TX 77004	$2000	All art students with completion of one year's course work in art at TSU may apply	Four years	Annually
Texas State Technical Institute, PO Box 11016, Amarillo, TX 79111	Varies (tuition)	Senior year students of program (CAA) at Texas State Technical Institute	One or two quarters	Annually
Texas Tech University, Department of Art, Box 4720, Lubbock, TX 79409	Variable	All undergraduate and graduate art students	One or two semesters	Each semester
Three Schools, New School of Art, 296 Brunswick Ave, Toronto, ON M5S 2M7, Canada	Up to $200	Students who have completed one year or more	One year	Annually
Louis Comfort Tiffany Foundation,* 4 Robin Hill Rd, Great Neck, NY 11024	$2000 (max)	US citizens of demonstrated talent	One year	Annually
Toledo Museum of Art,* 2445 Monroe Street, PO Box 1013, Toledo, OH 43697	Variable	Graduate students	One year	Annually
Toronto School of Art, 225 Brunswick Ave, Toronto, ON M5S 2M6, Canada	Variable	Students chosen by staff	One year	Beginning of each school year-Sept
Margaret Fort Trahern Gallery,* Austin Peay State University, Art Department, Clarksville, TN 37040	Variable	High school art seniors in central Tennessee	One year	Annually
Traphagen School of Fashion, 257 Park Ave S, New York, NY 10010	$2465 Famous Alumni Scholarship	Second year students	One year	Annually
	$2465 School Art League, New York City Scholarship	First year students		Annually
	$2465 National Scholastic Magazine Scholarship	First year students		Annually
	$2465	First year students (two years) Flemington Fur Co. Competition (open to high school juniors and seniors in NY, NJ, CT, DE, MD and PA)		Annually
Above scholarships are renewable upon performance each year				
Truro Center for the Arts at Castle Hill, Inc, Castle Rd, Box 756, Truro, MA 02666	4 working scholarships in exchange for tuition; no housing-ceramacists preferred	Preferably between 17 and 21 years	June 21-Sept 7	Annually
Tucson Museum of Art, Attn: M. E. Thompson, 235 W Alameda, Tucson, AZ 85701	$2000	Talented needy and minority students	One year	Annually

OFFERED BY	AMOUNT	OPEN TO	DURATION	WHEN OFFERED
Tufts University,* Fine Arts Dept, 11 Talbot Ave, Medford, MA 02155	Variable	According to need and ability		Annually
Tullahoma Fine Arts Center, 401 S Jackson, Tulahoma, TN 37388	Tuition	Motlow Community College art major	One year	Annually
Tusculum College,* Fine Arts Dept, Box 48, Greenville, TN 37743	$400-$800	Students in upper 40% of their class who show leadership talent, art talent	One year	Annually
Umpqua Community College,* Dept. of Art, PO Box 967, Roseburg, OR 97470	$132	New or returning art majors	One term	Annually
US Government Grants for Graduate Study Abroad under the Fulbright-Hays Act. Write: Study Abroad Programs, Institute of International Education, 809 United Nations Plaza, New York, NY 10017	Variable	Graduate students who are U.S. citizens with B.A. degree or in the creative and performing arts, 4 years of professional study and/or experience, and who have a knowledge of the language of the country for which the application is made.	One year	Annually
University of Alabama, Dept of Art, PO Box 1247, Huntsville, AL 35807	$768	Art major with 2.0 average on 3.0 scale	One year	Annually
University of Alaska at Anchorage,* Dept of Art, 2533 Providence Ave, Anchorage, AK 99504	$250 plus state aid	All art students		Annually
University of Arizona,* College of Fine Arts, Department of Art, Tucson, AZ 85721	Variable	Students enrolled in Art program UA	One year	Annually
University of Arkansas,* Fayetteville, AR 72701	$2070-$2421 Assistantships	Graduate students	Two years or more	Annually
	$100-$300 scholarships	Sophomore, junior or senior art students enrolled in the Art Department at the University of Arkansas	One year	Annually
University of California, Santa Barbara,* Santa Barbara, CA 93106	Variable	Graduate students approved by the Art Department chairman	Academic year	Annually
University of Chicago, Cochrane-Woods Art Center, 5540 S Greenwood, Chicago, IL 60637	Full and partial tuition scholarships and, in rare cases, stipends	The best qualified entering and continuing graduate students	Academic year	Annually, Mid-Feb
University of Colorado at Boulder, Fine Arts Department, Boulder, CO 80309	In-state tuition (5)	Undergraduates	One year	Annually
	$2500 plus tuition waiver	Graduate students	One year	Annually
	Maria Elkin Award-$200	Fine Arts student	Academic year	
	Eve Drewelowe Award-$300	Student majoring in painting with preference given to female students	Academic year	Annually (renewable)
University of Delaware, Newark, DE 19711 (in cooperation with Winterthur Museum)	Up to ten fellowships covering tuition, travel, and a $4000 stipend	College graduates in one of the humanities, social sciences, or American studies	Two years	Annually
University of Denver School of Art, University Park, Denver, CO 80208	Variable; several $1500 annual, renewable "University Scholars" merit awards; graduate student assistantships in addition to scholarships	Graduate students, eligible when accepted for admission; undergraduate, one through the National Scholastic Competition, others.	Varying	Quarterly and annually for different types
University of Hartford, Hartford Art School,* 200 Bloomfield Ave, West Hartford, CT 06117	$1000	Competition scholarship award	One year, renewable	Annually
University of Idaho,* Department of Art & Architecture, Moscow, ID 83843	$400 (Novah Southon Tisdale Scholarship)	All majors in art, undergraduate and graduate, based on ability alone		Annually in the Spring for Fall semester
	$400 (Commemorative Art Scholarship)	Upper division undergraduates in art, based on need and ability		Annually in the Spring for Fall semester
University of Illinois, Urbana-Champaign, College of Fine and Applied Arts, 110 Architecture Bldg, Urbana, IL 61801	Kate Neal Kinley Memorial Fellowship-$3500	Graduates of the College of Fine and Applied Arts of the University of Illinois, Urbana-Champaign and to graduates of similar institutions of equal educational standing	One academic year	Annually
University of Iowa, School of Art and Art History, Iowa City, IA 52242	Graduate College Scholarships up to $2000	All scholarships listed available to graduate students and some undergraduate students	One year (renewable)	Annually
	Ford Foundation B.F.A. and M.F.A. Scholarships up to $1500			
	Paula P. Grahame Scholarship up to $1500			
	Kress Foundation Fellowship in Art History $3500, Travel Grants to $1200			
	Assistantship $3900-$4200			

OFFERED BY	AMOUNT	OPEN TO	DURATION	WHEN OFFERED
University of Kansas, School of Education, School of Fine Arts, 7306 Bailey Hall, Lawrence, KS 66045	Variable	Undergraduates in Art Education and graduate students in Art Education	One academic year (renewable)	Annually
University of Lethbridge, Department of Art, Lethbridge, AB, Canada	Variable	Qualified students		Annually
	Art Department Faculty $100	Full-time second/third year student - Art major; outstanding accomplishment in an area of Studio Art over at least one full year at the University		Annually
	George Varzari Sculpture Award $100	Full-time student currently enrolled in a sculpture course at the U of L - outstanding in area of sculpture. Works sculpted during current academic year		
University of Louisville, Allen R Hite Art Institute, Louisville, KY 40208	Variable (tuition only)	Art and art history students	One year (renewable)	Annually
University of Michigan, Ann Arbor,* History of Art Department, Ann Arbor, MI 48109	Charles L. Freer Scholarship in Oriental Art. Amounts vary up to $2400 plus fees	Graduate student beginning advanced work in Oriental art		Annually
	Charles L. Freer Fellowships in Oriental Art. $400 per month	Advanced graduate students in Oriental art—residence at Freer Gallery, Washington, DC	One year	Annually
	Samuel H. Kress Foundation Scholarship and Fellowship. Amounts vary up to $2400 plus fees	Advanced graduate students	One year	Annually
	Graduate Fellowships offered by Horace H. Rackham School of Graduate Studies. Amounts vary up to $2400 plus fees	Graduate students	One year	Annually
	Teaching Fellowships approx $4000 per academic year	Graduate students of the second year and beyond	One year	Annually
	Regional Museum Internships. Stipend approx $2500 plus fees	Advanced graduate students	One year	Annually
University of Minnesota, Duluth, Department of Art, 317 Humanities Bldg, Duluth, MN 55812	Assistantships and/or associateships	Graduate students	One year	Annually
	$100 scholarships (4)	Undergraduate	Summer session only	
	$100 awards (6)	Outstanding new freshmen art majors	Fall quarter only	
	$500 scholarships (11)	Undergraduate and/or graduate	One year	Annually
University of Minnesota, Minneapolis, Department of Studio Art, Minneapolis, MN 55455	Variable, up to $200 for materials	Qualified undergraduates	One year	Winter or Spring
	Up to $3500 plus tuition	Graduate students		Winter
University of Mississippi, Department of Art, Fine Arts Center, University, MS 38677	$1900 for half time; $3800 full assistantship (5-6 available)	Graduate students in art (MFA, MA)	Nine months	Annually
University of Nebraska-Lincoln, Department of Art, Woods Hall, Lincoln, NE 68588	Thomas Coleman Memorial Scholarship in Printmaking $150 each	Outstanding graduate and undergraduate student in prints	Singular	Annually
	Francis Vreeland Award in Art, 3 awards of $500 each	Outstanding graduate and undergraduate students in studio art	Singular	Annually
	Jean R. Faulkner Freshman Art Scholarship, 3 awards of $200 each	Identified creative potential during first year of study	Singular	Annually
	Jean R. Faulkner Student Exhibition Recognition Award, 6 awards of $100 each	Outstanding achievement by students represented in annual undergraduate exhibition	Singular	Annually
	Ruth Ann Sack Memorial Scholarship in Photography and Painting, $100 awards	Outstanding upper division students in photography and painting	Singular	Annually as income available
University of Nevada,* Department of Art, 4505 Maryland Parkway, Las Vegas, NV 89154	$1000	Entering freshmen only	Four years, renewable upon demonstration of satisfactory progress	Annually
University of New Mexico, College of Fine Arts, Albuquerque, NM 87131	$4300 and $4600	Graduate students	One academic year	Annually
University of North Carolina-Chapel Hill, Department of Art, 104 Ackland Art Center 003A, Chapel Hill, NC 27514	Emily Pollard Fellowship, $4000	Art history graduate students only	One year	Annually
	Samuel H. Kress Fellowship $6000			
	Rockefeller Foundation Fellowship, varies, $3500-$6000			

OFFERED BY	AMOUNT	OPEN TO	DURATION	WHEN OFFERED
University of North Carolina,* Dept of Art & Music, University Heights, Asheville, NC 28804	$300 (Norman Sultan Scholarship)	Outstanding student majoring in art with financial need	One year	Annually
University of North Carolina at Greensboro, Greensboro, NC 27412	Variable	University art students	Up to four years	Annually
	Howard Scholarship, variable		One year	Annually
	$900-$1000 graduate assistantships in the Art Dept.	Graduates	Semester	Semi-annually
University of Notre Dame, Graduate School, Art Department, Notre Dame, IN 46556	Tuition $3950 Stipend $2800	Teaching assistants chosen by faculty	Up to two years	Annually
University of Oregon,* School of Architecture and Applied Arts, Dept of Fine and Applied Arts, Eugene, OR 97403	$100-$300 (20 units)	Students with one year residence	One year	Annually
	$2500-$2800 (14 units) graduate assistantships	Qualified students at graduate level: nonresident must submit photographic exhibit of recent work (most reserved for 2nd year of residence)	One year	Annually
University of Pittsburgh,* Henry Clay Frick Fine Arts Dept, Pittsburgh, PA 15260	$3140-TA, $3350-TF, $3500-Mellon Tuition scholarships	Fine arts graduate students (art history)	One year, renewable	Annually
University of San Diego,* Art Department, Alcala Park, San Diego, CA 92110	$1500	Art students at University	One year	Annually
	Ainosuke Esaki Commemorative Scholar-$200 per semester	Full time art majors, junior and senior years		
University of Southern California, Idyllwild School of Music and the Arts, PO Box 38, Idyllwild, CA 92349	$20,000	Students with proven ability and need	Ten-week summer program	Annually
University of Southern California, School of Fine Arts, Watt Hall 103, University Park, Los Angeles, CA 90007	$3000-Yvonne M. Kramer Scholarship	Currently enrolled Fine Arts students	One year	Annually
	$6000-J. Paul Getty Memorial Scholarship	Graduate Student, Art History	One year	Annually
	Graduate teaching assistantships (tuition credit and stipend)-contact School of Fine Arts	Graduate students, Art History and Studio Art	One to three years	Annually
	Museum Studies Fellowships-contact School of Fine Arts	Graduate students, Museum Studies Program	One to three years	Annually
	Graduate Fellowships-contact USC Graduate School, ADM 353, USC, Los Angeles, CA 90007	Graduate students	Generally one to three years	Annually
University of Tennessee-Knoxville, Department of Art, 927 Volunteer Blvd, Knoxville, TN 37916	Variable	Tennessee high school seniors planning to work towards an art major at UT-K	One year	Each March
	Variable	Undergraduate students who are enrolled	Annual	Each March
	Variable	Students who are applying to the Graduate School for admission and are planning to work for the MFA degree in the art department	Annual	Each April
University of Texas at Austin, Department of Art, 23rd and San Jacinto, Austin, TX 78712	Studio-Ford Foundation grants, varying amounts; student assistantships; all levels teaching assistantships, general scholarships, varying amounts			Semi-annually
University of Texas at San Antonio, Art Department, 4242 Piedras Dr E, Suite 250, San Antonio, TX 78284	$100 to $500	Art students in good standing	One semester	Each semester
University of Texas of the Permian Basin, Faculty of Art, Odessa, TX 79762	$800	Qualified students	One year	Annually
University of Utah,* Art Dept AAC 161, Salt Lake City, UT 84112	$100	Docents	One year	Annually
University of Washington,* School of Art, DM-10, Seattle, WA 98195	Approx $40,000	Art majors	One year and quarterly	Annually and quarterly
University of Waterloo, Waterloo, ON N2L 3G1, Canada	$1500	Outstanding students entering first year in the faculty of Arts	Two years ($750 each year)	Annually
University of Windsor,* School of Visual Arts, Huron Church Road at College, Windsor, ON, Canada N9B 3P4	Variable	Fine Arts students, other university students	One year	Annually

OFFERED BY	AMOUNT	OPEN TO	DURATION	WHEN OFFERED
University of Wisconsin-Eau Claire,* Dept of Art, Park and Garfield Aves, Eau Claire, WI 54701	Variable	Qualified students	One year	Annually
University of Wyoming,* Art Dept, University Station, Box 3138, Laramie, WY 82071	$1950	Both in-state and out-of-state students	One year (renewable)	Annually
Valley City State College, Art Department, Valley City, ND 58072	$300	Any full time art major	One year	Annually
Vancouver Community College, Langara Campus,* Dept of Fine Arts, 100 W 49th Ave, Vancouver, BC V5Y 2Z6, Canada	$15-$30	Any art student taking any academic and studio courses	One year	Annually
Ventura College, Fine Arts Department, 4667 Telegraph Rd, Ventura CA 93003	Various amounts	Ventura College Art Students only		Annually
Villa Montalvo Center for the Arts,* Montalvo Rd, P.O. Box 158, Saratoga, CA 95070	$75 single per month, $90 double per month (a limited number of resident scholarships)	Qualified artists with specific projects	Three months (may be extended an additional three months)	
Virginia Museum of Fine Arts,* Boulevard & Grove, Richmond, VA 23221	Student Fellowship $1500 Graduate Fellowship $3600 Professional Fellowship $2400	Virginians who were born in the State, or who have resided in it for a period of at least five years; must be involved in the arts.	One year	Annually, Deadline Apr 1
Virginia Polytechnic Institute and State University, Blacksburg, VA 24061	$150	Art majors who are rising seniors	One year	Annually
	$300	Any class	One year	Annually
Visual Art's Center of the Children's Aid Society, 209 Sullivan St, New York, NY 10012	Variable	Depending on economic situation	One year	Semi-annually
Waldorf College,* Art Department, Forest City, IA 50436	Variable with need	Art majors	One year	Annually
Washington and Lee University,* Dept of Fine Arts, Lexington, VA 24450	Varies according to need	Art majors, college men only	One year (renewable up to four years)	Annually
Washington State University,* Fine Arts Dept, Pullman, WA 99164	$200-$500	Art majors	One year	Annually
Washington University, St Louis, MO 63130	$225-$5350	Full-time students in the School of Fine Arts	One year (usually renewable)	Annually
Wayland Baptist College Department of Art, Box 54, 1900 W Seventh, Plainview, TX 79072	Various amounts	Everyone majoring or minoring in art	Semester	Semi-annually
	Ted Bell Memorial Art Award, $25-$200	Everyone majoring or minoring in art	Semester	Annually
Weber State College, Art Department 2001, Ogden, UT 84404	Tuition waiver	All art majors	One year	Annually
Wenatchee Valley College,* Art Dept, 1300 5th St, Wenatchee, WA 98801	$225(4)	Best qualified applicants		
Wesleyan College, Forsyth Rd, Macon, GA 31201	From title to full tuition	Any female who has made application and submits a portofolio	Until student leaves Wesleyan	Annually, before June
Western Illinois University Art Department, West Adams, Macomb, IL 61455	(4) Assistantships, $315 per month with summer tuition waiver	Graduate applicants with required credentials	One to one and a half years plus summer	Annually or semi-annually
	Tuition waivers (5 to 10) Talent grants $100 to $300 each (4 to 10)	Students matriculating or new students with outstanding records or portfolios	Varies with availability	Annually or semi-annually
Western Montana College,* Art Dept, 710 S Atlantic, Dillon, MT 59725	$100	A promising art student in second, third or fourth year at WMC	One year	Annually
Western Wyoming College Art Department, Rock Springs, WY 82901	Tuition	High school graduates with strong interest in the arts	One year (renewable for two years)	Annually
West Georgia College,* Art Department, Carrollton, GA 30117	Various	Art majors	One year	Annually
Westmar College, Art Department, Le Mars, IA 51031	Variable	Those of outstanding artistic ability and those who can demonstrate financial need		Annually
West Shore Community College,* Div of Humanities of Fine Arts, 3000 N Stiles Rd, Scottville, MI 49454	$150-$500	Qualified full-time talented art students	One year	Annually
West Texas State University, Department of Art, Box 16, WT Station, Canyon, TX 79016	Up to $500	High School seniors and transfer students	One year	Annually

OFFERED BY	AMOUNT	OPEN TO	DURATION	WHEN OFFERED
West Virginia University, Art Department, Morgantown, WV 26506	$2412	MFA degree students	One year (renewable)	Annually
Whitworth College,* Art Dept, W Hawthorne Rd, Spokane, WA 99251	Maximum $200	Art majors, students enrolling with art emphasis, undeclared majors	One year	Annually
Williams College, Department of Art, Williamstown, MA 01267	$3000 Hubbard Hutchinson Memorial Scholarship	Williams senior for two years of graduate work	Two years at $3000 a year	Annually
	Cadwallader Evans III Memorial Scholarship	Williams student beginning junior year and majoring in English or Art	One year (may be extended second year)	Annually
	Edith Weston Andrews Scholarship	Williams student majoring in art or music	One year (may be extended second year)	Annually
	Beatrice Stone Scholarship	Williams student majoring in art or music	One year (may be extended second year)	Annually
William Woods College, Fulton, MO 65251	$300 and up	Art majors	One year (renewable)	Annually
Windward Artists Guild, PO Box 851, Kailua, HI 96734	$100	High school students of Windward Oahu		Annually
Henry Francis du Pont Winterthur Museum, Winterthur, DE 19735	Variable	Graduate Students in art conservation and connoisseurship	Two or three years	Annually
Wittenberg University, Springfield, OH 45501	$4000-$6000	All art students	One year	Annually
Catherine Lorillard Wolfe Art Club,* 802 Broadway, New York, NY 10003	$100 each	Art Students League and National School of Design students	One year	Annually
Worcester Craft Center, 25 Sagamore Rd, Worcester, MA 01605	$60	People in need	Ten week semester	Annually
	Up to $300	People in need	18 week semester, full time program	Annually
Wright State University, Dept of Art and Art History, Dayton, OH 45435	Variable, $350 minimum	Art majors	Variable, one year minimum	Annually
Wyoming Council on the Arts, State of Wyoming, Cheyenne, WY 82002	$4000	Residents of Wyoming, over 18, not full-time student		Annually
Yale Center for British Art and British Studies, Box 2120 Yale Station, New Haven, CT 06520	Open	Advanced scholars in British studies	Two-fourteen weeks	Annually in Nov
Yale University,* School of Art, 180 York St, New Haven, CT 06520	Per need	Eligible students	Academic year	Annually
Young Harris College, Department of Art, Young Harris, Ga 30582	$420 (4)	Art majors	One year	Annually
Joseph Young/Art in Architecture, 1434 Spaulding Ave, Los Angeles, CA 90019	Tuition-free grant	Qualified students who enroll and study with Joseph Young	One yar	Annually

Open Exhibitions

National, Regional and State-Wide

ALABAMA

WATERCOLOR SOCIETY OF ALABAMA ANNUAL JURIED COMPETITION, Birmingham. Annual, Nov 9-Dec 14. All aqueous media applied to paper. Open to all US artists. Cash and purchase awards. October deadline. For further information write Donna Leigh Jackins, 3209 Pinehurst Dr, Birmingham, AL 35226.

ALASKA

ALL ALASKA JURIED EXHIBITION,* Anchorage. Annual, Feb, Anchorage; Mar, Fairbanks; Apr, Juneau. Paintings, prints, drawings, sculpture, & photography. Open to Alaska residents only. Jury, cash awards. No fee, two items per category. Entries due Jan. For further information write Anchorage Historical & Fine Arts Museum, 701 West Seventh Ave, Anchorage, AK 99501.

EARTH, FIRE AND FIBER CRAFT DESIGN JURIED EXHIBIT,* Anchorage. Annual, Oct, Nov, Fairbanks; Dec, Juneau. Open to all crafts media, pottery, jewelry, metal, wood, weaving, etc. Open to Alaska residents only. Juried, cash awards. No fee, two items per category. For further information write Anchorage Historical and Fine Arts Museum, 121 W Seventh Ave, Anchorage, AK 99501.

ARIZONA

ANNUAL NORTHLIGHT GALLERY FOUR CORNERS EXHIBITION,* Tempe, AZ. Annual, Jan-Feb. Photographs. Open to artists in AZ, CO, UT, and NM. Juried, purchase awards. Fee $2 per entry. Entries due Nov 10. For further information write Northlight Gallery, Arizona State University, Art Dept, Tempe, AZ 85281.

DOUGLAS ART ASSOCIATION TWO FLAGS ART FESTIVAL. Annual, May. Open to all artists of US & Mex. Cash awards, prizes & purchase awards. Entry fee $3, limit two, 20% comn. For further information write Douglas Art Association, Box 256, 300 11th St, Douglas, AZ 85607.

HEARD MUSEUM GUILD,* Phoenix. Annual, Nov-Dec. All original arts & crafts. Open to Indians of NAm, Indian students & those of Indian descent. Cash awards & ribbons. Fee 20% comn. Entry forms & work due Oct 9-Nov 6. For further information write Chmn, Heard Museum Guild Indian Arts & Crafts Exhibit, 22 E Monte Vista Rd, Phoenix, AZ 85004.

TUCSON MUSEUM OF ART/ARIZONA BIENNIAL. Held even numbered year Mar-Apr. Painting, sculpture, graphics, drawings and photography. Open to Ariz. residents. Jury, purchase and exhibition awards totaling $3,000. Fee $4 per entry. For entry due dates and further information write Arizona Biennial, Tucson Museum of Art, Attn. M. E. Thompson, 235 W Alameda, Tucson, AZ 85701.

TUCSON MUSEUM OF ART/ARIZONA CRAFTS. Biennial, odd numbered years, Mar-Apr. All craft media. Open to Arizona residents. Jury, purchase, cash and exhibition awards totaling $3,000. Fee $4 per entry. For entry due dates and further information write Arizona Crafts, Tucson Museum of Art, Attn. M. E. Thompson, 235 W Alameda, Tucson, AZ 85701.

ARKANSAS

ARKANSAS ARTS CENTER DELTA ART EXHIBITION, Little Rock. Annual, Oct-Nov. All paintings & sculpture (not over 500 pounds). Open to artists born in or residing in Ark, La, Miss, Mo, Okla, Tenn & Tex. Jury, $1000 Grand Award, $3000 purchase awards. Fee $5

per entry, limit two. For further information write Townsend Wolfe, The Arkansas Arts Center, MacArthur Park, PO Box 2137, Little Rock, AR 72203.

ARKANSAS ARTS CENTER PRINTS, DRAWINGS & CRAFTS EXHIBITION, Little Rock. Annual, May-June. Prints in all media; drawings in all media (except watercolors); photographs in color and/or monochrome; crafts in metal, clay, textile, glass, wood, plastics & combined media. Open to artists born in or residing in Ark, La, Miss, Mo, Okla, Tenn & Tex. Jury, awards & $2000 purchase prizes. Fee $5 for each entry, limit two. Dates for entry cards and work due to be announced. For further information write Townsend Wolfe, Director, the Arkansas Arts Center, MacArthur Park, PO Box 2137, Little Rock, AR 72203.

ARKANSAS ARTS CENTER TOYS DESIGNED BY ARTISTS EXHIBITION, Little Rock. Annual, Dec-Jan. Toys in all media. Open to all artists. $1000 in purchase awards. Fee $5 per entry, limit 3. Jury. Dates for entry cards and work due to be announced. For further information write Townsend Wolfe, Director, The Arkansas Arts Center, MacArthur Park, PO Box 2137, Little Rock, AR 72203.

FORT SMITH ART CENTER. Annual, Mar. Painting, watercolor, drawing. Open to artists of Ark, Kans, La, Mo. Okla, Miss, Tenn & Tex. Jury, prizes & purchase awards. Fee $5. Entry cards & work due Feb 20. For further information write Registrar, Fort Smith Art Center, 423 N Sixth St, Fort Smith, AR 72901.

CALIFORNIA

ALL-CALIFORNIA PRINT EXHIBITION,* Los Angeles. Annual, Jan. All prints. Open to living Calif artists. Jury, over $1500 awards. Fee, limit on entries. Fees, forms & work due Nov 18. For further information write Betty Anderson, Los Angeles Printmaking Society, 1028 Mission St, South Pasadena, CA 91030.

ANNUAL DELTA ART SHOW,* Antioch. Annual, Oct. Painting, watercolor, graphics, drawing, print, stitchery, two-dimensional collage (no photographs). Juried, purchase awards. Fee $3 entry. For further information write Delta Art Annual, PO Box 116, Antioch, CA 94509.

ANNUAL NORTHERN CALIFORNIA OPEN SHOW,* Sacramento. Annual, Nov. All media with size and weight limits. Open to California residents. Juried, cash awards. Fee $3.50. For further information write Mary Kay Extrom, 2711 Ione St, Sacramento, CA 95821.

ANNUAL PHOTOGRAPHY COMPETITION,* Richmond. Annual, Nov. Photography. Open to California residents only. Juried, purchase awards. Entries due Oct 10. For further information write Annual: Photography, Richmond Art Center, Civic Center Plaza, Richmond, CA 94804.

INK AND CLAY,* Pomona. Annual, Jan-Feb. Ink, ceramic ware or sculpture. Juried, purchase awards. Fee $7 for one or two entries. For further information write Art Department, California State Polytechnic University, 3801 W Temple Ave, Pomona, CA 91768.

MANY MEDIA MINI EXHIBITION, Redlands. Annual, Oct. All media, original work, total size not to exceed 15 inches in any direction (no photography). Open to all Calif artists. Fee $4 per entry, limit three. For further information write Redlands Art Association, 12 E Vine St, Redlands, CA 92373.

OLIVE HYDE ART GALLERY ANNUAL TEXTILE COMPETITION. Annual, Spring. Textiles. Open to any artist working in predominately fiber media. Juried, awards. Fee $3 per item, limit 3. Work must be hand delivered. For further information write Olive Hyde Art Gallery, City of Fremont, Dept of Recreation, PO Box 5006, Fremont, CA 94538.

SAN BERNARDINO ART ASSOCIATION INLAND EXHIBITION.* Annual, Oct. Oil, acrylic, watercolor, mixed, collage, graphics (no sculpture or photography). Open to all California artists. Cash awards & purchase awards. Fee $3 per entry, limit two, 30% comn. Entry cards & work due Sept 30. For further information write San Bernardino Art Association, PO Box 2272, San Bernardino, CA 92406.

SAN FRANCISCO ANNUAL ARTS FESTIVAL. Open to artists of the nine Bay Area counties. Purchase awards. For further information write Elio Benvenuto, Arts Commission—City and County of San Francisco, 165 Grove St, San Francisco, CA 94102.

SANTA CRUZ ART LEAGUE. Annual, Apr. Oil, watercolor & mixed media, representational art only. Open to all Calif residents. Jury. Fee $4 per entry, limit three in each medium. For further information write Santa Cruz Art League, 526 Broadway, Santa Cruz, CA 95060.

TRADITIONAL ARTISTS ANNUAL EXHIBITION,* Redlands. Annual, Nov-Dec. Representational painting, watercolor, drawing, graphics, sculpture. To be held in San Bernardino County Museum. Juried. Fee $5 per entry, limit 3. For further information write Dorothy Hanna, Exhibition Chairman, 174 Tamarisk, Rialto, CA 92376.

WATERCOLOR XI,* Riverside. Annual, Apr, at Riverside Art Center & Museum. Transparent watercolor. Open to all California artists who submit paintings in transparent watercolor. Juried, with $350, $250, $150 awards, and other cash awards, and honorable mentions. Fee $4 per painting, total of three, one hung. Entries due mid-March, date to be announced. For further information write Elizabeth Hopkins, Pres, Watercolor West, PO Box 213, Redlands, CA 92373.

COLORADO

FOOTHILLS ART CENTER/NORTH AMERICAN SCULPTURE EXHIBITION, Golden. Annual, Apr-May. Sculpture in a permanent media. Open to any living artist in the US, Mexico or Canada. Juried by slides, $5000 in cash awards. Details not yet confirmed. For further information write Marian Metsopoulos, Foothills Art Center, 809 15th St, Golden, CO 80401.

FOOTHILLS ART CENTER/REGIONAL OIL EXHIBITION, Golden. Annual, May-June. Oil. Open to states surrounding Colorado. Juried by slides, with cash awards. Details not yet confirmed. For further information write Marian Metsopoulos, Foothills Art Center, 809 15th St, Golden, CO 80401.

FOOTHILLS ART CENTER/ROCKY MOUNTAIN NATIONAL WATERMEDIA EXHIBITION, Golden. Annual, Aug-Sept. Watermedia on paper. Open to all artists living in the US. Juried by slides, with $9000 cash prizes. Details not yet confirmed. For further information write Marian Metsopoulos, Foothills Art Center, 809 15th St, Golden, CO 80401.

CONNECTICUT

HUDSON VALLEY ART ASSOCIATION, INC, White Plains. Annual, first week of May. School of realism only; oil, watercolors, graphics, sculpture, pastels. Open to all artists, over 18 years, in this school of art. Double juried show, juried for selection and prizes, monetary and gold medals (not in pastels) in each media. Fee $10. Entries due week prior to exhibition. For further information write Joan Rudman, Secretary, 274 Quarry Road, Stamford, CT 06903.

NEW HAVEN PAINT AND CLAY CLUB. Annual, Mar-Apr. Oil, watercolor, acrylic, graphics & sculpture. Open to artists from the New Eng states & NY. Prizes & purchase awards. Fee $7 for first entry, $5 for second, 15% comn. Entry cards & work due Feb 29th. For further information write Donna Infantino, 34 Sachem Rd, Branford, CT 06405.

SILVERMINE GUILD OF ARTISTS NATIONAL PRINT EXHIBITION, New Canaan. Biennial Mar-Apr. All print media. Open to all artists. Jury, purchase prizes. Fee $10 first entry, $5 second entry, two works per artist allowed. For further information write Exhib Secy, Silvermine Guild of Artists, Inc. 1037 Silvermine Rd, New Canaan, CT 06840.

SILVERMINE GUILD OF ARTISTS NEW ENGLAND EXHIBITION OF PAINTING AND SCULPTURE, New Canaan. Annual, May-June. All painting & sculpture. Open to artists of the six New England States plus NY, NJ & Pa. Jury; more than $10,000 in cash awards. Fee. For further information write Exhib Secy, Silvermine Guild of Artists, Inc, 1037 Silvermine Rd, New Canaan, CT 06840.

SLATER MEMORIAL MUSEUM, Norwich. Annual, Mar-Apr. Sculpture, painting, drawing and prints. Open to all resident Conn artists. Jury, prizes. Fee $5 per piece, limit two; sculpture limited to 200 pounds. For further information write The Slater Memorial Museum, 108 Crescent St. Norwich, CT 06360.

DELAWARE

DELAWARE ART MUSEUMS CONTEMPORARY CRAFTS EXHIBITION, Wilmington. Biennial, Nov-Dec. Ceramics, fibers, metals, wood, leather, and glass; must be original designs executed by the entrants. Open to craftsmen in Delaware and Northeastern US (includes Md, DC, NJ, Pa, NY, and New England). Invitational-juried by slides, with cash prizes awarded by judges and purchase prize made by the Museum. Fee; limit of three works per person. Details not yet established, make inquiries in August. For further information contact Lial A. Jones, Education Department, Delaware Art Museum, 2301 Kentmere Parkway, Wilmington, DE 19806. Phone: (302) 571-9594.

DISTRICT OF COLUMBIA

ANNUAL EXHIBITION, MINIATURE SOCIETY OF WASHINGTON,* DC. Annual, Nov. Painting, graphics, sculpture, carving, with various size limitations. Cash awards. Fee, nonmembers, $10 for 3 entries. Entries due Sept 8. For further information write Margaret Wisdon, 5812 Massachusetts Ave, NW, Washington, DC 20016.

SUMI-E SOCIETY OF AMERICA EXHIBITION, Washington, DC. Fall. Oriental brush painting only; subjects must be original. Open to all artists. Jury, prizes. Fee $20 for non-members, limit 2. For further information write Frank H Spink, Jr, 5158 Piedmont Place, Annandale, VA 22003.

FLORIDA

BOYNTON BEACH FESTIVAL OF THE ARTS ANNUAL, Boynton Beach. Annual, held first weekend in Mar. Oil, watercolors, ceramics, sculpture, graphics, photography-textiles, crafts, mixed media, jewelry. Open to all original artwork, professional and amateur. Juried, submit three slides/photographs, over $1000 in prizes and ribbons. Fee $20 professional, $15 amateur. Entries due February 15. For further information write Eleanor Krusell, 128 E Ocean Ave, Boynton Beach, FL 33435.

FALL FESTIVAL OF ARTS AND CRAFTS, Panama City. Annual, Nov, Indoor, Municipal Auditorium. All media, must be original arts and crafts. Open to national. Fee $20. For further information write Chairman, Fall Festival, Panama Art Assocation, PO Box 883, Panama City, FL 32401.

FLORIDA GULF COAST ANNUAL JURIED COMPETITION,* Clearwater. Annual, Oct-Nov. Drawing, painting, graphics, photographs. Open to Florida artists. Juried, cash awards. Fee $12. Entry due Oct 2. For further information write Florida Gulf Coast Art Center, 222 Ponce de Leon Blvd, Belleair, FL 33516.

MIAMI GRAPHICS BIENNIAL,* Miami. Biennial. Graphics. Open to all artists in the US. Juried with honor, purchase awards. Fee $10. For further information write to Metropolitan Museum & Art Centers, 1212 Anastasia Ave, Coral Gables, FL 33134.

MIAMI INTERNATIONAL PRINT BIENNIAL.* March-May. Juried. Entry due Nov 1. For further information write Miami International Print Biennial, PO Box 440826, Miami, FL 33144.

NATIONAL CAPE CORAL ANNUAL ART EXHIBITION.* Annual, Jan. Painting, print, drawing, sculpture, watercolor, collage. Open to all US artists. Juried, cash awards. Fee $15 for 3 slides, three slides per work maximum. For further information write Cape Coral Art League, c/o Julie Anzelmo, 4417 SE Ninth Ave, Cape Coral, FL 33904.

NATIONAL MINIATURE ART SHOW ANNUAL,* Clearwater. Annual, Jan. All media, fine art and sculpture, no crafts. Open to all artists in US and abroad. Juried, $1000 in prizes. Fee $7 for up to three works; $11 for up to six. Entry cards and checks by November 18, works due November 25. For further information write Mr. Leslie Chepren, 10993 Dorothy Lane, Largo, FL 33540.

SOCIETY OF THE FOUR ARTS EXHIBITION OF CONTEMPORARY AMERICAN PAINTINGS, Palm Beach. Annual, Dec. Oils, watercolor, drawings, mixed, & flat collages completed since Jan. Open to artists residing in the US. Cash awards. Fee $3, limit 2 entries (fee refunded if entry accepted); comn 10%. Specific dates on which entry cards & work are due are announced in prospectus available upon request in Sept. For further information write The Society of the Four Arts, Four Arts Plaza, Palm Beach, FL 33480.

GEORGIA

ATLANTA PLAYHOUSE THEATRE AND GEORGIA TECH STUDENT INTERNATIONAL DOGWOOD FESTIVAL ART SHOW, Atlanta. Annual, Mar-Apr (Atlanta Dogwood Festival). Any hanging work of art suitable; oils, tempera, drawings, graphics, sculptures, collages, textiles, sculpture, and photography. Open to all artists in the US/international. Juried by slides, judged for awards, with purchase awards and prizes. Fee $10. Entries due February. For further information write Ida S Borochoff, Artistic Director, Atlanta Playhouse Theatre, Ltd, 3450 Old Plantation Rd NW, Atlanta, GA 30327.

OUTDOORS IN GOERGIA ANNUAL WILDLIFE SHOW,* Atlanta. Annual, Oct. Painting (oils and acrylics), watercolor, drawing (pen and ink/charcoal/pencil/pastel), prints (engravings/woodcuts/etchings), photography, sculpture. Open to wildlife artists in Georgia. Juried, cash prizes for first place, ribbons for second and third place. Fee $25 to reserve 5 x 10 ft space. Entries due after April 20. For further information write Liz Carmichael Jones, Georgia Department of Natural Resources, Room 720, 270 Washington St, SW, Atlanta, GA 30334.

HAWAII

ARTISTS OF HAWAII, Honolulu. Annual, Dec. All-media. Open to all artists residing in Hawaii. Juror. Fee $3 per entry, limited to three. Slide entries due by Sept 30. For further information write Selden Washington, Asst Dir, Honolulu Academy of Arts, 900 S Beretania St, Honolulu, HI 96814.

HAWAII NATIONAL PRINT EXHIBITION,* Honolulu. Biennial, Sept-Oct. All media except monoprints. Open to all artists living in the US. Jury. Fee $8 per artist, three entries per artist. Entries due no later than July 1. For further information write Honolulu Academy of Arts, 900 S Beretania St, Honolulu, HI 96814.

ILLINOIS

ART INSTITUTE OF CHICAGO. Biennial. All media, not over 7 x 10 x 5 ft or weigh over 1000 pounds. Open to artists, 18 or over, legal residents of 130 mile radius of Chicago. Jury, awards. Fee none. For further information write Painting & Sculpture Dept, The Art Institute of Chicago, Michigan & Adams, Chicago, IL 60603.

NORTH SHORE ART LEAGUE NEW HORIZONS IN ART, Chicago. Annual, May. Painting, sculpture, graphics, photog. Open to Ill artists. Cash awards, purchase awards & ribbons. Fee 15% comn. Entry cards & work due early May. For further information write North Shore Art League, 620 Lincoln Ave, Winnetka, IL 60093.

ROCKFORD AND VICINITY ANNUAL JURIED SHOW. Annual Oct-Nov. Oil, watercolor, sculpture and graphic arts. Open to artists within 200 miles of Rockford. Fee $10 per entry (two pieces), $5 to members. Entries due in late October. For further information, write Rockford Art Association, 737 N Main St, Rockford, IL 61103.

SOCIETY OF TYPOGRAPHIC ARTS, STA 100. Annual. Books, brochures, announcements, invitations, stationery, annual reports, house organs, calendars, catalogs, posters, manuals, corporate graphics, packages, logos and trademarks. Fee $15 per entry for non members, $10 per entry for members. Entry due March 1. For further information write STA 100, Society of Typographic Arts, 54 E Erie St, Chicago, IL 60611.

INDIANA

ANDERSON FINE ARTS CENTER WINTER SHOW, Anderson. Annual, Jan-Feb. Watercolors and prints. Open to artists currently residing in Ind, Ill, Ky, Ohio and Mich. Juried by a professional outside the region, $1000 in cash and purchase awards. Fee $5 for two entries. Entry forms due December 23, works due first week in January. For further information write Executive Director, Anderson Fine Arts Center, 226 W Eighth St, Anderson, IN 46016.

BALL STATE UNIVERSITY DRAWING & SMALL SCULPTURE SHOW, Muncie. Annual, May-June. Drawings & small sculpture. Open to all artists in the United States. One judge, awards. Sculptures judged preliminarily by slides which are due around February 1. (Actual date varies slightly from year to year). Drawings must be sent to the Art Gal-

lery for judging. Due around end of March; actual date varies slightly from year to year also. For further information & prospectus write Art Gallery, Ball State University, Muncie, IN 47306.

EVANSVILLE MUSEUM OF ARTS & SCIENCE MID-STATES ART EXHIBITION. Annual, Nov. Painting, sculpture, watercolor, graphic arts, collage & mobiles (no photographs). Open to artists within a radius of 200 miles from Evansville or any resident of the State of Indiana. Jury, awards. Handling fee is $5 for one entry or $8 for limit of two entries. Entries due in Sept. For further information write Art Comt, Evansville Museum of Arts & Science, 411 SE Riverside Dr, Evansville, IN 47713.

EVANSVILLE MUSEUM OF ARTS & SCIENCE MID-STATES CRAFT EXHIBITION. Annual, Feb. Ceramics, textiles, metal work, wood, enamel, glass & others. Open to artists within a radius of 200 miles from Evansville or any resident of the State of Indiana. Jury, awards. Fee $5 for three objects or less. Entries due Jan. For further information write Craft Comt, Evansville Museum of Arts & Science, 411 SE Riverside Dr, Evansville, IN 47713.

INDIANAPOLIS MUSEUM OF ART INDIANA ARTISTS EXHIBITION AND INDIANA CRAFTS EXHIBITION. Biennial, Aug-Sept. Painting & sculpture, works on paper, textiles, wood, glass, ceramics, metalwork, and mixed media. Open to artists who reside or have resided in Indiana. Jury, awards. Fee $5 per entry, limit two per artist. Entries due early or mid-June. For further information write Registrar, Indianapolis Museum of Art, 1200 W 38th St, Indianapolis, IN 46208.

INDIANAPOLIS MUSEUM OF ART INDIANA ARTISTS EXHIBITION AND INDIANA CRAFTS EXHIBITION. Biennial, Aug-Sept. Painting and sculpture, works on paper, textiles, wood, glass, ceramics, metalwork, and mixed media. Open to past or present Indiana residents. Jury, awards. Fee $5 per artist, limit two. Entries due early or mid-June. For further information write Registrar, Indianapolis Museum of Art, 1200 W 38th St, Indianapolis, IN 46208.

LAFAYETTE ART CENTER FIESTA. Annual, Aug-Sept. All media and crafts. Open to all midwest artists and craftsmen. Juried, over $600 in prizes. Fee $20. Entry slides of work due by Aug 15. For further information write Lafayette, IN 47901.

MICHIANA REGIONAL BIENNIAL ART EXHIBITION, South Bend. Biennial. Painting, sculpture, graphics & crafts. Open to artists in Ill, Ken, OH, Mich & Ind, or former residents. Jury, awards. Fee $7, limited to two entries. For further information write Art Center Inc, 120 S Saint Joseph St, South Bend, IN 46601.

WABASH VALLEY EXHIBITION, Terre Haute. Annual, Mar. All media. Open to artists within a 160 mile radius of Terre Haute. Jury, Fee $5 for first entry, $4 for second entry, $3 for third entry, limit to three. Entries due Feb. For further information write Curator, The Sheldon Swope Art Gallery, 25 S Seventh St, Terre Haute, IN 47807.

IOWA

DES MOINES ART CENTER ANNUAL. Annual, Spring. Paintings, drawings, prints, sculpture, crafts. Open to anyone living in Iowa above high school age. Juried, best work $250, 1 adult $100 and a student $50 in sculpture, prints-drawings, and crafts. No fee. For further information write Des Moines Art Center, Greenwood Park, Des Moines, IA 50312.

IOWA CRAFTS ANNUAL, Mason City. Annual, Oct-Nov-Dec. Open to any and all craft media, such as clay, fiber, metals, and others. Open to all artists, craftspersons residing within the State of Iowa. Juried by submission of the work, up to $800 in cash awards. No fee. Entry deadline three weeks prior to opening of show. For further information write Richard Leet, Director, Charles H MacNider Museum, 303 Second St SE, Mason City, IA 50401.

NORWEGIAN-AMERICAN MUSEUM NATIONAL ROSEMALING EXHIBITION, Decorah. Annual, July. Rose painting on wood. Open to anyone who has been a resident of the US for last five years. Jury, $25 blue ribbon, $10 white ribbon. Fee $2 per entry. Entries due July 15. For further information write Norwegian-American Museum, 502 W Water St, Decorah, IA 52101.

SIOUX CITY ART CENTER. Annual, Fall. Paintings. Open to residents of Iowa, Nebr, Minn & SDak. One-man jury, up to $1200 in purchase & cash awards. Entries due Sept-Oct. For further information write Dir, Sioux City Art Center, 513 Nebraska St, Sioux City, IA 51101.

KANSAS

KANSAS WATERCOLOR SOCIETY TRI-STATE EXHIBITION, Wichita. Annual, April-May. Primarily transparent aqueous on paper. Open to all artists living in Kansas, Missouri, or Oklahoma. Cash awards, prizes, and purchase awards. For further information write Barbara Bulloch, Pres, Kansas Watercolor Society, 10414 E Harry, Wichita, KS 67207

KENTUCKY

J B SPEED ART MUSEUM ANNUAL, Louisville. Annual, Sept. In annual rotation in following order: graphics, painting, sculpture, crafts. Open to artists in Kentucky, Indiana, Ohio, Illinois, Missouri, Tennessee, Virginia, West Virginia. Juried, no special awards, purchase commitments. No fee. Entries due August 2. For further information write Reva Crumpler, J B Speed Art Museum, PO Box 8345, Louisville, KY 40208.

LOUISIANA

LOUISIANA WATERCOLOR SOCIETY INTERNATIONAL, Baton Rouge. Annual, Nov-Dec. Water based, recent original paintings on paper. Open to all artists. Cash awards and purchase prizes. Fee $5 per entry, no limit to number of entries. Slides and entry fees due Oct 1. For further information, write Roma Quartana, President, 235 Hollywood Dr, Metairie, LA 70005.

NEW ORLEANS MUSEUM OF ART. Triennial, Fall. Focus on contemporary art by prof artists from thirteen-state region of Southeastern US. Single juror, purchase awards. No fee. For further information write New Orleans Triennial, New Orleans Museum of Art, PO Box 19123, Lelong Ave, City Park, New Orleans, LA 70179.

MAINE

OGUNQUIT ART CENTER NATIONAL PAINTING EXHIBITION. Annual, June-Sept. Oil, watercolor, mixed (originals only). Open to all US artists. Cash awards. Fee $12, 25% comn. Entry cards due May 10 & work due June 7. For further information write Mrs F Nims, The Ogunquit Art Center, Hoyt's Lane, Ogunquit, ME 03907.

WILLIAM A FARNSWORTH ART MUSEUM OPEN SHOW, Rockland. Annual, Feb-Apr. All media included. Open to all resident Maine artists. Juried, prizes and awards. No fee. Entries due approximately February 15-24. For further information write Marius B Peladeau, Director, William A Farnsworth Library and Art Museum, Box 466, Rockland, ME 04841.

MARYLAND

ACADEMY OF THE ARTS MARYLAND ART EXHIBITION,* Easton. Annual, Apr-May. All painting, collages, graphics, sculpture. Open to artists born or residing in Maryland, students at Maryland art schools and members of the Academy. Jury, cash prizes & purchase awards. No fee. Entry cards due Apr 9 & work due Apr 14 & 15. For further information write The Academy of the Arts, PO Box 605, Easton, MD 21601.

BALTIMORE MUSEUM OF ART BIENNIAL EXHIBITION. Biennial, during the even year. All media (slides or photographs of work not acceptable). Open to artists born or currently residing in Md. Jury, prizes & awards. No fee. Entries due as announced, usually 3 months before exhibition. For further information write Alice C Steinbach, Dir Pub Info, Baltimore Museum of Art, Art Museum Dr, Baltimore, MD 21218.

CUMBERLAND VALLEY ANNUAL PHOTOGRAPHIC SALON, Hagerstown. Annual, Feb. Photographs. Open to residents & former residents of the Cumberland Valley region. Jury, prizes & awards. Fee $5. Entries due Jan 15. For further information write Washington County Museum of Fine Arts, PO Box 423, Hagerstown, MD 21740.

CUMBERLAND VALLEY ARTISTS ANNUAL EXHIBITION, Hagerstown. Annual, June. Open media. Open to residents & former residents of the Cumberland Valley region. Jury, prizes & awards. Fee $10. Entries due May 15. For further information write Washington County Museum of Fine Arts, PO Box 423, Hagerstown, MD 21740.

MASSACHUSETTS

BOSTON PRINTMAKERS.* Annual, location & dates change yearly. All print media except monotypes. Open to all American and Canadian printmakers. Jury, awards. Fee $5 each, limit two, 33⅓% Comn. For further information write Mrs S M Rantz, Secy, 299 High Rock St, Dept A, Needham, MA 02192.

GREATER FALL RIVER ART ASSOCIATION NATIONAL.* Annual, May. Painting, graphics, sculpture, pottery, blown glass, textiles. Open to all artists in the US & Canada. Jury, prizes & purchase awards. Fee $5 per entry. Entry cards & slides due Apr 12. For further information write Bernice Goldsmith, 80 Belmont St, Fall River, MA 02720.

MARION ART CENTER BISTATE SHOW.* Annual. Aug-Sept. Painting, print, sculpture, photography. Open to artists of Massachusetts & Rhode Island. Jury, prizes. Fee $5 for two entries. Entry cards & fee due Aug 15 & work due Aug 23. For further information write Marion Art Center, Marion, MA 02738.

NEW ENGLAND ARTISTS TRADITIONAL OPEN SHOW,* Fall River. Annual. Paintings, graphics. Jury, cash awards. Fee $3. Entries due Nov. For further information write Mrs Edward A Doyle, Dir, 80 Belmont St, Fall River, MA 02720.

SPRINGFIELD ART LEAGUE NATIONAL EXHIBITION. Annual, Apr-May. Painting, mixed, graphics, sculpture. Open to all artists residing in US. Jury, cash awards. Fee $8. Entry cards & work due Mar 29. For further information write Sally A Johnson, Exhib Chairwoman, 131 Maple St, Longmeadow, MA 01106.

MICHIGAN

HARTLAND ART COUNCIL ART SHOW. Annual, June. Open to all artists. Jury, prizes & purchase awards. Fee. For further information write Hartland Art Council, Box 126, Hartland, MI 48029.

MID-MICHIGAN ANNUAL EXHIBITION, Midland. Annual, Feb. All media & mixed media (painting, drawing, prints, sculpture, plastics, ceramics, textiles, jewelry, enameling, metalwork, woodwork, photography). Open to Mich artists 18 years and over, only original work completed within the past 2 yrs. Jury, prizes, & awards. Fee $15 per artist, limit three entries; $10 fee for MAC members. Entries due Jan. For further information write the Midland Art Council of Midland Center for the Arts, Inc, 1801 West St. Andrews, Midland, MI 48640.

MINNESOTA

ROCHESTER ART CENTER. Annual, June. All media. Open to artists and craftspeople of Minnesota. Non-juried, no prizes. Fee $12 for space rental. Entries due May 26. For further information write to B J Shigaki, Dir, 320 E Center, Rochester, MN 55901.

WEST/ART AND THE LAW. Annual, June. Two dimensional works in all media. Open to living American artists working in the US. Juried, $25,000 in purchase awards. No fee. Entries due Mar 17-Apr 4. For further information write West/Art and the Law, Minnesota Museum of Art, St. Peter at Kellogg, Saint Paul, MN 55102.

WHITE BEAR ARTS COUNCIL & LAKEWOOD COMMUNITY COLLEGE NORTHERN LIGHTS,* White Bear Lake. Annual, Apr. Paintings, sculpture, drawings, no prints. Open to artists in Minnesota, Wisconsin, Iowa, North Dakota and South Dakota. Juried, prizes, ribbons, money awards and purchase awards. Fee $5 first entry, $3 second entry, two entries per artist. Entries due approximately two weeks before show, date to be decided. For further information write White Bear Arts Council, Box 8715, White Bear Lake, MN 55110.

MISSISSIPPI

LAUREN ROGERS MUSEUM OF ART BIENNIAL, Laurel. May. All media painting competition, no sculpture. Open to residents of Miss, Tenn, WVa, Ky, NC, SC, Va, Ga, Fla, Ark, Tex. Juried, purchase awards with top award of $900, other lesser awards, together totaling $3000. Fee $5, maximum of three entries (color slides). Entries due March 1. For further information write Biennial, Lauren Rogers Museum of Art, PO Box 1108, Laurel, MS 39440.

MISSOURI

NATIONAL WILDLIFE ART SHOW (formerly Midwest Wildlife Art Show), Kansas City. Annual, Mar. Acrylics, drawings, oils, pastels, sculpture, watercolors, decoy carvings and wood carvings. Open to professional wildlife artists of the US and Canada. Juried, ribbons. Fee and donated original piece of artist's work to the Sponsor Ducks Unlimited. Entries due November 15. For further information write William A Anderson, Jr, Director, PO Box 26008, City Center Square, Kansas City, MO 64196.

WATERCOLOR USA, Springfield. Annual, late Spring, early Summer. Any aquamedia (paint composed of water-soluble pigment) executed on paper or a paper-like support. Open to living, adult artists, 18 years of age or older, residing in the US. Jury, approximately $10,000 in cash, purchase awards and patron purchases. Handling fee $6. Entry deadline varies from year to year. For further information write William C Landwehr, Dir, Springfield Art Museum, 1111 E Brookside Dr, Springfield, MO 65807.

NEBRASKA

JOSLYN ART MUSEUM BIENNIAL, Omaha. Biennial, held in even-numbered yrs, late winter or spring. Painting, sculpture, graphics. Open to artists in Ark, Colo, Ill, Ind, Iowa, Kans, La, Mich, Minn, Mo, Mont, Nebr, NMex, NDak, Ohio, Okla, SDak, Tex, Wisc & Wyo. Jury, awards. Entries due as announced. For further information write Joslyn Biennial, Joslyn Art Museum, 2200 Dodge St, Omaha, NE 68102.

NORTH PLATTE VALLEY ARTISTS' GUILD, Scottsbluff. Annual, Apr. All media. Open to residents of Mont, Nebr, NDak, SDak & Wyo. Juried, prizes, purchase awards & ribbons. Fee $5 per entry for adults & $1.50 for youths; 30% Comn. Entry cards due Mar 21, work due Mar 28. For further information write North Platte Valley Artists' Guild, PO Box 1041, Scottsbluff, NE 69361.

NEW JERSEY

ART CENTER OF NEW JERSEY, East Orange. Annual, Feb. Oil, watercolor, graphics, sculpture. Open to artists of Conn, NJ, NY & Pa. Jury, prizes. Fee $6 for one, $10 for two entries; 25% comn. For further information write Art Center of New Jersey, 16 Washington St, East Orange, NJ 07017.

HUNTERDON ART CENTER NATIONAL PRINT EXHIBITION, Clinton. Annual, Mar-Apr. All print media except monotype. Open to all artists in the US. Jury, purchase awards. Fee $10 for one or two prints includes insurance & return of work. For further information write A S Marsh, Hunterdon Art Center, 7 Center St, Clinton, NJ 08809.

MINIATURE ART SOCIETY OF NEW JERSEY,* Nutley. Annual, May. Original miniature art work (no crafts). Open to all artists. Jury, prizes & purchase awards. Fee $8, limit three (members seven). Entry cards due Feb 13, work due Feb 23. For further information write Nutley Art Center, 200 Chestnut St, Nutley, NJ 07110.

NEW JERSEY WATERCOLOR SOCIETY, Alternate yrs Morris Museum, Morristown & Monmouth Museum, Lincroft. Annual, Nov-Dec. Watercolor, casein, tempera. Open to all present or former residents of NJ. Jury, awards. Fee subject to yearly decision of board. For further information write June Benson, 71 Old Orchard Court, Cedar Grove, NJ 07009.

WESTFIELD ART ASSOCIATION,* Cranford. Annual, Mar-Apr. All painting, original work only. Open to all New Jersey residents. Jury, prizes & cash awards. Fee $5 per entry. Work due Mar 18. For further information write Mrs Elven Sheahan, 721 Clark St, Westfield, NJ 07090.

NEW MEXICO

MUSEUM OF ALBUQUERQUE.* Biennial. Arts and crafts. Open to artists and craftspeople of New Mexico. Entry due May. For further information write Ellen J Landis, Curator of Art, Museum of Albuquerque, PO Box 1293, Albuquerque, NM 87103.

MUSEUM OF NEW MEXICO,* Santa Fe. Biennial (New Mexico Biennial held alternate years), Feb-Mar Apr-May. All media. Open to artists of Southwest. Jury, awards. For further information write Museum of Fine Arts, Museum of New Mexico, PO Box 2087, Santa Fe, NM 87501.

NEW MEXICO ART LEAGUE SMALL PAINTING SHOW,* Albuquerque. Annual, Feb. All media. Open to all artists. Jury, prizes. Fee $6 per entry, limit two. Entry cards and work due Jan 10. For further information write New Mexico Art League, Old Town Gallery, 400 Romero St NW, Albuquerque, NM 87104.

NEW MEXICO ARTS AND CRAFTS FAIR, Albuquerque. Annual, last weekend in June. All media except home arts or crafts. Open to all NMex artists & craftsmen 18 yrs and older. Jury. Fee $60 each booth; $8 entry fee. Entry forms & 3 samples of work due mid-February. For further information write New Mexico Arts & Crafts Fair, 2745 San Mateo, NE, Suite G, Albuquerque, NM 87110.

NEW YORK

ALLIED ARTISTS OF AMERICA INC. Annual, Sept-Oct. Oil, acrylics, water media, sculpture, pastel. Open to all artists. Juried, over $10,000 in cash awards, plus medals. Fee $10 for one slide, 20% comn. Entries due May 5. For further information write (enclose self-addressed stamped envelope) Reta Soloway, Corres. Secretary, 145 Lexington Ave, Franklin Square, NY 11010.

AMERICAN WATERCOLOR SOCIETY,* New York. Annual, Apr. Watercolor, watermedia. Jury, cash awards with medals. Fee $8. Submission can be by slides. For further information write The American Watercolor Society, 1083 Fifth Ave, New York, NY 10028.

ART DIRECTORS CLUB, New York. Annual Exhibition of Advertising & Editorial Art & Design, Spring. Open to advertising or editorial materials, promotion, posters, packaging & others. Jury, medals & certificates. Fee. Entries due Dec. For further information write The Art Directors Club, 488 Madison Ave, New York, NY 10022.

AUDUBON ARTISTS, New York. Annual, Mar-Apr, at National Arts Club. Oil, aquamedia, mixed media, sculpture, graphics. Jury. Awards $4000 and ten medals. Fee $10. Slides due Feb 1. For further information write Audubon Artists, 225 W 34th St, Suite 1302, New York, NY 10001.

CHAUTAUQUA EXHIBITION OF AMERICAN ART.* Annual, July. Oil, acrylic, watercolor, prints, drawing, mixed media. Open to all artists residents of US & territories. Jury, cash prizes. Fee $6 for one entry, $10 for two. Entry slides (juried by slide only) due Apr 8 & work due May 31. For further information write Chautauqua Art Association, Box 1365, Chautauqua, NY 14722.

COOPERSTOWN ART ASSOCIATION NATIONAL EXHIBITION.* Annual, July-Aug. Painting, graphics, sculpture & crafts (no photography). Open to any adult in the US. $3000 in prizes. Fee $7.50 each entry, 20% comn. Mailed entries due in the hands of agent by June 7. Hand delivered entries June 15, 16 and 17 only. For further information write Cooperstown Art Association, 22 Main St, Cooperstown, NY 13326.

EVERSON MUSEUM OF ART NATIONAL CERAMIC EXHIBITION,* Syracuse. Biennial, Nov-Dec. Ceramics. Open to potters & enamelists in the US & Canada. Jury, purchase prizes. Fee. For further information write Everson Museum of Art, 401 Harrison St, Syracuse, NY 13202.

KNICKERBOCKER ARTISTS EXHIBITION,* New York. Annual, Oct. Oil, watercolor, acrylic, casein, graphics, sculpture. Open to all artists. Jury, prizes. Fee $10. Work due Oct 16. For further information write Ann Kovach, 100-36 Bellaire Place, Bellaire, NY 11429.

LONG BEACH ART ASSOCIATION. Annual, May. All media. Open to adults. Cash awards and ribbons. Fee $6 per entry, $10 for two. Entry cards and work due April 26. For further information write Long Beach Art Association, PO Box 70, Island Park, NY 11558.

NATIONAL ACADEMY OF DESIGN, New York. Annual, Feb-Mar. Oil, sculpture, watercolors, graphics. Open to all artists. Jury, awards. No fee. For further information write (requesting prospectus) National Academy of Design, 1083 Fifth Ave, New York, NY 10028.

NATIONAL ART LEAGUE SPRING EXHIBITION,* Douglaston. Annual. May. Oil, watercolor, casein, pastels, black/whites, graphics, and small sculpture. Open to all artists and sculptors. Juried, cash awards, prizes and ribbons. Fee $7 non members $5 members; 20% comn. For further information, write National Art League, Inc, 44-21 Douglaston Parkway, Douglaston, NY 11363.

NATIONAL ARTS CLUB OPEN WATERCOLOR EXHIBITION, New York. Annual, Feb. Watercolor only. Open to all. Juried, cash awards, material awards, one-man show awards. Fee $10. Work due Jan 31st. For further information write Moses Worthman, AWS, 3027 Brighton Fifth St, Brooklyn, NY 11235.

NATIONAL SCULPTURE SOCIETY, New York. Annual, Feb. Sculpture only. Open to all American sculptors on a juried basis. Jury prizes & awards. No fee. Write for prospectus approx Jan 1. For further information write National Sculpture Society, 15 E 26th St, New York, NY 10010.

NATIONAL SOCIETY OF PAINTERS IN CASEIN & ACRYLIC, New York. Annual, Mar. Casein and acrylic. Open to all artists. Jury, $2500 cash awards & medals. Fee $10. Slides due Jan 15. For further information write Lily Shuff, 155 West 68th St, New York, NY 10023.

PASTEL SOCIETY OF AMERICA NATIONAL JURIED ALL PASTEL SHOW, New York. Annual, Sept-Oct. Pastel only. Open to all artists. Juried, $4000 in cash prizes, plus material awards, scholarships. Fee $10 first entry, $5 second, limit two. Entry due September 10, out-of-towners may send slides, deadline July 1. For further information write Richard Pionk, Chairman, 1349 Lexington Ave, New York, NY 10028.

SOCIETY OF AMERICAN GRAPHIC ARTISTS,* New York. Biennial. All prints except monotype. Open to all printmakers. Jury, awards. Fee $5, limit one (30 inches maximum). For further information write Society of American Graphic Artists, 1083 Fifth Ave, New York, NY 10028.

WOLF AND MARY BRAUN FUND YOUNG DESIGNERS COMPETITION,* New York, NY. Annual. Open to students of product package design in credited schools in the United States and Canada. Jury, awards. For further information write W Braun Company, 260 Fifth Ave, New York, NY 10001.

CATHERINE LORILLARD WOLFE ART CLUB, INC, ANNUAL OPEN EXHIBITION, New York. Annual, December. Original oils, watercolors, pastels, acrylics, graphics, and sculpture. Open to all women artists of professional standing. Juried, cash awards, medals. Fee $12, commission. For further information and prospectus write Adrienne Potter, 520 Seventh St, Palisades Park, NJ 07650.

NORTH CAROLINA

CHARLOTTE PRINTMAKERS SOCIETY ANNUAL PRINT COMPETITION AND EXHIBITION.* Annual, Dec. Prizes and purchase awards. Entry due Nov 1. For further information write Paul J Harcharik, Charlotte Printmakers Society, 110 E Seventh St, Charlotte, NC 28202.

NORTH CAROLINA ARTISTS EXHIBITION, Raleigh. Annual, Apr. Painting, graphics, sculpture, photography, crafts. Open to natives & residents of NC. Cash awards, prizes & purchase awards. Fee $5 per artist, limit two works. Entry cards & work due February. For further information write Head, Exhibitions, North Carolina Museum of Art, 107 E Morgan St, Raleigh, NC 27611.

SOUTHEASTERN CENTER FOR CONTEMPORARY ART, Winston-Salem. Annual competition - media as specified. Open to all artists, 18 years & older, residing in the 11 southeastern states. Jury, purchase awards. Fee $6. For further information write Southeastern Center for Contemporary Art (SECCA), 750 Marguerite Dr, Winston-Salem, NC 27106.

NORTH DAKOTA

MINOT STATE COLLEGE NATIONAL PRINT & DRAWING EXHIBITION. Annual, Feb. All prints, drawings. Open to all US artists. Purchase awards. Fee; two slide entries. Slides due Dec 8. For further information write National Print & Drawing Exhibition, Art Department, Minot State College, Minot, ND 58701.

NATIONAL ART EXHIBITION BIENNIAL,* Valley City. Biennial, Apr. All media. Open to all artists. Juried, approximately $1500 in prizes. Fee $5, limit to two works per artist. Entries due March 18, no slides required. For further information write 2nd Crossing Gallery, Box 1319, Valley City State College, Valley City, ND 58072.

NORTH DAKOTA PRINT & DRAWING EXHIBITION, Grand Forks. Annual, Apr. All prints & drawings. Open to all US artists. Jury, purchase awards. Fee $7. Work due Mar 1. For further information write North Dakota Annual, Visual Arts Dept, University of North Dakota, Grand Forks, ND 58202.

OHIO

BUTLER INSTITUTE OF AMERICAN ART MIDYEAR SHOW, Youngstown. Annual, National, July-Aug. Oil, watercolor, acrylic, casein. Open to artists of the US. Jury, awards. Fee $10 for one to four slides. Entry cards and slides due Apr 27. For further information write Butler Institute of American Art, 524 Wick Ave, Youngstown, OH 44502.

MARIETTA COLLEGE CRAFTS NATIONAL. Annual. Crafts & sculpture. Open to craftspeople in the US. Jury, $5500 in awards & prizes. Fee $10. Slides due Sept 13. For further information write Arthur Howard Winer, Dir, MCCN, Marietta College, Marietta, OH 45750.

MARIETTA NATIONAL (formerly Mainstreams). Annual, Apr-May. Open to all painters & sculptors in US. Jury, prizes & purchase awards. Fee $10, limit three. Entry cards due Feb 9th. For further information write Arthur N Winer, Dir, Marietta National, Marietta College, Marietta, OH 45750.

MASSILLON MUSEUM OHIO FINE ARTS EXHIBITION. Biennial, Mar. Oil, watercolor, polymer, acrylic. Open to residents of Ohio & former residents. Jury, prizes & pruchase awards. Fee $5. Work due Feb 3. For further information write John Klassen. The Massillon Museum, 212 Lincoln Way E, Massillon, OH 44646.

OHIO ARTISTS & CRAFTSMEN SHOW, Massillon. Biennial, July-Aug. Print, drawing, photography, all crafts & sculpture. Open to all present & former residents of Ohio. Prizes & purchase awards. Fee $5, 10% comn. Work due June 13. For further information write John Klassen, The Massillon Museum, 212 Lincoln Way E, Massillon, OH 44646.

OHIO CERAMIC, SCULPTURE & CRAFT SHOW, Youngstown. Annual, Jan-Feb. Ceramic, enamel, sculpture and craft. Open to present & former Ohio residents. Jury, purchase awards. Entry fee. Entries due Dec 14. For further information write Butler Institute of American Art, 524 Wick Ave, Youngstown, OH 44502.

OKLAHOMA

GREEN COUNTRY ART ASSOCIATION DOGWOOD ART FESTIVAL,* Poteau. Annual, Easter-Mother's Day. Paintings & sculpture only. Open to artists of Arkansas, Kansas, Missouri, Oklahoma & Texas. Jury. Fee. Entry cards due Apr 2, work due Apr 14. For further information write Green Country Art Association, 1825 E 15th St, Tulsa, OK 74104.

OKLAHOMA ART CENTER EIGHT STATE EXHIBITION OF PAINTING & SCULPTURE, Oklahoma City. Biennial, Sept-Oct. Painting & sculpture. Open to residents of Ark, Colo, Kans, La, Mo, NMex, Okla & Tex. Jury, five purchase awards. Fee $10. Entries due by Aug. For further information write Oklahoma Art Center, 3113 Pershing Blvd, Oklahoma City, OK 73107.

OKLAHOMA ART CENTER NATIONAL PRINT & DRAWING EXHIBITION, Oklahoma City. Annual, Apr. Prints & drawings. Open to any resident of the US. Jury, awards. Fee $10 for three works. For further information write Oklahoma Art Center, 3113 Pershing Blvd, Oklahoma City, OK 73107.

PENNSYLVANIA

CARNEGIE INSTITUTE THREE RIVERS ARTS FESTIVAL, Pittsburgh. Annual, June. Painting, sculpture, crafts, photographs, banners & prints. Open to all artists within Western Pa and surrounding communities. Juried visual arts. Fee, 25% comn. Entry cards & slides due Mar 19. For further information write John Jay, Exec Dir, Three Rivers Arts Festival, 4400 Forbes Ave, Pittsburgh, PA 15213.

ERIE ART CENTER/PHOTONATIONAL. Biennial, odd years, June-July. Open to all US artists. Juried. Purchase Awards. Fee $5 per photo. Entries due April. For further information write Photonational, Erie Art Center, 338 W 6th St, Erie, PA 16507.

PRINT CLUB BIENNIAL INTERNATIONAL OPEN EXHIBITION, Philadelphia. Biennial, Spring. Prints (limited edition only). Open to all. Juried, purchase awards; prizes become part of The Print Club collection at the Philadelphia Museum of Art. Fee $7. Entry details to be announced. For further information write Ofelia Garcia, Director, The Print Club, 1614 Latimer St, Philadelphia, PA 19103.

WASHINGTON & JEFFERSON COLLEGE NATIONAL PAINTING SHOW, Washington. Annual, Mar-Apr. All painting. Open to any US artist, 18 yrs old. Prizes & purchase awards. Fee $5 for one or two slide entries. Entry cards & slides due Jan, work due Mar. For further information write Paul B Edwards, Art Dept, Washington & Jefferson College, Washington, PA 15301.

RHODE ISLAND

ART ASSOCIATION OF NEWPORT.* Annual, July. Oil, watercolor, prints, drawings, photographs (alternate with small sculpture). Open to all American artists. Jury, awards. Fee $7 ($7 for 2 photograghs). Entry due early June. For further information write Art Association of Newport, 76 Bellevue Ave, Newport, RI 02840.

PROVIDENCE ART CLUB. Three open shows every year, scheduled at different times & varied from season to season; for instance, an open small sculpture show, an open drawing or print show, or perhaps a painting or craft show. For further information write Mrs Tore Dalenius, Providence Art Club, 11 Thomas St, Providence, RI 02903.

PROVIDENCE WATERCOLOR CLUB.* Annual, Oct-Nov. Watercolor. Open to New England artists. Cash awards, prizes & ribbons. Fee $8. Work due Oct 14. For further information write Providence Watercolor Club, 6 Thomas St, Providence, RI 02906.

SOUTH COUNTRY ART ASSOCIATION ANNUAL OPEN SHOW, Kingston. Annual, Apr. All media. Open to all professional artists. Jury, cash awards. Fee $3 per entry, limit 3 per artist. Entries due first Fri & Sat in Apr. For further information write South Country Art Association, Helme House, 1319 Kingstown, RI 02881.

SOUTH CAROLINA

ARTISTIC SASS. Annual, write for schedule. Clay, glass, metal, wood, fiber (incl wearables), paper (incl photography) and mixed media. Open to artists over 18 years of age. Purchase awards, one man shows. Fee $10. Entry due Feb 1. For further information write R L Tarchinski, Artistic Sass, PO Box 6005, Hilton Head, SC 29928.

SOUTHERN WATERCOLOR SOCIETY ANNUAL EXHIBITION. Annual, Feb to be held in Mississippi. Watercolor. Open to all artists living in 18 southern states, plus Washington, DC. Juried, $3000 awards. Fee $10 members, $25 non-members. Slides due November 15. For further information write Southern Watercolor Society, 6025 Lakeshore Dr, Columbia, SC 29206.

TENNESSEE

ANNUAL PAPER AND CLAY EXHIBITION,* Memphis. Annual, Feb-Mar. Drawing, prints, cast paper, ceramics, mixed media including paper and clay. Juried, awards. Fee $5, 2 entries. For further information write Nancy Sharpe, Art Dept, Memphis State Univ, Memphis, TN 38152 (enclose SASE).

BROOKS MEMORIAL ART GALLERY MID-SOUTH EXHIBITION,* Memphis. Biennial, date for next exhibition not set. Paintings, drawings, sculpture, prints. Open to artists residing within 250 air miles of Memphis. Jury, awards. For further information write Mid-South Exhibition, Brooks Memorial Art Gallery, Overton Park, Memphis, TN 38112.

DULIN NATIONAL PRINT & DRAWING COMPETITION, Knoxville. Annual, May. Prints & drawings. Open to all artists living & working in the US. Prizes. Fee $5. Entry cards due mid-Mar, work due later Mar. For further information write Dulin Gallery of Art, 3100 Kingston Pike, Knoxville, TN 37919.

MISSISSIPPI RIVER CRAFT SHOW,* Memphis. Biennial, Sept-Oct. Open to craftsmen residing within the ten mid-continent states bordering the Mississippi River. For further information write Mississippi River Craft Show, Brooks Memorial Art Gallery, Overton Park, Memphis, TN 38112.

TENNESSEE ALL-STATE ARTISTS EXHIBITION,* Nashville. Annual, Nov. Oil, mixed, pastel, watercolor, graphics & sculpture. Open to all artists residing in Tennessee. Purchase awards. Fee $3 per entry; 10% comn. Entry cards & work due Sept 15-Oct 13. For further information write Watkins Institute, Sixth & Church, Nashville, TN 37219.

TENNESSEE ART LEAGUE & PARTHENON OF NASHVILLE CENTRAL SOUTH ART EXHIBITION. Annual, June. Painting, graphics, sculpture. Open to all artists of Ala, Ark, Ga, Ky, Miss, NC, SC, Tenn, Va & other areas within 300 miles of Nashville. Jury, awards and ribbons. Fee $5 per entry, limit 5. For further information write Tennessee Art League, 3011 Poston Ave, Nashville, TN 37203.

TEXAS

ABILENE FINE ARTS MUSEUM. Annual, Feb. Painting only. Open to all artists. Juried. Prizes awarded. For further information write Abilene Fine Arts Museum, PO Box 1858, Abilene TX 79604.

THE AMARILLO COMPETITION. Biennial, Dec. Any two-dimensional work. Open to all artists in Tex, NMex, Okla, Colo and Kan. Juried, purchase prizes and awards variable. Fee $5 per entry. Entries due October. For further information write Jerry Daviee, Curator, Amarillo Art Center, Box 447, Amarillo, TX 79178.

DEL MAR COLLEGE DRAWING & SMALL SCULPTURE SHOW, Corpus Christi. Annual, Apr. Any drawing or small sculpture. Open to all US artists. Jury, prizes & purchase awards. Fee $10 for one or two entries; all entries must conform to parcel post size. All drawings returned prepaid, sculpture collect. For further information write Joseph A Cain, Chmn, Dept of Fine Arts, Del Mar College, Corpus Christi, TX 78404.

EL PASO MUSEUM OF ART NATIONAL SUN CARNIVAL. Biennial, Dec. All painting. Open to any US citizen residing in the US and its territories. Jury, pruchase awards. For further information write Bill Rakocy, Curator of Collections, El Paso Museum of Art, 1211 Montana, El Paso, TX 79902.

HILL COUNTRY ARTS FOUNDATION ANNUAL JURIED ART EXHIBITION. Annual, Apr. All media painting & sculpture. Open to all persons residing in US. Juried, $1000 awards (total). Fee $5 per entry, limit 3. Entries due Apr 4-5. For further information write Hill Country Arts Foundation, PO Box 176, Ingram, TX 78025.

HILL COUNTRY ARTS FOUNDATION BIANNUAL GRAPHICS/ PHOTOGRAPHY EXHIBIT. Biannual, May-June. All media graphics and photography. Open to all persons residing in the US. Juried, $1000 total awards. Fee $5 per entry, limit three. Entries due May 2-3. For further information write Hill Country Arts Foundation, PO Box 176, Ingram, TX 78025.

RIO GRANDE VALLEY ARTS & CRAFTS EXPOSITION, Brownsville. Annual, Nov. All media. Open to all artists & craftsmen. For further information write Brownsville Art League, PO Box 3404, Brownsville, TX 78520.

TEXAS FINE ARTS ASSOCIATION ANNUAL EXHIBITION, Austin. Annual, May-June. Oil, acrylic, watercolor, drawing, sculpture & mixed media. Open to all artists residing in US. Jury, prizes, cash awards & purchase awards of approximately $5000. Fee $5 for non-members, $3 for members. Slides due Feb 1, work due Apr. For further information write Texas Fine Arts Association, PO Box 5023, Austin, TX 78763.

TEXAS WATERCOLOR SOCIETY EXHIBITION,* San Antonio. Annual, May. Transparent or opaque watercolor on paper; entries must be framed under plastic. Open to present and former residents of Texas. Cash awards, purchase awards. Fee $7.50 for painting for non-members, 10% comn. Entry cards & work due Jan 10. For further information write Texas Watercolor Society, 127 Canterbury Hill, San Antonio, TX 78209.

WEST TEXAS NATIONAL WATERCOLOR SHOW,* Lubbock. Annual, Dec-Jan. Watercolor. Open to all artists in US. Over $3500 in purchase prizes & awards. Fee $5 per entry, no limit. All will be by slides only; deadline for slides April 20. For further information write The Museum, Texas Tech University, PO Box 4499, Lubbock, TX 79409.

WORKS ON PAPER ANNUAL EXHIBITION,* San Marcos. Annual, Nov. Media on or of paper. Open to all US artists. Juried. Fee $10 per entry, limit three. For further information write Mark Todd, Art Dept, Southwest Texas State Univeristy, San Marcos, TX 78666.

UTAH

SPRINGVILLE MUSEUM OF ART ANNUAL NATIONAL APRIL SHOW. Annual, Apr. Paintings, drawings and prints. Open to all artists in the US. Juried, approximately $2000 cash prizes plus purchase awards. Fee $4 per work. Entries are pre-juried by slides. Prospectus available. For further information write Springville Museum of Art, 126 E 400th South, Springville, UT 84663.

UTAH STATEWIDE COMPETITION AND EXHIBIT, Salt Lake City. Annual, June through Labor Day. Painting, drawing, watercolor, sculpture, ceramics. Open to residents of Utah. Jury, $1000 purchase awards, other awards as merited. Entries due approx May 15 (varies each year). For further information write Utah Arts Council, 617 East South Temple, Salt Lake City, UT 84102.

VIRGINIA

IRENE LEACHE MEMORIAL EXHIBITION,* Norfolk. Biennial, Mar-Apr (even years). All painting & drawing media (pastels not acceptable). Open to artists residing in Virginia, North Carolina, South Carolina, Georgia, Maryland, West Virginia and District of Columbia. Jury, cash awards. Fee $10; limit three; 20% comn. Entry & cards due Jan 12. For further information write Irene Leache Memorial Exhibition, Chrysler Museum of Norfolk, Olney Rd & Mowbray Arch, Norfolk, VA 23510.

RICHMOND CRAFT FAIR.* Annual, Nov. US designer crafts, no oil/painting/kits, etc. Open to US designer craftsmen. Juried, 5 color slides, $2500 in purchase prize, and cash awards. Fee $3 slide, $30 booth, 15% comn. Entry slides due June 1. For further information write Ruth T Summers, Dir, Hand Work Shop, Inc, 7 N 6th St, Richmond, VA 23219.

ROANOKE FINE ARTS CENTER JURIED ARTIST EXHIBITION.* Annual, Nov. All media, except craft. Open to Virginia artists. Juried, purchase prizes and Certificates of Distinction. Fee $10, limit of three entries. For further information write Roanoke Fine Arts Center, 301 23rd St, SW, Roanoke, VA 24014.

VIRGINIA ARTISTS, Richmond. Biennial, May-June (odd years). Original paintings, drawings, watercolor, collages & sculpture. Jury, awards. Limit three works. Entries due Jan 1. For further information write Virginia Museum of Fine Arts, Boulevard & Grove Aves, Richmond, VA 23221.

VIRGINIA CRAFTSMEN,* Richmond. Biennial, Mar-Apr. Personally designed crafts in metal, textile, wood, ceramics & leather. Open to natives and residents of Virginia and those former residents who lived in Virginia for three years. Jury, awards. Limit of three works. Entries due by Jan. For further information write Virginia Museum of Fine Arts, Boulevard & Grove Aves, Richmond, VA 23221.

VIRGINIA DESIGNERS, Richmond. Biennial, Jan-Feb. Open to professional designers who are natives and residents of Va and those former residents who lived in Va for three years. Jury, awards. No fee, limit of eight entries. Entries due by Nov. For further information write Virginia Museum of Fine Arts, Boulevard & Grove Aves, Richmond, VA 23221.

VIRGINIA PHOTOGRAPHERS, Richmond. Biennial, May-June. Monochrome & color photographic prints. Open to natives & residents of Va & those former residents who live in Va for three years. Jury, awards. No entry fee, limit five prints. Entries by Feb 15. For further information write Virginia Museum of Fine Arts, Boulevard & Grove Aves, Richmond, VA 23221.

WASHINGTON

JURIED EXHIBITION OF PHOTOGRAPHIC ART ANNUAL,* Richland. Annual, Sept-Oct. Photography. Open to US. Juried, cash awards. Fee $3 per print, limit 3; 20% comn. For further information write John Clement, 313 Bernard, Richland, WA 99352.

NEW PHOTOGRAPHICS, Ellensburg. Annual, Apr-May. Photography. Open internationally. Juried, no prizes. No fee. Entry slides due Mar. For further information write Central Washington University, Art Department, Ellensburg, WA 98926.

NORTHWEST CRAFTS EXHIBITION,* Seattle. Biennial, Oct-Nov (odd years). Crafts in all media. Open to craftspeople presently working or residing in the states of Washington, Oregon, Idaho, Montana, Wyoming, and Alaska. Juried with awards. No entry fee. Entries due

September. For further information write Henry Art Gallery, University of Washington, Seattle, WA 98195.

NORTHWEST WATERCOLOR SOCIETY EXHIBITION, Bellevue. Annual, May. Water based painting on paper. Open to residents of Alaska, Idaho, Mont, Ore, Wash & BC. Cash, merchandise, & purchase awards. Fee $5, 30% comn. For further information or prospectus write Northwest Watercolor Society, 420 Tenth Ave, Kirkland, WA 98033.

WEST VIRGINIA

HUNTINGTON GALLERIES—EXHIBITION 280: PAINTING, SCULPTURE AND CRAFTS. Biennial, Mar-Apr. Open to artists above high school age, living within 280 miles of Huntington. Jury, awards. Fee. Slide entries due Dec, accepted work due Jan. For further information write Exhibition 280, Program Coordinator, Huntington Galleries, 2033 McCoy Rd, Huntington, WV 25701.

WISCONSIN

LAKEFRONT FESTIVAL OF ARTS,* Milwaukee. Annual. June. Multi-media. Open to professional artists and craftsmen from across the country. Juried, $5000 in prizes. Fee $8. Entries due mid-March. For further information write Milwaukee Art Center, 750 N Lincoln Memorial Dr, Milwaukee, WI 53202.

STEVENS POINT FINE ARTS EXHIBITION.* Annual, Oct. Painting, drawing graphics. Open to all artists residing in Wisconsin. Jury, $500 top award, other cash & purchase awards. Fee $10. Entry cards & work due Oct 21. For further information write Mrs James Delzell, 1124 Ridge Rd, Stevens Point, WI 54481.

WYOMING

WESTERN STATES ART EXHIBITION,* Cody. Annual, June-July. Oil, watercolor, graphics, pastels, sculpture, ceramics & other (all work must be suitable for hanging). Open to all artists. Cash awards & ribbons. Fee $5 prof, $3.50 amateur for each work, limit three. For further information write Cody County Art League, PO Box 1524, Cody, WY 82414.

BRITISH COLUMBIA

MUSEUM OF NORTHERN BRITISH COLUMBIA, PRINCE RUPERT MUSEUM ART GALLERY.* Annual, and biennial, Summer, late Spring, Christmas. Mixed, mainly oil, tempera, etc but includes sculpture in different media and crafts. Open to local and regional artists. Juried for photography or school art. For further information write Museum Art Gallery Coordinator, Box 669, Prince Rupert, BC V8J 3S1, Canada.

ONTARIO

SOUTHWEST 40, Windsor. Annual, March. All media. Open to artists of the southwestern Ont region. Jury prizes. Fee $3. Entries due Feb 17. For further information write The Art Gallery of Windsor, 445 Riverside Dr W, Windsor, ON N9A 6T8, Canada.

WESTERN ONTARIO EXHIBITION,* London. Annual, May. All painting media, sculpture, prints, drawings, wall hangings (batik or woven). Open to all residents of Southwestern Ontario. Jury, prizes & awards. No fee. Entries due early Apr. For further information write Secretary, Annual Western Ontario Exhibition, London Art Gallery, 305 Queen's Ave, London, ON N6B 1X2, Canada.

QUEBEC

CONCOURS D'ESTAMPE ET DE DESSIN QUEBECOIS, Sherbrooke. Biennial, June-Aug. Prints, drawings, all media. Open to all artists residing in Quebec. Juried, $3000 in prizes. No fee. Entries due February 28. For further information write Graham Cantieni Directeur Artistique, Centre Culturel, Universite de Sherbrooke, Sherbrooke, PQ J1K 2R1, Canada.

Traveling Exhibition Booking Agencies

ALBERTA ART FOUNDATION, 11th Floor, CN Tower, 10004-104 Ave, Edmonton, AB, T7J OK1, Canada. *Coordr/Consultant* W Tin Ng
Exhibits—Printmakers of Alberta—19 prints by contemporary artists. Other exhibitions can be arranged if interested parties write and indicate space available. Requests giving an advance notice of 4 months would be appreciated. No rental fee. Transportation arrangements: the Foundation will pre-pay one way and the borrower is responsible for the cost of returning the exhibitions. Catalogs available.

ALABAMA ART LEAGUE,* Montgomery Museum of Fine Arts, 440 South McDonough St, Montgomery, AL 36104. *Pres* A Phillip Coley.
Exhibit—approx 25-30 drawings, prints and small paintings selected from the annual juried exhibit by juror. No rental fee; in-state, pulled via trailer by Art League member; out-of-state, arrangements can be made. Catalog available.

AMARILLO ART CENTER, 2200 S Van Buren, Box 447, Amarillo, TX 79178. *Dir* Thomas A Livesay.
Exhibits—American Images, photographs from the Farm Security Administration; currently the exhibit is circulating with assistance from the National Endowment for the Humanities. Full description in *Humanities* magazine, Spring, 1977. Rental fee $150 through 1980; $250 after Jan 1981. Catalogs available.

AMERICAN ABSTRACT ARTISTS,* 1110 Park Ave, New York, NY 10028. *Pres* Judith Rothschild
Traveling shows available. No set rental fees.

AMERICAN FEDERATION OF ARTS, 41 E 65th St, New York, NY 10021. *Dir* Wilder Green.
Approximately 30 exhibitions circulated in the US and abroad—Painting, sculpture, graphic arts, photography, design and crafts. Exhibitions and catalogues organized by AFA with guest curators for museums, colleges, schools and art centers.

THE AMERICAN INSTITUTE OF GRAPHIC ARTS, 1059 Third Ave, New York, NY 10021. *Exec Dir* Caroline Hightower; *Coordr, Traveling Exhibitions* Glenngo Allen King.
Exhibits—The work of Ivan Chermayeff and Thomas Gelsmar. Consists of 20 photo-panels representing a broad spectrum of their work. Each panel is 46 x 67 x 9/16 inches and weighs 22 pounds. Rental fee is $150 to non-members and $100 to members of AIGA. Labeling information is provided. Exhibitor is responsible for insurance and shipping costs to next destination.
Posters 1973-1978—Posters from that period representing a brilliant visual spectrum of American culture and consumer concerns. Contains 170 pieces. Fee varies for members and non-members.
Traveling Slide Exhibitions—John Berg at CBS; Best Books; The Caricatures of David Levine; Communicating With Children; Communication Graphics; Covers; Environmental Design: Sinage and Graphics; Federal Design Response; Insides '78; John Lustig 1915-1955; James McMullan, Socio-Journalism; Mass/Comm, Mass/Trans; Portraits; Symbol Signs; Bradbury Thompson, AIGA Medalist 1975; Wit; Henry Wolfe, AIGA Medalist 1976. Brochure available.

AMERICAN WATERCOLOR SOCIETY, 14 E 90th St, New York, NY 10028. *Chmn Traveling Exhibitions* Dale Meyers.
Exhibits—One exhibition of fifty paintings is selected by the Jury of Awards from our annual exhibitions for a one-year circuit. The exhibition is framed. Several prizewinners from the annual are included. The framed show weighs about 1500 pounds. The AWS annuals are all juried, member and non-member, and are held each April in New York. Requests cannot be considered until the following September. Rental fee of $200 per week (two week minimum) booking. Exhibiting organizations pay on-going shipping. AWS carries limited insurance during the circuit. Two of the Annual Exhibition Catalogs (containing traveling exhibition listings and itineraries) are provided, plus publicity information and several black and white photographs of prize winning paintings.

ANCHORAGE HISTORICAL AND FINE ARTS MUSEUM, 121 W. Seventh Ave, Anchorage, AK 99501. *Dir* R L Shalkop.
Circulation of exhibitions in Alaska only. No rental fee; transportation variable. No catalogs available.

ARKANSAS ARTS CENTER, State Services, PO Box 2137, Little Rock, AR 72203. *Contact* Patti Maguire.
Exhibits—Facade by Louise Nevelson; DisFarmer: The Heber Springs Portraits 1939-1946; Untitled Etchings by Donald Judd; George Fisher Cartoons; Landscape; Young Arkansas Artists; Inez Whitfield Watercolors; Old Roots, New Directions: Arkansas Blues Today; Shape; Human Images in Prints; Ten West Coast Artists; Texture; Crafts; Watercolor: Works by Robert Andrew Parker; Toys Designed by Artists; Japanese Prints; Twenty Works on Paper; How to Kill; Ways of Seeing: An Exhibit for the Visually Impaired; Meyer Shapiro Portfolio; Arkansas Weavers' Work; Prints by Evan Lindquist and Ed Bernstein. Rental fees, out of state, $50 - $250. Shipping charges are extra. Catalogues are available for Works by Evan Lindquist and Ed Bernstein. Panels of text accompany other exhibitions. Additional exhibit information is available upon request.

ARKANSAS STATE UNIVERSITY, Drawer AAAA, Art Department, State University, AR 72467. *Coordinator of Traveling Exhibitions* Donn Hedman.
Faculty Traveling Exhibit—11 participating artists, 50 two-dimensional pieces—oils, watercolors, prints, drawings; 25 three-dimensional pieces—sculpture, ceramics, jewelry. Works range from traditional to contemporary. No rental fee, shipping one way. Catalogs available.

ART GALLERY OF ONTARIO, EXTENSION SERVICES, Grange Park, Toronto, ON M5T 1G4, Canada. *Head, Extension Services* Nancy Hushion.
Exhibits—Artists with their Work; A Canadian Survey; Selected Works from the Collection of Imperial Oil Limited; Coming Out: Six Generations of Women, photography by Susan Trow: Louis Comtois: Paintings 1974-1979; Contact 1979-1980; Contact 1980-1981; Drawings from Punch; Equipment for Eternity: Egyptian Arts and Crafts of the New Kingdom 1570 to 1085 B.C.; Figures and Portraits in the Thirties and Forties; Folk Art Treasures of Quebec; Hogarth's London; Humorist Walter Trier: A Selection from the Trier-Fodor Foundation Gift; Ketubah: Jewish Marriage Contracts; Master Prints from the Presgrave Collection; Prints by David Hockney; Sculpture of the 60's; Selected Impressions: Recent Acquisitions of Master Prints from the Fifteenth to the Twentieth Century. Rental fees vary.

ART IN ARCHITECTURE, 1434 S Spaulding Ave, Los Angeles, CA 90019. *Exec Dir* Millicent Young
Exhibit—Joseph Young's Triforium. 50 working drawings, photographs and technical studies outlining the designing, prefabrication and construction of the City of Los Angeles million dollar art symbol. Completed in 1975 by Joseph Young, one of America's most controversial architectural artists, the 60 ft high Triforium is the world's first major permanent polyphonoptic sculpture that was built between 1969 and 1975. Rental fee for 30 days $600, plus airfreight costs and insurance from previous exhibitor; exhibition can be accompanied by personal presentation by artist. Catalogs, posters, brochures and advance pr available.

ASSOCIATED AMERICAN ARTISTS,* 663 Fifth Ave, New York, NY 10022. *Dir* Sylvan Cole. *Traveling Exhibitions* Robert Koo.
Original prints in all media by artists of many countries. Etchings, lithographs, woodcuts, serigraphs, intaglios, stencils, in black and white, and in color.
Group Exhibitions—American Master Prints; Authors! Authors!; Prints by Jack Coughlin and Sidney Chafetz; New Talent in Printmaking.
One-Man Shows—John Taylor Arms, Mario Avati, Milton Avery, Will Barnet, Thomas Hart Benton, John Steuart Curry, Fritz Eichenberg, Lyonel Feininger, Rockwell Kent, Armin Landeck, Raphael Soyer, Paul Wunderlich.
Private and public organizations and institutions having facilities for the care of the fine prints eligible. Rental fees from $100 to $250. For additional information, please write or call 212-755-4211.

ASSOCIATION OF SCIENCE-TECHNOLOGY CENTERS (ASTC), 1016 16th St, NW, Washington, DC 20036. *Traveling Exhibitions* Sheila Grinell, Dana Perry.
Exhibits—Museum quality exhibitions on science, technology, arts-and-science, natural history, and general culture. Exhibition formats included are photography shows, art work and artifact collections and "hands-on" exhibits emphasizing viewer participation. Offerings include: Vasarely-29 works by the master of optical art; Tangata-33 large, color photographs of Maori carvings from New Zealand; People of the Cedar-41 contemporary Northwest Coast Indian crafts; The Many Faces of Fuji-65 photographs of Japan's symbolic mountain by Koyo Okada. Rental fees are charged for exhibitions, and exhibitors are responsible for the cost of inbound shipping unless otherwise specified. Shipping arrangements are made by ASTC. ASTC Travel Exhibition Service Catalog available free; call 202-452-0655.

BALL STATE UNIVERSITY ART GALLERY, Muncie, IN 47306. *Assist to Dir* Dolores Terhune.
Exhibits—Indiana Printmakers II—An exhibit made possible with the support of a grant from the Indiana Arts Commission and the National Endowment for the Arts, will be available for travel throughout Indiana from October, 1980 through September, 1982. The only cost to the exhibitor will be transportation of the exhibit one way. Catalog available.

BALTIMORE MUSEUM OF ART, Art Museum Drive, Traveling Exhibitions, Baltimore, MD 21218. *Dir of Educ* Susan S Badder.
Exhibits—Barye's Animals; Fellowship Exhibition II; Landscape Observed and Transformed; Montage of Dreams Deferred; Prints By a Sculptor: Richard Hunt; The Romance of Travel. Six to seven exhibitions per year, approximately 30 pieces in each. Rental fee $75 per 4-week booking; includes transportation, installation, printed brochures and posters. Catalogs available.

BALZEKAS MUSEUM OF LITHUANIAN CULTURE, 4012 Archer Ave, Chicago, IL 60632. *Pres* Stanley Balzekas, Jr.
Six small portable cases which include history, maps, and some memorabilia on Lithuania dating back 300 years. Rental fee is $150 plus transportation.

THE BRONX COUNTY HISTORICAL SOCIETY, 3266 Bainbridge Ave, Bronx, NY 10467. *Dir* G Hermalyn.
Exhibits—The Bronx River; 30 pieces. Faces of Edgar Allan Poe; 40 pieces. No rental fee. Transportation and insurance paid by borrower.

BURCHFIELD CENTER-WESTERN NEW YORK FORUM FOR AMERICAN ART, State University of New York College at Buffalo, 1300 Elmwood Ave, Buffalo, NY 14222. *Dir* Edna M Lindemann.
Exhibit—Charles Burchfield, His Painting and Related Work. The exhibition includes 50 works by the American watercolorist, mostly works from the Burchfield Center Permanent Collection. The works include 14 paintings, 26 drawings, sketches and doodles, seven wallpapers, including two original tempera designs and five wallpapers printed by the Birge Company, and three woodcuts, drawn by Burchfield and cut by Julius J Lankes. Rental fee $1750, plus transportation and insurance. In New York State travel arrangements may be made through the Gallery Association of New York State; others by arrangement. Catalogs are included in rental fee.

C W POST ART GALLERY,* C W Post College, Long Island University, Greenvale, NY 11548. *Dir* Joan Vita Miller.
Exhibits—Gertrude Stein and her Friends. A photographic exhibition consisting of 28 (30 x 40) photographic enlargements from Yale University's Beinecke Rare Book and Manuscript Library. The collection gives the viewer insight into the stimulating world of art and literature of an era inhabited by such luminaries as Picasso, Matisse, Braque, Renoir, Gris, Picabia and Vellotton. Fifty illustrated catalogs (20 pages) with an introduction by James Mellow, former New York Times art critic will be included.

C W Post Permanent Collection. An exhibition of contemporary graphics selected from the permanent collection represents a variety of styles comprising 20th century printmaking. No catalog available.
Rental fee is $250 per month. Transportation to be arranged.

JOHN C CALHOUN STATE COMMUNITY COLLEGE, The Art Gallery, Highway 31 North, Room 237-Fine Arts Bldg, Decature, AL 35602. *Dir* Helen Austin.
Exhibits—25 framed student photographs; 105 lineal feet.
The Classic Ideal in Nineteenth Century Tennessee Valley Architecture (available after Jan, 1981). The rental fee varies from $150 to $350 per show. Transportation and insurance costs must be prepaid by host. Catalog available.

CAMPBELL MUSEUM, Campbell Place, Camden, NJ 08101. *Museum Asst* Bess Brock.
Exhibit—18th & 19th century porcelain and soup tureens and accompanying catalogues. No rental fee. All transportation costs paid by Campbell Museum.

CENTER FOR CREATIVE PHOTOGRAPHY, 843 East University Blvd, Tucson, AZ 85719. *Center Asst/Exhib* Marnie Gillett.
Exhibits—Ansel Adams: A Survey. 40 framed prints personally selected by Adams to represent his long and distinguished career in photography. 100 running feet. Rental fee $500 per month.
Ansel Adams—Photographs of the Southwest: 1928-1968. 100 framed prints. This exhibition is a landmark as it culminates 40 years of work by Adams in the Southwest states. 200 running feet. Rental fee $1,000 per month.
Wynn Bullock—A retrospective selection of 50 framed prints (1939-1973) including many of Bullock's most well-known nude images, realistic nature studies, and negative abstractions. Rental fee $600 per month.
Harry Callahan—Photographs in Color by Harry Callahan. Callahan selected this exhibit of 53 dye transfer prints representing his Kodachrome images made between 1946 and 1978. Exhibition catalog available at $5.00 each with a 40% discount to renting institutions. Rental fee $600 per month.
Photography of the Fifties—100 framed photographs by American photographers done in the 1950's. Guest curated by Helen Gee. Catalog available at $8.95 each with a 40% discount to renting institutions. Rental fee $2,500 per month.

CHEROKEE NATIONAL MUSEUM, PO Box 515, TSA-LA-GI, Tahlequah, OK 74464. *Exec VPres* M A Hagerstrand.
Exhibits—Cherokee History and Culture; limited Indian Art on the Trail of Tears theme. Temporary exhibitions arranged with small institutions to their needs and desires and our capabilities and schedule. Rental fees arranged for each exhibit. No catalogs available.

CHINESE CULTURE FOUNDATION OF SAN FRANCISCO, 750 Kearny St, San Francisco, CA 94108. *Registrar* Greg Soone.
Exhibits—"Locke: A Chinese Community on the Sacramento Delta" by James Motlow. 45 photographs framed (16x20 inches) with and introductory panel and accompanying descriptive labels in both English & Chinese. Rental fee $250 plus shipping costs to next destination. No catalog available.

CLEMSON UNIVERSITY,* College of Architecture, Rudolph Lee Gallery, PO Box 992, Clemson, SC 29631. *Coordinator of Educational Media and Exhibits* Tom Dimond.
Exhibits—Foundry Art, 50 wooden patterns for industrial machines; photographs demonstrating casting process; SC Architecture, 114 black and white photo murals describing 300 years of South Carolina architecture. Rental fee and transportation arrangements on request.

DELAWARE ART MUSEUM,* 2301 Kentmere Parkway, Wilmington, DE 19806. *Coordinator Traveling Exhibitions* Susan Hall Brooks.
Three types of loan material available to the public—exhibitions (mounted reproductions ready for hanging); portfolios (slightly smaller pictures suitable for classroom); and slides (for supplementing your exhibition, class lecture). The material includes photography, reproductions, original works of art, records of recent exhibitions. Please call or write for additional information. No rental fee for in-state schools; out-of-state institutions annual fee of $25, mailing charges additional. Catalogs available.

DE SAISSET ART GALLERY & MUSEUM, University of Santa Clara, Santa Clara, CA 95053. *Dir* Brigid S Barton.
Exhibits—John Altoon Drawings—75 drawings chosen from the Altoon estate traveling through Western Association of Art Museums. Catalogue. Fee $1480 for members of WAAM; $1925 for non-members.
Contemporary Hand-Colored Photographs—Work by 20 artists of the Western United States. Catalogue. Fees to be announced.

EDMONTON ART GALLERY,* 2 Sir Winston Churchill Square, Edmonton, AB, Canada T5J 2C1. *Exten Cur* Ray Quellet.
Exhibits—William Tilland—Landscpae Photographs (28 photographs 14 x 18, 42 running feet); rental fee $150.
William Leroy Stevenson (26 oil paintings, most 24 x 30, 120 running feet); rental fee $200.
Violet Owen—Drawings and Paintings (20 works, 100 running feet); rental fee $150.
Alan Reynolds—Drawings by a Sculptor (20 drawings, 4 photographs, 16 x 20, 100 running feet); rental fee $100.
Signey Tillim—Adam and Eve Drawings (38 works 14 x 18, 80 running feet); rental fee $200.
The John Henry Hinton Photographs—China 1894-1918 (70 prints from original negatives, framed 14 x 18, 210 running feet); rental fee $200.
Rental fees, as noted with each exhibit. Crates provided. Exhibiting center pays one-way shipping charges. Insurance cost included in rental fee. Catalogs or posters available.

EDO COMPREHENSIVE EXHIBITION SERVICES, 453 Sycamore Road, Santa Monica, CA 90402. William Osmun. Tel: 213-454-8041.
Exhibits—Amish Quilts, about 1880-1930; Jasper Johns/Screenprints, 1968-1978; Herbert Bayer: Photographic Works, 1925-1936; Pictures of a Floating World, Japanese Woodcuts, late 18th-mid-19th centuries; The Graham Nash Collection, 19th & 20th Century Photographs; Earthworks-Land Reclamation as Sculpture; The Bizarre Imagery of Yoshitoshi; The Sensuous Line, Indian Drawings of the 17th, 18th and 19th centuries from the Paul F Walter Collection; Navajo Blankets 1850's-1890's from the collection of Anthony Berlant; Brooke Alexander, A Decade of Print Publishing, 1968-1978; Indonesian Textiles. Rental fees $850—$3,000; participant pays one-way transportation. Catalogs available.

ESMARK, INC, 55 E Monroe, Chicago, IL 60603. *Mgr Corporate Affairs* Liz Sode.
Exhibits—A collection of Currier & Ives prints capturing early American life—650 original Currier & Ives lithographs and memorabilia broken into four groups, each providing a cross-section of Currier & Ives works. They are loaned by contract as complete units.
The Legacy of Currier & Ives is a 16mm sound and color 23 minute film providing an extraordinary perspective of the nation's growth during its westward expansion. Over 200 prints from the Esmark Collection are shown in this movie which is made available for use in classrooms and meetings of civic and service organizations.

FISK UNIVERSITY MUSEUM, 18th & Jackson Sts, PO Box 2, Nashville, TN 37203. *Cur* R Hall.
Exhibits—William H Johnson exhibit (matted, 17 prints); Works by Contemporary Afro-Americans (20 paintings, prints & photographs); Works on Paper (17 prints & drawings by Afro-Americans). Rental fee and transportation paid for by exhibitor.

FLORIDA ARTIST GROUP, INC,* c/o Art Department, Stetson University, Deland, FL 32720. *Chmn Art Dept* Fred Messersmith.
Jury chosen Annual Exhibition of Members Show (34—45 entries) is available following the Spring Exhibition (May). Also, from the local areas other traveling exhibitions are available throughout the year (includes paintings, graphics, sculpture, assemblages). No rental fees; self-financed, hopefully, with help from the galleries and museums. Catalogs available for the Spring Annual.

FOLGER SHAKESPEARE LIBRARY,* 201 East Capitol St, SE, Washington DC, 20003. *Dir* O B Hardison, Jr.
Exhibit—Shakespeare: The Globe and The World.

FORT HAYS STATE UNIVERSITY, Department of Art, Hays, KS 67601. *Chmn* John C Thorns, Jr.
Varied exhibitions available depending upon the desire of the individual renting the exhibition. Rental fee: $50 plus shipping charges. No catalog available.

FREEDMAN GALLERY-ALBRIGHT COLLEGE, 13th & Exeter Sts, Reading, PA 19603. Tel 215-921-2381, Ext 337. *Dir* Marilyn A Zeitlin.
Exhibits—Janet Fish Show—200 running feet. Paintings & pastels. Available 1980-81. Rental fee $2000. Private or Artransport. Catalog available.
Architects as Artists—12 artists, including Aldo Rossi, Michael Graves, John Hejduk. Rental fee $1200. Transportation by private truck. Catalog available.

FRENCH CULTURAL SERVICES, Exhibitions Department, 972 Fifth Ave, New York, NY 10021. Tel 212-570-4400.
Photography Exhibits—Andre Villers: "Diurnes", a photographic (black and white) and montage essay done in collaboration with Picasso; Etienne Bertrand Weill—Metaforms (color and black & white); Collection Kahn—Autochromes, first color photographs (Tonkin, Ireland); Americans in France—Margi Ide Brockmon, Richard W Golden; Jaydie Putterman; French Photography 1975-1976—50 black and white photographs; Color from France—Philippe de Croix, Florence Gruere, Jean-Philippe Jourdrin, Lilian Rovers; Photographie Actuelle En France 1978—A selection of works by French photographers, representing today's trends in French photography, 52 Black and white photographs; A Certain Image of French Photography—50 black and white photographs assembled by The Foundation Nationale de la Photographie, by 25 well and lesser-known photographers; The Concrete Eye—60 black & white and color photographs by Michel DeLaborde, Jean-Claude Gautrand, Bernard Plossu and Yan Rocher; Philippe Salaun and D. H. Seylan-Two French Photographers—40 photographs; The Sky of the Earth-Jean-Marie Chourgnoz—50 black and white photographs.
Documentary Exhibits—Pictures of American Independence (from the collection of the Chateay of Blerancourt)—64 photographic panels; Victor Segalen 1878-1919—115 photographs; 19th & Early 20th Century French Illustrators (The Artine Artinian Collection)—30 original drawings; Posters of the 1980's—original turn-of-the-century posters from France; Tendencies of French Contemporary Architecture—96 photographs; Churches and Cathedrals—81 black and white photographs; Cinema—80 years of French movies; Le Metropolitain—68 black and white and color photographs about the Paris subway—yesterday, today, and tomorrow; Six Looks—The National Art and Culture Center—Georges Pompidou seen by six French contemporary photographers, 68 black and white photographs; French Cheeses and Wines—34 panels, with accompanying texts by Roy de Groot; Traditional Crafts—A photographic survey, 23 color illustrated panels; The Paris Opera—34 photographs mounted on cardboard; The French Novel Since 1945—photographs of, and about, contemporary French writers, 60 masonite panels; Maurice Ravel 1875-1937—A survey of the French composer's life, 80 black and white photographs; Jules Verne 1828-1905—16 black and white illustrated panels; Nadar 1820-1910—55 black and white photographs mounted on cardboard; Colette—The most famous French woman writer of her day, 73 black and white and color photographs; George Sand 1804-1876—112 black and white and color photographs; Moliere 1622-1673—77 black and white photographs and 22 text panels; Max Jacob 1876-1944—68 black and white and color photographs; Jean-Jacques Rousseau 1712-1778—95 black and white photographs; Voltaire 1694-1778—49 black and white and color photographs.
No rental fees, but one-way shipping costs plus insurance paid by exhibitor. Press releases available upon request. Catalog available.

GALERIE D'ART DU CENTRE CULTUREL, Universite de Sherbrooke, Sherbrooke, PQ J1K 2R1, Canada. *Dir* Graham Cantieni.
Exhibits—Artists of the Eastern Townships. 30 works on paper by members of the Regroupement des Artistes des Coulours de l'Est. Rental fee $200, plus transportation one way or to next center. No catalog available.

GALERIE RESTIGOUCHE GALLERY, 39 Andrew St, PO Box 674, Campbellton, NB E3N 3H1, Canada. *Dir & Curator* Paul Soucy.
Exhibits—Couleurs d'Acadie—Color photographs of brightly painted houses phenomena. 120 running feet. No rental fee. Borrower pays cost of transportation both ways. Catalog available.
Young Sculpture and Painting—Four contemporary artists from Montreal. 1500 square feet; 150 running feet. Rental fee $400 for one or two months, plus transportation to next center. Catalog available.
Two Maritime Sculptors—Luc Charette, environmental sculptor; Jacques Martin, wood sculptures. 1500 square feet. Rental fee $250 for one or two months, plus transportation to next center. Catalog available.

GUND COLLECTION OF WESTERN ART, One Erieview Plaza, Cleveland, OH 44114 (Mailing address: 14 Nassau St, PO Box 449, Princeton, NJ 08540). *Exec Dir* Diane Mitnaul.
Exhibit—Late 19th and early 20th century American Western Art (emphasis on Frederic S Remington, Charles M Russell; includes several Bierstadts, Farneys, A J Millers), 70 pieces. Collection is loaned to any interested museum or facility which meets security standards. No rental fee; exhibitor pays cost of insurance and shipping. Catalog available.

HOFSTRA UNIVERSITY,* Emily Lowe Gallery, Hempstead, NY 11550. *Dir* Kevin E Consey.
Exhibit—The Art of Boxing, 18th, 19th and 20th century prints, drawings, paintings and sculpture with boxing as the subject matter. Included are works by Riggs, Bellows, Cruikshank, Rowlandson, Currier & Ives, and Nieman, a total of 57 works. Rental fee of $500 for 6-8 week period; includes 100 catalogs.

HUDSON RIVER MUSEUM,* 511 Warburton Ave, Trevor Park on Hudson, Yonkers, NY 10701. *Dir* Richard Koshalek.
Exhibit—Lee Friedlander—Photographs, 150 black and white photographs with an illustrated book (137 black and white reproductions). Rental fee is $1,000 for a four week period. Photographs are framed under plexiglas and will be crated for shipping. Included in the fee are 25 free copies of the book, all expenses of insurance and crating and one-way transportation. Framed size of each photograph is 14 x 18 inches.

ILLINOIS STATE UNIVERSITY,* University Museums, Normal, IL 61761. *Dir* Roslyn A Walker-Oni.
Two exhibits—Development of the Figure Concept in Graphic Art Work by Children from Different Countries, 65 originals, requiring display space of 180-240 running feet, insurance $650; The Development of Spatial Relations in the Graphic Art Work by Children from Different Countries, 59 originals requiring display space of 180-240 running feet, insurance $590.
Rental fee: $100 plus return transportation. Explanatory text includes script, a list notating age, sex, size, country, title and accession number.

INDEPENDENT CURATORS INCORPORATED, 799 Broadway, New York, NY 10003. *Exec Dir* Susan Sollins; *Asst Dir* Anne Cohen DePietro; *Coordr* Patricia Reville.
Specialists in exhibitions of contemporary art and photography which are circulated throughout the US and abroad. Also offering educational consulting services.
Exhibits—(Partial listing) Supershow!—An introduction to contemporary art for children and adults. Painting, sculpture, video, and sonic art by 19 artists, including Cecile Abish, Mark di Suvero, Nancy Graves, Red Grooms, Claes Oldenburg, and Barbara Zucker. Three specially commissioned works. Rental fee $7500 (for a 6 to 8 week booking).
Collaborations and Amplifications—Explores collaborative efforts between visual artists and performing artists as well as sets and costumes created by visual artists who also perform in their own pieces. Costumes, props, sets, working drawings, and maquettes by 11 artists such as Eleanor Antin, Roger Brown, Jasper Johns, Joan Jonas, Alex Katz, Ann Wilson and Robert Wilson. Rental fee $2500.
Masks—Forty one works, including over 100 masks, made by 18 contemporary maskmakers. Focuses on selected variety of individual developments and explorations on the subject of masks. Some pieces were created for use in performance situations; others were never intended to be worn. Artists include Niki Edson, Robert Harding, Manuel Neri, Peter Schumann, Elke Solomon, and Jeff Way. Rental fee $1200.
Some Color Photographs—In the 1960's and 1970's American artists and photographers such as Jan Groover, Hans Namuth, Edward Ruscha, Lucas Samaras, and Eve Sonneman began to create color photographs intended to be viewed as art objects. Included are pieces by photographers trained in the tradition of black and white work as well as those who have achieved recognition primarily for their work in color. 30 works by 30 artists. Rental fee $700.
Mapped Art: Charts, Routes, Regions—Documents increasing use of maps and cartographic activity. Classified into three basic categories: charts, routes, and regions. Includes a wide variety of approaches and interpretations by artists such as John Cage, Agnes Denes, Dick Higgins, Susan Kaprov, Piero Manzoni, Joanne Snitzer, Michelle Stuart, and Roger Welch. Rental fee to be determined. Rental fees stated above are for 4-week period except where indicated. Exhibitor pays incoming shipping. Catalogues available.

INDIANA UNIVERSITY AT SOUTH BEND, 1700 Mishawaka Ave, South Bend, IN 46615. *Project Coordr* Janice Langland.
Exhibits—Four Figurative Artists—Two painters, a sculptor, and a printmaker are equally represented in this 40-piece exhibition of figurative art. This exhibition is designed to fit in an Econoline van and comes in crates small enough for two people to handle without special equipment. No rental fee, but borrower is responsible for insuring the work for $30,000. Transportation by Econoline van is the responsibility of the gallery. Catalog available.

INSTITUTE OF AMERICAN INDIAN ARTS MUSEUM, Cerrillos Rd, Santa Fe, NM 87501. *Dir* Charles Dailey
Exhibits—One With the Earth—Major traveling exhibit of Native American Indian arts and crafts, which includes 110 items; self-contained exhibit with pedestals, plastic cases, panels systems and plastic labels. Available for 3-5 week showings; request exhibitor to have a Native American Group as regional co-sponsor. Rental fee $600, plus gasoline.
Selections from the BIA/IAIA Collections. Four traveling exhibitions of paintings by contemporary Native American artists. Borrower pays only for transportation both ways.

INTERNATIONAL EXCHANGE PRINT EXHIBITIONS, Portland Art Museum, 1219 SW Park Ave, Portland, OR 97205. Tel: 503-226-2811. *Cur Prints & Drawings* Gordon W Gilkey.
Exhibits of about 100 each contemporary original graphic arts from abroad with new exhibits imported each year. Prorated expenses plus one-way transportation. Catalogs on request.

INTERNATIONAL EXHIBITIONS FOUNDATION, 1729 H St, NW, Suite 310, Washington, DC 20006. Tel: 202-298-7010. *President* Mrs John A Pope.
Organizes and circulates major art exhibitions throughout the United States, Canada and Europe. Exhibitions in the field of painting, drawings, prints, photographs, architecture, sculpture, folk art and decorative arts are available. Approximately 50 percent are special loan exhibitions from abroad, usually the first of their kind. All exhibitions are accompanied by scholarly catalogues published by the Foundation for the museums participating in the tours. Many exhibitions are also supplemented by educational, interpretive materials such as slides, films, photomurals, etc. Exhibitions are available to museums and university and college galleries for a wide range of rental fees plus transportation charges to the next exhibitor.

INTERNATIONAL MUSEUM OF PHOTOGRAPHY, 900 East Ave, Rochester, NY 14607. Tel: 716-271-3361. *Dir* Robert Doherty.
Exhibits—Contemporary Photographers VII; Lewis Hine; Arnold Newman; Contemporary Photographers VIII: Gary Metz, Stuart Rome, Tyrone Georgiou, Richard Margolis, Carla Steiger, and David Goldes; The Humane Propagandist: Roy Stryker; Kentucky Documentary Project: Ted Wathen, Bob Hower, and Bill Burke; Stephen Livick; My Land, My People: Arthur Rothstein; Barbara Morgan: Photomontages; A Panorama of the American Movie Still Photograph; Photo/Graphics; The Photographer's Hand; Steichen: A Centennial Tribute; West of the Rockies; Mark Cohen; Gary Hallman; Josef Sudek; Carl Toth. Rental for one month periods; cost includes insurance and one-way transportation. Slide sets relating to the history of photography are also available. For further information on exhibitions or slides write to the museum's Office of Extension Activities, above address.

KIAH MUSEUM,* 505 West 36th St, Savannah, GA 30311. *Asst Cur* Nancy H Walker.
Headquarters for National Conference of Artists student traveling shows. These projects have been spearheaded at the Kiah Museum with student NCA members taking part from at least 20 states and 17 foreign countries. Some of the art received in exchange from foreign students, and from each other, has been matted, acetate covered and organized.
Exhibits—International Student Artists Show, 52 pieces of acrylics, pencil, pen and inks, lithographs and watercolors from 18 countries; Hawaiian Show, 25 pieces of tree bark, shell and sand designs; African Collection, 35 pieces of watercolors, pen and inks, and crayons from Mawuli School, HoGhana, West Africa; American Collection, 30 pieces of watercolors, lithographs, pencil sketches, pen and inks and mixed media. No rental fees, but exhibitor is responsible for transportation and insurance expenses. Catalogs available.

LEIGH YAWKEY WOODSON ART MUSEUM, Franklin & 12th Sts, Wausau, WI 54401. *Dir* David J Wagner.
Exhibits—Americans in Glass 1978—Contemporary studio glass represented by 57 pieces. Rental fee $975 to members, $1265 to non-members. Contact Western Association of Art Museums, 270 Sutter St, San Francisco, CA 94108. Tel 415-392-9222. Catalog available.
Americans in Glass 1981—Contemporary studio glass. Contact Western Association of Art Museums, 270 Sutter St, San Francisco, CA 94108. Tel 415-392-9222. Catalog available.
Wisconsin's New Deal Art—75 works executed in Wisconsin under the Federal Projects of the New Deal Era. Rental fee $500 plus freight from previous exhibitor. Contact Leigh Yawkey Woodson Art Museum. Catalog available.

LOUISIANA STATE MUSEUM, 751 Chartres St, New Orleans, LA 70116. *Chief Curator* Vaughn L Glasgow.
Exhibits—Played With Immense Success—New Orleans and Louisiana music 1840-1940. 350 music sheets (many illustrated), approximately 100 objects (instruments, memorabilia) and sound tape. LP recordings available for gift shop sale. 46 panels and 3 cases, high security. Exhibition mounted in cooperation with Smithsonian Institution Traveling Exhibition Service. As arranged by Smithsonian Institution Traveling Exhibition Service: $850 rental fee plus out-bound shipment. Catalog in publication.

MENDEL ART GALLERY, 950 Spadina Crescent E, Saskatoon, SK S7K 3L6, Canada. *Dir & Curator* Allan MacKay.
Exhibits—Brian Wood Photographic Exhibition, Frank Nulf/Charles Ringness Recent Work Exhibition, Courtney Milne Exhibition, Wynona Mulcaster. Rental fee and transportation arrangements negotiable. Catalogs available for all except Wynona Mulcaster.

MIDTOWN GALLERIES, INC, 11 E 57th St, New York, NY 10022. *Dir* Mrs Alan D Gruskin.
Exhibitions arranged for group or one man shows of drawings, watercolors, oils by contemporary American artists. Available to museums, universities, colleges and art centers. Rental fees plus transportation. Rental fee cancelled upon museum purchase. Inquiries invited.

MIDWEST MUSEUM OF AMERICAN ART, PO Box 1812, Elkhart, IN 46515. *Dir* Mark J Meister.
Exhibits—Midwest Photo 81—Midwestern states juried photography exhibition. 75-100 photographs by established as well as young art photographers. Rental fee $400. Borrower pays insurance and out-going shipping. Catalog available.
American Masters of Photography—30 vintage photographs by Alfred Stieglitz, Edward Steichen, Walter Evans, Edward Weston, Imogen

Cunningham, Berenice Abbot, Edward Curtis, Arnold Guethe, Clarence White, W Eugene Smith, Ansel Adams, Minot White. $200 rental fee; borrower pays insurance and out-going shipping. Illustrated checklist available.

MORRIS-JUMEL MANSION, West 160 St & Edgecombe Ave, New York, NY 10032. *Exec Dir* Jane Sullivan Crowley.
Exhibits—Slide Presentations—The Royal Visit; Restoration of Morris Jumel; Morris-Jumel Colonial Herb Garden; NYC's Historical Heritage. Rental fee is a donation to Morris-Jumel Mansion.

LE MUSEE D'ART DE JOLIETTE, 145 Wilfrid-Corbeil St, Joliette, PQ J6E 3Z3. *Animator* Carmen Delorme-Toupin.
Exhibits—Twenty-Two Painters from the End of XIXth Century—Canadian painters such as Suzon-Cote, Leduc, Emily Carr, Edwin Holgate, William Brymner.
Joliette Museum of Art Collection—Twenty-two paintings, twenty-two panels, nine boxes and lights. The exhibition is offered without any rental fee to organizations, schools, libraries, city halls, cultural centers of Joliette area.

THE MUSEUM OF CARTOON ART, Comly Ave, Port Chester, NY 10573. *Dir* Charles Green
Exhibit—Cartoons in America. The cartoons in the collection were reproduced from woodcuts, engravings, lithographs, original art and printed pages. Cartoons were selected for their effective and timely reflection of following social themes: Settling the Land, The American Character, The Melting Pot, American Ingenuity, In Defense of Freedom, The Rights of the People, The American Dream, Social Problems, Great American Pastimes. Rental fee $1000 for two weeks; special rates for nonprofit organizations.

MUSEUM OF EARLY SOUTHERN DECORATIVE ARTS, 924 S Main St, (Mailing Add: Drawer F, Salem Station, Winston-Salem, NC 27101). *Asst to Dir* E Bryding Adams.
Photographs of objects of Southern origin made previous to 1821 in private collections throughout the South. Photographs mounted on masonite and formica panels. Rental fee $450 plus transportation one way. Brochure available.

MUSEUM OF FINE ARTS, 255 Beach Drive North, St Petersburg, FL 33701. *Asst Dir* Alan DuBois.
Exhibits—Twentieth Century American Photography—up to 70 framed images including works by such photographers as Abbott, Adams, Avedon, Bourke-White, Bullock, Callahan, Caponigro, Cunningham, Evans, Frank, Friedlander, Haas, Halsman, Morgan, Newman, Penn, Porter, Kertesz, Laughlin, Siskind, Sommer, W E Smith, H H Smith, Steichen, Strand, B Weston, E Weston, Vestal, White, Uelsman, and others. Sizes range from 9 x 12 to 30 x 40 inches. No rental fee to qualified museums; shipping and insurance expenses are borne by the borrower. Catalogs in preparation.

MUSEUM OF HOLOGRAPHY, 11 Mercer St, New York, NY 10013. Tel 212-753-7478. *Traveling Exhibitions Serv* Paul D Barefoot.
Exhibits—Through the Looking Glass—An exhibition of three-dimensional images made with lasers. Based on the museum's inaugural exhibition of the same name and includes more than 25 examples of state-of-the-art holography, selected for artistic and technical merit. It is the first major and largest exhibition of holography available for wide circulation and provides a thorough introduction to this new art form made with lasers. Rental fee $1500 per week (4 week minimum), plus transportation expense. Camera-ready artwork of catalog provided.

MUSEUM OF MODERN ART, 11 W 53rd St, New York, NY 10019. *Exhibition Program: Coordinator of Exhibitions* Richard L Palmer; *Admin Asst* Marie Frost.
A number of exhibitions directed by members of the Museum's curatorial staff are offered to other qualified museums on a participating basis. These exhibitions are generally either full-scale projects or reduced versions of shows initially presented at The Museum of Modern Art. Although exhibitions are not necessarily available at all times in all media, the traveling program does cover the entire range of the Museum's New York program-painting, sculpture, drawings, prints, photography, architecture and design. Participating fees usually begin at $750 for smaller exhibitions and range up to several thousand dollars for major exhibitions. Tour participants are also asked to cover prorated transport costs.
International Program: Dir, International Prog Waldo Rasmussen.
The primary function of the program is to encourage cultural exchange in all the visual arts on a broad international level. Exhibitions of painting, sculpture, drawings, prints, photography, architecture, design, and film are circulated by the Museum to foreign countries under the auspices of The International Council of The Museum of Modern Art. Exhibitions representing art of other countries or cultures are also pre-

pared for showing in the U.S. Rental fee plus transportation from preceding exhibitor. Programs with overseas libraries and visiting foreign specialists.
Circulating Film Program: Circulation Associate Bob Summers.
Films and programs are drawn from the Museum's international archive of films as well as being distributed on behalf of independent producers; these are made available for rental and, in some cases, for lease. The films exemplify or illustrate the history, development, and technical diversity of the motion picture. Programming assistance is available upon request. Rental or lease fee plus shipping and handling costs. Catalogues and supplements list more than 900 titles ranging from films of the 1890's to recent independent productions.

MUSEUM OF THE AMERICAN INDIAN/HEYE FOUNDATION, Broadway at 155th St, New York, NY. *Registrar* David Fawcett.
Exhibits—The Ancestors: Native Artisans of the Americas—This is an exhibition of materials showing seven different craft systems and the cultures in which they developed. Five hundred pieces were selected and represent cultures of North, Central, and South America. Catalog available.
Iroquois Silver—This is an exhibition of silver ornaments and utilitarian objects of the Iroquois people. It is due to travel to several museums in New York State including Indian museums: The schedule for this exhibition is being handled by the Gallery Associations of New York State. Tel 315-824-2510. Catalog in preparation.

NATIONAL FILM BOARD, Still Photography Division, Tunney's Pasture, Ottawa, ON, K1A ON1, Canada. *Exec Producer* Maureen Cumbers.
The Still Photography Division exhibits the work of contemporary Canadian photographers. Over 100 traveling exhibitions. No rental fee. Transportation inside Canada-the exhibitor shares the carriers' charges with the NFB; outside Canada-the exhibitor is responsible for transportation costs. Catalogue available.

NEWFOUNDLAND MUSEUM, Duckworth St, Saint John's, NF, Canada. *Extension Officer* Elizabeth Brown.
Exhibits—Newfoundland Photography 1849-1949—An exhibition of modern contact prints taken from early glass plate negatives in the Museum's collection. Rental fee $500 includes transportation and insurance costs. Catalog available.
Grass Work of Labrador—An exhibition of approx 90 objects made of grass, such as baskets, mats, toys, cradles, by the Indians of Northern Labrador. Photographs are included. Catalog available.

NEW HARMONY GALLERY OF CONTEMPORARY ART, Main St, New Harmony, IN 47631. *Dir* John P Begley.
Exhibits—New Harmony Imprints—An exhibition of original graphics published and printed in New Harmony, Indiana under the sponsorship of the New Harmony Gallery and the New Harmony Print Workshop. Size can vary from ten to thirty framed works by different artists who have worked in residence. Included are Richard Meier, Gary H Brown, Stephen Pace, Bil Whorrall, John and Marilyn Torre-Whitesell, Darryl Halbrooks and others. The exhibit is intended to expose the individual artists and the non-profit publisher who runs this residency program, and help support continued efforts. Exhibitor pays transportation costs and is expected to sell or buy at least one of the exhibited works, which are for sale. Proceeds are returned to the program to pay future residencies. Gallery will deliver or can ship, as show is framed and boxed. No catalog available.

NEW ORLEANS MUSEUM OF ART, PO Box 19123, City Park, New Orleans, LA 70179. *Assoc Curator, Traveling Exhib* Renee Rodrigue Ryan.
Exhibits—Early Views of the Vieux Carre: Paintings by William Woodward—21 paintings plus didactic panel. 3 crates; 80 running feet. Rental fee $100 within Louisiana; $200 outside Louisiana. Exhibitor pays transportation costs. The New Orleans Museum of Art insures all traveling exhibitions; exhibitor is responsible for first $100 of each claim. Catalog available.
Hard Times: Photographs from the Farm Security Administration, 1935-1942—Works by John Collier, Jack Delano, Walker Evans, Theo Jung, Dorothea Lange, Russell Lee, Carl Mydans, Arthur Rothstein, Ben Shahn, John Vachon, and Marion Post Wolcott are included. 42 photographs plus didactic panel. 3 crates; 120 running feet. Rental fee $125 inside Louisiana; $250 outside Louisiana. Exhibitor pays transportation costs.
Maya Rubbings by Merle Greene Robertson—Original rubbings of relief sculptures. 25 rubbings plus didactic materials. 6 crates; 100 running feet. Rental fee $125 within Louisiana; $250 outside Louisiana. Exhibitor pays transportation costs.
New Orleans Jazz Funerals: Photographs by Leo Touchet—New Orleans Jazz Funerals is divided into three phases (the Funerals and Procession, the Spectators, and the Second Line) presenting a complete documentation of this disappearing New Orleans phenomenon. 43 photographs plus didactic panel. 4 crates; 155 running feet. Rental fee $100 within Louis-

iana; $200 outside Louisiana. Exhibitor pays transportation costs.

Thirty Years of J L Steg: 1948-1978—Internationally renowned print-making professor of Newcomb College, Tulane University. His prints are included in the permanent collections of the Museum of Modern Art, New York City; the Library of Congress, Washington, DC; the National Collection of Fine Arts, Smithsonian Institution; as well as more than 60 international museums and institutions. 59 graphic works. 7 crates; 250 running feet. Rental fee $200 within Louisiana; $400 outside Louisiana. Exhibitor pays transportation costs.

Miserere by Georges Rouault—25 prints plus didactic panel, 15 black & white posters included. 2 creates; 100 running feet. Rental fee $200 within Louisiana; $400 outside Louisiana. Lighting conditions at the proposed exhibition facility are to be approved by NOMA prior to scheduling this exhibition. Exhibitor pays transportation costs.

Bayou Country: The Land of the Cajuns—Watercolors by Charles H Reinike. 35 watercolors plus didactic panel. 2 crates; 85 running feet. Rental fee $100 within Louisiana; $200 outside Louisiana. Exhibitor pays transportation costs.

Exhibition Posters from the Smithsonian Institution Traveling Exhibition Service—Fifteen posters SITES make up this exhibition. This exhibition should be of special interest to facilities with limited security and limited financial resources. 1 crate; 40 running feet. Rental fee $50 within Louisiana; $100 outside Louisiana. Transportation may be arranged by exhibitor.

Exhibition Posters from the New Orleans Museum of Art—Thirteen colorful posters from outstanding past and future exhibitions at the New Orleans Museum of Art. This exhibition should be of special interest to facilities with limited security and limited financial resources. 1 crate; 35 running feet. Rental fee $50 within Louisiana; $100 outside Louisiana. Transportation may be arranged by exhibitor.

Traveling exhibitions catalog available.

NEWPORT HARBOR ART MUSEUM, 850 San Clemente Dr, Newport Beach, CA 92660. *Director* Thomas H Garver; *Curator of Exhibitions and Collections* Betty Turnbull.

Organizes and circulates exhibitions of the art of our time, with the emphasis on American art of the last 30 years. Exhibitions are usually circulated by letter directly to other art institutions, but inquiries are always encouraged from any museum looking for exhibitions dealing with painting, sculpture and photography, with an emphasis on modern and contemporary art.

OAKLAND UNIVERSITY, Meadow Brook Art Gallery, Rochester, MI 48063. *Cur* Kiichi Usui.

Exhibits—Art in Architecture—42 photographic murals, 32 wall labels; 5 boxes for transportation. The exhibition was originally presented with the cooperation of the General Services Administration, Washington, DC; funded by Michigan Council for the Arts. No rental fee, but exhibitor is responsible for transportation and insurance coverage in the amount of $11,535.

Winoru Yamasaki slide presentation—160 slides (2 Carousel trays) and recorded tape. Rental fee $35. The exhibitor is responsible for transportation and insurance. Catalogs available at printers' cost of $1.75.

OLD BERGEN ART GUILD, 43 W 33rd St, Bayonne, NJ 07002. *Dir* William D Gorman; *Assoc Dir* Jan Gary.

Over 70 group and one-man traveling exhibits—Oils, watercolors, caseins and graphics in all styles by contemporary American artists. Available to museums, art centers, universities, colleges, and libraries. No fee, except for one-way express charge. Send stamped, addressed envelope for free catalog.

OWATONNA ARTS CENTER, PO Box 134, Owatonna, MN 55060. *Cur* Silvan Durben.

Exhibits—The Marianne Young World Costume Collection. This collection includes 98 garments from 25 countries and is complete with accessories such as hats, jewelry, gloves and boots. The collection includes caftans, saris, coats, kimonos and French originals. Examples of the gowns in the collection include: a dress from South Africa made completely of white ostrich feathers; a long gown from Pakistan covered with mirrors held in place by embroidery; a bright blue poncho cape from Bali (used in formal dances) which is painted in gold, yellow and shocking pink; a wine-red caracul skin coat from Afghanistan is embroidered in gold with black caracul edging. The costumes, all in her own petite size, were collected by Marianne Young during 50 years of travel. Rental fee is $400; transportation is negotiable. Brochure available on request.

PORTLAND ART MUSEUM, 1219 SW Park Ave, Portland, OR 97205. *Dir* Donald Jenkins; *Cur* Dr William Chiego.

Exhibits—Turkish Miniatures and Related Decorative Arts-from the collection of Edwin Binney III. Turkish miniature paintings and manuscripts; also includes examples of ceramics, textiles, and metal work. Rental fee under $10,000. Catalogs available.

PRATT MANHATTAN CENTER GALLERY,* 160 Lexington Ave, New York, NY 10016. *Dir* Andrew Stasik.

Exhibition of graphic arts—original prints, available to art schools, universities, art associations. Current shows—Contemporary Graphic Protest and the Grand Tradition; A Survey of Intaglio Printmaking; Photography in Printmaking; Sixth International Miniature Print Exhibition; The Presidency—Irreverent and Relevant; Five Contemporary Masters of the Black and White Print; The Black Experience in prints; The Figure and Machine in the Print Today; Monotypes; Contemporary Serigraphs; New Directions in Printmaking; The Collagraph—A New Print Medium; Contemporary American Fine Arts Posters; Puerto Rican Graphics; Against the Wall; Doris Lanier; Forerunners of the American Print Renaissance 1920 - 1950; The Butcher, the Baker, the Candlestick Maker; Images of Labor; Funny? Minimum rental fee.

ROTHMANS OF PALL MALL CANADA LIMITED, 75 Dufflaw Rd, Toronto, ON, Canada, M6A 2W4. Tel: 416-789-7711. *Contact* Alan R Hanlon.

Exhibits—Contemporary Canadian paintings, prints, drawings, and Eskimo sculpture-approx 350 works. Works from the collection available for circulating exhibitions to major public institutions in Canada. Presently circulating is Los Mayas, on a two-year tour schedule including 14 museums.

SANFORD MUSEUM AND PLANETARIUM,* 117 East Willow, Cherokee, IA 51012. Tel: 712-225-3922. *Dir* Robert W Hoge.

Virginia Herrick Quilt Block Exhibit—a large collection of quilt block patterns (some common and uncommon); Oscillons—electronic abstractions by Ben Laposky—photographs of works completed by one of the pioneers of computer art in North America and the world; Midwest Indians and Frontier Photography—early photographs of Indians connected with Iowa and the surrounding states, 1869 - 1900. Rental fee plus shipping charges to be paid by exhibitor.

SEGY GALLERY, 50 W 57th St, New York, NY 10019. *Dir* Ladislas Segy.

Exhibits—African sculptures, masks, statues, some utensils; in wood ivory and bronze. 30 African sculptures for 3 week period. Five circuits each season. Rental fee $450 for 3 weeks; insurance and one way transportation included. Art and science museums, art departments and galleries of universities and colleges, college Student Unions, art clubs, libraries and others eligible. Catalog available on request. Mr. Segy is available for lectures on African and Modern Art. Conditions upon request.

SMITHSONIAN INSTITUTION TRAVELING EXHIBITION SERVICE (SITES), Washington, DC 20560. *Actg Dir* Eileen Rose; *Admin Officer* Antonio Diez; *Program Officer* Anne R Gossett.

150 exhibitions—Architecture, cultural history, decorative arts, design, environment, paintings, prints & drawings, photography, science & technology. Available to educational, scientific, cultural and on occasion, commercial institutions. Educational materials and program activities supplement the exhibits. Catalogs, posters and brochures accompany specific exhibits. Annual catalog "Update" available on request. Quarterly newsletter "Siteline" available now.

SOCIETY OF AMERICAN GRAPHIC ARTISTS,* 1083 Fifth Ave, New York, NY 10028. Tel: 212-289-1507. *Pres* Stanley Kaplan.

55th SAGA National Traveling Print Exhibition (147 prints); 56th SAGA National Traveling Print Exhibition (50 prints). Rental fee $100 for one month; 50 catalogs to each institution.

MAURICE SPERTUS MUSEUM OF JUDAICA, 618 S Michigan Ave, Chicago, IL 60605. *Museum Registrar* Mary Larkin.

Exhibitions—The Jews of Sandor, 25 photographs, 1 lead photograph, 1 map panel, 1 synagogue floor plan panel and label copy. This photographic essay details the lives of the Jews of Sandor, an agrarian village in Iraqi Kurdistan, which ceased to exist as a unit when its people emigrated to Israel in 1950. The exhibition reveals life in this agrarian community, which until its assimilation into Israeli society, had changed little since Babylonian times. Rental fee $250 including insurance and 10 catalogs for 3 months. Additional catalogs $1.00 (selling price $1.50). Transportation costs will be borne by borrower.

The Jews of Yemen, 71 photographs, 1 map, 8 panels of explanatory copy; 1 eight-track cartridge of Yemenite dance music. This photographic essay depicts the sudden flight of the Jews from Yemen/Aden to Israel and reveals this largely unfamiliar aspect of Jewish culture. The majority of the photographs were taken in Aden and Israel during the period 1949-1950 in the course of Operation Magic Carpet. The remainder document certain aspects of the Yemenite Jews in Israel from 1950 to 1960. Rental fee of $750 (includes insurance) for 3 months. Catalogs available for $9.50 (selling price $12.00) Transportation charges extra. Additional components-a film of Boi Temen Dance Festival, approx 25 min in length; cost $50. Special arrangements may be made to borrow a limited number of pertinent artifacts (jewelry, textiles, household objects).

David Bennett: Illustrations to the Bible—Exhibit of 85 linoleum-cut prints (43 color, 42 black & white) depicting various Biblical themes. Highlighted are two series detailing the Story of Esther and the Story of Joseph. 35 prints, labels for each; 225 running feet. Rental fee $950 (including insurance) for 3 months. Transportation charges additional.
Faith & Form: Synagogue Architecture in Illinois—Photographic essay consisting of 145 black and white photographs surveying synagogue architecture in Illinois. This exhibition, surveying over 120 years of synagogue design, illustrates how Jewish communities in Illinois participated in and contributed to the broader crosscurrents of 19th & 20th century American architecture. Featured are structures by Adler & Sullivan, Alfred S. Alschuler and Minoru Yamasaki. 145 photographs with label copy. Rental fee of $1250 for 3 months includes insurance. 25 catalogs included (selling price $10). Transportation charges extra.

TEXAS FINE ARTS ASSOCIATION, 3809 W 35th St, Austin, TX 78703. *Exec Dir* Mrs John D Haltom.
Approximately 7 exhibitions containing 19-20 paintings each. Travel throughout Texas only. Rental fee $100, plus outgoing freight. Catalogs and biographic material available.

TUSKEGEE INSTITUTE,* George W Carver Museum, Tuskegee, AL 36088. *Dir Art Gallery* Stefania Jarkowski.
Exhibits—William H Johnson, Black artist, 20 works in oil, gouache, watercolor and ink collection of 35 contemporary Polish posters, all posters are matted and covered with acetate; collection of 48 watercolors by the contemporary leading artists of Poland, all paintings are matted and covered with acetate. No catalogs available.

UNIVERSITY OF ILLINOIS, Continuing Education and Public Service/Visual Arts, 123 Fine Arts Building, Champaign, IL 61820. *Prof* Ted Zernich.
Exhibitions—Drawing—approx 100 running feet; Graphic Design—approx 150 running feet; Instructional Materials—average 60 feet; Painting—approx 200 running feet; Photography—approx 60 ,running feet; Printmaking—approx 60 running feet; Sculpture—approx 2000 square feet. Rental fee of $40 provides 10 weeks of exhibition materials over 12 months. Participating institutions pay all shipping and insurance costs. Catalogs available.

UNIVERSITY OF MARYLAND ART GALLERY, Art-Sociology Building, College Park, MD 20742. *Dir* Edith A Tonelli.
Exhibits—Treasury Department Mural Studies from the 1930s and 1940s—120 sketches and finished studies in many media. A selection of this extensive collection can be arranged for exhibition. Other exhibition regularly organized by members of the art history faculty. Ancient to contemporary. Rental fee and transportation arranged. Full catalog for Treasury Department Mural Studies available.

UNIVERSITY OF MISSOURI-SAINT LOUIS, Art Department, 8001 Natural Bridge Rd, Saint Louis, MO 63121. *Chairperson* Sylvia Walters.
Available exhibitions change each year. These tend to be photographic in content. No rental fee. Borrower must provide all transportation and insurance. Renting institutions must also provide high security exhibition space.

UNIVERSITY OF NEW MEXICO, UNIVERSITY ART MUSEUM, Fine Arts Center 1017, Albuquerque, NM 87131. *Asst Dir* Anne McCauley.
Exhibits—Martin Chambi (1891-1973) Photographer of Cuzco—75 photographs in traveling exhibition. Chambi's work constitutes one of the few comprehensive records of all aspects of Cuzco culture, including the following: archaeological remains, Inca and pre-Inca; landscape; 20th century anthropology showing Indian customs, ceremonies and dress of many Indian communities around Cuzco; the city of Cuzco, the colonial architecture, as well as its contemporary life and people. Rental fee is $750. Booking institution pays shipping one way. Catalog available.

UNIVERSITY OF REGINA, Norman Mackenzie Art Gallery, Regina, SK, S4S 0A2, Canada.
Exhibitions are for circulation only within Canada. Exhibitions developed by the extension department's Community Program are exhibited throughout the province.

VAN ARSDALE ASSOCIATES, INC, PO Box 1965, Winter Park; FL 32790. *Pres* Dorothy T Van Arsdale.
Exhibits—Approx 20 exhibitions of painting, sculpture, drawings, prints, photographs, textiles, both foreign and American, usually about 25 to 50 pieces. Rental fees from $240 to $600 for 4-week booking period. The exhibitor is responsible for outgoing shipping. Annual catalog available plus occasional exhibition catalogs.

VIRGINIA POLYTECHNIC INSTITUTE AND STATE UNIVERSITY, Owens Hall, Department of Art, Blacksburg, VA 24061. *Head Dept* Prof John Link.
Faculty exhibition. No rental fee, but borrower must pay freight both ways and insurance. No catalog.

WASHINGTON PROJECT FOR THE ARTS, 1227 G St NW, Washington, DC 20005. *Exec Dir* Al Nodal.
Exhibit—Metarealities, an exhibition of paintings by seven Washington area artists; focuses on a group of painters who represent a specifically indigenous mode that has evolved during the past decade in the Nation's Capital. The work in this exhibition demands a lot from the viewer; it is analogous to poetry whereas the more easily accessible variety relates to prose. Rental fee $1000, plus two-way shipping.

WASHINGTON STATE ART SERVICES. Museum 'of Art, Washington State University, Pullman, WA 99164. *Dir* Sanford S. Shaman
Wide range of two-dimensional art objects. Each exhibit includes approx 20 - 30 art works ranging from works on paper to special installations. Rental fee available on request. Catalogs for certain exhibits.

WESTERN ASSOCIATION OF ART MUSEUMS, 270 Sutter St, San Francisco, CA 94108. Department of Traveling Exhibitions.
Approximately 30-50 exhibits of varied media, exhibition themes. Rental fees range from $300-$3000. Catalog upon request.

WESTMINSTER COLLEGE ART GALLERY,* New Wilmington, PA 16142. *Gallery Dir* Robert Godfrey.
Exhibits—The Figure in Recent American Painting, 24 large to medium size paintings; In Praise of Space - The Landscape in American Art, 58 large to small size paintings, drawings, watercolors by contemporary painters; The Figure in Recent American Drawings, 50 framed drawings by 25 contemporary artists; Recent American Narrative Painting; The Portrait in Recent American Painting. Rental fee approx $700 within a 500 mile radius and includes transportation, insurance, installation (if requested) and 100 catalogs.

PETER AND CATHARINE WHYTE FOUNDATION - PETER WHYTE GALLERY, 111 Bear St, Box 160, Banff, AB T0L 0C0, Canada *Curator* Anne F Ewen.
Exhibits—Permanent Collection—Painting, photographs, prints and drawings from the Permanent Collection on request. Local & regional artists on request. Approx 14 to 60 works in shows depending on request. Rental fee is usually $75; terms negotiable. Borrowing institution is responsible for cost of shipping & insurance.
In Mountain Light: The Photographs of Byron Harmon 1906-1934—Contains 60 photographs. Fee negotiable. Catalogue available.

THE WINNIPEG ART GALLERY, 300 Memorial Blvd, Winnipeg, MB, R3C 1V1, Canada. *Assoc Cur, Exten Servs* Donald DeGrow.
Exhibits—H Eric Bergman: Wood Engravings; British Watercolours; Salvador Dali: "Aliyah"; Modern European Graphics; W J Phillips: Woodcuts and Wood Engravings; Baker Lake Prints and Print Drawings; The Catch; Contemporary Canadian Graphics; L L Fitzgerald: The Development of an Artist; Steranko: A Graphic Narrative; Christiane Pflug: Drawings; Waiting: Photographs by Clayton Bailey; Artists in the Community; 19th Century European Landscape; Sketch Book: Watercolours by Nicolas Howard McGachen. Rental fees vary from $50 to $800 and include insurance and may include transportation depending on the exhibition. Catalogues and brochures may also be included, but this varies.

THE WINE MUSEUM OF SAN FRANCISCO, 633 Beach St, San Francisco, CA 94109. Tel 415-673-6990. *Dir* Ernest G Mittelberger.
Exhibits—"500 Years Of Wine in the Arts"—120 original prints, drawings and watercolors from the Christian Brothers Collection at The Wine Museum of San Francisco. The size of the exhibition is 172 linear feet, not counting distance between frames. The exhibition is in metal frames with plexiglass, ready to hang. Caption is contained in each frame. The framed prints are packed in five crates with screw-on lids; total weight 1342 lbs. Rental fee $150, which covers all organizational costs, including wall-to-wall insurance. Fee also includes 1000 visitor folders. Each borrower is responsible for outgoing shipping costs. Should freight costs exceed $100, excess can be charged back to the Wine Museum.

IV INDEXES

Organization

Personnel

Subject

Organization Index

Aarhus Art Museum, see Aarhus Kunstmuseum, Aarhus Denmark

Aarhus Kunstmuseum, Aarhus Art Museum, Aarhus Denmark

Abbot Hall Art Gallery, Cumbria England

Abilene Christian University, Art Dept, Abilene TX (S)

Abilene Fine Arts Museum, Abilene TX

Abingdon Square Painters, Inc, New York NY (S)

Academie Royale des Beaux-Arts, Royal Academy of Fine Arts, Brussels, Brussels Belgium (S)

Academie van Beeldende Kunsten, Academy of Fine Arts, Rotterdam Netherlands (S)

Academy of Art College, San Francisco CA (S)

Academy of Fine Arts, see Accademia di Belle Arti, Perugia Italy (S)

Academy of Fine Arts, see Akademie der Bildenden Künste, Munich Germany, Federal Republic of (S)

Academy of Fine Arts, see Akademie Vytvarnych Umeni, Praha Czechoslovakia (S)

Academy of Fine Arts in Nuremberg, see Akademie der Bildenden Künste in Nürnberg, Nuremberg Germany, Federal Republic of (S)

Academy of Fine Arts of Brera, see Accademia di Belle Arti di Brera, Milan Italy (S)

Academy of Professional Artists, Saint Louis MO

Academy of the Arts, Easton MD

Academy of the Museum of Conceptual Art, San Francisco CA

Accademia de Belle Artie Liceo Artistico, Academy of Fine Arts, Rome Italy (S)

Accademia de Belle Arti Ravenna Italia, Academy of Fine Arts, Ravenna Italy (S)

Accademia di Belle Arti, Academy of Fine Arts, Perugia Italy (S)

Accademia di Belle Arti di Brera, Academy of Fine Arts of Brera, Milan Italy (S)

Accademia di Belle Arti e Liceo Artistico, Florence Italy (S)

Accademia di Belle Arti e Liceo Artistico, Academy of Fine Arts, Bologna Italy (S)

Accademia di Belle Arti e Liceo Artistico, Academy of Fine Arts, Venice Italy (S)

Accademia de Belle Arti e Liceo Artistico, Academy of Fine Arts, Naples Italy (S)

Louise Sloss Ackerman Fine Arts Library, see San Francisco Museum of Modern Art, San Francisco CA

The Ackland Art Museum, see University of North Carolina, Chapel Hill NC

Adam House, see Glasgow Museums and Art Galleries, Glasgow Scotland

Adams National Historic Site, Quincy MA

Adamy's Plastics & Mold-Making Workshops, Larchmont NY (S)

Addison Gallery of American Art, see Phillips Academy, Andover MA

Adelphi University, Fine Arts Library, Garden City NY

Adelphi University, Department of Art and Art History, Garden City NY (S)

Adirondack Lakes Center for the Arts, Blue Mountain Lake NY

Adirondack Museum of the Adirondack Historical Association, Blue Mountain Lake NY

Administration Gallery, see University of Nebraska-Omaha Art Galleries, Omaha NE

Adrian College, Art Department, Adrian MI (S)

Advocates for the Arts, Los Angeles CA

Aegean School of Fine Arts, Paros Cyclades Greece (S)

Agecroft Association, Richmond VA

Ages of Man Fellowship, Amenia NY

Agnes Scott College, Department of Art, Decatur GA (S)

A I R Gallery, New York NY

Akademia Sztuk Pieknych, Academy of Fine Arts, Warsaw Poland (S)

Akademia Sztuk Pieknych, Academy of Fine Arts, Cracow Poland (S)

Akademie der Bildenden Künste, Academy of Fine Arts, Munich Germany, Federal Republic of (S)

Akademie der Bildenden Künste in Nürnberg, Academy of Fine Arts in Nuremberg, Nuremberg Germany, Federal Republic of (S)

Akademie Vytvarnych Umeni, Academy of Fine Arts, Praha Czechoslovakia (S)

Akron Art Institute, Akron OH

Alabama A & M University, Art Education Department, Huntsville AL (S)

Alabama Department of Archives and History Museum, Montgomery AL

Alabama Museum of Photography, Birmingham AL

Alaska Artists Guild, Anchorage AK

Alaska Association for the Arts, Fairbanks AK

Alaska State Museum, Juneau AK

Albany Institute of History and Art, Albany NY

Alberta Art Foundation, Edmonton AB

Alberta College of Art, Southern Alberta Institute of Technology, Calgary AB (S)

Alberta College of Art, see Alberta Society of Artists, Calgary AB

Alberta College of Art Gallery, Calgary AB

Alberta Society of Artists, Alberta College of Art, Calgary AB

Albertina Graphic Art Collection, see Graphische Sammlung Albertina, Vienna Austria

Albertus Magnus College, Art Department, New Haven CT (S)

Albion College, Bobbitt Visual Arts Center, Albion MI

Albion College, Department of Visual Arts, Albion MI (S)

Albrecht Art Museum, Saint Joseph MO

Albright College, Freedman Gallery, Reading PA

Albright College, Department of Art, Reading PA (S)

Albright-Knox Art Gallery, Buffalo Fine Arts Academy, Buffalo NY

Albuquerque Arts Council, Albuquerque NM

Albuquerque Museum of Art, History and Science, Albuquerque NM

Albuquerque Public Library, Albuquerque NM

Alcan Smelters and Chemicals Limited, Montreal PQ

Alcorn State University, Department of Fine Arts, Lorman MS (S)

Aldrich Museum of Contemporary Art, Ridgefield CT

Alexandria Museum Visual Art Center, see Central Louisiana Art Association, Alexandria LA

Alice Lloyd College, Art Department, Pippa Passes KY (S)

Alkmaar Municipal Museum, see Stedelijk Museum Alkmaar, Alkmaar Netherlands

Allan Hancock College, Fine Arts Department, Santa Maria CA (S)

Allegany Community College, Cumberland MD (S)

Allegheny College, Bowman, Megahan and Penelec Galleries, Meadville PA

Allegheny College, Art Department, Meadville PA (S)

Allen County Community College, Art Department, Iola KS (S)

Allende Institute, see Instituto Allende, San Mexico (S)

Allen Memorial Art Museum, see Oberlin College, Oberlin OH

Allentown Art Museum, Allentown PA

Allied Artists of America, Inc, New York NY

Allied Arts Council of Lethbridge, Bowman Arts Center, Lethbridge AB

Allied Arts Council of the Yakima Valley, Yakima WA

Allied Arts of Seattle, Inc, Seattle WA

All Saints' Museum, see Museum zu Allerheiligen, Schaffhausen Switzerland

Lyman Allyn Museum, New London CT

Alma College, Department of Art and Design, Alma MI (S)

Alte Pinakothek, see Bayerischen Staatsgemaldesammlungen, Munich Germany, Federal Republic of

Archbishop Alter Library, see College of Mount Saint Joseph on the Ohio, Mount Saint Joseph OH

Alumnae Centennial Library, see Saint Mary's College, Notre Dame IN

Alverno College, Art Department, Milwaukee WI (S)

Alverno College Gallery, Milwaukee WI

Alvin Community College, Art Dept, Alvin TX (S)

Amarillo Art Center, Amarillo TX

Amarillo Art Center Association, see Amarillo Art Center, Amarillo TX

Amarillo College, Art Dept, Amarillo TX (S)

Ambrosian Picture Gallery, see Pinacoteca Ambrosiana, Milan Italy

American Abstract Artists, Summit NJ

American Academy and Institute of Arts and Letters, New York NY

American Academy in Rome, Rome Italy (S)

American Academy in Rome, New York NY

American Academy in Rome Library, Rome Italy

American Academy of Art, Chicago IL (S)

American Antiquarian Society, Worcester MA

American Artists Professional League, Inc, New York NY

American Arts Documentation Centre, see University of Exeter, Exeter England

American Association of Museums, Washington DC

American Association of University Women, Washington DC

American Baptist Historical Society, Rochester NY

American Center for Students and Artists, Paris France (S)

American Ceramic Society, Columbus OH

American Classical College, Albuquerque NM (S)

American Color Print Society, Philadelphia PA

American Council for the Arts, New York NY

American Council for the Arts in Education, Baltimore MD

American Craft Council, New York NY

American Craft Council Library, see American Craft Museum, New York NY

American Craft Museum, New York NY

American Federation of Arts, New York NY

American Fine Arts Society, New York NY

American Institute for Conservation of Historic and Artistic Works (AIC), Washington DC

American Institute of Architects, Washington DC

American Institute of Architects Foundation, Washington DC

American Institute of Graphic Arts, New York NY

American International Sculptors Symposiums, Inc, New York NY

American Jewish Historical Society, Waltham MA

American Museum in Britain, Bath England

American Museum of Natural History, New York NY

American Numismatic Association, Colorado Springs CO

American Numismatic Society, New York NY

American Red Cross, Washington DC

American River College, Department of Art, Sacramento CA (S)

American School of Art, Palace of Fontainebleau, Fontainebleau France (S)

American Society for Aesthetics, Greenvale NY

American Society of Artists, Inc, Chicago IL

American Society of Bookplate Collectors and Designers, Alhambra CA

American Society of Contemporary Artists, New York NY

American Stained Glass Institute, Santa Fe NM (S)

American Swedish Historical Foundations Museum, Philadelphia PA

American Swedish Institute, Minneapolis MN

American University, Department of Art, Washington DC (S)

American University, Watkins Art Gallery, Washington DC

American University of Beirut, Archaeological Museum, Beirut Lebanon

American Watercolor Society, New York NY

Amerind Foundation, Inc, Dragoon AZ

AmeriTrust Company, Cleveland OH

Amherst College, Dept of Fine Arts, Amherst MA (S)

Amherst College, Amherst MA

Amsterdam, Plaza and Main Galleries, see Lincoln Center for the Performing Arts, New York NY

Anacostia Neighborhood Museum, Washington DC

Anchorage Historical and Fine Arts Museum, Anchorage AK

Ancient and Honorable Artillery Company of Massachusetts, Boston MA

Anderson College, Art Dept, Anderson IN (S)

Anderson County Arts Council, Anderson SC

Anderson Fine Arts Center, Anderson IN

Anderson Gallery, see Virginia Commonwealth University, Richmond VA

Anderson House Museum, Society of the Cincinnati, Washington DC

Anderson Learning Center, see Nasson College, Springvale ME

Anderson Park Art Gallery, Invercargill New Zealand

And-Or, Resources in Contemporary Arts, Seattle WA

Andrew-Safford House, see Essex Institute, Salem MA

Andrews University, Berrien Springs MI (S)

Andruss Library, see Bloomsburg State College, Bloomsburg PA

Angelo State University, Art and Music Department, San Angelo TX (S)

Angelo State University, Houston Harte University Center, San Angelo TX

Anglo-American Art Museum, see Louisiana State University, Baton Rouge LA

Anna Maria College, Department of Art, Paxton MA (S)

Anna Maria College, Saint Luke's Gallery, Paxton MA

Ann Arbor Art Association, Ann Arbor MI

Antelope Valley College, Lancaster CA (S)

Antioch College, Department of Art, Yellow Springs OH (S)

Antioch College, Noyes, Read and Gray Galleries, Yellow Springs OH

Antiquarian and Numismatic Society of Montreal, see Chateau de Ramezay, Montreal PQ

Antonelli School of Photography, Philadelphia PA (S)

Appalachian State University, Department of Art, Boone NC (S)

Aquinas College, Art Department, Grand Rapids MI (S)

Aquinas Library, see Rosary College, Florence Italy

Arbor Lodge State Historical Park, see Game and Parks Commission, Nebraska City NE

Archaeological Institute of America, New York NY

Archaeological Museum, Taxila Pakistan

Archaeological Museums of Istanbul, see Istanbul Arkeoloji Müzeleri, Istanbul Turkey

Architects Association of New Brunswick, Saint John NB

Architectural League of New York, New York NY

Archive of Contemporary Latin American Art, see Museum of Modern Art of Latin America, Washington DC

Archive of Old Spanish Missions, Diocese of Monterey, see Carmel Mission Basilica, Carmel CA

Archives of American Art, Smithsonian Institution, New York NY

Arco Center for Visual Art, Los Angeles CA

Arizona Artist Guild, Phoenix AZ

The Arizona Bank, Phoenix AZ

Arizona Commission on the Arts, Phoenix AZ

Arizona State University, Tempe AZ

Arizona State University, Tempe AZ (S)

Arizona Watercolor Association, Phoenix AZ

Arkansas Arts Center, Little Rock AR

Arkansas Arts Center, Little Rock AR (S)

Arkansas State University, Department of Art, State University AR (S)

Arkansas State University Art Gallery, Jonesboro, State University AR

Arkansas Tech University, Department of Art, Russellville AR (S)

Arkansas Territorial Restoration, Little Rock AR

Armeria Reale, Turin Italy

Armstrong Gallery, see Cornell College, Mount Vernon IA

Armstrong Museum of Art and Archaeology, see Olivet College, Olivet MI

Arnot Art Museum, Elmira NY

Arrowmont School of Arts and Crafts, Gatlinburg TN (S)

Art Academy of Cincinnati, Cincinnati OH (S)

Art and Education Council of Greater Saint Louis, Saint Louis MO

Art Association of Harrisburg, Harrisburg PA

Art Association of Jacksonville, David Strawn Art Gallery, Jacksonville IL

Art Association of Newport, Newport RI

Art Association of Richmond, Richmond IN

Art Association School, Spartanburg SC (S)

Art Barn, Greenwich CT

Art Center, Mount Clemens MI

Art Center, Waco TX

Art Center Association, Louisville KY

Art Center College of Design, James Lemont Fogg Memorial Library, Pasadena CA

Art Center College of Design, Pasadena CA (S)

Art Center, Inc, South Bend IN

Art Centre of New Jersey, East Orange NJ

Art Commission of the City of New York, New York NY

Art Complex Museum at Duxbury, Duxbury MA

Art Dealers Association of America, Inc, New York NY

Art Directors Club, Inc, New York NY

Artemisa Gallery, Chicago IL

Art Gallery, see John C Calhoun State Community College, Decatur AL

Art Gallery, see North Texas State University, Denton TX

Art Gallery, see LeMoyne College, Syracuse NY

Art Gallery, see San Jose State University, San Jose CA

Art Gallery of Brant, Inc, Brantford ON

Art Gallery of Greater Victoria, Victoria BC

Art Gallery of Hamilton, Hamilton ON

Art Gallery of New South Wales, Sydney Australia

Art Gallery of Nova Scotia, Halifax NS

Art Gallery of Ontario, Toronto ON

Art Gallery of Peterborough, Peterborough ON

Art Gallery of South Australia, Adelaide Australia

Art Gallery of the Academy of Fine Arts, see Gemaldegalerie der Akademie der Bildenden Kunste in Wien, Vienna Austria

Art Gallery of Western Australia, Perth Australia

Art Gallery of Windsor, Windsor ON

Art Gallery Society of Contemporary Art, Rawalpindi Gallery of Modern Art, Rawalpindi Pakistan

Art In Architecture - Joseph Young, Los Angeles CA (S)

Art in Architecture - Joseph Young Library, Los Angeles CA

Art Information Center, Inc, New York NY

Art Institute of Boston, Boston MA (S)

Art Institute of Boston, Gallery West, Gallery East, Boston MA

Art Institute of Chicago, Chicago IL

Art Institute of Fort Lauderdale, Fort Lauderdale FL

Art Institute of Fort Lauderdale, Fort Lauderdale FL (S)

Art Institute of Houston, Houston TX (S)

Art Institute of Philadelphia, Philadelphia PA (S)
Art Institute of Pittsburgh, Pittsburgh PA (S)
Art Institute of Pittsburgh Gallery, Pittsburgh PA
Art Instruction Schools, Minneapolis MN (S)
Artist-Craftsmen of New York, New York NY
Artists Association of Nantucket, Kenneth Taylor Gallery, Nantucket MA
Artists Coalition of Texas, Dallas TX
Artists Equity Association, Inc, Washington DC
Artists' Fellowship, Inc, New York NY
Artists Gallery, Vancouver BC
Artists Guild Inc of New York, New York NY
Artists Guild of Chicago, Chicago IL
Artists Space, New York NY
Artists Technical Institute, New York NY
Artist Studio Centers, Inc, New York NY (S)
Artists Welfare Fund, Inc, see New York Artists Equity Association, Inc, New York NY
Artists Workshop, see Three Schools, Toronto ON (S)
Art League of Houston, Houston TX
Art League of Manatee County, Bradenton FL
Art Libraries Society-North America, Iowa City IA
Art Metropole, Toronto ON
Art Museum, see Kunstmuseum, Winterthur Switzerland
Art Museum of Northern Jutland, see Nordjyllands Kunstmuseum, Aalborg Denmark
Art Museum of South Texas, Corpus Christi TX
Art Museum of the City of Bonn, see Stadtishces Kunstmuseum Bonn, Bonn Germany, Federal Republic of
Art of the American Peoples Museum, see Museo de Arte Popular Americano, Santiago Chile
Art Patrons League of Mobile, Mobile AL
Art Research Center, Kansas City MO
Arts and Crafts Association, Inc, Winston-Salem NC (S)
Arts and Crafts Association of Meriden Inc, Meriden CT
Arts and Crafts Center of Pittsburgh, Pittsburgh PA
Arts and Humanities Council of Tuscaloosa County, Inc, Tuscaloosa AL
Arts and Letters Club of Toronto, Toronto ON
Arts and Science Center, Nashua NH (S)
Arts and Science Center, Nashua NH
Arts Center of the Ozarks, see Council of Ozark Artists and Craftsmen, Inc, Springdale AR
Art School of the Crafts Guild, Holland MI (S)
Arts Club of Chicago, Chicago IL
Arts Club of Washington, James Monroe House, Washington DC
Arts Council, Inc, Winston-Salem NC
Arts Council of Spartanburg County, Inc, Spartanburg SC
Arts Council of the Mid-Columbia Region, Richland WA
Arts Council of Topeka, Topeka KS
Arts for Living Center, Burlington IA
Arts, Limited, Baltimore MD
Arts Place II, see Oklahoma Art Center, Oklahoma City OK
Art Students League of New York, New York NY (S)
Art Students League of New York, New York NY
Artworlds Center for Creative Arts, Ann Arbor MI
Asbury College, Student Center Gallery, Wilmore KY
Asbury College, Art Dept, Wilmore KY (S)
Asheville Art Museum, Asheville NC
Ashland College, Art Department, Ashland OH (S)
Ashland College Arts and Humanities Gallery, Ashland OH
Ashland Oil, Inc, Ashland KY
Ashmolean Museum of Art and Archaeology, see Oxford University, Oxford England
Ashtabula Arts Center, Ashtabula OH
Asia Foundation Gallery, The Asia Foundation, San Francisco CA
Asia House Gallery, see Asia Society, Inc, New York NY

Asian Art Museum of San Francisco, Avery Brundage Collection, San Francisco CA
Asian Collection, see Saint John's University, Jamaica NY
Asia Society, Inc, Asia House Gallery, New York NY
Assembly House, see Essex Institute, Salem MA
Associated Artists of New Jersey, Pittstown NJ
Associated Artists of Pittsburgh Arts and Crafts Center, Pittsburgh PA
Associated Artists of Winston-Salem, Winston-Salem NC
Associates of the Art Commission, Inc, see Art Commission of the City of New York, New York NY
Association des Musees Canadiens, see Canadian Museums Association, Ottawa ON
Association for the Preservation of Virgina Antiquities, Richmond VA
Association of American Editorial Cartoonists, Oklahoma City OK
Association of Art Museum Directors, Savannah GA
Association of Canadian Industrial Designers, Ontario, Toronto ON
Association of Collegiate Schools of Architecture, Washington DC
Association of Honolulu Artists, Honolulu HI
Association of Medical Illustrators, Los Angeles CA
Assumption College, Department of Fine Arts and Music, Worcester MA (S)
Atelje Mestrovic, see Galerije Grada Zagreba, Zagreb Yugoslavia
Ateneo Puertorriqueno, San Juan PR
Athenaeum Music and Arts Library, see Library Association of La Jolla, La Jolla CA
Athenaeum of Philadelphia, Philadelphia PA
Athens State College, Art Department, Athens AL (S)
Atkins Museum of Fine Art, see William Rockhill Nelson Gallery of Art, Kansas City MO
Lee Atkyns Studio-Gallery, Duncansville PA
Atlanta Area Technical School, Department of Commercial Art, Atlanta GA (S)
Atlanta Art Workers Coalition, Atlanta GA
Atlanta College of Art, Atlanta GA (S)
Atlanta College of Art Library, Atlanta GA
Atlanta Museum, Atlanta GA
Atlanta Public Library, Fine Arts Department, Atlanta GA
Atlantic Christian College, Art Dept, Wilson NC (S)
Atlantic Christian College, Case Art Gallery, Wilson NC
Atlantic Gallery, New York NY
Atlinson Art Gallery, see Sefton Metropolitan Borough, Southport England
Attleboro Museum, Center for the Arts, Attleboro MA
Atwood Center Gallery Lounge, see Saint Cloud State University, Saint Cloud MN
Auburn University, Department of Art, Auburn AL (S)
Auburn University at Montgomery, Art Department, Montgomery AL (S)
Auckland City Art Gallery, Auckland New Zealand
Eleanor Dean Audigier Art Collection, see University of Tennessee, Knoxville TN
Audubon Artists, Inc, New York NY
John James Audubon Museum, see Audubon State Park, Henderson KY
Audubon State Park, John James Audubon Museum, Henderson KY
Audubon Wildlife Sanctuary, Audubon PA
Auerbach Art Library, see Wadsworth Atheneum, Hartford CT
Augsburg College, Art Department, Minneapolis MN (S)

Augusta College, Department of Fine Arts, Augusta GA (S)
Augustana College, Bergendorf Fine Arts Gallery, Rock Island IL
Augustana College, Art Department, Sioux Falls SD (S)
Augustana College, Center for Western Studies, Sioux Falls SD
Augustana College, Art Department, Rock Island IL (S)
Augusta Richmond County Museum, Augusta GA
Aurora College, Art Department, Aurora IL (S)
Austin Arts Center, see Trinity College, Hartford CT
Austin College, Ida Green Gallery, Sherman TX
Austin College, Art Department, Sherman TX (S)
Austin Community College, Dept of Commercial Art & Fine Arts, Austin TX (S)
Austin Peay State University, Margaret Fort Trahern Gallery, Clarksville TN
Austin Peay State University, Dept of Art, Clarksville TN (S)
Austrian Gallery, see Osterreichische Galerie, Vienna Austria
Averett College, Art Department, Danville VA (S)
Avery Architectural and Fine Arts Library, see Columbia University, New York NY
Avila College, Art Gallery, Kansas City MO
Avila College, Art Department, Kansas City MO (S)
Azusa Pacific College, Art Dept, Azusa CA (S)
Babcock Art Library, see Sweet Briar College, Sweet Briar VA
Babson Library Art Gallery, see Springfield College, Springfield MA
Bacone College Museum, Muskogee OK
Bakersfield College, Art Department, Bakersfield CA (S)
Baker University, Department of Art, Baldwin City KS (S)
Baldwin Hotel Museum Annex, see Klamath County Museum, Klamath Falls OR
Baldwin Room (Canadian History Department), see Metropolitan Toronto Library Board, Toronto ON
Baldwin-Wallace College, Department of Art, Berea OH (S)
Baldwin-Wallace College Art Gallery, Berea OH
Ball State University, Art Department, Muncie IN (S)
Ball State University, Muncie IN
Baltimore Maritime Museum, Baltimore MD
Baltimore Museum of Art, Baltimore MD
Balzekas Museum of Lithuanian Culture, Chicago IL
Balzekas Museum Research Library, see Balzekas Museum of Lithuanian Culture, Chicago IL
Banff Centre, Walter Phillips Gallery, Banff AB
Banff Centre School of Fine Arts, Banff AB (S)
Bank of America, San Francisco CA
Bank of Maryville, Maryville TN
Bank of Mississippi, Tupelo MS
Bank of Oklahoma, Tulsa OK
Edward M Bannister Gallery, see Rhode Island College, Providence RI
Baptist College at Charleston, Department of Art, Charleston SC (S)
Barat College, Dept of Art, Lake Forest IL (S)
Barber-Scotia College, Art Department, Concord NC (S)
Bard College, William Cooper Procter Art Center, Annandale-on-Hudson NY
Bard College, Annandale-on-Hudson NY (S)
Bardo National Museum, see Musee National du Bardo, Le Bardo Tunisia
Barna Pottery, Santa Fe NM (S)
Barnard College, see Columbia University, New York NY (S)
The Barn Gallery, see Ogunquit Art Association, Ogunquit ME
Barry College, Department of Art, Miami Shores FL (S)
Basilian Fathers, Mundare AB
Bassist Institute Museum, Portland OR
Bass Museum of Art, Miami Beach FL
Bates College, Treat Gallery, Lewiston ME
Bates College, Art Dept, Lewiston ME (S)
Battle Creek Civic Art Center, Battle Creek MI

Brazosport College, Art Department, Lake Jackson TX (S)

Breezewood Foundation Museum and Garden, Monkton MD

Bremen Art Gallery, see Kunsthalle Bremen, Bremen Germany, Federal Republic of

Anne Bremer Memorial Library, see San Francisco Art Institute, San Francisco CA

Brenau College, Art Department, Gainesville GA (S)

Brera Picture Gallery, see Pinacoteca di Brera, Milan Italy

Brescia College, Art Department, Owensboro KY (S)

Brevard Art Center and Museum, Inc, Melbourne FL

Brevard College, Div of Fine Arts, Brevard NC (S)

Brevard College, Coltrane Art Center, Brevard NC

Brewton-Parker College, Visual Arts, Mount Vernon GA (S)

Briar Cliff College, Gallery 147, Sioux City IA

Briar Cliff College, Art Department, Sioux City IA (S)

Brick Store Museum, Kennebunk ME

Bridgeport Art League, Bridgeport CT

Bridgestone Bijutsukan, Bridgestone Museum of Art, Tokyo Japan

Bridgestone Museum of Art, see Bridgestone Bijutsukan, Tokyo Japan

Bridgewater State College, Art Department, Bridgewater MA (S)

Margaret M Bridwell Art Library, see University of Louisville, Louisville KY

Brigham City Museum-Gallery, Brigham City UT

Brigham Young University, Department of Art and Design, Provo UT (S)

Brigham Young University, Provo UT

Brighton Polytechnic, Faculty of Art and Design, Brighton England (S)

Bristol Art Museum, Bristol RI

Bristol Campus Center, see Hamilton College, Clinton NY

British Library, Reference Division, London England

British Museum, London England

British School at Rome, Rome Italy (S)

Brockton Art Center, Brockton MA

Brockton Art Center, Art Workshops, Brockton MA (S)

Brockton Public Library System, Municipal Art Gallery, Brockton MA

Saidye Bronfman Centre, Montreal PQ

Silas Bronson Library, Waterbury CT

Bronx Museum of the Arts, Bronx NY

Bronxville Public Library, Bronxville NY

Brookgreen Gardens, Murrells Inlet SC

Brookline Art Society, see Brookline Public Library, Brookline MA

Brookline Public Library, Brookline MA

Brooklyn Museum, Brooklyn NY

Brooklyn Museum Art School, Brooklyn NY (S)

Brooklyn Public Library, Art and Music Division, Brooklyn NY

Brooks Memorial Art Gallery, Memphis TN

Broome County Historical Library, see Roberson Center, Binghamton NY

Jay R Broussard Memorial Galleries, Baton Rouge LA

Annmary Brown Memorial Gallery, see Brown University, Providence RI

Brown County Art Gallery Association Inc, Nashville IN

Browne Hall Gallery, see Western Illinois University, Macomb IL

Armstrong Browning Library, see Baylor University, Waco TX

Jean Brown Archive, see Tyringham Institute, Tyringham MA

John Brown House, see Rhode Island Historical Society, Providence RI

Brownson Art Gallery, see Manhattanville College, Purchase NY

Brownsville Art League Museum, Brownsville TX

Topham Brown Gallery, see Vernon Art Association, Vernon BC

Brown University, Department of Art, Providence RI (S)

Brown University, Providence RI

Bruce Museum, Greenwich CT

Avery Brundage Collection, see Asian Art Museum of San Francisco, San Francisco CA

Brunnier Gallery, see Iowa State University, Ames IA

Richard F Brush Art Gallery, see St Lawrence University, Canton NY

Bryn Mawr College, Department of the History of Art, Bryn Mawr PA (S)

Bryn Mawr College, Art and Archaeology Library, Bryn Mawr PA

Buchanan Arts and Crafts Inc, Buchanan Dam TX

Buck Hill Art Association, Buck Hill Falls PA

Bucknell University, Department of Art, Lewisburg PA (S)

Bucknell University, Ellen Clarke Bertrand Library, Lewisburg PA

Bucks County Community College, Fine Arts Department, Newton PA (S)

Bucks County Community College, Newtown PA

Bucks County Historical Society Mercer Museum, Doylestown PA

Buffalo and Erie County Public Library, Buffalo NY

Buffalo Bill Memorial Association, Cody WY

Bundy Art Gallery, Waitsfield VT

Burchfield Center, Buffalo NY

Bureau of Museums and Historic Sites, see Division of Historical and Cultural Affairs, Dover DE

Burgmuseum, see Saltzburger Museum Carolino Augusteum, Salzburg Austria

Thomas Burke Memorial Washington State Museum, see University of Washington, Seattle WA

Burlington County Historical Society, Burlington NJ

Burnaby Art Gallery, Burnaby BC

Burnley School of Professional Art, Inc, Seattle WA (S)

Burpee Art Museum, see Rockford Art Association, Rockford IL

Burroughs Wellcome Company, Research Triangle Park NC

Busch-Reisinger Museum, see Harvard University, Cambridge MA

Bush House, and Bush Barn Art Center, see Salem Art Association, Salem OR

Buten Museum of Wedgwood, Merion PA

Butera School of Art, Boston MA (S)

Butler County Community College, Art Department, El Dorado KS (S)

Butler Institute of American Art, Youngstown OH

Butte Community College, Humanities Division (III), Oroville CA (S)

Byzantine Museum, Athens Greece

Cabrillo College, Visual Arts Division, Aptos CA (S)

Cabrini College, Department of Fine Arts, Radnor PA (S)

Caldwell College, Art Department, Caldwell NJ (S)

Caldwell College Art Gallery, Caldwell NJ

Calgary Artists Society, Calgary AB

California College of Arts and Crafts, Oakland CA (S)

California College of Arts & Crafts, Meyer Library, Oakland CA

California Historical Society, San Francisco CA

California Institute of Technology, Baxter Art Gallery, Pasadena CA

California Institute of the Arts, School of Art, Valencia CA (S)

California Institute of the Arts Library, Valencia CA

California Lutheran College, Art Department, Thousand Oaks CA (S)

California Museum of Science and Industry, Los Angeles CA

California Polytechnic State University at San Luis Obispo, Art Department, San Luis Obispo CA (S)

California State College, Department of Art, California PA (S)

California State College at San Bernardino, Fine Arts Department, San Bernardino CA (S)

California State College San Bernardino, College Art Galleries, San Bernardino CA

California State College, Sonoma, Department of Art, Rohnert Park CA (S)

California State College, Stanislaus, Turlock CA

California State College, Stanislaus, Art Department, Turlock CA (S)

California State Fair and Exposition Art Show, Sacramento CA

California State Polytechnic University, Pomona, Art Department, Pomona CA (S)

California State University at Long Beach, Art Department, Long Beach CA (S)

California State University, Chico, Art Gallery, Chico CA

California State University, Chico, Art Dept, Chico CA (S)

California State University, Dominguez Hills, School of Humanities & Fine Arts, Carson CA (S)

California State University, Fresno, Art Department, Fresno CA (S)

California State University Fullerton, Art Gallery, Fullerton CA

California State University, Fullerton, Art Department, Fullerton CA (S)

California State University, Hayward, Art Department, Hayward CA (S)

California State University, Long Beach, Long Beach CA

California State University, Los Angeles, Fine Arts Gallery, Los Angeles CA

California State University, Los Angeles, Art Department, Los Angeles CA (S)

California State University, Northridge, Department of Art-Two Dimensional Media, Northridge CA (S)

California State University, Northridge, Fine Arts Gallery, Northridge CA

California State University, Sacramento, Department of Art, Sacramento CA (S)

California State University, Sacramento, Library, Humanities Reference Media Services Ctr, Sacramento CA

Eleanor Calvert Memorial Library, see Kitchener-Waterloo Art Gallery, Kitchener ON

Calvert Marine Museum, Solomons MD

Calvin College, Art Dept, Grand Rapids MI (S)

Calvin College Center Art Gallery, Grand Rapids MI

Cambridge Art Association, Cambridge MA

Cambridge Public Library and Arts Centre, Cambridge ON

Camden County College, Department of Art, Blackwood NJ (S)

Cameron University, Art Department, Lawton OK (S)

Grace Campbell Gallery, see John M Cuelenaere Library, Prince Albert SK

Campbell Museum, Camden NJ

Sarah Campbell Blaffer Gallery, see University of Houston, Houston TX

Campbellsville College, Fine Arts Division, Campbellsville KY (S)

Campus Martius Museum and Ohio River Museum, Marietta OH

Canadian Artists' Representation, Winnipeg MB

Canadiana Sport Art Collection, Ottawa ON

Canadian Conference of the Arts, Ottawa ON

Canadian Crafts Council, Canadien de l'Artisanat, Ottawa ON

Canadian Crafts Council, Conseil Canadien de l'Artisanat, Ottawa ON

Canadian Guild of Crafts, Quebec, see Guilde Canadianne des Mietiers d'Art, Quebec, Montreal PQ

Canadian Museums Association, Association des Musees Canadiens, Ottawa ON

Canadian Society for Education Through Art, Regina SK

Canadian Society of Painters in Watercolour, Toronto ON

Canajoharie Library and Art Gallery, Canajoharie NY

Canton Art Institute, Canton OH

Canton Art Instutute, Canton OH (S)

Danforth Museum, Framingham MA

Danforth Museum School, Framingham MA (S)

Danville Museum of Fine Arts and History, see Virginia Museum, Danville VA

Martin D'Arcy Gallery of Art, see Loyala University of Chigago, Chicago IL

DAR Museum, National Society Daughters of the American Revolution, Washington DC

Dartington College of Arts, Library and Resources Centre, Devon England

Dartmouth College, Department of Art, Hanover NH (S)

Dartmouth College Museum & Galleries, Hanover NH

Dartmouth Heritage Museum, Dartmouth NS

Dauphin Allied Arts Centre, Dauphin MB

Davenport Municipal Art Gallery, Davenport IA

Davidson College, Art Dept, Davidson NC (S)

Davidson College Art Gallery, Davidson NC

Davidson County Community College, Language-Fine Arts Dept, Lexington NC (S)

Davis and Elkins College, Department of Art, Elkins WV (S)

H F Davis Memorial Library, see Colby Community College, Colby KS

John B Davis Gallery of Fine Art, see Idaho State University, Pocatello ID

Davison Art Center, see Wesleyan University, Middletown CT

Shelby Cullom Davis Museum of the Performing Arts and: The Library and Museum of the Performing Arts, at Lincoln Center, see New York Public Library, Museum NY

Gisela Dawley Art Studio, Simi Valley CA (S)

Dawson Creek Museum Art Gallery, see South Peace Art Society, Dawson Creek BC

Dayton Art Institute, Dayton OH

Dayton Hudson Corporation, Minneapolis MN

Deadwood Gulch Art Gallery, Deadwood SD

Dean Junior College, Visual and Performing Arts Department, Franklin MA (S)

De Anza College, Art Department, Cupertino CA (S)

Decatur House, Washington DC

Decker Gallery, see Maryland Institute College of Art, Baltimore MD

DeCordova and Dana Museum and Park, Lincoln MA

Dedham Historical Society, Dedham MA

Deere & Company, Moline IL

Deerfield Academy, Hilson Gallery, Deerfield MA

Delaware Art Museum, Wilmington DE

Delaware County Community College, Communications and Humanities House, Media PA (S)

Delaware State College, Department of Art and Art Education, Dover DE (S)

Delgado College, Department of Fine Arts, New Orleans LA (S)

Isaac Delgado Museum, see New Orleans Museum of Art, New Orleans LA

Del Mar College, Department of Art Gallery, Corpus Christi TX

Del Mar College, Department of Art, Corpus Christi TX (S)

Delta College, Art Department, University Center MI (S)

Delta State University, Fielding L Wright Art Center, Cleveland MS

Delta State University, Department of Art, Cleveland MS (S)

DeLuce Gallery, see Northwest Missouri State University, Maryville MO

Deming Luna Mimbres Museum, Deming NM

Den Grafiski HoJskole, Graphic College of Denmark, Copenhagen Denmark (S)

Denison University, Department of Art, Granville OH (S)

Denison University Art Gallery, Granville OH

Denver Art Museum, Frederic H Douglas Library, Denver CO

Denver Public Library, Denver CO

Department of Culture, Government of the Province of Alberta, Edmonton AB

Department of Manuscripts and Printed Books, see University of Cambridge, Cambridge England

Department of State, Diplomatic Reception Rooms, Washington DC

DePaul University, Department of Art, Chicago IL (S)

DePauw University, Art Department, Greencastle IN (S)

Dept of Art, see Hamline University Galleries, Saint Paul MN

DeRicci Gallery, see Edgewood College, Madison WI

de Saisset Art Gallery and Museum, see University of Santa Clara, Santa Clara CA

Desert Caballeros Western Museum, Wickenburg AZ

Alfred O Deshong Museum, Chester PA

Des Moines Area Community College, Art Department, Boone IA (S)

Des Moines Art Center, Des Moines IA

Det Danske Kunstindustrimuseum, Museum of Decorative Art, Copenhagen Denmark

Det Kongelige Danske Kunstakademi, The Royal Danish Academy of Fine Arts, Copenhagen Denmark (S)

Det Kongelige Danske Kunstakademi Bibliotek, Copenhagen Denmark

Detroit Institute of Arts, Detroit MI

Detroit Public Library, Fine Arts Department, Detroit MI

John Dewey Library, see Johnson State College, Johnson VT

DeWitt Cultural Center, see Hope College, Holland MI

M H de Young Memorial Museum and California Palace of the Legion of Honor, see Fine Arts Museums of San Francisco

De Young Museum Art School, San Francisco CA (S)

Dezign House III, Cleveland OH

Diablo Valley College Museum, Pleasant Hill CA

Diamond M Foundation Museum, Snyder TX

Dickinson College, Fine Arts Department, Carlisle PA (S)

Dickinson State College, Mind's Eye Gallery, Dickinson ND

Dickinson State College, Department of Art, Dickinson ND (S)

Dimock Gallery, see George Washington University Museum & Art Galleries, Washington DC

Dimond Slide Library, see University of New Hampshire, Durham NH

Division of Historical and Cultural Affairs, Bureau of Museums and Historic Sites, Dover DE

Dixie College, Southwestern Utah Art Gallery, Saint George UT

Dixie College, Art Department, Saint George UT (S)

Dixon Gallery and Gardens, Memphis TN

Doane College, Dept of Art, Crete NE (S)

Dobler Room, see Central Wyoming College, Riverton WY

Dom Jana Matejki, see Muzeum Narodowe w Krakowie, Cracow Poland

Doncaster Museum and Art Gallery, Doncaster England

Eva Brook Donly Museum, Simcoe ON

Donnell Library Center Art Library, see New York Public Library, New York NY

Dorian Gallery, see Galleria Doria Pamphilj, Rome Italy

Dorval Cultural Centre, Dorval PQ

Doshi Center for Contemporary Art, Harrisburg PA

Douglas Art Association, Little Gallery, Douglas AZ

Frederic H Douglas Library, see Denver Art Museum, Denver CO

Douglass College, see Rutgers, the State University of New Jersey, New Brunswick NJ (S)

Grace A Dow Memorial Library, Midland MI

Dowling College, Department of Art, Oakdale NY (S)

Downey Museum of Art, Downey CA

Downtown Minot Art Gallery, see Minot Art Gallery, Minot ND

Drake University, Art Department, Des Moines IA (S)

The Drawing Society, New York NY

Dreisbach Art Gallery, Mountainhome PA (S)

Drew University, College Art Gallery, Madison NJ

Drew University, Art Department, Madison NJ (S)

Drexel University, Department of Design, Philadelphia PA (S)

Drexel University Art Gallery and Museum Collection, Philadelphia PA

Felix J Dreyfous Library, see New Orleans Museum of Art, New Orleans LA

Doris and Henry Dreyfuss Study Center, see Cooper-Hewitt Museum, New York NY

Drury College, Art, Art History & Architecture Dept, Springfield MO (S)

Dubuque Art Association, Old Jail Gallery, Dubuque IA

Duke University, Department of Art, Durham NC (S)

Duke University Museum of Art, Durham NC

Dulin Gallery of Art, Knoxville TN

Dulwich Picture Gallery, London England

Dumbarton Oaks Research Library and Collections, see Harvard University, Washington DC

Dundee Museums and Art Gallery, Dundee Scotland

Dundurn Castle, Hamilton ON

Dunedin Fine Arts and Cultural Center, Dunedin FL (S)

Dunedin Public Art Gallery, Dunedin New Zealand

Dunlot Art Gallery, see Regina Public Library, Regina SK

DuPage Art League, Wheaton IL

Durand Art Collection, see Yankton College, Yankton SD

Durban Art Gallery, Durban South Africa, Republic of

DuSable Museum of African American History, Chicago IL

Dutchess Community College, Department of Visual Arts, Poughkeepsie NY (S)

Dwelling Sculpture Institute, Sierra Madre CA

Clara M Eagle Gallery, see Murray State University, Murray KY

Earlham College, Art Department, Richmond IN (S)

Earlham College, Leeds Gallery, Richmond IN

East Carolina University, Wellington B Gray Gallery, Greenville NC

East Carolina University, School of Art, Greenville NC (S)

East Central Junior College, Art Department, Decatur MS (S)

East Central Junior College, Art Dept, Union MO (S)

East Central University, Art Department, Ada OK (S)

Eastern Arizona College, Thatcher AZ (S)

Eastern Connecticut State College, Art Department, Willimantic CT (S)

Eastern Illinois University, Paul Turner Sargent Gallery, Charleston IL

Eastern Illinois University, Art Department, Charleston IL (S)

Eastern Kentucky University, Art Department, Richmond KY (S)

Eastern Michigan University, Sill Gallery, Ypsilanti MI

Eastern Michigan University, Dept of Art, Ypsilanti MI (S)

Eastern Montana College, Art Dept, Billings MT (S)

Eastern New Mexico University, Art Gallery, Portales NM

Eastern New Mexico University, Department of Art & Education, Portales NM (S)

Eastern Oregon State College, La Grande OR (S)

Eastern Washington State Historical Society, Cheney Cowles Memorial Museum, Spokane WA

Eastern Washington University, Department of Art, Cheney WA (S)

Eastern Wyoming College, Art Department, Torrington WY (S)

East Los Angeles College, Art Department, Monterey Park CA (S)

East Mississippi Junior College, Art Department, Scooba MS (S)

East Tennessee State University, Johnson City TN

Jonathan Fisher Memorial, Inc, see Parson Fisher House, Blue Hill ME

Fisk University, Art Dept, Nashville TN (S)

Fisk University Museum, Nashville TN

Fitchburg Art Museum, Fitchburg MA

Fitzwilliam Museum, see University of Cambridge, Cambridge England

Five Civilized Tribes Museum, Muskogee OK

Flagler College, Visual Arts Department, Saint Augustine FL (S)

Henry Morrison Flagler Museum, Palm Beach FL

Flamingo Gallery, see Clark County Library District, Las Vegas NV

Flathead Indian Museum, Saint Ignatius MT

Flathead Valley Art Association, see Hockaday Center for the Arts, Kalispell MT

Samuel S Fleisher Art Memorial, see Philadelphia Museum of Art, Philadelphia PA

Samuel S Fleisher Art Memorial, Philadelphia PA (S)

Robert Hull Fleming Museum, see University of Vermont, Burlington VT

Flint Institute of Arts, Flint MI

Flint Public Library, Fine Arts Department, Flint MI

Florence Museum, Florence SC

Florida A&M University, Department of Visual Arts & Humanities, Tallahassee FL (S)

Florida Artist Group Inc, Englewood FL

Florida Atlantic University, Art Department, Boca Raton FL (S)

Florida Atlantic University Art Gallery, Boca Raton FL

Florida Folklife Program, White Springs FL

Florida Gulf Coast Art Center, Inc, Clearwater FL (S)

Florida Gulf Coast Art Center, Inc, Clearwater FL

Florida International University, Visual Arts Department, Miami FL (S)

Florida International University Library, Art Department, Miami FL

Florida Junior College at Jacksonville, South Campus, Art Department, Jacksonville FL (S)

Florida School of the Arts, Visual Arts, Palatka FL (S)

Florida Southern College, Melvin Art Gallery, Lakeland FL

Florida Southern College, Art Department, Lakeland FL (S)

Florida State University, Tallahassee FL (S)

Florida State University, Art Gallery, Tallahassee FL

Roswell P Flower Memorial Library, Watertown NY

Floyd County Museum, New Albany IN

Henry N Flynt Library, see Historic Deerfield Inc, Deerfield MA

James Lemont Fogg Memorial Library, see Art Center College of Design, Pasadena CA

William Hayes Fogg Art Museum, see Harvard University, Cambridge MA

Fogler Library, see University of Maine at Orono, Orono ME

Folger Shakespeare Library, Washington DC

Fontbonne College, Department of Art, Clayton MO (S)

Fontbonne College, Art Department, Saint Louis MO (S)

Foothills Art Center, Inc, Golden CO (S)

Foothills Art Center, Inc, Golden CO

Forbes Library, Northampton MA

Forbes Street Gallery, see Carnegie-Mellon University, Pittsburgh PA

Fordham University, New York NY (S)

Forest Lawn Museum, Glendale CA

Fort Hays State University, Department of Art, Hays KS (S)

Fort Hays State University, Visual Arts Center, Hays KS

Fort Hill, see Clemson University, Clemson SC

Fort Lauderdale Museum of the Arts, Fort Lauderdale FL

Fort Lauderdale Museum of the Arts, Art School, Fort Lauderdale FL (S)

Fortman Studios Florence, Florence Italy (S)

Fort Meade Museum, Fort Meade MD

Fort Smith Art Center, Fort Smith AR

Fort Steilacoom Community College, Fine Arts Department, Tacoma WA (S)

Fort Ticonderoga Museum, Ticonderoga NY

Fort Wayne Fine Arts Foundation, Inc, Fort Wayne IN

Fort Wayne Museum of Art, Fort Wayne IN

Fort Worth Art Museum, Fort Worth TX

The Fort Worth National Bank, Fort Worth TX

Fort Worth Public Library, Fort Worth TX

Fort Wright College, Art Gallery, Spokane WA

Fort Wright College of the Holy Names, School of Art, Spokane WA (S)

Foster Caddell's Art School, Voluntown CT (S)

Stephen Foster State Folk Culture Center, see Florida Folklife Program, White Springs FL

Foundation for Today's Art, Nexus Gallery, Philadelphia PA

Foundation The Free Academy for Fine Arts, see Stichting de Vrije Academie Voor Beeldende Kunsten, The Netherlands (S)

Founders' Gallery, see University of San Diego, San Diego CA

Fourteen Sculptors Gallery, see Cultural Council Foundation, New York NY

Francis E Fowler Jr Foundation Museum, Beverly Hills CA

Framingham State College, Art Department, Framingham MA (S)

Franciscan Monastery, Holy Land of America, Washington DC

Franklin and Marshall College, Art Department, Lancaster PA (S)

Franklin College, Art Department, Franklin IN (S)

Franklin Furnace Archive, Inc, New York NY

Franklin Mint Corp Museum, Franklin Center PA

Franklin Pierce College, Art Department, Rindge NH (S)

Frank Phillips College, Art Department, Borger TX (S)

Frans Halsmuseum, Frans Hals Museum, Haarlem Netherlands

Simon Fraser Gallery, see Simon Fraser University, Burnaby BC

Fredericton National Exhibition Centre, Fredericton NB

Freedman Gallery, see Albright College, Reading PA

Free Library of Philadelphia, Philadelphia PA

Freeport Art Museum, see Highland Area Arts Council, Freeport IL

Free Public Library, Art and Music Department, Trenton NJ

Free Public Library of Elizabeth, Fine Arts Dept, Elizabeth NJ

Freer Gallery of Art, Washington DC

French Art Colony, Inc, Gallipolis OH

French Institute-Alliance Francaise Library, New York NY

Fresno Arts Center, Fresno CA

Fresno City College, Art Department, Fresno CA (S)

Frick Art Museum, Pittsburgh PA

Frick Art Reference Library, New York NY

Frick Collection, New York NY

Henry Clay Frick Fine Arts Library, see University of Pittsburgh, Pittsburgh PA

Lee M Friedman Memorial Library, see American Jewish Historical Society, Waltham MA

Friends of Photography, Carmel CA

Friends of the Arts and Sciences, Hilton Leech Studio, Sarasota FL (S)

Friends of the Whitney Museum of American Art, see Whitney Museum of American Art, New York NY

Friends of the Wright Art Center, see Beloit College, Beloit WI

Friends University, Art Department, Wichita KS (S)

Fries Museum, Leeuwarden Netherlands

Alfred Fromm Rare Wine Books Library, see Wine Museum of San Francisco, San Francisco CA

Frontier Times Museum, Bandera TX

Frostburg State College, Department of Art & Art Education, Frostburg MD (S)

Frostburg State College, Fine Arts Gallery I, Frostburg MD

Fruitlands Museums, Harvard MA

Charles and Emma Frye Art Museum, Seattle WA

Eugene R Fuller Gallery of Art, see Beaver College, Glenside PA

Fuller Lodge Art Center, Los Alamos NM

Fullerton College, Fine Arts and Art Department, Fullerton CA (S)

Fulton-Hayden Memorial Library, see Amerind Foundation, Inc, Dragoon AZ

Furman University, Department of Art, Greenville SC (S)

Gable Advertising Art School, Division of Advertising Design School, Inc, Cincinnati OH (S)

Galeria de la Raza, Studio 24, San Francisco CA

Galeria Venezuela, New York NY

Galerie Restigouche Gallery, Campbellton NB

Galerija Benko Horvat, see Galerije Grada Zagreba, Zagreb Yugoslavia

Galerije Grada Zagreba, City Art Galleries, Zagreb Yugoslavia

Galesburg Civic Art Center, Galesburg IL

Galleria Borghese, Borghese Gallery, Rome Italy

Galleria Degli Uffizi, Uffizi Gallery, Florence Italy

Galleria di Palazzo Bianco, White Palace Gallery, Genoa Italy

Galleria Doria Pamphilj, Dorian Gallery, Rome Italy

Galleria e Museo del Palazzo Ducale, Gallery and Museum of the Palazzo Ducale, Mantua Italy

Galleria, Museo e Medagliere Eslense, Este Gallery and Museum, Modena Italy

Galleria Nazionale d'Arte Antica - Palazzo Barberini, National Gallery in Barberini Palace, Rome Italy

Galleria Nazionale d'Arte Antica - Palazzo Corsini, see Galleria Nazionale d'Arte Antica - Palazzo Barberini, Rome Italy

Galleria Nazionale dell'Umbria, Umbrian National Gallery, Perugia Italy

Galleria Palatina, Palatine Gallery, Florence Italy

Galleria Sabauda, Turin Italy

Gallerie d'Art de l'Universite de Moncton, Moncton NB

Galleries of Ivy School of Professional Art, Pittsburgh PA

Galleries of the Claremont Colleges, Claremont CA

Gallery and Museum of the Palazzo Ducale, see Galleria e Museo del Palazzo Ducale, Mantua Italy

Gallery East, see College of Eastern Utah, Price UT

Gallery of DuPont Hall, see Washington and Lee University, Lexington VA

Gallery of Impressionists, see Musee du Jeu de Paume, Paris France

Gallery of Prehistoric Paintings, New York NY

Gallery on the Roof, see Saskatchewan Power Corporation, Regina SK

Gallery Stratford, Stratford ON

Gallery 147, see Briar Cliff College, Sioux City IA

Gallery 76, see Wenatchee Valley College, Wenatchee WA

Gallup Museum of Indian Arts, Church Rock NM

Game and Parks Commission, Arbor Lodge State Historical Park, Nebraska City NE

Gananoque Historical Museum, Gananoque ON

Gardiner Art Gallery, see Oklahoma State University, Stillwater OK

Isabella Stewart Gardner Museum, Boston MA

Gardner-Pingree House, see Essex Institute, Salem MA

Gaston College, Art Department, Dallas NC (S)

Gaston County Art and History Museum, Dallas NC

Gavilan College, Art Department, Gilroy CA (S)

Gavilan College, Art Gallery, Gilroy CA

Helen Palmer Geisel Library, see La Jolla Museum of Contemporary Art, La Jolla CA

Gemaldegalerie der Akademie der Bildenden Kunste in Wien, Art Gallery of the Academy of Fine Arts, Vienna Austria

Gemeentemuseum Arnhem, Municipal Museum of Arnhem, Arnhem Netherlands

General Mills, Inc, Minneapolis MN

General Services Administration, Washington DC

Geneva Schools of Art, see Ecoles d'Art de Geneve, Geneva Switzerland (S)

George Brown College of Applied Arts and Technology, Toronto ON (S)

George Mason University, Department of Fine and Performing Arts, Fairfax VA (S)

George Peabody College for Teachers, Cohen Memorial Museum of Art, Nashville TN

George Peabody College for Teachers, Art Faculty Department, Nashville TN (S)

Georgetown College, Art Department, Georgetown KY (S)

Georgetown University, Art and History Museum, Washington DC

Georgetown University, Department of Fine Arts, Washington DC (S)

George Washington University, Department of Art, Washington DC (S)

George Washington University Museum & Art Galleries, Washington DC

Georgia Institute of Technology, College of Architecture Library, Atlanta GA

Georgia Institute of Technology, College of Architecture, Atlanta GA (S)

Georgia Museum of Art, see University of Georgia, Athens GA

Georgian College of Applied Arts and Technology, Georgian Learning Resources Centre, Barrie ON

Georgian Court College, Department of Art, Lakewood NJ (S)

Georgian Court College Gallery, Lakewood NJ

Georgian House, see City Art Gallery, Bristol England

Georgia Southern College, Department of Art, Statesboro GA (S)

Georgia State University, Arthur I and Irma L Harris Reading Room and Visual Resource Library, Atlanta GA

Georgia State University, Atlanta GA (S)

Germain School of Photography, New York NY (S)

Germanic National Museum, see Germanisches National Museum, Nuremberg Germany, Federal Republic of

Germanisches National Museum, Germanic National Museum, Nuremberg Germany, Federal Republic of

Gerrit Rietveld Academie, Amsterdam Netherlands (S)

J Paul Getty Museum, Malibu CA

Gettysburg College, Department of Art, Gettysburg PA (S)

Ghana National Museum, Accra Ghana

Ghost Ranch Visitor Center, Abiquiu NM

Gibbes Art Gallery, see Carolina Art Association, Charleston SC

Gibbes Art Gallery School, Charleston SC (S)

Gibson Library, see Imperial Calcasieu Museum, Lake Charles LA

Gibson Society, Inc, Boston MA

Thomas Gilcrease Institute of American History and Art, Tulsa OK

Genevieve and Donald Gilmore Art Center, see Kalamazoo Institute of Arts, Kalamazoo MI

Gilpin County Arts Association, Central City CO

Adam L Gimbel Library, see Parsons School of Design, New York NY

Glasgow Museums and Art Galleries, Kelvingrove Art Gallery and Museum, Glasgow Scotland

Glassboro State College, Department of Art, Glassboro NJ (S)

Alfred C Glassell Junior School of Art, see Museum of Fine Arts, Houston TX (S)

Alfred C Glassell Jr School of Art Library, see Museum of Fine Arts, Houston, Houston TX

Glenbow Museum, Calgary AB

Glendale College, Department of Fine Arts, Glendale CA (S)

Glendale Federal Savings, Glendale CA

Glendenning Gallery, see Utah State Division of Fine Arts, Salt Lake City UT

Glenhyrst Arts Council of Brantford Inc, Brantford ON

Glenville State College, Department of Art, Glenville WV (S)

Glessner House, see Chicago Architecture Foundation, Chicago IL

Charles B Goddard Center for the Visual and Performing Arts, Ardmore OK

Goetz Art School, Bedford Hills NY (S)

Gogebic Community College, Art Department, Ironwood MI (S)

Golden State Mutual Life, Los Angeles CA

Golden West College, Arts, Humanities and Social Sciences Institute, Huntington Beach CA (S)

Goldsboro Art Center, Goldsboro NC (S)

Morris Goldstein Library, see Judah L Magnes Memorial Museum, Berkeley CA

Robert Goldwater Library of Primitive Art, see Metropolitan Museum of Art, New York NY

Gonzaga University, Department of Art, Spokane WA (S)

Gonzaga University, AD Gallery, Spokane WA

Donald B Gordon Memorial Library, see Palm Beach County Parks and Recreation Department, Delray Beach FL

Goshen College, Art Department, Goshen IN (S)

Gothenburg Art Gallery, see Göteborg Konstmuseum, Gothenburg Sweden

Goucher College, Art Department, Towson MD (S)

Goucher College, Kraushaar Auditorium Lobby Gallery, Towson MD

Government Employees Insurance Company, Washington DC

Grace College, Department of Art, Winona Lake IN (S)

Graceland College, Art Department, Lamoni IA (S)

Graduate Program in Art History, see Rutgers, the State University of New Jersey, New Brunswick NJ (S)

Graduate School of Fine Arts at Schifanoia Villa, see Rosary College, Florence Italy (S)

Grand Canyon College, Art Department, Phoenix AZ (S)

Grand Central Art Galleries, Inc, New York NY

Grand Marais Art Colony, Grand Marais MN (S)

Grand Prairie Art Council, Inc, Stuttgart AR

Grand Rapids Art Museum, Grand Rapids MI

Grand Rapids Junior College, Art Dept, Grand Rapids MI (S)

Grand Rapids Public Library, Music and Art Department, Grand Rapids MI

Grand Valley State Colleges, Art Department, Allendale MI (S)

Grange Art Gallery and Museum, see Royal Pavilion, Art Gallery and Museums, Brighton England

Graphic College of Denmark, see Den Grafiski HoJskole, Copenhagen Denmark (S)

Graphische Sammlung Albertina, Albertina Graphic Art Collection, Vienna Austria

Graves Art Gallery, see Sheffield City Art Galleries, Sheffield England

Grayson County College, Art Department, Denison TX (S)

Wellington B Gray Gallery, see East Carolina University, Greenville NC

Graziano Studios of Fine Arts Inc, Summer Art Workshop, RD 3, Plainfield NJ (S)

Greater Fall River Art Association, Fall River MA

Greater Gary Arts Council, Gary IN

Great Lakes Historical Society, Vermilion OH

Greco-Roman Museum, Alexandria Egypt

Greenfield Community College, Art Department, Greenfield MA (S)

Greenfield Village and Henry Ford Museum, Dearborn MI

Green Hill Art Gallery, Greensboro NC

Ida Green Gallery, see Austin College, Sherman TX

Green Mountain College, Department of Art, Poultney VT (S)

Greensboro College, Department of Art, Greensboro NC (S)

Greenville Art Center, Greenville NC

Greenville College, Dept of Art, Greenville IL (S)

Greenville College, Richard W Bock Sculpture Collection, Greenville IL

Greenville County Museum of Art, Museum School of Art, Greenville SC (S)

Greenville County Museum of Art, Greenville SC

Greenwich Art Society and Art Center, Greenwich CT

Greenwich House Pottery, New York NY (S)

Grey Art Gallery and Study Center, see New York University, New York NY

Grinnell College, Department of Art, Grinnell IA (S)

Grinstead Gallery, see Central Missouri State University, Warrensburg MO

The Grisons Museum of Art, see Bündner Kunstmuseum Chur, Chur Switzerland

Grolier Club Library, New York NY

Groningen Museum, see Groningen Museum voor Stad en Land, Groningen Netherlands

Groningen Museum voor Stad en Land, Groningen Museum, Groningen Netherlands

Grossmont College, Art Department, El Cajon CA (S)

Grossmont Community College Gallery, El Cajon CA

M Grumbacher Inc, New York NY

Grunwald Center for the Graphic Arts, see University of California, Los Angeles, Los Angeles CA

Göteborg Konstmuseum, Gothenburg Art Gallery, Gothenburg Sweden

John Simon Guggenheim Memorial Foundation, New York NY

Solomon R Guggenheim Museum, New York NY

Guilde Canadianne des Mietiers d'Art, Quebec, Canadian Guild of Crafts, Quebec, Montreal PQ

Guild Hall of East Hampton, Inc, Museum Section, East Hampton NY

Guild of Book Workers, New York NY

Guild of Boston Artists, Boston MA

Guild of South Carolina Artists, Columbia SC

Guilford Technical Institute, Commercial Art Dept, Jamestown NC (S)

Gulf Coast Community College, Division of Fine Arts, Panama City FL (S)

Jessica Gund Memorial Library, see Cleveland Institute of Art, Cleveland OH

Emery A Gunnin Architectural Library, see Clemson University, Clemson SC

Gunston Hall Plantation, Lorton VA

Gustavus Adolphus College, Art Department, Saint Peter MN (S)

Haags Gemeentemuseum, Municipal Museum of The Hague, The Hague Netherlands

Haaretz Museum, Tel-Aviv Israel

Haas Gallery of Art, see Bloomsburg State College, Bloomsburg PA

Haber School of Sculpture, Roslyn NY (S)

Haggs Castle, see Glasgow Museums and Art Galleries, Glasgow Scotland

Hagley Museum, Eleutherian Mills-Hagley Foundation, Greenville DE

Hale Hoikeike, see Maui Historical Society, Wailuku HI

Eisner Hall Art Gallery, see City College of the City of New York, New York NY

Hallmark Cards, Inc, Kansas City MO

Hall of Fame of the Trotter, Goshen NY

Stan Hywet Hall Foundation, Inc, Akron OH

Hallwalls Gallery, Buffalo NY

Frans Hals Museum, see Frans Halsmuseum, Haarlem Netherlands

Hamburg Art Museum, see Hamburger Kunsthalle, Hamburg Germany, Federal Republic of

Hamburger Kunsthalle, Hamburg Art Museum, Hamburg Germany, Federal Republic of

Hamilton Art Gallery, see Elmira College, Elmira NY

Hamilton College, Art Department, Clinton NY (S)

Hamilton College, Edward W Root Art Center, Clinton NY

Hamline University, Art Department, Saint Paul MN (S)

Hamline University Galleries, Dept of Art, Saint Paul MN

Hammond-Harwood House, Annapolis MD

Hammond Museum, Museum of the Humanities, North Salem NY

Hammond Museum, Inc, Gloucester MA

Hampshire County Public Library, Romney WV

Hampton Center for Arts and Humanities, Hampton VA

Hampton Institute, Art Department, Hampton VA (S)

Hampton Institute, College Museum, Hampton VA

Japanese Folk Art Museum, see Nihon Mingei Kan, Tokyo Japan

Japan House Gallery, see Japan Society, Inc, New York NY

Japan Society, Inc, New York NY

Javeriana University Faculty of Architecture and Design, see Universidad Javeriana, Bogota Colombia (S)

John Jay Homestead, Katonah NY

Jay-Rollins Library, see McMurry College, Abilene TX

Jefferds Tavern, see Society for the Preservation of Historic Landmarks, York ME

Jefferson Community College, Fine Arts, Louisville KY (S)

Jefferson Community College, Art Department, Watertown NY (S)

Jefferson Davis State Junior College, Art Department, Brewton AL (S)

Thomas Jefferson Memorial Foundation, see Monticello, Charlottesville VA

Jekyll Island National Historic Landmark, Jekyll Island GA

Arthur D Jenkins Library, see Textile Museum, Washington DC

Jersey City Museum Association, Jersey City NJ

Jersey City Public Library, Fine Arts Department, Jersey City NJ

Jersey City State College, Art Department, Jersey City NJ (S)

Jersey City State College, Courtney Art Gallery, Jersey City NJ

The Jewelry Institute, Metro New York Academy, New York NY (S)

The Jewelry Institute, New England Academy, Providence RI (S)

Jewish Community Center, Center Lobby Gallery, Long Beach CA

Jewish Museum, New York NY

Joe Kubert School of Cartoon and Graphic Art Inc, Dover NJ (S)

Johannesburg Art Gallery, Johannesburg South Africa, Republic of

John Brown University, Art Department, Siloam Springs AR (S)

John C Calhoun State Community College, Art Gallery, Decatur AL

John C Calhoun State Community College, Art Department, Decatur AL (S)

John Jay College of Criminal Justice, Department of Art, Music and Philosophy, New York NY (S)

John McCrady Art School of New Orleans, New Orleans LA (S)

Johns Hopkins University, Baltimore MD

Johns Hopkins University, Baltimore MD (S)

Johnson County Community College, Communications-Arts Division, Overland Park KS (S)

Grace Phillips Johnson Art Gallery, see Phillips University, Enid OK

Herbert F Johnson Museum of Art, see Cornell University, Ithaca NY

Johnson-Humrickhouse Museum, Coshocton OH

Jay Johnson, America's Folk Heritage Gallery, New York NY

John Graver Johnson Collection, see Philadelphia Museum of Art, Philadelphia PA

Johnson State College, Art Department, Johnson VT (S)

Johnson State College, John Dewey Library, Johnson VT

Johnston National Scouting Museum, North Brunswick NJ

Joliet Junior College, Art Dept, Joliet IL (S)

Joliet Junior College, Laura A Sprague Art Gallery, Joliet IL

Jones County Junior College, Art Department, Ellisville MS (S)

John Paul Jones House, Portsmouth NH

Jones Library, see Brevard College, Brevard NC

Jones Library, Inc, Amherst MA

Nettie Marie Jones Fine Arts Library, see Lake Placid School of Art Gallery, Lake Placid NY

Jonson Gallery, see University of New Mexico, Albuquerque NM

Jordan Historical Museum of The Twenty, Jordan ON

Jorgensen Gallery, see University of Connecticut, Storrs CT

Joseloff Gallery, see University of Hartford, West Hartford CT

Joslyn Art Museum, Omaha NE

Judson Baptist College, Department of Fine Arts, Portland OR (S)

Judson College, Division of Fine Arts, Marion AL (S)

Judson College, Division of Fine Arts, Elgin IL (S)

Juniata College, Department of Art, Huntingdon PA (S)

Junior Art Gallery, Louisville KY

Junior Arts Center, Los Angeles CA

Junior Center of Art and Science, Oakland CA

Junior College of Albany, Fine Arts Division, Albany NY (S)

Kalamazoo College, Art Department, Kalamazoo MI (S)

Kalamazoo Institute of Arts, Genevieve and Donald Gilmore Art Center, Kalamazoo MI

Kalamazoo Institute of Arts, Kalamazoo MI (S)

Kalamazoo Valley Community College, Department of Art, Kalamazoo MI (S)

Kalamunda Museum of Western Art, Somers MT

Kanazawa Bijutsu Kogei Daigaku, Kanazawa Municipal College of Fine and Industrial Arts, Kanazawa City Japan (S)

Kanazawa Municipal College of Fine and Industrial Arts, see Kanazawa Bijutsu Kogei Daigaku, Kanazawa City Japan (S)

Kansas City Art Institute, Charlotte Crosby Kemper Gallery, Kansas City MO

Kansas City Art Institute, Kansas City MO (S)

Kansas City Public Library, Art & Music Department, Kansas City MO

Kansas State Historial Society Museum, Topeka KS

Kansas State University, Paul Weigel Library, Manhattan KS

Kansas State University, Manhattan KS (S)

Kansas Watercolor Society, Wichita KS

Kansas Wesleyan University, Art Department, Salina KS (S)

Kapiolani Community College, Diamond Head Campus, Honolulu HI (S)

Kappa Pi International Honorary Art Fraternity, Birmingham AL

Katonah Gallery, Katonah NY

Kauai Community College, Department of Art, Lihue HI (S)

Kauai Museum, Lihue HI

Kauai Regional Library, Lihue HI

Kauffman Gallery, see Shippensburg State College, Shippensburg PA

Kaysville Community Art League, LeConte Stewart Art Gallery, Kaysville UT

Kean College of New Jersey, Fine Arts Department, Union NJ (S)

Kean College of New Jersey, Union NJ

Kearney State College, Dept of Art, Kearney NE (S)

Keene State College, Thorne-Sagendorph Art Gallery, Keene NH

Kellogg Community College, Arts Department, Battle Creek MI (S)

Kelly-Griggs House Museum, Red Bluff CA

Kelowna Centennial Museum and National Exhibit Centre, Kelowna BC

Kelsey Museum of Ancient and Medieval Archaeology, see University of Michigan Museum of Art, Ann Arbor MI

Kelvingrove Art Gallery and Museum, see Glasgow Museums and Art Galleries, Glasgow Scotland

Annie S Kemerer Museum, Bethlehem PA

Charlotte Crosby Kemper Gallery, see Kansas City Art Institute, Kansas City MO

Kemper Group, Long Grove IL

Kendall Art Gallery, see San Angelo Art Club, San Angelo TX

Kendall School of Design, Grand Rapids MI (S)

Kendall Whaling Museum, Sharon MA

Kennebec Valley Art Association, Harlow Gallery, Hallowell ME

John F Kennedy Center for the Performing Arts, Washington DC

John F Kennedy Library and Museum, Dorchester MA

Kennedy-King College, see City Colleges of Chicago, Chicago IL (S)

Kenosha Public Museum, Kenosha WI

Kent Art Association, Inc Gallery, Kent CT

Kent Library, see Southeast Missouri State University, Cape Girardeau MO

Kent State University, School of Art, Kent OH (S)

Kent State University, Kent OH

Kentucky Guild of Artists and Craftsmen Inc, Berea KY

Kentucky Historical Society Museum, Frankfort KY

Kentucky Library, see Western Kentucky University, Bowling Green KY

Kentucky Museum, see Western Kentucky University, Bowling Green KY

Kentucky State University, Jackson Hall Gallery, Frankfort KY

Kentucky Wesleyan College, Department of Fine Arts, Owensboro KY (S)

Kenyon College, Colburn Gallery, Gambier OH

Kenyon College, Art Department, Gambier OH (S)

Keokuk Art Center, Keokuk IA

Kern County Museum, Bakersfield CA

Maude I Kerns Art Center, Henry Korn Gallery, Eugene OR

Kestner-Museum, Hannover Germany, Federal Republic of

Ketterer Art Center, Bozeman MT

Keystone Junior College, Art Department, LaPlume PA (S)

Keystone Junior College Library, Art Section, Factoryville PA

Key West Art and Historical Society, Key West FL

Kiah Museum, Savannah GA

Kiehle Gallery, see Saint Cloud State University, Saint Cloud MN

Kilcawley Center Art Gallery, see Youngstown State University, Youngstown OH

Kilgore College, Department Art and Art Education, Kilgore TX (S)

Fiske Kimball Fine Arts Library, see University of Virginia, Charlottesville VA

Kimbell Art Museum, Fort Worth TX

King County Arts Commission, Seattle WA

Emma B King Library, see Shaker Museum, Old Chatham NY

King George VI Art Gallery, Port South Africa, Republic of

Kingsborough Community College, Department of Art, Brooklyn NY (S)

Kingsport Fine Arts Center, Kingsport TN

Kipp Gallery, see Indiana University of Pennsylvania, Indiana PA

Kirkland Art Center, Clinton NY

Kirkland Gallery, see Millikin University, Decatur IL

Kirkwood Community College, Department of Fine Arts, Cedar Rapids IA (S)

Kitchener-Waterloo Art Gallery, Kitchener ON

Kittredge Art Gallery, see University of Puget Sound, Tacoma WA

Klamath Art Gallery, see Klamath Falls Art Association, Klamath Falls OR

Klamath County Museum, Klamath Falls OR

Klamath Falls Art Association, Klamath Art Gallery, Klamath Falls OR

Paul Klapper Library, see Queens College of the City University of New York, Flushing NY

Allen Knight Maritime Museum, see Monterey History and Art Association, Monterey CA

Kobenhavns Bymuseum, Copenhagen City Museum, Copenhagen Denmark

Koenig Art Gallery, see Concordia College, Seward NE

Kohler Art Library, see University of Wisconsin, Madison WI

Kohler Company, Kohler WI

John Michael Kohler Arts Center, Sheboygan WI

Kokuritsu Seiyo Bijutsukan, see National Museum of Western Art, Tokyo Japan

Koninklijke Academie Van Beeldende Kunsten, Royal Academy of Fine Arts, The Hague Netherlands (S)

Koninklijk Kabinet van Schilderijen, Royal Picture Gallery, The Hague Netherlands

Koninklijk Museum voor Schone Kunsten, Royal Museum of Fine Arts, Antwerp Belgium

Konservator der Kunstdenkmaler, Dusseldorf Germany, Federal Republic of

Kootenay School of Art and Gallery, Nelson BC

Henry Korn Gallery, see Maude I Kerns Art Center, Eugene OR

Koshare Indian Museum, Inc, La Junta CO

Koyasan Reihokan, Museum of Buddhist Art, Wakayama Japan

Krannert Art Museum, see University of Illinois, Champaign IL

Krannert Gallery, see University of Evansville, Evansville IN

Krasl Art Center, see Saint Joseph Art Association Inc, Saint Joseph MI

Kraushaar Auditorium Lobby Gallery, see Goucher College, Towson MD

Kresge Art Center, see Michigan State University, East Lansing MI

Kress Foundation Department of Art History, see University of Kansas, Lawrence KS (S)

Kroller-Muller State Museum, see Ryksmuseum Kroller-Muller, Otterlo Netherlands

Kronquist Craft Gallery, see Milwaukee Area Technical College, Milwaukee WI

Kungl Konsthogskolan, College of Fine Arts in Stockholm, Stockholm Sweden (S)

Kungl Myntkabinettet Statens Museum För Mynt Medalj Och Penninghistoria, Royal Coin Cabinet, National Museum of Monetary History, Stockholm Sweden

Kunstgewerbemuseum der Stadt Köln, see Museen der Stadt Köln, Cologne Germany, Federal Republic of

Kunsthalle Bremen, Bremen Art Gallery, Bremen Germany, Federal Republic of

Kunsthaus Zurich, Museum of Fine Arts, Zurich Switzerland

Kunsthistorisches Museum, Museum of Fine Arts, Vienna Austria

Kunstindustrimuseet I Oslo, Oslo Museum of Applied Art, Oslo Norway

Kunstmuseum, Art Museum, Winterthur Switzerland

Kunstmuseum Bern, Museum of Fine Arts Berne, Berne Switzerland

Kunstmuseum Solothurn, Solothurn Art Museum, Solothurn Switzerland

Kutztown State College, Kutztown PA

Kyoto City University of Fine Arts, School of Art, Kyoto Japan (S)

Kyoto Kokuritsu Kindai Bijutsukan, National Museum of Modern Art, Kyoto, Kyoto Japan

La Casa del Libro, House of Books, San Juan PR

Ladies Library and Art Association, Independence KS

Ladycliff College, Art Department, Highland Falls NY (S)

Lafayette Art Center, Lafayette IN

Lafayette College, Department of Art, Easton PA (S)

La Grange College, Art Department, La Grange GA (S)

Laguna Beach Museum of Art, Laguna Beach CA

Laguna Beach School of Art, Laguna Beach CA (S)

Laguna Gloria Art Museum, Austin TX

Lahaina Arts Society, Lahaina HI

Lahore Museum, Lahore Pakistan

Laing Art Gallery and Museum, see Tyne and Wear County Council Museums, Newcastle England

La Jolla Museum of Contemporary Art, La Jolla CA

Lake City Community College, Art Department, Lake City FL (S)

Lake County Civic Center Association, Inc, Heritage Museum and Gallery, Leadville CO

Lake Erie College-Garfield Senior College, Art Department, Painesville OH (S)

Lake Forest College, Dept of Art, Lake Forest IL (S)

Lake Forest Library, Lake Forest IL

Lakehead University, Department of Fine Art, Thunder Bay ON (S)

Lake Michigan College, Department of Art, Benton Harbor MI (S)

Lake Placid School of Art, Lake Placid NY (S)

Lake Placid School of Art Gallery, Lake Placid NY

Lake Tahoe Community College, Art Department, South Lake Tahoe CA (S)

Lakeview Gallery, see Saint Francis College, Fort Wayne IN

Lakeview Museum of Arts and Sciences, Peoria IL

Lalit Kala Akademi, National Academy of Art, New India

La Mamelle Inc, San Francisco CA

Lamar University, Art Department, Beaumont TX (S)

Lambuth College, Department of Art, Jackson TN (S)

Lamont Gallery, see Phillips Exeter Academy, Exeter NH

Lampe Gallery of Fine Art, Lampe School of Art, New Orleans LA

Lampe School of Art, see Lampe Gallery of Fine Art, New Orleans LA

Herbert H Lamson Library, see Plymouth State College, Plymouth NH

Lancaster County Art Association, Lancaster PA

Clara Lander Library, see Winnipeg Art Gallery, Winnipeg MB

Lander College, Dept of Fine Arts, Greenwood SC (S)

Landmark Center, see Minnesota Museum of Art, Saint Paul MN

Lane Community College, Art and Applied Design Department, Eugene OR (S)

Henry S Lane Home, Crawfordsville IN

Laney College, Art Department, Oakland CA (S)

Laney College Library, Art Section, Oakland CA

Lang Art Gallery of Scripps College, see Galleries of the Claremont Colleges, Claremont CA

Langston University, Art Department, Langston OK (S)

Langston University Art Gallery, Langston OK

Lansing Art Gallery, Lansing MI

Lansing Community College, Performing & Creative Arts Dept, Lansing MI (S)

Laramie County Community College, Division of Humanities, Cheyenne WY (S)

La Roche College, Division of Graphic Arts & Design, Pittsburgh PA (S)

B F Larsen Gallery, see Brigham Young University, Provo UT

La Salle College, Department of Fine Arts, Philadelphia PA (S)

La Salle College Art Gallery, Philadelphia PA

Lasell Junior College, Art Department, Auburndale MA (S)

La Societe des Arts de Chicoutimi, Chicoutimi PQ

La Societe des Decorateurs-Ensembliers du Quebec, Interior Decorators' Society of Quebec, Montreal PQ

Las Vegas Art League, Las Vegas Art Museum, Las Vegas NV

L'Atelier, The Sculpture Workshop, Philadelphia PA (S)

Laughner Brothers, Inc, Indianapolis IN

Laumeier Sculpture Park, see Saint Louis County Department of Parks and Recreation, Saint Louis MO

Laurentian University, Sudbury ON

Laurier House, see Public Archives of Canada, Ottawa ON

Lausanne College of Art and Design, Lausanne Switzerland (S)

Lawrence University, Department of Art, Appleton WI (S)

Irene Leache Memorial, Norfolk VA

League of New Hampshire Craftsmen, Concord NH

Leatherstocking Brush and Palette Club Inc, Cooperstown NY

LeBrun Library, see Montclair Art Museum, Montclair NJ

Le Centre d'Art de Perce, Perce PQ

Lee Chapel and Museum, see Washington and Lee University, Lexington VA

Lee County Library, Tupelo MS

Leeds Art Galleries, Leeds England

Leeds Gallery, see Earlham College, Richmond IN

Lee Hall Gallery, see Northern Michigan University, Marquette MI

Harold B Lee Library, see Brigham Young University, Provo UT

Leelanau Summer Art School, Leland MI (S)

Rudolph E Lee Gallery, see Clemson University, Clemson SC

Leeward Community College, Arts and Humanities Division, Pearl City HI (S)

Legislative Building Art Gallery, Regina SK

Lehigh University, Department of Art and Architecture, Bethlehem PA (S)

Lehigh University Galleries, Bethlehem PA

Robert Lehman Collection Library, see Metropolitan Museum of Art, New York NY

Leicester Polytechnic, Faculty of Art and Design, Leicester England (S)

Leicestershire Museums, Art Galleries and Records Service, Leicestershire Museum and Art Gallery, Leicester England

Lemoyne Art Center, Tallahassee FL (S)

Lemoyne Art Foundation, Tallahassee FL

Le Moyne College, Art Department, Syracuse NY (S)

LeMoyne College, Art Gallery, Syracuse NY

Le Musee Regional de Rimouski, Rimouski PQ

Lenbach House City Gallery, see Stadtische Gallerie im Lanbachhaus, Munich Germany, Federal Republic of

Lenoir Rhyne College, Department of Art, Hickory NC (S)

Paul J Leonard Library, see San Francisco State University, San Francisco CA

Anna Leonowens Gallery, see Nova Scotia College of Art and Design, Halifax NS

LeSueur County Historical Society Museum, Elysian MN

Lewis and Clark College, Department of Art, Portland OR (S)

Lewis and Clark Community College, Art Dept, Godfrey IL (S)

Lewis-Clark State College, Art Department, Lewiston ID (S)

G Pillow Lewis Memorial Library, see Memphis Academy of Arts, Memphis TN

John and Ada Lewis Memorial Library, see University of Pennsylvania, Philadelphia PA

Irene Lewisohn Costume Reference Library, see Metropolitan Museum of Art, New York NY

Lexington Art League, Inc, Lexington KY

Lexington Public Library, Lexington KY

Leyden Municipal Museum, see Stedelijk Museum de Lakenhal, Leiden Netherlands

Liberty Hall Museum, Frankfort KY

Liberty Life Insurance Company, Greenville SC

Library Association of La Jolla, Athenaeum Music and Arts Library, La Jolla CA

Library Company of Philadelphia, Philadelphia PA

Library of Congress, Washington DC

Library of Royal Academy of Letters, History and Antiquities, see Statens Historiska Museum, Stockholm Sweden

Library of the Estonian State Art Institute, Tallinn Ussr

Licking County Art Association Gallery, Newark OH

Liebieghaus, Museum Alter Plastik, Museum of Sculpture, Frankfurt Germany, Federal Republic of

Liege Museums of Archeology and Decorative Arts, see Musees d'Archeologie et d'Arts Decoratifs, Liege Belgium

Lighthouse Gallery, Tequesta FL

Lillehammer Art Museum, see Lillehammer Bys Malerisamling, Lillehammer Norway

Lillehammer Bys Malerisamling, Lillehammer Art Museum, Lillehammer Norway

Limestone College, Art Department, Gaffney SC (S)

Lincoln Center for the Performing Arts, New York NY

Lincoln Community Arts Council, Lincoln NE

Lincoln County Cultural and Historical Association, Wiscasset ME

Lincoln County Fire Museum, see Lincoln County Cultural and Historical Association, Wiscasset ME

Lincoln County Museum, see Lincoln County Cultural and Historical Association, Wiscasset ME

Louis A Warren Lincoln Library and Museum, see Lincoln National Life Foundation, Inc, Fort Wayne IN

Lincoln Memorial Shrine, Redlands CA

Lincoln Memorial University, Department of Fine Arts, Harrogate TN (S)

Lincoln National Life Foundation, Inc, Louis A Warren Lincoln Library and Museum, Fort Wayne IN

Lincolnshire Museums, Usher Gallery, Lincoln England

Lincoln University, Art Department, Jefferson City MO (S)

Lindenwood Colleges, Harry D Hendren Gallery, Saint Charles MO

Lindenwood Colleges, Art Dept, Saint Charles MO (S)

Linfield College, Art Department, McMinnville OR (S)

Linn Benton Community College, Art Department, Albany OR (S)

Listasafn Einars Jonssonar, National Einar Jonsson Gallery, Reykjavik Iceland

Litchfield Historical Society, Litchfield CT

E H Little Gallery, see Memphis State University, Memphis TN

Little Firehouse Studio, see Southeast Arkansas Arts and Science Center, Pine Bluff AR (S)

Little Gallery, see Black Hills Art Center, Spearfish SD

Little Gallery, Studio Angelico, see Siena Heights College, Adrian MI

Livingston College, see Rutgers, the State University of New Jersey, New Brunswick NJ (S)

Livingston University, Division of Fine Arts, Livingston AL (S)

Lizzadro Museum of Lapidary Art, Elmhurst IL

James Lloyd Library, see Yankton College, Yankton SD

Lloydminster Barr Colony Museum Committee, Lloydminster SK

L & N Railroad Depot Gallery, see Singing River Art Association Inc, Pascagoula MS

Loch Haven Art Center, Inc, Orlando FL

Lockwood-Mathews Mansion Museum, Norwalk CT

Lockwood Memorial Library, see State University of New York at Buffalo, Buffalo NY

Loma Linda University, La Sierra Campus, Art Department, Riverside CA (S)

Jack London State Historic Park, Glen Ellen CA

London Regional Art Gallery, London ON

Long Beach Art Association, Long Beach NY

Long Beach City College, Department of Art, Long Beach CA (S)

Long Beach Museum of Art, Long Beach CA

Long Beach Public Library, Long Beach NY

Long Beach Public Library, Long Beach CA

Long Branch Historical Museum, Long Branch NJ

Longfellow National Historic Site, Cambridge MA

Longfellow's Wayside Inn, South Sudbury MA

Long Island Historical Society, Brooklyn NY

Long Island University, Brooklyn Center Art Department, Brooklyn NY (S)

Longview Museum and Arts Center, Longview TX

Longwood College, Department of Art, Farmville VA (S)

Longwood College, Bedford Gallery, Farmville VA

Loop College, see City Colleges of Chicago, Chicago IL (S)

Lopez Memorial Museum, Manila Philippines

Loretto Heights College, Department of Art, Denver CO (S)

Loretto-Hilton Center Gallery, see Webster College, St Louis MO

Los Alamos Arts Council, Los Alamos NM

Los Angeles Art Association and Galleries, Los Angeles CA

Los Angeles City College, Department of Art, Los Angeles CA (S)

Los Angeles County Museum of Art, Los Angeles CA

Los Angeles Harbor College, Art Department, Wilmington CA (S)

Los Angeles Harbor College Art Gallery, Wilmington CA

Los Angeles Institute of Contemporary Art, Los Angeles CA

Los Angeles Public Library, Art and Music Department, Los Angeles CA

Los Angeles Trade-Technical College Library, Los Angeles CA

Lotos Club, New York NY

Louisiana Arts and Science Center, Baton Rouge LA

Louisiana College, Dept of Art, Pineville LA (S)

Louisiana Historical Association, Confederate Museum, New Orleans LA

Louisiana Historical Center Library, see Louisiana State Museum, New Orleans LA

Louisiana Museum of Modern Art, Humlebaek Denmark

Louisiana State Exhibit Museum, Shreveport LA

Louisiana State Museum, New Orleans LA

Louisiana State University, Department of Fine Arts, Baton Rouge LA (S)

Louisiana State University, Baton Rouge LA

Louisiana Tech University, School of Art & Architecture, Ruston LA (S)

Louisville School of Art, Anchorage KY (S)

Louisville School of Art Gallery, Anchorage KY

Lourdes College, Art Department, Sylvania OH (S)

Louvre Museum, see Musee du Louvre, Paris France

Lovejoy Library, see Southern Illinois University, Edwardsville IL

Lovelace Medical Foundation, Art Collection, Albuquerque NM

Loveland Museum, Loveland CO

Love Library, see University of Nebraska Lincoln, Lincoln NE

Lovely Lane Museum, see United Methodist Historical Society, Baltimore MD

Lowe Art Museum, see University of Miami, Coral Gables FL

Emily Lowe Gallery, see Hofstra University, Hempstead NY

Joe and Emily Lowe Art Gallery, see Syracuse University, Syracuse NY

Lowell Art Association, Whistler House and Parker Gallery, Lowell MA

Lower Columbia College, Longview WA (S)

R H Lowie Museum of Anthropology, see University of California, Berkeley CA

Loyala University of Chigago, Martin D'Arcy Gallery of Art, Chicago IL

Loyola Marymount University, Art Gallery, Los Angeles CA

Loyola Marymount University, Department of Art, Los Angeles CA (S)

Loyola University of Chicago, Fine Arts Department, Chicago IL (S)

Loyola University of New Orleans, Department of Visual Arts, New Orleans LA (S)

Lubbock Art Association, Inc, Lubbock TX

Lumpkin Library, see Blackburn College, Carlinville IL

L'Universite Laval, Ecole des Arts Visuels de L'Universite Laval, Quebec PQ

Jeannette Lusk Library Collection, see South Dakota State University, Brookings SD

Lutheran Brethren Schools, Fergus Falls MN (S)

Lutheran Brotherhood, Minneapolis MN

Luther College, Art Department, Decorah IA (S)

Lyceum Club and Women's Art Association of Canada, Toronto ON

Lycoming College, Art Department, Williamsport PA (S)

Lycoming College Gallery, Williamsport PA

Lye-Tapley Shoe Shop (1830) and Vaughan Doll House, see Essex Institute, Salem MA

Lyme Art Association, Inc, Old Lyme CT

Lyme Historical Society, Inc, Old Lyme CT

Lynchburg College, Art Department, Lynchburg VA (S)

Lynchburg Fine Arts Center Inc, Lynchburg VA

Lyndhurst, Tarrytown NY

Lynnwood Arts Centre, Simcoe ON

Harrye Lyons Design Library, see North Carolina State University, Raleigh NC

Mabee-Gerrer Museum, see Saint Gregory's Abbey and College, Shawnee OK

MacAlester College, Department of Art, Saint Paul MN (S)

Macalester College Galleries, St Paul MN

MacArthur Memorial, Norfolk VA

Macdonald Steward Art Centre, Guelph ON

MacDonald-Steward Library, see Society of the Montreal Military and Maritime Museum, Montreal PQ

Norman Mackenzie Art Gallery Resource Centre, see University of Regina, Regina SK

Norman Mackenzie Art Gallery, see University of Regina, Regina SK

Mack Library, see Bob Jones University, Greenville SC

Mack Trucks Art Reference Library, see Allentown Art Museum, Allentown PA

MacMurray College, Art Department, Jacksonville IL (S)

Charles H MacNider Museum, Mason City IA

Macomb County Community College, Art Department, Warren MI (S)

Madison Area Technical College, Communication Arts, Madison WI (S)

Madison Art Center, Madison WI

Madison County Historical Society, Oneida NY

Madison Public Library, Madison WI

Madonna College, Art Dept, Livonia MI (S)

Judah L Magnes Memorial Museum, Western Jewish History Center, Berkeley CA

Magyar Nemzeti Galeria, Hungarian National Gallery, Budapest Hungary

Maharaja Sayajirao University of Baroda, Faculty of Fine Arts, Baroda India (S)

Mahoney Library, see College of Saint Elizabeth, Convent Station NJ

Maine Art Gallery, Old Academy, see Lincoln County Cultural and Historical Association, Wiscasset ME

Maine Coast Artists, Rockport ME

Maine Historical Society, Portland ME

Maine Maritime Museum, Bath ME

Mainline Center of the Arts, Haverford PA (S)

Main Line Center of the Arts, Haverford PA

Maitland Art Center Research Studio, Maitland FL

Malcolm X College, see City Colleges of Chicago, Chicago IL (S)

Malden Bridge School of Art, Malden Bridge NY (S)

Malden Public Library, Malden MA

Malone College, Department of Art, Canton OH (S)

Maltwood Art Museum and Gallery, see University of Victoria, Victoria BC

Man and His World, see Pavilion of Humour, Montreal PQ

Manatee Junior College, Department of Art, Bradenton FL (S)

Manchester City Art Galleries, Manchester England

Manchester City Library, Manchester NH

Manchester College, Art Department, North Manchester IN (S)

Manchester Community College, Fine Arts Department, Manchester CT (S)

Manchester Historic Association, Manchester NH

Manchester Institute of Arts and Sciences, Manchester NH (S)

Manchester Institute of Arts and Sciences Gallery, Manchester NH

Manchester Polytechnic, Faculty of Art and Design, Manchester England (S)

Mandeville Art Gallery, see University of California-San Diego, La Jolla CA

Manhattan College, School of Arts and Sciences, Bronx NY (S)

Manhattanville College, Brownson Art Gallery, Purchase NY

Manhattanville College, Art Department, Purchase NY (S)

Joseph Manigault House, see Charleston Museum, Charleston SC

Manitoba Association of Architects, Winnipeg MB

New York Institute of Photography, New York NY (S)

New York Institute of Technology, Fine Arts Department, Old Westbury NY (S)

New York Institute of Technology Gallery, Old Westbury NY

New York Public Library, New York NY

New York School of Interior Design, New York NY (S)

New York School of Interior Design Library, New York NY

New York Society of Architects, New York NY

New York State College of Ceramics at Alfred University, Scholes Library of Ceramics, Alfred NY

New York State College of Ceramics at Alfred University, Division of Art & Design, Alfred NY (S)

New York State College of Human Ecology, see Cornell University, Ithaca NY (S)

New York State Historical Association, Cooperstown NY

New York State Library, Manuscripts and Special Collections, Albany NY

New York State Museum, Albany NY

New York Studio School of Drawing, Painting and Sculpture, New York NY (S)

New York University, New York NY

New York University, Institute of Fine Arts, New York NY (S)

Nexus Gallery, see Foundation for Today's Art, Philadelphia PA

Elizabet Ney Museum, Austin TX

Niagara County Community College, Fine Arts Div, Sanborn NY (S)

Niagara County Community College Art Gallery, Sanborn NY

Nicholls State University, Dept of Art, Thibodaux LA (S)

Nichols Gallery, see Mankato State University, Mankato MN

The Nickle Arts Museum, see University of Calgary, Calgary AB

Nicolaysen Art Museum, Casper WY

Nihon Mingei Kan, Japanese Folk Art Museum, Tokyo Japan

Nijmeegs Museum Commanderie van Saint Jan, Nijmegen Netherlands

Nikolaj Pavlovic Higher Institute of Fine Arts, Sofia Bulgaria (S)

92nd Street YMHA-YWHA, Weill Art Gallery, New York NY

NMHT Branch of Smithsonian Institution Libraries, see National Museum of History and Technology, Washington DC

Nobles County Art Center Gallery, Worthington MN

Harry Nohr Art Gallery, see University of Wisconsin, Platteville WI

No Man's Land Historical Society, Goodwell OK

Nook Farm Research Library, see Mark Twain Memorial, Hartford CT

Noord-Brabants Museum, Hertogenbosch Netherlands

Nordiska Museet, Scandinavian Museum, Stockholm Sweden

Nordjyllands Kunstmuseum, Art Museum of Northern Jutland, Aalborg Denmark

Nordstrand Visual Arts Gallery, see Wayne State College, Wayne NE

Norfolk State College, Fine Arts Department, Norfolk VA (S)

Norsk Folkemuseum, Norwegian Folk Museum, Oslo Norway

Norsk Sjöfartsmuseum, Norwegian Maritime Museum, Oslo Norway

Northampton County Area Community College, Art Department, Bethlehem PA (S)

North Arkansas Community College, Art Department, Harrison AR (S)

North Bohemian Gallery of Fine Arts, see Severoceska Galerie Vytvarneho Umeni, Litomerice Czechoslovakia

North Canton Public Library, Little Art Gallery, North Canton OH

North Carolina Agricultural and Technical State University, Art Department, Greensboro NC (S)

North Carolina Art Society, Raleigh NC

North Carolina Central University, Museum of Art, Durham NC

North Carolina Central University, Art Dept, Durham NC (S)

North Carolina Museum of Art, Department of Cultural Resources, Raleigh NC

North Carolina Museums Council, Raleigh NC

North Carolina State University, Harrye Lyons Design Library, Raleigh NC

North Carolina State University at Raleigh, School of Design, Raleigh NC (S)

North Country Museum of Arts, Park Rapids MN

North Dakota State School of Science, Department of Art, Wahpeton ND (S)

Northeastern Illinois University, Art Department, Chicago IL (S)

Northeastern Junior College, Department of Art, Sterling CO (S)

Northeastern Nevada Museum, Elko NV

Northeastern Oklahoma A & M College, Art Department, Miami OK (S)

Northeastern Oklahoma State University, Tahlequah OK (S)

Northeast Louisiana University, Department of Art, Monroe LA (S)

Northeast Mississippi Junior College, Art Department, Booneville MS (S)

Northeast Missouri State University, Art Department, Kirksville MO (S)

Northeast Technical Community College, Dept of Art, Norfolk NE (S)

Northern Arizona University, Art Department, Flagstaff AZ (S)

Northern Arizona University, Art Gallery, Flagstaff AZ

Northern Illinois University, Swen Parson Gallery and Gallery 200, De Kalb IL

Northern Illinois University, Department of Art, De Kalb IL (S)

Northern Kentucky University, Fine Arts Department, Highland Heights KY (S)

Northern Kentucky University Gallery, Highland Heights KY

Northern Michigan University, Lee Hall Gallery, Marquette MI

Northern Michigan University, Dept of Art & Design, Marquette MI (S)

Northern Montana College, Department of Art, Havre MT (S)

Northern State College, Art Dept, Aberdeen SD (S)

Northern Virginia Community College, Art Department, Annandale VA (S)

Northern Virginia Fine Arts Association, Alexandria VA

Northestern Illinois University, North River Community Gallery, Chicago IL

North Hennepin Community College, Art Department, Minneapolis MN (S)

North Hennepin Community College, Art Gallery, Brooklyn Park MN

North Iowa Area Community College, Department of Art, Mason City IA (S)

North Park College, Art Department, Chicago IL (S)

Northport-East Northport Public Library, Northport NY

North River Community Gallery, see Northestern Illinois University, Chicago IL

North Seattle Community College, Art Department, Seattle WA (S)

North Shore Art League, Winnetka IL

North Shore Art League, Winnetka IL (S)

North Shore Arts Associaiton, Inc, Gloucester MA

North Texas State University, Art Department, Denton TX (S)

North Texas State University, Art Gallery, Denton TX

Northwest Community College, Powell WY (S)

Northwestern College, Ramaker Library Art Gallery, Orange City IA

Northwestern College, Art Department, Orange City IA (S)

Northwestern Michigan College, Art Dept, Traverse City MI (S)

Northwestern Michigan College, Mark Osterlin Library, Traverse City MI

Northwestern Oklahoma State University, Art Department, Alva OK (S)

Northwestern State University of Louisiana, Dept of Art, Natchitoches LA (S)

Northwestern University, Evanston IL

Northwestern University, Evanston, Evanston IL (S)

Northwest Kansas Cultural Arts Center, see Colby Community College, Colby KS

Northwest Missouri State University, Dept of Art, Maryville MO (S)

Northwest Missouri State University, DeLuce Gallery, Maryville MO

Northwest Nazarene College, Art Department, Nampa ID (S)

Norton Gallery and School of Art, West Palm Beach FL

R W Norton Art Gallery, Shreveport LA

Norwegian-American Museum, see Vesterheim, Decorah IA

Norwegian Folk Museum, see Norsk Folkemuseum, Oslo Norway

Norwegian Maritime Museum, see Norsk Sjöfartsmuseum, Oslo Norway

Norwich Art School, Norwich Free Academy, Art Dept, Norwich CT (S)

Norwich Free Academy, Slater Memorial Museum & Converse Art Gallery, Norwich CT

Notre Dame College, Art Department, Saint Louis MO (S)

Notre Dame College, Art Department, Manchester NH (S)

Nova Scotia Association of Architects, Halifax NS

Nova Scotia College of Art and Design, Halifax NS (S)

Nova Scotia College of Art and Design, Anna Leonowens Gallery, Halifax NS

Nova Scotia Technical College, Faculty of Architecture, Halifax NS (S)

Noyes, Read and Gray Galleries, see Antioch College, Yellow Springs OH

Nutana Collegiate Institute, Memorial Library and Art Gallery, Saskatoon SK

Nutley Art Center, Nutley NJ (S)

Ny Carlsberg Glyptothek, Carlsberg Gallery, Copenhagen Denmark

Oak Hall, Niagara Falls ON

Oakland City College, Division of Fine Arts, Oakland City IN (S)

Oakland City College Library, Art Department, Oakland City IN

Oakland Museum, Oakland CA

Oakland Public Library, Fine Arts Section, Oakland CA

Oakland University, Meadow Brook Art Gallery, Rochester MI

Oakland University, Dept of Art & Art History, Rochester MI (S)

Oak Ridge Community Art Center, Oak Ridge TN

Oakville Centennial-Gairloch Galleries, Oakville ON

Oatlands, Leesburg VA

Oberlin College, Department of Art, Oberlin OH (S)

Oberlin College, Allen Memorial Art Museum, Oberlin OH

Occidental College, Art Department, Los Angeles CA (S)

Occidental College Gallery, Los Angeles CA

Ocean City Arts Center, Ocean City NJ

Ocean City School of Art, Ocean City NJ (S)

Ocean County College, Humanities Department, Toms River NJ (S)

Octagon Center for the Arts, Ames IA

Mayo Hayes O'Donnell Library, see Monterey History and Art Association, Monterey CA

Offentliche Kunstsammlung-Kunstmuseum Basel, Museum of Fine Arts, Basel Switzerland

Oglebay Institute, Stifel Fine Arts Center, Wheeling WV

Oglebay Institute Mansion Museum, Wheeling WV

Oglebay Institute Mansion Museum Committee, see Oglebay Institute Mansion Museum, Wheeling WV

Providence Athenaeum, Providence RI

Providence College, Department of Fine Arts, Providence RI (S)

Providence Public Library, Art and Music Dept, Providence RI

Providence Water Color Club, Providence RI

Provincetown Art Association and Museum, Provincetown MA

Provincial Archives of Alberta, see Department of Culture, Government of the Province of Alberta, Edmonton AB

Provincial Archives of British Columbia, Victoria BC

Provincial Archives of Manitoba, Winnipeg MB

Provincial Museum of Alberta, see Department of Culture, Government of the Province of Alberta, Edmonton AB

Public Archives of Canada, Ottawa ON

Public Archives of Nova Scotia, Halifax NS

Public Art Fund, Inc, New York NY

Public Library of Charlotte and Mecklenburg County Charlotte NC

Public Library of Cincinnati and Hamilton County, Art and Music Department, Cincinnati OH

Public Library of Columbus and Franklin County, Humanities, Fine Arts and Recreation Division, Columbus OH

Public Library of Fort Wayne and Allen County, Fort Wayne IN

Public Library of the District of Columbia, Washington DC

Purdue University, Gallery I, Gallery II, Union Gallery & Stewart Center Gallery, West Lafayette IN

Purdue University Calumet Campus, Department of Creative Arts, Hammond IN (S)

Purdue University, Calumet Campus, Bicentennial Library Gallery, Hammond IN

Purdue University, Lafayette, Department of Creative Arts, Art & Design Section, West Lafayette IN (S)

George Putnam University Center, see Willamette University, Salem OR

Putnam Museum, Davenport IA

Quachita Baptist University, Department of Art, Arkadelphia AR (S)

Quapaw Quarter Association, Inc, Villa Marre, Little Rock AR

Queensborough Community College, Department of Art and Design, Bayside NY (S)

Queensborough Community College Library, Bayside NY

Queens Borough Public Library, Art and Music Division, Jamaica NY

Queens College, Art Dept, Charlotte NC (S)

Queens College of the City University of New York, Art Collection, Flushing NY

Queen's Gallery, London England

Queensland Art Gallery, Brisbane Australia

Queens Museum, Flushing NY

Queen's University, Department of Art, Kingston ON (S)

Queen's University, Agnes Etherington Art Centre, Kingston ON

Queen Victoria Museum and Art Gallery, Tasmania Australia

Ellen S Quillin Memorial Library, see San Antonio Museum Association, Inc, San Antonio TX

Quincy Art Center, Quincy IL

Quincy College, Dept of Art, Quincy IL (S)

Quincy College, Art Gallery, Quincy IL

Quincy Society of Fine Arts, Quincy IL

Racine Art Association, Racine WI

Racolta delle Stampe Achille Bertarelli, see Museo d'Arte Antica, Milan Italy

Radford University, Art Department, Radford VA (S)

Rahr-West Museum and Civic Center, Manitowoc WI

Rainier National Bank, Seattle WA

J K Ralston Museum and Art Center, Sidney MT

Willo Ralston Library for Historical Research, see J K Ralston Museum and Art Center, Sidney MT

Ralyn Art Center, Lakewood NJ (S)

Ramaker Library Art Gallery, see Northwestern College, Orange City IA

Ramat Hanegev College, Yeroham Israel (S)

Josephine D Randall Junior Museum, San Francisco CA

Jasper Rand Art Museum, see Westfield Athenaeum, Westfield MA

Randolph-Macon Woman's College, Department of Art, Lynchburg VA (S)

Randolph-Macon Womans College, Art Gallery, Lynchburg VA

Leah Ransburg Art Gallery, see Indiana Central University, Indianapolis IN

Elmer E Rasmuson Library, see University of Alaska, Fairbanks AK

Rautenstrach-Joest-Museum, see Museen der Stadt Köln, Cologne Germany, Federal Republic of

Rawalpindi Gallery of Modern Art, see Art Gallery Society of Contemporary Art, Rawalpindi Pakistan

Ray-Vogue School of Design, Chicago IL (S)

Reading Public Museum and Art Gallery, Reading PA

Red Deer College, Department of Art and Design, Red Deer AB (S)

Redding Museum & Art Center, Redding CA

Redlands Art Association, Redlands CA

Red Lodge, see City Art Gallery, Bristol England

Red River Valley Museum, Vernon TX

Redwood Library and Athenaeum, Newport RI

Carroll Reece Museum, see East Tennessee State University, Johnson City TN

Reed College, Department of Art, Portland OR (S)

Reed College Art Gallery, Portland OR

Martha Stecher Reed Art Library, see Akron Art Institute, Akron OH

Regina Public Library, Dunlot Art Gallery, Regina SK

Regional Museum of Nuevo Leon, see Museo Regional de Nuevo Leon, Monterrey Mexico

Region of Peel Museum and Art Gallery, Brampton ON

Regis College, L J Walters Jr Gallery, Weston MA

Regis College, Department of Art, Weston MA (S)

Rehoboth Art League, Inc, Rehoboth Beach DE

Rehoboth Art League, Inc, Rehoboth Beach DE (S)

Religious Americana Museum, Ringoes NJ

Rembrandthouse Museum, see Museum Het Rembrandthuis, Amsterdam Netherlands

Remington Art Museum, Ogdensburg NY

Rensselaer County Historical Society, Troy NY

Rensselaer Newman Foundation Chapel and Cultural Center, Troy NY

Rensselaer Polytechnic Institute, Troy NY (S)

John B Rentmeister Western Americana Library, see Brigham City Museum-Gallery, Brigham City UT

Renwick Gallery, see National Collection of Fine Arts, Washington DC

Revoltella Civic Museum-Gallery of Modern Art, see Civico Museo Revoltella-Galleria d'Arte Moderna, Trieste Italy

Reynolda House, Inc, Winston-Salem NC

R J Reynolds Industries, Inc, Winston-Salem NC

Rheinisches Landesmuseum Bonn, Rhineland Museum, Bonn Germany, Federal Republic of

Rhineland Museum, see Rheinisches Landesmuseum Bonn, Bonn Germany, Federal Republic of

Rhode Island College, Art Department, Providence RI (S)

Rhode Island College, Edward M Bannister Gallery, Providence RI

Rhode Island Historical Society, Providence RI

Rhode Island Junior College, Department of Art, Warwick RI (S)

Rhode Island Junior College, Art Department Gallery, Warwick RI

Rhode Island School of Design, Museum of Art, Providence RI

Rhode Island School of Design, Providence RI (S)

Rice University, Institute for the Arts, Rice Museum, Houston TX

Rice University, Department of Art and Art History, Houston TX (S)

Richard Bland College, Art Department, Petersburg VA (S)

Richard Gallery and Almond Tea Gallery, Divisions of Studios of Jack Richard, Cuyahoga Falls OH

Richardson Memorial Library, see Saint Louis Art Museum, Saint Louis MO

Studios of Jack Richard Creative School of Design, Cuyahoga Falls OH (S)

Richland Art Workshop of the Columbia Museum of Art, Columbia SC (S)

Richmond Art Center, Richmond CA

Richmond Arts Centre, Richmond BC

Richmond Public Library, Richmond VA

Ricker Library of Architecture and Art, see University of Illinois at Urbana-Champaign, Urbana IL

Ricks College, Department of Art, Rexburg ID (S)

Rider College, Department of Fine Arts, Lawrenceville NJ (S)

Rider College, Lawrenceville NJ

Ridgewood School of Art and Design, Ridgewood NJ (S)

Rijksakademie Van Beeldende Kunsten, State Academy of Fine Arts, Amsterdam Netherlands (S)

Rijksmuseum, State Museum, Amsterdam Netherlands

Rijksmuseum Vincent Van Gogh, Vincent Van Gogh State Museum, Amsterdam Netherlands

Rinehart School of Sculpture, see Maryland Institute, Baltimore MD (S)

Ring House Gallery, see University of Alberta, Edmonton AB

John and Mable Ringling Museum of Art, Sarasota FL

Ringling School of Art, Sarasota FL (S)

Ringling School of Art Library, Sarasota FL

Ringwood Manor House Museum, Ringwood NJ

Rio Hondo College, Fine Arts Department, Whittier CA (S)

Rio Hondo College Art Gallery, Whittier CA

Ripon College, Art Department, Ripon WI (S)

Ripon College Art Gallery, Ripon WI

Riverside Art Center and Museum, Riverside CA

Riverside City College, Department of Art, Riverside CA (S)

Riverside County Art and Cultural Center, Edward-Dean Museum of Decorative Arts, Cherry Valley CA

River Vale Public Library, River Vale NJ

Rivier College, Art Department, Nashua NH (S)

Römisch-Germanisches Museum, see Museen der Stadt Köln, Cologne Germany, Federal Republic of

Roanoke College, Art Department, Salem VA (S)

Roanoke Fine Arts Center, Roanoke VA

Roberson Center, Binghamton NY

Roberson Center for the Arts and Sciences, Binghamton NY (S)

Ken Roberts Gallery, see New Mexico Art League, Albuquerque NM

Roberts Room, see Towson State University, Towson MD

Mary S Robinson Art Library, see Foothills Art Center, Inc, Golden CO

Rochester Art Center, Rochester MN

Rochester Community College, Art Department, Rochester MN (S)

Rochester Historical Society, Rochester NY

Rochester Institute of Technology, Rochester NY (S)

Abby Aldrich Rockefeller Folk Art Center, Williamsburg VA

M C Rockefeller Arts Center Gallery, see State University of New York College at Fredonia, Fredonia NY

Rockford Art Association, Burpee Art Museum, Rockford IL

Rockford College, Department of Fine Arts, Rockford IL (S)

Rockland Community College, Art Department, Suffern NY (S)

Rockport Art Association, Rockport MA

Rock Valley College, Dept of Art, Rockford IL (S)

Rockwell-Corning Museum, Corning NY

Rockwell International Corporation, Pittsburgh PA

Rocky Mountain College, Art Dept, Billings MT (S)

Rocky Mountain School of Art, Denver CO (S)

Rocky Mountain School of Art Gallery, Denver CO

Rocky Mount Arts and Crafts Center, Rocky Mount NC

University of Arizona, Tucson AZ
University of Arizona, Department of Art, Tucson AZ (S)
University of Arkansas, Fayetteville AR
University of Arkansas, Art Slide Library, Little Rock AR
University of Arkansas, Art Department, Fayetteville AR (S)
University of Arkansas at Little Rock, Department of Art, Little Rock AR (S)
University of Auckland, Fine Arts Library, Auckland New Zealand
University of Auckland, School of Fine Arts, Auckland New Zealand (S)
University of Bridgeport, Art Department, Bridgeport CT (S)
University of Bridgeport, Magnus Wahlstrom Library, Bridgeport CT
University of British Columbia, Vancouver BC
University of British Columbia, Vancouver BC (S)
University of Calgary, Department of Art, Calgary AB (S)
University of Calgary, The Nickle Arts Museum, Calgary AB
University of California, University Art Galleries and California Museum of Photography, Riverside CA
University of California, Davis CA
University of California, Berkeley CA
University of California at Santa Cruz, Art Board of Studies, Santa Cruz CA (S)
University of California, Berkeley, Department of Art, Berkeley CA (S)
University of California, Davis, Art Department, Davis CA (S)
University of California, Irvine, Studio Art Department, Irvine CA (S)
University of California Irvine Art Gallery, Irvine CA
University of California, Los Angeles, Los Angeles CA
University of California, Los Angeles, Department of Art, Los Angeles CA (S)
University of California, Riverside, Riverside CA (S)
University of California-San Diego, La Jolla CA
University of California, San Diego, Visual Arts Department, La Jolla CA (S)
University of California, Santa Barbara, Art Department, Santa Barbara CA (S)
University of California, Santa Barbara, Santa Barbara CA
University of Cambridge, Fitzwilliam Museum, Cambridge England
University of Central Arkansas, Art Department, Conway AR (S)
University of Charleston, Art Department, Charleston WV (S)
University of Chicago, Department of Art History & Committee on Art & Design, Chicago IL (S)
University of Chicago, Chicago IL
University of Cincinnati, Cincinnati OH
University of Cincinnati, College of Design, Architecture and Art, Cincinnati OH (S)
University of Colorado, Boulder CO (S)
University of Colorado Art Galleries, Boulder CO
University of Colorado at Denver, Department of Fine Arts, Denver CO (S)
University of Connecticut, Storrs CT
University of Connecticut, Art Department, Storrs CT (S)
University of Dayton, Fine Arts Division, Dayton OH (S)
University of Delaware, Newark DE
University of Delaware, Department of Art, Newark DE (S)
University of Denver, School of Art, Denver CO (S)
University of Evansville, Art Dept, Evansville IN (S)
University of Evansville, Evansville IN
University of Exeter, American Arts Documentation Centre, Exeter England
University of Florida, Department of Art, Gainesville FL (S)
University of Florida, Gainesville FL
University of Georgia, Athens GA
University of Georgia, Franklin College of Arts and Sciences, Division of Fine Arts, Athens GA (S)

University of Gothenburg, School of Crafts and Design, Gothenburg Sweden (S)
University of Guelph, Fine Art Department, Guelph ON (S)
University of Hartford, Joseloff Gallery, West Hartford CT
University of Hawaii at Manoa, Art Gallery, Honolulu HI
University of Hawaii at Manoa, Department of Art, Honolulu HI (S)
University of Houston, Sarah Campbell Blaffer Gallery, Houston TX
University of Houston, Department of Art, Houston TX (S)
University of Idaho, Department of Art and Architecture, Moscow ID (S)
University of Idaho Museum, Moscow ID
University of Illinois, Champaign IL
University of Illinois at Chicago Circle, College of Architecture, Art & Urban Sciences, Chicago IL (S)
University of Illinois at the Medical Center, Dept of Biocommunication Arts-Medical Art, Chicago IL (S)
University of Illinois at Urbana-Champaign, World Heritage Museum, Urbana IL
University of Illinois, Urbana-Champaign, College of Fine and Applied Arts, Champaign IL (S)
University of Iowa, Iowa City IA
University of Iowa, School of Art and Art History, Iowa City IA (S)
University of Kansas, School of Fine Arts, Lawrence KS (S)
University of Kentucky, Lexington KY
University of Kentucky, Department of Art, Lexington KY (S)
University of La Verne, La Verne CA (S)
University of Lethbridge, Department of Art, Lethbridge AB (S)
University of Lethbridge Art Gallery, Lethbridge AB
University of Louisville, Louisville KY
University of Louisville, Allen R Hite Art Institute, Louisville KY (S)
University of Lowell, Department of Art, Lowell MA (S)
University of Maine, Art Department, Orono ME (S)
University of Maine at Augusta, Division of Arts and Humanities, Augusta ME (S)
University of Maine at Augusta Gallery, Augusta ME
University of Maine at Machias Art Gallery, Machias ME
University of Maine at Orono, Art Collection, Orono ME
University of Manchester, Whitworth Art Gallery, Manchester England
University of Manitoba, Winnipeg MB (S)
University of Manitoba Gallery III, Winnipeg MB
University of Mary Hardin-Baylor, Department of Fine Arts, Belton TX (S)
University of Maryland, Art Gallery, College Park MD
University of Maryland, Art Dept, College Park MD (S)
University of Maryland Baltimore County, Visual Arts Department, Catonsville MD (S)
University of Massachusetts, Amherst, Amherst MA (S)
University of Massachusetts, Amherst, Amherst MA
University of Miami, Department of Art, Coral Gables FL (S)
University of Miami, Lowe Art Museum, Coral Gables FL
University of Michigan, Ann Arbor, Ann Arbor MI (S)
University of Michigan Museum of Art, Ann Arbor MI
University of Minnesota, Minneapolis MN
University of Minnesota, Department of Design, Saint Paul MN (S)
University of Minnesota, Tweed Museum of Art, Duluth MN
University of Minnesota, Student Center Galleries, Saint Paul MN

University of Minnesota, Duluth, Art Dept, Duluth MN (S)
University of Minnesota, Minneapolis, Minneapolis MN (S)
University of Minnesota, Morris, Humanities Department, Morris MN (S)
University of Mississippi, University Museums, Oxford MS
University of Mississippi, University Gallery, University MS
University of Mississippi, Department of Art, University MS (S)
University of Missouri, Columbia MO
University of Missouri, Columbia MO (S)
University of Missouri-Kansas City, Dept of Art & Art History, Kansas City MO (S)
University of Missouri, Saint Louis, Gallery 210, Saint Louis MO
University of Missouri-Saint Louis, Art Dept, Saint Louis MO (S)
University of Montana, Gallery of Visual Arts, Missoula MT
University of Montana, Dept of Art, Missoula MT (S)
University of Montevallo, The Gallery, Montevallo AL
University of Montevallo, College of Fine Arts, Montevallo AL (S)
University of Nebraska at Omaha, Dept of Art, Omaha NE (S)
University of Nebraska Lincoln, Lincoln NE
University of Nebraska-Lincoln, Department of Art, Lincoln NE (S)
University of Nebraska-Omaha Art Galleries, Omaha NE
University of Nevada, Las Vegas, Department of Art, Las Vegas NV (S)
University of Nevada, Las Vegas, Art Gallery, Las Vegas NV
University of Nevada, Reno, Art Department, Reno NV (S)
University of New Brunswick, Art Education Section, Fredericton NB (S)
University of New Brunswick Art Centre, Fredericton NB
University of New Hampshire, University Art Galleries, Durham NH
University of New Hampshire, Department of the Arts, Durham NH (S)
University of New Haven, Department of Fine Arts, West Haven CT (S)
University of New Mexico, Albuquerque NM
University of New Mexico, Albuquerque NM (S)
University of New Orleans, Dept of Fine Arts, New Orleans LA (S)
University of New Orleans, Fine Arts Gallery, New Orleans LA
University of North Alabama, Department of Art, Florence AL (S)
University of North Carolina, Chapel Hill NC
University of North Carolina at Asheville, Dept of Art & Music, Asheville NC (S)
University of North Carolina at Chapel Hill, Art Department, Chapel Hill NC (S)
University of North Carolina at Greensboro, Chinqua-Penn Plantation House, Reidsville NC
University of North Carolina at Greensboro, Weatherspoon Art Gallery, Greensboro NC
University of North Carolina at Greensboro, Art Dept, Greensboro NC (S)
University of North Carolina at Wilmington, Art Department, Wilmington NC (S)
University of North Carolina-Charlotte, Creative Arts Dept, Charlotte NC (S)
University of North Dakota, Visual Arts Department, Grand Forks ND (S)
University of North Dakota Art Galleries, Grand Forks ND
University of Northern Colorado, John Mariani Art Gallery, Greeley CO
University of Northern Colorado, Department of Fine Arts, Greeley CO (S)
University of Northern Iowa, Department of Art, Cedar Falls IA (S)

Vassar College Art Gallery, Poughkeepsie NY

Vassar College, Art Department, Poughkeepsie NY (S)

Vatican Museums and Galleries, see Monumenti Musei e Gallerie Pontificie, Vatican City Italy

Vaudreuil Historial Museum, see Musee Historique de Vaudreuil, Woodstock PQ

Venice Painting, Drawing and Sculpture Studio, Inc, Venice CA (S)

Ventura College, Fine Arts Division, Ventura CA (S)

Verde Valley Art Association, Inc, Jerome AZ

Vermilion Community College, Art Department, Ely MN (S)

Vermilion County Museum Society, Danville IL

Vermont College of Norwich University, Philosophy, Religion and Fine Arts Department, Montpelier VT (S)

Vermont State Craft Center at Frog Hollow, Middlebury VT

Vernon Art Association, Topham Brown Gallery, Vernon BC

Vesper George School of Art, Boston MA (S)

Vesterheim, Norwegian-American Museum, Decorah IA

Vestlandske Kunstindustrimuseum, Western Norway Museum of Applied Art, Bergen Norway

Victoria and Albert Museum, London England

Victoria College, Victoria TX (S)

Victoria Mansion and Morse Libby Mansion, see Victoria Society of Maine Women, Portland ME

Victorian College of the Arts, School of Art, Melbourne Australia

Victoria Society of Maine Women, Victoria Mansion and Morse Libby Mansion, Portland ME

Victor Valley College, Art Department, Victorville CA (S)

Victor Valley College Library, Victorville CA

Michael Victor II Art Library, see Springfield Art Association of Edwards Place, Springfield IL

Villa Maria College of Buffalo, Art Department, Buffalo NY (S)

Villa Marre, see Quapaw Quarter Association, Inc, Little Rock AR

Villa Montalvo Center for the Arts, Saratoga CA

Villanova University, Department of Art and Art History, Villanova PA (S)

Vincennes University, Art Department, Vincennes IN (S)

Vincennes University, Art Slide Library, Vincennes IN

Virginia Beach Arts Center, Virginia Beach VA

Virginia Commonwealth University, School of the Arts, Richmond VA (S)

Virginia Commonwealth University, Richmond VA

Virginia Historical Society, Richmond VA

Virginia Intermont College, Fine Arts Department, Bristol VA (S)

Virginia Museum, Danville Museum of Fine Arts and History, Danville VA

Virginia Museum of Fine Arts, Richmond VA

Virginia Polytechnic Institute and State University, Blacksburg VA

Virginia State College, Fine Arts Department, Petersburg VA (S)

Virginia Tech, Department of Art, Blacksburg VA (S)

Virginia Wesleyan College, Art Department of the Humanities Division, Norfolk VA (S)

Virginia Western Community College, Commercial Art, Fine Art & Photography, Roanoke VA (S)

Visual Artists and Galleries Association, Inc, New York NY

Visual Artists and Galleries Association, Inc, New York NY

Visual Arts Center, see Fort Hays State University, Hays KS

Visual Arts Ontario, Toronto ON

Visual Studies Workshop, Rochester NY

Viterbo College, Art Department, La Crosse WI (S)

Viterbo College Art Gallery, La Crosse WI

Vizcaya Museum and Gardens, see Dade County Art Museum, Miami FL

Vysoka Skola Umeleckoprumyslova, Academy of Applied Arts, Prague Czechoslovakia (S)

Wabash College, Art Department, Crawfordsville IN (S)

Wachovia Bank & Trust Company, NA, Winston-Salem NC

Wadsworth Atheneum, Hartford CT

Wagner College, Department of Art, Staten Island NY (S)

Magnus Wahlstrom Library, see University of Bridgeport, Bridgeport CT

Wake Forest University, Department of Art, Winston-Salem NC (S)

Waldorf College, Art Department, Forest City IA (S)

Walker Art Center, Minneapolis MN

Walker Art Gallery, Liverpool England

Henry R Walker Jr Memorial Art Library, see Evansville Museum of Arts and Science, Evansville IN

Walker Museum, Fairlee VT

Wallace Collection, London England

Willoughby Wallace Memorial Library, Stony Creek CT

Wallingford Art League, Wallingford CT

Wallraf-Richartz-Museum, Museum Ludwig, see Museen der Stadt Köln, Cologne Germany, Federal Republic of

Walnut Creek Civic Arts Gallery, Walnut Creek CA

Walters Art Gallery, Baltimore MD

L J Walters Jr Gallery, see Regis College, Weston MA

Clarence Ward Art Library, see Oberlin College, Oberlin OH

John Ward House, see Essex Institute, Salem MA

Ward-Nasse Gallery, New York NY

Warwick Arts Foundation, Warwick RI

Washburn University, Mulvane Art Center, Topeka KS

Washburn University of Topeka, Department of Art, Topeka KS (S)

Washington and Jefferson College, Art Department, Washington PA (S)

Washington and Jefferson College, Commons Gallery, Washington PA

Washington and Lee University, Lexington VA

Washington and Lee University, Department of Fine Arts, Lexington VA (S)

Washington Art Association, Washington Depot CT

Washington County Museum of Fine Arts, Hagerstown MD

Washington National Insurance Company, Evanston IL

Washington State Historical Society, Tacoma WA

Washington State University, Museum of Art, Pullman WA

Washington State University, Fine Arts Department, Pullman WA (S)

Washington University, Saint Louis MO

Washington University, Saint Louis MO (S)

Waterloo Art Association, Waterloo IA

Waterloo Municipal Galleries, Waterloo IA

Waterville Historical Association, Waterville ME

Watkins Art Gallery, see American University, Washington DC

Watkins Institute, School for Adults, Nashville TN (S)

Watkins Institute, Nashville TN

Watson Gallery, see Wheaton College, Norton MA

Thomas J Watson Library, see Metropolitan Museum of Art, New York NY

Waubonsee Community College, Sugar Grove IL (S)

Wawel State Collections of Art, see Panstwowe Zbiory Sztuki na Wawelu, Cracow Poland

Wayland Baptist College, Department of Art & Music, Plainview TX (S)

Wayne Art Center, Wayne PA

Wayne Art Center, Wayne PA (S)

Waynesburg College, Department of Fine Arts, Waynesburg PA (S)

Wayne State College, Nordstrand Visual Arts Gallery, Wayne NE

Wayne State College, Art Department, Wayne NE (S)

Wayne State University, Community Arts Gallery, Detroit MI

Wayne State University, Department of Art and Art History, Detroit MI (S)

Weatherford College, Department of Humanities and Art, Weatherford TX (S)

Weatherspoon Art Gallery, see University of North Carolina at Greensboro, Greensboro NC

Weber State College, Art Department 2001, Ogden UT (S)

Webster College, Loretto-Hilton Center Gallery, St Louis MO

Webster College, Art Dept, Webster Groves MO (S)

Weidler Art Gallery, see Westmar College, LeMars IA

Paul Weigel Library, see Kansas State University, Manhattan KS

Weil Art Gallery, see Corpus Christi State University, Corpus Christi TX

Weill Art Gallery, see 92nd Street YMHA-YWHA, New York NY

Wellesley College, Wellesley MA

Wellesley College, Art Department, Wellesley MA (S)

Wellington Museum, London England

Wells College, Department of Art & Art History, Aurora NY (S)

Welsh Folk Museum, Saint Fagans Wales

Wenatchee Valley College, Gallery 76, Wenatchee WA

Wenatchee Valley College, Art Department, Wenatchee WA (S)

David Wender Library, see School of Holography, Chicago IL

Wenham Historical Association and Museum, Inc, Wenham MA

T T Wentworth, Jr Museum, Pensacola FL

Wesleyan College, Art Department, Macon GA (S)

Wesleyan University, Davison Art Center, Middletown CT

Wesleyan University, Art Department, Middletown CT (S)

West Baton Rouge Museum, Port Allen LA

West Bend Gallery of Fine Arts, West Bend WI

Westbrook College, Joan Whitney Payson Gallery of Art, Portland ME

Westchester Art Workshop, White Plains NY (S)

Westerly Public Library, Westerly RI

Western Association of Art Museums, San Francisco CA

Western Association of Art Museums, San Francisco CA

Western Canada Art Association Inc, Burnaby BC

Western Carolina University, Dept of Art, Cullowhee NC (S)

Western Colorado Center for the Arts, Inc, Grand Junction CO

Western Connecticut State College, Danbury CT (S)

Western Illinois University, Browne Hall Gallery, Macomb IL

Western Illinois University, Dept of Art, Macomb IL (S)

Western Jewish History Center, see Judah L Magnes Memorial Museum, Berkeley CA

Western Kentucky University, Bowling Green KY

Western Kentucky University, Art Department, Bowling Green KY (S)

Western Maryland College, Gallery One, Westminster MD

Western Maryland College, Art Dept, Westminster MD (S)

Western Michigan University, Department of Art, Kalamazoo MI (S)

Western Montana College, Art Dept, Dillon MT (S)

Western Montana College, Art Gallery, Dillon MT

Western New Mexico University, Dept of Fine Art, Art Div, Silver City NM (S)

Western Norway Museum of Applied Art, see Vestlandske Kunstindustrimuseum, Bergen Norway

Western Reserve Historical Society, Cleveland OH

Western State College, Quigley Hall Art Gallery, Gunnison CO

Western State College of Colorado, Department of Art, Gunnison CO (S)

Western States Arts Foundation, Denver CO

Western States Arts Foundation, Denver CO

Western Washington University, Art Department, Bellingham WA (S)

Western Wisconsin Technical Institute, Graphics Division, LACrosse WI (S)

Western Woodcarvings, Custer SD

Personnel Index

Individuals affiliated with art schools are indicated by "S".

Aach, Herb, *Pres*, Artists Technical Institute, New York NY

Aaron, Hetty Ventura, *Communications Officer*, London Regional Art Gallery, London ON

Aaseng, Lenore, *Asst Cur*, University of Minnesota, University Gallery, Minneapolis MN

Aasma, Karin, *Cur Exhib*, Rohsska Konstslojdmuseet, Rohss Museum of Arts and Crafts, Gothenburg Sweden

Abaze, Ramsay F K, *Librn*, Ghana National Museum, Library, Accra Ghana

Abbe, Elizabeth, *Librn*, Connecticut Historical Society, Library, Hartford CT

Abbe, Ronald, *Assoc Cur*, Housatonic Community College, Housatonic Museum of Art, Bridgeport CT

Abberger, Nancy, *Secy & Dir of Gallery Activities*, Morse Gallery of Art, Boulder FL

Abbey, Rita Deanin, *Prof*, University of Nevada, Las Vegas, Department of Art, Las Vegas NV (S)

Abbott, Lilly R, *Asst Treas*, Association of Honolulu Artists, Honolulu HI

Abbott, Sidney M, *Cur*, Ancient and Honorable Artillery Company of Massachusetts, Boston MA

Abd el Saniyeh Abd el, Saniyeh, *Sub-Dir*, Egyptian Museum, Cairo Egypt

Abee, Thelma M, *Asst to Dir*, Hickory Museum of Art, Inc, Hickory NC

Abel, Lorene, *Secy*, Pottstown Area Artists' Guild, Pottstown PA

Abeles, Sigmund, *Prof*, University of New Hampshire, Department of the Arts, Durham NH (S)

Abell, Richard, *Assoc Prof*, University of Minnesota, Department of Design, Saint Paul MN (S)

Abello, Juana L, *Chief Librn*, University of Santo Tomas, Library, Manila Philippines

Abelman, Arthur F, *Pres*, Sculpture Center, New York NY

Aberl, Caryl, *Volunteer Coordr*, Metropolitan Museum and Art Centers, Coral Gables FL

Abid, Ann B, *Librn*, Saint Louis Art Museum, Richardson Memorial Library, Saint Louis MO

Abita, Salvatore, *Dir Museo Villa Pignatelli*, Museo de Capodimonte, Mount Capodi Museum, Naples Italy

Abou-Ghazi, Dia, *Dir General of Museum*, Egyptian Museum, Cairo Egypt

Abou-Ghazi, Dia, *Dir*, Egyptian Museum, Library, Cairo Egypt

Aboyoussef, Sayed, *Lectr*, Georgian Court College, Department of Art, Lakewood NJ (S)

Abraham, Richard, *Head Dept*, Platte Technical Community College, Creative and Social Cluster, Columbus NE (S)

Abrahamson, Roy, *Chmn Art Educ*, Southern Illinois University, School of Art, Carbondale IL (S)

Abrams, Jean, *Coordr*, Mississippi Delta Junior College, Department of Fine Arts, Moorhead MS (S)

Abrams, Joe, *Chmn*, Mississippi Delta Junior College, Department of Fine Arts, Moorhead MS (S)

Abshier, Ann, *Public Relations*, Milwaukee Art Center, Milwaukee WI

Acero, Raul, *Instr*, Inter American University of Puerto Rico, Department of Performing Arts, San German PR (S)

Achenbach, Nancy F, *Exec Dir*, Northern Virginia Fine Arts Association, Alexandria VA

Achilles, Rolf, *Registrar*, University of Chicago, David and Alfred Smart Gallery, Chicago IL

Achofield, Peggy, *Pres*, Craftsmen's Association of British Columbia, Vancouver BC

Achuff, James, *Head Ceramics*, Chautauqua Institution, Chautauqua NY (S)

Acker, Vern, *Prof*, Eastern New Mexico University, Department of Art & Education, Portales NM (S)

Ackerman, Andrew, *Dir of Education*, Jewish Museum, New York NY

Ackerman, Ethel Ann, *Programs Dir*, Southern Oregon Historical Society, Jacksonville Museum, Jacksonville OR

Ackerman, Gerald M, *Chmn Dept*, Pomona College, Art Department, Claremont CA (S)

Ackerman, Ray, *Pres Omniplex Board of Trustees*, Omniplex, Oklahoma City OK

Ackerman, Robert, *Dean*, Drew University, College Art Gallery, Madison NJ

Ackerman, Rudy S, *Chmn Dept*, Moravian College, Department of Art, Bethlehem PA (S)

Ackley, Mark W, *Instructor*, University of Mississippi, Department of Art, University MS (S)

Ackley, Randall, *VPres*, Southeast Alaska Regional Arts Council, Inc, Sitka AK

Acorn, Eleanor, *Head Librn*, John M Cuelenaere Library, Grace Campbell Gallery, Prince Albert SK

Acorn, John Thomson, *Head Dept*, Clemson University, Department of History & Visual Studies, Clemson SC (S)

Acquavella, William, *VPres*, Art Dealers Association of America, Inc, New York NY

Adachi, Kenji, *Dir*, Tokyo Kokuritsu Kindai Bujutsukan, National Museum of Modern Art, Tokyo, Tokyo Japan

Adair, Charlene, *Secy*, Five Civilized Tribes Museum, Muskogee OK

Adams, Anne, *Registrar*, Amon Carter Museum of Western Art, Fort Worth TX

Adams, Ansel, *Chmn*, Friends of Photography, Carmel CA

Adams, Barbara, *Cur Education*, Polk Public Museum, Lakeland FL

Adams, Bebo, *Administrative Asst*, Canton Art Instutute, Canton OH (S)

Adams, Betty, *Instr*, Saint Mary's College, Raleigh NC (S)

Adams, Bryding, *Asst to Dir*, Museum of Early Southern Decorative Arts, Old Salem Inc, Winston-Salem NC

Adams, Charles, *Chmn Dept*, Central Florida Community College, Humanities Department, Ocala FL (S)

Adams, Clinton, *Dir*, University of New Mexico, Tamarind Institute, Albuquerque NM (S)

Adams, Clinton, *Acting Dir*, University of New Mexico, University Art Museum, Albuquerque NM

Adams, Douglas, *Assoc Prof*, Morehead State University, Art Department, Morehead KY (S)

Adams, Fletcher, *Dir*, Vesper George School of Art, Boston MA (S)

Adams, Fletcher P, *Secy*, Boston Watercolor Society, Scituate MA

Adams, James R C, *Head Dept*, Manchester College, Art Department, North Manchester IN (S)

Adams, Jon W, *In Charge Art Coll*, Rainier National Bank, Seattle WA

Adams, Karen, *Chairperson Fine Arts*, Roanoke College, Art Department, Salem VA (S)

Adams, Kenneth D, *Admin Asst*, Canton Art Institute, Canton OH

Adams, Leila, *Librn*, Fort Worth Art Museum, Fort Worth Art Museum Library, Fort Worth TX

Adams, Lowell, *Dir*, Oklahoma Art Center, Oklahoma City OK

Adams, M K, *Assoc Dir*, Oklahoma Art Center, Oklahoma Art Center Library, Oklahoma City OK

Adams, Margaret B, *Dir & Cur*, Presidio of Monterey Army Museum, Monterey CA

Adams, Mary Kathryn, *Assoc Dir*, Oklahoma Art Center, Oklahoma City OK

Adams, Nicholas, *Chmn Dept*, Lehigh University, Department of Art and Architecture, Bethlehem PA (S)

Adams, Robert, *Asst Prof*, Alabama A & M University, Art Education Department, Huntsville AL (S)

Adams, Roger, *Lectr*, Nazareth College of Rochester, Art Department, Rochester NY (S)

Adams, Roger J, *Chmn*, State University of New York College at Brockport, Department of Art, Brockport NY (S)

Adams, Roxana, *Secy*, Southeast Alaska Regional Arts Council, Inc, Sitka AK

Adams, Russell, *Instr*, University of Albuquerque, Art Department, Albuquerque NM (S)

Adams, Sarah, *Library Asst*, Lake Placid School of Art Gallery, Nettie Marie Jones Fine Arts Library, Lake Placid NY

Adams, Simeon, *VPres*, Gaston County Art and History Museum, Dallas NC

Adams, Suzanne, *Instructor*, Peters Valley Craft Center, Layton NJ (S)

Adams, Vaughn P, *Chmn Design Sciences*, Arizona State University, College of Architecture, Tempe AZ (S)

Adams, Virginia, *Assoc Prof*, College of Notre Dame of Maryland, Art Dept, Baltimore MD (S)

Adams, Wesley A, *Deputy Dir Finance & Administration*, Winterthur Museum and Gardens, Winterthur DE

Adamski, Irene, *Lectr*, Villa Maria College of Buffalo, Art Department, Buffalo NY (S)

Adamson, Jim, *Instr*, Sierra College, Art Department, Rocklin CA (S)

Adamy, George E, *Dir*, Adamy's Plastics & Mold-Making Workshops, Larchmont NY (S)

Addison, Laurel, *Cur Asst*, State University of New York College at Purchase, Neuberger Museum, Purchase NY

Addiss, Stephen, *Grad Advisor*, University of Kansas, Kress Foundation Department of Art History, Lawrence KS (S)

Addiss, Stephen, *Adjunct Cur of Japanese Art*, New Orleans Museum of Art, Isaac Delgado Museum, New Orleans LA

Addkison, Andry, *Instructor*, California College of Arts and Crafts, Oakland CA (S)

Addleson, E S J, *Cur*, Durban Art Gallery, Durban South Africa, Republic of

Adelman, Jean, *Librn*, University of Pennsylvania, John and Ada Lewis Memorial Library, Philadelphia PA

Adelmann, Arthur R, *Prof*, Weber State College, Art Department 2001, Ogden UT (S)

Adhemar, Helene, *Cur Orangerie & Jeu de Paume Galleries*, Musee du Louvre, Louvre Museum, Paris France

Adkins, Cary, *Instructor*, Grand Canyon College, Art Department, Phoenix AZ (S)

Adkins, Margie, *Asst Prof*, West Texas State University, Art Department, Canyon TX (S)

Adkins, Marjorie R, *Chief Fine Arts Division*, Chicago Public Library, Art Section, Fine Arts Division, Chicago IL

Adleman, Susan I, *Secy*, Annie S Kemerer Museum, Bethlehem PA

Adler, Sebastian, *Dir*, La Jolla Museum of Contemporary Art, La Jolla CA

Adlin, Nelson, *Prof*, Community College of Baltimore, Dept of Fine & Applied Arts, Baltimore MD (S)

Adnet, Jacques, *Dir*, Ecole Nationale Superieure des Arts Decoraties, National College of Decorative Arts, Paris France (S)

Adney, Carol, *Cur*, Indiana University - Purdue University at Indianapolis, Herron School of Art, Art Gallery, Indianapolis IN

Adolph, Hubert, *Cur*, Osterreichische Galerie, Austrian Gallery, Vienna Austria

Agard, J, *Chmn*, Green Mountain College, Department of Art, Poultney VT (S)

Agee, Sheila, *Asst Dir*, South Dakota State University, South Dakota Memorial Art Center, Brookings SD

Agha, Zubeida, *Executive Dir*, Art Gallery Society of Contemporary Art, Rawalpindi Gallery of Modern Art, Rawalpindi Pakistan

Aglio, Henry, *Instr*, Parkersburg Community College, Art Department, Parkersburg WV (S)

Agnew, Charles, *Coordr Interior Design*, Art Institute of Philadelphia, Philadelphia PA (S)

Agnew, L Jack, *Assoc Prof*, Sullivan County Community College, Div of Commercial Art and Photography, Loch Sheldrake NY (S)

Agorsah, E K, *Archaeology Keeper*, Ghana National Museum, Accra Ghana

Agostini, Peter, *Prof*, University of North Carolina at Greensboro, Art Dept, Greensboro NC (S)

Agueros, Jack, *Dir*, El Museo del Barrio, New York NY

Aguet, Henry, *Chmn Commercial Art & Design*, Herron School of Art, Indiana University-Purdue University, Indianapolis, Indianapolis IN (S)

Aguglia, Robert, *Cur*, Roberson Center, Binghamton NY

Aguilar, Maria Elena, *Circulation Supv*, Art Center College of Design, James Lemont Fogg Memorial Library, Pasadena CA

Aguirre, Jesse, *Pres*, Mexican Museum, San Francisco CA

Agullo, Manolo, *Instructor*, Arkansas Arts Center, Little Rock AR (S)

Ahearn, Mary M, *Mgr Tavern Door Card Shop*, Rockport Art Association, Rockport MA

Ahmad, Sufi, *Assoc Prof*, Saint Francis College, Art Department, Fort Wayne IN (S)

Ahmadi, Reza, *Instructor*, Central Missouri State University, Art Department, Warrensburg MO (S)

Ahmedi, Hong Kyung Elizabeth, *Librn*, New York Institute of Technology Gallery, Art & Architectural Library, Old Westbury NY

Ahmerd, Bashir, *Librn Clerk*, Lahore Museum, Library, Lahore Pakistan

Aho, Charles, *Adjunct Instr*, Le Moyne College, Art Department, Syracuse NY (S)

Ahrens, Henry, *Prof*, Trenton State College, Art Department, Trenton NJ (S)

Ahrens, Kent, *Asst Prof*, Georgetown University, Department of Fine Arts, Washington DC (S)

Ahysen, Harry J, *Assoc Prof*, Sam Houston State University, Art Department, Huntsville TX (S)

Aichele, K Porter, *Vis Asst Prof*, Bernard M Baruch College of the City University of New York, Art Department, New York NY (S)

Aiches, Alan, *Dir*, Saint John's Art Gallery, Wilmington NC

Aidlin, Jerome, *Instr*, Cleveland Institute of Art, Cleveland OH (S)

Aiken, Joyce, *Chmn*, California State University, Fresno, Art Department, Fresno CA (S)

Aiken, O S, *Treas*, Florence Museum, Florence SC

Aird, David, *Dir*, Musee Historique de Vaudreuil, Vaudreuil Historial Museum, Woodstock PQ

Aistars, John, *Dir Art Prog*, Cazenovia College, Chapman Art Center Gallery, Cazenovia NY

Aistars, John, *Dir*, Cazenovia College, Art Program, Cazenovia NY (S)

Aitken, George T, *Supt*, Williams College, Museum of Art, Williamstown MA

Akagawa, Kinji, *Acting Chmn Fine Arts*, Minneapolis College of Art and Design, Minneapolis MN (S)

Aker, George, *Pres*, Sierra Arts Foundation, Reno NV

Akin, Dennis, *Chmn Fine Arts Dept*, Dickinson College, Fine Arts Department, Carlisle PA (S)

Akinshegun, Riua, *Handicapped Services Coordr*, Junior Arts Center, Los Angeles CA

Akus, Julian, *Chmn*, Eastern Connecticut State College, Art Department, Willimantic CT (S)

Alatriste, Gabriel, *Instr*, University of the Americas, Graphic Arts and Design Dept, Cholula Mexico (S)

Albacete, M J, *Assoc Dir*, Canton Art Institute, Canton OH

Albacete, Manuel J, *Assoc Dir*, Canton Art Instutute, Canton OH (S)

Alber, Zofia, *Far Eastern Art*, Muzeum Narodowe w Krakowie, National Museum in Cracow, Cracow Poland

Alberici, Clelia, *Dir*, Museo d'Arte Antica, Civiche Raccolte de Arte Applicata, Milan Italy

Alberici, Clelia, *Dir*, Museo d'Arte Antica, Racolta delle Stampe Achille Bertarelli, Milan Italy

Albert, Portia, *Head Librn*, Kansas State Historial Society Museum, Library, Topeka KS

Albi, Giuseppe, *Chmn*, Alberta Art Foundation, Edmonton AB

Albrecht, Joseph H, *Pres*, Kenneth C Beck Center for the Cultural Arts, Lakewood OH

Albright, Ripley, *Asst Cur Prints & Drawings*, Brooklyn Museum, Brooklyn NY

Alcorn, Kathryn, *Chmn*, Central State University, Art Department, Edmond OK (S)

Aldao, Federico, *Dir*, Museo Nacional de Arte Decorativo, National Museum of Decorative Art, Buenos Aires Argentina

Alderett, R, *Instructor*, Golden West College, Arts, Humanities and Social Sciences Institute, Huntington Beach CA (S)

Alderman, Bissell, *Pres*, Sharon Arts Center, Inc, Sharon NH

Aldern, Robert, *Prof*, University of South Dakota, Dept of Art, Vermillion SD (S)

Alderson, William T, *Dir Museum Studies & Art Conservation*, University of Delaware, University Gallery, Newark DE

Aldrich, Ann, *Treas*, South County Art Association, Kingston RI

Aldrich, Larry, *Founder & Pres*, Soho Center for Visual Artists, f the Performing Arts, at Lincoln Center New York

Aldridge, C Clay, *Registrar*, National Infantry Museum, Fort Benning GA

Alesch, Eugene, *Assoc Prof*, Texas Tech University, Department of Art, Lubbock TX (S)

Alexander, Annette, *Instructor*, Your Heritage House, Inc, Detroit MI

Alexander, James, *Asst Prof*, University of Alabama in Birmingham, Department of Art, Birmingham AL (S)

Alexander, Jerry, *Lectr*, California State Polytechnic University, Pomona, Art Department, Pomona CA (S)

Alexander, Joy, *Asst Cur*, University of Michigan Museum of Art, Slide and Photograph Collection, Ann Arbor MI

Alexander, Robin, *Asst Prof Art*, Eastern Oregon State College, La Grande OR (S)

Alexander, Sandi, *Museum Asst*, Portsmouth Museums and Community Arts Center, Petersburg VA

Alexander, Sharon, *Secy*, University of Minnesota, Tweed Museum of Art, Duluth MN

Alexander, Suzanne, *Asst to Cur*, Courtauld Institute Galleries, London England

Alexick, David, *Prof*, Christopher Newport College, Fine and Performing Arts, Newport News VA (S)

Alexson, F, *Pres*, Saskatoon Gallery and Conservatory Corporation, Saskatoon SK

Alfano, Domenic, *Adjunct Instructor*, New York Institute of Technology, Fine Arts Department, Old Westbury NY (S)

Alford, Constance, *Asst Prof*, Alcorn State University, Department of Fine Arts, Lorman MS (S)

Alford, Helen, *Prof*, Linfield College, Art Department, McMinnville OR (S)

Alfredson, Alfred, *Pres*, Palette and Chisel Academy of Fine Arts Gallery, Chicago IL

Al-Hilali, Neda, *Assoc Prof*, Scripps College, Art Department, Claremont CA (S)

Ali, Hakim, *Dir William Grant Still Community Arts Center*, City of Los Angeles, Municipal Arts Dept, Los Angeles CA

Ali, Nusrat, *Display Officer*, Lahore Museum, Lahore Pakistan

Alibrandi, Gaetano, *Instr*, Danforth Museum School, Framingham MA (S)

Alinari, Luca, *Vis Artist*, Studio Art Centers International, Florence Italy (S)

Alinder, James, *Executive Dir*, Friends of Photography, Carmel CA

Alipranti, Marie, *Admin Coordr*, Farmington Valley Arts Center, Avon CT

Alisauskas, Ona, *Gallery Mgr*, Mississauga Library System, Mississauga ON

Alkema, Chester, *Chairperson Dept*, Grand Valley State Colleges, Art Department, Allendale MI (S)

Allan, George, *Pres*, Lahaina Arts Society, Lahaina HI

Allan, Gerald, *Basic Studies*, Minneapolis College of Art and Design, Minneapolis MN (S)

Allan, Ruth, *Instructor*, Wenatchee Valley College, Art Department, Wenatchee WA (S)

Allara, Pamela, *Asst Prof*, Tufts University, Fine Arts Department, Medford MA (S)

Allard, L Doug, *Owner*, Flathead Indian Museum, Saint Ignatius MT

Allemann, Hans, *Co-Chairperson Graphic Design*, Philadelphia College of Art, Philadelphia PA (S)

Allen, Carl M, *Dir Gallery*, Ashland College Arts and Humanities Gallery, Ashland OH

Allen, Charles, *VPres*, Yarmouth County Historical Society Museum, Yarmouth NS

Allen, Clyde, *Chmn*, Chabot College, Humanities Division, Hayward CA (S)

Allen, F Robert, *Chmn Dept*, Saint Louis Community College at Meramec, Art Dept, Saint Louis MO (S)

Allen, Fred R, *Instructor*, Saint Louis Community College at Meramec, Art Dept, Saint Louis MO (S)

Allen, Georgia K, *Executive Dir*, Arts Council of Spartanburg County, Inc, Spartanburg SC

Allen, Homer, *Chmn Art Dept*, Kentucky State University, Jackson Hall Gallery, Frankfort KY

Allen, J Clyff, *Dir & Preparator*, Brigham Young University, B F Larsen Gallery, Provo UT

Allen, James A, *Assoc Prof*, Daemen College, Art Department, Amherst NY (S)

Allen, Jean, *VPres*, Marin Society of Artists Inc, Ross CA

Allen, Jean S, *Instr*, Haskell Indian Junior College, Art Department, Lawrence KS (S)

Allen, Jere H, *Asst Prof*, University of Mississippi, Department of Art, University MS (S)

Allen, Jerry, *Visual Arts Coordr*, King County Arts Commission, Seattle WA

Allen, Kay, *Admin Asst*, University of Southern California, University Galleries, Los Angeles CA

Allen, Kenneth, *University Pres*, University of Maine at Orono, Art Collection, Orono ME

Allen, Margaret, *Fine Arts Reference Librn*, Grace A Dow Memorial Library, Midland MI

Allen, Margaret, *Secy*, University of Western Ontario, McIntosh Art Gallery, London ON

Allen, Mary Zane, *Gallery Mgr*, University of Wisconsin, Union Art Gallery, Milwaukee WI

Allen, Max I, *Prof*, Manchester College, Art Department, North Manchester IN (S)

Allen, Michael G, *Pres Bd Trustees*, Silvermine Guild School of the Arts, New Canaan CT

Allen, N F, *Secy*, Hill Country Arts Foundation, Ingram TX

Allen, Nancy S, *Librn*, Museum of Fine Arts, William Morris Hunt Memorial Library, Boston MA

Allen, Paul F, *Asst Prof*, Concordia College, Art Department, Moorhead MN (S)

Allen, Phyllis G, *Librn*, Pioneer Museum and Haggin Galleries, Petzinger Memorial Library, Stockton CA

Allen, Phyllis G, *Registrar*, Pioneer Museum and Haggin Galleries, Stockton CA

Allen, Raymond, *Asst Prof*, Middle Tennessee State University, Art Dept, Murfreesboro TN (S)

Allen, Reginald, *Cur of Gilbert & Sullivan Coll*, Pierpont Morgan Library, New York NY

Allen, Terry, *Prof*, California State University, Fresno, Art Department, Fresno CA (S)

Allen, Timothy S, *Dir*, Central Louisiana Art Association, Alexandria Museum Visual Art Center, Alexandria LA

Allentuck, Marcia E, *Prof*, City University of New York, PhD Program in Art History, New York NY (S)

Alley, James, *Instructor*, Interlochen Arts Academy, Dept of Visual Art, Interlochen MI (S)

Alley, Jon, *Instructor*, Bucks County Community College, Fine Arts Department, Newton PA (S)

Alley, Perry, *Treas*, Hudson Valley Art Association, Watertown NY

Allgood, C H, *Dir Exhib*, Memphis State University, E H Little Gallery, Memphis TN

Allgrove, Joan, *Keeper of Textiles*, University of Manchester, Whitworth Art Gallery, Manchester England

Alling, Clarence, *Gallery Dir*, Waterloo Municipal Galleries, Waterloo IA

Allison, Clement, *Chmn Creative Arts*, Tusculum College, Fine Arts Department, Greeneville TN (S)

Allison, Donn C, *Co-Dir*, Zigler Museum, Jennings LA

Allison, Frances H, *Co-Dir*, Zigler Museum, Jennings LA

Allison, Glenn, *Cur*, University of British Columbia, Fine Arts Gallery, Vancouver BC

Allison, Michael, *Community Outreach Coordr*, Southern Alleghenies Museum of Art, Loretto PA

Allison, Patricia, *VPres*, Woodmere Art Gallery, Philadelphia PA

Allison, Zoe, *VPres & Gallery Coordr*, Columbus College, Experimental Gallery, Columbus GA

Allodi, M, *VPres & Asst Cur*, Royal Ontario Museum, Canadiana Gallery, Toronto ON

Alloway, Lawrence, *Dir*, State University of New York at Stony Brook Art Gallery, Stony Brook NY

Alloway, Lawrence, *Prof*, State University of New York at Stony Brook, Art Department, Stony Brook NY (S)

Allred, Rayma, *Secy*, Springville Museum of Art, Springville UT

Allworth, Christopher, *Pres*, Yarmouth County Historical Society Museum, Yarmouth NS

Allyn, Robert, *VPres*, Owatonna Arts Center, Owatonna MN

Almanza, Miguel, *Asst Prof*, Bethel College, Dept of Art, North Newton KS (S)

Almquist, Robert, *Discipline Coordr*, Lewis-Clark State College, Art Department, Lewiston ID (S)

Alston, Robert, *Department of Art Chmn*, Southern Oregon College, Central Art Gallery, Ashland OR

Altemose, Pamela, *Instructor*, Ocean City School of Art, Ocean City NJ (S)

Alter, Forrest, *Head Art, Music & Drama Dept*, Flint Public Library, Fine Arts Department, Flint MI

Altman, Patricia B, *Cur of Textiles & Folk Art*, University of California, Los Angeles, Museum of Cultural History, Los Angeles CA

Alton, Susanna D, *Exhib Coordr*, American Federation of Arts, New York NY

Altschuler, Franz, *Asst Prof*, Morehead State University, Art Department, Morehead KY (S)

Alvare, Carlos J, *Assoc Prof*, Lehigh University, Department of Art and Architecture, Bethlehem PA (S)

Alvarez, Janice P, *Gallery Dir*, Saint Mary's College of California, Hearst Art Gallery, Moraga CA

Alway, Richard, *Warden*, University of Toronto, Hart House, Toronto ON

Amateau, Michele, *Vis Prof*, Minneapolis College of Art and Design, Minneapolis MN (S)

Ambach, Gordon, *Pres*, State Education Department, State University of New York, Albany NY

Ambatsis, Jannis, *Librn*, Kungl Myntkabinettet Statens Museum För Mynt Medalj Och Penninghistoria, Numismatic Section, Stockholm Sweden

Ambrose, Charles E, *Dir of Gallery, Cur of Museum & Permanent Coll*, Mississippi University for Women, Art Gallery and Museum, Columbus MS

Ambrose, Charles E, *Chmn*, Mississippi University for Women, Art Department, Columbus MS (S)

Ambrose, Gordon, *Caretaker & Watchman*, Moose Jaw Art Museum and National Exhibition Centre, Moose Jaw SK

Ambrosiani, Bjorn, *Keeper of Museum Department*, Statens Historiska Museum, Museum of National Antiquities, Stockholm Sweden

Ambrosino, Thomas, *Instructor*, Sullivan County Community College, Div of Commercial Art and Photography, Loch Sheldrake NY (S)

Ambrosio, Katie, *Mgr*, Carmel Mission Basilica, Carmel CA

Ameen, Lula, *Asst Prof*, Nicholls State University, Dept of Art, Thibodaux LA (S)

Amend, Gene, *Pres*, Artists Coalition of Texas, Dallas TX

Ames, Amyas, *Chmn of Board*, Lincoln Center for the Performing Arts, Amsterdam, Plaza and Main Galleries, New York NY

Ames, M M, *Dir*, University of British Columbia, Museum of Anthropology, Vancouver BC

Ames, Madge, *Treas*, Kennebec Valley Art Association, Harlow Gallery, Hallowell ME

Ames, Samuel B, *Asst Prof*, Rhode Island College, Art Department, Providence RI (S)

Ames, Walter, *Chmn Bd*, Timken Art Gallery, San Diego CA

Amico, Leonard N, *Asst Dir*, University of Illinois, Krannert Art Museum, Champaign IL

Amiet, Pierre, *Cur Oriental Antiquities*, Musee du Louvre, Louvre Museum, Paris France

Amiot, Theresa, *Chmn Dept*, College of Our Lady of the Elms, Department of Art, Chicopee MA (S)

Amir-Fazli, Homa, *Assoc Prof*, University of Minnesota, Department of Design, Saint Paul MN (S)

Amirsoltani, Karen, *Dept Head*, Ray-Vogue School of Design, Chicago IL (S)

Amissah-Arthur, J D, *Admin Secy*, Ghana National Museum, Accra Ghana

Ammerman, William, *Prof*, University of Wisconsin-River Falls, Art Department, River Falls WI (S)

Ammons, Betty, *Asst Librn*, United Methodist Historical Society, Library, Baltimore MD

Amoroso, L Louis, *Sr VPres*, AmeriTrust Company, Cleveland OH

Amory Jr, Robert, *Secy & Gen Counsel*, National Gallery of Art, Washington DC

Amos, Robert, *Asst Dir*, Art Gallery of Greater Victoria, Library, Victoria BC

Amrhein, John K, *College Librn*, Kutztown State College, Rohrbach Library, Kutztown PA

Amundson, Dale, *Vice-Representative*, Canadian Artists' Representation, Winnipeg MB

Amundson, Debra, *In Charge Art Program*, Lutheran Brotherhood, Minneapolis MN

Amussen, Theodore S, *Editor*, National Gallery of Art, Washington DC

Amylon, Kristin A, *Supv Museum Coll*, Rockwell-Corning Museum, Corning NY

Amyx, Chester, *Chmn Fine Arts Div*, Cuesta College, Art Department, San Luis Obispo CA (S)

Ananian, Elissa, *Prof*, Salem State College, Art Department, Salem MA (S)

Anawalt, Patricia, *Consulting Cur of Costumes & Textiles*, University of California, Los Angeles, Museum of Cultural History, Los Angeles CA

Anazawa, Kazuo, *Deputy Dir*, Tokyo Kokuritsu Kindai Bujutsukan, National Museum of Modern Art, Tokyo, Tokyo Japan

Ancona, Richard, *Instructor*, Villa Maria College of Buffalo, Art Department, Buffalo NY (S)

an der Heiderr, Rüdiger, *Cur Flemish Paintings*, Bayerischen Staatsgemaldesammlungen, Bavarian State Galleries of Art, Munich Germany, Federal Republic of

Anderle, Donald, *Chief*, New York Public Library, Art and Architecture Division, New York NY

Andersen, Greta, *Assoc Conservator*, Harvard University, William Hayes Fogg Art Museum, Cambridge MA

Andersen, Jeffrey W, *Dir*, Lyme Historical Society, Inc, Old Lyme CT

Andersen, Marion, *Secy*, Mid-America Arts Alliance, Kansas City MO

Anderson, A Douglas, *Dir Educational Services*, University of Nebraska Lincoln, Sheldon Memorial Art Gallery, Lincoln NE

Anderson, Altona, *Secy*, Center for the Visual Arts, Oakland CA

Anderson, Arthur, *Chmn*, York College of the City University of New York, Fine and Performing Arts, Jamaica NY (S)

Anderson, Barb, *Secy*, Lansing Art Gallery, Lansing MI

Anderson, Berneal, *Registrar*, Joslyn Art Museum, Omaha NE

Anderson, Betsy, *Lectr*, Saint Joseph's College, Fine Arts Program, Philadelphia PA (S)

Anderson, Bradley, *Dir Childrens Theatre*, Arkansas Arts Center, Little Rock AR

Anderson, Bradley, *Dir of Theatre*, Arkansas Arts Center, Little Rock AR (S)

Anderson, Charles R, *Head Dept*, Castleton State College, Art Department, Castleton VT (S)

Anderson, Cheryl, *Cur Educ Service*, Shaker Community, Inc, Pittsfield MA

Anderson, Dennis A, *Treas*, Muttart Gallery Associates, Calgary AB

Anderson, Donald B, *Pres Board Trustees*, Roswell Museum and Art Center, Roswell NM

Anderson, Donald P, *Dir*, University of Louisville, Allen R Hite Art Institute, Louisville KY

Anderson, Donald P, *Dir*, University of Louisville, Allen R Hite Art Institute, Louisville KY (S)

Anderson, Eric, *Prof*, University of North Carolina-Charlotte, Creative Arts Dept, Charlotte NC (S)

Anderson, Evelyn E, *Assoc Prof*, Sam Houston State University, Art Department, Huntsville TX (S)

Anderson, Gary, *Chmn*, Transylvania University, Studio Arts Department, Lexington KY (S)

Anderson, Glen Dale, *Chmn*, Southern Utah State College, Department of Art, Cedar City UT (S)

Anderson, Hale, *Asst Prof*, University of Northern Iowa, Department of Art, Cedar Falls IA (S)

Anderson, Herbert T, *Chmn Dept*, Chamberlayne Junior College, Department of Graphic and Applied Arts, Boston MA (S)

Anderson, James C, *Cur*, University of Louisville, University of Louisville Photographic Archives, Louisville KY

Anderson, Jean, *Secy*, Arts for Living Center, Burlington IA

Anderson, Jeffrey C, *Asst Prof*, George Washington University, Department of Art, Washington DC (S)

Anderson, Joan, *Cataloger*, California Institute of the Arts Library, Valencia CA

Anderson, John H, *Chmn*, Columbus College, Department of Art, Columbus GA (S)

Anderson, Jon, *Prof*, Utah State University, Department of Art, Logan UT (S)

Anderson, Kent, *Pres*, National Art Education Association, Reston VA

Anderson, Larry, *Assoc Prof*, California State University, Fresno, Art Department, Fresno CA (S)

Anderson, Lennart, *Instructor*, Oxbow Summer Art Workshops, Saugatuck MI (S)

Anderson, Leon, *Assoc Prof*, Saint Louis Community College at Forest Park, Dept of Art, Saint Louis MO (S)

Anderson, Lyle, *Instr*, Illinois Central College, Art and Humanities Department, East Peoria IL (S)

Anderson, Marian, *Vice Chmn*, Nebraska Arts Council Library, Omaha NE

Anderson, Mark, *Instructor*, Texas A & I University, Art Department, Kingsville TX (S)

Anderson, Martin, *Instr*, Lake Placid School of Art, Lake Placid NY (S)

Anderson, Mel, *Pres*, Saint Mary's College of California, Hearst Art Gallery, Moraga CA

Anderson, Neil, *Instr*, Bucknell University, Department of Art, Lewisburg PA (S)

Anderson, Othello, *Treas*, N.A.M.E. Gallery, Chicago IL

Anderson, Patricia, *Dir Library*, Englewood Library, Englewood NJ

Anderson, Patricia McGraw, *Dir*, University of Maine at Augusta Gallery, Augusta ME

Anderson, Paul L, *Cur Exhib*, Church of Jesus Christ of Latter-Day Saints, Information Center and Museum, Arts and Sites Division, Salt Lake City UT

Anderson, Richard E, *Pres*, Aldrich Museum of Contemporary Art, Ridgefield CT

Anderson, Robert, *Prof*, West Virginia University, Division of Art, Morgantown WV (S)

Anderson, Robert, *VPres*, Sioux City Art Center, Sioux City IA

Anderson, Robert C, *Mgr State Park Authority*, Jekyll Island National Historic Landmark, Jekyll Island GA

Anderson, Ross, *Cur of Collections & Education*, Everson Museum of Art, Syracuse NY

Anderson, Ruth M, *Cur Costume*, Hispanic Society of America Museum, New York NY

Anderson, Terrell, *Admin Asst for CETA Programs*, Los Angeles Institute of Contemporary Art, Los Angeles CA

Anderson, Tom, *Pres of Board of Dir*, Nobles County Art Center Gallery, Worthington MN

Anderson, William, *Asst Prof*, Savannah State College, Department of Fine Arts, Savannah GA (S)

Anderson, William, *Museum Archives Coordr*, Richmond Arts Centre, Richmond BC

Anderson Jr, L Price, *Cur*, University of California, Richard L Nelson Gallery, Davis CA

Andrade, Bruno, *Instructor*, Stephens College, Art Department, Columbia MO (S)

Andrea, Martha, *Instr*, Colby-Sawyer College, Art Department, New London NH (S)

Andreescu, Irina, *Vis Asst Prof*, Emory University, Art History Department, Atlanta GA (S)

Andres, Glenn, *Asst Dir*, Middlebury College, Johnson Gallery, Middlebury VT

Andres, Glenn M, *Chmn*, Middlebury College, Department of Art, Middlebury VT (S)

Andres, Michael, *Chmn*, Syracuse University, College of Visual and Performing Arts, Syracuse NY (S)

Andrew, Carl, *Cur Art*, Tasmanian Museum and Art Gallery, Hobart Australia

Andrews, Gail C, *Cur Decorative Arts*, Birmingham Museum of Art, Birmingham AL

Andrews, John F, *Dir Research Activities*, Folger Shakespeare Library, Washington DC

Andrews, Jon Philip, *In Charge Art Coll*, Westinghouse Electric Corporation, Pittsburgh PA

Andrews, Keith, *Keeper of Prints & Drawings*, National Galleries of Scotland, National Gallery of Scotland, Edinburgh Scotland

Andrews, Martha, *Coordr Inventory of American Paintings*, National Collection of Fine Arts, Washington DC

Andrews, Mary, *Librn*, Peter and Catharine Whyte Foundation, Peter Whyte Gallery Library, Banff AB

Andrews, Nancy, *Librn*, San Diego Museum of Art, Art Reference Library, San Diego CA

Andrews Jr, Fred A, *Pres*, Providence Art Club, Providence RI

Andrews-Zike, Lysbeth, *Ref Librn*, New Haven Colony Historical Society, Reference Library, New Haven CT

Andriola, Thom, *Dir Stables Gallery*, Taos Art Association Inc, Taos NM

Andrus, Beryl, *Young People's Coordr*, Clark County Library District, Las Vegas NV

Andrus, Donald F, *Cur*, Concordia University, Sir George Williams Art Galleries, Montreal PQ

Andrus, Jeanette, *Asst*, Pemaquid Group of Artists, Lewiston ME

Andruss, Edgar, *Mem & Museum Shop*, Museum of Fine Arts of Saint Petersburg, Florida, Inc, Saint Petersburg FL

Andursky, Myrna, *Instr*, Virginia Wesleyan College, Art Department of the Humanities Division, Norfolk VA (S)

Angeline, M, *Chairperson Art Dept*, Madonna College, Art Dept, Livonia MI (S)

Anglin, B, *Prof*, Christopher Newport College, Fine and Performing Arts, Newport News VA (S)

Anglin, Barbara, *Technical Services Librn*, Lee County Library, Tupelo MS

Anhalt, David, *Instructor*, Arkansas Arts Center, Little Rock AR (S)

Anhalt, Lenore, *Art Librn*, Shelter Rock Public Library, Albertson NY

Anker, Peter M, *Museum Dir*, Vestlandske Kunstindustrimuseum, Western Norway Museum of Applied Art, Bergen Norway

Anklam, Cissy, *Supv Public Services*, Mississippi Museum of Art, Jackson MS

Anne, Shirley, *Education & Extension Officer*, Laurentian University, Art Gallery, Sudbury ON

Anne, Shirley, *Education & Extension Officer*, Laurentian University, Museum and Arts Centre, Sudbury ON

Annino, Sam, *Asst Prof*, Springfield College, Department of Visual and Performing Arts, Springfield MA (S)

Annis, Norman, *Head Dept*, Southwest Missouri State University, Dept of Art, Springfield MO (S)

Anstee, J, *Cur*, Abbot Hall Art Gallery, Cumbria England

Anstis, Elisa, *Gallery Asst*, Burnaby Art Gallery, Burnaby BC

Anthony, Lawrence K, *Chmn Dept*, Southwestern at Memphis, Dept of Art, Memphis TN (S)

Antin, David, *Dept Chmn*, University of California, San Diego, Visual Arts Department, La Jolla CA (S)

Antin, Eleanor, *Assoc Prof*, University of California, San Diego, Visual Arts Department, La Jolla CA (S)

Antolik, Jerry, *Instructor*, Central Wyoming College, Art Center, Riverton WY (S)

Antonacci, Rafael H, *Sound Coordr*, Centro de Arte y Communicacion, Center of Art and Communication, Buenos Argentina

Antone, Bernie, *Asst Registrar*, Sierra Nevada Museum of Art, Reno NV

Antones, Juan Barbeta, *Dir*, Museo de Arte Moderno, Museum of Modern Art, Barcelona Spain

Anzelewsky, Fedja, *Dir*, Staatliche Museen Preussischer Kulturbesitz, Department of Prints and Drawings, Berlin Germany, Federal Republic of

Apking, Steve H, *Pres*, Dulin Gallery of Art, Knoxville TN

Appel, Keith, *Chmn*, University of Alaska at Anchorage, Department of Art, Anchorage AK (S)

Appel, Susan, *Asst Prof*, Phillips University, Department of Art, Enid OK (S)

Appel, Wallace H, *Secy-Treas*, Industrial Designers Society of America, Washington DC

Appell, William, *Pres*, Columbia County Historical Society, House of History and Van Alen House, Kinderhook NY

Apperson, George, *Asst Prof*, Southwestern at Memphis, Dept of Art, Memphis TN (S)

Apperson, George, *Cur*, Southwestern At Memphis, Jessie L Clough Art Memorial for Teaching, Memphis TN

Applegate, William H, *Asst Dir*, State Historical Society of Wisconsin, Madison WI

Appleman, David, *Instructor*, Bob Jones University, School of Fine Arts, Greenville SC (S)

Appleton, Clyde, *Assoc Prof*, University of North Carolina-Charlotte, Creative Arts Dept, Charlotte NC (S)

Applewhite, Robert A, *Dir*, Phoenix Art Museum, Phoenix AZ

Appleyard, Ronald, *Deputy Dir*, Art Gallery of South Australia, Adelaide Australia

Aragones, Sergio, *Vis Lectr*, Joe Kubert School of Cartoon and Graphic Art Inc, Dover NJ (S)

Arbuckle, Robert, *Dir*, Pennsylvania State University at New Kensington, New Kensington PA (S)

Arcadipone, Diana, *Assoc Dir*, Louisville School of Art Gallery, Anchorage KY

Arcadipone, Diana, *Assoc Dir*, Louisville School of Art, Anchorage KY (S)

Archambeau, Robert W, *Chmn Ceramics*, University of Manitoba, School of Art, Winnipeg MB (S)

Archer, Mary Lee, *Admin Asst*, Wichita Art Museum, Wichita KS

Archer, Nancy, *Bookmobile Librn*, Mexico-Audrain County Library, Mexico MO

Archibald, Robert, *Dir*, Montana Historical Society, Helena MT

Archibald, Thomas L, *Secy*, Stowe-Day Foundation, Hartford CT

Ardren, Robert K, *Chief Public Information*, John and Mable Ringling Museum of Art, Sarasota FL

Arellanes, Audrey Spencer, *Dir & Ed*, American Society of Bookplate Collectors and Designers, Alhambra CA

Arens, Norine M, *Admin Asst*, University of Oregon, Musuem of Art, Eugene OR

Arensberg, Charles C, *Chmn of Board*, Pittsburgh History and Landmarks Foundation, Old Post Office Museum, Pittsburgh PA

Arentz, Donald, *Asst Prof of Philosophy*, LeMoyne College, Art Gallery, Syracuse NY

Arguelles, Jose, *Assoc Prof*, University of Colorado at Denver, Department of Fine Arts, Denver CO (S)

Argyropoulos, Andy, *Assoc Prof*, Western Michigan University, Department of Art, Kalamazoo MI (S)

Ari, Donna B, *Dir Education*, Indianapolis Museum of Art, Indianapolis IN

Arie, Eizenberg, *Dir*, Municipality of Beit-Shan, Municipal Beit-Shan-Museum, Beit-Shan Israel

Ariss, Herbert, *Instr*, Southampton Art School, Southampton ON (S)

Arkus, Leon A, *Dir*, Carnegie Institute, Museum of Art, Pittsburgh PA

Arlen, Angie, *Instructor*, Mainline Center of the Arts, Haverford PA (S)

Armentrout, Sandra S, *Cur Registrar*, Brick Store Museum, Kennebunk ME

Armitage-Besman, Louise, *Asst*, Parry Sound Public Library, Parry Sound ON

Armstrong, Carl H, *Dir*, Indiana State Museum, Indianapolis IN

Armstrong, Elizabeth, *Dir*, California Institute of the Arts Library, Valencia CA

Armstrong, Gary, *Treas*, Spectrum, Friends of Fine Art, Inc, Toledo OH

Armstrong, Herbert E, *Pres*, Philadelphia Sketch Club Inc, Philadelphia PA

Armstrong, Kathryn, *Prof*, Sonoma State University, Art Department, Rohnert Park CA (S)

Armstrong, Lilian, *Prof*, Wellesley College, Art Department, Wellesley MA (S)

Armstrong, M E, *Lectr*, Trinity College, Department of Fine Arts, Washington DC (S)

Armstrong, Neil, *Manager School Fine Arts*, Banff Centre School of Fine Arts, Banff AB (S)

Armstrong, Robert L, *Chmn*, University of West Florida, Art Gallery, Pensacola FL

Armstrong, Robert L, *Chmn*, University of West Florida, Department of Art, Pensacola FL (S)

Armstrong, Rodney, *Dir & Librn*, Boston Athenaeum, Boston MA

Armstrong III, Thomas N, *Dir*, Whitney Museum of American Art, New York NY

Arnall, Lori, *Coordr Atrium Gallery*, Salt Lake City Public Library, Fine Arts Department, Salt Lake City UT

Arneson, Wendell, *Asst Prof*, St Olaf College, Art Department, Northfield MN (S)

Arnest, Bernard, *Chmn*, Colorado College, Department of Art, Colorado Springs CO (S)

Arnheim, Rudolf, *Pres*, American Society for Aesthetics, Greenvale NY

Arnold, Alice W, *Accountant*, Pine Castle Center of the Arts, Inc, Orlando FL

Arnold, Anna Bing, *Secy*, Los Angeles County Museum of Art, Los Angeles CA

Arnold, Isaac, *Chmn Board*, Museum of Fine Arts, Houston, Houston TX

Arnold, Joan, *Cataloger*, School of Visual Arts Library, New York NY

Arnold, Klaus, *Rector*, Staatliche Akademie der Bildenden Künste, State Academy of Fine Arts, Karlsruhe Germany, Federal Republic of (S)

Arnold, Leon, *Acting Dir*, Natural History Museum of Los Angeles County, Los Angeles CA

Arnold, Paul B, *Prof*, Oberlin College, Department of Art, Oberlin OH (S)

Arnold, Paul B, *Pres*, National Association of Schools of Art, Reston VA

Arnold, Ralph, *Assoc Prof*, Loyola University of Chicago, Fine Arts Department, Chicago IL (S)

Arnold, Richard, *Dir*, University of Washington, School of Art, Seattle WA (S)

Arnold, Robert, *Assoc Prof*, Ohio State University, Department of Art Education, Columbus OH (S)

Arnott, Julie, *Circulation Supv*, Washington University, Art and Architecture Library, Saint Louis MO

Arnowitz, Burt, *Video Cur*, Academy of the Museum of Conceptual Art, San Francisco CA

Aronson, David, *Prof*, Boston University, School of Visual Arts, Boston MA (S)

Aronson, Steven, *Dir Film Prog*, American Federation of Arts, New York NY

Arrazola, Javier, *Librn*, University of Santo Tomas, Library, Manila Philippines

Arredondo Jr, JR, *Coordr University Art Exhib*, Texas A & M University, Art Exhibits, College Station TX

Arrington, Gerald C, *Assoc Prof*, Concord College, Art Department, Athens WV (S)

Arroyo, Miguel G, *Dir*, Museo de Bellas Artes, Museum of Fine Arts, Caracas Venezuela

Arsenault, Kathleen, *Catalogue Librn*, Minneapolis College of Art and Design, Library and Media Center, Minneapolis MN

Arsenault, Wendell, *Chmn Dept of Graphic Design*, New England School of Art and Design, Boston MA (S)

Arslan, Ermanno, *Dir*, Museo d'Arte Antica, Museo di Milano, Milan Italy

Arslan, Ermanno, *Dir*, Museo d'Arte Antica, Raccolte Archaeologiche e Numismatiche, Milan Italy

Artasanchez, Pamela Maquard de, *Chmn*, University of the Americas, Graphic Arts and Design Dept, Cholula Mexico (S)

Artel, Linda, *Film Consultant*, University of California, Pacific Film Archive, Berkeley CA

Arth, Malcom, *Co-Dir*, Museum Management Institute, San Francisco CA (S)

Arthur, Kathleen, *Asst Prof*, James Madison University, Department of Art, Harrisonburg VA (S)

Arthur, Maude, *Treas*, Henry S Lane Home, Crawfordsville IN

Arthur, Revington, *Head Painting & Drawing*, Chautauqua Institution, Chautauqua NY (S)

Artzberger, John A, *Museum Dir*, Oglebay Institute Mansion Museum, Wheeling WV

Arvanites, Constantine, *Prof*, Boston State College, Art Department, Boston MA (S)

Arz, Leopoldine, *Registrar*, Walters Art Gallery, Baltimore MD

Asano, Toru, *Cur Painting*, Tokyo Kokuritsu Kindai Bujutsukan, National Museum of Modern Art, Tokyo, Tokyo Japan

Ascher, Celia, *In Charge Art Coll*, McCrory Corporation, New York NY

Asencio hijo, V Jaime, *Assoc Prof*, Inter American University of Puerto Rico, Department of Performing Arts, San German PR (S)

Asgari, Nusin, *Cur Department of Greek & Roman Antiquities*, Istanbul Arkeoloji Müzeleri, Archaeological Museums of Istanbul, Istanbul Turkey

Asghar, Muhammad, *Librn*, Lahore Museum, Library, Lahore Pakistan

Ash, Carla Caccamise, *In Charge Art Coll*, Joseph E Seagram & Sons, Inc, New York NY

Ashe, Mary, *Art & Music*, San Francisco Public Library, Art and Music Department, San Francisco CA

Asher, Frederick M, *Chmn*, University of Minnesota, Minneapolis, Art History, Minneapolis MN (S)

Asher, Martha, *Registrar*, Sterling and Francine Clark Art Institute, Williamstown MA

Ashley, Diane, *Village Dir*, Jekyll Island National Historic Landmark, Jekyll Island GA

Ashley, Gary, *Pres of Board of Trustees*, Western Colorado Center for the Arts, Inc, Grand Junction CO

Ashley, Paul, *Chmn Undergrad Div*, School of the Art Institute of Chicago, Chicago IL (S)

Ashley-Smith, J, *Keeper Conservation*, Victoria and Albert Museum, London England

Ashton, Marvin J, *Chmn Board*, Polynesian Cultural Center, Laie HI

Ashton, Pearl F, *Asst Treas*, Providence Water Color Club, Providence RI

Ashton, Rick J, *Asst Dir*, Public Library of Fort Wayne and Allen County, Fort Wayne IN

Ashton, Robin, *Chief Conservator*, Montreal Museum of Fine Arts, Montreal PQ

Ash III, Richard M, *Prof*, Midwestern State University, Department of Art, Wichita Falls TX (S)

Asihene, Emmanuel V, *Chmn Dept*, Clark College, Department of Art, Atlanta GA (S)

Asimakos, John, *Assoc Prof*, Mount Allison University, Fine Arts Department, Sackville NB (S)

Askan, Marie, *Instructor*, College of Santa Fe, Visual Arts Dept, Santa Fe NM (S)

Askren, Pat, *Fibre Dept Coordr*, Banff Centre School of Fine Arts, Banff AB (S)

Astrop, William B, *Pres Bd of Sponsors*, High Museum of Art, Atlanta GA

Astrua, Paola Lojacono, *Librn*, Galleria Sabauda, Biblioteca, Turin Italy

Aszling, Jill, *Registrar*, Cornell University, Herbert F Johnson Museum of Art, Ithaca NY

Atcheson, George, *Assoc Prof*, State University of New York College at Cortland, Art Department, Cortland NY (S)

Atcheson, Susie Walker, *Asst Cur*, Art Museum of South Texas, Library, Corpus Christi TX

Atherly, Mary, *Registrar & Secy*, Iowa State University, Brunnier Gallery, Ames IA

Atil, Esin, *Assoc Cur Near Eastern Art*, Freer Gallery of Art, Washington DC

Atkins, Charles K, *Dir*, Santa Cruz Public Library, Art, Music, Film Department, Santa Cruz CA

Atkins, Hannah, *Coordr Afro-American Gallery Kirkpatrick Center*, Omniplex, Oklahoma City OK

Atkinson, Betty, *Secy*, Alaska Artists Guild, Anchorage AK

Atkinson, James W, *VPres*, Birmingham-Bloomfield Art Association, Birmingham MI

Atkinson, Tracy, *Dir*, Wadsworth Atheneum, Hartford CT

Atkyns, Lee, *Dir*, Lee Atkyns Studio-Gallery, Duncansville PA

Aton, Steve, *Dir of Development and Public Relations*, Brockton Art Center, Brockton MA

Attrill, M V, *Keeper of Art*, Plymouth City Museum and Art Gallery, Plymouth England

Atwood, Raymond R, *Instructor*, Iowa Central Community College, Department of Art, Fort Dodge IA (S)

Atz, Anne, *Correspondence Secy*, Florida Artist Group Inc, Englewood FL

Au, Jerene, *Instr*, Maryville College, Art Department, Saint Louis MO (S)

Aubin, L, *Secy*, Musee d'Art de Saint-Laurent, Saint-Laurent PQ

Aubry, Diane, *Asst*, Musee du Quebec, Bibliotheque des Art, Quebec PQ

Auchstetter, Rosann, *Slide Librn*, Art Institute of Chicago, Ryerson and Burnham Libraries, Chicago IL

Auduns, Jon, *Chmn*, Listasafn Einars Jonssonar, National Einar Jonsson Gallery, Reykjavik Iceland

Auerbach, Seymour, *Prof*, Catholic University of America, Department of Architecture & Planning, Washington DC (S)

Augspurger, Roger, *Instr*, Platte Technical Community College, Creative and Social Cluster, Columbus NE (S)

August, Sandra, *Instr*, Cleveland Institute of Art, Cleveland OH (S)

Augusztiny, Roxana, *Registrar*, University of Washington, Thomas Burke Memorial Washington State Museum, Seattle WA

Auker, Alfred Van, *Prof*, Pierce College, Art Department, Woodland Hills CA (S)

Aulbur, Mark, *Pres*, Mexico-Audrain County Library, Mexico MO

Auld, Alasdair A, *Dir*, Glasgow Museums and Art Galleries, Kelvingrove Art Gallery and Museum, Glasgow Scotland

Aunspaugh, Richard, *Chmn*, Young Harris College, Department of Art, Young Harris GA (S)

Aurand, Charles H, *Dean College Creative Arts*, Northern Arizona University, Art Gallery, Flagstaff AZ

Aurenhammer, Hans, *Dir*, Osterreichische Galerie, Austrian Gallery, Vienna Austria

Austell, Joseph R, *Dir*, Wilkes Community College, Arts and Science Division, Wilkesboro NC (S)

Austen, Ian, *Chmn Craft Div*, Nova Scotia College of Art and Design, Halifax NS (S)

Austerman, Louis C, *Pres*, Cincinnati Art Club, Cincinnati OH

Austin, Helen C, *Instr*, John C Calhoun State Community College, Art Department, Decatur AL (S)

Austin, Helen C, *Dir*, John C Calhoun State Community College, Art Gallery, Decatur AL

Austin, Howard, *Instructor*, Milwaukee Area Technical College, Graphic & Applied Arts Div, Milwaukee WI (S)

Austin, Jerry, *Asst Prof*, Kearney State College, Dept of Art, Kearney NE (S)

Austin, William, *Cur Exhibits*, Institute of the Great Plains, Museum of the Great Plains, Lawton OK

Auth, Susan, *Cur Classical*, Newark Museum, Newark NJ

Autio, Rudy, *Vis Prof*, Victor Valley College, Art Department, Victorville CA (S)

Autio, Rudy, *Prof*, University of Montana, Dept of Art, Missoula MT (S)

Avara, Emma, *Bus Mgr*, Amarillo Art Center, Amarillo TX

Avdzej, Tamara, *Acquisitions Librn*, Kean College of New Jersey, Nancy Thompson Library, Union NJ

Averill, Chris, *Site Mgr*, Schuyler Mansion, Albany NY

Averill, Norman, *Instr*, Northwestern Michigan College, Art Dept, Traverse City MI (S)

Aversperg, Ruth, *Cultural Dir*, Pointe Claire Cultural Centre, Pointe Claire PQ

Avery, Millie, *VPres*, Copper Village Museum and Arts Center, Anaconda MT

Avery, Ruth, *Corresp Secy*, Lyme Art Association, Inc, Old Lyme CT

Avgikos, Jan, *Visual Coll Cur*, Atlanta College of Art Library, Atlanta GA

Awad, Lamia, *Secy*, American University of Beirut, Archaeological Museum, Beirut Lebanon

Axel, Helen, *VPres*, Hunterdon Art Center, Clinton NJ

Axelrod, Dee, *Vis Prof*, Minneapolis College of Art and Design, Minneapolis MN (S)

Axman, Milos, *Rector*, Akademie Vytvarnych Umeni, Academy of Fine Arts, Praha Czechoslavakia (S)

Axthelm, Kenneth, *Chief AV Division*, Brooklyn Public Library, Art and Music Division, Brooklyn NY

Ayers, J G, *Keeper Far Eastern Department*, Victoria and Albert Museum, London England

Ayers, Laura E, *Gallery Dir*, Sumter Gallery of Art, Sumter SC

Aylward, Roger, *Admins*, National Portrait Gallery, London England

Ayres, Larry M, *Chmn Dept*, University of California, Santa Barbara, Art Department, Santa Barbara CA (S)

Azevedo, Carlos de, *Lectr*, Miami University, Art Department, Oxford OH (S)

Azzaro, Samuel, *Secy*, League of New Hampshire Craftsmen, Concord NH

Baagoe, Thomas, *Librn*, Rohsska Konstslojdmuseet, Library, Gothenburg Sweden

Baagoe, Thomas, *Cur Coll*, Rohsska Konstslojdmuseet, Rohss Museum of Arts and Crafts, Gothenburg Sweden

Babbitt, Helen, *Assoc Prof*, Northeast Missouri State University, Art Department, Kirksville MO (S)

Babin, Pierre, *Pres*, Federation des Quebecoise des Services Socio-Culturels, Montreal PQ

Babisch, Joseph, *Assoc Prof*, Youngstown State University, Art Department, Youngstown OH (S)

Bace, Jill B, *Registrar*, University of Michigan Museum of Art, Kelsey Museum of Ancient and Medieval Archaeology, Ann Arbor MI

Bach, Dirk, *Head Art History*, Rhode Island School of Design, Providence RI (S)

Bach, Robert, *Instructor*, Northwestern Michigan College, Art Dept, Traverse City MI (S)

Bache, Bill, *Treas*, Lafayette Art Center, Lafayette IN

Bachman, Eve, *Development Officer*, Portland Art Association, Portland OR

Backlund, Caroline H, *Reader Services Librn*, National Gallery of Art, Library, Washington DC

Baco, Luis E, *Assoc Dir*, University of Puerto Rico, Mayaguez, Department of Humanities, Mayaguez PR (S)

Bacon, Eleanor, *Second VPres*, Toledo Federation of Art Societies, Toledo OH

Bacon, Mardges, *Asst Prof*, Trinity College, Department of Fine Arts, Hartford CT (S)

Bacon, Reba, *Pres*, Cumberland Art Society, Cookeville Art Center, Cookeville TN

Bacot, H Parrott, *Cur*, Louisiana State University, Anglo-American Art Museum, Baton Rouge LA

Badder, Susan, *Chmn Education Division*, Baltimore Museum of Art, Baltimore MD

Baden, Linda, *Editor*, Indiana University, Art Museum, Bloomington IN

Bader, Julia, *Asst Dir*, Art Center Association, Louisville KY

Badre, Leila, *Dir*, American University of Beirut, Archaeological Museum, Beirut Lebanon

Baer, Gerhard, *Dir*, Museum für Völkerkunde und Schweizerisches Museum für Volkskunde Basel, Museum of Ethnological Collections and Folklore, Basel Switzerland

Baer, Robert S, *Exec Secy*, Museum of Fine Arts of Saint Petersburg, Florida, Inc, Saint Petersburg FL

Baez, Felix Rodriguez, *Dir of School*, Institute of Puerto Rican Culture, Escuela de Artes Plasticas, Mayaguez PR

Baez, Myanda, *Prof*, Institute of Puerto Rican Culture, Escuela de Artes Plasticas, Mayaguez PR (S)

Bagby, William, *VPres*, Headley-Whitney Museum, Lexington KY

Bageris, John, *Chmn Fine Arts Dept*, Art Institute of Boston, Boston MA (S)

Bagley, Bill, *Assoc Prof*, Texas Tech University, Department of Art, Lubbock TX (S)

Bagley, Marian, *Prof*, University of Minnesota, Department of Design, Saint Paul MN (S)

Bagnall, William A, *Exec Dir*, DeCordova and Dana Museum and Park, Lincoln MA

Bahm, Glenn A, *VPres*, Art League of Houston, Houston TX

Bahnassi, Afif, *General Dir*, National Museum of Damascus, Damascus Syria

Bahnsen, Shirley, *Head Dept*, Mount Saint Clare College, Art Department, Clinton IA (S)

Bahr, David, *Gallery Dir*, Community College of Baltimore, Art Gallery, Baltimore MD

Bahr, David, *Assoc Prof*, Community College of Baltimore, Dept of Fine & Applied Arts, Baltimore MD (S)

Baier, Georgia, *Asst to the Dir*, Beaumont Art Museum, Beaumont TX

Baigell, Matthew, *Chmn*, Rutgers, the State University of New Jersey, Rutgers College, New Brunswick NJ (S)

Baigell, Matthew, *Prof*, Rutgers, the State University of New Jersey, Graduate Program in Art History, New Brunswick NJ (S)

Bailey, Bruce E, *Exec Dir*, Saint Bernard Foundation and Monastery, Miami Beach FL

Bailey, Elizabeth, *Instructor*, Wesleyan College, Art Department, Macon GA (S)

Bailey, Jane Terry, *Cur Burmese Art*, Denison University Art Gallery, Granville OH

Bailey, Jerry, *Chmn Metals*, Pan American University, Art Department, Edinburg TX (S)

Bailey, Marsha, *Asst Prof*, California State College, Sonoma, Department of Art, Rohnert Park CA (S)

Bailey, Martha, *Mgr Museum Shop*, Glenbow Museum, Calgary AB

Bailey, Richard C, *Dir*, Kern County Museum, Bakersfield CA

Bailey, Robert, *Crafts Dept Dir*, American Stained Glass Institute, Hobbs NM (S)

Bailey, Robert J, *Dir Historic Preservation*, Mississippi Department of Archives and History, Jackson MS

Bailey, Rodger, *Vpres*, Monterey Peninsula Museum of Art, Monterey CA

Bailey, Roger, *Assoc Prof*, Saint Laurence University, Department of Fine Arts, Canton NY (S)

Bailey, Terry, *Vis Prof*, Denison University, Department of Art, Granville OH (S)

Bailey, Walter J, *Chmn*, Baker University, Department of Art, Baldwin City KS (S)

Bailey, William, *Prof*, Yale University, School of Art, New Haven CT (S)

Bailey, William, *Artist in Res*, Viterbo College, Art Department, La Crosse WI (S)

Bailey, Willis, *Cur Oriental Art*, Zanesville Art Center, Zanesville OH

Bailin, Hella, *Treas*, Associated Artists of New Jersey, Pittstown NJ

Baillargeon, S, *Pres*, Peres Redemptoristes, Sainte Anne de Beaupre PQ

Bain, A, *Instr*, Selkirk College, Kootenay School of Art Division, Nelson BC (S)

Bain, Margaret, *Assoc Prof*, Daemen College, Art Department, Amherst NY (S)

Baines, Jean-Marie, *Asst to Dir*, Contemporary Arts Center, Cincinnati OH

Bair, Lavon H, *Admin & Financial Officer*, University of Pennsylvania, University Museum, Philadelphia PA

Bair, Miles, *Dir School of Art*, Illinois Wesleyan University, Merwin Gallery, Bloomington IL

Bair, Miles, *Dir*, Illinois Wesleyan University, School of Art, Bloomington IL (S)

Baird, John, *Photographer*, Art Research Center, Kansas City MO

Baird, Josiah L M, *Prof*, Pikeville College, Fine Arts Dept, Pikeville KY (S)

Baird, Mary Jane, *Instructor*, Delta State University, Department of Art, Cleveland MS (S)

Baird, Ted, *Head Dept Art*, Long Beach City College, Department of Art, Long Beach CA (S)

Baird, Thomas P, *Prof*, Trinity College, Department of Fine Arts, Hartford CT (S)

Bajko, Daria, *Admin Dir*, Ukrainian Museum, New York NY

Bajko, O, *Secy*, Ukrainian Museum, New York NY

Bak, Bronislaw, *Assoc Prof*, Georgia Southern College, Department of Art, Statesboro GA (S)

Bak, Elaine, *Asst Librn*, Long Island Historical Society, Library, Brooklyn NY

Bakanowsky, Lou J, *Chmn*, Harvard University, Carpenter Center for the Visual Arts, Cambridge MA

Bakanowsky, Louis, *Chmn Dept*, Harvard University, Department of Visual and Environmental Studies, Cambridge MA (S)

Bakar, Hugh, *Pres*, Monroe City-County Fine Arts Council, Monroe MI

Baker, Carl, *Asst Librn & Cataloger*, Art Center College of Design, James Lemont Fogg Memorial Library, Pasadena CA

Baker, Cassandra, *Dept of Education*, Columbia Museums of Art and Science, Columbia SC

Baker, Charles, *Chief of Exhibits*, Tennessee State Museum, Nashville TN

Baker, Charles L, *Dir*, Maitland Art Center Research Studio, Maitland FL

Baker, Danny, *Lectr*, Saint Joseph's College, Fine Arts Program, Philadelphia PA (S)

Baker, Edward R, *Chmn*, Orange Coast College, Division of Fine Arts, Costa Mesa CA (S)

Baker, Gary, *Prof*, Polk Community College, Division of Communications and Fine Arts, Winter Haven FL (S)

Baker, Gary E, *Cur*, Oglebay Institute Mansion Museum, Wheeling WV

Baker, Howard H (Senator), *VChmn*, United States Senate Commission on Art and Antiquities, Washington DC

Baker, James, *Instructor*, Providence College, Department of Fine Arts, Providence RI (S)

Baker, June, *Cur*, Santa Cruz Art League, Inc, Santa Cruz CA

Baker, Lee J, *Pres*, Columbia Museums of Art and Science, Columbia SC

Baker, Lee J, *Pres*, Columbia Museums of Art and Science, Columbia Art Association, Columbia SC

Baker, Marilyn, *Chmn Art History*, University of Manitoba, School of Art, Winnipeg MB (S)

Baker, Mary E, *Dir & Cur*, Houston Antique Museum, Chattanooga TN

Baker, North, *Pres*, California Historical Society, San Francisco CA

Baker, Roger, *Instr*, Clark College, Art Department, Vancouver WA (S)

Baker, T R, *Assoc Prof*, Arkansas State University, Department of Art, State University AR (S)

Baker, Tom, *Asst Preparator and Designer*, University of Kentucky, Art Museum, Lexington KY

Baker, W S, *Secy*, Civic Fine Arts Association Museum, Sioux Falls SD

Baker, William, *Cur*, Massachusetts Institute of Technology, Hart Nautical Museum, Cambridge MA

Baker, William, *Dir Div Humanities*, Philadelphia Community College, Department of Fine Arts, Philadelphia PA (S)

Baker, William, *Cur of Military History*, Tennessee State Museum, Nashville TN

Bakes, Alan, *Chmn Board*, Visual Arts Ontario, Toronto ON

Bakirer, Ömür, *Vis Prof*, Irish International Arts Centre, Castle Matrix, Rathkeale Ireland (S)

Balch, Manya, *Asst Cur*, Hofstra University, Emily Lowe Gallery, Hempstead NY

Balderacchi, Arthur, *Chmn*, University of New Hampshire, Department of the Arts, Durham NH (S)

Balderson, Lance, *Instructor*, Ocean City School of Art, Ocean City NJ (S)

Baldewiez, Elizabeth, *Asst Prof*, Saint Laurence University, Department of Fine Arts, Canton NY (S)

Baldridge, Mark S, *Asst Prof*, Longwood College, Department of Art, Farmville VA (S)

Baldwin, Ben, *Pres*, Maui Historical Society, Hale Hoikeike, Wailuku HI

Baldwin, Harold L, *Cur*, Middle Tennessee State University, Photographic Gallery, Murfreesboro TN

Baldwin, Helen D, *Gallery Dir*, Vanderbilt University, Art Gallery, Department of Fine Arts, Nashville TN

Baldwin, Joann, *Executive Secy*, William Rockhill Nelson Gallery of Art, Friends of Art, Kansas City MO

Baldwin, Robert A, *Assoc Prof*, Vanderbilt University, Dept of Fine Arts, Nashville TN (S)

Baldwin, Russell W, *Gallery Dir*, Palomar Community College, Boehm Gallery, San Marcos CA

Bale, Ken, *Head Found Studies*, Saint Martins School of Art, London England (S)

Balen, Samuel T, *Executive Dir*, National Council of Architectural Registration Boards, Washington DC

Bales, Richard, *Asst to Dir Music*, National Gallery of Art, Washington DC

Balestrieri, Madonna, *Instructor*, Cardinal Stritch College, Art Department, Milwaukee WI (S)

Balf, Oliver, *Instr*, Montserrat School of Visual Art, Beverly MA (S)

Balken, William R, *Gallery Supt & Preparator*, University of Utah, Utah Museum of Fine Arts, Salt Lake City UT

Balkman, Kathy, *Art Dir*, Federal Reserve Bank of Minneapolis, Minneapolis MN

Ball, Carlton, *Instr*, Tacoma Community College, Art Department, Tacoma WA (S)

Ball, George W, *Chmn Board of Trustees, Asia Society, Inc*, Asia Society, Inc, Asia House Gallery, New York NY

Ballaine, Jerrold, *Assoc Prof*, University of California, Berkeley, Department of Art, Berkeley CA (S)

Ballance, Stephen, *Instructor*, Northwestern Michigan College, Art Dept, Traverse City MI (S)

Ballay, Joseph, *Head*, Carnegie-Mellon University, Department of Design, Pittsburgh PA (S)

Ballentine, Don M, *Head Dept*, Atlanta Area Technical School, Department of Commercial Art, Atlanta GA (S)

Ballinger, Barbara, *Clerical Asst*, Ball State University, Architecture Library, Muncie IN

Ballinger, K A, *Pres*, Anderson Park Art Gallery, Invercargill New Zealand

Balogh, Anthony, *Instructor*, Madonna College, Art Dept, Livonia MI (S)

Balossi, John, *Instructor*, University of Puerto Rico, Department of Fine Arts, Mayaguez PR (S)

Balsiger, B, *Instructor*, Indiana University of Pennsylvania, Department of Art and Art Education, Indiana PA (S)

Baltadonis, John V, *Secy*, Philadelphia Sketch Club Inc, Philadelphia PA

Baltramaitis, Casimir, *VPres*, Balzekas Museum of Lithuanian Culture, Chicago IL

Baltus, J Ado, *Dir*, Ecole des Arts et Metiers d'Etterbeek, Brussels Belgium (S)

Balusek, William C, *Instructor*, San Jacinto College, Art Department, Pasadena TX (S)

Balzekas Jr, Stanley, *Secy*, Chicago Public Library, Cultural Center, Chicago IL

Balzekas Jr, Stanley, *Pres*, Balzekas Museum of Lithuanian Culture, Chicago IL

Balzekas III, Stanley, *Secy*, Balzekas Museum of Lithuanian Culture, Chicago IL

Bamford, Joseph, *VPres*, Fairbanks Museum and Planetarium, Saint Johnsbury VT

Banach, Jerzy, *Polish Iconography*, Muzeum Narodowe w Krakowie, National Museum in Cracow, Cracow Poland

Banai, M, *Archaeologist*, Museum of Ancient Art, Haifa Israel

Bancroft, Ann, *Librn*, Museum of New Mexico, Museum of International Folk Art Library, Santa Fe NM

Banda, Juan Jose Barragan, *Instructor*, University of Puerto Rico, Department of Fine Arts, Mayaguez PR (S)

Bandes, Susan, *Asst Prof*, Sweet Briar College, Art History Department, Sweet Briar VA (S)

Bandy, Mary Lea, *Acting Dir Dept Film*, Museum of Modern Art, New York NY

Bandy, Nancy, *Vis Prof*, Victoria College, Victoria TX (S)

Bania, Edward J, *Dir*, Evanston Art Center, Evanston IL

Banks, Janette, *Chmn Art Educ*, Moore College of Art, Philadelphia PA (S)

Banks, John, *Asst Prof*, Northwest Community College, Powell WY (S)

Banks, Paul N, *Pres*, American Institute for Conservation of Historic and Artistic Works (AIC), Washington DC

Banks, R K, *Dean*, University of Waterloo, Fine Arts Department, Waterloo ON (S)

Bannerjee, N R, *Dir*, National Museum of INdia, New Delhi India

Banning, Robert J, *VPres*, California Historical Society, San Francisco CA

Bannister, Barbara, *Office Mgr*, Brevard Art Center and Museum, Inc, Melbourne FL

Banta, Charles, *Secy - Treas*, Portland Center for the Visual Arts, Portland OR

Bantens, Robert J, *Asst Prof*, University of South Alabama, Department of Art, Mobile AL (S)

Banting, Donna, *Asst for Public Information*, New Orleans Museum of Art, Isaac Delgado Museum, New Orleans LA

Baptie, Sue M, *Dir*, Vancouver City Archives and Library, Vancouver BC

Baptist, Francis C, *Prof*, Clarion State College, Department of Art, Clarion PA (S)

Baracchini, Clara, *Dir*, Pinacoteca Nazionale, National Picture Gallery, Lucca Italy

Barazani, Morris, *Dir School Art & Design*, University of Illinois at Chicago Circle, College of Architecture, Art & Urban Sciences, Chicago IL (S)

Barbash, Steven, *Prof*, State University of New York College at Cortland, Art Department, Cortland NY (S)

Barbeau, Lynn, *Asst Cur*, Macdonald Steward Art Centre, Guelph ON

Barber, Catherine, *Assoc Librn*, Missouri Historical Society, Library, Saint Louis MO

Barber, William D, *Dir*, Region of Peel Museum and Art Gallery, Brampton ON

Barbic, Vesna, *Chief Cur*, Galerije Grada Zagreba, Atelje Mestrovic, Zagreb Yugoslavia

Barbier, Nicole, *Cur*, Musee des Beaux-Arts, Rennes France

Barbour, Dolly, *Pres*, Buchanan Arts and Crafts Inc, Buchanan Dam TX

Barclay, John T, *Pres*, Colorado Institute of Art, Denver CO (S)

Barde, Alex, *Assoc Prof*, Pittsburg State University, Art Department, Pittsburg KS (S)

Bardes, Leo N, *Div Dir*, College of San Mateo, Fine Arts Division, San Mateo CA (S)

Bardi, D M, *Dir*, Museu de Arte de Sao Paulo, Sao Paulo Art Museum, Sao Paulo Brazil

Bardwell, John, *VPres*, Society for the Preservation of Historic Landmarks, York ME

Barefoot, Paul D, *Dir Traveling Exhibition Services*, Museum of Holography, New York NY

Barela, Albert, *Painting & Drawing Coordr*, San Jose State University, Art Department, San Jose CA (S)

Baremore Jr, R E, *Dir*, Louisiana State Exhibit Museum, Shreveport LA

Baren, Paul, *Adminr*, Katonah Gallery, Katonah NY

Barker, Ann G, *Dir*, Fuller Lodge Art Center, Los Alamos NM

Barker, Garny, *Executive Dir*, Kentucky Guild of Artists and Craftsmen Inc, Berea KY

Barker, Jimmy H, *Asst Prof*, Sam Houston State University, Art Department, Huntsville TX (S)

Barker, Laurence, *Vis Prof*, Cleveland Institute of Art, Cleveland OH (S)

Barker, R Mildred, *Cur Manuscripts*, Shaker Museum, Poland Spring ME

Barker, Walter, *Assoc Prof*, University of North Carolina at Greensboro, Art Dept, Greensboro NC (S)

Barksdale, A Beverly, *General Mgr*, Cleveland Museum of Art, Cleveland OH

Barksdale, E, *VPres*, Farmington Valley Arts Center, Avon CT

Barlett, Peter, *Cur Natural History*, Bower's Museum, Santa Ana CA

Barlow, P J, *Head Dept History of Art and Complementary Studies*, City of Birmingham Polytechnic, Birmingham England (S)

Barna, Iris, *Dir*, Barna Pottery, Santa Fe NM (S)

Barnard, Robert, *Prof*, University of North Carolina at Chapel Hill, Art Department, Chapel Hill NC (S)

Barnes, Barry R, *Head Dept*, College of the Siskiyous, Art Department, Weed CA (S)

Barnes, Debbie, *Adjunct Instr*, Campbellsville College, Fine Arts Division, Campbellsville KY (S)

Barnes, Gary, *Asst Prof*, Arkansas Tech University, Department of Art, Russellville AR (S)

Barnes, Jairus B, *Dir History Museum*, Western Reserve Historical Society, Cleveland OH

Barnes, Kathy Chan, *Festivals Committee Dir*, American Society of Artists, Inc, Chicago IL

Barnes, Mary, *Instructor*, State University of New York College at Potsdam, Department of Fine Arts, Potsdam NY (S)

Barnes, Patricia P, *Registrar*, Montclair Art Museum, Art School, Montclair NJ (S)

Barnes, Sharron, *Assoc Prof*, Gulf Coast Community College, Division of Fine Arts, Panama City FL (S)

Barnes, Ted, *Asst Prof*, Campbellsville College, Fine Arts Division, Campbellsville KY (S)

Barnes, W D, *Asst Prof*, College of William and Mary, Department of Fine Arts, Williamsburg VA (S)

Barnes Jr, Carl F, *Pres*, International Center of Medieval Art, Inc, New York NY

Barnes Jr, Carl F, *Prof*, Oakland University, Dept of Art & Art History, Rochester MI (S)

Barnet, Richard, *Assoc Prof*, College of Mount Saint Vincent, Fine Arts Department, Riverdale NY (S)

Barnett, Cefni, *Cur & Keeper of Antiquities*, Newport Museum and Art Gallery, Newport Wales

Barnett, Ed Willis, *Pres & Cur*, Alabama Museum of Photography, Birmingham AL

Barnett, John D, *Asst Cur*, United States Navy, Combat Art Gallery, Washington DC

Barnett, Loretta, *Instr*, Colby-Sawyer College, Art Department, New London NH (S)

Barnett, Peter, *Asst Prof*, Earlham College, Art Department, Richmond IN (S)

Barnett, Vivian Endicott, *Assoc Cur*, Solomon R Guggenheim Museum, New York NY

Barnette, Charles R, *In Charge Art Coll*, Blount Inc, Montgomery AL

Barnhart, Peggy, *Accountant*, Art Center, Inc, South Bend IN

Barnitz, Downing, *Assoc Prof*, Florida Southern College, Art Department, Lakeland FL (S)

Barnum, Charles, *Pres*, Historical Society of Quincy and Adams County, Quincy IL

Barnwell, Ed, *Chief Cur*, Greenville County Museum of Art, Greenville SC

Barnwell, John, *Pres*, Miniature Art Society of New Jersey, Nutley NJ

Baro, Gene, *Consultant Cur Prints & Drawings*, Brooklyn Museum, Brooklyn NY

Baron, Judy Goldsmith, *Painter*, Regis College, Department of Art, Weston MA (S)

Barons, Richard, *Cur*, Roberson Center, Binghamton NY

Barr, David, *Prof*, Macomb County Community College, Art Department, Warren MI (S)

Barr, Donald, *Assoc Prof*, School of the Ozarks, Department of Art, Point Lookout MO (S)

Barr, Linda, *Librn & Archivist*, McMichael Canadian Collection, Library, Kleinburg ON

Barrachini, Clara, *Dir*, Museo Nazionale di Villa Guinigi, National Museum of Villa Guinigi, Lucca Italy

Barraclough, Dennis W, *Chmn Dept*, Daemen College, Art Department, Amherst NY (S)

Barradas, Manuel, *Instructor*, Harriet FeBland Art Workshop, New York NY (S)

Barradell, D, *Cur*, Lloydminster Barr Colony Museum Committee, Lloydminster SK

Barrager, Roberta, *Assoc Prof*, Pierce College, Art Department, Woodland Hills CA (S)

Barratt, D R, *Cur Exhib*, Queen Victoria Museum and Art Gallery, Tasmania Australia

Barreto, Ricardo, *Admin & Cur Asst*, Intermuseum Conservation Association, Oberlin OH

Barrett, Barbara, *Dir*, Toronto School of Art, Toronto ON (S)

Barrett, Eugene, *Dept Chmn*, Portland Community College, Department of Fine Arts, Portland OR (S)

Barrett, Jonathan, *Pres*, Architectural League of New York, New York NY

Barrett, Mary, *Prof*, University of Wisconsin-River Falls, Art Department, River Falls WI (S)

Barrett, Rhoda, *Acting Chief Education & Cultural Affairs Div*, National Museum of Man, Ottawa ON

Barrett, T R, *Head Art Dept*, Saint Paul's School, Sheldon Library, Concord NH

Barrett, Thomas R, *Head Dept*, Saint Paul's School, Art Department, Concord NH (S)

Barrett, Thomas R, *Head Art Dept*, Saint Paul's School, Art Center in Hargate, Concord NH

Barrick, Ken, *Prof*, New Mexico State University, Art Dept, Las Cruces NM (S)

Barrie, Dennis, *Dir*, Archives of American Art, Midwest Area Center, New York NY

Barrio-Garay, J L, *Chmn*, University of Western Ontario, Department of Visual Arts, London ON (S)

Barrish, A Jos, *Assoc Prof*, University of Dayton, Fine Arts Division, Dayton OH (S)

Barrish, Esther, *Assoc Prof*, Jersey City State College, Art Department, Jersey City NJ (S)

Barron, Ida W, *Exec Dir*, Key West Art and Historical Society, Key West FL

Barrows, Stanley, *Chmn Interior Design*, Fashion Institute of Technology, New York NY (S)

Barry, A Meredith, *Secy*, Visual Arts Ontario, Toronto ON

Barry, Robert E, *Coordr Gallery*, Southeastern Massachusetts University, College of Visual and Performing Arts, North Dartmouth MA (S)

Barsan, Mabel, *Secy*, Saint Mary's Romanian Orthodox Church, Romanian Ethnic Museum, Cleveland OH

Barsch, Virginia, *Assoc Prof*, Moorhead State University, Department of Art, Moorhead MN (S)

Barske, Diane, *Publicity*, Alaska Artists Guild, Anchorage AK

Barter, Judith, *Cur*, Amherst College, Amherst MA

Barth, Charles, *Chmn Dept*, Mount Mercy College, Art Department, Cedar Rapids IA (S)

Barth, Miles, *Cur of Coll*, International Center of Photography, New York NY

Bartholomew, Martha L, *Program Coordr*, Muckenthaler Cultural Center, Fullerton CA

Bartholomew, Robert P, *Prof*, University of Wisconsin, Madison, School of Family Resources and Consumer Sciences, Madison WI (S)

Bartholomew, Terese Tse, *Cur Indian Art*, Asian Art Museum of San Francisco, Avery Brundage Collection, San Francisco CA

Bartko, George, *Assoc Prof*, Saint Louis Community College at Florissant Valley, Department of Art, Ferguson MO (S)

Bartle, Dorothy B, *Cur Coins & Fri Museum*, Newark Museum, Newark NJ

Bartle, Wilmot T, *Admin Asst*, Newark Museum, Newark NJ

Bartlebaugh, Eloise, *Public Relations Coordr*, The Bradford Museum, Niles IL

Bartlett, Christopher, *Instructor*, Maryland College of Art and Design, Silver Spring MD (S)

Bartlett, Christopher, *Dir*, Towson State University, The Holtzman Art Gallery, Towson MD

Bartlett, Don, *Chmn Dept*, University of Missouri, Art Department, Columbia MO (S)

Bartlett, Ellism, *1st VPres*, Society of Animal Artists, Inc, Bronx NY

Bartlett, Frank, *Secy*, Waterville Historical Association, Waterville ME

Bartlett, Jack, *Asst Prof*, Mississippi State University, Art Department, Mississippi State MS (S)

Bartley, Anne, *Pres*, American Council for the Arts, New York NY

Bartner, Howard C, *Instr*, Johns Hopkins University, School of Medicine, Department of Art as Applied to Medicine, Baltimore MD (S)

Bartnick, Harry, *Chmn Painting Dept*, Lake Placid School of Art, Lake Placid NY (S)

Bartolo, Maria de Lourdes, *Dir*, Museu National de Arte Contemporanea, National Museum of Contemporary Art, Lisbon Portugal

Barton, Brigid S, *Dir*, University of Santa Clara, Library, Santa Clara CA

Barton, Brigid S, *Asst Prof*, University of Santa Clara, Fine Arts Department, Santa Clara CA (S)

Barton, Brigid S, *Dir*, University of Santa Clara, de Saisset Art Gallery and Museum, Santa Clara CA

Barton, Bruce Walter, *Prof*, University of Montana, Dept of Art, Missoula MT (S)

Barton, Linda, *Gallery Coordr*, Foundation for Today's Art, Nexus Gallery, Philadelphia PA

Barton, Paul, *Central Reference Librn*, University of Arizona, Main Library, Tucson AZ

Barton, Ruth, *Reference Librn*, Detroit Public Library, Fine Arts Department, Detroit MI

Baruzzi, Peter B, *Chmn*, Skidmore College, Department of Art, Saratoga Springs NY (S)

Basch, Odile, *Mgr Cultural Affairs*, Philip Morris Incorporated, New York NY

Bascom, Mansfield, *Dir*, Wharton Esherick Museum, Paoli PA

Bascom, Ruth E, *Pres*, Wharton Esherick Museum, Paoli PA

Bascom, William, *Dir*, University of California, R H Lowie Museum of Anthropology, Berkeley CA

Basicevic, Dimitrije, *Cur*, Galerije Grada Zagreba, Centar za Fotografija, Film i Televiziju, Zagreb Yugoslavia

Basile, Ken, *Dir*, Salisbury State College, Wildfowl Art Museum, Salisbury MD

Basiuk, Emil, *Pres*, Ukrainian National Museum & Library, Chicago IL

Bass, Reba, *Folklorist*, Craft and Folk Art Museum, Los Angeles CA

Bassett, Douglas A, *Dir*, National Museum of Wales, Cardiff Wales

Bassett, Hilary D, *Registrar*, Indianapolis Museum of Art, Indianapolis IN

Bassett, Jerry, *Exhib Coordr*, University of South Florida, University Galleries, Tampa FL

Bassett, Mary, *Librn*, Brandywine River Museum, Library, Chadds Ford PA

Bassham, Ben, *Div Coordr Art History*, Kent State University, School of Art, Kent OH (S)

Bassist, Donald H, *Pres*, Bassist Institute Museum, Portland OR

Bass Jr, Harry W, *Pres*, American Numismatic Society, New York NY

Basta, Mounir, *Dir*, Coptic Museum, Cairo Egypt

Bastedo, Philip, *Treas*, American Academy in Rome, New York NY

Bastian, Susan, *Registrar*, University of Notre Dame, Snite Museum of Art, Notre Dame IN

Basu, Sukanta, *Restorer*, National Gallery of Modern Art, New India

Batchelor, Anthony, *Instructor*, Art Academy of Cincinnati, Cincinnati OH (S)

Batchelor, Elizabeth, *Conservator*, Cincinnati Art Museum, Cincinnati OH

Batdorff, Jon, *Asst Prof*, Johnson State College, Art Department, Johnson VT (S)

Bates, Dorothy, *Instructor*, Charles Stewart Mott Community College, Fine Arts Division, Flint MI (S)

Bates, Henry E, *City Librn*, Milwaukee Public Library, Art and Music Department, Milwaukee WI

Bates, Pat Martin, *Assoc Prof*, University of Victoria, Department of Visual Arts, Victoria BC (S)

Batis, Robert, *Dir*, Charles B Goddard Center for the Visual and Performing Arts, Ardmore OK

Batista, Tomas, *Prof*, Institute of Puerto Rican Culture, Escuela de Artes Plasticas, Mayaguez PR (S)

Batson, Darrell, *Regional Service Librn*, Clark County Library District, Las Vegas NV

Battis, Cynthia J, *Supv Loan Dept*, Brookline Public Library, Brookline MA

Battisti, Eugenio, *Evan Pugh Prof*, Pennsylvania State University, University Park, Department of Art History, University Park PA (S)

Battisto, Caroline T, *Instructor*, Norwich Art School, Norwich Free Academy, Art Dept, Norwich CT (S)

Batty, Ellen, *Circulation Librn*, Athenaeum of Philadelphia, Philadelphia PA

Batty, John T, *Asst Dir*, Stockbridge Historical Society, Inc, Stockbridge MA

Batur, Sabahattin, *Dir*, Topkapi Saray Museum, Istanbul Turkey

Batzka, Stephen, *Asst Prof*, Manchester College, Art Department, North Manchester IN (S)

Baudouin, F, *Dir*, Museum Mayer van den Bergh, Antwerp Belgium

Baudouin, F, *Cur*, Openluchtmuseum voor Beeldhouwkunst, Middelheim, Open Air Museum for Sculpture Middelheim, Antwerp Belgium

Baudouin, Frans, *Keeper Art Historical Museum*, Rubenianum, Antwerp Belgium

Bauer, Ann, *Dir*, Vermilion County Museum Society, Danville IL

Bauer, I, *Cur Folk Art*, Bayerisches Nationalmuseum, Bavarian National Museum, Munich Germany, Federal Republic of

Bauer, Lynn, *VChmn*, Municipal Art Commission, Kansas City MO

Bauer, Margaret, *Education Prog Coordr*, Burchfield Center, Buffalo NY

Bauer, Margrit, *Cur*, Museum fur Kunstandwerk, Museum of Arts and Crafts, Frankfurt Germany, Federal Republic of

Bauer, Richard G, *Dir*, Capital University, Schumacher Gallery, Columbus OH

Bauer, Sophie, *Exchange Librn*, Stadelsches Kunstinstitut, Bibliothek, Frankfurt Germany, Federal Republic of

Bauerle, Babette, *Library Asst*, Bryn Mawr College, Art and Archaeology Library, Bryn Mawr PA

Baum, Gerald, *Cataloguer & Archivist*, Saint Louis Art Museum, Richardson Memorial Library, Saint Louis MO

Baum, Peter, *Dir*, Wolfgang-Gurlitt-Museum, Neue Galerie der Stadt Linz, Linz Austria

Bauman, Lorraine, *Cur of Education*, Fetherston Foundation, Packwood House Museum, Lewisburg PA

Bauman, Phil, *Business Mgr*, San Antonio Museum Association, Inc, San Antonio TX

Baumann, Edward, *Assoc Prof*, University of Missouri, Art History and Archaeology Department, Columbia MO (S)

Baumann, Richard, *Cur Renaissance & Modern ARt*, University of Missouri, Museum of Art and Archaeology, Columbia MO

Baumanu, F, *Dir*, Kunsthaus Zurich, Museum of Fine Arts, Zurich Switzerland

Baumgartel, Marguerite, *Assoc Prof*, University of Kansas, Department of Visual Arts Education, Lawrence KS (S)

Baumgartner, Victor, *Dir*, Cornish Institutue of Allied Arts, Cornish Gallery, Seattle WA

Bauske, Clay R, *Dir*, Missouri State Museum, Jefferson City MO

Bavolar, Thomas A, *Treas*, New Jersey Watercolor Society, Little Silver NJ

Baxter, James P, *Pres*, Art Institute of Chicago, Woman's Board, Chicago IL

Baxter, James P, *Pres*, Arts Club of Chicago, Chicago IL

Baxter, William Hubbard, *Chmn*, Birmingham-Southern College, Art Department, Birmingham AL (S)

Bay, Robert, *Prof*, Saint Louis Community College at Florissant Valley, Department of Art, Ferguson MO (S)

Bayard, Ivy, *Librn*, Temple University, Tyler School of Art Library, Philadelphia PA

Baybrooke, Valerie V, *Dir*, University of Mississippi, University Museums, Oxford MS

Bayer, Jeff, *VPres*, Southeastern College Art Conference, Chapel Hill NC

Bayer, Jeffrey J, *Chmn Dept*, University of Alabama in Huntsville, Department of Art, Huntsville AL (S)

Bayersdorfer Jr, Frederick S, *Dir*, Portsmouth Museums and Community Arts Center, Petersburg VA

Bayle, Robert O, *Prog Chmn*, Texas State Technical Institute, Department of Commercial Art, Amarillo TX (S)

Bayless, Stephen, *Head Dept*, Georgia Southern College, Department of Art, Statesboro GA (S)

Bayley, Christopher T, *Secy*, Corporate Council for the Arts, Seattle WA

Bayliss, George V, *Dean School*, University of Michigan, Ann Arbor, School of Art, Ann Arbor MI (S)

Bays, Barbara, *Program Dir*, Parkersburg Art Center, Parkersburg WV

Bayuzick, Dennis, *Asst Prof*, University of Wisconsin-Parkside, Art Discipline, Kenosha WI (S)

Beach, Dorothy, *Librn*, Trinity College Library, Washington DC

Beach, Robert M, *Dir*, Tome Parish Museum, Tome NM

Beadle, Paul J, *Prof*, University of Auckland, School of Fine Arts, Auckland New Zealand (S)

Beakley, Martha, *Prof*, Anderson College, Art Dept, Anderson IN (S)

Beal, Bill, *Reference Librn*, College of Southern Idaho, Library, Twin Falls ID

Beal, Graham W J, *Chief Cur*, Walker Art Center, Minneapolis MN

Beale, Arthur, *Chief Conservator*, Harvard University, William Hayes Fogg Art Museum, Cambridge MA

Beale, H B, *Treas*, Chester County Historical Society, West Chester PA

Beall, Mary, *Head Programming Dept*, Englewood Library, Englewood NJ

Bealmer, William, *Executive dir*, Springfield Art Association of Edwards Place, Springfield IL

Beam, Cheryl, *Office Mgr*, Joslyn Art Museum, Omaha NE

Beam, Kenneth M, *Assoc Dir*, North Carolina Museum of Art, Department of Cultural Resources, Raleigh NC

Beam, Philip C, *Instr*, Bowdoin College, Art Department, Brunswick ME (S)

Beamer, Karl, *Asst Prof*, Bloomsburg State College, Department of Art, Bloomsburg PA (S)

Bean, Jacob, *Cur Drawings*, Metropolitan Museum of Art, New York NY

Bean, Janet R, *Dir*, Chicago Public Library, Cultural Center, Chicago IL

Bear, Marcelle, *Treas*, Florida Artist Group Inc, Englewood FL

Beard, Albert, *Secy*, United States Figure Skating Hall of Fame and Museum, Colorado Springs CO

Beard, Olive, *Pres*, Williams County Historical Society, Williston ND

Bearden, Jacqueline, *Admin Asst*, Saint Augustine Historical Society, Library, Saint Augustine FL

Beardman, John, *Assoc Prof*, Oakland University, Dept of Art & Art History, Rochester MI (S)

Beardsley, Ed, *Instructor*, Umpqua Community College, Art Department, Roseburg OR (S)

Beardsley, Rosemary, *VPres*, Wayne Art Center, Wayne PA

Beardsley, Stephen, *Secy*, Floyd County Museum, New Albany IN

Beardsley Jr, Theodore S, *Dir*, Hispanic Society of America Museum, New York NY

Beare, Sarah, *Gallery Services Officer*, University of Manchester, Whitworth Art Gallery, Manchester England

Bear Jr, James A, *Cur-Dir*, Monticello, Thomas Jefferson Memorial Foundation, Charlottesville VA

Bearnson, Dorothy, *Prof*, University of Utah, Art Department, Salt Lake City UT (S)

Beasley, Jack, *Asst Prof*, University of North Carolina-Charlotte, Creative Arts Dept, Charlotte NC (S)

Beasley, Richard, *Instructor*, Northern Arizona University, Art Department, Flagstaff AZ (S)

Beatson, Gilbert R, *Pres*, Royal Architectural Institute of Canada, Ottawa ON

Beattie, Brent, *Chief Preparator*, Burnaby Art Gallery, Burnaby BC

Beatty, Norman G, *Dir Public Affairs*, Colonial Williamsburg Foundation, Williamsburg VA

Beaty, Shawn, *Library Asst*, Georgia Institute of Technology, College of Architecture Library, Atlanta GA

Beauchamp, Toni, *Asst Dir*, University of Houston, Sarah Campbell Blaffer Gallery, Houston TX

Beaudette, Margaret, *Chmn*, Elizabeth Seton College, Art Department, Yonkers NY (S)

Beaudoin, Paul-Emile, *Dir*, Musee Kateri Tekakwitha, Cahughnawaga PQ

Beaudoin-Ross, Jacqueline, *Cur Costume*, McGill University, McCord Museum, Montreal PQ

Beaumont, Maria Alice, *Dir*, Museu Nacional de Arte Antiga, National Museum of Ancient Art, Lisbon Portugal

Beaver, Albert P, *Head Photography*, Rhode Island School of Design, Providence RI (S)

Beaver, Susan, *Coordr*, Eye Level Gallery, Halifax NS

Bebee, Andrea K, *Librn*, University of Washington, Costume and Textile Study Center Library, Seattle WA

Becher, Liselotte, *Librn*, Staatliche Graphische Sammlung, Library, Munich Germany, Federal Republic of

Beck, Dorys L, *Asst to Dir*, Fresno Arts Center, Fresno CA

Beck, Helen, *Registrar*, Fetherston Foundation, Packwood House Museum, Lewisburg PA

Beck, Herbert, *Dir*, Liebieghaus, Museum Alter Plastik, Museum of Sculpture, Frankfurt Germany, Federal Republic of

Beck, James H, *Dir Grad Studies*, Columbia University, Department of Art History and Archaeology, New York NY (S)

Beck, Lon L, *Asst Prof*, Miami University, Art Department, Oxford OH (S)

Beck, Mary, *Executive Dir*, Hoosier Salon Patrons Association, Hoosier Salon Art Gallery, Indianapolis IN

Beckelman, John, *Asst Prof*, Coe College, Department of Art, Cedar Rapids IA (S)

Becker, Johanna, *Instructor*, College of Saint Benedict, Art Department, Saint Joseph MN (S)

Becker, Loren, *Pres*, Art Association of Jacksonville, David Strawn Art Gallery, Jacksonville IL

Becker, O F, *Acting Head Dept*, Savannah State College, Department of Fine Arts, Savannah GA (S)

Becker Jr, Ward S, *Secy*, New Haven Colony Historical Society, New Haven CT

Beckett, Jack, *Mgr Physical Plant*, Art Gallery of Ontario, Toronto ON

Beckman, Thomas, *Registrar*, Milwaukee Art Center, Milwaukee WI

Beckwith, Alice K, *Dir*, Pittsburgh Plan for Art Gallery, Pittsburgh PA

Beckwith, Diane V, *Secy*, Sweetwater Community Fine Arts Center, Rock Springs WY

Beebe, Mary, *Librn*, Portland Center for the Visual Arts, Library, Portland OR

Beebe, Mary, *VPres*, Western Association of Art Museums, San Francisco CA

Beebe, Mary L, *Executive Dir*, Portland Center for the Visual Arts, Portland OR

Beech, Olive Ann, *Chmn of Board*, Wichita Art Association Inc, Wichita KS

Beedle, R K, *Dir Restoration*, Jekyll Island National Historic Landmark, Jekyll Island GA

Beeke, Jim, *VPrincipal*, Nutana Collegiate Institute, Memorial Library and Art Gallery, Saskatoon SK

Beelke, R G, *Head Dept*, Purdue University, Lafayette, Department of Creative Arts, Art & Design Section, West Lafayette IN (S)

Beelke, Ralph, *Head Dept Creative Arts*, Purdue University, Gallery I, Gallery II, Union Gallery & Stewart Center Gallery, West Lafayette IN

Beeman, Carol, *Treas*, Douglas Art Association, Little Gallery, Douglas AZ

Beene, Patricia C, *Undergrad Admissions*, Southern Illinois University, School of Art, Carbondale IL (S)

Beer, Kenneth J, *Assoc Prof*, James Madison University, Department of Art, Harrisonburg VA (S)

Beer, Michael, *Vis Prof*, Aegean School of Fine Arts, Paros Cyclades Greece (S)

Beer, Ruth, *Asst Prof*, University of Victoria, Department of Visual Arts, Victoria BC (S)

Beeren, W A L, *Dir*, Museum Boymans-Van Beuningen, Rotterdam Netherlands

Beerman, Herbert, *Instructor*, Montclair Art Museum, Art School, Montclair NJ (S)

Beers, Nancy, *Cur Fine Arts*, Sunrise Foundation, Inc, Charleston WV

Beetem, Robert, *Prof*, University of Wisconsin, Madison, Department of Art, Madison WI (S)

Beg, Tahira A, *Keeper Coins & Medals*, Lahore Museum, Lahore Pakistan

Beggs, Alan, *Librn II*, Yonkers Public Library, Fine Arts Department, Yonkers NY

Begley, John, *Lectr*, University of Evansville, Art Dept, Evansville IN (S)

Beglo, Jo, *Reference and Coll Development Librn - Fine Arts and Architecture*, University of Waterloo, Dana Porter Arts Library, Waterloo ON

Behl, Wolfgang, *Prof*, Hartford Art School of the University of Hartford, West Hartford CT (S)

Behlke, David, *Chairperson*, Valley City State College, Art Department, Valley City ND (S)

Behrens, Fred, *Head Dept*, Columbia State Community College, Dept of Art, Columbia TN (S)

Beiersdorfer, Ann, *Dir*, Edgecliff College, Emery Galleries, Cincinnati OH

Beiersdorfer, Ann, *Chairperson Dept*, Edgecliff College, Department of Art, Cincinnati OH (S)

Beihl, Fred, *Pres*, William Rockhill Nelson Gallery of Art, Friends of Art, Kansas City MO

Beim, Elizabeth, *Development Officer*, Museum of the American Indian, New York NY

Bek, Bozo, *Chief Cur*, Galerije Grada Zagreba, Galerija Suvremene Umjetnosti, Zagreb Yugoslavia

Belas, Stuart, *Instructor*, Johnson County Community College, Communications-Arts Division, Overland Park KS (S)

Belding, Camilla, *Exec Secy*, Pen and Brush, Inc, New York NY

Belfi, John, *Instr*, Joe Kubert School of Cartoon and Graphic Art Inc, Dover NJ (S)

Belfort-Chalat, Jacqueline, *Dir*, Le Moyne College, Art Department, Syracuse NY (S)

Belhumeur, Roland J, *Acting Chmn Fine Arts Div*, Rhode Island School of Design, Providence RI (S)

Beling, Helen, *VPres Members*, Sculptors Guild, Inc, New York NY

Belisle, James, *Asst Prof*, University of Toronto, Department of Landscape Architecture, Toronto ON (S)

Beljon, J J, *Dir*, Koninklijke Academie Van Beeldende Kunsten, Royal Academy of Fine Arts, The Hague Netherlands (S)

Belknap, Robert, *Chmn Dept*, Glendale College, Department of Fine Arts, Glendale CA (S)

Bell, Allyn R, *VPres*, Historical Society of Pennsylvania, Philadelphia PA

Bell, Audrey, *Departmental Secy*, University of Alberta, Ring House Gallery, Edmonton AB

Bell, Byron, *Treas*, National Institute for Architectural Education, New York NY

Bell, Eugene, *Instr*, Cuyahoga Valley Art Center, Cuyahoga Falls OH (S)

Bell, Eunice, *Asst to Dir*, Ocean City Arts Center, Ocean City NJ

Bell, Garth, *Instructor*, Saint Louis Community College at Meramec, Art Dept, Saint Louis MO (S)

Bell, Gayle, *Second VPres*, Douglas Art Association, Little Gallery, Douglas AZ

Bell, James M, *Dir*, Fort Wayne Museum of Art, Fort Wayne IN

Bell, Kathy, *Instructor*, Bob Jones University, School of Fine Arts, Greenville SC (S)

Bell, Lucille, *Secy Bd of Dir*, New Muse Community Museum of Brooklyn, Inc, Brooklyn NY

Bell, Malcolm, *Chmn*, University of Virginia, McIntire Department of Art, Charlottesville VA (S)

Bell, Margaret, *Cur Decorative Art*, Art Gallery of Greater Victoria, Victoria BC

Bell, Michael, *Asst Dir Public Programs*, National Gallery of Canada, Ottawa ON

Bell, Pat Marian, *Registrar*, Studio Museum in Harlem, New York NY

Bell, Patrick, *Museum Technician*, Brockton Art Center, Brockton MA

Bell, R, *Cur Crafts*, Art Gallery of Western Australia, Perth Australia

Bell, Robert, *Instructor*, Umpqua Community College, Art Department, Roseburg OR (S)

Bell, Vern, *Executive Dir*, Saskatchewan Arts Board, Regina SK

Bell, Wanda, *Cur*, El Paso Museum of Art, Cavalry Museum, El Paso TX

Bell, Wanda, *Cur History*, El Paso Museum of Art, El Paso TX

Bell, Winnie, *Librn*, Harding University, Beaumont Memorial Library, Searcy AR

Bellah, Don, *Chmn*, Northwestern Oklahoma State University, Art Department, Alva OK (S)

Bellah, Donald W, *Dean*, Texas Wesleyan College, Department of Art, Fort Worth TX (S)

Bellingham, Susan, *Special Coll Librn*, University of Waterloo, Dana Porter Arts Library, Waterloo ON

Bellis, Cathy, *Vice Chmn*, Fine Arts Museums of San Francisco, The Museum Society, n of Honor co

Bellman, David, *Chief Cur*, McGill University, McCord Museum, Montreal PQ

Belloli, Jay, *Cur Modern Art*, Detroit Institute of Arts, Detroit MI

Belous, Russell, *Chief Cur*, Historic Pensacola Preservation Board, West Florida Museum of History, Pensacola FL

Belschner, Richard, *Financial Secy*, Public Library of Fort Wayne and Allen County, Fort Wayne IN

Belser, D C H, *Secy*, Columbia Museums of Art and Science, Columbia Art Association, Columbia SC

Belson, Anne M, *In Charge Art Collection*, Federal Reserve Bank of Boston, Boston MA

Beltran, Richard, *Dean*, Pels School of Art, New York NY (S)

Belz, Carl I, *Dir*, Brandeis University, Rose Art Museum, Waltham MA

Bena, Peter J, *Gallery Mgr*, University of Massachusetts, Amherst, University Gallery, Amherst MA

Benavides, Rodrigo, *Instructor*, Del Mar College, Department of Art, Corpus Christi TX (S)

Bencetie, Steve, *Prof*, Mansfield State College, Art Department, Mansfield PA (S)

Bench, Laura, *Instructor*, Seton Hill College, Department of Art, Greensburg PA (S)

Benckenstein, Eunice R, *VChmn*, Stark Museum of Art, Orange TX

Benda, Ric, *First VPres*, North Shore Art League, Winnetka IL

Ben-David, Channa, *Secy*, Museum of Japanese Art, Haifa Israel

Bendel, Donald, *Instructor*, Northern Arizona University, Art Department, Flagstaff AZ (S)

Bender, Betty W, *Dir*, Spokane Public Library, Spokane WA

Benedetti, Joan M, *Librn*, Craft and Folk Art Museum, Library and Media Resource Center, Los Angeles CA

Benedict, Judith, *Designer*, State University of New York at Oswego, Tyler Art Gallery, Oswego NY

Benedict, Mary Jane, *Librn*, Louisville School of Art Gallery, Library, Anchorage KY

Benes, Vladimir, *Deputy Dir*, Narodni Galerie v Prague, National Gallery of Prague, Prague Czechoslovakia

Benet Jr, Hugh, *VPres*, Star-Spangled Banner Flag House Association, Baltimore MD

Bengtz, Lillian E, *Assoc Dir*, Art Complex Museum at Duxbury, Duxbury MA

Benham, Caroline E, *Cur*, Cape Ann Historical Association, Gloucester MA

Benham, Sarah, *Gallery Dir*, Swain School of Design, William W Crapo Gallery, New Bedford MA

Benio, Pauleve, *Instructor*, Adrian College, Art Department, Adrian MI (S)

Benjamin, Carl, *Prof*, Pomona College, Art Department, Claremont CA (S)

Bennehoof, June, *Art Gallery Coordr*, Youngstown State University, Kilcawley Center Art Gallery, Youngstown OH

Bennet, Anna, *Cur in Charge Department Textiles*, Fine Arts Museums of San Francisco, M H de Young Memorial Museum and California Palace of the Legion of Honor

Bennett, Charles G, *Librn*, Bennington Museum, Library, Bennington VT

Bennett, K Sharon, *Librn*, Charleston Museum, Library, Charleston SC

Bennett, Leonie S, *Head*, Lasell Junior College, Art Department, Auburndale MA (S)

Bennett, Lloyd, *Asst Prof*, Xavier University of Louisiana, Department of Fine Arts, New Orleans LA (S)

Bennett, Margaret, *Head Membership*, University of Rochester, Memorial Art Gallery, Rochester NY

Bennett, Mary G, *Keeper British Art*, Walker Art Gallery, Liverpool England

Bennett, Paul, *Dir*, Gallery Stratford, Stratford ON

Benson, Bill, *Pres*, Red River Valley Museum, Vernon TX

Benson, Guy H, *Chmn*, Sullins College, Art Department, Bristol VA (S)

Benson, Jack, *Prof*, University of Massachusetts, Amherst, Art History Prog, Amherst MA (S)

Benson, John G, *Treas*, Hill Country Arts Foundation, Ingram TX

Benson, June, *Correspondence Secy*, New Jersey Watercolor Society, Little Silver NJ

Benson, Martha, *Dir*, Octagon Center for the Arts, Ames IA

Benson, Maxine, *Cur Documentary Resources*, Colorado Historical Society, Colorado Heritage Center, Denver CO

Benson, Skip, *Instructor*, California College of Arts and Crafts, Oakland CA (S)

Bentein, M R, *Asst Cur*, Openluchtmuseum voor Beeldhouwkunst, Middelheim, Open Air Museum for Sculpture Middelheim, Antwerp Belgium

Bentic, Ronald, *Chmn Div*, Wingate College, Division of Fine Arts, Wingate NC (S)

Bentley, James R, *Secy & Cur Manuscript*, Filson Club, Louisville KY

Bentley, T Keilor, *Dir*, Mount Allison University, Owens Art Gallery, Sackville NB

Bentz, Harry D, *Chmn Art Dept*, Shippensburg State College, Art Department, Shippensburg PA (S)

Bentz, Harry D, *Dir*, Shippensburg State College, Kauffman Gallery, Shippensburg PA

Benvenuto, Elio, *Visual Arts Dir*, San Francisco City and County Art Commission, San Francisco CA

Benz, Lee, *Instr*, Illinois Central College, Art and Humanities Department, East Peoria IL (S)

Berard, Guy, *Assoc Prof*, Saint Laurence University, Department of Fine Arts, Canton NY (S)

Berckenhagen, Ekhart, *Dir*, Staatliche Museen Preussischer Kulturbesitz, Kunstbibliothek, Berlin Germany, Federal Republic of

Berckenhagen, Ekhart, *Dir*, Staatliche Museen Preussischer Kulturbesitz, Art Library and Lipperheide Costume Library, Berlin Germany, Federal Republic of

Berendsen, Olga, *Prof*, Rutgers, the State University of New Jersey, Graduate Program in Art History, New Brunswick NJ (S)

Berenson, Bertram, *Dean*, University of Cincinnati, College of Design, Architecture and Art, Cincinnati OH (S)

Berenson, Linda, *Dir Sales Shop*, Colorado Springs Fine Arts Center, Colorado Springs CO

Berern, Stephen, *Dir Galleries*, Florida School of the Arts, Visual Arts, Palatka FL (S)

Beresford, Michael, *Asst Prof*, Webster College, Art Dept, Webster Groves MO (S)

Berezin, Ellen R, *Cur of Education*, Worcester Art Museum, Worcester MA

Berg, H, *Chmn Photography*, Fashion Institute of Technology, New York NY (S)

Berg, Henry, *Deputy Dir*, Solomon R Guggenheim Museum, New York NY

Berg, Jonas, *Keeper Industrial & Social History Department*, Nordiska Museet, Scandinavian Museum, Stockholm Sweden

Berg, Keith, *Pres*, Huntsville Art League and Museum Association Inc, Huntsville AL

Berg, Knut, *Dir*, Nasjonalgalleriet, National Gallery, Oslo Norway

Berg, Marie Gabrielle, *Asst Prof*, Marymount College of Virginia, Arts & Sciences Division, Arlington VA (S)

Berg, Mona, *Gallery Dir*, Purdue University, Gallery I, Gallery II, Union Gallery & Stewart Center Gallery, West Lafayette IN

Berg, Robert, *Grad Coordr*, San Diego State University, Department of Art, San Diego CA (S)

Berg, Ronald, *Academic Dean*, Concordia College, Fine Arts Galleries, Milwaukee WI

Berge, Louise, *Asst Cur Classical Art*, Art Institute of Chicago, Chicago IL

Bergen, Donald M, *Pres*, Hopewell Museum, Hopewell NJ

Berger, Howard R, *Pres*, Monmouth Museum and Cultural Center, Lincroft NJ

Berger, Jerry A, *Cur Collections*, University of Wyoming, Art Museum, Laramie WY

Berger, M, *Sr Library Asst*, McGill University, Blackader-Lauterman Library of Architecture and Arts, Montreal PQ

Berger, Markel Bruce, *Chmn Grad Prog*, Rutgers, the State University of New Jersey, Mason Gross School of the Arts, New Brunswick NJ (S)

Berger, Patricia, *Asst Prof*, University of Southern California, School of Fine Arts, Los Angeles CA (S)

Berger, Richard, *Chmn Sculpture Dept*, San Francisco Art Institute, San Francisco CA (S)

Berger, Ronald, *Instructor*, College of Santa Fe, Visual Arts Dept, Santa Fe NM (S)

Berger-Hughes, Mary Lee, *Exec Asst*, Textile Museum, Washington DC

Bergeron, Suzanne, *Secy to Dir*, Bowdoin College, Museum of Art & Peary-MacMillan Arctic Museum, Brunswick ME

Bergethon, K Roald, *Pres*, Buck Hill Art Association, Buck Hill Falls PA

Bergh, Erik, *Dir*, Turun Taidemuseo, Turku Art Museum, Turku Finland

Bergh, Helen, *Cur of Education*, Dacotah Prairie Museum, Aberdeen SD

Bergin, Robert P, *Treas*, John Simon Guggenheim Memorial Foundation, New York NY

Bergman, Edward A, *Pres*, Art Institute of Chicago, Print and Drawing Club, Chicago IL

Bergman, Ingrid, *Keeper Textiles & Costume*, Nordiska Museet, Scandinavian Museum, Stockholm Sweden

Bergman, Joseph, *Instr*, Siena Heights College, Art Department, Adrian MI (S)

Bergmann, R, *Assoc Prof*, McGill University, Department of Art History, Montreal PQ (S)

Berkey, Erna L, *VPres*, Kenneth C Beck Center for the Cultural Arts, Lakewood OH

Berkhofer, George H, *Executive Dir & Cur Museum*, Clark County Historical Society, Springfield OH

Berkley, Richard L, *Chmn*, Municipal Art Commission, Kansas City MO

Berkley, Robert J, *Dir*, Nasson College, Anderson Learning Center, Springvale ME

Berkowitz, Rita, *Art Instr*, School of Fashion Design, Boston MA (S)

Berkowitz, Roger M, *Cur Decorative Arts*, Toledo Museum of Art, Toledo OH

Berle, Kathy, *First VPres*, Artist-Craftsmen of New York, New York NY

Berlo, Janet, *Asst Prof*, University of Missouri-Saint Louis, Art Dept, Saint Louis MO (S)

Berman, Bernard, *Pres Board Trustees*, Allentown Art Museum, Allentown PA

Berman, Nancy, *Dir*, Hebrew Union College, Skirball Museum, Los Angeles CA

Bermingham, Peter, *Dir & Chief Cur*, University of Arizona, Museum of Art, Tucson AZ

Bernal, Christine, *Admin Asst*, Millicent Rogers Museum, Taos NM

Bernal, Rudy, *Preparator*, University of Chicago, David and Alfred Smart Gallery, Chicago IL

Bernard, H, *Coordr Interior Design*, Kean College of New Jersey, Fine Arts Department, Union NJ (S)

Bernard, Virginia Bilmazes, *Librn*, Haverhill Public Library, Haverhill MA

Bernardi, Rosemarie T, *Instructor*, University of Alabama in Huntsville, Department of Art, Huntsville AL (S)

Bernatowicz, Rita, *Instructor*, Castleton State College, Art Department, Castleton VT (S)

Bernbach, Cathy, *Slide Librn*, Hebrew Union College, Skirball Museum, Los Angeles CA

Berneche, Joanne, *Instructor*, William Woods-Westminster Colleges, Art Department, Fulton MO (S)

Bernhardt, Gerda, *Librn*, Staten Island Ferry Maritime Museum, Library, Staten Island NY

Bernstein, Edward C, *Asst Prof*, University of Arkansas, Art Department, Fayetteville AR (S)

Bernstein, Gerald S, *Chmn*, Brandeis University, Department of Fine Arts, Waltham MA (S)

Bernstein, Joanne, *Asst Prof*, Mills College, Art Department, Oakland CA (S)

Bernstein, Marcia, *Adminr Dir*, N.A.M.E. Gallery, Chicago IL

Berreth, David, *Dir*, Miami University Art Museum, Oxford OH

Berreth, David S, *Asst Dir*, University of Wisconsin, Elvehjem Art Center, Madison WI

Berry, Alice, *Assoc Prof*, South Dakota State University, Art Dept, Brookings SD (S)

Berry, Betty, *Primary Faculty*, Quachita Baptist University, Department of Art, Arkadelphia AR (S)

Berry, Dorothy M, *Dir*, Mills House Visual Arts Complex, Garden Grove CA

Berry, Ethan, *Instr*, Montserrat School of Visual Art, Beverly MA (S)

Berry, John, *Dir*, Society of Environmental Graphics Designers, Chicago IL

Berry, Margaret, *Asst Prof*, Lenoir Rhyne College, Department of Art, Hickory NC (S)

Berry, Michele K, *Secy*, Society of North American Artists, Inc, Omaha NE

Berry, Nancy, *Cur Educ*, Southern Methodist University, Meadows Museum, Dallas TX

Berry, Rosann S, *Executive Secy*, Society of Architectural Historians, Philadelphia PA

Berryman, Cara, *Exhib Coordr*, Wilkes College, Sordoni Art Gallery, Wilkes-Barre PA

Bersch, Mary John, *Prof*, College of Notre Dame of Maryland, Art Dept, Baltimore MD (S)

Bertagnolli, Janet L, *Registrar*, Illinois State University, Center for the Visual Arts Gallery, Normal IL

Bertelli, Carlo, *Dir*, Pinacoteca di Brera, Brera Picture Gallery, Milan Italy

Bertelli, Ilaria Toesca, *Dir*, Galleria e Museo del Palazzo Ducale, Gallery and Museum of the Palazzo Ducale, Mantua Italy

Bertheux, W, *Head Department Applied Art*, Stedlijk Museum-Amsterdam, Municipal Museum, Amsterdam Netherlands

Berthold, Fred, *Acting Chmn*, Dartmouth College, Department of Art, Hanover NH (S)

Bertolli, Robert, *Prof*, Boston State College, Art Department, Boston MA (S)

Bertolo, Diane, *Asst to Dir*, Hallwalls Gallery, Buffalo NY

Bertolotto, Claudio, *Staff Member*, Armeria Reale, Turin Italy

Bertolotto, Claudio, *Staff Member*, Galleria Sabauda, Turin Italy

Bertos, R, *Chmn*, McGill University, Department of Art History, Montreal PQ (S)

Bertram, Helge, *Dir School Painting, Sculpture and Graphic Arts*, Det Kongelige Danske Kunstakademi, The Royal Danish Academy of Fine Arts, Copenhagen Denmark (S)

Bertrand, J Rayburn, *Pres Foundation*, University of Southwestern Louisiana, Art Center for Southwestern Louisiana, Lafayette LA

Beryi, Luciano, *Dir*, Galleria Degli Uffizi, Uffizi Gallery, Florence Italy

Bessette, Don, *Instructor*, Junior College of Albany, Fine Arts Division, Albany NY (S)

Best, Harold, *Admin Dir*, Wheaton College, Dept of Art, Wheaton IL (S)

Best, William R, *Chief Cur & Dir*, Bennington Museum, Bennington VT

Bethany, Adeline, *Chmn Dept*, Cabrini College, Department of Fine Arts, Radnor PA (S)

Bethel, Audrey, *Dir*, Arts and Crafts Center of Pittsburgh, Pittsburgh PA

Betsch, William E, *Chmn*, University of Miami, Department of Art, Coral Gables FL (S)

Bettenbender, John, *Dean*, Rutgers, the State University of New Jersey, Mason Gross School of the Arts, New Brunswick NJ (S)

Bettinson, Brenda, *Chmn*, Pace University, Department of Art & Design, Pleasantville NY (S)

Bex, Florent, *Dir*, Internationaal Cultureel Centrum, International Cultural Centre, Antwerp Belgium

Beye, P, *Dir*, Staatsgalerie Stuttgart, Stuttgart Germany, Federal Republic of

Bezwinska, Yadwiga, *Documents*, Muzeum Narodowe w Krakowie, National Museum in Cracow, Cracow Poland

Bhowmik, S K, *Dir*, Museum and Picture Gallery, Baroda India

Biaggi, Jacqueline, *Cur*, El Museo del Barrio, New York NY

Biagi, Luigi, *Dir*, Accademia di Belle Arti e Liceo Artistico, Florence Italy (S)

Bianchi, Robert, *Assoc Cur Egyptian & Classical Art*, Brooklyn Museum, Brooklyn NY

Bianco, Thelma Roper, *Head*, Maryville College, Division of Fine Arts, Art Section, Maryville TN (S)

Biantoo, Bary, *Lectr*, Villa Maria College of Buffalo, Art Department, Buffalo NY (S)

Biascoechea, Carmen, *Dean Fine Arts School*, El Museo del Barrio, New York NY

Bibler, Richard, *Instructor*, Monterey Peninsula College, Art Department, Monterey CA (S)

Bibler, Robert, *Instructor*, Chemeketa Community College, Department of Humanities & Social Science, Salem OR (S)

Bibly, L B, *Instructor*, Chamberlayne Junior College, Department of Graphic and Applied Arts, Boston MA (S)

Bice, Megan, *Education Cur*, Art Gallery of Windsor, Windsor ON

Bickel, John, *VPres Planning*, Cedar Rapids Art Center, Cedar Rapids IA

Bickford, Christopher, *Asst Dir*, Connecticut Historical Society, Hartford CT

Bicknell, Robert E, *Chmn*, Wayland Baptist College, Department of Art & Music, Plainview TX (S)

Biddle, James, *Pres*, National Trust for Historic Preservation, Washington DC

Biddle, Martin, *Dir*, University of Pennsylvania, University Museum, Philadelphia PA

Biddle Jr, Livingston L, *Chmn*, National Endowment for the Arts, Washington DC

Bienemann, Bruce, *Dir*, Sioux City Art Center, Sioux City IA

Bienemann, Bruce, *Dir*, Sioux City Art Center, Sioux City IA (S)

Bieringa, L H, *Dir*, National Art Gallery of New Zealand, Wellington New Zealand

Biers, Jane C, *Cur Ancient Art*, University of Missouri, Museum of Art and Archaeology, Columbia MO

Biers, William R, *Chmn*, University of Missouri, Art History and Archaeology Department, Columbia MO (S)

Biesboer, P, *Cur Ancient Art*, Frans Halsmuseum, Frans Hals Museum, Haarlem Netherlands

Bigazzi, Anna, *Library Asst*, University of Hartford, Anne Bunce Cheney Library, West Hartford CT

Bigelow, David, *Asst Prof*, Middle Tennessee State University, Art Dept, Murfreesboro TN (S)

Biggers, John T, *Head Dept*, Texas Southern University, Department of Art, Houston TX (S)

Bigham, Darrell, *Pres Bd Dir*, Evansville Museum of Arts and Science, Evansville IN

Bigler, Steve, *Asst Prof*, University of Northern Iowa, Department of Art, Cedar Falls IA (S)

Bilaitis, Richard J, *Dir*, Wayne State University, Community Arts Gallery, Detroit MI

Bilinski, Donald, *Dir*, Polish Museum of America, Chicago IL

Bilisolij, F N, *VPres*, Irene Leache Memorial, Norfolk VA

Bilk, Marjorie, *Librn*, Moore College of Art Gallery, Library, Philadelphia PA

Billeter, E, *Asst Dir*, Kunsthaus Zurich, Museum of Fine Arts, Zurich Switzerland

Billings, Loren, *Dir*, School of Holography, David Wender Library, Chicago IL

Billings, Loren, *Pres*, School of Holography, Fine Arts Research and Holographic Center Museum, Chicago IL

Billings, Robert, *Secy*, School of Holography, Fine Arts Research and Holographic Center Museum, Chicago IL

Billings, Robert H, *Humanities & Fine Arts Chmn*, Los Angeles Harbor College, Art Department, Wilmington CA (S)

Billmeyer Jr, Fred W, *Secy*, Inter-Society Color Council, Troy NY

Binai, Paul F, *Cur Exhib*, Carnegie Institute, Museum of Art, Pittsburgh PA

Bindler, Nathan, *Assoc Prof*, Augusta College, Department of Fine Arts, Augusta GA (S)

Binegger, Uli, *Art-Cur in Charge of Serigraphed Reproductions*, Muiska-Museum, Munich Germany, Federal Republic of

Bingaman, Elizabeth, *Films Specialist*, Minneapolis Public Library and Information Center, Art, Music and Film Dept, Minneapolis MN

Bingenheimer, Robert, *Adjunct Assoc*, Wright State University, Art Department, Dayton OH (S)

Bingham, Olivia, *Secy*, Crossett Art League, Crossett AR

Binkley, Donald, *Coordr Exhib Omniplex*, Omniplex, Oklahoma City OK

Binks, Ronald, *Div Dir*, University of Texas at San Antonio, Division of Art and Design, San Antonio TX (S)

Binns, Patti, *Secy*, Kern County Museum, Bakersfield CA

Bippes, Bill, *Dir*, Spring Arbor College, Art Department, Spring Arbor MI (S)

Birch, Cathy, *Cataloguing Asst*, Rockwell-Corning Museum, Corning NY

Birch, Jeffery, *Cur Exhib*, Charlotte Nature Museum, Inc, Charlotte NC

Birckhead, Toni, *Pres*, Contemporary Arts Center, Cincinnati OH

Bird, Richard, *Head Dept*, Ricks College, Department of Art, Rexburg ID (S)

Birdsall, James, *Treas*, Owatonna Arts Center, Owatonna MN

Birdsall, Virginia, *Performing Art Chmn*, Owatonna Arts Center, Owatonna MN

Birgili, Turhan, *Cur Photography*, Istanbul Arkeoloji Müzeleri, Archaeological Museums of Istanbul, Istanbul Turkey

Birmingham, Mary, *Librn*, Bethany Lutheran College, Memorial Library, Mankato MN

Birnbaum, Mildred, *Pres*, Art Barn, Greenwich CT

Birnie, Adelaide R, *Bursar*, Montclair Art Museum, Montclair NJ

Birnie-Danzker, Jo-Anne, *Cur*, Vancouver Art Gallery, Vancouver BC

Bisaillon, Blaise, *Dir*, Forbes Library, Northampton MA

Bisaillon, Ed, *Dir*, Hastings Museum, Hastings NE

Bishop, Barbara L, *Chmn*, Longwood College, Department of Art, Farmville VA (S)

Bishop, Barbara L, *Chmn of Art Dept & Dir*, Longwood College, Bedford Gallery, Farmville VA

Bishop, Beverly, *Assoc Archivist*, Missouri Historical Society, Saint Louis MO

Bishop, Budd, *Pres*, Intermuseum Conservation Association, Oberlin OH

Bishop, Bud Harris, *Dir*, Columbus Museum of Art, Columbus OH

Bishop, Carol, *Chmn Fine & Applied Art*, Solano Community College, Department of Fine & Applied Art, Suisun City CA (S)

Bishop, Janice, *Admin Asst*, Ontario Association of Art Galleries, Toronto ON

Bishop, M E, *Registrar*, Queen's Gallery, London England

Bishop, Minor, *Secy*, Fine Arts Federation of New York, New York NY

Bishop, Robert, *Dir*, Museum of American Folk Art, New York NY

Biskaps, O, *Prof*, Nova Scotia Technical College, Faculty of Architecture, Halifax NS (S)

Bissietta, G F, *Coordr*, Accademia di Belle Arti, Academy of Fine Arts, Perugia Italy (S)

Bisson, Yvette, *Prof*, College Saint-Louis-Maillet, Department of Visual Arts, Edmundston NB (S)

Bittel, Anne, *Membership Secy*, New Orleans Museum of Art, Isaac Delgado Museum, New Orleans LA

Bittman, Hilde, *VPres*, South Peace Art Society, Dawson Creek Museum Art Gallery, Dawson Creek BC

Bittoni, Renato, *Vis Artist*, Studio Art Centers International, Florence Italy (S)

Bitz, Gwen, *Asst Registrar*, Walker Art Center, Minneapolis MN

Bivens, Carol D, *Downtown Gallery Curator*, Roanoke Fine Arts Center, Roanoke VA

Bivins Jr, John, *Publications Dir*, Museum of Early Southern Decorative Arts, Old Salem Inc, Winston-Salem NC

Bixenman, Betty, *Chmn Dept Fashion Design*, Woodbury University, Professional Arts Division, Los Angeles CA (S)

Bixler, Harvey R, *Cur*, Liberty Hall Museum, Frankfort KY

Bjerre, Henrik, *Acting for Chief Restorer*, Statens Museum for Kunst, Department of Painting and Sculpture, Copenhagen Denmark

Bjone, Helen, *VPres*, SVACA - Sheyenne Valley Arts and Crafts Association, Bjarne Ness Gallery, Fort Ransom ND

Bjorkland, Marilyn, *Registrar*, Minneapolis Institute of Arts, Minneapolis MN

Bjorklund, Patricia, *Instructor*, Chamberlayne Junior College, Department of Graphic and Applied Arts, Boston MA (S)

Bjorkman, Donald, *Assoc Prof*, California Polytechnic State University at San Luis Obispo, Art Department, San Luis Obispo CA (S)

Bjornsson, Arni, *Cur*, Thjodminjasafn, National Museum of Iceland, Rrykjavik Iceland

Björkvik, Halvard, *Dir*, Norsk Folkemuseum, Norwegian Folk Museum, Oslo Norway

Bjurlin, Marvin, *Prof*, State University College, Department of Art, Fredonia NY (S)

Bjurström, Per, *Dir*, Nationalmuseum, Stockholm Sweden

Black, Anna, *VPres*, Burlington County Historical Society, Burlington NJ

Black, Craig C, *Co-Dir*, Museum Management Institute, San Francisco CA (S)

Black, Francis, *Cur*, Schuyler-Hamilton House, Morristown NJ

Black, Jack, *Board Chmn*, Fayette Art Museum, Fayette AL

Black, James R, *Instr*, Schoolcraft College, Department of Art, Livonia MI (S)

Black, John, *Assoc Prof*, Central Virginia Community College, Division of Humanities, Lynchburg VA (S)

Black, Mary, *Cur Painting & Sculpture*, New York Historical Society, New York NY

Black, Patti Carr, *Dir Old Capitol Museum*, Mississippi Department of Archives and History, Jackson MS

Black, Richard, *Prof*, Drake University, Art Department, Des Moines IA (S)

Black, Sallie, *Co-Cur*, Historical Society of Bloomfield, New Jersey, Bloomfield NJ

Blackbeard, Bill, *Dir*, San Francisco Academy of Comic Art Library, San Francisco CA

Blackburn, Bob, *Publications*, Oklahoma Historical Society, Central Museum, Oklahoma City OK

Blackburn, J Glenn, *Chmn*, Clinch Valley College of the University of Virginia, Humanities Department, Wise VA (S)

Blackburn, R, *Chief Librn*, University of Toronto, Fine Arts Library, Toronto ON

Blackburn, Robert, *Dir*, Printmaking Workshop, New York NY

Blackhurst, Phillip, *Chmn*, University of Kansas, Department of Visual Communications, Lawrence KS (S)

Blackim, Dave, *Chmn*, Hutchinson Community Junior College, Art Department, Hutchinson KS (S)

Blackmun, Barbara, *Instructor*, San Diego Mesa College, Art Department, San Diego CA (S)

Blackney, Richard W, *Instructor*, Valencia Community College, Art Department, Orlando FL (S)

Blacksberg, Leslie, *Cataloger*, Hebrew Union College, Skirball Museum, Los Angeles CA

Blackwell, J V, *Chmn Dept*, University of Nebraska at Omaha, Dept of Art, Omaha NE (S)

Blackwood, C Roy, *Asst Prof*, Southeastern Louisiana University, Dept of Visual Arts, Hammond LA (S)

Blackwood, David, *VPres*, Royal Canadian Academy of Arts, Toronto ON

Blade, Timothy, *Asst Prof*, University of Minnesota, Department of Design, Saint Paul MN (S)

Blaesing, William, *Cur Exhib*, Racine Art Association, Charles A Wustum Museum of Fine Arts, Racine WI

Blagdon, Sharon, *Graphic Designer*, Brockton Art Center, Brockton MA

Blain, Bradley, *Cur*, Kitchener-Waterloo Art Gallery, Kitchener ON

Blain, Paul, *Education Officer*, Kitchener-Waterloo Art Gallery, Kitchener ON

Blain, Sandra J, *Dir*, Arrowmont School of Arts and Crafts, Gatlinburg TN (S)

Blain, Wilfred, *Admin Officer*, Ottawa Public Library, Ottawa ON

Blair, C, *Keeper Metalwork*, Victoria and Albert Museum, London England

Blair, Carl, *Instructor*, Bob Jones University, School of Fine Arts, Greenville SC (S)

Blair, Cetta, *Secy*, Sioux City Art Center, Sioux City IA

Blair, Jean, *Second VPres*, Monmouth Museum and Cultural Center, Lincroft NJ

Blair, Laurel G, *Cur*, Blair Museum of Lithophanes and Carved Waxes, Springfield OH

Blair, Mary, *Pres*, Brattleboro Museum and Art Center, Brattleboro VT

Blaisdell, Phillip, *Instr*, Joe Kubert School of Cartoon and Graphic Art Inc, Dover NJ (S)

Blake, Hortense, *Dir*, Clinton Art Association Gallery, Clinton IA

Blake, Peter, *Chmn Grad Studies*, Catholic University of America, Department of Architecture & Planning, Washington DC (S)

Blakely, Glen, *Instructor*, Dixie College, Art Department, Saint George UT (S)

Blakely, Phyllis R, *Assoc Archivist*, Public Archives of Nova Scotia, Halifax NS

Blakemore, Robbie G, *Head Dept*, University of Tennessee, Knoxville, Interior Design Department, Knoxville TN (S)

Blalock, Dorothy, *VPres*, Nicholas Roerich Museum, New York NY

Blanchard, Henry J, *Dir*, Centre Cultural de Shawinigan, Shawinigan PQ

Blanchet, Martta, *Dir*, Rockport Art Association, Rockport MA

Blanco, Ricardo, *Industrial Design*, Centro de Arte y Communicacion, Center of Art and Communication, Buenos Argentina

Blaney, Joseph, *Exec Deputy*, State Education Department, State University of New York, Albany NY

Blanton, Paul, *Head Dept*, University of Idaho, Department of Art and Architecture, Moscow ID (S)

Blasage, Margaret, *Dir Publications*, Art Institute of Chicago, Chicago IL

Blasdel, Hugo G, *Exec Dir*, National Architectural Accrediting Board, Inc, Washington DC

Blaskovich, Mary, *Admin Asst*, Copper Village Museum and Arts Center, Anaconda MT

Blason, Mirella, *Librn*, Museo Civico di Padua, Biblioteca, Padua Italy

Blaustein, Marcia, *Head Painting Dept*, Kalamazoo Institute of Arts, Kalamazoo MI (S)

Blazy, Diane, *Gallery Dir*, Lexington Public Library, Lexington KY

Blebtreu, Hermann K, *Dir*, Museum of Northern Arizona, Flagstaff AZ

Blechman, Nancy, *Adminr*, International Center of Photography, New York NY

Bledsoe, Jane K, *Administrative Dir*, California State University, Long Beach, The Art Museum and Galleries, Long Beach CA

Bleich, Marlene, *Information Specialist*, Los Angeles Institute of Contemporary Art, Los Angeles CA

Blench, Brian J R, *Keeper of Decorative Art*, Glasgow Museums and Art Galleries, Kelvingrove Art Gallery and Museum, Glasgow Scotland

Blenderman, Al, *Pres*, Sioux City Art Center, Sioux City IA

Blijenburg, F, *Asst*, Haags Gemeentemuseum, Art Library, The Hague Netherlands

Blindheim, Charlotte, *Head Viking Age Department*, Universitetets Samling av Nordiske Oldsaker, University Museum of National Antiquities, Oslo Norway

Blindheim, Martin, *Head Medieval Age Department*, Universitetets Samling av Nordiske Oldsaker, University Museum of National Antiquities, Oslo Norway

Bliss, Harry E, *Assoc Prof*, Palomar College, Art Department, San Marcos TX (S)

Blitz, Roberta, *Fine Arts Librn*, Adelphi University, Fine Arts Library, Garden City NY

Blitzer, Charles, *Asst Secy for Art & History*, Smithsonian Institution, Washington DC

Blix, Bill, *Instr*, Lane Community College, Art and Applied Design Department, Eugene OR (S)

Blizard, William, *Chmn Dept*, Springfield College, Department of Visual and Performing Arts, Springfield MA (S)

Blizzard, Alan, *Chmn Dept*, Scripps College, Art Department, Claremont CA (S)

Bloch, E Maurice, *Dir & Cur*, University of California, Los Angeles, Grunwald Center for the Graphic Arts, Los Angeles CA

Bloch, Milton J, *Dir*, Mint Museum of Art, Charlotte NC

Bloch, Peter, *Dir*, Staatliche Museen Preussischer Kulturbesitz, Department of Sculpture, Berlin Germany, Federal Republic of

Block, Bart, *Asst Program Coordr*, Texas A & M University, Memorial Student Center Arts Committee, College Station TX

Block, R M, *Chief Librn*, Medicine Hat Public Library, Medicine Hat AB

Blocker, Martha G, *Head Librn*, Indianapolis Museum of Art, Stout Reference Library, Indianapolis IN

Blocker, Merrie, *Dir Outreach Educ*, DeCordova and Dana Museum and Park, Lincoln MA

Blodau, Carol, *Instr*, Irish International Arts Centre, Castle Matrix, Rathkeale Ireland (S)

Blodau, Dietrich, *Instr*, Irish International Arts Centre, Castle Matrix, Rathkeale Ireland (S)

Blodgett, Fritz, *Instr*, Sierra College, Art Department, Rocklin CA (S)

Blogg, Irene, *Pres*, Sculptor's Society of Canada, Toronto ON

Blokhuis, S M, *Head Education Department*, Stedelijk Museum de Lakenhal, Leyden Municipal Museum, Leiden Netherlands

Blom, Billie, *Executive Secy*, Museum of the Arts Foundation, Missoula Museum of the Arts, Missoula MT

Blomstrann, Lois L, *Asst to Dir*, New Britain Museum of American Art, New Britain CT

Bloom, Leslye, *Asst Prof*, University of Evansville, Art Dept, Evansville IN (S)

Bloom, Miriam, *Asst Prof*, Colgate University, Department of Fine Arts, Hamilton NY (S)

Bloom, William, *Pres*, Artworlds Center for Creative Arts, Ann Arbor MI

Bloomer, Carolyn, *Asst Prof*, Monmouth College, Department of Art, West Long Branch NJ (S)

Bloomer, Harlan, *Gallery Dir*, Mankato State University, Nichols Gallery, Mankato MN

Bloomer, Jerry M, *Secy Registrar*, R W Norton Art Gallery, Shreveport LA

Bloomer, Jerry M, *Librn*, R W Norton Art Gallery, Library, Shreveport LA

Bloomer, Mary, *Instructor*, Your Heritage House, Inc, Detroit MI

Blosser, John, *Head Dept*, Hesston College, Hesston KS (S)

Blottiere, Sylvie, *Asst Cur*, Musee des Beaux-Arts, Rennes France

Blouin, Jean Charles, *Faculty Dean of Arts*, Universite Laval Cite Universitaire, School of Visual Arts, Quebec PQ (S)

Blouin, Patrick, *Pres*, Order of Architects of Quebec, Montreal PQ

Blovits, Larry, *Assoc Prof*, Aquinas College, Art Department, Grand Rapids MI (S)

Blum, Shirley N, *Chmn*, State University of New York College at Purchase, Department of Art History, Purchase NY (S)

Blum, Zevi, *Assoc Prof*, Cornell University, Department of Art, Ithaca NY (S)

Blumberg, Donald, *Vis Prof*, San Jose State University, Art Department, San Jose CA (S)

Blume, Peter F, *Cur*, Allentown Art Museum, Allentown PA

Blumenburg, Betty, *Secy*, Council of Delaware Artists, Wilmington DE

Blumenthal, Arthur, *Cur*, Dartmouth College Museum & Galleries, Hanover NH

Blumenthal, Elizabeth, *Instr*, Johns Hopkins University, School of Medicine, Department of Art as Applied to Medicine, Baltimore MD (S)

Blumenthal, Lyn, *Video Data Bank*, School of the Art Institute of Chicago Library, Chicago IL

Blundell, Harry, *Dir of Theatre*, Council of Ozark Artists and Craftsmen, Inc, Arts Center of the Ozarks, Springdale AR

Blundell, Kathi, *Prog Dir*, Council of Ozark Artists and Craftsmen, Inc, Arts Center of the Ozarks, Springdale AR

Blunk Jr, Robert, *Acting Chairperson*, Pittsburg State University, Art Department, Pittsburg KS (S)

Blyer, Verna R, *Administrative Secy*, Canton Art Instutute, Canton OH (S)

Boak, Gale H, *Asst Prof*, California State College, Department of Art, California PA (S)

Boardman, Gerard, *Librn*, South Street Seaport Museum, Library, New York NY

Boardman, J, *Cur Cast Gallery*, Oxford University, Ashmolean Museum of Art and Archaeology, Oxford England

Boardman, Patricia Hanify, *Art Therapist*, Regis College, Department of Art, Weston MA (S)

Boardman, Richard W, *Prof*, Fortman Studios Florence, Florence Italy (S)

Boatner, James, *Dir*, Philadelphia Art Alliance, Philadelphia PA

Boaz, William, *Instr*, Chapman College, Art Department, Orange CA (S)

Bob, Murray L, *Dir*, James Prendergast Library Association, Jamestown NY

Bobak, Bruno, *Dir*, University of New Brunswick Art Centre, Fredericton NB

Bobick, Bruce, *Chmn*, West Georgia College, Art Department, Carrollton GA (S)

Bobo, Paul, *Librn*, Spencer Museum of Art, Art Library, Lawrence KS

Bock, Henning, *Dir*, Staatliche Museen Preussischer Kulturbesitz, Picture Gallery, Berlin Germany, Federal Republic of

Bockstoce, John R, *Cur Ethnology*, New Bedford Whaling Museum, New Bedford MA

Bockwith, Wendy, *Instructor*, La Roche College, Division of Graphic Arts & Design, Pittsburgh PA (S)

Bodem, Dennis R, *Dir*, Jesse Besser Museum, Alpena MI

Bodine, Paul, *Asst Prof*, Eastern Illinois University, Art Department, Charleston IL (S)

Bodnar-Balahutrak, Lydia, *Instructor*, San Jacinto College North, Art Department, Houston TX (S)

Bodnar III, Peter David, *Instructor*, Louisville School of Art, Anchorage KY (S)

Boe, Alf, *Dir*, City of Oslo Art Collection, Munch Museum, Oslo Norway

Boecking Jr, H E, *Treas*, Oklahoma Art Center, Oklahoma City OK

Boegen, Anne, *Coordr Work with Children and Young Adults*, Miami-Dade Public Library, Miami FL

Boehm, Ann, *Acting Dir Midland Art Council*, Midland Center for the Arts, Midland MI (S)

Boehme, Sarah E, *Cur of Collections*, Stark Museum of Art, Orange TX

Boehmer, Ron, *Art Coordr*, Lynchburg Fine Arts Center Inc, Lynchburg VA

Boelke, Walter, *Instr*, Western Connecticut State College, Danbury CT (S)

Boem, Ann, *Pres & Acting Dir*, Midland Art Council of the Midland Center for the Arts, Midland MI

Boenden, Liselotte, *Library Asst*, Emily Carr College of Art Library, Vancouver BC

Boerlin, Paul-Henry, *Cur Paintings*, Offentliche Kunstsammlung-Kunstmuseum Basel, Museum of Fine Arts, Basel Switzerland

Boersma, J W, *Cur Archaeology*, Groningen Museum voor Stad en Land, Groningen Museum, Groningen Netherlands

Boesch, William, *Librn*, Portsmouth Athenaeum NR, Inc 1817, Library, Portsmouth NH

Boesser, Pauline, *Secy*, Saskatchewan Power Corporation, Gallery on the Roof, Regina SK

Boethius, Lena, *Asst Cur Deposit*, Göteborg Konstmuseum, Gothenburg Art Gallery, Gothenburg Sweden

Boeve, Edgar G, *Assoc Prof*, Calvin College, Art Dept, Grand Rapids MI (S)

Bogdanovitch, George, *Prof*, Denison University, Department of Art, Granville OH (S)

Boger, Lynn, *Store Mgr*, Tampa Museum, Tampa FL

Boggs, Arlene A, *Secy & Registrar*, Illinois State University, University Museums, Normal IL

Boggs, Arlene A, *Librn*, Illinois State University, Museum Library, Normal IL

Boggs, Jean Sutherland, *Dir*, Philadelphia Museum of Art, Philadelphia PA

Bogh, Lone, *Restorer*, Statens Museum for Kunst, Department of Painting and Sculpture, Copenhagen Denmark

Bogin, Sandy, *Slide Librn*, Hebrew Union College, Skirball Museum, Los Angeles CA

Bogle, Andrew, *Sr Cur*, Auckland City Art Gallery, Auckland New Zealand

Bogle, Jon, *Co-Dir*, Lycoming College Gallery, Williamsport PA

Bogle, Jon Robert, *Asst Prof*, Lycoming College, Art Department, Williamsport PA (S)

Bogle, Michael, *Textile Conservator*, Merrimack Valley Textile Museum, North Andover MA

Bohanon, Gloria, *Asst Prof*, Los Angeles City College, Department of Art, Los Angeles CA (S)

Bohaska, Dave, *Registrar*, Calvert Marine Museum, Solomons MD

Bohrnstedt, Wayne R, *Dean Division*, University of Redlands, Department of Art, Redlands CA (S)

Boileau, Andree, *Mgr*, Musee Historique de Vaudreuil, Vaudreuil Historial Museum, Woodstock PQ

Boiten, E A J, *Cur Medieval & Later History*, Groningen Museum voor Stad en Land, Groningen Museum, Groningen Netherlands

Bol, Peter C, *Staff*, Liebieghaus, Museum Alter Plastik, Museum of Sculpture, Frankfurt Germany, Federal Republic of

Bolan, Suzanne, *Dir*, The Rosenbach Museum and Library, Philadelphia PA

Boland, Dory, *Secy*, Bristol Art Museum, Bristol RI

Boland, Robert M, *Prof*, Berkshire Community College, Department of Fine Arts and Visual Communication, Pittsfield MA (S)

Bolas, Gerald D, *Dir*, Washington University, Gallery of Art, Saint Louis MO

Bolden, Joyce, *Chmn*, Alcorn State University, Department of Fine Arts, Lorman MS (S)

Bolden, Mary, *Acting Pres*, Plastic Club, Art Club for Women, Philadelphia PA

Bolding, Paul, *Dir*, Artists Gallery, Vancouver BC

Bolding, Paul, *Dir*, Artists Gallery, Art Library Service, Vancouver BC

Bolduc, Pauline, *Dept Head Technical Service*, New Bedford Free Public Library, New Bedford MA

Bolen, Jack, *Assoc Prof*, Kingsborough Community College, Department of Art, Brooklyn NY (S)

Boles, Michael F, *Instr*, Paris Junior College, Art Department, Paris TX (S)

Boles, Pat, *Instructor*, Monterey Peninsula College, Art Department, Monterey CA (S)

Bolge, George S, *Dir*, Fort Lauderdale Museum of the Arts, Fort Lauderdale FL

Bolge, George S, *Dir*, Fort Lauderdale Museum of the Arts, Art School, Fort Lauderdale FL (S)

Bolin, Judith, *Office Mgr*, San Jose Museum of Art, San Jose CA

Bolker, Henry, *Chmn Stewart Hall*, Pointe Claire Cultural Centre, Pointe Claire PQ

Bollek, Rosel, *Cur*, Stadtische Gallerie im Lanbachhaus, Lenbach House City Gallery, Munich Germany, Federal Republic of

Bollen, Sharon Kesterson, *Asst Prof*, College of Mount Saint Joseph, Art Department, Mount Saint Joseph OH (S)

Bolley, James R, *Mgr*, World Museum & Art Centre, Osborn Foundation, Tulsa OK

Bolliger, Irene, *Librn Coordr*, Ontario Crafts Council, Craft Resource Centre, Toronto ON

Bolliger, Irene, *Coordr Craft Resource Centre*, Ontario Crafts Council, Toronto ON

Bolner, Clifton, *Secy*, San Antonio Museum Association, Inc, San Antonio TX

Bolomey, Roger, *Prof*, California State University, Fresno, Art Department, Fresno CA (S)

Bolton, Bruce D, *Mgr*, Society of the Montreal Military and Maritime Museum, Saint Helen's Island Museum, Montreal PQ

Bolton, J W, *Acting Cur & Treas*, Museum, Greenwood SC

Bolton-Smith, Robin, *Assoc Cur 18th & 19th Century Painting & Sculpture*, National Collection of Fine Arts, Washington DC

Boltz, Shirley, *Pub Relations Coordr*, Indiana State Museum, Indianapolis IN

Bolz, Sarah, *Cur*, Elizabet Ney Museum, Austin TX

Bomasuto, Marilyn, *Art Gallery Asst*, State University of New York College at Fredonia, M C Rockefeller Arts Center Gallery, Fredonia NY

Bomnert, Thomas, *Instructor*, Charles Stewart Mott Community College, Fine Arts Division, Flint MI (S)

Bond, Arthur, *Head Art Dept*, John C Calhoun State Community College, Art Gallery, Decatur AL

Bond, Arthur, *Head Dept*, John C Calhoun State Community College, Art Department, Decatur AL (S)

Bond, Barbara, *Executive Dir*, York Institute Museum, Saco ME

Bond, Carolyn, *Dir*, Redding Museum & Art Center, Redding CA

Bond, Elisabeth, *Area Coordr*, Northern Illinois University, Department of Art, De Kalb IL (S)

Bond, Randall, *Librn*, Syracuse University, Library, Syracuse NY

Bond, Randall I, *Art Librn*, Ernest Stevenson Bird Library, Syracuse NY

Bondar, Marilyn, *Education Officer*, Art Gallery of Peterborough, Peterborough ON

Bondurant, Francis G, *Cataloger*, New York University, Stephen Chan Library of Fine Arts, New York NY

Bonebrake, John C, *Secy*, Cleveland Museum of Art, Print Club of Cleveland, Cleveland OH

Bonifay, William, *Instructor*, Milwaukee Area Technical College, Graphic & Applied Arts Div, Milwaukee WI (S)

Bonin, Joseph, *Treas*, New Orleans Museum of Art, Isaac Delgado Museum, New Orleans LA

Bonnal, J P, *Asst Conservator*, Musee Saint-Denis, Reims France

Bonner, Evelyn K, *Dir Library Services*, Sheldon Jackson College, Stratton Library, Sitka AK

Bonner, Robert, *Corresp Secy*, Monterey Peninsula Museum of Art, Monterey CA

Bonsanti, Giorgio, *Dir*, Galleria, Museo e Medagliere Eslense, Este Gallery and Museum, Modena Italy

Bonsanti, Giorgio, *Dir*, Museo di S Marco, Florence Italy

Bonte, Genevieve, *Conservator*, Union Centrale des Arts Decoratifs, Bibliotheque des Arts Decoratifs, Paris France

Bontrager, Jerry, *Asst Prof*, Greensboro College, Department of Art, Greensboro NC (S)

Bonzelaar, Helen, *Asst Prof*, Calvin College, Art Dept, Grand Rapids MI (S)

Boodnick, Allan, *Chmn*, Cerritos College, Art Department, Norwalk CA (S)

Boodro, Michael, *Asst Dir for Public Affairs*, New York University, Grey Art Gallery and Study Center, New York NY

Bookbinder, Judith, *Instr*, Danforth Museum School, Framingham MA (S)

Booke, Elizabeth M, *Pres*, Arts Council, Inc, Winston-Salem NC

Boone, Edward J, *Archivist*, MacArthur Memorial, MacArthur Memorial Library and Archives, Norfolk VA

Boone, Garret, *Chmn Dept*, Earlham College, Art Department, Richmond IN (S)

Boone, Garret J, *Chmn Art Dept*, Earlham College, Leeds Gallery, Richmond IN

Boone, Katherine B, *Registrar*, Polk Public Museum, Lakeland FL

Boone, Mary McDowell, *Chmn*, Liberty Hall Museum, Frankfort KY

Boone Jr, Edward J, *Archivist*, MacArthur Memorial, Norfolk VA

Boonstra, Harry, *Librn*, Hope College, Van Zoeren Library, Holland MI

Boorstin, Daniel J, *Librn of Congress*, Library of Congress, Washington DC

Booth, Bill R, *Head Dept*, Morehead State University, Art Department, Morehead KY (S)

Booth, Bill R, *Head Dept Art*, Morehead State University, Claypool-Young Art Gallery, Morehead KY

Booth, Bob, *Instructor*, State University College, Department of Art, Fredonia NY (S)

Booth, Elizabeth C, *Librn*, University of Pittsburgh, Henry Clay Frick Fine Arts Library, Pittsburgh PA

Booth, Gordon, *Public Manager*, National Gallery, London England

Booth, Louise A T, *Instr*, Morehead State University, Art Department, Morehead KY (S)

Booth, M A, *Secy*, Orange County Community of Museums and Galleries, Goshen NY

Booth, Malcolm, *Secy*, Orange County Community of Museums and Galleries, Library, Goshen NY

Booth, Ronald, *Prof*, University of North Carolina-Charlotte, Creative Arts Dept, Charlotte NC (S)

Boothby, Norman, *Prof*, Tulane University, Newcomb College, New Orleans LA (S)

Bopp, Emery, *Chmn*, Bob Jones University, School of Fine Arts, Greenville SC (S)

Boppel, Todd, *Prof*, University of Wisconsin-Stout, Art Department, Menomonie WI (S)

Borchardt, H, *VPres & Dir*, Lovis Corinth Memorial Foundation, Inc, New York NY

Borchert, Gary, *Instructor*, Oklahoma State University, School of Technical Training, Okmulgee OK (S)

Borchett-Lere, Debra, *Gallery Coordr*, Los Angeles Institute of Contemporary Art, Los Angeles CA

Bordaz, Robert, *Pres*, Union Centrale des Arts Decoratifs, Musee des Arts Decoratifs, Paris France

Bordeaux, Jean-Luc, *Dir*, California State University, Northridge, Fine Arts Gallery, Northridge CA

Bordeaux, Tom, *Pres*, Meridian Museum of Art, Meridian MS

Borden, Jeanne, *Librn*, Rhode Island School of Design, Library, Providence RI

Borden, Sidney, *Dir*, Institute of Lettering and Design, Chicago IL (S)

Borger, Hugo, *Dir*, Museen der Stadt Köln, Römisch-Germanisches Museum, Cologne Germany, Federal Republic of

Borger, Hugo, *Dir*, Museen der Stadt Köln, Kölnisches Stadtmuseum im Zeughaus, Cologne Germany, Federal Republic of

Borman, Charles, *Assoc Chmn*, California State University, Los Angeles, Art Department, Los Angeles CA (S)

Borman, R, *Cur*, Gemeentemuseum Arnhem, Municipal Museum of Arnhem, Arnhem Netherlands

Born, Richard, *Acting Cur*, University of Chicago, David and Alfred Smart Gallery, Chicago IL

Born, Richard, *Asst Dir*, University of Chicago, Bergman Gallery, Chicago IL

Bornarth, Philip W, *Fine Arts*, Rochester Institute of Technology, School of Art and Design, Rochester NY (S)

Borne, Susan Terry, *Slide Cur*, University of Arkansas, Art Slide Library, Little Rock AR

Bornhuetter, Robert, *Area Coordr*, Northern Illinois University, Department of Art, De Kalb IL (S)

Borman, D C, *Admin Dir*, Walker Art Center, Minneapolis MN

Borstein, Elena, *Instr*, York College of the City University of New York, Fine and Performing Arts, Jamaica NY (S)

Bortner, Selma, *Instructor*, Bucks County Community College, Fine Arts Department, Newton PA (S)

Bos, Dianne, *Education Officer*, Oakville Centennial-Gairloch Galleries, Oakville ON

Bosanko, Pamela A, *Executive Dir*, South Arkansas Art Center, El Dorado AR

Boschma, C, *Dir*, Fries Museum, Leeuwarden Netherlands

Bosco, Bob, *Instr*, Creighton University, Fine and Performing Arts Department, Omaha NE (S)

Bose, Arwin, *Assoc Prof*, Herbert H Lehman College, Art Department, Bronx NY (S)

Boser, Renee, *Cur Africa & Textiles*, Museum für Völkerkunde und Schweizerisches Museum für Volkskunde Basel, Museum of Ethnological Collections and Folklore, Basel Switzerland

Bosmans, J A, *VDir*, Fries Museum, Leeuwarden Netherlands

Bosson, Jack, *Pres*, 55 Mercer, New York NY

Bostwick, Elizabeth, *Librn*, Huntington Galleries, Library, Huntington WV

Boterf, C A, *Chmn*, Rice University, Department of Art and Art History, Houston TX (S)

Bothe, Jeane, *Cur Special Coll*, Institute of the Great Plains, Research Library, Lawton OK

Bothen, Claes, *Pres*, American Swedish Historical Foundations Museum, Philadelphia PA

Bothmer, Bernard V, *Chmn of Dept Egyptian & Classical Art, Keeper of the Wilbour Coll*, Brooklyn Museum, Brooklyn NY

Botkin, John, *Assoc Prof*, Delaware County Community College, Communications and Humanities House, Media PA (S)

Bott, Gerhard, *General Dir*, Museen der Stadt Köln, Wallraf-Richartz-Museum, Museum Ludwig, Cologne Germany, Federal Republic of

Bott, John, *Instr*, Colby-Sawyer College, Art Department, New London NH (S)

Bott, Patricia Allen, *Secy*, Society of Animal Artists, Inc, Bronx NY

Bott, William C, *Treas*, Attleboro Museum, Center for the Arts, Attleboro MA

Bottwin, Richard, *Instr*, Temple University, Art Department, Philadelphia PA (S)

Botwinick, Michael, *Dir*, Brooklyn Museum, Brooklyn NY

Bouchard, Leo, *Instructor*, Junior College of Albany, Fine Arts Division, Albany NY (S)

Boucher, Micheline M, *Library Technician*, Canadian Museums Association, Library, Ottawa ON

Bouchonville, Ruella, *Instructor*, Edgewood College, Art Department, Madison WI (S)

Boudreau, Elizabeth S, *Asst to the Dir*, State University of New York at Stony Brook Art Gallery, Stony Brook NY

Boudreau, Joseph W, *Asst Prof*, University of Minnesota, Duluth, Art Dept, Duluth MN (S)

Bouillette, Diane, *Instructor*, Oberlin College, Department of Art, Oberlin OH (S)

Bouler, Sheryl B, *Supv*, Newark Museum, Junior Museum, Newark NJ

Boulet, Roger H, *Dir*, Art Gallery of Greater Victoria, Victoria BC

Bouloukos, Athanasios, *Chmn Critical Studies*, Massachusetts College of Art, Boston MA (S)

Boulton, Jack, *VPres & Dir Art Program*, The Chase Manhattan Bank, NA, New York NY

Boulware, William, *Adjunct Prof*, Southwestern College, Winfield KS (S)

Boumphrey, R S, *VPres*, Abbot Hall Art Gallery, Cumbria England

Bourassa, R, *Graphics Supv*, Saskatchewan Power Corporation, Gallery on the Roof, Regina SK

Bourdeau, LaVonne, *Pres*, Galesburg Civic Art Center, Galesburg IL

Bourek, Vickie, *Instructor*, East Tennessee State University, Fine Arts Dept, Johnson City TN (S)

Bourque, Lise, *Prof*, College Saint-Louis-Maillet, Department of Visual Arts, Edmundston NB (S)

Bouslough, Ray, *Arts Specialist*, Davenport Municipal Art Gallery, Davenport IA

Bousquet, Jean, *Supv Music and Arts Services*, Berkshire Athenaeum, Pittsfield MA

Bouton, Margaret I, *Cur Education*, National Gallery of Art, Washington DC

Boux, Rene, *Fine Arts Subject Specialist*, University of Bridgeport, Magnus Wahlstrom Library, Bridgeport CT

Bovey, John A, *Provincial Archivist*, Provincial Archives of British Columbia, Victoria BC

Bovey, John A, *Archivist*, Provincial Archives of Manitoba, Winnipeg MB

Bowden, Karen, *Pres*, Society for the Preservation of Historic Landmarks, York ME

Bowe, Martin, *Dir*, Newfoundland Museum, Saint John's NF

Bowen, Charles, *Dean of Educ*, Cooper School of Art, Cooper Gallery, Cleveland OH

Bowen, Constance L, *Cur Modern Art*, Indiana University, Art Museum, Bloomington IN

Bowen, E V, *Secy*, Bowne House, Flushing NY

Bowen, Janet, *VPres*, Anderson County Arts Council, Anderson SC

Bowen, Susan, *Administrator*, School of the Art Association of Newport, Newport RI (S)

Bower, Gerald, *Assoc Prof*, Louisiana State University, Department of Fine Arts, Baton Rouge LA (S)

Bower, Nancy, *Cultural Affairs Committee*, Springfield College, Babson Library Art Gallery, Springfield MA

Bowerman, John, *Pres*, Henry S Lane Home, Crawfordsville IN

Bowers, Bruce, *Instructor*, Hiram College, Art Department, Hiram OH (S)

Bowers, John, *Lectr*, Notre Dame College, Art Department, Manchester NH (S)

Bowers, Paul, *Assoc Prof*, State University College, Department of Art, Fredonia NY (S)

Bowers, Shirlie, *Prof*, Saint Gregorys Junior College, Department of Art, Shawnee OK (S)

Bowker, Alvin, *Chmn Cultural Affairs*, University of Maine at Machias Art Gallery, Machias ME

Bowlen, Kennard, *Pres*, Custom House Maritime Museum, Newburyport MA

Bowling, Gary, *Instructor*, Sioux City Art Center, Sioux City IA (S)

Bowling, Gary R, *Head Dept*, Westmar College, Art Department, LeMars IA (S)

Bowman, Carl G, *Pres & Exec Dir*, Maritime Museum Association of San Diego, San Diego CA

Bowman, Dean B, *Prof*, Concordia College, Art Department, Moorhead MN (S)

Bowman, J, *Treas*, Kitchener-Waterloo Art Gallery, Kitchener ON

Bowman, Jeff R, *Chmn*, University of Southern Mississippi, Department of Art, Hattiesburg MS (S)

Bowman, Ken, *Instr*, Blackhawk Mountain School of Art, Black Hawk CO (S)

Bowman, Peter, *Asst Prof*, Southwestern at Memphis, Dept of Art, Memphis TN (S)

Bowman, Stanley, *Chmn Dept*, Cornell University, Department of Art, Ithaca NY (S)

Bowne, James D, *Dir*, Everhart Museum of Natural History, Science and Art, Scranton PA

Bowness, Alan, *Dir*, Tate Gallery, London England

Bowsfield, Blaire L, *Secy*, Lloydminster Barr Colony Museum Committee, Lloydminster SK

Box, Fred, *Public Information*, South Carolina Arts Commission, Columbia SC

Box, Harold, *Dean*, University of Texas, School of Architecture, Austin TX (S)

Box-Pope, Patrice, *Asst Chmn*, William Carey College, Art Department, Hattiesburg MS (S)

Boyce, Gerald G, *Dir*, Indiana Central University, Leah Ransburg Art Gallery, Indianapolis IN

Boyce, Gerald G, *Chmn Dept*, Indiana Central University, Fine Arts Department, Indianapolis IN (S)

Boyce, Louise, *Instr*, Tracey-Warner School, Philadelphia PA (S)

Boyce, Robert, *Asst Prof*, University of Wisconsin-Stevens Point, Department of Art, Stevens Point WI (S)

Boyce, William G, *Dir*, University of Minnesota, Tweed Museum of Art, Duluth MN

Boyce, William G, *Prof*, University of Minnesota, Duluth, Art Dept, Duluth MN (S)

Boyce Jr, Joel Lynn, *Coordr*, Umpqua Community College, Art Department, Roseburg OR (S)

Boyd, Amy S, *Dir*, Imperial Calcasieu Museum, Lake Charles LA

Boyd, B, *Conservator Prints & Watercolors*, City Art Gallery, Bristol England

Boyd, Evelyn, *Department Head*, Cuyahoga Community College, Department of Art, Cleveland OH (S)

Boyd, James D, *Dir*, Dundee Museums and Art Gallery, Dundee Scotland

Boyd, Jane, *Instr*, Cuyahoga Valley Art Center, Cuyahoga Falls OH (S)

Boyd, Julia, *Institute for Contemporary Art Suvp*, Virginia Museum of Fine Arts, Richmond VA

Boyd, Karen W, *Instructor*, Murray State University, Art Department, Murray KY (S)

Boyd, Pamela, *Public Programs Coordr*, Quapaw Quarter Association, Inc, Villa Marre, Little Rock AR

Boyd, Phillip, *Asst Preparator*, Contemporary Arts Center, Cincinnati OH

Boyd, Sterling, *Chief Programs*, North Carolina Museum of Art, Department of Cultural Resources, Raleigh NC

Boyd, Virginia T, *Asst Prof*, University of Wisconsin, Madison, School of Family Resources and Consumer Sciences, Madison WI (S)

Boyens, Charles, *Assoc Prof*, Jersey City State College, Art Department, Jersey City NJ (S)

Boyer, Fred, *Pres Board of Dir*, Copper Village Museum and Arts Center, Anaconda MT

Boyer, Leonard, *First VPres*, Berks Art Alliance, Reading PA

Boyer, Lillian, *Pres*, Lexington Art League, Inc, Lexington KY

Boyer, Ruth, *Instructor*, California College of Arts and Crafts, Oakland CA (S)

Boyesen, Lars Rostrup, *Dir*, Statens Museum for Kunst, Department of Painting and Sculpture, Copenhagen Denmark

Boyesen, L Rostrup, *Dir*, Nordjyllands Kunstmuseum, Art Museum of Northern Jutland, Aalborg Denmark

Boylan, Patrick J, *Dir of Museums and Art Galleries*, Leicestershire Museums, Art Galleries and Records Service, Leicestershire Museum and Art Gallery, Leicester England

Boyle, Bernard M, *Chmn Planning*, Arizona State University, College of Architecture, Tempe AZ (S)

Boyle, Richard J, *Dir*, Pennsylvania Academy of the Fine Arts, Philadelphia PA

Boyle, Ruth, *Bookstore Mgr*, Laguna Beach Museum of Art, Laguna Beach CA

Boyle, William J S, *Exec Dir*, Visual Arts Ontario, Toronto ON

Boynton, Charles, *Treas*, Salt Lake Art Center, Salt Lake City UT

Boynton, Jack, *Assoc Prof*, University of Saint Thomas, Art Department, Houston TX (S)

Boynton, Wyman P, *VPres*, John Paul Jones House, Portsmouth NH

Boyt, Patrick E, *Second VPres*, Beaumont Art Museum, Beaumont TX

Boyt, Richard, *Instructor*, Crowder College, Dept of Art, Neosho MO (S)

Braasem, W A, *Dir*, Westfries Museum, Hoorn Netherlands

Brabander, W H, *Deputy Managing Dir*, Stedlijk Museum-Amsterdam, Municipal Museum, Amsterdam Netherlands

Brabant, Joan, *Registrar*, Ontario College of Art, Toronto ON (S)

Bracewell, Shirley, *Community Program Head*, University of Regina, Norman Mackenzie Art Gallery, Regina SK

Brach, Philip L, *Adjunct Assoc Prof*, Catholic University of America, Department of Architecture & Planning, Washington DC (S)

Brackenridge, R Douglas, *Pres*, Presbyterian Historical Society, Philadelphia PA

Brackett, Cynthia, *Treas*, Pemaquid Group of Artists, Lewiston ME

Bradbury, Barbara, *Treas*, Greenwich Art Society and Art Center, Greenwich CT

Bradbury, Ellen, *Dir*, Museum of New Mexico, Museum of Fine Arts, Santa Fe NM

Bradbury, Ellen, *Dir Fine Arts*, Museum of New Mexico, Santa Fe NM

Bradbury, S A, *Keeper of Decorative Art*, Stoke-on-District Council, City Museum and Art Gallery, Hanley England

Bradford, Colleen H, *Chmn*, Brigham City Museum-Gallery, Brigham City UT

Bradford, Roberta, *Asst Librn*, Stowe-Day Foundation, Stowe-Day Library, Hartford CT

Bradford, William, *Academic Asst*, Courtauld Institute Galleries, London England

Bradley, Barbara, *Dir Illustration*, Academy of Art College, San Francisco CA (S)

Bradley, Byron, *Instructor*, Grand Marais Art Colony, Grand Marais MN (S)

Bradley, Douglas, *Cur*, University of Notre Dame, Snite Museum of Art, Notre Dame IN

Bradley, Kim, *Dir*, Portland State University, White Gallery, Portland OR

Bradley, R T, *Dir*, Sarnia Public Library and Art Gallery, Sarnia ON

Bradley, Sarah, *Asst Dir, Asia House Gallery*, Asia Society, Inc, Asia House Gallery, New York NY

Bradley, Tony, *Instructor*, University of North Carolina at Asheville, Dept of Art & Music, Asheville NC (S)

Bradley-Johnson, Gayle, *Prof*, North Park College, Art Department, Chicago IL (S)

Bradman, Susan, *Pres*, Burlington County Historical Society, Burlington NJ

Bradshaw, Bertram F, *Instr*, University of North Carolina at Wilmington, Art Department, Wilmington NC (S)

Bradshaw, Glenn R, *In Charge Undergrad Painting*, University of Illinois, Urbana-Champaign, Department of Art and Design, Champaign IL (S)

Bradshaw, Larry, *Assoc Prof*, University of Nebraska at Omaha, Dept of Art, Omaha NE (S)

Bradshaw, William T, *Head Dept*, University of California, Riverside, Program in Art, Riverside CA (S)

Bradt, Bernice, *Publicity & Public Relations*, The Robert McLaughlin Gallery, Oshawa ON

Bradway, Wallace, *Museum Registrar*, Art Institute of Chicago, Chicago IL

Bragg, Nicholas B, *Executive Dir*, Reynolda House, Inc, Winston-Salem NC

Braham, Allan, *Keeper*, National Gallery, London England

Braig, Kathryn B, *Asst to Librn*, Mariners Museum, Library, Newport News VA

Braithewaite, Elena, *Instructor*, Traphagen School of Fashion, New York NY (S)

Braithwaite, Noreen, *Pres*, Redding Museum & Art Center, Redding CA

Brakke, Michael, *VPres*, N.A.M.E. Gallery, Chicago IL

Bramante, Vanni, *Vis Artist*, Studio Art Centers International, Florence Italy (S)

Bramhall, Helen, *Secy*, Boca Raton Center for the Arts, Inc, Boca Raton FL

Bramson, Phyllis, *Coordr Fine Arts*, Columbia College, Art Department, Chicago IL (S)

Brand, Barbara A, *Admin*, Hammond-Harwood House, Annapolis MD

Brandenburg, Kurt E, *Exec Dir*, Chester County Historical Society, West Chester PA

Brandin, Donald N, *Chmn*, Art and Education Council of Greater Saint Louis, Saint Louis MO

Brandon, David S, *Cur & Dir*, Loveland Museum, Loveland CO

Brandon, Elinore, *Chmn Illustration*, Fashion Institute of Technology, New York NY (S)

Brandon, Kenneth, *Head Dept*, Otero Junior College, Art Department, La Junta CO (S)

Brandson, Lorraine, *Asst Cur*, Eskimo Museum, Churchill MB

Brandt, Rex, *Co-Dir*, Brandt Painting Workshops, Corona Del Mar CA (S)

Branham, Richard, *Chmn*, University of Kansas, Department of Design, Lawrence KS (S)

Brannen, Alison, *Instr*, Toronto School of Art, Toronto ON (S)

Brannon, Revelie, *Cur*, Clemson University, Fort Hill, Clemson SC

Branson, Edward V, *Instructor*, Yavapai College, Art Department, Prescott AZ (S)

Brant, Mary, *Mgr Community Arts Center*, Fort Wayne Fine Arts Foundation, Inc, Fort Wayne IN

Brantigan, Lisa, *Lectr*, Oakland University, Dept of Art & Art History, Rochester MI (S)

Brantley, Michael W, *Education Services*, North Carolina Museum of Art, Department of Cultural Resources, Raleigh NC

Branton, William Coleman, *Pres*, Jackson County Historical Society, Independence MO

Braselton Jr, W M, *Secy*, Brevard Art Center and Museum, Inc, Melbourne FL

Brassill, Jo Ann, *Prof*, University of Southern Colorado, Belmont Campus, Department of Art, Pueblo CO (S)

Brathe, Elhe, *Public Relations*, Stadtishces Kunstmuseum Bonn, Art Museum of the City of Bonn, Bonn Germany, Federal Republic of

Bratton, June, *Exhib Chmn*, San Angelo Art Club, Kendall Art Gallery, San Angelo TX

Braucht, June Elder, *Dir*, Monterey Peninsula Museum of Art, Monterey CA

Brauer, David, *Art Historian*, Museum of Fine Arts, Alfred C Glassell Junior School of Art, Houston TX (S)

Brauer, Fred, *Chmn Div*, Concordia College, Art Department, Saint Paul MN (S)

Brauer, James, *Chmn*, Concordia College, Bronxville NY (S)

Brauer, Richard, *Dir*, Valparaiso University, University Art Galleries and Collections, Valparaiso IN

Braun, C Allan, *Pres*, Southwest Museum, Los Angeles CA

Braun, David, *Instr*, Virginia Intermont College, Fine Arts Department, Bristol VA (S)

Braun, Suzan, *Assoc Prof*, Eastern Illinois University, Art Department, Charleston IL (S)

Braunlein, John H, *Dir*, Madison County Historical Society, Oneida NY

Braunstein, Mark M, *Librn*, Rosenthal Art Slides, Chicago IL

Bravakis, Olivia, *Asst Cur*, Wood Art Gallery, Montpelier VT

Bray, Connie, *Secy*, Hickory Museum of Art, Inc, Hickory NC

Bray, Jim, *Assoc Prof*, Phillips University, Department of Art, Enid OK (S)

Brayer, M Yves, *Keeper of Art*, Musee Marmottan, Paris France

Brazil, Judy, *Instructor*, Johnson County Community College, Communications-Arts Division, Overland Park KS (S)

Brazton, Anne, *Art Librn*, Ohio University, Fine Arts Library, Athens OH

Brealey, John, *Conservator Paintings*, Metropolitan Museum of Art, New York NY

Brechner, Michael, *Preparator*, University of Kentucky, Art Museum, Lexington KY

Breckenridge, James, *Prof*, Northwestern University, Evanston, Department of Art History, Evanston IL (S)

Breckenridge, James D, *Pres*, Midwest Art History Society, Evanston IL

Breckenridge, Mary, *Instructor*, College of Wooster, Department of Art, Wooster OH (S)

Breed, Charles A, *Chmn Dept*, Delta College, Art Department, University Center MI (S)

Breedlove, Marcia, *VPres*, Lubbock Art Association, Inc, Lubbock TX

Breen, Ed, *Vis Prof*, Marion College, Art Department, Marion IN (S)

Breeskin, Adelyn D, *Consultant 20th Century Painting & Sculpture*, National Collection of Fine Arts, Washington DC

Breil, Ruth, *Asst Prof*, Trenton State College, Art Department, Trenton NJ (S)

Breimayer, M Phyllis, *Asst Prof*, Georgian Court College, Department of Art, Lakewood NJ (S)

Breitberg, Sara, *Israeli Art*, Tel Aviv Museum, Tel-Aviv Israel

Breitenbach, William J, *Assoc Prof*, Sam Houston State University, Art Department, Huntsville TX (S)

Breithaupt, E M, *Dir*, Ripon College Art Gallery, Ripon WI

Breithaupt, Erwin, *Chmn*, Ripon College, Art Department, Ripon WI (S)

Bremer, Alicia, *Publicity Dir*, Utah Travel Council, Salt Lake City UT

Bremer, J, *Cur*, Municipal van Abbemuseum, Eindhoven Municipal Museum, Eindhoven Netherlands

Brener, Roland, *Assoc Prof*, University of Victoria, Department of Visual Arts, Victoria BC (S)

Brennan, Francis E, *Secy*, American Federation of Arts, New York NY

Brennan, Sandra, *Cur*, Ogunquit Art Association, The Barn Gallery, Ogunquit ME

Brennen, Ray R, *Secy*, Annie S Kemerer Museum, Bethlehem PA

Brenner, Jean, *Instr*, Marian College, Art Department, Eau Claire WI (S)

Brenner, M Diane, *Museum Archivist*, Anchorage Historical and Fine Arts Museum, Archives, Anchorage AK

Brent, Allen R, *Dir*, Louisiana Arts and Science Center, Baton Rouge LA

Breslau, Leo, *Pres*, National Art League, Douglaston NY

Breslow, Elaine, *Development*, Pennsylvania Academy of the Fine Arts, Philadelphia PA

Breton, Arthur, *Cur Manuscripts*, Archives of American Art, Smithsonian Institution, New York NY

Brettell, Ruthann, *Asst to Exec VPres*, American Numismatic Association, Colorado Springs CO

Bretz, Robert, *Librn*, Visual Studies Workshop, Research Center, Rochester NY

Breucker, Roland, *Vis Prof*, College Saint-Louis-Maillet, Department of Visual Arts, Edmundston NB (S)

Brew, Stan, *Superintendent*, University of Rochester, Memorial Art Gallery, Rochester NY

Brewer, Donald, *Dir*, University of Southern California, University Galleries, Los Angeles CA

Brewer, Phillip, *Chmn of Board*, Columbus Museum of Arts and Sciences, Columbus GA

Brewster, Janie, *Assoc Prof*, School of the Ozarks, Department of Art, Point Lookout MO (S)

Brewster III, Albert J, *Secy*, Stan Hywet Hall Foundation, Inc, Akron OH

Brezzo, Steven L, *Acting Dir*, San Diego Museum of Art, San Diego CA

Brian, Fred, *Instructor*, Illinois Wesleyan University, School of Art, Bloomington IL (S)

Brice, John, *Dir*, Hockaday Center for the Arts, Flathead Valley Art Association, Kalispell MT

Bricker, Norman, *Exec Secy*, Muckenthaler Cultural Center, Fullerton CA

Brickman, Ernest, *Pres*, Association of Honolulu Artists, Honolulu HI

Bridgeford, Robert G, *Dir*, Portland Children's Museum, Portland OR

Bridges, Tammy, *Library Asst*, Winnipeg Art Gallery, Clara Lander Library, Winnipeg MB

Briggs, Gordon, *VPres*, Brattleboro Museum and Art Center, Brattleboro VT

Briggs, Margaret, *Librn*, Kansas State Historial Society Museum, Library, Topeka KS

Briggs, Mignon, *Secy*, Art Gallery of Windsor, Windsor ON

Briggs, Peter S, *Registrar*, University of New Mexico, University Art Museum, Albuquerque NM

Bright, Alfred, *Assoc Prof*, Youngstown State University, Art Department, Youngstown OH (S)

Bright, Peggy, *Assoc Prof*, Texas Tech University, Department of Art, Lubbock TX (S)

Briley, John B, *Mgr*, Campus Martius Museum and Ohio River Museum, Marietta OH

Brill, Frederick, *Chmn Faculty Painting*, British School at Rome, Rome Italy (S)

Brill, Frederick, *Principal*, Chelsea School of Art, London England (S)

Brill, Margaret, *Asst Prof*, Corning Community College, Division of Humanities, Corning NY (S)

Brill, Marilyn, *VPres Programs*, Miniature Art Society of New Jersey, Nutley NJ

Brill, Norma, *Secy*, Mid-Southern Watercolorists, Little Rock AR

Brill, Robert H, *Research Scientist*, Corning Museum of Glass, Corning NY

Brill, Wayne, *Instructor*, Interlochen Arts Academy, Dept of Visual Art, Interlochen MI (S)

Brindle, Laurie A, *Gallery Asst*, Palomar Community College, Boehm Gallery, San Marcos CA

Bringle, Edwina, *Asst Prof*, University of North Carolina-Charlotte, Creative Arts Dept, Charlotte NC (S)

Brink, Quido, *VPres*, Wisconsin Painters and Sculptors, Inc, Milwaukee WI

Brinker, Helmut, *Cur East Asia*, Museum Rietberg Zurich, Zurich Switzerland

Brinkerhoff, Dericksen M, *Prof*, University of California, Riverside, Art History Department, Riverside CA (S)

Brinkgreve, C, *Asst Education Department*, Frans Halsmuseum, Frans Hals Museum, Haarlem Netherlands

Brinkman, John A, *Dir*, University of Chicago, Oriental Institute, Chicago IL

Brinton, Harry, *Dir*, Jacksonville Public Library, Art and Music Department, Jacksonville FL

Brisch, Klaus, *Dir*, Staatliche Museen Preussischer Kulturbesitz, Museum of Islamic Art and Antiquities, Berlin Germany, Federal Republic of

Brisson, Gerard, *Guide*, Musee d'Art de Joliette, Joliette PQ

Brisson, Harriet E, *Chmn*, Rhode Island College, Art Department, Providence RI (S)

Brisson, Robert A, *Treas*, New York Society of Architects, f the Performing Arts, at Lincoln Center New York

Bristol, Lillian, *Coordr Public Relations*, Montclair Art Museum, Montclair NJ

Bristow, James, *Admin Officer*, Winnipeg Art Gallery, Winnipeg MB

Bristow, Julia, *Art Chmn*, Irene Leache Memorial, Norfolk VA

Bristow, William A, *Prof*, Trinity University, Department of Art, San Antonio TX (S)

Bristowe, C Gordon G, *Asst Dir Admin & Facilities*, Royal Ontario Museum, Toronto ON

Britko, Stephen, *Studio Mgr*, University of New Mexico, Tamarind Institute, Albuquerque NM (S)

Britko, Steve, *Instructor*, Oxbow Summer Art Workshops, Saugatuck MI (S)

Britt, Sam Glenn, *Assoc Prof*, Delta State University, Department of Art, Cleveland MS (S)

Britton, Clark, *Chmn Graphic Design*, Wichita State University, Division of Art, Wichita KS (S)

Britton, Neil, *Asst Prof*, Virginia Wesleyan College, Art Department of the Humanities Division, Norfolk VA (S)

Britz, Kevin, *Exhibits Technician*, Institute of the Great Plains, Museum of the Great Plains, Lawton OK

Brkich, Lazar, *Cur European Folk Art*, Milwaukee Public Museum, Milwaukee WI

Broderick, Catherine, *Instr*, Vancouver Community College, Langara Campus, Department of Fine Arts, Vancouver BC (S)

Broderick, James, *Chmn*, Texas Tech University, Department of Art, Lubbock TX (S)

Brodeur, Danyelle, *Coordr*, Dorval Cultural Centre, Dorval PQ

Brodeur, Michael, *Instr*, Rivier College, Art Department, Nashua NH (S)

Brodhead, Wendy, *Asst Dir & Registrar*, California Institute of Technology, Baxter Art Gallery, Pasadena CA

Brodsky, Judith K, *Chmn Dept*, Rutgers University, Newark, Art Department, Newark NJ (S)

Brodsky, Stanley, *Prof*, School of the Arts, C W Post Center of Long Island University, Art Department, Greenvale NY (S)

Brody, Catherine T, *Acting Chief Librn*, New York City Community College, Namm Hall Library and Learning Resource Center, Brooklyn NY

Broekema, Andrew J, *Dean, College of the Arts*, Ohio State University, Gallery of Fine Arts, Columbus OH

Broekema, Andrew J, *Dean Col*, Ohio State University, College of the Arts, Columbus OH (S)

Brokaw, Dorothy, *Adminr*, Maryhill Museum of Art, Goldendale WA

Bromley, Allyn, *Instructor*, Leeward Community College, Arts and Humanities Division, Pearl City HI (S)

Broner, Mathew, *Assoc Prof*, Manhattanville College, Art Department, Purchase NY (S)

Bronkema, Jim, *Executive Dir*, Embarcadero Center Management, San Francisco CA

Bronnon, Ron, *Art Research Consultant*, Auckland City Art Gallery, Art Research Library, Auckland New Zealand

Bronowski, V, *Cur*, Musees Communaux Beaux-Arts et Archeologie, Community Museum of Fine Arts and Archaeology, Verviers Belgium

Brons, Marianne, *Asst*, Statens Museum for Kunst, Department of Painting and Sculpture, Copenhagen Denmark

Bronson, A A, *Secy & Treas*, Art Metropole, Toronto ON

Bronson, Marty, *Dir*, Fashion Institute of Technology, Galleries, New York NY

Bronzan, Sharon, *Instr*, Portland Community College, Department of Fine Arts, Portland OR (S)

Brooke, Anna, *Librn*, Hirshhorn Museum and Sculpture Garden, Library, Washington DC

Brooke, David S, *Dir*, Sterling and Francine Clark Art Institute, Williamstown MA

Brookes, Allan, *Asst Prof*, University of Northern Iowa, Department of Art, Cedar Falls IA (S)

Brookhart, Doris I, *Head Dept*, John Brown University, Art Department, Siloam Springs AR (S)

Brookhouse, Jon, *Instr*, Suomi College, Fine Arts Department, Hancock MI (S)

Brooking, Dolores, *Dir Educ*, Spencer Museum of Art, Lawrence KS

Brooks, Doug, *Chmn*, Phoenix College, Department of Art and Photography, Phoenix AZ (S)

Brooks, James, *Instructor*, Fairmont State College, Art Department, Fairmont WV (S)

Brooks, James, *Instructor*, Bob Jones University, School of Fine Arts, Greenville SC (S)

Brooks, John B, *Cur Crafts & Education*, Pennsylvania Farm Museum of Landis Valley, Lancaster PA

Brooks, John H, *Assoc Dir*, Sterling and Francine Clark Art Institute, Williamstown MA

Brooks, Mary Anna, *Instructor*, Milwaukee Area Technical College, Graphic & Applied Arts Div, Milwaukee WI (S)

Brooks, Wendell, *Asst Prof*, Trenton State College, Art Department, Trenton NJ (S)

Bross, John, *Instructor*, Greenfield Community College, Art Department, Greenfield MA (S)

Bross Jr, John A, *Pres*, Art Institute of Chicago, Old Masters Society, Chicago IL

Brothby, Janette J, *Admin Asst*, Wesleyan University, Davison Art Center, Middletown CT

Brothers, Betty, *Assoc Prof*, College of Mount Saint Joseph, Art Department, Mount Saint Joseph OH (S)

Brothers, Darrell, *Prof*, Thomas More College, Art Department, Fort Mitchell KY (S)

Brouch, Virginia M, *Chairperson*, Florida State University, Art Education Craft Design, Tallahassee FL (S)

Broude, Norma, *Assoc Prof*, American University, Department of Art, Washington DC (S)

Broudo, J David, *Head Dept*, Endicott College, Art Dept, Beverly MA (S)

Brouillet, Johanne, *Promotions*, University of Sherbrooke Cultural Center, Art Gallery, Sherbrooke PQ

Broun, Elizabeth, *Cur Prints & Drawings*, Spencer Museum of Art, Lawrence KS

Broussal, Roger, *Chief Conservator*, Bay Area Art Conservation Guild, San Francisco CA

Brouwer, Val, *VPres*, West Vancouver Visual Arts Society, West Vancouver BC

Brown, Alan, *Treas*, Maui Historical Society, Hale Hoikeike, Wailuku HI

Brown, Ann Barton, *Cur Coll*, Brandywine River Museum, Chadds Ford PA

Brown, Barbara, *Pres*, Dallas Public Library, Dallas Print and Drawing Society, Dallas TX

Brown, Barbara M, *Cur Education & Acting Cur Decorative Arts*, Milwaukee Art Center, Milwaukee WI

Brown, C Dudley, *VPres*, Arts Club of Washington, James Monroe House, Washington DC

Brown, Carole R, *Asst Prof*, Elmhurst College, Art Department, Elmhurst IL (S)

Brown, Caroline, *Display*, National Portrait Gallery, London England

Brown, Carolyn, *Bookstore Mgr*, Contemporary Arts Center, Cincinnati OH

Brown, Carroll, *Lectr*, Cardinal Stritch College, Art Department, Milwaukee WI (S)

Brown, C Gaskell, *Keeper of Archaeology*, Plymouth City Museum and Art Gallery, Plymouth England

Brown, Charles R, *Chmn*, San Jacinto College, Art Department, Pasadena TX (S)

Brown, Charlotte, *Secy*, Quapaw Quarter Association, Inc, Villa Marre, Little Rock AR

Brown, David Alan, *Cur Early Italian Painting*, National Gallery of Art, Washington DC

Brown, Dick, *Exten Head*, Topeka Public Library, Topeka KS

Brown, Dion K, *Dir*, Polk Community College, Division of Communications and Fine Arts, Winter Haven FL (S)

Brown, Don Robert, *Instructor*, Chamberlayne Junior College, Department of Graphic and Applied Arts, Boston MA (S)

Brown, Edward, *Chmn*, Atlantic Christian College, Art Dept, Wilson NC (S)

Brown, Edward, *Museum Dir*, Atlantic Christian College, Case Art Gallery, Wilson NC

Brown, Elizabeth, *Dir of Library*, College of Mount Saint Joseph on the Ohio, Archbishop Alter Library, Mount Saint Joseph OH

Brown, Elizabeth B, *Librn*, Montgomery Museum of Fine Arts, Library, Montgomery AL

Brown, Ellsworth, *Dir*, Tennessee State Museum, Nashville TN

Brown, Frances R, *Chmn*, Five Civilized Tribes Museum, Library, Muskogee OK

Brown, Gaye L, *Dir Publications*, Worcester Art Museum, Worcester MA

Brown, Georgina, *Executive Dir*, Lake County Civic Center Association, Inc, Heritage Museum and Gallery, Leadville CO

Brown, Gerald F, *Executive Dir*, Paint 'N Palette Club, Anamosa IA

Brown, Harold, *Cur Emeritus*, Maine Maritime Museum, Archives Library, Bath ME

Brown, Howard, *Prof*, Metropolitan State College, Art Department, Denver CO (S)

Brown, Ida, *Sales Mgr*, Rockwell-Corning Museum, Corning NY

Brown, J Carter, *Chmn*, Commission of Fine Arts, Washington DC

Brown, J Carter, *Dir*, National Gallery of Art, Washington DC

Brown, Jack Perry, *Librn*, Cleveland Museum of Art, Library, Cleveland OH

Brown, James, *Supt*, Longfellow National Historic Site, Cambridge MA

Brown, James M, *Dir*, Society of the Four Arts, Palm Beach FL

Brown, Jennings, *Dean*, Antelope Valley College, Lancaster CA (S)

Brown, John M, *General Mgr*, Bellingrath Gardens and Home, Theodore AL

Brown, Joseph, *Artist-in-Res*, Creighton University, Fine and Performing Arts Department, Omaha NE (S)

Brown, Judy, *Cur Art*, Valley National Bank of Arizona, Phoenix AZ

Brown, Katherine T, *Prof*, Rice University, Department of Art and Art History, Houston TX (S)

Brown, Kenneth David, *Head Dept*, Newberry College, Department of Art, Newberry SC (S)

Brown, Kevin, *Registrar*, Plains Art Museum, Rourke Art Gallery, Moorhead MN

Brown, Leonard, *Dir*, Tyringham Institute, Jean Brown Archive, Tyringham MA

Brown, Marion, *Asst Prof*, University of Wisconsin, Madison, School of Family Resources and Consumer Sciences, Madison WI (S)

Brown, Mary-Lou, *Head Training & Standards*, Canadian Museums Association, Association des Musees Canadiens, Ottawa ON

Brown, Mildred B, *Pres*, Paint 'N Palette Club, Anamosa IA

Brown, Milton W, *Res Prof*, City University of New York, PhD Program in Art History, New York NY (S)

Brown, Moreau D, *Chmn*, Lockwood-Mathews Mansion Museum, Norwalk CT

Brown, Myrtle, *Library Technician*, Charleston Museum, Library, Charleston SC

Brown, Peter T, *Vis Lectr*, Rice University, Department of Art and Art History, Houston TX (S)

Brown, Quentin James, *Equipment Technician*, California State University Fullerton, Art Gallery, Fullerton CA

Brown, R, *Chmn*, University of California, Los Angeles, Department of Art, Los Angeles CA (S)

Brown, Reynolds, *Adjunct Instructor*, Auburn University at Montgomery, Art Department, Montgomery AL (S)

Brown, Robert, *Dir*, Archives of American Art, New England Area Center, New York NY

Brown, Robert, *Chmn*, Lincoln Memorial University, Department of Fine Arts, Harrogate TN (S)

Brown, Robert E, *Asst Prof*, University of Nevada, Las Vegas, Department of Art, Las Vegas NV (S)

Brown, Robert W, *Prof*, Glendale College, Department of Fine Arts, Glendale CA (S)

Brown, Russell, *Bursar*, Royal College of Art Gallery, London England

Brown, Sarah R, *Pres*, Marion Art Center, Marion MA

Brown, Shirley, *Planning*, Huntsville Art League and Museum Association Inc, Huntsville AL

Brown, Susan G, *Asst Prof*, Richard Bland College, Art Department, Petersburg VA (S)

Brown, Terry, *Cur*, Society of Illustrators, New York NY

Brown, Thack, *In Charge Art Coll*, Burroughs Wellcome Company, Research Triangle Park NC

Brown, Theodore M, *Prof*, Cornell University, Department of the History of Art, Ithaca NY (S)

Brown, Thomas, *Chmn*, Quincy College, Dept of Art, Quincy IL (S)

Brown, Vee, *Instructor*, Young Harris College, Department of Art, Young Harris GA (S)

Brown, Warren D, *Prof*, Southwestern College, Winfield KS (S)

Brown, William, *Area Coordr*, Northern Illinois University, Department of Art, De Kalb IL (S)

Brown, William, *Cur Glass*, Zanesville Art Center, Zanesville OH

Brown, William J, *Dir*, Fairbanks Museum and Planetarium, Saint Johnsbury VT

Brown, William J, *Dir*, Penland School of Crafts, Penland NC (S)

Brown, William M, *Head Dept*, Dutchess Community College, Department of Visual Arts, Poughkeepsie NY (S)

Brown, William W, *Secy*, Mattatuck Historical Society, Mattatuck Museum, Waterbury CT

Brown, William Archie, *Affiliate*, Emory University, Art History Department, Atlanta GA (S)

Brown, Yvonne S, *Coll Development*, Chicago Public Library, Art Section, Fine Arts Division, Chicago IL

Browne, Charles C, *Asst Dir for Public Programs*, Fairbanks Museum and Planetarium, Saint Johnsbury VT

Browne, Cynthia E, *Cataloger*, New Jersey Historical Society Museum, Library, Newark NJ

Browne, Joseph P, *Dir*, University of Portland, Wilson W Clark Memorial Library, Portland OR

Browne, Norman, *Chmn Art Educ*, Pan American University, Art Department, Edinburg TX (S)

Browne, Patti, *Exec Dir*, Municipal Art Commission, Kansas City MO

Browne, Tom Martin, *Pres*, Center for the Visual Arts, Oakland CA

Brownell, Penelope, *Asst Prof*, University of British Columbia, Department of Fine Arts, Vancouver BC (S)

Brownfield, John P, *Chmn Dept*, University of Redlands, Department of Art, Redlands CA (S)

Browning, Anthony S E, *Deputy Dir*, Glasgow Museums and Art Galleries, Kelvingrove Art Gallery and Museum, Glasgow Scotland

Brown Jr, Bennie, *Librn & Archivist*, Gunston Hall Plantation, Library, Lorton VA

Brown Jr, W L Lyons, *Pres Board Governor*, J B Speed Art Museum, Louisville KY

Brownlee, Richard S, *Dir*, State Historical Society of Missouri, Columbia MO

Bumpass, Terry, *Prof*, New Mexico Junior College, Art Department, Hobbs NM (S)

Bunce, Frederick W, *Prof*, South Dakota State University, Art Dept, Brookings SD (S)

Bunce, William, *Dir*, University of Wisconsin, Kohler Art Library, Madison WI

Bunck, John, *Pres*, Concordia College, Fine Arts Galleries, Milwaukee WI

Bunge, Chris, *Asst Prof*, Denison University, Department of Art, Granville OH (S)

Bunker, George R, *Chmn*, University of Houston, Department of Art, Houston TX (S)

Bunn, Ann, *Cur Educ*, Contemporary Arts Museum, Houston TX

Bunnell, Peter C, *Pres*, Friends of Photography, Carmel CA

Bunse, Don, *Prof*, University of Montana, Dept of Art, Missoula MT (S)

Burback, William, *Dir Dept Education*, Museum of Modern Art, New York NY

Burcaw, G Ellis, *Dir*, University of Idaho Museum, Moscow ID

Burch, J Lindsey, *Instr*, Johns Hopkins University, School of Medicine, Department of Art as Applied to Medicine, Baltimore MD (S)

Burch, Marlyn, *Pres*, Arts Council of Topeka, Topeka KS

Burchett, Jayme, *Asst Prof*, School of the Ozarks, Department of Art, Point Lookout MO (S)

Burchett, Kenneth F, *Chmn*, School of the Ozarks, Department of Art, Point Lookout MO (S)

Burdayron, Linda, *Animator*, Dorval Cultural Centre, Dorval PQ

Burden, Shirley, *VPres*, Los Angeles Art Association and Galleries, Los Angeles CA

Burdick, Marjorie Z, *Secy*, University of Florida, University Gallery, Gainesville FL

Burford, James, *Asst Prof*, Mount Vernon College, Art Department, Washington DC (S)

Burgart, Herbert, *Pres*, Moore College of Art, Philadelphia PA (S)

Burger, Gary C, *Dir*, Berkshire Museum, Pittsfield MA

Burger, W Carl, *VPres for North Jersey*, Federated Art Associations of New Jersey, Inc, Westfield NJ

Burger, W Carl, *Pres*, Associated Artists of New Jersey, Pittstown NJ

Burgess, Hugh, *Dean*, Arizona State University, College of Architecture, Tempe AZ (S)

Burgess, James L, *Asst Prof*, Salisbury State College, Art Dept, Salisbury MD (S)

Burgess, Larry E, *Cur*, Lincoln Memorial Shrine, Redlands CA

Burghardt, James H, *Librn*, Multnomah County Library, Henry Failing Art and Music Department, Portland OR

Burk, C William, *Dir*, Southern Oregon Historical Society, Jacksonville Museum, Jacksonville OR

Burk, George, *Cur*, Nasson College, Anderson Learning Center, Springvale ME

Burke, Daniel, *Acting Dir*, Mercyhurst College, Department of Art, Erie PA (S)

Burke, Diane C, *Secy*, Guild of Book Workers, New York NY

Burke, Elizabeth, *Head Dept*, Union College, Art Department, Barbourville KY (S)

Burke, Jim, *Prof*, Louisiana State University, Department of Fine Arts, Baton Rouge LA (S)

Burke, Michael, *Lectr*, Lake Forest College, Dept of Art, Lake Forest IL (S)

Burke, William J, *Assoc Prof*, Florida International University, Visual Arts Department, Miami FL (S)

Burkett, M E, *Dir*, Abbot Hall Art Gallery, Cumbria England

Burkhalter, Sue, *Membership Secy*, San Antonio Museum Association, Inc, San Antonio TX

Burkhardt, Mary Ann, *Librn*, Rocky Mountain School of Art Gallery, Library, Denver CO

Burkhart, Ardath, *Pres*, Hoosier Salon Patrons Association, Hoosier Salon Art Gallery, Indianapolis IN

Burkhart, Linda, *Admin Asst*, Sanford Museum and Planetarium, Cherokee IA

Burko, Diane, *Asst Prof*, Philadelphia Community College, Department of Fine Arts, Philadelphia PA (S)

Burleigh, Joan, *Librn*, Mendocino Art Center, Library, Mendocino CA

Burley, William, *Treas*, Boothbay Region Art Gallery, Boothbay Harbor ME

Burley, William, *Treas*, Lincoln County Cultural and Historical Association, Maine Art Gallery, Old Academy, Wiscasset ME

Burman, Valerie, *Instr*, Western Wisconsin Technical Institute, Graphics Division, LACrosse WI (S)

Burn, Emilie E, *Head*, Jacksonville State University, Art Department, Pelham, Jacksonville AL (S)

Burn, Rosemary B, *Asst Librn*, Dartington College of Arts, Library and Resources Centre, Devon England

Burnell, Rosalind, *Asst Coordr*, Prince George Art Gallery, Prince George BC

Burnett, Virgil, *Prof*, University of Waterloo, Fine Arts Department, Waterloo ON (S)

Burnham, Bonnie, *Executive Dir*, International Foundation for Art Research, Inc, New York NY

Burnham, Dahl C, *Treas*, Pioneer Museum and Haggin Galleries, Stockton CA

Burnham, J Wesley, *Chmn Dept*, Northwestern University, Evanston, Department of Art, Evanston IL (S)

Burningham, Charlene, *Asst Prof*, University of Minnesota, Department of Design, Saint Paul MN (S)

Burnley, Gary M, *Asst Prof*, Lehigh University, Department of Art and Architecture, Bethlehem PA (S)

Burnley, Pamela, *Vis Prof*, Brewton-Parker College, Visual Arts, Mount Vernon GA (S)

Burns, A Lee, *Instructor*, Smith College, Art Department, Northampton MA (S)

Burns, Charles, *Business Mgr*, Brandywine River Museum, Chadds Ford PA

Burns, Jane, *Secy*, Midwest Museum of American Art, Elkhart IN

Burns, J Bradley, *Coordr of Exhib*, Hunter Museum of Art, Chattanooga TN

Burns, Joan E, *Prin Art Librn*, Newark Public Library, Newark NJ

Burns, L, *Cur*, Oak Hall, Niagara Falls ON

Burns, Maxine, *Secy*, York University Art Gallery, Downsview ON

Burns, Michael, *Asst Prof*, Avila College, Art Department, Kansas City MO (S)

Burns, R, *Pres*, Association of Collegiate Schools of Architecture, Washington DC

Burns, Richard, *Pres*, Society of Environmental Graphics Designers, Chicago IL

Burns, Richard D, *Pres*, Midwest Museum of American Art, Elkhart IN

Burns, Robert L, *Supt*, Scotts Bluff National Monument, Gering NE

Burns, William A, *Dir*, Florence Museum, Florence SC

Burns, William K, *Asst Prof*, Seton Hall University, Department of Art and Music, South Orange NJ (S)

Burnside, Wesley M, *Dir of Art Acquisitions*, Brigham Young University, B F Larsen Gallery, Provo UT

Burnstad, Helen, *Chairperson Div*, Nebraska Western College, Div of Language & Arts, Scottsbluff NE (S)

Burollet, Therese, *Dir*, Musee Cognacq-Jay, Cognacq-Jay Museum, Paris France

Burris, George, *Chmn Liberal Arts*, Kansas City Art Institute, Kansas City MO (S)

Burroughs, Charles G, *Cur*, DuSable Museum of African American History, Chicago IL

Burroughs, Margaret T, *Dir*, DuSable Museum of African American History, Chicago IL

Burshears, J F, *Dir*, Koshare Indian Museum, Inc, La Junta CO

Burson, Nancy, *Secy*, Scripps College, Clark Humanities Museum, Claremont CA

Burt, Clyde, *Assoc Prof*, Indiana University-Purdue University, Department of Fine Arts, Fort Wayne IN (S)

Burt, Elizabeth P, *Exec Dir*, Art Barn, Greenwich CT

Burt, Joan, *Chmn Dept Design*, Ontario College of Art, Toronto ON (S)

Burt, Ruth, *Supv of Standards*, League of New Hampshire Craftsmen, Concord NH

Burt, Valencia, *Pres Mills House Volunteers*, Mills House Visual Arts Complex, Garden Grove CA

Burton, Douglas, *Asst Prof*, Lenoir Rhyne College, Department of Art, Hickory NC (S)

Burton, Fred, *Instructor*, Midwestern State University, Department of Art, Wichita Falls TX (S)

Burton, Lewis, *Instructor*, Austin Peay State University, Dept of Art, Clarksville TN (S)

Burton, Lewis B, *Cur*, Austin Peay State University, Margaret Fort Trahern Gallery, Clarksville TN

Busch, Gunter, *Dir*, Kunsthalle Bremen, Bremen Art Gallery, Bremen Germany, Federal Republic of

Busch, P, *Dir*, California State University, Chico, Library, Chico CA

Buschen, John, *Chmn*, University of Wisconsin-River Falls, Art Department, River Falls WI (S)

Bush, Edward A, *Dir of Educational Services*, Museum of Holography, New York NY

Bush, Ernie, *Instr*, Dallas Baptist College, Department of Art, Dallas TX (S)

Bush, Martin H, *Dir*, Wichita State University, Edwin A Ulrich Museum of Art, Wichita KS

Bush, Renee, *Exhib Cur*, Southern Oregon Historical Society, Jacksonville Museum, Jacksonville OR

Bush, Robert D, *Asst Dir*, Historic New Orleans Collection, Kemper and Leila Williams Foundation, New Orleans LA

Bush, Teresia, *Coordr Exhib*, New Muse Community Museum of Brooklyn, Inc, Brooklyn NY

Bush, Terry M, *Dir McLean County Arts Center*, McLean County Art Association, Bloomington IL

Bushnell, Marietta P, *Librn*, Pennsylvania Academy of the Fine Arts, Library, Philadelphia PA

Buster, General William R, *Dir*, Kentucky Historical Society Museum, Frankfort KY

Butcher, Cynthia Jones, *Dir*, Kirkland Art Center, Clinton NY

Butcher, Larry, *Asst Prof*, Delta College, Art Department, University Center MI (S)

Buten, David, *Dir*, Buten Museum of Wedgwood, Merion PA

Buten, Harry M, *Pres*, Buten Museum of Wedgwood, Merion PA

Butera, Anne Fabbri, *Cur*, Alfred O Deshong Museum, Chester PA

Butera, Joseph L, *Dir*, Butera School of Art, Boston MA (S)

Butkus, Jim, *Dir*, Creighton University Art Gallery, Omaha NE

Butler, Charles R, *Chmn of the Board*, Fine Arts Museum of the South, Mobile AL

Butler, Colin, *Instructor*, Peters Valley Craft Center, Layton NJ (S)

Butler, Joseph G, *Dir & Pres*, Butler Institute of American Art, Youngstown OH

Butler, Joseph T, *Cur*, Sleepy Hollow Restorations Inc, Tarrytown NY

Butler, Marigene, *Conservator*, Philadelphia Museum of Art, Philadelphia PA

Butler, Marion, *Mgr Art Program*, Illinois Bell, Chicago IL

Butler, Robert B, *Chmn Dept*, Miami University, Art Department, Oxford OH (S)

Butler, Tom, *Asst Dir*, Sioux City Art Center, Sioux City IA (S)

Butler, Tom, *Asst Dir*, Sioux City Art Center, Sioux City IA

Butorac, Frank G, *Dir*, Mercer County Community College Gallery, Trenton NJ

Butterbaugh, Irene, *Sales Mgr*, Walters Art Gallery, Baltimore MD

Butterfield, Thomas F, *Dir Arts*, Virginia Polytechnic Institute and State University, Squires Art Gallery, Blacksburg VA

Butts III, H Daniel, *Dir*, Mansfield Art Center, Mansfield Fine Arts Guild Inc, Mansfield OH

Butz, Richard A, *Instructor*, Portland School of Art, Portland ME (S)

Canby, Jeanny Vorys, *Cur of Egyptian and Ancient Near Eastern Art*, Walters Art Gallery, Baltimore MD

Cancel, Luis R, *Dir*, Bronx Museum of the Arts, Bronx NY

Candau, Eugenie, *Librn*, San Francisco Museum of Modern Art, Louise Sloss Ackerman Fine Arts Library, San Francisco CA

Candelari, Paolina, *Dir*, Rosary College, Aquinas Library, Florence Italy

Canedy, Norman W, *Prof*, University of Minnesota, Minneapolis, Art History, Minneapolis MN (S)

Canepa, Jack, *Assoc Prof*, Webster College, Art Dept, Webster Groves MO (S)

Cangialosi, Russell, *Prof*, Los Angeles City College, Department of Art, Los Angeles CA (S)

Cankilioglu, Teoman, *Cur Islamic Coins*, Istanbul Arkeoloji Müzeleri, Archaeological Museums of Istanbul, Istanbul Turkey

Cannamela, Laura, *Slide Librn*, Worcester Art Museum, Worcester MA

Canning, Thomas, *Librn*, West Virginia University, Creative Arts Center Library, Morgantown WV

Cannon, Hilda, *Pres*, Kauai Museum, Lihue HI

Cannon-Brookes, P, *Keeper of Art*, National Museum of Wales, Cardiff Wales

Cano, Margarita, *Art Librn*, Miami-Dade Public Library, Miami FL

Canova, Bruno, *Vis Artist*, Studio Art Centers International, Florence Italy (S)

Canowan Jr, John J, *Pres*, Springfield City Library, Art Department, Springfield MA

Cansino, Felicia, *Art Coordr*, Crocker National Bank, Saint Paul CA

Cantelupe, Eugene, *Prof*, Wright State University, Art Department, Dayton OH (S)

Cantieni, Graham, *Art Dir*, University of Sherbrooke Cultural Center, Art Gallery, Sherbrooke PQ

Cantini, Virgil D, *Chmn*, University of Pittsburgh, Department of Studio Arts, Pittsburgh PA (S)

Cantlin, Katherine, *Recording Secy*, Art Centre of New Jersey, East Orange NJ

Cantone, Grace, *Prof*, Adelphi University, Department of Art and Art History, Garden City NY (S)

Cantor, Dorothy, *Educ Dir*, Mattatuck Historical Society, Mattatuck Museum, Waterbury CT

Canzani, Joseph V, *Pres*, Columbus College of Art and Design, Columbus OH (S)

Capa, Cornell, *Executive Dir*, International Center of Photography, New York NY

Capen, Elizabeth, *VPres*, Old State House, Hartford CT

Capers, Charlotte, *Dir Information and Education*, Mississippi Department of Archives and History, Jackson MS

Caplan, Jerry, *Co-Dir*, Chatham College Art Gallery, Pittsburgh PA

Caplow, Harriet, *Prof*, Indiana State University, Department of Humanities, Terre Haute IN (S)

Capo, Larry, *Chmn*, Rider College, Department of Fine Arts, Lawrenceville NJ (S)

Caponi, Anthony, *Head Dept*, MacAlester College, Department of Art, Saint Paul MN (S)

Capozzi, John, *Asst Art Cur*, Saint Bonaventure University Art Collection, Saint Bonaventure NY

Cappuccio, Thomas, *Assoc Prof*, Northern Michigan University, Dept of Art & Design, Marquette MI (S)

Caravaglia, Angelo, *Prof*, University of Utah, Art Department, Salt Lake City UT (S)

Carayanni, Evdoxia, *Restorer*, National Pinakothiki and Alexander Soutzos Museum, Athens Greece

Carboni, Clara, *Prog Coordr*, Fortman Studios Florence, Florence Italy (S)

Carbonneau, Richard J, *VPres of Board*, Racine Art Association, Racine WI

Carbotti, Richard, *Instructor*, Roger Williams College, Art Department, Bristol RI (S)

Carcaba, Hubert W, *VPres*, Saint Augustine Historical Society, Oldest House and Museums, Saint Augustine FL

Carchman, JoAnn, *Dir Community Services*, Princeton University, Art Museum, Princeton NJ

Carden, Micki, *Public Relations Coordr*, Miami-Dade Public Library, Miami FL

Carder, James M, *Instr*, Mount Vernon College, Art Department, Washington DC (S)

Carder, Robert, *Instr*, Seward County Community College, Art Department, Liberal KS (S)

Cardiff, Gene, *Cur Natural History*, San Bernardino County Museum and Satellites, Fine Arts Institute, Redlands CA

Cardile, Paul, *Asst Prof*, Denison University, Department of Art, Granville OH (S)

Cardile, Paul J, *Dir*, Denison University Art Gallery, Granville OH

Cardman, Cecilia, *First VPres*, Catharine Lorillard Wolfe Art Club, Inc, New York NY

Cardon, Patrick, *Adminr Curatorial Affairs*, Brooklyn Museum, Brooklyn NY

Cardy, B, *Keeper Conservation*, Manchester City Art Galleries, Manchester England

Carew, Roberta, *Admin Asst*, Valentine Museum, Richmond VA

Carey, John T, *Prof*, University of West Florida, Department of Art, Pensacola FL (S)

Carey, Melissa, *Development Dir*, Institute of Contemporary Art, Boston MA

Carey, Philip, *Cur*, Roberson Center, Binghamton NY

Carey, Thomas, *Instructor*, College of Saint Benedict, Art Department, Saint Joseph MN (S)

Caric, Olga, *Librn*, Museum of Modern Art, Library, Belgrade Yugoslavia

Carini, Anselmo, *Assoc Cur Prints & Drawings*, Art Institute of Chicago, Chicago IL

Carini, Dino, *Vis Artist*, Studio Art Centers International, Florence Italy (S)

Carlander, John, *Head Dept*, Augustana College, Art Department, Sioux Falls SD (S)

Carlberg, Norman, *Sculptor-in-Res*, Maryland Institute, Rinehart School of Sculpture, Baltimore MD (S)

Carlbon, Larry, *Pres*, Hunterdon Art Center, Clinton NJ

Carley, James P, *First VPres*, Rochester Historical Society, Rochester NY

Carling, Philip C, *First VPres*, Monmouth Museum and Cultural Center, Lincroft NJ

Carlisle, Dianna, *Cur & Adminr*, R Tait McKenzie Memorial Museum, Almonte ON

Carlisle, Nancy, *Cur*, Bates College, Treat Gallery, Lewiston ME

Carlos, Edward, *Chmn Dept*, University of the South, Dept of Fine Arts, Sewanee TN (S)

Carlos, Edward, *Dir*, University of the South Gallery of Fine Arts, Sewanee TN

Carlsen, Charles, *Biology Lab*, Exploratorium, San Francisco CA

Carlsgaard, Lynn, *Asst Prof*, Northern State College, Art Dept, Aberdeen SD (S)

Carlson, Cynthia, *Co-Chairperson Painting & Drawing*, Philadelphia College of Art, Philadelphia PA (S)

Carlson, Eleanor, *Chairperson Music Dept*, Southeastern Massachusetts University, College of Visual and Performing Arts, North Dartmouth MA (S)

Carlson, Eric, *Assoc Prof*, State University of New York College at Purchase, Department of Art History, Purchase NY (S)

Carlson, Pam, *Pres*, Eccles Community Art Center, Ogden UT

Carlson, Richard, *Cur Educ*, Hudson River Museum, Yonkers NY

Carlson, Robert E, *Secy*, Chester County Historical Society, West Chester PA

Carlson, Victor, *Cur Prints and Drawings*, Baltimore Museum of Art, Baltimore MD

Carmean Jr, E A, *Cur 20th Century Art*, National Gallery of Art, Washington DC

Carmichael, Jae, *Pres*, National Watercolor Society, Pasadena CA

Carmichael, James H (Pete), *Instructor*, Friends of the Arts and Sciences, Hilton Leech Studio, Sarasota FL (S)

Carmichael, Marion, *Catalogue Librn*, Stowe-Day Foundation, Stowe-Day Library, Hartford CT

Carmichael, Wade, *Exhib Design Coordr*, Indiana State Museum, Indianapolis IN

Carneghi, Donna, *Admn Asst*, San Jose Museum of Art, San Jose CA

Carner, Ann L, *Admin*, Arts and Science Center, Nashua NH

Carney, John, *Chairperson Dept*, Western Michigan University, Department of Art, Kalamazoo MI (S)

Carney, Karen, *Librn*, Simon's Rock of Bard College, Library, Great Barrington MA

Carniglia, Steven C, *VPres*, American Ceramic Society, Columbus OH

Caron, Gerald, *VPres*, Mystic Art Association, Inc, Mystic CT

Caron, Joseph F, *Dept Head*, Allen County Community College, Art Department, Iola KS (S)

Carpenter, Bruce, *VPres*, Western Illinois University, Browne Hall Gallery, Macomb IL

Carpenter, Candace, *Dir*, Palo Alto Cultural Center, Palo Alto CA

Carpenter, Emily, *Dir*, Metropolitan Arts Commission, Portland OR

Carpenter, Gilbert, *Prof*, University of North Carolina at Greensboro, Art Dept, Greensboro NC (S)

Carpenter, Gilbert F, *Dir*, University of North Carolina at Greensboro, Weatherspoon Art Gallery, Greensboro NC

Carpenter, Harlow, *Dir*, Bundy Art Gallery, Waitsfield VT

Carpenter, James M, *Chmn Dept*, Colby College, Art Dept, Waterville ME (S)

Carpenter, Rob, *Instructor*, Nicholls State University, Dept of Art, Thibodaux LA (S)

Carpentier, Andre, *Cur*, Pavilion of Humour, Man and His World, Montreal PQ

Carpentier, Paul, *Conservator & Ethnographer*, Musee du Quebec, Quebec PQ

Carper, Dolorita, *Instr*, Marian College, Art Department, Indianapolis IN (S)

Carps, Bea, *Asst Cur Education*, Brooks Memorial Art Gallery, Memphis TN

Carr, Carol, *Secy*, Wallingford Art League, Wallingford CT

Carr, Carolyn Kinder, *Cur of Art*, Akron Art Institute, Akron OH

Carr, Frances A, *Archivist*, Shaker Museum, Poland Spring ME

Carr, J Revell, *Dir*, Mystic Seaport Museum, Inc, Mystic CT

Carr, J Revell, *Dir*, Mystic Seaport Museum, Inc, Children's Museum, Mystic CT

Carrero, Jaime, *Asst Prof*, Inter American University of Puerto Rico, Department of Performing Arts, San German PR (S)

Carr-Harris, Ian, *Dir*, Ontario College of Art, Library, Audio-Visual Centre, Toronto ON

Carrick, Betty, *Secy*, Redding Museum & Art Center, Redding CA

Carrie, Evaline V, *Dir*, McGroarty Cultural Art Center, Tujunga CA (S)

Carriere, Lisette, *Registrar*, Historic New Orleans Collection, Kemper and Leila Williams Foundation, New Orleans LA

Carrillo, Alfred, *Asst Prof*, Pierce College, Art Department, Woodland Hills CA (S)

Carrillo, Carmen, *Hispanic Community Coordr*, Mexican Museum, San Francisco CA

Carroll, Betty Jo, *Interim Dir*, Augusta Richmond County Museum, Augusta GA

Carroll, Constance J, *Assoc Cur Educ*, Schenectady Museum, Schenectady NY

Carroll, Michael, *Asst Dir Finance & Admin*, National Gallery of Canada, Ottawa ON

Carroll, Nancy, *Public Relations*, Ashtabula Arts Center, Ashtabula OH

Carroll, Richard S, *Dir*, John and Mable Ringling Museum of Art, Sarasota FL

Carroll, Theresa A, *Town Librn*, Brookline Public Library, Brookline MA

Carrott, Richard G, *Chmn*, University of California, Riverside, Art History Department, Riverside CA (S)

Carson, Barbara E, *Supv*, Morris-Butler Museum of High Victorian Decorative Arts, Indianapolis IN

Carson, Edmund, *Dir*, Art Gallery of New South Wales, Sydney Australia

Carson, Elizabeth, *Instr*, Aegean School of Fine Arts, Paros Cyclades Greece (S)

Carson, Leta, *Chairperson*, Fairmont State College, Art Department, Fairmont WV (S)

Carson, Mearl, *Supv*, Palo Alto Junior Museum, Palo Alto CA

Carson, Samuel G, *Pres*, Toledo Museum of Art, Toledo OH

Carson, Sydney, *Instructor*, California College of Arts and Crafts, Oakland CA (S)

Carswell, John, *Cur*, University of Chicago, Oriental Institute, Chicago IL

Cart, Cynthia K, *Registrar*, Evansville Museum of Arts and Science, Evansville IN

Cart, E, *Secy*, Florence Museum, Florence SC

Carter, Curtis L, *Dir*, Marquette University, Marquette Fine Art Collection, Milwaukee WI

Carter, Denny T, *Cur Painting*, Cincinnati Art Museum, Cincinnati OH

Carter, Don R M, *Exec Dir*, Sierra Arts Foundation, Reno NV

Carter, Doris, *Prof*, Worcester State College, Art Department, Worcester MA (S)

Carter, Dwight, *Instructor*, Chamberlayne Junior College, Department of Graphic and Applied Arts, Boston MA (S)

Carter, Eltse B, *Chmn Humanities Div*, Northern Virginia Community College, Art Department, Annandale VA (S)

Carter, Granville W, *Pres*, National Sculpture Society, New York NY

Carter, Hope, *VPres*, Princeton Art Association, Princeton NJ

Carter, Jack, *Acting Dir*, University of California, Los Angeles, Frederick S Wight Art Gallery, Los Angeles CA

Carter, Judy Jerstad, *Reference Librn*, Palomar Community College, Fine Arts Library, San Marcos CA

Carter, Rand, *Assoc Prof*, Hamilton College, Art Department, Clinton NY (S)

Carter, Robert, *Chmn*, Jamestown College, Art Department, Jamestown ND (S)

Carter, Yvonne, *Asst Prof*, University of the District of Columbia, Art Department, Washington DC (S)

Carter Jr, Charles Hill, *Owner*, Shirley Plantation, Charles City VA

Cartesegna, Giorgio Dondi e Marisa, *Staff Member*, Armeria Reale, Turin Italy

Cartland, John, *Treas*, Museum of Contemporary Art, Chicago IL

Cartmell, Peter, *Pres*, New Jersey Historical Society Museum, Newark NJ

CArtmell, Robert, *Assoc Prof*, State University of New York at Albany, Art Department, Albany NY (S)

Cartwright, AnnaBelle, *Cur of Exhibits*, Putnam Museum, Davenport IA

Cartwright, James, *Pres of Board*, Oshkosh Public Museum, Oshkosh WI

Cartwright, Joseph L, *Dir*, Putnam Museum, Davenport IA

Cartwright, Rick, *Asst Prof*, Saint Francis College, Art Department, Fort Wayne IN (S)

Carty, J M, *First VPres*, Kitchener-Waterloo Art Gallery, Kitchener ON

Caruso, Gordon, *Instr*, Vancouver Community College, Langara Campus, Department of Fine Arts, Vancouver BC (S)

Carver, Mary E, *Cur Asst & Registrar*, J B Speed Art Museum, Louisville KY

Carver, Melvin, *Prof*, North Carolina Central University, Art Dept, Durham NC (S)

Cary, Richard, *Instr*, Lincoln Memorial University, Department of Fine Arts, Harrogate TN (S)

Casa, Sal, *Vis Prof*, Butte Community College, Humanities Division (III), Oroville CA (S)

Casale, Jacqueline, *Asst Prof*, Worcester State College, Art Department, Worcester MA (S)

Casamar, Manuel, *Cur*, Museo Romantico, Museum of the Romantic Epoch, Madrid Spain

Casanova, Aldo, *Prof*, Scripps College, Art Department, Claremont CA (S)

Casas, Mel, *Chmn*, San Antonio College, Art Department, San Antonio TX (S)

Case, H J, *Keeper Department Antiquities*, Oxford University, Ashmolean Museum of Art and Archaeology, Oxford England

Case, Robert, *Dir of Jekyll Island Authority*, Jekyll Island National Historic Landmark, Jekyll Island GA

Casebier, Rodney, *Instructor*, William Woods-Westminster Colleges, Art Department, Fulton MO (S)

Casey, Grace, *Executive Dir*, New Hampshire Art Association, Inc, Manchester NH

Casey, Jack, *Executive Dir*, San Antonio Art League, San Antonio TX

Casey, Jean, *Reference*, Mason City Public Library, Mason City IA

Casey, Warren V, *Prof*, Texas Woman's University, Department of Art, Denton TX (S)

Cash, Tim, *Cur*, University of Alabama in Huntsville, Gallery of Art, Huntsville AL

Casher, Theodore P, *Instructor*, Dean Junior College, Visual and Performing Arts Department, Franklin MA (S)

Caskey, Robert, *Instructor*, Charles Stewart Mott Community College, Fine Arts Division, Flint MI (S)

Caskey, Tamara, *Librn*, Galleries of Ivy School of Professional Art, Library, Pittsburgh PA

Casler, Sally, *Asst Dir*, Boise Gallery of Art, Boise ID

Cason, Robert A, *Museum Cur*, Alabama Department of Archives and History Museum, Montgomery AL

Casper, Geraldine, *Cur*, Bergstrom Art Center and Museum, Neenah WI

Cass, David B, *Asst Cur*, Sterling and Francine Clark Art Institute, Williamstown MA

Cassady, Dick, *Area Chmn Art History*, Pasadena City College, Art Department, Pasadena CA (S)

Cassedy, David, *Librn & Registrar*, Museums at Stony Brook, Kate Strong Historical Library, Stony Brook NY

Cassel, Barbara, *In Charge Art Coll*, Glendale Federal Savings, Glendale CA

Casselman, Robert C, *Assoc Dir*, Museum of Fine Arts, Boston MA

Cassels, Charlotte, *Chmn*, South Carolina Arts Commission, Columbia SC

Cassill, Carroll, *Instr*, Cleveland Institute of Art, Cleveland OH (S)

Cassino, Barbara, *Asst Prof*, University of Northern Iowa, Department of Art, Cedar Falls IA (S)

Cassino, Michael, *Chmn Art Dept*, Adrian College, Art Department, Adrian MI (S)

Casstevens, Kenneth, *Assoc Prof*, University of Texas at Tyler, Department of Art, Tyler TX (S)

Cast, David J, *Dir Undergrad Studies*, Yale University, Department of the History of Art, New Haven CT (S)

Castellani, John A, *Resident Dir*, Mount Vernon, Mount Vernon VA

Castelli, Leo, *Pres*, Art Dealers Association of America, Inc, New York NY

Castile, Rand, *Dir*, Japan Society, Inc, Japan House Gallery, New York NY

Castille, Noemi, *Head Anthropological Department*, Museo Nacional de Antropologia, National Museum of Anthropology, Mexico Mexico

Castleberry, David, *Crafts Coordr*, San Jose State University, Art Department, San Jose CA (S)

Castleman, Darlene, *VPres*, Coquille Valley Art Association, Coquille OR

Castleman, Riva, *Dir Prints & Illustrated Books*, Museum of Modern Art, New York NY

Castro, A, *Asst Prof*, George Mason University, Department of Fine and Performing Arts, Fairfax VA (S)

Castro, Catarina Maria, *Cur*, Museu Nacional de Soares dos Reis, National Museum of Soares Dos Reis, Oporto Portugal

Caswell, Fay, *Treas*, Buchanan Arts and Crafts Inc, Buchanan Dam TX

Caswell, James O, *Assoc Prof*, University of British Columbia, Department of Fine Arts, Vancouver BC (S)

Catalano, James J, *Chmn Printmaking Dept*, Lake Placid School of Art, Lake Placid NY (S)

Catalano, Kathleen, *Cur*, Longfellow National Historic Site, Cambridge MA

Cataldi, Pat, *Conservator*, United States Figure Skating Hall of Fame and Museum, Colorado Springs CO

Catan, Paul, *Pres*, Rensselaer Newman Foundation Chapel and Cultural Center, Troy NY

Catan-Rose, Richard, *Dir*, Catan-Rose Institute of Art, Forest Hills NY (S)

Cate, Phillip Dennis, *Dir & Cur Prints*, Rutgers University, Art Gallery, New Brunswick NJ

Cates, Mary, *Recording Secy*, Arts Club of Washington, James Monroe House, Washington DC

Cathcart, Linda L, *Dir*, Contemporary Arts Museum, Houston TX

Cathers, James, *Instructor*, Roger Williams College, Art Department, Bristol RI (S)

Cathey, Charles W, *Registrar*, Carnegie Institute, Museum of Art, Pittsburgh PA

Catron, Patricia, *Dir*, Springfield Art Center, Springfield OH

Catron, Patricia D'Arcy, *Dir*, Springfield Art Center, Springfield OH (S)

Catterall, John, *Dir School*, Montana State University, School of Art, Bozeman MT (S)

Caulk, Douglas, *Museum Mgr*, State University of New York College at Purchase, Neuberger Museum, Purchase NY

Causa, Raffaello, *Dir*, Museo de Capodimonte, Mount Capodi Museum, Naples Italy

Cauthen, Gene, *Dir Fine Arts Gallery*, Mount Wachusett Community College, Art Galleries, Gardner MA

Cauthorn, Jess D, *Dir*, Burnley School of Professional Art, Inc, Seattle WA (S)

Cavalier, Carolyn, *Instructor*, Factory of Visual Art, Seattle WA (S)

Cavallo, Adolph, *Cur Costume & Textiles*, Philadelphia Museum of Art, Philadelphia PA

Cavanagh, Carroll J, *Assoc Secy & Assoc Gen Counsel*, National Gallery of Art, Washington DC

Cavanaugh, Carroll, *Dir*, Craft Center Museum, Wilton CT

Cavanaugh, Tom, *Prof*, Louisiana State University, Department of Fine Arts, Baton Rouge LA (S)

Cavano, Robert, *VPres*, Cleveland Museum of Art, Print Club of Cleveland, Cleveland OH

Caver, Ralph, *Prof*, Texarkana Community College, Art Department, Texarkana TX (S)

Caver, William, *Chmn*, Texarkana Community College, Art Department, Texarkana TX (S)

Caviness, Madeline H, *Chmn Fine Arts Dept*, Tufts University, Fine Arts Department, Medford MA (S)

Cawood, Hobart G, *Supt*, Independence National Historical Park, Philadelphia PA

Cayton, David, *Chmn Two-Dimensional Studies*, Bowling Green State University, School of Art, Bowling Green OH (S)

Cazelles, Raymond, *Conservator of Coll*, Institut de France, Musee Conde, Paris France

Cazort, Mary, *Cur Drawings*, National Gallery of Canada, Ottawa ON

Cecere, Jim, *Prof*, Mansfield State College, Art Department, Mansfield PA (S)

Cellini, Nicholas, *Fine Arts Librn*, Beverly Hills Public Library, Fine Arts Library, Beverly Hills CA

Cerny, Charlene, *Cur American & Latin American Coll*, Museum of New Mexico, Museum of International Folk Art, Santa Fe NM

Cervantes, James, *Cur Military History*, Heritage Plantation of Sandwich, Sandwich MA

Cervene, Richard, *Prof*, Grinnell College, Department of Art, Grinnell IA (S)

Cervenka, Barbara, *Instr*, Siena Heights College, Art Department, Adrian MI (S)

Cevc, Anica, *Dir*, Narodna Galerija, National Art Gallery, Ljubljana Yugoslavia

Chabaud, M Andre, *Dir*, Musee du Louvre, Louvre Museum, Paris France

Chadick, Ellen, *Head Dept*, Art Institute of Houston, Houston TX (S)

Chafee, Richard, *Asst Prof*, Connecticut College, Department of Art History, New London CT (S)

Chaffee, Tom, *Asst Prof*, Arkansas State University, Department of Art, State University AR (S)

Chaikin, Hand, *Dir*, Verde Valley Art Association, Inc, Jerome AZ

Challinor, David, *Asst Secy Science*, Smithsonian Institution, Washington DC

Challis, A Thomas, *Librn*, Southern Utah State College, Library, Cedar City UT

Chalmers, Joan, *VPres*, Canadian Crafts Council, Conseil Canadien de l'Artisanat, Ottawa ON

Chalmers Jr, E Laurence, *Pres*, Art Institute of Chicago, Chicago IL

Chamberlain, Betty, *Dir*, Art Information Center, Inc, New York NY

Chamberlain, Charles F, *Chmn Ceramics*, East Carolina University, School of Art, Greenville NC (S)

Chamberlain, E, *Keeper Prints*, University of Cambridge, Fitzwilliam Museum, Cambridge England

Chamberlain, Ken, *Head Librn*, Emily Carr College of Art Library, Vancouver BC

Chamberlain, Merle, *Asst Librn & Archivist*, Philadelphia Museum of Art, Marian Angell Boyer and Francis Boyer Library, Philadelphia PA

Chamberlain, Owen, *Instr*, Portland Community College, Department of Fine Arts, Portland OR (S)

Chamberlain, Peter, *Instructor*, Elmira College, Art Department, Elmira NY (S)

Chamberlin, Marsha, *Executive Dir*, Ann Arbor Art Association, Ann Arbor MI

Chamberlin, Wesley, *Assoc Chmn*, San Francisco State University, Art Department, San Francisco CA (S)

Chambers, Bruce W, *Acting Dir*, University of Rochester, Memorial Art Gallery, Rochester NY

Chambers-Hartz, Jill, *Exhib Coordr*, Cornell University, Herbert F Johnson Museum of Art, Ithaca NY

Champa, Kermit S, *Chmn*, Brown University, Department of Art, Providence RI (S)

Champlin, C Curtis, *Business Adminr*, San Diego Museum of Art, San Diego CA

Chan, Shu-Park, *VPres*, Triton Museum of Art, Santa Clara CA

Chandler, Barbara, *Registrar*, Philadelphia Museum of Art, Philadelphia PA

Chandler, Clay, *Pres*, Omaha Children's Museum, Inc, Omaha NE

Chandler, William L, *Chmn*, Concordia College, Art Department, Milwaukee WI (S)

Chandler, William L, *Cur*, Concordia College, Fine Arts Galleries, Milwaukee WI

Chandra, Pramod, *Prof*, University of Chicago, Department of Art History & Committee on Art & Design, Chicago IL (S)

Chaney, Jim, *Gallery Dir*, Kutztown State College, Sharadin Art Gallery, Kutztown PA

Chang, John R, *Deputy Dir*, Vancouver City Archives and Library, Vancouver BC

Chang, Peter, *Cur Department Rare Books & Documents*, National Palace Museum, Taipei China, Republic of

Chang, T L, *Pres*, National Taiwan Academy of Arts, Taipei China, Republic of (S)

Chanlatte, Luis A, *Cur Archaeology*, University of Puerto Rico, Museum of Archaeology, History and Art, Rio Piedras PR

Chao-shen, Chiang, *Deputy Dir & Cur Department Calligraphy & Painting*, National Palace Museum, Taipei China, Republic of

Chapin, Leslie A, *Treas*, Westfield Athenaeum, Jasper Rand Art Museum, Westfield MA

Chapklin, Pam, *Instructor*, Cazenovia College, Art Program, Cazenovia NY (S)

Chaplin, George, *Dir Studio Arts Program*, Trinity College, Austin Arts Center, Hartford CT

Chaplin, George, *Dir Studio Arts Prog*, Trinity College, Department of Fine Arts, Hartford CT (S)

Chapman, Allan D, *Museum Librn*, Metropolitan Museum of Art, Robert Goldwater Library of Primitive Art, New York NY

Chapman, B, *Cur Painting & Asst Cur Historical Coll* Art Gallery of Western Australia, Perth Australia

Chapman, George, *Asst Prof*, Trenton State College, Art Department, Trenton NJ (S)

Chapman, S Vannort, *VPres*, Star-Spangled Banner Flag House Association, Baltimore MD

Chapman, Wesley G, *Chmn Dept Art*, Southern Oregon State College, Department of Art, Ashland OR (S)

Chapnick, Ronald, *Secy*, Fine ARts Association, School of Fine Arts, Willoughby OH

Chappell, Berkley W, *Chmn Dept*, Oregon State University, Department of Art, Corvallis OR (S)

Chappell, Miles, *Chmn*, College of William and Mary, Department of Fine Arts Gallery, Williamsburg VA

Chappell, Miles, *Chmn*, College of William and Mary, Department of Fine Arts, Williamsburg VA (S)

Chappell, Sally Kitt, *Chmn Dept*, DePaul University, Department of Art, Chicago IL (S)

Chapu, Philippe, *Cur*, Musee National des Monuments Francais, National Museum of French Sculpture and Murals, Paris France

Charland, William, *Prof*, New Mexico State University, Art Dept, Las Cruces NM (S)

Charles, Jenny, *CETA Librn*, Springfield Art Association of Edwards Place, Michael Victor II Art Library, Springfield IL

Charles, Peter, *Prof*, West Virginia University, Division of Art, Morgantown WV (S)

Charley, Alfred B, *Assoc Prof*, Clarion State College, Department of Art, Clarion PA (S)

Charlton, R I H, *Public Officer*, Oxford University, Ashmolean Museum of Art and Archaeology, Oxford England

Charron, Daniel C, *Instructor*, Norwich Art School, Norwich Free Academy, Art Dept, Norwich CT (S)

Chase, David, *Pres Board of Trustees*, Museum of Northern Arizona, Flagstaff AZ

Chase, W T, *Head Conservator, Technical Laboratory*, Freer Gallery of Art, Washington DC

Chasteen, James, *Pres*, John C Calhoun State Community College, Art Gallery, Decatur AL

Chatti, Orville K, *Chmn*, Skagit Valley College, Department of Art, Mount Vernon WA (S)

Chavez, Lita, *Instructor*, Southwestern School of Art, Albuquerque NM (S)

Chavez, Olga Joffre, *Asst Dir*, Museo Nacional de Arqueologia, National Museum, La Paz Bolivia

Chaw, Gladys, *Chief Librn*, College of San Mateo Library, San Mateo CA

Cheatham, Frank, *Prof*, Texas Tech University, Department of Art, Lubbock TX (S)

Cheever, David, *Chmn Executive Committee*, Arts and Science Center, Nashua NH

Cheevers, James W, *Senior Cur*, United States Naval Academy Museum, Annapolis MD

Cheezem, James, *Pres*, Museum, Greenwood SC

Chegwidden, Dennis, *Prof*, Hutchinson Community Junior College, Art Department, Hutchinson KS (S)

Chehab, Emir Maurice, *Dir & Chief Cur*, Musee National, National Museum of Lebanon, Beirut Lebanon

Chelimsky, Oscar, *Instructor*, Maryland College of Art and Design, Silver Spring MD (S)

Chellemi, Lee, *Gallery Dir*, Saint Augustine Art Association Gallery, Saint Augustine FL

Cheney, Iris, *Prof*, University of Massachusetts, Amherst, Art History Prog, Amherst MA (S)

Cheney, Kenneth D, *Chmn Humanities Div*, Linn Benton Community College, Art Department, Albany OR (S)

Cheney, Liana, *Asst Prof*, University of Lowell, Department of Art, Lowell MA (S)

Cheney, Rowland, *Chmn*, San Joaquin Delta College, Art Department, Stockton CA (S)

Chenoweth, Mary, *Assoc Prof*, Colorado College, Department of Art, Colorado Springs CO (S)

Chepp, Mark, *Cur of Collections*, University of Wisconsin, Department of Art History Gallery, Milwaukee WI

Chernow, Burt, *Chmn*, Housatonic Community College, Art Department, Bridgeport CT (S)

Chernow, Burt, *Dir*, Housatonic Community College, Housatonic Museum of Art, Bridgeport CT

Cherrington, Mary B, *Secy*, French Art Colony, Inc, Gallipolis OH

Cherry, Sheldon, *Pres*, Vancouver Art Gallery, Vancouver BC

Cherry, Terry, *Chmn*, East Mississippi Junior College, Art Department, Scooba MS (S)

Chessler, Abbie, *Gallery Asst*, Arts, Limited, Baltimore MD

Chester, Jan, *Business Mgr*, Institute of Contemporary Art, Boston MA

Chester, Janie K, *Dir*, Saginaw Art Museum, Saginaw MI

Chetham, Charles, *Dir & Chief Cur*, Smith College, Museum of Art, Northampton MA

Chevallier, B, *Cur*, Musee National du Chateau de Fontainebleau, National Museum of Fontainebleau, Fontainebleau France

Chevian, Margaret, *Asst*, Providence Public Library, Art and Music Dept, Providence RI

Chew, Paul A, *Dir*, Westmoreland County Museum of Art, Greensburg PA

Chianese, Umberto, *Asst Supt*, Museo de Capodimonte, Mount Capodi Museum, Naples Italy

Chiang, Vivian, *Acting Dir*, Chinese Culture Foundation, Chinese Culture Center Gallery, San Francisco CA

Chiarini, Marco, *Dir*, Galleria Palatina, Palatine Gallery, Florence Italy

Chiarito, Robert, *Vis Lectr*, California State College, Stanislaus, Art Department, Turlock CA (S)

Chiba-Cohen, Judith, *Cur European Coll*, Museum of New Mexico, Museum of International Folk Art, Santa Fe NM

Chick, Lucille, *Staff Secy*, Southern Artists Association, Fine Arts Center, Hot Springs AR

Chickanzeff, S, *Catalog Librn*, San Francisco Art Institute, Anne Bremer Memorial Library, San Francisco CA

Chieffo, Clifford, *Prof*, Georgetown University, Department of Fine Arts, Washington DC (S)

Chieffo, Clifford T, *Cur*, Georgetown University, Art and History Museum, Washington DC

Chieffo, Patricia H, *Assoc Cur*, Georgetown University, Art and History Museum, Washington DC

Chiego, William, *Cur*, Portland Art Association, Portland OR

Chihuly, Dale, *Head Glass*, Rhode Island School of Design, Providence RI (S)

Child, Kent, *Chmn Humanities Div*, Gavilan College, Art Department, Gilroy CA (S)

Child, Kent, *Gallery Advisor & Humanities Division Dir*, Gavilan College, Art Gallery, Gilroy CA

Child, Tim, *Gallery Education Coordr*, Thames Arts Centre, Chatham ON

Childs, Elizabeth, *Cur of General Coll*, Valentine Museum, Richmond VA

Childs, Suse C, *Librn*, Metropolitan Museum of Art, Cloisters Library, New York NY

Chilla, Benigna, *Instr*, Berkshire Community College, Department of Fine Arts and Visual Communication, Pittsfield MA (S)

Chillman, Helen, *Slide & Photograph*, Yale University, Art and Architecture Library, New Haven CT

Chilton, W P, *Pres of Board*, Hermitage Foundation Museum, Norfolk VA

Chin, Cecilia H, *Assoc Librn and Head Reference Dept*, Art Institute of Chicago, Ryerson and Burnham Libraries, Chicago IL

Ching-hung, Wang, *Head Librn*, National Palace Museum, Library, Taipei China, Republic of

Chiolo, Jim, *Exhib Preparator*, Museum of the Southwest, Midland TX

Chipley, Sheila M, *Asst Prof*, Concord College, Art Department, Athens WV (S)

Chiro, Lily, *Admin*, Cultural Initiative, Toronto ON

Chism, Robert H, *Chmn*, Butler County Community College, Art Department, El Dorado KS (S)

Chlebak, George F, *Head Dept*, Kansas Wesleyan University, Art Department, Salina KS (S)

Chmura, Helen, *Instr*, Lourdes College, Art Department, Sylvania OH (S)

Choate, Jerry, *Instructor*, Northeastern Oklahoma State University, Tahlequah OK (S)

Chodkowski, Henry J, *Prof*, University of Louisville, Allen R Hite Art Institute, Louisville KY (S)

Choi, Sunu, *Dir-General*, National Museum of Korea, Seoul Korea

Chong, Yagmo, *Chief Cur*, National Museum of Korea, Seoul Korea

Chouteau, Thomas F, *Chmn Dept*, Saint Ambrose College, Art Department, Davenport IA (S)

Choy, Weng Yang, *Cur of Art*, National Museum Art Gallery, Singapore Singapore, Republic of

Chrisman, Diane S, *Deputy Dir Public Services*, Buffalo and Erie County Public Library, Buffalo NY

Christ, Ron, *Grad Coordr*, Wichita State University, Division of Art, Wichita KS (S)

Christensen, John, *Instr*, Taft College, Division of Performing Arts, Taft CA (S)

Christensen, Kathleen E, *Staff Asst*, University of New Mexico, University Art Museum, Albuquerque NM

Christensen, Robert C, *Dir Education & Special Programs*, Charles H MacNider Museum, Mason City IA

Christensen, Ruth, *Librn*, Southwest Museum, Braun Research Library, Los Angeles CA

Christensen, V A, *Dir*, Spiva Art Center, Inc, Joplin MO

Christenson, Alice, *Secy*, Calgary Artists Society, Calgary AB

Christenson, Dorothy, *Executive Secy*, Boca Raton Center for the Arts, Inc, Boca Raton FL

Christenson, Elroy, *Instructor*, North Seattle Community College, Art Department, Seattle WA (S)

Christenson, John, *Instr*, Mount San Jacinto College, Art Department, San Jacinto CA (S)

Christian, Emmitt, *Prof*, State University College, Department of Art, Fredonia NY (S)

Christiani, Jane, *Head of Education Department*, Winnipeg Art Gallery, Winnipeg MB

Christiansen, J, *Cur Greek & Roman Art*, Ny Carlsberg Glyptothek, Carlsberg Gallery, Copenhagen Denmark

Christianson, John, *Dir in Charge of Academic Relations*, Vesterheim, Norwegian-American Museum, Decorah IA

Christie, H, *Chmn Display Design*, Fashion Institute of Technology, New York NY (S)

Christie, Robert, *Gallery Supv*, University of Saskatchewan, Gordon Snelgrove Art Gallery, Saskatoon SK

Christin, J J, *Secy*, Rockwell International Corporation, Pittsburgh PA

Christison, Muriel B, *Dir*, University of Illinois, Krannert Art Museum, Champaign IL

Christoph, Peter, *Manuscripts and Special Coll*, New York State Library, Manuscripts and Special Collections, Albany NY

Christopher, William, *Pres*, Art Association of Richmond, Richmond IN

Christophersen, Betty, *VPres*, Paint 'N Palette Club, Anamosa IA

Chruscick, Tadeusz, *Dir*, Muzeum Narodowe w Krakowie, National Museum in Cracow, Cracow Poland

Chrysler Jr, Walter P, *Pres Board of Trustees*, Chrysler Museum, Norfolk VA

Chu, Petra T D, *Chmn*, Seton Hall University, Department of Art and Music, South Orange NJ (S)

Chu, Petra Ten-Doesschate, *Dir*, Seton Hall University, Student Center Art Gallery, South Orange NJ

Chumley, Gail, *Secy to Dir*, Brooks Memorial Art Gallery, Memphis TN

Chumley, Jere L, *Dept Coordr*, Cleveland State Community College, Department of Art, Cleveland TN (S)

Church, Elsa, *Cur*, Schenectady County Historical Society, Schenectady NY

Church, Jack, *Pres*, Key West Art and Historical Society, Key West FL

Church, John, *Instructor*, Interlochen Arts Academy, Dept of Visual Art, Interlochen MI (S)

Churches, Roger, *Chmn*, Loma Linda University, La Sierra Campus, Art Department, Riverside CA (S)

Churchill, Angola, *Chmn*, New York University, Department of Art Education & Div of Creative Arts, New York NY (S)

Churchill, Donald, *Instr*, Kilgore College, Department Art and Art Education, Kilgore TX (S)

Churdar, Janice, *Staff Supv*, Bob Jones University, Greenville SC

Churn, Sherry, *Asst Prof*, Brenau College, Art Department, Gainesville GA (S)

Chusid, J, *Asst Dir & Journal Managing Ed*, Association of Collegiate Schools of Architecture, Washington DC

Cialdella, Gary, *Head Photography Dept*, Kalamazoo Institute of Arts, Kalamazoo MI (S)

Ciampa, Rose, *Secy*, Queens Museum, Flushing NY

Ciampoli, Judith, *Cur Pictures*, Missouri Historical Society, Saint Louis MO

Cianfoni, Emilio, *Conservator*, Dade County Art Museum, Vizcaya Museum and Gardens, Miami FL

Cifka, Brigitta, *Head Modern Art*, Szepmuveszet Museum, Museum of Fine Arts, Budapest Hungary

Cimental, Virginia, *Pres*, Marian Osborne Cunningham Art Gallery, Bakersfield CA

Cindric, Mike, *Asst Chmn Undergrad Study*, University of North Carolina at Chapel Hill, Art Department, Chapel Hill NC (S)

Cinelli, Michael J, *Head Dept*, Northern Michigan University, Dept of Art & Design, Marquette MI (S)

Cini, Joyce, *Dir*, Jacque Marchais Center of Tibetan Arts, Inc, Staten Island NY

Cipriano, Zenaida D, *Chief Librn*, Lopez Memorial Museum, Library, Manila Philippines

Cischkiewicz, Stanislaw, *Deputy Dir*, Panstwowe Zbiory Sztuki na Wawelu, Wawel State Collections of Art, Cracow Poland

Cisneros, Dorothy, *Asst Librn*, Huntington Free Library and Reading Room, Depository Library for the Museum of the American Indian, Bronx NY

Cissell, Michael, *Student Dir*, University of Alabama in Huntsville, Gallery of Art, Huntsville AL

Citrin, Sharon, *Cur*, Gallery of Prehistoric Paintings, New York NY

Claflin, Susan, *Instructor*, Clayworks, New York NY (S)

Clahassey, Patricia, *Chmn*, College of Saint Rose, Division of Art, Albany NY (S)

Clain-Stefanelli, Elvira, *Art Advisory Board*, Society of Medalists, Danbury CT

Clancy, Justine, *Slide Cur*, University of Southern California, Architecture and Fine Arts Library, Los Angeles CA

Clancy, Patrick, *Instructor*, Colgate University, Department of Fine Arts, Hamilton NY (S)

Clapp, Nick, *Instructor*, William Woods-Westminster Colleges, Art Department, Fulton MO (S)

Clapp, Robert T, *Secy*, Providence Athenaeum, Library, Providence RI

Clapp, Roger T, *Secy*, Providence Athenaeum, Providence RI

Clarien, Gary, *Workshop Supv*, Palo Alto Cultural Center, Palo Alto CA

Clark, Alan B, *Dir*, Albuquerque Public Library, Albuquerque NM

Clark, Alson, *Librn*, University of Southern California, Architecture and Fine Arts Library, Los Angeles CA

Clark, A McFadyen, *Chief Canadian Ethnology Service*, National Museum of Man, Ottawa ON

Clark, Barbara A, *Museum Dir*, Las Vegas Art League, Las Vegas Art Museum, Las Vegas NV

Clark, Bede, *Instructor*, Dunedin Fine Arts and Cultural Center, Dunedin FL (S)

Clark, Bob, *Head Dept*, Southwestern Technical College, Commercial Art & Advertising Design Dept, Sylva NC (S)

Clark, Carol, *Cur Paintings*, Amon Carter Museum of Western Art, Fort Worth TX

Clark, Carroll, *Editor Office of Publications*, National Collection of Fine Arts, Washington DC

Clark, Charles E, *VPres*, New Hampshire Historical Society, Concord NH

Clark, Gary F, *Asst Prof*, Bloomsburg State College, Department of Art, Bloomsburg PA (S)

Clark, Howard, *Instructor*, Oxbow Summer Art Workshops, Saugatuck MI (S)

Clark, Ian Christie, *Secy General*, National Museums of Canada, Ottawa ON

Clark, Jack, *Dir*, Bruce Museum, Greenwich CT

Clark, James M, *Chmn*, Blackburn College, Department of Art, Carlinville IL (S)

Clark, Jane, *Dir Educ*, South Street Seaport Museum, New York NY

Clark, Joan, *VPres Programs*, Cedar Rapids Art Center, Cedar Rapids IA

Clark, Kathryn, *Instructor*, Oxbow Summer Art Workshops, Saugatuck MI (S)

Clark, Marcia, *Registrar*, Fort Worth Art Museum, Fort Worth TX

Clark, Margy, *Secy*, Kingsport Fine Arts Center, Kingsport TN

Clark, Mark A, *Cur Decorative Arts*, Chrysler Museum, Norfolk VA

Clark, Mary Ann, *Chmn Dept*, Northeast Technical Community College, Dept of Art, Norfolk NE (S)

Clark, Mary Ellen, *Business Mgr*, Owensboro Museum of Fine Art, Owensboro KY

Clark, Mel L, *Assoc Prof*, Graceland College, Art Department, Lamoni IA (S)

Clark, Neill, *Instructor*, Atlanta College of Art, Atlanta GA (S)

Clark, Neill W, *Pres*, Hickory Museum of Art, Inc, Hickory NC

Clark, Pat, *Assoc Prof*, University of Wisconsin-River Falls, Art Department, River Falls WI (S)

Clark, Phyllis Blair, *Asst Mus Dir*, College of Wooster Art Center Museum, Wooster OH

Clark, Ralph T, *Prof*, Utah State University, Department of Art, Logan UT (S)

Clark, Roberta Carter, *Pres*, New Jersey Watercolor Society, Little Silver NJ

Clark, Robert Sterling, *Vis Prof*, Williams College, Department of Art, Williamstown MA (S)

Clark, Tommy, *Instructor*, Campbellsville College, Fine Arts Division, Campbellsville KY (S)

Clark, Winnifred, *Reference Librn*, Detroit Public Library, Fine Arts Department, Detroit MI

Clarke, A S, *Keeper Department of Natural History*, Royal Scottish Museum, Edinburgh Scotland

Clarke, D V, *Asst Dir*, Leicester Polytechnic, Faculty of Art and Design, Leicester England (S)

Clarke, Jude, *Cur*, Vernon Art Association, Topham Brown Gallery, Vernon BC

Clarke, Michael, *Asst Keeper Prints*, University of Manchester, Whitworth Art Gallery, Manchester England

Clark Jr, Edward F, *County Executive ,Hon*, Hudson County Court House, Board of Chosen Freeholders, Jersey City NJ

Clarkson, John, *Prof*, West Virginia University, Division of Art, Morgantown WV (S)

Clarkson, John D, *Cur CAC Galleries*, West Virginia University, Galleries A and B, Morgantown WV

Clarkson, John D, *Cur Art and Dir Acquisition*, West Virginia University, Creative Arts Center and Gallery, Morgantown WV

Claus, William, *Instructor*, Junior College of Albany, Fine Arts Division, Albany NY (S)

Clausen, Robert, *Instr*, Rochester Community College, Art Department, Rochester MN (S)

Claxton-Oldfield, Patricia, *Librn*, The Robert McLaughlin Gallery, Library, Oshawa ON

Clay, Langdon F, *Asst Dir*, University of Rochester, Memorial Art Gallery, Rochester NY

Clayton, John M, *University Archivist & Dir Permanent Coll*, University of Delaware, University Art Collections, Newark DE

Clearwater, Jim, *Gallery Mgr*, New York University, Grey Art Gallery and Study Center, New York NY

Cleary, John R, *Instructor*, Salisbury State College, Art Dept, Salisbury MD (S)

Cleary, John R, *Gallery Dir*, Salisbury State College, College Gallery, Salisbury MD

Cleary, Manon, *Assoc Prof*, University of the District of Columbia, Art Department, Washington DC (S)

Cleaver, M, *Reference Librn*, San Francisco Art Institute, Anne Bremer Memorial Library, San Francisco CA

Clee, Paul, *Instr*, Tacoma Community College, Art Department, Tacoma WA (S)

Clemans, H, *Instructor*, Golden West College, Arts, Humanities and Social Sciences Institute, Huntington Beach CA (S)

Clement, Adele, *Secy*, Essex Art Association, Inc, Essex CT

Clement, Claudia, *Librn*, And-Or, Resources in Contemporary Arts, Seattle WA

Clement, Constance, *Asst Dir Publications & Information*, Yale University, Yale Center for British Art, New Haven CT

Clement, Dixie, *Manager Kirkpatrick Center*, Omniplex, Oklahoma City OK

Clement, J William, *Pres*, Virginia Museum, Danville Museum of Fine Arts and History, Danville VA

Clemente, Vincent, *Instr*, Utica College of Syracuse University, Division of Humanities, Utica NY (S)

Clementi, Anthony, *Adjunct Instructor*, New York Institute of Technology, Fine Arts Department, Old Westbury NY (S)

Clement Jr, Robert L, *VPres*, Charleston Museum, Charleston SC

Clements, Nora, *Secy*, Society for the Preservation of Historic Landmarks, York ME

Clements, Richard, *Pres*, Oklahoma Art Center, Oklahoma City OK

Clemes, Patricia, *Instr*, Toronto School of Art, Toronto ON (S)

Clemmer, John, *Chmn*, Tulane University, Newcomb College, New Orleans LA (S)

Clemmer, John, *Chmn Art Department*, Tulane University, Newcomb Art Department Exhibition Gallery, New Orleans LA

Clervi, Paul, *Asst Prof*, William Woods-Westminster Colleges, Art Department, Fulton MO (S)

Clervi, Paul, *Dir*, William Woods College, Art Gallery, Fulton MO

Cleveland, Helen B, *Pres & Advisor Dir*, Chautauqua Gallery of Art, Chautauqua NY

Cleveland, Joanne, *Instructor*, Wayne Art Center, Wayne PA (S)

Cleveland, Luana, *Secy*, Women's Interart Center, Inc, Interart Gallery, New York NY

Cleveland, R Earl, *Chmn Dept*, Carson-Newman College, Art Dept, Jefferson City TN (S)

Cleveland, William W F, *Dean of Fine Arts*, De Anza College, Art Department, Cupertino CA (S)

Cleveland Jr, John H, *Executive Dir*, Greater Gary Arts Council, Gary IN

Cleverdon, John H, *Prof*, University of South Alabama, Department of Art, Mobile AL (S)

Clewell, E B, *Cur*, Moravian Historical Society, Whitefield House Museum, Nazareth PA

Clewell, Heather A, *Secy & Archivist*, Fetherston Foundation, Packwood House Museum, Lewisburg PA

Clifford, Deborah, *Vice Chmn of Board*, Vermont State Craft Center at Frog Hollow, Middlebury VT

Clifford, Ethel, *Admin Asst*, Haystack Mountain School of Crafts Gallery, Deer Isle ME

Clifford, Kenneth, *Assoc Prof*, Mississippi State University, Art Department, Mississippi State MS (S)

Clifford, Lynne, *Asst to Dir*, Region of Peel Museum and Art Gallery, Brampton ON

Clifford, Paul A, *Cur Pre-Columbian Coll*, Duke University Museum of Art, Durham NC

Clifford, T P P, *Dir*, Manchester City Art Galleries, Manchester England

Clifton, Betty, *Faculty Dir*, Eliot McMurrough School of Art, Melbourne FL (S)

Clifton, Darleen, *Photo Technician*, Institute of the Great Plains, Museum of the Great Plains, Lawton OK

Cline, Dale K, *VPres*, Hickory Museum of Art, Inc, Hickory NC

Cline, Kay, *Museum on Wheels Dir*, Monterey Peninsula Museum of Art, Monterey CA

Cline Jr, Fred A, *Librn*, Asian Art Museum of San Francisco, Library, San Francisco CA

Clinkinbeard, Al, *Chmn*, San Jacinto College North, Art Department, Houston TX (S)

Clinton, Barbara, *Coordr of Public Relations*, Currier Gallery of Art, Manchester NH

Clisby, Roger D, *Chief Cur*, Crocker Art Museum, Sacramento CA

Clodfelter, E Scott, *Business Mgr*, Portland Art Association, Portland OR

Close, Patrick, *Dir*, Photographers Gallery, Saskatoon SK

Clothier, George B, *Treas*, Philadelphia Museum of Art, Samuel S Fleisher Art Memorial, Philadelphia PA

Cloudsley, Donald, *Deputy Dir Support Services*, Buffalo and Erie County Public Library, Buffalo NY

Clough, Charles, *VPRes*, Hallwalls Gallery, Buffalo NY

Clovis, John, *Instructor*, Fairmont State College, Art Department, Fairmont WV (S)

Clowes, Allen W, *Cur*, Indianapolis Museum of Art, Clowes Fund Collection, Indianapolis IN

Clunie, Margaret B, *Cur*, Bowdoin College, Museum of Art & Peary-MacMillan Arctic Museum, Brunswick ME

Coates, Ann S, *Cur Slides*, University of Louisville, Slide Collection, Louisville KY

Coates, F Del, *Chmn Industrial Design*, Center for Creative Studies—College of Art and Design, Detroit MI (S)

Coates, Ross, *Chmn*, Washington State University, Fine Arts Department, Pullman WA (S)

Coats, Marvin S, *Lectr*, Wake Forest University, Department of Art, Winston-Salem NC (S)

Cobb, John L, *Chmn*, Eastern Oregon State College, La Grande OR (S)

Coblentz, Patricia L, *Asst Dir*, Museum of American Folk Art, New York NY

Coburn, Bette Lee, *Pres Elect*, Guild of South Carolina Artists, Columbia SC

Coburn, Dwight, *Instructor*, Factory of Visual Art, Seattle WA (S)

Cochran, Malcolm, *Exhib Coordr*, Dartmouth College Museum & Galleries, Hanover NH

Cochran, Thomas C, *VPres*, Historical Society of Pennsylvania, Philadelphia PA

Cockey III, Thomas B, *Chmn House Committee*, Mount Clare Mansion, Baltimore MD

Coddington, Dabney M, *Cur Education*, Tryon Palace Restoration Complex, New Bern NC

Codell, Julie F, *Asst Prof*, University of Montana, Dept of Art, Missoula MT (S)

Cody, John V, *Prof*, Boston State College, Art Department, Boston MA (S)

Coe, Beverly, *Executive Secy*, Tampa Museum, Tampa FL

Coe, Henry H R, *Chmn*, Buffalo Bill Memorial Association, Cody WY

Coe, Katherine, *Publicist*, Heard Museum, Phoenix AZ

Coe, Mildred M, *Exec Dir*, Hickory Museum of Art, Inc, Hickory NC

Coe, Ralph T, *Lectr*, University of Kansas, Kress Foundation Department of Art History, Lawrence KS (S)

Coe, Ralph T, *Dir*, William Rockhill Nelson Gallery of Art, Atkins Museum of Fine Art, Kansas City MO

Coe, William R, *Cur American Section*, University of Pennsylvania, University Museum, Philadelphia PA

Coerr, DeRenne, *Registrar de Young Museum*, Fine Arts Museums of San Francisco, M H de Young Memorial Museum and California Palace of the Legion of Honor

Cofer, Alene N, *Assoc Dir*, Mariners Museum, Newport News VA

Coffee, Baxter, *Instructor*, Del Mar College, Department of Art, Corpus Christi TX (S)

Coffee, Mary, *Instr*, Portland Community College, Department of Fine Arts, Portland OR (S)

Coffey, Bettye, *Clerical Hostess*, Red River Valley Museum, Vernon TX

Coffey, John W, *Acting Dir*, Williams College, Museum of Art, Williamstown MA

Coffin, David, *Prof*, Princeton University, Department of Art and Archaeology, Princeton NJ (S)

Coffin, Douglas, *Instructor*, College of Santa Fe, Visual Arts Dept, Santa Fe NM (S)

Coffman, Gloria, *Asst Librn*, Maryland College of Art and Design Library, Silver Spring MD

Coffman, Michael, *Program Developer*, Jacksonville Museum of Arts and Sciences, Jacksonville FL

Coffman, Terrence J, *Pres*, Maryland College of Art and Design, Silver Spring MD (S)

Cofrances, Humbert, *Pres*, Frederick Thompson Foundation, Inc, New York NY

Coggins, Jack, *Pres*, Berks Art Alliance, Reading PA

Coghlan, Gladys M, *Dir of Libraries*, Historical Society of Delaware, Library, Wilmington DE

Cogswell, Dean, *Pres*, Wenham Historical Association and Museum, Inc, Wenham MA

Cohan, Allan L, *Coordr*, Ulster County Community College, Visual Arts Gallery, Stone Ridge NY

Cohan, Jack, *Mgr Jorgensen Auditorium*, University of Connecticut, Jorgensen Gallery, Storrs CT

Cohan, Zara, *Gallery Dir*, Kean College of New Jersey, Union NJ

Cohen, Allan, *Head Dept*, Ulster County Community College, Department of Visual Arts, Stone Ridge NY (S)

Cohen, Charles E, *Chmn*, University of Chicago, Department of Art History & Committee on Art & Design, Chicago IL (S)

Cohen, Edwin, *Head Dept Art*, Purdue University Calumet Campus, Department of Creative Arts, Hammond IN (S)

Cohen, Faye, *Pres*, Main Line Center of the Arts, Haverford PA

Cohen, George, *Assoc Prof*, Hofstra University, Department of Art History, Hempstead NY (S)

Cohen, Harold, *Prof*, University of California, San Diego, Visual Arts Department, La Jolla CA (S)

Cohen, Janet, *Adjunct Instructor*, New York Institute of Technology, Fine Arts Department, Old Westbury NY (S)

Cohen, Kathleen, *Chmn*, San Jose State University, Art Department, San Jose CA (S)

Cohen, Mitchell, *Registrar*, Davenport Municipal Art Gallery, Davenport IA

Cohen, Phyllis, *Dir Art Therapy*, Dean Junior College, Visual and Performing Arts Department, Franklin MA (S)

Cohen, Ronald, *Asst Prof*, University of Chicago, Department of Art History & Committee on Art & Design, Chicago IL (S)

Cohen. PhD, Edwin, *Head Dept Art*, Purdue University, Calumet Campus, Bicentennial Library Gallery, Hammond IN

Cohn, Anna R, *Dir*, B'nai B'rith Exhibit Hall, Washington DC

Cohn, Marjorie, *Assoc Conservator*, Harvard University, William Hayes Fogg Art Museum, Cambridge MA

Cohn, Shelley, *Education Coordr*, Arizona Commission on the Arts, Phoenix AZ

Cohodas, Marvin, *Asst Prof*, University of British Columbia, Department of Fine Arts, Vancouver BC (S)

Coiner, Maynard R, *Head Dept*, Concord College, Art Department, Athens WV (S)

Coke, Charles V, *Assoc Prof*, Northwestern State University of Louisiana, Dept of Art, Natchitoches LA (S)

Coker, Alyce B, *Asst Prof*, University of Minnesota, Duluth, Art Dept, Duluth MN (S)

Coker, John, *Dir Fine Arts Events*, University of South Florida, University Galleries, Tampa FL

Coker, Robert R, *Treas*, Brookgreen Gardens, Murrells Inlet SC

Colacicchi, Piero, *Instr*, Studio Art Centers International, Florence Italy (S)

Colarusso, Corrinne, *Foundation Chmn*, Atlanta College of Art, Atlanta GA (S)

Colbert, Betty, *Instr*, University of Albuquerque, Art Department, Albuquerque NM (S)

Colby, Victor, *Prof*, Cornell University, Department of Art, Ithaca NY (S)

Colchado, Jose, *Art Educ Coordr*, San Jose State University, Art Department, San Jose CA (S)

Colchin, Helen, *Head Fine Arts Dept*, Public Library of Fort Wayne and Allen County, Fort Wayne IN

Cole, Alan, *Chmn of Board*, Association of Medical Illustrators, Los Angeles CA

Cole, Casdiss Ann, *Instructor*, Peters Valley Craft Center, Layton NJ (S)

Cole, David C, *Cur*, Fort Meade Museum, Fort Meade MD

Cole, Elise, *Cur Art Education*, Ella Sharp Museum, Jackson MI

Cole, Frederic, *VPres*, Key West Art and Historical Society, Key West FL

Cole, Harold D, *Chmn Div*, Baldwin-Wallace College, Department of Art, Berea OH (S)

Cole, Howson W, *Librn*, Virginia Historical Society, Library, Richmond VA

Cole, Robert, *Foundation Studies*, Rochester Institute of Technology, School of Art and Design, Rochester NY (S)

Coleburn, Sue, *Bookstore Mgr*, Brandywine River Museum, Chadds Ford PA

Coleman, Elizabeth A, *Cur Costumes & Textiles*, Brooklyn Museum, Brooklyn NY

Coleman, Henry, *Assoc Prof*, College of William and Mary, Department of Fine Arts, Williamsburg VA (S)

Coleman, Loring, *VPres*, Concord Art Association, Concord MA

Coleman, Myrlan, *Head Dept of Art*, Weatherford College, Department of Humanities and Art, Weatherford TX (S)

Coleman, Norman, *Historic Site Asst*, Schuyler Mansion, Albany NY

Coleman, Reginald, *Instr*, College of Lake County, Art Department, Grayslake IL (S)

Coleman, Thomas F, *Chmn*, Indiana University, Bloomington, Department of Fine Arts, Bloomington IN (S)

Coles, Arlo, *Instructor*, Ricks College, Department of Art, Rexburg ID (S)

Coles, William H, *Pres*, Carolina Art Association, Gibbes Art Gallery, Charleston SC

Colevechio, X G, *Head Dept*, Saint Norbert College, Art Department, De Pere WI (S)

Coley, Betty A, *Librn*, Baylor University, Armstrong Browning Library, Waco TX

Coley, Philip, *Asst Prof*, Auburn University at Montgomery, Art Department, Montgomery AL (S)

Colin, Elena, *Lectr*, Institute for American Universities, Fine Arts in Aix, Avignon and Canterbury, Aix-en-Provence France (S)

Colin, M, *Office Mgr*, Association of Collegiate Schools of Architecture, Washington DC

Colin, Ralph F, *Admin VPres & Counsel*, Art Dealers Association of America, Inc, New York NY

Colket, Meredith, *Exec Dir*, Western Reserve Historical Society, Cleveland OH

Colleck, Philip, *VPres*, National Antique and Art Dealers Association of America, New York NY

Collens, David R, *Dir*, Storm King Art Center, Mountainville NY

Collet, Lee, *Instructor*, Muskegon Community College, Dept of Creative & Performing Arts, Muskegon MI (S)

Collett, Joan, *Librn*, Saint Louis Public Library, Saint Louis MO

Collette, Alfred T, *Dir*, Syracuse University, Art Collection, Syracuse NY

Collier, Glenn W, *VPres*, Springfield Art Center, Springfield OH

Collier, Hilma Greggerson, *Dir*, Carrizo Art and Craft Workshops, Ruidoso NM (S)

Collier, Natalee, *Head Performing Arts Dept*, Long Beach Public Library, Long Beach CA

Collier, Ralph, *Pres*, Campbell Museum, Camden NJ

Collier, Ric, *Secy*, Western Association of Art Museums, San Francisco CA

Collier, Richard L, *Dir*, Boise Gallery of Art, Boise ID

Collier, Will, *Prof*, Santa Rosa Junior College, Art Department, Santa Rosa CA (S)

Collings, Betty, *Dir*, Ohio State University, Gallery of Fine Arts, Columbus OH

Collingwood, Peter, *Visiting Prof*, University of Minnesota, Duluth, Art Dept, Duluth MN (S)

Collins, Alan, *Prof*, Loma Linda University, La Sierra Campus, Art Department, Riverside CA (S)

Collins, Barbara H, *Asst Dir*, New Bedford Whaling Museum, New Bedford MA

Collins, Christiane C, *Head Librn*, Parsons School of Design, Adam L Gimbel Library, New York NY

Collins, David M, *Bus Adminr*, Frick Collection, New York NY

Collins, Delmar L, *Mgr*, Will Rogers Memorial and Museum, Claremore OK

Collins, Harvey A, *Chmn Dept*, Olivet Nazarene College, Dept of Art, Kankakee IL (S)

Collins, Howard, *VChmn Dept*, University of Nebraska-Lincoln, Department of Art, Lincoln NE (S)

Collins, J W, *Pres*, Bank of Mississippi, Tupelo MS

Collins, Jesse, *Instructor*, Junior College of Albany, Fine Arts Division, Albany NY (S)

Collins, Jim, *Prof*, University of Tennessee at Chattanooga, Department of Art, Chattanooga TN (S)

Collins, Joel, *Asst Prof*, Mount Union College, Department of Art, Alliance OH (S)

Collins, M Regina, *Chmn*, Mount Mary College, Tower Gallery, Milwaukee WI

Collins, Marcia, *Librn*, University of Missouri, Art Archaeology and Music Library, Columbia MO

Collins, Margaret, *Instructor*, Madonna College, Art Dept, Livonia MI (S)

Collins, Marianne, *Public Affairs Coordr*, Solomon R Guggenheim Museum, New York NY

Collins, Marie, *Office Mgr*, Art League of Manatee County, Bradenton FL

Collins, Reba, *Cur-Librn*, Will Rogers Memorial and Museum, Library, Claremore OK

Collins, Reba Neighbors, *Cur*, Will Rogers Memorial and Museum, Claremore OK

Collins, Regine, *Chmn*, Mount Mary College, Art Department, Milwaukee WI (S)

Collins, Ruth, *Reference*, Santa Cruz Public Library, Art, Music, Film Department, Santa Cruz CA

Collins, Susan, *Asst Dir*, Westerly Public Library, Westerly RI

Collins, Thom, *Instructor*, Peters Valley Craft Center, Layton NJ (S)

Collins, William C, *Dir*, Portland School of Art, Portland ME (S)

Collins Jr, Johan R, *Pres*, Adirondack Lakes Center for the Arts, Blue Mountain Lake NY

Collinson, Helen, *Cur*, University of Alberta, Ring House Gallery, Edmonton AB

Coll Vidal, Rosa G, *Pres*, Museo Historico de Puerto Rico Inc, Santurce PR

Colozzi, Carl, *Asst Dir*, Philadelphia Museum of Art, Philadelphia PA

Colporaal, J, *Pres*, Nationaal Glasmuseum, Leerdam Netherlands

Colson, Chester, *Prof*, Wilkes College, Department of Art, Wilkes-Barre PA (S)

Colt, Priscilla, *Dir*, University of Kentucky, Art Museum, Lexington KY

Colvert, Richard, *Secy*, Charles B Goddard Center for the Visual and Performing Arts, Ardmore OK

Colvig, Richard, *Sr Librn in Charge*, Oakland Public Library, Fine Arts Section, Oakland CA

Colwill, Stiles T, *Gallery Cur*, Maryland Historical Society Museum, Baltimore MD

Colyer, Darrell, *Exhib Coordr*, University of Alberta, Ring House Gallery, Edmonton AB

Comas, Genoveva, *Assoc Prof*, Inter American University of Puerto Rico, Department of Performing Arts, San German PR (S)

Combs, Richard, *Business Mgr*, Chicago Architecture Foundation, Glessner House, Chicago IL

Comer, Eugenia, *Asst Prof*, Augusta College, Department of Fine Arts, Augusta GA (S)

Comiskey, Ernest D, *Prof*, West Liberty State College, Art Department, West Liberty WV (S)

Compton, J R, *Editor & Publisher*, Artists Coalition of Texas, Dallas TX

Compton, Julie M, *Head Fine Arts Department*, Atlanta Public Library, Fine Arts Department, Atlanta GA

Compton Jr, Beverley C, *Pres*, Municipal Art Society of Baltimore City, Baltimore MD

Comstock, Gregory, *Coordr Artisan Center*, Jamestown Community College, Art Department, Jamestown NY (S)

Comstock, Jane, *Visiting Instructor*, University of Colorado at Denver, Department of Fine Arts, Denver CO (S)

Comtois, George, *Dir*, Manchester Historic Association, Manchester NH

Conan, Vivian, *Dir*, Port Chester Public Library, Port Chester NY

Conant, Howard, *Dept Head*, University of Arizona, Department of Art, Tucson AZ (S)

Conant, Mary, *Pres*, Marblehead Arts Association, Inc, Marblehead MA

Conaway, James, *Prof*, Hamline University, Art Department, Saint Paul MN (S)

Conaway, James, *Exhib Dir*, Hamline University Galleries, Dept of Art, Saint Paul MN

Concha, Jerry, *Chmn Drawing & Painting*, De Young Museum Art School, San Francisco CA (S)

Condax, Philip, *Equipment*, International Museum of Photography at George Eastman House, Rochester NY

Condit, Carl W, *Chmn Dept*, Northwestern University, Evanston, Department of Art History, Evanston IL (S)

Condit, Cecelia, *Instructor*, University of South Dakota, Dept of Art, Vermillion SD (S)

Conesa, Lilliam, *Supv Processing Center*, Miami-Dade Public Library, Miami FL

Conforti, Michael, *Cur Sculpture & Decorative Arts*, Fine Arts Museums of San Francisco, M H de Young Memorial Museum and California Palace of the Legion of Honor

Conger, Clement E, *Cur*, White House, Washington DC

Conger, Clement E, *Cur*, Department of State, Diplomatic Reception Rooms, Washington DC

Conger, John T, *Mgr Personnel*, Metropolitan Museum of Art, New York NY

Conger, William, *Assoc Prof*, DePaul University, Department of Art, Chicago IL (S)

Conley, B, *Instructor*, Golden West College, Arts, Humanities and Social Sciences Institute, Huntington Beach CA (S)

Conlon, F S, *Dir*, USS North Carolina Battleship Memorial, Wilmington NC

Conlon, James E, *Prof*, University of South Alabama, Department of Art, Mobile AL (S)

Conn, Richard, *Cur Native Arts Department*, Denver Art Museum, Frederic H Douglas Library, Denver CO

Connah, Neill W, *Assoc Prof*, Georgia Institute of Technology, College of Architecture, Atlanta GA (S)

Connell, Stephen, *Assoc Prof*, University of Montana, Dept of Art, Missoula MT (S)

Connelly, James L, *Assoc Prof*, University of Kansas, Kress Foundation Department of Art History, Lawrence KS (S)

Connelly, Michael, *Cur*, Yellowstone Art Center, Billings MT

Conner, Ann Louise, *Asst Prof*, University of North Carolina at Wilmington, Art Department, Wilmington NC (S)

Conner, Laurence, *Chmn*, Marycrest College, Art Department, Davenport IA (S)

Conner, M Rebecca, *Head Dept*, Saint Mary College, Art Department, Leavenworth KS (S)

Conner, Neppie, *Chmn Dept*, University of Arkansas, Art Department, Fayetteville AR (S)

Conner, Will, *General Mgr*, Mid-America Arts Alliance, Kansas City MO

Conners, Holly, *Asst Cur Paintings & Sculpture*, Brooklyn Museum, Brooklyn NY

Connett, Dee M, *Head Dept*, Friends University, Art Department, Wichita KS (S)

Connolly, Agnes R, *Auditor*, Solomon R Guggenheim Museum, New York NY

Connolly, A L J, *Head Dept Communication Arts & Design*, Manchester Polytechnic, Faculty of Art and Design, Manchester England (S)

Connolly, Bruce E, *Head Technical Services*, New York State College of Ceramics at Alfred University, Scholes Library of Ceramics, Alfred NY

Connolly, Felicia, *Office Admin*, Wenham Historical Association and Museum, Inc, Wenham MA

Connolly, G Florence, *Cur of Fine Arts*, Boston Public Library, Fine Arts Department, Boston MA

Connolly, Thomas, *Treas*, Artists Guild Inc of New York, New York NY

Connor, Catherine, *Asst Prof*, Fontbonne College, Art Department, Saint Louis MO (S)

Connor, Catherine, *Asst Prof*, Fontbonne College, Department of Art, Clayton MO (S)

Connor, George, *Pres Board Trustees*, Louisiana Arts and Science Center, Baton Rouge LA

Connors, Cathy Chance, *Membership Dir*, Studio Museum in Harlem, New York NY

Connors, Dorothy, *Adminr*, Metropolitan Museum and Art Centers, Coral Gables FL

Connors, Jeanne, *Asst Prof*, Community College of Allegheny County, Boyce Campus, Art Department, Monroeville PA (S)

Connors, Laura, *Drama*, Ashtabula Arts Center, Ashtabula OH

Conover, James H, *Assoc Dean*, Ohio University, School of Art, Athens OH (S)

Conover, Robert, *Library Dir*, Pasadena Public Library, Pasadena CA

Conrad, A, *Dir*, Art Instruction Schools, Minneapolis MN (S)

Conrad, Frances M, *Dir*, Shelter Rock Public Library, Albertson NY

Conrad, Kurt, *Cur Ethnology*, Saltzburger Museum Carolino Augusteum, Salzburg Museum, Salzburg Austria

Conrad, Sadie, *Secy*, Kelowna Centennial Museum and National Exhibit Centre, Kelowna BC

Conrad, Theodore, *VPres*, Jersey City Museum Association, Jersey City NJ

Conrad, William S, *Asst Prof*, University of Mississippi, Department of Art, University MS (S)

Conragan, A Kirk, *Dir*, Josephine D Randall Junior Museum, San Francisco CA

Conroy, Joseph, *Asst Prof*, Camden County College, Department of Art, Blackwood NJ (S)

Consey, Kevin E, *Dir*, Hofstra University, Emily Lowe Gallery, Hempstead NY

Constable, Giles, *Dir*, Harvard University, Dumbarton Oaks Research Library and Collections, Washington DC

Constantine, Greg, *Chmn*, Andrews University, Berrien Springs MI (S)

Constantine, H F, *Dir*, Sheffield City Art Galleries, Sheffield England

Constantine, Jay, *Instr*, Aurora College, Art Department, Aurora IL (S)

Constantine, John, *Acting Chmn Dept*, North Seattle Community College, Art Department, Seattle WA (S)

Contensou, Bernadette, *Conservator in Chief*, Musee d'Art Moderne de la Ville de Paris, Paris France

Conway, Gregg, *Chmn Dept*, Paris American Academy, Paris France (S)

Conway, Wallace, *Cur Exhibits*, New Jersey State Museum, Trenton NJ

Cook, Alan M, *Keeper of Public Services*, University of Pennsylvania, University Museum, Philadelphia PA

Cook, Bonnie, *Registrar*, San Jose State University, Union Gallery, San Jose CA

Cook, Christopher C, *Dir*, Phillips Academy, Addison Gallery of American Art, Andover MA

Cook, Douglas, *Head Dept Theatre and Film*, Pennsylvania State University, University Park, College of Arts and Architecture, University Park PA (S)

Cook, Gary A, *Instr*, Wake Forest University, Department of Art, Winston-Salem NC (S)

Cook, John, *Asst Prof*, Bloomsburg State College, Department of Art, Bloomsburg PA (S)

Cook, Lloyd, *Asst Chmn*, Texas State Technical Institute, Department of Commercial Art, Amarillo TX (S)

Cook, Mary, *Museum Secy*, University of Oklahoma, Museum of Art, Norman OK

Cook, Nancy, *Instr*, College of Lake County, Art Department, Grayslake IL (S)

Cook, Ralph B, *Chmn*, West Virginia Wesleyan College, Department of Fine Arts, Buckhannon WV (S)

Cook, Sterling, *Cur*, Miami University Art Museum, Oxford OH

Cook, W H, *Admin VPres*, Transco Companies Inc, Houston TX

Cooke, A Martin, *Class Supv*, Richmond Art Center, Library, Richmond CA

Cooke, Constance B, *Acting Dir*, Queens Borough Public Library, Art and Music Division, Jamaica NY

Cooke, Edwy F, *Dir*, Concordia University, Sir George Williams Art Galleries, Montreal PQ

Cooke, S Tucker, *Prof*, University of North Carolina at Asheville, Dept of Art & Music, Asheville NC (S)

Cook-Endres, Barbara, *Secy*, Manitoba Society of Artists, Winnipeg MB

Cooker, Rae, *Studios*, Midland Art Council of the Midland Center for the Arts, Midland MI

Cooker, Rae, *Studio Coordr*, Midland Center for the Arts, Midland MI (S)

Cook Jr, John F, *Dir*, Bloomsburg State College, Haas Gallery of Art, Bloomsburg PA

Cooley, Marior, *Instr*, Miami University, Art Department, Oxford OH (S)

Coolidge, Lawrence, *Chmn Trustees*, Longfellow's Wayside Inn, South Sudbury MA

Coomes, Charles, *Treas*, Saint Augustine Historical Society, Oldest House and Museums, Saint Augustine FL

Coon, A W, *VPres of the Board*, R W Norton Art Gallery, Shreveport LA

Coon, Robert, *Chmn Art Dept*, Kean College of New Jersey, Union NJ

Coon, Robert B, *Chmn Fine Arts Dept*, Kean College of New Jersey, Fine Arts Department, Union NJ (S)

Coones, R C, *Instructor*, Northeastern Oklahoma State University, Tahlequah OK (S)

Cooney, Betty, *Library Technician*, University of Colorado Art Galleries, Art and Architecture Library, Boulder CO

Cooney, John, *Vis Prof*, Case Western Reserve University, Department of Art, Cleveland OH (S)

Coonrod, Craig T, *Coordr*, Rhode Island College, Edward M Bannister Gallery, Providence RI

Cooper, Bobby, *Div Head*, Utica Junior College, Humanities Division, Utica MS (S)

Cooper, Brian, *Registrar*, Royal College of Art Gallery, London England

Cooper, Frederick A, *Prof*, University of Minnesota, Minneapolis, Art History, Minneapolis MN (S)

Cooper, Kathleen, *Cur Educ*, Indiana State Museum, Indianapolis IN

Cooper, Ken, *Community Services Dir*, Gavilan College, Art Gallery, Gilroy CA

Cooper, Margo, *Instr*, Mount San Jacinto College, Art Department, San Jacinto CA (S)

Cooper, Mark, *Mgr Photograph Studio*, Metropolitan Museum of Art, New York NY

Cooper, Willard, *Chmn Dept*, Centenary College of Louisiana, Department of Art, Shreveport LA (S)

Cooper, Willard, *Cur*, Centenary College of Louisiana, Meadows Museum of Art, Shreveport LA

Cooperman, Evelyn, *Librn*, San Diego Public Library, Art & Music Section, San Diego CA

Cope, Johnnye Louise, *Humanities Librn*, North Texas State University, Willis Library, Humanities Division, Denton TX

Copeland, Betty, *Assoc Prof*, Cleveland State University, Art Department, Cincinnati OH (S)

Copeland, Karen, *Education Cur*, Craft and Folk Art Museum, Los Angeles CA

Copeland, Lee G, *Dean*, University of Pennsylvania, Graduate School of Fine Arts, Philadelphia PA (S)

Copely, William N, *Asst Librn*, New Hampshire Historical Society, Library, Concord NH

Coplan, Robin, *Dir*, Maryland Institute College of Art, Decker Gallery, Baltimore MD

Copley, Joseph P, *Cur*, Portsmouth Athenaeum NR, Inc 1817, Portsmouth NH

Coppe, Bunny, *Member Chmn*, Florida Artist Group Inc, Englewood FL

Corbacho, Antonio Sancho, *Dir*, Escuela Superior de Bellas Artes de Santa Isabel de Hungria de Seville, Seville School of Fine Arts, Seville Spain (S)

Corbeil, John W, *Assoc Prof*, Pierce College, Art Department, Woodland Hills CA (S)

Corbelletti, Raniero, *Head Dept Archit*, Pennsylvania State University, University Park, College of Arts and Architecture, University Park PA (S)

Corbin, David C, *Pres*, Stan Hywet Hall Foundation, Inc, Akron OH

Corbin, George, *Asst Prof*, Herbert H Lehman College, Art Department, Bronx NY (S)

Corbin, Jeff, *Dir*, Society of Environmental Graphics Designers, Chicago IL

Corcoran, Frank, *Asst Dir Pub Prog*, National Museum of Man, Ottawa ON

Cordell, Howard, *Dir*, Florida International University Library, Art Department, Miami FL

Cordes, Christopher, *Asst Prof*, University of Rhode Island, Department of Art, Kingston RI (S)

Cordier, Claude, *Conservator*, Musee du Petit Palais, Centre International de Documentation et de Recherche, Avignon France

Cordiner, William, *Assoc Prof*, University of Northern Colorado, Department of Fine Arts, Greeley CO (S)

Corey, Constance, *Acting Asst Librn*, Arizona State University, Hayden Library, Tempe AZ

Corey, Peter L, *Dir, Cur*, Sheldon Jackson College, Sheldon Jackson Museum, Sitka AK

Corinth, Thomas, *Secy*, Lovis Corinth Memorial Foundation, Inc, New York NY

Corle, Karen, *Secy*, Erie Art Center, Erie PA

Corlette, Suzanne, *Cur Cultural History*, New Jersey State Museum, Trenton NJ

Corley, Suber, *VPres*, Cultural Initiative, Toronto ON

Cormack, Malcolm, *Cur Paintings*, Yale University, Yale Center for British Art, New Haven CT

Cormican, John, *Chairperson Div*, Utica College of Syracuse University, Division of Humanities, Utica NY (S)

Cormier, George Anne, *Slide Librn*, San Antonio Museum Association, Inc, Ellen S Quillin Memorial Library, San Antonio TX

Corn, Wanda, *Assoc Prof*, Mills College, Art Department, Oakland CA (S)

Cornelius, Phil, *Area Chmn Ceramics*, Pasadena City College, Art Department, Pasadena CA (S)

Cornell, David, *Librn*, Archie Bray Foundation, Library, Helena MT

Cornell, Dorothy, *Dir*, River Vale Public Library, River Vale NJ

Corning, George, *Pres*, Art Centre of New Jersey, East Orange NJ

Corning, Mary L, *Office Admin*, Wenham Historical Association and Museum, Inc, Wenham MA

Corning, Mary L, *Librn*, Wenham Historical Association and Museum, Inc, Timothy Pickering Library, Wenham MA

Cornman, Maura, *Assoc Cur Conservation*, University of Missouri, Museum of Art and Archaeology, Columbia MO

Corno, Gene, *Instructor*, Mesa Community College, Department of Art, Mesa AZ (S)

Corpier, Leslee N, *Asst Prof*, Mary Baldwin College, Department of Art, Staunton VA (S)

Corr, Jim, *Dir*, Western Montana College, Art Gallery, Dillon MT

Corr, Martha, *Museum Shop Mgr*, Virginia Museum, Danville Museum of Fine Arts and History, Danville VA

Correas, Horacio E, *Dir*, Museo Municipal de Bellas Artes Juan B Castagnino, Municipal Museum of Fine Arts, Rosario Argentina

Correro, Guido, *Assoc Prof*, Herkimer County Community College, Humanities Division, Herkimer NY (S)

Corrigan, Paul J, *Instructor*, Modesto Junior College, Arts Humanities and Speech Division, Modesto CA (S)

Corrigan, Robert W, *Dean*, University of Wisconsin-Milwaukee, Department of Art, Milwaukee WI (S)

Corrigan, Ruth R, *Dir of University Libraries*, Carnegie-Mellon University, Hunt Library, Pittsburgh PA

Cory, Ken, *Librn*, Western Montana College, Library, Dillon MT

Cossitt, F D, *Instr*, Virginia Wesleyan College, Art Department of the Humanities Division, Norfolk VA (S)

Cost, James S, *Instr*, Texas State Technical Institute, Department of Commercial Art, Amarillo TX (S)

Costa, Germana Maria Camarao, *Librn*, Museu de Arte Moderna, Library, Rio Brazil

Costa, Theodore, *Captain and Historian*, Staten Island Ferry Maritime Museum, Staten Island NY

Costantini, Mary, *Chmn Dept*, Caldwell College, Art Department, Caldwell NJ (S)

Costello, Michael, *Instructor*, University of Lowell, Department of Art, Lowell MA (S)

Costigan, Constance C, *Asst Prof*, George Washington University, Department of Art, Washington DC (S)

Cote, Jean-Guy, *Pres Board Dir & Pres Executive Committee*, Le Musee Regional de Rimouski, Rimouski PQ

Cote, Philip, *Chmn Holoyoke Historical Commission*, City of Holyoke Museum-Wistariahurst, Holyoke MA

Cothren, Michael, *Asst Prof*, Swarthmore College, Department of Art, Swarthmore PA (S)

Cotner, Lloyd, *Asst Prof*, Williamsport Area Community College, Department of Engineering and Design, Williamsport PA (S)

Cotton, Juanita, *Asst Prof*, Langston University, Art Department, Langston OK (S)

Cottrill, Tom, *Chmn*, Northeastern Oklahoma State University, Tahlequah OK (S)

Couch, Urban, *Chmn Art Department*, West Virginia University, Galleries A and B, Morgantown WV

Couch, Urban, *Chmn*, West Virginia University, Division of Art, Morgantown WV (S)

Coughlin, Joann, *Pres*, Coos Art Museum, Coos Bay OR

Coulling, S H, *Executive Dir*, Oglebay Institute Mansion Museum, Wheeling WV

Coulling, Stanley H, *Executive Dir*, Oglebay Institute, Stifel Fine Arts Center, Wheeling WV

Coulter, Gary E, *Chmn Dept*, Hastings College, Art Dept, Hastings NE (S)

Coulter, Jerry L, *Prof*, James Madison University, Department of Art, Harrisonburg VA (S)

Coupe, Walter, *VPres*, Providence Art Club, Providence RI

Couper, James M, *Assoc Prof*, Florida International University, Visual Arts Department, Miami FL (S)

Couper, Richard W, *Pres*, New York Public Library, New York NY

Courad, John, *Instructor*, San Diego Mesa College, Art Department, San Diego CA (S)

Courter, Gary, *Instructor*, Umpqua Community College, Art Department, Roseburg OR (S)

Courtney, Kathleen, *Lectr*, Mount Marty College, Art Dept, Yankton SD (S)

Courtney, Keith, *Community Relations*, Art Gallery of Hamilton, Hamilton ON

Courtney, R Howard, *Sales & Rental Chmn*, Peoria Art Guild, Peoria IL

Coutermarsh, Eva, *Admin Asst*, Dartmouth College Museum & Galleries, Hanover NH

Coutu, Paul, *Technician*, Musee d'Art de Joliette, Joliette PQ

Couture, Marie, *Chmn Dept*, Rivier College, Art Department, Nashua NH (S)

Couture, Theresa, *Instr*, Rivier College, Art Department, Nashua NH (S)

Couturier, Darrell J, *Assoc Dir*, Couturier Galerie, Stamford CT

Couturier, Marion B, *Dir*, Couturier Galerie, Stamford CT

Couvee, D H, *Dir*, Frans Halsmuseum, Frans Hals Museum, Haarlem Netherlands

Couvee-Jampoller, L, *Cur*, Rijksmuseum Vincent Van Gogh, Vincent Van Gogh State Museum, Amsterdam Netherlands

Couwenbergh, P M, *Librn*, Stedelijk Museum de Lakenhal, Library, Leiden Netherlands

Covatta, Annette, *Prog Dir*, American Council for the Arts, New York NY

Coverstone, Jean L, *Head Dept*, Grace College, Department of Art, Winona Lake IN (S)

Covey, Victor C B, *Sr Conservator*, National Gallery of Art, Washington DC

Cowan, Lenore, *Cur*, New York Public Library, Picture Collection, New York NY

Cowan, Merrilea, *Cur Archaeology*, Division of Historical and Cultural Affairs, Bureau of Museums and Historic Sites, Dover DE

Cowan, Natalie J, *Head Librn*, California Historical Society, Library, San Francisco CA

Cowardin III, Samuel P, *Assoc Prof*, Clark University, Art Program, Worcester MA (S)

Cowden, Dorothy, *Dir*, University of Tampa, Department of Art, Tampa FL (S)

Cowen, Daniel J, *Instructor*, West Liberty State College, Art Department, West Liberty WV (S)

Cowles, Charles, *Cur*, Seattle Art Museum, Modern Art Pavilion, Seattle WA

Cowles, Gardner, *VChmn*, Museum of Modern Art, New York NY

Cowley, Edward, *Prof*, State University of New York at Albany, Art Department, Albany NY (S)

Cox, Allyn, *Secy*, Art Commission of the City of New York, Associates of the Art Commission, Inc, New York NY

Cox, Angela, *Education Officer*, National Portrait Gallery, London England

Cox, Beverly, *Cur Exhib*, National Portrait Gallery, Washington DC

Cox, David N, *Assoc Prof*, Weber State College, Art Department 2001, Ogden UT (S)

Cox, James D, *Galleries Dir*, Grand Central Art Galleries, Inc, New York NY

Cox, Kathryn D, *Registrar*, Frick Art Museum, Pittsburgh PA

Cox, Lorraine, *Treas*, National Hall of Fame for Famous American Indians, Anadarko OK

Cox, Lynn, *Instructor*, Springfield College, Department of Visual and Performing Arts, Springfield MA (S)

Cox, Marvel, *Instructor*, Sioux City Art Center, Sioux City IA (S)

Cox, Pat, *First VPres*, National Watercolor Society, Pasadena CA

Cox, Robert, *Instructor*, Wayne Art Center, Wayne PA (S)

Coxwell, Roy, *Pres*, Desert Caballeros Western Museum, Wickenburg AZ

Cox III, Joseph L, *Assoc Prof*, Miami University, Art Department, Oxford OH (S)

Coy, Katherine V, *Asst Cur of Prints & Education*, University of California, University Art Galleries and California Museum of Photography, Riverside CA

Coyne, Alice, *Correspondence Secy*, New Hampshire Art Association, Inc, Manchester NH

Cozzi, Ciriaco, *Pres*, Provincetown Art Association and Museum, Provincetown MA

Cozzie, Anthony F, *Dir*, Roswell P Flower Memorial Library, Watertown NY

Crabb, Patrick, *Instructor*, Santa Ana College, Art Department, Santa Ana CA (S)

Crabb, Ted, *Dir & Secy*, University of Wisconsin, Memorial Union Gallery, Madison WI

Crafford, D, *Professional Asst*, Pretoria Art Museum, Pretoria South Africa, Republic of

Craford, Jane, *Slide Bank Dir & Special Studies Program Dir*, Portland Center for the Visual Arts, Portland OR

Craft, Douglas, *Instr*, College of New Rochelle, Art Department, New Rochelle NY (S)

Craig, Albert K, *Librn*, Alabama Department of Archives and History Museum, Library, Montgomery AL

Craig, Christina, *Asst Prof*, Trenton State College, Art Department, Trenton NJ (S)

Craig, Dan, *Instructor*, Northeast Technical Community College, Dept of Art, Norfolk NE (S)

Craig, Glenn, *Sr Librn*, Edinburgh College of Art Library, Edinburgh Scotland

Craig, Jack, *VPres*, Art Gallery of Nova Scotia, Halifax NS

Craig, Kenneth, *Prog Coordr*, Alberta College of Art, Southern Alberta Institute of Technology, Calgary AB (S)

Crain, John W, *Dir*, Dallas Historical Society, Dallas TX

Crain, Kathleen, *Librn*, University of Southwestern Louisiana, Art Center Library, Lafayette LA

Crain, Sally, *VPres*, Cumberland Art Society, Cookeville Art Center, Cookeville TN

Crain, Steve, *Adjunct Instructor*, Lamar University, Art Department, Beaumont TX (S)

Cram, Joanna, *Secy*, Community Arts Council of Vancouver, Vancouver BC

Cramer, Richard, *Gallery Dir*, Temple University, Tyler School of Art-Galleries, Philadelphia PA

Cramer, Richard D, *Head Dept*, University of California, Davis, Art Department, Davis CA (S)

Crandall, James, *Asst Prof*, Pierce College, Art Department, Woodland Hills CA (S)

Crandall, William, *Instructor*, Milwaukee Area Technical College, Graphic & Applied Arts Div, Milwaukee WI (S)

Crane, Charles, *Assoc Prof*, University of Lethbridge, Department of Art, Lethbridge AB (S)

Crane, Diane, *Instructor*, Viterbo College, Art Department, La Crosse WI (S)

Crane, Howard, *Chmn Dept*, Ohio State University, Department of the History of Art, Columbus OH (S)

Crane, Michael, *Dir*, San Jose State University, Art Gallery, San Jose CA

Crane, Robert B, *Dir Corporate Affairs*, Emerson Electric Company, Saint Louis MO

Crane, Ruth, *Registrar*, Fairbanks Museum and Planetarium, Saint Johnsbury VT

Crane, Tim, *Assoc Prof*, Viterbo College, Art Department, La Crosse WI (S)

Cranford, June, *Secy & Registrar*, Rocky Mountain School of Art Gallery, Denver CO

Crangle, William, *Pres*, Canajoharie Library and Art Gallery, Canajoharie NY

Crary Jr, Miner D, *Chairman Board Trustees*, Heckscher Museum, Huntington NY

Crask, R M, *Assoc Prof*, Jefferson Community College, Fine Arts, Louisville KY (S)

Craven, David, *Asst Prof*, State University of New York College at Cortland, Art Department, Cortland NY (S)

Craven, Jayne, *Head Art & Music Department*, Public Library of Cincinnati and Hamilton County, Art and Music Department, Cincinnati OH

Craven Jr, Roy C, *Dir*, University of Florida, University Gallery, Gainesville FL

Crawford, David, *Chmn of Board*, Vermont State Craft Center at Frog Hollow, Middlebury VT

Crawford, Donald D, *Dir*, Lauren Rogers Library and Museum of Art, Laurel MS

Crawford, J J, *Pres*, Strasburg Museum, Strasburg VA

Crawford, Jon, *Instructor*, Ivy School of Professional Art, Downtown Annex, Pittsburgh PA (S)

Crawford, Margaret, *Assoc Prof*, Nazareth College of Rochester, Art Department, Rochester NY (S)

Crawford, Nancy L, *Exec Secy*, Eliot McMurrough School of Art, Melbourne FL (S)

Crawford, Robert, *Dir*, Ridgewood School of Art and Design, Ridgewood NJ (S)

Crawford, Spencer, *Instructor*, East Tennessee State University, Fine Arts Dept, Johnson City TN (S)

Crawford, Vaughn E, *Cur in Charge Ancient Near Eastern Art*, Metropolitan Museum of Art, New York NY

Crawley, Nona, *Secy*, Historical Society of Quincy and Adams County, Quincy IL

Crawshay, William, *Pres*, National Museum of Wales, Cardiff Wales

Creagan, Daniel A, *Chmn*, Spring Hill College, Fine Arts Department, Mobile AL (S)

Creager, Ann, *Conservator*, National Collection of Fine Arts, Washington DC

Creager, Marile, *Asst Dir*, Tacoma Public Library, Handforth Gallery, Tacoma WA

Creamer, George, *Asst Prof*, Wright State University, Art Department, Dayton OH (S)

Creech, Franklin U, *Head*, Gaston College, Art Department, Dallas NC (S)

Creek, Isaac, *Instr*, Bowie State College, Department of Fine and Performing Arts, Bowie MD (S)

Creel, Dana S, *Pres*, Sleepy Hollow Restorations Inc, Tarrytown NY

Crelly, William R, *Prof*, Emory University, Art History Department, Atlanta GA (S)

Crenascol, Louis de, *Prof*, Seton Hall University, Department of Art and Music, South Orange NJ (S)

Crepeau, Pierre, *Chief Canadian Centre for Folk Culture Studies*, National Museum of Man, Ottawa ON

Crepin, Simone, *Asst Librn*, Royal Academy of Fine Arts, Bibliotheque Artistique, Brussels Belgium

Cress, George, *Dir*, University of Tennessee at Chattanooga Art Gallery, Chattanooga TN

Cress, George, *Head*, University of Tennessee at Chattanooga, Department of Art, Chattanooga TN (S)

Cresswell, Pearl, *Asst to Cur*, Fisk University Museum, Nashville TN

Crestreet, Cynthia Ann, *Chmn*, Saint Mary-of-the-Woods College, Art Department, Saint Mary-of-the-Woods IN (S)

Crewe Jr, Leonard C, *Pres*, Maryland Historical Society Museum, Baltimore MD

Crew Jr, Roger T, *Research Asst*, MacArthur Memorial, MacArthur Memorial Library and Archives, Norfolk VA

Crew Jr, Roger T, *Research Asst*, MacArthur Memorial, Norfolk VA

Crews, Polly, *Dir*, Fort Smith Art Center, Fort Smith AR

Cribb-Carsley, Pamela, *Programs Coordr*, Ontario Association of Art Galleries, Toronto ON

Cridge, Edmund, *Head Media Services*, University of Alaska, Elmer E Rasmuson Library, Fairbanks AK

Crighton, R, *Keeper Applied Arts*, University of Cambridge, Fitzwilliam Museum, Cambridge England

Crimmins, Gerald, *Chmn Sculpture&/Metalsmithing*, Moore College of Art, Philadelphia PA (S)

Crisp, Lynn, *Library Asst*, North Carolina State University, Harrye Lyons Design Library, Raleigh NC

Crispino, Luigi, *Chmn Dept*, Franklin College, Art Department, Franklin IN (S)

Critchfield, Harry, *Instructor*, California College of Arts and Crafts, Oakland CA (S)

Crittall, John, *Treas*, Royal College of Art Gallery, London England

Croake, Richard, *Coordr Public Programs*, University of Michigan Museum of Art, Alumni Memorial Hall Museum, Ann Arbor MI

Crocket, David S *Acting Dept Head*, Lafayette College, Department of Art, Easton PA (S)

Crockett, Alan, *Vis Asst Prof*, Texas Tech University, Department of Art, Lubbock TX (S)

Crockett, Richard B, *Pres Board Dir*, Plains Art Museum, Main Gallery, Moorhead MN

Crockett, Ted, *Treas*, Salisbury State College, Wildfowl Art Museum, Salisbury MD

Croft, Dorothy, *Chmn*, Presidential Museum, Odessa TX

Croft, Michael, *Coordr Three-Dimentional Areas*, University of Arizona, Department of Art, Tucson AZ (S)

Croft, Rebecca, *Head Information Center*, Lexington Public Library, Lexington KY

Croft, Thomas, *Asst*, Cathedral Museum of Religious Art, New York NY

Crogahn, Robert, *Asst Prof*, University of North Carolina-Charlotte, Creative Arts Dept, Charlotte NC (S)

Croke, Carolyn, *Chief Librn*, Woodstock Art Gallery, Woodstock ON

Cromwell, L, *Head*, University of Calgary, Department of Art, Calgary AB (S)

Cromwell-Lacy, Sherry, *Dir*, Kansas City Art Institute, Charlotte Crosby Kemper Gallery, Kansas City MO

Cronk, Frank, *Assoc Prof*, University of Idaho, Department of Art and Architecture, Moscow ID (S)

Crook, J, *Head Dept Three-Dimensional Design*, Brighton Polytechnic, Faculty of Art and Design, Brighton England (S)

Crooker, M J A, *Assoc Prof*, Mount Allison University, Fine Arts Department, Sackville NB (S)

Crosby, Peter, *Secy*, Fairbanks Museum and Planetarium, Saint Johnsbury VT

Crosby, Ranice W, *Dir Dept*, Johns Hopkins University, School of Medicine, Department of Art as Applied to Medicine, Baltimore MD (S)

Cross, F K, *Dir*, Attleboro Museum, Center for the Arts, Attleboro MA

Cross, Kenneth, *Honorary Treas*, Community Arts Council of Vancouver, Vancouver BC

Crossin, A L, *Pres Manitoba Historicas Society*, Manitoba Historical Society, Dalnavert - MacDonald House Museum, Winnipeg MB

Cross Jr, Frank Moore, *Dir*, Harvard University, Harvard Semitic Museum, Cambridge MA

Crossnoe, Thomas G, *Chmn*, Midwestern State University, Department of Art, Wichita Falls TX (S)

Croton, Lynn, *Prof*, School of the Arts, C W Post Center of Long Island University, Art Department, Greenvale NY (S)

Crouse, Barbara B, *Dir*, Art Association of Jacksonville, David Strawn Art Gallery, Jacksonville IL

Crouse, Jack W, *Instructor*, Olympic College, Art Department, Bremerton WA (S)

Crouse, Michael G, *Asst Dir*, Art Association of Jacksonville, David Strawn Art Gallery, Jacksonville IL

Crow, Kenneth V, *Instructor*, Olympic College, Art Department, Bremerton WA (S)

Crow, Martha, *Dir*, Avila College, Art Gallery, Kansas City MO

Crow, Martha, *Instr*, Avila College, Art Department, Kansas City MO (S)

Crowder, Charles, *Dir Music*, Phillips Collection, Washington DC

Crowe, Edith, *Art Reference Librn*, San Jose State University, Art Department Library, San Jose CA

Crowell, Andrea, *Admin Secy*, Sierra Nevada Museum of Art, Reno NV

Crowell, Cathy Cherry, *Instr*, Newberry College, Department of Art, Newberry SC (S)

Crowell, Richard B, *VPres*, Central Louisiana Art Association, Alexandria Museum Visual Art Center, Alexandria LA

Crowfoot, H L, *Dir*, Jordan Historical Museum of The Twenty, Jordan ON

Crowley, Jane Sullivan, *Dir*, Morris-Jumel Mansion, New York NY

Crowley, Pat, *Dir*, Texas Christian University, Student Center Gallery, Ft Worth TX

Crown, Ruth, *Secy*, Federated Art Associations of New Jersey, Inc, Westfield NJ

Crown III, William, *Treas*, Florida Gulf Coast Art Center, Inc, Clearwater FL

Croy, Robert, *Design & Exhib Dir*, Owensboro Museum of Fine Art, Owensboro KY

Croydon, Michael, *Prof*, Lake Forest College, Dept of Art, Lake Forest IL (S)

Crozier, John, *Librn*, Santa Barbara Museum of Art, Library, Santa Barbara CA

Cruger, George, *Head Communications Division*, Virginia Museum of Fine Arts, Richmond VA

Cruise, J E, *Dir*, Royal Ontario Museum, Canadiana Gallery, Toronto ON

Cruise, James E, *Dir*, Royal Ontario Museum, Toronto ON

Crumet, Helen, *Main Gallery Chairperson*, Licking County Art Association Gallery, Newark OH

Crumpler, Reva, *Communications Officer*, J B Speed Art Museum, Louisville KY

Cruser, Patricia, *Assoc Dean Liberal Arts*, Philadelphia College of Art, Philadelphia PA (S)

Crutchfield, Vonnie, *Secy*, Laguna Beach Museum of Art, Laguna Beach CA

Cruz, Lucy, *Pres of Board*, Harwood Foundation of the University of New Mexico, Taos NM

Cruz, Maria Socorro, *Prof*, Institute of Puerto Rican Culture, Escuela de Artes Plasticas, Mayaguez PR (S)

Cubbs, Joanne, *Lectr*, Cardinal Stritch College, Art Department, Milwaukee WI (S)

Cucksey, Roger, *Keeper of Art*, Newport Museum and Art Gallery, Newport Wales

Cuddy, Joan, *Slide Librn*, Alberta College of Art Gallery, Library, Calgary AB

Cudecki, Edwin, *Pres*, Polish Museum of America, Chicago IL

Cullen, John, *Asst to Dir*, California State University, Los Angeles, Fine Arts Gallery, Los Angeles CA

Culley, Paul T, *Head Technical Reference*, New York State College of Ceramics at Alfred University, Scholes Library of Ceramics, Alfred NY

Culley, Robert, *Div Coordr Painting*, Kent State University, School of Art, Kent OH (S)

Culver, R Neal, *Treas*, Dulin Gallery of Art, Knoxville TN

Culverwell, Albert H, *Dir*, Eastern Washington State Historical Society, Cheney Cowles Memorial Museum, Spokane WA

Cumbers, Maureen, *Executive Producer*, National Film Board of Canada, Still Photography Division, Photo Gallery, Ottawa ON

Cumings, Frederick J, *Dir*, Detroit Institute of Arts, Detroit MI

Cumming, Doug, *Assoc Prof*, University of Wisconsin-Stout, Art Department, Menomonie WI (S)

Cumming, Glen E, *Dir*, Art Gallery of Hamilton, Hamilton ON

Cumming, Moira, *Secy*, Huntsville Art League and Museum Association Inc, Huntsville AL

Cumming, Robert, *Assoc Prof*, Hartford Art School of the University of Hartford, West Hartford CT (S)

Cumming, William, *Instructor*, Burnley School of Professional Art, Inc, Seattle WA (S)

Cummings, Abbott L, *Exec Dir*, Society for the Preservation of New England Antiquities, Boston MA

Cummings, Frederick J, *Executive Dir*, Detroit Institute of Arts, Detroit Institute of Art Founders Society, Detroit MI

Cummings, George, *Instructor*, Portland Art Museum, Museum Art School, Portland OR (S)

Cummings, Hildegard, *Exhib Coordr*, University of Connecticut, William Benton Museum of Art, Storrs CT

Cummings, John B, *Treas*, Roberson Center, Binghamton NY

Cummings, Paul, *Pres*, The Drawing Society, New York NY

Cummings, Paul, *Cur*, Whitney Museum of American Art, New York NY

Cummins, Karen, *Asst Dir*, New Jersey State Museum, Trenton NJ

Cundiff, Linda, *Instr*, Parkersburg Community College, Art Department, Parkersburg WV (S)

Cunliffe, Nanette, *Instructor*, Rehoboth Art League, Inc, Rehoboth Beach DE (S)

Cunningham, Carole, *Registrar*, University of Michigan Museum of Art, Alumni Memorial Hall Museum, Ann Arbor MI

Cunningham, Jan, *Admin Asst*, Southeast Alaska Regional Arts Council, Inc, Sitka AK

Cunningham, John, *Instructor*, Ohio Visual Art Institute, Cincinnati OH (S)

Cunningham, John, *Pres*, Carmel Art Institute, Carmel CA (S)

Cunningham, Judy, *Dir of Museum School*, Philbrook Art Center, Tulsa OK

Cunningham, Linda, *Asst Prof*, Franklin and Marshall College, Art Department, Lancaster PA (S)

Cunningham, Mem, *VPres*, Artists Coalition of Texas, Dallas TX

Cunningham, Robert, *Asst Dir*, Queensland Art Gallery, Brisbane Australia

Cunningham, Roland C, *Conservator*, Wadsworth Atheneum, Hartford CT

Cunningham, Shirley, *Museum Asst*, Ships of The Sea Museum, Savannah GA

Curfman, John, *Prof*, Colorado State University, Department of Art, Fort Collins CO (S)

Curini, Walter, *Vis Prof*, Fortman Studios Florence, Florence Italy (S)

Curlee, Barbara B, *Chmn*, Northeast Mississippi Junior College, Art Department, Booneville MS (S)

Curran, Joan, *Instr*, Bucknell University, Department of Art, Lewisburg PA (S)

Curri, Claudio B, *Instr*, Studio Art Centers International, Florence Italy (S)

Currie, William, *Dir and Pres*, Hallwalls Gallery, Buffalo NY

Currier, Mary Ann, *Instructor*, Louisville School of Art, Anchorage KY (S)

Currier, Prescott, *Pres*, Lincoln County Cultural and Historical Association, Wiscasset ME

Curry, Brian, *Business Mgr*, League of New Hampshire Craftsmen, Concord NH

Curry, Crossan H, *Assoc Prof*, Miami University, Art Department, Oxford OH (S)

Curry, D, *Keeper of National History*, Plymouth City Museum and Art Gallery, Plymouth England

Curry, David, *Instructor*, Sacramento City College, Art Department, Sacramento CA (S)

Curry, Gwen, *Instr*, University of Victoria, Department of Visual Arts, Victoria BC (S)

Curry, W G, *Pres*, Art Gallery of Windsor, Windsor ON

Curtis, Brian, *Asst Prof*, Hillsdale College, Art Dept, Hillsdale MI (S)

Curtis, Frances, *Gallery Hostess*, Pemaquid Group of Artists, Lewiston ME

Curtis, George H, *Asst Dir*, Harry S Truman Library and Museum, Independence MO

Curtis, Howard W, *Cur*, Haverhill Public Library, Haverhill MA

Curtis, John O, *Dir Cur Dept*, Old Sturbridge Village, Sturbridge MA

Curtis, Nelson, *Prof*, University of Idaho, Department of Art and Architecture, Moscow ID (S)

Curtis, Philip H, *Cur Decorative Arts*, Newark Museum, Newark NJ

Curtis, Roger, *Treas*, North Shore Arts Associaiton, Inc, Gloucester MA

Curtis, Samuel L, *Chmn Dept*, Cheyney State College, Department of Art, Cheyney PA (S)

Curtis, Sandra J, *Area Collector*, Archives of American Art, Texas Area Center: Museum of Fine Arts, New York NY

Curtis, Verna, *Asst Cur*, Milwaukee Art Center, Milwaukee WI

Curtis, Walter D, *Asst Prof*, University of Arkansas, Art Department, Fayetteville AR (S)

Curtis, Winifred, *Secy*, North Shore Arts Associaiton, Inc, Gloucester MA

Curtiss, Harold M, *Pres*, Sheldon Art Museum, Middlebury VT

Cushing, Barbara, *Assoc Prof*, University of Maine, Art Department, Orono ME (S)

Cushing, John D, *Librn*, Massachusetts Historical Society, Library, Boston MA

Cushing, Stanley E, *Librn*, Guild of Book Workers, Library, New York NY

Cusick, Jessica, *Project Coordr*, Public Art Fund, Inc, New York NY

Custer, Austin, *Education Coordr*, Anderson Fine Arts Center, Anderson IN

Cutler, Anthony, *Prof*, Pennsylvania State University, University Park, Department of Art History, University Park PA (S)

Cymbalsity, B, *Pres*, Ukrainian Museum, New York NY

Cyr, Paul, *Dept Head Genealogy & Whaling Coll*, New Bedford Free Public Library, New Bedford MA

Czainuki, James, *Asst Prof*, State University of New York College at Potsdam, Department of Fine Arts, Potsdam NY (S)

Czarniecki III, M J, *Dir*, Mississippi Museum of Art, Jackson MS

Czartoryska, Urszula, *Cur*, Muzeum Sztuki, Lodz Poland

Czerner, Olgierd, *Dir*, Ministry of Culture and Art, Museum of Architecture in Wroclaw, Wroclaw Poland

Czestochowski, Joseph, *Dir*, Cedar Rapids Art Center, Cedar Rapids IA

Czichos, Raymond L, *Dir*, Pioneer Town, Wimberley TX

Czuma, Stansilaw, *Cur Indian Art*, Cleveland Museum of Art, Cleveland OH

Dabash, Adrian G, *Instructor*, Providence College, Department of Fine Arts, Providence RI (S)

Dachman, Linda, *Public Information Mgr*, San Francisco Art Institute, San Francisco CA

daCosta-Nunes, Hedy, *Instructor*, Monmouth College, Department of Art, West Long Branch NJ (S)

Dagel, Linda, *Dir*, Muscatine Art Center, Muscatine IA

Dagenais, Margaret, *Prof*, Loyola University of Chicago, Fine Arts Department, Chicago IL (S)

Daggett, Bradford, *Pres*, Art Institute of Pittsburgh, Pittsburgh PA (S)

Daggett, Bradford, *Pres*, Art Institute of Pittsburgh Gallery, Pittsburgh PA

D'Agostino, Peter, *Asst Prof*, Wright State University, Art Department, Dayton OH (S)

Dahlen, Marilyn, *Secy*, Coquille Valley Art Association, Coquille OR

Dahlquist, Marcy, *Chmn Communications*, Minneapolis Institute of Arts, Minneapolis MN

Dahlstrom, Nancy, *Assoc Prof*, Hollins College, Art Department, Hollins VA (S)

Dahoda, Peter, *Prof*, Miami University, Art Department, Oxford OH (S)

Daigle, Jean, *Dir*, Gallerie d'Art de l'Universite de Moncton, Moncton NB

Dailey, Charles, *Dir*, Institute of American Indian Arts Museum, Santa Fe NM

Dailey, Charles A, *Dir*, Institute of American Indian Arts, Santa Fe NM (S)

Dailey, Dan, *Chmn Fine Arts-3D*, Massachusetts College of Art, Boston MA (S)

Dailey, William, *Assoc Prof*, University of North Carolina-Charlotte, Creative Arts Dept, Charlotte NC (S)

Dainton, Fred, *Chmn British Library Board*, British Library, Reference Division, London England

Daitzman, Eleanor, *Admin Dir*, Main Line Center of the Arts, Haverford PA

Daitzman, Eleanor, *Admin Dir*, Mainline Center of the Arts, Haverford PA (S)

Daives, James, *Dean*, Nova Scotia College of Art and Design, Anna Leonowens Gallery, Halifax NS

Dake, Dennis, *Coordr Art Educ*, Iowa State University, Department of Design, Ames IA (S)

Dale, Libby, *Community Relations Officer*, First National Bank, Fort Collins CO

Dale, Linda, *Information Officer*, Newfoundland Museum, Saint John's NF

Dale, Marianne, *Library Asst*, North Carolina State University, Harrye Lyons Design Library, Raleigh NC

Dale, Sharon, *Instructor*, Allegheny College, Art Department, Meadville PA (S)

Dalenius, Majory, *Gallery Secy*, Providence Art Club, Providence RI

Daley, Lee, *Owner*, Danforth Museum School, Framingham MA (S)

Dallavis, Olive Louise, *Pres*, Avila College, Art Gallery, Kansas City MO

Dalton, Mary, *Public Relations*, Midland Art Council of the Midland Center for the Arts, Midland MI

Dalton, Nancy C, *Secy*, Westfield Athenaeum, Jasper Rand Art Museum, Westfield MA

Daltrop, Georg, *Cur for Classical Art (Greek & Roman Sculpture)*, Monumenti Musei e Gallerie Pontificie, Vatican Museums and Galleries, Vatican City Italy

DaLuiso, Florence S, *Art Librn*, State University of New York at Buffalo, Lockwood Memorial Library, Buffalo NY

Daly, Charles, *Instr*, College of New Rochelle, Art Department, New Rochelle NY (S)

Daly, Florence, *VPres*, Kennebec Valley Art Association, Harlow Gallery, Hallowell ME

Daly, Russell, *Chmn Sculpture*, Swain School of Design, New Bedford MA (S)

Daly, Stephen, *Asst Prof*, University of Texas at San Antonio, Division of Art and Design, San Antonio TX (S)

Dalzotto, Eugene, *Prof*, Bemidji State University, Art Department, Bemidji MN (S)

D'Amato, Juliana, *Prof*, Albertus Magnus College, Art Department, New Haven CT (S)

Dambach, Charles F, *Executive Dir*, National Assembly of Community Arts Agencies, Washington DC

D'Ambrosio, Domenica, *Staff Member*, Armeria Reale, Turin Italy

Damianos, Sylvester, *Pres*, Pittsburgh Plan for Art Gallery, Pittsburgh PA

Damico, Chris, *Instructor*, Ocean City School of Art, Ocean City NJ (S)

Damm, Judith, *Asst Chmn Advertising Design*, Art Institute of Fort Lauderdale, Fort Lauderdale FL (S)

Damon, Alan, *Assoc Prof*, New York City Community College of the City University of New York, Department of Art and Advertising Design, Brooklyn NY (S)

Damon, T A, *Dir*, United States Navy Memorial Museum, Washington DC

Damron, John, *Recording Secy*, American Artists Professional League, Inc, New York NY

Dancy, Sherrie, *Instr*, Wilkes Community College, Arts and Science Division, Wilkesboro NC (S)

Dandignac, Pat, *Editor-in-Chief American Craft Magazine*, American Craft Council, New York NY

D'Andrea, Jeanne, *Cur Exhib and Publications*, Los Angeles County Museum of Art, Los Angeles CA

Dane, William J, *Supv Art & Music Department*, Newark Public Library, Newark NJ

Danforth, Charles D, *Chmn Div*, University of Maine at Augusta, Division of Arts and Humanities, Augusta ME (S)

D'Angelo, George A, *Pres*, Philadelphia Art Alliance, Philadelphia PA

D'Angelo, Maria J, *Assoc Prof*, Mount Aloysius Junior College, Art Department, Cresson PA (S)

Daniel, Betty, *Library Records*, Washington University, Art and Architecture Library, Saint Louis MO

Daniel, Fred, *Gallery Asst*, California State University, Los Angeles, Fine Arts Gallery, Los Angeles CA

Daniel, Keith, *Chmn*, Assumption College, Department of Fine Arts and Music, Worcester MA (S)

Daniel, Suzanne, *Asst Prof*, Morgan State University, Department of Art, Baltimore MD (S)

Daniels, Dan, *In Charge Art Coll & Dir Public Relations*, M Grumbacher Inc, New York NY

Daniels, John P, *Head Education & State Service,* John and Mable Ringling Museum of Art, Sarasota FL

Daniels, Ronald B, *Chief Public Services,* Bucknell University, Ellen Clarke Bertrand Library, Lewisburg PA

Danielson, Cornelia, *Adjunct Lectr,* Manhattan College, School of Arts and Sciences, Bronx NY (S)

Danielson, J Deering, *Chmn Board Governors,* Metropolitan Museum and Art Centers, Coral Gables FL

Danielson, Phyllis I, *Dir,* Kendall School of Design, Grand Rapids MI (S)

Danner, Katharine, *Dir,* Southern Oregon College, Stevenson Union Art Gallery, Ashland OR

Dannials, Earnie, *Program Advisor,* University of Southwestern Louisiana, Union Art Gallery, Lafayette LA

Danoff, I Michael, *Assoc Dir,* Milwaukee Art Center, Milwaukee WI

Dantzic, Cynthia, *Dir,* Long Island University, Brooklyn Center Art Department, Brooklyn NY (S)

Danziger, Lucy, *VPres,* Museum of American Folk Art, New York NY

Daoud, Rihab, *Librn,* National Museum of Damascus, Library, Damascus Syria

Dar, Saifur Rahman, *Dir,* Lahore Museum, Lahore Pakistan

Dardess, Betty, *Pres,* Tennessee Valley Art Center, Tuscumbia AL

d'Argence, Rene Yvon Lefebvre, *Dir & Chief Cur,* Asian Art Museum of San Francisco, Avery Brundage Collection, San Francisco CA

D'Arista, Robert, *Chmn,* American University, Watkins Art Gallery, Washington DC

D'Arista, Robert, *Chmn Dept,* American University, Department of Art, Washington DC (S)

Darke, M H, *Head Dept Environmental Design,* Manchester Polytechnic, Faculty of Art and Design, Manchester England (S)

Darling, Janina, *Instructor,* Eastern Illinois University, Art Department, Charleston IL (S)

Darling, Sharon, *Cur Decorative Arts,* Chicago Historical Society, Chicago IL

D'Arms, John, *Dir,* American Academy in Rome, New York NY

D'Arms, John H, *Dir,* American Academy in Rome, Rome Italy (S)

Darrow, Paul, *Prof,* Scripps College, Art Department, Claremont CA (S)

Darst, Lise, *Museum Cur,* Rosenberg Library, Galveston TX

Daste, Nowell A, *Head Dept,* McNeese State University, Department of Visual Arts, Lake Charles LA (S)

Dattel, Michael, *Dir Advertising/Graphic Design,* Academy of Art College, San Francisco CA (S)

Daube, Leon, *Pres,* Charles B Goddard Center for the Visual and Performing Arts, Ardmore OK

Daugherty, Charles, *Prof,* Pomona College, Art Department, Claremont CA (S)

Daugherty, Frances P, *Chmn Art History,* East Carolina University, School of Art, Greenville NC (S)

Daugherty, Marshall, *Chmn,* Mercer University, Art Department, Macon GA (S)

Daum, Timothy, *Asst Art Librn,* Ohio University, Fine Arts Library, Athens OH

Daval, M Jean-Luc, *10Head,* Ecoles d'Art de Geneve, Ecole Superieure D'Art Visuel, Geneva Switzerland (S)

D'Avanzo, Suzanne H, *Instructor,* Providence College, Department of Fine Arts, Providence RI (S)

Dave, Teresa, *Instructor,* Gable Advertising Art School, Division of Advertising Design School, Inc, Cincinnati OH (S)

Davenport, Patricia, *Cur Educ,* El Paso Museum of Art, El Paso TX

Davern, Jeremyn, *Public Affairs Dir,* Grand Central Art Galleries, Inc, New York NY

Davezac, Bertrand, *Vis Lectr,* Rice University, Department of Art and Art History, Houston TX (S)

Davi, Susan A, *Reference Librn (Art & Art History),* University of Delaware, Morris Library, Newark DE

David, Agnes, *Pres,* Associated Artists of Winston-Salem, Winston-Salem NC

David, Honore S, *Chmn Education Dept,* Dayton Art Institute, Dayton OH

Davidock, Peter, *Registrar,* National Gallery of Art, Washington DC

Davidson, Bernice, *Research Cur,* Frick Collection, New York NY

Davidson, Carl Melvin, *Dean College Fine & Communication Arts,* Loyola Marymount University, Department of Art, Los Angeles CA (S)

Davidson, Karen, *Staff Asst,* Harvard University, Busch-Reisinger Museum, Cambridge MA

Davidson, Kay M, *Instructor,* Leeward Community College, Arts and Humanities Division, Pearl City HI (S)

Davidson, Marilyn, *Secy,* Windward Artists Guild, Kailua HI

Davidson, Paul, *Vis Prof,* Oral Roberts University, Fine Arts Department, Tulsa OK (S)

Davidson-Powers, Cynthia, *Public Information Officer,* Akron Art Institute, Akron OH

Daviee, Jerry M, *Cur of Art,* Amarillo Art Center, Amarillo TX

Davies, Betse, *Registrar,* University of Utah, Utah Museum of Fine Arts, Salt Lake City UT

Davies, Cynthia, *Cur Harvey Coll,* Heard Museum, Phoenix AZ

Davies, Hugh M, *Dir,* University of Massachusetts, Amherst, University Gallery, Amherst MA

Davies, James, *Pres,* Swain School of Design, William W Crapo Gallery, New Bedford MA

Davies, James R, *Pres,* Swain School of Design, New Bedford MA (S)

Davila, Arturo, *Prof,* Institute of Puerto Rican Culture, Escuela de Artes Plasticas, Mayaguez PR (S)

Davila, Arturo V, *Dir,* University of Puerto Rico, Museum of Archaeology, History and Art, Rio Piedras PR

Davis, Ann Marie, *Dir,* Tyringham Art Galleries, Tyringham MA

Davis, Art, *Asst Prof,* Grace College, Department of Art, Winona Lake IN (S)

Davis, Ben, *Video Chmn,* Atlanta College of Art, Atlanta GA (S)

Davis, Charles B, *Pres,* Federated Arts Council of Richmond, Inc, Richmond VA

Davis, C Malcolm, *Pres,* Newark Museum, Newark NJ

Davis, Colonius, *Prof,* Southampton College of Long Island University, Fine Arts Division, Southampton NY (S)

Davis, Constance, *Asst Prof,* McNeese State University, Department of Visual Arts, Lake Charles LA (S)

Davis, Cynthia, *VPres,* Second Street Gallery, Charlottesville VA

Davis, D Jack, *Head Dept,* North Texas State University, Art Department, Denton TX (S)

Davis, Darwin R, *Dir,* Battle Creek Civic Art Center, Battle Creek MI

Davis, David, *Division Chmn,* Fordham University, New York NY (S)

Davis, Don F, *Chmn Dept,* Southern Illinois University at Edwardsville, Department of Art and Design, Edwardsville IL (S)

Davis, Donald, *Dir,* Tyringham Art Galleries, Tyringham MA

Davis, Dustin P, *Gallery Dir,* Frostburg State College, Fine Arts Gallery I, Frostburg MD

Davis, Frank R, *Treas,* Philadelphia Sketch Club Inc, Philadelphia PA

Davis, Jack, *Chmn Dept,* Beaver College, Department of Fine Arts, Glenside PA (S)

Davis, Jack, *Chmn Dept Fine Arts,* Beaver College, Eugene R Fuller Gallery of Art, Glenside PA

Davis, Joan C, *Dir,* Bob Jones University, Greenville SC

Davis, John E, *Lectr,* Ladycliff College, Art Department, Highland Falls NY (S)

Davis, John R, *Gallery Cur,* McLean County Art Association, Bloomington IL

Davis, Keith F, *Cur,* Hallmark Cards, Inc, Hallmark Collections, Kansas City MO

Davis, Larry H, *Assoc Prof,* Midwestern State University, Department of Art, Wichita Falls TX (S)

Davis, Lee Baxter, *Chmn Graphics,* East Texas State University, Department of Art, Commerce TX (S)

Davis, Margaret, *Photographer,* Southern Oregon Historical Society, Jacksonville Museum, Jacksonville OR

Davis, Marilyn, *Controller,* Seattle Art Museum, Seattle WA

Davis, Mary, *Librn,* University of Kentucky, Art Library, Lexington KY

Davis, Mary B, *Librn,* Huntington Free Library and Reading Room, Depository Library for the Museum of the American Indian, Bronx NY

Davis, Michael, *Instr,* Mount Saint Mary's College, Art Department, Los Angeles CA (S)

Davis, Norma, *Secy,* Los Alamos Arts Council, Los Alamos NM

Davis, Patty Morton, *Dir,* Pacific Grove Art Center, Pacific Grove CA

Davis, Paul, *Instructor,* Saginaw Valley State College, Dept of Art & Design, University Center MI (S)

Davis, Paul, *Prof,* University of Utah, Art Department, Salt Lake City UT (S)

Davis, Richard, *Sculpture Coordr,* North Texas State University, Art Department, Denton TX (S)

Davis, Richard P, *Secy,* Everson Museum of Art, Syracuse NY

Davis, Robert S, *Pres,* Providence Athenaeum, Providence RI

DAvis, Robert S, *Pres,* Providence Athenaeum, Library, Providence RI

Davis, Sue, *Secy,* Waterloo Art Association, Waterloo IA

Davis, Susan, *Asst Prof,* Loma Linda University, La Sierra Campus, Art Department, Riverside CA (S)

Davis, Trudy, *Librn,* Woodrow Wilson Birthplace Foundation, Library, Staunton VA

Davis, Virginia Irby, *Asst Prof,* Lynchburg College, Art Department, Lynchburg VA (S)

Davis, W M, *VPres,* New England School of Art and Design, Boston MA (S)

Davis, Wayne, *Instructor,* Rudolph Schaeffer School of Design, San Francisco CA (S)

Davis, Wes, *Dir,* Angelo State University, Houston Harte University Center, San Angelo TX

Davis, William D, *Asst Dir,* Pennsylvania State University, Museum of Art, University Park PA

Davis, Willis H, *Assoc Prof,* Miami University, Art Department, Oxford OH (S)

Davis, Willis Bing, *Chmn,* Central State University, Department of Art, Wilberforce OH (S)

Davis Jr, Colis, *Dir Photography,* Hampton Center for Arts and Humanities, Hampton VA

Davis Jr, H Chace, *Treas,* Peale Museum, Baltimore MD

Daw, Robert H, *Fine Arts Chmn,* Topeka Public Library, Topeka KS

Dawkins, Jimmie, *Asst Prof,* Alabama A & M University, Art Education Department, Huntsville AL (S)

Dawley, Gisela, *Owner,* Gisela Dawley Art Studio, Simi Valley CA (S)

Dawson, Bess, *Dir,* Mississippi Art Colony, Meridian MS

Dawson, John M, *Dir of Libraries,* University of Delaware, Morris Library, Newark DE

Dawson, Robert, *VPres Public Affairs,* Greenfield Village and Henry Ford Museum, Dearborn MI

Dawson, Schyular, *Instructor,* Ocean City School of Art, Ocean City NJ (S)

Day, Angela, *Secy,* University of Exeter, American Arts Documentation Centre, Exeter England

Day, Ben, *Assoc Prof,* Boston University, School of Visual Arts, Boston MA (S)

Day, David, *Instructor*, Wayne Art Center, Wayne PA (S)

Day, Gary, *Asst Prof*, University of Nebraska at Omaha, Dept of Art, Omaha NE (S)

Day, Holliday T, *Cur of American Art*, Joslyn Art Museum, Omaha NE

Day, J Dennis, *Dir*, Salt Lake City Public Library, Fine Arts Department, Salt Lake City UT

Day, Jean, *Secy*, Coos Art Museum, Coos Bay OR

Day, John A, *Chmn Dept*, University of South Dakota, Dept of Art, Vermillion SD (S)

Day, John A, *Dir*, University of South Dakota Art Galleries, Vermillion SD

Day, Maurice, *VPres*, Pemaquid Group of Artists, Lewiston ME

Day, Stan, *Head*, University of Saskatchewan, Saskatoon Campus, Department of Art, Saskatoon SK (S)

Day, Steve, *Preservation Dir*, Oklahoma Historical Society, Central Museum, Oklahoma City OK

Day, William, *Deputy Dir*, Studio Museum in Harlem, New York NY

Day Jr, Philip A, *Acting Chmn*, Westminster College, Department of Art, Salt Lake City UT (S)

Dayton, Gary A, *Librn & Archivist*, Burchfield Center, Burchfield Center Resource Room, Buffalo NY

Dayton, Gary A, *Registrar*, Burchfield Center, Buffalo NY

Deaderickm, Joseph, *Prof*, University of Wyoming, Art Department, Laramie WY (S)

Deal, Joe, *Cur of Collections*, University of California, University Art Galleries and California Museum of Photography, Riverside CA

Deal, Joe M, *Asst Prof*, University of California, Riverside, Program in Art, Riverside CA (S)

Deal, Mary Lou, *Staff*, Hand Work Shop, Inc, Richmond VA

Deal, Ronald, *Treas*, Hickory Museum of Art, Inc, Hickory NC

Deale, Vail, *Dir & Librn*, Beloit College, Morse Library, Beloit WI

Dean, Bruce, *Instr*, Lane Community College, Art and Applied Design Department, Eugene OR (S)

Dean, Doug, *Asst Dir*, Southwestern School of Art, Albuquerque NM (S)

Dean, Grant, *Past-Chmn*, Special Libraries Association, Museum, Arts and Humanities Division, New York NY

Dean, Harvey A, *Dir*, East Tennessee State University, Carroll Reece Museum, Johnson City TN

Dean, James, *Cur of Art*, National Air and Space Museum, Washington DC

Dean, Lina, *Instructor*, Interlochen Arts Academy, Dept of Visual Art, Interlochen MI (S)

Dean, Richard, *Asst Prof*, Dean Junior College, Visual and Performing Arts Department, Franklin MA (S)

Dean, Sonia, *Asst Dir*, National Gallery of Victoria, Melbourne Australia

Deane, John C, *VPres*, Sierra Nevada Museum of Art, Reno NV

Dear, Adelaide, *Secy*, Jersey City Museum Association, Jersey City NJ

de Araujo, Alicia Torres, *Dir*, Museo de Arte—Jose Luis Bello y Gonzales, Museum of Art, Puebla Mexico

Dearborn, Mona, *Keeper Catalog of American Portraits*, National Portrait Gallery, Washington DC

Deardorf, Catherine, *Membership*, Blanden Memorial Art Gallery, Fort Dodge IA

Dearsley-Vernon, Ann, *Dir Education*, Chrysler Museum, Norfolk VA

de Artasanchez, Pamela M, *Chairperson*, Universidad de las Americas, Galeria de Arte, Cholula Mexico

Dearth, Robert, *Dir Office Cultural Affairs Oakland Univ*, Oakland University, Meadow Brook Art Gallery, Rochester MI

de Ayoroa, Jane Harmon, *Exhib Coordr*, Museum of Modern Art of Latin America, Washington DC

de Bary, Catherine, *Newsletter Editor*, Women in the Arts Foundation, Inc, New York NY

Debbaut, J, *Cur*, Municipal van Abbemuseum, Eindhoven Municipal Museum, Eindhoven Netherlands

de Bengoechea Niebla, D Javier, *Dir*, Museo de Bellas Artes, Museum of Fine Arts, Bilbao Spain

de Beurs, Frederica, *Art Librn*, Malden Public Library, Malden MA

de Bisthoven, A Janssens, *Dir*, Stedelyke Musea, City Museums, Bruges Belgium

de Bluyne, J I H, *Secy*, Nationaal Glasmuseum, Leerdam Netherlands

DeBoer, Roy H, *Chmn*, Rutgers, the State University of New Jersey, Cook College, Department of Landscape Architecture, New Brunswick NJ (S)

de Bruijn, J G, *Librn*, Teylers Museum, Library, Haarlem Netherlands

Debs, Barbara Knowles, *Pres*, Manhattanville College, Brownson Art Gallery, Purchase NY

DeCandido, Grace Anne, *Reference Librn & Cataloguer*, Parsons School of Design, Adam L Gimbel Library, New York NY

DeCato, Carolyn Clark, *Registrar*, Walker Art Center, Minneapolis MN

de Cecilia, Janet, *Asst Prof*, New York Institute of Technology, Fine Arts Department, Old Westbury NY (S)

de Chero, Peter, *Chmn*, National Assembly of State Arts Agencies, Washington DC

Decker, Bernhard, *Staff*, Liebieghaus, Museum Alter Plastik, Museum of Sculpture, Frankfurt Germany, Federal Republic of

Decker, David O, *Assoc Prof*, University of Maine, Art Department, Orono ME (S)

Decker, Geri, *Librn*, University of Notre Dame, Architecture Library, Notre Dame IN

de Clapp, Anne, *Chmn*, Wellesley College, Art Department, Wellesley MA (S)

DeConcini, Barbara, *Academic Chmn*, Atlanta College of Art, Atlanta GA (S)

DeConcini, Dino, *Chmn*, Arizona Commission on the Arts, Phoenix AZ

de Coninck, Suzanne, *Secy*, Musee d'Art Moderne de la Ville de Paris, Paris France

Decoteau, Pamela, *Asst Chmn Dept*, Southern Illinois University at Edwardsville, Department of Art and Design, Edwardsville IL (S)

de Cruz, Adele, *Conservator*, North Carolina Museum of Art, Department of Cultural Resources, Raleigh NC

de Deo, M, *Chmn*, Thomas More College, Art Department, Fort Mitchell KY (S)

Dedrick, Philip, *Chmn Dept Fine Arts*, Rockford College, Department of Fine Arts, Rockford IL (S)

de Duncan, Gloria, *Instr*, Inter American University of Puerto Rico, Department of Performing Arts, San German PR (S)

Dee, Elaine Evans, *Cur Drawings & Prints*, Cooper-Hewitt Museum, Smithsonian Institution National Museum of Design, New York NY

Deemer, Jean, *Instr*, Cuyahoga Valley Art Center, Cuyahoga Falls OH (S)

Deering, Roger, *Dir*, Roger Deering School of Outdoor Painting, Kennebunkport ME (S)

Deering, Ronald F, *Cur*, Southern Baptist Seminary Museum, Louisville KY

Deering, Winifred, *Registrar & Secy*, Roger Deering School of Outdoor Painting, Kennebunkport ME (S)

Deese, Rupert, *Instructor*, Cuesta College, Art Department, San Luis Obispo CA (S)

de Fato, Elizabeth, *Librn*, Seattle Art Museum, Library, Seattle WA

DeFazio, Raymond, *Instructor*, Seton Hill College, Department of Art, Greensburg PA (S)

DeFeo, J, *Asst Prof*, California State College, Sonoma, Department of Art, Rohnert Park CA (S)

DeFrancis, Marjorie U, *Adminr*, Art Center, Mount Clemens MI

de Gary, Marie Noele, *Cur*, Union Centrale des Arts Decoratifs, Musee des Arts Decoratifs, Paris France

DeGeest, Boyd, *Instr*, Western Wisconsin Technical Institute, Graphics Division, LACrosse WI (S)

de Gerenday, Laci, *Secy*, National Sculpture Society, New York NY

Degio, Michel, *Treas*, La Societe des Decorateurs-Ensembliers du Quebec, Interior Decorators' Society of Quebec, Montreal PQ

de Goyer, Kirk, *Acting Dir*, University of California, University Art Galleries and California Museum of Photography, Riverside CA

De Grada, Raffaele, *Dir*, Accademia de Belle Arti Ravenna Italia, Academy of Fine Arts, Ravenna Italy (S)

de Graffenried, Gaines, *Cur*, Texas Ranger Hall of Fame and Museum, Waco TX

de Grassi, Leonard, *Prof*, Glendale College, Department of Fine Arts, Glendale CA (S)

de Gregorio, Vincent J, *Chmn*, Elizabeth City State University, Department of Art, Elizabeth City NC (S)

de Grey, Roger, *Principal*, City and Guilds of London Art School, London England (S)

de Groot, J R, *Cur*, Gemeentemuseum Arnhem, Municipal Museum of Arnhem, Arnhem Netherlands

de Groër, M, *Cur Objects d'Art*, Musee du Louvre, Louvre Museum, Paris France

Degse, Rogena, *Asst Prof*, Ohio State University, Department of Art Education, Columbus OH (S)

de Gurza, Aurea Ruiz, *Cur*, Museo de San Carlos, Museum of San Carlos, Mexico Mexico

de Gurza, Aurea Ruiz, *Librn*, Museo de San Carlos, Biblioteca, Mexico Mexico

de Guy, Carmen Vazquez, *Instr*, Inter American University of Puerto Rico, Department of Performing Arts, San German PR (S)

de Haan, Andy, *Cur*, Territorial Statehouse, Fillmore UT

De Hahn, Mary, *Vice Chmn*, Mid-America Arts Alliance, Kansas City MO

Dehoney, Martyvonne, *Chmn Art Dept*, Drew University, College Art Gallery, Madison NJ

Dehoney, Martyvonne, *Chmn Dept*, Drew University, Art Department, Madison NJ (S)

Deighton, Edwin J, *Asst Dir*, University of Oklahoma, Museum of Art, Norman OK

de Irezabal, Pilar de la Fuente, *Cur Museography*, Museo de San Carlos, Museum of San Carlos, Mexico Mexico

De Jong, Joline, *Assoc Prof*, Central College, Art Department, Pella IA (S)

de Jong, Klaas, *Dir*, Academie van Beeldende Kunsten, Academy of Fine Arts, Rotterdam Netherlands (S)

De Katch, Joan, *Secy*, Artists Guild Inc of New York, New York NY

deKramer, John, *Assoc Prof*, Pierce College, Art Department, Woodland Hills CA (S)

Delabano, Barney, *Cur Exhib*, Dallas Museum of Fine Arts, Dallas TX

Delafield, David, *Prof*, University of Northern Iowa, Department of Art, Cedar Falls IA (S)

Delaiti, Nancy, *Chmn Dept*, Berkshire Community College, Department of Fine Arts and Visual Communication, Pittsfield MA (S)

Delamar, Nancy, *Art Librn*, Arkansas Arts Center, Elizabeth Prewitt Taylor Memorial Library, Little Rock AR

Delaney, Barry Leo, *Cur of Art*, Staten Island Institute of Arts and Sciences, Staten Island NY

Delaney, Caldwell, *Dir*, Museum of the City of Mobile, Mobile AL

Delaney, Jan, *Coordr Gallery Services & Mem Secy*, London Regional Art Gallery, London ON

Delaney, Richard, *Assoc Prof*, California State University, Fresno, Art Department, Fresno CA (S)

DeLany, W S, *Pres*, Truxtun-Decatur Naval Museum, Washington DC

de Laris, Margarita A, *Head Public Relations*, Museo Nacional de Antropologia, National Museum of Anthropology, Mexico Mexico

de la Sota MacMahon, D Patricio, *Pres*, Museo de Bellas Artes, Museum of Fine Arts, Bilbao Spain

Delehanty, Suzanne, *Dir*, State University of New York College at Purchase, Neuberger Museum, Purchase NY

Deleu, Monique, *Librn*, Royal Academy of Fine Arts, Bibliotheque Artistique, Brussels Belgium

Delgado, Alfonso, *Head Construction*, Universidad Javeriana, Javeriana University Faculty of Architecture and Design, Bogota Colombia (S)

Delgado, O'Siris, *Pres Board Trusts*, Ateneo Puertorriqueno, San Juan PR

Delivorrias, Angleos, *Dir*, Benaki Museum, Athens Greece

Dell, Roger, *Cur Gallery Program*, Honolulu Academy of Arts, Honolulu HI

Dellaripa, Filomena, *Instructor*, Samuel S Fleisher Art Memorial, Philadelphia PA (S)

Delliho, Lawrence, *Asst Prof*, Camden County College, Department of Art, Blackwood NJ (S)

Dellis, Arlene B, *Registrar*, University of Miami, Lowe Art Museum, Coral Gables FL

Delluva, Patricia, *Registrar*, Allentown Art Museum, Allentown PA

Delmastro, Sherry, *Educational Asst*, Southern Illinois University Museum and Art Galleries, Carbondale IL

De Longa, Leonard, *Prof*, Mount Holyoke College, Art Department, South Hadley MA (S)

de Looper, Willem, *Assoc Cur*, Phillips Collection, Washington DC

Delorme, Carmen, *Animator*, Musee d'Art de Joliette, Library, Joliette PQ

DeLorme, Carmen, *Animator*, Musee d'Art de Joliette, Joliette PQ

de Loye, Georges, *Chief Cur*, Musee du Petit Palais, Avignon France

del Pedregal, Patricio Court, *Dir*, Museo de Arte Popular Americano, Art of the American Peoples Museum, Santiago Chile

DeLuca, Richard, *Cur*, Roberson Center, Binghamton NY

Deluca Jr, Ben J, *Executive Dir*, Hammond Museum, Inc, Gloucester MA

DeLue, Donald, *First VPres*, Council of American Artist Societies, New York NY

DelValle, Helen, *VPres*, American Society of Artists, Inc, Chicago IL

Delvca, Joe, *Prof*, Western Michigan University, Department of Art, Kalamazoo MI (S)

DeMarco, Marco, *Instr*, Cleveland Institute of Art, Cleveland OH (S)

de Margerie, Emmanuel Jacquin, *Dir*, Ecole du Louvre, School of the Louvre, Paris France (S)

de Martini, Vega, *Librn*, Museo de Capodimonte, Library, Naples Italy

de Matos, Rosalia Avalos , *Dir*, Museo Nacional de la Cultura Peruana, National Museum of Peruvian Culture, Lima Peru

Dembicki, Diane, *Cur*, Ponca City Cultural Center Museum, Ponca City OK

Dembrowski, Valerie F, *Controller*, Southwest Museum, Los Angeles CA

Demby, Patricia A, *Asst Dir*, Peters Valley Craft Center, Layton NJ (S)

de Medina, Federico Dietz, *Cur Archaeology*, Museo Nacional de Arqueologia, National Museum, La Paz Bolivia

DeMelim, John, *Prof*, Rhode Island College, Art Department, Providence RI (S)

DeMelim Jr, John, *VPres*, Providence Water Color Club, Providence RI

de Menil, John, *Dir*, Rice University, Institute for the Arts, Rice Museum, Houston TX

de Merindol, Christian, *Keeper*, Musee National des Monuments Francais, National Museum of French Sculpture and Murals, Paris France

Demeritt Jr, Dwight, *Pres*, Long Island Historical Society, Brooklyn NY

Demers, Christian, *Dir*, University of Quebec, Trois Rivieres, Fine Arts Section, Trois Rivieres PQ (S)

Demers, Edmund, *Prof*, Eisenhower College, Seneca Falls NY (S)

Demetrion, James T, *Dir*, Des Moines Art Center, Des Moines IA

DeMeyer, Tracy, *Office Coordr*, Arts Council of the Mid-Columbia Region, Richland WA

de Michelli, A, *Pres*, Accademia di Belle Arti di Brera, Academy of Fine Arts of Brera, Milan Italy (S)

D'Emilio, Sandra, *Cur*, Museum of New Mexico, Museum of Fine Arts, Santa Fe NM

de Moleiro, Prisca Dale, *Secy*, Museo de Bellas Artes, Museum of Fine Arts, Caracas Venezuela

de Monchaux, Paul, *Chmn Faculty Sculpture*, British School at Rome, Rome Italy (S)

de Montebello, Philippe, *Dir*, Metropolitan Museum of Art, New York NY

DeMore, Charles, *Pres*, United States Figure Skating Hall of Fame and Museum, Colorado Springs CO

DeMoss, Max, *Instr*, Mount San Jacinto College, Art Department, San Jacinto CA (S)

DeMots, Lois, *Instr*, Siena Heights College, Art Department, Adrian MI (S)

Dempsey, Bruce H, *Dir*, Jacksonville Art Museum, Jacksonville FL

Dempsey, Charles, *Chmn Dept*, Bryn Mawr College, Department of the History of Art, Bryn Mawr PA (S)

Dempsey, Connie, *Cur Education*, Paine Art Center and Arboretum, Oshkosh WI

Dempsey, H A, *Chief Cur*, Glenbow Museum, Calgary AB

Dempsey, John P, *Assoc Prof*, University of Alabama in Huntsville, Department of Art, Huntsville AL (S)

de Nave, F, *Asst Dir*, Stedelijk Prentenkabinet, Municipal Gallery of Graphic Arts, Antwerp Belgium

de Nave, F, *Asst Dir*, Museum Plantin-Moretus, Plantin-Moretus Museum, Antwerp Belgium

den Blaauwen, A L, *Dir Decorative Art*, Rijksmuseum, State Museum, Amsterdam Netherlands

Denby, Greg, *Preparatorial*, University of Notre Dame, Snite Museum of Art, Notre Dame IN

Dengate, James, *Cur Numismatics*, University of Illinois at Urbana-Champaign, World Heritage Museum, Urbana IL

Dengler, Eartha, *Asst Librn*, Merrimack Valley Textile Museum, Library, North Andover MA

Denison, Cara D, *Assoc Cur Drawings and Prints*, Pierpont Morgan Library, New York NY

Denman, R, *Adminr*, Museum of Northern British Columbia, Prince Rupert Museum Art Gallery, Prince Rupert BC

Dennard, William, *Instr*, Museum of Fine Arts, Alfred C Glassell Junior School of Art, Houston TX (S)

Dennett, Bernie, *Dept Head*, Ray-Vogue School of Design, Chicago IL (S)

Denning, Catherine, *Research Asst*, Brown University, Annmary Brown Memorial Gallery, Providence RI

Dennis, David, *Installation Coordr*, University of Iowa, Museum of Art, Iowa City IA

Dennis, James, *Prof*, University of Wisconsin, Madison, Department of Art, Madison WI (S)

Dennis, Paulette, *Asst Treas*, Greater Fall River Art Association, Fall River MA

Dennis, Terry, *Instr*, Rochester Community College, Art Department, Rochester MN (S)

Dennison, Keith E, *Dir*, Pioneer Museum and Haggin Galleries, Stockton CA

Dennison, Nan, *Asst to Dir*, Henry Morrison Flagler Museum, Palm Beach FL

Denny, Walter B, *Assoc Prof*, University of Massachusetts, Amherst, Art History Prog, Amherst MA (S)

Denny Jr, Paul, *Assoc Prof*, Phillips University, Department of Art, Enid OK (S)

Denton, Lynn, *Lectr*, Saint Joseph's College, Fine Arts Program, Philadelphia PA (S)

Denton, Mark, *Dir Neighborhood Art Program*, San Francisco City and County Art Commission, San Francisco CA

Denton, Spencer, *Dir*, Five Civilized Tribes Museum, Library, Muskogee OK

Denton, Spencer, *Dir*, Five Civilized Tribes Museum, Muskogee OK

Dentzel, Carl, *Pres Cultural Heritage Board*, City of Los Angeles, Municipal Arts Dept, Los Angeles CA

Dentzel, Carl S, *Dir*, Southwest Museum, Los Angeles CA

De Paolis, Gloria, *Asst Prof*, Pennsylvania State University, Fayette Campus, Department of Art, Uniontown PA (S)

dePencier, H, *Cur Asst*, Royal Ontario Museum, Canadiana Gallery, Toronto ON

dePeyster, James A, *VPres*, Society of the Four Arts, Palm Beach FL

de Pierola, Consuelo Sanz-Pastor y Fernandez, *Dir of Found of the Museum*, Museo Cerralbo, Madrid Spain

DePillars, Murry N, *Dean*, Virginia Commonwealth University, School of the Arts, Richmond VA (S)

de Poorter, Nora, *Asst Keeper*, Rubenianum, Antwerp Belgium

DePopolo, Margaret, *Librn*, Massachusetts Institute of Technology, Rotch Library of Architecture and Planning, Cambridge MA

Derbes, Anne, *Lectr*, Hood College, Department of Art, Frederick MD (S)

Derer, F J, *Executive Secy*, West Bend Gallery of Fine Arts, West Bend WI

Derga, Malinda, *Secy*, Paint 'N Palette Club, Anamosa IA

Derkowski, Jerzy, *Vice Rector*, Panstwowa Wyzsza Szkola Sztuk Plastycznych, Higher School of Art and Design, Lodz Poland (S)

Dern, James, *Secy*, Canajoharie Library and Art Gallery, Canajoharie NY

de Roo, Rene, *Cur*, Musees Royaux d'Art et d'Histoire, Royal Museums of Art and History, Brussels Belgium

Derrevere, William, *Instr*, Tulsa Junior College, Art Department, Tulsa OK (S)

DeRuiter, Garret, *Assoc Prof*, Eastern Illinois University, Art Department, Charleston IL (S)

de St Amand, Francyne, *Cur*, Women's Interart Center, Inc, Interart Gallery, New York NY

de Savoye, Janni, *Exec Asst*, Visual Arts Ontario, Toronto ON

des Grange, Jane, *Dir*, Hartwick College Fine Art Gallery, Yager Museum, Oneonta NY

Deshaies, Ruth Dryden, *Chmn Art Prog*, Tallahassee Community College, Art Department, Tallahassee FL (S)

Deshayes, J, *Dir*, Universite de Paris I a la Sorbonne, Institut d'Art et d'Archeologie, Paris France (S)

de Silva, P, *Dir*, Colombo National Museum, Colombo Sri Lanka

DeSisso, Janet, *Asst Dir*, Store Front Museum, Jamaica NY

Desloover, Rose E, *Assoc Prof*, Marygrove College, Dept of Art & Art History, Detroit MI (S)

de Sosa, Elsa Rosenthal, *Librn*, Escuela Superior de Bellas Artes Ernesto de la Carcova, Enrique Prince Library, Buenos Argentina

De Sota, Raoul, *Assoc Prof*, Los Angeles City College, Department of Art, Los Angeles CA (S)

Desportes, Ulysse, *Head Dept*, Mary Baldwin College, Department of Art, Staunton VA (S)

DesRoches, Joseph, *Pres*, Warwick Arts Foundation, Warwick RI

DesRosiers, Roger, *Dean School*, Washington University, School of Fine Arts, Saint Louis MO (S)

Dessureault, Pierre, *Producer*, National Film Board of Canada, Still Photography Division, Photo Gallery, Ottawa ON

D'Estout, Marc, *Asst Dir*, Triton Museum of Art, Santa Clara CA

de Suduiraut, S Guillot, *Asst Conservator*, Musee des Beaux-Arts, Museum of Fine Arts, Tours France

de Taranco, Felipe Maria Garin Orlitz, *Dir*, Escuela Superior de Bellas Artes de San Carlos, Valencia School of Fine Arts, Valencia Spain (S)

de Temple, Jean, *Asst Dir*, Ottawa Public Library, Ottawa ON

Detmer, Howard F, *Pres*, Victoria Society of Maine Women, Victoria Mansion and Morse Libby Mansion, Portland ME

Detmers, William, *Chmn Art Educ*, Herron School of Art, Indiana University-Purdue University, Indianapolis, Indianapolis IN (S)

Detro, Leroy, *Mgr de Young Bookshop*, Fine Arts Museums of San Francisco, The Museum Society, n of Honor co

Deutsch, Sanna, *Registrar*, Honolulu Academy of Arts, Honolulu HI

DeVeau, Winifred, *Art Dir*, Port Chester Public Library, Port Chester NY

de Vecsey, Esther, *Cur*, College of Wooster Art Center Museum, Wooster OH

de Villechenon, M N Pinot, *Chief Conservator*, Musee des Beaux-Arts, Museum of Fine Arts, Tours France

Devine, Elizabeth, *Instructor*, Edgewood College, Art Department, Madison WI (S)

Devine, Marge Duffy, *Scribe*, National Cartoonists Society, Brooklyn NY

DeVinny, Douglas, *Asst Prof*, University of Wisconsin-Parkside, Art Discipline, Kenosha WI (S)

DeVinny, Douglas T, *Asst Prof*, Mesa College, Art Department, Grand Junction CO (S)

Devito, Connie, *Instr*, Bowie State College, Department of Fine and Performing Arts, Bowie MD (S)

Devlin, Mary K, *Technical Services Librn*, University of Portland, Wilson W Clark Memorial Library, Portland OR

Devlin, Richard, *Chmn Dept*, Carlow College, Art Department, Pittsburgh PA (S)

Devlin, Violet K, *Art Librn*, Rider College, Franklin F Moore Library and Art Room, Lawrenceville NJ

DeVore, Richard, *Prof*, Colorado State University, Department of Art, Fort Collins CO (S)

de Vues Robbi, H D, *Board of Trustees*, Teylers Museum, Haarlem Netherlands

Dew, James, *Prof*, University of Montana, Dept of Art, Missoula MT (S)

Dew, Roderick, *Librn*, Colorado Springs Fine Arts Center, Library, Colorado Springs CO

DeWall, Beth, *Cur Slides & Photographs*, Cincinnati Art Museum, Cincinnati OH

Dewdney, Eric, *Programs Coordr*, Cambridge Public Library and Arts Centre, Cambridge ON

Dewey, Paul E, *Chmn*, Whitman College, Art Department, Walla Walla WA (S)

Dewey, Priscilla B, *Dir*, Charles River Creative Arts Program, Dover MA (S)

Dewey, Richard, *Librn Aga Khan Program for Islamic Architecture*, Massachusetts Institute of Technology, Rotch Library of Architecture and Planning, Cambridge MA

Dewey II, Tom, *Asst Prof*, University of Mississippi, Department of Art, University MS (S)

de Wilde, E L L, *Dir*, Stedlijk Museum-Amsterdam, Municipal Museum, Amsterdam Netherlands

DeWitt Jr, Ward, *Pres*, Tennessee Historical Society, Nashville TN

Deyell, Daniel, *Dir & Cur*, Muttart Gallery Associates, Calgary AB

Dhaemers, Robert A, *Prof*, Mills College, Art Department, Oakland CA (S)

d'Harnoncourt, Anne, *Cur 20th Century Art*, Philadelphia Museum of Art, Philadelphia PA

Diamond, Joan, *Asst Prof*, Hollins College, Art Department, Hollins VA (S)

Diamond, Larry, *Vis Asst Prof*, University of Toronto, Department of Landscape Architecture, Toronto ON (S)

Di Bartolomeo, R E, *Secy*, Oglebay Institute Mansion Museum, Oglebay Institute Mansion Museum Committee, Wheeling WV

Dibble, Charles, *Acting Chmn*, Syracuse University, College of Visual and Performing Arts, Syracuse NY (S)

Dibble, George S, *Emeritus Prof*, University of Utah, Art Department, Salt Lake City UT (S)

Dibble, Thomas Reilly, *Dir*, Southern Vermont Art Center, Manchester VT

Dibble, V C, *Vis Prof*, Parkersburg Community College, Art Department, Parkersburg WV (S)

DiBella, Joseph, *Asst Prof*, Mary Washington College, Art Department, Fredericksburg VA (S)

di Benedetto, Nancy, *Administrative Dean*, New York School of Interior Design, New York NY (S)

Dibert, Rita, *Asst Prof*, Pomona College, Art Department, Claremont CA (S)

DiBiaso, Jay Richard, *Cur*, University of Miami, Lowe Art Museum, Coral Gables FL

DiBlasi, Pauline, *Graphic Designer*, American Federation of Arts, New York NY

Dice, Elizabeth J, *Assoc Prof*, Mississippi University for Women, Art Department, Columbus MS (S)

DiCicco, Jon, *Instructor*, Providence College, Department of Fine Arts, Providence RI (S)

Dickenhof, John, *Area Chmn Crafts*, Pasadena City College, Art Department, Pasadena CA (S)

Dickenson, Sara, *Asst Prof*, Southern University in New Orleans, Art Dept, New Orleans LA (S)

Dickenson, Victoria, *Cur Coll*, Newfoundland Museum, Saint John's NF

Dickerson, Amina, *Program Dir*, Museum of African Art, Washington DC

Dickerson, K, *Prog Coordr*, Alberta College of Art, Southern Alberta Institute of Technology, Calgary AB (S)

Dickerson, R E, *Chmn*, Humboldt State University, Art Department, Arcata CA (S)

Dickerson, Vera M, *Instr*, Virginia Western Community College, Commercial Art, Fine Art & Photography, Roanoke VA (S)

Dickey, T, *Coordr Exhib & Educational Programs*, University of Alaska, Museum, Fairbanks AK

Dickey, Terry, *Treas*, Alaska Association for the Arts, Fairbanks AK

Dickinson, Frank Holdsworth, *Asst Dir*, Dunedin Public Art Gallery, Dunedin New Zealand

Dickinson, Stirling, *Pres*, Instituto Allende, Allende Institute, San Mexico (S)

Dickinson, Susan, *Executive Secy*, Rodman Hall Arts Centre, Saint Catharines ON

Dickson, David W D, *Pres*, Montclair State College, Gallery One, Upper Montclair NJ

Dickson, Donna, *VChmn*, Wyoming Council on the Arts, Cheyenne WY

Dickson, Doris J, *Dir*, Henry B Plant Museum, Tampa FL

Dickson, Janet S, *Cur Education*, Yale University, Art Gallery, New Haven CT

Diechome, Benoit, *Pres*, La Societe des Decorateurs-Ensembliers du Quebec, Interior Decorators' Society of Quebec, Montreal PQ

Dieckman, Suzanne, *Instr*, Creighton University, Fine and Performing Arts Department, Omaha NE (S)

Diehl, George K, *Chmn Dept Fine Arts*, La Salle College, Department of Fine Arts, Philadelphia PA (S)

Dierfeldt, Jerome, *Exhib Specialist*, Hastings Museum, Hastings NE

Dietemann, Dave, *MFA Coordr*, Colorado State University, Department of Art, Fort Collins CO (S)

Dieterly, Richard, *Secy*, Hunterdon Art Center, Clinton NJ

Dietrich, Bruce L, *Dir*, Reading Public Museum and Art Gallery, Reading PA

Dietrich, Daryl, *Chmn Div of Humanities*, Wenatchee Valley College, Art Department, Wenatchee WA (S)

Dietrich, Gerhard, *Staff*, Museen der Stadt Köln, Kunstgewerbemuseum der Stadt Köln, Cologne Germany, Federal Republic of

Dietsch, Elaine, *Registrar*, Santa Barbara Museum of Art, Santa Barbara CA

Dietz, Charles, *Dir*, Zanesville Art Center, Zanesville OH

Dietz, Judy, *Acting Registrar*, Art Gallery of Nova Scotia, Halifax NS

Diez, Raul, *Secy*, Museo Romantico, Museum of the Romantic Epoch, Madrid Spain

Diez, William E, *Second VPres*, Rochester Historical Society, Rochester NY

Diffily, John A, *Dir Education*, Amon Carter Museum of Western Art, Fort Worth TX

DiGiovanni, Robert, *Prof*, Boston State College, Art Department, Boston MA (S)

DiGiusto, Gerald, *Prof*, State University of New York College at Cortland, Art Department, Cortland NY (S)

Di Julio, Max, *Prog Dir*, Loretto Heights College, Department of Art, Denver CO (S)

Dillard, Jane, *Asst Prof*, University of North Carolina-Charlotte, Creative Arts Dept, Charlotte NC (S)

Dillenbeck, Mildred, *Dir*, Remington Art Museum, Ogdensburg NY

Diller, J David, *Head Arts Dept*, James Madison University, Sawhill Gallery, Harrisonburg VA

Diller, J David, *Head Dept*, James Madison University, Department of Art, Harrisonburg VA (S)

Dillon, Dougals, *Chmn Board Trustees*, Metropolitan Museum of Art, New York NY

Dillon, John, *Asst Prof*, Chadron State College, Div of Fine Arts, Chadron NE (S)

Dillon, John, *Assoc Prof*, University of Alabama in Birmingham, Department of Art, Birmingham AL (S)

Dillon, Michael, *Cur of Exhib*, Tyler Museum of Art, Tyler TX

Dillon, Mildred, *VPres*, American Color Print Society, Philadelphia PA

Dillon, Monika, *Public Affairs*, Museum of the City of New York, New York NY

Dillon, Phyllis, *Conservator*, Museum of the American Indian, New York NY

Dillon, Virginia, *Circulation Dept Head*, Wichita Public Library, Wichita KS

Dillow, Nancy, *Chief Cur*, Winnipeg Art Gallery, Winnipeg MB

Dimant, Enrique, *Courses & Conferences*, Centro de Arte y Communicacion, Center of Art and Communication, Buenos Argentina

DiMattia Jr, Ernest A, *Dir*, Ferguson Library, Stamford CT

DiMattio, Vincent, *Assoc Prof*, Monmouth College, Department of Art, West Long Branch NJ (S)

Dimond, Thomas, *Asst Prof Art*, Eastern Oregon State College, La Grande OR (S)

Dimond, Tom, *Coordr Educational Media & Exhib*, Clemson University, Rudolph E Lee Gallery, Clemson SC

Dimor, Phillip, *Dept Head AV*, New Bedford Free Public Library, New Bedford MA

Dines, Nicholas, *Dir MLA Prog*, University of Massachusetts, Amherst, College of Food and Natural Resources, Amherst MA (S)

Dings, Marjorie, *Admin Asst Friends of Art*, Wellesley College, Museum, Wellesley MA

Dinkelspiel, Edgar N, *Pres*, Long Branch Historical Museum, Long Branch NJ

Dinneen, Marie de Sales, *Chmn of Dept*, Regis College, Department of Art, Weston MA (S)

Dinsmore, John N, *Assoc Prof*, Kearney State College, Dept of Art, Kearney NE (S)

Dinsmore, Marianne, *Librn*, Lyman Allyn Museum, Library, New London CT

Dinsmorg, Grant, *Instructor*, La Roche College, Division of Graphic Arts & Design, Pittsburgh PA (S)

DiPerna Jr, Frank, *Chmn Photography*, Corcoran School of Art, Washington DC (S)

Di Peso, Charles C, *Foundation Dir*, Amerind Foundation, Inc, Dragoon AZ

Dippel, R M, *Head Department Painting & Sculpture*, Stedlijk Museum-Amsterdam, Municipal Museum, Amsterdam Netherlands

Dippolito, Frank, *Art Dept Chmn*, Tacoma Community College, Art Department, Tacoma WA (S)

Dirks, John, *Asst Dir*, Museum of Art of Ogunquit, Ogunquit ME

Disbro, William, *Chmn*, Jamestown Community College, Art Department, Jamestown NY (S)

DiSegi, Mary Ann, *Second VPres*, Berks Art Alliance, Reading PA

Dishman, Darral A, *Dir Dept*, Missouri Southern State College, Dept of Art, Joplin MO (S)

Disney, Russell, *Treas*, Canadian Conference of the Arts, Ottawa ON

DiTeresa, Neil, *Assoc Prof*, Berea College, Art Department, Berea KY (S)

Dittman, Reidar, *Assoc Prof*, St Olaf College, Art Department, Northfield MN (S)

Dittmar, Thelma, *Registrar*, Canton Art Instutute, Canton OH (S)

Divelbess, Diane, *Prof*, California State Polytechnic University, Pomona, Art Department, Pomona CA (S)

Divelbiss, Maggie, *Development Mgr*, Sangre De Cristo Arts & Conference Center, Pueblo CO

Divers, Dorothy, *Assoc Prof*, St Olaf College, Art Department, Northfield MN (S)

Dix, Ursus, *Acting Head Restoration & Conservation Lab*, National Gallery of Canada, Ottawa ON

Dixon, Bob, *Asst Prof*, Sangamon State University, Creative Arts Program, Springfield IL (S)

Dixon, Carol, *Publicity*, Greenwich Art Society and Art Center, Greenwich CT

Dixon, Daniel L, *Museum Mgr*, Omaha Children's Museum, Inc, Omaha NE

Dixon, Jenny, *Acting Dir*, Public Art Fund, Inc, New York NY

Dixon, Joycelyn, *Staff Specialist*, Pacific Northwest Bell, Seattle WA

Dixon, Ken, *Assoc Prof*, Texas Tech University, Department of Art, Lubbock TX (S)

Dixon, Stewart S, *VPres*, Chicago Historical Society, Chicago IL

Dixon Jr, Albert G, *Dir*, San Jose Museum of Art, San Jose CA

Dixon Jr, F Eugene, *Pres*, Philadelphia Art Commission, Philadelphia PA

Doak, Banton S, *Assoc Prof*, Florida Southern College, Art Department, Lakeland FL (S)

Doak, Gale L, *Instructor*, Florida Southern College, Art Department, Lakeland FL (S)

Doane, John, *Instructor*, California State College, Sonoma, Department of Art, Rohnert Park CA (S)

Dobbins, Kathleen, *Slide Librn*, University of Virginia, Fiske Kimball Fine Arts Library, Charlottesville VA

Dobbins, Nancy, *Hostess*, Baylor University, Armstrong Browning Library, Waco TX

Dobbs, Gigi, *Exhib Prog Dir*, Western Association of Art Museums, San Francisco CA

Dobbs, John, *Assoc Prof*, John Jay College of Criminal Justice, Department of Art, Music and Philosophy, New York NY (S)

Dobbs, W A, *Pres*, Singing River Art Association Inc, L & N Railroad Depot Gallery, Pascagoula MS

Dobe, William, *Instructor*, Notre Dame College, Art Department, Manchester NH (S)

Dobereiner, John, *Prof*, University of Victoria, Department of Visual Arts, Victoria BC (S)

Dobereiner, Wendy, *Asst Prof*, University of British Columbia, Department of Fine Arts, Vancouver BC (S)

Dobkin, John, *Dir*, National Academy School of Fine Arts, New York NY (S)

Dobkin, John H, *Dir*, National Academy of Design, New York NY

Dobkin, John H, *Dir*, National Academy of Design, New York NY (S)

Dobrowolski, Fred, *Lectr*, Notre Dame College, Art Department, Manchester NH (S)

Dobrowolsky, Stanley, *Secy*, Taras H Schevchenko Museum and Memorial Park Foundation, Oakville ON

Docktor, Gail, *Public Relations Officer*, Fine Arts Museums of San Francisco, M H de Young Memorial Museum and California Palace of the Legion of Honor, n of Honor co

Doctor, Antonio P, *Dir*, University of Windsor, School of Visual Arts, Windsor ON (S)

Doctorow, Erica, *Head Fine Arts Library*, Adelphi University, Fine Arts Library, Garden City NY

Dodd, Irene, *Head Dept*, Valdosta State College, Department of Art, Valdosta GA (S)

Dodd, Irene, *Head Art Department*, Valdosta State College, Art Gallery, Valdosta GA

Dodge, Deborah, *Admin Asst*, Wichita State University, Edwin A Ulrich Museum of Art, Wichita KS

Dodge, Ernest S, *Dir*, Peabody Museum of Salem, Salem MA

Dodge, Robert, *Instructor*, Bucks County Community College, Fine Arts Department, Newton PA (S)

Dodson, Robert G, *Dir*, Saint Gregory's Abbey and College, Mabee-Gerrer Museum, Shawnee OK

Dodson, Roy E, *Prof*, Sul Ross State University, Department of Art, Alpine TX (S)

Dodwell, C R, *Dir*, University of Manchester, Whitworth Art Gallery, Manchester England

Dodworth, Allen Stevens, *Dir*, Salt Lake Art Center, Salt Lake City UT

Doe, Donald B, *Asst Prof*, University of Nebraska at Omaha, Dept of Art, Omaha NE (S)

Doe, Donald Bartlett, *Gallery Dir*, University of Nebraska-Omaha Art Galleries, New Gallery, Omaha NE

Doedon, Kathy, *Secy*, Custer County Art Center, Miles City MT

Doelger, William E P, *Secy-Treas*, Society of the Four Arts, Palm Beach FL

Doelle, E, *Librn*, McGill University, Blackader-Lauterman Library of Architecture and Arts, Montreal PQ

D'Oench, Ellen G, *Cur*, Wesleyan University, Davison Art Center, Middletown CT

Doerfler, Roy D, *Instructor*, Nebraska Western College, Div of Language & Arts, Scottsbluff NE (S)

Doering, Colette, *Asst Prof*, Avila College, Art Department, Kansas City MO (S)

Doeringer, Suzannah, *Deputy Dir*, Harvard University, William Hayes Fogg Art Museum, Cambridge MA

Doerzbach, Cindy, *Cur*, Salisbury State College, Wildfowl Art Museum, Salisbury MD

Doherty, Ann, *Development Dir*, International Center of Photography, New York NY

Doherty, Roger, *Cur Buildings & Sites*, Colorado Historical Society, Colorado Heritage Center, Denver CO

Dohn, Helen, *Secy*, Virginia Museum of Fine Arts, Richmond VA

Dohnalova, Marie, *Librn*, Moravska Galerie v Brne, Library, Brno Czechoslovakia

Doig, Thomas G, *Administrator*, Concord Antiquarian Society Museum, Concord MA

Doiron, Jeannette, *Chmn*, Beaumont Arts Council, Beaumont TX

Dolan, Douglas C, *Exec Dir*, Historical Society of York County, York PA

Dolan, Kate, *Asst Prof*, Denison University, Department of Art, Granville OH (S)

Dolan, Mary, *Dir*, Copper Village Museum and Arts Center, Anaconda MT

Dole, Algar, *Instructor*, Austin Peay State University, Dept of Art, Clarksville TN (S)

Dole, John S, *Treas & Gen Counsel*, Council of American Artist Societies, New York NY

Dolkart, Ruth M, *Adminr*, Jewish Museum, New York NY

Doll, Donald A, *Chmn Fine & Performing Arts Dept*, Creighton University Art Gallery, Omaha NE

Doll, Donald A, *Chmn Dept*, Creighton University, Fine and Performing Arts Department, Omaha NE (S)

Doll, Nancy, *Dir*, Keene State College, Thorne-Sagendorph Art Gallery, Keene NH

Dolphin, Mary, *Asst Prof*, Worcester State College, Art Department, Worcester MA (S)

Domas, Joseph J, *Secy*, Religious Americana Museum, Ringoes NJ

Domas, Joseph J, *Cur*, Religious Americana Museum, Ringoes NJ

Dominguez, Frank, *Instructor*, Bucks County Community College, Fine Arts Department, Newton PA (S)

Doms, Keith, *Dir Library*, Free Library of Philadelphia, Art Department, Philadelphia PA

Donahue, Michael, *Chmn*, Temple Junior College, Art Department, Temple TX (S)

Donahue, Rodney, *Asst Instr*, University of the District of Columbia, Art Department, Washington DC (S)

Donald, Anne, *Keeper of Fine Art*, Glasgow Museums and Art Galleries, Kelvingrove Art Gallery and Museum, Glasgow Scotland

Donaldson, David, *Cur*, Morse Gallery of Art, Boulder FL

Donaldson, Marjory, *Cur*, University of New Brunswick Art Centre, Fredericton NB

Donaldson, P, *Instructor*, Golden West College, Arts, Humanities and Social Sciences Institute, Huntington Beach CA (S)

Donaldson, Shirley, *Gallery Dir*, Coe College, Art Galleries, Cedar Rapids IA

Donaldson, Shirley, *Gallery Dir*, Coe College, Department of Art, Cedar Rapids IA (S)

Donaldson, Thomas E, *Assoc Prof*, Cleveland State University, Art Department, Cincinnati OH (S)

Donato, James, *Instructor*, Antonelli School of Photography, Philadelphia PA

Donbaz, Veysel, *Cur Cuneiform Tablet Coll*, Istanbul Arkeoloji Müzeleri, Archaeological Museums of Istanbul, Istanbul Turkey

Dondy, Emanuel, *Library Dir*, Mount Vernon Public Library, Fine Art Department, Mount Vernon NY

Dongilla, Thomas, *Instructor*, Indiana University of Pennsylvania, Department of Art and Art Education, Indiana PA (S)

Donlan, Alberta F, *Librn*, Museum of New Mexico, Museum of Fine Arts Library, Santa Fe NM

Donley, Marge, *Instructor*, Southwestern Oklahoma State University, Art Department, Weatherford OK (S)

Donley, Robert, *Assoc Prof*, DePaul University, Department of Art, Chicago IL (S)

Donnan, Christopher B, *Dir*, University of California, Los Angeles, Museum of Cultural History, Los Angeles CA

Donnelly, James, *VPres*, Arts and Crafts Association of Meriden Inc, Meriden CT

Donoghue, F J, *Doll Cur*, Wenham Historical Association and Museum, Inc, Wenham MA

Donohue, Katherine, *Librn*, Natural History Museum of Los Angeles County, Library, Los Angeles CA

Donovan, Mary Louise, *Pres*, Southern Tier Arts Association, Inc, Elmira NY

Donovan, Robert G, *VPres Educ*, International Correspondence Schools, School of Interior Design, Scranton PA (S)

Donze, Sara Lee, *Library Dir*, North Canton Public Library, Little Art Gallery, North Canton OH

Doogan, Margaret, *Coordr Graphic Design*, University of Arizona, Department of Art, Tucson AZ (S)

Dooley Jr, Edwin L, *Dir*, Virginia Historical Society, Richmond VA

Doolittle Jr, Roy W, *Secy*, Albright-Knox Art Gallery, Buffalo Fine Arts Academy, Buffalo NY

Dopita, A, *Security*, Blanden Memorial Art Gallery, Fort Dodge IA

Doppelfeld, Dieter, *Treasurer*, Alaska Artists Guild, Anchorage AK

Doran, Faye, *Assoc Prof*, Harding University, Department of Art, Searcy AR (S)

Doran, James, *Chmn Dept*, Ocean County College, Humanities Department, Toms River NJ (S)

Doran, Megan, *Asst Cur*, University of British Columbia, Fine Arts Gallery, Vancouver BC

Dorholt, Kingsly, *Dir*, Saint Cloud State University, Kiehle Gallery, Saint Cloud MN

Dorn, Gordon J, *Workshop Dir*, Oxbow Summer Art Workshops, Saugatuck MI (S)

Dornemann, Rudolph, *Cur of History*, Milwaukee Public Museum, Milwaukee WI

Dorsey, Dia M, *Development Officer*, Seattle Art Museum, Seattle WA

Dorsey, Michael, *Asst Prof*, Mississippi State University, Art Department, Mississippi State MS (S)

D'Orsi, Sybil, *Treas*, Catharine Lorillard Wolfe Art Club, Inc, New York NY

Dortch, Mike, *Regional Park Supt*, William S Hart Museum, Newhall CA

Dortch, Willie Jo, *Bookkeeper Secy*, Virginia Beach Arts Center, Virginia Beach VA

Dorval, Karen A, *Head Fine Arts Department*, Springfield City Library, Art Department, Springfield MA

Dotson, Esther G, *Assoc Prof*, Cornell University, Department of the History of Art, Ithaca NY (S)

Duckworth, Marilyn, *Audiovisual Coordr*, New Orleans Museum of Art, Isaac Delgado Museum, New Orleans LA

Ducommun, Charles E, *VPres*, Los Angeles County Museum of Art, Los Angeles CA

Duda, Donald L, *Assoc Prof*, Dickinson State College, Department of Art, Dickinson ND (S)

Dudley, David, *Dir Upper Midwest Conservation Assoc*, Minneapolis Institute of Arts, Minneapolis MN

Dudley, Janice Stafford, *Secy*, MacArthur Memorial, Norfolk VA

Dudley, Peter, *Instructor*, Greenfield Community College, Art Department, Greenfield MA (S)

Due, Patricia, *Gallery Shop Dir*, Ann Arbor Art Association, Ann Arbor MI

Duel, Doris C, *Library Technical Asst*, Palomar Community College, Fine Arts Library, San Marcos CA

Duenyas, Ester, *Education Cur*, Hebrew Union College, Skirball Museum, Los Angeles CA

Dufault, Ron, *Gallery Cur*, University of Minnesota, Student Center Galleries, Saint Paul MN

Duff, James H, *Dir*, Brandywine River Museum, Chadds Ford PA

Duff, Kenneth R, *Pres*, Art League of Houston, Houston TX

Duffek, Robert, *Instructor*, Mohawk Valley Community College, Advertising Design and Production, Utica NY (S)

Duffey, Judith, *Instructor*, Western Carolina University, Dept of Art, Cullowhee NC (S)

Duffin, Dianna, *Chmn*, Pikeville College, Fine Arts Dept, Pikeville KY (S)

Duffy, Brian, *Lectr*, Villa Maria College of Buffalo, Art Department, Buffalo NY (S)

Duffy, Mary, *Admin Asst*, Museum of Holography, Reference Library, New York NY

Duffy, Valerie N, *Admin Asst*, William A Farnsworth Library and Art Museum, Rockland ME

Dufort, Robert, *Chairperson Dept Art*, Schoolcraft College, Department of Art, Livonia MI (S)

Dufour, Lydia A, *Cur Iconography*, Hispanic Society of America Museum, New York NY

Dufour, Paul, *Prof*, Louisiana State University, Department of Fine Arts, Baton Rouge LA (S)

Dugan, Alan, *Instructor*, Truro Center for the Arts at Castle Hill, Inc, Truro MA (S)

Dugan, George, *Assoc Prof*, State University of New York College at Cortland, Art Department, Cortland NY (S)

Dugdale, James, *Instructor,* Joliet Junior College, Art Dept, Joliet IL (S)

Duggan, Lynn, *Instructor*, Nazareth College of Rochester, Art Department, Rochester NY (S)

Duhaime, Lucie, *Treas*, New Hampshire Art Association, Inc, Manchester NH

Duhme Jr, H Richard, *Head Sculpture*, Chautauqua Institution, Chautauqua NY (S)

Duke, Carl F, *Head Dept*, Pensacola Junior College, Department of Visual Arts, Pensacola FL (S)

Duke, Carol, *Chmn*, King County Arts Commission, Seattle WA

Dull, Elizabeth, *Assoc Prof*, Western Michigan University, Art History Division, Kalamazoo MI (S)

Dumas, Josephine, *Secy*, Mid-Hudson Arts and Science Center, Poughkeepsie NY

Dumbleton, Duane D, *Chmn Div Fine Arts & Humanities*, Florida Junior College at Jacksonville, South Campus, Art Department, Jacksonville FL (S)

duMont, Ann W, *Asst Cur & Registrar*, Pocumtuck Valley Memorial Association, Memorial Hall, Deerfield MA

Dumpis, Benita, *Conservator*, University of California, Los Angeles, Museum of Cultural History, Los Angeles CA

Dunaway, Bob A, *Chmn*, Hinds Junior College, Department of Art, Raymond MS (S)

Dunaway, Bob A, *Dir*, Hinds Junior College, Marie Hull Gallery, Raymond MS

Dunaway, Sherry R, *Secy-Registrar*, University of Texas at Arlington, University Art Gallery, Arlington TX

Dunbar, Burton L, *Chmn*, University of Missouri-Kansas City, Dept of Art & Art History, Kansas City MO (S)

Dunbar, Frank, *Secy Board of Trustees*, Royal Ontario Museum, Toronto ON

Dunbar, Philip H, *Cur*, Connecticut Historical Society, Hartford CT

Dunbeck, Helen, *Dir Business Services*, Museum of Contemporary Art, Chicago IL

Duncan, A Baker, *Chmn*, San Antonio Museum Association, Inc, San Antonio TX

Duncan, Donald, *Assoc Prof*, Ohio State University, Department of Art Education, Columbus OH (S)

Duncan, Richard, *Asst Prof*, Florida International University, Visual Arts Department, Miami FL (S)

Duncan, Susan G, *Mgr Library Services*, Hallmark Cards, Inc, Creative Library, Kansas City MO

Dundin, John, *Prof*, Catholic University of America, Department of Architecture & Planning, Washington DC (S)

Dunifon, Don, *Assoc Prof*, Wittenberg University, Art Department, Springfield OH (S)

Dunkelman, Martha, *Asst Prof*, Wright State University, Art Department, Dayton OH (S)

Dunkle, Alvin, *Dir*, Thiel College, Sampson Art Gallery, Greenville PA

Dunkle, Alvin S, *Chmn Dept*, Thiel College, Department of Art, Greenville PA (S)

Dunkum, Patricia, *Secy*, Museum of the Arts Foundation, Missoula Museum of the Arts, Missoula MT

Dunlap, Barbara, *Co-Chief of Archives & Art Library*, City College of the City of New York, Morris Raphael Cohen Library, New York NY

Dunlap, Kenneth, *Instructor*, Ivy School of Professional Art, Downtown Annex, Pittsburgh PA (S)

Dunlevy, Raymond E, *Chmn*, California State College, Department of Art, California PA (S)

Dunlop, Donna, *Asst to Art Librn*, Rutgers University, Art Library, New Brunswick NJ

Dunn, David W, *Dir & Cur*, Fetherston Foundation, Packwood House Museum, Lewisburg PA

Dunn, Ed, *Prof*, Western New Mexico University, Dept of Fine Art, Art Div, Silver City NM (S)

Dunn, Elaine, *Gallery Asst*, Dixon Gallery and Gardens, Memphis TN

Dunn, McChesney S, *Asst Dir*, Southeastern Center for Contemporary Art, Winston-Salem NC

Dunn, Sandra, *Asst Coordr*, Ontario Crafts Council, Craft Resource Centre, Toronto ON

Dunn, Warren, *Instr*, Clark College, Art Department, Vancouver WA (S)

Dunnigam, Mary C, *Librn*, University of Virginia, Fiske Kimball Fine Arts Library, Charlottesville VA

Dunwiddie, Charlotte, *VPres*, National Sculpture Society, New York NY

Duparc, F J, *Asst*, Koninklijk Kabinet van Schilderijen, Royal Picture Gallery, The Hague Netherlands

Dupepe, F Clancy, *Pres*, Louisiana State Museum, New Orleans LA

Dupie, Pauline, *Second VPres*, La Societe des Decorateurs-Ensembliers du Quebec, Interior Decorators' Society of Quebec, Montreal PQ

Dupraz, Claude, *Head Industrial Design Dept*, Lausanne College of Art and Design, Lausanne Switzerland

Dupree, Michael, *Prof*, West Virginia University, Division of Art, Morgantown WV (S)

Durham, David, *Instructor*, Saint Louis Community College at Meramec, Art Dept, Saint Louis MO (S)

Durham, James, *Head Dept*, Okaloosa-Walton Junior College, Dept of Fine & Performing Arts, Niceville FL (S)

Durian-Ress, S, *Cur Textiles*, Bayerisches Nationalmuseum, Bavarian National Museum, Munich Germany, Federal Republic of

Durkan, Lisa, *Coordr of Public Information & Special Events*, Brooks Memorial Art Gallery, Memphis TN

Durkee, Stephen, *Prof*, Framingham State College, Art Department, Framingham MA (S)

Durkin, Silvan A, *Cur*, Owatonna Arts Center, Owatonna MN

Durland, Don, *Prof*, Texas Tech University, Department of Art, Lubbock TX (S)

Durrant, George D, *Assoc Prof*, Palomar College, Art Department, San Marcos TX (S)

Dursum, Brian A, *Asst to Dir & Cur of Oriental Art*, University of Miami, Lowe Art Museum, Coral Gables FL

Duseck, Bernard, *Prof*, California Polytechnic State University at San Luis Obispo, Art Department, San Luis Obispo CA (S)

Dusendschon, Noel, *Prof*, Indiana University-Purdue University, Department of Fine Arts, Fort Wayne IN (S)

Dustin, John, *Humanities & Fine Arts Librn*, Southern Illinois University, Lovejoy Library, Edwardsville IL

Dutton, Richard, *Dept Head*, Indian Hills Community College, Ottumwa Heights Campus, Dept of Art, Ottumwa IA (S)

Dutton, Richard H, *Head Dept*, Indian Hills Community College, Department of Art, Centerville IA (S)

Dvorak, Anna, *Librn*, North Carolina Museum of Art, Library, Raleigh NC

D'Vorzon, Berenice, *Assoc Prof*, Wilkes College, Department of Art, Wilkes-Barre PA (S)

Dwight, Edward H, *Dir*, Munson-Williams-Proctor Institute, Museum of Art, Utica NY

Dworkin, Ellen, *Asst Librn*, Brand Library and Art Center, Glendale CA

Dwyer, Donald, *Prof*, School of the Arts, C W Post Center of Long Island University, Art Department, Greenvale NY (S)

Dwyer, Eugene J, *Chmn*, Kenyon College, Art Department, Gambier OH (S)

Dwyer, Janet, *Asst Librn*, Wellesley College, Art Library, Wellesley MA

Dwyer, Jayne, *Pres*, Ogunquit Art Association, The Barn Gallery, Ogunquit ME

Dwyer, Kathy L, *Exec Dir*, Federated Arts Council of Richmond, Inc, Richmond VA

Dwyer, Melva J, *Head Librn*, University of British Columbia, Fine Arts Division Library, Vancouver BC

Dwyer, William E, *Pres*, Historic Deerfield Inc, Deerfield MA

Dyck, Walter, *Prof*, Johnson State College, Art Department, Johnson VT (S)

Dyer, Saskia, *VPres*, Coos Art Museum, Coos Bay OR

Dyke, Elmarie, *Pres*, Pacific Grove Art Center, Pacific Grove CA

Dykes, D W, *Secy*, National Museum of Wales, Cardiff Wales

Dykes, Stephen, *Deputy Dir for Admin*, Fine Arts Museums of San Francisco, M H de Young Memorial Museum and California Palace of the Legion of Honor

Dynneson, Donald, *Prof*, Concordia College, Art Department, Seward NE (S)

Dyson Jr, Robert H, *Pres*, Archaeological Institute of America, New York NY

Dzikowski, Barbara, *Executive Secy*, Art Center, Inc, South Bend IN

Eads, Hannah, *Asst Prof*, Eastern Illinois University, Art Department, Charleston IL (S)

Eager, George, *Asst Dir*, Museum of the American Indian, New York NY

Eager, Gerald, *Head Dept*, Bucknell University, Department of Art, Lewisburg PA (S)

Eagerman, Suzanne, *Lectr*, Trinity College, Department of Fine Arts, Washington DC (S)

Eagerton, Robert, *Chmn Printmaking*, Herron School of Art, Indiana University-Purdue University, Indianapolis, Indianapolis IN (S)

Eakins, E, *Pres Board of Trustees*, Burnaby Art Gallery, Burnaby BC

Eakins, Joyce, *Dir*, Colorado Women's College, Lyle True Gallery, Denver CO

Eakins, Joyce, *Vis Prof*, Colorado Women's College, Department of Art, Denver CO (S)

Eis, Ruth, *Cur*, Judah L Magnes Memorial Museum, Western Jewish History Center, Berkeley CA

Eisen, Sylvia, *Dir*, Long Beach Public Library, Long Beach NY

Eisenman, Alvin, *Prof*, Yale University, School of Art, New Haven CT (S)

Eisgrau, Evelyn, *VPres & Action Chmn*, Women in the Arts Foundation, Inc, New York NY

Eisler, Sue, *Chairperson Dept*, Saint Louis Community College at Florissant Valley, Department of Art, Ferguson MO (S)

Eisman, Hy, *Instr*, Joe Kubert School of Cartoon and Graphic Art Inc, Dover NJ (S)

Eiteljorg, Harrison, *Chmn Board of Trustees*, Indianapolis Museum of Art, Indianapolis IN

Eitner, Lorenz, *Chmn Dept Art*, Stanford University, Department of Art, Stanford CA (S)

Eitner, Lorenz, *Dir*, Stanford University, T W Stanford Art Gallery & Museum of Art, Stanford CA

Ekdahl, Janis, *Librn*, Vassar College Art Gallery, Art Library, Poughkeepsie NY

Ekedal, Ellen, *Dir*, Loyola Marymount University, Art Gallery, Los Angeles CA

Eknoian, Gerald, *Instructor*, De Anza College, Art Department, Cupertino CA (S)

Ela, Janet, *Cur*, Madison Art Center, Madison WI

Elam, Leslie A, *Dir & Secy*, American Numismatic Society, New York NY

Elder III, William Voss, *Chmn Curatorial Div & Cur Decorative Arts*, Baltimore Museum of Art, Baltimore MD

Eldot, Eleanor, *Music & Art Librn*, Queensborough Community College Library, Bayside NY

Eldred, Dale, *Chmn Sculpture*, Kansas City Art Institute, Kansas City MO (S)

Eldredge, Bruce B, *Dir*, Schenectady Museum, Schenectady NY

Eldredge, Charles, *Assoc Prof*, University of Kansas, Kress Foundation Department of Art History, Lawrence KS (S)

Eldredge, Charles C, *Dir*, Spencer Museum of Art, Lawrence KS

Elert, Samuel, *Head Fashion Dept*, Paris American Academy, Paris France (S)

Eley, L, *Librn*, University of Regina, Fine Arts Library, Regina SK

Eley, Margaret, *Dir*, California Historical Society, El Molino Viejo, San Francisco CA

Elfvin, John T, *VPres*, Albright-Knox Art Gallery, Buffalo Fine Arts Academy, Buffalo NY

Elgavish, J, *Dir*, Museum of Ancient Art, Haifa Israel

El Ghiriani, Youseff, *Dir*, Greco-Roman Museum, Alexandria Egypt

Elias, Clifford E, *Secy*, Merrimack Valley Textile Museum, North Andover MA

Elias, Margery M, *Assoc*, Dezign House III, Cleveland OH

Elias, Ramon J, *Dir*, Dezign House III, Cleveland OH

Eliason, Linda, *Chairperson*, William Penn College, Art Department, Oskaloosa IA (S)

Eliet, Leslie Ann, *Registrar*, Colgate University, Picker Art Gallery, Hamilton NY

Eliscur, Frank, *Art Advisory Board*, Society of Medalists, Danbury CT

Elkin, P Bush, *Secy*, Dallas Public Library, Dallas Print and Drawing Society, Dallas TX

Elkington, Richard N, *Chmn*, Providence College, Department of Fine Arts, Providence RI (S)

Elkins, Bettye, *VPres*, Ann Arbor Art Association, Ann Arbor MI

Elks, Hazel Hulbert, *Library Dir*, Free Public Library of Elizabeth, Fine Arts Dept, Elizabeth NJ

Ellinger, Bruce, *Instr*, Madison Area Technical College, Communication Arts, Madison WI (S)

Elliott, David, *Dir of Museum*, Museum of Modern Art Oxford, Oxford England

Elliott, James, *Dir*, University of California, University Art Museum, Berkeley CA

Elliott, James, *VPres*, Licking County Art Association Gallery, Newark OH

Elliott, L Gene, *Librn*, Bob Jones University, Mack Library, Greenville SC

Elliott, Robbin, *Executive VPres*, Royal Architectural Institute of Canada, Ottawa ON

Elliott, Roger, *Asst Prof*, Central Virginia Community College, Division of Humanities, Lynchburg VA (S)

Elliott, Willoughby, *Chairperson Fine Art*, Southeastern Massachusetts University, College of Visual and Performing Arts, North Dartmouth MA (S)

Elliott Jr, J H, *Dir*, Atlanta Museum, Atlanta GA

Ellis, Charles, *Coordr Commercial Art*, Art Institute of Philadelphia, Philadelphia PA (S)

Ellis, Donald, *Dir of Exhib*, University of Manitoba Gallery III, Faculty of Architecture Exhibition Centre, Winnipeg MB

Ellis, Edwin C, *Prof*, Central Missouri State University, Art Department, Warrensburg MO (S)

Ellis, George R, *Asst Dir & Cur Africa, Oceania & Indonesia*, University of California, Los Angeles, Museum of Cultural History, Los Angeles CA

Ellis, Nancy L, *Registrar*, University of California, Los Angeles, Museum of Cultural History, Los Angeles CA

Ellis, Richard, *2nd VPres*, Society of Animal Artists, Inc, Bronx NY

Ellis, W F, *Dir*, Art Gallery of Western Australia, Perth Australia

Ellis Jr, Robert H, *Cur*, Kendall Whaling Museum, Sharon MA

Ellison, Joan, *Asst Dir*, San Francisco City and County Art Commission, San Francisco CA

Ellison, Rosemary, *Cur*, Southern Plains Indian Museum, Anadarko OK

Ellison, Rosemary, *Acting Cur*, Museum of the Plains Indian, Browning MT

Ellmore, Dennis, *Asst Prof*, Los Angeles City College, Department of Art, Los Angeles CA (S)

Elrod, James, *Assoc Librn & Head, Technical Processes*, California Institute of the Arts Library, Valencia CA

Elsey, George M, *Pres*, American Red Cross, Washington DC

Elsner, Larry, *Prof*, Utah State University, Department of Art, Logan UT (S)

Elson, James, *Chmn*, High Point College, Fine Arts Department, High Point NC (S)

Elvestrom, Michael D, *Dir*, University of Wisconsin Center-Medford, Art Department, Medford WI (S)

Elwell, George R, *Prof*, Pacific Lutheran University, Department of Art, Tacoma WA (S)

Ely, Robert V, *VPres*, Roswell Museum and Art Center, Roswell NM

Elzea, Rowland P, *Acting Dir & Cur*, Delaware Art Museum, Wilmington DE

Elzinga, G, *Cur Archaeology & Prints & Drawings*, Fries Museum, Leeuwarden Netherlands

Emanuelli, Sharon, *Asst to Prog Dir*, Craft and Folk Art Museum, Los Angeles CA

Embree, Gisela, *Treas*, Santa Cruz Art League, Inc, Santa Cruz CA

Embrey, Carl, *Instr*, San Antonio Art Institute, San Antonio TX (S)

Emden, Miriam, *Head Membership Dept*, Solomon R Guggenheim Museum, New York NY

Emerick, Judson, *Asst Prof*, Pomona College, Art Department, Claremont CA (S)

Emerson, John M, *Pres*, Canadian Society for Education Through Art, Regina SK

Emerson, Roberta Shinn, *Dir*, Huntington Galleries, Huntington WV

Emerson, William R, *Dir*, Franklin D Roosevelt Library and Museum, Hyde Park NY

Emery, Irene, *Cur Emeritus*, Textile Museum, Washington DC

Emil, Arthur D, *VPres*, American Federation of Arts, New York NY

Emison, Elizabeth, *Instr*, Union University, Department of Art, Jackson TN (S)

Emmerich, Carl, *Prof*, Eastern Illinois University, Art Department, Charleston IL (S)

Emmerman, Linda, *Gallery Dir*, Northeast Missouri State University, Art Department, Kirksville MO (S)

Emmert, Richard, *Gallery Mgr*, Gilpin County Arts Association, Central City CO

Emmett, Joseph O, *Treas*, Cincinnati Art Club, Cincinnati OH

Emont, Deborah, *Cur of Collections*, Brooks Memorial Art Gallery, Memphis TN

Endacott, Pamela, *Instructor*, Smith College, Art Department, Northampton MA (S)

Endegama, P, *Cur Anthropology*, Colombo National Museum, Colombo Sri Lanka

Eng, James, *Instr*, Danforth Museum School, Framingham MA (S)

Eng, Seok Chee, *Asst Cur*, National Museum Art Gallery, Singapore Singapore, Republic of

Engebretson, James, *Instructor*, University of Wisconsin-River Falls, Art Department, River Falls WI (S)

Engel, Charlene, *Asst Prof*, Moravian College, Department of Art, Bethlehem PA (S)

Engel, Helen Vanden, *Music Librn*, Grand Rapids Public Library, Music and Art Department, Grand Rapids MI

Engel, Margaret, *Secy*, Pittsburgh Plan for Art Gallery, Pittsburgh PA

Engel, William, *Pres*, Riverside Art Center and Museum, Riverside CA

Engelhardt, Jim, *Asst Prof*, University of Idaho, Department of Art and Architecture, Moscow ID (S)

Engelmann, Lothar K, *Dean*, Rochester Institute of Technology, College of Graphic Arts and Photography, Rochester NY (S)

Engelsma, S Wille, *Cur Textiles*, Fries Museum, Leeuwarden Netherlands

Engel II, Michael, *Pres*, Artists' Fellowship, Inc, New York NY

Engeman, Richard H, *Librn*, Southern Oregon Historical Society, Library, Jacksonville OR

Engerman, Jeanne, *Asst Librn*, Washington State Historical Society, Hewitt Memorial Library, Tacoma WA

Englar, Jerry, *Assoc Prof*, University of Toronto, Department of Landscape Architecture, Toronto ON (S)

Engle, G W, *Adminr*, Colorado Springs Fine Arts Center, Colorado Springs CO

Engle, Nanene, *Assoc Prof*, University of Evansville, Art Dept, Evansville IN (S)

Engler, Christine, *Recording Secy*, Society of American Graphic Artists, New York NY

Engler, Toby, *Asst to Dir*, Tucson Museum of Art, Tucson AZ

Engleson, Richard, *Dir Arts & Science*, Southwestern Community College, Art Department, Creston IA (S)

English, Joseph G, *Adminr*, National Gallery of Art, Washington DC

English, Peter, *Instructor*, Pels School of Art, New York NY (S)

Engman, Robert, *Chmn*, University of Pennsylvania, Department of Fine Arts, Philadelphia PA (S)

Enman, Tom K, *Dir*, Laguna Beach Museum of Art, Laguna Beach CA

Ensor, John H, *Treas*, Star-Spangled Banner Flag House Association, Baltimore MD

Enyeart, James, *Dir*, Center for Creative Photography, Tucson AZ

Enyeart, James L, *VPres*, Friends of Photography, Carmel CA

Epke, William P, *Dir Corporate Support*, Equitable Life Assurance Society, New York NY

Eppridge, Theresa, *Head Dept*, College of New Rochelle, Art Department, New Rochelle NY (S)

Epstein, Ann, *Asst Prof*, Duke University, Department of Art, Durham NC (S)

Epstein, Eva, *Dir Institute*, Saidye Bronfman Centre, Montreal PQ

Epstein, Mary, *Head Dept*, Drexel University, Department of Design, Philadelphia PA (S)

Erb, Sandra, *Secy to Dir*, San Diego Museum of Art, San Diego CA

Erbes, Roslyn, *Prof*, Indiana State University, Department of Humanities, Terre Haute IN (S)

Ercilla, Jorge Guillermo Luna, *Regent & Prof*, Escuela Superior de Bellas Artes Ernesto de la Carcova, National Superior School of Fine Arts Ernesto de la Carcova, Buenos Argentina

Erdal, Behcet, *Cur Laboratory Preservation*, Istanbul Arkeoloji Müzeleri, Archaeological Museums of Istanbul, Istanbul Turkey

Erdle, Rob, *Dir*, Chautauqua Gallery of Art, Chautauqua NY

Erdossy, Alan, *Dir*, Sharon Arts Center, Inc, Sharon NH

Erdossy, Alan, *Dir*, Sharon Arts Center, Peterborough NH (S)

Erhart, K Patricia, *Asst Prof*, University of Southern California, School of Fine Arts, Los Angeles CA (S)

Eri, Gyöngyi, *Deputy Dir General*, Magyar Nemzeti Galeria, Hungarian National Gallery, Budapest Hungary

Erichsen, John, *Asst Cur*, Kobenhavns Bymuseum, Copenhagen City Museum, Copenhagen Denmark

Erickson, Ann, *Assoc Prof*, University of Minnesota, Department of Design, Saint Paul MN (S)

Erickson, Johanna, *Instr*, Danforth Museum School, Framingham MA (S)

Erickson, Jon T, *Cur Coll*, Heard Museum, Phoenix AZ

Erikson, Marianne, *Asst Cur Textiles*, Rohsska Konstslojdmuseet, Rohss Museum of Arts and Crafts, Gothenburg Sweden

Erkin, Annette E, *Librn*, Phoenix Art Museum, Art Research Library, Phoenix AZ

Erlebacher, Walter, *Chairperson Sculpture*, Philadelphia College of Art, Philadelphia PA (S)

Ermoyan, Arpi, *Executive Dir*, Society of Illustrators, New York NY

Erney, Richard A, *Dir*, State Historical Society of Wisconsin, Madison WI

Ernst, E Urban, *Pres*, Pioneer Museum and Haggin Galleries, Stockton CA

Eroman, Mariella, *Instr*, Silver Lake College, Art Department, Manitowoc WI (S)

Errickson, Betsy, *Asst Cur*, Hopewell Museum, Hopewell NJ

Ertas, Adam, *Instructor*, College of DuPage, Humanities Div, Glen Ellyn IL (S)

Erten, Yücel, *Asst Dir*, Istanbul Arkeoloji Müzeleri, Archaeological Museums of Istanbul, Istanbul Turkey

Erwin, Saralee, *Instr*, Danforth Museum School, Framingham MA (S)

Esbensen, Leonard, *Asst Prof*, Mount Saint Mary's College, Art Department, Los Angeles CA (S)

Esch, Joan, *Asst Prof*, Mount Holyoke College, Art Department, South Hadley MA (S)

Eschberger, Denise, *Education Coordr*, Museum of the Southwest, Midland TX

Escher, S Firmin, *Dean of Fine Art*, College of Saint Benedict, Art Department, Saint Joseph MN (S)

Eshelman, Ralph E, *Dir*, Calvert Marine Museum, Solomons MD

Eshoo, Robert, *Supv The Currier Art Center*, Currier Gallery of Art, Manchester NH

Eshoo, Virginia, *Coordr of Membership*, Currier Gallery of Art, Manchester NH

Eskew, Doyle, *Assoc Prof*, Prince George's Community College, Art Department, Largo MD (S)

Eskind, Andrew, *Asst Dir*, International Museum of Photography at George Eastman House, Rochester NY

Esmerian, Ralph, *Chmn*, Museum of American Folk Art, New York NY

Esparza, Roberto, *Community Relations Coordr*, San Antonio Museum Association, Inc, San Antonio TX

Espey, Jule Adele, *Asst Prof*, Our Lady of the Lake University, Department of Art, San Antonio TX (S)

Espina, Dennisse, *Production Asst*, Asheville Art Museum, Asheville NC

Espinoso, Victoria, *Prof*, Institute of Puerto Rican Culture, Escuela de Artes Plasticas, Mayaguez PR (S)

Esquibel, George A, *Subject Area Rep*, Sacramento City College, Art Department, Sacramento CA (S)

Essar, Gary, *Asst Cur*, Regina Public Library, Dunlot Art Gallery, Regina SK

Essers, Volkmar, *Cur*, Konservator der Kunstdenkmaler, Dusseldorf Germany, Federal Republic of

Estabrook, Reed, *Assoc Prof*, University of Northern Iowa, Department of Art, Cedar Falls IA (S)

Esterly, Freda, *Cur*, Staten Island Institute of Arts and Sciences, Staten Island Museum, Staten Island NY (S)

Esterly, Freda Mulcahy, *Museum Lectr*, Staten Island Institute of Arts and Sciences, Staten Island NY

Esteros, Gertrude, *Head Dept*, University of Minnesota, Department of Design, Saint Paul MN (S)

Estes, Jim, *Asst Prof*, Missouri Western State College, Art Department, Saint Joseph MO (S)

Estes, Rosemary N, *Archivist*, Museum of Early Southern Decorative Arts, Old Salem Inc, Winston-Salem NC

Eszlary, E, *Head Old Sculpture*, Szepmuveszet Museum, Museum of Fine Arts, Budapest Hungary

Ethier, L, *Pres*, Musee d'Art de Saint-Laurent, Saint-Laurent PQ

Etier, Marc, *Vis Prof*, East Central University, Art Department, Ada OK (S)

Etter, Juanita, *Asst Mgr*, Campus Martius Museum and Ohio River Museum, Marietta OH

Euell, Julian, *Asst Secy for Public Service*, Smithsonian Institution, Washington DC

Eugene, Robert, *Adminr*, Princeton Antiques Bookservice, Art Marketing Reference Library, Atlantic City NJ

Evans, Bruce, *VPres*, Intermuseum Conservation Association, Oberlin OH

Evans, Bruce H, *Dir*, Dayton Art Institute, Dayton OH

Evans, Charles F, *Head Dept*, Winona State University, Art Department, Winona MN (S)

Evans, Christine, *Second VPres*, Association of Honolulu Artists, Honolulu HI

Evans, Constance, *Assoc Prof*, Southampton College of Long Island University, Fine Arts Division, Southampton NY (S)

Evans, Deborah L, *Dir*, Annie S Kemerer Museum, Bethlehem PA

Evans, Donald, *Assoc Prof*, Vanderbilt University, Dept of Fine Arts, Nashville TN (S)

Evans, Dorinda, *Asst Prof*, Emory University, Art History Department, Atlanta GA (S)

Evans, Dorothy G, *Exec Dir*, School Art League of New York City, Brooklyn NY

Evans, Elaine A, *Cur Coll*, University of Tennessee, Frank H McClung Museum, Knoxville TN

Evans, Elspeth, *Archive & Library*, National Portrait Gallery, London England

Evans, Emily, *Librn*, Portland Art Association, Museum Library, Portland OR

Evans, Fran, *Librn*, Prince George Art Gallery, Library, Prince George BC

Evans, Fydella, *Registrar*, Percy H Whiting Art Center, Fairhope AL

Evans, Garth, *Visiting Artist*, Mount Holyoke College, Art Department, South Hadley MA (S)

Evans, Howard M, *Dir*, Haystack Mountain School of Crafts Gallery, Deer Isle ME

Evans, Howard M, *Dir*, Haystack Mountain School of Crafts, Deer Isle ME (S)

Evans, Jack P, *Treas*, Montgomery Museum of Fine Arts, Montgomery AL

Evans, John S, *Sales Mgr*, Grand Central Art Galleries, Inc, New York NY

Evans, Josephine, *Membership*, Pennsylvania Academy of the Fine Arts, Philadelphia PA

Evans, Linda E, *Executive Dir*, Center for the Visual Arts, Oakland CA

Evans, Nancy Goyne, *Registrar*, Winterthur Museum and Gardens, Winterthur DE

Evans, Peggy B, *Gallery*, French Art Colony, Inc, Gallipolis OH

Evans, Ric, *Coordr*, Wenatchee Valley College, Gallery 76, Wenatchee WA

Evans, Richard, *Prof*, University of Wyoming, Art Department, Laramie WY (S)

Evans, Robert G, *Vice Chmn Board & Chmn Membership Committee*, Kansas City Art Institute, Charlotte Crosby Kemper Gallery, Kansas City MO

Evans, Robert J, *Cur Art*, Illinois State Museum of Natural History and Art, Springfield IL

Evans, Rojean, *Public Relations*, Oregon School of Arts and Crafts, Hoffman Gallery, Portland OR

Evans, W Donald, *Chmn*, Lynchburg College, Art Department, Lynchburg VA (S)

Evarts, Wilbur, *Executive Dir*, Paint 'N Palette Club, Anamosa IA

Evelyn, Douglas E, *Deputy Dir*, National Museum of History and Technology, Smithsonian Institution, Washington DC

Even, Robert L, *Chmn Dept Art*, Northern Illinois University, Department of Art, De Kalb IL (S)

Even, Robert L, *Chmn Dept*, Northern Illinois University, Swen Parson Gallery and Gallery 200, De Kalb IL

Everett, Russell, *Adjunct Instr*, Auburn University at Montgomery, Art Department, Montgomery AL (S)

Everett, Sally, *Asst Prof*, Metropolitan State College, Art Department, Denver CO (S)

Everts, Connor, *Head Graphics Dept*, Cranbrook Academy of Art, Bloomfield Hills MI (S)

Everts, Connor, *Vis Prof*, Sun Valley Center for the Arts & Humanities, Department of Fine Art, Sun Valley ID (S)

Eves, Bruce, *Publicity*, Cultural Initiative, Toronto ON

Evett, Philip J, *Assoc Prof*, Trinity University, Department of Art, San Antonio TX (S)

Ewald, G, *Dir*, Staatsgalerie Stuttgart, Stuttgart Germany, Federal Republic of

Ewens, Mary, *Dean*, Rosary College, Graduate School of Fine Arts at Schifanoia Villa, Florence Italy (S)

Ewens, Polly, *Chmn Foundations Dept*, Milwaukee School of the Arts, Milwaukee WI (S)

Ewing, Bayard, *Pres Board of Trustees*, American Federation of Arts, New York NY

Ewing, George, *Dir*, Museum of New Mexico, Santa Fe NM

Ewing, Reid, *Pres*, Morse Gallery of Art, Boulder FL

Ewing, Tom, *Instructor*, Mainline Center of the Arts, Haverford PA (S)

Ewing, William, *Dir Exhib*, International Center of Photography, New York NY

Eyerly, Pauline, *Cur of Ed*, Portland Art Association, Portland OR

Eyre, Bill, *Cultural Programs Coordr*, Hampton Center for Arts and Humanities, Hampton VA

Eysselinck, Walter, *Head*, Carnegie-Mellon University, Department of Drama, Pittsburgh PA (S)

Fabbri, Nancy Rash, *Assoc Prof*, Connecticut College, Department of Art History, New London CT (S)

Faber, David, *Prof*, West Virginia University, Division of Art, Morgantown WV (S)

Faber, Tobias, *Dir School Archit*, Det Kongelige Danske Kunstakademi, The Royal Danish Academy of Fine Arts, Copenhagen Denmark (S)

Fabiano, Daniel, *Assoc Prof*, University of Wisconsin-Stevens Point, Department of Art, Stevens Point WI (S)

Fabregas, Rafael, *Pres*, La Casa del Libro, House of Books, San Juan PR

Fabrycki, William, *Chmn Dept*, Joliet Junior College, Art Dept, Joliet IL (S)

Faccinto, Victor, *Gallery Dir*, Wake Forest University, Department of Art, Winston-Salem NC (S)

Fagaly, William A, *Chief Cur*, New Orleans Museum of Art, Isaac Delgado Museum, New Orleans LA

Fagen, Henry, *Dir*, Converse College, Milliken Art Gallery, Spartanburg SC

Fagen Jr, Henry, *Chmn Dept*, Converse College, Art Dept, Spartanburg SC (S)

Faggioli, Renzo, *Ceramist-in-Residence*, Moravian College, Department of Art, Bethlehem PA (S)

Fahlen, Charles, *Chmn Printmaking*, Moore College of Art, Philadelphia PA (S)

Fahy, Barbara M, *Assoc Prof*, Albright College, Department of Art, Reading PA (S)

Fahy, Everett, *Dir*, Frick Collection, New York NY

Faichney, John, *Art Librn*, Cultural Initiative, Library, Toronto ON

Faichney, John, *Librn*, Cultural Initiative, Cultural Initiative Archives, Toronto ON

Faichney, John, *Secy*, Cultural Initiative, Toronto ON

Faill, Carol E, *Executive Dir*, Doshi Center for Contemporary Art, Harrisburg PA

Fain, Barnet, *Chmn Museum Council*, Rhode Island School of Design, Museum of Art, Providence RI

Fain, Yonia, *Asst Prof*, Hofstra University, Department of Art History, Hempstead NY (S)

Fair, Barry, *Registrar*, London Regional Art Gallery, London ON

Fair, Beth, *Vol Coordinator*, Palo Alto Cultural Center, Palo Alto CA

Fairbanks, Evelyn, *Executive Dir ,10*, Metropolitan Cultural Arts Center, Minneapolis MN

Fairbanks, Jonathan, *Cur American Decorative Arts*, Museum of Fine Arts, Boston MA

Fairbanks, Justin, *Head*, Eastern Arizona College, Thatcher AZ (S)

Fairchild, Isabel S, *Dir*, Central Connecticut State College Museum, New Britain CT

Faircloth, Norman D, *Head*, Guilford Technical Institute, Commercial Art Dept, Jamestown NC (S)

Fairhead, Patricia, *Instr*, Toronto School of Art, Toronto ON (S)

Faison, Barbara A, *Admin Officer*, National Portrait Gallery, Washington DC

Fales, Haliburton, *Secy*, Pierpont Morgan Library, New York NY

Falgoust, Hymel G, *Prof*, Southeastern Louisiana University, Dept of Visual Arts, Hammond LA (S)

Falk, Lorne, *Asst Cur*, Banff Centre, Walter Phillips Gallery, Banff AB

Falk, Toby, *Museum Educ Coordr*, Tucson Museum of Art, Tucson AZ

Falkenheim, Jacqueline V, *Asst Prof*, Cornell University, Department of the History of Art, Ithaca NY (S)

Falkner, Etta, *Librn*, Old Sturbridge Village, Research Library, Sturbridge MA

Faller, Marion, *Instructor*, Colgate University, Department of Fine Arts, Hamilton NY (S)

Fames, William C W, *Chmn of Board*, Salmagundi Club, New York NY

Famolari, Toni, *Instructor*, Wayne Art Center, Wayne PA (S)

Fan, Manya, *Secy*, Lafayette Art Center, Lafayette IN

Fanani, Dom, *Instructor*, Millersville State College, Art Department, Millersville PA (S)

Fanata, Katherine, *Circulation*, Long Beach Public Library, Long Beach NY

Fancher, Oliver, *Asst Prof*, Middle Tennessee State University, Art Dept, Murfreesboro TN (S)

Fane, Diana, *Asst Cur African, Oceanic & New World Cultures*, Brooklyn Museum, Brooklyn NY

Fannin, Bill, *Cur*, Missouri State Museum, Jefferson City MO

Fanta, Fran, *Dir of Public Relations*, University of Chicago, David and Alfred Smart Gallery, Chicago IL

Fantauzzi, Dan, *Instr*, Youngstown State University, Art Department, Youngstown OH (S)

Faralli, Adelaide, *Chmn Advertising Design*, Moore College of Art, Philadelphia PA (S)

Farber, Lola, *Library Asst*, University of Colorado Art Galleries, Art and Architecture Library, Boulder CO

Farber, Manny, *Prof*, University of California, San Diego, Visual Arts Department, La Jolla CA (S)

Farias, Laura, *Asst Prof*, Texas Tech University, Department of Art, Lubbock TX (S)

Farinella, Paul J, *Pres*, Munson-Williams-Proctor Institute, Museum of Art, Utica NY

Faris, Brunel D, *Chmn*, Oklahoma City University, Art Department, Oklahoma City OK (S)

Faris, Peter K, *Dir*, Western Colorado Center for the Arts, Inc, Grand Junction CO

Farkas, Ray Lynn, *VPres*, Wallingford Art League, Wallingford CT

Farley, Authur Leonard, *Prof*, Mississippi State University, Art Department, Mississippi State MS (S)

Farlow, Susan, *Asst*, Wellesley College, Art Library, Wellesley MA

Farmer, Barthwell, *Chmn Art History*, Edinboro State College, Art Department, Edinboro PA (S)

Farmer, Betsy, *Instructor*, Shippensburg State College, Art Department, Shippensburg PA (S)

Farmer, Gregory, *Cur*, Connecticut Valley Historical Museum, Springfield MA

Farmer, Guss, *Asst Prof*, Southwestern University, Art Department, Georgetown TX (S)

Farmer, Susan, *Asst Prof*, Silver Lake College, Art Department, Manitowoc WI (S)

Farnam, Anne, *Cur*, Essex Institute, Salem MA

Farnsley, Charles P, *Pres*, Filson Club, Reference and Research Library, Louisville KY

Farooq, A A, *Custodian*, Archaeological Museum, Taxila Pakistan

Farooqi, Anis, *Deputy Keeper Education*, National Gallery of Modern Art, New India

Farquharson, Alexander, *Instr*, Boston Center for Adult Education, Boston MA (S)

Farquharson, Marion, *Instructor*, Rehoboth Art League, Inc, Rehoboth Beach DE (S)

Farr, Dennis, *Dir*, Birmingham Museums and Art Gallery, Birmingham England

Farr, Dorothy, *Cur*, Queen's University, Agnes Etherington Art Centre, Kingston ON

Farr, Frederick S, *Chmn Monterey Council*, Casa Amesti, Monterey CA

Farr, Mary G, *Museum Coordr*, Kenneth C Beck Center for the Cultural Arts, Lakewood OH

Farrar, Elaine W, *Instructor*, Yavapai College, Art Department, Prescott AZ (S)

Farrell, A, *Instr*, Selkirk College, Kootenay School of Art Division, Nelson BC (S)

Farrell, Eugene, *Science Assoc*, Harvard University, William Hayes Fogg Art Museum, Cambridge MA

Farrell, Patricia, *Docent*, Saint Anselm's College, Manchester NH

Farrell, Peggy, *Vis Prof*, Carroll College, Art Department, Waukesha WI (S)

Farrell-Ward, Lorna, *Cur*, Vancouver Art Gallery, Vancouver BC

Farrior, Patti, *Secy Registrar*, North Carolina Central University, Museum of Art, Durham NC

Faryniak, Karen, *Instructor*, Mohawk Valley Community College, Advertising Design and Production, Utica NY (S)

Fasanelli, James, *Assoc Prof*, University of Maryland Baltimore County, Visual Arts Department, Catonsville MD (S)

Fash, William L, *Dean*, Georgia Institute of Technology, College of Architecture, Atlanta GA (S)

Fasman, Marjorie, *Chmn Bd Trustees*, Junior Arts Center, Los Angeles CA

Fasoldt, Sarah, *Gallery Mgr*, Maine Coast Artists, Rockport ME

Fassett, Brian R, *Asst Prof*, Northeast Louisiana University, Department of Art, Monroe LA (S)

Fasulo, Marijo, *Asst Dir*, State University of New York at Albany, University Art Gallery, Albany NY

Faude, Wilson H, *Exec Dir*, Old State House, Hartford CT

Faudie, Fred, *Chairperson Dept*, University of Lowell, Department of Art, Lowell MA (S)

Faulkner, Lloyd E, *Chairperson Div*, Modesto Junior College, Arts Humanities and Speech Division, Modesto CA (S)

Faul, Karene, *Instr*, College of Saint Rose, Division of Art, Albany NY (S)

Faunce, Sarah C, *Cur & Dept Head Paintings & Sculpture*, Brooklyn Museum, Brooklyn NY

Fausett, Dean, *Pres*, National Society of Mural Painters, Inc, New York NY

Fava, Anna Serena, *Dir*, Museo Civico di Torino, Municipal Museum, Turin Italy

Favell, Gene H, *Pres*, Favell Museum of Western Art & Indian Artifacts, Klamath Falls OR

Favell, Winifred L, *VPres & Treas*, Favell Museum of Western Art & Indian Artifacts, Klamath Falls OR

Faviere, Jean, *Conservation*, Musee des Beaux-Arts, Museum of Fine Arts, Strasbourg France

Fawcett, David, *Registrar*, Museum of the American Indian, New York NY

Fawcett, Joyce, *Dir*, Deming Luna Mimbres Museum, Deming NM

Fawcett, W Peyton, *Librn*, Field Museum of Natural History, Library, Chicago IL

Fawcett Jr, R Richard, *Treas*, Canton Art Institute, Canton OH

Fawkes, Judith, *Lectr*, Lewis and Clark College, Department of Art, Portland OR (S)

Fay, Kathy, *Art Instr*, School of Fashion Design, Boston MA (S)

Fay, Peter, *Head Librn*, John F Kennedy Center for the Performing Arts, Performing Arts Library, Washington DC

Faymann, Lynn G, *Pres Board of Trustees*, La Jolla Museum of Contemporary Art, La Jolla CA

Fazekas, Andre, *Instructor*, Ivy School of Professional Art, Downtown Annex, Pittsburgh PA (S)

Fazzini, Richard, *Cur Egyptian & Classical Art*, Brooklyn Museum, Brooklyn NY

Featherstone, David, *Executive Asst*, Friends of Photography, Carmel CA

Feaux, Shirley, *VPres*, Huntsville Art League and Museum Association Inc, Huntsville AL

FeBland, Harriet, *Dir*, Harriet FeBland Art Workshop, New York NY (S)

Fechter, Earl, *Asst Prof*, Vermont College of Norwich University, Philosophy, Religion and Fine Arts Department, Montpelier VT (S)

Federico, Frank, *Instructor*, Dunedin Fine Arts and Cultural Center, Dunedin FL (S)

Federico, Jean Taylor, *Cur*, DAR Museum, National Society Daughters of the American Revolution, Washington DC

Federighi, Christine, *Instructor*, University of Miami, Department of Art, Coral Gables FL (S)

Feeney, John, *Historic Site Mgr*, Mills Mansion State Historic Site, Staatsburg NY

Feeny, Lawrence, *Assoc Prof*, Mississippi University for Women, Art Department, Columbus MS (S)

Feeny, William, *Instr*, Madison Area Technical College, Communication Arts, Madison WI (S)

Feher, Joseph, *Cur*, Honolulu Academy of Arts, Studio Program, Honolulu HI (S)

Feher, Joseph, *Senior Cur & Cur Graphic Arts & Studio Programmer*, Honolulu Academy of Arts, Honolulu HI

Fehm Jr, Sherwood A, *Adj Cur Art History*, Southern Illinois University Museum and Art Galleries, Carbondale IL

Feichtmeir, Karl, *Manuscripts*, California Historical Society, Library, San Francisco CA

Feidt, Thorpe, *Instr*, Montserrat School of Visual Art, Beverly MA (S)

Feigenbaum, Rita, *Registrar*, Jewish Museum, New York NY

Feinblatt, Ebria, *Sr Cur of Prints and Drawings*, Los Angeles County Museum of Art, Los Angeles CA

Feiner, Lynn, *Recording Secy*, South County Art Association, Kingston RI

Feint, Donald, *Supt*, Cornell University, Herbert F Johnson Museum of Art, Ithaca NY

Felber, Leland, *Instructor*, Milwaukee Area Technical College, Graphic & Applied Arts Div, Milwaukee WI (S)

Felder, Paul, *Asst Prof*, Lehigh University, Department of Art and Architecture, Bethlehem PA (S)

Feldman, Arthur M, *Dir*, Spertus Museum of Judaica, Chicago IL

Feldman, Edmund B, *Pres-Elect*, National Art Education Association, Reston VA

Feldman, Eugene P, *Resident Dir*, DuSable Museum of African American History, Chicago IL

Feldman, Nan, *Instr*, Danforth Museum School, Framingham MA (S)

Fell, Kathleen, *Instructor*, Ocean City School of Art, Ocean City NJ (S)

Felling, Bill, *Pres*, Oak Ridge Community Art Center, Oak Ridge TN

Fellows, Helen, *Cur Coll*, Loveland Museum, Loveland CO

Felter, James Warren, *Chmn*, Western Canada Art Association Inc, Burnaby BC

Felter, James Warren, *Dir*, Simon Fraser University, Simon Fraser Gallery, Burnaby BC

Fenderson, Michael, *Dir Human Servs*, Mills House Visual Arts Complex, Garden Grove CA

Fenimore, Ronald, *Coordr Advertising Design*, Iowa State University, Department of Design, Ames IA (S)

Fennimore, Patricia, *Head Childrens Department*, Springfield Free Public Library, Donald B Palmer Museum, Springfield NJ

Fenton, Julia A, *Dir*, Atlanta Art Workers Coalition, Information Resource Center, Atlanta GA

Fenton, T, *Dir*, Edmonton Art Gallery, Edmonton AB

Ferazza, Mario, *Asst Cur for Modern Religious Art Coll*, Monumenti Musei e Gallerie Pontificie, Vatican Museums and Galleries, Vatican City Italy

Ferber, Elise V H, *Head Art Information Service*, National Gallery of Art, Washington DC

Ferber, Lee, *Prof*, Drake University, Art Department, Des Moines IA (S)

Ferber, Linda, *Cur Paintings & Sculpture*, Brooklyn Museum, Brooklyn NY

Ferber, Stanley, *Chmn Dept*, State University of New York at Binghamton, Department of Art History, Binghamton NY (S)

Ferbitta, Angelo, *Chmn Gallery*, Art Institute of Boston, Gallery West, Gallery East, Boston MA

Ferdinandy, Magdalana, *Instructor*, University of Puerto Rico, Department of Fine Arts, Mayaguez PR (S)

Ference, Cynthia K, *Dir*, Green Hill Art Gallery, Greensboro NC

Ferguson, Carra, *Chmn*, Georgetown University, Department of Fine Arts, Washington DC (S)

Ferguson, Charles B, *Dir*, New Britain Museum of American Art, New Britain CT

Ferguson, Charles C, *Chmn*, Macdonald Steward Art Centre, Guelph ON

Ferguson, John, *Instructor*, Saint Louis Community College at Meramec, Art Dept, Saint Louis MO (S)

Ferguson, Ken, *Business Mgr*, Art Gallery of Windsor, Windsor ON

Ferguson, Ken, *Vis Prof*, Cochise College, Art Department, Douglas AZ (S)

Ferguson, Kenneth, *Chmn Crafts*, Kansas City Art Institute, Kansas City MO (S)

Ferguson, Lorna, *Cur*, Tatham Art Gallery, Pietermaritzburg South Africa, Republic of

Ferguson, Marie D, *Adminr*, Dayton Art Institute, Dayton OH

Ferguson, Robert, *Asst Cur*, Jersey City Museum Association, Jersey City NJ

Ferguson, Robert J, *Chmn Dept*, Henry Ford Community College, Art Dept, Dearborn MI (S)

Ferguson, Rodney, *Asst Prof*, Southern University in New Orleans, Art Dept, New Orleans LA (S)

Fergusson, Peter J, *Prof*, Wellesley College, Art Department, Wellesley MA (S)

Fernandez, Nell, *Admin Dir*, Instituto Allende, Allende Institute, San Mexico (S)

Fernandez, Rafael A, *Cur Prints & Drawings*, Sterling and Francine Clark Art Institute, Williamstown MA

Ferng, Hou-Ran, *Librn*, Saint John's University, Asian Collection, Jamaica NY

Ferrara, Luciana, *Second Dir*, Galleria Borghese, Borghese Gallery, Rome Italy

Ferrario, Frank, *Instr*, Fontbonne College, Art Department, Saint Louis MO (S)

Ferrario, Frank, *Instructor*, Fontbonne College, Department of Art, Clayton MO (S)

Ferrario, Paula, *Serials and Rare Books*, Washington University, Art and Architecture Library, Saint Louis MO

Ferren, Rae, *Assoc Cur*, Guild Hall of East Hampton, Inc, Museum Section, East Hampton NY

Ferrer, Miguel A, *Treas*, La Casa del Libro, House of Books, San Juan PR

Ferrini, Azio J, *VPres*, Portsmouth Athenaeum NR, Inc 1817, Portsmouth NH

Ferris, Margaret G, *Instr*, Virginia Western Community College, Commercial Art, Fine Art & Photography, Roanoke VA (S)

Ferroni, Juan, *Head Archit*, Universidad Javeriana, Javeriana University Faculty of Architecture and Design, Bogota Colombia (S)

Ferrulli, Helen, *Educ Cur*, Whitney Museum of American Art, New York NY

Ferst, Richard, *Vice Chmn*, Please Touch Museum, Philadelphia PA

Fessler, M Thomasita, *Head Dept*, Cardinal Stritch College, Art Department, Milwaukee WI (S)

Fetchko, Peter, *Asst Dir*, Peabody Museum of Salem, Salem MA

Ffolliott, Sheila, *Asst Prof*, George Mason University, Department of Fine and Performing Arts, Fairfax VA (S)

Fiandaca, Fred, *Asst Prof*, Framingham State College, Art Department, Framingham MA (S)

Ficken, Dale, *Assoc Prof*, Fort Hays State University, Department of Art, Hays KS (S)

Fidler, Spencer, *Prof*, New Mexico State University, Art Dept, Las Cruces NM (S)

Fiebich-Ripke, Annemarie, *Cur Restoration*, Saltzburger Museum Carolino Augusteum, Salzburg Museum, Salzburg Austria

Fiedler, Buddy, *Dir*, Carnegie-Mellon University, Forbes Street Gallery, Pittsburgh PA

Fiedler, Joseph, *Instructor*, Ivy School of Professional Art, Downtown Annex, Pittsburgh PA (S)

Fiehler, Joann, *Asst Prof*, University of Dayton, Fine Arts Division, Dayton OH (S)

Field, Charles, *Prof*, University of Texas at San Antonio, Division of Art and Design, San Antonio TX (S)

Field, Frank E, *Pres*, Art Students League of New York, New York NY

Field, Grace, *Libr Clerk*, University of Rochester, Memorial Art Gallery Library, Rochester NY

Field, M Theophane, *Chmn*, Sacred Heart College, Department of Art, Belmont NC (S)

Field, Philip, *Chmn Printmaking*, Pan American University, Art Department, Edinburg TX (S)

Field, Richard, *Dir*, University of Wisconsin, Harry Nohr Art Gallery, Platteville WI

Field, Richard S, *Cur Prints, Drawings & Watercolors*, Yale University, Art Gallery, New Haven CT

Fields, Patricia, *Prof*, Linfield College, Art Department, McMinnville OR (S)

Fife, Ed, *Assoc Prof*, University of Toronto, Department of Landscape Architecture, Toronto ON (S)

Fifield, Mary L, *Chmn Dept*, Saint Louis Community College at Forest Park, Dept of Art, Saint Louis MO (S)

Figueroa, Paul C, *Cur Education*, Carolina Art Association, Gibbes Art Gallery, Charleston SC

Figundio, Alice, *Librn*, University of Chicago, Research Archives, Chicago IL

Fikus, Vivian Noyes, *Dir*, Nutley Art Center, Nutley NJ (S)

Filby, Don, *Instructor*, Friends University, Art Department, Wichita KS (S)

File, M Jeanne, *Prof*, Daemen College, Art Department, Amherst NY (S)

Filkosky, Josefa, *Instructor*, Seton Hill College, Department of Art, Greensburg PA (S)

Finch, Robert, *Instructor*, Mainline Center of the Arts, Haverford PA (S)

Findkoglu, Zeki, *Asst Prof*, University of the District of Columbia, Art Department, Washington DC (S)

Findley, Jerry, *Asst Dir*, Southern Oregon College, Stevenson Union Art Gallery, Ashland OR

Fine, Ruth, *VPres*, Print Club, Philadelphia PA

Finegan, Don, *Prof*, University of Northern Iowa, Department of Art, Cedar Falls IA (S)

Fingesten, Peter, *Chmn*, Pace University, Art and Music Department, New York NY (S)

Fink, Eleanor, *Chief Office Visual Resources*, National Collection of Fine Arts, Washington DC

Fink, Herbert, *Printmaker-Drawer*, Southern Illinois University, School of Art, Carbondale IL (S)

Fink, Jack, *Prof*, Nassau Community College, Art Department, Garden City NY (S)

Fink, Lois M, *Research Cur*, National Collection of Fine Arts, Washington DC

Fink, Morton, *Head Spec Studies*, Rhode Island School of Design, Providence RI (S)

Finkel, Kenneth, *Cur of Prints*, Library Company of Philadelphia, Philadelphia PA

Finkel, Tina I, *Pres*, Duke University Museum of Art, Union Graphic Arts Committee, Durham NC

Finkelpearl, Katherine D, *Librn*, Wellesley College, Art Library, Wellesley MA

Finley, Gregg, *Cur Canadian History*, New Brunswick Museum, Saint John NB

Finley Jr, Fred S, *Pres*, Wind River Valley Artists Guild, Dubois WY

Finney, W D, *Pres Board Trustees*, Oklahoma Historical Society, Central Museum, Oklahoma City OK

Finsen, Hanne, *Dir*, Ordrupgaard Collection, Charlottenlund Denmark

Fiorello, Joseph, *Prof*, Boston State College, Art Department, Boston MA (S)

Fiorentino, Francis, *Instr*, Utica College of Syracuse University, Division of Humanities, Utica NY (S)

Fiorio, M T, *Cojservator*, Civica Galleria d'Arte Moderna, Milan Italy

Firestone, Evan R, *Head Dept*, Western Carolina University, Dept of Art, Cullowhee NC (S)

Firth, Edith G, *Head Canadian History Department*, Metropolitan Toronto Library Board, Baldwin Room (Canadian History Department), Toronto ON

Fisch, Robert W, *Cur Arms & Armor*, United States Military Academy, West Point Museum, West Point NY

Fischer, Alice S, *Executive Secy*, Fine Arts Museums of San Francisco, The Museum Society, n of Honor co

Fischer, Barbara, *Children's Room Dept Head*, Wichita Public Library, Wichita KS

Fischer, Billie, *Instr*, Kalamazoo College, Art Department, Kalamazoo MI (S)

Fischer, Eberhard, *Dir*, Museum Rietberg Zurich, Zurich Switzerland

Fischer, Erik, *Keeper*, Statens Museum for Kunst, Den Kongelige Kobberstiksamling, Copenhagen Denmark

Fischer, F, *Chmn of Board*, University of Victoria, Maltwood Art Museum and Gallery, Victoria BC

Fischer, Henry G, *Lila Acheson Wallace Cur Egyptology*, Metropolitan Museum of Art, New York NY

Fischer, Martin, *Head Dept*, Toronto Art Therapy Institute, Toronto ON (S)

Fischer, Robert L, *Secy*, Grand Prairie Art Council, Inc, Stuttgart AR

Fischer, Stephen, *Instr*, Waynesburg College, Department of Fine Arts, Waynesburg PA (S)

Fish, Mary E, *Dir Creative Arts Department*, Oglebay Institute, Stifel Fine Arts Center, Wheeling WV

Fisher, Alleene Lowery, *Dir*, Art School of the Crafts Guild, Holland MI (S)

Fisher, Arlene, *Pres*, Lancaster County Art Association, Lancaster PA

Fisher, B C, *Owner*, Westover, Charles City VA

Fisher, F S, *Mgr*, Westover, Charles City VA

Fisher, Frederick J, *Dir*, Hyde Collection, Glens Falls NY

Fisher, James, *Dir*, Elizabet Ney Museum, Austin TX

Fisher, Jay, *Asst Cur Prints and Drawings*, Baltimore Museum of Art, Baltimore MD

Fisher, John C, *Secy*, Louisiana State University, Anglo-American Art Museum, Baton Rouge LA

Fisher, John J, *Journal Ed*, American Society for Aesthetics, Greenvale NY

Fisher, Mac, *Instructor*, Samuel S Fleisher Art Memorial, Philadelphia PA (S)

Fisher, Marlene, *Dean of Faculty*, Manhattanville College, Brownson Art Gallery, Purchase NY

Fisher, Nora, *Cur Textiles*, Museum of New Mexico, Museum of International Folk Art, Santa Fe NM

Fisher, Rosemary, *Instructor*, Arkansas Arts Center, Little Rock AR (S)

Fisher, Suzanne, *Division Head*, Public Library of Columbus and Franklin County, Humanities, Fine Arts and Recreation Division, Columbus OH

Fisher, Sylvia, *Pres Board of Dir*, Asheville Art Museum, Asheville NC

Fisher-Page, Margot, *Dir*, Oakville Centennial-Gairloch Galleries, Oakville ON

Fishman, Katherine, *Asst Prof*, Wright State University, Art Department, Dayton OH (S)

Fisk, Pat, *Instructor*, Del Mar College, Department of Art, Corpus Christi TX (S)

Fiske, Patricia L, *Asst Cur Old World*, Textile Museum, Washington DC

Fiske, Timothy, *Assoc Dir*, Minneapolis Institute of Arts, Minneapolis MN

Fitch, Daniel, *Vis Prof*, Harrisburg Area Community College, Division of Communication and the Arts, Harrisburg PA (S)

Fitch, George, *Fine Arts Coordr*, Tunxis Community College, Graphic Design & Applied Arts Dept, Farmington CT (S)

Fitchett, Claiborne, *Secy*, Irene Leache Memorial, Norfolk VA

Fite, Nancy, *DirChildrens Museum*, Arts and Science Center, Nashua NH

Fittipaldi, Teodore, *Dir*, Museo Nazionale di San Martino, National Museum, Naples Italy

Fittipaldi, Teodore, *Supv & Dir Museo S Martino*, Museo de Capodimonte, Mount Capodi Museum, Naples Italy

Fitzgerald, Dori B, *Membership & Education Coordr*, Roanoke Fine Arts Center, Roanoke VA

Fitzgerald, Harriet, *Dir*, Abingdon Square Painters, Inc, New York NY (S)

Fitzgerald, May, *Librn*, Whitney Museum of American Art, Library, New York NY

Fitzgerald, Oscar, *Assoc Dir*, United States Navy Memorial Museum, Washington DC

Fitzmaurice, Robert M, *Chmn*, Inter American University of Puerto Rico, Department of Performing Arts, San German PR (S)

Fitzpatrick, Philip, *Instructor*, Lamar University, Art Department, Beaumont TX (S)

Fitzpatrick, Robert, *Pres*, California Institute of the Arts, School of Art, Valencia CA (S)

Fitz-Simons, Linda, *Head Dept*, Peace College, Art Department, Raleigh NC (S)

Fix, John R, *Instructor*, Norwich Art School, Norwich Free Academy, Art Dept, Norwich CT (S)

Flach, Victor, *Prof*, University of Wyoming, Art Department, Laramie WY (S)

Flack, C E, *Admin Asst*, Rome Historical Society, Rome Information and Cultural Center, Rome NY

Flagg, Thomas J, *Dean*, Howard University, Department of Art, Washington DC (S)

Flaherty, Joe, *Coordr Book Distribution*, Visual Studies Workshop, Rochester NY

Flaherty, Michael, *Craftshop Dir*, University of Southwestern Louisiana, Union Art Gallery, Lafayette LA

Flam, Jack, *Assoc Prof*, City University of New York, PhD Program in Art History, New York NY (S)

Flanagan, Jeanne, *Dir*, College of Saint Rose Art Gallery, Albany NY

Flanagan III, E Michael, *Cur Exhib & Registrar*, Midwest Museum of American Art, Elkhart IN

Flanigan, James F, *Chmn*, University of Notre Dame, Department of Art, Notre Dame IN (S)

Flannery, Louis, *Chief Librn*, Oregon Historical Society, Library, Portland OR

Flannery, Michael J, *Interlibrary Loan Librn*, Plymouth State College, Herbert H Lamson Library, Plymouth NH

Flansburg, Margaret, *Dir Education*, Oklahoma Museum of Art, Oklahoma City OK

Flavin, Patricia, *Clerical Officer*, Hugh Lane Municipal Gallery of Modern Art, Dublin Ireland

Fleck, Paul D, *Pres*, Ontario College of Art, Toronto ON (S)

Fleck, Paul D, *Pres*, Ontario College of Art, Gallery 76, Toronto ON

Fleck, Rudolf, *Asst Prof*, Loyola Marymount University, Department of Art, Los Angeles CA (S)

Fleischer, Roland E, *Prof*, Pennsylvania State University, University Park, Department of Art History, University Park PA (S)

Fleischmann, Libby, *Librn*, Judah L Magnes Memorial Museum, Morris Goldstein Library, Berkeley CA

Fleming, Joel, *Pres*, Everson Museum of Art, Syracuse NY

Fleming, Margaret, *VPres*, Art Gallery of Peterborough, Peterborough ON

Fleming, Martha, *Dir Film & Video*, Art Metropole, Toronto ON

Fletcher, David, *Dir*, Rensselaer Newman Foundation Chapel and Cultural Center, Troy NY

Fletcher, Donald B, *Pres*, Redwood Library and Athenaeum, Newport RI

Fletcher, Dudty, *Instr*, Danforth Museum School, Framingham MA (S)

Fletcher, Marilyn, *Secy*, Providence Art Club, Providence RI

Fletcher, Martha, *Conservator*, University of Washington, Costume and Textile Study Center, Seattle WA

Fletcher, P R, *Head Dept Printing Technol*, Manchester Polytechnic, Faculty of Art and Design, Manchester England (S)

Flexner, Craig, *Registrar*, Hudson River Museum, Yonkers NY

Flexner, John, *Librn*, Harwood Foundation of the University of New Mexico, Library, Taos NM

Flick, Hugh M, *Pres*, Plymouth Antiquarian Society, Plymouth MA

Flinn, Elizabeth, *Assoc Museum Educator*, Metropolitan Museum of Art, Junior Museum, New York NY

Flint, Janet, *Treas*, Print Council of America, Washington DC

Flint, Janet A, *Cur Prints & Drawings*, National Collection of Fine Arts, Washington DC

Flint, Peter, *Vis Prof*, Porterville Community College, Department of Fine Arts, Porterville CA (S)

Flint, Robert, *Treas*, Civic Fine Arts Association Museum, Sioux Falls SD

Floberg, John F, *Chmn Contributions*, The Firestone Tire & Rubber Company, Akron OH

Flodstrom, Sven, *Pres*, Swedish American Museum Association of Chicago, Chicago IL

Flom, K Christine, *Cur*, Hartwick College Fine Art Gallery, Oneonta NY

Florenza, Blanche, *Secy*, Art Directors Club, Inc, New York NY

Florillo, Ciro, *Asst Supt*, Museo de Capodimonte, Mount Capodi Museum, Naples Italy

Flowers, Thomas E, *Prof*, Furman University, Department of Art, Greenville SC (S)

Flowers II, H D, *Chairperson Dept*, Bowie State College, Department of Fine and Performing Arts, Bowie MD (S)

Floyd, Margaret, *Asst Prof*, Tufts University, Fine Arts Department, Medford MA (S)

Flumiani, C M, *Pres*, Classical School Gallery, Albuquerque NM

Flumiani, C M, *Pres*, American Classical College, Albuquerque NM (S)

Flynn, Barbara, *Head Audio-visual Center*, Chicago Public Library, Cultural Center, Chicago IL

Flynn, Barbara, *Supervisor Librn*, Ontario City Library, Ontario CA

Flynn, Brendan, *Keeper Art*, Central Art Gallery, Wolverhampton England

Flynn, Charles, *Instr*, Virginia Wesleyan College, Art Department of the Humanities Division, Norfolk VA (S)

Flynn, Charles, *Instructor*, Virginia State College, Fine Arts Department, Petersburg VA (S)

Flynn, Elisabeth L, *Assoc Prof*, Longwood College, Department of Art, Farmville VA (S)

Flynt Jr, Henry N, *VPres*, Historic Deerfield Inc, Deerfield MA

Foedisch, Cathryne, *Admin Asst*, Buten Museum of Wedgwood, Merion PA

Fogarty, Cheryl, *Instructor*, Mohawk Valley Community College, Advertising Design and Production, Utica NY (S)

Fogel, D, *VPres*, Nicholas Roerich Museum, New York NY

Fogleman, James K, *Pres*, American Institute of Graphic Arts, New York NY

Fohrman, Darcie, *Cur Exhib*, San Diego Museum of Art, San Diego CA

Folda, Jaroslav, *Prof*, University of North Carolina at Chapel Hill, Art Department, Chapel Hill NC (S)

Foley, Kathy Kelsey, *Dir*, Northwestern University, Mary & Leigh Block Gallery, Evanston IL

Foley, Patricia, *Admin Dir*, Please Touch Museum, Philadelphia PA

Foley, Suzanne, *Chief Cur*, San Francisco Museum of Modern Art, San Francisco CA

Foley, Vincent P, *Dir Wyoming State Archives, Museums and Historical Department*, Wyoming State Art Gallery, Cheyenne WY

Follis, John, *Dir*, Society of Environmental Graphics Designers, Chicago IL

Folsom, Karl L, *Preparator*, Wine Museum of San Francisco, San Francisco CA

Fomerand, Raissa, *Librn*, Sleepy Hollow Restorations Inc, Library, Tarrytown NY

Fominaya, Eloy, *Head Dept*, Augusta College, Department of Fine Arts, Augusta GA (S)

Fones, Sue Anne, *Dir*, Galesburg Civic Art Center, Galesburg IL

Fong, Wen, *Special Consultant for Far Eastern Affairs*, Metropolitan Museum of Art, New York NY

Fong, Wen, *Chmn Prog Chinese and Japanese Art and Archaeology*, Princeton University, Department of Art and Archaeology, Princeton NJ (S)

Font, Frances, *Librn*, Museo de Arte Moderno, Library, Barcelona Spain

Fontein, Jan, *Dir*, Museum of Fine Arts, Boston MA

Foote, Annemarie, *Cur America*, Museum für Völkerkunde und Schweizerisches Museum für Volkskunde Basel, Museum of Ethnological Collections and Folklore, Basel Switzerland

Foote, Vincent M, *Dir Product Design Prog*, North Carolina State University at Raleigh, School of Design, Raleigh NC (S)

Forbes, Barbara, *Asst Prof*, Florida International University, Visual Arts Department, Miami FL (S)

Forbes, Donna M, *Dir*, Yellowstone Art Center, Billings MT

Forbes, Gaylord, *Instructor*, De Anza College, Art Department, Cupertino CA (S)

Forbes, H A Crosby, *Cur*, Museum of the American China Trade, Milton MA

Forbes, Wayne, *Instr*, Illinois Central College, Art and Humanities Department, East Peoria IL (S)

Force, Debra J, *Dir & Cur*, INA Corporation, Philadelphia PA

Force, Roland W, *Dir*, Museum of the American Indian, New York NY

Ford, Beth M, *Instructor*, Florida Southern College, Art Department, Lakeland FL (S)

Ford, Charles, *Exhib Coordr*, Jay R Broussard Memorial Galleries, Baton Rouge LA

Ford, Colin, *Asst Keeper*, National Portrait Gallery, London England

Ford, C Richard, *Secy*, Oklahoma Art Center, Oklahoma City OK

Ford, Harry X, *Pres*, California College of Arts and Crafts, Oakland CA (S)

Ford, Janice B, *Asst Prof*, Pikeville College, Fine Arts Dept, Pikeville KY (S)

Ford, Margaret, *Instructor*, Factory of Visual Art, Seattle WA (S)

Ford, Peggy A, *Dir*, University of Northern Colorado, John Mariani Art Gallery, Greeley CO

Ford, Richard E, *Dir & Cur*, John Woodman Higgins Armory, Worcester MA

Ford, Richard E, *Dir*, John Woodman Higgins Armory, Library, Worcester MA

Ford, Sharon, *Dept Chmn*, Santa Ana College, Art Department, Santa Ana CA (S)

Foreman, Mary D, *Dir*, Percy H Whiting Art Center, Fairhope AL

Forero, Diego, *Architecture Coordr*, Centro de Arte y Communicacion, Center of Art and Communication, Buenos Argentina

Foresman, Margaret, *Second VPres*, Key West Art and Historical Society, Key West FL

Forester, Alice, *VPres*, Leigh Yawkey Woodson Art Museum, Inc, Wausau WI

Forge, Andrew, *Dean*, Yale University, School of Art, New Haven CT (S)

Formo, Peter L, *VPres*, Amerind Foundation, Inc, Dragoon AZ

Formosa, Gerald, *Instr*, Vancouver Community College, Langara Campus, Department of Fine Arts, Vancouver BC (S)

Forrest, Erik, *Dir*, Ohio University, School of Art, Athens OH (S)

Forrest, Erik, *Dir*, Ohio University, Seigfred Gallery, Athens OH

Forrest, James T, *Prof*, University of Wyoming, Art Department, Laramie WY (S)

Forrest, James T, *Dir*, University of Wyoming, Art Museum, Laramie WY

Forrest, James Taylor, *Dir*, Bradford Brinton Memorial Ranch Museum, Big Horn WY

Forrest, K, *Community Program Officer*, University of Regina, Norman Mackenzie Art Gallery, Regina SK

Forrester, R A, *Head Dept Archit*, University of Manitoba, Faculty of Architecture, Winnipeg MB (S)

Forrester, Vivien, *House Mgr*, University of North Carolina at Greensboro, Chinqua-Penn Plantation House, Reidsville NC

Forsey, William C, *Dir*, London Regional Art Gallery, London ON

Forster, Art, *Instructor*, Wayne Art Center, Wayne PA (S)

Forster, Patricia, *Librn*, National Gallery of Victoria, Library, Melbourne Australia

Forster, Peter E, *Asst Dean*, University of Manitoba, Faculty of Architecture, Winnipeg MB (S)

Forster-Hahn, Francoise, *Assoc Prof*, University of California, Riverside, Art History Department, Riverside CA (S)

Forsyth, Ilene, *Vis Prof*, University of Pittsburgh, Henry Clay Frick Fine Arts Department, Pittsburgh PA (S)

Forte, Leo, *Pres*, Fortman Studios Florence, Florence Italy (S)

Fortenberry, Paul, *Instructor*, Pels School of Art, New York NY (S)

Fortson, Kay, *Pres*, Kimbell Art Museum, Fort Worth TX

Fosdick, Sina, *Exec VPres*, Nicholas Roerich Museum, New York NY

Foskey, Randall, *Dir Press Bureau*, Colonial Williamsburg Foundation, Williamsburg VA

Foss, Randi, *Librn*, Norsk Folkemuseum, Norsk Folkemuseums Bibliotek, Oslo Norway

Fossi, Mazzino, *Librn*, Galleria, Museo e Medagliere Eslense, Biblioteca della Soprintendenza, Modena Italy

Foster, April, *Instructor*, Art Academy of Cincinnati, Cincinnati OH (S)

Foster, Arthur J, *Secy*, American Fine Arts Society, New York NY

Foster, Brian, *Mgr Cultural Arts Center*, Colby Community College, Northwest Kansas Cultural Arts Center, Colby KS

Foster, David, *Chmn Art Dept*, Lake Tahoe Community College, Art Department, South Lake Tahoe CA (S)

Foster, David G, *Dept Head*, University of Oregon, Department of Fine & Applied Arts, Eugene OR (S)

Foster, Doris, *Visual Arts Coordr*, Fine ARts Association, School of Fine Arts, Willoughby OH

Foster, Doris, *Visual Arts Coordr & Gallery Dir*, School of Fine Arts, Visual Arts Department, Willoughby OH (S)

Foster, Elaine, *Prof*, Jersey City State College, Art Department, Jersey City NJ (S)

Foster, G W, *Secy*, Hoosier Salon Patrons Association, Hoosier Salon Art Gallery, Indianapolis IN

Foster, Guthrie, *Dean of Students*, Atlanta College of Art, Atlanta GA (S)

Foster, James W, *Dir*, Honolulu Academy of Arts, Honolulu HI

Foster, Ken, *Instructor*, Muskegon Community College, Dept of Creative & Performing Arts, Muskegon MI (S)

Foster, Lee, *Admin Asst*, Chinese Culture Foundation, Chinese Culture Center Gallery, San Francisco CA

Foster, Mary Sue, *Chmn Art Educ*, Wichita State University, Division of Art, Wichita KS (S)

Foster, Roger W, *VPres*, Fitchburg Art Museum, Fitchburg MA

Foster, Ruth Sullivan, *Pres*, Colonel Black Mansion, Ellsworth ME

Fostervoll, Kari, *Conservator Textiles*, Kunstindustrimuseet I Oslo, Oslo Museum of Applied Art, Oslo Norway

Fouch, Doris, *Dir*, Tubac Center of the Arts, Santa Cruz Valley Art Association, Tubac AZ

Fouche, Ruth C, *In Charge of Art Coll*, Bank of Maryville, Maryville TN

Foujita, Shin-ichiro, *Cur*, Ohara Bijitsukan, Ohara Museum of Art, Kurashiki Japan

Fountain, Gail, *Assoc Prof*, University of Wisconsin-Stevens Point, Department of Art, Stevens Point WI (S)

Fournier, Marguerite, *Secy*, Gallerie d'Art de l'Universite de Moncton, Moncton NB

Fowle, William C, *Chmn Dept*, Mercersburg Academy, Department of Fine Arts, Mercersburg PA (S)

Fowler, Albert W, *Asst Dir*, Swarthmore College, Friends Historical Library, Swarthmore PA

Fowler, Harry W, *VPres*, American Numismatic Society, New York NY

Fowler, Theodore, *Librn*, Washington Art Association, Library, Washington Depot CT

Fox, Carol, *Asst to Dir*, National Gallery of Art, Washington DC

Fox, Frank, *Chmn Design Div*, Nova Scotia College of Art and Design, Halifax NS (S)

Fox, Jan Marshall, *Art Coordr*, University of Wisconsin, Memorial Union Gallery, Madison WI

Fox, John, *Instr*, Community College of the Finger Lakes, Visual & Performing Arts Department, Canandaigua NY (S)

Fox, Judith Woos, *Asst Dir*, Wellesley College, Museum, Wellesley MA

Fox, Katie, *Asst Cur*, Salisbury State College, Wildfowl Art Museum, Salisbury MD

Fox, Michael, *Business Mgr*, Heard Museum, Phoenix AZ

Fox, Randall, *Supt*, Game and Parks Commission, Arbor Lodge State Historical Park, Nebraska City NE

Fox, Thurman O, *Dir Museum*, State Historical Society of Wisconsin, Madison WI

Foy, Elizabeth J, *Admin Asst*, National Gallery of Art, Washington DC

Fraccio, William, *Instructor*, Propersi Galleries and School of Art Inc, Greenwich CT (S)

Fraccio, William, *Asst Chmn*, Propersi School of Art Inc Galleries, Greenwich CT

Fraenkel, Richard, *Chairperson*, University of Rhode Island, Department of Art, Kingston RI (S)

Fraher, David J, *Dir of Programs*, Wyoming Council on the Arts, Cheyenne WY

Francell, Larry, *Dir*, Wichita Falls Museum and Art Center, Wichita Falls TX

Francell, Larry, *Librn*, Wichita Falls Museum and Art Center, Library, Wichita Falls TX

Francis, Cortez, *Chmn*, Manatee Junior College, Department of Art, Bradenton FL (S)

Francis, Helen C, *Library and Museum Dir*, Springfield Free Public Library, Donald B Palmer Museum, Springfield NJ

Francis, Nancy E, *Librn*, Kitchener-Waterloo Art Gallery, Eleanor Calvert Memorial Library, Kitchener ON

Francis, Tom, *Painting Chmn*, Atlanta College of Art, Atlanta GA (S)

Franck, Barbara, *Admin Secy*, Washington University, Gallery of Art, Saint Louis MO

Franco, Robert, *Dir*, Silvermine Guild School of the Arts, New Canaan CT (S)

Franco, Robert, *School Dir*, Silvermine Guild School of the Arts, New Canaan CT

Frandrup, Dennis, *Instructor*, College of Saint Benedict, Art Department, Saint Joseph MN (S)

Frandsen, Doris, *Dir Exhib*, Waterloo Art Association, Waterloo IA

Frandsen, Jan Würtz, *Asst Keeper*, Statens Museum for Kunst, Den Kongelige Kobberstiksamling, Copenhagen Denmark

Franjevic, Jack N, *Head Dept*, College of Great Falls, Dept of Art, Great Falls MT (S)

Frank, Ann, *Fine Arts Librn*, Manchester City Library, Manchester NH

Frank, Barbara, *Asst Cur Slide Libr*, University of California, University Art Galleries and California Museum of Photography, Riverside CA

Frank, David, *Assoc Prof*, Mississippi University for Women, Art Department, Columbus MS (S)

Frank, Richard, *Asst Prof*, Augusta College, Department of Fine Arts, Augusta GA (S)

Frank, Robert, *Instructor*, Pels School of Art, New York NY (S)

Frankel, Dextra, *Dir*, California State University Fullerton, Art Gallery, Fullerton CA

Frankel, Robert H, *Asst Dir*, Phoenix Art Museum, Phoenix AZ

Franklin, Abigail, *Mgr Dir*, Women's Interart Center, Inc, Interart Gallery, New York NY

Franklin, Carole, *Music Librn*, Pennsylvania State University, Pattee Library, University Park PA

Franklin, Edith, *First VPres*, Toledo Federation of Art Societies, Toledo OH

Franklin, Evelyn, *Instructor*, University of Minnesota, Department of Design, Saint Paul MN (S)

Franklin, Gilbert, *Dean Fine Arts and Design Div*, Rhode Island School of Design, Providence RI (S)

Franklin, Hardy R, *Dir Libr*, Public Library of the District of Columbia, Art Division, Washington DC

Franklin, Martha, *Assoc Librn*, Kalamazoo Institute of Arts, Library, Kalamazoo MI

Franklin, Patt, *Assoc Prof ,Jeanna/Bearce, MFA E03 ,Assoc Prof*, University of Southern Maine, Art Dept, Gorham ME (S)

Frankova, A, *Chief of Department Expositions*, Statni Zidovske Muzeum, State Jewish Museum, Prague Czechoslovakia

Frankowiak, Robert, *Asst Art Dir*, Milwaukee Public Museum, Milwaukee WI

Frankston, Leon, *Asst Prof*, Nassau Community College, Art Department, Garden City NY (S)

Frantz, Barry, *Instructor*, Cuesta College, Art Department, San Luis Obispo CA (S)

Frantz, John C, *Dir*, San Francisco Public Library, Art and Music Department, San Francisco CA

Frappier, Gilles, *Dir*, Ottawa Public Library, Ottawa ON

Frase, John M, *Prof*, George Peabody College for Teachers, Art Faculty Department, Nashville TN (S)

Fraser, Alan, *Research Cur*, Indianapolis Museum of Art, Clowes Fund Collection, Indianapolis IN

Fraser, Ted, *Cur*, Art Gallery of Windsor, Windsor ON

Frattallone, Joe, *Assoc Prof*, Western Michigan University, Department of Art, Kalamazoo MI (S)

Frauchiger, Fritz A, *Cur*, Arco Center for Visual Art, Los Angeles CA

Fraunfelter, George, *Adj Cur Geology*, Southern Illinois University Museum and Art Galleries, Carbondale IL

Frayher, Mary, *Secy*, Guild Hall of East Hampton, Inc, Museum Section, East Hampton NY

Frazar, Stanton M, *Dir*, Historic New Orleans Collection, Kemper and Leila Williams Foundation, New Orleans LA

Fraze, Denny, *Chmn*, Amarillo College, Art Dept, Amarillo TX (S)

Frazer, Alan D, *Cur - Registrar*, New Jersey Historical Society Museum, Newark NJ

Frazer, Alfred, *Chmn*, Columbia University, Graduate Department, New York NY (S)

Frazer, John, *Prof*, Wesleyan University, Art Department, Middletown CT (S)

Frazier, Alton V, *Dir*, Utah Travel Council, Salt Lake City UT

Frazier, Gillian, *Instr*, Danforth Museum School, Framingham MA (S)

Frazier, William, *Asst Prof*, Mary Baldwin College, Department of Art, Staunton VA (S)

Frazier, William, *Exhib Coordr*, University of Houston, Sarah Campbell Blaffer Gallery, Houston TX

Frederick, Anne P, *Instr*, University of Richmond, Department of Art, Richmond VA (S)

Fredericks, Evelyn, *Librn*, Institute of American Indian Arts Museum, Library, Santa Fe NM

Fredericks, Marshall M, *Second VPres*, Brookgreen Gardens, Murrells Inlet SC

Fredericksen, Burton, *Cur of Paintings*, J Paul Getty Museum, Malibu CA

Fredlund, Björn, *Cur Old Masters Department*, Göteborg Konstmuseum, Gothenburg Art Gallery, Gothenburg Sweden

Fredrick, Charles, *Assoc Prof*, California State Polytechnic University, Pomona, Art Department, Pomona CA (S)

Fredrickson, B M, *Assoc Dir*, Joslyn Art Museum, Omaha NE

Free, Robert M, *Asst Dir*, University of Washington, Thomas Burke Memorial Washington State Museum, Seattle WA

Freed, Donald, *VPres*, New York Society of Architects, f the Performing Arts, at Lincoln Center New York

Freed, Reva, *Second VPres*, Artist-Craftsmen of New York, New York NY

Freedman, Ben, *Prof*, West Virginia University, Division of Art, Morgantown WV (S)

Freedman, Doris, *Pres*, Public Art Fund, Inc, New York NY

Freedman, Doris C, *Pres*, Municipal Art Society of New York, New York NY

Freedman, Jacob B, *Executive Dir*, Prospect Hospital, Bronx NY

Freeman, David, *Assoc Prof*, Winthrop College, Department of Art, Rock Hill SC (S)

Freeman, Gary, *Chmn Sculpture*, Herron School of Art, Indiana University-Purdue University, Indianapolis, Indianapolis IN (S)

Freeman, John, *Instructor*, Del Mar College, Department of Art, Corpus Christi TX (S)

Freeman, John, *Asst Prof*, University of Wisconsin-Superior, Department of Art, Superior WI (S)

Freeman, June, *Dir State Services*, Arkansas Arts Center, Little Rock AR

Freeman, Mark, *VPres*, New York Artists Equity Association, Inc, New York NY

Freeman, Mark, *Pres*, National Society of Painters in Casein and Acrylic, Inc, New York NY

Freeman, Nan B, *Asst Prof*, Wellesley College, Art Department, Wellesley MA (S)

Freeman, Rob, *Gallery Technician*, Macdonald Steward Art Centre, Guelph ON

Freeman, Tina, *Cur of Photography*, New Orleans Museum of Art, Isaac Delgado Museum, New Orleans LA

Freer, Harvey, *Dir Coll*, Maryhill Museum of Art, Goldendale WA

Freer, Raymond A, *Chmn*, Anderson College, Art Dept, Anderson IN (S)

Fregin, Nancy J, *Pres*, American Society of Artists, Inc, Chicago IL

Freitag, Wolfgang , *Librn*, Harvard University, Fine Arts Library, Cambridge MA

Freivogel, Max, *Dir*, Museum zu Allerheiligen, All Saints' Museum, Schaffhausen Switzerland

Frel, Jiri, *Vis Prof*, University of Southern California, School of Fine Arts, Los Angeles CA (S)

Frel, Jiri, *Cur of Antiquities*, J Paul Getty Museum, Malibu CA

French, Denney, *Secy*, Art Association of Richmond, Richmond IN

French, Ray H, *Prof*, DePauw University, Art Department, Greencastle IN (S)

French, Ronald L, *Dir*, Gable Advertising Art School, Division of Advertising Design School, Inc, Cincinnati OH (S)

French, Stephen, *Printmaking & Photography Coordr*, San Jose State University, Art Department, San Jose CA (S)

Frendel, Yvonne, *Head Librn*, Nationalmuseum, Library, Stockholm Sweden

Frenguelli, P, *Dir*, Accademia di Belle Arti, Academy of Fine Arts, Perugia Italy (S)

Freshley, Katherine T, *Librn*, Textile Museum, Arthur D Jenkins Library, Washington DC

Frets, Paul W, *Prof*, Radford University, Art Department, Radford VA (S)

Freudenheim, Susan, *Coordr of Education*, Fort Worth Art Museum, Fort Worth TX

Freundlich, August L, *Dean*, Syracuse University, College of Visual and Performing Arts, Syracuse NY (S)

Frey, Carroll, *Instructor*, Community College of Baltimore, Dept of Fine & Applied Arts, Baltimore MD (S)

Frey, Mary, *Instructor*, Hartford Art School of the University of Hartford, West Hartford CT (S)

Frey, Viola, *Instructor*, California College of Arts and Crafts, Oakland CA (S)

Friary, Donald R, *Executive Dir & Secy*, Historic Deerfield Inc, Deerfield MA

Fricke, Michele, *Gallery Dir*, Saint Mary's College, Moreau Gallery Three, Notre Dame IN

Frick II, Henry Clay, *Pres*, Frick Collection, New York NY

Fridley, Russell W, *Dir*, Minnesota Historical Society, St Paul MN

Friedberg, Arthur L, *Executive Dir*, American Ceramic Society, Columbus OH

Friedel, Helmut, *Cur*, Stadtische Gallerie im Lanbachhaus, Lenbach House City Gallery, Munich Germany, Federal Republic of

Friedenberg, Elizabeth, *Adjunct Prof*, Centenary College of Louisiana, Department of Art, Shreveport LA (S)

Friedhoff, Beverly, *Office Mgr*, Civic Fine Arts Association Museum, Sioux Falls SD

Friedman, Betty, *Executive Dir*, Farmington Valley Arts Center, Avon CT

Friedman, Estelle, *Instructor*, Santa Ana College, Art Department, Santa Ana CA (S)

Friedman, J Roger, *Pres*, Lotos Club, New York NY

Friedman, Joan, *Education Specialist*, Hofstra University, Emily Lowe Gallery, Hempstead NY

Friedman, Joan, *Cur Rare Books*, Yale University, Yale Center for British Art, New Haven CT

Friedman, John, *Chmn Photography*, De Young Museum Art School, San Francisco CA (S)

Friedman, Kenneth S, *Executive Dir*, Institute for Advanced Studies in Contemporary Art, New York NY

Friedman, Martin, *Dir*, Walker Art Center, Minneapolis MN

Friedman, Mildred S, *Cur Design*, Walker Art Center, Minneapolis MN

Friedman, Mira, *Cur*, Tel Aviv Museum, Tel-Aviv Israel

Frields, Gary Q, *Chmn Art Dept*, Kilgore College, Department Art and Art Education, Kilgore TX (S)

Friesen, Paul, *Assoc Prof*, Bethel College, Dept of Art, North Newton KS (S)

Frietag, Wolfgang, *Chmn of Board*, Art Libraries Society-North America, Iowa City IA

Frinta, Mojimir, *Prof*, State University of New York at Albany, Art Department, Albany NY (S)

Frinta, Mojmir, *Art Historian*, State University of New York at Albany, Art Department Slide Library, Albany NY (S)

Frisch, Susan, *Program Asst*, Chesterwood, Chesterwood Library, Stockbridge MA

Fritsch, John, *Instr*, Madison Area Technical College, Communication Arts, Madison WI (S)

Fritschi, Ingeborg, *VPres*, Nicholas Roerich Museum, New York NY

Fritzmann, Frank J, *Gallery Coordr*, Northeastern Illinois University, North River Community Gallery, Chicago IL

Frizzelle, Jack, *Mgr Public Information*, Metropolitan Museum of Art, New York NY

Froehlich, Olga, *Asst*, Artists Gallery, Vancouver BC

Froehlich, Olga, *Asst Dir & Cur*, Artists Gallery, Art Library Service, Vancouver BC

Froelich, Susan, *Exhibit Gallery Dir*, Ann Arbor Art Association, Ann Arbor MI

Frohlich, Gebhard, *Chmn*, Loyola University of New Orleans, Department of Visual Arts, New Orleans LA (S)

Frohn, Ann, *Secy*, Santa Cruz Art League, Inc, Santa Cruz CA

Frohock, Edith, *Assoc Prof*, University of Alabama in Birmingham, Department of Art, Birmingham AL (S)

Froiland, Sven G, *Pres*, Augustana College, Center for Western Studies, Sioux Falls SD

Frolik, James, *VPres*, Chinese Culture Foundation, Chinese Culture Center Gallery, San Francisco CA

Frombach, Ernest, *Assoc Prof*, Mansfield State College, Art Department, Mansfield PA (S)

Fromer, Seymour, *Dir*, Judah L Magnes Memorial Museum, Western Jewish History Center, Berkeley CA

Fronmuller, Regina Marie, *Head Dept*, Springfield College in Illinois, Dept of Art, Springfield IL (S)

Fronton, Andre, *Registrar*, National Gallery of Canada, Ottawa ON

Frost, F Daniel, *Pres*, Los Angeles County Museum of Art, Los Angeles CA

Frost, J William, *Dir*, Swarthmore College, Friends Historical Library, Swarthmore PA

Frost, Richard I, *Cur Buffalo Bill Museum*, Buffalo Bill Memorial Association, Cody WY

Frost, Robert, *VPres*, Washington Art Association, Washington Depot CT

Fry, Edward, *Vis Prof*, University of Pittsburgh, Henry Clay Frick Fine Arts Department, Pittsburgh PA (S)

Fry, George, *Dir of Crafts*, New Brunswick Craft School and Centre Gallery, Federicton NB

Fry, George F, *Dir*, New Brunswick Craft School and Centre, Fredericton NB (S)

Fryberger, Betsy G, *Cur of Prints & Drawings*, Stanford University, T W Stanford Art Gallery & Museum of Art, Stanford CA

Frymer, Carol, *Library Technician*, Art Gallery of Ontario, Edward P Taylor Reference Library, Toronto ON

Fu, Shen, *Assoc Cur Chinese Art*, Freer Gallery of Art, Washington DC

Fuchs, Angelee, *Dir*, Notre Dame College, Art Department, Saint Louis MO (S)

Fuchs, M Angelee, *Instr*, Mount Mary College, Art Department, Milwaukee WI (S)

Fuchs, M Tharsilla, *Prof*, Our Lady of the Lake University, Department of Art, San Antonio TX (S)

Fuchs, R H, *Dir*, Municipal van Abbemuseum, Eindhoven Municipal Museum, Eindhoven Netherlands

Fudge, John R, *Assoc Prof*, University of Colorado at Denver, Department of Fine Arts, Denver CO (S)

Fuentes, Tina, *Instructor*, Southwestern School of Art, Albuquerque NM (S)

Fuerstein, Carol, *Ed*, Solomon R Guggenheim Museum, New York NY

Fuerstein, Saul, *Preparator*, Solomon R Guggenheim Museum, New York NY

Fuertsch, Maureen, *Dir*, New Mexico Art League, Ken Roberts Gallery, Albuquerque NM

Fugitt, Patricia, *Gallery & Artmobile Cur*, South Texas Artmobile, Corpus Christi TX

Fujii, Hisae, *Cur Prints & Drawing*, Tokyo Kokuritsu Kindai Bujutsukan, National Museum of Modern Art, Tokyo, Tokyo Japan

Fujimura, Tamio, *Instr*, Studio Art Centers International, Florence Italy (S)

Fukunaga, Shigeki, *Cur*, Kyoto Kokuritsu Kindai Bijutsukan, National Museum of Modern Art, Kyoto, Kyoto Japan

Fulgoni, John, *Assoc Prof*, Dean Junior College, Visual and Performing Arts Department, Franklin MA (S)

Fullam, Agatha, *Asst Cur*, Waterville Historical Association, Waterville ME

Fuller, Benjamin, *Dir Resource Development & Cur*, Mystic Seaport Museum, Inc, Mystic CT

Fuller, George, *Head Dept Interior Design*, University of Manitoba, Faculty of Architecture, Winnipeg MB (S)

Fuller, James, *Prof*, Scripps College, Art Department, Claremont CA (S)

Fuller, Richard, *Assoc Prof*, Wilkes College, Department of Art, Wilkes-Barre PA (S)

Fuller, Robert S, *Chmn*, Randolph-Macon Woman's College, Department of Art, Lynchburg VA (S)

Fullinwider, Sylvia, *Secy*, Ogunquit Art Association, The Barn Gallery, Ogunquit ME

Fulton, Ken, *Head Dept*, Northwest Community College, Powell WY (S)

Fulton, William Duncan, *Pres*, Amerind Foundation, Inc, Dragoon AZ

Fumagalli, Orazio, *Prof*, University of Wisconsin-Stout, Art Department, Menomonie WI (S)

Funderburk, Brent, *Asst Prof*, Nebraska Wesleyan University, Art Dept, Lincoln NE (S)

Funk, Roger, *Chmn Department of Art*, Michigan State University, Kresge Art Center, East Lansing MI

Funk, Roger L, *Chmn Dept*, Michigan State University, Dept of Art, East Lansing MI (S)

Funk, Ruth, *Fine Arts*, Martin Memorial Library, York PA

Funk, Ruth, *Instructor*, Junior College of Albany, Fine Arts Division, Albany NY (S)

Funk, Tom, *Prof*, Ocean County College, Humanities Department, Toms River NJ (S)

Funk, Verne, *Prof*, Texas Tech University, Department of Art, Lubbock TX (S)

Furches, Harry, *Instructor*, Murray State University, Art Department, Murray KY (S)

Furlong, Cindy, *Conservation Asst*, Visual Studies Workshop, Research Center, Rochester NY

Furstenberg, James H, *Cur Program Development*, Honolulu Academy of Arts, Honolulu HI

Fuschman, Larry, *Assoc Prof*, College of Mount Saint Vincent, Fine Arts Department, Riverdale NY (S)

Fusco, Peter, *Cur of European Sculpture*, Los Angeles County Museum of Art, Los Angeles CA

Fusconi, Giulia, *Asst*, Instituto Nazionale per la Grafica, Rome Italy

Futernick, Robert, *Conservator Paper*, Fine Arts Museums of San Francisco, M H de Young Memorial Museum and California Palace of the Legion of Honor, n of Honor co

Fu-tsung, Chiang, *Dir*, National Palace Museum, Taipei China, Republic of

Fyfe, Jo, *Dept Chmn*, Spokane Falls Community College, Creative & Performing Arts, Spokane WA (S)

Fyfe, Jo, *Chmn Visual Arts Department*, Spokane Falls Community College Fine Art Gallery, Spokane WA

Gabay, Y, *Dir Theater Museum*, Haaretz Museum, Tel-Aviv Israel

Gabe, Ronald C, *Pres*, Art Metropole, Toronto ON

Gabel, Marlene, *Dir*, Contemporary Crafts Association and Gallery, Portland OR

Gabhart, Ann, *Dir*, Wellesley College, Museum, Wellesley MA

Gabin, George, *Instr*, Montserrat School of Visual Art, Beverly MA (S)

Gaboda, James J, *Chmn*, Hofstra University, Department of Fine Arts, Hempstead NY (S)

Gabor, Eszter, *Head Art Historian*, Szepmuveszet Museum, Library, Budapest Hungary

Gaborit, M Jean Rene, *Cur Sculptures*, Musee du Louvre, Louvre Museum, Paris France

Gabriel, Robert A, *Exec Dir*, Brevard Art Center and Museum, Inc, Melbourne FL

Gacke, Terry L, *Dir*, Carrie McLain Museum, Nome AK

Gadd, Emily, *Slide Cur*, Montana State University, Creative Arts Library, Bozeman MT

Gaffney, Gary, *Instructor*, Art Academy of Cincinnati, Cincinnati OH (S)

Gaffney, Thomas L, *Acting Dir*, Maine Historical Society, Portland ME

Gage, Frances, *Instr*, Toronto School of Art, Toronto ON (S)

Gagne, Jocelyne, *Secy*, Pavilion of Humour, Man and His World, Montreal PQ

Gagne, W Arthur, *Adminr*, Worcester Art Museum, Worcester MA

Gagnon, Celine, *Pres*, Institut des Arts au Saguenay, National Exhibition Center, Jonquiere PQ

Gagnon, Claire, *Conservator*, Musee des Augustines de l'Hotel Dieu of Quebec, Quebec PQ

Gahran, Hazel Ward, *Mgr Museum Shop*, Kauai Museum, Lihue HI

Gahran, Robert A, *Dir*, Kauai Museum, Lihue HI

Gailis, Charles R, *Pres*, Haystack Mountain School of Crafts Gallery, Deer Isle ME

Gaines, Charles, *Prof*, California State University, Fresno, Art Department, Fresno CA (S)

Gaines, Edith B, *Dir Annual Programs*, Art Institute of Chicago, Chicago IL

Gaines, Ervin J, *Dir*, Cleveland Public Library, Cleveland OH

Gaines, Joel, *Adjunct Asst Prof*, Le Moyne College, Art Department, Syracuse NY (S)

Gaines, Tom, *Chmn*, Centre College of Kentucky, Art Department, Danville KY (S)

Gaines, William, *Programs Dir*, Virginia Museum of Fine Arts, Richmond VA

Gaither, James L, *Acting Head*, Casper College, Casper WY (S)

Gajdycz, Lesia, *Public Relations*, Ukrainian Museum, New York NY

Galantic, Ivan, *Assoc Prof*, Tufts University, Fine Arts Department, Medford MA (S)

Galavaris, G, *Prof*, McGill University, Department of Art History, Montreal PQ (S)

Galban, Victoria S, *Asst Cur Research*, Metropolitan Museum of Art, Robert Lehman Collection Library, New York NY

Gale, Margaret, *VPres*, Art Metropole, Toronto ON

Gale, Rebecca, *Secy*, Eccles Community Art Center, Ogden UT

Galembo, Phyllis, *Asst Prof*, State University of New York at Albany, Art Department, Albany NY (S)

Galis, Diana, *Adjunct Prof*, Franklin and Marshall College, Art Department, Lancaster PA (S)

Gallagher, Cynthia, *Adjunct Instructor*, New York Institute of Technology, Fine Arts Department, Old Westbury NY (S)

Gallagher, Jerome, *Head Dept*, Yankton College, Dept of Art, Yankton SD (S)

Gallagher, Jerome E, *Cur*, Yankton College, Durand Art Collection, Yankton SD

Gallagher, Pat, *Dir*, Oklahoma Art Center, Arts Place II, Oklahoma City OK

Gallagher, Paul, *Dir*, Johnson State College, John Dewey Library, Johnson VT

Gallagher, Robert, *Secy*, Montgomery Museum of Fine Arts, Montgomery AL

Gallander, Cathleen S, *Dir*, Art Museum of South Texas, Corpus Christi TX

Gallanos, Alma, *Asst Instr*, Stevenson Academy of Traditional Painting, Sea Cliff NY (S)

Gallatin, Gaile, *Dir Educ*, Davenport Municipal Art Gallery, Davenport IA

Gallatin, Gaile, *Head Art Dept*, Simpson College Art Gallery, Indianola IA

Gallatin, Gaile, *Chairperson Dept*, Simpson College, Art Department, Indianola IA (S)

Galles, Kathy, *Secy*, Keokuk Art Center, Keokuk IA

Gallinger, Janice, *Dir Library Services*, Plymouth State College, Herbert H Lamson Library, Plymouth NH

Gallo, Frank, *In Charge Sculpture*, University of Illinois, Urbana-Champaign, Department of Art and Design, Champaign IL (S)

Galloway, C, *VPres*, Rockford Art Association, Burpee Art Museum, Rockford IL

Galloway, Helen, *Assoc Prof*, Saint Mary's College, Art Department, Winona MN (S)

Galloway, Mary F, *Secy*, Columbia Museums of Art and Science, Columbia Science Museum, Columbia SC

Galloway, R Dean, *Librn*, California State College, Stanislaus, Vache Library, Turlock CA

Gallwitz, Klaus, *Dir*, Stadelsches Kunstinstitut, Staedel Art Institute, Frankfurt Germany, Federal Republic of

Galther, Edmund B, *Dir*, Museum of the National Center of Afro-American Artists, Boston MA

Gamble, Linda, *Business Mgr*, Montana Historical Society, Helena MT

Gamboa, Fernando, *Dir*, Museo de Arte Moderno, Museum of Modern Art, Mexico City Mexico

Gambsky, George, *Head Photography*, Chautauqua Institution, Chautauqua NY (S)

Gamlin, Sandi, *Admin Asst*, University of Kentucky, Art Museum, Lexington KY

Gandhi, Shri M N, *Keeper Art & Archaeological Sections*, Museum and Picture Gallery, Baroda India

Gannon, Catherine B, *Adult Service Librn*, Jones Library, Inc, Amherst MA

Gannon, Ellen, *Lectr*, Ladycliff College, Art Department, Highland Falls NY (S)

Gansworth, George, *Instructor*, Mainline Center of the Arts, Haverford PA (S)

Gant, Sally, *Educ Coordr*, Museum of Early Southern Decorative Arts, Old Salem Inc, Winston-Salem NC

Gantle, Thorn, *Secy-Treas & Dir*, Intermuseum Conservation Association, Oberlin OH

Gantner, Theo, *Cur Europe*, Museum für Völkerkunde und Schweizerisches Museum für Volkskunde Basel, Museum of Ethnological Collections and Folklore, Basel Switzerland

Gantt, Richard, *Instr*, Averett College, Art Department, Danville VA (S)

Gantz, Carroll M, *Pres*, Industrial Designers Society of America, Washington DC

Ganz, Howard, *Chmn*, Miracosta College, Creative Arts Department, Oceanside CA (S)

Ganzel, Agneta, *Instr*, Lourdes College, Art Department, Sylvania OH (S)

Garas, Klara, *Dir-General*, Szepmuveszet Museum, Museum of Fine Arts, Budapest Hungary

Garbee, Robert H, *Pres*, Association for the Preservation of Virgina Antiquities, Richmond VA

Garberi, M, *Dir*, Civica Galleria d'Arte Moderna, Milan Italy

Garberi, Mercedes, *Dir*, Museo d'Arte Antica, Museum of Ancient Art, Milan Italy

Garbolinski, Wiestaw, *Rector*, Panstwowa Wyzsza Szkola Sztuk Plastycznych, Higher School of Art and Design, Lodz Poland (S)

Garcia, Donna Marie, *District Adminr*, Kauai Regional Library, Lihue HI

Garcia, Hector, *Assoc Prof*, Indiana University-Purdue University, Department of Fine Arts, Fort Wayne IN (S)

Garcia, Ofelia, *Dir*, Print Club, Philadelphia PA

Gardner, Allan R, *Instructor*, Portland School of Art, Portland ME (S)

Gardner, Byron, *Prof*, Portland State University, Department of Art and Architecture, Portland OR (S)

Gardner, Cyril, *Instructor*, Mainline Center of the Arts, Haverford PA (S)

Gardner, Elizabeth E, *Cur European Paintings*, Metropolitan Museum of Art, New York NY

Gardner, Frederick, *Head, Public Services*, California Institute of the Arts Library, Valencia CA

Gardner, Jack, *Admin*, Clark County Library District, Las Vegas NV

Gardner, Joan, *Asst Prof*, University of New Haven, Department of Fine Arts, West Haven CT (S)

Gardner, Norman, *VPres*, Kent Art Association, Inc Gallery, Kent CT

Gardner, Robert, *Sr Lectr*, Harvard University, Department of Visual and Environmental Studies, Cambridge MA (S)

Gardner, Robert G, *Dir & Sr Lecturer-Visual Studies*, Harvard University, Carpenter Center for the Visual Arts, Cambridge MA

Garff, Jan, *Asst Keeper*, Statens Museum for Kunst, Den Kongelige Kobberstiksamling, Copenhagen Denmark

Garfield, Alan, *Instr*, Creighton University, Fine and Performing Arts Department, Omaha NE (S)

Garfield, Alan, *Dir*, Saint Joseph Art Association Inc, Krasl Art Center, Saint Joseph MI

Gargan, R, *Secy*, Dartmouth Heritage Museum, Dartmouth NS

Garhart, Martin, *Assoc Prof*, Kenyon College, Art Department, Gambier OH (S)

Gariepy, Luce, *Asst*, Musee du Quebec, Bibliotheque des Art, Quebec PQ

Garland, Patricia, *Assoc Conservator*, Wadsworth Atheneum, Hartford CT

Garland, Peter, *Assoc Prof*, Smith College, Art Department, Northampton MA (S)

Garlick, K J, *Keeper Western Art*, Oxford University, Ashmolean Museum of Art and Archaeology, Oxford England

Garmhausen, Winona, *Dir Dept*, College of Santa Fe, Visual Arts Dept, Santa Fe NM (S)

Garnder, Mara, *Education Coordr*, Center for Inter-American Relations Art Gallery, New York NY

Garner, Edna, *VPres*, DuPage Art League, Wheaton IL

Garner, Nancy E, *Instructor*, Providence College, Department of Fine Arts, Providence RI (S)

Garrard, Mary D, *Prof*, American University, Department of Art, Washington DC (S)

Garret, Sally, *Education Coordr*, Hand Work Shop, Inc, Richmond VA

Garrett, Katherine, *Registrar*, Stanford University, T W Stanford Art Gallery & Museum of Art, Stanford CA

Garrett, Sid, *Prof*, Louisiana State University, Department of Fine Arts, Baton Rouge LA (S)

Garrett, Stephen, *Dir*, J Paul Getty Museum, Malibu CA

Garrison, Clayton, *Dean*, University of California, Irvine, Studio Art Department, Irvine CA (S)

Garrison, Douglas, *Office Mgr*, Birmingham-Bloomfield Art Association, Birmingham MI

Garrison, J Richie, *Dir of Education*, Historic Deerfield Inc, Deerfield MA

Garrison, Jim, *Chmn Dept Art*, Mesa Community College, Department of Art, Mesa AZ (S)

Garrone, Giovanna Galante, *Dir*, Galleria Sabauda, Turin Italy

Garside, Anne, *Editor of Publications*, Walters Art Gallery, Baltimore MD

Garson, Inex, *Cur*, Hirshhorn Museum and Sculpture Garden, Washington DC

Garte, Edna, *Cur*, University of Minnesota, Tweed Museum of Art, Duluth MN

Garte, Edna J, *Asst Prof*, University of Minnesota, Duluth, Art Dept, Duluth MN (S)

Garten, Clifford, *Instructor*, Hamline University, Art Department, Saint Paul MN (S)

Gartenberg, Gerald, *Admin*, John and Mable Ringling Museum of Art, Sarasota FL

Garth, C Tyrell, *First VPres*, Beaumont Art Museum, Beaumont TX

Garthwaite, Ernest, *Instr*, York College of the City University of New York, Fine and Performing Arts, Jamaica NY (S)

Gartner, Carol B, *Chmn*, Pace University, White Plains, Division of Arts and Letters, White Plains NY (S)

Garver, Thomas H, *Dir*, Newport Harbor Art Museum, Newport Beach CA

Garver, Thomas H, *Pres*, Western Association of Art Museums, San Francisco CA

Garvey, Colleen, *Prof*, University of Wisconsin-Stevens Point, Department of Art, Stevens Point WI (S)

Garvie, Peter M, *Dean*, University of Texas, Department of Art, Austin TX (S)

Garvin, James L, *Cur*, New Hampshire Historical Society, Concord NH

Garza, Carmen Lomas, *Cur & Education Coordinator*, Galeria de la Raza, Studio 24, San Francisco CA

Garza, Lynne, *Asst Librn & Reference*, Detroit Institute of Arts, Research Library, Detroit MI

Garzio, Angelo, *Prof*, Kansas State University, Art Department, Manhattan KS (S)

Garzon-Blanco, Armando, *Head Dept*, Nicholls State University, Dept of Art, Thibodaux LA (S)

Gasc, Nadine, *Cur*, Union Centrale des Arts Decoratifs, Musee des Arts Decoratifs, Paris France

Gaskin, Leroy, *Cur Ceramics & Sculpture*, Smith-Mason Gallery and Museum, Washington DC

Gasparovic, Ljerka, *Cur*, Strossmayerova Galerija Starih Majstora Jugoslavenske Akademije Znanosti I Umjetnosti, Strossmayer's Gallery of Old Masters of the Yugoslavia Academy of Sciences and Arts, Zagreb Yugoslavia

Gasparro, Frank, *Instructor*, Samuel S Fleisher Art Memorial, Philadelphia PA (S)

Gass, Adney, *Instr*, Citrus Community College, Art Department, Azusa CA (S)

Gast, Michael, *Pres*, Artists Equity Association, Inc, Washington DC

Gates, Alice, *Secy*, Old Gaol Museum, York ME

Gates, Elaine, *Assoc Prof*, Hood College, Department of Art, Frederick MD (S)

Gates, H I, *Asst Prof*, George Washington University, Department of Art, Washington DC (S)

Gates, Helen, *Assoc Librn*, Arizona State University, Hayden Library, Tempe AZ

Gates, Jay, *Dir*, Brooks Memorial Art Gallery, Memphis TN

Gates, Kathryn, *Registrar*, Portland Art Association, Portland OR

Gates, Tom, *Chmn Art History*, De Young Museum Art School, San Francisco CA (S)

Gatewood, Maud F, *Coordr*, Averett College, Art Department, Danville VA (S)

Gatley, Ian, *Assoc Prof Art*, Eastern Oregon State College, La Grande OR (S)

Gatty, Arthur, *Dir Governor's School for the Arts*, Pennsylvania Department of Education, Arts in Education Program, Harrisburg PA

Gaudieri, Alexander V J, *Dir*, Telfair Academy of Arts and Sciences Inc, Savannah GA

Gaudieri, Millicent Hall, *Executive Secy*, Association of Art Museum Directors, Savannah GA

Gaudreau, Therest Marie, *Acquisitions*, Trinity College Library, Washington DC

Gaughan, Tom, *Instructor*, Samuel S Fleisher Art Memorial, Philadelphia PA (S)

Gauss, V, *Cur Prints & Drawings 19th - 20th Century*, Staatsgalerie Stuttgart, Stuttgart Germany, Federal Republic of

Gauvreau, Robert G, *Instructor*, Modesto Junior College, Arts Humanities and Speech Division, Modesto CA (S)

Gaver, Eleanor C, *Librn*, Carolina Art Association, Library, Charleston SC

Gavin, Carney E S, *Cur*, Harvard University, Harvard Semitic Museum, Cambridge MA

Gaw, George, *Acting Communication Design Chmn*, Art Center College of Design, Pasadena CA (S)

Gawley, Irwin, *VPres*, Montclair State College, Gallery One, Upper Montclair NJ

Gawman, Ann, *Pres Board of Dir*, Kitchener-Waterloo Art Gallery, Kitchener ON

Gawron, Carol, *Supv Traveling Libraries*, Miami-Dade Public Library, Miami FL

Gay, Charles, *Treas*, Eureka Springs Guild of Artists and Crafts People, Eureka Springs AR

Gaydos, Tim, *Instructor*, Montclair Art Museum, Art School, Montclair NJ (S)

Gayle, Margot, *Pres*, Fine Arts Federation of New York, New York NY

Gayner, Esther K, *Corresponding Secy*, New York Artists Equity Association, Inc, New York NY

Gazda, Elaine K, *Asst Cur*, University of Michigan Museum of Art, Kelsey Museum of Ancient and Medieval Archaeology, Ann Arbor MI

Gazurian, Garo, *Prof*, Pierce College, Art Department, Woodland Hills CA (S)

Gealt, Adelheid, *Cur Western Art to 1800*, Indiana University, Art Museum, Bloomington IN

Geary, Ray, *Head Graphic Design*, Virginia Museum of Fine Arts, Richmond VA

Gebel, Ruth, *Cur Exhibits*, Albuquerque Museum of Art, History and Science, Albuquerque NM

Gebhard, David, *Dir*, University of California, Santa Barbara, Art Museum, Santa Barbara CA

Gebhard, David, *First VPres*, Society of Architectural Historians, Philadelphia PA

Gebhart, Nan, *Periodicals Librn*, Ringling School of Art Library, Sarasota FL

Geddes, Robert L, *Dean*, Princeton University, School of Architecture and Urban Planning, Princeton NJ (S)

Gedeon, Cindy, *Cur Asst*, University of California, Los Angeles, Grunwald Center for the Graphic Arts, Los Angeles CA

Gee, Kunkil, *Dir Puyo Museum*, National Museum of Korea, Seoul Korea

Geelhaar, Christian, *Cur 19th & 20th Century Paintings*, Offentliche Kunstsammlung-Kunstmuseum Basel, Museum of Fine Arts, Basel Switzerland

Geerlings, M A, *Secy*, Ryksmuseum Kroller-Muller, Kroller-Muller State Museum, Otterlo Netherlands

Geeslin, L Gaddis, *Prof*, Sam Houston State University, Art Department, Huntsville TX (S)

Gehner, Robert, *Assoc prof*, University of North Carolina-Charlotte, Creative Arts Dept, Charlotte NC (S)

Gehring, Brent, *Instructor*, Ricks College, Department of Art, Rexburg ID (S)

Gehrm, Barbara, *Secy*, Salisbury State College, Wildfowl Art Museum, Salisbury MD

Geibert, Ron, *Vis Prof*, Nebraska Wesleyan University, Art Dept, Lincoln NE (S)

Geiger, Gail, *Asst Prof*, University of Wisconsin, Madison, Department of Art, Madison WI (S)

Geiger, William S, *Secy*, Woodmere Art Gallery, Philadelphia PA

Geimer, Mary, *Instructor*, Purdue University Calumet Campus, Department of Creative Arts, Hammond IN (S)

Geinzer, Eugene M, *Asst Prof*, Georgetown University, Department of Fine Arts, Washington DC (S)

Geis, M Christina, *Dir*, Georgian Court College Gallery, Lakewood NJ

Geis, M Christina, *Head Dept*, Georgian Court College, Department of Art, Lakewood NJ (S)

Geischer, Geraldine, *Instructor*, Milwaukee Area Technical College, Graphic & Applied Arts Div, Milwaukee WI (S)

Geise, Ina, *Secy*, Tennessee Valley Art Center, Tuscumbia AL

Geissler, H, *Cur Prints & Drawings 15th - 18th Century*, Staatsgalerie Stuttgart, Stuttgart Germany, Federal Republic of

Gekiere, Madeleine, *Prof*, City College of the City of New York, Art Department, New York NY (S)

Gelburd, Gail, *Art Cur*, Morris Museum of Arts and Sciences, Morristown NJ

Gelick, Michael, *Dir School Architecture*, University of Illinois at Chicago Circle, College of Architecture, Art & Urban Sciences, Chicago IL (S)

Gelinas, Andre A, *Pres*, Fitchburg Art Museum, Fitchburg MA

Gellman, Lola B, *Chmn*, Queensborough Community College, Department of Art and Design, Bayside NY (S)

Gellman, Marianne, *Photography Coordr*, North Texas State University, Art Department, Denton TX (S)

Gelman, Janet, *Cur Education*, George Walter Vincent Smith Art Museum, Springfield MA

Geltner, Frank, *Prog Consultant*, University of Oregon, Erb Memorial Union Art Gallery, Eugene OR

Genter, Anne S, *Secy*, Pittsburgh History and Landmarks Foundation, Old Post Office Museum, Pittsburgh PA

Gentry, James, *Asst Dir*, Southern Highland Handicraft Guild, Asheville NC

Gentry, Susannah, *Secy*, Jackson County Historical Society, Independence MO

George, Amanda, *Prof*, Fortman Studios Florence, Florence Italy (S)

George, David, *Head Fine Arts*, Truett-McConnell College, Fine Arts Department, Cleveland GA (S)

George, Gloria, *Secy*, West Hills Unitarian Fellowship, Portland OR

George, Gordon, *Treas*, San Antonio Museum Association, Inc, San Antonio TX

George, Judith P, *Prof*, Miami University, Art Department, Oxford OH (S)

George, Rick, *Exec Dir*, South Carolina Arts Commission, Columbia SC

George, Tom, *Chmn*, Salisbury State College, Wildfowl Art Museum, Salisbury MD

Georgel, M, *Staff*, Musee des Beaux-Arts de Dijon, Museum of Fine Arts, Dijon France

Georgias, Andrew, *Asst Prof*, Glendale College, Department of Fine Arts, Glendale CA (S)

Georlett, Joyce, *Dir of Development*, Putnam Museum, Davenport IA

Gepts, G, *Dir & Cur*, Koninklijk Museum voor Schone Kunsten, Royal Museum of Fine Arts, Antwerp Belgium

Gerard, John, *Cur of Coll*, Cranbrook Academy of Art Museum, Bloomfield Hills MI

Gerard, Stacie, *Asst*, Clark University, Little Center Gallery, Worcester MA

Gerardia, Helen, *Treas*, Society of American Graphic Artists, New York NY

Gerardia, Helen, *Recording Secy*, New York Artists Equity Association, Inc, New York NY

Gerardine, M, *Dir*, Caldwell College Art Gallery, Caldwell NJ

Gerbens, Martin L, *Slide Cur*, Ringling School of Art Library, Sarasota FL

Gerde, Priscilla M, *Department Head Community Relations*, Eli Lilly and Company, Indianapolis IN

Gerdine, Peter C, *Acquisitions Librn*, Plymouth State College, Herbert H Lamson Library, Plymouth NH

Gerdts, William H, *Chmn Exec Committee*, City University of New York, PhD Program in Art History, New York NY (S)

Gerecke, Kent, *Head Dept City Planning*, University of Manitoba, Faculty of Architecture, Winnipeg MB (S)

Gergen, Paul, *Treas*, Octagon Center for the Arts, Ames IA

Gerhart, Susan, *Librn & Hostess*, Benzonia Public Library, Benzonia MI

Gerkens, Gerhard, *Asst Cur*, Kunsthalle Bremen, Bremen Art Gallery, Bremen Germany, Federal Republic of

Gerling, Stephen E, *Coordr*, University of Connecticut, Jorgensen Gallery, Storrs CT

German, Barbara, *Librn*, Traphagen School of Fashion, Library, New York NY

Gernand, John, *Registrar & Archivist*, Phillips Collection, Washington DC

Gerrier, Arthur J, *Manuscripts Asst*, Maine Historical Society, Library, Portland ME

Gers, Muriel L, *Librn*, Walters Art Gallery, Library, Baltimore MD

Gershowitz, Paul, *Dir*, Mid-Hudson Arts and Science Center, Poughkeepsie NY

Gerszi, Terez, *Head Prints & Drawings*, Szepmuveszet Museum, Museum of Fine Arts, Budapest Hungary

Gertjejansen, Doyle, *Assoc Prof*, University of New Orleans, Dept of Fine Arts, New Orleans LA (S)

Gesen, Carl G, *VPres*, New Hampshire Historical Society, Concord NH

Geske, Norman A, *Dir*, University of Nebraska Lincoln, Sheldon Memorial Art Gallery, Lincoln NE

Gesterfield, Kathryn J, *Dir*, Illinois State Library, Springfield IL

Gettinger, Ed, *Head Dept*, University of South Dakota, Springfield, Springfield SD (S)

Getty, Nilda C, *Prof*, Colorado State University, Department of Art, Fort Collins CO (S)

Getty, Ron, *Cur of Cultural History*, Glenbow Museum, Calgary AB

Gevins, Jack, *Instructor*, Bucks County Community College, Fine Arts Department, Newton PA (S)

Geyer, George E, *Instructor*, Santa Ana College, Art Department, Santa Ana CA (S)

Geyer, Juan, *Educ Coordr*, Junior Arts Center, Los Angeles CA

Ghal, Muhammad, *Librn Asst*, Lahore Museum, Library, Lahore Pakistan

Ghannam, Edward, *Instructor*, University of Miami, Department of Art, Coral Gables FL (S)

Ghattas, Antoine, *Secy*, Order of Architects of Quebec, Montreal PQ

Ghelli, Giuliano, *Vis Artist*, Studio Art Centers International, Florence Italy (S)

Ghez, M Oscar, *Pres & Founder*, Musee d'Art Moderne, Modern Art Museum, Geneva Switzerland

Ghez, Susanne, *Dir*, University of Chicago, Bergman Gallery, Chicago IL

Ghigna, Nancy Holmes, *Dir*, Yuma Art Center, Yuma AZ

Ghiz, Ronald, *Assoc Prof*, University of Maine, Art Department, Orono ME (S)

Giaccone, T, *Chmn Advertising Design*, Fashion Institute of Technology, New York NY (S)

Gibbons, Hugh, *Prof*, Texas Tech University, Department of Art, Lubbock TX (S)

Gibbons, Jerry, *Chmn*, Southern Baptist College, Dept of Art, College City AR (S)

Gibbons, M, *Registrar*, National College of Art and Design, Dublin Ireland (S)

Gibbs, Barbara, *Deputy Dir*, Portland Art Association, Portland OR

Gibbs, Bonnie, *Cur*, Principia College, School of Nations Museum, Elsah IL

Gibbs, Cora Lee, *Cur Education*, Rhode Island School of Design, Museum of Art, Providence RI

Gibbs, Donald T, *Librn*, Redwood Library and Athenaeum, Newport RI

Gibian, J Catherine, *Asst Prof*, State University of New York College at Cortland, Art Department, Cortland NY (S)

Gibson, Ellery, *Instructor*, Northern Arizona University, Art Department, Flagstaff AZ (S)

Gibson, James S, *Assoc Prof*, Middle Tennessee State University, Art Dept, Murfreesboro TN (S)

Gibson, Jim, *Chmn*, Northern State College, Art Dept, Aberdeen SD (S)

Gibson, Joyce, *Head Extension & Education*, Glenbow Museum, Calgary AB

Gibson, Kurt, *Cur Exhib*, Polk Public Museum, Lakeland FL

Gibson, M, *Extension Officer*, Saskatoon Gallery and Conservatory Corporation, Saskatoon SK

Gibson, Robin, *Asst Keeper*, National Portrait Gallery, London England

Gibson, William, *House Chmn*, Plastic Club, Art Club for Women, Philadelphia PA

Gidard, Sara, *Instructor*, Chamberlayne Junior College, Department of Graphic and Applied Arts, Boston MA (S)

Gidley, Mick, *Dir*, University of Exeter, American Arts Documentation Centre, Exeter England

Gieber, P Terry, *Instr Art*, Southwestern Community College, Art Department, Creston IA (S)

Giencke, Kathleen, *Exhibits Designer*, Southern Illinois University Museum and Art Galleries, Carbondale IL

Gierut, Bernadine, *Asst to Dir*, Spertus Museum of Judaica, Chicago IL

Giese, David, *Asst Prof*, University of Idaho, Department of Art and Architecture, Moscow ID (S)

Giesy, Alene, *Circ Dept Head*, Topeka Public Library, Topeka KS

Gifford, A M, *Dean Applied Arts*, Ryerson Polytechnical Institute Library, Toronto ON

Gifford, Lynn, *Membership*, Plains Art Museum, Main Gallery, Moorhead MN

Gikas, Chris, *Chmn Dept*, Eastern New Mexico University, Department of Art & Education, Portales NM (S)

Gikas, Chris, *Dir*, Eastern New Mexico University, Art Gallery, Portales NM

Gilbedt, Christopher, *Principal Keeper*, Leeds Art Galleries, Leeds England

Gilbert, Albert, *Pres*, Society of Animal Artists, Inc, Bronx NY

Gilbert, Creighton E, *Prof*, Cornell University, Department of the History of Art, Ithaca NY (S)

Gilbert, Gail R, *Art Librn*, University of Louisville, Allen R Hite Art Institute, Louisville KY

Gilbert, Gail R, *Head Art Library*, University of Louisville, Margaret M Bridwell Art Library, Louisville KY

Gilbert, James, *Instr*, Pontiac Art Center, Pontiac MI (S)

Gilbert, Jean, *Technical Processes*, Ponca City Library, Ponca City OK

Gilbert, W Herbert, *Assoc Prof*, University of British Columbia, Department of Fine Arts, Vancouver BC (S)

Gilborn, Craig A, *Dir*, Adirondack Museum of the Adirondack Historical Association, Blue Mountain Lake NY

Gilbreth, T S, *Dir*, Diamond M Foundation Museum, Snyder TX

Gilden, Anita, *Asst Librn*, Albright-Knox Art Gallery, Art Reference Library, Buffalo NY

Giles, Timothy B, *Librn*, Dartington College of Arts, Library and Resources Centre, Devon England

Gilfoy, Peggy S, *Cur Textiles and Ethnographic Art*, Indianapolis Museum of Art, Indianapolis IN

Gilkey, Gordon, *Cur of Prints & Drawings*, Portland Art Association, Portland OR

Gill, Andrew J, *Exec Dir*, New Muse Community Museum of Brooklyn, Inc, Brooklyn NY

Gill, Charles, *Instructor*, California College of Arts and Crafts, Oakland CA (S)

Gill, Johanna, *Chmn Media*, Massachusetts College of Art, Boston MA (S)

Gill, Mohinder, *Prof*, North Carolina Central University, Art Dept, Durham NC (S)

Gill, Mohinder S, *Assoc Prof*, Elizabeth City State University, Department of Art, Elizabeth City NC (S)

Gill, Phyllis, *Admin Asst Art Galleries*, University of California, University Art Galleries and California Museum of Photography, Riverside CA

Gill, Sarah, *Prof*, Santa Rosa Junior College, Art Department, Santa Rosa CA (S)

Gill, Thomas, *Dir*, Chemeketa Community College, Department of Humanities & Social Science, Salem OR (S)

Gill, Ursula, *Instructor*, Maryland College of Art and Design, Silver Spring MD (S)

Gillard, Frank M, *Treas*, Maritime Art Association, Summerside PE

Gillespie, Bruce, *Treas*, Wayne Art Center, Wayne PA

Gillespie, Gary, *Prof*, Glenville State College, Department of Art, Glenville WV (S)

Gillespie, Martha, *Secy*, Roswell Museum and Art Center, Roswell NM

Gillespie, Nancy, *Dir & Cur*, Iowa State University, Brunnier Gallery, Ames IA

Gillette, Gerald W, *Research Historian*, Presbyterian Historical Society, Philadelphia PA

Gilley, Alma, *Financial Officer*, Wichita Art Museum, Wichita KS

Gilliam, Betty J, *Assoc Prof*, Clinch Valley College of the University of Virginia, Humanities Department, Wise VA (S)

Gilliam, Scott, *Instructor*, Atlanta College of Art, Atlanta GA (S)

Gilliatt, Michael, *Asst Prof*, Virginia State College, Fine Arts Department, Petersburg VA (S)

Gillies, Sue, *Asst Librn*, New York Historical Society, Library, New York NY

Gillis, Jean, *Cur Botanical Science*, Heritage Plantation of Sandwich, Sandwich MA

Gillis, Verna, *Pres & Executive Dir*, American International Sculptors Symposiums, Inc, New York NY

Gillis Jr, Gaylord W, *VPres*, Detroit Institute of Arts, Detroit Institute of Art Founders Society, Detroit MI

Gilman, John, *VPres*, Sculpture Center, New York NY

Gilmer, J Mel, *Pres*, Sturdivant Hall, Selma AL

Gilmor, Jane, *Asst Prof*, Mount Mercy College, Art Department, Cedar Rapids IA (S)

Gilmor, Jane E, *Dir*, Mount Mercy College, McAuley Gallery, Cedar Rapids IA

Gilmore, Thomas J, *Assoc Prof*, Miami University, Art Department, Oxford OH (S)

Gilmore-Bryan, Janet, *Visual Arts Dir*, Brewton-Parker College, Visual Arts, Mount Vernon GA (S)

Gilot, Francoise, *Chmn Painting & Drawing Workshops*, University of Southern California, Idyllwild Campus, Idyllwild School of Music and the Arts, Idyllwild CA (S)

Gil-Roberts, H, *Pres*, Lyme Art Association, Inc, Old Lyme CT

Gilroy, William, *VPres*, South County Art Association, Kingston RI

Gilson, Jake, *Chmn*, Mount Saint Mary's College, Art Department, Los Angeles CA (S)

Gilstrap, Sara, *Instructor*, Midland College, Art Department, Midland TX (S)

Gimbel, Pat, *Asst Dir*, University of North Dakota Art Galleries, Grand Forks ND

Gimse, Malcolm, *Asst Prof*, St Olaf College, Art Department, Northfield MN (S)

Gingles, Bill, *Dir*, Brenau College, Art Department, Gainesville GA (S)

Gingrich, John, *Chmn*, University of La Verne, La Verne CA (S)

Ginthner, Delores, *Asst Prof*, University of Minnesota, Department of Design, Saint Paul MN (S)

Giopulos, Peter, *Assoc Dean College*, Rochester Institute of Technology, College of Fine and Applied Arts, Rochester NY (S)

Giopulos, Peter, *Dir*, Rochester Institute of Technology, School of Art and Design, Rochester NY (S)

Giordano, Enrico, *Assoc Prof*, College of Mount Saint Vincent, Fine Arts Department, Riverdale NY (S)

Gipe, Thomas D, *Head Sculpture*, Southern Illinois University at Edwardsville, Department of Art and Design, Edwardsville IL (S)

Gippetti, Louis, *Instr*, Danforth Museum School, Framingham MA (S)

Gipstein, Edward, *Docent*, Lyman Allyn Museum, New London CT

Girdler Jr, Reynolds, *First VPres*, School Art League of New York City, Brooklyn NY

Gisiger, Hansjörg, *Head Fine Arts*, Lausanne College of Art and Design, Lausanne Switzerland (S)

Gispert, Pedro J, *Cur Art*, University of Puerto Rico, Museum of Archaeology, History and Art, Rio Piedras PR

Gitner, Fred J, *Librn*, French Institute-Alliance Francaise Library, New York NY

Gittins, Alvin, *Prof*, University of Utah, Art Department, Salt Lake City UT (S)

Giuntini, Gilles, *Asst Prof*, Hartford Art School of the University of Hartford, West Hartford CT (S)

Givins, Marjorie, *Librn*, Polk Public Museum, Library, Lakeland FL

Givler, David, *Assoc Dir*, Wright State University, Fine Arts Gallery, Dayton OH

Givler, David, *Adjunct Assoc*, Wright State University, Art Department, Dayton OH (S)

Gladstone, Caroline Thierman, *Vol Guides Coordr*, Philadelphia Museum of Art, Philadelphia PA

Glaesemer, Jürgen, *Cur*, Kunstmuseum Bern, Museum of Fine Arts Berne, Berne Switzerland

Glaser, Michael, *Chmn*, Saint Mary's College of Maryland, Arts & Letters Div, Saint Mary's City MD (S)

Glaser, Walter, *Prof*, California State Polytechnic University, Pomona, Art Department, Pomona CA (S)

Glasgow, Lukman, *Dir*, Downey Museum of Art, Downey CA

Glasgow, Vaughn, *Chief Cur*, Louisiana State Museum, New Orleans LA

Glasmann, Richard, *VPres*, Eccles Community Art Center, Ogden UT

Glaspy, Sugar, *Adminr*, Dallas Historical Society, Research Center Library, Dallas TX

Glasrud, Barbara, *Chmn*, Concordia College, Art Department, Moorhead MN (S)

Glass, Corrie, *Pres*, Artists Guild of Chicago, Chicago IL

Glassman, Jerome, *Pres*, Mitchell Museum, Mount Vernon IL

Glasson, Lloyd, *Assoc Prof*, Hartford Art School of the University of Hartford, West Hartford CT (S)

Glattley, Charles D, *Secy*, Sierra Arts Foundation, Reno NV

Glavin, Ellen Marie, *Prof*, Emmanuel College, Art Department, Boston MA (S)

Glazer, Jean, *Prof*, Portland State University, Department of Art and Architecture, Portland OR (S)

Glazer, Robert, *Assoc Prof*, University of North Carolina-Charlotte, Creative Arts Dept, Charlotte NC (S)

Gleason, Dale L, *Division Chmn*, Bellevue Community College, Division of Creative Arts, Bellevue WA (S)

Gleason, Katherine, *Secy*, State University of New York at Binghamton, University Art Gallery, Binghamton NY

Gleason, Ron, *Dir*, Tyler Museum of Art, Tyler TX

Gleeson, Larry, *Art History Coordr*, North Texas State University, Art Department, Denton TX (S)

Gleeson, M, *Executive Dir*, Artists Guild of Chicago, Chicago IL

Glen, T, *Assoc Prof*, McGill University, Department of Art History, Montreal PQ (S)

Glenn, Constance W, *Dir*, California State University, Long Beach, The Art Museum and Galleries, Long Beach CA

Glenn, Dixie, *Instr*, University of Kansas, Department of Visual Arts Education, Lawrence KS (S)

Glenn, Edna, *Assoc Prof*, Texas Tech University, Department of Art, Lubbock TX (S)

Glick, David, *VPres Education*, Greenfield Village and Henry Ford Museum, Dearborn MI

Glick, Lucy, *Secy*, Pennsylvania Academy of the Fine Arts, Fellowship of the Pennsylvania Academy of the Fine Arts, Philadelphia PA

Glicksman, Gretchen, *Registrar*, University of California, University Art Museum, Berkeley CA

Glidden, Germain G, *Dir*, National Art Museum of Sports, Inc, New York NY

Glidden, Robert, *VPres*, American Council for the Arts in Education, Baltimore MD

Glier, Nancy, *Membership & Gallery Coordr*, Contemporary Arts Center, Cincinnati OH

Glob, P V, *Dir*, Nationalmuseet, National Museum, Copenhagen Denmark

Globus, Dorothy Twining, *Exhib Coordr*, Cooper-Hewitt Museum, Smithsonian Institution National Museum of Design, New York NY

Glover, Jack N, *Cur*, Sunset Trading Post Old West Museum, Sunset TX

Glover, Tom, *Instructor*, Amarillo College, Art Dept, Amarillo TX (S)

Gluhman, Joseph W, *Head Dept*, Western Kentucky University, Art Department, Bowling Green KY (S)

Glusberg, Jorge, *Pres*, Centro de Arte y Communicacion, Center of Art and Communication, Buenos Argentina

Glusberg, Leonardo, *VPres*, Centro de Arte y Communicacion, Center of Art and Communication, Buenos Argentina

Glynn, Lucille, *Secy*, Hutchinson Art Association, Hutchinson KS

Gnat, Raymond, *Dir*, Indianapolis Marion County Public Library, Indianapolis IN

Goad, Albert W, *Chmn*, Ashland College Arts and Humanities Gallery, Ashland OH

Goad, Albert W, *Chmn*, Ashland College, Art Department, Ashland OH (S)

Gobar, Anne, *Cur*, Headley-Whitney Museum, Library, Lexington KY

Gobar, Anne, *Cur*, Headley-Whitney Museum, Lexington KY

Goberis, Theodora S, *Instructor*, Norwich Art School, Norwich Free Academy, Art Dept, Norwich CT (S)

Gochenoor, Carol, *Admin Dir*, Brattleboro Museum and Art Center, Brattleboro VT

Gockerell, N, *Cur Folk Art*, Bayerisches Nationalmuseum, Bavarian National Museum, Munich Germany, Federal Republic of

Godbolt, Fred B, *Pres Emeritus*, Kelly-Griggs House Museum, Pasadena CA

Godfrey, Robert, *Dir*, Westminster College Art Gallery, New Wilmington PA

Godlewski, Henry, *Asst Prof*, Mohawk Valley Community College, Advertising Design and Production, Utica NY (S)

Godwin, Marilyn O, *Pres*, Pensacola Museum of Art, Pensacola FL

Goehlich, John, *Dept Head*, Ray-Vogue School of Design, Chicago IL (S)

Goelet, Robert G, *Pres*, New York Historical Society, New York NY

Goelet, Robert G, *Pres*, American Museum of Natural History, New York NY

Goepper, Roger, *Dir*, Museen der Stadt Köln, Museum für Ostasiatische Kunst, Cologne Germany, Federal Republic of

Goetemann, Gordon, *Instructor*, College of Saint Benedict, Art Department, Saint Joseph MN (S)

Goetz, Edith, *Instructor*, Goetz Art School, Bedford Hills NY (S)

Goetz, Richard V, *Dir*, Goetz Art School, Bedford Hills NY (S)

Goetz, Robert C, *Treas*, National Gallery of Art, Washington DC

Goff, Lila J, *Asst to Dir for Libraries and Museum Coll*, Minnesota Historical Society, St Paul MN

Goff, Lloyd Lozes, *Secy*, National Society of Mural Painters, Inc, New York NY

Goffen, Rona, *Asst Prof*, Duke University, Department of Art, Durham NC (S)

Gogel, Ken, *Prof*, University of Northern Iowa, Department of Art, Cedar Falls IA (S)

Goheen, Ellen R, *Cur 20th Century Art*, William Rockhill Nelson Gallery of Art, Atkins Museum of Fine Art, Kansas City MO

Goings, Ralph, *Vis Prof*, Utica College of Syracuse University, Division of Humanities, Utica NY (S)

Goins, Ralph Michael, *Asst Prof*, University of North Carolina at Wilmington, Art Department, Wilmington NC (S)

Gold, Harvey, *Admin*, Pennsylvania Academy of the Fine Arts, Philadelphia PA

Gold, Howard, *Assoc Prof*, Middle Tennessee State University, Art Dept, Murfreesboro TN (S)

Gold, Marvin, *VPres*, Erie Art Center, Erie PA

Gold, Peter, *Cur Coll*, Indiana University, University Museum, Bloomington IN

Gold, Sharon, *Vis Prof*, University of Texas at San Antonio, Division of Art and Design, San Antonio TX (S)

Goldberg, Gisela, *Cur Old German Paintings*, Bayerischen Staatsgemaldesammlungen, Bavarian State Galleries of Art, Munich Germany, Federal Republic of

Goldberg, Kenneth P, *Asst Librn*, Cleveland Institute of Art, Jessica Gund Memorial Library, Cleveland OH

Goldberg, Rochelle, *Head Readers Services*, School of the Art Institute of Chicago Library, Chicago IL

Goldcamp, Alice, *Education Dir*, Butler Institute of American Art, Youngstown OH

Golden, Harvey, *Dir Continuing Education*, Saidye Bronfman Centre, Montreal PQ

Golden, Morton, *Deputy Dir Admin*, Los Angeles County Museum of Art, Los Angeles CA

Golden, Nancy, *VPres*, New Mexico Art League, Ken Roberts Gallery, Albuquerque NM

Goldhammer, Peter, *VPres*, New York Society of Architects, f the Performing Arts, at Lincoln Center New York

Goldin, Leon, *Chmn Div*, Columbia University, Division of Painting and Sculpture, New York NY (S)

Golding, Robert D, *Instructor*, Antonelli School of Photography, Philadelphia PA (S)

Goldman, Max, *VPres*, La Casa del Libro, House of Books, San Juan PR

Goldman, Saul, *Video Officer*, Cultural Initiative, Toronto ON

Goldman, Stewart, *Instructor*, Art Academy of Cincinnati, Cincinnati OH (S)

Goldner, George, *In Charge*, J Paul Getty Museum, Photo Archives, Malibu CA

Goldsmith, Benedict, *Dir of Exhibits*, Maine Coast Artists, Rockport ME

Goldsmith, Cathy, *Head*, Art Gallery of Ontario, Edward P Taylor Audio-Visual Centre, Toronto ON

Goldsmith, Zina, *Gallery Dir*, Beaver College, Eugene R Fuller Gallery of Art, Glenside PA

Goldstein, Alan, *Instructor*, Bucks County Community College, Fine Arts Department, Newton PA (S)

Goldstein, Carl, *Assoc Prof*, University of North Carolina at Greensboro, Art Dept, Greensboro NC (S)

Goldstein, Elsie, *Treas*, Arizona Watercolor Association, Phoenix AZ

Goldstein, Gladys, *Assoc Prof*, College of Notre Dame of Maryland, Art Dept, Baltimore MD (S)

Goldstein, Howard, *Prof*, Trenton State College, Art Department, Trenton NJ (S)

Goldstein, Jack, *Instructor*, Hartford Art School of the University of Hartford, West Hartford CT (S)

Goldstein, Milton, *Prof*, Adelphi University, Department of Art and Art History, Garden City NY (S)

Goldstein, Nathan, *Chmn Found Dept*, Art Institute of Boston, Boston MA (S)

Goldstein, Sidney M, *Cur Ancient Glass*, Corning Museum of Glass, Corning NY

Goldstein, Vivian, *Trustee*, Foundation for Today's Art, Nexus Gallery, Philadelphia PA

Goldwater, Marge, *Cur*, Fort Worth Art Museum, Fort Worth TX

Goldworm, Judith, *Asst to Dir*, Lehigh University Galleries, Bethlehem PA

Golfman, Eleanor, *Treas*, Manitoba Society of Artists, Winnipeg MB

Golub, Leon, *Prof*, Rutgers, the State University of New Jersey, Mason Gross School of the Arts, New Brunswick NJ (S)

Gomez, R V J, *Head*, University of Regina, Department of Visual Arts, Regina SK (S)

Gomez-Moreno, Carmen, *Cur Medieval Art*, Metropolitan Museum of Art, New York NY

Gomez-Moreno, Maria Elena, *Dir*, Museo Romantico, Museum of the Romantic Epoch, Madrid Spain

Gomez-Moreno, Maria Elena, *Dir*, Casa y Museo del Greco, El Greco's House and Museum, Toledo Spain

Gomez-Sicre, Jose, *Dir*, Museum of Modern Art of Latin America, Washington DC

Gontesky, Michael, *Asst Prof*, Mount Marty College, Art Dept, Yankton SD (S)

Gonzales, Alex, *Instructor*, Monterey Peninsula College, Art Department, Monterey CA (S)

Gonzales, Camille, *Technical Asst*, Santa Monica College Art Gallery, Santa Monica CA

Gonzalez, Xavier, *Instructor*, Truro Center for the Arts at Castle Hill, Inc, Truro MA (S)

Good, Bruce, *Instr*, Brazosport College, Art Department, Lake Jackson TX (S)

Good, Vernon L, *Pres*, Council of Delaware Artists, Wilmington DE

Goodale, Carol, *Instr*, Pontiac Art Center, Pontiac MI (S)

Goodale, Carol S, *Educ Coordr*, Pontiac Art Center, Pontiac MI

Goodfriend, Janet R, *Dir*, Studio School of Art and Design, Philadelphia PA (S)

Goodhue, Timothy, *Registrar*, Yale University, Yale Center for British Art, New Haven CT

Gooding, Kenneth, *Dir Auto Museum*, Western Reserve Historical Society, Cleveland OH

Goodlett, Henry, *Pres*, Central Florida Community College Art Collection, Ocala FL

Goodman, Bernard, *Asst Supt*, Independence National Historical Park, Philadelphia PA

Goodman, Bert, *Vis Prof*, Mount Vernon Nazarene College, Art Department, Mount Vernon OH (S)

Goodman, Helen J, *Executive Secy*, Carnegie Institute, Museum of Art, Pittsburgh PA

Goodman, Susan, *Chief Cur*, Jewish Museum, New York NY

Goodman, Wayne, *Instructor*, Ocean City School of Art, Ocean City NJ (S)

Goodmen, Iris, *Coordr of Public Relations*, Springfield Free Public Library, Donald B Palmer Museum, Springfield NJ

Goodnough, Joan, *Adminr Asst to Dir*, Moose Jaw Art Museum and National Exhibition Centre, Moose Jaw SK

Goodreau, D A, *Chmn*, Carleton University, Department of Art History, Ottawa ON (S)

Goodrich, Margaret, *Librn*, Denver Art Museum, Frederic H Douglas Library, Denver CO

Goodridge, Edythe, *Cur*, Memorial University Newfoundland, Art Gallery, Saint John's NF

Goodridge, Laurence W, *Instructor*, Art Academy of Cincinnati, Cincinnati OH (S)

Goodspeed, Barbara, *Pres*, Kent Art Association, Inc Gallery, Kent CT

Goodwin, David, *Instructor*, Coe College, Department of Art, Cedar Rapids IA (S)

Goodwin, John A, *VPres*, Lowell Art Association, Whistler House and Parker Gallery, Lowell MA

Goodyear, John Lake, *Prof*, Rutgers, the State University of New Jersey, Mason Gross School of the Arts, New Brunswick NJ (S)

Goodyear Jr, Frank H, *Cur*, Pennsylvania Academy of the Fine Arts, Philadelphia PA

Goosey, Jim, *Construction Specialist*, Montana State University, Museum of the Rockies, Bozeman MT

Goossen, Eugene C, *Prof*, City University of New York, PhD Program in Art History, New York NY (S)

Gorbey, Judie, *Supvr Guest Relations*, Franklin Mint Corp Museum, Franklin Center PA

Gordon, Albert C, *Dir*, Washington and Lee University, Gallery of DuPont Hall, Lexington VA

Gordon, Alden R, *Asst Prof*, Trinity College, Department of Fine Arts, Hartford CT (S)

Gordon, Amorita, *Asst Dir*, Lauren Rogers Library and Museum of Art, Laurel MS

Gordon, Anne M, *Librn*, Long Island Historical Society, Library, Brooklyn NY

Gordon, Anne W, *Librn in Charge*, Carnegie Library of Pittsburgh, Pittsburgh PA

Gordon, Ayala, *Cur Youth Wing*, Israel Museum, Jerusalem Israel

Gordon, Carol, *Cur Decorative Arts*, Munson-Williams-Proctor Institute, Museum of Art, Utica NY

Gordon, Diana, *Museum Dir*, The Bradford Museum, Niles IL

Gordon, Donald, *Prof*, University of Pittsburgh, Henry Clay Frick Fine Arts Department, Pittsburgh PA (S)

Gordon, G Lynn, *Chmn*, Radford University, Art Department, Radford VA (S)

Gordon, John, *Instructor*, Sioux City Art Center, Sioux City IA (S)

Gordon, Joy L, *Dir*, Danforth Museum, Framingham MA

Gordon, Lida, *Instructor*, Louisville School of Art, Anchorage KY (S)

Gordon, Martha, *Asst Prof*, Tarrant County Junior College, Northeast Campus, Hurst TX (S)

Gordon, Thomas L, *Chmn*, Ohio Northern University, Department of Art, Ada OH (S)

Gore, Jefferson A, *Cur Fine Arts*, Reading Public Museum and Art Gallery, Reading PA

Gore, Kenneth L, *VPres*, Guild of Boston Artists, Boston MA

Gore, Samuel M, *Head Dept*, Mississippi College, Art Department, Clinton MS (S)

Gore, Tom, *Cur*, Open Space Gallery, Secession Gallery of Photography, Victoria BC

Gorecki, Claudia, *Secy*, Wisconsin Painters and Sculptors, Inc, Milwaukee WI

Gorecki, Claudia M, *Assoc Prof*, Cardinal Stritch College, Art Department, Milwaukee WI (S)

Goridey, Frances, *Secy*, Yarmouth County Historical Society Museum, Yarmouth NS

Gorini, Giovanni, *Dir*, Museo Civico di Padua, Municipal Museum, Padua Italy

Gorka, Paul, *Instructor*, Wayne Art Center, Wayne PA (S)

Gorman, James G, *Coordr*, Vincennes University, Art Department, Vincennes IN (S)

Gorman, Joan H, *Cur*, Brandywine River Museum, Chadds Ford PA

Gorman, Mary B, *Librn*, Vincennes University, Art Slide Library, Vincennes IN

Gorman, William D, *Pres*, Allied Artists of America, Inc, New York NY

Gormley, Brian, *Dir*, Lake Placid School of Art, Lake Placid NY (S)

Gorney, Diane E, *Admin Coordr*, Women's Art Registry of Minnesota, Minneapolis MN

Gorny, Anthony, *Asst Prof*, Temple University, Art Department, Philadelphia PA (S)

Gorove, Margaret, *Chmn*, University of Mississippi, Department of Art, University MS (S)

Gorove, Margaret, *Dir*, University of Mississippi, University Gallery, University MS

Gorrostiza, D Manuel Llano, *Secy*, Museo de Bellas Artes, Museum of Fine Arts, Bilbao Spain

Gorton, Tonda, *Arts Services Coordr*, Arizona Commission on the Arts, Phoenix AZ

Goshorn, Robert M, *Pres*, Chester County Historical Society, West Chester PA

Gosley, G S, *Dir*, Dartmouth Heritage Museum, Dartmouth NS

Gosselin, Claude, *Dir of Exhib*, Musee d'Art Contemporain, Montreal PQ

Gostin, Arlene, *Chairperson Educ*, Philadelphia College of Art, Philadelphia PA (S)

Gothberg, Ed, *Instructor*, Casper College, Casper WY (S)

Gottfried, Herbert, *Chmn*, Oklahoma State University, Art Department, Stillwater OK (S)

Gottlieb, Darcy, *Instr*, International Fine Arts College, Miami FL (S)

Gottlieb, Gerald, *Cur Early Children's Books*, Pierpont Morgan Library, New York NY

Gottliets, Robert A, *Executive Dir*, Art Center Association, Louisville KY

Gottschalk, Roger, *Chmn*, University of Wisconsin-Platteville, Department of Fine Art, Platteville WI (S)

Gottselig, Len, *Library & Archives*, Glenbow Museum, Library, Calgary AB

Gould, Emilie W, *Site Mgr*, John Jay Homestead, Katonah NY

Gould, I O, *Archivist*, New Haven Colony Historical Society, Reference Library, New Haven CT

Gouma-Peterson, Thalia, *Prof*, College of Wooster, Department of Art, Wooster OH (S)

Gourley III, Hugh J, *Dir*, Colby Museum of Art, Waterville ME

Gous, Julian, *Asst Prof Officer*, King George VI Art Gallery, Port South Africa, Republic of

Govier, Victor M, *Exhib Program Dir*, Anacostia Neighborhood Museum, Washington DC

Gowans, Alan, *Chmn*, University of Victoria, Department of History in Art, Victoria BC (S)

Gowen, Michael, *Collections Mgr*, University of California, Los Angeles, Museum of Cultural History, Los Angeles CA

Gowen, Rebecca, *Asst Prof*, University of Southern California, School of Fine Arts, Los Angeles CA (S)

Gower, Dorothy, *VPres*, Vernon Art Association, Topham Brown Gallery, Vernon BC

Gowin, Emmett, *Vis Prof*, Johnson State College, Art Department, Johnson VT (S)

Gowing, Lawrence, *Dir*, Slade School of Fine Art, London England (S)

Graas, T, *Cur*, Noord-Brabants Museum, Hertogenbosch Netherlands

Grabar, Oleg, *Chmn Dept*, Harvard University, Department of Fine Arts, Cambridge MA (S)

Grabarski, Sam W, *Dir*, Quincy Society of Fine Arts, Quincy IL

Grabowicz, Oksana, *Cur*, Ukrainian Museum, New York NY

Grabowski, Irena, *Arms & Armour*, Muzeum Narodowe w Krakowie, National Museum in Cracow, Cracow Poland

Guenther, Bruce, *Assoc Cur*, Seattle Art Museum, Modern Art Pavilion, Seattle WA

Guenthler, John R, *Asst Prof*, Indiana University Southeast, Fine Arts Department, New Albany IN (S)

Guerin, Charles, *Dir Exhib & Physical Plant*, Colorado Springs Fine Arts Center, Colorado Springs CO

Guernica, Rudy, *School Slide Service*, School of the Art Institute of Chicago Library, Chicago IL

Guernsey, Terry, *Lectr*, University of Victoria, Department of History in Art, Victoria BC (S)

Guerra, Luis, *Head Dept*, Austin Community College, Dept of Commercial Art & Fine Arts, Austin TX (S)

Guerra, Mary Ellen, *Research Assoc, Art Theft Archive*, International Foundation for Art Research, Inc, New York NY

Guertin, Joseph, *Instructor*, Portland School of Art, Portland ME (S)

Guest, Tim, *Archivist*, Art Metropole, Toronto ON

Guest, Tim, *Archivist*, Art Metropole, Library, Toronto ON

Gueury, Marie-Claire, *Asst Cur*, Musees d'Archeologie et d'Arts Decoratifs, Liege Museums of Archeology and Decorative Arts, Liege Belgium

Guffin, Raymond L, *Asst Prof*, Stillman College, Stillman Art Gallery and Art Department, Tuscaloosa AL (S)

Gugell, Gwen, *Instructor*, Springfield College, Department of Visual and Performing Arts, Springfield MA (S)

Guido, Nelida Maria Luisa, *Secy*, Escuela Superior de Bellas Artes Ernesto de la Carcova, National Superior School of Fine Arts Ernesto de la Carcova, Buenos Argentina

Guidos, Patricia, *Instructor*, Antonelli School of Photography, Philadelphia PA (S)

Guilford II, Ben J, *Asst Dir*, Miami-Dade Public Library, Miami FL

Guill, Kenneth, *Asst Prof*, Georgia Southern College, Department of Art, Statesboro GA (S)

Guillaume, Harry, *Prof*, University of Northern Iowa, Department of Art, Cedar Falls IA (S)

Guillermety, Jose Buscaglia, *Instructor*, University of Puerto Rico, Department of Fine Arts, Mayaguez PR (S)

Guilmain, Jacques, *Prof*, State University of New York at Stony Brook, Art Department, Stony Brook NY (S)

Gulbranson, Rex, *Visual Arts Coordr*, Arizona Commission on the Arts, Phoenix AZ

Gulliver, Adelaide C, *Pres*, Museum of the National Center of Afro-American Artists, Boston MA

Gummere, Judy, *Circulation Head*, Lake Forest Library, Lake Forest IL

Gunaris, Zofia, *Mgr*, Ministry of Culture and Art, Museum of Architecture in Wroclaw, Wroclaw Poland

Gunasinghe, Siri, *Prof*, University of Victoria, Department of History in Art, Victoria BC (S)

Gundersheimer, Herman, *Lectr*, La Salle College, Department of Fine Arts, Philadelphia PA (S)

Gunderson, Barry, *Asst Prof*, Kenyon College, Art Department, Gambier OH (S)

Gunderson, Karen, *Acting Chmn*, College of Mount Saint Vincent, Fine Arts Department, Riverdale NY (S)

Gunn, Norman, *Pres*, Central Louisiana Art Association, Alexandria Museum Visual Art Center, Alexandria LA

Gunnerson, Don, *Planning & Design*, Licking County Art Association Gallery, Newark OH

Gunnion, Vernon S, *Cur Collections*, Pennsylvania Farm Museum of Landis Valley, Lancaster PA

Gunstone, Antony J H, *Dir*, Lincolnshire Museums, Usher Gallery, Lincoln England

Gunter, Virginia, *Dir*, Massachusetts Institute of Technology, Compton Gallery, Cambridge MA

Gunther, Charles F, *Dir Art Educ*, University of Toledo, Department of Art, Art Education and Art History, Toledo OH (S)

Gunther, Charles F, *Asst Dir Education*, Toledo Museum of Art, Toledo OH

Gunther, Charles F, *Asst Dir*, Toledo Museum of Art, School of Design, Toledo OH (S)

Gunther, Gloria, *Treas*, Prince George Art Gallery, Prince George BC

Guraedy, J Bruce, *Head Dept*, East Central Junior College, Art Department, Decatur MS (S)

Guralnik, Nehama, *European & American Art*, Tel Aviv Museum, Tel-Aviv Israel

Gursoy, Ahmet, *Pres*, Federation of Modern Painters and Sculptors, New York NY

Gussow, Alan, *Vis Prof*, Santa Rosa Junior College, Art Department, Santa Rosa CA (S)

Gussow, Roy, *Pres*, Sculptors Guild, Inc, New York NY

Gust, Otto, *Secy*, Craft Center Museum, Wilton CT

Gustaferro, Colleen, *Second VPres*, Arizona Watercolor Association, Phoenix AZ

Gustafson, Dwight, *Dean*, Bob Jones University, School of Fine Arts, Greenville SC (S)

Gustafson, Louise, *Pres*, Arts Council of the Mid-Columbia Region, Richland WA

Gustafson, R David, *Chmn*, Rock Valley College, Dept of Art, Rockford IL (S)

Gustavson, Robert E, *Executive Dir*, Corporate Council for the Arts, Seattle WA

Gustin, Mickey, *Dir*, Factory of Visual Art, Seattle WA (S)

Guston, Philip, *Prof*, Boston University, School of Visual Arts, Boston MA (S)

Gustow, Hazel, *Library Dir*, Philadelphia College of Art Gallery, Library, Philadelphia PA

Gutekunst, B, *Head Humanities Division*, Catholic University of America, Humanities Division, Mullen Library, Washington DC

Guthrie, C Willis, *Prof*, Carroll College, Art Department, Waukesha WI (S)

Guthrie, Robert M, *Exhib Dir*, Fredericton National Exhibition Centre, Fredericton NB

Gutierrez, Enrique Garcia, *Head Dept*, University of Puerto Rico, Department of Fine Arts, Mayaguez PR (S)

Gutierrez, Luis, *Instr*, San Jose City College, School of Fine Arts, San Jose CA (S)

Gutierrez-Solana, Carlos, *Cur*, Queens Museum, Flushing NY

Gutridge, Delbert R, *Registrar*, Cleveland Museum of Art, Cleveland OH

Gutteridge, Mary, *Assoc Librn*, Sheldon Jackson College, Stratton Library, Sitka AK

Guyatt, Richard, *Rector & VProvost*, Royal College of Art Gallery, London England

Guyatt, Richard, *Rector*, Royal College of Art, London England (S)

Guy Jr, John H, *Regent*, Mount Vernon, Mount Vernon VA

Guzak, Karen, *Instructor*, Factory of Visual Art, Seattle WA (S)

Guzman, Diane, *Librn*, Brooklyn Museum, Wilbour Library of Egyptology, Brooklyn NY

Guzman, Gabriela, *Head Promotion Department*, Museo Nacional de Antropologia, National Museum of Anthropology, Mexico Mexico

Guzzetti, Alfred, *Prof*, Harvard University, Department of Visual and Environmental Studies, Cambridge MA (S)

Gyer, Jack, *Cur*, Yosemite Museum Collections, Yosemite National Park CA

Gyllensvard, Bo, *Dir*, Ostasiatiska Museet, Museum of Far Eastern Antiquities, Stockholm Sweden

Gza, Israel Cavazos, *Cur*, Museo Regional de Nuevo Leon, Regional Museum of Nuevo Leon, Monterrey Mexico

Haag, J, *Cur Conservation*, Bayerisches Nationalmuseum, Bavarian National Museum, Munich Germany, Federal Republic of

Haagensen, Lynn, *Asst Prof*, University of Idaho, Department of Art and Architecture, Moscow ID (S)

Haarer, Ann, *Chmn Dept*, College of Saint Elizabeth, Art Department, Convent Station NJ (S)

Haas, David, *Assoc Prof*, University of Northern Colorado, Department of Fine Arts, Greeley CO (S)

Haas, Edward, *Chief Cur*, Louisiana State Museum, New Orleans LA

Haas, Pauline, *Coordr*, Whitworth College, Art Department, Spokane WA (S)

Haas, Susanne, *Cur Prehistory & India*, Museum für Völkerkunde und Schweizerisches Museum für Volkskunde Basel, Museum of Ethnological Collections and Folklore, Basel Switzerland

Habel, Dorothy, *Asst Prof*, University of Nebraska at Omaha, Dept of Art, Omaha NE (S)

Haber, Mortimer N, *Dir*, Haber School of Sculpture, Roslyn NY (S)

Haberman, David, *Assoc Prof*, Cuyahoga Community College, Department of Art, Cleveland OH (S)

Habershaw, David, *VPres*, Bristol Art Museum, Bristol RI

Habraken, N John, *Head Dept Architecture*, Massachusetts Institute of Technology, School of Architecture and Planning, Cambridge MA (S)

Habst, Gail J, *Communications Officer*, Visual Arts Ontario, Toronto ON

Hachey, Paul A, *Asst Cur*, Beaverbrook Art Gallery, Fredericton NB

Hack, Janet S, *Graphics Designer*, Hall of Fame of the Trotter, Goshen NY

Hackenbroch, Yvonne, *Consultant Sculpture & Decorative Art*, Metropolitan Museum of Art, New York NY

Hacker, Susan, *Asst Prof*, Webster College, Art Dept, Webster Groves MO (S)

Hackett, David, *Lectr*, Cardinal Stritch College, Art Department, Milwaukee WI (S)

Hackett, Joan, *Art Education Coordr*, Museum of Art, Science and Industry, Bridgeport CT

Hackett, Susie, *VPres*, Alaska Association for the Arts, Fairbanks AK

Hacking, Gary E, *Dir*, Presidential Museum, Odessa TX

Hackler, Robert, *Pres Board of Trustees*, Anderson Fine Arts Center, Anderson IN

Hackley, Martha, *Mgr Sales & Info*, Frick Collection, New York NY

Haddaway, William C, *Art Librn*, Dallas Public Library, Fine Arts Division, Dallas TX

Hadler, Mona, *Assoc Prof*, City University of New York, PhD Program in Art History, New York NY (S)

Hadley, Rollin van N, *Dir*, Isabella Stewart Gardner Museum, Boston MA

Hadwin, Millie, *Dir*, Ella Sharp Museum, Jackson MI

Hadzi, Dimitri, *Prof*, Harvard University, Department of Visual and Environmental Studies, Cambridge MA (S)

Hadzi, Martha Leeb, *Chmn*, Mount Holyoke College, Art Department, South Hadley MA (S)

Hafer, Ardyth, *Pres*, Los Alamos Arts Council, Los Alamos NM

Hagan, Jane, *Librn*, Brand Library and Art Center, Glendale CA

Hagan, Kathy, *Chmn Three-Dimensional and Crafts Studies*, Bowling Green State University, School of Art, Bowling Green OH (S)

Hagelberg, Richard, *Pres*, Greater Gary Arts Council, Gary IN

Hagelberger, Richard, *Asst Prof*, Wittenberg University, Art Department, Springfield OH (S)

Hageman, Lee, *Chmn Dept Art*, Northwest Missouri State University, DeLuce Gallery, Maryville MO

Hageman, Lee, *Chmn Dept*, Northwest Missouri State University, Dept of Art, Maryville MO (S)

Hagen, Charles, *Editor Afterimage*, Visual Studies Workshop, Rochester NY

Hagen, Gary, *Assoc Prof*, University of Wisconsin-Stevens Point, Department of Art, Stevens Point WI (S)

Hager, Hellmut, *Dept Chmn*, Pennsylvania State University, University Park, Department of Art History, University Park PA (S)

Hager, Hellmut, *Head Dept Art History*, Pennsylvania State University, University Park, College of Arts and Architecture, University Park PA (S)

Hager, Kristi, *Asst Prof*, University of Santa Clara, Fine Arts Department, Santa Clara CA (S)

Hager, Michael W, *Dir*, Montana State University, Museum of the Rockies, Bozeman MT

Hammon, Margaret, *Pres*, Muckenthaler Cultural Center, Fullerton CA

Hammond, Jack, *Instructor*, Maryland College of Art and Design, Silver Spring MD (S)

Hammond, Natalie Hays, *Dir*, Hammond Museum, Museum of the Humanities, North Salem NY

Hammond, Ruth, *Dir of Information Services*, Ontario College of Art, Toronto ON (S)

Hammond Jr, Lyman H, *Dir*, MacArthur Memorial, Norfolk VA

Hamoy, Carol, *Publicity Chmn & Funding Chmn*, Women in the Arts Foundation, Inc, New York NY

Hampson, Katherine, *Secy*, Verde Valley Art Association, Inc, Jerome AZ

Hampton, Grace, *Chmn*, Jackson State University, Department of Art, Jackson MS (S)

Hancock, Marga Rose, *Acting Dir*, Allied Arts of Seattle, Inc, Seattle WA

Hancock, Paula, *Cur Educ*, High Museum of Art, Atlanta GA

Hancox, William J, *Executive Dir*, Confederation Centre Art Gallery and Museum, Charlottetown PE

Hand, John, *Cur Northern European Painting*, National Gallery of Art, Washington DC

Handleman, David, *Pres Meadow Brook Gallery Assocs*, Oakland University, Meadow Brook Art Gallery, Rochester MI

Handy, Susan, *Museum Shop Mgr*, Rhode Island School of Design, Museum of Art, Providence RI

Hanes, James, *Asst Prof*, La Salle College, Department of Fine Arts, Philadelphia PA (S)

Hanes, John W, *Chmn*, National Museum of Racing, Inc, Saratoga Springs NY

Hanford, Sharon, *Cur*, Salem Art Association, Bush House, and Bush Barn Art Center, Salem OR

Hanft, Margie, *Film Librn*, California Institute of the Arts Library, Valencia CA

Hanger, Jim, *Instructor*, Mary Baldwin College, Department of Art, Staunton VA (S)

Hankamer, Roberta, *Secy Treas*, Special Libraries Association, Museum, Arts and Humanities Division, New York NY

Hankel, Wayne, *Pres*, SVACA - Sheyenne Valley Arts and Crafts Association, Bjarne Ness Gallery, Fort Ransom ND

Hankin, Stephen, *Asst Prof*, University of Wisconsin-Stevens Point, Department of Art, Stevens Point WI (S)

Hanlon, Alan R, *Dir Rothmans Art Program*, Rothmans of Pall Mall Canada Limited, Toronto ON

Hanna, James, *Asst Prof*, Texas Tech University, Department of Art, Lubbock TX (S)

Hanna, Katherine, *Dir*, Taft Museum, Cincinnati OH

Hanna, Martha, *Producer*, National Film Board of Canada, Still Photography Division, Photo Gallery, Ottawa ON

Hanna, Paul, *Asst Chmn*, Texas Tech University, Department of Art, Lubbock TX (S)

Hannan, William, *Assoc Prof*, Black Hawk College, Art Dept, Moline IL (S)

Hanners, Roger, *Chmn Balch House*, Beverly Historical Society, Beverly MA

Hanniford, Sultana, *Recording Secy*, Lyme Art Association, Inc, Old Lyme CT

Hannon, William J, *Chmn Design*, Massachusetts College of Art, Boston MA (S)

Hansen, A, *Pres*, Rodman Hall Arts Centre, Saint Catharines ON

Hansen, Arthur, *Treas*, Jersey City Museum Association, Jersey City NJ

Hansen, Borge, *Dir*, Louisiana Museum of Modern Art, Humlebaek Denmark

Hansen, Chris, *Instructor*, Milwaukee Area Technical College, Graphic & Applied Arts Div, Milwaukee WI (S)

Hansen, Gail, *Educational Chmn*, Huntsville Art League and Museum Association Inc, Huntsville AL

Hansen, Gaylen C, *Prof*, Washington State University, Fine Arts Department, Pullman WA (S)

Hansen, Harry, *Chmn Studio*, University of South Carolina, Department of Art, Columbia SC (S)

Hansen, James L, *Prof*, Portland State University, Department of Art and Architecture, Portland OR (S)

Hansen, Jonathon, *Asst Dir*, Lansing Art Gallery, Lansing MI

Hanson, Elloyd, *Instructor*, Truro Center for the Arts at Castle Hill, Inc, Truro MA (S)

Hanson, Philip, *Instructor*, Oxbow Summer Art Workshops, Saugatuck MI (S)

Hanson, Sandra, *VPres*, Quapaw Quarter Association, Inc, Villa Marre, Little Rock AR

Hanson, Wesley T, *Chmn*, International Museum of Photography at George Eastman House, Rochester NY

Hanssen, Peter, *Assoc Prof*, Kingsborough Community College, Department of Art, Brooklyn NY (S)

Haq, Sylvia S, *Librn*, Munson-Williams-Proctor Institute, Art Reference Library, Utica NY

Har, Lorraine, *Chmn Textile Design*, Fashion Institute of Technology, New York NY (S)

Hara, Teruo, *Assoc Prof*, Mary Washington College, Art Department, Fredericksburg VA (S)

Harasimowicz, Alan, *Preparator*, Southern Illinois University Museum and Art Galleries, Carbondale IL

Harbach, Merle S, *Dir Education*, Columbus Museum of Art, Columbus OH

Harbison, Craig, *Dir*, University of Massachusetts, Amherst, Art History Prog, Amherst MA (S)

Harbour, June, *Executive Secy*, Washington State University, Museum of Art, Pullman WA

Harbour Jr, John W, *Exec Dir*, Sleepy Hollow Restorations Inc, Tarrytown NY

Hard, Michael W, *Treas*, Amerind Foundation, Inc, Dragoon AZ

Hardberger, Linda M, *Librn*, San Antonio Museum Association, Inc, Ellen S Quillin Memorial Library, San Antonio TX

Harden, Larry, *Lectr*, Trinity College, Department of Fine Arts, Washington DC (S)

Hardie, P, *Cur Oriental Art*, City Art Gallery, Bristol England

Hardiman, George W, *In Charge Art Educ*, University of Illinois, Urbana-Champaign, Department of Art and Design, Champaign IL (S)

Hardison Jr, O B, *Dir*, Folger Shakespeare Library, Washington DC

Hardman, Jack N, *Dir*, Burnaby Art Gallery, Burnaby BC

Hardwig, Scott, *Asst Prof*, Roanoke College, Art Department, Salem VA (S)

Hardy, Frances, *Instructor*, Mississippi University for Women, Art Department, Columbus MS (S)

Haren, John Van, *Dept Head*, Eastern Michigan University, Sill Gallery, Ypsilanti MI

Hargrove, June E, *Assoc Prof*, Cleveland State University, Art Department, Cincinnati OH (S)

Harjo, Pauline, *Admin Asst*, Bacone College Museum, Muskogee OK

Harker, Suzanne, *Asst Prof*, Mount Mary College, Art Department, Milwaukee WI (S)

Harkins, Dennis, *Dir Photography*, Art Institute of Fort Lauderdale, Fort Lauderdale FL (S)

Harkness, Mary Lou, *Librn*, University of South Florida, Library, Tampa FL

Harlan, Calvin, *Assoc Prof*, University of New Orleans, Dept of Fine Arts, New Orleans LA (S)

Harlan, Mary L, *Cur of Exhib*, Columbus Museum of Art, Columbus OH

Harlan, Roger, *Exec Secy*, Rockford Art Association, Burpee Art Museum, Rockford IL

Harlan, Susan, *Instructor*, Brenau College, Art Department, Gainesville GA (S)

Harle, J C, *Keeper Depart Eastern Art*, Oxford University, Ashmolean Museum of Art and Archaeology, Oxford England

Harless, Ida, *Temporary Instructor*, Sam Houston State University, Art Department, Huntsville TX (S)

Harley, James, *Instr*, Bowdoin College, Art Department, Brunswick ME (S)

Harlow, Ann, *Asst to the Dir*, Mills College, Art Gallery, Oakland CA

Harlow, Bonnie K, *Registrar*, Saint Joseph Museum, Saint Joseph MO

Harlow, Thompson R, *Dir*, Connecticut Historical Society, Hartford CT

Harmon, Jean, *Asst Prof*, Missouri Western State College, Art Department, Saint Joseph MO (S)

Harmon, Robert, *Instr*, Studio School of Art and Design, Philadelphia PA (S)

Harms, Gudrun, *Librn*, Konservator der Kunstdenkmaler, Library, Dusseldorf Germany, Federal Republic of

Harms, Martin, *Dir Architecture*, North Carolina State University at Raleigh, School of Design, Raleigh NC (S)

Harney, Jean, *Recording Secy*, Arizona Artist Guild, Phoenix AZ

Harper, Ann Boyce, *Asst Dir for Admin*, Baltimore Museum of Art, Baltimore MD

Harper, Carolyn, *Docent Chairperson*, Licking County Art Association Gallery, Newark OH

Harper, Eleanor, *Secy*, Rockport Art Association, Rockport MA

Harper, Elsie, *Library Asst for Slides*, Georgia Institute of Technology, College of Architecture Library, Atlanta GA

Harper, George D, *Instructor*, Glenville State College, Department of Art, Glenville WV (S)

Harper, Grady, *Prof*, Northwestern State University of Louisiana, Dept of Art, Natchitoches LA (S)

Harper, John, *Arts Cur*, Redding Museum & Art Center, Redding CA

Harper, Prudence Oliver, *Cur Ancient Near Eastern Art*, Metropolitan Museum of Art, New York NY

Harper, Robert, *Instructor*, California College of Arts and Crafts, Oakland CA (S)

Harper, Robert L, *Head Librn*, California College of Arts & Crafts, Meyer Library, Oakland CA

Harpole, Patricia, *Chief Reference Librn*, Minnesota Historical Society, Library, St Paul MN

Harprath, Richard, *Cur*, Staatliche Graphische Sammlung, National Graphic Collection, Munich Germany, Federal Republic of

Harrel, Ralph, *Dean*, Southwest Texas State University, Department of Art, San Marcos TX (S)

Harrington, William T, *Cur*, East Windsor Historical Society Inc, Scantic Academy Museum, West Hartford CT

Harrington, William T, *Cur*, East Windsor Historical Society Inc, Scantic Academy Museum, West Hartford CT

Harris, A Peter, *Dir*, Rodman Hall Arts Centre, Saint Catharines ON

Harris, Allyn O, *Prof*, Community College of Baltimore, Dept of Fine & Applied Arts, Baltimore MD (S)

Harris, Carolyn, *Librn*, College of the Ozarks Library, Clarksville AR

Harris, Charley M, *Cur Education*, Pensacola Museum of Art, Pensacola FL

Harris, Conley, *Assoc Prof*, University of New Hampshire, Department of the Arts, Durham NH (S)

Harris, Cynthia, *Asst Prof*, Mary Baldwin College, Department of Art, Staunton VA (S)

Harris, David, *Dir of Arts & Sciences*, Indian Hills Community College, Ottumwa Heights Campus, Dept of Art, Ottumwa IA (S)

Harris, David J, *Instructor*, North Seattle Community College, Art Department, Seattle WA (S)

Harris, Dorothy, *Asst Prof*, Jersey City State College, Art Department, Jersey City NJ (S)

Harris, Edwin, *Assoc Prof*, University of Northern Iowa, Department of Art, Cedar Falls IA (S)

Harris, Erdman, *Pres*, Hill-Stead Museum, Farmington CT

Harris, Gene E, *Registrar*, Brandywine River Museum, Chadds Ford PA

Harris, Harry A, *Dir*, Woodmere Art Gallery, Philadelphia PA

Harris, J Carver, *Mgr*, Saint Augustine Historical Society, Library, Saint Augustine FL

Harris, Jean C, *Prof*, Mount Holyoke College, Art Department, South Hadley MA (S)

Harris, Jean C, *Dir*, Mount Holyoke College Art Museum, South Hadley MA

Harris, Jeanne, *Assoc Cur Oriental Art*, William Rockhill Nelson Gallery of Art, Atkins Museum of Fine Art, Kansas City MO

Harris, John M, *Dir*, Tippecanoe County Historical Museum, Lafayette IN

Harris, Louis, *Chmn*, American Council for the Arts, New York NY

Harris, Paul Rogers, *Dir*, Art Center, Waco TX

Harris, Randall, *Asst Prof*, University of Mississippi, Department of Art, University MS (S)

Harris, Ronn, *Theatre Mgr*, Portsmouth Museums and Community Arts Center, Petersburg VA

Harris, Wilhelmina S, *Supt*, Adams National Historic Site, Quincy MA

Harris, Willard R, *Chmn*, State University of New York, University Center at Buffalo, Department of Art and Art History, Buffalo NY (S)

Harrison, Carole, *Assoc Prof*, State University College, Department of Art, Fredonia NY (S)

Harrison, Cheryl, *Instructor*, Brevard College, Div of Fine Arts, Brevard NC (S)

Harrison, Donald, *Pres*, Washington Art Association, Washington Depot CT

Harrison, Ed, *Pres Bd of Governors*, Natural History Museum of Los Angeles County, Los Angeles CA

Harrison, Edward E, *Pres*, Fairfield Historical Society, Fairfield CT

Harrison, Honey, *Librn*, Museum of Fine Arts, Houston, Alfred C Glassell Jr School of Art Library, Houston TX

Harrison, Joseph R, *Chmn Board Trustees*, Metropolitan Museum and Art Centers, Coral Gables FL

Harrison, Julia, *Cur of Ethnology*, Glenbow Museum, Calgary AB

Harrison, Mark S, *Head Industrial Design*, Rhode Island School of Design, Providence RI (S)

Harrison, Newton, *Prof*, University of California, San Diego, Visual Arts Department, La Jolla CA (S)

Harrison, Richard, *Instructor*, Rehoboth Art League, Inc, Rehoboth Beach DE (S)

Harrison, Richard D, *VPres*, Oklahoma Art Center, Oklahoma City OK

Harrison, Ruth, *Admin Asst*, Hunterdon Art Center, Clinton NJ

Harrison, Tony, *Lectr*, Columbia University, Division of Painting and Sculpture, New York NY (S)

Harrow, Arthur, *VPres*, Artists' Fellowship, Inc, New York NY

Hart, Allen M, *Dir*, Children's Aid Society, New York NY (S)

Hart, Arnold, *Instr*, Okaloosa-Walton Junior College, Dept of Fine & Performing Arts, Niceville FL (S)

Hart, E J, *Adminr & Head Archivist*, Peter and Catharine Whyte Foundation, Peter Whyte Gallery, Banff AB

Hart, Evelyn L, *Head*, Enoch Pratt Free Library of Baltimore City, George Peabody Branch, Baltimore MD

Hart, Larry, *Pres*, Schenectady County Historical Society, Schenectady NY

Hart, Robert A, *Dir*, Santa Barbara Public Library, Faulkner Memorial Art Wing, Santa Barbara CA

Hart, Robert G, *General Mgr*, United States Department of the Interior, Indian Arts and Crafts Board, Washington DC

Hart, Vincent, *Lectr*, Georgian Court College, Department of Art, Lakewood NJ (S)

Harten, Jürgen, *Dir*, Städtische Kunsthalle, City Art Gallery, Dusseldorf Germany, Federal Republic of

Harter, Donald, *Asst Prof*, Midwestern State University, Department of Art, Wichita Falls TX (S)

Harter, Donald R, *Chmn*, Niagara County Community College, Fine Arts Div, Sanborn NY (S)

Harter, Harry H, *Chmn Dept Fine Arts*, Maryville College Fine Arts Center Gallery, Maryville TN

Hartgen, Vincent A, *Cur*, University of Maine at Orono, Art Collection, Orono ME

Hartgen, Vincent A, *Prof*, University of Maine, Art Department, Orono ME (S)

Hartig, Thomas H, *Executive Dir*, Woodrow Wilson Birthplace Foundation, Staunton VA

Hartigan, Grace, *Artist-in-Res*, Maryland Institute, Hoffberger School of Painting, Baltimore MD (S)

Hartley, Paul, *Chmn Drawing & Painting ,*, East Carolina University, School of Art, Greenville NC (S)

Hartman, Eleanor C, *Librn*, Los Angeles County Museum of Art, Library, Los Angeles CA

Hartman, James, *Cur Historic Preservation*, Colorado Historical Society, Colorado Heritage Center, Denver CO

Hartman, Joan M, *Dir of Membership & Public Information*, Jewish Museum, New York NY

Hartman, Mary, *Service Librn*, Sweet Briar College, Babcock Art Library, Sweet Briar VA

Hartman, Russell P, *Acting Dir*, Navajo Tribal Museum, Window Rock AZ

Hartman, Terry L, *Instructor*, Modesto Junior College, Arts Humanities and Speech Division, Modesto CA (S)

Hartmann, Hans, *Dir*, Bündner Kunstmuseum Chur, The Grisons Museum of Art, Chur Switzerland

Hartog, Simon H den, *Dir*, Gerrit Rietveld Academie, Amsterdam Netherlands (S)

Hartsook, Jane, *Dir*, Greenwich House Pottery, New York NY (S)

Hartwell, Carroll T, *Cur Photography*, Minneapolis Institute of Arts, Minneapolis MN

Harvath Jr, John, *Head, Fine Arts & Recreation*, Houston Public Library, Houston TX

Harvey, Bunny, *Asst Prof*, Wellesley College, Art Department, Wellesley MA (S)

Harvey, Clifford, *Prof*, West Virginia University, Division of Art, Morgantown WV (S)

Harvey, Donald, *Prof*, University of Victoria, Department of Visual Arts, Victoria BC (S)

Harvey, Donald E, *Dir*, University of Akron, University Galleries, Akron OH

Harvey, Georgia, *Registrar*, Hebrew Union College, Skirball Museum, Los Angeles CA

Harvey, J, *Gallery Secy*, Abbot Hall Art Gallery, Cumbria England

Harvey, Karen J, *Librn*, Smith College, Hillyer Art Library, Northampton MA

Harvey, Marjorie, *Asst Cur & Registrar*, Akron Art Institute, Akron OH

Harvey, Mary, *Tour Exhib Coordr*, University of Minnesota, University Gallery, Minneapolis MN

Harvey, Nancy E, *Asst Division Chief*, Chicago Public Library, Art Section, Fine Arts Division, Chicago IL

Harvey, Page, *Instructor*, Brenau College, Art Department, Gainesville GA (S)

Harvey, Robin, *Comptroller*, Museum of Holography, New York NY

Harvey, Virginia I, *Cur*, University of Washington, Costume and Textile Study Center, Seattle WA

Harwick, Eugene, *Assoc Prof*, Fort Hays State University, Department of Art, Hays KS (S)

Harwick, Joanne, *Assoc Prof*, Fort Hays State University, Department of Art, Hays KS (S)

Harycki, Jill, *Asst to Dir*, University of Wisconsin, Allen Priebe Gallery, Oshkosh WI

Hasbury, S, *Art Documentalist*, National Gallery of Canada, Library, Ottawa ON

Hasebe, Mitsuhiko, *Cur Ceramics*, Tokyo Kokuritsu Kindai Bujutsukan, Crafts Gallery, Tokyo Japan

Hasen, Irwin, *Instr*, Joe Kubert School of Cartoon and Graphic Art Inc, Dover NJ (S)

Hasenmuller, Christine, *Assoc Prof*, Vanderbilt University, Dept of Fine Arts, Nashville TN (S)

Hasenyager, Shirley, *Treas*, Windward Artists Guild, Kailua HI

Haskell, Barbara, *Cur*, Whitney Museum of American Art, New York NY

Haskell, Ruth, *Secy*, Ashtabula Arts Center, Ashtabula OH

Haskett, William R, *Chmn*, McLennan Community College, Fine Arts Department, Waco TX (S)

Haskins, John, *Prof*, University of Pittsburgh, Henry Clay Frick Fine Arts Department, Pittsburgh PA (S)

Haslan, K, *Secy*, Royal Ontario Museum, Canadiana Gallery, Toronto ON

Hassan, Gaylord, *Coordr of Cultural Arts*, New Muse Community Museum of Brooklyn, Inc, Brooklyn NY

Hasselbach, Gloria, *Instructor*, Goldsboro Art Center, Goldsboro NC (S)

Hassenpflug, Earl, *Chmn*, Otterbein College, Department of Visual Arts, Westerville OH (S)

Hassold, Edith, *Art History Librn*, Duke University Museum of Art, East Campus Library, Durham NC

Hassrick, Peter, *Chmn*, Wyoming Council on the Arts, Cheyenne WY

Hassrick, Peter H, *Dir*, Buffalo Bill Memorial Association, Cody WY

Hastie, Reid, *Prof*, Texas Tech University, Department of Art, Lubbock TX (S)

Haswell, Hollee, *Librn*, Worcester Art Museum, Library, Worcester MA

Hatch, Bab, *Dir Admin*, Laguna Gloria Art Museum, Austin TX

Hatch, John, *Prof*, University of New Hampshire, Department of the Arts, Durham NH (S)

Hategan, Vasile, *Dir*, Saint Mary's Romanian Orthodox Church, Romanian Ethnic Museum, Cleveland OH

Hatfield, Rab, *Vis Prof*, Syracuse University, Department of Art History, Syracuse NY (S)

Hathaway, Carol J, *Coordr*, Roger Williams College, Art Department, Bristol RI (S)

Hathaway, Lucinda, *Instructor*, Ocean City School of Art, Ocean City NJ (S)

Hathaway, Walter M, *Dir*, Columbia Museums of Art and Science, Columbia SC

Hatie, George D, *Pres*, American Numismatic Association, Colorado Springs CO

Hatmaker, Paul, *Treas*, Strasburg Museum, Strasburg VA

Hatzenbuehler, Camille, *Board Pres*, Chicago Public Library, Cultural Center, Chicago IL

Hauber, Brenda, *Registrar*, Oshkosh Public Museum, Oshkosh WI

Hauberg, John H, *Chmn of Board*, Seattle Art Museum, Seattle WA

Hauck, Alice H, *Instructor*, Providence College, Department of Fine Arts, Providence RI (S)

Hauge, Ole, *Chmn of the Board*, Vestlandske Kunstindustrimuseum, Western Norway Museum of Applied Art, Bergen Norway

Haugerud, James S, *Registrar*, United States Senate Commission on Art and Antiquities, Washington DC

Haught, Mary, *Secy*, State University of New York College at Potsdam, Brainerd Art Gallery, Potsdam NY

Haulicek, William, *Cur of Educ*, Riverside Art Center and Museum, Riverside CA

Haupt, Margaret, *Registrar*, Art Gallery of Hamilton, Hamilton ON

Haupt, Margaret, *Registrar*, Art Gallery of Hamilton, Muriel Isabel Bostwich Library, Hamilton ON

Haupt, Shirley, *Assoc Prof*, University of Northern Iowa, Department of Art, Cedar Falls IA (S)

Hauser, Brigitta, *Cur Education Department*, Museum für Völkerkunde und Schweizerisches Museum für Volkskunde Basel, Museum of Ethnological Collections and Folklore, Basel Switzerland

Hauser, Robert A, *Museum Conservator*, Merrimack Valley Textile Museum, North Andover MA

Hausman, Jerome H, *Pres*, Minneapolis College of Art and Design, Minneapolis MN (S)

Hausmann, Albert Charles, *Asst Prof*, University of North Alabama, Department of Art, Florence AL (S)

Hausrath, Joan, *Asst Prof*, Bridgewater State College, Art Department, Bridgewater MA (S)

Havas, Edwin, *Instructor*, Montclair Art Museum, Art School, Montclair NJ (S)

Havas, Edwin, *Asst Prof*, Seton Hall University, Department of Art and Music, South Orange NJ (S)

Havas, Sandra H, *Dir*, Eccles Community Art Center, Ogden UT

Havel, Joseph, *Instructor*, Austin College, Art Department, Sherman TX (S)

Havel, Lynn B, *Instr*, Butler County Community College, Art Department, El Dorado KS (S)

Havens, Neil, *Prof*, Rice University, Department of Art and Art History, Houston TX (S)

Havens, Walter, *Admin*, Favell Museum of Western Art & Indian Artifacts, Klamath Falls OR

Haver, Ronald, *Dir of Film Programs*, Los Angeles County Museum of Art, Los Angeles CA

Havill, Jeffrey, *Assoc Prof*, Alma College, Department of Art and Design, Alma MI (S)

Havis, C Kenneth, *Gallery Dir*, North Texas State University, Art Gallery, Denton TX

Havlena, Jarmila, *Prof*, Los Angeles Harbor College, Art Department, Wilmington CA (S)

Hawcroft, Francis W, *Principal Keeper*, University of Manchester, Whitworth Art Gallery, Manchester England

Hawkes, Elizabeth, *Asst Cur & Cur John Sloan Archives*, Delaware Art Museum, Wilmington DE

Hawkes, Mary, *Secy*, Pocumtuck Valley Memorial Association, Memorial Hall, Deerfield MA

Hawkins, Ashton, *VPres, Secy & Counsel*, Metropolitan Museum of Art, New York NY

Hawkins, Gregory W, *Chmn*, Eastern Washington University, Department of Art, Cheney WA (S)

Hawkins, John, *Assoc Prof*, Queensborough Community College, Department of Art and Design, Bayside NY (S)

Hawkins, Lewis, *Instructor*, Maryland College of Art and Design, Silver Spring MD (S)

Hawkins, Linda, *Program Coordr*, Artworlds Center for Creative Arts, Ann Arbor MI

Hawkins, Rebecca, *Asst Prof*, James Madison University, Department of Art, Harrisonburg VA (S)

Hawkins, Thomas, *Gallery Dir*, Rio Hondo College Art Gallery, Whittier CA

Hawley, Barbara, *Prof*, Cape Cod Community College, Art Dept, West Barnstable MA (S)

Hawley, Henry, *Chief Cur Later Western Art*, Cleveland Museum of Art, Cleveland OH

Hawley, Jean, *Instructor*, Southwestern School of Art, Albuquerque NM (S)

Haworth, Julia C, *Exec Secy*, Tennessee Botanical Gardens and Fine Arts Center, Inc, Nashville TN

Hawthrush, Virginia, *Treas*, Leatherstocking Brush and Palette Club Inc, Cooperstown NY

Haxthausen, Charles W, *Asst Cur*, Harvard University, Busch-Reisinger Museum, Cambridge MA

Hay, H James, *Assoc Prof*, Olivet College, Art Dept, Olivet MI (S)

Hay, Ike, *Instructor*, Millersville State College, Art Department, Millersville PA (S)

Hayano, Carl, *Grad Coordr*, Northern Illinois University, Department of Art, De Kalb IL (S)

Hayashida, Richard, *Instructor*, Leeward Community College, Arts and Humanities Division, Pearl City HI (S)

Haycock, Charles M, *Chmn*, Madison Area Technical College, Communication Arts, Madison WI (S)

Haycock, Everett, *Prof*, Ohio Wesleyan University, Fine Arts Department, Delaware OH (S)

Hayden, Robert, *Asst Dir Operations*, Brooklyn Museum, Brooklyn NY

Haydu, John R, *Asst Prof*, Central Missouri State University, Art Department, Warrensburg MO (S)

Hayes, Bonnie, *Asst Prof*, Beaver College, Department of Fine Arts, Glenside PA (S)

Hayes, Charles, *Prof*, Metropolitan State College, Art Department, Denver CO (S)

Hayes, Dorothy, *Assoc Prof*, New York City Community College of the City University of New York, Department of Art and Advertising Design, Brooklyn NY (S)

Hayes, George, *Asst Prof*, Shorter College, Art Department, Rome GA (S)

Hayes, Joann, *Instr*, Madison Area Technical College, Communication Arts, Madison WI (S)

Hayes, John, *Dir*, National Portrait Gallery, London England

Hayes, Lynn, *Assoc Prof*, Brazosport College, Art Department, Lake Jackson TX (S)

Hayes, Richard, *Dir of Permanent Collection*, Thiel College, Sampson Art Gallery, Greenville PA

Hayes, Richard E, *Asst Prof*, Northeast Louisiana University, Department of Art, Monroe LA (S)

Hayes, Richard L, *Assoc Prof*, Thiel College, Department of Art, Greenville PA (S)

Hayes, Ron, *VPres*, Ogunquit Art Association, The Barn Gallery, Ogunquit ME

Haylett Jr, R C, *Vice Chmn*, Oglebay Institute Mansion Museum, Oglebay Institute Mansion Museum Committee, Wheeling WV

Haymaker, James, *Dir*, Pfeiffer College, Art Program, Misenheimer NC (S)

Haynes, Douglas, *Chmn*, University of Alberta, Department of Art and Design, Edmonton AB (S)

Haynes, N Fred, *Pres*, Museum of Arts and History, Port Huron MI

Haynes, R, *Head Dept Art History*, Brighton Polytechnic, Faculty of Art and Design, Brighton England (S)

Haynie, Sonya, *Lectr*, University of Texas of Permian Basin, Art Discipline, Odessa TX (S)

Hayter, Stanley William, *Board Dir Member*, Art Information Center, Inc, New York NY

Hayward, Jan, *Cur*, Metropolitan Museum of Art, Cloisters, New York NY

Hayward, Nancy, *Pres*, Maude I Kerns Art Center, Henry Korn Gallery, Eugene OR

Hazar, Julie, *Development Dir*, Hudson River Museum, Yonkers NY

Hazelgrove, Nancy, *Instr*, Toronto School of Art, Toronto ON (S)

Hazlehurst, F Hamilton, *Chmn*, Vanderbilt University, Art Gallery, Department of Fine Arts, Nashville TN

Hazlehurst, F Hamilton, *Chmn Dept*, Vanderbilt University, Dept of Fine Arts, Nashville TN (S)

Heacock, Walter J, *General Dir*, Hagley Museum, Eleutherian Mills-Hagley Foundation, Washington DE

Head, Albert B, *Dir*, Jay R Broussard Memorial Galleries, Baton Rouge LA

Head, Robert W, *Chmn*, Murray State University, Art Department, Murray KY (S)

Head, Robert W, *Chmn*, Murray State University, Clara M Eagle Gallery, Murray KY

Heald, Betty, *Asst Prof*, Ohio Wesleyan University, Fine Arts Department, Delaware OH (S)

Heald, Geneva, *Pres*, Santa Cruz Art League, Inc, Santa Cruz CA

Healey, Ruth, *Gallery Dir*, Russell Sage College, New Gallery, Troy NY

Heaney, Howell J, *Rare Book Librn*, Free Library of Philadelphia, Rare Book Department, Philadelphia PA

Heard, J, *Instructor*, Golden West College, Arts, Humanities and Social Sciences Institute, Huntington Beach CA (S)

Hearn, Barbara, *Archivist*, Winterthur Museum and Gardens, Library, Winterthur DE

Hearn, M F, *Prof*, University of Pittsburgh, Henry Clay Frick Fine Arts Department, Pittsburgh PA (S)

Heath, Donald F, *Chmn*, Phillips University, Department of Art, Enid OK (S)

Heatherington, Donald, *Pres*, Historical Society of Early American Decoration, Inc, Cooperstown NY

Heaton, William B, *VPres*, Michigan Artrain, Inc, Detroit MI

Hebblethwaite, Norman, *Chief Librn*, Cambridge Public Library and Arts Centre, Cambridge ON

Hebert, Annabelle, *Dir*, Provincetown Art Association and Museum, Provincetown MA

Heck, Hiram, *Pres Board Trustees*, Zanesville Art Center, Zanesville OH

Heckman, Keith, *Pres*, Lincoln Community Arts Council, Lincoln NE

Heckman, Philip, *VPres*, University of Nebraska Lincoln, Nebraska Art Association, Lincoln NE

Heckman, Steve, *Head Art Dept*, Seward County Community College, Art Department, Liberal KS (S)

Hecksher, Morrison H, *Cur American Decorative Art*, Metropolitan Museum of Art, New York NY

Hedberg, Gregory H, *Cur Paintings*, Minneapolis Institute of Arts, Minneapolis MN

Heden, Karl-Gustaf, *Dir*, Göteborg Konstmuseum, Gothenburg Art Gallery, Gothenburg Sweden

Hedergott, Bodo, *Chief Cur*, Herzog Anton Ulrich-Museum, Medieval Section: Burg Dankwarderode, Brunswick Germany, Federal Republic of

Hedin, Thomas F, *Asst Prof*, University of Minnesota, Duluth, Art Dept, Duluth MN (S)

Hedley, R, *Dir*, Trent Polytechnic, School of Art and Design, Nottingham England (S)

Hedman, Donn, *Asst Prof*, Arkansas State University, Department of Art, State University AR (S)

Hedman, Teri Jo, *VPres*, Alaska Artists Guild, Anchorage AK

Hedrick, Basil C, *Asst Dir*, Illinois State Museum of Natural History and Art, Springfield IL

Hedvall, Anders, *Head Librn*, Statens Historiska Museum, Library of Royal Academy of Letters, History and Antiquities, Stockholm Sweden

Heefner, William F, *Pres*, Bucks County Historical Society Mercer Museum, Doylestown PA

Heepke, Carol, *Education Coordr*, Brockton Art Center, Brockton MA

Heeschen, Carl F, *Prof*, Allegheny College, Art Department, Meadville PA (S)

Heffner, Jane E, *Development Officer*, Whitney Museum of American Art, New York NY

Heflin, Patricia, *Staff Asst*, Department of State, Diplomatic Reception Rooms, Washington DC

Hefting, P H, *Cur*, Ryksmuseum Kroller-Muller, Kroller-Muller State Museum, Otterlo Netherlands

Heftman, Lily, *Area Chairperson Apparel Arts*, Pasadena City College, Art Department, Pasadena CA (S)

Hegarty, Kevin, *Dir*, Tacoma Public Library, Handforth Gallery, Tacoma WA

Hegarty, Melinda, *Instructor*, Eastern Illinois University, Art Department, Charleston IL (S)

Höegh, Hans, *Pres*, Kunstindustrimuseet I Oslo, Oslo Museum of Applied Art, Oslo Norway

Hehman, Jennifer, *Cur*, Ohio State University, Visual Resource Collection, Department of History of Art, Columbus OH

Heiberger, Jeannette, *Instructor*, Maryland College of Art and Design, Silver Spring MD (S)

Heide, Cynthia, *Dir of Corporate Affairs*, Benson & Hedges (Canada) Inc, Montreal PQ

Heidel, Frederick H, *Prof*, Portland State University, Department of Art and Architecture, Portland OR (S)

Heideman, Susan, *Instructor*, Smith College, Art Department, Northampton MA (S)

Heikenen, Patricia, *Publications & Public Relations*, Minnesota Museum of Art, Saint Paul MN

Heil, Harry, *Dir*, Western State College, Quigley Hall Art Gallery, Gunnison CO

Heilmann, Clinstof, *Cur 19th Century Art*, Bayerischen Staatsgemaldesammlungen, Bavarian State Galleries of Art, Munich Germany, Federal Republic of

Heilmeyer, Wolf-D, *Dir*, Staatliche Museen Preussischer Kulturbesitz, Greek and Roman Antiquities, Berlin Germany, Federal Republic of

Heiloms, May, *Honorary Life Pres*, Painters and Sculptors Society of New Jersey, Inc, New York NY

Heimberg, Bruno, *Restoration Department*, Bayerischen Staatsgemaldesammlungen, Bavarian State Galleries of Art, Munich Germany, Federal Republic of

Hein, Don, *Cur Art Education*, Art Gallery of South Australia, Adelaide Australia

Hein, Max, *Prof*, Santa Rosa Junior College, Art Department, Santa Rosa CA (S)

Heinemann, Ernest, *Librn*, Haaretz Museum, Central Library, Tel-Aviv Israel

Heinmiller, Carl, *VPres*, Sheldon Museum and Cultural Center, Haines AK

Heins, Valerie, *Mem Secy*, Allentown Art Museum, Allentown PA

Heintz, David, *Instructor*, California College of Arts and Crafts, Oakland CA (S)

Heinz, Susan, *Exec Dir*, Palos Verdes Art Center, Rancho Palos Verdes CA

Heisch, John, *Dir Reference Library*, Oklahoma Historical Society, Library, Oklahoma City OK

Heiser, Richard, *Librn*, Navajo Tribal Museum, Navajo Nation Library, Window Rock AZ

Heisinger, Kathryn, *Cur European Decorative Arts after 1700*, Philadelphia Museum of Art, Philadelphia PA

Heit, Dorothea, *Vis Prof*, Oral Roberts University, Fine Arts Department, Tulsa OK (S)

Helfrich, Paul, *Assoc Prof*, College of William and Mary, Department of Fine Arts, Williamsburg VA (S)

Helgesen, Aina, *Adminr*, Statens Kunstakademi, State Art Academy, Oslo Norway (S)

Hellberg, Ray W, *Head*, Utah State University, Department of Art, Logan UT (S)

Hellebrand, Nancy, *Instructor*, Bucks County Community College, Fine Arts Department, Newton PA (S)

Hellen, Joan E, *Dir*, Museum of the Southwest, Midland TX

Heller, John, *Assoc Prof*, Bridgewater State College, Art Department, Bridgewater MA (S)

Heller, Jules, *Dean College of Fine Arts*, Arizona State University, Department of Art, Tempe AZ (S)

Heller, Peter, *Assoc Prof*, Johnson State College, Art Department, Johnson VT (S)

Heller, Reinhold, *Prof*, University of Chicago, Department of Art History & Committee on Art & Design, Chicago IL (S)

Heller, Tobie, *Librn*, Palm Beach County Parks and Recreation Department, Donald B Gordon Memorial Library, Delray Beach FL

Hellier, Bob, *Preparator*, Tampa Museum, Tampa FL

Helliesen, Sidsel, *Keeper Prints & Drawings*, Nasjonalgalleriet, National Gallery, Oslo Norway

Helliwell, Eleanor, *Corresp Secy*, Seattle Weaver's Guild, Seattle WA

Helm, Edwin, *Instructor*, Langston University, Art Department, Langston OK (S)

Helm, Robert, *Assoc Prof*, Washington State University, Fine Arts Department, Pullman WA (S)

Helman, Phoebe, *Adjunct Assoc Prof*, New York Institute of Technology, Fine Arts Department, Old Westbury NY (S)

Helmer, Bonnie, *Teacher*, Venice Painting, Drawing and Sculpture Studio, Inc, Venice CA (S)

Helmich, John, *Asst Dir Financial Aide*, Brooklyn Museum, Brooklyn NY

Helmken, Deborah, *Asst Dir*, Ships of The Sea Museum, Savannah GA

Helms, Roy H, *Executive Dir*, National Assembly of State Arts Agencies, Washington DC

Helsell, Charles, *Cur*, University of Minnesota, University Gallery, Minneapolis MN

Helseth, W Joseph, *Instructor*, Dalton Junior College, Division of Humanities, Dalton GA (S)

Helsted, Dyveke, *Dir*, Thorvaldsen Museum, Copenhagen Denmark

Helvey, Kenneth W, *Chmn*, Fullerton College, Fine Arts and Art Department, Fullerton CA (S)

Helzer, Richard, *Instr*, Portland Community College, Department of Fine Arts, Portland OR (S)

Hemdahl-Owen, Ann, *Asst Prof*, Jefferson Community College, Fine Arts, Louisville KY (S)

Hempel, Gordon, *Secy*, Artists Guild of Chicago, Chicago IL

Hemus, Sharon, *Activities Coordr*, San Diego Museum of Art, San Diego CA

Hench, Robert, *Gallery Dir*, University of Southern Colorado, Pueblo CO

Hench, Robert, *Assoc Prof*, University of Southern Colorado, Belmont Campus, Department of Art, Pueblo CO (S)

Hendershot, Jim, *Asst Prof*, St John's University, Art Department, Collegeville MN (S)

Henderson, J Welles, *Pres*, Philadelphia Maritime Museum, Philadelphia PA

Henderson, J J, *Asst Dir*, Birmingham Museums and Art Gallery, Birmingham England

Henderson, J T, *Cur*, Woodstock Art Gallery, Woodstock ON

Henderson, John T, *Pres*, Jefferson Community College, Art Department, Watertown NY (S)

Henderson, Lana T, *Chmn*, North Carolina Central University, Art Dept, Durham NC (S)

Henderson, Lyman, *Treas*, Visual Arts Ontario, Toronto ON

Henderson, Maren, *Assoc Prof*, California State Polytechnic University, Pomona, Art Department, Pomona CA (S)

Henderson, Paul, *Cur*, Scripps College, Clark Humanities Museum, Claremont CA

Henderson, Robbin, *Dir & Cur*, Berkeley Art Center, Berkeley CA

Henderson, Robert, *Head Library & Museum of the Performing Arts*, New York Public Library, Shelby Cullom Davis Museum of the Performing Arts and: The Library and Museum of the Performing Arts, at Lincoln Center, Museum NY

Henderson, Robert M, *Chief*, Lincoln Center for the Performing Arts, Library, New York NY

Henderson, Susan, *Vis Prof*, Oral Roberts University, Fine Arts Department, Tulsa OK (S)

Henderson, Thomas, *Assoc Prof*, Mount Allison University, Fine Arts Department, Sackville NB (S)

Hendrick, Barbara, *Mgr Publications*, Long Beach Museum of Art, Long Beach CA

Hendricks, Barkley L, *Assoc Prof*, Connecticut College, Department of Art, New London CT (S)

Hendricks, Bartlett, *Cur Science*, Berkshire Museum, Pittsfield MA

Hendrickson, Torval E, *Chmn*, Western Wisconsin Technical Institute, Graphics Division, LACrosse WI (S)

Hendrickx, James, *Instr*, Mount Vernon Nazarene College, Art Department, Mount Vernon OH (S)

Hendrix, James P, *VPres*, Green Hill Art Gallery, Greensboro NC

Hendry, Joyce, *Instructor*, De Anza College, Art Department, Cupertino CA (S)

Henes, Ernst L, *Museum Dir*, Spirit of '76 Museum, Southern Lorain County Historical Society, Wellington OH

Henes, Margaret, *Secy*, Spirit of '76 Museum, Southern Lorain County Historical Society, Wellington OH

Hengst, Timothy, *Instr*, Johns Hopkins University, School of Medicine, Department of Art as Applied to Medicine, Baltimore MD (S)

Henkel, Margot A, *Executive Dir*, New York Society of Architects, f the Performing Arts, at Lincoln Center New York

Henle, Jane, *Asst Prof*, Marymount College, Art Department, Tarrytown NY (S)

Henners, Noel W, *Dir*, National Air and Space Museum, Washington DC

Hennessey, William J, *Dir*, Vassar College Art Gallery, Poughkeepsie NY

Hennesy, Janet, *Asst Librn*, Minneapolis College of Art and Design, Library and Media Center, Minneapolis MN

Henning, Darrell, *Cur*, Vesterheim, Norwegian-American Museum, Decorah IA

Henning, Edward B, *Chief Cur Modern Art*, Cleveland Museum of Art, Cleveland OH

Henning, Jeff, *Visual Arts Coordr*, Ashtabula Arts Center, Ashtabula OH

Henning, K Louise, *Reference Librn*, University of Wisconsin, Kohler Art Library, Madison WI

Henning, Roni, *Master Printer*, New York Institute of Technology, Fine Arts Department, Old Westbury NY (S)

Henning, William, *Cur Fine Arts Coll*, Colorado Springs Fine Arts Center, Colorado Springs CO

Henri, Phyllis, *Public Information*, Art Research Center, Kansas City MO

Henricks, Duane Ed, *Documents & Reference Librn*, Southeast Missouri State University, Kent Library, Cape Girardeau MO

Henry, Anneliese, *Secy*, Second Street Gallery, Charlottesville VA

Henry, Clarice, *Art Librn*, Hewlett-Woodmere Public Library, Hewlett NY

Henry, Esther, *Pres*, Academy of the Arts, Easton MD

Henry, Fred, *Asst Prof*, Southern Arkansas University, Department of Fine Arts, Magnolia AR (S)

Henry, Jean, *Chmn*, University of New Haven, Department of Fine Arts, West Haven CT (S)

Henry, Joseph, *Cur*, Craft Center Museum, Wilton CT

Henry, Joseph R, *VPres*, Art Center College of Design, Pasadena CA (S)

Henry, Lawrence, *Division Dir*, Division of Historical and Cultural Affairs, Bureau of Museums and Historic Sites, Dover DE

Henry, Nancy, *Public Information*, Museum of the American Indian, New York NY

Henry, Penelope, *Librn*, Parrish Art Museum, Aline B Saarinen Library, Southampton NY

Henry, Penelope, *Registrar*, Parrish Art Museum, Southampton NY

Henry, Sara, *Asst Prof*, Drew University, Art Department, Madison NJ (S)

Henry III, John B, *Dir Coll & Exhib*, Mississippi Museum of Art, Jackson MS

Hensche, Henry, *Dir*, Cape School of Art, Provincetown MA (S)

Henschen, Eva, *Cur Education*, Thorvaldsen Museum, Copenhagen Denmark

Hensler, D C, *Head Dept Fine Art*, Manchester Polytechnic, Faculty of Art and Design, Manchester England (S)

Hensler, Ruth, *Instructor*, Saint Louis Community College at Meramec, Art Dept, Saint Louis MO (S)

Hensley, Fred Owen, *Asst Prof*, University of North Alabama, Department of Art, Florence AL (S)

Hensley, Paul, *Archivist*, Mariners Museum, Library, Newport News VA

Henson, Jim, *Executive Dir*, Red River Valley Museum, Vernon TX

Henson, Joan, *Instr*, Clark College, Art Department, Vancouver WA (S)

Hentchel, Fred, *Instr*, Illinois Central College, Art and Humanities Department, East Peoria IL (S)

Henze, F E, *Secy*, Rome Historical Society, Rome Information and Cultural Center, Rome NY

Hepburn, Charles M, *Dean of Studies*, College of Great Falls, Dept of Art, Great Falls MT (S)

Hepburn, Tony, *Head Dept*, New York State College of Ceramics at Alfred University, Division of Art & Design, Alfred NY (S)

Hepler, Frank C, *Pres*, New Haven Colony Historical Society, New Haven CT

Hepner, Edward J, *Site Supt*, Bishop Hill Historic Site, Bishop Hill IL

Herban, Mathew, *Assoc Prof*, Ohio State University, Department of the History of Art, Columbus OH (S)

Herberg, Mayde, *Instructor*, Santa Ana College, Art Department, Santa Ana CA (S)

Herbert, Al, *Prof*, Macomb County Community College, Art Department, Warren MI (S)

Herbert, Albert, *Head Painting & Sculpture*, Saint Martins School of Art, London England (S)

Herdeg, John A, *Pres*, Winterthur Museum and Gardens, Winterthur DE

Heredia, Ruben, *Vis Prof*, Butte Community College, Humanities Division (III), Oroville CA (S)

Heredia, Victor, *Dir Display and Design*, School of Holography, Fine Arts Research and Holographic Center Museum, Chicago IL

Herger, Dorothy, *Instr*, Solano Community College, Department of Fine & Applied Art, Suisun City CA (S)

Herman, Lloyd E, *Dir*, National Collection of Fine Arts, Renwick Gallery, Washington DC

Herman, Susan, *Asst Prof*, California State University, Fresno, Art Department, Fresno CA (S)

Hermann, Kathy, *Instructor*, Taylor University, Art Department, Upland IN (S)

Hermant, Sydney M, *Chmn Board of Trustees*, Royal Ontario Museum, Toronto ON

Hermel, Sidney H, *Recording Secy*, Artists' Fellowship, Inc, New York NY

Hernandez, Jo Farb, *Librn*, Triton Museum of Art, Library, Santa Clara CA

Hernandez, Jo Farb, *Dir*, Triton Museum of Art, Santa Clara CA

Hernandez, Samuel R, *Asst Prof*, University of Santa Clara, Fine Arts Department, Santa Clara CA (S)

Herod, Dave D, *Senior Cur Anthropologist*, University of California, R H Lowie Museum of Anthropology, Berkeley CA

Herold, Donald G, *Dir*, Charleston Museum, Charleston SC

Herr, Marcianne, *Cur of Education*, Akron Art Institute, Akron OH

Herreman, Marilyn, *Art Education*, Licking County Art Association Gallery, Newark OH

Herrero, Susana, *Instructor*, University of Puerto Rico, Department of Fine Arts, Mayaguez PR (S)

Herrick, Daniel, *VPres Finance & Treas*, Metropolitan Museum of Art, New York NY

Herrick, Esther, *Chmn Hale House*, Beverly Historical Society, Beverly MA

Herrick, Fred R, *Dir*, Springfield Art & Historical Society, Springfield VT

Herrick, Fred R, *Librn*, Springfield Art & Historical Society, Library, Springfield VT

Herrick, Melissa, *Registrar*, University of Minnesota, University Gallery, Minneapolis MN

Herriges, Malanie, *Librn*, Milwaukee School of the Arts, Library, Milwaukee WI

Herring, Jack W, *Dir*, Baylor University, Armstrong Browning Library, Waco TX

Herring, Pam, *Office Mgr*, Carson County Square House Museum, Panhandle TX

Herrington, Marie Opolzer, *Asst for Clippings*, Nationalmuseum, Library, Stockholm Sweden

Herrington, Thomas E, *Preparator*, New Orleans Museum of Art, Isaac Delgado Museum, New Orleans LA

Herrold, David, *Asst Prof*, DePauw University, Art Department, Greencastle IN (S)

Herscher, Irenaeus, *Art Cur*, Saint Bonaventure University Art Collection, Saint Bonaventure NY

Hershberger, Abner, *Chmn*, Goshen College, Art Department, Goshen IN (S)

Hershey, Michael, *Instructor*, Doane College, Dept of Art, Crete NE (S)

Hershey, Nona, *Vis Instr*, Temple Abroad of Temple University, Rome Italy (S)

Hertel, C H, *Prof Art*, Pitzer College, Department of Art, Claremont CA (S)

Hertzi, Joseph R, *Dir*, Canton Art Institute, Canton OH

Hertzi, Joseph R, *Dir*, Canton Art Instutute, Canton OH (S)

Hertzman, Gay M, *Chief Cur*, North Carolina Museum of Art, Department of Cultural Resources, Raleigh NC

Herzbrun, Helene M, *Prof*, American University, Department of Art, Washington DC (S)

Herzman, Diane, *Exec Dir*, Art Directors Club, Inc, New York NY

Heslin, James J, *Dir*, New York Historical Society, New York NY

Hess, Honee, *Cur of Education*, University of Iowa, Museum of Art, Iowa City IA

Hess, Stanley, *Prof*, Drake University, Art Department, Des Moines IA (S)

Hessemer, Betty, *Instructor*, Rehoboth Art League, Inc, Rehoboth Beach DE (S)

Hester, Charles, *Treas*, Newport Harbor Art Museum, Newport Beach CA

Hester, Warren, *Pres*, Coppini Academy of Fine Arts, San Antonio TX

Heth, Susan, *Registrar*, University of Alberta, Ring House Gallery, Edmonton AB

Heubner, M Rosemarita, *Assoc Prof*, Mount Mary College, Art Department, Milwaukee WI (S)

Heuler, Henry J, *Assoc Prof*, University of West Florida, Department of Art, Pensacola FL (S)

Heuler, Judith A, *Asst Prof*, University of West Florida, Department of Art, Pensacola FL (S)

Heuser, Jay, *Technical Dir*, Art Research Center, Kansas City MO

Hewitt, Clarissa, *Asst Prof*, California Polytechnic State University at San Luis Obispo, Art Department, San Luis Obispo CA (S)

Hewitt, Duncan, *Assoc Prof*, University of Southern Maine, Art Dept, Gorham ME (S)

Hewitt, Linda V, *Asst Dir*, Isabella Stewart Gardner Museum, Boston MA

Hext, Charles R, *Asst Prof*, Sul Ross State University, Department of Art, Alpine TX (S)

Heyduck, Bill, *Prof*, Eastern Illinois University, Art Department, Charleston IL (S)

Heyman, Therese, *Sr Cur Prints & Photographs*, Oakland Museum, Oakland CA

Heywood, John, *Facility Adminr*, University of Calgary, The Nickle Arts Museum, Calgary AB

Hibbard, James, *Prof*, Portland State University, Department of Art and Architecture, Portland OR (S)

Hibbard, Stephen T, *Pres*, Gibson Society, Inc, Boston MA

Hibbs, Vivian A, *Cur Archaeology*, Hispanic Society of America Museum, New York NY

Hichman, Ronald D, *Dir*, Phoenix Art Museum, Phoenix AZ

Hickerson, Wanda, *Library Asst*, New Orleans Museum of Art, Felix J Dreyfous Library, New Orleans LA

Hickie, Philip, *Head Div Design*, National Art School, Department of Technical Education, Darlinghurst Australia (S)

Hicklin, Barbara Roe, *Pres*, Alberta Society of Artists, Alberta College of Art, Calgary AB

Hickman, David, *Pres*, Mid-America College Art Association, Houston TX

Hickman, Helen C, *Pres*, Stained Glass Association of America, Bronxville NY

Hickman, Patricia, *Chmn Textiles*, De Young Museum Art School, San Francisco CA (S)

Hickman, Theresa, *Mem Secy*, Norton Gallery and School of Art, West Palm Beach FL

Hicks, D W, *Pres*, Frontier Times Museum, Bandera TX

Hicks, Ellen C, *Ed*, American Association of Museums, Washington DC

Hicks, Gloria, *Instructor*, Your Heritage House, Inc, Detroit MI

Hicks, Herbert A, *Dept Chmn*, University of Lethbridge, Department of Art, Lethbridge AB (S)

Hicks, James H, *Slide Librn*, Portland Art Association, Museum Library, Portland OR

Hicks, Jennifer, *Membership Coordr*, Millicent Rogers Museum, Taos NM

Hicks, John, *Prof*, Drake University, Art Department, Des Moines IA (S)

Hicks, Leon, *Assoc Prof*, Webster College, Art Dept, Webster Groves MO (S)

Hicks, Margaret, *Dir*, Navarro College, Art Department, Corsicana TX (S)

Hicks, Nancy, *Admin Mgr*, National Assembly of Community Arts Agencies, Washington DC

Hicks, Ron, *Instructor*, Johnson County Community College, Communications-Arts Division, Overland Park KS (S)

Hickson, Howard, *Dir*, Northeastern Nevada Museum, Elko NV

Hidemark, Elisabet, *Keeper Domestic Life Department*, Nordiska Museet, Scandinavian Museum, Stockholm Sweden

Hielkema, Arthur, *Librn*, Northwestern College, Library, Orange City IA

Hiers, C, *Head*, Auburn University, Department of Art, Auburn AL (S)

Hiester, Jan, *Registrar*, Charleston Museum, Charleston SC

Hiester, John, *Asst Prof*, Jamestown Community College, Art Department, Jamestown NY (S)

Hietbrink, Elaine, *Secy*, South Dakota State University, South Dakota Memorial Art Center, Brookings SD

Higa, Kazuo, *Chmn*, Los Angeles City College, Department of Art, Los Angeles CA (S)

Higa, Yosh, *Assoc Prof*, Southampton College of Long Island University, Fine Arts Division, Southampton NY (S)

Higgins, Edward, *Assoc Prof*, Mercyhurst College, Department of Art, Erie PA (S)

Higgins, Janet, *Asst Prof*, Middle Tennessee State University, Art Dept, Murfreesboro TN (S)

Higgins, John J, *Secy*, Rochester Historical Society, Rochester NY

Higgins, John J, *Dir of Finance*, Museum of Fine Arts, Boston MA

High, Charles, *Instructor*, Your Heritage House, Inc, Detroit MI

Hightower, Caroline, *Exec Dir*, American Institute of Graphic Arts, New York NY

Hightower, John B, *Pres*, South Street Seaport Museum, New York NY

Hiigel, Lewis, *Dean Fine Arts*, El Camino College Art Gallery, Torrance CA

Hiigel, Lewis E, *Dean Div*, El Camino College, Division of Fine Arts, Los Angeles CA (S)

Hilaize, Francois, *Keeper*, Musee National des Monuments Francais, National Museum of French Sculpture and Murals, Paris France

Hildebrand, Sam, *Instr*, Claremore College, Art Department, Claremore OK (S)

Hildreth, Joseph, *Assoc Prof*, State University of New York College at Potsdam, Department of Fine Arts, Potsdam NY (S)

Hiles, Bruce, *Registrar*, University of Southern California, University Galleries, Los Angeles CA

Hill, C C, *Dir*, Kingsport Fine Arts Center, Kingsport TN

Hill, Charles, *Cur*, Los Angeles Institute of Contemporary Art, Downtown Gallery, Los Angeles CA

Hill, Charles, *Cur Post Confederation Canadian Art*, National Gallery of Canada, Ottawa ON

Hill, Cindy, *Secy*, Pensacola Junior College, Visual Arts Gallery, Pensacola FL

Hill, Darrell, *Instructor*, John Brown University, Art Department, Siloam Springs AR (S)

Hill, Dorothy M, *Education Specialist*, Omaha Children's Museum, Inc, Omaha NE

Hill, Edward G, *Head Dept*, Wilberforce University, Art Department, Wilberforce OH (S)

Hill, Esther, *Assoc Prof*, University of North Carolina-Charlotte, Creative Arts Dept, Charlotte NC (S)

Hill, Gail, *Secy & Office Mgr*, Lynnwood Arts Centre, Simcoe ON

Hill, Harold W, *Chmn*, Texas Lutheran College, Department of Visual Arts, Seguin TX (S)

Hill, James Berry, *Secy*, National Antique and Art Dealers Association of America, New York NY

Hill, Larry, *Treas*, Vernon Art Association, Topham Brown Gallery, Vernon BC

Hill, Lisa, *Museum Cur*, The Bradford Museum, Niles IL

Hill, Marie, *Secy*, Vernon Art Association, Topham Brown Gallery, Vernon BC

Hill, Nicholas, *Asst Prof*, Bethany College, Lindsborg KS (S)

Hill, Patricia, *Secy*, Roberson Center, Binghamton NY

Hill, Peter, *Prof*, University of Nebraska at Omaha, Dept of Art, Omaha NE (S)

Hill, Richard, *Drawing Chmn*, Atlanta College of Art, Atlanta GA (S)

Hill, Thelma, *Instr*, Morgan State University, Department of Art, Baltimore MD (S)

Hill, Warren H, *Superintendent*, Roosevelt-Vanderbilt National Historic Sites, Hyde Park NY

Hill, William M, *Dir*, Santa Monica College Art Gallery, Santa Monica CA

Hillbruner, Fred, *Head Technical Services*, School of the Art Institute of Chicago Library, Chicago IL

Hiller, Jack, *Chmn*, Valparaiso University, University Art Galleries and Collections, Valparaiso IN

Hiller, Sandra, *Librn*, Museum of the Southwest, Library, Midland TX

Hiller, Sandra J, *Registrar*, Museum of the Southwest, Midland TX

Hilliard, Elbert R, *Dir*, Mississippi Department of Archives and History, Jackson MS

Hilliard, Glenn, *Legal VPres*, Liberty Life Insurance Company, Greenville SC

Hilliard, Patsy Jo, *Secy*, Fine Arts Museums of San Francisco, The Museum Society, n of Honor co

Hilligoss, Martha, *Chief Art Dept*, Saint Louis Public Library, Saint Louis MO

Hillix, Virginia, *Education Dir*, Art Research Center, Kansas City MO

Hillman, Arthur, *Instructor*, Simon's Rock of Bard College, Studio Arts Department, Great Barrington MA (S)

Hillman, Raymond, *Cur of History*, Pioneer Museum and Haggin Galleries, Stockton CA

Hills, Patricia, *Cur*, Whitney Museum of American Art, New York NY

Hilschenz, Helga, *Cur*, Kestner-Museum, Hannover Germany, Federal Republic of

Hilson, M Douglas, *In Charge Grad Painting*, University of Illinois, Urbana-Champaign, Department of Art and Design, Champaign IL (S)

Hilt, Lyda, *Librn Genealogical Section*, Tippecanoe County Historical Museum, Alameda McCollough Library, Lafayette IN

Hilt, Lyda, *Cur of Genealogy*, Tippecanoe County Historical Museum, Lafayette IN

Hime, Gary D, *Asst Librn*, Wichita Public Library, Wichita KS

Himmel, Betty, *Dir*, Katonah Gallery, Katonah NY

Himmelheber, G, *Cur Furniture*, Bayerisches Nationalmuseum, Bavarian National Museum, Munich Germany, Federal Republic of

Hinckley, William P, *Pres*, Parson Fisher House, Jonathan Fisher Memorial, Inc, Blue Hill ME

Hine, Lela M, *Cur & Registrar*, Hermitage Foundation Museum, Norfolk VA

Hines, Adrienne G, *Chmn*, Federated Arts Council of Richmond, Inc, Richmond VA

Hines, Charles, *Instructor*, Dunedin Fine Arts and Cultural Center, Dunedin FL (S)

Hines, Felrath, *Sr Conservator*, National Portrait Gallery, Washington DC

Hines, James, *Prof*, Christopher Newport College, Fine and Performing Arts, Newport News VA (S)

Hines, Norman, *Prof*, Pomona College, Art Department, Claremont CA (S)

Hinkhouse, Jim, *Prof*, Fort Hays State University, Department of Art, Hays KS (S)

Hinkle, Joseph, *Secy*, Museum of the American China Trade, Milton MA

Hinshaw, Edwin, *Secy*, Carson County Square House Museum, Panhandle TX

Hinson, Tom E, *Assoc Cur Modern Art*, Cleveland Museum of Art, Cleveland OH

Hios, Theo, *VPres*, Federation of Modern Painters and Sculptors, New York NY

Hipsley, Vicky, *Cur Entomology*, San Bernardino County Museum and Satellites, Fine Arts Institute, Redlands CA

Hirsch, Adrienne, *Deputy Dir*, Arizona Commission on the Arts, Phoenix AZ

Hirsch, Barron, *Chmn Dept*, Saginaw Valley State College, Dept of Art & Design, University Center MI (S)

Hirsch, Betty Wurth, *Dir*, Museum of the American China Trade, Milton MA

Hirsch, Sharon Latchaw, *Asst Prof*, Dickinson College, Fine Arts Department, Carlisle PA (S)

Hirschfeld, Jonathan, *Teacher*, Venice Painting, Drawing and Sculpture Studio, Inc, Venice CA (S)

Hirschfield, James, *Instructor*, Factory of Visual Art, Seattle WA (S)

Hirschl, Milton, *Prof*, Pierce College, Art Department, Woodland Hills CA (S)

Hirschl, Norman, *VPres*, Art Dealers Association of America, Inc, New York NY

Hirshbein, Omus, *Performing Arts Dir*, 92nd Street YMHA-YWHA, Weill Art Gallery, New York NY

Hirshler, Eric E, *Prof*, Denison University, Department of Art, Granville OH (S)

Hitchcock, D Michael, *Asst Prof*, George Washington University, Department of Art, Washington DC (S)

Hitchcock, Evelyn, *Gallery Dir*, University Art Gallery of California State University at Dominguez Hills, Dominguez Hills CA

Hitchcock, Howard G, *Chmn*, California State University at Long Beach, Art Department, Long Beach CA (S)

Hitchcock, P, *Chmn*, California State University, Sacramento, Department of Art, Sacramento CA (S)

Hitchings, Gladys, *Librn*, Davenport Municipal Art Gallery, Art Reference Library, Davenport IA

Hitchings, Sinclair H, *Keeper of Prints*, Boston Public Library, Albert H Wiggin Gallery (Prints), Boston MA

Hitch Jr, Henry C, *VPres*, No Man's Land Historical Society, Goodwell OK

Hite, Madeline, *Cur Education*, Division of Historical and Cultural Affairs, Bureau of Museums and Historic Sites, Dover DE

Hitt, Terry, *Instr*, University of Dayton, Fine Arts Division, Dayton OH (S)

Hittle, Sheila, *Membership Secy*, San Diego Museum of Art, San Diego CA

Hökby, N G, *Head Art Education Department*, Nationalmuseum, Stockholm Sweden

Hlad, Richard, *Assoc Prof*, Tarrant County Junior College, Northeast Campus, Hurst TX (S)

Hlusicka, Jiri, *Art Historian & Dir*, Moravska Galerie v Brne, Moravian Gallery at Brno, Brno Czechoslovakia

Öhman, Nina, *Cur*, Nationalmuseum, Moderna Museet, Stockholm Sweden

Ho, Abraham P, *Cur*, Saint John's University, Chung-Cheng Art Gallery, Jamaica NY

Ho, Fran, *Assoc Prof*, Washington State University, Fine Arts Department, Pullman WA (S)

Ho, Wai-Kam, *Cur Chinese Art*, Cleveland Museum of Art, Cleveland OH

Hoadley, Adele, *Correspondence Secy*, Berks Art Alliance, Reading PA

Hoadley, Bruce, *Instructor*, Truro Center for the Arts at Castle Hill, Inc, Truro MA (S)

Hoagland, Joan, *Head Fine Arts Dept*, Cleveland Public Library, Cleveland OH

Hoar, Bill, *Asst Prof*, Northern State College, Art Dept, Aberdeen SD (S)

Hoard, Eric B, *Treas*, Rochester Historical Society, Rochester NY

Hoare, Gabriel Mary, *Assoc Prof*, Webster College, Art Dept, Webster Groves MO (S)

Hobbs, Franklin W, *First Regent*, Gunston Hall Plantation, Lorton VA

Hobbs, Joe F, *Dir*, University of Oklahoma, School of Art, Norman OK (S)

Hobbs, Orodon, *Pres*, Sarasota Art Association, Sarasota FL

Hobbs, Robert, *Adjunct Cur Modern Art*, Cornell University, Herbert F Johnson Museum of Art, Ithaca NY

Hobbs, Robert C, *Asst Prof*, Cornell University, Department of the History of Art, Ithaca NY (S)

Hobbs, Robert D, *Chmn*, Clarion State College, Department of Art, Clarion PA (S)

Hobday, John, *National Dir*, Canadian Conference of the Arts, Ottawa ON

Hobgood, Wade, *Instructor*, Western Carolina University, Dept of Art, Cullowhee NC (S)

Hobin, James R, *Librn*, Albany Institute of History and Art, McKinney Library, Albany NY

Hoblitzell, Alan P, *Treas*, Municipal Art Society of Baltimore City, Baltimore MD

Hobrecht, Hilary, *Pastor Reverend*, Mission San Miguel, San Miguel CA

Hobson, David L, *Secy*, Springfield Art Center, Springfield OH

Hobson, Kitty A, *Archivist*, Oshkosh Public Museum, Library, Oshkosh WI

Hochstetler, T Max, *Instructor*, Austin Peay State University, Dept of Art, Clarksville TN (S)

Hockenhull, Jo, *Asst Prof*, Washington State University, Fine Arts Department, Pullman WA (S)

Hocker, Bea Carrillo, *Education Coordr*, Mexican Museum, San Francisco CA

Hockett, Roland L, *Assoc Prof*, Gulf Coast Community College, Division of Fine Arts, Panama City FL (S)

Hockschild, H K, *Pres*, Adirondack Museum of the Adirondack Historical Association, Blue Mountain Lake NY

Hodge, A W, *Head School Industrial Design*, Leicester Polytechnic, Faculty of Art and Design, Leicester England (S)

Hodge, Bill, *Pres*, Ontario Crafts Council, Toronto ON

Hodge, David, *Dir*, University of Wisconsin, Allen Priebe Gallery, Oshkosh WI

Hodge, G Stuart, *Dir*, Flint Institute of Arts, Flint MI

Hodge, Karen, *Dir*, Boulder Center for the Visual Arts, Boulder CO

Hodgell, Lois, *Coordr*, University of Minnesota, Morris, Humanities Department, Morris MN (S)

Hodges, Jeanne B, *Pres*, American Institute of Architects Foundation, Washington DC

Hodgson, James, *Acquisitions Librn*, Harvard University, Fine Arts Library, Cambridge MA

Hoell, Peter, *Instructor*, Saint Louis Community College at Meramec, Art Dept, Saint Louis MO (S)

Hoermann, Barbara, *Library Asst*, University of California, Art Department Library, Davis CA

Hoernschemeyer, Craig, *Instructor*, Albion College, Department of Visual Arts, Albion MI (S)

Hoesing, Joletta, *Special Projects*, Omaha Children's Museum, Inc, Omaha NE

Hoetink, H R, *Dir*, Koninklijk Kabinet van Schilderijen, Royal Picture Gallery, The Hague Netherlands

Hoffa, Harlan, *Acting Dir School Visual Arts*, Pennsylvania State University, University Park, College of Arts and Architecture, University Park PA (S)

Hoffman, Gregory, *Chmn*, International Fine Arts College, Miami FL (S)

Hoffman, Jo Lynn, *Dir Development*, Laguna Gloria Art Museum, Austin TX

Hoffman, Kathy, *Asst Prof*, Bradford College, Art Department, Bradford MA (S)

Hoffman, Kristen, *Lectr*, Trinity College, Department of Fine Arts, Washington DC (S)

Hoffman, L G, *Dir*, Davenport Municipal Art Gallery, Davenport IA

Hoffman, Laurence, *Chief Conservator*, Hirshhorn Museum and Sculpture Garden, Washington DC

Hoffman, Lee M, *Prof*, University of South Alabama, Department of Art, Mobile AL (S)

Hoffman, Margit, *Assoc Librn*, Nationalmuseum, Library, Stockholm Sweden

Hoffman, Marilyn, *Dir*, Brockton Art Center, Brockton MA

Hoffman, Marilyn F, *Dir*, Brockton Art Center, Art Workshops, Brockton MA (S)

Hoffman, Michael, *Advisor Alfred Stieglitz Center*, Philadelphia Museum of Art, Philadelphia PA

Hoffman, Nancy, *Asst Prof*, Hartford Art School of the University of Hartford, West Hartford CT (S)

Hoffman, Neil, *Dean*, Otis Art Institute of Parsons School of Design, Los Angeles CA (S)

Hoffman, William, *Chmn*, Rutgers University, Camden, Art Department, Camden NJ (S)

Hoffman, William, *Business & Technical Dept Head*, Wichita Public Library, Wichita KS

Hoffmann, John, *Dir Research*, School of Holography, Fine Arts Research and Holographic Center Museum, Chicago IL

Hoffmann, Lynn, *Cataloger*, Oshkosh Public Museum, Oshkosh WI

Hoffmann, Sally, *Public Service*, Spencer Museum of Art, Lawrence KS

Hoffmeister, Donald F, *Dir*, University of Illinois, Museum of Natural History, Champaign IL

Hoffsis, Bev, *Secy*, Main Line Center of the Arts, Haverford PA

Hoffstot, Barbara, *VPres*, Pittsburgh History and Landmarks Foundation, Old Post Office Museum, Pittsburgh PA

Hofheinz, Rudolf, *Instr*, Virginia Western Community College, Commercial Art, Fine Art & Photography, Roanoke VA (S)

Hofmann, Werner, *Dr Werner/Hofmann*

Hofshire, Sheri, *VPres*, Omaha Children's Museum, Inc, Omaha NE

Hofstede, Peter, *Librn*, Groningen Museum voor Stad en Land, Library, Groningen Netherlands

Hofstede, Peter, *Scientific Asst*, Groningen Museum voor Stad en Land, Groningen Museum, Groningen Netherlands

Hofstetter, Mary, *Financial Aid Officer*, Ontario College of Art, Toronto ON (S)

Hogan, Dan, *VPres*, Oklahoma Art Center, Oklahoma City OK

Hogan, Dana, *Instr*, Mount San Jacinto College, Art Department, San Jacinto CA (S)

Hogan, Gary, *Assoc Prof*, Hartford Art School of the University of Hartford, West Hartford CT (S)

Hogan, James, *Assoc Prof*, Saint Louis Community College at Forest Park, Dept of Art, Saint Louis MO (S)

Hoge, Robert W, *Dir*, Sanford Museum and Planetarium, Cherokee IA

Hogg, Alyson, *Librn*, Art Gallery of Western Australia, Library, Perth Australia

Hogge, J R, *Pres*, Carson County Square House Museum, Panhandle TX

Hogsett, Ted C, *Dir*, Southwestern School of Art, Albuquerque NM (S)

Hohby, Susan, *Secy & Coordr*, Chilliwack Arts Council, Chilliwack BC

Hohl, Robert, *Reference Librn*, Saint Mary's College, Alumnae Centennial Library, Notre Dame IN

Hohmann, John J, *Dir*, Michigan Artrain, Inc, Detroit MI

Hohn, Hubert, *Photography Dept Head*, Banff Centre School of Fine Arts, Banff AB (S)

Hoke, Elizabeth G, *Librn*, Wadsworth Atheneum, Auerbach Art Library, Hartford CT

Hoke, Montee, *Asst Prof*, Southwestern Oklahoma State University, Art Department, Weatherford OK (S)

Holahan, Elizabeth G, *Pres*, Rochester Historical Society, Rochester NY

Holahan, Mary, *Registrar*, Delaware Art Museum, Wilmington DE

Holak, Resa, *Asst to Librn*, Munson-Williams-Proctor Institute, Art Reference Library, Utica NY

Holcombe, Anna, *Instructor*, Illinois Wesleyan University, School of Art, Bloomington IL (S)

Holden, Don, *VPres*, Ages of Man Fellowship, Amenia NY

Holder, Charles, *Instructor*, Dunedin Fine Arts and Cultural Center, Dunedin FL (S)

Holder, Thomas J, *Chmn Dept*, University of Nevada, Las Vegas, Department of Art, Las Vegas NV (S)

Holechek, John L, *Educ Coordinator*, McLean County Art Association, Bloomington IL

Holladay, Harlan H, *Prof*, Saint Laurence University, Department of Fine Arts, Canton NY (S)

Holland, Flanders, *Asst Dir*, Norton Gallery and School of Art, West Palm Beach FL

Holland, Jay, *Chmn Fine Arts*, Center for Creative Studies—College of Art and Design, Detroit MI (S)

Holland, John Boyd, *Assoc Prof*, Moorhead State University, Department of Art, Moorhead MN (S)

Holland, Joyce, *Librn*, Brandon Allied Arts Council, Brandon Allied Arts Center Library, Brandon MB

Holland, Sarah, *Pres*, San Angelo Art Club, Kendall Art Gallery, San Angelo TX

Hollenhorst, Bernice, *Head Librn*, Saint Mary's College, Alumnae Centennial Library, Notre Dame IN

Holley, William H, *Chmn Art Educ*, East Carolina University, School of Art, Greenville NC (S)

Holliday, Ardis, *Dir*, Westerly Public Library, Westerly RI

Holliday, Clayton S, *Dir*, King George VI Art Gallery, Port South Africa, Republic of

Holliday, Judith, *Librn*, Cornell University, Fine Arts Library, Ithaca NY

Hollingsworth, Harry W, *VPres*, Antonelli School of Photography, Philadelphia PA (S)

Hollis, Edna, *Chmn Div Communications & Humanities*, Lewis and Clark Community College, Art Dept, Godfrey IL (S)

Holloway, Peter, *Instr*, Irish International Arts Centre, Castle Matrix, Rathkeale Ireland (S)

Holloway, R J, *Dir*, William Humphreys Art Gallery, Library, Kimberley South Africa, Republic of

Holloway, R J, *Cur*, William Humphreys Art Gallery, Kimberley South Africa, Republic of

Holloway, W Martin, *Coordr Visual Commun*, Kean College of New Jersey, Fine Arts Department, Union NJ (S)

Hollowell, David, *Assoc Prof*, Fontbonne College, Art Department, Saint Louis MO (S)

Hollowell, David, *Asst Prof*, Fontbonne College, Department of Art, Clayton MO (S)

Hollstein, Dell K, *Pres*, Fayetteville Museum of Art, Inc, Fayetteville NC

Holm, Bill, *Cur Northwest Coast Indian Art*, University of Washington, Thomas Burke Memorial Washington State Museum, Seattle WA

Holman, Thomas, *Cur*, Norton Gallery and School of Art, West Palm Beach FL

Holmberg, Harry E, *Chmn Div*, Chadron State College, Div of Fine Arts, Chadron NE (S)

Holmberg, Harry E, *Coordr*, Chadron State College, Arts Gallery, Chadron NE

Holmes, Barry, *Chmn Dept*, Vancouver Community College, Langara Campus, Department of Fine Arts, Vancouver BC (S)

Holmes, David V, *Asst Prof*, University of Wisconsin-Parkside, Art Discipline, Kenosha WI (S)

Holmes, Diana, *Instructor*, Art Academy of Cincinnati, Cincinnati OH (S)

Holmes, Emily, *Instructor*, Friends of the Arts and Sciences, Hilton Leech Studio, Sarasota FL (S)

Holmes, J, *Cur Asst*, Royal Ontario Museum, Canadiana Gallery, Toronto ON

Holmes, Judith, *Secy*, Oakland University, Meadow Brook Art Gallery, Rochester MI

Holmes, Larry, *Coordr Foundations*, University of Delaware, Department of Art, Newark DE (S)

Holmes, Oakley N, *Assoc Prof*, Jacksonville State University, Art Department, Pelham, Jacksonville AL (S)

Holmes, Peggy, *Assoc Dir Main Adult Servs*, Long Beach Public Library, Long Beach CA

Holmes, Tony, *Instr*, College of Lake County, Art Department, Grayslake IL (S)

Holmes, Wendy, *Asst Prof*, University of Rhode Island, Department of Art, Kingston RI (S)

Holmes, Wendy, *Instructor*, Peters Valley Craft Center, Layton NJ (S)

Holmes, Wilbur T, *Exec Dir*, Newport Historical Society, Newport RI

Holmgren, Doreen, *Coordr*, University of Wisconsin, Elvehjem Art Center, Madison WI

Holmns, LeRoy F, *Chmn*, North Carolina Agricultural and Technical State University, Art Department, Greensboro NC (S)

Holmquist, Carolyn, *Art & Music Librn*, Seattle Public Library, Seattle WA

Holmquist, Julie, *Dir*, Alverno College Gallery, Milwaukee WI

Holmquist, June, *Asst Dir*, Minnesota Historical Society, St Paul MN

Holo, Selma, *Cur*, Norton Simon Museum, Pasadena CA

Holohan, Ronald, *Chmn*, Illinois Central College, Art and Humanities Department, East Peoria IL (S)

Holownia, Thaddeus, *Lectr*, Mount Allison University, Fine Arts Department, Sackville NB (S)

Holroyd, Ruth, *Head Weaving*, Chautauqua Institution, Chautauqua NY (S)

Holsheiser, Harold, *Secy*, Mexico-Audrain County Library, Mexico MO

Holsing, Marilyn, *Asst Prof*, Temple University, Art Department, Philadelphia PA (S)

Holst, V, *Cur 19th Century*, Staatsgalerie Stuttgart, Stuttgart Germany, Federal Republic of

Holt, Jane B, *Hostess*, Centre Hill Mansion, Petersburg VA

Holt, Joan, *Ed Bulletin*, Metropolitan Museum of Art, New York NY

Holt, Martha, *Gallery Dir*, Allegheny College, Art Department, Meadville PA (S)

Holt, Martha A, *Gallery Dir*, Allegheny College, Bowman, Megahan and Penelec Galleries, Meadville PA

Holt, R J, *Dir*, Chesapeake Bay Maritime Museum, Saint Michaels MD

Holt, Ruth, *Vis Prof*, John C Calhoun State Community College, Art Department, Decatur AL (S)

Holte, Norman, *Pres*, Bethany Lutheran College, Memorial Library, Mankato MN

Holtgrewe, Douglas, *Instructor*, Elmira College, Art Department, Elmira NY (S)

Holton, Mark, *Cur*, Confederation Centre Art Gallery and Museum, Charlottetown PE

Holton, Susan, *Librn*, American Institute of Architects, Library, Washington DC

Holtzer, Esther Rachel, *Education Asst*, Minnesota Museum of Art, Saint Paul MN

Holverson, John, *Dir*, Portland Museum of Art, Portland ME

Holvey, Sam, *Chmn Visual Communications*, Corcoran School of Art, Washington DC (S)

Holzman, David, *Instr*, Western Connecticut State College, Danbury CT (S)

Holzrichter, Elmer, *Asst Prof*, Kearney State College, Dept of Art, Kearney NE (S)

Homan, Ralph, *Instructor*, College of the Sequoias, Art Department, Visalia CA (S)

Homecki, Adam, *Manuscripts*, Muzeum Narodowe w Krakowie, National Museum in Cracow, Cracow Poland

Homes, Philip C, *Executive Dir*, Peters Valley Craft Center Library, Layton NJ

Homes, Philip C, *Exec Dir*, Peters Valley Craft Center, Layton NJ (S)

Honadel, Rand, *Cur*, Ketterer Art Center, Bozeman MT

Honig, Mervin, *Secy*, Audubon Artists, Inc, New York NY

Honig, Sylvia, *Asst Prof*, Trenton State College, Art Department, Trenton NJ (S)

Honisch, Dieter, *Dir*, Staatliche Museen Preussischer Kulturbesitz, Nationalgalerie, Berlin Germany, Federal Republic of

Honsa, Vlasta, *Reference*, Clark County Library District, Las Vegas NV

Hood, Gail, *Instructor*, Southeastern Louisiana University, Dept of Visual Arts, Hammond LA (S)

Hood, Gary, *Cur*, Wichita State University, Edwin A Ulrich Museum of Art, Wichita KS

Hood, Graham S, *Dir & Cur Coll*, Colonial Williamsburg Foundation, Williamsburg VA

Hood, H, *VPres*, Madison County Historical Society, Oneida NY

Hood, Kenneth, *Deputy Dir*, National Gallery of Victoria, Melbourne Australia

Hood, Mary Bryan, *Dir*, Owensboro Museum of Fine Art, Owensboro KY

Hood, Paul, *Development Dir*, Virginia Museum of Fine Arts, Richmond VA

Hood, Richard, *Pres*, American Color Print Society, Philadelphia PA

Hood, William, *Asst Prof*, Oberlin College, Department of Art, Oberlin OH (S)

Hoogendonk, M, *Cur Modern Art*, Frans Halsmuseum, Frans Hals Museum, Haarlem Netherlands

Hoogs, Barbara F, *Keeper, Lending Coll*, Honolulu Academy of Arts, Honolulu HI

Hooi, Christopher, *Dir*, National Museum Art Gallery, Singapore Singapore, Republic of

Hooks, Earl, *Chmn Dept*, Fisk University, Art Dept, Nashville TN (S)

Hooks, Earl J, *Dir*, Fisk University Museum, Nashville TN

Hookway, H T, *Chief Executive*, British Library, Reference Division, London England

Hoole, John, *Asst Dir*, Museum of Modern Art Oxford, Oxford England

Hooper, Rosemary, *Coordr Printmaking*, University of Delaware, Department of Art, Newark DE (S)

Hooper-Greenhill, Eilean, *Education*, National Portrait Gallery, London England

Hooper Jr, James A, *Asst Prof*, McNeese State University, Department of Visual Arts, Lake Charles LA (S)

Hoopes, Marian Buck, *Instructor*, Springfield College in Illinois, Dept of Art, Springfield IL (S)

Hooten, Joseph, *Instructor*, Long Beach City College, Department of Art, Long Beach CA (S)

Hoover, H Earl, *Pres*, Palm Springs Desert Museum, Inc, Palm Springs CA

Hoover, Martha, *Program Advisor*, University of Southwestern Louisiana, Union Art Gallery, Lafayette LA

Hoover, Richard, *Co-Chmn*, North Canton Public Library, Little Art Gallery, North Canton OH

Hoover, Robert, *Secy*, Octagon Center for the Arts, Ames IA

Hoover, Susan, *Instr*, University of Northern Colorado, Department of Fine Arts, Greeley CO (S)

Hoozee, Robert, *Asst*, Museum voor Schone Kunsten, Ghent Belgium

Hopcraft, Timothy, *Controller*, Art Gallery of Ontario, Toronto ON

Hope, Louise, *Gallery Exhibits Chmn*, Huntsville Art League and Museum Association Inc, Huntsville AL

Hope, Samuel, *Exec Dir*, National Association of Schools of Art, Reston VA

Hopkins, Carolyn, *Board Pres*, Lake Placid School of Art Gallery, Lake Placid NY

Hopkins, Elizabeth, *VPres*, San Bernardino County Museum and Satellites, Fine Arts Institute, Redlands CA

Hopkins, Floy, *Secy*, Lubbock Art Association, Inc, Lubbock TX

Hopkins, Henry T, *Dir*, San Francisco Museum of Modern Art, San Francisco CA

Hopkins, Joe, *Chmn*, Sullivan County Community College, Div of Commercial Art and Photography, Loch Sheldrake NY (S)

Hopkins, Joseph W, *Exhib Coordr*, University of Tennessee, Frank H McClung Museum, Knoxville TN

Hopkins, Ruth, *Vis Instr*, Judson College, Division of Fine Arts, Elgin IL (S)

Hopkins, Susan, *VPres*, Wayne Art Center, Wayne PA

Hopkins, William, *Instructor*, Ocean City School of Art, Ocean City NJ (S)

Hopper, James, *Chmn*, Mount Union College, Department of Art, Alliance OH (S)

Hopper, Robert, *Asst Keeper Art*, University of Manchester, Whitworth Art Gallery, Manchester England

Hoppin, Martha, *Asst Prof*, University of Massachusetts, Amherst, Art History Prog, Amherst MA (S)

Hopps, Bud, *Dir Public Relations*, California Museum of Science and Industry, Los Angeles CA

Hopton, Leslie, *Museum Educator*, Kelowna Centennial Museum and National Exhibit Centre, Kelowna BC

Horlbeck, Frank, *Prof*, University of Wisconsin, Madison, Department of Art, Madison WI (S)

Horn, Burce, *Instructor*, Northern Arizona University, Art Department, Flagstaff AZ (S)

Horn, Joe, *VPres*, Saint Augustine Art Association Gallery, Saint Augustine FL

Horn, Samuel, *Secy*, New York Society of Architects, f the Performing Arts, at Lincoln Center New York

Hornack, Curtis, *Exec Dir*, Yaddo, Saratoga Springs NY (S)

Hornaday, Richard, *Chmn*, California State University, Chico, Art Gallery, Chico CA

Hornaday, Richard, *Chmn*, California State University, Chico, Art Dept, Chico CA (S)

Horner, Thomas H, *Pres*, Canton Art Institute, Canton OH

Horovitz, Lee, *Pres*, Ojai Valley Art Center, Ojai CA

Horowitz, Harvy, *Librn*, Hebrew Union College, Frances Henry Library, Los Angeles CA

Horowitz, Marvin, *Assoc Prof*, New York Institute of Technology, Fine Arts Department, Old Westbury NY (S)

Horrell, Deborah, *Instructor*, Factory of Visual Art, Seattle WA (S)

Horrocks, Sandra, *Public Relations Mgr*, Philadelphia Museum of Art, Philadelphia PA

Horse Capture, George P, *Cur Plains Indian Museum*, Buffalo Bill Memorial Association, Cody WY

Horsey, Ann, *Cur Coll*, Division of Historical and Cultural Affairs, Bureau of Museums and Historic Sites, Dover DE

Horsfield, Kate, *Video Data Bank*, School of the Art Institute of Chicago Library, Chicago IL

Horste, Kathryn, *Asst Prof*, Colgate University, Department of Fine Arts, Hamilton NY (S)

Hortenburg, Larry, *Instructor*, Austin Peay State University, Dept of Art, Clarksville TN (S)

Hortian, Serena, *Dir*, Scalamandre Museum of Textiles, New York NY

Horton, Christopher, *Assoc Prof*, Hartford Art School of the University of Hartford, West Hartford CT (S)

Horton, Frank L, *Dir*, Museum of Early Southern Decorative Arts, Old Salem Inc, Winston-Salem NC

Horton, Gary M, *Dean*, Houston Baptist College, Department of Art, Houston TX (S)

Horton, Kay, *Asst Prof*, University of Nebraska Lincoln, Architecture Library, Lincoln NE

Horton, Luci, *First VPres*, Greater Gary Arts Council, Gary IN

Horuitz, Suzanne, *Trustee*, Foundation for Today's Art, Nexus Gallery, Philadelphia PA

Horvat, Krisjohn O, *Asst Prof*, Rhode Island College, Art Department, Providence RI (S)

Horvath, David, *Asst Cur*, University of Louisville, University of Louisville Photographic Archives, Louisville KY

Horvitz, Suzanne, *VPres in Charge Art*, Philadelphia Art Alliance, Philadelphia PA

Horwedel, Lowell, *VPres*, Lafayette Art Center, Lafayette IN

Hosch, Heinz L, *Chmn*, York College of Pennsylvania, Department of Humanities and Fine Arts, York PA (S)

Hoskin, John, *Head School Fine Art*, Leicester Polytechnic, Faculty of Art and Design, Leicester England (S)

Hoskins, Alice, *Education Officer*, Art Gallery of Nova Scotia, Halifax NS

Hospodar, Emil W, *Head*, University of Illinois at the Medical Center, Dept of Biocommunication Arts-Medical Art, Chicago IL (S)

Hossler, Marguerite, *Chmn Dept Commercial Art*, Woodbury University, Professional Arts Division, Los Angeles CA (S)

Hotchkiss, Horace L, *Cur Corbit-Sharp & Wilson-Warner Houses*, Winterthur Museum and Gardens, Historic Odessa, Winterthur DE

Hotka, Ray, *Exhibit Chmn*, The Dalles Art Association, The Dalles OR

Houde, Jean-Luc, *Asst Dir*, Centre Cultural de Shawinigan, Shawinigan PQ

Houeman, Alice, *Conservator*, Alaska State Museum, Juneau AK

Hough, Frances D, *VPres*, Gilpin County Arts Association, Central City CO

Hough, Samuel J, *Cur*, Brown University, Annmary Brown Memorial Gallery, Providence RI

Houghland, W D, *Instr*, College of William and Mary, Department of Fine Arts, Williamsburg VA (S)

Houghton, Barbara, *Asst Prof*, Metropolitan State College, Art Department, Denver CO (S)

Houlas, Robin, *Asst Mgr*, Salvador Dali Museum, Beachwood OH

Houle, Elyse, *Secy*, Musee d'Art de Joliette, Library, Joliette PQ

Houle, Elyse, *Secy*, Musee d'Art de Joliette, Joliette PQ

Houle, Pierre, *Admin Dir*, Institut des Arts au Saguenay, National Exhibition Center, Jonquiere PQ

Houlihan, Patrick T, *Dir*, Heard Museum, Phoenix AZ

Houllahan, Roberta, *Instructor*, Rhode Island College, Art Department, Providence RI (S)

Houmes, Chris, *Assoc Dir*, Museum of York County, Rock Hill SC

House, Gloria Gilmore, *Secy*, International Center of Medieval Art, Inc, New York NY

Houseman, Bette, *Exhib Designer*, Calvert Marine Museum, Solomons MD

Housman, Russell, *Prof*, Nassau Community College, Art Department, Garden City NY (S)

Houston, Blanche V, *Cataloguer*, Frick Art Reference Library, New York NY

Houze, Barbara, *Instructor*, Colgate University, Department of Fine Arts, Hamilton NY (S)

Hoven, Tore, *Mgr*, Seattle Art Museum, Modern Art Pavilion, Seattle WA

Hover, Jesse, *Chairperson*, City College of San Francisco, Art Department, San Francisco CA (S)

Hoverstadt, G W, *Head Dept Visual Studies*, Manchester Polytechnic, Faculty of Art and Design, Manchester England (S)

Howard, Cecil, *Prof*, Western New Mexico University, Dept of Fine Art, Art Div, Silver City NM (S)

Howard, Dan F, *Chmn Dept*, University of Nebraska-Lincoln, Department of Art, Lincoln NE (S)

Howard, Elizabeth, *Pres*, National Assembly of Community Arts Agencies, Washington DC

Howard, Jamie, *Pres*, Columbus College, Experimental Gallery, Columbus GA

Howard, Jean, *Instructor*, Johnson County Community College, Communications-Arts Division, Overland Park KS (S)

Howard, Jonas A, *Chmn Dept*, Indiana University Southeast, Fine Arts Department, New Albany IN (S)

Howard, Kathryn, *Photographer*, Art Research Center, Kansas City MO

Howard, Nikki, *Instructor*, Ohio Visual Art Institute, Cincinnati OH (S)

Howard, Norma, *Vice Chmn*, Nicolaysen Art Museum, Casper WY

Howard, Richard, *Instr*, Mount Vernon College, Art Department, Washington DC (S)

Howard, Robert, *Prof*, University of North Carolina at Chapel Hill, Art Department, Chapel Hill NC (S)

Howard Jr, Milo B, *Dir*, Alabama Department of Archives and History Museum, Montgomery AL

Howarth, Anthony J, *Cur*, Southampton Art Gallery and Museum Service, Southampton England

Howarth, Shirles, *Dir*, Tampa Museum, Library, Tampa FL

Howarth, Shirley R, *Dir*, Tampa Museum, Tampa FL

Howat, John K, *Cur American Paintings & Sculpture*, Metropolitan Museum of Art, New York NY

Howe, Katherine, *Assoc Cur*, Museum of Fine Arts, Houston, Houston TX

Howe, Raymond, *Cur Education*, New Jersey State Museum, Trenton NJ

Howell, Charles, *Cur Entomology*, San Bernardino County Museum and Satellites, Fine Arts Institute, Redlands CA

Howell, Joseph, *Secy & Registrar*, Zanesville Art Center, Zanesville OH

Howell, Joseph, *Librn*, Zanesville Art Center, Library, Zanesville OH

Howell, Robert, *Assoc Prof*, California Polytechnic State University at San Luis Obispo, Art Department, San Luis Obispo CA (S)

Howell, Robert, *Asst Prof*, McMurry College, Art Dept, Abilene TX (S)

Howell, Sally, *Dir*, Willamette University, George Putnam University Center, Salem OR

Howell, Steven, *Instr*, Johnson State College, Art Department, Johnson VT (S)

Howell, Tom, *Prof*, Porterville Community College, Department of Fine Arts, Porterville CA (S)

Howerton, Glen E, *Prof*, Furman University, Department of Art, Greenville SC (S)

Howes, Lorraine, *Head Apparel Design*, Rhode Island School of Design, Providence RI (S)

Howes, Michael, *Instructor*, Nicholls State University, Dept of Art, Thibodaux LA (S)

Howett, John, *Chmn*, Emory University, Art History Department, Atlanta GA (S)

Howie, Bob, *Vis Prof*, Oral Roberts University, Fine Arts Department, Tulsa OK (S)

Howkins, Mary Ball, *Asst Prof*, Rhode Island College, Art Department, Providence RI (S)

Howland, Cindy, *Treas*, Redding Museum & Art Center, Redding CA

Howland Jr, Harold, *Temporary Managing Dir*, The Jewelry Institute, New England Academy, Providence RI (S)

Howlett, Dorn, *Chmn Art Educ*, Edinboro State College, Art Department, Edinboro PA (S)

Howrigan, Roger, *Instr*, Saint Thomas Aquinas College, Art Department, Sparkhill NY (S)

Howsare, Susan, *Acting Chmn*, Waynesburg College, Department of Fine Arts, Waynesburg PA (S)

Howton, Bea, *Recording Secy*, Key West Art and Historical Society, Key West FL

Howze, Jim, *Prof*, Texas Tech University, Department of Art, Lubbock TX (S)

Hoy, Harold, *Instr*, Lane Community College, Art and Applied Design Department, Eugene OR (S)

Hoyle, Pamela, *Print Dept Cur*, Boston Athenaeum, Boston MA

Hoyle, William, *Pres*, Greater Fall River Art Association, Fall River MA

Hoyman, Lisa, *Childrens Room*, Mason City Public Library, Mason City IA

Härtel, Herbert, *Dir*, Staatliche Museen Preussischer Kulturbesitz, Museum of Indian Art, Berlin Germany, Federal Republic of

Hruska, Dorothy Irene, *Co-Dir & Muzeologist*, LeSueur County Historical Society Museum, Elysian MN

Hruska, James E, *Pres & Dir*, LeSueur County Historical Society Museum, Elysian MN

Hruska, Robert J, *Asst Dir & Cur Anthropology*, Oshkosh Public Museum, Oshkosh WI

Hrusovsky, Paul, *Instructor*, Webster College, Art Dept, Webster Groves MO (S)

Hsu, F Richard, *Pres & Dir*, China Institute in America, China House Gallery, New York NY

Huacuja, Jose Chavez, *Instr*, University of the Americas, Graphic Arts and Design Dept, Cholula Mexico (S)

Hubbard, George D, *Pres*, Peale Museum, Baltimore MD

Hubbard, Howard W, *Chief Public Relations Division*, Enoch Pratt Free Library of Baltimore City, Baltimore MD

Hubbard, John D, *Assoc Prof*, Northern Michigan University, Dept of Art & Design, Marquette MI (S)

Hubbard, Marguerite B, *Acting Cur Museum*, Franklin D Roosevelt Library and Museum, Hyde Park NY

Hubbard, Tom, *Instructor*, Ohio Visual Art Institute, Cincinnati OH (S)

Hubbard, William, *VPres*, Pocumtuck Valley Memorial Association, Memorial Hall, Deerfield MA

Hubbuch, Myrt W, *Asst Prof*, University of North Alabama, Department of Art, Florence AL (S)

Huber, Catherine, *Dir Musee Enfants*, Musee d'Art Moderne de la Ville de Paris, Paris France

Huber, Leonard V, *Pres*, Louisiana Historical Association, Confederate Museum, New Orleans LA

Huber, R, *Instructor*, Golden West College, Arts, Humanities and Social Sciences Institute, Huntington Beach CA (S)

Huber, Robert L, *Coordr Fine and Performing Arts*, Ocean County College, Humanities Department, Toms River NJ (S)

Huberman, Brian, *Lectr*, Rice University, Department of Art and Art History, Houston TX (S)

Hubert, Rebecca. *AV Librn*, Houston Public Library, Houston TX

Hubert, Rebecca, *AV Librn*, Anna Maria College, Saint Luke's Gallery, Paxton MA

Hubler, Mary Jane, *Asst*, Lincoln National Life Foundation, Inc, Louis A Warren Lincoln Library and Museum, Fort Wayne IN

Hubley, Loretta, *Instructor*, Madonna College, Art Dept, Livonia MI (S)

Huchard, Viviane, *Conservator*, Musee des Beaux-Arts, Museum of Fine Arts, Angers France

Huchel, Frederick M, *Dir*, Brigham City Museum-Gallery, Brigham City UT

Hucker, Robert, *Treas*, Amarillo Art Center, Amarillo Art Center Association, Amarillo TX

Huddlestone, Ralph, *Instr*, Utah Technical College at Salt Lake, Commercial Art Department, Salt Lake City UT (S)

Hudek, Janan, *Admin Asst*, McLean County Art Association, Bloomington IL

Hudon, Paul, *Supv Education Services*, Merrimack Valley Textile Museum, North Andover MA

Hudson, Andrew, *Chmn Complementary Studies*, Corcoran School of Art, Washington DC (S)

Hudson, Donna M, *Secy & Bookkeeper*, Lynchburg Fine Arts Center Inc, Lynchburg VA

Hudson, Jack, *VPres*, French Art Colony, Inc, Gallipolis OH

Hudson, Nancy, *Asst Dir*, Clark County Library District, Las Vegas NV

Hudson, Ralph M, *VPres*, Kappa Pi International Honorary Art Fraternity, Birmingham AL

Hudson, Samuel, *Asst Prof*, Nazareth College of Rochester, Art Department, Rochester NY (S)

Hudson, Tom, *Dean*, Emily Carr College of Art, Vancouver BC (S)

Huebner, Gregory, *Chmn*, Wabash College, Art Department, Crawfordsville IN (S)

Huemer, Frances, *Prof*, University of North Carolina at Chapel Hill, Art Department, Chapel Hill NC (S)

Huey, Joyce, *Dir Support Services*, South Carolina Arts Commission, Columbia SC

Huey, Norma, *Exec Dir*, Women's City Club of Cleveland, Cleveland OH

Huff, Cecile C, *Assoc Prof*, Prince George's Community College, Art Department, Largo MD (S)

Huff, Cynthia, *Admin Asst to Dir*, University of Notre Dame, Snite Museum of Art, Notre Dame IN

Huffman, Kathy, *Cur*, Long Beach Museum of Art, Long Beach CA

Huffman, Lorilee, *Registrar*, Southern Illinois University Museum and Art Galleries, Carbondale IL

Huffstot, John, *Asst Cur*, University of Missouri, Museum of Art and Archaeology, Columbia MO

Hughes, Danny R, *Asst Executive Dir*, Arts Council of Spartanburg County, Inc, Spartanburg SC

Hughes, Graham, *Art Dir*, Worshipful Company of Goldsmiths, London England

Hughes, Inez H, *Dir*, Harrison County Historical Museum, Marshall TX

Hughes, John, *Assoc Prof*, Missouri Western State College, Art Department, Saint Joseph MO (S)

Hughes, John T, *Gallery Coordr*, Missouri Western State College, Fine Arts Gallery, Saint Joseph MO

Hughes, Mai, *Clerical Asst*, Museum of the Southwest, Midland TX

Hughes, Martha, *Cur*, Elizabet Ney Museum, Austin TX

Hughes, Max, *Vice Chmn*, Salisbury State College, Wildfowl Art Museum, Salisbury MD

Hughes, P, *Asst to Dir*, Wallace Collection, London England

Hughes, Paul J, *First VPres*, Greater Fall River Art Association, Fall River MA

Hughes, Phillip Samuel, *Under Secy*, Smithsonian Institution, Washington DC

Hughes, Polly, *Prof*, Western New Mexico University, Dept of Fine Art, Art Div, Silver City NM (S)

Hughitt, Robert, *Instr*, Portland Community College, Department of Fine Arts, Portland OR (S)

Hughson, John, *Chmn*, State University College, Department of Art, Fredonia NY (S)

Hugo, Joan, *Librn*, Otis Art Institute of Parsons School of Design Gallery, Library, Los Angeles CA

Hugunin, Jim, *Instructor*, California Lutheran College, Art Department, Thousand Oaks CA (S)

Huhtala, Eugene, *Comptroller*, Western Reserve Historical Society, Cleveland OH

Huisman, Carl J, *Assoc Prof*, Calvin College, Art Dept, Grand Rapids MI (S)

Huitson, John, *Deputy Dir*, American Museum in Britain, Bath England

Hulbert, Bette, *Cur Collections*, Alaska State Museum, Juneau AK

Hulbert, James C, *Assoc Prof*, Palomar College, Art Department, San Marcos TX (S)

Hulet, Grant M, *Instr*, Utah Technical College at Salt Lake, Commercial Art Department, Salt Lake City UT (S)

Hulitar, Philip, *Vpres*, Society of the Four Arts, Palm Beach FL

Hull, David, *Librn*, National Maritime Museum, Library, San Francisco CA

Hull, Joan C, *Dir*, New Jersey Historical Society Museum, Newark NJ

Hull, John, *Assoc Prof*, Marymount College, Art Department, Tarrytown NY (S)

Hull, P, *Mgr Learning Resources*, Georgian College of Applied Arts and Technology, Georgian Learning Resources Centre, Barrie ON

Hull, William, *Dir*, Pennsylvania State University, Museum of Art, University Park PA

Hulmer, Eric C, *Cur*, Butler Institute of American Art, Youngstown OH

Humble, Doug, *Galleries Mgr*, Galleries of the Claremont Colleges, Claremont CA

Humelsine, Carlisle H, *VPres*, National Gallery of Art, Washington DC

Hummel, Charles F, *Deputy Dir Collections*, Winterthur Museum and Gardens, Winterthur DE

Hummel, Lisa, *Registrar*, Virginia Museum of Fine Arts, Richmond VA

Humphrey, David R, *Dean*, Florida School of the Arts, Visual Arts, Palatka FL (S)

Humphrey, Deborah, *Office Mgr*, Marin Society of Artists Inc, Ross CA

Humphrey, Don, *Chief Cur*, Museum of New Mexico, Museum of Fine Arts, Santa Fe NM

Humphrey, G, *Pres*, South Peace Art Society, Dawson Creek Museum Art Gallery, Dawson Creek BC

Humphrey, James, *Chmn Advertising Design*, Pan American University, Art Department, Edinburg TX (S)

Humphrey, John H, *Asst Cur*, University of Michigan Museum of Art, Kelsey Museum of Ancient and Medieval Archaeology, Ann Arbor MI

Humphrey, Rita S, *Admin Asst*, Baylor University, Armstrong Browning Library, Waco TX

Humphrey, Rosemary, *Secy*, Ashtabula Arts Center, Ashtabula OH

Humphrey, Tom, *Librn*, Central Wyoming College, Central Wyoming College Library, Riverton WY

Humphreys, Bill, *Secy*, Salisbury State College, Wildfowl Art Museum, Salisbury MD

Hundley, Deborah, *Gallery Mgr*, Virginia Museum, Danville Museum of Fine Arts and History, Danville VA

Hungerford, Constance Cain, *Asst Prof*, Swarthmore College, Department of Art, Swarthmore PA (S)

Hunke, Susan, *Asst Dir*, Plains Art Museum, Main Gallery, Moorhead MN

Hunnicutt, Evelyn, *Treas*, Coquille Valley Art Association, Coquille OR

Hunsberger, Charles W, *Dir*, Clark County Library District, Las Vegas NV

Hunt, Carol, *Registrar*, Putnam Museum, Davenport IA

Hunt, Carole, *Secy*, Strasburg Museum, Strasburg VA

Hunt, David C, *Dir*, Museum of the Arts Foundation, Missoula Museum of the Arts, Missoula MT

Hunt, Diana K, *Admin*, Art Institute of Pittsburgh Gallery, Resource Center, Pittsburgh PA

Irwin, Arthur, *Coordr Professional Art*, City College of San Francisco, Art Department, San Francisco CA (S)

Irwin, Barbara S, *Library Dir*, New Jersey Historical Society Museum, Library, Newark NJ

Irwin, G, *Head Dept Fine Art*, Brighton Polytechnic, Faculty of Art and Design, Brighton England (S)

Irwin, Margaret, American Museum in Britain, Library, Bath England

Isaacs, Avrom, *VPres*, Professional Art Dealers Association of Canada, Toronto ON

Isaacs, Claire, *Dir Junior Arts Center*, City of Los Angeles, Municipal Arts Dept, Los Angeles CA

Isaacs, Claire, *Dir*, Junior Arts Center, Los Angeles CA

Isaacson, Gene L, *Instructor*, Santa Ana College, Art Department, Santa Ana CA (S)

Isaksson, Olov, *Dir*, Statens Historiska Museum, Museum of National Antiquities, Stockholm Sweden

Iselin, Lewis, *Pres*, Louis Comfort Tiffany Foundation, Great Neck NY

Ishibashi, Shojiro, *Pres*, Bridgestone Bijutsukan, Bridgestone Museum of Art, Tokyo Japan

Ishikawa, Joseph, *Dir of Gallery*, Michigan State University, Kresge Art Center, East Lansing MI

Isola, M Catelli, *Dir*, Instituto Nazionale per la Grafica, Rome Italy

Isoline, Charles, *Communication Design*, Baylor University, Department of Fine Arts, Waco TX (S)

Isphording, Eduard, *Asst*, Germanisches National Museum, Bibliothek, Nuremberg Germany, Federal Republic of

Israel, Eliot, *Pres*, Roosevelt Public Library Art Workshop Gallery, Roosevelt NY

Italiano, Joan N, *Chmn*, College of the Holy Cross, Department of Fine Arts, Worcester MA (S)

Italiano, Lisa, *Asst Cur Education*, George Walter Vincent Smith Art Museum, Springfield MA

Itatani, Michiko, *Pres*, N.A.M.E. Gallery, Chicago IL

Itkonen, Kerttu, *Librn*, Suomen Kansallismuseo, National Board of Antiquities and Historical Monuments Library, Helsinki Finland

Itman, Leszek, *Dir*, Muzeum Narodowe we Wroclawiu, National Museum, Wroclaw Poland

Ittmann, John, *Cur Prints & Drawings*, Minneapolis Institute of Arts, Minneapolis MN

Iverson, Thomas L, *Instr*, Dallas Baptist College, Department of Art, Dallas TX (S)

Ives, Colta Feller, *Cur in Charge Prints & Photographs*, Metropolitan Museum of Art, New York NY

Ivey, Nancy, *Gallery Shop Mgr*, Madison Art Center, Madison WI

Ivins, Mildred, *Chmn Fashion Illustration*, Moore College of Art, Philadelphia PA (S)

Ivory, Paul W, *Adminr*, Chesterwood, Stockbridge MA

Ivy, Margaret, *Dir*, St Mary's University of San Antonio, Department of Fine Arts, San Antonio TX (S)

Iwaskai, Yoshikazu, *Chief Cur Fine Art Department & Cur Sculpture*, Tokyo Kokuritsu Kindai Bujutsukan, National Museum of Modern Art, Tokyo, Tokyo Japan

Izquierdo, Manuel, *Instructor*, Portland Art Museum, Museum Art School, Portland OR (S)

Jachimowicz, Elizabeth, *Cur Costumes*, Chicago Historical Society, Chicago IL

Jack, Ann L, *Dir*, College of Marin, Art Gallery, Kentfield CA

Jack, Marlene, *Asst Prof*, College of William and Mary, Department of Fine Arts, Williamsburg VA (S)

Jack, Meredith M, *Instructor*, Lamar University, Art Department, Beaumont TX (S)

Jackson, A, *Instructor*, Golden West College, Arts, Humanities and Social Sciences Institute, Huntington Beach CA (S)

Jackson, Anke tom Dieck, *Educ Dir*, Parrish Art Museum, Southampton NY

Jackson, Arnold, *Secy*, American Society of Artists, Inc, Chicago IL

Jackson, B, *Secy-Registrar*, University of Victoria, Maltwood Art Museum and Gallery, Victoria BC

Jackson, Gay, *Program Coordr*, Huntington Galleries, Huntington WV

Jackson, Gene E, *Prof*, Sam Houston State University, Art Department, Huntsville TX (S)

Jackson, Gregg, *Grants & Memorial Liaison*, Indiana State Museum, Indianapolis IN

Jackson, Herb, *Chmn*, Davidson College, Art Dept, Davidson NC (S)

Jackson, Herb, *Dir*, Davidson College Art Gallery, Davidson NC

Jackson, Jack, *Art Librn*, Boston Athenaeum, Boston MA

Jackson, Marg, *Education & Extension*, The Robert McLaughlin Gallery, Oshawa ON

Jackson, Martin, *Instructor*, Samuel S Fleisher Art Memorial, Philadelphia PA (S)

Jackson, Richard, *Instructor*, Murray State University, Art Department, Murray KY (S)

Jackson, Richard G, *Gallery Dir*, Murray State University, Clara M Eagle Gallery, Murray KY

Jackson, Rosemary, *Pres & Dir*, Museum of Holography, New York NY

Jackson, Ward, *Archivist*, Solomon R Guggenheim Museum, New York NY

Jackson, Ward, *Membership Chmn*, American Abstract Artists, Summit NJ

Jackson, William, *Chairperson Studio Arts Dept*, Simon's Rock of Bard College, Studio Arts Department, Great Barrington MA (S)

Jackson, William, *Chmn Art Dept*, Simon's Rock of Bard College, Great Barrington MA (S)

Jacob, Sabine, *Asst*, Herzog Anton Ulrich-Museum, Medieval Section: Burg Dankwarderode, Brunswick Germany, Federal Republic of

Jacobs, Ellen, *Assoc Prof*, Florida International University, Visual Arts Department, Miami FL (S)

Jacobs, Elliott, *VPres*, Atlantic Gallery, New York NY

Jacobs, Harold, *Chmn Painting*, Moore College of Art, Philadelphia PA (S)

Jacobs, John H, *Dir*, Pasadena City College, Art Gallery, Pasadena CA

Jacobs, John R, *Chmn Dept*, Rio Hondo College, Fine Arts Department, Whittier CA (S)

Jacobs, Peter A, *Chmn*, Colorado State University, Department of Art, Fort Collins CO (S)

Jacobs, Stan, *Chmn*, Midland College, Art Department, Midland TX (S)

Jacobsen, Florence S, *Dir*, Church of Jesus Christ of Latter-Day Saints, Information Center and Museum, Arts and Sites Division, Salt Lake City UT

Jacobsen, Lolli, *Dir Textile Arts*, Mendocino Art Center, Inc, Mendocino CA (S)

Jacobsen, Muriel, *Pres Board of Dir*, Maryhill Museum of Art, Goldendale WA

Jacobsen, Robert, *Cur Oriental Arts*, Minneapolis Institute of Arts, Minneapolis MN

Jacobsen, Ruth, *Slide Registry Chmn*, Women in the Arts Foundation, Inc, New York NY

Jacobson, Larry, *Coordr*, Advocates for the Arts, Los Angeles CA

Jacobson, Lee, *Instructor*, Chemeketa Community College, Department of Humanities & Social Science, Salem OR (S)

Jacobson, R I, *Chmn*, Carleton College, Department of Art History, Northfield MN (S)

Jacobson, Selma, *Second VPres, Archivist & Board of Dir*, Swedish American Museum Association of Chicago, Chicago IL

Jacobson, Thora E, *Adminr*, Philadelphia Museum of Art, Samuel S Fleisher Art Memorial, Philadelphia PA

Jacobson, Thora E, *Administrator*, Samuel S Fleisher Art Memorial, Philadelphia PA (S)

Jacobson, Warren, *Prof*, University of the South, Dept of Fine Arts, Sewanee TN (S)

Jacoby, R B, *VPres*, Mississippi Art Colony, Meridian MS

Jacoby, Thomas J, *Head*, University of Connecticut, Art and Design Library, Storrs CT

Jacomo, Edward, *Assoc Prof*, Alma College, Department of Art and Design, Alma MI (S)

Jacqmin, Alice, *First Asst*, Houston Public Library, Houston TX

Jacqmin, Alice, *First Asst*, Anna Maria College, Saint Luke's Gallery, Paxton MA

Jacques, Annie, *Conservateur*, Ecole Nle Superieure des Beaux-Arts, La Bibliotheque, Paris France

Jacques, Michael, *Asst Prof*, Emmanuel College, Art Department, Boston MA (S)

Jaffar, S M, *Cur*, Peshawar Museum, Peshawar Pakistan

Jaffe, A M, *Dir*, University of Cambridge, Fitzwilliam Museum, Cambridge England

Jaffe, Amanda, *Asst Prof*, Ohio Wesleyan University, Fine Arts Department, Delaware OH (S)

Jaffe, Hilde W, *Acting Dean*, Fashion Institute of Technology, New York NY (S)

Jaffe, Richard, *VPres*, Print Club, Philadelphia PA

Jahnigan, Debra, *Instructor*, Rehoboth Art League, Inc, Rehoboth Beach DE (S)

Jahos, Catherine, *Program Adminr*, Monmouth Museum and Cultural Center, Lincroft NJ

Jakob, Fred, *Supt*, Frick Collection, New York NY

Jakobsen, Kristian, *Dir*, Aarhus Kunstmuseum, Aarhus Art Museum, Aarhus Denmark

Jakstas, Alfred, *Conservator*, Art Institute of Chicago, Chicago IL

Jalet, Vanessa, *Dir Coordr*, Solomon R Guggenheim Museum, New York NY

Jameikis, Brone, *Keeper AV Center*, Honolulu Academy of Arts, Honolulu HI

James, Earl, *Adminr*, Decatur House, Washington DC

James, Earl, *Adminr*, Woodrow Wilson House, Washington DC

James, Henry, *Librn*, Sweet Briar College, Babcock Art Library, Sweet Briar VA

James, Jeanne, *Vis Prof*, Nebraska Wesleyan University, Art Dept, Lincoln NE (S)

James, Leslie, *Schools Service Officer*, Newport Museum and Art Gallery, Newport Wales

James, Philip, *Asst Prof*, James Madison University, Department of Art, Harrisonburg VA (S)

James, Sally, *Chmn*, Bemidji State University, Art Department, Bemidji MN (S)

Jameson, Collin, *Corresp Secy*, Key West Art and Historical Society, Key West FL

Jamieson, Charles F, *Assoc Prof*, Maryville College, Art Department, Saint Louis MO (S)

Jamison, Bill, *Executive Dir*, Western States Arts Foundation, Denver CO

Jamnik, Irmgard, *Cur*, Brant County Museum, Brantford ON

Jandova, Libuse, *Deputy Dir & Chief Graphic Art Coll*, Narodni Galerie v Prague, National Gallery of Prague, Prague Czechoslovakia

Janes, Gale, *Educ Head*, Tacoma Art Museum, Tacoma WA

Janick, Richard N, *Chairperson Dept Art*, Monterey Peninsula College, Art Department, Monterey CA (S)

Janis, Eugenia P, *Assoc Prof*, Wellesley College, Art Department, Wellesley MA (S)

Jankowski, Edward, *Asst Prof*, Monmouth College, Department of Art, West Long Branch NJ (S)

Janowicz, Jacqueline, *Gift Shop*, Rome Art and Community Center, Rome NY

Jansen, Catherine, *Instructor*, Bucks County Community College, Fine Arts Department, Newton PA (S)

Jansen, Charles, *Asst Prof*, Middle Tennessee State University, Art Dept, Murfreesboro TN (S)

Jansky, Rollin, *Chmn*, University of Wisconsin-Parkside, Art Discipline, Kenosha WI (S)

Janson, Anthony F, *Senior Cur*, Indianapolis Museum of Art, Indianapolis IN

Janssen, P L A, *Dir*, Gemeentemuseum Arnhem, Municipal Museum of Arnhem, Arnhem Netherlands

Janssen, Walter, *Department Dir*, Rheinisches Landesmuseum Bonn, Rhineland Museum, Bonn Germany, Federal Republic of

Jaramillo, Gloria, *Registrar*, Mexican Museum, San Francisco CA

Jarden, Richards, *Head Sculpture*, Rhode Island School of Design, Providence RI (S)

Jardine, Don, *Assoc Dir*, Art Instruction Schools, Minneapolis MN (S)

Jareckie, Stephen B, *Registrar & Cur Photography*, Worcester Art Museum, Worcester MA

Jared, Dorothy, *Secy*, University of Louisville, Allen R Hite Art Institute, Louisville KY

Jarkowski, Joseph, *Prof*, West Shore Community College, Div of Humanities & Fine Arts, Scottville MI (S)

Jarkowski, Stefania, *Art Gallery Dir*, Tuskegee Institute, George Washington Carver Museum, Tuskegee AL

Jaros, Miroslav, *Dir*, Statni Zidovske Muzeum, State Jewish Museum, Prague Czechoslovakia

Jarrett, James R, *Secy*, National Institute for Architectural Education, New York NY

Jaskevich, Jane, *Prof*, Polk Community College, Division of Communications and Fine Arts, Winter Haven FL (S)

Jasmin, Bernard, *Dir Visual Arts*, Universite Laval Cite Universitaire, School of Visual Arts, Quebec PQ (S)

Jasper, A Ben, *Head Art Dept*, Augustana College, Bergendorf Fine Arts Gallery, Rock Island IL

Jasper, Alvin Ben, *Chmn Dept*, Augustana College, Art Department, Rock Island IL (S)

Jay, Nancy, *Instr*, Valencia Community College, Art Department, Orlando FL (S)

Jaynes, Rebecca, *Comptroller*, Mississippi Museum of Art, Jackson MS

Jean-Bart, Gabrielle, *Instructor*, Traphagen School of Fashion, New York NY (S)

Jedrey, Micheline, *Assoc Librn*, Massachusetts Institute of Technology, Rotch Library of Architecture and Planning, Cambridge MA

Jefferies, J H, *Pres Board of Dir*, Museum of Northern British Columbia, Prince Rupert Museum Art Gallery, Prince Rupert BC

Jeffery, Antony, *Coordr Education Services*, London Regional Art Gallery, London ON

Jeffords Jr, Walter M, *VPres*, National Museum of Racing, Inc, Saratoga Springs NY

Jeffress, Charles, *Assoc Prof*, Louisiana College, Dept of Art, Pineville LA (S)

Jeffries, William W, *Dir*, United States Naval Academy Museum, Annapolis MD

Jeker, Werner, *Head Graphic Design Dept*, Lausanne College of Art and Design, Lausanne Switzerland (S)

Jendrzejewski, Amy Delap, *Asst Prof*, Vincennes University, Art Department, Vincennes IN (S)

Jenkins, Basil W R, *Cur*, Francis E Fowler Jr Foundation Museum, Beverly Hills CA

Jenkins, Donald, *Dir*, Portland Art Association, Portland OR

Jenkins, Edward C, *Treas*, Buck Hill Art Association, Buck Hill Falls PA

Jenkins, Harold R, *Librn*, Kansas City Public Library, Art & Music Department, Kansas City MO

Jenkins, Harvey C, *Chmn*, Fayetteville State University, Fayetteville NC (S)

Jenkins, Norma P H, *Librn*, Corning Museum of Glass, Corning Museum of Glass Library, Corning NY

Jenkins, Peter, *Clerk*, Worshipful Company of Goldsmiths, London England

Jenkins, Robert, *Instr*, Citrus Community College, Art Department, Azusa CA (S)

Jenkins, Stephen, *Preparator*, Contemporary Arts Center, Cincinnati OH

Jenkins, Suzanne, *Registrar*, National Portrait Gallery, Washington DC

Jenkins, Virginia, *Dir*, Central Michigan University, University Art Gallery, Mount Pleasant MI

Jenks, George M, *Librn*, Bucknell University, Ellen Clarke Bertrand Library, Lewisburg PA

Jennerjahn, W P, *Prof*, Adelphi University, Department of Art and Art History, Garden City NY (S)

Jennings, Edward, *Cur*, Talladega College, Savery Art Gallery, Talladega AL

Jennings, James W, *Dir*, Virginia Museum, Danville Museum of Fine Arts and History, Danville VA

Jennings, JoAnne, *Operations Mgr*, Quapaw Quarter Association, Inc, Villa Marre, Little Rock AR

Jennings, W Croft, *Chmn Museum Commission*, Columbia Museums of Art and Science, Columbia SC

Jensch, Anne, *Dir*, Maude Kerns Art Center School, Eugene OR (S)

Jensch, Anne, *Dir*, Maude I Kerns Art Center, Henry Korn Gallery, Eugene OR

Jensen, Carl, *Asst Prof*, University of Southern Colorado, Belmont Campus, Department of Art, Pueblo CO (S)

Jensen, David, *Dir of Installations*, Fort Worth Art Museum, Fort Worth TX

Jensen, James F, *Asst Cur Western Art & Publications Ed*, Honolulu Academy of Arts, Honolulu HI

Jensen, Janet M, *Personnel Coordr*, Peoria Art Guild, Peoria IL

Jensen, Knud W, *Dir*, Louisiana Museum of Modern Art, Humlebaek Denmark

Jensen, Molly, *Membership Coordr*, Tampa Museum, Tampa FL

Jensen, Olive, *Assoc Prof*, Texas Tech University, Department of Art, Lubbock TX (S)

Jensen, Robert, *Graphic Designer*, Walker Art Center, Minneapolis MN

Jensen, Robert A, *Assoc Prof*, Calvin College, Art Dept, Grand Rapids MI (S)

Jensen, William M, *Art History*, Baylor University, Department of Fine Arts, Waco TX (S)

Jeong, T H, *Dir Development*, School of Holography, Fine Arts Research and Holographic Center Museum, Chicago IL

Jepdrzejewski, Andrew, *Instructor*, Vincennes University, Art Department, Vincennes IN (S)

Jeppson, Gabrilla, *Asst Dir Cultural Affairs & Programs*, Harvard University, William Hayes Fogg Art Museum, Cambridge MA

Jergens, Robert, *Instr*, Cleveland Institute of Art, Cleveland OH (S)

Jerman, Majda, *Cur Exhib*, Moderna Galerija, Modern Art Gallery, Ljubljana Yugoslavia

Jerome, Andre, *Exhib*, Musee d'Art de Saint-Laurent, Saint-Laurent PQ

Jerry, Sylvester, *Education*, Racine Art Association, Racine WI

Jessiman, John, *Prof*, State University of New York College at Cortland, Art Department, Cortland NY (S)

Jessop, Gerald, *Dir*, Moose Jaw Art Museum and National Exhibition Centre, Moose Jaw SK

Jeswald, Joseph, *Dir*, Montserrat School of Visual Art, Beverly MA (S)

Jewesson, Kenneth R, *Dir*, Museum of Fine Arts, Alfred C Glassell Junior School of Art, Houston TX (S)

Jiggetts, Joseph, *Chmn Bd of Dir*, New Muse Community Museum of Brooklyn, Inc, Brooklyn NY

Jillings, Bess, *Public Relations*, University of Regina, Norman Mackenzie Art Gallery, Regina SK

Jimenez, Elizabeth, *Asst*, Museo de San Carlos, Biblioteca, Mexico Mexico

Jipson, James W, *Chmn*, Villa Maria College of Buffalo, Art Department, Buffalo NY (S)

Jircik, Nancy L, *Acting Chmn*, University of Saint Thomas, Art Department, Houston TX (S)

Jiversen, Bettina Byrd, *Chairperson*, Eureka Springs Guild of Artists and Crafts People, Eureka Springs AR

Joachim, Harold, *Cur Prints & Drawings*, Art Institute of Chicago, Chicago IL

Joanice, Mary, *Librn*, Briar Cliff College, Library, Sioux City IA

Jobb, Andor P, *Asst Prof*, Clarion State College, Hazel Sanford Gallery, Clarion PA

Joel, Abraham, *Head Conservator*, Detroit Institute of Arts, Detroit MI

Joglar, Raul, *Adminr*, Institute of Puerto Rican Culture, Museo de Bellas Artes, San Juan PR

Johannesen, Ole Ronning, *Chief Executive*, Lillehammer Bys Malerisamling, Lillehammer Art Museum, Lillehammer Norway

Johanson, George, *Instructor*, Portland Art Museum, Museum Art School, Portland OR (S)

John, Paul, *Exhibit Specialist*, Bower's Museum, Santa Ana CA

Johnes, Marjorie, *Head Cataloguer*, Saint Mary's College, Alumnae Centennial Library, Notre Dame IN

Johnson, Ann, *Periodicals Librn*, Saint Mary's College, Alumnae Centennial Library, Notre Dame IN

Johnson, Arthur H, *Cur*, University of New Mexico, Jonson Gallery, Albuquerque NM

Johnson, Betty, *Asst Prof*, University of Northern Colorado, Department of Fine Arts, Greeley CO (S)

Johnson, Bruce, *Kemble Coll*, California Historical Society, Library, San Francisco CA

Johnson, Byron, *Cur History*, Albuquerque Museum of Art, History and Science, Albuquerque NM

Johnson, Caryle, *Prof*, North Carolina Central University, Art Dept, Durham NC (S)

Johnson, Cathryne, *Cur Publications*, Colorado Historical Society, Colorado Heritage Center, Denver CO

Johnson, Cletus, *Asst Prof*, School of the Ozarks, Department of Art, Point Lookout MO (S)

Johnson, Dale R, *Assoc Prof*, Bethel College, Department of Art, Saint Paul MN (S)

Johnson, David, *Prog Dir*, Youngstown State University, Kilcawley Center Art Gallery, Youngstown OH

Johnson, David, *Acting Chairperson*, Indiana State University, Department of Humanities, Terre Haute IN (S)

Johnson, David, *Chmn*, Bethel College, Department of Art, Saint Paul MN (S)

Johnson, David S, *Head Dept*, Judson Baptist College, Department of Fine Arts, Portland OR (S)

Johnson, Don, *Head Dept*, Cochise College, Art Department, Douglas AZ (S)

Johnson, Dorothy E, *Pres*, Historical Society of Bloomfield, New Jersey, Bloomfield NJ

Johnson, Douglas, *Asst Prof*, University of Wisconsin-River Falls, Art Department, River Falls WI (S)

Johnson, Edith, *Secy & Treas*, Swedish American Museum Association of Chicago, Chicago IL

Johnson, Edna, *Dir*, Southampton Art School, Southampton ON (S)

Johnson, Ellen H, *Honorary Cur Modern Art*, Oberlin College, Allen Memorial Art Museum, Oberlin OH

Johnson, Elma, *Instructor*, University of North Carolina at Asheville, Dept of Art & Music, Asheville NC (S)

Johnson, Eric, *Pres*, West Hills Unitarian Fellowship, Portland OR

Johnson, Eugene, *Prof*, Bethel College, Department of Art, Saint Paul MN (S)

Johnson, Eugene J, *Chmn Dept*, Williams College, Department of Art, Williamstown MA (S)

Johnson, Evert A, *Cur Art*, Southern Illinois University Museum and Art Galleries, Carbondale IL

Johnson, George, *Exhib Designer*, University of California, Los Angeles, Museum of Cultural History, Los Angeles CA

Johnson, Gerald C, *Assoc Prof*, University of Colorado at Denver, Department of Fine Arts, Denver CO (S)

Johnson, Haynes, *Pres*, Stamford Museum and Nature Center, Stamford CT

Johnson, Ilse, *Assoc Prof*, Trenton State College, Art Department, Trenton NJ (S)

Johnson, James K, *Dept Chmn*, Eastern Illinois University, Art Department, Charleston IL (S)

Johnson, Jan, *Asst Librn*, Sweet Briar College, Babcock Art Library, Sweet Briar VA

Johnson, Jay, *Owner*, Jay Johnson, America's Folk Heritage Gallery, New York NY

Johnson, Jean H, *In Charge Art Coll*, Southeast Banking Corporation, Miami FL

Johnson, Josephine, *Second VPres*, Greater Gary Arts Council, Gary IN

Johnson, K A, *Asst Prof*, University of Nebraska Lincoln, Love Library, Lincoln NE

Johnson, Katherine King, *Chmn of Board*, Rutland Area Art Association, Inc, Chaffee Art Gallery, Rutland VT

Johnson, Kathryn C, *Acting Chmn Education*, Minneapolis Institute of Arts, Minneapolis MN

Johnson, Lester, *Chairperson*, Cypress College, Cypress CA (S)

Johnson, Lincoln F, *Chmn*, Goucher College, Art Department, Towson MD (S)

Johnson, Lincoln F, *Chmn Dept*, Goucher College, Kraushaar Auditorium Lobby Gallery, Towson MD

Johnson, Lois, *Secy*, Print Club, Philadelphia PA

Johnson, Lois, *VPres*, American Color Print Society, Philadelphia PA

Johnson, Louis W, *Adjunct Assoc Prof*, Catholic University of America, Department of Architecture & Planning, Washington DC (S)

Johnson, Lynne, *Instr*, Rivier College, Art Department, Nashua NH (S)

Johnson, Maurice, *Educ Chmn*, Art Association School, Spartanburg SC (S)

Johnson, Michael, *Instructor*, Murray State University, Art Department, Murray KY (S)

Johnson, Michael, *Instructor*, Santa Ana College, Art Department, Santa Ana CA (S)

Johnson, Millard, *Pres*, Phelps County Historical Society Museum, Holdrege NE

Johnson, Moira, *Education Officer*, National Art Gallery of New Zealand, Wellington New Zealand

Johnson, Nancy, *Research Librn*, American Academy and Institute of Arts and Letters, Library, New York NY

Johnson, Nancy Porter, *Dir Foundation*, University of Southwestern Louisiana, Art Center for Southwestern Louisiana, Lafayette LA

Johnson, Nota, *Instr*, Tulsa Junior College, Art Department, Tulsa OK (S)

Johnson, Pamela, *Asst Dir Programs*, American Association of Museums, Washington DC

Johnson, Paul, *Education Officer*, Sarjeant Gallery, Wanganui New Zealand

Johnson, Peter, *Asst Prof*, Smith College, Art Department, Northampton MA (S)

Johnson, Peter, *Instr*, Butler County Community College, Art Department, El Dorado KS (S)

Johnson, Philip, *Assoc Prof*, Black Hawk College, Art Dept, Moline IL (S)

Johnson, Rebecca, *Admin Asst*, Augustana College, Center for Western Studies, Sioux Falls SD

Johnson, Richard, *Pres*, Boothbay Region Art Gallery, Boothbay Harbor ME

Johnson, Richard A, *Chmn*, University of New Orleans, Dept of Fine Arts, New Orleans LA (S)

Johnson, Richard A, *Chmn Fine Arts*, University of New Orleans, Fine Arts Gallery, New Orleans LA

Johnson, Richard A, *Gallery Dir*, University of New Orleans, Fine Arts Gallery, New Orleans LA

Johnson, Robert F, *Cur Prints & Drawings*, Fine Arts Museums of San Francisco, M H de Young Memorial Museum and California Palace of the Legion of Honor

Johnson, Rodell, *VPres*, New Jersey Watercolor Society, Little Silver NJ

Johnson, Roger, *Chmn & Dir*, Lincoln County Cultural and Historical Association, Maine Art Gallery, Old Academy, Wiscasset ME

Johnson, Rosemary, *Cur Visual Art*, Supplementary Educational Center, Art Gallery, Salisbury NC

Johnson, Ruth Carter, *Pres*, Amon Carter Museum of Western Art, Fort Worth TX

Johnson, Susan, *Instructor*, Art Institute of Houston, Houston TX (S)

Johnson, Terence, *Chmn Studio Div*, Nova Scotia College of Art and Design, Halifax NS (S)

Johnson, Thano, *Instructor*, College of Marin, Department of Art, Kentfield CA (S)

Johnson, Theodore E, *Dir*, Shaker Museum, Poland Spring ME

Johnson, Theodore E, *Librn*, Shaker Museum, Shaker Library, Poland Spring ME

Johnson, Tom, *Instructor*, College of Marin, Department of Art, Kentfield CA (S)

Johnson, Wallace N, *Asst Prof*, Winona State University, Art Department, Winona MN (S)

Johnson, Walter C, *Asst Dir*, The Rosenbach Museum and Library, Philadelphia PA

Johnson, William R, *Chief Art & Music Division*, Brooklyn Public Library, Art and Music Division, Brooklyn NY

Johnson, Yankee, *Executive Dir*, King County Arts Commission, Seattle WA

Johnson Jr, Charles W, *Chmn*, University of Richmond, Department of Art, Richmond VA (S)

Johnson Sr, David, *Dir Visual Arts*, Benedict College, Visual Art Studies, Columbia SC (S)

Johnsson, Ulf G, *Head Royal Castles Coll*, Nationalmuseum, Stockholm Sweden

Johnsson, Ulf G, *Cur*, Svenska Statens Portrahsamling, Swedish State Portrait Gallery, Gothenburg Sweden

Johnston, Alexa, *Cur of New Zealand Paintings and Sculpture*, Auckland City Art Gallery, Auckland New Zealand

Johnston, Anne, *Public Information Officer*, Western Kentucky University, Kentucky Museum, Bowling Green KY

Johnston, Catherine, *Gallery Asst*, Simon Fraser University, Simon Fraser Gallery, Burnaby BC

Johnston, Gordon E, *Display Supv*, Department of Culture, Government of the Province of Alberta, Provincial Museum of Alberta, Edmonton AB

Johnston, James, *Prof*, Macomb County Community College, Art Department, Warren MI (S)

Johnston, Lilla, *Secy*, South Arkansas Art Center, El Dorado AR

Johnston, Maxine, *Pres*, Scottsdale Artists' League, Scottsdale AZ

Johnston, Patricia, *Dir of Gallery*, University of Montevallo, The Gallery, Montevallo AL

Johnston, Peggy, *Pres*, Mid-Southern Watercolorists, Little Rock AR

Johnston, Phillip, *Chief Cur & Cur Decorative Arts*, Wadsworth Atheneum, Hartford CT

Johnston, Richard, *Assoc Prof*, University of Utah, Art Department, Salt Lake City UT (S)

Johnston, Robert H, *Dir*, Rochester Institute of Technology, School of American Craftsmen, Rochester NY (S)

Johnston, Robert H, *Dean College*, Rochester Institute of Technology, College of Fine and Applied Arts, Rochester NY (S)

Johnston, Robert P, *Chmn*, Western Michigan University, Art History Division, Kalamazoo MI (S)

Johnston, Sona, *Assoc Cur Painting and Sculpture*, Baltimore Museum of Art, Baltimore MD

Johnston, Thomas V, *Head Dept*, California Polytechnic State University at San Luis Obispo, Art Department, San Luis Obispo CA (S)

Johnston, W Robert, *Registrar*, National Collection of Fine Arts, Washington DC

Johnston, William R, *Asst Dir*, Walters Art Gallery, Baltimore MD

Johnstone, Martha, *Pres*, Keokuk Art Center, Keokuk IA

Johonsen, L, *Dir*, Ny Carlsberg Glyptothek, Carlsberg Gallery, Copenhagen Denmark

Jolles, Arnold H, *Dir*, Seattle Art Museum, Seattle WA

Jolley, Milt, *Asst Dir*, Utah Travel Council, Salt Lake City UT

Jolly, Robert, *Head*, Presbyterian College, Fine Arts Department, Clinton SC (S)

Jolly, Robert, *Assoc Prof of Art*, Presbyterian College, James H Thomason Library, Clinton SC

Jolly, Robert, *Chmn*, Tennessee Wesleyan College, Department of Art, Athens TN (S)

Joly, Cyril M, *Pres*, Waterville Historical Association, Waterville ME

Jonas, Allen A, *Chmn Dept*, Bluefield State College, Art Department, Bluefield WV (S)

Jones, Allan L, *Chmn*, Antioch College, Department of Art, Yellow Springs OH (S)

Jones, Anne, *Executive Secy*, Wichita Falls Museum and Art Center, Wichita Falls TX

Jones, Annette D, *Education Coordr*, Tampa Museum, Tampa FL

Jones, Anthony, *Chmn*, Texas Christian University, Art Department, Fort Worth TX (S)

Jones, Benjamin, *Asst Prof*, Jersey City State College, Art Department, Jersey City NJ (S)

Jones, Betsy B, *Assoc Dir & Cur of Paintings*, Smith College, Museum of Art, Northampton MA

Jones, Betty, *Office Secy*, Virginia Museum, Danville Museum of Fine Arts and History, Danville VA

Jones, Bob, *Chmn of the Board*, Bob Jones University, Greenville SC

Jones, Brian H, *Asst Prof*, Indiana University Southeast, Fine Arts Department, New Albany IN (S)

Jones, Charles J, *Assoc Prof*, Saint Louis Community College at Florissant Valley, Department of Art, Ferguson MO (S)

Jones, Charlott, *Asst Prof*, Arkansas State University, Department of Art, State University AR (S)

Jones, Dancy, *Admin Asst*, Tennessee State Museum, Nashville TN

Jones, David, *Dir*, Tucson Museum of Art School, Tucson AZ (S)

Jones, David L, *Cur Educ*, Tucson Museum of Art, Tucson AZ

Jones, Don, *VPres*, Western Association of Art Museums, San Francisco CA

Jones, Frances F, *Cur Coll*, Princeton University, Art Museum, Princeton NJ

Jones, Frank, *Assoc Prof*, Palomar College, Art Department, San Marcos TX (S)

Jones, Frederick N, *Instructor*, Guilford Technical Institute, Commercial Art Dept, Jamestown NC (S)

Jones, Gail, *Secy*, University of Notre Dame, Snite Museum of Art, Notre Dame IN

Jones, Gerard, *Secy*, Louis Comfort Tiffany Foundation, Great Neck NY

Jones, Harold, *Secy*, Singing River Art Association Inc, L & N Railroad Depot Gallery, Pascagoula MS

Jones, Harold, *Coordr Photography*, University of Arizona, Department of Art, Tucson AZ (S)

Jones, Harvey L, *Deputy Cur Art*, Oakland Museum, Oakland CA

Jones, Herbert A, *Pres*, Albany Institute of History and Art, Albany NY

Jones, Howard, *Prof*, University of New Orleans, Dept of Fine Arts, New Orleans LA (S)

Jones, J T, *Publications Mgr*, Birmingham Museums and Art Gallery, Birmingham England

Jones, James, *Pres*, Calgary Artists Society, Calgary AB

Jones, James E, *Assoc Prof*, Morgan State University, Department of Art, Baltimore MD (S)

Jones, Jameson J, *Pres*, Memphis Academy of Arts, Frank T Tobey Gallery, Memphis TN

Jones, Jameson M, *Pres*, Memphis Academy of Arts, Memphis TN (S)

Jones, J Kenneth, *Cur Decorative Arts*, Charleston Museum, Charleston SC

Jones, Johanna, *Secy*, Taos Art Association Inc, Taos NM

Jones, John L, *Chmn*, Fine Arts Museums of San Francisco, The Museum Society, n of Honor co

Jones, Judy Voss, *Instructor*, Converse College, Art Dept, Spartanburg SC (S)

Jones, Julie, *Cur Primitive Art*, Metropolitan Museum of Art, New York NY

Jones, Justin, *Staff Asst*, Saint Gregory's Abbey and College, Mabee-Gerrer Museum, Shawnee OK

Jones, Leigh Rehner, *Historic Site Mgr*, Palisades Interstate Park Commission, Senate House State Historic Site, Kingston NY

Jones, Lewis, *Vis Prof*, University of South Carolina, Department of Art, Columbia SC (S)

Jones, Linda, *Asst Dir & Cur Educ*, Loveland Museum, Loveland CO

Jones, Lora W, *Dir Community Affairs*, E R Squibb & Sons, Inc, Princeton NJ

Jones, Maedine, *Asst Cur*, Plains Indians & Pioneer Historical Foundation, Pioneer Museum & Art Center, Woodward OK

Jones, Margaret, *Correspondence Secy*, Coppini Academy of Fine Arts, San Antonio TX

Jones, Marvin H, *Assoc Prof*, Cleveland State University, Art Department, Cincinnati OH (S)

Jones, Melissa, *Cur of Education*, Gaston County Art and History Museum, Dallas NC

Jones, Michael, *Dir*, Wright State University, Fine Arts Gallery, Dayton OH

Jones, Michael, *Adjunct Assoc*, Wright State University, Art Department, Dayton OH (S)

Jones, Pauline, *Sales Gallery Mgr*, Amarillo Art Center, Amarillo TX

Jones, Phyllis, *Secy*, Virginia Museum, Danville Museum of Fine Arts and History, Danville VA

Jones, R L, *Chmn*, Shepherd College, Art Department, Shepherdstown WV (S)

Jones, Robert, *Instructor*, Northeast Missouri State University, Art Department, Kirksville MO (S)

Jones, Roder H, *Assoc Prof*, Morehead State University, Art Department, Morehead KY (S)

Jones, Ron, *Prof*, University of the South, Dept of Fine Arts, Sewanee TN (S)

Jones, Timothy, *Pres*, Manchester Historic Association, Manchester NH

Jones, Wallace, *Finance*, Plastic Club, Art Club for Women, Philadelphia PA

Jones, Warren E, *Vice Chmn Board Trustees*, McMichael Canadian Collection, Kleinburg ON

Jones, William E, *Cur of Decorative Arts*, Los Angeles County Museum of Art, Los Angeles CA

Jones, Yvonne, *Keeper Applied Art*, Central Art Gallery, Wolverhampton England

Jongue, Serge, *Asst Cur*, Pavilion of Humour, Man and His World, Montreal PQ

Jonson, Raymond, *Dir*, University of New Mexico, Jonson Gallery, Albuquerque NM

Jonsson, Halldor J, *Cur*, Thjodminjasafn, National Museum of Iceland, Rrykjavik Iceland

Joosten, E, *Deputy Dir*, Ryksmuseum Kroller-Muller, Kroller-Muller State Museum, Otterlo Netherlands

Joosten, J M, *Research Cur*, Stedlijk Museum-Amsterdam, Municipal Museum, Amsterdam Netherlands

Joost-Gaugier, Christiane L, *Head Dept*, New Mexico State University, Art Dept, Las Cruces NM (S)

Joppien, Rüdiger, *Staff*, Museen der Stadt Köln, Kunstgewerbemuseum der Stadt Köln, Cologne Germany, Federal Republic of

Jordan, Dan, *Vis Prof*, Marion College, Art Department, Marion IN (S)

Jordan, H Glenn, *Executive Dir*, Oklahoma Historical Society, Central Museum, Oklahoma City OK

Jordan, I Douglas, *Instr*, Utah Technical College at Salt Lake, Commercial Art Department, Salt Lake City UT (S)

Jordan, Jack, *Head Dept*, Southern University in New Orleans, Art Dept, New Orleans LA (S)

Jordan, James W, *Assoc Prof*, Antioch College, Department of Art, Yellow Springs OH (S)

Jordan, Jim, *Film Dept Chmn*, Art Center College of Design, Pasadena CA (S)

Jordan, Julia, *Dir*, Rocky Mount Arts and Crafts Center, Rocky Mount NC

Jordan, Marie, *Slide Librn*, Art Center College of Design, James Lemont Fogg Memorial Library, Pasadena CA

Jordan, William B, *Dir*, Southern Methodist University, Meadows Museum, Dallas TX

Jordan, William B, *Dir of Meadows Museum*, Southern Methodist University, Division of Art and Art History, Dallas TX (S)

Jordan, William B, *Dir*, Southern Methodist University, University Gallery, Dallas TX

Jordre, Emma M, *Prog Coordr*, University of Wisconsin, Madison, School of Family Resources and Consumer Sciences, Madison WI (S)

Jorgensen, David, *Instructor*, Salve Regina the Newport College, Art Department, Newport RI (S)

Jorgensen, Sandra, *Chairperson Art Dept*, Elmhurst College, Art Department, Elmhurst IL (S)

Jorgenson, Dean Dale, *Head Div Fine Arts*, Northeast Missouri State University, Art Department, Kirksville MO

Jorgenson, Lynn, *Western Assoc of Art Museums Exec Dir*, Museum Management Institute, San Francisco CA (S)

Jorgenson, Lynn, *Executive Dir*, Western Association of Art Museums, San Francisco CA

Jornaes, Bjarne, *Cur*, Thorvaldsen Museum, Copenhagen Denmark

Joseph, Bruce, *Intrepretations*, Oklahoma Historical Society, Central Museum, Oklahoma City OK

Joseph, Philip M, *Asst Prof*, Miami University, Art Department, Oxford OH (S)

Josephs, John, *Chmn*, Artists Guild Inc of New York, New York NY

Joslin, Elizabeth, *Admin*, Bundy Art Gallery, Waitsfield VT

Joslyn, Cathie, *Asst Prof*, Clarion State College, Department of Art, Clarion PA (S)

Joubert, Jean, *Registrar & Preparator*, Wichita Falls Museum and Art Center, Wichita Falls TX

Joundi, Adman, *Cur*, National Museum of Damascus, Damascus Syria

Jovine, Marcel, *Art Advisory Board*, Society of Medalists, Danbury CT

Joyal, Me Serge, *VPres*, Musee d'Art de Joliette, Joliette PQ

Joyaux, Alain, *Asst Dir*, Flint Institute of Arts, Flint MI

Joyce, Henry, *Cur Satellite Galleries*, Bronx Museum of the Arts, Bronx NY

Joyce, Kathleen, *Assoc Prof*, Rocky Mountain College, Art Dept, Billings MT (S)

Joyner, Charles, *Dir Design Fundamentals*, North Carolina State University at Raleigh, School of Design, Raleigh NC (S)

Joyner, Marjorie Hake, *Librn*, Ball State University, Architecture Library, Muncie IN

Jörg, C J A, *Cur Oriental Ceramics*, Groningen Museum voor Stad en Land, Groningen Museum, Groningen Netherlands

Ju, I-Hsiung, *Prof*, Washington and Lee University, Department of Fine Arts, Lexington VA (S)

Judkins, Helen, *Art Gallery Dir*, Pointe Claire Cultural Centre, Pointe Claire PQ

Judkins, W O, *Prof*, McGill University, Department of Art History, Montreal PQ (S)

Judson, Jay Richard, *Chmn*, University of North Carolina at Chapel Hill, Art Department, Chapel Hill NC (S)

Judson, J Richard, *Prof*, University of North Carolina at Chapel Hill, Art Department, Chapel Hill NC (S)

Judson, William, *Cur Film Section*, Carnegie Institute, Museum of Art, Pittsburgh PA

Juhasz, Elaine, *Assoc Prof*, Youngstown State University, Art Department, Youngstown OH (S)

Julian, Joanne, *Head Dept*, College of the Canyons, Art Department, Valencia CA (S)

Julio, Pat T, *Dept Head*, Western State College, Quigley Hall Art Gallery, Gunnison CO

Jumonville, Florence, *Librn*, Historic New Orleans Collection, Library, New Orleans LA

Jung, Michael, *Chmn Dept*, Denison University, Department of Art, Granville OH (S)

Jungblut, Fran, *Secy*, DuPage Art League, Wheaton IL

Jungels, Robert, *Acting Head Film*, Rhode Island School of Design, Providence RI (S)

Juristo, Michelle S, *Asst Cur*, University of South Florida, University Galleries, Tampa FL

Jussel, Christian, *Treas*, National Antique and Art Dealers Association of America, New York NY

Justmann, C Robert, *Pres*, Dubuque Art Association, Old Jail Gallery, Dubuque IA

K, Harold, *Co-Dir*, Museum Management Institute, San Francisco CA (S)

Kaasa, W H, *Secy*, Alberta Art Foundation, Edmonton AB

Kaaver, Del, *VPres*, Hutchinson Art Association, Hutchinson KS

Kabelac, Ursula, *Librn Asst*, Hamburger Kunsthalle, Bibliothek der Hamburger Kunsthalle, Hamburg Germany, Federal Republic of

Kabriel, J Ronald, *Asst Prof*, Catholic University of America, Department of Architecture & Planning, Washington DC (S)

Kachel, Harold S, *Museum Dir*, No Man's Land Historical Society, Goodwell OK

Kachel, Joan Overton, *Cur & Secy*, No Man's Land Historical Society, Goodwell OK

Kadish, Skip, *Instructor*, Monterey Peninsula College, Art Department, Monterey CA (S)

Kaericher, John, *Coll Coordr*, Northwestern College, Ramaker Library Art Gallery, Orange City IA

Kaericher, John, *Chmn Dept*, Northwestern College, Art Department, Orange City IA (S)

Kaganoff, Nathan M, *Librn*, American Jewish Historical Society, Lee M Friedman Memorial Library, Waltham MA

Kagle, Joe, *Dir*, Southeast Arkansas Arts and Science Center, Pine Bluff AR

Kagle, Joseph L, *Dir*, Southeast Arkansas Arts and Science Center, Little Firehouse Studio, Pine Bluff AR (S)

Kahan, Mitchell D, *Cur*, Montgomery Museum of Fine Arts, Montgomery AL

Kahler, Richard F, *Pres*, Rome Historical Society, Rome Information and Cultural Center, Rome NY

Kahmeyer, Ray, *Assoc Prof*, Bethany College, Lindsborg KS (S)

Kahn, H Peter, *Prof*, Cornell University, Department of the History of Art, Ithaca NY (S)

Kahn, Herbert, *Cur*, Exchange National Bank of Chicago, Chicago IL

Kahr, Madlyn, *Prof*, University of California, San Diego, Visual Arts Department, La Jolla CA (S)

Kain, Jay D, *Chmn Dept*, Mansfield State College, Art Department, Mansfield PA (S)

Kakis, Juris, *Chmn Dept*, Ohio Dominican College, Art Department, Columbus OH (S)

Kakudo, Yoshiko, *Cur Japanese Art*, Asian Art Museum of San Francisco, Avery Brundage Collection, San Francisco CA

Kakutani, Mitsuo, *Artist-in-Res*, Earlham College, Art Department, Richmond IN (S)

Kalb, Marty, *Assoc Prof*, Ohio Wesleyan University, Fine Arts Department, Delaware OH (S)

Kalbacher, Billie, *Office Mgr*, Guild Hall of East Hampton, Inc, Museum Section, East Hampton NY

Kale, Louise, *Registrar*, College of William and Mary, Department of Fine Arts Gallery, Williamsburg VA

Kalenberg, Angel, *Dir*, Museo Nacional de Artes Plasticas, National Museum of Fine Arts, Montevideo Uruguay

Kaleshefski, Martha Rochester, *Asst Prof*, College Misericordia, Art Department, Dallas PA (S)

Kaleshefski, Ralph G, *Chmn Dept*, College Misericordia, Art Department, Dallas PA (S)

Kalk, Joan, *Lectr*, Felician College, Art Department, Chicago IL (S)

Kalla, Ron, *Asst Prof*, Beaver College, Department of Fine Arts, Glenside PA (S)

Kallenberger, Klaus, *Assoc Prof*, Middle Tennessee State University, Art Dept, Murfreesboro TN (S)

Kamansky, David, *Dir*, Pacific - Asia Museum, Pasadena CA

Kamber, Andre, *Conservator*, Kunstmuseum Solothurn, Solothurn Art Museum, Solothurn Switzerland

Kaminsky, Vera, *Coordr Fibers*, University of Delaware, Department of Art, Newark DE (S)

Kamm, Keith, *Bibliographer*, Athenaeum of Philadelphia, Philadelphia PA

Kamon, Yasuo, *Executive Dir*, Bridgestone Bijutsukan, Bridgestone Museum of Art, Tokyo Japan

Kampen, Michael, *Assoc Prof*, University of North Carolina-Charlotte, Creative Arts Dept, Charlotte NC (S)

Kampen, Natalie, *Asst Prof*, University of Rhode Island, Department of Art, Kingston RI (S)

Kampen, Owen, *Instr*, Madison Area Technical College, Communication Arts, Madison WI (S)

Kampiziones, Andrew, *Board Pres*, Florence Museum, Florence SC

Kamrowski, Gerome, *Exhib Dir*, University of Michigan Museum of Art, Slusser Gallery, Ann Arbor MI

Kan, Michael, *Cur Ethnographic Art*, Detroit Institute of Arts, Detroit MI

Kane, Jean DuVal, *Dir Coll*, Valentine Museum, Richmond VA

Kane, Lila, *Instructor*, Springfield College, Department of Visual and Performing Arts, Springfield MA (S)

Kane, Marian, *Asst Cur*, Madison Art Center, Madison WI

Kane, Susan, *Asst Prof*, Oberlin College, Department of Art, Oberlin OH (S)

Kaneko, James S, *Chmn*, American River College, Department of Art, Sacramento CA (S)

Kaneko, John H, *Instr*, American River College, Department of Art, Sacramento CA (S)

Kaneko, Jun, *Head Ceramics Dept*, Cranbrook Academy of Art, Bloomfield Hills MI (S)

Kang, Ingu, *Cur in Charge of Archaeology*, National Museum of Korea, Seoul Korea

Kang, Shin Theke, *Cur*, University of Illinois, World Heritage Museum, Champaign IL

Kangas, Gene, *Assoc Prof*, Cleveland State University, Art Department, Cincinnati OH (S)

Kaniaris, Peter, *Instructor*, Albion College, Department of Visual Arts, Albion MI (S)

Kanowicz, Dina McDonald, *Dir*, High Plains Museum, Library, McCook NE

Kanwischer, Ed, *Instr*, College of Lake County, Art Department, Grayslake IL (S)

Kaplan, Alice M, *Exec VPres*, Museum of American Folk Art, New York NY

Kaplan, Joyce, *Treas*, Artist-Craftsmen of New York, New York NY

Kaplan, Julius, *Chmn Art Dept*, California State College San Bernardino, College Art Galleries, San Bernardino CA

Kaplan, Julius, *Chmn Dept*, California State College at San Bernardino, Fine Arts Department, San Bernardino CA (S)

Kaplan, Leon, *Asst to the Dir*, Arkansas Arts Center, Little Rock AR

Kaplan, Stanley, *Prof*, Nassau Community College, Art Department, Garden City NY (S)

Kappen, Larry, *Instructor*, Monterey Peninsula College, Art Department, Monterey CA (S)

Kaprielian, Walter, *VPres*, Art Directors Club, Inc, New York NY

Kaprow, Allan, *Prof*, University of California, San Diego, Visual Arts Department, La Jolla CA (S)

Karabatsos, Lewis, *Pres*, Lowell Art Association, Whistler House and Parker Gallery, Lowell MA

Karalis, Constantine, *Dir*, Pratt Institute, School of Architecture, Brooklyn NY (S)

Karatzas, Steven, *Chmn Dept*, Linfield College, Art Department, McMinnville OR (S)

Karberg, Richard, *Assoc Prof*, Cuyahoga Community College, Department of Art, Cleveland OH (S)

Kardon, Janet, *Dir*, University of Pennsylvania, Institute of Contemporary Art, Philadelphia PA

Karl, Maggie, *Dir*, Coos Art Museum, Coos Bay OR

Karlin, Renata, *Dir*, Henry Street Settlement Arts for Living Center, New York NY (S)

Karlstrom, Paul, *Dir*, Archives of American Art, West Coast Area Center; de Young Museum, New York NY

Karmel, Karen, *Asst Cur Educ*, Midwest Museum of American Art, Elkhart IN

Karo, Jerzy, *Head School Graphics*, Leicester Polytechnic, Faculty of Art and Design, Leicester England (S)

Karoblis, Dalija, *Asst Town Librn*, Brookline Public Library, Brookline MA

Karolyi, Janet, *Secy*, California State University, Chico, Art Gallery, Chico CA

Karow, Betty, *Librn*, Milwaukee Art Center, Library, Milwaukee WI

Karpel, Eli, *Prof*, Pierce College, Art Department, Woodland Hills CA (S)

Karpowicz, Terrence, *VPres*, N.A.M.E. Gallery, Chicago IL

Karr, Ina, *Treas*, Lyme Art Association, Inc, Old Lyme CT

Karraker, Jack, *Chmn Dept*, Kearney State College, Dept of Art, Kearney NE (S)

Karsina, James, *Assoc Prof*, Aquinas College, Art Department, Grand Rapids MI (S)

Karterud, Arvin, *Cur*, Lyman Allyn Museum, New London CT

Karther, Alex, *Asst Prof*, Texas Tech University, Department of Art, Lubbock TX (S)

Karunanayake, C I, *Librn*, Colombo National Museum, Library, Colombo Sri Lanka

Karwosia, Richard, *Assoc Prof*, New York City Community College of the City University of New York, Department of Art and Advertising Design, Brooklyn NY (S)

Kasakaitis, Jurgis, *Head Librn*, Balzekas Museum of Lithuanian Culture, Balzekas Museum Research Library, Chicago IL

Kasal, Robert, *Prof*, Portland State University, Department of Art and Architecture, Portland OR (S)

Kasper, Sandy, *Music Coordr*, Ashtabula Arts Center, Ashtabula OH

Kass, Emily, *Acting Cur Education*, Walker Art Center, Minneapolis MN

Kassel, Barbara, *Asst Prof*, Colby College, Art Dept, Waterville ME (S)

Kassenaar, J, *VPres*, Winnipeg Art Gallery, Winnipeg MB

Kassiday, Sharlene, *Instructor*, Joliet Junior College, Art Dept, Joliet IL (S)

Kasson, Michael, *Head of Maintenance Dept*, Topeka Public Library, Gallery of Fine Arts, Topeka KS

Kassoy, Bernard, *Instructor*, Harriet FeBland Art Workshop, New York NY (S)

Kassoy, Hortense, *Instructor*, Harriet FeBland Art Workshop, New York NY (S)

Katopis, Beverly, *Librn I*, Yonkers Public Library, Fine Arts Department, Yonkers NY

Katsaros, Aliki, *Asst to the Dir*, Fitchburg Art Museum, Fitchburg MA

Katsiff, Bruce, *Chairperson Dept*, Bucks County Community College, Fine Arts Department, Newton PA (S)

Katsiff, Bruce, *Chairperson*, Bucks County Community College, Newtown PA

Katter, Eldon, *Gallery Coordr*, Kutztown State College, Sharadin Art Gallery, Kutztown PA

Katz, Alice, *Asst Prof*, University of Illinois at the Medical Center, Dept of Biocommunication Arts-Medical Art, Chicago IL (S)

Katz, Guiliana, *Lectr*, Toronto Art Therapy Institute, Toronto ON (S)

Katz, Janet, *Prog Coordr*, Queens Museum, Flushing NY

Katz, Karl, *Chmn Special Projects*, Metropolitan Museum of Art, New York NY

Katz, Mel, *VPres*, Portland Center for the Visual Arts, Portland OR

Katz, Melvin, *Prof*, Portland State University, Department of Art and Architecture, Portland OR (S)

Katz, Robert I, *Head Drawing*, Southern Illinois University at Edwardsville, Department of Art and Design, Edwardsville IL (S)

Katz, Theodore, *Chief Division Educ*, Philadelphia Museum of Art, Philadelphia PA

Katzive, David H, *Asst Dir Education & Program Development*, Brooklyn Museum, Brooklyn NY

Kauffman, C, *Keeper Paintings, Prints, Drawings & Photographs*, Victoria and Albert Museum, London England

Kaufman, Barbara, *Asst Prof*, Seton Hall University, Department of Art and Music, South Orange NJ (S)

Kaufman, Barbara W, *Cur Exhib*, Seton Hall University, Student Center Art Gallery, South Orange NJ

Kaufman, Irving, *Prof*, City College of the City of New York, Art Department, New York NY (S)

Kaufman, James C, *Assoc Prof*, Miami University, Art Department, Oxford OH (S)

Kaufman, Jane, *Chief Cataloguer*, Harvard University, Fine Arts Library, Cambridge MA

Kaufman, Suzanne, *Instructor*, Rock Valley College, Dept of Art, Rockford IL (S)

Kaufmann, Christian, *Cur Oceania*, Museum für Völkerkunde und Schweizerisches Museum für Volkskunde Basel, Museum of Ethnological Collections and Folklore, Basel Switzerland

Kaufmann, Robert C, *Librn*, Cooper-Hewitt Museum, Doris and Henry Dreyfuss Study Center, New York NY

Kaul, Marlin, *Assoc Prof*, Bemidji State University, Art Department, Bemidji MN (S)

Kaulitz, Garry, *Instructor*, Louisville School of Art, Anchorage KY (S)

Kawakita, Michiaki, *Dir*, Kyoto Kokuritsu Kindai Bijutsukan, National Museum of Modern Art, Kyoto, Kyoto Japan

Kay, Susan, *Assoc Prof*, College of Mount Saint Vincent, Fine Arts Department, Riverdale NY (S)

Kaya, Douglas, *Head Div*, Leeward Community College, Arts and Humanities Division, Pearl City HI (S)

Kaye, George, *Treas*, School Art League of New York City, Brooklyn NY

Kays, William Keith, *Dir of Museum School*, Sierra Nevada Museum of Art, Reno NV

Kayser, Thomas A, *Dir Art Center*, Kalamazoo Institute of Arts, Genevieve and Donald Gilmore Art Center, Kalamazoo MI

Keam, Grace S, *Reference Librn*, Cincinnati Art Museum, Library, Cincinnati OH

Keane, Patricia E, *Head Art Section*, Chicago Public Library, Art Section, Fine Arts Division, Chicago IL

Keane, Terence, *Cur*, Elizabet Ney Museum, Austin TX

Kearney, John, *Dir*, Contemporary Art Workshop, Chicago IL

Kearney, John W, *Dir*, Contemporary Art Workshop, Chicago IL (S)

Kearney, Lynn, *Admin Dir*, Contemporary Art Workshop, Chicago IL

Kearney, Lynn, *Admin Dir*, Contemporary Art Workshop, Chicago IL (S)

Kearns, Jerry L, *Reference Section*, Library of Congress, Washington DC

Kearns, Lola, *Dir Arts in Special Education Project*, Pennsylvania Department of Education, Arts in Education Program, Harrisburg PA

Kearse, Dieter Morris, *Dir Planning & Development*, New Museum, New York NY

Keator, David, *Instructor*, Louisville School of Art, Anchorage KY (S)

Keats, Norman, *Prof*, University of Wisconsin-Stevens Point, Department of Art, Stevens Point WI (S)

Keaveney, R, *Cur*, National Gallery of Ireland, Dublin Ireland

Keaveney, Sydney Starr, *Art and Architecture Librn*, Pratt Institute Library, Brooklyn NY

Kebrle, John, *Second VPres*, Stained Glass Association of America, Bronxville NY

Keech, John, *Asst Prof*, Arkansas State University, Department of Art, State University AR (S)

Keech, John, *Chmn Exhib*, Arkansas State University Art Gallery, Jonesboro, Springdale AR

Keefe, Gerald, *VPres*, Florida Gulf Coast Art Center, Inc, Clearwater FL

Keefe, Katharine Lee, *Cur*, University of North Carolina, The Ackland Art Museum, Chapel Hill NC

Keegan, Dan, *Asst Prof*, Graceland College, Art Department, Lamoni IA (S)

Keel, Chad, *Vis Prof*, Nebraska Wesleyan University, Art Dept, Lincoln NE (S)

Keeler, David, *Chief Office of Exhib & Design*, National Collection of Fine Arts, Washington DC

Keeley, Shelagh, *Cur Asst*, York University Art Gallery, Downsview ON

Keeling, Henry C, *Coordr*, University of Charleston, Art Department, Charleston WV (S)

Keen, Betty, *Registrar*, Birmingham Museum of Art, Birmingham AL

Keene, Paul, *Instructor*, Bucks County Community College, Fine Arts Department, Newton PA (S)

Keene, R, *Asst Dir*, Johannesburg Art Gallery, Johannesburg South Africa, Republic of

Keener, Scott, *Secy*, University of North Carolina at Greensboro, Weatherspoon Art Gallery, Greensboro NC

Keener, William G, *Acting Dir*, Ohio Historical Society, Columbus OH

Keeney, Allen L, *Dir*, Sweetwater Community Fine Arts Center, Rock Springs WY

Keens, Bill, *Ed*, American Council for the Arts, New York NY

Keiser, Dale, *Second VPres*, Toledo Artists' Club, Toledo OH

Keith, Douglas S, *VPres*, Great Lakes Historical Society, Vermilion OH

Keith, Marie C, *Asst Librn & Indexer of Photographs*, Frick Art Reference Library, New York NY

Kelder, Diane, *Prof*, City University of New York, PhD Program in Art History, New York NY (S)

Kelemen, Boris, *Dir*, Galerije Grada Zagreba, City Art Galleries, Zagreb Yugoslavia

Kelemen, Boris, *Chief Cur*, Galerije Grada Zagreba, Galerija Primitivne Umjetnosti, Zagreb Yugoslavia

Kelleher, Radford D, *Publisher*, Metropolitan Museum of Art, New York NY

Keller, Douglas, *Head Dept*, Coffeyville Community Junior College, Art Department, Coffeyville KS (S)

Keller, John, *Instructor*, Harding University, Department of Art, Searcy AR (S)

Keller, Marjorie, *Asst Prof*, University of Rhode Island, Department of Art, Kingston RI (S)

Keller, Steven, *Asst to the Dean*, Hartford Art School of the University of Hartford, West Hartford CT (S)

Kellett, Mary, *Librn*, Joslyn Art Museum, Art Reference Library, Omaha NE

Kelley, C Regina, *Asst Prof*, University of Maine, Art Department, Orono ME (S)

Kelley, Cecilia, *Instr*, Schoolcraft College, Department of Art, Livonia MI (S)

Kelley, Donald C, *Art GAllery Dir*, Boston Athenaeum, Boston MA

Kelley, Geraldine, *Prog Educational Services Coordr*, Southern Illinois University Museum and Art Galleries, Carbondale IL

Kelley, Helen, *Prof*, California Polytechnic State University at San Luis Obispo, Art Department, San Luis Obispo CA (S)

Kelley, John, *Photo Technician*, University of South Carolina, Slide Library, Columbia SC

Kelley, Leo, *Chmn Liberal Arts*, Swain School of Design, New Bedford MA (S)

Kelley, Terry, *Instructor*, Your Heritage House, Inc, Detroit MI

Kellough, Booth, *Pres & Dir Art Exhib*, West Baton Rouge Museum, Port Allen LA

Kelly, Amanda, *Accountant*, Artworlds Center for Creative Arts, Ann Arbor MI

Kelly, Ardie L, *Librn*, Mariners Museum, Library, Newport News VA

Kelly, Charlotte, *Cur Slide & Photograph Library & Art History Teaching Coll*, University of Delaware, University Art Collections, Newark DE

Kelly, Clyde, *Prof*, Los Angeles City College, Department of Art, Los Angeles CA (S)

Kelly, Columba, *Chmn*, Saint Meinrad College, Department of Art, Saint Meinrad IN (S)

Kelly, Elinor, *Librn*, Eastern Washington State Historical Society, Library, Spokane WA

Kelly, J H, *Keeper of Social History*, Stoke-on-District Council, City Museum and Art Gallery, Hanley England

Kelly, James, *Chief Researcher*, Tennessee State Museum, Nashville TN

Kelly, Lloyd L, *Pres of the Board*, Roberson Center, Binghamton NY

Kelly, Margaret, *Recording Secy*, Florida Artist Group Inc, Englewood FL

Kelly, M Teresita, *Instructor*, Edgewood College, Art Department, Madison WI (S)

Kelly, Perry, *Assoc Prof*, Western Carolina University, Dept of Art, Cullowhee NC (S)

Kelly, Vincent N, *Instructor*, Yavapai College, Art Department, Prescott AZ (S)

Kelly, William, *Dean School Art*, Victorian College of the Arts, School of Art, Melbourne Australia (S)

Kelly, William, *Assoc Prof*, Bemidji State University, Art Department, Bemidji MN (S)

Kelm, Don, *Chmn*, Northern Kentucky University, Fine Arts Department, Highland Heights KY (S)

Kelsey, Darwin P, *VPres Museum Admin*, Old Sturbridge Village, Sturbridge MA

Kelson, H Eugene, *Adminr*, National Collection of Fine Arts, Washington DC

Kemeny, Lydia, *Head Fashion Design*, Saint Martins School of Art, London England (S)

Kemp, Betty R, *Dir*, Lee County Library, Tupelo MS

Kemp, Paul, *Crafts*, Baylor University, Department of Fine Arts, Waco TX (S)

Kemp, Sheldon, *Field Representative*, Lansing Art Gallery, Lansing MI

Kempf, Beth, *Secy*, Wayne Art Center, Wayne PA

Kempf, Nancy, *Librn*, Omniplex, Florence O Wilson Library, Oklahoma City OK

Kempff, Katinka, *Asst Dir*, Pretoria Art Museum, Pretoria South Africa, Republic of

Kenamore, Jane, *Cur Special Coll*, Rosenberg Library, Galveston TX

Kendall, Thomas, *Head Ceramics Dept*, Kalamazoo Institute of Arts, Kalamazoo MI (S)

Kendall, William, *Asst Prof*, Bridgewater State College, Art Department, Bridgewater MA (S)

Kendrick, Diane, *Instr*, Averett College, Art Department, Danville VA (S)

Kenealy, Mary, *Artist-in-Residence*, Trinity College, Department of Fine Arts, Hartford CT (S)

Keneklis, James, *Business Mgr*, Brockton Art Center, Brockton MA

Kenfield, John F, *Assoc Prof*, Rutgers, the State University of New Jersey, Graduate Program in Art History, New Brunswick NJ (S)

Kennard, Clande L, *Assoc Prof*, Southwestern University, Art Department, Georgetown TX (S)

Kennard, Mary Ed, *Gift Shop Mgr*, Ships of The Sea Museum, Savannah GA

Kennedy, Arlene, *Exhib Coordr*, University of Western Ontario, McIntosh Art Gallery, London ON

Kennedy, Dorothy, *Secy*, Galesburg Civic Art Center, Galesburg IL

Kennedy, Garry Neill, *Pres*, Nova Scotia College of Art and Design, Anna Leonowens Gallery, Halifax NS

Kennedy, Garry Neill, *Pres*, Nova Scotia College of Art and Design, Halifax NS (S)

Kennedy, Geene, *Dir*, Grossmont Community College Gallery, El Cajon CA

Kennedy, James E, *Head*, University of South Alabama, Ethnic American Slide Library, Mobile AL

Kennedy, James E, *Chmn*, University of South Alabama, Department of Art, Mobile AL (S)

Kennedy, Patrick, *Instr*, Orange County Community College, Art Department, Middletown NY (S)

Kennedy, Richard, *Instructor*, University of North Carolina-Charlotte, Creative Arts Dept, Charlotte NC (S)

Kennedy, Robert, *Prof*, North Carolina Central University, Art Dept, Durham NC (S)

Kennedy, Roger G, *Dir*, National Museum of History and Technology, Smithsonian Institution, Washington DC

Kennedy, Ronald, *Asst Prof*, Southeastern Louisiana University, Dept of Visual Arts, Hammond LA (S)

Kenney, Chris, *Archivist of the Keystone Mast Collection*, University of California, University Art Galleries and California Museum of Photography, Riverside CA

Kenney, Jody, *Dir*, Shelburne Museum, Shelburne VT

Kenney, Marilyn, *Secy*, Penobscot Marine Museum, Searsport ME

Kenniston, Francis W, *Assoc Chairperson Studio Art*, Florida State University, Art Department, Tallahassee FL (S)

Kennon, Arthur, *Ed*, Kappa Pi International Honorary Art Fraternity, Birmingham AL

Kenny, Aidea J, *Chairperson Div*, Passaic County Community College, Division of Humanities, Paterson NJ (S)

Kenny, Edith, *Chmn Dept*, Marygrove College, Dept of Art & Art History, Detroit MI (S)

Kenny, Ellen, *Dir*, College of New Rochelle, Castle Gallery, New Rochelle NY

Kenny, Margaret, *Acting Chief Librn*, City College of the City of New York, Morris Raphael Cohen Library, New York NY

Kent, Marilyn, *Dir*, University of Tennessee, University of Tennessee Exhibits Committee, Knoxville TN

Kent, Renee, *Slide Librn*, Sarah Lawrence College Library, Bronxville NY

Kent, Sherman, *Dir Education Omniplex*, Omniplex, Oklahoma City OK

Kenyon, Richard A, *Assoc Prof*, Rhode Island College, Art Department, Providence RI (S)

Kepachar, Frances, *VPres*, Virginia Museum, Danville Museum of Fine Arts and History, Danville VA

Kepes, Katherine, *Librn*, Carnegie Library of Pittsburgh, Pittsburgh PA

Kepon, Barbara, *Pres*, Humboldt Arts Council, Eureka CA

Keppel, Marilyn, *In Charge Art Coll*, First and Merchants National Bank, Richmond VA

Kerametli, Can, *Dir*, Turk ve Islam Eserleri Muzesi, Museum of Turkish and Islamic Art, Istanbul Turkey

Kermer, Wolfgang, *Rector*, Staatliche Akademie der Bildenden Künste, State Academy of Fine Arts, Stuttgart Germany, Federal Republic of (S)

Kern, Barbara J, *Head Art & Music Dept*, Multnomah County Library, Henry Failing Art and Music Department, Portland OR

Kern, Norval, *Art Department Chairman*, Trenton State College, Holman Gallery, Trenton NJ

Kern, Norval C, *Chmn Dept*, Trenton State College, Art Department, Trenton NJ (S)

Kernan, Kerri, *Chmn*, Texas A & M University, Memorial Student Center Arts Committee, College Station TX

Kernell, Gunnel, *Asst Cur*, Rohsska Konstslojdmuseet, Rohss Museum of Arts and Crafts, Gothenburg Sweden

Kerr, Donald A, *Prof*, Grand Valley State Colleges, Art Department, Allendale MI (S)

Kerr, Ken, *VChmn*, Midland Art Council of the Midland Center for the Arts, Midland MI

Kerr, Myrtle, *Treas*, Kappa Pi International Honorary Art Fraternity, Birmingham AL

Kerr, Warren, *Pres*, Klamath Falls Art Association, Klamath Art Gallery, Klamath Falls OR

Kerrigan, Elsie, *Adminr*, Glenhyrst Arts Council of Brantford Inc, Brantford ON

Kerrigan, Thomas L, *Assoc Prof*, University of Minnesota, Duluth, Art Dept, Duluth MN (S)

Kershner, Rita E, *Secy*, Washington County Museum of Fine Arts, Hagerstown MD

Kerslake, John, *Asst Keeper*, National Portrait Gallery, London England

Kerslake, Kenneth A, *Prof*, University of Florida, Department of Art, Gainesville FL (S)

Kerslake, Phyllis, *VPres*, Hartland Art Council, Hartland MI

Kersting, Irene, *Admin Asst*, Albuquerque Museum of Art, History and Science, Albuquerque NM

Kesler, Karen, *Executive Dir*, Mendocino Art Center, Mendocino CA

Kesler, Karen A, *Executive Dir*, Mendocino Art Center, Inc, Mendocino CA (S)

Kessler, Fred, *Secy*, Fetherston Foundation, Packwood House Museum, Lewisburg PA

Kessler, Herbert L, *Chmn*, Johns Hopkins University, Department of the History of Art, Baltimore MD (S)

Kessler, John W, *Pres*, Columbus Museum of Art, Columbus OH

Kester, Lee, *Gift Shop Mgr*, Paine Art Center and Arboretum, Oshkosh WI

Ketchum, James R, *Cur*, United States Senate Commission on Art and Antiquities, Washington DC

Ketner, David, *Assoc Prof*, University of Rhode Island, Department of Art, Kingston RI (S)

Kettering, Alison, *Asst Prof*, Swarthmore College, Department of Art, Swarthmore PA (S)

Kettler, Kerwin E, *Academic Dean*, New York School of Interior Design, New York NY (S)

Kettlewell, James, *Cur*, Hyde Collection, Glens Falls NY

Key, Margaret A, *Registrar*, Bower's Museum, Santa Ana CA

Keyes, Jonathan M, *VPres*, Concord Antiquarian Society Museum, Concord MA

Keyes, Richard, *Instructor*, Long Beach City College, Department of Art, Long Beach CA (S)

Keyew, David, *Prof*, Pacific Lutheran University, Department of Art, Tacoma WA (S)

Keziere, Russell, *Vanguard Ed*, Vancouver Art Gallery, Vancouver BC

Khandalavala, Karl J, *Chmn*, Lalit Kala Akademi, National Academy of Art, New India

Khoury, J, *Librn*, American University of Beirut, Library, Beirut Lebanon

Khuri-Majoli, Pauline, *Prof*, Loyola Marymount University, Department of Art, Los Angeles CA (S)

Khurshid, Zarina, *Public Relations Officer*, Lahore Museum, Lahore Pakistan

Kiah, Virginia J, *Dir & Founder*, Kiah Museum, Savannah GA

Kiang, Dawson, *Assoc Prof*, Pennsylvania State University, University Park, Department of Art History, University Park PA (S)

Kickham, Joanne, *Membership Secy*, Museum of the American China Trade, Milton MA

Kidane, Girma, *Museum Cur*, University of Addis Ababa, Museum of the Institute of Ethiopian Studies, Addis Ababa Ethiopia

Kidd, Mary Jane, *Dir Galleries*, Edinboro State College, Art Department, Edinboro PA (S)

Kiefer, Catherine Rudy, *Exec Secy*, Frick Art Museum, Pittsburgh PA

Kieffer, Elizabeth, *Secy*, Williams College, Museum of Art, Williamstown MA

Kiel, Martha, *Instructor*, Hardin-Simmons University, Art Dept, Abilene TX (S)

Kietzman, William, *Slide Librn*, Plymouth State College, Herbert H Lamson Library, Plymouth NH

Kievets, Dennis, *Assoc Prof*, Hiram College, Art Department, Hiram OH (S)

Kihl, Harold, *Secy*, Washington Art Association, Washington Depot CT

Kiihne, Raymond R, *Asst Prof*, Winona State University, Art Department, Winona MN (S)

Kilbourne, John D, *Dir*, Anderson House Museum, Society of the Cincinnati, Washington DC

Kildou, Virginia L, *Chmn Dept*, Heidelberg College, Department of Art, Tiffin OH (S)

Killoran, Maureen, *Asst*, Worcester Art Museum, Library, Worcester MA

Killy, E James, *Asst Prof*, Miami University, Art Department, Oxford OH (S)

Kilmurry, Irene, *Prof*, Cardinal Stritch College, Art Department, Milwaukee WI (S)

Kim, Chung S, *Librn*, Ryerson Polytechnical Institute Library, Architecture Library, Toronto ON

Kimball, Lee, *Library Coordr*, Art Gallery of Ontario, Edward P Taylor Reference Library, Toronto ON

Kimball, Mary Ellen, *Instr Art*, Southwestern Community College, Art Department, Creston IA (S)

Kimble, Warren, *Asst Prof*, Castleton State College, Art Department, Castleton VT (S)

Kimbrell, Leonard B, *Head Dept*, Portland State University, Department of Art and Architecture, Portland OR (S)

Kimbrough, Joseph, *Dir*, Minneapolis Public Library and Information Center, Art, Music and Film Dept, Minneapolis MN

Kimmel, Jim, *Treas*, Lubbock Art Association, Inc, Lubbock TX

Kimmel, K N, *Dept Chmn*, Salisbury State College, College Gallery, Salisbury MD

Kimmel, Kent N, *Chmn*, Salisbury State College, Art Dept, Salisbury MD (S)

Kimmitt, J S, *Exec Secy*, United States Senate Commission on Art and Antiquities, Washington DC

Kinard, John R, *Dir*, Anacostia Neighborhood Museum, Washington DC

Kincaid, Clarence, *Prof*, Texas Tech University, Department of Art, Lubbock TX (S)

Kinch, Bruce, *Chmn Photography Dept*, Art Institute of Boston, Boston MA (S)

Kindermann, Helmmo, *Chmn Photography Dept*, Lake Placid School of Art, Lake Placid NY (S)

Kindred, Louise, *Librn*, Middletown Fine Arts Center, Library, Middletown OH

King, Barbara N, *Secy*, Kenneth C Beck Center for the Cultural Arts, Lakewood OH

King, Bruce, *Asst Dir*, Valentine Museum, Richmond VA

King, Claudia L, *Instr*, University of Nevada, Las Vegas, Department of Art, Las Vegas NV (S)

King, Constance, *Music Dir*, Pine Castle Center of the Arts, Inc, Orlando FL

King, D, *Keeper Textiles*, Victoria and Albert Museum, London England

King, Gerald, *Assoc Prof*, Prince George's Community College, Art Department, Largo MD (S)

King, Jack, *Asst Prof*, Augusta College, Department of Fine Arts, Augusta GA (S)

King, Kim, *Librn*, Victor Valley College Library, Victorville CA

King, Mary Elizabeth, *Keeper of Coll*, University of Pennsylvania, University Museum, Philadelphia PA

King, Max, *Graphic Designer*, Craft and Folk Art Museum, Los Angeles CA

King, Muriel, *Librn*, Winnipeg Sketch Club, Library, Winnipeg MB

King, Patrick, *Asst Cur*, Indiana University - Purdue University at Indianapolis, Herron School of Art, Art Gallery, Indianapolis IN

King, Susan, *Instr*, Howard College, Art Department, Big Spring TX (S)

King Jr, Charles H, *Cataloger*, National Collection of Fine Arts, Library of the National Collection of Fine Arts and the National Portrait Gallery, Washington DC

Kingmans, H, *Educational Officer*, Fries Museum, Leeuwarden Netherlands

Kingsland Jr, Herbert, *Treas*, Vermont State Craft Center at Frog Hollow, Middlebury VT

Kingsley, Betty, *Corresponding Secy*, Historical Society of Bloomfield, New Jersey, Bloomfield NJ

Kingsley, Robert, *Asst Prof*, DePauw University, Art Department, Greencastle IN (S)

Kington, Brent, *Chmn of Metals*, Southern Illinois University, School of Art, Carbondale IL (S)

Kinkead, Duncan, *Asst Prof*, Duke University, Department of Art, Durham NC (S)

Kinnaird, Richard, *Asst Chmn Studio Art*, University of North Carolina at Chapel Hill, Art Department, Chapel Hill NC (S)

Kinney, Gilbert H, *Pres*, Archives of American Art, Smithsonian Institution, New York NY

Kinney, Mary T, *Dean*, Columbus College of Art and Design, Columbus OH (S)

Kinnie, Frances Bartlett, *Dean*, Jacksonville University, Department of Art, Jacksonville FL (S)

Kinoshita, Masao, *Dir*, Ohio State University, School of Architecture, Columbus OH (S)

Kinsella, Doris, *Asst Prof*, Hartford Art School of the University of Hartford, West Hartford CT (S)

Kinsinger, Patti, *Exhib Coordr*, Public Library of Columbus and Franklin County, Humanities, Fine Arts and Recreation Division, Columbus OH

Kinsman, Robert D, *Dir*, Sheldon Swope Art Gallery, Terre Haute IN

Kintzler, David, *Asst Dir*, Housatonic Community College, Housatonic Museum of Art, Bridgeport CT

Kinz, Lance, *Dir*, University of Cincinnati, Tangeman Fine Arts Gallery, Cincinnati OH

Kinzie, Christie, *Museum Asst*, Ships of The Sea Museum, Savannah GA

Kiper, Carol, *Vis Prof*, Oral Roberts University, Fine Arts Department, Tulsa OK (S)

Kipilii, Mary Lu, *Head AV Unit*, Hawaii State Library, Fine Arts-Audiovisual Section, Honolulu HI

Kirby, Grant, *Head of Department*, Auckland City Art Gallery, Auckland New Zealand

Kirby, Kent, *Chmn*, Alma College, Department of Art and Design, Alma MI (S)

Kirby, Peggy Jo, *Registrar*, North Carolina Museum of Art, Department of Cultural Resources, Raleigh NC

Kirk, Harry, *Instructor*, Shippensburg State College, Art Department, Shippensburg PA (S)

Kirk, John, *Prof*, Shoreline Community College, Humanities Division, Seattle WA (S)

Kirk, Martha Ann, *Instr*, Incarnate Word College, Humanities and Fine Arts, San Antonio TX (S)

Kirker, Anne, *Cur Prints & Drawings*, National Art Gallery of New Zealand, Wellington New Zealand

Kirking, Clayton, *Dir Handforth Gallery*, Tacoma Public Library, Handforth Gallery, Tacoma WA

Kirkland, Starr, *Circulation-Periodicals Librn*, Atlanta College of Art Library, Atlanta GA

Kirkman, Dale, *Pres*, Phillips County Museum, Helena AR

Kirkpatrick, John E, *Pres Board of Governors Kirkpatrick Center*, Omniplex, Oklahoma City OK

Kirkpatrick, Nancy, *Adminr*, Hirshhorn Museum and Sculpture Garden, Washington DC

Kirschenbaum, Jules, *Prof*, Drake University, Art Department, Des Moines IA (S)

Kirshenbaum, Morris B, *Dir*, Galleries of Ivy School of Professional Art, Pittsburgh PA

Kirshner, Judith Russi, *Cur*, Museum of Contemporary Art, Chicago IL

Kirstel, Harvey, *Asst Prof*, University of Maryland Baltimore County, Visual Arts Department, Catonsville MD (S)

Kiser, Kimmerly, *Asst Prof*, Wright State University, Art Department, Dayton OH (S)

Kishimoto, Yuji, *VPres*, Blacksburg Regional Art Association, Blacksburg VA

Kiskadden, Robert M, *Asst Dean*, Wichita State University, Division of Art, Wichita KS (S)

Kissinger, Beverly, *Instructor*, Mississippi University for Women, Art Department, Columbus MS (S)

Kistemaker, J, *Cur Physics*, Teylers Museum, Haarlem Netherlands

Kisthardt, James N, *Head Art and Music Dept*, Free Public Library, Art and Music Department, Trenton NJ

Kitao, T Kaori, *Chairperson Dept Art*, Swarthmore College, Department of Art, Swarthmore PA (S)

Kittle, Barbara, *Librn*, University of Arizona, Fine Arts Library, Tucson AZ

Kittleson, Lars, *Prof*, Pacific Lutheran University, Department of Art, Tacoma WA (S)

Kitzing, Erna, *Bookeeper*, Springfield Free Public Library, Donald B Palmer Museum, Springfield NJ

Kivircik, Havva, *Librn*, Istanbul Arkeoloji Müzeleri, Library, Istanbul Turkey

Kiyooka, Roy, *Prof*, University of British Columbia, Department of Fine Arts, Vancouver BC (S)

Kiyuan, Michael, *Treas*, Association of Honolulu Artists, Honolulu HI

Kizik, Roger, *Preparator*, Brandeis University, Rose Art Museum, Waltham MA

Kjelson, Beth, *Dir*, Minot Art Gallery, Minot Art Association, Minot ND

Klapproth, R, *Cur Nederlandish Painting*, Staatsgalerie Stuttgart, Stuttgart Germany, Federal Republic of

Klassen, John, *Education*, Massillon Museum, Massillon OH

Klauner, Friderike, *Dir*, Kunsthistorisches Museum, Museum of Fine Arts, Vienna Austria

Klaven, Marvin L, *Chmn Art Dept*, Millikin University, Art Dept, Decatur IL (S)

Klaven, Marvin L, *Dir*, Millikin University, Kirkland Gallery, Decatur IL

Kleeman, Kay, *Executive Dir*, Meadville Council on the Arts, Meadville PA

Kleeman, Richard, *Head Dept*, Allegheny College, Art Department, Meadville PA (S)

Klein, Arthur, *Chmn of the Board*, Philadelphia Art Alliance, Philadelphia PA

Klein, Carol, *Instructor*, Ivy School of Professional Art, Downtown Annex, Pittsburgh PA (S)

Klein, Leanne, *Registrar*, Minnesota Museum of Art, Saint Paul MN

Klein, Leanne, *Librn*, Minnesota Museum of Art, Library, Saint Paul MN

Klein, R M, *Secy*, Please Touch Museum, Philadelphia PA

Klein, Victor L, *Pres*, Birmingham-Bloomfield Art Association, Birmingham MI

Kleinenbroich, Helmut, *Librn*, Staatliche Kunstakodemie Dusseldorf - Bibliothek, Dusseldorf Germany, Federal Republic of

Kleinschmidt, Robert, *Assoc Prof*, University of Utah, Art Department, Salt Lake City UT (S)

Kleinsmith, Gene, *Chmn Dept*, Victor Valley College, Art Department, Victorville CA (S)

Klemm, Jean Agnes, *Instr*, Siena Heights College, Art Department, Adrian MI (S)

Klemm, Jeannine, *Dir*, Siena Heights College, Little Gallery, Studio Angelico, Adrian MI

Klemm, Jeannine, *Chairperson Dept*, Siena Heights College, Art Department, Adrian MI (S)

Klemmer, Virginia, *Gallery Dir*, Sarasota Art Association, Sarasota FL

Klenk, William, *Prof*, University of Rhode Island, Department of Art, Kingston RI (S)

Klep, Rolf, *Dir*, Columbia River Maritime Museum, Astoria OR

Klepac, L, *Deputy Dir*, Art Gallery of Western Australia, Perth Australia

Klesse, Brigitte, *Dir*, Museen der Stadt Köln, Kunstgewerbemuseum der Stadt Köln, Cologne Germany, Federal Republic of

Klesse, Brigitte, *Dir*, Museen der Stadt Köln, Kunstgewerbemuseum, Cologne Germany, Federal Republic of

Klessman, Ruediger, *Dir*, Herzog Anton Ulrich-Museum, Medieval Section: Burg Dankwarderode, Brunswick Germany, Federal Republic of

Klett, Mark C, *Instr*, Sun Valley Center for the Arts & Humanities, Department of Fine Art, Sun Valley ID (S)

Kliman, Eve, *Asst Prof*, University of Waterloo, Fine Arts Department, Waterloo ON (S)

Klimiades, Mario N, *Librn*, Amerind Foundation, Inc, Fulton-Hayden Memorial Library, Dragoon AZ

Klimschmidt, Irene, *Asst*, Stadistshces Kunstmuseum Bonn, Art Museum of the City of Bonn, Bonn Germany, Federal Republic of

Kline, Irving, *Adjunct Instr*, Delaware County Community College, Communications and Humanities House, Media PA (S)

Kline, Naomi, *Cur*, Hammond Museum, Inc, Gloucester MA

Klingman, Berry, *Printmaking*, Baylor University, Department of Fine Arts, Waco TX (S)

Klish-Ginsberg, Rene, *Registrar*, United States Military Academy, West Point Museum, West Point NY

Klobe, Tom, *Dir*, University of Hawaii at Manoa, Art Gallery, Honolulu HI

Klomburg, Robert, *Planetarium Dir*, Hudson River Museum, Yonkers NY

Klonis, Stewart, *Executive Dir*, Art Students League of New York, New York NY

Klonis, Stewart, *Pres*, American Fine Arts Society, New York NY

Klonis, Stewart, *Exec Dir*, Art Students League of New York, New York NY (S)

Klopfenstein, Philip A, *Dir*, Montgomery Museum of Fine Arts, Montgomery AL

Klopfer, M, *Art Ed*, Lovis Corinth Memorial Foundation, Inc, New York NY

Klosinska, Janina, *Icons*, Muzeum Narodowe w Krakowie, National Museum in Cracow, Cracow Poland

Kluge, Gordon, *Chmn Printamking Dept*, San Francisco Art Institute, San Francisco CA (S)

Klukas, Arnold, *Asst Prof*, Bridgewater State College, Art Department, Bridgewater MA (S)

Klyberg, Albert T, *Dir*, Rhode Island Historical Society, Providence RI

Kmiecinska-Kaczmarek, Teresa, *Cur*, Muzeum Sztuki, Lodz Poland

Knachel, Philip A, *Assoc Dir*, Folger Shakespeare Library, Washington DC

Knapikowa, Marta, *Mgr*, Muzeum Narodowe w Krakowie, Biblioteka, Cracow Poland

Knapp, Candace, *Vis Prof*, Temple Junior College, Art Department, Temple TX (S)

Knapp, Dick, *Instr*, University of Albuquerque, Art Department, Albuquerque NM (S)

Knapp, Ronald, *VPres*, Springfield Art & Historical Society, Springfield VT

Knapp, S, *VPres*, Montana State University, Fine Arts Gallery, Bozeman MT

Knaub, Donald E, *Dir Civic Arts*, Muckenthaler Cultural Center, Fullerton CA

Knaub, Donald E, *Dir*, Huntsville Museum of Art, Huntsville AL

Knauber, Ann, *Membership Coordr*, Fine Arts Museums of San Francisco, The Museum Society, n of Honor co

Knecht, Samuel, *Acting Dir*, Hillsdale College, Art Dept, Hillsdale MI (S)

Kneebone, Sidney, *Head Librn*, City College of the City of New York, Morris Raphael Cohen Library, New York NY

Kneedler, Franklin, *Deputy Dir*, Mystic Seaport Museum, Inc, Mystic CT

Kneisel, Stephen, *Asst Supv*, Newark Museum, Junior Museum, Newark NJ

Knevel, Ken, *Pres*, Lafayette Art Center, Lafayette IN

Knickmeyer, Henry, *Dir Grad Prog*, Fontbonne College, Department of Art, Clayton MO (S)

Knickmeyer, Henry, *Dir Grad Prog*, Fontbonne College, Art Department, Saint Louis MO (S)

Knight, Allegra, *Secy*, Vassar College Art Gallery, Poughkeepsie NY

Knight, Mary Ann, *First Asst Music and Arts Services*, Berkshire Athenaeum, Pittsfield MA

Knight, Myra, *Head Art & Music Department*, Richmond Public Library, Richmond VA

Knipe, Jan, *Instructor*, Viterbo College, Art Department, La Crosse WI (S)

Knipe, Jim, *Asst Prof*, Viterbo College, Art Department, La Crosse WI (S)

Knipple, Kathleen, *Instr*, Studio Art Centers International, Florence Italy (S)

Knisley, Rhoda, *Prof*, Spring Arbor College, Art Department, Spring Arbor MI (S)

Knobler, Nathan, *Dean of Faculty*, Philadelphia College of Art Gallery, Philadelphia PA

Knobler, Nathan, *Dean Faculty*, Philadelphia College of Art, Philadelphia PA (S)

Knodel, Gerhardt, *Head Fiber Dept*, Cranbrook Academy of Art, Bloomfield Hills MI (S)

Knoerr, Margaret, *Reference Librn*, Duke University Museum of Art, East Campus Library, Durham NC

Knoeset, Erwin W H, *Treas*, Saint Louis Artists' Guild, Saint Louis MO

Knoop, Cary, *Assoc Prof*, Eastern Illinois University, Art Department, Charleston IL (S)

Knop, Christine, *Registrar*, Philbrook Art Center, Tulsa OK

Knott, Elen, *Development Asst*, Reynolda House, Inc, Winston-Salem NC

Knott, Elen, *Librn*, Reynolda House, Inc, Library, Winston-Salem NC

Knott, Robert, *Chmn*, Wake Forest University, Department of Art, Winston-Salem NC (S)

Know, Seymour H, *Chmn*, Albright-Knox Art Gallery, Buffalo Fine Arts Academy, Buffalo NY

Knowles, C W, *Pres*, Kelowna Centennial Museum and National Exhibit Centre, Kelowna BC

Knowles, Judith, *Dir Div Fine Arts*, Shasta College, Art Department, Fine Arts Division, Redding CA (S)

Knowles, Penny, *Cur Education*, Santa Barbara Museum of Art, Santa Barbara CA

Knowlton, John H B, *Prof*, Connecticut College, Department of Art History, New London CT (S)

Knox, George, *Acting Head*, University of British Columbia, Department of Fine Arts, Vancouver BC (S)

Knox, Northrup R, *VPres*, Albright-Knox Art Gallery, Buffalo Fine Arts Academy, Buffalo NY

Knox, Rich, *Instr*, Western Wisconsin Technical Institute, Graphics Division, LACrosse WI (S)

Knudson, Elizabeth, *Librn*, University of Utah, Owen Library, Salt Lake City UT

Knuth, Priscilla, *Managing Editor*, Oregon Historical Society, Library, Portland OR

Knutson, Michael, *Asst Prof*, Swarthmore College, Department of Art, Swarthmore PA (S)

Knutson, Norman, *Assoc Prof*, Adrian College, Art Department, Adrian MI (S)

Knutson, Wayne, *Dean*, University of South Dakota, Dept of Art, Vermillion SD (S)

Koberg, William, *Preparator*, Phillips Collection, Washington DC

Kobrynich, Bill, *Dir Interior Design*, Art Institute of Fort Lauderdale, Fort Lauderdale FL (S)

Koch, Bruno, *Prof*, Christopher Newport College, Fine and Performing Arts, Newport News VA (S)

Koch, Cynthia, *Dir*, Old Barracks, Trenton NJ

Koch, Erik, *Chmn*, Schiller College, Europe University, Art Department, Strasbourg France (S)

Koch, George, *Secy*, Artists Equity Association, Inc, Washington DC

Koch, Janet L, *Conservator*, New Jersey Historical Society Museum, Library, Newark NJ

Koch, Robert, *Prof*, Princeton University, Department of Art and Archaeology, Princeton NJ (S)

Kocher, E G, *Executive Dir*, West Bend Gallery of Fine Arts, West Bend WI

Kocher, Robert L, *Prof*, Coe College, Department of Art, Cedar Rapids IA (S)

Kocher, Sandra, *Chairperson*, Worcester State College, Art Department, Worcester MA (S)

Kocherthaler, Mina, *VPres*, National Society of Painters in Casein and Acrylic, Inc, New York NY

Kochka, Al, *Dir*, Sangre De Cristo Arts & Conference Center, Pueblo CO

Koe, Pamela, *Admin Asst-Registrar*, University of California, Santa Barbara, Art Museum, Santa Barbara CA

Koebbeman, Skip, *Instructor*, Louisville School of Art, Anchorage KY (S)

Koel, Ottilia, *Librn & Manuscripts Cur*, New Haven Colony Historical Society, Reference Library, New Haven CT

Koella, Rudolf, *Cur*, Kunstmuseum, Art Museum, Winterthur Switzerland

Koenig, Robert j, *Dir*, Montclair Art Museum, Montclair NJ

Koeninger, Kay, *Registrar*, Galleries of the Claremont Colleges, Claremont CA

Koepplin, Dieter, *Cur Prints & Drawings*, Offentliche Kunstsammlung-Kunstmuseum Basel, Museum of Fine Arts, Basel Switzerland

Koerlin, Ernest, *Assoc Prof*, Wright State University, Art Department, Dayton OH (S)

Koerner, Mark, *Chmn Design Dept*, Milwaukee School of the Arts, Milwaukee WI (S)

Koester, Olaf, *Cur*, Statens Museum for Kunst, Department of Painting and Sculpture, Copenhagen Denmark

Koga, James, *Instructor*, Honolulu Academy of Arts, Studio Program, Honolulu HI (S)

Kogel, Albert, *Prof*, Cochise College, Art Department, Douglas AZ (S)

Kohl, Barbara H, *Head Adult Services*, Brookline Public Library, Brookline MA

Kohler, Edith, *Pres & Dir*, Middletown Fine Arts Center, Middletown OH

Kohler, Ruth, *Dir*, John Michael Kohler Arts Center, Sheboygan WI

Kohlmann, Theodor, *Dir*, Staatliche Museen Preussischer Kulturbesitz, Museum of German Ethnology, Berlin Germany, Federal Republic of

Kohlschreiber, Molly Haines, *Instr*, Victor Valley College, Art Department, Victorville CA (S)

Kohn, Bernard A, *Treas*, American Color Print Society, Philadelphia PA

Kohn, Ira, *Cur Exhib*, Western Kentucky University, Kentucky Museum, Bowling Green KY

Kohn, Judith, *Instructor*, Ocean City School of Art, Ocean City NJ (S)

Koike, Masahiro, *Cur Education & Public Relations*, Tokyo Kokuritsu Kindai Bujutsukan, National Museum of Modern Art, Tokyo, Tokyo Japan

Koiwa, Kensuke, *Admin Chief*, Tokyo Kokuritsu Kindai Bujutsukan, National Museum of Modern Art, Tokyo, Tokyo Japan

Koke, Richard J, *Cur Museum*, New York Historical Society, New York NY

Kola, Vaino, *Chmn Dept*, Wheaton College, Art Department, Norton MA (S)

Kolarik, Ruth, *Instructor*, Colorado College, Department of Art, Colorado Springs CO (S)

Kolch, David, *Conservator*, Lyman Allyn Museum, New London CT

Koller, Johann, *Restoration Department*, Bayerischen Staatsgemaldesammlungen, Bavarian State Galleries of Art, Munich Germany, Federal Republic of

Kolltveit, Bard, *Cur*, Norsk Sjöfartsmuseum, Norwegian Maritime Museum, Oslo Norway

Kolltveit, Marit, *Librn*, Vestlandske Kunstindustrimuseum, Library, Bergen Norway

Kolowrat, Elizabeth, *Museum Educ*, Pennsylvania Academy of the Fine Arts, Philadelphia PA

Kolpan, Gerald, *Instructor*, Mainline Center of the Arts, Haverford PA (S)

Komal, Dennis, *Dir*, San Diego State University, Art Gallery, San Diego CA

Komives, Ralph, *Instructor*, Stephens College, Art Department, Columbia MO (S)

Kondos, Gregory, *Instructor*, Sacramento City College, Art Department, Sacramento CA (S)

Kongshaug, Steve H, *Cur*, Schofield Barracks, Tropic Lightning Historical Center, Honolulu HI

Konieczny, Marian, *Rector*, Akademia Sztuk Pieknych, Academy of Fine Arts, Cracow Poland (S)

Konopka, Joseph, *VPres*, Associated Artists of New Jersey, Pittstown NJ

Konrad, Anton, *Conservator*, Museo de Arte de Ponce, Ponce Art Museum, Ponce PR

Koo, Rosalyn, *Pres*, Chinese Culture Foundation, Chinese Culture Center Gallery, San Francisco CA

Koob, Katherine R, *Asst Cur Textiles*, Merrimack Valley Textile Museum, North Andover MA

Koomar, John, *Asst Dir*, Studio School of Art and Design, Philadelphia PA (S)

Koons, Darrel, *Instructor*, Bob Jones University, School of Fine Arts, Greenville SC (S)

Koontz, Sondra, *State-Wide Film Service*, Wichita Public Library, Wichita KS

Koos, John, *Prof*, New York City Community College of the City University of New York, Department of Art and Advertising Design, Brooklyn NY (S)

Koos, Kathleen, *Teacher & Education Asst*, Minnesota Museum of Art, Saint Paul MN

Kooyman, Olga, *Assoc Prof*, Los Angeles City College, Department of Art, Los Angeles CA (S)

Koozer, Don, *Art Librn*, University of Oklahoma, Art Library, Norman OK

Kopff, Maria, *Polish Painting & Sculpture of the 14th - 18th Centuries*, Muzeum Narodowe w Krakowie, National Museum in Cracow, Cracow Poland

Koppeis, Francis, *Innkeeper*, Longfellow's Wayside Inn, South Sudbury MA

Kopytoff, Igor, *Cur African Ethnology*, University of Pennsylvania, University Museum, Philadelphia PA

Koras, George, *Prof*, State University of New York at Stony Brook, Art Department, Stony Brook NY (S)

Kord, Victor, *Chmn*, University of Wisconsin, Madison, Department of Art, Madison WI (S)

Kordich, Diane D, *Asst Prof*, Northern Michigan University, Dept of Art & Design, Marquette MI (S)

Korey, Marie, *Cur of Printed Books*, Library Company of Philadelphia, Philadelphia PA

Korneitchouk, Ursula, *Asst to Dir*, Cleveland Museum of Art, Cleveland OH

Kornitnik, Mary, *Finance Officer*, Sweetwater Community Fine Arts Center, Rock Springs WY

Kornowski, Walter L, *Chmn*, Bethany College, Art Department, Bethany WV (S)

Kornwold, J D, *Assoc Prof*, College of William and Mary, Department of Fine Arts, Williamsburg VA (S)

Korshak, Yvonne, *Chmn*, Adelphi University, Department of Art and Art History, Garden City NY (S)

Kortum, Karl, *Chief Cur*, National Maritime Museum, San Francisco CA

Korzenik, Diana, *Chmn Art Educ*, Massachusetts College of Art, Boston MA (S)

Kosan, Julius T, *Chmn Art Dept*, Bowling Green State University, Art Department, Huron OH (S)

Koschatzky, Walter, *Dir*, Graphische Sammlung Albertina, Albertina Graphic Art Collection, Vienna Austria

Kosche, Eugene R, *Cur Military & Mechanical Arts*, Bennington Museum, Bennington VT

Kosh, Neil, *Chmn*, Temple University, Art Department, Philadelphia PA (S)

Koshalek, Richard, *Dir*, Hudson River Museum, Yonkers NY

Kosher, Helene, *Cur Slide Libr*, University of California, University Art Galleries and California Museum of Photography, Riverside CA

Koshute, Joseph, *Art Dir*, Patterson Library, Westfield NY

Kosich, Frank, *Pres*, Women's City Club of Cleveland, Cleveland OH

Kosics, Theresa, *Secy*, Southern Artists Association, Fine Arts Center, Hot Springs AR

Kosik, Edwin M, *Chmn Trustees*, Everhart Museum of Natural History, Science and Art, Scranton PA

Koslosky, Robert, *Asst Prof*, Bloomsburg State College, Department of Art, Bloomsburg PA (S)

Kosmer, Ellen, *Prof*, Worcester State College, Art Department, Worcester MA (S)

Kosterman, Wayne J, *Secy*, Society of Environmental Graphics Designers, Chicago IL

Kotalik, Jiri, *Pres*, Narodni Galerie v Prague, National Gallery of Prague, Prague Czechoslovakia

Kotik, Charlotta, *Assoc Cur*, Albright-Knox Art Gallery, Buffalo Fine Arts Academy, Buffalo NY

Kotun, H Paul, *Dir*, Washington County Museum of Fine Arts, Hagerstown MD

Kouris, Sharon Wells, *Chmn Dept*, Barat College, Dept of Art, Lake Forest IL (S)

Koursaros, Harry G, *Assoc Prof*, Albright College, Department of Art, Reading PA (S)

Kovacs, B Jeanne, *Pres*, Wallingford Art League, Wallingford CT

Kovacs, Katherine M, *Archivist*, Corcoran Gallery of Art, Library, Washington DC

Kowal, Calvin, *Instructor*, Art Academy of Cincinnati, Cincinnati OH (S)

Kowal, David, *Instructor*, Emmanuel College, Art Department, Boston MA (S)

Kowalek, Jon W, *Dir*, Tacoma Art Museum, Tacoma WA

Kowalke, Kit, *Chmn*, Honolulu Community College, Department of Art, Department of Commercial Art, Department of Graphic Art, Honolulu HI (S)

Kowall, Thomas W, *Dir Student Services*, Emily Carr College of Art, Vancouver BC (S)

Kowalska, Irena, *Mgr*, Muzeum Narodowe w Krakowie, Biblioteka, Cracow Poland

Kowalski, Lee, *Public Relations*, Vernon Art Association, Topham Brown Gallery, Vernon BC

Kowski, Robert, *Chmn Dept*, Greensboro College, Department of Art, Greensboro NC (S)

Kowsky, Francis R, *Chmn*, State University of New York College at Buffalo, Fine Arts Department, Buffalo NY (S)

Kozar, W J, *Asst Dir Admin*, National Museum of Man, Ottawa ON

Kozloff, Arielle P, *Assoc Cur in Charge Ancient Art*, Cleveland Museum of Art, Cleveland OH

Kozlowski, Deirdre Lee, *Instr*, Mount Mary College, Art Department, Milwaukee WI (S)

Kozuszek, Larry, *Asst Prof*, Saint Louis Community College at Florissant Valley, Department of Art, Ferguson MO (S)

Kpenig, Robert J, *Dir*, Montclair Art Museum, Art School, Montclair NJ (S)

Kraay, C M, *Keeper Heberden Coin Room*, Oxford University, Ashmolean Museum of Art and Archaeology, Oxford England

Kraemer, Pat, *Instr*, Rochester Community College, Art Department, Rochester MN (S)

Kraetschmer, Diana, *Reference Librn*, University of British Columbia, Fine Arts Division Library, Vancouver BC

Kraft, Regina, *Assoc Prof*, Elizabeth Seton College, Art Department, Yonkers NY (S)

Krainak, Paul, *VPres*, N.A.M.E. Gallery, Chicago IL

Krakel, Dean, *Exec Dir*, National Cowboy Hall of Fame and Western Heritage Center, Oklahoma City OK

Kramer, Edith, *Asst Programmer*, University of California, Pacific Film Archive, Berkeley CA

Kramer, Graham, *Secy*, Central Louisiana Art Association, Alexandria Museum Visual Art Center, Alexandria LA

Kramer, Steve, *Chmn*, Ellsworth Community College, Department of Fine Arts, Iowa Falls IA (S)

Kramers, George, *Head Dept*, Frostburg State College, Department of Art & Art Education, Frostburg MD (S)

Kramrisch, Stella, *Cur Emeritus Indian Art*, Philadelphia Museum of Art, Philadelphia PA

Kraning, Alan, *Instr*, Western Wisconsin Technical Institute, Graphics Division, LACrosse WI (S)

Krantz, P J, *Coordr Fine Arts*, Jefferson Community College, Fine Arts, Louisville KY (S)

Krashes, Barbara, *VPres*, Federation of Modern Painters and Sculptors, New York NY

Krasner, Bonnie, *Pres*, Jewish Community Center, Center Lobby Gallery, Long Beach CA

Krasu, Fred, *Treas*, Art Barn, Greenwich CT

Kraus, Shirley, *Gallery Dir*, Art Barn, Greenwich CT

Krause, Carol, *Dir Education*, Please Touch Museum, Philadelphia PA

Krause, Lawrence, *Instr*, Cleveland Institute of Art, Cleveland OH (S)

Krause, Martin F, *Asst Cur Prints & Drawings*, Indianapolis Museum of Art, Indianapolis IN

Krauss, Rosalind, *Prof*, City University of New York, PhD Program in Art History, New York NY (S)

Krausz, Peter Thomas, *Cur*, Saidye Bronfman Centre, Montreal PQ

Krauth, Harald, *Assoc Prof*, Vermont College of Norwich University, Philosophy, Religion and Fine Arts Department, Montpelier VT (S)

Kraver, Ronald, *Vis Lectr*, University of North Carolina at Chapel Hill, Art Department, Chapel Hill NC (S)

Kravitz, E Walter, *Assoc Prof*, George Mason University, Department of Fine and Performing Arts, Fairfax VA (S)

Kraywinkel, Howard, *Dir Museum Photography*, Art Institute of Chicago, Chicago IL

Krebs, Harry, *Assoc Prof*, Dickinson College, Fine Arts Department, Carlisle PA (S)

Krebs, Jerry H, *Asst Prof*, Radford University, Art Department, Radford VA (S)

Krebs, Rose, *Prof*, School of the Arts, C W Post Center of Long Island University, Art Department, Greenvale NY (S)

Kreeger, David Lloyd, *Pres*, Corcoran Gallery of Art, Washington DC

Kreiberg, Henrik, *Dir*, Sunbury Shores Arts and Nature Centre, Inc, Saint Andrews NB

Kreidl, Detlev, *Asst Dir*, Museum Moderner Kunst, Museum of Modern Art, Vienna Austria

Kreisberg, Luisa, *Dir Public Information*, Museum of Modern Art, New York NY

Kreiter, James W, *Cur Art*, Neville Public Museum, Green Bay WI

Krejcarek, Philip, *Asst Prof*, Carroll College, Art Department, Waukesha WI (S)

Kremer, E, *Treas*, Association of Collegiate Schools of Architecture, Washington DC

Kreneck, Lynwood, *Prof*, Texas Tech University, Department of Art, Lubbock TX (S)

Kressy, Christopher, *Head Dept*, Plymouth State College, Art Department, Plymouth NH (S)

Kresta, S, *Instr*, Selkirk College, Kootenay School of Art Division, Nelson BC (S)

Kreuger, Patricia A, *Program Dir*, Saint Cloud State University, Atwood Center Gallery Lounge, Saint Cloud MN

Kricke, Norbert, *Dir*, Staatliche Kunstakademie, Dusseldorf, Hochschule für Bildende Künste, Dusseldorf Germany, Federal Republic of

Krieg, William F, *Dir & VPres Collector Relations*, Franklin Mint Corp Museum, Franklin Center PA

Krieger, Kurt, *Dir*, Staatliche Museen Preussischer Kulturbesitz, Museum of Ethnology, Berlin Germany, Federal Republic of

Kriek, K J, *Dir*, Stedelijk Museum Alkmaar, Alkmaar Municipal Museum, Alkmaar Netherlands

Krimstein, Jordan, *Instr*, Blackhawk Mountain School of Art, Black Hawk CO (S)

Krishan, Bal, *Sr Librn*, National Museum of INdia, Library, New Delhi India

Kriss-Rettenbeck, L, *General Dir*, Bayerisches Nationalmuseum, Bavarian National Museum, Munich Germany, Federal Republic of

Kristovich, Brook B, *Arts & Crafts Dir*, Yugtarvik Regional Museum, Bethel AK

Krochman, Kay, *Division Head*, Dallas Public Library, Fine Arts Division, Dallas TX

Krody, Barron, *Instructor*, Art Academy of Cincinnati, Cincinnati OH (S)

Kroeker, Leon, *Head Dept*, Oral Roberts University, Fine Arts Department, Tulsa OK (S)

Kroese, H E Stenfert, *Board of Trustees*, Teylers Museum, Haarlem Netherlands

Kroll, Morton, *Vice Chmn*, King County Arts Commission, Seattle WA

Krommenhoek, Hans, *Instructor*, Milwaukee Area Technical College, Graphic & Applied Arts Div, Milwaukee WI (S)

Kronenberg, Ann, *Treas*, Women in the Arts Foundation, Inc, New York NY

Kronenberg, John L, *Assoc Dean*, Rochester Institute of Technology, College of Graphic Arts and Photography, Rochester NY (S)

Kronewetter, Justin, *Chmn & Dir of Exhib*, Ohio Wesleyan University, Department of Fine Arts Gallery, Delaware OH

Kronewetter, Justin, *Chmn*, Ohio Wesleyan University, Fine Arts Department, Delaware OH (S)

Kronstedt, Richard, *Dir*, Minneapolis College of Art and Design, Library and Media Center, Minneapolis MN

Kroop, Bernie, *Instructional Asst*, Sullivan County Community College, Div of Commercial Art and Photography, Loch Sheldrake NY (S)

Krouse, Drew, *Head Dept*, Kalamazoo Valley Community College, Department of Art, Kalamazoo MI (S)

Krudo, Shlomo, *VPres*, Artists Guild of Chicago, Chicago IL

Krueger, Donald W, *Dir*, Clark University, Little Center Gallery, Worcester MA

Krueger, Donald W, *Chmn Art Prog & Dept Visual & Performing Arts*, Clark University, Art Program, Worcester MA (S)

Krueger, Fred, *Second VPres Exhibitions*, Arizona Artist Guild, Phoenix AZ

Krueger, Lothar, *Prof*, University of Arkansas, Art Department, Fayetteville AR (S)

Krueger, Pamela, *Dir*, Laurentian University, Museum and Arts Centre, Sudbury ON

Krueger, Pamela, *Dir*, Laurentian University, Art Gallery, Sudbury ON (S)

Krueger, Pamela, *VPres*, Ontario Association of Art Galleries, Toronto ON

Krueger, Rodney, *Instr*, Fresno City College, Art Department, Fresno CA (S)

Kruetzman, William E, *Technician*, J B Speed Art Museum, Louisville KY

Krug, Harry E, *Prof*, Pittsburg State University, Art Department, Pittsburg KS (S)

Krulick, Janet, *Cur of Education*, Beaumont Art Museum, Beaumont TX

Krulik, Barbara, *Asst*, National Academy of Design, New York NY

Krumor, Sekul, *Rektor*, Nikolaj Pavlovic Higher Institute of Fine Arts, Sofia Bulgaria (S)

Krumrein, John, *Assoc Prof*, Prince George's Community College, Art Department, Largo MD (S)

Kruse, Donald, *Assoc Prof*, Indiana University-Purdue University, Department of Fine Arts, Fort Wayne IN (S)

Kruse, Gerald, *Asst Prof*, South Dakota State University, Art Dept, Brookings SD (S)

Krush, Beth, *Chmn Illustration*, Moore College of Art, Philadelphia PA (S)

Krushenick, John, *Asst Dir*, Morris Museum of Arts and Sciences, Morristown NJ

Krutza, June, *Prof*, Eastern Illinois University, Art Department, Charleston IL (S)

Kryzsko, Karen, *Head Dept*, Saint Mary's College, Art Department, Winona MN (S)

Krzisnik, Zoran, *Dir*, Moderna Galerija, Modern Art Gallery, Ljubljana Yugoslavia

Köse, Ismail H, *Asst Dir*, Istanbul Arkeoloji Müzeleri, Archaeological Museums of Istanbul, Istanbul Turkey

Kuan, Baulu, *Instructor*, College of Saint Benedict, Art Department, Saint Joseph MN (S)

Kubert, Joe, *Pres*, Joe Kubert School of Cartoon and Graphic Art Inc, Dover NJ (S)

Kubly, Don, *Pres*, Art Center College of Design, Pasadena CA (S)

Kubris, Valdes, *Assoc Prof*, New York Institute of Technology, Fine Arts Department, Old Westbury NY (S)

Kuch, Harry G, *Pres*, Woodmere Art Gallery, Philadelphia PA

Kuchar, Kathleen, *Prof*, Fort Hays State University, Department of Art, Hays KS (S)

Kuchel, Konrad G, *Coordr Loans*, American Federation of Arts, New York NY

Kuchlich, Betty, *Program Consultant*, Xerox Corporation, Art Collection, Stamford CT

Kuchta, Ronald A, *Dir*, Everson Museum of Art, Syracuse NY

Kuckreja, Karen, *Instr*, Taft College, Division of Performing Arts, Taft CA (S)

Kudlawiec, Dennis P, *Chmn*, Livingston University, Division of Fine Arts, Livingston AL (S)

Kudo, Kazuaki, *Dir*, Tokyo-To Bijutsukan, Tokyo Metropolitan Art Museum, Tokyo Japan

Kudron, Georgeann, *Dir of Educ*, Des Moines Art Center, Des Moines IA

Kuehn, Claire, *Archivist & Librn*, Panhandle-Plains Historical Society Museum, Library, Canyon TX

Kuehn, Gary, *Assoc Prof*, Rutgers, the State University of New Jersey, Mason Gross School of the Arts, New Brunswick NJ (S)

Kuehne, R E, *VPres*, Orange County Community of Museums and Galleries, Goshen NY

Kuehne, Richard E, *Dir Museum*, United States Military Academy, West Point Museum, West Point NY

Kuentz, Pierre, *Instr*, Schiller College, Europe University, Art Department, Strasbourg France (S)

Kugler, Richard C, *Dir*, New Bedford Whaling Museum, New Bedford MA

Kuhl, Condon, *Chairperson Dept*, Drake University, Art Department, Des Moines IA (S)

Kuhlman, Barbara, *Prof*, State University of New York College at Cortland, Art Department, Cortland NY (S)

Kuhn, Annette, *Adminr*, Art Commission of the City of New York, New York NY

Kuhrmann, Dieter, *Dir*, Staatliche Graphische Sammlung, National Graphic Collection, Munich Germany, Federal Republic of

Kuiper, James, *Dir of Exhib*, Calvin College Center Art Gallery, Grand Rapids MI

Kuiper, James, *Instructor*, Calvin College, Art Dept, Grand Rapids MI (S)

Kuiper, John, *Acting Dir*, International Museum of Photography at George Eastman House, Rochester NY

Kujundzic, Zeljko, *Chmn Dept*, Pennsylvania State University, Fayette Campus, Department of Art, Uniontown PA (S)

Kulik, David, *Asst Prof*, Daemen College, Art Department, Amherst NY (S)

Kulla, Linda Claire, *Cur Educ*, Missouri Historical Society, Saint Louis MO

Kultzen, Rolf, *Cur Italian Paintings*, Bayerischen Staatsgemaldesammlungen, Bavarian State Galleries of Art, Munich Germany, Federal Republic of

Kulzer, S Linda, *VPres*, College of Saint Benedict, Art Gallery, Saint Joseph MN

Kumnick, Charles, *Asst Prof*, Trenton State College, Art Department, Trenton NJ (S)

Kumpan, Mariam, *Asst Librn*, Haaretz Museum, Central Library, Tel-Aviv Israel

Kuna, Magdalene, *Pres*, Quincy Art Center, Quincy IL

Kunda, Judith Lea, *Dir Art Gallery*, Los Angeles Harbor College Art Gallery, Wilmington CA

Kunkel, Jerry W, *Chmn*, University of Colorado, Boulder CO (S)

Kunstler, Phyllis, *Childrens Librn*, Port Chester Public Library, Port Chester NY

Kuntz, David L, *Exhibits Designer*, Illinois State University, University Museums, Normal IL

Kuo, James K Y, *Prof*, Daemen College, Art Department, Amherst NY (S)

Kuony, John H, *Dir & Cur Art*, Oshkosh Public Museum, Oshkosh WI

Kupferman, Norman, *Adult Services*, Long Beach Public Library, Long Beach NY

Kur, Mitchell, *Treas*, Danforth Museum, Framingham MA

Kurata, Bunsaku, *Dir*, Nara Kokuritsu Hakubutsukan, Nara National Museum, Nara-shi Japan

Kurcbart, Maria, *Asst Prof*, Hartford Art School of the University of Hartford, West Hartford CT (S)

Kureshi, B A, *Chmn*, Lahore Museum, Lahore Pakistan

Kurka, Donald F, *Head Dept Art*, University of Tennessee, Knoxville, Department of Art, Knoxville TN (S)

Kurneta, Anthony, *Visiting Lectr*, College of the Holy Cross, Department of Fine Arts, Worcester MA (S)

Kuronen, Dennis, *Asst Prof*, Beaver College, Department of Fine Arts, Glenside PA (S)

Kurriger, Patricia, *Instructor*, College of DuPage, Humanities Div, Glen Ellyn IL (S)

Kurth, Burton O, *Pres*, Art Gallery of Greater Victoria, Victoria BC

Kurth, Constance S, *Admin Asst & Prog Dir*, University of Vermont, Robert Hull Fleming Museum, Burlington VT

Kurtz, Stephen G, *Principal*, Phillips Exeter Academy, Lamont Gallery, Exeter NH

Kuruna, Daniel, *Acting Chmn Art Dept*, Western Illinois University, Browne Hall Gallery, Macomb IL

Kuruna, Daniel L, *Chmn Dept*, Western Illinois University, Dept of Art, Macomb IL (S)

Kurz, Kathe, *Lectr*, Carroll College, Art Department, Waukesha WI (S)

Kusama, Tetsuo, *Asst Prof*, Utah State University, Department of Art, Logan UT (S)

Kuspit, Donald B, *Chmn*, State University of New York at Stony Brook, Art Department, Stony Brook NY (S)

Kusti, Nicholas, *Cur*, Historic Burlington County Prison Museum, Mount Holly NJ

Kutcher, Emily, *Admin*, Dauphin Allied Arts Centre, Dauphin MB

Kutchera, Dean, *VPres*, Palm Beach County Parks and Recreation Department, Morikami Museum of Japanese Culture, Delray Beach FL

Kutchins, Laurie, *Information Officer*, Wyoming Council on the Arts, Cheyenne WY

Kuthy, Sandor, *Cur*, Kunstmuseum Bern, Museum of Fine Arts Berne, Berne Switzerland

Kutschera, Volker, *Cur Theatrical Sciences & Public Relations*, Saltzburger Museum Carolino Augusteum, Salzburg Museum, Salzburg Austria

Kutsky, Irene, *Instr*, College of New Rochelle, Art Department, New Rochelle NY (S)

Kuwayama, George, *Sr Cur of Far Eastern Art*, Los Angeles County Museum of Art, Los Angeles CA (S)

Kuykendall, Karen Tucker, *Cur Education*, Florida Gulf Coast Art Center, Inc, Clearwater FL

Kvaran, Olafur, *Dir*, Listasafn Einars Jonssonar, National Einar Jonsson Museum, Reykjavik Iceland

Kwiecinski, Chet, *Dir*, Abilene Fine Arts Museum, Abilene TX

Laas, Maria, *Secy*, Omaha Children's Museum, Inc, Omaha NE

Lab, Walter F, *Instructor*, Modesto Junior College, Arts Humanities and Speech Division, Modesto CA (S)

Labaree, Benjamin, *Munson Institute Dir*, Mystic Seaport Museum, Inc, Mystic CT

LaBarge, Dave, *Instr*, Siena Heights College, Art Department, Adrian MI (S)

LaBelle, Marguarite, *Asst Prof*, Jersey City State College, Art Department, Jersey City NJ (S)

Laberge, Craig, *Exhib Coordr*, McGill University, McCord Museum, Montreal PQ

Labiche, Walter A, *Dir*, New Orleans Art Institute, New Orleans LA (S)

Labot, Tony, *Preparator*, Academy of the Museum of Conceptual Art, San Francisco CA

Labuhn, Erda, *Cur*, Diablo Valley College Museum, Pleasant Hill CA

Lacey, James R, *Acting Dir*, Historical Society of Delaware, Read House, The Strand, Wilmington DE

Lachapelle, Pierre, *Secy*, Canadian Museums Association, Association des Musees Canadiens, Ottawa ON

Lackaff, Deanna S, *Dir of Development & Public Relations*, Museum of the American China Trade, Milton MA

Lackey, Elaine, *Pres Board Trustees*, Mendocino Art Center, Mendocino CA

Laclotte, Michel, *Cur Paintings*, Musee du Louvre, Louvre Museum, Paris France

Laclotte, Michel, *Chief Cur*, Musee du Jeu de Paume, Gallery of Impressionists, Paris France

Lacouture, Felipe, *Dir*, Museo Nacional de Historia, National Hisotrical Museum, Mexico City Mexico

Ladd, Pauline, *Assoc Prof*, Rhode Island College, Art Department, Providence RI (S)

Ladely, Dan, *Dir Sheldon Film Theatre*, University of Nebraska Lincoln, Sheldon Memorial Art Gallery, Lincoln NE

Laderman, Gabriel, *Artist in Res*, Viterbo College, Art Department, La Crosse WI (S)

Ladis, Andrew, *Instructor*, Austin Peay State University, Dept of Art, Clarksville TN (S)

Ladish, Mary, *Cur Asst*, Marquette University, Marquette Fine Art Collection, Milwaukee WI

Ladnowska, Janina, *Cur*, Muzeum Sztuki, Lodz Poland

LaFantasie, Glenn, *Ed, Roger Williams Corresp*, Rhode Island Historical Society, Providence RI

Lafferty, Anna, *Graphic Design Coordr*, Tunxis Community College, Graphic Design & Applied Arts Dept, Farmington CT (S)

Lafferty, Frederick W, *Recording Secy*, Maryland Historical Society Museum, Baltimore MD

Laflamme, Carole, *Secy-Accountant*, Galerie Restigouche Gallery, Campbellton NB

LaFollette, Curtis K, *Assoc Prof*, Rhode Island College, Art Department, Providence RI (S)

Lafon, Dee J, *Chmn*, East Central University, Art Department, Ada OK (S)

LaFond, Robert, *Registrar*, Princeton University, Art Museum, Princeton NJ

Lafortune, F, *Chief Librn*, Musee du Quebec, Bibliotheque des Art, Quebec PQ

LaFrance, Gene, *VPres*, LeSueur County Historical Society Museum, Elysian MN

LaFreniere, Isabel, *Pres & Cur*, Rockport Art Association, Rockport MA

Lagerberg, Don, *Chmn Dept*, California State University, Fullerton, Art Department, Fullerton CA (S)

Lagerqvist, Lars O, *Deputy Keeper*, Kungl Myntkabinettet Statens Museum För Mynt Medalj Och Penninghistoria, Royal Coin Cabinet, National Museum of Monetary History, Stockholm Sweden

Lago, Armando M, *Adjunct Assoc Prof*, Catholic University of America, Department of Architecture & Planning, Washington DC (S)

Lagoria, Georgianna, *Gallery Coordr*, University of Santa Clara, de Saisset Art Gallery and Museum, Santa Clara CA

Lagrue, Catherine, *Asst Conservator*, Musee des Beaux-Arts, Museum of Fine Arts, Angers France

Lahaye, Francois, *Dir*, Centre Culturel de Trois Rivieres, Trois Rivieres PQ

Lahiri, Subrata, *Assoc Prof*, University of Arkansas, Art Department, Fayetteville AR (S)

Lahr, J Stephen, *Asst Prof*, University of Nebraska at Omaha, Dept of Art, Omaha NE (S)

Laidlaw, Ann, *Prof*, Hollins College, Art Department, Hollins VA (S)

Laine, Osmo, *VPres*, Turun Taidemuseo, Turku Art Museum, Turku Finland

Laing, Aileen H, *Chmn Dept*, Sweet Briar College, Art History Department, Sweet Briar VA (S)

Laing, Richard H, *Dean*, East Carolina University, Wellington B Gray Gallery, Greenville NC

Laing, Richard H, *Dean*, East Carolina University, School of Art, Greenville NC (S)

Laird, W David, *Univrsity Librn*, University of Arizona, Main Library, Tucson AZ

Lake, Jerry L, *Asst Prof*, George Washington University, Department of Art, Washington DC (S)

Lake, Lucinda, *Librn*, Center for the Visual Arts, Slide Library, Oakland CA

Lake, Mary M, *Dir*, Peninsula Fine Arts Center, Newport News VA

Laker, Philip, *Instructor*, Northwest Missouri State University, Dept of Art, Maryville MO (S)

Lakins, Claire, *Education*, Hastings County Museum, Belleville ON

Lakoff, Walter, *VPres*, Art Association of Richmond, Richmond IN

Lally, Franca P, *Asst Dir*, Caravan of East and West, Inc, Caravan House Galleries, New York NY

Lally, John, *Gallery Dir*, Caravan of East and West, Inc, Caravan House Galleries, New York NY

Lalonde, Marcel, *Dir*, Saint Joseph's Oratory, Montreal PQ

La Malfa, James, *Head Dept*, University of Wisconsin Center, Marinette WI (S)

Lamarche, Jeanette, *Admin*, Pointe Claire Cultural Centre, Pointe Claire PQ

Lamarche-Ouellet, Helene, *Chief Educ Officer*, Montreal Museum of Fine Arts, School of Art and Design, Montreal PQ (S)

Lambert, Anne, *Cur Education*, University of Wisconsin, Elvehjem Art Center, Madison WI

Lambert, Don, *Exec Dir*, Arts Council of Topeka, Topeka KS

Lambert, Nancy Sifferd, *Art & Architecture Librn*, Yale University, Art and Architecture Library, New Haven CT

Lambert, Rose, *Librn*, Louisiana State Museum, Louisiana Historical Center Library, New Orleans LA

Lambert, W E, *Asst Prof*, Del Mar College, Department of Art, Corpus Christi TX (S)

Lambl, Chris, *Instructor*, Ivy School of Professional Art, Downtown Annex, Pittsburgh PA (S)

Lambrecht, Eleni, *Treas*, Hartland Art Council, Hartland MI

Lammers, George, *VPres*, Canadian Museums Association, Association des Musees Canadiens, Ottawa ON

Lammon, Dwight P, *Deputy Dir Collections*, Corning Museum of Glass, Corning NY

Lamon, Evelyn, *Chief of Operations*, Portland Art Association, Portland OR

Lamont, Bridget, *Assoc Dir Library Development*, Illinois State Library, Springfield IL

Lamoureux, Richard E, *Asst Prof*, Assumption College, Department of Fine Arts and Music, Worcester MA (S)

Lampe, Frederick, *Co-Owner*, Lampe Gallery of Fine Art, Lampe School of Art, New Orleans LA

Lampe, George, *Dir*, Stichting de Vrije Academie Voor Beeldende Kunsten, Foundation The Free Academy for Fine Arts, The Netherlands (S)

Lampe, June, *Co-Owner*, Lampe Gallery of Fine Art, Lampe School of Art, New Orleans LA

Lampe, William, *Preparator*, University of Minnesota, University Gallery, Minneapolis MN

Lamph, John, *Assoc Prof*, Mary Washington College, Art Department, Fredericksburg VA (S)

Lancaster, John, *Instructor*, Malden Bridge School of Art, Malden Bridge NY (S)

Lancaster, Madeline E, *Pres*, Springfield Historical Society, Springfield NJ

Lancaster, Michael, *Instructor*, Malden Bridge School of Art, Malden Bridge NY (S)

Lancman, Eli, *Dir*, Museum of Japanese Art, Haifa Israel

Land, Norman, *Assoc Prof*, University of Missouri, Art History and Archaeology Department, Columbia MO (S)

Land, Shirley, *Publicity Dir*, Silvermine Guild School of the Arts, New Canaan CT

Landa, Robin, *Instructor*, Elizabeth Seton College, Art Department, Yonkers NY (S)

Landau, E, *Dir Institute for Promotion Art & Science*, Haaretz Museum, Tel-Aviv Israel

Landau, Laureen, *Instructor*, Sacramento City College, Art Department, Sacramento CA (S)

Landau, Zuki, *Chief Librn*, School of Visual Arts Library, New York NY

Landess, Susan, *Public Relations Dir*, Denver Art Museum, Frederic H Douglas Library, Denver CO

Landfear, Adele, *Recording Secy*, Miniature Art Society of New Jersey, Nutley NJ

Landis, Ellen, *Cur Art*, Albuquerque Museum of Art, History and Science, Albuquerque NM

Landreau, Anthony N, *Cur Education*, Carnegie Institute, Museum of Art, Pittsburgh PA

Landry, Dorothy, *Asst Custodian*, West Baton Rouge Museum, Port Allen LA

Landry, Lionel, *Executive VPres, Asia Society, Inc*, Asia Society, Inc, Asia House Gallery, New York NY

Landry, Marguerite, *Secy*, University of Southwestern Louisiana, Art Center for Southwestern Louisiana, Lafayette LA

Landsley, Patrick, *Registrar*, Concordia University, Sir George Williams Art Galleries, Montreal PQ

Landwehr, William C, *Dir*, Springfield Art Museum, Springfield MO

Lane, Bob, *Dir*, Society of Environmental Graphics Designers, Chicago IL

Lane, Carl A, *Keeper of Manuscripts*, New Jersey Historical Society Museum, Library, Newark NJ

Lane, Jean C, *Chairperson*, Jersey City State College, Art Department, Jersey City NJ (S)

Lane, Kevin, *Dir & Education Dir*, Merrick Art Gallery, New Brighton PA

Lane, Leonard, *Treas*, Arts for Living Center, Burlington IA

Lane, Madeleine, *Assoc Prof*, Adelphi University, Department of Art and Art History, Garden City NY (S)

Lane Jr, C Gardner, *Dir*, Penobscot Marine Museum, Searsport ME

Lang, Alyce, *Asst Dir*, Old Barracks, Trenton NJ

Lang, James, *Lectr*, La Salle College, Department of Fine Arts, Philadelphia PA (S)

Lang, R Park, *Asst Prof*, Southwestern Oklahoma State University, Art Department, Weatherford OK (S)

Lang, Rodger, *Prof*, Metropolitan State College, Art Department, Denver CO (S)

Lang, Thomas, *Assoc Prof*, Webster College, Art Dept, Webster Groves MO (S)

Langan, L V, *Chmn*, Sarnia Public Library and Art Gallery, Sarnia ON

Langberg, Harald, *Keeper Danish Prehistoric Coll*, Nationalmuseet, National Museum, Copenhagen Denmark

Lange, Jim, *Secy & Treas*, Association of American Editorial Cartoonists, Oklahoma City OK

Lange, Linda, *Registrar*, Beaumont Art Museum, Beaumont TX

Lange, Patricia, *Assoc Librn*, University of Maryland, Art Library, College Park MD

Lange, Yvonne, *Dir*, Museum of New Mexico, Museum of International Folk Art, Santa Fe NM

Langford, Martha, *Producer*, National Film Board of Canada, Still Photography Division, Photo Gallery, Ottawa ON

Langhart, Nicholas, *Adminr*, Museums at Stony Brook, Stony Brook NY

Langland, Harold, *Assoc Prof*, Indiana University at South Bend, Fine Arts Department, South Bend IN (S)

Langley, Pepper, *Master Woodcarver*, Calvert Marine Museum, Solomons MD

Langoussis, Andrew, *Prof*, Rockford College, Department of Fine Arts, Rockford IL (S)

Langstadt, R, *Lectr*, McGill University, Department of Art History, Montreal PQ (S)

Langston, Linda, *Coordinating Cur*, Palo Alto Cultural Center, Palo Alto CA

Lanier, David, *Assoc Prof*, University of the District of Columbia, Art Department, Washington DC (S)

Lanier, Steven L, *Development Dir*, Worcester Art Museum, Worcester MA

Lansbury, Edgar, *VPres*, Nicholas Roerich Museum, New York NY

Lansdown, Robert R, *Dir*, Woolaroc Museum, Bartlesville OK

Lantzy, Don, *Dir*, Temple Abroad of Temple University, Rome Italy (S)

Lao, Lincoln, *Instr*, Schoolcraft College, Department of Art, Livonia MI (S)

LaPaglia, Peter, *Cur of Collections*, Tennessee State Museum, Nashville TN

LaPalme, Robert, *Dir*, Pavilion of Humour, Man and His World, Montreal PQ

Lape, Jane M, *Cur*, Fort Ticonderoga Museum, Ticonderoga NY

Lape, Jane M, *Librn*, Fort Ticonderoga Museum, Library, Ticonderoga NY

Lapierre, Raymond C, *Secy*, Musee d'Art de Joliette, Joliette PQ

La Plante, Roy, *Instructor*, Wayne Art Center, Wayne PA (S)

LaPointe, Madeleine, *Library Technician*, Sheridan College School of Applied Arts and Technology, School of Crafts and Design Library, Mississauga ON

Lapp, Maurice, *Prof*, Santa Rosa Junior College, Art Department, Santa Rosa CA (S)

Lappen, Jon, *Pres Municipal Arts Commission*, City of Los Angeles, Municipal Arts Dept, Los Angeles CA

Lapsansky, Phillip, *Chief of Reference*, Library Company of Philadelphia, Philadelphia PA

Laracuente, Mahir, *Prof*, Catholic University of Puerto Rico, Department of History & Fine Arts, Ponce PR (S)

La Regina, A, *Dir*, Museo Nazionale Romano, National Museum of Rome, Rome Italy

Large, Freda M, *Executive Secy*, Architects Association of New Brunswick, Saint John NB

Larimer, Jan, *Chmn Board*, Nicolaysen Art Museum, Casper WY

Larkin, Alan, *Asst Prof*, Indiana University at South Bend, Fine Arts Department, South Bend IN (S)

Larkin, Eugene, *Prof*, University of Minnesota, Department of Design, Saint Paul MN (S)

Larkin, Frank Y, *VPres*, Museum of Modern Art, New York NY

Larkin, James S, *VPres*, Alabama Museum of Photography, Birmingham AL

Larkin, Jean T, *Membership Coordr*, Worcester Art Museum, Worcester MA

Larkin, Mary, *Registrar*, Spertus Museum of Judaica, Chicago IL

Larmer, Oscar V, *Prof*, Kansas State University, Art Department, Manhattan KS (S)

Larned, Ronald, *Chmn*, Rollins College, Department of Art, Main Campus, Winter Park FL (S)

La Rocca, E, *Staff*, Musei Capitolini, Museum of Sculpture, Rome Italy

Larochelle, Pierre, *Dir*, L'Universite Laval, Ecole des Arts Visuels de L'Universite Laval, Quebec PQ

LaRoux, Leonard, *Instr*, College of Saint Rose, Division of Art, Albany NY (S)

LaRow, Magdalen, *Head Dept*, Nazareth College of Rochester, Art Department, Rochester NY (S)

LaRowe, Betsy, *Instructor*, Laramie County Community College, Division of Humanities, Cheyenne WY (S)

Larsen, D, *Cur*, University of Alaska, Museum, Fairbanks AK

Larsen, Jack Lenor, *Vice Chmn*, American Craft Council, New York NY

Larsen, Jack Lenor, *Chmn of Board*, Haystack Mountain School of Crafts Gallery, Deer Isle ME

Larsen, Maria, *Registrar*, Shaker Museum, Old Chatham NY

Larsen, Richard, *Chmn*, Lloydminster Barr Colony Museum Committee, Lloydminster SK

Larsen, Susan, *Asst Prof*, University of Southern California, School of Fine Arts, Los Angeles CA (S)

Larsen, William, *Librn*, Southwest Craft Center, Library, San Antonio TX

Larson, Arthur D, *Asst Dir Admin*, Museum of Fine Arts, Boston MA

Larson, Blaine, *Chmn Fourth Year*, Corcoran School of Art, Washington DC (S)

Larson, Gail, *Dir*, Idaho State University, John B Davis Gallery of Fine Art, Pocatello ID

Larson, J Russell, *Assoc Prof*, Whitworth College, Art Department, Spokane WA (S)

Larson, Mike, *Prof*, Shoreline Community College, Humanities Division, Seattle WA (S)

Larson, Neil G, *Dir*, Litchfield Historical Society, Litchfield CT

Larson, Paul W, *Dir*, University of Minnesota, Student Center Galleries, Saint Paul MN

Larson, Sidney, *Cur*, State Historical Society of Missouri, Columbia MO

La Rue, James, *Instructor*, Harding University, Department of Art, Searcy AR (S)

LaSalle, Barbara, *Registrar*, Brooklyn Museum, Brooklyn NY

Lasansky, Leonardo, *Prof*, Hamline University, Art Department, Saint Paul MN (S)

Lasansky, William, *Instr*, Bucknell University, Department of Art, Lewisburg PA (S)

Lasbury, Lee, *Pres*, Florida Artist Group Inc, Englewood FL

Lasch, Robert, *Pres*, Tubac Center of the Arts, Santa Cruz Valley Art Association, Tubac AZ

LaScola, Cathy, *Head Public Information*, J Paul Getty Museum, Malibu CA

Lash, Ken, *Prof*, University of Northern Iowa, Department of Art, Cedar Falls IA (S)

Laske, Lyle, *Prof*, Moorhead State University, Department of Art, Moorhead MN (S)

Laskin, Harriette C F, *Art Coordr*, Tidewater Community College, Art Department, Portsmouth VA (S)

Laskin Jr, Myron, *Research Cur European Art*, National Gallery of Canada, Ottawa ON

Lasko, Peter, *Dir*, Courtauld Institute Galleries, London England

Laskovski, Peter, *Dir*, Shaker Museum, Old Chatham NY

Lassen, Erik, *Dir*, Det Danske Kunstindustrimuseum, Museum of Decorative Art, Copenhagen Denmark

Lassiter, Frances, *Prof*, New York Institute of Technology, Fine Arts Department, Old Westbury NY (S)

Lasuchin, Michael, *Chairperson Printmaking*, Philadelphia College of Art, Philadelphia PA (S)

Laszczoki, Marisha, *Asst Librn*, Craft and Folk Art Museum, Library and Media Resource Center, Los Angeles CA

Latcher, Mary Ellen, *Historic Site Asst*, Schuyler Mansion, Albany NY

Latham, Dorothy, *Secy*, Green Hill Art Gallery, Greensboro NC

Lathrop, Welland, *Instructor*, Rudolph Schaeffer School of Design, San Francisco CA (S)

Latka, Nick, *Instructor*, University of Southern Colorado, Belmont Campus, Department of Art, Pueblo CO (S)

Latocha, Sue, *Instructor*, Joliet Junior College, Art Dept, Joliet IL (S)

Latta, George, *Emeritus Prof*, William Woods-Westminster Colleges, Art Department, Fulton MO (S)

Latta, Peter, *Exhib Officer*, Mount Saint Vincent University Art Gallery, Halifax NS

Lattimore, Walter, *Asst Prof*, University of the District of Columbia, Art Department, Washington DC (S)

Lattin, Floyd, *Secy of Museum*, Solomon R Guggenheim Museum, New York NY

Latzel, Ruth, *Librn*, Hamburger Kunsthalle, Bibliothek der Hamburger Kunsthalle, Hamburg Germany, Federal Republic of

Latzko, Walter, *Staff Asst*, Hall of Fame of the Trotter, Goshen NY

Lau, Jean, *Gallery Shop Dir*, Ann Arbor Art Association, Ann Arbor MI

Lau, Jo, *Admin Secy*, University of Michigan Museum of Art, Alumni Memorial Hall Museum, Ann Arbor MI

Laub, David, *VPres*, Boca Raton Center for the Arts, Inc, Boca Raton FL

Laubenstein, Richard, *Instructor*, Ohio Visual Art Institute, Cincinnati OH (S)

Lauder, Ronald, *VPres*, Museum of American Folk Art, New York NY

Laufer, Marilyn, *Mem Secy*, Sioux City Art Center, Sioux City IA

Laughlin, Thomas C, *Registrar*, Museum of Fine Arts of Saint Petersburg, Florida, Inc, Saint Petersburg FL

Laughner, Charles, *Pres*, Laughner Brothers, Inc, Indianapolis IN

Laurent, John, *Prof*, University of New Hampshire, Department of the Arts, Durham NH (S)

Laurent, John, *Chmn Committee*, Old Gaol Museum, York ME

Laurette, Patrick, *Asst Cur*, Art Gallery of Nova Scotia, Halifax NS

Lauriane, Mary, *Art Dir*, Felician College, Art Department, Chicago IL (S)

Laurin, Fernand, *Technician*, Musee d'Art de Joliette, Joliette PQ

Laury, Frank, *Prof*, California State University, Fresno, Art Department, Fresno CA (S)

Lauvao, Fa'ailoilo, *Cur*, Jean P Haydon Museum, Pago Pago, American Samoa PI

Lauver, James, *Asst Prof*, Northern State College, Art Dept, Aberdeen SD (S)

Lavallee, G, *VPres*, Musee d'Art de Saint-Laurent, Saint-Laurent PQ

Lavallee, Gerard, *Dir & Cur*, Musee d'Art de Saint-Laurent, Saint-Laurent PQ

Laver, Samuel, *Assoc Dir*, Buten Museum of Wedgwood, Merion PA

Laverty, Peter, *Head Div Fine Arts*, National Art School, Department of Technical Education, Darlinghurst Australia (S)

LaVoy, Walter J, *Chmn Dept*, Central Connecticut State College, Department of Art, New Britain CT (S)

Law, Aaron, *Chmn Found Prog*, Herron School of Art, Indiana University-Purdue University, Indianapolis, Indianapolis IN (S)

Lawall, David B, *Cur*, University of Virginia, Art Museum, Charlottesville VA

Lawder, Standish, *Assoc Prof*, University of California, San Diego, Visual Arts Department, La Jolla CA (S)

Lawhorn, James C, *Adminr*, Huntington Galleries, Huntington WV

Lawless, Benjamin W, *Asst Dir for Exhibits*, National Museum of History and Technology, Smithsonian Institution, Washington DC

Lawless, Jane, *Art & Music Librn*, Malden Public Library, Malden MA

Lawless, Ken, *Mgr Dir Center for Music, Drama & Art*, Lake Placid School of Art Gallery, Lake Placid NY

Lawless, Ramsay, *Pres Bd of Mgrs*, University of Rochester, Memorial Art Gallery, Rochester NY

Lawner, Ruth, *Publishing Editor*, Spencer Museum of Art, Lawrence KS

Lawrence, Camille, *Instructor*, Davidson County Community College, Language-Fine Arts Dept, Lexington NC (S)

Lawrence, Charles D, *Cur*, United States Navy, Combat Art Gallery, Washington DC

Lawrence, David, *Head Dept*, San Bernardino Valley College, Art Department, San Bernardino CA (S)

Lawrence, Frances, *Business Mgr*, Birmingham-Bloomfield Art Association, Birmingham MI

Lawrence, Helen, *Librn*, Southern Methodist University, Art Library, Dallas TX

Lawrence, Jacob, *Board Dir Member*, Art Information Center, Inc, New York NY

Lawrence, John, *Asst Cur*, Historic New Orleans Collection, Kemper and Leila Williams Foundation, New Orleans LA

Lawrence, John D, *Head Dept*, La Grange College, Art Department, La Grange GA (S)

Lawrence, Kitty, *Asst Cur*, Dixon Gallery and Gardens, Memphis TN

Lawrence, Robert M, *Secy*, American Institute of Architects, Washington DC

Lawrence, William A, *Treas*, Concord Antiquarian Society Museum, Concord MA

Lawson, Edward P, *Chief Education Dept*, Hirshhorn Museum and Sculpture Garden, Washington DC

Lawson, John, *Corresp Secy*, San Bernadino Art Association, Inc, San Bernadino CA

Lawson, John, *Treas*, San Bernadino Art Association, Inc, San Bernadino CA

Lawson, Noel G, *Prof*, Radford University, Art Department, Radford VA (S)

Lawson, Pam F, *Asst Prof*, Radford University, Art Department, Radford VA (S)

Lawson, Stephen, *Prof*, West Virginia University, Division of Art, Morgantown WV (S)

Lawton, Maria, *Dir*, Boca Raton Center for the Arts, Inc, Boca Raton FL

Lawton, Mary S, *Acting Chmn Fine Arts Dept*, Loyola University of Chicago, Fine Arts Department, Chicago IL (S)

Lawton, Thomas, *Dir*, Freer Gallery of Art, Washington DC

Lazar, Howard, *Coordr Street Artist Program*, San Francisco City and County Art Commission, San Francisco CA

Lazaridis, Paul, *Dir Ephore of Byzantine Antiquities*, Byzantine Museum, Athens Greece

Lazarus, Diane, *Exec Dir*, Hunterdon Art Center, Clinton NJ

Lazarus, William, *Cur of Sciences*, Columbia Museums of Art and Science, Columbia Science Museum, Columbia SC

Lazarus H, Alan H, *Chairman*, William Paterson College, Art Department, Wayne NJ (S)

Lazarus IV, Fred, *Pres*, Maryland Institute College of Art, Decker Gallery, Baltimore MD

Lazarus IV, Fred, *Pres*, Maryland Institute, College of Art, Baltimore MD (S)

Lazelle, Pat, *Instructor*, Southwestern Oklahoma State University, Art Department, Weatherford OK (S)

Lazerek, John, *Treas*, Mystic Art Association, Inc, Mystic CT

Lazor, Gloria, *Dir*, Clinton Historical Museum Village, Clinton NJ

Lazorik, Wayne R, *Chmn*, University of New Mexico, Department of Art, Albuquerque NM (S)

Lazzaro, Richard, *Chmn*, University of Wisconsin, Art Department Gallery, Madison WI

Lücke, H K, *Chmn*, University of Toronto, Department of Fine Art, Toronto ON (S)

Lea, Stanley E, *Prof*, Sam Houston State University, Art Department, Huntsville TX (S)

Leach, David, *Asst Prof*, Wright State University, Art Department, Dayton OH (S)

Leach, Ellis, *Secy*, Victoria Society of Maine Women, Victoria Mansion and Morse Libby Mansion, Portland ME

Leach, Frederick D, *Head Dept*, Hamline University, Art Department, Saint Paul MN (S)

Leach, Mary E, *Pres*, Owatonna Arts Center, Owatonna MN

Leach, Richard, *Prof*, Albion College, Department of Visual Arts, Albion MI (S)

Leach, Sandford B, *Exec VPres*, Rehoboth Art League, Inc, Rehoboth Beach DE

Leach Jr, Maurice D, *Librn*, Washington and Lee University, McCormick Library, Lexington VA

Leader, Garnet R, *Pres*, Kappa Pi International Honorary Art Fraternity, Birmingham AL

Leadingham, Jo, *Gallery Coordr*, Kentucky State University, Jackson Hall Gallery, Frankfort KY

Leaf, Roy, *VPres*, Skowhegan School of Painting and Sculpture, Portland ME (S)

Leahy, John Louise, *Assoc Prof*, Marygrove College, Dept of Art & Art History, Detroit MI (S)

Leake, A J, *Cur*, Naval Amphibious Museum, Norfolk VA

Leake, Carol, *Instructor*, Southeastern Louisiana University, Dept of Visual Arts, Hammond LA (S)

Leake, Carol S, *Chmn Board of Trustees*, Lee County Library, Tupelo MS

Leake, James C, *Secy*, Cherokee National Historical Society, Inc, Tahlequah OK

Leaman, Ellen, *Education Cur*, Historic New Orleans Collection, Kemper and Leila Williams Foundation, New Orleans LA

Learmonth, G S, *Keeper Conservation*, Birmingham Museums and Art Gallery, Birmingham England

Learner, Vickie, *Preparator*, Bergen Community Museum, Paramus NJ

Leary, Edward F, *Dir*, Boston University, School of Visual Arts, Boston MA (S)

Leary, Melody A, *Instructor*, Norwich Art School, Norwich Free Academy, Art Dept, Norwich CT (S)

Leary, Thomas, *Prof*, Salem State College, Art Department, Salem MA (S)

Leavitt, Thomas W, *Dir*, Merrimack Valley Textile Museum, North Andover MA

Leavitt, Thomas W, *Prof*, Cornell University, Department of the History of Art, Ithaca NY (S)

Leavitt, Thomas W, *Dir*, Cornell University, Herbert F Johnson Museum of Art, Ithaca NY

Lebeck, Steven, *Coordr Graphic Design*, Florida School of the Arts, Visual Arts, Palatka FL (S)

LeBlanc, Sylvia, *Treas*, Huntsville Art League and Museum Association Inc, Huntsville AL

LeBreton, E F, *VPres*, Louisiana State Museum, New Orleans LA

Lecavalier, Fernand, *Pastor & Dir*, Musee de L'Eglise Notre-Dame, Montreal PQ

Ledbetter, Roseanne, *Secy*, Western Illinois University, Browne Hall Gallery, Macomb IL

Lederer, Bertha V B, *Coordr Fine Arts Activities*, State University of New York College at Geneseo, Fine Arts Gallery, Geneseo NY

Lederer, Kurt L, *Dir*, Academy of the Arts, Easton MD

LeDoux, David, *Prof*, Middle Tennessee State University, Art Dept, Murfreesboro TN (S)

LeDuc, Paul, *Artistic Cur*, Saint Joseph's Oratory, Montreal PQ

Lee, Christopher G, *Dir*, Columbus Chapel, Boal Mansion and Museum, Boalsburg PA

Lee, Ellen W, *Assoc Cur Painting & Sculpture*, Indianapolis Museum of Art, Indianapolis IN

Lee, Esther, *Asst Head Art & Music Division*, Queens Borough Public Library, Art and Music Division, Jamaica NY

Lee, Hon Ching, *Dir Gallery*, Rockford College, Department of Fine Arts, Rockford IL (S)

Lee, Hyosoo, *Technical Services Librn*, Cleveland Institute of Art, Jessica Gund Memorial Library, Cleveland OH

Lee, Jean Gordon, *Cur Far Eastern Art*, Philadelphia Museum of Art, Philadelphia PA

Lee, Kyung, *Instructor*, Philadelphia Community College, Department of Fine Arts, Philadelphia PA (S)

Lee, Marielow, *Admin Secy*, Davenport Municipal Art Gallery, Davenport IA

Lee, Marijane, *Secy*, Chinese Culture Foundation, Chinese Culture Center Gallery, San Francisco CA

Lee, Mathilde Boal, *Dir*, Columbus Chapel, Boal Mansion and Museum, Boalsburg PA

Lee, Nanyong, *Cur in Charge of Registrar*, National Museum of Korea, Seoul Korea

Lee, Rebekah E, *Asst Dir*, Fayetteville Museum of Art, Inc, Fayetteville NC

Lee, Robert, *Chmn Fine arts*, Hartnell College, Art and Photography Departments, Salinas CA (S)

Lee, Robert J, *Assoc Prof*, Marymount College, Art Department, Tarrytown NY (S)

Lee, Roland, *Instructor*, Dixie College, Art Department, Saint George UT (S)

Lee, Sherman E, *Dir & Chief Cur Oriental Art*, Cleveland Museum of Art, Cleveland OH

Lee, Stanley, *Instr*, Indiana University-Purdue University, Department of Fine Arts, Fort Wayne IN (S)

Lee, Thomas P, *Cur Painting*, Fine Arts Museums of San Francisco, M H de Young Memorial Museum and California Palace of the Legion of Honor, n of Honor co

Lee, William, *Instructor*, Elmira College, Art Department, Elmira NY (S)

Lee, Wynn, *Dir & Cur*, Mark Twain Memorial, Hartford CT

Leeam, Arch, *Chmn*, St Olaf College, Art Department, Northfield MN (S)

Lee-Bevier, Kip, *Dir of Visitor Services*, Wine Museum of San Francisco, San Francisco CA

Leece, Curtis, *Instructor*, Saginaw Valley State College, Dept of Art & Design, University Center MI (S)

Leece, Gayle, *Instructor*, Saginaw Valley State College, Dept of Art & Design, University Center MI (S)

Leeds, Jo Alice, *Asst Prof*, University of North Carolina at Greensboro, Art Dept, Greensboro NC (S)

Leeds, Temme Barkin, *Cur*, Georgia State University, Arthur I and Irma L Harris Reading Room and Visual Resource Library, Atlanta GA

Leedy Jr, Walter C, *Assoc Prof*, Cleveland State University, Art Department, Cincinnati OH (S)

Leek, Thomas A, *Dir*, Southern Utah State College, Braithwaite Fine Arts Gallery, Cedar City UT

Lee-Mills, Rowe, *Instr*, Claremore College, Art Department, Claremore OK (S)

Leeper, Jeannette, *Curator*, Laguna Beach Museum of Art, Laguna Beach CA

Leeper, John P, *Librn*, Marion Koogler McNay Art Institute, Library, San Antonio TX

Leeper, John Palmer, *Dir*, Marion Koogler McNay Art Institute, San Antonio TX

Lees, Gary P, *Asst Prof*, Johns Hopkins University, School of Medicine, Department of Art as Applied to Medicine, Baltimore MD (S)

Lees Jr, Avon, *Pres*, Tobe-Coburn School for Fashion Careers, Ltd, New York NY (S)

Leet, Richard E, *Dir*, Charles H MacNider Museum, Mason City IA

Leete, William, *Prof*, University of Rhode Island, Department of Art, Kingston RI (S)

Leete, William C, *Asst Prof*, Northern Michigan University, Dept of Art & Design, Marquette MI (S)

Leeuw, R A, *Dir*, Stedelijk Museum het Prinsenhof, Het Prinsenhof State Museum, Delft Netherlands

Lee III, Tennent, *Chmn Board*, Huntsville Museum of Art, Huntsville AL

Lefebre, George, *Custodian*, West Baton Rouge Museum, Port Allen LA

Lefebure, Amelie, *Asst to Museum*, Institut de France, Musee Conde, Paris France

LeFevre, Geraldine, *Asst Dir*, San Antonio Public Library, San Antonio TX

Lefevre, Jerry, *Instructor*, School of the Associated Arts, Saint Paul MN (S)

Leff, Alix, *Instructor*, Clayworks, New York NY (S)

Leffler, William I, *Treas*, Museum of American Folk Art, New York NY

Legakis, Brian, *Asst Prof*, Wake Forest University, Department of Art, Winston-Salem NC (S)

Legentil, Danielle, *Research*, Musee d'Art de Saint-Laurent, Saint-Laurent PQ

Legner, Anton, *Dir*, Museen der Stadt Köln, Schnutgen-Museum, Cologne Germany, Federal Republic of

Legrand, C, *Asst Conservator*, Musee des Beaux-Arts, Museum of Fine Arts, Tours France

Legrand, Francine-Claire, *Cur Modern Art*, Musees Royaux des Beaux-Arts de Belgique, Royal Museums of Fine Arts of Belgium, Brussels Belgium

Lehder, Diane, *Instr*, Xavier University of Louisiana, Department of Fine Arts, New Orleans LA (S)

Lehman, Arnold L, *Dir*, Baltimore Museum of Art, Baltimore MD

Lehman, Arnold L, *Dir*, Metropolitan Museum and Art Centers, Coral Gables FL

Lehman, Mark, *Asst Prof*, Trenton State College, Art Department, Trenton NJ (S)

Lehnert, Pamela, *Instr*, Peace College, Art Department, Raleigh NC (S)

Lehnert, Thompson, *Div Coordr Art Educ*, Kent State University, School of Art, Kent OH (S)

Lehrer, Leonard, *Chmn*, Arizona State University, Department of Art, Tempe AZ (S)

Leiber, Gerson, *Pres*, Society of American Graphic Artists, New York NY

Leiberman, Richard, *Instructor*, Mainline Center of the Arts, Haverford PA (S)

Leibert, Peter, *Chmn*, Connecticut College, Department of Art, New London CT (S)

Leider, Karen, *Cataloger*, Trinity College Library, Washington DC

Leifer, Elizabeth, *Instr*, Suomi College, Fine Arts Department, Hancock MI (S)

Leighton, D S R, *Dir Banff Centre*, Banff Centre School of Fine Arts, Banff AB (S)

Leijon, Per-Olow, *Cur*, Ostasiatiska Museet, Museum of Far Eastern Antiquities, Stockholm Sweden

Leinhardt, Lynne, *Instructor*, Factory of Visual Art, Seattle WA (S)

Leippe, Harry M, *Prof*, New Mexico Highlands University, Dept of Fine Arts, Las Vegas NM (S)

Leipzig, Arthur, *Prof*, School of the Arts, C W Post Center of Long Island University, Art Department, Greenvale NY (S)

Leisure, Hoyt B, *VPres*, Los Angeles County Museum of Art, Los Angeles CA

Leite, Alicia Dantas, *Head Librn*, Museu de Arte Moderna, Library, Rio Brazil

Leith, Chris, *Chmn Art Dept*, Emma Willard School Arts Division, Troy NY (S)

Leja, Michael, *Cur*, Brandeis University, Rose Art Museum, Waltham MA

Lekberg, Barbara, *VPres*, Sculpture Center, New York NY

Lem, Wu Chien, *Asst Prof*, University of South Dakota, Dept of Art, Vermillion SD (S)

Lema, Joseph, *Instr*, Utah Technical College at Salt Lake, Commercial Art Department, Salt Lake City UT (S)

Leman, Jack, *Instructor*, Oxbow Summer Art Workshops, Saugatuck MI (S)

Lemay, Charles, *Lectr*, Notre Dame College, Art Department, Manchester NH (S)

Lemieux, Louis, *Dir*, National Museums of Canada, National Museum of Natural Sciences, Ottawa ON

Leming Jr, John W, *Pres*, Annie S Kemerer Museum, Bethlehem PA

Lemmens, G T M, *Dir*, Nijmeegs Museum Commanderie van Saint Jan, Nijmegen Netherlands

Lemmerman, Harold, *Prof*, Jersey City State College, Art Department, Jersey City NJ (S)

Lemmerman, Harold, *Dir*, Jersey City State College, Courtney Art Gallery, Jersey City NJ

Lemoine, Pierre, *Cur*, Musee National du Chateau de Versailles, National Museum of the Chateau of Versailles, Versailles France

Lemon, James, *Dir*, Art Association of Richmond, Richmond IN

Lemon, Thomas, *Instructor*, Chamberlayne Junior College, Department of Graphic and Applied Arts, Boston MA (S)

Lenertz, John, *Instructor*, School of the Associated Arts, Saint Paul MN (S)

Lennig, Arthur, *Assoc Prof*, State University of New York at Albany, Art Department, Albany NY (S)

Lenon, Timothy, *Assoc Conservator*, Art Institute of Chicago, Chicago IL

Lent, Donald, *Chmn*, Bates College, Art Dept, Lewiston ME (S)

Lentel, Allota, *Registrar*, Heritage Plantation of Sandwich, Sandwich MA

Lenz, Christian, *Cur German Baroque Paintings*, Bayerischen Staatsgemaldesammlungen, Bavarian State Galleries of Art, Munich Germany, Federal Republic of

Leon, Clinton J, *Instr*, Haskell Indian Junior College, Art Department, Lawrence KS (S)

Leon, Dennis, *Instructor*, California College of Arts and Crafts, Oakland CA (S)

Leonard, Carol, *Activities Coordr*, New Orleans Museum of Art, Isaac Delgado Museum, New Orleans LA

Leonard, Dorothy, *Dir*, Kansas State University, Paul Weigel Library, Manhattan KS

Leonard, Glen M, *Asst Dir*, Church of Jesus Christ of Latter-Day Saints, Information Center and Museum, Arts and Sites Division, Salt Lake City UT

Leonard, Joanne, *Lectr*, Mills College, Art Department, Oakland CA (S)

Leonard, Marion K, *Supt Historical Properties*, Sloane-Stanley Museum, West Hartford CT

Leonard, Rebecca, *Secy*, Atlantic Gallery, New York NY

Leondar, Arnold, *Chmn*, Tarrant County Junior College, Northeast Campus, Hurst TX (S)

Leonelli, Marie-Claude, *Dir*, Musee du Petit Palais, Centre International de Documentation et de Recherche, Avignon France

Leopold, J H, *Scientific Asst Silver*, Groningen Museum voor Stad en Land, Groningen Museum, Groningen Netherlands

Lepine, Micheline, *Technical Asst to Dir*, Burchfield Center, Buffalo NY

Lepore, James, *Assoc Prof*, Youngstown State University, Art Department, Youngstown OH (S)

Lepper, Rita, *Pres*, South County Art Association, Kingston RI

Lepper, Rita C, *Chmn*, Rhode Island Junior College, Department of Art, Warwick RI (S)

Lepper, Rita C, *Chmn*, Rhode Island Junior College, Art Department Gallery, Warwick RI

Leppien, Helmut R, *Dir*, Museen der Stadt Köln, Kunsthalle, Cologne Germany, Federal Republic of

Lerand, Laura, *Secy*, Visual Arts Ontario, Toronto ON

Lerner, Abram, *Dir*, Hirshhorn Museum and Sculpture Garden, Washington DC

Lerner, Alexandra, *Trustee*, Foundation for Today's Art, Nexus Gallery, Philadelphia PA

Lerner, Martin, *Research Fellow Far Eastern Art*, Metropolitan Museum of Art, New York NY

LeRoy, Bruce, *Dir*, Washington State Historical Society, Tacoma WA

LeRoy, Harold M, *Pres*, American Society of Contemporary Artists, Brooklyn NY

Leroy, Louis, *Expansion Arts Coordr*, Arizona Commission on the Arts, Phoenix AZ

Leroy, Maurice, *Prof*, Academie Royale des Beaux-Arts, Royal Academy of Fine Arts, Brussels, Brussels Belgium

Leser, Robert, *VPres*, Nicholas Roerich Museum, New York NY

Lesher, Melinda K, *Asst Prof*, Davidson College, Art Dept, Davidson NC (S)

LeShock, Ed, *Instructor*, Radford University, Art Department, Radford VA (S)

Lesko, Diane M, *Instructor*, Lycoming College, Art Department, Williamsport PA (S)

Lesley, Miriam L, *Head Art Dept*, Free Library of Philadelphia, Art Department, Philadelphia PA

Leslie, Jane E H, *Research Ancient Art*, Indiana University, Art Museum, Bloomington IN

Leslie, Nicholas, *Instr*, Studio School of Art and Design, Philadelphia PA (S)

Lessard, Elizabeth B, *Librn*, Manchester Historic Association, Manchester NH

Lessmann, Johanna, *Asst*, Herzog Anton Ulrich-Museum, Medieval Section: Burg Dankwarderode, Brunswick Germany, Federal Republic of

Lester Jr, William Carey, *Instructor*, Delta State University, Department of Art, Cleveland MS (S)

Lesynski, Loris, *Instr*, Toronto School of Art, Toronto ON (S)

Letchworth, Francis, *Museum Artist*, Woolaroc Museum, Bartlesville OK

Lethert, Helen M, *Dir Public Relations*, Art Institute of Chicago, Chicago IL

Letocha, Louise, *Dir*, Musee d'Art Contemporain, Montreal PQ

Letourneau, Fernande, *VPres*, Musee Historique de Vaudreuil, Vaudreuil Historial Museum, Woodstock PQ

Letson, Kathleen J, *Admin Asst*, Wright State University, Fine Arts Gallery, Dayton OH

Lett, James, *Exhibits Specialist*, National Infantry Museum, Fort Benning GA

Lettis, Donald R, *Academy Dean*, Massachusetts College of Art, Boston MA (S)

Leufert, Gerd, *Cur Prints & Drawings*, Museo de Bellas Artes, Museum of Fine Arts, Caracas Venezuela

Leuy, James, *Dir*, Harwood Foundation of the University of New Mexico, Library, Taos NM

LeVan, Marie, *Secy*, Arts and Crafts Association of Meriden Inc, Meriden CT

LeVander, Bernhard W, *Pres*, American Swedish Institute, Minneapolis MN

Leven, Arline, *Asst Cur*, Washington University, Gallery of Art, Saint Louis MO

Levenson, Harvey R, *Chairperson*, La Roche College, Division of Graphic Arts & Design, Pittsburgh PA (S)

LeVeque, Ann, *Museum Cur*, Rhode Island Historical Society, Providence RI

Leverette, Carlton, *Assoc Prof*, Community College of Baltimore, Dept of Fine & Applied Arts, Baltimore MD (S)

Levesque, A, *Librn*, Gallerie d'Art de l'Universite de Moncton, Champlain Library, Moncton NB

Levesque, Michel, *Secy*, Institut des Arts au Saguenay, National Exhibition Center, Jonquiere PQ

Levey, Michael, *Dir*, National Gallery, London England

Levi, Julian, *Art Workshops Dir*, New School for Social Research Art Center Gallery, New York NY

Levie, S H, *Dir General*, Rijksmuseum Vincent Van Gogh, Vincent Van Gogh State Museum, Amsterdam Netherlands

Levie, S H, *Dir General*, Rijksmuseum, State Museum, Amsterdam Netherlands

Levin, Esther, *Placement Officer*, Ontario College of Art, Toronto ON (S)

Levin, Gail, *Cur*, Whitney Museum of American Art, New York NY

Levin, Gail, *Vis Prof*, City University of New York, PhD Program in Art History, New York NY (S)

Levin, Inabelle, *Asst Prof*, Case Western Reserve University, Department of Art, Cleveland OH (S)

Levin, Karen, *Dir*, Omaha Children's Museum, Inc, Omaha NE

Levin, Mary Jean Redon, *Asst to Dir*, Hermitage Foundation Museum, Norfolk VA

Levin, Ruth, *Registrar*, Bennington Museum, Bennington VT

Levine, Arnold E, *VPres & Treas*, Des Moines Art Center, Des Moines IA

Levine, David, *Pres*, Art Commission of the City of New York, Associates of the Art Commission, Inc, New York NY

Levine, Frederick, *Asst Prof*, Northwestern University, Evanston, Department of Art History, Evanston IL (S)

Levine, Gillian, *Cur*, Institute of Contemporary Art, Boston MA

Levine, Julius S, *Assoc Prof*, Catholic University of America, Department of Architecture & Planning, Washington DC (S)

Levine, Phyllis, *Public Information Dir*, International Center of Photography, New York NY

Levinson, Budd, *Chmn*, Guild Hall of East Hampton, Inc, Museum Section, East Hampton NY

Levinson, Robert A, *Chmn Board of Governors*, Brooklyn Museum, Brooklyn NY

Levitin, Susan, *Cur in Charge Exhib*, Fine Arts Museums of San Francisco, M H de Young Memorial Museum and California Palace of the Legion of Honor

Levitt, Isabell, *Prof*, North Carolina Central University, Art Dept, Durham NC (S)

Levitt, James, *Pres of Board*, Potsdam Public Museum, Potsdam NY

Levitt, M R, *Chief Instr*, Selkirk College, Kootenay School of Art Division, Nelson BC (S)

Levitt Jr, William, *Chmn*, Wagner College, Department of Art, Staten Island NY (S)

Levra, Ray, *Prof*, Cochise College, Art Department, Douglas AZ (S)

Levsen, Mildred, *Secy*, Springfield Historical Society, Springfield NJ

Levy, A, *Head Dept Textiles-Fashion*, Manchester Polytechnic, Faculty of Art and Design, Manchester England (S)

Levy, David C, *Dean*, Parsons School of Design, New York NY (S)

Levy, James, *Dir*, Harwood Foundation of the University of New Mexico, Taos NM

Levy, Reynold, *Exec Dir*, 92nd Street YMHA-YWHA, Weill Art Gallery, New York NY

Levy, Richard W, *First VPres*, New Orleans Museum of Art, Isaac Delgado Museum, New Orleans LA

Levy, S Arthur, *Librn*, Buten Museum of Wedgwood, Library, Merion PA

Lew, Eileen, *Chmn Children's Classes*, De Young Museum Art School, San Francisco CA (S)

Lew, Robert F, *Real Estate Adminr*, Pittsburgh National Bank, Pittsburgh PA

Lew, William, *Instructor*, Murray State University, Art Department, Murray KY (S)

Lewandowski, Edmund D, *Chmn*, Winthrop College, Department of Art, Rock Hill SC (S)

Lewandowski, Edmund D, *Dir*, Winthrop College Gallery of Art, Rock Hill SC

Lewandowski, Felicia, *Instructor*, Radford University, Art Department, Radford VA (S)

Lewicki, James, *Prof*, School of the Arts, C W Post Center of Long Island University, Art Department, Greenvale NY (S)

LeWinter, Stephen S, *Asst Prof*, University of Tennessee at Chattanooga, Department of Art, Chattanooga TN (S)

Lewis, A B, *Honorary Cur Millington-Barnard Coll*, University of Mississippi, University Museums, Oxford MS

Lewis, Albert J, *Instructor*, San Diego Mesa College, Art Department, San Diego CA (S)

Lewis, Arnold, *Dir*, College of Wooster Art Center Museum, Wooster OH

Lewis, Arnold, *Prof*, College of Wooster, Department of Art, Wooster OH (S)

Lewis, Carolyn K, *Asst Prof*, University of New Orleans, Dept of Fine Arts, New Orleans LA (S)

Lewis, Dorothy H, *Instructor*, Rehoboth Art League, Inc, Rehoboth Beach DE (S)

Lewis, Elma, *Artistic Dir*, Museum of the National Center of Afro-American Artists, Boston MA

Lewis, Harold H, *Secy*, Historical Society of Pennsylvania, Philadelphia PA

Lewis, J Thomas, *Pres*, New Orleans Museum of Art, Isaac Delgado Museum, New Orleans LA

Lewis, James E, *Dir*, Morgan State University Gallery of Art, Baltimore MD

Lewis, James S, *Prof*, Morgan State University, Department of Art, Baltimore MD (S)

Lewis, John I, *Instructor*, Rehoboth Art League, Inc, Rehoboth Beach DE (S)

Lewis, Joyce, *Pres*, Blacksburg Regional Art Association, Blacksburg VA

Lewis, Louise, *Assoc Dir*, California State University, Northridge, Fine Arts Gallery, Northridge CA

Lewis, Louise L, *Assoc Prof*, Gulf Coast Community College, Division of Fine Arts, Panama City FL (S)

Lewis, Marcia, *Instructor*, Long Beach City College, Department of Art, Long Beach CA (S)

Lewis, Michael H, *Chmn*, University of Maine, Art Department, Orono ME (S)

Lewis, Monty, *Dir*, Coronado School of Fine Arts, Coronado CA (S)

Lewis, Peggy, *Pres*, Allied Arts Council of the Yakima Valley, Yakima WA

Lewis, Phillip, *Chmn Anthropology*, Field Museum of Natural History, Chicago IL

Lewis, Raeford, *Dir*, Central Missouri State University, Grinstead Gallery, Warrensburg MO

Lewis, Raeford W, *Instructor*, Central Missouri State University, Art Department, Warrensburg MO (S)

Lewis, Ralph M, *Dir*, Rosicrucian Egyptian Museum and Art Gallery, San Jose CA

Lewis, Robert, *Instr*, Maryville College, Art Department, Saint Louis MO (S)

Lewis, Samella, *Pres*, Scripps College, Clark Humanities Museum, Claremont CA

Lewis, Susan, *Librn*, Boston Architectural Center, Library, Boston MA

Lewis, Tharten, *Managing Dir*, Dundurn Castle, Hamilton ON

Lewis, Virginia E, *Dir*, Frick Art Museum, Pittsburgh PA

Lewis Jr, Douglas, *Cur Sculpture*, National Gallery of Art, Washington DC

Lewisohn, Jeanne F, *VPres*, Guild of Book Workers, New York NY

Lewitin, Marguerite A L, *Pres*, Women's Interart Center, Inc, Interart Gallery, New York NY

Lewnadowski, Michaeline, *Instructor*, Salve Regina the Newport College, Art Department, Newport RI (S)

Leys, Dale, *Instructor*, Murray State University, Art Department, Murray KY (S)

Lezama, Jorge E, *Rector & Prof*, Escuela Superior de Bellas Artes Ernesto de la Carcova, National Superior School of Fine Arts Ernesto de la Carcova, Buenos Argentina

Li, Chu-tsing, *Prof*, University of Kansas, Kress Foundation Department of Art History, Lawrence KS (S)

Li, Yuk-Wong, *Instructor*, Honolulu Academy of Arts, Studio Program, Honolulu HI (S)

Liakos, J Dimitri, *Area Coordr*, Northern Illinois University, Department of Art, De Kalb IL (S)

Libby, Gary Russell, *Dir*, Museum of Arts and Sciences, Cuban Museum, Planetarium, Daytona Beach FL

Liberski, Benon, *Vice Rector*, Panstwowa Wyzsza Szkola Sztuk Plastycznych, Higher School of Art and Design, Lodz Poland (S)

Libeskind, Daniel, *Head Architecture Dept*, Cranbrook Academy of Art, Bloomfield Hills MI (S)

Libhart, Myles, *Dir of Museums, Exhib & Publications*, United States Department of the Interior, Indian Arts and Crafts Board, Washington DC

Libin, Laurence, *Assoc Cur in Charge Musical Instruments*, Metropolitan Museum of Art, New York NY

Licht, Ira, *Dir*, University of Miami, Lowe Art Museum, Coral Gables FL

Licht, Margherita, *Instr*, Studio Art Centers International, Florence Italy (S)

Liddiard, Jean, *Press & Public Relations*, National Portrait Gallery, London England

Liddle, Nancy, *Dir*, State University of New York at Albany, University Art Gallery, Albany NY

Lidh, William R, *Asst Prof*, Western Carolina University, Dept of Art, Cullowhee NC (S)

Lie, Inger Marie Kvaal, *Cur*, Kunstindustrimuseet I Oslo, Oslo Museum of Applied Art, Oslo Norway

Lieberman, Ralph, *Asst Prof*, Hamilton College, Art Department, Clinton NY (S)

Lieberman, William S, *Dir Drawings*, Museum of Modern Art, New York NY

Liebermen, William, *Chmn Department 20th Century Art*, Metropolitan Museum of Art, New York NY

Liebert, H W, *Pres*, Grolier Club Library, New York NY

Liebling, Jerry, *Artist in Res*, Viterbo College, Art Department, La Crosse WI (S)

Liebman, Steve, *Asst Prof*, Hamilton College, Art Department, Clinton NY (S)

Lief, Philip, *Instr*, Berkshire Community College, Department of Fine Arts and Visual Communication, Pittsfield MA (S)

Lien, Lary, *Chairperson Dept*, Interlochen Arts Academy, Dept of Visual Art, Interlochen MI (S)

Lierheimer, Violet, *Acquisitions Librn*, Mexico-Audrain County Library, Mexico MO

Lierley, Mary, *Asst Prof*, Kearney State College, Dept of Art, Kearney NE (S)

Lifschitz, Ed, *Acad Coordr*, Museum of African Art, Washington DC

Lifson, Hank, *Head Dept*, Cornell College, Art Department, Mount Vernon IA (S)

Lifson, Hank, *Dir Gallery & Chmn Dept of Art*, Cornell College, Armstrong Gallery, Mount Vernon IA

Light, Frank, *Pres*, Emerald Empire Arts Association, Springfield OR

Light, Marie, *Cur*, University of Michigan Museum of Art, Slide and Photograph Collection, Ann Arbor MI

Light, Raymond E, *Dean*, University of Wisconsin-Whitewater, Department of Art, Whitewater WI (S)

Lightbown, R W, *Keeper*, Victoria and Albert Museum, National Art Library, London England

Lightfoot, Mark, *Coordr*, Prince George Art Gallery, Prince George BC

Lignell, Ellen, *Librn*, Montana State University, Creative Arts Library, Bozeman MT

Ligo, Larry L, *Asst Prof*, Davidson College, Art Dept, Davidson NC (S)

Likes, James, *Asst Supt*, Bishop Hill Historic Site, Bishop Hill IL

Lile, Thomas C, *Dir of Squires*, Virginia Polytechnic Institute and State University, Squires Art Gallery, Blacksburg VA

Lillen, Jody L, *Dir*, Nicolaysen Art Museum, Casper WY

Lillich, Meredith, *Instr*, Syracuse University, Department of Art History, Syracuse NY (S)

Lilly, Marnee, *Asst Cur Coll*, Maine Maritime Museum, Bath ME

Lilyquist, Christine, *Cur Egyptian Art*, Metropolitan Museum of Art, New York NY

Lim, K W, *Head Department Asiatic Art*, Rijksmuseum, State Museum, Amsterdam Netherlands

Lima, Isabel Navarro, *Secy*, Museo de Arte—Jose Luis Bello y Gonzales, Museum of Art, Puebla Mexico

Limondjian, Hilde, *Program Mgr Concerts & Lectures*, Metropolitan Museum of Art, New York NY

Limonte, Naomi, *Secy*, American Color Print Society, Philadelphia PA

Limpert, John, *Dir Membership & Development*, Museum of Modern Art, New York NY

Lin, Henry H, *Dean*, Ohio University, School of Art, Athens OH (S)

Lin, Henry H, *Dir*, Ohio University, Anthony G Trisolini Memorial Gallery, Athens OH

Lincer, Kathy, *Librn*, Cochise College Library, Douglas AZ

Lincoln, Crawford, *Pres*, Old Sturbridge Village, Sturbridge MA

Lindborg, Henry L, *Chmn Arts & Letters*, Marian College, Art Department, Eau Claire WI (S)

Lindeman, Kathryn B, *Writer & Editor*, Smithsonian Institution, Washington DC

Lindemann, Edna M, *Dir*, Burchfield Center, Buffalo NY

Lindemann, Hans K, *Owner & Founder*, Museum of American Treasures, National City CA

Lindenheim, Diane, *Instructor*, Bucks County Community College, Fine Arts Department, Newton PA (S)

London, Laurence, *Managing Dir*, Charles B Goddard Center for the Visual and Performing Arts, Ardmore OK

London, Peter, *Chairperson Art Educ*, Southeastern Massachusetts University, College of Visual and Performing Arts, North Dartmouth MA (S)

London, Phyllis, *Lectr*, Regis College, Department of Art, Weston MA (S)

Londono, Jorge, *Head Urban Studies*, Universidad Javeriana, Javeriana University Faculty of Architecture and Design, Bogota Colombia (S)

Lone, Mary, *Assoc Prof*, Texarkana Community College, Art Department, Texarkana TX (S)

Lonergan, Mary Ann, *Instructor*, Briar Cliff College, Art Department, Sioux City IA (S)

Long, Charles, *Public Information Officer*, Fine Arts Museums of San Francisco, M H de Young Memorial Museum and California Palace of the Legion of Honor

Long, Charles, *Museum Consultant*, San Antonio Art League, San Antonio TX

Long, Clarence W, *Pres Board of Trustees*, Indianapolis Museum of Art, Indianapolis IN

Long, Elizabeth, *Admin Dir*, Lighthouse Gallery, Tequesta FL

Long, Glenn A, *Executive Dir*, Sunrise Foundation, Inc, Charleston WV

Long, Herbert S, *Pres*, Hill Country Arts Foundation, Ingram TX

Long, John M, *Dean School of Fine Arts*, Troy State University, Department of Art, Troy AL (S)

Long, Judith Jackson, *Art & Music Librn*, Brookline Public Library, Brookline MA

Long, Katherine H, *Pres*, Louisiana State University, Anglo-American Art Museum, Baton Rouge LA

Long, Melba LeGrande, *Instructor*, Converse College, Art Dept, Spartanburg SC (S)

Long, Nancy, *Gallery Mgr & Public Relations*, Morse Gallery of Art, Boulder FL

Long, Noyer C, *Chmn*, Appalachian State University, Department of Art, Boone NC (S)

Long, Phillip, *VPres*, Contemporary Arts Center, Cincinnati OH

Long, Rose-Carol, *Assoc Prof*, City University of New York, PhD Program in Art History, New York NY (S)

Long, Walter K, *Dir*, Cayuga Museum of History and Art, Auburn NY

Long, Willia, *Cur Old Capitol*, Kentucky Historical Society Museum, Frankfort KY

Longen, Leonarda, *Instructor & Res Artist*, Mount Marty College, Art Dept, Yankton SD (S)

Longhauser, William, *Chairperson Graphic Design*, Philadelphia College of Art, Philadelphia PA (S)

Longin, Tom, *Dean*, Ithaca College, Art Department, Ithaca NY (S)

Longley, Pat, *VPRes Publicity*, Miniature Art Society of New Jersey, Nutley NJ

Longo, Morris T, *Chairman Hon*, Hudson County Court House, Board of Chosen Freeholders, Jersey City NJ

Longstreet, Margarita, *Secy*, Willard House and Clock Museum, Inc, Grafton MA

Longstreet, Stephen, *Pres*, Los Angeles Art Association and Galleries, Los Angeles CA

Longsworth, Charles R, *Pres*, Colonial Williamsburg Foundation, Williamsburg VA

Longsworth, Ellen, *Asst Prof*, Bradford College, Art Department, Bradford MA (S)

Lonier, Teresa, *Instructor*, East Tennessee State University, Fine Arts Dept, Johnson City TN (S)

Loo, Edna, *Corresponding Secy*, Association of Honolulu Artists, Honolulu HI

Loomis, Shirley, *VPres*, Pence Gallery, Davis CA

Loomis, Suzanne M, *Dir*, Sierra Nevada Museum of Art, Reno NV

Loomis, Tom, *Asst Prof*, Mansfield State College, Art Department, Mansfield PA (S)

Looney, M O, *Pres*, Missouri Western State College, Fine Arts Gallery, Saint Joseph MO

Looney, Robert F, *Head*, Free Library of Philadelphia, Print and Picture Department, Philadelphia PA

Lopez, Jesse, *Production Mgr*, Rice University, Institute for the Arts, Rice Museum, Houston TX

Lopez, Jorge Martinez, *Dir*, Universidad de Guadalajara, Cursos de Verano Cursos de Invierno, Guadalajara Mexico (S)

Lopez, Oscar M, *Pres*, Lopez Memorial Museum, Manila Philippines

Lopez, Trinidad, *Prof*, New Mexico State University, Art Dept, Las Cruces NM (S)

Lopez Del Compo, Rafael, *Prof*, Institute of Puerto Rican Culture, Escuela de Artes Plasticas, Mayaguez PR (S)

LoPresti, Maryellen, *Librn*, North Carolina State University, Harrye Lyons Design Library, Raleigh NC

Lord, Eileen, *Prof*, University of Bridgeport, Art Department, Bridgeport CT (S)

Lord, Florence S, *Coordr*, Kenyon College, Colburn Gallery, Gambier OH

Lord, J V, *Head Dept Visual Communication*, Brighton Polytechnic, Faculty of Art and Design, Brighton England (S)

Lord, Linda, *Registrar*, Manchester Institute of Arts and Sciences Gallery, Manchester NH

Lord, Linda, *Registrar*, Manchester Institute of Arts and Sciences, Manchester NH (S)

Lorenc, E Terry, *Asst Instructor*, Jamestown Community College, Art Department, Jamestown NY (S)

Lorenson, Joan, *Curatorial Registrar*, Montclair Art Museum, Montclair NJ

Lorentz, Stanislaw, *Dir*, Muzeum Narodowe, National Museum, Warsaw Poland

Lorenz, Hella, *Cur*, Suermondt-Ludwig-Museum der Stadt Aachen, Aachen Germany, Federal Republic of

Lorenzana, Katherine Harper, *Asst Prof*, Loyola Marymount University, Department of Art, Los Angeles CA (S)

Lorenzetti, Constanza, *Dir*, Accademie de Belle Arti e Liceo Artistico, Academy of Fine Arts, Naples Italy (S)

Loriaux, Maurice, *Head Dept*, American Stained Glass Institute, Hobbs NM (S)

Lorriman, Hugh, *VPres*, Lynnwood Arts Centre, Simcoe ON

Loscalzo, Michael, *Art Music Librn*, Bayonne Free Public Library, Art Department, Bayonne NJ

Lotreck, Annelaine, *Librn*, Willoughby Wallace Memorial Library, Stony Creek CT

Lottes, John W, *Pres*, Kansas City Art Institute, Kansas City MO (S)

Louca, Nick, *Instr*, Aegean School of Fine Arts, Paros Cyclades Greece (S)

Louchheim, Stuart F, *Chmn*, Philadelphia Museum of Art, Samuel S Fleisher Art Memorial, Philadelphia PA

Loud, Dana, *Library Asst*, Lake Placid School of Art Gallery, Nettie Marie Jones Fine Arts Library, Lake Placid NY

Loudon, Helen, *Secy*, Marin Society of Artists Inc, Ross CA

Louer, Albert O, *Public Relations*, Indianapolis Museum of Art, Indianapolis IN

Loughran, Bernice, *Prof*, California Polytechnic State University at San Luis Obispo, Art Department, San Luis Obispo CA (S)

Louie, Reagan, *Chmn Photography Dept*, San Francisco Art Institute, San Francisco CA (S)

Louis, William, *Chmn Fine Arts*, Avila College, Art Gallery, Kansas City MO

Louis, William J, *Chmn*, Avila College, Art Department, Kansas City MO (S)

Lourido, Delia, *Librn*, Ateneo Puertorriqueno, Library, San Juan PR

Lovato, Manuelita, *Cur Functions*, Institute of American Indian Arts Museum, Santa Fe NM

Love, Frances, *Dir*, University of Southwestern Louisiana, Art Center for Southwestern Louisiana, Lafayette LA

Love, Josephine Harreld, *Dir*, Your Heritage House, Inc, Detroit MI

Love, Marion, *Head Dept*, Lenoir Rhyne College, Department of Art, Hickory NC (S)

Loveday, Amos, *Chief Educ Division*, Ohio Historical Society, Columbus OH

Lovejoy, Carolyn, *Librn*, Rockwell-Corning Museum, Library, Corning NY

Lovejoy, Carolyn, *Admin Asst*, Rockwell-Corning Museum, Corning NY

Loveless, Jim, *Prof*, Colgate University, Department of Fine Arts, Hamilton NY (S)

Lovett, Peggy, *Instr*, Marian College, Art Department, Indianapolis IN (S)

Lovette, Joanne P, *Chairperson*, Indiana University of Pennsylvania, Department of Art and Art Education, Indiana PA (S)

Low, Markus J, *In Charge Art Coll*, Ciba-Geigy Corporation, Ardsley NY

Low, Theodore L, *Dir of Education*, Walters Art Gallery, Baltimore MD

Lowe, Elmer, *Gift Shop Coordr*, Salisbury State College, Wildfowl Art Museum, Salisbury MD

Lowe, Elsie T, *Secy*, Palette and Chisel Academy of Fine Arts Gallery, Chicago IL

Lowe, Harry, *Asst Dir*, National Collection of Fine Arts, Washington DC

Lowe, J Michael, *Chmn*, Saint Laurence University, Department of Fine Arts, Canton NY (S)

Lowe, Patricia A, *Secy*, Will Rogers Memorial and Museum, Claremore OK

Lowe, Rolland, *VPres*, Chinese Culture Foundation, Chinese Culture Center Gallery, San Francisco CA

Lowenthal, Ruth, *Dir*, Colby Community College, H F Davis Memorial Library, Colby KS

Lower, W J, *Dept Chmn*, Troy State University, Department of Art, Troy AL (S)

Lowery, Clifford B, *Pres Board Dir*, Green Hill Art Gallery, Greensboro NC

Lowing, Robert, *Instructor*, Millersville State College, Art Department, Millersville PA (S)

Lowrance, Miriam A, *Head Dept*, Sul Ross State University, Department of Art, Alpine TX (S)

Lowrie, Pamela B, *Instructor*, College of DuPage, Humanities Div, Glen Ellyn IL (S)

Lowry, Keith, *Prof*, Kearney State College, Dept of Art, Kearney NE (S)

Lowy, George, *Dir*, Pratt Institute Library, Brooklyn NY

Loy, John, *Instr*, Utica College of Syracuse University, Division of Humanities, Utica NY (S)

Loyd, Corinne, *Asst Dir*, Ashtabula Arts Center, Ashtabula OH

Loyd, Jan, *Asst Prof*, University of North Carolina-Charlotte, Creative Arts Dept, Charlotte NC (S)

Lubar, Sheldon B, *Pres Board Trustees*, Milwaukee Art Center, Milwaukee WI

Lubbers, Lee, *Instr*, Creighton University, Fine and Performing Arts Department, Omaha NE (S)

Lube, Neal, *VPres*, Safety Harbor Museum of History and Fine Arts, Safety Harbor FL

Lubetkin, Robert, *Pres Bd of Trustees*, Des Moines Art Center, Des Moines IA

Lucas, James, *Assoc Prof*, Youngstown State University, Art Department, Youngstown OH (S)

Lucas, Margaret O, *Grad Studies Coordr*, North Texas State University, Art Department, Denton TX (S)

Lucas, Sheri, *Cur Asst*, Contemporary Arts Center, Cincinnati OH

Lucas, Walter, *Keeper of Natural Sciences & Social & Industrial History*, Newport Museum and Art Gallery, Newport Wales

Luce, Richard, *Asst to Library Dir*, Boulder Public Library and Gallery, Boulder CO

Luchars, Margaret, *Library Technician*, Cooper-Hewitt Museum, Doris and Henry Dreyfuss Study Center, New York NY

Luchechko, John, *Asst Dir Reader Services*, Jersey City State College, Forrest A Irwin Library, Jersey City NJ

Luchman, Stewart, *Assoc Prof*, Bethel College, Department of Art, Saint Paul MN (S)

Luchs, Alison, *Prof*, Syracuse University, Department of Art History, Syracuse NY (S)

Lucia, Michael C, *In Charge Art Coll*, Sears Roebuck and Company, Chicago IL

Lucius, Terrell, *Coordr Exhib*, Minneapolis Institute of Arts, Minneapolis MN

Luck, Meredith, *Assoc Prof*, Union University, Department of Art, Jackson TN (S)

Luckert, Walter, *Technician*, State University of New York at Binghamton, University Art Gallery, Binghamton NY

Luckett, Helen, *Keeper of Education*, Southampton Art Gallery and Museum Service, Southampton England

Luckey, James, *VPres*, Maui Historical Society, Hale Hoikeike, Wailuku HI

Luckner, Kurt T, *Cur Ancient Art*, Toledo Museum of Art, Toledo OH

Ludden, Franklin, *Prof*, Ohio State University, Department of the History of Art, Columbus OH (S)

Luddy, Tony, *Cur Film*, University of California, Pacific Film Archive, Berkeley CA

Ludgin, Donald, *Secy*, Museum of Contemporary Art, Chicago IL

Ludke, Rae, *VPres*, Phoenix Art Museum, Phoenix AZ

Ludmer, Joyce P, *Art Librn*, University of California, Los Angeles, Art Library, Los Angeles CA

Ludwig, Coy L, *Dir*, State University of New York at Oswego, Tyler Art Gallery, Oswego NY

Lue, Joanne, *Admin Asst*, State University of New York at Albany, University Art Gallery, Albany NY

Lueb, Miriam Dorothy, *Dir Library System*, Our Lady of the Lake University, Saint Florence Library, San Antonio TX

Luecking, Stephen, *Asst Prof*, DePaul University, Department of Art, Chicago IL (S)

Luedtke, John, *Cur Oriental, Classical and Decorative Art*, Milwaukee Public Museum, Milwaukee WI

Luehrman, Richard A, *Head Dept*, Central Missouri State University, Art Department, Warrensburg MO (S)

Lugo, Anthony J, *Assoc Prof*, Palomar College, Art Department, San Marcos TX (S)

Lukasiewicz, Ronald, *Preparator*, University of Georgia, Georgia Museum of Art, Athens GA

Lukomsky, O, *Librn*, Ukrainian Museum of Canada, Library, Edmonton AB

Lukosius, Richard, *Prof*, Connecticut College, Department of Art, New London CT (S)

Lumpkin, Farnese, *Asst Prof*, Savannah State College, Department of Fine Arts, Savannah GA (S)

Lumsden, Ian G, *Cur*, Beaverbrook Art Gallery, Fredericton NB

Luna, Mario, *Lectr*, University of Victoria, Department of History in Art, Victoria BC (S)

Lund, David, *Asst Prof*, Columbia University, Division of Painting and Sculpture, New York NY (S)

Lund, Hakon, *Dir*, Det Kongelige Danske Kunstakademi Bibliotek, Copenhagen Denmark

Lund, Marlene, *Executive Dir*, Southeast Alaska Regional Arts Council, Inc, Sitka AK

Lund, Nils-Ole, *Rector*, School of Architecture in Aarhus, Aarhus Denmark (S)

Lund, Richard, *Instructor*, College of DuPage, Humanities Div, Glen Ellyn IL (S)

Lund, Sally, *Pres*, Erie Art Center, Erie PA

Lundberg, Erveen C, *Librn*, John Woodman Higgins Armory, Library, Worcester MA

Lunde, Joel, *Head Dept*, Lutheran Brethren Schools, Fergus Falls MN (S)

Lunde, Mary Lee, *Asst Prof*, State University College, Department of Art, Fredonia NY (S)

Lungren, Glenn, *In Charge Art Coll*, First Security Bank of Idaho, Boise ID

Lunsford, John, *Cur*, Dallas Museum of Fine Arts, Dallas TX

Lunt, Wilhelmina V, *Cur*, Historical Society of Old Newbury, Cushing House Museum, Newburyport MA

Lupori, Peter, *Chmn*, College of Saint Catherine, Visual Arts Department, Saint Paul MN (S)

Lurie, Ann T, *Assoc Cur Paintings*, Cleveland Museum of Art, Cleveland OH

Lurie, David J, *Asst Prof*, University of Nevada, Las Vegas, Department of Art, Las Vegas NV (S)

Lurie, Nancy, *Cur Anthropology*, Milwaukee Public Museum, Milwaukee WI

Lussier, Rick, *Third VPres*, Arizona Watercolor Association, Phoenix AZ

Lustosa, Helosia Aleixo, *Executive Dir*, Museu de Arte Moderna, Museum of Modern Art, Rio Brazil

Lutchmansingh, Larry, *Chmn*, Bowdoin College, Art Department, Brunswick ME (S)

Luthi, Louise, *Instructor*, Stephens College, Art Department, Columbia MO (S)

Luthy, Dorothy, *Secy*, The Dalles Art Association, The Dalles OR

Lutjeans, Phyllis, *Cur Education*, Newport Harbor Art Museum, Newport Beach CA

Lykins, Jere, *Asst Prof*, Berry College, Art Department, Mount Berry GA (S)

Lyle, John, *Prof*, Mount Saint Mary's College, Fine Arts Department, Emmitsburg MD (S)

Lyman, Thomas W, *Prof*, Emory University, Art History Department, Atlanta GA (S)

Lyman Jr, Henry Hawkins, *Instructor*, Fort Wright College of the Holy Names, School of Art, Spokane WA (S)

Lynagh, Patricia, *Media Center Librn*, Cleveland Institute of Art, Jessica Gund Memorial Library, Cleveland OH

Lynch, Kenneth, *Pres*, Craft Center Museum, Wilton CT

Lynn, Vanessa, *Dir*, Pratt Institute Library, Brooklyn NY

Lyon, Elizabeth T, *Cur*, Centre Hill Mansion, Petersburg VA

Lyon, Robert, *Instructor*, Millersville State College, Art Department, Millersville PA (S)

Lyons, Bettina, *Cur Historic Sites*, Tucson Museum of Art, Tucson AZ

Lyons, Ian R, *Exec Dir*, Pontiac Art Center, Pontiac MI (S)

Lyons, Joan, *Coordr Print Shop*, Visual Studies Workshop, Rochester NY

Lyons, Judith, *Instr*, Hood College, Department of Art, Frederick MD (S)

Lyons, Lisa, *Cur*, Walker Art Center, Minneapolis MN

Lyons, Lynda, *Exploratorium Mgr*, University of California, Los Angeles, Exploratorium, University Student Union, Los Angeles CA

Lyons, Nathan, *Dir*, Visual Studies Workshop, Rochester NY

Lyster, Patricia M, *Instructor*, Emmanuel College, Art Department, Boston MA (S)

Lytal, Billy, *Dir*, Mississippi College Library, Art Department, Clinton MS

Lytwyn, Nancy L, *Asst Prof*, Salisbury State College, Art Dept, Salisbury MD (S)

Ma, Hans Brill, *Librn*, Royal College of Art Gallery, College Library, London England

MA, Idie Payne, *Ceramic Coordr*, Butte Community College, Humanities Division (III), Oroville CA (S)

Maag, Albert, *Dir*, Capital University, Library, Columbus OH

Maakestad, John, *Prof*, St Olaf College, Art Department, Northfield MN (S)

Maass, R Andrew, *Dir*, Tucson Museum of Art, Tucson AZ

Maass, R Andrew, *Exec Dir*, Fresno Arts Center, Fresno CA

Mabbott, Margaret, *Secy*, Wind River Valley Artists Guild, Dubois WY

Mabille, Gerard, *Cur*, Union Centrale des Arts Decoratifs, Musee des Arts Decoratifs, Paris France

Mabry, Mary, *Chmn Art Educ*, Bowling Green State University, School of Art, Bowling Green OH (S)

MacAdam, Bonnie, *Cur*, Lyme Historical Society, Inc, Old Lyme CT

MacAdam, Bonnie, *Librn*, Lyme Historical Society, Inc, Lyme Historical Society Archives, Old Lyme CT

MacAdams, Dick, *Pres*, Spectrum, Friends of Fine Art, Inc, Toledo OH

Macandrew, Hugh, *Keeper National Gallery of Scotland*, National Galleries of Scotland, National Gallery of Scotland, Edinburgh Scotland

Macaulay, Betty, *Librn*, Banff Centre, Library, Banff AB

Macaulay, Thomas, *Acting Chairer*, Wright State University, Art Department, Dayton OH (S)

MacBeath, George, *Pres*, Canadian Museums Association, Association des Musees Canadiens, Ottawa ON

MacBoggs, Mayo, *Instructor*, Converse College, Art Dept, Spartanburg SC (S)

MacCampbell, James C, *Dir Libraries*, University of Maine at Orono, Fogler Library, Orono ME

MacCarthy, John Peters, *Pres*, Art and Education Council of Greater Saint Louis, Saint Louis MO

Macco, Michela Di, *Staff Member*, Galleria Sabauda, Turin Italy

MacDonald, Alex, *Mgr Public Affairs*, Art Gallery of Ontario, Toronto ON

MacDonald, Ann, *Executive Dir*, Community Arts Council of Vancouver, Vancouver BC

MacDonald, Bruce, *Vis Lectr*, Tufts University, Fine Arts Department, Medford MA (S)

MacDonald, Bruce K, *Dean*, School of the Museum of Fine Arts, Boston MA (S)

MacDonald, C A, *VPres*, Litchfield Historical Society, Litchfield CT

MacDonald, George, *Senior Archaeologist*, National Museum of Man, Ottawa ON

MacDonald, Judy, *Registrar*, Confederation Centre Art Gallery and Museum, Charlottetown PE

MacDonald, Lee, *Acting Dir*, Cambridge Art Association, Cambridge MA

Macdonald, Robert R, *Dir*, Louisiana State Museum, New Orleans LA

MacDonald, William A, *Prof*, George Washington University, Department of Art, Washington DC (S)

Macdonell, Cameron, *VPres*, Southern Tier Arts Association, Inc, Elmira NY

MacDougall, E Bruce, *Head*, University of Massachusetts, Amherst, College of Food and Natural Resources, Amherst MA (S)

MacDougall, Susan, *Asst Dir*, Phillips Exeter Academy, Lamont Gallery, Exeter NH

MacEachron, David, *Pres Japan Society*, Japan Society, Inc, Japan House Gallery, New York NY

MacFarlane, G Edward, *Lectr*, University of Victoria, Department of History in Art, Victoria BC (S)

MacGillivray, Vera, *Dir*, Fine Arts Center of Clinton, Clinton IL

MacGregor, D O, *Dir*, Selkirk College, Kootenay School of Art Division, Nelson BC (S)

MacGregor, Janet, *Personal Asst & Secy*, Confederation Centre Art Gallery and Museum, Charlottetown PE

MacGregor, Nancy, *Assoc Prof*, Ohio State University, Department of Art Education, Columbus OH (S)

Mach, Edward L, *Pres*, Rutland Area Art Association, Inc, Chaffee Art Gallery, Rutland VT

Mach, John, *Asst Prof*, Savannah State College, Department of Fine Arts, Savannah GA (S)

Machado, Rodolfo, *Head Archit Dept*, Rhode Island School of Design, Providence RI (S)

Machek, Frank, *Chmn Department Visual Arts*, Albion College, Bobbitt Visual Arts Center, Albion MI

Machek, Frank, *Chmn Dept Visual Arts*, Albion College, Department of Visual Arts, Albion MI (S)

Machizukir, Tomie, *Librn*, Japan Society, Inc, Library, New York NY

Macht, Carol, *Sr Cur & Cur Decorative Arts*, Cincinnati Art Museum, Cincinnati OH

Mack, Laura, *Librn*, Museum of Holography, Reference Library, New York NY

Mack, Laura, *Dir of Information Services*, Museum of Holography, New York NY

Mack, Rodger, *Acting Chmn*, Syracuse University, College of Visual and Performing Arts, Syracuse NY (S)

MacKay, Allan, *Dir & Cur*, Saskatoon Gallery and Conservatory Corporation, Saskatoon SK

MacKay, Don, *Assoc Prof*, University of Waterloo, Fine Arts Department, Waterloo ON (S)

MacKeeman, Robert, *Dir*, Nova Scotia College of Art and Design, Anna Leonowens Gallery, Halifax NS

MacKenzie, Donald, *Chmn*, College of Wooster, Department of Art, Wooster OH (S)

Mackey, Karl A, *Managing Dir*, Kenneth C Beck Center for the Cultural Arts, Lakewood OH

Mackie, G, *Instr*, Selkirk College, Kootenay School of Art Division, Nelson BC (S)

Mackie, Louise W, *Cur Old World*, Textile Museum, Washington DC

Mackie, Murray, *Pres*, Chilliwack Arts Council, Chilliwack BC

MacKillop, Roderick, *Assoc Prof*, University of North Carolina-Charlotte, Creative Arts Dept, Charlotte NC (S)

Macklin, A D, *Head Dept*, Virginia State College, Fine Arts Department, Petersburg VA (S)

Macknight, H, *Recording Secy*, Lyceum Club and Women's Art Association of Canada, Toronto ON

MacLean, Kathryn, *Cultural Coordr*, Richmond Arts Centre, Richmond BC

MacLeish, Bruce, *Cur*, Plymouth Antiquarian Society, Plymouth MA

MacLeish, Bruce, *Cur*, Western Kentucky University, Kentucky Museum, Bowling Green KY

MacLeish, Patricia, *Registrar*, Western Kentucky University, Kentucky Museum, Bowling Green KY

MacLennan, H K, *Chmn of the Board*, Desert Caballeros Western Museum, Wickenburg AZ

MacLeod, Robert, *Chmn*, Confederation Centre Art Gallery and Museum, Charlottetown PE

Macmaster, W T, *Assoc Dir*, Rome Historical Society, Rome Information and Cultural Center, Rome NY

MacMillan, Ladd, *Cur Arts & Crafts*, Heritage Plantation of Sandwich, Sandwich MA

MacMillan, Laurie, *Information Dir*, Utah Travel Council, Salt Lake City UT

MacNutt, Glenn, *VPres*, Boston Watercolor Society, Scituate MA

Macomber Jr, William B, *Pres*, Metropolitan Museum of Art, New York NY

MacTavish, Alison M, *Cur Octagon*, American Institute of Architects Foundation, Washington DC

MacTavish, Alison M, *Librn*, American Institute of Architects Foundation, Library, Washington DC

MacWilliam, Mary, *Assoc Dir*, San Francisco State University, Paul J Leonard Library, San Francisco CA

Madden, Charles F, *Admin*, Webster College, Loretto-Hilton Center Gallery, St Louis MO

Madden, Daniel, *Pres*, Ashtabula Arts Center, Ashtabula OH

Madden, J Robert, *Prof*, Lamar University, Art Department, Beaumont TX (S)

Madden, Lois, *Executive Secy*, Art Center Association, Louisville KY

Maddick, Russell, *Assoc Prof*, Youngstown State University, Art Department, Youngstown OH (S)

Maddox, Gene, *Instructor*, College of the Sequoias, Art Department, Visalia CA (S)

Maddox, Georgia, *Resident Hostess*, Willard House and Clock Museum, Inc, Grafton MA

Maddox, Jerald C, *Coll Planner & Coordr*, Library of Congress, Washington DC

Maddox, Jerrold, *Head Dept*, Kansas State University, Art Department, Manhattan KS (S)

Maddux Jr, Sam, *2nd VPres*, San Antonio Museum Association, Inc, San Antonio TX

Mader, Daniel, *Assoc Prof*, College of Mount Saint Joseph, Art Department, Mount Saint Joseph OH (S)

Madigan, Richard A, *Dir*, Norton Gallery and School of Art, West Palm Beach FL

Madison, James, *Second VPres*, Southeastern College Art Conference, Chapel Hill NC

Madonia, Ann C, *Cur*, Davenport Municipal Art Gallery, Davenport IA

Madrigal, August, *Prof*, University of Bridgeport, Art Department, Bridgeport CT (S)

Maffeo, Edward, *Assoc Prof*, University of New Haven, Department of Fine Arts, West Haven CT (S)

Magavern, Samuel D, *Pres*, Albright-Knox Art Gallery, Buffalo Fine Arts Academy, Buffalo NY

Magavern II, William J, *Treas*, Albright-Knox Art Gallery, Buffalo Fine Arts Academy, Buffalo NY

Magdanz-Robbins, Christine, *Exhib, Education & Circulation Coordr*, Western Association of Art Museums, San Francisco CA

Magdolf, Samuel, *Second VPres*, School Art League of New York City, Brooklyn NY

Magee, Eileen, *Program Coordr*, Athenaeum of Philadelphia, Philadelphia PA

Maggiolo, Allison, *Secy*, Art Center Association, Louisville KY

Magill, Betty, *Secy*, Ball State University, Art Gallery, Muncie IN

Magnan, Oscar, *Dir*, Saint Peter's College Art Gallery, Jersey City NJ

Magnan, Oscar G, *Chmn*, Saint Peter's College, Fine Arts Department, Jersey City NJ (S)

Magnanimi, Giuseppina, *Dir*, Galleria Nazionale d'Arte Antica - Palazzo Barberini, National Gallery in Barberini Palace, Rome Italy

Magnanimi, Giuseppina, *Dir*, Galleria Nazionale d'Arte Antica - Palazzo Barberini, Galleria Nazionale d'Arte Antica - Palazzo Corsini, Rome Italy

Magnusson, B, *Head Prints & Drawings Dept*, Nationalmuseum, Stockholm Sweden

Magnusson, Filkand Thor, *Dir*, Thjodminjasafn, National Museum of Iceland, Rrykjavik Iceland

Magowan, Robert A, *VPres*, Society of the Four Arts, Palm Beach FL

Magri, Phyllis, *Instructor*, Chamberlayne Junior College, Department of Graphic and Applied Arts, Boston MA (S)

Magruder, Ralph, *Instructor*, Texas A & I University, Art Department, Kingsville TX (S)

Maguire, Myra, *Head Pre-Dipl Studies*, National College of Art and Design, Dublin Ireland (S)

Maguire, William, *Asst Prof*, Florida International University, Visual Arts Department, Miami FL (S)

Mahan, Robert B, *Instructor*, Guilford Technical Institute, Commercial Art Dept, Jamestown NC (S)

Mahe, John, *Cur*, Historic New Orleans Collection, Kemper and Leila Williams Foundation, New Orleans LA

Maher, John R, *Pres*, Portsmouth Athenaeum NR, Inc 1817, Portsmouth NH

Mahey, John, *Chief Cur*, Philbrook Art Center, Tulsa OK

Mahler, R, *VChmn*, Oakville Centennial-Gairloch Galleries, Oakville ON

Mahlmann, John J, *Exec Dir*, National Art Education Association, Reston VA

Mahmoud, Samira Hanafy, *Librn*, Greco-Roman Museum, Library, Alexandria Egypt

Mahon, Bonnie H, *Public Information Coordr*, Columbus Museum of Art, Columbus OH

Mahoney, Charles A, *Pres*, Boston Watercolor Society, Scituate MA

Mahoney, Charles A, *Pres*, Guild of Boston Artists, Boston MA

Mahoney, Eleanor, *Instr*, Danforth Museum School, Framingham MA (S)

Mahoney, Eugene, *Dir*, Game and Parks Commission, Arbor Lodge State Historical Park, Nebraska City NE

Mahoney, Michael, *Chmn Dept Fine Arts*, Trinity College, Austin Arts Center, Hartford CT

Mahoney, Michael, *Instructor*, Your Heritage House, Inc, Detroit MI

Mahoney, Michael R T, *Chmn*, Trinity College, Department of Fine Arts, Hartford CT (S)

Mahy, Gordon, *Assoc Prof*, Mars Hill College, Mars Hill NC (S)

Maidment, Ian, *Cur Presentations*, Art Gallery of South Australia, Adelaide Australia

Maidoff, Jules, *Dir*, Studio Art Centers International, Florence Italy (S)

Maier, Manfred, *Vis Prof*, Ball State University, Art Department, Muncie IN (S)

Main, Jo Ann, *Instr*, University of Albuquerque, Art Department, Albuquerque NM (S)

Maines, Clark, *Asst Prof*, Wesleyan University, Art Department, Middletown CT (S)

Maize, Shirley, *Arts Coordinator*, Tennessee Valley Art Center, Tuscumbia AL

Majeske, Robert, *Instr*, Illinois Central College, Art and Humanities Department, East Peoria IL (S)

Majeski, Thomas H, *Prof*, University of Nebraska at Omaha, Dept of Art, Omaha NE (S)

Major, Lillian, *Cur*, Columbus Chapel, Boal Mansion and Museum, Boalsburg PA

Makov, Susan, *Asst Prof*, Weber State College, Art Department 2001, Ogden UT (S)

Makow, Yoram, *Chmn*, California State Polytechnic University, Pomona, Art Department, Pomona CA (S)

Malek, Greg, *Tour Guide*, Will Rogers Memorial and Museum, Claremore OK

Malgeri, Dina G, *Librn*, Malden Public Library, Malden MA

Malin, Edward, *Instructor*, Portland Art Museum, Museum Art School, Portland OR (S)

Malinjod, M Claude, *Head*, Ecoles d'Art de Geneve, Ecole des Arts Decoratifs, Geneva Switzerland (S)

Malke, Lutz S, *Cur*, Stadelsches Kunstinstitut, Staedel Art Institute, Frankfurt Germany, Federal Republic of

Mallekote, W N, *Admin*, Westfries Museum, Hoorn Netherlands

Mallet, J V G, *Keeper Ceramics*, Victoria and Albert Museum, London England

Mallory, Clifford D, *Pres*, Mystic Seaport Museum, Inc, Mystic CT

Mallory, Nina, *Assoc Prof*, State University of New York at Stony Brook, Art Department, Stony Brook NY (S)

Malm, Eric S, *Secy*, Brookgreen Gardens, Murrells Inlet SC

Malmanger, Magne, *Keeper Paintings*, Nasjonalgalleriet, National Gallery, Oslo Norway

Malmquist, A Keith, *Prof*, Bemidji State University, Art Department, Bemidji MN (S)

Malone, Delores, *Secy*, Fine Arts Museums of San Francisco, M H de Young Memorial Museum and California Palace of the Legion of Honor

Malone, Lee, *Dir*, Museum of Fine Arts of Saint Petersburg, Florida, Inc, Art Reference Library, Saint Petersburg FL

Malone, Robert J, *Secy*, New York Historical Society, New York NY

Malone, Robert R, *Head Printmaking*, Southern Illinois University at Edwardsville, Department of Art and Design, Edwardsville IL (S)

Maloney, Patricia, *Instructor*, Washington and Jefferson College, Art Department, Washington PA (S)

Maloubier, Jacques, *Instructor*, Propersi Galleries and School of Art Inc, Greenwich CT (S)

Malpass, Leslie, *Pres*, Western Illinois University, Browne Hall Gallery, Macomb IL

Manchester, Ellen, *Dir Photography*, Sun Valley Center for the Arts & Humanities, Department of Fine Art, Sun Valley ID (S)

Mancinelli, Fabrizio, *Cur for Medieval & Modern Art*, Monumenti Musei e Gallerie Pontificie, Vatican Museums and Galleries, Vatican City Italy

Mandel, Howard, *VPres*, New York Artists Equity Association, Inc, New York NY

Mandel, Howard, *VPres*, National Society of Painters in Casein and Acrylic, Inc, New York NY

Mandel, Howard, *VPres*, Audubon Artists, Inc, New York NY

Mandle, Roger, *Dir*, Toledo Museum of Art, Toledo OH

Mangio, Rosanne, *Dir*, Rustic Canyon Arts and Crafts Center, Los Angeles City Dept of Recreation and Parks, Santa Monica CA

Mango, Charles L, *Dir Museum of Fine Art*, Nassau County Museum of Fine Art, Roslyn NY

Mangold, Robert, *Prof*, Metropolitan State College, Art Department, Denver CO (S)

Mangulis, Ingrida, *Prof*, Salem State College, Art Department, Salem MA (S)

Mangum, William, *Assoc Prof*, Salem College, Art Department, Winston-Salem NC (S)

Manhart, Marcia, *Asst Dir*, Philbrook Art Center, Tulsa OK

Manheim, Emily M, *VPres*, National Antique and Art Dealers Association of America, New York NY

Manilla, Morton, *Chmn Educ Committee*, Toronto Art Therapy Institute, Toronto ON (S)

Manilow, Lewis, *Pres*, Museum of Contemporary Art, Chicago IL

Manley, Kathy, *Public Relations*, Artworlds Center for Creative Arts, Ann Arbor MI

Manly, Isaac V, *Pres*, North Carolina Art Society, Raleigh NC

Manly, J Alden, *Librn*, Saint Paul's School, Sheldon Library, Concord NH

Mann, Elaine E, *Dir*, National Museum of Racing, Inc, Saratoga Springs NY

Mann, Jack, *Asst Prof*, Wittenberg University, Art Department, Springfield OH (S)

Mann, Linda K, *Dir*, J K Ralston Museum and Art Center, Sidney MT

Mann, Richard, *Dir*, Cathedral Museum of Religious Art, New York NY

Mann, Virginia, *Gallery Dir*, Silvermine Guild School of the Arts, New Canaan CT

Mann, Vivian, *Cur of Judaica*, Jewish Museum, New York NY

Mannheimer, Marc, *Asst Prof*, Bradford College, Art Department, Bradford MA (S)

Manning, James, *Sr Keeper - Keeper of Conservation*, Plymouth City Museum and Art Gallery, Plymouth England

Manning, James L, *Public Relations and Grants*, Southern Tier Arts Association, Inc, Elmira NY

Manning, John, *Dir Munson-Williams-Proctor School of Art*, Utica College of Syracuse University, Division of Humanities, Utica NY (S)

Manning, John R, *Dir*, Munson-Williams-Proctor Institute, School of Art, Utica NY (S)

Manning, Larry, *Instructor*, Jefferson Davis State Junior College, Art Department, Brewton AL (S)

Manning, Les, *Ceramics Dept Head*, Banff Centre School of Fine Arts, Banff AB (S)

Manning, Peter, *Dean*, Nova Scotia Technical College, Faculty of Architecture, Halifax NS (S)

Manning, Polly, *Membership*, Licking County Art Association Gallery, Newark OH

Manning, Robert F, *Dept Chmn*, Manchester Community College, Fine Arts Department, Manchester CT (S)

Mannino, James, *Instructor*, Mohawk Valley Community College, Advertising Design and Production, Utica NY (S)

Manns, Suzanne, *Instr*, Museum of Fine Arts, Alfred C Glassell Junior School of Art, Houston TX (S)

Manou, Dorothy, *Public Relations Dir*, Buten Museum of Wedgwood, Merion PA

Mansfield, Joehugh, *Pres*, Creek Council House and Museum, Okmulgee OK

Mansfield, Patricia K, *Assoc Prof*, University of Wisconsin, Madison, School of Family Resources and Consumer Sciences, Madison WI (S)

Manske, Leo, *Pres*, Guild of South Carolina Artists, Columbia SC

Manson, Martha L, *Cur*, San Jose Museum of Art, San Jose CA

Mantel, Barbara F, *Asst to Dir*, Ohio University, Anthony G Trisolini Memorial Gallery, Athens OH

Mantie, Eugene, *Audiovisual Media Coordr*, Nation Portrait Gallery, Washington DC

Manuel, Mary, *Head Technical Services*, Springfield Free Public Library, Donald B Palmer Museum, Springfield NJ

Manusos, Mary, *Gallery Dir*, Ohio University, Seigfred Gallery, Athens OH

Manzella, David B, *Chmn Grad Studies Div*, Rhode Island School of Design, Providence RI (S)

Maortua, Jose A, *Prof*, Morehead State University, Art Department, Morehead KY (S)

Maounis, John, *Photograph Librarian*, National Maritime Museum, San Francisco CA

Map, Thomas, *Dir Committee*, University of Chicago, Department of Art History & Committee on Art & Design, Chicago IL (S)

Mapes, Jean, *Registrar*, Philadelphia College of Textiles and Science, Paley Design Center, Philadelphia PA

Maples, Jerry, *Pres*, Cedar Rapids Art Center, Cedar Rapids IA

Mapp, Thomas, *Dir*, University of Chicago, Lorado Taft Midway Studios, Chicago IL

Mara, Elaine, *Instructor*, Emma Willard School Arts Division, Troy NY (S)

Maradiaga, Ralph, *Co-Dir*, Galeria de la Raza, Studio 24, San Francisco CA

Marandel, Patrice, *Cur*, Museum of Fine Arts, Houston, Houston TX

Marantz, Kenneth A, *Chmn Dept*, Ohio State University, Department of Art Education, Columbus OH (S)

Marble, Fran, *Librn*, Allied Arts Council of the Yakima Valley, Warehouse Gallery, Yakima WA

Marcellus, Robert, *Instructor*, College of the Sequoias, Art Department, Visalia CA (S)

March, Paula, *Registrar Legion of Honor*, Fine Arts Museums of San Francisco, M H de Young Memorial Museum and California Palace of the Legion of Honor

Marchant, Sylvia L, *Dir of Education*, Greenville County Museum of Art, Greenville SC

Marchini, Julie, *Asst Dir*, Montclair State College, Gallery One, Upper Montclair NJ

Marcik, John, *Librn*, Saint Bonaventure University Art Collection, Friedsam Memorial Library, Saint Bonaventure NY

Marconi, Nello, *Chief Design & Production*, National Portrait Gallery, Washington DC

Marcou, George T, *Assoc Prof*, Catholic University of America, Department of Architecture & Planning, Washington DC (S)

Marcoux, Alice, *Head Textile Design*, Rhode Island School of Design, Providence RI (S)

Marcus, George, *Publicity Editor*, Philadelphia Museum of Art, Philadelphia PA

Marcus, Peter, *Chairperson Two-Dimensional Dept*, Washington University, School of Fine Arts, Saint Louis MO (S)

Marcus, Richard, *Librn & Dir*, Spertus Museum of Judaica, Helen Asher and Norman Asher Library of Spartus College, Chicago IL

Marcus, Sharon, *Curriculum Dir*, Oregon School of Arts and Crafts, Hoffman Gallery, Portland OR

Marcus, Shelly, *Lectr*, California State Polytechnic University, Pomona, Art Department, Pomona CA (S)

Marcus, Stanley, *Chmn*, University of Texas of Permian Basin, Art Discipline, Odessa TX (S)

Marcusen, Richard B, *Instructor*, Yavapai College, Art Department, Prescott AZ (S)

Marcy, Jean F, *Librn*, Saint Johnsbury Athenaeum, Saint Johnsbury VT

Marden, Anne, *VPres*, Waterville Historical Association, Waterville ME

Marder, Estelle, *Chmn Volunteer Service*, Asheville Art Museum, Asheville NC

Marder, Tod, *Asst Prof*, Rutgers, the State University of New Jersey, Graduate Program in Art History, New Brunswick NJ (S)

Marein, Shirley, *Assoc Prof*, New York Institute of Technology, Fine Arts Department, Old Westbury NY (S)

Marek, Bernie, *Instr*, Colorado Women's College, Department of Art, Denver CO (S)

Marforell, Antonio, *Prof*, Institute of Puerto Rican Culture, Escuela de Artes Plasticas, Mayaguez PR (S)

Margolis, Abby, *Membership*, California Historical Society, San Francisco CA

Margolis, Ann, *Pres*, League of New Hampshire Craftsmen, Concord NH

Margolis, Marianne, *Cur*, International Museum of Photography at George Eastman House, Rochester NY

Margolis, Richard, *Lectr*, Nazareth College of Rochester, Art Department, Rochester NY (S)

Marincola, Paula, *Asst to Dir*, University of Pennsylvania, Institute of Contemporary Art, Philadelphia PA

Maringoni, Martino, *Instr*, Studio Art Centers International, Florence Italy (S)

Marino, Lucilla, *Librn*, American Academy in Rome Library, Rome Italy

Marion, Marjorie, *Chmn Div*, College of St Francis, Art Department, Joliet IL (S)

Marion, Oliver, *Pres*, Gilbert Stuart Birthplace, Saunderstown RI

Marioni, Tom, *Dir*, Academy of the Museum of Conceptual Art, San Francisco CA

Maris, Arno, *Chmn Dept*, Westfield State College, Art Department, Westfield MA (S)

Mark, Joseph, *Instructor*, Williamsport Area Community College, Department of Engineering and Design, Williamsport PA (S)

Marker, David G, *Provost*, Hope College, DeWitt Cultural Center, Holland MI

Markham, Nancy, *Cur Formal Education*, Colorado Historical Society, Colorado Heritage Center, Denver CO

Markhoff, Alex, *Asst Prof*, State University of New York at Albany, Art Department, Albany NY (S)

Markrich, Lilo, *Museum Shop Mgr*, Textile Museum, Washington DC

Marks, Arthur S, *Asst Chmn Grad Study*, University of North Carolina at Chapel Hill, Art Department, Chapel Hill NC (S)

Marks, Richard, *Keeper of Burrell Collection*, Glasgow Museums and Art Galleries, Kelvingrove Art Gallery and Museum, Glasgow Scotland

Marks, Robert C, *Dean*, Harrington Institute of Interior Design, Chicago IL (S)

Marks, Robert W, *VPres*, Carolina Art Association, Gibbes Art Gallery, Charleston SC

Marks, Sandi, *Instructor*, San Jacinto College, Art Department, Pasadena TX (S)

Marks, William L, *Vice Chmn Board*, Huntsville Museum of Art, Huntsville AL

Markson, Eileen, *Head Librn*, Bryn Mawr College, Art and Archaeology Library, Bryn Mawr PA

Markussen, Ase, *Head Librn*, Kunstindustrimuseet I Oslo, Library, Oslo Norway

Markwordt, Judith S, *Staff Asst*, Duke University Museum of Art, Durham NC

Marlin, William, *Chmn Dept*, Camden County College, Department of Art, Blackwood NJ (S)

Marling, Karal Ann, *Assoc Prof*, University of Minnesota, Minneapolis, Art History, Minneapolis MN (S)

Marlow, Jessie, *Clerical Hostess*, Red River Valley Museum, Vernon TX

Marlow, K, *Dir*, Brandon Allied Arts Council, Brandon MB

Marlowe, Willie, *Chairwoman*, Junior College of Albany, Fine Arts Division, Albany NY (S)

Marois, R, *Chief Archaeological Survey of Canada*, National Museum of Man, Ottawa ON

Marom, Naama, *Librn*, Israel Museum, Library for Art and Archaeology, Jerusalem Israel

Maronde, Doreen, *Head Dept*, Kirkwood Community College, Department of Fine Arts, Cedar Rapids IA (S)

Marquardt, Emil, *Sr Secy*, Florida Gulf Coast Art Center, Inc, Clearwater FL

Marquess, Joyce O, *Asst Prof*, University of Wisconsin, Madison, School of Family Resources and Consumer Sciences, Madison WI (S)

Marras, Amerigo, *Pres & Art Dir*, Cultural Initiative, Toronto ON

Marron, Donald B, *VPres*, Museum of Modern Art, New York NY

Marrs, Robert E, *VPres Admin Affairs*, Art Institute of Chicago, Chicago IL

Mars, Marilyn, *Executive Dir*, Second Street Gallery, Charlottesville VA

Marsh, Anne Steele, *Secy*, Associated Artists of New Jersey, Pittstown NJ

Marsh, E Thomas, *Prof*, University of Louisville, Allen R Hite Art Institute, Louisville KY (S)

Marsh, Robert, *Assoc Prof*, Averett College, Art Department, Danville VA (S)

Marshal, Robert L, *Chmn*, Brigham Young University, Department of Art and Design, Provo UT (S)

Marshall, Gordon, *Asst Librn*, Library Company of Philadelphia, Philadelphia PA

Marshall, Grant, *Dir*, Arts for Living Center, Burlington IA

Marshall, Joseph W, *Librn*, Franklin D Roosevelt Library and Museum, Library, Hyde Park NY

Marshall, Richard, *Cur*, Whitney Museum of American Art, New York NY

Marshall, Thomas, *Asst Prof*, Atlantic Christian College, Art Dept, Wilson NC (S)

Marshman, Robert B, *Assoc Prof*, University of West Florida, Department of Art, Pensacola FL (S)

Marston, R E, *Librn & Arts Services Officer*, Sefton Metropolitan Borough, Atlinson Art Gallery, Southport England

Marstrander, Sverre, *Dir*, Universitetets Samling av Nordiske Oldsaker, University Museum of National Antiquities, Oslo Norway

Marten, Skip, *Instructor*, Ohio Visual Art Institute, Cincinnati OH (S)

Martens, Chris, *Asst Prof*, South Dakota State University, Art Dept, Brookings SD (S)

Martens, Irmelin, *Head Stone & Bronze Age Department*, Universitetets Samling av Nordiske Oldsaker, University Museum of National Antiquities, Oslo Norway

Martens, Margareta, *Librn*, Ostasiatiska Museet, Library, Stockholm Sweden

Marter, Joan, *Asst Prof*, Rutgers, the State University of New Jersey, Graduate Program in Art History, New Brunswick NJ (S)

Marti, M, *Asst Dir Business Admin*, Kunsthaus Zurich, Museum of Fine Arts, Zurich Switzerland

Martin, Alvin, *Asst Prof*, University of Texas at San Antonio, Division of Art and Design, San Antonio TX (S)

Martin, Anne, *Instructor*, Fontbonne College, Department of Art, Clayton MO (S)

Martin, Anthony, *Asst Prof*, Kingsborough Community College, Department of Art, Brooklyn NY (S)

Martin, Benjamin, *Chairperson Environmental Design*, Philadelphia College of Art, Philadelphia PA (S)

Martin, C Max, *Park Supt*, Territorial Statehouse, Fillmore UT

Martin, Don, *Instr*, Flagler College, Visual Arts Department, Saint Augustine FL (S)

Martin, Eric, *Dean*, California Institute of the Arts, School of Art, Valencia CA (S)

Martin, Frances, *Research Cur*, Evansville Museum of Arts and Science, Evansville IN

Martin, Fred, *Literary Chmn*, Irene Leache Memorial, Norfolk VA

Martin, Gene, *Dir*, Daniel Boone Regional Library, Columbia MO

Martin, Gerry J, *Secy-Treas*, American Council for the Arts in Education, Baltimore MD

Martin, Gloria, *Lectr*, Notre Dame College, Art Department, Manchester NH (S)

Martin, Gordon P, *University Librn*, California State University, Sacramento, Library, Humanities Reference Media Services Ctr, Sacramento CA

Martin, Harold T, *Pres*, Art Institute of Chicago, Antiquarian Society, Chicago IL

Martin, Hugh, *Dir*, Star-Spangled Banner Flag House Association, Baltimore MD

Martin, Irene, *Asst Dir*, Southern Methodist University, Meadows Museum, Dallas TX

Martin, Jaques, *Prof*, College Saint-Louis-Maillet, Department of Visual Arts, Edmundston NB (S)

Martin, Jean, *Librn*, Vancouver Art Gallery, Library, Vancouver BC

Martin, John, *Prof*, Princeton University, Department of Art and Archaeology, Princeton NJ (S)

Martin, John, *Prof*, Wesleyan University, Art Department, Middletown CT (S)

Martin, John H, *Deputy Dir Admin*, Corning Museum of Glass, Corning NY

Martin, John Rupert, *Secy*, College Art Association of America, New York NY

Martin, Kate, *Registrar*, National Art Gallery of New Zealand, Wellington New Zealand

Martin, Kenneth R, *Dir*, Kendall Whaling Museum, Sharon MA

Martin, Laura B, *Asst Dir*, Roberson Center, Binghamton NY

Martin, Loretta, *Asst Cur Coll*, El Paso Museum of Art, El Paso TX

Martin, Marne, *Librn*, Instituto Allende Library, San Mexico

Martin, Mary Alice, *Slide Cur*, Memphis State University, Art History Slide Library, Memphis TN

Martin, Máry Belle, *Prof*, Northeast Missouri State University, Art Department, Kirksville MO (S)

Martin, Michel, *Conservator Contemporary Art*, Musee du Quebec, Quebec PQ

Martin, Roger, *Instr*, Montserrat School of Visual Art, Beverly MA (S)

Martin, Rosanne, *Slide Librn*, Montclair State College, Slide Library, Upper Montclair NJ

Martin, Ruth, *Head Art, Music, Recreation Dept*, Memphis-Shelby County Public Library and Information Center, Department of Art, Music and Recreation, Memphis TN

Martin, Shirley, *Corresp Secy*, Greater Fall River Art Association, Fall River MA

Martin, Susan, *Secy*, Adirondack Lakes Center for the Arts, Blue Mountain Lake NY

Martin, Susan K, *Dir*, Johns Hopkins University, Milton S Eisenhower Library Galleries, Baltimore MD

Martin, Suzanne, *Asst Prof*, Colorado Women's College, Department of Art, Denver CO (S)

Martin, Thomas, *Asst Prof*, New York Institute of Technology, Fine Arts Department, Old Westbury NY (S)

Martin, Timothy, *Instructor*, Junior College of Albany, Fine Arts Division, Albany NY (S)

Martin, Tom, *Cur of Exhibits*, Museum of the American Indian, New York NY

Martin, Vernon, *Dept Head*, Hartford Public Library, Hartford CT

Martin, W S, *Chmn Management Committee*, Manitoba Historical Society, Dalnavert - MacDonald House Museum, Winnipeg MB

Martindale Jr, Wallace S, *Treas*, Woodmere Art Gallery, Philadelphia PA

Martinez, Manny, *Prof*, Cochise College, Art Department, Douglas AZ (S)

Martinez, Mari, *Supv Information*, Mississippi Museum of Art, Jackson MS

Martinez, Maria, *Instructor*, University of Southern California, Idyllwild Campus, Idyllwild School of Music and the Arts, Idyllwild CA (S)

Martino, Babette, *Instructor*, Mohawk Valley Community College, Advertising Design and Production, Utica NY (S)

Martinsen, Richard, *Chmn*, Sheridan College, Art Department, Sheridan WY (S)

Martinson, Frances S, *VPres & Secy*, Museum of American Folk Art, New York NY

Martinson, Robert, *Librn*, Housatonic Community College, Library, Bridgeport CT

Maruo, Sadamu, *Chief Film Center*, Tokyo Kokuritsu Kindai Bujutsukan, National Film Center, Tokyo Japan

Marus, Lilian, *Executive Secy*, National Institute for Architectural Education, New York NY

Marvin, James C, *Dir*, Topeka Public Library, Topeka KS

Marvin, Miranda C, *Assoc Prof*, Wellesley College, Art Department, Wellesley MA (S)

Marxhansen, Ben, *Assoc Prof*, Concordia College, Art Department, Saint Paul MN (S)

Marxhausen, Renhold P, *Prof*, Concordia College, Art Department, Seward NE (S)

Maryon, Edward, *Prof*, University of Utah, Art Department, Salt Lake City UT (S)

Marzahn, Bruce, *Asst Prof*, Daemen College, Art Department, Amherst NY (S)

Marzan, Alberta, *Fashion Design Coordr*, North Texas State University, Art Department, Denton TX (S)

Marzio, Peter C, *Dir*, Corcoran Gallery of Art, Washington DC

Marzkiw, Dori, *Gallery Secy*, Palomar Community College, Boehm Gallery, San Marcos CA

Maser, Edward, *Prof*, University of Chicago, Department of Art History & Committee on Art & Design, Chicago IL (S)

Maser, Edward A, *Dir*, University of Chicago, David and Alfred Smart Gallery, Chicago IL

Masin, Jiri, *Chief Ancient Art Coll*, Narodni Galerie v Prague, National Gallery of Prague, Prague Czechoslovakia

Masling, Annette, *Librn*, Albright-Knox Art Gallery, Art Reference Library, Buffalo NY

Masog, John, *Secy*, North Country Museum of Arts, Park Rapids MN

Mason, Baniel, *Head Art Dept*, Bethany College, Lindsborg KS (S)

Mason, Daniel, *Department Head*, Bethany College, Mingenback Art Center, Lindsborg KS

Mason, Debby Dale, *Coordr of Museum Information*, Tennessee State Museum, Nashville TN

Mason, Elizabeth, *Prof*, Harding University, Department of Art, Searcy AR (S)

Mason, Helen S, *Dir*, Smith-Mason Gallery and Museum, Washington DC

Mason, Henry Lea, *Pres*, Arts Club of Washington, James Monroe House, Washington DC

Mason, John, *Pres*, Octagon Center for the Arts, Ames IA

Mason, Phillip, *Prof*, Fisk University, Art Dept, Nashville TN (S)

Mason, Rainer M, *Cur*, Musee d'Art et d'Histoire, Museum of Art and History, Geneva Switzerland

Mason, Tal, *Chmn Dept Art*, Florida Atlantic University Art Gallery, Boca Raton FL

Mason, Terry, *First VPres*, Douglas Art Association, Little Gallery, Douglas AZ

Mason Jr, Charles E, *Honorary Cur of Prints*, Boston Athenaeum, Boston MA

Mason Jr, Francis S, *Asst Dir*, Pierpont Morgan Library, New York NY

Massaguer, Margarida, *Librn*, Museo de Arte Moderno, Library, Barcelona Spain

Massar, Phyllis, *Art & Music Librn*, Ferguson Library, Stamford CT

Massaroni, Dino, *Instr*, Cuyahoga Valley Art Center, Cuyahoga Falls OH (S)

Massee, Judy, *Chmn Division of Arts*, Reed College Art Gallery, Portland OR

Massey, Arleta, *Secy*, San Angelo Art Club, Kendall Art Gallery, San Angelo TX

Massey, Geoffrey, *VPres*, Vancouver Art Gallery, Vancouver BC

Massey, Robert, *Vis Prof*, Cochise College, Art Department, Douglas AZ (S)

Massiczek, Albert, *Dir*, Gemaldegalerie der Akademie der Bildenden Kunste in Wien, Kupferstichkabinett der Akademie der Bildenden Kunste, Vienna Austria

Massin, Eugene, *Instructor*, University of Miami, Department of Art, Coral Gables FL (S)

Masters, Ann D, *Cur*, Roanoke Fine Arts Center, Roanoke VA

Masters, Leslie, *Asst Dir*, Birmingham-Bloomfield Art Association, Birmingham MI

Masterson, William, *Preparator*, University of New Mexico, University Art Museum, Albuquerque NM

Mastroianni, Umberto, *Prof*, Accademia di Belle Arti e Liceo Artistico, Academy of Fine Arts, Bologna Italy (S)

Masun, Phil, *Instructor*, William Jewell College, Art Dept, Liberty MO (S)

Mates, Julian, *Dean*, School of the Arts, C W Post Center of Long Island University, Art Department, Greenvale NY (S)

Mates, Robert E, *Photographer*, Solomon R Guggenheim Museum, New York NY

Mather, Christine, *Cur Spanish Colonial Coll*, Museum of New Mexico, Museum of International Folk Art, Santa Fe NM

Mather II, Charles E, *Pres*, National Museum of Racing, Inc, Saratoga Springs NY

Mathews, Glynice, *Instructor*, Friends University, Art Department, Wichita KS (S)

Mathews, Nancy Mowll, *Cur*, Randolph-Macon Womans College, Art Gallery, Lynchburg VA

Mathey, Francois, *Chief Cur*, Union Centrale des Arts Decoratifs, Musee des Arts Decoratifs, Paris France

Mathiasson, Kurt, *First VPres & Mgr*, Swedish American Museum Association of Chicago, Chicago IL

Mathis, Doyle, *VPres*, Berry College, Art Department, Mount Berry GA

Mathisen, Raymond, *Pres Board Trustees*, Metropolitan Museum and Art Centers, Coral Gables FL

Maticevic, Davor, *Cur*, Galerije Grada Zagreba, Galerija Suvremene Umjetnosti, Zagreb Yugoslavia

Mato, Daniel, *Dir Exhib*, University of Manitoba Gallery III, Winnipeg MB

Matos, Sandra, *Asst Cur*, Safety Harbor Museum of History and Fine Arts, Safety Harbor FL

Matranga, Frank P, *Assoc Prof*, Los Angeles Harbor College, Art Department, Wilmington CA (S)

Matsch, Robert, *VPres*, Arts for Living Center, Burlington IA

Matson, Judy, *Pub Information Dir*, Hudson River Museum, Yonkers NY

Matsumoto, Moritaka, *Asst Prof*, University of British Columbia, Department of Fine Arts, Vancouver BC (S)

Matter, Mercedes, *Dean*, New York Studio School of Drawing, Painting and Sculpture, New York NY (S)

Matthews, George G, *Pres & Trustee*, Henry Morrison Flagler Museum, Palm Beach FL

Matthews, Harriett, *Assoc Prof*, Colby College, Art Dept, Waterville ME (S)

Matthews, J Eugene, *Chmn Board Dir*, Sumter Gallery of Art, Sumter SC

Matthews, Mary, *Asst Prof*, College of Saint Teresa, Art Department, Winona MN (S)

Matthews, Molly, *Secy*, University of New Orleans, Fine Arts Gallery, New Orleans LA

Matthews, Nicks, *VPres Arts Division & Exhibit Chmn*, Council of Ozark Artists and Craftsmen, Inc, Arts Center of the Ozarks, Springdale AR

Matthews, T, *VPres*, University of Victoria, Maltwood Art Museum and Gallery, Victoria BC

Matthias, Susan M, *Asst Prof*, Indiana University Southeast, Fine Arts Department, New Albany IN (S)

Mattingly, James T, *Art Coordr*, Oregon College of Education, Creative Arts Department, Visual Arts, Monmouth OR (S)

Mattingly, James T, *Coordr of Art*, Oregon College of Education Galleries, Monmouth OR

Mattson, Robert, *Head Dept*, Willmar Community College, Willmar MN (S)

Mattus, Mary Ann, *Secy*, Blacksburg Regional Art Association, Blacksburg VA

Mattusch, Carol C, *Asst Prof*, George Mason University, Department of Fine and Performing Arts, Fairfax VA (S)

Matus, Theodore P, *Asst Prof*, Western Carolina University, Dept of Art, Cullowhee NC (S)

Matusiewicz, Daniel A, *Dir Admin, Sales & Security*, Mississippi Museum of Art, Jackson MS

Mauck, Marchita, *Assoc Prof*, Louisiana State University, Department of Fine Arts, Baton Rouge LA (S)

Maughelli, Mary, *Prof*, California State University, Fresno, Art Department, Fresno CA (S)

Mau Jean, Didier, *Instructor*, Umpqua Community College, Art Department, Roseburg OR (S)

Mauner, George L, *Prof*, Pennsylvania State University, University Park, Department of Art History, University Park PA (S)

Mauren, Paul, *Instr*, College of Saint Rose, Division of Art, Albany NY (S)

Maurer, Evan, *Cur Primitive Art*, Art Institute of Chicago, Chicago IL

Maurer, Sherry, *Cur*, Cedar Rapids Art Center, Cedar Rapids IA

Maurice, K, *Cur Clocks*, Bayerisches Nationalmuseum, Bavarian National Museum, Munich Germany, Federal Republic of

Mauro, Arthur V, *Pres*, Winnipeg Art Gallery, Winnipeg MB

Maut, K Frank V, *Cur 20th Century*, Staatsgalerie Stuttgart, Stuttgart Germany, Federal Republic of

Mauthe, Ernest, *Assoc Prof*, Mercyhurst College, Department of Art, Erie PA (S)

Maveety, Patrick, *Dir of Oriental Art*, Stanford University, T W Stanford Art Gallery & Museum of Art, Stanford CA

Maves, David W, *Chmn*, College of Charleston, Fine Arts Department, Charleston SC (S)

Mavigliano, George, *Chmn Art History*, Southern Illinois University, School of Art, Carbondale IL (S)

Mavroudis, Demetrios, *Assoc Prof*, University of Richmond, Department of Art, Richmond VA (S)

Mawn, Peter R, *Cur*, Museum of Art of Ogunquit, Ogunquit ME

Mawson, Robert, *Asst Adminr*, Woodrow Wilson House, Washington DC

Mawson, Robert, *Asst Adminr*, Decatur House, Washington DC

Maxey, Diane, *Corresponding Secy*, Arizona Artist Guild, Phoenix AZ

Maxwell, Allan, *Asst Prof*, Wilkes College, Department of Art, Wilkes-Barre PA (S)

Maxwell, William, *Instr*, College of New Rochelle, Art Department, New Rochelle NY (S)

May, A Hyatt, *Pres*, Hispanic Society of America Museum, New York NY

May, Florence L, *Cur Textiles*, Hispanic Society of America Museum, New York NY

May, James M, *Asst Prof*, Kearney State College, Dept of Art, Kearney NE (S)

May, Juanita, *Dir School*, Metropolitan Museum and Art Centers, Coral Gables FL

May, Larry, *Instructor*, Art Academy of Cincinnati, Cincinnati OH (S)

May, Laurie, *Executive Secy*, Craft and Folk Art Museum, Los Angeles CA

May, Susan L, *Interpretive Programs Asst*, Schuyler Mansion, Albany NY

Mayall, Myrtle, *Secy*, West Vancouver Visual Arts Society, West Vancouver BC

Mayer, Bena F, *VPres & Secy*, Artists Technical Institute, New York NY

Mayer, Charles, *Asst Prof*, Indiana State University, Department of Humanities, Terre Haute IN (S)

Mayer, Daniel D, *Cur Exhib*, New York State Historical Association, Fenimore House, Cooperstown NY

Mayer, Herbert, *Dir*, Mayer School of Fashion Design, Art Department, New York NY (S)

Mayer, Jessie, *Pres*, Essex Art Association, Inc, Essex CT

Mayer, Joseph, *Assoc Prof*, Prince George's Community College, Art Department, Largo MD (S)

Mayer, Joyce, *Executive Secy*, Buffalo Bill Memorial Association, Cody WY

Mayer, Martin, *Cur*, Suermondt-Ludwig-Museum der Stadt Aachen, Aachen Germany, Federal Republic of

Mayer, Ralph, *Dir*, Artists Technical Institute, New York NY

Mayer, Rick, *Chief Exhib Preparator*, Ohio State University, Gallery of Fine Arts, Columbus OH

Mayes, Steven L, *Head Dept*, West Texas State University, Art Department, Canyon TX (S)

Mayhall, Dorothy, *Dir*, Aldrich Museum of Contemporary Art, Ridgefield CT

Mayhew, Edgar, *Prof*, Connecticut College, Department of Art History, New London CT (S)

Mayhew, Edgar DeN, *Dir*, Lyman Allyn Museum, New London CT

Maylone, R Russell, *Cur Special Coll*, Northwestern University, Library, Art Collection, Evanston IL

Maynard, Gladys, *Instructor*, Chamberlayne Junior College, Department of Graphic and Applied Arts, Boston MA (S)

Maynard, Louise, *Secy*, Southwest Museum, Los Angeles CA

Maynard, Lucille, *Treas*, Greater Fall River Art Association, Fall River MA

Maynard, Maureen, *Executive Dir*, Warwick Arts Foundation, Warwick RI

Maynard, Neil, *Pres*, Grand Prairie Art Council, Inc, Stuttgart AR

Maynard, Veronica, *Secy*, National Assembly of Community Arts Agencies, Washington DC

Maynard, William, *Chmn Fine Arts*, New England School of Art and Design, Boston MA (S)

Mayo, Marty, *Cur*, Contemporary Arts Museum, Houston TX

Mayo, Noel, *Chairperson Industrial Design*, Philadelphia College of Art, Philadelphia PA (S)

Mayor, A Hyatt, *First VPres*, Brookgreen Gardens, Murrells Inlet SC

Mayor, Robin C, *Prin*, Emily Carr College of Art, Vancouver BC (S)

Mays, Clarence C, *Head Dept*, Virginia Western Community College, Commercial Art, Fine Art & Photography, Roanoke VA (S)

Mays, Louis, *Treas*, Tennessee Valley Art Center, Tuscumbia AL

Maytham, Thomas N, *Dir*, Denver Art Museum, Frederic H Douglas Library, Denver CO

Maza, Herbert, *Pres*, Institute for American Universities, Fine Arts in Aix, Avignon and Canterbury, Aix-en-Provence France (S)

Mazeika, George, *Registrar*, University of Connecticut, William Benton Museum of Art, Storrs CT

Maze Jr, Clarence, *Pres*, Richard Bland College, Art Department, Petersburg VA (S)

Mazonowicz, Douglas, *Dir*, Gallery of Prehistoric Paintings, New York NY

Mazur, Alexander, *Pres*, Bridgeport Art League, Bridgeport CT

Mazur, Robert, *Chmn Grad Studies*, Bowling Green State University, School of Art, Bowling Green OH (S)

Mazurek, Wanda, *Cur*, East Windsor Historical Society Inc, Scantic Academy Museum, West Hartford CT

Mazurkewicz, James, *Instr*, Cleveland Institute of Art, Cleveland OH (S)

Mazzola, John W, *Pres*, Lincoln Center for the Performing Arts, Amsterdam, Plaza and Main Galleries, New York NY

McAfee, Michael J, *Cur History*, United States Military Academy, West Point Museum, West Point NY

McAleer, J Philip, *Prof*, Nova Scotia Technical College, Faculty of Architecture, Halifax NS (S)

McAlexander, Kent, *Assoc Prof*, Northeast Missouri State University, Art Department, Kirksville MO (S)

McAlister, Richard A, *Instructor*, Providence College, Department of Fine Arts, Providence RI (S)

McAlister, Roger Cornell, *Chmn Dept*, Lane Community College, Art and Applied Design Department, Eugene OR (S)

McAllister, Gerry, *Dir*, University of California-San Diego, Mandeville Art Gallery, La Jolla CA

McAllister, Lewis, *Chmn*, Mount Saint Mary's College, Fine Arts Department, Emmitsburg MD (S)

McAlpine, Barbara, *Asst to Dir*, California State University Fullerton, Art Gallery, Fullerton CA

McAlpine, David, *Treas*, Monterey Peninsula Museum of Art, Monterey CA

McArt, Craig J, *Environmental Design*, Rochester Institute of Technology, School of Art and Design, Rochester NY (S)

McArthur, Kenneth S, *Managing Dir*, Eva Brook Donly Museum, Simcoe ON

McBeth, James R, *Prof*, Weber State College, Art Department 2001, Ogden UT (S)

McBratney, Deborah, *Executive Dir*, Anderson Fine Arts Center, Anderson IN

McBride, Alex, *Chmn Dept*, Juniata College, Department of Art, Huntingdon PA (S)

McBride, Clyde M, *Trustee*, Religious Americana Museum, Ringoes NJ

McBride, Ronald O, *Instructor*, Dalton Junior College, Division of Humanities, Dalton GA (S)

McBurney, William Craig, *Exec Dir*, Hoyt Institute of Fine Arts, New Castle PA

McCabe, Cynthia, *Cur*, Hirshhorn Museum and Sculpture Garden, Washington DC

McCabe, Maureen, *Assoc Prof*, Connecticut College, Department of Art, New London CT (S)

McCabe, William, *Prof*, Connecticut College, Department of Art, New London CT (S)

McCaffrey, Rosanne, *Assoc Cur*, Historic New Orleans Collection, Kemper and Leila Williams Foundation, New Orleans LA

McCain, J W, *VPres*, Safety Harbor Museum of History and Fine Arts, Safety Harbor FL

McCain, John, *VPres*, Katonah Gallery, Katonah NY

McCallum, Ian, *Dir & Cur*, American Museum in Britain, Bath England

McCann, David, *Registrar*, Fine Arts Museum of the South, Mobile AL

McCann, William J, *Dir*, California Museum of Science and Industry, Los Angeles CA

McCarren, Paul, *Instructor*, Georgetown University, Department of Fine Arts, Washington DC (S)

McCarroll, B J, *Gallery Dir*, University of Lethbridge Art Gallery, Lethbridge AB

McCarroll, Bill, *Asst Prof*, University of Lethbridge, Department of Art, Lethbridge AB (S)

McCartan, Edward, *Instr*, College of Saint Rose, Division of Art, Albany NY (S)

McCarthy, Bridget Beattie, *Executive Dir*, Oregon School of Arts and Crafts, Hoffman Gallery, Portland OR

McCarthy, Bridget Beattie, *Dir*, Oregon School of Arts and Crafts, Portland OR (S)

McCarthy, Dennis, *Prof*, Benedictine College, Art Department, Atchison KS (S)

McCarthy, Eibhlin, *Registrar*, National Gallery of Ireland, Dublin Ireland

McCarthy, Joe, *Senior Adviser*, Pennsylvania Department of Education, Arts in Education Program, Harrisburg PA

McCarthy, John R, *Treas*, Artists' Fellowship, Inc, New York NY

McCarthy, Paul, *Head Archives*, University of Alaska, Elmer E Rasmuson Library, Fairbanks AK

McCarty, Lorraine, *Instr*, Pontiac Art Center, Pontiac MI (S)

McCarty, Michael, *Instructor*, Utica Junior College, Humanities Division, Utica MS (S)

McCarty, Timothy L, *Asst Dir for Programming*, University of Minnesota, Student Center Galleries, Saint Paul MN

McCary, Jill, *Cur Educ*, Central Louisiana Art Association, Alexandria Museum Visual Art Center, Alexandria LA

McCauley, Elizabeth Anne, *Asst Dir*, University of New Mexico, University Art Museum, Albuquerque NM

McCauley, Gardiner, *Dir & Head Art Dept*, Stephens College, Lewis James and Nellie Stratton Davis Art Gallery, Columbia MO

McCauley, Gardiner R, *Head Dept*, Stephens College, Art Department, Columbia MO (S)

McCauley, Nancy P, *Instructor*, Stephens College, Art Department, Columbia MO (S)

McCauley, Nicholas, *Art Librn*, Houston Public Library, Houston TX

McCauley, Nicholas, *Art Librn*, Anna Maria College, Saint Luke's Gallery, Paxton MA

McCauley, Robert, *Prof*, Rockford College, Department of Fine Arts, Rockford IL (S)

McChesney, Jenny, *Asst Dir Operations*, Carnegie-Mellon University, Forbes Street Gallery, Pittsburgh PA

McClain, Matthew, *Cur & Admin*, University of Pennsylvania, Institute of Contemporary Art, Philadelphia PA

McClain, San, *Pres*, Alaska Artists Guild, Anchorage AK

McClanahan, John, *Painting*, Baylor University, Department of Fine Arts, Waco TX (S)

McCleary, George, *Secy*, Springfield Art Center, Springfield OH

McCleary, Mary, *Dir*, Stephen F Austin State University, Art Gallery, Nacogdoches TX

McCleary, Peter, *Chmn*, University of Pennsylvania, Department of Architecture, Philadelphia PA (S)

McClellan, Douglas, *Chmn*, University of California at Santa Cruz, Art Board of Studies, Santa Cruz CA (S)

McClelland, Steve, *Instructor*, Factory of Visual Art, Seattle WA (S)

McClendon, Joan, *Cur of Education*, Wichita Falls Museum and Art Center, Wichita Falls TX

McClintory, Donald, *Pres*, Art Center Association, Louisville KY

McCloud, Darlene, *Dir*, Municipal Art Society of New York, The Information Exchange, New York NY

McClung, Millard, *Assoc Dir*, Oregon Historical Society, Portland OR

McClure, Nell, *Dir*, Minnesota Museum of Art, Art School, Education Division, Saint Paul MN (S)

McClure, Nell H, *Acting Dir Education*, Minnesota Museum of Art, Saint Paul MN

McCoal, Patric, *Head Humanities*, Saint Gregorys Junior College, Department of Art, Shawnee OK (S)

McColley, Sutherland, *Dir*, Dulin Gallery of Art, Knoxville TN

McCollough, Ed, *Instructor*, Illinois Wesleyan University, School of Art, Bloomington IL (S)

McCollum, Michael, *Chmn Art Department*, University of Nevada, Las Vegas, Art Gallery, Las Vegas NV

McCollum, Michael L, *Assoc Prof*, University of Nevada, Las Vegas, Department of Art, Las Vegas NV (S)

McComb, Ron, *Librn*, Cornish Institutue of Allied Arts, Poncho Library, Seattle WA

McCombs, Bruce, *Asst Prof*, Hope College, Art Department, Holland MI (S)

McCone, Michael, *Deputy Dir*, San Francisco Museum of Modern Art, San Francisco CA

McConnell, Fraiser, *Asst Librn*, California College of Arts & Crafts, Meyer Library, Oakland CA

McConnell, Gordon, *Cur*, Art Center, Waco TX

McCord, Jane M, *Head Dept*, Shorter College, Art Department, Rome GA (S)

McCord, Marie M, *Chmn*, Oakland City College, Division of Fine Arts, Oakland City IN (S)

McCorison, Marcus A, *Dir*, American Antiquarian Society, Worcester MA

McCormick, Charles James, *Chmn*, Georgetown College, Art Department, Georgetown KY (S)

McCormick, James, *Head Dept*, University of Wisconsin-Stout, Art Department, Menomonie WI (S)

McCormick, John, *Assoc Prof*, Delta College, Art Department, University Center MI (S)

McCormick, W F, *Pres*, Leigh Yawkey Woodson Art Museum, Inc, Wausau WI

McCourt, Mike, *Art Cur*, Montana Historical Society, Library, Helena MT

McCoy, Elinor Sue, *Asst Cur Educational Services*, University of Utah, Utah Museum of Fine Arts, Salt Lake City UT

McCoy, Evelyn, *Special Programs Adminr*, Arkansas Arts Center, Elizabeth Prewitt Taylor Memorial Library, Little Rock AR

McCoy, Evelyn, *Dir Special Projects*, Arkansas Arts Center, Little Rock AR

McCoy, Frank, *Art Department Chmn*, University of Montevallo, The Gallery, Montevallo AL

McCoy, Garnett, *Archivist*, Archives of American Art, Washington Center, New York NY

McCoy, Grace, *Instr*, Claremore College, Art Department, Claremore OK (S)

McCoy, Katherine, *Assoc Head Design Dept*, Cranbrook Academy of Art, Bloomfield Hills MI (S)

McCoy, L Frank, *Chmn*, University of Montevallo, College of Fine Arts, Montevallo AL (S)

McCoy, Michael, *Assoc Head Design Dept*, Cranbrook Academy of Art, Bloomfield Hills MI (S)

McCoy, Sally, *Instructor*, La Roche College, Division of Graphic Arts & Design, Pittsburgh PA (S)

McCracken, Patrick, *Cur Education*, Albuquerque Museum of Art, History and Science, Albuquerque NM

McCracken, Peggie, *Cur Kirkpatrick Center*, Omniplex, Oklahoma City OK

McCrady, Carolyn, *Secy*, Greater Gary Arts Council, Gary IN

McCrady, Howard, *Treas*, Phoenix Art Museum, Phoenix AZ

McCray, Dorothy, *Prof*, Western New Mexico University, Dept of Fine Art, Art Div, Silver City NM (S)

McCray, Mogie, *Dir of Education*, Carson County Square House Museum, Panhandle TX

McCready, Eric, *Dir*, University of Texas at Austin, University Art Museum, Austin TX

McCready, Eric S, *Dir*, University of Wisconsin, Elvehjem Art Center, Madison WI

McCready, Reyburn R, *Librn*, University of Oregon, School of Architecture and Allied Arts Library, Eugene OR

McCreath, William, *Chmn*, Montclair State College, Fine Arts Department, Montclair NJ (S)

McCreaty, William, *Chmn Fine Arts Department*, Montclair State College, Gallery One, Upper Montclair NJ

McCue, Gerald M, *Dean*, Harvard University, Graduate School of Design, Departments of Architecture, City and Regional Planning, Landscape Archit and Urban Design Prog, Cambridge MA (S)

McCue, Harry, *Chmn*, Ithaca College, Art Department, Ithaca NY (S)

McCuistion, Fred, *Pres*, Council of Ozark Artists and Craftsmen, Inc, Arts Center of the Ozarks, Springdale AR

McCuistion, John, *Dir*, University of Puget Sound, Kittredge Art Gallery, Tacoma WA

McCuistion, John, *Chmn*, University of Puget Sound, Art Department, Tacoma WA (S)

McCulloch-Lovell, Ellen, *Secy*, National Assembly of State Arts Agencies, Washington DC

McCullough, Joseph, *Secy*, Cleveland Institute of Art, Cleveland Art Association, Cleveland OH

McCullough, Joseph, *Pres*, Cleveland Institute of Art, Cleveland OH (S)

McCullough, Joseph, *Pres*, Cleveland Institute of Art, Cleveland OH

McCurdy, Daniel, *Registrar*, University of California, University Art Galleries and California Museum of Photography, Riverside CA

McCutchen, Ann, *VPres*, Tennessee Valley Art Center, Tuscumbia AL

McCutchen, Kathryn, *Cur Asst*, Department of State, Diplomatic Reception Rooms, Washington DC

McDaniel, Dennis K, *Dir*, Peale Museum, Baltimore MD

McDermand, Robert V, *Coordr Public Services*, Plymouth State College, Herbert H Lamson Library, Plymouth NH

McDermott, Betty, *Asst for Special Projects*, New Orleans Museum of Art, Isaac Delgado Museum, New Orleans LA

McDermott, M J, *Librn-Tutor*, National Gallery of Zimbabwe Rhodesia, Thomas Meikle Library, Salisbury Zimbahwe Rhodesia

McDermott, Mary Ellen, *Instr*, Cleveland Institute of Art, Cleveland OH (S)

McDermott, Nancy, *Development Officer*, Solomon R Guggenheim Museum, New York NY

McDonald, Barbara, *Prog Coordr*, King County Arts Commission, Seattle WA

McDonald, Eloise E, *Librn*, University of Arkansas, Fine Arts Library, Fayetteville AR

McDonald, Robert, *Coordr Art*, Cape Cod Community College, Art Dept, West Barnstable MA (S)

McDonald, Robert, *Sr Cur*, La Jolla Museum of Contemporary Art, La Jolla CA

McDonnell, Patricia, *Western Assoc of Art Museums Professional Training Coordr*, Museum Management Institute, San Francisco CA (S)

McDonough, Reginald, *Superior Reverend*, Mission San Miguel, San Miguel CA

McDougal Jr, O J, *Pres Board Trustees*, Hastings Museum, Hastings NE

McDougall, Tom, *Assoc Prof*, California State University, Fresno, Art Department, Fresno CA (S)

McDowell, H Woodward, *Treas*, Presbyterian Historical Society, Philadelphia PA

McDowell, James, *Assoc*, College of Our Lady of the Elms, Department of Art, Chicopee MA (S)

McDowell, Paul, *Asst Prof*, Eastern Illinois University, Art Department, Charleston IL (S)

McDowell, Peggy, *Assoc Prof*, University of New Orleans, Dept of Fine Arts, New Orleans LA (S)

McElhaney, Penny, *Instructor*, Grand Canyon College, Art Department, Phoenix AZ (S)

McElroy, R E, *VPres*, Control Data Arts International, Saint Paul MN

McEndarfer, Ed, *Asst Prof*, Northeast Missouri State University, Art Department, Kirksville MO (S)

McEroy, Georgett, *VPres*, Willard House and Clock Museum, Inc, Grafton MA

McEvilley, Thomas, *Vis Lectr*, Rice University, Department of Art and Art History, Houston TX (S)

McEwen, Amy V, *Assoc Dir*, China Institute in America, China House Gallery, New York NY

McFadden, David, *Cur Decorative Arts*, Cooper-Hewitt Museum, Smithsonian Institution National Museum of Design, New York NY

McFadden, James L, *Asst Prof*, South Carolina State College, Art Program, Orangeburg SC (S)

McFarland, Clairvaux, *Assoc Prof*, College of Saint Teresa, Art Department, Winona MN (S)

McFarland, Jean, *Asst Prof*, Winthrop College, Department of Art, Rock Hill SC (S)

McFarland, William, *VPres*, Lexington Art League, Inc, Lexington KY

McFarlane, Len, *Technician*, University of British Columbia, Museum of Anthropology, Vancouver BC

McFee, Doris, *Head Librn*, Chappell Memorial Library and Art Gallery, Chappell NE

McFeetors, J, *Pres*, Manitoba Association of Architects, Winnipeg MB

McGaha, Jerry, *Museum Dir*, United States Figure Skating Hall of Fame and Museum, Colorado Springs CO

McGarry, Patricia, *Secy*, Farmington Valley Arts Center, Avon CT

McGarvey, Jayne, *Treas*, Kent Art Association, Inc Gallery, Kent CT

McGeary, George L, *Chmn Fine Arts Dept*, Manhattan College, School of Arts and Sciences, Bronx NY (S)

McGee, Melvin C, *Secy*, Buffalo Bill Memorial Association, Cody WY

McGee, Michael L, *Bus Mgr*, Oklahoma Museum of Art, Oklahoma City OK

McGee, Thomas, *Pres*, Farmington Valley Arts Center, Avon CT

McGee, William, *Chmn*, Herbert H Lehman College, Art Department, Bronx NY (S)

McGee, Winston, *Chmn of Art Dept*, California State College, Stanislaus, Art Gallery, Turlock CA

McGee, Winston, *Chmn Dept*, California State College, Stanislaus, Art Department, Turlock CA (S)

McGehee, Terry, *Instr*, Agnes Scott College, Department of Art, Decatur GA (S)

McGeorge, Pauline, *Assoc Prof*, University of Lethbridge, Department of Art, Lethbridge AB (S)

McGhan, Rena, *Cur*, Sioux Indian Museum, Rapid City SD

McGinnis, Darrell, *Prof*, Fort Hays State University, Department of Art, Hays KS (S)

McGinnis, Mark, *Asst Prof*, Northern State College, Art Dept, Aberdeen SD (S)

McGough, Charles, *Dir*, East Texas State University, Little Gallery, Commerce TX

McGough, Charles E, *Head Dept*, East Texas State University, Department of Art, Commerce TX (S)

McGovern, Anna, *Head of the Library Committee*, Danforth Museum, Library, Framingham MA

McGowan, James K, *Chmn*, University of North Carolina at Wilmington, Art Department, Wilmington NC (S)

McGowan, Kathryn, *VPres*, Artworlds Center for Creative Arts, Ann Arbor MI

McGrath, Don, *VPres*, William Rockhill Nelson Gallery of Art, Friends of Art, Kansas City MO

McGraw, William R, *Chmn Dept*, Youngstown State University, Art Department, Youngstown OH (S)

McGreevy, Susan, *Dir*, Wheelwright Museum, Santa Fe NM

McGregor, R B, *Acting Dir*, Hawkes Bay Art Gallery and Museum, Napier New Zealand

McGregor, Rob Roy, *Corresponding Secy*, Concord Antiquarian Society Museum, Concord MA

McGuigan, Ann, *Asst Cur*, Washington State University, Museum of Art, Pullman WA

McGuiness, Brendan, *Rector Msgr*, San Carlos Cathedral, Monterey CA

McGuire, David J, *Chmn*, Cabrillo College, Visual Arts Division, Aptos CA (S)

McGuire, James, *Educ Coordinator*, Lyman Allyn Museum, New London CT

McGuire, Michael C, *Dean of Educ*, Central Academy of Commercial Art, Cincinnati OH (S)

McGuire, Samuel B, *Instructor*, Central Academy of Commercial Art, Cincinnati OH (S)

McHarg, Ian L, *Chmn*, University of Pennsylvania, Department of Landscape Architecture and Regional Planning, Philadelphia PA (S)

McHenry, Nadine, *Vis Prof*, Nebraska Wesleyan University, Art Dept, Lincoln NE (S)

McHugh, Owen, *Coordr Two-Dimensional Design*, Columbia College, Art Department, Chicago IL (S)

McHugh, Patricia W, *First Asst Fine Arts Department*, Detroit Public Library, Fine Arts Department, Detroit MI

McHugh, Patricia Tool, *Instructor*, Sacramento City College, Art Department, Sacramento CA (S)

McIlhenny, John, *Park Historian & Admin Supv*, Robert W Ryerss Library and Museum, Philadelphia PA

McIllhenny, Henry P, *Chmn*, Philadelphia Museum of Art, Philadelphia PA

McIlvain, Barbara L, *VPres for South Jersey*, Federated Art Associations of New Jersey, Inc, Westfield NJ

McIlvain, Douglas L, *Assoc Prof*, Georgian Court College, Department of Art, Lakewood NJ (S)

McIlvain, Isabel, *Prof*, Washington and Lee University, Department of Fine Arts, Lexington VA (S)

McIntire, Letha E, *Instructor*, Trinity University, Department of Art, San Antonio TX (S)

McIntosh, Ellen, *Dir*, Lynnwood Arts Centre, Simcoe ON

McIntosh, Gail, *Pres*, Second Street Gallery, Charlottesville VA

McIntyre, Nancy J, *Dir*, Lemoyne Art Foundation, Tallahassee FL

McIntyre, Nancy J, *Dir*, Lemoyne Art Center, Tallahassee FL (S)

McIntyre, P F, *Cur Fine Art*, Queen Victoria Museum and Art Gallery, Tasmania Australia

McIntyre, Ralph, *Treas*, Roswell Museum and Art Center, Roswell NM

McKannay, Ludmila, *Instr*, Danforth Museum School, Framingham MA (S)

McKay, Allan, *Secy & Treas*, Western Canada Art Association Inc, Burnaby BC

McKay, Claudine, *Prof*, Xavier University of Louisiana, Department of Fine Arts, New Orleans LA (S)

McKay, Gerry, *Secy*, Amarillo Art Center, Amarillo Art Center Association, Amarillo TX

McKay, Renee, *VPres*, New York Artists Equity Association, Inc, New York NY

McKay, Renee, *Pres*, Audubon Artists, Inc, New York NY

McKean, Hugh F, *Dir*, Morse Gallery of Art, Boulder FL

McKee, Clyde V, *Secy*, Stark Museum of Art, Orange TX

McKee, Fred, *Instructor*, Miles Community College, Dept of Fine Arts & Humanities, Miles City MT (S)

McKee, Joel, *Admin*, Clark County Library District, Las Vegas NV

McKee, John, *Instr*, Bowdoin College, Art Department, Brunswick ME (S)

McKeel, Ellen, *Secy*, Polk Public Museum, Lakeland FL

McKemie, William, *Asst Secy Treas & Cur*, Agecroft Association, Richmond VA

McKenna, George L, *Registrar & Cur Prints*, William Rockhill Nelson Gallery of Art, Atkins Museum of Fine Art, Kansas City MO

McKenna, John V, *Executive Dir*, Fort Wayne Fine Arts Foundation, Inc, Fort Wayne IN

McKenna, Maureen, *Cur Asst*, Illinois State Museum of Natural History and Art, Springfield IL

McKenna, William, *Asst Prof of Philosophy*, LeMoyne College, Art Gallery, Syracuse NY

McKenney, Kathryn, *Slides*, Winterthur Museum and Gardens, Library, Winterthur DE

McKenzie, Jack H, *Dean*, University of Illinois, Urbana-Champaign, College of Fine and Applied Arts, Champaign IL (S)

McKenzie, Louise, *Personnel*, Boca Raton Center for the Arts, Inc, Library of the Center, Boca Raton FL

McKenzie, W P, *VPres*, Civic Fine Arts Association Museum, Sioux Falls SD

McKenzie, Warren, *Vis Prof*, Victor Valley College, Art Department, Victorville CA (S)

McKenzie, Wilfred, *Asst Prof*, Winona State University, Art Department, Winona MN (S)

McKeon, Laura, *Instructor*, Lake Forest College, Dept of Art, Lake Forest IL (S)

McKeon, William E, *VPres*, Marblehead Arts Association, Inc, Marblehead MA

McKerrow, Ann, *Registrar*, Saint Louis County Department of Parks and Recreation, Laumeier Sculpture Park, Saint Louis MO

McKibben, Gael May, *Asst to Dir*, Westbrook College, Joan Whitney Payson Gallery of Art, Portland ME

McKibben, W Alex, *Assoc Prof*, Miami University, Art Department, Oxford OH (S)

McKibbin, Robert H, *Asst Prof*, Grinnell College, Department of Art, Grinnell IA (S)

McKie, Donald, *Art Librn*, University of California-San Diego, Central University Library, La Jolla CA

McKillop, Susan, *Prof*, Sonoma State University, Art Department, Rohnert Park CA (S)

McKillop, Susan, *Asst Prof*, California State College, Sonoma, Department of Art, Rohnert Park CA (S)

McKinley, June, *Instructor*, Del Mar College, Department of Art, Corpus Christi TX (S)

McKinney, Brian, *Personnel*, Art Institute of Fort Lauderdale, Fort Lauderdale FL

McKinney, Claude E, *Dean*, North Carolina State University at Raleigh, School of Design, Raleigh NC (S)

McKinney, Helen, *Librn*, Society of the Four Arts, Library, Palm Beach FL

McKinney, Ramsey, *VPres*, Art Patrons League of Mobile, Mobile AL

McKinster, Karen, *Secy*, Asheville Art Museum, Asheville NC

McKinstry III, John, *Secy & Operations Mgr*, Headley-Whitney Museum, Lexington KY

McLachlan, Elizabeth Parker, *Dir Prog*, Rutgers, the State University of New Jersey, Graduate Program in Art History, New Brunswick NJ (S)

McLanahan, Alexander K, *Pres*, Museum of Fine Arts, Houston, Houston TX

McLaney, Patricia, *Asst Prof*, University of North Carolina-Charlotte, Creative Arts Dept, Charlotte NC (S)

McLaren, Ross, *Film Officer*, Cultural Initiative, Toronto ON

McLarty, Jack, *Instructor*, Portland Art Museum, Museum Art School, Portland OR (S)

McLary, David, *Cur Exhib*, Indiana State Museum, Indianapolis IN

McLaughlin, Charles, *Exec Dir*, McAllen International Museum, McAllen TX

McLaughlin, Eleanor, *Supv Branches*, Miami-Dade Public Library, Miami FL

McLaughlin, James, *Cur*, Phillips Collection, Washington DC

McLaughlin, Willie, *Secy*, Museum, Greenwood SC

McLaughlin Jr, E S, *Pres*, Art Patrons League of Mobile, Mobile AL

McLay, Peter, *Installations Officer & Designer*, University of Waterloo, Arts Centre Gallery, Waterloo ON

McLean, Barrie, *Lectr*, University of Victoria, Department of History in Art, Victoria BC (S)

McLean, Harriet, *Exec Dir*, Boston Center for Adult Education, Boston MA (S)

McLean, Jessica P, *Instructor*, Georgia Institute of Technology, College of Architecture, Atlanta GA (S)

McLean, Linda, *Interpretive Programs Asst*, Olana Historic Site, Hudson NY

McLean, Peter, *Assoc Prof*, Hartford Art School of the University of Hartford, West Hartford CT (S)

McLean, Robert, *Dept Head*, Contra Costa College, Department of Art, San Pablo CA (S)

McLemore, Cosy, *Cur of Education*, Dallas Historical Society, Dallas TX

McLennan, Bill, *Designer*, University of British Columbia, Museum of Anthropology, Vancouver BC

McLeod, Phyllis A, *Dir*, Fayetteville Museum of Art, Inc, Fayetteville NC

McMahan, Patricia, *Dir DeCordova School*, DeCordova and Dana Museum and Park, Lincoln MA

McMahon, James, *Prof*, Manatee Junior College, Department of Art, Bradenton FL (S)

McManus, G Louis, *Supt*, Sterling and Francine Clark Art Institute, Williamstown MA

McMenomy, Robert, *Instructor*, Long Beach City College, Department of Art, Long Beach CA (S)

McMichael, Robert, *Dir*, McMichael Canadian Collection, Kleinburg ON

McMillan, Adell, *Dir*, University of Oregon, Erb Memorial Union Art Gallery, Eugene OR

McMillan, David, *Chmn Photography*, University of Manitoba, School of Art, Winnipeg MB (S)

McMillan, Konrad, *Instr*, Taft College, Division of Performing Arts, Taft CA (S)

McMillan, R Bruce, *Dir*, Illinois State Museum of Natural History and Art, Springfield IL

McMillan, Robert W, *Coordr Painting & Drawing*, University of Arizona, Department of Art, Tucson AZ (S)

McMorris, Penny, *Cur Asst*, Owens-Corning Fiberglas Corporation, Toledo OH

McNally, Dennis, *Lectr*, Saint Joseph's College, Fine Arts Program, Philadelphia PA (S)

McNally, Dorothy, *Asst to Dir*, Newark Museum, Newark NJ

McNally, Sheila J, *Prof*, University of Minnesota, Minneapolis, Art History, Minneapolis MN (S)

McNamara, Thomas, *Controller*, Museum of the City of New York, New York NY

McNamee, Harriet, *Cur*, Towson State University, Roberts Room, Towson MD

McNamee, Mary S, *Cur of Coll*, Evansville Museum of Arts and Science, Evansville IN

McNaught, William, *Dir*, Archives of American Art, New York Area Center, New York NY

McNealy, Terry A, *Librn*, Bucks County Historical Society Mercer Museum, Spruance Library, Doylestown PA

McNeely, Robert, *Instructor*, William Jewell College, Art Dept, Liberty MO (S)

McNeice, J, *Librn Barrie Campus*, Georgian College of Applied Arts and Technology, Georgian Learning Resources Centre, Barrie ON

McNeil, David K, *Dir*, Thames Arts Centre, Chatham ON

McNeil, Donald B, *Art Cur*, General Mills, Inc, Minneapolis MN

McNeil, Henry, *Pres & Chmn of Board*, Pennsylvania Academy of the Fine Arts, Philadelphia PA

McNiff, Philip J, *Dir & Librn*, Boston Public Library, Central Library, Boston MA

McNulty, Kneeland, *Cur Prints, Drawings & Photographs*, Philadelphia Museum of Art, Philadelphia PA

McParland, Maighread, *Restorer Paper*, National Gallery of Ireland, Dublin Ireland

McPhail, Donald W, *Pres*, Print Club, Philadelphia PA

McPheeters, E K, *Dean*, Auburn University, Department of Art, Auburn AL (S)

McPherson, C R, *VPres*, Wilmington Trust Company, Wilmington DE

McQuarrie, Pam, *Sales Shop Mgr*, Salt Lake Art Center, Salt Lake City UT

McQuay, Paul L, *Dir Dept*, Williamsport Area Community College, Department of Engineering and Design, Williamsport PA (S)

McQueen, Patricia, *Registrar*, Rice University, Institute for the Arts, Rice Museum, Houston TX

McQuillan, Frances, *Instructor*, Montclair Art Museum, Art School, Montclair NJ (S)

McQuire, Patrick F, *Assoc Prof*, Morgan State University, Department of Art, Baltimore MD (S)

McRae, Donald C, *Dean Col*, University of New Mexico, College of Fine Arts, Albuquerque NM (S)

McRaven Jr, Donald B, *Assoc Prof*, Moorhead State University, Department of Art, Moorhead MN (S)

McRoberts, Jerry, *Asst Prof*, Eastern Illinois University, Art Department, Charleston IL (S)

McRoberts, Michele, *Instructor*, Roger Williams College, Art Department, Bristol RI (S)

McVickar, Malcolm, *Pres*, Marin Society of Artists Inc, Ross CA

McWhirter, David, *Vis Lectr*, University of Toronto, Department of Landscape Architecture, Toronto ON (S)

McWhorter, Jean, *Supervisor*, Richland Art Workshop of the Columbia Museum of Art, Columbia SC (S)

McWilliams, David Jackson, *Dir*, La Casa del Libro, House of Books, San Juan PR

McWilliams, Harvey, *Instr*, University of Richmond, Department of Art, Richmond VA (S)

Mead, Katherine H, *Cur Coll*, Santa Barbara Museum of Art, Santa Barbara CA

Mead, Mary, *Instr*, Danforth Museum School, Framingham MA (S)

Meader, Robert F W, *Librn*, Shaker Community, Inc, Hancock Shaker Village Library, Pittsfield MA

Meaders, James M, *Head Dept*, Erskine College, Department of Art, Due West SC (S)

Meadow, Robert, *Instructor*, Peters Valley Craft Center, Layton NJ (S)

Meads, A, *Prog Coordr*, Alberta College of Art, Southern Alberta Institute of Technology, Calgary AB (S)

Meakin, Alexander C, *Pres*, Great Lakes Historical Society, Vermilion OH

Meaney, Judith, *Asst Prof*, Catholic University of America, Department of Architecture & Planning, Washington DC (S)

Means, Beverley H, *Librn*, Columbia Museums of Art and Science, Library, Columbia SC

Means, Beverley H, *Asst Cur & Registrar*, Columbia Museums of Art and Science, Columbia SC

Meany, Philip K, *Assoc Prof*, University of Minnesota, Duluth, Art Dept, Duluth MN (S)

Mear, Margaret, *Asst Prof*, Saint Mary's College, Art Department, Winona MN (S)

Mears, Frederick W, *Pres*, Concord Antiquarian Society Museum, Concord MA

Medina, Dennis, *Museum Cur*, Dwight D Eisenhower Presidential Library, Abilene KS

Meditz, Walter, *VPres*, Buck Hill Art Association, Buck Hill Falls PA

Meehan, William, *Chmn*, DePauw University, Art Department, Greencastle IN (S)

Meek, William E, *Instructor*, Texas Woman's University, Department of Art, Denton TX (S)

Meeker, Barbara, *Instructor*, Purdue University Calumet Campus, Department of Creative Arts, Hammond IN (S)

Meeker, Barbara M, *Chmn Gallery Committee*, Purdue University, Calumet Campus, Bicentennial Library Gallery, Hammond IN

Meeker Jr, David Olan, *Exec VPres*, American Institute of Architects, Washington DC

Megee, Lucile K, *Pres*, Rehoboth Art League, Inc, Rehoboth Beach DE

Meglin, Joellen, *Instr*, Creighton University, Fine and Performing Arts Department, Omaha NE (S)

Megna, Ralph J, *Executive Dir*, Quapaw Quarter Association, Inc, Villa Marre, Little Rock AR

Meibos, Joleen, *Secy*, Brigham Young University, B F Larsen Gallery, Provo UT

Meier, Nikolaus, *Librn*, Offentliche Kunstsammlung-Kunstmuseum Basel, Library, Basel Switzerland

Meigham, Melissa, *Registrar*, American Federation of Arts, New York NY

Meilhac, Pierre, *Secy*, Union Centrale des Arts Decoratifs, Musee des Arts Decoratifs, Paris France

Meinhardt, Nevin, *Dir Advertising Design*, Art Institute of Fort Lauderdale, Fort Lauderdale FL (S)

Meiritt, H J, *Chmn*, Art Gallery of Brant, Inc, Brantford ON

Meister, Mark J, *Dir*, Midwest Museum of American Art, Elkhart IN

Mejer, Robert Lee, *Gallery Dir*, Quincy College, Art Gallery, Quincy IL

Melander, Torben, *Cur Archaeology*, Thorvaldsen Museum, Copenhagen Denmark

Melberg, Jerald, *Cur of Exhib*, Mint Museum of Art, Charlotte NC

Melim, Susan, *Asst Cur Exhib*, Fine Arts Museums of San Francisco, M H de Young Memorial Museum and California Palace of the Legion of Honor

Meline, Elva, *Cur*, San Fernando Valley Historical Society, Mission Hills CA

Mellen, Frances P, *Cur*, Concord Art Association, Concord MA

Mellick, James D, *Head Art Dept*, Houghton College, Art Department, Houghton NY (S)

Mellinger, Sydney S, *Librn*, Lake Forest Library, Lake Forest IL

Mellink, Machteld, *VPres*, Archaeological Institute of America, New York NY

Mellish, Raoul, *Dir*, Queensland Art Gallery, Brisbane Australia

Mellon, Paul, *Chmn Board of Trustees*, National Gallery of Art, Washington DC

Meloy, Margaret, *Instructor*, Louisville School of Art, Anchorage KY (S)

Melson, Robert, *Asst Prof*, University of Chicago, Department of Art History & Committee on Art & Design, Chicago IL (S)

Melton, Burt, *VPres*, Fayetteville Museum of Art, Inc, Fayetteville NC

Melton, Nancy, *Assoc Dir*, Mariners Museum, Newport News VA

Melton, Willard, *Instructor*, Sacramento City College, Art Department, Sacramento CA (S)

Memmesheimer, Paul, *Dir*, Konservator der Kunstdenkmaler, Dusseldorf Germany, Federal Republic of

Menard, Lloyd, *Asst Prof*, University of South Dakota, Dept of Art, Vermillion SD (S)

Menard, Michael J, *Archivist*, Museum of Western Colorado Archives, Grand Junction CO

Menaro, Glenn, *Dir Student Union*, University of Southwestern Louisiana, Union Art Gallery, Lafayette LA

Menase, Ljerka, *Cur Documentation*, Moderna Galerija, Modern Art Gallery, Ljubljana Yugoslavia

Mende, Ursula, *Asst*, Germanisches National Museum, Bibliothek, Nuremberg Germany, Federal Republic of

Mendel, Robin, *Young Adult Librn*, Port Chester Public Library, Port Chester NY

Mendenhall, Bethany, *Assoc Librn*, J Paul Getty Museum, Research Library, Malibu CA

Mendez, Charles, *Instructor*, Maryland College of Art and Design, Silver Spring MD (S)

Mendlow, Philip, *Dean*, Ivy School of Professional Art, Downtown Annex, Pittsburgh PA (S)

Mendoza, Cristina, *Cur*, Museo de Arte Moderno, Museum of Modern Art, Barcelona Spain

Mendoza, Margot, *Secy*, McLean County Art Association, Bloomington IL

Mendro, Donna, *Recordings Librn*, Dallas Public Library, Fine Arts Division, Dallas TX

Menear, William H, *Dir*, Hewlett-Woodmere Public Library, Hewlett NY

Menger, Linda, *Lectr*, Delta College, Art Department, University Center MI (S)

Menges, Edward, *Prof*, Saint Louis Community College at Florissant Valley, Department of Art, Ferguson MO (S)

Mennen, Muriel, *Treas*, Wisconsin Painters and Sculptors, Inc, Milwaukee WI

Menocal, Narciso, *Asst Prof*, University of Wisconsin, Madison, Department of Art, Madison WI (S)

Menzies, Neal, *Asst Librn*, Otis Art Institute of Parsons School of Design Gallery, Library, Los Angeles CA

Mercader, Yolanda, *Librn*, Museo Nacional de Antropologia, Library, Mexico Mexico

Mercier, Guy, *Educatives Services*, Musee du Quebec, Quebec PQ

Meredith, A, *Museum Education Officer*, Birmingham Museums and Art Gallery, Birmingham England

Meredith, Georgette, *Dir*, University of Illinois, World Heritage Museum, Champaign IL

Meredith, Howard L, *Dir*, Bacone College Museum, Muskogee OK

Meredith, Jacquie, *Exhib*, National Portrait Gallery, London England

Merians, Melvin, *Chmn Friends of the Neuberger Museum*, State University of New York College at Purchase, Neuberger Museum, Purchase NY

Merig, J, *Secy*, Art Patrons League of Mobile, Mobile AL

Merino-Antolinez, Jesus M, *Jesus M/Merino-Antolinez*

Merle, Michel, *Asst Prof*, Worcester State College, Art Department, Worcester MA (S)

Merley, Bruce, *Asst to Dir*, Fine Arts Museums of San Francisco, M H de Young Memorial Museum and California Palace of the Legion of Honor, n of

Merman, Toby, *Chmn Dept Interior Design*, Woodbury University, Professional Arts Division, Los Angeles CA (S)

Merrell, C Phelps, *Supt*, Norton Gallery and School of Art, West Palm Beach FL

Merrick, Gail, *Instructor*, Burnley School of Professional Art, Inc, Seattle WA (S)

Merrick, Robert S, *Trustee*, Merrick Art Gallery, New Brighton PA

Merrill, Nancy O, *Cur Glass*, Chrysler Museum, Norfolk VA

Merrill, Pam, *Exhib Coordr*, Palos Verdes Art Center, Rancho Palos Verdes CA

Merriman, Mira P, *Chmn Art History*, Wichita State University, Division of Art, Wichita KS (S)

Merritt, Helen, *Asst Chairperson Dept*, Northern Illinois University, Department of Art, De Kalb IL (S)

Merrow, John, *Executive Secy*, Marblehead Historical Society, Marblehead MA

Merwin, Mary M, *Dir*, Massillon Museum, Massillon OH

Merwin, Nancy S, *Pres*, McLean County Art Association, Bloomington IL

Merz, Helen, *Librn*, Schweizerisches Landesmuseum, Library, Zurich Switzerland

Mesa, Antonio, *Instructor*, Arkansas Arts Center, Little Rock AR (S)

Meseguer, Ines B, *Secy*, Escuela Superior de Bellas Artes de la Nacion Ernesto de la Carcova, National Superior School of Fine Arts Ernesto de la Carcova, Buenos Aires Argentina (S)

Meshorer, Yaakov, *Chief Cur Bronfman Archaeological Museum*, Israel Museum, Jerusalem Israel

Messer, Thomas M, *Dir*, Solomon R Guggenheim Museum, New York NY

Messersmith, Fred, *Head Dept*, Stetson University, Art Department, De Land FL (S)

Messersmith, Fred, *Dir*, Stetson University, Art Gallery, Deland FL

Messineo Jr, Len, *Art & Music Dept Head*, Wichita Public Library, Wichita KS

Mester Jr, Clark, *Instr*, Bowie State College, Department of Fine and Performing Arts, Bowie MD (S)

Meszaros, Imre, *Librn*, Washington University, Art and Architecture Library, Saint Louis MO

Metcalf, C E, *Museums & Historical Sites*, Oklahoma Historical Society, Central Museum, Oklahoma City OK

Metcalf, Charles W, *Chmn*, Liberty Hall Museum, Orlando Brown House Frankfort KY

Metcalf, William E, *Chief Cur*, American Numismatic Society, New York NY

Metcalfe, Dorothy, *Information Department*, Vancouver Art Gallery, Vancouver BC

Metcoff, Don, *Librn*, American Society of Artists, Inc, Library, Chicago IL

Metsopoulos, Marian J, *Exec Dir*, Foothills Art Center, Inc, Golden CO (S)

Metsopoulos, Marian J, *Executive Dir*, Foothills Art Center, Inc, Golden CO

Mettier, Jack, *Chmn Div*, Taft College, Division of Performing Arts, Taft CA (S)

Metz, Carolyn J, *Head*, Indianapolis Museum of Art, Slide Collection, Indianapolis IN

Metz, Rinda M, *Prof*, Chowan College, Division of Art, Murfreesboro NC (S)

Metzger, Robert, *Art Dir*, Stamford Museum and Nature Center, Stamford CT

Metzke, John, *Cultural Affairs Coordr*, Central Wyoming College, Dobler Room, Riverton WY

Metzker, Dale, *Asst Prof*, Williamsport Area Community College, Department of Engineering and Design, Williamsport PA (S)

Meunier, Brian A, *Instr*, Swarthmore College, Department of Art, Swarthmore PA (S)

Mew, T J, *Chmn*, Berry College, Art Department, Mount Berry GA (S)

Mew III, T J, *Chmn*, Berry College, Art Department, Mount Berry GA

Mew III, T J, *Chmn*, Berry College, Moon Library, Mount Berry GA

Meyer, Barbara, *Chmn*, Mary Washington College, Art Department, Fredericksburg VA (S)

Meyer, Bernice L, *Adminr*, University of Rochester, Memorial Art Gallery, Rochester NY

Meyer, Charles E, *Prof*, Western Michigan University, Department of Art, Kalamazoo MI (S)

Meyer, Charles E, *Prof*, Western Michigan University, Art History Division, Kalamazoo MI (S)

Meyer, David, *Instructor*, Eastern Arizona College, Thatcher AZ (S)

Meyer, Eileen, *Second VPres*, Marian Osborne Cunningham Art Gallery, Bakersfield CA

Meyer, Franz, *Dir*, Offentliche Kunstsammlung-Kunstmuseum Basel, Museum of Fine Arts, Basel Switzerland

Meyer, Inga, *Pres*, New Rochelle Public Library, New Rochelle Art Association, New Rochelle NY

Meyer, Joan, *Head Reference Department*, Springfield Free Public Library, Donald B Palmer Museum, Springfield NJ

Meyer, Judy, *Supvr*, Kent State University, Architecture and Urban Studies Library, Kent OH

Meyer, Loretta, *Membership Secy*, Westmoreland County Museum of Art, Greensburg PA

Meyer, Marie D, *Dir Education*, Old State House, Hartford CT

Meyer, Meir, *Dir of Public Affairs*, Israel Museum, Jerusalem Israel

Meyer, Roberta, *Instr*, Madison Area Technical College, Communication Arts, Madison WI (S)

Meyer, Ursula, *Prof*, Herbert H Lehman College, Art Department, Bronx NY (S)

Meyer, Valerie D, *Head Fine Arts Library*, University of Michigan Museum of Art, Fine Arts Library, Ann Arbor MI

Meyers, Dan, *Business Mgr*, International Museum of Photography at George Eastman House, Rochester NY

Meyers, Donald E, *Chmn*, Mesa College, Art Department, Grand Junction CO (S)

Meyers, Emily, *Educ Asst*, Children's Museum of History, Natural History and Science, Utica NY

Meyers, Francis, *Instr*, Cleveland Institute of Art, Cleveland OH (S)

Meyers, Judith, *Asst Dir*, School Art League of New York City, Brooklyn NY

Miakush, Jerry, *Cur*, Ukrainian National Museum & Library, Chicago IL

Michael, John, *Prof*, Miami University, Art Department, Oxford OH (S)

Michael, Simon, *Head Dept*, Simon Michael School of Fine Arts, Rockport TX (S)

Michaelides, C, *Dean School*, Washington University, School of Architecture, Saint Louis MO (S)

Michaels, Henry, *Instr*, Western Wisconsin Technical Institute, Graphics Division, LACrosse WI (S)

Michaels, Paul, *Instr*, Tacoma Community College, Art Department, Tacoma WA (S)

Michaels, Rebecca, *Programs Coordr*, Anderson County Arts Council, Anderson SC

Michaely, Alina, *Dir Fine Arts School*, Saidye Bronfman Centre, Montreal PQ

Michala, Mollie, *Affiliate*, Emory University, Art History Department, Atlanta GA (S)

Michalowski, Kazimierz, *VDir*, Muzeum Narodowe, National Museum, Warsaw Poland

Michaud, Beverly, *Office Mgr*, Palo Alto Cultural Center, Palo Alto CA

Michaux, Henry G, *Assoc Prof*, South Carolina State College, Art Program, Orangeburg SC (S)

Michel, Delbert, *Assoc Prof*, Hope College, Art Department, Holland MI (S)

Micheli, Julio, *Head Dept*, Catholic University of Puerto Rico, Department of History & Fine Arts, Ponce PR (S)

Michels, Eileen, *Chmn*, College of Saint Thomas, Department of Art, Saint Paul MN (S)

Michelsen, P, *Keeper Open-air Museum at Sorgenfri*, Nationalmuseet, National Museum, Copenhagen Denmark

Mickey, Susan B, *Education Coordr*, Southeastern Center for Contemporary Art, Winston-Salem NC

Midani, Akram, *Dean*, Carnegie-Mellon University, College of Fine Arts, Pittsburgh PA (S)

Middaugh, Robert, *Cur*, The First National Bank of Chicago, Chicago IL

Middlebrook, David, *Ceramics Coordr*, San Jose State University, Art Department, San Jose CA (S)

Middlebrook, Robert, *VPres*, Washington Art Association, Washington Depot CT

Middlestadt, Larry, *Instr*, Toronto School of Art, Toronto ON (S)

Middleton, David, *Lectr*, Centenary College of Louisiana, Department of Art, Shreveport LA (S)

Middleton, Janet, *Librn*, Tasmanian Museum and Art Gallery, Library, Hobart Australia

Miele, Joh, *Curriculum Chmn Fashion Illustration*, Art Institute of Fort Lauderdale, Fort Lauderdale FL (S)

Mier, Norman, *Dept Head*, Ray-Vogue School of Design, Chicago IL (S)

Mihailovic, Olivera, *Cur*, University of Chicago, Art Slide Collection, Chicago IL

Mihal, Milan, *Assoc Prof*, Vanderbilt University, Dept of Fine Arts, Nashville TN (S)

Mike, Carol, *Film & Video Coordr*, Los Angeles Institute of Contemporary Art, Los Angeles CA

Miki, Tamon, *Chief Cur Project and Reference Materials Department*, Tokyo Kokuritsu Kindai Bujutsukan, National Museum of Modern Art, Tokyo, Tokyo Japan

Mikus, Eleanore, *Asst Prof*, Cornell University, Department of Art, Ithaca NY (S)

Milan, George, *Dir Bureau of Music*, City of Los Angeles, Municipal Arts Dept, Los Angeles CA

Milbank, W H, *Dir*, Sarjeant Gallery, Wanganui New Zealand

Milbrath, Harold A, *Head Dept*, Milwaukee Area Technical College, Graphic & Applied Arts Div, Milwaukee WI (S)

Milejszo, C, *Prog Coordr*, Alberta College of Art, Southern Alberta Institute of Technology, Calgary AB (S)

Miles, Carol, *Asst*, Arts Council of the Mid-Columbia Region, Richland WA

Miles, Grady Garfield, *Prof*, Barber-Scotia College, Art Department, Concord NC (S)

Miles, J, *Head Dept Fashion and Textiles*, Brighton Polytechnic, Faculty of Art and Design, Brighton England (S)

Miles, James B, *Chmn*, Palm Beach Junior College, Department of Art, Lake Worth FL (S)

Miles, Pamela, *Mgr*, University of South Florida, University Galleries, Tampa FL

Miles, W C, *Prof*, New Mexico State University, Art Dept, Las Cruces NM (S)

Miley, Les, *Chmn Art Dept*, University of Evansville, Krannert Gallery, Evansville IN

Miley, Mimi, *Cur Educ*, Allentown Art Museum, Allentown PA

Miley Jr, Leslie, *Chmn Dept*, University of Evansville, Art Dept, Evansville IN (S)

Milford, Howard, *Treas*, Stan Hywet Hall Foundation, Inc, Akron OH

Milford, Judith, *Secy*, Paducah Art Guild, Paducah KY

Milhau, Denis, *Cur*, Musee des Augustins, Museum of Augustins, Toulouse France

Milhoan, Randy, *Dir*, Colorado Mountain College, Summervail Workshop for Art & Critical Studies, Vail CO (S)

Milkovich, Michael, *Dir*, Dixon Gallery and Gardens, Memphis TN

Milks, Marte E, *Executive Dir*, Lansing Art Gallery, Lansing MI

Millard, Charles, *Chief Cur*, Hirshhorn Museum and Sculpture Garden, Washington DC

Millard, Richard, *First VPres*, Stained Glass Association of America, Bronxville NY

Millau, Dan, *VPres*, Saint Mary's Romanian Orthodox Church, Romanian Ethnic Museum, Cleveland OH

Miller, A, *Vol Librn*, Dade County Art Museum, Library, Miami FL

Miller, Alan C, *Librn*, University of Oregon, School of Architecture and Allied Arts Library, Eugene OR

Miller, Archibald M, *Chmn*, University of Rochester, Department of Fine Arts, Rochester NY (S)

Miller, Arthur, *Instructor*, Lower Columbia College, Longview WA (S)

Miller, Benjamin T, *Dir*, Southern Illinois University, School of Art, Carbondale IL (S)

Miller, Bill, *VPres*, Morse Gallery of Art, Boulder FL

Miller, Bob, *Admin Asst Exhibit Design*, Exploratorium, San Francisco CA

Miller, Bobbie, *Secy*, San Bernardino County Museum and Satellites, Fine Arts Institute, Redlands CA

Miller, Constance, *Secy*, Pioneer Museum and Haggin Galleries, Stockton CA

Miller, Dan, *Instructor*, Wayne Art Center, Wayne PA (S)

Miller, David, *Dir*, Skidmore College, Art Gallery, Saratoga Springs NY

Miller, David A, *Admin*, Historic Burlington County Prison Museum, Mansion at Smithville, Mount Holly NJ

Miller, Don, *Asst Prof*, University of Wisconsin-River Falls, Art Department, River Falls WI (S)

Miller, Donald, *3rd VPres*, Society of Animal Artists, Inc, Bronx NY

Miller, Donna, *Instructor*, Weatherford College, Department of Humanities and Art, Weatherford TX (S)

Miller, Eleanor, *Secy*, Boothbay Region Art Gallery, Boothbay Harbor ME

Miller, Elizabeth, *Coordr Drawing & Painting*, Iowa State University, Department of Design, Ames IA (S)

Miller, Emil, *Prof*, Glendale College, Department of Fine Arts, Glendale CA (S)

Miller, Eugene, *Special Events Coordr*, Junior Arts Center, Los Angeles CA

Miller, Georgia, *Secy*, Safety Harbor Museum of History and Fine Arts, Safety Harbor FL

Miller, Glen, *Instructor*, College of Marin, Department of Art, Kentfield CA (S)

Miller, Hester, *Head Fine Arts Dept*, Albuquerque Public Library, Albuquerque NM

Miller, J Robert, *Lectr*, McMurry College, Art Dept, Abilene TX (S)

Miller, J Brough, *Chmn*, Texas Woman's University, Department of Art, Denton TX (S)

Miller, James R, *Cur*, Safety Harbor Museum of History and Fine Arts, Safety Harbor FL

Miller, Jean J, *Art Librn*, University of Hartford, Anne Bunce Cheney Library, West Hartford CT

Miller, Joan Vita, *Dir*, C W Post Center of Long Island University, Art Gallery, Greenvale NY

Miller, Joseph, *Prof*, Catholic University of America, Department of Architecture & Planning, Washington DC (S)

Miller, Judy, *Asst Prof*, Austin College, Art Department, Sherman TX (S)

Miller, K R, *Dir*, Mitchell Museum, Library, Mount Vernon IL

Miller, Kenneth R, *Exec VPres*, Mitchell Museum, Mount Vernon IL

Miller, L Don, *Pres*, Arizona Artist Guild, Phoenix AZ

Miller, Laurence, *Dir*, Laguna Gloria Art Museum, Austin TX

Miller, Lawrence K, *Pres*, Shaker Community, Inc, Pittsfield MA

Miller, Lee Anne, *Chmn*, Wayne State University, Department of Art and Art History, Detroit MI (S)

Miller, Lenore D, *Cur*, George Washington University Museum & Art Galleries, Washington DC

Miller, Lillian B, *Historian American Culture*, National Portrait Gallery, Washington DC

Miller, Margaret, *Asst Prof*, Colby College, Art Dept, Waterville ME (S)

Miller, Margaret A, *Dir*, University of South Florida, University Galleries, Tampa FL

Miller, Marion G, *Asst Prof*, Mount Holyoke College, Art Department, South Hadley MA (S)

Miller, Marjorie, *Art Librn*, Fashion Institute of Technology, Library, New York NY

Miller, Mark, *Dir*, Arizona State University, Memorial Union Gallery, Tempe AZ

Miller, Marlan, *Instructor*, Mesa Community College, Department of Art, Mesa AZ (S)

Miller, Marlene, *Instr*, Illinois Central College, Art and Humanities Department, East Peoria IL (S)

Miller, Marlene, *Instructor*, Bucks County Community College, Fine Arts Department, Newton PA (S)

Miller, Mary M, *Librn*, Springfield Art Center, Library, Springfield OH

Miller, Mary Richardson, *Instructor*, Wayne Art Center, Wayne PA (S)

Miller, Nancy Ann, *Instructor*, Your Heritage House, Inc, Detroit MI

Miller, R C, *Chmn*, Oglebay Institute Mansion Museum, Oglebay Institute Mansion Museum Committee, Wheeling WV

Miller, Ralph, *Pres*, Spirit of '76 Museum, Southern Lorain County Historical Society, Wellington OH

Miller, Richard M, *VPres Exhib & Special Programs*, Sculptors Guild, Inc, New York NY

Miller, Robert, *Dept Head*, Ray-Vogue School of Design, Chicago IL (S)

Miller, Rose Shechet, *Instr*, Danforth Museum School, Framingham MA (S)

Miller, Ruby, *Secy*, Mitchell Museum, Mount Vernon IL

Miller, Rus A, *Pres*, Pocumtuck Valley Memorial Association, Memorial Hall, Deerfield MA

Miller, Samual C, *Dir*, Newark Museum, Newark NJ

Miller, Sandra, *Instructor*, Ocean City School of Art, Ocean City NJ (S)

Miller, Valerie, *Supv Art School*, Carolina Art Association, Gibbes Art Gallery, Charleston SC

Miller, Valerie, *Dir*, Gibbes Art Gallery School, Charleston SC (S)

Miller, William B, *Prof*, Colby College, Art Dept, Waterville ME (S)

Miller, William B, *Cur*, Waterville Historical Association, Waterville ME

Miller, William B, *Librn*, Presbyterian Historical Society, Library, Philadelphia PA

Miller, William B, *Mgr*, Presbyterian Historical Society, Philadelphia PA

Miller-Keller, Andrea, *Cur of Matrix*, Wadsworth Atheneum, Hartford CT

Milley, John C, *Chief Cur*, Independence National Historical Park, Philadelphia PA

Millin, Aimee, *Secy*, Canadian Society of Painters in Watercolour, Toronto ON

Millis, Judith A, *Head Fiber & Fabric*, Southern Illinois University at Edwardsville, Department of Art and Design, Edwardsville IL (S)

Mills, David, *Asst Dir*, Newfoundland Museum, Saint John's NF

Mills, Fred V, *Chmn Art Dept*, Illinois State University, Art Dept, Normal IL (S)

Mills, G G, *Chmn*, Oakville Centennial-Gairloch Galleries, Oakville ON

Mills, James, *Assoc Prof*, East Tennessee State University, Fine Arts Dept, Johnson City TN (S)

Mills, Jane, *Secy*, Columbia County Historical Society, House of History and Van Alen House, Kinderhook NY

Mills, Lawrence, *Head Dept*, Central College, Art Department, Pella IA (S)

Mills, Majorie, *First VPres*, San Bernadino Art Association, Inc, San Bernadino CA

Mills, Margaret M, *Exec Dir*, American Academy and Institute of Arts and Letters, New York NY

Mills, Paul C, *Dir*, Santa Barbara Museum of Art, Santa Barbara CA

Mills, Richard, *Asst Prof*, Auburn University at Montgomery, Art Department, Montgomery AL (S)

Millspaugh, Martin L, *VPres*, Peale Museum, Baltimore MD

Millstein, Barbara, *Assoc Cur Sculpture Garden*, Brooklyn Museum, Brooklyn NY

Milne, Audrey, *Cur*, York Institute Museum, Saco ME

Milne, Norman F, *Clerk*, Currier Gallery of Art, Manchester NH

Milne, Robert D, *VPres*, Cleveland Museum of Art, Print Club of Cleveland, Cleveland OH

Milner, F J, *Education Officer*, Walker Art Gallery, Liverpool England

Milner, Sue, *Head Dept*, Eastern Wyoming College, Art Department, Torrington WY (S)

Milonadis, K, *Vis Prof*, Hobart School of Welding Technology, Troy OH (S)

Milosevich, Joe, *Gallery Dir*, Joliet Junior College, Laura A Sprague Art Gallery, Joliet IL

Milosevich, Joe, *Instructor*, Joliet Junior College, Art Dept, Joliet IL (S)

Milrad, Aaron M, *Admin VPres*, Professional Art Dealers Association of Canada, Toronto ON

Milrany, Donna, *Asst Dir*, Portland Center for the Visual Arts, Portland OR

Milrod, Linda J, *Dir*, Dalhousie University, Art Gallery, Halifax NS

Mims, Hazel, *Secy*, Fine Arts Museum of the South, Mobile AL

Mims, Michael, *Area Chmn Photography*, Pasadena City College, Art Department, Pasadena CA (S)

Mims, Thomas E, *Asst Prof*, University of North Alabama, Department of Art, Florence AL (S)

Miner, Laura Lynn, *In Charge Art Coll*, Citibank, NA, New York NY

Minicki, Josephine, *Librn*, South African National Gallery, Library, Cape South Africa, Republic of

Minnick, John D, *Pres*, Topeka Art Guild, Topeka KS

Mino, Yutaka, *Cur Oriental Art*, Indianapolis Museum of Art, Indianapolis IN

Minor, Charlotte, *Art Coordr*, Federal Reserve Bank of Richmond, Richmond VA

Minot, Michael, *Instr*, Vancouver Community College, Langara Campus, Department of Fine Arts, Vancouver BC (S)

Minott, Lorraine, *Cur,* Please Touch Museum, Philadelphia PA

Minschey, Bill, *Prof,* California State University, Fresno, Art Department, Fresno CA (S)

Mintich, Mary, *Assoc Prof,* Winthrop College, Department of Art, Rock Hill SC (S)

Mintz, Donald, *Dean,* Montclair State College, Gallery One, Upper Montclair NJ

Mintz, Donald, *Dean,* Montclair State College, Fine Arts Department, Montclair NJ (S)

Minutillo, Richard, *Cur,* Brockton Art Center, Brockton MA

Miodonska, Barbara, *Polish Illuminated Manuscripts,* Muzeum Narodowe w Krakowie, National Museum in Cracow, Cracow Poland

Miotke, Anne, *Instructor,* Art Academy of Cincinnati, Cincinnati OH (S)

Miranda, Gregorio Cordero, *Dir,* Museo Nacional de Arqueologia, National Museum, La Paz Bolivia

Mirzaoff, Gus, *Treas,* Key West Art and Historical Society, Key West FL

Miseho, Ivan R, *Instr,* Orange County Community College, Art Department, Middletown NY (S)

Misfeldt, Willard, *Chmn Art History,* Bowling Green State University, School of Art, Bowling Green OH (S)

Mitchell, Alex F, *Chmn Dept,* Lake Forest College, Dept of Art, Lake Forest IL (S)

Mitchell, Annette, *Lectr,* Notre Dame College, Art Department, Manchester NH (S)

Mitchell, Beresford, *Chmn Dept Commun & Design,* Ontario College of Art, Toronto ON (S)

Mitchell, C, *Instructor,* Golden West College, Arts, Humanities and Social Sciences Institute, Huntington Beach CA (S)

Mitchell, Douglas, *Prof,* Cape Cod Community College, Art Dept, West Barnstable MA (S)

Mitchell, Eugene W, *Asst Dir Admin,* Dallas Museum of Fine Arts, Dallas TX

Mitchell, Fred, *Vis Prof,* Utica College of Syracuse University, Division of Humanities, Utica NY (S)

Mitchell, Jannie, *First VPres,* Arizona Watercolor Association, Phoenix AZ

Mitchell, Judith L, *In Charge Art Coll,* The Third National Bank and Trust Company, Dayton OH

Mitchell, Kenneth Eugene, *Head Dept,* Colby Community College, Visual Arts Department, Colby KS (S)

Mitchell, Lee, *Lectr,* Villa Maria College of Buffalo, Art Department, Buffalo NY (S)

Mitchell, M F, *VPres,* Saskatoon Gallery and Conservatory Corporation, Saskatoon SK

Mitchell, Mary Virginia, *Asst Prof,* Longwood College, Department of Art, Farmville VA (S)

Mitchell, R E, *Assoc Prof,* Arkansas State University, Department of Art, State University AR (S)

Mitchell, Ramona, *Lectr,* Lake Forest College, Dept of Art, Lake Forest IL (S)

Mitchell, Richard, *Assoc Prof,* Youngstown State University, Art Department, Youngstown OH (S)

Mitchell, Robin, *Registrar,* University of Kentucky, Art Museum, Lexington KY

Mitchell, Stanley A, *Prof,* Chowan College, Division of Art, Murfreesboro NC (S)

Mitchell, Suzanne, *Cur Oriental Art,* Detroit Institute of Arts, Detroit MI

Mitchell, Vicki L, *Instr,* Colby Community College, Visual Arts Department, Colby KS (S)

Mitsuda, Mary, *Asst Dir,* Contemporary Arts Center of Hawaii, Honolulu HI

Mittelberger, Ernest G, *Dir,* Wine Museum of San Francisco, San Francisco CA

Mittelgluck, Eugene L, *Dir,* New Rochelle Public Library, New Rochelle NY

Mittman, Sima, *Assoc Dir Performing Arts,* 92nd Street YMHA-YWHA, Weill Art Gallery, New York NY

Miyazaki, Hiroshi, *Instructor,* San Diego Mesa College, Art Department, San Diego CA (S)

Mizui, Yasuo, *Instructor,* Sarah Lawrence College, Village des Arts en France du Sarah Lawrence College, Locoste France (S)

Mladenka, Dorcas, *Asst Prof,* Our Lady of the Lake University, Department of Art, San Antonio TX (S)

Mölder, A, *Dean,* Eesti Nsv Riiklik Kunstiinstituut, Tallinn Ussr (S)

Mo, Charles l, *Registrar,* New Orleans Museum of Art, Isaac Delgado Museum, New Orleans LA

Mochon, Anne, *Asst Prof,* University of Massachusetts, Amherst, Art History Prog, Amherst MA (S)

Mocsanyi, Paul, *Dir,* New School for Social Research Art Center Gallery, Collectors Institute of the New School, New York NY

Mocsanyi, Paul, *Dir Art Center,* New School for Social Research Art Center Gallery, New York NY

Moczulska, Koystyna, *Greek & Roman Art,* Muzeum Narodowe w Krakowie, National Museum in Cracow, Cracow Poland

Mode, Robert L, *Assoc Prof,* Vanderbilt University, Dept of Fine Arts, Nashville TN (S)

Model, Elisabeth, *Secy,* Federation of Modern Painters and Sculptors, New York NY

Moehring, Eugene P, *Cur Exhibits,* Southern Illinois University Museum and Art Galleries, Carbondale IL

Moeller, Robert C, *Cur European Decorative Arts & Sculpture,* Museum of Fine Arts, Boston MA

Moen, George J, *Dir,* Youth Cultural Center, Waco TX

Moerman, I W L, *Cur History,* Stedelijk Museum de Lakenhal, Leyden Municipal Museum, Leiden Netherlands

Moes, Robert, *Cur Oriental Art,* Brooklyn Museum, Brooklyn NY

Moeser, J, *Dean,* University of Kansas, School of Fine Arts, Lawrence KS (S)

Moffett, Kenworth, *Cur Contemporary Art,* Museum of Fine Arts, Boston MA

Moffitt, Elizabeth, *Prof,* University of New Haven, Department of Fine Arts, West Haven CT (S)

Moffitt, John, *Prof,* New Mexico State University, Art Dept, Las Cruces NM (S)

Mognetti, Elisabeth, *Conservator,* Musee du Petit Palais, Avignon France

Mohamed, John, *Instructor,* Purdue University Calumet Campus, Department of Creative Arts, Hammond IN (S)

Mohsen, Mohammed A, *Dir,* Egyptian Museum, Cairo Egypt

Moisan, Micheline, *Assoc Cur Dept Prints and Drawings,* Montreal Museum of Fine Arts, Montreal PQ

Mol, J De, *Dir,* Nationaal Hoger Instituut Voor Bouwkunst en Stedebouw, National Higher Institute of Architecture and Town Planning), Antwerp Belgium (S)

Mol, Janet M, *Instructor,* Norwich Art School, Norwich Free Academy, Art Dept, Norwich CT (S)

Molaug, SVen, *Dir,* Norsk Sjöfartsmuseum, Norwegian Maritime Museum, Oslo Norway

Moldenhauer, R, *Business Mgr,* Saskatoon Gallery and Conservatory Corporation, Saskatoon SK

Moldenhauer, Roger, *Archivist & Librn,* Concordia Historical Institute, Library, Saint Louis MO

Moldovan, George, *Assoc Prof,* East Tennessee State University, Fine Arts Dept, Johnson City TN (S)

Moldovan, George, *Dir Exhibitions,* East Tennessee State University, Elizabeth Slocum Gallery, Johnson City TN

Moldroski, Al, *Assoc Prof,* Eastern Illinois University, Art Department, Charleston IL (S)

Molen, Larry Ter, *VPres Develop & Public Relations,* Art Institute of Chicago, Chicago IL

Molfino, Alessandra Mottola, *Dir,* Museo Poldi Pezzoli, Poldi Pezzoli Museum, Milan Italy

Molner, Frank, *Instructor,* Santa Ana College, Art Department, Santa Ana CA (S)

Molten, Carol, *Instructional Media Specialist,* University of South Carolina, Slide Library, Columbia SC

Moltesen, M, *Cur Greek & Roman Art,* Ny Carlsberg Glyptothek, Carlsberg Gallery, Copenhagen Denmark

Monaco, Theresa, *Chairperson Dept,* Emmanuel College, Art Department, Boston MA (S)

Monaghan, Keith, *Prof,* Washington State University, Fine Arts Department, Pullman WA (S)

Monaghan, Susan, *Asst to the Dir,* Ann Arbor Art Association, Ann Arbor MI

Monberg, Torben, *Keeper Ethnographic Coll,* Nationalmuseet, National Museum, Copenhagen Denmark

Mondrus, Martin, *Prof,* Glendale College, Department of Fine Arts, Glendale CA (S)

Monge, Federico Berreda Y, *Instructor,* University of Puerto Rico, Department of Fine Arts, Mayaguez PR (S)

Mongi, Ennaifer, *Dir,* Musee National du Bardo, Bardo National Museum, Le Bardo Tunisia

Monies, Leif, *Dir,* Den Grafiski HoJskole, Graphic College of Denmark, Copenhagen Denmark (S)

Monk, Neils-Henry, *In charge,* University of Gothenburg, School of Crafts and Design, Gothenburg Sweden (S)

Monkhouse, Christopher, *Cur Decorative Arts,* Rhode Island School of Design, Museum of Art, Providence RI

Monkhouse, Valerie, *Chief Librn,* National Museums of Canada, Library, Ottawa ON

Monkman, Betty C, *Registrar,* White House, Washington DC

Monnier-Raball, Jacques, *Principal,* Lausanne College of Art and Design, Lausanne Switzerland (S)

Monroe, Betty Iverson, *Assoc Prof,* Northwestern University, Evanston, Department of Art History, Evanston IL (S)

Monroe, Dan, *Deputy Dir,* Alaska State Museum, Juneau AK

Monroe, Michael, *Cur,* National Collection of Fine Arts, Renwick Gallery, Washington DC

Monroe, P Jensen, *Supv Museum Prog,* Rockwell-Corning Museum, Corning NY

Monroe, P S, *Second VPres,* San Bernadino Art Association, Inc, San Bernadino CA

Monsma, Marvin, *Librn,* Calvin College Center Art Gallery, Library, Grand Rapids MI

Monson, Ed, *Recording Secy,* SVACA - Sheyenne Valley Arts and Crafts Association, Bjarne Ness Gallery, Fort Ransom ND

Monson, James P, *Asst Prof,* College of the Holy Cross, Department of Fine Arts, Worcester MA (S)

Monson, Richard D, *Assoc Prof,* Central Missouri State University, Art Department, Warrensburg MO (S)

Montague, Prudence D, *Pres,* Northern Virginia Fine Arts Association, Alexandria VA

Monteferrante, Sally, *Instructor,* Community College of Baltimore, Dept of Fine & Applied Arts, Baltimore MD (S)

Montenero, Giulio, *Dir,* Civico Museo Revoltella-Galleria d'Arte Moderna, Revoltella Civic Museum-Gallery of Modern Art, Trieste Italy

Montes, Amelia, *Secy,* Centro de Arte y Communicacion, Center of Art and Communication, Buenos Argentina

Montgomery, Colleen, *Registrar,* University of Vermont, Robert Hull Fleming Museum, Burlington VT

Montgomery, Edward K, *Asst Prof,* Miami University, Art Department, Oxford OH (S)

Montgomery, George R, *Secy,* Louisiana State Museum, New Orleans LA

Montgomery, Katherine, *Instructor,* Davidson County Community College, Language-Fine Arts Dept, Lexington NC (S)

Montgomery, Küllike, *Asst Cur Graphics & Drawings,* Göteborg Konstmuseum, Gothenburg Art Gallery, Gothenburg Sweden

Montgomery, L A D, *Treas,* Pennsylvania Academy of the Fine Arts, Fellowship of the Pennsylvania Academy of the Fine Arts, Philadelphia PA

Montgomery, Robert P, *Head Dept,* John Jay College of Criminal Justice, Department of Art, Music and Philosophy, New York NY (S)

Montgomery, Sue B, *Assoc Prof,* Oral Roberts University, Fine Arts Department, Tulsa OK (S)

Monti, E Tittoni, *Staff,* Musei Capitolini, Museum of Sculpture, Rome Italy

Montilla, Cynthia, *Librn & Registrar*, The Turner Museum, Denver CO

Monton, Pat, *Instr*, West Shore Community College, Div of Humanities & Fine Arts, Scottville MI (S)

Montoya, Gustavo, *Preparator*, Craft and Folk Art Museum, Los Angeles CA

Montplaisir, Isabelle, *Librn*, Musee d'Art Contemporain, Bibliotheque, Montreal PQ

Montverde, Mildred, *Assoc Prof*, University of Southern Colorado, Belmont Campus, Department of Art, Pueblo CO (S)

Moody, Barbara, *Instr*, Montserrat School of Visual Art, Beverly MA (S)

Moody, Margaret J, *Registrar*, Dartmouth College Museum & Galleries, Hanover NH

Moody Jr, James W, *Dir*, Historic Pensacola Preservation Board, West Florida Museum of History, Pensacola FL

Moon, Caroline, *Museum Coordr*, Iowa State Education Association, Salisbury House, Des Moines IA

Moon, Marvin, *Assoc Prof*, Texas Tech University, Department of Art, Lubbock TX (S)

Moon, Warren, *Assoc Prof*, University of Wisconsin, Madison, Department of Art, Madison WI (S)

Moone, Charles L, *Prof*, University of Colorado at Denver, Department of Fine Arts, Denver CO (S)

Moonelio, Judith, *Prof*, Rockford College, Department of Fine Arts, Rockford IL (S)

Mooney, Ann Austin, *Art Library Asst*, College of Mount Saint Joseph on the Ohio, Archbishop Alter Library, Mount Saint Joseph OH

Mooney, James E, *Dir*, Historical Society of Pennsylvania, Philadelphia PA

Moore, A W, *Keeper of Fine Art*, Sefton Metropolitan Borough, Atlinson Art Gallery, Southport England

Moore, Alfred A, *Chmn*, Contemporary Arts Center, Cincinnati OH

Moore, Barry E, *Cur International Coll of Child Art*, Illinois State University, University Museums, Normal IL

Moore, Benjamin F, *Asst Cur of Education*, Telfair Academy of Arts and Sciences Inc, Savannah GA

Moore, Blanche, *Asst to Dir*, Print Club, Philadelphia PA

Moore, Craig, *Prof*, Taylor University, Art Department, Upland IN (S)

Moore, Donald Everett, *Acting Chmn*, Mitchell Community College, Visual Art Dept, Statesville NC (S)

Moore, Elfrida B, *Secy*, Carolina Art Association, Gibbes Art Gallery, Charleston SC

Moore, Ethel, *Cur*, University of Georgia, Georgia Museum of Art, Athens GA

Moore, Everett L, *Dir*, Woodbury University Library, Los Angeles CA

Moore, Herbert, *Business Mgr*, Columbus Museum of Art, Columbus OH

Moore, James C, *Dir*, Albuquerque Museum of Art, History and Science, Albuquerque NM

Moore, Kathleen, *Asst Supt*, Game and Parks Commission, Arbor Lodge State Historical Park, Nebraska City NE

Moore, Kathleen, *Asst to Art Librn*, University of Louisville, Margaret M Bridwell Art Library, Louisville KY

Moore, L A, *Dir*, Plainfield Public Library, Plainfield NJ

Moore, Micahel, *Instructor*, Fort Wright College of the Holy Names, School of Art, Spokane WA (S)

Moore, Michael G, *Chmn*, University of Southern Maine, Art Dept, Gorham ME (S)

Moore, Nicholas K, *VPres*, Columbia Museums of Art and Science, Columbia SC

Moore, Nicholas K, *VPres*, Columbia Museums of Art and Science, Columbia Art Association, Columbia SC

Moore, Russell J, *Dir*, Long Beach Museum of Art, Long Beach CA

Moore, Stephen, *Dir & Cur*, San Jose State University, Union Gallery, San Jose CA

Moore, Turner, *Secy*, Star-Spangled Banner Flag House Association, Baltimore MD

Moorhead, Richard, *VPres Board Dir*, Plains Art Museum, Main Gallery, Moorhead MN

Moorhead, Robert, *Dir*, Deerfield Academy, Hilson Gallery, Deerfield MA

Moorhead, Tracy, *Registrar*, Plains Art Museum, Main Gallery, Moorhead MN

Moosleitner, Fritz, *Cur Prehistory*, Saltzburger Museum Carolino Augusteum, Salzburg Museum, Salzburg Austria

Mooz, R Peter, *Dir*, Virginia Museum of Fine Arts, Richmond VA

Moppett, G, *Asst Cur*, Saskatoon Gallery and Conservatory Corporation, Saskatoon SK

Morais, LeRoy, *Chmn*, University of Maryland Baltimore County, Visual Arts Department, Catonsville MD (S)

Morales, Luis M Rodirquez, *Executive Dir*, Institute of Puerto Rican Culture, Museo de Bellas Artes, San Juan PR

Morales, Luis M Rodriquez, *Exec Dir*, Instituto de Cultura Puertorriquena, Institute of Puerto Rican Culture, San Juan PR

Morales, Martha, *In Charge*, American Institute for Conservation of Historic and Artistic Works (AIC), Library, Washington DC

Morales, Raymond, *Asst Prof*, University of Utah, Art Department, Salt Lake City UT (S)

Moran, Diane D, *Asst Prof*, Sweet Briar College, Art History Department, Sweet Briar VA (S)

Moran, Henry, *Executive Dir*, Mid-America Arts Alliance, Kansas City MO

Moran, Jose, *Instructor*, California State College at San Bernardino, Fine Arts Department, San Bernardino CA (S)

Moran, Lois, *Executive Dir of Council*, American Craft Council, New York NY

Moran, Ruth H, *Dir Business Affairs*, Minnesota Museum of Art, Saint Paul MN

Morand, Kathleen, *Head Dept*, Queen's University, Department of Art, Kingston ON (S)

Morand, Mabel H, *Pres*, National Association of Women Artists, Inc, New York NY

Morandi, Thomas, *Assoc Prof Art*, Eastern Oregon State College, La Grande OR (S)

Morawetz, Bruno, *Board Pres*, Art Gallery of Peterborough, Peterborough ON

Morbey, Mary Leigh, *Dir of Gallery*, University of Maine at Machias Art Gallery, Machias ME

Morehart, Mary, *Assoc Prof*, University of British Columbia, Department of Fine Arts, Vancouver BC (S)

Morehead, Kathleen, *Chmn of Trustee Committee*, George Walter Vincent Smith Art Museum, Springfield MA

Morehouse, Dorothy V, *Dir*, Monmouth Museum and Cultural Center, Lincroft NJ

Morehouse, William, *Chairperson*, California State College, Sonoma, Department of Art, Rohnert Park CA (S)

Morehouse, William, *Dept Chairperson*, Sonoma State University, Art Department, Rohnert Park CA (S)

Moreland, David, *Assoc Prof*, University of Idaho, Department of Art and Architecture, Moscow ID (S)

Morel-Hall, Sylvie, *Acting Chief Nat Prog Div*, National Museum of Man, Ottawa ON

Morello, Samuel E, *Chmn Dept*, Charles Stewart Mott Community College, Fine Arts Division, Flint MI (S)

Morgan, Andrew, *Instructor*, University of Miami, Department of Art, Coral Gables FL (S)

Morgan, Charlene, *Admin Asst*, Ontario Association of Art Galleries, Resource Centre, Toronto ON

Morgan, Charlene, *Admin Asst*, Ontario Association of Art Galleries, Toronto ON

Morgan, Connie, *Office Admin*, West Hills Unitarian Fellowship, Portland OR

Morgan, Edward A, *Pres Board Trustees*, Huntington Free Library and Reading Room, Depository Library for the Museum of the American Indian, Bronx NY

Morgan, H S, *Pres*, Pierpont Morgan Library, New York NY

Morgan, Helen, *Assoc Prof*, South Dakota State University, Art Dept, Brookings SD (S)

Morgan, Hubert V, *Pres*, Danbury Scott-Fanton Museum and Historical Society, Inc, Danbury CT

Morgan, Jane Hale, *Library Dir*, Detroit Public Library, Fine Arts Department, Detroit MI

Morgan, Jim, *Instructor*, Goldsboro Art Center, Goldsboro NC (S)

Morgan, Madel, *Dir Archives & Library*, Mississippi Department of Archives and History, Jackson MS

Morgan, Mavera, *Prof*, University of the District of Columbia, Art Department, Washington DC (S)

Morgan, Peter, *Head School Fashion and Textile Design*, Leicester Polytechnic, Faculty of Art and Design, Leicester England (S)

Morgan, W P, *Dir & Cur*, Regina Public Library, Dunlot Art Gallery, Regina SK

Morgan, Wayne J, *Genl Mgr*, Fort Ticonderoga Museum, Ticonderoga NY

Morgan, William, *Assoc Prof*, University of Wisconsin-Superior, Department of Art, Superior WI (S)

Morganstern, James, *Asst Prof*, Ohio State University, Department of the History of Art, Columbus OH (S)

Moriarty, Peter, *Lectr*, Johnson State College, Art Department, Johnson VT (S)

Morin, Thomas, *Art Dept Chmn*, University of Akron, University Galleries, Akron OH

Morin, Thomas, *Dept Head*, University of Akron, Department of Art, Akron OH (S)

Morkholm, Otto, *Keeper Royal Coll of Coins & Medals*, Nationalmuseet, National Museum, Copenhagen Denmark

Morley, John, *Dir*, Royal Pavilion, Art Gallery and Museums, Brighton England

Morningstar, William, *Instructor*, Berea College, Art Department, Berea KY (S)

Morrin, Peter, *Cur of 20th Century Art*, High Museum of Art, Atlanta GA

Morris, Daniel, *Asst Prof*, Waynesburg College, Department of Fine Arts, Waynesburg PA (S)

Morris, Edward S, *Keeper Foreign Art*, Walker Art Gallery, Liverpool England

Morris, Gerald E, *Librn*, Mystic Seaport Museum, Inc, G W Blunt White Library, Mystic CT

Morris, Gwin, *Pres*, Harrison County Historical Museum, Marshall TX

Morris, Henry, *Chmn Memorial Hall Committee*, Louisiana Historical Association, Confederate Museum, New Orleans LA

Morris, Homer, *Assoc Dean*, Harford Community College, Humanities Div, Bel Air MD (S)

Morris, Jerry W, *Assoc Prof*, Miami University, Art Department, Oxford OH (S)

Morris, Joyce, *Secy*, Berry College, Art Department, Mount Berry GA

Morris, Judy, *Pres*, Rogue Valley Art Association, Medford OR

Morris, Kay T, *Registrar*, Hunter Museum of Art, Chattanooga TN

Morris, Lorainne, *Secy*, University of Minnesota, Tweed Museum of Art, Duluth MN

Morris, Pat, *Publications*, Art Gallery of Windsor, Windsor ON

Morris, Phillip S, *Dean*, Memphis Academy of Arts, Memphis TN (S)

Morris, Robert, *Prof*, University of Bridgeport, Art Department, Bridgeport CT (S)

Morris, Ron, *Instr*, Danforth Museum School, Framingham MA (S)

Morris, Terry, *Pres*, Allied Arts Council of Lethbridge, Bowman Arts Center, Lethbridge AB

Morrisey, Bob, *Prof*, Polk Community College, Division of Communications and Fine Arts, Winter Haven FL (S)

Morris Jr, Jack A, *Executive Dir*, Greenville County Museum of Art, Greenville SC

Morrison, Ann, *Education*, Vancouver Art Gallery, Vancouver BC

Morrison, Barry, *Cur*, Banff Centre, Walter Phillips Gallery, Banff AB

Morrison, Maureen, *Secy*, Kauai Museum, Lihue HI

Morrison, M Christine, *Librn*, National Endowment for the Arts, Library, Washington DC

Morrison, Pam, *Office Mgr*, Northeastern Nevada Museum, Elko NV

Morrison, Phil, *Installations Dir*, California State University, Northridge, Fine Arts Gallery, Northridge CA

Morrison, Philip R, *Dir*, Hermitage Foundation Museum, Norfolk VA

Morrison, Robert, *Chmn Dept*, Rocky Mountain College, Art Dept, Billings MT (S)

Morrison, Robert J, *Chmn Dept*, University of Nevada, Reno, Art Department, Reno NV (S)

Morrison, Sue, *Chmn Design Dept*, Art Institute of Boston, Boston MA (S)

Morrissey, Blair, *Chairperson Dept*, Muskegon Community College, Dept of Creative & Performing Arts, Muskegon MI (S)

Morrisson, Stan, *Head Sign Painting*, Butera School of Art, Boston MA (S)

Morrow, Jeanne, *Pres*, Abingdon Square Painters, Inc, New York NY (S)

Morrow, John A, *Pres*, Arts and Letters Club of Toronto, Toronto ON

Morrow, Joseph, *Cur Material Culture*, Colorado Historical Society, Colorado Heritage Center, Denver CO

Morrow, Lori, *Photographs*, Montana Historical Society, Library, Helena MT

Morrow, Terry, *Prof*, Texas Tech University, Department of Art, Lubbock TX (S)

Morrow, Tony, *VPres*, Adirondack Lakes Center for the Arts, Blue Mountain Lake NY

Morsches, Richard, *VPres Operations*, Metropolitan Museum of Art, New York NY

Morsching, Carol, *Secy*, LeSueur County Historical Society Museum, Elysian MN

Morse, A Reynolds, *Pres*, Salvador Dali Museum, Beachwood OH

Morse, Irma P, *Pres*, Arts and Crafts Association of Meriden Inc, Meriden CT

Morse, James, *Secy*, Artworlds Center for Creative Arts, Ann Arbor MI

Morse, Shirlie, *Clerk*, Detroit Public Library, Fine Arts Department, Detroit MI

Mortenson, K, *Instructor*, Golden West College, Arts, Humanities and Social Sciences Institute, Huntington Beach CA (S)

Mortimer, Ann, *Pres*, Canadian Crafts Council, Conseil Canadien de l'Artisanat, Ottawa ON

Morton, Robert, *Prof*, Portland State University, Department of Art and Architecture, Portland OR (S)

Mosby, Dewey F, *Cur European Art*, Detroit Institute of Arts, Detroit MI

Moseley, Michael, *Instr*, Youngstown State University, Art Department, Youngstown OH (S)

Moser, Joann, *Acting Dir & Cur Collections*, University of Iowa, Museum of Art, Iowa City IA

Moser, Margaret, *Librn*, Allegheny College, Lawrence Lee Pelliter Library, Meadville PA

Moser, Rex, *Dir Museum Education*, Art Institute of Chicago, Chicago IL

Moses, Arthur, *Assoc*, College of Our Lady of the Elms, Department of Art, Chicopee MA (S)

Moses, B J, *Instructor*, Arkansas Arts Center, Little Rock AR (S)

Moses, Eva W, *Asst Librn*, R W Norton Art Gallery, Library, Shreveport LA

Moshenson, Edna, *Graphics*, Tel Aviv Museum, Tel-Aviv Israel

Mosley, Kim, *Asst Prof*, Saint Louis Community College at Florissant Valley, Department of Art, Ferguson MO (S)

Mosley, Michael, *Asst Prof*, University of North Carolina-Charlotte, Creative Arts Dept, Charlotte NC (S)

Moss, Betty, *Secy*, Sculptor's Society of Canada, Toronto ON

Moss, Dixie, *Sr Arts Coordr*, Lincoln Community Arts Council, Lincoln NE

Moss, Helen, *Development Officer*, Fine Arts Museums of San Francisco, M H de Young Memorial Museum and California Palace of the Legion of Honor

Moss, Jacqueline, *Cur Education*, Aldrich Museum of Contemporary Art, Ridgefield CT

Moss, James E, *Exec Dir & Secy*, California Historical Society, San Francisco CA

Moss, Joe, *Coordr Sculpture*, University of Delaware, Department of Art, Newark DE (S)

Moss, Marsha, *Pres*, Cheltenham Art Centre, Cheltenham PA (S)

Moss, Michael E, *Cur Art*, United States Military Academy, West Point Museum, West Point NY

Moss, Paulette, *Secy*, Midland Art Council of the Midland Center for the Arts, Midland MI

Moss, William W, *Chief Archivist*, John F Kennedy Library and Museum, Dorchester MA

Moss Jr, Roger W, *Dir*, Athenaeum of Philadelphia, Philadelphia PA

Mossop, J, *Head, Paintings, Drawings and Prints*, Provincial Archives of British Columbia, Victoria BC

Mott, Margaret, *Affiliate*, Emory University, Art History Department, Atlanta GA (S)

Motta, Edson, *Dir & Prof*, Museu Nacional de Belas Artes, National Museum of Fine Arts, Rio Brazil

Motz, Leslie, *Assoc Prof*, Indiana University-Purdue University, Department of Fine Arts, Fort Wayne IN (S)

Moubayed, Sylvia, *Executive Dir*, Providence Athenaeum, Library, Providence RI

Moubry, Veronica, *Secy*, Shippensburg State College, Kauffman Gallery, Shippensburg PA

Moulton, Frank, *Pres*, New Hampshire Art Association, Inc, Manchester NH

Moulton, Rosalind, *Instructor*, Stephens College, Art Department, Columbia MO (S)

Moulton, Susan, *Chairperson*, California State College, Sonoma, Department of Art, Rohnert Park CA (S)

Moulton, Susan, *Acting Gallery Dir*, Sonoma State College Art Gallery, Rohnert Park CA

Moulton, Susan, *Prof*, Sonoma State University, Art Department, Rohnert Park CA (S)

Mountcastle, Howard, *Childrens Librn*, Mexico-Audrain County Library, Mexico MO

Mountford, A R, *Dir*, Stoke-on-District Council, City Museum and Art Gallery, Hanley England

Mountjoy, Edie, *Secy*, Art Gallery of Brant, Inc, Brantford ON

Mountsier III, Silas R, *2nd VPres*, Lotos Club, New York NY

Mourao, Rui, *Dir*, Museu da Inconfidencia, History of Democratic Ideals and Culture in Minas Gerais, Ouro Brazil

Mousel, Carol, *VPres*, Sierra Arts Foundation, Reno NV

Mousseau, P J, *Assoc Prof*, Moorhead State University, Department of Art, Moorhead MN (S)

Moybayed, Sylvia, *Exec Dir*, Providence Athenaeum, Providence RI

Mozley, Anita V, *Cur of Photography*, Stanford University, T W Stanford Art Gallery & Museum of Art, Stanford CA

Mruskovic, Stefan, *Dir*, Slovenska Narodna Galeria, Slovak National Gallery, Bratislava Czechoslovakia

Mudge, Nina R, *Cur*, Sheldon Art Museum, Middlebury VT

Muehsam, Gerd, *Art Bibliographer*, Queens College of the City University of New York, Art Collection, Flushing NY

Mueller, Dorothy, *Librn*, Philadelphia Maritime Museum, Library, Philadelphia PA

Mueller, Gary V, *Asst Prof*, Pacific University in Oregon, Department of Fine Arts, Forest Grove OR (S)

Mueller, Jean, *Membership & Vol Coordr*, University of Utah, Utah Museum of Fine Arts, Salt Lake City UT

Mueller, John, *Instr*, Concordia College, Art Department, Saint Paul MN (S)

Mueller, Louis, *Acting Head Jewelry & Light Metal*, Rhode Island School of Design, Providence RI (S)

Mueller, Martha A, *Head Readers Services*, New York State College of Ceramics at Alfred University, Scholes Library of Ceramics, Alfred NY

Mueller-Hauck, Janni, *Dir*, Staatliche Museen Preussischer Kulturbesitz, Education Department, Berlin Germany, Federal Republic of

Mugnaini, Joseph, *Instructor*, University of Southern California, Idyllwild Campus, Idyllwild School of Music and the Arts, Idyllwild CA (S)

Muhlberger, Richard, *Dir*, George Walter Vincent Smith Art Museum, Springfield MA

Muhlert, Jan Keene, *Dir*, Amon Carter Museum of Western Art, Fort Worth TX

Muick, Paul C, *Prof*, Mary Washington College, Art Department, Fredericksburg VA (S)

Muirhead, Robert Bruce, *Chmn*, Hamilton College, Art Department, Clinton NY (S)

Mujino, Margaret, *Office Mgr & Admin Asst*, Propersi School of Art Inc Galleries, Greenwich CT

Muldavin, Phyllis, *Asst Prof*, Los Angeles City College, Department of Art, Los Angeles CA (S)

Mulder, A, *Secy*, Manitoba Historical Society, Dalnavert - MacDonald House Museum, Winnipeg MB

Mulder, Char, *Secy*, Hope College, DeWitt Cultural Center, Holland MI

Mulgrew, John, *Prof*, Pace University, Department of Art & Design, Pleasantville NY (S)

Mulhearn, Flora, *Asst Prof*, College Misericordia, Art Department, Dallas PA (S)

Mullen, James, *Pres*, Cooperstown Art Association, Cooperstown NY

Mullen, James, *Chmn*, State University of New York College at Oneonta, Department of Art, Oneonta NY (S)

Mullen, James M, *Chmn Art Dept*, State University of New York College at Oneonta, Oneonta NY (S)

Mullen, Joseph, *Comptroller*, Shelburne Museum, Shelburne VT

Mullen, Philip, *Artist in Res*, University of South Carolina, Department of Art, Columbia SC (S)

Mullen, Ray, *Instructor*, Kirkwood Community College, Department of Fine Arts, Cedar Rapids IA (S)

Mullen, Robert, *Asst Prof*, University of Texas at San Antonio, Division of Art and Design, San Antonio TX (S)

Muller, Doris, *Asst Prof*, Jersey City State College, Art Department, Jersey City NJ (S)

Muller, Helen, *Prof*, Nassau Community College, Art Department, Garden City NY (S)

Muller, Jeffrey, *Instr*, Bowdoin College, Art Department, Brunswick ME (S)

Muller, Joan L, *Dir*, Virginia Commonwealth University, School of The Arts Library, Richmond VA

Muller, Karen, *Head Technical Services*, Art Institute of Chicago, Ryerson and Burnham Libraries, Chicago IL

Muller, Martin, *Music Department*, Centro de Arte y Communicacion, Center of Art and Communication, Buenos Argentina

Muller, Mary M, *Adminr*, Carolina Art Association, Gibbes Art Gallery, Charleston SC

Muller, Norman E, *Conservator*, Worcester Art Museum, Worcester MA

Muller, Priscilla E, *Cur Mus Paintings & Metalwork*, Hispanic Society of America Museum, New York NY

Muller, Robert, *Chief Librn*, Queens College of the City University of New York, Art Collection, Flushing NY

Muller, Sheila, *Asst Prof*, University of Utah, Art Department, Salt Lake City UT (S)

Muller Jr, J Frederick, *Secy*, New Orleans Museum of Art, Isaac Delgado Museum, New Orleans LA

Mulliner, Gayle, *Membership Secy*, Madison Art Center, Madison WI

Mullins, P Joseph, *Dir*, Parkersburg Art Center, Parkersburg WV

Mullis, Don, *Instructor*, Vincennes University, Art Department, Vincennes IN (S)

Mulloy, Betty, *Librn*, Lauren Rogers Library and Museum of Art, Laurel MS

Mulvany, John, *Chairperson Art & Photography Depts*, Columbia College, Art Department, Chicago IL (S)

Mumm, Dianne, *Educ Coordr*, Sioux City Art Center, Sioux City IA (S)

Mumm, Dianne, *Educ Coordr*, Sioux City Art Center, Sioux City IA

Mundt, Alice, *Cur Japanese Prints*, Worcester Art Museum, Worcester MA

Mundy, E James, *Asst Prof*, Mount Holyoke College, Art Department, South Hadley MA (S)

Mundy, Jane McKee, *Adminr*, Lynchburg Fine Arts Center Inc, Lynchburg VA

Munee, James C, *Assoc Prof*, Kansas State University, Art Department, Manhattan KS (S)

Munford, M B, *Asst Cur Decorative Arts*, Baltimore Museum of Art, Baltimore MD

Munford, Melinda Brady, *Asst Cur*, Parrish Art Museum, Southampton NY

Munford, Robert, *Assoc Prof*, Southampton College of Long Island University, Fine Arts Division, Southampton NY (S)

Munhall, Edgar, *Cur*, Frick Collection, New York NY

Munie, Marsha, *Instr*, Gettysburg College, Department of Art, Gettysburg PA (S)

Munns, Lynn, *Instructor*, Casper College, Casper WY (S)

Muno, Rich, *Managing Dir*, National Cowboy Hall of Fame and Western Heritage Center, Oklahoma City OK

Munoz, Gilbert, *Instructor*, Texas A & I University, Art Department, Kingsville TX (S)

Munoz, Ramon, *Head Means of Expression*, Universidad Javeriana, Javeriana University Faculty of Architecture and Design, Bogota Colombia (S)

Munoz, Teresa, *Asst Prof*, Loyola Marymount University, Department of Art, Los Angeles CA (S)

Munro, Alan, *Dir*, Alaska State Museum, Juneau AK

Munro, Maralin, *Secy*, Art Gallery of Peterborough, Peterborough ON

Munro, Peter, *Dir*, Kestner-Museum, Hannover Germany, Federal Republic of

Munsch, Gene, *Conservator Furniture*, Fine Arts Museums of San Francisco, M H de Young Memorial Museum and California Palace of the Legion of Honor

Munson, Paul, *Instructor*, Radford University, Art Department, Radford VA (S)

Munson, Richard, *Chmn*, University of Northern Colorado, Department of Fine Arts, Greeley CO (S)

Muntz, Ursula, *Asst Sales Gallery Mgr*, Amarillo Art Center, Amarillo TX

Munves, Edward, *Pres*, National Antique and Art Dealers Association of America, New York NY

Munz, Willette M, *Department Chmn*, University of Texas at El Paso, El Paso TX

Munz, Willette M, *Head Dept*, University of Texas at El Paso, Department of Art, El Paso TX (S)

Munzenrider, Claire, *Conservator*, Museum of New Mexico, Museum of International Folk Art, Santa Fe NM

Murata, Hiroshi, *Asst Prof*, Trenton State College, Art Department, Trenton NJ (S)

Murchie, John, *Dir*, Nova Scotia College of Art and Design, Library, Halifax NS

Murdock, John, *VPres*, Wind River Valley Artists Guild, Dubois WY

Murdock, Robert A, *Exec Dir*, Association for the Preservation of Virgina Antiquities, Richmond VA

Murdock, Robert M, *Dir*, Grand Rapids Art Museum, Grand Rapids MI

Murdock, William, *Dir*, Pace University, Pace University Library, Briarcliff Manor NY

Murdy, Jean, *Secy*, Custom House Maritime Museum, Newburyport MA

Murenko, Tania, *Recording Secy*, Community Arts Council of Vancouver, Vancouver BC

Murkett Jr, Philip T, *First VPres*, Montgomery Museum of Fine Arts, Montgomery AL

Muro, George, *Head*, Allan Hancock College, Fine Arts Department, Santa Maria CA (S)

Murphy, Barbara, *Registrar*, United States Figure Skating Hall of Fame and Museum, Colorado Springs CO

Murphy, Christine, *Assoc Prof*, College of Mount Saint Vincent, Fine Arts Department, Riverdale NY (S)

Murphy, Donn, *Prof*, Georgetown University, Department of Fine Arts, Washington DC (S)

Murphy, H D, *Treas*, Desert Caballeros Western Museum, Wickenburg AZ

Murphy, J P, *Chmn*, Rockland Community College, Art Department, Suffern NY (S)

Murphy, John Cullen, *Pres*, National Cartoonists Society, Brooklyn NY

Murphy, John Satre, *Assoc Prof*, University of Wisconsin-Parkside, Art Discipline, Kenosha WI (S)

Murphy, Joseph S, *Pres*, Bennington College, Bennington VT (S)

Murphy, Kenneth, *Instructor*, Mohawk Valley Community College, Advertising Design and Production, Utica NY (S)

Murphy, Margaret-ann, *Dir*, Craft Students League of the YWCA, New York NY (S)

Murphy, Mary-Kate, *Librn*, Maine Historical Society, Library, Portland ME

Murphy, Patrick, *Asst Prof*, Williamsport Area Community College, Department of Engineering and Design, Williamsport PA (S)

Murphy, Rivers C, *Prof*, Northwestern State University of Louisiana, Dept of Art, Natchitoches LA (S)

Murray, Ann H, *Dir*, Wheaton College, Watson Gallery, Norton MA

Murray, Don E, *Assoc Prof*, University of Florida, Department of Art, Gainesville FL (S)

Murray, Donald R, *Chmn Div*, Malone College, Department of Art, Canton OH (S)

Murray, Gale, *Asst Prof*, Colorado College, Department of Art, Colorado Springs CO (S)

Murray, Jim, *Gallery Dir*, Mount Saint Mary's College Fine Arts Gallery, Los Angeles CA

Murray, Jim, *Assoc Prof*, Mount Saint Mary's College, Art Department, Los Angeles CA (S)

Murray, Joan, *Dir*, The Robert McLaughlin Gallery, Oshawa ON

Murray, John, *Chmn*, New York Institute of Technology, Fine Arts Department, Old Westbury NY (S)

Murray, John, *Associate Dir Fine Arts Dept*, New York Institute of Technology Gallery, Old Westbury NY

Murray, L, *Chief Cur Canadian War Museum*, National Museum of Man, Ottawa ON

Murray, L F, *Cur*, National Museums of Canada, Canadian War Museum, Ottawa ON

Murray, Neale, *Chmn Dept*, North Park College, Art Department, Chicago IL (S)

Murray, Richard V, *Dir*, Birmingham Museum of Art, Birmingham AL

Murray, Robert, *Instructor*, New York School of Interior Design, New York NY (S)

Murray, Robin B, *Dir and Head Serials Section*, New York State College of Ceramics at Alfred University, Scholes Library of Ceramics, Alfred NY

Murray, Timothy G, *Assoc Prof*, Brevard College, Div of Fine Arts, Brevard NC (S)

Murray, Tom, *Dir*, Brevard College, Coltrane Art Center, Brevard NC

Murray, William, *Asst Prof*, Northeast Missouri State University, Art Department, Kirksville MO (S)

Murray Jr, Robinson, *Librn*, Essex Institute, Salem MA

Murrow, Nila West, *Head Dept*, Bethany Nazarene College, Art Department, Bethany OH (S)

Musgrave, Jean E, *Registrar*, Hall of Fame of the Trotter, Goshen NY

Musgrove, Stephen W, *Asst Dir*, Mint Museum of Art, Charlotte NC

Musial, Tom, *Board Chmn*, Rahr-West Museum and Civic Center, Manitowoc WI

Musselman, Jamie, *Instr*, Moravian College, Department of Art, Bethlehem PA (S)

Must, Raymond, *Associate Prof*, Wright State University, Art Department, Dayton OH (S)

Muston, Harvey, *Dir*, Craft Center Museum, Wilton CT

Musy, J, *Dir*, Ecole Nationale Superieure des Beaux-Arts, National College of Fine Arts, Paris France (S)

Muth, Tom J, *Asst Dir*, Topeka Public Library, Topeka KS

Mutt, E, *Head of Library*, Library of the Estonian State Art Institute, Tallinn Ussr

Muysson, William, *Assoc Cur*, Queen's University, Agnes Etherington Art Centre, Kingston ON

Muzii, Rossana, *Supv & Dir Drawings & Prints*, Museo de Capodimonte, Mount Capodi Museum, Naples Italy

Myers, Adele, *Instr*, Saint Thomas Aquinas College, Art Department, Sparkhill NY (S)

Myers, Fred A, *Dir*, Thomas Gilcrease Institute of American History and Art, Tulsa OK

Myers, Frederick, *Assoc Prof*, University of Northern Colorado, Department of Fine Arts, Greeley CO (S)

Myers, Jack, *Instructor*, Portland Art Museum, Museum Art School, Portland OR (S)

Myers, Jo, *Head Dept*, Des Moines Area Community College, Art Department, Boone IA (S)

Myers, Legh, *Secy*, Sculptors Guild, Inc, New York NY

Myers, Lynn, *Cur Art Gallery*, University of South Carolina, McKissick Museums, Columbia SC

Myers, Lynn Robertson, *Admin Asst*, Guild of South Carolina Artists, Columbia SC

Myers, Margaret, *Librn Asst*, Heard Museum, Heard Museum Library, Phoenix AZ

Myers, Richard, *Grad Coordr*, Kent State University, School of Art, Kent OH (S)

Myers, Robert, *Instr*, Ellsworth Community College, Department of Fine Arts, Iowa Falls IA (S)

Myers, V, *Secy*, Macdonald Steward Art Centre, Guelph ON

Myers Jr, Earl B, *Pres*, Ladies Library and Art Association, Independence KS

Myhre, Eric J, *Pres*, Montana Historical Society, Helena MT

Myles, K A, *Asst Dir*, Ghana National Museum, Accra Ghana

Myron, Robert, *Chmn*, Hofstra University, Department of Art History, Hempstead NY (S)

Naab, Michael, *Cur*, Columbia River Maritime Museum, Astoria OR

Naberezny, Jon, *Prof*, Youngstown State University, Art Department, Youngstown OH (S)

Nabholz, Marie-Louise, *Cur East Asia*, Museum für Völkerkunde und Schweizerisches Museum für Volkskunde Basel, Museum of Ethnological Collections and Folklore, Basel Switzerland

Nachumi, Annette, *Area Liaison*, Women in the Arts Foundation, Inc, New York NY

Nadel, Joshua, *Prof*, University of Maine at Augusta, Division of Arts and Humanities, Augusta ME (S)

Naeve, Milo M, *Cur American Art*, Art Institute of Chicago, Chicago IL

Nagar, Sarla, *Assoc Cur South Asian Art*, University of Missouri, Museum of Art and Archaeology, Columbia MO

Nagel, John, *Instructor*, Saint Louis Community College at Meramec, Art Dept, Saint Louis MO (S)

Nagel, Stewart, *Assoc Prof*, Bloomsburg State College, Department of Art, Bloomsburg PA (S)

Nager, Arthur, *Assoc Prof*, University of Bridgeport, Art Department, Bridgeport CT (S)

Nagle, Ron, *Visiting Lucie Stern Prof*, Mills College, Art Department, Oakland CA (S)

Nagle, Virginia, *Assoc Prof*, University of Minnesota, Department of Design, Saint Paul MN (S)

Naguib, Mustafa, *Dir*, Naguib School of Sculpture, Inc, Glen Ellyn IL (S)

Nagy, Klara Lovass, *Asst Cur*, Potsdam Public Museum, Potsdam NY

Nagy, Margaret, *Instructor*, Mississippi University for Women, Art Department, Columbus MS (S)

Nagy, Martin, *Recording Secy*, Spectrum, Friends of Fine Art, Inc, Toledo OH

Nair, Vijay, *Librn*, Adirondack Museum of the Adirondack Historical Association, Library, Blue Mountain Lake NY

Najmi, Virginia, *Cur Coll*, Lakeview Museum of Arts and Sciences, Peoria IL

Nakashima, Tom, *Prof*, West Virginia University, Division of Art, Morgantown WV (S)

Nama, George, *VPres*, Society of American Graphic Artists, New York NY

Name, Eniro, *Asst to Dir*, Universidad de las Americas, Library, Cholula Mexico

Namer, Rosella, *Librn*, Viterbo College Art Gallery, Zoeller Fine Arts Library, La Crosse WI

Nance, Archie L, *VPres*, The Fort Worth National Bank, Fort Worth TX

Nantais-Picher, Lise, *Dir*, Musee du Quebec, Quebec PQ

Naos, Theodore, *Assoc Prof*, Catholic University of America, Department of Architecture & Planning, Washington DC (S)

Narad, Regina L, *Executive Secy*, Westmoreland County Museum of Art, Greensburg PA

Nartker, John, *Chmn*, College of Mount Saint Joseph, Art Department, Mount Saint Joseph OH (S)

Nasby, Judith, *Dir*, Macdonald Steward Art Centre, Guelph ON

Nasca, Veronica, *Secy*, Museum of Cartoon Art, Port Chester NY

Nasgaard, Roald, *Chief Cur*, Art Gallery of Ontario, Toronto ON

Nash, Les, *Instructor*, Louisville School of Art, Anchorage KY (S)

Nashner, Barbara A, *Cur Education*, The Rosenbach Museum and Library, Philadelphia PA

Naso, Albert, *Chmn*, Bakersfield College, Art Department, Bakersfield CA (S)

Nason, James, *Cur Ethnology & Anthropology*, University of Washington, Thomas Burke Memorial Washington State Museum, Seattle WA

Naspo, Diana, *Instructor*, Montclair Art Museum, Art School, Montclair NJ (S)

Nassar, Mahasen, *Sub-Dir*, Egyptian Museum, Cairo Egypt

Nasse, Harry, *Dir*, Ward-Nasse Gallery, New York NY

Nasta, Linda, *Educational Liaison*, Bergen Community Museum, Paramus NJ

Natalini, Bob, *Instructor*, Peters Valley Craft Center, Layton NJ (S)

Natapoff, Flora, *Sr Lectr*, Harvard University, Department of Visual and Environmental Studies, Cambridge MA (S)

Nathanson, Carol, *Asst Prof*, Case Western Reserve University, Department of Art, Cleveland OH (S)

Nathanson, Carol, *Assoc Prof*, Wright State University, Art Department, Dayton OH (S)

Nathanson, Marjorie Frankel, *Cur History*, Southern Illinois University Museum and Art Galleries, Carbondale IL

Nathorst-Böös, Ernst, *Asst Keeper*, Kungl Myntkabinettet Statens Museum För Mynt Medalj Och Penninghistoria, Royal Coin Cabinet, National Museum of Monetary History, Stockholm Sweden

Nation, Morna, *Instructor*, Wharton County Junior College, Art Department, Wharton TX (S)

Nauert, Patricia, *Registrar*, Los Angeles County Museum of Art, Los Angeles CA

Naujoks, Robert, *Instructor*, Mount Mercy College, Art Department, Cedar Rapids IA (S)

Naumer, Helmuth J, *Executive Dir*, San Antonio Museum Association, Inc, San Antonio TX

Nava, John, *Chmn Art & Exhib Dir*, University of Redlands, Peppers Art Center and Gallery, Redlands CA

Navin, Jane, *Coordr Interior Design*, Iowa State University, Department of Design, Ames IA (S)

Navone, Edward, *Asst Dir*, Washburn University, Mulvane Art Center, Topeka KS

Navot, S, *Secy Haartz Museum*, Haaretz Museum, Tel-Aviv Israel

Navrat, Den, *Gallery Supv*, Dickinson State College, Mind's Eye Gallery, Dickinson ND

Navrat, Dennis Edward, *Prof*, Dickinson State College, Department of Art, Dickinson ND (S)

Navratil, Amy, *Librn*, Norton Simon Museum, Library, Pasadena CA

Navratil, Barbara, *Secy*, New Mexico Art League, Ken Roberts Gallery, Albuquerque NM

Nawrocki, Thomas, *Assoc Prof*, Mississippi University for Women, Art Department, Columbus MS (S)

Nawrot, Andrzej, *Head Dept Industrial Design*, Panstwowa Wyzsza Szkola Sztuk Plastycznych, Higher School of Art and Design, Lodz Poland (S)

Naylor, Charles E, *Treas*, Dallas Public Library, Dallas Print and Drawing Society, Dallas TX

Naylor, Geoffrey J, *Prof*, University of Florida, Department of Art, Gainesville FL (S)

Neaher, Nancy C, *Asst Prof*, Cornell University, Department of the History of Art, Ithaca NY (S)

Neal, George, *Instr*, Marian College, Art Department, Indianapolis IN (S)

Neal, Harold, *Instructor*, Ivy School of Professional Art, Downtown Annex, Pittsburgh PA (S)

Neal, Thomas, *Div Chmn*, Laramie County Community College, Division of Humanities, Cheyenne WY (S)

Near, Pinkney, *Chief Cur*, Virginia Museum of Fine Arts, Richmond VA

Neary, Patrick, *Cur Exhib*, Heard Museum, Phoenix AZ

Nebelong, Bent, *Mayor*, Thorvaldsen Museum, Copenhagen Denmark

Needham, Harry T, *Exec VPres and Cur*, Desert Caballeros Western Museum, Wickenburg AZ

Needham, Paul, *Cur Printed Books and Bindings*, Pierpont Morgan Library, New York NY

Needle, Bill, *Chairperson Dept Art*, Southeast Missouri State University, Department of Art, Cape Girardeau MO (S)

Neeld, Peter, *Keeper of Local History*, Central Art Gallery, Wolverhampton England

Neely, Ester, *Activities Consultant*, University of Minnesota, Student Center Galleries, Saint Paul MN

Neely Jr, Mark E, *Dir*, Lincoln National Life Foundation, Inc, Louis A Warren Lincoln Library and Museum, Fort Wayne IN

Neerincx, R, *Cur*, Gemeentemuseum Arnhem, Municipal Museum of Arnhem, Arnhem Netherlands

Neff, George, *Chmn Dept*, Glassboro State College, Department of Art, Glassboro NJ (S)

Neff, John H, *Dir*, Museum of Contemporary Art, Chicago IL

Neff, Mary, *Coordr*, Marian College, Art Department, Eau Claire WI (S)

Neff, William B, *Bulletin Ed*, Special Libraries Association, Museum, Arts and Humanities Division, New York NY

Negley, Nancy B, *Pres*, San Antonio Museum Association, Inc, San Antonio TX

Neidhardt, C R, *Dir*, Austin College, Ida Green Gallery, Sherman TX

Neidhardt, Carl R, *Chmn*, Austin College, Art Department, Sherman TX (S)

Neil, Milton, *Instr*, Joe Kubert School of Cartoon and Graphic Art Inc, Dover NJ (S)

Neild, Nancy, *Secy*, Beaumont Art Museum, Beaumont TX

Neill, Mary G, *Cur Oriental Art*, Yale University, Art Gallery, New Haven CT

Neils, Jenifer, *Vis Lectr*, University of North Carolina at Chapel Hill, Art Department, Chapel Hill NC (S)

Neiswender, Barbara H, *Adminr*, New Orleans Museum of Art, Isaac Delgado Museum, New Orleans LA

Nellermoe, John, *Chmn Dept*, Waldorf College, Art Department, Forest City IA (S)

Nelsen, Kenneth, *Asst Prof*, Northwest Missouri State University, Dept of Art, Maryville MO (S)

Nelson, Burton R, *Cur Exhib*, Hastings Museum, Hastings NE

Nelson, Carey Boone, *Pres*, Catharine Lorillard Wolfe Art Club, Inc, New York NY

Nelson, Carolyn, *Programs Dir*, Centenary College of Louisiana, Meadows Museum of Art, Shreveport LA

Nelson, Dan, *Asst Dir*, Bradford Brinton Memorial Ranch Museum, Big Horn WY

Nelson, Donald K, *Dir Libraries*, Brigham Young University, Harold B Lee Library, Provo UT

Nelson, Gary, *Instructor*, Burnley School of Professional Art, Inc, Seattle WA (S)

Nelson, Harold, *Assoc Cur American & Contemporary Art & Registrar*, University of Missouri, Museum of Art and Archaeology, Columbia MO

Nelson, James E, *Chmn*, Grand Canyon College, Art Department, Phoenix AZ (S)

Nelson, Jane, *Librn*, Fine Arts Museums of San Francisco, Library, n of Honor co

Nelson, Jane, *Asst Prof*, Missouri Western State College, Art Department, Saint Joseph MO (S)

Nelson, Jean, *Lectr*, Notre Dame College, Art Department, Manchester NH (S)

Nelson, Jeffrey, *Prof*, Butte Community College, Humanities Division (III), Oroville CA (S)

Nelson, Jon, *Asst to Dir*, University of Nebraska Lincoln, Sheldon Memorial Art Gallery, Lincoln NE

Nelson, Joyce, *Mgr Tweed Museum Gift Shop*, University of Minnesota, Tweed Museum of Art, Duluth MN

Nelson, Ken, *Instr*, Wilkes Community College, Arts and Science Division, Wilkesboro NC (S)

Nelson, L, *Security*, Blanden Memorial Art Gallery, Fort Dodge IA

Nelson, Laurel, *Dir*, Westmar College, Weidler Art Gallery, LeMars IA

Nelson, Lawrence B, *Division Dir*, Chipola Junior College, Art Department, Marianna FL (S)

Nelson, Lila, *Textiles Cur*, Vesterheim, Norwegian-American Museum, Decorah IA

Nelson, Linda, *Librn*, Museum of Fine Arts, Houston, Museum Library, Houston TX

Nelson, Marion J, *Prof*, University of Minnesota, Minneapolis, Art History, Minneapolis MN (S)

Nelson, Marion John, *Dir*, Vesterheim, Norwegian-American Museum, Decorah IA

Nelson, Nina, *Dance Coordr*, Ashtabula Arts Center, Ashtabula OH

Nelson, Osea, *Asst Dir*, Bradford Brinton Memorial Ranch Museum, Big Horn WY

Nelson, Richard, *Asst Cur*, Muskegon Museum of Art, Muskegon MI

Nelson, Robert, *VPres*, Missouri Western State College, Fine Arts Gallery, Saint Joseph MO

Nelson, Robert A, *Instructor*, Millersville State College, Art Department, Millersville PA (S)

Nelson, Ronald E, *Historian*, Bishop Hill Historic Site, Bishop Hill IL

Nelson, Sally, *Chmn*, Phillips County Community College, Department of English and Fine Arts, Helena AR (S)

Nemethy, Vicky, *Office Mgr*, Saint Joseph Art Association Inc, Krasl Art Center, Saint Joseph MI

Nepean, Donald, *Supv Creative & Performing Arts Department*, Spokane Falls Community College Fine Art Gallery, Spokane WA

Nepean, Donald, *Chmn*, Spokane Falls Community College, Creative & Performing Arts, Spokane WA (S)

Neprud, K, *Lectr*, California Lutheran College, Art Department, Thousand Oaks CA (S)

Nesbit, G H H, *Head Dept*, Port Elizabeth Technikon, Department of Art and Design of the Port, Port South Africa, Republic of (S)

Nesbit, Thomas, *Librn*, University of Rochester, Memorial Art Gallery Library, Rochester NY

Ness, Bjarne, *Exec Secy*, SVACA - Sheyenne Valley Arts and Crafts Association, Bjarne Ness Gallery, Fort Ransom ND

Nessim, Lalla Halim, *Librn*, Greco-Roman Museum, Library, Alexandria Egypt

Ness Jr, John H, *Executive Secy*, United Methodist Church Commission on Archives and History, Lake Junaluska NC

Netsky, Ron, *Asst Prof*, Nazareth College of Rochester, Art Department, Rochester NY (S)

Neufeld, Harold, *Treas Board of Dir*, Lake County Civic Center Association, Inc, Heritage Museum and Gallery, Leadville CO

Nordell, Marilyn, *Instructor*, Burnley School of Professional Art, Inc, Seattle WA (S)

Nordin, Rob, *Asst Dir*, Utah Travel Council, Salt Lake City UT

Nordland, Gerald, *Dir*, Milwaukee Art Center, Milwaukee WI

Nordmeyer, Jim, *Instructor*, Dunedin Fine Arts and Cultural Center, Dunedin FL (S)

Nordstrom, Marlene, *Lectr*, University of Wisconsin-Superior, Department of Art, Superior WI (S)

Norick, Frank A, *Asst Dir*, University of California, R H Lowie Museum of Anthropology, Berkeley CA

Norman, Jan, *Instr*, Avila College, Art Department, Kansas City MO (S)

Norman, P Roussel, *Second VPres*, New Orleans Museum of Art, Isaac Delgado Museum, New Orleans LA

Normand, Marc, *Program Coordr*, Manchester Institute of Arts and Sciences Gallery, Manchester NH

Normand, Marc, *Program Coordr*, Manchester Institute of Arts and Sciences, Manchester NH (S)

Norris, Andrea, *Chief Cur*, University of Texas at Austin, University Art Museum, Austin TX

Norris, Marianne, *Secy*, Muttart Gallery Associates, Calgary AB

Norris, Ross, *Assoc Prof*, Ohio State University, Department of Art Education, Columbus OH (S)

Norris, Sally, *Librn*, Tacoma Art Museum, Library, Tacoma WA

North, C Murray, *Dean College Fine Arts*, University of Nebraska-Omaha Art Galleries, New Gallery, Omaha NE

North, John, *Dir*, Ryerson Polytechnical Institute Library, Toronto ON

North, Kenda, *Special Projects Dir*, University of California, University Art Galleries and California Museum of Photography, Riverside CA

North, Kenda, *Lectr*, University of California, Riverside, Program in Art, Riverside CA (S)

North, P B, *Asst Prof*, George Mason University, Department of Fine and Performing Arts, Fairfax VA (S)

North, Stanley, *Dir*, Beaupre, A Creative and Performing Arts Center, Stockbridge MA (S)

Northcutt, Jane, *Dir*, Ponca City Library, Ponca City OK

Northcutt, John, *Archaeologist*, Institute of the Great Plains, Museum of the Great Plains, Lawton OK

Northern, Tamara, *Cur of Anthropology*, Dartmouth College Museum & Galleries, Hanover NH

Northup, Marjorie, *Cur of Education*, Reynolda House, Inc, Winston-Salem NC

Norton, Agatha A, *Prof*, University of Wisconsin, Madison, School of Family Resources and Consumer Sciences, Madison WI (S)

Norton, C D, *Pres*, Lighthouse Gallery, Tequesta FL

Norton, Paul, *Prof*, University of Massachusetts, Amherst, Art History Prog, Amherst MA (S)

Norton Jr, Richard W, *Pres of the Board*, R W Norton Art Gallery, Shreveport LA

Norvella, David, *Instr*, Howard College, Art Department, Big Spring TX (S)

Norwood, Malcolm M, *Chmn Dept*, Delta State University, Fielding L Wright Art Center, Cleveland MS

Norwood, Malcolm M, *Chmn*, Delta State University, Department of Art, Cleveland MS (S)

Notenboom, W, *Asst*, Haags Gemeentemuseum, Art Library, The Hague Netherlands

Nottage, James H, *Asst Museum Dir*, Kansas State Historial Society Museum, Topeka KS

Nottage, Mary Ellen Hennessey, *Cur of Decorative Art*, Kansas State Historial Society Museum, Topeka KS

Nottingham, Walter, *Artist in Res*, Viterbo College, Art Department, La Crosse WI (S)

Nottingham, Walter, *Prof*, University of Wisconsin-River Falls, Art Department, River Falls WI (S)

Nouvel, Odile, *Cur*, Union Centrale des Arts Decoratifs, Musee des Arts Decoratifs, Paris France

Novack, Frank T, *Head Dept*, Norwich Art School, Norwich Free Academy, Art Dept, Norwich CT (S)

Novak, Barbara, *Dept Art History*, Columbia University, Barnard College, New York NY (S)

Novak, Philip, *Asst Dir*, Stamford Museum and Nature Center, Stamford CT

Nowicki, David, *Secy*, Associated Artists of Pittsburgh Arts and Crafts Center, Pittsburgh PA

Noyes, Marie E, *Asst to Dir*, Norwich Free Academy, Slater Memorial Museum & Converse Art Gallery, Norwich CT

Noyes, Nancy, *Admin Secy*, Carnegie Institute, Museum of Art, Pittsburgh PA

Noyes, Sandy, *Instructor*, Peters Valley Craft Center, Layton NJ (S)

Noyes Fikus, Vivian, *Secy*, Miniature Art Society of New Jersey, Nutley NJ

Nozynski, John H, *Deputy Dir for Development*, Walters Art Gallery, Baltimore MD

Nuell, Lon, *Chmn Art Dept*, Middle Tennessee State University, Art Dept, Murfreesboro TN (S)

Nugent, Patricia M, *Chmn Div*, Rosemont College, Division of the Arts, Rosemont PA (S)

Nugent, Robert, *Dir*, Jersey City State College, Forrest A Irwin Library, Jersey City NJ

Nunn, Willie, *Specialist*, Elizabet Ney Museum, Austin TX

Nunoo, R B, *Dir*, Ghana National Museum, Accra Ghana

Nurik, Tracey, *Intern*, Clark University, Little Center Gallery, Worcester MA

Nurton, Marti, *Cur Education*, Paine Art Center and Arboretum, Oshkosh WI

Nutt, Ginny, *VPres*, Waterloo Art Association, Waterloo IA

Nutter, Daniel L, *Dir*, Southwestern College, Memorial Library, Winfield KS

Nutting, Anne C, *Head Art & Music Division*, Berkeley Public Library, Berkeley CA

Nuvolo, Giorgio Ascani, *Dir*, Accademia di Belle Arti, Academy of Fine Arts, Perugia Italy (S)

Nuwer, Alice, *School Asst*, Sierra Nevada Museum of Art, Reno NV

Nuzum, Thomas, *Instructor*, Charles Stewart Mott Community College, Fine Arts Division, Flint MI (S)

Nuzzolese, Ellen, *Asst Secy & Treas*, Hall of Fame of the Trotter, Goshen NY

Nyce, Fletcher E, *Secy*, Cincinnati Institute of Fine Arts, Cincinnati OH

Nyenhuis, Jacob E, *Dean Arts & Humanities*, Hope College, DeWitt Cultural Center, Holland MI

Nygren, Edward J, *Cur*, Corcoran Gallery of Art, Washington DC

Nyzio, Anthony, *Pres*, Attleboro Museum, Center for the Arts, Attleboro MA

Oagley, Howard, *Assoc Prof*, University of Evansville, Art Dept, Evansville IN (S)

Oakes, John Warren, *Dir*, Western Kentucky University, Ivan Wilson Center for Fine Arts Gallery, Bowling Green KY

Oakes, Patricia, *Executive Dir*, Villa Montalvo Center for the Arts, Saratoga CA

Oakley, Rhoda, *Prof*, University of Maine at Augusta, Division of Arts and Humanities, Augusta ME (S)

Oakley, Stephen, *AsstDir*, Lemoyne Art Foundation, Tallahassee FL

Oas, Luke, *Instructor*, Murray State University, Art Department, Murray KY (S)

Oberhausen, Judy, *Cur*, Art Center, Inc, South Bend IN

Oberhuber, Oswald, *Rector*, Hochschule Für Angewandte Kunst in Wien, University of Applied Art in Vienna, Vienna Austria (S)

O'Brien, Marcia E, *Dir Office of Cultural Development*, Nassau County Museum of Fine Art, Roslyn NY

O'Brien, Maureen C, *Cur*, Montclair Art Museum, Montclair NJ

O'Brien, Paddy, *Asst Dir & Cur*, London Regional Art Gallery, London ON

Obschruff, Helga, *Asst to Librn*, Konservator der Kunstdenkmaler, Library, Dusseldorf Germany, Federal Republic of

Ocepek, Louis, *Prof*, Portland State University, Department of Art and Architecture, Portland OR (S)

Ockenga, Starr, *Dir*, Massachusetts Institute of Technology, Creative Photography Gallery, Cambridge MA

Ockerse, Thomas, *Chmn Design Div*, Rhode Island School of Design, Providence RI (S)

O'Clair, Robert, *Librn*, Manhattanville College, Manhattanville Library, Purchase NY

O'Connell, Charles, *VPres*, Attleboro Museum, Center for the Arts, Attleboro MA

O'Connor, Andrew, *Restorer Painting*, National Gallery of Ireland, Dublin Ireland

O'Connor, John A, *Assoc Prof*, University of Florida, Department of Art, Gainesville FL (S)

O'Connor, Molly M, *Librn*, Dartmouth College Museum & Galleries, Sherman Art Library, Hanover NH

O'Connor, Stanley J, *Prof*, Cornell University, Department of the History of Art, Ithaca NY (S)

O'Connor, Thom, *Prof*, State University of New York at Albany, Art Department, Albany NY (S)

Oddi, Arch Vincenzo, *Dir*, Galleria di Palazzo Bianco, White Palace Gallery, Genoa Italy

Oddy, Revel, *Keeper Department of Art & Archaeology*, Royal Scottish Museum, Edinburgh Scotland

Odelberg, Maj, *Head Education Department*, Statens Historiska Museum, Museum of National Antiquities, Stockholm Sweden

Odenweller, Theodore, *Exhib Designer*, University of Illinois at Urbana-Champaign, World Heritage Museum, Urbana IL

Odevseff, Barbara, *Registrar*, Wichita Art Museum, Wichita KS

Odom, Dorothy, *Secy*, Doshi Center for Contemporary Art, Harrisburg PA

Odom, Ralph L, *Chmn*, Philander Smith College, Department of Art, Little Rock AR (S)

O'Donal, Rory, *Executive Dir*, Ontario Association of Art Galleries, Toronto ON

O'Donnell, Ellen, *Asst Dir*, Provincetown Art Association and Museum, Provincetown MA

O'Donnell, Margaret M, *Instr*, College of Saint Rose, Division of Art, Albany NY (S)

O'Donnell, Patricia Chapin, *Dir*, Philadelphia College of Textiles and Science, Paley Design Center, Philadelphia PA

O'Driscoll, Sean, *Dir*, Irish International Arts Centre, Castle Matrix, Rathkeale Ireland (S)

Oehlschlaeger, Frank, *Prof*, Notre Dame College, Art Department, Manchester NH (S)

Oeschger, Ramon E, *Instr*, San Jose City College, School of Fine Arts, San Jose CA (S)

Oeste, Luella, *Librn*, Edmonton Art Gallery, Library, Edmonton AB

Oestreich, Nelson E, *Head Dept*, Westminster College, Art Department, New Wilmington PA (S)

Oettel, Russell L, *Chmn Dept*, Indiana University-Purdue University, Department of Fine Arts, Fort Wayne IN (S)

Oexmann, Joan, *Secy*, Lexington Art League, Inc, Lexington KY

Offenbacher, Hurley, *Construction Mgr*, National Gallery of Art, Washington DC

Offner, Elliot Melville, *Prof*, Smith College, Art Department, Northampton MA (S)

Offutt, Florence S, *Chmn Dept*, Porterville Community College, Department of Fine Arts, Porterville CA (S)

Ofm, Christian, *Local Minister*, Mission San Luis Rey Museum, San Luis Rey CA

Ofm, Marion, *Mgr*, Mission San Luis Rey Museum, San Luis Rey CA

Ogborn, Elizabeth, *Keeper of Art*, Southampton Art Gallery and Museum Service, Southampton England

Ogden, R Lynn, *Executive Dir*, Canadian Museums Association, Association des Musees Canadiens, Ottawa ON

Ogdin Jr, George L, *Chrm*, Dulin Gallery of Art, Knoxville TN

Oggier, Brigitte, *Librn*, School of Fine Arts Library, Geneva Switzerland

Ogle, Philip, *Instructor*, School of the Associated Arts, Saint Paul MN (S)

O'Gorman, James F, *Prof*, Wellesley College, Art Department, Wellesley MA (S)

O'Gorman, Laurel, *Conservator & Preparator*, Minnesota Museum of Art, Saint Paul MN

Ogura, Tadao, *Chief Cur*, Kyoto Kokuritsu Kindai Bijutsukan, National Museum of Modern Art, Kyoto, Kyoto Japan

O'Halloran, B C, *Chmn*, Incarnate Word College, Humanities and Fine Arts, San Antonio TX (S)

O'Hara, Anne, *Adjunct Prof*, Tougaloo College, Art Department, Tougaloo MS (S)

O'Hara, Arthur N, *Business Mgr*, Great Lakes Historical Society, Vermilion OH

O'Hara, Bruce, *Photographer*, Tougaloo College, Art Collection, Tougaloo MS

O'Hara, Bruce, *Asst Prof*, Tougaloo College, Art Department, Tougaloo MS (S)

O'Hara, Kathleen, *Lectr*, Johnson State College, Art Department, Johnson VT (S)

O'Hara, Rosalie, *Instructor*, Seton Hill College, Department of Art, Greensburg PA (S)

O'Hare, Marita, *Executive Dir*, Architectural League of New York, New York NY

O'Hayes, Patrick, *Secy*, Newport Historical Society, Newport RI

O'Hear III, James, *Asst Chmn Undergrad Studies*, Catholic University of America, Department of Architecture & Planning, Washington DC (S)

O'Hern, Dianne, *Asst Prof*, Southern Arkansas University, Department of Fine Arts, Magnolia AR (S)

O'Heron, Susan, *Gallery Asst*, Lynnwood Arts Centre, Simcoe ON

Ohlin, Betty E, *Asst Prof*, Rhode Island College, Art Department, Providence RI (S)

Ohm, Annaliese, *Dir*, Museum fur Kunstandwerk, Museum of Arts and Crafts, Frankfurt Germany, Federal Republic of

Oikawa-Picante, Teri, *Conservator Painting*, Fine Arts Museums of San Francisco, M H de Young Memorial Museum and California Palace of the Legion of Honor, n of Honor co

OJalvo, David, *Cur-Dir*, Musee des Beaux-Arts, Museum of Fine Arts, Orleans France

Okazaki, Arthur, *Assoc Prof*, Washington State University, Fine Arts Department, Pullman WA (S)

O'Keeffe, Judith, *Educator*, Burnaby Art Gallery, Burnaby BC

O'Keeffe, Patric, *Instr*, Marian College, Art Department, Indianapolis IN (S)

O'Kelley, Doramae, *Vis Prof*, Adrian College, Art Department, Adrian MI (S)

Okie, Richardson B, *Chmn Board Trustees*, Minnesota Museum of Art, Saint Paul MN

Oklinetzky, Sam, *Dir*, University of Oklahoma, Museum of Art, Norman OK

Oko, Andrew J, *Cur*, Art Gallery of Hamilton, Hamilton ON

O'Konski, R, *Instr*, Catholic University of America, Department of Architecture & Planning, Washington DC (S)

Olafsson, Prudmundur, *Cur*, Thjodminjasafn, National Museum of Iceland, Rrykjavik Iceland

Olander, William, *Cur Modern Art*, Oberlin College, Allen Memorial Art Museum, Oberlin OH

Olcay, Nekriman, *Cur Non-Islamic Coins*, Istanbul Arkeoloji Müzeleri, Archaeological Museums of Istanbul, Istanbul Turkey

Oldacht, Linda, *Asst Librn*, Mount Wachusett Community College, Library, Gardner MA

Oldaker, William B, *Assoc Prof*, West Virginia Wesleyan College, Department of Fine Arts, Buckhannon WV (S)

Oldenburg, Richard E, *Dir Museum*, Museum of Modern Art, New York NY

O'Leary, Daniel J, *Asst Dir Admin*, Cooper-Hewitt Museum, Smithsonian Institution National Museum of Design, New York NY

O'Leary, Dennis, *Dir*, Montana State University, Fine Arts Gallery, Bozeman MT

O'Leary, Mary, *Secy*, Princeton Art Association, Princeton NJ

O'Leary, Thomas M, *Pres*, Boca Raton Center for the Arts, Inc, Boca Raton FL

Olejarz, Harold, *Board of Dir*, Cultural Council Foundation, Fourteen Sculptors Gallery, New York NY

O'Lenick, David, *Dir*, Brooklyn Museum Art School, Brooklyn NY (S)

Olin, Ferris, *Art Librn*, Rutgers University, Art Library, New Brunswick NJ

Oliver, Celia Y, *Registrar*, Shelburne Museum, Shelburne VT

Oliver, Cornelia, *Prof*, Mary Washington College, Art Department, Fredericksburg VA (S)

Oliver, F Duane, *Asst Prof*, Western Carolina University, Dept of Art, Cullowhee NC (S)

Oliver, John A, *Asst Dir*, Flint Public Library, Fine Arts Department, Flint MI

Oliver, Loren, *Chmn Studio Art*, Sweet Briar College, Art History Department, Sweet Briar VA (S)

Oliver, Michael, *Instructor*, Friends University, Art Department, Wichita KS (S)

Oliver, Richard B, *Cur Architecture & Design*, Cooper-Hewitt Museum, Smithsonian Institution National Museum of Design, New York NY

Oliver, Samuel F, *Dir*, Museo Nacional de Bellas Artes, National Museum of Fine Arts, Buenos Aires Argentina

Olivera, Nathan, *Vis Prof*, Santa Rosa Junior College, Art Department, Santa Rosa CA (S)

Oliver Jr, Andrew, *Dir*, Textile Museum, Washington DC

Olney, Susan Faxon, *Dir*, University of New Hampshire, University Art Galleries, Durham NH

O'Looney, James, *Asst Prof*, Mohawk Valley Community College, Advertising Design and Production, Utica NY (S)

Olpin, Robert S, *Chairperson*, University of Utah, Art Department, Salt Lake City UT (S)

Olpin, Robert S, *Dir*, University of Utah, Owen Library, Salt Lake City UT

Olsen, Dennis, *Instr*, Studio Art Centers International, Florence Italy (S)

Olsen, Harald P, *Cur*, Statens Museum for Kunst, Department of Painting and Sculpture Library, Copenhagen Denmark

Olsen, Mel, *Chmn*, University of Wisconsin-Superior, Department of Art, Superior WI (S)

Olsen, Paul, *Instructor*, Mississippi University for Women, Art Department, Columbus MS (S)

Olsen, Valerie Loupe, *Cur of Prints and Drawings*, New Orleans Museum of Art, Isaac Delgado Museum, New Orleans LA

Olson, Edna M, *Secy of Board*, Racine Art Association, Racine WI

Olson, George, *Asst Prof*, College of Wooster, Department of Art, Wooster OH (S)

Olson, Gerald, *Dir*, Dixie College, Southwestern Utah Art Gallery, Saint George UT

Olson, Gerald, *Head Dept*, Dixie College, Art Department, Saint George UT (S)

Olson, James C, *Chmn*, Mid-America Arts Alliance, Kansas City MO

Olson, Janis, *Registrar*, Whatcom Museum of History and Art, Bellingham WA

Olson, Jay, *Chmn*, Sioux Falls College, Department of Art, Sioux Falls SD (S)

Olson Jr, Joseph, *Assoc Prof*, Georgia Southern College, Department of Art, Statesboro GA (S)

Olsson, Helen, *Libr Asst*, Newark Museum, Library, Newark NJ

Olszewski, Edward J, *Assoc Prof*, Case Western Reserve University, Department of Art, Cleveland OH (S)

Olszewski, Edward J, *VPres & Secy*, Midwest Art History Society, Evanston IL

Olvera, Karen, *Slide Librn*, North Texas State University, Art Slide Library, Denton TX

O'Malley, Lynda W, *Cur & Caretaker*, South County Art Association, Kingston RI

O'Malley, William, *Instructor*, Charles Stewart Mott Community College, Fine Arts Division, Flint MI (S)

Oman, Richard G, *Cur Coll*, Church of Jesus Christ of Latter-Day Saints, Information Center and Museum, Arts and Sites Division, Salt Lake City UT

O'Marchadha, Domhnall, *Acting Dir*, National College of Art and Design, Dublin Ireland (S)

O'Meara, Virginia, *Assoc Prof*, Maryville College, Art Department, Saint Louis MO (S)

Omelia, John F, *Asst Prof*, Manhattan College, School of Arts and Sciences, Bronx NY (S)

Omick, Robert, *Chmn Dept*, Western New Mexico University, Dept of Fine Art, Art Div, Silver City NM (S)

O'Neal, Eugene, *Instr*, Elizabeth City State University, Department of Art, Elizabeth City NC (S)

O'Neal, Mary Lois, *Head Dept*, Grayson County College, Art Department, Denison TX (S)

O'Neal, R Ronald, *Head Dept*, Wiley College, Department of Fine Arts, Marshall TX (S)

O'Neil, John, *Prof*, Rice University, Department of Art and Art History, Houston TX (S)

Oneil, John, *Chmn*, University of South Carolina, Department of Art, Columbia SC (S)

O'Neili, Robert, *Prof*, Lamar University, Art Department, Beaumont TX (S)

O'Neill, John P, *Ed-in-Chief*, Metropolitan Museum of Art, New York NY

O'Neill, Kathleen, *Mgr Museum Shop*, Philadelphia Museum of Art, Philadelphia PA

O'Neill, Mary Jo, *Dir*, Riverside County Art and Cultural Center, Edward-Dean Museum of Decorative Arts, Cherry Valley CA

Onorato, Ronald J, *Asst Prof*, University of Rhode Island, Department of Art, Kingston RI (S)

Onorato, Ronald J, *Dir Exhib*, University of Rhode Island Gallery, Kingston RI

Opar, Barbara A, *Architecture Librn*, Ernest Stevenson Bird Library, Syracuse NY

Oppenheimer, Frank, *Dir*, Exploratorium, San Francisco CA

Opper, Michael, *Prof*, California State University, Fresno, Art Department, Fresno CA (S)

Oppermann, Kathleen, *Admin Asst*, Chesterwood, Stockbridge MA

Oppler, Ellen, *Instr*, Syracuse University, Department of Art History, Syracuse NY (S)

Opstad, Lauritz, *Dir*, Kunstindustrimuseet I Oslo, Oslo Museum of Applied Art, Oslo Norway

Orchard, Sharon, *Librn*, Coquille Valley Art Association, Library, Coquille OR

Ordos, Joseph, *Assoc Prof*, University of Minnesota, Department of Design, Saint Paul MN (S)

O'Riordan, C, *Keeper Natural History Division*, National Museum of Ireland, Dublin Ireland

O'Riordan, I W, *Asst Keeper of Art*, Plymouth City Museum and Art Gallery, Plymouth England

Orlando, Tom, *Cur Special Coll*, Chicago Public Library, Cultural Center, Chicago IL

Orling, Anne, *Pres*, Professional Artists Guild, Roslyn Heights NY

Ormand, Mark, *Education Coordr Programs*, Metropolitan Museum and Art Centers, Coral Gables FL

Ormond, Richard, *Deputy Dir*, National Portrait Gallery, London England

Ornelas, Al, *VPres*, School of Holography, Fine Arts Research and Holographic Center Museum, Chicago IL

Ornstein-van Slooten, Eva, *Cur*, Museum Het Rembrandthuis, Rembrandthouse Museum, Amsterdam Netherlands

O'Rourke, Alice, *Prof*, Edgewood College, Art Department, Madison WI (S)

O'Rourke, Alice, *Pres*, Edgewood College, DeRicci Gallery, Madison WI

O'Rourke, James, *Dir & Secy Board Dir*, Plains Art Museum, Main Gallery, Moorhead MN

Orr, Carol, *Pres*, Museum of the Arts Foundation, Missoula Museum of the Arts, Missoula MT

Orr, Loren, *Chmn Division*, Sierra College, Art Department, Rocklin CA (S)

Orr, Robert, *Lectr*, Lake Forest College, Dept of Art, Lake Forest IL (S)

Orsnes, Mogens, *Keeper Danish Prehistoric Coll*, Nationalmuseet, National Museum, Copenhagen Denmark

Ortbals, John, *Asst Prof*, Saint Louis Community College at Florissant Valley, Department of Art, Ferguson MO (S)

Orth, Fredrich, *Chmn Dept Art*, San Diego State University, Art Gallery, San Diego CA

Orth, Fredrick, *Chmn*, San Diego State University, Department of Art, San Diego CA (S)

Ortlip, Paul, *Instructor*, Montclair Art Museum, Art School, Montclair NJ (S)

Ortman, George, *Head Painting Dept*, Cranbrook Academy of Art, Bloomfield Hills MI (S)

Ortolano, Darby, *Instructor*, Clayworks, New York NY (S)

Orton, C H, *Cur of Numismatics*, University of Calgary, The Nickle Arts Museum, Calgary AB

Orwin, Franklin, *Pres Board Trustees*, Chicago Architecture Foundation, Glessner House, Chicago IL

Ory, Norma R, *Dean Junior School*, Museum of Fine Arts, Alfred C Glassell Junior School of Art, Houston TX (S)

Osawa, Mamoru, *Pres*, Kanazawa Bijutsu Kogei Daigaku, Kanazawa Municipal College of Fine and Industrial Arts, Kanazawa City Japan (S)

Osborn, Daisy, *Founder*, World Museum & Art Centre, Osborn Foundation, Tulsa OK

Osborn, Lillian, *Secy*, East Windsor Historical Society Inc, Scantic Academy Museum, West Hartford CT

Osborn, T L, *Founder*, World Museum & Art Centre, Osborn Foundation, Tulsa OK

Osborne, Carol, *Asst Dir*, Stanford University, T W Stanford Art Gallery & Museum of Art, Stanford CA

Osborne, Don, *Asst Prof*, Bethany College, Lindsborg KS (S)

Osborne, John, *Chmn Printmaking*, Swain School of Design, New Bedford MA (S)

Osborne, Leon H, *Chmn*, Fresno City College, Art Department, Fresno CA (S)

Osbun, Biddy, *Dir*, Ships of The Sea Museum, Savannah GA

Osbun, Jack, *Asst Prof*, Wittenberg University, Art Department, Springfield OH (S)

Oshinsky, Sybil, *Instr*, Pontiac Art Center, Pontiac MI (S)

Osler, William, *Secy*, Arts and Letters Club of Toronto, Toronto ON

Osman, Randolph, *Gallery & Museum Dir*, East Carolina University, Wellington B Gray Gallery, Greenville NC

Osman, Siham A, *Asst Prof*, York College of Pennsylvania, Department of Humanities and Fine Arts, York PA (S)

Ossa, Nena, *Cur*, Museo Nacional de Bellas Artes, National Museum of Fine Arts, Santiago Chile

Ossa, Wilhelm, *Instructor*, Casper College, Casper WY (S)

Osted, Hans, *Pres*, Manitoba Society of Artists, Winnipeg MB

Osten, Owen K, *Photographer & Publisher*, Plains Art Museum, Main Gallery, Moorhead MN

Ostermeyer, Denis, *Prof*, Shoreline Community College, Humanities Division, Seattle WA (S)

Ostiguy, Jean-Rene, *Research Cur Canadian Art*, National Gallery of Canada, Ottawa ON

Ostrom, James E, *Accountant*, California Historical Society, San Francisco CA

Ostrov, Lyn, *Instr*, Bowie State College, Department of Fine and Performing Arts, Bowie MD (S)

Ostrow, Mindy, *Gallery Asst*, State University of New York at Oswego, Tyler Art Gallery, Oswego NY

Ostrow, Stephen E, *Dean*, University of Southern California, School of Fine Arts, Los Angeles CA (S)

O'Sullivan, John C, *Keeper Folklife*, National Museum of Ireland, Dublin Ireland

O'Sullivan, N, *Education Officer*, National Gallery of Ireland, Dublin Ireland

Oszuscik, Philippe, *Asst Prof*, University of South Alabama, Department of Art, Mobile AL (S)

Otis, Leone, *Education Cur*, Montclair Art Museum, Montclair NJ

Otis, Leone, *Children's Instructor*, Montclair Art Museum, Art School, Montclair NJ (S)

O'Toole, Dorothea Barrick, *Prof*, Mount Saint Mary's College, Fine Arts Department, Emmitsburg MD (S)

Otremba, Geraldine M, *Deputy Dir of Operations & Center Liaison with the Library of Congress*, John F Kennedy Center for the Performing Arts, Performing Arts Library, Washington DC

Ott, A K, *Secy*, Bündner Kunstmuseum Chur, The Grisons Museum of Art, Chur Switzerland

Ott, John Harlow, *Dir*, Shaker Community, Inc, Pittsfield MA

Ott, Joyce Mary, *VPres*, Association of Honolulu Artists, Honolulu HI

Ott, Judith L, *Dept Chmn*, Johnson State College, Art Department, Johnson VT (S)

Ott, Wendell, *Dir*, Roswell Museum and Art Center, Roswell NM

Ottensmeyer, David J, *Chief Executive Officer*, Lovelace Medical Foundation, Art Collection, Albuquerque NM

Otter, Janet, *Instr*, Judson Baptist College, Department of Fine Arts, Portland OR (S)

Otto, Martha, *Head Archaeology*, Ohio Historical Society, Columbus OH

Otton, Bill, *College of Arts & Humanities Dir*, South Texas Artmobile, Corpus Christi TX

Otton, William, *Dir*, Corpus Christi State University, Weil Art Gallery, Corpus Christi TX

Ou, Mie Shu, *Instr*, University of Albuquerque, Art Department, Albuquerque NM (S)

Oughton, Larry, *Asst Prof*, Delta College, Art Department, University Center MI (S)

Ourbre, Hayward L, *Chmn*, Winston-Salem State University, Art Department, Winston-Salem NC (S)

Oursel, Herve, *Conservator*, Musee des Beaux-Arts de Lille, Museum of Fine Arts, Lille France

Outterbridge, John, *Dir Watts Towers Arts Center*, City of Los Angeles, Municipal Arts Dept, Los Angeles CA

Overby, Osmund, *Prof*, University of Missouri, Art History and Archaeology Department, Columbia MO (S)

Overby, Osmund, *Dir*, University of Missouri, Museum of Art and Archaeology, Columbia MO

Overduin, H, *Deputy Dir & Head Educative Department*, Haags Gemeentemuseum, Municipal Museum of The Hague, The Hague Netherlands

Overland, Carlton E, *Cur Coll*, University of Wisconsin, Elvehjem Art Center, Madison WI

Overly, Dan, *Executive Dir*, Craftmen's Guild of Mississippi, Columbus MS

Overvoorde, Chris Stoffel, *Chmn Dept*, Calvin College, Art Dept, Grand Rapids MI (S)

Owczarski, Marian, *Dir*, Orchard Lake School Galeria, Orchard Lake MI

Owen, John, *Exhib Designer*, University of Vermont, Robert Hull Fleming Museum, Burlington VT

Owen, T M, *Cur*, Welsh Folk Museum, Saint Fagans Wales

Owens, David, *Instr*, Okaloosa-Walton Junior College, Dept of Fine & Performing Arts, Niceville FL (S)

Owens, George A, *Pres*, Tougaloo College, Art Collection, Tougaloo MS

Owens, Geraldine, *Library Asst*, Walker Art Center, Library, Minneapolis MN

Owens, Gwendolyn, *Asst Cur*, Cornell University, Herbert F Johnson Museum of Art, Ithaca NY

Owens, Gwendolyn, *Asst Cur*, Cornell University, Museum Library, Ithaca NY

Owens, Helen McKenzie, *Pres*, Kelly-Griggs House Museum, Pasadena CA

Owens, John, *Pres*, Arts and Humanities Council of Tuscaloosa County, Inc, Tuscaloosa AL

Owens, Kenneth, *Instr*, Fresno City College, Art Department, Fresno CA (S)

Owens, Nell, *Pres*, Portage and District Arts Council, Portage la Prairie MB

Owens, Paul, *Performing Art Dir*, Southeast Arkansas Arts and Science Center, Pine Bluff AR

Owens, Wallace, *Chmn*, Langston University Art Gallery, Langston OK

Owens, Wallace, *Chmn*, Langston University, Art Department, Langston OK (S)

Ownbey, Ronald B, *Chmn*, Mount San Antonio College, Art Department, Walnut CA (S)

Ownby, Joanna, *Registrar*, Crocker Art Museum, Sacramento CA

Oxenaar, R W D, *Dir*, Ryksmuseum Kroller-Muller, Kroller-Muller State Museum, Otterlo Netherlands

Oxhammar, Greger, *Head Administration Department*, Nordiska Museet, Scandinavian Museum, Stockholm Sweden

Ozegovic, Jack, *Instructor*, Northwestern Michigan College, Art Dept, Traverse City MI (S)

Ozmin, M J, *Head Design*, National College of Art and Design, Dublin Ireland (S)

P-Jobb, Andor S, *Asst Prof*, Clarion State College, Department of Art, Clarion PA (S)

Paarlberg, Mildred, *Cur of Coll*, Tippecanoe County Historical Museum, Lafayette IN

Paasche, Norman, *Assoc Prof*, Lewis and Clark College, Department of Art, Portland OR (S)

Pabst, Sophie, *Librn*, Rijksmuseum Vincent Van Gogh, Library, Amsterdam Netherlands

Pace, Gary, *Museum Guide*, The Parthenon, Memphis TN

Pace, Stephen, *Assoc Prof*, American University, Department of Art, Washington DC (S)

Pacheco, Fisico Arturo Romano, *Dir*, Museo Nacional de Antropologia, National Museum of Anthropology, Mexico Mexico

Pachter, Marc, *Historian*, National Portrait Gallery, Washington DC

Pachucki, Romek, *Art Conservator*, Tasmanian Museum and Art Gallery, Hobart Australia

Pacini, Marina E, *Recorder*, Minnesota Museum of Art, Saint Paul MN

Packard, Daniel, *Assoc Prof*, University of South Dakota, Dept of Art, Vermillion SD (S)

Packard, Helen, *Secy*, Toledo Artists' Club, Toledo OH

Packard, Sandra P, *Assoc Prof*, Miami University, Art Department, Oxford OH (S)

Padden, Anne, *Admin Asst*, Cranbrook Academy of Art Museum, Bloomfield Hills MI

Paddison, Sara, *Instructor*, Goldsboro Art Center, Goldsboro NC (S)

Padgett, James, *Instr*, Wilberforce University, Art Department, Wilberforce OH (S)

Padgett, Michael, *Gallery Dir*, University of Wisconsin, Gallery 101, River Falls WI

Padgett, R Paul, *Asst Prof*, West Liberty State College, Art Department, West Liberty WV (S)

Page, A N, *Acting Pres*, Salisbury State College, College Gallery, Salisbury MD

Page, Addison Franklin, *Dir & Cur*, J B Speed Art Museum, Louisville KY

Page, J D, *Gallery Preparator*, Los Angeles Institute of Contemporary Art, Los Angeles CA

Page, John, *Prof*, University of Northern Iowa, Department of Art, Cedar Falls IA (S)

Page, John F, *Dir & Secy*, New Hampshire Historical Society, Concord NH

Page, Marcia, *Registrar*, Craft and Folk Art Museum, Los Angeles CA

Page, Richard K, *Dir*, Philadelphia Maritime Museum, Philadelphia PA

Page, Suzanne, *Dir*, Musee d'Art Moderne de la Ville de Paris, Paris France

Paggie, Michael, *Office Mgr*, Madison Art Center, Madison WI

Paier, Edward T, *Pres*, Paier School of Art, Inc, Hamden CT (S)

Paige, Robert, *Asst Prof*, Philadelphia Community College, Department of Fine Arts, Philadelphia PA (S)

Paine, Roberta, *Museum Educator*, Metropolitan Museum of Art, Junior Museum, New York NY

Paine, Thelma, *Dept Head Reference*, New Bedford Free Public Library, New Bedford MA

Paine, Wesley M, *Dir*, The Parthenon, Memphis TN

Parrino, George, *Acad Dir*, San Antonio Art Institute, San Antonio TX (S)

Parris, Nina, *Cur*, University of Vermont, Robert Hull Fleming Museum, Burlington VT

Parris, Nina, *Chief Cur*, Columbia Museums of Art and Science, Columbia SC

Parris, Peggy, *Instructor*, Sioux City Art Center, Sioux City IA (S)

Parrish, LaRayne, *Cur*, Wheelwright Museum, Santa Fe NM

Parry, Anita, *Secy*, Burlington County Historical Society, Burlington NJ

Parry, Pamela Jeffcott, *Executive Secy*, Art Libraries Society-North America, Iowa City IA

Parsens, Merribell, *Chmn-Curatorial Liaison for Education*, Metropolitan Museum of Art, New York NY

Parshall, Robert, *Assoc Prof*, University of Illinois at the Medical Center, Dept of Biocommunication Arts-Medical Art, Chicago IL (S)

Parson, Leon, *Instructor*, Ricks College, Department of Art, Rexburg ID (S)

Parsons, David G, *Prof*, Rice University, Department of Art and Art History, Houston TX (S)

Parsons, Jean, *Instructor*, Interlochen Arts Academy, Dept of Visual Art, Interlochen MI (S)

Parsons, Jerry, *Chmn*, Prince George's Community College, Art Department, Largo MD (S)

Parsons, June C, *Mgr*, Oklahoma Art Center, Arts Place II, Oklahoma City OK

Parsons, Kermit C, *Dean Col*, Cornell University, Department of Art, Ithaca NY (S)

Parsons, Norma, *Librn*, Birmingham Public Library, Art and Music Department, Birmingham AL

Parsons, Peggy, *Gift Shop Coordr*, Salisbury State College, Wildfowl Art Museum, Salisbury MD

Parton, Ralf, *Prof*, California State College, Stanislaus, Art Department, Turlock CA (S)

Partridge, Donald B, *Pres*, Philadelphia College of Textiles and Science, School of Textiles, Philadelphia PA (S)

Partridge, Virginia P, *Asst Cur*, New York State Historical Association, Farmers' Museum, Inc, Cooperstown NY

Pascale, Mark, *Asst Prof*, University of Missouri-Saint Louis, Art Dept, Saint Louis MO (S)

Paschall, JoAnne, *Dir*, Atlanta College of Art Library, Atlanta GA

Paskus, Ben, *Instructor*, Illinois Wesleyan University, School of Art, Bloomington IL (S)

Pasley, Bruce, *Asst Prof*, Saint Louis Community College at Forest Park, Dept of Art, Saint Louis MO (S)

Pasquali, Dino, *Vis Artist*, Studio Art Centers International, Florence Italy (S)

Passage, George W, *Pres*, Mariners Museum, Newport News VA

Passeri, Leonardo, *Instr*, Studio Art Centers International, Florence Italy (S)

Passi, Conte Ing Alessandro, *Pres*, Accademia di Belle Arti e Liceo Artistico, Academy of Fine Arts, Venice Italy (S)

Patano, Tony, *Coordr Interior Design*, Columbia College, Art Department, Chicago IL (S)

Paterson, Ian, *Asst Dir*, Oakville Centennial-Gairloch Galleries, Oakville ON

Paterson, John A, *Secy*, Canadian Conference of the Arts, Ottawa ON

Patitucci, Joe, *Instr*, American River College, Department of Art, Sacramento CA (S)

Patnode, J Scott, *Dir*, Gonzaga University, AD Gallery, Spokane WA

Patnode, J Scott, *Chmn*, Gonzaga University, Department of Art, Spokane WA (S)

Patrick, Brian, *Asst Prof*, University of Utah, Art Department, Salt Lake City UT (S)

Patrick, Darryl, *Dept Head*, Sam Houston State University, Art Department, Huntsville TX (S)

Patrick, Peggy, *Asst Dir*, Des Moines Art Center, Des Moines IA

Pattemore, A, *Secy*, Rodman Hall Arts Centre, Saint Catharines ON

Patten, Barbara, *Instructor*, Spring Hill College, Fine Arts Department, Mobile AL (S)

Patten, Carol D, *Cur*, Stockbridge Mission House Association, Stockbridge MA

Patten, Lloyd L, *Assoc Prof*, University of South Alabama, Department of Art, Mobile AL (S)

Patten, Ray, *Chmn Dept*, Pearl River Junior College, Fine Arts Department, Poplarville MS (S)

Pattengale, Paul F, *Pres*, Saint Louis Artists' Guild, Saint Louis MO

Patterson, Curtis, *Sculpture Chmn*, Atlanta College of Art, Atlanta GA (S)

Patterson, David, *Mgr Public Relations & Membership*, Cleveland Museum of Art, Cleveland OH

Patterson, Flo, *Secy*, Central Iowa Art Association, Inc, Marshalltown IA

Patterson, James, *Community Coordr*, Michigan Artrain, Inc, Detroit MI

Patterson, M J, *Cur*, Museum of Northern British Columbia, Prince Rupert Museum Art Gallery, Prince Rupert BC

Patterson, Michele, *Library Asst*, University of North Carolina, Art Library, Chapel Hill NC

Patterson, Nancy-Lou, *Assoc Prof*, University of Waterloo, Fine Arts Department, Waterloo ON (S)

Patterson, Pearl, *Secy*, Buchanan Arts and Crafts Inc, Buchanan Dam TX

Patterson, W D M, *Treas*, West Vancouver Visual Arts Society, West Vancouver BC

Patterson, Willis R, *Head Dept*, Central Wyoming College, Art Center, Riverton WY (S)

Patterson III, W Calvin, *Pres*, Michigan Artrain, Inc, Detroit MI

Pattison, Christie R, *Lectr*, University of North Carolina at Wilmington, Art Department, Wilmington NC (S)

Patton, Glenn N, *Prof*, Trinity University, Department of Art, San Antonio TX (S)

Patton, M Ellen, *Asst Prof*, Miami University, Art Department, Oxford OH (S)

Patton, Pat, *Pres*, Prescott Fine Arts Association, Prescott AZ

Paukert, Karel, *Cur Musical Arts*, Cleveland Museum of Art, Cleveland OH

Paul, Arthur, *VPres, Corporate Art & Graphics Dir*, Playboy Enterprises, Inc, Chicago IL

Paul, Natalie, *Asst Prof*, Northern Michigan University, Dept of Art & Design, Marquette MI (S)

Paul, Paddy, *Executive Secy*, Sunbury Shores Arts and Nature Centre, Inc, Saint Andrews NB

Paul, Richard, *Chmn Faculty Gallery Comt*, Purdue University, Gallery I, Gallery II, Union Gallery & Stewart Center Gallery, West Lafayette IN

Paulin, Richard C, *Dir*, University of Oregon, Musuem of Art, Eugene OR

Paul Jr, William D, *Dir*, University of Georgia, Georgia Museum of Art, Athens GA

Paull, James F, *Dir*, University of the Pacific, University Center Gallery, Stockton CA

Paull, Joy, *Business Mgr*, University of Regina, Norman Mackenzie Art Gallery, Regina SK

Pauls, James, *Asst Prof*, Northeast Missouri State University, Art Department, Kirksville MO (S)

Paulsen, Richard, *Instr*, Elmhurst College, Art Department, Elmhurst IL (S)

Paulson, Alan, *Asst Prof*, Gettysburg College, Department of Art, Gettysburg PA (S)

Paulson, Congdon E, *VPres*, University of Nebraska Lincoln, Nebraska Art Association, Lincoln NE

Paulson, Peter J, *Dir*, New York State Library, Manuscripts and Special Collections, Albany NY

Paulson, Robert, *Chmn Two-Dimensional Design*, Southern Illinois University, School of Art, Carbondale IL (S)

Paulson, Suzanne, *Docent Chmn*, Laguna Beach Museum of Art, Laguna Beach CA

Pauwels, Henri, *Cur Ancient Art*, Musees Royaux des Beaux-Arts de Belgique, Royal Museums of Fine Arts of Belgium, Brussels Belgium

Pav, John, *Prof*, East Tennessee State University, Fine Arts Dept, Johnson City TN (S)

Pavia, Raymond F, *VChmn*, National Institute for Architectural Education, New York NY

Pawel, Nancy, *Lectr*, Incarnate Word College, Humanities and Fine Arts, San Antonio TX (S)

Paxson, R C, *Head Dept*, Troy State University, Department of Art, Troy AL (S)

Paxton, T A, *Treas*, Paducah Art Guild, Paducah KY

Payne, J Couric, *Mgr Book Store*, San Diego Museum of Art, San Diego CA

Payne, Jacqueline, *Library Technician*, Sheridan College of Applied Arts and Technology, Visual Arts Library, Oakville ON

Payne, William J, *Dean*, University of Georgia, Franklin College of Arts and Sciences, Division of Fine Arts, Athens GA (S)

Payne, Woodward, *Instructor*, Mesa Community College, Department of Art, Mesa AZ (S)

Payton, Martin, *Instr*, Xavier University of Louisiana, Department of Fine Arts, New Orleans LA (S)

Paz, Samuel, *Conservator*, Museo Nacional de Bellas Artes, National Museum of Fine Arts, Buenos Aires Argentina

Pazi, M, *Asst Dir*, Topkapi Saray Museum, Istanbul Turkey

Peabody, Veeva, *Asst Cur*, Desert Caballeros Western Museum, Wickenburg AZ

Peace, Bernie K, *Chmn*, West Liberty State College, Art Department, West Liberty WV (S)

Pearce, Dan M, *Instr*, Elizabeth City State University, Department of Art, Elizabeth City NC (S)

Pearce, Mary L, *Head Dept*, Rehoboth Art League, Inc, Rehoboth Beach DE (S)

Pearlman, Kay, *Sr Librn Technical Services*, Ontario City Library, Ontario CA

Pearlstein, Seymour, *Assoc Prof*, New York City Community College of the City University of New York, Department of Art and Advertising Design, Brooklyn NY (S)

Pears, David, *Chmn Council of Management*, Museum of Modern Art Oxford, Oxford England

Pearse, Harold, *Chmn Art Educ Div*, Nova Scotia College of Art and Design, Halifax NS (S)

Pearson, Clifton, *Secy Board*, Huntsville Museum of Art, Huntsville AL

Pearson, Clifton, *Head Dept*, Alabama A & M University, Art Education Department, Huntsville AL (S)

Pearson, Frank C, *Chmn*, Dickinson State College, Department of Art, Dickinson ND (S)

Pearson, Jim, *Asst Prof*, Vincennes University, Art Department, Vincennes IN (S)

Pearson, John, *Assoc Prof*, Oberlin College, Department of Art, Oberlin OH (S)

Pearson, Waynn, *Sr Librn Adult Services*, Ontario City Library, Ontario CA

Pease, David, *Dean*, Temple University, Tyler School of Art-Galleries, Philadelphia PA

Pease, David, *Dean*, Tyler School of Art of Temple University, Philadelphia PA (S)

Pebworth, Charles A, *Prof*, Sam Houston State University, Art Department, Huntsville TX (S)

Peck, Louis A, *Chmn*, Boise State University, Art Department, Boise ID (S)

Peck, Margaret, *Asst*, Tucson Museum of Art, Tucson Museum of Art Library, Tucson AZ

Peck, William H, *Cur Ancient*, Detroit Institute of Arts, Detroit MI

Peckenpaugh, C W, *Chmn Fine Arts Dept*, Milwaukee School of the Arts, Milwaukee WI (S)

Peckham, Anita, *Recording Secy*, Seattle Weaver's Guild, Seattle WA

Peckham, Nicholas, *Instructor*, Stephens College, Art Department, Columbia MO (S)

Pecoraro, Sal, *Instructor*, De Anza College, Art Department, Cupertino CA (S)

Pedersen, Margaret, *Pres*, Southern Artists Association, Fine Arts Center, Hot Springs AR

Pedersen, Marit Lande, *Museum Lectr*, City of Oslo Art Collection, Munch Museum, Oslo Norway

Pederson, Ronald, *Instructor*, Calvin College, Art Dept, Grand Rapids MI (S)

Pedley, John G, *Dir*, University of Michigan Museum of Art, Kelsey Museum of Ancient and Medieval Archaeology, Ann Arbor MI

Peebles, David, *Pres*, Peninsula Fine Arts Center, Newport News VA

Peebles, Phoebe, *Archivist*, Harvard University, William Hayes Fogg Art Museum, Cambridge MA

Peek, Charles, *Asst Dir*, USS North Carolina Battleship Memorial, Wilmington NC

Peeno, Sherman, *Secy*, Cincinnati Art Club, Cincinnati OH

Peetz, John E, *Dir & Chief Exec Officer*, Oakland Museum, Oakland CA

Pegden, N A, *Asst Dir Arts*, Leicestershire Museums, Art Galleries and Records Service, Leicestershire Museum and Art Gallery, Leicester England

Peine, Mary Jane, *Prof Emeritus of Art*, Marian College, Art Department, Indianapolis IN

Peirce, John, *Newsletter*, Alaska Artists Guild, Anchorage AK

Peirce, Robert, *Editor*, Portland Art Association, Portland OR

Peithman, Russell I, *Exec Dir*, Charlotte Nature Museum, Inc, Charlotte NC

Pekarsky, Mel, *Assoc Prof*, State University of New York at Stony Brook, Art Department, Stony Brook NY (S)

Peladeau, Marius B, *Dir*, William A Farnsworth Library and Art Museum, Rockland ME

Pelehach, Patricia, *Asst to Dir*, Buten Museum of Wedgwood, Merion PA

Pelfrey, Robert, *Instructor*, Cuesta College, Art Department, San Luis Obispo CA (S)

Pelham, Alfred M, *Treas*, Detroit Institute of Arts, Detroit Institute of Art Founders Society, Detroit MI

Pelham, Robert, *Instructor*, Friends of the Arts and Sciences, Hilton Leech Studio, Sarasota FL (S)

Pell, John G, *Pres*, Fort Ticonderoga Museum, Ticonderoga NY

Pell, John H G, *VPres*, Plymouth Antiquarian Society, Plymouth MA

Pelletier, Brenda, *Registrar*, Bowdoin College, Museum of Art & Peary-MacMillan Arctic Museum, Brunswick ME

Pelletier, Jacqueline, *Chef de Bibliotheque*, Universite de Montreal, Bibliotheque d'Amenagement, Montreal PQ

Pelli, Cesar, *Dean*, Yale University, School of Architecture, New Haven CT (S)

Pellicciaro, Marid, *Prof*, Washington and Lee University, Department of Fine Arts, Lexington VA (S)

Pels, Albert, *Dir*, Pels School of Art, New York NY (S)

Pelton, Margaret M, *Chmn Dept*, Miami-Dade Community College Campuses, Art Department, Miami FL (S)

Pelton, Richard M, *Pres*, Munson Gallery, New Haven CT

Peltz, Margaret, *Secy*, Fine Arts Center of Clinton, Clinton IL

Pelzel, Thomas O, *Assoc Prof*, University of California, Riverside, Art History Department, Riverside CA (S)

Penay, Lucinao J, *Assoc Prof*, American University, Department of Art, Washington DC (S)

Pence, Nina, *Chmn Exhib*, Klamath Falls Art Association, Klamath Art Gallery, Klamath Falls OR

Pendell, David, *Asst Prof*, University of Utah, Art Department, Salt Lake City UT (S)

Pendergraft, Norman, *Prof*, North Carolina Central University, Art Dept, Durham NC (S)

Pendergraft, Norman E, *Dir*, North Carolina Central University, Museum of Art, Durham NC

Pendleton, Eldridge H, *Dir & Cur Coll*, Old Gaol Museum, York ME

Pendley, Barry, *Instructor*, Laramie County Community College, Division of Humanities, Cheyenne WY (S)

Pendley, Wilbur, *Asst Prof*, Trenton State College, Art Department, Trenton NJ (S)

Penhallow, David, *Cur*, Kauai Museum, Lihue HI

Peniston, Robert C, *Dir*, Washington and Lee University, Lee Chapel and Museum, Lexington VA

Penkowski, Giuseppe, *Cur for Ethnographical Coll*, Monumenti Musei e Gallerie Pontificie, Vatican Museums and Galleries, Vatican City Italy

Pennington, Nancy, *Secy*, Licking County Art Association Gallery, Newark OH

Pennington, W J, *Pres*, Corporate Council for the Arts, Seattle WA

Penny, Karen, *Asst Program Coordr*, Texas A & M University, Memorial Student Center Arts Committee, College Station TX

Penzes, Eva, *Scientific Secy*, Magyar Nemzeti Galeria, Hungarian National Gallery, Budapest Hungary

Pepe, Marie Huper, *Chmn*, Agnes Scott College, Department of Art, Decatur GA (S)

Pepich, Bruce, *Art Dir*, Racine Art Association, Charles A Wustum Museum of Fine Arts, Racine WI

Pepich, Bruce, *Art Project Dir*, Racine Art Association, Racine WI

Pepper, Terence, *Photographs*, National Portrait Gallery, London England

Peragine, Dan, *Vis Prof*, Nebraska Wesleyan University, Art Dept, Lincoln NE (S)

Peralta Ramos, Inga, *Pres*, Millicent Rogers Museum, Taos NM

Percival, H V T, *Officer in Charge*, Wellington Museum, London England

Percival, Robert, *Cur Art*, New Brunswick Museum, Saint John NB

Pere, Dorothy, *Pres*, Pennsylvania Academy of the Fine Arts, Fellowship of the Pennsylvania Academy of the Fine Arts, Philadelphia PA

Pere, Dorothy, *Instructor*, Ocean City School of Art, Ocean City NJ (S)

Pereira, Vera Monteiro, *Chief Librn*, Museu Nacional de Belas Artes, Library, Rio Brazil

Perez, Arq Ignacio Cabral, *Instr*, University of the Americas, Graphic Arts and Design Dept, Cholula Mexico (S)

Perez, J Esteban, *Installation Designer*, Center for Inter-American Relations Art Gallery, New York NY

Perez, Vincent, *Instructor*, California College of Arts and Crafts, Oakland CA (S)

Perinchief, Morris, *Asst Prof*, Dickinson College, Fine Arts Department, Carlisle PA (S)

Perkins, Anne Newhold, *Staff Artist*, Richmond Public Library, Richmond VA

Perkins, Constance M, *Chmn*, Occidental College, Art Department, Los Angeles CA (S)

Perkins, Constance M, *Dir*, Occidental College Gallery, Los Angeles CA

Perkins, Dean, *Asst Prof*, Vermont College of Norwich University, Philosophy, Religion and Fine Arts Department, Montpelier VT (S)

Perkins, Dorothy, *Cur*, University of Massachusetts, Amherst, Art Slide Library, Amherst MA

Perkins, Elizabeth, *Cur Museum*, Kentucky Historical Society Museum, Frankfort KY

Perkins, G Holmes, *Chmn Grad Group*, University of Pennsylvania, Department of Architecture, Philadelphia PA (S)

Perkins, Helen D, *VPres*, Stowe-Day Foundation, Hartford CT

Perkins, Robert E, *Pres*, Ringling School of Art, Sarasota FL (S)

Perkins, Ron, *Principal*, Nutana Collegiate Institute, Memorial Library and Art Gallery, Saskatoon SK

Perkins, Tim, *Media Center Dir*, Minneapolis College of Art and Design, Library and Media Center, Minneapolis MN

Perkis, Roselaine, *Asst Prof*, Ladycliff College, Art Department, Highland Falls NY (S)

Perlman, Bennard B, *Chmn*, Community College of Baltimore, Dept of Fine & Applied Arts, Baltimore MD (S)

Perlman, Raymond, *In Charge Graphic Design*, University of Illinois, Urbana-Champaign, Department of Art and Design, Champaign IL (S)

Perlmutter, Jack, *Chmn Printmaking*, Corcoran School of Art, Washington DC (S)

Pernish, Paul, *Instructor*, Contra Costa College, Department of Art, San Pablo CA (S)

Perri, John, *Assoc Prof*, University of Wisconsin-Stout, Art Department, Menomonie WI (S)

Perrin, Deborah, *Gallery Asst*, Arco Center for Visual Art, Los Angeles CA

Perrin, Joseph S, *Head Dept*, Georgia State University, Atlanta GA (S)

Perrin, Louise H M, *Library Asst*, Historic Deerfield Inc, Henry N Flynt Library, Deerfield MA

Perrine, Rebecca, *Library Asst*, Virginia Historical Society, Library, Richmond VA

Perron, Robert, *Pres*, Beverly Historical Society, Beverly MA

Perrot, Paul N, *Asst Secy for Museum Programs*, Smithsonian Institution, Washington DC

Perrucio, Joseph, *Asst Admin*, Thousand Islands Museum Craft School, Clayton NY (S)

Perry, Charles E, *Asst Humanities Librn*, North Texas State University, Willis Library, Humanities Division, Denton TX

Perry, Deborah L, *Second VChmn*, Guild Hall of East Hampton, Inc, Museum Section, East Hampton NY

Perry, Donald, *Chmn*, Emporia State University, Department of Art, Emporia KS (S)

Perry, Doug, *Executive*, Arts and Humanities Council of Tuscaloosa County, Inc, Tuscaloosa AL

Perry, Lallah M, *Asst Prof*, Delta State University, Department of Art, Cleveland MS (S)

Perry, Pamela, *Asst Cur*, Regina Public Library, Dunlot Art Gallery, Regina SK

Perry Jr, Roger N, *Pres*, John Woodman Higgins Armory, Worcester MA

Persegati, Walter, *Secy-Treas*, Monumenti Musei e Gallerie Pontificie, Vatican Museums and Galleries, Vatican City Italy

Persoons, Guido, *Prof*, Bibliotheek Nationaal Hoger Instituut voor Bouwkunst en Stedebouw, Antwerp Belgium

Perucchi, U, *VDir Graphic Coll & Library*, Kunsthaus Zurich, Library, Zurich Switzerland

Petch, H, *Pres*, University of Victoria, Maltwood Art Museum and Gallery, Victoria BC

Peter, Max, *Dir & Exhibits Chmn*, College of Idaho, Blatchley Gallery, Caldwell ID

Peterdi, Gabor, *Prof*, Yale University, School of Art, New Haven CT (S)

Peterman, Ben, *Vis Prof*, Sam Houston State University, Art Department, Huntsville TX (S)

Peters, Evelyn, *Chmn of Board*, Buchanan Arts and Crafts Inc, Buchanan Dam TX

Peters, F Warren, *Librn*, Detroit Institute of Arts, Research Library, Detroit MI

Peters, H C, *Executive Secy*, Manitoba Association of Architects, Winnipeg MB

Peters, Jean, *Dir Public Relations*, Paine Art Center and Arboretum, Oshkosh WI

Peters, Larry D, *Dir*, Topeka Public Library, Gallery of Fine Arts, Topeka KS

Peters, Muriel N, *Librn*, Dedham Historical Society, Dedham MA

Peters, R, *VPres*, Association of Collegiate Schools of Architecture, Washington DC

Peters, Wallace, *Assoc Prof*, Philadelphia Community College, Department of Fine Arts, Philadelphia PA (S)

Peters, Walter C, *Pres Board Trustees*, Zigler Museum, Jennings LA

Petersen, A J, *Head Department Prints & Drawings*, Stedlijk Museum-Amsterdam, Municipal Museum, Amsterdam Netherlands

Petersen, Daniel W, *Instructor*, Modesto Junior College, Arts Humanities and Speech Division, Modesto CA (S)

Petersen, Leonard, *Asst Prof*, University of Wisconsin-Superior, Department of Art, Superior WI (S)

Petersen, Nancy A, *Exec Asst*, Timken Art Gallery, San Diego CA

Petersen, Peter, *Cur of Education*, Putnam Museum, Davenport IA

Petersen, Robert J, *Business Mgr*, Cincinnati Art Museum, Cincinnati OH

Petersen, Wayne L, *Promotion Dir*, Augustana College, Center for Western Studies, Sioux Falls SD

Peterson, A E S, *Recording Secy*, Providence Water Color Club, Providence RI

Pines, Philip A, *Pres*, Orange County Community of Museums and Galleries, Goshen NY

Pines, Philip A, *Dir*, Hall of Fame of the Trotter, Goshen NY

Pinkerton, Clayton, *Acting Cur*, Richmond Art Center, Richmond CA

Pinkney, Helen L, *Librn*, Dayton Art Institute, Library, Dayton OH

Pinkston, Howell, *Art Dept Chmn*, Pierce College, Art Department, Woodland Hills CA (S)

Pinsky, A, *Dean Faculty*, Concordia University - Sir George Williams Campus, Faculty of Fine Arts, Montreal PQ (S)

Pinsky, Alfred, *Dean Faculty Fine Arts*, Concordia University, Sir George Williams Campus, Department of Fine Arts, Montreal PQ (S)

Pinson, Patricia, *Assoc Prof*, Union University, Department of Art, Jackson TN (S)

Pinto, Doralisa Duarte, *Librn*, Museo Nacional de Bellas Artes, Library, Santiago Chile

Pinto, James, *Dean Fine Arts and Crafts*, Instituto Allende, Allende Institute, San Mexico (S)

Pinto, Sandra, *Dir*, Galleria Palatina, Galleria d'Arte Moderna, Florence Italy

Piotrowski, R, *Head*, Northern Arizona University, Art Department, Flagstaff AZ (S)

Piper, D T, *Dir*, Oxford University, Ashmolean Museum of Art and Archaeology, Oxford England

Piper, Peter, *Instructor*, Laramie County Community College, Division of Humanities, Cheyenne WY (S)

Pique, Jean Pierre, *Chmn Interior Design & Dec*, Traphagen School of Fashion, New York NY (S)

Pisano, Edward, *Security*, Brooklyn Museum, Brooklyn NY

Pisano, Ronald G, *Dir*, Parrish Art Museum, Southampton NY

Piskoti, James, *Prof*, California State College, Stanislaus, Art Department, Turlock CA (S)

Pisney, Raymond, *Dir*, Missouri Historical Society, Saint Louis MO

Pisney, Raymond F, *Dir*, Woodrow Wilson Birthplace Foundation, Staunton VA

Pistorius, Nancy, *Asst Head Fine Arts Library*, University of New Mexico, Fine Arts Library, Albuquerque NM

Pite, Stephen, *Coordr Acad Advancement*, School of Visual Arts, New York NY (S)

Pitkin, Orleonok, *Co-Chairman*, Portland Center for the Visual Arts, Portland OR

Pitman, Ursula, *Exhib Interpreter*, Fitchburg Art Museum, Fitchburg MA

Pitner, Ed, *Chmn*, Parkersburg Community College, Art Department, Parkersburg WV (S)

Pitre, Marc, *Cur*, Gallerie d'Art de l'Universite de Moncton, Moncton NB

Pitt, Paul, *Asst Prof*, Harding University, Department of Art, Searcy AR (S)

Pitter, Pauline O, *Secy*, Pine Castle Center of the Arts, Inc, Orlando FL

Pittman, David, *Artmobile Coordr*, Virginia Museum of Fine Arts, Richmond VA

Pitts, Margaret, *VPres*, Vancouver Art Gallery, Vancouver BC

Pitts, Terence R, *Librn*, Center for Creative Photography, Library, Tucson AZ

Pitts, Terence R, *Cur & Libr Photography Archive*, Center for Creative Photography, Tucson AZ

Pitts, Tom, *Asst Prof*, Berry College, Art Department, Mount Berry GA (S)

Piwonka, Ruth, *Exec Dir*, Columbia County Historical Society, House of History and Van Alen House, Kinderhook NY

Pizanti, E, *Librn*, Museum of Ancient Art, Library, Haifa Israel

Pizzat, Joseph, *Prof*, Mercyhurst College, Department of Art, Erie PA (S)

Place, Bradley E, *Head Dept*, University of Tulsa, Department of Art, Tulsa OK (S)

Placzek, Adolf K, *Pres*, Society of Architectural Historians, Philadelphia PA

Placzek, Adolf K, *Librn*, Columbia University, Avery Architectural and Fine Arts Library, New York NY

Plahter, Leif, *Chief Restorer*, Nasjonalgalleriet, National Gallery, Oslo Norway

Plaisted, Lola P, *Development Officer*, Minnesota Museum of Art, Saint Paul MN

Planchet, Paul, *Pres*, North Shore Arts Associaiton, Inc, Gloucester MA

Plank, Marcella, *Cur*, Plains Indians & Pioneer Historical Foundation, Pioneer Museum & Art Center, Woodward OK

Platais, Maris, *Pres*, Concord Art Association, Concord MA

Platais, Maris, *Secy*, Guild of Boston Artists, Boston MA

Platou, Ralph V, *Chief Cur*, Historic New Orleans Collection, Kemper and Leila Williams Foundation, New Orleans LA

Platt, John H, *Head Librn*, Historical Society of Pennsylvania, Philadelphia PA

Platt Jr, Geoffrey, *VPres*, National Assembly of Community Arts Agencies, Washington DC

Pleer, Ilmar, *Dir*, Johnston National Scouting Museum, North Brunswick NJ

Pletcher, Robert E, *Assoc Prof*, George Peabody College for Teachers, Art Faculty Department, Nashville TN (S)

Pletscher, Josephine, *Head Fine Arts Division*, Pasadena Public Library, Pasadena CA

Ploeger, Fred, *Cur Art*, Eastern Washington State Historical Society, Cheney Cowles Memorial Museum, Spokane WA

Plogman, Bernard E, *Head Dept*, University of Dayton, Fine Arts Division, Dayton OH (S)

Plominska, M, *Head of Education Department*, Muzeum Narodowe, National Museum, Warsaw Poland

Plosky, Charles, *Asst Prof*, Jersey City State College, Art Department, Jersey City NJ (S)

Plous, Phyllis, *Cur*, University of California, Santa Barbara, Art Museum, Santa Barbara CA

Plum, Joel, *Head of Dept*, Wesleyan College, Art Department, Macon GA (S)

Plumb, James, *Cur*, Academy of the Arts, Easton MD

Plume, Clarence, *Secy*, Palm Beach County Parks and Recreation Department, Morikami Museum of Japanese Culture, Delray Beach FL

Plummer, Carlton, *Assoc Prof*, University of Lowell, Department of Art, Lowell MA (S)

Plummer, Jean, *Librn*, Craftsmen's Association of British Columbia, Library, Vancouver BC

Plummer, John, *Prof*, Princeton University, Department of Art and Archaeology, Princeton NJ (S)

Plummer, John H, *Cur Medieval and Renaissance Manuscripts*, Pierpont Morgan Library, New York NY

Plummer, R, *Dean Faculty*, Brighton Polytechnic, Faculty of Art and Design, Brighton England (S)

Podles, Mary Smith, *Cur Renaissance and Baroque Art*, Walters Art Gallery, Baltimore MD

Poe, Robert Harold, *Coordr Visual Arts*, Lander College, Dept of Fine Arts, Greenwood SC (S)

Poesch, Jessie, *Prof*, Tulane University, Newcomb College, New Orleans LA (S)

Pogany, G E, *Dir General*, Magyar Nemzeti Galeria, Hungarian National Gallery, Budapest Hungary

Pogue, Larry, *Head Dept*, East Central Junior College, Art Dept, Union MO (S)

Pogue, Stephanie, *Assoc Prof*, Fisk University, Art Dept, Nashville TN (S)

Pohl, Skip, *Asst Dir*, San Bernardino County Museum and Satellites, Fine Arts Institute, Redlands CA

Pohlman, Lynette, *Asst Dir & Asst Cur*, Iowa State University, Brunnier Gallery, Ames IA

Poirier, Lynne F, *Chief Cur*, Bucks County Historical Society Mercer Museum, Doylestown PA

Pokinski, Deborah, *Instr*, Hamilton College, Art Department, Clinton NY (S)

Pokross, David R, *Chmn Executive Council*, American Jewish Historical Society, Waltham MA

Polan, Louise, *Cur Exhib*, Huntington Galleries, Huntington WV

Polch, Karel, *Executive Secy*, Fairmount Park Art Association, Philadelphia PA

Poleshuck, Walter, *Assoc Dir Finance & Development*, American Federation of Arts, New York NY

Poleskie, Steve, *Assoc Prof*, Cornell University, Department of Art, Ithaca NY (S)

Poling, Clark V, *Assoc Prof*, Emory University, Art History Department, Atlanta GA (S)

Poling, John, *Admin Asst*, Anderson Fine Arts Center, Anderson IN

Poling, John, *Librn*, Anderson Fine Arts Center, Library, Anderson IN

Polito, Ronald, *Chairperson*, Boston State College, Art Department, Boston MA (S)

Polk III, Andrew, *Instr*, Wake Forest University, Department of Art, Winston-Salem NC (S)

Pollans, Albert A, *Treas*, Beaumont Art Museum, Beaumont TX

Pollard, G, *Keeper Coins & Medals*, University of Cambridge, Fitzwilliam Museum, Cambridge England

Pollard, Nathaniel, *Academic Dean*, Tougaloo College, Art Collection, Tougaloo MS

Pollini, John, *Archaeological Coll Cur*, Johns Hopkins University, Archaeological Collection, Baltimore MD

Pollock, Ann, *Cur*, Vancouver Art Gallery, Vancouver BC

Pollock, Luella, *Librn*, Reed College Art Gallery, Eric V Hauser Memorial Library, Portland OR

Polo, Romulo, *Head Industrial Design*, Universidad Javeriana, Javeriana University Faculty of Architecture and Design, Bogota Colombia (S)

Polshek, James Stewart, *Dean*, Columbia University, School of Architecture and Planning, New York NY (S)

Polster, Joanne, *Librn*, American Craft Council, American Craft Council Library, New York NY

Polster, Joanne, *Librn*, American Craft Museum, American Craft Council Library, New York NY

Polster, Nancy, *Coordr Design*, Iowa State University, Department of Design, Ames IA (S)

Polston, John, *Chmn*, Sinclair Community College, Department of Art, Dayton OH (S)

Pomar, Teresa, *Dir*, Museo Nacional de Artes e Industrias Populares, National Museum of Crafts and Popular Industries, Mexico Mexico

Pomarede, F, *Conservator*, Musee Saint-Denis, Reims France

Pomeroy, Stacy F, *Cur*, Rensselaer County Historical Society, Troy NY

Pond, Freda, *Mem Chmn*, Women in the Arts Foundation, Inc, New York NY

Pond, Jeanne C, *Asst Cur of Education*, Worcester Art Museum, Worcester MA

Pons, Neus, *Librn*, Museo de Arte Moderno, Library, Barcelona Spain

Ponsat, Claude, *Chmn*, Saint John'S University, Department of Fine Arts, Jamaica NY (S)

Poole, Jerry D, *Head Dept*, University of Central Arkansas, Art Department, Conway AR (S)

Poole, M, *Secy*, South Peace Art Society, Dawson Creek Museum Art Gallery, Dawson Creek BC

Poon, Vivian, *Treas*, Southeast Alaska Regional Arts Council, Inc, Sitka AK

Poor, Robert, *Assoc Prof*, University of Minnesota, Minneapolis, Art History, Minneapolis MN (S)

Pope, Richard C, *Assoc Prof*, University of Alabama in Huntsville, Department of Art, Huntsville AL (S)

Popov, H, *Dir*, State Museum of Oriental Art, Moscow Ussr

Popovic, Tanya, *Chairperson & Librn*, LeMoyne College, Art Gallery, Syracuse NY

Popovich, Ljubica D, *Assoc Prof*, Vanderbilt University, Dept of Fine Arts, Nashville TN (S)

Popp, Janet E, *Secy*, Capital University, Schumacher Gallery, Columbus OH

Poppe, Mary, *Museum Receptionist & Shop Mgr*, Bowdoin College, Museum of Art & Peary-MacMillan Arctic Museum, Brunswick ME

Porada, Edith, *Honorary Cur Seals and Tablets*, Pierpont Morgan Library, New York NY

Poras, E Linda, *Instr*, Danforth Museum School, Framingham MA (S)

Porcelli, Carolyn, *Development Assoc*, Solomon R Guggenheim Museum, New York NY

Poritsky, Raphael, *Instr*, Cleveland Institute of Art, Cleveland OH (S)

Porps, Ernest O, *Assoc Prof*, University of Colorado at Denver, Department of Fine Arts, Denver CO (S)

Porten, Virginia B, *Business Mgr*, Roanoke Fine Arts Center, Roanoke VA

Porter, Anastasia, *Corresp Secy*, Lowell Art Association, Whistler House and Parker Gallery, Lowell MA

Porter, Arthur, *Lecture Chmn*, Irene Leache Memorial, Norfolk VA

Porter, Bob, *Publications Mgr*, American Council for the Arts, New York NY

Porter, Dean A, *Dir*, University of Notre Dame, Snite Museum of Art, Notre Dame IN

Porter, Elmer J, *Secy*, Kappa Pi International Honorary Art Fraternity, Birmingham AL

Porter, Elwin, *Dir*, South Florida Art Institute of Hollywood, Hollywood FL (S)

Porter, George D, *Comptroller*, John and Mable Ringling Museum of Art, Sarasota FL

Porter, Jeanne Chenault, *Assoc Prof*, Pennsylvania State University, University Park, Department of Art History, University Park PA (S)

Porter, Jerry, *Dir Omniplex*, Omniplex, Oklahoma City OK

Porter, Richard, *Registrar*, Pennsylvania State University, Museum of Art, University Park PA

Porter, Thomas, *Instr*, Virginia Western Community College, Commercial Art, Fine Art & Photography, Roanoke VA (S)

Porter, W Hubert, *Acting Dir*, American Baptist Historical Society, Rochester NY

Porter, William L, *Dean*, Massachusetts Institute of Technology, School of Architecture and Planning, Cambridge MA (S)

Portland, Jack, *Lectr*, Lewis and Clark College, Department of Art, Portland OR (S)

Poser, Mimi, *Public Affairs Officer*, Solomon R Guggenheim Museum, New York NY

Poska, Roland, *Instructor*, Oxbow Summer Art Workshops, Saugatuck MI (S)

Posner, David, *Instructor*, Georgia Southern College, Department of Art, Statesboro GA (S)

Posniak, Richard, *Chmn Sculpture&/Metalsmithing*, Moore College of Art, Philadelphia PA (S)

Possanzini, Rag Albertina, *Dir*, Accademia di Belle Arti, Academy of Fine Arts, Perugia Italy (S)

Post, Jerry L, *Head Dept*, Allegany Community College, Cumberland MD (S)

Poster, Amy, *Assoc Cur Oriental Art*, Brooklyn Museum, Brooklyn NY

Postler, Jan, *Registrar*, Montana State University, Museum of the Rockies, Bozeman MT

Potemska, Maria, *Restorer*, Muzeum Sztuki, Lodz Poland

Potter, Ted, *Dir*, Southeastern Center for Contemporary Art, Winston-Salem NC

Pottruff, Richard, *Dir*, Art Gallery of Brant, Inc, Brantford ON

Potts, Charles, *Photography Dept Chmn*, Art Center College of Design, Pasadena CA (S)

Potts, Connie, *Exhib Designer*, Hastings County Museum, Belleville ON

Potts, Don, *Asst Prof*, California State College, Sonoma, Department of Art, Rohnert Park CA (S)

Potvin, Earl F, *Prof*, College of Saint Teresa, Art Department, Winona MN (S)

Poulin, Jacques, *Dir*, Chateau de Ramezay, Antiquarian and Numismatic Society of Montreal, Montreal PQ

Poulos, Anna, *Head Dept*, College of Saint Teresa, Art Department, Winona MN (S)

Poulos, Basilios, *Asst Prof*, Rice University, Department of Art and Art History, Houston TX (S)

Pounds, Joseph, *Cur*, Franciscan Monastery, Holy Land of America, Washington DC

Poussaint, Alvin, *Secy*, Museum of the National Center of Afro-American Artists, Boston MA

Powell, David, *Asst Prof*, Bradford College, Art Department, Bradford MA (S)

Powell, Dean, *Pres*, Artists Guild Inc of New York, New York NY

Powell, Donald, *Bibliographer*, Tucson Museum of Art, Tucson Museum of Art Library, Tucson AZ

Powell, Earl A, *Dir*, Los Angeles County Museum of Art, Los Angeles CA

Powell, George E, *Chmn Board of Governors*, Kansas City Art Institute, Charlotte Crosby Kemper Gallery, Kansas City MO

Powell, JoAnne, *Registrar*, Indiana University, University Museum, Bloomington IN

Powell, Robert, *Instructor*, Ricks College, Department of Art, Rexburg ID (S)

Powell III, Earl A, *Executive Cur*, National Gallery of Art, Washington DC

Powelson, Rosemary, *Instructor*, Lower Columbia College, Longview WA (S)

Powers, Carolyn, *Asst Prof*, New Mexico Highlands University, Dept of Fine Arts, Las Vegas NM (S)

Powers, David F, *Cur*, John F Kennedy Library and Museum, Dorchester MA

Powers, H Burton, *Pres*, Stowe-Day Foundation, Hartford CT

Powers, Judith B, *Managing Dir*, Florida Gulf Coast Art Center, Inc, Clearwater FL (S)

Powers, Judith Boodon, *Managing Dir*, Florida Gulf Coast Art Center, Inc, Clearwater FL

Powers, Karen, *Admin Asst*, Amarillo Art Center, Amarillo TX

Powers, Phylis, *Mem Secy*, Oklahoma Museum of Art, Oklahoma City OK

Pramuk, Mary Vlcek, *Cur*, West Baton Rouge Museum, Port Allen LA

Pransky, Shirley, *Instructor*, Boston Center for Adult Education, Boston MA (S)

Pratt, Gail, *Fund Development & Public Relations Officer*, Honolulu Academy of Arts, Honolulu HI

Pratt, Jean A, *Instr*, American River College, Department of Art, Sacramento CA (S)

Pratt, Judith, *Lectr*, Trinity College, Department of Fine Arts, Washington DC (S)

Pratt, Laura C, *Head Librn*, Maryland College of Art and Design Library, Silver Spring MD

Pratt, Vernon, *Asst Prof*, Duke University, Department of Art, Durham NC (S)

Pratt, William C, *Dir*, Irwin City Art Foundation, Masur Museum of Art, Monroe LA

Preato, Robert R, *Dir American Masters Dept*, Grand Central Art Galleries, Inc, New York NY

Prebandier, Leon, *Dean*, Lausanne College of Art and Design, Lausanne Switzerland (S)

Preble, Michael, *Cur of Exhib & Coll*, Huntsville Museum of Art, Huntsville AL

Preddy, Jane, *Cur*, Trinity University, Department of Art Slide Collection, San Antonio TX

Pregno, Adrienne, *Chmn*, Ladycliff College, Art Department, Highland Falls NY (S)

Preisner, Olga, *Cur*, Pennsylvania State University, Museum of Art, University Park PA

Preketes, Beryl, *Recording Secy*, Toledo Federation of Art Societies, Toledo OH

Prendeville, Jet M, *Art Librn*, Rice University, Library, Houston TX

Prentiss, Bard, *Asst Prof*, State University of New York College at Cortland, Art Department, Cortland NY (S)

Prentiss, Margo, *Secy Registrar*, Albrecht Art Museum, Saint Joseph MO

Prescott, Kenneth, *Chmn*, University of Texas - Austin, Art Department, Austin TX (S)

Press, Barbara, *Public Information & Publications Officer*, Heckscher Museum, Huntington NY

Press, Nancy S, *Coordr Education & Cur Crafts*, Cornell University, Herbert F Johnson Museum of Art, Ithaca NY

Pressing, Kirk L, *Supv Central Services*, Milwaukee Public Library, Art and Music Department, Milwaukee WI

Pressly, William, *Dir Grad Studies*, Yale University, Department of the History of Art, New Haven CT (S)

Pressman, Lenore, *Prof*, North Park College, Art Department, Chicago IL (S)

Presteich, Larry, *Instructor*, Northeastern Junior College, Department of Art, Sterling CO (S)

Prestiano, Robert, *Coordr*, Angelo State University, Art and Music Department, San Angelo TX (S)

Preston, Ruth, *Restoration Coordr*, Southern Oregon Historical Society, Jacksonville Museum, Jacksonville OR

Preston, Steve, *Head Librn*, College of Southern Idaho, Library, Twin Falls ID

Preston Jr, Herbert R, *VPres*, Star-Spangled Banner Flag House Association, Baltimore MD

Prestwich, Linda, *Cur and Dir*, Highland Area Arts Council, Freeport Art Museum, Freeport IL

Preszler, Robert E, *Cur*, Washington County Museum of Fine Arts, Hagerstown MD

Preusser, Frank, *Restoration Department*, Bayerischen Staatsgemaldesammlungen, Bavarian State Galleries of Art, Munich Germany, Federal Republic of

Prevost, Candace, *Asst to Dir*, Dallas Historical Society, Dallas TX

Prewitt, Diana, *Cur Education*, Brooks Memorial Art Gallery, Memphis TN

Price, Brett, *Instr*, Chapman College, Art Department, Orange CA (S)

Price, Charles, *Chmn*, Connecticut College, Department of Art History, New London CT (S)

Price, Geraldine, *Adv Dir*, Santa Fe Workshops of Contemporary Art, Santa Fe NM (S)

Price, James E, *Dir*, Ohio Visual Art Institute, Cincinnati OH (S)

Price, Joan, *Assoc Prof*, City College of the City of New York, Art Department, New York NY (S)

Price, Larry, *Asst Librn*, Berkshire Athenaeum, Pittsfield MA

Price, Michael, *Prof*, Hamline University, Art Department, Saint Paul MN (S)

Price, Monroe E, *Dir*, Advocates for the Arts, Los Angeles CA

Price, Pam, *Asst Prof*, University of Texas of Permian Basin, Art Discipline, Odessa TX (S)

Price, Priscilla, *Admin Asst*, State University of New York at New Paltz, College Art Gallery, New Paltz NY

Price, Priscilla B, *Registrar*, Corning Museum of Glass, Corning NY

Price, Walter W, *Dir*, Gunston Hall Plantation, Lorton VA

Price, Windsor M, *Pres*, Skaneateles Library Association, Skaneateles NY

Prichett, Peter P, *VPres*, Annie S Kemerer Museum, Bethlehem PA

Prier, Carol Molly, *Lectr*, Mills College, Art Department, Oakland CA (S)

Priest, Terri, *Asst Prof*, College of the Holy Cross, Department of Fine Arts, Worcester MA (S)

Primm, Joan, *Cur of Education*, Bower's Museum, Santa Ana CA

Prince, Nancy Moyer, *Head Dept*, Pan American University, Art Department, Edinburg TX (S)

Prince, Roger O, *Dir*, Wooster Community Art Center, Danbury CT

Prindle, William, *Pres*, American Ceramic Society, Columbus OH

Prins, Johanna W, *Slide Curator*, Ernest Stevenson Bird Library, Syracuse NY

Prinster, Inez Dillon, *Asst Archivist*, Museum of Western Colorado Archives, Grand Junction CO

Prip, John A, *Head Jewelry and Light Metals*, Rhode Island School of Design, Providence RI (S)

Prislin, Jill, *Fine Arts Chmn*, West Hills Unitarian Fellowship, Portland OR

Pritchard, C William, *Mgr Business Operations*, Iowa State Education Association, Salisbury House, Des Moines IA

Pritchard, Mary, *Art Cur*, Ashland Oil, Inc, Phoenix KY

Privratsky, Grace, *Chmn*, North Country Museum of Arts, Park Rapids MN

Probert, Richard, *Chmn*, Muskingum College, Art Department, New Concord OH (S)

Procario, Saverio, *Deputy Dir Admin*, Sleepy Hollow Restorations Inc, Tarrytown NY

Prochazka, Vaclav, *Chief Modern Art Coll*, Narodni Galerie v Prague, National Gallery of Prague, Prague Czechoslovakia

Proctor, Fred, *Treas*, Princeton Art Association, Princeton NJ

Proctor, Letitia, *Librn*, Brooks Memorial Art Gallery, Library, Memphis TN

Proctor, Valerie, *Cur*, Public Archives of Canada, Laurier House, Ottawa ON

Prodinger, Freidrike, *Dir Ethnology, History of Civilization, Arts and Crafts*, Saltzburger Museum Carolino Augusteum, Salzburg Museum, Salzburg Austria

Prokop, Clifton A, *Instr*, Keystone Junior College, Art Department, Cleveland PA (S)

Prokop, Peter, *Pres & Cur*, Taras H Schevchenko Museum and Memorial Park Foundation, Oakville ON

Prokopoff, Stephen S, *Dir*, Institute of Contemporary Art, Boston MA

Prol, Elbertus, *Cur*, Ringwood Manor House Museum, Ringwood NJ

Proper, David R, *Librn*, Historic Deerfield Inc, Henry N Flynt Library, Deerfield MA

Propersi, August, *Dir*, Propersi Galleries and School of Art Inc, Greenwich CT (S)

Propersi, August, *Pres & Dir*, Propersi School of Art Inc Galleries, Greenwich CT

Propersi, Joann, *VPres*, Propersi School of Art Inc Galleries, Greenwich CT

Prose, Maryruth, *Cur Education*, Institute of the Great Plains, Museum of the Great Plains, Lawton OK

Proske, Beatrice G, *Cur Emer Sculpture*, Hispanic Society of America Museum, New York NY

Pross, Lester F, *Chmn*, Berea College, Art Department, Berea KY (S)

Pross, Lester F, *Chmn Art Dept*, Berea College, Art Department Gallery, Berea KY

Protic, Miodrag B, *Dir*, Museum of Modern Art, Belgrade Yugoslavia

Provencher, Alfred, *Assoc Prof*, Monmouth College, Department of Art, West Long Branch NJ (S)

Provenzano, Linda, *Librn*, University of California, Pacific Film Archive, Berkeley CA

Proweller, William, *Prof*, State University College, Department of Art, Fredonia NY (S)

Pruce, Marilyn, *Registrar*, Rutgers University, Art Gallery, New Brunswick NJ

Prucha, John J, *VPres*, Everson Museum of Art, Syracuse NY

Pruette, Patricia, *Secy & Receptionist*, Museum of Early Southern Decorative Arts, Old Salem Inc, Winston-Salem NC

Pruner, Gary L, *Instr*, American River College, Department of Art, Sacramento CA (S)

Pryor, Jerome, *Head Dept*, Xavier University, Fine Arts Department, Cincinnati OH (S)

Ptacek, Gerald P, *Pres of Board*, Racine Art Association, Racine WI

Ptasinski, Margaret, *Children's Librn*, Long Beach Public Library, Long Beach NY

Puccineli, Lydia, *Cur Coll*, Museum of African Art, Washington DC

Puerta, Fabio, *Head Advertising Art*, Universidad Javeriana, Javeriana University Faculty of Architecture and Design, Bogota Colombia (S)

Puffer, John, *Instructor*, Kirkwood Community College, Department of Fine Arts, Cedar Rapids IA (S)

Pugen, Dianne, *Instr*, Toronto School of Art, Toronto ON (S)

Pugh, Mary, *Secy*, Hampshire County Public Library, Romney WV

Pugh, Simon, *Head Complementary Studies*, Saint Martins School of Art, London England (S)

Pujol, Elliott, *Assoc Prof*, Kansas State University, Art Department, Manhattan KS (S)

Pulas, Arthur, *Chmn*, Syracuse University, College of Visual and Performing Arts, Syracuse NY (S)

Pulford, E B, *Prof*, Mount Allison University, Fine Arts Department, Sackville NB (S)

Pullium, Bruce, *Secy*, Fayetteville Museum of Art, Inc, Fayetteville NC

Pulsifer, Dorothy, *Asst Prof*, Bridgewater State College, Art Department, Bridgewater MA (S)

Pultorak, Marceil, *Chairperson*, Carroll College, Art Department, Waukesha WI (S)

Pum, Robert, *Head Dept*, University of Wisconsin-Green Bay, Visual Arts Discipline, Green Bay WI (S)

Pumplin, Paula L, *Reference Librn*, Frick Art Reference Library, New York NY

Punnet, Nan, *VPres*, Midland Art Council of the Midland Center for the Arts, Midland MI

Punt, Rodney L, *General Mgr*, City of Los Angeles, Municipal Arts Dept, Los Angeles CA

Purdy, David, *Chmn Dept*, Columbia Junior College, Department of Physical Creative & Performing Arts, Columbia CA (S)

Purdy, Henry, *Dir*, Holland College, School of Visual Arts, Charlottetown PE (S)

Purdy, Henry, *Dir*, Holland College, School of Visual Arts Library, West Royalty PE

Purdy, P, *VPres Board of Dir*, Museum of Northern British Columbia, Prince Rupert Museum Art Gallery, Prince Rupert BC

Purdy, Polly, *Secy*, Maui Historical Society, Hale Hoikeike, Wailuku HI

Purrington, Philip F, *Sr Cur*, New Bedford Whaling Museum, New Bedford MA

Pursell, Clay, *Instr*, Maryville College, Art Department, Saint Louis MO (S)

Purvis, Susan, *Instructor*, Arkansas Arts Center, Little Rock AR (S)

Puryear, Thomas, *Chairperson Art History*, Southeastern Massachusetts University, College of Visual and Performing Arts, North Dartmouth MA (S)

Pusic, Marija, *Head of Documentation*, Museum of Modern Art, Belgrade Yugoslavia

Putar, Radoslav, *Chief Cur*, Galerije Grada Zagreba, Galerija Benko Horvat, Zagreb Yugoslavia

Putman, Eve, *Office Secy*, Charles B Goddard Center for the Visual and Performing Arts, Ardmore OK

Putney, Elizabeth, *Assoc Educ*, Museum of Early Southern Decorative Arts, Old Salem Inc, Winston-Salem NC

Putney, Janice, *Distribution*, Electronic Arts Intermix, Inc, New York NY

Puvogel, Renate, *Librn*, Suermondt-Ludwig-Museum der Stadt Aachen, Library, Aachen Germany, Federal Republic of

Pyle, Gene J, *Asst Prof*, Morehead State University, Art Department, Morehead KY (S)

Pyles, Linda, *VPres*, The Dalles Art Association, The Dalles OR

Quader, Walter, *Instructor*, Ivy School of Professional Art, Downtown Annex, Pittsburgh PA (S)

Qually, Ingolf J, *Chmn*, Gettysburg College, Department of Art, Gettysburg PA (S)

Quandt, Elizabeth, *Chmn Dept*, Santa Rosa Junior College, Art Department, Santa Rosa CA (S)

Quaresma, Maria Clementina, *Cur*, Museu Nacional de Soares dos Reis, National Museum of Soares Dos Reis, Oporto Portugal

Queen, John, *Assoc Prof*, Texas Tech University, Department of Art, Lubbock TX (S)

Queen, Louise, *Admin Asst*, United Methodist Church Commission on Archives and History, Lake Junaluska NC

Quick, Betsy, *Exhib Coordr*, University of California, Los Angeles, Museum of Cultural History, Los Angeles CA

Quick, Birney M, *Head Dept*, Grand Marais Art Colony, Grand Marais MN (S)

Quick, Edward, *Registrar*, Montgomery Museum of Fine Arts, Montgomery AL

Quick, Michael , *Cur of American Art*, Los Angeles County Museum of Art, Los Angeles CA

Quick, Richard, *Museum Asst*, Rahr-West Museum and Civic Center, Manitowoc WI

Quigley, Gerard, *Visiting Lectr*, College of the Holy Cross, Department of Fine Arts, Worcester MA (S)

Quimby, George I, *Dir*, University of Washington, Thomas Burke Memorial Washington State Museum, Seattle WA

Quimby, Ian M G, *Editor Publications Office*, Winterthur Museum and Gardens, Winterthur DE

Quinlan, Sandra, *Pres*, New Mexico Art League, Ken Roberts Gallery, Albuquerque NM

Quinn, Ann, *Cur of Education*, San Bernardino County Museum and Satellites, Fine Arts Institute, Redlands CA

Quinn, James, *Assoc Prof*, University of Mississippi, Department of Art, University MS (S)

Quinn, Patrick J, *Dean*, Rensselaer Polytechnic Institute, School of Architecture, Troy NY (S)

Quinn, Robert G, *Pres*, Beaumont Art Museum, Beaumont TX

Quinn, Robert M, *Coordr Art History*, University of Arizona, Department of Art, Tucson AZ (S)

Quinn, Thomas, *Pres Governor's Board*, Olana Historic Site, Hudson NY

Quinsac, Annie, *Instr*, University of South Carolina, Department of Art, Columbia SC (S)

Quintal, Margaret, *Dir*, Oscar Howe Art Center, Mitchell SD

Quirarte, Jacinto, *Prof*, University of Texas at San Antonio, Division of Art and Design, San Antonio TX (S)

Quirk, James, *Assoc Prof*, Northern Michigan University, Dept of Art & Design, Marquette MI (S)

Quirk, Marie S, *Museum Dir*, City of Holyoke Museum-Wistariahurst, Holyoke MA

Quirke, Lillian, *Instructor*, De Anza College, Art Department, Cupertino CA (S)

Raab, Tom, *Instructor*, Georgia Southern College, Department of Art, Statesboro GA (S)

Raasch, L, *Dir*, Art Institute of Chicago, Junior Museum, Chicago IL

Rabben, Anne Lise, *Librn*, Nasjonalgalleriet, Library, Oslo Norway

Rabe, Fred, *Assoc Prof*, Weber State College, Art Department 2001, Ogden UT (S)

Rabinovich, Lidia, *Librn*, Centro de Arte y Communicacion, Library, Buenos Argentina

Rabis, James, *Librn*, Fairfield Public Library and Museum, Fairfield Art Association, Fairfield IA

Rackley, William, *Assoc Prof*, University of North Carolina-Charlotte, Creative Arts Dept, Charlotte NC (S)

Racz, Andre, *Prof*, Columbia University, Division of Painting and Sculpture, New York NY (S)

Raczkowski, Lucia, *Asst to Dir*, The Robert McLaughlin Gallery, Oshawa ON

Radan, George, *Prof*, Villanova University, Department of Art and Art History, Villanova PA (S)

Raday, Maria, *VPres*, Main Line Center of the Arts, Haverford PA

Radcliffe, A, *Keeper Architecture & Sculpture*, Victoria and Albert Museum, London England

Radde, Bruce, *Art History Coordr*, San Jose State University, Art Department, San Jose CA (S)

Radecki, Martin J, *Conservator*, Indianapolis Museum of Art, Indianapolis IN

Radell, Sheila, *Childrens Dept Head*, Topeka Public Library, Topeka KS

Rademachery, Richard J, *Head Librn*, Wichita Public Library, Wichita KS

Rademaker, Pierre, *Assoc Prof*, California Polytechnic State University at San Luis Obispo, Art Department, San Luis Obispo CA (S)

Radice, Anne Imelda, *Architectural Historian*, United States Capitol Museum, Washington DC

Radich, Anthony J, *Admin Dir*, Virginia Beach Arts Center, Virginia Beach VA

Radner, Rogene, *Cur*, Lahaina Arts Society, Lahaina HI

Radosh, Sondra M, *Asst Dir*, Jones Library, Inc, Amherst MA

Radysh, Jeanne, *Dept Head*, Ray-Vogue School of Design, Chicago IL (S)

Raedeke, Paul, *Dir Photography*, Academy of Art College, San Francisco CA (S)

Raedler, Dorothy F, *Dir*, St Croix School of the Arts, Inc, Christansted Saint Croix VI (S)

Raetsch, Fred, *Secy*, Anderson County Arts Council, Anderson SC

Ragan, Robert, *Pres*, Gaston County Art and History Museum, Dallas NC

Raggio, Olga, *Chmn Sculpture & Decorative Arts*, Metropolitan Museum of Art, New York NY

Rago, Juliet, *Assoc Prof*, Loyola University of Chicago, Fine Arts Department, Chicago IL (S)

Ragouzis, Perry, *Coordr Teacher Cert*, Colorado State University, Department of Art, Fort Collins CO (S)

Raguin, Virginia C, *Asst Prof*, College of the Holy Cross, Department of Fine Arts, Worcester MA (S)

Rahja, Virginia, *Dir*, School of the Associated Arts, Saint Paul MN (S)

Rahjd, Virginia, *Dir*, School of the Associated Arts Galleries, Saint Paul MN

Rahner, Tom, *Chmn*, Flagler College, Visual Arts Department, Saint Augustine FL (S)

Raia, Frank, *Dir Education*, Art Institute of Fort Lauderdale, Fort Lauderdale FL (S)

Raible, Alton, *Instructor*, College of Marin, Department of Art, Kentfield CA (S)

Rainer, Otto, *Admin*, Saltzburger Museum Carolino Augusteum, Salzburg Museum, Salzburg Austria

Raines, Kevin, *Instructor*, Moravian College, Department of Art, Bethlehem PA (S)

Rainforth, Denis, *Technician*, Sarjeant Gallery, Wanganui New Zealand

Raisanen, Bobbi, *Dance Coordr*, Ashtabula Arts Center, Ashtabula OH

Raiser, Anna, *Instructor*, Greenville College, Dept of Art, Greenville IL (S)

Raiser, C Lane, *Asst Prof*, Greenville College, Dept of Art, Greenville IL (S)

Rajam, Margaret, *Prof*, West Virginia University, Division of Art, Morgantown WV (S)

Rakocy, William, *Cur Coll*, El Paso Museum of Art, El Paso TX

Ralph, Karl E, *Asst to Dean, Business Affairs*, Indiana University - Purdue University at Indianapolis, Herron School of Art, Art Gallery, Indianapolis IN

Ralston, Penny, *Pres*, South Arkansas Art Center, El Dorado AR

Ramade, Patrick, *Asst Cur*, Musee des Beaux-Arts, Rennes France

Ramage, Andrew, *Assoc Prof*, Cornell University, Department of the History of Art, Ithaca NY (S)

Ramage, Edward D, *Asst Librn*, Skaneateles Library Association, Library, Skaneateles NY

Ramage, William, *Instructor*, Castleton State College, Art Department, Castleton VT (S)

Rambeau, Roberta, *Secy & Budget Officer*, University of Santa Clara, de Saisset Art Gallery and Museum, Santa Clara CA

Ramberg, Chris, *Instructor*, Oxbow Summer Art Workshops, Saugatuck MI (S)

Ramberg, W Dodd, *Prof*, Catholic University of America, Department of Architecture & Planning, Washington DC (S)

Ramirez, Adrian N, *Prof*, Catholic University of Puerto Rico, Department of History & Fine Arts, Ponce PR (S)

Ramke, Grace, *Assoc Prof*, McNeese State University, Department of Visual Arts, Lake Charles LA (S)

Ramos, Carolyn, *Instr*, Citrus Community College, Art Department, Azusa CA (S)

Ramsaran, Helen, *Assoc Prof*, John Jay College of Criminal Justice, Department of Art, Music and Philosophy, New York NY (S)

Ramsauer, Joseph F, *Chmn Dept*, Black Hawk College, Art Dept, Moline IL (S)

Ramsay, George, *Assoc Prof*, Wittenberg University, Art Department, Springfield OH (S)

Ramsay, Jane, *Records Researcher*, Presbyterian Historical Society, Philadelphia PA

Ramsay Sr, Charles, *Instr*, Oral Roberts University, Fine Arts Department, Tulsa OK (S)

Ramsdell, F A, *Secy*, Potsdam Public Museum, Potsdam NY

Ramsey, Robert David, *Chmn*, College of Notre Dame, Department of Art, Belmont CA (S)

Ramseyer, Urs, *Cur Indonesia*, Museum für Völkerkunde und Schweizerisches Museum für Volkskunde Basel, Museum of Ethnological Collections and Folklore, Basel Switzerland

Ramstedt Jr, Nils W, *Asst Prof*, University of Nevada, Las Vegas, Department of Art, Las Vegas NV (S)

Ranalli, Daniel, *Dir*, Truro Center for the Arts at Castle Hill, Inc, Truro MA (S)

Rand, Evelyn, *Children's Librn*, Society of the Four Arts, Library, Palm Beach FL

Rand, Harry, *Cur 20th Century Painting & Sculpture*, National Collection of Fine Arts, Washington DC

Randall, Lilian M C, *Cur of Manuscripts and Rare Books*, Walters Art Gallery, Baltimore MD

Randall Jr, Richard H, *Dir*, Walters Art Gallery, Baltimore MD

Randazzo, Angelo, *Exec Dir*, Manchester Institute of Arts and Sciences, Manchester NH (S)

Randazzo, Angelo, *Exec Dir*, Manchester Institute of Arts and Sciences Gallery, Manchester NH

Randel, Jo Stewart, *Dir*, Carson County Square House Museum, Panhandle TX

Rand Jr, Olan A, *Asst Prof*, Northwestern University, Evanston, Department of Art History, Evanston IL (S)

Randolfe, Anita, *Librn*, New York Chamber of Commerce and Industry, Library, New York NY

Randolph, James, *Secy*, Oklahoma Museum of Art, Oklahoma City OK

Randolph, Mary Ellen, *Assoc Prof*, Hood College, Department of Art, Frederick MD (S)

Rands, Robert L, *Adj Cur Archaeology*, Southern Illinois University Museum and Art Galleries, Carbondale IL

Raneo, Frank, *Chmn Fashion Illustration*, New England School of Art and Design, Boston MA (S)

Rang, Christina, *In-House Gallery Chmn*, Women in the Arts Foundation, Inc, New York NY

Rankin, Allan, *Pres*, Maritime Art Association, Summerside PE

Rankin, Barbara, *Corresp Secy*, Association of Medical Illustrators, Los Angeles CA

Rankin, Gratia, *Exhib Coordr*, San Jose State University, Union Gallery, San Jose CA

Rankin, Joseph T, *Cur*, New York Public Library, Spencer Collection, New York NY

Rankin, Marjorie E, *Dean*, Drexel University, Department of Design, Philadelphia PA (S)

Ransom, Charles, *Instr*, Portland Community College, Department of Fine Arts, Portland OR (S)

Ransom, Gordon, *Head Graphic Design*, Saint Martins School of Art, London England (S)

Rapp, Brigid, *Librn*, National Trust for Historic Preservation, Library, Washington DC

Rapp, Martin, *Dir Dept Publication*, Museum of Modern Art, New York NY

Rappaport, Susan, *Public Information*, Pennsylvania Academy of the Fine Arts, Philadelphia PA

Rapson, Ralph E, *Head*, University of Minnesota, Minneapolis, School of Architecture and Landscape Architecture, Minneapolis MN (S)

Raquel, Alba, *Secy*, Museo Historico de Puerto Rico Inc, Santurce PR

Rasch, Arthur Robert, *Chmn Communication Arts*, East Carolina University, School of Art, Greenville NC (S)

Rash, Dillman A, *Chmn Board of Governors*, J B Speed Art Museum, Louisville KY

Rasmussen, Gail, *Exec Dir*, Artists Equity Association, Inc, Washington DC

Rasmussen, Gerald E, *Dir*, Stamford Museum and Nature Center, Stamford CT

Rasmussen, H, *Keeper Danish Folk Museum*, Nationalmuseet, National Museum, Copenhagen Denmark

Rasmussen, Keith, *Printmaking Chmn*, Atlanta College of Art, Atlanta GA (S)

Rasmussen, Marie, *Instructor*, Umpqua Community College, Art Department, Roseburg OR (S)

Rasmussen, Theodore, *Head Dept*, Iowa Wesleyan College, Art Department, Mount Pleasant IA (S)

Rasmussen, Waldo, *Dir International Prog*, Museum of Modern Art, New York NY

Rastede, Kent, *Asst Dir*, University of Nebraska-Omaha Art Galleries, New Gallery, Omaha NE

Ratcliff, Gary L, *Asst Prof*, Northeast Louisiana University, Department of Art, Monroe LA (S)

Ratcliffe, Jefferson, *Cur*, Sturdivant Hall, Selma AL

Rathbun, Joan Nachbaur, *Dir*, Longview Museum and Arts Center, Longview TX

Rathbun, William Jay, *Asian Art Cur*, Seattle Art Museum, Seattle WA

Ratner, Hindy, *Extension Cur*, University of British Columbia, Museum of Anthropology, Vancouver BC

Rattenbury, Richard, *Cur Winchester Museum*, Buffalo Bill Memorial Association, Cody WY

Rattner, Carl, *Chmn*, Saint Thomas Aquinas College, Art Department, Sparkhill NY (S)

Rattray, Alexander, *Head Landscape Archit*, University of Manitoba, Faculty of Architecture, Winnipeg MB (S)

Ratzenberger, Katharine M, *Asst Librn*, National Collection of Fine Arts, Library of the National Collection of Fine Arts and the National Portrait Gallery, Washington DC

Rauch, John V, *Prof*, Northern Michigan University, Dept of Art & Design, Marquette MI (S)

Raupt, Florita, *Cur Museum Coll*, Traphagen School of Fashion, Museum Collection, New York NY

Rauschenberg, Bradford L, *Librn*, Museum of Early Southern Decorative Arts, Library, Winston-Salem NC

Ravel, Nahum, *Executive Dir*, Saidye Bronfman Centre, Montreal PQ

Ravenel, Gaillard F, *Chief Design & Installation*, National Gallery of Art, Washington DC

Ravin, Yoram, *Dir General*, Israel Museum, Jerusalem Israel

Raw, Carl J, *Chmn*, County College of Morris, Art Department, Dover NJ (S)

Rawlings, John, *Instructor*, Northwest Community College, Powell WY (S)

Rawls, William A, *Dir Theatre*, Rocky Mount Arts and Crafts Center, Rocky Mount NC

Rawson, G H, *Pres*, Lyceum Club and Women's Art Association of Canada, Toronto ON

Rawson, Hufty E, *Prof*, Catholic University of Puerto Rico, Department of History & Fine Arts, Ponce PR (S)

Ray, Clyde, *VPres*, Spirit of '76 Museum, Southern Lorain County Historical Society, Wellington OH

Ray, Don, *VPres*, Muttart Gallery Associates, Calgary AB

Ray, Geeta, *Librn*, National Gallery of Modern Art, Reference Library, New India

Ray, Glen A, *Coordr Arts*, Old Dominion University Gallery, Norfolk VA

Ray, Gordan B, *Pres*, John Simon Guggenheim Memorial Foundation, New York NY

Ray, Jim, *Dir*, Albrecht Art Museum, Saint Joseph MO

Ray, Lawrence, *Dir Interior Design*, Lambuth College, Department of Art, Jackson TN (S)

Ray, Leanna W, *Museum Guide*, Tomoka State Park Museum, Ormond Beach FL

Ray, Marlene, *Secy*, Museum of the Southwest, Midland TX

Ray, Sunil C, *Dir*, Indian Museum, Calcutta India

Ray, Timothy, *Assoc Prof*, Moorhead State University, Department of Art, Moorhead MN (S)

Ray, Wade, *Dir*, Ray-Vogue School of Design, Chicago IL (S)

Raybon, Phares, *Chmn*, Quachita Baptist University, Department of Art, Arkadelphia AR (S)

Rayburn, Pat, *Pres*, The Dalles Art Association, The Dalles OR

Rayen, James W, *Prof*, Wellesley College, Art Department, Wellesley MA (S)

Raymond, Dana M, *Secy*, Archives of American Art, Smithsonian Institution, New York NY

Raymond, Dana M, *Secy*, Guild Hall of East Hampton, Inc, Museum Section, East Hampton NY

Raymond, Glenn T, *Chmn*, Grand Rapids Junior College, Art Dept, Grand Rapids MI (S)

Raymond, Robert E, *Pres Board Dir*, Zanesville Art Center, Zanesville OH

Raz, Robert, *Dir Library*, Grand Rapids Public Library, Music and Art Department, Grand Rapids MI

Razadi, Camille, *AV Librn*, Beverly Hills Public Library, Fine Arts Library, Beverly Hills CA

Rücker, Elisabeth, *Dir*, Germanisches National Museum, Bibliothek, Nuremberg Germany, Federal Republic of

Rea, Jacqueline, *Co-Supv Picture Librr*, Cooper-Hewitt Museum, Doris and Henry Dreyfuss Study Center, New York NY

Rea, W H, *Horticulturist*, Tryon Palace Restoration Complex, New Bern NC

Read, Donna, *Assoc Prof*, Texas Tech University, Department of Art, Lubbock TX (S)

Rea Jr, Philip L, *Regent*, Schuyler-Hamilton House, Morristown NJ

Reardon, Michael J, *Dir*, Blackhawk Mountain School of Art Gallery, Blackhawk CO

Reardon, Michael J, *Executive Dir*, Blackhawk Mountain School of Art, Black Hawk CO (S)

Rearwin, K R, *VPres*, Timken Art Gallery, San Diego CA

Reber, Joseph E, *Secy*, Montana Historical Society, Helena MT

Reboli, John P, *Assoc Prof*, College of the Holy Cross, Department of Fine Arts, Worcester MA (S)

Rechtman, Elisheva, *Librn*, Israel Museum, Library for Art and Archaeology, Jerusalem Israel

Rector, Lois, *Instructor*, Dunedin Fine Arts and Cultural Center, Dunedin FL (S)

Rector, Robert, *Assoc Prof*, Northwestern State University of Louisiana, Dept of Art, Natchitoches LA (S)

Redd, Richard J, *Prof*, Lehigh University, Department of Art and Architecture, Bethlehem PA (S)

Redden, Nigel, *Dir Performing Arts*, Walker Art Center, Minneapolis MN

Reddix, Roscoe, *Asst Prof*, Southern University in New Orleans, Art Dept, New Orleans LA (S)

Redfearn, Jerome, *Chmn*, Kentucky Wesleyan College, Department of Fine Arts, Owensboro KY (S)

Redfern, Alan, *Pres*, High Plains Museum, McCook NE

Redlin, Dorothy, *Library Technician*, Saskatchewan Photographic Art Division, Photographic Art Library, Regina SK

Redling, Lisa, *Dir Admissions*, Ringling School of Art, Sarasota FL (S)

Redman, W A, *Chief Admin Officer*, Alcan Smelters and Chemicals Limited, Montreal PQ

Redmond, Arlene, *Recording Secy*, Lowell Art Association, Whistler House and Parker Gallery, Lowell MA

Redmond, Charles R, *Secy of Foundation*, Times Mirror Company, Los Angeles CA

Ree, Roland, *Assoc Prof*, University of North Carolina-Charlotte, Creative Arts Dept, Charlotte NC (S)

Reeck, Edna, *Gallery Dir*, Waterloo Art Association, Waterloo IA

Reed, Alan, *Instructor*, St John's University, Art Department, Collegeville MN (S)

Reed, Berry C, *Assoc Prof*, Palomar College, Art Department, San Marcos TX (S)

Reed, Carl, *Asst Prof*, Colorado College, Department of Art, Colorado Springs CO (S)

Reed, Harold, *Chmn*, Salem College, Art Department, Salem WV (S)

Reed, Howard B, *Assoc Dir*, Fairbanks Museum and Planetarium, Saint Johnsbury VT

Reed, Jesse F, *Chmn*, Davis and Elkins College, Department of Art, Elkins WV (S)

Reed, Larry W, *Div Head*, Campbellsville College, Fine Arts Division, Campbellsville KY (S)

Reed, Nancy, *Assoc Prof*, Texas Tech University, Department of Art, Lubbock TX (S)

Reed, R B, *Chmn Dept*, Purdue University, Lafayette, Department of Creative Arts, Art & Design Section, West Lafayette IN (S)

Reed, Ralph, *Lectr*, Mills College, Art Department, Oakland CA (S)

Reed, Raymond D, *Dean*, Texas A & M University, College of Architecture and Environmental Design, College Station TX (S)

Reed, Richard S, *Dir*, Fruitlands Museums, Harvard MA

Reed, Robert B, *Chmn Art & Design*, Purdue University, Gallery I, Gallery II, Union Gallery & Stewart Center Gallery, West Lafayette IN

Rees, Philip, *Art Librn*, University of North Carolina, Art Library, Chapel Hill NC

Reese, Anne O, *Librn*, Toledo Museum of Art, Library, Toledo OH

Reese, Brenda, *Dir Neighborhood Arts*, Arkansas Arts Center, Little Rock AR

Reese, Gary, *Chief Librn*, Tacoma Public Library, Handforth Gallery, Tacoma WA

Reese Jr, Jesse C, *Executive Dir*, Arts Council, Inc, Winston-Salem NC

Reeve, Gordon, *Chmn Sculpture*, University of Manitoba, School of Art, Winnipeg MB (S)

Reeve, James K, *Dir*, Oklahoma Museum of Art, Oklahoma City OK

Reeves, Charles M, *VPres*, North Carolina Art Society, Raleigh NC

Reeves, Robert L, *VPres*, Stan Hywet Hall Foundation, Inc, Akron OH

Reff, Theodore, *Vis Prof*, University of Missouri, Art History and Archaeology Department, Columbia MO (S)

Regan, Franklin F, *Pres*, Bowne House, Flushing NY

Reger, Lawrence L, *Dir*, American Association of Museums, Washington DC

Regier, Kathleen J, *Chairperson Dept*, Webster College, Art Dept, Webster Groves MO (S)

Regier, Robert W, *Chmn*, Bethel College, Dept of Art, North Newton KS (S)

Rehmani, F M Anjum, *Keeper Muslim Period Coll*, Lahore Museum, Lahore Pakistan

Rehnberg, Mats, *Chmn The Institute of Ethnology*, Nordiska Museet, Scandinavian Museum, Stockholm Sweden

Reich, Shirley, *Secy*, Triton Museum of Art, Santa Clara CA

Reichel, Lorna, *Adjunct Prof*, Roanoke College, Art Department, Salem VA (S)

Reichert, Don, *Chmn Painting*, University of Manitoba, School of Art, Winnipeg MB (S)

Reichlin, Elinor, *Librn*, Society for the Preservation of New England Antiquities, Library, Boston MA

Reid, Ellie, *Pres*, Minneapolis Institute of Arts, Friend of the Institute, Minneapolis MN

Reid, Jo, *Educ Dir*, Coos Art Museum, Coos Bay OR (S)

Reid, Joan, *Cur*, Vassar College Art Gallery, Poughkeepsie NY

Reid, Lawry, *Chairperson Dept*, Dean Junior College, Visual and Performing Arts Department, Franklin MA (S)

Reid, Richard S, *Dir*, Belmont, Gari Melchers Memorial Gallery, Fredericksburg VA

Reid, Robert, *Vis Prof*, Drew University, Art Department, Madison NJ (S)

Reid, Robert, *Dir*, Summit Art Center, Inc, Summit NJ

Reid, Wilma, *Community Relations*, College of New Rochelle, Castle Gallery, New Rochelle NY

Reid Jr, Bryan S, *Secy*, Chicago Historical Society, Chicago IL

Reif, F David, *Assoc Prof*, University of Wyoming, Art Department, Laramie WY (S)

Reiff, Daniel, *Prof*, State University College, Department of Art, Fredonia NY (S)

Reiling, Susan W, *Cur Coll*, Dade County Art Museum, Vizcaya Museum and Gardens, Miami FL

Reilly, Carol, *Lectr*, Georgian Court College, Department of Art, Lakewood NJ (S)

Reilly, Jerry M, *Instructor*, Modesto Junior College, Arts Humanities and Speech Division, Modesto CA (S)

Reilly, Maggie, *Asst Dir*, Ward-Nasse Gallery, New York NY

Reily, Bill, *Assoc Prof*, Incarnate Word College, Humanities and Fine Arts, San Antonio TX (S)

Reimer, Jean, *Secy*, Marian Osborne Cunningham Art Gallery, Bakersfield CA

Reina, Charles, *Asst Prof*, Nassau Community College, Art Department, Garden City NY (S)

Reina, Ruben E, *Cur Latin American Ethnology*, University of Pennsylvania, University Museum, Philadelphia PA

Reinert, Elsie, *VPres*, North Shore Arts Associaiton, Inc, Gloucester MA

Reinhard, Jane, *Instructor*, Millersville State College, Art Department, Millersville PA (S)

Reinhardt, Richard H, *Co-Chairperson Crafts*, Philadelphia College of Art, Philadelphia PA (S)

Reinhart, Margaret, *Prof*, Avila College, Art Department, Kansas City MO (S)

Reinhold, Allen, *Instr*, Utah Technical College at Salt Lake, Commercial Art Department, Salt Lake City UT (S)

Reinholtz, Richard, *Assoc Prof*, University of Montana, Dept of Art, Missoula MT (S)

Reinits, Judy, *VPres*, Bay Area Art Conservation Guild, San Francisco CA

Reinke, Bernnett, *Librn*, Dickinson State College, Stoxen Library, Dickinson ND

Reinold, Marlinde, *Librn*, Stadelsches Kunstinstitut, Bibliothek, Frankfurt Germany, Federal Republic of

Reinowski, Laura, *Prof*, Temple Junior College, Art Department, Temple TX (S)

Reis, Joseph J, *Head Extension Prog Development*, National Gallery of Art, Washington DC

Reischer, Phyllis, *Educ Coordr*, Metropolitan Museum and Art Centers, Coral Gables FL

Reisinger, Landon C, *Librn*, Historical Society of York County, Library, York PA

Reit, Karen, *Head of Dept*, Bethany Lutheran College, Art Department, Mankato MN (S)

Reitz, Don, *Vis Prof*, Victor Valley College, Art Department, Victorville CA (S)

Reitzel, William, *VPres*, Newport Historical Society, Newport RI

Reizen, Sandra, *Secy*, Rensselaer County Historical Society, Troy NY

Relemen, Frank, *Dir Abstract Design*, American Stained Glass Institute, Hobbs NM (S)

Remington, Marie, *Adjunct Lectr*, Indiana University at South Bend, Fine Arts Department, South Bend IN (S)

Remsen, I B, *Pres*, Ann Arbor Art Association, Ann Arbor MI

Remsing, Joseph G, *Instructor*, Modesto Junior College, Arts Humanities and Speech Division, Modesto CA (S)

Renaud, William, *Clerk*, Greater Fall River Art Association, Fall River MA

Renforth, John, *Membership Dir*, Corporate Council for the Arts, Seattle WA

Renfrow, William, *Assoc Prof*, Texas A & I University, Art Department, Kingsville TX (S)

Renger, Konrad, *Cur*, Staatliche Graphische Sammlung, National Graphic Collection, Munich Germany, Federal Republic of

Renner, S Emanuel, *Pres*, College of Saint Benedict, Art Gallery, Saint Joseph MN

Rennie, Dorothy B, *Exhib & Publications*, North Carolina Museum of Art, Department of Cultural Resources, Raleigh NC

Renwick, Allison, *Instr*, Portland Community College, Department of Fine Arts, Portland OR (S)

Reott, Steve, *Instructor*, California College of Arts and Crafts, Oakland CA (S)

Replogle, Jean, *Exec Dir*, Association of Medical Illustrators, Los Angeles CA

Replogle, Rex, *Assoc Prof*, Kansas State University, Art Department, Manhattan KS (S)

Repper, George, *1st VPres*, Lotos Club, New York NY

Repplier, Cynthia, *Coordinator Visitor Services*, Brandywine River Museum, Chadds Ford PA

Reshower, Joe de Cassares, *Lectr*, Georgia Institute of Technology, College of Architecture, Atlanta GA (S)

Resnikoff, Florence, *Instructor*, California College of Arts and Crafts, Oakland CA (S)

Retana, Graciela Reyes, *Dir*, Museo de San Carlos, Museum of San Carlos, Mexico Mexico

Retfalvi, A, *Librn*, University of Toronto, Fine Arts Library, Toronto ON

Reuben, Don S, *Pres*, Art Institute of Chicago, Textile Society, Chicago IL

Reusswig, William, *Visual Communication Chmn*, Atlanta College of Art, Atlanta GA (S)

Reuter, Anneliese, *Dir Education*, Staatliche Kunsthalle, State Art Gallery, Karlshruhe Germany, Federal Republic of

Reuter, Laurel J, *Dir & Head Cur*, University of North Dakota Art Galleries, Grand Forks ND

Reuther, Belinda, *Cur*, Louisiana Historical Association, Confederate Museum, New Orleans LA

Reutlinger, Dagmar E, *Cur Coll*, Worcester Art Museum, Worcester MA

Reutz, John, *Secy*, Gilpin County Arts Association, Central City CO

Revicki, Robert, *Adviser*, Pennsylvania Department of Education, Arts in Education Program, Harrisburg PA

Revor, M Remy, *Prof*, Mount Mary College, Art Department, Milwaukee WI (S)

Rewald, John, *Prof*, City University of New York, PhD Program in Art History, New York NY (S)

Rexroth, Nancy, *Asst Prof*, Wright State University, Art Department, Dayton OH (S)

Rexroth, Nancy, *Instr*, Antioch College, Department of Art, Yellow Springs OH (S)

Reyes, Felipe, *Asst Prof*, University of Texas at San Antonio, Division of Art and Design, San Antonio TX (S)

Reyes, Lawney, *Art & Design Officer*, Seattle-First National Bank, Seattle WA

Reyman, Janusz, *Polish Coins*, Muzeum Narodowe w Krakowie, National Museum in Cracow, Cracow Poland

Reynard, Kenneth D, *Fleet Capt*, Maritime Museum Association of San Diego, San Diego CA

Reynolds, Allie, *Pres*, National Hall of Fame for Famous American Indians, Anadarko OK

Reynolds, Don L, *Asst Dir & Cur Pony Express Stables*, Saint Joseph Museum, Saint Joseph MO

Reynolds, Gary, *Cur*, New York University, Grey Art Gallery and Study Center, New York NY

Reynolds, Harold M, *Asst Prof*, Central Missouri State University, Art Department, Warrensburg MO (S)

Reynolds, Neil, *Pres Board of Dir*, Lake County Civic Center Association, Inc, Heritage Museum and Gallery, Leadville CO

Reynolds, Robert, *Prof*, California Polytechnic State University at San Luis Obispo, Art Department, San Luis Obispo CA (S)

Reynolds, Robert, *Cur Geology*, San Bernardino County Museum and Satellites, Fine Arts Institute, Redlands CA

Reynolds, Ron, *Asst Prof*, Arkansas Tech University, Department of Art, Russellville AR (S)

Reynolds, Stephen, *Assoc Prof*, University of Texas at San Antonio, Division of Art and Design, San Antonio TX (S)

Reynolds, Thomas J, *Registrar*, Germain School of Photography, New York NY (S)

Reynolds, Valrae, *Cur Oriental Coll*, Newark Museum, Newark NJ

Reynolds, Wiley R, *VPres*, Society of the Four Arts, Palm Beach FL

Rezac, Roselyn, *Coordr*, University of Minnesota, Coffman Union Gallery, Minneapolis MN

Rüger, Christoph B, *Dir*, Rheinisches Landesmuseum Bonn, Rhineland Museum, Bonn Germany, Federal Republic of

Rhea, Richard, *Instr*, Tacoma Community College, Art Department, Tacoma WA (S)

Rhein, Donna E, *Librn*, Dallas Museum of Fine Arts, Library, Dallas TX

Rhie, Marilyn M, *Lectr*, Mount Holyoke College, Art Department, South Hadley MA (S)

Rhinehart, Paula, *Exec Secy*, Riverside Art Center and Museum, Riverside CA

Rhoades, Leonard N, *Treas*, Portsmouth Athenaeum NR, Inc 1817, Portsmouth NH

Rhoads, Larry, *Cur Asst*, Illinois State Museum of Natural History and Art, Springfield IL

Rhodes, Adam, *Treas*, Haystack Mountain School of Crafts Gallery, Deer Isle ME

Rhodes, Curtis, *Assoc Prof*, Western Michigan University, Department of Art, Kalamazoo MI (S)

Rhodes, David, *Pres*, School of Visual Arts, New York NY (S)

Rhodes, Glenda, *Head Fine Arts Department*, Salt Lake City Public Library, Fine Arts Department, Salt Lake City UT

Rhodes, Herbert C, *Dir*, Supplementary Educational Center, Art Gallery, Salisbury NC

Rhodes, Jane, *Secy*, Newport Harbor Art Museum, Newport Beach CA

Rhodes, Jim, *Adult Serv Dept*, Topeka Public Library, Topeka KS

Rhodes, Reilly P, *Dir*, Bower's Museum, Santa Ana CA

Rhodes, Silas H, *Chmn*, School of Visual Arts, New York NY (S)

Ricard, Jack, *Dir*, Arizona Watercolor Association, Phoenix AZ

Ricciardi, Dana, *Registrar*, Museum of the American China Trade, Milton MA

Ricciardi, Dana D, *Archivist*, Museum of the American China Trade, Library and Archives, Milton MA

Ricciotti, Dominic, *Asst Prof*, University of Arkansas, Art Department, Fayetteville AR (S)

Rice, Antony, *Asst Prof*, Wesleyan College, Art Department, Macon GA (S)

Rice, Danielle, *Cur of Education*, Wadsworth Atheneum, Hartford CT

Rice, Ed, *Dir*, Gertrude Herbert Memorial Institute of Art, Augusta GA

Rice, Jacquelin, *Head Ceramics*, Rhode Island School of Design, Providence RI (S)

Rice, Nancy, *Instr*, Maryville College, Art Department, Saint Louis MO (S)

Rice, Norman, *Instructor*, Ivy School of Professional Art, Downtown Annex, Pittsburgh PA (S)

Rice, Norman S, *Dir*, Albany Institute of History and Art, Albany NY

Rice, Roberta, *Asst Prof*, University of North Carolina at Greensboro, Art Dept, Greensboro NC (S)

Ricehill, Ernest, *Instructor*, Sioux City Art Center, Sioux City IA (S)

Ricehill Jr, Ernest, *Cur*, Sioux City Art Center, Sioux City IA

Rich, Joseph, *Div Chairperson*, Butte Community College, Humanities Division (III), Oroville CA (S)

Rich, Robert E, *VPres*, Albright-Knox Art Gallery, Buffalo Fine Arts Academy, Buffalo NY

Richard, Jack, *Dir*, Richard Gallery and Almond Tea Gallery, Divisions of Studios of Jack Richard, Cuyahoga Falls OH

Richard, Jack, *Dir*, Studios of Jack Richard Creative School of Design, Cuyahoga Falls OH (S)

Richard, Jim, *Assoc Prof*, University of New Orleans, Dept of Fine Arts, New Orleans LA (S)

Richard, Oscar G, *Dir*, Louisiana State University, Anglo-American Art Museum, Baton Rouge LA

Richard, Paul, *Cur Coll*, Indiana State Museum, Indianapolis IN

Richard, Violet, *Gallery Dir*, Southern Artists Association, Fine Arts Center, Hot Springs AR

Richards, Bruce, *VPres*, Southern Artists Association, Fine Arts Center, Hot Springs AR

Richards, Chuck, *Custodian*, Gibson Society, Inc, Boston MA

Richards, Dick, *Cur Decorative Arts*, Art Gallery of South Australia, Adelaide Australia

Richards, Karl, *Chmn Dept*, Arkansas State University, Department of Art, State University AR (S)

Richards, Karl, *Chmn Department of Art*, Arkansas State University Art Gallery, Jonesboro, Springdale AR

Richards, L W, *Asst Prof*, Nova Scotia Technical College, Faculty of Architecture, Halifax NS (S)

Richards, Lee, *Prof*, New Mexico State University, Art Dept, Las Cruces NM (S)

Richards, Louise S, *Cur Prints & Drawings*, Cleveland Museum of Art, Cleveland OH

Richards, Milton, *Head Dept*, Mohawk Valley Community College, Advertising Design and Production, Utica NY (S)

Richards, Nancy, *Asst Administrator & Cur*, Lyndhurst, Tarrytown NY

Richards, Nancy E, *Cur*, Winterthur Museum and Gardens, Winterthur DE

Richards, Pam, *Custodian*, Gibson Society, Inc, Boston MA

Richards, Peter, *Artist Coordr*, Exploratorium, San Francisco CA

Richards, Richard, *Prof*, Assumption College, Department of Fine Arts and Music, Worcester MA (S)

Richards, Valerie, *Librn*, University of Auckland, Fine Arts Library, Auckland New Zealand

Richardson, Brenda, *Asst Dir of Art*, Baltimore Museum of Art, Baltimore MD

Richardson, Francis, *Assoc Prof*, Ohio State University, Department of the History of Art, Columbus OH (S)

Richardson, Gail, *Librn*, La Jolla Museum of Contemporary Art, Helen Palmer Geisel Library, La Jolla CA

Richardson, Gordon, *Asst Prof*, University of Dayton, Fine Arts Division, Dayton OH (S)

Richardson, James, *Conservator*, Ella Sharp Museum, Jackson MI

Richardson, John A, *Head Art History*, Southern Illinois University at Edwardsville, Department of Art and Design, Edwardsville IL (S)

Richardson, Katherine W, *Asst to Dir*, Essex Institute, Salem MA

Richardson, Thomas W, *Secy*, Phoenix Art Museum, Phoenix AZ

Richardson, Wallace, *Chmn*, Nebraska Arts Council Library, Omaha NE

Richardt, George, *Pres Board*, The Parthenon, Memphis TN

Richelien, Judith, *Librn*, Phillips Collection, Library, Washington DC

Richenburg, Robert, *Prof*, Ithaca College, Art Department, Ithaca NY (S)

Richeson, Joan, *Instructor*, Mount Saint Clare College, Art Department, Clinton IA (S)

Richman, Gary, *Asst Prof*, University of Rhode Island, Department of Art, Kingston RI (S)

Richman, Irwin, *Prof*, Pennsylvania State University, Capitol Campus, Department of Humanities, Middletown PA (S)

Richman, Roberta, *Coordr*, Hera Educational Foundation, Hera Gallery, Wakefield RI

Richmond, Bill, *Gallery Coordr*, University of Evansville, Krannert Gallery, Evansville IN

Richmond, Neal W, *Art Librn and Cur*, Queens College of the City University of New York, Art Collection, Flushing NY

Richmond, William, *Asst Prof*, University of Evansville, Art Dept, Evansville IN (S)

Richter, John, *VPres*, Art Centre of New Jersey, East Orange NJ

Richter, Mischa, *VPres*, Provincetown Art Association and Museum, Provincetown MA

Rickels, Robert E, *Chmn Art Dept*, Concordia College, Art Department, Saint Paul MN (S)

Ricketts, Nancy, *Library Asst In Charge of Interlibrary Loan & Periodicals*, Sheldon Jackson College, Stratton Library, Sitka AK

Ridder, Daniel H, *Treas*, Los Angeles County Museum of Art, Los Angeles CA

Riddle, Verna B, *Library Dir*, Kansas City Art Institute, Library, Kansas City MO

Ridenhower, Elizabeth, *Prof*, Trinity University, Department of Art, San Antonio TX (S)

Rider, Marianna, *Cur*, Stradling Museum of the Horse, Inc, Patagonia AZ

Ridge, A D, *Provincial Archivist*, Department of Culture, Government of the Province of Alberta, Provincial Archives of Alberta, Edmonton AB

Ridgway, William C, *Chmn Bd Trustees*, Mystic Seaport Museum, Inc, Mystic CT

Ridington, Thomas, *Asst Prof*, La Salle College, Department of Fine Arts, Philadelphia PA (S)

Ridington, Thomas, *Cur*, La Salle College Art Gallery, Philadelphia PA

Ridley, Bob, *Instr*, Sierra College, Art Department, Rocklin CA (S)

Ried, Megan, *Cur of Design & Displays*, Dacotah Prairie Museum, Aberdeen SD

Riederer, Josef, *Dir*, Staatliche Museen Preussischer Kulturbesitz, Rathgen-Research-Laboratory, Berlin Germany, Federal Republic of

Riedinger, Robert J, *Correspondence Secy*, Artists' Fellowship, Inc, New York NY

Rieger, Sonja, *Asst Prof*, University of Alabama in Birmingham, Department of Art, Birmingham AL (S)

Riel, Pamela, *Educ Coordr*, Manchester Institute of Arts and Sciences Gallery, Manchester NH

Riel, Pamela, *Educational Coordr*, Manchester Institute of Arts and Sciences, Manchester NH (S)

Rifai, Maggie, *Admin Asst & Secy*, Kentucky Guild of Artists and Craftsmen Inc, Berea KY

Riffle, Brenda, *Librn*, Hampshire County Public Library, Romney WV

Rigby, Bruce, *Asst Prof*, Trenton State College, Art Department, Trenton NJ (S)

Rigdon, Jerry, *Pres*, Arts for Living Center, Burlington IA

Riggins, Lois, *Cur of Education*, Tennessee State Museum, Nashville TN

Riggs, Cynthia, *Comptroller*, Huntington Galleries, Huntington WV

Riggs, Don, *Head Librn*, Arizona State University, Howe Architecture Library, Tempe AZ

Riggs, Don, *Chief Librn*, Arizona State University, Hayden Library, Tempe AZ

Riggs, George W, *Asst Adminr*, National Gallery of Art, Washington DC

Riggs, Timothy A, *Cur Prints & Drawings*, Worcester Art Museum, Worcester MA

Rights, Edith A, *Librn*, Montclair Art Museum, LeBrun Library, Montclair NJ

Rigsby, Joe, *Instructor*, Murray State University, Art Department, Murray KY (S)

Riisön, Thale, *Cur*, Vestlandske Kunstindustrimuseum, Western Norway Museum of Applied Art, Bergen Norway

Riksen, Ron, *Chmn Visual Communications*, Kendall School of Design, Grand Rapids MI (S)

Riley, Carroll L, *Adj Cur Anthropology*, Southern Illinois University Museum and Art Galleries, Carbondale IL

Riley, Dot, *Pres*, Lansing Art Gallery, Lansing MI

Riley, Judith C, *Registrar*, Chrysler Museum, Norfolk VA

Riley, Orrin, *Conservator*, Solomon R Guggenheim Museum, New York NY

Rindlisbacher, David, *Asst Prof*, West Texas State University, Art Department, Canyon TX (S)

Rinehart, Michael, *Librn*, Sterling and Francine Clark Art Institute, Clark Art Institute Library, Williamstown MA

Ring, Eduardo, *Cur*, Centro de Arte y Communicacion, Center of Art and Communication, Buenos Argentina

Ringsmuth, Charles R, *Assoc Prof*, Corning Community College, Division of Humanities, Corning NY (S)

Rini, Theresa, *Asst Librn*, Old Sturbridge Village, Research Library, Sturbridge MA

Rink, Bernard C, *Library Dir*, Northwestern Michigan College, Mark Osterlin Library, Traverse City MI

Riordain, A B O, *Dir*, National Museum of Ireland, Dublin Ireland

Riordan, Claudia, *Researcher*, Northeastern Nevada Museum, Elko NV

Riordan, John, *Prof*, State University of New York College at Potsdam, Department of Fine Arts, Potsdam NY (S)

Riordan, Mary, *Dir*, Muskegon Museum of Art, Muskegon MI

Riorden, Virginia, *Asst Comptroller*, Sterling and Francine Clark Art Institute, Williamstown MA

Riordon, Bernard, *Secy & Cur*, Art Gallery of Nova Scotia, Halifax NS

Rios, John, *Prof*, Texas Woman's University, Department of Art, Denton TX (S)

Ripley, S Dillon, *Secy*, Smithsonian Institution, Washington DC

Rippe, Peter, *Executive Dir*, Roanoke Fine Arts Center, Roanoke VA

Ripper, Stephen, *Instructor*, Bucks County Community College, Fine Arts Department, Newton PA (S)

Rippeteau, Bruce, *State Archaeolgist*, Colorado Historical Society, Colorado Heritage Center, Denver CO

Ripton, Michael J, *Dir Bureau of Museum*, Pennsylvania Historical and Museum Commission, Harrisburg PA

Risatti, Howard, *Asst Prof*, University of Alabama in Birmingham, Department of Art, Birmingham AL (S)

Riser, Harry, *First VPres*, Hoosier Salon Patrons Association, Hoosier Salon Art Gallery, Indianapolis IN

Rishel, Joseph, *Cur Paintings before 1900*, Philadelphia Museum of Art, Philadelphia PA

Rishel, Joseph J, *Cur*, Philadelphia Museum of Art, John Graver Johnson Collection, Philadelphia PA

Rising, Joan, *Art Historian*, Greenfield Community College, Art Department, Greenfield MA (S)

Risley, John, *Chmn*, Wesleyan University, Art Department, Middletown CT (S)

Riss, Murray, *Asst Prof*, Southwestern at Memphis, Dept of Art, Memphis TN (S)

Risseeuw, John, *Asst Prof*, University of South Dakota, Dept of Art, Vermillion SD (S)

Ristine, James D, *Exhib*, Minnesota Museum of Art, Saint Paul MN

Ritch, Andrew J, *VPres*, Hill Country Arts Foundation, Ingram TX

Ritchie, Adam B, *Deputy Dir*, Dundee Museums and Art Gallery, Dundee Scotland

Ritchie, Andrew C, *Board Dir Member*, Art Information Center, Inc, New York NY

Ritchie, Grace, *Asst Cur J M W Turner Collection*, Indianapolis Museum of Art, Indianapolis IN

Ritchie, Ross, *Exhibitions Designer*, Auckland City Art Gallery, Auckland New Zealand

Ritchie, Verna Ford, *Librn*, University of Northern Iowa, Art and Music Dept Library, Cedar Falls IA

Ritscher, Carol, *Secy*, Palos Verdes Art Center, Rancho Palos Verdes CA

Ritter, E W, *Pres*, Brevard Art Center and Museum, Inc, Melbourne FL

Ritter, Josef, *Instructor*, Cazenovia College, Art Program, Cazenovia NY (S)

Ritter, Robert, *Dir Public Relations*, Greenfield Village and Henry Ford Museum, Dearborn MI

Ritterskamp, John P, *Assoc Prof*, Antioch College, Department of Art, Yellow Springs OH (S)

Rivard, Nancy, *Cur American Art*, Detroit Institute of Arts, Detroit MI

Rivera-Torres, Carmen, *Admin Asst*, Bronx Museum of the Arts, Bronx NY

Rivero, Gullermo, *Asst to Dir*, Universidad de las Americas, Library, Cholula Mexico

Rivoire, Helena G, *Chief Technical Services*, Bucknell University, Ellen Clarke Bertrand Library, Lewisburg PA

Roach, Juanetta, *Librn*, Tougaloo College, Library, Tougaloo MS

Roach-Higgins, Mary, *Prof*, University of Wisconsin, Madison, School of Family Resources and Consumer Sciences, Madison WI (S)

Robbert, Paul, *Prof*, Western Michigan University, Department of Art, Kalamazoo MI (S)

Robbins, Anne, *Asst Prof*, Southwestern at Memphis, Dept of Art, Memphis TN (S)

Robbins, Caroline, *VPres*, Historical Society of Pennsylvania, Philadelphia PA

Robbins, Phyllis Y, *Instr*, American River College, Department of Art, Sacramento CA (S)

Robbins, Warren M, *Dir*, Museum of African Art, Washington DC

Robbins, William R, *Dir*, Brant County Museum, Brantford ON

Robels, Hella, *Cur Engravings*, Museen der Stadt Köln, Wallraf-Richartz-Museum, Museum Ludwig, Cologne Germany, Federal Republic of

Roberds, Gene, *Coordr Fine Art*, Florida School of the Arts, Visual Arts, Palatka FL (S)

Roberson, Samuel, *Chmn Art History*, Herron School of Art, Indiana University-Purdue University, Indianapolis, Indianapolis IN (S)

Robert Jr, Henry Flood, *Dir*, Joslyn Art Museum, Omaha NE

Roberts, Charles, *Treas*, Erie Art Center, Erie PA

Roberts, Cynthia, *Slide Cur*, School of Visual Arts Library, New York NY

Roberts, George, *Prof*, University of Idaho, Department of Art and Architecture, Moscow ID (S)

Roberts, Helene, *Cur Visual Coll*, Harvard University, Fine Arts Library, Cambridge MA

Roberts, Laura, *Cur Education*, Rhode Island Historical Society, Providence RI

Roberts, Lois, *Treas*, South Peace Art Society, Dawson Creek Museum Art Gallery, Dawson Creek BC

Roberts, Louis, *Pres*, Artists Association of Nantucket, Kenneth Taylor Gallery, Nantucket MA

Roberts, Mary C, *Assoc Prof*, Northwestern State University of Louisiana, Dept of Art, Natchitoches LA (S)

Roberts, Maureen, *Gallery Coordr*, Philadelphia College of Textiles and Science, Paley Design Center, Philadelphia PA

Roberts, Ruth, *Cur*, Shaker Museum, Old Chatham NY

Roberts, Sally, *Vis Assoc Prof*, Drew University, Art Department, Madison NJ (S)

Robertshaw, Mary Jane, *Instr*, College of New Rochelle, Art Department, New Rochelle NY (S)

Roberts-Jones, Philippe, *Dir*, Musees Royaux des Beaux-Arts de Belgique, Royal Museums of Fine Arts of Belgium, Brussels Belgium

Robertson, Charles M, *pres*, School Art League of New York City, Brooklyn NY

Robertson, Cheryl, *Asst Cur Decorative Arts & Prairie Archives*, Milwaukee Art Center, Milwaukee WI

Robertson, Donald, *Assoc Prof*, Northwest Missouri State University, Dept of Art, Maryville MO (S)

Robertson, Donald, *Prof*, Tulane University, Newcomb College, New Orleans LA (S)

Robertson, George H, *Pres*, Mohawk Valley Community College, Advertising Design and Production, Utica NY (S)

Robertson, Joan E, *Art Cur*, Kemper Group, Long Grove IL

Robertson, Joe Chris, *Chmn*, Mars Hill College, Mars Hill NC (S)

Robertson, John K, *Pres*, Professional Art Dealers Association of Canada, Toronto ON

Robertson, Johnye, *Instr*, Paris Junior College, Art Department, Paris TX (S)

Robertson, Roderick, *Asst Prof*, Saint Mary's College, Art Department, Winona MN (S)

Roberts III, Percival R, *Chmn Dept of Art*, Bloomsburg State College, Haas Gallery of Art, Bloomsburg PA

Roberts III, Percival R, *Chmn Dept*, Bloomsburg State College, Department of Art, Bloomsburg PA (S)

Robidoux, Omer, *Dir*, Eskimo Museum, Churchill MB

Robins, Marty, *Asst Prof*, Texas Tech University, Department of Art, Lubbock TX (S)

Robinson, D, *Keeper Paintings & Drawings*, University of Cambridge, Fitzwilliam Museum, Cambridge England

Robinson, Don D, *Chmn Dept*, Harding University, Department of Art, Searcy AR (S)

Robinson, Douglas, *Registrar*, Hirshhorn Museum and Sculpture Garden, Washington DC

Robinson, Eric, *Mgr*, Delaware Art Museum, Downtown Gallery, Wilmington DE

Robinson, Francis W, *Cur Emeritus Medieval Art*, Detroit Institute of Arts, Detroit MI

Robinson, Franklin, *Dir*, Rhode Island School of Design, Museum of Art, Providence RI

Robinson, George, *Assoc Prof,* Bethel College, Department of Art, Saint Paul MN (S)

Robinson, Grove, *Chmn Dept Art,* Union University, Department of Art, Jackson TN (S)

Robinson, Henry S, *Prof,* Case Western Reserve University, Department of Art, Cleveland OH (S)

Robinson, Joyce, *Dir Educational Prog,* Colorado Springs Fine Arts Center, Colorado Springs CO

Robinson, Lilien F, *Chmn,* George Washington University, Department of Art, Washington DC (S)

Robinson, Mary Ann, *Chmn Art Dept,* McPherson College, McPherson KS

Robinson, Mary Ann, *Chmn,* McPherson College, Art Department, McPherson KS (S)

Robinson, Orvetta, *Librn,* Illinois State Museum of Natural History and Art, Library, Springfield IL

Robinson, P, *Dir Science Museum,* Birmingham Museums and Art Gallery, Birmingham England

Robinson, Ralph, *Treas,* Gaston County Art and History Museum, Dallas NC

Robinson, Roger W, *Dir,* Willard House and Clock Museum, Inc, Grafton MA

Robinson, Roger W, *Pres,* Willard House and Clock Museum, Inc, Grafton MA

Robinson, Susan Barnes, *Asst Prof,* Loyola Marymount University, Department of Art, Los Angeles CA (S)

Robinson, William A, *Dir,* University of Houston, Sarah Campbell Blaffer Gallery, Houston TX

Robinson Jr, E B, *Chmn Board of Trustees,* Mississippi Museum of Art, Jackson MS

Robischon, Helen, *Library Asst,* University of Southern California, Architecture and Fine Arts Library, Los Angeles CA

Robishaw, Richard, *Asst Prof,* Springfield College, Department of Visual and Performing Arts, Springfield MA (S)

Robison, Andrew, *Pres,* Print Council of America, Washington DC

Robison, Charles, *Chmn Art and Music,* Angelo State University, Art and Music Department, San Angelo TX (S)

Robison, Joan, *Librn,* Baltimore Museum of Art, Library, Baltimore MD

Robison Jr, Andrew, *Cur Prints & Drawings,* National Gallery of Art, Washington DC

Roche, Valerie, *Instr,* Creighton University, Fine and Performing Arts Department, Omaha NE (S)

Rocher-Jauneau, Madeleine, *Chief Cur,* Musee des Beaux-Arts, Palais Saint Pierre, Museum of Fine Arts, Lyon France

Rochette, Edward C, *Exec VPres,* American Numismatic Association, Colorado Springs CO

Rochford, Paul A, *Prof,* Hiram College, Art Department, Hiram OH (S)

Rock, John, *Asst Dir,* Oregon State University, Fairbanks Gallery, Corvallis OR

Rockefeller, David, *VChmn,* Museum of Modern Art, New York NY

Rockefeller III, John D, *Pres,* Museum of Modern Art, New York NY

Rock Jr, William, *Chmn,* University of Toronto, Department of Landscape Architecture, Toronto ON (S)

Rockmuller, Rebecca, *Chief of Public Services,* Hewlett-Woodmere Public Library, Hewlett NY

Rod, Donald O, *Dir,* University of Northern Iowa, Art and Music Dept Library, Cedar Falls IA

Rodbard, Betty, *Treas,* National Watercolor Society, Pasadena CA

Rode, Meredith, *Prof,* University of the District of Columbia, Art Department, Washington DC (S)

Rode, Penny, *Instructor,* Ivy School of Professional Art, Downtown Annex, Pittsburgh PA (S)

Roderick, Carolyn, *Librn,* French Art Colony, Inc, Library, Gallipolis OH

Rodgers, David, *Cur,* Central Art Gallery, Wolverhampton England

Rodgers, Jack A, *Exec Dir,* San Antonio Art Institute, San Antonio TX (S)

Rodgers, Linda, *Pres,* Wayne Art Center, Wayne PA

Rodgers, Linda, *Pres,* Wayne Art Center, Wayne PA (S)

Rodgers, Mary M, *Asst to Dir,* Wine Museum of San Francisco, San Francisco CA

Rodgers, Mary M, *Librn,* Wine Museum of San Francisco, Alfred Fromm Rare Wine Books Library, San Francisco CA

Rodino, Simonetta Prosperi, *Asst,* Instituto Nazionale per la Grafica, Rome Italy

Rodrigues, Richard, *Coordr Fine Arts,* City College of San Francisco, Art Department, San Francisco CA (S)

Rodriquez, Carlos, *Dir,* National Museum of Colonial Art of the Casa de la Cultura Educatoriana, Quito Ecuador

Rodriquez, Peter, *Founder & Dir,* Mexican Museum, San Francisco CA

Rodwell, Marianne, *Lectr,* Cardinal Stritch College, Art Department, Milwaukee WI (S)

Roe, Albert S, *Prof,* Cornell University, Department of the History of Art, Ithaca NY (S)

Roe, Ruth, *Librn,* Newport Harbor Art Museum, Library, Newport Beach CA

Roebuck, Rhonda, *Asst Prof,* Jacksonville State University, Art Department, Pelham, Jacksonville AL (S)

Roerich, Svetoslav, *VPres,* Nicholas Roerich Museum, New York NY

Roese, Ronnie, *Cur of Exhib,* Dallas Historical Society, Dallas TX

Roeyer, Mark, *Exhib Designer,* Spencer Museum of Art, Lawrence KS

Rogan, Robert C, *Head Dept,* Lamar University, Art Department, Beaumont TX (S)

Rogers, Charles B, *Dir,* Rogers House Museum Gallery, Ellsworth KS

Rogers, Elizabeth, *Secy,* Leatherstocking Brush and Palette Club Inc, Cooperstown NY

Rogers, Francis D, *VPres,* Art Commission of the City of New York, Associates of the Art Commission, Inc, New York NY

Rogers, Gail, *Executive Dir,* Craftsmen's Association of British Columbia, Vancouver BC

Rogers, George P, *First VPres,* Arts Club of Chicago, Chicago IL

Rogers, Jac, *Dept Chmn,* Spokane Falls Community College, Creative & Performing Arts, Spokane WA (S)

Rogers, James W, *Asst Prof,* Glenville State College, Department of Art, Glenville WV (S)

Rogers, John L, *Head Dept,* Aurora College, Art Department, Aurora IL (S)

Rogers, Les, *Historian,* Alaska Association for the Arts, Fairbanks AK

Rogers, Malcolm, *Asst Keeper Archive & Library,* National Portrait Gallery, Library, London England

Rogers, Marjorie, *Museum Education,* University of California, Los Angeles, Museum of Cultural History, Los Angeles CA

Rogers, Millard F, *Dir,* Cincinnati Art Museum, Cincinnati OH

Rogers, Riley, *Dir,* Fine Arts Club, Second Crossing Gallery, Valley City ND

Rogers, Robert, *Asst Prof,* Queensborough Community College, Department of Art and Design, Bayside NY (S)

Rogers, Samuel S, *Pres,* Merrimack Valley Textile Museum, North Andover MA

Rogers, Warren, *Pres,* Society of Illustrators, New York NY

Roger-Smith, Karreen, *Public Relations Coordr,* University of Rochester, Memorial Art Gallery, Rochester NY

Rogerson, Terry V, *Asst Gallery Supt & Preparator,* University of Utah, Utah Museum of Fine Arts, Salt Lake City UT

Rogge, Steve, *Dir,* Mason City Public Library, Mason City IA

Rogoff, Anita, *Assoc Prof,* Case Western Reserve University, Department of Art, Cleveland OH (S)

Rohlfing, Christian, *Asst Dir for Coll,* Cooper-Hewitt Museum, Smithsonian Institution National Museum of Design, New York NY

Rohm, Robert H, *Prof,* University of Rhode Island, Department of Art, Kingston RI (S)

Rohmoser, Albin, *Cur Art History,* Saltzburger Museum Carolino Augusteum, Salzburg Museum, Salzburg Austria

Rohn, David, *Vis Instr,* Drew University, Art Department, Madison NJ (S)

Rohozynsky, K, *VPres,* Ukrainian Museum, New York NY

Roizen, Moises, *Chmn,* West Valley College, Art Department, Saratoga CA (S)

Roland, George, *Prof,* Allegheny College, Art Department, Meadville PA (S)

Rolfing, Sue, *Secy,* Hockaday Center for the Arts, Flathead Valley Art Association, Kalispell MT

Roller, Gilbert, *Head Art Dept,* Asbury College, Student Center Gallery, Wilmore KY

Roller, Gilbert, *Div Head,* Asbury College, Art Dept, Wilmore KY (S)

Roller, Marion, *Chmn Design Dept,* Traphagen School of Fashion, New York NY (S)

Roller, Russell, *Chmn,* Northeastern Illinois University, Art Department, Chicago IL (S)

Roller, Russell, *Dept Chmn,* Northestern Illinois University, North River Community Gallery, Chicago IL

Roller, Terry, *Instructor,* Eastern Illinois University, Art Department, Charleston IL (S)

Rollins, Caroline, *Membership, Sales & Information,* Yale University, Art Gallery, New Haven CT

Rollman-Shay, Charlotte, *Instructor,* Oxbow Summer Art Workshops, Saugatuck MI (S)

Rollman-Shay, Ed, *Instructor,* Oxbow Summer Art Workshops, Saugatuck MI (S)

Roloff, Daphne, *Dir of Libraries,* Art Institute of Chicago, Ryerson and Burnham Libraries, Chicago IL

Roloff, Daphne, *Chmn-elect,* Special Libraries Association, Museum, Arts and Humanities Division, New York NY

Roloff, Daphne, *Dir Libraries,* Art Institute of Chicago, Chicago IL

Rolujo, Takatsugu, *Chief Cur,* Bridgestone Bijutsukan, Bridgestone Museum of Art, Tokyo Japan

Romancito, Rick, *Audio-Visual Coordr,* Millicent Rogers Museum, Taos NM

Romanek, V, *Asst Prof,* Pennsylvania State University, Fayette Campus, Department of Art, Uniontown PA (S)

Romano, Giovanni, *Pres,* Galleria Sabauda, Turin Italy

Romano, Giovanni, *Pres,* Armeria Reale, Turin Italy

Romano, James, *Asst Cur Egyptian & Classical Art,* Brooklyn Museum, Brooklyn NY

Romano, Salvatore, *Asst Prof,* Herbert H Lehman College, Art Department, Bronx NY (S)

Romano, Umberto, *Dir,* Umberto Romano School of Creative Art, New York NY (S)

Rombout, Luke, *Dir,* Vancouver Art Gallery, Vancouver BC

Romero, Ernest S, *Pres,* Taos Art Association Inc, Taos NM

Rompf, Julienne, *Prof,* Marian College, Art Department, Eau Claire WI (S)

Ronberg, Jim, *Artist in Res,* Sun Valley Center for the Arts & Humanities, Department of Fine Art, Sun Valley ID (S)

Roncalli, Francesco, *Cur Etruscan Antiquities (Etruscan Museum),* Monumenti Musei e Gallerie Pontificie, Vatican Museums and Galleries, Vatican City Italy

Ronte, Dieter, *Cur Engravings,* Museen der Stadt Köln, Wallraf-Richartz-Museum, Museum Ludwig, Cologne Germany, Federal Republic of

Ronte, Dieter, *Dir,* Museum Moderner Kunst, Museum of Modern Art, Vienna Austria

Rooney, Andrew A, *Pres,* Lockwood-Mathews Mansion Museum, Norwalk CT

Rooney, Judity M, *Cur,* Museum of Fine Arts, Houston, Houston TX

Rooney, Paul M, *Dir,* Buffalo and Erie County Public Library, Buffalo NY

Rooney, Thomas P, *Chmn,* Catholic University of America, Department of Art, Washington DC (S)

Roos, Gabrielle, *Assoc Prof,* City College of the City of New York, Art Department, New York NY (S)

Roosevelt, Anna C, *Cur South America*, Museum of the American Indian, New York NY

Root, Margaret C, *Asst Cur*, University of Michigan Museum of Art, Kelsey Museum of Ancient and Medieval Archaeology, Ann Arbor MI

Root, Stanley, *Pres*, Philadelphia Museum of Art, Women's Committee, Philadelphia PA

Roozen, Mary Louise, *In Charge Art Coll*, The Marine Corporation, Milwaukee WI

Ropko, Frederick, *Assoc Prof*, University of the District of Columbia, Art Department, Washington DC (S)

Rorem, Jan, *Assoc Prof*, Black Hawk College, Art Dept, Moline IL (S)

Rorimer, Anne, *Assoc Cur 20th Century Painting & Sculpture*, Art Institute of Chicago, Chicago IL

Rorup, Marianne, *Librn*, Statens Museum for Kunst, Department of Prints and Drawings Library, Copenhagen Denmark

Rosa, Joyce, *Prof*, School of the Arts, C W Post Center of Long Island University, Art Department, Greenvale NY (S)

Rosand, David, *Chmn*, Columbia University, Department of Art History and Archaeology, New York NY (S)

Rosati, Angelo V, *Prof*, Rhode Island College, Art Department, Providence RI (S)

Rose, Jack, *Dir Fashion*, Art Institute of Fort Lauderdale, Fort Lauderdale FL (S)

Rose, Jeanne, *Corresp Secy*, Arts Club of Washington, James Monroe House, Washington DC

Rose, Knuse, *Rector*, Statens Kunstakademi, State Art Academy, Oslo Norway (S)

Rose, Larry, *Instructor*, Oklahoma State University, School of Technical Training, Okmulgee OK (S)

Rose, Margaret, *Acquisitions Librn*, Art Center College of Design, James Lemont Fogg Memorial Library, Pasadena CA

Rose, P D, *Head Dept Combined Arts*, Brighton Polytechnic, Faculty of Art and Design, Brighton England (S)

Rose, Patricia, *Assoc Chairperson Art History*, Florida State University, Art Department, Tallahassee FL (S)

Rose, Richard, *Cur*, Hartwick College Fine Art Gallery, Yager Museum, Oneonta NY

Rose, Roger C, *Cur Education*, San Diego Museum of Art, San Diego CA

Rose, Timothy G, *Dir*, Springville Museum of Art, Springville UT

Roseberg, Carl, *Prof*, College of William and Mary, Department of Fine Arts, Williamsburg VA (S)

Roseberry, Helen, *Registrar*, East Tennessee State University, Carroll Reece Museum, Johnson City TN

Rosegrant, Julie, *Treas*, Brattleboro Museum and Art Center, Brattleboro VT

Rosemfeld, Myra Nan, *Research Cur*, Montreal Museum of Fine Arts, Montreal PQ

Rosen, Barry H, *Dir & Archivist*, University of South Carolina, McKissick Museums, Columbia SC

Rosen, James M, *Prof*, Santa Rosa Junior College, Art Department, Santa Rosa CA (S)

Rosen, Steven W, *Chief Cur*, Columbus Museum of Art, Columbus OH

Rosenbaum, Allen, *Acting Dir*, Princeton University, Art Museum, Princeton NJ

Rosenberg, Amy, *Asst Cur*, University of Michigan Museum of Art, Kelsey Museum of Ancient and Medieval Archaeology, Ann Arbor MI

Rosenberg, Barry A, *Asst Prof*, Miami University, Art Department, Oxford OH (S)

Rosenberg, Herbert, *Asst Prof*, Jersey City State College, Art Department, Jersey City NJ (S)

Rosenberg, Kay, *Asst Prof*, Bradford College, Art Department, Bradford MA (S)

Rosenberg, Marcia, *School Administrator*, Danforth Museum School, Framingham MA (S)

Rosenberg, Marti, *Coordr of Tennessee State Museum Association Inc*, Tennessee State Museum, Nashville TN

Rosenberg, Paul B, *Pres Board of Trustees*, Danforth Museum, Framingham MA

Rosenberger, James, *Audience & Program Development Dir*, Contemporary Arts Center, Cincinnati OH

Rosenberger, Pat, *Executive Dir*, Valley Art Center Inc, Clarkston WA

Rosenblatt, Arthur, *VPres Architecture & Planning*, Metropolitan Museum of Art, New York NY

Rosenfeld, Edie, *Instr*, Spring Arbor College, Art Department, Spring Arbor MI (S)

Rosenfeld, L, *Cur Coll*, Edinboro State College, Art Department, Edinboro PA (S)

Rosenfield, Ethel, *Instr*, Toronto School of Art, Toronto ON (S)

Rosenfield, Rachel, *Assoc Cur*, Portland Art Association, Portland OR

Rosenstein, Harris, *Exec Adminr*, Rice University, Institute for the Arts, Rice Museum, Houston TX

Rosensweig, Larry, *Cur*, Palm Beach County Parks and Recreation Department, Morikami Museum of Japanese Culture, Delray Beach FL

Rosenthal, Donald A, *Cur of Coll*, University of Rochester, Memorial Art Gallery, Rochester NY

Rosenthal, Earl, *Prof*, University of Chicago, Department of Art History & Committee on Art & Design, Chicago IL (S)

Rosenthal, Gertrude, *Consultant for Western Art*, Honolulu Academy of Arts, Honolulu HI

Rosenthal, John W, *Dir*, Rosenthal Art Slides, Chicago IL

Rosenthal, Mark, *Cur of Coll*, University of California, University Art Museum, Berkeley CA

Rosenthal, Robert, *Assoc Prof*, Hanover College, Department of Art, Hanover IN (S)

Rosenzweig, Harry, *Dir*, Montclair State College, Gallery One, Upper Montclair NJ

Rosevear, Carol, *Librn*, New Brunswick Museum, Library, Saint John NB

Rosing, Larry, *Chmn Visual Arts*, Rutgers, the State University of New Jersey, Mason Gross School of the Arts, New Brunswick NJ (S)

Roskill, Mark, *Prof*, University of Massachusetts, Amherst, Art History Prog, Amherst MA (S)

Roskopp, Joanne, *Pres Bd of Trustees*, Art Center, Mount Clemens MI

Roskos, George, *Prof*, Pacific Lutheran University, Department of Art, Tacoma WA (S)

Rosnow, Nancy, *Asst Prof*, New Mexico Highlands University, Dept of Fine Arts, Las Vegas NM (S)

Rosoff, Sidney, *Secy*, American Craft Council, New York NY

Rosofsky, Seymour, *Instr*, Blackhawk Mountain School of Art, Black Hawk CO (S)

Ross, Alex, *Librn*, Stanford University, Art Library of the Stanford University Libraries, Stanford CA

Ross, Barbara T, *Custodian Prints & Drawings*, Princeton University, Art Museum, Princeton NJ

Ross, David, *Dir*, New Brunswick Museum, Saint John NB

Ross, David, *Chief Cur*, University of California, University Art Museum, Berkeley CA

Ross, Douglas, *Chmn Graduate Committee*, University of Nebraska-Lincoln, Department of Art, Lincoln NE (S)

Ross, F, *Instructor*, Indiana University of Pennsylvania, Department of Art and Art Education, Indiana PA (S)

Ross, Fernande, *Registrar*, Yale University, Art Gallery, New Haven CT

Ross, Gavin T N, *Acting Principal*, Edinburgh College of Art, Edinburgh Scotland (S)

Ross, Jack, *Dean*, Humber College of Applied Arts and Technology, Creative and Communication Arts Division, Rexdale ON (S)

Ross, Joanna H, *Chmn Dept*, Lambuth College, Department of Art, Jackson TN (S)

Ross, John, *Prof*, Manhattanville College, Art Department, Purchase NY (S)

Ross, Joseph B, *Asst Prof*, Saint Mary's College of Maryland, Arts & Letters Div, Saint Mary's City MD (S)

Ross, Judy, *Photographer-in-Residence*, Moravian College, Department of Art, Bethlehem PA (S)

Ross, Louis, *Asst Prof*, Trenton State College, Art Department, Trenton NJ (S)

Ross, Lynda, *Asst Prof*, University of Montana, Dept of Art, Missoula MT (S)

Ross, Mary Anne, *Instructor*, Delta State University, Department of Art, Cleveland MS (S)

Ross, Novelene, *Cur of Education*, Wichita Art Museum, Library, Wichita KS

Ross, Robert F, *Asst Prof*, University of Arkansas, Art Department, Fayetteville AR (S)

Rossbach, Paul R, *Dir Public Relations*, San Antonio Museum Association, Inc, San Antonio TX

Rossiter, Margaret, *Asst Prof*, Sangamon State University, Creative Arts Program, Springfield IL (S)

Rossol, Monona, *Pres*, Artist-Craftsmen of New York, New York NY

Roster, Laila, *Dir*, Contemporary Arts Center of Hawaii, Honolulu HI

Rostworowski, Marek, *European Painting of the 15th - 17th Centuries*, Muzeum Narodowe w Krakowie, National Museum in Cracow, Cracow Poland

Rosvall, Margareta, *First Library Asst*, Nationalmuseum, Library, Stockholm Sweden

Roth, Elizabeth, *Keeper of Prints*, New York Public Library, Prints Division, New York NY

Roth, Leland M, *Asst Prof*, Northwestern University, Evanston, Department of Art History, Evanston IL (S)

Roth, Mardee, *VPres*, Alaska Association for the Arts, Fairbanks AK

Roth, Moira, *Assoc Prof*, University of California, San Diego, Visual Arts Department, La Jolla CA (S)

Rothe, Janet, *Cur Collections*, Paine Art Center and Arboretum, Oshkosh WI

Rothenberg, Jack, *Chmn*, City College of the City of New York, Art Department, New York NY (S)

Rotherberg, Jacob, *Chmn Art Department*, City College of the City of New York, Eisner Hall Art Gallery, New York NY

Rothholz, Peter, *Chmn*, Queens Museum, Flushing NY

Rothman, Joseph, *VPres*, New York Artists Equity Association, Inc, New York NY

Rothrock, Ilse S, *Librn*, Kimbell Art Museum, Library, Fort Worth TX

Rothstein, Laura, *Pres*, Kennebec Valley Art Association, Harlow Gallery, Hallowell ME

Rotramel, Betty, *Secy*, Eureka Springs Guild of Artists and Crafts People, Eureka Springs AR

Rotterdam, Paul, *Sr Lectr*, Harvard University, Department of Visual and Environmental Studies, Cambridge MA (S)

Rotterdam, Paul, *Vis Prof*, University of Texas at San Antonio, Division of Art and Design, San Antonio TX (S)

Rottermund, Andrzej, *VDir*, Muzeum Narodowe, National Museum, Warsaw Poland

Roudzens, Mark, *Prof*, Salem State College, Art Department, Salem MA (S)

Rouillard, Paul R, *Secy-Treas*, National Museum of Racing, Inc, Saratoga Springs NY

Roulet, Ann, *Pres*, Cleveland Institute of Art, Cleveland Art Association, Cleveland OH

Roulston, P, *Resource Centre*, University of Regina, Norman Mackenzie Art Gallery, Regina SK

Roulston, Pat, *Librn*, University of Regina, Norman Mackenzie Art Gallery Resource Centre, Regina SK

Rounds, Earl, *Treas*, Bristol Art Museum, Bristol RI

Rounsavall, Cathryn, *Instructor*, Arkansas Arts Center, Little Rock AR (S)

Rourke, Orland J, *Asst Prof*, Concordia College, Art Department, Moorhead MN (S)

Rouse, Jeffrey P, *Registrar*, Westmoreland County Museum of Art, Greensburg PA

Rouse, John R, *Dir & Cur*, Wichita Art Association Inc, Wichita KS

Rouse, John R, *Dir*, School of the Wichita Art Association, Wichita KS (S)

Rouse, John R, *Dir*, Wichita Art Association Inc, Maude Schollenberger Memorial Library, Wichita KS

Rouse, Terrie, *Cur*, Studio Museum in Harlem, New York NY

Rousek, Marie, *Librn*, College of Saint Elizabeth, Mahoney Library, Convent Station NJ

Roush, Jack, *Public Information Coordr*, Millicent Rogers Museum, Taos NM

Rousseau, Irene, *Pres*, American Abstract Artists, Summit NJ

Rousseve, Numa, *Prof Emeritus*, Xavier University of Louisiana, Department of Fine Arts, New Orleans LA (S)

Roux, Emmanuel, *Mgr*, Lotos Club, New York NY

Rovetti, Paul F, *Dir*, University of Connecticut, William Benton Museum of Art, Storrs CT

Row, Brian G, *Chmn*, Southwest Texas State University, Department of Art, San Marcos TX (S)

Rowan, George, *Assoc Prof*, University of New Orleans, Dept of Fine Arts, New Orleans LA (S)

Rowan, Gerald, *Prog Coordr*, Northampton County Area Community College, Art Department, Bethlehem PA (S)

Rowan, Herman, *Chmn Dept*, University of Minnesota, Minneapolis, Department of Studio Art, Minneapolis MN (S)

Rowan, Madeline Bronsdon, *Cur of Ethnology & Public Programming*, University of British Columbia, Museum of Anthropology, Vancouver BC

Rowan, Odessa W, *Corresponding Secy*, Spectrum, Friends of Fine Art, Inc, Toledo OH

Rowe, Ann P, *Asst Cur New World*, Textile Museum, Washington DC

Rowe, Bobby Louise, *Asst Prof*, Middle Tennessee State University, Art Dept, Murfreesboro TN (S)

Rowe, Donald, *Chmn*, Olivet College, Art Dept, Olivet MI (S)

Rowe, Donald F, *Dir*, Loyala University of Chigago, Martin D'Arcy Gallery of Art, Chicago IL

Rowe, M Jessica, *Dir*, Blanden Memorial Art Gallery, Fort Dodge IA

Rowe, Reginald M, *Instr*, San Antonio Art Institute, San Antonio TX (S)

Rowe, Ria, *Admin Officer*, University of British Columbia, Museum of Anthropology, Vancouver BC

Rowe, Robert, *Dir*, Leeds Art Galleries, Leeds England

Rowe, William Thomas, *Assoc Prof*, Saint Mary's College of Maryland, Arts & Letters Div, Saint Mary's City MD (S)

Rowell, Edwin W, *Cur*, Historical Society of Early American Decoration, Inc, Cooperstown NY

Rowell, Margit, *Cur*, Solomon R Guggenheim Museum, New York NY

Rowinski, L J, *Dir*, University of Alaska, Museum, Fairbanks AK

Rowland, Elden, *Instructor*, Friends of the Arts and Sciences, Hilton Leech Studio, Sarasota FL (S)

Rowland, Katherine L, *Consultant Special Projects*, Friends of the Arts and Sciences, Hilton Leech Studio, Sarasota FL (S)

Rowley, Susan, *Instructor*, Nazareth College of Rochester, Art Department, Rochester NY (S)

Rowlison, Eric, *Dir*, National Gallery of Victoria, Melbourne Australia

Roworth, Wendy, *Asst Prof*, University of Rhode Island, Department of Art, Kingston RI (S)

Roy, Barbara, *Catalog Librn*, Presbyterian Historical Society, Philadelphia PA

Roy, Carmen, *Senior Scientist Canadian Centre for Folk Culture Studies*, National Museum of Man, Ottawa ON

Roy, James, *Chmn*, Saint Cloud State University, Department of Art, Saint Cloud MN (S)

Roy, Jeanne, *Supvr*, Musee des Augustines de l'Hotel Dieu of Quebec, Quebec PQ

Roy, Margery, *Admin Asst*, Mount Holyoke College Art Museum, South Hadley MA

Roy, Rob, *Chairperson Dept*, Suomi College, Fine Arts Department, Hancock MI (S)

Royce, Diana, *Head Librn*, Stowe-Day Foundation, Stowe-Day Library, Hartford CT

Roycroft, R, *Community Program Officer*, University of Regina, Norman Mackenzie Art Gallery, Regina SK

Royster, Kenneth L, *Asst Prof*, Morgan State University, Department of Art, Baltimore MD (S)

Rozen, Melvyn J, *Assoc Prof*, Ohio Dominican College, Art Department, Columbus OH (S)

Rozene, Janette, *Reference Librn*, Museum of Modern Art, Library, New York NY

Rozman, Joseph, *Asst Prof*, Mount Mary College, Art Department, Milwaukee WI (S)

Rozman, Ksenija, *Asst*, Narodna Galerija, National Art Gallery, Ljubljana Yugoslavia

Rozniatowski, David William, *Chief Librn*, Winnipeg Art Gallery, Clara Lander Library, Winnipeg MB

Rozsa, Eva, *Librn*, Magyar Nemzeti Galeria, Library, Budapest Hungary

Ruan, Judith, *Dir*, City of Brampton Public Library and Art Gallery, Belleville ON

Rubasamen, Grace, *Gallery Mgr*, Mendocino Art Center, Mendocino CA

Rubenstein, Benay, *Secy*, American International Sculptors Symposiums, Inc, New York NY

Rubenstein, Meridel, *Instructor*, College of Santa Fe, Visual Arts Dept, Santa Fe NM (S)

Rubin, David S, *Asst Dir*, Galleries of the Claremont Colleges, Claremont CA

Rubin, Virginia, *Executive Asst*, Exploratorium, San Francisco CA

Rubin, William, *Dir Painting & Sculpture Coll*, Museum of Modern Art, New York NY

Rubins, Geoffrey, *Lectr*, Institute for American Universities, Fine Arts in Aix, Avignon and Canterbury, Aix-en-Provence France (S)

Rudasill Jr, Leroy U, *Chmn*, Southern Seminary Junior College, Buena Vista VA (S)

Rudberg, Peggy, *Slide Librn*, Minneapolis College of Art and Design, Library and Media Center, Minneapolis MN

Rudell, Joan Marie, *Dir*, Black Hills Art Center, Little Gallery, Spearfish SD

Rudenstine, Angelica, *Research Cur*, Solomon R Guggenheim Museum, New York NY

Rudman, Joan, *Secy*, Hudson Valley Art Association, Watertown NY

Rudy, Andrea, *Vistors Center Adminr*, Stowe-Day Foundation, Hartford CT

Rueckert, R, *Cur Ceramics and Glass*, Bayerisches Nationalmuseum, Bavarian National Museum, Munich Germany, Federal Republic of

Rueschhoff, Philip H, *Chmn Dept*, University of Kansas, Department of Visual Arts Education, Lawrence KS (S)

Ruff, Eric, *Cur*, Yarmouth County Historical Society Museum, Yarmouth NS

Ruffer, David G, *Pres*, Albright College, Freedman Gallery, Reading PA

Ruffle, John, *Keeper Archaeology*, Birmingham Museums and Art Gallery, Birmingham England

Ruffo, Joseph M, *Head Dept*, University of Northern Iowa, Department of Art, Cedar Falls IA (S)

Ruffolo Jr, Robert E, *Pres*, Princeton Antiques Bookservice, Art Marketing Reference Library, Atlantic City NJ

Rufo, Christy R, *Pres*, New England School of Art and Design, Boston MA (S)

Rufty, Al, *Pres*, Arts and Crafts Association, Inc, Winston-Salem NC (S)

Ruggles, John R, *VPres*, Dulin Gallery of Art, Knoxville TN

Ruhmer, Eberhard, *Cur 19th Century Art*, Bayerischen Staatsgemaldesammlungen, Bavarian State Galleries of Art, Munich Germany, Federal Republic of

Ruiz, Noemi, *Assoc Chmn*, Inter American University of Puerto Rico, Department of Performing Arts, San German PR (S)

Ruiz-Avila, Hugo, *Registrar*, University of Iowa, Museum of Art, Iowa City IA

Rumford, Beatrix T, *Dir*, Abby Aldrich Rockefeller Folk Art Center, Williamsburg VA

Runestad, Cornell, *Division Chmn of Fine Arts*, Wayne State College, Nordstrand Visual Arts Gallery, Wayne NE

Runestad, Cornell, *Div Chmn*, Wayne State College, Art Department, Wayne NE (S)

Runke, Henry M, *Head Dept*, University of Wisconsin-Stevens Point, Department of Art, Stevens Point WI (S)

Runner, Larry D, *Asst Prof*, Mesa College, Art Department, Grand Junction CO (S)

Runyon, Betty V, *Dir Visitor Services*, Minnesota Museum of Art, Saint Paul MN

Runyon, John M, *Chmn*, Corning Community College, Division of Humanities, Corning NY (S)

Rupe, Bonnie, *Acquisitions Dept Head*, Wichita Public Library, Wichita KS

Rus, Alexandra, *Dir*, Muzeul de Arta Cluj-Napoca, Museum of Art, Cluj-Napoca Romania

Rush, Jean C, *Coordr Art Educ*, University of Arizona, Department of Art, Tucson AZ (S)

Rush, Lucile, *Librn*, Saint Joseph Museum, Library, Saint Joseph MO

Rushton, Brian, *Publications & Marketing Services Mgr*, Brooklyn Museum, Brooklyn NY

Rusk, Ann, *Division Head*, Yuba College, Fine Arts Division, Marysville CA (S)

Ruskin, Laurie, *Treas*, Eccles Community Art Center, Ogden UT

Rusnell, Wesley A, *Registrar & Cur*, Roswell Museum and Art Center, Roswell NM

Russell, Don, *Coordr Summer Institute*, Visual Studies Workshop, Rochester NY

Russell, H, *Instructor*, Indiana University of Pennsylvania, Department of Art and Art Education, Indiana PA (S)

Russell, Jennifer, *Cur*, Whitney Museum of American Art, New York NY

Russell, John, *Lectr*, John Jay College of Criminal Justice, Department of Art, Music and Philosophy, New York NY (S)

Russell, John I, *Educ Coordr*, Worcester Craft Center, Worcester MA (S)

Russell, John I, *Exhib Coordr*, Worcester Craft Center Gallery, Worcester MA

Russell, Kent dur, *Cur Art*, Museum of Art, Science and Industry, Bridgeport CT

Russell, Marilyn Miller, *Asst Curator*, Frick Art Museum, Pittsburgh PA

Russell, Nancy, *Secy*, Sculpture Center, New York NY

Russell, Reba, *Cur of Education*, Dixon Gallery and Gardens, Memphis TN

Russell, Robert, *Assoc Prof*, Jersey City State College, Art Department, Jersey City NJ (S)

Russell, Robert, *Assoc Prof*, Pittsburg State University, Art Department, Pittsburg KS (S)

Russell, Stella, *Chmn*, Nassau Community College, Art Department, Garden City NY (S)

Russell, Thomas, *Instructor*, Roger Williams College, Art Department, Bristol RI (S)

Russell, William, *Corresponding Secy*, Gilpin County Arts Association, Central City CO

Russo, Alexander, *Chairperson*, Hood College, Department of Art, Frederick MD (S)

Russom, J Michael, *Asst Prof*, Assumption College, Department of Fine Arts and Music, Worcester MA (S)

Rust, David E, *Cur French Painting*, National Gallery of Art, Washington DC

Rust, Edwin C, *Dir Emeritus*, Memphis Academy of Arts, Frank T Tobey Gallery, Memphis TN

Rust, Joe C, *Secy*, San Antonio Art League, San Antonio TX

Ruston, Shelley, *Asst Dir Activities*, Santa Barbara Museum of Art, Santa Barbara CA

Rutherford, Margaret, *Corresponding Secy*, Arts for Living Center, Burlington IA

Rutkowski, Walter E, *Head Dept*, Louisiana State University, Department of Fine Arts, Baton Rouge LA (S)

Rutkowski, Walter E, *Head Department*, Louisiana State University, Department of Fine Arts, Baton Rouge LA

Rutledge, Patricia P, *Librn*, Cincinnati Art Museum, Library, Cincinnati OH

Rutledge, Ruth, *Instr*, Victor Valley College, Art Department, Victorville CA (S)

Rutz, Harold, *Chmn*, Concordia Lutheran College, Department of Fine Arts, Austin TX (S)

Ruus, Inge, *Curatorial Asst*, University of British Columbia, Museum of Anthropology, Vancouver BC

Ruwadi, Raymond, *Clerk & Treas*, Massillon Museum, Massillon OH

Ruyle, Kermit, *Instructor*, Saint Louis Community College at Florissant Valley, Department of Art, Ferguson MO (S)

Ruzicka, Francis A, *Head Dept*, University of Georgia, Franklin College of Arts and Sciences, Division of Fine Arts, Athens GA (S)

Ryan, Carolyn, *Field Archivist*, New Jersey Historical Society Museum, Library, Newark NJ

Ryan, David, *Dir*, Fort Worth Art Museum, Fort Worth TX

Ryan, James, *Historic Site Mgr*, Olana Historic Site, Hudson NY

Ryan, M F, *Keeper Antiquities*, National Museum of Ireland, Dublin Ireland

Ryan, Martin, *Assoc Prof*, Monmouth College, Department of Art, West Long Branch NJ (S)

Ryan, Noel, *Chief Librn*, Mississauga Library System, Mississauga ON

Ryan, Renee Rodrique, *Asst Registrar, Cur of Traveling Exhib*, New Orleans Museum of Art, Isaac Delgado Museum, New Orleans LA

Ryan, William V, *Librn*, Bloomsburg State College, Andruss Library, Bloomsburg PA

Ryan, Wilma, *Pres*, Coquille Valley Art Association, Coquille OR

Rybak, Natalia, *Development Officer*, Ukrainian Museum, New York NY

Ryberg, H Theodore, *Dir*, University of Alaska, Elmer E Rasmuson Library, Fairbanks AK

Rychlewski, Karen, *Assoc Prof*, West Liberty State College, Art Department, West Liberty WV (S)

Ryden, Kenneth G, *Assoc Prof*, Greenville College, Dept of Art, Greenville IL (S)

Ryndel, Nils, *Cur Modern Department*, Göteborg Konstmuseum, Gothenburg Art Gallery, Gothenburg Sweden

Rypsam, Russell, *Historian*, Artists' Fellowship, Inc, New York NY

Ryska, Jaroslav, *Asst Prof*, Youngstown State University, Art Department, Youngstown OH (S)

Ryskamp, Charles, *Dir*, Pierpont Morgan Library, New York NY

Ryuto, Setsuko, *Admin Asst*, Pioneer Museum and Haggin Galleries, Stockton CA

Saaltink, H W, *Sr Research Asst*, Westfries Museum, Hoorn Netherlands

Saari, Sandra, *Chmn*, Eisenhower College, Seneca Falls NY (S)

Saavedra, E Michale Schanches, *Cur of Library Materials*, Valentine Museum, Library, Richmond VA

Sabel, Jim, *Pres*, Montgomery Museum of Fine Arts, Montgomery AL

Sacher, Pamela, *Instructor*, Greenfield Community College, Art Department, Greenfield MA (S)

Sachs, Steven F, *Asst Prof*, Catholic University of America, Department of Architecture & Planning, Washington DC (S)

Sachs, William R, *Pres*, New York Society of Architects, f the Performing Arts, at Lincoln Center New York

Sachs II, Samuel, *Dir*, Minneapolis Institute of Arts, Minneapolis MN

Sack, Suzanne P, *Conservator*, Brooklyn Museum, Brooklyn NY

Sackerlotzky, Rotraud, *Gallery Coordr*, Trenton State College, Holman Gallery, Trenton NJ

Sadek, George, *Dean*, Cooper Union School of Art, New York NY (S)

Sadek, V, *Deputy Dir*, Statni Zidovske Muzeum, State Jewish Museum, Prague Czechoslovakia

Sadik, Marvin, *Dir*, National Portrait Gallery, Washington DC

Saether, Jan, *Chmn Painting Dept*, Venice Painting, Drawing and Sculpture Studio, Inc, Venice CA (S)

Safarik, Eduard A, *Dir*, Galleria Doria Pamphilj, Dorian Gallery, Rome Italy

Safford, Merritt, *Conservator Prints & Drawings*, Metropolitan Museum of Art, New York NY

Sagan, Bruce, *VPres*, Chicago Public Library, Cultural Center, Chicago IL

Sage, Diane, *Special Projects Officer*, Ontario Association of Art Galleries, Toronto ON

Sage, Konrad, *Dir*, Hochschule der Künste Berlin, Berlin College of Art, Berlin Germany, Federal Republic of (S)

Sager, Donald J, *Commissioner*, Chicago Public Library, Art Section, Fine Arts Division, Chicago IL

Sagonic, Livio, *Instr*, Drew University, Art Department, Madison NJ (S)

Sahlstrand, James, *Dir Art Gallery*, Central Washington University, Sara Spurgeon Gallery, Ellensburg WA

Sahni, S K, *Deputy Keeper Art Coll*, National Gallery of Modern Art, New India

Saillant, Michele, *Asst*, Rhode Island College, Edward M Bannister Gallery, Providence RI

Sain, Robert, *Dir Development*, Walker Art Center, Minneapolis MN

St Jean, George, *Librn*, Monterey History and Art Association, Museum Library, Monterey CA

St John, Richard, *Chmn Studio Arts*, Wichita State University, Division of Art, Wichita KS (S)

St John, S C, *Controller*, San Francisco Museum of Modern Art, San Francisco CA

St John, Steve, *Chief Cur & Registrar*, Central Louisiana Art Association, Alexandria Museum Visual Art Center, Alexandria LA

St John, Terry, *Vis Prof*, Santa Rosa Junior College, Art Department, Santa Rosa CA (S)

St John, Wayne L, *Chmn*, Southern Illinois University, Department of Design, Carbondale IL (S)

St Florian, Friedrich, *Dean Archit Div*, Rhode Island School of Design, Providence RI (S)

St-Gelais, Helene, *VPres*, Institut des Arts au Saguenay, National Exhibition Center, Jonquiere PQ

St German, Lee, *Secy & Asst to Dir*, Bruce Museum, Greenwich CT

St Pierr, Normand, *Chief Librn*, Public Archives of Canada, Public Archives Library, Ottawa ON

St Pierre, Carolyn, *Prof*, Boston State College, Art Department, Boston MA (S)

Saito, Deborah, *Library Asst In Charge of Circulation & State Documents*, Sheldon Jackson College, Stratton Library, Sitka AK

Saito, Mike, *Instructor*, Factory of Visual Art, Seattle WA (S)

Sajbel, Ed, *Art Dept Chmn*, University of Southern Colorado, Pueblo CO

Sajbel, Edward R, *Chmn*, University of Southern Colorado, Belmont Campus, Department of Art, Pueblo CO (S)

Sakaguchi, Ben, *Area Chmn Studio Art*, Pasadena City College, Art Department, Pasadena CA (S)

Sakakeeny, Donna Tryon, *Assoc Prof*, Palomar College, Art Department, San Marcos TX (S)

Sakazume, Katsuyuki, *Instructor*, Peters Valley Craft Center, Layton NJ (S)

Salam, Heliede, *Asst Prof*, Radford University, Art Department, Radford VA (S)

Salan, Jean, *Deputy Dir*, Museum of African Art, Washington DC

Salanty, David, *Pres*, Saint Mary's Romanian Orthodox Church, Romanian Ethnic Museum, Cleveland OH

Salberg, Lester, *Instructor*, Rock Valley College, Dept of Art, Rockford IL (S)

Salcedo, Alberto Santibanez, *Dir*, Museo de Arte, Museum of Art, Lima Peru

Salcedo, Jaime, *Head History*, Universidad Javeriana, Javeriana University Faculty of Architecture and Design, Bogota Colombia (S)

Sale, Russell, *Asst Prof*, Wake Forest University, Department of Art, Winston-Salem NC (S)

Saleh, Moh, *First Sub-Dir*, Egyptian Museum, Cairo Egypt

Salet, Francis, *Dir*, Musee de Cluny, Cluny Museum, Paris France

Salgado, Ronald, *Gallery Dir*, Muckenthaler Cultural Center, Fullerton CA

Salisbury, Ralph F, *Dir*, Ralyn Art Center, Lakewood NJ (S)

Salisian, Steve, *Instr*, San Jose City College, School of Fine Arts, San Jose CA (S)

Sallaberry, Carlos A, *Dir Architectural Department*, Centro de Arte y Communicacion, Center of Art and Communication, Buenos Argentina

Salley, Claude B, *Instructor*, Hardin-Simmons University, Art Dept, Abilene TX (S)

Salley, Jo Dean, *Instructor*, Hardin-Simmons University, Art Dept, Abilene TX (S)

Salmon, Eugene N, *Assoc Humanities Reference Librn*, California State University, Sacramento, Library, Humanities Reference Media Services Ctr, Sacramento CA

Salmon, H Morrey, *Treas*, National Museum of Wales, Cardiff Wales

Salmon, Larry, *Cur Textiles*, Museum of Fine Arts, Boston MA

Salo, Carol, *Instr*, Suomi College, Fine Arts Department, Hancock MI (S)

Salomon, Judith, *Instr*, Cleveland Institute of Art, Cleveland OH (S)

Salter, Peter, *Instructor*, Stephens College, Art Department, Columbia MO (S)

Saltmarche, Kenneth, *Dir*, Art Gallery of Windsor, Windsor ON

Saltzman, Marvin, *Prof*, University of North Carolina at Chapel Hill, Art Department, Chapel Hill NC (S)

Salveson, Doug, *Assoc Prof*, Findlay College, Art Department, Findlay OH (S)

Salveson, Douglas, *Dir*, Findlay College, Egner Fine Arts Center, Findlay OH

Salyer, Ruth Osgood, *Admin Dir*, Laguna Beach School of Art, Laguna Beach CA (S)

Salzillo, Marjorie, *Instr*, Utica College of Syracuse University, Division of Humanities, Utica NY (S)

Salzillo, William, *Assoc Prof*, Hamilton College, Art Department, Clinton NY (S)

Salzman, Stanley, *Dir Education*, National Institute for Architectural Education, New York NY

Samford, Michael, *Cur*, George Peabody College for Teachers, Cohen Memorial Museum of Art, Nashville TN

Samford, Michael, *Assoc Prof*, George Peabody College for Teachers, Art Faculty Department, Nashville TN (S)

Sammarjano, Vito, *Prof*, Salem State College, Art Department, Salem MA (S)

Samoyault, Jean-Pierre, *Cur*, Musee National du Chateau de Fontainebleau, National Museum of Fontainebleau, Fontainebleau France

Sampics, Robert, *Chmn Board*, Metropolitan Cultural Arts Center, Minneapolis MN

Sample, George, *Asst Prof*, Central Missouri State University, Art Department, Warrensburg MO (S)

Samples, R McCartney, *Asst Dir Education & Communication*, Royal Ontario Museum, Toronto ON

Samples-Kelley, Gerri, *Dir*, Floyd County Museum, New Albany IN

Sampson, Rose, *Treas*, Galesburg Civic Art Center, Galesburg IL

Samter, Virginia, *Pres*, Evanston Art Center, Evanston IL

Samuel, Evelyn K, *Dir*, New York University, Stephen Chan Library of Fine Arts, New York NY

Samuelson, Fred, *Head Grad Studies*, Instituto Allende, Allende Institute, San Mexico (S)

Samuelson, Jerry, *Dean Sch Arts*, California State University, Fullerton, Art Department, Fullerton CA (S)

Samuelson, Rich, *Dir & Pres*, Atlantic Gallery, New York NY

San, Juk, *Instructor*, Rudolph Schaeffer School of Design, San Francisco CA (S)

Sanchez, Beatrice Rivas, *Academic Dean*, Maryland College of Art and Design, Silver Spring MD (S)

Sanchez, Laura, *Cur*, Anderson Fine Arts Center, Anderson IN

Sand, Mary, *Dir*, North Dakota State School of Science, Department of Art, Wahpeton ND (S)

Sandelin, Lee, *Art Librn*, San Diego State University, Love Library and Art Department Slide Library, San Diego CA

Sanden, Michael, *Educ Dir*, Oklahoma Art Center, Oklahoma Art Center Annex, Oklahoma City OK

Sanders, Albert E, *Cur Natural History*, Charleston Museum, Charleston SC

Sanders, Robert, *Cur Herpetology*, San Bernardino County Museum and Satellites, Fine Arts Institute, Redlands CA

Sanders, Scott, *Deputy Dir*, South Carolina Arts Commission, Columbia SC

Sanders, Sue, *Secy*, Museum of York County, Rock Hill SC

Sanders, Val G, *Assoc Prof*, Palomar College, Art Department, San Marcos TX (S)

Sanderson, Bob, *VPres*, Community Arts Council of Vancouver, Vancouver BC

Sandison, Patricia A, *Secy*, Longview Museum and Arts Center, Longview TX

Sandler, Irving, *Assoc Prof*, State University of New York College at Purchase, Department of Art History, Purchase NY (S)

Sandler, Lucy Freeman, *VPres*, College Art Association of America, New York NY

Sandler, Mark, *Art Department Chmn*, State University of New York College at Potsdam, Brainerd Art Gallery, Potsdam NY

Sandler, Mark H, *Chmn*, State University of New York College at Potsdam, Department of Fine Arts, Potsdam NY (S)

Sandmann, Herbert, *Prof*, University of Wisconsin-Stevens Point, Department of Art, Stevens Point WI (S)

Sandon, Flo, *Instr*, Rochester Community College, Art Department, Rochester MN (S)

Sandoz, M Andre, *Pres*, Musee des Beaux-Arts et Societe des Amis des Arts, Museum of Fine Arts, La Switzerland

Sands, John O, *Asst Dir for Coll*, Mariners Museum, Newport News VA

Sandvik, Trond, *Dir Educ*, Tennessee Botanical Gardens and Fine Arts Center, Nashville TN (S)

Sandweiss, Martha, *Cur Photographic Coll*, Amon Carter Museum of Western Art, Fort Worth TX

Sanford, Cynthia, *Trustee & Cur*, Jersey City Museum Association, Jersey City NJ

Sanger, Helen, *Librn*, Frick Art Reference Library, New York NY

Sanguinetti, E F, *Dir*, University of Utah, Utah Museum of Fine Arts, Salt Lake City UT

San Jose, Julio M, *Dean*, Virginia Polytechnic Institute and State University, Architecture Library, Blacksburg VA

Sankowsky, Itzhaic, *Instructor*, Mainline Center of the Arts, Haverford PA (S)

San Martin, Maria L, *Dir*, Escuela Nacional de Bellas Artes Manuel Belgrano, National School of Fine Arts Manuel Belgrano, Buenos Aires Argentina (S)

Sanpera, M Carmen Farie, *Cur*, Museo de Arte Cataluna, Museum of Ancient Art, Barcelona Spain

Santi, Francesco, *Dir*, Galleria Nazionale dell'Umbria, Umbrian National Gallery, Perugia Italy

Santomasso, Eugene A, *Asst Prof*, City University of New York, PhD Program in Art History, New York NY (S)

Santucci, Renato, *Video Coordr*, Centro de Arte y Communicacion, Center of Art and Communication, Buenos Argentina

Saper, Arnold, *Chmn Printmaking*, University of Manitoba, School of Art, Winnipeg MB (S)

Sapino, Cheryl, *Instr*, Danforth Museum School, Framingham MA (S)

Sarda, Rafael, *Public Relations Coordr*, Museum of Modern Art of Latin America, Washington DC

Sargent, C H, *Dir*, Watkins Institute, Nashville TN

Sargent, Eliot, *Chmn Antiquarian House*, Plymouth Antiquarian Society, Plymouth MA

Sargent, William, *Asst Cur*, Museum of the American China Trade, Milton MA

Sarkany, Tamas, *Asst Keeper*, Kungl Myntkabinettet Statens Museum För Mynt Medalj Och Penninghistoria, Royal Coin Cabinet, National Museum of Monetary History, Stockholm Sweden

Sarn, John, *Faculty Advisor*, University of Alabama in Huntsville, Gallery of Art, Huntsville AL

Sarn, John A, *Asst Prof*, University of Alabama in Huntsville, Department of Art, Huntsville AL (S)

Saromines, Barbara, *Instructor*, Leeward Community College, Arts and Humanities Division, Pearl City HI (S)

Sartor, Joe D, *Asst Prof*, Morehead State University, Art Department, Morehead KY (S)

Sartre, Josiane, *Conservator*, Union Centrale des Arts Decoratifs, Bibliotheque des Arts Decoratifs, Paris France

Sasowsky, Norman, *Coordr Art Educ*, University of Delaware, Department of Art, Newark DE (S)

Sassoon, Steven, *VPres*, Monterey Peninsula Museum of Art, Monterey CA

Satter, Michelle, *Communications*, Institute of Contemporary Art, Boston MA

Satz, Arthur, *Pres*, New York School of Interior Design, New York NY (S)

Sauberli, Ronald, *Library Asst*, Illinois State Museum of Natural History and Art, Library, Springfield IL

Sauer, Louis, *Head*, Carnegie-Mellon University, Department of Architecture, Pittsburgh PA (S)

Sauer, Richard, *Instr*, Danforth Museum School, Framingham MA (S)

Saul, John V, *Cur & Mgr*, Frontier Times Museum, Bandera TX

Saule, Vigeo, *Prof*, Bernard M Baruch College of the City University of New York, Art Department, New York NY (S)

Saunders, Eleanor, *Asst Prof*, State University of New York College at Purchase, Department of Art History, Purchase NY (S)

Saunders, J D, *Prof*, University of Auckland, School of Fine Arts, Auckland New Zealand (S)

Saunders, Joan, *Gallery Coordr*, University of Hartford, Joseloff Gallery, West Hartford CT

Saunders, Phyllis, *Prof*, Passaic County Community College, Division of Humanities, Paterson NJ (S)

Saunders, Richard, *Cur American Paintings, Sculpture, Drawings & Prints*, Wadsworth Atheneum, Hartford CT

Sauvageau, Susan, *Asst Prof*, Eisenhower College, Seneca Falls NY (S)

Savage, James, *Dir*, School of Fine Arts, Visual Arts Department, Willoughby OH (S)

Savage, James J, *Executive Dir*, Fine ARts Association, School of Fine Arts, Willoughby OH

Savage, Karen, *Chmn Grad Div*, School of the Art Institute of Chicago, Chicago IL (S)

Savage, Martena, *Mgr*, Flathead Indian Museum, Saint Ignatius MT

Savage, Roger, *Pres*, Eye Level Gallery, Halifax NS

Savage, William, *Education Museums*, University of South Carolina, McKissick Museums, Columbia SC

Savill, R J, *Asst to Dir*, Wallace Collection, London England

Savinar, Barbara, *Registrar*, Oakland Museum, Oakland CA

Saw, James T, *Chmn*, Palomar College, Art Department, San Marcos TX (S)

Sawa, Ryuken, *Head Dept*, Kyoto City University of Fine Arts, School of Art, Kyoto Japan (S)

Sawchak, M, *Secy*, Ukrainian Museum, New York NY

Sawka, Michaleen, *Cur Secy*, San Diego Museum of Art, San Diego CA

Sawruk, Polli, *Asst Dir*, Muhlenberg College Center for the Arts, Allentown PA

Sawycky, Roman, *Asst Dir*, Free Public Library of Elizabeth, Fine Arts Dept, Elizabeth NJ

Sawyer, Alan, *Prof*, University of British Columbia, Department of Fine Arts, Vancouver BC (S)

Sawyer III, Henry W, *VPres*, Fairmount Park Art Association, Philadelphia PA

Saxe, Edward L, *Dir Admin*, Museum of Modern Art, New York NY

Sayad, Homer E, *VPres*, Art and Education Council of Greater Saint Louis, Saint Louis MO

Saylor, Harold D, *Pres*, Historical Society of Pennsylvania, Philadelphia PA

Sayre, C Franklin, *Asst Prof*, Oakland University, Dept of Art & Art History, Rochester MI (S)

Sayre, Eleanor A, *Cur Prints & Drawings*, Museum of Fine Arts, Boston MA

Sayre, Suzanne, *Instructor*, William Woods-Westminster Colleges, Art Department, Fulton MO (S)

Scafati, M, *VPres*, Brevard Art Center and Museum, Inc, Melbourne FL

Scafetta, Stefano, *Conservator*, National Collection of Fine Arts, Washington DC

Scaggs, Donald, *Printmaking Coordr*, North Texas State University, Art Department, Denton TX (S)

Scaife, Richard M, *Chmn Museum of Art Committee*, Carnegie Institute, Museum of Art, Pittsburgh PA

Scala, Joseph, *Dir*, Syracuse University, College of Visual and Performing Arts, Syracuse NY (S)

Scala, Joseph A, *Dir*, Syracuse University, Joe and Emily Lowe Art Gallery, Syracuse NY

Scalamandre, Franco, *Founder & Pres*, Scalamandre Museum of Textiles, New York NY

Scalise, James W, *Chmn Archit*, Arizona State University, College of Architecture, Tempe AZ (S)

Scanga, Italo, *Prof*, University of California, San Diego, Visual Arts Department, La Jolla CA (S)

Scannell, Joseph E, *Chmn*, Saint Anselm's College, Department of Fine Arts, Manchester NH (S)

Scannell, Joseph E, *Assoc Dir*, Saint Anselm's College, Manchester NH

Scannell, Joseph S, *Asst Prof*, College of the Holy Cross, Department of Fine Arts, Worcester MA (S)

Scarborough, Cleve K, *Dir*, Hunter Museum of Art, Chattanooga TN

Scarlet, Peter, *Dir Sonoma Film Institute*, Sonoma State University, Art Department, Rohnert Park CA (S)

Scarlett, Robert, *Librn*, Memphis Academy of Arts, G Pillow Lewis Memorial Library, Memphis TN

Scarratt, Irene, *Pres*, Sunbury Shores Arts and Nature Centre, Inc, Saint Andrews NB

Schaad, Dee, *Asst Prof*, Indiana Central University, Fine Arts Department, Indianapolis IN (S)

Schaber, Ken, *Asst Prof*, Lake Michigan College, Department of Art, Benton Harbor MI (S)

Schade, William, *Instructor*, Junior College of Albany, Fine Arts Division, Albany NY (S)

Schaedler, A, *Cur Sculpture & Paintings*, Bayerisches Nationalmuseum, Bavarian National Museum, Munich Germany, Federal Republic of

Schaefer, Jean O, *Asst Prof*, University of Wyoming, Art Department, Laramie WY (S)

Schaefer, Peter, *Public Information Officer*, Museums at Stony Brook, Stony Brook NY

Schaefer, Ronald, *Chmn*, University of North Dakota, Visual Arts Department, Grand Forks ND (S)

Schaefer Jr, Fred, *Instructor*, Williamsport Area Community College, Department of Engineering and Design, Williamsport PA (S)

Schaeffer, Marilyn, *Assoc Prof*, New York City Community College of the City University of New York, Department of Art and Advertising Design, Brooklyn NY (S)

Schaeffer, Rudolph, *Dir*, Rudolph Schaeffer School of Design, San Francisco CA (S)

Schaeffer, William D, *Pres*, Inter-Society Color Council, Troy NY

Schaffer, Dale, *Mgr*, Western Woodcarvings, Custer SD

Schaffer, Gloria, *Mgr*, Western Woodcarvings, Custer SD

Schaffer, Jo, *Cur*, State University of New York College at Cortland, Art Slide Library, Cortland NY

Schaller, Ralph, *Asst Prof*, Loyola University of Chicago, Fine Arts Department, Chicago IL (S)

Schalliol, David, *Cur Exhib*, Indiana University, University Museum, Bloomington IN

Schaltenbrand, Philip, *Asst Prof*, California State College, Department of Art, California PA (S)

Schantz, Michael W, *Asst to Dir*, University of California, Los Angeles, Grunwald Center for the Graphic Arts, Los Angeles CA

Schar, Stuart, *Dir*, Kent State University, School of Art, Kent OH (S)

Scharff, Carol, *Instructor*, University of Northern Iowa, Department of Art, Cedar Falls IA (S)

Schatz, Charlotte, *Instructor*, Bucks County Community College, Fine Arts Department, Newton PA (S)

Schauer, Mary, *Assoc Cur*, Neville Public Museum, Green Bay WI

Schauer, Rudolph I, *Prof*, University of Minnesota, Duluth, Art Dept, Duluth MN (S)

Scheele, William F, *Dir & Secy Board*, Columbus Museum of Arts and Sciences, Columbus GA

Scheer, Malcolm E, *Librn*, New York School of Interior Design Library, New York NY

Scheffler, Patricia, *Head Librn*, Interlochen Center for the Arts, Interlochen Arts Academy Library, Interlochen MI

Scheidt, Patricia M, *Dir*, Arts Club of Chicago, Chicago IL

Schele, Linda, *Assoc Prof*, University of South Alabama, Department of Art, Mobile AL (S)

Schelfler, Gisela, *Cur*, Staatliche Graphische Sammlung, National Graphic Collection, Munich Germany, Federal Republic of

Schell, Deborah, *Librn*, Saginaw Art Museum, Library, Saginaw MI

Schell, Edwin, *Executive Secy*, United Methodist Historical Society, Lovely Lane Museum, Baltimore MD

Schell, Edwin, *Librn*, United Methodist Historical Society, Library, Baltimore MD

Schellstede, Eloise J, *Pres*, Schellstede Gallery of Fine Arts, Tulsa OK

Schellstede, Richard L, *VPres & Dir*, Schellstede Gallery of Fine Arts, Tulsa OK

Scheps, Marc, *Dir & Chief Cur*, Tel Aviv Museum, Tel-Aviv Israel

Scher, Linda E, *Corresp Secy*, Salmagundi Club, New York NY

Scherer, Herbert G, *Librn*, University of Minnesota, Art Library, Minneapolis MN

Scherpereel, R, *Chmn*, Texas A and I University, Art Gallery, Kingville TX

Scherpereel, Richard, *Chmn*, Texas A & I University, Art Department, Kingsville TX (S)

Scherz, Barbara, *Receptionist*, Madison Art Center, Madison WI

Schetzsle, Letha, *Registrar*, Denison University Art Gallery, Granville OH

Schick, Marjorie, *Assoc Prof*, Pittsburg State University, Art Department, Pittsburg KS (S)

Schier, Peter E, *Chmn*, University of Bridgeport, Art Department, Bridgeport CT (S)

Schiferl, Ellen, *Instructor*, Fort Hays State University, Department of Art, Hays KS (S)

Schiff, Jean, *Asst Prof*, Metropolitan State College, Art Department, Denver CO (S)

Schiffner, R, *Instructor*, Golden West College, Arts, Humanities and Social Sciences Institute, Huntington Beach CA (S)

Schild, Curt, *Cur*, Rosicrucian Egyptian Museum and Art Gallery, San Jose CA

Schimansky, Dobrila-Donya, *Museum Librn*, Metropolitan Museum of Art, Thomas J Watson Library, New York NY

Schimmelman, Janice C, *Visiting Instr*, Oakland University, Dept of Art & Art History, Rochester MI (S)

Schlageter, Robert W, *Dir*, Cummer Gallery of Art, DeEtte Holden Cummer Museum Foundation, Jacksonville FL

Schlansky, Delia, *Slide Cur*, California State University, Sacramento, Library, Humanities Reference Media Services Ctr, Sacramento CA

Schlawin, Judy, *Instr*, Winona State University, Art Department, Winona MN (S)

Schleif, Corine, *Instr*, Maryville College, Art Department, Saint Louis MO (S)

Schleif, Thomas S, *Cur*, Leigh Yawkey Woodson Art Museum, Inc, Wausau WI

Schlesinger, Stephen L, *Secy*, John Simon Guggenheim Memorial Foundation, New York NY

Schlieder, Katharine J, *Admin Asst*, Rome Art and Community Center, Rome NY

Schling, Dorothy T, *Dir*, Danbury Scott-Fanton Museum and Historical Society, Inc, Danbury CT

Schloss, Stuart, *Treas*, Contemporary Arts Center, Cincinnati OH

Schlossberg, Leon, *Asst Prof*, Johns Hopkins University, School of Medicine, Department of Art as Applied to Medicine, Baltimore MD (S)

Schlosser, Mary C, *Pres*, Guild of Book Workers, New York NY

Schlosser, Tom, *Chmn Dept*, College of Saint Mary, Art Department, Omaha NE (S)

Schlotterback, Thomas, *Chmn*, Western Washington University, Art Department, Bellingham WA (S)

Schlump, John O, *Chmn*, Wittenberg University, Art Department, Springfield OH (S)

Schluntz, R, *Exec Dir*, Association of Collegiate Schools of Architecture, Washington DC

Schmaljohn, Russell, *Asst Prof*, Northwest Missouri State University, Dept of Art, Maryville MO (S)

Schmidt, Bill, *Vis Asst Prof*, University of Maryland Baltimore County, Visual Arts Department, Catonsville MD (S)

Schmidt, Eberhard, *VPres*, Boothbay Region Art Gallery, Boothbay Harbor ME

Schmidt, Herbert F, *Mgr Design*, Metropolitan Museum of Art, New York NY

Schmidt, Kathleen, *Instructor*, Northeastern Oklahoma State University, Tahlequah OK (S)

Schmidt, Martin F, *Librn*, Filson Club, Reference and Research Library, Louisville KY

Schmidt, Maurice, *Assoc Prof*, Texas A & I University, Art Department, Kingsville TX (S)

Schmidt, Myron, *Asst Prof*, Dean Junior College, Visual and Performing Arts Department, Franklin MA (S)

Schmidt, Norman, *Chmn Graphic Design*, University of Manitoba, School of Art, Winnipeg MB (S)

Schmidt, Valentine L, *Librn*, John and Mable Ringling Museum of Art, Art Research Library, Sarasota FL

Schmitt, Annegrit, *National Cur*, Staatliche Graphische Sammlung, National Graphic Collection, Munich Germany, Federal Republic of

Schmitt, Marilyn, *Instructor*, University of Miami, Department of Art, Coral Gables FL (S)

Schmitt, Tom, *Asst Dir*, Metropolitan Museum and Art Centers, Coral Gables FL

Schmutzhart, Berthold, *Chmn Sculpture*, Corcoran School of Art, Washington DC (S)

Schmutzhart, Slaithong, *Instr*, Mount Vernon College, Art Department, Washington DC (S)

Schnabel, David J, *Chmn Dept*, Pasadena City College, Art Department, Pasadena CA (S)

Schönberger, Arno, *Chief Dir*, Germanisches National Museum, Germanic National Museum, Nuremberg Germany, Federal Republic of

Schneider, Gail K, *Editor & Librn*, Staten Island Institute of Arts and Sciences, Staten Island NY

Schneider, Hugo, *Dir*, Schweizerisches Landesmuseum, Swiss National Museum, Zurich Switzerland

Schneider, Jane, *Board of Dir*, Cultural Council Foundation, Fourteen Sculptors Gallery, New York NY

Schneider, Janet, *Dir*, Queens Museum, Flushing NY

Schneider, Jenny, *VDir*, Schweizerisches Landesmuseum, Swiss National Museum, Zurich Switzerland

Schneider, Laurie, *Prof*, John Jay College of Criminal Justice, Department of Art, Music and Philosophy, New York NY (S)

Schneider, Richard, *Prof*, University of Wisconsin-Stevens Point, Department of Art, Stevens Point WI (S)

Schneider, Richard D, *Assoc Prof*, Cleveland State University, Art Department, Cincinnati OH (S)

Schneider, Robert M, *VPres*, Xerox Corporation, Art Collection, Stamford CT

Schneiderman, Richard, *Cur Graphic Arts*, University of Georgia, Georgia Museum of Art, Athens GA

Schnell, Lloyd, *Chmn Photography*, Kansas City Art Institute, Kansas City MO (S)

Schnell, Ronald, *Chmn Dept*, Tougaloo College, Art Department, Tougaloo MS (S)

Schnepper, Mark A, *Cur Exhib*, Evansville Museum of Arts and Science, Evansville IN

Schnirel, James, *Dean*, Utah Technical College at Salt Lake, Commercial Art Department, Salt Lake City UT (S)

Schnorr, Emil, *Adjunct Prof*, Springfield College, Department of Visual and Performing Arts, Springfield MA (S)

Schnorr, Emil G, *Conservator*, George Walter Vincent Smith Art Museum, Springfield MA

Schnorrenberg, John M, *Chmn Dept*, University of Alabama in Birmingham, Department of Art, Birmingham AL (S)

Schnorrenburg, John, *Pres*, Southeastern College Art Conference, Chapel Hill NC

Schoeberlein, Elizabeth, *Assoc Prof*, Colorado Women's College, Department of Art, Denver CO (S)

Schoedel, J Dan, *Chairperson Board of Trustees*, Spokane Public Library, Spokane WA

Schoen, Myron E, *Dir*, Union of American Hebrew Congregations, Synagogue Art and Architectural Library, New York NY

Schoene, Kathleen S, *Librn*, Missouri Historical Society, Library, Saint Louis MO

Schoenfeld, William, *Prof*, Ocean County College, Humanities Department, Toms River NJ (S)

Schoenheider, Charles, *VPres*, Peoria Art Guild, Peoria IL

Schofield, Barbara, *Public Relations*, State University of New York College at Purchase, Neuberger Museum, Purchase NY

Schofield, Ellice, *Cur*, Stowe-Day Foundation, Hartford CT

Schofield, Peg, *Lectr*, Saint Joseph's College, Fine Arts Program, Philadelphia PA (S)

Scholder, Fritz, *Instructor*, University of Southern California, Idyllwild Campus, Idyllwild School of Music and the Arts, Idyllwild CA (S)

Scholder, Larry, *Chmn*, Southern Methodist University, Division of Art and Art History, Dallas TX (S)

Scholfield, Helen, *Secy*, Leigh Yawkey Woodson Art Museum, Inc, Wausau WI

Scholl, Neil, *Photographer in Res*, New York Institute of Technology, Fine Arts Department, Old Westbury NY (S)

Schoonover, Daniel, *Library Asst*, Metropolitan Museum of Art, Cloisters Library, New York NY

Schorgl, Thomas B, *Dir*, Art Center, Inc, South Bend IN

Schorr, David, *Assoc Prof*, Wesleyan University, Art Department, Middletown CT (S)

Schory, Karen, *Instructor*, Johnson County Community College, Communications-Arts Division, Overland Park KS (S)

Schott, Gene A, *Dir*, Heritage Plantation of Sandwich, Sandwich MA

Schou-Christensen, Jorg Jorgen, *Keeper*, Det Danske Kunstindustrimuseum, Museum of Decorative Art, Copenhagen Denmark

Schrader, Jack, *Cur*, Metropolitan Museum of Art, Cloisters, New York NY

Schrader-Hooker, Charlotte, *Prof*, Longwood College, Department of Art, Farmville VA (S)

Schrank Jr, H Paul, *Librn*, University of North Dakota Art Galleries, Bierce Library, Grand Forks ND

Schrank Jr, H Paul, *Librn*, University of Akron, Bierce Library Art Department, Akron OH

Schreckengost, Viktor, *Instr*, Cleveland Institute of Art, Cleveland OH (S)

Schreiber, Beverly, *Gallery Dir*, Jewish Community Center, Center Lobby Gallery, Long Beach CA

Schreiber, Frank, *Head Dept*, North Hennepin Community College, Art Department, Minneapolis MN (S)

Schreiber, Judith, *Dir Public Relations*, Colorado Springs Fine Arts Center, Colorado Springs CO

Schreiberova, Katarina, *Chief Department Nonprofessional Art*, Slovenska Narodna Galeria, Slovak National Gallery, Bratislava Czechoslovakia

Schremmer, Harold, *Visiting Prof*, Portland School of Art, Portland ME (S)

Schrock, Eileen, *VPres*, Phelps County Historical Society Museum, Holdrege NE

Schroeder, George S, *Chmn*, Hiram College, Art Department, Hiram OH (S)

Schroeder, Howard S, *Instructor*, Rehoboth Art League, Inc, Rehoboth Beach DE (S)

Schroeder, Lee, *Assoc Prof*, Hanover College, Department of Art, Hanover IN (S)

Schroeder, Lynn, *Coordr Printmaking*, University of Arizona, Department of Art, Tucson AZ (S)

Schroeder, Susan, *Instructor*, Hiram College, Art Department, Hiram OH (S)

Schubert, Terrance, *Asst Prof*, University of Wisconsin-River Falls, Art Department, River Falls WI (S)

Schug, Albert, *Librn*, Museen der Stadt Köln, Kunst und Museumsbibliothek, Cologne Germany, Federal Republic of

Schug, Albert, *Librn*, Museen der Stadt Köln, Wallraf-Richartz-Museum Bibliothek, Cologne Germany, Federal Republic of

Schuld, James, *Instr*, Portland Community College, Department of Fine Arts, Portland OR (S)

Schuler, Hans C, *Dir*, Schuler School of Fine Arts, Baltimore MD (S)

Schulman, Barbara, *Asst Prof*, Weber State College, Art Department 2001, Ogden UT (S)

Schulman, Robert, *Pres*, Federal Design Council, Washington DC

Schulman, William, *Assoc Prof*, University of Wisconsin-Stout, Art Department, Menomonie WI (S)

Schulner, Diane, *Instr*, International Fine Arts College, Miami FL (S)

Schulter, Margildis, *Asst Cur*, Kestner-Museum, Hannover Germany, Federal Republic of

Schultz, Bernie, *Prof*, West Virginia University, Division of Art, Morgantown WV (S)

Schultz, Douglas G, *Cur*, Albright-Knox Art Gallery, Buffalo Fine Arts Academy, Buffalo NY

Schultz, Jody, *Instructor*, Highland Community College, Freeport IL (S)

Schultz, LeRoy, *Asst Prof*, Southwestern Oklahoma State University, Art Department, Weatherford OK (S)

Schultz, Sharon L, *Deputy Dir*, Center for Inter-American Relations Art Gallery, New York NY

Schultz, Stanly, *Pres*, Old State House, Hartford CT

Schultz, William, *Head National History*, Ohio Historical Society, Columbus OH

Schultze, Jurgen, *Cur*, Kunsthalle Bremen, Bremen Art Gallery, Bremen Germany, Federal Republic of

Schultze, Raymond W, *Prof*, Kearney State College, Dept of Art, Kearney NE (S)

Schulz, Charles A, *Studio Dir*, Art Association of Harrisburg, Harrisburg PA

Schulze, Franz, *Prof*, Lake Forest College, Dept of Art, Lake Forest IL (S)

Schulz-Hoffmann, Carla, *Cur 20th Century Art*, Bayerischen Staatsgemaldesammlungen, Bavarian State Galleries of Art, Munich Germany, Federal Republic of

Schumacher, Herb, *Prof*, University of Northern Colorado, Department of Fine Arts, Greeley CO (S)

Schumacher, Tom, *VPres*, Verde Valley Art Association, Inc, Jerome AZ

Schupbach, Theresa, *Instr*, Kenyon College, Art Department, Gambier OH (S)

Schuster, Adeline, *Librn*, Harrington Institute of Interior Design Library, Chicago IL

Schutte, Richard, *Treas*, Valley Art Center Inc, Clarkston WA

Schutte, Thomas F, *Pres*, Philadelphia College of Art, Philadelphia PA (S)

Schutte, Thomas F, *Pres*, Philadelphia College of Art Gallery, Philadelphia PA

Schutz, Edward E, *Head Dept*, Northeast Louisiana University, Department of Art, Monroe LA (S)

Schuyler, Jane, *Instr*, York College of the City University of New York, Fine and Performing Arts, Jamaica NY (S)

Schuyler, Robert, *Assoc Cur in charge American Historical Archaeology*, University of Pennsylvania, University Museum, Philadelphia PA

Schwab, Bernard, *Dir*, Madison Public Library, Madison WI

Schwab, Norman, *Assoc Prof*, Mount Saint Mary's College, Art Department, Los Angeles CA (S)

Schwabach, James Bruce, *Instructor*, Herkimer County Community College, Humanities Division, Herkimer NY (S)

Schwacha, Ruth, *Treas*, Art Centre of New Jersey, East Orange NJ

Schwartz, Carole, *Asst Librn & Museum Archivist*, Cincinnati Art Museum, Library, Cincinnati OH

Schwartz, Douglas W, *Pres*, School of American Research, Santa Fe NM

Schwartz, Ellen, *Librn*, Crocker Art Museum, Library, Sacramento CA

Schwartz, Gregory, *Curatorial Asst*, Dartmouth College Museum & Galleries, Hanover NH

Schwartz, Judith, *Public Relations Mgr*, Brooklyn Museum, Brooklyn NY

Schwartz, Judith, *Dir*, University of Toronto, Hart House, Toronto ON

Schwartz, Marta, *Librn III & Head Department*, Yonkers Public Library, Fine Arts Department, Yonkers NY

Schwartz, Stephen H, *Dir*, Kenosha Public Museum, Kenosha WI

Schwarz, Jack, *Chmn Dept*, Biola College, Art Department, La Mirada CA (S)

Schwarz, Joseph, *Head Dept*, Auburn University at Montgomery, Art Department, Montgomery AL (S)

Schwarz, William, *Assoc Prof*, University of Illinois at the Medical Center, Dept of Biocommunication Arts-Medical Art, Chicago IL (S)

Schwatz, Alan E, *Secy*, Detroit Institute of Arts, Detroit Institute of Art Founders Society, Detroit MI

Schwebel, Renata M, *Executive VPres*, Sculptors Guild, Inc, New York NY

Schweighauser, Virginia L, *Museum Secy*, East Tennessee State University, Carroll Reece Museum, Johnson City TN

Schweiss, Ruth Keller, *Executive Dir*, Academy of Professional Artists, Saint Louis MO

Schweitzer, Mary de Paul, *Coordr*, Marian College, Art Department, Indianapolis IN (S)

Schweizer, Paul D, *Dir*, St Lawrence University, Richard F Brush Art Gallery, Canton NY

Schweizer, Paul D, *Asst Prof*, Saint Laurence University, Department of Fine Arts, Canton NY (S)

Schwenk III, J W, *Dir*, Jackson County Historical Society, 1859 Jail Museum and Marshall's House, Independence MO

Schwermer, Sabine, *Librn*, Staatliche Kunsthalle, Library, Karlshruhe Germany, Federal Republic of

Schwidder, Ernst, *Prof*, Pacific Lutheran University, Department of Art, Tacoma WA (S)

Schwieger, C R, *Chmn*, Minot State College, Division of Fine Arts, Minot ND (S)

Schwing, Charles E, *Pres*, American Institute of Architects, Washington DC

Scillia, Diane, *Admin Asst*, Chrysler Museum, Norfolk VA

Scioli, Don, *Lectr*, Saint Joseph's College, Fine Arts Program, Philadelphia PA (S)

Sciotti, Angela M, *Library Dir*, Swain School of Design, Library, New Bedford MA

Scoones, Nancy, *Adminr*, Cornell University, Herbert F Johnson Museum of Art, Ithaca NY

Scorsone, Dora J, *Secy*, State University of New York College at Geneseo, Fine Arts Gallery, Geneseo NY

Scott, Charles C, *Prof*, Glenville State College, Department of Art, Glenville WV (S)

Scott, David W, *Planning Consult*, National Gallery of Art, Washington DC

Scott, Floyd, *Cur Exhib*, Carson County Square House Museum, Panhandle TX

Scott, G Richard, *Academic Dean*, Avila College, Art Gallery, Kansas City MO

Scott, Hilda, *Consulting Librn*, Norton Gallery and School of Art, Library, West Palm Beach FL

Scott, James, *Instructor*, Burnley School of Professional Art, Inc, Seattle WA (S)

Scott, Jim, *Exhib Preparator*, Ohio State University, Gallery of Fine Arts, Columbus OH

Scott, John, *Adjunct Cur*, Museum of Fine Arts, Houston, Houston TX

Scott, John F, *Asst Prof*, Rice University, Department of Art and Art History, Houston TX (S)

Scott, John T, *Chmn*, Xavier University of Louisiana, Department of Fine Arts, New Orleans LA (S)

Scott, Oliver Patrick, *Chmn*, Morgan State University, Department of Art, Baltimore MD (S)

Scott, P F, *Pres*, Abbot Hall Art Gallery, Cumbria England

Scott, Paul, *Instr*, Montserrat School of Visual Art, Beverly MA (S)

Scott, Pete, *Exhibit Supv*, California State Fair and Exposition Art Show, Sacramento CA

Scott, T, *Head Dept Art*, City of Birmingham Polytechnic, Birmingham England (S)

Scott, Violet A, *Cur Art Center*, Honolulu Academy of Arts, Honolulu HI

Scott, Walter D, *Executive VPres*, The Pillsbury Company, Minneapolis MN

Scottez, Annie, *Asst*, Musee des Beaux-Arts de Lille, Museum of Fine Arts, Lille France

Scott-Gibson, Herbert, *Museum Education Community Education*, Metropolitan Museum of Art, New York NY

Scourfield, E, *Keeper Family and Rural Life*, Welsh Folk Museum, Saint Fagans Wales

Scranton, Robert, *Vis Prof*, Emory University, Art History Department, Atlanta GA (S)

Scripture, P F, *VPres*, Rome Historical Society, Rome Information and Cultural Center, Rome NY

Scroggins, Clyde, *Rental Mgr*, University of Minnesota, University Gallery, Minneapolis MN

Scucchi, Robie, *Asst Prof*, Mississippi State University, Art Department, Mississippi State MS (S)

Scudder, Rogers, *Dir of Library*, American Academy in Rome Library, Rome Italy

Scull III, Ward, *VPres*, Peninsula Fine Arts Center, Newport News VA

Scutt, W H, *Archaeological Asst*, Plymouth City Museum and Art Gallery, Plymouth England

Sdunek, Bruce, *Pres*, Hartland Art Council, Hartland MI

Seabold, Tom, *Dir*, Keokuk Art Center, Keokuk IA

Seace, Barry W, *Asst Prof*, Mount Holyoke College, Art Department, South Hadley MA (S)

Seager, Pamela L, *Dir of Administrative Services*, California Historical Society, San Francisco CA

Seagrave, Edmund O, *Assoc Mgr*, University of Connecticut, Jorgensen Gallery, Storrs CT

Seah, Gek Eng, *Librn*, National Museum Art Gallery, Library, Singapore Singapore, Republic of

Seal, Leila B, *Coordr of Museum Services*, Museum of the Southwest, Midland TX

Seal, Robert H, *1st VPres*, San Antonio Museum Association, Inc, San Antonio TX

Seaman, Anne T, *Librn*, Honolulu Academy of Arts, Library, Honolulu HI

Seamans, Warren A, *Dir*, Massachusetts Institute of Technology, Historical Collections, Cambridge MA

Searing, Helen, *Chairperson Art Dept*, Smith College, Art Department, Northampton MA (S)

Searle, Annie, *Public Relations Mgr*, Seattle Art Museum, Seattle WA

Searles, Rose, *Head Circulation Department*, Springfield Free Public Library, Donald B Palmer Museum, Springfield NJ

Secor, W Fielding, *VPres*, Mattatuck Historical Society, Mattatuck Museum, Waterbury CT

Seddon, Brian Abell, *Keeper Natural History*, Birmingham Museums and Art Gallery, Birmingham England

Seeley, A Mae, *Dir*, Staten Island Institute of Arts and Sciences, Staten Island NY

Seeley, J, *Asst Prof*, Wesleyan University, Art Department, Middletown CT (S)

Seelhorst, R C, *Instructor*, Indiana University of Pennsylvania, Department of Art and Art Education, Indiana PA (S)

Seelye, Eugene A, *Assoc Prof*, Clarion State College, Department of Art, Clarion PA (S)

Seeman, Becky, *Instructor*, College of Wooster, Department of Art, Wooster OH (S)

Segal, Arline, *Cur Arts*, The Rosenbach Museum and Library, Philadelphia PA

Segerson, Marge, *Librn*, Museum of Arts and Sciences, Library, Daytona Beach FL

Segger, Martin, *Dir & Cur*, University of Victoria, Maltwood Art Museum and Gallery, Victoria BC

Segger, Martin J, *Lectr*, University of Victoria, Department of History in Art, Victoria BC (S)

Segoviano, Jose Luis Mercado, *Head Dept*, Escuela de Artes Decorativas, School of Decorative Arts, Madrid Spain (S)

Seherr-Thoss, H C, *Pres*, Litchfield Historical Society, Litchfield CT

Sehrai, Fidaullah, *Dir*, Peshawar Museum, Peshawar Pakistan

Seibert, Donald C, *Dept Head*, Ernest Stevenson Bird Library, Syracuse NY

Seibert, Marzie, *Vol Services*, Rockwell-Corning Museum, Corning NY

Seidel, Linda, *Assoc Prof*, University of Chicago, Department of Art History & Committee on Art & Design, Chicago IL (S)

Seifert, Johannes, *Librn*, Rheinisches Landesmuseum Bonn, Library, Bonn Germany, Federal Republic of

Seitchik, Carol, *Dir*, Muse Art Gallery, Philadelphia PA

Seitz, John, *VPres*, Associated Artists of Pittsburgh Arts and Crafts Center, Pittsburgh PA

Seiz, John, *Instructor*, Springfield College in Illinois, Dept of Art, Springfield IL (S)

Sekino, Tad, *Chmn Ceramics*, De Young Museum Art School, San Francisco CA (S)

Sekler, Eduard F, *Prof*, Harvard University, Department of Visual and Environmental Studies, Cambridge MA (S)

Selby, Pat, *Pres*, Cuyahoga Valley Art Center, Cuyahoga Falls OH (S)

Selby, Roger L, *Dir*, Winnipeg Art Gallery, Winnipeg MB

Seley, Beverly, *Prof*, Grand Valley State Colleges, Art Department, Allendale MI (S)

Seley, Jason, *Prof*, Cornell University, Department of Art, Ithaca NY (S)

Seligman, T K, *Deputy Dir Education & Exhib*, Fine Arts Museums of San Francisco, M H de Young Memorial Museum and California Palace of the Legion of Honor, n of Honor co

Seligsohn, Valerie, *Assoc Prof*, Philadelphia Community College, Department of Fine Arts, Philadelphia PA (S)

Sellars, Judith, *Librn*, Museum of New Mexico, Museum of International Folk Art Library, Santa Fe NM

Selle, Thomas, *Lectr*, Carroll College, Art Department, Waukesha WI (S)

Sellers, Boris, *Mgr*, Detroit Institute of Arts, Detroit Institute of Art Founders Society, Detroit MI

Sellers, Joan, *Dir of Performing Arts*, Mid-Hudson Arts and Science Center, Poughkeepsie NY

Sellers, John, *Chmn*, Syracuse University, College of Visual and Performing Arts, Syracuse NY (S)

Sellin, David, *Chief Cur*, United States Capitol Museum, Washington DC

Selter, Dan, *Instr*, Transylvania University, Studio Arts Department, Lexington KY (S)

Selvar, Jane Cumming, *Dir*, Bronxville Public Library, Bronxville NY

Selzi, Paul, *Chmn Art Gallery*, Fairfield Public Library and Museum, Fairfield Art Association, Fairfield IA

Semerad, Marjorie, *Chmn*, Russell Sage College, Visual and Performing Arts Department, Troy NY (S)

Semeraro, Claudia Marino, *Librn*, Museu de Arte de Sao Paulo, Library, Sao Paulo Brazil

Semler, Evelyn, *Reference Librn*, Pierpont Morgan Library, New York NY

Semmel, Marsha K, *Art Historian & Promotion*, Taft Museum, Cincinnati OH

Semper, Rob, *Admin Asst*, Exploratorium, San Francisco CA

Sendra, Eloisa, *Cur*, Museo de Arte Moderno, Museum of Modern Art, Barcelona Spain

Senior, P A, *Dir*, Johannesburg Art Gallery, Johannesburg South Africa, Republic of

Seniw, N, *Pres*, Ukrainian Museum of Canada, Edmonton AB

Senner, Eileen, *Gallery Chmn*, Oregon College of Education Galleries, Monmouth OR

Sennett, Arthur, *Prof*, State University of New York College at Potsdam, Department of Fine Arts, Potsdam NY (S)

Senti, Marvel, *Pres*, Hutchinson Art Association, Hutchinson KS

Senungetuk, Ronald, *Dept Head & Prof*, University of Alaska, Department of Art, Fairbanks AK (S)

Sepessy, Joan L, *Asst Librn*, Toledo Museum of Art, Library, Toledo OH

Sepulveda, Teresa, *Head Ethnographical Department*, Museo Nacional de Antropologia, National Museum of Anthropology, Mexico Mexico

Serafine, Joseph, *VPres*, United States Figure Skating Hall of Fame and Museum, Colorado Springs CO

Serafy, Jean, *Chmn*, Texas Southmost College, Fine Arts Department, Brownsville TX (S)

Serenco, Henry, *Assoc Prof*, University of Nebraska at Omaha, Dept of Art, Omaha NE (S)

Serette, David W, *Cur Graphic Arts & Photography*, Shaker Museum, Poland Spring ME

Serfaty, Gail F, *Asst Cur*, Department of State, Diplomatic Reception Rooms, Washington DC

Serisawa, Sueo, *Instructor*, University of Southern California, Idyllwild Campus, Idyllwild School of Music and the Arts, Idyllwild CA (S)

Serra, Ing Mario, *Pres*, Accademia di Belle Arti, Academy of Fine Arts, Perugia Italy (S)

Serra, Rosanna Maggio, *Cur Modern Art Collection*, Museo Civico di Torino, Municipal Museum, Turin Italy

Seruey, Margueite, *Secy*, La Societe des Decorateurs-Ensembliers du Quebec, Interior Decorators' Society of Quebec, Montreal PQ

Serullaz, Maurice, *Cur Drawings*, Musee du Louvre, Louvre Museum, Paris France

Sever, Ziya, *Chmn*, Alvin Community College, Art Dept, Alvin TX (S)

Severa, Joan, *Cur of Textiles*, State Historical Society of Wisconsin, Madison WI

Severens, Martha R, *Cur Collection*, Carolina Art Association, Gibbes Art Gallery, Charleston SC

Sevigny, Maurice J, *Dir*, Bowling Green State University, School of Art, Bowling Green OH (S)

Sevy, Barbara, *Librn*, Philadelphia Museum of Art, Marian Angell Boyer and Francis Boyer Library, Philadelphia PA

Seward, Claude, *Instr*, Orange County Community College, Art Department, Middletown NY (S)

Sewell, Darrel, *Cur American Art*, Philadelphia Museum of Art, Philadelphia PA

Sewell, Jack, *Cur Oriental Art*, Art Institute of Chicago, Chicago IL

Sewell, Jack, *Secy Treas*, Art Institute of Chicago, Orientals, Chicago IL

Sexauer, Donald R, *Chmn Printmaking*, East Carolina University, School of Art, Greenville NC (S)

Sexauer, William, *VPres*, Historical Society of Quincy and Adams County, Quincy IL

Sexton, Irwin, *Dir*, San Antonio Public Library, San Antonio TX

Sextone, Dick, *Instructor*, Peters Valley Craft Center, Layton NJ (S)

Seyfert, Anna Mary, *Pres*, Arizona Watercolor Association, Phoenix AZ

Seyffert, A, *Professional Asst*, Pretoria Art Museum, Pretoria South Africa, Republic of

Seylaz, Paul, *Dir & Cur*, Musee des Beaux-Arts et Societe des Amis des Arts, Museum of Fine Arts, La Switzerland

Sgouros, Thomas, *Head Illustration*, Rhode Island School of Design, Providence RI (S)

Shackelford, Bruce M, *Dir*, Creek Council House and Museum, Okmulgee OK

Shackelford, Bruce M, *Cur-Dir*, Creek Council House and Museum, Creek Council House Library, Okmulgee OK

Shackelford, Marjorie, *Development Officer*, San Antonio Museum Association, Inc, San Antonio TX

Shadbolt, Douglas, *Dir*, University of British Columbia, School of Architecture, Vancouver BC (S)

Shady, Kathy J, *Asst Librn*, Chester County Historical Society, Library, West Chester PA

Shafer, Stan, *Chmn*, College of Saint Benedict, Art Department, Saint Joseph MN (S)

Shafer, Stanley, *Chmn of Art Dept & Gallery Dir*, College of Saint Benedict, Art Gallery, Saint Joseph MN

Shaffer, Diane, *Asst Prof*, Aquinas College, Art Department, Grand Rapids MI (S)

Shaffer, Ellen, *Cur*, Silverado Museum, Saint Helena CA

Shaffer, Jeanne, *Chmn*, Huntingdon College, Dept of Visual and Performing Arts, Montgomery AL (S)

Shaffer, Kenneth, *Chmn*, Mount Vernon Nazarene College, Art Department, Mount Vernon OH (S)

Shaffstall, James W, *Chmn*, Hanover College, Department of Art, Hanover IN (S)

Shainswit, Lisa, *Public Appearance Chmn*, Women in the Arts Foundation, Inc, New York NY

Shalkop, R L, *Dir*, Anchorage Historical and Fine Arts Museum, Anchorage AK

Shaman, Floyd D, *Asst Prof*, Delta State University, Department of Art, Cleveland MS (S)

Shaman, Sanford S, *Dir*, Washington State University, Museum of Art, Pullman WA

Shaman, Sanford Sivitz, *Dir*, University of Northern Iowa, Gallery of Art, Cedar Falls IA

Shane, Audrey, *Archivist*, University of British Columbia, Museum of Anthropology, Vancouver BC

Shaneour, Michael, *Dir*, Custer County Art Center, Miles City MT

Shaner, Carol, *Exhibits Librn*, Sarah Lawrence College Library, Bronxville NY

Shangraw, Clarence F, *Sr Cur*, Asian Art Museum of San Francisco, Avery Brundage Collection, San Francisco CA

Shankel, Carol, *Public Relations*, Spencer Museum of Art, Lawrence KS

Shannahan, John W, *Dir*, Sloane-Stanley Museum, West Hartford CT

Shannon, Joseph, *Chief Exhib*, Hirshhorn Museum and Sculpture Garden, Washington DC

Shannon, Joseph, *Prof*, Trenton State College, Art Department, Trenton NJ (S)

Shannon, Mary R, *Cur*, Rochester Historical Society, Rochester NY

Shannon, Zella, *Assoc Dir*, Minneapolis Public Library and Information Center, Art, Music and Film Dept, Minneapolis MN

Shapiro, Babe, *Artist-in-Res*, Maryland Institute, Mount Royal School of Painting, Baltimore MD (S)

Shapiro, Charlotte, *Park Houses*, Philadelphia Museum of Art, Philadelphia PA

Shapiro, F, *Chmn Fine Arts*, Fashion Institute of Technology, New York NY (S)

Shapiro, Irving, *Dir*, American Academy of Art, Chicago IL (S)

Shapiro, Laurie, *Dir Education*, Mid-Hudson Arts and Science Center, Poughkeepsie NY

Shapiro, Michael, *Chief Bureau of Museums and Historic Sites*, Division of Historical and Cultural Affairs, Bureau of Museums and Historic Sites, Dover DE

Shapiro, Stephen, *Pres*, Bay Area Art Conservation Guild, San Francisco CA

Sharp, Ellen, *Graphic Arts*, Detroit Institute of Arts, Detroit MI

Sharp, Kenton, *Instr*, Montserrat School of Visual Art, Beverly MA (S)

Sharp, L G, *Dir*, Museum of Applied Arts and Sciences, Sydney Australia

Sharp, Renata, *Executive Secy*, Städtische Kunsthalle, City Art Gallery, Dusseldorf Germany, Federal Republic of

Sharpe, Bruce, *Dean*, Pratt Institute, School of Art and Design, Brooklyn NY (S)

Sharpe, David C, *Acting Chmn Archit*, Illinois Institute of Technology, College of Architecture, Planning and Design, Department of Architecture, Chicago IL (S)

Sharpe, Janet R, *Progress Consultant*, Angelo State University, Houston Harte University Center, San Angelo TX

Sharpe, K, *Keeper*, South London Art Gallery, London England

Sharpe, Sara, *Treas*, Plastic Club, Art Club for Women, Philadelphia PA

Sharrow, Sheba, *Instructor*, Millersville State College, Art Department, Millersville PA (S)

Shatto, Gloria, *Pres*, Berry College, Art Department, Mount Berry GA

Shaughnessy, Marie, *Funding*, Alaska Artists Guild, Anchorage AK

Shaughnessy, Robert, *Prof*, Southampton College of Long Island University, Fine Arts Division, Southampton NY (S)

Shaver, Shirlee, *Asst Prof*, Texas Woman's University, Department of Art, Denton TX (S)

Shaver-Crandell, Anne, *Assoc Prof*, City College of the City of New York, Art Department, New York NY (S)

Shaviro, Sol, *Chmn Board*, Bronx Museum of the Arts, Bronx NY

Shaw, Audrey, *Admin Secy*, Association of Canadian Industrial Designers, Ontario, Toronto ON

Shaw, Courtney, *Head Art Library*, University of Maryland, Art Library, College Park MD

Shaw, Luke A, *Dept Coordr*, Coppin State College, Art Dept, Baltimore MD (S)

Shaw, Mary M, *Dir*, Johnson-Humrickhouse Museum, Coshocton OH

Shaw, Maxine, *Secy*, Vancouver Art Gallery, Vancouver BC

Shaw, Sarah, *Asst*, Providence Public Library, Art and Music Dept, Providence RI

Shaw, Wayne L, *Chmn Art Dept*, Belleville Area College, Art Department, Belleville IL (S)

Shaw Jr, H Allen, *Instructor*, Oklahoma State University, School of Technical Training, Okmulgee OK (S)

Shawl, William, *Acad Dean*, Golden West College, Arts, Humanities and Social Sciences Institute, Huntington Beach CA (S)

Shea, David, *Tres*, Hoosier Salon Patrons Association, Hoosier Salon Art Gallery, Indianapolis IN

Shea, John Martin, *Pres*, Newport Harbor Art Museum, Newport Beach CA

Shea, Liliosa, *Assoc Prof*, Notre Dame College, Art Department, Manchester NH (S)

Shea, William G, *Admin Asst*, Portsmouth Museums and Community Arts Center, Petersburg VA

Sheaks, Barclay, *Head Dept*, Virginia Wesleyan College, Art Department of the Humanities Division, Norfolk VA (S)

Shealor, Walter H, *VPres*, Canton Art Institute, Canton OH

Sheardy, Robert, *Instructor*, Muskegon Community College, Dept of Creative & Performing Arts, Muskegon MI (S)

Shearer, Elizabeth, *Pres*, Cleveland Museum of Art, Print Club of Cleveland, Cleveland OH

Shearer, Linda, *Asst Cur*, Solomon R Guggenheim Museum, New York NY

Shear Jr, T Leslie, *Chmn Prog in Classical Archaeology*, Princeton University, Department of Art and Archaeology, Princeton NJ (S)

Shearman, John, *Chmn Dept*, Princeton University, Department of Art and Archaeology, Princeton NJ (S)

Shearouse Jr, Henry G, *Librn*, Denver Public Library, Denver CO

Shears, Edith D, *Pres*, Toledo Artists' Club, Toledo OH

Sheffield, Clinton A, *Assoc Prof*, Dickinson State College, Department of Art, Dickinson ND (S)

Sheffield, John T, *Treas*, Wichita Art Association Inc, Wichita KS

Sheingorn, Pamela, *Assoc Prof*, Bernard M Baruch College of the City University of New York, Art Department, New York NY (S)

Shekore, Mark, *Assoc Prof*, Northern State College, Art Dept, Aberdeen SD (S)

Shelbourn, Sherry, *Admis Officer*, Scotts Bluff National Monument, Gering NE

Sheldon, James L, *Cur Photography*, Phillips Academy, Addison Gallery of American Art, Andover MA

Shellito, Jean, *Secy*, Kansas Watercolor Society, Wichita KS

Shellman, Feay, *Cur of Coll*, Telfair Academy of Arts and Sciences Inc, Savannah GA

Shelly, Barbara, *Instr*, Vancouver Community College, Langara Campus, Department of Fine Arts, Vancouver BC (S)

Shelton, Margaret, *Secy*, Ann Arbor Art Association, Ann Arbor MI

Shen-Dar, Judith, *Cur*, Museum of Modern Art, Haifa Israel

Shenk, Wilbur, *VPres*, Ashtabula Arts Center, Ashtabula OH

Shenon, Michael, *Design Coordr*, San Jose State University, Art Department, San Jose CA (S)

Sheon, Aaron, *Prof*, University of Pittsburgh, Henry Clay Frick Fine Arts Department, Pittsburgh PA (S)

Shepard, Fred, *Preparator*, University of Santa Clara, de Saisset Art Gallery and Museum, Santa Clara CA

Shepard, Fred, *Instructor*, Murray State University, Art Department, Murray KY (S)

Shepard, Willard, *Secy*, Lyman Allyn Museum, New London CT

Shephard, Dorothy G, *Cur Textiles*, Cleveland Museum of Art, Cleveland OH

Shepherd, Jeani, *Curatorial Asst*, Illinois State University, University Museums, Normal IL

Shepherd, Murray, *University Librn*, University of Waterloo, Dana Porter Arts Library, Waterloo ON

Shepler, Joseph, *Co-Dir*, Chatham College Art Gallery, Pittsburgh PA

Shepler, Martha, *Instructor*, La Roche College, Division of Graphic Arts & Design, Pittsburgh PA (S)

Shepp, Alan, *Chmn*, California State University, Hayward, Art Department, Hayward CA (S)

Sheppard, Carl D, *Prof*, University of Minnesota, Minneapolis, Art History, Minneapolis MN (S)

Sheppard, Carl D, *Treas*, International Center of Medieval Art, Inc, New York NY

Sheppard, John, *Dir Public Relations*, Brandywine River Museum, Chadds Ford PA

Sheppard, Margaret, *Pres*, Eliot McMurrough School of Art, Melbourne FL (S)

Sheppard, Roger, *Publications*, National Portrait Gallery, London England

Sheridan, Helen, *Head Librn*, Kalamazoo Institute of Arts, Library, Kalamazoo MI

Sherker, Michael, *Assoc Prof*, Kingsborough Community College, Department of Art, Brooklyn NY (S)

Sherlock, David, *Deputy Dir*, National College of Art and Design, Dublin Ireland (S)

Sherman, Cindy, *Dir*, Artists Space, Unaffiliated Artists File, New York NY

Sherman, Cindy, *Program Coordr*, Artists Space, Committee for the Visual Arts, Inc, New York NY

Sherman, Helen, *Assoc Prof*, Marygrove College, Dept of Art & Art History, Detroit MI (S)

Sherman, Meg, *Chmn Design*, Swain School of Design, New Bedford MA (S)

Sherman, Paul T, *Admin Services Librn*, New York City Community College, Namm Hall Library and Learning Resource Center, Brooklyn NY

Sherman, Randi, *Educational Coordr*, Spertus Museum of Judaica, Chicago IL

Sherman, Roger, *Cur*, Plains Art Museum, Main Gallery, Moorhead MN

Sherman, Thomas L, *Dir of Development*, Delaware Art Museum, Wilmington DE

Sherman, William A, *Pres*, Newport Historical Society, Newport RI

Shermoe, Raymond, *Executive Dir*, Civic Fine Arts Association Museum, Sioux Falls SD

Sherpick, William E, *Chmn*, Farmington Museum, Stanley-Whitman House, Farmington CT

Sherrill, Marjorie, *Development Coordr*, Tucson Museum of Art, Tucson AZ

Sherwin, Brian, *Pres*, Fine ARts Association, School of Fine Arts, Willoughby OH

Sherwood, Richard E, *Chmn*, Los Angeles County Museum of Art, Los Angeles CA

Shestack, Alan, *Dir*, Yale University, Art Gallery, New Haven CT

Shewhake, Mitzi, *Asst Prof*, Winston-Salem State University, Art Department, Winston-Salem NC (S)

Shickman, Allan, *Asst Prof*, University of Northern Iowa, Department of Art, Cedar Falls IA (S)

Shield, Jan G, *Asst Prof*, Pacific University in Oregon, Department of Fine Arts, Forest Grove OR (S)

Shields, C D, *In Charge Art Program*, The Standard Oil Company (Ohio), Cleveland OH

Shields, Charles A, *Secy*, Litchfield Historical Society, Litchfield CT

Shields, Mildren, *Secy*, Racine Art Association, Racine WI

Shiels, L F, *Secy*, Canadian Artists' Representation, Winnipeg MB

Shiff, Richard, *Assoc Prof*, University of North Carolina at Chapel Hill, Art Department, Chapel Hill NC (S)

Shigaki, Betty Jean, *Dir*, Rochester Art Center, Rochester MN

Shih, Hsio-Yen, *Dir*, National Museums of Canada, National Gallery of Canada, Ottawa ON

Shih, Hsio-Yen, *Dir*, National Gallery of Canada, Ottawa ON

Shimada, Norio, *Cur*, Bridgestone Bijutsukan, Bridgestone Museum of Art, Tokyo Japan

Shimizu, Yoshiaki, *Assoc Cur Japanese Art*, Freer Gallery of Art, Washington DC

Shin, Hyun, *Asst Prof*, University of Northern Colorado, Department of Fine Arts, Greeley CO (S)

Shindelbower, Daniel N, *Chmn*, Eastern Kentucky University, Art Department, Richmond KY (S)

Shine, Carolyn R, *Cur Costumes, Textiles, Tribal Arts*, Cincinnati Art Museum, Cincinnati OH

Shipley, Roger, *Co-Dir*, Lycoming College Gallery, Williamsport PA

Shipley, Roger Douglas, *Chmn Dept*, Lycoming College, Art Department, Williamsport PA (S)

Shireman, Candace, *Supv Art Area*, Cleveland State University, Library - Art Area, Cleveland OH

Shires, Bill, *Instructor*, West Texas State University, Art Department, Canyon TX (S)

Shirk, S, *Dean*, Albright College, Freedman Gallery, Reading PA

Shirley, Karen, *Chmn*, Antioch College, Noyes, Read and Gray Galleries, Yellow Springs OH

Shirley, Karen, *Assoc Prof*, Antioch College, Department of Art, Yellow Springs OH (S)

Shishido, Miles, *Chmn Div*, Pacific University in Oregon, Department of Fine Arts, Forest Grove OR (S)

Shissler, Barbara, *Cur Education*, National Collection of Fine Arts, Washington DC

Shlomberg, Karen Ann, *Program Dir*, Farmington Valley Arts Center, Avon CT

Shoemaker, George R, *Chmn Art Dept*, Edinboro State College, Art Department, Edinboro PA (S)

Shoja, Jafar, *Instr*, Rivier College, Art Department, Nashua NH (S)

Sholl, Betty, *Treas*, The Dalles Art Association, The Dalles OR

Shook, Larry, *Head Dept*, Victoria College, Victoria TX (S)

Shoolroy, Clifton, *Treas*, Sierra Nevada Museum of Art, Reno NV

Shooter, Tom, *Instructor*, Boston Center for Adult Education, Boston MA (S)

Shopmaker, Laurence, *Asst Dir*, State University of New York College at Purchase, Neuberger Museum, Purchase NY

Shores, Ken, *Prof*, Lewis and Clark College, Department of Art, Portland OR (S)

Shorr, Phil, *Pres*, Art Institute of Chicago, Society for Contemporary Arts, Chicago IL

Short, Ian, *Chmn Two-Dimensional Area*, Edinboro State College, Art Department, Edinboro PA (S)

Showman, Richard K, *Ed, Nathanael Green Papers*, Rhode Island Historical Society, Providence RI

Shri, R K, *Keeper Gandhi, Art and Architecture*, Museum and Picture Gallery, Baroda India

Shroff, Piroja, *Instructor*, California College of Arts and Crafts, Oakland CA (S)

Shrum, L Vance, *Asst to Dir*, Cummer Gallery of Art, DeEtte Holden Cummer Museum Foundation, Jacksonville FL

Shubert, Joseph, *State Librn-Assoc Commissioner for Libraries*, New York State Library, Manuscripts and Special Collections, Albany NY

Shuck, Patrick, *Instructor*, Saint Louis Community College at Meramec, Art Dept, Saint Louis MO (S)

Shuemaker, Ira, *Interior Design Coordr*, North Texas State University, Art Department, Denton TX (S)

Shuff, Lily, *Secy*, National Society of Painters in Casein and Acrylic, Inc, New York NY

Shuffleburg, David, *Clerk*, Springfield Art & Historical Society, Springfield VT

Shulansky, Ruth, *Membership Coordr*, Old State House, Hartford CT

Shull, Carl, *Prof*, Eastern Illinois University, Art Department, Charleston IL (S)

Shuman, Geraldine S, *Museum Coordr*, Hastings Museum, Hastings NE

Shumway, Floyd M, *Dir*, New Haven Colony Historical Society, New Haven CT

Shust, Maria, *Dir*, Ukrainian Museum, New York NY

Shuttleworth, Winifred, *Secy*, Cedar Rapids Art Center, Cedar Rapids IA

Sibley, Carter, *Asst Dir Finance & Development*, Huntsville Museum of Art, Huntsville AL

Sichova, N, *Art Secy*, State Museum of Oriental Art, Moscow Ussr

Sickman, Laurence, *Dir Emeritus*, William Rockhill Nelson Gallery of Art, Atkins Museum of Fine Art, Kansas City MO

Sickman, Laurence, *Lectr*, University of Kansas, Kress Foundation Department of Art History, Lawrence KS (S)

Sida, Roberto Garibay, *Master Plastic Arts*, Escuela Nacional de Artes Plasticas, National School of Plastic Arts, Mexico City Mexico (S)

Siddens, Vera Jo, *Asst Prof*, University of Northern Iowa, Department of Art, Cedar Falls IA (S)

Sidey, Tessa, *Art Asst*, York City Art Gallery, York England

Sidky, Nadia Sayed, *Librn*, Greco-Roman Museum, Library, Alexandria Egypt

Sidler, Helen A, *Executive Dir*, Albuquerque Arts Council, Albuquerque NM

Sidman, Howard F, *Chmn Dept*, MacMurray College, Art Department, Jacksonville IL (S)

Sido, Lee, *Asst Prof*, Wabash College, Art Department, Crawfordsville IN (S)

Sidrow, Sigred, *Librn*, Jacque Marchais Center of Tibetan Arts, Inc, Library, Staten Island NY

Siebecker, Dorothy, *Cataloger*, Tucson Museum of Art, Tucson Museum of Art Library, Tucson AZ

Siebel, Julia, *Secy*, Friends of Photography, Carmel CA

Siebenheller, William, *Pres*, Staten Island Institute of Arts and Sciences, Staten Island NY

Sieber, Robert N, *Dir*, Pennsylvania Farm Museum of Landis Valley, Lancaster PA

Sieg, Robert, *Instructor*, East Central University, Art Department, Ada OK (S)

Siegel, Ernest, *Dir*, Enoch Pratt Free Library of Baltimore City, Baltimore MD

Siegel, Larry, *Pres of Board*, Yellowstone Art Center, Billings MT

Siegner, Dwight, *Lectr*, Mount Allison University, Fine Arts Department, Sackville NB (S)

Siegriest, Louis, *Vis Prof*, Santa Rosa Junior College, Art Department, Santa Rosa CA (S)

Siekevitz, Rebecca, *Supervising Librn*, New York Public Library, Donnell Library Center Art Library, New York NY

Siersma, Betsy, *Registrar*, University of Massachusetts, Amherst, University Gallery, Amherst MA

Sifford, Harlan L, *Librn*, University of Iowa, Art Library, Iowa City IA

Sihare, L P, *Dir*, National Gallery of Modern Art, New India

Sikora, Zdzislaw, *Instructor*, Wesleyan College, Art Department, Macon GA (S)

Silberman, Arthur, *Dir*, Native American Painting Reference Library, Oklahoma City OK

Silberstein-Storfer, Muriel R, *Pres*, Art Commission of the City of New York, New York NY

Siler, Patrick, *Asst Prof*, Washington State University, Fine Arts Department, Pullman WA (S)

Silhan, William A, *Assoc Prof*, University of West Florida, Department of Art, Pensacola FL (S)

Sills, Walter O, *Instructor*, Laramie County Community College, Division of Humanities, Cheyenne WY (S)

Silva, Joseph L, *Treas*, Corporate Council for the Arts, Seattle WA

Silver, Arthur, *Prof*, School of the Arts, C W Post Center of Long Island University, Art Department, Greenvale NY (S)

Silver, Daniel Jeremy, *Dir*, Temple Museum of Jewish Religious Art and Music, Cleveland OH

Silver, Thomas C, *Assoc Prof*, Cleveland State University, Art Department, Cincinnati OH (S)

Silverberg, David, *Prof*, Mount Allison University, Fine Arts Department, Sackville NB (S)

Silverman, Harold, *Instructor*, Traphagen School of Fashion, New York NY (S)

Silverthorne, Holly, *Instructor*, Wayne Art Center, Wayne PA (S)

Simakas, Lula, *Instructor*, Madonna College, Art Dept, Livonia MI (S)

Siman, Rebecca H, *Dir*, Burlington County Historical Society, Burlington NJ

Sime, John, *Pres*, Three Schools, Toronto ON (S)

Simerly, Robert, *Institute Dir*, Museum Management Institute, San Francisco CA (S)

Simkin, Phillips, *Instr*, York College of the City University of New York, Fine and Performing Arts, Jamaica NY (S)

Simmons, Betty Jo, *Exec Dir*, Salem Art Association, Bush House, and Bush Barn Art Center, Salem OR

Simmons, Charles B, *Executive Dir*, Henry Morrison Flagler Museum, Palm Beach FL

Simmons, Harold C, *Chmn*, Baylor University, Department of Fine Arts, Waco TX (S)

Simmons, John H, *Chmn Dept*, Drury College, Art, Art History & Architecture Dept, Springfield MO (S)

Simmons, Terry K, *Exhib Chmn*, Delta State University, Fielding L Wright Art Center, Cleveland MS

Simmons, Terry Kay, *Asst Prof*, Delta State University, Department of Art, Cleveland MS (S)

Simon, Barbara, *Secy*, University of Nebraska Lincoln, Nebraska Art Association, Lincoln NE

Simon, Carol, *Registrar*, Beloit College, Theodore Lyman Wright Art Center, Beloit WI

Simon, David L, *Chmn*, State University of New York College at Cortland, Art Slide Library, Cortland NY

Simon, David L, *Chmn*, State University of New York College at Cortland, Art Department, Cortland NY (S)

Simon, Elizabeth, *Asst Prof*, Daemen College, Art Department, Amherst NY (S)

Simon, Herbert, *Assoc Prof*, Wilkes College, Department of Art, Wilkes-Barre PA (S)

Simon, Liz, *Dir*, Daemen College, Dun Scotus Gallery, Amherst NY

Simon, Lois, *Recording Secy*, North Shore Art League, Winnetka IL

Simon, Robert, *Chmn Acad Studies*, Art Institute of Boston, Boston MA (S)

Simon, Sidney, *Prof*, University of Minnesota, Minneapolis, Art History, Minneapolis MN (S)

Simon, Sidney, *Instructor*, Truro Center for the Arts at Castle Hill, Inc, Truro MA (S)

Simonds, M E, *Cur*, Hastings County Museum, Belleville ON

Simonoff, Arnold, *Chmn*, School of the Arts, C W Post Center of Long Island University, Art Department, Greenvale NY (S)

Simons, Anneke Prins, *Prof*, Jersey City State College, Art Department, Jersey City NJ (S)

Simons, Chris, *Prof*, Shoreline Community College, Humanities Division, Seattle WA (S)

Simons, Phil, *Assoc Prof*, Porterville Community College, Department of Fine Arts, Porterville CA (S)

Simonsen, Vibeke, *Interior Design Consultant*, Champion International Corporation, Stamford CT

Simota, Jan, *Rector*, Vysoka Skola Umeleckoprumyslova, Academy of Applied Arts, Prague Czechoslovakia (S)

Simpson, Dale, *Pres*, Glenhyrst Arts Council of Brantford Inc, Brantford ON

Simpson, Derrol, *Pres*, Gananoque Historical Museum, Gananoque ON

Simpson, Ian, *Principal*, Saint Martins School of Art, London England (S)

Simpson, James, *Instructor*, Long Beach City College, Department of Art, Long Beach CA (S)

Simpson, Pamela H, *Head Dept*, Washington and Lee University, Department of Fine Arts, Lexington VA (S)

Simpson, Ruth D, *Cur Archeaology*, San Bernardino County Museum and Satellites, Fine Arts Institute, Redlands CA

Simpson, William Kelly, *Cur Egyptian Art*, Museum of Fine Arts, Boston MA

Sims, Judith, *Dir Prog*, Laguna Gloria Art Museum, Austin TX

Sims, Patterson, *Cur*, Whitney Museum of American Art, New York NY

Sinagra, Attilio, *Instructor*, Ocean City School of Art, Ocean City NJ (S)

Sinail, Eve, *Prof*, West Virginia University, Division of Art, Morgantown WV (S)

Sinclair, Iain, *Dir*, Three Schools, New School of Art, Toronto ON (S)

Sinclair, Jane, *Instr*, Chapman College, Art Department, Orange CA (S)

Sinclair, Susan, *Librn*, Isabella Stewart Gardner Museum, Library, Boston MA

Sing, Lillian, *Secy*, Chinese Culture Foundation, Chinese Culture Center Gallery, San Francisco CA

Singeling, B, *Public Relations*, Stedelijk Museum het Prinsenhof, Het Prinsenhof State Museum, Delft Netherlands

Singer, Arnold, *Prof*, Cornell University, Department of Art, Ithaca NY (S)

Singer, Clyde, *Assoc Dir*, Butler Institute of American Art, Youngstown OH

Singer, Stuart M, *Chmn Applied Arts & Design*, Catonsville Community College, Art & Applied Art Dept, Catonsville MD (S)

Singerman, Tjimkje, *Gallery Asst*, California State University, Northridge, Fine Arts Gallery, Northridge CA

Singiser, George W, *VPres*, Rensselaer County Historical Society, Troy NY

Singletary, Terry L, *Guard Preparator*, North Carolina Central University, Museum of Art, Durham NC

Singstock, Allen, *Arboretum Mgr*, Paine Art Center and Arboretum, Oshkosh WI

Sinkevitch, Alice, *Mgr*, Chicago Architecture Foundation, ArchiCenter, Chicago IL

Sintz, Edward F, *Dir*, Miami-Dade Public Library, Miami FL

Sinyda, Angela, *Bookkeeper*, Studio Museum in Harlem, New York NY

Sioui, Anne-Marie, *Dir of Traveling Exhib*, Musee d'Art Contemporain, Montreal PQ

Sipiora, Leonard P, *Dir*, El Paso Museum of Art, El Paso TX

Sirotkovic, Jakov, *Pres*, Strossmayerova Galerija Starih Majstora Jugoslavenske Akademije Znanosti I Umjetnosti, Strossmayer's Gallery of Old Masters of the Yugoslavia Academy of Sciences and Arts, Zagreb Yugoslavia

Siskind, Elli, *Instr*, Marian College, Art Department, Indianapolis IN (S)

Sisler, Rebecca, *Executive Dir*, Royal Canadian Academy of Arts, Toronto ON

Sisserson, Helen, *Asst Prof*, Nassau Community College, Art Department, Garden City NY (S)

Sisson, Jacqueline D, *Head Librn*, Ohio State University, Fine Arts Library, Columbus OH

Sittenfeld, Paul George, *Pres*, Cincinnati Institute of Fine Arts, Cincinnati OH

Sittner, S Scott, *Instructor*, Indian Hills Community College, Department of Art, Centerville IA (S)

Sitton, Robert, *Dir Film Study Center*, Portland Art Association, Portland OR

Sitton, Robert, *Dir*, Portland Art Association, Northwest Film Study Center, Portland OR

Sivers, Cora, *Cur of Marghab Collection*, South Dakota State University, South Dakota Memorial Art Center, Brookings SD

Sivulich, Kenneth G, *Dir*, Erie District Library Center, Erie PA

Sjoeberg, Lars, *Asst Keeper*, Svenska Statens Portrahsamling, Swedish State Portrait Gallery, Gothenburg Sweden

Sjövold, Aase Bay, *Cur*, Kunstindustrimuseet I Oslo, Oslo Museum of Applied Art, Oslo Norway

Skeie, Penny Sue, *Admin Secy & Bookkeeper*, Blanden Memorial Art Gallery, Fort Dodge IA

Skelley, Robert C, *Prof*, University of Florida, Department of Art, Gainesville FL (S)

Skelton, R, *Keeper Indian Art*, Victoria and Albert Museum, London England

Skidmore, Margaret, *Development Officer*, Museum of Fine Arts, Houston, Houston TX

Skiles, Jackie, *Public Appearance Chm*, Women in the Arts Foundation, Inc, New York NY

Skilliter, Lowell, *Treas*, Toledo Artists' Club, Toledo OH

Skinner, David E, *VPres*, Corporate Council for the Arts, Seattle WA

Skinner, Robert, *Prof*, Southampton College of Long Island University, Fine Arts Division, Southampton NY (S)

Skjelstad, Lucy, *Dir*, Oregon State University, Horner Museum, Corvallis OR

Skjerven, Astrid, *Librn*, Kunstindustrimuseet I Oslo, Library, Oslo Norway

Skorton, Ron, *Instructor*, Emma Willard School Arts Division, Troy NY (S)

Skovgaard, Bente, *Chief Cur*, Statens Museum for Kunst, Department of Painting and Sculpture, Copenhagen Denmark

Skowronek, Stefan, *Ancient Coins*, Muzeum Narodowe w Krakowie, National Museum in Cracow, Cracow Poland

Skramstad Jr, Harold K, *Dir*, Chicago Historical Society, Chicago IL

Skuja, Lucija, *Head Music & Art Dept*, Grand Rapids Public Library, Music and Art Department, Grand Rapids MI

Skuse, Virginia, *Cur*, Rochester Historical Society, Rochester NY

Skvarla, Diane K, *Museum Specialist*, United States Senate Commission on Art and Antiquities, Washington DC

Skydell, Ceil, *Mgr of Museum Shop*, Jewish Museum, New York NY

Slade, Rona, *Chmn Foundation & Second Year*, Corcoran School of Art, Washington DC (S)

Slade, Roy, *Dir Museum*, Cranbrook Academy of Art Museum, Bloomfield Hills MI

Slade, Roy, *Pres*, Cranbrook Academy of Art, Bloomfield Hills MI (S)

Slaney, Steven, *Designer of Exhib*, University of California, Santa Barbara, Art Museum, Santa Barbara CA

Slate, Joseph, *Prof*, Kenyon College, Art Department, Gambier OH (S)

Slater, Robert S, *Pres*, Palm Beach County Parks and Recreation Department, Morikami Museum of Japanese Culture, Delray Beach FL

Slater, Van E, *Assoc Prof*, Compton Community College, Compton CA (S)

Slattum, Jerry, *Asst Prof*, California Lutheran College, Art Department, Thousand Oaks CA (S)

Slaugenhop, Ann, *Secy*, Red River Valley Museum, Vernon TX

Slaughter, Neill, *Instr*, Temple University, Art Department, Philadelphia PA (S)

Slavin III, Richard E, *Administrator*, Lyndhurst, Tarrytown NY

Slayton, Ronald, *Cur*, Wood Art Gallery, Montpelier VT

Slee, David W, *Technician*, University of Michigan Museum of Art, Kelsey Museum of Ancient and Medieval Archaeology, Ann Arbor MI

Slee, Jacquelynn, *Asst to Dir*, University of Michigan Museum of Art, Alumni Memorial Hall Museum, Ann Arbor MI

Sleight, Frederick W, *Exec Dir*, Palm Springs Desert Museum, Inc, Palm Springs CA

Slemmons, Rod, *Cur*, Whatcom Museum of History and Art, Bellingham WA

Slenker, Elizabeth, *Instr*, Saint Thomas Aquinas College, Art Department, Sparkhill NY (S)

Slive, Seymour, *Dir*, Harvard University, William Hayes Fogg Art Museum, Cambridge MA

Sloan, Susan, *Asst Dir Public Relations*, Carnegie-Mellon University, Forbes Street Gallery, Pittsburgh PA

Sloan, Thomas L, *Asst Prof*, Northwestern University, Evanston, Department of Art History, Evanston IL (S)

Sloane, Eric, *Art Advisory Board*, Society of Medalists, Danbury CT

Slobodkina, Esphyr, *Treas*, American Abstract Artists, Summit NJ

Slocum, Richard, *Dir*, Our Lady of the Lake University, Department of Art, San Antonio TX (S)

Slomann, Wencke, *Head Early Iron Age Department*, Universitetets Samling av Nordiske Oldsaker, University Museum of National Antiquities, Oslo Norway

Sloshberg, Leah P, *Dir*, New Jersey State Museum, Trenton NJ

Slottman, Helen, *First VPres*, Pen and Brush, Inc, New York NY

Slouffman, Jim, *Instructor*, Ohio Visual Art Institute, Cincinnati OH (S)

Slowe, V A J, *Deputy Dir*, Abbot Hall Art Gallery, Cumbria England

Slusarski, Peter, *Asst Prof*, Eisenhower College, Seneca Falls NY (S)

Sluzas, Raymund, *Instr*, Catholic University of America, Department of Architecture & Planning, Washington DC (S)

Small, Carol, *Instr*, Gettysburg College, Department of Art, Gettysburg PA (S)

Smallenberg, Harry, *Chmn General Studies*, Center for Creative Studies—College of Art and Design, Detroit MI (S)

Smalley, David, *Prof*, Connecticut College, Department of Art, New London CT (S)

Smalley, Gayle, *Prof*, California State University, Fresno, Art Department, Fresno CA (S)

Smalley, Stephen, *Chmn*, Bridgewater State College, Art Department, Bridgewater MA (S)

Smallman, Carol, *Exec Assts*, Archaeological Institute of America, New York NY

Smar, Joyce, *Supv Music*, Toledo Museum of Art, Toledo OH

Smart, John K, *Pres*, Licking County Art Association Gallery, Newark OH

Smart, Wini, *Recording Secy*, New Jersey Watercolor Society, Little Silver NJ

Smedley, Geoffrey, *Prof*, University of British Columbia, Department of Fine Arts, Vancouver BC (S)

Smerczak, Janet E, *Lending Dept*, Newark Museum, Newark NJ

Smet, Dany, *Librn*, Internationaal Cultureel Centrum, Library, Antwerp Belgium

Smigocki, Stephen, *Instructor*, Fairmont State College, Art Department, Fairmont WV (S)

Smiter, Janine, *Chief Information Services*, National Gallery of Canada, Ottawa ON

Smith, Albert H, *Asst Prof*, Georgia Institute of Technology, College of Architecture, Atlanta GA (S)

Smith, Alex, *Dir*, Manchester Polytechnic, Faculty of Art and Design, Manchester England (S)

Smith, Allen C, *Cur Coll*, Arnot Art Museum, Elmira NY

Smith, Ann, *Dir*, Mattatuck Historical Society, Mattatuck Museum, Waterbury CT

Smith, Ann Cote, *Dir*, Copper King Mansion, Butte MT

Smith, Arthur, *Prof*, Salem State College, Art Department, Salem MA (S)

Smith, Arthur E, *Prof*, University of Minnesota, Duluth, Art Dept, Duluth MN (S)

Smith, B J, *Dir*, Oklahoma State University, Gardiner Art Gallery, Stillwater OK

Smith, Bob, *Dir*, Los Angeles Institute of Contemporary Art, Los Angeles CA

Smith, Brydon, *Asst Dir Coll & Research*, National Gallery of Canada, Ottawa ON

Smith, Carey, *Asst Framer*, Kalamunda Museum of Western Art, Somers MT

Smith, Cecil, *Pres*, Kalamunda Museum of Western Art, Somers MT

Smith, Charles Lee, *Secy & Treas*, North Carolina Art Society, Raleigh NC

Smith, Claude, *Prof*, Western New Mexico University, Dept of Fine Art, Art Div, Silver City NM (S)

Smith, Craig, *Asst Prof*, Metropolitan State College, Art Department, Denver CO (S)

Smith, Cubert, *Chmn*, West Virginia State College, Art Department, Institute WV (S)

Smith, D, *Art Technician*, Durban Art Gallery, Durban South Africa, Republic of

Smith, Darold, *Assoc Prof*, West Texas State University, Art Department, Canyon TX (S)

Smith, David, *Visual Arts Coordr*, Mid-America Arts Alliance, Kansas City MO

Smith, David, *Chmn Painting*, Swain School of Design, New Bedford MA (S)

Smith, David L, *Assoc Prof*, University of Wisconsin-Stevens Point, Department of Art, Stevens Point WI (S)

Smith, D C F, *Librn*, Royal Scottish Museum, Library, Edinburgh Scotland

Smith, Diane, *Instructor*, Art Academy of Cincinnati, Cincinnati OH (S)

Smith, Donald C, *Secy*, Canton Art Institute, Canton OH

Smith, Donald C, *Prof*, Rhode Island College, Art Department, Providence RI (S)

Smith, Donna Ridley, *Asst Humanities Reference Librn*, California State University, Sacramento, Library, Humanities Reference Media Services Ctr, Sacramento CA

Smith, Dorothy V, *Librn*, Leatherstocking Brush and Palette Club Inc, Cooperstown Art Association Workroom, Cooperstown NY

Smith, Douglas Campbell, *Assoc Prof*, Central Oregon Community College, Department of Art, Bend OR (S)

Smith, Elinore, *Slide Librarian*, Tucson Museum of Art, Tucson Museum of Art Library, Tucson AZ

Smith, Elizabeth D, *Pres*, Verde Valley Art Association, Inc, Jerome AZ

Smith, Faith, *Adjunct Instr*, Delaware County Community College, Communications and Humanities House, Media PA (S)

Smith, Frank Anthony, *Prof*, University of Utah, Art Department, Salt Lake City UT (S)

Smith, Frederick T, *Asst Prof*, University of Minnesota, Minneapolis, Art History, Minneapolis MN (S)

Smith, Gary, *Cur*, Missouri Historical Society, Saint Louis MO

Smith, Gary T, *Dir*, Hartnell College Gallery, Salinas CA

Smith, George, *Asst Prof*, University of the District of Columbia, Art Department, Washington DC (S)

Smith, George M, *Adminr*, Woodlawn Plantation, Mount Vernon VA

Smith, George M, *Adminr*, Pope-Leighey House, Mount Vernon VA

Smith, Gerald, *Dir*, San Bernardino County Museum and Satellites, Fine Arts Institute, Redlands CA

Smith, Gladys, *Asst Librn*, Chappell Memorial Library and Art Gallery, Chappell NE

Smith, Gregory Allgire, *Asst Dir*, Akron Art Institute, Akron OH

Smith, Harriet Ross, *Receptionist*, Virginia Beach Arts Center, Virginia Beach VA

Smith, Hilda S, *Ceramics*, Baylor University, Department of Fine Arts, Waco TX (S)

Smith, Iras, *Librn*, Fine Arts Museum of the South, Library, Mobile AL

Smith, J Kellum, *Secy*, American Academy in Rome, New York NY

Smith, J Vivian, *Publicity*, Licking County Art Association Gallery, Newark OH

Smith, J B, *Dir*, Baylor University, Baylor Art Museum, Waco TX

Smith, Jack, *Div Coordr Crafts*, Kent State University, School of Art, Kent OH (S)

Smith, James, *Asst Prof*, University of Missouri-Saint Louis, Art Dept, Saint Louis MO (S)

Smith, James E, *Assoc Prof*, Western Carolina University, Dept of Art, Cullowhee NC (S)

Smith, James L, *Pres*, Waterloo Art Association, Waterloo IA

Smith, James G E, *Cur North America*, Museum of the American Indian, New York NY

Smith, James Morton, *Dir*, Winterthur Museum and Gardens, Winterthur DE

Smith, Janet Carl, *Coordr of Programs & Exhibits*, Chicago Public Library, Cultural Center, Chicago IL

Smith, Jean, *Arts & Architecture Librn*, Pennsylvania State University, Pattee Library, University Park PA

Smith, Jean, *Secy*, Sheldon Museum and Cultural Center, Haines AK

Smith, Jerry R, *Assoc Dean Instruction*, Delaware County Community College, Communications and Humanities House, Media PA (S)

Smith, Jo Ann, *Dir*, Elmira College, Hamilton Art Gallery, Elmira NY

Smith, Joann, *Instructor*, Elmira College, Art Department, Elmira NY (S)

Smith, John P, *Asst Prof*, University of New Orleans, Dept of Fine Arts, New Orleans LA (S)

Smith, John W, *Asst Prof*, University of Arkansas, Art Department, Fayetteville AR (S)

Smith, Joyce, *Pres*, Douglas Art Association, Little Gallery, Douglas AZ

Smith, Karl, *Interim Dir*, Mexico-Audrain County Library, Mexico MO

Smith, Kent, *Asst Cur*, Long Beach Museum of Art, Long Beach CA

Smith, La Priel, *Museum Attendant*, Kalamunda Museum of Western Art, Somers MT

Smith, Louise, *Educational Chmn*, Huntsville Art League and Museum Association Inc, Huntsville AL

Smith, Luther, *In Charge Photography*, University of Illinois, Urbana-Champaign, Department of Art and Design, Champaign IL (S)

Smith, Maggie, *Recording Secy*, Kent Art Association, Inc Gallery, Kent CT

Smith, Margaret Supplee, *Assoc Prof*, Wake Forest University, Department of Art, Winston-Salem NC (S)

Smith, Marie, *Mem Secy*, Rockport Art Association, Rockport MA

Smith, Marie W, *VPres*, Kalamunda Museum of Western Art, Somers MT

Smith, Marion Kay, *Staff Asst*, Southeastern College Art Conference, Chapel Hill NC

Smith, Mark S, *Instructor*, Texas Woman's University, Department of Art, Denton TX (S)

Smith, Mark Lesly, *Chmn*, Southwestern University, Art Department, Georgetown TX (S)

Smith, Melvin T, *Dir*, Utah Division of State History, Salt Lake City UT

Smith, Merrill W, *Visual Coll Librn*, Massachusetts Institute of Technology, Rotch Library of Architecture and Planning, Cambridge MA

Smith, Michael D, *Executive VPres*, Saint Paul - Ramsey Arts and Science Council, Saint Paul MN

Smith, Michael H, *Dir*, California Institute of Technology, Baxter Art Gallery, Pasadena CA

Smith, Michael J, *Head Painting*, Southern Illinois University at Edwardsville, Department of Art and Design, Edwardsville IL (S)

Smith, Mimi, *Secy*, 55 Mercer, New York NY

Smith, Moishe, *Prof*, Utah State University, Department of Art, Logan UT (S)

Smith, Nancy, *Children's Instructor*, Montclair Art Museum, Art School, Montclair NJ (S)

Smith, Nancy, *Prof*, Boston University, School of Visual Arts, Boston MA (S)

Smith, Neville, *Dir Development*, Colorado Springs Fine Arts Center, Colorado Springs CO

Smith, Noble, *Asst Dir*, Philadelphia Museum of Art, Philadelphia PA

Smith, Paul, *VPres*, Louis Comfort Tiffany Foundation, Great Neck NY

Smith, Paul J, *Dir*, American Craft Museum, New York NY

Smith, Peter, *Head Publications & Communications*, National Gallery of Canada, Ottawa ON

Smith, Philip Oliver, *Prof*, Rice University, Department of Art and Art History, Houston TX (S)

Smith, Priscilla, *Librn*, Freer Gallery of Art, Library, Washington DC

Smith, R, *Asst Dir*, University Club Library, New York NY

Smith, Raychelle R, *Museum Attendant*, Kalamunda Museum of Western Art, Somers MT

Smith, Richard, *Exhibition Coordr*, State University of New York at Stony Brook Art Gallery, Stony Brook NY

Smith, Richard, *VPres*, Floyd County Museum, New Albany IN

Smith, Robert, *Chief Main Library*, Memphis-Shelby County Public Library and Information Center, Department of Art, Music and Recreation, Memphis TN

Smith, Robert Ross, *Deputy Dir*, Copper King Mansion, Butte MT

Smith, Rockwell L, *Secy*, Kalamunda Museum of Western Art, Somers MT

Smith, Sheila, *Co-Supv Picture Library*, Cooper-Hewitt Museum, Doris and Henry Dreyfuss Study Center, New York NY

Smith, Stancil M, *Asst Adminr*, Pope-Leighey House, Mount Vernon VA

Smith, Stancil M, *Asst Adminr*, Woodlawn Plantation, Mount Vernon VA

Smith, Stephen L, *Framer*, Kalamunda Museum of Western Art, Somers MT

Smith, Steven P, *Artists in Residence Coordr*, Wyoming Council on the Arts, Cheyenne WY

Smith, Susan, *Instructor*, Castleton State College, Art Department, Castleton VT (S)

Smith, Susan, *Registrar*, University of Houston, Sarah Campbell Blaffer Gallery, Houston TX

Smith, Thomas G, *Head Junior Dept*, Berkshire Museum, Pittsfield MA

Smith, Thomas R, *Head*, University of New Brunswick, Art Education Section, Fredericton NB (S)

Smith, Tobi, *Dir Develop*, Los Angeles Institute of Contemporary Art, Los Angeles CA

Smith, Virginia, *Asst Prof*, Bernard M Baruch College of the City University of New York, Art Department, New York NY (S)

Smith, Virginia R, *Picture Coll Librn*, Chicago Public Library, Art Section, Fine Arts Division, Chicago IL

Smith, W E, *Pres*, Rensselaer County Historical Society, Troy NY

Smith, W I, *Dominion Archivist*, Public Archives of Canada, Public Archives Library, Ottawa ON

Smith, Walter, *Prof*, Pierce College, Art Department, Woodland Hills CA (S)

Smith, Walter G, *Chmn*, Utah State Division of Fine Arts, Glendenning Gallery, Salt Lake City UT

Smith, Willard, *Instructor*, College of DuPage, Humanities Div, Glen Ellyn IL (S)

Smith, William, *Head Acquisitions Department*, University of Alaska, Elmer E Rasmuson Library, Fairbanks AK

Smith, William B, *Pres*, Fine Arts Center of Clinton, Clinton IL

Smith Jr, Hugh J, *Research Assoc*, New Orleans Museum of Art, Isaac Delgado Museum, New Orleans LA

Smith Jr, Robert H, *Secy*, Old State House, Hartford CT

Smith-Robison, Cathy, *Instr*, Cleveland State Community College, Department of Art, Cleveland TN (S)

Smith III, Donald, *Development Dir*, Please Touch Museum, Philadelphia PA

Smith III, Ira, *Dir*, Pennsylvania Historical and Museum Commission, William Penn Memorial Museum, Harrisburg PA

Smits, Kathy, *Secy*, Bergstrom Art Center and Museum, Neenah WI

Smock, Andrew, *Instructor*, Purdue University Calumet Campus, Department of Creative Arts, Hammond IN (S)

Smock, Jean, *Adminr*, Newport Harbor Art Museum, Newport Beach CA

Smolko, John, *Instr*, Cuyahoga Valley Art Center, Cuyahoga Falls OH (S)

Smullin, Frank, *Instr*, Duke University, Department of Art, Durham NC (S)

Smyavois, Arleigh, *Instr*, Kalamazoo Valley Community College, Department of Art, Kalamazoo MI (S)

Smyth, David, *Vis Prof*, Ithaca College, Art Department, Ithaca NY (S)

Smythe, James E, *Chmn*, Pepperdine University, Humanities-Fine Arts Division, Malibu CA (S)

Smythe, Nancy C, *VPres*, Carolina Art Association, Gibbes Art Gallery, Charleston SC

Sneed, Richard, *Dean Acad Affairs*, Santa Ana College, Art Department, Santa Ana CA (S)

Snell, Joseph W, *Executive Dir*, Kansas State Historial Society Museum, Topeka KS

Snellenberger, Earl, *Assoc Prof*, Indiana Central University, Fine Arts Department, Indianapolis IN (S)

Snider, Jane Anne, *Asst Librn*, Indiana University - Purdue University at Indianapolis, Herron School of Art Library, Indianapolis IN

Sninsky, Anna Marie, *Pres*, Associated Artists of Pittsburgh Arts and Crafts Center, Pittsburgh PA

Snipper, Martin, *Dir Cultural Affairs*, San Francisco City and County Art Commission, San Francisco CA

Snodgrass, John, *Treas*, Charles B Goddard Center for the Visual and Performing Arts, Ardmore OK

Snodgrass, Robert, *Pres*, Clark County Historical Society, Springfield OH

Snoeckx, Maria, *Chief Asst*, Museum Smidt van Gelder, Smidt van Gelder Museum, Antwerp Belgium

Snooks, A Nancy, *Asst*, Pierce College, Art Department, Woodland Hills CA (S)

Snouffer, Kitsy, *VPres*, West Hills Unitarian Fellowship, Portland OR

Snow, Anthony E, *Deputy Dir Communications*, Corning Museum of Glass, Corning NY

Snow, Anthony E, *Dir*, Rockwell-Corning Museum, Corning NY

Snow, Maryly, *Librn*, University of California, Visual Aids Collection, Berkeley CA

Snow, Ralph L, *Exec Dir*, Maine Maritime Museum, Bath ME

Snow, V Douglas, *Prof*, University of Utah, Art Department, Salt Lake City UT (S)

Snowden, Mary, *Instructor*, California College of Arts and Crafts, Oakland CA (S)

Snowden, Pennell, *Cur*, Muchnic Foundation and Atchison Art Association, Muchnic Gallery, Atchison KS

Snug, Peggy, *Corresponding Secy*, Toledo Federation of Art Societies, Toledo OH

Snyder, Barry, *Instructor*, Fairmont State College, Art Department, Fairmont WV (S)

Snyder, Bill, *Chmn*, Laney College, Art Department, Oakland CA (S)

Snyder, Dean, *Instructor*, California College of Arts and Crafts, Oakland CA (S)

Snyder, Dennis, *Chmn*, Idaho State University, Department of Art, Pocatello ID (S)

Speirs, W B, *Asst Provincial Archivist*, Department of Culture, Government of the Province of Alberta, Provincial Archives of Alberta, Edmonton AB

Spellman, Peter, *Instr*, Montserrat School of Visual Art, Beverly MA (S)

Spence, George, *Pres*, Creative Arts Guild, Dalton GA

Spence, Joseph R, *Chmn*, University of North Carolina-Charlotte, Creative Arts Dept, Charlotte NC (S)

Spence, Karen, *Library Asst*, University of California, Art Department Library, Davis CA

Spencer, Anne, *Cur Ethnology*, Newark Museum, Newark NJ

Spencer, Avery, *Mem Secy*, Berkshire Museum, Pittsfield MA

Spencer, Bea, *Secy*, Owatonna Arts Center, Owatonna MN

Spencer, Charlotte, *Instructor*, Roger Williams College, Art Department, Bristol RI (S)

Spencer, Helen, *Tech Serv Head*, Topeka Public Library, Topeka KS

Spencer, Howard D, *Cur of Coll-Exhib*, Wichita Art Museum, Wichita KS

Spencer, John M, *Bldg Mgr*, Owatonna Arts Center, Owatonna MN

Spencer. John R, *Chmn Dept*, Duke University, Department of Art, Durham NC (S)

Spencer, Patricia, *Lectr*, University of Wisconsin-Superior, Department of Art, Superior WI (S)

Spencer, Reid, *VPres Board of Trustees*, Chrysler Museum, Norfolk VA

Sperber, Barbara, *Business Officer*, Queens Museum, Flushing NY

Sperr, Portra, *Executive Dir*, Please Touch Museum, Philadelphia PA

Speyer, A James, *Cur 20th Century Painting & Sculpture*, Art Institute of Chicago, Chicago IL

Spicer, John B, *Instructor*, Jefferson Davis State Junior College, Art Department, Brewton AL (S)

Spielma, Carol Anne, *Chmn*, Please Touch Museum, Philadelphia PA

Spigel, Bernice, *Dir*, Creative Arts Guild, Dalton GA

Spillane, Robert, *Deputy Commissioner for Elementary, Secondary and Continuing Educ*, State Education Department, State University of New York, Albany NY

Spillman, Jane Shadel, *Cur American Glass*, Corning Museum of Glass, Corning NY

Spilman, Craig, *Instr*, Lane Community College, Art and Applied Design Department, Eugene OR (S)

Spinar, Melvin, *Assoc Prof*, South Dakota State University, Art Dept, Brookings SD (S)

Spinosa, Nicola, *Supv & Dir Museo Villa Floridiana*, Museo de Capodimonte, Mount Capodi Museum, Naples Italy

Spinski, Victor, *Coordr Ceramics*, University of Delaware, Department of Art, Newark DE (S)

Spinx, Jack C, *Chief Exhib, Loans & Registration*, National Gallery of Art, Washington DC

Spiro, Anna L, *Instructor*, Central Missouri State University, Art Department, Warrensburg MO (S)

Spiro, Stephen B, *Cur*, University of Notre Dame, Snite Museum of Art, Notre Dame IN

Spivey, Towana, *Cur Anthropology*, Institute of the Great Plains, Museum of the Great Plains, Lawton OK

Spivy, Mary P, *Dir*, Farmington Museum, Stanley-Whitman House, Farmington CT

Spohn, Charles L, *Dean School Fine Arts*, Miami University, Art Department, Oxford OH (S)

Sponberg, Lars, *Prof*, North Park College, Art Department, Chicago IL (S)

Sporer, Francis, *Asst Prof*, William Woods-Westminster Colleges, Art Department, Fulton MO (S)

Sprague, Brian L, *Instructor*, Lewis-Clark State College, Art Department, Lewiston ID (S)

Sprague, Mary, *Instructor*, Saint Louis Community College at Meramec, Art Dept, Saint Louis MO (S)

Sprague Jr, Norman, *VPres*, Southwest Museum, Los Angeles CA

Spratlin, Samuel A, *Financial Secy*, Berkshire Museum, Pittsfield MA

Spratt, Albert, *Personnel*, Mississauga Library System, Central Library, Art Division, Mississauga ON

Sprigg, June, *Cur Coll*, Shaker Community, Inc, Pittsfield MA

Spriggs, Betty, *Talking Books for the Blind*, Wichita Public Library, Wichita KS

Spring, Ernest, *First VPres*, Toledo Artists' Club, Toledo OH

Spring, W D, *Chmn*, University of Minnesota, Morris, Humanities Department, Morris MN (S)

Springer, Frank, *Secy*, National Cartoonists Society, Brooklyn NY

Springer, John, *Pres*, Community Arts Council of Vancouver, Vancouver BC

Springer Jr, Homer L, *Assoc Prof*, Longwood College, Department of Art, Farmville VA (S)

Springfeldt, Björn, *Chief Cur*, Nationalmuseum, Moderna Museet, Stockholm Sweden

Sprouls, Patricia, *Recording Secy*, Catharine Lorillard Wolfe Art Club, Inc, New York NY

Sprout, Francis, *Asst Prof*, Metropolitan State College, Art Department, Denver CO (S)

Spurgin, John E, *Chmn*, Mankato State University, Art Department, Mankato MN (S)

Spurlock, William, *Cur Exhib*, Santa Barbara Museum of Art, Santa Barbara CA

Spyers-Duran, Peter, *Dir*, California State University, Long Beach, Library, Long Beach CA

Squier, Jack L, *Prof*, Cornell University, Department of Art, Ithaca NY (S)

Squyres, Earl E, *Office Mgr*, Cherokee National Historical Society, Inc, Tahlequah OK

Sreen, Alfred E, *Dir*, Texas Woman's University Art Gallery, Denton TX

Staber, Rinny, *Instructor*, Peters Valley Craft Center, Layton NJ (S)

Staccioli, Sara, *Dir*, Galleria Borghese, Borghese Gallery, Rome Italy

Stach, Leonard R, *Chmn*, University of Wisconsin-La Crosse, Art Department, La Crosse WI (S)

Stachura, Jozef, *Instructor*, Ivy School of Professional Art, Downtown Annex, Pittsburgh PA (S)

Stack, Edward W, *Secy*, Plymouth Antiquarian Society, Plymouth MA

Stackhouse, Robert, *Chmn Third Year*, Corcoran School of Art, Washington DC (S)

Stacy, Betty, *Librn*, Virginia Museum of Fine Arts, Library, Richmond VA

Staffne, Dennis, *Asst Prof*, Northern Michigan University, Dept of Art & Design, Marquette MI (S)

Stafford, Beverly B, *Librn*, Oregon School of Arts and Crafts, Library, Portland OR

Stafford, Beverly B, *Librn*, School of the Arts and Crafts Society of Portland, Library, Portland OR

Stafford, Elizabeth, *Secy*, Brattleboro Museum and Art Center, Brattleboro VT

Stafford, F Eugene, *Instructor*, Guilford Technical Institute, Commercial Art Dept, Jamestown NC (S)

Stageman, Charles, *Chmn Dept*, Haverford College, Fine Arts Department, Haverford PA (S)

Stahl, Carol, *Dir*, Bergen Community Museum, Paramus NJ

Stahl, Judith R, *Art Dir*, Louisiana State University, Union Art Gallery, Baton Rouge LA

Stainback, Charles, *Coordr Exhib*, Visual Studies Workshop, Rochester NY

Staiti, Paul J, *Asst Prof*, Mount Holyoke College, Art Department, South Hadley MA (S)

Staky, Early, *Assoc Prof*, University of Saint Thomas, Art Department, Houston TX (S)

Stallings Jr, Robert L, *Chmn*, Tryon Palace Restoration Complex, New Bern NC

Stallions, Jewel, *Dir*, Oak Ridge Community Art Center, Oak Ridge TN

Stambaugh, Rex, *Asst Prof*, Winthrop College, Department of Art, Rock Hill SC (S)

Stampfle, Felice, *Cur Drawings and Prints*, Pierpont Morgan Library, New York NY

Stanczak, Julian, *Instr*, Cleveland Institute of Art, Cleveland OH (S)

Standley, Ray, *Treas*, Beverly Historical Society, Beverly MA

Stanforth, Melvin S, *Chmn Interior Design*, East Carolina University, School of Art, Greenville NC (S)

Stanger, Janet, *Secy*, Artists Coalition of Texas, Dallas TX

Stanis, Elaine-Carol, *Cur of Children's Literature*, Rutgers University, Art Gallery, New Brunswick NJ

Stanislawski, Barbara, *Mgr Coll*, School of American Research, Santa Fe NM

Stanislawski, Ryszard, *Dir*, Muzeum Sztuki, Lodz Poland

Stankieqica, Richard, *Prof*, State University of New York at Albany, Art Department, Albany NY (S)

Stankiewicz, Mary Ann, *Asst Prof*, University of Maine, Art Department, Orono ME (S)

Stanley, Henry, *Chmn*, Metropolitan Arts Commission, Portland OR

Stanley, Janet L, *Librn*, Museum of African Art, Library, Washington DC

Stanley, Keith, *Cur Classical Coll*, Duke University Museum of Art, Durham NC

Stanley-Baker, P Richard, *Asst Prof*, University of Victoria, Department of History in Art, Victoria BC (S)

Stansbury, George, *Chmn*, University of Mary Hardin-Baylor, Department of Fine Arts, Belton TX

Stanton, Alden O, *Pres*, Morris-Jumel Mansion, New York NY

Stanton, Frank, *Prof*, Saint Louis Community College at Florissant Valley, Department of Art, Ferguson MO (S)

Stanton, Jane T, *Instructor*, Art Academy of Cincinnati, Cincinnati OH (S)

Stanton, Kathe Kertz, *Public Information*, Walker Art Center, Minneapolis MN

Stapleton, Ann, *Chmn*, Jackson County Historical Society, John Wornall House, Independence MO

Stapleton, Scott O, *Asst Art Library*, University of Chicago, Art Library, Chicago IL

Stapp, William F, *Cur Photographs*, National Portrait Gallery, Washington DC

Stark, J W, *Dir Art Exhib and Special Asst to the Pres for Development of Cultural Programs*, Texas A & M University, Art Exhibits, College Station TX

Stark, Nelda C, *Chmn*, Stark Museum of Art, Orange TX

Stark, Robert, *Museum Adminr*, Oregon Historical Society, Portland OR

Stark, Shirley, *Chmn*, Chatham College, Department of Art, Pittsburgh PA (S)

Stark, Shirley, *Co-Dir*, Chatham College Art Gallery, Pittsburgh PA

Starks, Linda, *Secy*, Art Institute of Chicago, Chicago IL

Starr, Kenneth, *Pres*, American Association of Museums, Washington DC

Starr, Kenneth, *Dir*, Milwaukee Public Museum, Milwaukee WI

Stars, W K, *Dir*, Duke University Museum of Art, Durham NC

Stars, W K, *Assoc Prof*, Duke University, Department of Art, Durham NC (S)

Stasik, Andrew, *Dir*, Pratt Institute, Pratt Manhattan Center Gallery, New York NY

Statlander, Raymond, *Asst Prof*, Jersey City State College, Art Department, Jersey City NJ (S)

Staub, Geraldine Peterson, *Cur*, Drexel University Art Gallery and Museum Collection, Philadelphia PA

Stauder, Catherine, *Researcher*, Kauai Museum, Lihue HI

Stauder, M Stephanie, *Chmn*, Edgewood College, Art Department, Madison WI (S)

Stauder, M Stephanie, *Art Department Chmn*, Edgewood College, DeRicci Gallery, Madison WI

Staven, Leland, *Cur*, Agnes Scott College, Dalton Gallery, Decatur GA

Stavropoulos, Theo, *Assoc Prof*, Herbert H Lehman College, Art Department, Bronx NY (S)

StClair, Guy, *Dir*, University Club Library, New York NY

Steadman, David, *Assoc Prof*, Pomona College, Art Department, Claremont CA (S)

Steadman, David, *Research Cur*, Norton Simon Museum, Pasadena CA

Steadman, David W, *Dir*, Galleries of the Claremont Colleges, Claremont CA

Steadman, Kent, *Instr*, Fresno City College, Art Department, Fresno CA (S)

Steadman, Thomas, *Asst Prof*, Georgia Southern College, Department of Art, Statesboro GA (S)

Steans, Joan, *Asst Prof*, Jersey City State College, Art Department, Jersey City NJ (S)

Stearns, Robert, *Dir*, Contemporary Arts Center, Cincinnati OH

Stecle, Elizabeth, *VPres*, League of New Hampshire Craftsmen, Concord NH

Steed, Mary Ann, *Business Mgr*, Sunrise Foundation, Inc, Charleston WV

Steeger, Henry, *Acad Exec Dean*, Tunxis Community College, Graphic Design & Applied Arts Dept, Farmington CT (S)

Steel, Joan, *Librn*, Saskatoon Gallery and Conservatory Corporation, Library, Saskatoon SK

Steel, Lavar, *Chmn*, College of Southern Idaho, Art Department, Twin Falls ID (S)

Steel, La Var, *Chmn Art Dept*, College of Southern Idaho, Art Gallery, Twin Falls ID

Steel, Virginia Oberlin, *Dir*, Rutgers University, Stedman Art Gallery, Camden NJ

Steele, Craig, *Asst Dir*, Rocky Mountain School of Art Gallery, Denver CO

Steele, James, *Dir Fine Arts*, Hampton Center for Arts and Humanities, Hampton VA

Steele, John, *Assoc Prof*, East Tennessee State University, Fine Arts Dept, Johnson City TN (S)

Steele, Philip J, *Dir*, Rocky Mountain School of Art Gallery, Denver CO

Steele, Ray W, *Dir*, C M Russell Museum, Great Falls MT

Steele, Victoria, *Belt Library Asst*, University of California, Los Angeles, Elmer Belt Library of Vinciana, Los Angeles CA

Steen, Albert, *Cur*, Kunstindustrimuseet I Oslo, Oslo Museum of Applied Art, Oslo Norway

Steen, Linda, *Acting Dir Development & Public Relations*, Dayton Art Institute, Dayton OH

Steenberg, Gerald W, *Librn*, St Paul Public Library, Saint Paul MN

Steenbock, Frauke, *Dir*, Staatliche Museen Preussischer Kulturbesitz, Museums Library, Berlin Germany, Federal Republic of

Steensland, Ronald, *Dir*, Lexington Public Library, Lexington KY

Steere Jr, Frank W, *Asst Treas*, Stan Hywet Hall Foundation, Inc, Akron OH

Steffens, Louise, *Exec Asst*, Phillips Collection, Washington DC

Steg, James, *Prof*, Tulane University, Newcomb College, New Orleans LA (S)

Steger, Scott, *Chmn Art Committee*, Angelo State University, Houston Harte University Center, San Angelo TX

Steidl, Rose, *Chmn Dept*, Cornell University, New York State College of Human Ecology, Ithaca NY (S)

Steigleder, Linda, *Registrar*, Everson Museum of Art, Syracuse NY

Stein, Albert, *Admin Aide*, Bower's Museum, Santa Ana CA

Stein, Claire A, *Executive Dir*, National Sculpture Society, New York NY

Stein, Edwin E, *Dean*, University of Hartford, Joseloff Gallery, West Hartford CT

Stein, Edwin E, *Dean*, Hartford Art School of the University of Hartford, West Hartford CT (S)

Stein, Margaret, *Instructor*, Greenfield Community College, Art Department, Greenfield MA (S)

Stein, Michael, *Assoc Cur*, Housatonic Community College, Housatonic Museum of Art, Bridgeport CT

Stein, Robert, *Co-Chairperson Illustration*, Philadelphia College of Art, Philadelphia PA (S)

Stein, Virginia, *Librn*, Eastern Michigan University, Art Department Book Collection, Ypsilanti MI

Steinaa, Eva, *Librn*, Det Danske Kunstindustrimuseum, Library, Copenhagen Denmark

Steinberg, Ronald M, *Prof*, Rhode Island College, Art Department, Providence RI (S)

Steinfeldt, Cecilia, *Sr Cur of History & Decorative Arts*, San Antonio Museum Association, Inc, San Antonio TX

Steingraber, E, *Dir*, Bayerischen Staatsgemaldesammlungen, Bavarian State Galleries of Art, Munich Germany, Federal Republic of

Steinhauser, Judy, *Chmn Photography*, Moore College of Art, Philadelphia PA (S)

Steininger, Dwight F, *VPres*, Brown County Art Gallery Association Inc, Nashville IN

Steinman, Steve, *Board of Dir*, Cultural Council Foundation, Fourteen Sculptors Gallery, New York NY

Steiro, Carol, *Cur Coll*, Museum of New Mexico, Museum of International Folk Art, Santa Fe NM

Stele-Mozina, Melita, *Cur Museum Coll*, Moderna Galerija, Modern Art Gallery, Ljubljana Yugoslavia

Stemmler, Dicrk, *Dir*, Stadtishces Kunstmuseum Bonn, Art Museum of the City of Bonn, Bonn Germany, Federal Republic of

Stemple, Colette, *Instr*, Lake Placid School of Art, Lake Placid NY (S)

Stene, Larry, *Instructor*, Bemidji State University, Art Department, Bemidji MN (S)

Stensrude, Richard J, *Dept Coordr*, Clark College, Art Department, Vancouver WA (S)

Stephan, Joanne, *Record Secy*, Berks Art Alliance, Reading PA

Stephanian, C, *Media Dir*, San Francisco Art Institute, Anne Bremer Memorial Library, San Francisco CA

Stephany, Jaromir, *Assoc Prof*, University of Maryland Baltimore County, Visual Arts Department, Catonsville MD (S)

Stephen, Barbara, *Assoc Dir*, Royal Ontario Museum, Toronto ON

Stephen, Francis, *Prof*, Texas Tech University, Department of Art, Lubbock TX (S)

Stephens, Arial A, *Dir*, Public Library of Charlotte and Mecklenburg County, Charlotte NC

Stephens, Marjorie, *Registrar*, Brooklyn Museum Art School, Brooklyn NY (S)

Stephens, Michael, *Cur and Registrar*, Millicent Rogers Museum, Taos NM

Stephens, Michael, *Coordr*, Art Research Center, Kansas City MO

Stephens, Press, *Instructor*, Central Wyoming College, Art Center, Riverton WY (S)

Stephens, Richard A, *Pres*, Academy of Art College, San Francisco CA (S)

Stephens, William B, *Chmn*, University of Texas at Tyler, Department of Art, Tyler TX (S)

Stephenson, Ann, *Dean Fine Arts Div*, Southwestern Community College, Art Gallery, Chula Vista CA

Stephenson, Carolynn, *Registrar*, Louisville School of Art Gallery, Anchorage KY

Stephenson, Christie, *Bibliographer*, University of Virginia, Fiske Kimball Fine Arts Library, Charlottesville VA

Stephenson, Robert E, *Librn*, Virginia Polytechnic Institute and State University, Architecture Library, Blacksburg VA

Sterhan, Cob, *Pro-Provost*, Royal College of Art Gallery, London England

Sterling, William H, *Chmn*, Wilkes College, Department of Art, Wilkes-Barre PA (S)

Sterling, William H, *Dir*, Wilkes College, Sordoni Art Gallery, Wilkes-Barre PA

Stern, Fred, *Assoc Prof*, University of Maryland Baltimore County, Visual Arts Department, Catonsville MD (S)

Stern, Howard, *VPres*, Mid-Southern Watercolorists, Little Rock AR

Stern, Milton R, *Institute Advisor*, Museum Management Institute, San Francisco CA (S)

Stern, Wilma, *Vis Asst Prof*, Pennsylvania State University, University Park, Department of Art History, University Park PA (S)

Sterritt, James, *Chairperson Three-Dimensional Dept*, Washington University, School of Fine Arts, Saint Louis MO (S)

Sterud, Eugene L, *Exec Dir*, Archaeological Institute of America, New York NY

Stevanov, Zoran, *Dir of Exhib*, Fort Hays State University, Visual Arts Center, Hays KS

Stevanov, Zoran, *Assoc Prof*, Fort Hays State University, Department of Art, Hays KS (S)

Steven, Faye, *Secy*, Phelps County Historical Society Museum, Holdrege NE

Steven, Leland, *Assoc Prof*, Agnes Scott College, Department of Art, Decatur GA (S)

Stevens, Elizabeth, *Exec Dir*, Louis Comfort Tiffany Foundation, Great Neck NY

Stevens, George F, *Secy & Dir*, Oregon State University, Memorial Union Art Gallery, Corvallis OR

Stevens, Harold, *Prof*, School of the Arts, C W Post Center of Long Island University, Art Department, Greenvale NY (S)

Stevens, John E, *Asst Prof*, Manchester Community College, Fine Arts Department, Manchester CT (S)

Stevens, Lynnette, *Periodical Librn*, LeMoyne College, Art Gallery, Syracuse NY

Stevens, Martha, *Cur Education*, Alaska State Museum, Juneau AK

Stevens, Martha, *Cur of Education*, Alaska State Museum, Library, Juneau AK

Stevens, Nancy, *Museum Shop Mgr*, Old State House, Hartford CT

Stevens, Richard, *Dir Education*, School of Holography, Fine Arts Research and Holographic Center Museum, Chicago IL

Stevens, Robert, *Rare Books Librn*, Rosenberg Library, Galveston TX

Stevens, Roger L, *Chmn of the Board of Trustees*, John F Kennedy Center for the Performing Arts, Washington DC

Stevens, Suzanne Howes, *Asst Prof*, Manchester Community College, Fine Arts Department, Manchester CT (S)

Stevens, Timothy J, *Dir*, Walker Art Gallery, Liverpool England

Stevens Jr, Edward John, *Dir*, Newark School of Fine and Industrial Art, Newark NJ (S)

Stevenson, A Brockie, *Chmn Drawing & Design*, Corcoran School of Art, Washington DC (S)

Stevenson, Harold Ransom, *Head Dept*, Stevenson Academy of Traditional Painting, Sea Cliff NY (S)

Stevenson, Irene D, *Cir Librn*, Society of the Four Arts, Library, Palm Beach FL

Stevenson, John R, *Pres*, National Gallery of Art, Washington DC

Stevenson, Lori, *Student Dir*, Thiel College, Sampson Art Gallery, Greenville PA

Stevenson, Marsha, *Reference Librn*, University of Pittsburgh, Henry Clay Frick Fine Arts Library, Pittsburgh PA

Stevenson, S, *Instr*, Selkirk College, Kootenay School of Art Division, Nelson BC (S)

Stevenson, Trish, *Instructor*, Northeast Technical Community College, Dept of Art, Norfolk NE (S)

Stewart, Albert, *Dir*, Florida State University, Art Gallery, Tallahassee FL

Stewart, Ann, *Librn*, National Gallery of Ireland, Art Reference Library, Dublin Ireland

Stewart, Beth, *Secy*, Midland Art Council of the Midland Center for the Arts, Midland MI

Stewart, Charles A, *Dean*, Howard Payne University, Department of Art, Brownwood TX (S)

Stewart, Clara M, *Corresp Secy*, Providence Water Color Club, Providence RI

Stewart, Donald F, *Dir*, Baltimore Maritime Museum, Baltimore MD

Stewart, Dorothy, *VPres*, Florida Artist Group Inc, Englewood FL

Stewart, Duncan E, *Asst Prof*, University of West Florida, Department of Art, Pensacola FL (S)

Stewart, Duncan E, *Dir*, University of West Florida, Art Gallery, Pensacola FL

Stewart, Frank, *Pres*, Muttart Gallery Associates, Calgary AB

Stewart, Hannah, *Asst Prof*, University of Saint Thomas, Art Department, Houston TX (S)

Stewart, Jack, *Chmn*, Indiana State University, Art Department, Terre Haute IN (S)

Stewart, Jack, *Chmn Art Dept*, Indiana State University, Turman Gallery, Terre Haute IN

Stewart, James, *Cur Historic Buildings*, Division of Historical and Cultural Affairs, Bureau of Museums and Historic Sites, Dover DE

Stewart, Jarvis, *Prof*, Ohio Wesleyan University, Fine Arts Department, Delaware OH (S)

Stewart, Jason, *Preparator*, State University of New York at Albany, University Art Gallery, Albany NY

Stewart, Jean C, *Asst Cur Collection*, Carolina Art Association, Gibbes Art Gallery, Charleston SC

Stewart, John, *Dean*, University of Montevallo, College of Fine Arts, Montevallo AL (S)

Stewart, John R, *Chmn Dept*, Oregon State University, Department of Architecture and Landscape Architecture, Corvallis OR (S)

Stewart, Marlene, *Head-Circulation*, Ponca City Library, Ponca City OK

Stewart, Maureen, *Adminr*, New Museum, New York NY

Stewart, Milo V, *Assoc Dir & Chief Education*, Plymouth Antiquarian Society, Plymouth MA

Stewart, Milo V, *Assoc Dir and Chief Educ*, New York State Historical Association, Fenimore House, Cooperstown NY

Stewart, Priscilla, *Prof*, Manatee Junior College, Department of Art, Bradenton FL (S)

Stewart, Robert, *VPres*, Octagon Center for the Arts, Ames IA

Stewart, Robert, *Photography Chmn*, Atlanta College of Art, Atlanta GA (S)

Stewart, Robert G, *Cur Paintings & Sculpture*, National Portrait Gallery, Washington DC

Stewart, Ruth Chambers, *Exec Secy*, Rehoboth Art League, Inc, Rehoboth Beach DE

Stewart, Wes, *Photographer Technician*, Museum of Early Southern Decorative Arts, Old Salem Inc, Winston-Salem NC

Stewart, William G, *General Manager*, Willet Stained Glass Studios, Philadelphia PA

Stewner, Annette, *Librn*, Hamburger Kunsthalle, Bibliothek der Hamburger Kunsthalle, Hamburg Germany, Federal Republic of

Steyaert, John, *Asst Prof*, University of Minnesota, Minneapolis, Art History, Minneapolis MN (S)

Stiassni, Christine, *Dir*, Museum of Art, Science and Industry, Bridgeport CT

Stibbe, Katherine Campbell, *Pres*, Nicholas Roerich Museum, New York NY

Stickler, Jim, *Instructor*, Murray State University, Art Department, Murray KY (S)

Stickles, Robert, *Chmn Dept of Interior Design*, New England School of Art and Design, Boston MA (S)

Stickney, Jess, *VPres*, Custer County Art Center, Miles City MT

Stieglitz, Mary G, *Prof*, University of Wisconsin, Madison, School of Family Resources and Consumer Sciences, Madison WI (S)

Stiles, Lois Kent, *Chief Art Div*, Public Library of the District of Columbia, Art Division, Washington DC

Stiles, Mary, *Dir*, Sculpture Center, New York NY

Stiles, Mary, *Dir*, Sculpture Center, New York NY (S)

Stillman, Damie, *Second VPres*, Society of Architectural Historians, Philadelphia PA

Stillman, Diane B, *Cur of Education*, Delaware Art Museum, Wilmington DE

Stillman, George, *Chmn*, Central Washington University, Department of Art, Ellensburg WA (S)

Stillman, George, *Chmn Art Department*, Central Washington University, Sara Spurgeon Gallery, Ellensburg WA

Stimson II, William A, *Treas*, Fine Arts Museums of San Francisco, The Museum Society

Stiner, Jim, *Dir Public Affairs*, Kohler Company, Kohler WI

Stirnaman, Glen, *Secy*, San Bernadino Art Association, Inc, San Bernadino CA

Stites, Mary Henry, *Secy*, Moravian Historical Society, Whitefield House Museum, Nazareth PA

Stites, M Elizabeth, *Librn*, Maryland College of Art and Design Library, Silver Spring MD

Stith, Nancy W, *Librn*, American Numismatic Association, Library, Colorado Springs CO

Stitt, Susan, *Dir*, Museums at Stony Brook, Stony Brook NY

Stobo Jr, William G, *Instr*, Tidewater Community College, Art Department, Portsmouth VA (S)

Stockdale, Louise L, *Mgr*, Gunston Hall Plantation, Lorton VA

Stockli, Helen, *Corresponding Secy*, Kent Art Association, Inc Gallery, Kent CT

Stockly, Elizabeth, *Dir*, Art Center College of Design, James Lemont Fogg Memorial Library, Pasadena CA

Stockwell, Ross, *Chairperson*, San Diego Mesa College, Art Department, San Diego CA (S)

Stoddard, Donna M, *Coordr Art*, Florida Southern College, Melvin Art Gallery, Lakeland FL

Stoddard, Donna M, *Coordr Dept*, Florida Southern College, Art Department, Lakeland FL (S)

Stoddard, F Don, *Executive Dir*, United States Figure Skating Hall of Fame and Museum, Colorado Springs CO

Stoddard, Stanford C, *Chmn of Board*, Detroit Institute of Arts, Detroit Institute of Art Founders Society, Detroit MI

Stodola, Mark, *Pres*, Quapaw Quarter Association, Inc, Villa Marre, Little Rock AR

Stoelzel, Martin C, *Chmn Dept*, College of Marin, Department of Art, Kentfield CA (S)

Stoesser, Elise, *Cur Asst*, Regina Public Library, Dunlot Art Gallery, Regina SK

Stoker, Eloise, *Asst Prof*, Incarnate Word College, Humanities and Fine Arts, San Antonio TX (S)

Stoker, Jim, *Assoc Prof*, Trinity University, Department of Art, San Antonio TX (S)

Stokes, Charlotte, *Asst Prof*, Oakland University, Dept of Art & Art History, Rochester MI (S)

Stokes, Thomas L, *Chmn Board of Trustees*, Chrysler Museum, Norfolk VA

Stokstad, Marilyn, *Research Cur*, Spencer Museum of Art, Lawrence KS

Stokstad, Marilyn, *Prof*, University of Kansas, Kress Foundation Department of Art History, Lawrence KS (S)

Stoll, Robert, *Co-Chairman*, Portland Center for the Visual Arts, Portland OR

Stolot, Franziszek, *Deputy Dir Polish Art of 16th - 18th Centuries*, Muzeum Narodowe w Krakowie, National Museum in Cracow, Cracow Poland

Stolz, Merton, *Treas*, Providence Athenaeum, Library, Providence RI

Stolz, Merton P, *Treas*, Providence Athenaeum, Providence RI

Stone, Carolyn, *Chmn Art Education*, Delta State University, Fielding L Wright Art Center, Cleveland MS

Stone, Carolyn Rea, *Assoc Prof*, Delta State University, Department of Art, Cleveland MS (S)

Stone, Dorris, *Exec Secy*, Watkins Institute, Nashville TN

Stone, Earl E, *Dir*, Monterey History and Art Association, Allen Knight Maritime Museum, Monterey CA

Stone, Gretchen Knowles, *Cur*, Guild of Boston Artists, Boston MA

Stone, Isabel, *Secy*, Plastic Club, Art Club for Women, Philadelphia PA

Stone, Julie, *Education Coordr*, Lynnwood Arts Centre, Simcoe ON

Stone, K Gordon, *Assoc Museum Librn*, Metropolitan Museum of Art, Irene Lewisohn Costume Reference Library, New York NY

Stone, K G, *Pres*, San Bernadino Art Association, Inc, San Bernadino CA

Stone, Linda, *Cur Art*, Woolaroc Museum, Bartlesville OK

Stoneham, John, *Librn*, Maryland Institute College of Art, Library, Baltimore MD

Stonehill, John J, *Chmn Board*, National Institute for Architectural Education, New York NY

Stone Jr, William F, *Recording Secy*, Monterey Peninsula Museum of Art, Monterey CA

Stones, M Alison, *Assoc Prof*, University of Minnesota, Minneapolis, Art History, Minneapolis MN (S)

Stong, Roy, *Dir*, Victoria and Albert Museum, London England

Stonum, Paul T, *Executive VPres & Dir*, National Hall of Fame for Famous American Indians, Anadarko OK

Stonum, Sally, *Secy*, National Hall of Fame for Famous American Indians, Anadarko OK

Storer, C A, *Chmn Board Trustees*, Zigler Museum, Jennings LA

Storer, J D, *Keeper Department of Technology*, Royal Scottish Museum, Edinburgh Scotland

Storey, Gwen, *Asst Cur*, Scripps College, Clark Humanities Museum, Claremont CA

Storey, Jackson Grey, *Pres*, Central Academy of Commercial Art, Cincinnati OH (S)

Storr, Annie V F, *Dir*, Westbrook College, Joan Whitney Payson Gallery of Art, Portland ME

Story, Lewis W, *Assoc Dir*, Denver Art Museum, Frederic H Douglas Library, Denver CO

Story, William E, *Dir*, Ball State University, Art Gallery, Muncie IN

Stotz, Virginia, *Coordr Art History*, Kean College of New Jersey, Fine Arts Department, Union NJ (S)

Stoughton, Gen, *Librn*, Oak Ridge Community Art Center, Library, Oak Ridge TN

Stoughton, Michael, *Asst Prof*, University of Minnesota, Minneapolis, Art History, Minneapolis MN (S)

Stout, Kenneth, *Assoc Prof*, Fontbonne College, Art Department, Saint Louis MO (S)

Stout, Kenneth, *Assoc Prof*, Fontbonne College, Department of Art, Clayton MO (S)

Stover, Edwin L, *Dir Instr*, San Jose City College, School of Fine Arts, San Jose CA (S)

Stover, Richard, *Head Dept*, Riverside City College, Department of Art, Riverside CA (S)

Stowe, Dalton, *Secy*, Gaston County Art and History Museum, Dallas NC

Stow III, James P, *Pres*, Westfield Athenaeum, Jasper Rand Art Museum, Westfield MA

Strachota, J, *Instructor*, Milwaukee Area Technical College, Graphic & Applied Arts Div, Milwaukee WI (S)

Strachota, John, *Gallery Dir*, Milwaukee Area Technical College, Kronquist Craft Gallery, Milwaukee WI

Stradling, Anne C, *Dir*, Stradling Museum of the Horse, Inc, Patagonia AZ

Straight, Elsie H, *Head Librn*, Ringling School of Art Library, Sarasota FL

Straight, Robert, *Asst Prof*, Connecticut College, Department of Art, New London CT (S)

Strand, Elizabeth, *Prof*, Concordia College, Art Department, Moorhead MN (S)

Strandberg, Kevin, *Instructor*, Illinois Wesleyan University, School of Art, Bloomington IL (S)

Strater, Henry, *Dir*, Museum of Art of Ogunquit, Ogunquit ME

Straton, Eileen, *Assoc Prof*, Oral Roberts University, Fine Arts Department, Tulsa OK (S)

Stratton, Marcel C, *Assoc Prof*, Moorhead State University, Department of Art, Moorhead MN (S)

Straub, Dale, *Prof*, Williamsport Area Community College, Department of Engineering and Design, Williamsport PA (S)

Strauss, Helen, *Asst*, Pemaquid Group of Artists, Lewiston ME

Strauss, Melvin, *Pres*, Cornish Institute, Seattle WA (S)

Strawn, Jarrett W, *Head Dept*, Beloit College, Department of Art, Beloit WI (S)

Strawn, Martha, *Asst Prof*, University of North Carolina-Charlotte, Creative Arts Dept, Charlotte NC (S)

Strawn, Mel, *Dir*, University of Denver, School of Art, Denver CO (S)

Sunman, Barbara P, *Treas*, Providence Water Color Club, Providence RI

Sunu, Chol, *Librn*, National Museum of Korea, Library, Seoul Korea

Suren, M, *Cur*, Municipal van Abbemuseum, Eindhoven Municipal Museum, Eindhoven Netherlands

Surkamer, Susie, *Dir Arts Development*, South Carolina Arts Commission, Columbia SC

Surtees, Ursula, *Dir & Cur*, Kelowna Centennial Museum and National Exhibit Centre, Kelowna BC

Susi, Frank, *Instr*, Cuyahoga Valley Art Center, Cuyahoga Falls OH (S)

Susovski, Marijan, *Cur*, Galerije Grada Zagreba, Galerija Suvremene Umjetnosti, Zagreb Yugoslavia

Susovski, Marijan, *Librn*, Galerije Grada Zagreba, Gallery of Contemporary Art Library, Zagreb Yugoslavia

Susskind, Lawrence, *Head Dept Urban Studies and Planning*, Massachusetts Institute of Technology, School of Architecture and Planning, Cambridge MA (S)

Sussman, Elisabeth, *Cur*, Institute of Contemporary Art, Boston MA

Sussman, Gary, *School Dir*, Sculpture Center, New York NY

Sussman, Margaret, *Pres*, Pen and Brush, Inc, New York NY

Suter, Sherwood E, *Head Dept*, McMurry College, Art Dept, Abilene TX (S)

Suter, Sherwood E, *Dept Chmn & Gallery Dir*, McMurry College, Ryan Fine Arts Center, Abilene TX

Sutherland, A J, *Pres Bd*, Timken Art Gallery, San Diego CA

Sutherland, Adair R, *Assoc Dir*, San Antonio Museum Association, Inc, San Antonio TX

Sutherland, Martha, *Gallery Coordinator*, University of Arkansas, Fine Arts Center Gallery, Fayetteville AR

Sutter, Carolyn, *Dir Libr Servs*, Long Beach Public Library, Long Beach CA

Sutter, James, *Prof*, State University of New York College at Potsdam, Department of Fine Arts, Potsdam NY (S)

Suttle, Betty, *Librn*, Millicent Rogers Museum, Library, Taos NM

Sutton, B Lee, *Lectr*, Centenary College of Louisiana, Department of Art, Shreveport LA (S)

Sutton, Bernice, *Pres*, Winnipeg Sketch Club, Winnipeg MB

Sutton, Judith, *Assoc Dir*, Public Library of Charlotte and Mecklenburg County, Charlotte NC

Svaren, Jacqueline, *Instr*, Portland Community College, Department of Fine Arts, Portland OR (S)

Svaren, Russell, *Instr*, Portland Community College, Department of Fine Arts, Portland OR (S)

Svedlow, Andrew, *Educational Cur*, Bruce Museum, Greenwich CT

Svendsen, Louise Averiil, *Sr Cur*, Solomon R Guggenheim Museum, New York NY

Swahn, Jan Öjvind, *Librn-in-Chief*, Nordiska Museet, Library, Stockholm Sweden

Swaim, Darlene, *Instructor*, Mesa Community College, Department of Art, Mesa AZ (S)

Swain, Robert, *Pres*, Ontario Association of Art Galleries, Toronto ON

Swain, Robert F, *Dir*, Queen's University, Agnes Etherington Art Centre, Kingston ON

Swan, Genell, *Dir*, Marian Osborne Cunningham Art Gallery, Bakersfield CA

Swanberg, Randall, *VPres*, Montana Historical Society, Helena MT

Swank, Scott T, *Deputy Dir Interpretation*, Winterthur Museum and Gardens, Winterthur DE

Swanson, Dean R, *Dir*, Minnesota Museum of Art, Saint Paul MN

Swanson, Mary, *Adjunct Instr*, College of Saint Thomas, Department of Art, Saint Paul MN (S)

Swanson, Roy, *Prof*, Hutchinson Community Junior College, Art Department, Hutchinson KS (S)

Swanson, Thoma, *Chmn*, Albertus Magnus College, Art Department, New Haven CT (S)

Swartz, Henry, *Undergrad Coordr*, North Texas State University, Art Department, Denton TX (S)

Swarz, Sahl, *Asst Prof*, Columbia University, Division of Painting and Sculpture, New York NY (S)

Swearingen, Eugene, *Chmn Executive Committee*, Bank of Oklahoma, Tulsa OK

Sweatt, Lilla, *Slide Cur*, San Diego State University, Love Library and Art Department Slide Library, San Diego CA

Sweeney, Dennis, *Instr*, Montserrat School of Visual Art, Beverly MA (S)

Sweeney, Gray, *Asst Prof*, Grand Valley State Colleges, Art Department, Allendale MI (S)

Sweeney, John A H, *Asst to the Dir*, Winterthur Museum and Gardens, Winterthur DE

Sweeney, Kent, *Pres Board of Dir*, Art Gallery of Nova Scotia, Halifax NS

Sweeney, Mary Sue, *Program & Publicity*, Newark Museum, Newark NJ

Sweeney, Patricia, *Librn*, Birmingham Public Library, Art and Music Department, Birmingham AL

Sweeney, Richard, *Dir*, Public Library of Columbus and Franklin County, Humanities, Fine Arts and Recreation Division, Columbus OH

Sweeney, Robert, *Chmn Dept*, Amherst College, Dept of Fine Arts, Amherst MA (S)

Sweet, Douglass, *Instructor*, San Jacinto College, Art Department, Pasadena TX (S)

Sweeting, Sharon Howe, *Chmn*, Special Libraries Association, Museum, Arts and Humanities Division, New York NY

Sweet Jr, Ernest A, *Treas*, Currier Gallery of Art, Manchester NH

Swenson, Inga Christine, *Acting Asst Cur Prints*, Smith College, Museum of Art, Northampton MA

Swenson, Ronald, *Dean*, School of the Associated Arts, Saint Paul MN (S)

Swenson, Ronald, *Dean*, School of the Associated Arts Galleries, Saint Paul MN

Swenson, Sandra, *Chmn Art History*, Pan American University, Art Department, Edinburg TX (S)

Swerdfager, Bruce, *Pres Bd of Trustees*, Gallery Stratford, Stratford ON

Swift, June M, *Executive Secy*, Saint Joseph Museum, Saint Joseph MO

Swimmer, Ross O, *Pres*, Cherokee National Historical Society, Inc, Tahlequah OK

Swinton, Elizabeth, *Lectr*, Tufts University, Fine Arts Department, Medford MA (S)

Switlick, Viola, *Secy*, Monroe City-County Fine Arts Council, Monroe MI

Swords, Cramer, *Gallery Dir*, Central Florida Community College Art Collection, Ocala FL

Swoyer, David, *Cur of Education*, New Orleans Museum of Art, Isaac Delgado Museum, New Orleans LA

Sykes, Lawrence F, *Prof*, Rhode Island College, Art Department, Providence RI (S)

Sykes, Ronald, *Instructor*, Millersville State College, Art Department, Millersville PA (S)

Sykora, T A, *Secy*, Great Lakes Historical Society, Vermilion OH

Symington, Martha F, *Secy*, Frick Collection, New York NY

Symns, Edith M, *Dir of Gallery*, Hutchinson Art Association, Hutchinson KS

Symons, Evelyn, *Cur*, Gananoque Historical Museum, Gananoque ON

Synder, R Brant, *Treas*, Norton Gallery and School of Art, West Palm Beach FL

Syverson, John, *Instr*, Western Wisconsin Technical Institute, Graphics Division, LACrosse WI (S)

Szablowski, Jerzy, *Dir*, Panstwowe Zbiory Sztuki na Wawelu, Wawel State Collections of Art, Cracow Poland

Szabo, Albert, *Prof*, Harvard University, Department of Visual and Environmental Studies, Cambridge MA (S)

Szabo, George, *Cur Robert Lehman Coll*, Metropolitan Museum of Art, New York NY

Szabo, Matyas, *Keeper Field Research & Archives*, Nordiska Museet, Scandinavian Museum, Stockholm Sweden

Szainer, Armand, *Asst Prof*, Notre Dame College, Art Department, Manchester NH (S)

Szarkowski, John, *Dir Dept Photography*, Museum of Modern Art, New York NY

Szege, Balint, *Deputy Dir General*, Magyar Nemzeti Galeria, Hungarian National Gallery, Budapest Hungary

Szeitz, P R, *Chmn*, Moorhead State University, Department of Art, Moorhead MN (S)

Szelepin, Malgorzata, *Mgr*, Ministry of Culture and Art, Museum of Architecture in Wroclaw, Wroclaw Poland

Szentlekey, T, *Deputy Dir*, Szepmuveszet Museum, Museum of Fine Arts, Budapest Hungary

Szereszewski, Yaffa, *Chief Librn*, Israel Museum, Library for Art and Archaeology, Jerusalem Israel

Szilagyi, Eve, *Instr*, Pontiac Art Center, Pontiac MI (S)

Szilagyi, J Gy, *Head Greek & Roman Antiquities*, Szepmuveszet Museum, Museum of Fine Arts, Budapest Hungary

Sznajderman, Marius, *Dir*, Galeria Venezuela, New York NY

Szuszitzky, Blanche, *Treas*, North Country Museum of Arts, Park Rapids MN

Szynaka, Edward M, *Dir*, Grace A Dow Memorial Library, Midland MI

Tabakoff, Sheila K, *Dir*, Kent State University, School of Art Gallery, Kent OH

Tacang, Lee, *Instructor*, De Anza College, Art Department, Cupertino CA (S)

Tacha, Athena, *Assoc Prof*, Oberlin College, Department of Art, Oberlin OH (S)

Tack, A Catherine, *Librn*, Carnegie Library of Pittsburgh, Pittsburgh PA

Tade, George T, *Dean*, Texas Christian University, Art Department, Fort Worth TX (S)

Tadlock, Marvin, *Instr*, Virginia Intermont College, Fine Arts Department, Bristol VA (S)

Tadmor, Gabriel, *Dir*, Museum of Modern Art, Haifa Israel

Tafoya, Guadalupe, *Bilingual Coordr*, Millicent Rogers Museum, Taos NM

Taggart, Ross, *Lectr*, University of Kansas, Kress Foundation Department of Art History, Lawrence KS (S)

Taggart, Ross E, *Sr Cur*, William Rockhill Nelson Gallery of Art, Atkins Museum of Fine Art, Kansas City MO

Tai, Jane S, *Asst Dir & Dir Exhib*, American Federation of Arts, New York NY

Takach, Mary H, *Dir*, Pensacola Museum of Art, Pensacola FL

Takacs, M H, *Head Old Pictures*, Szepmuveszet Museum, Museum of Fine Arts, Budapest Hungary

Takahara, Takeshi, *Asst Prof*, Grand Valley State Colleges, Art Department, Allendale MI (S)

Takizawa, Yashushi, *Cur Planning & International Exchange*, Tokyo Kokuritsu Kindai Bujutsukan, National Museum of Modern Art, Tokyo, Tokyo Japan

Talbot, Jarold D, *Cur*, Hill-Stead Museum, Farmington CT

Talbot, Phillips, *Pres, Asia Society, Inc*, Asia Society, Inc, Asia House Gallery, New York NY

Talbot, William, *Executive Secy*, Washington Art Association, Washington Depot CT

Talbot, William S, *Assoc Cur Paintings*, Cleveland Museum of Art, Cleveland OH

Talbott, Edward L, *Assoc Prof*, Miami University, Art Department, Oxford OH (S)

Talerice, Eric, *Vis Prof*, Carroll College, Art Department, Waukesha WI (S)

Taliaferro, Ray, *Pres Commission*, San Francisco City and County Art Commission, San Francisco CA

Taliano, A, *VPres*, Rodman Hall Arts Centre, Saint Catharines ON

Talini, Stefania, *Prof*, Fortman Studios Florence, Florence Italy (S)

Talley, Dan R, *Gallery Cur*, Atlanta Art Workers Coalition, Atlanta GA

Talley, Dwight, *Supt of Grounds*, University of North Carolina at Greensboro, Chinqua-Penn Plantation House, Reidsville NC

Talley, Lilburn, *Pres*, Belle Grove, Middletown VA

Talmadge, Linda L, *Asst*, Ohio State University, Fine Arts Library, Columbus OH

Tal-Mason, Sydney, *Chairperson*, Florida Atlantic University, Art Department, Boca Raton FL (S)

Tam, L C S, *Cur*, Hong Kong Museum of Art, Edinburgh Place Hong Kong

Tamayo, Daisy, *Sr Art Librn*, Free Public Library of Elizabeth, Fine Arts Dept, Elizabeth NJ

Tamerlis, Victor, *Treas*, Sculpture Center, New York NY

Tamplin, Illi-Maria, *Dir*, Art Gallery of Peterborough, Peterborough ON

Tamura, Ruth, *Cur Exten Services*, Honolulu Academy of Arts, Honolulu HI

Tanabe, Takao, *Art Dept Head*, Banff Centre School of Fine Arts, Banff AB (S)

Tandy, Jean C, *Coordinator Dept Art*, Mount Wachusett Community College, Art Galleries, Gardner MA

Tanis, Steven, *Coordr Drawing & Painting*, University of Delaware, Department of Art, Newark DE (S)

Tanis, Thomas P, *Secy*, Buck Hill Art Association, Buck Hill Falls PA

Tank, Frida, *Librn*, City of Oslo Art Collection, Library, Oslo Norway

Tannberg, Kersti, *Fine Arts Librn Liaison*, Wheaton College, Fine Arts Collection, Norton MA

Tanner, Daniel, *Technical Dir*, University of California, Pacific Film Archive, Berkeley CA

Tanner, Estelle, *Pres*, State University of New York College at Purchase, Neuberger Museum, Purchase NY

Tanous, Joe, *Instructor*, Monterey Peninsula College, Art Department, Monterey CA (S)

Tanselle, G Thomas, *VPres*, John Simon Guggenheim Memorial Foundation, New York NY

Tansey, Luraine, *Instr*, San Jose City College, School of Fine Arts, San Jose CA (S)

Tanzola, Mona, *Prof*, Western New Mexico University, Dept of Fine Art, Art Div, Silver City NM (S)

Taplin, Franklin P, *Dir*, Westfield Athenaeum, Jasper Rand Art Museum, Westfield MA

Taradash, Meryl, *Instructor*, Montclair Art Museum, Art School, Montclair NJ (S)

Tarantal, Stephen, *Co-Chairperson Illustration*, Philadelphia College of Art, Philadelphia PA (S)

Tarbox, Gurdon L, *Dir*, Brookgreen Gardens, Murrells Inlet SC

Tarbox Jr, Gurdon L, *Librn*, Brookgreen Gardens, Library, Murrells Inlet SC

Tardo, Barbara, *Assoc Prof*, Southeastern Louisiana University, Dept of Visual Arts, Hammond LA (S)

Tarnowski, Thomas, *Instructor*, Johnson County Community College, Communications-Arts Division, Overland Park KS (S)

Tarter, O W, *Instructor*, West Texas State University, Art Department, Canyon TX (S)

Tarvas, P, *Asst Rector*, Eesti Nsv Riiklik Kunstiinstituut, Tallinn Ussr (S)

Tasch, Linda, *Newsletter Editor*, Millicent Rogers Museum, Taos NM

Tasse, M Jeanne, *Chmn Art Dept*, Marietta College, Grover M Hermann Fine Arts Center, Marietta OH

Tasse, M Jeanne, *Chmn*, Marietta College, Art Department, Marietta OH (S)

Tassell, C B, *Dir*, Queen Victoria Museum and Art Gallery, Tasmania Australia

Taszycka, Maria, *Polish Costumes & Textiles*, Muzeum Narodowe w Krakowie, National Museum in Cracow, Cracow Poland

Tate, Henry A, *Prof*, Chamberlayne Junior College, Department of Graphic and Applied Arts, Boston MA (S)

Tate, John, *Asst Art*, Dartmouth Heritage Museum, Dartmouth NS

Tate, LaDeane V, *Instructor*, Olympic College, Art Department, Bremerton WA (S)

Tatham, David, *Chmn*, Syracuse University, Department of Art History, Syracuse NY (S)

Tatman, Sandra, *Architectural Librn*, Athenaeum of Philadelphia, Philadelphia PA

Tator, Marie A, *Asst Prof*, Salisbury State College, Art Dept, Salisbury MD (S)

Tatum, George B, *Pres*, Lyme Historical Society, Inc, Old Lyme CT

Taubin, William, *Pres*, Art Directors Club, Inc, New York NY

Taulbee, Kathryn, *Registrar*, Cincinnati Art Museum, Cincinnati OH

Tawn, Robert, *Asst Prof*, Nassau Community College, Art Department, Garden City NY (S)

Taylor, Anita, *Chmn*, George Mason University, Department of Fine and Performing Arts, Fairfax VA (S)

Taylor, Ben, *Chmn Museum Committee*, Fairfield Public Library and Museum, Fairfield Art Association, Fairfield IA

Taylor, Bob, *Pres*, Association of American Editorial Cartoonists, Oklahoma City OK

Taylor, Brent, *Ceramics Technician*, Victor Valley College, Art Department, Victorville CA (S)

Taylor, Brett, *Dir*, Aegean School of Fine Arts, Paros Cyclades Greece (S)

Taylor, Carolyn, *Secy*, Southern Illinois University Museum and Art Galleries, Carbondale IL

Taylor, Cecil, *Dir*, Artworlds Center for Creative Arts, Ann Arbor MI

Taylor, Charles, *Preparator of Exhib*, Philbrook Art Center, Tulsa OK

Taylor, Cynthia, *Prof*, Manatee Junior College, Department of Art, Bradenton FL (S)

Taylor, David G, *Cur*, McMaster University Art Gallery, Hamilton ON

Taylor, Donald R, *Dir*, Tryon Palace Restoration Complex, New Bern NC

Taylor, Elizabeth H, *Assoc Dir*, Hammond Museum, Museum of the Humanities, North Salem NY

Taylor, Eric, *Preparator*, Whatcom Museum of History and Art, Bellingham WA

Taylor, Frances, *Executive Dir*, Ocean City Arts Center, Ocean City NJ

Taylor, Frances J, *Executive Dir*, Ocean City School of Art, Ocean City NJ (S)

Taylor, George, *VPres*, Plastic Club, Art Club for Women, Philadelphia PA

Taylor, Howard J, *Asst Dir*, Philadelphia Maritime Museum, Philadelphia PA

Taylor, Hugh A, *Provincial Archivist*, Public Archives of Nova Scotia, Halifax NS

Taylor, Hugh H, *Prof*, Washington and Jefferson College, Art Department, Washington PA (S)

Taylor, Ira M, *Chmn*, Hardin-Simmons University, Art Dept, Abilene TX (S)

Taylor, J, *Secy*, Anderson Park Art Gallery, Invercargill New Zealand

Taylor, J Allyn, *Chmn Board Turstees*, McMichael Canadian Collection, Kleinburg ON

Taylor, James, *Manuscripts & Microfilm*, Winterthur Museum and Gardens, Library, Winterthur DE

Taylor, Jean F, *Asst Prof*, Northeast Louisiana University, Department of Art, Monroe LA (S)

Taylor, Jeanne, *Instructor*, Dunedin Fine Arts and Cultural Center, Dunedin FL (S)

Taylor, John A, *Pres*, Oklahoma Museum of Art, Oklahoma City OK

Taylor, John Lloyd, *Dir*, University of Wisconsin, School of Fine Arts Galleries, Milwaukee WI

Taylor, Joseph, *Cur*, Liberty Hall Museum, Orlando Brown House 202 Wilkinson St, Frankfort KY

Taylor, Joshua C, *Pres*, College Art Association of America, New York NY

Taylor, Joshua C, *Dir*, National Collection of Fine Arts, Washington DC

Taylor, Kendall, *Gallery Dir*, State University of New York College at Potsdam, Department of Fine Arts, Potsdam NY (S)

Taylor, Kendall, *Gallery Dir*, State University of New York College at Potsdam, Brainerd Art Gallery, Potsdam NY

Taylor, Lisa, *Dir*, Cooper-Hewitt Museum, Smithsonian Institution National Museum of Design, New York NY

Taylor, M P, *Grad Advisor*, University of Texas - Austin, Art Department, Austin TX (S)

Taylor, Mack, *Instructor*, La Roche College, Division of Graphic Arts & Design, Pittsburgh PA (S)

Taylor, Marcia, *Asst Prof*, Trenton State College, Art Department, Trenton NJ (S)

Taylor, Marilyn S, *Conservator and Cur Coll*, Saint Joseph Museum, Saint Joseph MO

Taylor, Mary Jane, *Instructor*, Brenau College, Art Department, Gainesville GA (S)

Taylor, Michael, *Dir*, George Peabody College for Teachers, Cohen Memorial Museum of Art, Nashville TN

Taylor, Michael D, *Assoc Prof*, University of Missouri-Saint Louis, Art Dept, Saint Louis MO (S)

Taylor, Michael L, *Chmn*, George Peabody College for Teachers, Art Faculty Department, Nashville TN (S)

Taylor, P W, *Deputy Cur*, South London Art Gallery, London England

Taylor, Philip, *Instr*, Studio School of Art and Design, Philadelphia PA (S)

Taylor, Rene, *Dir*, Museo de Arte de Ponce, Ponce Art Museum, Ponce PR

Taylor, Richard, *VPres*, Museum of American Folk Art, New York NY

Taylor, Richard, *Pres*, Independence Community Junior College, Fine Arts Department, Independence KS (S)

Taylor, Rod A, *Head Dept*, Norfolk State College, Fine Arts Department, Norfolk VA (S)

Taylor, Sally, *Admis Asst*, Jacksonville Museum of Arts and Sciences, Jacksonville FL

Taylor, Shirley, *Admin Secy*, Hebrew Union College, Skirball Museum, Los Angeles CA

Taylor, Susan, *Development Coordr*, Tampa Museum, Tampa FL

Taylor, Tom, *Coordr Crafts*, Columbia College, Art Department, Chicago IL (S)

Taylor, Veda, *Co-Chmn & Secy*, Valley Art Center Inc, Clarkston WA

Taylor, Warren, *Instructor*, Midland College, Art Department, Midland TX (S)

Taylor, Will, *Cur Art Coll*, Lovelace Medical Foundation, Art Collection, Albuquerque NM

Taylor, William, *Asst Prof*, University of the District of Columbia, Art Department, Washington DC (S)

Taylor Jr, Herman W, *Prof*, Washington and Lee University, Department of Fine Arts, Lexington VA (S)

Taylor Jr, W E, *Dir*, National Museum of Man, Ottawa ON

Taylor Jr, W E, *Dir*, National Museums of Canada, National Museum of Man, Ottawa ON

Taylor Jr, William C, *Business Mgr*, Arts Council of Spartanburg County, Inc, Spartanburg SC

Teahan, John, *Keeper Art*, National Museum of Ireland, Dublin Ireland

Teahan, John W, *Asst Librn*, Wadsworth Atheneum, Auerbach Art Library, Hartford CT

Tebble, Norman, *Dir*, Royal Scottish Museum, Edinburgh Scotland

Teczar, Steven, *Instr*, Maryville College, Art Department, Saint Louis MO (S)

Teed, Truman, *Chmn Art Educ*, University of South Carolina, Department of Art, Columbia SC (S)

Teholiz, Leo, *Head Dept*, West Shore Community College, Div of Humanities & Fine Arts, Scottville MI (S)

Teichert, Gayl, *Gallery Clerk*, University of Montana, Gallery of Visual Arts, Missoula MT

Teichman, Carmela, *Librn*, Israel Museum, Library for Art and Archaeology, Jerusalem Israel

Teilhet, Jehanne, *Lectr*, University of California, San Diego, Visual Arts Department, La Jolla CA (S)

Teilman, Herdis Bull, *Cur Painting & Sculpture*, Carnegie Institute, Museum of Art, Pittsburgh PA

Teis, Daniel K, *Chmn*, University of Delaware, Department of Art, Newark DE (S)

Teitz, Richard Stuart, *Dir*, Worcester Art Museum, Worcester MA

Teixeira, Laurie, *Security Officer*, Auckland City Art Gallery, Auckland New Zealand

Teixeira, Maria Emilia Amaral, *Dir*, Museu Nacional de Soares dos Reis, National Museum of Soares Dos Reis, Oporto Portugal

Telford, Elizabeth S, *Registrar*, John and Mable Ringling Museum of Art, Sarasota FL

Teller, Gus, *Deputy Dir Operations*, Fine Arts Museums of San Francisco, M H de Young Memorial Museum and California Palace of the Legion of Honor

Temme, Norman, *Ed*, Stained Glass Association of America, Bronxville NY

Temple, Seth, *Pres*, San Antonio Art League, San Antonio TX

Temple, Tom, *Assoc Prof*, Central Oregon Community College, Department of Art, Bend OR (S)

Templer, Joan, *Lectr*, Georgia Institute of Technology, College of Architecture, Atlanta GA (S)

Templeton, Judy, *Secy*, Columbus College, Experimental Gallery, Columbus GA

Templeton, Orion A, *Pres*, Lynchburg Fine Arts Center Inc, Lynchburg VA

Templin, Vivian, *Readers Services*, Trinity College Library, Washington DC

Tenabe, Gabriel S, *Cur*, Morgan State University Gallery of Art, Baltimore MD

Tennent, Elaine, *Dir*, Tennent Art Foundation Gallery, Honolulu HI

Tennent, John H, *VPres*, Bowne House, Flushing NY

Tenney, Nancy, *Admin Asst*, Dartmouth College Museum & Galleries, Hanover NH

Teoli, Alfred, *Assoc Prof*, University of Illinois at the Medical Center, Dept of Biocommunication Arts-Medical Art, Chicago IL (S)

Terenzio, Stephanie, *Asst Dir*, University of Connecticut, William Benton Museum of Art, Storrs CT

Tereshko, Daniel, *Assoc Prof*, Moravian College, Department of Art, Bethlehem PA (S)

Terhune, Anne, *Instr*, College of New Rochelle, Art Department, New Rochelle NY (S)

Terhune, Dolores, *Asst to Dir*, Ball State University, Art Gallery, Muncie IN

Terrell, James A, *Chmn*, Southwestern Oklahoma State University, Art Department, Weatherford OK (S)

Terrell, Richard, *Head Dept*, Doane College, Dept of Art, Crete NE (S)

Terrill, Evelyn B, *Exhib Chmn*, West Baton Rouge Museum, Port Allen LA

Terrill, Martha, *Cur*, Transco Companies Inc, Houston TX

Terry, George, *Cur Historical Collection*, University of South Carolina, McKissick Museums, Columbia SC

Tersteeg, William, *Instr*, Keystone Junior College, Art Department, Cleveland PA (S)

Teslow, Pamela, *Cur*, North Country Museum of Arts, Park Rapids MN

Tester, Louise C, *Executive Dir*, Arizona Commission on the Arts, Phoenix AZ

Teter, Keith, *Industrial Design Chmn*, Art Center College of Design, Pasadena CA (S)

Tetrau, Richard, *Librn*, Saint Peter's College Art Gallery, College Library, Art Section, Jersey City NJ

Tetreault, Eva, *Admin Secy*, Federation des Quebecoise des Services Socio-Culturels, Montreal PQ

Tetreault Jr, Theodore J, *Park Manager*, Harkness Memorial State Park, Waterford CT

Tettleton, Robert L, *Prof*, University of Mississippi, Department of Art, University MS (S)

Teufel, Nicolette, *Registrar*, Heard Museum, Phoenix AZ

Thal, Nelson, *Pres*, Toledo Federation of Art Societies, Toledo OH

Thal, Nelson, *VPres*, Spectrum, Friends of Fine Art, Inc, Toledo OH

Thalacker, Donald W, *Dir Fine Arts Program*, General Services Administration, Washington DC

Thaler, Donald M, *Pres*, French Art Colony, Inc, Gallipolis OH

Thaler, Janice M, *Acting Dir*, French Art Colony, Inc, Gallipolis OH

Thayed, Fred, *Asst Prof*, Radford University, Art Department, Radford VA (S)

Thayer, Cornelia, *Instructor*, Emma Willard School Arts Division, Troy NY (S)

Thayer, Russell, *Assoc Prof*, Delta College, Art Department, University Center MI (S)

Thayn, Florence H, *Art Reference*, United States Capitol Museum, Art Reference Library, Washington DC

Theel, Marcia M, *Office Mgr*, Leigh Yawkey Woodson Art Museum, Inc, Wausau WI

Thein, John, *Instr*, Creighton University, Fine and Performing Arts Department, Omaha NE (S)

Theis, Andrew, *Instr*, Studio School of Art and Design, Philadelphia PA (S)

Thelin, Valfred, *Treas*, Ogunquit Art Association, The Barn Gallery, Ogunquit ME

Theobald, Sharon A, *Dir*, Lafayette Art Center, Lafayette IN

Theodore, Crystal, *Prof*, James Madison University, Department of Art, Harrisonburg VA (S)

Theodore, Josephine, *Executive Secy*, University of Utah, Utah Museum of Fine Arts, Salt Lake City UT

Theriault, Jean-Guy, *Animator*, Institut des Arts au Saguenay, National Exhibition Center, Jonquiere PQ

Theriault, Lucien, *Pres*, Musee Historique de Vaudreuil, Vaudreuil Historial Museum, Woodstock PQ

Theriault, Normand, *Cur Contemporary Canadian Art*, Montreal Museum of Fine Arts, Montreal PQ

Theuer, Otto, *Acting Dir Cur*, Minnesota Museum of Art, Saint Paul MN

Thibault, Claude, *Conservator Ancient Art*, Musee du Quebec, Quebec PQ

Thibault, H Donald, *Associate Dir Student Activities*, Rider College, Rider College Art Gallery, Lawrenceville NJ

Thibeault, Leopold, *Preparator*, Galerie Restigouche Gallery, Campbellton NB

Thieband, Wayne, *Vis Prof*, Santa Rosa Junior College, Art Department, Santa Rosa CA (S)

Thiebeige, Claude, *First VPres*, La Societe des Decorateurs-Ensembliers du Quebec, Interior Decorators' Society of Quebec, Montreal PQ

Thiedeman, Michael, *Assoc Prof*, West Virginia Wesleyan College, Department of Fine Arts, Buckhannon WV (S)

Thielen, Greg G, *Cur of Coll & Registrar*, Springfield Art Museum, Springfield MO

Thiem, G, *Dir Department of Prints & Drawings*, Staatsgalerie Stuttgart, Stuttgart Germany, Federal Republic of

Thiras, Antoinette, *Registrar*, Phillips Academy, Addison Gallery of American Art, Andover MA

Thisdlae, Hector, *Admin Asst*, Musee d'Art Contemporain, Montreal PQ

Thivierge, Jean-Marie, *Conservateur*, Musee du Seminaire de Quebec, Quebec PQ

Thogerson, Gary, *Librn*, J K Ralston Museum and Art Center, Willo Ralston Library for Historical Research, Sidney MT

Thom, Ian, *Cur of Contemporary Art*, Art Gallery of Greater Victoria, Victoria BC

Thomas, Anne W, *Secy*, Southeastern College Art Conference, Chapel Hill NC

Thomas, C David, *Instructor*, Emmanuel College, Art Department, Boston MA (S)

Thomas, Curtis R, *Adminr*, Shadows-on-the-Teche, New Iberia LA

Thomas, David, *Dir*, Art Gallery of South Australia, Adelaide Australia

Thomas, Ed, *Instructor*, Springfield College, Department of Visual and Performing Arts, Springfield MA (S)

Thomas, Elaine, *Dept Chmn*, Tuskegee Institute, Art Department, Tuskegee Institute AL (S)

Thomas, Elaine F, *Dir & Cur*, Tuskegee Institute, George Washington Carver Museum, Tuskegee AL

Thomas, Elaine G, *Dir*, International Correspondence Schools, School of Interior Design, Scranton PA (S)

Thomas, George, *Dir*, Whatcom Museum of History and Art, Bellingham WA

Thomas, Hess, *Cur 20th Century Art*, Metropolitan Museum of Art, New York NY

Thomas, Homer, *Prof*, University of Missouri, Art History and Archaeology Department, Columbia MO (S)

Thomas, James, *Deputy Dir Admin*, American Association of Museums, Washington DC

Thomas, James A, *Maintenance*, Tryon Palace Restoration Complex, New Bern NC

Thomas, Jean, *Instructor*, Emmanuel College, Art Department, Boston MA (S)

Thomas, Jean, *First VPres Membership*, Arizona Artist Guild, Phoenix AZ

Thomas, Jesse, *VPres*, Prescott Fine Arts Association, Prescott AZ

Thomas, Jill, *REgistrar*, University of Mississippi, University Museums, Oxford MS

Thomas, John L, *Pres*, Thomas College Gallery, Waterville ME

Thomas, John Z, *Asst Prof*, Hanover College, Department of Art, Hanover IN (S)

Thomas, Lewis, *Mgr Legion Bookshop*, Fine Arts Museums of San Francisco, The Museum Society

Thomas, Linda, *Registrar*, Museum of Fine Arts, Boston MA

Thomas, Paul, *Planning Chmn*, Illinois Institute of Technology, College of Architecture, Planning and Design, Department of Architecture, Chicago IL (S)

Thomas, Peter G, *Dean*, Corcoran School of Art, Washington DC (S)

Thomas, Ralph R, *Asst Dean & Dir Admissions*, Indiana University - Purdue University at Indianapolis, Herron School of Art, Art Gallery, Indianapolis IN

Thomas, Richard C, *Head Metalsmithing Dept*, Cranbrook Academy of Art, Bloomfield Hills MI (S)

Thomas, Ronald, *Instructor*, Saint Louis Community College at Meramec, Art Dept, Saint Louis MO (S)

Thomas, Sam, *Asst Prof*, Mansfield State College, Art Department, Mansfield PA (S)

Thomas, Sidney, *Instr*, Syracuse University, Department of Art History, Syracuse NY (S)

Thomas, Troy, *Instructor*, Pennsylvania State University, Capitol Campus, Department of Humanities, Middletown PA (S)

Thomas, William, *Prof*, West Virginia University, Division of Art, Morgantown WV (S)

Thomas, William Radford, *Chmn Dept*, East Tennessee State University, Fine Arts Dept, Johnson City TN (S)

Thomas, W Radford, *Chmn Art Dept*, East Tennessee State University, Elizabeth Slocum Gallery, Johnson City TN

Thomas Jr, Minor Wine, *Dir and Chief Cur*, New York State Historical Association, Fenimore House, Cooperstown NY

Thomas Jr, Minor Wine, *Dir & Chief Cur*, New York State Historical Association, Farmers' Museum, Inc, Cooperstown NY

Thomason, Barbara, *Lectr*, California State Polytechnic University, Pomona, Art Department, Pomona CA (S)

Thomason, Roger, *Crafts Coordr*, North Texas State University, Art Department, Denton TX (S)

Thompson, Ann, *Exten Service Coordr*, Clark County Library District, Las Vegas NV

Thompson, Audrey, *Pres*, Prince George Art Gallery, Prince George BC

Thompson, B, *VPres*, Manitoba Historical Society, Dalnavert - MacDonald House Museum, Winnipeg MB

Thompson, Charles, *Asst Prof*, East Tennessee State University, Fine Arts Dept, Johnson City TN (S)

Thompson, Charles, *Library Dir*, Patterson Library, Westfield NY

Thompson, Colin, *Dir*, National Galleries of Scotland, National Gallery of Scotland, Edinburgh Scotland

Thompson, Conway Betty, *Asst Prof*, Longwood College, Department of Art, Farmville VA (S)

Thompson, Eleanor, *Printed Books & Periodicals*, Winterthur Museum and Gardens, Library, Winterthur DE

Thompson, Eleanor E, *Dir*, Wenham Historical Association and Museum, Inc, Wenham MA

Thompson, Elwood N, *Pres*, University of Nebraska Lincoln, Nebraska Art Association, Lincoln NE

Thompson, Ernest, *VPres*, Pemaquid Group of Artists, Lewiston ME

Thompson, Ernest T, *Instructor*, Portland School of Art, Portland ME (S)

Thompson, Florence, *Secy*, Pemaquid Group of Artists, Lewiston ME

Thompson, Frederick, *Executive Dir*, Frederick Thompson Foundation, Inc, New York NY

Thompson, H E, *Dean*, University of Manitoba, Faculty of Architecture, Winnipeg MB (S)

Thompson, Helen, *Prof*, New Mexico Highlands University, Dept of Fine Arts, Las Vegas NM (S)

Thompson, J Paul, *Instructor*, Olivet Nazarene College, Dept of Art, Kankakee IL (S)

Thompson, Jack, *Chmn Ceramic Design*, Moore College of Art, Philadelphia PA (S)

Thompson, James E, *Dir*, Charles B Goddard Center for the Visual and Performing Arts, Ardmore OK

Thompson, Jeanine, *Adminr*, Artists Coalition of Texas, Dallas TX

Thompson, Jill, *Instructor*, Northwestern Michigan College, Art Dept, Traverse City MI (S)

Thompson, J M A, *Dir of County Museums*, Tyne and Wear County Council Museums, Laing Art Gallery and Museum, Newcastle England

Thompson, Joanne, *Lectr*, University of Santa Clara, Fine Arts Department, Santa Clara CA (S)

Thompson, John R, *Chmn Ceramics Dept*, Lake Placid School of Art, Lake Placid NY (S)

Thompson, Joseph B, *Pres*, Antonelli School of Photography, Philadelphia PA (S)

Thompson, Kaye, *Secy*, Las Vegas Art League, Las Vegas Art Museum, Las Vegas NV

Thompson, Lewis, *Prof*, Hollins College, Art Department, Hollins VA (S)

Thompson, Lise, *VPres*, Alaska Artists Guild, Anchorage AK

Thompson, Lou, *Instr*, Colby-Sawyer College, Art Department, New London NH (S)

Thompson, M E, *Bus Secy*, Tucson Museum of Art, Tucson AZ

Thompson, Marsi, *Pub Relations Dir*, National Cowboy Hall of Fame and Western Heritage Center, Oklahoma City OK

Thompson, Meera, *Asst*, Metropolitan Museum of Art, Junior Museum, New York NY

Thompson, Melissa, *Business Mgr*, Portland Center for the Visual Arts, Portland OR

Thompson, Mercedes, *Prof*, North Carolina Central University, Art Dept, Durham NC (S)

Thompson, Morley P, *Pres*, Taft Museum, Cincinnati OH

Thompson, Philip, *Chmn*, Augsburg College, Art Department, Minneapolis MN (S)

Thompson, Robert, *Pres*, Percy H Whiting Art Center, Fairhope AL

Thompson, Stuart R, *Chmn Dept*, Seton Hill College, Department of Art, Greensburg PA (S)

Thompson, Walter, *Dir*, Bradley University, Art Dept, Peoria IL (S)

Thompson, William F, *Dir Research*, State Historical Society of Wisconsin, Madison WI

Thompson Jr, Harold W, *Dir*, Free Public Library, Art and Music Department, Trenton NJ

Thomsen, Robert E, *Prof*, Glendale College, Department of Fine Arts, Glendale CA (S)

Thomson, Garry, *Scientific Adviser*, National Gallery, London England

Thomson, Pat, *Educ Dir*, Contemporary Arts Center, Cincinnati OH

Thorburn, Dan, *Preparator*, Art Gallery of Hamilton, Hamilton ON

Thorburn, Rick, *Pres*, Vernon Art Association, Topham Brown Gallery, Vernon BC

Thorkildsen, Jean, *Cur*, Schenectady County Historical Society, Schenectady NY

Thorn, James C, *Assoc Prof*, Northwestern State University of Louisiana, Dept of Art, Natchitoches LA (S)

Thornberry, Nancye, *Dir*, Polk Public Museum, Lakeland FL

Thorne, Frank, *Vis Lectr*, Joe Kubert School of Cartoon and Graphic Art Inc, Dover NJ (S)

Thorne, J W, *Secy*, Skaneateles Library Association, Skaneateles NY

Thornhill, Gay, *VPres*, Singing River Art Association Inc, L & N Railroad Depot Gallery, Pascagoula MS

Thorns Jr, John C, *Chmn*, Fort Hays State University, Department of Art, Hays KS (S)

Thorns Jr, John C, *Chmn Art Dept*, Fort Hays State University, Visual Arts Center, Hays KS

Thornton, P K, *Keeper Furniture*, Victoria and Albert Museum, London England

Thornton, Richard, *Head Dept*, University of Connecticut, Art Department, Storrs CT (S)

Thorp, Grant, *Instructor*, East Central University, Art Department, Ada OK (S)

Thorpe, F, *Chief History Division*, National Museum of Man, Ottawa ON

Thorpe, Gordon L, *Lectr*, University of California, Riverside, Program in Art, Riverside CA (S)

Thorpe, James, *Dir*, Huntington Library, Art Gallery and Botanical Gardens, San Marino CA

Thorpe, James, *Assoc Prof*, State University of New York College at Cortland, Art Department, Cortland NY (S)

Thorstvedt, Else Marie, *Librn*, Norsk Sjöfartsmuseum, Library, Oslo Norway

Thrall, Arthur, *Chmn*, Lawrence University, Department of Art, Appleton WI (S)

Thrall, Flicka, *VPres*, East Windsor Historical Society Inc, Scantic Academy Museum, West Hartford CT

Thrash, James R, *Library Dir*, Salisbury State College, Blackwell Library, Art Department, Salisbury MD

Threatt, Thomas K, *Asst*, Fort Worth Public Library, Fort Worth TX

Throm, Qurentia P, *Dept Chmn*, Valencia Community College, Art Department, Orlando FL (S)

Thue, Oscar, *Keeper Sculpture*, Nasjonalgalleriet, National Gallery, Oslo Norway

Thurheimer, David C, *Dir*, Brick Store Museum, Kennebunk ME

Thurlow, Alan, *Asst Prof*, Mississippi University for Women, Art Department, Columbus MS (S)

Thurlow, Fearn, *Cur Painting & Sculpture*, Newark Museum, Newark NJ

Thurman, Christa C Mayer, *Cur Textiles*, Art Institute of Chicago, Chicago IL

Thurman, Henry L, *Acting Dir*, Southern University A & M College, Division of Architecture, Baton Rouge LA (S)

Thurman, Melvena, *Preservation Dir*, Oklahoma Historical Society, Central Museum, Oklahoma City OK

Thurmond, Macel, *Executive Secy*, Utah Travel Council, Salt Lake City UT

Thursz, Frederic, *Prof*, Kingsborough Community College, Department of Art, Brooklyn NY (S)

Tibbetts, Tyler, *Treas*, Keokuk Art Center, Keokuk IA

Tiberia, Vitaliano, *Asst Supt*, Museo de Capodimonte, Mount Capodi Museum, Naples Italy

Tibesar, Leo J, *Acting Cur*, Catholic Historical Society of Saint Paul, Saint Paul MN

Tidd, Patrick, *Instructor*, Contra Costa College, Department of Art, San Pablo CA (S)

Tidemann, Viola, *Reference Dept Head*, Wichita Public Library, Wichita KS

Tieken, Theodore, *Pres*, Chicago Historical Society, Chicago IL

Tiemann, Robert E, *Assoc Prof*, Trinity University, Department of Art, San Antonio TX (S)

Tierney, Lennox, *Prof*, University of Utah, Art Department, Salt Lake City UT (S)

Tiessen, George, *Chmn*, University of Victoria, Department of Visual Arts, Victoria BC (S)

Tietz, William, *Pres*, Montana State University, Fine Arts Gallery, Bozeman MT

Tiff, Georgiana, *Head Arts & Recreation Dept*, Denver Public Library, Denver CO

Tilghman, Douglas, *Asst Dir Admin*, Spencer Museum of Art, Lawrence KS

Tilghman, Romalyn, *Secy*, National Assembly of Community Arts Agencies, Washington DC

Till, C M, *Acting Dir*, National Gallery of Zimbabwe Rhodesia, Salisbury Zimbahwe Rhodesia

Tilley, Harriette, *Secy, Receptionist, Bookkeeper*, Children's Museum of History, Natural History and Science, Utica NY

Tilley, Lewis, *Prof*, University of Southern Colorado, Belmont Campus, Department of Art, Pueblo CO (S)

Timmerman, Mary Jane, *Instructor*, Murray State University, Art Department, Murray KY (S)

Timms, Peter, *Dir*, Fitchburg Art Museum, Fitchburg MA

Tinelli, Stephen D, *Assoc Prof*, West Virginia Wesleyan College, Department of Fine Arts, Buckhannon WV (S)

Tinley, Glenn, *Head Design Department*, Winnipeg Art Gallery, Winnipeg MB

Tinnin, Janet, *Secy*, Meridian Museum of Art, Meridian MS

Tinsley, Earl M, *Dean of Col*, Cottey College, Fine Arts Div, Nevada MO (S)

Tinsley, Walter R, *In Charge Art Coll*, Government Employees Insurance Company, Los Angeles MD

Titchener, S W, *Town Clerk*, Stoke-on-District Council, City Museum and Art Gallery, Hanley England

Titus, William, *Registrar*, Heckscher Museum, Huntington NY

Tiura, Oliver, *Dir*, Lakehead University, Department of Fine Art, Thunder Bay ON (S)

Tlicker, John Oren, *Chmn*, Syracuse University, College of Visual and Performing Arts, Syracuse NY (S)

Toadvine, Jane E, *Sr Instr*, Miami University, Art Department, Oxford OH (S)

Toal, Harold T, *Chmn of the Board*, Bass Museum of Art, Miami Beach FL

Tobin, Edgar, *Pres*, Marion Koogler McNay Art Institute, San Antonio TX

Tobin, Linda, *Dir*, University of California, Memorial Union Art Gallery, Davis CA

Tobol, Carol, *10 Research Asst*, Kendall Whaling Museum, Library, Sharon MA

Todaro, Frank, *Building & Grounds Supt*, R W Norton Art Gallery, Shreveport LA

Todd, Barbara, *Cur of Education*, Rodman Hall Arts Centre, Saint Catharines ON

Todd, Hugh, *Librn*, Litchfield Historical Society, Ingraham Memorial Research Library, Litchfield CT

Todd, Ken P, *Treas*, King County Arts Commission, Seattle WA

Toennis, Barbara J, *Instructor*, Central Academy of Commercial Art, Cincinnati OH (S)

Toffel, Alvin E, *Pres*, Norton Simon Museum, Pasadena CA

Toland, Stel, *Cur Asst*, Oakland University, Meadow Brook Art Gallery, Rochester MI

Tolles Jr, Bryant F, *Dir*, Essex Institute, Salem MA

Tolmatch, Elaine, *Registrar*, Montreal Museum of Fine Arts, Montreal PQ

Tomasch, Otto H, *Instr*, York College of Pennsylvania, Department of Humanities and Fine Arts, York PA (S)

Tomasini, Wallace J, *Dir*, University of Iowa, School of Art and Art History, Iowa City IA (S)

Tomasita, Mary, *Head Department*, Cardinal Stritch College, Milwaukee WI

Tomayko, Vicky, *Asst Prof*, Connecticut College, Department of Art, New London CT (S)

Tomiyama, Hideo, *Chief Cur*, National Museum of Western Art, Kokuritsu Seiyo Bijutsukan, Tokyo Japan

Tomlinson, D, *Head Dept Fashion and Textiles*, City of Birmingham Polytechnic, Birmingham England (S)

Tomlinson, Tom, *Exec Dir*, Allied Arts Council of the Yakima Valley, Yakima WA

Tommi, Josee, *Dir*, Le Centre d'Art de Perce, Perce PQ

Tomsic, Walt, *Chmn*, Pacific Lutheran University, Department of Art, Tacoma WA (S)

Tomsik, C S, *Controller & Corporate Secy*, Glenbow Museum, Calgary AB

Tonelli, Edith A, *Dir*, University of Maryland, Art Gallery, College Park MD

Toner, Rochele, *Assoc Prof*, Temple University, Art Department, Philadelphia PA (S)

Toner, William H, *Dir Public Relations*, Worcester Art Museum, Worcester MA

Tooman, Judy, *Pres*, Ponca City Art Association, Ponca City OK

Toon, J, *Historical Resources Librn*, Department of Culture, Government of the Province of Alberta, Provincial Archives of Alberta, Edmonton AB

Toperoff, Sam, *Assoc Prof*, Hofstra University, Department of Art History, Hempstead NY (S)

Toperzer, Tom R, *Dir*, Illinois State University, Center for the Visual Arts Gallery, Normal IL

Topolski, Andy, *Instructor*, Villa Maria College of Buffalo, Art Department, Buffalo NY (S)

Toquero, Jose Lazcarro, *Instr*, University of the Americas, Graphic Arts and Design Dept, Cholula Mexico (S)

Torcoletti, Enzo, *Treas*, Saint Augustine Art Association Gallery, Saint Augustine FL

Torcoletti, Enzo, *Asst Prof*, Flagler College, Visual Arts Department, Saint Augustine FL (S)

Tormey, John L, *VPres*, Stan Hywet Hall Foundation, Inc, Akron OH

Tornheim, N, *Instructor*, Golden West College, Arts, Humanities and Social Sciences Institute, Huntington Beach CA (S)

Torreano, John, *Vis Prof*, New Mexico State University, Art Dept, Las Cruces NM (S)

Torrence, Dave, *Chmn County Museum Board*, J K Ralston Museum and Art Center, Sidney MT

Torrenti, Thomas, *VPres*, Lyme Art Association, Inc, Old Lyme CT

Torres, Dorothy, *Asst Dir*, San Jose State University, Union Gallery, San Jose CA

Torrini, Rudolph E, *Chmn Dept*, Fontbonne College, Art Department, Saint Louis MO (S)

Torrini, Rudolph E, *Chmn Dept*, Fontbonne College, Department of Art, Clayton MO (S)

Torroelia, Isabelle, *Head Art Dept*, School of Fashion Design, Boston MA (S)

Toscano, James V, *Pres*, Minnesota Museum of Art, Saint Paul MN

Tostenrud, Don B, *Chmn & Chief Executive Officer*, The Arizona Bank, Phoenix AZ

Toth, Carl, *Head Photography Dept*, Cranbrook Academy of Art, Bloomfield Hills MI (S)

Toth, Judith, *Lectr*, Oakland University, Dept of Art & Art History, Rochester MI (S)

Toth, Richard, *Head*, Utah State University, Department of Landscape Architecture, Logan UT (S)

Touhey, John F, *Dir*, Fashion Institute of Technology, Library, New York NY

Touhey, Paula, *Cur Education*, Kenosha Public Museum, Kenosha WI

Toupin, Jacques, *Dir*, Musee d'Art de Joliette, Joliette PQ

Toupin, Juanita, *Librn*, Montreal Museum of Fine Arts, Library, Montreal PQ

Toureiere, Michel, *Dir*, Ecole Nationale Superieure des Arts Decoratives, National College of Decorative Arts, Paris France (S)

Tournon-Branley, M, *Fine Arts Dir*, American School of Art, Palace of Fontainebleau, Fontainebleau France (S)

Tourville, Lettie, *Dir*, Hamilton College, Edward W Root Art Center, Clinton NY

Toutant, Eileen, *Asst to Cur*, University of Louisville, Slide Collection, Louisville KY

Tovar, Francisco Gil, *Dir*, Colombian Institute of Culture, Museum of Colonial Art, Bogota Colombia

Tovish, Harold, *Prof*, Boston University, School of Visual Arts, Boston MA (S)

Tow, Terry, *Coordr Crafts*, Iowa State University, Department of Design, Ames IA (S)

Towe, Kelly, *Instructor*, Ohio Visual Art Institute, Cincinnati OH (S)

Tower, A Wesley, *Head Div*, Culver-Stockton College, Division of Fine Arts, Canton MO (S)

Town, Vernon, *Instructor*, Murray State University, Art Department, Murray KY (S)

Townes, Jack, *Dir*, School of the Arts and Crafts Society of Portland, Hoffman Gallery, Portland OR

Townley, Frances, *VPres*, Kent Art Association, Inc Gallery, Kent CT

Townsend, Arthur, *State Historic Preservation Officer*, Colorado Historical Society, Colorado Heritage Center, Denver CO

Townsend, Carol, *Assoc Prof*, Daemen College, Art Department, Amherst NY (S)

Townsend, Sally O C, *Dir Education*, Newark Museum, Newark NJ

Townsend, Samuel, *Librn*, Skaneateles Library Association, Library, Skaneateles NY

Townsend, Vera B, *Assoc Prof*, University of Missouri, Art History and Archaeology Department, Columbia MO (S)

Toy, Randy, *Exhibitions Preparator*, Brooks Memorial Art Gallery, Memphis TN

Toy Jr, Ernest, *Librn*, California State University Fullerton, Library, Fullerton CA

Tozer, Jane, *Keeper Costume*, Manchester City Art Galleries, Manchester England

Tracey, Donald, *Instr*, Tacoma Community College, Art Department, Tacoma WA (S)

Trachtman, Philip, *Pres*, Art Institute of Philadelphia, Philadelphia PA (S)

Tracy, Berry B, *Cur in Charge American Decorative Arts*, Metropolitan Museum of Art, New York NY

Tracy, Regina, *Dir & Cur*, Custom House Maritime Museum, Newburyport MA

Trafford, Hal, *Head Commercial Art*, Butera School of Art, Boston MA (S)

Trakis, Louis, *Head Dept*, Manhattanville College, Art Department, Purchase NY (S)

Trank, Lynn, *Prof*, Eastern Illinois University, Art Department, Charleston IL (S)

Transatti, Peggy, *Dir*, Clark County Library District, Flamingo Gallery, Las Vegas NV

Trapp, Claude W, *Pres*, Headley-Whitney Museum, Lexington KY

Trapp, Frank, *Dir*, Amherst College, Amherst MA

Trapp, Kenneth R, *Cur*, Cincinnati Art Museum, Cincinnati OH (S)

Trapp, Roy, *Museum Supv*, University of South Florida, University Galleries, Tampa FL

Trappeniers, M, *Cur*, Noord-Brabants Museum, Hertogenbosch Netherlands

Trassati, Joseph A, *Bldg Supt*, Berkshire Museum, Pittsfield MA

Trattner, Alfred, *Librn Fine Arts*, Jersey City Public Library, Fine Arts Department, Jersey City NJ

Trau, Robert A, *Instructor*, Central Academy of Commercial Art, Cincinnati OH (S)

Travis, David, *Assoc Cur Photography*, Art Institute of Chicago, Chicago IL

Treadway, Beth, *Instructor*, Pace University, Department of Art & Design, Pleasantville NY (S)

Treadway, Beth A, *Gallery Dir*, Pace University, The Art Gallery, Briarcliff Manor NY

Treadwell, Helen, *Pres*, United States Committee of the International Association of Art, Inc, New York NY

Treanor, Dennis, *Cur Arts & Crafts*, Josephine D Randall Junior Museum, San Francisco CA

Tredennick, Dorothy, *Prof*, Berea College, Art Department, Berea KY (S)

Tree, Walter Fox, *Prof*, Boston State College, Art Department, Boston MA (S)

Treese, William R, *Head Arts Library*, University of California, Santa Barbara, Arts Library, Santa Barbara CA

Trefry, Philippe, *Asst*, Musee du Quebec, Bibliotheque des Art, Quebec PQ

Tremaine, Laurine, *Librn*, Parry Sound Public Library, Parry Sound ON

Trembath, J, *Education Officer*, Durban Art Gallery, Durban South Africa, Republic of

Tremper, Yolanda, *Secy*, Bergen Community Museum, Paramus NJ

Trepp, George, *Asst Dir*, Long Beach Public Library, Long Beach NY

Tresler, George W, *Pres*, Cody Country Art League, Cody WY

Treuter, Lirl, *Coordr of Art*, Fort Worth Public Library, Fort Worth TX

Trevellyan, Vernon, *Chmn Design*, Cornish Institute, Seattle WA (S)

Trevithick, Claudia, *Special Projects*, University of Southwestern Louisiana, Art Center for Southwestern Louisiana, Lafayette LA

Triano, Anthony, *Asst Prof*, Seton Hall University, Department of Art and Music, South Orange NJ (S)

Tribble, Genevieve, *Librn*, Art Complex Museum at Duxbury, Duxbury MA

Tribble, Genevieve M, *Librn*, Art Complex Museum at Duxbury, Library, Duxbury MA

Triggs, Stanley, *Cur Photography*, McGill University, McCord Museum, Montreal PQ

Trimberger, Christine, *Chmn Arts & Humanities Div*, Alverno College, Art Department, Milwaukee WI (S)

Tringale, Vincent J, *Prof*, Boston State College, Art Department, Boston MA (S)

Triplette, Laurie D, *In Charge Art Coll*, R J Reynolds Industries, Inc, Winston-Salem NC

Tripp, Powell, *Chmn Advertising Design*, Center for Creative Studies—College of Art and Design, Detroit MI (S)

Tripp, Wendell, *Ed Assoc & Chief Library Service*, New York State Historical Association, Library, Cooperstown NY

Trippy, Don, *Pres*, Las Vegas Art League, Las Vegas Art Museum, Las Vegas NV

Trissel, James, *Prof*, Colorado College, Department of Art, Colorado Springs CO (S)

Tritschler, Thomas, *Chmn Dept*, University of Guelph, Fine Art Department, Guelph ON (S)

Trivers, Mollie, *Community Development Coordr*, Arizona Commission on the Arts, Phoenix AZ

Trivigno, Pat, *Prof*, Tulane University, Newcomb College, New Orleans LA (S)

Trnek, Renate, *Asst*, Gemaldegalerie der Akademie der Bildenden Kunste in Wien, Art Gallery of the Academy of Fine Arts, Vienna Austria

Troemel, Jean, *Secy*, Saint Augustine Art Association Gallery, Saint Augustine FL

Trojanova, Eva, *Chief Department Graphic Art*, Slovenska Narodna Galeria, Slovak National Gallery, Bratislava Czechoslovakia

Trolle, Jorgen, *Pres*, Det Danske Kunstindustrimuseum, Museum of Decorative Art, Copenhagen Denmark

Trop-Blumberg, Sandra, *Asst Dir*, Everson Museum of Art, Syracuse NY

Troutman, Maralynn, *Cur Education*, Loch Haven Art Center, Inc, Orlando FL

Troutman, Philip, *Cur Coll*, Courtauld Institute Galleries, London England

Trovato, Joseph S, *Asst to Dir*, Munson-Williams-Proctor Institute, Museum of Art, Utica NY

Trowell, Ian, *Pres*, Ontario Society of Artists, Toronto ON

Troy, John, *Chmn of Board*, Tennessee Valley Art Center, Tuscumbia AL

Troyen, Aimee, *Asst Cur Prints & Drawings*, Fine Arts Museums of San Francisco, M H de Young Memorial Museum and California Palace of the Legion of Honor

Truax, Harold R, *Prof*, Miami University, Art Department, Oxford OH (S)

Trubner, Henry, *Asian Art Cur*, Seattle Art Museum, Seattle WA

Trudel, Jean, *Dir*, Montreal Museum of Fine Arts, Montreal PQ

Trudell, Don, *Instr*, Madison Area Technical College, Communication Arts, Madison WI (S)

Trueb, Verena, *Secy*, Offentliche Kunstsammlung-Kunstmuseum Basel, Museum of Fine Arts, Basel Switzerland

Trueblood, Franklin D, *Secy*, Arts Club of Chicago, Chicago IL

Truettner, William H, *Cur 18th & 19th Century Painting & Sculpture*, National Collection of Fine Arts, Washington DC

Truex, Duane P, *Dir*, Roberson Center for the Arts and Sciences, Binghamton NY (S)

Truex, Duane P, *Dir*, Roberson Center, Binghamton NY

Trujillo, Rupert A, *Dean*, Harwood Foundation of the University of New Mexico, Taos NM

Trumbore, Bertha, *Pres*, Pottstown Area Artists' Guild, Pottstown PA

Truplo, Charles, *Chief Bureau of Art Educ*, State Education Department, State University of New York, Albany NY

Tryba, John, *Assoc Prof*, Cardinal Stritch College, Art Department, Milwaukee WI (S)

Tryba, Mildred, *Instructor*, Cardinal Stritch College, Art Department, Milwaukee WI (S)

Tryloff, Robin, *Executive Dir*, Nebraska Arts Council Library, Omaha NE

Trythall, Gilvert, *Dean*, West Virginia University, Galleries A and B, Morgantown WV

Tsakona, Pitsa, *Librn*, Benaki Museum, Library, Athens Greece

Tschinkel, Paul, *Assoc Prof*, Queensborough Community College, Department of Art and Design, Bayside NY (S)

Tschudy, Karen, *Librn*, Cleveland Institute of Art, Jessica Gund Memorial Library, Cleveland OH

Tse, Stephen, *Chmn*, Big Bend Community College, Art Department, Moses Lake WA (S)

Tuboden, G, *Cur 20th Century*, Staatsgalerie Stuttgart, Stuttgart Germany, Federal Republic of

Tuchman, Barbara W, *Pres*, American Academy and Institute of Arts and Letters, New York NY

Tuchman, Maurice, *Sr Cur of Modern Art*, Los Angeles County Museum of Art, Los Angeles CA

Tuck, Brooke, *Secy*, Hartland Art Council, Hartland MI

Tucker, Anne, *Cur of Photography*, Museum of Fine Arts, Houston, Houston TX

Tucker, David, *VPres*, Mid-Hudson Arts and Science Center, Poughkeepsie NY

Tucker, James E, *Cur*, University of North Carolina at Greensboro, Weatherspoon Art Gallery, Greensboro NC

Tucker, Louis L, *Dir*, Massachusetts Historical Society, Boston MA

Tucker, Marcia, *Dir*, New Museum, New York NY

Tucker, Margaret, *Supv Media Center*, Mississippi Museum of Art, Jackson MS

Tucker, Margaret, *Media Center Supv*, Mississippi Museum of Art, Media Center Library, Jackson MS

Tucker, Marty, *Artist in Res*, Viterbo College, Art Department, La Crosse WI (S)

Tucker, Pat, *Secy*, Maude I Kerns Art Center, Henry Korn Gallery, Eugene OR

Tufts, Roger, *Instructor*, Tarrant County Junior College, Northeast Campus, Hurst TX (S)

Tuhey, Ned, *Instructor*, Mesa Community College, Department of Art, Mesa AZ (S)

Tuiasosopo, Palauni, *Chmn Board of Trustees*, Jean P Haydon Museum, Pago Pago, American Samoa PI

Tulanowski, Elaine, *Asst Prof*, College Misericordia, Art Department, Dallas PA (S)

Tulokas, Maria, *Acting Head Textile Design*, Rhode Island School of Design, Providence RI (S)

Tumolo, Camille, *Cur Education*, Heard Museum, Phoenix AZ

Tunis, Roselyn, *Cur*, Roberson Center, Binghamton NY

Turbiville, Matilda, *Social Dir*, Virginia Museum, Danville Museum of Fine Arts and History, Danville VA

Turk, Rudy H, *Dir*, Arizona State University, University Art Collections, Tempe AZ

Turlington, Lucy B, *In Charge Art Coll*, United Virginia Bank, Richmond VA

Turnbull, Betty, *Cur Exhib & Col*, Newport Harbor Art Museum, Newport Beach CA

Turnbull, Christine, *Treas*, Toledo Federation of Art Societies, Toledo OH

Turnbull, Krista, *Preparator*, University of Washington, Costume and Textile Study Center, Seattle WA

Turnbull, Lucy, *Honorary Cur of Classics*, University of Mississippi, University Museums, Oxford MS

Turnbull, Paula, *Chmn*, Fort Wright College of the Holy Names, School of Art, Spokane WA (S)

Turnbull, Paula M, *Chmn*, Fort Wright College, Art Gallery, Spokane WA

Turner, Anne M, *Dir*, Jones Library, Inc, Amherst MA

Turner, A Richard, *Chmn*, New York University, Institute of Fine Arts, New York NY (S)

Turner, A Richard, *Prof*, Grinnell College, Department of Art, Grinnell IA (S)

Turner, Arthur, *Instr*, Museum of Fine Arts, Alfred C Glassell Junior School of Art, Houston TX (S)

Turner, Bruce F, *Chmn*, Wharton County Junior College, Art Department, Wharton TX (S)

Turner, David, *Cur of Education*, Amarillo Art Center, Amarillo TX

Turner, Diana, *Cur Educ*, Asian Art Museum of San Francisco, Avery Brundage Collection, San Francisco CA

Turner, Evan H, *Dir*, University of North Carolina, The Ackland Art Museum, Chapel Hill NC

Turner, Harvey, *Instructor*, Grand Marais Art Colony, Grand Marais MN (S)

Turner, Helen Mary, *Head Dept*, Maple Woods Community College, Dept of Art & Art History, Kansas City MO (S)

Turner, J Rigbie, *Asst Cur Autograph and Music Manuscripts*, Pierpont Morgan Library, New York NY

Turner, James, *Instr*, Bucknell University, Department of Art, Lewisburg PA (S)

Turner, Judith, *Librn*, Milwaukee Public Museum, Library, Milwaukee WI

Turner, Richard, *Chairperson*, Chapman College, Art Department, Orange CA (S)

Turner, Robert B, *Assoc Prof*, University of Northern Colorado, Department of Fine Arts, Greeley CO (S)

Turner, Thomas, *Asst Prof*, University of North Carolina-Charlotte, Creative Arts Dept, Charlotte NC (S)

Turner, William K, *Dean*, Tulane University, School of Architecture, New Orleans LA (S)

Turnure, James, *VPres*, Fetherston Foundation, Packwood House Museum, Lewisburg PA

Turpin, J, *Head History of Art*, National College of Art and Design, Dublin Ireland (S)

Turpin, Thomas D, *Assoc Prof*, University of Arkansas, Art Department, Fayetteville AR (S)

Turzanski, Ludwik, *Chmn*, University of Colorado at Denver, Department of Fine Arts, Denver CO (S)

Tuthill, Barbara A, *Supv Librn*, San Diego Public Library, Art & Music Section, San Diego CA

Tutt, George E, *Chmn Div Fine Arts & Head Art Dept*, William Woods-Westminster Colleges, Art Department, Fulton MO (S)

Tuttle, Ilene, *Museum on Wheels Coordr*, Monterey Peninsula Museum of Art, Monterey CA

Tvrdik, Valerie, *Editor & Cur*, University of Minnesota, University Gallery, Minneapolis MN

Twarogowski, Leroy, *Asst Chmn*, Colorado State University, Department of Art, Fort Collins CO (S)

Tweedie, Henrietta, *Treas*, DuPage Art League, Wheaton IL

Tweedy, Joan, *Asst Prof*, University of North Carolina-Charlotte, Creative Arts Dept, Charlotte NC (S)

Twery, Thelma L, *Asst Prof*, Lynchburg College, Art Department, Lynchburg VA (S)

Twiddy, Raymond, *Assoc Prof*, Sweet Briar College, Art History Department, Sweet Briar VA (S)

Twiggs, Leo F, *Dir*, South Carolina State College, Art Program, Orangeburg SC (S)

Twining, David C, *Dir Development & Communication*, Western Reserve Historical Society, Cleveland OH

Twiston-Davies, W A, *VPres*, National Museum of Wales, Cardiff Wales

Tworkov, Jack, *Exhib*, Spokane Falls Community College Fine Art Gallery, Spokane WA

Tye, William, *Educ Coordr*, Kalamazoo Institute of Arts, Kalamazoo MI (S)

Tyger, Barbara, *Dir*, San Francisco Academy of Comic Art Library, San Francisco CA

Tyler, Ron, *Dir Publ & Cur History*, Amon Carter Museum of Western Art, Fort Worth TX

Tym, Eva, *Secy*, Muttart Gallery Associates, Calgary AB

Tyne, Janet, *Chmn Metal Arts*, De Young Museum Art School, San Francisco CA (S)

Tyre, Dan, *Secy*, School Art League of New York City, Brooklyn NY

Tyrie, Harold Joffre, *Secy*, Dunedin Public Art Gallery, Dunedin New Zealand

Tysinger, Joan, *Asst*, Georgia State University, Arthur I and Irma L Harris Reading Room and Visual Resource Library, Atlanta GA

Ubans, Juris, *Assoc Prof*, University of Southern Maine, Art Dept, Gorham ME (S)

Uchiyama, Tadashi, *Dir*, National Museum of Western Art, Kokuritsu Seiyo Bijutsukan, Tokyo Japan

Uchiyama, Takeo, *Cur*, Kyoto Kokuritsu Kindai Bijutsukan, National Museum of Modern Art, Kyoto, Kyoto Japan

Udell, Seymour, *Secy*, Lotos Club, New York NY

Udvardy, John, *Acting Chmn Freshman Foundation Division*, Rhode Island School of Design, Providence RI (S)

Ueda, Osamu, *Assoc Cur Oriental Art*, Art Institute of Chicago, Chicago IL

Uelsmann, Jerry N, *Graduate Research Prof*, University of Florida, Department of Art, Gainesville FL (S)

Uhde, Jan, *Asst Prof*, University of Waterloo, Fine Arts Department, Waterloo ON (S)

Uhlir, James R, *Pres*, Allied Arts of Seattle, Inc, Seattle WA

Ulbricht, J, *Undergrad Advisor*, University of Texas - Austin, Art Department, Austin TX (S)

Ulen, Sarah M, *Registrar*, Indiana University, Art Museum, Bloomington IN

Ulloa, Jorge, *Head Archit Drafting*, Universidad Javeriana, Javeriana University Faculty of Architecture and Design, Bogota Colombia (S)

Ulrich, Dee, *Registrar*, Southwest Museum, Los Angeles CA

Ulrich, Edwin A, *Dir*, Edwin A Ulrich Museum, Hyde Park NY

Ulrich, Edwin A, *Dir*, Edwin A Ulrich Museum, Library, Hyde Park NY

Ulrich, R, *Asst Prof*, Youngstown State University, Art Department, Youngstown OH (S)

Ultan, Roslye, *Cur Permanent Collection*, Hamline University Galleries, Dept of Art, Saint Paul MN

Umehara, Takeshi, *Dir*, Kyoto City University of Fine Arts, School of Art, Kyoto Japan (S)

Umen, Harry, *Asst Prof*, Notre Dame College, Art Department, Manchester NH (S)

Umlauf, Karl, *Chmn Painting*, East Texas State University, Department of Art, Commerce TX (S)

Umpleby, Isabelle, *Registrar*, Huntington Galleries, Huntington WV

Underbrink, Robert, *Head Librn*, Blackburn College, Lumpkin Library, Carlinville IL

Undergill, E H, *Chief Instr*, Selkirk College, Kootenay School of Art Division, Nelson BC (S)

Undergill, E H, *Gallery Curator & Dir*, Kootenay School of Art and Gallery, Nelson BC

Underwood, Barbara, *Admin Asst*, University of California, Los Angeles, Museum of Cultural History, Los Angeles CA

Underwood, Genevieve, *Assoc Prof Art & Chmn Dept*, Loyola Marymount University, Department of Art, Los Angeles CA (S)

Underwood, Sandra L, *Instructor*, Saint Mary's College of Maryland, Arts & Letters Div, Saint Mary's City MD (S)

Unger, Howard, *Prof*, Ocean County College, Humanities Department, Toms River NJ (S)

Unger, Miss P, *Public Relations Officer in Charge Activities & Members Origanization*, Haaretz Museum, Tel-Aviv Israel

Unger, William, *Prof*, Northeast Missouri State University, Art Department, Kirksville MO (S)

Ungerleider-Mayerson, Joy, *Dir*, Jewish Museum, New York NY

Unruh, Melvin, *Assoc Prof*, Bethany Nazarene College, Art Department, Bethany OH (S)

Unseld, Teresa, *Asst Prof*, Winston-Salem State University, Art Department, Winston-Salem NC (S)

Unser, Carlene, *Dir*, Viterbo College Art Gallery, La Crosse WI

Unser, Carlene, *Chmn*, Viterbo College, Art Department, La Crosse WI (S)

Unsworth, Jean, *Prof*, Loyola University of Chicago, Fine Arts Department, Chicago IL (S)

Upchurch, John D, *Chmn*, Brevard College, Div of Fine Arts, Brevard NC (S)

Upchurch Jr, W K, *Second VPres*, Montgomery Museum of Fine Arts, Montgomery AL

Upston, Louise, *Exhib Officer*, National Art Gallery of New Zealand, Wellington New Zealand

Upton, Jan, *Business Mgr*, Dallas Historical Society, Dallas TX

Upton, Richard F, *Pres*, New Hampshire Historical Society, Concord NH

Urbach, Zsuzsanna, *Head Old Pictures*, Szepmuveszet Museum, Museum of Fine Arts, Budapest Hungary

Urban, Janos, *Head General Artistic Studies*, Lausanne College of Art and Design, Lausanne Switzerland (S)

Urban, Richard, *Asst Prof*, University of Alabama in Birmingham, Department of Art, Birmingham AL (S)

Urban, Thomas, *Craft Center Coordr*, University of Oregon, Erb Memorial Union Art Gallery, Eugene OR

Urbanek, Sherrl, *Cashier-Receptionist*, Joslyn Art Museum, Omaha NE

Urbani, Giovanni, *Dir*, Instituto Centrale del Restauro, Central Institute for the Restoration of Works of Art, Rome Italy (S)

Urbscheit, Lawrence, *Prof Emeritus*, State University College, Department of Art, Fredonia NY (S)

Urner, Phil, *Treas*, Marian Osborne Cunningham Art Gallery, Bakersfield CA

Urquhart, A M, *Chmn Dept*, University of Waterloo, Fine Arts Department, Waterloo ON (S)

Urquhart, Kenneth T, *Head Library & Archives*, Historic New Orleans Collection, Library, New Orleans LA

Urry, Audrey, *Recording Secy*, Arizona Watercolor Association, Phoenix AZ

Ursprung, Will, *Instructor*, Wayne Art Center, Wayne PA (S)

Usher, Elizabeth R, *Chief Librn*, Metropolitan Museum of Art, Thomas J Watson Library, New York NY

Usui, Kiichi, *Cur*, Oakland University, Meadow Brook Art Gallery, Rochester MI

Utech, Franklin R, *Chmn*, University of Wisconsin-Oshkosh, Department of Art, Oshkosh WI (S)

Utterbach, Rosalie, *Chmn Div*, Woodbury University, Professional Arts Division, Los Angeles CA (S)

Utzinger, Robert C, *Dir School*, Montana State University, School of Architecture, Bozeman MT (S)

Uyemura, Ken, *Instructor*, University of Miami, Department of Art, Coral Gables FL (S)

Uzunoglu, Edibe, *Cur Museum of Ancient Orient*, Istanbul Arkeoloji Müzeleri, Archaeological Museums of Istanbul, Istanbul Turkey

Vacca, Johanna D, *Instructor*, Norwich Art School, Norwich Free Academy, Art Dept, Norwich CT (S)

Vachon, Marc, *Instr*, Danforth Museum School, Framingham MA (S)

Vaculik, Karol, *Chief Department Slovak & European Art to 19th Century*, Slovenska Narodna Galeria, Slovak National Gallery, Bratislava Czechoslovakia

Valcarcel, Luis E, *Pres*, Museo Nacional de la Cultura Peruana, National Museum of Peruvian Culture, Lima Peru

Valdes, Karen, *Dir Cur*, Miami-Dade Community College, South Campus, Art Gallery, Miami FL

Valdez, Frank, *Asst Secy*, San Antonio Museum Association, Inc, San Antonio TX

Valentine, Lanci, *Dir Public Affairs*, Art Complex Museum at Duxbury, Duxbury MA

Valentine, Milfred, *Chmn*, Jones County Junior College, Art Department, Ellisville MS (S)

Valentini, Livio Orazio, *Vis Artist*, Studio Art Centers International, Florence Italy (S)

Valerio, James, *Assoc Prof*, Cornell University, Department of Art, Ithaca NY (S)

Valery, Francois, *Pres*, American School of Art, Palace of Fontainebleau, Fontainebleau France (S)

Valk, Will, *Lectr*, Coe College, Department of Art, Cedar Rapids IA (S)

Valley, Jerry, *Chmn Three-Dimensional Area*, Edinboro State College, Art Department, Edinboro PA (S)

Vallibhatama, Srisakra, *Asst Prof*, Cornell University, Department of the History of Art, Ithaca NY (S)

Van Alstine, John, *Asst Prof*, University of Wyoming, Art Department, Laramie WY (S)

Vanarelli, Mario, *Rector*, Escuela Superior de Bellas Artes de la Nacion Ernesto de la Carcova, National Superior School of Fine Arts Ernesto de la Carcova, Buenos Aires Argentina (S)

Vanbianchi, Peggy, *Instructor*, Factory of Visual Art, Seattle WA (S)

Van Bodegraven, A, *Treas*, Albright College, Freedman Gallery, Reading PA

van Borssum Buisman, J H, *Deputy Cur Art Coll*, Teylers Museum, Haarlem Netherlands

van Boven, M M A, *Dir*, Noord-Brabants Museum, Hertogenbosch Netherlands

Van Buitenen, Georgette, *Dir*, University of Illinois at Urbana-Champaign, World Heritage Museum, Urbana IL

van Buren, Anne, *Asst Prof*, Tufts University, Fine Arts Department, Medford MA (S)

Vance, Alex, *Dir*, Bergstrom Art Center and Museum, Neenah WI

Vance, Carl, *Deputy Dir*, Santa Barbara Museum of Art, Santa Barbara CA

Vance Jr, Joseph, *Treas*, Society of Animal Artists, Inc, Bronx NY

Vanco, John, *Exec Dir*, Erie Art Center, Erie PA

van Crimpen, H, *Cur*, Rijksmuseum Vincent Van Gogh, Vincent Van Gogh State Museum, Amsterdam Netherlands

van Damme, Joan, *Instr*, Toronto School of Art, Toronto ON (S)

Vandeboncoeur, Guy, *Cur*, Society of the Montreal Military and Maritime Museum, Saint Helen's Island Museum, Montreal PQ

Vandegrift, David, *Assoc Prof*, Marygrove College, Dept of Art & Art History, Detroit MI (S)

van den Berk, Aloys, *Librn*, Municipal van Abbemuseum, Library, Eindhoven Netherlands

Vandendaele, Richard, *Dir*, Academie Royale des Beaux-Arts, Institute Superieur d'Architecture Victor Horta, Brussels Belgium (S)

VanDerBeek, Stan, *Prof*, University of Maryland Baltimore County, Visual Arts Department, Catonsville MD (S)

van der Grinten, J, *Cur Modern Art*, Nijmeegs Museum Commanderie van Saint Jan, Nijmegen Netherlands

Vanderhill, Marlene, *Secy*, Calvin College Center Art Gallery, Grand Rapids MI

Van Derhill, Rein, *Asst Prof*, Northwestern College, Art Department, Orange City IA (S)

Van Derhill, Rein, *Exhib Coordr*, Northwestern College, Ramaker Library Art Gallery, Orange City IA

van der Kemp, Gerald, *Cur*, Musee National du Chateau de Versailles, National Museum of the Chateau of Versailles, Versailles France

Vandermade, James S, *Pres*, Montclair Art Museum, Montclair NJ

van der Mast, W M, *Head History Department*, Haags Gemeentemuseum, Municipal Museum of The Hague, The Hague Netherlands

Vandermeer, Jos, *Instructor*, University of North Carolina at Asheville, Dept of Art & Music, Asheville NC (S)

van der Meulen, Jan, *Chmn*, Cleveland State University, Art Department, Cincinnati OH (S)

Vanderstrappen, Harrie, *Prof*, University of Chicago, Department of Art History & Committee on Art & Design, Chicago IL (S)

van der Vossen-Delbruck, E, *Librn*, Rijksmuseum, Library, Amsterdam Netherlands

Vanderway, Richard, *Education Coordr*, Whatcom Museum of History and Art, Bellingham WA

Vander Weg, Phillip, *Asst Prof*, Middle Tennessee State University, Art Dept, Murfreesboro TN (S)

Van Der Wege, Robert, *Asst Dir*, University of Minnesota, University Gallery, Minneapolis MN

van der Wolk, J, *Dir*, Rijksmuseum Vincent Van Gogh, Vincent Van Gogh State Museum, Amsterdam Netherlands

van der Woud, A, *Cur*, Ryksmuseum Kroller-Muller, Kroller-Muller State Museum, Otterlo Netherlands

van Donme, B J, *Exec Asst*, Brooklyn Museum, Brooklyn NY

Van Doren, Marcia, *VPres*, Wenatchee Valley College, Gallery 76, Wenatchee WA

Van Duke, Fred, *Instr*, Utah Technical College at Salt Lake, Commercial Art Department, Salt Lake City UT (S)

Van Duzer, Bert, *VPres*, Leatherstocking Brush and Palette Club Inc, Cooperstown NY

van Eijle, R, *Secy General*, Rijksmuseum, State Museum, Amsterdam Netherlands

Van Enkevort, Renata, *Secy*, Alaska Association for the Arts, Fairbanks AK

van Everdingen, Arie, *Chmn Dept*, Monmouth College, Department of Art, West Long Branch NJ (S)

Vanfelt, Elizabeth, *Art Dir*, Hill Country Arts Foundation, Ingram TX (S)

van Gelder, H E, *Cur Coins & Medals*, Teylers Museum, Haarlem Netherlands

Vanger, Lee, *Librn*, Ships of The Sea Museum, Library, Savannah GA

VanGilder, Caron, *Executive Dir*, Ashtabula Arts Center, Ashtabula OH

van Ginkel, Blanche Lemco, *Dir*, University of Toronto, School of Architecture, Toronto ON (S)

Vango, Eugene, *Asst Prof*, Virginia State College, Fine Arts Department, Petersburg VA (S)

van Golberdinge, D, *Education Department*, Nijmeegs Museum Commanderie van Saint Jan, Nijmegen Netherlands

van Grootheest, T, *Head Communication Department*, Stedlijk Museum-Amsterdam, Municipal Museum, Amsterdam Netherlands

Van Halsema, Brenda, *Instructor*, Calvin College, Art Dept, Grand Rapids MI (S)

Van Haren, John E, *Head Dept*, Eastern Michigan University, Dept of Art, Ypsilanti MI (S)

Van Hoesen, Lois, *Reference Supv*, Brookline Public Library, Brookline MA

Van Hooft, Gordon, *Asst Commissioner for General Education & Curricular Services*, State Education Department, State University of New York, Albany NY

Van Horn, Chalmer, *Assoc Prof*, Williamsport Area Community College, Department of Engineering and Design, Williamsport PA (S)

Van Horn, David, *Instr*, Siena Heights College, Art Department, Adrian MI (S)

Van Horn, Donald, *Asst Prof*, University of Texas at Tyler, Department of Art, Tyler TX (S)

Van Horn, Henry, *Exec Secy*, Mansfield Art Center, Mansfield Fine Arts Guild Inc, Mansfield OH

VanHorn, Walter, *Cur of Coll*, Anchorage Historical and Fine Arts Museum, Anchorage AK

van Kooten, C, *Cur*, Gemeentemuseum Arnhem, Municipal Museum of Arnhem, Arnhem Netherlands

Van Laar, Timothy, *Instructor*, Calvin College, Art Dept, Grand Rapids MI (S)

van Leeuwen, J M, *Adminr*, Stedelijk Museum de Lakenhal, Leyden Municipal Museum, Leiden Netherlands

Van Loen, Alfred, *Prof*, School of the Arts, C W Post Center of Long Island University, Art Department, Greenvale NY (S)

van Loenen Martinet, J, *Deputy Dir*, Stedlijk Museum-Amsterdam, Municipal Museum, Amsterdam Netherlands

Van Looy, Glenn, *Asst*, Internationaal Cultureel Centrum, International Cultural Centre, Antwerp Belgium

Vann, Lowell C, *Chmn*, Samford University, Art Department, Birmingham AL (S)

van Niekerk, Raymund H, *Dir*, South African National Gallery, Cape South Africa, Republic of

Van Nort, Mary, *Head Librn*, Keystone Junior College Library, Art Section, Factoryville PA

van Nouhuys, L, *Board of Trustees*, Teylers Museum, Haarlem Netherlands

van Oosterwijk, Cecile, *Asst Cur*, Museum Het Rembrandthuis, Rembrandthouse Museum, Amsterdam Netherlands

Van Orden, Stuart, *Head Dept*, Christopher Newport College, Fine and Performing Arts, Newport News VA (S)

VanPelt, Elizabeth, *Art Dir*, Hill Country Arts Foundation, Ingram TX

Van Riper, Tracy, *Education Dir*, Philipse Manor Hall State Historic Site, Yonkers NY

Van Roose, Monique, *Asst*, Museum voor Schone Kunsten, Ghent Belgium

Van Schaack, Eric, *Chmn*, Colgate University, Department of Fine Arts, Hamilton NY (S)

Van Scoy, Burton B, *Program Specialist*, Brevard Art Center and Museum, Inc, Melbourne FL

VanSuchtelen, Adrian, *Assoc Prof*, Utah State University, Department of Art, Logan UT (S)

Van Tassel, Harold, *Pres*, Summit Art Center, Inc, Summit NJ

Van Tassell, Katherine, *Asst Registrar*, Minnesota Museum of Art, Saint Paul MN

van Thiel, P J J, *Dir Department Paintings*, Rijksmuseum, State Museum, Amsterdam Netherlands

Van Valen, Julie, *Asst Librn*, Beloit College, Morse Library, Beloit WI

Van Veen, Felicia, *Treas*, Artists Technical Institute, New York NY

van Velzen, T, *Dir*, Haags Gemeentemuseum, Municipal Museum of The Hague, The Hague Netherlands

van Velzen, T, *Dir*, Haags Gemeentemuseum, Museum Bredius, The Hague Netherlands

VanVoorst, Philip, *Assoc Prof*, Northwest Missouri State University, Dept of Art, Maryville MO (S)

Van Wagoner, Richard J, *Chmn*, Weber State College, Art Department 2001, Ogden UT (S)

Van Why, Joseph S, *Dir*, Stowe-Day Foundation, Hartford CT

Van Why, Joseph S, *Dir*, Stowe-Day Foundation, Stowe-Day Library, Hartford CT

Van Wormer, Mark, *Instructor*, Emma Willard School Arts Division, Troy NY (S)

Van Wylen, Gordon, *Pres*, Hope College, DeWitt Cultural Center, Holland MI

Vanyslova, Marcala, *Head of the Service*, Narodni Galerie v Prague, Library, Prague Czechoslovakia

VanZandt, Paul, *Chmn Dept*, Pembroke State University, Art Dept, Pembroke NC (S)

VanZanten, David T, *Secy*, Society of Architectural Historians, Philadelphia PA

Vappi, Nancy, *Pres*, Museum of the American China Trade, Milton MA

Vares, J, *Rector*, Eesti Nsv Riiklik Kunstiinstituut, Tallinn Ussr (S)

Varga, Edit, *Head Egyptian Antiquities*, Szepmuveszet Museum, Museum of Fine Arts, Budapest Hungary

Varian, Elayne H, *Cur Contemporary Art*, John and Mable Ringling Museum of Art, Sarasota FL

Varley, Christopher, *Canada Art*, Edmonton Art Gallery, Edmonton AB

Varney, Ginny, *Rentals Coordinator*, Sangre De Cristo Arts & Conference Center, Pueblo CO

Varriano, John L, *Assoc Prof*, Mount Holyoke College, Art Department, South Hadley MA (S)

Varrum, John P, *Chmn*, Northern Montana College, Department of Art, Havre MT (S)

Vascovitch, Joanne M, *Instructor*, Chamberlayne Junior College, Department of Graphic and Applied Arts, Boston MA (S)

Vaskys, Petras, *Co-Chairperson Crafts*, Philadelphia College of Art, Philadelphia PA (S)

Vasquez, Leah, *Admin Asst*, University of California Irvine Art Gallery, Irvine CA

Vasquez, Mario, *Head Museographical Department*, Museo Nacional de Antropologia, National Museum of Anthropology, Mexico Mexico

Vasseur, Dominique, *Asst Cur European Painting & Registrar*, Dayton Art Institute, Dayton OH

Vatasiano, Virgil, *Pres Scientific Council*, Muzeul de Arta Cluj-Napoca, Museum of Art, Cluj-Napoca Romania

Vaugel, Martine Olga, *Chmn Sculpture Dept*, Venice Painting, Drawing and Sculpture Studio, Inc, Venice CA (S)

Vaughan, Alan, *Asst Prof*, George Peabody College for Teachers, Art Faculty Department, Nashville TN (S)

Vaughan, J Terrell, *Pres*, Missouri Historical Society, Saint Louis MO

Vaughan, Mack, *Advertising Design Coordr*, North Texas State University, Art Department, Denton TX (S)

Vaughan, Thomas, *Dir*, Oregon Historical Society, Portland OR

Vaughn, Robert A, *Executive Dir*, Alaska Association for the Arts, Fairbanks AK

Vaux, Richard, *Assoc Prof*, Adelphi University, Department of Art and Art History, Garden City NY (S)

Vazquez, Paul, *Assoc Prof*, University of Bridgeport, Art Department, Bridgeport CT (S)

Vazquez, Sandra B de, *Instr*, University of the Americas, Graphic Arts and Design Dept, Cholula Mexico (S)

v-d Walle, T Y, *Archaeology Department*, Westfries Museum, Hoorn Netherlands

Veater, David M, *Cur Education*, Huntington Galleries, Huntington WV

Vega, Ed, *Dept Head*, University of Albuquerque, Art Department, Albuquerque NM (S)

Vegeler, Robert H, *Dir*, Public Library of Fort Wayne and Allen County, Fort Wayne IN

Velasquez, Geraldine, *Lectr*, Georgian Court College, Department of Art, Lakewood NJ (S)

Velde, Jeanne E, *Instr*, Kilgore College, Department Art and Art Education, Kilgore TX (S)

Veldhuis, Joyce, *Instr*, Ulster County Community College, Department of Visual Arts, Stone Ridge NY (S)

Velesikova, Berta, *Dir*, Severoceska Galerie Vytvarneho Umeni, North Bohemian Gallery of Fine Arts, Litomerice Czechoslovakia

Velick, Harry, *Secy*, Birmingham-Bloomfield Art Association, Birmingham MI

Velous, Mary, *Secy*, Nicolaysen Art Museum, Casper WY

Venable, S J, *VPres*, Lansing Art Gallery, Lansing MI

Vencenza, Bottino, *Dir*, Accademia de Belle Artie Liceo Artistico, Academy of Fine Arts, Rome Italy (S)

Venegas, Haydee, *Asst to Dir*, Museo de Arte de Ponce, Ponce Art Museum, Ponce PR

Veneziani, Patricia, *Head Art Music & Theatre Dept*, Silas Bronson Library, Waterbury CT

Venner, Tom, *Instr*, Siena Heights College, Art Department, Adrian MI (S)

Venters, Roy, *Asst Dir*, Contemporary Arts Center of Hawaii, Honolulu HI

Ventimiglia, John T, *Instructor*, Portland School of Art, Portland ME (S)

Vera, Victor, *Secy*, Museo Nacional de Arqueologia, National Museum, La Paz Bolivia

Verano, Pedro P Polo, *Acad Dean*, Universidad Javeriana, Javeriana University Faculty of Architecture and Design, Bogota Colombia (S)

Verb, Lois, *Pres*, North Shore Art League, Winnetka IL

Verb, Lois, *Pres*, North Shore Art League, Winnetka IL (S)

Verdugo, Rene, *Registrar*, Tucson Museum of Art, Tucson AZ

VerHague, James, *Communication Design*, Rochester Institute of Technology, School of Art and Design, Rochester NY (S)

Vermeersch, V, *Cur*, Stedelyke Musea, City Museums, Bruges Belgium

Vermeule, Cornelius C, *Cur Classical Art*, Museum of Fine Arts, Boston MA

Verney, Katherine, *Assoc Prof*, Villa Maria College of Buffalo, Art Department, Buffalo NY (S)

Vernez-Moudon, A, *Secy*, Association of Collegiate Schools of Architecture, Washington DC

Vernon, Carol, *Asst Prof*, Southwestern Oregon Community College, Visual Arts Department, Coos Bay OR (S)

Vernon, Marlene, *Advisor*, University of Minnesota, Coffman Union Gallery, Minneapolis MN

Vernon, Mary, *Chmn*, Southern Methodist University, Division of Art and Art History, Dallas TX (S)

Versaci, Nancy R, *Dir*, Brown University, Bell Gallery, Providence RI

Versweyveld, Judith, *Exec Dir*, Vermont State Craft Center at Frog Hollow, Middlebury VT

Verworn, Charles, *Chief Custodian*, Rodman Hall Arts Centre, Saint Catharines ON

Vest, John, *Asst Admin*, Favell Museum of Western Art & Indian Artifacts, Klamath Falls OR

Vey, Horst, *Dir*, Staatliche Kunsthalle, State Art Gallery, Karlsruhe Germany, Federal Republic of

Viana, Maria Teresa, *Cur*, Museu Nacional de Soares dos Reis, National Museum of Soares Dos Reis, Oporto Portugal

Vickers, Robert, *Prof*, Hope College, Art Department, Holland MI (S)

Victor, Mary O'Neill, *Dir*, Fine Arts Museum of the South, Mobile AL

Viener, Saul, *Pres*, American Jewish Historical Society, Waltham MA

Viera, Ricardo, *Dir Exhib & Coll*, Lehigh University Galleries, Bethlehem PA

Viera, Ricardo, *Assoc Prof*, Lehigh University, Department of Art and Architecture, Bethlehem PA (S)

Vieser, Milford A, *Chmn of the Board*, New Jersey Historical Society Museum, Newark NJ

Vigiletti, Robert, *Chmn Photography*, Center for Creative Studies—College of Art and Design, Detroit MI (S)

Vigtel, Gudmund, *Dir*, High Museum of Art, Atlanta GA

Vigurs, P F, *Keeper of Fine Art*, Stoke-on-District Council, City Museum and Art Gallery, Hanley England

Vilcek, Marcia, *Assoc Cur Central Catalog*, Metropolitan Museum of Art, New York NY

Vilcins, M, *Reference Librn*, National Gallery of Canada, Library, Ottawa ON

Vilk, Kathleen, *Instructor*, Chamberlayne Junior College, Department of Graphic and Applied Arts, Boston MA (S)

Villa, Carlos, *Chmn Painting Dept*, San Francisco Art Institute, San Francisco CA (S)

Villafine, Josefina, *VPres*, Museo Historico de Puerto Rico Inc, Santurce PR

Villard, Francois, *Cur Greek & Roman Antiquities*, Musee du Louvre, Louvre Museum, Paris France

Vincent, Don, *Librn*, University of New Hampshire, Dimond Slide Library, Durham NH

Vincent, Ellen, *Instructor*, Maryland College of Art and Design, Silver Spring MD (S)

Vincent, Joseph G, *Dir*, Rome Historical Society, Rome Information and Cultural Center, Rome NY

Vinson, Alda, *Instr*, Lane Community College, Art and Applied Design Department, Eugene OR (S)

Vint, Virginia H, *Prof*, Winona State University, Art Department, Winona MN (S)

Vinton, William C, *Asst Dir Museum Education*, Fairbanks Museum and Planetarium, Saint Johnsbury VT

Viola, Carol J, *Chairperson*, Waubonsee Community College, Sugar Grove IL (S)

VisGirda, Rimas T, *Instructor*, Bemidji State University, Art Department, Bemidji MN (S)

Vislosky, R J, *Instructor*, Indiana University of Pennsylvania, Department of Art and Art Education, Indiana PA (S)

Visser, Mary, *Instr*, Southwestern University, Art Department, Georgetown TX (S)

Visser-Rapp, Susan, *Registrar*, Columbus Museum of Art, Columbus OH

Vitagliano, Maria, *Instructor*, Chamberlayne Junior College, Department of Graphic and Applied Arts, Boston MA (S)

Vizzini, Michael, *Chmn Crafts*, Center for Creative Studies—College of Art and Design, Detroit MI (S)

Vlack, Don, *Dir Shelby Cullon Davis Museum of the Performing Arts*, New York Public Library, Shelby Cullom Davis Museum of the Performing Arts and: The Library and Museum of the Performing Arts, at Lincoln Center, Museum NY

Vocelka, Mary, *Librn*, Yosemite Museum Collections, Library, Yosemite National Park CA

Vodicka, Julia R, *Dir*, Hampton Institute, College Museum, Hampton VA

Voelker, Cecilia, *Asst Prof*, Augusta College, Department of Fine Arts, Augusta GA (S)

Voelkle, William M, *Assoc Cur Medieval & Renaissance Manuscripts*, Pierpont Morgan Library, New York NY

Voet, L, *Dir*, Stedelijk Prentenkabinet, Municipal Gallery of Graphic Arts, Antwerp Belgium

Voet, L, *Dir*, Museum Plantin-Moretus, Plantin-Moretus Museum, Antwerp Belgium

Vogel, Carl D, *Pres*, Hochschule für Bildende Künste, College of Fine Arts, Hamburg Germany, Federal Republic of (S)

Vogel, Kevin, *VPres*, Dallas Public Library, Dallas Print and Drawing Society, Dallas TX

Vogler, Cheryl, *Library Asst & Slide Collection*, Saint Louis Art Museum, Richardson Memorial Library, Saint Louis MO

Voglsamer, Günther, *Prof*, Akademie der Bildenden Künste in Nürnberg, Academy of Fine Arts in Nuremberg, Nuremberg Germany, Federal Republic of (S)

Vogt, Joel, *Instr*, Avila College, Art Department, Kansas City MO (S)

Vogt, John, *Assoc Prof*, Kansas State University, Art Department, Manhattan KS (S)

Vogt, Margaret, *Registrar*, Massillon Museum, Massillon OH

Vogt, Peter, *Chmn*, Burchfield Center, Buffalo NY

Vogtle, Joseph S, *Treas*, Everson Museum of Art, Syracuse NY

Voinovich, George S, *Secy*, Women's City Club of Cleveland, Cleveland OH

Volant, Jacques, *Cur*, Eskimo Museum, Churchill MB

Volk, Beverly T, *Exec Dir*, Philadelphia Art Commission, Philadelphia PA

Volk, Jane, *Pres*, Norton Gallery and School of Art, West Palm Beach FL

Volk, P, *Cur Sculpture & Paintings*, Bayerisches Nationalmuseum, Bavarian National Museum, Munich Germany, Federal Republic of

Volk, Sylvia P, *Education Prog Coordr*, Burchfield Center, Buffalo NY

Volkert, James, *Art Cur*, Junior Arts Center, Los Angeles CA

Volkes, Ann, *Editing Post Production Facility*, Electronic Arts Intermix, Inc, New York NY

vonBarann, L, *VPres*, Doshi Center for Contemporary Art, Harrisburg PA

von Barann, Lawrence, *Vis Prof*, Harrisburg Area Community College, Division of Communication and the Arts, Harrisburg PA (S)

von Berckefeldt, Susan, *Mus Serv*, Crocker Art Museum, Sacramento CA

Von Blon, Philip, *Chmn Board*, Walker Art Center, Minneapolis MN

von Bock, Gisela Reineking, *Vice-Dir*, Museen der Stadt Köln, Kunstgewerbemuseum der Stadt Köln, Cologne Germany, Federal Republic of

von Borries, Johann Eckart, *Dir Engraving*, Staatliche Kunsthalle, State Art Gallery, Karlsruhe Germany, Federal Republic of

von Bothmer, Dietrich, *Chmn Greek & Roman Art*, Metropolitan Museum of Art, New York NY

von Frankenberg, Gisela, *Librn*, Muiska-Museum, LIbrary, Munich Germany, Federal Republic of

von Frankenberg, Gisela, *Pres*, Muiska-Museum, Munich Germany, Federal Republic of

von Gagern, Axel, *Dir*, Museen der Stadt Köln, Rautenstrach-Joest-Museum, Cologne Germany, Federal Republic of

von Gagern, Axel, *Dir*, Museen der Stadt Köln, Rautenstrach-Joest-Museum Bibliothek, Cologne Germany, Federal Republic of

von Heusinger, Christian, *Cur*, Herzog Anton Ulrich-Museum, Medieval Section: Burg Dankwarderode, Brunswick Germany, Federal Republic of

von Hohenzollern, J G Prinz, *Cur French Paintings*, Bayerischen Staatsgemaldesammlungen, Bavarian State Galleries of Art, Munich Germany, Federal Republic of

von Mueller, Adriaan, *Dir*, Staatliche Museen Preussischer Kulturbesitz, Museum of Pre-history and Proto-history, Berlin Germany, Federal Republic of

von Rague, Beatrix, *Dir*, Staatliche Museen Preussischer Kulturbesitz, Museum of Far Eastern Art, Berlin Germany, Federal Republic of

vonSchlegell, David, *Assoc Prof*, Yale University, School of Art, New Haven CT (S)

von Sonnenburg, Hubert Falkner, *Dir Restoration Department*, Bayerischen Staatsgemaldesammlungen, Bavarian State Galleries of Art, Munich Germany, Federal Republic of

von Wodtke, Charlotte B, *Cur Education*, Albright-Knox Art Gallery, Buffalo Fine Arts Academy, Buffalo NY

Voos, William J, *Pres*, Atlanta College of Art, Atlanta GA (S)

Voris, Anna M, *Cur Spanish Painting*, National Gallery of Art, Washington DC

Voris, Peter, *Prof*, New Mexico State University, Art Dept, Las Cruces NM (S)

Vosbeck, R Randall, *First VPres*, American Institute of Architects, Washington DC

Voss, Bill, *Instructor*, Mesa Community College, Department of Art, Mesa AZ (S)

Voss, James, *Chmn Fine Arts*, Saint Clair County Community College, Fine Arts Department, Port Huron MI (S)

Votaw, Barbara, *Conservator*, Bob Jones University, Greenville SC

Voulkos, Peter, *Vis Prof*, Tulane University, Newcomb College, New Orleans LA (S)

Vousden, Robin, *Exhibitions Officer*, University of Manchester, Whitworth Art Gallery, Manchester England

Vrhunc, Polonca, *Asst*, Narodna Galerija, National Art Gallery, Ljubljana Yugoslavia

Vries, P I M, *Adjunct-Dir & Cur Paintings & Drawings*, Groningen Museum voor Stad en Land, Groningen Museum, Groningen Netherlands

Vrijland, C W D, *Board of Trustees*, Teylers Museum, Haarlem Netherlands

Vroom, N R A, *Dir*, Rijksakademie Van Beeldende Kunsten, State Academy of Fine Arts, Amsterdam Netherlands (S)

Vroom, W H, *Head Department Dutch History*, Rijksmuseum, State Museum, Amsterdam Netherlands

Vruwink, John, *Assoc Prof*, Central College, Art Department, Pella IA (S)

Vuoristo, Osmo, *Dir*, Suomen Kansallismuseo, National Museum of Finland, Helsinki Finland

Waaler, Diane, *Registrar*, University of Illinois, Krannert Art Museum, Champaign IL

Wada, Wes, *Assoc Prof*, College of Southern Idaho, Art Department, Twin Falls ID (S)

Waddell, Carol, *Librn Historical Section*, Tippecanoe County Historical Museum, Alameda McCollough Library, Lafayette IN

Waddell, Carol N, *Asst Dir*, Tippecanoe County Historical Museum, Lafayette IN

Waddell, Roberta, *Cur of Prints*, Toledo Museum of Art, Toledo OH

Waddington, Susan R, *Head*, Providence Public Library, Art and Music Dept, Providence RI

Wade, J P, *Cur Arts*, Museum of Applied Arts and Sciences, Sydney Australia

Wade, John, *Assoc Prof*, Temple University, Art Department, Philadelphia PA (S)

Wade, Joyce, *Secy*, Pence Gallery, Davis CA

Wadley, William, *Prof*, University of the South, Dept of Fine Arts, Sewanee TN (S)

Wadsworth, Anne, *Librn*, William A Farnsworth Library and Art Museum, William A Farnsworth Library, Rockland ME

Wadsworth, Burton R, *Pres*, East Windsor Historical Society Inc, Scantic Academy Museum, West Hartford CT

Wadsworth, Dorothy, *Coordr Commercial Art Prog*, Johnson County Community College, Communications-Arts Division, Overland Park KS (S)

Waehrer, Anita, *Instr*, San Diego Mesa College, Art Department, San Diego CA (S)

Waetzoldt, Stephan, *Dir*, Staatliche Museen Preussischer Kulturbesitz, State Museums, Foundation for Prussian Cultural Treasures, Berlin Germany, Federal Republic of

Wageman, Virginia, *Dir Public Relations*, Princeton University, Art Museum, Princeton NJ

Wagenknecht, Robert, *Dir*, Springfield City Library, Art Department, Springfield MA

Wagman Jr, N E, *Chmn Dept*, Salem State College, Art Department, Salem MA (S)

Wagner, Barbara, *Assoc Cur*, University of Michigan Museum of Art, Slide and Photograph Collection, Ann Arbor MI

Wagner, Carolyn, *Dir*, California Historical Society, History Center, San Francisco CA

Wagner, Carolyn Ditte, *Dir for Southern California*, California Historical Society, San Francisco CA

Wagner, David J, *Dir*, Leigh Yawkey Woodson Art Museum, Inc, Wausau WI

Wagner, Hugo, *Dir*, Kunstmuseum Bern, Museum of Fine Arts Berne, Berne Switzerland

Wagner, Nora, *Education Dir*, Mexican Museum, San Francisco CA

Wagner, Norman, *Instructor*, Atlanta College of Art, Atlanta GA (S)

Wagner, Wesley, *Asst Prof*, Bethany College, Art Department, Bethany WV (S)

Wagstaff, Marge, *Secy*, Reynolda House, Inc, Winston-Salem NC

Wahl, Connie, *VPres*, Council of Delaware Artists, Wilmington DE

Wahl, Jane, *Reference Librn*, University of Portland, Wilson W Clark Memorial Library, Portland OR

Waiek, Yenusz, *Italian Painting*, Muzeum Narodowe w Krakowie, National Museum in Cracow, Cracow Poland

Wain-Hobson, D, *Dean Faculty*, Manchester Polytechnic, Faculty of Art and Design, Manchester England (S)

Wait Jr, Newman E, *Pres*, Yaddo, Saratoga Springs NY (S)

Wakeford, Mary, *Secy*, Hofstra University, Emily Lowe Gallery, Hempstead NY

Wakeman, Phil, *Instructor*, Louisville School of Art, Anchorage KY (S)

Wakerlin, Ruth, *Pres*, Association of Medical Illustrators, Los Angeles CA

Walberg, G F, *Education Department*, Frans Halsmuseum, Frans Hals Museum, Haarlem Netherlands

Walch, John, *Assoc Conservators*, Saint Gregory's Abbey and College, Mabee-Gerrer Museum, Shawnee OK

Walchli, Nancy A, *Admin Asst*, Yale University, Department of the History of Art, New Haven CT (S)

Wald, Palmer, *Adminr*, Whitney Museum of American Art, New York NY

Walden, Peggy, *Instr*, University of Albuquerque, Art Department, Albuquerque NM (S)

Walden, Robert Jerry, *Asst Prof*, Delta State University, Department of Art, Cleveland MS (S)

Waldfogel, Melvin, *Prof*, University of Minnesota, Minneapolis, Art History, Minneapolis MN (S)

Waldfogel, Melvin, *Acting Dir*, University of Minnesota, University Gallery, Minneapolis MN

Waldman, Diane, *Cur Exhib*, Solomon R Guggenheim Museum, New York NY

Waldron, Ethna, *Cur*, Hugh Lane Municipal Gallery of Modern Art, Dublin Ireland

Waldron, Shirley A, *Publicity Coordr*, Ocean City Arts Center, Ocean City NJ

Walenkamp, J H C, *Cur Minerals & Fossils*, Teylers Museum, Haarlem Netherlands

Wales, Alice A, *VPres*, Roberson Center, Binghamton NY

Walker, Alan, *VPres*, Jesse Besser Museum, Alpena MI

Walker, Barbara, *Assoc Prof*, Southeastern Louisiana University, Dept of Visual Arts, Hammond LA (S)

Walker, Beverly, *Secy REceptionist*, Remington Art Museum, Ogdensburg NY

Walker, Brian, *Dir*, Museum of Cartoon Art, Port Chester NY

Walker, Charles, *Instructor*, De Anza College, Art Department, Cupertino CA (S)

Walker, Daniel S, *Cur Ancient, Near and Far Eastern Arts*, Cincinnati Art Museum, Cincinnati OH

Walker, E K, *Chmn*, George Brown College of Applied Arts and Technology, Toronto ON (S)

Walker, Edith G Bradley, *Dir*, Greenville Art Center, Greenville NC

Walker, J Charles, *Div Coordr Design*, Kent State University, School of Art, Kent OH (S)

Walker, Joe, *Chmn*, New Mexico Junior College, Art Department, Hobbs NM (S)

Walker, Keith, *Asst Prof*, University of Santa Clara, Fine Arts Department, Santa Clara CA (S)

Walker, Larry, *Chmn*, University of the Pacific, Department of Art, Stockton CA (S)

Walker, Linda B, *Adminr*, Art Museum of South Texas, Corpus Christi TX

Walker, Lyn, *Prof*, William Jewell College, Art Dept, Liberty MO (S)

Walker, Merle D, *Dir*, League of New Hampshire Craftsmen, Concord NH

Walker, Mort, *Pres*, Museum of Cartoon Art, Port Chester NY

Walker, Nancy H, *Asst Cur*, Kiah Museum, Savannah GA

Walker, Noel Gahagan, *Asst Dir*, Walker Museum, Fairlee VT

Walker, Patricia, *Instr*, Danforth Museum School, Framingham MA (S)

Walker, Raymond, *Prof*, Jersey City State College, Art Department, Jersey City NJ (S)

Walker, Ronald, *Chairperson Photography & Film*, Philadelphia College of Art, Philadelphia PA (S)

Walker, William B, *Chief Librn*, National Collection of Fine Arts, Library of the National Collection of Fine Arts and the National Portrait Gallery, Washington DC

Walker, William B, *Librn*, National Portrait Gallery, Washington DC

Walker-Oni, Roslyn A, *Dir*, Illinois State University, University Museums, Normal IL

Walker II, Herbert Brooks, *Dir*, Walker Museum, Fairlee VT

Walkinshaw, Allan, *Asst Cur & Registrar*, The Robert McLaughlin Gallery, Oshawa ON

Wall, Brent, *Instr*, Aurora College, Art Department, Aurora IL (S)

Wall, Constance, *Asst Librn & Cataloguer*, Detroit Institute of Arts, Research Library, Detroit MI

Wall, Margaret, *Education Specialist*, Tryon Palace Restoration Complex, New Bern NC

Wallace, Anthony F C, *Cur North American Ethnology*, University of Pennsylvania, University Museum, Philadelphia PA

Wallace, Betty, *Head Dept*, Nebraska Wesleyan University, Art Dept, Lincoln NE (S)

Wallace, Betty, *Dir*, Nebraska Wesleyan University, Elder Gallery, Lincoln NE

Wallace, Dee, *Librn*, University of Illinois at Urbana-Champaign, Ricker Library of Architecture and Art, Urbana IL

Wallace, G, *Chmn Dept*, McMaster University, Department of Art and Art History, Hamilton ON (S)

Wallace, George, *Dir*, McMaster University Art Gallery, Hamilton ON

Wallace, Howard A, *Dir*, Naval Amphibious Museum, Norfolk VA

Wallace, John, *Instructor*, Truro Center for the Arts at Castle Hill, Inc, Truro MA (S)

Wallace, Leonard R, *Chmn Dept*, Orange County Community College, Art Department, Middletown NY (S)

Wallace, Richard W, *Prof*, Wellesley College, Art Department, Wellesley MA (S)

Wallace, Victoria, *Dir*, Northport-East Northport Public Library, Northport NY

Wallens, Nancy G, *Reference Librn*, Lake Forest Library, Lake Forest IL

Waller, Bret, *Dir*, University of Michigan Museum of Art, Alumni Memorial Hall Museum, Ann Arbor MI

Waller, M, *Keeper*, Royal Pavilion, Art Gallery and Museums, Grange Art Gallery and Museum, Brighton England

Waller, Richard, *Community Gallery Coordr*, Brooklyn Museum, Brooklyn NY

Wallin, Franklin, *Pres College*, Earlham College, Leeds Gallery, Richmond IN

Wallin, Hans Erik, *Cur*, Louisiana Museum of Modern Art, Humlebaek Denmark

Wallis, C Lamar, *Dir*, Memphis-Shelby County Public Library and Information Center, Department of Art, Music and Recreation, Memphis TN

Wallis, Hal, *Secy*, Palm Springs Desert Museum, Inc, Palm Springs CA

Wallis, Harriett, *Instructor*, Springfield College, Department of Visual and Performing Arts, Springfield MA (S)

Wallis, Mel R, *Instructor*, Olympic College, Art Department, Bremerton WA (S)

Walls, Michael, *Dir*, Virginia Commonwealth University, Anderson Gallery, Richmond VA

Walls, Roger James, *Pres*, Saskatchewan Association of Architects, Saskatoon SK

Wallschlaeger, Charles A, *Chmn Dept*, Ohio State University, Department of Industrial Design, Columbus OH (S)

Wally, Tony, *Community Arts Development Coordr*, King County Arts Commission, Seattle WA

Walplock, Kenneth, *Asst Prof*, Queensborough Community College, Department of Art and Design, Bayside NY (S)

Walsh, Barbara B, *Mellon Asst Prof*, Vanderbilt University, Dept of Fine Arts, Nashville TN (S)

Walsh, Bee, *Pres*, San Bernardino County Museum and Satellites, Fine Arts Institute, Redlands CA

Walsh, Breffny A, *Dir*, Rensselaer County Historical Society, Troy NY

Walsh, Dawna Hamm, *Asst Prof*, Dallas Baptist College, Department of Art, Dallas TX (S)

Walsh, James, *Cur Exhib*, Schenectady Museum, Schenectady NY

Walsh, John R, *In Charge Art Coll*, The Indiana National Bank, Indianapolis IN

Walsh, Richard K, *Pres*, Oregon College of Art, Ashland OR (S)

Walsh, Sue, *Asst Cur Decorative Arts*, Dayton Art Institute, Dayton OH

Walsh, Thomas, *Chmn Sculpture*, Southern Illinois University, School of Art, Carbondale IL (S)

Walsh Jr, Albert J, *Coordr*, Butte Community College, Humanities Division (III), Oroville CA (S)

Walson, John, *Instructor*, Muskegon Community College, Dept of Creative & Performing Arts, Muskegon MI (S)

Walter, Charles Thomas, *Asst Prof*, Bloomsburg State College, Department of Art, Bloomsburg PA (S)

Walter, Elizabeth, *Instr*, University of North Alabama, Department of Art, Florence AL (S)

Walters, Denzil, *Chmn*, Shoreline Community College, Humanities Division, Seattle WA (S)

Walters, Don, *Chmn Dept*, Western Montana College, Art Dept, Dillon MT (S)

Walters, Janet S, *Asst VPres*, Wachovia Bank & Trust Company, NA, Winston-Salem NC

Walters, Louisella, *Dir*, Regis College, L J Walters Jr Gallery, Weston MA

Walters, Louisella, *Prof*, Regis College, Department of Art, Weston MA (S)

Walters, Sylvia S, *Chmn Art Department*, University of Missouri, Saint Louis, Gallery 210, Saint Louis MO

Walters, Sylvia Solochek, *Chairperson Dept*, University of Missouri-Saint Louis, Art Dept, Saint Louis MO (S)

Walters, Walter H, *Dean*, Pennsylvania State University, University Park, College of Arts and Architecture, University Park PA (S)

Waltershausen, George L, *Chmn Dept*, Monmouth College, Dept of Art, Monmouth IL (S)

Walther, Karen, *Registrar*, Northeastern Nevada Museum, Elko NV

Walton, James M, *Pres*, Carnegie Institute, Museum of Art, Pittsburgh PA

Walton, Jeri, *Museum Asst*, Montana State University, Museum of the Rockies, Bozeman MT

Walton, John, *Principal*, Heatherley School of Fine Art, OW Ashbumham School, London England (S)

Walton, K, *Asst Cur Applied Art*, City Art Gallery, Bristol England

Walton, Nancy M, *Dir*, Junior Center of Art and Science, Oakland CA

Walton, Thomas, *Instr*, Catholic University of America, Department of Architecture & Planning, Washington DC (S)

Walton, William, *Chmn Printmaking*, Moore College of Art, Philadelphia PA (S)

Walusis, Michael, *Assoc Prof*, Youngstown State University, Art Department, Youngstown OH (S)

Walz, Arzella, *Secy*, Ponca City Art Association, Ponca City OK

Walz, Clark, *Dir*, Dacotah Prairie Museum, Aberdeen SD

Walz, Clark, *Dir*, Dacotah Prairie Museum, Historical Research Center Library, Aberdeen SD

Wambaug, Robert, *Dir*, Chief Plenty Coups State Monument, Pryor MT

Wands, Robert, *Asst Prof*, University of Southern Colorado, Belmont Campus, Department of Art, Pueblo CO (S)

Wanserski, Martin, *Asst Prof*, University of South Dakota, Dept of Art, Vermillion SD (S)

Wantland, Mary Jo, *Coordr Indian Gallery Kirkpatrick Center*, Omniplex, Oklahoma City OK

Wantz, John A, *Instructor*, College of DuPage, Humanities Div, Glen Ellyn IL (S)

Wantz, Justine, *Asst Prof*, Loyola University of Chicago, Fine Arts Department, Chicago IL (S)

Wantz, Richard G, *Pres Board of Trustees*, Washington County Museum of Fine Arts, Hagerstown MD

Warburg, Stephanie, *Instructor*, Chamberlayne Junior College, Department of Graphic and Applied Arts, Boston MA (S)

Warburton, Austen, *Pres*, Triton Museum of Art, Santa Clara CA

Ward, Bill, *Instructor*, University of Miami, Department of Art, Coral Gables FL (S)

Ward, Christine W, *Manuscripts Librn*, Albany Institute of History and Art, McKinney Library, Albany NY

Ward, Elaine, *Chairperson*, University of Minnesota, Coffman Union Gallery, Minneapolis MN

Ward, Jan R, *Asst Prof*, Del Mar College, Department of Art, Corpus Christi TX (S)

Ward, Jeffrey C, *Pres*, Art Institute of Chicago, Auxiliary Board, Chicago IL

Ward, John L, *Assoc Prof*, University of Florida, Department of Art, Gainesville FL (S)

Ward, Joseph, *Chmn*, Baptist College at Charleston, Department of Art, Charleston SC (S)

Ward, Karl, *Pres Chilkat Valley Historical Society*, Sheldon Museum and Cultural Center, Haines AK

Ward, Lyle, *Head Art Dept*, College of the Ozarks Library, Clarksville AR

Ward, Lyle, *Head Art Dept*, College of the Ozarks, Department of Art, Clarksville AR (S)

Ward, Marietta M, *Librn*, University of Washington, Art Library, Seattle WA

Ward, Mary M, *Exec Dir*, Princeton Art Association, Princeton NJ

Ward, Melinda, *Dir Learning Museum Program*, Walker Art Center, Minneapolis MN

Ward, N Jeanne, *Instructor*, Guilford Technical Institute, Commercial Art Dept, Jamestown NC (S)

Ward, N W, *Asst Prof*, George Mason University, Department of Fine and Performing Arts, Fairfax VA (S)

Ward, Phillip A, *Prof*, University of Florida, Department of Art, Gainesville FL (S)

Ward, Robert, *Instr*, Bowie State College, Department of Fine and Performing Arts, Bowie MD (S)

Ward, Robert G, *Assoc Prof*, Northeast Louisiana University, Department of Art, Monroe LA (S)

Ward, William, *Teacher*, Philadelphia Maritime Museum, Philadelphia PA

Ward, William E, *Asst in East Indian Art & Museum Designer*, Cleveland Museum of Art, Cleveland OH

Warden, Cynthia Lee, *Supv Coll & Registrar*, Mississippi Museum of Art, Jackson MS

Wardlaw, George, *Chmn Dept*, University of Massachusetts, Amherst, College of Arts and Sciences, Amherst MA (S)

Wardlaw, Tom, *Pres*, Lynnwood Arts Centre, Simcoe ON

Wardwell, Allen, *Dir, Asia House Gallery*, Asia Society, Inc, Asia House Gallery, New York NY

Warehall, Bill, *Instructor*, California State College at San Bernardino, Fine Arts Department, San Bernardino CA (S)

Warehall, Bill, *Vis Prof*, Victor Valley College, Art Department, Victorville CA (S)

Waren, Stanley, *VPres*, Women's Interart Center, Inc, Interart Gallery, New York NY

Warfield, Darlene, *Head of Circulation*, Clark County Library District, Las Vegas NV

Warford, Fred R, *Dir*, Claremore College, Art Department, Claremore OK (S)

Waricher, George, *Instructor*, Shippensburg State College, Art Department, Shippensburg PA (S)

Wark, Robert R, *Cur Art Coll*, Huntington Library, Art Gallery and Botanical Gardens, San Marino CA

Warmus, William, *Asst Cur 20th Century Glass*, Corning Museum of Glass, Corning NY

Warner, Deborah, *Chmn Textile Design*, Moore College of Art, Philadelphia PA (S)

Warner, Douglas, *Instructor*, Charles Stewart Mott Community College, Fine Arts Division, Flint MI (S)

Warner, H, *Instructor*, Golden West College, Arts, Humanities and Social Sciences Institute, Huntington Beach CA (S)

Warner, Lewis H, *Pres*, Tracey-Warner School, Philadelphia PA (S)

Warner, Mary, *Prof in Charge*, University of Montana, Gallery of Visual Arts, Missoula MT

Warner, Mary, *Asst Prof*, University of Montana, Dept of Art, Missoula MT (S)

Warner III, John, *Treas*, Fine Arts Center of Clinton, Clinton IL

Warnick, Lucy Brown, *Gallery Dir*, Rogue Valley Art Association, Medford OR

Warp, Harold, *Pres*, Pioneer Village, Minden NE

Warr, Nemo, *Photographer*, Detroit Institute of Arts, Detroit MI

Warren, Bee, *Librn*, DeCordova and Dana Museum and Park, DeCordova Museum Library, Lincoln MA

Warren, Betty, *Dir*, Malden Bridge School of Art, Malden Bridge NY (S)

Warren, George, *Pres*, Atlanta Art Workers Coalition, Atlanta GA

Warren, Marlea, *Head Art, Music, Films Dept*, Minneapolis Public Library and Information Center, Art, Music and Film Dept, Minneapolis MN

Warren, Millard, *Instr*, Studio School of Art and Design, Philadelphia PA (S)

Warren, Ralph, *Dir of Gallery*, Bowling Green State University, Fine Arts Gallery, Bowling Green OH

Warren, Russell, *Instructor*, Davidson College, Art Dept, Davidson NC (S)

Warren, Skelly, *Prof*, Christopher Newport College, Fine and Performing Arts, Newport News VA (S)

Warren, Tom, *Pres*, Wenatchee Valley College, Gallery 76, Wenatchee WA

Warrington, Joanna, *Secy*, Towson State University, The Holtzman Art Gallery, Towson MD

Warrington, John W, *Chmn*, Taft Museum, Cincinnati OH

Warshasky, Stanford, *Dir*, Silas Bronson Library, Waterbury CT

Warwick, Katherine, *Asst to Dir Public Information*, National Gallery of Art, Washington DC

Wasgatt, Mary K, *Membership Secy*, William A Farnsworth Library and Art Museum, Rockland ME

Washburn, Gordon B, *Chmn Art Committee*, China Institute in America, China House Gallery, New York NY

Washington, Bisa, *Art Asst*, Newark Museum, Junior Museum, Newark NJ

Washington, Selden, *Asst Dir*, Honolulu Academy of Arts, Honolulu HI

Wasiluk, Elizabeth S, *Cur Astronomy*, Hastings Museum, Hastings NE

Wass, Betty, *Asst Prof*, University of Wisconsin, Madison, School of Family Resources and Consumer Sciences, Madison WI (S)

Wasserman, L Katherine, *Treas*, Triton Museum of Art, Santa Clara CA

Wasserman, Rose, *Chairperson*, Pratt-Phoenix School of Design, Associate Degree Department, New York NY (S)

Watcke, Thomas C, *Head Dept*, Albright College, Department of Art, Reading PA (S)

Waterman, Kate, *Public Relations*, Rhode Island Historical Society, Providence RI

Waters, Arnold, *Pres*, Fairbanks Museum and Planetarium, Saint Johnsbury VT

Waters, Deborah D, *Decorative Arts Photographic Collections*, Winterthur Museum and Gardens, Library, Winterthur DE

Waters, Sara, *Asst Prof*, Texas Tech University, Department of Art, Lubbock TX (S)

Waterston, C D, *Keeper Department of Geology*, Royal Scottish Museum, Edinburgh Scotland

Waterston, Harry, *Pres*, New York Artists Equity Association, Inc, New York NY

Waterton, Eric C, *Art Dir*, Department of Culture, Government of the Province of Alberta, Provincial Museum of Alberta, Edmonton AB

Watkins, Ben, *Prof*, Eastern Illinois University, Art Department, Charleston IL (S)

Watkins, John P, *Pres*, California State College, Department of Art, California PA (S)

Watkins, Ragland, *Assoc Dir Gallery*, Artists Space, New York NY

Watkins, Ruth Nagle, *Chmn*, College of Notre Dame of Maryland, Art Dept, Baltimore MD (S)

Watkinson, Patricia, *Cur*, Washington State University, Museum of Art, Pullman WA

Watral, James, *Chmn Ceramics*, East Texas State University, Department of Art, Commerce TX (S)

Watrous, John, *Prof*, Santa Rosa Junior College, Art Department, Santa Rosa CA (S)

Watson, Clarissa H, *Dir*, Country Art Gallery, Locust Valley NY

Watson, Edwin W, *Exec Dir*, Belle Grove, Middletown VA

Watson, Herb, *Visual Designer*, University of British Columbia, Museum of Anthropology, Vancouver BC

Watson, Jan, *Asst Prof*, Bradford College, Art Department, Bradford MA (S)

Watson, Jennifer, *Asst Cur & Registrar*, The Robert McLaughlin Gallery, Oshawa ON

Watson, John, *VPres*, Art Centre of New Jersey, East Orange NJ

Watson, Katharine J, *Dir*, Bowdoin College, Museum of Art & Peary-MacMillan Arctic Museum, Brunswick ME

Watson, Lorraine, *Head Teaching Staff*, Ocean City School of Art, Ocean City NJ (S)

Watson, Paulette Skirbunt, *Dir*, James Monroe Law Office - Museum and Memorial Library, Fredericksburg VA

Watson, Ronald, *Chmn Dept*, Aquinas College, Art Department, Grand Rapids MI (S)

Watson, Scott, *Registrar*, Vancouver Art Gallery, Vancouver BC

Watson, Wendy, *Chief Cur*, Mount Holyoke College Art Museum, South Hadley MA

Watt, Virginia J, *Managing Dir*, Guilde Canadianne des Mietiers d'Art, Quebec, Canadian Guild of Crafts, Quebec, Montreal PQ

Wattenmaker, Richard J, *Dir*, Chrysler Museum, Norfolk VA

Watts, Chris, *Chmn Fine Arts*, Cornish Institute, Seattle WA (S)

Watts, Jare, *Dir*, Universidad de las Americas, Library, Cholula Mexico

Watts, Melvin E, *Cur*, Currier Gallery of Art, Manchester NH

Watts, R Michael, *Dir*, Paducah Art Guild, Paducah KY

Watts, Roland S, *Assoc Prof*, Winston-Salem State University, Art Department, Winston-Salem NC (S)

Waufle, Alan D, *Dir*, Gaston County Art and History Museum, Dallas NC

Waugh, Carlisle J, *Head Dept*, Oklahoma State University, School of Technical Training, Okmulgee OK (S)

Wavell, Joan B, *Adminr*, Rollins College, George D and Harriet W Cornell Fine Arts Center Museum, Winter Park FL

Wax, Bernard, *Dir*, American Jewish Historical Society, Waltham MA

Waxman, Joanne, *Librn*, Portland School of Art Library, Portland ME

Waxman, S, *Secy*, McMaster University Art Gallery, Hamilton ON

Way, Gordon, *Dir*, Cody Country Art League, Cody WY

Wayne, James M, *Instr*, San Jose City College, School of Fine Arts, San Jose CA (S)

Wayne, Sam, *Instructor*, Saint Louis Community College at Meramec, Art Dept, Saint Louis MO (S)

Wdowka, Wanda, *Dir*, Traphagen School of Fashion, New York NY (S)

Weare, Shane, *Prof*, Sonoma State University, Art Department, Rohnert Park CA (S)

Weare, Shane, *Assoc Prof*, California State College, Sonoma, Department of Art, Rohnert Park CA (S)

Weaver, Anna, *Librn*, University of Florida, Architecture and Fine Arts Library, Gainesville FL

Weaver, George, *VPres*, Chautauqua Gallery of Art, Chautauqua NY

Weaver, Howard S, *Dir*, Yale University, School of Art, New Haven CT (S)

Weaver, James D, *Cur Education*, Springfield Art Museum, Springfield MO

Weaver, Judy, *Administrative Asst*, Montana State University, Museum of the Rockies, Bozeman MT

Weaver, L E, *Chmn Art Dept*, University of Lethbridge Art Gallery, Lethbridge AB

Weaver, Larry E, *Assoc Dean Div Fine Arts*, University of Lethbridge, Department of Art, Lethbridge AB (S)

Weaver, Marguerite, *Secy-Treas*, Hill-Stead Museum, Farmington CT

Weaver, Mary Catharine, *Dir*, Martin Memorial Library, York PA

Weaver, Paula, *Asst Prof*, University of the District of Columbia, Art Department, Washington DC (S)

Webb, Beth R, *Mus and Art Librn*, Brigham Young University, Harold B Lee Library, Provo UT

Webb, Brian, *Asst Prof*, Vermont College of Norwich University, Philosophy, Religion and Fine Arts Department, Montpelier VT (S)

Webb, Edward, *Cur Historic Houses*, Charleston Museum, Charleston SC

Webb, Robert, *Treas*, Adirondack Lakes Center for the Arts, Blue Mountain Lake NY

Webber, E Leland, *Pres & Dir*, Field Museum of Natural History, Chicago IL

Webber, Elizabeth, *Chmn Cabot House Museum & Library*, Beverly Historical Society, Beverly MA

Webber, Larry Jan, *Assoc Prof*, Mississippi State University, Art Department, Mississippi State MS (S)

Webber, Nancy E, *Asst Prof*, Los Angeles Harbor College, Art Department, Wilmington CA (S)

Webby, Ernest J, *Dir*, Brockton Public Library System, Municipal Art Gallery, Brockton MA

Weber, Arthur, *Dean*, Herron School of Art, Indiana University-Purdue University, Indianapolis, Indianapolis IN (S)

Weber, Arthur H, *Dean*, Indiana University - Purdue University at Indianapolis, Herron School of Art, Art Gallery, Indianapolis IN

Weber, B M A, *Chmn Dept*, California Lutheran College, Art Department, Thousand Oaks CA (S)

Weber, Bruce, *Cur*, University of Kentucky, Art Museum, Lexington KY

Weber, Dorothy M, *Executive Dir*, Visual Artists and Galleries Association, Inc, New York NY

Weber, John, *Assoc Prof*, Elmhurst College, Art Department, Elmhurst IL (S)

Weber, Kathleen, *Chmn*, Howard College, Art Department, Big Spring TX (S)

Weber, Louis, *Assoc Prof*, University of Dayton, Fine Arts Division, Dayton OH (S)

Weber, Michael, *Assoc Dir*, Museum of New Mexico, Santa Fe NM

Weber, Robert C, *Div of Arts*, Davis and Elkins College, Department of Art, Elkins WV (S)

Weberg, Lorraine, *Art Librn*, Fashion Institute of Technology, Library, New York NY

Webernick, Gary, *Cur of Exhibits*, Anchorage Historical and Fine Arts Museum, Anchorage AK

Webster, Christopher R, *Exec Secy*, North Carolina Art Society, Raleigh NC

Webster, D B, *Pres & Cur*, Royal Ontario Museum, Canadiana Gallery, Toronto ON

Webster, Laurence, *VPres*, Rockport Art Association, Rockport MA

Webster, M, *Instructor*, Northern Arizona University, Art Department, Flagstaff AZ (S)

Webster, Paul, *Lectr*, Oakland University, Dept of Art & Art History, Rochester MI (S)

Webster, Sally, *Dir*, A I R Gallery, New York NY

Wechsler, Jeffrey, *Cur Painting & Sculpture*, Rutgers University, Art Gallery, New Brunswick NJ

Wedell, Maida, *Instructor*, Laramie County Community College, Division of Humanities, Cheyenne WY (S)

Wedow, Marian B, *Dir*, Rome Art and Community Center, Rome NY

Weekly, Nancy, *Asst Gallery Dir*, State University College, Department of Art, Fredonia NY (S)

Weekly, Nancy, *Art Gallery Dir*, State University of New York College at Fredonia, M C Rockefeller Arts Center Gallery, Fredonia NY

Weeks, Dennis W, *Dir of Prog*, Saint Joseph's College, Fine Arts Program, Philadelphia PA (S)

Weeks, Edward F, *Cur*, Birmingham Museum of Art, Birmingham AL

Weeks, James, *Prof*, Boston University, School of Visual Arts, Boston MA (S)

Weeks, Kenneth, *Instr*, Portland Community College, Department of Fine Arts, Portland OR (S)

Weer, Barry D, *Asst Dir*, Illinois State University, Center for the Visual Arts Gallery, Normal IL

Wees, Beth Carver, *Asst Cur*, Sterling and Francine Clark Art Institute, Williamstown MA

Wees, J Dustin, *Photograph & Slide Librn*, Sterling and Francine Clark Art Institute, Williamstown MA

Wegner, Maxeen, *Second VPres*, Coos Art Museum, Coos Bay OR

Wegner, Nadene, *Instructor*, Louisville School of Art, Anchorage KY (S)

Wegner, Theresa, *Photographer*, Minnesota Museum of Art, Saint Paul MN

Weidensee, Victor, *Chmn*, Black Hills State College, Art Department, Spearfish SD (S)

Weidl, Beverly, *Cur*, Hopewell Museum, Hopewell NJ

Weidman, James F, *Development Officer*, Huntington Galleries, Huntington WV

Weidmann, Daniel, *Graphic Designer*, Brooklyn Museum, Brooklyn NY

Weidner, Gregory J, *Curatorial Asst*, Pittsburgh History and Landmarks Foundation, Old Post Office Museum, Pittsburgh PA

Weidner, Marsha, *Instructor*, Oberlin College, Department of Art, Oberlin OH (S)

Weidner Jr, H G, *VPres*, Women's City Club of Cleveland, Cleveland OH

Weiffenbach, Jean-Edith V, *Dir Exhib & Cur Permanent Coll*, University of Colorado Art Galleries, Boulder CO

Weigel, Jan, *Designer*, Taft Museum, Cincinnati OH

Weil, Meg, *Treas*, New York Artists Equity Association, Inc, New York NY

Weil, Norman, *Asst Prof*, Northwest Missouri State University, Dept of Art, Maryville MO (S)

Weil, Rose R, *Exec Secy*, College Art Association of America, New York NY

Weil, Stephen, *Deputy Dir*, Hirshhorn Museum and Sculpture Garden, Washington DC

Weil, Steven E, *Co-Dir*, Museum Management Institute, San Francisco CA (S)

Weiler, Melody, *Instructor*, Murray State University, Art Department, Murray KY (S)

Weill, Alan, *Conservator*, Union Centrale des Arts Decoratifs, Musee de l'Affiche, Paris France

Weimerskirch, Robert, *Instr*, Museum of Fine Arts, Alfred C Glassell Junior School of Art, Houston TX (S)

Wein, Frances, *Ed*, National Portrait Gallery, Washington DC

Weinberg, Alison, *Treas*, Verde Valley Art Association, Inc, Jerome AZ

Weinberg, Ephraim, *Dean*, Pennsylvania Academy of the Fine Arts, Philadelphia PA (S)

Weinberg, H Barbara, *Assoc Prof*, City University of New York, PhD Program in Art History, New York NY (S)

Weinberg, Susan, *Registrar*, Detroit Institute of Arts, Detroit MI

Weinberger, Oscar, *Treas*, Guild Hall of East Hampton, Inc, Museum Section, East Hampton NY

Weinbrecht, Ruby, *Chmn Libr Committee*, James Monroe Law Office - Museum and Memorial Library, Library, Fredericksburg VA

Weiner, Abe, *Instructor*, Ivy School of Professional Art, Downtown Annex, Pittsburgh PA (S)

Weingarden, Lauren, *Vis Lectr*, University of North Carolina at Chapel Hill, Art Department, Chapel Hill NC (S)

Weingartner, Fannia, *Editor*, Chicago Historical Society, Chicago IL

Weinger, Paul, *Second VPres*, North Shore Art League, Winnetka IL

Weingrod, Carmi, *Slide Cur*, University of Oregon, School of Architecture and Allied Arts Library, Eugene OR

Weinhardt Jr, Carl J, *Dir*, Dade County Art Museum, Vizcaya Museum and Gardens, Miami FL

Weinland, Richard, *Treas*, Katonah Gallery, Katonah NY

Weinman, Albert, *Art Advisory Board*, Society of Medalists, Danbury CT

Weinrich, Peter H, *Exec Dir*, Canadian Crafts Council, Conseil Canadien de l'Artisanat, Ottawa ON

Weinschenk, Franz, *Dean*, Fresno City College, Art Department, Fresno CA (S)

Weinstein, Alan, *Vis Prof*, University of Texas at San Antonio, Division of Art and Design, San Antonio TX (S)

Weinstein, Joyce, *Coordr*, Women in the Arts Foundation, Inc, New York NY

Weinstein, Joyce, *Pres*, Women in the Arts Foundation, Inc, New York NY

Weinstein, M, *Treas*, Lovis Corinth Memorial Foundation, Inc, New York NY

Weintraub, Linda, *Gallery Dir*, Muhlenberg College Center for the Arts, Allentown PA

Weir, Stan, *Vis Prof*, Oral Roberts University, Fine Arts Department, Tulsa OK (S)

Weirich, David, *Instr*, Mount San Jacinto College, Art Department, San Jacinto CA (S)

Weis, Anne, *Asst Prof*, University of Pittsburgh, Henry Clay Frick Fine Arts Department, Pittsburgh PA (S)

Weis, Helene H, *Librn*, Willet Stained Glass Studios, Library, Philadelphia PA

Weisberg, Charlene, *Instructor*, University of Southern California, Idyllwild Campus, Idyllwild School of Music and the Arts, Idyllwild CA (S)

Weisberg, Gabriel P, *Cur Education*, Cleveland Museum of Art, Cleveland OH

Weisberg, Rebecca, *Museum Liaison Chmn*, Women in the Arts Foundation, Inc, New York NY

Weisenburger, Patricia, *Asst Dir*, Kansas State University, Paul Weigel Library, Manhattan KS

Weiser, Kurt, *Resident Dir*, Archie Bray Foundation, Helena MT

Weisflog, Donald, *Prof*, Anderson College, Art Dept, Anderson IN (S)

Weisl Jr, Edwin L, *Pres*, International Foundation for Art Research, Inc, New York NY

Weisman, Gustav, *Chmn Dept Exp Art*, Ontario College of Art, Toronto ON (S)

Weisman, James H, *Theatre Dir*, Hill Country Arts Foundation, Ingram TX

Weisman, Judy, *Chief, Education and Public Programs*, Chicago Historical Society, Chicago IL

Weiss, Anton, *Art Dir*, Watkins Institute, Nashville TN

Weiss, Evelyn, *Cur Modern Art*, Museen der Stadt Köln, Wallraf-Richartz-Museum, Museum Ludwig, Cologne Germany, Federal Republic of

Weiss, Gilbert H, *Instructor*, Antonelli School of Photography, Philadelphia PA (S)

Weiss, Harvey, *Asst Prof*, Adelphi University, Department of Art and Art History, Garden City NY (S)

Weiss, John, *Coordr Photography*, University of Delaware, Department of Art, Newark DE (S)

Weiss, Milton, *Instructor*, Ivy School of Professional Art, Downtown Annex, Pittsburgh PA (S)

Weiss, Murray, *Artist in Res*, Viterbo College, Art Department, La Crosse WI (S)

Weiss, Nathan, *Pres*, Kean College of New Jersey, Union NJ

Weisser, Terry Drayman, *Dir of Conservation Dept*, Walters Art Gallery, Baltimore MD

Weisz, Helen, *Instructor*, Bucks County Community College, Fine Arts Department, Newton PA (S)

Weitz, Stephen, *Instr*, Temple University, Art Department, Philadelphia PA (S)

Weitzel, Robert D, *Dean*, Cleveland Institute of Art, Cleveland OH

Weitzmann, Kurt, *Consultative Cur*, Metropolitan Museum of Art, Cloisters, New York NY

Welbur, Beverly Zisla, *Assoc Dir*, Saint Anselm's College, Manchester NH

Welch, Bill, *Instructor*, Oklahoma State University, School of Technical Training, Okmulgee OK (S)

Welch, Ileana, *Dir Cultural Heritage*, City of Los Angeles, Municipal Arts Dept, Los Angeles CA

Welch, Paul, *Chmn Dept*, Northwestern Michigan College, Art Dept, Traverse City MI (S)

Welch, Robert B, *Chmn*, Limestone College, Art Department, Gaffney SC (S)

Welch, S Anthony, *Assoc Prof*, University of Victoria, Department of History in Art, Victoria BC (S)

Welch, Stuart Cary, *Consultant Department Islamic Art*, Metropolitan Museum of Art, New York NY

Welch, Sue C, *Librn*, Schenectady Museum, Library, Schenectady NY

Welcome, Jennie, *Secy*, Douglas Art Association, Little Gallery, Douglas AZ

Welden, Larry, *Instructor*, Sacramento City College, Art Department, Sacramento CA (S)

Welesehuk, Damien, *Dir*, Basilian Fathers, Mundare AB

Wellington, Margot, *Executive Dir*, Municipal Art Society of New York, New York NY

Welliver, Jackie, *Instructor*, Williamsport Area Community College, Department of Engineering and Design, Williamsport PA (S)

Welliver, Neil G, *Chmn*, University of Pennsylvania, Department of Fine Arts, Philadelphia PA (S)

Wells, Augusta, *Secy*, Lighthouse Gallery, Tequesta FL

Wells, Carol, *Instructor*, Villa Maria College of Buffalo, Art Department, Buffalo NY (S)

Wells, Charles, *Archivist*, Klamath County Museum, Klamath Falls OR

Wells, James L, *Cur Graphics*, Smith-Mason Gallery and Museum, Washington DC

Wells, Rufus, *Asst Prof*, University of the District of Columbia, Art Department, Washington DC (S)

Wells, Vern, *Area Chmn Art History*, Pasadena City College, Art Department, Pasadena CA (S)

Welsh, Alexandra, *Cur of Robinson Coll*, United States Naval Academy Museum, Annapolis MD

Welsh, Constance, *Lectr*, University of North Carolina-Charlotte, Creative Arts Dept, Charlotte NC (S)

Welsh Jr, Peter C, *Cur of Art*, Kansas State Historial Society Museum, Topeka KS

Welu, James Q, *Assoc Cur*, Worcester Art Museum, Worcester MA

Welu, William, *Chmn Dept Art*, Briar Cliff College, Gallery 147, Sioux City IA

Welu, William J, *Chairperson*, Briar Cliff College, Art Department, Sioux City IA (S)

Wendel, Charlotte, *Development Officer*, San Jose Museum of Art, San Jose CA

Wender, D, *Dir Development*, School of Holography, Fine Arts Research and Holographic Center Museum, Chicago IL

Wender, David, *In Charge*, School of Holography, David Wender Library, Chicago IL

Wendland, Betty, *Asst Dir*, University of Illinois at Urbana-Champaign, World Heritage Museum, Urbana IL

Weng, Siegfried, *Dir Emeritus*, Evansville Museum of Arts and Science, Evansville IN

Wengenroth, Richard, *Chmn*, Bernard M Baruch College of the City University of New York, Art Department, New York NY (S)

Wengler, Jane, *Instructor*, Oxbow Summer Art Workshops, Saugatuck MI (S)

Wenig-Horswell, Judy, *Asst Prof*, Goshen College, Art Department, Goshen IN (S)

Wentworth, T W, *Deputy Dir & Secy*, T T Wentworth, Jr Museum, Pensacola FL

Wentworth Jr, T T, *Dir & Cur*, T T Wentworth, Jr Museum, Pensacola FL

Wentz, Manfred, *Prof*, University of Wisconsin, Madison, School of Family Resources and Consumer Sciences, Madison WI (S)

Werk, Horst, *Asst Prof*, Corning Community College, Division of Humanities, Corning NY (S)

Werndli, Phillip A, *Dir*, Florida Folklife Program, White Springs FL

Werner, Don, *Designer*, Museum of the American Indian, New York NY

Werner, Judy, *Young Adult*, Mason City Public Library, Mason City IA

Werner, Susan, *Cur Asst*, Wheaton College, Watson Gallery, Norton MA

Werness, Hope B, *Vis Lectr*, California State College, Stanislaus, Art Department, Turlock CA (S)

Wernig, Raymond, *VChmn*, Stan Hywet Hall Foundation, Inc, Akron OH

Wert, Ned O, *Chmn Exhib*, Indiana University of Pennsylvania, Kipp Gallery, Indiana PA

Werth, A J, *Dir*, Pretoria Art Museum, Pretoria South Africa, Republic of

Wertheim, Earl, *Asst Prof*, Sullivan County Community College, Div of Commercial Art and Photography, Loch Sheldrake NY (S)

Wertz, Andrew W, *Dir*, Hamilton College, Bristol Campus Center, Clinton NY

Wesaw, Sallie, *Instructor*, Central Wyoming College, Art Center, Riverton WY (S)

Wescoat, Bonna B, *Library Cur*, Beaumont Art Museum, Library, Beaumont TX

Wesle, Janet, *Programmer & Exhib*, Minnesota Museum of Art, Saint Paul MN

Wesp, Erwin O, *Exhib Chmn*, Coppini Academy of Fine Arts, San Antonio TX

Wessel, Frederick, *Asst Prof*, Hartford Art School of the University of Hartford, West Hartford CT (S)

Wessels, Henry, *Assoc Prof*, California Polytechnic State University at San Luis Obispo, Art Department, San Luis Obispo CA (S)

Wessetsky, V, *Head Egyptian Antiquities*, Szepmuveszet Museum, Museum of Fine Arts, Budapest Hungary

Wessling, Schneider, *Pres*, Akademie der Bildenden Künste, Academy of Fine Arts, Munich Germany, Federal Republic of (S)

West, Bruce, *Lectr*, Lewis and Clark College, Department of Art, Portland OR (S)

West, Elizabeth, *Coordr*, Art League of Houston, Houston TX

West, Harvey, *Dir*, University of Washington, Henry Art Gallery, Seattle WA

West, Jean, *Arts Workshop*, Newark Museum, Newark NJ

West, Mary Ellen, *Acting Head Librn*, Ohio Historical Society, Archives and Library, Columbus OH

West, Richard, *VPres*, Historical Society of Bloomfield, New Jersey, Bloomfield NJ

West, Richard Vincent, *Dir*, Crocker Art Museum, Sacramento CA

West, Sharon, *Head Catalog Department*, University of Alaska, Elmer E Rasmuson Library, Fairbanks AK

Westberg, Alma, *Art & Music Librn*, Santa Cruz Public Library, Art, Music, Film Department, Santa Cruz CA

Westergaard, Hanne, *Cur*, Statens Museum for Kunst, Department of Painting and Sculpture, Copenhagen Denmark

Westergard, Jim, *Coordr Art and Design*, Red Deer College, Department of Art and Design, Red Deer AB (S)

Westermark, Ulla, *Keeper*, Kungl Myntkabinettet Statens Museum För Mynt Medalj Och Penninghistoria, Royal Coin Cabinet, National Museum of Monetary History, Stockholm Sweden

Westermeyer, Eleanore, *Librn*, Herzog Anton Ulrich-Museum, Library, Brunswick Germany, Federal Republic of

Western, Dominique C, *Cur Exhib*, Division of Historical and Cultural Affairs, Bureau of Museums and Historic Sites, Dover DE

Westers, A, *Head Department of Decorative Arts*, Haags Gemeentemuseum, Municipal Museum of The Hague, The Hague Netherlands

Westervelt, Alice, *Museum Shop Mgr*, Rhode Island School of Design, Museum of Art, Providence RI

Westervelt, Robert F, *Assoc Prof*, Agnes Scott College, Department of Art, Decatur GA (S)

Westfall, Mid, *Secy*, Humboldt Arts Council, Eureka CA

Westhafer, Dorothy H, *Gallery Dir*, Niagara County Community College Art Gallery, Sanborn NY

Westheimer, Jerome M, *VPres*, Oklahoma Art Center, Oklahoma City OK

Westin, Robert H, *Chmn*, University of Florida, Department of Art, Gainesville FL (S)

Westin, Sandra, *Public Affairs Officer*, National Portrait Gallery, Washington DC

Weston, Norman B, *Pres*, Detroit Institute of Arts, Detroit Institute of Art Founders Society, Detroit MI

Weston, Robert T, *Art Museum Adminr*, Detroit Institute of Arts, Detroit MI

Wetherbee, Nathaniel, *Secy*, Marblehead Arts Association, Inc, Marblehead MA

Wetherbee Jr, Ralph H, *Chmn Board*, Springfield Art Center, Springfield OH

Wettersten, Ansel, *Cur Capricorn Asunder Gallery*, San Francisco City and County Art Commission, San Francisco CA

Wettre, Hakan, *Cur Exhib Department*, Göteborg Konstmuseum, Gothenburg Art Gallery, Gothenburg Sweden

Wetzel, Gail, *Instr*, Aegean School of Fine Arts, Paros Cyclades Greece (S)

Wewer, William J, *Executive Dir*, Pennsylvania Historical and Museum Commission, Harrisburg PA

Weyerhaeuser, Charles A, *Museum Dir*, Art Complex Museum at Duxbury, Duxbury MA

Weyl, Martin, *Chief Cur Arts*, Israel Museum, Jerusalem Israel

Whaley, Bill, *Executive Dir*, Taos Art Association Inc, Taos NM

Whang, Ji Hyun, *Librn*, Museen der Stadt Köln, Museum für Ostasiatische Kunst Bibliothek, Cologne Germany, Federal Republic of

Wharton, D W, *Dir*, Sun Valley Center for the Arts & Humanities, Department of Fine Art, Sun Valley ID (S)

Wharton, Hugh D, *Business Mgr*, Historic Deerfield Inc, Deerfield MA

Wharton, John, *Dir*, Phillips Exeter Academy, Lamont Gallery, Exeter NH

Wheadon, Lynn, *Treas*, Calgary Artists Society, Calgary AB

Wheat, Gilbert, *Instructor*, College of Marin, Department of Art, Kentfield CA (S)

Wheatley, Kim, *Slide Librn*, Munson-Williams-Proctor Institute, Art Reference Library, Utica NY

Wheatley, Richard, *Instr*, Wilberforce University, Art Department, Wilberforce OH (S)

Wheeler, Catherine, *Head of Public Relations*, Winterthur Museum and Gardens, Winterthur DE

Wheeler, Claire, *Admin Asst*, Shaker Museum, Old Chatham NY

Wheeler, Coleman, *Prof*, North Arkansas Community College, Art Department, Harrison AR (S)

Wheeler, Elbert, *Instr*, Phillips University, Department of Art, Enid OK (S)

Wheeler, Gary, *Asst Prof*, Miami University, Art Department, Oxford OH (S)

Wheeler, Mark, *Pres*, Art Institute of Fort Lauderdale, Fort Lauderdale FL (S)

Wheeler, Meme, *Instr*, Phillips University, Department of Art, Enid OK (S)

Wheeler, Richard, *Asst Prof*, Denison University, Department of Art, Granville OH (S)

Wheeler, Robert, *VPres Coll*, Greenfield Village and Henry Ford Museum, Dearborn MI

Wheeler, Robert C, *Assoc Dir*, Minnesota Historical Society, St Paul MN

Wheelock, Gary, *Dir Development & Community Relations*, Newport Harbor Art Museum, Newport Beach CA

Wheelock Jr, Arthur K, *Cur Dutch & Flemish Painting*, National Gallery of Art, Washington DC

Whelan, Janet, *VPres*, Warwick Arts Foundation, Warwick RI

Whelan, L, *Secy*, Saskatoon Gallery and Conservatory Corporation, Saskatoon SK

Whelchel, David, *Registrar*, Washington State University, Museum of Art, Pullman WA

Whetstone, Nita, *Adjunct Instr*, Auburn University at Montgomery, Art Department, Montgomery AL (S)

Whiddon, Henry, *Painting & Drawing Coordr*, North Texas State University, Art Department, Denton TX (S)

Whipkey, Harry E, *Dir Bureau Archives & History*, Pennsylvania Historical and Museum Commission, Harrisburg PA

Whipple, Enez, *Dir*, Guild Hall of East Hampton, Inc, Museum Section, East Hampton NY

Whitacre, Steven, *Chmn Found*, Kansas City Art Institute, Kansas City MO (S)

Whitaker, Tom J, *Chmn*, Prestonsburg Community College, Art Department, Prestonsburg KY (S)

Whitaker Jr, Richard R, *Dean*, University of Illinois at Chicago Circle, College of Architecture, Art & Urban Sciences, Chicago IL (S)

Whitbeck, Gary, *Dir*, Rahr-West Museum and Civic Center, Manitowoc WI

Whitbeck Jr, Carl G, *VPres*, Columbia County Historical Society, House of History and Van Alen House, Kinderhook NY

Whitcomb, Morton C, *Secy*, Colonel Black Mansion, Ellsworth ME

Whitcomb, Therese T, *Dir*, University of San Diego, Founders' Gallery, San Diego CA

Whitcomb, Therese Truitt, *Chmn*, University of San Diego, Art Department, San Diego CA (S)

White, Albert, *Secy*, Professional Art Dealers Association of Canada, Toronto ON

White, Amos, *Instr*, Bowie State College, Department of Fine and Performing Arts, Bowie MD (S)

White, Barbara, *Asst Prof*, Tufts University, Fine Arts Department, Medford MA (S)

White, Barbara, *Instructor*, Charles Stewart Mott Community College, Fine Arts Division, Flint MI (S)

White, Benjamin, *Asst to Exhib Coordr*, Dartmouth College Museum & Galleries, Hanover NH

Wilkinson, Betty F, *Librn & Registrar*, Art Gallery of Windsor, Reference Library, Windsor ON

Wilkinson, Irene, *Head Technical Services*, Brookline Public Library, Brookline MA

Wilkinson, P Chauvin, *Chmn Empire Bedroom Coll*, West Baton Rouge Museum, Port Allen LA

Wilkinson, William D, *Dir*, Mariners Museum, Newport News VA

Willenson, Elaine Kaye, *Dir*, Germain School of Photography, New York NY (S)

Willet, E Crosby, *Pres*, Willet Stained Glass Studios, Philadelphia PA

Willet, Henry Lee, *Chmn*, Willet Stained Glass Studios, Philadelphia PA

Willey, Joella, *Secy*, Prescott Fine Arts Association, Prescott AZ

Williams, Althea B, *Deputy Cur of Education*, Norton Simon Museum, Pasadena CA

Williams, Ann, *Asst Prof*, Beaver College, Department of Fine Arts, Glenside PA (S)

Williams, Ardelia, *Head Dept*, Marion College, Art Department, Marion IN (S)

Williams, Bruce, *Instr*, Chapman College, Art Department, Orange CA (S)

Williams, C E, *Art Dir*, Plains Indians & Pioneer Historical Foundation, Pioneer Museum & Art Center, Woodward OK

Williams, Carolyn, *Exec Cur & Acting Dir*, Asheville Art Museum, Asheville NC

Williams, Casey, *Instr*, Museum of Fine Arts, Alfred C Glassell Junior School of Art, Houston TX (S)

Williams, Charlene, *Business Mgr*, Lemoyne Art Foundation, Tallahassee FL

Williams, Charles, *Extension Supv*, Department of Culture, Government of the Province of Alberta, Provincial Museum of Alberta, Edmonton AB

Williams, Clarence, *VPres*, Carson County Square House Museum, Panhandle TX

Williams, Ethelynn, *Head of Reference*, New Rochelle Public Library, New Rochelle NY

Williams, Frances S, *Pres*, Polk Public Museum, Lakeland FL

Williams, H L, *Chmn*, Florida A&M University, Department of Visual Arts & Humanities, Tallahassee FL (S)

Williams, Haydn, *Pres*, Asia Foundation Gallery, The Asia Foundation, San Francisco CA

Williams, Hiram D, *Prof*, University of Florida, Department of Art, Gainesville FL (S)

Williams, Irving, *Pres*, Fetherston Foundation, Packwood House Museum, Lewisburg PA

Williams, James M, *Dir*, Johnson County Community College, Communications-Arts Division, Overland Park KS (S)

Williams, Jane, *Agent*, Richard Gallery and Almond Tea Gallery, Divisions of Studios of Jack Richard, Cuyahoga Falls OH

Williams, Jane, *Dir*, Creative School of Design Library, Cuyahoga Falls OH

Williams, Jo Ella, *Asst Prof*, Northeast Louisiana University, Department of Art, Monroe LA (S)

Williams, John, *Chmn*, University of Pittsburgh, Henry Clay Frick Fine Arts Department, Pittsburgh PA (S)

Williams, John C, *Pres & Dir*, Agecroft Association, Richmond VA

Williams, Keven, *Cur Exhibitions*, Kenosha Public Museum, Kenosha WI

Williams, Lewis C, *Pres*, Cleveland Museum of Art, Cleveland OH

Williams, Lorraine, *Cur Archaeology-Ethnology*, New Jersey State Museum, Trenton NJ

Williams, Lucia, *Exec Asst to Dir*, Wadsworth Atheneum, Hartford CT

Williams, Margaret Click, *Chmn Dept*, Saint Mary's College, Raleigh NC (S)

Williams, Martha, *Budget Officer*, Harvard University, William Hayes Fogg Art Museum, Cambridge MA

Williams, Mary Beth, *Admin Asst to Dir*, Springfield Art Museum, Springfield MO

Williams, Mary Jane, *Registrar*, Arizona State University, University Art Collections, Tempe AZ

Williams, Marylou S, *Dir & Cur*, Beloit College, Theodore Lyman Wright Art Center, Beloit WI

Williams, Maudine B, *Head Librn*, Indiana University - Purdue University at Indianapolis, Herron School of Art Library, Indianapolis IN

Williams, Randy, *Dir*, Arts and Crafts Association, Inc, Winston-Salem NC (S)

Williams, Rev H, *Pres*, Moravian Historical Society, Whitefield House Museum, Nazareth PA

Williams, Richard, *Chmn Foundations*, University of Manitoba, School of Art, Winnipeg MB (S)

Williams, Richmond, *Dir*, Hagley Museum, Eleutherian Mills Historical Library, Washington DE

Williams, Roberta L, *Exec Dir*, Junior Art Gallery, Louisville KY

Williams, Roger, *Dir*, Art Academy of Cincinnati, Cincinnati OH (S)

Williams, Roger, *Adjunct Assoc Prof*, New York Institute of Technology, Fine Arts Department, Old Westbury NY (S)

Williams, Ruth, *Asst Librn*, Beloit College, Morse Library, Beloit WI

Williams, Sally, *Cur Lion's Gallery of the Senses*, Wadsworth Atheneum, Hartford CT

Williams, Sheri, *Gallery Chmn*, Texas A & M University, Memorial Student Center Arts Committee, College Station TX

Williams, Stephen R, *Dir*, Museum of Arts and History, Port Huron MI

Williams, Susan, *Exhib Preparator*, Ohio State University, Gallery of Fine Arts, Columbus OH

Williams, Susan, *Registrar*, Corcoran Gallery of Art, Washington DC

Williams, Sylvia, *Cur African, Oceanic & New World Cultures*, Brooklyn Museum, Brooklyn NY

Williams, W, *Instructor*, Northern Arizona University, Art Department, Flagstaff AZ (S)

Williams, Wayne, *Prof*, Community College of the Finger Lakes, Visual & Performing Arts Department, Canandaigua NY (S)

Williams, Winifred S, *Assoc Prof*, Texas Woman's University, Department of Art, Denton TX (S)

Williamson, Anne K, *Cur*, Jones Library, Inc, Amherst MA

Williamson, David, *Dir Educ*, Octagon Center for the Arts, Ames IA

Williamson, James, *Head Education Services*, Art Gallery of Ontario, Toronto ON

Williamson, Moncrieff, *Dir*, Confederation Centre Art Gallery and Museum, Charlottetown PE

Williamson, Preston, *Instr*, Studio School of Art and Design, Philadelphia PA (S)

Willingham, John, *Pres*, Southeastern Center for Contemporary Art, Winston-Salem NC

Willis, William H, *Pres*, Art Institute of Boston, Gallery West, Gallery East, Boston MA

Willis Jr, William H, *Pres*, Art Institute of Boston, Boston MA (S)

Willoughby, Sue, *VPres*, Ontario Crafts Council, Toronto ON

Wills Jr, J Robert, *Dean*, University of Kentucky, Department of Art, Lexington KY (S)

Wilmerding, John, *Cur American Art & Sr Cur*, National Gallery of Art, Washington DC

Wilson, A, *Dir General Reference Division*, British Library, Reference Division, London England

Wilson, A D P, *Dir*, City Art Gallery, Bristol England

Wilson, Ann Hysmith, *Secy*, Saint Louis Artists' Guild, Saint Louis MO

Wilson, B K, *Pres Elect*, Arts for Living Center, Burlington IA

Wilson, Betty, *Instructor*, College of Marin, Department of Art, Kentfield CA (S)

Wilson, Bob, *Instructor*, Ohio Visual Art Institute, Cincinnati OH (S)

Wilson, Chris, *Asst Prof*, Atlantic Christian College, Art Dept, Wilson NC (S)

Wilson, D M, *Dir*, British Museum, London England

Wilson, Don, *Vis Prof*, Oral Roberts University, Fine Arts Department, Tulsa OK (S)

Wilson, Don W, *Assoc Dir*, State Historical Society of Wisconsin, Madison WI

Wilson, Forrest, *Chmn Undergrad Studies*, Catholic University of America, Department of Architecture & Planning, Washington DC (S)

Wilson, Fred, *Instructor*, Arkansas Arts Center, Little Rock AR (S)

Wilson, Gillian, *Cur of Decorative Arts*, J Paul Getty Museum, Malibu CA

Wilson, Helen, *Secy*, Jesse Besser Museum, Alpena MI

Wilson, Hugh Allen, *Chmn*, Union College, Department of the Arts, Schenectady NY (S)

Wilson, Jack, *Asst to Exhib Coordr*, Dartmouth College Museum & Galleries, Hanover NH

Wilson, Jackie, *Dir of Development*, Amarillo Art Center, Amarillo TX

Wilson, Jane, *Educ Dir & Registrar*, Owensboro Museum of Fine Art, Owensboro KY

Wilson, Jay M, *Pres Board of Trustees*, Walters Art Gallery, Baltimore MD

Wilson, John L, *Pres Board of Trustees*, Hoyt Institute of Fine Arts, New Castle PA

Wilson, John M, *Chmn Art Dept*, Hope College, Art Department, Holland MI (S)

Wilson, John M, *Chmn*, Hope College, DeWitt Cultural Center, Holland MI

Wilson, John R, *Prof*, Butte Community College, Humanities Division (III), Oroville CA (S)

Wilson, Karen, *Educ Coordr*, Parkersburg Art Center, Parkersburg WV

Wilson, Kenneth T, *Assoc Prof*, Bloomsburg State College, Department of Art, Bloomsburg PA (S)

Wilson, Lucy, *Art Librn*, Laney College Library, Art Section, Oakland CA

Wilson, Lucy P, *Business Mgr*, Southeastern Center for Contemporary Art, Winston-Salem NC

Wilson, Lysbeth, *Asst Librn*, University of Illinois at Urbana-Champaign, Ricker Library of Architecture and Art, Urbana IL

Wilson, Marc, *Lectr*, University of Kansas, Kress Foundation Department of Art History, Lawrence KS (S)

Wilson, Marc F, *Cur Oriental Art*, William Rockhill Nelson Gallery of Art, Atkins Museum of Fine Art, Kansas City MO

Wilson, Margaret, *Treas*, Essex Art Association, Inc, Essex CT

Wilson, Martha, *Executive Dir*, Franklin Furnace Archive, Inc, New York NY

Wilson, Mary, *Asst Prof*, University of Missouri-Saint Louis, Art Dept, Saint Louis MO (S)

Wilson, Mary, *In Charge Art Coll*, The Bendix Corporation, Southfield MI

Wilson, Owen, *Business Adminr*, Ontario College of Art, Toronto ON (S)

Wilson, Patsy, *Dir Library Services*, Coake County College Library, Art Department, Gainesville TX

Wilson, Reginald, *Chmn of Board*, Your Heritage House, Inc, Detroit MI

Wilson, Sally D, *Pres & Chmn*, Bristol Art Museum, Bristol RI

Wilson, Stanley, *Assoc Prof*, California State Polytechnic University, Pomona, Art Department, Pomona CA (S)

Wilson, Steve, *Dir*, Institute of the Great Plains, Museum of the Great Plains, Lawton OK

Wilson, Wayne, *Display Coordr*, Kelowna Centennial Museum and National Exhibit Centre, Kelowna BC

Wilson, William, *Prof*, State University of New York at Albany, Art Department, Albany NY (S)

Wilson, William H, *Cur of Collections*, John and Mable Ringling Museum of Art, Sarasota FL

Wilton, Andrew, *Cur Prints & Drawings*, Yale University, Yale Center for British Art, New Haven CT

Wilvers, Ed, *Head Dept*, Arkansas Tech University, Department of Art, Russellville AR (S)

Wimbush, Sarah, *Archive & Library*, National Portrait Gallery, London England

Wimmer, Charles, *Assoc Prof*, University of Wisconsin-Stout, Art Department, Menomonie WI (S)

Winans, Martha, *Educational Cur*, La Jolla Museum of Contemporary Art, La Jolla CA

Windham, Richard, *Treas*, Green Hill Art Gallery, Greensboro NC

Wineberg, P J, *Asst Public Relations*, Ashtabula Arts Center, Ashtabula OH

Wineland, Gene, *Chmn*, Pratt Community College, Art Department, Pratt KS (S)

Wineman, Nada, *Cur Coll*, Jacksonville Museum of Arts and Sciences, Jacksonville FL

Winer, Alan, *Asst Dir*, Visual Studies Workshop, Rochester NY

Winer, Donald, *Pres*, Doshi Center for Contemporary Art, Harrisburg PA

Winer, Donald A, *Cur of Fine Arts*, Pennsylvania Historical and Museum Commission, William Penn Memorial Museum, Harrisburg PA

Winer, Helene, *Executive Dir*, Artists Space, New York NY

Winer, Jane, *Head Dept*, University of South Carolina at Aiken, Aiken SC (S)

Winfield, Rodney M, *Prof*, Maryville College, Art Department, Saint Louis MO (S)

Wing, James A, *Asst Prof*, Gogebic Community College, Art Department, Ironwood MI (S)

Wing, Stephen, *Prof*, Mars Hill College, Mars Hill NC (S)

Wink, Jon D, *Chmn*, Stephen F Austin State University, Art Department, Nacogdoches TX (S)

Winker, Dietmar R, *Chmn*, Illinois Institute of Technology, Institute of Design, Chicago IL (S)

Winkler, Dietmar R, *Dean Col*, Southeastern Massachusetts University, College of Visual and Performing Arts, North Dartmouth MA (S)

Winkler, Eldon, *Pres*, American Council for the Arts in Education, Baltimore MD

Winkler, Paul, *Asst Dir*, Museum of New Mexico, Museum of International Folk Art, Santa Fe NM

Winland, Carol, *Pres*, Hampshire County Public Library, Romney WV

Winningham, Geoffrey, *Prof*, Rice University, Department of Art and Art History, Houston TX (S)

Winokur, James, *VPres*, Pittsburgh Plan for Art Gallery, Pittsburgh PA

Winqvist, M, *Head Department of Long-term Loans & Traveling Exhib*, Nationalmuseum, Stockholm Sweden

Winsand, Orvill, *Head*, Carnegie-Mellon University, Department of Art, Pittsburgh PA (S)

Winsett, Merrill, *Chmn of the Board of Trustees*, Amarillo Art Center, Amarillo Art Center Association, Amarillo TX

Winslow, John R, *Assoc Prof*, Catholic University of America, Department of Art, Washington DC (S)

Winter, Gerald G, *Instructor*, University of Miami, Department of Art, Coral Gables FL (S)

Winter, R B, *Secy*, Oxford University, Ashmolean Museum of Art and Archaeology, Oxford England

Winter, W J, *Secy*, Saint Augustine Historical Society, Oldest House and Museums, Saint Augustine FL

Winter, William F, *Pres Board Trustees*, Mississippi Department of Archives and History, Jackson MS

Winterich, Otto C, *Treas*, Stained Glass Association of America, Bronxville NY

Winters, John L, *Assoc Prof*, University of Mississippi, Department of Art, University MS (S)

Winters, Nathan, *Asst Prof*, University of Utah, Art Department, Salt Lake City UT (S)

Wintgens, D, *Cur Modern Art*, Stedelijk Museum de Lakenhal, Leyden Municipal Museum, Leiden Netherlands

Winther, Annemarie, *Asst Cur*, Kunsthalle Bremen, Bremen Art Gallery, Bremen Germany, Federal Republic of

Wioko, Gerhard M, *Chmn*, Holyoke Community College, Department of Art, Holyoke MA (S)

Wipfler, Heinz, *Asst Prof*, Queensborough Community College, Department of Art and Design, Bayside NY (S)

Wirgin, Jan, *Cur*, Ostasiatiska Museet, Museum of Far Eastern Antiquities, Stockholm Sweden

Wirtz, Virginia, *Mus Dir*, Maui Historical Society, Hale Hoikeike, Wailuku HI

Wirz, Dadi, *Asst Prof*, Rice University, Department of Art and Art History, Houston TX (S)

Wisdom, John Minor, *Chief Cur*, Museum of Fine Arts, Houston, Houston TX

Wisdon, Karen, *Art Prof Adminr*, American Stained Glass Institute, Hobbs NM (S)

Wise, Howard, *Pres*, Electronic Arts Intermix, Inc, New York NY

Wise, Lawrence, *Chmn of Fine Arts*, New Mexico Highlands University Art Gallery, Las Vegas NM

Wise, Loren E, *Chmn Dept*, New Mexico Highlands University, Dept of Fine Arts, Las Vegas NM (S)

Wise, R Gordon, *Dir*, Millersville State College, Art Department, Millersville PA (S)

Wise, Susan, *Asst Cur Earlier Paintings & Sculpture*, Art Institute of Chicago, Chicago IL

Wiseman, Howard, *VPres*, Springfield Historical Society, Springfield NJ

Wisherd, Susan, *Chmn*, State University of New York College at New Paltz, Art Education Department, New Paltz NY (S)

Wisnewski, Mary Ward, *Dir*, Spartanburg County Art Association, Spartanburg SC

Wisniowska, Zofia, *Chief Librn*, Muzeum Narodowe, Library, Warsaw Poland

Wisnosky, John, *Chmn Department Art*, University of Hawaii at Manoa, Art Gallery, Honolulu HI

Wisnosky, John, *Chmn*, University of Hawaii at Manoa, Department of Art, Honolulu HI (S)

Wissink, Rita, *Instructor*, Wayne Art Center, Wayne PA (S)

Wistar, Caroline, *Asst Cur*, La Salle College Art Gallery, Philadelphia PA

Witherow, Dale, *Asst Prof*, Mansfield State College, Art Department, Mansfield PA (S)

Withrow, W J, *Dir*, Art Gallery of Ontario, Toronto ON

Witt, David, *Cur*, Harwood Foundation of the University of New Mexico, Taos NM

Witt, E C, *Cur Applied Art*, City Art Gallery, Bristol England

Witt, Ruth E, *Asst Dir*, University of Missouri, Museum of Art and Archaeology, Columbia MO

Witt, Walter, *Instr*, Fresno City College, Art Department, Fresno CA (S)

Wittenberg, Alice E, *Pres*, Walker Art Center, Minneapolis MN

Wittershiem, John, *Instr*, Siena Heights College, Art Department, Adrian MI (S)

Witthoft, Brucia, *Instr*, Framingham State College, Art Department, Framingham MA (S)

Wittmann, Harold M, *Asst Dir*, Fine Arts Museum of the South, Mobile AL

Wittmer, Marcilene, *Instructor*, University of Miami, Department of Art, Coral Gables FL (S)

Witts, Noel, *Head School Expressive Arts*, Leicester Polytechnic, Faculty of Art and Design, Leicester England (S)

Witz, Herbert E, *Pres*, Star-Spangled Banner Flag House Association, Baltimore MD

Witzmann, Hugh, *Head Dept*, St John's University, Art Department, Collegeville MN (S)

Wixon, William D, *Chmn Department Medieval Art*, Metropolitan Museum of Art, New York NY

Wlodarczyk, Joyce Anne, *Instr*, Inter American University of Puerto Rico, Department of Performing Arts, San German PR (S)

W'Niemeijer, J, *Dir Printroom*, Rijksmuseum, State Museum, Amsterdam Netherlands

Wnuk, Martin, *Asst Prof*, Kearney State College, Dept of Art, Kearney NE (S)

Woerner, Sylvia, *Pres*, Leatherstocking Brush and Palette Club Inc, Cooperstown NY

Woitena, Ben, *Instr*, Museum of Fine Arts, Alfred C Glassell Junior School of Art, Houston TX (S)

Wojcik, Gary, *Asst Prof*, Ithaca College, Art Department, Ithaca NY (S)

Wolanin, Barbara, *Instructor*, Trinity College, Department of Fine Arts, Washington DC (S)

Wolber, Paul, *Prof*, Spring Arbor College, Art Department, Spring Arbor MI (S)

Wolcott, Edward, *Treas*, Irene Leache Memorial, Norfolk VA

Wold, William, *Assoc Prof*, University of South Dakota, Dept of Art, Vermillion SD (S)

Woldbye, Vibeke, *Keeper*, Det Danske Kunstindustrimuseum, Museum of Decorative Art, Copenhagen Denmark

Wolf, Arthur H, *Dir*, Millicent Rogers Museum, Taos NM

Wolf, John H, *Chmn of the Board*, Woodmere Art Gallery, Philadelphia PA

Wolf, Karen, *Instr*, Marian College, Art Department, Indianapolis IN (S)

Wolf, Marian, *Asst Librn*, Solomon R Guggenheim Museum, Library, New York NY

Wolf, Patricia, *Cur of Education*, Anchorage Historical and Fine Arts Museum, Anchorage AK

Wolf, Sara, *Librn*, Mint Museum of Art, Library, Charlotte NC

Wolf, Tom, *Cur*, Bard College, William Cooper Procter Art Center, Annandale-on-Hudson NY

Wolfe, Judith, *Cur*, Guild Hall of East Hampton, Inc, Museum Section, East Hampton NY

Wolfe, Townsend, *Exec Dir*, Arkansas Arts Center, Little Rock AR

Wolfe Jr, Robert, *Prof*, Miami University, Art Department, Oxford OH (S)

Wolfe III, Townsend D, *Exec Dir*, Arkansas Arts Center, Little Rock AR

Wolfram, William R, *Head Dept*, Concordia College, Art Department, Seward NE (S)

Wolfson, Rhoda, *Program Dir*, Jewish Community Center, Center Lobby Gallery, Long Beach CA

Wolf II, Edwin, *Librn*, Library Company of Philadelphia, Philadelphia PA

Wolf III, William W, *Chmn Dept*, Grinnell College, Department of Art, Grinnell IA (S)

Wolkow, Beverly, *Exec Dir*, Iowa State Education Association, Salisbury House, Des Moines IA

Woll, Gerd, *Cur*, City of Oslo Art Collection, Munch Museum, Oslo Norway

Wollowitz, Charles, *Adjunct Asst Prof*, Le Moyne College, Art Department, Syracuse NY (S)

Wolsk, Nancy, *Coordr*, Transylvania College, Morlan Gallery, Lexington KY

Wolter, Ted, *Asst Dir Kirkland Gallery & Art Prof*, Millikin University, Kirkland Gallery, Decatur IL

Womack, Noel, *Pres*, Mississippi Museum of Art, Jackson MS

Womack, William, *Instructor*, Southwestern at Memphis, Dept of Art, Memphis TN (S)

Wong, Eddie, *Cur*, University of Wisconsin-Stout, Gallery 209, Menomonie WI

Wong, Florence, *Vice Chmn*, Fine Arts Museums of San Francisco, The Museum Society, n of Honor co

Wong, Jason D, *Cur*, Syracuse University, Joe and Emily Lowe Art Gallery, Syracuse NY

Wood, Arthur M, *Chmn Board of Trustees*, Art Institute of Chicago, Chicago IL

Wood, Barbara, *Dir*, Three Schools, Artists Workshop, Toronto ON (S)

Wood, Clifford P, *Sr Asst Humanities Reference Librn*, California State University, Sacramento, Library, Humanities Reference Media Services Ctr, Sacramento CA

Wood, Dan, *Dept Head*, Vermilion Community College, Art Department, Ely MN (S)

Wood, David H, *Dir*, Stockbridge Historical Society, Inc, Stockbridge MA

Wood, James N, *Dir*, Art Institute of Chicago, Chicago IL

Wood, John J, *Deputy Dir*, Minnesota Historical Society, St Paul MN

Wood, Katharine M, *Chief Reference Librn*, University of Delaware, Morris Library, Newark DE

Wood, Leonard E, *Instructor*, Independence Community Junior College, Fine Arts Department, Independence KS (S)

Wood, Marcia J, *Instr*, Kalamazoo College, Art Department, Kalamazoo MI (S)

Wood, Mathilde, *Instr*, Danforth Museum School, Framingham MA (S)

Wood, Richard H, *Keeper of Art*, Lincolnshire Museums, Usher Gallery, Lincoln England

Wood, Roger H, *Asst Prof*, University of Mississippi, Department of Art, University MS (S)

Wood, Steve, *Artist-in-Residence*, Trinity College, Department of Fine Arts, Hartford CT (S)

Wood, William P, *Pres*, Philadelphia Museum of Art, Philadelphia PA

Woodall, William, *Admin*, Joslyn Art Museum, Omaha NE

Woodburn, Steven, *Adjunct Assoc Prof*, New York Institute of Technology, Fine Arts Department, Old Westbury NY (S)

Woodell, Bill, *Asst Dir*, Southeast Arkansas Arts and Science Center, Pine Bluff AR

Wooden, Howard E, *Dir*, Wichita Art Museum, Wichita KS

Woodfall, Amy, *Whistler House Dir*, Lowell Art Association, Whistler House and Parker Gallery, Lowell MA

Woodford, Don, *Instructor*, California State College at San Bernardino, Fine Arts Department, San Bernardino CA (S)

Woodgate-Jones, Katharine, *Conservator*, Auckland City Art Gallery, Auckland New Zealand

Woodger, Carol, *Reference Librn*, Port Chester Public Library, Port Chester NY

Woodhouse, Anne, *Cur Decorative Arts*, State Historical Society of Wisconsin, Madison WI

Woodington, Walter, *Cur*, Royal Academy Schools, Royal Academy of Arts, London England

Woodruff, Marian D, *Dir of Education*, Currier Gallery of Art, Manchester NH

Woods, Arlene, *Head Dept*, Salve Regina the Newport College, Art Department, Newport RI (S)

Woods, Michael, *Dir Fine Art*, Academy of Art College, San Francisco CA (S)

Woods, Michael, *Prof*, University of Maine at Augusta, Division of Arts and Humanities, Augusta ME (S)

Woods, Paula, *Cur of Educ*, Tippecanoe County Historical Museum, Lafayette IN

Woods, Yvette, *Instructor*, Saint Louis Community College at Meramec, Art Dept, Saint Louis MO (S)

Woodson, Doris, *Asst Prof*, Virginia State College, Fine Arts Department, Petersburg VA (S)

Woodward, Crystal, *Instructor*, Sarah Lawrence College, Village des Arts en France du Sarah Lawrence College, Locoste France (S)

Woodward, Emily M, *Grants & Accessibility Coordr*, University of California, Los Angeles, Museum of Cultural History, Los Angeles CA

Woodward, Gary, *Assoc Prof*, Kansas State University, Art Department, Manhattan KS (S)

Woodward, Kesler, *Cur Visual Arts*, Alaska State Museum, Juneau AK

Woodward, Roland H, *Museum Cur*, Historical Society of Delaware, Read House, The Strand, Wilmington DE

Woody, Elsbeth, *Asst Prof*, Bernard M Baruch College of the City University of New York, Art Department, New York NY (S)

Woody, Gorman, *VPres*, Santa Cruz Art League, Inc, Santa Cruz CA

Woody, Howard, *Instr*, University of South Carolina, Department of Art, Columbia SC (S)

Woolard, Robert W, *Publication Dir*, University of California, Los Angeles, Museum of Cultural History, Los Angeles CA

Woolfenden, William E, *Dir*, Archives of American Art, Smithsonian Institution, New York NY

Woolley, John, *Adminr & Technical Dir*, Trinity College, Austin Arts Center, Hartford CT

Woolson, Lawrence B, *Treas*, Springfield Art & Historical Society, Springfield VT

Woolson, Lawrence B, *Pres*, Springfield Art & Historical Society, Springfield VT

Woolworth, Helen, *Pres*, Community Gallery of Lancaster County, Lancaster PA

Wooster, Laurence, *Assoc Prof*, Pittsburg State University, Art Department, Pittsburg KS (S)

Wordell, Edmund M, *Librn*, Newport Historical Society, Library, Newport RI

Worden, Stuart, *Secy*, Dulin Gallery of Art, Knoxville TN

Workman, Reginald, *Coordr Music*, New Muse Community Museum of Brooklyn, Inc, Brooklyn NY

Workman, Robert, *Asst Cur*, Wichita State University, Edwin A Ulrich Museum of Art, Wichita KS

Wormhoundt, Pearl, *Assoc Prof*, William Penn College, Art Department, Oskaloosa IA (S)

Worrall, Helen V, *Assoc Prof*, Miami University, Art Department, Oxford OH (S)

Worrell, Robert, *Instructor*, Ricks College, Department of Art, Rexburg ID (S)

Worsham, Charles E, *Asst Prof*, Lynchburg College, Art Department, Lynchburg VA (S)

Worsley, Dorcas, *Librn*, Tucson Museum of Art, Tucson Museum of Art Library, Tucson AZ

Worsley, Kae, *Exec Secy*, Nova Scotia Association of Architects, Halifax NS

Worst, Harry A, *Prog Dir Art*, Lansing Community College, Performing & Creative Arts Dept, Lansing MI (S)

Worteck, Susan, *Registrar*, University of Maryland, Art Gallery, College Park MD

Worth, Carl, *Cur*, Walnut Creek Civic Arts Gallery, Turlock CA

Worth, Peter, *Chief Acad Advisor*, University of Nebraska-Lincoln, Department of Art, Lincoln NE (S)

Worth, Tim, *Cur*, Manitoba Historical Society, Dalnavert - MacDonald House Museum, Winnipeg MB

Worthen, Bill, *Dir*, Arkansas Territorial Restoration, Little Rock AR

Worthington, Courtenay P, *Pres*, Dedham Historical Society, Dedham MA

Worthington, Netter, *Dean School*, United States International University, School of Performing and Visual Arts, San Diego CA (S)

Worthman, Moses, *VPres*, Allied Artists of America, Inc, New York NY

Wortz, Melinda, *Chmn*, University of California, Irvine, Studio Art Department, Irvine CA (S)

Wortz, Melinda, *Dir*, University of California Irvine Art Gallery, Irvine CA

Wosika, Kathy, *Instr*, Fresno City College, Art Department, Fresno CA (S)

Wost, David, *Instructor*, Sioux City Art Center, Sioux City IA (S)

Woudhuysen, P, *Librn*, University of Cambridge, Department of Manuscripts and Printed Books, Cambridge England

Woudhuysen, P, *Keeper Manuscripts & Printed Books*, University of Cambridge, Fitzwilliam Museum, Cambridge England

Wouthuyzen, E, *Asst Education Department*, Frans Halsmuseum, Frans Hals Museum, Haarlem Netherlands

Wray, Dick, *Instr*, Museum of Fine Arts, Alfred C Glassell Junior School of Art, Houston TX (S)

Wray, George T, *Chmn*, University of Idaho, Department of Art and Architecture, Moscow ID (S)

Wright, C Bagley, *Pres of Board*, Seattle Art Museum, Seattle WA

Wright, David W, *Registrar*, Pierpont Morgan Library, New York NY

Wright, Donald H, *Pres*, Cooper School of Art, Cooper Gallery, Cleveland OH

Wright, Frank C, *Pres*, Council of American Artist Societies, New York NY

Wright, Gerry, *Genealogy*, California Historical Society, Library, San Francisco CA

Wright, Helena, *Librn*, Merrimack Valley Textile Museum, Library, North Andover MA

Wright, James, *Head Fine Arts Library*, University of New Mexico, Fine Arts Library, Albuquerque NM

Wright, Jay, *Dir*, Philbrook Art Center, Tulsa OK

Wright, Michael, *Instructor*, California College of Arts and Crafts, Oakland CA (S)

Wright, Nancy, *Secy*, Vermont State Craft Center at Frog Hollow, Middlebury VT

Wright, Nina, *In Charge Art Program*, Ruder & Finn Fine Arts, New York NY

Wright, Pal T, *Dir*, Ottawa University, Department of Art, Ottawa KS (S)

Wright, Patricia, *Cataloger*, Sweet Briar College, Babcock Art Library, Sweet Briar VA

Wright, Sally, *Secy*, Art Gallery of Peterborough, Peterborough ON

Wright, Stanley Marc, *Dir*, Wright School of Art, Stowe VT (S)

Wright, Vincent, *Prof*, School of the Arts, C W Post Center of Long Island University, Art Department, Greenvale NY (S)

Wright, Virgina M, *Curatorial Asst*, Illinois State University, University Museums, Normal IL

Wright, Virginia L, *Reference Librn*, Corning Museum of Glass, Corning Museum of Glass Library, Corning NY

Wright, W Pope, *Asst Prof*, University of Wisconsin-Superior, Department of Art, Superior WI (S)

Wright, William, *Assoc Dean*, New York Studio School of Drawing, Painting and Sculpture, New York NY (S)

Wrigley, Clifford S, *Prof*, Boston State College, Art Department, Boston MA (S)

Wriston, Barbara, *Dir Museum Education*, Art Institute of Chicago, Chicago IL

Wroblewski, Peggy, *Reference Librn*, University of British Columbia, Fine Arts Division Library, Vancouver BC

Wrolstad, Merald E, *Ed Museum Publications*, Cleveland Museum of Art, Cleveland OH

Wroth, William, *Cur Taylor Mus*, Colorado Springs Fine Arts Center, Colorado Springs CO

Wu, Dorothea, *Head, Art & Music Division*, Queens Borough Public Library, Art and Music Division, Jamaica NY

Wu, Marshall, *Cur of Asian Art*, University of Michigan Museum of Art, Alumni Memorial Hall Museum, Ann Arbor MI

Wu, Marshall P, *Cur Asian Art*, Honolulu Academy of Arts, Honolulu HI

Wu, William, *Lectr*, Mills College, Art Department, Oakland CA (S)

Wulfing, Peter, *VPres*, Keokuk Art Center, Keokuk IA

Wurdemann, Helen, *Dir*, Los Angeles Art Association and Galleries, Los Angeles CA

Wurfbain, M L, *Dir*, Stedelijk Museum de Lakenhal, Leyden Municipal Museum, Leiden Netherlands

Wurmfeld, Sanford, *Chmn Art Dept*, Hunter College, Art Department, New York NY (S)

Wurtele, C Angus, *VPres*, Walker Art Center, Minneapolis MN

Wurtele, Margaret, *Arts Grants Adminr*, Dayton Hudson Corporation, Minneapolis MN

Wyant, Katherine F, *Dir - Cur*, Potsdam Public Museum, Potsdam NY

Wyatt, Stanley, *Prof*, City College of the City of New York, Art Department, New York NY (S)

Wyatt, Susan, *Assoc Dir Services*, Artists Space, New York NY

Wyatt, Susan, *Assoc Dir*, Artists Space, Unaffiliated Artists File, New York NY

Wyckoff, Donald L, *Assoc Dean*, Southampton College of Long Island University, Fine Arts Division, Southampton NY (S)

Wyckoff, Sylvia, *Chmn*, Syracuse University, College of Visual and Performing Arts, Syracuse NY (S)

Wydick, Judy, *Pres*, Pence Gallery, Davis CA

Wyle, Edith R, *Prog Dir*, Craft and Folk Art Museum, Los Angeles CA

Wylo, Martin, *Chief Restorer*, National Gallery, London England

Wyngaard, Susan, *Dir*, International Museum of Photography at George Eastman House, Archives, Rochester NY

Wynn, Marie, *Prof*, Southampton College of Long Island University, Fine Arts Division, Southampton NY (S)

Wynn, Nancy, *Division Chmn*, Wells College, Department of Art & Art History, Aurora NY (S)

Wynne, Brian J, *Exec Dir*, Industrial Designers Society of America, Washington DC

Wynne, Michael, *Asst Dir*, National Gallery of Ireland, Dublin Ireland

Subject Index

Major subjects are listed first, followed by named collections.

AFRICAN ART

Albion College, Bobbitt Visual Arts Center, Albion MI
Baltimore Museum of Art, Baltimore MD
Bower's Museum, Santa Ana CA
Brandeis University, Rose Art Museum, Waltham MA
Dallas Museum of Fine Arts, Dallas TX
Detroit Institute of Arts, Detroit MI
Durban Art Gallery, Durban South Africa, Republic of
Everhart Museum of Natural History, Science and Art, Scranton PA
Everson Museum of Art, Syracuse NY
Fine Arts Museum of the South, Mobile AL
Fisk University Museum, Nashville TN
Flint Institute of Arts, Flint MI
Florence Museum, Florence SC
Galleries of the Claremont Colleges, Claremont CA
Hampton Institute, College Museum, Hampton VA
Heard Museum, Phoenix AZ
High Museum of Art, Atlanta GA
Hofstra University, Emily Lowe Gallery, Hempstead NY
Howard University Gallery of Art, Washington DC
William Humphreys Art Gallery, Kimberley South Africa, Republic of
Illinois State University, University Museums, Normal IL
Johannesburg Art Gallery, Johannesburg South Africa, Republic of
King George VI Art Gallery, Port South Africa, Republic of
Loch Haven Art Center, Inc, Orlando FL
Marietta College, Grover M Hermann Fine Arts Center, Marietta OH
Milwaukee Public Museum, Milwaukee WI
Minneapolis Institute of Arts, Minneapolis MN
Minnesota Museum of Art, Saint Paul MN
Montreal Museum of Fine Arts, Montreal PQ
Muscatine Art Center, Muscatine IA
Museum, Greenwood SC
Museum of the Philadelphia Civic Center, Philadelphia PA
Museum of the United States Department of the Interior, Washington DC
Museum Rietberg Zurich, Zurich Switzerland
New Muse Community Museum of Brooklyn, Inc, Brooklyn NY
New Orleans Museum of Art, Isaac Delgado Museum, New Orleans LA
North Carolina Central University, Museum of Art, Durham NC
North Carolina Museum of Art, Department of Cultural Resources, Raleigh NC
North Country Museum of Arts, Park Rapids MN
Norwich Free Academy, Slater Memorial Museum & Converse Art Gallery, Norwich CT
Omniplex, Oklahoma City OK
Philbrook Art Center, Tulsa OK

Plains Art Museum, Rourke Art Gallery, Moorhead MN
Plains Art Museum, Main Gallery, Moorhead MN
Pretoria Art Museum, Pretoria South Africa, Republic of
Putnam Museum, Davenport IA
St Lawrence University, Richard F Brush Art Gallery, Canton NY
Schenectady Museum, Schenectady NY
South African National Gallery, Cape South Africa, Republic of
State University of New York College at Purchase, Neuberger Museum, Purchase NY
Tatham Art Gallery, Pietermaritzburg South Africa, Republic of
Topeka Public Library, Topeka KS
University of Delaware, University Art Collections, Newark DE
University of Idaho Museum, Moscow ID
University of Iowa, Museum of Art, Iowa City IA
University of Kentucky, Art Museum, Lexington KY
University of Maryland, Art Gallery, College Park MD
University of Miami, Lowe Art Museum, Coral Gables FL
University of Michigan Museum of Art, Alumni Memorial Hall Museum, Ann Arbor MI
University of Notre Dame, Snite Museum of Art, Notre Dame IN
University of Oklahoma, Museum of Art, Norman OK
University of Oregon, Musuem of Art, Eugene OR
University of Santa Clara, de Saisset Art Gallery and Museum, Santa Clara CA
University of South Florida, University Galleries, Tampa FL
University of Wisconsin-Stout, Gallery 209, Menomonie WI
Williams College, Museum of Art, Williamstown MA

AFRO-AMERICAN ART

DuSable Museum of African American History, Chicago IL
Fisk University Museum, Nashville TN
Florence Museum, Florence SC
Hampton Institute, College Museum, Hampton VA
Howard University Gallery of Art, Washington DC
Museum of the National Center of Afro-American Artists, Boston MA
New Muse Community Museum of Brooklyn, Inc, Brooklyn NY
Scripps College, Clark Humanities Museum, Claremont CA
Store Front Museum, Jamaica NY
Studio Museum in Harlem, New York NY

AMERICAN INDIAN ART

Amerind Foundation, Inc, Dragoon AZ
Anchorage Historical and Fine Arts Museum, Anchorage AK
Atlanta Museum, Atlanta GA
Bacone College Museum, Muskogee OK
Birmingham Museum of Art, Birmingham AL
Bower's Museum, Santa Ana CA
Brandeis University, Rose Art Museum, Waltham MA
Bruce Museum, Greenwich CT
Butler Institute of American Art, Youngstown OH
Carmel Mission Basilica, Carmel CA
Cayuga Museum of History and Art, Auburn NY
Chief Plenty Coups State Monument, Pryor MT
Colby Museum of Art, Waterville ME
Colorado Springs Fine Arts Center, Colorado Springs CO
Dacotah Prairie Museum, Aberdeen SD
Denver Art Museum, Frederic H Douglas Library, Denver CO
Desert Caballeros Western Museum, Wickenburg AZ
Evansville Museum of Arts and Science, Evansville IN
Everhart Museum of Natural History, Science and Art, Scranton PA
Favell Museum of Western Art & Indian Artifacts, Klamath Falls OR
Five Civilized Tribes Museum, Muskogee OK
Flathead Indian Museum, Saint Ignatius MT
Fort Lauderdale Museum of the Arts, Fort Lauderdale FL
Fruitlands Museums, Harvard MA
Gallup Museum of Indian Arts, Church Rock NM
Thomas Gilcrease Institute of American History and Art, Tulsa OK
Hampton Institute, College Museum, Hampton VA
Hartwick College Fine Art Gallery, Yager Museum, Oneonta NY
Harwood Foundation of the University of New Mexico, Taos NM
Hastings Museum, Hastings NE
Heard Museum, Phoenix AZ
Heritage Plantation of Sandwich, Sandwich MA
Historic Burlington County Prison Museum, Mount Holly NJ
Illinois State University, University Museums, Normal IL
Institute of American Indian Arts Museum, Santa Fe NM
Johnson-Humrickhouse Museum, Coshocton OH
Joslyn Art Museum, Omaha NE
Kelly-Griggs House Museum, Pasadena CA
Kiah Museum, Savannah GA
Koshare Indian Museum, Inc, La Junta CO
Legislative Building Art Gallery, Regina SK
Louisiana Arts and Science Center, Baton Rouge LA
Maryhill Museum of Art, Goldendale WA
Milwaukee Public Museum, Milwaukee WI
Minneapolis Institute of Arts, Minneapolis MN

AMERICAN WESTERN ART

ANTHROPOLOGY

ANTIQUITIES - ASSYRIAN

ANTIQUITIES - BYZANTINE

ANTIQUITIES - EGYPTIAN

Heritage Museum, Urbana IL
University of Michigan Museum of Art, Kelsey
Museum of Ancient and Medieval Archaeology,
Ann Arbor MI
University of Missouri, Museum of Art and
Archaeology, Columbia MO
University of North Carolina, The Ackland Art
Museum, Chapel Hill NC
University of Rochester, Memorial Art Gallery,
Rochester NY
University of Utah, Utah Museum of Fine Arts, Salt
Lake City UT
University of Wisconsin, Elvehjem Art Center,
Madison WI
Walters Art Gallery, Baltimore MD
Worcester Art Museum, Worcester MA

ANTIQUITIES - ETRUSCAN

Kestner-Museum, Hannover Germany, Federal
Republic of
Metropolitan Museum of Art, New York NY
Musee du Petit Palais, Municipal Museum, Paris
France
Newark Museum, Newark NJ
Ny Carlsberg Glyptothek, Carlsberg Gallery,
Copenhagen Denmark
Thorvaldsen Museum, Copenhagen Denmark
University of Chicago, Oriental Institute, Chicago IL
University of Missouri, Museum of Art and
Archaeology, Columbia MO
Vassar College Art Gallery, Poughkeepsie NY
Walters Art Gallery, Baltimore MD

ANTIQUITIES - GREEK

Baltimore Museum of Art, Baltimore MD
Beloit College, Theodore Lyman Wright Art Center,
Beloit WI
Benaki Museum, Athens Greece
Berkshire Museum, Pittsfield MA
Bowdoin College, Museum of Art &
Peary-MacMillan Arctic Museum, Brunswick ME
British Museum, London England
Chrysler Museum, Norfolk VA
Cincinnati Art Museum, Cincinnati OH
Cleveland Museum of Art, Cleveland OH
Corcoran Gallery of Art, Washington DC
Courtauld Institute Galleries, London England
Cyprus Museum, Nicosia Cyprus
Fine Arts Museums of San Francisco, M H de
Young Memorial Museum and California Palace of
the Legion of Honor, n of Honor co
Isabella Stewart Gardner Museum, Boston MA
J Paul Getty Museum, Malibu CA
Greco-Roman Museum, Alexandria Egypt
Hammond Museum, Inc, Gloucester MA
Harvard University, William Hayes Fogg Art
Museum, Cambridge MA
Herzog Anton Ulrich-Museum, Medieval Section:
Burg Dankwarderode, Brunswick Germany,
Federal Republic of
James Madison University, Sawhill Gallery,
Harrisonburg VA
Kestner-Museum, Hannover Germany, Federal
Republic of
Metropolitan Museum of Art, New York NY
Milwaukee Art Center, Milwaukee WI
Minneapolis Institute of Arts, Minneapolis MN
Monumenti Musei e Gallerie Pontificie, Vatican
Museums and Galleries, Vatican City Italy
Mount Holyoke College Art Museum, South Hadley
MA
Munson-Williams-Proctor Institute, Museum of Art,
Utica NY
Musee des Beaus-Arts, Palais Saint Pierre, Museum
of Fine Arts, Lyon France
Musee du Petit Palais, Municipal Museum, Paris
France
Musees Royaux d'Art et d'Histoire, Royal Museums
of Art and History, Brussels Belgium
Museum of Fine Arts, Boston MA
Museum of Fine Arts, Houston, Houston TX

Muzeum Narodowe, National Museum, Warsaw
Poland
Narodni Galerie v Prague, National Gallery of
Prague, Prague Czechoslovakia
National Gallery of Ireland, Dublin Ireland
National Museum of Damascus, Damascus Syria
Newark Museum, Newark NJ
Ny Carlsberg Glyptothek, Carlsberg Gallery,
Copenhagen Denmark
Portland Art Association, Museum, Portland OR
Princeton University, Art Museum, Princeton NJ
Queens College of the City University of New York,
Art Collection, Flushing NY
Queen's University, Agnes Etherington Art Centre,
Kingston ON
Rhode Island School of Design, Museum of Art,
Providence RI
Royal Pavilion, Art Gallery and Museums, Art
Gallery and Museum, Brighton England
Saginaw Art Museum, Saginaw MI
Saint Gregory's Abbey and College, Mabee-Gerrer
Museum, Shawnee OK
Santa Barbara Museum of Art, Santa Barbara CA
Seattle Art Museum, Seattle WA
Spencer Museum of Art, Lawrence KS
Staten Island Institute of Arts and Sciences, Staten
Island NY
Szepmuveszet Museum, Museum of Fine Arts,
Budapest Hungary
Tel Aviv Museum, Tel-Aviv Israel
Thorvaldsen Museum, Copenhagen Denmark
Toledo Museum of Art, Toledo OH
University of Cambridge, Fitzwilliam Museum,
Cambridge England
University of Chicago, David and Alfred Smart
Gallery, Chicago IL
University of Illinois, World Heritage Museum,
Champaign IL
University of Illinois at Urbana-Champaign, World
Heritage Museum, Urbana IL
University of Michigan Museum of Art, Kelsey
Museum of Ancient and Medieval Archaeology,
Ann Arbor MI
University of Michigan Museum of Art, Alumni
Memorial Hall Museum, Ann Arbor MI
University of Mississippi, University Museums,
Oxford MS
University of Missouri, Museum of Art and
Archaeology, Columbia MO
University of Vermont, Robert Hull Fleming
Museum, Burlington VT
University of Wisconsin, Elvehjem Art Center,
Madison WI
Vassar College Art Gallery, Poughkeepsie NY
Virginia Museum of Fine Arts, Richmond VA
Walters Art Gallery, Baltimore MD
Williams College, Museum of Art, Williamstown MA
Yale University, Art Gallery, New Haven CT

ANTIQUITIES - ORIENTAL

Atlanta Museum, Atlanta GA
Cincinnati Art Museum, Cincinnati OH
Detroit Institute of Arts, Detroit MI
Harvard University, William Hayes Fogg Art
Museum, Cambridge MA
Kunsthistorisches Museum, Museum of Fine Arts,
Vienna Austria
Musees Royaux d'Art et d'Histoire, Royal Museums
of Art and History, Brussels Belgium
Museum of Fine Arts, Springfield MA
National Museum of Damascus, Damascus Syria
Northwestern College, Ramaker Library Art Gallery,
Orange City IA
Plains Art Museum, Main Gallery, Moorhead MN
Staten Island Institute of Arts and Sciences, Staten
Island NY
Toledo Museum of Art, Toledo OH
University of Illinois, World Heritage Museum,
Champaign IL
Worcester Art Museum, Worcester MA

ANTIQUITIES - PERSIAN

Bob Jones University, Greenville SC
British Museum, London England
Cincinnati Art Museum, Cincinnati OH
Detroit Institute of Arts, Detroit MI
Metropolitan Museum of Art, New York NY
Munson-Williams-Proctor Institute, Museum of Art,
Utica NY
Plains Art Museum, Rourke Art Gallery, Moorhead
MN
Plains Art Museum, Main Gallery, Moorhead MN
University of Chicago, Oriental Institute, Chicago IL
University of Missouri, Museum of Art and
Archaeology, Columbia MO
Walters Art Gallery, Baltimore MD

ANTIQUITIES - ROMAN

Baltimore Museum of Art, Baltimore MD
Berkshire Museum, Pittsfield MA
Bob Jones University, Greenville SC
Bowdoin College, Museum of Art &
Peary-MacMillan Arctic Museum, Brunswick ME
British Museum, London England
Chrysler Museum, Norfolk VA
Cincinnati Art Museum, Cincinnati OH
Cleveland Museum of Art, Cleveland OH
Courtauld Institute Galleries, London England
Cyprus Museum, Nicosia Cyprus
Dade County Art Museum, Vizcaya Museum and
Gardens, Miami FL
Detroit Institute of Arts, Detroit MI
Fine Arts Museums of San Francisco, M H de
Young Memorial Museum and California Palace of
the Legion of Honor, n of Honor co
Franciscan Monastery, Holy Land of America,
Washington DC
Galleria Degli Uffizi, Uffizi Gallery, Florence Italy
Galleria e Museo del Palazzo Ducale, Gallery and
Museum of the Palazzo Ducale, Mantua Italy
Isabella Stewart Gardner Museum, Boston MA
J Paul Getty Museum, Malibu CA
Greco-Roman Museum, Alexandria Egypt
Hammond Museum, Inc, Gloucester MA
Harvard University, William Hayes Fogg Art
Museum, Cambridge MA
Herzog Anton Ulrich-Museum, Medieval Section:
Burg Dankwarderode, Brunswick Germany,
Federal Republic of
James Madison University, Sawhill Gallery,
Harrisonburg VA
Johns Hopkins University, Archaeological Collection,
Baltimore MD
Kestner-Museum, Hannover Germany, Federal
Republic of
Metropolitan Museum of Art, New York NY
Milwaukee Art Center, Milwaukee WI
Minneapolis Institute of Arts, Minneapolis MN
Monumenti Musei e Gallerie Pontificie, Vatican
Museums and Galleries, Vatican City Italy
Mount Holyoke College Art Museum, South Hadley
MA
Musee des Beaus-Arts, Palais Saint Pierre, Museum
of Fine Arts, Lyon France
Musee du Petit Palais, Municipal Museum, Paris
France
Musee National, National Museum of Lebanon,
Beirut Lebanon
Musees Communaux Beaux-Arts et Archeologie,
Community Museum of Fine Arts and
Archaeology, Verviers Belgium
Musei Capitolini, Museum of Sculpture, Rome Italy
Museo Civico di Torino, Municipal Museum, Turin
Italy
Museo de Bellas Artes, Museum of Fine Arts, Bilbao
Spain
Museo Nazionale di San Martino, National Museum,
Naples Italy
Museo Nazionale di Villa Guinigi, National Museum
of Villa Guinigi, Lucca Italy
Museum and Picture Gallery, Baroda India
Museum of Fine Arts, Boston MA
Museum of Fine Arts, Houston, Houston TX

ARCHAEOLOGY

ARCHITECTURE

ASIAN ART

BAROQUE ART

Gables FL
University of Notre Dame, Snite Museum of Art, Notre Dame IN

BRONZES

American University of Beirut, Archaeological Museum, Beirut Lebanon
Anderson House Museum, Society of the Cincinnati, Washington DC
Atlanta Museum, Atlanta GA
Baltimore Museum of Art, Baltimore MD
Bayerisches Nationalmuseum, Bavarian National Museum, Munich Germany, Federal Republic of
Chesterwood, Stockbridge MA
College of Wooster Art Center Museum, Wooster OH
Concordia College, Fine Arts Galleries, Milwaukee WI
Corcoran Gallery of Art, Washington DC
Dade County Art Museum, Vizcaya Museum and Gardens, Miami FL
Diamond M Foundation Museum, Snyder TX
Franciscan Monastery, Holy Land of America, Washington DC
Franklin Mint Corp Museum, Franklin Center PA
Freer Gallery of Art, Washington DC
Frick Collection, New York NY
Hall of Fame of the Trotter, Goshen NY
Harvard University, William Hayes Fogg Art Museum, Cambridge MA
Hermitage Foundation Museum, Norfolk VA
Indianapolis Museum of Art, Indianapolis IN
Indian Museum, Calcutta India
Kansas State Historial Society Museum, Topeka KS
Loyala University of Chigago, Martin D'Arcy Gallery of Art, Chicago IL
Musee du Petit Palais, Municipal Museum, Paris France
Museen der Stadt Köln, Museum für Ostasiatische Kunst, Cologne Germany, Federal Republic of
Musei Capitolini, Museum of Sculpture, Rome Italy
Museo Civico di Padua, Municipal Museum, Padua Italy
Museo d'Arte Antica, Civiche Raccolte de Arte Applicata, Milan Italy
Museo Nazionale di San Martino, National Museum, Naples Italy
Museo Nazionale Romano, National Museum of Rome, Rome Italy
Museo Poldi Pezzoli, Poldi Pezzoli Museum, Milan Italy
Museum fur Kunstandwerk, Museum of Arts and Crafts, Frankfurt Germany, Federal Republic of
National Cowboy Hall of Fame and Western Heritage Center, Oklahoma City OK
National Hall of Fame for Famous American Indians, Anadarko OK
National Museum of INdia, New Delhi India
National Museum of Korea, Seoul Korea
National Museum of Racing, Inc, Saratoga Springs NY
William Rockhill Nelson Gallery of Art, Atkins Museum of Fine Art, Kansas City MO
Norton Gallery and School of Art, West Palm Beach FL
Oxford University, Ashmolean Museum of Art and Archaeology, Oxford England
Plymouth City Museum and Art Gallery, Plymouth England
Portland Art Association, Museum, Portland OR
Princeton University, Art Museum, Princeton NJ
Queens College of the City University of New York, Art Collection, Flushing NY
Remington Art Museum, Ogdensburg NY
Rockwell-Corning Museum, Corning NY
Rollins College, George D and Harriet W Cornell Fine Arts Center Museum, Winter Park FL
Saint Louis Art Museum, Saint Louis MO
Springville Museum of Art, Springville UT
Thorvaldsen Museum, Copenhagen Denmark
University of Iowa, Museum of Art, Iowa City IA
University of Michigan Museum of Art, Kelsey Museum of Ancient and Medieval Archaeology,

Ann Arbor MI
University of Southwestern Louisiana, Art Center for Southwestern Louisiana, Lafayette LA
Victoria and Albert Museum, London England
Virginia Museum, Danville Museum of Fine Arts and History, Danville VA
Virginia Museum of Fine Arts, Richmond VA
Wadsworth Atheneum, Hartford CT
World Museum & Art Centre, Osborn Foundation, Tulsa OK

CALLIGRAPHY

La Casa del Libro, House of Books, San Juan PR
Lahore Museum, Lahore Pakistan
National Museum of Korea, Seoul Korea
Saint John's University, Chung-Cheng Art Gallery, Jamaica NY
George Walter Vincent Smith Art Museum, Springfield MA
Topkapi Saray Museum, Istanbul Turkey

CARPETS & RUGS

Dade County Art Museum, Vizcaya Museum and Gardens, Miami FL
Department of State, Diplomatic Reception Rooms, Washington DC
Det Danske Kunstindustrimuseum, Museum of Decorative Art, Copenhagen Denmark
Hermitage Foundation Museum, Norfolk VA
Huntington Galleries, Huntington WV
Iowa State Education Association, Salisbury House, Des Moines IA
Museo Poldi Pezzoli, Poldi Pezzoli Museum, Milan Italy
Museu Nacional de Arte Antiga, National Museum of Ancient Art, Lisbon Portugal
National Museum of Pakistan, Karachi Pakistan
Panstwowe Zbiory Sztuki na Wawelu, Wawel State Collections of Art, Cracow Poland
Portland Art Association, Museum, Portland OR
The Rosenbach Museum and Library, Philadelphia PA
Sierra Nevada Museum of Art, Reno NV
George Walter Vincent Smith Art Museum, Springfield MA
State Museum of Oriental Art, Moscow Ussr
Topkapi Saray Museum, Istanbul Turkey
Turk ve Islam Eserleri Muzesi, Museum of Turkish and Islamic Art, Istanbul Turkey
Victoria and Albert Museum, London England
Woodmere Art Gallery, Philadelphia PA

CARTOONS

Hartwick College Fine Art Gallery, Oneonta NY
Herbert Hoover Presidential Library, West Branch IA
Kansas State Historial Society Museum, Topeka KS
Pavilion of Humour, Man and His World, Montreal PQ
Harry S Truman Library and Museum, Independence MO

CERAMICS

Albany Institute of History and Art, Albany NY
Albion College, Bobbitt Visual Arts Center, Albion MI
American Swedish Institute, Minneapolis MN
Anderson House Museum, Society of the Cincinnati, Washington DC
Art Gallery of Western Australia, Perth Australia
Baltimore Museum of Art, Baltimore MD
Bayerisches Nationalmuseum, Bavarian National Museum, Munich Germany, Federal Republic of
Berea College, Art Department Gallery, Berea KY
Birmingham Museums and Art Gallery, Birmingham England
Brandeis University, Rose Art Museum,

Waltham MA
Buten Museum of Wedgwood, Merion PA
Butler Institute of American Art, Youngstown OH
California State Fair and Exposition Art Show, Sacramento CA
California State University, Chico, Art Gallery, Chico CA
Calvin College Center Art Gallery, Grand Rapids MI
Charleston Museum, Charleston SC
Chester County Historical Society, West Chester PA
City Art Gallery, Bristol England
Cleveland Museum of Art, Cleveland OH
College of Saint Benedict, Art Gallery, Saint Joseph MN
Columbus Museum of Art, Columbus OH
Concordia College, Koenig Art Gallery, Seward NE
Cranbrook Academy of Art Museum, Bloomfield Hills MI
Creighton University Art Gallery, Omaha NE
DAR Museum, National Society Daughters of the American Revolution, Washington DC
Doncaster Museum and Art Gallery, Doncaster England
Drexel University Art Gallery and Museum Collection, Philadelphia PA
Durban Art Gallery, Durban South Africa, Republic of
Ella Sharp Museum, Jackson MI
Essex Institute, Salem MA
Everson Museum of Art, Syracuse NY
Franciscan Monastery, Holy Land of America, Washington DC
Fries Museum, Leeuwarden Netherlands
George Peabody College for Teachers, Cohen Memorial Museum of Art, Nashville TN
Goucher College, Kraushaar Auditorium Lobby Gallery, Towson MD
Groningen Museum voor Stad en Land, Groningen Museum, Groningen Netherlands
Haaretz Museum, Tel-Aviv Israel
Harrison County Historical Museum, Marshall TX
Harvard University, William Hayes Fogg Art Museum, Cambridge MA
Haystack Mountain School of Crafts Gallery, Deer Isle ME
Historic Deerfield Inc, Deerfield MA
Honolulu Academy of Arts, Honolulu HI
Indianapolis Museum of Art, Indianapolis IN
Indian Museum, Calcutta India
Institut de France, Musee Conde, Paris France
Institute of American Indian Arts Museum, Santa Fe NM
Iowa State University, Brunnier Gallery, Ames IA
Jacksonville Art Museum, Jacksonville FL
Johannesburg Art Gallery, Johannesburg South Africa, Republic of
King George VI Art Gallery, Port South Africa, Republic of
Kunsthistorisches Museum, Museum of Fine Arts, Vienna Austria
Kunstindustrimuseet I Oslo, Oslo Museum of Applied Art, Oslo Norway
Leeds Art Galleries, Leeds England
Lemoyne Art Foundation, Tallahassee FL
Lincolnshire Museums, Usher Gallery, Lincoln England
Mercer County Community College Gallery, Trenton NJ
Minnesota Museum of Art, Saint Paul MN
James Monroe Law Office - Museum and Memorial Library, Fredericksburg VA
Moravska Galerie v Brne, Moravian Gallery at Brno, Brno Czechoslovakia
Mount Saint Vincent University Art Gallery, Halifax NS
Municipality of Beit-Shan, Municipal Beit-Shan-Museum, Beit-Shan Israel
Musee d'Art de Saint-Laurent, Saint-Laurent PQ
Musee des Beaus-Arts, Palais Saint Pierre, Museum of Fine Arts, Lyon France
Musee des Beaux-Arts de Lille, Museum of Fine Arts, Lille France
Musee du Petit Palais, Municipal Museum, Paris France

COINS & MEDALS

COSTUMES

CRAFTS

Tempe AZ
Bucks County Historical Society Mercer Museum, Doylestown PA
College of Saint Benedict, Art Gallery, Saint Joseph MN
Confederation Centre Art Gallery and Museum, Charlottetown PE
Contemporary Crafts Association and Gallery, Portland OR
Craft and Folk Art Museum, Los Angeles CA
Craft Center Museum, Wilton CT
East Tennessee State University, Carroll Reece Museum, Johnson City TN
Evansville Museum of Arts and Science, Evansville IN
Favell Museum of Western Art & Indian Artifacts, Klamath Falls OR
Fine Arts Museum of the South, Mobile AL
Greenfield Village and Henry Ford Museum, Dearborn MI
Institute of American Indian Arts Museum, Santa Fe NM
Kyoto Kokuritsu Kindai Bijutsukan, National Museum of Modern Art, Kyoto, Kyoto Japan
Long Beach Museum of Art, Long Beach CA
Marietta College, Grover M Hermann Fine Arts Center, Marietta OH
Massillon Museum, Massillon OH
Carrie McLain Museum, Nome AK
Milwaukee Area Technical College, Kronquist Craft Gallery, Milwaukee WI
Minnesota Museum of Art, Saint Paul MN
Minot Art Gallery, Minot Art Association, Minot ND
Moose Jaw Art Museum and National Exhibition Centre, Moose Jaw SK
Museen der Stadt Köln, Kunstgewerbemuseum, Cologne Germany, Federal Republic of
Museo Cerralbo, Madrid Spain
Museo Nacional de Arqueologia, National Museum, La Paz Bolivia
Museum of the Plains Indian, Browning MT
Mystic Seaport Museum, Inc, Mystic CT
New Bedford Whaling Museum, New Bedford MA
Noord-Brabants Museum, Hertogenbosch Netherlands
Nordiska Museet, Scandinavian Museum, Stockholm Sweden
Oakland Museum, Oakland CA
Principia College, School of Nations Museum, Elsah IL
Lauren Rogers Library and Museum of Art, Laurel MS
San Diego State University, Art Gallery, San Diego CA
Taras H Schevchenko Museum and Memorial Park Foundation, Oakville ON
Schweizerisches Landesmuseum, Swiss National Museum, Zurich Switzerland
Sioux Indian Museum, Rapid City SD
Southern Plains Indian Museum, Anadarko OK
Southwest Museum, Los Angeles CA
Tacoma Art Museum, Tacoma WA
Tokyo Kokuritsu Kindai Bujutsukan, National Museum of Modern Art, Tokyo, Tokyo Japan
Tokyo-To Bijutsukan, Tokyo Metropolitan Art Museum, Tokyo Japan
Ukrainian Museum of Canada, Edmonton AB
Vermont State Craft Center at Frog Hollow, Middlebury VT
Vestlandske Kunstindustrimuseum, Western Norway Museum of Applied Art, Bergen Norway
Worcester Craft Center Gallery, Worcester MA
World Museum & Art Centre, Osborn Foundation, Tulsa OK

DECORATIVE ARTS

Albuquerque Museum of Art, History and Science, Albuquerque NM
Lyman Allyn Museum, New London CT
Arkansas Arts Center, Little Rock AR
Art Gallery of Greater Victoria, Victoria BC
Art Institute of Chicago, Chicago IL

Athenaeum of Philadelphia, Philadelphia PA
Atlanta Museum, Atlanta GA
Augusta Richmond County Museum, Augusta GA
Baltimore Museum of Art, Baltimore MD
Bayerisches Nationalmuseum, Bavarian National Museum, Munich Germany, Federal Republic of
Beaumont Art Museum, Beaumont TX
Beloit College, Theodore Lyman Wright Art Center, Beloit WI
Bower's Museum, Santa Ana CA
Bowne House, Flushing NY
Campus Martius Museum and Ohio River Museum, Marietta OH
Canton Art Institute, Canton OH
Carnegie Institute, Museum of Art, Pittsburgh PA
Center for Inter-American Relations Art Gallery, New York NY
Charleston Museum, Charleston SC
Chesterwood, Stockbridge MA
Chicago Historical Society, Chicago IL
Church of Jesus Christ of Latter-Day Saints, Information Center and Museum, Arts and Sites Division, Salt Lake City UT
Cincinnati Art Museum, Cincinnati OH
City of Oslo Art Collection, Munch Museum, Oslo Norway
Cleveland Museum of Art, Cleveland OH
College of the Americas, Museum of the Americas, Brookfield VT
Colombian Institute of Culture, Museum of Colonial Art, Bogota Colombia
Columbia County Historical Society, House of History and Van Alen House, Kinderhook NY
Columbia Museums of Art and Science, Columbia SC
Connecticut Valley Historical Museum, Springfield MA
Cooper-Hewitt Museum, Smithsonian Institution National Museum of Design, New York NY
Cranbrook Academy of Art Museum, Bloomfield Hills MI
Crocker Art Museum, Sacramento CA
Cummer Gallery of Art, DeEtte Holden Cummer Museum Foundation, Jacksonville FL
Currier Gallery of Art, Manchester NH
Custom House Maritime Museum, Newburyport MA
Deming Luna Mimbres Museum, Deming NM
Department of Culture, Government of the Province of Alberta, Provincial Museum of Alberta, Edmonton AB
Det Danske Kunstindustrimuseum, Museum of Decorative Art, Copenhagen Denmark
Detroit Institute of Arts, Detroit MI
Division of Historical and Cultural Affairs, Bureau of Museums and Historic Sites, Dover DE
Drexel University Art Gallery and Museum Collection, Philadelphia PA
El Paso Museum of Art, El Paso TX
Evansville Museum of Arts and Science, Evansville IN
Farmington Museum, Stanley-Whitman House, Farmington CT
William A Farnsworth Library and Art Museum, Rockland ME
Fetherston Foundation, Packwood House Museum, Lewisburg PA
Fine Arts Museum of the South, Mobile AL
Fine Arts Museums of San Francisco, M H de Young Memorial Museum and California Palace of the Legion of Honor, n of Honor co
Flint Institute of Arts, Flint MI
Francis E Fowler Jr Foundation Museum, Beverly Hills CA
Gemeentemuseum Arnhem, Municipal Museum of Arnhem, Arnhem Netherlands
J Paul Getty Museum, Malibu CA
Grand Rapids Art Museum, Grand Rapids MI
Greenfield Village and Henry Ford Museum, Dearborn MI
Gunston Hall Plantation, Lorton VA
Haags Gemeentemuseum, Municipal Museum of The Hague, The Hague Netherlands
Harvard University, Dumbarton Oaks Research Library and Collections, Washington DC
Harvard University, William Hayes Fogg Art

Museum, Cambridge MA
Hermitage Foundation Museum, Norfolk VA
Herzog Anton Ulrich-Museum, Medieval Section: Burg Dankwarderode, Brunswick Germany, Federal Republic of
High Museum of Art, Atlanta GA
Hispanic Society of America Museum, New York NY
Historical Society of Early American Decoration, Inc, Cooperstown NY
Historic Deerfield Inc, Deerfield MA
Honolulu Academy of Arts, Honolulu HI
Hudson River Museum, Yonkers NY
Huntington Galleries, Huntington WV
Huntington Library, Art Gallery and Botanical Gardens, San Marino CA
Illinois State Museum of Natural History and Art, Springfield IL
Illinois State University, University Museums, Normal IL
Independence National Historical Park, Philadelphia PA
Indianapolis Museum of Art, Indianapolis IN
Johnson-Humrickhouse Museum, Coshocton OH
Joslyn Art Museum, Omaha NE
Annie S Kemerer Museum, Bethlehem PA
Leeds Art Galleries, Leeds England
Leicestershire Museums, Art Galleries and Records Service, Leicestershire Museum and Art Gallery, Leicester England
Litchfield Historical Society, Litchfield CT
Longfellow's Wayside Inn, South Sudbury MA
Los Angeles County Museum of Art, Los Angeles CA
Louisiana State Museum, New Orleans LA
Louisiana State University, Anglo-American Art Museum, Baton Rouge LA
L'Universite Laval, Ecole des Arts Visuels de L'Universite Laval, Quebec PQ
Macdonald Steward Art Centre, Guelph ON
Madison County Historical Society, Oneida NY
Marquette University, Marquette Fine Art Collection, Milwaukee WI
McGill University, McCord Museum, Montreal PQ
Metropolitan Museum of Art, New York NY
Miami University Art Museum, Oxford OH
Minneapolis Institute of Arts, Minneapolis MN
Mint Museum of Art, Charlotte NC
Montreal Museum of Fine Arts, Montreal PQ
Morris-Butler Museum of High Victorian Decorative Arts, Indianapolis IN
Morris Museum of Arts and Sciences, Morristown NJ
Mount Clare Mansion, Baltimore MD
Munson-Williams-Proctor Institute, Museum of Art, Utica NY
Muscatine Art Center, Muscatine IA
Musee du Louvre, Louvre Museum, Paris France
Musees d'Archeologie et d'Arts Decoratifs, Liege Museums of Archeology and Decorative Arts, Liege Belgium
Museo Nacional de Arte Decorativo, National Museum of Decorative Art, Buenos Aires Argentina
Museo Poldi Pezzoli, Poldi Pezzoli Museum, Milan Italy
Museo Romantico, Museum of the Romantic Epoch, Madrid Spain
Museum Mayer van den Bergh, Antwerp Belgium
Museum of American Folk Art, New York NY
Museum of Arts and History, Port Huron MI
Museum of Arts and Sciences, Cuban Museum, Planetarium, Daytona Beach FL
Museum of Early Southern Decorative Arts, Old Salem Inc, Winston-Salem NC
Museum of Fine Arts, Boston MA
Museum of Fine Arts, Houston, Houston TX
Museum of Fine Arts of Saint Petersburg, Florida, Inc, Saint Petersburg FL
Museum of the American China Trade, Milton MA
Museum of the American Indian, New York NY
Museum of the City of New York, New York NY
Museums at Stony Brook, Stony Brook NY
Museu Nacional de Arte Antiga, National Museum of Ancient Art, Lisbon Portugal

McMaster University Art Gallery, Hamilton ON
Meridian Museum of Art, Meridian MS
Middlebury College, Johnson Gallery, Middlebury VT
Millikin University, Kirkland Gallery, Decatur IL
Mills College, Art Gallery, Oakland CA
Ministry of Culture and Art, Museum of Architecture in Wroclaw, Wroclaw Poland
Minneapolis Institute of Arts, Minneapolis MN
Minnesota Museum of Art, Saint Paul MN
Mississippi University for Women, Art Gallery and Museum, Columbus MS
Montclair Art Museum, Montclair NJ
Mount Holyoke College Art Museum, South Hadley MA
Muiska-Museum, Munich Germany, Federal Republic of
Munson-Williams-Proctor Institute, Museum of Art, Utica NY
Musee de L'Oeuvre Notre Dame, Cathedral Museum, Strasbourg France
Musee des Beaus-Arts, Palais Saint Pierre, Museum of Fine Arts, Lyon France
Musee des Beaux-Arts, Rennes France
Musee du Louvre, Louvre Museum, Paris France
Musee du Petit Palais, Municipal Museum, Paris France
Museo Cerralbo, Madrid Spain
Museo d'Arte Antica, Museum of Ancient Art, Milan Italy
Museo de Bellas Artes, Museum of Fine Arts, Caracas Venezuela
Museo de Capodimonte, Mount Capodi Museum, Naples Italy
Museo del Prado, National Museum of Paintings and Sculpture, Madrid Spain
Museo Nacional de Artes Plasticas, National Museum of Fine Arts, Montevideo Uruguay
Museum Boymans-Van Beuningen, Rotterdam Netherlands
Museum Het Rembrandthuis, Rembrandthouse Museum, Amsterdam Netherlands
Museum of American Folk Art, New York NY
Museum of Arts and Sciences, Inc, Macon GA
Museum of Fine Arts of Saint Petersburg, Florida, Inc, Saint Petersburg FL
Museum of Modern Art, Belgrade Yugoslavia
Museum of Modern Art, Haifa Israel
Museum of Modern Art, New York NY
Museum voor Schone Kunsten, Ghent Belgium
Muzeum Narodowe, National Museum, Warsaw Poland
Nasjonalgalleriet, National Gallery, Oslo Norway
National Air and Space Museum, Washington DC
National Collection of Fine Arts, Washington DC
National Galleries of Scotland, National Gallery of Scotland, Edinburgh Scotland
National Pinakothiki and Alexander Soutzos Museum, Athens Greece
National Portrait Gallery, London England
New Haven Colony Historical Society, New Haven CT
Newport Museum and Art Gallery, Newport Wales
Oakland Museum, Oakland CA
Offentliche Kunstsammlung-Kunstmuseum Basel, Museum of Fine Arts, Basel Switzerland
Oklahoma Art Center, Oklahoma City OK
Olana Historic Site, Hudson NY
Owensboro Museum of Fine Art, Owensboro KY
Oxford University, Ashmolean Museum of Art and Archaeology, Oxford England
Pavilion of Humour, Man and His World, Montreal PQ
Pennsylvania Academy of the Fine Arts, Philadelphia PA
Pennsylvania State University, Museum of Art, University Park PA
Phillips Academy, Addison Gallery of American Art, Andover MA
Pinacoteca di Brera, Brera Picture Gallery, Milan Italy
Plains Art Museum, Main Gallery, Moorhead MN
Plymouth City Museum and Art Gallery, Plymouth England
Portland Art Association, Museum, Portland OR

Quincy College, Art Gallery, Quincy IL
Reed College Art Gallery, Portland OR
Rijksmuseum, State Museum, Amsterdam Netherlands
John and Mable Ringling Museum of Art, Sarasota FL
Roberson Center, Binghamton NY
The Rosenbach Museum and Library, Philadelphia PA
Saint Louis Art Museum, Saint Louis MO
Saltzburger Museum Carolino Augusteum, Salzburg Museum, Salzburg Austria
San Jose Museum of Art, San Jose CA
Santa Barbara Museum of Art, Santa Barbara CA
Sefton Metropolitan Borough, Atlinson Art Gallery, Southport England
Shaker Museum, Poland Spring ME
Slovenska Narodna Galeria, Slovak National Gallery, Bratislava Czechoslovakia
Smith College, Museum of Art, Northampton MA
South African National Gallery, Cape South Africa, Republic of
Southern Alleghenies Museum of Art, Loretto PA
Southern Illinois University Museum and Art Galleries, Carbondale IL
South London Art Gallery, London England
Springfield Art Museum, Springfield MO
Staatliche Graphische Sammlung, National Graphic Collection, Munich Germany, Federal Republic of
Stadelsches Kunstinstitut, Staedel Art Institute, Frankfurt Germany, Federal Republic of
Stadtische Gallerie im Lanbachhaus, Lenbach House City Gallery, Munich Germany, Federal Republic of
Staten Island Ferry Maritime Museum, Staten Island NY
Statens Museum for Kunst, Den Kongelige Kobberstiksamling, Copenhagen Denmark
State University of New York at Albany, University Art Gallery, Albany NY
State University of New York College at Potsdam, Brainerd Art Gallery, Potsdam NY
State University of New York College at Purchase, Neuberger Museum, Purchase NY
Stedlijk Museum-Amsterdam, Municipal Museum, Amsterdam Netherlands
Szepmuveszet Museum, Museum of Fine Arts, Budapest Hungary
Telfair Academy of Arts and Sciences Inc, Savannah GA
Teylers Museum, Haarlem Netherlands
Thorvaldsen Museum, Copenhagen Denmark
Tokyo Kokuritsu Kindai Bujutsukan, National Museum of Modern Art, Tokyo, Tokyo Japan
Turun Taidemuseo, Turku Art Museum, Turku Finland
Ulster County Community College, Visual Arts Gallery, Stone Ridge NY
United States Naval Academy Museum, Annapolis MD
University of California, Los Angeles, Grunwald Center for the Graphic Arts, Los Angeles CA
University of Cambridge, Fitzwilliam Museum, Cambridge England
University of Colorado Art Galleries, Boulder CO
University of Georgia, Georgia Museum of Art, Athens GA
University of Illinois, Krannert Art Museum, Champaign IL
University of Iowa, Museum of Art, Iowa City IA
University of Louisville, Allen R Hite Art Institute, Louisville KY
University of Manchester, Whitworth Art Gallery, Manchester England
University of Massachusetts, Amherst, University Gallery, Amherst MA
University of Minnesota, University Gallery, Minneapolis MN
University of Mississippi, University Museums, Oxford MS
University of Missouri, Museum of Art and Archaeology, Columbia MO
University of Nebraska Lincoln, Sheldon Memorial Art Gallery, Lincoln NE
University of New Mexico, University Art Museum, Albuquerque NM
University of North Carolina, The Ackland Art Museum, Chapel Hill NC
University of North Carolina at Greensboro, Weatherspoon Art Gallery, Greensboro NC
University of Notre Dame, Snite Museum of Art, Notre Dame IN
University of Pittsburgh, University Art Gallery, Pittsburgh PA
University of Southern Colorado, Pueblo CO
University of South Florida, University Galleries, Tampa FL
University of Texas at Austin, University Art Museum, Austin TX
University of Vermont, Robert Hull Fleming Museum, Burlington VT
University of Washington, Henry Art Gallery, Seattle WA
University of Wisconsin, Allen Priebe Gallery, Oshkosh WI
University of Wisconsin-Stout, Gallery 209, Menomonie WI
Valparaiso University, University Art Galleries and Collections, Valparaiso IN
Vassar College Art Gallery, Poughkeepsie NY
Victoria and Albert Museum, London England
Wadsworth Atheneum, Hartford CT
Walker Art Gallery, Liverpool England
Washington County Museum of Fine Arts, Hagerstown MD
Westminster College Art Gallery, New Wilmington PA
Whitney Museum of American Art, New York NY
Wichita Art Museum, Wichita KS
Williams College, Museum of Art, Williamstown MA
Wolfgang-Gurlitt-Museum, Neue Galerie der Stadt Linz, Linz Austria
York City Art Gallery, York England

EMBROIDERY

Baltimore Museum of Art, Baltimore MD
Historic Deerfield Inc, Deerfield MA
Topkapi Saray Museum, Istanbul Turkey
Ukrainian National Museum & Library, Chicago IL
Victoria and Albert Museum, London England
West Baton Rouge Museum, Port Allen LA

ENAMELS

California State Fair and Exposition Art Show, Sacramento CA
Indian Museum, Calcutta India
Loyala University of Chigago, Martin D'Arcy Gallery of Art, Chicago IL
Manchester City Art Galleries, Manchester England
Museo de Arte—Jose Luis Bello y Gonzales, Museum of Art, Puebla Mexico
National Museum of Wales, Cardiff Wales
Victoria and Albert Museum, London England

ESKIMO ART

Alaska State Museum, Juneau AK
Anchorage Historical and Fine Arts Museum, Anchorage AK
Art Gallery of Western Australia, Perth Australia
Beaumont Art Museum, Beaumont TX
Eskimo Museum, Churchill MB
Johnson-Humrickhouse Museum, Coshocton OH
Louisiana Arts and Science Center, Baton Rouge LA
Macdonald Steward Art Centre, Guelph ON
Carrie McLain Museum, Nome AK
Museum of the United States Department of the Interior, Washington DC
Portland Art Association, Museum, Portland OR
University of Idaho Museum, Moscow ID
Winnipeg Art Gallery, Winnipeg MB
Yugtarvik Regional Museum, Bethel AK

Gardens, San Marino CA
Hyde Collection, Glens Falls NY
Indianapolis Museum of Art, Indianapolis IN
Iowa State University, Brunnier Gallery, Ames IA
Jekyll Island National Historic Landmark, Jekyll
 Island GA
Kelly-Griggs House Museum, Pasadena CA
Kiah Museum, Savannah GA
Kunstindustrimuseet I Oslo, Oslo Museum of
 Applied Art, Oslo Norway
Longfellow's Wayside Inn, South Sudbury MA
Lyndhurst, Tarrytown NY
Maryhill Museum of Art, Goldendale WA
Minnesota Museum of Art, Saint Paul MN
James Monroe Law Office - Museum and Memorial
 Library, Fredericksburg VA
Moravska Galerie v Brne, Moravian Gallery at Brno,
 Brno Czechoslovakia
Morris-Butler Museum of High Victorian Decorative
 Arts, Indianapolis IN
Mount Clare Mansion, Baltimore MD
Mount Mary College, Tower Gallery, Milwaukee WI
Mount Vernon, Mount Vernon VA
Musee d'Art de Saint-Laurent, Saint-Laurent PQ
Musee des Beaus-Arts, Palais Saint Pierre, Museum
 of Fine Arts, Lyon France
Musee des Beaux-Arts de Dijon, Museum of Fine
 Arts, Dijon France
Musee du Petit Palais, Municipal Museum, Paris
 France
Musee du Quebec, Quebec PQ
Musee du Seminaire de Quebec, Quebec PQ
Musee Historique de Vaudreuil, Vaudreuil Historial
 Museum, Woodstock PQ
Musee National du Chateau de Fontainebleau,
 National Museum of Fontainebleau, Fontainebleau
 France
Musee National du Chateau de Versailles, National
 Museum of the Chateau de Versailles, Versailles
 France
Musees Royaux d'Art et d'Histoire, Royal Museums
 of Art and History, Brussels Belgium
Museo Cerralbo, Madrid Spain
Museo de Arte, Museum of Art, Lima Peru
Museo Romantico, Museum of the Romantic Epoch,
 Madrid Spain
Museu da Inconfidencia, History of Democratic
 Ideals and Culture in Minas Gerais, Ouro Brazil
Museum Boymans-Van Beuningen, Rotterdam
 Netherlands
Museum fur Kunstandwerk, Museum of Arts and
 Crafts, Frankfurt Germany, Federal Republic of
Museum Mayer van den Bergh, Antwerp Belgium
Museum of American Folk Art, New York NY
Museum of Arts and Sciences, Cuban Museum,
 Planetarium, Daytona Beach FL
Museum of Art, Science and Industry, Bridgeport
 CT
Museum of Early Southern Decorative Arts, Old
 Salem Inc, Winston-Salem NC
Museum of the American China Trade, Milton MA
Museu Nacional de Arte Antiga, National Museum
 of Ancient Art, Lisbon Portugal
Museu Nacional de Soares dos Reis, National
 Museum of Soares Dos Reis, Oporto Portugal
National Trust for Historic Preservation, Washington
 DC
William Rockhill Nelson Gallery of Art, Atkins
 Museum of Fine Art, Kansas City MO
New Bedford Whaling Museum, New Bedford MA
Norwich Free Academy, Slater Memorial Museum &
 Converse Art Gallery, Norwich CT
Oatlands, Leesburg VA
Olana Historic Site, Hudson NY
Old Gaol Museum, York ME
Panstwowe Zbiory Sztuki na Wawelu, Wawel State
 Collections of Art, Cracow Poland
Philadelphia Museum of Art, Philadelphia PA
Philbrook Art Center, Tulsa OK
Henry B Plant Museum, Tampa FL
Quapaw Quarter Association, Inc, Villa Marre, Little
 Rock AR
Remington Art Museum, Ogdensburg NY
Rhode Island School of Design, Museum of Art,
 Providence RI

Roberson Center, Binghamton NY
Rohsska Konstslojdmuseet, Rohss Museum of Arts
 and Crafts, Gothenburg Sweden
Rosicrucian Egyptian Museum and Art Gallery, San
 Jose CA
Royal Pavilion, Art Gallery and Museums,
 Thomas-Stanford Museum, Preston Manor,
 Brighton England
Saltzburger Museum Carolino Augusteum, Salzburg
 Museum, Salzburg Austria
San Diego Museum of Art, San Diego CA
Schweizerisches Landesmuseum, Swiss National
 Museum, Zurich Switzerland
Shaker Museum, Poland Spring ME
Shirley Plantation, Charles City VA
Stedelyke Musea, City Museums, Bruges Belgium
Stedlijk Museum-Amsterdam, Municipal Museum,
 Amsterdam Netherlands
Taft Museum, Cincinnati OH
Topkapi Saray Museum, Istanbul Turkey
University of Alberta, Ring House Gallery,
 Edmonton AB
University of Cambridge, Fitzwilliam Museum,
 Cambridge England
University of North Carolina at Greensboro,
 Chinqua-Penn Plantation House, Reidsville NC
University of San Diego, Founders' Gallery, San
 Diego CA
University of Santa Clara, de Saisset Art Gallery and
 Museum, Santa Clara CA
University of Tennessee, Frank H McClung Museum,
 Knoxville TN
University of Tennessee, Eleanor Dean Audigier Art
 Collection, Knoxville TN
University of Utah, Utah Museum of Fine Arts, Salt
 Lake City UT
University of Wisconsin, Elvehjem Art Center,
 Madison WI
Vestlandske Kunstindustrimuseum, Western Norway
 Museum of Applied Art, Bergen Norway
Victoria and Albert Museum, London England
Virginia Museum of Fine Arts, Richmond VA
Wallace Collection, London England
Wellington Museum, London England
White House, Washington DC
Woodmere Art Gallery, Philadelphia PA
World Museum & Art Centre, Osborn Foundation,
 Tulsa OK

GLASS

Abbot Hall Art Gallery, Cumbria England
Albany Institute of History and Art, Albany NY
Albion College, Bobbitt Visual Arts Center, Albion
 MI
American Swedish Institute, Minneapolis MN
American University of Beirut, Archaeological
 Museum, Beirut Lebanon
Art Gallery of Western Australia, Perth Australia
Ball State University, Art Gallery, Muncie IN
Baltimore Museum of Art, Baltimore MD
Bayerisches Nationalmuseum, Bavarian National
 Museum, Munich Germany, Federal Republic of
Bennington Museum, Bennington VT
Bergstrom Art Center and Museum, Neenah WI
Bower's Museum, Santa Ana CA
Brigham City Museum-Gallery, Brigham City UT
Brockton Art Center, Brockton MA
Brooks Memorial Art Gallery, Memphis TN
Charleston Museum, Charleston SC
Chrysler Museum, Norfolk VA
City Art Gallery, Bristol England
Columbus Chapel, Boal Mansion and Museum,
 Boalsburg PA
Cooper-Hewitt Museum, Smithsonian Institution
 National Museum of Design, New York NY
Coptic Museum, Cairo Egypt
Corning Museum of Glass, Corning NY
Currier Gallery of Art, Manchester NH
Dartmouth Heritage Museum, Dartmouth NS
Doncaster Museum and Art Gallery, Doncaster
 England
Everhart Museum of Natural History, Science and
 Art, Scranton PA

Flint Institute of Arts, Flint MI
Franciscan Monastery, Holy Land of America,
 Washington DC
Freer Gallery of Art, Washington DC
Haaretz Museum, Tel-Aviv Israel
Hammond-Harwood House, Annapolis MD
Harvard University, Harvard Semitic Museum,
 Cambridge MA
Hastings Museum, Hastings NE
Historic Burlington County Prison Museum, Mount
 Holly NJ
Houston Antique Museum, Chattanooga TN
Iowa State University, Brunnier Gallery, Ames IA
Istanbul Arkeoloji Müzeleri, Archaeological
 Museums of Istanbul, Istanbul Turkey
Kunstindustrimuseet I Oslo, Oslo Museum of
 Applied Art, Oslo Norway
Lincolnshire Museums, Usher Gallery, Lincoln
 England
Manchester City Art Galleries, Manchester England
Maryland Historical Society Museum, Baltimore MD
Mitchell Museum, Mount Vernon IL
Montreal Museum of Fine Arts, Montreal PQ
Moravska Galerie v Brne, Moravian Gallery at Brno,
 Brno Czechoslovakia
Mount Clare Mansion, Baltimore MD
Musee de L'Oeuvre Notre Dame, Cathedral
 Museum, Strasbourg France
Musees d'Archeologie et d'Arts Decoratifs, Liege
 Museums of Archeology and Decorative Arts,
 Liege Belgium
Musees Royaux d'Art et d'Histoire, Royal Museums
 of Art and History, Brussels Belgium
Museo de Capodimonte, Mount Capodi Museum,
 Naples Italy
Museo Nazionale Romano, National Museum of
 Rome, Rome Italy
Museum, Greenwood SC
Museum Boymans-Van Beuningen, Rotterdam
 Netherlands
Museum fur Kunstandwerk, Museum of Arts and
 Crafts, Frankfurt Germany, Federal Republic of
Museum of Applied Arts and Sciences, Sydney
 Australia
Museu Nacional de Soares dos Reis, National
 Museum of Soares Dos Reis, Oporto Portugal
Muzeum Narodowe we Wroclawiu, National
 Museum, Wroclaw Poland
Nationaal Glasmuseum, Leerdam Netherlands
National Gallery of Victoria, Melbourne Australia
National Museum of History and Technology,
 Smithsonian Institution, Washington DC
National Museum of Pakistan, Karachi Pakistan
Newark Museum, Newark NJ
Oglebay Institute Mansion Museum, Wheeling WV
Oshkosh Public Museum, Oshkosh WI
Philadelphia Museum of Art, Philadelphia PA
Phillips County Museum, Helena AR
Portland Museum of Art, Portland ME
Potsdam Public Museum, Potsdam NY
Principia College, School of Nations Museum, Elsah
 IL
Queens College of the City University of New York,
 Art Collection, Flushing NY
Rahr-West Museum and Civic Center, Manitowoc
 WI
Remington Art Museum, Ogdensburg NY
Royal Pavilion, Art Gallery and Museums,
 Thomas-Stanford Museum, Preston Manor,
 Brighton England
Sefton Metropolitan Borough, Atlinson Art Gallery,
 Southport England
Sierra Nevada Museum of Art, Reno NV
Stark Museum of Art, Orange TX
State University of New York College at Geneseo,
 Fine Arts Gallery, Geneseo NY
Stedelijk Museum de Lakenhal, Leyden Municipal
 Museum, Leiden Netherlands
Stedlijk Museum-Amsterdam, Municipal Museum,
 Amsterdam Netherlands
Österreichisches Museum für angewandte Kunst,
 Vienna Austria
Toledo Museum of Art, Toledo OH
Topeka Public Library, Topeka KS
Triton Museum of Art, Santa Clara CA

Eva Brook Donly Museum, Simcoe ON
East Tennessee State University, Carroll Reece Museum, Johnson City TN
Floyd County Museum, New Albany IN
Fort Ticonderoga Museum, Ticonderoga NY
Gananoque Historical Museum, Gananoque ON
Germanisches National Museum, Germanic National Museum, Nuremberg Germany, Federal Republic of
Thomas Gilcrease Institute of American History and Art, Tulsa OK
Glenbow Museum, Calgary AB
Great Lakes Historical Society, Vermilion OH
Harrison County Historical Museum, Marshall TX
Historical Society of Bloomfield, New Jersey, Bloomfield NJ
Historical Society of Old Newbury, Cushing House Museum, Newburyport MA
Historical Society of Quincy and Adams County, Quincy IL
Historisches Museum, Historical Museum, Saint Switzerland
Indian Museum, Calcutta India
Institute of the Great Plains, Museum of the Great Plains, Lawton OK
John Paul Jones House, Portsmouth NH
Jordan Historical Museum of The Twenty, Jordan ON
Kansas State Historial Society Museum, Topeka KS
Kentucky Historical Society Museum, Frankfort KY
Klamath County Museum, Klamath Falls OR
Long Branch Historical Museum, Long Branch NJ
Louisiana State Exhibit Museum, Shreveport LA
Loveland Museum, Loveland CO
Missouri Historical Society, Saint Louis MO
Missouri State Museum, Jefferson City MO
Moravian Historical Society, Whitefield House Museum, Nazareth PA
Muscatine Art Center, Muscatine IA
Museum of Northern British Columbia, Prince Rupert Museum Art Gallery, Prince Rupert BC
Museum of the American Indian, New York NY
National Museum of Man, Ottawa ON
Naval Amphibious Museum, Norfolk VA
Newfoundland Museum, Saint John's NF
No Man's Land Historical Museum, Goodwell OK
Norsk Folkemuseum, Norwegian Folk Museum, Oslo Norway
Northeastern Nevada Museum, Elko NV
Oklahoma Historical Society, Central Museum, Oklahoma City OK
Old Gaol Museum, York ME
Phelps County Historical Society Museum, Holdrege NE
Philipse Manor Hall State Historic Site, Yonkers NY
Pioneer Village, Minden NE
Pittsburgh History and Landmarks Foundation, Old Post Office Museum, Pittsburgh PA
Ringwood Manor House Museum, Ringwood NJ
Rome Historical Society, Rome Information and Cultural Center, Rome NY
Franklin D Roosevelt Library and Museum, Hyde Park NY
Safety Harbor Museum of History and Fine Arts, Safety Harbor FL
Saint Bernard Foundation and Monastery, Miami Beach FL
Saint-Gaudens National Historic Site, Concord NH
Saint Louis County Historical Society, Duluth MN
Schofield Barracks, Tropic Lightning Historical Center, Honolulu HI
Schweizerisches Landesmuseum, Swiss National Museum, Zurich Switzerland
Scotts Bluff National Monument, Gering NE
Sheldon Art Museum, Middlebury VT
Society of the Montreal Military and Maritime Museum, Saint Helen's Island Museum, Montreal PQ
Southern Oregon Historical Society, Jacksonville Museum, Jacksonville OR
State Historical Society of Wisconsin, Madison WI
Statni Zidovske Muzeum, State Jewish Museum, Prague Czechoslovakia
Sunset Trading Post Old West Museum, Sunset TX
Tennessee State Museum, Nashville TN

Ukrainian Museum of Canada, Edmonton AB
USS North Carolina Battleship Memorial, Wilmington NC
Van Cortlandt Museum, Bronx NY
Waterville Historical Association, Waterville ME
Western Reserve Historical Society, Cleveland OH
Williams County Historical Society, Williston ND
Woodrow Wilson Birthplace Foundation, Staunton VA
York Institute Museum, Saco ME

IVORY

Bayerisches Nationalmuseum, Bavarian National Museum, Munich Germany, Federal Republic of
Bruce Museum, Greenwich CT
Coptic Museum, Cairo Egypt
Diamond M Foundation Museum, Snyder TX
Galleria Nazionale dell'Umbria, Umbrian National Gallery, Perugia Italy
Harvard University, Dumbarton Oaks Research Library and Collections, Washington DC
Indian Museum, Calcutta India
Iowa State University, Brunnier Gallery, Ames IA
Loyala University of Chigago, Martin D'Arcy Gallery of Art, Chicago IL
Mitchell Museum, Mount Vernon IL
Museum, Greenwood SC
Museum of Applied Arts and Sciences, Sydney Australia
Omniplex, Oklahoma City OK
Rahr-West Museum and Civic Center, Manitowoc WI
Robert W Ryerss Library and Museum, Philadelphia PA
Saint Bonaventure University Art Collection, Saint Bonaventure NY
Saint John's University, Chung-Cheng Art Gallery, Jamaica NY
Sheffield City Art Galleries, Mappin Art Gallery, Sheffield England
University of Michigan Museum of Art, Kelsey Museum of Ancient and Medieval Archaeology, Ann Arbor MI
University of Santa Clara, de Saisset Art Gallery and Museum, Santa Clara CA
Yugtarvik Regional Museum, Bethel AK

JADE

Diamond M Foundation Museum, Snyder TX
Freer Gallery of Art, Washington DC
Harvard University, William Hayes Fogg Art Museum, Cambridge MA
Hermitage Foundation Museum, Norfolk VA
Indianapolis Museum of Art, Indianapolis IN
Mitchell Museum, Mount Vernon IL
Norton Gallery and School of Art, West Palm Beach FL
Roswell Museum and Art Center, Roswell NM
Saint Bonaventure University Art Collection, Saint Bonaventure NY
Saint John's University, Chung-Cheng Art Gallery, Jamaica NY
Seattle Art Museum, Seattle WA
Virginia Museum of Fine Arts, Richmond VA
Washington County Museum of Fine Arts, Hagerstown MD

JEWELRY

Baltimore Museum of Art, Baltimore MD
Benaki Museum, Athens Greece
Det Danske Kunstindustrimuseum, Museum of Decorative Art, Copenhagen Denmark
Doncaster Museum and Art Gallery, Doncaster England
Egyptian Museum, Cairo Egypt
Franciscan Monastery, Holy Land of America, Washington DC
Harvard University, Dumbarton Oaks Research Library and Collections, Washington DC

Haystack Mountain School of Crafts Gallery, Deer Isle ME
Institute of American Indian Arts Museum, Santa Fe NM
Kunsthistorisches Museum, Museum of Fine Arts, Vienna Austria
Milwaukee Public Museum, Milwaukee WI
James Monroe Law Office - Museum and Memorial Library, Fredericksburg VA
Moravska Galerie v Brne, Moravian Gallery at Brno, Brno Czechoslovakia
Musee National, National Museum of Lebanon, Beirut Lebanon
Museo del Prado, National Museum of Paintings and Sculpture, Madrid Spain
Museu Nacional de Soares dos Reis, National Museum of Soares Dos Reis, Oporto Portugal
Panstwowe Zbiory Sztuki na Wawelu, Wawel State Collections of Art, Cracow Poland
Rollins College, George D and Harriet W Cornell Fine Arts Center Museum, Winter Park FL
Schweizerisches Landesmuseum, Swiss National Museum, Zurich Switzerland
Southwestern At Memphis, Jessie L Clough Art Memorial for Teaching, Memphis TN
Taft Museum, Cincinnati OH
Valentine Museum, Richmond VA
Victoria and Albert Museum, London England
Virginia Museum of Fine Arts, Richmond VA

JUDAICA

American Jewish Historical Society, Waltham MA
B'nai B'rith Exhibit Hall, Library, Washington DC
Haaretz Museum, Tel-Aviv Israel
Hebrew Union College, Skirball Museum, Los Angeles CA
Jewish Community Center, Center Lobby Gallery, Long Beach CA
Jewish Museum, New York NY
Judah L Magnes Memorial Museum, Western Jewish History Center, Berkeley CA
92nd Street YMHA-YWHA, Weill Art Gallery, New York NY
Spertus Museum of Judaica, Chicago IL
Statni Zidovske Muzeum, State Jewish Museum, Prague Czechoslovakia
Tel Aviv Museum, Tel-Aviv Israel
Temple Museum of Jewish Religious Art and Music, Cleveland OH

LACES

Baltimore Museum of Art, Baltimore MD
Cooper-Hewitt Museum, Smithsonian Institution National Museum of Design, New York NY
George Peabody College for Teachers, Cohen Memorial Museum of Art, Nashville TN
Montreal Museum of Fine Arts, Montreal PQ
Musees Royaux d'Art et d'Histoire, Royal Museums of Art and History, Brussels Belgium
Museo de Arte—Jose Luis Bello y Gonzales, Museum of Art, Puebla Mexico
University of Washington, Costume and Textile Study Center, Seattle WA
Victoria and Albert Museum, London England
Washington County Museum of Fine Arts, Hagerstown MD

LANDSCAPES

University of Southern California, University Galleries, Los Angeles CA
University of Washington, Henry Art Gallery, Seattle WA

LATIN AMERICAN ART

Arizona State University, University Art Collections, Tempe AZ
Institute of Puerto Rican Culture, Museo de Bellas

Artes, San Juan PR
Metropolitan Museum and Art Centers, Coral Gables FL
Museo de Arte Popular Americano, Art of the American Peoples Museum, Santiago Chile
Museo de Bellas Artes, Museum of Fine Arts, Caracas Venezuela
Museo Municipal de Bellas Artes Juan B Castagnino, Municipal Museum of Fine Arts, Rosario Argentina
Museo Nacional de Bellas Artes, National Museum of Fine Arts, Buenos Aires Argentina
Museu de Arte Moderna, Museum of Modern Art, Rio Brazil
University of Florida, University Gallery, Gainesville FL

MANUSCRIPTS

American Jewish Historical Society, Waltham MA
Brigham Young University, B F Larsen Gallery, Provo UT
Chicago Historical Society, Chicago IL
Coptic Museum, Cairo Egypt
Freer Gallery of Art, Washington DC
Haverhill Public Library, Haverhill MA
Institut de France, Musee Conde, Paris France
Kestner-Museum, Hannover Germany, Federal Republic of
Litchfield Historical Society, Ingraham Memorial Research Library, Litchfield CT
Judah L Magnes Memorial Museum, Western Jewish History Center, Berkeley CA
Musee de L'Eglise Notre-Dame, Montreal PQ
Museo di S Marco, Florence Italy
Museum fur Kunstandwerk, Museum of Arts and Crafts, Frankfurt Germany, Federal Republic of
Oklahoma Museum of Art, Oklahoma City OK
Old Gaol Museum, York ME
Plymouth City Museum and Art Gallery, Plymouth England
The Rosenbach Museum and Library, Philadelphia PA
United States Naval Academy Museum, Annapolis MD
University of Cambridge, Fitzwilliam Museum, Cambridge England
University of Michigan Museum of Art, Alumni Memorial Hall Museum, Ann Arbor MI
Washington County Museum of Fine Arts, Hagerstown MD

MARINE PAINTING

Baltimore Maritime Museum, Baltimore MD
Butler Institute of American Art, Youngstown OH
Columbia River Maritime Museum, Astoria OR
Harvard University, Busch-Reisinger Museum, Cambridge MA
Maine Maritime Museum, Bath ME
Maritime Museum Association of San Diego, San Diego CA
Massachusetts Institute of Technology, Hart Nautical Museum, Cambridge MA
Mystic Seaport Museum, Inc, Mystic CT
National Maritime Museum, San Francisco CA
Norsk Sjöfartsmuseum, Norwegian Maritime Museum, Oslo Norway
Peabody Museum of Salem, Salem MA
Penobscot Marine Museum, Searsport ME
Truxtun-Decatur Naval Museum, Washington DC
United States Navy Memorial Museum, Washington DC
Wichita State University, Edwin A Ulrich Museum of Art, Wichita KS
Yarmouth County Historical Society Museum, Yarmouth NS

MEDIEVAL ART

Galleria e Museo del Palazzo Ducale, Gallery and Museum of the Palazzo Ducale, Mantua Italy
Hammond Museum, Inc, Gloucester MA
Herzog Anton Ulrich-Museum, Medieval Section: Burg Dankwarderode, Brunswick Germany, Federal Republic of
Marion Koogler McNay Art Institute, San Antonio TX
Metropolitan Museum of Art, New York NY
Monterey History and Art Association, Allen Knight Maritime Museum, Monterey CA
Musee de Cluny, Cluny Museum, Paris France
Museum of Fine Arts, Houston, Houston TX
Muzeum Narodowe we Wroclawiu, National Museum, Wroclaw Poland
Osterreichische Galerie, Austrian Gallery, Vienna Austria
Rensselaer Newman Foundation Chapel and Cultural Center, Troy NY
Saint Mary's College of California, Hearst Art Gallery, Moraga CA
Saltzburger Museum Carolino Augusteum, Salzburg Museum, Salzburg Austria
Toledo Museum of Art, Toledo OH
University of Illinois, Krannert Art Museum, Champaign IL
University of Rochester, Memorial Art Gallery, Rochester NY
University of Vermont, Robert Hull Fleming Museum, Burlington VT
University of Wisconsin, Elvehjem Art Center, Madison WI
Vassar College Art Gallery, Poughkeepsie NY
Williams College, Museum of Art, Williamstown MA
Worcester Art Museum, Worcester MA

METALWORK

Bayerisches Nationalmuseum, Bavarian National Museum, Munich Germany, Federal Republic of
City Art Gallery, Bristol England
Freer Gallery of Art, Washington DC
Harvard University, Dumbarton Oaks Research Library and Collections, Washington DC
Istanbul Arkeoloji Müzeleri, Archaeological Museums of Istanbul, Istanbul Turkey
Jay Johnson, America's Folk Heritage Gallery, New York NY
Maryland Historical Society Museum, Baltimore MD
Musee d'Art de Saint-Laurent, Saint-Laurent PQ
Museo de Arte, Museum of Art, Lima Peru
Museo Poldi Pezzoli, Poldi Pezzoli Museum, Milan Italy
Museum fur Kunstandwerk, Museum of Arts and Crafts, Frankfurt Germany, Federal Republic of
Museum of Applied Arts and Sciences, Sydney Australia
Museum of Early Southern Decorative Arts, Old Salem Inc, Winston-Salem NC
National Gallery of Victoria, Melbourne Australia
Oxford University, Ashmolean Museum of Art and Archaeology, Oxford England
Pioneer Town, Wimberley TX
Principia College, School of Nations Museum, Elsah IL
Rohsska Konstslojdmuseet, Rohss Museum of Arts and Crafts, Gothenburg Sweden
Saint Clair County Community College, Jack R Hennesey Art Galleries, Port Huron MI
Shaker Museum, Poland Spring ME
Southern Illinois University Museum and Art Galleries, Carbondale IL
Southwestern At Memphis, Jessie L Clough Art Memorial for Teaching, Memphis TN
Österreichisches Museum für angewandte Kunst, Vienna Austria
Turk ve Islam Eserleri Muzesi, Museum of Turkish and Islamic Art, Istanbul Turkey
United States Naval Academy Museum, Annapolis MD
University of Cambridge, Fitzwilliam Museum, Cambridge England

Vestlandske Kunstindustrimuseum, Western Norway Museum of Applied Art, Bergen Norway
Victoria and Albert Museum, London England
Wallace Collection, London England

MEXICAN ART

Center for Inter-American Relations Art Gallery, New York NY
Craft and Folk Art Museum, Los Angeles CA
El Paso Museum of Art, El Paso TX
Fresno Arts Center, Fresno CA
McAllen International Museum, McAllen TX
Mercer County Community College Gallery, Trenton NJ
Museo de Arte Moderno, Museum of Modern Art, Mexico City Mexico
Museo del Estado de Taliseo, National Museum, Guadalajara Mexico
Museum of New Mexico, Museum of International Folk Art, Santa Fe NM
Museum of New Mexico, Museum of Fine Arts, Santa Fe NM
Phoenix Art Museum, Phoenix AZ
University of Houston, Sarah Campbell Blaffer Gallery, Houston TX
Wichita Art Museum, Wichita KS

MINIATURES

Carolina Art Association, Gibbes Art Gallery, Charleston SC
Graphische Sammlung Albertina, Albertina Graphic Art Collection, Vienna Austria
Indian Museum, Calcutta India
King George VI Art Gallery, Port South Africa, Republic of
Lahore Museum, Lahore Pakistan
Musee Cognacq-Jay, Cognacq-Jay Museum, Paris France
Museo de Arte—Jose Luis Bello y Gonzales, Museum of Art, Puebla Mexico
National Collection of Fine Arts, Washington DC
National Museum of Pakistan, Karachi Pakistan
National Portrait Gallery, London England
New Jersey Historical Society Museum, Newark NJ
New Orleans Museum of Art, Isaac Delgado Museum, New Orleans LA
R W Norton Art Gallery, Shreveport LA
Oxford University, Ashmolean Museum of Art and Archaeology, Oxford England
Portland Art Association, Museum, Portland OR
Saint Bonaventure University Art Collection, Saint Bonaventure NY
Topkapi Saray Museum, Istanbul Turkey
University of Cincinnati, Tangeman Fine Arts Gallery, Cincinnati OH
Victoria and Albert Museum, London England
Wallace Collection, London England

MOSAICS

Baltimore Museum of Art, Baltimore MD
Harvard University, Dumbarton Oaks Research Library and Collections, Washington DC
Municipality of Beit-Shan, Municipal Beit-Shan-Museum, Beit-Shan Israel
Musee National, National Museum of Lebanon, Beirut Lebanon
Museo Nazionale di San Martino, National Museum, Naples Italy
Museo Nazionale di Villa Guinigi, National Museum of Villa Guinigi, Lucca Italy
Museo Nazionale Romano, National Museum of Rome, Rome Italy
Worcester Art Museum, Worcester MA

ORIENTAL ART

Allentown Art Museum, Allentown PA
Anderson House Museum, Society of the Cincinnati, Washington DC
Art Complex Museum at Duxbury, Duxbury MA
Art Gallery of Greater Victoria, Victoria BC
Art Institute of Chicago, Chicago IL
Asian Art Museum of San Francisco, Avery Brundage Collection, San Francisco CA
Baltimore Museum of Art, Baltimore MD
Bates College, Treat Gallery, Lewiston ME
Beloit College, Theodore Lyman Wright Art Center, Beloit WI
Benaki Museum, Athens Greece
Berkshire Museum, Pittsfield MA
Blanden Memorial Art Gallery, Fort Dodge IA
Boise Gallery of Art, Boise ID
British Museum, London England
Brooks Memorial Art Gallery, Memphis TN
Bruce Museum, Greenwich CT
California State University, Chico, Art Gallery, Chico CA
Carnegie Institute, Museum of Art, Pittsburgh PA
Carolina Art Association, Gibbes Art Gallery, Charleston SC
Central Art Gallery, Wolverhampton England
China Institute in America, China House Gallery, New York NY
Chrysler Museum, Norfolk VA
City Art Gallery, Bristol England
City of Holyoke Museum-Wistariahurst, Holyoke MA
Cleveland Museum of Art, Cleveland OH
Colby Museum of Art, Waterville ME
College of William and Mary, Department of Fine Arts Gallery, Williamsburg VA
College of Wooster Art Center Museum, Wooster OH
Columbus Museum of Art, Columbus OH
Craft and Folk Art Museum, Los Angeles CA
Cummer Gallery of Art, DeEtte Holden Cummer Museum Foundation, Jacksonville FL
Dayton Art Institute, Dayton OH
Deadwood Gulch Art Gallery, Deadwood SD
Denver Art Museum, Frederic H Douglas Library, Denver CO
Alfred O Deshong Museum, Chester PA
Det Danske Kunstindustrimuseum, Museum of Decorative Art, Copenhagen Denmark
Drexel University Art Gallery and Museum Collection, Philadelphia PA
Durban Art Gallery, Durban South Africa, Republic of
Evansville Museum of Arts and Science, Evansville IN
Everhart Museum of Natural History, Science and Art, Scranton PA
Everson Museum of Art, Syracuse NY
Fine Arts Museum of the South, Mobile AL
Flint Institute of Arts, Flint MI
Florence Museum, Florence SC
Francis E Fowler Jr Foundation Museum, Beverly Hills CA
Fresno Arts Center, Fresno CA
Galleries of the Claremont Colleges, Claremont CA
Isabella Stewart Gardner Museum, Boston MA
Greenville College, Richard W Bock Sculpture Collection, Greenville IL
Hammond-Harwood House, Annapolis MD
Headley-Whitney Museum, Lexington KY
Hermitage Foundation Museum, Norfolk VA
High Museum of Art, Atlanta GA
Hofstra University, Emily Lowe Gallery, Hempstead NY
Honolulu Academy of Arts, Honolulu HI
Indianapolis Museum of Art, Indianapolis IN
Johnson-Humrickhouse Museum, Coshocton OH
Kenosha Public Museum, Kenosha WI
King George VI Art Gallery, Port South Africa, Republic of
Kunsthalle Bremen, Bremen Art Gallery, Bremen Germany, Federal Republic of
Kunsthistorisches Museum, Museum of Fine Arts, Vienna Austria

Leeds Art Galleries, Leeds England
Leicestershire Museums, Art Galleries and Records Service, Leicestershire Museum and Art Gallery, Leicester England
Metropolitan Museum and Art Centers, Coral Gables FL
Minneapolis Institute of Arts, Minneapolis MN
Moravska Galerie v Brne, Moravian Gallery at Brno, Brno Czechoslovakia
Mount Clare Mansion, Baltimore MD
Musee du Seminaire de Quebec, Quebec PQ
Museum of Fine Arts, Boston MA
Museum of Fine Arts, Springfield MA
Museum of Fine Arts, Houston, Houston TX
Museum of Japanese Art, Haifa Israel
Museum of the American China Trade, Milton MA
Museum of the Philadelphia Civic Center, Philadelphia PA
Museum of the Southwest, Midland TX
Museum Rietberg Zurich, Zurich Switzerland
Museu Nacional de Arte Antiga, National Museum of Ancient Art, Lisbon Portugal
Muskegon Museum of Art, Muskegon MI
Narodni Galerie v Prague, National Gallery of Prague, Prague Czechoslovakia
William Rockhill Nelson Gallery of Art, Atkins Museum of Fine Art, Kansas City MO
Newark Museum, Newark NJ
Norton Gallery and School of Art, West Palm Beach FL
Norwich Free Academy, Slater Memorial Museum & Converse Art Gallery, Norwich CT
Oregon State University, Horner Museum, Corvallis OR
Oxford University, Ashmolean Museum of Art and Archaeology, Oxford England
Pacific - Asia Museum, Pasadena CA
Panstwowe Zbiory Sztuki na Wawelu, Wawel State Collections of Art, Cracow Poland
Parrish Art Museum, Southampton NY
Pennsylvania State University, Museum of Art, University Park PA
Philadelphia Museum of Art, Philadelphia PA
Philbrook Art Center, Tulsa OK
Phoenix Art Museum, Phoenix AZ
Plains Art Museum, Main Gallery, Moorhead MN
Henry B Plant Museum, Tampa FL
Portland Art Association, Museum, Portland OR
Potsdam Public Museum, Potsdam NY
Princeton University, Art Museum, Princeton NJ
Rhode Island Historical Society, John Brown House, Providence RI
Rhode Island School of Design, Museum of Art, Providence RI
Roswell Museum and Art Center, Roswell NM
Royal Pavilion, Art Gallery and Museums, Brighton England
Saginaw Art Museum, Saginaw MI
Saint Francis College, Lakeview Gallery, Fort Wayne IN
Saint John's University, Chung-Cheng Art Gallery, Jamaica NY
St Lawrence University, Richard F Brush Art Gallery, Canton NY
Saint Louis Art Museum, Saint Louis MO
San Diego Museum of Art, San Diego CA
Santa Barbara Museum of Art, Santa Barbara CA
Scripps College, Clark Humanities Museum, Claremont CA
Seattle Art Museum, Seattle WA
Sheffield City Art Galleries, Mappin Art Gallery, Sheffield England
George Walter Vincent Smith Art Museum, Springfield MA
Sonoma State College Art Gallery, Rohnert Park CA
Spencer Museum of Art, Lawrence KS
Stanford University, T W Stanford Art Gallery & Museum of Art, Stanford CA
State Museum of Oriental Art, Moscow Ussr
State University of New York at New Paltz, College Art Gallery, New Paltz NY
Österreichisches Museum für angewandte Kunst, Vienna Austria
Taft Museum, Cincinnati OH
Tallahassee Junior Museum, Tallahassee FL

Topkapi Saray Museum, Istanbul Turkey
Tucson Museum of Art, Tucson AZ
University of Cambridge, Fitzwilliam Museum, Cambridge England
University of Chicago, David and Alfred Smart Gallery, Chicago IL
University of Florida, University Gallery, Gainesville FL
University of Illinois, Krannert Art Museum, Champaign IL
University of Miami, Lowe Art Museum, Coral Gables FL
University of Missouri, Museum of Art and Archaeology, Columbia MO
University of North Carolina at Greensboro, Chinqua-Penn Plantation House, Reidsville NC
University of Notre Dame, Snite Museum of Art, Notre Dame IN
University of Oregon, Musuem of Art, Eugene OR
University of Regina, Norman Mackenzie Art Gallery, Regina SK
University of Vermont, Robert Hull Fleming Museum, Burlington VT
University of Wisconsin, School of Fine Arts Galleries, Milwaukee WI
Vanderbilt University, Art Gallery, Department of Fine Arts, Nashville TN
Vassar College Art Gallery, Poughkeepsie NY
Vestlandske Kunstindustrimuseum, Western Norway Museum of Applied Art, Bergen Norway
Virginia Museum, Danville Museum of Fine Arts and History, Danville VA
Wadsworth Atheneum, Hartford CT
Walker Museum, Fairlee VT
Washington and Lee University, Gallery of DuPont Hall, Lexington VA
Washington County Museum of Fine Arts, Hagerstown MD
Wesleyan University, Davison Art Center, Middletown CT
Williams College, Museum of Art, Williamstown MA
Woodmere Art Gallery, Philadelphia PA
World Museum & Art Centre, Osborn Foundation, Tulsa OK

PAINTING - AMERICAN

Abilene Fine Arts Museum, Abilene TX
Albany Institute of History and Art, Albany NY
Alberta College of Art Gallery, Calgary AB
Albrecht Art Museum, Saint Joseph MO
Albright College, Freedman Gallery, Reading PA
Albright-Knox Art Gallery, Buffalo Fine Arts Academy, Buffalo NY
Allegheny College, Bowman, Megahan and Penelec Galleries, Meadville PA
Allentown Art Museum, Allentown PA
Lyman Allyn Museum, New London CT
American University, Watkins Art Gallery, Washington DC
Anderson House Museum, Society of the Cincinnati, Washington DC
Arizona State University, University Art Collections, Tempe AZ
Arkansas Arts Center, Little Rock AR
Art Gallery of Nova Scotia, Halifax NS
Art Gallery of Ontario, Toronto ON
Art Institute of Chicago, Chicago IL
Atlanta Museum, Atlanta GA
Attleboro Museum, Center for the Arts, Attleboro MA
Auckland City Art Gallery, Auckland New Zealand
Augusta Richmond County Museum, Augusta GA
Baldwin-Wallace College Art Gallery, Berea OH
Ball State University, Art Gallery, Muncie IN
Baltimore Museum of Art, Baltimore MD
Bard College, William Cooper Procter Art Center, Annandale-on-Hudson NY
Bates College, Treat Gallery, Lewiston ME
Beaumont Art Museum, Beaumont TX
Belmont, Gari Melchers Memorial Gallery, Fredericksburg VA
Beloit College, Theodore Lyman Wright Art Center, Beloit WI

Museums at Stony Brook, Stony Brook NY
Muskegon Museum of Art, Muskegon MI
National Air and Space Museum, Washington DC
National Gallery of Ireland, Dublin Ireland
Nebraska Wesleyan University, Elder Gallery, Lincoln NE
Newark Museum, Newark NJ
New Bedford Whaling Museum, New Bedford MA
New Britain Museum of American Art, New Britain CT
New Haven Colony Historical Society, New Haven CT
New Jersey State Museum, Trenton NJ
New Orleans Museum of Art, Isaac Delgado Museum, New Orleans LA
Newport Harbor Art Museum, Newport Beach CA
New York University, Grey Art Gallery and Study Center, New York NY
North Carolina Central University, Museum of Art, Durham NC
North Carolina Museum of Art, Department of Cultural Resources, Raleigh NC
Norton Gallery and School of Art, West Palm Beach FL
R W Norton Art Gallery, Shreveport LA
Norwich Free Academy, Slater Memorial Museum & Converse Art Gallery, Norwich CT
Oakland Museum, Oakland CA
Oberlin College, Allen Memorial Art Museum, Oberlin OH
Offentliche Kunstsammlung-Kunstmuseum Basel, Museum of Fine Arts, Basel Switzerland
Ohara Bijitsukan, Ohara Museum of Art, Kurashiki Japan
Oklahoma Museum of Art, Oklahoma City OK
Olana Historic Site, Hudson NY
Omniplex, Oklahoma City OK
Owensboro Museum of Fine Art, Owensboro KY
Panhandle-Plains Historical Society Museum, Canyon TX
Parrish Art Museum, Southampton NY
The Parthenon, Memphis TN
Peale Museum, Baltimore MD
Pennsylvania Academy of the Fine Arts, Philadelphia PA
Pennsylvania State University, Museum of Art, University Park PA
Philadelphia Museum of Art, Philadelphia PA
Philbrook Art Center, Tulsa OK
Phillips Academy, Addison Gallery of American Art, Andover MA
Phillips County Museum, Helena AR
Pioneer Museum and Haggin Galleries, Stockton CA
Portland Museum of Art, Portland ME
Portsmouth Athenaeum NR, Inc 1817, Portsmouth NH
Princeton University, Art Museum, Princeton NJ
Purdue University, Gallery I, Gallery II, Union Gallery & Stewart Center Gallery, West Lafayette IN
Racine Art Association, Charles A Wustum Museum of Fine Arts, Racine WI
Rahr-West Museum and Civic Center, Manitowoc WI
Randolph-Macon Womans College, Art Gallery, Lynchburg VA
Reading Public Museum and Art Gallery, Reading PA
Reed College Art Gallery, Portland OR
Remington Art Museum, Ogdensburg NY
Reynolda House, Inc, Winston-Salem NC
Rhode Island School of Design, Museum of Art, Providence RI
Roberson Center, Binghamton NY
Rockwell-Corning Museum, Corning NY
Rogers House Museum Gallery, Ellsworth KS
Lauren Rogers Library and Museum of Art, Laurel MS
Rollins College, George D and Harriet W Cornell Fine Arts Center Museum, Winter Park FL
Robert W Ryerss Library and Museum of Art, Philadelphia PA
Saginaw Art Museum, Saginaw MI
Saint Bonaventure University Art Collection, Saint Bonaventure NY

Saint Clair County Community College, Jack R Hennesey Art Galleries, Port Huron MI
Saint Gregory's Abbey and College, Mabee-Gerrer Museum, Shawnee OK
Saint John's Art Gallery, Wilmington NC
Saint Johnsbury Athenaeum, Saint Johnsbury VT
St Lawrence University, Richard F Brush Art Gallery, Canton NY
Saint Louis Art Museum, Saint Louis MO
San Diego Museum of Art, San Diego CA
San Diego State University, Art Gallery, San Diego CA
San Francisco Museum of Modern Art, San Francisco CA
San Jose Museum of Art, San Jose CA
San Jose State University, Union Gallery, San Jose CA
Santa Barbara Museum of Art, Santa Barbara CA
Schenectady Museum, Schenectady NY
Seattle Art Museum, Seattle WA
Shelburne Museum, Shelburne VT
Silverado Museum, Saint Helena CA
Norton Simon Museum, Pasadena CA
Smith College, Museum of Art, Northampton MA
George Walter Vincent Smith Art Museum, Springfield MA
Smith-Mason Gallery and Museum, Washington DC
South Dakota State University, South Dakota Memorial Art Center, Brookings SD
Southern Alleghenies Museum of Art, Loretto PA
Southern Illinois University Museum and Art Galleries, Carbondale IL
Southern Utah State College, Braithwaite Fine Arts Gallery, Cedar City UT
Spencer Museum of Art, Lawrence KS
Springfield Art Museum, Springfield MO
Springville Museum of Art, Springville UT
Staten Island Institute of Arts and Sciences, Staten Island NY
State University of New York at Albany, University Art Gallery, Albany NY
State University of New York at New Paltz, College Art Gallery, New Paltz NY
State University of New York at Oswego, Tyler Art Gallery, Oswego NY
State University of New York College at Geneseo, Fine Arts Gallery, Geneseo NY
State University of New York College at Potsdam, Brainerd Art Gallery, Potsdam NY
State University of New York College at Purchase, Neuberger Museum, Purchase NY
Stedlijk Museum-Amsterdam, Municipal Museum, Amsterdam Netherlands
Stephens College, Lewis James and Nellie Stratton Davis Art Gallery, Columbia MO
Stetson University, Art Gallery, Deland FL
SVACA - Sheyenne Valley Arts and Crafts Association, Bjarne Ness Gallery, Fort Ransom ND
Tacoma Art Museum, Tacoma WA
Tasmanian Museum and Art Gallery, Hobart Australia
Tel Aviv Museum, Tel-Aviv Israel
Timken Art Gallery, San Diego CA
Toledo Museum of Art, Toledo OH
Tomoka State Park Museum, Ormond Beach FL
Topeka Public Library, Topeka KS
Triton Museum of Art, Santa Clara CA
Tryon Palace Restoration Complex, New Bern NC
Tucson Museum of Art, Tucson AZ
Edwin A Ulrich Museum, Hyde Park NY
Ulster County Community College, Visual Arts Gallery, Stone Ridge NY
United States Capitol Museum, Washington DC
United States Naval Academy Museum, Annapolis MD
United States Navy Memorial Museum, Washington DC
University of Alberta, Ring House Gallery, Edmonton AB
University of Chicago, David and Alfred Smart Gallery, Chicago IL
University of Colorado Art Galleries, Boulder CO
University of Connecticut, William Benton Museum of Art, Storrs CT

University of Delaware, University Art Collections, Newark DE
University of Florida, University Gallery, Gainesville FL
University of Georgia, Georgia Museum of Art, Athens GA
University of Illinois, Krannert Art Museum, Champaign IL
University of Iowa, Museum of Art, Iowa City IA
University of Kentucky, Art Museum, Lexington KY
University of Maryland, Art Gallery, College Park MD
University of Minnesota, Tweed Museum of Art, Duluth MN
University of Minnesota, University Gallery, Minneapolis MN
University of Nebraska Lincoln, Sheldon Memorial Art Gallery, Lincoln NE
University of New Mexico, University Art Museum, Albuquerque NM
University of North Carolina, The Ackland Art Museum, Chapel Hill NC
University of North Carolina at Greensboro, Weatherspoon Art Gallery, Greensboro NC
University of Northern Iowa, Gallery of Art, Cedar Falls IA
University of Notre Dame, Snite Museum of Art, Notre Dame IN
University of Pittsburgh, University Art Gallery, Pittsburgh PA
University of Santa Clara, de Saisset Art Gallery and Museum, Santa Clara CA
University of Southern California, University Galleries, Los Angeles CA
University of South Florida, University Galleries, Tampa FL
University of Southwestern Louisiana, Art Center for Southwestern Louisiana, Lafayette LA
University of Texas at Austin, University Art Museum, Austin TX
University of Wisconsin, Elvehjem Art Center, Madison WI
University of Wisconsin, Memorial Union Gallery, Madison WI
University of Wisconsin, School of Fine Arts Galleries, Milwaukee WI
University of Wisconsin-Stout, Gallery 209, Menomonie WI
Utah Division of State History, Salt Lake City UT
Valentine Museum, Richmond VA
Valparaiso University, University Art Galleries and Collections, Valparaiso IN
Vancouver Art Gallery, Vancouver BC
Vassar College Art Gallery, Poughkeepsie NY
Villa Montalvo Center for the Arts, Saratoga CA
Virginia Commonwealth University, Anderson Gallery, Richmond VA
Wadsworth Atheneum, Hartford CT
Walker Art Center, Minneapolis MN
Walker Museum, Fairlee VT
Washburn University, Mulvane Art Center, Topeka KS
Washington County Museum of Fine Arts, Hagerstown MD
Westbrook College, Joan Whitney Payson Gallery of Art, Portland ME
Western State College, Quigley Hall Art Gallery, Gunnison CO
Westminster College Art Gallery, New Wilmington PA
Westmoreland County Museum of Art, Greensburg PA
White House, Washington DC
Whitney Museum of American Art, New York NY
Wichita Art Museum, Wichita KS
Wichita State University, Edwin A Ulrich Museum of Art, Wichita KS
Williams College, Museum of Art, Williamstown MA
Winnipeg Art Gallery, Winnipeg MB
Wood Art Gallery, Montpelier VT
Woodmere Art Gallery, Philadelphia PA
Worcester Art Museum, Worcester MA
Yale University, Art Gallery, New Haven CT
York Institute Museum, Saco ME
Zigler Museum, Jennings LA

PAINTING - AUSTRALIAN

Art Gallery of New South Wales, Sydney Australia
Art Gallery of South Australia, Adelaide Australia
Art Gallery of Western Australia, Perth Australia
Auckland City Art Gallery, Auckland New Zealand
National Art Gallery of New Zealand, Wellington
   New Zealand
National Gallery of Victoria, Melbourne Australia
Queensland Art Gallery, Brisbane Australia
Queen Victoria Museum and Art Gallery, Tasmania
   Australia
Tasmanian Museum and Art Gallery, Hobart
   Australia

PAINTING - BRITISH

Abbot Hall Art Gallery, Cumbria England
Albany Institute of History and Art, Albany NY
Arnot Art Museum, Elmira NY
Baltimore Museum of Art, Baltimore MD
Bates College, Treat Gallery, Lewiston ME
Beaverbrook Art Gallery, Fredericton NB
Birmingham Museums and Art Gallery, Birmingham
   England
Bowdoin College, Museum of Art &
   Peary-MacMillan Arctic Museum, Brunswick ME
Central Art Gallery, Wolverhampton England
City Art Gallery, Bristol England
College of the Americas, Museum of the Americas,
   Brookfield VT
Corcoran Gallery of Art, Washington DC
Courtauld Institute Galleries, London England
Davenport Municipal Art Gallery, Davenport IA
Delaware Art Museum, Wilmington DE
Dulwich Picture Gallery, London England
Dundee Museums and Art Gallery, Dundee Scotland
Glasgow Museums and Art Galleries, Kelvingrove
   Art Gallery and Museum, Glasgow Scotland
Gunston Hall Plantation, Lorton VA
Hugh Lane Municipal Gallery of Modern Art,
   Dublin Ireland
William Humphreys Art Gallery, Kimberley South
   Africa, Republic of
Huntington Library, Art Gallery and Botanical
   Gardens, San Marino CA
Johannesburg Art Gallery, Johannesburg South
   Africa, Republic of
King George VI Art Gallery, Port South Africa,
   Republic of
Leeds Art Galleries, Leeds England
Leicestershire Museums, Art Galleries and Records
   Service, Leicestershire Museum and Art Gallery,
   Leicester England
Lincolnshire Museums, Usher Gallery, Lincoln
   England
Louisiana State University, Anglo-American Art
   Museum, Baton Rouge LA
Manchester City Art Galleries, Manchester England
Mint Museum of Art, Charlotte NC
Montreal Museum of Fine Arts, Montreal PQ
Museo de San Carlos, Museum of San Carlos,
   Mexico Mexico
Museu de Arte de Sao Paulo, Sao Paulo Art
   Museum, Sao Paulo Brazil
Museum of Fine Arts, Springfield MA
Museum of Modern Art, Haifa Israel
National Art Gallery of New Zealand, Wellington
   New Zealand
National Galleries of Scotland, National Gallery of
   Scotland, Edinburgh Scotland
National Galleries of Scotland, Scottish National
   Gallery of Modern Art, Edinburgh Scotland
National Gallery, London England
National Gallery of Ireland, Dublin Ireland
National Gallery of Victoria, Melbourne Australia
National Museum of Wales, Cardiff Wales
National Portrait Gallery, London England
New Orleans Museum of Art, Isaac Delgado
   Museum, New Orleans LA
Newport Museum and Art Gallery, Newport Wales
Owensboro Museum of Fine Art, Owensboro KY
Oxford University, Ashmolean Museum of Art and
   Archaeology, Oxford England

Pennsylvania State University, Museum of Art,
   University Park PA
Plymouth City Museum and Art Gallery, Plymouth
   England
Princeton University, Art Museum, Princeton NJ
The Rosenbach Museum and Library, Philadelphia
   PA
Royal Pavilion, Art Gallery and Museums,
   Thomas-Stanford Museum, Preston Manor,
   Brighton England
San Diego Museum of Art, San Diego CA
Sefton Metropolitan Borough, Atlinson Art Gallery,
   Southport England
Sheffield City Art Galleries, Mappin Art Gallery,
   Sheffield England
South London Art Gallery, London England
Tate Gallery, London England
Tatham Art Gallery, Pietermaritzburg South Africa,
   Republic of
Tyne and Wear County Council Museums, Laing Art
   Gallery and Museum, Newcastle England
University of Cambridge, Fitzwilliam Museum,
   Cambridge England
University of Florida, University Gallery, Gainesville
   FL
University of Manchester, Whitworth Art Gallery,
   Manchester England
University of Notre Dame, Snite Museum of Art,
   Notre Dame IN
University of Southern California, University
   Galleries, Los Angeles CA
University of Utah, Utah Museum of Fine Arts, Salt
   Lake City UT
Walker Art Gallery, Liverpool England
Walters Art Gallery, Baltimore MD
Wellington Museum, London England
Westmoreland County Museum of Art, Greensburg
   PA
Worcester Art Museum, Worcester MA
Yale University, Yale Center for British Art, New
   Haven CT
York City Art Gallery, York England

PAINTING - CANADIAN

L'Universite Laval, Ecole des Arts Visuels de
   L'Universite Laval, Quebec PQ
McGill University, McCord Museum, Montreal PQ
Montreal Museum of Fine Arts, Montreal PQ

PAINTING - DUTCH

Arnot Art Museum, Elmira NY
Bates College, Treat Gallery, Lewiston ME
Brooks Memorial Art Gallery, Memphis TN
Calvin College Center Art Gallery, Grand Rapids
   MI
Chrysler Museum, Norfolk VA
Sterling and Francine Clark Art Institute,
   Williamstown MA
Corcoran Gallery of Art, Washington DC
Durban Art Gallery, Durban South Africa, Republic
   of
Evansville Museum of Arts and Science, Evansville
   IN
Frans Halsmuseum, Frans Hals Museum, Haarlem
   Netherlands
Fries Museum, Leeuwarden Netherlands
Isabella Stewart Gardner Museum, Boston MA
Gemeentemuseum Arnhem, Municipal Museum of
   Arnhem, Arnhem Netherlands
Glasgow Museums and Art Galleries, Kelvingrove
   Art Gallery and Museum, Glasgow Scotland
Groningen Museum voor Stad en Land, Groningen
   Museum, Groningen Netherlands
Göteborg Konstmuseum, Gothenburg Art Gallery,
   Gothenburg Sweden
Haags Gemeentemuseum, Municipal Museum of The
   Hague, The Hague Netherlands
William Humphreys Art Gallery, Kimberley South
   Africa, Republic of
Johannesburg Art Gallery, Johannesburg South
   Africa, Republic of

Koninklijk Kabinet van Schilderijen, Royal Picture
   Gallery, The Hague Netherlands
Kunstmuseum Bern, Museum of Fine Arts Berne,
   Berne Switzerland
Manchester City Art Galleries, Manchester England
Michaelis Collection, Cape Province South Africa,
   Republic of
Montreal Museum of Fine Arts, Montreal PQ
Municipal van Abbemuseum, Eindhoven Municipal
   Museum, Eindhoven Netherlands
Musee des Beaus-Arts, Palais Saint Pierre, Museum
   of Fine Arts, Lyon France
Musee des Beaux-Arts, Museum of Fine Arts,
   Angers France
Museo de San Carlos, Museum of San Carlos,
   Mexico Mexico
Museu de Arte de Sao Paulo, Sao Paulo Art
   Museum, Sao Paulo Brazil
Museum Boymans-Van Beuningen, Rotterdam
   Netherlands
Museum Het Rembrandthuis, Rembrandthouse
   Museum, Amsterdam Netherlands
Museum of Fine Arts, Springfield MA
Museu Nacional de Belas Artes, National Museum of
   Fine Arts, Rio Brazil
National Gallery, London England
National Gallery of Ireland, Dublin Ireland
Nijmeegs Museum Commanderie van Saint Jan,
   Nijmegen Netherlands
Noord-Brabants Museum, Hertogenbosch
   Netherlands
Offentliche Kunstsammlung-Kunstmuseum Basel,
   Museum of Fine Arts, Basel Switzerland
Oxford University, Ashmolean Museum of Art and
   Archaeology, Oxford England
Pretoria Art Museum, Pretoria South Africa,
   Republic of
Rijksmuseum, State Museum, Amsterdam
   Netherlands
Rijksmuseum Vincent Van Gogh, Vincent Van Gogh
   State Museum, Amsterdam Netherlands
Ryksmuseum Kroller-Muller, Kroller-Muller State
   Museum, Otterlo Netherlands
San Diego Museum of Art, San Diego CA
Sheffield City Art Galleries, Mappin Art Gallery,
   Sheffield England
Slovenska Narodna Galeria, Slovak National Gallery,
   Bratislava Czechoslovakia
Staatliche Kunsthalle, State Art Gallery, Karlshruhe
   Germany, Federal Republic of
Stadelsches Kunstinstitut, Staedel Art Institute,
   Frankfurt Germany, Federal Republic of
Statens Museum for Kunst, Department of Painting
   and Sculpture, Copenhagen Denmark
Stedelijk Museum Alkmaar, Alkmaar Municipal
   Museum, Alkmaar Netherlands
Stedelijk Museum de Lakenhal, Leyden Municipal
   Museum, Leiden Netherlands
Stedelijk Museum het Prinsenhof, Het Prinsenhof
   State Museum, Delft Netherlands
Strossmayerova Galerija Starih Majstora
   Jugoslavenske Akademije Znanosti I Umjetnosti,
   Strossmayer's Gallery of Old Masters of the
   Yugoslavia Academy of Sciences and Arts, Zagreb
   Yugoslavia
Tel Aviv Museum, Tel-Aviv Israel
Teylers Museum, Haarlem Netherlands
Timken Art Gallery, San Diego CA
University of California, Santa Barbara, Art
   Museum, Santa Barbara CA
University of Southern California, University
   Galleries, Los Angeles CA
Westfries Museum, Hoorn Netherlands
Worcester Art Museum, Worcester MA

PAINTING - EUROPEAN

Albright-Knox Art Gallery, Buffalo Fine Arts
   Academy, Buffalo NY
Allentown Art Museum, Allentown PA
American University, Watkins Art Gallery,
   Washington DC
Art Complex Museum at Duxbury, Duxbury MA
Art Gallery of Greater Victoria, Victoria BC

Art Gallery of Ontario, Toronto ON
Auckland City Art Gallery, Auckland New Zealand
Bates College, Treat Gallery, Lewiston ME
Bayerischen Staatsgemaldesammlungen, Neue Pinakothek, Munich Germany, Federal Republic of
Bayerischen Staatsgemaldesammlungen, Alte Pinakothek, Munich Germany, Federal Republic of
Bayerischen Staatsgemaldesammlungen, Staatsgalerie Moderne-Kunst, Munich Germany, Federal Republic of
Bayerisches Nationalmuseum, Bavarian National Museum, Munich Germany, Federal Republic of
Beloit College, Theodore Lyman Wright Art Center, Beloit WI
Berkshire Museum, Pittsfield MA
Birmingham Museums and Art Gallery, Birmingham England
Blanden Memorial Art Gallery, Fort Dodge IA
Bündner Kunstmuseum Chur, The Grisons Museum of Art, Chur Switzerland
Bob Jones University, Greenville SC
Boise Gallery of Art, Boise ID
Bowdoin College, Museum of Art & Peary-MacMillan Arctic Museum, Brunswick ME
Brockton Art Center, Brockton MA
Brown University, Bell Gallery, Providence RI
Bruce Museum, Greenwich CT
Carnegie Institute, Museum of Art, Pittsburgh PA
Cincinnati Art Museum, Cincinnati OH
Cleveland Museum of Art, Cleveland OH
Columbia Museums of Art and Science, Columbia SC
Columbus Museum of Art, Columbus OH
Columbus Museum of Arts and Sciences, Columbus GA
Corcoran Gallery of Art, Washington DC
Cornell University, Herbert F Johnson Museum of Art, Ithaca NY
Country Art Gallery, Locust Valley NY
Cummer Gallery of Art, DeEtte Holden Cummer Museum Foundation, Jacksonville FL
Currier Gallery of Art, Manchester NH
Dallas Museum of Fine Arts, Dallas TX
Danforth Museum, Framingham MA
Davenport Municipal Art Gallery, Davenport IA
Dayton Art Institute, Dayton OH
Denver Art Museum, Frederic H Douglas Library, Denver CO
Alfred O Deshong Museum, Chester PA
Detroit Institute of Arts, Detroit MI
Dezign House III, Cleveland OH
Dixon Gallery and Gardens, Memphis TN
Doncaster Museum and Art Gallery, Doncaster England
Dulwich Picture Gallery, London England
Edmonton Art Gallery, Edmonton AB
Evansville Museum of Arts and Science, Evansville IN
Everhart Museum of Natural History, Science and Art, Scranton PA
Fairbanks Museum and Planetarium, Saint Johnsbury VT
William A Farnsworth Library and Art Museum, Rockland ME
Fine Arts Museums of San Francisco, M H de Young Memorial Museum and California Palace of the Legion of Honor, n of Honor co
Flint Institute of Arts, Flint MI
Frick Collection, New York NY
Galerije Grada Zagreba, Galerija Suvremene Umjetnosti, Zagreb Yugoslavia
George Peabody College for Teachers, Cohen Memorial Museum of Art, Nashville TN
J Paul Getty Museum, Malibu CA
Grand Rapids Art Museum, Grand Rapids MI
Solomon R Guggenheim Museum, New York NY
Hamburger Kunsthalle, Hamburg Art Museum, Hamburg Germany, Federal Republic of
Harvard University, Busch-Reisinger Museum, Cambridge MA
Harvard University, William Hayes Fogg Art Museum, Cambridge MA
Headley-Whitney Museum, Lexington KY
Gertrude Herbert Memorial Institute of Art, Augusta GA

Herzog Anton Ulrich-Museum, Medieval Section: Burg Dankwarderode, Brunswick Germany, Federal Republic of
High Museum of Art, Atlanta GA
Hirshhorn Museum and Sculpture Garden, Washington DC
Hofstra University, Emily Lowe Gallery, Hempstead NY
Honolulu Academy of Arts, Honolulu HI
Huntington Galleries, Huntington WV
Hyde Collection, Glens Falls NY
Indianapolis Museum of Art, Indianapolis IN
Joslyn Art Museum, Omaha NE
Kunsthalle Bremen, Bremen Art Gallery, Bremen Germany, Federal Republic of
Kunstmuseum Bern, Museum of Fine Arts Berne, Berne Switzerland
La Salle College Art Gallery, Philadelphia PA
Leeds Art Galleries, Leeds England
Leicestershire Museums, Art Galleries and Records Service, Leicestershire Museum and Art Gallery, Leicester England
Le Musee Regional de Rimouski, Rimouski PQ
Los Angeles County Museum of Art, Los Angeles CA
Magyar Nemzeti Galeria, Hungarian National Gallery, Budapest Hungary
Maryhill Museum of Art, Goldendale WA
McMaster University Art Gallery, Hamilton ON
Merrick Art Gallery, New Brighton PA
Metropolitan Museum of Art, New York NY
Milwaukee Art Center, Milwaukee WI
Minneapolis Institute of Arts, Minneapolis MN
Mint Museum of Art, Charlotte NC
Moderna Galerija, Modern Art Gallery, Ljubljana Yugoslavia
Mount Holyoke College Art Museum, South Hadley MA
Munson-Williams-Proctor Institute, Museum of Art, Utica NY
Musee d'Art de Joliette, Joliette PQ
Musee de L'Oeuvre Notre Dame, Cathedral Museum, Strasbourg France
Musee des Beaux-Arts, Museum of Fine Arts, Strasbourg France
Musee des Beaux-Arts de Lille, Museum of Fine Arts, Lille France
Musee des Beaux-Arts et Societe des Amis des Arts, Museum of Fine Arts, La Switzerland
Museo de Bellas Artes, Museum of Fine Arts, Caracas Venezuela
Museo Municipal de Bellas Artes Juan B Castagnino, Municipal Museum of Fine Arts, Rosario Argentina
Museo Nacional de Artes Plasticas, National Museum of Fine Arts, Montevideo Uruguay
Museo Nacional de Bellas Artes, National Museum of Fine Arts, Buenos Aires Argentina
Museo Nazionale di San Matteo, Saint Matteo National Museum, Pisa Italy
Museum and Picture Gallery, Baroda India
Museum Mayer van den Bergh, Antwerp Belgium
Museum of Arts and Sciences, Inc, Macon GA
Museum of Fine Arts, Springfield MA
Museum of Fine Arts, Houston, Houston TX
Museum of Modern Art, Belgrade Yugoslavia
Museum voor Schone Kunsten, Ghent Belgium
Museu Nacional de Arte Antiga, National Museum of Ancient Art, Lisbon Portugal
Muskegon Museum of Art, Muskegon MI
Muzeul de Arta Cluj-Napoca, Museum of Art, Cluj-Napoca Romania
Muzeum Narodowe, National Museum, Warsaw Poland
Narodna Galerija, National Art Gallery, Ljubljana Yugoslavia
Narodni Galerie v Prague, National Gallery of Prague, Prague Czechoslovakia
Nasjonalgalleriet, National Gallery, Oslo Norway
National Art Gallery of New Zealand, Wellington New Zealand
National Gallery of Victoria, Melbourne Australia
National Museum of Western Art, Kokuritsu Seiyo Bijutsukan, Tokyo Japan
National Pinakothiki and Alexander Soutzos

Museum, Athens Greece
New Orleans Museum of Art, Isaac Delgado Museum, New Orleans LA
New York University, Grey Art Gallery and Study Center, New York NY
North Carolina Museum of Art, Department of Cultural Resources, Raleigh NC
North Country Museum of Arts, Park Rapids MN
Northwestern College, Ramaker Library Art Gallery, Orange City IA
Norton Gallery and School of Art, West Palm Beach FL
R W Norton Art Gallery, Shreveport LA
Offentliche Kunstsammlung-Kunstmuseum Basel, Museum of Fine Arts, Basel Switzerland
Ohara Bijitsukan, Ohara Museum of Art, Kurashiki Japan
Oklahoma Museum of Art, Oklahoma City OK
Panstwowe Zbiory Sztuki na Wawelu, Wawel State Collections of Art, Cracow Poland
Philadelphia Museum of Art, Philadelphia PA
Philbrook Art Center, Tulsa OK
Pioneer Museum and Haggin Galleries, Stockton CA
Portland Museum of Art, Portland ME
Princeton University, Art Museum, Princeton NJ
Queens College of the City University of New York, Art Collection, Flushing NY
Queensland Art Gallery, Brisbane Australia
Reading Public Museum and Art Gallery, Reading PA
Remington Art Museum, Ogdensburg NY
John and Mable Ringling Museum of Art, Sarasota FL
Lauren Rogers Library and Museum of Art, Laurel MS
Rollins College, George D and Harriet W Cornell Fine Arts Center Museum, Winter Park FL
Saginaw Art Museum, Saginaw MI
Saint Gregory's Abbey and College, Mabee-Gerrer Museum, Shawnee OK
Saint Louis Art Museum, Saint Louis MO
San Diego Museum of Art, San Diego CA
Santa Barbara Museum of Art, Santa Barbara CA
Sarjeant Gallery, Wanganui New Zealand
Sarjeant Gallery, Wanganui New Zealand
Seattle Art Museum, Seattle WA
Severoceska Galerie Vytvarneho Umeni, North Bohemian Gallery of Fine Arts, Litomerice Czechoslovakia
Shelburne Museum, Shelburne VT
Slovenska Narodna Galeria, Slovak National Gallery, Bratislava Czechoslovakia
Smith College, Museum of Art, Northampton MA
George Walter Vincent Smith Art Museum, Springfield MA
South African National Gallery, Cape South Africa, Republic of
Southern Illinois University Museum and Art Galleries, Carbondale IL
Spencer Museum of Art, Lawrence KS
Springville Museum of Art, Springville UT
Staatsgalerie Stuttgart, Stuttgart Germany, Federal Republic of
Stadelsches Kunstinstitut, Staedel Art Institute, Frankfurt Germany, Federal Republic of
State University of New York College at Purchase, Neuberger Museum, Purchase NY
Stedlijk Museum-Amsterdam, Municipal Museum, Amsterdam Netherlands
Szepmuveszet Museum, Museum of Fine Arts, Budapest Hungary
Tacoma Art Museum, Tacoma WA
Taft Museum, Cincinnati OH
Tel Aviv Museum, Tel-Aviv Israel
Thorvaldsen Museum, Copenhagen Denmark
Toledo Museum of Art, Toledo OH
Tucson Museum of Art, Tucson AZ
University of Chicago, David and Alfred Smart Gallery, Chicago IL
University of Cincinnati, Tangeman Fine Arts Gallery, Cincinnati OH
University of Connecticut, William Benton Museum of Art, Storrs CT
University of Illinois, Krannert Art Museum, Champaign IL

University of Iowa, Museum of Art, Iowa City IA
University of Kentucky, Art Museum, Lexington KY
University of Missouri, Museum of Art and Archaeology, Columbia MO
University of North Carolina, The Ackland Art Museum, Chapel Hill NC
University of North Carolina at Greensboro, Weatherspoon Art Gallery, Greensboro NC
University of Northern Iowa, Gallery of Art, Cedar Falls IA
University of Notre Dame, Snite Museum of Art, Notre Dame IN
University of Oklahoma, Museum of Art, Norman OK
University of Wisconsin, Elvehjem Art Center, Madison WI
Vancouver Art Gallery, Vancouver BC
Vanderbilt University, Art Gallery, Department of Fine Arts, Nashville TN
Vassar College Art Gallery, Poughkeepsie NY
Victoria and Albert Museum, London England
Virginia Museum of Fine Arts, Richmond VA
Wadsworth Atheneum, Hartford CT
Wallace Collection, London England
Walters Art Gallery, Baltimore MD
Washburn University, Mulvane Art Center, Topeka KS
Washington and Lee University, Gallery of DuPont Hall, Lexington VA
Westbrook College, Joan Whitney Payson Gallery of Art, Portland ME
Westmoreland County Museum of Art, Greensburg PA
Wichita State University, Edwin A Ulrich Museum of Art, Wichita KS
Wilkes College, Sordoni Art Gallery, Wilkes-Barre PA
Williams College, Museum of Art, Williamstown MA
Wolfgang-Gurlitt-Museum, Neue Galerie der Stadt Linz, Linz Austria
Woodmere Art Gallery, Philadelphia PA
Yale University, Art Gallery, New Haven CT
York City Art Gallery, York England
Zigler Museum, Jennings LA

PAINTING - FLEMISH

Arnot Art Museum, Elmira NY
Brooks Memorial Art Gallery, Memphis TN
Capital University, Schumacher Gallery, Columbus OH
Chrysler Museum, Norfolk VA
Sterling and Francine Clark Art Institute, Williamstown MA
Clemson University, Fort Hill, Clemson SC
Columbus Chapel, Boal Mansion and Museum, Boalsburg PA
Corcoran Gallery of Art, Washington DC
Dundee Museums and Art Gallery, Dundee Scotland
Durban Art Gallery, Durban South Africa, Republic of
Evansville Museum of Arts and Science, Evansville IN
Frick Art Museum, Pittsburgh PA
Galleria di Palazzo Bianco, White Palace Gallery, Genoa Italy
Galleria Nazionale d'Arte Antica - Palazzo Barberini, National Gallery in Barberini Palace, Rome Italy
Galleria Sabauda, Turin Italy
Isabella Stewart Gardner Museum, Boston MA
Glasgow Museums and Art Galleries, Kelvingrove Art Gallery and Museum, Glasgow Scotland
Göteborg Konstmuseum, Gothenburg Art Gallery, Gothenburg Sweden
William Humphreys Art Gallery, Kimberley South Africa, Republic of
Koninklijk Kabinet van Schilderijen, Royal Picture Gallery, The Hague Netherlands
Koninklijk Museum voor Schone Kunsten, Royal Museum of Fine Arts, Antwerp Belgium
Michaelis Collection, Cape Province South Africa, Republic of
Musee des Augustins, Museum of Augustins,

Toulouse France
Musee des Beaus-Arts, Palais Saint Pierre, Museum of Fine Arts, Lyon France
Museo de San Carlos, Museum of San Carlos, Mexico Mexico
Museu de Arte de Sao Paulo, Sao Paulo Art Museum, Sao Paulo Brazil
Museum Mayer van den Bergh, Antwerp Belgium
National Gallery of Ireland, Dublin Ireland
Oxford University, Ashmolean Museum of Art and Archaeology, Oxford England
San Diego Museum of Art, San Diego CA
Slovenska Narodna Galeria, Slovak National Gallery, Bratislava Czechoslovakia
Staatliche Kunsthalle, State Art Gallery, Karlshruhe Germany, Federal Republic of
Stadelsches Kunstinstitut, Staedel Art Institute, Frankfurt Germany, Federal Republic of
Statens Museum for Kunst, Department of Painting and Sculpture, Copenhagen Denmark
Stedelyke Musea, City Museums, Bruges Belgium
Strossmayerova Galerija Starih Majstora Jugoslavenske Akademije Znanosti I Umjetnosti, Strossmayer's Gallery of Old Masters of the Yugoslavia Academy of Sciences and Arts, Zagreb Yugoslavia
University of Southern California, University Galleries, Los Angeles CA
Virginia Museum of Fine Arts, Richmond VA
Worcester Art Museum, Worcester MA

PAINTING - FRENCH

Arnot Art Museum, Elmira NY
Art Institute of Chicago, Chicago IL
Baltimore Museum of Art, Baltimore MD
Bates College, Treat Gallery, Lewiston ME
Chrysler Museum, Norfolk VA
Sterling and Francine Clark Art Institute, Williamstown MA
Corcoran Gallery of Art, Washington DC
Courtauld Institute Galleries, London England
Davenport Municipal Art Gallery, Davenport IA
Dixon Gallery and Gardens, Memphis TN
Drexel University Art Gallery and Museum Collection, Philadelphia PA
Dulwich Picture Gallery, London England
Durban Art Gallery, Durban South Africa, Republic of
Frick Art Museum, Pittsburgh PA
Galleria Sabauda, Turin Italy
Isabella Stewart Gardner Museum, Boston MA
Glasgow Museums and Art Galleries, Kelvingrove Art Gallery and Museum, Glasgow Scotland
Grand Rapids Art Museum, Grand Rapids MI
Göteborg Konstmuseum, Gothenburg Art Gallery, Gothenburg Sweden
Hill-Stead Museum, Farmington CT
Hugh Lane Municipal Gallery of Modern Art, Dublin Ireland
William Humphreys Art Gallery, Kimberley South Africa, Republic of
Institut de France, Musee Conde, Paris France
Johannesburg Art Gallery, Johannesburg South Africa, Republic of
Kunsthalle Bremen, Bremen Art Gallery, Bremen Germany, Federal Republic of
Kunstmuseum, Art Museum, Winterthur Switzerland
Kunstmuseum Bern, Museum of Fine Arts Berne, Berne Switzerland
Marion Koogler McNay Art Institute, San Antonio TX
Montreal Museum of Fine Arts, Montreal PQ
Musee Cognacq-Jay, Cognacq-Jay Museum, Paris France
Musee des Augustins, Museum of Augustins, Toulouse France
Musee des Beaus-Arts, Palais Saint Pierre, Museum of Fine Arts, Lyon France
Musee des Beaux-Arts, Rennes France
Musee des Beaux-Arts, Museum of Fine Arts, Orleans France
Musee des Beaux-Arts, Museum of Fine Arts, Strasbourg France

Musee des Beaux-Arts, Museum of Fine Arts, Angers France
Musee des Beaux-Arts de Dijon, Museum of Fine Arts, Dijon France
Musee du Louvre, Louvre Museum, Paris France
Musee du Petit Palais, Avignon France
Musee Marmottan, Paris France
Musee National du Chateau de Fontainebleau, National Museum of Fontainebleau, Fontainebleau France
Musee National du Chateau de Versailles, National Museum of the Chateau of Versailles, Versailles France
Musee Saint-Denis, Reims France
Museo de San Carlos, Museum of San Carlos, Mexico Mexico
Museu de Arte de Sao Paulo, Sao Paulo Art Museum, Sao Paulo Brazil
Museum Boymans-Van Beuningen, Rotterdam Netherlands
Museum of Fine Arts, Springfield MA
Museum of Modern Art, Haifa Israel
Museu Nacional de Belas Artes, National Museum of Fine Arts, Rio Brazil
National Gallery, London England
National Gallery of Ireland, Dublin Ireland
National Museum of Wales, Cardiff Wales
Norton Gallery and School of Art, West Palm Beach FL
Ny Carlsberg Glyptothek, Carlsberg Gallery, Copenhagen Denmark
Ordrupgaard Collection, Charlottenlund Denmark
Oxford University, Ashmolean Museum of Art and Archaeology, Oxford England
Pioneer Museum and Haggin Galleries, Stockton CA
Saint Louis Art Museum, Saint Louis MO
Sheffield City Art Galleries, Mappin Art Gallery, Sheffield England
Strossmayerova Galerija Starih Majstora Jugoslavenske Akademije Znanosti I Umjetnosti, Strossmayer's Gallery of Old Masters of the Yugoslavia Academy of Sciences and Arts, Zagreb Yugoslavia
Tatham Art Gallery, Pietermaritzburg South Africa, Republic of
Tel Aviv Museum, Tel-Aviv Israel
Telfair Academy of Arts and Sciences Inc, Savannah GA
Timken Art Gallery, San Diego CA
University of California, Santa Barbara, Art Museum, Santa Barbara CA
University of Notre Dame, Snite Museum of Art, Notre Dame IN
University of Rochester, Memorial Art Gallery, Rochester NY
University of Southern California, University Galleries, Los Angeles CA
Wallace Collection, London England
Worcester Art Museum, Worcester MA

PAINTING - GERMAN

Arnot Art Museum, Elmira NY
Columbus Chapel, Boal Mansion and Museum, Boalsburg PA
Davenport Municipal Art Gallery, Davenport IA
Drexel University Art Gallery and Museum Collection, Philadelphia PA
Gemaldegalerie der Akademie der Bildenden Kunste in Wien, Art Gallery of the Academy of Fine Arts, Vienna Austria
Germanisches National Museum, Germanic National Museum, Nuremberg Germany, Federal Republic of
Grand Rapids Art Museum, Grand Rapids MI
Kunsthalle Bremen, Bremen Art Gallery, Bremen Germany, Federal Republic of
Kunsthaus Zurich, Museum of Fine Arts, Zurich Switzerland
Kunstmuseum, Art Museum, Winterthur Switzerland
Milwaukee Art Center, Milwaukee WI
Muiska-Museum, Munich Germany, Federal Republic of
Museen der Stadt Köln, Wallraf-Richartz-Museum,

Museum Ludwig, Cologne Germany, Federal
Republic of
Museu de Arte de Sao Paulo, Sao Paulo Art
Museum, Sao Paulo Brazil
Museum of Modern Art, Haifa Israel
National Gallery, London England
National Gallery of Ireland, Dublin Ireland
Offentliche Kunstsammlung-Kunstmuseum Basel,
Museum of Fine Arts, Basel Switzerland
Saint Louis Art Museum, Saint Louis MO
Spencer Museum of Art, Lawrence KS
Staatliche Kunsthalle, State Art Gallery, Karlshruhe
Germany, Federal Republic of
Stadelsches Kunstinstitut, Staedel Art Institute,
Frankfurt Germany, Federal Republic of
Stadtische Gallerie im Lanbachhaus, Lenbach House
City Gallery, Munich Germany, Federal Republic
of
Stadtishces Kunstmuseum Bonn, Art Museum of the
City of Bonn, Bonn Germany, Federal Republic of
Strossmayerova Galerija Starih Majstora
Jugoslavenske Akademije Znanosti I Umjetnosti,
Strossmayer's Gallery of Old Masters of the
Yugoslavia Academy of Sciences and Arts, Zagreb
Yugoslavia
Suermondt-Ludwig-Museum der Stadt Aachen,
Aachen Germany, Federal Republic of
Telfair Academy of Arts and Sciences Inc, Savannah
GA

PAINTING - ISRAELI

Museum of Modern Art, Haifa Israel
Tel Aviv Museum, Tel-Aviv Israel

PAINTING - ITALIAN

Arnot Art Museum, Elmira NY
Ball State University, Art Gallery, Muncie IN
Bates College, Treat Gallery, Lewiston ME
Brooks Memorial Art Gallery, Memphis TN
Bruce Museum, Greenwich CT
Canton Art Institute, Canton OH
Chrysler Museum, Norfolk VA
Civica Galleria d'Arte Moderna, Milan Italy
Civico Museo Revoltella-Galleria d'Arte Moderna,
Revoltella Civic Museum-Gallery of Modern Art,
Trieste Italy
Sterling and Francine Clark Art Institute,
Williamstown MA
Classical School Gallery, Albuquerque NM
Columbia Museums of Art and Science, Columbia
SC
Columbus Chapel, Boal Mansion and Museum,
Boalsburg PA
Dulwich Picture Gallery, London England
Dundee Museums and Art Gallery, Dundee Scotland
Frick Art Museum, Pittsburgh PA
Frick Collection, New York NY
Galleria Borghese, Borghese Gallery, Rome Italy
Galleria Degli Uffizi, Uffizi Gallery, Florence Italy
Galleria di Palazzo Bianco, White Palace Gallery,
Genoa Italy
Galleria Doria Pamphilj, Dorian Gallery, Rome Italy
Galleria Nazionale d'Arte Antica - Palazzo
Barberini, National Gallery in Barberini Palace,
Rome Italy
Galleria Nazionale dell'Umbria, Umbrian National
Gallery, Perugia Italy
Galleria Palatina, Palatine Gallery, Florence Italy
Galleria Sabauda, Turin Italy
Galleries of the Claremont Colleges, Claremont CA
Isabella Stewart Gardner Museum, Boston MA
George Peabody College for Teachers, Cohen
Memorial Museum of Art, Nashville TN
Glasgow Museums and Art Galleries, Kelvingrove
Art Gallery and Museum, Glasgow Scotland
Grand Rapids Art Museum, Grand Rapids MI
Howard University Gallery of Art, Washington DC
Hyde Collection, Glens Falls NY
Indianapolis Museum of Art, Clowes Fund
Collection, Indianapolis IN
Kunstmuseum, Art Museum, Winterthur Switzerland

Kunstmuseum Bern, Museum of Fine Arts Berne,
Berne Switzerland
Musee des Augustins, Museum of Augustins,
Toulouse France
Musee des Beaus-Arts, Palais Saint Pierre, Museum
of Fine Arts, Lyon France
Musee des Beaux-Arts, Museum of Fine Arts,
Angers France
Musee du Petit Palais, Avignon France
Museo Civico di Padua, Municipal Museum, Padua
Italy
Museo Civico di Torino, Municipal Museum, Turin
Italy
Museo d'Arte Antica, Museo di Milano, Milan Italy
Museo d'Arte Antica, Museum of Ancient Art,
Milan Italy
Museo de Capodimonte, Mount Capodi Museum,
Naples Italy
Museo de San Carlos, Museum of San Carlos,
Mexico Mexico
Museo di S Marco, Florence Italy
Museo Nazionale di San Martino, National Museum,
Naples Italy
Museo Nazionale di San Matteo, Saint Matteo
National Museum, Pisa Italy
Museo Nazionale G A Sanna, G A Sanna National
Museum, Sassari Italy
Museo Poldi Pezzoli, Poldi Pezzoli Museum, Milan
Italy
Museu de Arte de Sao Paulo, Sao Paulo Art
Museum, Sao Paulo Brazil
Museum and Picture Gallery, Baroda India
Museum Boymans-Van Beuningen, Rotterdam
Netherlands
Museum of Fine Arts, Springfield MA
Museu Nacional de Belas Artes, National Museum of
Fine Arts, Rio Brazil
National Gallery, London England
National Gallery of Ireland, Dublin Ireland
Oxford University, Ashmolean Museum of Art and
Archaeology, Oxford England
Parrish Art Museum, Southampton NY
Philbrook Art Center, Tulsa OK
Pinacoteca Ambrosiana, Ambrosian Picture Gallery,
Milan Italy
Pinacoteca di Brera, Brera Picture Gallery, Milan
Italy
Portland Art Association, Museum, Portland OR
San Diego Museum of Art, San Diego CA
Sheffield City Art Galleries, Mappin Art Gallery,
Sheffield England
Stadelsches Kunstinstitut, Staedel Art Institute,
Frankfurt Germany, Federal Republic of
Statens Museum for Kunst, Department of Painting
and Sculpture, Copenhagen Denmark
State University of New York College at Potsdam,
Brainerd Art Gallery, Potsdam NY
Strossmayerova Galerija Starih Majstora
Jugoslavenske Akademije Znanosti I Umjetnosti,
Strossmayer's Gallery of Old Masters of the
Yugoslavia Academy of Sciences and Arts, Zagreb
Yugoslavia
Tel Aviv Museum, Tel-Aviv Israel
Timken Art Gallery, San Diego CA
University of Arizona, Museum of Art, Tucson AZ
University of California, Santa Barbara, Art
Museum, Santa Barbara CA
University of Notre Dame, Snite Museum of Art,
Notre Dame IN
University of Southern California, University
Galleries, Los Angeles CA
University of Tennessee, Eleanor Dean Audigier Art
Collection, Knoxville TN
University of Utah, Utah Museum of Fine Arts, Salt
Lake City UT
Vanderbilt University, Art Gallery, Department of
Fine Arts, Nashville TN
Vassar College Art Gallery, Poughkeepsie NY
Virginia Museum of Fine Arts, Richmond VA

PAINTING - JAPANESE

Bridgestone Bijutsukan, Bridgestone Museum of Art,
Tokyo Japan
Calvin College Center Art Gallery, Grand Rapids
MI
Cleveland Museum of Art, Cleveland OH
Hofstra University, Emily Lowe Gallery, Hempstead
NY
Honolulu Academy of Arts, Honolulu HI
Japan Society, Inc, Japan House Gallery, New York
NY
Kyoto Kokuritsu Kindai Bijutsukan, National
Museum of Modern Art, Kyoto, Kyoto Japan
Museum of Japanese Art, Haifa Israel
National Museum of Western Art, Kokuritsu Seiyo
Bijutsukan, Tokyo Japan
New Orleans Museum of Art, Isaac Delgado
Museum, New Orleans LA
Ohara Bijitsukan, Ohara Museum of Art, Kurashiki
Japan
Palm Beach County Parks and Recreation
Department, Morikami Museum of Japanese
Culture, Delray Beach FL
Saint John's University, Chung-Cheng Art Gallery,
Jamaica NY
Seattle Art Museum, Seattle WA
State University of New York College at Potsdam,
Brainerd Art Gallery, Potsdam NY
Tokyo Kokuritsu Kindai Bujutsukan, National
Museum of Modern Art, Tokyo, Tokyo Japan
Tokyo-To Bijutsukan, Tokyo Metropolitan Art
Museum, Tokyo Japan

PAINTING - NEW ZEALANDER

Anderson Park Art Gallery, Invercargill New
Zealand
Auckland City Art Gallery, Auckland New Zealand
Hawkes Bay Art Gallery and Museum, Napier New
Zealand
Sarjeant Gallery, Wanganui New Zealand

PAINTING - POLISH

Muzeum Narodowe, National Museum, Warsaw
Poland
Muzeum Narodowe we Wroclawiu, National
Museum, Wroclaw Poland
Muzeum Narodowe w Krakowie, National Museum
in Cracow, Cracow Poland
Orchard Lake School Galeria, Orchard Lake MI
Polish Museum of America, Research Library,
Chicago IL
Polish Museum of America, Chicago IL

PAINTING - RUSSIAN

Concordia College, Fine Arts Galleries, Milwaukee
WI
Francis E Fowler Jr Foundation Museum, Beverly
Hills CA
National Gallery of Ireland, Dublin Ireland
University of Wisconsin, Elvehjem Art Center,
Madison WI

PAINTING - SCANDINAVIAN

American Swedish Historical Foundations Museum,
Philadelphia PA
American Swedish Institute, Minneapolis MN
City of Oslo Art Collection, Munch Museum, Oslo
Norway
Göteborg Konstmuseum, Gothenburg Art Gallery,
Gothenburg Sweden
Lillehammer Bys Malerisamling, Lillehammer Art
Museum, Lillehammer Norway
Louisiana Museum of Modern Art, Humlebaek
Denmark
Nasjonalgalleriet, National Gallery, Oslo Norway
Nationalmuseum, Moderna Museet, Stockholm

Sweden
Nordjyllands Kunstmuseum, Art Museum of
   Northern Jutland, Aalborg Denmark
Ny Carlsberg Glyptothek, Carlsberg Gallery,
   Copenhagen Denmark
Ordrupgaard Collection, Charlottenlund Denmark
Statens Museum for Kunst, Department of Painting
   and Sculpture, Copenhagen Denmark
Turun Taidemuseo, Turku Art Museum, Turku
   Finland
Universitetets Samling av Nordiske Oldsaker,
   University Museum of National Antiquities, Oslo
   Norway

PAINTING - SPANISH

Arnot Art Museum, Elmira NY
Canton Art Institute, Canton OH
Casa y Museo del Greco, El Greco's House and
   Museum, Toledo Spain
Columbus Chapel, Boal Mansion and Museum,
   Boalsburg PA
Montreal Museum of Fine Arts, Montreal PQ
Musee des Augustins, Museum of Augustins,
   Toulouse France
Musee des Beaus-Arts, Palais Saint Pierre, Museum
   of Fine Arts, Lyon France
Musee des Beaux-Arts, Museum of Fine Arts,
   Angers France
Museo Cerralbo, Madrid Spain
Museo de Arte Cataluna, Museum of Ancient Art,
   Barcelona Spain
Museo de Bellas Artes, Museum of Fine Arts, Bilbao
   Spain
Museo del Prado, National Museum of Paintings and
   Sculpture, Madrid Spain
Museo de San Carlos, Museum of San Carlos,
   Mexico Mexico
Museo Nacional de Bellas Artes, National Museum
   of Fine Arts, Santiago Chile
Museo Romantico, Museum of the Romantic Epoch,
   Madrid Spain
Museu de Arte de Sao Paulo, Sao Paulo Art
   Museum, Sao Paulo Brazil
National Gallery, London England
National Gallery of Ireland, Dublin Ireland
San Diego Museum of Art, San Diego CA
Sheffield City Art Galleries, Mappin Art Gallery,
   Sheffield England
Southern Methodist University, Meadows Museum,
   Dallas TX
Timken Art Gallery, San Diego CA

PERIOD ROOMS

Adams National Historic Site, Quincy MA
Allentown Art Museum, Allentown PA
American Museum in Britain, Bath England
Brick Store Museum, Kennebunk ME
Centre Hill Mansion, Petersburg VA
Chateau de Ramezay, Antiquarian and Numismatic
   Society of Montreal, Montreal PQ
Chester County Historical Society, West Chester PA
Chicago Architecture Foundation, Glessner House,
   Chicago IL
Cincinnati Art Museum, Cincinnati OH
City of Holyoke Museum-Wistariahurst, Holyoke
   MA
Clemson University, Fort Hill, Clemson SC
Cliveden, Philadelphia PA
Colonel Black Mansion, Ellsworth ME
Concord Antiquarian Society Museum, Concord MA
Copper King Mansion, Butte MT
Creek Council House and Museum, Okmulgee OK
Decatur House, Washington DC
Department of State, Diplomatic Reception Rooms,
   Washington DC
Desert Caballeros Western Museum, Wickenburg AZ
Division of Historical and Cultural Affairs, Bureau of
   Museums and Historic Sites, Dover DE
Dundurn Castle, Hamilton ON
East Tennessee State University, Carroll Reece
   Museum, Johnson City TN

Walter Elwood Museum and Art Gallery,
   Amsterdam NY
Farmington Museum, Stanley-Whitman House,
   Farmington CT
Henry Morrison Flagler Museum, Palm Beach FL
Frans Halsmuseum, Frans Hals Museum, Haarlem
   Netherlands
Frick Art Museum, Pittsburgh PA
Gananoque Historical Museum, Gananoque ON
Gibson Society, Inc, Boston MA
Stan Hywet Hall Foundation, Inc, Akron OH
Hopewell Museum, Hopewell NJ
Independence National Historical Park, Philadelphia
   PA
Indianapolis Museum of Art, Indianapolis IN
Israel Museum, Jerusalem Israel
John Jay Homestead, Katonah NY
John Paul Jones House, Portsmouth NH
Jordan Historical Museum of The Twenty, Jordan
   ON
Kansas State Historial Society Museum, Topeka KS
Kentucky Historical Society Museum, Frankfort KY
Henry S Lane Home, Crawfordsville IN
Liberty Hall Museum, Frankfort KY
Longfellow National Historic Site, Cambridge MA
Longfellow's Wayside Inn, South Sudbury MA
Loveland Museum, Loveland CO
Manitoba Historical Society, Dalnavert - MacDonald
   House Museum, Winnipeg MB
Mills Mansion State Historic Site, Staatsburg NY
Minneapolis Institute of Arts, Minneapolis MN
Monticello, Thomas Jefferson Memorial Foundation,
   Charlottesville VA
Morris-Jumel Mansion, New York NY
Mount Vernon, Mount Vernon VA
Muchnic Foundation and Atchison Art Association,
   Muchnic Gallery, Atchison KS
Musee de L'Oeuvre Notre Dame, Cathedral
   Museum, Strasbourg France
Museum of Fine Arts, Boston MA
William Rockhill Nelson Gallery of Art, Atkins
   Museum of Fine Art, Kansas City MO
Nordiska Museet, Scandinavian Museum, Stockholm
   Sweden
Norsk Folkemuseum, Norwegian Folk Museum, Oslo
   Norway
Oatlands, Leesburg VA
Oglebay Institute Mansion Museum, Wheeling WV
Old Barracks, Trenton NJ
Pennsylvania Historical and Museum Commission,
   Harrisburg PA
Phelps County Historical Society Museum, Holdrege
   NE
Philadelphia Museum of Art, Philadelphia PA
Public Archives of Canada, Laurier House, Ottawa
   ON
Rhode Island Historical Society, John Brown House,
   Providence RI
Robert W Ryerss Library and Museum, Philadelphia
   PA
Saint Augustine Historical Society, Oldest House and
   Museums, Saint Augustine FL
Schuyler-Hamilton House, Morristown NJ
Schuyler Mansion, Albany NY
Shaker Community, Inc, Pittsfield MA
Shelburne Museum, Shelburne VT
Sheldon Art Museum, Middlebury VT
Society for the Preservation of Historic Landmarks,
   Elizabeth Perkins House, York ME
State Historical Society of Wisconsin, Madison WI
Stedelijk Museum de Lakenhal, Leyden Municipal
   Museum, Leiden Netherlands
Stockbridge Mission House Association, Stockbridge
   MA
Sturdivant Hall, Selma AL
Telfair Academy of Arts and Sciences Inc, Savannah
   GA
Tippecanoe County Historical Museum, Lafayette IN
University of the South Gallery of Fine Arts,
   Sewanee TN
Vermilion County Museum Society, Danville IL
Western Reserve Historical Society, Cleveland OH
Westfries Museum, Hoorn Netherlands
Woodrow Wilson House, Washington DC

PEWTER

Albany Institute of History and Art, Albany NY
Essex Institute, Salem MA
Franklin Mint Corp Museum, Franklin Center PA
Historic Deerfield Inc, Deerfield MA
Litchfield Historical Society, Litchfield CT
Museum Boymans-Van Beuningen, Rotterdam
   Netherlands
Museum fur Kunstandwerk, Museum of Arts and
   Crafts, Frankfurt Germany, Federal Republic of
New Haven Colony Historical Society, New Haven
   CT
Oglebay Institute Mansion Museum, Wheeling WV
Schweizerisches Landesmuseum, Swiss National
   Museum, Zurich Switzerland
Stedelijk Museum de Lakenhal, Leyden Municipal
   Museum, Leiden Netherlands

PHOTOGRAPHY

Alabama Museum of Photography, Birmingham AL
Alberta College of Art Gallery, Calgary AB
Albrecht Art Museum, Saint Joseph MO
Albright College, Freedman Gallery, Reading PA
Albuquerque Museum of Art, History and Science,
   Albuquerque NM
Amarillo Art Center, Amarillo TX
Art Institute of Chicago, Chicago IL
Auckland City Art Gallery, Auckland New Zealand
Beaumont Art Museum, Beaumont TX
Berea College, Art Department Gallery, Berea KY
Jesse Besser Museum, Alpena MI
California State Fair and Exposition Art Show,
   Sacramento CA
Carnegie Institute, Museum of Art, Pittsburgh PA
Amon Carter Museum of Western Art, Fort Worth
   TX
Center for Creative Photography, Tucson AZ
Cincinnati Art Museum, Cincinnati OH
Corcoran Gallery of Art, Washington DC
Cornell University, Herbert F Johnson Museum of
   Art, Ithaca NY
Creighton University Art Gallery, Omaha NE
Crocker Art Museum, Sacramento CA
DuSable Museum of African American History,
   Chicago IL
Edmonton Art Gallery, Edmonton AB
Galerije Grada Zagreba, Galerija Suvremene
   Umjetnosti, Zagreb Yugoslavia
Galleries of the Claremont Colleges, Claremont CA
Gemaldegalerie der Akademie der Bildenden Kunste
   in Wien, Kupferstichkabinett der Akademie der
   Bildenden Kunste, Vienna Austria
George Washington University Museum & Art
   Galleries, Washington DC
Grossmont Community College Gallery, El Cajon
   CA
Guild Hall of East Hampton, Inc, Museum Section,
   East Hampton NY
Harvard University, William Hayes Fogg Art
   Museum, Cambridge MA
Haverhill Public Library, Haverhill MA
High Museum of Art, Atlanta GA
Historic New Orleans Collection, Kemper and Leila
   Williams Foundation, New Orleans LA
Hofstra University, Emily Lowe Gallery, Hempstead
   NY
Hudson River Museum, Yonkers NY
Illinois State Museum of Natural History and Art,
   Springfield IL
Institute of American Indian Arts Museum, Santa Fe
   NM
International Center of Photography, New York NY
International Museum of Photography at George
   Eastman House, Rochester NY
Kalamazoo Institute of Arts, Genevieve and Donald
   Gilmore Art Center, Kalamazoo MI
Kobenhavns Bymuseum, Copenhagen City Museum,
   Copenhagen Denmark
Lehigh University Galleries, Bethlehem PA
Library of Congress, Washington DC
Louisiana Arts and Science Center, Baton Rouge LA
Louisiana State Museum, New Orleans LA

Meridian Museum of Art, Meridian MS
Merrimack Valley Textile Museum, North Andover MA
Miami-Dade Community College, South Campus, Art Gallery, Miami FL
Middle Tennessee State University, Photographic Gallery, Murfreesboro TN
Midwest Museum of American Art, Elkhart IN
Mills College, Art Gallery, Oakland CA
Minneapolis Institute of Arts, Minneapolis MN
Monterey Peninsula Museum of Art, Monterey CA
Moravska Galerie v Brne, Moravian Gallery at Brno, Brno Czechoslavakia
Muiska-Museum, Munich Germany, Federal Republic of
Museo Nazionale di Villa Guinigi, National Museum of Villa Guinigi, Lucca Italy
Museum, Greenwood SC
Museum of Fine Arts, Houston, Houston TX
Museum of Holography, New York NY
Museum of Modern Art, New York NY
Museum of the City of New York, New York NY
National Film Board of Canada, Still Photography Division, Photo Gallery, Ottawa ON
National Gallery of Victoria, Melbourne Australia
National Maritime Museum, San Francisco CA
National Museum of History and Technology, Smithsonian Institution, Washington DC
National Portrait Gallery, London England
New Orleans Museum of Art, Isaac Delgado Museum, New Orleans LA
Newport Harbor Art Museum, Newport Beach CA
Oakland Museum, Oakland CA
Ohio Wesleyan University, Department of Fine Arts Gallery, Delaware OH
Olana Historic Site, Hudson NY
Open Space Gallery, Secession Gallery of Photography, Victoria BC
Peale Museum, Baltimore MD
Phillips Academy, Addison Gallery of American Art, Andover MA
Photographers Gallery, Saskatoon SK
Pinacoteca Nazionale, National Picture Gallery, Lucca Italy
Plains Art Museum, Main Gallery, Moorhead MN
Polk Public Museum, Lakeland FL
Potsdam Public Museum, Potsdam NY
Roberson Center, Binghamton NY
Saint Anselm's College, Manchester NH
St Lawrence University, Richard F Brush Art Gallery, Canton NY
Saint Louis Art Museum, Saint Louis MO
San Francisco Museum of Modern Art, San Francisco CA
School of Holography, Fine Arts Research and Holographic Center Museum, Chicago IL
Silverado Museum, Saint Helena CA
Smith College, Museum of Art, Northampton MA
Southern Illinois University Museum and Art Galleries, Carbondale IL
State Historical Society of Wisconsin, Madison WI
State University of New York College at Purchase, Neuberger Museum, Purchase NY
Stedlijk Museum-Amsterdam, Municipal Museum, Amsterdam Netherlands
Studio Museum in Harlem, New York NY
Swedish American Museum Association of Chicago, Chicago IL
Tasmanian Museum and Art Gallery, Hobart Australia
Territorial Statehouse, Fillmore UT
Truxtun-Decatur Naval Museum, Washington DC
Ulster County Community College, Visual Arts Gallery, Stone Ridge NY
United Methodist Historical Society, Lovely Lane Museum, Baltimore MD
University of Calgary, The Nickle Arts Museum, Calgary AB
University of California, University Art Galleries and California Museum of Photography, Riverside CA
University of Colorado Art Galleries, Boulder CO
University of Florida, University Gallery, Gainesville FL
University of Iowa, Museum of Art, Iowa City IA
University of Massachusetts, Amherst, University Gallery, Amherst MA
University of Nebraska Lincoln, Sheldon Memorial Art Gallery, Lincoln NE
University of New Mexico, University Art Museum, Albuquerque NM
University of Notre Dame, Snite Museum of Art, Notre Dame IN
University of Oklahoma, Museum of Art, Norman OK
University of Santa Clara, de Saisset Art Gallery and Museum, Santa Clara CA
University of South Florida, University Galleries, Tampa FL
University of Washington, Henry Art Gallery, Seattle WA
University of West Florida, Art Gallery, Pensacola FL
University of Wisconsin, School of Fine Arts Galleries, Milwaukee WI
Valentine Museum, Richmond VA
Walker Art Center, Minneapolis MN
Whatcom Museum of History and Art, Bellingham WA
Yosemite Museum Collections, Yosemite National Park CA

PORCELAIN

Abbot Hall Art Gallery, Cumbria England
Allentown Art Museum, Allentown PA
American Swedish Institute, Minneapolis MN
Atlanta Museum, Atlanta GA
Baltimore Museum of Art, Baltimore MD
Bayerisches Nationalmuseum, Bavarian National Museum, Munich Germany, Federal Republic of
Beaverbrook Art Gallery, Fredericton NB
Bellingrath Gardens and Home, Theodore AL
Benaki Museum, Athens Greece
Brooks Memorial Art Gallery, Memphis TN
Bruce Museum, Greenwich CT
City Art Gallery, Bristol England
Sterling and Francine Clark Art Institute, Williamstown MA
College of Wooster Art Center Museum, Wooster OH
Cranbrook Academy of Art Museum, Bloomfield Hills MI
Cummer Gallery of Art, DeEtte Holden Cummer Museum Foundation, Jacksonville FL
Department of State, Diplomatic Reception Rooms, Washington DC
Det Danske Kunstindustrimuseum, Museum of Decorative Art, Copenhagen Denmark
Dixon Gallery and Gardens, Memphis TN
Ella Sharp Museum, Jackson MI
Everson Museum of Art, Syracuse NY
Franklin Mint Corp Museum, Franklin Center PA
Frick Art Museum, Pittsburgh PA
Frick Collection, New York NY
Gemeentemuseum Arnhem, Municipal Museum of Arnhem, Arnhem Netherlands
Haags Gemeentemuseum, Municipal Museum of The Hague, The Hague Netherlands
Hammond-Harwood House, Annapolis MD
Headley-Whitney Museum, Lexington KY
Hill-Stead Museum, Farmington CT
Herbert Hoover Presidential Library, West Branch IA
Indianapolis Museum of Art, Indianapolis IN
Jacksonville Art Museum, Jacksonville FL
Lehigh University Galleries, Bethlehem PA
Maryland Historical Society Museum, Baltimore MD
Montreal Museum of Fine Arts, Montreal PQ
Mount Clare Mansion, Baltimore MD
Museo d'Arte Antica, Civiche Raccolte de Arte Applicata, Milan Italy
Museo de Arte—Jose Luis Bello y Gonzales, Museum of Art, Puebla Mexico
Museo de Bellas Artes, Museum of Fine Arts, Caracas Venezuela
Museo de Capodimonte, Mount Capodi Museum, Naples Italy
Museo Nazionale di San Martino, National Museum, Naples Italy
Museum of Fine Arts, Boston MA
Museum of the American China Trade, Milton MA
Museu Nacional de Soares dos Reis, National Museum of Soares Dos Reis, Oporto Portugal
National Museum of Wales, Cardiff Wales
Norton Gallery and School of Art, West Palm Beach FL
Parrish Art Museum, Southampton NY
Philadelphia Museum of Art, Philadelphia PA
Henry B Plant Museum, Tampa FL
Plymouth City Museum and Art Gallery, Plymouth England
Remington Art Museum, Ogdensburg NY
Rhode Island School of Design, Museum of Art, Providence RI
Riverside County Art and Cultural Center, Edward-Dean Museum of Decorative Arts, Cherry Valley CA
The Rosenbach Museum and Library, Philadelphia PA
Robert W Ryerss Library and Museum, Philadelphia PA
Saint Bonaventure University Art Collection, Saint Bonaventure NY
Saint John's University, Chung-Cheng Art Gallery, Jamaica NY
Saint Louis Art Museum, Saint Louis MO
Seattle Art Museum, Seattle WA
Ships of The Sea Museum, Savannah GA
Stark Museum of Art, Orange TX
Stedelyke Musea, City Museums, Bruges Belgium
Österreichisches Museum für angewandte Kunst, Vienna Austria
Taft Museum, Cincinnati OH
Topkapi Saray Museum, Istanbul Turkey
University of Notre Dame, Snite Museum of Art, Notre Dame IN
University of Tennessee, Eleanor Dean Audigier Art Collection, Knoxville TN
Virginia Museum, Danville Museum of Fine Arts and History, Danville VA
Virginia Museum of Fine Arts, Richmond VA
Wadsworth Atheneum, Hartford CT
Wallace Collection, London England
Washington and Lee University, Gallery of DuPont Hall, Lexington VA
Wellington Museum, London England
T T Wentworth, Jr Museum, Pensacola FL
White House, Washington DC
Wichita Art Museum, Wichita KS
Woodmere Art Gallery, Philadelphia PA
World Museum & Art Centre, Osborn Foundation, Tulsa OK

PORTRAITS

Baltimore Museum of Art, Baltimore MD
Bowdoin College, Museum of Art & Peary-MacMillan Arctic Museum, Brunswick ME
Canton Art Institute, Canton OH
Carolina Art Association, Gibbes Art Gallery, Charleston SC
Everson Museum of Art, Syracuse NY
Historical Society of Quincy and Adams County, Quincy IL
Huntington Galleries, Huntington WV
Independence National Historical Park, Philadelphia PA
Indianapolis Museum of Art, Indianapolis IN
John Jay Homestead, Katonah NY
Jekyll Island National Historic Landmark, Jekyll Island GA
Kunstmuseum, Art Museum, Winterthur Switzerland
Legislative Building Art Gallery, Regina SK
Lincoln Center for the Performing Arts, Amsterdam, Plaza and Main Galleries, New York NY
Lincoln National Life Foundation, Inc, Louis A Warren Lincoln Library and Museum, Fort Wayne IN
James Monroe Law Office - Museum and Memorial Library, Fredericksburg VA
Musee des Beaux-Arts, Museum of Fine Arts, Orleans France
Musee Historique de Vaudreuil, Vaudreuil Historial

Istanbul Arkeoloji Müzeleri, Archaeological
Museums of Istanbul, Istanbul Turkey
Lahore Museum, Lahore Pakistan
Maryhill Museum of Art, Goldendale WA
Metropolitan Museum of Art, New York NY
Montreal Museum of Fine Arts, Montreal PQ
Musee National, National Museum of Lebanon,
Beirut Lebanon
Musees d'Archeologie et d'Arts Decoratifs, Liege
Museums of Archeology and Decorative Arts,
Liege Belgium
Museum of Fine Arts, Springfield MA
Museum of Fine Arts, Houston, Houston TX
Museum zu Allerheiligen, All Saints' Museum,
Schaffhausen Switzerland
National Museum of INdia, New Delhi India
National Museum of Pakistan, Karachi Pakistan
Olivet College, Armstrong Museum of Art and
Archaeology, Olivet MI
Rheinisches Landesmuseum Bonn, Rhineland
Museum, Bonn Germany, Federal Republic of
Seattle Art Museum, Seattle WA
Southwest Museum, Los Angeles CA
Staten Island Institute of Arts and Sciences, Staten
Island NY
Statens Historiska Museum, Museum of National
Antiquities, Stockholm Sweden
State University of New York at New Paltz, College
Art Gallery, New Paltz NY
Stephens College, Lewis James and Nellie Stratton
Davis Art Gallery, Columbia MO
University of Missouri, Museum of Art and
Archaeology, Columbia MO
University of Rochester, Memorial Art Gallery,
Rochester NY
World Museum & Art Centre, Osborn Foundation,
Tulsa OK

PRINTS

Abilene Fine Arts Museum, Abilene TX
Albion College, Bobbitt Visual Arts Center, Albion
MI
Albrecht Art Museum, Saint Joseph MO
Albright College, Freedman Gallery, Reading PA
Albright-Knox Art Gallery, Buffalo Fine Arts
Academy, Buffalo NY
Aldrich Museum of Contemporary Art, Ridgefield
CT
Lyman Allyn Museum, New London CT
Arizona State University, University Art Collections,
Tempe AZ
Arkansas Arts Center, Little Rock AR
Art Gallery of Brant, Inc, Brantford ON
Art Gallery of Nova Scotia, Halifax NS
Art Gallery of South Australia, Adelaide Australia
Art Gallery of Western Australia, Perth Australia
Art Institute of Chicago, Chicago IL
Art Museum of South Texas, Corpus Christi TX
Attleboro Museum, Center for the Arts, Attleboro
MA
Auckland City Art Gallery, Auckland New Zealand
Augustana College, Bergendorf Fine Arts Gallery,
Rock Island IL
Baldwin-Wallace College Art Gallery, Berea OH
Ball State University, Art Gallery, Muncie IN
Baltimore Museum of Art, Baltimore MD
Bard College, William Cooper Procter Art Center,
Annandale-on-Hudson NY
Bates College, Treat Gallery, Lewiston ME
Baylor University, Baylor Art Museum, Waco TX
Beaverbrook Art Gallery, Fredericton NB
Belmont, Gari Melchers Memorial Gallery,
Fredericksburg VA
Beloit College, Theodore Lyman Wright Art Center,
Beloit WI
Berea College, Art Department Gallery, Berea KY
Jesse Besser Museum, Alpena MI
Bowdoin College, Museum of Art &
Peary-MacMillan Arctic Museum, Brunswick ME
Brandeis University, Rose Art Museum, Waltham
MA
Brevard College, Coltrane Art Center, Brevard NC
Brigham Young University, B F Larsen Gallery,

Provo UT
British Museum, London England
Brown University, Bell Gallery, Providence RI
Burnaby Art Gallery, Burnaby BC
Butler Institute of American Art, Youngstown OH
California State Fair and Exposition Art Show,
Sacramento CA
Calvin College Center Art Gallery, Grand Rapids
MI
Capital University, Schumacher Gallery, Columbus
OH
Carnegie Institute, Museum of Art, Pittsburgh PA
Carolina Art Association, Gibbes Art Gallery,
Charleston SC
Amon Carter Museum of Western Art, Fort Worth
TX
Cincinnati Art Museum, Cincinnati OH
City College of the City of New York, Eisner Hall
Art Gallery, New York NY
College of Eastern Utah, Gallery East, Price UT
College of Idaho, Blatchley Gallery, Caldwell ID
College of Saint Benedict, Art Gallery, Saint Joseph
MN
College of Wooster Art Center Museum, Wooster
OH
Columbus Museum of Art, Columbus OH
Columbus Museum of Arts and Sciences, Columbus
GA
Concordia College, Koenig Art Gallery, Seward NE
Confederation Centre Art Gallery and Museum,
Charlottetown PE
Cooper-Hewitt Museum, Smithsonian Institution
National Museum of Design, New York NY
Coos Art Museum, Coos Bay OR
Cranbrook Academy of Art Museum, Bloomfield
Hills MI
Crocker Art Museum, Sacramento CA
Danforth Museum, Framingham MA
DAR Museum, National Society Daughters of the
American Revolution, Washington DC
Diamond M Foundation Museum, Snyder TX
Drew University, College Art Gallery, Madison NJ
Dundee Museums and Art Gallery, Dundee Scotland
DuSable Museum of African American History,
Chicago IL
East Tennessee State University, Carroll Reece
Museum, Johnson City TN
Ella Sharp Museum, Jackson MI
Wharton Esherick Museum, Paoli PA
Everhart Museum of Natural History, Science and
Art, Scranton PA
Findlay College, Egner Fine Arts Center, Findlay
OH
Fine Arts Museum of the South, Mobile AL
Fitchburg Art Museum, Fitchburg MA
Fort Hays State University, Visual Arts Center, Hays
KS
Fort Wayne Museum of Art, Fort Wayne IN
Frick Collection, New York NY
Fries Museum, Leeuwarden Netherlands
Frostburg State College, Fine Arts Gallery I,
Frostburg MD
Gemaldegalerie der Akademie der Bildenden Kunste
in Wien, Kupferstichkabinett der Akademie der
Bildenden Kunste, Vienna Austria
Gemeentemuseum Arnhem, Municipal Museum of
Arnhem, Arnhem Netherlands
George Washington University Museum & Art
Galleries, Washington DC
Gonzaga University, AD Gallery, Spokane WA
Goucher College, Kraushaar Auditorium Lobby
Gallery, Towson MD
Grand Rapids Art Museum, Grand Rapids MI
Graphische Sammlung Albertina, Albertina Graphic
Art Collection, Vienna Austria
Groningen Museum voor Stad en Land, Groningen
Museum, Groningen Netherlands
Grossmont Community College Gallery, El Cajon
CA
Göteborg Konstmuseum, Gothenburg Art Gallery,
Gothenburg Sweden
Solomon R Guggenheim Museum, New York NY
Guild Hall of East Hampton, Inc, Museum Section,
East Hampton NY
Haags Gemeentemuseum, Municipal Museum of The

Hague, The Hague Netherlands
Hall of Fame of the Trotter, Goshen NY
Hamburger Kunsthalle, Hamburg Art Museum,
Hamburg Germany, Federal Republic of
Hammond-Harwood House, Annapolis MD
Hartwick College Fine Art Gallery, Oneonta NY
Harvard University, William Hayes Fogg Art
Museum, Cambridge MA
Haverhill Public Library, Haverhill MA
Heckscher Museum, Huntington NY
Herzog Anton Ulrich-Museum, Medieval Section:
Burg Dankwarderode, Brunswick Germany,
Federal Republic of
Highland Area Arts Council, Freeport Art Museum,
Freeport IL
High Museum of Art, Atlanta GA
Hill-Stead Museum, Farmington CT
Historic New Orleans Collection, Kemper and Leila
Williams Foundation, New Orleans LA
Honolulu Academy of Arts, Honolulu HI
Howard University Gallery of Art, Washington DC
Hunter Museum of Art, Chattanooga TN
Huntington Galleries, Huntington WV
Hyde Collection, Glens Falls NY
Illinois Wesleyan University, Merwin Gallery,
Bloomington IL
Indianapolis Museum of Art, Indianapolis IN
Indiana University, Art Museum, Bloomington IN
Jacksonville Art Museum, Jacksonville FL
Johannesburg Art Gallery, Johannesburg South
Africa, Republic of
Johnson-Humrickhouse Museum, Coshocton OH
Keene State College, Thorne-Sagendorph Art
Gallery, Keene NH
Kendall Whaling Museum, Sharon MA
Kent State University, School of Art Gallery, Kent
OH
Kunsthalle Bremen, Bremen Art Gallery, Bremen
Germany, Federal Republic of
Kunstmuseum, Art Museum, Winterthur Switzerland
Kyoto Kokuritsu Kindai Bijutsukan, National
Museum of Modern Art, Kyoto, Kyoto Japan
La Casa del Libro, House of Books, San Juan PR
La Salle College Art Gallery, Philadelphia PA
Leeds Art Galleries, Leeds England
Library of Congress, Washington DC
Lindenwood Colleges, Harry D Hendren Gallery,
Saint Charles MO
Long Beach Museum of Art, Long Beach CA
Longfellow's Wayside Inn, South Sudbury MA
Los Angeles County Museum of Art, Los Angeles
CA
Lycoming College Gallery, Williamsport PA
Macdonald Steward Art Centre, Guelph ON
Madison Art Center, Madison WI
Judah L Magnes Memorial Museum, Western Jewish
History Center, Berkeley CA
Marquette University, Marquette Fine Art
Collection, Milwaukee WI
Maryville College Fine Arts Center Gallery,
Maryville TN
Massachusetts Institute of Technology, MIT
Committee on Visual Arts (Hayden Gallery and
MIT Permanent Collection), Cambridge MA
McAllen International Museum, McAllen TX
McGill University, McCord Museum, Montreal PQ
The Robert McLaughlin Gallery, Oshawa ON
McMaster University Art Gallery, Hamilton ON
Marion Koogler McNay Art Institute, San Antonio
TX
McPherson College, McPherson KS
Meridian Museum of Art, Meridian MS
Merrimack Valley Textile Museum, North Andover
MA
Miami-Dade Community College, South Campus,
Art Gallery, Miami FL
Miami University Art Museum, Oxford OH
Michigan State University, Kresge Art Center, East
Lansing MI
Middlebury College, Johnson Gallery, Middlebury
VT
Millikin University, Kirkland Gallery, Decatur IL
Mills College, Art Gallery, Oakland CA
Minneapolis Institute of Arts, Minneapolis MN
Minnesota Museum of Art, Saint Paul MN

FL

University of Wisconsin, Allen Priebe Gallery, Oshkosh WI
University of Wisconsin, Memorial Union Gallery, Madison WI
University of Wisconsin, School of Fine Arts Galleries, Milwaukee WI
University of Wisconsin-Stout, Gallery 209, Menomonie WI
Utah Division of State History, Salt Lake City UT
Valentine Museum, Richmond VA
Valparaiso University, University Art Galleries and Collections, Valparaiso IN
Vanderbilt University, Art Gallery, Department of Fine Arts, Nashville TN
Victoria and Albert Museum, London England
Virginia Commonwealth University, Anderson Gallery, Richmond VA
Virginia Museum, Danville Museum of Fine Arts and History, Danville VA
Wadsworth Atheneum, Hartford CT
Walker Art Gallery, Liverpool England
Walker Museum, Fairlee VT
Washburn University, Mulvane Art Center, Topeka KS
Washington County Museum of Fine Arts, Hagerstown MD
Wayne State College, Nordstrand Visual Arts Gallery, Wayne NE
Wesleyan University, Davison Art Center, Middletown CT
Western State College, Quigley Hall Art Gallery, Gunnison CO
Westminster College Art Gallery, New Wilmington PA
Westmoreland County Museum of Art, Greensburg PA
White House, Washington DC
Whitney Museum of American Art, New York NY
Wichita Falls Museum and Art Center, Wichita Falls TX
Williams College, Museum of Art, Williamstown MA
Wolfgang-Gurlitt-Museum, Neue Galerie der Stadt Linz, Linz Austria
Worcester Art Museum, Worcester MA
York City Art Gallery, York England

RELIGIOUS ART

Bass Museum of Art, Miami Beach FL
Benaki Museum, Athens Greece
Bob Jones University, Greenville SC
Breezewood Foundation Museum and Garden, Monkton MD
Byzantine Museum, Athens Greece
Cathedral Museum of Religious Art, New York NY
Catholic Historical Society of Saint Paul, Saint Paul MN
Church of Jesus Christ of Latter-Day Saints, Information Center and Museum, Arts and Sites Division, Salt Lake City UT
Concordia Historical Institute, Saint Louis MO
Coptic Museum, Cairo Egypt
Franciscan Monastery, Holy Land of America, Washington DC
Georgetown University, Art and History Museum, Washington DC
Harvard University, Dumbarton Oaks Research Library and Collections, Washington DC
Koyasan Reihokan, Museum of Buddhist Art, Wakayama Japan
Los Angeles County Museum of Art, Los Angeles CA
Louisiana Arts and Science Center, Baton Rouge LA
Mission San Luis Rey Museum, San Luis Rey CA
Mission San Miguel, San Miguel CA
Monumenti Musei e Gallerie Pontificie, Vatican Museums and Galleries, Vatican City Italy
Moravian Historical Society, Whitefield House Museum, Nazareth PA
Musee d'Art de Joliette, Joliette PQ
Musee de L'Eglise Notre-Dame, Montreal PQ
Musee Kateri Tekakwitha, Cahughnawaga PQ
Museen der Stadt Köln, Kölnisches Stadtmuseum im

Zeughaus, Cologne Germany, Federal Republic of
Museen der Stadt Köln, Schnutgen-Museum, Cologne Germany, Federal Republic of
Museo de Arte, Museum of Art, Lima Peru
Museo de Arte—Jose Luis Bello y Gonzales, Museum of Art, Puebla Mexico
Museu da Inconfidencia, History of Democratic Ideals and Culture in Minas Gerais, Ouro Brazil
Nara Kokuritsu Hakubutsukan, Nara National Museum, Nara-shi Japan
Nasjonalgalleriet, National Gallery, Oslo Norway
National Museum of Korea, Seoul Korea
Newark Museum, Newark NJ
Noord-Brabants Museum, Hertogenbosch Netherlands
Peres Redemptoristes, Sainte Anne de Beaupre PQ
Peshawar Museum, Peshawar Pakistan
Philadelphia Museum of Art, Philadelphia PA
Religious Americana Museum, Ringoes NJ
Rensselaer Newman Foundation Chapel and Cultural Center, Troy NY
Millicent Rogers Museum, Taos NM
Saint Bernard Foundation and Monastery, Miami Beach FL
Saint Mary's College of California, Hearst Art Gallery, Moraga CA
San Carlos Cathedral, Monterey CA
Southern Baptist Seminary Museum, Louisville KY
Timken Art Gallery, San Diego CA
Tome Parish Museum, Tome NM
United Methodist Church Commission on Archives and History, Lake Junaluska NC
United Methodist Historical Society, Lovely Lane Museum, Baltimore MD
Universitetets Samling av Nordiske Oldsaker, University Museum of National Antiquities, Oslo Norway
University of Addis Ababa, Museum of the Institute of Ethiopian Studies, Addis Ababa Ethiopia
University of Wisconsin, Elvehjem Art Center, Madison WI
University of Wisconsin, Department of Art History Gallery, Milwaukee WI
Valparaiso University, University Art Galleries and Collections, Valparaiso IN

RENAISSANCE ART

Ball State University, Art Gallery, Muncie IN
Baltimore Museum of Art, Baltimore MD
Berea College, Art Department Gallery, Berea KY
Brooks Memorial Art Gallery, Memphis TN
City College of the City of New York, Eisner Hall Art Gallery, New York NY
Columbia Museums of Art and Science, Columbia SC
El Paso Museum of Art, El Paso TX
Flint Institute of Arts, Flint MI
Frick Collection, New York NY
Galleria e Museo del Palazzo Ducale, Gallery and Museum of the Palazzo Ducale, Mantua Italy
Galleries of the Claremont Colleges, Claremont CA
George Peabody College for Teachers, Cohen Memorial Museum of Art, Nashville TN
Grand Rapids Art Museum, Grand Rapids MI
Hammond Museum, Inc, Gloucester MA
Hartwick College Fine Art Gallery, Oneonta NY
Harvard University, Busch-Reisinger Museum, Cambridge MA
Gertrude Herbert Memorial Institute of Art, Augusta GA
Honolulu Academy of Arts, Honolulu HI
Howard University Gallery of Art, Washington DC
Indianapolis Museum of Art, Clowes Fund Collection, Indianapolis IN
Mint Museum of Art, Charlotte NC
Musee de L'Oeuvre Notre Dame, Cathedral Museum, Strasbourg France
Museo de Bellas Artes, Museum of Fine Arts, Bilbao Spain
Museo de Capodimonte, Mount Capodi Museum, Naples Italy
New Orleans Museum of Art, Isaac Delgado Museum, New Orleans LA

Panstwowe Zbiory Sztuki na Wawelu, Wawel State Collections of Art, Cracow Poland
Parrish Art Museum, Southampton NY
Philadelphia Museum of Art, Philadelphia PA
Philbrook Art Center, Tulsa OK
Portland Art Association, Museum, Portland OR
San Diego Museum of Art, San Diego CA
Severoceska Galerie Vytvarneho Umeni, North Bohemian Gallery of Fine Arts, Litomerice Czechoslovakia
Taft Museum, Cincinnati OH
University of Arizona, Museum of Art, Tucson AZ
University of Rochester, Memorial Art Gallery, Rochester NY
University of Utah, Utah Museum of Fine Arts, Salt Lake City UT
University of Wisconsin, Elvehjem Art Center, Madison WI
Vanderbilt University, Art Gallery, Department of Fine Arts, Nashville TN
Virginia Museum of Fine Arts, Richmond VA

RESTORATIONS

Huntington Galleries, Huntington WV

SCRIMSHAW

Heritage Plantation of Sandwich, Sandwich MA
Kendall Whaling Museum, Sharon MA
New Bedford Whaling Museum, New Bedford MA
Ships of The Sea Museum, Savannah GA

SCULPTURE

Abbot Hall Art Gallery, Cumbria England
Albany Institute of History and Art, Albany NY
Albright College, Freedman Gallery, Reading PA
Albright-Knox Art Gallery, Buffalo Fine Arts Academy, Buffalo NY
Lyman Allyn Museum, New London CT
American Swedish Institute, Minneapolis MN
American University of Beirut, Archaeological Museum, Beirut Lebanon
Anderson House Museum, Society of the Cincinnati, Washington DC
Archaeological Museum, Taxila Pakistan
Arizona State University, University Art Collections, Tempe AZ
Art Gallery of Nova Scotia, Halifax NS
Art Gallery of Ontario, Toronto ON
Art Gallery of South Australia, Adelaide Australia
Art Gallery of Western Australia, Perth Australia
Art Institute of Chicago, Chicago IL
Atlanta Museum, Atlanta GA
Auckland City Art Gallery, Auckland New Zealand
Augusta Richmond County Museum, Augusta GA
Baldwin-Wallace College Art Gallery, Berea OH
Baltimore Museum of Art, Baltimore MD
Bard College, William Cooper Procter Art Center, Annandale-on-Hudson NY
Bass Museum of Art, Miami Beach FL
Bayerischen Staatsgemaldesammlungen, Neue Pinakothek, Munich Germany, Federal Republic of
Bayerischen Staatsgemaldesammlungen, Staatsgalerie Moderne-Kunst, Munich Germany, Federal Republic of
Bayerisches Nationalmuseum, Bavarian National Museum, Munich Germany, Federal Republic of
Baylor University, Baylor Art Museum, Waco TX
Beaumont Art Museum, Beaumont TX
Beaverbrook Art Gallery, Fredericton NB
Beloit College, Theodore Lyman Wright Art Center, Beloit WI
Bergstrom Art Center and Museum, Neenah WI
Berkshire Museum, Pittsfield MA
Blanden Memorial Art Gallery, Fort Dodge IA
Bob Jones University, Greenville SC
Boise Gallery of Art, Boise ID
Bridgestone Bijutsukan, Bridgestone Museum of Art, Tokyo Japan
Brigham Young University, B F Larsen Gallery,

Republic of
Museo Civico di Padua, Municipal Museum, Padua
Italy
Museo Civico di Torino, Municipal Museum, Turin
Italy
Museo d'Arte Antica, Civiche Raccolte de Arte
Applicata, Milan Italy
Museo d'Arte Antica, Museum of Ancient Art,
Milan Italy
Museo de Arte, Museum of Art, Lima Peru
Museo de Arte Cataluna, Museum of Ancient Art,
Barcelona Spain
Museo de Arte—Jose Luis Bello y Gonzales,
Museum of Art, Puebla Mexico
Museo de Bellas Artes, Museum of Fine Arts,
Caracas Venezuela
Museo del Prado, National Museum of Paintings and
Sculpture, Madrid Spain
Museo de San Carlos, Museum of San Carlos,
Mexico Mexico
Museo Municipal de Bellas Artes Juan B Castagnino,
Municipal Museum of Fine Arts, Rosario
Argentina
Museo Nacional de Artes Plasticas, National
Museum of Fine Arts, Montevideo Uruguay
Museo Nacional de Bellas Artes, National Museum
of Fine Arts, Santiago Chile
Museo Nacional de Bellas Artes, National Museum
of Fine Arts, Buenos Aires Argentina
Museo Nazionale di San Martino, National Museum,
Naples Italy
Museo Nazionale di San Matteo, Saint Matteo
National Museum, Pisa Italy
Museo Nazionale di Villa Guinigi, National Museum
of Villa Guinigi, Lucca Italy
Museo Nazionale G A Sanna, G A Sanna National
Museum, Sassari Italy
Museo Nazionale Romano, National Museum of
Rome, Rome Italy
Museu de Arte de Sao Paulo, Sao Paulo Art
Museum, Sao Paulo Brazil
Museum Mayer van den Bergh, Antwerp Belgium
Museum of American Folk Art, New York NY
Museum of Art of Ogunquit, Ogunquit ME
Museum of Arts and Sciences, Inc, Macon GA
Museum of Fine Arts, Boston MA
Museum of Fine Arts, Springfield MA
Museum of Fine Arts, Houston, Houston TX
Museum of Fine Arts of Saint Petersburg, Florida,
Inc, Saint Petersburg FL
Museum of Modern Art, Belgrade Yugoslavia
Museum of Modern Art, Haifa Israel
Museum of Modern Art, New York NY
Museum of the United States Department of the
Interior, Washington DC
Museum Rietberg Zurich, Zurich Switzerland
Museum voor Schone Kunsten, Ghent Belgium
Museu Nacional de Arte Antiga, National Museum
of Ancient Art, Lisbon Portugal
Museu Nacional de Soares dos Reis, National
Museum of Soares Dos Reis, Oporto Portugal
Muzeul de Arta Cluj-Napoca, Museum of Art,
Cluj-Napoca Romania
Muzeum Narodowe, National Museum, Warsaw
Poland
Muzeum Narodowe we Wroclawiu, National
Museum, Wroclaw Poland
Muzeum Narodowe w Krakowie, National Museum
in Cracow, Cracow Poland
Nara Kokuritsu Hakubutsukan, Nara National
Museum, Nara-shi Japan
Narodna Galerija, National Art Gallery, Ljubljana
Yugoslavia
Narodni Galerie v Prague, National Gallery of
Prague, Prague Czechoslovakia
Nasjonalgalleriet, National Gallery, Oslo Norway
Nassau County Museum of Fine Art, Roslyn NY
National Air and Space Museum, Washington DC
National Collection of Fine Arts, Washington DC
National Galleries of Scotland, Scottish National
Gallery of Modern Art, Edinburgh Scotland
National Galleries of Scotland, National Gallery of
Scotland, Edinburgh Scotland
National Gallery of Modern Art, New India
Nationalmuseum, Moderna Museet, Stockholm

Sweden
National Museum of INdia, New Delhi India
National Museum of Korea, Seoul Korea
National Museum of Pakistan, Karachi Pakistan
National Museum of Western Art, Kokuritsu Seiyo
Bijutsukan, Tokyo Japan
National Pinakothiki and Alexander Soutzos
Museum, Athens Greece
National Portrait Gallery, London England
Nebraska Wesleyan University, Elder Gallery,
Lincoln NE
William Rockhill Nelson Gallery of Art, Atkins
Museum of Fine Art, Kansas City MO
Newark Museum, Newark NJ
New Orleans Museum of Art, Isaac Delgado
Museum, New Orleans LA
Newport Museum and Art Gallery, Newport Wales
New School for Social Research Art Center Gallery,
New York NY
Elizabet Ney Museum, Austin TX
Noord-Brabants Museum, Hertogenbosch
Netherlands
Nordjyllands Kunstmuseum, Art Museum of
Northern Jutland, Aalborg Denmark
North Carolina Museum of Art, Department of
Cultural Resources, Raleigh NC
Northwestern College, Ramaker Library Art Gallery,
Orange City IA
Norton Gallery and School of Art, West Palm Beach
FL
R W Norton Art Gallery, Shreveport LA
Ny Carlsberg Glyptothek, Carlsberg Gallery,
Copenhagen Denmark
Oakland Museum, Oakland CA
Oberlin College, Allen Memorial Art Museum,
Oberlin OH
Ohara Bijitsukan, Ohara Museum of Art, Kurashiki
Japan
Oklahoma Art Center, Oklahoma City OK
Olivet College, Armstrong Museum of Art and
Archaeology, Olivet MI
Openluchtmuseum voor Beeldhouwkunst,
Middelheim, Open Air Museum for Sculpture
Middelheim, Antwerp Belgium
Oxford University, Ashmolean Museum of Art and
Archaeology, Oxford England
Pennsylvania Academy of the Fine Arts, Philadelphia
PA
Pennsylvania State University, Museum of Art,
University Park PA
Philbrook Art Center, Tulsa OK
Phillips Academy, Addison Gallery of American Art,
Andover MA
Phoenix Art Museum, Phoenix AZ
Pioneer Town, Wimberley TX
Plains Art Museum, Main Gallery, Moorhead MN
Ponca City Cultural Center Museum, Ponca City
OK
Portland Art Association, Museum, Portland OR
Portland Museum of Art, Portland ME
Purdue University, Gallery I, Gallery II, Union
Gallery & Stewart Center Gallery, West Lafayette
IN
Queensland Art Gallery, Brisbane Australia
Queen's University, Agnes Etherington Art Centre,
Kingston ON
Red River Valley Museum, Vernon TX
Reed College Art Gallery, Portland OR
Remington Art Museum, Ogdensburg NY
Rensselaer Newman Foundation Chapel and Cultural
Center, Troy NY
Rijksmuseum, State Museum, Amsterdam
Netherlands
John and Mable Ringling Museum of Art, Sarasota
FL
Robert W Ryerss Library and Museum, Philadelphia
PA
Ryksmuseum Kroller-Muller, Kroller-Muller State
Museum, Otterlo Netherlands
Saginaw Art Museum, Saginaw MI
Saint Clair County Community College, Jack R
Hennesey Art Galleries, Port Huron MI
Saint Johnsbury Athenaeum, Saint Johnsbury VT
St Lawrence University, Richard F Brush Art
Gallery, Canton NY

Saint Louis Art Museum, Saint Louis MO
Saint Louis County Department of Parks and
Recreation, Laumeier Sculpture Park, Saint Louis
MO
Saint Mary's College of California, Hearst Art
Gallery, Moraga CA
San Carlos Cathedral, Monterey CA
San Diego Museum of Art, San Diego CA
San Diego State University, Art Gallery, San Diego
CA
San Francisco Museum of Modern Art, San
Francisco CA
San Jose Museum of Art, San Jose CA
San Jose State University, Union Gallery, San Jose
CA
Santa Barbara Museum of Art, Santa Barbara CA
Scripps College, Clark Humanities Museum,
Claremont CA
Sefton Metropolitan Borough, Atlinson Art Gallery,
Southport England
Severoceska Galerie Vytvarneho Umeni, North
Bohemian Gallery of Fine Arts, Litomerice
Czechoslovakia
Sheffield City Art Galleries, Mappin Art Gallery,
Sheffield England
Silverado Museum, Saint Helena CA
Norton Simon Museum, Pasadena CA
Slovenska Narodna Galeria, Slovak National Gallery,
Bratislava Czechoslovakia
Smith-Mason Gallery and Museum, Washington DC
South African National Gallery, Cape South Africa,
Republic of
Southern Alleghenies Museum of Art, Loretto PA
Southern Illinois University Museum and Art
Galleries, Carbondale IL
Springfield Art Museum, Springfield MO
Stanford University, T W Stanford Art Gallery &
Museum of Art, Stanford CA
Staten Island Institute of Arts and Sciences, Staten
Island NY
Statens Museum for Kunst, Department of Painting
and Sculpture, Copenhagen Denmark
State University of New York at Albany, University
Art Gallery, Albany NY
State University of New York College at Fredonia,
M C Rockefeller Arts Center Gallery, Fredonia
NY
State University of New York College at Geneseo,
Fine Arts Gallery, Geneseo NY
State University of New York College at Potsdam,
Brainerd Art Gallery, Potsdam NY
State University of New York College at Purchase,
Neuberger Museum, Purchase NY
Stedelijk Museum Alkmaar, Alkmaar Municipal
Museum, Alkmaar Netherlands
Stedelijk Museum de Lakenhal, Leyden Municipal
Museum, Leiden Netherlands
Stedelyke Musea, City Museums, Bruges Belgium
Stedlijk Museum-Amsterdam, Municipal Museum,
Amsterdam Netherlands
Stephens College, Lewis James and Nellie Stratton
Davis Art Gallery, Columbia MO
Storm King Art Center, Mountainville NY
Strossmayerova Galerija Starih Majstora
Jugoslavenske Akademije Znanosti I Umjetnosti,
Strossmayer's Gallery of Old Masters of the
Yugoslavia Academy of Sciences and Arts, Zagreb
Yugoslavia
Studio Museum in Harlem, New York NY
Suermondt-Ludwig-Museum der Stadt Aachen,
Aachen Germany, Federal Republic of
Szepmuveszet Museum, Museum of Fine Arts,
Budapest Hungary
Tacoma Art Museum, Tacoma WA
Tate Gallery, London England
Tatham Art Gallery, Pietermaritzburg South Africa,
Republic of
Thorvaldsen Museum, Copenhagen Denmark
Tokyo Kokuritsu Kindai Bujutsukan, National
Museum of Modern Art, Tokyo, Tokyo Japan
Tokyo-To Bijutsukan, Tokyo Metropolitan Art
Museum, Tokyo Japan
Toledo Museum of Art, Toledo OH
Tomoka State Park Museum, Ormond Beach FL
Triton Museum of Art, Santa Clara CA

Tucson Museum of Art, Tucson AZ
Turk ve Islam Eserleri Muzesi, Museum of Turkish and Islamic Art, Istanbul Turkey
Turun Taidemuseo, Turku Art Museum, Turku Finland
Tyringham Art Galleries, Tyringham MA
Ulster County Community College, Visual Arts Gallery, Stone Ridge NY
United States Capitol Museum, Washington DC
United States Naval Academy Museum, Annapolis MD
University of Alberta, Ring House Gallery, Edmonton AB
University of Arizona, Museum of Art, Tucson AZ
University of Calgary, The Nickle Arts Museum, Calgary AB
University of California, Los Angeles, Frederick S Wight Art Gallery, Los Angeles CA
University of Cambridge, Fitzwilliam Museum, Cambridge England
University of Chicago, David and Alfred Smart Gallery, Chicago IL
University of Colorado Art Galleries, Boulder CO
University of Connecticut, William Benton Museum of Art, Storrs CT
University of Delaware, University Art Collections, Newark DE
University of Iowa, Museum of Art, Iowa City IA
University of Kentucky, Art Museum, Lexington KY
University of Manchester, Whitworth Art Gallery, Manchester England
University of Maryland, Art Gallery, College Park MD
University of Michigan Museum of Art, Kelsey Museum of Ancient and Medieval Archaeology, Ann Arbor MI
University of Michigan Museum of Art, Alumni Memorial Hall Museum, Ann Arbor MI
University of Minnesota, Tweed Museum of Art, Duluth MN
University of Minnesota, University Gallery, Minneapolis MN
University of Missouri, Museum of Art and Archaeology, Columbia MO
University of Nebraska Lincoln, Sheldon Memorial Art Gallery, Lincoln NE
University of New Mexico, University Art Museum, Albuquerque NM
University of North Carolina, The Ackland Art Museum, Chapel Hill NC
University of North Carolina at Greensboro, Weatherspoon Art Gallery, Greensboro NC
University of Notre Dame, Snite Museum of Art, Notre Dame IN
University of Pittsburgh, University Art Gallery, Pittsburgh PA
University of San Diego, Founders' Gallery, San Diego CA
University of Santa Clara, de Saisset Art Gallery and Museum, Santa Clara CA
University of South Florida, University Galleries, Tampa FL
University of Southwestern Louisiana, Art Center for Southwestern Louisiana, Lafayette LA
University of Tennessee, Eleanor Dean Audigier Art Collection, Knoxville TN
University of Wisconsin, School of Fine Arts Galleries, Milwaukee WI
University of Wisconsin, Elvehjem Art Center, Madison WI
University of Wisconsin, Memorial Union Gallery, Madison WI
University of Wisconsin-Stout, Gallery 209, Menomonie WI
Utah Division of State History, Salt Lake City UT
Valentine Museum, Richmond VA
Vancouver Art Gallery, Vancouver BC
Vassar College Art Gallery, Poughkeepsie NY
Victoria and Albert Museum, London England
Villa Montalvo Center for the Arts, Saratoga CA
Virginia Museum of Fine Arts, Richmond VA
Walker Art Center, Minneapolis MN
Walker Art Gallery, Liverpool England
Walker Museum, Fairlee VT
Wallace Collection, London England

Washburn University, Mulvane Art Center, Topeka KS
Washington County Museum of Fine Arts, Hagerstown MD
Wellington Museum, London England
Western Woodcarvings, Custer SD
Westmoreland County Museum of Art, Greensburg PA
White House, Washington DC
Whitney Museum of American Art, New York NY
Wichita Art Museum, Wichita KS
Wichita State University, Edwin A Ulrich Museum of Art, Wichita KS
Wilkes College, Sordoni Art Gallery, Wilkes-Barre PA
Williams College, Museum of Art, Williamstown MA
Winnipeg Art Gallery, Winnipeg MB
Wolfgang-Gurlitt-Museum, Neue Galerie der Stadt Linz, Linz Austria
Woodmere Art Gallery, Philadelphia PA
World Museum & Art Centre, Osborn Foundation, Tulsa OK
Yale University, Art Gallery, New Haven CT
York Institute Museum, Saco ME
Zigler Museum, Jennings LA

SILVER

Albany Institute of History and Art, Albany NY
Allentown Art Museum, Allentown PA
Art Gallery of Western Australia, Perth Australia
Baltimore Museum of Art, Baltimore MD
Berea College, Art Department Gallery, Berea KY
Berkshire Museum, Pittsfield MA
Birmingham Museum of Art, Birmingham AL
Birmingham Museums and Art Gallery, Birmingham England
City Art Gallery, Bristol England
Sterling and Francine Clark Art Institute, Williamstown MA
Colombian Institute of Culture, Museum of Colonial Art, Bogota Colombia
Currier Gallery of Art, Manchester NH
Department of State, Diplomatic Reception Rooms, Washington DC
Det Danske Kunstindustrimuseum, Museum of Decorative Art, Copenhagen Denmark
Detroit Institute of Arts, Detroit MI
Doncaster Museum and Art Gallery, Doncaster England
Essex Institute, Salem MA
Francis E Fowler Jr Foundation Museum, Beverly Hills CA
Franciscan Monastery, Holy Land of America, Washington DC
Frans Halsmuseum, Frans Hals Museum, Haarlem Netherlands
Frick Art Museum, Pittsburgh PA
Fries Museum, Leeuwarden Netherlands
Gemeentemuseum Arnhem, Municipal Museum of Arnhem, Arnhem Netherlands
George Peabody College for Teachers, Cohen Memorial Museum of Art, Nashville TN
Groningen Museum voor Stad en Land, Groningen Museum, Groningen Netherlands
Hammond-Harwood House, Annapolis MD
Harvard University, William Hayes Fogg Art Museum, Cambridge MA
Hill-Stead Museum, Farmington CT
Historic Deerfield Inc, Deerfield MA
Huntington Galleries, Huntington WV
Kunstindustrimuseet I Oslo, Oslo Museum of Applied Art, Oslo Norway
Leeds Art Galleries, Leeds England
Le Musee Regional de Rimouski, Rimouski PQ
Lincolnshire Museums, Usher Gallery, Lincoln England
Litchfield Historical Society, Litchfield CT
Louisiana State University, Anglo-American Art Museum, Baton Rouge LA
Loyala University of Chigago, Martin D'Arcy Gallery of Art, Chicago IL
Manchester City Art Galleries, Manchester England
Maryland Historical Society Museum, Baltimore MD

Mitchell Museum, Mount Vernon IL
James Monroe Law Office - Museum and Memorial Library, Fredericksburg VA
Montclair Art Museum, Montclair NJ
Mount Clare Mansion, Baltimore MD
Musee Cognacq-Jay, Cognacq-Jay Museum, Paris France
Musee d'Art de Saint-Laurent, Saint-Laurent PQ
Musee de L'Eglise Notre-Dame, Montreal PQ
Musee de L'Oeuvre Notre Dame, Cathedral Museum, Strasbourg France
Musees Royaux d'Art et d'Histoire, Royal Museums of Art and History, Brussels Belgium
Museo de Arte Popular Americano, Art of the American Peoples Museum, Santiago Chile
Museu da Inconfidencia, History of Democratic Ideals and Culture in Minas Gerais, Ouro Brazil
Museum Boymans-Van Beuningen, Rotterdam Netherlands
Museum fur Kunstandwerk, Museum of Arts and Crafts, Frankfurt Germany, Federal Republic of
Museum of Arts and Sciences, Cuban Museum, Planetarium, Daytona Beach FL
Museum of Fine Arts, Boston MA
Museum of the American China Trade, Milton MA
National Museum of Wales, Cardiff Wales
New Haven Colony Historical Society, New Haven CT
R W Norton Art Gallery, Shreveport LA
Philadelphia Museum of Art, Philadelphia PA
Plymouth City Museum and Art Gallery, Plymouth England
Portland Art Association, Museum, Portland OR
Remington Art Museum, Ogdensburg NY
Lauren Rogers Library and Museum of Art, Laurel MS
Rohsska Konstslojdmuseet, Rohss Museum of Arts and Crafts, Gothenburg Sweden
The Rosenbach Museum and Library, Philadelphia PA
Royal Pavilion, Art Gallery and Museums, Thomas-Stanford Museum, Preston Manor, Brighton England
San Diego Museum of Art, San Diego CA
Shirley Plantation, Charles City VA
Spertus Museum of Judaica, Chicago IL
Statni Zidovske Muzeum, State Jewish Museum, Prague Czechoslovakia
Stedelijk Museum Alkmaar, Alkmaar Municipal Museum, Alkmaar Netherlands
Stedelijk Museum de Lakenhal, Leyden Municipal Museum, Leiden Netherlands
Stedelijk Museum het Prinsenhof, Het Prinsenhof State Museum, Delft Netherlands
United States Naval Academy Museum, Annapolis MD
University of Iowa, Museum of Art, Iowa City IA
University of Santa Clara, de Saisset Art Gallery and Museum, Santa Clara CA
University of South Carolina, McKissick Museums, Columbia SC
University of Southwestern Louisiana, Art Center for Southwestern Louisiana, Lafayette LA
University of Tennessee, Eleanor Dean Audigier Art Collection, Knoxville TN
University of Utah, Utah Museum of Fine Arts, Salt Lake City UT
Valentine Museum, Richmond VA
Vestlandske Kunstindustrimuseum, Western Norway Museum of Applied Art, Bergen Norway
Victoria and Albert Museum, London England
Virginia Museum of Fine Arts, Richmond VA
Wadsworth Atheneum, Hartford CT
Wellington Museum, London England
Westfries Museum, Hoorn Netherlands
Yale University, Art Gallery, New Haven CT

SOUTHWESTERN ART

Amerind Foundation, Inc, Dragoon AZ
Colorado Springs Fine Arts Center, Colorado Springs CO
Douglas Art Association, Little Gallery, Douglas AZ
Harwood Foundation of the University of New

Mexico, Taos NM
Heard Museum, Phoenix AZ
Northern Arizona University, Art Gallery, Flagstaff AZ
Roswell Museum and Art Center, Roswell NM
Yuma Art Center, Yuma AZ

STAINED GLASS

Art Institute of Chicago, Chicago IL
Bayerisches Nationalmuseum, Bavarian National Museum, Munich Germany, Federal Republic of
Corcoran Gallery of Art, Washington DC
John Woodman Higgins Armory, Worcester MA
Jekyll Island National Historic Landmark, Jekyll Island GA
Musee de L'Oeuvre Notre Dame, Cathedral Museum, Strasbourg France
Victoria and Albert Museum, London England
Willet Stained Glass Studios, Library, Philadelphia PA

TAPESTRIES

American Swedish Institute, Minneapolis MN
Anderson House Museum, Society of the Cincinnati, Washington DC
Baltimore Museum of Art, Baltimore MD
Bayerisches Nationalmuseum, Bavarian National Museum, Munich Germany, Federal Republic of
College of Wooster Art Center Museum, Wooster OH
Corcoran Gallery of Art, Washington DC
Cummer Gallery of Art, DeEtte Holden Cummer Museum Foundation, Jacksonville FL
Dade County Art Museum, Vizcaya Museum and Gardens, Miami FL
Det Danske Kunstindustrimuseum, Museum of Decorative Art, Copenhagen Denmark
Frick Art Museum, Pittsburgh PA
Galleria di Palazzo Bianco, White Palace Gallery, Genoa Italy
George Peabody College for Teachers, Cohen Memorial Museum of Art, Nashville TN
John Woodman Higgins Armory, Worcester MA
Hill-Stead Museum, Farmington CT
Hyde Collection, Glens Falls NY
Iowa State Education Association, Salisbury House, Des Moines IA
Leeds Art Galleries, Leeds England
Musee du Petit Palais, Municipal Museum, Paris France
Musees Royaux d'Art et d'Histoire, Royal Museums of Art and History, Brussels Belgium
Musei Capitolini, Museum of Sculpture, Rome Italy
Museo di Capodimonte, Mount Capodi Museum, Naples Italy
Museo Nazionale di San Matteo, Saint Matteo National Museum, Pisa Italy
Museum of Fine Arts, Boston MA
Museum of Modern Art, Belgrade Yugoslavia
National Museum of Wales, Cardiff Wales
R W Norton Art Gallery, Shreveport LA
Panstwowe Zbiory Sztuki na Wawelu, Wawel State Collections of Art, Cracow Poland
Philadelphia Museum of Art, Philadelphia PA
Norton Simon Museum, Pasadena CA
Stedelijk Museum de Lakenhal, Leyden Municipal Museum, Leiden Netherlands
Stedelijk Museum het Prinsenhof, Het Prinsenhof State Museum, Delft Netherlands
Stedelyke Musea, City Museums, Bruges Belgium
Österreichisches Museum für angewandte Kunst, Vienna Austria
University of Houston, Sarah Campbell Blaffer Gallery, Houston TX
University of San Diego, Founders' Gallery, San Diego CA
University of Santa Clara, de Saisset Art Gallery and Museum, Santa Clara CA
University of Utah, Utah Museum of Fine Arts, Salt Lake City UT
Victoria and Albert Museum, London England
Virginia Museum of Fine Arts, Richmond VA
Wadsworth Atheneum, Hartford CT

TEXTILES

Allentown Art Museum, Allentown PA
American Swedish Institute, Minneapolis MN
Art Institute of Chicago, Chicago IL
Baltimore Museum of Art, Baltimore MD
Balzekas Museum of Lithuanian Culture, Chicago IL
Berea College, Art Department Gallery, Berea KY
Birmingham Museums and Art Gallery, Birmingham England
Bower's Museum, Santa Ana CA
Brooks Memorial Art Gallery, Memphis TN
California State Fair and Exposition Art Show, Sacramento CA
Calvin College Center Art Gallery, Grand Rapids MI
Charleston Museum, Charleston SC
Cincinnati Art Museum, Cincinnati OH
Cleveland Museum of Art, Cleveland OH
Cooper-Hewitt Museum, Smithsonian Institution National Museum of Design, New York NY
Coptic Museum, Cairo Egypt
Cranbrook Academy of Art Museum, Bloomfield Hills MI
Currier Gallery of Art, Manchester NH
Denver Art Museum, Frederic H Douglas Library, Denver CO
Det Danske Kunstindustrimuseum, Museum of Decorative Art, Copenhagen Denmark
Detroit Institute of Arts, Detroit MI
Drexel University Art Gallery and Museum Collection, Philadelphia PA
Flint Institute of Arts, Flint MI
Fries Museum, Leeuwarden Netherlands
Gaston County Art and History Museum, Dallas NC
Germanisches National Museum, Germanic National Museum, Nuremberg Germany, Federal Republic of
Goucher College, Kraushaar Auditorium Lobby Gallery, Towson MD
Haags Gemeentemuseum, Municipal Museum of The Hague, The Hague Netherlands
Harvard University, Dumbarton Oaks Research Library and Collections, Washington DC
Highland Area Arts Council, Freeport Art Museum, Freeport IL
Historic Deerfield Inc, Deerfield MA
Honolulu Academy of Arts, Honolulu HI
Indianapolis Museum of Art, Indianapolis IN
Indian Museum, Calcutta India
Institute of American Indian Arts Museum, Santa Fe NM
Jewish Museum, New York NY
Johannesburg Art Gallery, Johannesburg South Africa, Republic of
Kunstindustrimuseet I Oslo, Oslo Museum of Applied Art, Oslo Norway
Litchfield Historical Society, Litchfield CT
Los Angeles County Museum of Art, Los Angeles CA
Loyala University of Chigago, Martin D'Arcy Gallery of Art, Chicago IL
Maryland Historical Society Museum, Baltimore MD
Merrimack Valley Textile Museum, North Andover MA
Minnesota Museum of Art, Saint Paul MN
Musee d'Art de Saint-Laurent, Saint-Laurent PQ
Musees Royaux d'Art et d'Histoire, Royal Museums of Art and History, Brussels Belgium
Museo d'Arte Antica, Civiche Raccolte di Arte Applicata, Milan Italy
Museo Nazionale di Villa Guinigi, National Museum of Villa Guinigi, Lucca Italy
Museum fur Kunstandwerk, Museum of Arts and Crafts, Frankfurt Germany, Federal Republic of
Museum Mayer van den Bergh, Antwerp Belgium
Museum of American Folk Art, New York NY
Museum of Applied Arts and Sciences, Sydney Australia
Museum of Fine Arts, Boston MA
Museum of New Mexico, Museum of International Folk Art, Santa Fe NM
Museum of the American China Trade, Milton MA
Museums at Stony Brook, Stony Brook NY
Muzeum Narodowe w Krakowie, National Museum in Cracow, Cracow Poland
National Gallery of Victoria, Melbourne Australia
National Museum of History and Technology, Smithsonian Institution, Washington DC
Norwich Free Academy, Slater Memorial Museum & Converse Art Gallery, Norwich CT
Olana Historic Site, Hudson NY
Palm Beach County Parks and Recreation Department, Morikami Museum of Japanese Culture, Delray Beach FL
Philadelphia College of Textiles and Science, Paley Design Center, Philadelphia PA
Principia College, School of Nations Museum, Elsah IL
Quapaw Quarter Association, Inc, Villa Marre, Little Rock AR
Rhode Island School of Design, Museum of Art, Providence RI
Rohsska Konstslojdmuseet, Rohss Museum of Arts and Crafts, Gothenburg Sweden
Saginaw Art Museum, Saginaw MI
Scalamandre Museum of Textiles, New York NY
Schenectady Museum, Schenectady NY
Scripps College, Clark Humanities Museum, Claremont CA
Shaker Museum, Poland Spring ME
Shelburne Museum, Shelburne VT
Smith-Mason Gallery and Museum, Washington DC
Southwestern At Memphis, Jessie L Clough Art Memorial for Teaching, Memphis TN
Spertus Museum of Judaica, Chicago IL
State Museum of Oriental Art, Moscow Ussr
Statni Zidovske Muzeum, State Jewish Museum, Prague Czechoslovakia
Stedelyke Musea, City Museums, Bruges Belgium
Stedlijk Museum-Amsterdam, Municipal Museum, Amsterdam Netherlands
Österreichisches Museum für angewandte Kunst, Vienna Austria
Textile Museum, Washington DC
University of Alberta, Ring House Gallery, Edmonton AB
University of California, Los Angeles, Museum of Cultural History, Los Angeles CA
University of Cambridge, Fitzwilliam Museum, Cambridge England
University of Manchester, Whitworth Art Gallery, Manchester England
University of Miami, Lowe Art Museum, Coral Gables FL
University of Michigan Museum of Art, Kelsey Museum of Ancient and Medieval Archaeology, Ann Arbor MI
University of San Diego, Founders' Gallery, San Diego CA
University of Washington, Costume and Textile Study Center, Seattle WA
Vestlandske Kunstindustrimuseum, Western Norway Museum of Applied Art, Bergen Norway

WATERCOLORS

Brevard College, Coltrane Art Center, Brevard NC
Butler Institute of American Art, Youngstown OH
California Historical Society, San Francisco CA
California State Fair and Exposition Art Show, Sacramento CA
Central Art Gallery, Wolverhampton England
Corcoran Gallery of Art, Washington DC
Dundee Museums and Art Gallery, Dundee Scotland
Graphische Sammlung Albertina, Albertina Graphic Art Collection, Vienna Austria
Göteborg Konstmuseum, Gothenburg Art Gallery, Gothenburg Sweden
Harkness Memorial State Park, Waterford CT
Howard University Gallery of Art, Washington DC
Indianapolis Museum of Art, Indianapolis IN
Joslyn Art Museum, Omaha NE
Kalamazoo Institute of Arts, Genevieve and Donald Gilmore Art Center, Kalamazoo MI

Collections

Alfred I Barton Collection

University of Miami, Lowe Art Museum, Coral Gables FL

Bernard Baruch Silver Collection

University of South Carolina, McKissick Museums, Columbia SC

Anoine Louis Barye Collection of Bronzes

Corcoran Gallery of Art, Washington DC

Bauhaus Archives

Harvard University, Busch-Reisinger Museum, Cambridge MA

Ellen H Bayard Painting Collection

Baltimore Museum of Art, Baltimore MD

Elizabeth Palmer Bayler Collection of Textiles

University of Washington, Costume and Textile Study Center, Seattle WA

Behrick Collection

California State University, Chico, Art Gallery, Chico CA

Zoe Beiler Paintings Collection

Dickinson State College, Mind's Eye Gallery, Dickinson ND

Thomas E Benesch Memorial Drawing Collection

Baltimore Museum of Art, Baltimore MD

Bennington Pottery Collection

Bennington Museum, Bennington VT

Roloff Beny Collection

University of Calgary, The Nickle Arts Museum, Calgary AB

Evangeline Bergstrom Paperweight Collection

Bergstrom Art Center and Museum, Neenah WI

Berman Collection

Lehigh University Galleries, Bethlehem PA

Bernat Oriental Collection

Colby Museum of Art, Waterville ME

Harry A Bernstein Memorial Painting Collection

Baltimore Museum of Art, Baltimore MD

Bertha Schaefer Bequest Collection

University of Nebraska Lincoln, Sheldon Memorial Art Gallery, Lincoln NE

Mary Duke Biddle Gallery for the Blind

North Carolina Museum of Art, Department of Cultural Resources, Raleigh NC

Albert Bierstadt Collection

National Cowboy Hall of Fame and Western Heritage Center, Oklahoma City OK

Biggs Sculpture Collection

Red River Valley Museum, Vernon TX

Bingham Collection

University of California, University Art Galleries and California Museum of Photography, Riverside CA

Vyvyan Blackford Collection

Fort Hays State University, Visual Arts Center, Hays KS

Edwin M Blake Memorial

Trinity College, Austin Arts Center, Hartford CT

A Aubrey Bodine Collection

Peale Museum, Baltimore MD

Bodmer Collection

Joslyn Art Museum, Omaha NE

Boehm Collection

Bellingrath Gardens and Home, Theodore AL

Frederick T Bonham Collection

University of Tennessee, Frank H McClung Museum, Knoxville TN

Bradley Collection

Milwaukee Art Center, Milwaukee WI

Henry D Bradley Memorial Print Collection

Albrecht Art Museum, Saint Joseph MO

Branch Collection of Renaissance Art

Virginia Museum of Fine Arts, Richmond VA

Constantin Brancusi Sculpture Collection

Solomon R Guggenheim Museum, New York NY

Rex Brasher Collection

Harkness Memorial State Park, Waterford CT

Saidye & Samuel Bronfman Collection of Canadian Art

Montreal Museum of Fine Arts, Montreal PQ

Ailsa Mellon Bruce Collection of Decorative Arts

Carnegie Institute, Museum of Art, Pittsburgh PA
Virginia Museum of Fine Arts, Richmond VA

Buddhist Art Collection

Jacque Marchais Center of Tibetan Arts, Inc, Staten Island NY

Burnap English Pottery Collection

Potsdam Public Museum, Potsdam NY

James F Byrnes Collection

University of South Carolina, McKissick Museums, Columbia SC

Caballeria Collection of Oils

Southwest Museum, Los Angeles CA

Edward Joseph Callagher III American Paintings Collection

Baltimore Museum of Art, Baltimore MD

Forrest C Campbell Print Collection

Albrecht Art Museum, Saint Joseph MO

B G Canton Gallery

Stanford University, T W Stanford Art Gallery & Museum of Art, Stanford CA

Carder Steuben Glass Collection

Rockwell-Corning Museum, Corning NY

Carney Ceramics Collection

Parrish Art Museum, Southampton NY

Emily Carr Collection

Vancouver Art Gallery, Vancouver BC

Carrington Collection of Chinese Art

Rhode Island Historical Society, John Brown House, Providence RI

John H Cassell Collection of Political Cartoons

Hartwick College Fine Art Gallery, Oneonta NY

Gregorio Vasquez Ceballos Collection

Colombian Institute of Culture, Museum of Colonial Art, Bogota Colombia

Chagall Graphics Collection

San Jose State University, Art Gallery, San Jose CA

Mark Chagall Stained Glass Collection

Art Institute of Chicago, Chicago IL

Conrad Wise Chapman Oils Collection

Valentine Museum, Richmond VA

Daniel Chester French Home

Chesterwood, Stockbridge MA

Child Art Collection

Illinois State University, University Museums, Normal IL

Choate Lace Collection

University of Washington, Costume and Textile Study Center, Seattle WA

Christian Brothers Collection

Wine Museum of San Francisco, San Francisco CA

Frederic Edwin Church Collection

Olana Historic Site, Hudson NY

Civil War Collection

Chicago Historical Society, Chicago IL
Historic New Orleans Collection, Kemper and Leila Williams Foundation, New Orleans LA
Kiah Museum, Savannah GA
Library of Congress, Washington DC
Muscatine Art Center, Muscatine IA
Museum of Arts and History, Port Huron MI

Clarendon Portrait Collection

Plymouth City Museum and Art Gallery, Plymouth England

Clark European Collection

Corcoran Gallery of Art, Washington DC

Laura A Clubb Collection of Paintings

Philbrook Art Center, Tulsa OK

Coe Collection

Coe College, Art Galleries, Cedar Rapids IA

Colsa Collection

Saint Mary's Romanian Orthodox Church, Romanian Ethnic Museum, Cleveland OH

Cone Collection of French Art

Baltimore Museum of Art, Baltimore MD

Marvin Cone Oils Collection

Coe College, Art Galleries, Cedar Rapids IA

Copeland Collection

Delaware Art Museum, Wilmington DE

Cotter Collection

Saint Mary's College, Moreau Gallery Three, Notre Dame IN

Cottonian Collection

Plymouth City Museum and Art Gallery, Plymouth England

Samuel Courtauld Collection of French Paintings

Courtauld Institute Galleries, London England

Cowan Collection

The Parthenon, Memphis TN

Crozier Collection of Chinese Art

Philadelphia Museum of Art, Philadelphia PA

Cummings Collection

Colby Museum of Art, Waterville ME

Currier and Ives Lithograph Collection

Diamond M Foundation Museum, Snyder TX

Charles Cutts Collection

Sierra Nevada Museum of Art, Reno NV

Cybis Collection

Mercer County Community College Gallery, Trenton NJ

Elise Agnus Daingerfield 18th Century Collection

Baltimore Museum of Art, Baltimore MD

Cyrus Dallin Bronze Collection

Springville Museum of Art, Springville UT

Dana Collection

University of Montana, Gallery of Visual Arts, Missoula MT

David Robinson Collection of Antiquities

University of Mississippi, University Museums, Oxford MS

Davies Collection of Old Masters

National Museum of Wales, Cardiff Wales

Nellie Stratton Davis Art Gallery

Stephens College, Lewis James and Nellie Stratton Davis Art Gallery, Columbia MO

Norman Davis Collection of Classical Art

Seattle Art Museum, Seattle WA

D'Berger Collection

University of Santa Clara, de Saisset Art Gallery and Museum, Santa Clara CA

Frank E Delano Gallery of African Art

Museum, Greenwood SC

Agnes Delano Watercolor and Print Collection

Howard University Gallery of Art, Washington DC

Edmond de Rothschild Collection

Musee du Louvre, Louvre Museum, Paris France

De Winton Collection of Porcelain

National Museum of Wales, Cardiff Wales

I A Dinerstein Collection

Milwaukee Public Museum, Milwaukee WI

Maynard Dixon Collection

Brigham Young University, B F Larsen Gallery, Provo UT

F B Doane Collection of Western American Art

Frontier Times Museum, Bandera TX

Dorflinger Glass Collection

Everhart Museum of Natural History, Science and Art, Scranton PA

Doughty Bird Collection

Reynolda House, Inc, Winston-Salem NC

Doughty Porcelain Collection

Parrish Art Museum, Southampton NY

Marie Dressler Collection

Kiah Museum, Savannah GA

Anthony J Drexel Collection of 19th Century Paintings

Drexel University Art Gallery and Museum Collection, Philadelphia PA

Driebe Collection of Paintings

Lehigh University Galleries, Bethlehem PA

Dunbarton Print Collection

Saint Mary's College, Moreau Gallery Three, Notre Dame IN

Dunnigan Collection of Etchings

Parrish Art Museum, Southampton NY

Harvey Dunn Paintings Collection

South Dakota State University, South Dakota Memorial Art Center, Brookings SD

Hanson Rawlings Duval Jr Memorial Collection

Baltimore Museum of Art, Baltimore MD

Clara M Eagle Gallery Coll

Murray State University, Clara M Eagle Gallery, Murray KY

James Earle Collection of Western Art

National Cowboy Hall of Fame and Western Heritage Center, Oklahoma City OK

Henry Eichheim Collection

Santa Barbara Museum of Art, Santa Barbara CA

Abram Eisenberg French Painting Collection

Baltimore Museum of Art, Baltimore MD

Elkins Collection of Old Masters

Philadelphia Museum of Art, Philadelphia PA

Elliott Collection of 20th Century European Art

University of Iowa, Museum of Art, Iowa City IA

Jacob Epstein Old Masters Collection

Baltimore Museum of Art, Baltimore MD

Esso Collection

University of Miami, Lowe Art Museum, Coral Gables FL

European Prehistory

University of Missouri, Art Archaeology and Music Library, Columbia MO

Eustis Collection of Furniture

Oatlands, Leesburg VA

Florence Naftzger Evans Collection of Porcelain

Wichita Art Museum, Wichita KS

Mrs Arthur Kelly Evans Collection of Pottery and Porcelain

Virginia Museum of Fine Arts, Richmond VA

Walker Evans Collection

University of California, University Art Galleries and California Museum of Photography, Riverside CA

William T Evans Collection

National Collection of Fine Arts, Washington DC

Peter Carl Faberge Collection of Czarist Jewels

Virginia Museum of Fine Arts, Richmond VA

Fairbanks Collection of Paintings

Fort Wayne Museum of Art, Fort Wayne IN

Daniel Farber Photography Collection

Jesse Besser Museum, Alpena MI

Lyonel Feininger Archives

Harvard University, Busch-Reisinger Museum, Cambridge MA

Dexter M Ferry Collection

Vassar College Art Gallery, Poughkeepsie NY

Clark Field Collection of American Indian Crafts

Philbrook Art Center, Tulsa OK

Elizabeth Parke Firestone Collection of French Silver

Detroit Institute of Arts, Detroit MI

Fisher Collection

Parson Fisher House, Jonathan Fisher Memorial, Inc, Blue Hill ME

Fisher Memorial Collection

Beloit College, Theodore Lyman Wright Art Center, Beloit WI

Flagg Tanning Corporation Collection

Milwaukee Art Center, Milwaukee WI

Charles & Katherine Fleetwood Pre-Columbian Collection

University of Houston, Sarah Campbell Blaffer Gallery, Houston TX

Julius Fleischman Collection

University of Cincinnati, Tangeman Fine Arts Gallery, Cincinnati OH

Frank M Hall Collection

University of Nebraska Lincoln, Sheldon Memorial Art Gallery, Lincoln NE

Simon Fraser Collection

Simon Fraser University, Simon Fraser Gallery, Burnaby BC

Laura G Fraser Studio Collection of Western Art

National Cowboy Hall of Fame and Western Heritage Center, Oklahoma City OK

Toni Frissell Collection

Library of Congress, Washington DC

Roger Fry Collection

Courtauld Institute Galleries, London England

Eugene Fuller Memorial Collection of Chinese Jades

Seattle Art Museum, Seattle WA

Edward J Gallagher Jr Collection

University of Arizona, Museum of Art, Tucson AZ

Gallatin Collection

Philadelphia Museum of Art, Philadelphia PA

Gallier Architectural Drawings Collection

Historic New Orleans Collection, Kemper and Leila Williams Foundation, New Orleans LA

Gambier-Parry Collection of Old Masters

Courtauld Institute Galleries, London England

Eugene Garbaty Collection

University of Washington, Costume and Textile Study Center, Seattle WA

Garfield Collection

Sonoma State College Art Gallery, Rohnert Park CA

William Randolph Hearst Collection of Arms & Armour

Detroit Institute of Arts, Detroit MI

Heeramaneck Collection of Asian Art

Virginia Museum of Fine Arts, Richmond VA

Heeramaneck Collection of Primitive Art

Seattle Art Museum, Seattle WA

Edward F Heyne Pre-Columbian Collection

University of Houston, Sarah Campbell Blaffer Gallery, Houston TX

Abby Williams Hill Collection

University of Puget Sound, Kittredge Art Gallery, Tacoma WA

Freeman Hinckley Oriental Collection

Bates College, Treat Gallery, Lewiston ME

Hinkhouse Contemporary Art Collection

Coe College, Art Galleries, Cedar Rapids IA

Hirsch Collection of Oriental Rugs

Portland Art Association, Museum, Portland OR

Joseph H Hirshhorn Collection

Hirshhorn Museum and Sculpture Garden, Washington DC

Hispanic Collection

Hispanic Society of America Museum, New York NY
Library of Congress, Washington DC

Morris Henry Hobbs Print Collection

Historic New Orleans Collection, Kemper and Leila Williams Foundation, New Orleans LA

Roy Hofheinz Tapestry Collection

University of Houston, Sarah Campbell Blaffer Gallery, Houston TX

Holden Collection

Cleveland Museum of Art, Cleveland OH

Willitts J Hole Collection

University of California, Los Angeles, Frederick S Wight Art Gallery, Los Angeles CA

Oliver Wendell Holmes Stereographic Collection

Canton Art Institute, Canton OH

Winslow Homer Collection

Bowdoin College, Museum of Art & Peary-MacMillan Arctic Museum, Brunswick ME
Colby Museum of Art, Waterville ME

Winslow Homer Woodcut Collection

State Capitol Museum, Olympia WA

Samuel Houghton Great Basin Collection

Sierra Nevada Museum of Art, Reno NV

J Harry Howard Gemstone Collection

University of South Carolina, McKissick Museums, Columbia SC

Oscar Howe Collection

University of South Dakota Art Galleries, Vermillion SD

Anna C Hoyt Collection of Old Masters

Vanderbilt University, Art Gallery, Department of Fine Arts, Nashville TN

Gardiner Greene Hubbard Endowment Collection of Prints

Library of Congress, Washington DC

Winifred Kimball Hudnut Collection

University of Utah, Utah Museum of Fine Arts, Salt Lake City UT

J Marvin Hunter Western Americana Collection

Frontier Times Museum, Bandera TX

Charles & Elsa Hutzler Memorial Collection of Contemporary Sculpture

Baltimore Museum of Art, Baltimore MD

International Collection of Child Art

Illinois State University, University Museums, Normal IL

Isaacson Porcelain Collection

Seattle Art Museum, Seattle WA

Harry L Jackson Print Coll

Murray State University, Clara M Eagle Gallery, Murray KY

Jackson Silver Collection

National Museum of Wales, Cardiff Wales

Mary Frick Jacobs European Art Collection

Baltimore Museum of Art, Baltimore MD

Jarves Collection of Italian Paintings

Yale University, Art Gallery, New Haven CT

Jette Collection

Colby Museum of Art, Waterville ME

E Johnson Collection

Saint Louis County Historical Society, Duluth MN

John G Johnson Collection of Old Masters

Philadelphia Museum of Art, Philadelphia PA

S C Johnson & Son Collection

National Collection of Fine Arts, Washington DC

F B Johnston Collection

Library of Congress, Washington DC

Harriet Lane Johnston Collection

National Collection of Fine Arts, Washington DC

T Catesby Jones Collection of 20th Century European Art

Virginia Museum of Fine Arts, Richmond VA

Sylvan Lehman Joseph Print Collection

Bates College, Treat Gallery, Lewiston ME

Eugene S Juda Memorial Engravings Collection

Albrecht Art Museum, Saint Joseph MO

Vasily Kandinsky Collection

Solomon R Guggenheim Museum, New York NY

Kardian Collection of Mexican Art

Wichita Art Museum, Wichita KS

William Keith Paintings Collection

Saint Mary's College of California, Hearst Art Gallery, Moraga CA

Kelsey Collection

Mercer County Community College Gallery, Trenton NJ

Kemper Collection of American Paintings

Albrecht Art Museum, Saint Joseph MO

Lord Lee of Fareham Collection of Old Masters

Courtauld Institute Galleries, London England

George A Lucas Collection

Baltimore Museum of Art, Baltimore MD

MacQuoid Collection

Royal Pavilion, Art Gallery and Museums, Thomas-Stanford Museum, Preston Manor, Brighton England

Ernst Mahler Collection of Germanic Glass

Bergstrom Art Center and Museum, Neenah WI

Elmer Majolica Collection

Triton Museum of Art, Santa Clara CA

Maltwood Decorative Art Collection

University of Victoria, Maltwood Art Museum and Gallery, Victoria BC

Richard Mandell Collection

University of South Carolina, McKissick Museums, Columbia SC

Ralph C Marcove Collection of Oriental Art

Pennsylvania State University, Museum of Art, University Park PA

Marghab Linens Collection

South Dakota State University, South Dakota Memorial Art Center, Brookings SD

Marie Hull Collection

Delta State University, Fielding L Wright Art Center, Cleveland MS

John Marin Collection

Colby Museum of Art, Waterville ME

John and Norma Marin Collection

University of Maine at Machias Art Gallery, Machias ME

Markley Collection of Ancient Peruvian Ceramics

Pennsylvania State University, Museum of Art, University Park PA

Marks Collection of Pre-Columbian Art

East Tennessee State University, Carroll Reece Museum, Johnson City TN

Jacob Marks Memorial Collection

Memphis Academy of Arts, Frank T Tobey Gallery, Memphis TN

William H Marlatt Collection

Cleveland Museum of Art, Cleveland OH

Fred Dana Marsh Collection

Tomoka State Park Museum, Ormond Beach FL

Martinez-Canas Collection of Latin American Paintings

Metropolitan Museum and Art Centers, Coral Gables FL

Matsukata Collection

National Museum of Western Art, Kokuritsu Seiyo Bijutsukan, Tokyo Japan

Saidie A May Collection

Baltimore Museum of Art, Baltimore MD

McCrellis Doll Collection

Rhode Island Historical Society, John Brown House, Providence RI

McFadden Collection of Old Masters

Philadelphia Museum of Art, Philadelphia PA

McLanahan Memorial Collection

Baltimore Museum of Art, Baltimore MD

George F McMurray Collection

Trinity College, Austin Arts Center, Hartford CT

Paul McPharlin Collection of Theatre & Graphic Arts

Detroit Institute of Arts, Detroit MI

Meissen Porcelain Collection

Cummer Gallery of Art, DeEtte Holden Cummer Museum Foundation, Jacksonville FL
Virginia Museum of Fine Arts, Richmond VA

Conger Metcalf Collection

Coe College, Art Galleries, Cedar Rapids IA

Michael Silver Collection

University of Utah, Utah Museum of Fine Arts, Salt Lake City UT

Michener Collection of American Paintings

University of Texas at Austin, University Art Museum, Austin TX

Military Art Collection

Fort Meade Museum, Fort Meade MD
National Infantry Museum, Fort Benning GA
United States Military Academy, West Point Museum, West Point NY

Samuel & Tobie Miller Collection

Baltimore Museum of Art, Baltimore MD

Millet Collection

Wesleyan University, Davison Art Center, Middletown CT

Millington-Barnard Collection

University of Mississippi, University Museums, Oxford MS

Albert K Mitchell Russell-Remington Collection

National Cowboy Hall of Fame and Western Heritage Center, Oklahoma City OK

Molinari Coin Collection

Bowdoin College, Museum of Art & Peary-MacMillan Arctic Museum, Brunswick ME

Marianne Moore Archive Coll

The Rosenbach Museum and Library, Philadelphia PA

Moore Collection

University of Illinois, Krannert Art Museum, Champaign IL

Grace Moore Collection

University of Tennessee, Frank H McClung Museum, Knoxville TN

Henry Moore Sculpture Collection

Art Gallery of Ontario, Toronto ON

Thomas Moran Collection

National Cowboy Hall of Fame and Western Heritage Center, Oklahoma City OK

J P Morgan Collection

Wadsworth Atheneum, Hartford CT

Morgenroth Collection of Renaissance Medals

University of California, Santa Barbara, Art Museum, Santa Barbara CA

Mormon Collection

Church of Jesus Christ of Latter-Day Saints, Information Center and Museum, Arts and Sites Division, Salt Lake City UT

Howard J Morrison Jr Osteological Collection

Kiah Museum, Savannah GA

Morse Collection

Beloit College, Theodore Lyman Wright Art Center, Beloit WI

William Moser Collection of African Art

Fort Wayne Museum of Art, Fort Wayne IN

William Sidney Mount Collection

Museums at Stony Brook, Stony Brook NY

Arnold Mountfort Collection

University of Santa Clara, de Saisset Art Gallery and Museum, Santa Clara CA

Mourot Collection of Meissen Porcelain

Virginia Museum of Fine Arts, Richmond VA

General Munthe Collection of Chinese Art

Vestlandske Kunstindustrimuseum, Western Norway Museum of Applied Art, Bergen Norway

Roland P Murdock Collection of American Art

Wichita Art Museum, Wichita KS

Gwen Houston Naftzger Collection of Porcelain Birds

Wichita Art Museum, Wichita KS

L S and Ilda L Naftzger Collection of Prints and Drawings

Wichita Art Museum, Wichita KS

M C Naftzger Collection of Russell Paintings

Wichita Art Museum, Wichita KS

Nance Collection of Pottery and Porcelain

National Museum of Wales, Cardiff Wales

Nause & Graff Print Collection

Northern Illinois University, Swen Parson Gallery and Gallery 200, De Kalb IL

Near Eastern and Mediterranean Art and Archaeology

University of Missouri, Art Archaeology and Music Library, Columbia MO

Carl Netzaw Collection of Antique Jewelry

Milwaukee Public Museum, Milwaukee WI

Neuhoff Collection of English Furniture

Columbia Museums of Art and Science, Columbia SC

Newcomb Pottery Collection

West Baton Rouge Museum, Port Allen LA

Niblack Collection of Woodcarvings

Western Woodcarvings, Custer SD

Andrei Nitecki African Art Collections

Syracuse University, Art Collection, Syracuse NY

Harry T Norton Collection of Glass

Montreal Museum of Fine Arts, Montreal PQ

Alice B Nunn Silver Collection

Portland Art Association, Museum, Portland OR

Wallace Nutting Collection

Wadsworth Atheneum, Hartford CT

Olsen Collection

University of Illinois, Krannert Art Museum, Champaign IL

Oppenheimer Collection of Gothic and Medieval Art

Marion Koogler McNay Art Institute, San Antonio TX

Paperweight Collection

Muscatine Art Center, Muscatine IA

Parish Collection of Furniture

Remington Art Museum, Ogdensburg NY

Samuel Parrish Collection of Renaissance Art

Parrish Art Museum, Southampton NY

J G D'Arch Paul Collection

Baltimore Museum of Art, Baltimore MD

John Barton Payne Collection

Virginia Museum of Fine Arts, Richmond VA

Peabody Institute Collection

Baltimore Museum of Art, Baltimore MD

Adelaide Pearson Collection

Colby Museum of Art, Waterville ME

Samuel Pees Contemporary Painting Collection

Allegheny College, Bowman, Megahan and Penelec Galleries, Meadville PA

Pendleton Collection

Kelly-Griggs House Museum, Pasadena CA

Pendleton House Decorative Arts Collection

Rhode Island School of Design, Museum of Art, Providence RI

Joseph Pennell Collection

George Washington University Museum & Art Galleries, Washington DC

Pennell Endowment Collection of Prints

Library of Congress, Washington DC

Ferdinand Perret Art Reference Library

National Collection of Fine Arts, Library of the National Collection of Fine Arts and the National Portrait Gallery, Washington DC

Mel Pfaelzer Surrealist Collection

Northern Illinois University, Swen Parson Gallery and Gallery 200, De Kalb IL

Leonard Pfeiffer Collection

University of Arizona, Museum of Art, Tucson AZ

Phelps Collection

Delaware Art Museum, Wilmington DE

Walter J Phillips Collection

Banff Centre, Walter Phillips Gallery, Banff AB

Phillips Portrait Collection

Parrish Art Museum, Southampton NY

Duncan Phyfe Furniture Collection

Taft Museum, Cincinnati OH

Albert Pilavin Collection of 20th Century American Arts

Rhode Island School of Design, Museum of Art, Providence RI

Lucile Pillow Porcelain Collection

Montreal Museum of Fine Arts, Montreal PQ

Pitkin Collection of Oriental Art

Beloit College, Theodore Lyman Wright Art Center, Beloit WI

Poindexter Collection

University of Montana, Gallery of Visual Arts, Missoula MT

William J Pollock Collection of American Indian Art

Colby Museum of Art, Waterville ME

Lillian Thomas Pratt Collection of Czarist Jewels

Virginia Museum of Fine Arts, Richmond VA

Elisabeth Severance Prentiss Collection

Cleveland Museum of Art, Cleveland OH

William Henry Price Memorial Collection of Oil Paintings

Oregon State University, Memorial Union Art Gallery, Corvallis OR

Pulsifer Collection of Winslow Homer

Colby Museum of Art, Waterville ME

Putnam Collection

Timken Art Gallery, San Diego CA

Quaker Art Collection

Swarthmore College, Friends Historical Library, Swarthmore PA

Freda & Clara Radoff Mexican Print Collection

University of Houston, Sarah Campbell Blaffer Gallery, Houston TX

Natacha Rambova Egyptian Collection

University of Utah, Utah Museum of Fine Arts, Salt Lake City UT

Rand Collection of American Indian Art

Montclair Art Museum, Montclair NJ

Raoul Collection

University of California, University Art Galleries and California Museum of Photography, Riverside CA

Rasmussen Collection of Eskimo Arts

Portland Art Association, Museum, Portland OR

Ray American Indian Collection

Red River Valley Museum, Vernon TX

Ruth Reeves Asian-Indian Folk Art Collection

Syracuse University, Art Collection, Syracuse NY

Frederic Remington Collection

Bradford Brinton Memorial Ranch Museum, Big Horn WY
Buffalo Bill Memorial Association, Cody WY
R W Norton Art Gallery, Shreveport LA

Frederick Remington Collection

St Lawrence University, Richard F Brush Art Gallery, Canton NY

Renaissance Art History

University of Missouri, Art Archaeology and Music Library, Columbia MO

Richards Coin Collection

Hastings Museum, Hastings NE

General Lawrason Riggs Collection

Baltimore Museum of Art, Baltimore MD

Rindisbacher Watercolor Collection

United States Military Academy, West Point Museum, West Point NY

William Ritschel Collection

Monterey Peninsula Museum of Art, Monterey CA

David Roberts Collection

Riverside County Art and Cultural Center, Edward-Dean Museum of Decorative Arts, Cherry Valley CA

Roberts Sculpture Collection

Portland Art Association, Museum, Portland OR

Marion Sharp Robinson Collection

University of Utah, Utah Museum of Fine Arts, Salt Lake City UT

Abby Aldrich Rockefeller Collection of Japanese Art

Rhode Island School of Design, Museum of Art, Providence RI

Robert F Rockwell Foundation Collection

Rockwell-Corning Museum, Corning NY

Grace Rainey Rogers Collection

Cleveland Museum of Art, Cleveland OH

John Rogers Sculpture Collection

Saginaw Art Museum, Saginaw MI

Roland Art Collection

Pioneer Museum and Haggin Galleries, Petzinger Memorial Library, Stockton CA

Edward Rose Collection of Ceramics

Brandeis University, Rose Art Museum, Waltham MA

Ross Graphics Collection

Beloit College, Theodore Lyman Wright Art Center, Beloit WI

Guy Rowe Wax Drawings Collections

Angelo State University, Houston Harte University Center, San Angelo TX

Peter Paul Rubens Collection

John and Mable Ringling Museum of Art, Sarasota FL

C M Russell Bronze Collection

National Cowboy Hall of Fame and Western Heritage Center, Oklahoma City OK

Charles M Russell Collection

Bradford Brinton Memorial Ranch Museum, Big Horn WY
Buffalo Bill Memorial Association, Cody WY
William S Hart Museum, Newhall CA
R W Norton Art Gallery, Shreveport LA
C M Russell Museum, Great Falls MT

Charles M Russell Paintings

Wichita Art Museum, Wichita KS

Russell-Remington Collection

National Cowboy Hall of Fame and Western Heritage Center, Oklahoma City OK

Saint Joseph Photographic Collection

Albrecht Art Museum, Saint Joseph MO

Wilbur Sandison Photography Collection

Whatcom Museum of History and Art, Bellingham WA

Sandwich Glass Collection

Brockton Art Center, Brockton MA

Sargent Collection of American Indian Art

Montclair Art Museum, Montclair NJ

Sawhill Artifact Collection

James Madison University, Sawhill Gallery, Harrisonburg VA

Jonathan Sax Print Collection

University of Minnesota, Tweed Museum of Art, Duluth MN

Eugene Schaefer Collection of Ancient Glass

Newark Museum, Newark NJ

Schiller Oriental Collection

City Art Gallery, Bristol England

Alice F Schott Doll Collection

Santa Barbara Museum of Art, Santa Barbara CA

Schreyvogel Collection

National Cowboy Hall of Fame and Western Heritage Center, Oklahoma City OK

Schuette Woodland Indian Collection

Rahr-West Museum and Civic Center, Manitowoc WI

Schwartz Collection of Chinese Ivories

Rahr-West Museum and Civic Center, Manitowoc WI

Scotese Graphic Collection

Columbia Museums of Art and Science, Columbia SC

Philip Sears Sculpture Collection

Fruitlands Museums, Harvard MA

Seibels Collection

Columbia Museums of Art and Science, Columbia SC

John L Severance Collection

Cleveland Museum of Art, Cleveland OH

Shaker Collection

Art Complex Museum at Duxbury, Duxbury MA
Shaker Community, Inc, Pittsfield MA
Shaker Museum, Poland Spring ME
Shaker Museum, Old Chatham NY

Sharp Collection of Glass

Remington Art Museum, Ogdensburg NY

William Ludlow Sheppard Watercolor Collection

Valentine Museum, Richmond VA

David M Shoup Collection of Korean Pottery

Allegheny College, Bowman, Megahan and Penelec Galleries, Meadville PA

Franz W Sichel Collection of Glass

Wine Museum of San Francisco, San Francisco CA

B Simon Lithography Collection

Historic New Orleans Collection, Kemper and Leila Williams Foundation, New Orleans LA

Falk Simon Silver Collection

Rohsska Konstslojdmuseet, Rohss Museum of Arts and Crafts, Gothenburg Sweden

Singer Collection

Vestlandske Kunstindustrimuseum, Western Norway Museum of Applied Art, Bergen Norway

Sloan Collection

Valparaiso University, University Art Galleries and Collections, Valparaiso IN

Eric Sloan Collection

Sloane-Stanley Museum, West Hartford CT

Helen S Slosberg Collection of Oceanic Art

Brandeis University, Rose Art Museum, Waltham MA

Smith Collection of Watch Keys

Rollins College, George D and Harriet W Cornell Fine Arts Center Museum, Winter Park FL

C R Smith Collection of Western American Art

University of Texas at Austin, University Art Museum, Austin TX

Smith Painting Collection

Woodmere Art Gallery, Philadelphia PA

Smith-Paterson Memorial Collection

Delta State University, Fielding L Wright Art Center, Cleveland MS

Southeast Asian Artifact Collection

Illinois State University, University Museums, Normal IL

Anisoara Stan Collection

Saint Mary's Romanian Orthodox Church, Romanian Ethnic Museum, Cleveland OH

Stanford Family Collection

Stanford University, T W Stanford Art Gallery & Museum of Art, Stanford CA

Staples Collection of Indonesian Art

James Madison University, Sawhill Gallery, Harrisonburg VA

John Steele Print Collection

East Tennessee State University, Carroll Reece Museum, Johnson City TN

Stern Collection

Philadelphia Museum of Art, Philadelphia PA

Harold P Stern Collection of Oriental Art

Vanderbilt University, Art Gallery, Department of Fine Arts, Nashville TN

Stern-Davis Collection of Peruvian Painting

New Orleans Museum of Art, Isaac Delgado Museum, New Orleans LA

Stiegel Glass Collection

Philadelphia Museum of Art, Philadelphia PA

Alfred Stieglitz Collection

Fisk University Museum, Nashville TN

Clyfford Still Collection

San Francisco Museum of Modern Art, San Francisco CA

Thomas D Stimson Memorial Collection of Far Eastern Art

Seattle Art Museum, Seattle WA

Stoddard Collection of Greek Vases

Yale University, Art Gallery, New Haven CT

Ala Story Print Collection

University of California, Santa Barbara, Art Museum, Santa Barbara CA

Thomas Sully Gallery Collection

Longwood College, Bedford Gallery, Farmville VA

Sully Portrait Collection

United States Military Academy, West Point Museum, West Point NY

Tabor Collection of Oriental Art

Philbrook Art Center, Tulsa OK

Robert H Tannahill Collection of Impressionist & Post Impressionist Paintings

Detroit Institute of Arts, Detroit MI

Taylor Collection of Southwestern Art

Colorado Springs Fine Arts Center, Colorado Springs CO

Justin K Thannhauser Collection of Impressionist & Post-Impressionist Paintings

Solomon R Guggenheim Museum, New York NY

Thieme Collection of Paintings

Fort Wayne Museum of Art, Fort Wayne IN

Pyke Thompson Collection

National Museum of Wales, Cardiff Wales

Mary Thaw Thomson Collection of 17th Century French Engraving

Vassar College Art Gallery, Poughkeepsie NY

Thorne Miniature Collection

Art Institute of Chicago, Chicago IL

Tibetan Art Collection

Jacque Marchais Center of Tibetan Arts, Inc, Staten Island NY

Harriett Tidball Collection

University of Washington, Costume and Textile Study Center, Seattle WA

Tiffany Collection

Mark Twain Memorial, Hartford CT

Louis Comfort Tiffany Collection

Morse Gallery of Art, Boulder FL

Tiffany Glass Collection

Houston Antique Museum, Chattanooga TN

William Toben Memorial Collection

Albrecht Art Museum, Saint Joseph MO

Trees Collection

University of Illinois, Krannert Art Museum, Champaign IL

Trovwer Silver Collection

University of Utah, Utah Museum of Fine Arts, Salt Lake City UT

Tucker Porcelain Collection

Philadelphia Museum of Art, Philadelphia PA

J M W Turner Watercolor Collection

Indianapolis Museum of Art, Indianapolis IN

George P Tweed Memorial Collection of Paintings

University of Minnesota, Tweed Museum of Art, Duluth MN

Tylecote Glass Collection

Manchester City Art Galleries, Manchester England

Tyson Collection

Philadelphia Museum of Art, Philadelphia PA

Uhry Print Collection

High Museum of Art, Atlanta GA

Doris Ulmann Photography Collection

Berea College, Art Department Gallery, Berea KY

Ulrich Collection of Waugh Paintings

Wichita State University, Edwin A Ulrich Museum of Art, Wichita KS

James Ward Usher Collection

Lincolnshire Museums, Usher Gallery, Lincoln England

Edward Virginus Valentine Sculpture Collection

Valentine Museum, Richmond VA

Vanderpoel Collection

Norwich Free Academy, Slater Memorial Museum & Converse Art Gallery, Norwich CT

Van Ess Collection of Renaissance and Baroque Art

Hartwick College Fine Art Gallery, Oneonta NY

Van Gogh Collection

Ryksmuseum Kroller-Muller, Kroller-Muller State Museum, Otterlo Netherlands

Matthew Vassar Collection

Vassar College Art Gallery, Poughkeepsie NY

James Ven Der Zee Photography Collection

Studio Museum in Harlem, New York NY

Ellis Verink Photograph Collection

Polk Public Museum, Lakeland FL

Voertman Collection

North Texas State University, Art Gallery, Denton TX

Von Schleinitz Collection

Milwaukee Art Center, Milwaukee WI

J H Wade Collection

Cleveland Museum of Art, Cleveland OH

Walker Collection of French Impressionists

Corcoran Gallery of Art, Washington DC

Cloud Wampler Collection of Oriental Art

Everson Museum of Art, Syracuse NY

Felix M Warbur Collection of Medieval Sculpture

Vassar College Art Gallery, Poughkeepsie NY

Warren Collection of Classical Antiquities

Bowdoin College, Museum of Art & Peary-MacMillan Arctic Museum, Brunswick ME

Watkins Collection of American and European Paintings

American University, Watkins Art Gallery, Washington DC

William Watson Collection of Ceramics

Lemoyne Art Foundation, Tallahassee FL

Coulten Waugh Collection

Edwin A Ulrich Museum, Hyde Park NY

Frederick J Waugh Collection

Edwin A Ulrich Museum, Hyde Park NY

Samuel Bell Waugh Collection

Edwin A Ulrich Museum, Hyde Park NY

Frederick J Waugh Paintings

Wichita State University, Edwin A Ulrich Museum of Art, Wichita KS

Wax Collection

Blair Museum of Lithophanes and Carved Waxes, Springfield OH

John Wayne Kachina Collection

National Cowboy Hall of Fame and Western Heritage Center, Oklahoma City OK

Weatherhead Collection of Contemporary Graphics

Fort Wayne Museum of Art, Fort Wayne IN

Noah Webster Collection

New Haven Colony Historical Society, Reference Library, New Haven CT

Wedgwood Collection

Buten Museum of Wedgwood, Merion PA

Wedgwood Porcelain Collection

Henry B Plant Museum, Tampa FL

Wedgwood Pottery Collection

R W Norton Art Gallery, Shreveport LA

Teresa Jackson Weill Collection

Brandeis University, Rose Art Museum, Waltham MA

J Alden Weir Collection

Brigham Young University, B F Larsen Gallery, Provo UT

Benjamin West Collection

Bob Jones University, Greenville SC

Maurice Wetheim Collection

Harvard University, William Hayes Fogg Art Museum, Cambridge MA

Candace Wheeler Collection

Mark Twain Memorial, Hartford CT

Whittington Memorial Collection

Delta State University, Fielding L Wright Art Center, Cleveland MS

Bartlett Wicks Collection

University of Utah, Utah Museum of Fine Arts, Salt Lake City UT

Archibald M Willard Paintings Collection

Spirit of '76 Museum, Southern Lorain County Historical Society, Wellington OH

Will Collection of Paintings & Drawings

Jersey City Museum Association, Jersey City NJ

Willett Ceramics Collection

Royal Pavilion, Art Gallery and Museums, Art Gallery and Museum, Brighton England

Adolph D and Wilkins C Williams Collection

Virginia Museum of Fine Arts, Richmond VA

James McNeill Whistler Collection

Freer Gallery of Art, Washington DC

White Collection

Baltimore Museum of Art, Baltimore MD
Philadelphia Museum of Art, Philadelphia PA

Elizabeth White Collection

Sumter Gallery of Art, Sumter SC

White Silver Collection

Baltimore Museum of Art, Baltimore MD

Whitney Silver Collection

Montclair Art Museum, Montclair NJ

Ralph Wilson Collection

Lehigh University Galleries, Bethlehem PA

Wilstach Collection of Old Masters

Philadelphia Museum of Art, Philadelphia PA

Witter Bynner Collection of Chinese Art

Roswell Museum and Art Center, Roswell NM

Grant Wood Collection

Davenport Municipal Art Gallery, Davenport IA

William Woodward Collection

Baltimore Museum of Art, Baltimore MD

Theodore Wores Collection

Triton Museum of Art, Santa Clara CA

Frank Lloyd Wright Collection

Allentown Art Museum, Allentown PA

W Lloyd Wright Collection

George Washington University Museum & Art Galleries, Washington DC

Wurtzburger Collection

Baltimore Museum of Art, Baltimore MD

Andrew Wyeth Collection

Brandywine River Museum, Chadds Ford PA
Greenville County Museum of Art, Greenville SC

Mahonri Young Collection of Manuscripts

Brigham Young University, B F Larsen Gallery, Provo UT

Karl Zerbe Collection of Serigraphs

Lemoyne Art Foundation, Tallahassee FL